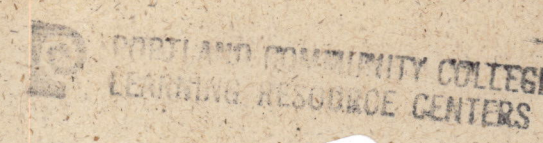

RAND McNALLY

ANNIVERSARY EDITION

The New International Atlas
Der Neue Internationale Atlas
El Nuevo Atlas Internacional
Le Nouvel Atlas International
O Nôvo Atlas Internacional

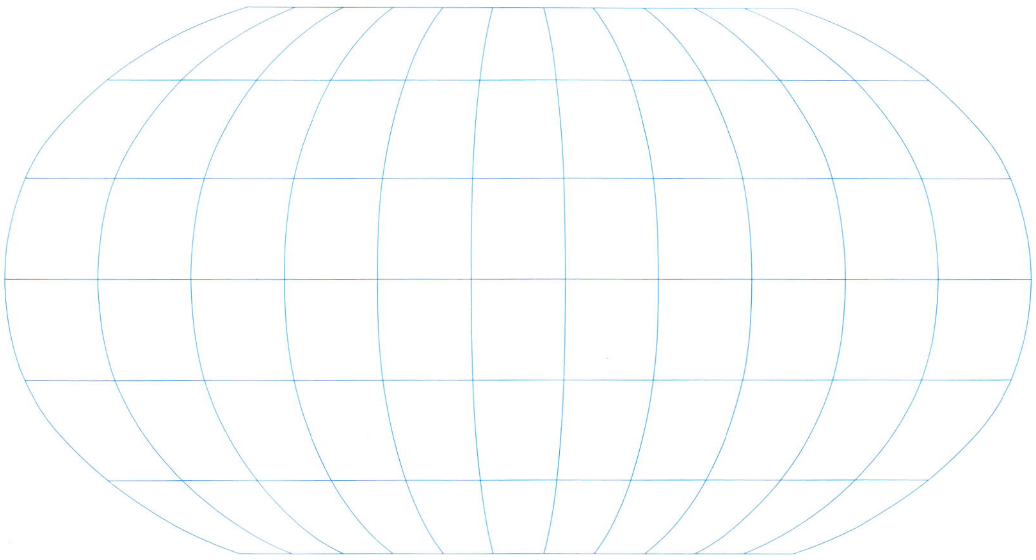

RAND McNALLY CHICAGO / NEW YORK / SAN FRANCISCO

ADVISERS AND CONSULTANTS

The editors wish to express their special appreciation to these geographers, cartographers, and regional specialists who assisted in the refinement of the basic concepts of the atlas or who participated in the review of many of the regional maps.

ALLGEMEINE UND KARTOGRAPHISCHE BERATER

Die Herausgeber möchten ihren besonderen Dank den Geographen, Kartographen und Landeskundlern aussprechen, die mitgeholfen haben bei der Klärung des Atlaskonzepts oder beteiligt waren an der Durchsicht vieler Regionalkarten.

ASESORES Y CONSULTORES

Los redactores quieren expresar su más profundo agradecimiento a los geógrafos, cartógrafos y especialistas en mapas regionales, que han colaborado en la determinación exacta de los conceptos básicos del atlas o que han participado en la revisión de gran número de los mapas regionales.

CONSEILLERS ET CONSULTANTS

Les éditeurs veulent exprimer ici leur gratitude aux géographes, cartographes et spécialistes régionaux qui ont collaboré à la mise au point de la conception de base de l'Atlas ou qui ont participé à la révision de nombreuses cartes régionales.

CONSELHEIROS E CONSULTORES

Os editores desejam expressar seu profundo agradecimento aos geógrafos, cartógrafos e especialistas regionais que assistiram no refinamento dos conceitos básicos do atlas ou que tenham participado na revisão de um grande número de mapas regionais.

Library of Congress Cataloging-in-Publication Data

Rand McNally and Company.
The new international atlas = Der neue internationale Atlas = El nuevo atlas internacional = Le nouvel atlas international = O nôvo atlas internacional. -- Anniversary ed.
p. cm.
English, French, German, Portuguese, and Spanish.
At head of title: Rand McNally.
Editorial and cartographic direction, Russell L. Voisin, Michael W. Dobson, Jon M. Leverenz.
Includes index.
ISBN 0-528-83548-3
1. Atlases. I. Title. II. Title: Neue internationale Atlas. III. Title: Nuevo atlas internacional. IV. Title: Nouvel atlas international. V. Title: Nôvo atlas internacional. VI. Title: Rand McNally, the new international atlas.
G1021.R23 1992 <G&M>
912--dc20 92-24030
CIP
MAP

International Planning Conference
Internationale Planungskonferenz
Conferencia Internacional de Consultores
Conférence Internationale de Planning
Conferência Internacional de Consultores

Dr. MANLIO CASTIGLIONI
Italy

Dr. ARCH C. GERLACH
United States

Dr. Ir. CORNELIS KOEMAN
Netherlands

Dr. ANDRÉ LIBAULT
Brazil

Brig. D. E. O. THACKWELL
United Kingdom

ROBERT J. VOSKUIL
United States

Dr. AKIRA WATANABE
Japan

Map Advisers
Kartographische Berater
Consejeros Cartográficos
Conseillers Cartographes
Conselheiros Cartográficos

Europe
Prof. Dr. EMIL MEYNEN
Germany

Dr. SANDOR RADO
Hungary

Asia
Dr. HISASHI SATO
Japan

Australia
R. O. BUCHANAN
United Kingdom

Anglo-America
Dr. ARCH C. GERLACH
United States

Latin America
Dr. ANDRÉ LIBAULT
Brazil

Dra. CONSUELO SOTO MORA
Mexico

Dr. JORGE A. VIVÓ ESCOTO
Mexico

Metropolitan Area Maps
Prof. HAROLD M. MAYER
United States

Rand McNally
Corporate Advisory Group
Thomas J. Hermes
Dennis O'Shea
Carl Mapes, Ph.D.
Bruce C. Ogilvie, Ph.D.
Paul T. Tiddens

The New International Atlas

Printed in the United States of America.

International Atlas Staff
Redaktion des Internationalen Atlasses
Personal del Atlas Internacional
Personnel de l'Atlas International
Redação do Atlas Internacional

RAND McNALLY

Publisher
Andrew McNally III
Andrew McNally IV

Editorial and Cartographic Direction
Russell L. Voisin
Michael W. Dobson, Ph.D.
Jon M. Leverenz

Art and Design Direction
Chris Arvetis
Gordon Hartshorne

Coordination
V. Patrick Healy
Arlen H. Winterfeld
John E. Zych

Geographic Research and Index
Susan Hudson
Keith Jennerjohn
Felix A. Lopez
Raymond T. Tobiaski
Richard L. Forstall (Consultant)

Cartographic Editorial
Robert K. Argersinger
Winifred V. Farbman

Cartographic Compilation
Ernest A. Dahl
Esther A. Grene
Lynn N. Jasmer
Han Sik Lee
Larry K. Tyler

Cartographic Production
Timothy J. Carter
Ronald Peters
Barbara Smith
Walter E. Erck
Joseph H. Funke
Ruthe Garner
Raymond J. Nitch

Composition and Typesetting
Sam Wilen
Rajani Veeramachaneni

Terrain Illustrators
Ivan Barcaba
Evelyn Mitchell
Mary Jo Schrader

MONDADORI McNALLY GmbH, Stuttgart

General Manager
Helmut Schaub
and Cartographic Staff

CARTOGRAPHIA, Budapest

Coordinator
Ervin Földi
and Cartographic Staff

ESSELTE MAP SERVICE, Stockholm

Editorial and Cartographic Direction
Paul R. Kraske,
Jürgen Jansch,
and Cartographic Staff

GEORGE PHILIP & SON, London

Editorial and Cartographic Direction
Harold Fullard,
A. G. Poynter,
and Cartographic Staff

TEIKOKU-SHOIN CO., LTD., Tokyo

Supervisor
Kimio Moriya
and Cartographic Staff

Foreword

THE HISTORY OF MAPS is as old as travel, discovery, and curiosity about the world. Since the earliest times, cartographers have served mariners with guidance for their explorations, monarchs with portraits of their territories, and scholars with a record of the earth's surface. Today, maps play an even more important role by providing men with the evidence of the ties which link the world's countries and peoples to one another.

The prime function of a map is to portray the earth's surface and the patterns of human occupance that have developed upon it. If a map were no more than an objective record, it would not need revision; however, a map is more than just a simple picture. Greatly reduced in scale from the reality it represents, it must abstract and generalize from that reality, selecting and interpreting the facts deemed to be of greatest significance. Thus, not only must cartography map new regions of the world, but it must also reflect a steady improvement in the techniques of portraying geographic information for the user.

The present century has offered a great challenge to map makers. Not only has it witnessed the increasing demand for specialized map information from governments, teachers, and scientists, it has also seen growing numbers of non-specialists eager to use maps in their business, for travel, or simply for enjoyment.

The Editors of *The International Atlas* feel, then, that a new work should be more than an updated version of older ones. The goal should be to produce an atlas of the greatest possible value and interest to a wide range of specialists and laymen. In this Foreword, we call the attention of users to several aspects which are new to the traditional framework of atlas publishing. The two most significant of these are the internationality of its planning and execution, and the designing of the maps as components of five distinctive series.

From the beginning, this Atlas has been international in concept, planning, editorial policy, and production. It was felt by Rand McNally & Company that there would be important gains in source material and expertise from the participation of organizations with previous cartographic experience in widely varying regions of the world. The advice and guidance of the senior personnel of these organizations has borne out this belief, although Rand McNally & Company as publisher has retained prime responsibility.

The editorial policies of the Atlas have been established with international use in mind, being designed for those whose native tongue is German, Spanish, French or Portuguese, as well as English. This international approach has been carried into the maps through the utilization of the metric system of measurement, and particularly by a strong emphasis on the use of local forms for geographic names. Essentially all names are in the local language, and English is used only for names of major features which extend across international borders. The names of countries appear on most of the maps both in English and in the locally official forms.

Generic terms for physical features (mountain, island, cape, etc.) also appear in their local forms, not in English. Short glossaries translating the most common of these terms appear in the margins of most maps. There is also a comprehensive glossary of all the generic terms. In the index to the Atlas, translation of generic terms is aided by the use of a system of symbols.

The coverage of the world's regions has also been planned with international utilization in mind. The space allotted to each region reflects its relative economic and cultural significance on the world scene, as well as its total population and area. There is an approximate balance between Anglo-America, Europe, and Asia, each with over one-fifth of the total map pages. Africa, Oceania, and Latin America together account for the remaining one-third. The index maps on pages xiii-xv show the map coverage according to scale.

The second of the Atlas' significant new aspects is the planning of the maps as components of five separate series. Each series has a distinctive style and content. In the first of these series, the continents are portrayed at 1:24,000,000 in natural colors, as they might appear from about 4,000 miles in space. The series also includes maps of the oceans at 1:48,000,000 and the world at 1:75,000,000.

In the next series, the major world regions are uniformly portrayed at 1:12,000,000 (190 miles to the inch). These maps are primarily political in style and content. The third series covers virtually the entire inhabited area of the earth at either 1:6,000,000 (95 miles to the inch), for the less dense regions, or 1:3,000,000 (47 miles to the inch), for Europe, most of North America, and the densest portions of South and East Asia. Physical and cultural detail are given approximately equal emphasis in this series.

In the fourth series, the scale of 1:1,000,000 (16 miles to the inch) has been used to portray key regions in each continent, selected for their exceptional importance, high population density, or complexity of development. The emphasis is on cultural detail, though shaded relief also appears. A final series maps the world's major urban areas at 1:300,000 (4.7 miles to the inch). This series emphasizes the complex patterns characteristic of large urban areas, omitting relief portrayal.

Each of the map series is comprehensive in a significant sense. The first three are territorially comprehensive, except for a few remote areas, and the last two are comprehensive for the most densely settled regions of the earth.

The sequence of maps in the Atlas begins with the series of world, continent, and ocean maps. Next are the three series of regional maps, arranged within major regions from smallest scale (1:12,000,000) to largest scale (1:1,000,000). The metropolitan map series (1:300,000) has been kept together in one section following the regional maps.

The individual map layouts have usually been planned to portray geographic and economic regions rather than individual countries. Thus there are maps of the Iberian Peninsula and of Southeastern Europe, but no separate maps of Portugal or Romania. In a few instances, this has necessitated the omission of some small portion of the region or country described in the map title. Inset maps have also been avoided, though exceptions have been made to portray some isolated islands or island groups.

The map symbols used for given features (Legend to Maps, pages x-xii) are generally alike on all of the map scales, though reduced in size on smaller scales. The symbols most often used have been arranged on page xi.

No aspect of map design has shown more dramatic advances in recent years than the cartographic rendering of relief. The Editors believe that the most effective method to depict this is the bird's-eye view or hill shading technique, which uses variation from light through dark tones to indicate slope and shape of relief features pictorially. This Atlas uses shaded relief on all but one of its five map series. On the 1:6,000,000 and 1:3,000,000 maps, it appears in combination with altitude tints, which show variations in elevation by means of light reflection, hue and intensity.

In the concluding portion of the Atlas are various tables and summaries for general reference. Next is the comprehensive glossary of geographic terms (pages 289-295). The World Information Table (pages 296-299) lists the area, population, and political status for each major political unit. The world's largest metropolitan areas are listed on page 300, followed by a comprehensive list of the world's major cities with population (pages 301-316). Finally, the Index provides map location references—map page, latitude and longitude—for more than 160,000 names.

Vorwort

DIE GESCHICHTE DER KARTE ist so alt wie das Reisen, die Entdeckungsfahrten und die Wissbegier über die Welt. Seit alten Zeiten haben Kartographen den Seefahrern mit Unterlagen für ihre Erkundungen gedient, den Herrschern Aufnahmen ihres Besitzes und den Gelehrten Darstellungen der Erdoberfläche geliefert. Heute spielen Karten eine noch bedeutendere Rolle, weil sie den Menschen vor Augen führen, wie eng die Länder und Völker der Welt miteinander verbunden sind.

Wichtigste Aufgabe einer Karte ist es, die Oberfläche der Erde und die vom Menschen geschaffenen Formen darzustellen. Wäre eine Karte nichts anderes als eine objektive Bestandsaufnahme, brauchte sie nicht bearbeitet zu werden; eine Karte ist jedoch mehr als nur ein Bild. Da sie eine vielfache Verkleinerung der Wirklichkeit wiedergibt, muss sie abstrahieren und durch Auswahl und Symbolisierung der wesentlichsten Tatsachen vereinfachen. So hat die Kartographie neue Regionen der Erde aufzunehmen und den neuesten Stand der Darstellung geographischer Informationen für den Benutzer aufzuzeigen.

Unser Jahrhundert bedeutet für die Kartographen eine grosse Herausforderung. Karten werden nicht nur in zunehmendem Masse von Regierungen, Wissenschaftlern und Pädagogen gefordert, sondern auch von interessierten Laien, die in ihrem Beruf, auf Reisen oder einfach zu ihrer Freude Karten benutzen.

Die Herausgeber des *Internationalen Atlas* meinen, dass ein neues Atlaswerk mehr sein sollte als nur die laufend gehaltene Ausgabe eines alten. Das Ziel sollte sein, einen Atlas von höchstem Gebrauchswert und Interesse sowohl für Fachleute als auch Laien zu schaffen.

In diesem Sinne möchten wir auf Besonderheiten hinweisen, die sich von dem traditionallen Aufbau eines Atlas wesentlich unterscheiden. Die beiden wichtigsten sind die Internationalität in Planung und Ausführung sowie die einheitliche Gestaltung der Karten zu fünf Gruppen.

Von Anfang an war dieser Atlas international in Planung, Redaktion und Herstellung. Rand McNally & Company war überzeugt, dass die Beteiligung von Partnern aus verschiedenen Teilen der Welt mit ihrer kartographischen Erfahrung einen grossen Gewinn an Quellen und Rat ergeben würde. Der Rat und die Mitarbeit dieser Fachleute haben diese Ansicht voll bestätigt, wobei Rand McNally als Verleger die letzte Entscheidung zufiel.

Die redaktionelle Bearbeitung des Atlas erfolgte mit Blick auf einen internationalen Interessentenkreis, vor allem aber für Benutzer, deren Muttersprache Deutsch, Spanisch, Französisch, Portugiesisch oder Englisch ist. Diese internationale Einstellung zeigt sich im Karteninhalt selbst, in der Benutzung des metrischen Masssystems und vor allem in der Bevorzugung der lokalen Schreibweise geographischer Namen. Grundsätzlich werden alle Namen in der Landessprache wiedergegeben; nur Namen grösserer Objekte, die sich über nationale Grenzen erstrecken, erscheinen in Englisch. Die Ländernamen stehen auf den meisten Karten sowohl in Englisch als auch in der offiziellen nationalen Form.

Namen für physische Objekte (Berg, Insel, Kap usw.) sind ebenfalls in ihrer lokalen Form wiedergegeben, nicht in Englisch. Die am häufigsten vorkommenden Begriffe stehen am Rande der meisten Karten erläutert. Der Atlas enthält ausserdem ein umfangreiches Verzeichnis aller Gattungsbegriffe. Im Register wird das Verständnis dieser Gattungsbegriffe durch ein System von Symbolen erleichtert.

Die Kartenausschnitte der verschiedenen Regionen der Erde wurden gleichfalls mit Blick auf einen internationalen Benutzerkreis gewählt. In diesem Atlas entspricht der einer Region zugemessene Kartenanteil ihrer relativen wirtschaftlichen und kulturellen Bedeutung in der Welt wie ihrer Gesamtbevölkerung und Fläche. Auf Anglo-Amerika, Europa und Asien entfällt mit je etwas mehr als einem Fünftel der Gesamtkartenzahl ungefähr der gleiche Anteil. Das verbleibende Drittel teilen sich Afrika, Australien, Ozeanien und Lateinamerika. Auf den Seiten XIII-XV sind die Karteausschnitte den Massstäben entsprechend auf Übersichtskarten ersichtlich.

Die zweite wesentliche Besonderheit des Atlas ist seine Gliederung der Karten in fünf charakteristische Gruppen. Jede Gruppe ist gekennzeichnet durch einen bestimmten Stil und Inhalt. In der ersten Gruppe werden die Kontinente (1:24 Mill.) abgebildet, wie sie sich aus einer ungefähren Entfernung von 6 500 km aus dem Weltraum darbieten. Diese Gruppe schliesst Karten der Ozeane (1:48 Mill.) und der Erde (1:75 Mill.) ein. In der folgenden Gruppe werden Grossregionen einheitlich (1:12 Mill.) dargestellt. Diese Karten sind in erster Linie politische Karten. Die dritte Serie deckt im wesentlichen das bewohnte Gebiet der Erde, entweder 1:6 Mill. für weniger dicht besiedelte Gebiete oder 1:3 Mill. für Europa, den Grossteil von Nordamerika und die dichtest besiedelten Teile Süd- und Ostasiens. Physische und kulturgeographische Einzelheiten werden in ungefähr gleichem Umfang wiedergegeben.

Für die vierte Gruppe wurde der Massstab 1:1 Mill. gewählt, um zentrale Räume jedes Kontinents abzubilden; sie sind entsprechend ihrer aussergewöhnlichen Bedeutung, hohen Bevölkerungsdichte oder komplexen Entwicklung gewählt. Betont werden kulturgeographische Einzelheiten, dazu enthalten die Karten eine Reliefschummerung. Die letzte Gruppe umfasst die bedeutendsten Stadtregionen der Erde (1:300 000). Diese Serie hebt das charakteristische, komplexe Gefüge grosser städtischer Ballungsgebiete hervor; auf Reliefdarstellung wurde verzichtet.

Jede der Kartenserien ist in sich abgeschlossen: Die ersten drei sind in bezug auf die Landflächen umfassend, ausgenommem einige entlegene Gebiete; die zwei letzten sind es hinsichtlich der Darstellung der dichtest besiedelten Räume der Erde.

Der Atlas beginnt mit der Gruppe der Welt-, Kontinent- und Ozeankarten. Es folgen drei Gruppen Regionalkarten, innerhalb jeder Grossregion geordnet vom kleinsten Massstab (1:12 Mill.) zum grössten (1:1 Mill.). Die Serie der Stadtregionen (1:300 000) wurde in einem einzigen Kapitel zusammengefasst, im Anschluss an die Regionalkarten.

Die Festlegung der einzelnen Kartenausschnitte zielte gewöhnlich mehr darauf ab, geographische und wirtschaftliche Regionen darzustellen als einzelne Staaten. Es gibt daher eine Karte der Iberischen Halbinsel oder von Südosteuropa, aber keine Einzelkarte von Portugal oder Rumänien. In einigen Fällen sind hierdurch kleinere Flächen des Landes oder der Region nicht erfasst, die im Kartentitel genannt sind. Die Verwendung von Einsatzkärtchen wurde möglichst vermieden, dennoch waren Ausnahmen erforderlich, um entlegene Inseln oder Inselgruppen darstellen zu können.

Die Kartensignaturen für bestimmte Objekte (Zeichenerklärung Seite X-XII) gleichen sich im allgemeinen in allen Massstäben, auch wenn sie in Karten kleinerer Massstäbe verkleinert sind. Die am häufigsten vorkommenden Signaturen sind auf Seite XI dargestellt.

Auf kaum einem Gebiet der Kartengestaltung gab es in den vergangenen Jahren so eindrucksvolle Fortschritte wie auf dem der Geländedarstellung. Die Herausgeber glauben, dass die wirkungsvollste Darstellungsmethode die Reliefschummerung ist. Sie benutzt Tonabstufungen von Hell zu Dunkel, um Neigungen und Geländeformen plastisch hervorzuheben. Dieser Atlas bringt die Schummerung bei vier der fünf Kartenserien. In den Karten 1:6 und 1:3 Mill. wird sie kombiniert mit farbigen Höhenschichten, die unterschiedliche Höhenlagen durch ihren Farb- und Tonwert abgestuft wiedergeben.

Der letzte Teil des Atlas enthält zahlreiche Tabellen und Übersichten. Auf Seite 289-295 folgt eine Zusammenstellung geographischer Begriffe. In einer Länderübersicht (Seite 296-299) sind Daten über Fläche, Bevölkerung und politischen Status der wichtigsten politischen Einheiten zusammengefasst. Die grössten Stadtregionen der Erde werden auf Seite 300 dargestellt. Weiter folgt eine umfangreiche Liste der wichtigsten Weltstädte mit Einwohnerzahlen (Seite 301-316). Im Register werden für über 160 000 Namen die Kartenseite sowie die geographische Länge und Breite aufgeführt.

Prefacio

La historia de los mapas es tan antigua como la de los viajes, los descubrimientos y la curiosidad del hombre por el mundo. Desde hace mucho tiempo los cartógrafos han proporcionado guías a los navegantes en sus exploraciones, descripciones de sus territorios a los monarcas y registros de la superficie de la tierra a los eruditos. Más importante todavía es el papel que desempeñan los mapas en la actualidad, proporcionando al hombre en todas partes prueba de los lazos que vinculan entre sí a los diferentes países y pueblos del globo.

La función primordial de un mapa es la representación de la superficie de la tierra y de los patrones de ocupación humana que se han desarrollado sobre ella. Si un mapa no fuera sino un registro objetivo, no necesitaría ser revisado; sin embargo, un mapa es algo más que una simple representación gráfica. Representando una realidad enormemente reducida a escala, el mapa, forzosamente, debe abstraer y generalizar de esa realidad, seleccionando e interpretando los hechos que se juzguen de mayor significación. En consecuencia, la cartografía no debe limitarse al trazo de mapas de las nuevas regiones del mundo, sino que debe reflejar en ellos un continuo adelanto en las técnicas de representación de la información geográfica en provecho de quien los utiliza.

El siglo actual ha venido a presentar a los cartógrafos una desafiante tarea. Es época que no sólo ha presenciado una creciente demanda de información cartográfica especializada por parte de los gobiernos, maestros y científicos, sino que durante ella ha surgido un público cada vez mayor de gentes no especializadas, ávidas de aprovechar los mapas en sus negocios y viajes o que los adquieren simplemente por placer.

Los directores del *Atlas Internacional* consideran, por lo tanto, que una nueva obra debe ser algo más que una versión al día de trabajos anteriores. El objetivo debe ser producir un atlas del mayor valor e interés posibles para un vasto número de especialistas y de legos en la materia. En este prefacio, queremos llamar la atención de quienes consulten esta obra sobre varias innovaciones introducidas en el diseño tradicional de un atlas. De ellas, las más significativas son la internacionalidad de su preparación, y el diseño de los mapas como componentes de cinco series con características propias.

Desde un principio, este atlas ha tenido carácter internacional en cuanto a su concepto básico, su planeamiento, política editorial y producción. Rand McNally y Compañía consideró que con la participación de organizaciones con experiencia en cartografía en una gran variedad de regiones del mundo, se obtendría importante progreso en cuanto a fuentes de material y de conocimientos. Esta creencia originó el asesoramiento y guía recibidos del personal directivo de estas organizaciones, aunque Rand McNally y Compañía ha retenido la responsabilidad principal como casa editora.

Las normas o política editorial del atlas se ha establecido teniendo en cuenta su uso internacional, y éste ha sido diseñado para el público de habla alemana, española, francesa, portuguesa e inglesa. Este carácter internacional se introdujo en los mapas mediante la utilización del sistema métrico y en particular, dando marcada preferencia al uso de vocablos locales en la nomenclatura. Virtualmente todo nombre se da en el idioma de la localidad, usándose el inglés únicamente en la identificación de elementos geográficos de mayor importancia que se extienden a través de las fronteras internacionales. En la mayoría de los mapas, los nombres de los países aparecen en inglés y en la forma oficial localmente utilizada.

Los términos genéricos de geografía física (montañas, islas, cabos, etc.), también aparecen en el idioma local, no en inglés. Al margen de la mayoría de los mapas se incluyen breves glosarios con la traducción de los más comunes de dichos términos. Se incluye también un glosario completo de los términos genéricos y en el índice del atlas, mediante un sistema de símbolos, se facilita la traducción de los mismos.

Igualmente, la amplitud que el atlas da a las distintas regiones del mundo, fue preparada con un criterio de utilización internacional. El espacio asignado a cada región refleja su posición económica y cultural relativa dentro del escenario mundial, así como su población y superficie. El resultado de esto ha sido el equilibrio aproximado resultante entre Angloamérica, Europa y Asia, ocupando, cada cual, más de la quinta parte del total de páginas dedicadas a mapas. Africa, Oceanía y América Latina juntas, cubren el resto del volumen. Los mapas índices, en las páginas xiii a xv, muestran, a escala, la extensión de las regiones que los mapas comprenden.

El segundo de los nuevo aspectos significativos del atlas, es el planeamiento de los mapas como componentes de cinco series separadas. Cada serie tiene un estilo y contenido propios. En la primera de estas series, los continentes están representados a una escala de 1:24 000 000, en colores naturales, como aparecerían al observar la tierra desde el espacio a una distancia de cerca de 6 500 kilómetros. La serie incluye también mapas de los océanos a escala 1:48 000 000 y del mundo a escala 1:75 000 000.

En la serie siguiente, las principales regiones del mundo están uniformemente representadas a escala 1:12 000 000 (120 km por cm). Estos mapas son básicamente políticos en su estilo y contenido. La tercera serie cubre prácticamente el total de la superficie habitada de la tierra, a una de dos escalas: 1:6 000 000 (60 km por cm), para las regiones menos densas, o 1:3 000 000 (30 km por cm), para Europa, la mayor parte de Norteamérica y las regiones de mayor densidad de población del Sur y Sureste de Asia. En esta serie se hace aproximadamente igual énfasis a los detalles de orden físico y cultural.

En la cuarta serie se ha usado la escala 1:1 000 000 (10 km por cm), para representar las regiones más notables en cada continente, seleccionadas por su excepcional importancia, alta densidad de población o complejidad de desarrollo. Acá, el énfasis es en el detalle cultural aunque también aparece el relieve utilizando la técnica de sombreado. La serie final la componen los mapas de las principales áreas urbanas del mundo a una escala de 1:300 000 (3 km por cm). Esta serie recalca los complejos patrones culturales característicos de las grandes áreas urbanas, omitiendo la representación del relieve.

Cada una de las series es en sí una serie integral desde el punto de vista de significación. Las tres primeras, con excepción de unas cuantas áreas remotas, son territorialmente completas; las dos últimas, son completas en cuanto a las regiones más densamente pobladas de la tierra.

La sucesión de los mapas en el atlas principia con la serie del mundo, los continentes y los océanos. Luego vienen las tres series de mapas regionales distribuídos dentro de cada región principal, de la escala menor, (1:12 000 000), a la escala mayor, (1:1 000 000). La serie de mapas de áreas metropolitanas (1:300 000), se ofrece en una sección, inmediatamente después de los mapas regionales.

En general, el trazado de cada mapa se hizo con miras a representar regiones geográficas y económicas, y no necesariamente países individuales. Así, el atlas contiene mapas de la Península Ibérica y de Europa Sudoriental, pero no mapas separados de Portugal o de Rumania. En unos pocos casos, esto impuso la necesidad de omitir alguna pequeña porción de la región o país descrito en el título del mapa. También se evitó la inserción de mapas detallando determinada área, aunque se hicieron excepciones para representar algunas islas o grupos de islas.

Los símbolos utilizados para ciertos elementos (Leyenda para Mapas, páginas x a xii), son en general similares en todas las escalas, aunque reducidos en tamaño en los mapas de escala más pequeña. Los usados más frecuentemente se encuentran en la página xi.

En ningún aspecto del diseño cartográfico se han hecho progresos tan notables en años recientes como en la representación del relieve del terreno. Los editores opinan, sin embargo, que el método más efectivo en este sentido es la vista a vuelo de pájaro o técnica de sombreado: la variación de tonos claros a obscuros indica gráficamente la pendiente y la configuración del relieve. Este atlas utiliza el sombreado en cuatro de las cinco series de mapas. En los mapas a escala 1:6 000 000 y 1:3 000 000, el sombreado se combina con tintes que indican los cambios de altitud mediante reflexión de la luz, colorido e intensidad variables.

En la última parte del atlas se ofrecen varias tablas y resúmenes para consulta. En seguida se encuentra un glosario completo de términos geográficos (páginas 289-295). La Tabla de Información Mundial, (páginas 296 a 299), muestra el área, la población y la situación de cada una de las principales unidades políticas. La lista de las áreas metropolitanas más grandes del mundo aparece en la página 300, y está seguida por una lista completa de las principales ciudades del mundo con indicación del número de habitantes, (páginas 301-316). Finalmente, el índice ofrece referencias para localizar en los mapas más de 160 000 nombres: página del mapa, latitud y longitud.

Avant-propos

L'histoire des cartes géographiques remonte aussi loin que celle des voyages, des découvertes et du sentiment de curiosité touchant le globe terrestre. Depuis les temps les plus reculés, les cartographes ont servi les marins en les aidant à s'orienter dans leurs voyages d'explorations, les monarques en leur fournissant des représentations de leurs territoires, les savants en les documentant sur la surface terrestre. De nos jours, les cartes jouent un rôle plus important encore, en ce qu'elles procurent aux hommes l'évidence tangible des liens joignant les uns aux autres peuples et nations du monde.

La fonction primordiale d'une carte consiste à représenter la surface du globe et la répartition des concentrations humaines qui s'y sont développées. Une carte ne fût-elle qu'un document objectif, point ne serait besoin de la réviser; mais justement, elle constitue bien davantage qu'une simple image. Considérablement réduite relativement à la réalité qu'elle représente, elle doit abstraire et généraliser à partir de cette réalité, par la sélection et l'interprétation des données jugées les plus significatives. De sorte que la cartographie doit non seulement établir les cartes des nouvelles régions du globe, mais il lui faut en outre refléter les progrès constants des techniques d'exposé de la documentation géographique à l'intention du lecteur.

Le siècle actuel a porté un défi suprême aux cartographes. Non seulement en ce que l'on y est témoin d'une demande toujours croissante de cartes à l'usage des spécialistes, de la part des gouvernements, des professeurs et des savants, mais aussi bien en ce que l'on y constate une proportion de plus en plus élevée de non-initiés avides d'utiliser des cartes de vulgarisation pour leurs affaires, leurs voyages, ou simplement leur plaisir.

Les Editeurs de *L'Atlas International* estiment, dès lors, qu'un nouvel ouvrage se doit d'être plus qu'une ancienne version mise à jour. Le but qu'ils se proposent consiste à sortir un atlas qui soit du plus haut intérêt et de la plus profonde valeur pour un vaste public de spécialistes et de profanes. Les Editeurs attirent l'attention des lecteurs sur plusieurs innovations apportées ici au cadre traditionnel de publication des atlas. Deux des plus significatives de ces innovations résident dans l'internationalisation de la conception et de l'exécution d'une part, d'autre part dans la disposition des cartes réparties en cinq séries distinctives.

Envisagé et entrepris sur un mode international dès le début, cet Atlas s'est développé selon une conception, une forme éditoriale et une réalisation du même ordre. Rand McNally & Company jugeait que de sérieux avantages—apports importants en matériaux de documentation et en connaissances spécialisées faisant autorité—résulteraient d'une collaboration avec des organisations possédant de longue date une expérience cartographique des régions les plus diversifiées du globe. Les avis et les opinions émanant du personnel de cadres de ces organisations ont corroboré iette conviction, encore que Rand McNally en tant que société d'édition en assume la responsabilité principale.

D'usage international, destiné à des lecteurs de langue allemande, espagnole, française ou portugaise, tout autant qu'anglaise, cet Atlas a dû être édité sous une forme qui tînt compte de sa raison d'être. Cette conception internationale de l'Atlas a été réalisée sur les cartes elles-mêmes avec d'une part l'utilisation du système métrique, avec d'autre part l'emploi délibéré des noms géographiques sous leur forme nationale. Essentiellement, tous les noms apparaissent sous leur forme nationale, l'anglais n'étant utilisé que pour les noms d'importantes structures du relief qui s'étendent par-delà les frontières internationales. Sur la plupart des cartes, les noms des pays apparaissent à la fois en anglais et sous leur forme nationale officielle.

Les termes génériques désignant des structures de relief (montagne, île, cap, etc.) apparaissent également sous leur forme nationale, et non pas en anglais. En marge de la plupart des cartes, de courtes listes lexicales donnent la traduction des plus communs de ces termes. En outre, un glossaire donne tous les termes génériques dont la traduction se trouve par ailleurs facilitée grâce au système de symboles décrit dans l'Index de l'Atlas.

La répartition des régions du globe a été également déterminée en tenant compte de l'usage international qu'il sera fait de l'Atlas. L'espace attribué à chaque région reflète son importance économique et culturelle relative dans le monde, aussi bien que sa superficie et sa population. Il y a un équilibre approximatif entre l'Amérique du Nord, l'Europe et l'Asie, chacune avec plus d'un cinquième de la totalité des pages. L'Afrique, l'Océanie et l'Amérique du Sud occupent le tiers restant. Les cartes index des pages xiii-xv présentent la répartition des cartes en fonction de l'échelle à laquelle elles sont reproduites.

La seconde des innovations importantes de cet Atlas réside dans la conception des cartes en tant qu'éléments constitutifs de cinq séries séparées. Style et contenu distinctifs caractérisent nettement chacune de ces cinq séries. Dans la première, les continents sont représentés à l'échelle de 1:24 000 000, en couleurs naturelles, tels qu'ils apparaîtraient, vus de l'espace, à 6 500 km. Cette série comprend également les cartes de océans à l'échelle de 1:48 000 000 et du monde à l'échelle de 1:75 000 000.

Dans la série suivante, les régions majeures du globe sont représentées de facon uniforme à l'échelle de 1:12 000 000 (120 km au cm). Par leur style et leur contenu, celles-ci sont essentiellement des cartes politiques. Dans la troisième série, virtuellement toute las surface habitée de la terre est représentée, soit à l'échelle de 1:6 000 000 (60 km au cm) pour les régions de moindre densité de population, soit à l'échelle de 1:3 000 000 (30 km au cm) pour l'Europe, la plus grande partie de l'Amérique du Nord et les portions de plus forte densité du Sud et de l'Est de l'Asie. Dans cette série, une importance à peu près égale a été accordée aux détails physiques et aux détails culturels.

Dans la quatrième série, l'échelle de 1:1 000 000 (10 km au cm) a été employée pour représenter certaines régions-clefs de chaque continent, choisies pour leur importance exceptionnelle, leur densité de population, ou la complexité de leur développement. L'accent porte sur les détails culturels, bien que le relief ombré apparaisse également. Une série finale souligne la répartition culturelle complexe, caractéristique des vastes zones urbaines, omettant le relief.

Chacune de ces séries est complète dans un mode significatif. Les trois premières sont complètes du point de vue territorial, exception faite de quelques lointaines contrées, et les deux dernières sont complètes en ce qui concerne les régions du globe de plus forte densité de population.

La succession des cartes de l'Atlas s'ouvre avec la série qui comprend les cartes du monde, des continents, et des océans. A sa suite, viennent les trois séries de cartes régionales disposées pour chaque région principale depuis les plus petites échelles (1:12 000 000), aux plus grandes (1:1 000 000). La série des cartes métropolitaines est groupée en une section qui fait suite aux cartes régionales.

La répartition individuelle des cartes a généralement été conçue en fonction des régions géographiques et économiques, plutôt qu'en fonction des frontières politiques nationales. De sorte qu'il y a des cartes de la Péninsule Ibérique et de l'Europe du Sud-Est, mais pas de cartes séparées pour le Portugal ou la Roumanie. Dans quelques cas, ceci a nécessité l'omission de quelque petite portion de la région ou du pays décrit dans le titre de la carte. Les insertions d'extensions ont également été évitées, encore que plusieurs exceptions aient été faites pour représenter certaines îles isolées ou certains groupes d'îles.

Les symboles employés sur les cartes sont en général identiques pour toutes les échelles de cartes, quoique de taille réduite sur les cartes à petite échelle. Les symboles les plus fréquemment employés ont été réunis à la page xi.

Aucun de aspects de la réalisation des cartes n'a fait de progrès plus prodigieux durant ces dernières années que la représentation cartographique du relief. Les Editeurs estiment que la méthode la plus efficace est celle de la "vue à vol d'oiseau", ou technique du relief ombré; celle-ci utilise toute la gamme des tons, des plus clairs aux plus foncés, pour indiquer picturalement l'inclinaison des pentes et la forme des structures du relief. Le relief ombré apparaît sur quatre des cinqu séries de cartes. Sur les cartes au 1:6 000 000ᵉ et au 1:3 000 000ᵉ, il apparaît en combinaison avec les teintes d'altitude qui indiquent les variations d'élévation au moyen de la réflexion de la lumière, de la nuance et de l'intensité.

Dans la dernière partie de l'Atlas, qui constitue sa conclusion, se trouvent divers tableaux de récapitulations et de références. A sa suite se trouve le lexique complet des termes géographiques (pages 289-295). Puis une table d'informations mondiales donne la liste de toutes les unités politiques principales, avec superficie, population et statut politique de chacune (pages 296-299). La liste des plus importants centres urbains du monde est à la page 300. A la suite de cette table se trouve une liste complète des principales villes du monde avec leur population (pages 301-316). Enfin, l'Index fournit des références de cartes—numéros de pages, longitude et latitude—pour permettre de situer plus de 160 000 noms géographiques.

Prefácio

A HISTÓRIA DOS MAPAS é tão antiga quanto as das viagens, descobertas, e curiosidades sobre o mundo. Desde os primórdios tempos, cartógrafos têm servido à marinheiros orientando-os em suas explorações, monarcas com reproduções dos seus territórios, e acadêmicos com o registro da superfície da terra. Hoje, os mapas têm um papel mais importante-ainda, fornecendo ao homem provas das ligações que unem os países e os povos do mundo.

A função fundamental do mapa é de retratar a superfície da terra e os padrões da ocupação humana que sobre ela se desenvolveu. Se o mapa não fosse nada mais que um registro objetivo, não necessitaria de revisão; contudo, um mapa é mais do que um simples retrato. Grandemente reduzido em escala, em relação à realidade que representa, ele deve absorver e ao mesmo tempo generalizar a realidade, selecionando e interpretando os fatos supostamente de maior significado. Portanto, não somente é preciso que o cartógrafo registre novas regiões do mundo, mas também tente refletir um melhoramento contínuo nas técnicas de retratamento de informação geográfica para o usuário.

O século atual tem oferecido um grande desafio para confeccionadores de mapas. Não há somente o testemunho da crescente demanda por mapas de informações especializadas, pelos governos, professores e cientistas, mas também tem-se notado um número crescente de leigos, ansiosos em usar mapas em seus negócios, viagens, ou simplesmente como-passatempo.

Os Editores do *Atlas Internacional* sentem, que um novo trabalho deveria ser mais do que uma versão renovada dos trabalhos anteriores. O objetivo deveria ser de produzir um atlas de máximo valor e interêsse possível, para uma grande gama de especialistas e leigos. Neste prefácio, chamamos a atenção dos usuários para os vários aspectos-que são novos para os esquemas tradicionais de publicação de atlas. Os dois mais significantes são: a internacionalidade do seu planejamento e execução, e o arranjo de mapas como componentes de cinco séries distintas.

Desde o início, o atlas tem sido internacional em conceito, planejamento, política editorial e produção. Rand McNally & Company sentiu que haveriam ganhos importantes na fonte de material e conhecimento, pela participação de organizações com experiências cartográficas anteriores, nas mais diversas regiões do mundo. O conselho e orientação do quadro pessoal dessas organizações têm comprovado esta crença, apesar da Rand McNally & Company, como editor, ter retido a responsabilidade principal.

As políticas editoriais do Atlas têm sido estabelecidas visando o uso internacional, sendo designado para aqueles cuja língua nativa é Alemão, Espanhol, Francês ou Português, bem como Inglês. Essa técnica internacional tem sido executada em mapas, através da utilização do sistema métrico de medidas, e particularmente, pela grande ênfase no uso dos estilos locais para nomes geográficos. Essencialmente, todos os nomes estão em linguagem local, e o Inglês é usado somente para nomes de acidentes geográficos importantes, que se extendam através de fronteiras internacionais. Os nomes dos países-aparecem na maioria dos mapas, em Inglês, e em linguagem oficial local.

Termos genéricos para características físicas (montanhas, ilhas, cabos, etc.) aparecem também nas suas formas locais, não em Inglês. Pequenos glossários traduzindo estes têrmos mais comuns aparecem nas margens da maioria dos mapas. Há também um glossário completo de todos os termos genéricos. No índice dos atlas, a tradução dos termos genéricos é auxiliada pelo uso de um sistema de símbolos.

A cobertura das regiões do mundo tem sido visando a utilização internacional. O espaço atribuído para cada região reflete seu relativo significado econômico e cultural no cenário mundial, bem como sua população e área. Há um balanço aproximado entre Anglo-América, Europa e Ásia, cada qual com mais de um quinto do total de páginas. África, Oceania e América Latina, juntos, contam com o restante um terço. O mapa índice nas páginas xiii-xv mostra a cobertura do mapa de acordo com a escala.

Um novo aspecto secundário do Atlas, é o planejamento de mapas como componentes de cinco séries separadas. Cada série tem um estilo e conteúdo distinto. Na primeira dessas séries, os continentes são ilustrados em 1:24 000 00 em cores naturais, tal como elas apareceriam a 6.500 km de espaço. A série também inclui mapas dos oceanos em 1:48 000 000 e do mundo em 1:75 000 000.

Na série seguinte, as regiões principais do mundo estão uniformemente ilustradas em 1:12 000 000 (120 km por cm). Estes mapas são principalmente políticos no estilo e conteúdo. A terceira série virtualmente, cobre toda a área habitada da terra em 1:6 000 000 (60 km por cm) para as regiões menos densas, ou 1:3 000 000 (47 km por cm) para Europa, maioria da América do Norte, e a mais densa porção do Sul e Leste da Ásia. É dado ênfase de igual valor aos detalhes físicos e culturais nesta série.

Na quarta série, a escala de 1:1 000 000 (10 km por cm) tem sido usada para ilustrar regiões chaves em cada continente, selecionado pela sua excepcional importância, alta densidade populacional ou complexidade de desenvolvimento. A ênfase está no detalhe cultural, apesar de relêvo sombreado também aparecer. A série final mapeia as principais áreas urbanas mundiais em 1:300 000 (3 km por cm). Esta série enfatiza padrões complexos característicos de grandes áreas urbanas, omitindo a ilustração do relêvo.

Cada série de mapas é completa em um determinado senso. As três primeiras são territorialmente completas, exceto as poucas áreas remotas, e as duas últimas são também completas para as regiões mais densamente habitadas da terra.

A sequência de mapas no Atlas começa com a série de mapas do mundo, continentes e oceanos. Em seguida, estão as três séries de mapas regionais, arranjados dentro de regiões principais de escala mínima (1:12 000 000) para escala máxima (1:1 000 000). As séries de mapas metropolitanos (1:300 000) têm sido mantidas juntas em uma secção seguindo os mapas regionais.

As apresentações individuais dos mapas têm sido normalmente planejadas para ilustrar regiões geográficas e econômicas em vez de países individuais. Portanto, existem mapas da Península Ibérica e do Sudeste Europeu, mas não existem mapas separados para Portugal ou Romênia. Em alguns casos, foi necessária a omissão de pequena porção de uma região ou país, descrito no título do mapa. Têm sido evitados os mapas embutidos, apesar de terem sido feitas exceções para ilustrar algumas ilhas ou grupos de ilhas isolados.

Os símbolos dos mapas usados para as características dadas (legendas para mapas, páginas x-xii) são geralmente semelhantes em todas as escalas dos mapas, apesar de serem reduzidos em tamanho nas escalas menores. Os símbolos mais usados foram dispostos na página xi.

Nenhum aspecto de apresentação de mapas, mostrou-se mais dramático recentemente, do que a reprodução cartográfica do relêvo. Os editores acreditam que o método mais efetivo para representá-lo é a reprodução vista do alto ou a técnica do sombreamento das colinas, que usa variações de tonalidades claras para escuras, para indicar o declive e a forma dos aspectos dos relêvos, por meio de ilustrações. Este Atlas usa relêvo sombreado em todas as cinco séries de mapas, com exceção de uma. Nos mapas de 1:6 000 000 e 1:3 000 000, aparece em combinação com variações de cores das altitudes, que mostram variações em elevação por meio de reflexão da luz, matiz e intensidade.

Na porção conclusiva do Atlas, estão várias tabelas e sumários para referências gerais. Em seguida, está um glossário completo de termos geográficos (páginas 289-295). A tabela de informação mundial (páginas 296-299). Registra a área, população e "status" político para cada unidade política principal. As maiores áreas metropolitanas do mundo, estão relacionadas na página 300. É seguido por uma lista completa das principais cidades do mundo, com as respectivas populações (páginas 301-316). Finalmente, o índice dá referências para a localização do mapa—página do mapa, latitude e longitude—com mais de 160 000 nomes.

SUMMARY OF CONTENTS

ADVISERS, CONTRIBUTORS, EDITORS AND STAFF ii
FOREWORD iii
SUMMARY OF CONTENTS vi
LIST OF MAPS vi–vii
LEGEND TO MAPS x–xii
WORLD AND REGIONAL INDEX MAPS xiii–xv
SELECTED MAP REFERENCES xvi
WORLD SCENE xvii–xl
MAPS (see *List of Maps,* vi–vii) 1–288
World, Ocean, and Continent Maps 1–19
Regional Maps 20–258
Metropolitan Area Maps 259–288
GLOSSARY AND ABBREVIATIONS OF GEOGRAPHICAL TERMS 289–295
WORLD INFORMATION TABLE 296–299
METROPOLITAN AREAS TABLE 300
POPULATIONS OF CITIES AND TOWNS 301–316
INDEX 317

INHALTSVERZEICHNIS

BERATER, MITARBEITER, HERAUSGEBER UND REDAKTION ii
VORWORT iii–iv
INHALTSVERZEICHNIS vi
KARTENVERZEICHNIS vii
ZEICHENERKLÄRUNG x–xii
WELT- UND REGIONALE INDEXKARTEN xiii–xv
REGISTER WICHTIGER GEOGRAPHISCHER NAMEN xvi
WELT-PANORAMA xvii–xl
KARTEN (siehe *Kartenverzeichnis,* vii) 1–288
Weltkarten, Karten der Ozeane und Erdteile 1–19
Regionalkarten 20–258
Karten von Stadtregionen 259–288
VERZEICHNIS UND ABKÜRZUNGEN GEOGRAPHISCHER BEGRIFFE 289–295
WELT-INFORMATIONSTABELLE 296–299
TABELLE DER STADTREGIONEN 300
EINWOHNERZAHLEN VON GROSS-STÄDTEN 301–316
REGISTER 317

SUMARIO DEL CONTENIDO

ASESORES, COLABORADORES, REDACTORES Y AYUDANTES ii
PREFACIO iv
SUMARIO DEL CONTENIDO vi
LISTA DE MAPAS vii–viii
LEYENDAS PARA MAPAS x–xii
INDICE DE LOS MAPAS DEL MUNDO Y REGIONALES xiii–xv
SELECCIONES DE REFERENCIAS DE LOS MAPAS xvi
PERSPECTIVA DEL MUNDO xvii–xl
MAPAS (véase *Lista de Mapas,* vii–viii) 1–288
Mapas del Mundo, Océanos y Continentes 1–19
Mapas Regionales 20–258
Mapas de las Áreas Metropolitanas 259–288
GLOSARIO Y ABREVIACIONES DE TÉRMINOS GEOGRÁFICOS 289–295
TABLA DE INFORMACIÓN MUNDIAL 296–299
TABLA DE LAS ÁREAS METROPOLITANAS 300
HABITANTES EN LAS CIUDADES Y POBLACIONES 301–316
INDICE 317

TABLE DES MATIÈRES

CONSEILLERS, COLLABORATEURS, RÉDACTEURS ET PERSONNEL ii
AVANT-PROPOS iv–v
TABLE DES MATIÈRES vi
LISTE DES CARTES viii–ix
LÉGENDE DES CARTES x–xii
INDEX DES CARTES DU MONDE ET DES CARTES RÉGIONALES xiii–xv
INDEX CARTOGRAPHIQUE ABRÉGÉ xvi
LE MONDE AUJOURD'HUI xvii–xl
CARTES (voir *Liste des Cartes,* viii–ix) 1–288
Cartes du Monde, des Océans et des Continents 1–19
Cartes Régionales 20–258
Cartes des Zones Métropolitaines 259–288
GLOSSAIRE ET ABRÉVIATIONS DE TERMES GÉOGRAPHIQUES 289–295
TABLE D'INFORMATIONS MONDIALES 296–299
TABLE DES ZONES MÉTROPOLITAINES 300
POPULATION DES GRANDS CENTRES ET DES VILLES 301–316
INDEX 317

SUMÁRIO

EDITORES, ASSESSORES E COLABORADORES ii
PREFÁCIO v
SUMÁRIO vi
LISTA DE MAPAS ix
LEGENDAS DOS MAPAS x–xii
ÍNDICE DES MAPAS DO MUNDO E REGIONAIS xiii–xv
REFERÊNCIAS A MAPAS SELECIONADAS xvi
PERSPECTIVA DO MUNDO xvii–xl
MAPAS (ver a *Lista de Mapas,* ix) 1–288
Mapas do mundo, dos oceanos e dos continentes 1–19
Mapas regionais 20–258
Mapas das áreas metropolitanas 259–288
GLOSSÁRIO E ABREVIAÇÕES DE TERMOS GEOGRÁFICOS 289–295
TABELA DE INFORMAÇÕES MUNDIAIS 296–299
TABELA DAS ÁREAS METROPOLITANAS 300
POPULAÇAÕ DOS CENTROS URBANOS 301–316
ÍNDICE 317

List of Maps

WORLD, OCEAN and CONTINENT MAPS

* Introduction 1
1:75 World: Political 2–3
1:75 World: Physical 4–5
1:48 Pacific and Indian Oceans 6–7
1:48 Atlantic Ocean 8
1:24 Antarctica 9
1:24 Europe and Africa 10–11
1:24 Asia 12–13
1:24 Australia and Oceania 14–15
1:24 North America 16–17
1:24 South America 18–19

REGIONAL MAPS

Introduction 20–21

Eurasia

1:12 Europe 22–23
1:6 Northern Europe 24–25
1:3 Southern Scandinavia 26–27
1:3 British Isles 28–29
1:3 Central Europe 30–31
1:3 France and the Alps 32–33
1:3 Spain and Portugal 34–35
1:3 Italy 36–37
1:3 Southeastern Europe 38–39
1:1 Stockholm - Karlstad 40
1:1 København - Malmö - Kiel 41
1:1 London - Birmingham - Cardiff 42–43
1:1 Dublin - Manchester - Newcastle upon Tyne 44–45
1:1 Glasgow - Edinburgh - Aberdeen 46–47
1:1 Dublin - Belfast - Cork 48–49
1:1 Paris - London - Bruxelles 50–51
1:1 Amsterdam - Düsseldorf - Hamburg 52–53
1:1 Berlin - Hamburg - Praha 54–55
1:1 Bruxelles - Frankfurt - Stuttgart 56–57
1:1 Zürich - Genève - Strasbourg 58–59
1:1 Nürnberg - München 60
1:3 Wien - Brno - Linz 61
1:1 Lyon - Marseille - Milano 62–63
1:1 München - Venezia - Firenze 64–65
1:1 Roma - Firenze - Napoli 66–67
1:1 Napoli - Messina - Bari 68–69
1:1 Palermo - Catania - Messina 70
1:1 Cagliari - Sassari 71
1:12 Northwest Asia 72–73
1:12 Northeast Asia 74–75
1:3 Baltic and Moscow Regions 76–77
1:3 Ukraine 78–79
1:3 Volga Region 80–81
1:1 Moskva - Tula - Tver' 82
1:1 Doneck - Lugansk - Rostov 83
1:3 Caucasus and Transcaucasia 84
1:3 Tashkent Region 85
1:6 Central Russia and Kazakhstan 86–87
1:6 Lake Baikal Region 88
1:6 Far Eastern Russia 89
1:12 China, Japan and Korea 90–91
1:3 Japan 92–93
1:1 Tōkyō - Nagoya - Kyōto 94–95
1:1 Ōsaka - Hiroshima - Fukuoka 96–97
1:3 Northeast China and Korea 98–99
1:3 East and Southeast China 100–101
1:6 Interior China 102–103
1:1 Shenyang -Fushun (Mukden - Fushun) 104
1:1 Beijing - Tianjin (Peking - Tientsin) 105
1:1 Shanghai - Nanjing (Shanghai - Nanking) 106
1:1 Chongqing - Chengdu (Chungking - Chengtu) 107
1:6 Southeast Asia 108–109
1:6 Burma, Thailand and Indochina 110–111
1:6 Malaysia and Western Indonesia 112–113
1:3 Malaya, Singapore and Northern Sumatra 114
1:3 Java • Lesser Sunda Islands 115
1:3 Philippines 116–117
1:12 India, Pakistan and Southwest Asia 118–119
1:6 Northern India and Pakistan 120–121
1:6 Southern India and Sri Lanka 122
1:3 Punjab and Kashmir 123
1:3 Ganges Lowland and Nepal 124–125
1:1 Calcutta - Dhaka - Jamshedpur 126–127
1:6 The Middle East 128–129
1:3 Turkey and Cyprus 130–131
1:1 Yerushalayim - Dimashq (Jerusalem - Damascus) 132–133

Africa

1:12 Western North Africa 134–135
1:12 Eastern North Africa 136–137
1:12 Southern Africa 138–139
1:6 Egypt and Sudan 140–141
1:1 Al-Qāhirah - As-Suways (Cairo - Suez) 142–143
1:6 Ethiopia, Somalia and Yemen 144–145
1:6 Libya and Chad 146–147
1:6 Northwestern Africa 148–149
1:6 West Africa 150–151
1:6 Western Congo Basin 152–153
1:6 East Africa and Eastern Congo Basin 154–155
1:6 Southern Africa and Madagascar 156–157
1:3 South Africa 158–159

Australia/Oceania

1:12 Australia 160–161
1:6 Western and Central Australia 162–163
1:6 Northern Australia and New Guinea 164–165
1:6 Eastern Australia 166–167
1:1 Perth • Adelaide 168
1:1 Melbourne - Geelong - Ballarat 169
1:1 Sydney - Newcastle 170
1:1 Brisbane • Canberra 171
1:3 New Zealand 172–173
Various Scales
Islands of the Pacific 174–175

Anglo America

1:12 Canada 176–177
1:12 United States 178–179
1:6 Alaska and Yukon 180–181
1:6 Southwestern Canada 182–183
1:6 South-Central Canada 184–185
1:6 Southeastern Canada 186–187
1:3 Northeastern United States 188–189
1:6 Great Lakes Region 190–191
1:6 Southeastern United States 192–193
1:6 Mississippi Valley 194–195
1:6 Southern Great Plains 196–197
1:6 Northern Great Plains 198–199
1:6 Southern Rocky Mountains 200–201
1:6 Northwestern United States 202–203
1:6 California and Nevada 204–205
1:1 Montréal - Québec 206
1:1 Boston - New York - Albany 207
1:1 New York - Philadelphia - Washington - Norfolk 208–209
1:1 New York - Buffalo 210–211
1:1 Toronto - Ottawa 212–213
1:1 Pittsburgh - Cleveland - Detroit 214–215
1:1 Chicago - Detroit - Milwaukee 216–217
1:1 Indianapolis - Cincinnati - Louisville 218
1:1 St. Louis - Springfield 219
1:1 Miami - Tampa - Orlando 220–221
1:1 Houston - Dallas - Austin 222–223
1:1 Vancouver - Seattle - Portland 224–225
1:1 San Francisco - Reno - Bakersfield 226–227
1:1 Los Angeles - San Diego 228
Various Scales
Hawaii 229

Latin America

1:12 Middle America 230–231
1:6 Mexico 232–233
1:3 Central Mexico 234–235
1:3 Central America 236–237
1:6 Caribbean Region 238–239
Various Scales
Islands of the West Indies 240–241
1:12 Northern South America 242–243
1:12 Southern South America 244–245
1:6 Colombia, Ecuador, Venezuela and Guyana 246–247
1:6 Peru, Bolivia and Western Brazil 248–249
1:6 Northeastern Brazil 250–251
1:6 Central Argentina and Chile 252–253
1:6 Southern Argentina and Chile 254
1:6 Southeastern Brazil 255
1:1 Rio de Janeiro - São Paulo 256–257
1:1 Buenos Aires - Montevideo 258

METROPOLITAN AREA MAPS (1:300,000)

Introduction 259
London 260
Paris 261
Manchester - Liverpool 262
Ruhr Area 263
Berlin • Wien • Budapest 264
Sankt Peterburg • Moskva 265
Madrid • Milano • Lisboa • Barcelona 266
Roma • Athínai • İstanbul • Tehrān 267
Tōkyō - Yokohama 268

*Scale in millions

Krung Thep (Bangkok) • Thanh Pho Ho Chi Minh (Saigon) • Jakarta • Shanghai • T'aipei • Manila 269
Ōsaka - Kōbe - Kyōto 270
Beijing (Peking) • Sŏul • Singapore • Hong Kong 271
Delhi • Bombay • Calcutta 272
Lagos • Kinshasa - Brazzaville • Al-Qāhirah (Cairo) • Johannesburg 273
Sydney • Melbourne 274
Montréal • Toronto 275
New York 276–277
Chicago 278
Cleveland • Pittsburgh 279
Los Angeles 280
Detroit - Windsor 281
San Francisco - Oakland - San Jose 282
Boston 283
Buffalo - Niagara Falls • Baltimore • Washington 284
Philadelphia 285
Ciudad de México • La Habana • Caracas • Lima • Santiago 286
Rio de Janeiro • São Paulo 287
Buenos Aires 288

Kartenverzeichnis

WELTKARTEN, KARTEN DER OZEANE UND ERDTEILE

* Einleitung 1
1:75 Erde: Politisch 2–3
1:75 Erde: Physisch 4–5
1:48 Pazifischer und Indischer Ozean 6–7
1:48 Atlantischer Ozean 8
1:24 Antarktis 9
1:24 Europa und Afrika 10–11
1:24 Asien 12–13
1:24 Australien und Ozeanien 14–15
1:24 Nordamerika 16–17
1:24 Südamerika 18–19

REGIONALKARTEN

Einleitung 20–21

Eurasien

1:12 Europa 22–23
1:6 Nordeuropa 24–25
1:3 Südskandinavien 26–27
1:3 Britische Inseln 28–29
1:3 Mitteleuropa 30–31
1:3 Frankreich und die Alpen 32–33
1:3 Spanien und Portugal 34–35
1:3 Italien 36–37
1:3 Südosteuropa 38–39
1:1 Stockholm - Karlstad 40
1:1 København - Malmö - Kiel 41
1:1 London - Birmingham - Cardiff 42–43
1:1 Dublin - Manchester - Newcastle upon Tyne 44–45
1:1 Glasgow - Edinburgh - Aberdeen 46–47
1:1 Dublin - Belfast - Cork 48–49
1:1 Paris - London - Bruxelles 50–51
1:1 Amsterdam - Düsseldorf - Hamburg 52–53
1:1 Berlin - Hamburg - Praha 54–55
1:1 Bruxelles - Frankfurt - Stuttgart 56–57
1:1 Zürich - Genève - Strasbourg 58–59
1:1 Nürnberg - München 60
1:3 Wien - Brno - Linz 61
1:1 Lyon - Marseille - Milano 62–63
1:1 München - Venezia - Firenze 64–65
1:1 Roma - Firenze - Napoli 66–67
1:1 Napoli - Messina - Bari 68–69
1:1 Palermo - Catania - Messina 70
1:1 Cagliari - Sassari 71
1:12 Nordwestasien 72–73
1:12 Nordostasien 74–75
1:3 Baltenland und Mittelrussland 76–77
1:3 Ukraine 78–79
1:3 Wolgagebiet 80–81
1:1 Moskva - Tula - Tver' 82
1:1 Doneck - Lugansk - Rostov 83
1:3 Kaukasus und Transkaukasien 84
1:3 Taschkentgebiet 85
1:6 Mittelrussland und Kasachstan 86–87
1:6 Baikalseegebiet 88
1:6 Russlands Ferne Osten 89
1:12 China, Japan und Korea 90–91
1:3 Japan 92–93
1:1 Tōkyō - Nagoya - Kyōto 94–95
1:1 Ōsaka - Hiroshima - Fukuoka 96–97
1:3 Nordostchina und Korea 98–99
1:3 Ost- und Südostchina 100–101
1:6 Innerchina 102–103
1:1 Shenyang -Fushun (Mukden - Fushun) 104
1:1 Beijing - Tianjin (Peking - Tientsin) 105
1:1 Shanghai - Nanjing (Shanghai - Nanking) 106
1:1 Chongqing - Chengdu (Chungking - Chengtu) 107
1:6 Südostasien 108–109
1:6 Burma, Thailand und Indochina 110–111
1:6 Malaysia und westliches Indonesien 112–113
1:3 Malaya, Singapur und Nordsumatra 114
1:3 Java • Kleine Sundainseln 115
1:3 Philippinen 116–117
1:12 Indien, Pakistan und Südwestasien 118–119
1:6 Nordindien und Pakistan 120–121
1:6 Südindien und Sri Lanka 122
1:3 Pandschab und Kaschmir 123
1:3 Gangestiefland und Nepal 124–125
1:1 Calcutta - Dhaka - Jamshedpur 126–127
1:6 Vorderasien 128–129
1:3 Türkei und Zypern 130–131
1:1 Yerushalayim - Dimashq (Jerusalem - Damascus) 132–133

Afrika

1:12 West Nordafrika 134–135
1:12 Ost Nordafrika 136–137
1:12 Südafrika 138–139
1:6 Ägypten und Sudan 140–141
1:1 Al-Qāhirah - As-Suways (Cairo - Suez) 142–143
1:6 Äthiopien, Somalia und Jemen 144–145
1:6 Libyen und Tschad 146–147
1:6 Nordwestafrika 148–149
1:6 Westafrika 150–151
1:6 Westliches Kongobecken 152–153
1:6 Ostafrika und Östliches Kongobecken 154–155
1:6 Südafrika und Madagaskar 156–157
1:3 Republik Südafrika 158–159

Australien/Ozeanien

1:12 Australien 160–161
1:6 West-und Mittelaustralien 162–163
1:6 Nordaustralien und Neuguinea 164–165
1:6 Ostaustralien 166–167
1:1 Perth • Adelaide 168
1:1 Melbourne - Geelong - Ballarat 169
1:1 Sydney - Newcastle 170
1:1 Brisbane • Canberra 171
1:3 Neuseeland 172-173
verschiedene Massstäbe
Pazifische Inseln 174–175

Anglo-Amerika

1:12 Kanada 176–177
1:12 Vereinigte Staaten 178–179
1:6 Alaska und Yukon 180–181
1:6 Südwestkanada 182–183
1:6 Südliches Mittelkanada 184–185
1:6 Südostkanada 186–187
1:3 Nordöstliche Vereinigte Staaten 188–189
1:6 Grosse Seen-Region 190–191
1:6 Südöstliche Vereinigte Staaten 192–193
1:6 Mississippi-Tiefland 194–195
1:6 Südliche Grosse Ebenen 196–197
1:6 Nördliche Grosse Ebenen 198–199
1:6 Südliches Felsengebirge 200–201
1:6 Nordwestliche Vereinigte Staaten 202–203
1:6 Kalifornien und Nevada 204–205
1:1 Montréal - Québec 206
1:1 Boston - New York - Albany 207
1:1 New York - Philadelphia - Washington - Norfolk 208–209
1:1 New York - Buffalo 210–211
1:1 Toronto - Ottawa 212–213
1:1 Pittsburgh - Cleveland - Detroit 214–215
1:1 Chicago - Detroit - Milwaukee 216–217
1:1 Indianapolis - Cincinnati - Louisville 218
1:1 St. Louis - Springfield 219
1:1 Miami - Tampa - Orlando 220–221
1:1 Houston - Dallas - Austin 222–223
1:1 Vancouver - Seattle - Portland 224–225
1:1 San Francisco - Reno - Bakersfield 226–227
1:1 Los Angeles - San Diego 228
verschiedene Massstäbe
Hawaii 229

Latein-Amerika

1:12 Mittelamerika 230–231
1:6 Mexiko 232–233
1:3 Mittelmexiko 234–235
1:3 Zentralamerika 236–237
1:6 Mittelamerikanische Inselwelt 238–239
verschiedene Massstäbe
Westindische Inseln 240–241
1:12 Südamerika, nördlicher Teil 242–243
1:12 Südamerika, südlicher Teil 244–245
1:6 Kolumbien, Ecuador, Venezuela und Guayana 246–247
1:6 Peru, Bolivien und westliches Brasilien 248–249
1:6 Nordostbrasilien 250–251
1:6 Mittelargentinien und Mittelchile 252–253
1:6 Südliches Argentinien und südliches Chile 254
1:6 Südostbrasilien 255
1:1 Rio de Janeiro - São Paulo 256–257
1:1 Buenos Aires - Montevideo 258

KARTEN VON STRADTREGIONEN (1:300 000)

Einleitung 259
London 260
Paris 261
Manchester - Liverpool 262
Ruhr Area 263
Berlin • Wien • Budapest 264
Sankt Peterburg • Moskva 265
Madrid • Milano • Lisboa • Barcelona 266
Roma • Athínai • İstanbul • Tehrān 267
Tōkyō - Yokohama 268
Krung Thep (Bangkok) • Thanh Pho Ho Chi Minh (Saigon) • Jakarta • Shanghai • T'aipei • Manila 269
Ōsaka - Kōbe - Kyōto 270
Beijing (Peking) • Sŏul • Singapore • Hong Kong 271
Delhi • Bombay • Calcutta 272
Lagos • Kinshasa - Brazzaville • Al-Qāhirah (Cairo) • Johannesburg 273
Sydney • Melbourne 274
Montréal • Toronto 275
New York 276–277
Chicago 278
Cleveland • Pittsburgh 279
Los Angeles 280
Detroit - Windsor 281
San Francisco - Oakland - San Jose 282
Boston 283
Buffalo - Niagara Falls • Baltimore • Washington 284
Philadelphia 285
Ciudad de México • La Habana • Caracas • Lima • Santiago 286
Rio de Janeiro • São Paulo 287
Buenos Aires 288

* Massstab in Millionen

Lista de Mapas

MAPAS DEL MUNDO, OCÉANOS Y CONTINENTES

* Introducción 1
1:75 Mundo: Político 2–3
1:75 Mundo: Físico 4–-5
1:48 Océanos Pacífico e Indico 6–7
1:48 Océano Atlántico 8
1:24 Antártida 9
1:24 Europa y África 10–11
1:24 Asia 12–13
1:24 Australia y Oceanía 14–15
1:24 América del Norte 16–17
1:24 América del Sur 18–19

MAPAS REGIONALES

Introducción 20–21

Eurasia

1:12 Europa 22–23
1:6 Europe Septentrional 24–25
1:3 Escandinavia Meridional 26–27
1:3 Islas Británicas 28–29
1:3 Europa Central 30–31
1:3 Francia y los Alpes 32–33
1:3 España y Portugal 34–35
1:3 Italia 36–37
1:3 Europa Sud-oriental 38–39
1:1 Stockholm - Karlstad 40
1:1 København - Malmö - Kiel 41
1:1 London - Birmingham - Cardiff 42–43
1:1 Dublin - Manchester - Newcastle upon Tyne 44–45
1:1 Glasgow - Edinburgh - Aberdeen 46–47
1:1 Dublin - Belfast - Cork 48–49
1:1 Paris - London - Bruxelles 50–51
1:1 Amsterdam - Düsseldorf - Hamburg 52–53
1:1 Berlin - Hamburg - Praha 54–55
1:1 Bruxelles - Frankfurt - Stuttgart 56–57
1:1 Zürich - Genève - Strasbourg 58–59
1:1 Nürnberg - München 60
1:3 Wien - Brno - Linz 61
1:1 Lyon - Marseille - Milano 62–63
1:1 München - Venezia - Firenze 64–65
1:1 Roma - Firenze - Napoli 66–67
1:1 Napoli - Messina - Bari 68–69
1:1 Palermo - Catania - Messina 70
1:1 Cagliari - Sassari 71
1:12 Asia Nor-occidental 72–73
1:12 Asia Nor-oriental 74–75
1:3 Regiones de Báltico y de Moscú 76–77
1:3 Ucrania 78–79
1:3 Región del Volga 80–81
1:1 Moskva - Tula - Tver' 82
1:1 Doneck - Lugansk - Rostov 83
1:3 Cáucaso y Transcaucasia 84
1:3 Región de Tachkent 85
1:6 Rusia Central e Kazajstan 86–87
1:6 Región del Lago Baikal 88

*Escala en millones

1:6 Extremo Oriente Ruso 89
1:12 China, Japón y Corea 90–91
1:3 Japón 92–93
1:1 Tōkyō - Nagoya - Kyōto 94–95
1:1 Ōsaka - Hiroshima - Fukuoka 96–97
1:3 China Nor-oriental y Corea 98–99
1:3 Este y Sudeste de la China 100–101
1:6 China Interior 102–103
1:1 Shenyang -Fushun (Mukden - Fushun) 104
1:1 Beijing - Tianjin (Peking - Tientsin) 105
1:1 Shanghai - Nanjing (Shanghai - Nanking) 106
1:1 Chongqing - Chengdu (Chungking - Chengtu) 107
1:6 Asia Sud-oriental 108–109
1:6 Birmania, Siam e Indochina 110–111
1:6 Malasia e Indonesia Occidental 112–113
1:3 Malaya, Singapur y Sumatra Septentrional 114
1:3 Java • Islas Menores de la Sonda 115
1:3 Filipinas 116–117
1:12 India, Pakistán y Asia Sud-occidental 118–119
1:6 India Septentrional y Pakistán 120–121
1:6 India Meridional y Sri Lanka 122
1:3 Punjab y Cachemira 123
1:3 Llanuras del Ganges y Nepal 124–125
1:1 Calcutta - Dhaka - Jamshedpur 126–127
1:6 El Medio Oriente 128–129
1:3 Turquía y Chipre 130–131
1:1 Yerushalayim - Dimashq (Jerusalem - Damascus) 132–133

África

1:12 Región Occidental de Africa Septentrional 134–135
1:12 Región Oriental de Africa Septentrional 136–137
1:12 África Meridional 138–139
1:6 Egipto y Sudán 140–141
1:1 Al-Qāhirah - As-Suways (Cairo - Suez) 142–143
1:6 Etiopía, Somalía y Yemen 144–145
1:6 Libia y el Chad 146–147
1:6 África Nor-occidental 148–149
1:6 África Occidental 150–151
1:6 Cuenca Occidental del Congo 152–153
1:6 África Oriental y Cuenca Oriental del Congo 154–155
1:6 África Meridional y Madagascar 156–157
1:3 Sudáfrica 158–159

Australia/Oceanía

1:12 Australia 160–161
1:6 Australia Centro-occidental 162–163
1:6 Australia Septentrional y Nueva Guinea 164–165
1:6 Australia Oriental 166–167
1:1 Perth • Adelaide 168
1:1 Melbourne - Geelong - Ballarat 169
1:1 Sydney - Newcastle 170
1:1 Brisbane • Canberra 171
1:3 Nueva Zelanda 172-173
Varias Escalas
Islas del Pacífico 174–175

América Anglosajona

1:12 Canadá 176–177
1:12 Estados Unidos 178–179
1:6 Alaska y Yukón 180–181
1:6 Canadá Sud-occidental 182–183
1:6 Centro Meridional del Canadá 184–185
1:6 Canadá Sud-oriental 186–187
1:3 Nor-este de los Estados Unidos 188–189
1:6 Región de los Grandes Lagos 190–191
1:6 Sud-este de los Estados Unidos 192–193
1:6 Valle del Misisipí 194–195
1:6 Grandes Llanos: zona meridional 196–197
1:6 Grandes Llanos: zona septentrional 198–199
1:6 Montañas Rocosas: zona meridional 200–201
1:6 Nor-oeste de los Estados Unidos 202–203
1:6 California y Nevada 204–205
1:1 Montréal - Québec 206
1:1 Boston - New York - Albany 207
1:1 New York - Philadelphia - Washington - Norfolk 208–209
1:1 New York - Buffalo 210–211
1:1 Toronto - Ottawa 212–213
1:1 Pittsburgh - Cleveland - Detroit 214–215
1:1 Chicago - Detroit - Milwaukee 216–217
1:1 Indianapolis - Cincinnati - Louisville 218
1:1 St. Louis - Springfield 219
1:1 Miami - Tampa - Orlando 220–221
1:1 Houston - Dallas - Austin 222–223
1:1 Vancouver - Seattle - Portland 224–225
1:1 San Francisco - Reno - Bakersfield 226–227
1:1 Los Angeles - San Diego 228
Varias Escalas
Hawaii 229

América Latina

1:12 México, Centroamérica y Las Antillas 230–231
1:6 México 232–233
1:3 México Central 234–235
1:3 América Central 236–237
1:6 Región del Caribe 238–239
Varias Escalas
Islas de las Antillas 240–241
1:12 América del Sur: zona septentrional 242–243
1:12 América del Sur: zona meridional 244–245
1:6 Colombia, Ecuador, Venezuela y Guyana 246–247
1:6 Perú, Bolivia y Brasil Occidental 248–249
1:6 Brasil Nor-oriental 250–251
1:6 Argentina y Chile: zonas centrales 252–253
1:6 Argentina y Chile: zonas meridionales 254
1:6 Brazil Sud-oriental 255
1:1 Rio de Janeiro - São Paulo 256–257
1:1 Buenos Aires - Montevideo 258

MAPAS DE LAS ÁREAS METROPOLITANAS (1:300 000)

Introducción 259
London 260
Paris 261
Manchester - Liverpool 262
Ruhr Area 263
Berlin • Wien • Budapest 264
Sankt Peterburg • Moskva 265
Madrid • Milano • Lisboa • Barcelona 266
Roma • Athínai • İstanbul • Tehrān 267
Tōkyō - Yokohama 268
Krung Thep (Bangkok) • Thanh Pho Ho Chi Minh (Saigon) • Jakarta • Shanghai • T'aipei • Manila 269
Ōsaka - Kōbe - Kyōto 270
Beijing (Peking) • Sŏul • Singapore • Hong Kong 271
Delhi • Bombay • Calcutta 272
Lagos • Kinshasa - Brazzaville • Al-Qāhirah (Cairo) • Johannesburg 273
Sydney • Melbourne 274
Montréal • Toronto 275
New York 276–277
Chicago 278
Cleveland • Pittsburgh 279
Los Angeles 280
Detroit - Windsor 281
San Francisco - Oakland - San Jose 282
Boston 283
Buffalo - Niagara Falls • Baltimore • Washington 284
Philadelphia 285
Ciudad de México • La Habana • Caracas • Lima • Santiago 286
Rio de Janeiro • São Paulo 287
Buenos Aires 288

*Escala en millones

Liste des Cartes

CARTES DU MONDE, DES OCÉANS ET DES CONTINENTS

* Introduction 1
1:75 Monde: Politique 2–3
1:75 Monde: Physique 4–5
1:48 Océans Pacifique et Indien 6–7
1:48 Océan Atlantique 8
1:24 Antarctique 9
1:24 Europe et Afrique 10–11
1:24 Asie 12–13
1:24 Australie et Océanie 14–15
1:24 Amérique du Nord 16–17
1:24 Amérique du Sud 18–19

CARTES RÉGIONALES

Introduction 20–21

Eurasie

1:12 Europe 22–23
1:6 Europe Septentrionale 24–25
1:3 Scandinavie Méridionale 26–27
1:3 Îles Britanniques 28–29
1:3 Europe Centrale 30–31
1:3 France et Alpes 32–33
1:3 Espagne et Portugal 34–35
1:3 Italie 36–37
1:3 Europe du Sud-Est 38–39
1:1 Stockholm Karlstad 40
1:1 København - Malmö - Kiel 41
1:1 London - Birmingham - Cardiff 42–43
1:1 Dublin - Manchester - Newcastle upon Tyne 44–45
1:1 Glasgow - Edinburgh - Aberdeen 46–47
1:1 Dublin - Belfast - Cork 48–49
1:1 Paris - London - Bruxelles 50–51
1:1 Amsterdam - Düsseldorf - Hamburg 52–53
1:1 Berlin - Hamburg - Praha 54–55
1:1 Bruxelles - Frankfurt - Stuttgart 56–57
1:1 Zürich - Genève - Strasbourg 58–59
1:1 Nürnberg - München 60
1:3 Wien - Brno - Linz 61
1:1 Lyon - Marseille - Milano 62–63
1:1 München - Venezia - Firenze 64–65
1:1 Roma - Firenze - Napoli 66–67
1:1 Napoli - Messina - Bari 68–69
1:1 Palermo - Catania - Messina 70
1:1 Cagliari - Sassari 71
1:12 Asie du Nord-Ouest 72–73
1:12 Asie du Nord-Est 74–75
1:3 Républiques Baltes et la Région de Moscou 76–77
1:3 Ukraine 78–79
1:3 Région de la Volga 80–81
1:1 Moskva - Tula - Tver' 82
1:1 Doneck - Lugansk - Rostov 83
1:3 Caucasie et Transcaucasie 84
1:3 Région de Tachkent 85
1:6 Russie Centrale et Kazakhstan 86–87
1:6 Région du Lac Baïkal 88
1:6 Extrême-Orient Russe 89
1:12 Chine, Japon et Corée 90–91
1:3 Japon 92–93
1:1 Tōkyō - Nagoya - Kyōto 94–95
1:1 Ōsaka - Hiroshima - Fukuoka 96–97
1:3 Nord-Est de la Chine et Corée 98–99
1:3 Chine de l'Est et du Sud-Est 100–101
1:6 Chine Intérieure 102–103
1:1 Shenyang -Fushun (Mukden - Fushun) 104
1:1 Beijing - Tianjin (Peking - Tientsin) 105
1:1 Shanghai - Nanjing (Shanghai - Nanking) 106
1:1 Chongqing - Chengdu (Chungking - Chengtu) 107
1:6 Asie du Sud-Est 108–109
1:6 Birmanie, Thaïlande et Indochine 110–111
1:6 Malaisie et Indonésie Occidentale 112–113
1:3 Malaya, Singapour et Sumatra Septentrional 114
1:3 Java • Petites Îles de la Sonde 115
1:3 Philippines 116–117
1:12 Inde, Pakistan et Asie du Sud-Ouest 118–119
1:6 Inde Septentrionale et Pakistan 120–121
1:6 Inde Méridionale et Sri Lanka 122
1:3 Punjab et Cachemire 123
1:3 Plaine du Gange et Népal 124–125
1:1 Calcutta - Dhaka - Jamshedpur 126–127
1:6 Le Moyen-Orient 128–129
1:3 Turquie et Chypre 130–131
1:1 Yerushalayim Dimashq (Jerusalem - Damascus) 132–133

Afrique

1:12 Afrique du Nord Occidentale 134–135
1:12 Afrique du Nord Orientale 136–137
1:12 Afrique Méridionale 138–139
1:6 Égypte et Soudan 140–141
1:1 Al-Qāhirah - As-Suways (Cairo - Suez) 142–143
1:6 Ethiopie, Somalie et Yemen 144–145
1:6 Libye et Tchad 146–147
1:6 Afrique du Nord-Ouest 148–149
1:6 Afrique Occidentale 150–151
1:6 Bassin du Congo, partie Occidentale 152–153
1:6 Afrique Orientale et Bassin du Congo, partie Orientale 154–155
1:6 Afrique Méridionale et Madagascar 156–157
1:3 Afrique du Sud 158–159

Australie/Océanie

1:12 Australie 160–161
1:6 Australie Occidentale et Centrale 162–163
1:6 Australie Septentrionale et Nouvelle Guinée 164–165
1:6 Australie Orientale 166–167
1:1 Perth • Adelaide 168
1:1 Melbourne - Geelong - Ballarat 169
1:1 Sydney - Newcastle 170
1:1 Brisbane • Canberra 171
1:3 Nouvelle Zélande 172–173
Echelles Variées
Îles du Pacifique 174–175

Amérique Anglo-Saxonne

1:12 Canada 176–177
1:12 États-Unis 178–179
1:6 Alaska et Yukon 180–181
1:6 Sud-Ouest du Canada 182–183
1:6 Canada Central, partie Méridionale 184–185
1:6 Sud-Est du Canada 186–187
1:3 Nord-Est des États-Unis 188–189
1:6 Région des Grands Lacs 190–191
1:6 Sud-Est des États-Unis 192–193
1:6 Vallée du Mississippi 194–195
1:6 Grandes Plaines, partie Méridionale 196–197
1:6 Grandes Plaines, partie Septentrionale 198–199
1:6 Montagnes Rocheuses, partie Méridionale 200–201
1:6 Nord-Ouest des États-Unis 202–203
1:6 Californie et Névada 204–205
1:1 Montréal - Québec 206

*Echelle en millions

1:1 Boston - New York - Albany 207
1:1 New York - Philadelphia - Washington - Norfolk 208–209
1:1 New York - Buffalo 210–211
1:1 Toronto - Ottawa 212–213
1:1 Pittsburgh - Cleveland - Detroit 214–215
1:1 Chicago - Detroit - Milwaukee 216–217
1:1 Indianapolis - Cincinnati - Louisville 218
1:1 St. Louis - Springfield 219
1:1 Miami - Tampa - Orlando 220–221
1:1 Houston - Dallas - Austin 222–223
1:1 Vancouver - Seattle - Portland 224–225
1:1 San Francisco - Reno - Bakersfield 226–227
1:1 Los Angeles - San Diego 228
Echelles Variées
Hawaï 229

Amérique Latine

1:12 Mexique, Amérique Centrale et Région des Caraïbes 230 –231
1:6 Mexique 232–233
1:3 Mexique Central 234–235
1:3 Amérique Centrale 236–237
1:6 Région des Caraïbes 238–239
Echelles Variées
Îles des Antilles 240–241
1:12 Amérique du Sud Septentrionale 242–243
1:12 Amérique du Sud Méridionale 244–245
1:6 Colombie, Équateur, Venezuela et Guyane 246–247
1:6 Pérou, Bolivie et Brésil Occidental 248–249
1:6 Nord-Est du Brésil 250–251
1:6 Argentine et Chili, parties Centrales 252–253
1:6 Argentine et Chili, parties Méridionales 254
1:6 Sud-Est du Brésil 255
1:1 Rio de Janeiro - São Paulo 256–257
1:1 Buenos Aires - Montevideo 258

CARTES DES ZONES MÉTROPOLITAINES (1:300 000)

Introduction 259
London 260
Paris 261
Manchester - Liverpool 262
Ruhr Area 263
Berlin • Wien • Budapest 264
Sankt Peterburg • Moskva 265
Madrid • Milano • Lisboa • Barcelona 266
Roma • Athínai • İstanbul • Tehrān 267
Tōkyō - Yokohama 268
Krung Thep (Bangkok) • Thanh Pho Ho Chi Minh (Saigon) • Jakarta • Shanghai • T'aipei • Manila 269
Ōsaka - Kōbe - Kyōto 270
Beijing (Peking) • Sŏul • Singapore • Hong Kong 271
Delhi • Bombay • Calcutta 272
Lagos • Kinshasa - Brazzaville • Al-Qāhirah (Cairo) • Johannesburg 273
Sydney • Melbourne 274
Montréal • Toronto 275
New York 276–277
Chicago 278
Cleveland • Pittsburgh 279
Los Angeles 280
Detroit - Windsor 281
San Francisco - Oakland - San Jose 282
Boston 283
Buffalo - Niagara Falls • Baltimore • Washington 284
Philadelphia 285
Ciudad de México • La Habana • Caracas • Lima • Santiago 286
Rio de Janeiro • São Paulo 287
Buenos Aires 288

* Echelle en millions

Lista de Mapas

MAPAS DO MUNDO, DOS OCEANOS E DOS CONTINENTES

* Introdução 1
1:75 Mundo: Político 2–3
1:75 Mundo: Físico 4–5
1:48 Oceanos Pacífico e Indico 6–7
1:48 Oceano Atlântico 8
1:24 Antártida 9
1:24 Europa e África 10–11
1:24 Ásia 12–13
1:24 Austrália e Oceania 14–15
1:24 América do Norte 16–17
1:24 América do Sul 18–19

MAPAS REGIONAIS

Introdução 20–21

Eurásia

1:12 Europa 22–23
1:6 Europa Setentrional 24–25
1:3 Escandinávia Meridional 26–27
1:3 Ilhas Britânicas 28–29
1:3 Europa Central 30–31
1:3 França e os Alpes 32–33
1:3 Espanha e Portugal 34–35
1:3 Itália 36–37
1:3 Europa Sul-oriental 38–39
1:1 Stockholm - Karlstad 40
1:1 København - Malmö - Kiel 41
1:1 London - Birmingham - Cardiff 42–43
1:1 Dublin - Manchester - Newcastle upon Tyne 44–45
1:1 Glasgow - Edinburgh - Aberdeen 46–47
1:1 Dublin - Belfast - Cork 48–49
1:1 Paris - London - Bruxelles 50–51
1:1 Amsterdam - Düsseldorf - Hamburg 52–53
1:1 Berlin - Hamburg - Praha 54–55
1:1 Bruxelles - Frankfurt - Stuttgart 56–57
1:1 Zürich - Genève - Strasbourg 58–59
1:1 Nürnberg - München 60
1:3 Wien - Brno - Linz 61
1:1 Lyon - Marseille - Milano 62–63
1:1 München - Venezia - Firenze 64–65
1:1 Roma - Firenze - Napoli 66–67
1:1 Napoli - Messina - Bari 68–69
1:1 Palermo - Catania - Messina 70
1:1 Cagliari - Sassari 71
1:12 Ásia do Norte Ocidental 72–73
1:12 Ásia do Norte Oriental 74–75
1:3 Regiões do Báltico e de Moscou 76–77
1:3 Ucrânia 78–79
1:3 Região do Volga 80–81
1:1 Moskva - Tula - Tver' 82
1:1 Doneck - Lugansk - Rostov 83
1:3 Cáucaso e Transcaucásia 84
1:3 Região do Taschkent 85
1:6 Rússia Central e Casaquistão 86–87
1:6 Região do Lago Baikal 88
1:6 Extremo Oriente Russo 89
1:12 China, Japão e Coréia 90–91
1:3 Japão 92–93
1:1 Tōkyō - Nagoya - Kyōto 94–95
1:1 Ōsaka - Hiroshima - Fukuoka 96–97
1:3 Nordeste da China e Coréia 98–99
1:3 Leste e Sudeste da China 100–101
1:6 China Interior 102–103
1:1 Shenyang -Fushun (Mukden - Fushun) 104
1:1 Beijing - Tianjin (Peking - Tientsin) 105
1:1 Shanghai - Nanjing (Shanghai - Nanking) 106
1:1 Chongqing - Chengdu (Chungking - Chengtu) 107
1:6 Sudeste Asiático 108–109
1:6 Birmânia, Tailândia e Indochina 110–111
1:6 Malásia e Indonésia Ocidental 112–113
1:3 Malaia, Cingapura e Sumatra Setentrional 114
1:3 Java • Ilhas Menores da Sonda 115
1:3 Filipinas 116–117
1:12 Índia, Paquistão e Ásia do Sudoeste 118–119
1:6 Índia Setentrional e Paquistão 120–121
1:6 Índia Meridional e Sri Lanka 122
1:3 Punjab e Cachemira 123
1:3 Planície do Ganges e Nepal 124–125
1:1 Calcutta - Dhaka - Jamshedpur 126–127
1:6 Oriente Médio 128–129
1:3 Turquia e Chipre 130–131
1:1 Yerushalayim - Dimashq (Jerusalem - Damascus) 132–133

África

1:12 África do Norte Ocidental 134–135
1:12 África do Norte Oriental 136–137
1:12 África Meridional 138–139
1:6 Egito e Sudão 140–141
1:1 Al-Qāhirah - As-Suways (Cairo - Suez) 142–143
1:6 Etiópia, Somália e Iêmen 144–145
1:6 Líbia e Tchad 146–147
1:6 África Norte-ocidental 148–149
1:6 África Ocidental 150–151
1:6 Bacia Ocidental do Congo 152–153
1:6 África Oriental e Bacia Oriental do Congo 154–155
1:6 África Meridional e Madagascar 156–157
1:3 África do Sul 158–159

Austrália/Oceania

1:12 Austrália 160–161
1:6 Austrália Ocidental e Central 162–163
1:6 Austrália Setentrional e Nova Guiné 164–165
1:6 Austrália Oriental 166–167
1:1 Perth • Adelaide 168
1:1 Melbourne - Geelong - Ballarat 169
1:1 Sydney - Newcastle 170
1:1 Brisbane • Canberra 171
1:3 Nova Zelândia 172–173
Várias Escalas
Ilhas do Pacífico 174–175

América Anglosaxônica

1:12 Canadá 176–177
1:12 Estados Unidos 178–179
1:6 Alasca e Yukon 180–181
1:6 Canadá: Sudoeste 182–183
1:6 Canadá Central, parte meridional 184–185
1:6 Canadá: Sudeste 186–187
1:3 Estados Unidos: Nordeste 188–189
1:6 Região dos Grandes Lagos 190–191
1:6 Estados Unidos: Sudeste 192–193
1:6 Vale do Mississippi 194–195
1:6 Grandes Planícies: zona meridional 196–197
1:6 Grandes Planícies: zona setentrional 198–199
1:6 Montanhas Rochosas: zona meridional 200–201
1:6 Noroeste dos Estados Unidos 202–203
1:6 Califórnia e Nevada 204–205
1:1 Montréal Québec 206
1:1 Boston - New York - Albany 207
1:1 New York - Philadelphia - Washington - Norfolk 208–209
1:1 New York - Buffalo 210–211
1:1 Toronto - Ottawa 212–213
1:1 Pittsburgh - Cleveland - Detroit 214–215
1:1 Chicago - Detroit - Milwaukee 216–217
1:1 Indianapolis - Cincinnati - Louisville 218
1:1 St. Louis - Springfield 219
1:1 Miami - Tampa - Orlando 220–221
1:1 Houston - Dallas - Austin 222–223
1:1 Vancouver - Seattle - Portland 224–225
1:1 San Francisco - Reno - Bakersfield 226–227
1:1 Los Angeles - San Diego 228
Várias Escalas
Havaí 229

América Latina

1:12 México, América Central e Antilhas 230–231
1:6 México 232–233
1:3 México Central 234–235
1:3 América Central 236–237
1:6 Região do Caribe 238–239
Várias Escalas
Ilhas do Caribe (Índias Ocidentais) 240–241
1:12 América do Sul: zona setentrional 242–243
1:12 América do Sul: zona meridional 244–245
1:6 Colômbia, Equador, Venezuela e Guiana 246–247
1:6 Peru, Bolívia e Brasil Ocidental 248–249
1:6 Brasil: Nordeste 250–251
1:6 Argentina e Chile: zonas centrais 252–253
1:6 Argentina e Chile: zonas meridionais 254
1:6 Brasil: Sudeste 255
1:1 Rio de Janeiro - São Paulo 256–257
1:1 Buenos Aires - Montevideo 258

MAPAS DAS ÁREAS METROPOLITANAS (1:300 000)

Introdução 259
London 260
Paris 261
Manchester - Liverpool 262
Ruhr Area 263
Berlin • Wien • Budapest 264
Sankt Peterburg • Moskva 265
Madrid • Milano • Lisboa • Barcelona 266
Roma • Athínai • İstanbul • Tehrān 267
Tōkyō - Yokohama 268
Krung Thep (Bangkok) • Thanh Pho Ho Chi Minh (Saigon) • Jakarta • Shanghai • T'aipei • Manila 69
Ōsaka - Kōbe - Kyōto 270
Beijing (Peking) • Sŏul • Singapore • Hong Kong 271
Delhi • Bombay • Calcutta 272
Lagos • Kinshasa - Brazzaville • Al-Qāhirah (Cairo) • Johannesburg 273
Sydney • Melbourne 274
Montréal • Toronto 275
New York 276–277
Chicago 278
Cleveland • Pittsburgh 279
Los Angeles 280
Detroit - Windsor 281
San Francisco - Oakland - San Jose 282
Boston 283
Buffalo - Niagara Falls • Baltimore • Washington 284
Philadelphia 285
Rio de Janeiro • São Paulo 287
Buenos Aires 288

*Escalas em milhões

Legend to Maps / Zeichenerklärung
Leyendas Para Mapas / Légende des Cartes / Legendas dos Mapas

The design and color of the map symbols are consistent throughout the Regional and Metropolitan Area maps, although the size of the symbol varies with scale. An asterisk marks those symbols which appear only on the 1:300,000 scale maps. Symbols for inhabited localities, boundaries, and capitals are given on page xi.

The symbol → 80-81 in the margin of a map directs the reader to a map of the adjoining area.

A separate legend on page 1 identifies the land and submarine features which appear on the World, Ocean, and Continent maps.

Der Entwurf und die Farbe der Kartensymbole sind einheitlich für alle Regionalkarten und Karten von Stadtregionen, während die Grösse des Symbols sich mit dem Massstab ändert. Ein Stern kennzeichnet diejenigen Symbole, welche nur auf den Karten im Massstab 1:300 000 erscheinen. Symbole für bewohnte Orte, für Grenzen und Hauptstädte sind auf Seite xi angeführt.

Kennzeichen → 80-81 am Rande einer Karte ist ein Hinweis für den Leser, die Karte eines angrenzenden Gebietes nachzuschlagen.

Eine andere Legende auf Seite 1 identifiziert die Land- und untermeerischen Phänomene, die auf den Weltkarten, Karten der Ozeane und Erdteile erscheinen.

El diseño y el color de los símbolos cartográficos son uniformes para todas los mapas regionales y de las áreas metropolitanas, aunque el tamaño del símbolo varía según la escala. Un asterisco distingue los símbolos que aparecen sólo en los mapas a 1:300 000. Los símbolos de lugares poblados, de límites y de capitales se hallan en la página xi.

El símbolo → 80-81 al margen de un mapa dirige al lector a un mapa del área adyacente.

Otra leyenda, en la página 1, identifica la topografía terrestre y submarina que se encuentra en los mapas del Mundo, Océanos y Continentes.

La couleur et la forme des symboles cartographiques des cartes régionales et des cartes des zones métropolitaines sont identiques, bien que la grandeur des signes varie selon l'échelle. Un astérisque accompagne les symboles qui n'apparaissent que sur les cartes au 1:300 000. La légende des signes conventionnels pour les lieux habités, les frontières et les capitales se trouve à la page xi.

Le symbole → 80-81 en marge d'une carte renvoie le lecteur à une carte de la région voisine.

Pour les cartes du monde, des océans et des continents une légende séparée, à la page 1, donne le sens des symboles représentant les paysages continentaux et les formes de relief sous-marin.

A cor e a forma dos símbolos cartográficos dos mapas regionais e das áreas metropolitanas são idênticos, ainda que a dimensão do símbolo varie segundo a escala. Um asterisco distingue os símbolos que só aparecem nos mapas da escala de 1:300 000. As legendas dos símbolos convencionais dos lugares povoados, fronteiras e capitais encontram-se à pág. xi.

O símbolo → 80-81 à margem de um mapa, remete o leitor a um mapa da região vizinha.

Nos mapas do mundo, dos oceanos e dos continentes uma legenda separada, na pág. 1, indica o sentido dos símbolos representativos das paisagens continentais e das formas do relevo submarino.

Hydrographic Features / Hydrographische Objekte / Elementos Hidrográficos / Données Hydrographiques / Acidentes Hidrográficos

Shoreline / Uferlinie
Línea costanera / Trait de côte
Linha costeira

Undefined or Fluctuating Shoreline
Unbestimmte oder Veränderliche Uferlinie
Línea costanera indefinida o fluctuante
Trait de côte indéfini ou fluctuant
Linha costeira indefinida ou flutuante

Amur
River, Stream / Fluss, Strom
Río, Corriente / Rivière, Cours d'eau
Rio, curso d'água

Intermittent Stream / Periodischer Fluss
Corriente intermitente / Cours d'eau périodique
Rio, curso d'água intermitente

SALTO ANGEL
Rapids, Falls / Stromschnellen, Wasserfälle
Rápidos, Cascadas / Rapides, Chutes d'eau
Corredeiras, quedas d'água

764
Depth of Water / Wassertiefe
Profundidad del agua / Profondeur bathymétrique
Profundidade da água

8428
Greatest Depth (Atlantic, Indian, Pacific oceans)
Grösste Tiefe (Atlantischer, Indischer, Pazifischer Ozean)
Profundidad más grande (Océanos Atlántico, Índico, Pacífico)
Profondeur maximum (océans Atlantique, Indien, Pacifique)
Profundidade máxima (oceanos Atlântico, Índico, Pacífico)

Canal du Midi
Navigable Canal / Schiffbarer Kanal
Canal navegable / Canal navigable
Canal navegável

Irrigation or Drainage Canal
Be- oder Entwässerungskanal
Canal de irrigación o desagüe
Canal d'irrigation ou de drainage
Canal de irrigação ou drenagem

Los Angeles Aqueduct
Aqueduct / Aquädukt
Acueducto / Aqueduc
Aqueduto

Pier, Breakwater / Landungsbrücke, Wellenbrecher
Embarcadero, Rompeolas / Jetée, Brise-lames
Cais, Quebra-mar

GREAT BARRIER REEF
Reef / Riff
Arrecife / Récif
Recife

Kumdah
Uninhabited Oasis / Unbewohnte Oase
Oasis deshabitado / Oasis inhabitée
Oásis desabitado

L. Victoria
Lake, Reservoir / See, Stausee
Lago, Embalse / Lac, Réservoir
Lago, reservatório (represa)

Intermittent Lake, Reservoir
Periodischer See, Stausee
Lago o Embalse intermitente
Lac ou Réservoir périodique
Lago, reservatório (represa) intermitente

Tuz Gölü
Salt Lake / Salzsee
Lago salado / Lac salé
Lago salgado

Dry Lake Bed / Trockener Seeboden
Lecho de lago seco / Fond de lac asséché
Leito de lago seco

The Everglades
Swamp / Sumpf
Pantano / Marais
Pântano

RIMO GLACIER
Glacier / Gletscher
Glaciar / Glacier
Geleira

(395)
Lake Surface Elevation
Seehöhe
Elevación del lago
Cote du niveau du lac
Altitude do nível do lago

Topographic Features / Topographische Objekte / Elementos Topográficos / Données Topographiques / Acidentes Topográficos

Matterhorn 4478
Elevation Above Sea Level
Höhe über dem Meeresspiegel
Elevatión sobre del nivel del mar
Cote au-dessus du niveau de la mer
Altitude acima do nível do mar

76
Elevation Below Sea Level
Höhe unter dem Meeresspiegel
Elevación bajo del nivel del mar
Cote au-dessous du niveau de la mer
Altitude abaixo do nível do mar

Mount Cook 3764
Highest Elevation in Country
Höchster Punkt des Landes
Elevación más alta en el país
Cote la plus élevée d'un pays
Altitude mais elevada de um país

133
Lowest Elevation in Country
Tiefster Punkt des Landes
Elevación más baja en el país
Cote la plus basse d'un pays
Altitude mais baixa de um país

(106)
Elevation of City
Höhenangabe einer Stadt
Elevación de ciudad
Altitude d'une ville
Altitude de uma cidade

Khyber Pass 1067
Mountain Pass / Pass
Paso / Col de montagne
Passo (de montanha)

Rock / Fels
Roca / Rocher
Rocha

Lava / Lava
Lava / Lave
Lava

Sand Area / Sandgebiet
Area de arena / Région sableuse, Erg
Região arenosa, Erg

Salt Flat / Salzebene
Salar / Dépression salée
Depressão salgada

Elevations and depths are given in meters
Höhen und Tiefen sind in Metern angegeben
Elevaciones y profundidades se dan en metros
Cotes et profondeurs sont indiquées en mètres
Altitudes e profundidades são apresentadas em metros

ANDES
KUNLUN SHAN
Mountain Range, Plateau, Valley, etc.
Gebirge, Hochebene, Tal, usw.
Sierra, Meseta, Valle, etc.
Chaîne de montagnes, Plateau, Vallée, etc.
Cadeia de montanhas. Planalto, Vale etc.

BAFFIN ISLAND
NUNIVAK ISLAND
Island
Insel
Isla
Île
Ilha

POLUOSTROV KAMČATKA
CABO DE HORNOS
Peninsula, Cape, Point, etc.
Halbinsel, Kap, Landspitze, usw.
Península, Cabo, Punta, etc.
Péninsule, Cap, Pointe, etc.
Península, Cabo, Ponta etc.

Highest Elevation and Lowest Elevation of a continent are underlined
Höchster und tiefster Punkt innerhalb eines Erdteils sind unterstrichen
Elevación más alta y más baja de un continente se subrayan
La cote la plus haute et la cote la plus basse d'un continent sont soulignées
As altitudes mais e menos elevadas de um continente são sublinhadas

Legend to Maps/Zeichenerklärung
Leyendas Para Mapas/Légende des Cartes/Legendas dos Mapas

Inhabited Localities / Bewohnte Orte / Lugares Poblados / Lieux Habités / Lugares Habitados

The symbol represents the number of inhabitants within the locality/Die Signatur entspricht der Einwohnerzahl des Ortes
El símbolo representa el número de habitantes dentro del lugar/Le symbole représente le nombre d'habitants de la localité
O símbolo representa o número de habitantes do lugar

1:300,000 1:1,000,000
1:3,000,000 1:6,000,000

- 0—10,000
- 10,000—25,000
- 25,000—100,000
- 100,000—250,000
- 250,000—1,000,000
- >1,000,000

1:12,000,000

- 0—50,000
- 50,000—100,000
- 100,000—250,000
- 250,000—1,000,000
- >1,000,000

1:24,000,000
1:48,000,000

- 0—100,000
- 100,000—1,500,000
- >1,500,000

The size of type indicates the relative economic and political importance of the locality
Die Schriftgrösse entspricht der relativen wirtschaftlichen und politischen Bedeutung des Ortes
El tamaño del tipo de imprenta indica la relativa importancia económica y política del lugar
La dimension des caractères indique l'importance économique et politique relative d'une localité
A dimensão dos caracteres tipográficos indica a importância econômica e política relativa do lugar

Écommoy Lisieux **Rouen**
Trouville Orléans **PARIS**

Hollywood *Westminster* — Section of a City, Neighborhood/Stadtteil, Nachbarschaft
Sección de una ciudad, Barrio/Arrondissement, Quartier
Seção de uma cidade, Bairro

Northland Center — * Major Shopping Center/Haupteinkaufszentrum/Mercado principal
Centre commercial important/Centro comercial importante

BYRD — Scientific Station/Wissenschaftliche Station/Estación científica
Station scientifique/Estação científica

Bi'r Safājah — Inhabited Oasis/Bewohnte Oase/Oasis habitado
Oasis habitée/Oásis habitado

Kumdah — Uninhabited Oasis/Unbewohnte Oase/Oasis deshabitado
Oasis inhabitée/Oásis desabitado

Urban Area (area of continuous industrial, commercial, and residential development)
Stadtgebiet (ausgedehntes industrie-, Geschäfts- und Wohngebiet)
Zona urbanizada (área de desarrollo industrial, comercial y residencial)
Zone urbanisée (zone d'occupation continue par des industries, des commerces, des habitations)
Zona urbanizada (área de ocupação contínua por indústrias, estabelecimentos comerciais e habitações)

* Major Industrial Area/Hauptindustriegebiet/Zona principal industrial
Région industrielle importante/Zona industrial importante

* Wooded Area/Wald/Área de bosque
Région boisée/Área verde

* Local Park or Recreational Area/Park oder Erholungsgebiet
Parque municipal o área de recreo/Parc municipal ou zone de loisirs
Parque municipal ou área de lazer

Political Boundaries / Politische Grenzen / Límites Políticos / Frontières Politiques / Fronteiras e Limites

International (First-order political unit) /**Staatsgrenze** (Politische Einheit erster Ordnung)
Internacionales (Unidad política de primer orden) /**Internationales** (Entités politiques de premier ordre)
Internacionais (Unidade política de primeiro nível)

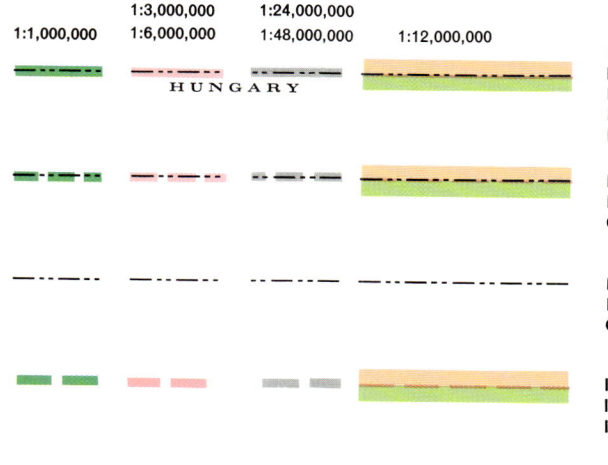

1:1,000,000 | 1:300,000 1:3,000,000 1:6,000,000 | 1:24,000,000 1:48,000,000 | 1:12,000,000

HUNGARY — Demarcated, Undemarcated, and Administrative
Markiert, unmarkiert, verwaltungstechnisch
Demarcado, No demarcado, y Administrativo
Délimitées, Non-délimitées, Administratives
Delimitados, Não delimitados, Administrativos

Disputed de facto/Umstritten de facto
Disputado de hecho/Contestées de facto
Contestados de fato

Disputed de jure/Umstritten de jure
Disputado de derecho/Contestées de jure
Contestados de direito

Indefinite or Undefined/Unklar oder Unbestimmt
Indefinido o No determinado/Imprécises ou Non définies
Imprecisos ou Não definidos

Demarcation Line/Demarkationslinie
Línea de demarcación/Ligne de démarcation
Linha de demarcação

Capitals of Political Units
Hauptstädte politischer Einheiten
Capitales de Unidades Políticas
Capitales d'Entités Politiques
Capitais de Unidades Políticas

BUDAPEST — Independent Nation
Unabhängiger Staat
Nación independiente
État indépendant
Estado independente

Cayenne — Dependency
(Colony, protectorate, etc.)
Abhängiges Gebiet
(Kolonie, Protektorat, usw.)
Dependencia
(Colonia, protectorado, etc.)
Territoire dépendant
(Colonie, protectorat, etc.)
Dependência
(Colônia, protetorado, etc.)

GALAPAGOS (Ecuador) — Administering Country
Verwaltender Staat
País administrador
Pays administrateur
País administrador

Internal/Verwaltungsgrenze/Internos/Intérieures/Limites Internos

PERNAMBUCO — **State, Province, etc.** (Second-order political unit)
Land, Provinz, usw. (Politische Einheit zweiter Ordnung)
Estado, Provincia, etc. (Unidad política de segundo orden)
État, Province, etc. (Subdivision administrative de deuxième ordre)
Estado, Província, etc. (Unidade política de segundo nível)

Recife — State, Province, etc./Land, Provinz, usw.
Estado, Provincia, etc./État, Province, etc.
Estado, Província, etc.

SIENA WESTCHESTER — **County, Oblast, etc.** (Third-order political unit)/**Grafschaft, Oblast, usw.** (Politische Einheit dritter Ordnung)
Condado, Oblast, etc. (Unidad política de tercer orden)
Comté, Oblast, etc. (Subdivision administrative de troisième ordre)
Condado, Oblast, etc. (Unidade política de terceiro nível)

Ambāla **Johnstown** — County, Oblast, etc./Grafschaft, Oblast, usw.
Condado, Oblast, etc./Comté, Oblast, etc.
Condado, Oblast, etc.

ISERLOHN — **Okrug, Kreis, etc.** (Fourth-order political unit)/**Okrug, Kreis, usw.** (Politische Einheit vierter Ordnung)
Okrug, Kreis, etc. (Unidad política de cuarto orden)
Okrug, Kreis, etc. (Subdivision administrative de quatrième ordre)
Okrug, Kreis, etc. (Unidade política de quarto nível)

Iserlohn — Okrug, Kreis, etc./Okrug, Kreis, usw.
Okrug, Kreis, etc./Okrug, Kreis, etc.
Okrug, Kreis, etc.

City or Municipality (may appear in combination with another boundary symbol)
Stadt oder Gemeinde (kann zusammen mit einem anderen Begrenzungssymbol erscheinen)
Ciudad o Municipio (puede aparecer en combinación con otro símbolo de límite)
Ville ou Municipalité (peut paraître en combinaison avec un autre symbole de limites politiques)
Cidade ou Municipalidade (Pode aparecer em combinação com outro símbolo de limite político)

NORMANDIE — **Historical Region** (No boundaries indicated)
Historische Landschaft (Grenzen werden nicht gezeigt)
Región Histórica (Sin indicación de límites)
Région Historique (Sans indication de frontières)
Região Histórica (Sem indicação de fronteiras)

Legend to Maps/Zeichenerklärung
Leyendas Para Mapas/Légende des Cartes/Legendas dos Mapas

Transportation /Verkehr /Transporte /Transports /Transporte

Road/Strasse/Camino/Route/Rodovia — 1:300,000 | 1:1,000,000 | 1:3,000,000 1:6,000,000 | 1:12,000,000

Primary/Erster Ordnung/Principal/de premier ordre/Principal — PASSAIC EXPWY. (I-80) | PENNSYLVANIA TURNPIKE

Secondary/Zweiter Ordnung/Secundario/de second ordre/Secundária — BERLINER RING

Tertiary/Dritter Ordnung/Terciario/de troisième ordre/Terciária

Minor Road, Trail/Weg, Pfad
Rodera, Vereda/Route secondaire, Piste/Caminho, trilha

Railway/Eisenbahn/Ferrocarril/Voie ferrée/Ferrovia

Primary/Hauptbahn/Principal/Principale/Principal — CANADIAN NATIONAL | SANTA FE

Secondary/Sonstige Bahn/Secundario/Secondaire/Secundária

*Rapid Transit/Schnellverkehr/Tránsito rápido/Métro/Trânsito rápido (metrô)

Airport/Flughafen/Aeropuerto/Aéroport/Aeroporto — LONDON (HEATHROW) AIRPORT | DULLES INTERNATIONAL AIRPORT

*Rail or Air Terminal/Bahnhof oder Flughafengebäude
Terminal ferroviaria o aéro/Gare ou aérogare
Terminal ferroviário ou aéreo (estação) — SÜD-BAHNHOF

REICHS-BRÜCKE — Bridge/Brücke/Puente/Pont/Ponte

GREAT ST. BERNARD TUNNEL — Tunnel/Tunnel/Túnel/Tunnel/Túnel

Houston Ship Channel — Shipping Channel/Schiffahrtsrinne
Canal marítimo/Chenal maritime
Canal marítimo

Canal du Midi — Navigable Canal/Schiffbarer Kanal
Canal navegable/Canal navigable
Canal navegável

Intracoastal Waterway/Küstenschiffahrtsweg
Via fluvial Intracostera/Canal côtier
Via costeira interna

TO MALMÖ — Ferry/Fähre
Balsadera/Bac
Balsa

Miscellaneous Cultural Features /Sonstige Objekte /Elementos Culturales Misceláneos
Éléments Culturels Divers /Acidentes Culturais Diversos

PARQUE NACIONAL LANÍN — National or State Park or Monument
National- oder Naturpark oder Denkmal
Parque o Monumento nacional o provincial
Parc ou Monument national ou régional
Parque ou Monumento nacional ou regional

EDISON NAT. HIST. SITE — National or State Historic(al) Site, Memorial
Historische Stätte, Gedenkstätte
Sitio histórico nacional o provincial, Monumento
Site historique national ou régional, Mémorial
Sítio histórico nacional ou regional, Monumento histórico

SEMINOLE IND. RES. — Indian Reservation/Indianerreservation
Reserva de indios/Réserve indienne
Reserva indígena

FORT DIX — Military Installation/Militäranlage
Instalación militar/Installation militaire
Instalação militar

GREENWOOD CEMETERY — * Cemetery/Friedhof
Cementerio/Cimetière/Cemitério

SORBONNE — Point of Interest (Battlefield, museum, temple, university, etc.)
Sehenswürdigkeit (Schlachtfeld, Museum, Tempel, Universität, usw.)
Punto de interés (Campo de batalla, museo, templo, universidad, etc.)
Curiosité (Champ de bataille, musée, temple, université, etc.)
Pontos de interesse (Campo de batalha, museu, templo, universidade, etc.)

STEPHANSDOM — Church, Monastery/Kirche, Kloster
Iglesia, Monasterio/Église, Monastère
Igreja, Mosteiro

UXMAL — Ruins/Ruinen/Ruinas/Ruines/Ruínas

WINDSOR CASTLE — Castle/Burg, Schloss/Castillo/Château/Castelo

* Lighthouse/Leuchtturm
Faro/Phare/Farol

ASWĀN DAM — Dam/Damm/Presa/Barrage
Represa (barragem)

* Lock/Schleuse/Esclusa
Écluse/Eclusa

Crib — * Water Intake Crib/Wasseraufnahmestation
Toma de agua/Prise d'eau/Captação de água

Quarry or Surface Mine
Steinbruch oder Tagebau
Cantera o Mina de hoyo abierto
Carrière ou Mine à ciel ouvert
Pedreira ou mina a céu aberto

Subsurface Mine/Bergwerk
Mina subterránea/Mine souterraine
Mina subterrânea

* Oil Well/Ölbohrturm
Pozo de petróleo/Puits de pétrole
Poço de petróleo

Metric-English Equivalents /Umrechnung metrischer Masse in englische Masse /Métrico-Equivalentes Ingleses
Equivalences métriques des mesures anglaises /Equivalentes métricos das medidas inglesas

Areas represented by one square centimeter at various map scales
Flächen die einem cm² in den verschiedenen Kartenmassstäben entsprechen
Áreas representados por un centímetro cuadrado a varias escalas de mapas
Surface représentée par un cm² aux échelles indiquées
Áreas representadas por cm² nas escalas indicadas nos mapas

Meter=3.28 feet
Kilometer=0.62 mile
Meter² (m²)=10.76 square feet
Kilometer² (km²)=0.39 square mile

	km²	square miles
1:300,000	9 km²	3.48 square miles
1:1,000,000	100 km²	39 square miles
1:3,000,000	900 km²	348 square miles
1:6,000,000	3,600 km²	1,390 square miles
1:12,000,000	14,400 km²	5,558 square miles
1:24,000,000	57,600 km²	22,234 square miles
1:48,000,000	230,400 km²	88,934 square miles

Elevation tints shown only on 1:3,000,000 and 1:6,000,000 scale maps
Höhenschichten erscheinen nur auf Karten im Massstab 1:3 000 000 und 1:6 000 000
Se indica las tintas de elevación sólo en los mapas de escala 1:3 000 000 y 1:6 000 000
Teintes hypsométriques exprimées seulement sur cartes à 1:3 000 000 et 1:6 000 000
Indicaram-se as graduações de cor hipsométricas somente nos mapas de escalas 1:3 000 000 e 1:6 000 000

Meters	Feet
6000	19685
4000	13124
3000	9843
2000	6562
1000	3281
500	1640
200	656
0	0
Land Below Sea Level 0	0
200	656
1000	3281
3000	9843
6000	19685
9000	29520

Alternate Names /Alternative Namensformen /Nombres Alternativos
Variantes Toponymiques /Variantes Toponímicas

MOSKVA
MOSCOW

Basel
Bâle

English or second official language names are shown in reduced size lettering
Englische Namen oder Namen in einer zweiten offiziellen Sprache erscheinen in kleineren Schriftgrössen
Los nombres en inglés o un segundo idioma oficial se muestran en tipo de imprenta mas pequeño
Les toponymes en anglais ou dans la seconde langue officielle sont indiqués en caractères plus petits
Os topônimos em inglês ou num segundo idioma oficial aparecem em tipologia menor

VOLGOGRAD
(STALINGRAD)

Ventura
(San Buenaventura)

Historical or other alternates in the local language are shown in parentheses
Historische oder alternative Namensformen einheimischen Sprache erscheinen in Klammern
Los nombres históricos y alternativos locales se muestran en paréntesis
Les noms historiques de lieux ou les variantes toponymiques locales sont mis entre parenthèses
Os topônimos históricos ou as variantes toponímicas locais aparecem entre parênteses

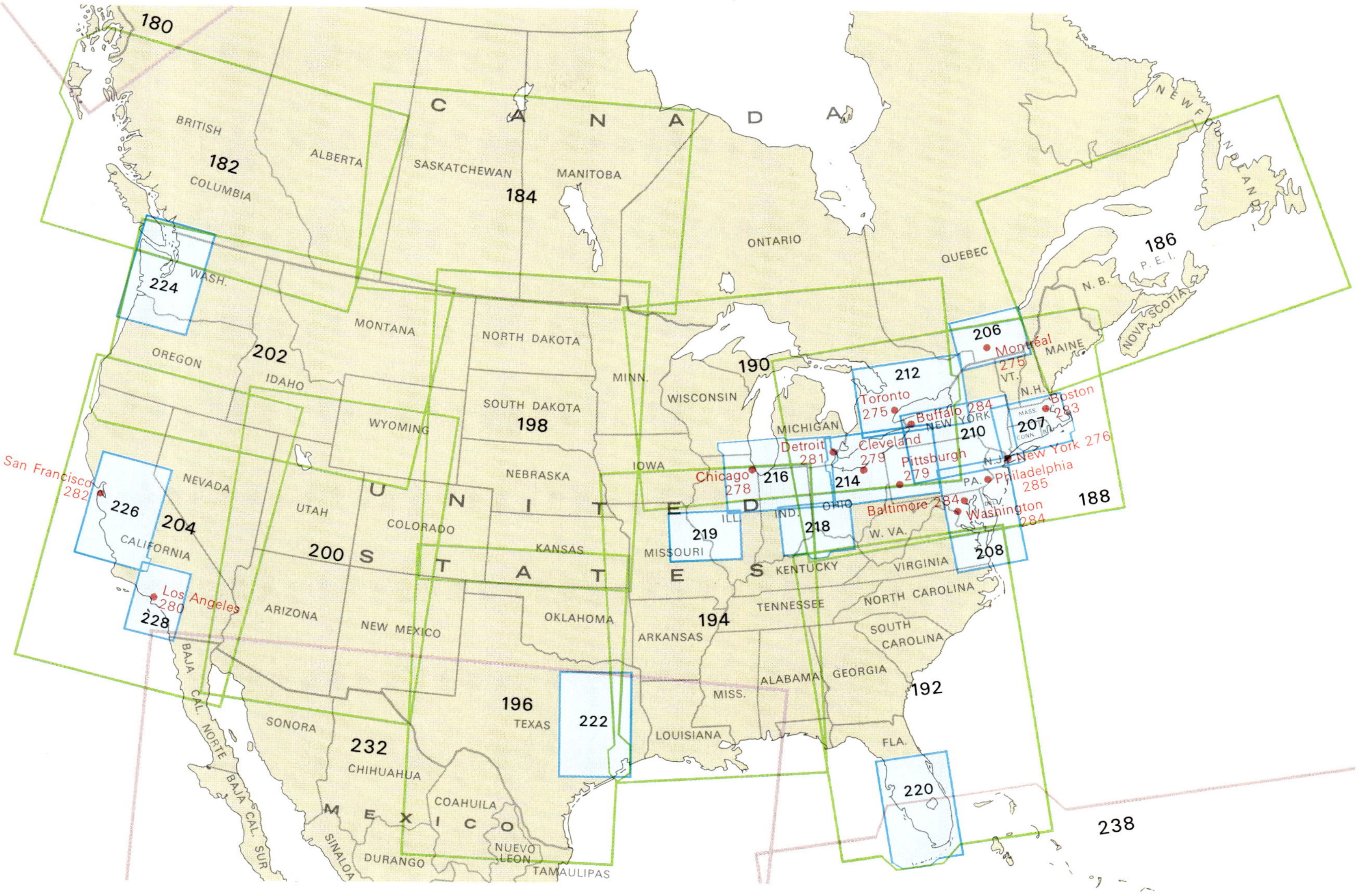
180
BRITISH COLUMBIA
182
ALBERTA
SASKATCHEWAN
MANITOBA
184
CANADA
ONTARIO
QUEBEC
NEWFOUNDLAND
186
P.E.I.
N.B.
NOVA SCOTIA
MAINE
224
WASH.
MONTANA
NORTH DAKOTA
202
OREGON
IDAHO
WYOMING
SOUTH DAKOTA
198
MINN.
WISCONSIN
190
MICHIGAN
212
Toronto 275
206
Montréal 275
VT.
N.H.
MASS.
CONN.
Boston 283
207
NEW YORK
210
Buffalo 284
Detroit 281
Cleveland 279
Pittsburgh 279
New York 276
N.J.
PA.
Philadelphia 285
216
214
Chicago 278
IOWA
NEBRASKA
NEVADA
UTAH
COLORADO
KANSAS
204
San Francisco 282
226
CALIFORNIA
200
UNITED STATES
219
ILL.
IND.
OHIO
218
W. VA.
Baltimore 284
Washington 284
188
208
MISSOURI
KENTUCKY
VIRGINIA
Los Angeles 280
228
ARIZONA
NEW MEXICO
OKLAHOMA
194
ARKANSAS
TENNESSEE
NORTH CAROLINA
SOUTH CAROLINA
GEORGIA
ALABAMA
MISS.
192
BAJA CAL. NORTE
SONORA
232
196
TEXAS
222
LOUISIANA
FLA.
220
CHIHUAHUA
COAHUILA
MEXICO
BAJA CAL. SUR
SINALOA
DURANGO
NUEVO LEON
TAMAULIPAS
238

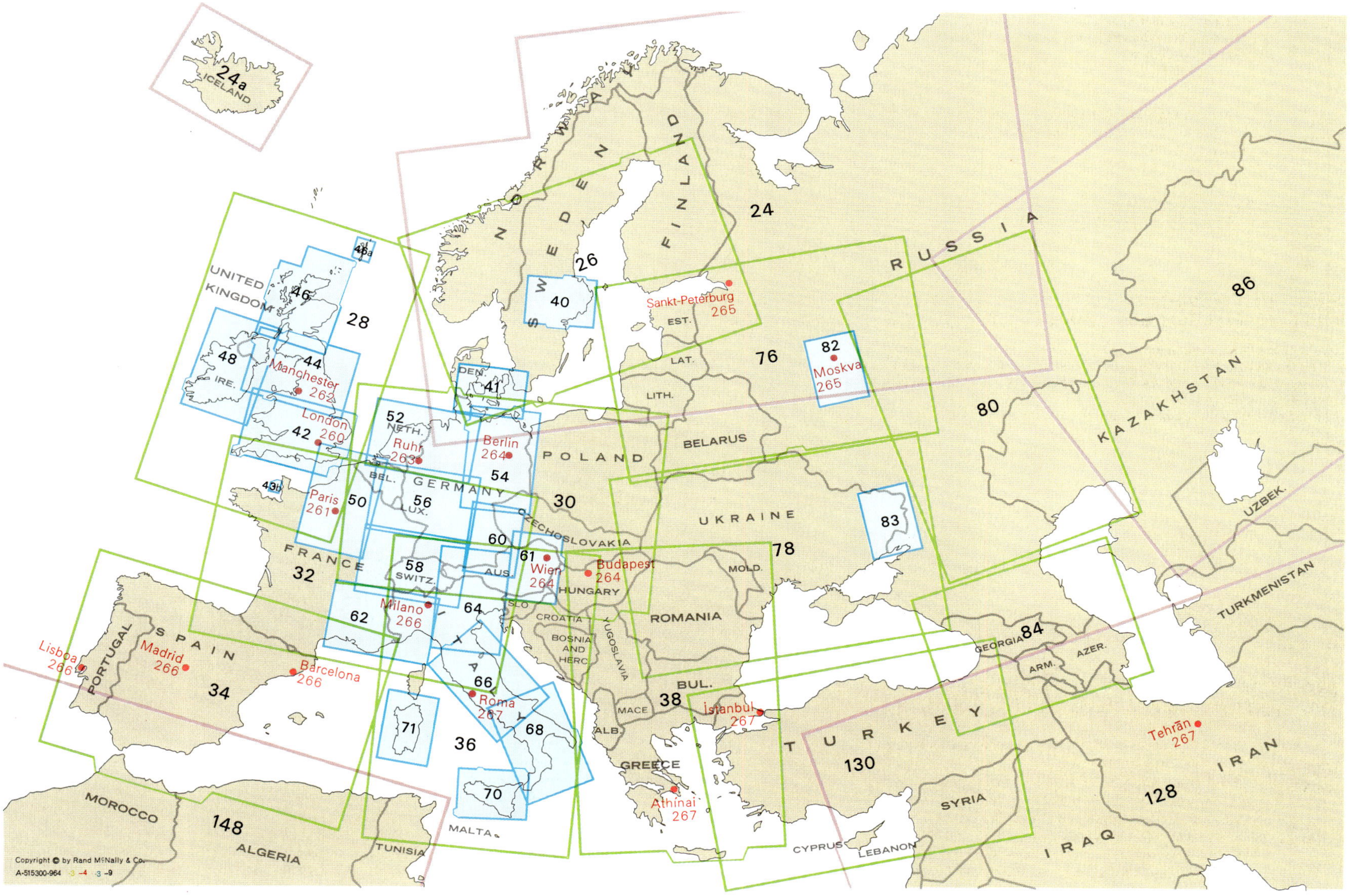
24a
ICELAND
NORWAY
SWEDEN
FINLAND
24
26
40
46a
UNITED KINGDOM
46
28
48
IRE.
44
Manchester 262
Sankt-Peterburg 265
EST.
LAT.
LITH.
76
RUSSIA
82
Moskva 265
86
80
KAZAKHSTAN
DEN.
41
52
NETH.
Ruhr 263
Berlin 264
London 260
42
54
POLAND
BELARUS
BEL.
GERMANY
56
LUX.
30
43b
Paris 261
50
UKRAINE
83
CZECHOSLOVAKIA
60
61
Wien 264
Budapest 264
AUS.
HUNGARY
78
MOLD.
FRANCE
32
58
SWITZ.
62
Milano 266
64
SLO.
CROATIA
BOSNIA AND HERC.
YUGOSLAVIA
ROMANIA
UZBEK.
TURKMENISTAN
GEORGIA
84
ARM.
AZER.
SPAIN
PORTUGAL
Lisboa 266
Madrid 266
Barcelona 266
34
ITALY
66
Roma 267
71
36
68
70
MACE
ALB.
BUL.
38
İstanbul 267
TURKEY
130
GREECE
Athinai 267
Tehrān 267
IRAN
128
SYRIA
IRAQ
CYPRUS
LEBANON
MALTA
TUNISIA
MOROCCO
148
ALGERIA
Copyright © by Rand McNally & Co.
A-515300-964

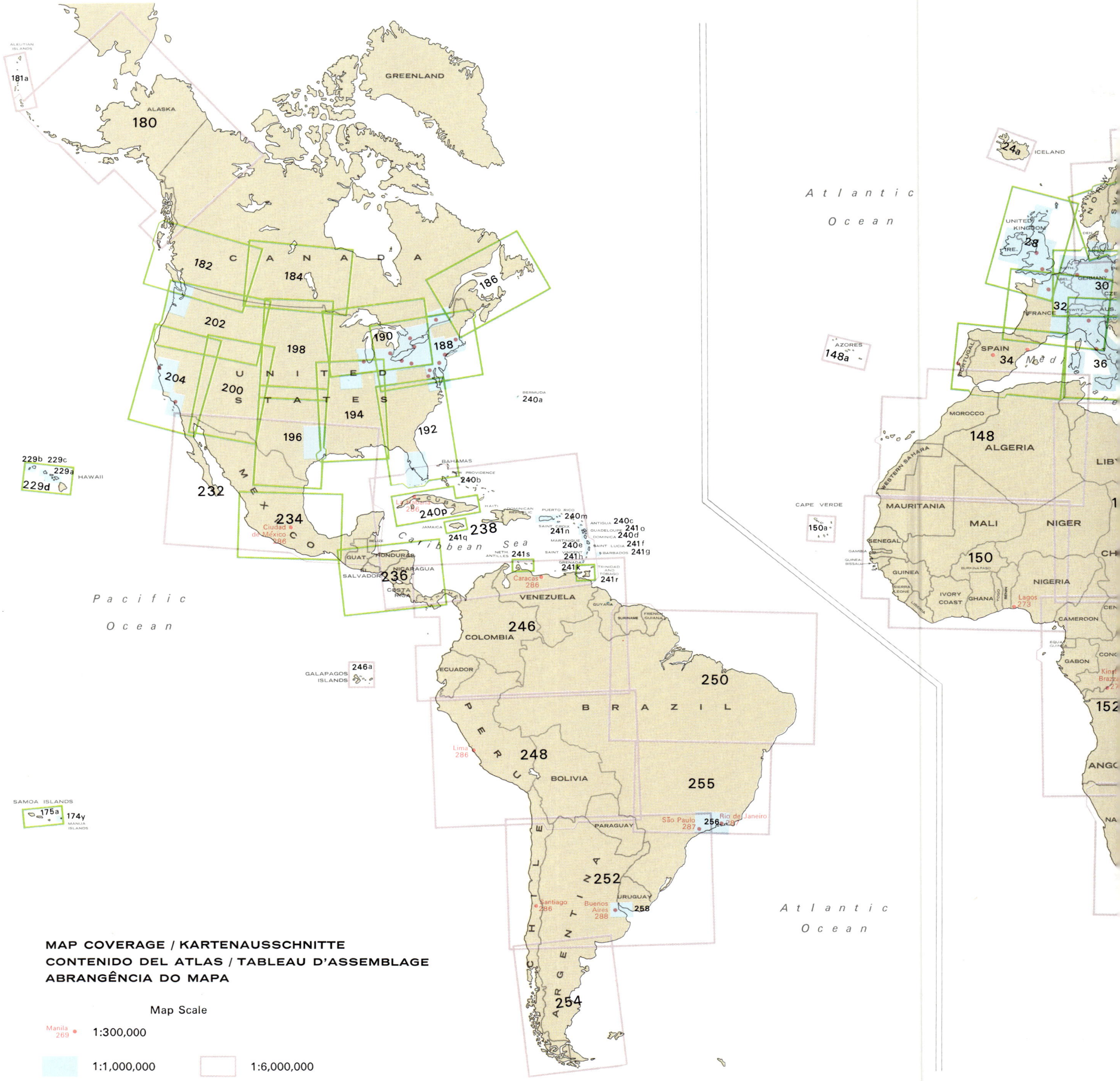

MAP COVERAGE / KARTENAUSSCHNITTE
CONTENIDO DEL ATLAS / TABLEAU D'ASSEMBLAGE
ABRANGÊNCIA DO MAPA

Map Scale

Manila 269 • 1:300,000

1:1,000,000 — 1:6,000,000

1:3,000,000 — 1:12,000,000

148 Page Reference / Seitenangabe
Página de Referencia / Page de Référence / Página de Referência

Enlarged maps of Anglo-America and Europe on page xiii.
Vergrösserte Karten von Anglo-Amerika und Europa auf Seite xiii.
Mapas aumentados de América Anglosajona y Europa, página xiii.
Cartes à grande échelle de l'Amérique anglo-saxonne et de l'Europe à la page xiii.
Mapas ampliados da América Anglo-saxônica e da Europa, página xiii.

World, Ocean, and Continent maps on pages 2-19.
Weltkarten, Karten der Ozeane und Erdteile auf Seiten 2-19.
Mapas del Mundo, Océanos y Continentes, páginas 2-19.
Cartes du Monde, des Océans et des Continents aux pages 2-19.
Mapas do Mundo, dos Oceanos e dos Continentes, páginas 2-19.

Additional Pacific Ocean Island maps on pages 174-175.
Zusätzliche Karten der Inseln des Pazifischen Ozeans auf Seite 174-175.
Mapas adicionales de las Islas del Océano Pacifico, páginas174-175.
Cartes supplémentaires des Îles de l'Océan Pacifique aux pages 174-175.
Mapas suplementares das ilhas do Oceano Pacífico, páginas 174-175.

RUSSIA
KAZAKHSTAN
MONGOLIA
CHINA
INDIA
PAKISTAN
AFGHANISTAN
IRAN
IRAQ
TURKEY
SYRIA
EGYPT
SUDAN
SAUDI ARABIA
OMAN
YEMEN
ETHIOPIA
SOMALIA
KENYA
TANZANIA
MOZAMBIQUE
MADAGASCAR
UKRAINE
TURKMENISTAN
UZBEKISTAN
NEPAL
BURMA
LAOS
THAILAND
CAMBODIA
MALAYSIA
INDONESIA
BORNEO
SUMATRA
JAVA
PHILIPPINES
TAIWAN
KOREA
JAPAN
PAPUA NEW GUINEA
NEW GUINEA
AUSTRALIA
TASMANIA
NEW ZEALAND
SOLOMON ISLANDS
NEW CALEDONIA
FIJI
SRI LANKA
Black Sea
Caspian Sea
Red Sea
Indian Ocean
Pacific Ocean
Tehrān 267
Delhi 272
Calcutta 272
Bombay 272
Beijing (Peking) 271
Shanghai
T'aipei
Hong Kong
Manila 269
Krung Thep (Bangkok) 269
Thanh-pho Ho Chi Minh (Saigon) 269
Singapore 271
Jakarta 269
Sydney 274
Melbourne
24 76 78 80 84 85 86 88 89 92 93b 94 96 98 100 102 104 105 106 107 110 112 114 115a 115b 116 120 122 123 124 126 128 130 132 140 142 144 154 157a 157b 157c 162 164 166 168a 168b 169 170 171a 171b 172 174m 175b 175c 175d 175e 175f 175g

176 178 230 242 244 22 72 74 90 118 134 136 138 108 160

Adriatic Sea 36-37
Aegean Sea 39
Afars and Issas, see Djibouti
Afghanistan 118-119
Africa 10-11
Alabama 195
Alaska 180-181
Albania 38-39
Alberta 184-185
Aleutian Islands 180-181
Algeria 148-149
Alps 33
American Samoa 175a
Andaman and Nicobar Islands 110-111
Andes 18-19
Andorra 35
Angola 152-153
Anguilla 239
Antarctica 9
Antigua and Barbuda 239
Appalachian Mountains 17
Arabian Peninsula 118
Arabian Sea 118-119
Aral Sea 86
Arctic Ocean 16
Argentina 244-245
Arizona 201
Arkansas 194-195
Armenia 84
Aruba 241s
Ascension 11
Asia 12-13
Asia Minor 23
Atlantic Ocean 8
Atlas Mountains 134-135
Australia 160-161
Australian Capital Territory 171b
Austria 30-31
Azerbaijan 84
Azores 148a
Bahamas 238-239
Bahrain 129
Baikal, Lake 88
Balearic Islands 35
Balkhash, Lake 87
Baltic Sea 24
Bangladesh 121
Barbados 241g
Belarus 76
Belgium 30
Belize 233
Bengal, Bay of 13
Benin 151
Bering Sea 16
Bermuda 240a
Bhutan 121
Bismarck Archipelago 165
Black Sea 23
Bolivia 248-249
Bophuthatswana 156-157
Borneo 112-113
Bosnia and Hercegovina 36
Botswana 156-157
Brazil 242-245
British Columbia 182-183
British Honduras, see Belize
British Solomon Islands, see Solomon Islands
British Virgin Islands 240m
Brunei 113
Bulgaria 38-39
Burkina Faso 150-151
Burma 110-111
Burundi 154
California 204-205
Cambodia 110-111
Cameroon 135
Canada 176-177
Canary Islands 148
Cape Verde 150a
Caribbean Sea 238-239
Caroline Islands 14-15
Caspian Sea 72
Cayman Islands 238
Celebes 113
Central African Republic 135
Central America 236-237
Ceylon, see Sri Lanka
Chad 146-147
Channel Islands 43b
Chile 244
China 90-91
Ciskei 159
Cocos (Keeling) Islands 13
Colombia 246-247
Colorado 199-201
Comoros 157a
Congo 152
Congo, Democratic Republic of the, see Zaire
Connecticut 207
Cook Islands 15
Corsica 36-37
Costa Rica 237
Crete 39
Croatia 36
Cuba 240p
Curacao 241s
Cyprus 130-131
Czechoslovakia 30-31
Dahomey, see Benin
Delaware 208-209
Denmark 26
Djibouti 144
Dominica 240d
Dominican Republic 239
Ecuador 246
Egypt 140
El Salvador 236
England 28-29
Equatorial Guinea 152
Erie, Lake 214-215
Estonia 76
Ethiopia 144-145
Europe 22-23
Faeroe Islands 22
Falkland Islands 254
Fiji 175g
Finland 24-25
Florida 193
France 32-33
French Guiana 250
French Polynesia 15
Gabon 152
Galapagos Islands 246a
Gambia 150
Georgia (U.S.) 192-193
Georgia 84
Germany 30-31
Ghana 151
Gibraltar 34
Gobi Desert 90-91
Great Britain, see United Kingdom
Great Lakes 190-191
Greece 39
Greenland 16
Grenada 241k
Guadeloupe 241o
Guam 174p
Guatemala 236
Guernsey 43b
Guinea 150
Guinea-Bissau 150
Guyana 247
Haiti 238-239
Hawaii 229d
Himalayas 120-121
Hispaniola 238-239
Holland, see Netherlands
Honduras 236-237
Hong Kong 271d
Hudson Bay 176-177
Hungary 31
Huron, Lake 191
Iceland 24a
Idaho 202-203
Illinois 190, 194
India 119
Indiana 194
Indian Ocean 6
Indonesia 108-109
Inner Mongolia 90-91
Iowa 190, 199
Iran 128-129
Iraq 128
Ireland 48-49
Isle of Man 44
Israel 132-133
Italy 36-37
Ivory Coast 150-151
Jamaica 241q
Japan 92-93
Java 115a
Jersey 43b
Jordan 128
Kansas 199
Kazakhstan 72-73
Kentucky 192, 194
Kenya 154
Kiribati 15
Korea, North 99
Korea, South 99
Kuwait 128
Kyrgyzstan 85
Labrador 177
Laos 110
Latvia 76
Lebanon 128
Lesotho 159
Liberia 150
Libya 146-147
Liechtenstein 59
Lithuania 76
Louisiana 195
Luxembourg 56
Macau 101
Macedonia 38-39
Madagascar 157b
Madeira Islands 148
Maine 186
Malagasy Republic, see Madagascar
Malawi 155
Malaysia 112-113
Maldives 13
Mali 134-135
Malta 37
Manchuria 89
Manitoba 184-185
Maritime Provinces 186-187
Marshall Islands 15
Martinique 240e
Maryland 188-189
Massachusetts 207
Mauritania 134
Mauritius 157c
Mayotte 157a
Mediterranean Sea 10
Melanesia 14-15
Mexico 232-233
Mexico, Gulf of 231-232
Michigan 190-191
Michigan, Lake 190-191
Micronesia, Federated States of 14-15
Middle East 128-129
Midway Islands 174g
Minnesota 190, 198
Mississippi 195
Missouri 194
Moldova 78
Monaco 63
Mongolia 90-91
Montana 198, 202-203
Montserrat 239
Morocco 148-149
Mozambique 138-139
Myanmar, see Burma
Namibia 156
Nauru 174b
Nebraska 199
Nepal 124-125
Netherlands 52-53
Netherlands Antilles 241s
Nevada 204-205
New Brunswick 186
New Caledonia 175f
Newfoundland 187
New Guinea 164-165
New Hampshire 189
New Hebrides, see Vanuatu
New Jersey 208, 211
New Mexico 196, 201
New South Wales 166-167
New York 188-189
New Zealand 172-173
Nicaragua 236-237
Niger 134-135
Nigeria 135
Niue 174v
Norfolk Island 174c
North America 16-17
North Carolina 192
North Dakota 198
Northern Ireland 48-49
Northern Mariana Islands 14
Northern Territory 160-161
North Sea 22
Northwest Territories 176-177
Norway 24-25
Nova Scotia 186-187
Nyasa, Lake 155
Ohio 188
Oklahoma 196
Oman 118
Ontario 176-177, 188-189
Ontario, Lake 212-213
Oregon 202
Orkney Islands 46
Pacific Ocean 6-7
Pakistan 120
Palau 14
Palestine 132-133
Panama 246
Papua New Guinea 165
Paraguay 249, 252-253
Pennsylvania 188-189
Persian Gulf 128-129
Peru 242
Philippines 116-117
Pitcairn 174e
Poland 31
Polynesia 15
Portugal 34
Portuguese Guinea, see Guinea-Bissau
Prince Edward Island 186
Puerto Rico 240m
Qatar 129
Quebec 177, 189
Queensland 161
Red Sea 137
Reunion 157c
Rhode Island 207
Rhodesia, see Zimbabwe
Rocky Mountains 16-17
Romania 38
Russia 72-75
Rwanda 154
Sahara Desert 134-135
St. Helena 11
St. Kitts and Nevis 239
St. Lucia 241f
St. Pierre and Miquelon 187
St. Vincent and the Grenadines 241h
San Marino 66
Sao Tome and Principe 152
Sardinia 71
Saskatchewan 184-185
Saudi Arabia 118
Scandinavia 24
Scotland 46-47
Senegal 150
Seychelles 139
Shetland Islands 46a
Siberia 74-75
Sicily 70
Sierra Leone 150
Singapore 271c
Sinkiang 90
Slovenia 36
Society Islands 15
Solomon Islands 175e
Somalia 144-145
South Africa 156-157
South America 18-19
South Australia 163
South Carolina 192
South China Sea 108
South Dakota 198-199
South Georgia 245
Southwest Africa, see Namibia
Spain 34-35
Spanish Sahara, see Western Sahara
Sri Lanka 122
Sudan 140-141
Sumatra 108
Superior, Lake 190-191
Suriname 250
Swaziland 159
Sweden 24
Switzerland 58-59
Syria 128
Taiwan 101
Tajikistan 72
Tanganyika, Lake 154-155
Tanzania 154-155
Tasmania 167
Tennessee 192, 194-195
Texas 196-197
Thailand 110-111
Tibet 90
Tierra del Fuego 254
Togo 151
Tokelau 15
Tonga 15
Transcaucasia 84
Transkei 159
Transvaal 156-157
Trinidad and Tobago 241r
Tristan da Cunha 8
Tunisia 149
Turkey 130-131
Turkmenistan 72
Turks and Caicos Islands 239
Tuvalu 15
Uganda 154
Ukraine 78-79
United Arab Emirates 129
United Kingdom 28-29
United States 178-179
Ural Mountains 72-73
Uruguay 253
Utah 200-201
Uzbekistan 72
Vanuatu 175f
Vatican City 267a
Venda 157
Venezuela 246-247
Vermont 189
Victoria 167
Victoria, Lake 154
Vietnam 110-111
Virginia 188, 192
Virgin Islands 240m
Wake Island 174a
Wales 29
Wallis and Futuna 15
Washington 202
Western Australia 162
Western Sahara 148
Western Samoa 175a
West Indies 238-239
West Virginia 188, 192
White Russia, see Belarus
White Sea 25
Wisconsin 190
Wyoming 198-200, 202
Yellow Sea 91
Yemen 118
Yugoslavia 38-39
Yukon 181
Zaire 138
Zambia 138-139
Zanzibar 154
Zimbabwe 155

World Scene

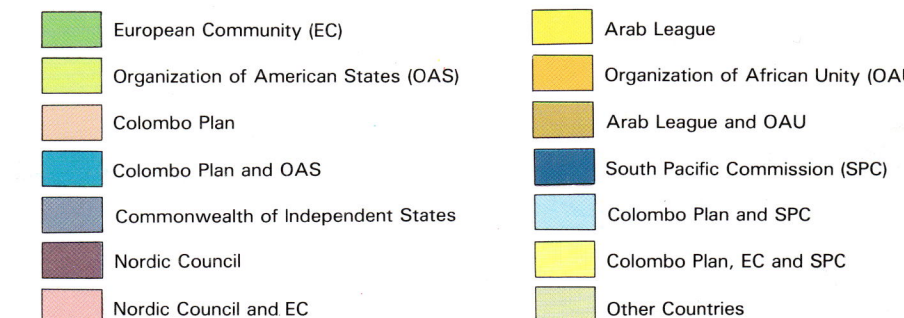

Intergovernmental Organizations: May 1, 1992

The admission of scores of new countries to the world community after World War II, indicated on the map above by the dates of their independence, created certain opportunities for these new countries that had formerly been the prerogative of a much smaller community of independent states. Until the 19th century, the countries to which international law was applicable was confined to the principal states of Europe and such others, like those of the Americas, as had asserted their independence and right to be treated as equals, or those older kingdoms and states like Siam and Ethiopia that had preserved their independence in an era of colonialism and had, perforce, to be treated as equals in treaty relationships. But equality as a matter of international law does not constitute equality of opportunity, identity of national interest, or safety from aggression. Consequently, despite the aims and achievements of the United Nations, there remains the need for intergovernmental organizations as a means for small *and* large countries to promote economic advancement, military security, or to assert their cultural identity with a stronger voice than a single country might possess. The organizations shown represent some of the principal regional and mutual-interest organizations created to advance those interests.

- European Community (EC)
- Organization of American States (OAS)
- Colombo Plan
- Colombo Plan and OAS
- Commonwealth of Independent States
- Nordic Council
- Nordic Council and EC
- Arab League
- Organization of African Unity (OAU)
- Arab League and OAU
- South Pacific Commission (SPC)
- Colombo Plan and SPC
- Colombo Plan, EC and SPC
- Other Countries

Seaward Claims

Common territorial sea claims

- 3 nautical miles
- 6 nautical miles
- 12 nautical miles

Less common claims

- 4 nautical miles
- 10 nautical miles
- Over 12 nautical miles
- Unusual claim

Other features

- Landlocked countries
- Continental shelf

Note: Territorial claims of outlying islands to their offshore waters are the same as those of the administering country.

The growth of international law on the legal status of the portions of the seas claimed by coastal states probably began in the early 17th century, when conflicting claims to parts of the high seas by colonial and exploring European sea powers induced the Dutch jurist Hugo Grotius to write *Mare liberum* (1609), on the concept of the "free, or open, sea." His work was answered in 1617-18 by John Selden's *Mare clausum*, proposing that the seas were as subject to property rights and claims as land areas. The first successful synthesis of the two positions was Cornelis van Bynkershoek's *De dominio maris* (1702) in which he suggested that the seaward limit of a national claim should be that of its effective land-based control (the distance of a cannon-shot, three nautical miles). Though never universally accepted, that standard persisted well into the twentieth century.

After World War II, however, both traditional sea-based economic activity—fishing, commercial navigation—and activities made newly possible or intensified by technological change—exploitation of the seabed, pollution, scientific investigation—led coastal states to make increasingly wider claims to both territorial seas, those wholly subject to national law, and to zones in which some, but not all, sovereign rights were claimed, usually to protect economic, but especially fishing, interests. The first Law of the Sea Conference in 1958 attempted under UN auspices to codify international law in these areas. More than 14 years later at the final meeting of the Third Conference, a text representing the efforts of some 150 countries was opened for signature on Dec. 10, 1982 as the *United Nations Convention on the Law of the Sea*. Accessions were deposited that day by 119 states to a document providing definitions, guidelines, procedures, and institutions to govern a wide range of maritime law and activities.

Among the subjects relating to sovereignty delimited by the Convention were sections defining the rights, jurisdiction, and duties of coastal states in matters relating to the territorial sea, the right of innocent passage, international straits, archipelagic (island) states, exclusive economic zones (EEZ's), the continental shelf, the high seas, as well as access to, and use of, areas of the sea beyond the jurisdiction of a single national power.

Territorial sea may be claimed up to a distance of 12 nautical miles (n.m.) from either the shoreline of a coastal state (measured from low water on navigational charts), or from a straight baseline defined by the state when its shoreline is very irregular, as is that of Norway. Waters directly connected to the sea behind this baseline are called internal waters, and include bays (which may be closed at the mouth by a single baseline if they are less than 24 n.m. wide, and river mouths and estuaries. A zone contiguous to the territorial sea not wider than 24 n.m. beyond the baselines defining the territorial sea is defined in which states may exercise *limited* control for customs, immigration, fiscal, or sanitary reasons. Another zone, defined in relation to the continental shelf (the seaward prolongation of the coastal landmass beneath the sea) permits extension of the national sovereignty over the seabed and subsoil of the zone to the edge of the continental margin (the lower termination of the continental slope and rise) for purposes of exploration, scientific study, or economic exploitation of either biological or mineral resources.

In areas of the seas where coastal states lie in close proximity, the seaward extension of a national boundary may necessitate the drawing or negotiation of an international boundary in the sea. Where claims permissible under the Convention overlap, as in the Persian Gulf, median lines must be drawn so as to accommodate each state's maximum claim without disadvantaging bordering states.

The table opposite provides a description of the nature of current national claims to territorial seas and of the economic, usually fishing, zones that have been declared *within* the permissible 200-n.m. limits of the potential EEZ permitted by the Convention.

Offshore zones

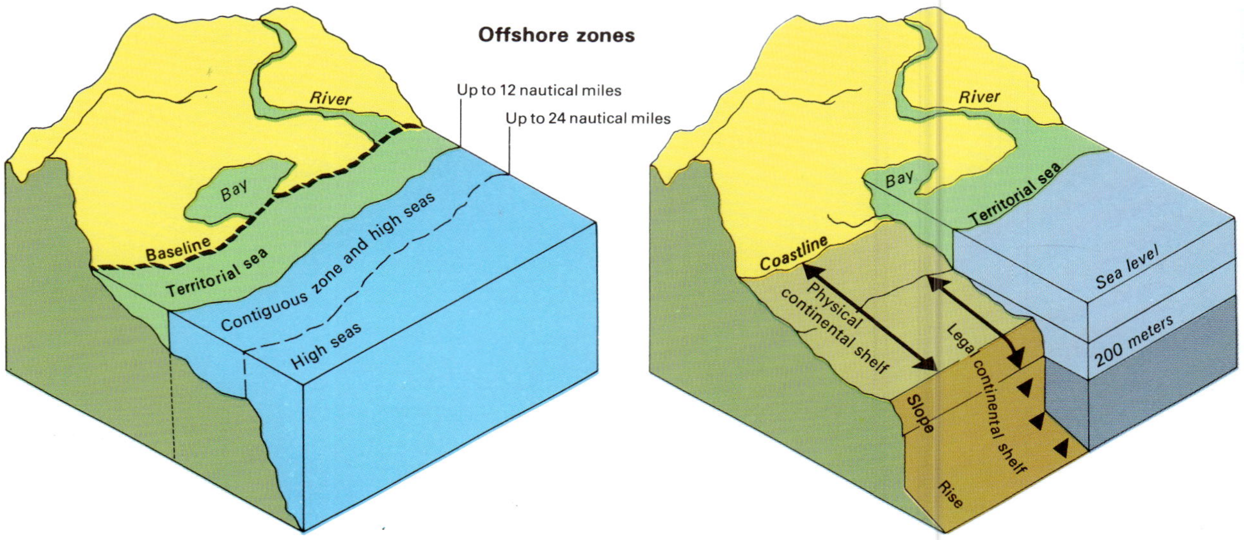

Irregular coastline of Norway

Norway measures its territorial sea from a straight baseline, which in general runs along the outer fringe of offshore islands and coastal promontories. The Law of the Sea Convention permits this type of claim in the case of highly irregular coastlines fringed with islands. In other cases the coastal features do not justify such claims to additional waters, and the claims may not be recognized.

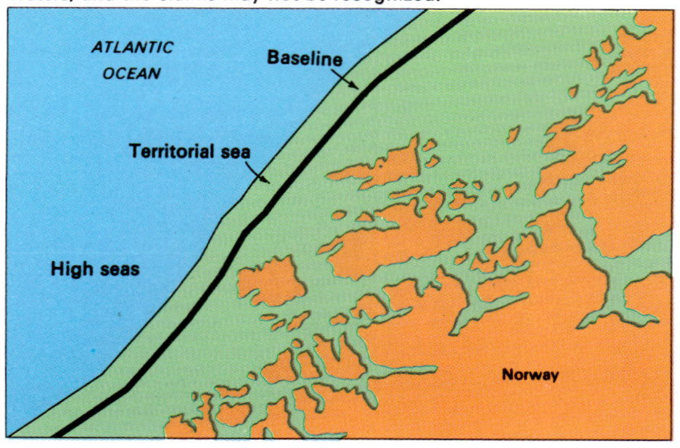

Overlapping claims in the Persian Gulf

The waters of the Persian Gulf are less than 200 meters in depth and the entire seabed is continental shelf. To determine the extent of jurisdiction that each state has over the resources of the seabed beyond its territorial sea, the Law of the Sea Convention provides for median lines, measured from the same baseline as the territorial sea. The median lines divide the continental shelf between opposite and adjacent states.

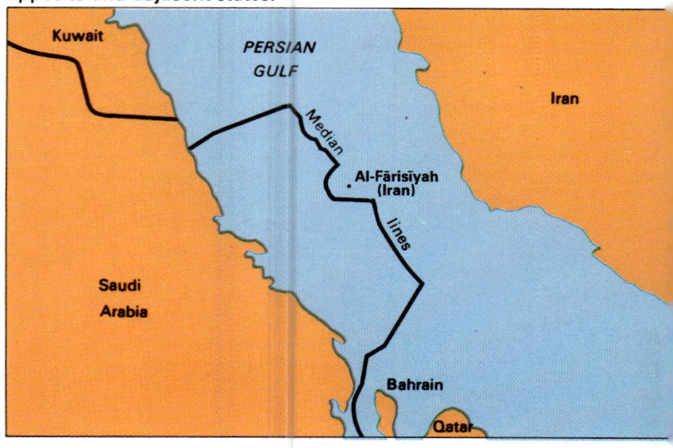

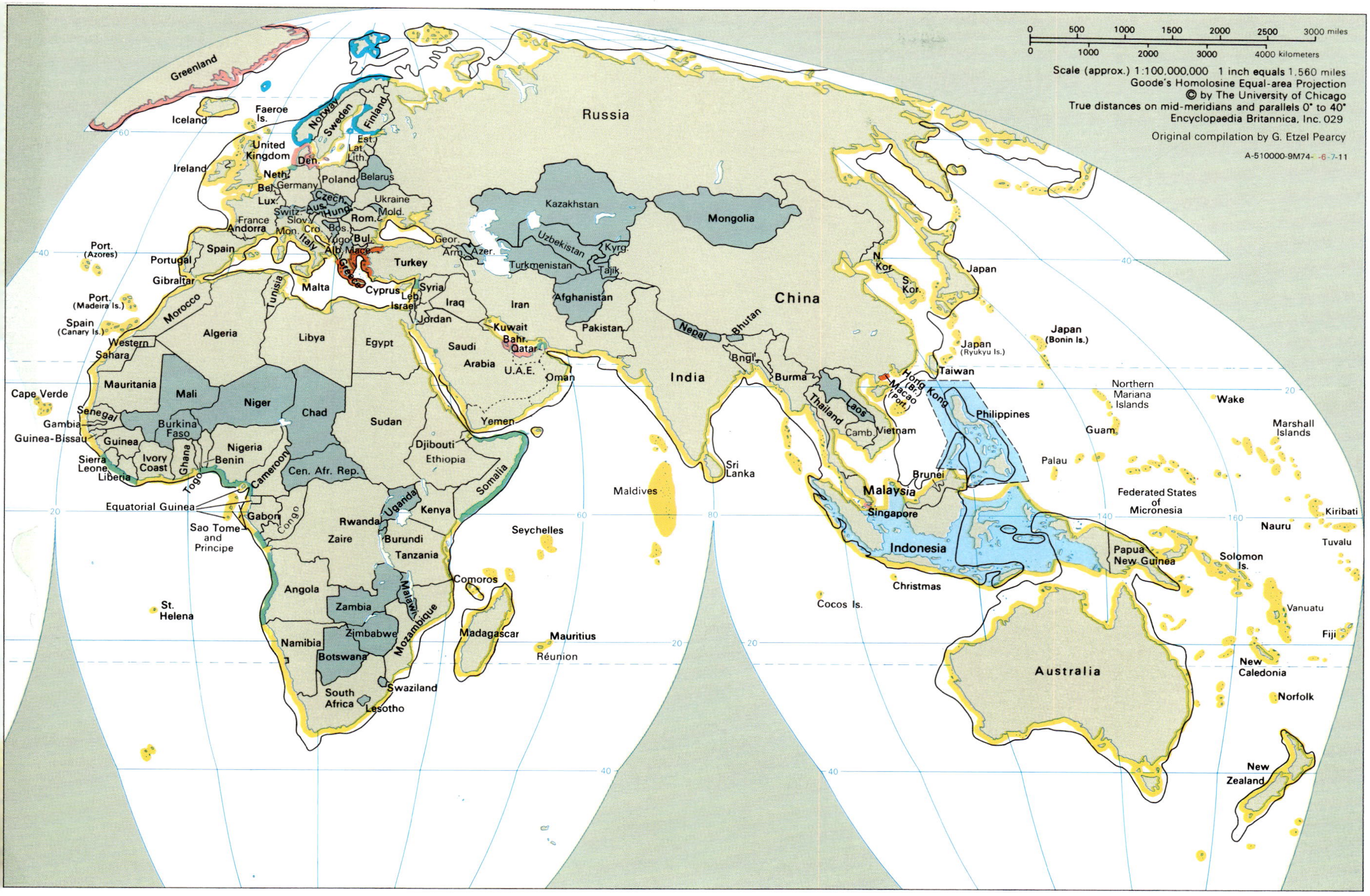

Political unit	Territorial sea claim*	Fishing claim*†
Albania	12 A	
Algeria	12 A	
Angola	20 A	200
Antigua and Barbuda	12	200 D
Argentina	12 A	200 D
Aruba	12 B	
Australia	12 A	200
Bahamas	3	200
Bahrain	3	
Bangladesh	12 A	200 D
Barbados	12	200 D
Belgium	12	E
Belize	3	
Benin	200	
Bermuda	3 B	200
Brazil	200 A	
Brunei	12	200
Bulgaria	12 A	200 D
Burma	12 A	200 D
Cambodia	12 A	200 D
Cameroon	50 A	
Canada	12 A	200
Cape Verde	12 C	200 D
Chile	12 A	200 D
China	12 A	
Colombia	12 A	200 D
Comoros	12 C	200 D
Congo	200	
Cook Islands	12 B	200 D
Costa Rica	12	200 D
Cuba	12 A	200 D
Cyprus	12	
Denmark	3 A	200
Djibouti	12	200 D
Dominica	12	200 D
Dominican Republic	6 A	200 D
Ecuador	200 A	
Egypt	12 A	200 D
El Salvador	200	
Equatorial Guinea	12	200 D
Ethiopia	12 A	
Faeroe Islands	3 B	200
Falkland Islands	3	200
Fiji	12 C	200 D
Finland	4 A	12
France	12 A	200 D
French Guiana	12 B	200 D
French Polynesia	12 B	200 D
Gabon	12	200 D
Gambia	12	200
Germany	3-16 A	200
Ghana	12	200 D
Gibraltar	3 B	

Political unit	Territorial sea claim*	Fishing claim*†
Greece	6	
Greenland	3 B	200
Grenada	12	200 D
Guatemala	12 A	200 D
Guinea	12 A	200 D
Guinea-Bissau	12 A	200 D
Guyana	12	200
Haiti	12 A	200 D
Honduras	12	200 D
Hong Kong	3 B	
Iceland	12 A	200 D
India	12	200 D
Indonesia	12 C	200 D
Iran	12 A	50
Iraq	12	
Ireland	12 A	200
Israel	12	
Italy	12	
Ivory Coast	12	200 D
Jamaica	12	
Japan	12	200
Jordan	3	
Kenya	12 A	200 D
Kiribati	12	200 D
Korea, North	12	200 D
Korea, South	12 A	
Kuwait	12 A	
Lebanon	12	
Liberia	200	
Libya	12 A	
Madagascar	12 A	200 D
Malaysia	12 A	200 D
Maldives	12	37-310 D
Malta	12 A	25
Marshall Islands	12	200 D
Mauritania	12 A	200 D
Mauritius	12 A	200 D
Mexico	12 A	200 D
Micronesia, Fed. States of	12	200 D
Monaco	12	
Morocco	12 A	200 D
Mozambique	12 A	200 D
Namibia	12	200 D
Nauru	12	200
Netherlands	12 A	200
Netherlands Antilles	12	
New Caledonia	12 B	200 D
New Zealand	12	200 D
Nicaragua	200	
Nigeria	30	200 D
Northern Mariana Islands	12 B	200 D
Norway	4 A	200 D

Political unit	Territorial sea claim*	Fishing claim*†
Oman	12 A	200 D
Pakistan	12	200 D
Palau	12 B	200 D
Panama	200 A	
Papua New Guinea	12 C	200
Peru	200	
Philippines		200 D
Poland	12 A	E
Portugal	12 A	200 D
Puerto Rico	12 B	200 D
Qatar	3	E
Romania	12	200 D
St. Kitts and Nevis	12	200 D
St. Lucia	12	200 D
St. Pierre and Miquelon	12 B	200 D
St. Vincent and the Grenadines	12	200 D
Sao Tome and Principe	12 C	200 D
Saudi Arabia	12 A	
Senegal	12 A	200 D
Seychelles	12	200 D
Sierra Leone	200	
Singapore	3	
Solomon Islands	12 C	200 D
Somalia	200 A	
South Africa	12	200
Soviet Union (former)	12 A	200 D
Spain	12 AC	200 D
Sri Lanka	12 A	200 D
Sudan	12 A	
Suriname	12	200 D
Sweden	12 A	E
Syria	35 A	
Taiwan	12	200 D
Tanzania	12 A	200 D
Thailand	12 A	200 D
Togo	30	200 D
Tonga	12 A	200 D
Trinidad and Tobago	12	200 D
Tunisia	12 A	
Turkey	6-12 A	12
Tuvalu	12	200 D
United Arab Emirates	3	F
United Kingdom	12 A	200
United States	12	200 D
Uruguay	200	
Vanuatu	12 C	200 D
Venezuela	12 A	200 D
Vietnam	12 A	200 D
Western Samoa	12	200 D
Yemen	12	
Yugoslavia	12 A	
Zaire	12	200 D

* Nautical miles
† When claim is beyond the territorial sea.
Data as of December 31, 1990.

A. Measured from a straight baseline.
B. Same as that of administering country.
C. Extends beyond a perimeter drawn around archipelago.

D. Exclusive economic zone.
E. Fishing rights extend to median line with neighboring countries.
F. Exclusive econ. zone extends to median line with neighboring countries.

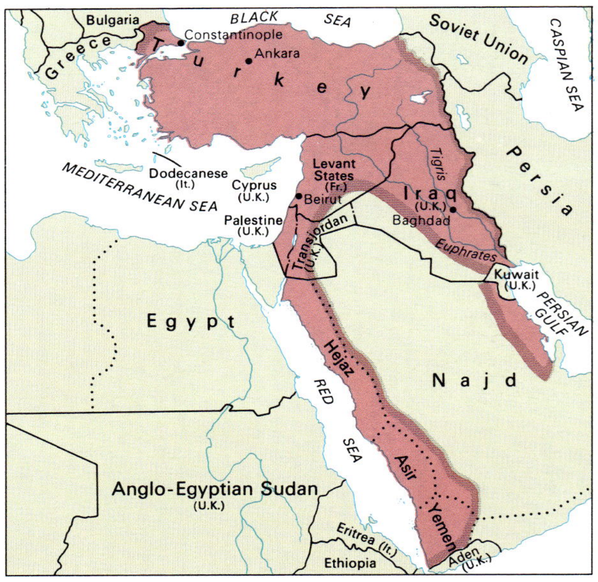

Dissolution of the Ottoman Empire

- Ottoman Empire 1913
- Administrative boundaries (1923) as a result of WW I settlements; dotted are indefinite

Dissolution of Austria-Hungary

- Austria-Hungary 1913
- Administrative boundaries (1923) as a result of WW I settlements

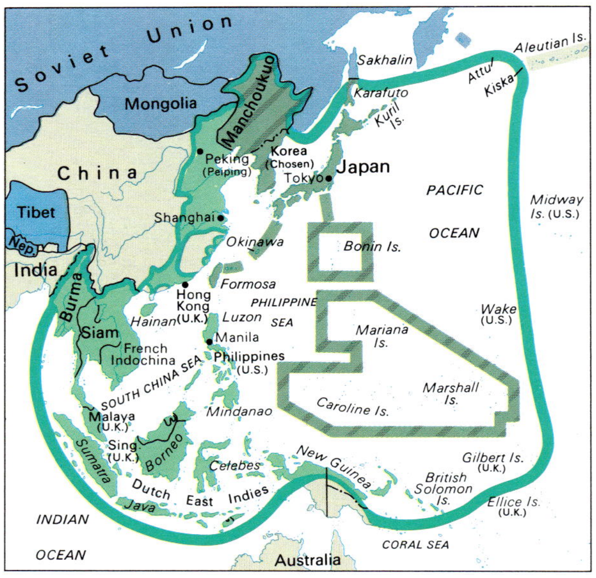

Japanese Expansion World War II

- Japan 1939
- Japanese dependencies 1939
- Maximum occupation
- Neutral states
- States joining Allies 1945

Axis Expansion World War II

- Germany 1939
- Other Axis Powers 1940-45
- Maximum occupation
- Neutral states
- States joining Allies 1943-45

*Occupied by Allies

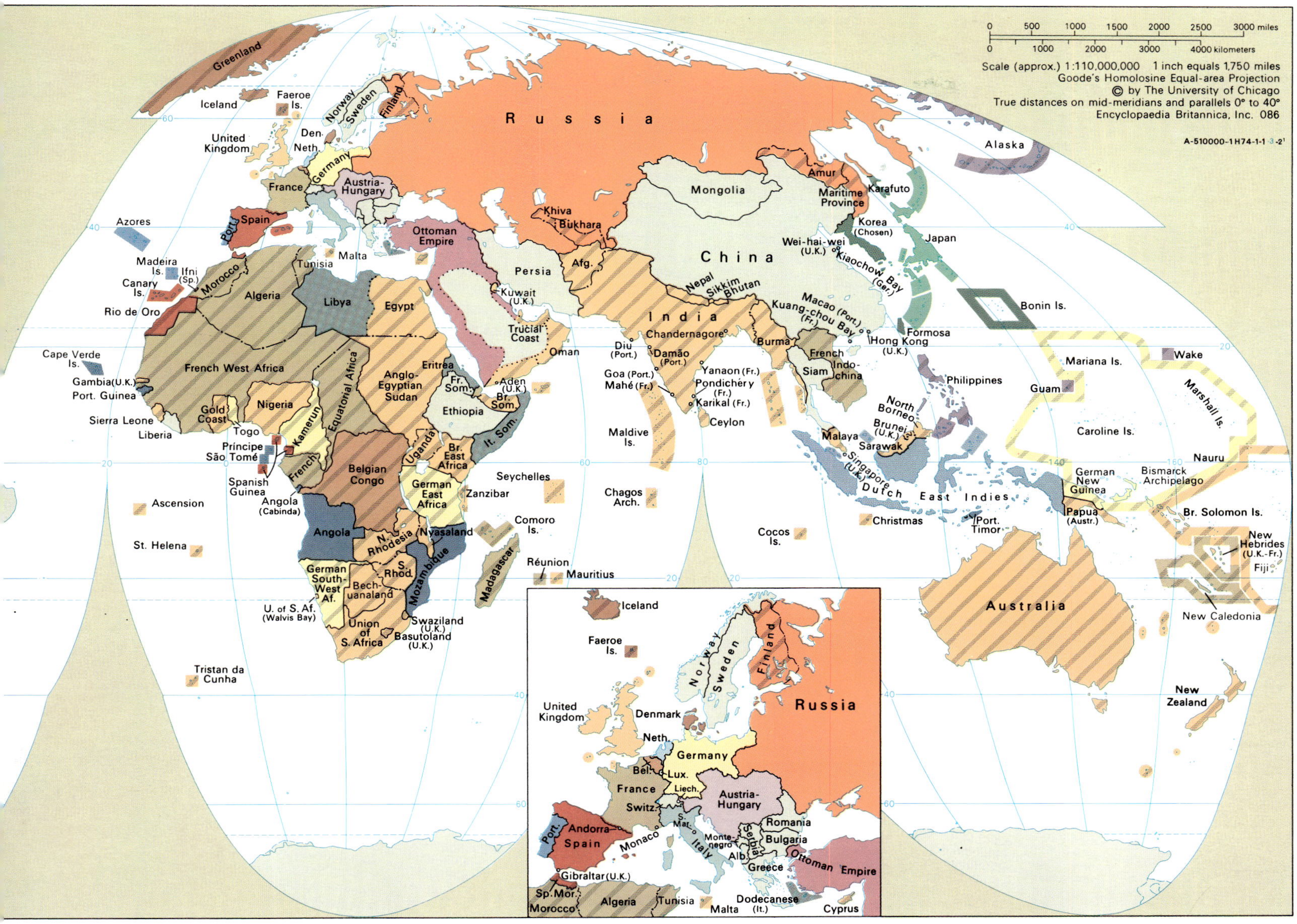

The World January 1, 1914

- United Kingdom
  - Related areas
- France
  - Related areas
- Portugal
  - Related areas
- Spain
  - Related areas
- Netherlands
  - Related areas
- Belgium
  - Related areas
- Germany
  - Related areas
- Denmark
  - Related areas
- Japan
  - Related areas
- Italy
  - Related areas
- United States
  - Related areas
- Ottoman Empire
- Russia
  - Related areas
- Austria-Hungary
- Countries without related areas
- Disputed areas
- Intercolonial boundary

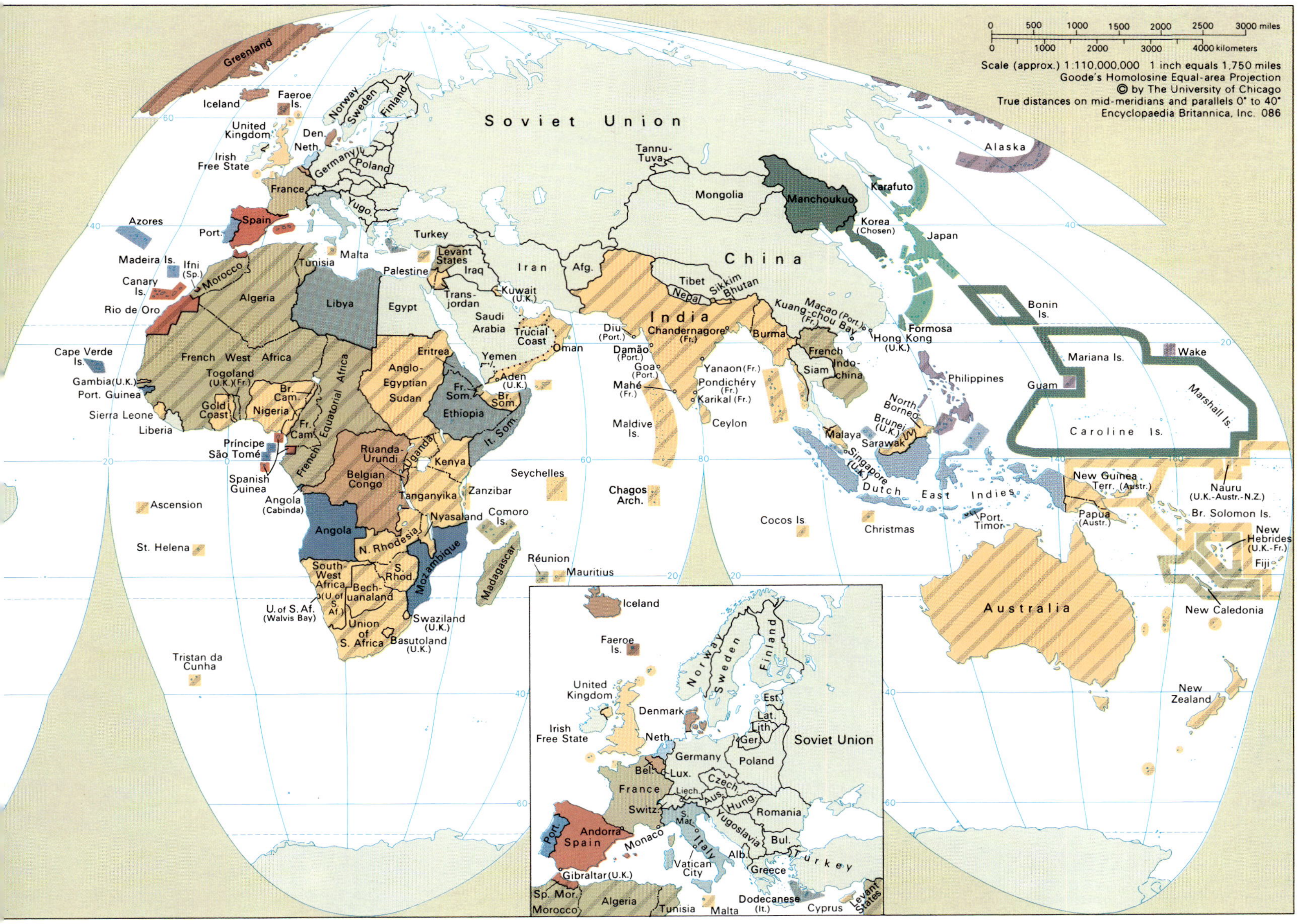

The World January 1, 1937

- United Kingdom
  - Related areas
- France
  - Related areas
- Portugal
  - Related areas
- Spain
  - Related areas
- Netherlands
  - Related areas
- Belgium
  - Related areas
- Denmark
  - Related areas
- Japan
  - Related areas
- Italy
  - Related areas
- United States
  - Related areas
- Countries without related areas
- Disputed areas
- Intercolonial boundary

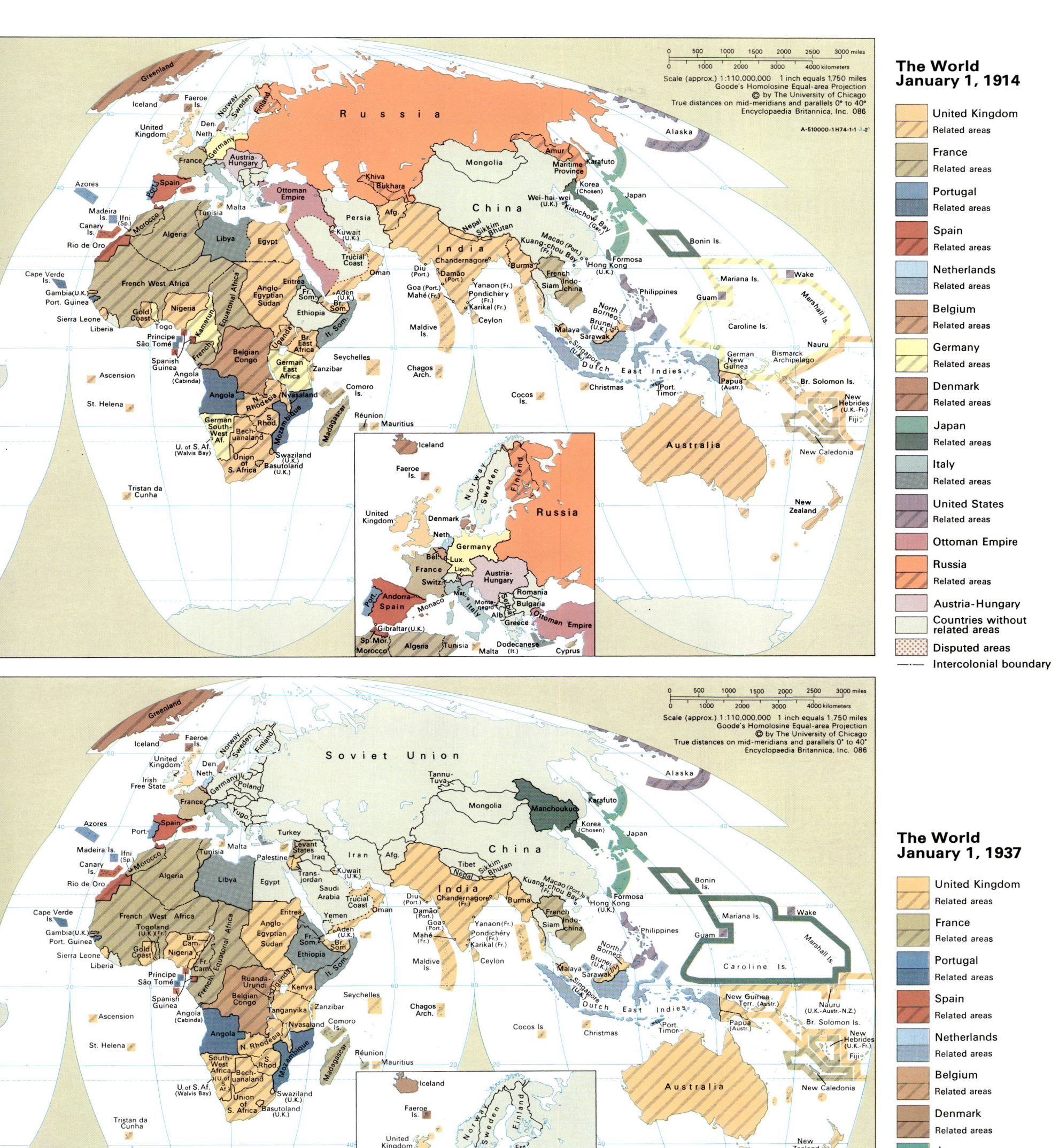

Population

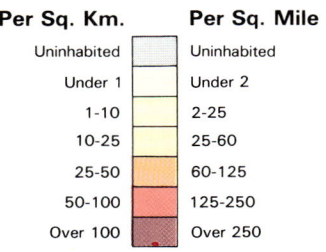

Per Sq. Km.	Per Sq. Mile
Uninhabited	Uninhabited
Under 1	Under 2
1-10	2-25
10-25	25-60
25-50	60-125
50-100	125-250
Over 100	Over 250

- ● Metropolitan areas over 2,000,000 population
- ○ Metropolitan areas 1,000,000 to 2,000,000 population

Some cities are identified by initial letter only.

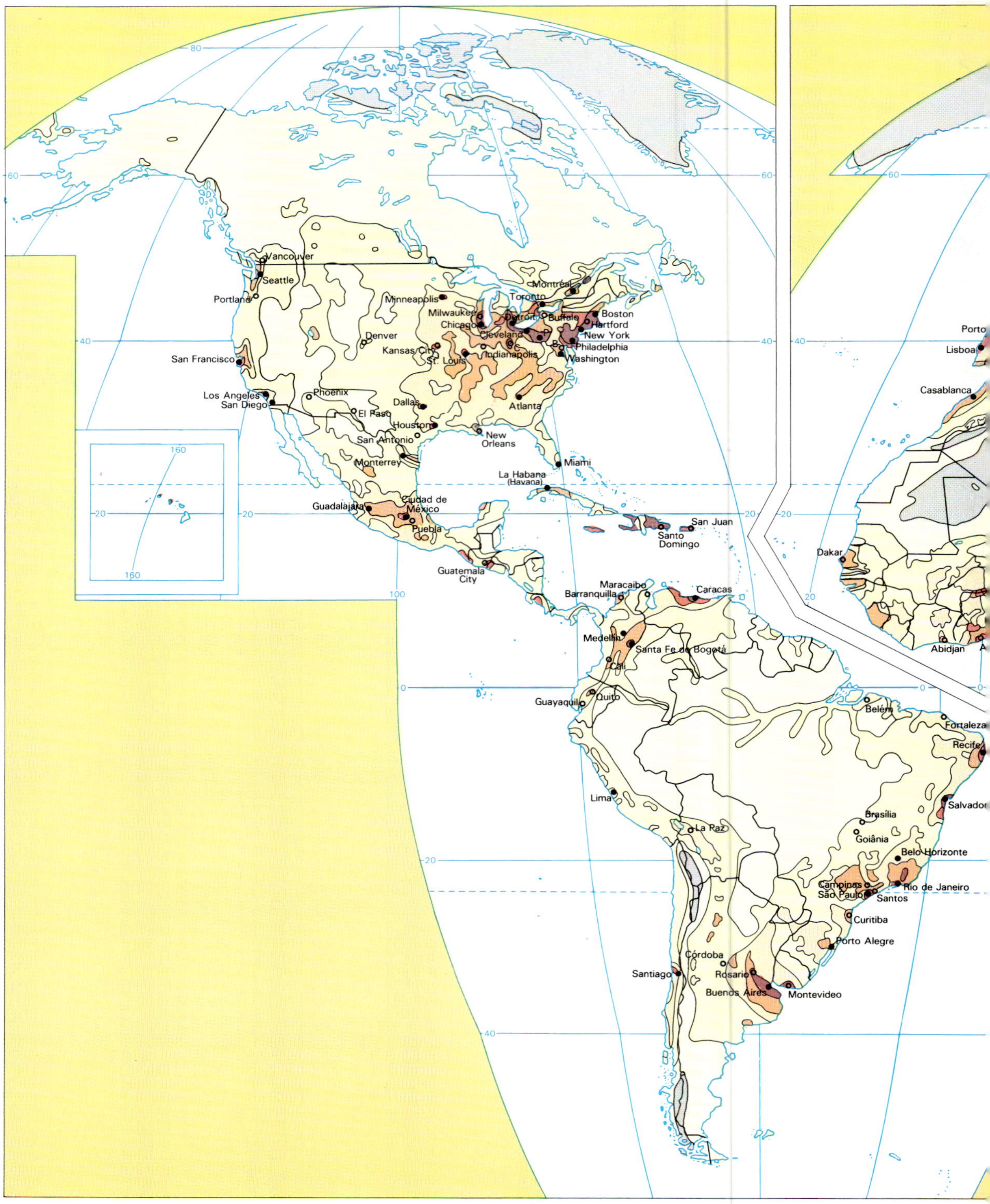

The numbers and distribution of human beings on their planet and the forms that their occupance takes are controlled by a variety of factors. The main population map opposite focuses on identifying the location and density of the most populous regions and cities of the earth. The Urbanization inset highlights the propensity of man to congregate in cities and the group of ''age pyramids'' below illustrates some of the diversity that is concealed within apparently simple population totals.

Population

The patterns of distribution shown display certain characteristics worldwide: relative densities decline with altitude (and the capacity of the land to support higher densities); settlement patterns follow rivers, or focus on harbours opening on large bodies of water connecting populous, economically interrelated areas; populations tend to fill up contiguous areas of similar topographical and climatic opportunity, whether in coastal plains, intermontane basins, along railroad right-of-ways, or in biologically and climatically defined regions of similar soil, vegatative response, or access from more populous areas.

The main map also identifies the largest cities of the world, distinguishing between those of 1-2 million and more than 2 million population. The selection of cities is determined by the concept of ''city proper,'' that is, usually the smallest contiguous civilly or adminstratively defined and named entity. The meaning of the concept in terms of local practice worldwide, however, is considerable. A city of 100,000 may in one country be a single social, economic, and administrative place, bound together fully by its transportation infrastructure and representing a single *urban* entity in its population's collective mind. A city of the same apparent size in another country, however, might represent something more nearly characterizable as 100 villages of 1,000 persons, pursuing separate economic activities in separate neighbourhoods, often poorly interconnected, sometimes still predominately rural in terms of economic activity, and perhaps not universally understood by its own people as the greater place seen by others.

Urbanization

The concept of ''urban'' exemplified on the inset map of urbanization is particularly elusive in international studies of population, as most countries have their own definition of the concept, appropriate to local conditions and discourse, but often unsuitable for international comparisons. It is that local concept which is mapped here. Size is a useful indicator as to whether a place is classifiable as ''urban,'' but as indicated above, the ''size'' of a place, even in the presence of administrative requirements may be misleading. Japan defines a place as ''urban'' if it has 50,000 or more population and meets certain criteria for their location within the city. A smaller country with a less hospitable landscape, like Iceland or Norway, might, by the same token, define a place as small as 200 as ''urban'' if it had predominately non-rural employment patterns, administrative function, or its houses were closer together than some set distance. The concept of ''metropolitan area,'' or urban areas contiguous with a central city that are economically dependent on it is also complex and interpreted differently throughout the world. The inset map of urbanization extends the city proper concept of the main map by showing metropolitan areas of more than 2 million. As can be seen from comparison of the two maps, sometimes high urbanization may correlate with relatively low numbers or densities of population. This occurs when the majority of a population lives in large settlements, rather than distributed across an entire landscape and may happen either because of localized economic and employment opportunities in the city, or because the countryside is unsuitable for agricultural or other exploitation. The strong correlation, however, is still between highly populous areas and large cities.

Age and sex composition

Among the characteristics of a population having the greatest significance both in terms of current needs and future trends, the age and sex composition of a population is perhaps the most important. Several examples are presented at the right of a graphic called an ''age pyramid,'' which summarizes the relative proportion of males and females in each age cohort of a population. These examples, drawn by five-year age groups, often illuminate the effects on the whole population of the recent history of the relative growth or diminution of smaller parts of the whole: war losses, emigration of the young for work abroad, natural causes like disasters. The origins of the concern of many countries and organizations with uncontrolled population growth may be inferred from examples like Brazil, where the high proportion of young people means enormous numbers (both absolutely and relatively) in or near their childbearing years resulting in growth rates for the total population that can outrun the far more difficult-to-attain economic growth rates that determine the relative prosperity of a country. Japan, on the other hand, shows a pattern typical of a demographically mature population, that is, a population which is growing slowly or not at all, resulting in lower, more predictable, and more economically supportable demographic rates, but also foreshadowing the movement of large numbers of its people into the pensionable and financially dependent age groups without large numbers of younger workers to support them. The Japanese example also shows, in a somewhat smoothed form, the effects of some of the viscissitudes of Twentieth century history on the relative size of certain age groups.

Age and sex composition

- Male
- Female

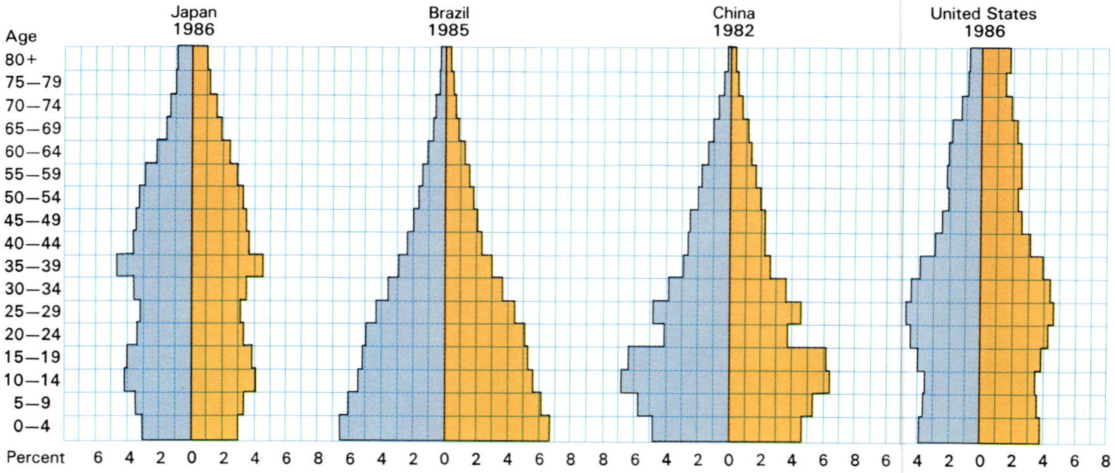

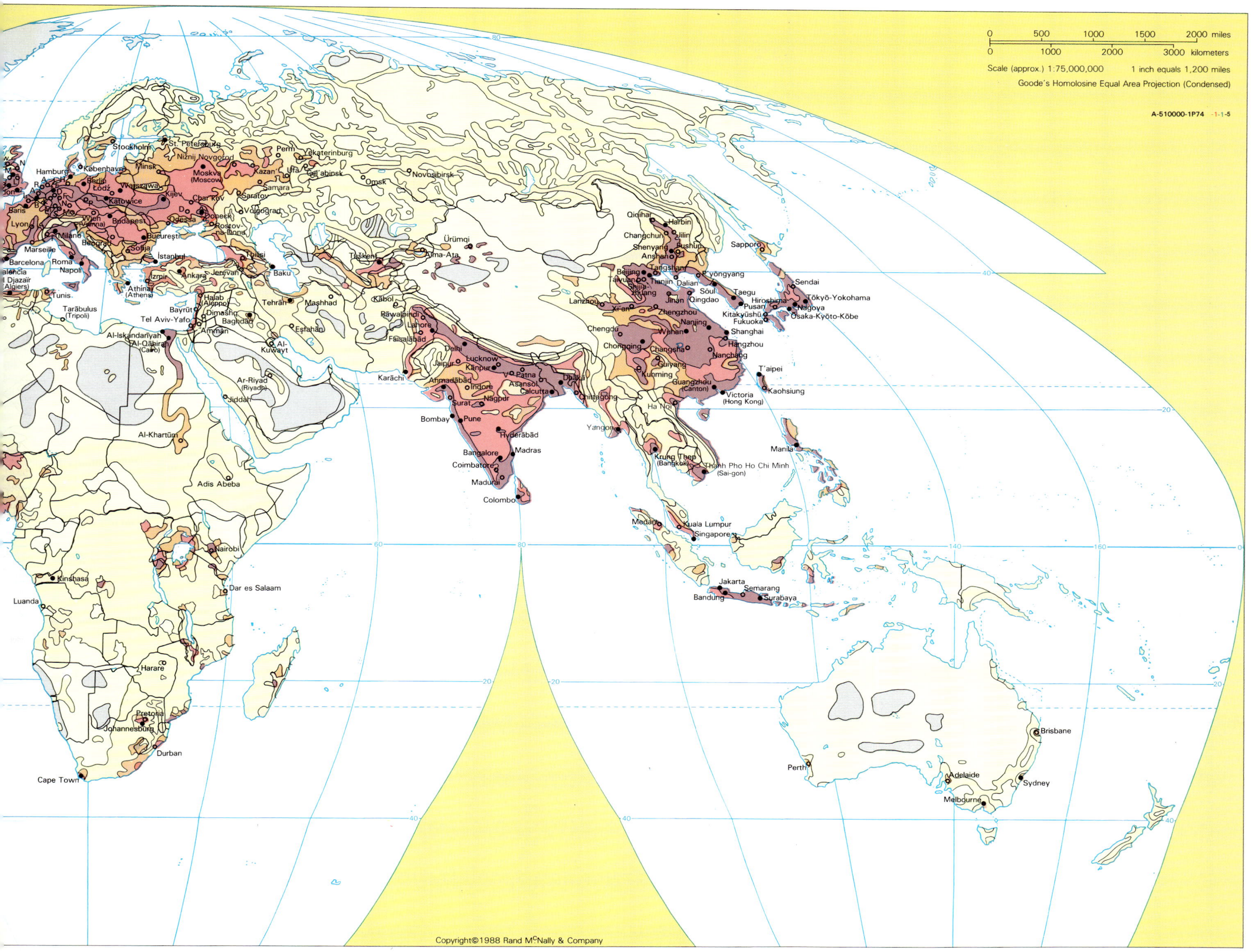

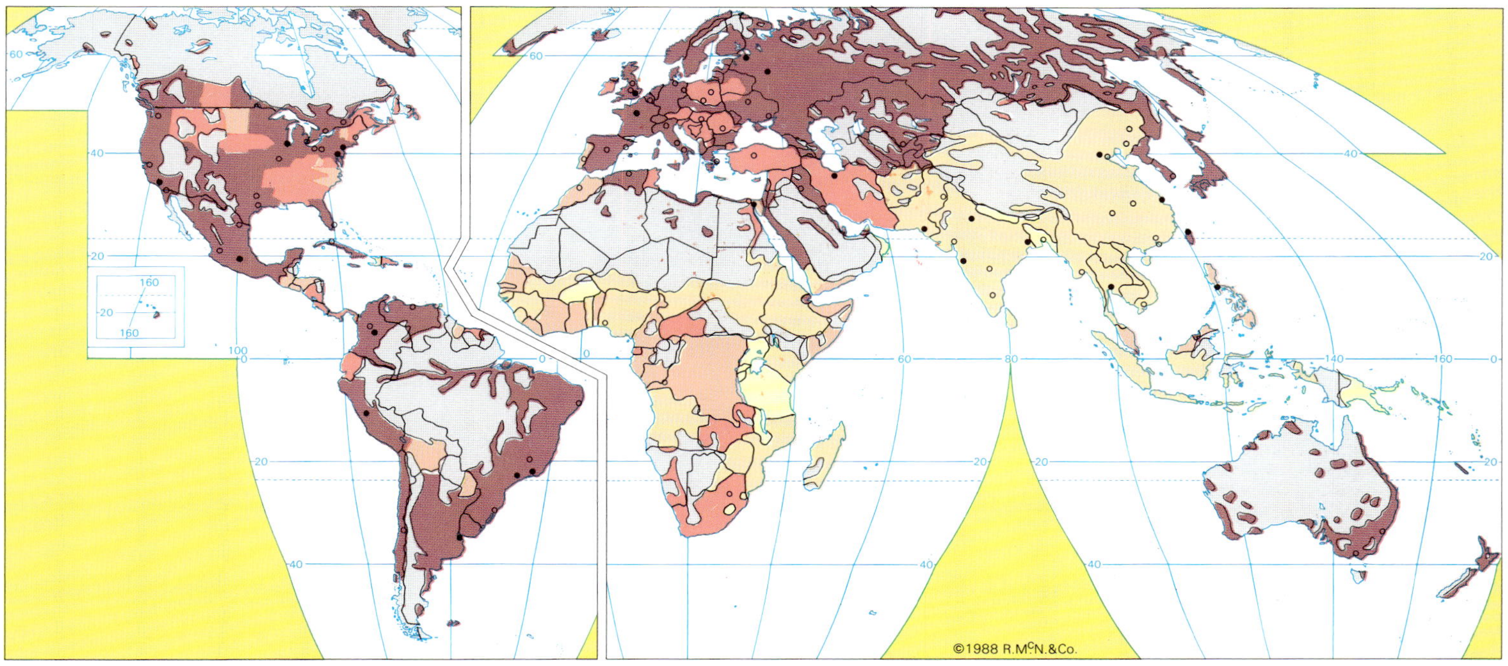

Urbanization

World Av. 42% →

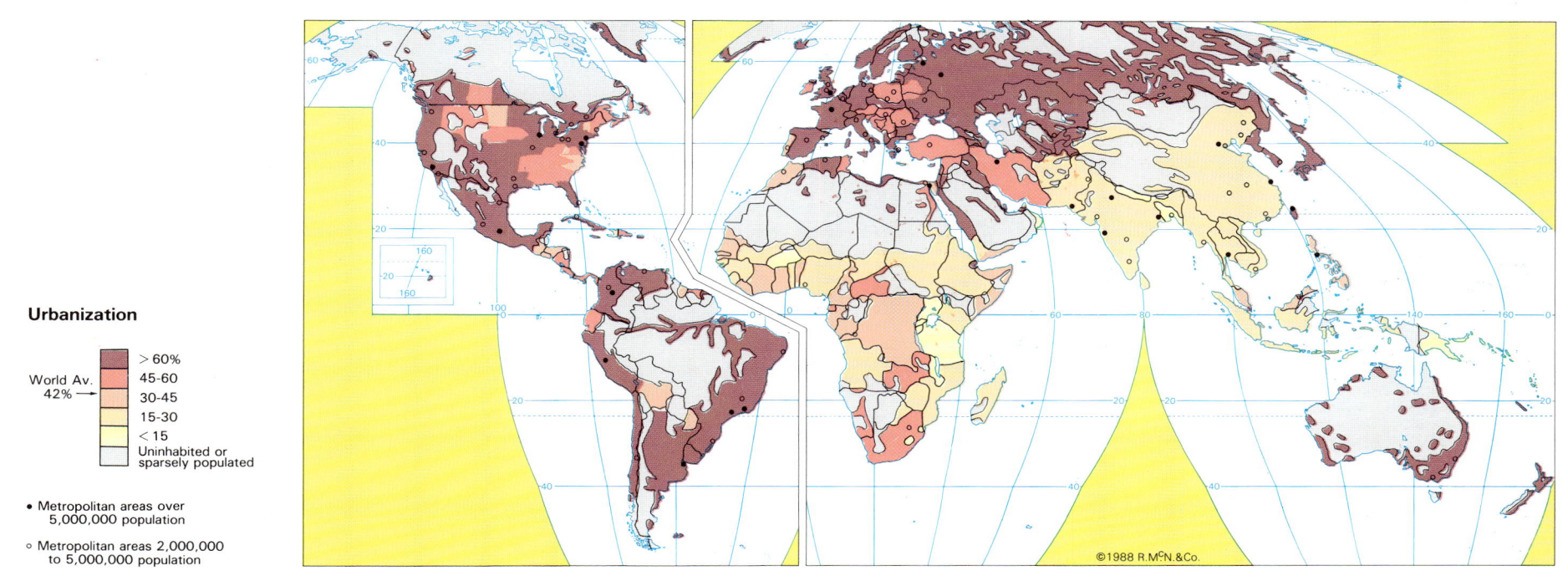

- > 60%
- 45-60
- 30-45
- 15-30
- < 15
- Uninhabited or sparsely populated

• Metropolitan areas over 5,000,000 population

○ Metropolitan areas 2,000,000 to 5,000,000 population

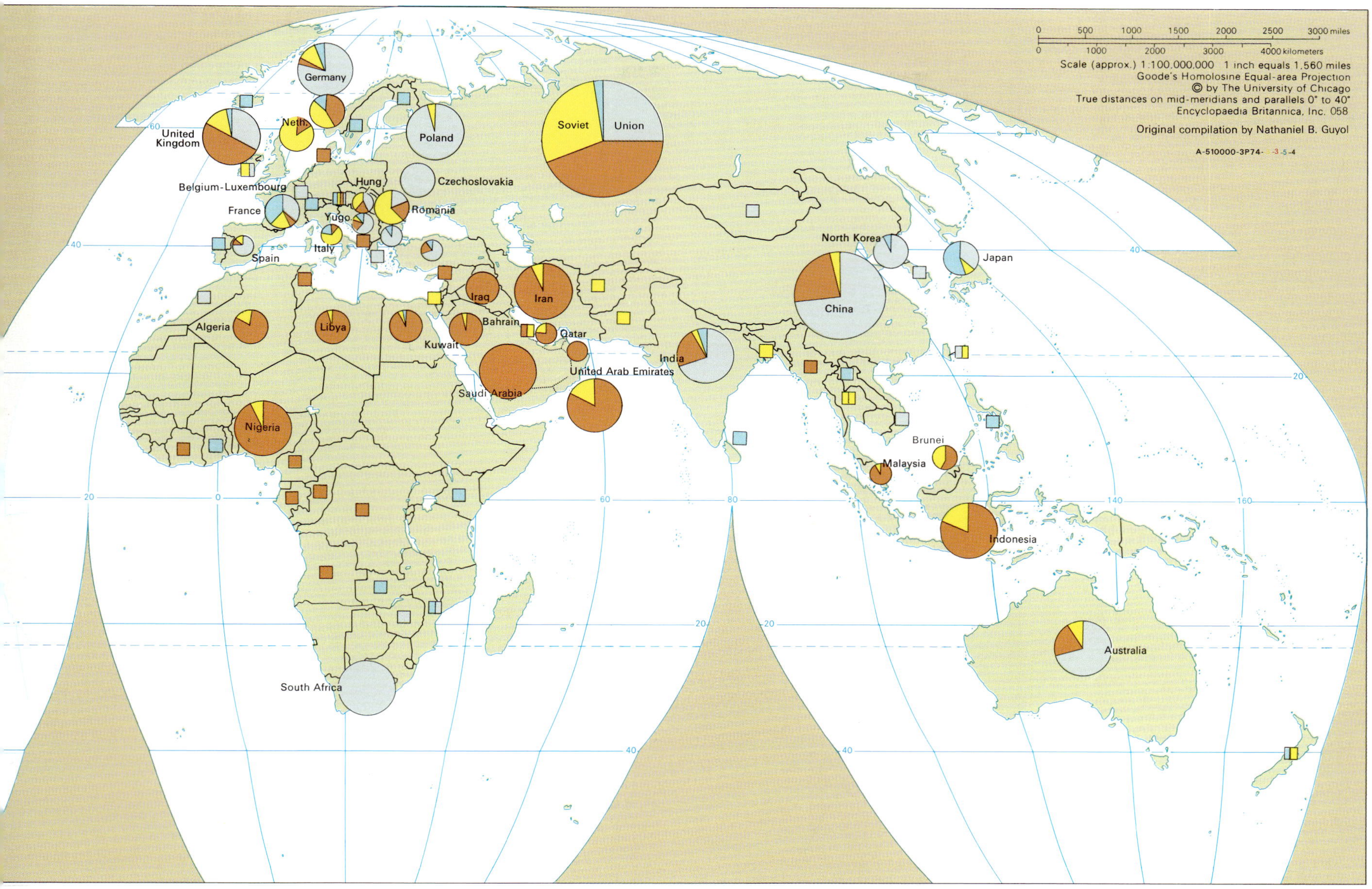

0 500 1000 1500 2000 2500 3000 miles
0 1000 2000 3000 4000 kilometers
Scale (approx.) 1:100,000,000 1 inch equals 1,560 miles
Goode's Homolosine Equal-area Projection
© by The University of Chicago
True distances on mid-meridians and parallels 0° to 40°
Encyclopaedia Britannica, Inc. 058
Original compilation by Nathaniel B. Guyol
A-510000-3P74- -3-5-4
Germany
United Kingdom
Neth.
Poland
Soviet Union
Czechoslovakia
Belgium-Luxembourg
Hung
France
Yugo.
Romania
Italy
Spain
North Korea
Japan
Iraq
Iran
China
Algeria
Libya
Bahrain
Qatar
Kuwait
India
United Arab Emirates
Saudi Arabia
Nigeria
Brunei
Malaysia
Indonesia
Australia
South Africa

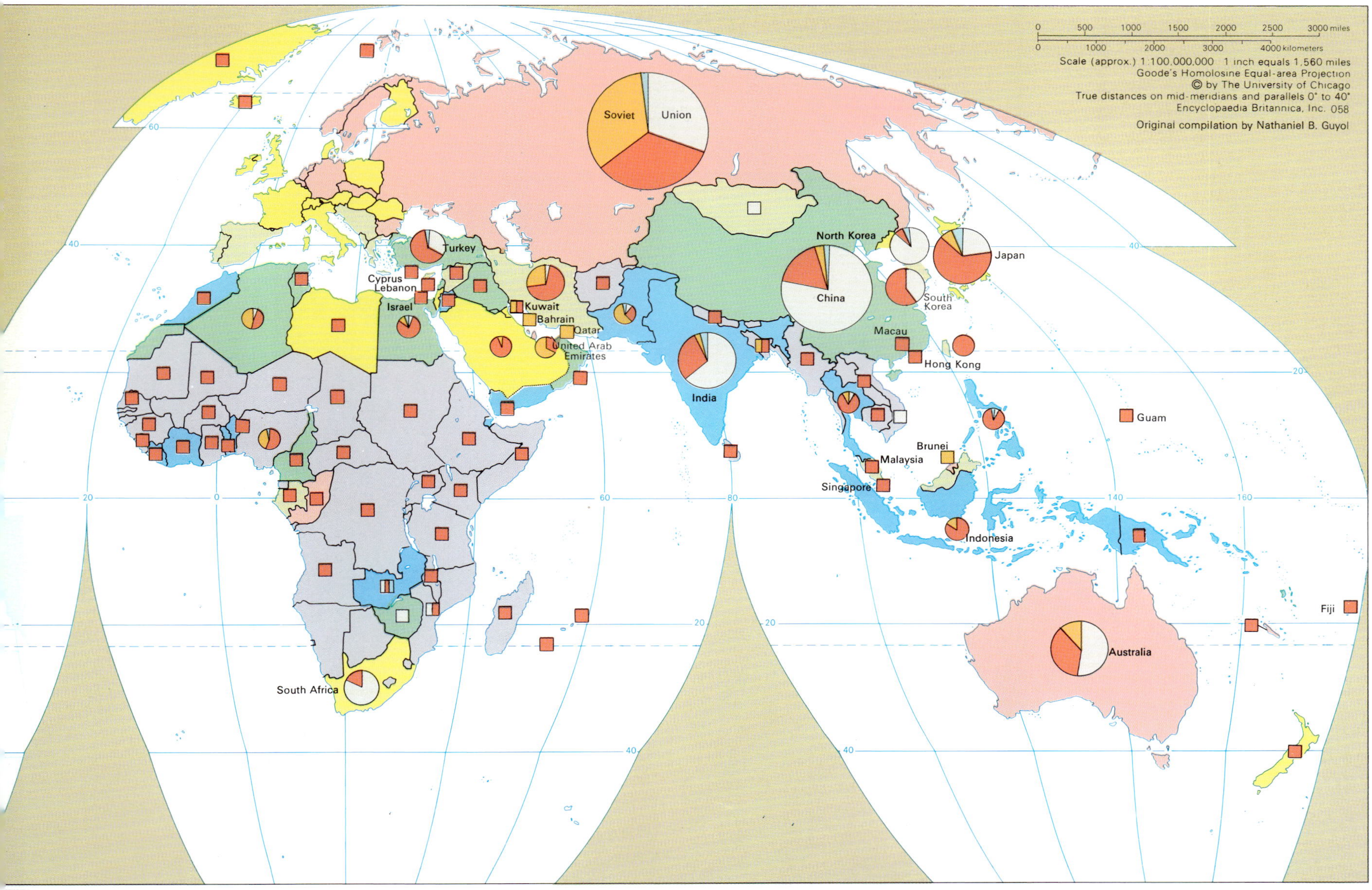

0 500 1000 1500 2000 2500 3000 miles
0 1000 2000 3000 4000 kilometers
Scale (approx.) 1:100,000,000 1 inch equals 1,560 miles
Goode's Homolosine Equal-area Projection
© by The University of Chicago
True distances on mid-meridians and parallels 0° to 40°
Encyclopaedia Britannica, Inc. 058
Original compilation by Nathaniel B. Guyol
Soviet Union
North Korea
Turkey
Japan
Cyprus
Lebanon
Israel
Kuwait
Bahrain
Qatar
United Arab Emirates
China
South Korea
Macau
Hong Kong
India
Guam
Brunei
Malaysia
Singapore
Indonesia
Fiji
Australia
South Africa

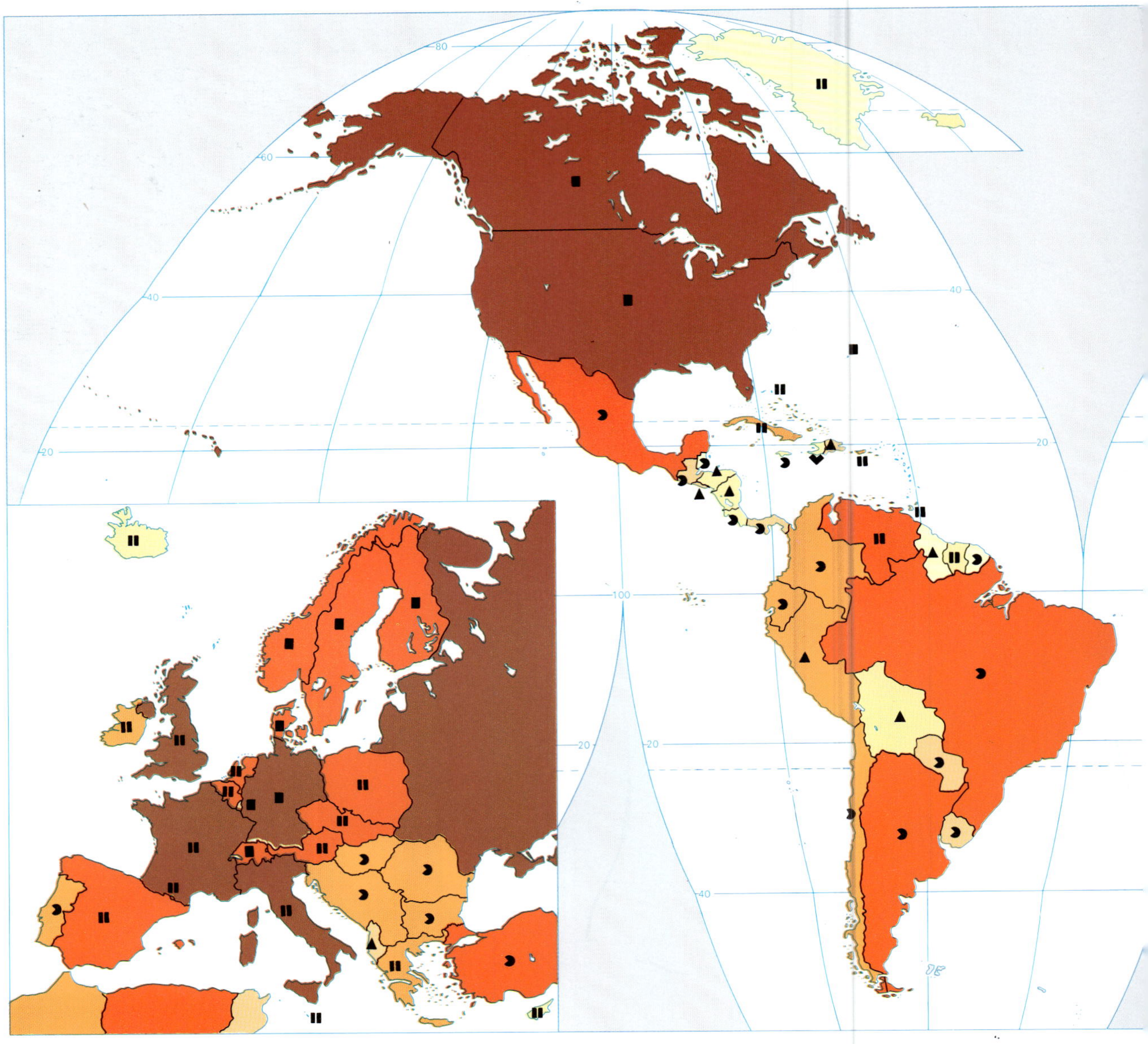

Gross National Product

Total per country at market price
In billions of U.S. dollars

Total per country	Number of countries
300–3,670	9
50–300	26
10–50	28
3–10	34
1–3	32
Less than 1	21
No data available	

Per capita
In U.S. dollars

Symbol	Per capita	Number of countries
■	10,000–22,300	19
▮▮	3,000–10,000	33
◗	1,000–3,000	32
▲	400–1,000	30
♥	200–400	27
●	Less than 200	15

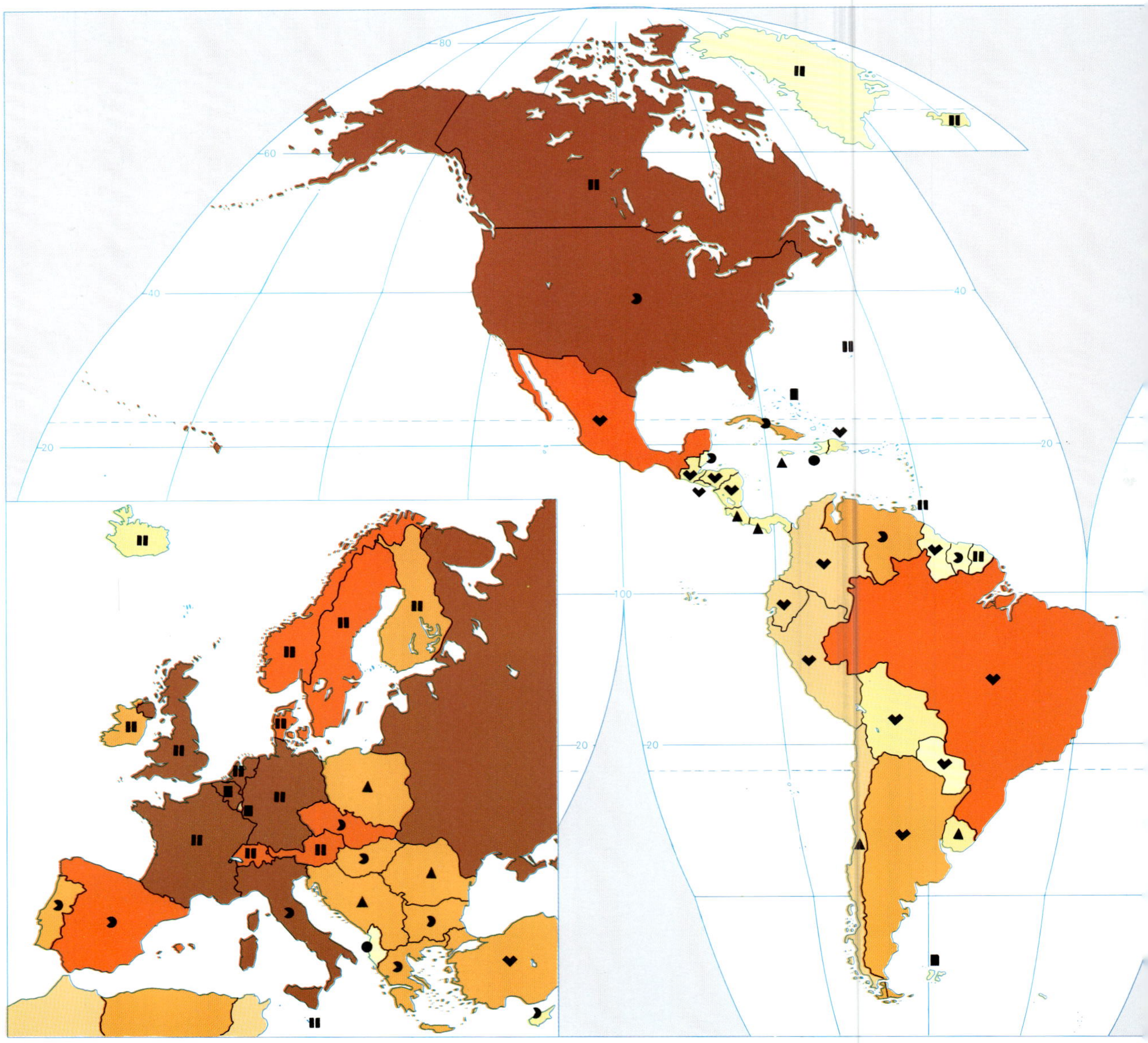

International Trade

Total per country
In billions of U.S. dollars

Total per country	Number of countries
100–560	10
30–100	18
10–30	25
3–10	19
1–3	33
Less than 1	46
No data available	

Per capita
In U.S. dollars

Symbol	Per capita	Number of countries
■	10,000–45,000	11
▮▮	3,000–10,000	25
◗	1,000–3,000	27
▲	500–1,000	18
♥	200–500	36
●	Less than 200	39

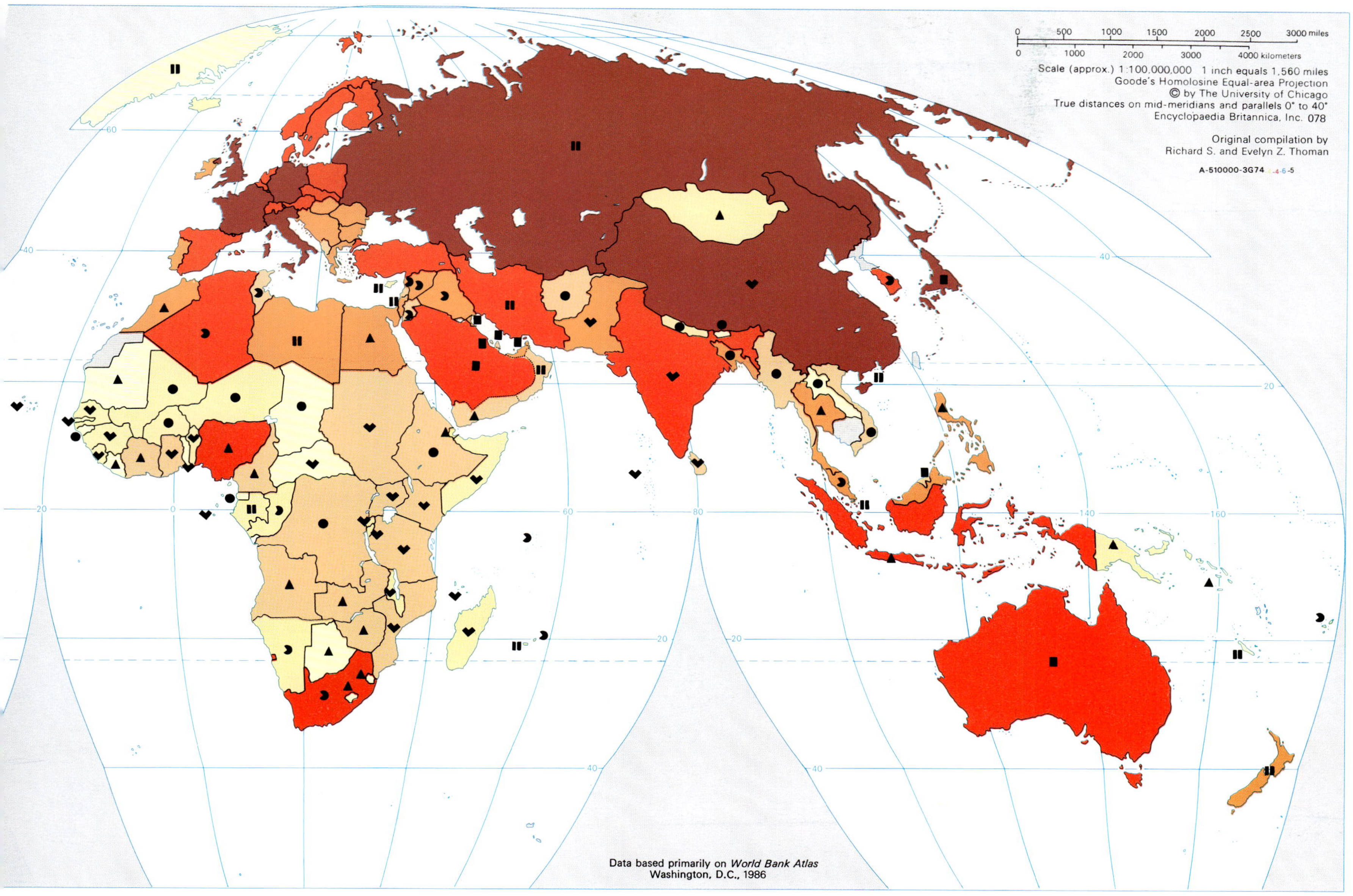
0 500 1000 1500 2000 2500 3000 miles
0 1000 2000 3000 4000 kilometers
Scale (approx.) 1:100,000,000 1 inch equals 1,560 miles
Goode's Homolosine Equal-area Projection
© by The University of Chicago
True distances on mid-meridians and parallels 0° to 40°
Encyclopaedia Britannica, Inc. 078
Original compilation by
Richard S. and Evelyn Z. Thoman
A-510000-3G74
Data based primarily on *World Bank Atlas*
Washington, D.C., 1986

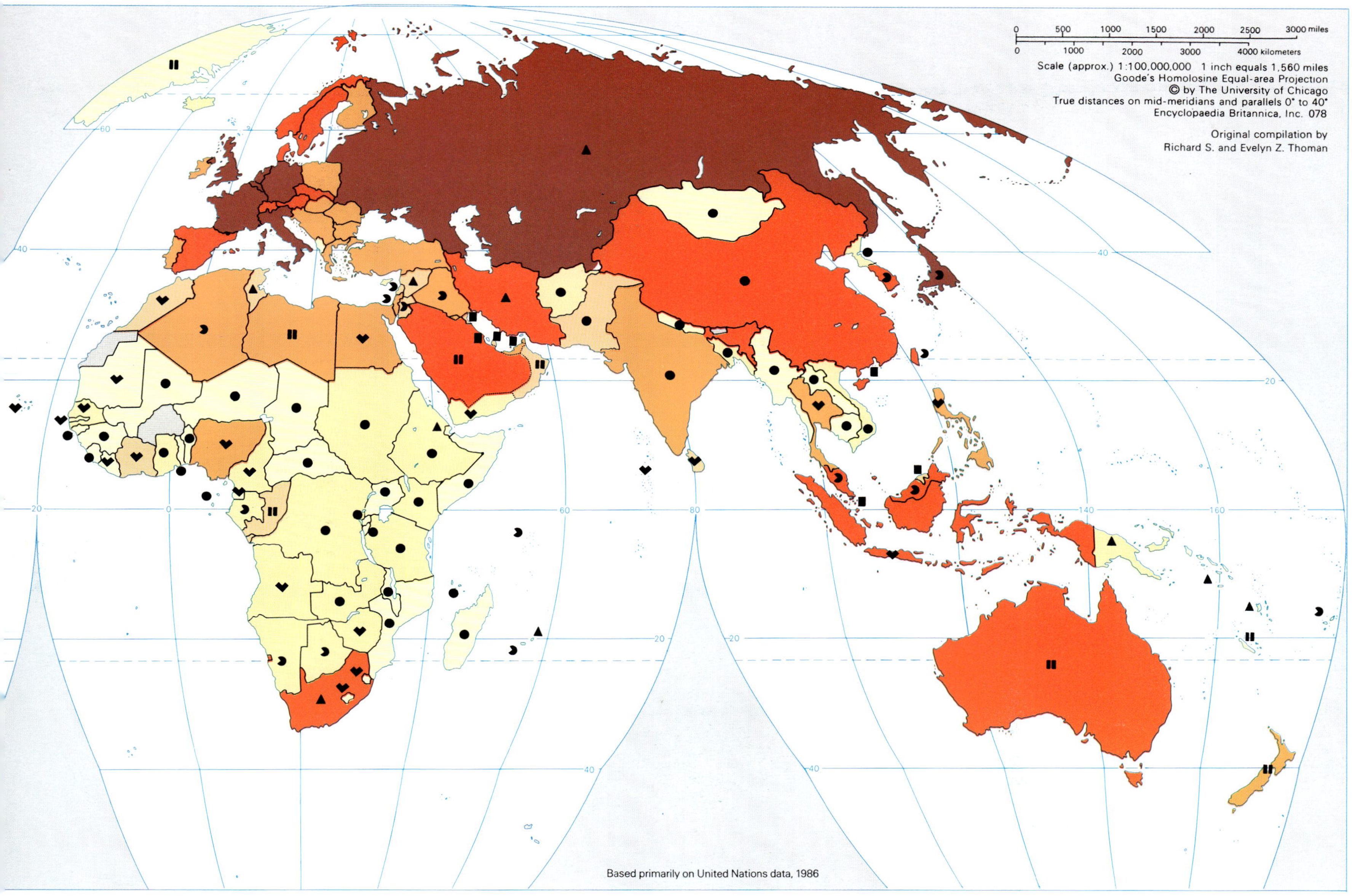
0 500 1000 1500 2000 2500 3000 miles
0 1000 2000 3000 4000 kilometers
Scale (approx.) 1:100,000,000 1 inch equals 1,560 miles
Goode's Homolosine Equal-area Projection
© by The University of Chicago
True distances on mid-meridians and parallels 0° to 40°
Encyclopaedia Britannica, Inc. 078
Original compilation by
Richard S. and Evelyn Z. Thoman
Based primarily on United Nations data, 1986

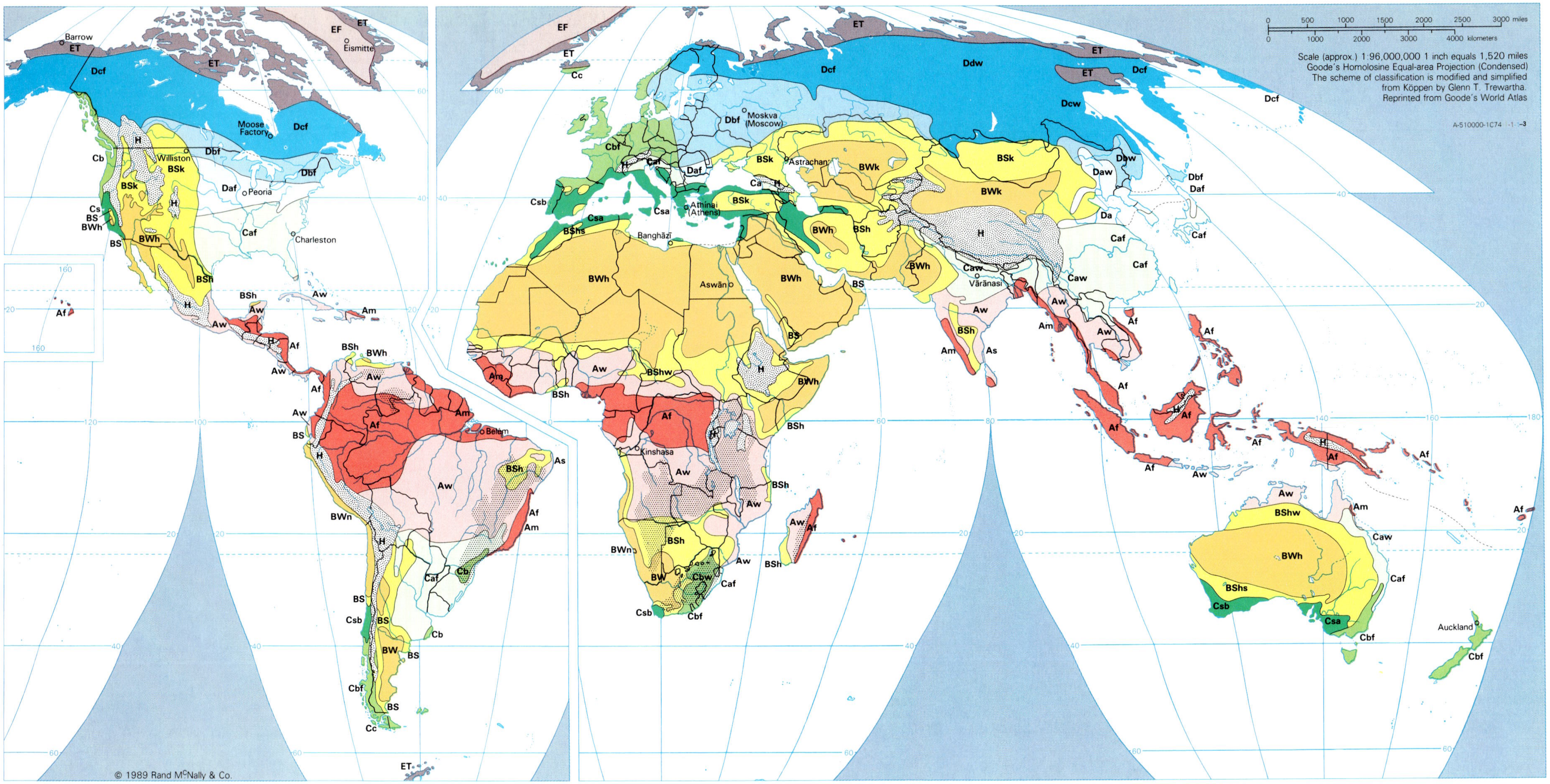

Climate

A. Tropical Rainy Climates
- Tropical Rainforest (**Af**, **Am**)
- Tropical Savanna (**Aw**)
  Cooler uplands stippled

B. Dry Climates
- Steppe (**BS**)
  Tropical and Subtropical Steppe (**BSh**)
  Middle latitude Steppe (**BSk**)
- Desert (**BW**)
  Tropical and Subtropical Desert (**BWh**)
  Middle latitude Desert (**BWk**)

C. Humid Mesothermal Climates
- Mediterranean or Dry Summer Subtropical (**Cs**)
- Humid Subtropical (**Ca**, warm summer)
- Marine West Coast (**Cb**, **Cc**, cool summer)

D. Humid Microthermal Climates
- Humid Continental, Warm Summer (**Da**)
- Humid Continental, Cool Summer (**Db**)
- Subarctic (**Dc**, **Dd**)

E. Polar Climates
- Tundra (**ET**)
- Ice Cap (**EF**)

H. Extensive Uplands

Undifferentiated Highlands

Two types of higher elevation climatic region are shown: (1) lower and flatter 'extensive uplands' areas above 2000 feet (600 meters), which, though cooler and wetter, contain no topographic barriers to climatic regions around them, and are thus classifiable with them; and (2) 'undifferentiated highlands,' mountainous regions of great elevation (forming barriers to regional atmospheric circulation) and great local relief, creating microclimates effectively unmappable at this scale.

Type Regions and Subtypes

A – Tropical forest climates: coolest month above 64.4°F. (18°C.).

B – Dry climates

BS – Steppe or semiarid climate.

BW – Desert or arid climate.

*C – Mesothermal forest climates: coldest month above 32°F. (0°C.) but below 64.4°F. (18°C.); warmest month above 50°F. (10°C.).

*D – Microthermal, snow-forest climates: coldest month below 32°F. (0°C.); warmest month above 50°F. (10°C.).

E – Polar climates: warmest month below 50°F. (10°C.).

ET – Tundra climate: warmest month below 50°F. (10°C.) but above 32°F. (0°C.).

EF – Perpetual frost: all months below 32°F. (0°C.).

a – Warmest month above 71.6°F. (22°C.).

b – Warmest month below 71.6°F. (22°C.).

c – Less than four months over 50°F. (10°C.).

d – Same as "c", but coldest month below -36.4°F. (-38°C.).

f – Constantly moist; precipitation all through the year.

*h – Hot and dry; all months above 32°F. (0°C.).

*k – Cold and dry; at least one month below 32°F. (0°C.)

m – Monsoon rain; short dry season, but total rainfall sufficient to support rainforest.

n – Frequent fog.

s – Dry season in summer.

w – Dry season in winter.

* Modification of Köppen definition

Curves show Fahrenheit temperature; vertical bars show precipitation in inches.

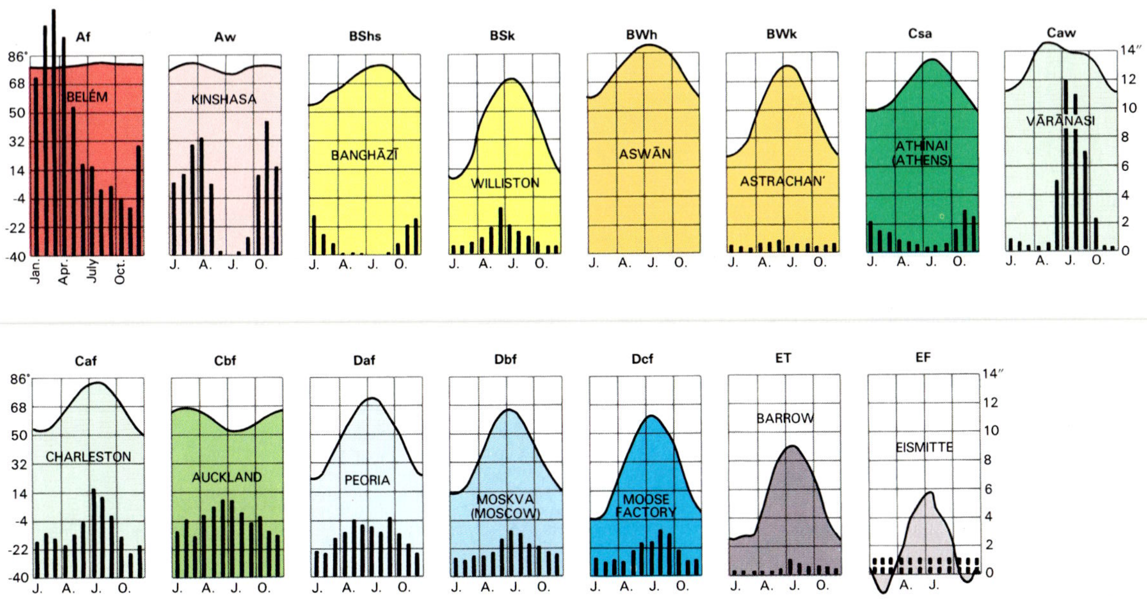

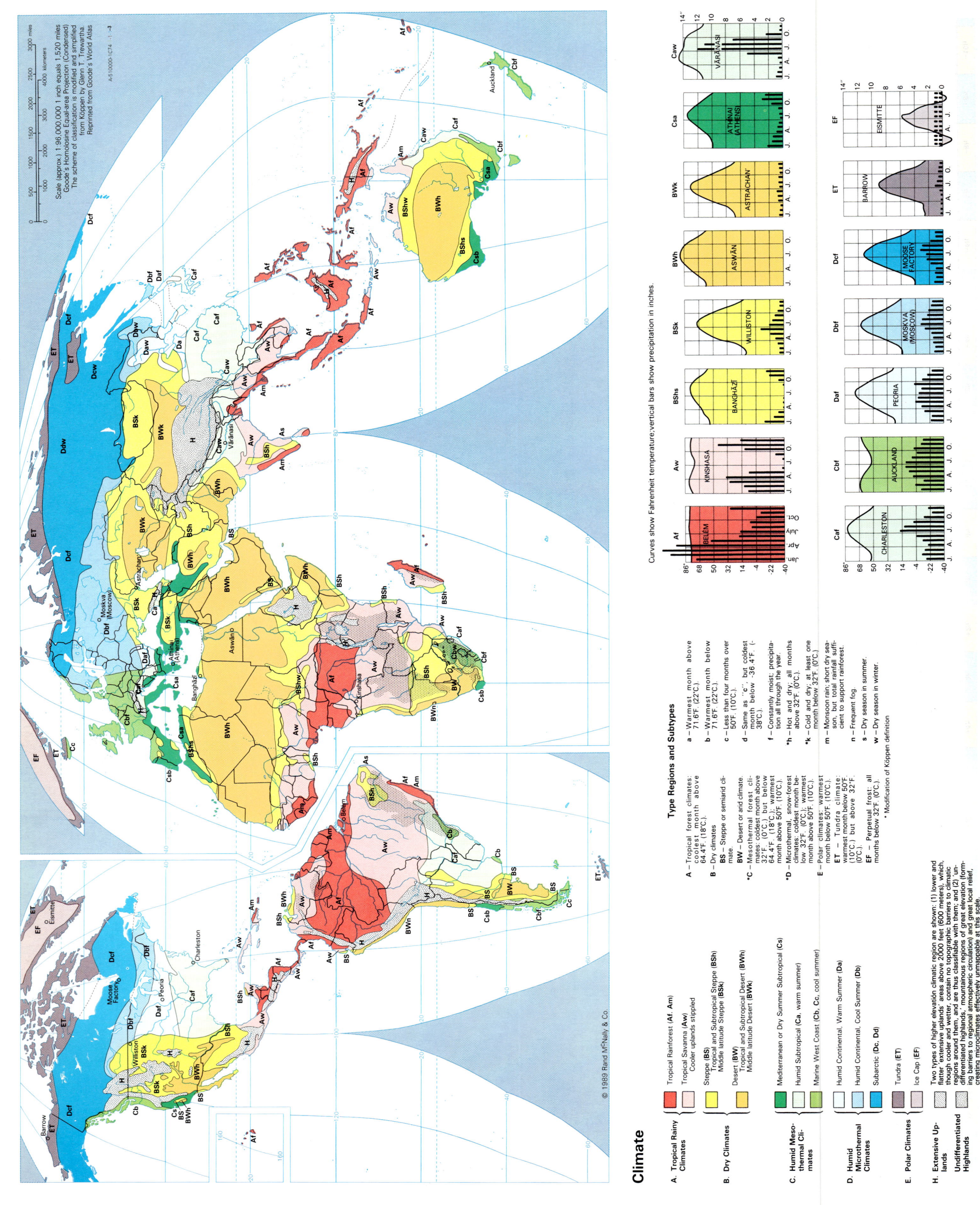

Time Zones

- Standard time zone of even-numbered hours from Greenwich time
- Standard time zone of odd-numbered hours from Greenwich time
- Time varies from the standard time zone by half an hour
- Time varies from the standard time zone by other than half an hour

h m hours, minutes

The standard time zone system, fixed by international agreement and by law in each country, is based on a theoretical division of the globe into 24 zones of 15° longitude each. The mid-meridian of each zone fixes the hour for the entire zone. The zero time zone extends 7½° east and 7½° west of the Greenwich meridian, 0° longitude. Since the earth rotates toward the east, time zones to the west of Greenwich are earlier, to the east, later.

Plus and minus hours at the top of the map are added to or subtracted from local time to find Greenwich time. Local standard time can be determined for any area in the world by adding one hour for each time zone counted in an easterly direction from one's own, or by subtracting one hour for each zone counted in a westerly direction. To separate one day from the next, the 180th meridian has been designated as the international date line. On both sides of the line the time of day is the same, but west of the line it is one day later than it is to the east.

Countries that adhere to the international zone system adopt the zone applicable to their location. Some countries, however, establish time zones based on political boundaries, or adopt the time zone of a neighboring unit. For all or part of the year some countries also advance their time by one hour, thereby utilizing more daylight hours each day.

Surface Configuration

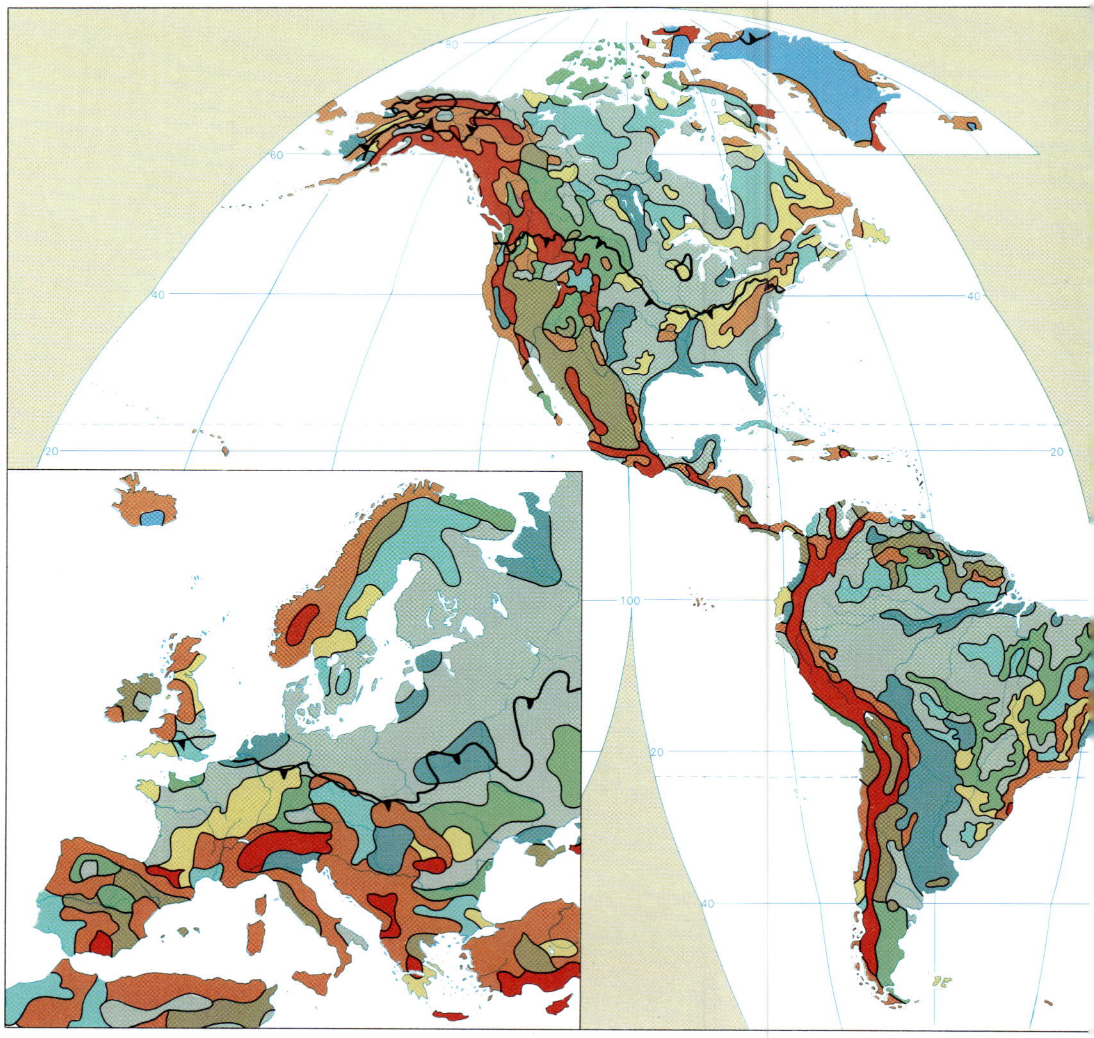

Smooth lands

- Level plains: nearly all slopes gentle; local relief less than 100 ft. (30 m.)
- Irregular plains: majority of slopes gentle; local relief 100-300 ft. (30-90 m.)

Broken lands

- Tablelands and plateaus: majority of slopes gentle, with the gentler slopes on the uplands; local relief more than 300 ft. (90 m.)
- Hill-studded plains: majority of slopes gentle, with the gentler slopes in the lowlands; local relief 300-1,000 ft. (90-300 m.)
- Mountain-studded plains: majority of slopes gentle, with the gentler slopes in the lowlands; local relief more than 1,000 ft. (300 m.)

Rough lands

- Hill lands: steeper slopes predominate; local relief less than 1,000 ft. (300 m.)
- Mountains: steeper slopes predominate; local relief 1,000-5,000 ft. (300-1,500 m.)
- Mountains of great relief: steeper slopes predominate; local relief more than 5,000 ft. (1,500 m.)

Other surfaces

- Ice caps: permanent ice
- Maximum extent of glaciation

Earth Structure and Tectonics

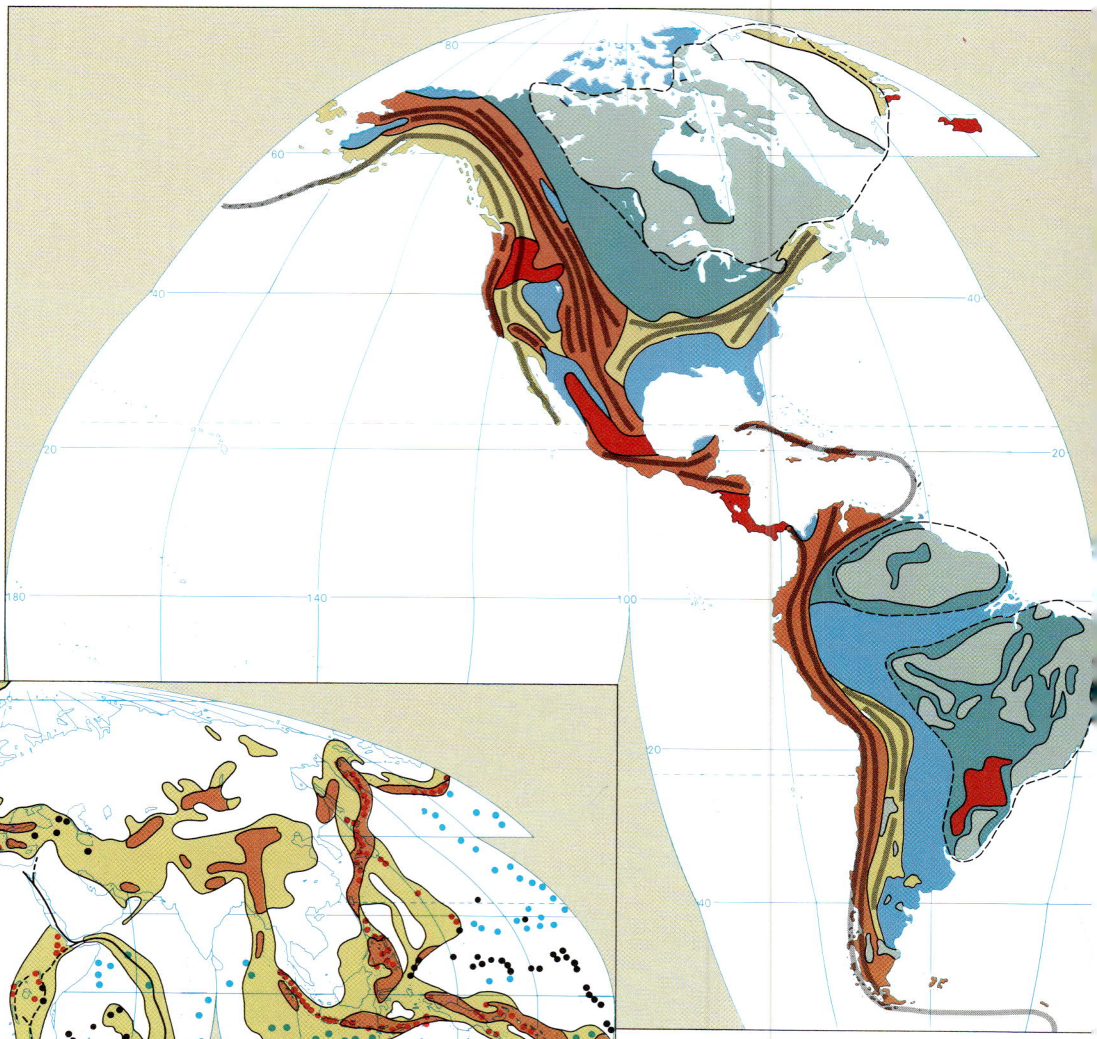

- Precambrian stable shield areas
- Exposed Precambrian rock
- Paleozoic and Mesozoic flat-lying sedimentary rocks
- Principal Paleozoic and Mesozoic folded areas
- Cenozoic sedimentary rocks
- Principal Cenozoic folded areas
- Lava plateaus
- Major trends of folding

Geologic time chart

Precambrian—from formation of the earth (at least 4 billion years ago) to 600 million years ago

Paleozoic—from 600 million to 200 million years ago

Mesozoic—from 200 million to 70 million years ago

Cenozoic—from 70 million years ago to present time

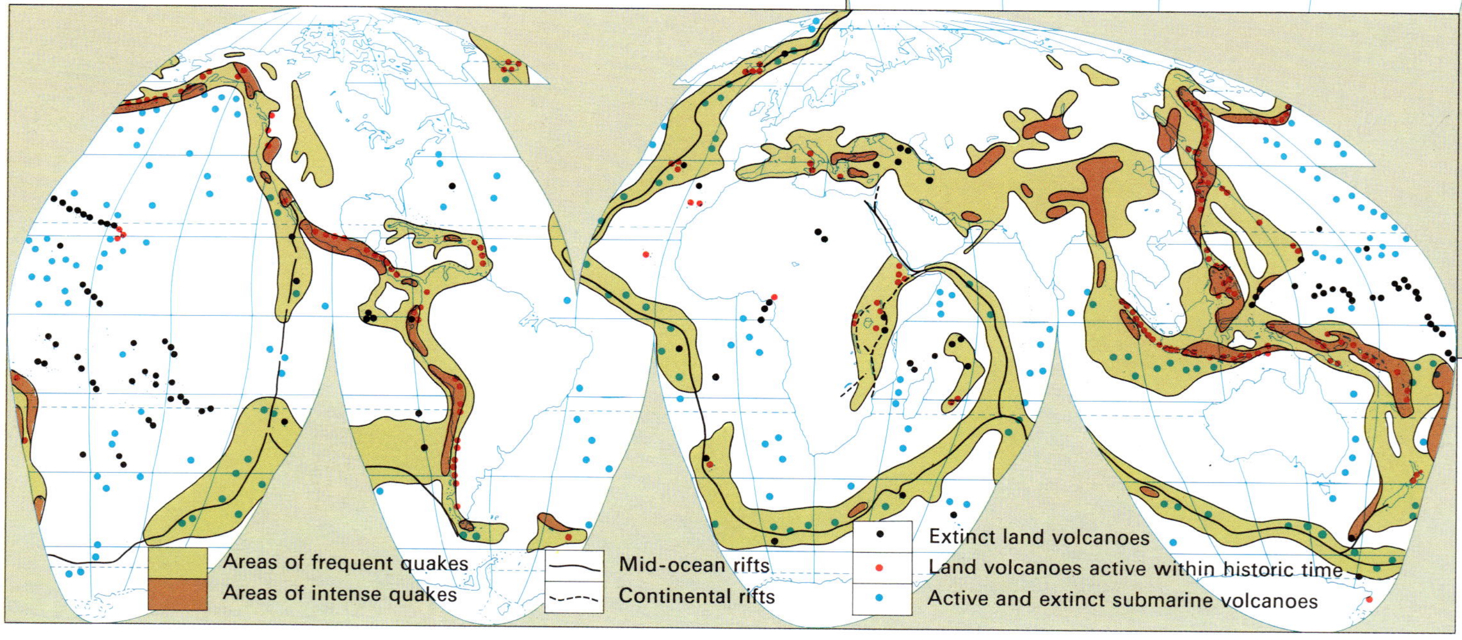

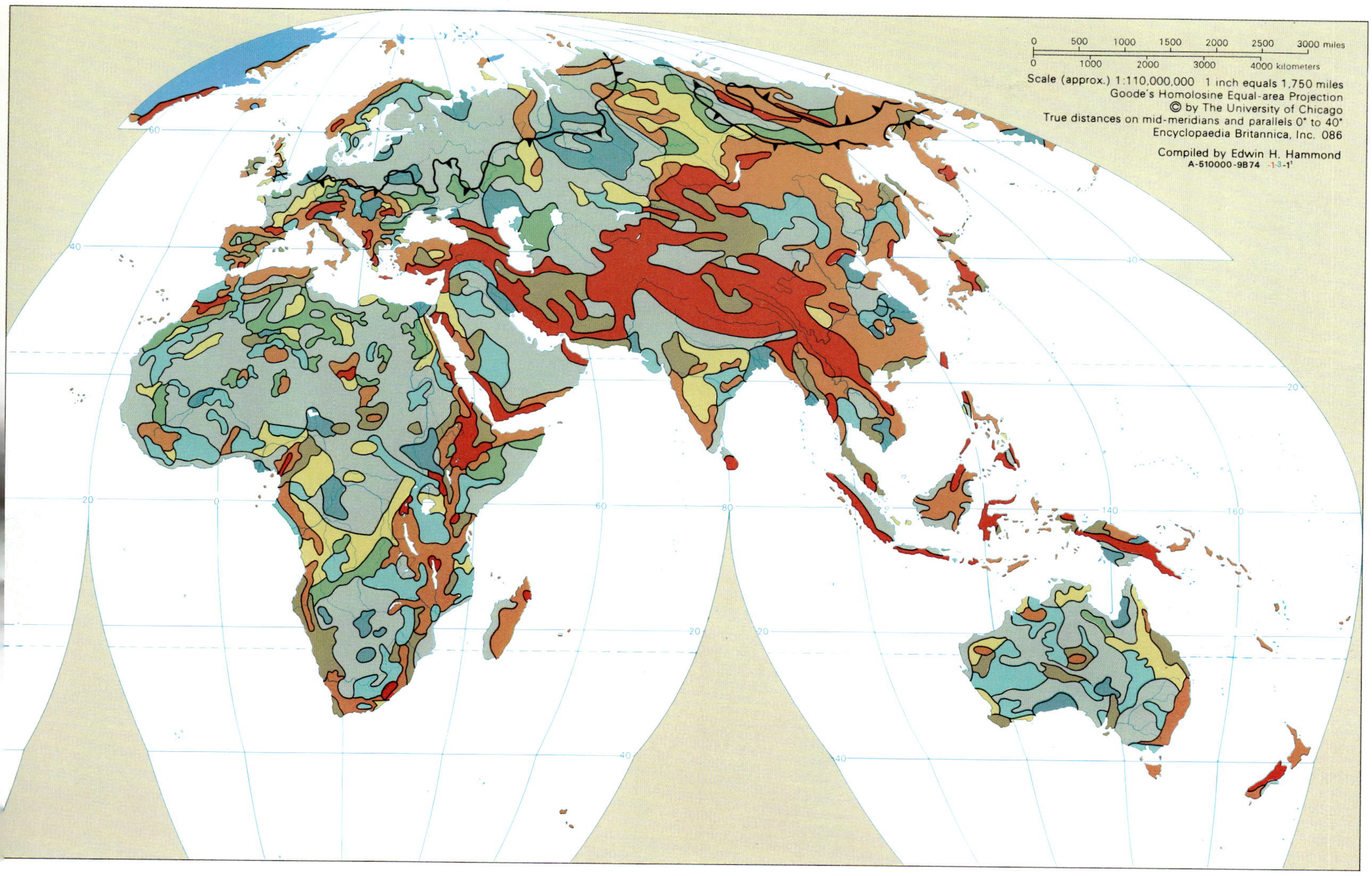

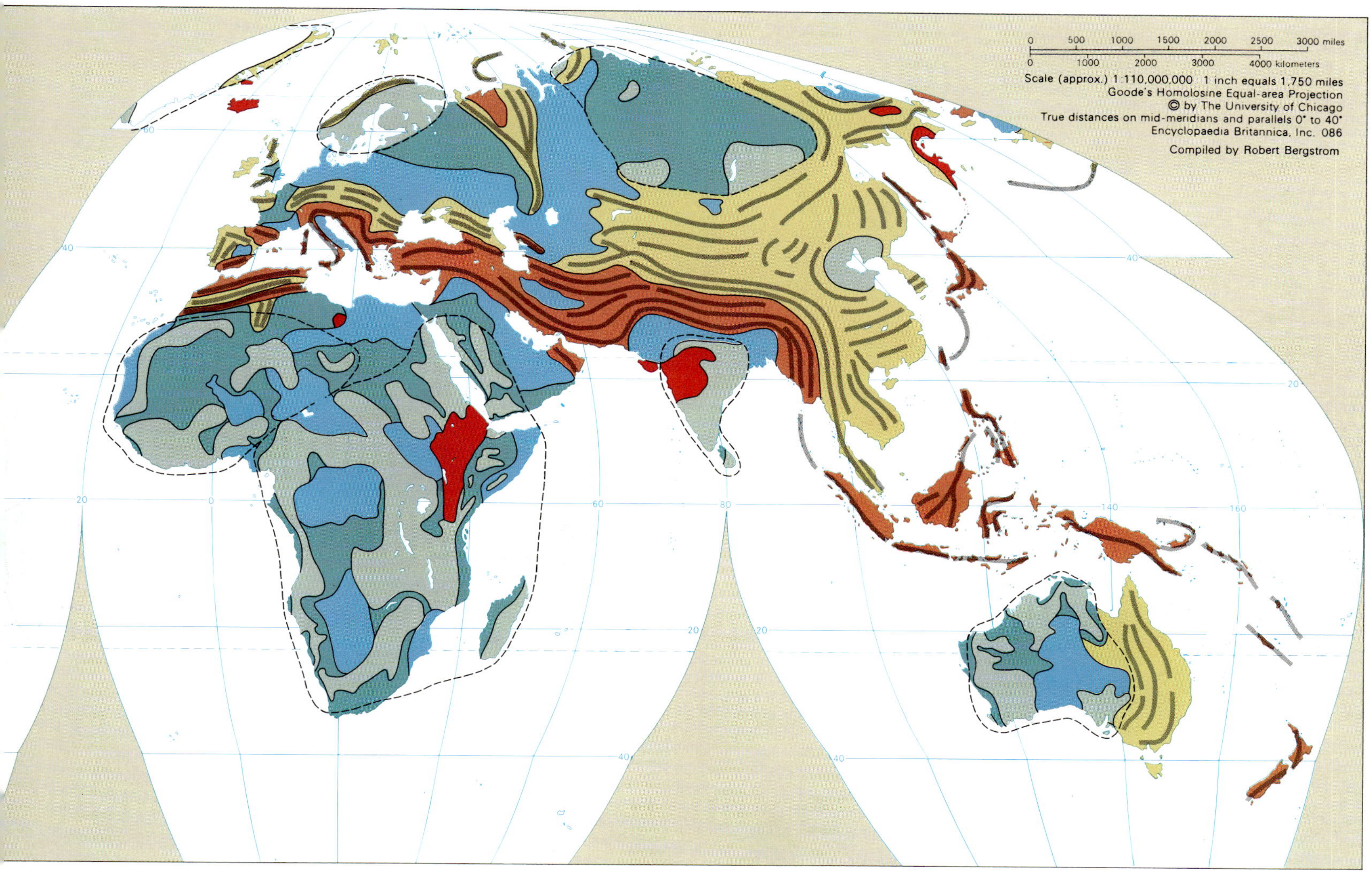

Development of the earth's structure

The earth is in process of constant transformation. Movements in the hot, dense interior of the earth result in folding and fracture of the crust and transfer of molten material to the surface. As a result, large structures such as mountain ranges, volcanoes, lava plateaus, and rift valleys are created. The forces that bring about these structural changes are called *tectonic forces.*

The present continents have developed from stable nuclei, or *shields*, of ancient (Precambrian) rock. Erosive forces such as water, wind, and ice have worn away particles of the rock, depositing them at the edges of the shields, where they have accumulated and ultimately become sedimentary rock. Subsequently, in plaees, these extensive areas of flat-lying rock have been elevated, folded, or warped, by the action of tectonic forces, to form mountains. The shape of these mountains has been altered by later erosion. Where the forces of erosion have been at work for a long time, the mountains tend to have a low relief and rounded contours, like the Appalachians. Mountains more recently formed are high and rugged, like the Himalayas.

The map above depicts some of the major geologic structures of the earth and identifies them according to the period of their formation. A geologic time chart is included in the legend. The inset map shows the most important areas of earthquakes, rifts, and volcanic activity. Comparison of all the maps will show the close correlation between present-day mountain systems, recent (Cenozoic) mountain-building, and the areas of frequent earthquakes and active volcanoes.

Natural Vegetation

Broad-leaved evergreen vegetation
- Broad-leaved evergreen forest
- Broad-leaved evergreen shrub formation
- Scattered broad-leaved evergreen shrubs
- Scattered broad-leaved evergreen dwarf shrubs

Broad-leaved deciduous vegetation
- Broad-leaved deciduous forest
- Broad-leaved deciduous shrub formation
- Scattered broad-leaved deciduous shrubs
- Scattered broad-leaved deciduous dwarf shrubs

Coniferous vegetation
- Needle-leaved evergreen forest
- Scattered needle-leaved evergreen trees
- Needle-leaved deciduous forest

Mixed vegetation without grass
- Forest of broad-leaved evergreen and deciduous trees
- Forest of broad-leaved and needle-leaved evergreen trees
- Broad-leaved deciduous forests with broad-leaved evergreen shrubs
- Forest of broad-leaved deciduous and needle-leaved evergreen trees

Mixed vegetation with grass
- Grassland with scattered broad-leaved evergreen trees
- Grassland with broad-leaved evergreen shrubs
- Grassland with scattered broad-leaved deciduous trees
- Grassland with broad-leaved deciduous shrubs

Grassland, tundra, barren
- Grassland
- Patches of grass
- Lichens and grasses
- Lichens and mosses
- Barren

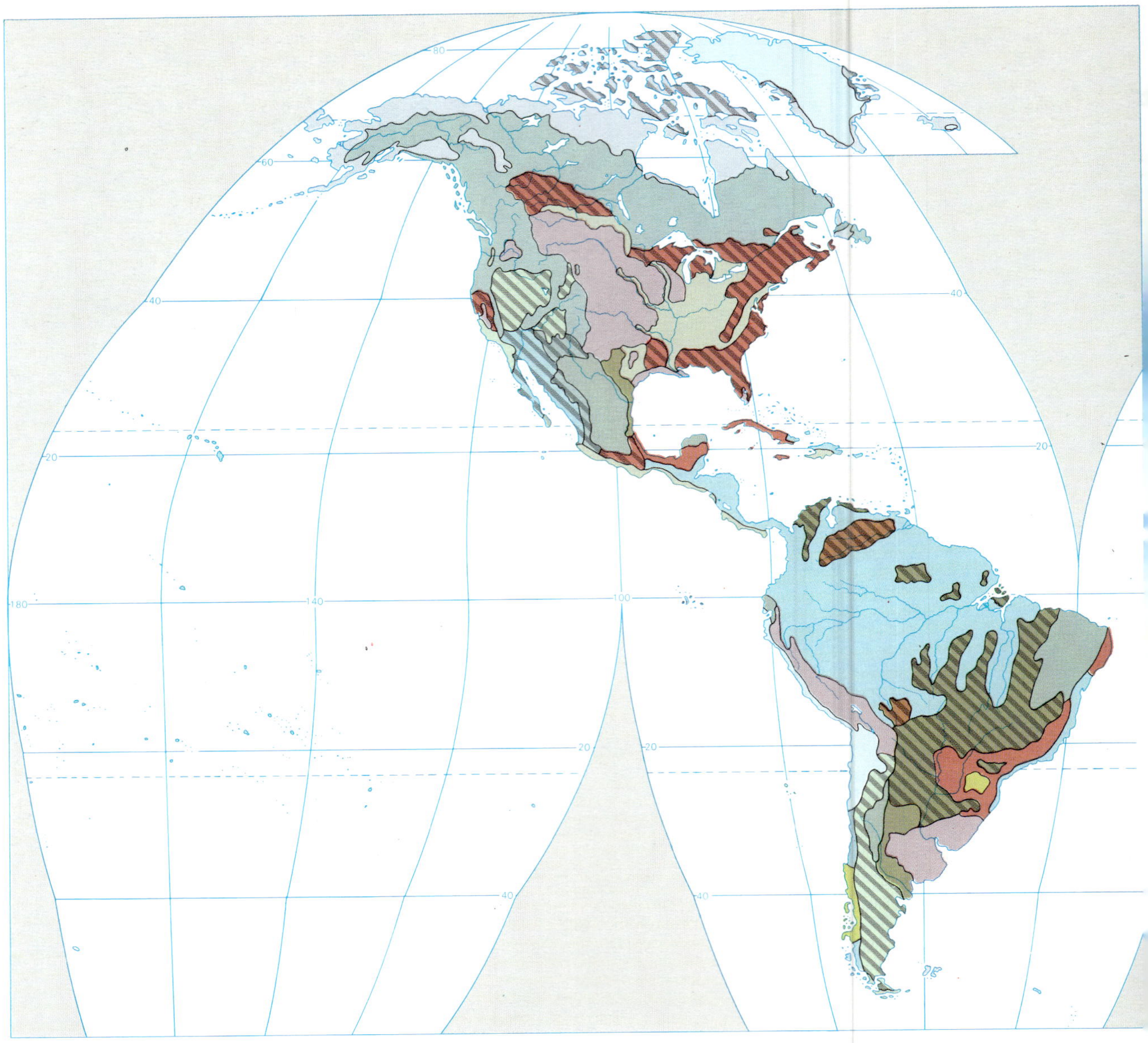

Soils

- Tundra soils of frigid climates; commonly with permanently frozen subsoil; supports dwarf shrubs, mosses, and lichens; some used for reindeer pasture
- Podzolic soils of humid, cool climates; covered with predominantly coniferous forest; some farming, mainly subsistence
- Podzolic soils of humid, temperate climates; originally covered with predominantly deciduous forest, much of it removed to accommodate extensive general farming, industry, and cities
- Podzolic soils of humid, warm climates; covered with coniferous or mixed forest; general farming
- Chernozemic soils of subhumid and semiarid, cool to tropical climates; supports mainly grasslands; extensive grain and livestock farming
- Latosolic soils of humid or wet-dry tropical and subtropical climates; supports forest or savanna; shifting cultivation with some plantation agriculture
- Grumusolic soils of humid to semiarid and temperate to tropical climates, with distinct wet and dry seasons; mainly grass-covered; livestock and grain farming
- Desertic soils of arid climates; includes many areas of shallow, stony soils; sparse cover of shrubs and grass, some suitable for grazing; fertile if irrigated; dry farming possible in some areas
- Mountain soils of all climates; shallow, stony; barren, grass-covered, or forested, depending on climate; includes many areas of other soils
- Alluvial soils of all climates; deposited by water in flood plains and deltas of rivers; intensive farming in most temperate and some tropical regions (many smaller areas not shown)
- Ice cap of polar regions

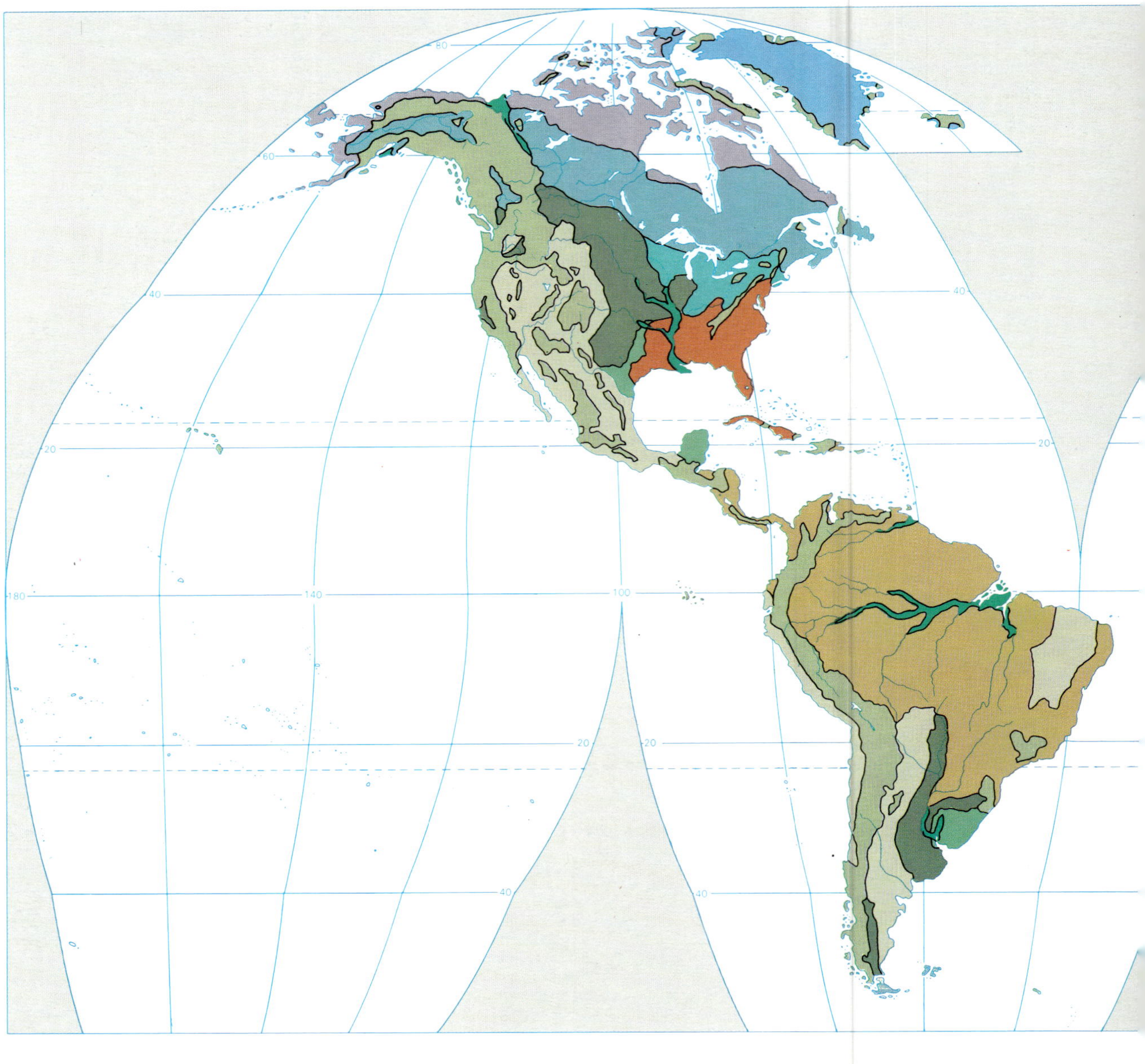

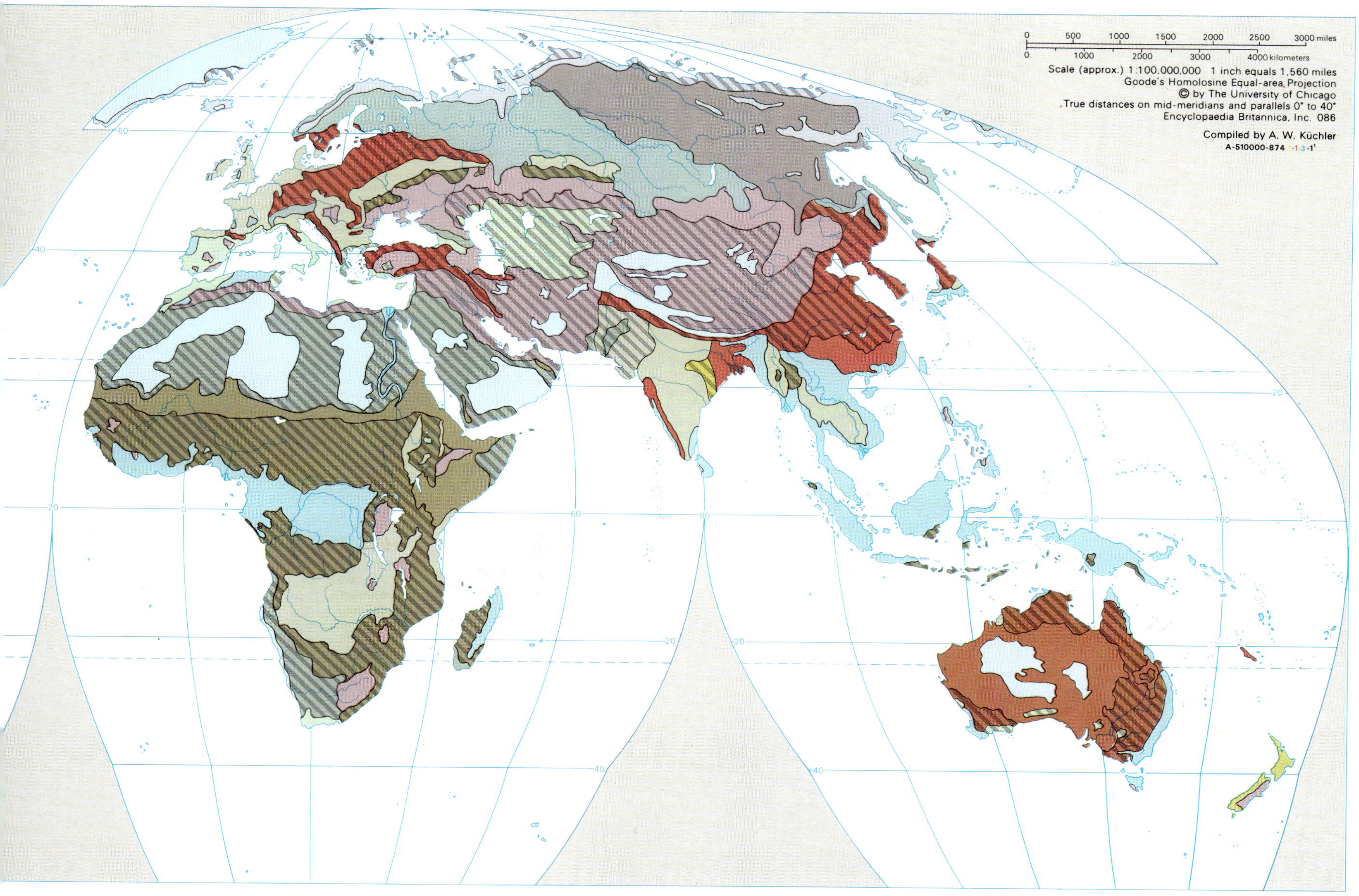
0 500 1000 1500 2000 2500 3000 miles
0 1000 2000 3000 4000 kilometers
Scale (approx.) 1:100,000,000 1 inch equals 1,560 miles
Goode's Homolosine Equal-area Projection
© by The University of Chicago
True distances on mid-meridians and parallels 0° to 40°
Encyclopaedia Britannica, Inc. 086
Compiled by A. W. Küchler
A-510000-874 -1-3-1

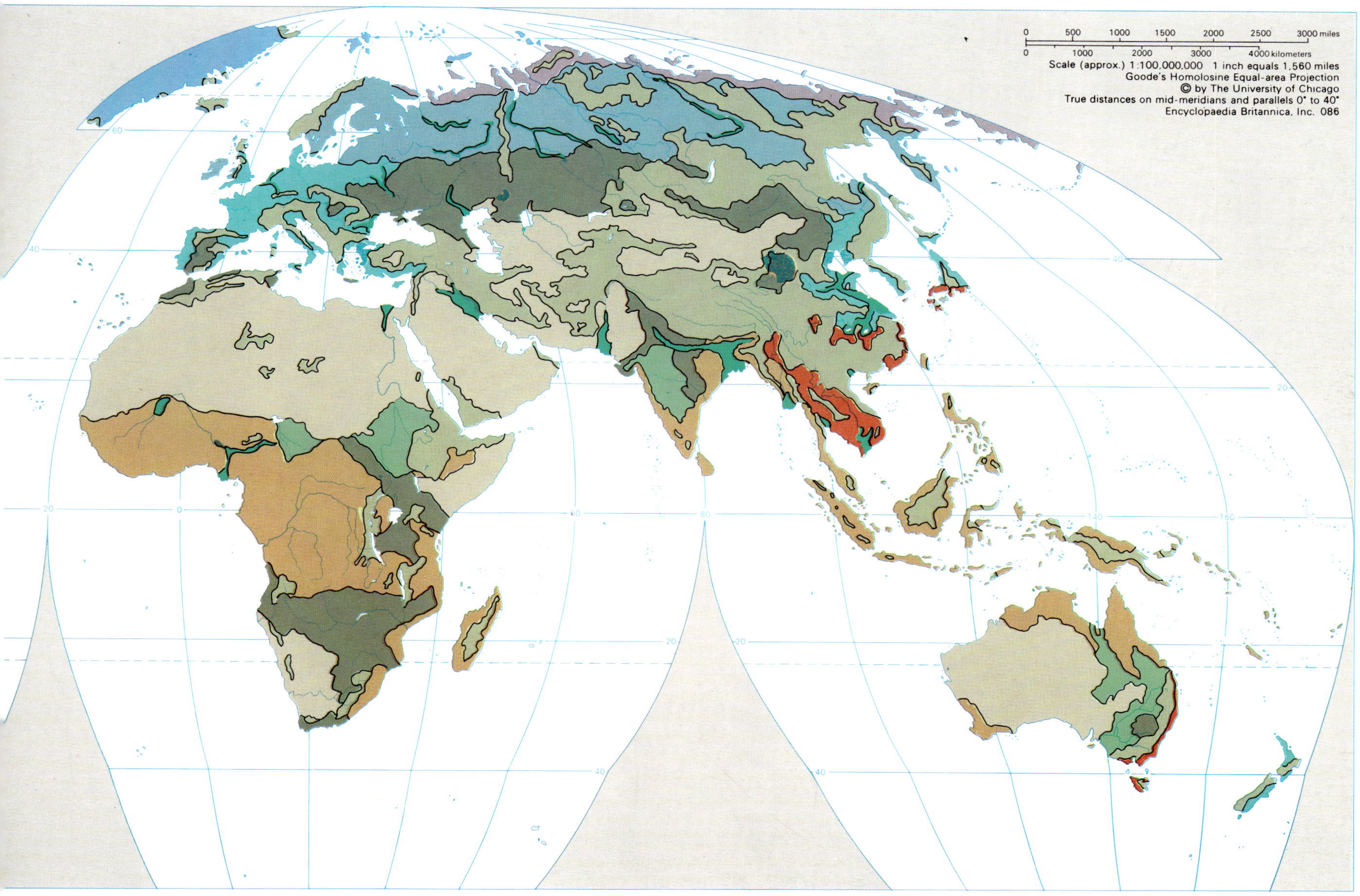
0 500 1000 1500 2000 2500 3000 miles
0 1000 2000 3000 4000 kilometers
Scale (approx.) 1:100,000,000 1 inch equals 1,560 miles
Goode's Homolosine Equal-area Projection
© by The University of Chicago
True distances on mid-meridians and parallels 0° to 40°
Encyclopaedia Britannica, Inc. 086

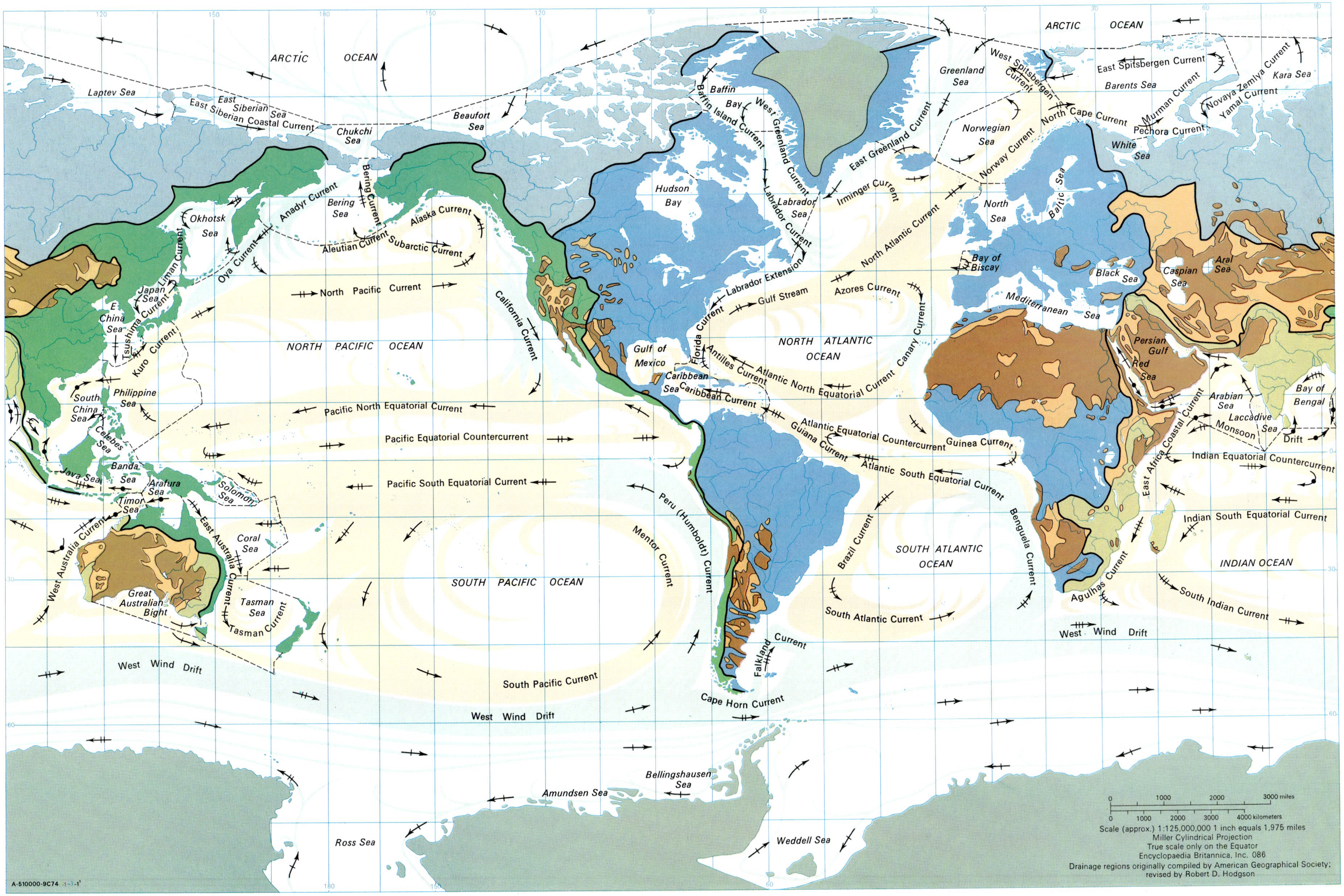

Drainage Regions and Ocean Currents

Currents during Northern Hemisphere winter

- Cold current
- Warm current
- Indicates a current that reverses direction during Northern Hemisphere summer

Speed of current
(1 knot=1 nautical mile[6,076 ft.] per hour)

- Less than 0.5 knots
- 0.5—0.8 knots
- Greater than 0.8 knots
- Limits of seas

Drainage regions
Surface drainage reaching an Ocean

- Outline of oceanic drainage regions
- Atlantic Ocean
- Pacific Ocean
- Indian Ocean
- Arctic Ocean

- Surface drainage not reaching an ocean
- Arid regions
- Ice cap

THIS SECTION OPENS with World Political and World Physical maps at the scale of 1:75,000,000. There follow maps of the Pacific, Indian, and Atlantic oceans at the scale 1:48,000,000, the largest scale at which the total expanse of these bodies of water could be portrayed. Finally, a series of continent relief maps at the scale of 1:24,000,000 show a global view of the earth as it would appear from about 4,000 miles in space. The Azimuthal Equal-Area projection is used for the 1:24,000,000 maps, the scale being approximately that of a globe 20 inches in diameter.

The colors of the continent maps portray the land areas as if viewed from space during the growing season, without regard to the fact that the growing seasons are not concurrent in all areas. Underwater features and varying water depths are represented by shaded relief and different color tones. The result is a strong physical portrait of the earth's major land and submarine forms. The legend below shows how these different kinds of terrain and vegetation have been represented. The names of physical features—plateaus, basins, mountain ranges, seas, rivers, lakes, gulfs, trenches, bays, islands—predominate on these maps.

DIESER KARTENTEIL BEGINNT mit politischen und physischen Weltkarten im Massstab 1:75 Millionen. Dann folgen Karten des Pazifischen, Indischen und Atlantischen Ozeans in 1:48 Millionen, dem grössten Massstab, in dem diese Wasserflächen in ihrer ganzen Ausdehnung abgebildet werden konnten. Schliesslich folgt eine Reihe von Reliefkarten der Erdteile in 1:24 Millionen. Sie geben eine Übersicht der Erde, wie sie aus einer Entfernung von ungefähr 6 400 Kilometer aus dem Weltraum gewonnen würde. Den Karten im Massstab 1:24 Millionen liegt ein flächentreuer azimutaler Entwurf zugrunde, dieser Massstab entspricht ungefähr dem eines Globus von 50 cm Durchmesser.

Die Farben der Erdteilkarten bilden jedes Landgebiet so ab, wie es in der Vegetationsperiode aus der Vogelperspektive erschiene, ohne zu berücksichtigen, dass die Vegetationsperioden nicht in allen Gebieten gleichzeitig eintreten. Die Gliederung des Meeresbodens und die unterschiedlichen Meerestiefen werden durch Schummerung und verschiedene Farbstufen dargestellt. Das Ergebnis ist eine anschauliche physische Darstellung der wichtigsten terrestrischen und untermeerischen Formen der Erde. Die untenstehende Zeichenerklärung zeigt, wie diese verschiedenen Geländeformen und Vegetationsgebiete veranschaulicht werden. Namen physischer Objekte—Hochebenen, Becken, Gebirgszüge, Meere, Flüsse, Seen, Buchten, Gräben, Inseln—herrschen in diesen Karten vor.

ESTA SECCIÓN DA PRINCIPIO con los Mapas Políticos y Físicos del Mundo, a una escala de 1:75 000 000. A continuación están los mapas de los océanos Pacífico, Indico y Atlántico a una escala de 1:48 000 000, que es la mayor escala utilizable para la representación de esas masas de agua en toda su extensión. Por último, una serie de mapas del relieve de los continentes, a una escala de 1:24 000 000, proporcionan una vista global de la tierra tal como se apreciaría desde el espacio a una distancia aproximada de 6 400 kilómetros. La proyección azimutal equiárea se usa, para los mapas de 1:24 000 000, a una escala según la cual la tierra se reduciría a un globo de unos 50 cm de diámetro.

Los colores utilizados en los mapas de los continentes representan las diversas regiones de la tierra tal como se verían desde el espacio durante la estación en que la vegetación se desarrolla, sin tomar en cuenta que este fenómeno no se produce simultáneamente en todas las áreas. Las estructuras características del fondo marino y las variaciones de profundidad de los océanos se representan mediante relieve sombreado y distintos matices de color. El resultado es una imagen elocuente de las formas terrestres y submarinas más notables del planeta. La leyenda abajo explica cómo se representan estos diferentes tipos de terreno y vegetación. En estos mapas predomina la nomenclatura de elementos físicos: mesetas, cuencas, sierras, mares, ríos, lagos, golfos, bahías, trincheras, islas.

CETTE PARTIE comprend d'abord des cartes du monde politique et du monde physique à l'échelle de 1:75 000 000. Viennent ensuite les cartes des océans Pacifique, Indien et Atlantique à l'échelle de 1:48 000 000, la plus grande échelle qui a permis la reproduction complète de ces étendues d'eau. Pour terminer, une série de cartes en relief des continents à l'échelle de 1:24 000 000 donne une vue globale de la terre, telle qu'elle apparaîtrait vue de l'espace à une distance d'environ 6 400 kilomètres. La projection azimutale équivalente a été utilisée pour les cartes au 1:24 000 000ᵉ, dont l'échelle équivaut à celle d'un globe de 50 cm de diamètre environ.

Les couleurs des cartes font apparaître les continents tels qu'on les verrait de l'espace, pendant la saison de croissance végétale, mais sans tenir compte du fait que cette saison n'apparaît pas partout simultanément. Le relief sous-marin est représenté par un estompage et la profondeur des océans par une variation de la couleur. Il en résulte une reproduction vigoureuse des principaux paysages continentaux et des principales formes sous-marines. La légende ci-dessous indique de quelle façon ils sont cartographiés. Les noms d'éléments topographiques tels que plateaux, bassins, chaînes de montagnes, mers, cours d'eau, lacs, golfes, baies, crêtes, îles et fosses océaniques, prédominent dans ces cartes.

ESTA SEÇÃO PRINCIPIA com os mapas políticos e físicos do Mundo, em escala de 1:75 000 000. Seguem-se os mapas dos oceanos Pacífico, Índico e Atlântico na escala de 1:48 000 000, a maior escala que se pode utilizar para a representação dessas massas de água em toda a sua extensão. Finalmente, uma série de mapas de relevo dos continentes, na escala de 1:24 000 000, proporciona uma visão global da Terra tal como apareceria do espaço a uma distância aproximada de cerca de 6 400 km. A projeção azimutal equiárea foi usada para os mapas da escala de 1:24 000 000, segundo a qual a Terra se apresentaria como um globo de cerca de 50 cm de diâmetro.

As cores utilizadas nos mapas dos continentes representam as massas terrestres tal como apareceriam vistas do espaço durante a estação do crescimento vegetal, sem levar em conta que este fenômeno não se produz simultaneamente em todas as regiões. As características do fundo do mar e as variações de profundidade das águas são representadas por um relevo sombreado e por diferentes matizes de cor. O resultado proporciona uma imagem física eloqüente das principais formas terrestres e submarinas da Terra. As legendas abaixo explicam como foram representados os diversos tipos de terreno e de vegetação. Nestes mapas predomina a nomenclatura dos elementos físicos: planaltos, bacias, cadeias de montanhas, mares, rios, lagos, golfos, baías, fossas, ilhas.

Land Features / Land Phänomene / Elementos de la Tierra
Paysages Continentaux / Acidentes Continentais

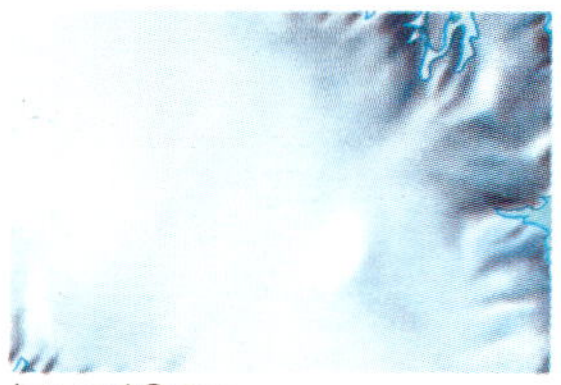

Ice and Snow
Eis und Schnee
Hielo y nieve
Glace et neige
Gelo e neve

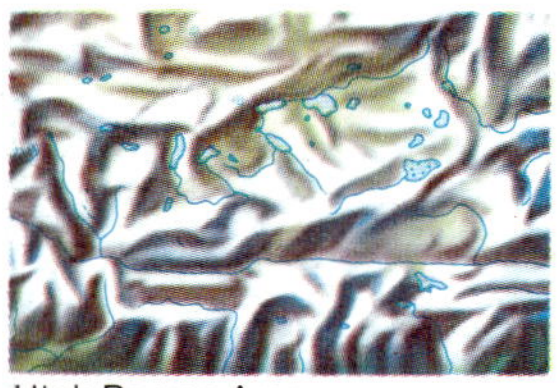

High Barren Area
Hochgebirgswüste
Alta zona árida
Région haute et aride
Alta zona árida

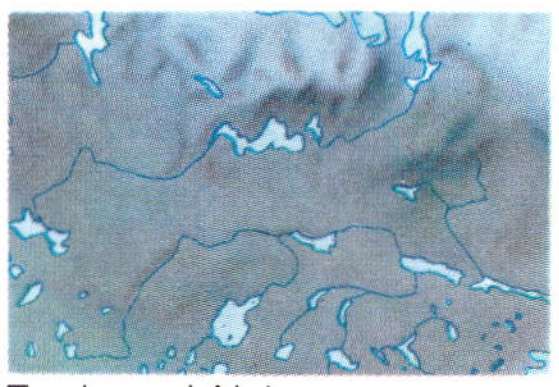

Tundra and Alpine
Tundra und Alpine Vegetation
Tundra y alpina
Toundra et végétation alpine
Tundra e vegetação alpina

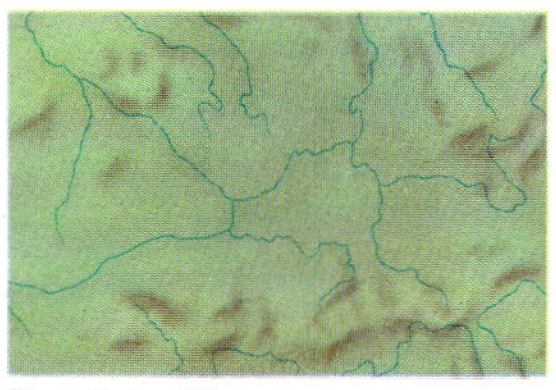

Needleleaf Trees
Nadelwälder
Coníferas
Forêt de conifères
Coníferas

Broadleaf Trees
Laubwälder
Árboles de hojas anchas
Forêt à feuilles caduques
Árvores de folhas caducas

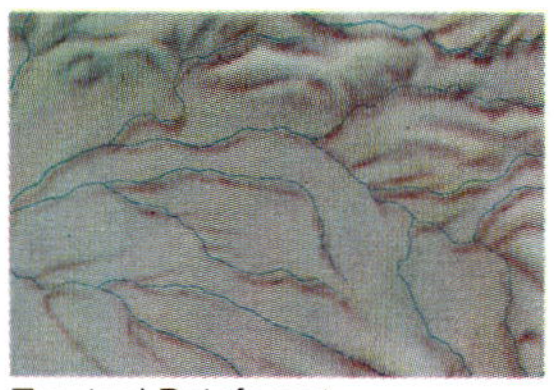

Tropical Rainforest
Tropischer Regenwald
Bosque tropical lluvioso
Forêt tropicale humide
Floresta tropical úmida

Grassland
Grasland
Pradera
Formations herbacées
Pradaria

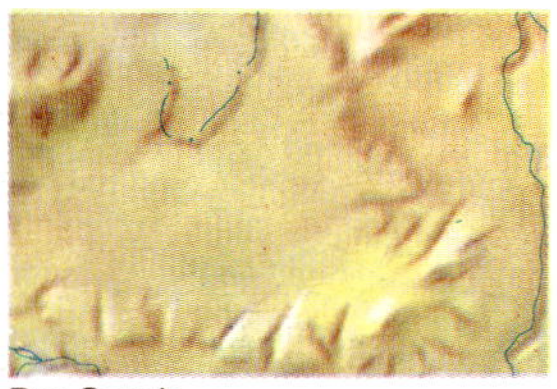

Dry Scrub
Trockenes Buschland
Matorral
Brousse sèche
Caatinga

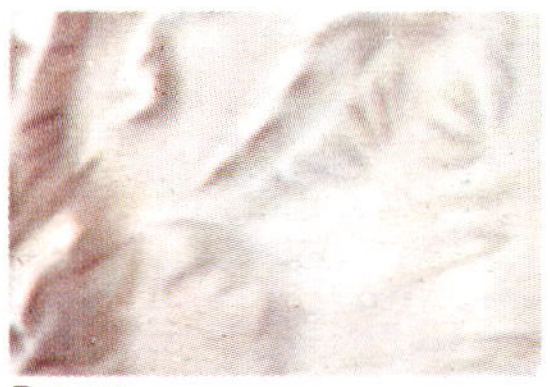

Desert
Wüste
Desierto
Désert
Deserto

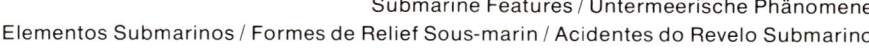

Submarine Features / Untermeerische Phänomene
Elementos Submarinos / Formes de Relief Sous-marin / Acidentes do Revelo Submarino

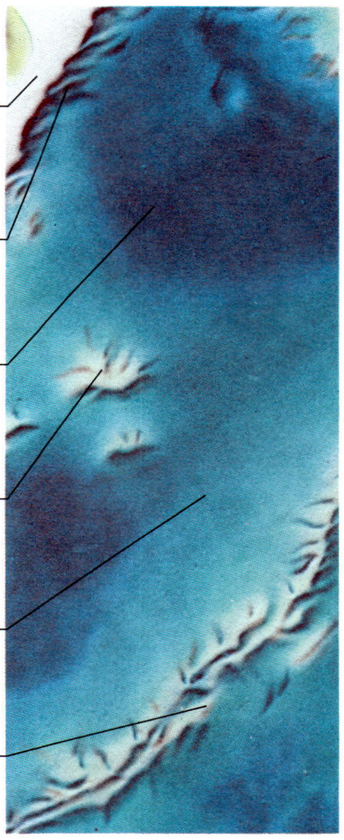

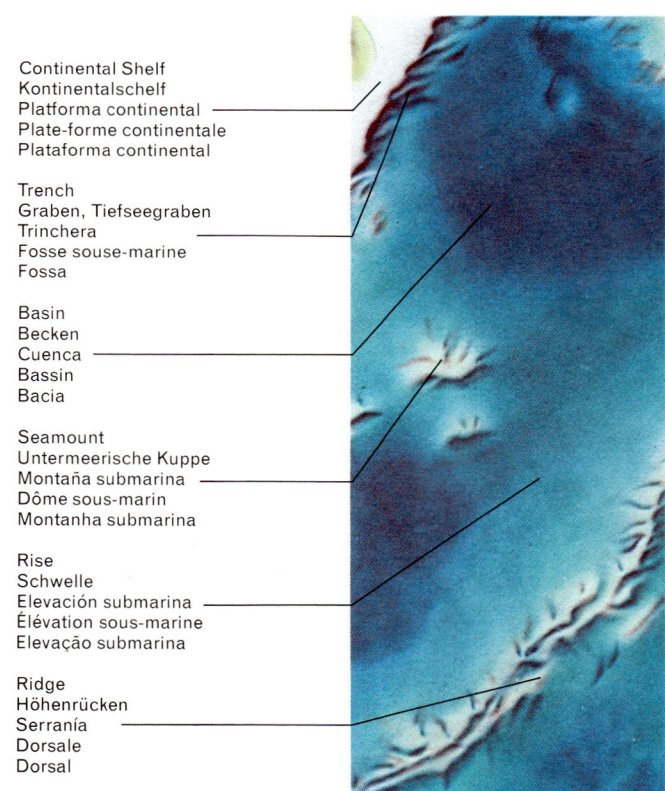

Continental Shelf
Kontinentalschelf
Platforma continental
Plate-forme continentale
Plataforma continental

Trench
Graben, Tiefseegraben
Trinchera
Fosse souse-marine
Fossa

Basin
Becken
Cuenca
Bassin
Bacia

Seamount
Untermeerische Kuppe
Montaña submarina
Dôme sous-marin
Montanha submarina

Rise
Schwelle
Elevación submarina
Élévation sous-marine
Elevação submarina

Ridge
Höhenrücken
Serranía
Dorsale
Dorsal

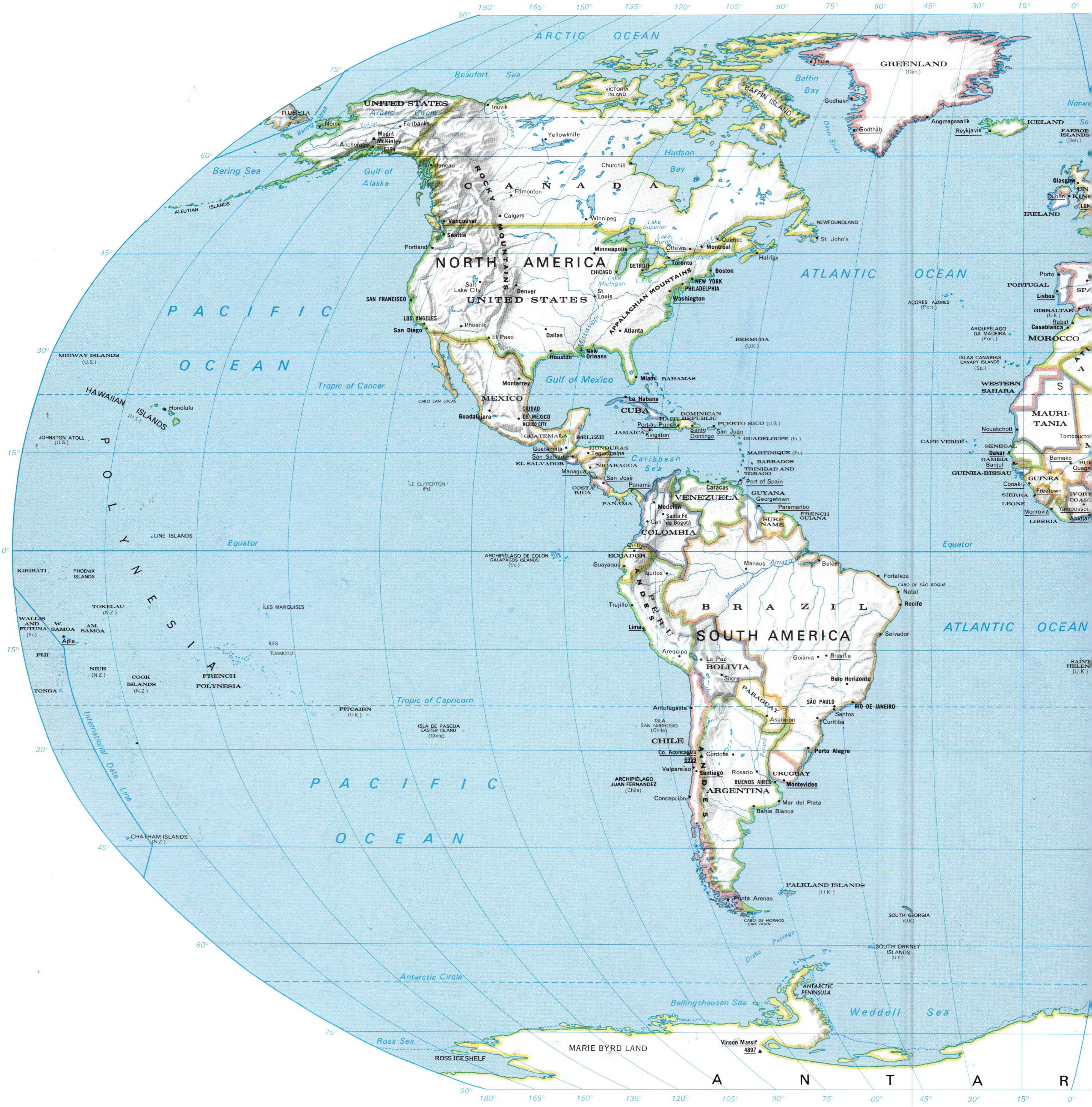
ARCTIC OCEAN
Beaufort Sea
GREENLAND
(Den.)
Thule
Baffin Bay
BAFFIN ISLAND
VICTORIA ISLAND
Godhavn
Godthåb
Angmagssalik
Reykjavik
ICELAND
FAEROE ISLANDS
(Den.)
RUSSIA
UNITED STATES
Arctic Circle
Nome
Fairbanks
Inuvik
Anchorage
Mount McKinley
6194
Yellowknife
Bering Sea
Gulf of Alaska
Hudson Bay
Churchill
Juneau
ROCKY MOUNTAINS
C A N A D A
Edmonton
ALEUTIAN ISLANDS
Calgary
Winnipeg
Vancouver
Seattle
Lake Superior
NEWFOUNDLAND
St. John's
Portland
Minneapolis
Lake Huron
Québec
Ottawa
Montreal
Toronto
Halifax
NORTH AMERICA
CHICAGO
DETROIT
Boston
Lake Michigan
Lake Ontario
L. Erie
NEW YORK
PHILADELPHIA
Washington
APPALACHIAN MOUNTAINS
Salt Lake City
Denver
UNITED STATES
St. Louis
SAN FRANCISCO
LOS ANGELES
San Diego
Phoenix
Atlanta
Mississippi
El Paso
Dallas
Rio Grande
Houston
New Orleans
ATLANTIC OCEAN
PACIFIC OCEAN
BERMUDA
(U.K.)
Miami
BAHAMAS
Gulf of Mexico
Monterrey
Tropic of Cancer
CABO SAN LUCAS
MEXICO
Guadalajara
CIUDAD DE MÉXICO
MEXICO CITY
La Habana
CUBA
DOMINICAN REPUBLIC
HAITI
PUERTO RICO (U.S.)
Port-au-Prince
Santo Domingo
San Juan
JAMAICA
Kingston
GUADELOUPE (Fr.)
MARTINIQUE (Fr.)
BARBADOS
TRINIDAD AND TOBAGO
Port of Spain
GUATEMALA
BELIZE
Guatemala
HONDURAS
Tegucigalpa
San Salvador
EL SALVADOR
NICARAGUA
Managua
Caribbean Sea
San José
COSTA RICA
Panamá
PANAMA
Caracas
VENEZUELA
GUYANA
Georgetown
Paramaribo
SURINAME
FRENCH GUIANA
Medellín
Santa Fe de Bogotá
Cali
COLOMBIA
Quito
ECUADOR
Guayaquil
Iquitos
Manaus
Amazon
Belém
Fortaleza
CABO DE SÃO ROQUE
Natal
Recife
Trujillo
PERU
ANDES
Lima
B R A Z I L
SOUTH AMERICA
Salvador
Arequipa
La Paz
BOLIVIA
Sucre
Goiânia
Brasília
Belo Horizonte
PARAGUAY
SÃO PAULO
RIO DE JANEIRO
Santos
Curitiba
Asunción
Antofagasta
ISLA SAN AMBROSIO
(Chile)
CHILE
Co. Aconcagua
6959
Córdoba
Porto Alegre
Valparaíso
Santiago
Rosario
URUGUAY
BUENOS AIRES
Montevideo
ARCHIPIÉLAGO JUAN FERNÁNDEZ
(Chile)
ARGENTINA
Concepción
Mar del Plata
Bahía Blanca
FALKLAND ISLANDS
(U.K.)
Punta Arenas
CABO DE HORNOS
CAPE HORN
SOUTH GEORGIA
(U.K.)
Drake Passage
SOUTH ORKNEY ISLANDS
(U.K.)
ANTARCTIC PENINSULA
Bellingshausen Sea
Weddell Sea
Antarctic Circle
Ross Sea
MARIE BYRD LAND
Vinson Massif
4897
ROSS ICE SHELF
A N T A R
MIDWAY ISLANDS
(U.S.)
HAWAIIAN ISLANDS
(U.S.)
Honolulu
JOHNSTON ATOLL
(U.S.)
P O L Y N E S I A
ÎLE CLIPPERTON
(Fr.)
LINE ISLANDS
Equator
ARCHIPIÉLAGO DE COLÓN
GALÁPAGOS ISLANDS
(Ec.)
KIRIBATI
PHOENIX ISLANDS
TOKELAU
(N.Z.)
ÎLES MARQUISES
WALLIS AND FUTUNA
(Fr.)
W. SAMOA
AM. SAMOA
Apia
ÎLES TUAMOTU
FIJI
NIUE
(N.Z.)
COOK ISLANDS
(N.Z.)
FRENCH POLYNESIA
TONGA
Tropic of Capricorn
PITCAIRN
(U.K.)
ISLA DE PASCUA
EASTER ISLAND
(Chile)
International Date Line
CHATHAM ISLANDS
(N.Z.)
Norwegian Sea
Glasgow
Dublin
IRELAND
PORTUGAL
Porto
Lisboa
AÇORES AZORES
(Port.)
GIBRALTAR
(U.K.)
Rabat
Casablanca
ARQUIPÉLAGO DA MADEIRA
(Port.)
MOROCCO
ISLAS CANARIAS
CANARY ISLANDS
(Sp.)
WESTERN SAHARA
MAURITANIA
Nouakchott
Tombouctou
CAPE VERDE
SENEGAL
Dakar
GAMBIA
Banjul
Bamako
GUINEA-BISSAU
GUINEA
Conakry
SIERRA LEONE
Freetown
Monrovia
LIBERIA
Abidjan
Yamoussoukro
SAINT HELENA
(U.K.)
180° 165° 150° 135° 120° 105° 90° 75° 60° 45° 30° 15° 0°
90° 75° 60° 45° 30° 15° 0° 15° 30° 45° 60° 75° 90°

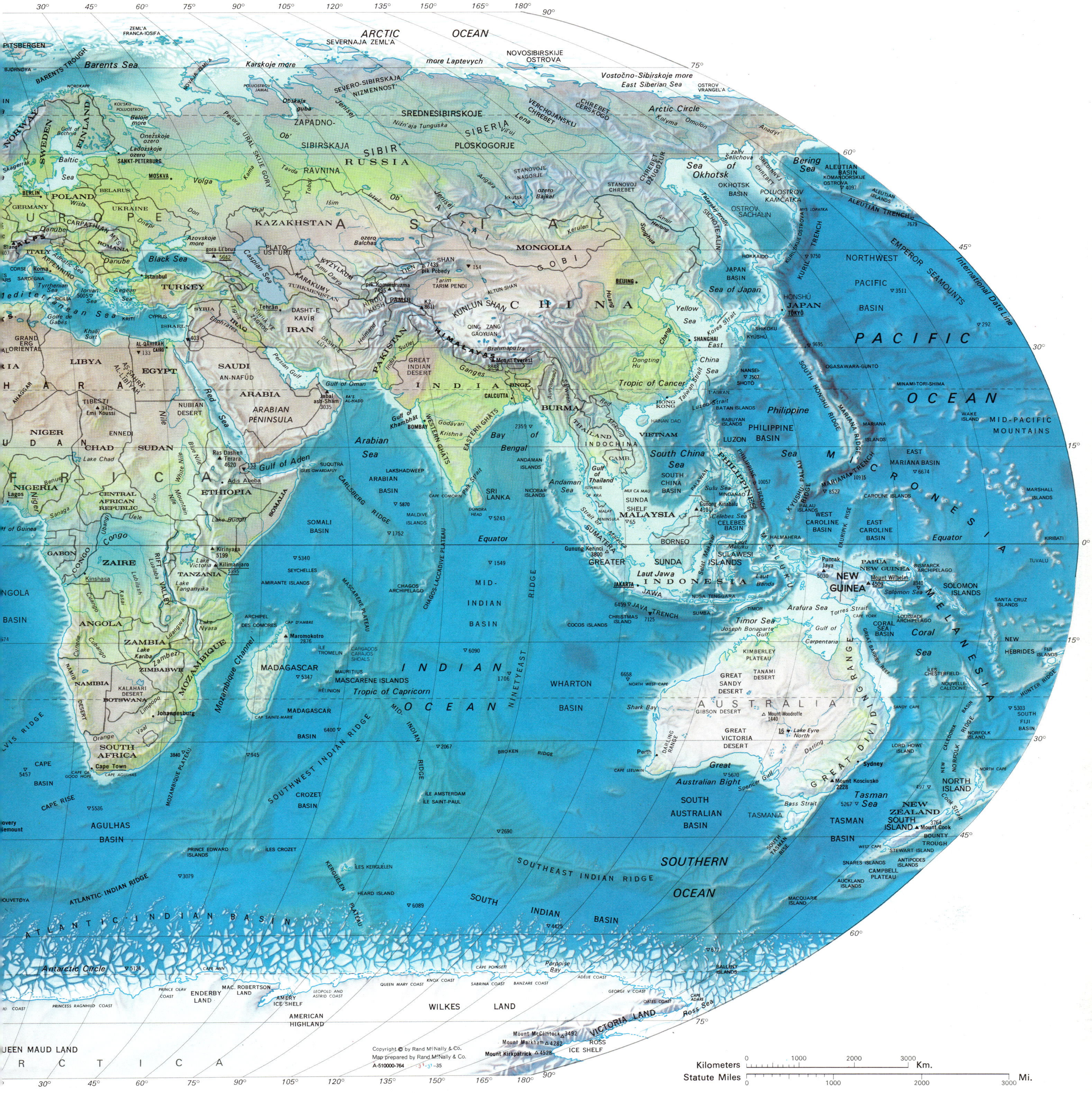

One centimeter represents 750 kilometers.
One inch represents approximately 1200 miles.
Robinson Projection
Scale 1:75,000,000

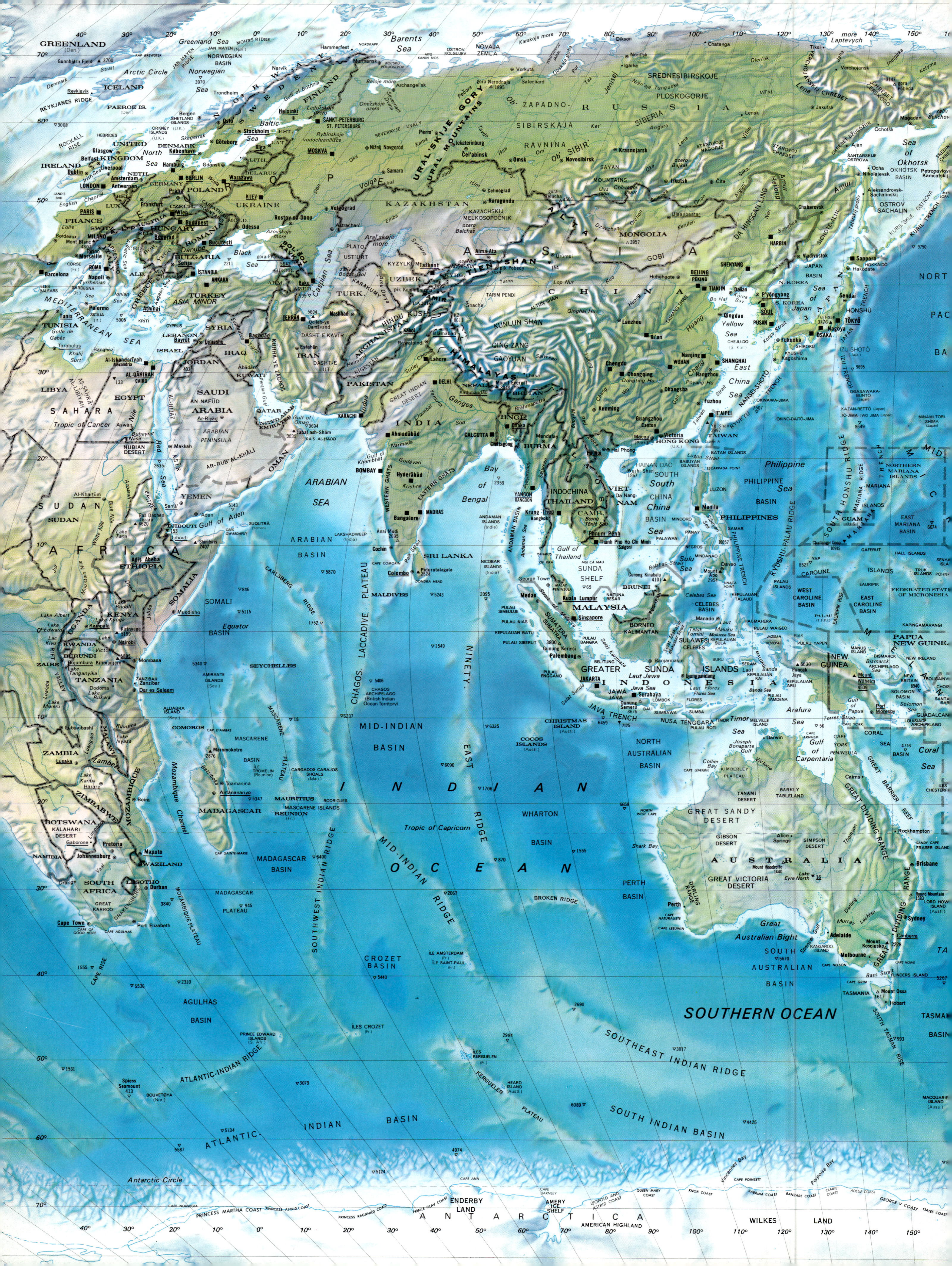
GREENLAND
Barents Sea
Greenland Sea
Norwegian Sea
NORWEGIAN BASIN
Arctic Circle
ICELAND
REYKJANES RIDGE
FAEROE IS.
Reykjavík
UNITED KINGDOM
IRELAND
North Sea
Baltic Sea
NORWAY
SWEDEN
FINLAND
DENMARK
København
Oslo
Stockholm
Helsinki
SANKT-PETERBURG
MOSKVA
LONDON
Dublin
PARIS
FRANCE
BERLIN
POLAND
Warszawa
UKRAINE
KIEV
HUNGARY
ROMANIA
BULGARIA
ROMA
MADRID
Barcelona
Black Sea
Caspian Sea
TURKEY
ASIA MINOR
ANKARA
ISTANBUL
MEDITERRANEAN SEA
TUNISIA
LIBYA
EGYPT
AL-QAHIRAH
SAHARA
Tropic of Cancer
SYRIA
IRAQ
JORDAN
ISRAEL
LEBANON
IRAN
TEHRAN
SAUDI ARABIA
AN-NAFUD
Ar-Riyad
ARABIAN PENINSULA
AR-RUB' AL-KHALI
YEMEN
OMAN
KUWAIT
QATAR
UNITED ARAB EMIRATES
Gulf of Oman
Gulf of Aden
AFGHANISTAN
PAKISTAN
KARACHI
HINDU KUSH
INDIA
DELHI
NEPAL
BHUTAN
BNGL.
CALCUTTA
BOMBAY
MADRAS
Bangalore
Hyderabad
Ahmadabad
SRI LANKA
Colombo
MALDIVES
ARABIAN SEA
ARABIAN BASIN
Bay of Bengal
URALSKIJE GORY
URAL MOUNTAINS
KAZAKHSTAN
UZBEK
TURK
Aral'skoje more
TIEN SHAN
KUNLUN SHAN
HIMALAYAS
TARIM PENDI
QING ZANG GAOYUAN
ZAPADNO-SIBIRSKAJA RAVNINA
SREDNESIBIRSKOJE PLOSKOGORJE
SIBERIA
RUSSIA
ASIA
ALTAI
MONGOLIA
GOBI
CHINA
BEIJING
SHANGHAI
Chongqing
Chengdu
Wuhan
Nanjing
Guangzhou
HONG KONG
TAIPEI
TAIWAN
DA HINGGAN LING
N. KOREA
S. KOREA
P'yongyang
SŎUL
Yellow Sea
East China Sea
South China Sea
Sea of Japan
JAPAN
TŌKYŌ
OSAKA
HONSHU
HOKKAIDO
Sapporo
Sea of Okhotsk
Laptevych more
Karskoje more
BURMA
THAILAND
INDOCHINA
VIETNAM
CAMB.
Gulf of Thailand
MALAYSIA
Singapore
BRUNEI
BORNEO
SUMATRA
JAKARTA
JAVA
Java Sea
GREATER SUNDA ISLANDS
SUNDA SHELF
INDONESIA
Celebes Sea
Sulu Sea
PHILIPPINES
Manila
Philippine Sea
PHILIPPINE BASIN
NEW GUINEA
PAPUA NEW GUINEA
Arafura Sea
Timor Sea
Coral Sea
Gulf of Carpentaria
AUSTRALIA
GREAT SANDY DESERT
GREAT VICTORIA DESERT
GIBSON DESERT
GREAT DIVIDING RANGE
GREAT BARRIER REEF
Perth
Adelaide
Melbourne
Sydney
Brisbane
Canberra
Hobart
TASMANIA
Great Australian Bight
NORTH AUSTRALIAN BASIN
PERTH BASIN
SOUTH AUSTRALIAN BASIN
WHARTON BASIN
JAVA TRENCH
AFRICA
SUDAN
ETHIOPIA
Adis Abeba
SOMALIA
KENYA
TANZANIA
ZAIRE
ZAMBIA
ZIMBABWE
MOZAMBIQUE
BOTSWANA
KALAHARI DESERT
NAMIBIA
SOUTH AFRICA
Johannesburg
Pretoria
Cape Town
Durban
Mozambique Channel
MADAGASCAR
Antananarivo
MAURITIUS
RÉUNION
SEYCHELLES
COMOROS
SOMALI BASIN
Equator
CARLSBERG RIDGE
CHAGOS-LACCADIVE PLATEAU
NINETY-EAST RIDGE
MID-INDIAN BASIN
MID-INDIAN RIDGE
INDIAN OCEAN
Tropic of Capricorn
MASCARENE BASIN
MADAGASCAR BASIN
SOUTHWEST INDIAN RIDGE
CROZET BASIN
AGULHAS BASIN
ATLANTIC-INDIAN RIDGE
ATLANTIC-INDIAN BASIN
SOUTHEAST INDIAN RIDGE
SOUTH INDIAN BASIN
SOUTHERN OCEAN
BROKEN RIDGE
KERGUELEN PLATEAU
Antarctic Circle
ANTARCTICA
ENDERBY LAND
AMERICAN HIGHLAND
WILKES LAND
PRINCESS MARTHA COAST

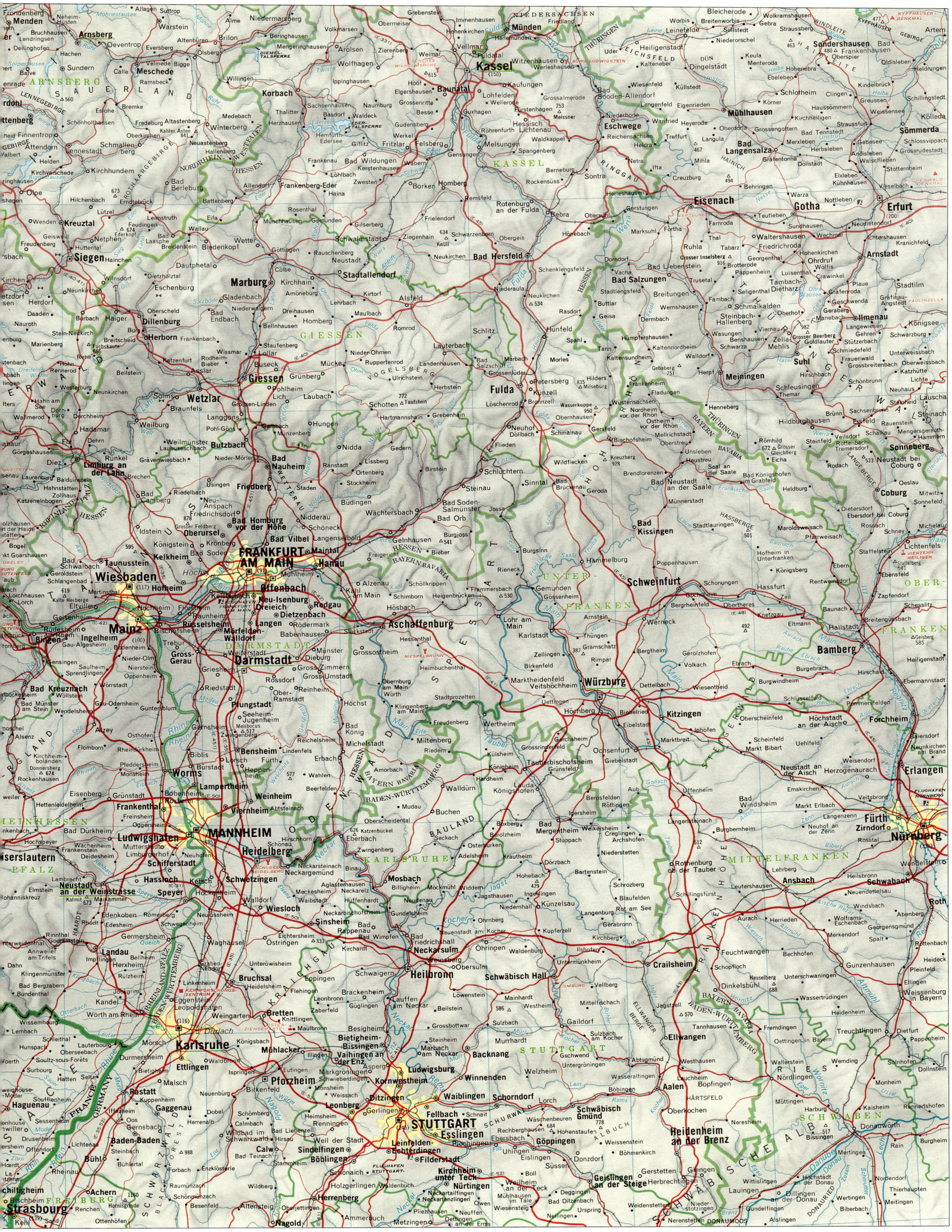

Map continues pages 54-55

Map continues page 60

Kilometers 0 10 20 30 40 50 Km.

Statute Miles 0 10 20 30 40 50 Mi.

Scale 1:1,000,000

One centimeter represents 10 kilometers.
One inch represents approximately 16 miles.
Lambert Conformal Conic Projection

Map continues pages 50-51

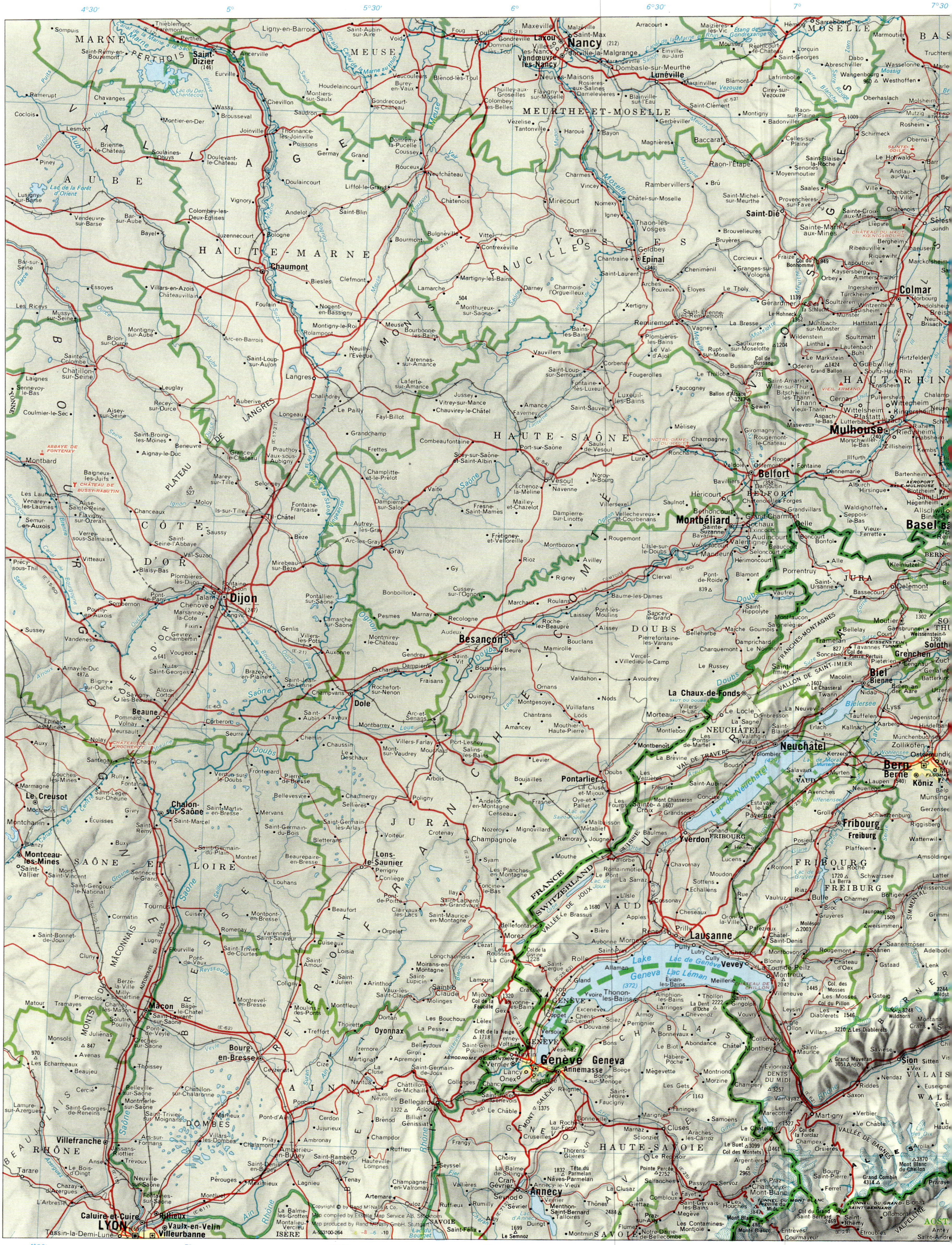

MAP FORM	col	Horn	lago	mont	passo	piz.-zo	See	Spitze	val
ENGLISH	pass	peak	lake	mount	pass	peak	lake	peak	valley
DEUTSCH	Pass	Horn	See	Berg	Pass	Gipfel	See	Spitze	Tal
ESPAÑOL	paso	pico	lago	monte	paso	pico	lago	pico	valle
FRANÇAIS	col	cime	lac	mont	col	cime	lac	cime	val
PORTUGUÊS	passo	pico	lago	monte	passo	pico	lago	pico	vale

Map continues pages 56-57

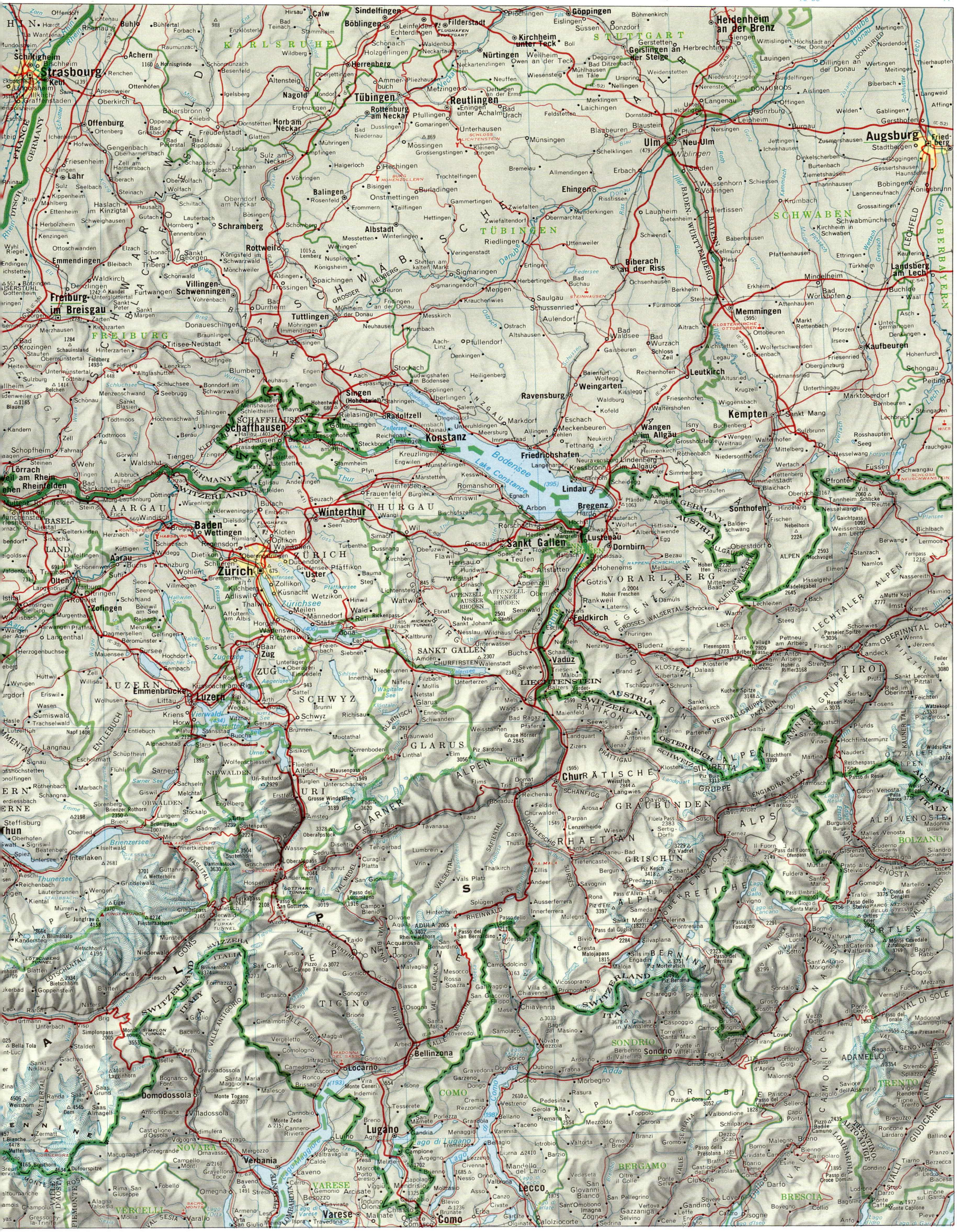

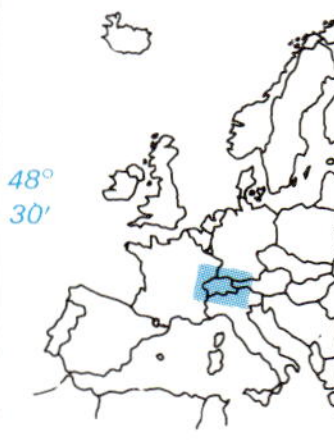

Map continues page 60

Map continues pages 64-65

Map continues pages 62-63

Kilometers 0 10 20 30 40 50 Km.

Statute Miles 0 10 20 30 40 50 Mi.

Scale 1:1,000,000

One centimeter represents 10 kilometers.
One inch represents approximately 16 miles.
Lambert Conformal Conic Projection

Map continues pages 54-55

Map continues pages 56-57

Map continues pages 58-59

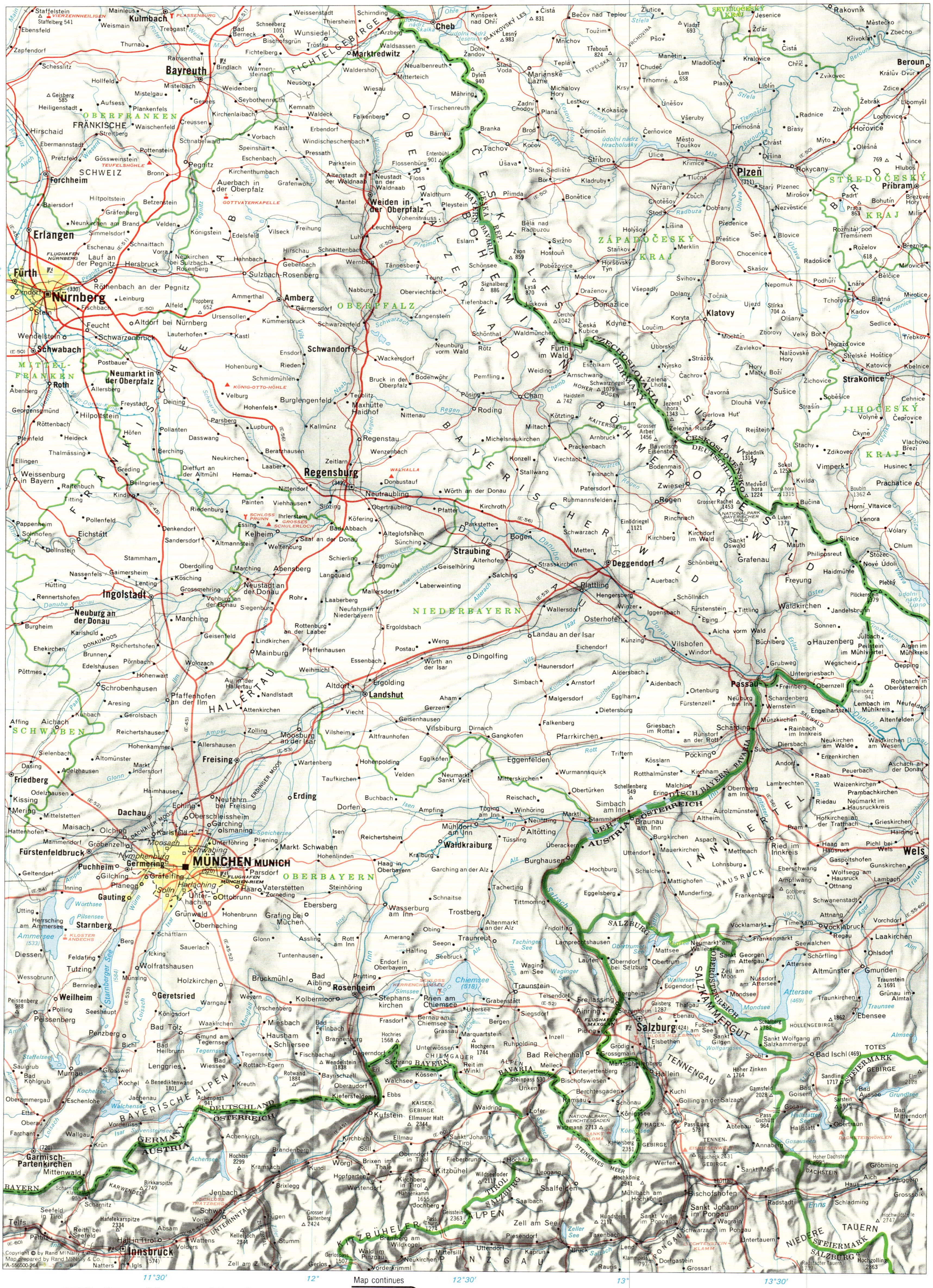

Map continues page 61

Map continues pages 64-65

DEUTSCH	Berg	Gebirge	Pass	Schloss	See
ENGLISH	mountain	range	pass	castle	lake
ESPAÑOL	montaña	sierra	paso	castillo	lago
FRANÇAIS	montagne	chaîne	col	château	lac
PORTUGUÊS	montanha	serra	passo	castelo	lago

Kilometers 0 10 20 30 40 50 Km.

Statute Miles 0 10 20 30 40 50 Mi.

Scale 1:1,000,000

One centimeter represents 10 kilometers.
One inch represents approximately 16 miles.
Modified Polyconic Projection

Map continues page 60

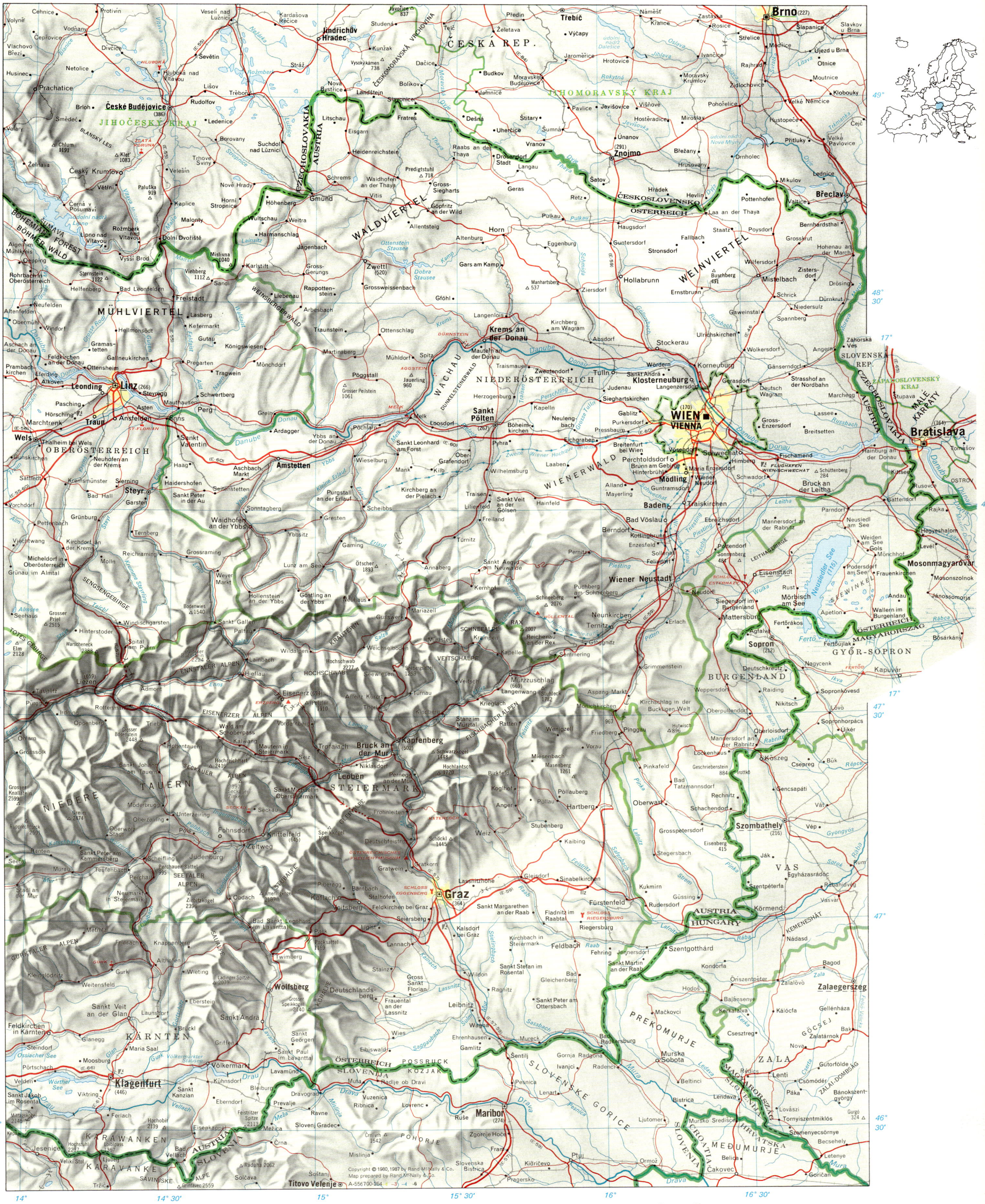

Map continues pages 64-65

DEUTSCH	Alpe, -n	Berg	Gebirge	Sattel	Schloss	Wald
ENGLISH	mountains	mountain	range	saddle	castle	forest; mountains
ESPAÑOL	montañas	montaña	sierra	paso	castillo	bosque; montañas
FRANÇAIS	montagnes	montagne	chaîne	col	château	forêt; montagnes
PORTUGUÊS	montanhas	montanha	serra	passo	castelo	Floresta; montanhas

Kilometers 0 10 20 30 40 50 Km.
Statute Miles 0 10 20 30 40 50 Mi.

Scale 1:1,000,000

One centimeter represents 10 kilometers.
One inch represents approximately 16 miles.

Lambert Conformal Conic Projection

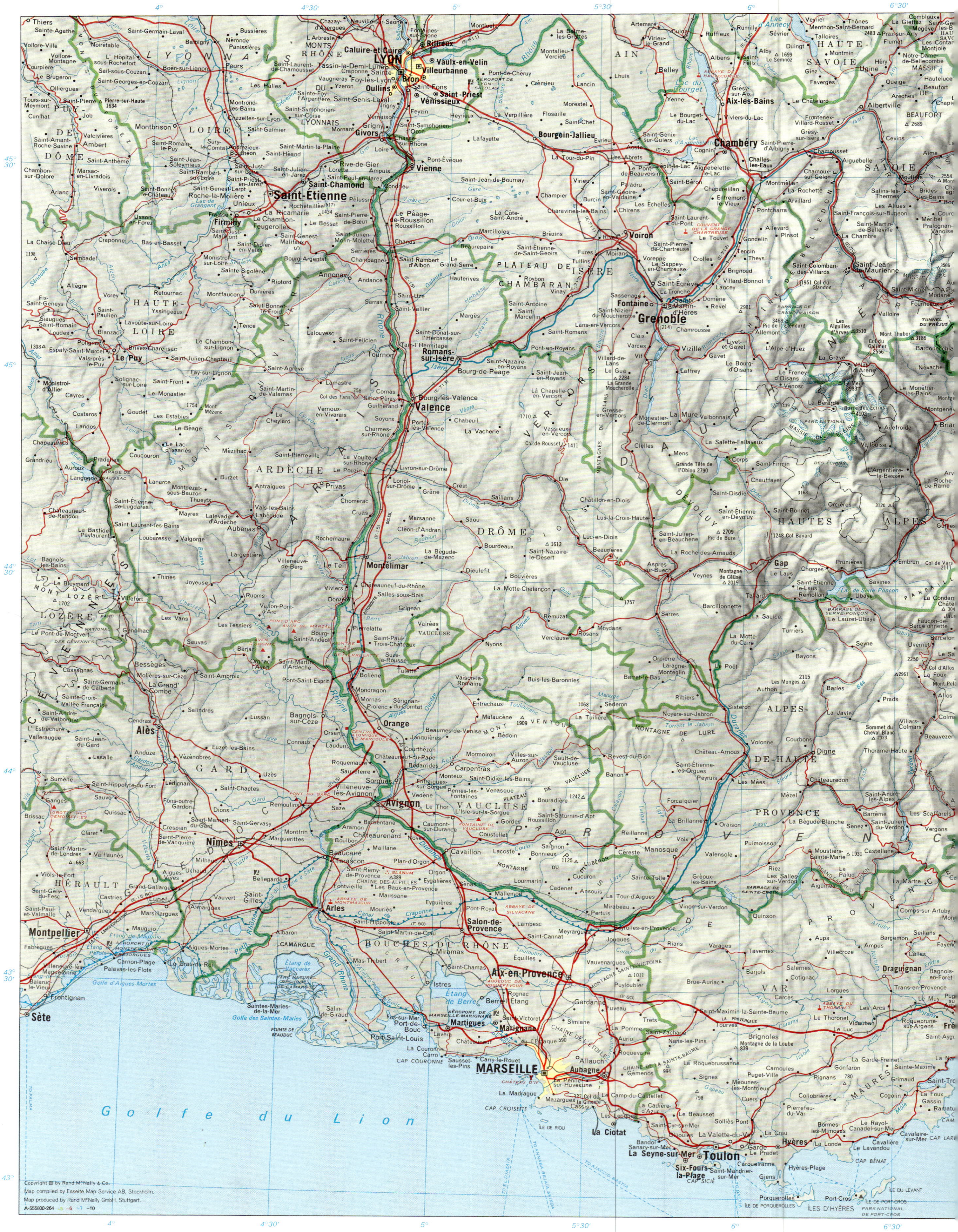

MAP FORM	abbaye	capo	col	île, i.	lac, l.	monte	passo	pic	val (-le)
ENGLISH	abbey	cape	pass	island	lake	mountain	pass	peak	valley
DEUTSCH	Abtei	Kap	Pass	Insel	See	Berg	Pass	Gipfel	Tal
ESPAÑOL	abadia	cabo	paso	isla	lago	montaña	paso	pico	valle
FRANÇAIS	abbaye	cap	col	île	lac	montagne	col	cime	val
PORTUGUÊS	abadia	cabo	passo	ilha	lago	montanha	passo	pico	vale

Map continues pages 58-59

Map continues pages 64-65

Kilometers 0 10 20 30 40 50 Km.

Statute Miles 0 10 20 30 40 50 Mi.

Scale 1:1,000,000

One centimeter represents 10 kilometers.
One inch represents approximately 16 miles.

Lambert Conformal Conic Projection

Map continues page 61

Map continues page 60

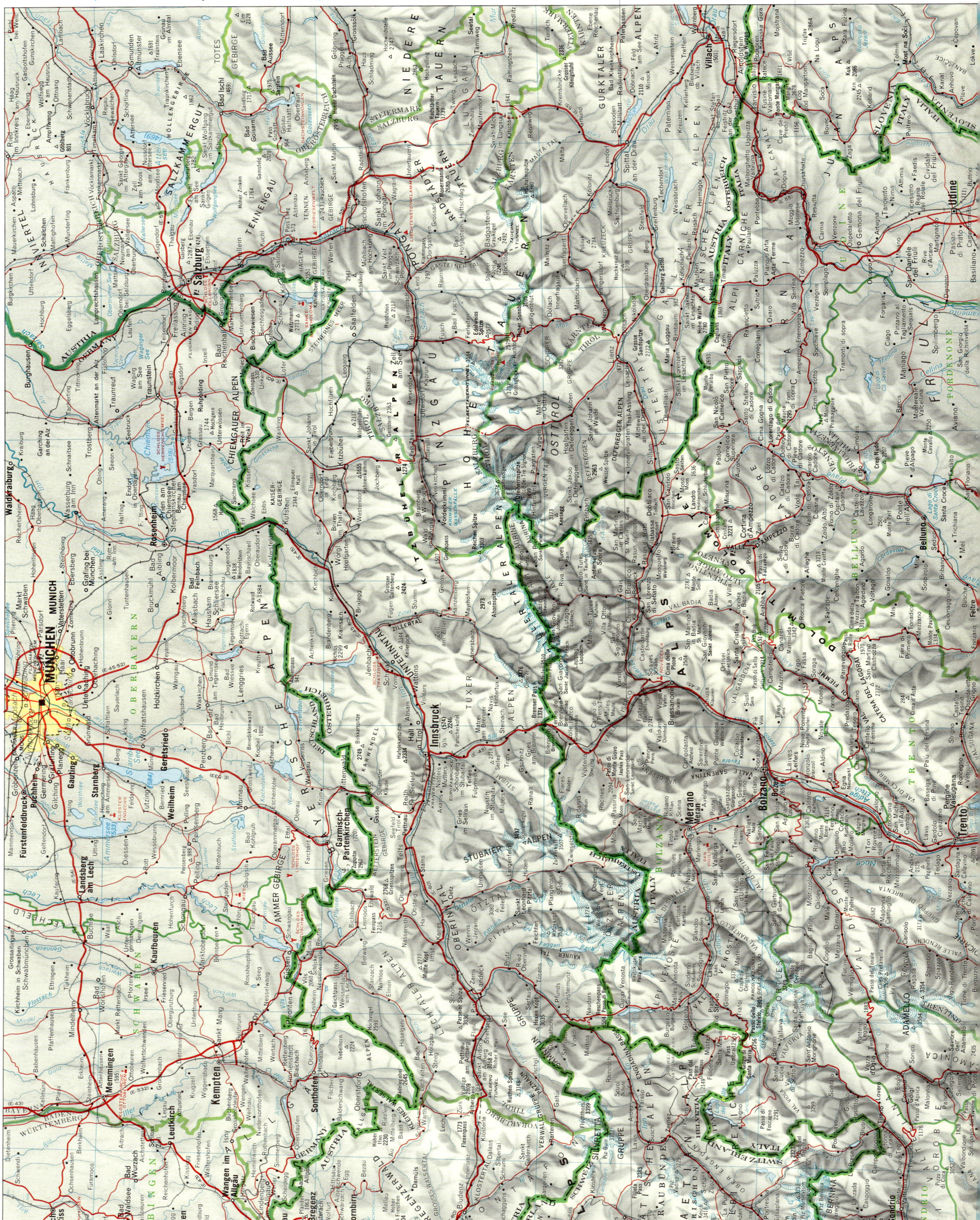

Map continues pages 58-59

ADRIATIC SEA
MARE ADRIATICO
Gulf of Venice
LIGURIAN SEA
MAR LIGURE
Map continues pages 66-67
Map continues pages 62-63
Scale 1:1,000,000
One centimeter represents 10 kilometers.
One inch represents approximately 16 miles.
Lambert Conformal Conic Projection

Map continues pages 64-65

MAP FORM	golfo	isola	lago	monte	monti	passo	punta
ENGLISH	gulf	island	lake	mountain	mountains	pass	point
DEUTSCH	Golf	Insel	See	Berg	Berge	Pass	Landspitze
ESPAÑOL	golfo	isla	lago	montaña	montañas	paso	punta
FRANÇAIS	golfe	île	lac	montagne	montagnes	col	pointe
PORTUGUÊS	golfo	ilha	lago	montanha	montanhas	passo	ponta

Map continues pages 68-69

Kilometers 0 10 20 30 40 50 Km.
Statute Miles 0 10 20 30 40 50 Mi.

Scale 1:1,000,000

One centimeter represents 10 kilometers.
One inch represents approximately 16 miles.
Lambert Conformal Conic Projection

Map continues pages 66-67

MAP FORM	capo	golfo	isola	lago	monte	monti	punta
ENGLISH	cape	gulf	island	lake	mountain	mountains	point
DEUTSCH	Kap	Golf	Insel	See	Berg	Berge	Landspitze
ESPAÑOL	cabo	golfo	isla	lago	montaña	montañas	punta
FRANÇAIS	cap	golfe	île	lac	montagne	montagnes	pointe
PORTUGUÊS	cabo	golfo	ilha	lago	montanha	montanhas	ponta

Map continues page 70

Kilometers 0 10 20 30 40 50 Km.
Statute Miles 0 10 20 30 40 50 Mi.

Scale 1:1,000,000

One centimeter represents 10 kilometers.
One inch represents approximately 16 miles.

Lambert Conformal Conic Projection

Map continues pages 68-69

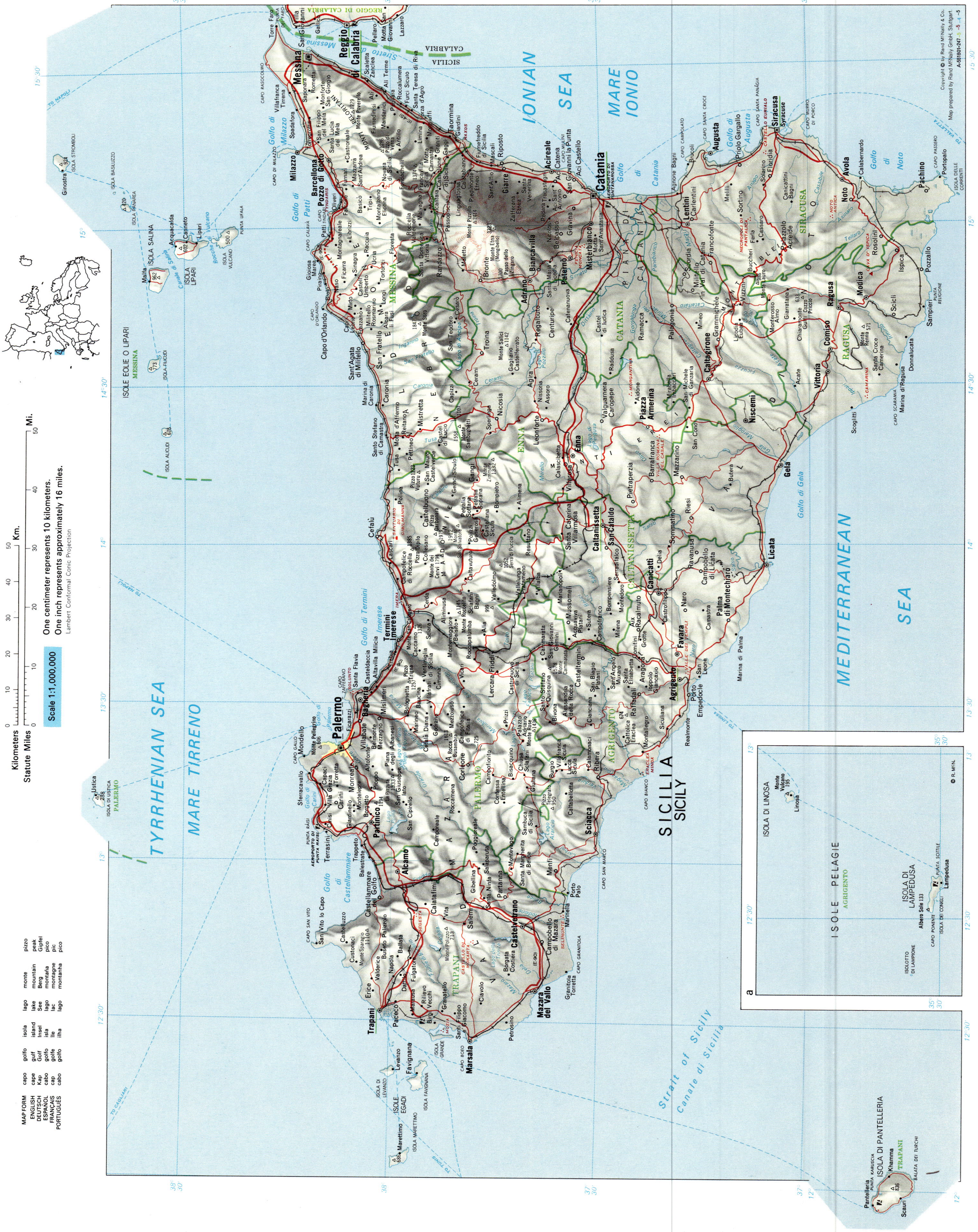

MAP FORM	capo	golfo	isola	lago, l.	monte
ENGLISH	cape	gulf	island	lake	mountain
DEUTSCH	Kap	Golf	Insel	See	Berg
ESPAÑOL	cabo	golfo	isla	lago	montaña
FRANÇAIS	cap	golfe	île	lac	montagne
PORTUGUÊS	cabo	golfo	ilha	lago	montanha

Kilometers 0 10 20 30 40 50 Km.

Statute Miles 0 10 20 30 40 50 Mi.

Scale 1:1,000,000

One centimeter represents 10 kilometers.

One inch represents approximately 16 miles.

Lambert Conformal Conic Projection

Map continues pages 22-23

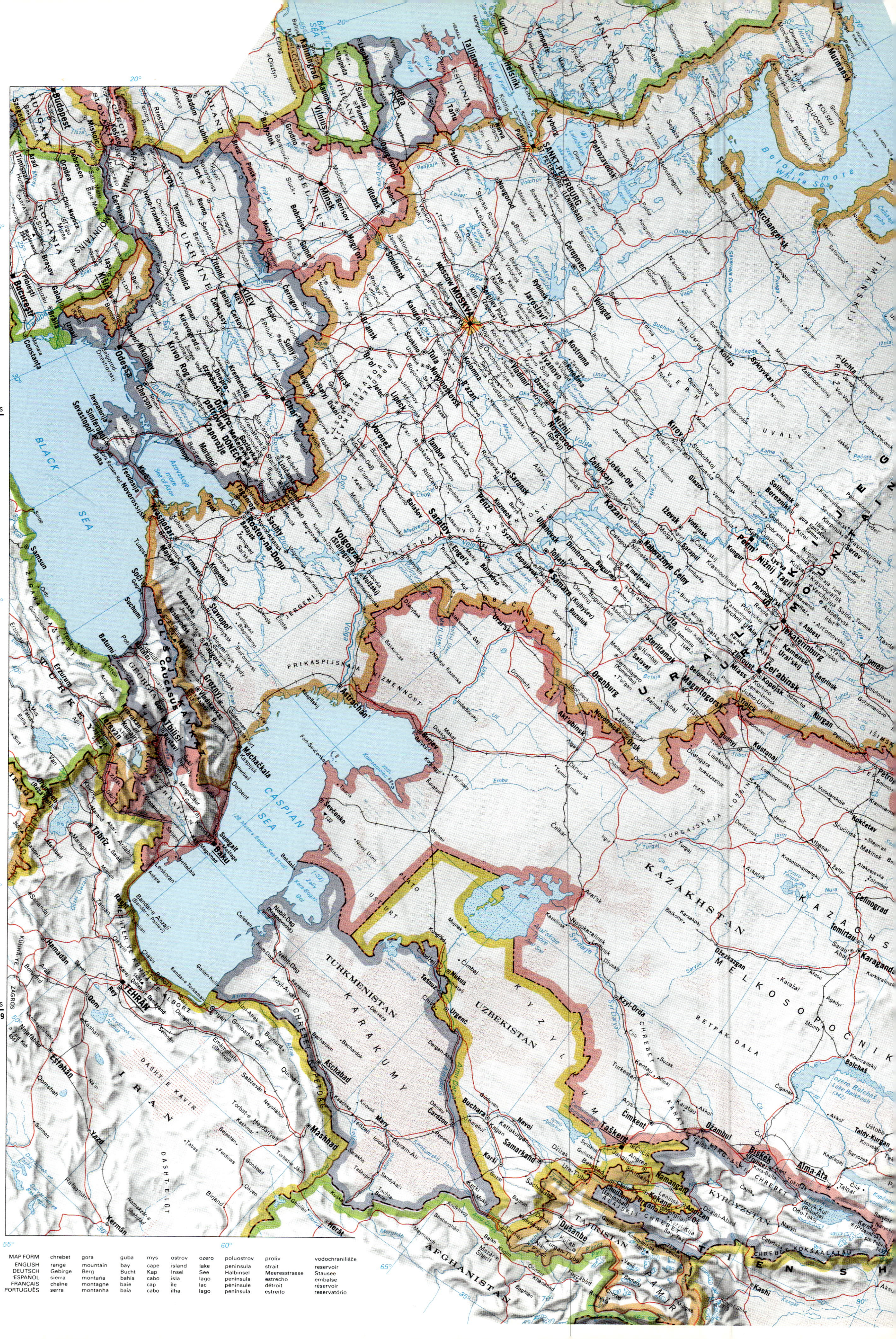

Map continues pages 118-119

MAP FORM	chrebet	gora	guba	mys	ostrov	ozero	poluostrov	proliv	vodochranilišče
ENGLISH	range	mountain	bay	cape	island	lake	peninsula	strait	reservoir
DEUTSCH	Gebirge	Berg	Bucht	Kap	Insel	See	Halbinsel	Meeresstrasse	Stausee
ESPAÑOL	sierra	montaña	bahía	cabo	isla	lago	península	estrecho	embalse
FRANÇAIS	chaîne	montagne	baie	cap	île	lac	péninsule	détroit	réservoir
PORTUGUÊS	serra	montanha	baía	cabo	ilha	lago	península	estreito	reservatório

Map continues pages 90-91

Kilometers 0 200 400 600 Km.
Statute Miles 0 200 400 600 Mi.

Scale 1:12,000,000

One centimeter represents 120 kilometers.
One inch represents approximately 190 miles.
Lambert Conformal Conic Projection

Map continues pages 72-73

Map continues pages 90-91

MAP FORM	chrebet	gora	guba	mys	ostrov	ozero	poluostrov	proliv	vodochranilišče
ENGLISH	range	mountain	bay	cape	island	lake	peninsula	strait	reservoir
DEUTSCH	Gebirge	Berg	Bucht	Kap	Insel	See	Halbinsel	Meeresstrasse	Stausee
ESPAÑOL	sierra	montaña	bahia	cabo	isla	lago	peninsula	estrecho	embalse
FRANÇAIS	chaîne	montagne	baie	cap	île	lac	péninsule	détroit	réservoir
PORTUGUÊS	serra	montanha	baia	cabo	ilha	lago	peninsula	estreito	reservatório

Kilometers 0 200 400 600 Km.
Statute Miles 0 200 400 600 Mi.

Scale 1:12,000,000

One centimeter represents 120 kilometers.
One inch represents approximately 190 miles.
Lambert Conformal Conic Projection

ALASKA
UNITED STATES
Bering Strait
SAINT LAWRENCE ISLAND
NUNIVAK ISLAND
Chukchi Sea
OSTROV VRANGEL'A
proliv Longa
EKIATAPSKIJ CHREBET
ČUKOTSKIJ POLUOSTROV
Anadyrskij zaliv
zaliv Kresta
Bering Sea
SAINT MATTHEW ISLAND
VOSTOČNO-SIBIRSKOJE MORE
EAST SIBERIAN SEA
OSTROVA DE-LONGA
NOVOSIBIRSKIJE OSTROVA
OSTROV KOTEL'NYJ
OSTROV BOL'ŠOJ L'ACHOVSKIJ
L'ACHOVSKIJE OSTROVA
OSTROV NOVAJA SIBIR'
proliv Sannikova
proliv Dmitrija Lapteva
MEDVEŽ'I OSTROVA
ANŽU
AN'UJSKIJ CHREBET
ANADYRSKOJE PLOSKOGORJE
KOLYMSKAJA NIZMENNOST'
JUKAGIRSKOJE PLOSKOGORJE
KOR'AKSKOJE NAGORJE
PENŽINSKIJ CHREBET
Janskij zaliv
Čokurdach
Srednekolymsk
Zyr'anka
Kolyma
Čerskij
Bilibino
Anadyr'
Penžinskaja guba
Gižiginskaja guba
zaliv Šelichova
MOMSKIJ CHREBET
CHREBET ČERSKOGO
CHREBET SUNTAR-CHAJATA
VERCHOJANSKIJ CHREBET
SIBERIA
CHREBET SETTE-DABAN
Verchojansk
Batagaj
Sangar
Jakutsk
Pokrovsk
Magadan
Ochotsk
Ajan
Nikolajevsk-na-Amure
ALDANSKOJE NAGORJE
STANOVOJ CHREBET
CHREBET DŽUGDŽUR
SEA OF OKHOTSK
OCHOTSKOJE MORE
ŠANTARSKIJE OSTROVA
OSTROV SACHALIN SAKHALIN
Južno-Sachalinsk
Tatarskij proliv
La Perouse Strait
POLUOSTROV KAMČATKA KAMCHATKA
SREDINNYJ CHREBET
Petropavlovsk-Kamčatskij
Ust'-Kamčatsk
KOMANDORSKIJE OSTROVA
Karaginskij zaliv
KURIL'SKIJE OSTROVA
KURIL ISLANDS
Pervyj Kuril'skij proliv
Habomai, Shikotan, Kunashiri, and Etorofu, occupied since 1945, are claimed by Japan pending a final peace treaty.
BUREINSKIJ CHREBET
SICHOTE-ALIN'
Komsomol'sk-na-Amure
Chabarovsk
Blagoveščensk
Svobodnyj
Tynda
Vladivostok
Ussurijsk
Nachodka
Sovetskaja Gavan'
DA HINGGAN LING
XIAO HINGGAN LING
NEI MONGGOL ZIZHIQU
INNER MONGOLIA
HEILONGJIANG
MANCHURIA
CHINA
Harbin
Qiqihar
Jiamusi
Mudanjiang
JILIN
HOKKAIDŌ
Sapporo
Asahikawa
Kushiro
Hakodate
Aomori
Hachinohe
Akita
Morioka
JAPAN
HONSHŪ
SEA OF JAPAN
PACIFIC OCEAN
Arctic Circle

Baltic and Moscow Regions / Baltenland und Mittelrussland / Regiones de Báltico y de Moscú
Républiques Baltes et la Région de Moscou / Regiões do Báltico e de Moscou

Map continues
pages 26-27

Map continues
pages 30-31

Meters	Feet
6000	19685
4000	13124
3000	9843
2000	6562
1000	3281
500	1640
200	656
0	0
Land Below Sea Level	
0	0
200	656
1000	3281
3000	9843
6000	19685
9000	29520

MAP FORM	gr'ada	ostrov, o.	ozero, o.	vodochranilišče, vdchr.	vozvyšennost', vozv.	zaliv	zapovednik, zapov.
ENGLISH	ridge	island	lake	reservoir	upland	gulf; bay	reserve
DEUTSCH	Höhenrücken	Insel	See	Stausee	Bergland	Golf; Bucht	Reservat
ESPAÑOL	lomerío	isla	lago	embalse	tierras altas	golfo; bahía	reserva
FRANÇAIS	crête	île	lac	réservoir	hautes terres	golfe; baie	réserve
PORTUGUÊS	cordilheira	ilha	lago	reservatório	terras altas	golfo; baía	reserva

Map continues pages 24-25

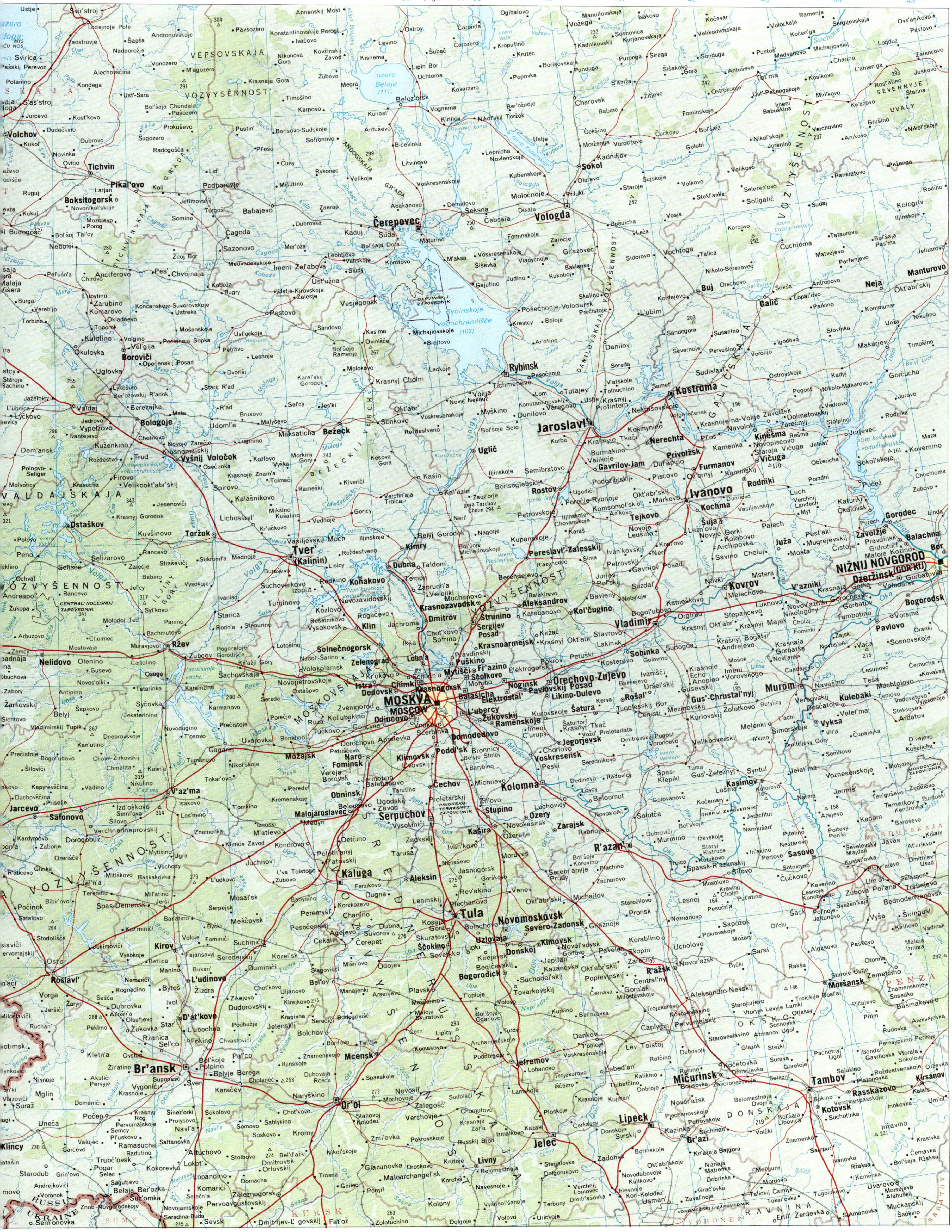

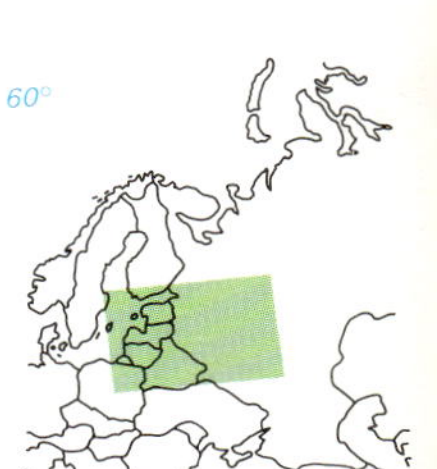

Map continues pages 80-81

Map continues pages 78-79

Kilometers 0 50 100 150 Km.
Statute Miles 0 50 100 150 Mi.

Scale 1:3,000,000

One centimeter represents 30 kilometers.
One inch represents approximately 47 miles.
Lambert Conformal Conic Projection

Map continues pages 30-31

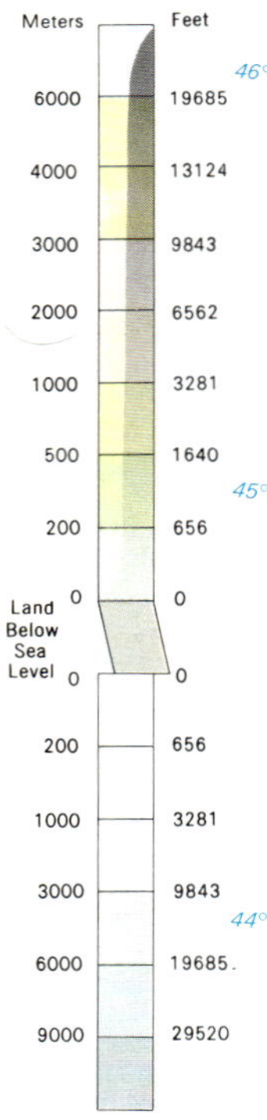

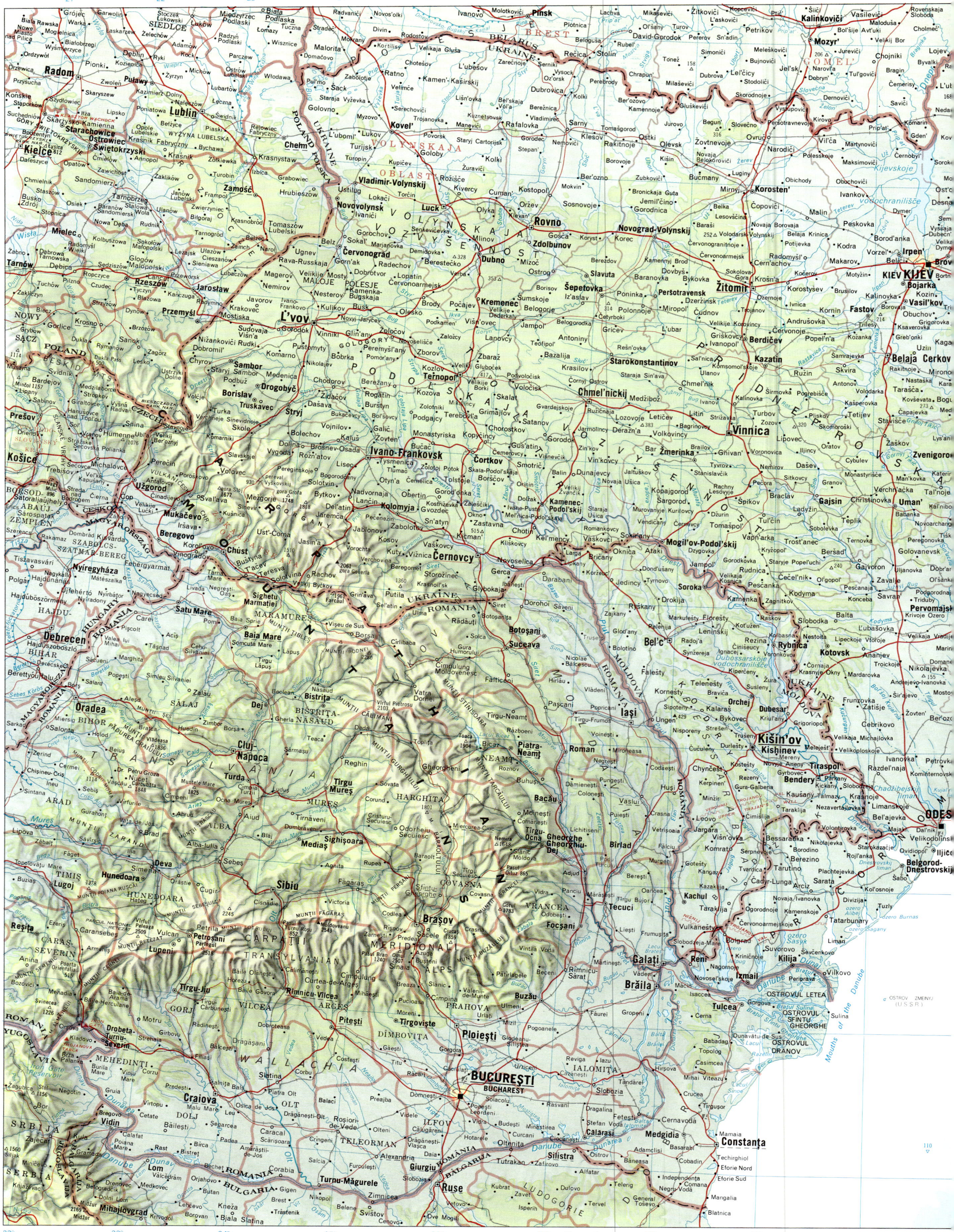

Map continues pages 38-39

MAP FORM	gora	liman	mys	nizmennost', nizm.	ozero	vozvyšennost', vozv.	zaliv
ENGLISH	mountain	bay	cape	plain	lake	upland	bay
DEUTSCH	Berg	Bucht	Kap	Ebene	See	Bergland	Bucht
ESPAÑOL	montaña	bahía	cabo	llanno	lago	tierras altas	bahía
FRANÇAIS	montagne	baie	cap	plaine	lac	hautes terres	baie
PORTUGUÊS	montanha	baía	cabo	planície	lago	terras altas	baía

Map continues pages 76-77

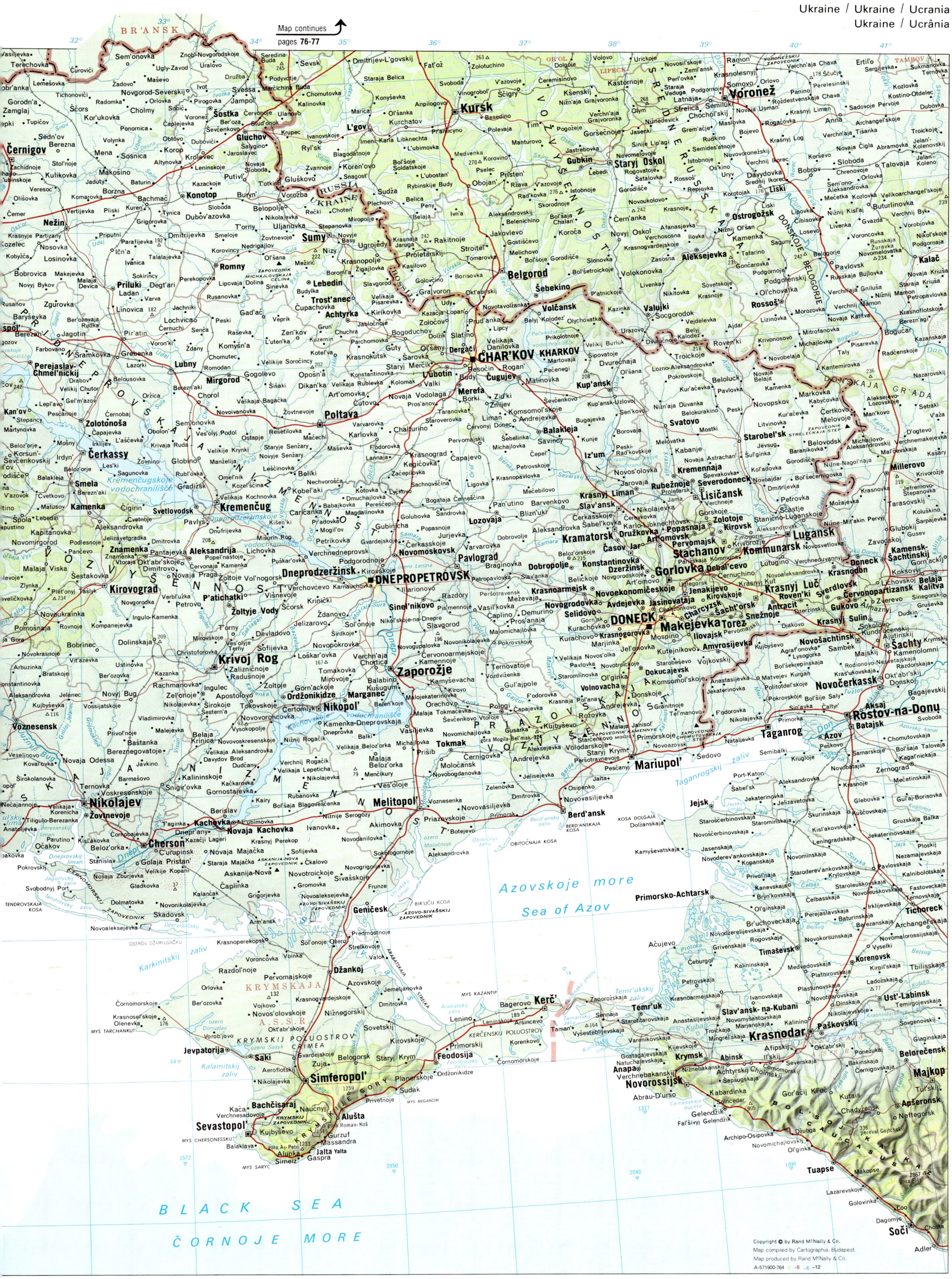

Map continues pages 80-81

Map continues page 84

Kilometers 0 50 100 150 Km.
Statute Miles 0 50 100 150 Mi.

Scale 1:3,000,000

One centimeter represents 30 kilometers.
One inch represents approximately 47 miles.
Lambert Conformal Conic Projection

Map continues pages 24-25

Map continues pages 76-77

Map continues pages 86-87

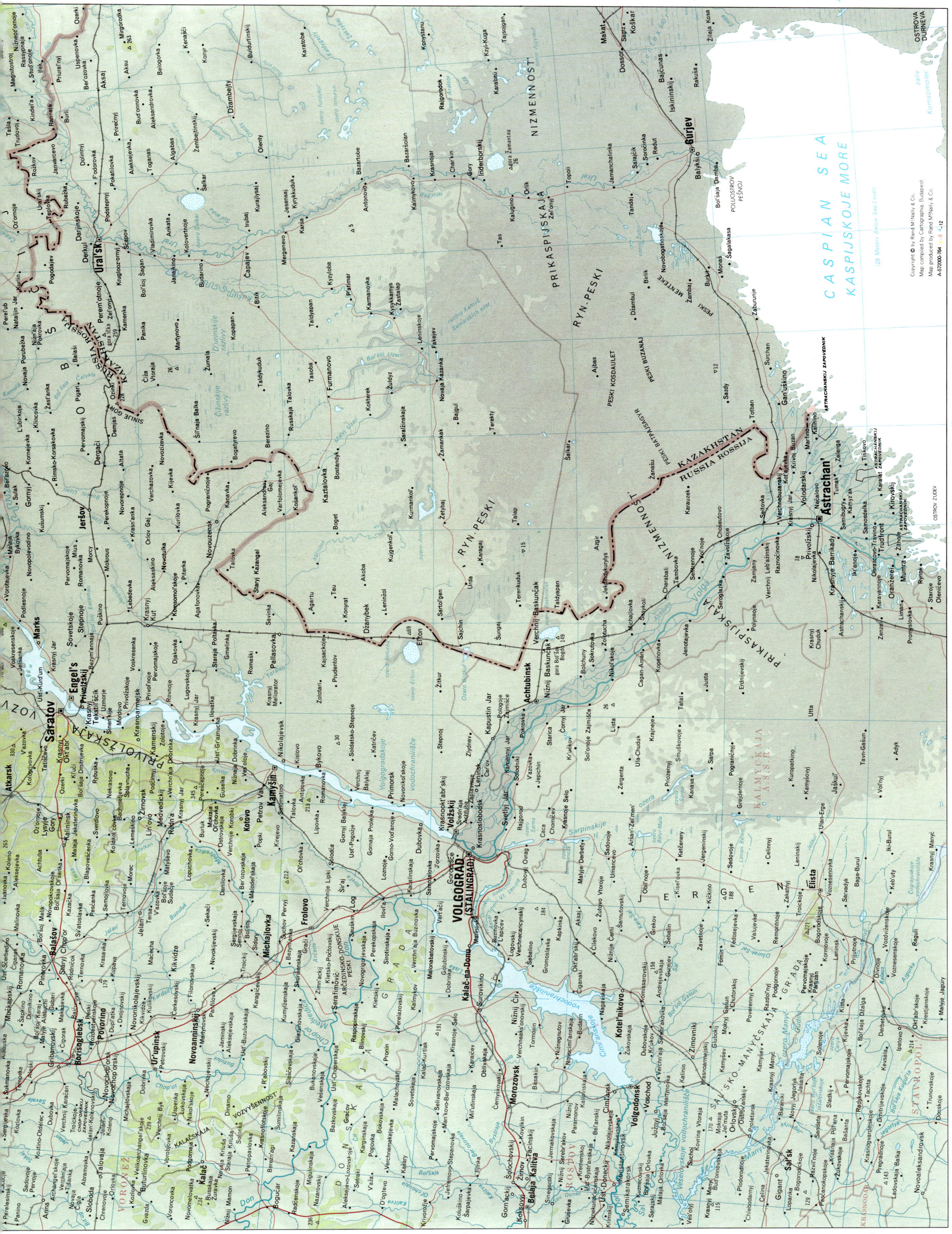

Map continues page 84

Map continues pages 78-79

Scale 1:3,000,000
One centimeter represents 30 kilometers.
One inch represents approximately 47 miles.
Lambert Conformal Conic Projection

Kilometers 0 50 100 150 Km.
Statute Miles 0 50 100 150 Mi.

MAPFORM	gory	ostrov	ozero	peski	vodochranilišče	vozvyšennost'	zapovednik
ENGLISH	mountains	island	lake	desert	reservoir	upland	reserve
DEUTSCH	Berge	Insel	See	Wüste	Stausee	Bergland	Reservat
ESPAÑOL	montañas	isla	lago	desierto	embalse	tierras altas	reserva
FRANÇAIS	montagnes	île	lac	désert	réservoir	hautes terres	réserve
PORTUGUÊS	montanhas	ilha	lago	deserto	reservatório	terras altas	reserva

Feet: 19685, 13124, 9843, 6562, 3281, 1640, 656, 0, 0, 656, 3281, 9843, 19685, 29520
Meters: 6000, 4000, 3000, 2000, 1000, 500, 200, 0, Land Below Sea Level, 0, 200, 1000, 3000, 6000, 9000

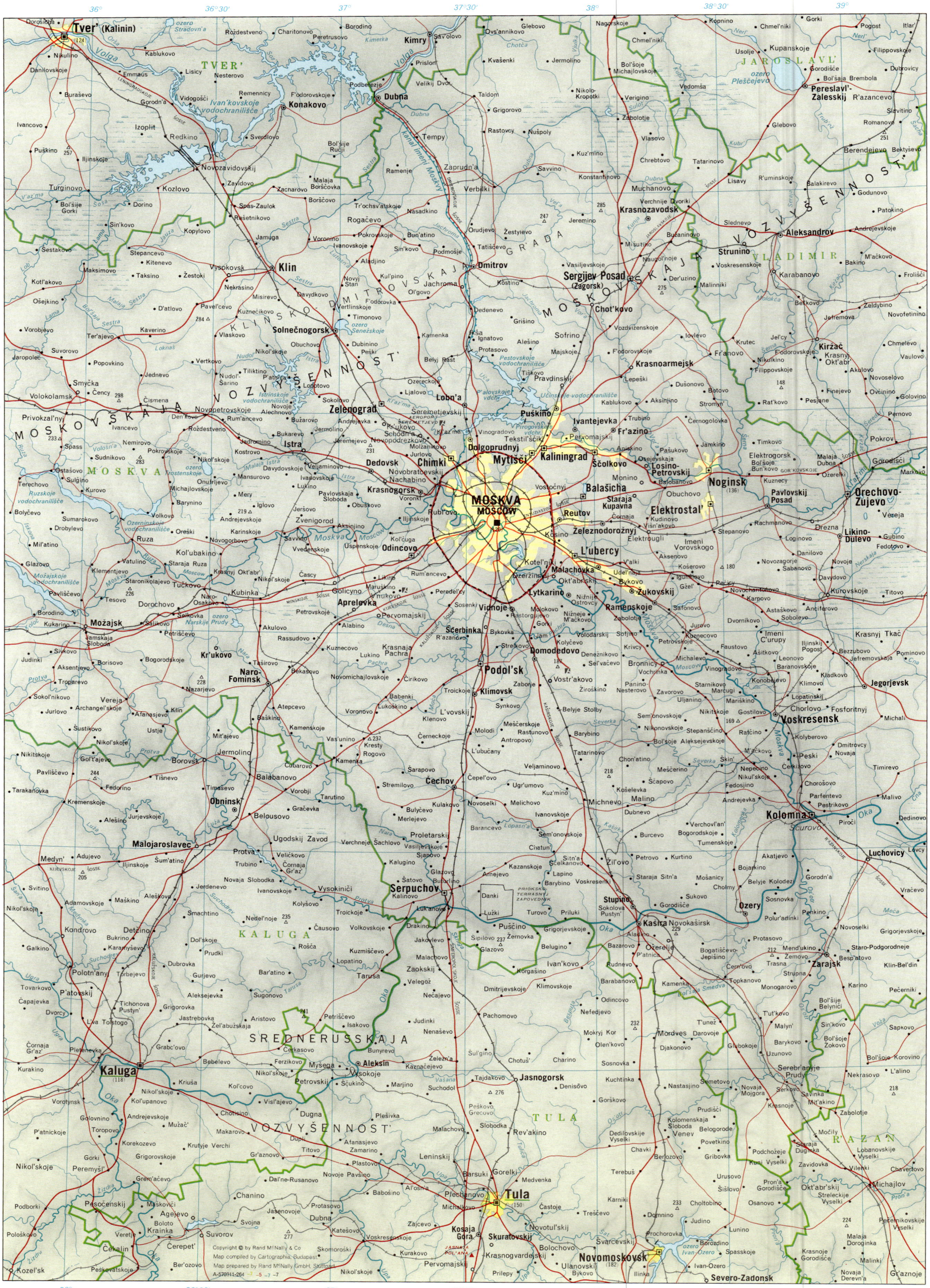

MAP FORM	gr'ada	ozero	vodochranilišče, vdchr.	vozvyšennost'	zapovednik
ENGLISH	ridge	lake	reservoir	upland	reserve
DEUTSCH	Hohenrücken	See	Stausee	Bergland	Reservat
ESPAÑOL	lomerío	lago	embalse	tierras altas	reserva
FRANÇAIS	crête	lac	réservoir	hautes terres	réserve
PORTUGUÊS	cordilheira	lago	reservatório	terras altas	reserva

Kilometers 0 10 20 30 40 50 Km.

Statute Miles 0 10 20 30 40 50 Mi.

Scale 1:1,000,000

One centimeter represents 10 kilometers.
One inch represents approximately 16 miles.

Lambert Conformal Conic Projection

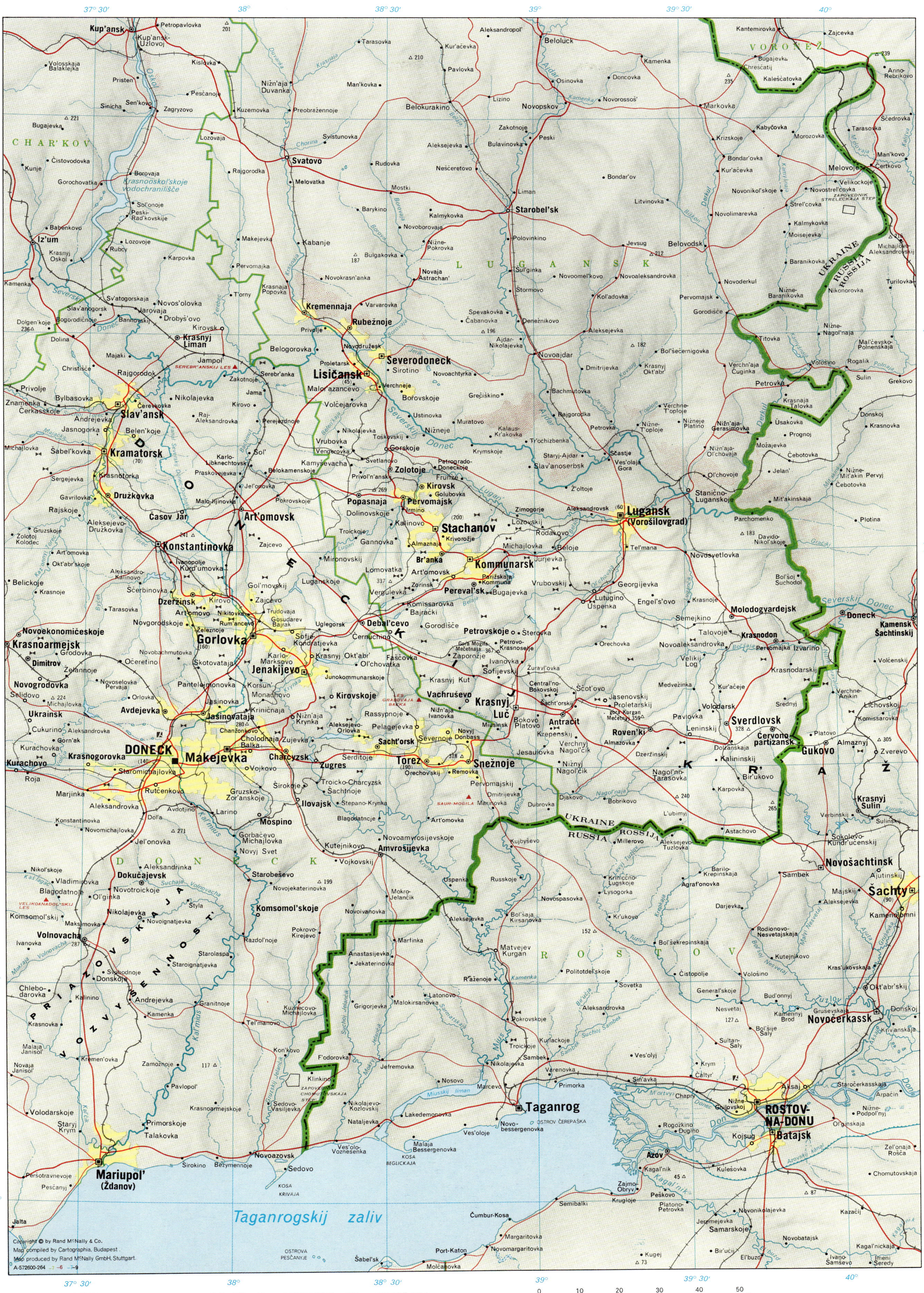

MAP FORM	kosa	ostrov, o.	vodochranilišče, vdchr.	vozvyšennost', vozv.	zaliv	zapovednik, zapov
ENGLISH	spit	island	reservoir	upland	bay	reserve
DEUTSCH	Landzunge	Insel	Stausee	Bergland	Bucht	Reservat
ESPAÑOL	lengua de tierra	isla	embalse	tierras altas	bahía	reserva
FRANÇAIS	flèche	île	réservoir	hautes terres	baie	réserve
PORTUGUÊS	ponta de terra	ilha	reservatório	terras altas	baía	reserva

Kilometers 0 10 20 30 40 50 Km.

Statute Miles 0 10 20 30 40 50 Mi.

Scale 1:1,000,000

One centimeter represents 10 kilometers.
One inch represents approximately 16 miles
Lambert Conformal Conic Projection

Caucasus and Transcaucasia / Kaukasus und Transkaukasien / Cáucaso y Transcaucasia
Caucasie et Transcaucasie / Cáucaso e Transcaucásia

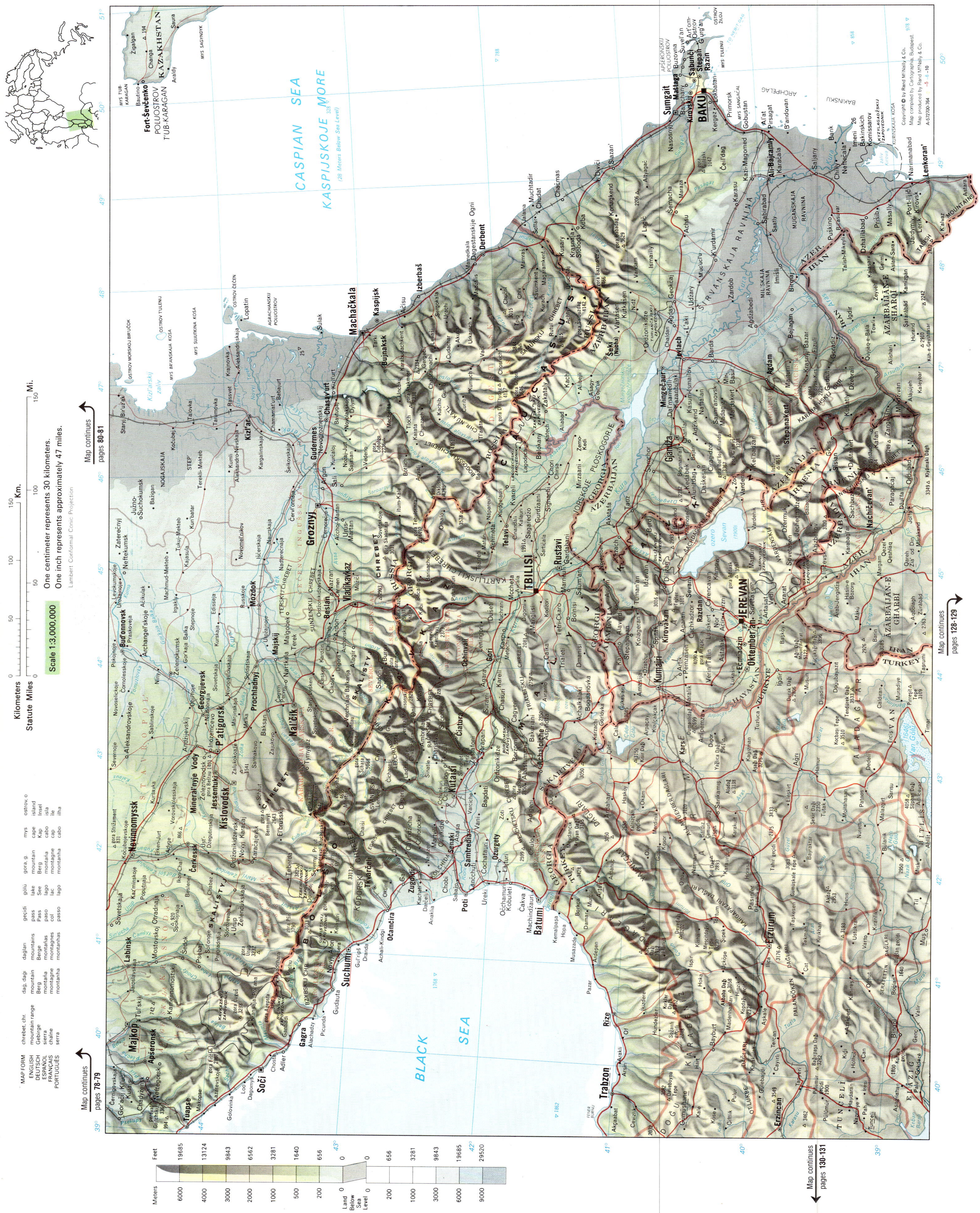

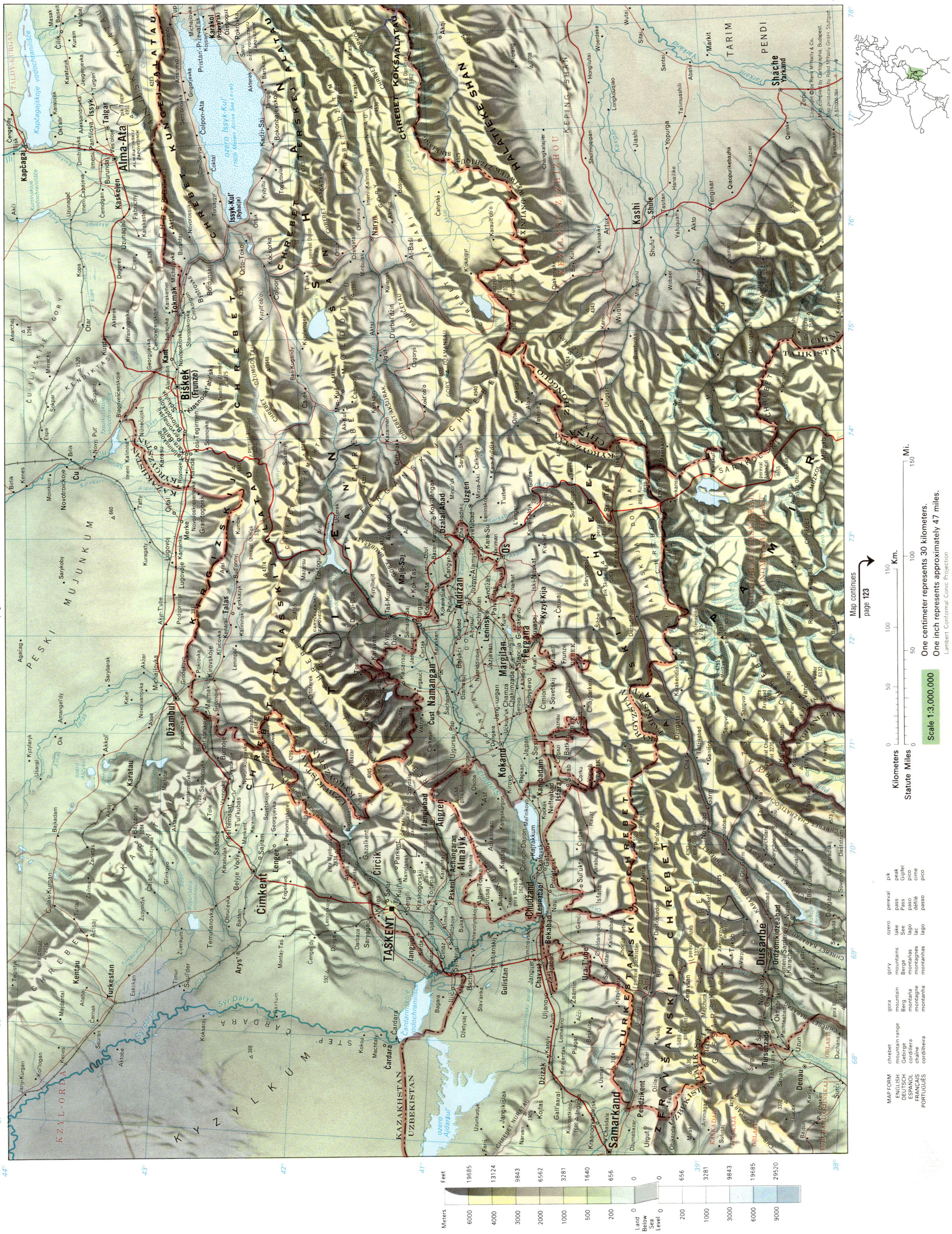
Map continues pages 86-87
Map continues page 123
Alma-Ata
Biškek (Frunze)
Taškent
Dušanbe
Samarkand
Kokand
Namangan
Andižan
Fergana
Oš
Kashi
Shache (Yarkand)
Issyk-Kul'
ozero Issyk-Kul'
Džambul
Čimkent
Turkestan
Kentau
Karatau
Syr Darya
KAZAKHSTAN
UZBEKISTAN
TAJIKISTAN
CHINA
PESKI MUJUNKUM
KYZYLKUM
TARIM PENDI
KEPING SHAN
Kilometers
Statute Miles
Km.
Mi.
One centimeter represents 30 kilometers.
One inch represents approximately 47 miles.
Scale 1:3,000,000
Lambert Conformal Conic Projection
Feet
Meters
19685
13124
9843
6562
3281
1640
656
0
6000
4000
3000
2000
1000
500
200
Land Below Sea Level
29520
9000
MAP FORM / ENGLISH / DEUTSCH / ESPAÑOL / FRANÇAIS / PORTUGUÊS
chrebet / mountain range / Gebirge / cordillera / chaîne / cordilheira
gora / mountain / Berg / montaña / montagne / montanha
gory / mountains / Berge / montañas / montagnes / montanhas
ozero / lake / See / lago / lac / lago
pereval / pass / Pass / paso / défilé / passo
pik / peak / Gipfel / pico / cime / pico

Central Russia and Kazakhstan / Mittelrussland und Kasachstan / Rusia Central e Kazajstan
Russie Centrale et Kazakhstan / Rússia Central e Casaquistão

Map continues pages 72-73

Map continues pages 24-25

Map continues pages 80-81

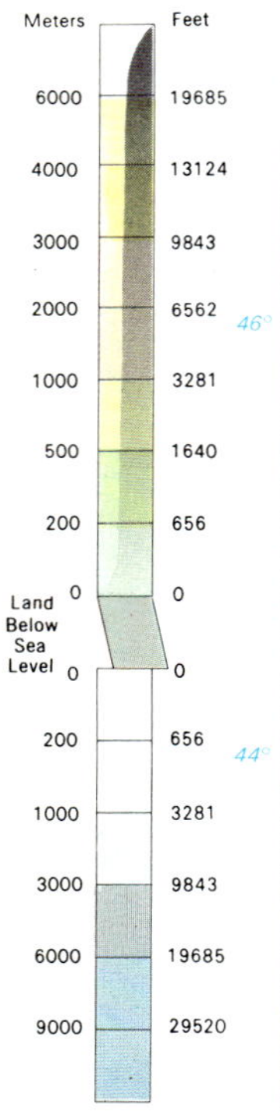

Map continues page 85

MAP FORM	chrebet	gora	hu	ozero	plato	porog
ENGLISH	mountain range	mountain	lake	lake	plateau	waterfall
DEUTSCH	Gebirge	Berg	See	See	Hochebene	Wasserfall
ESPAÑOL	cordillera	montaña	lago	lago	meseta	cascada
FRANÇAIS	chaîne	montagne	lac	lac	plateau	chute d'eau
PORTUGUÊS	cordilheira	montanha	lago	lago	planalto	queda d'água

Map continues page 88

Kilometers 0 100 200 300 Km.
Statute Miles 0 100 200 300 Mi.

Scale 1:6,000,000
One centimeter represents 60 kilometers.
One inch represents approximately 95 miles.
Lambert Conformal Conic Projection

Lake Baikal Region / Baikalseegebiet / Región del Lago Baikal
Région du Lac Baïkal / Região do Lago Baikal

Map continues page 89

MAP FORM	chrebet	gora	nuruu	nuur	ozero, o.	porog	uul
ENGLISH	mountain range	mountain	mountain range	lake	lake	waterfall	mountains
DEUTSCH	Gebirge	Berg	Gebirge	See	See	Wasserfall	Berge
ESPAÑOL	cordillera	montaña	cordillera	lago	lago	cascada	montañas
FRANÇAIS	chaîne	montagne	chaîne	lac	lac	chute d'eau	montagnes
PORTUGUÊS	cordilheira	montanha	cordilheira	lago	lago	queda d'água	montanhas

Scale 1:6,000,000

One centimeter represents 60 kilometers.
One inch represents approximately 95 miles.

Lambert Conformal Conic Projection

Kilometers 0 100 200 300 Km.
Statute Miles 0 100 200 300 Mi.

Map continues pages 74-75

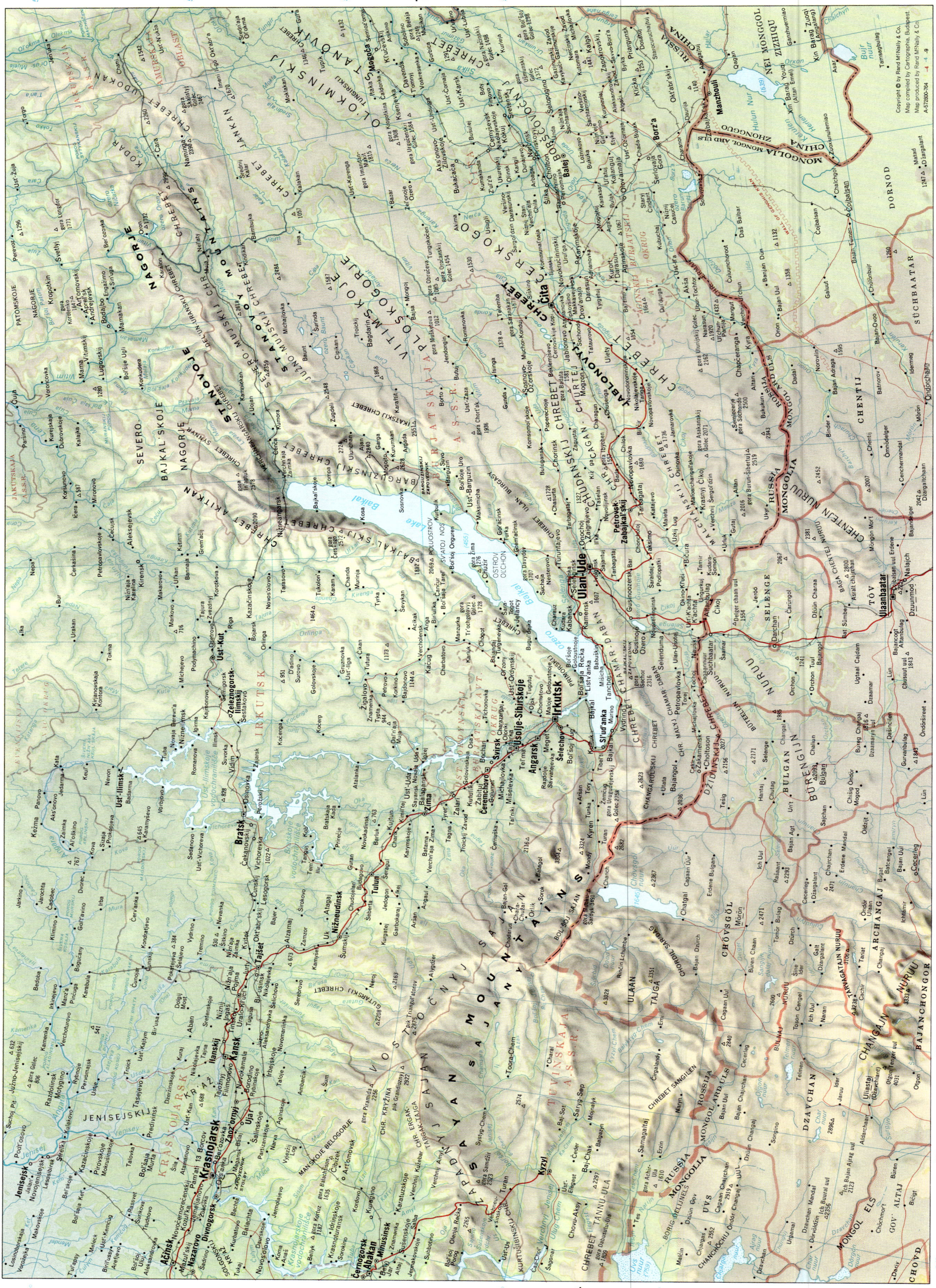

Map continues pages 102-103

Feet	Meters
19685	6000
13124	4000
9843	3000
6562	2000
3281	1000
1640	500
656	200
0	0
Land Below Sea Level	
656	200
3281	1000
9843	3000
19685	6000
29520	9000

Map continues pages 86-87

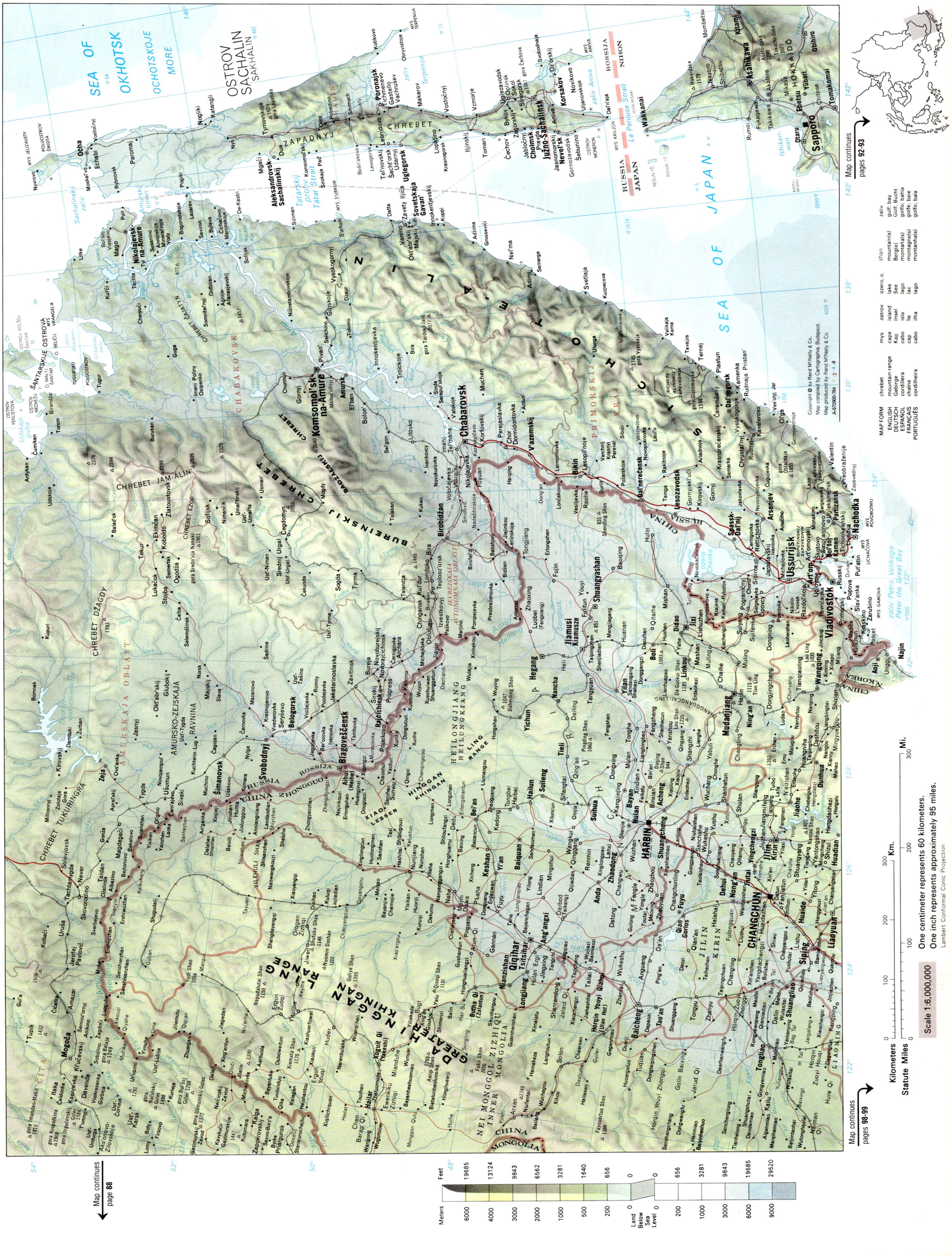
SEA OF OKHOTSK
OCHOTSKOJE MORE
OSTROV SACHALIN
SAKHALIN
SEA OF JAPAN
La Perouse Strait
Tatar Strait
HOKKAIDŌ
RUSSIA
JAPAN
CHINA
MONGOLIA
Chabarovsk
Komsomol'sk-na-Amure
Blagoveščensk
Vladivostok
Nachodka
Ussurijsk
Birobidžan
Harbin
Qiqihar
Changchun
Sapporo
Asahikawa
Južno-Sachalinsk
Jiamusi
Mudanjiang
Map continues pages 74-75
Map continues page 88
Map continues pages 92-93
Map continues pages 98-99
Scale 1:6,000,000
One centimeter represents 60 kilometers.
One inch represents approximately 95 miles.
Lambert Conformal Conic Projection
Kilometers
Statute Miles
Km.
Mi.
Meters
Feet
Land Below Sea Level
MAP FORM
ENGLISH
DEUTSCH
ESPAÑOL
FRANÇAIS
PORTUGUÊS
Copyright © by Rand McNally & Co.
Map compiled by Cartographia, Budapest.
Map produced by Rand McNally & Co.

Map continues pages 74-75

Map continues pages 118-119

MAP FORM	bandao	dao	hu	-jima	pendi	shan	-shima
ENGLISH	peninsula	island	lake	island	basin	mountain(s)	island
DEUTSCH	Halbinsel	Insel	See	Insel	Becken	Berg(e)	Insel
ESPAÑOL	península	isla	lago	isla	cuenca	montaña(s)	isla
FRANÇAIS	péninsule	île	lac	île	bassin	montagne(s)	île
PORTUGUÊS	península	ilha	lago	ilha	bacia	montanha(s)	ilha

Map continues pages 108-109

Kilometers 0 200 400 600 Km.
Statute Miles 0 200 400 600 Mi.

Scale 1:12,000,000
One centimeter represents 120 kilometers.
One inch represents approximately 190 miles.
Lambert Conformal Conic Projection

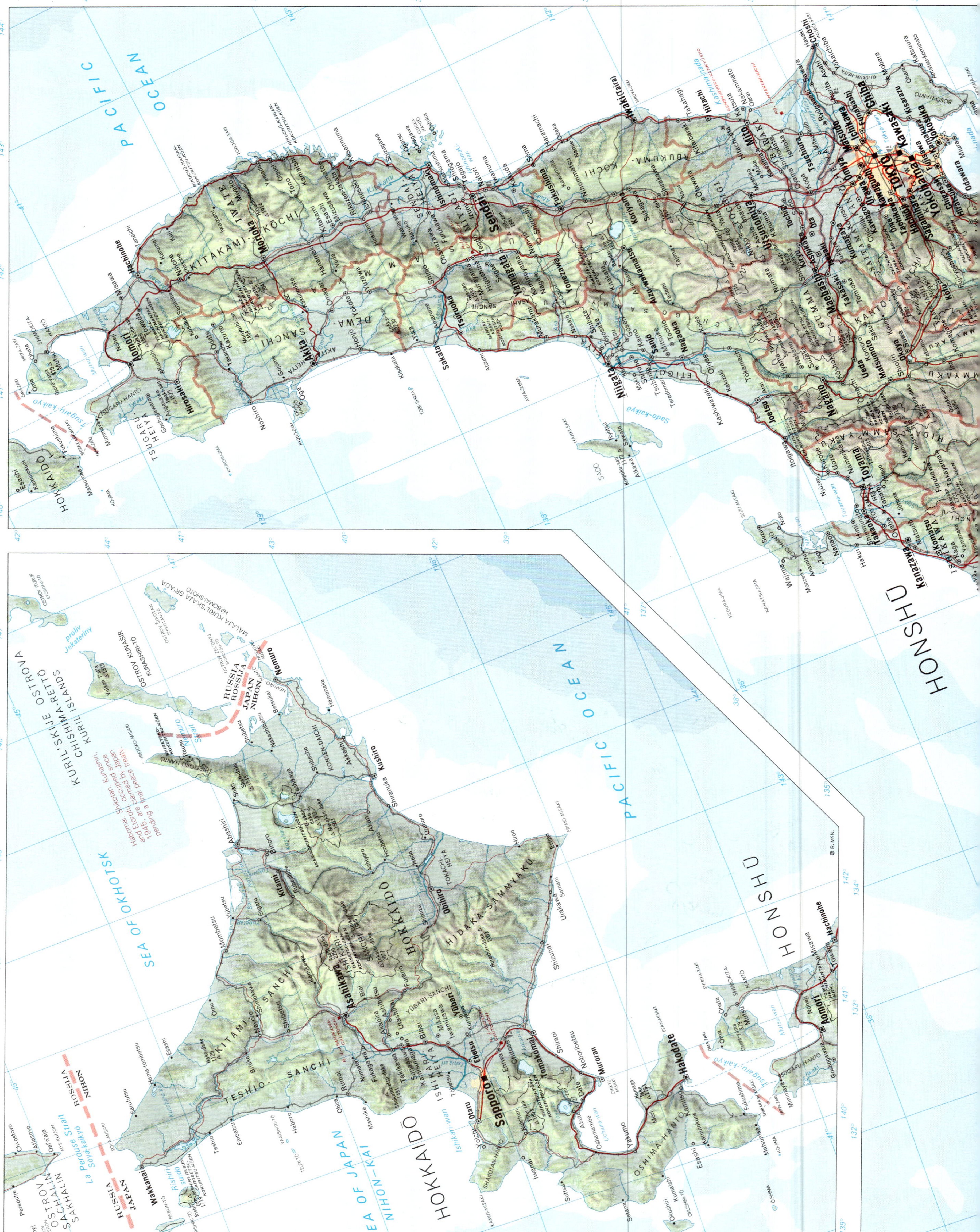
PACIFIC OCEAN
HONSHŪ
HOKKAIDŌ
SEA OF OKHOTSK
SEA OF JAPAN
NIHON-KAI
KURIL'SKIJE OSTROVA
CHISHIMA-RETTO
KURIL ISLANDS
OSTROV SACHALIN
SAKHALIN
La Perouse Strait
Sōya-kaikyō
RUSSIA
JAPAN
NIHON
Tōkyō
Sendai
Sapporo
Hakodate
Asahikawa
Niigata
Akita
Morioka
Aomori
Habomai, Shikotan, Kunashiri and Etorofu, occupied since 1945 are illegal by Japan. (claimed 'occupied by 1945 peace treaty' pending)

a

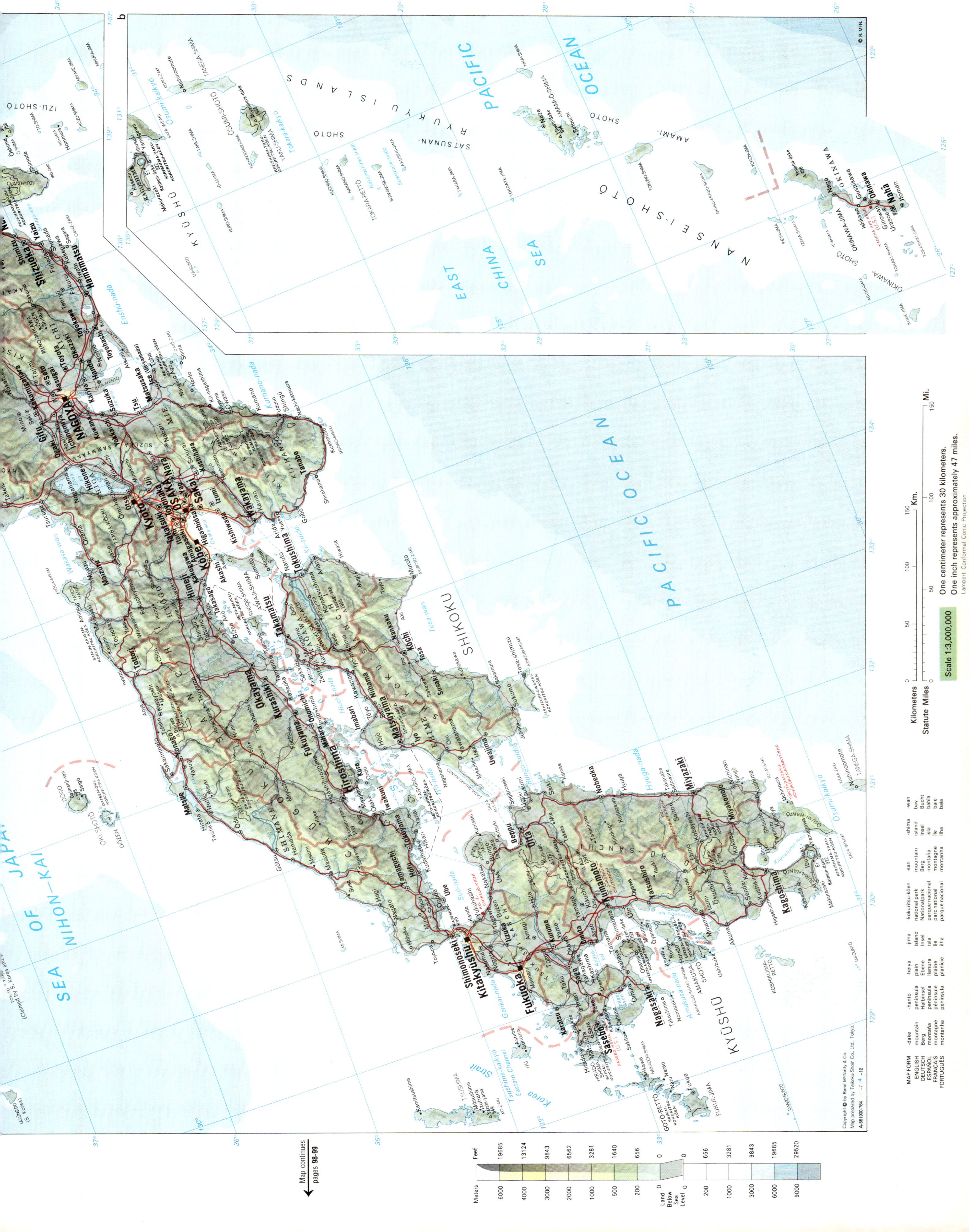
b
PACIFIC OCEAN
EAST CHINA SEA
SEA OF JAPAN
NIHON-KAI
RYUKYU ISLANDS
NANSEI-SHOTO
SATSUNAN-SHOTO
AMAMI-SHOTO
OKINAWA-SHOTO
KYŪSHŪ
SHIKOKU
OSAKA
KYOTO
NAGOYA
Kobe
Hiroshima
Fukuoka
Kitakyushu
Shimonoseki
Nagasaki
Kagoshima
Naha
Map continues pages 98-99
Kilometers
Statute Miles
Km.
Mi.
Scale 1:3,000,000
One centimeter represents 30 kilometers.
One inch represents approximately 47 miles.
Lambert Conformal Conic Projection
Meters
Feet
Land Below Sea Level
Copyright © by Rand McNally & Co.
Map prepared by Teikoku-Shoin Co., Ltd., Tokyo
MAP FORM
ENGLISH
DEUTSCH
ESPAÑOL
FRANÇAIS
PORTUGUÊS
-dake mountain Berg montaña montagne montanha
-hantō peninsula Halbinsel península péninsule península
-heiya plain Ebene llanura plaine planície
-jima island Insel isla île ilha
-kokuritsu-kōen national park Nationalpark parque nacional parc national parque nacional
-san mountain Berg montaña montagne montanha
-shima island Insel isla île ilha
-wan bay Bucht bahía baie baía

Map continues pages 96-97

MAP FORM	-dake	-hantō	-kokutei-kōen	-misaki	-san	-tōge	-wan	-yama	-zaki
ENGLISH	mountain	peninsula	national park	cape	mountain	pass	bay	mountain	point
DEUTSCH	Berg	Halbinsel	Nationalpark	Kap	Berg	Pass	Bucht	Berg	Landspitze
ESPAÑOL	montaña	península	parque nacional	cabo	montaña	paso	bahía	montaña	punta
FRANÇAIS	montagne	péninsule	parc national	cap	montagne	col	baie	montagne	pointe
PORTUGUÊS	montanha	península	parque nacional	cabo	montanha	passo	baía	montanha	ponta

Kilometers 0 10 20 30 40 50 Km.

Statute Miles 0 10 20 30 40 50 Mi.

Scale 1:1,000,000

One centimeter represents 10 kilometers.
One inch represents approximately 16 miles.
Lambert Conformal Conic Projection

MAP FORM	-jima	-misaki	-san	-sen	-shima	-tōge	-yama	-zen
ENGLISH	island	cape	mountain	mountain	island	pass	mountain	mountain
DEUTSCH	Insel	Kap	Berg	Berg	Insel	Pass	Berg	Berg
ESPAÑOL	isla	cabo	montaña	montaña	isla	paso	montaña	montaña
FRANÇAIS	île	cap	montagne	montagne	île	col	montagne	montagne
PORTUGUÊS	ilha	cabo	montanha	montanha	ilha	passo	montanha	montanha

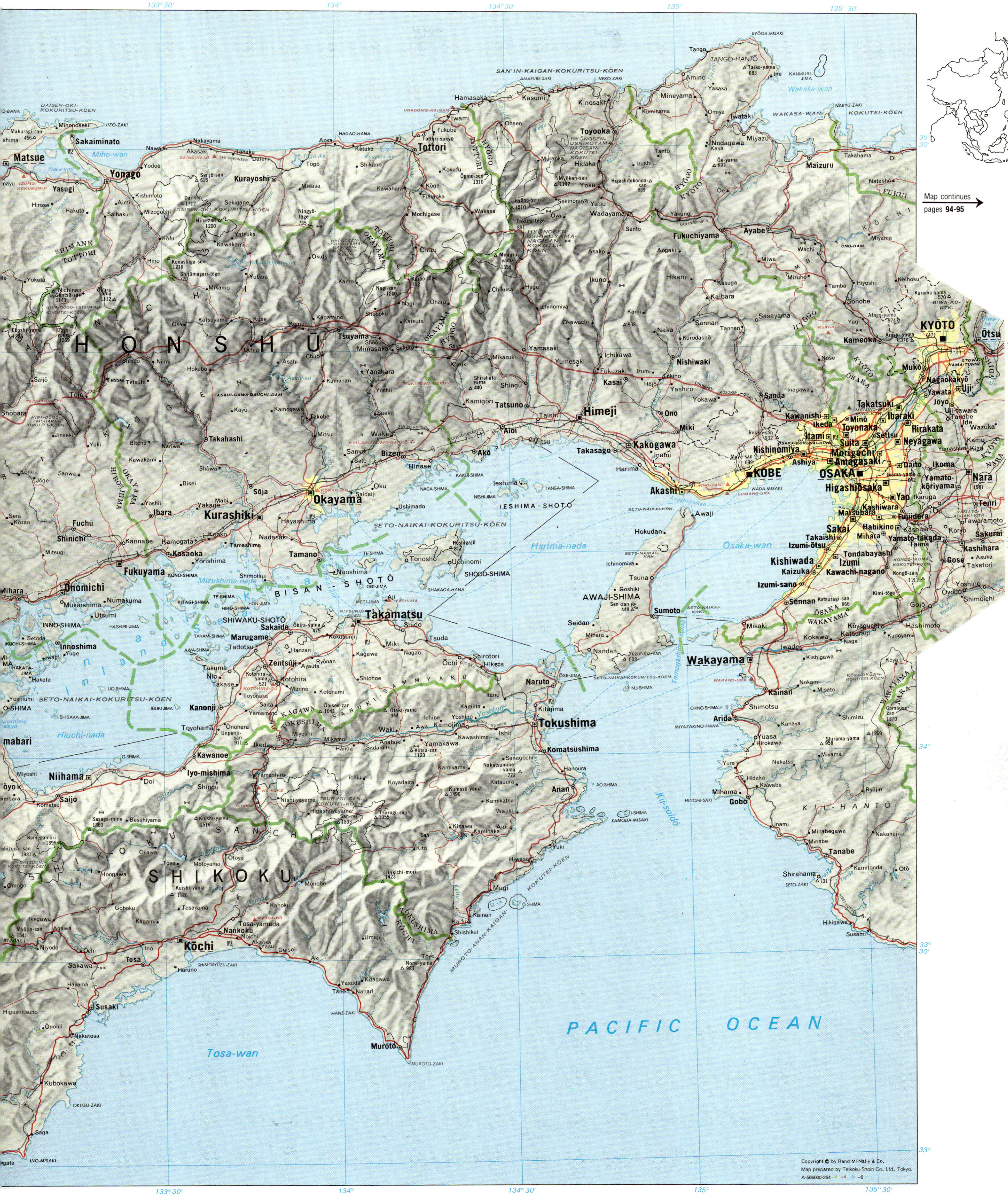

Kilometers 0 10 20 30 40 50 Km.

Statute Miles 0 10 20 30 40 50 Mi.

Scale 1:1,000,000

One centimeter represents 10 kilometers.
One inch represents approximately 16 miles.
Lambert Conformal Conic Projection

Northeast China and Korea / Nordostchina und Korea / China Nor-oriental y Corea
Nord-Est de la Chine et Corée / Nordeste da China e Coréia

Map continues pages 102-103

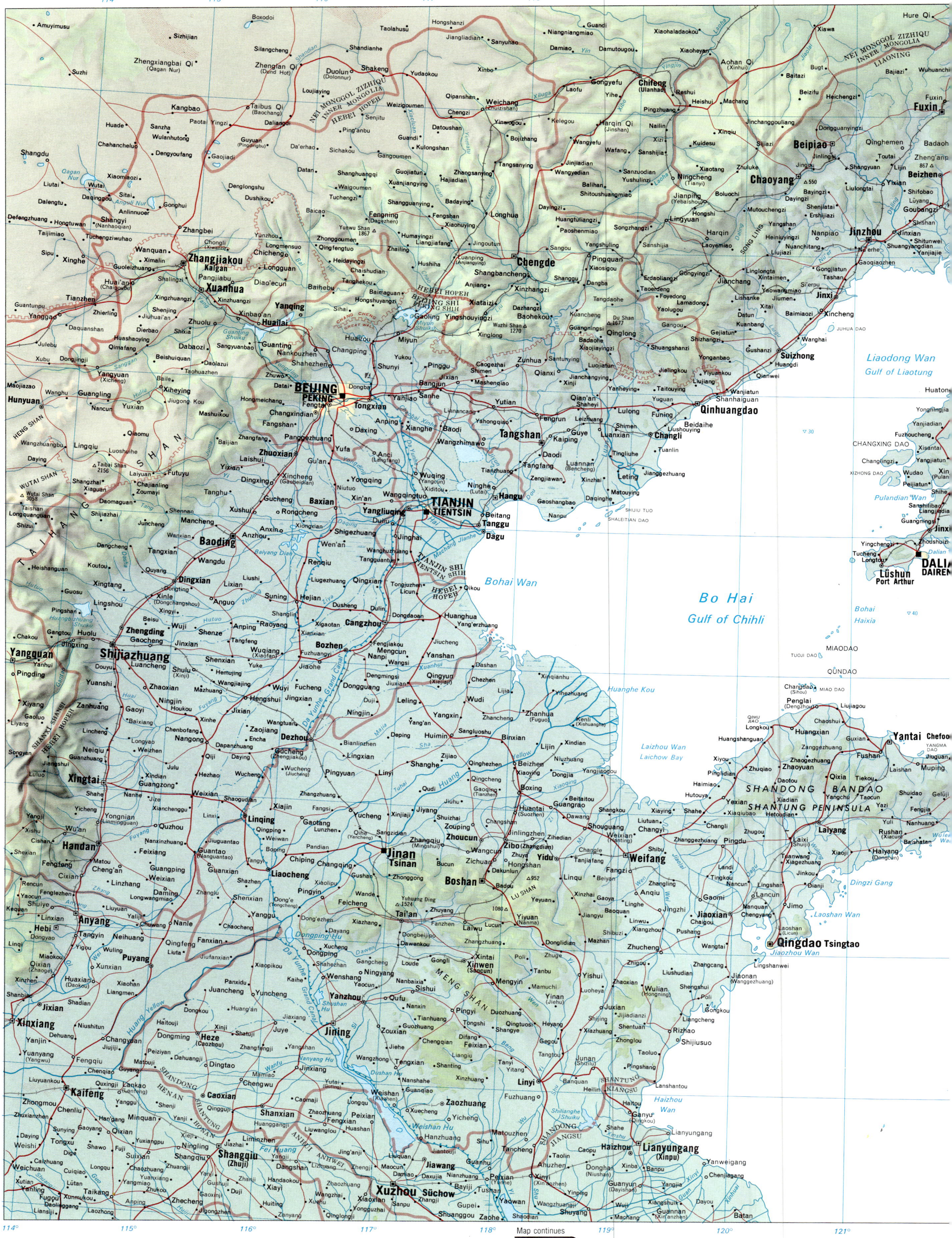

Meters	Feet
6000	19685
4000	13124
3000	9843
2000	6562
1000	3281
500	1640
200	656
0	0
Land Below Sea Level 0	0
200	656
1000	3281
3000	9843
6000	19685
9000	29520

Map continues pages 100-101

MAP FORM	dao	-do	-gang	hu	kukrip kongwŏn	-san	shan	wan
ENGLISH	island	island	river	lake	national park	mountain	mountain(s)	bay
DEUTSCH	Insel	Insel	Fluss	See	Nationalpark	Berg	Berg(e)	Bucht
ESPAÑOL	isla	isla	río	lago	parque nacional	montaña	montaña(s)	bahía
FRANÇAIS	île	île	rivière	lac	parc national	montagne	montagne(s)	baie
PORTUGUÊS	ilha	ilha	rio	lago	parque nacional	montanha	montanha(s)	baía

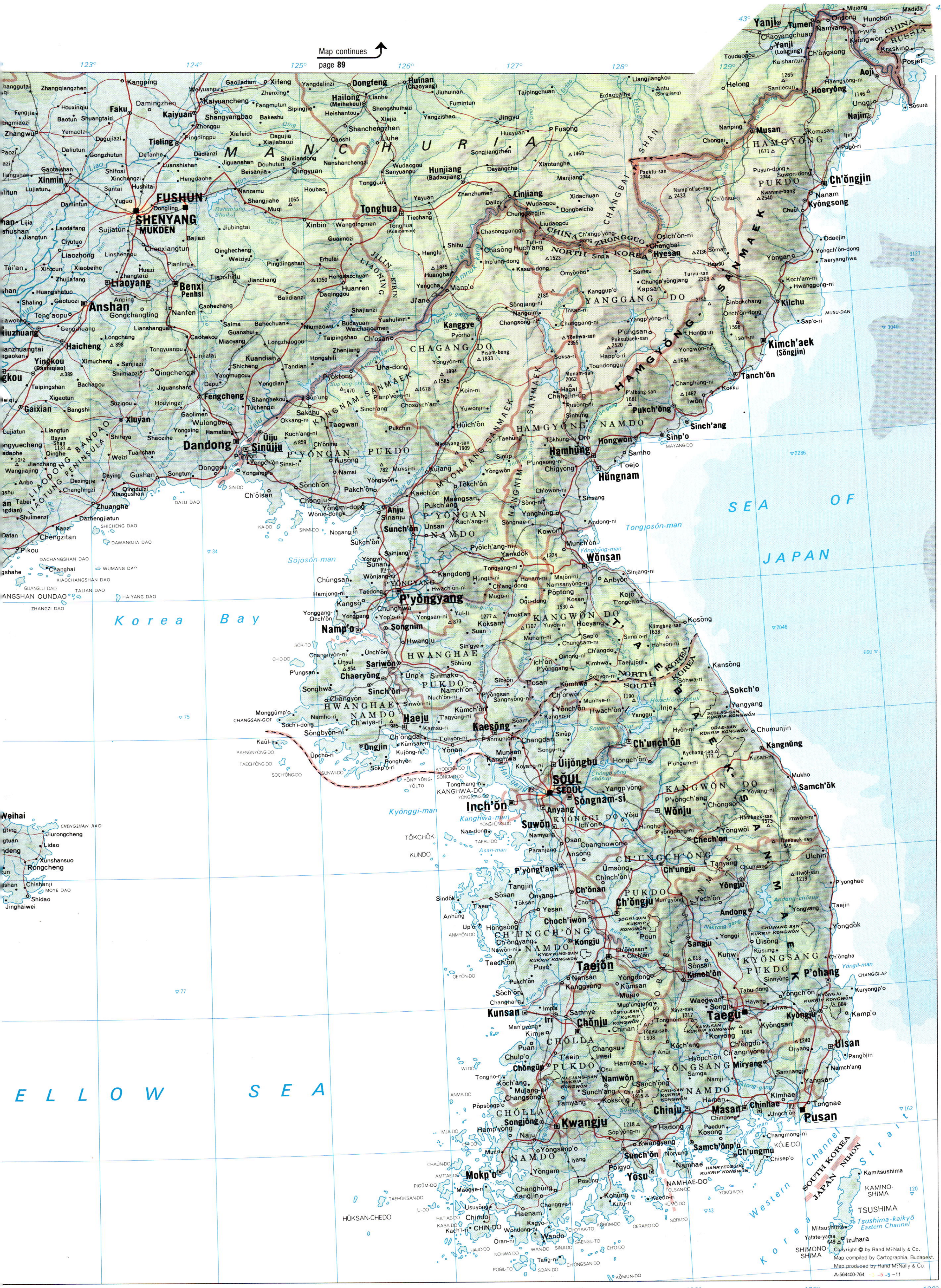

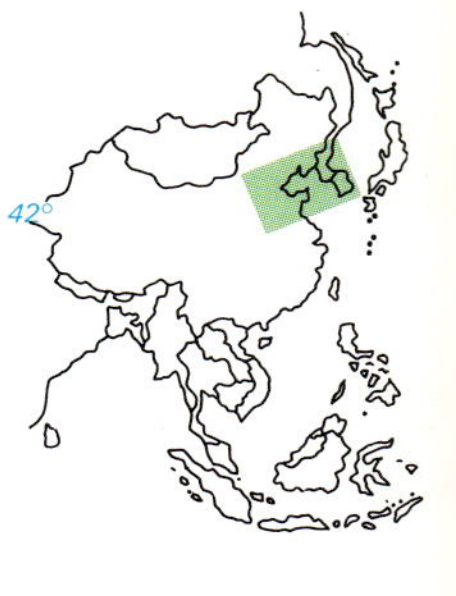

Kilometers 0 50 100 150 Km.

Statute Miles 0 50 100 150 Mi.

Scale 1:3,000,000

One centimeter represents 30 kilometers.

One inch represents approximately 47 miles.

Lambert Conformal Conic Projection

Map continues pages 98-99

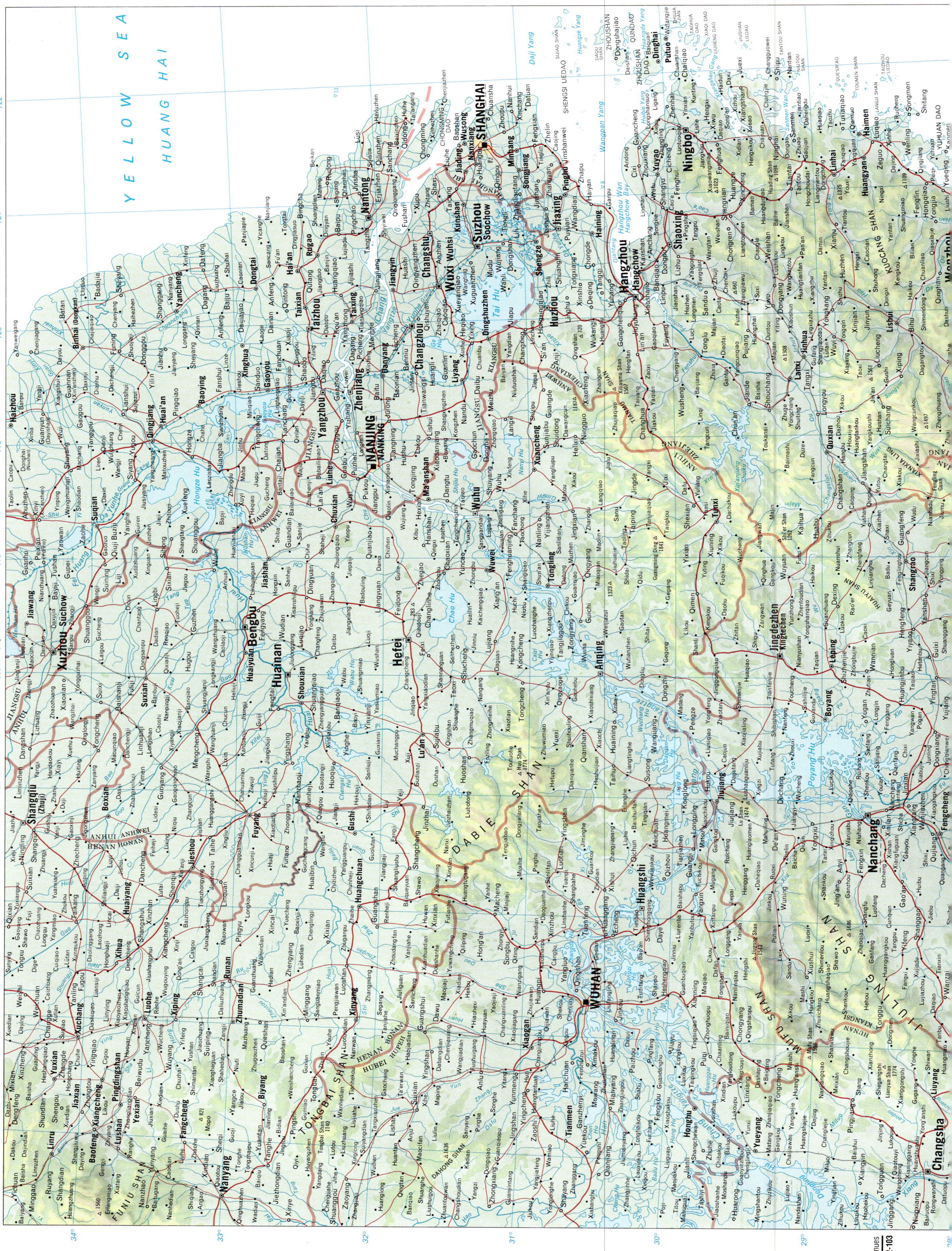

Map continues pages 102-103

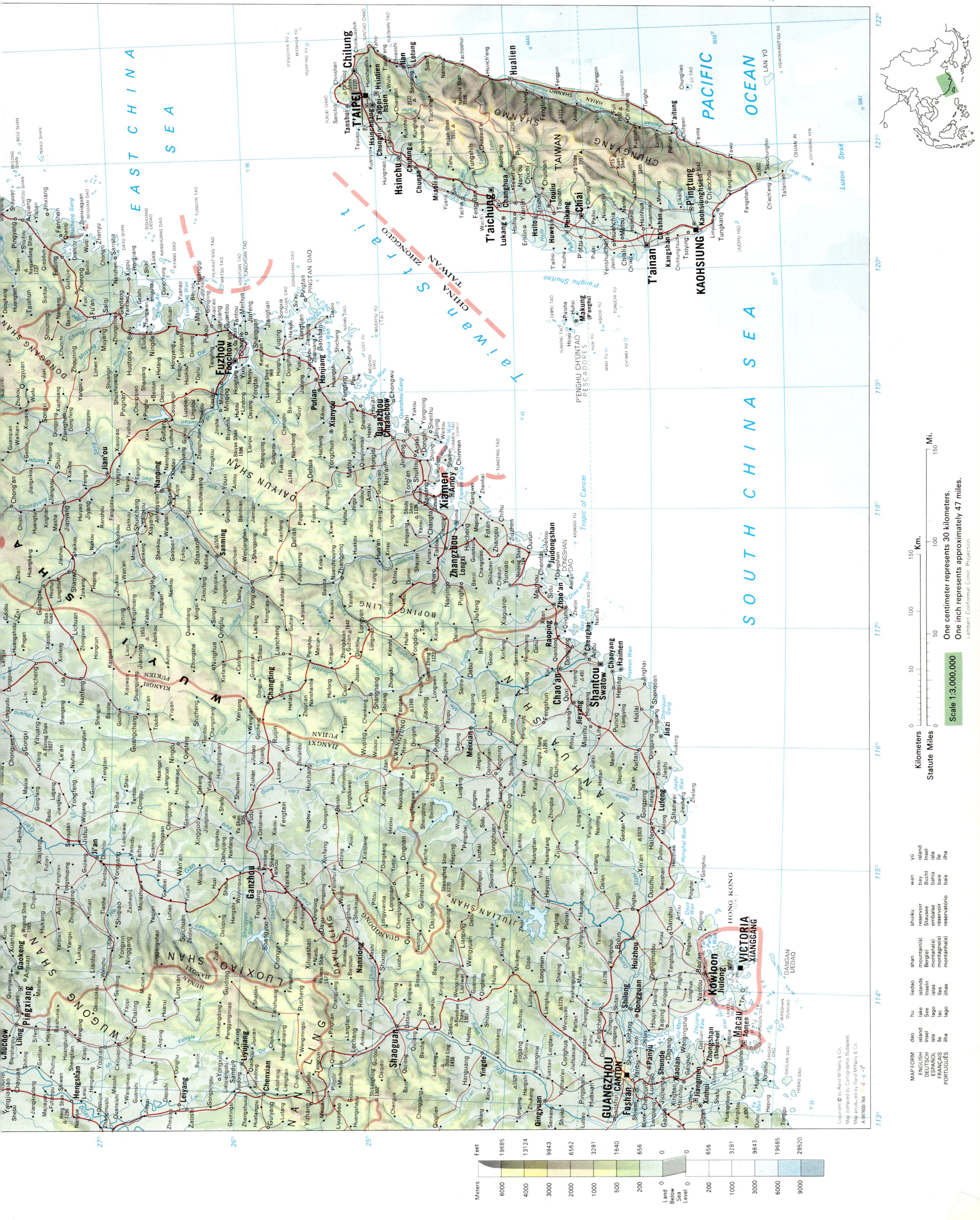
EAST CHINA SEA
Taiwan Strait
TAIWAN HAIXIA
CHINA ZHONGGUO
PACIFIC OCEAN
SOUTH CHINA SEA
Luzon Strait
TAIWAN
T'AIPEI
KAOHSIUNG
T'ainan
T'aichung
Chilung
Hualien
FUJIAN
JIANGXI
GUANGDONG
HUNAN
Fuzhou
Xiamen
Amoy
Quanzhou
Zhangzhou
Shantou
Swatow
Ganzhou
Shaoguan
GUANGZHOU
CANTON
Foshan
Kowloon
VICTORIA
HONG KONG
Macau
Nanping
Sanming
Putian
Meixian
WUYI SHAN
NAN LING
Tropic of Cancer
P'ENGHU CH'ÜNTAO
PESCADORES
Makung
Scale 1:3,000,000
One centimeter represents 30 kilometers.
One inch represents approximately 47 miles.
Kilometers
Statute Miles
Lambert Conformal Conic Projection
Feet
Meters
Land Below Sea Level
Copyright © by Rand McNally & Co.
Map compiled by Rand McNally & Co.
Map produced by Cartographia Budapest
MAP FORM
ENGLISH
DEUTSCH
ESPAÑOL
FRANÇAIS
PORTUGUÊS

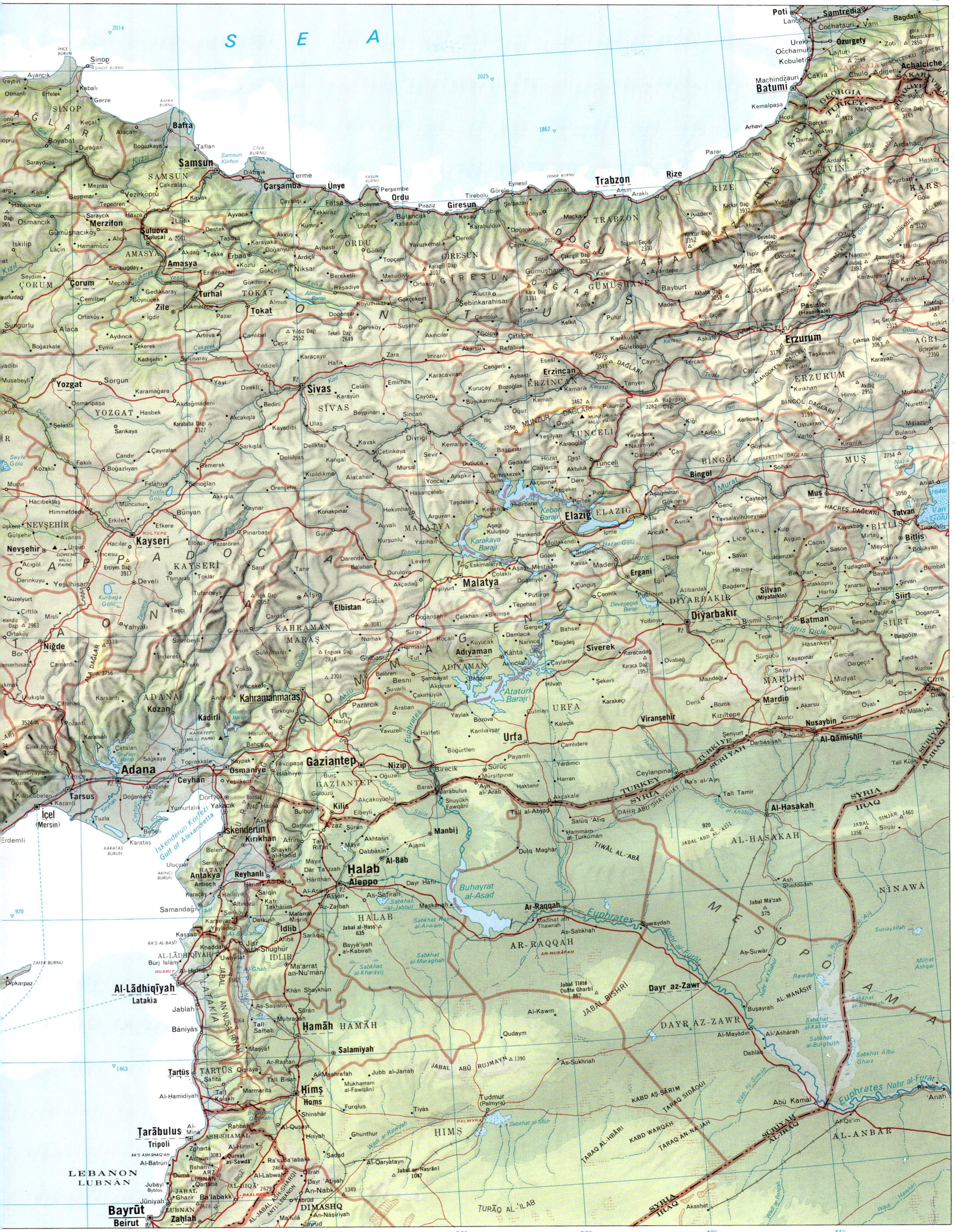

Map continues page 84

Map continues pages 128-129

Kilometers 0 50 100 150 Km.
Statute Miles 0 50 100 150 Mi.

Scale 1:3,000,000

One centimeter represents 30 kilometers.
One inch represents approximately 47 miles.
Conic Projection, Two Standard Parallels

MEDITERRANEAN
SEA
DIMASHQ DAMASCUS
Bayrūt
Yerushalayim Jerusalem
TEL AVIV-YAFO
'Ammān
Hefa
Area occupied by Israel.
(A) Area occupied by United Nations Disengagement Observer Force since 1974.
(B) Golan Heights area. Occupied by Israel since 1967. Unilaterally annexed by Israel, 1981.
(C) West Bank area. Unilaterally annexed by Jordan, 1950. Occupied by Israel since 1967. Status to be determined.
(D) East Jerusalem portion of West Bank. Unilaterally annexed by Israel, 1980.
(E) Gaza Strip. Occupied by Israel since 1967. Status to be determined.

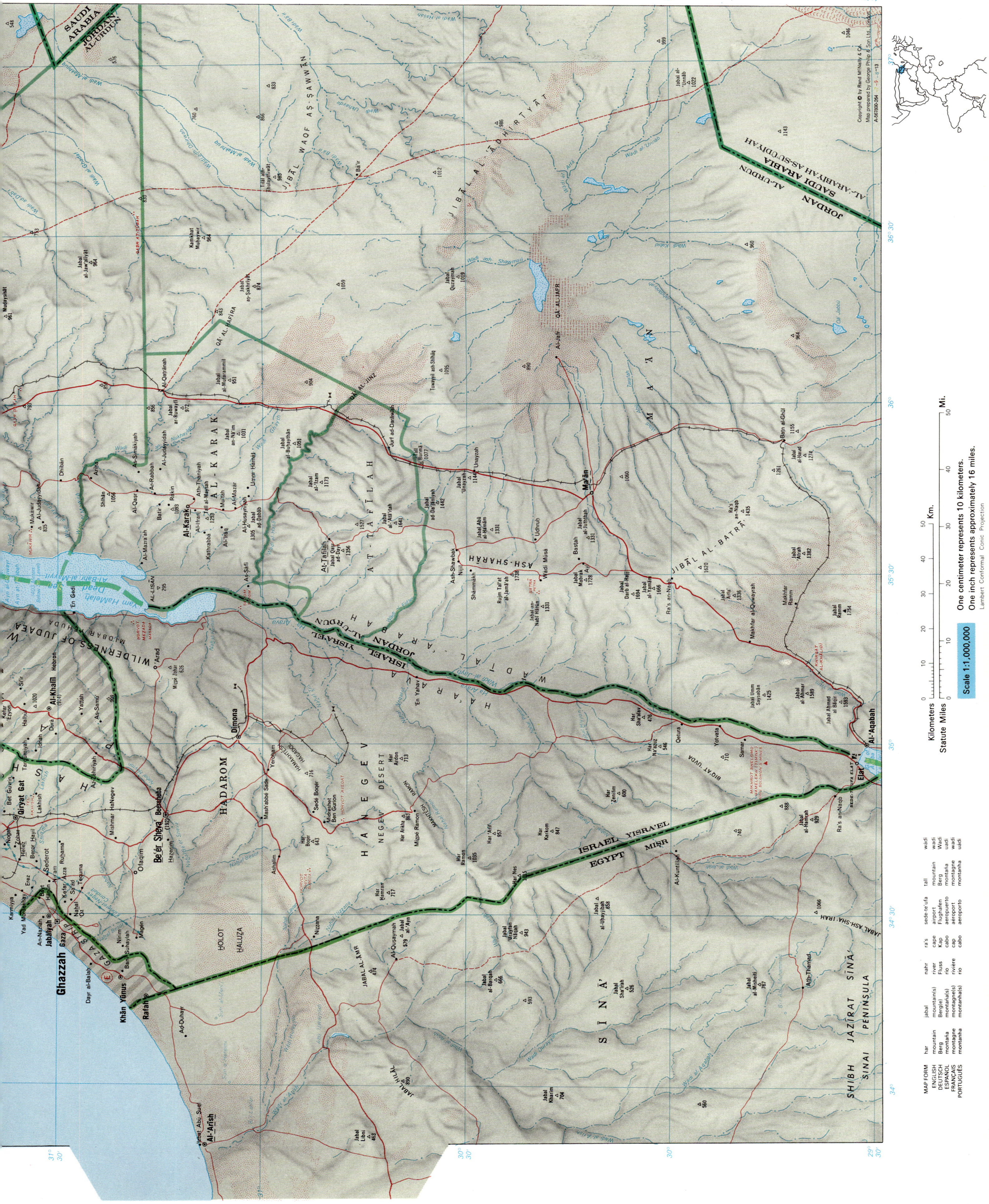
Scale 1:1,000,000
One centimeter represents 10 kilometers.
One inch represents approximately 16 miles.
Lambert Conformal Conic Projection
Kilometers
Statute Miles
JORDAN
AL-URDUN
SAUDI ARABIA
AL-'ARABIYAH AS-SU'ŪDIYAH
ISRAEL
YISRA'EL
EGYPT
MIṢR
HANEGEV
HADAROM
Ma'ān
Al-'Aqabah
Elat
Dimona
Be'ér Sheva
Ghazzah
Khān Yūnus
Al-'Arīsh

MAP FORM	bahr, baḥr	chott	jabal	lake	mountains	oued	wahât
ENGLISH	river, sea	salt marsh	mountain(s)	lake	mountains	wadi	oasis
DEUTSCH	Fluss, Meer	Salzmarsch	Berg(e)	See	Berge	Wadi	Oase
ESPAÑOL	río, mar	pantano salado	montaña(s)	lago	montañas	uadi	oasis
FRANÇAIS	rivière, mer	marais salé	montagne(s)	lac	montagnes	wadi	oasis
PORTUGUÊS	rio, mar	pântano salgado	montanha(s)	lago	montanhas	uádi	oásis

Map continues
pages 154-155

Map continues pages 156-157

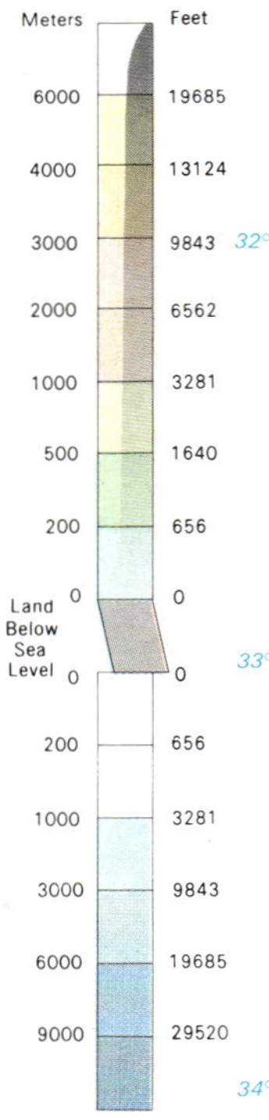

MAP FORM	bay	berge	cape	dam	game reserve	national park	pass	point
ENGLISH	bay	mountains	cape	dam	game reserve	national park	pass	point
DEUTSCH	Bucht	Berge	Kap	Damm	Wildpark	Nationalpark	Pass	Landspitze
ESPAÑOL	bahía	montañas	cabo	presa	vedado de caza	parque nacional	paso	punta
FRANÇAIS	baie	montagnes	cap	barrage	reserve à gibier	parc national	col	pointe
PORTUGUÊS	baía	montanhas	cabo	represa	reserva de caça	parque nacional	passo	ponta

Kilometers 0 50 100 150 Km.

Statute Miles 0 50 100 150 Mi.

Scale 1:3,000,000

One centimeter represents 30 kilometers.
One inch represents approximately 47 miles.

Lambert Conformal Conic Projection

Map continues
pages 108-109

ENGLISH	bay	cape	island	lake	mount	point	range	reef
DEUTSCH	Bucht	Kap	Insel	See	Berg	Landspitze	Gebirge	Riff
ESPAÑOL	bahía	cabo	isla	lago	montaña	punta	cordillera	arrecife
FRANÇAIS	baie	cap	île	lac	mont	pointe	chaîne	récif
PORTUGUÊS	baía	cabo	ilha	lago	monte	ponta	cordilheira	recife

Kilometers 0 200 400 600 Km.
Statute Miles 0 200 400 600 Mi.

Scale 1:12,000,000

One centimeter represents 120 kilometers.
One inch represents approximately 190 miles.

Lambert Conformal Conic Projection

Western and Central Australia / West-und Mittelaustralien / Australia Centro-occidental
Australie Occidentale et Centrale / Austrália Ocidental e Central

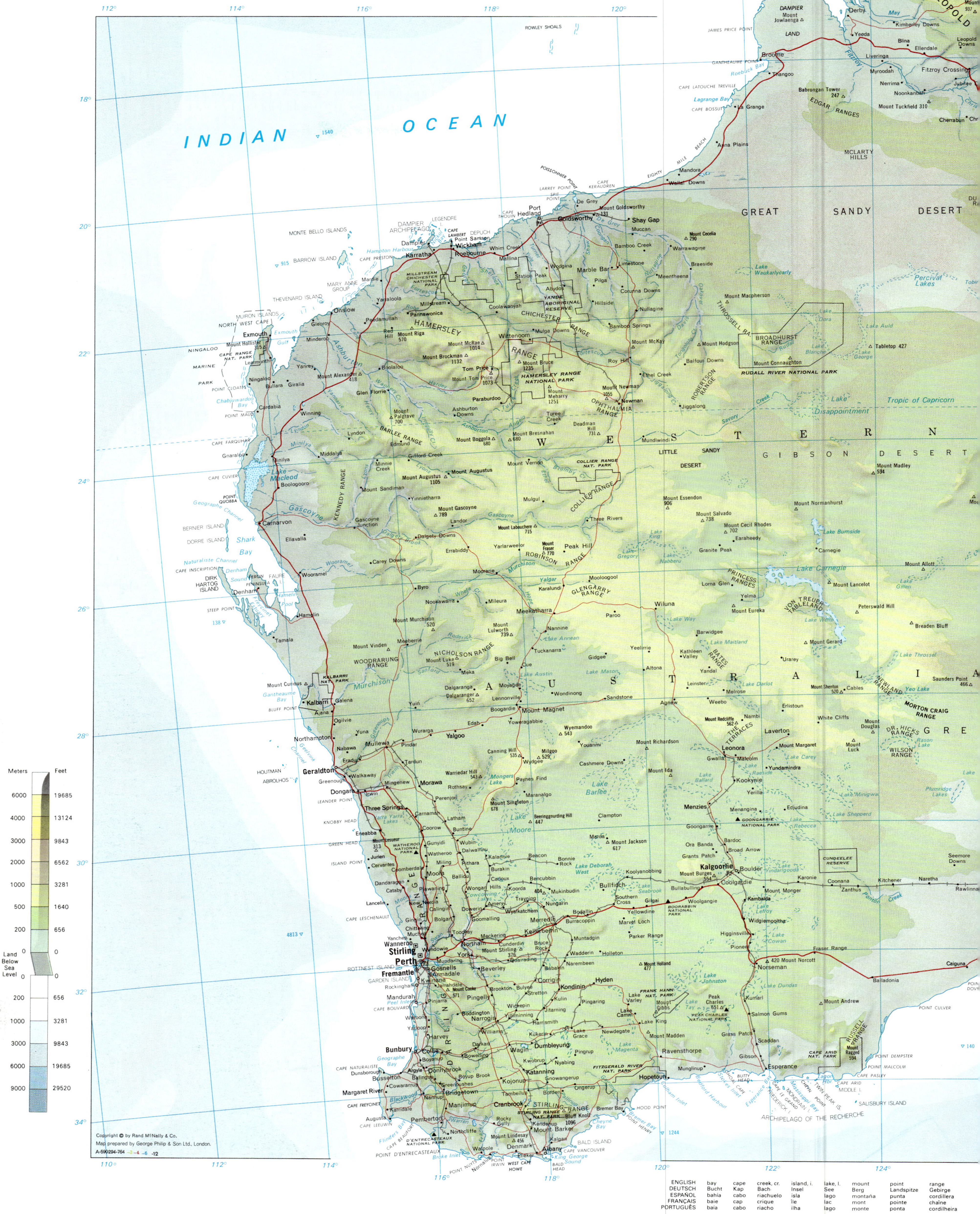

ENGLISH	bay	cape	creek, cr.	island, i.	lake, l.	mount	point	range
DEUTSCH	Bucht	Kap	Bach	Insel	See	Berg	Landspitze	Gebirge
ESPAÑOL	bahía	cabo	riachuelo	isla	lago	montaña	punta	cordillera
FRANÇAIS	baie	cap	crique	île	lac	mont	pointe	chaîne
PORTUGUÊS	baía	cabo	riacho	ilha	lago	monte	ponta	cordilheira

Map continues
pages 164-165

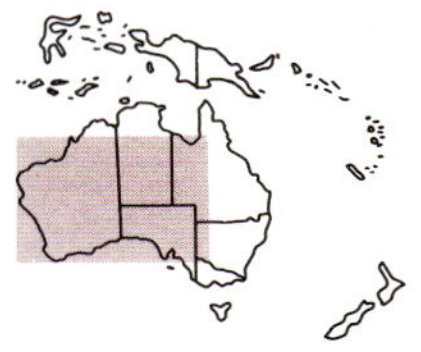

Map continues
pages 166-167

Kilometers 0 100 200 300 Km.
Statute Miles 0 100 200 300 Mi.

Scale 1:6,000,000

One centimeter represents 60 kilometers.
One inch represents approximately 95 miles.
Lambert Conformal Conic Projection

Map continues pages 112-113

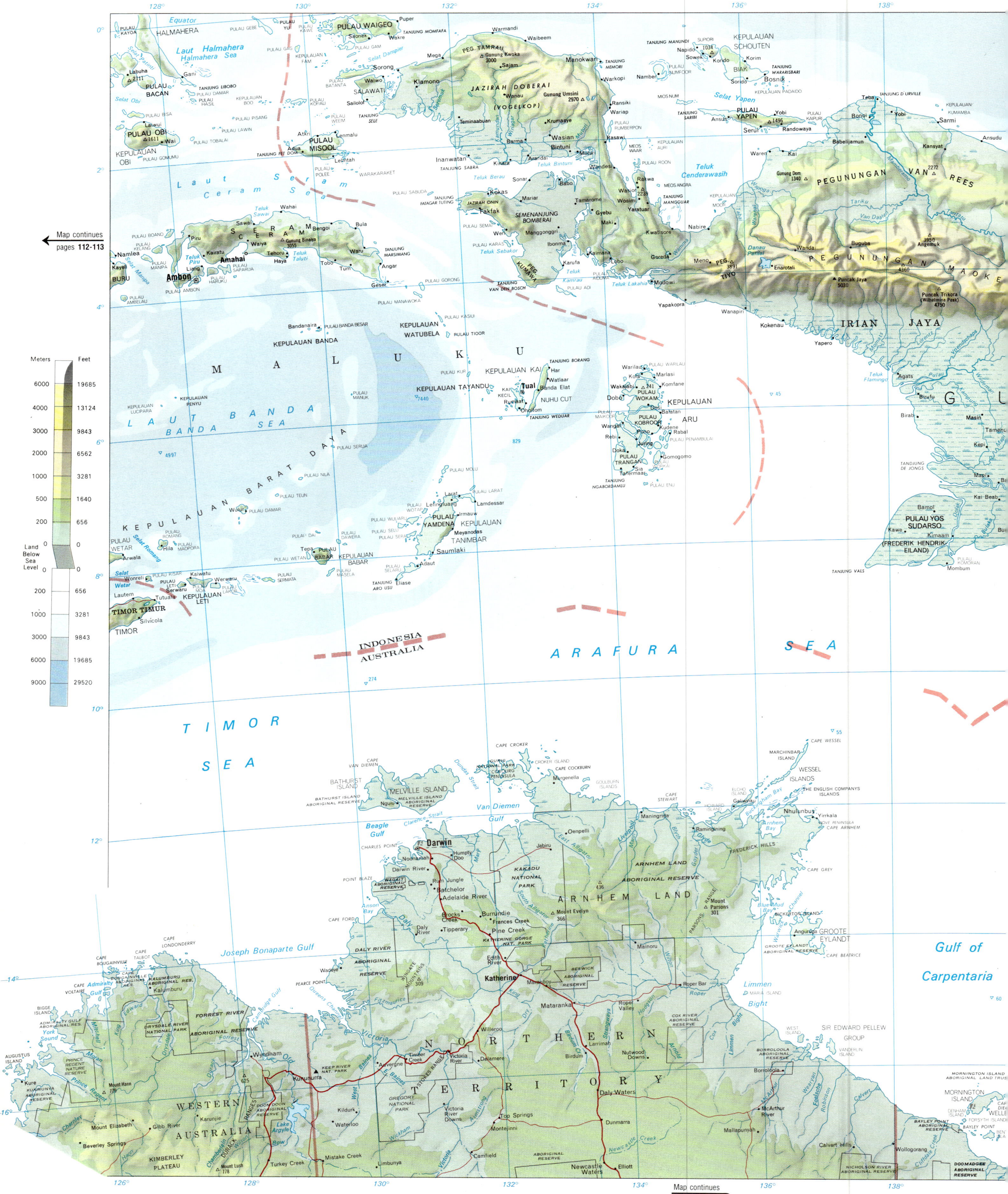

Map continues pages 162-163

MAP FORM	bay	cape	island	kepulauan	mount	pulau	range	tanjung
ENGLISH	bay	cape	island	islands	mount	island	range	cape
DEUTSCH	Bucht	Kap	Insel	Inseln	Berg	Insel	Gebirge	Kap
ESPAÑOL	bahía	cabo	isla	islas	montaña	isla	cordillera	cabo
FRANÇAIS	baie	cap	île	îles	mont	île	chaîne	cap
PORTUGUÊS	baía	cabo	ilha	ilhas	monte	ilha	cordilheira	cabo

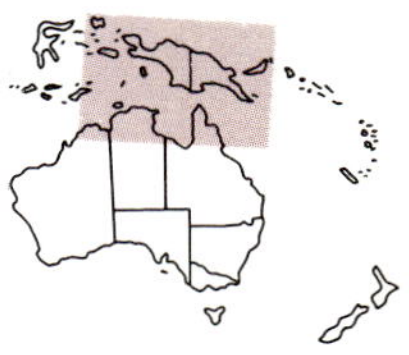

Map continues pages 166-167

Kilometers 0 100 200 300 Km.

Statute Miles 0 100 200 300 Mi.

Scale 1:6,000,000

One centimeter represents 60 kilometers.
One inch represents approximately 95 miles.
Lambert Conformal Conic Projection

Map continues
pages 176-177

Kilometers 0 200 400 600 Km.
Statute Miles 0 200 400 600 Mi.

Scale 1:12,000,000

One centimeter represents 120 kilometers.
One inch represents approximately 190 miles.
Albers Conical Equal-Area Projection

Alaska and Yukon / Alaska und Yukon / Alaska y Yukón
Alaska et Yukon / Alasca e Yukon

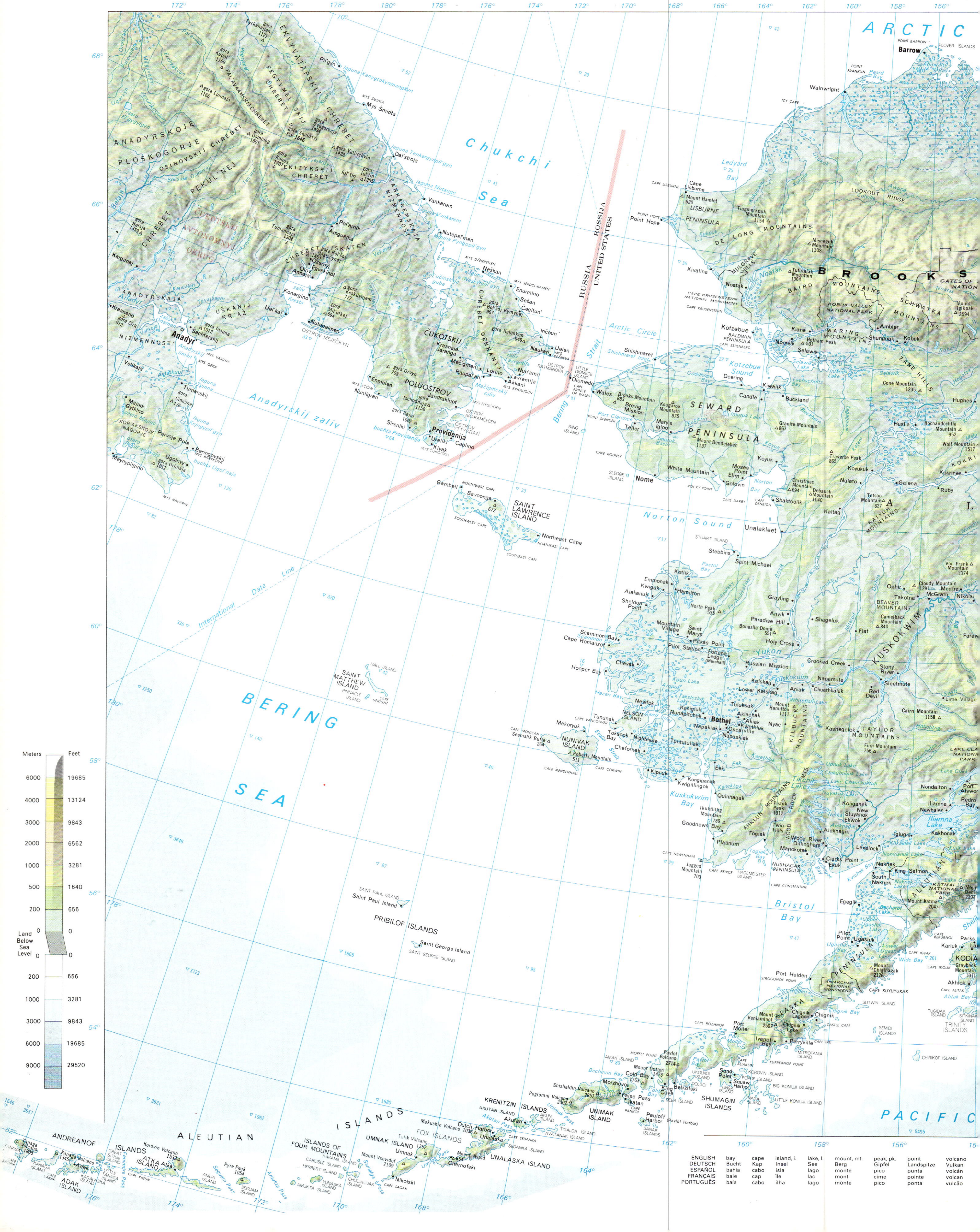

Map continues pages 176-177

Map continues pages 182-183

Kilometers 0 100 200 300 Km.
Statute Miles 0 100 200 300 Mi.

Scale 1:6,000,000

One centimeter represents 60 kilometers.
One inch represents approximately 95 miles.
Lambert Conformal Conic Projection

Southwestern Canada / Südwestkanada / Canadá Sud-occidental
Sud-Ouest du Canada / Canadá: Sudoeste

Map continues pages 180-181

ENGLISH	creek	Indian reserve	inlet	island	lake, l.	mountain	peak	provincial park	sound
DEUTSCH	Bach	Indianerreservation	Einfahrt	Insel	See	Berg	Gipfel	Provinz-Park	Sund
ESPAÑOL	riachuelo	reserva de Indios	abra	isla	lago	montaña	pico	parque de provincia	sonda
FRANÇAIS	crique	réserve indienne	bras de mer	île	lac	montagne	cime	parc provincial	détroit
PORTUGUÊS	riacho	reserva indígena	enseada	ilha	lago	montanha	pico	parque provincial	estreito

Map continues pages 184-185

Map continues pages 202-203

Kilometers 0 50 100 150 Km.
Statute Miles 0 50 100 150 Mi.

Scale 1:3,000,000
One centimeter represents 30 kilometers.
One inch represents approximately 47 miles.
Lambert Conformal Conic Projection

Map continues pages 182-183

Meters	Feet
6000	19685
4000	13124
3000	9843
2000	6562
1000	3281
500	1640
200	656
0	0
Land Below Sea Level 0	0
200	656
1000	3281
3000	9843
6000	19685
9000	29520

ENGLISH	creek, cr.	hills	Indian reserve	island, i.	lake, l.	provincial park
DEUTSCH	Bach	Hügel	Indianerreservation	Insel	See	Provinz-Park
ESPAÑOL	riachuelo	colinas	reserva de Indios	isla	lago	parque de provincia
FRANÇAIS	crique	collines	réserve indienne	île	lac	parc provincial
PORTUGUÊS	riacho	colinas	reserva indígena	ilha	lago	parque provincial

Map continues pages 202-203

Map continues pages 198-199

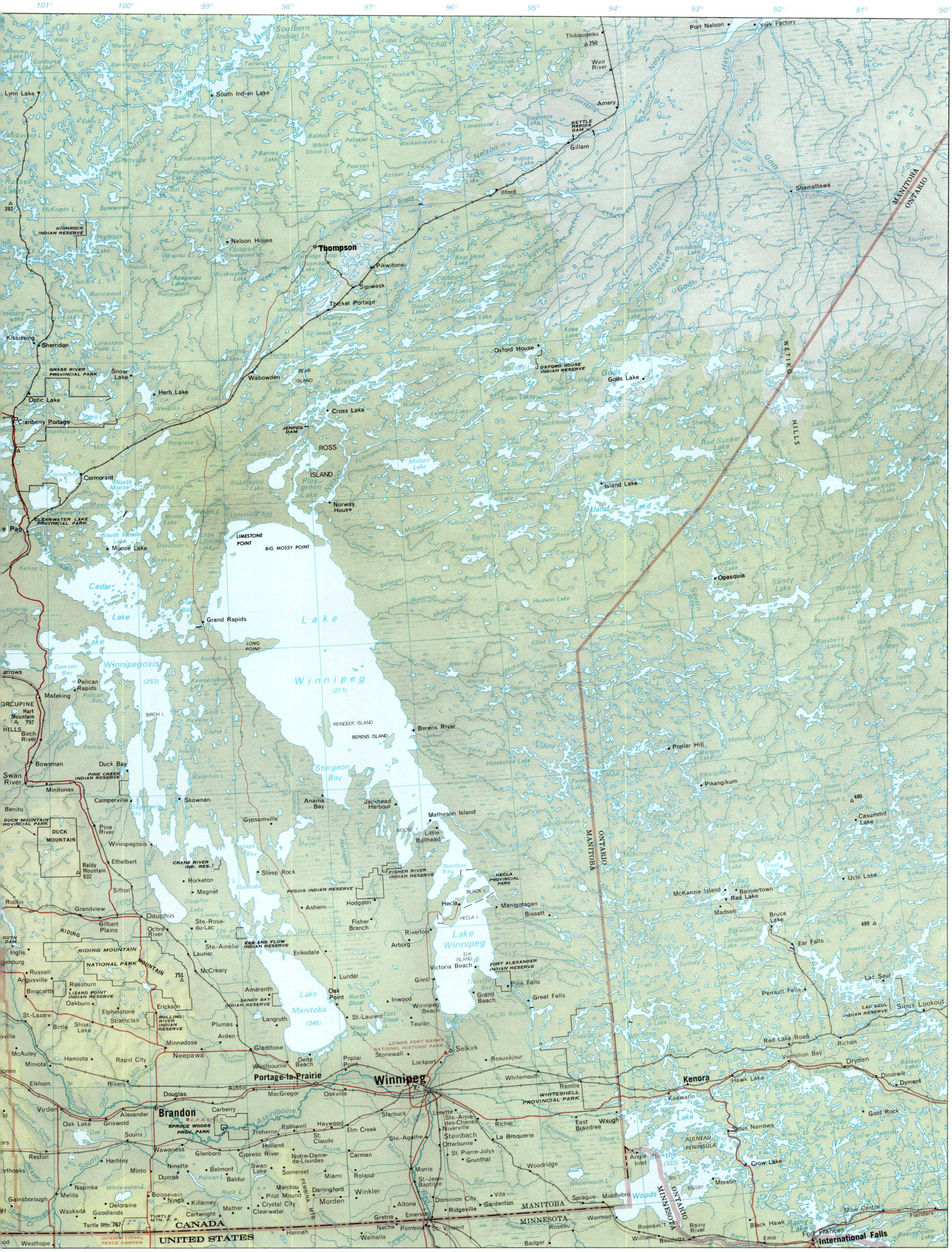

Map continues pages 190-191

Kilometers 0 50 100 150 Km.
Statute Miles 0 50 100 150 Mi.

Scale 1:3,000,000

One centimeter represents 30 kilometers.
One inch represents approximately 47 miles.
Lambert Conformal Conic Projection

Meters / Feet
6000 19685
4000 13124
3000 9843
2000 6562
1000 3281
500 1640
200 656
Land Below Sea Level 0 0
0 0
200 656
1000 3281
3000 9843
6000 19685
9000 29520

← Map continues pages 188-189

ENGLISH	bay	cape	dam	island	lake, l.	mountain	point	strait
DEUTSCH	Bucht	Kap	Damm	Insel	See	Berg	Landspitze	Meeresstrasse
ESPAÑOL	bahía	cabo	presa	isla	lago	montaña	punta	estrecho
FRANÇAIS	baie	cap	barrage	île	lac	montagne	pointe	détroit
PORTUGUÊS	baía	cabo	represa	ilha	lago	montanha	ponta	estreito

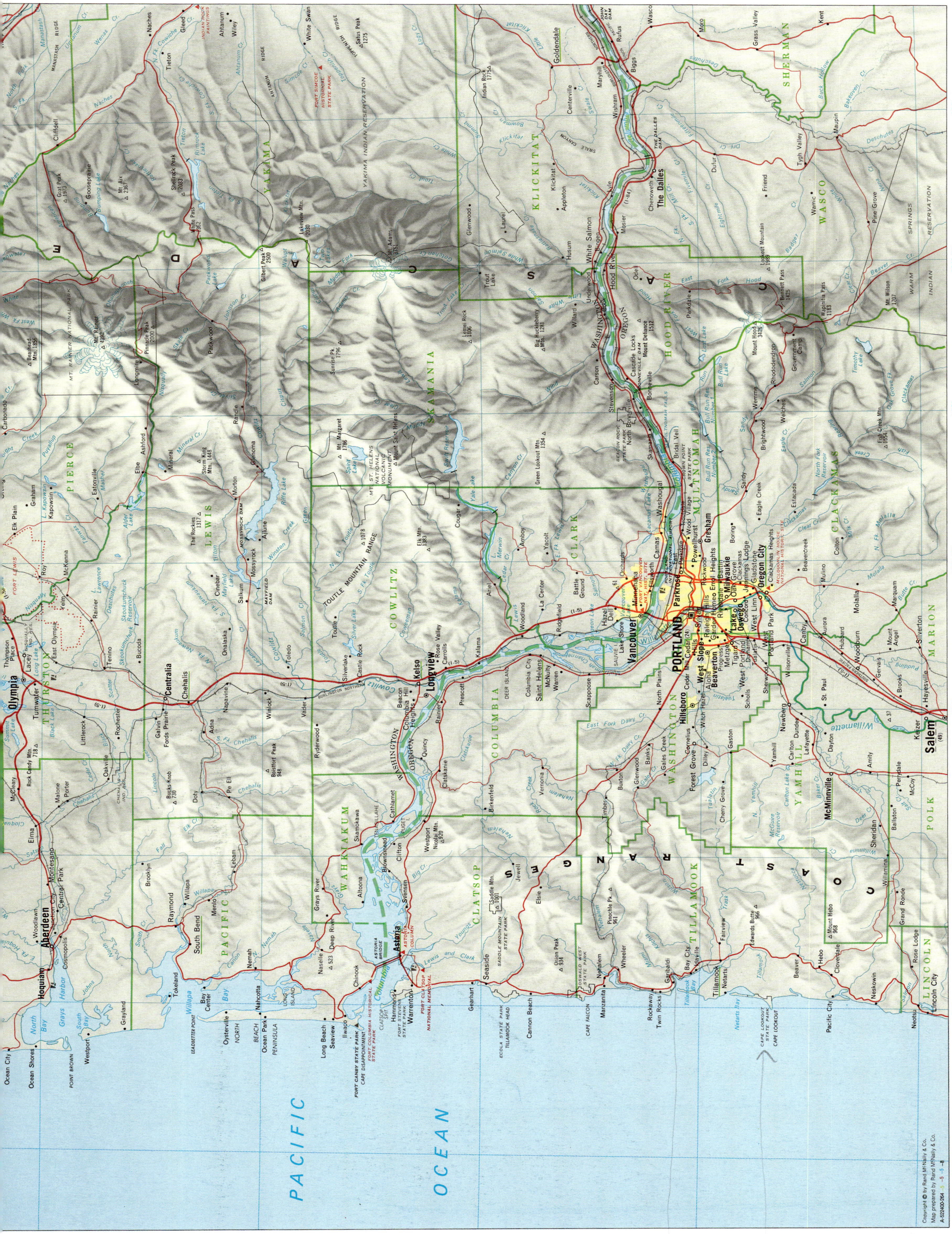

ENGLISH	bay	cape	channel	creek, cr.	island, i.	lake, l.	mount	peak	strait
DEUTSCH	Bucht	Kap	Kanal	Bach	Insel	See	Berg	Gipfel	Meeresstrasse
ESPAÑOL	bahía	cabo	canal	riachuelo	isla	lago	monte	pico	estrecho
FRANÇAIS	baie	cap	canal	ruisseau	île	lac	mont	cime	détroit
PORTUGUÊS	baía	cabo	canal	riacho	ilha	lago	monte	pico	estreito

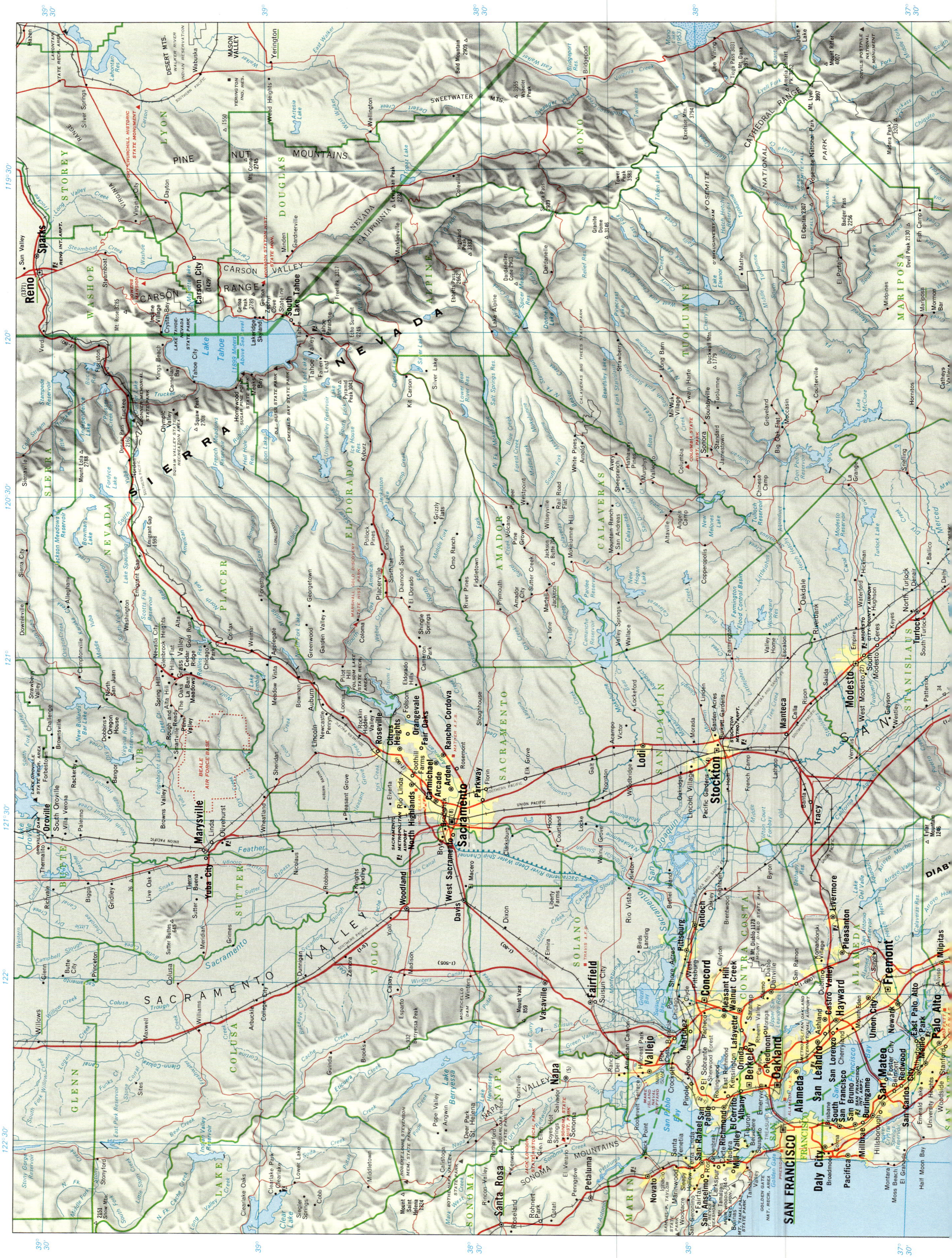

Reno
Sparks
Carson City
Lake Tahoe
South Lake Tahoe
SIERRA NEVADA
Sacramento
Stockton
Modesto
Lodi
Manteca
Tracy
Marysville
Yuba City
Oroville
Auburn
Placerville
Roseville
Woodland
Davis
Vacaville
Fairfield
Vallejo
Napa
Petaluma
Santa Rosa
Novato
San Rafael
Richmond
Berkeley
Oakland
Alameda
San Leandro
Hayward
Fremont
Livermore
Pleasanton
Concord
Walnut Creek
Antioch
Pittsburg
SAN FRANCISCO
Daly City
San Mateo
Palo Alto
Turlock
SACRAMENTO VALLEY
YOSEMITE NATIONAL PARK

Map continues page 228

ENGLISH	bay	canal	creek, cr.	lake, l.	mountain, mtn.	pass	range	reservoir	slough
DEUTSCH	Bucht	Kanal	Bach	See	Berg	Pass	Gebirge	Stausee	verlandene Wasserfläche
ESPAÑOL	bahía	canal	riachuelo	lago	montaña	paso	sierra	embalse	pantano
FRANÇAIS	baie	canal	crique	lac	montagne	col	chaîne	réservoir	fondrière
PORTUGUÊS	baía	canal	riacho	lago	montanha	passo	serra	reservatório	pântano

Kilometers 0 10 20 30 40 50 Km.
Statute Miles 0 10 20 30 40 50 Mi.

Scale 1:1,000,000

One centimeter represents 10 kilometers.
One inch represents approximately 16 miles.

Lambert Conformal Conic Projection

Map continues pages 226-227

ENGLISH	canyon	creek, cr.	lake, l.	mountain, mtn.	pass	peak	point	reservoir, res
DEUTSCH	Cañon	Bach	See	Berg	Pass	Gipfel	Landspitze	Stausee
ESPAÑOL	cañón	riachuelo	lago	montaña	paso	pico	punta	embalse
FRANÇAIS	canyon	crique	lac	montagne	col	cime	pointe	réservoir
PORTUGUÊS	canhão	riacho	lago	montanha	passo	pico	ponta	reservatório

Kilometers 0 10 20 30 40 50 Km.

Statute Miles 0 10 20 30 40 50 Mi.

Scale 1:1,000,000

One centimeter represents 10 kilometers.
One inch represents approximately 16 miles.

Lambert Conformal Conic Projection

a

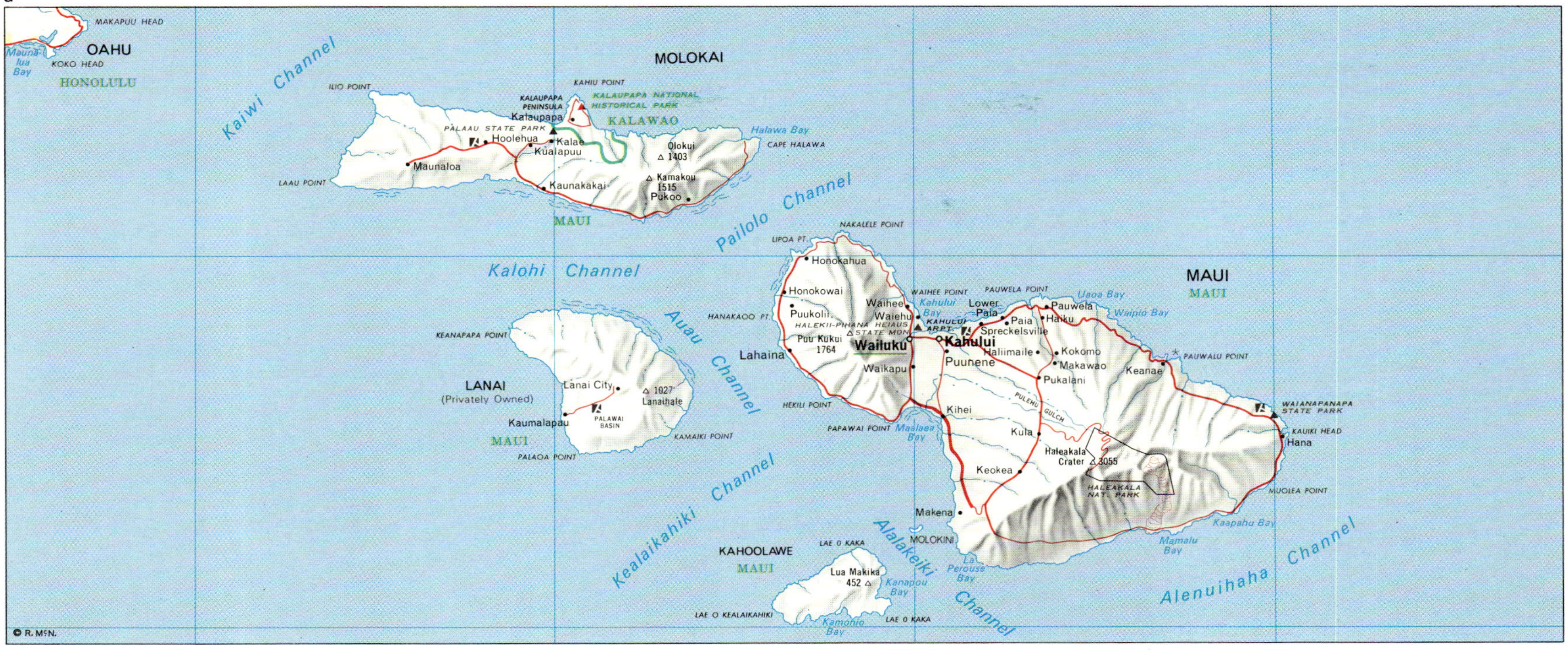

b

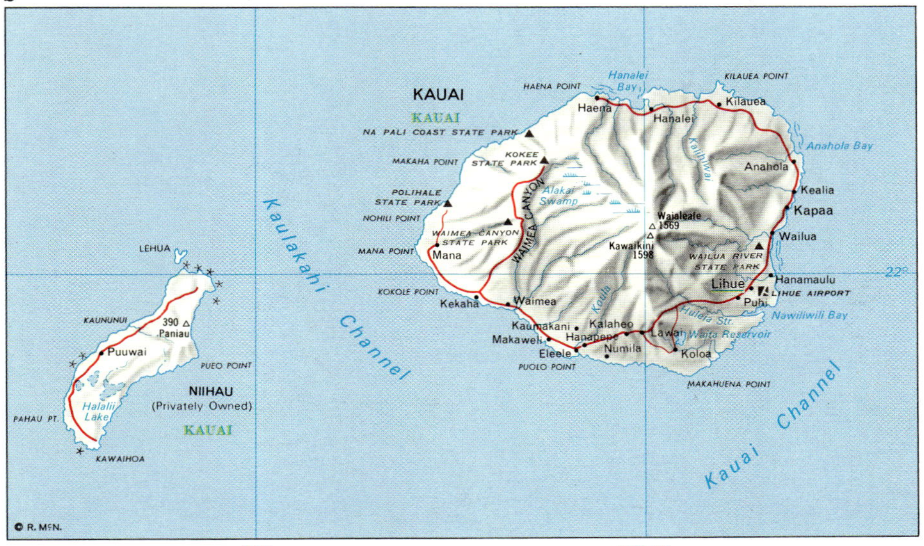

c

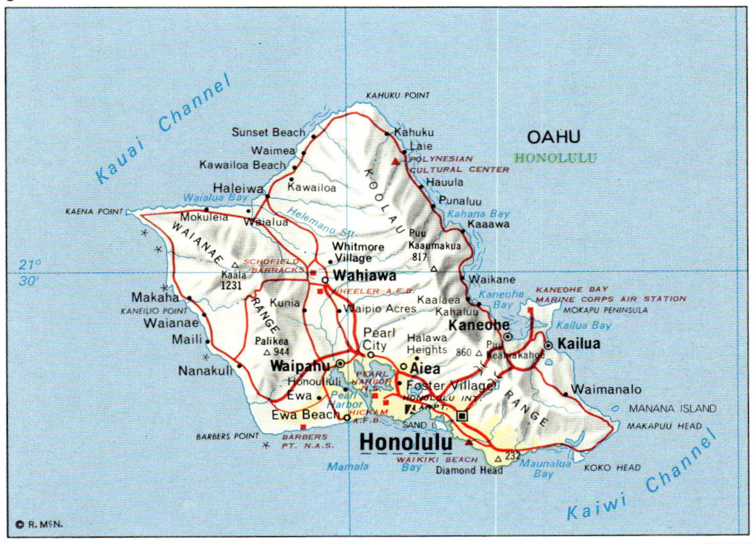

Kilometers 0 10 20 30 40 50 Km.
Statute Miles 0 10 20 30 40 50 Mi.

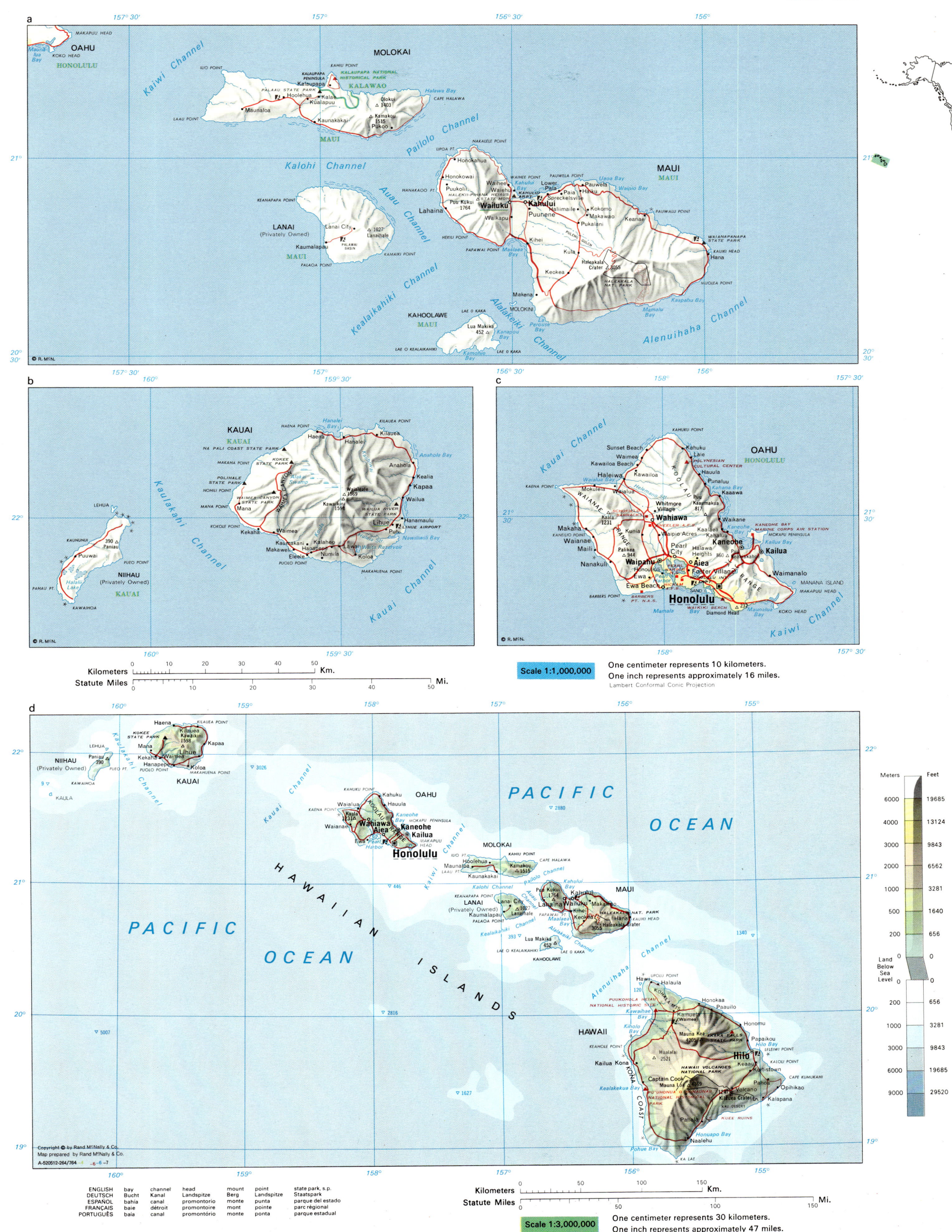

Scale 1:1,000,000
One centimeter represents 10 kilometers.
One inch represents approximately 16 miles.
Lambert Conformal Conic Projection

d

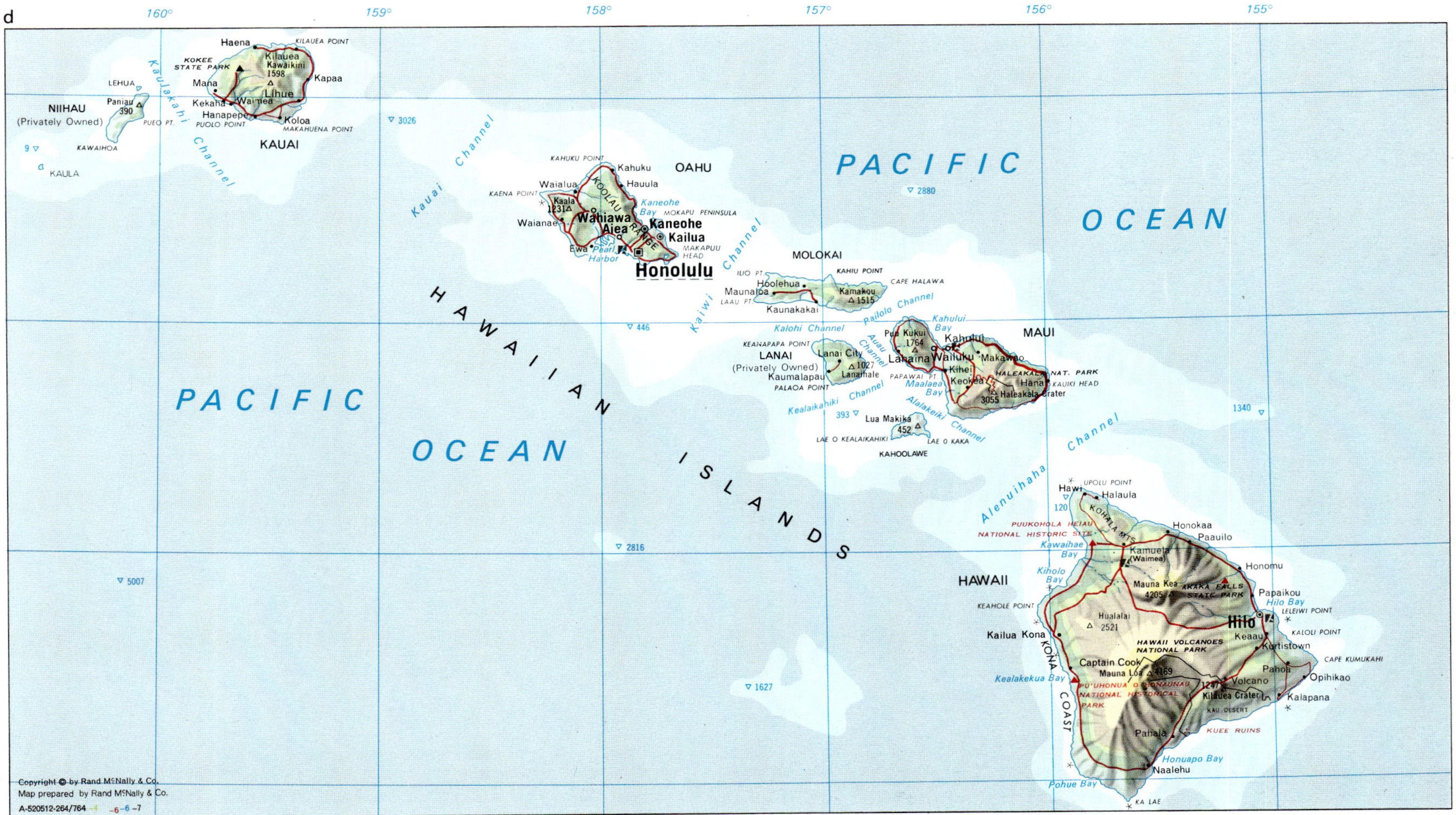

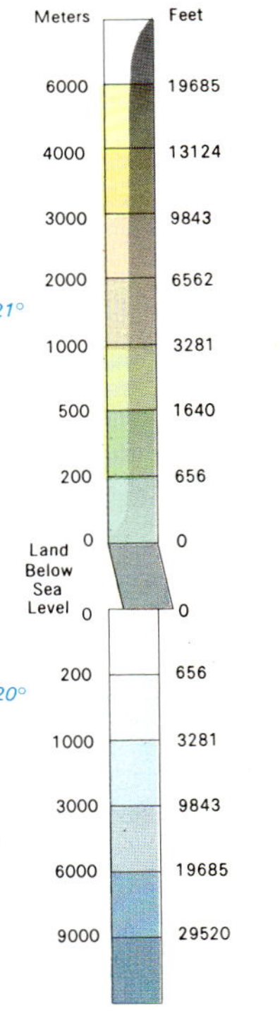

ENGLISH	bay	channel	head	mount	point	state park, s.p.
DEUTSCH	Bucht	Kanal	Landspitze	Berg	Landspitze	Staatspark
ESPAÑOL	bahía	canal	promontorio	monte	punta	parque del estado
FRANÇAIS	baie	canal	promontoire	mont	pointe	parc régional
PORTUGUÊS	baía	canal	promontório	monte	ponta	parque estadual

Kilometers 0 50 100 150 Km.
Statute Miles 0 50 100 150 Mi.

Scale 1:3,000,000
One centimeter represents 30 kilometers.
One inch represents approximately 47 miles.
Lambert Conformal Conic Projection

Map continues
pages 178-179

ESPAÑOL	cabo	cordillera	golfo	isla, i.	lago, l.	punta	sierra	volcán, vol.
ENGLISH	cape	mountains	gulf	island	lake	point	mountains	volcano
DEUTSCH	Kap	Berge	Golf	Insel	See	Landspitze	Berge	Vulkan
FRANÇAIS	cap	montagnes	golfe	île	lac	pointe	montagnes	volcan
PORTUGUÊS	cabo	cordilheira	golfo	ilha	lago	ponta	serra	vulcão

Map continues pages 242-243

Kilometers 0 200 400 600 Km.
Statute Miles 0 200 400 600 Mi.

Scale 1:12,000,000

One centimeter represents 120 kilometers.
One inch represents approximately 190 miles.
Oblique Conic Conformal Projection

Mexico / Mexiko / México
Mexique / México

ESPAÑOL	bahía	cerro	isla	laguna	presa	punta	río	sierra
ENGLISH	bay	mountain	island	lagoon	reservoir	point	river	mountains
DEUTSCH	Bucht	Berg	Insel	Haff	Stausee	Landspitze	Fluss	Berge
FRANÇAIS	baie	montagne	île	lagune	réservoir	pointe	rivière	montagnes
PORTUGUÊS	baía	montanha	ilha	laguna	reservatório	ponta	rio	serra

Kilometers 0 100 200 300 Km.
Statute Miles 0 100 200 300 Mi.

Scale 1:6,000,000

One centimeter represents 60 kilometers.
One inch represents approximately 95 miles.
Lambert Conformal Conic Projection

Map continues pages 238-239
Map continues pages 236-237

Central Mexico / Mittelmexiko / México Central
Mexique Central / México Central

Map continues pages 232-233

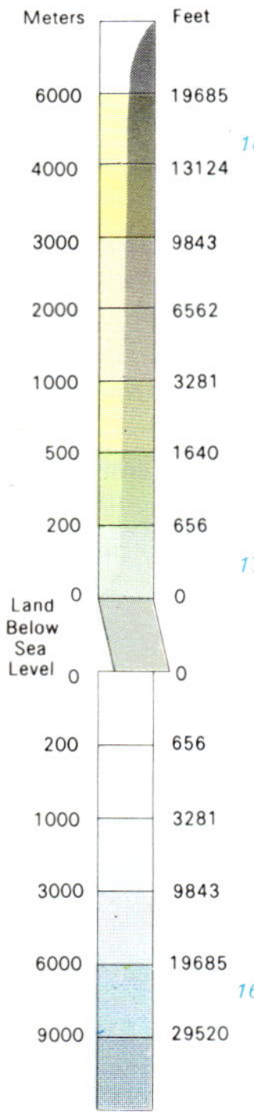

ESPAÑOL	arroyo	boca	cerro	lago	laguna	punta	río	sierra	volcán
ENGLISH	brook	entrance	butte	lake	lagoon	point	river	ranges	volcano
DEUTSCH	Bach	Einfahrt	Restberg	See	Haff	Landspitze	Fluss	Bergketten	Vulkan
FRANÇAIS	ruisseau	entrée	butte	lac	lagune	pointe	rivière	chaîne	volcan
PORTUGUÊS	riacho	entrada	cerro	lago	laguna	ponta	rio	serra	vulcão

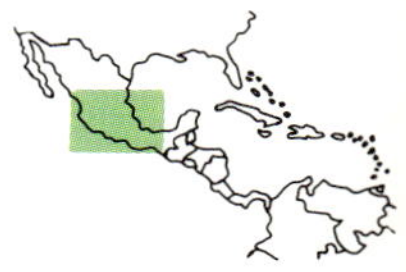

Map continues pages 232-233

Map continues pages 236-237

Kilometers 0 50 100 150 Km.
Statute Miles 0 50 100 150 Mi.

Scale 1:3,000,000

One centimeter represents 30 kilometers.
One inch represents approximately 47 miles.
Lambert Conformal Conic Projection

Map continues pages 232-233

Map continues pages 234-235

ESPAÑOL	bahia	cerro	cordillera	isla	lago	laguna	punta	sierra	volcán
ENGLISH	bay	mountain	mountains	island	lake	lagoon	point	mountains	volcano
DEUTSCH	Bucht	Berg	Berge	Insel	See	Haff	Landspitze	Berge	Vulkan
FRANÇAIS	baie	montagne	montagnes	île	lac	lagune	pointe	montagnes	volcan
PORTUGUÊS	baía	montanha	cordilheira	ilha	lago	laguna	ponta	serra	vulcão

Map continues pages 246-247

Kilometers 0 50 100 150 Km.

Statute Miles 0 50 100 150 Mi.

Scale 1:3,000,000

One centimeter represents 30 kilometers.
One inch represents approximately 47 miles.

Lambert Conformal Conic Projection

Caribbean Region / Mittelamerikanische Inselwelt / Región del Caribe
Région des Caraïbes / Região do Caribe

MAP FORM	bahía	cabo	cerro	channel	golfo	isla	passage	pico	punta
ENGLISH	bay	cape	mountain	channel	gulf	isle	passage	peak	point
DEUTSCH	Bucht	Kap	Berg	Kanal	Golf	Insel	Durchfahrt	Gipfel	Landspitze
ESPAÑOL	bahía	cabo	cerro	canal	golfo	isla	pasaje	pico	punta
FRANÇAIS	baie	cap	montagne	détroit	golfe	île	passage	cime	pointe
PORTUGUÊS	baía	cabo	montanha	canal	golfo	ilha	passagem	pico	ponta

Map continues pages 246-247

Kilometers 0 100 200 300 Km.

Statute Miles 0 100 200 300 Mi.

Scale 1:6,000,000

One centimeter represents 60 kilometers.
One inch represents approximately 95 miles.
Lambert Conformal Conic Projection

a

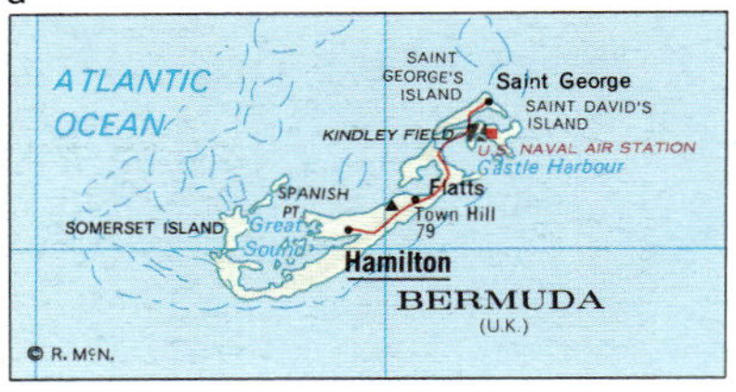

b

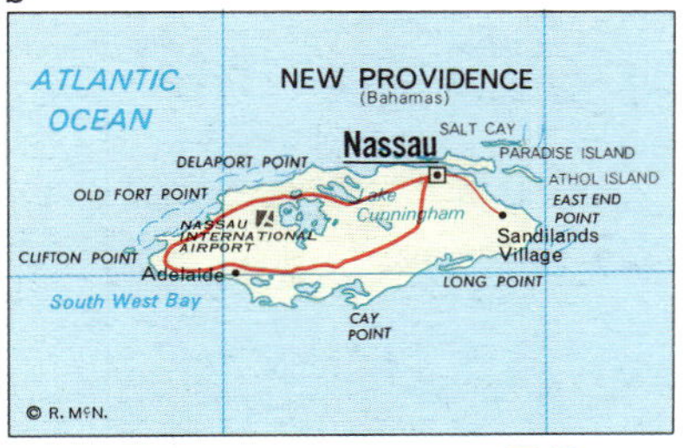

c

d

e

m

p

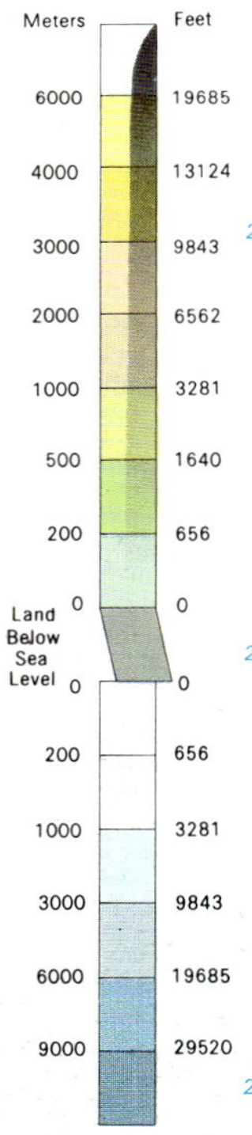

MAP FORM	bahía	cayo	channel	ensenada	golfo	island	mount	passage	point
ENGLISH	bay	cay	channel	bayou	gulf	island	mount	passage	point
DEUTSCH	Bucht	Klippe	Kanal	Altwasser	Golf	Insel	Berg	Durchfahrt	Landspitze
ESPAÑOL	bahía	cayo	canal	ensenada	golfo	isla	montaña	pasaje	punta
FRANÇAIS	baie	caye	détroit	bayou	golfe	île	mont	passage	pointe
PORTUGUÊS	baía	baixio	canal	enseada	golfo	ilha	montanha	passagem	ponta

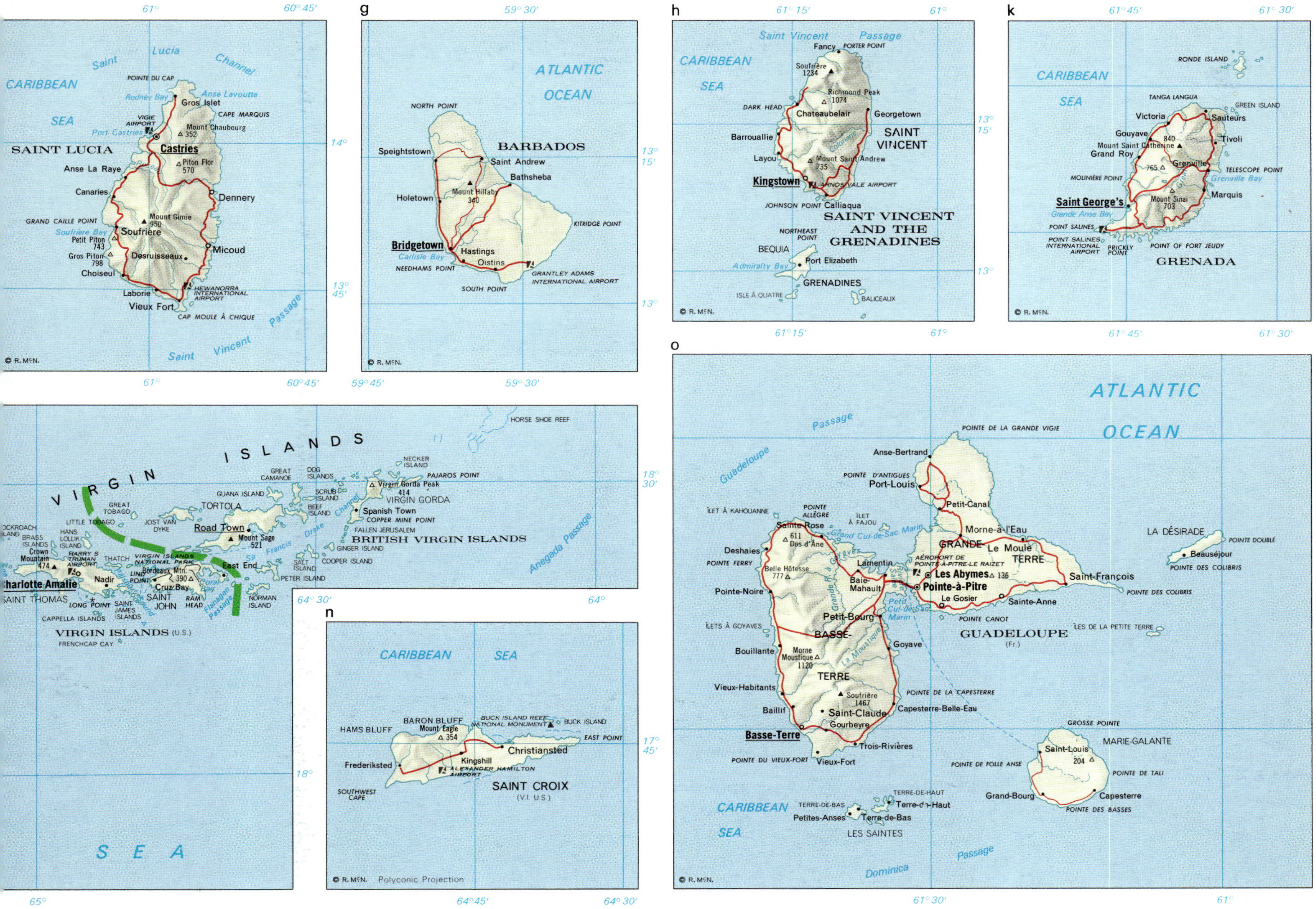

Kilometers 0 10 20 30 40 50 Km.
Statute Miles 0 10 20 30 40 50 Mi.

Scale 1:1,000,000
One centimeter represents 10 kilometers.
One inch represents approximately 16 miles.
Transverse Mercator Projection (except as noted)

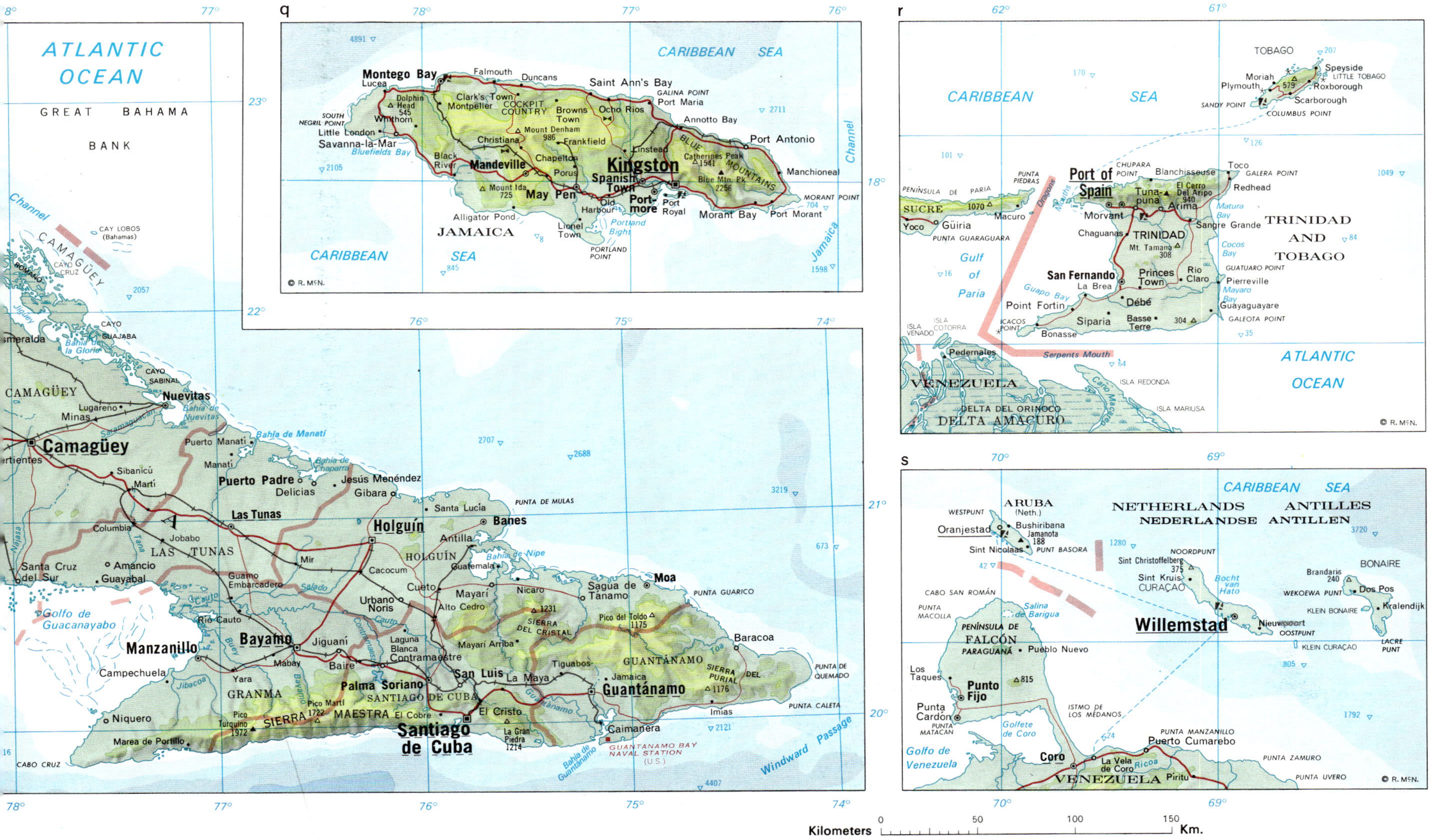

Kilometers 0 50 100 150 Km.
Statute Miles 0 50 100 150 Mi.

Scale 1:3,000,000
One centimeter represents 30 kilometers.
One inch represents approximately 47 miles.
Lambert Conformal Conic Projection

Map continues pages 230-231

Kilometers 0 200 400 600 Km.
Statute Miles 0 200 600 Mi.

Scale 1:12,000,000
One centimeter represents 120 kilometers.
One inch represents approximately 190 miles.
Oblique Conic Conformal Projection

Map continues pages 244-245

MAP FORM	cerro	cordillera	ilha	lago	nevado	peninsula	serra
ENGLISH	mountain	range	island	lake	mountain	peninsula	mountains
DEUTSCH	Berg	Gebirge	Insel	See	Berg	Halbinsel	Berge
ESPAÑOL	montaña	cordillera	isla	lago	montaña	península	montañas
FRANÇAIS	montagne	chaîne	île	lac	montagne	péninsule	montagnes
PORTUGUÊS	montanha	cordilheira	ilha	lago	montanha	península	montanhas

Map continues pages 242-243

MAP FORM	cerro, co.	golfo	ilha	isla	lago	lagoa	monte	salar
ENGLISH	butte	gulf	island	isle	lake	lake	mountain	saltflat
DEUTSCH	Restberg	Golf	Insel	Insel	See	See	Berg	Salzebene
ESPAÑOL	cerro	golfo	isla	isla	lago	lago	montaña	salobral
FRANÇAIS	butte	golfe	île	île	lac	lac	montagne	salina
PORTUGUÊS	colina	golfo	ilha	ilha	lago	lago	montanha	salina

Scale 1:12,000,000

One centimeter represents 120 kilometers.
One inch represents approximately 190 miles.
Oblique Conic Conformal Projection

Colombia, Ecuador, Venezuela and Guyana / Kolumbien, Ecuador, Venezuela und Guayana / Colombia, Ecuador, Venezuela y Guyana
Colombie, Équateur, Venezuela et Guyane / Colômbia, Equador, Venezuela e Guiana

Map continues pages 238-239

Map continues pages 248-249

MAP FORM	bahía	cabo	cerro, co.	golfo	igarapé	isla, i.	lago, l.	punta	volcán, vol.
ENGLISH	bay	cape	butte	gulf	river	island	lake	point	volcano
DEUTSCH	Bucht	Kap	Restberg	Golf	Fluss	Insel	See	Landspitze	Vulkan
ESPAÑOL	bahía	cabo	cerro	golfo	río	isla	lago	punta	volcán
FRANÇAIS	baie	cap	butte	golfe	rivière	île	lac	pointe	volcan
PORTUGUÊS	baía	cabo	colina	golfo	rio	ilha	lago	ponta	vulcão

Map continues
pages 238-239

Map continues
pages 250-251

Kilometers 0 100 200 300 Km
Statute Miles 0 100 200 300 Mi.

Scale 1:6,000,000

One centimeter represents 60 kilometers.
One inch represents approximately 95 miles.
Oblique Conic Conformal Projection

Peru, Bolivia and Western Brazil / Peru, Bolivien und westliches Brasilien / Perú, Bolivia y Brasil Occidental
Pérou, Bolivie et Brésil Occidental / Peru, Bolívia e Brasil Ocidental

MAP FORM	cerro	cordillera	isla, i.	lago, l.	nevado	punta	rio	serra
ENGLISH	mountain	mountains	island	lake	mountain	point	river	mountains
DEUTSCH	Berg	Berge	Insel	See	Berg	Landspitze	Fluss	Berge
ESPAÑOL	montaña	montañas	isla	lago	nevado	punta	rio	sierra
FRANÇAIS	montagne	montagnes	île	lac	montagne	pointe	rivière	montagnes
PORTUGUÊS	montanha	montanhas	ilha	lago	pico nevado	ponta	rio	serra

Map continues pages 246-247

Map continues pages 250-251

Map continues page 255

Map continues pages 252-253

Kilometers 0 100 200 300 Km.
Statute Miles 0 100 200 300 Mi.

Scale 1:6,000,000
One centimeter represents 60 kilometers.
One inch represents approximately 95 miles.
Oblique Conic Conformal Projection

a

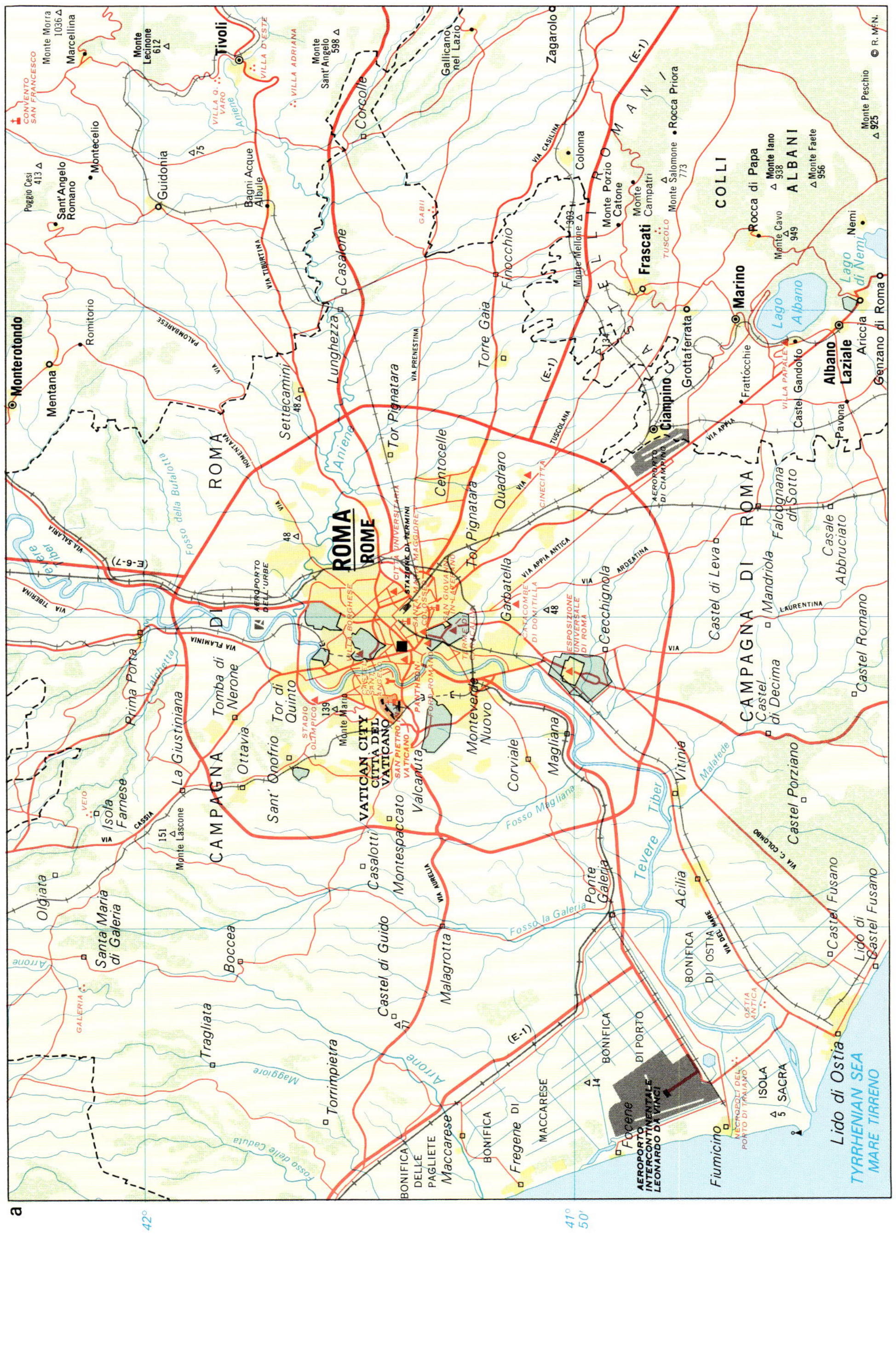

b

c

d

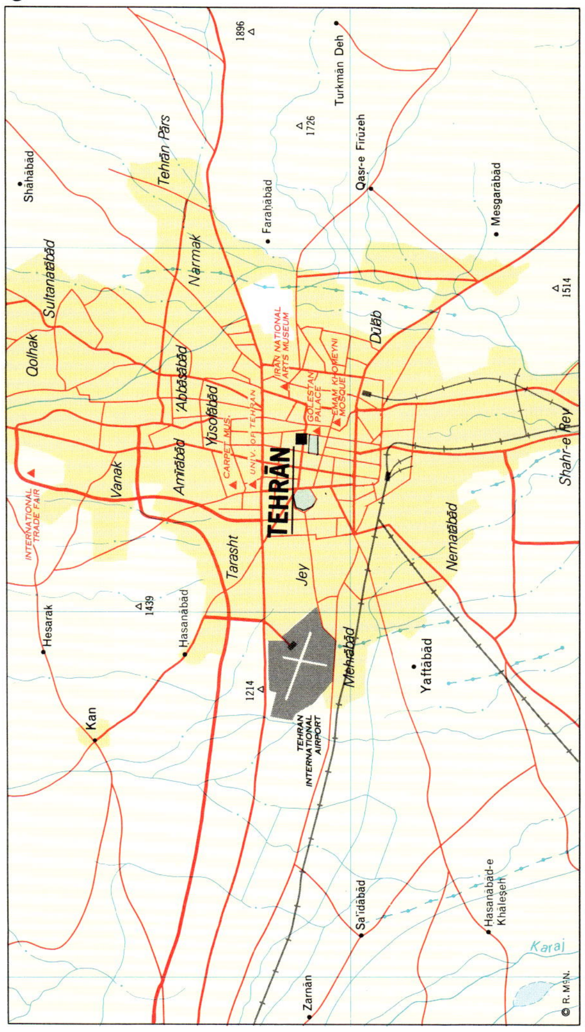

Kilometers 0 5 10 15 Km.
Statute Miles 0 5 10 15 Mi.
Scale 1:300,000
One centimeter represents 3 kilometers.
One inch represents approximately 4.7 miles.

	AREA (km²)	POPULATION
ROMA	2,000	3,250,000
ATHÍNAI	1,100	3,350,000
İSTANBUL	1,300	4,300,000
TEHRĀN	950	5,200,000

MAP FORM	ada	burnu	camii	deresi	fosso	moní	monte
ENGLISH	island	cape	mosque	river	brook	monastery	mount
DEUTSCH	Insel	Kap	Moschee	Fluss	Bach	Kloster	Berg
ESPAÑOL	isla	cabo	mezquita	río	arroyo	monasterio	monte
FRANÇAIS	île	cap	mosquée	rivière	ruisseau	monastère	mont
PORTUGUÊS	ilha	cabo	mesquita	rio	arroio	mosteiro	monte

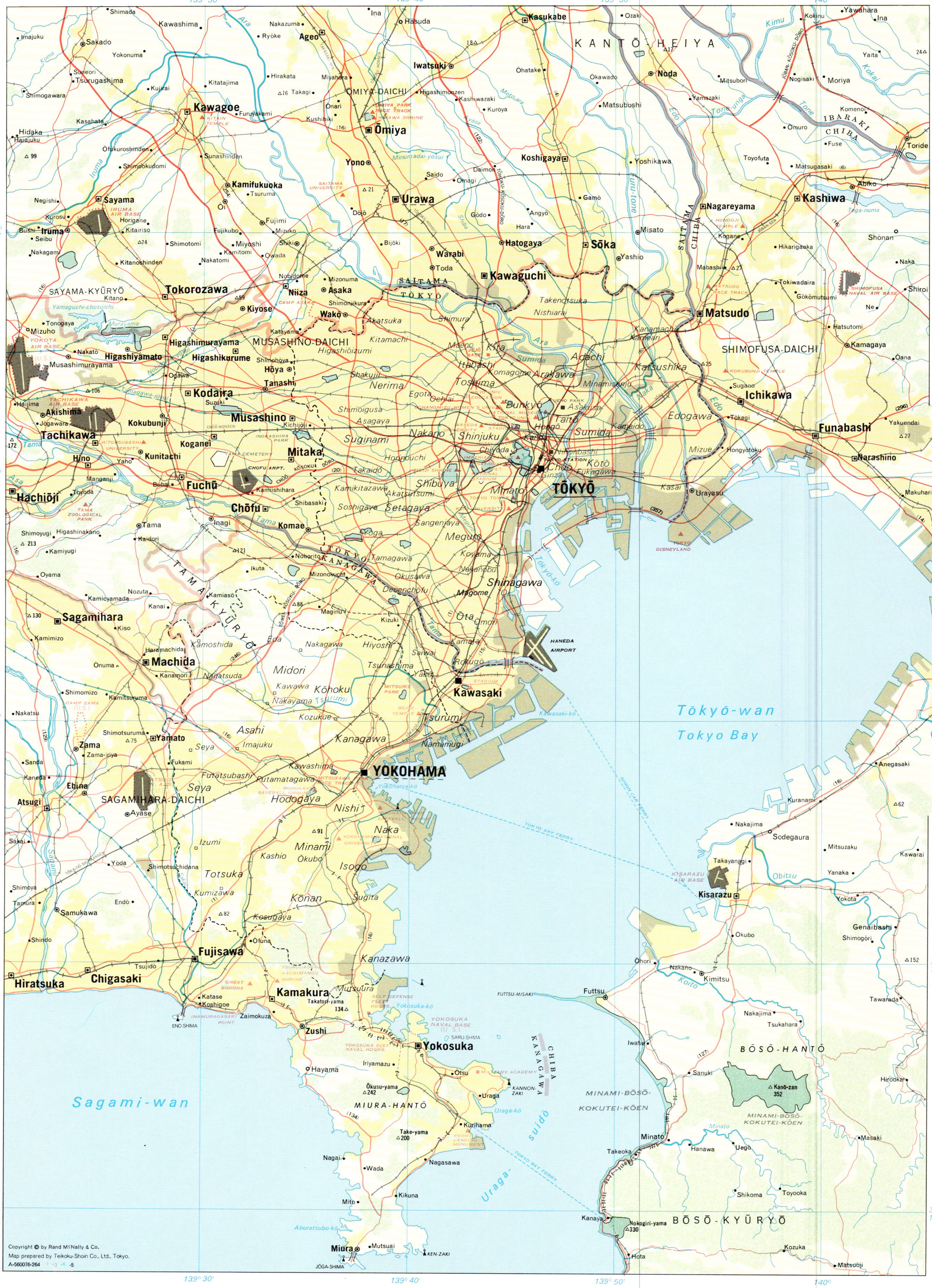

AREA (km²): 5,350
POPULATION: 24,350,000

MAP FORM	air base	camp	-daichi	-kō	-shima	temple	-yama
ENGLISH	air base	camp	plateau	harbor	island	temple	mountain
DEUTSCH	Luftstützpunkt	Lager	Hochebene	Hafen	Insel	Tempel	Berg
ESPAÑOL	base aérea	campo	meseta	puerto	isla	templo	montaña
FRANÇAIS	base aérienne	camp	plateau	port	île	temple	montagne
PORTUGUÊS	base aérea	campo	planalto	porto	ilha	templo	montanha

Kilometers 0 5 10 15 Km.
Statute Miles 0 5 10 15 Mi.

Scale 1:300,000

One centimeter represents 3 kilometers.
One inch represents approximately 4.7 miles.

a

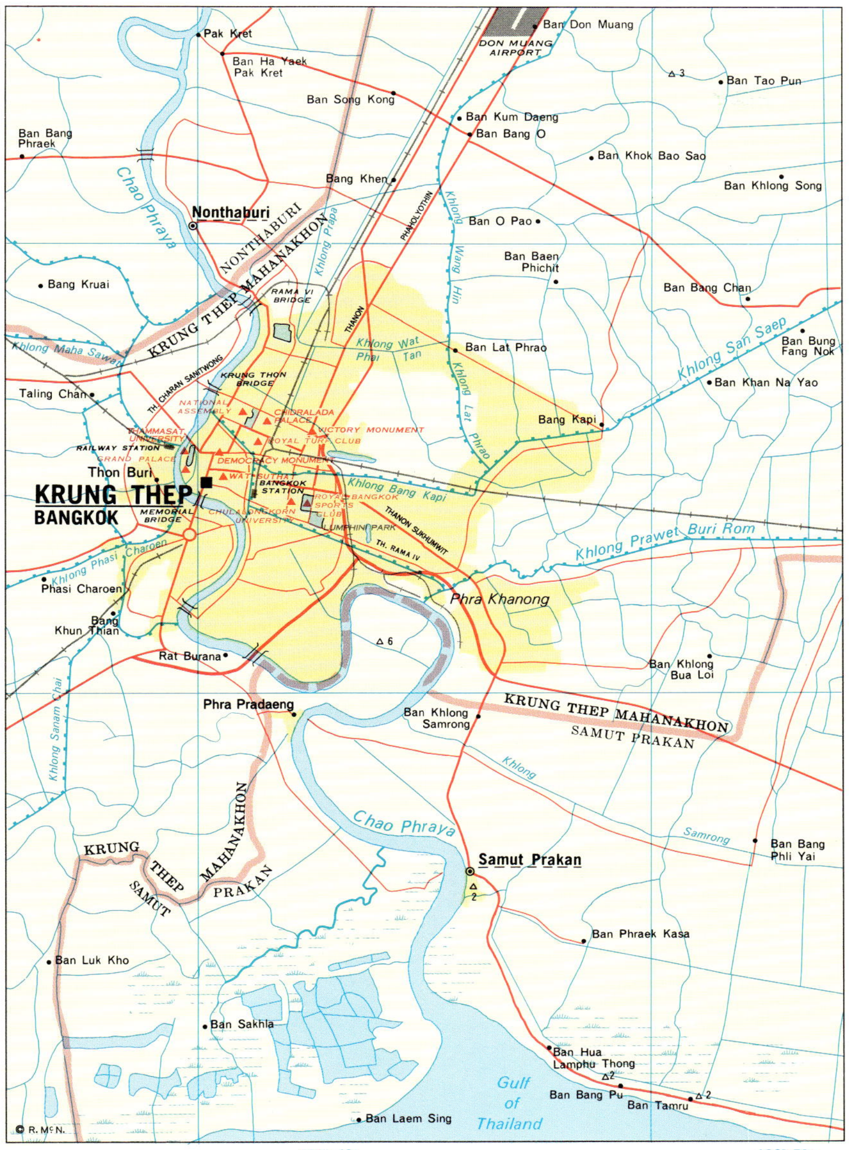

b

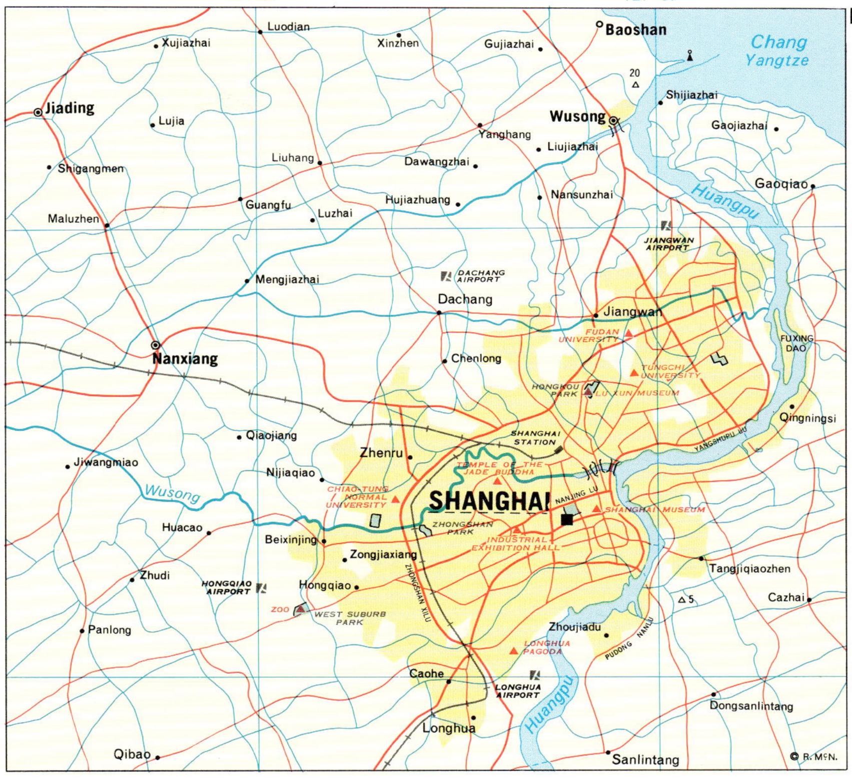

c

d

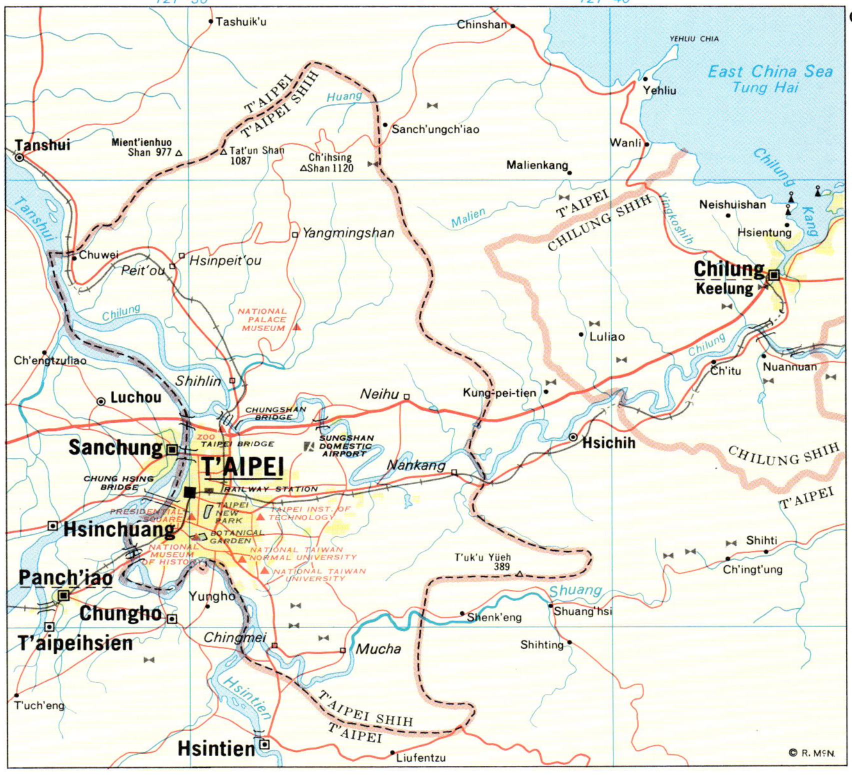

e

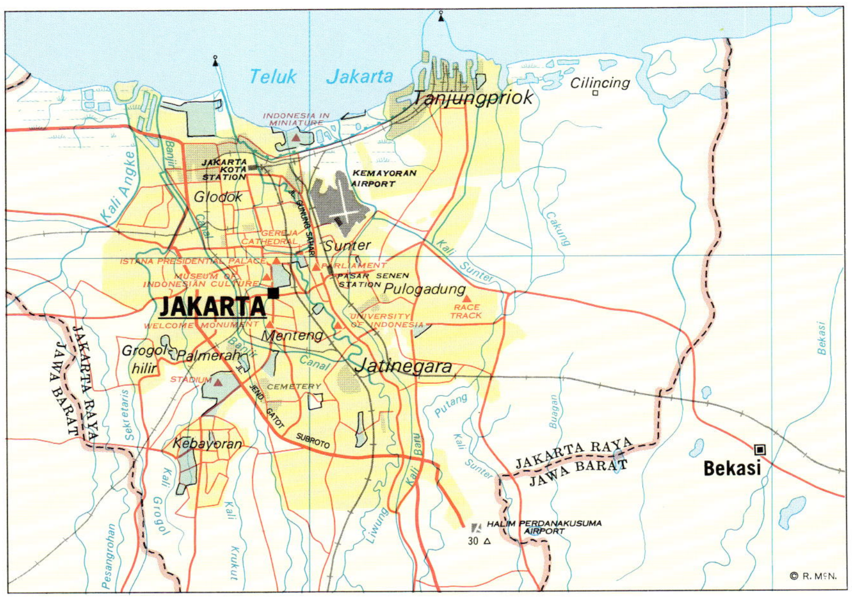

f

Map compiled by Cartographia, Budapest.
Map produced by Rand McNally & Co.
A-560051-264

	AREA (km²)	POPULATION
KRUNG THEP (BANGKOK)	1,450	5,300,000
SAI-GON	750	2,400,000
JAKARTA	700	6,450,000
SHANGHAI	1,000	8,400,000
T'AIPEI	950	4,125,000
MANILA	650	5,900,000

MAP FORM	kali	khlong	monument	shan
ENGLISH	stream	stream	monument	mountain
DEUTSCH	Bach	Bach	Denkmal	Berg
ESPAÑOL	corriente de agua	corriente de agua	monumento	montaña
FRANÇAIS	cours d'eau	cours d'eau	monument	montagne
PORTUGUÊS	corrente de água	corrente de água	monumento	montanha

Kilometers 0 5 10 15 Km.
Statute Miles 0 5 10 15 Mi.

Scale 1:300,000
One centimeter represents 3 kilometers.
One inch represents approximately 4.7 miles.

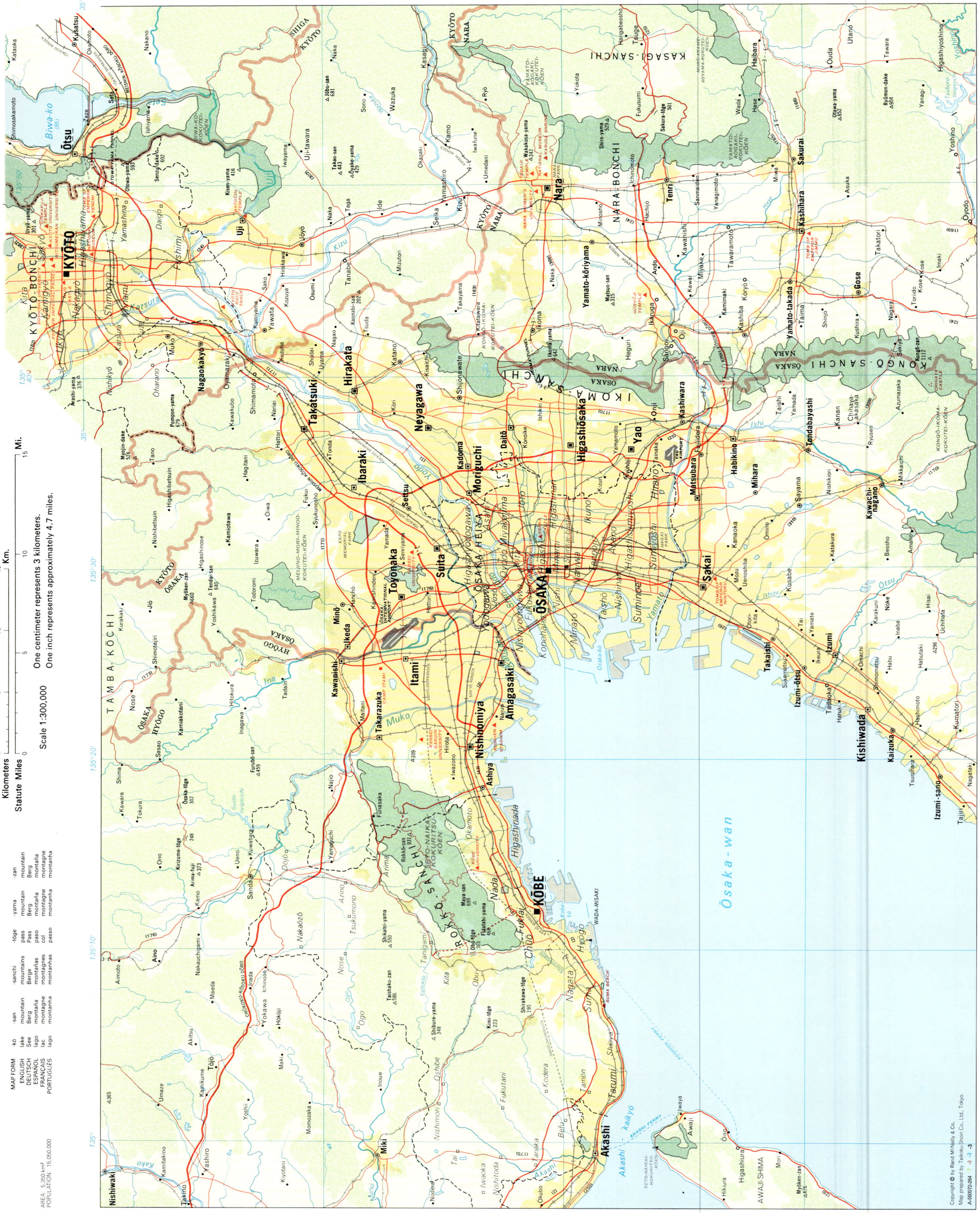
Kilometers 0 5 10 15 Km.
Statute Miles 0 5 10 15 Mi.
Scale 1:300,000
One centimeter represents 3 kilometers.
One inch represents approximately 4.7 miles.
MAP FORM -kō -san -sanchi -tōge -yama -zan
ENGLISH lake mountain mountains pass mountain mountain
DEUTSCH See Berg Berge Pass Berg Berg
ESPAÑOL lago montaña montañas paso montaña montaña
FRANÇAIS lac montagne montagnes col montagne montagne
PORTUGUÊS lago montanha montanhas passo montanha montanha
AREA 5,350 km²
POPULATION 15,050,000
Ōsaka-wan
Copyright © by Rand McNally & Co.
Map prepared by Teikoku-Shoin Co. Ltd., Tokyo.

a

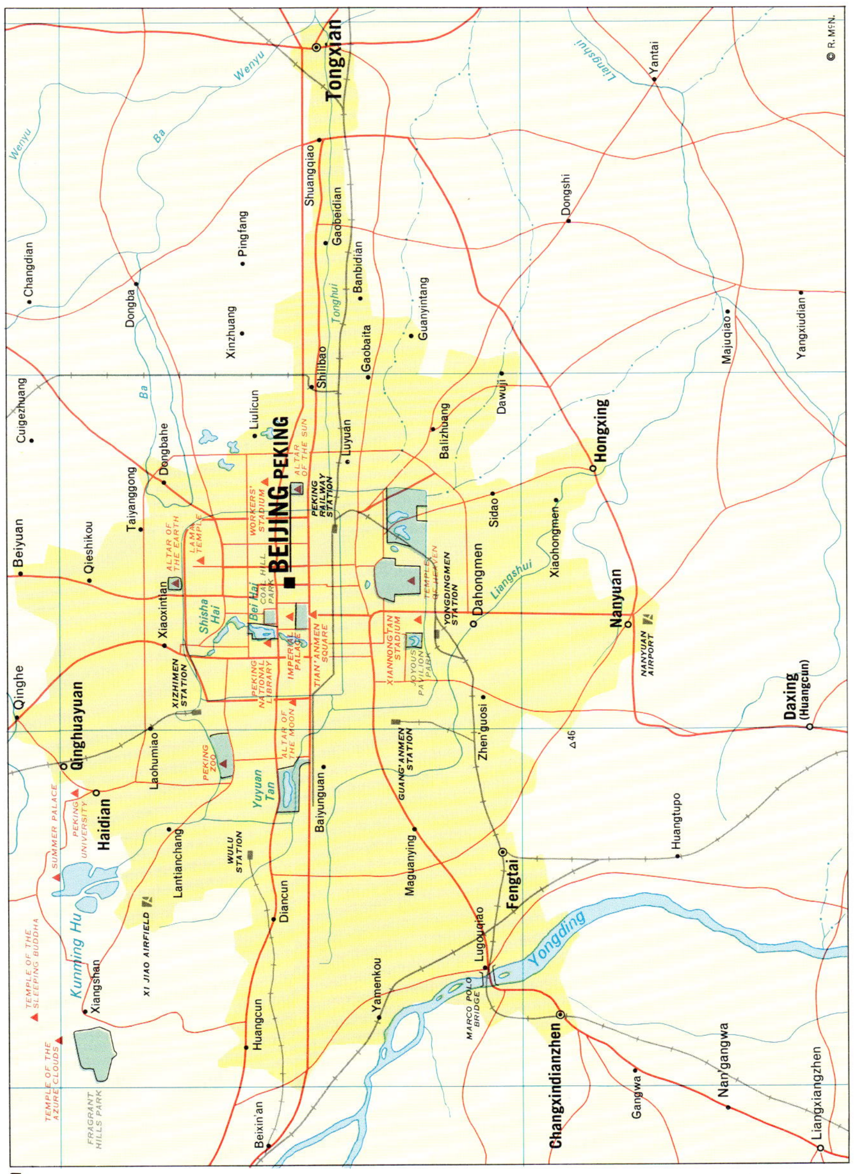

b

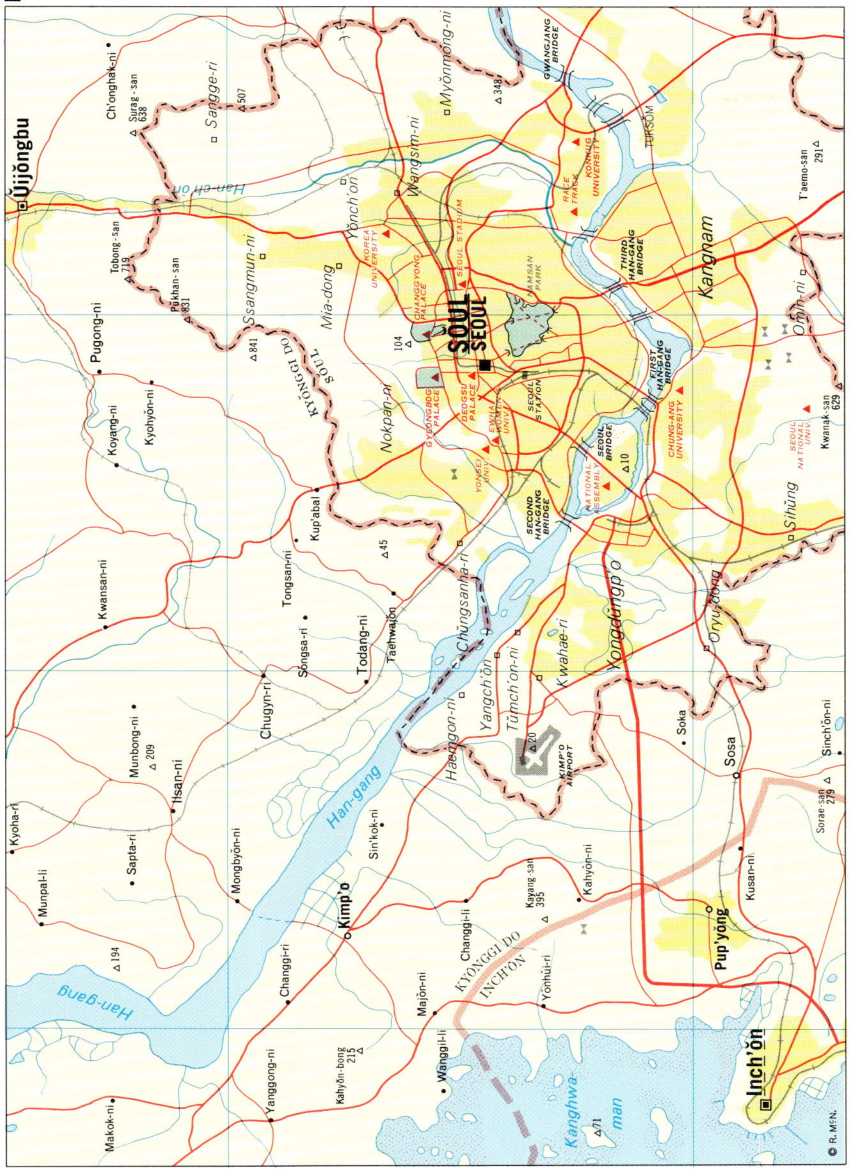

c

d

Scale 1:300,000

One centimeter represents 3 kilometers.
One inch represents approximately 4.7 miles.

	AREA (km²)	POPULATION
BEIJING (PEKING)	1,550	5,300,000
SŎUL	1,450	9,300,000
SINGAPORE	900	2,600,000
HONG KONG	650	4,450,000

MAP FORM	airport	chau	island	park	peak	reservoir	wan
ENGLISH	airport	island	island	park	peak	reservoir	bay
DEUTSCH	Flughafen	Insel	Insel	Park	Gipfel	Stausee	Bucht
ESPAÑOL	aeropuerto	isla	isla	parque	pico	estanque	bahía
FRANÇAIS	aéroport	île	île	parc	cime	réservoir	baie
PORTUGUÊS	aeroporto	ilha	ilha	parque	pico	reservatório	baía

	AREA (km²)	POPULATION
DELHI	1,400	5,500,000
BOMBAY	1,050	8,250,000
CALCUTTA	3,100	11,200,000

ENGLISH	DEUTSCH	ESPAÑOL	FRANÇAIS	PORTUGUÊS
airport	Flughafen	aeropuerto	aéroport	aeroporto
dock	Dock	muelle	quai	cais
island	Insel	isla	île	ilha
lake	See	lago	lac	lago
point	Punkt	punta	pointe	ponta
railroad station	Bahnhof	terminal ferroviaria	gare	estação ferroviária
road	Landstrasse	camino	route	rodovia
temple	Tempel	templo	temple	templo

Kilometers 0 5 10 15 Km.
Statute Miles 0 5 10 15 Mi.

Scale 1:300,000
One centimeter represents 3 kilometers.
One inch represents approximately 4.7 miles.

b

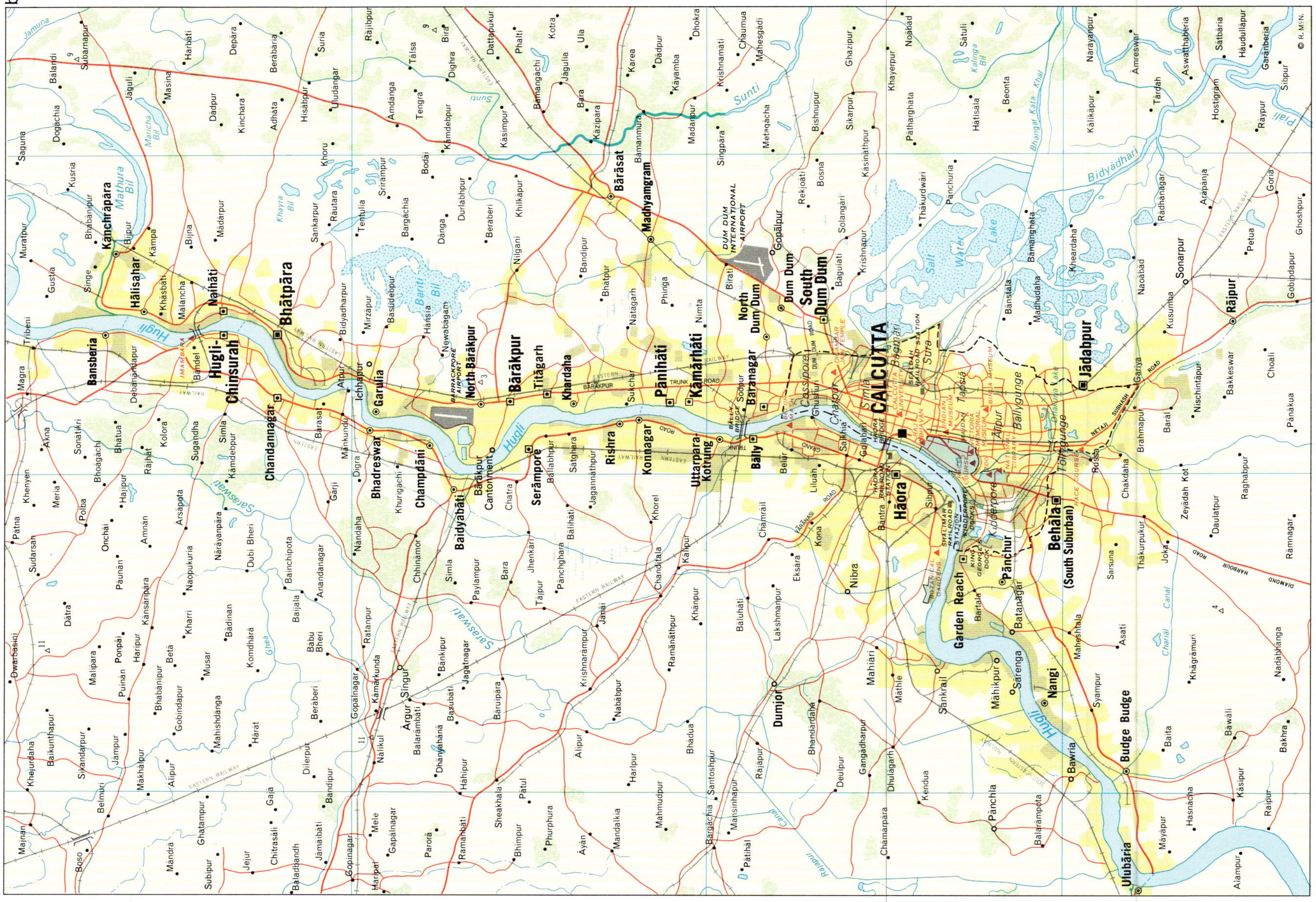

a

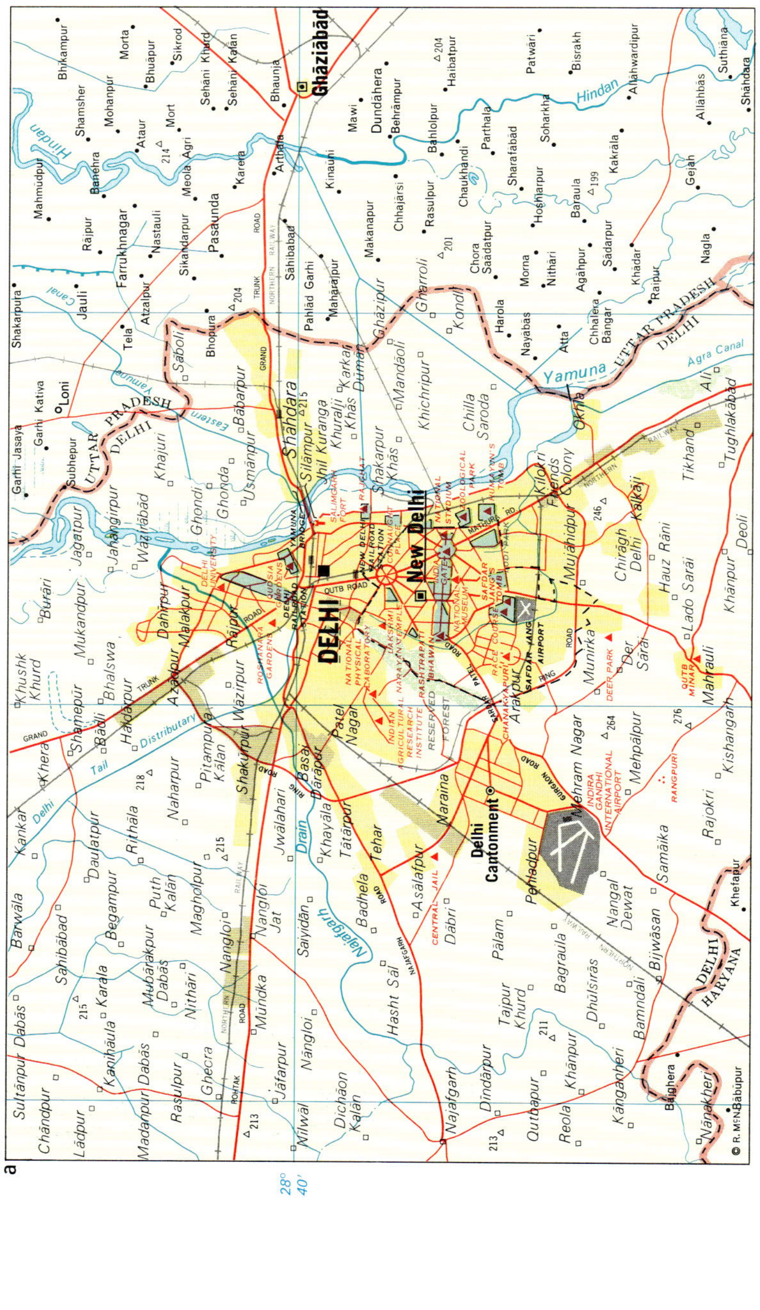

c

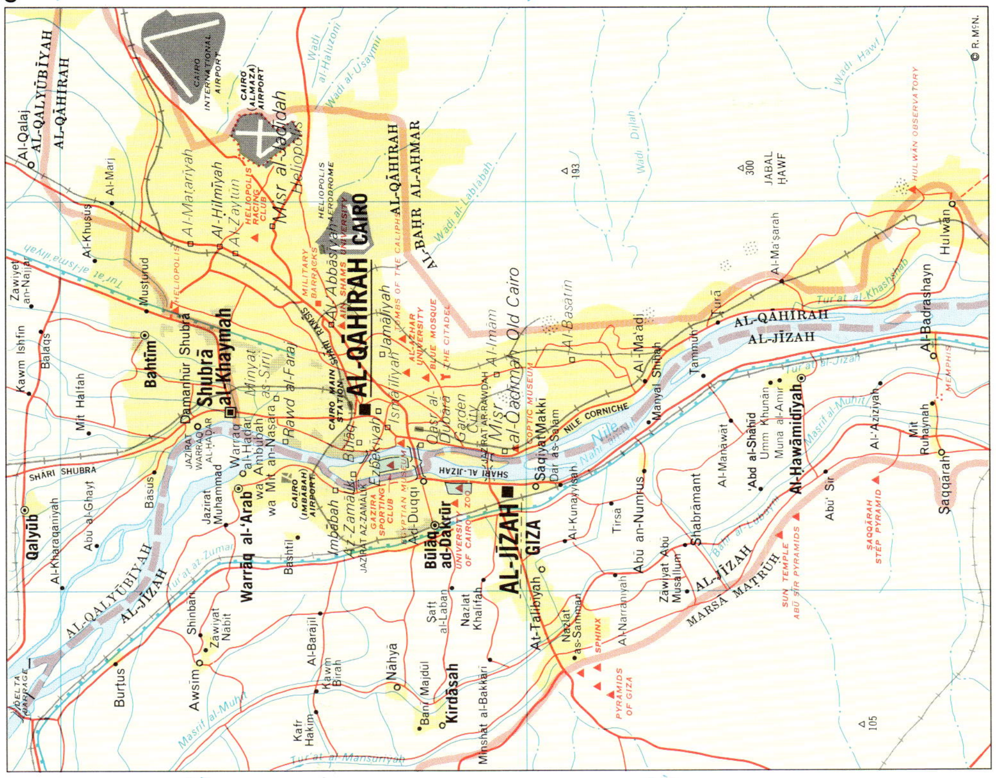

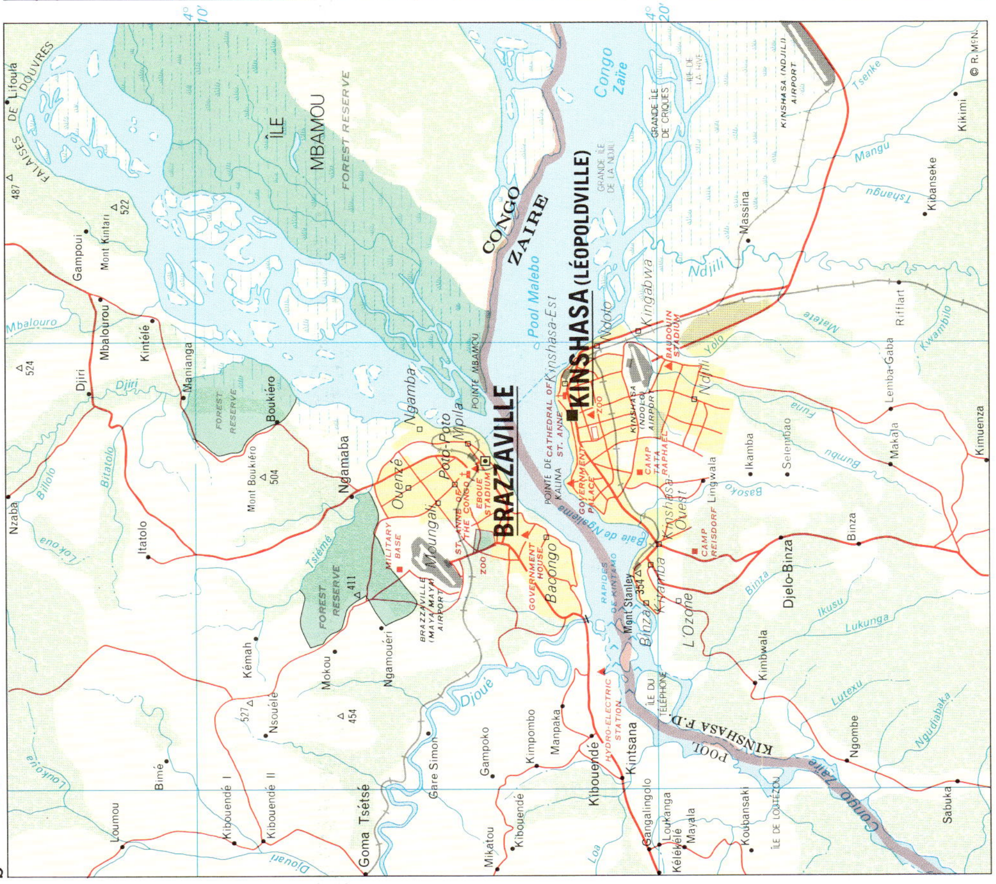

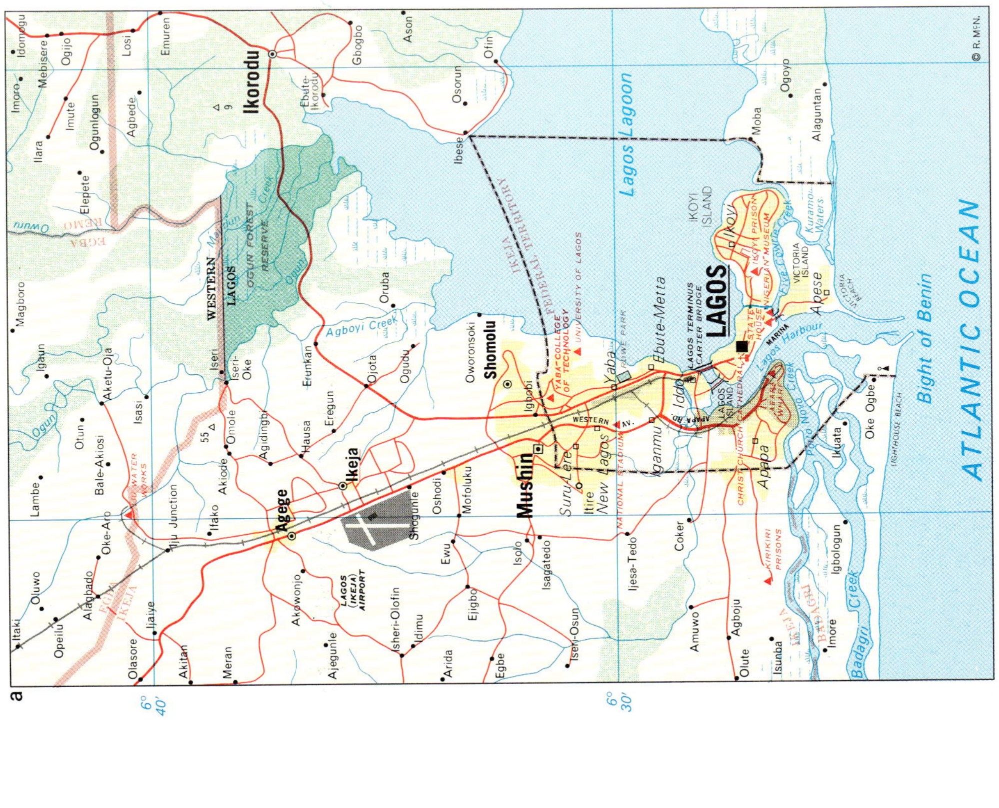

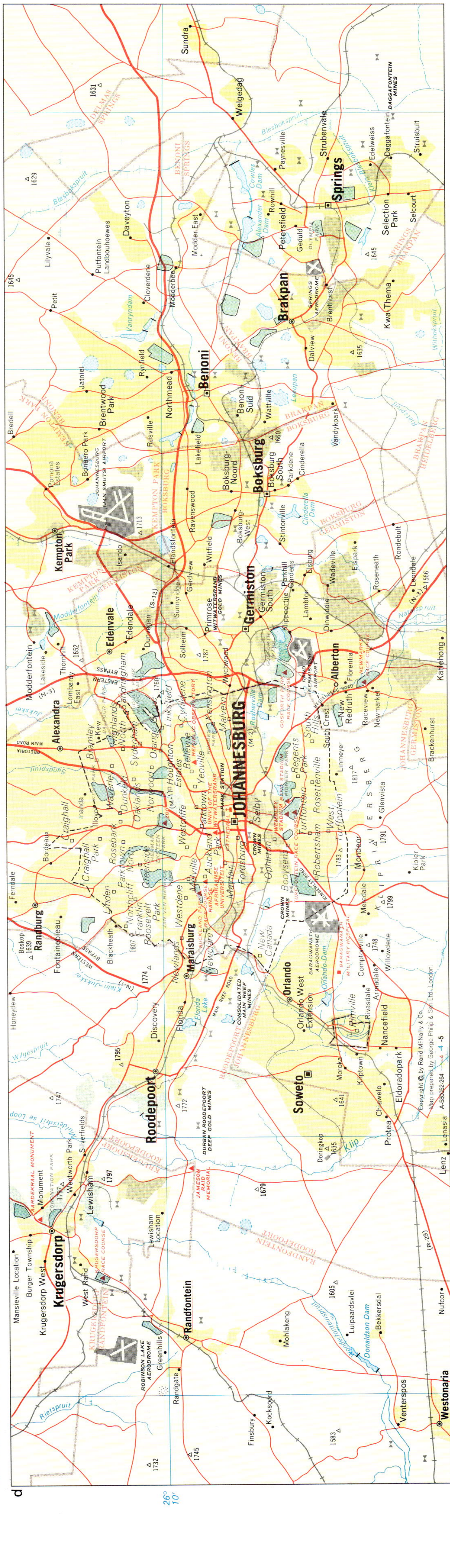

	AREA (km²)	POPULATION
LAGOS	750	2,400,000
KINSHASA-BRAZZAVILLE	1,150	2,750,000
AL-QĀHIRAH (CAIRO)	1,200	8,900,000
JOHANNESBURG	2,650	3,300,000

MAP FORM	airport	creek	dam	île	park	race course	tur'at	wadi
ENGLISH	airport	creek	dam	island	park	race course	canal	wadi
DEUTSCH	Flughafen	Bach	Damm	Insel	Park	Rennbahn	Kanal	Wadi
ESPAÑOL	aeropuerto	riachuelo	presa	isla	parque	hipódromo	canal	uadi
FRANÇAIS	aéroport	crique	barrage	île	parc	champ de course	canal	wadi
PORTUGUÊS	aeroporto	riacho	represa	ilha	parque	hipódromo	canal	uádi

Kilometers 0 5 10 15 Km.
Statute Miles 0 5 10 15 Mi.

Scale 1:300,000
One centimeter represents 3 kilometers.
One inch represents approximately 4.7 miles.

a

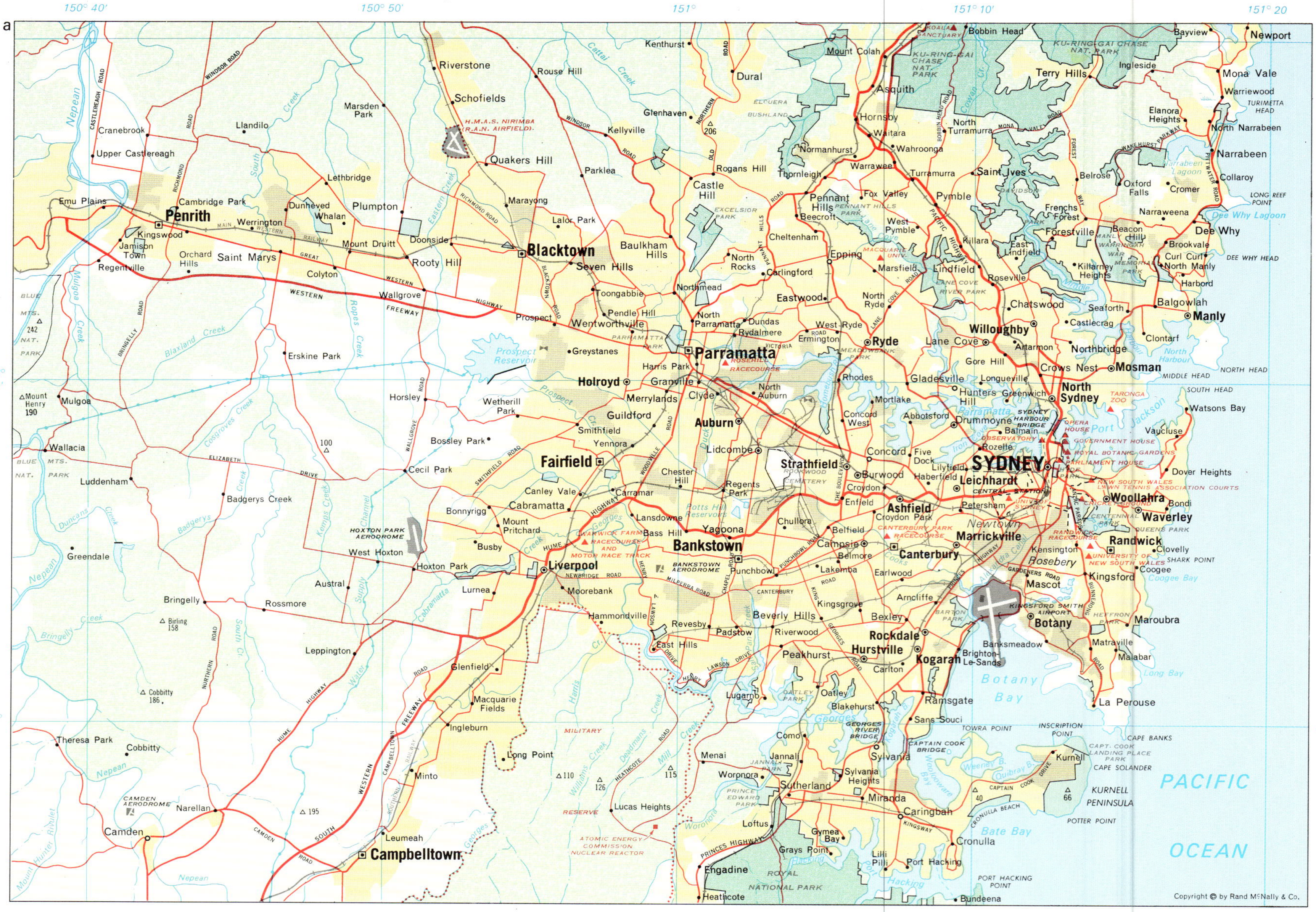

b

144° 40' 144° 50' 145° 145° 10' 145° 20'

	AREA (km²)	POPULATION
MELBOURNE	2,600	2,425,000
SYDNEY	2,800	2,850,000

ENGLISH	bay, b.	bridge	creek, cr.	highway	point	road
DEUTSCH	Bucht	Brücke	Bach	Landstrasse	Landspitze	Landstrasse
ESPAÑOL	bahía	puente	riachuelo	camino	punta	camino
FRANÇAIS	baie	pont	crique	route	pointe	route
PORTUGUÊS	baía	ponte	riacho	rodovia	ponta	rodovia

Kilometers 0 5 10 15 Km.

Statute Miles 0 5 10 15 Mi.

Scale 1:300,000

One centimeter represents 3 kilometers.
One inch represents approximately 4.7 miles.

a

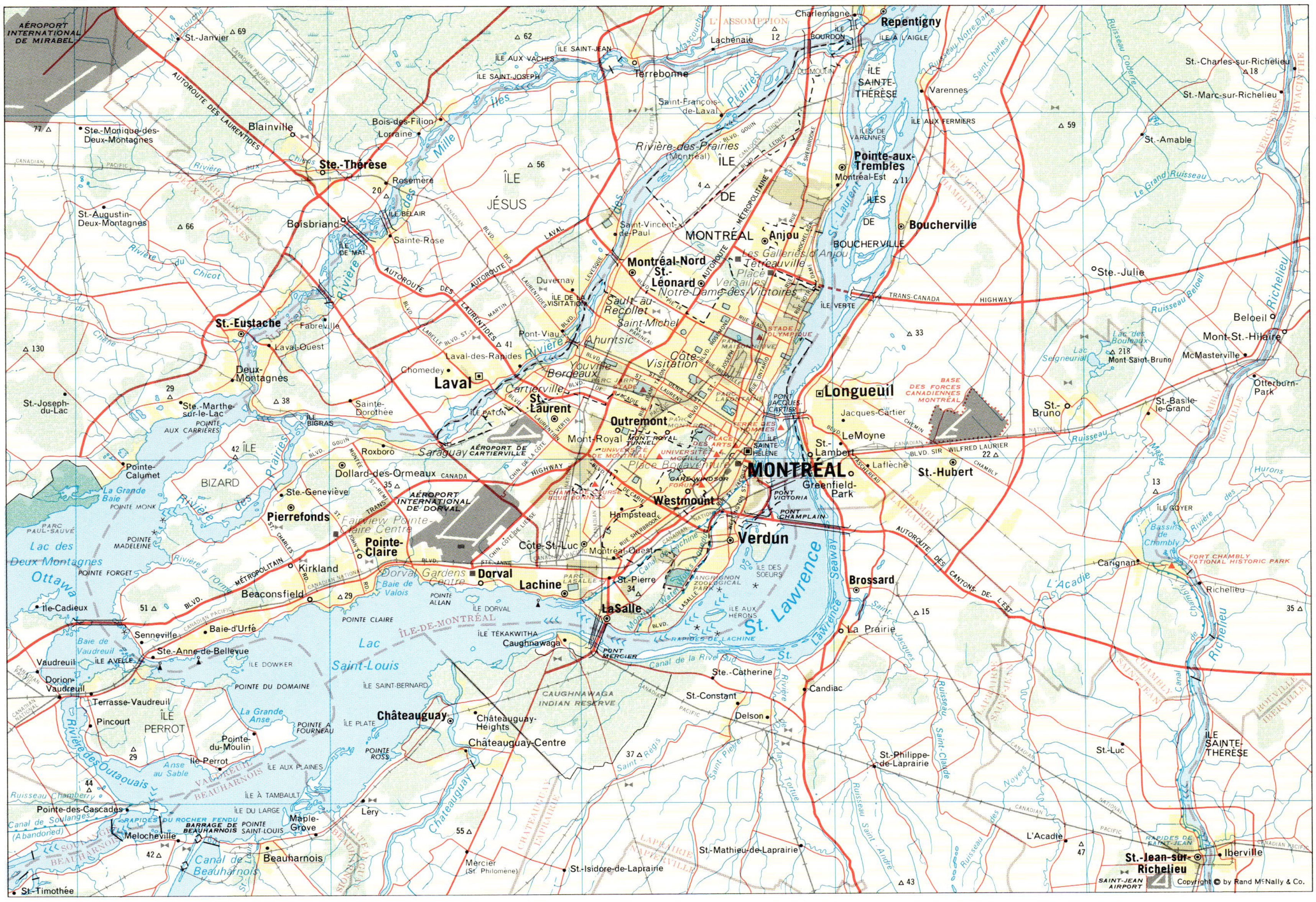

b

	AREA (km²)	POPULATION
MONTRÉAL	3,100	2,875,000
TORONTO	2,100	2,850,000

MAP FORM	île	park	rapides	rivière	ruisseau
ENGLISH	island	park	rapids	river	brook
DEUTSCH	Insel	Park	Stromschnellen	Fluss	Bach
ESPAÑOL	isla	parque	rápidos	río	arroyo
FRANÇAIS	île	parc	rapides	rivière	ruisseau
PORTUGUÊS	ilha	parque	rápidos	rio	arroio

Kilometers 0 5 10 15 Km.
Statute Miles 0 5 10 15 Mi.

Scale 1:300,000

One centimeter represents 3 kilometers.
One inch represents approximately 4.7 miles.

AREA: 8,900 km²
POPULATION: 15,800,000

ENGLISH	bay	brook, br.	creek	harbor	island	lake, l.	point	pond
DEUTSCH	Bucht	Bach	Bach	Hafen	Insel	See	Landspitze	Teich
ESPAÑOL	bahía	arroyo	riachuelo	puerto	isla	lago	punta	charca
FRANÇAIS	baie	ruisseau	crique	port	île	lac	pointe	étang
PORTUGUÊS	baía	arroio	riacho	porto	ilha	lago	ponta	lagoa

Kilometers 0 5 10 15 Km.

Statute Miles 0 5 10 15 Mi.

Scale 1:300,000

One centimeter represents 3 kilometers.
One inch represents approximately 4.7 miles.

AREA: 4,500 km²
POPULATION: 6,700,000

ENGLISH	airport	creek, cr.	harbor	lake, l.	park	woods
DEUTSCH	Flughafen	Bach	Hafen	See	Park	Gehölz
ESPAÑOL	aeropuerto	riachuelo	puerto	lago	parque	bosques
FRANÇAIS	aéroport	crique	port	lac	parc	bois
PORTUGUÊS	aeroporto	riacho	porto	lago	parque	bosques

Kilometers 0 5 10 15 Km.
Statute Miles 0 5 10 15 Mi.

Scale 1:300,000

One centimeter represents 3 kilometers.
One inch represents approximately 4.7 miles.

a

b

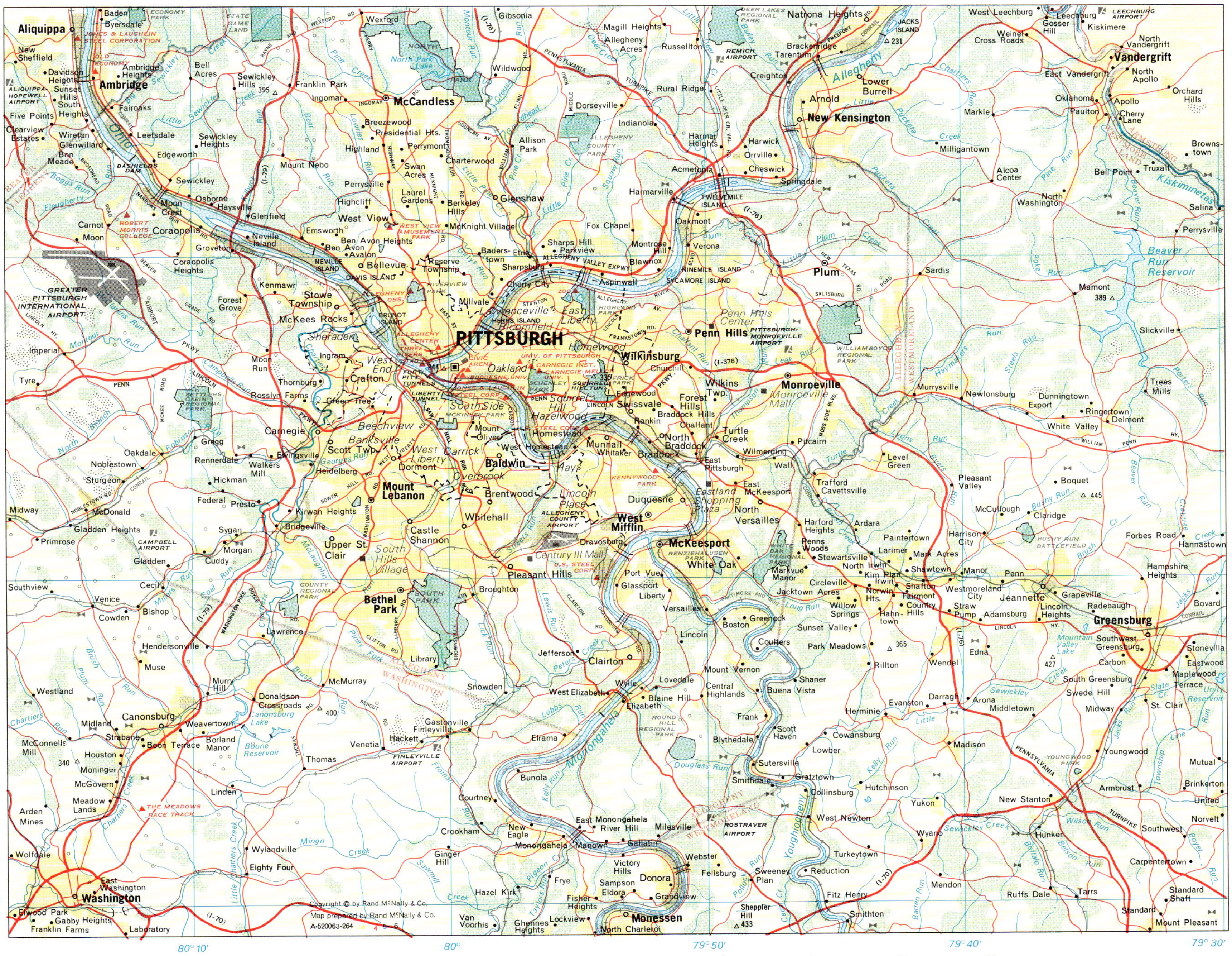

	AREA (km²)	POPULATION
CLEVELAND	1,900	1,850,000
PITTSBURGH	3,800	1,950,000

ENGLISH	creek, cr.	ditch	island	lake, l.	park	reservoir	run
DEUTSCH	Bach	Graben	Insel	See	Park	Stausee	Bach
ESPAÑOL	riachuelo	acequia	isla	lago	parque	embalse	arroyo
FRANÇAIS	crique	fossé	île	lac	parc	réservoir	ruisseau
PORTUGUÊS	riacho	fosso	ilha	lago	parque	reservatório	córrego

Kilometers 0 5 10 15 Km.

Statute Miles 0 5 10 15 Mi.

Scale 1:300,000

One centimeter represents 3 kilometers.
One inch represents approximately 4.7 miles.

ENGLISH	canyon	college	creek	dam	hills	mount	park	peak	reservoir
DEUTSCH	Cañon	College	Bach	Damm	Hügel	Berg	Park	Gipfel	Stausee
ESPAÑOL	cañón	escuela	riachuelo	diques	colinas	montaña	parque	pico	estanque
FRANÇAIS	canyon	collège	cirque	barrage	colline	mont	parc	cime	réservoir
PORTUGUÊS	canhão	colégio	riacho	represa	colinas	monte	parque	pico	reservatório

AREA 5,900 km²
POPULATION 8,375,000

Kilometers 0 5 10 15 Km.
Statute Miles 0 5 10 15 Mi.

Scale 1:300,000
One centimeter represents 3 kilometers.
One inch represents approximately 4.7 miles.

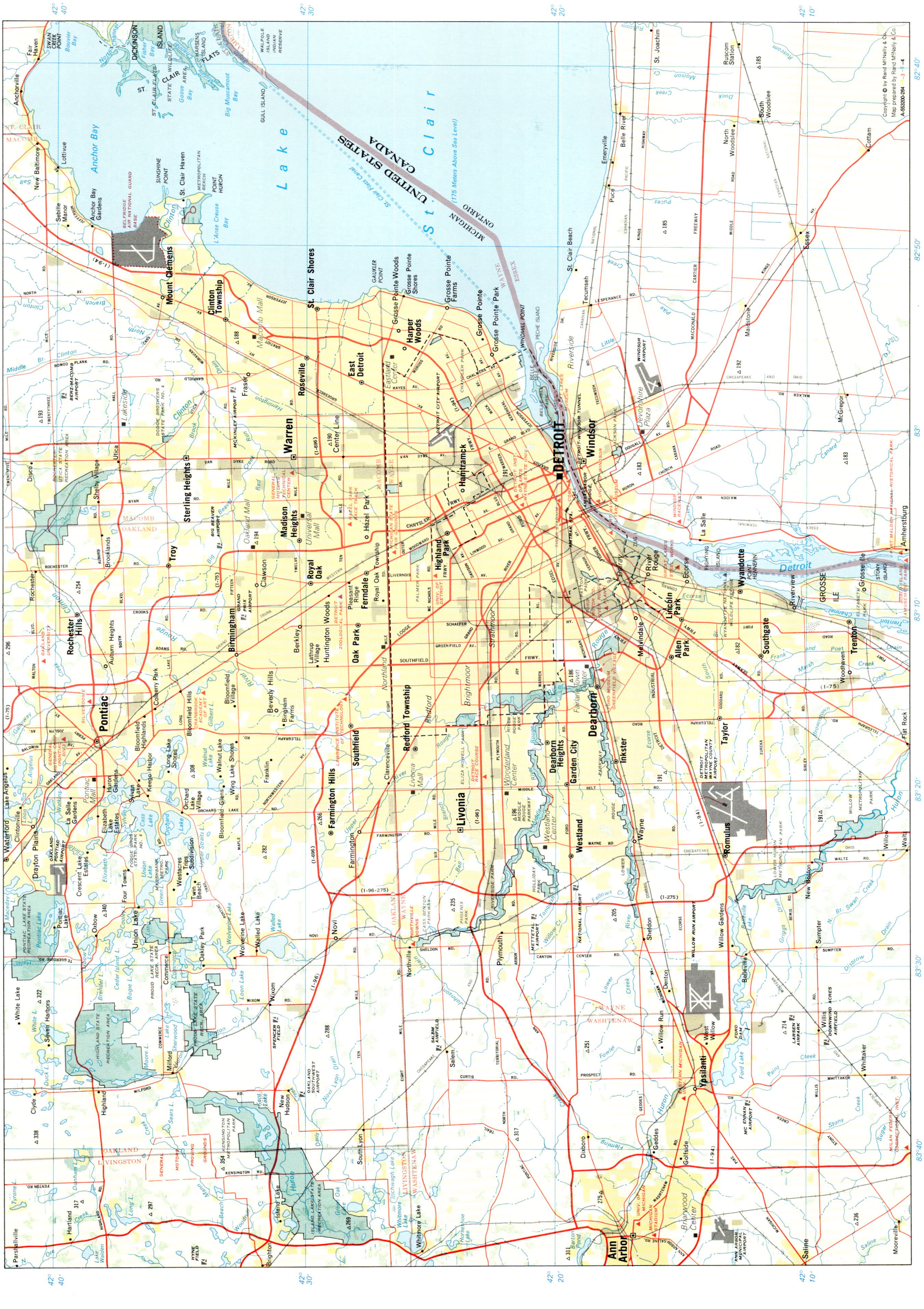

Scale 1:300,000
One centimeter represents 3 kilometers.
One inch represents approximately 4.7 miles.

Kilometers 0 5 10 15 Km.
Statute Miles 0 5 10 15 Mi.

ENGLISH	bay	channel	creek, cr.	island	lake, l.	point
DEUTSCH	Bucht	Kanal	Bach	Insel	See	Landspitze
ESPAÑOL	bahía	canal	riachuelo	isla	lago	punta
FRANÇAIS	baie	canal	crique	île	lac	pointe
PORTUGUÊS	baía	canal	riacho	ilha	lago	ponta

AREA 5,550 km²
POPULATION 4,425,000

ENGLISH	DEUTSCH	Map Form / Geographische Begriffe / Términos Geográficos / Termes Géographiques / Termos Geográficos	ESPAÑOL	FRANÇAIS	PORTUGUÊS
mountains	Gebirge	**serra** *Cat.*	montañas	montagnes	montanhas
range, mountain	Gebirge, Berg	**serra** *Port.*	sierra	chaîne, montagne	serra
ridge(s)	Höhenrücken	**serranía(s)** *Sp.*	serranía(s)	crête(s)	serrania(s)
island	Insel	**sha** *Ch.*	isla	île	ilha
rapids	Stromschnellen	**shallāl** *Ara.*	rápidos	rapides	rápidos
desert	Wüste	**shamo** *Ch.*	desierto	désert	deserto
mountain(s), island	Berg(e), Insel	**shan** *Ch.*	montaña(s), isla	montagne(s), île	montanha(s), ilha
pass	Pass	**shankou** *Ch.*	paso	col	passo
mountains	Berge	**shanmo** *Ch.*	montañas	montagnes	montanhas
bay	Bucht	**sharm** *Ara.*	bahía	baie	baía
peninsula	Halbinsel	**shibh jazīrat** *Ara.*	península	péninsule	península
island	Insel	**-shima** *Jpn.*	isla	île	ilha
reef	Riff	**-shō** *Jpn.*	arrecife	récif	recife
shoal(s)	Untiefe(n)	**shoal(s)** *Eng.*	bajo(s)	haut-fond(s)	baixio(s)
islands	Inseln	**-shotō** *Jpn.*	islas	îles	ilhas
shrine	Schrein	**shrine** *Eng.*	santuario	châsse	santuário
river	Fluss	**shui** *Ch.*	río	rivière	rio
reservoir	Stausee	**shuiku** *Ch.*	embalse	réservoir	reservatório
strait	Meeresstrasse	**shuitao** *Ch.*	estrecho	détroit	estreito
temple	Tempel	**si** *Ch.*	templo	temple	templo
range, ridge	Gebirge, Höhenrücken	**sierra** *Sp.*	sierra	chaîne, crête	serra
rapids	Stromschnellen	**šivera** *Rus.*	rápidos	rapides	rápidos
lake	See	**-sjø** *Nor.*	lago	lac	lago
lakes	Seen	**-sjöarna** *Swe.*	lagos	lacs	lagos
lake	See	**-sjøen** *Nor.*	lago	lac	lago
lake, bay	See, Bucht	**-sjön** *Swe.*	lago, bahía	lac, baie	lago, baía
island	Insel	**skär** *Swe.*	isla	île	ilha
forest	Wald	**-skog, -skogen** *Swe.*	bosque	forêt	floresta
mountain	Berg	**slieve** *Gae.*	montaña	montagne	montanha
castle	Schloss	**slot** *Du.*	castillo	château	castelo
castle	Schloss	**slott** *Swe.*	castillo	château	castelo
slough (swamp)	verlandende Wasserfläche	**slough** *Eng.*	pantano	fondrière	pântano, brejo
ridge	Höhenrücken	**snía., serranía** *Sp.*	serranía	crête	serrania
snowfield	Schneefeld	**snowfield** *Eng.*	ventisquero	champ de neige	campo de neve
lake	See	**-sø** *Dan.*	lago	lac	lago
sound	Sund	**sonda** *Sp.*	sonda	détroit	estreito
sound	Sund	**sound** *Eng.*	sonda	détroit	estreito
cave, tunnel	Höhle, Tunnel	**souterrain** *Fr.*	cueva, túnel	souterrain	caverna, túnel
state park	Naturpark	**s.p., state park** *Eng.*	parque provincial	parc régional	parque estadual
cave	Höhle	**špilja** *S./C.*	cueva	caverne	caverna
spit	Landzunge	**spit** *Eng.*	lengua de tierra	flèche	ponta de terra
peak	Spitze	**Spitze** *Ger.*	pico	cime	pico
spring	Quelle	**spr., spring** *Eng.*	manantial	source	fonte, manancial
square	Platz	**sq., square** *Eng.*	plaza	place	praça
range, ridge	Gebirge, Höhenrücken	**srra., sierra** *Sp.*	sierra	chaîne, crête	serra
saint	Sankt	**st., saint** *Eng., Fr.*	san, santa, santo	saint	são, santa, santo
street	Strasse	**st., street** *Eng.*	calle	rue	rua
saint	Sankt	**sta., santa** *Port., Sp.*	santa	sainte	santa
station	Bahnhof, Stützpunkt	**sta., station** *Eng., Fr.*	estación	station	estação
stadium	Stadion	**stad., stadium** *Eng.*	estadio	stade	estádio
stadium	Stadion	**stadio** *It.*	estadio	stade	estádio
stadium	Stadion	**Stadion** *Ger.*	estadio	stade	estádio
stadium	Stadion	**stadion** *Rus.*	estadio	stade	estádio
stadium	Stadion	**stadium** *Eng.*	estadio	stade	estádio
state beach	öffentlicher Badestrand	**state beach** *Eng.*	playa provincial	plage régionale	praia estadual
state forest	Wald in Gemeinbesitz	**state forest** *Eng.*	bosque provincial	forêt régionale	floresta estadual
state historical park	Park an historischer Stätte	**state historical park** *Eng.*	parque histórico provincial	parc historique régional	parque histórico estadual
state park	Naturpark	**state park** *Eng.*	parque provincial	parc régional	parque estadual
state recreation area	Ausflugsgebiet	**state recreation area** *Eng.*	zona de recreo provincial	zone récréative regionale	área de lazer estadual
station	Bahnhof, Stützpunkt	**station** *Eng., Fr.*	estación	station	estação
reservoir	Stausee	**Stausee** *Ger.*	embalse	réservoir	reservatório
station	Bahnhof, Stützpunkt	**stazione** *It.*	estación	station	estação
saint	Sankt	**ste., sainte** *Fr.*	santa	sainte	santa
mountains	Berge	**stěny** *Czech*	montañas	montagnes	montanhas
steppe	Steppe	**step'** *Rus.*	estepa	steppe	estepe
peak	Gipfel	**štít** *Slo.*	pico	cime	pico
saint	Sankt	**sto., santo** *Port., Sp.*	santo	saint	santo
strait(s)	Meeresstrasse	**strait(s)** *Eng.*	estrecho	détroit	estreito
stream	Strom	**stream** *Eng.*	corriente de agua	cours d'eau	curso d'água
street	Strasse	**street** *Eng.*	calle	rue	rua
strait	Meeresstrasse	**stretto** *It.*	estrecho	détroit	estreito
stream	Strom	**Strom** *Ger.*	corriente de agua	cours d'eau	curso d'água
stream	Strom	**-ström, -strömmen** *Swe.*	corriente de agua	cours d'eau	curso d'água
river	Fluss	**-su** *Kor.*	río	rivière	rio
channel	Kanal	**-suidō** *Jpn.*	canal, estrecho	canal, détroit	canal, estreito
sound	Sund	**Sund** *Ger.*	sonda	détroit	estreito
sound	Sund	**-sund** *Swe.*	sonda	détroit	estreito
swamp	Sumpf	**swamp** *Eng.*	pantano	marais	pântano
ridge	Höhenrücken	**syrt** *Tur.*	sierra	crête	serra
island	Insel	**sziget** *Hung.*	isla	île	ilha

T

ENGLISH	DEUTSCH	Map Form	ESPAÑOL	FRANÇAIS	PORTUGUÊS
tableland	Tafelland	**tableland** *Eng.*	mesa, altiplano	plateau	planalto
woods	Gehölz	**taillis** *Fr.*	bosque	taillis	bosque
reef	Riff	**taka** *Indon.*	arrecife	récif	recife
mountain	Berg	**-take** *Jpn.*	montaña	montagne	montanha
waterfall	Wasserfall	**-taki** *Jpn.*	cascada	chute d'eau	queda d'água
valley	Tal	**Tal** *Ger.*	valle	vallée	vale
mountain	Berg	**tall** *Ara.*	montaña	montagne	montanha
mountain, hill	Berg, Hügel	**tallat** *Ara.*	montaña, colina	montagne, colline	montanha, colina
hills	Hügel	**tallāt** *Ara.*	colinas	collines	colinas
dam	Talsperre	**Talsperre** *Ger.*	presa	barrage	represa
point	Landspitze	**-tangar, -tangi** *Ice.*	punta	pointe	ponta
cape	Kap	**tanjong** *Mal.*	cabo	cap	cabo
cape	Kap	**tanjung** *Indon.*	cabo	cap	cabo
island	Insel	**tao** *Ch.*	isla	île	ilha
hills	Hügel	**ṭaraq** *Ara.*	colinas	collines	colinas
lake	See	**tasek** *Mal.*	lago	lac	lago
lake	See	**tasik** *Indon.*	lago	lac	lago
plateau	Hochebene	**tassili** *Ber.*	meseta	plateau	planalto
mountain	Berg	**taung** *Bur.*	montaña	montagne	montanha
range	Gebirge	**taungdan** *Bur.*	sierra	chaîne	cordilheira
theatre	Theater	**teatro** *It., Sp.*	teatro	théâtre	teatro
bay	Bucht	**teluk** *Indon.*	bahía	baie	baía
temple	Tempel	**temple** *Eng., Fr.*	templo	temple	templo
church	Kirche	**templom** *Hung.*	iglesia	église	igreja
desert	Wüste	**ténéré** *Ber.*	desierto	désert	deserto
peak, hill	Gipfel, Hügel	**tepe, tepesi** *Tur.*	pico, colina	cime, colline	pico, colina
territory	Territorium	**territory** *Eng.*	territorio	territoire	território
lagoon	Lagune, Haff	**thale** *Thai*	laguna	lagune	laguna
mountains	Berge	**thiu khao** *Thai*	montañas	montagnes	montanhas
mountain	Berg	**-tind,-tinderne** *Nor.*	montaña	montagne	montanha
ridge	Höhenrücken	**ṭiwāl** *Ara.*	sierra	crête	serra
mountain	Berg	**-tjåkko, tjöure** *Lapp.*	montaña	montagne	montanha
island	Insel	**-to** *Kor.*	isla	île	ilha
island	Insel	**-tō** *Jpn.*	isla	île	ilha
lake	See	**tó** *Hung.*	lago	lac	lago
pass	Pass	**-tōge** *Jpn.*	paso	col	passo
island	Insel	**tokong** *Mal.*	isla	île	ilha
lake	See	**tônlé** *Cbd.*	lago	lac	lago
mountain torrent	Wildbach	**torrente** *It., Sp.*	torrente	torrent	torrente
tower	Turm	**tower** *Eng.*	torre	tour	torre
turnpike	gebühren-pflichtige Autobahn	**tpk., turnpike** *Eng.*	camino con peaje	grande route à péage	rodovia com pedágio
lake	See	**-träsk** *Swe.*	lago	lac	lago
trench	Tiefseegraben	**trench** *Eng.*	trinchera	tranchée	fossa submarina
trough	Tiefseegraben	**trough** *Eng.*	trinchera	tranchée	fossa submarina
volcano	Vulkan	**tulūl** *Ara.*	volcán	volcan	vulcão
tunnel	Tunnel	**túnel** *Sp.*	túnel	tunnel	túnel
tunnel	Tunnel	**tunnel** *Eng., Fr.*	túnel	tunnel	túnel
hill, mountain	Hügel, Berg	**-tunturi** *Finn.*	colina, montaña	colline, montagne	colina, montanha
island	Insel	**tuo** *Ch.*	isla	île	ilha
canal	Kanal	**tur'at** *Ara.*	canal	canal	canal
turnpike	gebühren-pflichtige Autobahn	**turnpike** *Eng.*	camino con peaje	grande route à péage	rodovia com pedágio

U-V

ENGLISH	DEUTSCH	Map Form	ESPAÑOL	FRANÇAIS	PORTUGUÊS
cape	Kap	**ujung** *Indon.*	cabo	cap	cabo
lagoon	Lagune, Haff	**-umi** *Jpn.*	laguna	lagune	laguna
United Nations	Vereinte Nationen	**U.N., United Nations** *Eng.*	Naciones Unidas	Nations Unies	Nações Unidas
canal	Kanal	**-unga** *Jpn.*	canal	canal	canal
university	Universität	**univ., universidad** *Sp.* **universidade università university**	universidad	université	universidade
university	Universität	**Universität** *Ger.*	universidad	université	universidade
university	Universität	**université** *Fr.*	universidad	université	universidade
university	Universität	**universitet** *Rus.*	universidad	université	universidade
upland	Bergland	**upland** *Eng.*	tierras altas	hautes terres	terras altas
lake	See	**-ura** *Jpn.*	lago	lac	lago
mountain(s)	Berg(e)	**uul** *Mong.*	montaṇa(s)	montagne(s)	montanha(s)
elevation(s)	Höhe(n)	**uval(y)** *Rus.*	altura(s)	élévation(s)	elevação(ões)
spring	Quelle	**'uyūn** *Ara.*	manantial	source	fonte, manancial
hill	Hügel	**-vaara** *Finn.*	colina	colline	colina
strait	Meeresstrasse	**väin** *Est.*	estrecho	détroit	estreito
valley	Tal	**val** *Fr., It.*	valle	val	vale
valley	Tal	**valle** *It., Sp.*	valle	vallée	vale
valley	Tal	**vallée** *Fr.*	valle	vallée	vale
waterfall	Wasserfall	**vallen** *Du.*	cascada	chute d'eau	queda d'água
valley	Tal	**valley** *Eng.*	valle	vallée	vale
valley	Tal	**vallon** *Fr.*	valle	vallon	vale
lake	See	**-vatn** *Ice., Nor.*	lago	lac	lago
lake	See	**-vatnet** *Nor.*	lago	lac	lago
lake	See	**-vattnett** *Swe.*	lago	lac	lago
reservoir	Stausee	**vdchr., vodochranilišče** *Rus.*	embalse	réservoir	reservatório
hills	Hügel	**-veden** *Swe.*	colinas	collines	colinas
upland	Bergland	**verch** *Rus.*	tierras altas	hautes terres	terras altas
lake	See	**-vesi** *Finn.*	lago	lac	lago
viaduct	Viadukt	**viaducto** *Sp.*	viaducto	viaduc	viaduto
plateau	Hochebene	**-vidda** *Nor.*	meseta	plateau	planalto
gulf	Golf	**-viken** *Swe.*	golfo	golfe	golfo
bay	Bucht	**vinh** *Viet.*	bahía	baie	baía
mountain	Berg	**vîrful** *Rom.*	montaña	montagne	montanha
airport	Flughafen	**vliegveld** *Du.*	aeropuerto	aéroport	aeroporto
channel	Kanal	**vliet** *Du.*	canal, estrecho	canal, détroit	canal, estreito
canal	Kanal	**vodnyj put'** *Rus.*	canal	canal	canal
reservoir	Stausee	**vodochranilišče** *Rus.*	embalse	réservoir	reservatório
railroad station	Bahnhof	**vokzal** *Rus.*	estación de ferrocarril	gare	estação ferroviária
volcano	Vulkan	**vol., volcán** *Sp.* **volcano**	volcán	volcan	vulcão
pass	Pass	**vorota** *Rus.*	paso	col	passo
upland	Bergland	**vozvyšennost'** *Rus.*	tierras altas	hautes terres	terras altas
mountain	Berg	**vrâh** *Blg.*	montaña	montagne	montanha
mountains	Berge	**vrchovina** *Czech, Slo.*	montañas	montagnes	montanhas
mountains	Berge	**vrchy** *Slo.*	montañas	montagnes	montanhas
peak	Gipfel	**vrh** *S./C.*	pico	cime	pico
volcano	Vulkan	**vulkan** *Rus.*	volcán	volcan	vulcão
bay	Bucht	**vung** *Viet.*	bahía	baie	baía
mountain, hill	Berg, Hügel	**-vuori** *Finn.*	montaña, colina	montagne, colline	montanha, colina

W-Z

ENGLISH	DEUTSCH	Map Form	ESPAÑOL	FRANÇAIS	PORTUGUÊS
west	West	**w., west** *Eng.*	oeste	ouest	oeste
marsh	Marsch	**wa** *Ch.*	pantano	marais	pântano
wadi	Wadi	**wādī** *Ara.*	uadi	wadi	uádi
oasis	Oase	**wāhat, wāhāt** *Ara.*	oasis	oasis	oásis
forest, mountains	Wald	**Wald** *Ger.*	bosque, montaṇas	forêt, montagnes	floresta, montanhas
bay	Bucht	**wan** *Ch., Jap.*	bahía	baie	baía
wash	Wadi	**wash** *Eng.*	uadi	wadi	uádi
waterfalls	Wasserfälle	**Wasserfälle** *Ger.*	cascadas	chutes d'eau	quedas d'água
water (lake, river)	Wasser (See, Fluss)	**water** *Eng.*	agua (lago, río)	eau (lac, rivière)	água (lago, rio)
waterway	Wasserstrasse	**waterway** *Eng.*	canal	canal	canal
pond	Weiher	**Weiher** *Ger.*	charca	étang	charco
well	Brunnen	**well** *Eng.*	pozo	puits	poço
bay	Wiek	**Wiek** *Ger.*	bahía	baie	baía
woods	Gehölz	**woods** *Eng.*	bosque	bois	bosque
water (lake, river)	Wasser (See, Fluss)	**wr., water** *Eng.*	agua (lago, río)	eau (lac, rivière)	água (lago, rio)
strait	Meeresstrasse	**xia** *Ch.*	estrecho	détroit	estreito
lake, sea	See, Meer	**yam** *Heb.*	lago, mar	lac, mer	lago, mar
mountain	Berg	**-yama** *Jpn.*	montaña	montagne	montanha
bay	Bucht	**yang** *Ch.*	bahía	baie	baía
peninsula	Halbinsel	**yarımadası** *Tur.*	península	péninsule	península
mountain	Berg	**yebel** *Ara.*	montaña	montagne	montanha
rock, island	Fels, Insel	**yen** *Ch.*	roca, isla	rocher, île	rochedo, ilha
mountains	Berge	**yoma** *Bur.*	montañas	montagnes	montanhas
island	Insel	**yu** *Ch.*	isla	île	ilha
lake	See	**yumco** *Tib.*	lago	lac	lago
canal	Kanal	**yunhe** *Ch.*	canal	canal	canal
intermittent lake	periodischer See	**zahrez** *Ara.*	lago intermitente	lac périodique	lago intermitente
point	Landspitze	**-zaki** *Jpn.*	punta	pointe	ponta
lagoon	Lagune, Haff	**zalew** *Pol.*	laguna	lagune	laguna
gulf, bay	Golf, Bucht	**zaliv** *Rus.*	golfo, bahía	golfe, baie	golfo, baía
reserve	Reservat	**zapov., zapovednik** *Rus.*	reserva	réserve	reserva
sea, lake	Meer, See	**zee** *Du.*	mar, lago	mer, lac	mar, lago
autonomous province	autonome Provinz	**zizhiqu** *Ch.*	provincia autónoma	province autonome	província autônoma
zoo	Zoo	**zoo** *Eng.*	parque zoológico	zoo	jardim zoológico

THIS TABLE gives the area, population, population density, capital, and political status for every country in the world. The political units listed are categorized by political status in the last column of the table, as follows: A—independent countries; B—internally independent political entities which are under the protection of another country in matters of defense and foreign affairs; C—colonies and other dependent political units; and D—the major administrative subdivisions of Australia, Canada, China, the United Kingdom, and the United States. For comparison, the table also includes the continents and the world. For units categorized B, the names of protecting countries are specified in the political-status column. For units categorized C, the names of administering countries are given in parentheses in the first column.

The populations are estimates for January 1, 1992, made by Rand McNally on the basis of official data, United Nations estimates, and other available information.

IN DIESER ÜBERSICHT sind Fläche, Bevölkerung, Bevölkerungsdichte, Hauptstadt und politischer Status für jedes Land der Erde aufgeführt. Die politischen Einheiten sind in der letzten Spalte der Tabelle nach ihrem politischen Status wie folgt gegliedert: A—souveräne Staaten; B—innenpolitisch unabhängige Länder unter der Protektion eines anderen Landes in Angelegenheiten der Aussenpolitik und Verteidigung; C—Kolonien oder anderweitig abhängige Gebiete; D—die wichtigsten Verwaltungseinheiten von Australien, Kanada, China, dem Vereinigten Königreich und den Vereinigten Staaten. Für Vergleiche enthält die Übersicht auch Angaben über die Kontinente und die Welt. Für die unter B eingestuften Einheiten ist der Name des Schutzstaates in der Spalte Politischer Status aufgeführt. Für die unter C eingestuften Gebiete steht der Name des die Verwaltung ausübenden Landes in Klammern in der ersten Spalte.

Die Bevölkerungsangaben sind Schätzungen zum 1. Januar 1992, die Rand McNally auf der Grundlage amtlicher Zahlen, Schätzungen der Vereinten Nationen und anderer zugänglicher Informationen berechnet hat.

EL CUADRO ABAJO incluye la extensión, población y densidad de población, la capital y el estado político de todos los países del mundo. Las entidades políticas nombradas están clasificadas de acuerdo a su estado político en la última columna de la tabla, de esta manera: A—países independientes; B—entidades políticas internamente independientes las cuales se encuentran bajo la protección de otro país en cuanto a asuntos de defensa nacional y relaciones con el extranjero; C—colonias y otras entidades políticas dependientes; y D—las mayores subdivisiones administrativas de Australia, Canadá, China, el Reino Unido, y los Estados Unidos. Para servir de medida comparativa, el cuadro también incluye los continentes y el mundo. Para las entidades de la clasificación B, los nombres de los países protectores están especificados en la columna de estado político. Para las unidades bajo la categoría C, los nombres de los países administradores se encuentran entre paréntesis en la primera columna.

Las poblaciones son los estimados de Rand McNally, tomados el 1o. de Enero de 1992, en base a datos oficiales, estimados de las Naciones Unidas y varias otras informaciones disponibles.

CETTE TABLE donne, pour chaque pays du monde, les renseignements suivants: superficie, population, densité de population, capitale, statut politique. Les entités politiques sont classées, selon leur statut, dans la dernière colonne du tableau: A—pays indépendants; B—entités politiques indépendants intérieurement, mais qui se trouvent sous la protection d'un autre pays pour leur défense et leurs relations extérieures; C—colonies et autres entités politiques dépendantes; D—principales subdivisions administratives de l'Australie, du Canada, de la Chine, du Royaume-Uni, des États-Unis. Pour permettre les comparaisons, la table comprend aussi les continents et le monde. Pour les entités politiques de la catégorie B, les noms des pays protecteurs sont spécifiés dans la colonne "statut politique". Pour celles de la catégorie C, les noms des pays administrateurs sont mis entre parenthèses dans la première colonne.

Les chiffres concernant la population sont des estimations au 1er janvier 1992, établies par Rand McNally, d'après les sources officielles, les estimations des Nations Unies et autres informations disponibles.

A TABELA que se segue apresenta a área, a população, a densidade demográfica, a capital e o estatuto político de todos os países do mundo. As unidades políticas relacionadas na tabela estão classificadas de acordo com o respectivo estatuto político na última coluna, do seguinte modo: A—países independentes; B—unidades políticas internamente independentes mas que se encontram sob a proteção de outro país no tocante a assuntos de defesa nacional e negócios extrenos; C—colônias e outras unidades políticas dependentes; e D—subdivisões administrativas principais da Austrália, Canadá, China, Reino Unido e Estados Unidos. Para fins de comparabilidade, a tabela também inclui os continentes e o mundo. No tocante ás unidades classificadas em B, os nomes dos países protetores estão especificados na coluna relativa ao estatuto político. Para as unidades da categoria C, os nomes dos países administradores figuram entre parênteses na primeira coluna.

Os dados relativos à população são estimativas de Rand McNally para 1 de janeiro de 1992, com base em dados oficiais, estimativas das Nações Unidas e outras informações disponíveis.

NAME / NAME / NOMBRE / NOM / NOME English / Englisch Inglés / Anglais / Inglês	Local / Einheimisch Local / Local / Local	AREA / FLÄCHE AREA / SUPERFICIE / ÁREA sq. km.	sq. mi.	POPULATION BEVÖLKERUNG POBLACIÓN POPULATION POPULAÇÃO	DENSITY PER BEVÖLKERUNGSDICHTE PRO / DENSIDAD POR DENSITÉ / DENSIDADE POR sq. km.	sq. mi.	CAPITAL HAUPSTADT CAPITAL CAPITALE CAPITAL	POLITICAL STATUS POLITISCHER STATUS ESTADO POLÍTICO STATUS POLITIQUE ESTATUTO POLÍTICO
†Afghanistan	Afghānestān	652,225	251,826	16,880,000	26	67	Kābol	A
Africa	. . .	30,300,000	11,700,000	694,000,000	23	59	. . .	. . .
Alabama, U.S.	Alabama	135,775	52,423	4,099,000	30	78	Montgomery	D
Alaska, U.S.	Alaska	1,700,139	656,424	560,000	0.3	0.9	Juneau	D
†Albania	Shqipëri	28,748	11,100	3,352,000	117	302	Tiranë	A
Alberta, Can.	Alberta	661,190	255,287	2,499,000	3.8	9.8	Edmonton	D
†Algeria	Algérie (French) / Djazaïr (Arabic)	2,381,741	919,595	26,360,000	11	29	El Djazaïr (Algiers)	A
American Samoa (U.S.)	American Samoa (English) / Amerika Samoa (Samoan)	199	77	49,000	246	636	Pago Pago	C
Andorra	Andorra	453	175	54,000	119	309	Andorra	B(Sp., Fr.)
†Angola	Angola	1,246,700	481,354	10,425,000	8.4	22	Luanda	A
Anguilla	Anguilla	91	35	7,000	77	200	The Valley	B(U.K.)
Anhwei, China	Anhui	139,000	53,668	58,250,000	419	1,085	Hefei	D
Antarctica	. . .	14,000,000	5,400,000	[1]	. . .	. . .	. . .	. . .
†Antigua and Barbuda	Antigua and Barbuda	443	171	64,000	144	374	St. John's	A
†Argentina	Argentina	2,780,092	1,073,400	32,860,000	12	31	Buenos Aires and Viedma[5]	A
Arizona, U.S.	Arizona	295,276	114,006	3,780,000	13	33	Phoenix	D
Arkansas, U.S.	Arkansas	137,742	53,182	2,383,000	17	45	Little Rock	D
Armenia	Hayastan	29,800	11,506	3,360,000	113	292	Jerevan	A
Aruba	Aruba	193	75	64,000	332	853	Oranjestad	B(Neth.)
Asia	. . .	44,900,000	17,300,000	3,331,500,000	74	193	. . .	. . .
†Australia	Australia	7,682,300	2,966,155	17,420,000	2.3	5.9	Canberra	A
Australian Capital Territory, Austl.	Australian Capital Territory	2,400	927	294,000	123	317	Canberra	D
†Austria	Österreich	83,855	32,377	7,681,000	92	237	Wien (Vienna)	A
Azerbaijan	Azerbajdžan	86,600	33,436	7,170,000	83	214	Baku (Baky)	A
†Bahamas	Bahamas	13,939	5,382	260,000	19	48	Nassau	A
†Bahrain	Al-Baḥrayn	691	267	546,000	790	2,045	Al-Manāmah	A
†Bangladesh	Bangladesh	143,998	55,598	118,000,000	819	2,122	Dhaka (Dacca)	A
†Barbados	Barbados	430	166	257,000	598	1,548	Bridgetown	A
†Belarus	Byelarus'	207,600	80,155	10,390,000	50	130	Minsk	A
†Belgium	Belgique (French) / België (Flemish)	30,518	11,783	9,932,000	325	843	Bruxelles (Brussels)	A
†Belize	Belize	22,963	8,866	232,000	10	26	Belmopan	A
†Benin	Bénin	112,600	43,475	4,914,000	44	113	Porto-Novo and Cotonou	A
Bermuda (U.K.)	Bermuda	54	21	60,000	1,111	2,857	Hamilton	C
†Bhutan	Druk-Yul	46,500	17,954	1,614,000	35	90	Thimphu	B(India)
†Bolivia	Bolivia	1,098,581	424,165	7,243,000	6.6	17	La Paz and Sucre	A
Bophuthatswana[2]	Bophuthatswana	40,509	15,641	3,500,000	86	224	Mmabatho	B(S. Afr.)
†Bosnia and Hercegovina	Bosna i Hercegovina	51,129	19,741	4,519,000	88	229	Sarajevo	A
†Botswana	Botswana	582,000	224,711	1,345,000	2.3	6.0	Gaborone	A
†Brazil	Brasil	8,511,965	3,286,488	156,750,000	18	48	Brasília	A
British Columbia, Can.	British Columbia (English) / Colombie-Britannique (French)	947,800	365,948	3,106,000	3.3	8.5	Victoria	D
British Indian Ocean Territory (U.K.)	British Indian Ocean Territory	60	23	[1]	. . .	. . .	. . .	C
British Virgin Islands (U.K.)	British Virgin Islands	153	59	14,000	92	237	Road Town	C
†Brunei	Brunei	5,765	2,226	411,000	71	185	Bandar Seri Begawan	A
†Bulgaria	Bâlgarija	110,912	42,823	8,902,000	80	208	Sofija (Sofia)	A
†Burkina Faso	Burkina Faso	274,200	105,869	9,510,000	35	90	Ouagadougou	A
†Burma	Myanmar	676,577	261,228	42,615,000	63	163	Yangon (Rangoon)	A
†Burundi	Burundi	27,830	10,745	5,924,000	213	551	Bujumbura	A
California, U.S.	California	424,002	163,707	30,680,000	72	187	Sacramento	D
†Cambodia	Kâmpŭchéa	181,035	69,898	8,543,000	47	122	Phnum Pénh (Phnom Penh)	A
†Cameroon	Cameroun (French) / Cameroon (English)	475,442	183,569	11,550,000	24	63	Yaoundé	A
†Canada	Canada	9,970,610	3,849,674	26,985,000	2.7	7.0	Ottawa	A
†Cape Verde	Cabo Verde	4,033	1,557	393,000	97	252	Praia	A
Cayman Islands (U.K.)	Cayman Islands	259	100	28,000	108	280	George Town	C
†Central African Republic	République centrafricaine	622,984	240,535	2,990,000	4.8	12	Bangui	A
†Chad	Tchad	1,284,000	495,755	5,178,000	4.0	10	N'Djamena	A
Chekiang, China	Zhejiang	101,800	39,305	45,255,000	445	1,151	Hangzhou	D
†Chile	Chile	756,626	292,135	13,395,000	18	46	Santiago	A
†China (excl. Taiwan)	Zhongguo	9,556,100	3,689,631	1,181,580,000	124	320	Beijing (Peking)	A
Christmas Island (Austl.)	Christmas Island	135	52	2,300	17	44	The Settlement	C
Ciskei[2]	Ciskei	7,760	2,996	2,500,000	322	834	Bisho	B(S. Afr.)
Cocos (Keeling) Islands (Austl.)	Cocos (Keeling) Islands	14	5.4	700	50	130	. . .	C
†Colombia	Colombia	1,141,748	440,831	33,170,000	29	75	Santa Fe de Bogotá	A
Colorado, U.S.	Colorado	269,620	104,100	3,356,000	12	32	Denver	D
†Comoros	Comores (French) / Al-Qumur (Arabic)	2,235	863	484,000	217	561	Moroni	A
†Congo	Congo	342,000	132,047	2,344,000	6.9	18	Brazzaville	A
Connecticut, U.S.	Connecticut	14,358	5,544	3,336,000	232	602	Hartford	D
Cook Islands	Cook Islands	236	91	18,000	76	198	Avarua	B(N.Z.)
†Costa Rica	Costa Rica	51,100	19,730	3,151,000	62	160	San José	A
†Croatia	Hrvatska	56,538	21,829	4,800,000	85	220	Zagreb	A
†Cuba	Cuba	110,861	42,804	10,785,000	97	252	La Habana (Havana)	A
†Cyprus (excl. North Cyprus)	Kípros (Greek) / Kıbrıs (Turkish)	5,896	2,276	713,000	121	313	Nicosia (Levkosía)	A
Cyprus, North	Ķuzey Kıbrıs	3,355	1,295	192,000	57	148	Nicosia (Lefkoşa)	A
†Czechoslovakia	Československo	127,899	49,382	15,755,000	123	319	Praha (Prague)	A

NAME / NAME / NOMBRE / NOM / NOME English / Englisch Inglés / Anglais / Inglês	 Local / Einheimisch Local / Local / Local	AREA / FLÄCHE AREA / SUPERFICIE / ÁREA sq. km.	 sq. mi.	POPULATION BEVÖLKERUNG POBLACIÓN POPULATION POPULAÇÃO	DENSITY PER BEVÖLKERUNGSDICHTE PRO / DENSIDAD POR DENSITÉ / DENSIDADE POR sq. km.	 sq. mi.	CAPITAL HAUPSTADT CAPITAL CAPITALE CAPITAL	POLITICAL STATUS POLITISCHER STATUS ESTADO POLÍTICO STATUS POLITIQUE ESTATUTO POLÍTICO
Delaware, U.S.	Delaware	6,447	2,489	679,000	105	273	Dover	D
†Denmark	Danmark	43,093	16,638	5,154,000	120	310	København (Copenhagen)	A
District of Columbia, U.S.	District of Columbia	177	68	611,000	3,452	8,985	Washington	D
†Djibouti	Djibouti	23,200	8,958	351,000	15	39	Djibouti	A
†Dominica	Dominica	790	305	87,000	110	285	Roseau	A
†Dominican Republic	República Dominicana	48,442	18,704	8,124,000	168	434	Santo Domingo	A
†Ecuador	Ecuador	283,561	109,484	10,880,000	38	99	Quito	A
†Egypt	Mişr	1,001,449	386,662	55,105,000	55	143	Al-Qāhirah (Cairo)	A
†El Salvador	El Salvador	21,041	8,124	5,473,000	260	674	San Salvador	A
England, U.K.	England	130,439	50,363	48,015,000	368	953	London	D
†Equatorial Guinea	Guinea Ecuatorial	28,051	10,831	384,000	14	35	Malabo	A
†Estonia	Eesti	45,100	17,413	1,606,000	36	92	Tallinn	A
†Ethiopia	Ityopiya	1,251,282	483,123	54,040,000	43	112	Adis Abeba	A
Europe	. . .	9,900,000	3,800,000	695,200,000	70	183	. . .	. . .
Faeroe Islands	Føroyar	1,399	540	48,000	34	89	Tórshavn	B(Den.)
Falkland Islands (U.K.)[3]	Falkland Islands	12,173	4,700	2,000	0.2	0.4	Stanley	C
†Fiji	Fiji (French / Viti (Fijian)	18,333	7,078	747,000	41	106	Suva	A
†Finland	Suomi (Finnish) / Finland (Swedish)	338,145	130,559	5,001,000	15	38	Helsinki (Helsingfors)	A
Florida, U.S.	Florida	170,313	65,758	13,360,000	78	203	Tallahassee	D
†France (excl. Overseas Departments)	France	547,026	211,208	57,010,000	104	270	Paris	A
French Guiana (Fr.)	Guyane française	91,000	35,135	104,000	1.1	3.0	Cayenne	C
French Polynesia (Fr.)	Polynésie française	4,000	1,544	198,000	50	128	Papeete	C
Fukien, China	Fujian	120,000	46,332	30,840,000	257	666	Fuzhou	D
†Gabon	Gabon	267,667	103,347	1,088,000	4.1	11	Libreville	A
†Gambia	Gambia	10,689	4,127	889,000	83	215	Banjul	A
Georgia, U.S.	Georgia	153,953	59,441	6,657,000	43	112	Atlanta	D
Georgia	Sakartvelo	69,700	26,911	5,550,000	80	206	Tbilisi	A
†Germany	Deutschland	356,955	137,822	79,710,000	223	578	Berlin and Bonn	A
†Ghana	Ghana	238,533	92,098	15,865,000	67	172	Accra	A
Gibraltar (U.K.)	Gibraltar	6.0	2.3	31,000	5,167	13,478	Gibraltar	C
†Greece	Ellás	131,990	50,962	10,285,000	78	202	Athínai (Athens)	A
Greenland	Kalaallit Nunaat (Eskimo) / Grønland (Danish)	2,175,600	840,004	57,000	. . .	0.1	Godthåb (Nuuk)	B(Den.)
†Grenada	Grenada	344	133	98,000	285	737	St. George's	A
Guadeloupe (incl. Dependencies) (Fr.)	Guadeloupe	1,780	687	346,000	194	504	Basse-Terre	C
Guam (U.S.)	Guam	541	209	147,000	272	703	Agana	C
†Guatemala	Guatemala	108,889	42,042	9,386,000	86	223	Guatemala	A
Guernsey (incl. Dependencies) (U.K.)	Guernsey	78	30	58,000	744	1,933	St. Peter Port	C
†Guinea	Guinée	245,857	94,926	7,553,000	31	80	Conakry	A
†Guinea-Bissau	Guiné-Bissau	36,125	13,948	1,036,000	29	74	Bissau	A
†Guyana	Guyana	214,969	83,000	748,000	3.5	9.0	Georgetown	A
Hainan, China	Hainan	34,000	13,127	7,090,000	209	540	Haikou	D
†Haiti	Haïti	27,750	10,714	6,361,000	229	594	Port-au-Prince	A
Hawaii, U.S.	Hawaii	28,313	10,932	1,133,000	40	104	Honolulu	D
Heilungkiang, China	Heilongjiang	469,000	181,082	37,690,000	80	208	Harbin	D
Honan, China	Henan	167,000	64,479	87,670,000	525	1,360	Zhengzhou	D
†Honduras	Honduras	112,088	43,277	5,342,000	48	123	Tegucigalpa	A
Hong Kong (U.K.)	Hong Kong (English) / Xianggang (Chinese)	1,072	414	5,874,000	5,479	14,188	Hong Kong (Victoria)	C
Hopeh, China	Hebei	190,000	73,359	62,860,000	331	857	Shijiazhuang	D
Hunan, China	Hunan	210,000	81,081	63,810,000	304	787	Changsha	D
†Hungary	Magyarország	93,033	35,920	10,555,000	113	294	Budapest	A
Hupeh, China	Hubei	187,400	72,356	56,360,000	301	779	Wuhan	D
†Iceland	Ísland	103,000	39,769	261,000	2.5	6.6	Reykjavík	A
Idaho, U.S.	Idaho	216,456	83,574	1,065,000	4.9	13	Boise	D
Illinois, U.S.	Illinois	150,007	57,918	11,575,000	77	200	Springfield	D
†India (incl. part of Jammu and Kashmir)	India (English) / Bharat (Hindi)	3,203,975	1,237,062	874,150,000	273	707	New Delhi	A
Indiana, U.S.	Indiana	94,328	36,420	5,615,000	60	154	Indianapolis	D
†Indonesia	Indonesia	1,948,732	752,410	195,300,000	100	260	Jakarta	A
Inner Mongolia, China	Nei Monggol	1,183,000	456,759	22,685,000	19	50	Hohhot	D
Iowa, U.S.	Iowa	145,754	56,276	2,801,000	19	50	Des Moines	D
†Iran	Īrān	1,638,057	632,457	60,000,000	37	95	Tehrān	A
†Iraq	Al-'Irāq	438,317	169,235	19,915,000	45	118	Baghdād	A
†Ireland	Ireland (English) / Éire (Gaelic)	70,285	27,137	3,484,000	50	128	Dublin (Baile Átha Cliath)	A
Isle of Man	Isle of Man	572	221	64,000	112	290	Douglas	B(U.K.)
†Israel	Yisra'el (Hebrew) / Isrā'īl (Arabic)	20,770	8,019	4,393,000	212	548	Yerushalayim (Jerusalem)	A
Israeli Occupied Areas[4]	. . .	7,632	2,947	1,789,000	234	607	. . .	. . .
†Italy	Italia	301,277	116,324	57,830,000	192	497	Roma (Rome)	A
†Ivory Coast	Côte d'Ivoire	322,500	124,518	13,240,000	41	106	Abidjan and Yamoussoukro[5]	A
†Jamaica	Jamaica	10,991	4,244	2,501,000	228	589	Kingston	A
†Japan	Nihon	377,801	145,870	124,270,000	329	852	Tōkyō	A
Jersey (U.K.)	Jersey	116	45	85,000	733	1,889	St. Helier	C
†Jordan	Al-Urdun	91,000	35,135	3,485,000	38	99	'Ammān	A
Kansas, U.S.	Kansas	213,110	82,282	2,517,000	12	31	Topeka	D
Kansu, China	Gansu	450,000	173,746	23,275,000	52	134	Lanzhou	D
Kazakhstan	Kazakhstan	2,717,300	1,049,156	16,880,000	6.2	16	Alma-Ata (Almaty)	A
Kentucky, U.S.	Kentucky	104,665	40,411	3,727,000	36	92	Frankfort	D
†Kenya	Kenya	582,646	224,961	25,695,000	44	114	Nairobi	A
Kiangsi, China	Jiangxi	166,600	64,325	39,110,000	235	608	Nanchang	D
Kiangsu, China	Jiangsu	102,600	39,614	69,830,000	681	1,763	Nanjing (Nanking)	D
Kiribati	Kiribati	811	313	72,000	89	230	Bairiki	A
Kirin, China	Jilin	187,000	72,201	25,760,000	138	357	Changchun	D
†Korea, North	Chosŏn-minjujuŭi-inmīn-konghwaguk	120,538	46,540	22,250,000	185	478	P'yŏngyang	A
†Korea, South	Taehan-min'guk	99,016	38,230	43,305,000	437	1,133	Sŏul (Seoul)	A
†Kuwait	Al-Kuwayt	17,818	6,880	2,244,000	126	326	Al-Kuwayt (Kuwait)	A
Kwangsi Chuang, China	Guangxi Zhuangzu	236,300	91,236	44,310,000	188	486	Nanning	D
Kwangtung, China	Guangdong	178,000	68,726	63,800,000	358	928	Guangzhou (Canton)	D
Kweichow, China	Guizhou	170,000	65,637	33,795,000	199	515	Guiyang	D
Kyrgyzstan	Kyrgyzstan	198,500	76,641	4,385,000	22	57	Biškek (Frunze)	A
†Laos	Lao	236,800	91,429	4,158,000	18	45	Viangchan (Vientiane)	A
†Latvia	Latvija	63,700	24,595	2,737,000	43	111	Rīga	A
†Lebanon	Lubnān	10,400	4,015	3,409,000	328	849	Bayrūt (Beirut)	A
†Lesotho	Lesotho	30,355	11,720	1,824,000	60	156	Maseru	A
Liaoning, China	Liaoning	145,700	56,255	41,590,000	285	739	Shenyang (Mukden)	D
†Liberia	Liberia	99,067	38,250	2,776,000	28	73	Monrovia	A
†Libya	Lībiyā	1,759,540	679,362	4,416,000	2.5	6.5	Tarābulus (Tripoli)	A
†Liechtenstein	Liechtenstein	160	62	28,000	175	452	Vaduz	A
†Lithuania	Lietuva	65,200	25,174	3,767,000	58	150	Vilnius	A
Louisiana, U.S.	Louisiana	134,275	51,843	4,251,000	32	82	Baton Rouge	D
†Luxembourg	Luxembourg (French) / Lezebuurg (Luxembourgish)	2,586	998	390,000	151	391	Luxembourg	A
Macau (Port.)	Macau	17	6.6	448,000	26,353	67,879	Macau	C
Macedonia	Makedonija	25,713	9,928	2,120,000	82	214	Skopje	A
†Madagascar	Madagasikara (Malagasy) / Madagascar (French)	587,041	226,658	12,380,000	21	55	Antananarivo	A
Maine, U.S.	Maine	91,653	35,387	1,252,000	14	35	Augusta	D
†Malawi	Malaŵi	118,484	45,747	9,523,000	80	208	Lilongwe	A
†Malaysia	Malaysia	334,758	129,251	18,200,000	54	141	Kuala Lumpur	A
†Maldives	Maldives	298	115	230,000	772	2,000	Male	A
†Mali	Mali	1,240,000	478,767	8,438,000	6.8	18	Bamako	A
†Malta	Malta	316	122	357,000	1,130	2,926	Valletta	A
Manitoba, Can.	Manitoba	649,950	250,947	1,129,000	1.7	4.5	Winnipeg	D
†Marshall Islands	Marshall Islands	181	70	49,000	271	700	Majuro (island)	A
Martinique (Fr.)	Martinique	1,100	425	347,000	315	816	Fort-de-France	C
Maryland, U.S.	Maryland	32,135	12,407	4,895,000	152	395	Annapolis	D
Massachusetts, U.S.	Massachusetts	27,337	10,555	6,107,000	223	579	Boston	D

NAME / NAME / NOMBRE / NOM / NOME English / Englisch Inglés / Anglais / Inglês	Local / Einheimisch Local / Local / Local	AREA / FLÄCHE AREA / SUPERFICIE / ÁREA sq. km.	sq. mi.	POPULATION BEVÖLKERUNG POBLACIÓN POPULATION POPULAÇÃO	DENSITY PER BEVÖLKERUNGSDICHTE PRO / DENSIDAD POR DENSITÉ / DENSIDADE POR sq. km.	sq. mi.	CAPITAL HAUPSTADT CAPITAL CAPITALE CAPITAL	POLITICAL STATUS POLITISCHER STATUS ESTADO POLÍTICO STATUS POLITIQUE ESTATUTO POLÍTICO
†Mauritania	Mauritanie (French) / Mūrītāniyā (Arabic)	1,025,520	395,956	2,028,000	2.0	5.1	Nouakchott	A
†Mauritius (incl. Dependencies)	Mauritius	2,040	788	1,085,000	532	1,377	Port Louis	A
Mayotte (Fr.)(6)	Mayotte	374	144	77,000	206	535	Dzaoudzi and Mamoudzou(5)	C
†Mexico	México	1,958,201	756,066	91,000,000	46	120	Ciudad de México (Mexico City)	A
Michigan, U.S.	Michigan	250,738	96,810	9,423,000	38	97	Lansing	D
†Micronesia, Federated States of	Federated States of Micronesia	702	271	109,000	155	402	Kolonia and Paliker(5)	A
Midway Islands (U.S.)	Midway Islands	5.2	2.0	500	96	250	. . .	C
Minnesota, U.S.	Minnesota	225,182	86,943	4,459,000	20	51	St. Paul	D
Mississippi, U.S.	Mississippi	125,443	48,434	2,604,000	21	54	Jackson	D
Missouri, U.S.	Missouri	180,546	69,709	5,200,000	29	75	Jefferson City	D
Moldova	Moldova	33,700	13,012	4,440,000	132	341	Kišin'ov (Chişinău)	A
Monaco	Monaco	1.9	0.7	30,000	15,789	42,857	Monaco	A
†Mongolia	Mongol Ard Uls	1,566,500	604,829	2,278,000	1.5	3.8	Ulaanbaatar (Ulan Bator)	A
Montana, U.S.	Montana	380,850	147,046	806,000	2.1	5.5	Helena	D
Montenegro, Yugo.	Crna Gora	13,812	5,333	647,000	47	121	Titograd	D
Montserrat (U.K.)	Montserrat	102	39	13,000	127	333	Plymouth	C
†Morocco (excl. Western Sahara)	Al-Magrib	446,550	172,414	26,470,000	59	154	Rabat	A
†Mozambique	Moçambique	799,380	308,642	15,460,000	19	50	Maputo	A
†Namibia (excl. Walvis Bay)	Namibia	823,144	317,818	1,548,000	1.9	4.9	Windhoek	A
Nauru	Nauru (English) / Naoero (Nauruan)	21	8.1	9,000	429	1,111	Yaren District	A
Nebraska, U.S.	Nebraska	200,358	77,358	1,615,000	8.1	21	Lincoln	D
†Nepal	Nepāl	147,181	56,827	19,845,000	135	349	Kāṭhmāṇḍau	A
†Netherlands	Nederland	41,785	16,133	15,065,000	361	934	Amsterdam and 's-Gravenhage (The Hague)	A
Netherlands Antilles	Nederlandse Antillen	800	309	190,000	238	615	Willemstad	B(Neth.)
Nevada, U.S.	Nevada	286,368	110,567	1,257,000	4.4	11	Carson City	D
New Brunswick, Can.	New Brunswick (English) / Nouveau-Brunswick (French)	73,440	28,355	743,000	10	26	Fredericton	D
New Caledonia (Fr.)	Nouvelle-Calédonie	19,058	7,358	174,000	9.1	24	Nouméa	C
Newfoundland, Can.	Newfoundland (English) / Terre-Neuve (French)	405,720	156,649	591,000	1.5	3.8	St. John's	D
New Hampshire, U.S.	New Hampshire	24,219	9,351	1,138,000	47	122	Concord	D
New Jersey, U.S.	New Jersey	22,590	8,722	7,850,000	347	900	Trenton	D
New Mexico, U.S.	New Mexico	314,939	121,598	1,550,000	4.9	13	Santa Fe	D
New South Wales, Austl.	New South Wales	801,600	309,500	5,930,000	7.4	19	Sydney	D
New York, U.S.	New York	141,089	54,475	18,260,000	129	335	Albany	D
†New Zealand	New Zealand	268,112	103,519	3,463,000	13	33	Wellington	A
†Nicaragua	Nicaragua	129,640	50,054	3,805,000	29	76	Managua	A
†Niger	Niger	1,267,000	489,191	8,113,000	6.4	17	Niamey	A
†Nigeria	Nigeria	923,768	356,669	124,300,000	135	349	Lagos and Abuja(5)	A
Ningsia Hui, China	Ningxia Huizu	66,400	25,637	4,845,000	73	189	Yinchuan	D
Niue	Niue	258	100	1,800	7.0	18	Alofi	B(N.Z.)
Norfolk Island (Austl.)	Norfolk Island	36	14	2,600	72	186	Kingston	C
North America	. . .	24,700,000	9,500,000	436,300,000	18	46	. . .	. . .
North Carolina, U.S.	North Carolina	139,397	53,821	6,770,000	49	126	Raleigh	D
North Dakota, U.S.	North Dakota	183,123	70,704	644,000	3.5	9.1	Bismarck	D
Northern Ireland, U.K.	Northern Ireland	14,121	5,452	1,596,000	113	293	Belfast	D
Northern Mariana Islands	Northern Mariana Islands	477	184	46,000	96	250	Saipan (island)	B(U.S.)
Northern Territory, Austl.	Northern Territory	1,346,200	519,771	160,000	0.1	0.3	Darwin	D
Northwest Territories, Can.	Northwest Territories (English) / Territoires du Nord-Ouest (French)	3,426,320	1,322,910	54,000	. . .	. . .	Yellowknife	D
†Norway (incl. Svalbard and Jan Mayen)	Norge	386,975	149,412	4,286,000	11	29	Oslo	A
Nova Scotia, Can.	Nova Scotia (English) / Nouvelle-Écosse (French)	55,490	21,425	920,000	17	43	Halifax	D
Oceania (incl. Australia)	. . .	8,500,000	3,300,000	27,300,000	3.2	8.3	. . .	. . .
Ohio, U.S.	Ohio	116,103	44,828	10,980,000	95	245	Columbus	D
Oklahoma, U.S.	Oklahoma	181,049	69,903	3,169,000	18	45	Oklahoma City	D
†Oman	ʿUmān	212,457	82,030	1,562,000	7.4	19	Masqaṭ (Muscat)	A
Ontario, Can.	Ontario	1,068,580	412,581	9,820,000	9.2	24	Toronto	D
Oregon, U.S.	Oregon	254,819	98,386	2,895,000	11	29	Salem	D
†Pakistan (incl. part of Jammu and Kashmir)	Pākistān	879,902	339,732	119,000,000	135	350	Islāmābād	A
Palau (Trust Territory)	Palau (English) / Belau (Palauan)	508	196	15,000	30	77	Koror and Melekeok(5)	B(U.S.)
†Panama	Panamá	75,517	29,157	2,503,000	33	86	Panamá	A
†Papua New Guinea	Papua New Guinea	462,840	178,704	3,960,000	8.6	22	Port Moresby	A
†Paraguay	Paraguay	406,752	157,048	4,871,000	12	31	Asunción	A
Peking, China	Beijing	16,800	6,487	11,700,000	696	1,804	Beijing (Peking)	D
Pennsylvania, U.S.	Pennsylvania	119,291	46,058	12,042,000	101	261	Harrisburg	D
†Peru	Perú	1,285,216	496,225	22,585,000	18	46	Lima	A
†Philippines	Philippines (English) / Pilipinas (Tagalog)	300,000	115,831	62,380,000	208	539	Manila	A
Pitcairn (incl. Dependencies) (U.K.)	Pitcairn	49	19	40	0.8	2.1	Adamstown	C
†Poland	Polska	312,683	120,728	37,840,000	121	313	Warszawa (Warsaw)	A
†Portugal	Portugal	91,985	35,516	10,410,000	113	293	Lisboa (Lisbon)	A
Prince Edward Island, Can.	Prince Edward Island (English) / Île-du Prince-Édouard (French)	5,660	2,185	134,000	24	61	Charlottetown	D
Puerto Rico	Puerto Rico	9,104	3,515	3,528,000	388	1,004	San Juan	B(U.S.)
†Qatar	Qaṭar	11,437	4,416	532,000	47	120	Ad-Dawḥah (Doha)	A
Quebec, Can.	Québec	1,540,680	594,860	6,911,000	4.5	12	Québec	D
Queensland, Austl.	Queensland	1,727,200	666,876	2,981,000	1.7	4.5	Brisbane	D
Reunion (Fr.)	Réunion	2,510	969	613,000	244	633	Saint-Denis	C
Rhode Island, U.S.	Rhode Island	4,002	1,545	1,019,000	255	660	Providence	D
†Romania	România	237,500	91,699	23,465,000	99	256	Bucureşti (Bucharest)	A
†Russia	Rossija	17,075,400	6,592,849	150,505,000	8.8	23	Moskva (Moscow)	A
†Rwanda	Rwanda	26,338	10,169	8,053,000	306	792	Kigali	A
St. Helena (incl. Dependencies) (U.K.)	St. Helena	314	121	7,000	22	58	Jamestown	C
†St. Kitts and Nevis	St. Kitts and Nevis	269	104	42,000	156	404	Basseterre	A
†St. Lucia	St. Lucia	616	238	155,000	252	651	Castries	A
St. Pierre and Miquelon (Fr.)	Saint-Pierre-et-Miquelon	242	93	6,000	25	65	Saint-Pierre	C
†St. Vincent and the Grenadines	St. Vincent and the Grenadines	388	150	115,000	296	767	Kingstown	A
†San Marino	San Marino	61	24	23,000	377	958	San Marino	A
†Sao Tome and Principe	São Tomé e Príncipe	964	372	130,000	135	349	São Tomé	A
Saskatchewan, Can.	Saskatchewan	652,330	251,866	1,052,000	1.6	4.2	Regina	D
†Saudi Arabia	Al-ʿArabīyah as-Suʿūdīyah	2,149,690	830,000	16,690,000	7.8	20	Ar-Riyāḍ (Riyadh)	A
Scotland, U.K.	Scotland	78,772	30,414	5,125,000	65	169	Edinburgh	D
†Senegal	Sénégal	196,712	75,951	7,569,000	38	100	Dakar	A
Serbia, Yugo.	Srbija	88,361	34,116	9,975,000	113	292	Beograd (Belgrade)	D
†Seychelles	Seychelles	453	175	69,000	152	394	Victoria	A
Shanghai, China	Shanghai	6,200	2,394	13,705,000	2,210	5,725	Shanghai	D
Shansi, China	Shanxi	156,000	60,232	29,895,000	192	496	Taiyuan	D
Shantung, China	Shandong	153,000	59,074	87,550,000	572	1,482	Jinan	D
Shensi, China	Shaanxi	205,000	79,151	34,030,000	166	430	Xi'an (Sian)	D
†Sierra Leone	Sierra Leone	72,325	27,925	4,330,000	60	155	Freetown	A
†Singapore	Singapore	636	246	3,062,000	4,814	12,447	Singapore	A
Sinkiang Uighur, China	Xinjiang Uygur	1,600,000	617,764	15,715,000	9.8	25	Ürümqi	D
†Slovenia	Slovenija	20,251	7,819	1,989,000	98	254	Ljubljana	A
†Solomon Islands	Solomon Islands	28,370	10,954	353,000	12	32	Honiara	A
†Somalia	Somaliya	637,657	246,201	6,823,000	11	28	Muqdisho (Mogadishu)	A

NAME / NAME / NOMBRE / NOM / NOME English / Englisch Inglés / Anglais / Inglês	Local / Einheimisch Local / Local / Local	AREA / FLÄCHE AREA / SUPERFICIE / ÁREA sq. km.	sq. mi.	POPULATION BEVÖLKERUNG POBLACIÓN POPULATION POPULAÇÃO	DENSITY PER BEVÖLKERUNGSDICHTE PRO / DENSIDAD POR DENSITÉ / DENSIDADE POR sq. km.	sq. mi.	CAPITAL HAUPSTADT CAPITAL CAPITALE CAPITAL	POLITICAL STATUS POLITISCHER STATUS ESTADO POLITICO STATUS POLITIQUE ESTATUTO POLITICO
†South Africa (incl. Walvis Bay)	South Africa (English) / Suid-Afrika (Afrikaans)	1,123,226	433,680	36,765,000	33	85	Pretoria, Cape Town, and Bloemfontein	A
South America	. . .	17,800,000	6,900,000	306,700,000	17	44	. . .	. . .
South Australia, Austl.	South Australia	984,000	379,925	1,465,000	1.5	3.9	Adelaide	D
South Carolina, U.S.	South Carolina	82,898	32,007	3,559,000	43	111	Columbia	D
South Dakota, U.S.	South Dakota	199,745	77,121	673,000	3.4	8.7	Pierre	D
South Georgia and the South Sandwich Islands (U.K.)	. . .	3,755	1,450	(1)	. . .	. . .	. . .	C
†Spain	España	504,750	194,885	39,465,000	78	203	Madrid	A
Spanish North Africa (Sp.)(7)	Plazas de Soberanía en el Norte de África	32	12	137,000	4,281	11,417	. . .	C
†Sri Lanka	Sri Lanka	64,652	24,962	17,530,000	271	702	Colombo and Sri Jayawardenapura	A
†Sudan	As-Sūdān	2,505,813	967,500	27,630,000	11	29	Al-Kharṭūm (Khartoum)	A
†Suriname	Suriname	163,820	63,251	405,000	2.5	6.4	Paramaribo	A
†Swaziland	Swaziland	17,364	6,704	875,000	50	131	Mbabane and Lobamba	A
†Sweden	Sverige	449,964	173,732	8,581,000	19	49	Stockholm	A
Switzerland	Schweiz (German) / Suisse (French) / Svizzera (Italian)	41,293	15,943	6,804,000	165	427	Bern (Berne)	A
†Syria	Sūrīyah	185,180	71,498	13,210,000	71	185	Dimashq (Damascus)	A
Szechwan, China	Sichuan	570,000	220,078	114,970,000	202	522	Chengdu	D
Taiwan	T'aiwan	36,002	13,900	20,785,000	577	1,495	T'aipei	A
Tajikistan	Tajikistan	143,100	55,251	5,210,000	36	94	Dušanbe	A
†Tanzania	Tanzania	945,087	364,900	27,325,000	29	75	Dar es Salaam and Dodoma(5)	A
Tasmania, Austl.	Tasmania	67,800	26,178	463,000	6.8	18	Hobart	D
Tennessee, U.S.	Tennessee	109,158	42,146	4,959,000	45	118	Nashville	D
Texas, U.S.	Texas	695,676	268,601	17,355,000	25	65	Austin	D
†Thailand	Prathet Thai	513,115	198,115	57,200,000	111	289	Krung Thep (Bangkok)	A
Tibet, China	Xizang	1,220,000	471,045	2,245,000	1.8	4.8	Lhasa	D
Tientsin, China	Tianjin	11,300	4,363	9,100,000	805	2,086	Tianjin (Tientsin)	D
†Togo	Togo	56,785	21,925	3,880,000	68	177	Lomé	A
Tokelau (N.Z.)	Tokelau	12	4.6	1,700	142	370	. . .	C
Tonga	Tonga	750	290	103,000	137	355	Nukuʻalofa	A
Transkei(2)	Transkei	43,553	16,816	4,200,000	96	250	Umtata	B(S. Afr.)
†Trinidad and Tobago	Trinidad and Tobago	5,128	1,980	1,293,000	252	653	Port of Spain	A
Tsinghai, China	Qinghai	720,000	277,994	4,725,000	6.6	17	Xining	D
†Tunisia	Tunisie (French) / Tunis (Arabic)	163,610	63,170	8,367,000	51	132	Tunis	A
†Turkey	Türkiye	779,452	300,948	58,850,000	76	196	Ankara	A
Turkmenistan	Turkmenistan	488,100	188,456	3,615,000	7.4	19	Aščhabad (Ashgabat)	A
Turks and Caicos Islands (U.K.)	Turks and Caicos Islands	500	193	12,000	24	62	Grand Turk	C
Tuvalu	Tuvalu	26	10	9,000	346	900	Funafuti	A
†Uganda	Uganda	241,139	93,104	18,485,000	77	199	Kampala	A
†Ukraine	Ukrayina	603,700	233,090	52,800,000	87	227	Kijev (Kiev)	A
†United Arab Emirates	Al-Imārāt al-ʻArabīyah al-Muttaḥidah	83,600	32,278	2,459,000	29	76	Abū Ẓaby (Abu Dhabi)	A
†United Kingdom	United Kingdom	244,100	94,248	57,630,000	236	611	London	A
†United States	United States	9,809,431	3,787,425	253,510,000	26	67	Washington	A
†Uruguay	Uruguay	177,414	68,500	3,130,000	18	46	Montevideo	A
Utah, U.S.	Utah	219,902	84,904	1,757,000	8.0	21	Salt Lake City	D
Uzbekistan	Ŭzbekiston	447,400	172,742	20,325,000	45	118	Taškent (Toshkent)	A
†Vanuatu	Vanuatu	12,190	4,707	153,000	13	33	Port Vila	A
Vatican City	Città del Vaticano	0.4	0.2	800	2,000	4,000	Città del Vaticano (Vatican City)	A
Venda(2)	Venda	6,198	2,393	925,000	149	387	Thohoyandou	B(S. Afr.)
†Venezuela	Venezuela	912,050	352,145	20,430,000	22	58	Caracas	A
Vermont, U.S.	Vermont	24,903	9,615	583,000	23	61	Montpelier	D
Victoria, Austl.	Victoria	227,600	87,877	4,455,000	20	51	Melbourne	D
†Vietnam	Viet Nam	331,689	128,066	68,310,000	206	533	Ha Noi	A
Virginia, U.S.	Virginia	110,771	42,769	6,333,000	57	148	Richmond	D
Virgin Islands (U.S.)	Virgin Islands	344	133	103,000	299	774	Charlotte Amalie	C
Wake Island (U.S.)	Wake Island	7.8	3.0	200	26	67	. . .	C
Wales, U.K.	Wales	20,768	8,019	2,894,000	139	361	Cardiff	D
Wallis and Futuna (Fr.)	Wallis et Futuna	255	98	17,000	67	173	Mata-Utu	C
Washington, U.S.	Washington	184,674	71,303	4,984,000	27	70	Olympia	D
Western Australia, Austl.	Western Australia	2,525,500	975,101	1,672,000	0.7	1.7	Perth	D
Western Sahara	. . .	266,000	102,703	200,000	0.8	1.9	El Aaiún (Laayone)	. . .
†Western Samoa	Western Samoa (English) / Samoa i Sisifo (Samoan)	2,831	1,093	192,000	68	176	Apia	A
West Virginia, U.S.	West Virginia	62,759	24,231	1,775,000	28	73	Charleston	D
Wisconsin, U.S.	Wisconsin	169,653	65,503	4,964,000	29	76	Madison	D
Wyoming, U.S.	Wyoming	253,349	97,818	448,000	1.8	4.6	Cheyenne	D
†Yemen	Al-Yaman	531,869	205,356	11,825,000	22	58	Ṣanʻāʼ	A
†Yugoslavia	Jugoslavija	102,173	39,449	10,622,000	104	269	Beograd (Belgrade)	A
Yukon Territory, Can.	Yukon Territory	483,450	186,661	26,000	0.1	0.1	Whitehorse	D
Yunnan, China	Yunnan	394,000	152,124	38,875,000	99	256	Kunming	D
†Zaire	Zaïre	2,345,095	905,446	38,475,000	16	42	Kinshasa	A
†Zambia	Zambia	752,614	290,586	8,201,000	11	28	Lusaka	A
†Zimbabwe	Zimbabwe	390,759	150,873	9,748,000	25	65	Harare (Salisbury)	A
WORLD	. . .	150,100,000	57,900,000	5,491,000,000	37	95	. . .	. . .

† Member of the United Nations (1991).
. . . None, or not applicable.
(1) No permanent population.
(2) Bophuthatswana, Ciskei, Transkei, and Venda are not recognized by the United Nations.
(3) Claimed by Argentina.
(4) Includes West Bank, Golan Heights, and Gaza Strip.
(5) Future capital.
(6) Claimed by Comoros.
(7) Comprises Ceuta, Melilla, and several small islands.

† Mitglied der Vereinten Nationen (1991).
. . . Kein(e), oder nicht anwendbar.
(1) Bevölkerungszahl schwankend.
(2) Bophuthatswana, Ciskei, Transkei und Venda von Vereinten Nationen nicht anerkannt.
(3) Von Argentinien beansprucht.
(4) Westufer, Golan-Höhen und Gazastreifen einbegriffen.
(5) Zukünftige Hauptstadt.
(6) Von Komoren beansprucht.
(7) Umfasst Ceuta, Melilla und mehrere kleine Inseln.

† Miembro de las Naciones Unidas (1991).
. . . Ninguno, o no se aplica.
(1) Sin población permanente.
(2) Bophuthatswana, Ciskei, Transkei y Venda no reconocido por las Naciones Unidas.
(3) Reclamado por la Argentina.
(4) Incluye la ribera oeste, las alturas de Golán y la franja de Gaza.
(5) Capital futura.
(6) Reclamado por las Comores.
(7) Comprende Ceuta, Melilla y various islas pequeñas.

† Membre des Nations Unies (1991).
. . . Pas d'information, ou pas applicable.
(1) Pas de population permanente.
(2) Bophuthatswana, Ciskei, Transkei et Venda non reconnaissent pas les Nations Unies.
(3) Revendiqué par l'Argentine.
(4) Y compris Cisjordanie, hauteurs de Golan et la bande de Gaza.
(5) Capitale future.
(6) Revendiqué par les Comores.
(7) Inclus Ceuta, Melilla et plusieurs petites îles.

† Membro das Nações Unidas (1991).
. . . Inexistente ou não aplicável.
(1) Sem população permanente.
(2) Bophuthatswana, Ciskei, Transkei e Venda não son reconhecido pelas Nações Unidas.
(3) Reivindicado pela Argentina.
(4) Incluindo a margem oeste, as colinas de Golan e a faixa de Gaza.
(5) Capital futuro.
(6) Reivindicado pelas Comores.
(7) Compreende Ceuta, Melilla e várias ilhas pequenas.

THIS TABLE lists the major metropolitan areas of the world according to their estimated population on January 1, 1992. For convenience in reference, the areas are grouped by major region with the total for each region given. The number of areas by population classification is given in parentheses with each size group.

For ease of comparison, each metropolitan area has been defined by Rand McNally according to consistent rules. A metropolitan area includes a central city, neighboring communities linked to it by continuous built-up areas, and more distant communities if the bulk of their population is supported by commuters to the central city. Some metropolitan areas have more than one central city; in such cases each central city is listed.

IN DIESER TABELLE sind die Hauptmetropolen der Welt verzeichnet, gemessen nach ihrer Bevölkerung, die nach dem Stand vom 1. Januar 1992 geschätzt wurde. Zur besseren Übersicht sind die Zonen nach grösseren Regionen gruppiert, wobei die Gesamtzahl für jede Region angegeben ist. Die Anzahl der Zonen ist nach Bevölkerung klassifiziert und in Klammern hinter denen nach Grössen sortierten Gruppen angegeben.

Zum einfacheren Vergleich ist jede Metropole von Rand McNally nach übereinstimmenden Massstäben definiert worden. Eine Metropole schliesst eine zentrale Stadt mit benachbarten Gemeinden, die mit ihr durch ununterbrochen bebaute Gebiete verbunden sind ein, sowie weiter entfernte Gemeinden, wenn der grösste Teil ihrer Bevölkerung von den Pendlern unterhalten wird. Einige Metropolen haben mehr als eine zentrale Stadt; in solchen Fällen ist jede dieser zentralen Städte angeführt.

ESTA TABLA indica las principales áreas metropolitanas del mundo, de acuerdo con su población calculada al 1 de enero de 1992. Para facilitar las referencias, las áreas se han agrupado por regiones principales, indicándose el total para cada región. El número de áreas, clasificadas por población, se indica entre paréntesis en los grupos de cada tamaño.

Para facilitar las comparaciones, Rand McNally ha definido cada área metropolitana de acuerdo con reglas consistentes. Un área metropolitana incluye una ciudad central, localidades vecinas vinculadas con ella mediante sectores construídos y contínuos, y localidades más distantes, si el grueso de su población lo constituye un núcleo que diariamente viaja a la ciudad central. Algunas áreas metropolitanas incluyen más de una ciudad central; en tales casos se indica cada una dichas ciudades.

CETTE TABLE contient la liste des aires métropolitaines les plus considérables dans le monde pour ce qui est du peuplement a la date du 1 er janvier 1992. Afin de faciliter la consultation, on a groupé les aires par grandes régions en indiquant la population totale pour chaque région, et, entre parenthéses, le nombre d'aires comprises dans celle-ci.

Afin de rendre plus faciles les comparaisons, Rand McNally a défini chaque aire métropolitaine selorègles cohérentes: une aire métropolitaine englobe une citè centrale ou métropole et l'environnement urbain continu qui s'y rattache; elle inclut également des agglomérations éloignées de la métropole lorsque la population de ces dernières est pour sa májorité constituée d'habitants se rendant quotidiennement dans la cité ou est situé le lieu de travail de ceux-ci. On trouvera quelques aires métropolitaines pourvues de plus d'une métropole. Dans ce cas, chaque métropole est mentionnée.

A TABELA que se segúe relaciona as principais áreas metropolitanas do mundo, de acordo com as respectivas populações, estimadas para 1 de janeiro de 1992. Para facilidade de referência, as áreas metropolitanas foram agrupadas dentro das regiões maiores, indicando-se, entre parênteses, os totais de cada região maior e o número de áreas metropolitanas, classificadas segundo a população, compreendidas em cada uma.

Para fins de comparabilidade, Rand McNally definiu cada área metropolitana de acordo com regras uniformes. Uma área metropolitana inclui uma cidade central, as localidades vizinhas ligadas a ela por áreas construídas contínuas, e as localidades mais distantes, desde que a maior parte de suas respectivas populações dependa economicamente da cidade central e que para ela viaje diariamente. Algumas áreas metropolitanas incluem mais de uma cidade central; em tais casos, indicam-se ambas as cidades.

CLASSIFICATION KLASSIFIZIERT CLASIFICADAS CLASSIFICATION CLASSIFICAÇÃO	ANGLO-AMERICA ANGLO-AMERIKA AMÉRICA ANGLOSAJONA AMÉRIQUE ANGLO-SAXONNE AMÉRICA ANGLO-SAXÔNICA	LATIN AMERICA LATEIN-AMERIKA AMÉRICA LATINA AMÉRIQUE LATINE AMÉRICA LATINA	WESTERN EUROPE WESTEUROPA EUROPA OCCIDENTAL EUROPE OCCIDENTALE EUROPA OCIDENTALE	EASTERN EUROPE-RUSSIA OSTEUROPA-RUSSLAND EUROPA ORIENTAL-RUSIA EUROPE ORIENTALE-RUSSIE EUROPA ORIENTAL-RÚSSIA	WEST ASIA WESTASIEN ASIA OCCIDENTAL ASIE OCCIDENTALE ÁSIA OCIDENTAL	EAST ASIA OSTASIEN ASIA ORIENTAL ASIE ORIENTALE ÁSIA ORIENTAL	AFRICA-OCEANIA AFRIKA-OZEANIEN AFRICA-OCEANÍA AFRIQUE-OCÉANIE ÁFRICA-OCEANIA
Over 15,000,000 (6)	New York	Ciudad de México (Mexico City) São Paulo				Ōsaka-Kōbe-Kyōto Sŏul (Seoul) Tōkyō-Yokohama	
10,000,000-15,000,000 (13)	Los Angeles	Buenos Aires Rio de Janeiro	London Paris	Moskva (Moscow)	Bombay Calcutta Delhi-New Delhi	Jakarta Manila Shanghai	Al-Qāhirah (Cairo)
5,000,000-10,000,000 (19)	Chicago Philadelphia-Trenton-Wilmington San Francisco-Oakland-San Jose	Lima Santa Fe de Bogotá Santiago	Essen-Dortmund-Duisburg (Ruhr Area)	Sankt-Peterburg (St. Petersburg)	Dhaka (Dacca) İstanbul Karāchi Madras Tehrān	Beijing (Peking) Krung Thep (Bangkok) Nagoya T'aipei Tianjin (Tientsin) Victoria (Hong Kong)	
3,000,000-5,000,000 (41)	Boston Dallas-Fort Worth Detroit-Windsor Houston Miami-Fort Lauderdale Montréal San Diego-Tijuana Toronto Washington	Belo Horizonte Caracas Guadalajara Porto Alegre Recife	Barcelona Berlin Madrid Milano (Milan) Napoli (Naples) Roma (Rome)	Athínai (Athens) Kijev (Kiev)	Ahmadābād Baghdād Bangalore Hyderābād Lahore	Guangzhou (Canton) Pusan Shenyang (Mukden) Singapore Thanh Pho Ho Chi Minh (Saigon) Wuhan Yangon (Rangoon)	Al-Iskandarīyah (Alexandria) Casablanca Johannesburg Kinshasa Lagos Melbourne Sydney
2,000,000-3,000,000 (55)	Atlanta Baltimore Cleveland Minneapolis-St. Paul Phoenix Pittsburgh St. Louis Seattle-Tacoma	Fortaleza La Habana (Havana) Medellín Monterrey Salvador San Juan Santo Domingo	Birmingham Bruxelles (Brussels) Frankfurt am Main Hamburg Lisboa (Lisbon) Manchester Stuttgart Wien (Vienna)	București (Bucharest) Budapest Char'kov (Kharkov) Doneck-Makejevka Katowice-Bytom-Gliwice Nižnij Novgorod (Gorkiy) Warszawa (Warsaw)	Ankara Baku Colombo Dimashq (Damascus) Kānpur Pune (Poona) Taškent	Bandung Changchun Chengdu (Chengtu) Chongqing (Chungking) Dalian (Dairen) Harbin Kuala Lumpur Nanjing (Nanking) P'yongyang Sapporo-Otaru Surabaya Taegu Xi'an (Sian)	Abidjan Al-Kharṭūm-Umm Durmān (Khartoum-Omdurman) Cape Town Durban El Djazaïr (Algiers)
1,500,000-2,000,000 (50)	Cincinnati Denver Vancouver	Brasília Cali Curitiba Guatemala Guayaquil Montevideo	Amsterdam Glasgow København (Copenhagen) Köln (Cologne) Leeds-Bradford Liverpool Mannheim München (Munich) Stockholm Torino (Turin)	Beograd (Belgrade) Dnepropetrovsk Jekaterinburg (Sverdlovsk) Minsk Novosibirsk	ʿAmman Ar-Riyad (Riyadh) Bayrūt (Beirut) Chittagong İzmir Jaipur Jiddah Kābol (Kabul) Lucknow Mashhad Nāgpur Rāwalpindi-Islāmābād Surat Tel Aviv-Yafo	Fukuoka Hiroshima-Kure Jinan (Tsinan) Kaohsiung Kitakyūshū-Shimonoseki Medan Qingdao (Tsingtao) Taiyuan	Accra Adis Abeba Dakar Nairobi
1,000,000-1,500,000 (116)	Buffalo-Niagara Falls-St. Catharines Columbus El Paso-Ciudad Juárez Hartford-New Britain Indianapolis Kansas City Milwaukee New Orleans Norfolk-Newport News Portland Riverside-San Bernardino Sacramento St. Petersburg-Clearwater San Antonio	Barranquilla Belém Campinas Córdoba Goiânia La Paz Manaus Maracaibo Puebla Quito Rosario San José Santos Valencia	Antwerpen (Antwerp) Dublin (Baile Átha Cliath) Düsseldorf Hannover Helsinki Lille-Roubaix Lyon Marseille Newcastle-Sunderland Nürnberg Porto Rotterdam Sevilla Valencia	Čel'abinsk (Chelyabinsk) Łódź Kazan' Krasnojarsk Odessa Omsk Perm Praha (Prague) Rīga Rostov-na-Donu Samara (Kuybyshev) Saratov Sofija (Sofia) Ufa Volgograd	Al-Kuwayt (Kuwait) Alma-Ata Asansol Bhopāl Cochin Coimbatore Esfahān Faisalabad Ḥalab (Aleppo) Indore Jerevan Ludhiāna Madurai Patna Shīrāz Tabrīz Tbilisi Vadodara Vārānasi (Benares) Vishākhapatnam	Anshan Baotou Benxi Changsha Fushun Guiyang Hangzhou Ha Noi Jilin (Kirin) Kunming Kwangju Lanzhou Nanchang Palembang Qiqihar (Tsitsihar) Semarang Sendai Shijiazhuang Shizuoka-Shimizu Taejŏn Tangshan Ürümqi Xuzhou Zhengzhou Zibo	Adelaide Brisbane Dar es Salaam Douala Harare Ibadan Kampala Luanda Maputo Perth Pretoria Rabat-Salé Ṭarābulus (Tripoli) Tunis
Total/Gesamtzahl Total/Total/Total (300)	39	39	41	31	54	65	31

ALL URBAN CENTERS of 50,000 or more population and many other important or well-known cities and towns are listed in the following table. The populations are from recent censuses (designated C) or official estimates (designated E) for the dates specified. For a few cities, only unofficial estimates are available (designated U). For comparison, the total population of each country is also given. For each country, the date stated for the total population also applies to the cities, except those for which another date is specified.

Population estimates for 1992 for countries may be found in the World Information Table.

A population figure in parentheses and preceded by a star (★) is the population of a city's entire metropolitan area. To permit meaningful comparisons of metropolitan areas, these have been defined by Rand McNally according to consistent rules (see introduction to Metropolitan Areas Table), and in some cases may differ somewhat from the officially recognized metropolitan areas. Where a town is located within the metropolitan area of another city, that city's name is given in parentheses preceded by a star (★). The capital of a country is denoted by CAPITAL letters.

ALLE STÄDTISCHEN ZENTREN mit 50 000 oder mehr Einwohnern und zahlreiche andere bedeutende oder bekannte Städte sind in der folgenden Tabelle zusammengestellt. Die Bevölkerungszahlen stammen von neuesten Zählungen (mit C gekennzeichnet) oder amtlichen Schätzungen (E) zu den angegebenen Zeitpunkten. Für einige wenige Städte waren lediglich inoffizielle Schätzungen erhältlich (U). Zu Vergleichszwecken ist ferner die Gesamtbevölkerung jedes Landes angegeben. Das Bezugsjahr für die Einwohnerzahl eines Landes betrifft auch die Städte mit Ausnahme jener, bei denen ein anderes Datum angegeben ist.

Schätzungen der Bevölkerungszahlen der Länder für 1992 finden sich in der Welt-Informationstabelle.

Bevölkerungszahlen in Klammern mit vorangestelltem Stern (★) beziehen sich auf die gesamte Stadtregion einer Stadt. Um sinnvolle Vergleiche von Stadtregionen zu ermöglichen, wurden diese von Rand McNally nach einheitlichen Regeln festgelegt (siehe Einleitung: Tabelle der Stadtregionen), weshalb sie in einigen Fällen etwas von der offiziellen Abgrenzung von Stadtregionen abweichen können. Ist eine Stadt in die Stadtregion einer anderen Grossstadt einbezogen, so wird der Name der Stadtregion mit vorangestelltem Stern (★) in Klammern aufgeführt. Die Hauptstadt eines Landes wird durch GROSSBUCHSTABEN hervorgehoben.

TODAS LOS CENTROS URBANOS de 50 000 habitantes o más y muchos otros de importancia así como bien conocidas ciudades y pueblos están incluídos en la tabla que se presenta a continuación. El número de habitantes indicados está tomado del censo más reciente (cifras identificadas con la letra C) o estimados oficiales (E) para las fechas especificadas. Para algunas ciudades, sólo existen informes no oficiales (U). Para medida de comparación, la población total de cada país se encuentra incluída también.

Para permitir una comparación, se da la población total de cada país, referente al mismo año que se usa para las ciudades principles, excepto para aquellas en las que se especifica otra fecha. El número de habitantes para 1992 para los países, se encuentra en la Tabla de Información Mundial.

La segunda cifra para la población que aparece en paréntesis y está precedida por una estrella (★) constituye la población de un área metropolitana entera. Para permitir comparaciones validas de áreas metropolitanas, éstas fueron definidas por Rand McNally siguiendo las reglas establecidas para estos propósitos (véase la Introducción a la Tabla de las Areas Metropolitanas), y en algunas ocasiones pueden ser un poco distintas de las áreas metropolitanas oficialmente reconocidas. Cuando una población se encuentra dentro de los límites de un área metropolitana de otra ciudad, el nombre de ésta se da entre paréntesis precedido por una (★). La capital de un país se indica con letras MAYÚSCULAS.

TOUTES LES VILLES de plus de 50 000 habitants et des villes moins peuplées, mais cèlèbres ou importantes, sont mentionnées dans la table ci-dessous. Les chiffres donnant la population proviennent de recensements récents (référence C), ou d'estimations officielles (référence E), aux dates indiquées. Pour quelques villes, on dispose seulement d'estimations non officielles (référence U). La population totale de chaque pays est également donnée, ce qui permet des comparaisons. Dans chaque pays, la date des renseignements est identique pour les villes et le pays, sauf indication contraire.

On trouvera dans la table d'informations mondiales les estimations de la population en 1992 pour chaque pays.

Les chiffres entre parenthèses, précédés d'une étoile (★), indiquent la population de l'ensemble de la zone métropolitaine. Pour permettre d'établir des comparaisons significatives entre les zones métropolitaines, ces dernières ont été définies selon des critères uniformes par Rand McNally & Company (voir l'introduction à la table des zones métropolitaines). Parfois, les limites des zones métropolitaines ainsi définies diffèrent des limites officielles. Quand une ville fait partie de la zone métropolitaine d'une autre ville, le nom de celle-ci, précédé d'une étoile (★), est mis entre parenthèses. Le nom des capitales de pays est écrit en lettres MAJUSCULES.

TODOS OS CENTROS URBANOS de 50 000 habitantes e mais, bem como muitas outras cidades e vilas importantes ou muito conhecidas figuram na tabela que se apresenta em sequida. Os dados relativos à população referem-se a censos recentes (identificadas com a letra C), ou a estimativas oficiais (E) nas datas indicadas. Para algumas cidades só existem estimativas não oficiais (U). Para fins de comparabilidade, apresenta-se também a população total de cada país.

Para cada país, a data de referência da população total aplica-se também às cidades exceto quando especificado em contrário. As estimativas da população dos países para 1992 encontra-se na *Tabela de informaçoes mundiais.*

Um dado de população apresentado entre parênteses e precedido por uma estrela (★), refere-se à população de toda a área metropolitana. Para fins de comparabilidade, as áreas metropolitanas foram definidas por Rand McNally segundo regras coerentes (ver a 'Introdução' à *Tabela das áreas metropolitanas),* e em certos casos podem ser um pouco diferentes das áreas metropolitanas oficialmente reconhecidas. Quando um centro urbano esta localizado dentro dos limites da área metropolitana de outro, seu nome figura entre parênteses precedido por uma estrela (★). A capital de um país é indicada por letras MAIÚSCULAS.

AFGHANISTAN / Afghānestān	
1988 E	17,672,000
Herāt	177,300
Jalālābād (1982E)	58,000
• KĀBOL	1,424,400
Kondūz (1982E)	57,000
Mazār-e Sharīf	130,600
Qandahār	225,500
ALBANIA / Shqipëri	
1989 C	3,182,400
Durrës	82,700
Elbasan	80,700
Korçë	63,600
Shkodër	79,900
• TIRANË	238,100
Vlorë	71,700
ALGERIA / Algérie / Djazaïr	
1987 C	23,038,942
Aïn el Beïda	61,997
Aïn Oussera	44,270
Aïn Témouchent	47,479
Annaba (Bône)	305,526
Bab Ezzouar (★El Djazaïr)	55,211
Barika	56,488
Batna	181,601
Béchar	107,311
Bejaïa (Bougie)	114,534
Beskra	128,281
Bordj Bou Arreridj	84,264
Bordj el Kiffan (★El Djazaïr)	61,035
Boufarik	41,305
Bou Saâda	66,688
Ech Cheliff (Orléansville)	129,976
El Boulaïda	170,935
• EL DJAZAÏR (ALGIERS) (★2,547,983)	1,507,241
El Djelfa	84,207
El Eulma	67,933
El Wad	70,073
Ghardaïa	89,415
Ghilizane	80,091
Guelma	77,821
Jijel	62,793
Khemis	55,335
Khenchla	69,743
Laghouat	67,214
Lemdiyya	85,195
Maghniyya	52,275
Messaad	47,460
Mestghanem	114,037
Mouaskar	64,691
M'Sila	65,805
Qacentina	440,842
Saïda	80,825
Sidi bel Abbès	152,778
Skikda	128,747
Souq Ahras	83,015
Stif	170,182
Tbessa	107,559
Tihert	95,821
Tilimsen	126,882
Tizi-Ouzou	61,163
Touggourt	70,645
Wahran	628,558
Wargla	81,721
AMERICAN SAMOA / Amerika Samoa	
1980 C	32,279
• PAGO PAGO	3,075
ANDORRA	
1991 E	54,507
• ANDORRA	20,437
ANGOLA	
1989 E	9,739,100
Benguela (1983E)	155,000
Huambo (Nova Lisboa) (1983E)	203,000
Lobito (1983E)	150,000
• LUANDA	1,459,900
Lubango (1984E)	95,915
Namibe (1981E)	100,000
ANGUILLA	
1984 C	6,680
South Hill	961
• THE VALLEY	1,042
ANTIGUA AND BARBUDA	
1977 E	72,000
• SAINT JOHN'S	24,359
ARGENTINA	
1980 C	27,947,446
Almirante Brown (★Buenos Aires)	331,919
Avellaneda (★Buenos Aires)	334,145
Bahía Blanca	223,818
Berazategui (★Buenos Aires)	201,862
Berisso (★Buenos Aires)	66,152
• BUENOS AIRES (★10,750,000)	2,922,829
Campana (★Buenos Aires)	54,832
Caseros (Tres de Febrero) (★Buenos Aires)	345,424
Comodoro Rivadavia	96,817
Concordia	94,222
Córdoba (★1,070,000)	993,055
Corrientes	180,612
Esteban Echeverría (★Buenos Aires)	188,923
Florencio Varela (★Buenos Aires)	173,452
Formosa	93,603
General San Martín (★Buenos Aires)	385,625
General Sarmiento (San Miguel) (★Buenos Aires)	502,926
Godoy Cruz (★Mendoza)	142,408
Gualeguaychú	51,400
Junín	62,458
Lanús (★Buenos Aires)	466,980
La Plata (★Buenos Aires)	477,175
La Rioja	67,043
Las Heras (★Mendoza)	101,579
Lomas de Zamora (★Buenos Aires)	510,130
Mar del Plata	414,696
Mendoza (★650,000)	119,088
Mercedes	50,992
Merlo (★Buenos Aires)	292,587
Moreno (★Buenos Aires)	194,440
Morón (★Buenos Aires)	598,420
Necochea	51,069
Neuquén	90,089
Olavarría	64,097
Paraná	161,638
Pergamino	68,612
Pilar (★Buenos Aires)	84,429
Posadas	143,889
Presidencia Roque Sáenz Peña	49,341
Punta Alta	56,620
Quilmes (★Buenos Aires)	446,587
Rafaela	53,273
Resistencia	220,104
Río Cuarto	110,254
Rosario (★1,045,000)	938,120
Salta	260,744
San Carlos de Bariloche	48,980
San Fernando (★Buenos Aires)	133,624
San Fernando del Valle de Catamarca (★90,000)	78,799
San Francisco (★58,536)	51,932
San Isidro (★Buenos Aires)	289,170
San Juan (★300,000)	118,046
San Justo (★Buenos Aires)	949,566
San Lorenzo (★Rosario)	96,891
San Luis	70,999
San Miguel de Tucumán (★525,000)	392,888
San Nicolás de los Arroyos	98,495
San Rafael	70,959
San Salvador de Jujuy	124,950
Santa Fe	292,165
Santiago del Estero (★200,000)	148,758
San Vincente (★Buenos Aires)	55,803
Tandil	79,429
Tigre (★Buenos Aires)	206,349
Trelew	52,372
Vicente López (★Buenos Aires)	291,072
Villa Krause (★San Juan)	66,693
Villa María	67,560
Villa Nueva (★Mendoza)	164,670
Zárate	67,143
ARMENIA / Hayastan	
1989 C	3,283,000
Abovjan (1987E)	53,000
Ečmiadzin (★Jerevan) (1987E)	53,000
• JEREVAN (★1,315,000)	1,199,000
Kirovakan (1987E)	169,000
Kumajri	120,000
Razdan (1987E)	56,000
ARUBA	
1987 E	64,763
• ORANJESTAD	19,800
AUSTRALIA	
1989 E	16,833,100
Adelaide (★1,036,747)	12,340
Albury (★66,530)	40,730
Auburn (★Sydney)	49,950
Ballarat (★80,090)	36,680
Bankstown (★Sydney)	158,750
Bayswater (★Perth)	46,426
Bendigo (★67,920)	32,050
Berwick (★Melbourne)	64,100
Blacktown (★Sydney)	210,900
Blue Mountains (★Sydney)	70,800
Box Hill (★Melbourne)	47,700
Brisbane (★1,273,511)	744,828
Broadmeadows (★Melbourne)	105,500
Brunswick (★Melbourne)	41,100
Camberwell (★Melbourne)	87,700
Campbelltown (★Sydney)	139,500
CANBERRA (★271,362) (1986C)	247,194
Canning (★Perth)	69,104
Canterbury (★Sydney)	135,200
Caulfield (★Melbourne)	70,100
Coburg (★Melbourne)	54,500
Cockburn (★Perth)	49,802
Coffs Harbour	47,890
Dandenong (★Melbourne)	59,400
Darwin (★73,300)	63,900
Doncaster (★Melbourne)	107,300
Enfield (★Adelaide)	64,058
Essendon (★Melbourne)	55,300
Fairfield (★Sydney)	176,350
Footscray (★Melbourne)	48,700
Frankston (★Melbourne)	90,500
Geelong (★148,980)	13,190
Gosford	126,600

▲ Population of an entire municipality, commune, or district, including rural area.
• Largest city in country.
★ Population or designation of the metropolitan area, including suburbs.
C Census. E Official estimate. U Unofficial estimate.

▲ Bevölkerung eines ganzen städtischen Verwaltungsgebietes, eines Kommunalbezirkes oder eines Distrikts, einschliesslich ländlicher Gebiete.
• Grösste Stadt des Landes.
★ Bevölkerung oder Bezeichnung der Stadtregion einschliesslich Vororte.
C Volkszählung. E Offizielle Schätzung. U Inoffizielle Schätzung.

▲ Población de un municipio, comuna o distrito entero, incluyendo sus áreas rurales.
• Ciudad más grande de un país.
★ Población o designación de un área metropolitana, incluyendo los suburbios.
C Censo. E Estimado oficial. U Estimado no oficial.

▲ Population d'une municipalité, d'une commune ou d'un district, zone rurale incluse.
• Ville la plus peuplée du pays.
★ Population de l'agglomération (ou nom de la zone métropolitaine englobante).
C Recensement. E Estimation officielle. U Estimation non officielle.

▲ População de um municipio, comuna ou distrito, inclusive as respectivas áreas rurais.
• Maior cidade de um país.
★ População ou indicação de uma área metropolitana.
C Censo. E Estimativa oficial. U Estimativa não oficial.

Gosnells (★Perth)	71,862
Heidelberg (★Melbourne)	63,500
Hobart (★181,210)	47,280
Holroyd (★Sydney)	82,500
Hurstville (★Sydney)	66,350
Ipswich (★Brisbane)	75,283
Keilor (★Melbourne)	103,700
Knox (★Melbourne)	121,300
Kogarah (★Sydney)	47,850
Lake Macquarie (★Newcastle)	161,700
Launceston (★92,350)	32,150
Leichhardt (★Sydney)	58,950
Liverpool (★Sydney)	99,750
Logan (★Brisbane)	142,222
Mackay (★50,885)	22,583
Malvern (★Melbourne)	43,400
Marion (★Adelaide)	74,631
Marrickville (★Sydney)	84,650
Melbourne (★3,039,100)	55,300
Melville (★Perth)	85,590
Mitcham (★Adelaide)	63,301
Moorabbin (★Melbourne)	98,900
Newcastle (★425,610)	130,940
Noarlunga (★Adelaide)	77,352
Northcote (★Melbourne)	49,100
North Sydney (★Sydney)	53,400
Nunawading (★Melbourne)	96,400
Oakleigh (★Melbourne)	57,600
Parramatta (★Sydney)	134,600
Penrith (★Sydney)	152,650
Perth (★1,158,387)	82,413
Prahran (★Melbourne)	43,900
Preston (★Melbourne)	82,000
Randwick (★Sydney)	119,200
Redcliffe (★Brisbane)	48,123
Rockdale (★Sydney)	88,200
Rockhampton (★61,694)	58,890
Ryde (★Sydney)	94,400
Saint Kilda (★Melbourne)	46,400
Salisbury (★Adelaide)	106,129
Shoalhaven	64,070
Southport (★254,861)	135,408
South Sydney (★Sydney)	74,100
Springvale (★Melbourne)	88,700
Stirling (★Perth)	181,556
Sunshine (★Melbourne)	97,700
• Sydney (★3,623,550)	9,800
Tea Tree Gully (★Adelaide)	82,324
Toowoomba	81,071
Townsville (★111,972)	83,339
Wagga Wagga	52,180
Wanneroo (★Perth)	163,324
Waverley (★Melbourne)	126,300
Waverley (★Sydney)	61,850
West Torrens (★Adelaide)	44,711
Willoughby (★Sydney)	53,950
Wollongong (★236,690)	174,770
Woodville (★Adelaide)	82,590
Woollahra (★Sydney)	53,850

AUSTRIA / Österreich

1981 C	7,555,338
Bruck an der Mur (★52,000)	15,068
Graz (★325,000)	243,166
Innsbruck (★185,000)	117,287
Klagenfurt (★115,000)	87,321
Leoben (★52,000)	31,989
Linz (★335,000)	199,910
Neunkirchen (★45,000)	10,764
Salzburg (★220,000)	139,426
Sankt Pölten (★67,000)	50,419
Steyr (★65,000)	38,942
Villach (★65,000)	52,692
Wels (★76,000)	51,060
• WIEN (VIENNA) (★1,875,000) (1988E)	1,482,800

AZERBAIJAN

1991 E	7,136,600
Ali-Bajramly	61,500
• BAKU (★2,020,000)	1,080,500
Gjandža	282,200
Mingečaur	90,900
Nachičevan'	61,700
Šeki (Nucha)	63,200
Stepanakert	55,200
Sumgait (★Baku)	236,200

BAHAMAS

1990 C	254,685
Freeport (▲171,542)	28,200
• NASSAU	141,000

BAHRAIN / Al-Baḥrayn

1981 C	350,798
• AL-MANĀMAH (★224,643)	115,054
Al-Muḥarraq (★Al-Manāmah)	57,688

BANGLADESH

1981 C	87,119,965
Barisāl	172,905
Begamganj	69,623
Bhairab Bāzār	63,563
Bogra	68,749
Brāhmanbāria	87,570
Chāndpur	85,656
Chittagong (★1,391,877)	980,000
Chuādanga	76,000
Comilla	184,132
• DHAKA (DACCA) (★3,430,312)	2,365,695
Dinājpur	96,718
Farīdpur	66,579
Gopālpur	31,725
Gulshan (★Dhaka)	215,444
Jamālpur	91,815
Jessore	148,927
Jhenida	47,953
Khulna	648,359
Kishorganj	52,302
Kurīgrām	47,641
Kushtia	74,892
Mādārīpur	63,917
Mīrpur (★Dhaka)	349,031
Mymensingh	190,991
Naogaon	52,975
Nārāyanganj (★Dhaka)	405,562
Narsinghdi	76,841
Nawābganj	87,724
Noākhāli	59,065
Pābna	109,065
Patuākhāli	48,121
Rājshāhi	253,740
Rangpur	153,174
Saidpur	126,608
Sātkhira	52,156
Sherpur	48,214
Sirājganj	106,774
Sītākunda (★Chittagong)	237,520
Sylhet	168,371
Tangail	77,518
Tongi (★Dhaka)	94,580

BARBADOS

1980 C	244,228
• BRIDGETOWN (★115,000)	7,466

BELARUS

1991 E	10,260,400
Baranoviči	166,700
Bobrujsk	223,000
Borisov	150,200
Brest	277,000
Gomel'	503,300
Grodno	284,800
Lida	95,000
• MINSK (★1,694,000)	1,633,600
Mogil'ov	363,000
Molodečno	93,500
Mozyr'	103,000
Novopolock	96,600
Orša	125,300
Pinsk	123,800
Polock	78,700
Rečica	69,400
Sluck	60,100
Soligorsk	96,000
Vitebsk	361,500
Žlobin	60,800
Žodino	56,000

BELGIUM / België / Belgique

1987 E	9,864,751
Aalst (Alost) (★Bruxelles)	77,113
Anderlecht (★Bruxelles)	88,849
Antwerpen (★1,100,000)	479,748
Bastogne (▲11,699)	6,900
Brugge (Bruges) (★223,000)	117,755
• BRUXELLES (★2,385,000)	136,920
Charleroi (★480,000)	209,395
Etterbeek (★Bruxelles)	44,240
Forest (★Bruxelles)	48,266
Genk (★Hasselt)	61,391
Gent (Gand) (★465,000)	233,856
Hasselt (★290,000)	65,563
Ixelles (★Bruxelles)	76,241
Kortrijk (Courtrai) (★202,000)	76,216
La Louvière (★147,000)	76,340
Leuven (Louvain) (★173,000)	84,583
Liège (Luik) (★750,000)	200,891
Mechelen (Malines) (★121,000)	75,808
Molenbeek-St.-Jean (★Bruxelles)	69,764
Mons (Bergen) (★242,000)	89,697
Mouscron (★Lille, France)	53,713
Namur (★147,000)	102,670
Oostende (Ostende) (★122,000)	68,318
Roeselare (Roulers)	51,963
Saint-Gilles (★Bruxelles)	42,482
Schaerbeek (★Bruxelles)	104,919
Seraing (★Liège)	61,731
Sint-Niklaas (Saint-Nicolas)	68,082
Spa	9,645
Tournai (Doornik) (▲66,998)	44,900
Uccle (★Bruxelles)	75,876
Verviers (★101,000)	53,498
Waterloo (★Bruxelles)	25,232
Woluwe-Saint-Lambert (Sint-Lambrechts-Woluwe) (★Bruxelles)	47,887

BELIZE

1990 C	184,340
• Belize City	43,621
BELMOPAN	5,256

BENIN / Bénin

1984 E	3,825,000
Abomey	53,000
• COTONOU	478,000
Natitingou (1975E)	51,000
Ouidah (1979E)	53,000
Parakou	92,000
PORTO-NOVO	164,000

BERMUDA

1985 E	56,000
• HAMILTON (★15,000)	1,676

BHUTAN / Druk-Yul

1982 E	1,333,000
• THIMPHU	12,000

BOLIVIA

1990 E	7,314,000
Cochabamba	413,300
• LA PAZ	1,125,600
Montero (1988E)	84,100
Oruro	207,700
Potosí	120,100
Santa Cruz de la Sierra	696,100
SUCRE	101,400
Tarija	74,600
Trinidad	51,900

BOPHUTHATSWANA

1987 E	1,819,242
• Ga-Rankuwa (1980C)	48,300
Mafikeng (★16,000) (1980C)	6,500
MMABATHO (★Mafikeng) (1977E)	9,062

BOSNIA AND HERCEGOVINA / Bosna i Hercegovina

1987 E	4,400,464
Banja Luka (▲193,890)	130,900
• SARAJEVO (▲479,688)	341,200
Tuzla (▲129,967)	67,300
Zenica (▲144,869)	67,500

BOTSWANA

1991 C	1,325,291
Francistown	65,026
• GABORONE	133,791
Selebi Phikwe	39,769

BRAZIL / Brasil

1985 E	135,564,395
Alagoinhas (▲116,959)	87,500
Alegrete (▲71,898)	56,700
Alvorada (★Porto Alegre) (1989E)	115,465
Americana	156,030
Anápolis	225,840
Apucarana (▲92,812)	73,700
Aracaju	360,013
Araçatuba	129,304
Araguari (▲96,035)	84,300
Arapiraca (▲147,879)	91,400
Araraquara (▲145,042)	87,500
Araras (▲71,652)	59,900
Araxá	61,418
Assis (▲74,238)	63,100
Atibaia (▲81,263) (1989E)	64,200
Bacabal (▲97,633) (1989E)	51,600
Bagé (▲106,155)	70,800
Barbacena (▲99,337)	80,200
Barra do Piraí (▲78,189)	55,700
Barra Mansa (★Volta Redonda)	149,200
Barretos	80,202
Bauru	220,105
Bayeux (★João Pessoa)	67,182
Belém (★1,295,000) (1989E)	1,190,017
Belford Roxo (★Rio de Janeiro)	340,700
Belo Horizonte (★3,340,000) (1989E)	2,339,039
Betim (★Belo Horizonte)	96,810
Birigui (▲71,527) (1989E)	63,660
Blumenau	192,074
Boa Vista (▲74,493) (1989E)	48,700
Botucatu (▲71,139)	62,600
Bragança Paulista (▲105,099)	76,300
BRASÍLIA (1989E)	1,803,478
Cabo (▲134,748) (1989E)	62,000
Caçapava (▲64,213)	56,600
Cáceres (▲92,370) (1989E)	51,700
Cachoeira do Sul (▲91,492)	58,900
Cachoeirinha (★Porto Alegre)	73,117
Cachoeiro de Itapemirim (▲138,156)	95,000
Campina Grande	279,929
Campinas (★1,290,000) (1989E)	946,035
Campo Grande	384,398
Campos (▲366,716)	187,900
Campos Elisios (★Rio de Janeiro)	188,200
Canoas (★Porto Alegre)	261,222
Carapicuíba (★São Paulo)	265,856
Carazinho (▲62,108)	48,500
Cariacica (★Vitória)	74,300
Carpina (▲71,753) (1989E)	48,000
Caruaru (▲190,794)	152,100
Cascavel (▲200,485)	123,100
Castanhal (▲89,703)	71,200
Cataguases (▲62,080) (1989E)	50,900
Catanduva (▲80,309)	71,400
Caucaia (★Fortaleza)	78,500
Cavaleiro (★Recife)	106,600
Caxias (▲148,230)	66,300
Caxias do Sul	266,809
Chapecó (▲100,997)	64,200
Coelho da Rocha (★Rio de Janeiro)	164,400
Colatina (▲106,260)	58,600
Colombo (★Curitiba)	65,900
Conselheiro Lafaiete	77,958
Contagem (★Belo Horizonte)	152,700
Corumbá (▲80,666)	65,800
Crato (▲86,371)	52,700
Criciúma (▲128,410)	85,900
Cruz Alta (▲71,817)	58,300
Cruzeiro	63,918
Cubatão (★Santos)	98,322
Cuiabá (▲1,815,000) (1989E)	1,390,967
Curitiba (★1,700,000)	1,279,205
Diadema (★São Paulo)	320,187
Divinópolis	139,940
Dourados (▲123,757)	89,200
Duque de Caxias (★Rio de Janeiro)	353,200
Embu (★São Paulo)	119,791
Erechim (▲70,709)	54,300
Esteio (★Porto Alegre)	58,964
Feira de Santana (▲355,201)	278,600
Ferraz de Vasconcelos (★São Paulo)	68,831
Florianópolis (★365,000)	178,400
Fortaleza (★2,040,000) (1989E)	1,763,546
Foz do Iguaçu (▲182,101)	124,900
Franca	182,820
Garanhuns	73,100
Goiânia (★1,130,000) (1989E)	6,038,187
Governador Valadares (▲216,957)	192,300
Guaratinguetá (▲93,534)	80,400
Guarujá (★Santos)	83,500
Guarulhos (★São Paulo)	571,700
Ijuí (▲82,064)	64,400
Ilhéus (▲145,810)	79,400
Imperatriz (▲235,453)	119,500
Ipatinga (★270,000)	149,100
Ipiíba (★Rio de Janeiro)	116,200
Itabira (▲81,771)	66,300
Itabuna (▲167,543)	142,200
Itajaí	104,232
Itajubá (▲69,675)	61,500
Itapecerica da Serra (★São Paulo)	65,500
Itapetininga (▲105,512)	76,700
Itapeva (▲92,122) (1989E)	51,400
Itapevi (★São Paulo)	66,825
Itaquaquecetuba (★São Paulo)	91,366
Itaquari (★Vitória)	163,900
Itatiba (▲58,508) (1989E)	49,700
Itaúna	61,446
Itú (▲92,786)	77,900
Ituiutaba (▲85,365)	74,900
Itumbiara (▲78,844)	57,200
Jaboatão (★Recife)	82,900
Jaboatão (★Recife) (1989E)	94,000
Jacareí	149,061
Jataí (▲65,383) (1989E)	49,700
Jaú (▲92,547)	74,500
Jequié (▲127,070)	92,100
João Monlevade (1989E)	60,731
João Pessoa (★550,000)	348,500
Joinvile	302,877
Juàzeiro (★Petrolina)	78,600
Juazeiro do Norte	159,806
Juiz de Fora	349,720
Jundiaí (▲313,652)	268,900
Lajes (▲143,246)	103,600
Lavras	52,100
Leme (▲65,006) (1989E)	55,900
Limeira	186,986
Linhares (▲122,453)	53,400
Lins (▲59,479) (1989E)	51,700
Londrina (▲346,676)	296,400
Lorena	63,230
Luziânia (▲98,408)	71,400
Macapá (▲168,839)	109,400
Maceió	482,195
Majé (▲225,398) (1989E)	49,600
Manaus (1989E)	1,089,962
Marabá (▲133,559)	92,700
Marília (▲136,187)	116,100
Maringá	196,871
Mauá (★São Paulo)	269,321
Mesquita (★Rio de Janeiro)	161,300
Mogi das Cruzes (▲255,636) (★ São Paulo) (1989E)	155,900
Mojiguaçu (▲91,994)	81,800
Mojimirim (▲63,313)	52,300
Monjolo (★Rio de Janeiro)	113,900
Montes Claros (▲214,472)	183,500
Mossoró (▲158,723)	128,300
Muriaé (▲80,466)	57,600
Muribeca dos Guararapes (★Recife) (1989E)	196,000
Natal	510,106
Neves (★Rio de Janeiro)	163,600
Nilópolis (★Rio de Janeiro)	112,800
Niterói (★Rio de Janeiro)	441,684
Nova Friburgo (▲143,529)	103,500
Nova Iguaçu (★Rio de Janeiro)	592,800
Novo Hamburgo (★Porto Alegre)	167,744
Olinda (★Recife)	316,600
Osasco (★São Paulo)	591,568
Ourinhos (▲65,841)	58,100
Paranaguá (▲94,809)	82,300
Paranavaí (▲75,511)	60,900
Parnaíba (▲116,206)	90,200
Parque Industrial (★Belo Horizonte)	228,400
Passo Fundo (▲137,843)	117,500
Passos (▲79,393)	65,500
Patos	74,298
Patos de Minas (▲99,027)	69,000
Paulo Afonso (▲86,182)	75,300
Pelotas (▲277,730)	210,300
Petrolina (★225,000)	92,100
Petrópolis (▲284,535) (★ Rio de Janeiro) (1989E)	173,600
Pindamonhangaba (▲86,990)	64,100
Pinheirinho (★Curitiba)	51,600
Piracicaba (▲252,079)	211,000
Poá (★São Paulo)	66,006
Poços de Caldas	100,004
Ponta Grossa	223,154
Porto Alegre (★2,850,000) (1989E)	1,371,313
Porto Velho (▲202,011)	152,700
Pouso Alegre (▲65,958)	58,300
Praia Grande (★Santos)	67,800
Presidente Prudente	155,883
Queimados (★Rio de Janeiro)	113,700
Recife (★2,880,000) (1989E)	1,352,024
Ribeirão Preto	383,125
Rio Branco (▲145,486)	109,800
Rio Claro	129,859
Rio de Janeiro (★11,050,000) (1989E)	6,011,181
Rio do Sul (1989E)	48,860
Rio Grande	164,221
Rio Verde (▲92,954)	59,400
Rondonópolis (▲101,642)	65,500
Salto (1989E)	59,561
Salvador (★2,275,000) (1989E)	2,000,387
Santa Bárbara d'Oeste	95,818
Santa Cruz do Sul (▲115,288)	60,300
Santa Maria (▲196,827)	163,900
Santana do Livramento (▲70,489)	60,100
Santarém (▲226,618)	120,800
Santa Rita (★João Pessoa)	60,100
Santa Rosa (▲66,925) (1989E)	51,500
Santo André (★São Paulo)	635,129
Santo Ângelo (▲107,559)	57,700
Santos (★1,165,000) (1989E)	483,314
São Bernardo do Campo (★São Paulo)	562,485
São Borja (▲71,317) (1989E)	50,600
São Caetano do Sul (★São Paulo)	171,005
São Carlos	140,383
São Gonçalo (★Rio de Janeiro)	262,400
São João da Boa Vista (▲61,653)	50,400
São João del-Rei (▲74,385)	61,400
São João de Meriti (★Rio de Janeiro)	241,700
São José do Rio Preto	229,221
São José dos Campos	372,578
São José dos Pinhais (★Curitiba)	64,100
São Leopoldo (★Porto Alegre)	114,065
São Lourenco da Mata (★Recife)	65,936
São Luís (★600,000)	227,900
• São Paulo (★16,925,000) (1989E)	10,997,473
São Vicente (★Santos)	239,778
Sapucaia do Sul (★Porto Alegre)	91,820
Sertãozinho (▲72,441) (1989E)	60,100
Sete Lagoas	121,418
Sete Pontes (★Rio de Janeiro)	72,300
Sobral (▲112,275)	69,400
Sorocaba	327,468
Susano (★São Paulo)	128,924
Taboão da Serra (★São Paulo)	122,112
Tatuí (▲69,358)	56,000
Taubaté	205,120
Teófilo Otoni (▲126,265)	82,700
Teresina (★525,000)	425,300
Teresópolis (▲115,859)	92,600
Timon (★Teresina)	68,300
Três Rios (▲93,902) (1989E)	61,900
Tubarão (▲82,082)	70,400
Tupã (▲65,867) (1989E)	51,400

▲ Population of an entire municipality, commune, or district, including rural area.
• Largest city in country.
★ Population or designation of the metropolitan area, including suburbs.
C Census. **E** Official estimate. **U** Unofficial estimate.

▲ Bevölkerung eines ganzen städtischen Verwaltungsgebietes, eines Kommunalbezirkes oder eines Distrikts, einschliesslich ländlicher Gebiete.
• Grösste Stadt des Landes.
★ Bevölkerung oder Bezeichnung der Stadtregion einschliesslich Vororte.
C Volkszählung. **E** Offizielle Schätzung. **U** Inoffizielle Schätzung.

Ubá (▲67,166) (1989E)	53,700
Uberaba	244,875
Uberlândia	312,024
Uruguaiana (▲105,862)	91,500
Varginha	74,630
Várzea Grande (▲124,188) (1989E)	64,600
Vicente de Carvalho (★Santos)	102,700
Vila Velha (★Vitória)	91,900
Vitória (★735,000)	201,500
Vitória da Conquista (▲198,150)	145,800
Vitória de Santo Antão (▲100,450)	67,800
Volta Redonda (★375,000)	219,267

BRITISH VIRGIN ISLANDS

1980 C	12,034
• ROAD TOWN	2,479

BRUNEI

1981 C	192,832
• BANDAR SERI BEGAWAN (★64,000)	22,777
Seria	23,415

BULGARIA / Bâlgarija

1989 E	8,986,636
Asenovgrad	
Blagoevgrad	74,236
Burgas	200,464
Dimitrovgrad	57,102
Dobrič	112,582
Gabrovo	80,930
Haskovo	93,609
Jambol	97,414
Kârdžali	58,995
Kazanlâk	63,776
Kjustendil	55,620
Loveč	50,872
Mihajlovgrad	55,203
Pazardžik	83,451
Pernik	97,930
Pleven	136,287
Plovdiv	364,162
Razgrad	56,494
Ruse	190,720
Silistra	56,907
Sliven	109,432
• SOFIJA (★1,205,000)	1,136,875
Stara Zagora	158,151
Šumen	107,973
Varna	306,300
Veliko Târnovo	71,709
Vidin	65,892
Vraca	81,992

BURKINA FASO

1985 C	7,964,705
Bobo Dioulasso	228,668
Koudougou	51,926
• OUAGADOUGOU	441,514
Ouahigouya	38,902

BURMA / Myanmar

1983 C	34,124,908
Bago (Pegu)	150,528
Chauk	51,437
Dawei (Tavoy)	69,882
Henzada	82,005
Kale	52,628
Lashio	88,590
Magway	54,881
Mandalay	532,949
Mawlamyine (Moulmein)	219,961
Maymyo	63,782
Meiktila	96,496
Mergui (Myeik)	88,600
Mogok	49,392
Monywa	106,843
Myingyan	77,060
Myitkyinā	56,427
Nyaunglebin	55,194
Pakokku	71,860
Pathein (Bassein)	144,096
Prome (Pyè)	83,332
Pyinmana	52,962
Sagaing	46,212
Shwebo	52,185
Sittwe (Akyab)	107,621
Taunggyi	108,231
Thaton	61,790
Toungoo	65,861
• YANGON (RANGOON) (★2,800,000)	2,705,039
Yenangyaung	62,582

BURUNDI

1990 C	5,356,266
• BUJUMBURA	226,628
Gitega	15,750

CAMBODIA / Kâmpŭchéa

1990 E	8,567,582
Bătdâmbâng	94,412
Kâmpóng Saôm	67,452
• PHNUM PÉNH	477,874
Prey Vêng	41,456
Siĕmréab	76,434
Sisŏphŏn	67,041
Ta Khmau	34,947

CAMEROON / Cameroun

1986 E	10,446,409
Bafoussam (1985E)	89,000
Bamenda (1985E)	72,000
• Douala	1,029,731
Foumban (1985E)	50,000
Garoua (1985E)	96,000
Kumba (1985E)	67,000
Maroua	103,653
Ngaoundéré (1985E)	61,000
Nkongsamba	123,149
YAOUNDÉ	653,670

CANADA

1986 C	25,354,064

CANADA: ALBERTA

1986 C	2,375,278
Calgary (★671,326)	636,104
Edmonton (★785,465)	573,982
Lethbridge	58,841
Medicine Hat (★50,734)	41,804
Red Deer	54,425

CANADA: BRITISH COLUMBIA

1986 C	2,889,207
Burnaby (★Vancouver)	145,161
Kamloops	61,773
Kelowna (★89,730)	61,213
Matsqui (★88,420)	51,449
Nanaimo (★60,420)	49,029
Prince George	67,621
Richmond (★Vancouver)	108,492
Vancouver (★1,380,729)	431,147
Victoria (★255,547)	66,303

CANADA: MANITOBA

1986 C	1,071,232
Winnipeg (★625,304)	594,551

CANADA: NEW BRUNSWICK

1986 C	710,422
Fredericton (★65,768)	44,352
Moncton (★102,084)	55,468
Saint John (★121,265)	76,381

CANADA: NEWFOUNDLAND

1986 C	568,349
Saint John's (★161,901)	96,216

CANADA: NORTHWEST TERRITORIES

1986 C	52,238
Yellowknife	11,753

CANADA: NOVA SCOTIA

1986 C	873,199
Dartmouth (★Halifax)	65,243
Halifax (★295,990)	113,577
Sydney (★119,470)	27,754

CANADA: ONTARIO

1986 C	9,113,515
Barrie (★67,703)	48,287
Brampton (★Toronto)	188,498
Brantford (★90,521)	76,146
Burlington (★Hamilton)	116,675
Cambridge (Galt) (★Kitchener)	79,920
Cornwall (★51,719)	46,425
East York (★Toronto)	101,085
Etobicoke (★Toronto)	302,973
Gloucester (★Ottawa)	89,810
Guelph (★85,962)	78,235
Hamilton (★557,029)	306,728
Kingston (★122,350)	55,050
Kitchener (★311,195)	150,604
London (★342,302)	269,140
Markham (★Toronto)	114,597
Mississauga (★Toronto)	374,005
Nepean (★Ottawa)	95,490
Niagara Falls (★Saint Catharines)	72,107
North Bay (★57,422)	50,623
North York (★Toronto)	556,297
Oakville (★Toronto)	87,107
Oshawa (★203,543)	123,651
OTTAWA (★819,263)	300,763
Peterborough (★87,083)	61,049
Saint Catharines (★343,258)	123,455
Sarnia (★85,700)	49,033
Sault Sainte Marie (★84,617)	80,905
ScarboroughToronto)	484,676
Sudbury (★148,877)	88,717
Thunder Bay (★122,217)	112,272
• Toronto (★3,427,168)	612,289
Vaughan (★Toronto)	65,058
Waterloo (★Kitchener)	58,718
Windsor (★253,988)	193,111
York (★Toronto)	135,401

CANADA: PRINCE EDWARD ISLAND

1986 C	126,646
Charlottetown (★53,868)	15,776

CANADA: QUÉBEC

1986 C	6,540,276
Beauport (★Québec)	62,869
Brossard (★Montréal)	57,441
Charlesbourg (★Québec)	68,996
Chicoutimi (★158,468)	61,083
Drummondville (★56,283)	36,020
Gatineau (★Ottawa)	81,244
Hull (★Ottawa)	58,722
Jonquière (★Chicoutimi)	58,467
La Salle (★Montréal)	75,621
Laval (★Montréal)	284,164
Longueuil (★Montréal)	125,441
Montréal (★2,921,357)	1,015,420
Montréal-Nord (★Montréal)	90,303
Québec (★603,267)	164,580
Sainte-Foy (★Québec)	69,615
Saint-Hubert (★Montréal)	66,218
Saint-Jean-sur-Richelieu (★59,958)	34,745
Saint-Laurent (★Montréal)	67,002
Saint-Léonard (★Montréal)	75,947
Shawinigan (★61,965)	21,470
Sherbrooke (★129,960)	74,438
Trois-Rivières (★128,888)	50,122
Verdun (★Montréal)	60,246

CANADA: SASKATCHEWAN

1986 C	1,010,198
Regina (★186,521)	175,064
Saskatoon (★200,665)	177,641

CANADA: YUKON

1986 C	23,504
Whitehorse	15,199

CAPE VERDE / Cabo Verde

1990 C	336,798
Mindelo	47,050
• PRAIA	61,797

CAYMAN ISLANDS

1988 E	25,900
• GEORGE TOWN	13,700

CENTRAL AFRICAN REPUBLIC / République centrafrique

1984 E	2,517,000
• BANGUI	473,817
Bouar (1982E)	48,000

CHAD / Tchad

1988 E	5,428,000
Abéché	40,000
Moundou	100,000
• N'DJAMENA	500,000
Sarh	76,835

CHILE

1982 C	11,329,736
Antofagasta	185,486
Apoquindo (★Santiago)	175,735
Arica	139,320
Calama	81,684
Cerrillos (★Santiago)	67,013
Cerro Navia (★Santiago)	137,777
Chillán	118,163
Concepción (★675,000)	267,891
Conchalí (★Santiago)	157,884
Copiapó	69,045
Coquimbo	62,186
Coronel (★Concepción)	65,918
Curicó	60,550
El Bosque (★Santiago)	143,717
Huechuraba (★Santiago)	56,313
Independencia (★Santiago)	86,724
Iquique	110,153
La Cisterna (★Santiago)	95,863
La Florida (★Santiago)	191,883
La Granja (★Santiago)	109,168
La Pintana (★Santiago)	73,932
La Reina (★Santiago)	80,452
La Serena	83,283
Las Rejas (★Santiago)	147,918
Linares	46,433
Lo Barnechea (★Santiago)	24,258
Lo Espejo (★Santiago)	124,462
Lo Prado (★Santiago)	103,575
Los Ángeles	70,529
Lota (★Concepción)	47,133
Macul (★Santiago)	113,100
Maipú (★Santiago)	114,117
Ñuñoa (★Santiago)	168,919
Osorno	95,286
Ovalle	43,023
Pedro Aguirre Cerda (★Santiago)	145,207
Peñalolén (★Santiago)	137,298
Providencia (★Santiago)	115,449
Pudahuel (★Santiago)	97,578
Puente Alto (★Santiago)	109,239
Puerto Montt	84,410
Punta Arenas	95,332
Quilpué (★Valparaíso)	84,136
Quinta Normal (★Santiago)	128,989
Rancagua	139,925
Recoleta (★Santiago)	164,292
Renca (★Santiago)	93,928
San Antonio	61,486
San Bernardo (★Santiago)	117,132
San Joaquín (★Santiago)	123,904
San Miguel (★Santiago)	88,764
San Ramón (★Santiago)	99,410
• SANTIAGO (★4,100,000)	232,667
Talca	128,544
Talcahuano (★Concepción)	202,368
Temuco	157,297
Valdivia	100,046
Vallenar	38,375
Valparaíso (★675,000)	265,355
Villa Alemana (★Valparaíso)	55,766
Viña del Mar (★Valparaíso)	244,899
Vitacura (★Santiago)	72,038

CHINA / Zhongguo

1988 E	1,103,983,000
Abagnar Qi (▲100,700) (1986E)	71,700
Acheng (1985E)	100,304
Aihui (▲135,000) (1986E)	76,700
Aksu (▲345,900) (1986E)	1,431,000
Altay (▲141,700) (1986E)	62,800
Anci (Langfang) (▲522,800) (1986E)	122,100
Anda (▲425,500) (1986E)	130,200
Ankang (1985E)	89,188
Anqing (▲433,900) (1986E)	213,200
Anshan	1,330,000
Anshun (▲214,700) (1986E)	128,800
Anyang (▲541,900) (1986E)	361,200
Baicheng (▲282,000) (1986E)	198,600
Baiquan (1985E)	50,996
Baiyin (▲301,900) (1986E)	157,100
Baoding (▲535,100) (1986E)	423,200
Baoji (▲359,500) (1986E)	286,200
Baoshan (▲688,400) (1986E)	52,300
Baotou (Paotow)	1,130,000
Baoying (1985E)	50,479
Bei'an (▲440,500) (1986E)	199,500
Beihai (▲175,900) (1986E)	119,000
BEIJING (PEKING) (★7,200,000)	6,710,000
Beipiao (▲603,700) (1986E)	180,900
Bengbu (▲612,600) (1986E)	403,900
Benxi (Penhsi)	860,000
Bijie (1985E)	54,871
Binxian (▲177,900) (1986E)	86,700
Binxian (1982C)	127,326
Boli (1985E)	61,990
Bose (▲271,400) (1986E)	82,000
Boshan (1975U)	100,000
Boxian (1985E)	63,222
Boxing (1982C)	57,554
Boyang (1985E)	60,688
Butha Qi (Zalantun) (▲389,500) (1986E)	111,300
Cangshan (Bianzhuang) (1982C)	79,334
Cangzhou (▲293,600) (1986E)	196,700
Changchun (▲2,000,000)	1,822,000
Changde (▲220,800) (1986E)	178,200
Changge (1982C)	67,002
Changji (▲233,400) (1986E)	110,500
Changqing (1982C)	65,094
Changsha	1,230,000
Changshou (1985E)	51,923
Changshu (▲998,000) (1986E)	281,300
Changtu (1985E)	49,937
Changyi (1982C)	64,513
Changzhi (▲463,400) (1986E)	273,000
Changzhou (Changchow) (1986E)	522,700
Chao'an (▲1,214,500) (1986E)	265,400
Chaoxian (▲739,500) (1986E)	116,800
Chaoyang, Guangdong prov. (1985E)	85,968
Chaoyang, Liaoning prov. (▲318,900) (1986E)	180,300
Chengde (▲330,400) (1986E)	226,600
Chengdu (Chengtu) (▲2,960,000)	1,884,000
Chenghai (1985E)	50,631
Chenxian (▲191,900) (1986E)	143,500
Chifeng (Ulanhad) (▲882,900) (1986E)	299,000
Chongqing (Chungking) (▲2,890,000)	2,502,000
Chuxian (▲365,000) (1986E)	113,300
Chuxiong (▲379,400) (1986E)	67,700
Da'an (1985E)	70,552
Dachangzhen (1975U)	50,000
Dalian (Dairen)	2,280,000
Dandong (1986E)	579,800
Daqing (▲880,000)	640,000
Dashiqiao (1985E)	68,898
Datong (1985E)	55,529
Datong (▲1,040,000)	810,000
Dawa (1985E)	142,581
Daxian (▲209,400) (1986E)	142,000
Dehui (1985E)	60,247
Dengfeng (1982C)	49,746
Deqing (1982C)	48,726
Deyang (▲753,400) (1986E)	184,800
Dezhou (▲276,200) (1986E)	161,300
Didao (1975U)	50,000
Dinghai (1985E)	50,161
Dongchuan (Xincun) (▲275,100) (1986E)	67,400
Dongguan (▲1,208,500) (1986E)	254,900
Dongsheng (▲121,300) (1986E)	57,500
Dongtai (1985E)	65,788
Dongying (▲514,400) (1986E)	178,100
Dukou (▲551,200) (1986E)	380,200
Dunhua (▲448,000) (1986E)	217,100
Duyun (▲386,600) (1986E)	123,800
Echeng (▲938,000) (1986E)	217,400
Enshi (▲679,000) (1986E)	84,300
Erenhot (1986E)	7,200
Ergun Zuoqi (1985E)	55,970
Feixian (1982C)	73,246
Fengcheng (1985E)	66,745
Foshan (▲312,700) (1986E)	243,500
Fujin (1985E)	60,948
Fuling (▲973,500) (1986E)	166,300
Fushun (Funan)	1,290,000
Fuxian (Wafangdian) (▲960,700) (1986E)	246,200
Fuxin	700,000
Fuyang (▲195,200) (1986E)	143,400
Fuyu, Heilongjiang prov. (1985E)	48,670
Fuyu, Jilin prov. (1985E)	98,373
Fuzhou, Fujian prov. (▲1,240,000)	910,000
Fuzhou, Jiangxi prov. (▲171,800) (1986E)	106,700
Gaixian (1985E)	67,587
Ganhe (1985E)	48,128
Ganzhou (▲346,000) (1986E)	191,600
Gaoqing (Tianzhen) (1982C)	70,411
Gaoyou (1985E)	57,844
Gejiu (Kokiu) (▲341,700) (1986E)	193,600
Golmud (1986E)	60,300
Gongchangling (1982C)	49,281
Guanghua (▲420,000) (1986E)	104,400
Guangyuan (▲805,500) (1986E)	162,200
Guangzhou (Canton) (▲3,420,000)	3,100,000
Guanxian, Shandong prov. (1982C)	49,782
Guanxian, Sichuan prov. (1985E)	65,039
Guilin (Kweilin) (▲457,500) (1986E)	324,200
Guixian (1985E)	61,970
Guiyang (Kweiyang) (▲1,430,000)	1,030,000
Haicheng (▲984,800) (1986E)	210,700
Haifeng (1985E)	50,401
Haikou (▲289,600) (1986E)	209,200
Hailar (▲163,549) (1986E)	180,000
Hailin (1985E)	58,909
Hailong (Meihekou) (▲534,200) (1986E)	117,500
Hailun (1985E)	83,448
Haiyang (Dongcun) (1982C)	77,098
Hami (Kumul) (▲270,300) (1986E)	146,400
Hancheng (▲304,200) (1986E)	66,600
Handan (▲1,030,000)	870,000
Hangu (1975U)	100,000
Hangzhou (Hangchow)	1,290,000
Hanzhong (▲415,000) (1986E)	151,700
Harbin	2,710,000
Hebi (▲321,600) (1986E)	158,500
Hechi (▲266,800) (1986E)	74,400
Hechuan (1985E)	65,237
Hefei (▲930,000)	740,000
Hegang (1986E)	588,300
Helong (1985E)	62,665
Hengshui (▲286,500) (1986E)	83,100
Hengyang (▲601,300) (1986E)	419,200
Heshan (▲109,600) (1986E)	42,000
Heze (Caozhou) (▲1,001,500) (1986E)	115,400
Hohhot (▲830,000)	670,000
Hongjiang (▲67,000) (1986E)	54,300
Horqin Youyi Qianqi (Ulan Hot) (▲192,100) (1986E)	129,100
Hotan (▲122,800) (1986E)	71,700
Houma (▲158,500) (1986E)	67,000
Huadian (1985E)	75,183
Huai'an (1985E)	65,673
Huaibei (▲447,200) (1986E)	252,100
Huaide (▲899,400) (1986E)	187,600
Huaihua (▲427,100) (1986E)	102,000
Huainan (▲1,110,000)	700,000
Huaiyin (Wangying) (▲382,500) (1986E)	201,700
Huanan (1985E)	66,596
Huanggang (1982C)	65,961

▲ Población de un municipio, comuna o distrito entero, incluyendo sus áreas rurales.
• Ciudad más grande de un país.
★ Población o designación de un área metropolitana, incluyendo los suburbios.
C Censo. **E** Estimado oficial. **U** Estimado no oficial.

▲ Population d'une municipalité, d'une commune ou d'un district, zone rurale incluse.
• Ville la plus peuplée du pays.
★ Population de l'agglomération (ou nom de la zone métropolitaine englobante).
C Recensement. **E** Estimation officielle. **U** Estimation non officielle.

▲ População de um município, comuna ou distrito, inclusive as respectivas áreas rurais.
• Maior cidade de um país.
★ População ou indicação de uma área metropolitana.
C Censo. **E** Estimativa oficial. **U** Estimativa não oficial.

Huangshi (▲431,713) (1986E)	451,900
Huayun (Huarong) (▲313,500) (1986E)	81,000
Huinan (Chaoyang) (1985E)	52,429
Huizhou (▲182,100) (1986E)	117,000
Hulan (1985E)	74,989
Hunjiang (Badaojiang) (▲687,700) (1986E)	442,600
Huzhou (▲964,400) (1986E)	208,500
Jiading (1985E)	60,718
Jiamusi (Kiamusze) (▲557,700) (1986E)	429,800
Ji'an (▲184,300) (1986E)	132,200
Jiangling (1985E)	77,887
Jiangmen (▲231,700) (1986E)	168,800
Jiangyin (1985E)	66,476
Jiangyou (1985E)	72,663
Jian'ou (1985E)	55,180
Jiaohe (1985E)	51,504
Jiaojiang (▲385,200) (1986E)	82,300
Jiaoxian (1985E)	51,869
Jiaozuo (▲509,900) (1986E)	335,400
Jiawang (1975U)	50,000
Jiaxing (▲686,500) (1986E)	210,200
Jiayuguan (▲102,100) (1986E)	73,800
Jiexiu (1985E)	51,300
Jieyang (1985E)	98,531
Jilin (Kirin)	1,200,000
Jinan (Tsinan) (▲2,140,000)	1,546,000
Jinchang (Baijiazui) (▲136,000) (1986E)	90,500
Jincheng (▲612,700) (1986E)	99,900
Jingdezhen (Kingtechen) (▲569,700) (1986E)	304,000
Jingmen (▲946,500) (1986E)	227,000
Jinhua (▲799,900) (1986E)	147,800
Jining, Nei Monggol prov. (1986E)	163,300
Jining, Shandong prov. (▲765,700) (1986E)	222,600
Jinshi (▲219,700) (1986E)	73,700
Jinxi (▲634,300) (1986E)	223,100
Jinxian (1985E)	95,761
Jinzhou (Chinchou) (▲810,000)	710,000
Jishou (▲194,500) (1986E)	59,500
Jishu (1985E)	75,587
Jiujiang (▲382,300) (1986E)	248,500
Jiuquan (Suzhou) (▲269,900) (1986E)	56,300
Jiutai (1985E)	63,021
Jixi (▲820,000)	700,000
Jixian (1985E)	59,725
Juancheng (1982C)	54,110
Junan (Shizilu) (1982C)	90,222
Junxian (▲423,400) (1986E)	97,000
Juxian (1982C)	51,666
Kaifeng (▲629,100) (1986E)	458,800
Kaili (▲342,100) (1986E)	96,600
Kaiping (1985E)	54,145
Kaiyuan (▲342,100) (1986E)	96,600
Kaiyuan (1985E)	85,762
Karamay (▲168,868) (1986E)	185,300
Kashi (▲194,500) (1986E)	146,300
Keshan (1985E)	65,088
Korla (▲219,000) (1986E)	129,400
Kunming (▲1,550,000)	1,310,000
Kunshan (1985E)	44,645
Kuqa (1985E)	63,847
Kuytun (1986E)	60,200
Laiwu (▲1,041,800) (1986E)	143,500
Langxiang (1985E)	64,658
Lanxi (1985E)	53,236
Lanxi (▲606,800) (1986E)	70,500
Lanzhou (Lanchow) (▲1,420,000)	1,297,000
Lechang (1986E)	56,913
Lengshuijiang (▲277,600) (1986E)	101,700
Lengshuitan (▲362,000) (1986E)	60,900
Leshan (▲972,300) (1986E)	307,300
Lhasa (▲107,700) (1986E)	84,400
Lianyungang (Xinpu) (▲459,400) (1986E)	288,000
Liaocheng (▲724,300) (1986E)	119,000
Liaoyang (▲576,900) (1986E)	442,600
Liaoyuan (▲771,577) (1986E)	370,400
Liling (▲856,300) (1986E)	107,100
Linfen (▲530,100) (1986E)	157,600
Lingling (▲515,300) (1986E)	72,700
Lingyuan (1985E)	66,825
Linhai (1985E)	52,653
Linhe (▲365,900) (1986E)	99,800
Linkou (1985E)	52,936
Linqing (▲603,000) (1986E)	87,000
Linqu (1982C)	84,196
Linxia (▲150,200) (1986E)	72,900
Linyi (▲1,365,000) (1986E)	190,000
Liuzhou	680,000
Longjiang (1985E)	51,156
Longyan (▲378,500) (1986E)	114,500
Loudi (▲254,300) (1986E)	84,200
Lu'an (▲163,400) (1986E)	122,600
Lufeng (1985E)	53,015
Luohe (▲159,100) (1986E)	102,300
Luoyang (Loyang) (▲1,090,000)	760,000
Luzhou (▲360,300) (1986E)	237,800
Ma'anshan (▲367,000) (1986E)	258,900
Manzhouli (1986E)	116,600
Maoming (▲434,900) (1986E)	118,600
Meixian (▲740,600) (1986E)	169,100
Mengyin (1982C)	70,602
Mianyang, Sichuan prov. (▲848,500) (1986E)	233,900
Minhang (1975U)	60,000
Mishan (1985E)	54,919
Mixian (1982C)	64,776
Mudanjiang (▲580,982)	650,000
Nahe (1985E)	49,725
N'aizishen (1985E)	51,982
Nancha (1975U)	50,000
Nanchang (▲1,260,000)	1,090,000
Nanchong (▲238,100) (1986E)	158,000
Nanjing (Nanking)	2,390,000
Nanning (▲1,000,000)	720,000
Nanpiao (1982C)	67,274
Nanping (▲420,800) (1986E)	157,100
Nantong (▲411,000) (1986E)	308,800
Nanyang (▲294,800) (1986E)	199,400
Neihuang (1982C)	56,039
Neijiang (▲298,500) (1986E)	191,100
Ning'an (1985E)	49,334
Ningbo (▲1,050,000)	570,000
Ningyang (1982C)	55,424
Nong'an (1985E)	55,966
Nunjiang (1985E)	59,276
Orogen Zizhiqi (1985E)	48,042
Panshan (▲343,100) (1986E)	248,100
Panshi (1985E)	59,270
Pingdingshan (▲819,900) (1986E)	363,200
Pingliang (▲362,500) (1986E)	85,400
Pingxiang, Jiangxi prov. (▲1,286,700) (1986E)	368,700
Pingyi (1982C)	89,373
Pingyin (1982C)	62,827
Potou (▲456,100) (1986E)	59,000
Puqi (1985E)	65,239
Putian (▲265,400) (1986E)	64,600
Putuo (1985E)	50,962
Puyang (▲1,086,100) (1986E)	131,000
Qian Gorlos (1985E)	79,494
Qingdao (Tsingtao)	1,300,000
Qinggang (1985E)	43,075
Qingjiang, Jiangsu prov. (▲246,617) (1982C)	150,000
Qingjiang, Jiangxi prov. (1985E)	42,698
Qingyuan (1985E)	51,756
Qinhuangdao (Chinwangtao) (▲436,000) (1986E)	307,500
Qinzhou (▲923,400) (1986E)	97,100
Qiqihar (Tsitsihar) (▲1,330,000)	1,180,000
Qitaihe (▲309,900) (1986E)	166,400
Qixia (1982C)	54,158
Qixian (1982C)	53,041
Quanzhou (Chuanchou) (▲436,000) (1986E)	157,000
Qujing (▲758,000) (1986E)	135,000
Quxian (▲704,800) (1986E)	124,000
Raoping (1985E)	54,831
Rizhao (▲970,300) (1986E)	93,300
Rongcheng (1982C)	52,878
Rugao (1985E)	50,643
Rui'an (1985E)	57,993
Sanmenxia (Shanxian) (▲150,000) (1986E)	79,000
Sanming (▲214,300) (1986E)	144,900
• Shanghai (★9,300,000)	7,220,000
Shangqiu (Zhuji) (▲199,400) (1986E)	135,400
Shangrao (▲142,500) (1986E)	113,000
Shangshui (1982C)	50,191
Shantou (Swatow) (▲790,000)	560,000
Shanwei (1985E)	61,234
Shaoguan (▲344,892) (1986E)	363,100
Shaowu (▲266,700) (1986E)	81,400
Shaoxing (▲250,900) (1986E)	167,100
Shaoyang (▲465,900) (1986E)	218,600
Shashi (1986E)	253,700
Shenxian (1982C)	50,208
Shenyang (Mukden) (▲4,370,000)	3,910,000
Shenzhen (▲231,900) (1986E)	189,600
Shiguaigou (1975U)	50,000
Shihezi (▲549,300) (1987E)	304,700
Shijiazhuang	1,220,000
Shiyan (▲332,600) (1986E)	227,300
Shizuishan (▲317,400) (1986E)	225,500
Shouguang (1982C)	83,400
Shuangcheng (1985E)	91,163
Shuangliao (1985E)	67,326
Shuangyashan (1986E)	427,300
Shuicheng (▲2,216,500) (1986E)	363,500
Shulan (1986E)	50,582
Shunde (1985E)	50,262
Siping (▲357,800) (1986E)	280,100
Sishui (1982C)	82,990
Songjiang (1985E)	71,864
Songjianghe (1985E)	53,023
Suifenhe (▲21,700) (1986E)	13,900
Suihua (▲732,100) (1986E)	200,400
Suileng (1985E)	68,399
Suining (▲1,174,900) (1986E)	118,500
Suixian (▲1,281,600) (1986E)	187,700
Suqian (1985E)	50,742
Suxian (▲218,600) (1986E)	123,300
Suzhou (Soochow)	740,000
Tai'an (▲1,325,400) (1986E)	215,900
Taiyuan (▲1,980,000)	1,700,000
Taizhou (▲210,800) (1987E)	143,200
Tancheng (1982C)	61,857
Tangshan (▲1,440,000)	1,080,000
Tao'an (1985E)	76,269
Tengxian (1985E)	53,254
Tianjin (Tientsin) (★5,540,000)	4,950,000
Tianshui (▲953,200) (1986E)	209,500
Tiefa (▲146,367) (1982C)	60,000
Tieli (1985E)	102,527
Tieling (▲454,100) (1986E)	326,100
Tongchuan (▲393,200) (1986E)	268,900
Tonghua (▲367,400) (1986E)	290,200
Tongliao (▲253,100) (1986E)	190,100
Tongling (▲216,400) (1986E)	182,900
Tongren (1985E)	50,307
Tongxian (1985E)	97,168
Tumen (▲99,700) (1986E)	77,600
Tunxi (▲104,500) (1986E)	61,800
Turpan (▲196,800) (1986E)	52,300
Ürümqi (▲1,147,300)	1,060,000
Wangkui (1985E)	52,021
Wangqing (1985E)	61,237
Wanxian (▲280,800) (1986E)	138,700
Weifang (▲1,042,200) (1986E)	312,500
Weihai (▲220,800) (1986E)	83,000
Weinan (▲699,400) (1986E)	111,300
Weishan (Xiazhen) (1982C)	57,932
Weixian (Hanting) (1982C)	50,180
Wenzhou (▲530,600) (1986E)	372,200
Wuchang (1985E)	64,403
Wuhai (1986E)	266,000
Wuhan	3,570,000
Wuhu (▲502,200) (1986E)	396,000
Wulian (Hongning) (1982C)	51,718
Wusong (1982C)	64,017
Wuwei (Liangzhou) (▲804,000) (1986E)	115,500
Wuxi (Wuhsi)	880,000
Wuzhong (▲402,400) (1986E)	48,600
Wuzhou (Wuchow) (▲261,500) (1986E)	194,800
Xiaguan (▲395,800) (1986E)	112,100
Xiamen (Amoy) (▲546,400) (1986E)	343,700
Xi'an (Sian) (▲2,580,000)	2,210,000
Xiangfan (▲421,200) (1986E)	314,900
Xiangtan (▲511,100) (1986E)	389,500
Xianning (▲402,200) (1986E)	122,200
Xianyang (▲641,800) (1986E)	285,900
Xiaogan (▲1,204,400) (1986E)	125,500
Xiaoshan (1985E)	63,074
Xichang (▲161,000) (1986E)	105,000
Xinghua (1985E)	75,573
Xinglongzhen (1982C)	52,961
Xingtai (▲350,800) (1986E)	265,600
Xinhui (1985E)	77,381
Xining (Sining)	620,000
Xinmin (1985E)	47,900
Xintai (▲1,157,300) (1986E)	171,400
Xinwen (Suncun) (1975U)	50,000
Xinxian (▲398,600) (1986E)	74,200
Xinxiang (▲540,500) (1986E)	411,000
Xinyang (▲234,200) (1986E)	169,100
Xinyu (▲610,600) (1986E)	140,200
Xuancheng (1985E)	52,387
Xuanhua (1975U)	140,000
Xuanwei (1982C)	70,081
Xuchang (▲247,200) (1986E)	167,800
Xuguit Qi (Yakeshi) (1986E)	390,000
Xuzhou (Süchow)	860,000
Yaan (▲277,600) (1986E)	89,200
Yan'an (▲259,800) (1986E)	86,700
Yancheng (▲1,251,400) (1986E)	258,400
Yangcheng (1982C)	57,255
Yangjiang (1986E)	91,433
Yangquan (▲478,900) (1986E)	295,100
Yangzhou (▲417,300) (1986E)	321,500
Yanji (▲216,900) (1986E)	175,000
Yanji (Longjing) (1985E)	55,035
Yanling (1982C)	52,679
Yantai (Chefoo) (▲717,300) (1986E)	327,000
Yanzhou (1985E)	48,972
Yaxian (Sanya) (▲321,700) (1986E)	70,500
Yi'an (1986E)	54,253
Yibin (Ipin) (▲636,500) (1986E)	218,800
Yichang (Ichang) (1986E)	410,500
Yichuan (1982C)	58,914
Yichun, Heilongjiang prov.	840,000
Yichun, Jiangxi prov. (▲770,200) (1986E)	132,600
Yidu (1985E)	54,838
Yilan (1985E)	50,436
Yima (▲84,800) (1986E)	53,700
Yinan (Jiehu) (1982C)	67,803
Yinchuan (▲396,900) (1986E)	268,200
Yingchengzi (1985E)	59,072
Yingkou (▲480,000) (1986E)	366,900
Yingtan (▲116,200) (1986E)	64,500
Yining (Kuldja) (▲232,000) (1986E)	153,200
Yiyang (▲365,000) (1986E)	155,300
Yiyuan (Nanma) (1982C)	53,800
Yong'an (▲269,000) (1986E)	105,100
Yongchuan (1985E)	70,444
Yuci (▲420,700) (1986E)	171,000
Yueyang (▲411,300) (1986E)	239,500
Yulin, Guangxi Zhuangzu prov. (▲1,228,800) (1986E)	115,600
Yulin, Shaanxi prov. (1985E)	51,610
Yumen (Laojunmiao) (▲160,100) (1986E)	84,300
Yuncheng, Shandong prov. (1982C)	54,262
Yuncheng, Shansi prov. (▲434,900) (1986E)	87,000
Yunyang (1982C)	54,903
Yushu (1985E)	57,222
Yuyao (▲772,700) (1986E)	169,700
Zaozhuang (▲1,592,000) (1986E)	292,200
Zhangjiakou (Kalgan) (▲640,000)	500,000
Zhangye (▲394,200) (1986E)	73,000
Zhangzhou (Longxi) (▲310,400) (1986E)	159,400
Zhanjiang (▲920,900) (1986E)	335,500
Zhaodong (1985E)	99,836
Zhaoqing (Gaoyao) (▲187,600) (1986E)	145,700
Zhaotong (▲546,600) (1986E)	77,500
Zhaoyuan (1985E)	42,426
Zhaoyuan (1982C)	56,389
Zhengzhou (Chengchow) (▲1,580,000)	1,150,000
Zhenjiang (1986E)	412,400
Zhongshan (Shiqizhen) (▲1,059,700) (1986E)	238,700
Zhoucun (1975U)	50,000
Zhoukouzhen (▲220,400) (1986E)	110,500
Zhuhai (▲155,000) (1986E)	88,800
Zhumadian (▲149,500) (1986E)	99,400
Zhuoxian (1985E)	54,523
Zhuzhou (Chuchow) (▲499,600) (1986E)	344,800
Zibo (Zhangdian) (▲2,370,000)	840,000
Zigong (Tzukung) (▲909,300) (1986E)	361,700
Zixing (▲334,300) (1986E)	97,100
Ziyang (1985E)	57,349
Zouping (1982C)	49,274
Zouxian (1985E)	61,578
Zunyi (▲347,600) (1986E)	236,600

CISKEI

1986 E	882,200
BISHO	2,850
• Mdantsane (★East London, S. Afr.)	242,823

COLOMBIA

1985 C	27,867,326
Armenia	187,130
Barrancabermeja	137,406
Barranquilla (★1,140,000)	899,781
Bello (★Medellín)	212,861
Bucaramanga (★550,000)	352,326
Buenaventura	160,342
Buga	82,992
Cali (★1,400,000)	1,350,565
Cartagena	531,426
Cartago	97,791
Ciénaga	56,860
Cúcuta (★445,000)	379,478
Dos Quebradas (★Pereira)	101,480
Duitama	56,390
Envigado (★Medellín)	91,391
Florencia	66,430
Floridablanca (★Bucaramanga)	143,824
Girardot	70,078
Ibagué	292,965
Itagüí (★Medellín)	137,623
Magangué	49,160
Maicao	46,033
Malambo (★Barranquilla)	52,584
Manizales (★330,000)	299,352
Medellín (★2,095,000)	1,468,089
Montería	157,466
Neiva	194,556
Ocaña	51,443
Palmira	175,186
Pasto	197,407
Pereira (★390,000)	233,271
Popayán	141,964
• SANTA FE DE BOGOTÁ (★4,260,000)	3,982,941
Santa Marta	177,922
Sincelejo	120,537
Soacha (★Santa Fe de Bogotá)	109,051
Sogamoso	64,437
Soledad (★Barranquilla)	165,791
Tuluá	99,721
Tunja	93,792
Valledupar	142,771
Villa Rosario (★Cúcuta)	63,615
Villavicencio	178,685
Zipaquirá	45,676

COMOROS / Al-Qumur / Comores

1990 E	452,742
• MORONI	23,432

CONGO

1989 C	2,188,367
• BRAZZAVILLE (1984C)	585,812
Dolisie	57,991
Pointe-Noire	350,139

COOK ISLANDS

1986 C	18,155
• AVARUA	9,678

COSTA RICA

1988 E	2,851,000
Alajuela (★34,556) (1984C)	29,273
Desamparados (★San José) (1984C)	43,352
Puerto Limón (★62,600)	40,400
Puntarenas (1984C)	29,224
• SAN JOSÉ (★670,000)	278,600

CROATIA / Hrvatska

1987 E	4,673,517
Osijek (★162,490)	106,800
Rijeka (★199,282)	166,400
Split	191,074
• ZAGREB	697,925

CUBA

1991 E	10,694,465
Bayamo	139,061
Camagüey	286,404
Cárdenas (▲84,590)	69,800
Cárdenas (1981C)	59,352
Ciego de Avila	101,620
Cienfuegos	136,233
Florida	51,442
Guantánamo	215,864
Holguín	236,967
• LA HABANA (HAVANA) (★2,210,000)	2,119,059
Las Tunas	126,678
Manzanillo	108,668
Matanzas	119,510
Morón	49,793
Palma Soriano (▲124,543)	66,600
Pinar del Río	136,303
Sancti Spíritus	97,522
Santa Clara	203,753
Santiago de Cuba	434,541

CYPRUS / Kıbrıs / Kípros

1982 C	512,097
Lárnax (Larnaca) (★48,330)	35,823
Lemesós (Limassol) (★107,161)	74,782
• NICOSIA (LEVKOSÍA) (★185,000)	48,221

CYPRUS, NORTH / Kuzey Kıbrıs

1985 E	160,287
Gazimağusa (Famagusta)	19,428
• NICOSIA (LEFKOŞA)	37,400

CZECHOSLOVAKIA / Československo

1990 E	15,661,734
Banská Bystrica	87,834
Bratislava (1991E)	444,482
Brno (★450,000)	392,285
České Budějovice (★114,000)	99,428
Chomutov (★80,000)	55,735
Děčín (★72,000)	56,034
Frýdek-Místek (★Ostrava)	66,791
Havířov (★Ostrava)	92,037
Hradec Králové (★113,000)	101,302
Jihlava	54,855
Karlovy Vary (Carlsbad)	58,039
Karviná (★Ostrava)	69,521
Kladno (★88,500)	73,347
Košice	237,099
Liberec (★175,000)	104,256
Martin	66,678
Mladá Boleslav	49,195
Most (★135,000)	71,360
Nitra	91,297
Olomouc (★126,000)	107,044
Opava (★77,500)	63,440
Ostrava (★760,000)	331,557
Pardubice	95,909
Plzeň (★210,000)	175,038
Poprad	53,039
• PRAHA (★1,325,000) (1991E)	1,215,076
Přerov	51,996
Prešov	90,121
Prievidza	52,624
Prostějov	52,074
Spišská Nová Ves	45,260
Teplice (★94,000)	55,287
Trenčín	57,813
Trnava	72,866
Ústí nad Labem (★115,000)	106,499
Žilina	97,508

▲ Population of an entire municipality, commune, or district, including rural area.
• Largest city in country.
★ Population or designation of the metropolitan area, including suburbs.
C Census. **E** Official estimate. **U** Unofficial estimate.

▲ Bevölkerung eines ganzen städtischen Verwaltungsgebietes, eines Kommunalbezirkes oder eines Distrikts, einschliesslich ländlicher Gebiete.
• Grösste Stadt des Landes.
★ Bevölkerung oder Bezeichnung der Stadtregion einschliesslich Vororte.
C Volkszählung. **E** Offizielle Schätzung. **U** Inoffizielle Schätzung.

Zlín (★124,000)	87,189

DENMARK / Danmark

1990 E	5,135,409
Ålborg (▲155,019)	114,000
Århus (▲261,437)	202,300
Ballerup (★København)	45,218
Esbjerg (▲81,504)	71,900
Fredericia (▲46,072)	28,400
Frederiksberg (★København)	85,611
Gentofte (★København)	65,303
Gladsakse (★København)	60,882
Helsingør (Elsinore) (★København)	56,701
Horsens (▲55,210)	47,300
Hvidovre (★København)	48,748
• KØBENHAVN (★1,685,000)	466,723
Kolding (▲57,285)	42,200
Kongens Lyngby (★København)	49,317
Odense (▲176,133)	140,100
Randers	61,020
Rønne	15,187
Roskilde (▲49,081) (★ København)	39,800
Vejle (▲51,263)	45,200

DJIBOUTI

1976 E	226,000
• DJIBOUTI	120,000

DOMINICA

1984 E	77,000
• ROSEAU	9,348

DOMINICAN REPUBLIC / República Dominicana

1990 E	7,169,800
Barahona	80,400
La Romana	147,800
La Vega	192,300
Mao	58,400
San Francisco de Macorís	165,300
San Juan [de la Maguana]	129,700
San Pedro de Macorís	144,300
Santiago [de los Caballeros]	489,500
• SANTO DOMINGO	2,411,900

ECUADOR

1990 C	9,622,608
Ambato	124,518
Babahoyo	50,249
Cuenca	195,738
Eloy Alfaro (★Guayaquil)	81,366
Esmeraldas	98,065
• Guayaquil	1,475,118
Ibarra	80,477
Loja	96,220
Machala	143,892
Manta	122,426
Milagro	93,010
Portoviejo	134,180
Quevedo	87,789
QUITO (★1,300,000)	1,094,318
Riobamba	92,664
Santo Domingo de los Colorados	114,048

EGYPT / Miṣr

1986 C	48,205,049
Abnūb	48,519
Abū Kabīr	69,509
Abū Tīj	48,711
Akhmīm	70,602
Al-'Arīsh	67,638
Al-Fayyūm	212,523
Al-Hawāmidīyah (★Al-Qāhirah)	73,060
Al-Iskandarīyah (Alexandria) (★3,350,000)	2,917,327
Al-Ismā'īlīyah (★235,000)	212,567
Al-Jīzah (Giza) (★Al-Qāhirah)	1,870,508
Al-Maḥallah al-Kubrā	358,844
Al-Manṣūrah (★375,000)	316,870
Al-Manzilah	55,090
Al-Maṭarīyah	74,554
Al-Minyā	179,136
• AL-QĀHIRAH (CAIRO) (★9,300,000)	6,052,836
Al-Qanāṭir al-Khayrīyah	48,909
Al-Uqṣur (Luxor)	125,404
Armant	54,650
Ashmūn	54,450
As-Sinbillāwayn	60,285
As-Suways (Suez)	326,820
Aswān	191,461
Asyūṭ	273,191
Az-Zaqāzīq	245,496
Bahtīm (★Al-Qāhirah)	275,807
Banhā	115,571
Banī Mazār	47,964
Banī Suwayf	151,813
Bilbays	96,540
Bilqās Qism Awwal	73,162
Biyalā	47,781
Būlāq ad-Dakrūr (★Al-Qāhirah)	148,787
Būr Sa'īd (Port Said)	399,793
Būsh	54,482
Damanhūr	190,840
Disūq	78,119
Dumyāṭ (Damietta)	89,498
Fāqūs	48,625
Hawsh 'Īsā (1980C)	53,619
Idkū	70,729
Jirjā	70,899
Kafr ad-Dawwār (★Al-Iskandarīyah)	195,102
Kafr ash-Shaykh	102,910
Kafr az-Zayyāt	58,061
Kawm Umbū	52,131
Maghāghah	50,807
Mallawī	99,062
Manfalūṭ	52,644
Marsā Maṭrūḥ	43,192
Minūf	69,883
Mīt Ghamr (★100,000)	92,253
Qalyūb	86,684
Qinā	119,794
Rashīd (Rosetta)	52,014
Rummānah	50,014

Samālūṭ	62,404
Sāqiyat Makkī	51,062
Sawhāj	132,965
Shibīn al-Kawm	132,751
Shubrā al-Khaymah (★Al-Qāhirah)	710,794
Sinnūris	55,323
Ṭahṭā	58,516
Ṭalkhā (★Al-Manṣūrah)	55,757
Ṭanṭā	334,505
Timā	47,223
Warrāq al-'Arab (★Al-Qāhirah)	127,108
Ziftā (★Mīt Ghamr)	69,050

EL SALVADOR

1985 E	5,337,896
Delgado (★San Salvador)	67,684
Mejicanos (★San Salvador)	91,465
Nueva San Salvador (★San Salvador)	53,688
San Miguel	88,520
• SAN SALVADOR (★920,000)	462,652
Santa Ana	137,879
Soyapango (★San Salvador)	60,000

EQUATORIAL GUINEA / Guinea Ecuatorial

1983 C	300,000
• MALABO	31,630

ESTONIA / Eesti

1991 E	1,581,800
Kohtla-Järve	74,700
Narva	83,000
Pärnu	54,200
• TALLINN	481,500
Tartu	115,300

ETHIOPIA / Ityopiya

1986 E	44,927,000
• ADIS ABEBA (★1,760,000) (1988E)	1,686,300
Akaki Beseka (★Adis Abeba)	59,000
Asmera (1988E)	319,353
Awasa (1984C)	36,169
Bahir Dar	60,000
Debre Zeyit	56,000
Dese	77,000
Dire Dawa	107,000
Gonder	88,000
Harer	68,000
Jima	67,000
Mekele	66,000
Mitsiwa (1984C)	15,441
Nazret	83,000

FAEROE ISLANDS / Føroyar

1990 E	47,946
• TÓRSHAVN	14,767

FALKLAND ISLANDS

1986 C	1,916
• STANLEY	1,200

FIJI

1986 C	715,375
Lautoka (★39,057)	28,728
• SUVA (★141,273)	69,665

FINLAND / Suomi

1989 E	4,954,359
Espoo (Esbo) (★Helsinki)	167,734
• HELSINKI (HELSINGFORS) (★1,040,000)	489,965
Jyväskylä (★93,000)	66,197
Kotka	57,181
Kouvola (★53,821)	31,890
Kuopio	79,495
Lahti (★108,000)	93,251
Lappeenranta	54,926
Oulu (★121,000)	98,933
Pori	76,789
Tampere (★241,000)	171,088
Turku (Åbo) (★228,000)	159,917
Vaasa (Vasa)	53,440
Vantaa (Vanda) (★Helsinki)	151,157

FRANCE

1990 C	56,614,493
Aix-en-Provence (★Marseille)	123,842
Ajaccio	58,315
Albi (★54,359)	46,579
Alès (★76,856)	41,037
Amiens (★156,120)	131,872
Angers (★208,282)	141,404
Angoulême (★102,908)	42,876
Annecy (★126,729)	49,644
Antibes (★Cannes)	63,248
Antony (★Paris)	57,771
Argenteuil (★Paris)	93,096
Arles (★54,309)	39,000
Armentières (★57,738)	25,219
Arras (★79,607)	38,983
Asnières [-sur-Seine] (★Paris)	71,850
Aubervilliers (★Paris)	67,557
Aulnay-sous-Bois (★Paris)	82,314
Avignon (★181,136)	86,939
Bastia (★52,446)	37,845
Bayonne (★164,378)	40,051
Beauvais (★57,704)	54,190
Belfort (★77,844)	50,125
Besançon (★122,623)	113,828
Béthune (★261,535)	24,556
Béziers (★76,304)	70,996
Blois (★65,132)	49,318
Bondy (★Paris)	46,676
Bordeaux (★760,000)	210,336
Boulogne-Billancourt (★Paris)	101,743
Boulogne-sur-Mer (★91,249)	43,678
Bourg-en-Bresse (★55,784)	40,972
Bourges (★94,731)	75,609
Brest (★201,480)	147,956
Brive-la-Gaillarde (★64,379)	49,765
Bruay-en-Artois (★Béthune)	24,927
Caen (★191,490)	112,846
Calais (★101,768)	75,309
Cambrai (★48,133)	33,092
Cannes (★335,647)	68,676
Carcassonne	43,470
Castres (★46,482)	44,812
Châlons-sur-Marne (★61,452)	48,423
Chalon-sur-Saône (★77,764)	54,575
Chambéry (★103,283)	54,120
Champigny-sur-Marne (★Paris)	79,486
Charleville-Mézières (★67,213)	57,008
Chartres (★85,933)	39,595
Châteauroux (★67,090)	50,969
Châtellerault (★36,298)	34,678
Cherbourg (★92,045)	27,121
Cholet	55,132
Clamart (★Paris)	47,227
Clermont-Ferrand (★254,416)	136,181
Clichy (★Paris)	48,030
Cognac (★27,468)	19,528
Colmar (★83,816)	63,498
Colombes (★Paris)	78,513
Compiègne (★67,057)	41,896
Courbevoie (★Paris)	65,389
Creil (★97,119)	31,956
Créteil (★Paris)	82,088
Denain (★Valenciennes)	19,544
Dieppe (★43,348)	35,894
Dijon (★230,451)	146,703
Douai (★199,562)	42,175
Drancy (★Paris)	60,707
Dunkerque (★190,879)	70,331
Elbeuf (★53,886)	16,604
Épinal (★62,140)	36,732
Épinay-sur-Seine (★Paris)	48,762
Évreux (★57,968)	49,103
Fontainebleau (★35,706)	15,714
Fontenay-sous-Bois (★Paris)	51,868
Forbach (★98,758)	27,076
Fréjus (★73,967)	41,486
Gennevilliers (★Paris)	44,818
Grenoble (★404,733)	150,758
Hagondange (★112,061)	8,222
Hayange (★Thionville)	15,638
Issy-les-Moulineaux (★Paris)	46,127
Ivry-sur-Seine (★Paris)	53,619
La Rochelle (★100,264)	71,094
La Seyne-sur-Mer (★Toulon)	59,968
Laval (★56,855)	50,473
Le Blanc-Mesnil (★Paris)	46,956
Le Havre (★253,627)	195,854
Le Mans (★189,107)	145,502
Lens (★323,174)	35,017
Le Puy (★43,499)	21,743
Levallois-Perret (★Paris)	47,548
Lille (★1,050,000)	172,142
Limoges (★170,065)	133,464
Longwy (★41,300)	15,439
Lorient (★115,488)	59,271
Lourdes	16,300
Lyon (★1,335,000)	415,487
Mâcon (★46,714)	37,275
Maisons-Alfort (★Paris)	53,375
Mantes-la-Jolie (★Paris)	45,087
Marseille (★1,225,000)	800,550
Martigues (★Marseille)	31,300
Maubeuge (★102,772)	34,989
Meaux (★63,006)	48,305
Melun (★107,705)	35,319
Menton (★Monaco, Monaco)	29,141
Mérignac (★Bordeaux)	57,273
Metz (★193,117)	119,594
Meudon (★Paris)	45,339
Montargis (★52,804)	15,020
Montbéliard (★117,510)	29,005
Montceau-les-Mines (★47,283)	22,999
Montluçon (★63,018)	44,248
Montpellier (★248,303)	207,996
Montreuil-sous-Bois (★Paris)	94,754
Moulins (★41,715)	22,799
Moyeuvre-Grande (★Hagondange)	9,203
Mulhouse (Mülhausen) (★223,856)	108,357
Nancy (★329,447)	99,351
Nanterre (★Paris)	84,565
Nantes (★496,078)	244,995
Neuilly-sur-Seine (★Paris)	61,768
Nevers (★58,915)	41,968
Nice (★516,740)	342,439
Nîmes (★138,527)	128,471
Niort (★65,792)	57,012
Noisy-le-Sec (★Paris)	36,309
Orléans (★243,153)	105,111
Orly (★Paris)	21,646
Pantin (★Paris)	47,303
• PARIS (★10,275,000)	2,152,423
Pau (★144,674)	82,157
Périgueux (★63,322)	30,280
Perpignan (★157,873)	105,983
Pessac (★Bordeaux)	51,055
Poissy (★Paris)	36,745
Poitiers (★107,625)	78,894
Quimper (★65,954)	59,437
Reims (★206,437)	180,620
Rennes (★245,065)	197,536
Roanne (★77,160)	41,756
Rodez (★39,017)	24,701
Romans-sur-Isère (★49,212)	32,734
Roubaix (★Lille)	97,746
Rouen (★380,161)	102,723
Rueil-Malmaison (★Paris)	66,401
Saint-Brieuc (★83,861)	44,752
Saint-Chamond (★81,795)	38,878
Saint-Denis (★Paris)	89,988
Saint-Dizier (★40,097)	33,552
Saint-Étienne (★313,338)	199,396
Saint-Lô (★2,760)	21,546
Saint-Malo	48,057
Saint-Maur-des-Fossés (★Paris)	77,206
Saint-Nazaire (★131,511)	64,812
Saint-Ouen (★Paris)	42,343
Saint-Quentin (★71,113)	60,644
Sarcelles (★Paris)	56,833
Sevran	48,478
Soissons (★46,168)	29,829
Strasbourg (★415,000)	252,338
Suresnes (★Paris)	35,998
Tarbes (★77,787)	47,566
Thionville (★132,413)	39,712
Toulon (★437,553)	167,619
Toulouse (★650,000)	358,688
Tourcoing (★Lille)	93,765
Tours (★282,152)	129,509
Troyes (★122,763)	59,255
Valence (★107,965)	63,437
Valenciennes (★338,392)	38,441
Vénissieux (★Lyon)	60,444
Verdun-sur-Meuse (★26,711)	20,753
Versailles (★Paris)	87,789
Vichy (★61,566)	27,714
Villefranche (★55,249)	29,542
Villejuif (★Paris)	48,405
Villeneuve-d'Ascq (★Lille)	65,320
Villeurbanne (★Lyon)	116,872
Vitry-sur-Seine (★Paris)	82,400
Wattrelos (★Lille)	43,675

FRENCH GUIANA / Guyane française

1982 C	73,022
• CAYENNE	38,091

FRENCH POLYNESIA / Polynésie française

1988 C	188,814
• PAPEETE (★80,000)	23,555

GABON

1985 E	1,312,000
Franceville	58,800
Lambaréné	49,500
• LIBREVILLE	235,700
Port Gentil	124,400

GAMBIA

1983 C	687,817
• BANJUL (★160,000)	44,188
Brikama	19,624

GEORGIA

1991 E	5,464,200
Batumi	137,500
Gori	70,100
Kutaisi	238,200
Poti	51,100
Rustavi (★Tbilisi)	161,900
Suchumi	120,000
• TBILISI (★1,460,000)	1,279,000
Zugdidi	50,600

GERMANY / Deutschland

1990 E	79,112,831
Aachen (★540,000)	236,987
Aalen (★78,000)	63,783
Ahlen	53,322
Albstadt	47,337
Alsdorf (★Aachen)	46,618
Altenburg	51,426
Amberg	42,660
Arnsberg (1989E)	73,912
Aschaffenburg (★150,000)	63,057
Augsburg (★420,000)	250,197
Baden-Baden	51,085
Bad Homburg (★Frankfurt am Main)	51,354
Bad Oeynhausen	45,029
Bad Salzuflen (★Herford)	51,991
Bamberg (★122,000)	69,980
Bautzen	50,627
Bayreuth (★87,000)	71,527
Berchtesgaden	7,720
Bergheim (★Köln)	57,239
Bergisch Gladbach (★Köln) (1989E)	101,983
Bergkamen (★Essen)	49,303
BERLIN (★4,150,000)	3,409,737
Bielefeld (★535,000)	315,096
Bitterfeld (★105,000)	20,017
Bocholt	68,244
Bochum (★Essen)	393,053
BONN (★575,000)	287,117
Bottrop (★Essen)	117,464
Brandenburg	93,441
Braunschweig (★320,000)	256,323
Bremen (★790,000)	544,327
Bremerhaven (★180,000)	129,357
Castrop-Rauxel (★Essen)	78,267
Celle	71,601
Chemnitz (★500,000)	301,918
Cottbus	128,943
Cuxhaven	55,637
Dachau (★München)	34,489
Darmstadt (★315,000)	137,537
Delmenhorst (★Bremen)	74,350
Dessau (★138,000)	101,262
Detmold	67,803
Dinslaken (★Essen)	64,481
Dormagen (★Köln)	56,917
Dorsten (★Essen)	76,929
Dortmund (★Essen)	594,058
Dresden (★870,000)	501,417
Duisburg (★Essen)	532,152
Düren (★108,000)	84,251
Düsseldorf (★1,225,000)	574,022
Eberswalde	54,332
Eisenach	47,027
Eisenhüttenstadt	52,393
Emden	50,090
Erfurt	217,035
Erlangen (★Nürnberg)	100,996
Eschweiler (★Aachen)	54,098
• Essen (★5,050,000)	624,445
Esslingen (★Stuttgart)	91,092
Euskirchen	48,561
Flensburg (★98,000)	86,582
Frankfurt am Main (★1,935,000)	635,151
Frankfurt an der Oder	87,126
Freiberg	49,840
Freiburg (★235,000)	187,767
Freital (★Dresden)	41,358
Friedrichshafen	53,493
Fulda (★74,000)	55,381
Fürth (★Nürnberg)	100,906
Garbsen (★Hannover)	60,013
Garmisch-Partenkirchen	26,413
Gelsenkirchen (★Essen)	289,791
Gera	132,257
Giessen (★155,000)	72,884
Gladbeck (★Essen)	79,533
Göppingen (★155,000)	53,997
Görlitz	74,766
Goslar (★72,000)	45,939
Gotha	56,715
Göttingen	120,242
Greifswald	68,270
Grevenbroich (★Düsseldorf)	60,047
Gummersbach	49,933
Gütersloh (★Bielefeld)	85,178

▲ Población de un municipio, comuna o distrito entero, incluyendo sus áreas rurales.
• Ciudad más grande de un país.
★ Población o designación de un área metropolitana, incluyendo los suburbios.
C Censo. **E** Estimado oficial. **U** Estimado no oficial.

▲ Population d'une municipalité, d'une commune ou d'un district, zone rurale incluse.
• Ville la plus peuplée du pays.
★ Population de l'agglomération (ou nom de la zone métropolitaine englobante).
C Recensement. **E** Estimation officielle. **U** Estimation non officielle.

▲ População de um municipio, comuna ou distrito, inclusive as respectivas áreas rurais.
• Maior cidade de um país.
★ População ou indicação de uma área metropolitana.
C Censo. **E** Estimativa oficial. **U** Estimativa não oficial.

Hagen (★Essen)	212,460
Halberstadt	46,851
Halle (★455,000)	230,728
Halle-Neustadt (★Halle)	90,956
Hamburg (★2,385,000)	1,626,220
Hameln (★65,000)	57,945
Hamm	179,109
Hanau (★Frankfurt am Main)	85,672
Hannover (★1,000,000)	505,872
Hattingen (★Essen)	57,209
Heidelberg (★Mannheim)	134,496
Heidenheim (★80,000)	49,504
Heilbronn (★245,000)	113,955
Herford (★120,000)	62,657
Herne (★Essen)	176,472
Herten (★Essen)	68,621
Hilden (★Düsseldorf)	54,273
Hildesheim (★126,000)	104,203
Hof	52,319
Hoyerswerda	67,881
Hürth (★Köln)	49,924
Ingolstadt (★145,000)	101,360
Iserlohn	94,695
Jena	105,825
Kaiserslautern (★130,000)	97,625
Karlsruhe (★505,000)	270,659
Kassel (★375,000)	191,598
Kempten (Allgäu)	61,075
Kerpen (★Köln)	56,091
Kiel (★325,000)	243,579
Kleve	45,235
Koblenz (★170,000)	107,938
Köln (★1,810,000)	946,280
Konstanz	73,853
Krefeld (★Essen)	240,208
Landshut	58,125
Langenfeld (★Düsseldorf)	51,971
Leipzig (★720,000)	530,010
Leverkusen (★Köln)	159,325
Lippstadt	61,413
Lübeck (★250,000)	212,932
Lüdenscheid	77,620
Ludwigsburg (★Stuttgart)	81,306
Ludwigshafen (★Mannheim)	159,567
Lüneburg	60,937
Lünen (★Essen)	86,363
Magdeburg (★400,000)	288,355
Mainz (★Wiesbaden)	177,062
Mannheim (★1,525,000)	305,974
Marburg	72,656
Marl (★Essen)	90,725
Meerbusch (★Düsseldorf)	51,166
Menden	55,500
Merseburg (★Halle)	44,367
Minden (★121,000)	76,321
Moers (★Essen)	103,521
Mönchengladbach (★410,000)	255,905
Mülheim an der Ruhr (★Essen)	176,149
München (Munich) (★1,900,000)	1,206,683
Münster	253,123
Neubrandenburg	90,953
Neumünster	80,294
Neunkirchen/Saar (★125,000)	51,277
Neuss (★Düsseldorf)	145,665
Neustadt an der Weinstrasse	51,232
Neu-Ulm (★Ulm)	45,835
Neuwied (★157,000)	61,290
Norderstedt (★Hamburg)	67,651
Nordhausen	48,089
Nordhorn	48,861
Nürnberg (★1,065,000)	485,717
Oberammergau	5,175
Oberhausen (★Essen)	222,419
Offenbach (★Frankfurt am Main)	113,990
Offenburg	52,480
Oldenburg	142,233
Osnabrück (★270,000)	161,317
Paderborn	116,604
Passau	49,846
Peine	45,975
Pforzheim (★230,000)	110,865
Pirmasens	47,178
Pirna (★Dresden)	43,486
Plauen	73,971
Potsdam (★Berlin)	141,430
Ratingen (★Düsseldorf)	90,672
Ravensburg (★75,000)	44,728
Recklinghausen (★Essen)	123,528
Regensburg (★180,000)	120,006
Remscheid (★Wuppertal)	121,786
Reutlingen (★170,000)	101,987
Rheine	69,736
Riesa	47,326
Rosenheim	55,074
Rostock	252,956
Rüsselsheim (★Wiesbaden)	58,849
Saarbrücken (★365,000)	190,466
Saarlouis (★115,000)	38,059
Salzgitter	112,689
Sankt Augustin (★Bonn)	50,983
Schwäbisch Gmünd	58,892
Schwedt	52,569
Schweinfurt (★105,000)	53,636
Schwerin	129,492
Schwerte (★Essen)	49,821
Siegburg (★175,000)	34,771
Siegen (★192,000)	107,039
Sindelfingen (★Stuttgart)	58,240
Solingen (★Wuppertal)	162,928
Stendal	50,717
Stolberg (★Aachen)	56,841
Stralsund	74,566
Stuttgart (★2,005,000)	570,699
Suhl	56,125
Trier (★122,000)	96,721
Troisdorf (★Siegburg)	63,371
Tübingen	78,643
Ulm (★215,000)	108,930
Unna (★Essen)	61,108
Velbert (★Essen)	88,651
Viersen (★Mönchengladbach)	76,669
Villingen-Schwenningen	77,174
Weimar	61,583
Wesel	59,100
Wetzlar (★96,000)	51,017
Wiesbaden (★790,000)	256,885
Wilhelmshaven (★122,000)	90,051
Wismar	57,173
Witten (★Essen)	104,701
Wittenberg	51,754
Wolfenbüttel (★Braunschweig)	51,413
Wolfsburg	126,708
Worms (★Mannheim)	75,326
Wuppertal (★845,000)	378,312
Würzburg (★195,000)	125,953
Zweibrücken (★100,000)	33,496
Zwickau (★180,000)	118,914

GHANA

1987 E	13,577,538
• ACCRA (★1,390,000)	949,113
Ashiaman (★Accra) (1984C)	49,427
Cape Coast (1984C)	86,620
Koforidua (1984C)	54,400
Kumasi (★540,000)	385,192
Obuasi (1984C)	60,146
Sekondi (★175,352) (1984C)	32,355
Tafo (★Kumasi) (1984C)	50,432
Takoradi (★Sekondi) (1984C)	61,527
Tamale (★168,091)	151,069
Tema (★Accra)	109,975
Teshie (★Accra) (1984C)	62,954

GIBRALTAR

1988 E	30,077
• GIBRALTAR	30,077

GREECE / Ellás

1981 C	9,740,417
Aiyáleo (★Athínai) (1991C)	79,560
Amaroúsion (★Athínai) (1991C)	63,619
Ampelókipoi (★Thessaloníki)	40,033
• ATHÍNAI (ATHENS) (★3,096,775) (1991E)	748,110
Áyios Dhimítrios (★Athínai) (1991C)	57,387
Ermoúpolis (★16,595)	13,876
Galátsion (★Athínai) (1991C)	56,972
Glifádha (★Athínai) (1991C)	62,310
Ilioúpolis (★Athínai) (1991C)	72,623
Ioánnina (1991C)	56,496
Iráklion (★110,958)	102,398
Kalámai (★43,235)	42,075
Kalamariá (★Thessaloníki)	51,676
Kallithéa (★Athínai) (1991C)	110,738
Kardhítsa	27,291
Kateríni (★39,895)	38,404
Kavála	56,375
Keratsínion (★Athínai) (1991C)	71,845
Khalándrion (★Athínai) (1991C)	72,286
Khalkís	44,867
Khaniá (★61,976)	47,451
Khíos (★29,742)	24,070
Koridhallós (★Athínai) (1991C)	63,033
Kórinthos (Corinth) (1991C)	28,903
Lárisa (★125,623) (1991C)	113,426
Návplion	10,609
Néa Ionía (★Athínai) (1991C)	60,364
Néa Liósia (★Athínai) (1991C)	78,029
Neápolis (★Thessaloníki)	31,464
Néa Smírni (★Athínai) (1991C)	69,319
Níkaia (★Athínai) (1991C)	87,924
Palaión Fáliron (★Athínai) (1991C)	60,974
Pátrai (★154,596)	142,163
Peristérion (★Athínai) (1991C)	145,854
Piraiévs (Piraeus) (★Athínai) (1991C)	169,622
Ródhos (Rhodes)	40,392
Spárti (Sparta) (★14,388)	12,975
Thessaloníki (Salonika) (★706,180)	406,413
Tríkala	40,857
Trípolis	21,311
Véroia	37,087
Víron (★Athínai) (1991C)	57,149
Vólos (★107,407)	71,378
Zográfos (★Athínai) (1991C)	78,570

GREENLAND / Grønland / Kalaallit Nunaat

1990 E	55,558
Egedesminde (Aasiaat)	3,308
• GODTHÅB (NUUK)	12,217
Holsteinsborg (Sisimiut)	4,871

GRENADA

1981 C	89,088
• SAINT GEORGE'S (★25,000)	4,788

GUADELOUPE

1982 C	328,400
BASSE-TERRE (★26,600)	13,656
Les Abymes (★Pointe-à-Pitre)	56,165
• Pointe-à-Pitre (★83,000)	25,310

GUAM

1990 C	133,152
• AGANA (★50,000)	1,139

GUATEMALA

1989 E	8,935,395
Escuintla	60,673
• GUATEMALA (★1,400,000)	1,057,210
Quetzaltenango	88,769

GUERNSEY

1986 C	55,482
• SAINT PETER PORT (★36,000)	16,085

GUINEA / Guinée

1986 E	6,225,000
• CONAKRY	800,000
Kankan	100,000
Kindia	80,000
Labé	110,000
Nzérékoré (1983C)	55,356

GUINEA-BISSAU / Guiné-Bissau

1988 E	945,000
• BISSAU	125,000

GUYANA

1983 E	918,000
• GEORGETOWN (★188,000)	78,500

HAITI / Haïti

1987 E	5,531,802
Cap-Haïtien	72,161
Gonaïves	37,034
• PORT-AU-PRINCE (★880,000)	797,000

HONDURAS

1988 C	4,376,839
Choluteca	53,799
El Progreso	55,523
La Ceiba	68,289
San Pedro Sula	279,356
• TEGUCIGALPA	551,606

HONG KONG

1986 C	5,395,997
Kowloon (Jiulong) (★Victoria)	774,781
Kwai Chung (★Victoria)	131,362
New Kowloon (Xinjiulong) (★Victoria)	1,526,910
Sha Tin (★Victoria)	355,810
Sheung Shui	87,206
Tai Po	119,679
Tsuen Wan (Quanwan) (★Victoria)	514,241
Tuen Mun (★Victoria)	262,458
• VICTORIA (★4,770,000) (1991C)	1,250,993
Yuen Long	75,740

HUNGARY / Magyarország

1991 C	10,354,842
Békéscsaba (▲67,691)	58,900
• BUDAPEST (★2,515,000)	2,018,035
Debrecen	213,927
Dunaújváros	58,874
Eger	62,474
Érd (★Budapest)	43,563
Győr	129,598
Hódmezővásárhely (▲51,180)	42,800
Kaposvár	71,368
Kecskemét (▲103,568)	82,000
Miskolc	194,033
Nagykanizsa	53,700
Nyíregyháza (▲114,596)	88,800
Ózd	43,020
Pécs	170,023
Salgótarján	47,500
Sopron	55,140
Szeged	176,135
Székesfehérvár	109,106
Szolnok	78,661
Szombathely	85,702
Tatabánya	73,854
Vác	33,858
Veszprém	64,277
Zalaegerszeg	62,357

ICELAND / Ísland

1991 E	255,708
Akureyri	14,174
• REYKJAVÍK (★145,980)	97,569

INDIA / Bharat

1991 C	844,324,222
Abohar	107,016
Achalpur	96,216
Ādilābād	84,233
Adītyapur (★Jamshedpur)	78,184
Ādoni	135,718
Agartala	157,636
Āgra (★955,684)	899,195
Āgra Cantonment (★Āgra)	49,975
Ahmadābād (★3,297,655)	2,872,865
Ahmadnagar (★221,710)	181,015
Āīzawl	154,343
Ajmer	401,930
Akola	327,946
Akot	65,670
Alandur (★Madras)	125,009
Alīgarh	479,978
Ālīpur Duār (★103,512)	65,945
Allahābād (★858,213)	806,447
Alleppey (★264,887)	174,606
Alwal (★Hyderābād)	66,064
Alwar (★211,162)	206,107
Amalner	76,406
Ambājogāi	57,054
Ambāla	119,535
Ambāla Cantonment (★Ambāla Sadar)	48,903
Ambāla Sadar (★139,615)	90,712
Ambāsamudram (★59,527)	33,860
Ambattur (★Madras)	223,332
Ambikāpur (★53,228)	50,278
Āmbūr	75,728
Amrāvati	433,746
Amreli (★69,279)	67,740
Amritsar	709,456
Amroha	136,893
Anakāpalle	84,362
Ānand (★168,776)	110,144
Anantapur	174,792
Anjār	51,207
Ara	156,871
Arakkonam	71,500
Arcot (★114,884)	45,193
Arni	54,881
Aruppukkottai	78,184
Asansol (★763,845)	261,836
Ashoknagar-Kalyangarh (★Hābra)	96,315
Āttūr	55,529
Auraiya	50,771
Aurangābād (★592,052)	572,034
Avadi (★Madras)	180,291
Āzamgarh	78,382
Badagara (★102,429)	72,441
Bāgalkot	76,819
Baharampur (★126,303)	115,036
Bahraich	135,352
Baidyabāti (★Calcutta)	90,601
Bālāghāt (★67,113)	62,164
Balāngīr	70,014
Bāleshwar (★102,504)	86,116
Ballarpur (★92,438)	83,511
Ballia	84,758
Bālly (★Calcutta)	73,265
Bālly (★Calcutta)	181,978
Balrāmpur	60,077
Bālurghāt (★126,199)	119,829
Bānda	97,227
Bangalore (★4,086,548)	2,650,659
Bangaon	79,433
Bānkura	114,927
Bansberia (★Calcutta)	93,447
Bānswāra (★67,952)	66,676
Bāpatla	62,688
Bārākpur (★Calcutta)	133,429
Bārān	57,703
Baranagar (★Calcutta)	223,770
Bārāsat (★Calcutta)	102,648
Baraut	67,673
Barddhamān	244,789
Bareilly (★607,652)	583,473
Bargarh	51,135
Bāripada (★68,895)	49,569
Bārmer	69,385
Bārsi	88,774
Basīrhāt	101,652
Basti	87,512
Batala (★106,062)	88,896
Bathinda	159,114
Beāwar (★106,715)	105,357
Begusarai (★83,907)	71,362
Bela	66,845
Belampalli	66,608
Belgaum (★401,619)	325,639
Bellary	245,758
Bettiah	92,583
Betūl	63,489
Bhadrak	76,390
Bhadrāvati (★149,131)	55,413
Bhadrāvati New Town (★Bhadrāvati)	74,864
Bhadreswar (★Calcutta)	72,414
Bhāgalpur (★261,855)	254,993
Bhandāra	71,762
Bharatpur (★156,844)	148,506
Bharūch (★138,246)	132,312
Bhātpāra (★Calcutta)	304,298
Bhavāni (★97,020)	35,202
Bhāvnagar (★403,521)	400,636
Bhawānipatna	51,014
Bhilai (★688,670)	389,601
Bhīlwāra	183,791
Bhīmavaram	125,495
Bhind	109,731
Bhiwandi (★391,670)	378,546
Bhiwāni	121,449
Bhopāl	1,063,662
Bhubaneshwar	411,542
Bhuj (★110,734)	91,901
Bhusāwal (★159,459)	144,804
Bīd	112,351
Bīdar (★130,804)	107,542
Bihār	200,976
Bijāpur (★193,038)	186,846
Bijnor (★73,570)	66,156
Bīkāner	415,355
Bilāspur (★233,570)	190,911
Birlapur (★65,333)	20,239
Birnagar (★92,108)	20,014
Bishnupur	56,119
Bodhan	64,386
Bodināyakkanūr	66,028
Bokāro Steel City (★415,686)	350,540
Bombay (★12,571,720)	9,909,547
Botād	64,491
Brahmapur	210,585
Brajrajnagar	69,548
Budaun	116,706
Budge Budge (★Calcutta)	73,361
Bulandshahr	126,737
Bulsār (★111,759)	57,903
Būndi	65,016
Burhānpur	172,809
• Calcutta (★11,605,833)	4,388,262
Calicut (★800,913)	419,531
Cannanore (★Tellicherry)	65,233
Chāībāsa	56,657
Chākdaha	74,780
Chakradharpur (★48,329)	33,263
Chālisgaon	77,346
Champdāni (★Calcutta)	98,818
Chandannagar (★Calcutta)	122,351
Chandausi	82,733
Chandīgarh (★574,646)	502,992
Chandrapur	225,841
Changanācheri	52,448
Channapatna	55,210
Chāpra	136,824
Chhatarpur (★75,515)	72,745
Chhindwāra (★96,852)	93,731
Chidambaram (★68,819)	58,927
Chikmagalūr	60,814
Chilakalūrupet	79,081
Chīrāla (★142,654)	80,837
Chitradurga (★103,345)	87,053
Chittaranjan (★58,338)	47,148
Chittoor	133,233
Chūru (★82,818)	82,430
Cochin (★1,139,543)	564,038
Coimbatore (★1,135,549)	853,402
Contai	53,425
Coonoor (★99,615)	47,100
Cuddalore	143,774
Cuddapah (★215,545)	121,422
Cuttack (★439,273)	402,390
Dabgram	146,917
Dabhoi	50,619
Dāhod (★96,568)	66,444
Dāltenganj	56,408
Damoh (★105,032)	95,553
Dānāpur (★Patna)	84,104
Darbhanga	218,274
Darjiling	73,088
Datia	65,565
Dāvangere (★287,114)	265,971
Dehra Dūn (★367,411)	270,028
Dehri	94,526
Delhi (★8,375,188)	7,174,755
Delhi Cantonment (★Delhi)	94,326
Deoband	62,461
Deoghar (★85,846)	76,322
Deolāli Cantonment (★Nāsik)	51,115
Deoria	81,943
Dewās	163,699
Dhamtari	69,273
Dhanbad (★817,549)	151,334
Dhār	59,089
Dharmapuri	59,070
Dharmavaram	78,747
Dhaulpur	68,524
Dhorāji (★79,414)	77,683
Dhrāngadhra	54,281
Dhuburi	65,861
Dhule	277,957
Dibrugarh (★123,885)	118,374
Dindigul	182,293
Dum Dum (★Calcutta)	40,942
Durg (★Bhilai)	150,513

▲ Population of an entire municipality, commune, or district, including rural area.
• Largest city in country.
★ Population or designation of the metropolitan area, including suburbs.
C Census. **E** Official estimate. **U** Unofficial estimate.

▲ Bevölkerung eines ganzen städtischen Verwaltungsgebietes, eines Kommunalbezirkes oder eines Distrikts, einschliesslich ländlicher Gebiete.
• Grösste Stadt des Landes.
★ Bevölkerung oder Bezeichnung der Stadtregion einschliesslich Vororte.
C Volkszählung. **E** Offizielle Schätzung. **U** Inoffizielle Schätzung.

Durgāpur	415,986
Elūru	212,918
Erode (★357,427)	158,774
Etah	78,424
Etāwah	124,032
Faizābād (★177,505)	125,012
Farīdābad New Township (★Delhi)	613,828
Farrukhābād (★207,783)	193,624
Fatehpur	117,203
Fathpur, Rājasthān state	66,398
Fīrozābād (★270,534)	215,089
Fīrozpur	77,505
Fīrozpur Cantonment	53,691
Gadag	133,918
Gandhidham	104,392
Gāndhinagar	121,746
Ganga Ghat	50,520
Gangānagar	161,377
Gangāpur (★68,982)	53,784
Gangāwati (★81,108)	64,807
Gangtok	24,971
Gārulia (★Calcutta)	80,872
Gaya (★293,971)	291,220
Ghāziābād (★519,508)	460,949
Ghāzīpur	77,069
Girīdīh	77,912
Godhra (★100,363)	96,514
Gonda	106,078
Gondal (★81,533)	80,506
Gondia	109,271
Gorakhpur	489,850
Gudivāda	101,635
Gudiyāttam (★89,966)	82,652
Gūdūr	55,962
Gulbarga (★309,962)	303,139
Guna (★	100,389
Guntakal	107,560
Guntūr	471,020
Gurdāspur	54,575
Gurgaon (★134,639)	120,790
Guruvayur (★118,626)	20,209
Guwāhāti	577,591
Gwalior (★720,068)	692,982
Hābra (★196,457)	100,142
Hājīpur	87,669
Haldwāni	102,744
Hālisahar (★Calcutta)	113,670
Hānsi	59,638
Hanumāngarh (★82,717)	78,504
Hāora (★Calcutta)	946,732
Hāpur	146,591
Hardoi	88,632
Haridwār (★188,961)	148,882
Harihar	66,660
Hassan (★108,458)	90,719
Hāthras	113,653
Hazārībāg	97,712
Hindupur	104,635
Hinganghāt	78,709
Hingoli	54,444
Hisār (★180,774)	172,873
Hoshiārpur	122,528
Hospet (★134,935)	96,499
Hubli-Dhārwār	647,640
Hugli-Chinsurah (★Calcutta)	142,388
Hyderābād (★4,280,261)	2,991,884
Ichalkaranji (★235,854)	214,835
Imphāl (★200,615)	196,268
Indore (★1,104,065)	1,086,673
Ingrāj Bāzār (★176,991)	139,018
Itārsi (★85,706)	78,700
Jabalpur (★887,188)	739,961
Jabalpur Cantonment (★Jabalpur)	56,742
Jagādhri (★Yamunānagar)	67,371
Jagdalpur (★84,553)	65,544
Jagtiāl	67,965
Jaipur (★1,514,425)	1,454,678
Jalandhar	519,530
Jālgaon	241,603
Jālna	174,958
Jalpāiguri	67,495
Jamālpur	86,123
Jammu (★223,361) (1981C)	206,135
Jamnagar (★365,464)	325,475
Jamshedpur (★834,535)	461,212
Jaora (★55,986)	54,960
Jaunpur	136,287
Jaypur	65,582
Jetpur (★95,290)	73,556
Jhānsi (★368,590)	301,304
Jharia (★Dhanbād)	69,542
Jhārsuguda	65,022
Jhunjhunūn	71,972
Jīnd	85,307
Jodhpur	648,621
Jorhāt (★111,584)	57,998
Jūnāgadh (★166,755)	130,132
Kadaiyanallūr	68,805
Kadiri	63,428
Kaithal	71,294
Kākināda (★327,407)	279,875
Kalamassery (★Cochin)	54,313
Kālol (★92,320)	81,916
Kalyān (★Bombay)	1,014,062
Kāmārhāti (★Calcutta)	266,625
Kambam	51,987
Kāmthi (★131,837)	78,586
Kānchipuram (★169,813)	145,028
Kānchrāpāra (★Calcutta)	100,059
Kānnangād (★118,180)	57,133
Kannauj	59,650
Kānpur (★2,111,284)	1,958,282
Kānpur Cantonment (★Kānpur)	93,109
Kapra (★Hyderābād)	87,607
Kapūrthala (1981C)	63,083
Karād	56,705
Kāraikkudi (★110,473)	71,599
Karauli	48,961
Karīmnagar	148,349
Karnāl (★176,120)	173,742
Karūr (★110,605)	73,428
Kārwār	51,011
Kāsaragod	50,123
Kāsganj	75,610
Kāshīpur	69,889
Katihār (★154,101)	135,348
Kātwa	55,535
Kāvali	65,804
Kāyankulam	67,170
Khadki Cantonment (★Pune)	78,046
Khambhāt (★89,813)	76,724
Khāmgaon	73,705
Khammam (★148,646)	127,812
Khandwa	145,111
Khanna	72,140
Kharagpur (★279,736)	189,101
Kharagpur Railway Settlement (★Kharagpur)	881,253
Khargone	66,776
Khurja	80,384
Kishanganj	64,462
Kishangarh Bās	81,944
Koch Bihār (★92,628)	71,028
Kohīma	53,122
Kolār	83,219
Kolār Gold Fields (★156,398)	72,481
Kolhāpur (★417,286)	405,118
Konnagar (★Calcutta)	62,214
Korba	124,365
Kota	536,444
Kot Kapūra	62,403
Kottagūdem (★102,061)	80,420
Kottayam (★166,178)	62,829
Kovilpatti	77,967
Krishnagiri	60,252
Krishnanagar	120,918
Kukatpalle (★Hyderābād)	185,378
Kulti (★Asansol)	108,930
Kumbakonam (★150,502)	139,449
Kundla (★65,732)	64,762
Kurasia (★71,638)	15,828
Kurichi (★Coimbatore)	63,688
Kurnool (★274,795)	236,313
Lādnūn	48,174
Lakhīmpur	79,549
Lalitpur	79,891
Lātūr	197,164
Lucknow (★1,642,134)	1,592,010
Lucknow Cantonment (★Lucknow)	50,124
Ludhiāna	1,012,062
Machilīpatnam (Bandar)	159,007
Madanapalle	73,729
Madgaon (Margao) (★72,070)	58,745
Mādhavaram (★Madras)	49,005
Madras (★5,361,468)	3,795,028
Madurai (★1,093,702)	951,696
Mahbūbnagar	116,775
Mahesāna (★109,540)	87,889
Mahoba	56,152
Mahuva (★63,837)	59,675
Mainpuri	76,696
Malappuram (★142,203)	49,690
Mālegaon	342,431
Māler Kotla	88,587
Malkajgiri (★Hyderābād)	126,066
Mancheriyal	52,626
Mandsaur	95,758
Mandya	119,970
Mangalore (★425,785)	272,819
Mango (★Jamshedpur)	110,024
Manjeri	69,335
Manmād	61,257
Mannārgudi	56,563
Mathura (★233,235)	226,850
Maunath Bhanjan	136,447
Māyūram	77,042
Medinīpur	125,098
Meerut (★846,954)	752,078
Meerut Cantonment (★Meerut)	94,876
Melappālaiyam (★Tirunelveli)	68,318
Mettuppālaiyam	63,217
Mhow (★83,649)	74,852
Mira Bhayandar (★Bombay)	175,372
Miraj (★Sāngli)	121,564
Miryalaguda	65,836
Mirzāpur	169,368
Modinagar (★124,197)	102,307
Moga (★110,867)	108,213
Mokāma	59,519
Morādābād (★432,434)	416,836
Morbi (★120,107)	90,349
Morena	147,095
Mormugao (★91,285)	83,209
Motihāri (★82,965)	77,440
Muktsar	66,377
Munger	150,042
Murwāra	163,390
Muzaffarnagar (★247,729)	240,057
Muzaffarpur	240,450
Mysore (★652,246)	480,006
Nadiād (★170,018)	166,852
Nagaon	93,324
Nāgappattinam (★99,024)	86,155
Nāgaur	68,088
Nagda	79,405
Nāgercoil	189,482
Nagīna	58,494
Nāgpur (★1,661,409)	1,622,225
Naihāti (★Calcutta)	132,032
Najībābād	66,842
Nalasopara (★Bombay)	67,548
Nalgonda	84,674
Nānded (★308,853)	274,626
Nandurbār	78,364
Nandyāl	120,171
Nangi (★Calcutta)	52,909
Narasapur	56,358
Narasaraopet	88,766
Nāshik (★722,139)	646,896
Navadwip (★156,117)	125,247
Navsāri (★190,019)	125,980
Nawābganj (★77,613)	64,719
Nawāda	53,075
Nedumangād	49,864
Neemuch (★90,460)	81,397
Nellore	316,445
New Bombay (★Bombay)	307,297
NEW DELHI (★Delhi)	294,149
Neyveli (★126,494)	117,471
Nirmal	57,777
Nizāmābād	240,924
North Bārākpur (★Calcutta)	100,513
North Dum Dum (★Calcutta)	151,298
Ongole (★128,128)	100,544
Orai	98,640
Osmānābād	67,980
Pālakodu	56,972
Palani (★75,948)	68,747
Pālanpur (★90,231)	80,620
Pālayankottai (★Tirunelveli)	97,662
Pālghāt (★179,695)	122,964
Pāli	136,797
Pallavaram (★Madras)	111,194
Palwal	59,127
Palwancha	52,892
Panaji (Panjim) (★85,199)	42,915
Pānchur (★Calcutta)	30,481
Pandharpur	79,798
Pānihāti (★Calcutta)	275,359
Pānīpat	191,010
Panruti	51,424
Paramakkudi	72,105
Parbhani	190,235
Parli	72,573
Pātan (★97,025)	96,109
Pathānkot (★147,130)	142,862
Patiāla (★268,521)	253,341
Patna (★1,098,572)	916,980
Pattukkottai	57,909
Payyannūr	64,011
Periyakulam	46,739
Petlād	48,546
Phagwāra (★88,855)	83,702
Pīlībhīt	106,329
Pimpri-Chinchwad (★Pune)	515,962
Pollāchi (★127,180)	87,012
Pondicherry (★401,337)	202,648
Ponmalai (★Tiruchchirāppalli)	70,196
Ponnāni	51,754
Ponnūru Nidubrolu	54,352
Porbandar (★160,043)	116,546
Port Blair	74,810
Proddatūr	133,860
Pudukkottai	98,619
Pune (Poona) (★2,485,014)	1,559,558
Pune Cantonment (★Pune)	81,978
Puri	124,835
Pūrnia (★135,995)	114,189
Puruliya	92,574
Quilon (★362,402)	139,717
Qutubullapur (★Hyderābād)	105,380
Rabkavi Banhatti	60,607
Rāe Bareli	130,101
Rāichūr (★170,500)	157,477
Raiganj (★159,675)	151,454
Raigarh (★92,569)	89,166
Raipur (★461,851)	437,887
Rājahmundry (★403,781)	326,071
Rājapālaiyam	114,042
Rajendranagar (★Hyderābād)	83,849
Rajhara-Jharandalli	55,928
Rājkot (★651,007)	556,137
Rāj Nāndgaon	125,394
Rājpur (★86,390)	61,121
Rājpura	70,886
Rāmanāthapuram	52,654
Rāmgarh (★82,186)	51,138
Rāmpur	242,752
Rānāghāt (★126,611)	64,244
Rānchi (★614,454)	598,498
Rānībennur	67,419
Rānīganj (★155,644)	62,014
Ratlām (★195,752)	183,370
Ratnāgiri	56,512
Raurkela (★398,692)	215,489
Raurkela Civil Township (★Raurkela)	140,192
Rāyagāda	48,352
Rewa	128,918
Rewāri	75,294
Rishra (★Calcutta)	102,649
Robertson Pet (★Kolār Gold Fields)	67,900
Rohtak	215,844
Roorkee (★90,116)	80,236
Rudrapur	61,067
Sāgar (★256,878)	195,106
Sahāranpur	373,904
Saharsa	80,071
Salem (★573,685)	363,934
Sambalpur (★192,917)	130,766
Sambhal	150,012
Sangamner	48,895
Sangareddi	50,098
Sāngli (★363,728)	193,181
Sangrūr	56,374
Sardārshahr	67,969
Sarni	84,201
Sāsarām	98,220
Sātāra	95,133
Satna (★160,191)	156,321
Sawāi Mādhopur (★77,561)	72,037
Secunderābād Cantonment (★Hyderābād)	167,461
Sehore	71,437
Seoni	64,302
Serampore (★Calcutta)	137,087
Serilungampalle (★Hyderābād)	72,648
Shahdol (★60,572)	55,554
Shāhjahānpur (★260,260)	237,663
Shāmli	70,347
Shāntipur	109,911
Shikohābād	63,240
Shiliguri	226,677
Shillong (★222,273)	130,691
Shimoga (★192,647)	178,882
Shivpuri	108,271
Shrirampur (★79,042)	71,356
Siddhapur (★51,586)	50,858
Sīkar	148,235
Silchar	115,045
Simla (★109,860)	81,463
Sindri (★Dhānbād)	72,349
Sircilla	50,012
Sirsa	112,542
Sītāpur	120,595
Siuri	54,274
Sivakāsi (★102,139)	65,556
Siwān	81,092
Solāpur (★620,499)	603,870
Sonīpat	142,992
South Dum Dum (★Calcutta)	230,507
Srīkākulam	88,684
Srikalahasti	61,575
Srīnagar (★606,002) (1981C)	594,775
Srīrangam (★Tiruchchirāppalli)	69,928
Srīvilliputtūr	68,543
Sujāngarh	70,393
Sultānpur	76,567
Sūrat (★1,517,076)	149,643
Surendranagar (★166,309)	105,973
Suriāpet	60,563
Tādepallegūdem	88,979
Tādpatri	71,043
Talipparamba	60,242
Tāmbaram (★Madras)	106,590
Tānda	69,989
Tanuku	62,877
Tellicherry (★463,951)	103,577
Tenāli	143,836
Tenkāsi	55,044
Tezpur	54,999
Thāna (★Bombay)	796,620
Thānesar	81,275
Thanjāvūr	200,216
Theni-Allinagaram	65,958
Thrippunithura (★Cochin)	51,032
Tīkamgarh	54,130
Tindivanam	61,715
Tinsukia	73,760
Tiruchchirāppalli (★711,120)	386,628
Tiruchengodu	62,903
Tirunelveli (★365,932)	135,762
Tirupati (★189,030)	174,393
Tiruppattūr	54,884
Tiruppur (★305,546)	235,076
Tiruvannāmalai	108,291
Tirūvottiyūr (★Madras)	167,851
Titāgarh (★Calcutta)	113,831
Tonk	100,020
Trichūr (★274,898)	73,849
Trivandrum (★825,682)	523,733
Trruchchendūr (★75,400)	27,363
Tumkūr (★179,497)	138,598
Tuticorin (★284,193)	205,105
Udagamandalam	81,726
Udaipur	307,682
Udamalpet	58,643
Udgīr	70,409
Ujjain	366,787
Ulhāsnagar (★Bombay)	368,822
Unnāo	107,246
Upleta	51,553
Uppal Kalan (★Hyderābād)	75,039
Uttarpara-Kotrung (★Calcutta)	100,867
Vadodara (★1,115,390)	1,021,084
Vālpārai	106,289
Vāniyambādi (★92,097)	72,282
Vārānasi (Benares) (★1,026,467)	925,962
Vasai (Bassein) (★83,572)	39,741
Veerappanchattiram (★Erode)	61,598
Vejalpur (★Ahmadābād)	89,053
Vellore (★304,713)	172,467
Verāval (★119,995)	93,826
Vidisha	92,917
Vijayawāda (★845,305)	701,351
Vikramasingapuram	49,034
Viluppuram	88,916
Viramgām	51,089
VirārBombay)	57,581
Virudunagar	70,951
Vishākhapatnam (★1,051,918)	750,024
Visnagar (★59,693)	57,834
Vizianagaram (★176,125)	159,461
Wadhwan (★Surendranager)	49,773
Warangal (★466,877)	446,760
Wardha	102,974
Wāshīm	49,133
Yamunānagar (★219,642)	144,250
Yavatmāl (★121,834)	108,591
Yemmiganur	65,118
INDONESIA	
1980 C	147,490,298
Ambon (▲207,702)	111,914
Balikpapan (▲279,852)	208,040
Banda Aceh (Kuturaja)	71,868
Bandung (★1,800,000) (1985E)	1,633,000
Banjarmasin (1983E)	424,000
Banyuwangi	90,378
Batang	49,328
Bekasi (★Jakarta)	144,290
Bengkulu (▲64,733)	32,478
Binjai	71,444
Blitar (★100,000)	78,503
Bogor (★560,000)	246,946
Bojonegoro	57,483
Bukittinggi (▲70,691)	55,577
Cianjur	105,655
Cibinong	87,580
Cilacap	127,017
Cimahi (★Bandung) (1971C)	72,367
Ciparay	66,854
Cirebon (★275,000)	223,504
Denpasar	159,233
Depok (★Jakarta)	126,693
Garut	145,624
Genteng	59,481
Gorontalo (▲97,610)	63,554
Gresik	86,418
● JAKARTA (★1,000,000) (1989E)	9,200,000
Jambi (▲230,046)	155,761
Jayapura (Sukarnapura)	60,641
Jember	171,284
Jombang	58,800
Karawang	72,195
Kediri (▲221,830)	176,261
Kisaran	58,129
Klangenang	64,013
Klaten	117,560
Kudus	154,478
Kupang	84,587
Langsa	16,426
Lumajang	58,495
Madiun (★180,000)	150,562
Magelang (★160,000)	123,358
Majalaya	87,474
Malang (1983E)	547,000
Manado	217,091
Mataram	210,485
Medan (1985E)	2,110,000
Mojokerto	68,849
Muncar	47,009
Padang (▲657,000) (1983E)	405,600
Padangsidempuan	56,984
Palangkaraya (▲60,447)	51,686
Palembang (1983E)	874,000
Pangkalpinang	90,078
Pare	47,262
Parepare (▲86,360)	62,865
Pasuruan (★125,000)	95,864
Pati	50,159
Pekalongan (★260,000)	132,413
Pekanbaru	186,199
Pemalang	72,663
Pematangsiantar (★175,000)	150,296
Ponorogo	55,523
Pontianak (1983E)	343,000

▲ Población de un municipio, comuna o distrito entero, incluyendo sus áreas rurales.
● Ciudad más grande de un país.
★ Población o designación de un área metropolitana, incluyendo los suburbios.
C Censo. **E** Estimado oficial. **U** Estimado no oficial.

▲ Population d'une municipalité, d'une commune ou d'un district, zone rurale incluse.
● Ville la plus peuplée du pays.
★ Population de l'agglomération (ou nom de la zone métropolitaine englobante).
C Recensement. **E** Estimation officielle. **U** Estimation non officielle.

▲ População de um municipio, comuna ou distrito, inclusive as respectivas áreas rurais.
● Maior cidade de um país.
★ População ou indicação de uma área metropolitana.
C Censo. **E** Estimativa oficial. **U** Estimativa não oficial.

Pringsewu	56,115
Probolinggo	100,296
Purwakarta	61,995
Purwokerto	143,787
Salatiga	85,740
Samarinda (▲264,012)	182,473
Semarang (1983E)	1,206,000
Serang	78,209
Sibolga	59,466
Sidoarjo	56,090
Singaraja	53,368
Singkawang	58,693
Situbondo	58,299
Sorong	52,041
Subang	52,041
Sukabumi (★225,000)	109,898
Surabaya (1985E)	2,345,000
Surakarta (★575,000) (1983E)	491,000
Taman	64,358
Tangerang	97,091
Tanjungkarang-Telukbetung (★375,000)	284,167
Tarakan	46,657
Tasikmalaya	192,267
Tebingtinggi (▲92,068)	69,569
Tegal (★340,000)	131,440
Tembilahan	52,140
Tuban	48,558
Tulungagung	91,585
Ujungpandang (Makasar) (1983E)	841,000
Yogyakarta (★510,000) (1983E)	421,000

IRAN / Īrān

1986 C	49,445,010
Ābādān (1976C)	296,081
Āghā Jārī (1982E)	64,000
Ahar (1982E)	52,000
Ahvāz	579,826
Āmol	118,242
Andīmeshk (1982E)	53,000
Arāk	265,349
Ardabīl	281,973
Bābol	115,320
Bākhtarān (Kermānshāh)	560,514
Bandar-e 'Abbās	201,642
Bandar-e Anzalī (Bandar-e Pahlavī) (1982E)	83,000
Bandar-e Būshehr	120,787
Bandar-e Māh Shahr (1982E)	88,000
Behbahān (1982E)	84,000
Bīrjand (1982E)	68,000
Bojnūrd (1982E)	82,000
Borāzjān (1982E)	53,000
Borūjerd	183,879
Dezfūl	151,420
Do Rūd (1982E)	52,000
Emāmshahr (Shāhrūd) (1982E)	68,000
Eşfahān (★1,175,000)	986,753
Eslāmābād (1982E)	71,000
Eslāmshahr (★Tehrān)	215,129
Fasā (1982E)	67,000
Gonbad-e Qābūs (1982E)	75,000
Gorgān	139,430
Hamadān	272,499
Īlām (1982E)	75,000
Jahrom (1982E)	68,000
Karaj (★Tehrān)	275,100
Kāshān	138,599
Kāzerūn (1982E)	63,000
Kermān	257,284
Khomeynīshahr (★Eşfahān)	104,647
Khorramābād	208,592
Khorramshahr (1976C)	146,706
Khvoy	115,343
Mahābād (1982E)	63,000
Malāyer	103,640
Marāgheh	100,679
Marand (1982E)	59,000
Marv Dasht (1982E)	72,000
Mashhad	1,463,508
Masjed-e Soleymān	104,787
Mīāndoāb (1982E)	52,000
Mīāneh (1982E)	57,000
Najafābād	129,058
Neyshābūr	109,258
Orūmīyeh (Reẕā'īyeh)	300,746
Qā'emshahr	109,288
Qazvīn	248,591
Qom	543,139
Qomsheh (1982E)	67,000
Qūchān (1982E)	61,000
Rafsanjān (1982E)	61,000
Rāmhormoz (1982E)	53,000
Rasht	290,897
Sabzevār	129,103
Sanandaj	204,537
Saqqez (1982E)	76,000
Sārī	141,020
Semnān (1982E)	54,000
Shahr-e Kord (1982E)	63,000
Shīrāz	848,289
Sīrjān (1982E)	67,000
Tabrīz	971,482
● TEHRĀN (★7,500,000)	6,042,584
Torbat-e Heydarīyeh (1982E)	62,000
Varāmīn (1982E)	51,000
Yazd	230,483
Zābol (1982E)	58,000
Zāhedān	281,923
Zanjān	215,261
Zarrīn Shahr (1982E)	69,000

IRAQ / Al 'Irāq

1985 E	15,584,987
Ad-Dīwānīyah (1970E)	62,300
Al-'Amārah	131,785
Al-Başrah	616,700
Al-Ḩillah	215,249
Al-Kūt	73,022
Al-Mawşil	570,926
An-Najaf	242,603
An-Nāşirīyah	138,842
Ar-Ramādī	137,388
As-Samāwah	75,293
As-Sulaymānīyah	279,424
● BAGHDĀD (1987C)	3,841,268
Ba'qūbah	114,516
Irbīl	333,903
Karbalā'	184,574
Kirkūk (1970E)	207,900
Sāmarrā'	20,002

IRELAND / Éire

1986 C	3,540,643
Cork (★173,694)	133,271
● DUBLIN (BAILE ÁTHA CLIATH) (★1,140,000)	502,749
Dún Laoghaire (★Dublin)	54,715
Galway	47,104
Limerick (★76,557)	56,279
Waterford (★41,054)	39,529

ISLE OF MAN

1986 C	64,282
● DOUGLAS (★28,500)	20,368

ISRAEL / Isrā'īl / Yisra'el

1991 E	4,713,800
Ashdod	83,900
Ashqelon	59,700
Bat Yam (★Tel Aviv-Yafo)	141,300
Be'ér Sheva (Beersheba)	122,000
Bene Beraq (★Tel Aviv-Yafo)	116,700
Elat	26,300
Giv'atayim (★Tel Aviv-Yafo)	46,600
Ḩefa (★450,000)	245,900
Herzliyya (★Tel Aviv-Yafo)	77,200
Ḩolon (★Tel Aviv-Yafo)	156,700
Kefar Sava (★Tel Aviv-Yafo)	61,100
Lod (Lydda) (★Tel Aviv-Yafo)	43,300
Nazerat (Nazareth) (★77,000)	53,600
Netanya (★Tel Aviv-Yafo)	132,200
Petah Tiqwa (★Tel Aviv-Yafo)	144,000
Ra'ananna (★Tel Aviv-Yafo)	53,600
Ramat Gan (★Tel Aviv-Yafo)	119,500
Rehovot (★Tel Aviv-Yafo)	80,300
Rishon LeZiyyon (★Tel Aviv-Yafo)	139,500
● Tel Aviv-Yafo (★1,735,000)	339,400
YERUSHALAYIM (AL-QUDS) (JERUSALEM) (★560,000)	524,500

ISRAELI OCCUPIED TERRITORIES

1991 E	1,704,900
Al-Quds (Jerusalem) (★Yerushalayim) (1976E)	90,000
Arīḩā (Jericho) (1967C)	6,829
Bayt Laḩm (Bethlehem) (1971E)	25,000
● Ghazzah (1967C)	118,272
Khān Yūnis (1967C)	52,997
Nābulus (1971E)	64,000
Rafaḩ (1967C)	49,812

ITALY / Italia

1987 E	57,290,519
Afragola (★Napoli)	59,397
Alessandria (▲96,014)	76,100
Altamura	54,784
Ancona	104,409
Andria	88,348
Arezzo (▲91,681)	74,200
Asti (▲75,459)	63,600
Avellino	56,407
Aversa (★Napoli)	57,827
Bari (★475,000)	362,524
Barletta	86,954
Benevento (▲65,661)	54,400
Bergamo (★345,000)	118,959
Biella	51,788
Bitonto	51,962
Bologna (★525,000)	432,406
Bolzano	101,515
Brescia	199,286
Brindisi	92,280
Busto Arsizio (★Milano)	78,056
Cagliari (★305,000)	220,574
Caltanissetta	62,352
Campobasso (▲50,801)	44,000
Carpi (▲60,614)	49,500
Carrara (★Massa)	69,229
Caserta	65,974
Casoria (★Napoli)	54,100
Castellammare di Stabia (★Napoli)	68,491
Catania (★550,000)	372,486
Catanzaro	102,558
Cava de'Tirreni (★Salerno)	52,028
Cerignola	53,463
Cesena (▲90,012)	72,600
Chieti	55,827
Cinisello Balsamo (★Milano)	78,917
Civitavecchia	50,806
Collegno (★Torino)	49,334
Cologno Monzese (★Milano)	52,554
Como (★165,000)	91,738
Cosenza (★150,000)	106,026
Cremona	76,979
Crotone (▲61,005)	53,600
Cuneo (▲55,878)	47,900
Empoli (▲43,940)	33,200
Ercolano (★Napoli)	62,783
Ferrara (▲143,950)	113,300
Firenze (★640,000)	425,835
Foggia	155,051
Foligno (▲53,568)	42,500
Forlì (▲110,482)	91,200
Gela	79,378
Genova (Genoa) (★805,000)	727,427
Giugliano in Campania (★Napoli)	51,187
Grosseto (▲70,592)	56,400
Imola (▲61,587)	48,200
Imperia	41,481
L'Aquila (▲66,438)	42,200
La Spezia (★185,000)	108,937
Latina (▲98,479)	67,800
Lecce	100,981
Lecco	48,844
Legnano (★Milano)	48,711
Livorno	174,065
Lucca	88,024
Manfredonia	57,707
Mantova (▲56,817)	49,000
Marsala	80,468
Massa (★145,000)	66,872
Matera	52,819
Messina	268,896
Mestre (★Venezia)	189,700
● Milano (Milan) (★3,750,000)	1,495,260
Modena	176,880
Molfetta	64,519
Moncalieri (★Torino)	62,306
Monza (★Milano)	122,064
Napoli (Naples) (★2,875,000)	1,204,211
Nicastro (▲67,562)	52,100
Nocera Inferiore	48,151
Novara	102,742
Padova (★270,000)	225,769
Palermo	723,732
Parma	175,842
Paternò	45,513
Pavia	82,065
Perugia (▲146,713)	106,700
Pesaro (▲90,336)	78,700
Pescara	131,027
Piacenza	105,626
Pisa	104,384
Pistoia (▲90,689)	76,800
Pordenone	50,825
Portici (★Napoli)	76,302
Potenza (▲67,114)	57,600
Pozzuoli (★Napoli)	65,000
Prato (★215,000)	164,595
Quartu Sant'Elena	52,838
Ragusa	67,748
Ravenna (▲136,016)	86,500
Reggio di Calabria	178,821
Reggio nell'Emilia (▲130,086)	107,300
Rho (★Milano)	50,876
Rimini (▲130,698)	114,600
Rivoli (★Torino)	50,786
ROMA (★3,175,000)	2,815,457
Salerno (★250,000)	154,848
San Benedetto del Tronto	45,397
San Giorgio a Cremano (★Napoli)	63,656
San Remo	60,797
San Severo	55,239
Sassari	120,152
Savona (★112,000)	62,300
Scandicci (★Firenze)	54,367
Sesto Fiorentino (★Firenze)	46,355
Sesto San Giovanni (★Milano)	91,624
Siena	59,712
Siracusa	122,857
Taranto	244,997
Teramo (▲52,378)	36,000
Terni (▲111,157)	94,500
Torino (★1,550,000)	1,035,565
Torre Annunziata (★Napoli)	57,508
Torre del Greco (★Napoli)	105,066
Trapani (▲73,083)	63,000
Trento (▲100,202)	81,500
Treviso	85,083
Trieste (Triest)	239,031
Udine (★126,000)	100,211
Varese	88,353
Venezia (Venice) (★420,000)	88,700
Vercelli	51,008
Verona	259,151
Viareggio (▲59,146)	50,300
Vicenza	110,449
Vigevano	62,671
Viterbo (▲59,267)	47,900
Vittoria	54,795

IVORY COAST / Côte d'Ivoire

1983 E	9,300,000
● ABIDJAN	1,950,000
Bouaké	275,000
Daloa (1986E)	120,000
Korhogo	125,000
Man (1986E)	59,000
YAMOUSSOUKRO	80,000

JAMAICA

1982 C	2,190,357
● KINGSTON (★770,000) (1987E)	646,400
Montego Bay	70,265
Portmore (★Kingston)	73,426
Spanish Town (★Kingston)	89,097

JAPAN / Nihon

1990 C	123,611,541
Abiko (★Tōkyō)	120,629
Ageo (★Tōkyō)	194,952
Aizu-wakamatsu	119,084
Akashi (★Ōsaka)	270,728
Akigawa (★Tōkyō)	50,388
Akishima (★Tōkyō)	105,375
Akita	302,359
Akō	51,131
Amagasaki (★Ōsaka)	498,998
Anan (▲59,045)	47,000
Anjō	142,217
Aomori	287,813
Arao (★Ōmuta)	59,508
Asahikawa	359,069
Asaka (★Tōkyō)	103,621
Ashikaga	167,687
Ashiya (★Ōsaka)	87,528
Atami	47,290
Atsugi (★Tōkyō)	197,292
Ayase (★Tōkyō)	77,926
Beppu	130,323
Bisai (★Nagoya)	55,881
Chiba (★Tōkyō)	829,467
Chichibu	60,916
Chigasaki (★Tōkyō)	201,672
Chikushino (★Fukuoka)	70,303
Chiryū (★Nagoya)	54,061
Chita (★Nagoya)	75,434
Chitose	78,947
Chōfu (★Tōkyō)	197,680
Chōshi	85,138
Daitō (★Ōsaka)	126,460
Dazaifu(★Fukuoka)	62,408
Ebetsu (★Sapporo)	97,201
Ebina (★Tōkyō)	105,816
Eniwa	55,613
Fuchū (★Tōkyō)	209,419
Fuchū	45,738
Fuchū	50,061
Fuji (★370,000)	222,500
Fujieda (★Shizuoka)	119,815
Fujiidera (★Ōsaka)	65,924
Fujimi (★Tōkyō)	94,858
Fujinomiya (★Fuji)	117,093
Fujioka (▲60,983)	50,100
Fujisawa (★Tōkyō)	350,335
Fuji-yoshida	54,802
Fukaya (▲94,023)	75,600
Fukuchiyama (▲66,506)	56,700
Fukui	252,750
Fukuoka (★1,750,000)	1,237,107
Fukushima	277,526
Fukuyama	365,615
Funabashi (★Tōkyō)	533,273
Furukawa (▲64,227)	51,200
Fussa (★Tōkyō)	58,053
Gamagōri	84,819
Gifu	410,318
Ginowan (1985C)	69,206
Ginowan	75,899
Gotemba	79,560
Gushikawa	54,026
Gyōda	83,181
Habikino (★Ōsaka)	115,035
Hachinohe	241,065
Hachiōji (★Tōkyō)	466,373
Hadano (★Tōkyō)	155,619
Hagi	50,619
Hakodate	307,251
Hamada	49,139
Hamakita	81,159
Hamamatsu	534,624
Hanamaki (▲70,514)	55,000
Handa (★Nagoya)	99,550
Hannō (★Tōkyō)	73,216
Hashima	61,460
Hasuda (★Tōkyō)	59,703
Hatogaya (★Tōkyō)	56,441
Hatsukaichi (★Hiroshima)	63,441
Hekinan	65,901
Higashihiroshima (★Hiroshima)	94,206
Higashikurume (★Tōkyō)	113,800
Higashimatsuyama	84,395
Higashimurayama (★Tōkyō)	134,002
Higashiōsaka (★Ōsaka)	518,251
Higashiyamato (★Tōkyō)	75,124
Hikari (★Tokuyama)	47,613
Hikone	99,518
Himeji (★660,000)	454,360
Himi (▲60,768)	51,400
Hino (★Tōkyō)	165,935
Hirakata (★Ōsaka)	390,790
Hiratsuka (★Tōkyō)	245,944
Hirosaki (▲174,710)	133,800
Hiroshima (★1,575,000)	1,085,677
Hita (▲64,694)	57,100
Hitachi	202,145
Hōfu	117,639
Honjō	59,094
Hōya (★Tōkyō)	95,148
Hyūga	58,448
Ibaraki (★Ōsaka)	254,080
Ichihara (★Tōkyō)	257,717
Ichikawa (★Tōkyō)	436,597
Ichinomiya (★Nagoya)	262,434
Ichinoseki (▲61,971)	50,100
Iida (▲91,859)	64,700
Iizuka (★110,000)	83,133
Ikeda (★Ōsaka)	104,219
Ikoma (★Ōsaka)	99,598
Imabari	123,114
Imari (▲60,887)	50,000
Ina (▲60,063)	49,500
Inagi (★Tōkyō)	58,593
Inazawa (★Nagoya)	96,277
Inuyama (★Nagoya)	69,803
Iruma (★Tōkyō)	137,585
Isahaya	90,678
Ise (Uji-yamada)	104,162
Isehara (★Tōkyō)	89,568
Isesaki	115,939
Ishinomaki	121,980
Itami (★Ōsaka)	186,132
Itō	71,223
Iwaki (Taira)	355,817
Iwakuni	109,534
Iwamizawa	80,423
Iwata	83,521
Iwatsuki (★Tōkyō)	106,462
Izumi (★Sendai)	124,216
Izumi (★Ōsaka)	146,105
Izumi-ōtsu (★Ōsaka)	67,037
Izumi-sano (★Ōsaka)	88,862
Izumo (▲82,680)	69,600
Joetsu	130,114
Jōyō (★Ōsaka)	84,770
Kadoma (★Ōsaka)	142,288
Kaga	69,199
Kagoshima	536,685
Kainan (★Wakayama)	48,598
Kaizuka (★Ōsaka)	79,236
Kakamigahara	129,682
Kakegawa (▲72,795)	59,000
Kakogawa (★Ōsaka)	239,803
Kamagaya (★Tōkyō)	95,052
Kamaishi	52,483
Kamakura (★Tōkyō)	174,299
Kameoka	85,283
Kamifukuoka (★Tōkyō)	58,753
Kanazawa	442,872
Kani (★Nagoya)	80,012
Kanoya (▲77,652)	61,500
Kanuma (▲90,044)	74,900
Karatsu (▲79,206)	70,500
Kariya (★Nagoya)	120,121
Kasai	51,789
Kasaoka (▲59,618)	52,700
Kashihara (★Ōsaka)	115,556
Kashiwa (★Tōkyō)	305,060
Kashiwara (★Ōsaka)	76,819
Kashiwazaki (▲88,309)	75,300
Kasuga (★Fukuoka)	88,703
Kasugai (★Nagoya)	266,599
Kasukabe (★Tōkyō)	188,809
Katano (★Ōsaka)	65,311
Katsuta	109,826
Kawachi-nagano (★Ōsaka)	108,770
Kawagoe (★Tōkyō)	304,860
Kawaguchi (★Tōkyō)	438,667
Kawanishi (★Ōsaka)	141,254
Kawasaki (★Tōkyō)	1,173,606
Kesennuma	65,578
Kimitsu (▲89,243)	76,100
Kiryū	126,443
Kisarazu	123,434
Kishiwada (★Ōsaka)	188,553
Kitaibaraki	51,092
Kitakyūshū (★1,525,000)	1,026,467
Kitami	107,247
Kitamoto (★Tōkyō)	63,933
Kiyose (★Tōkyō)	67,540
Kōbe (★Ōsaka)	1,477,423
Kōchi	317,090
Kodaira (★Tōkyō)	164,021
Kōfu	200,630

▲ Population of an entire municipality, commune, or district, including rural area.
● Largest city in country.
★ Population or designation of the metropolitan area, including suburbs.
C Census. **E** Official estimate. **U** Unofficial estimate.

▲ Bevölkerung eines ganzen städtischen Verwaltungsgebietes, eines Kommunalbezirkes oder eines Distrikts, einschliesslich ländlicher Gebiete.
● Grösste Stadt des Landes.
★ Bevölkerung oder Bezeichnung der Stadtregion einschliesslich Vororte.
C Volkszählung. **E** Offizielle Schätzung. **U** Inoffizielle Schätzung.

Koga (★Tōkyō)	58,227
Koganei (★Tōkyō)	105,888
Kokubunji (★Tōkyō)	100,958
Komae (★Tōkyō)	74,197
Komaki (★Nagoya)	124,441
Komatsu	106,072
Kōnan (★Nagoya)	93,836
Kōnosu (★Tōkyō)	72,436
Kōriyama	314,651
Koshigaya (★Tōkyō)	285,280
Kudamatsu (★Tokuyama)	53,029
Kuki (★Tōkyō)	66,852
Kumagaya	152,122
Kumamoto	579,305
Kunitachi (★Tōkyō)	65,830
Kurashiki	414,692
Kurayoshi (▲51,835)	42,700
Kure (★Hiroshima)	216,717
Kuroiso (▲52,346)	41,900
Kurume	228,350
Kusatsu (★Ōsaka)	94,766
Kushiro	205,640
Kuwana (★Nagoya)	97,911
Kyōto (★Ōsaka)	1,461,140
Machida (★Tōkyō)	349,030
Maebashi	286,261
Maizuru	96,329
Marugame	75,607
Matsubara (★Ōsaka)	135,921
Matsudo (★Tōkyō)	456,211
Matsue	142,931
Matsumoto	200,723
Matsusaka	118,727
Matsuyama	443,317
Mihara	85,518
Miki (★Ōsaka)	76,509
Minō (★Ōsaka)	122,133
Misato (★Tōkyō)	128,377
Mishima (★Numazu)	105,419
Mitaka (★Tōkyō)	165,555
Mito	234,970
Miura (★Tōkyō)	52,441
Miyako	58,505
Miyakonojō (▲130,155)	106,200
Miyazaki	287,367
Mobara	83,437
Moriguchi (★Ōsaka)	157,365
Morioka	235,440
Moriyama	58,561
Mukō (★Ōsaka)	52,932
Munakata	68,267
Muroran (★195,000)	117,852
Musashimurayama (★Tōkyō)	65,555
Musashino (★Tōkyō)	139,069
Mutsu	48,470
Nabari	68,933
Nagahama	55,482
Nagano	347,036
Nagaoka	185,938
Nagaokakyō (★Ōsaka)	77,193
Nagareyama (★Tōkyō)	140,059
Nagasaki	444,616
Nagoya (★4,800,000)	2,154,664
Naha	304,896
Nakama (★Kitakyūshū)	49,216
Nakatsu	66,383
Nakatsugawa	53,722
Nanao	50,101
Nara (★Ōsaka)	349,356
Narashino (★Tōkyō)	151,472
Narita	86,708
Naruto	64,577
Naze	46,309
Neyagawa (★Ōsaka)	256,521
Niigata	486,087
Niihama	129,151
Niitsu (▲64,005)	55,700
Niiza (★Tōkyō)	138,919
Nishinomiya (★Ōsaka)	426,919
Nishio	95,198
Nobeoka	130,615
Noboribetsu (★Muroran)	55,575
Noda (★Tōkyō)	114,476
Nōgata	62,532
Noshiro (▲55,915)	47,800
Numazu (★495,000)	211,731
Obihiro	167,389
Ōbu (★Nagoya)	69,721
Ōdate (▲68,196)	58,500
Odawara	193,415
Ōgaki	148,281
Ōita	408,502
Ōkawa	45,705
Okaya	59,854
Okayama	593,742
Okazaki	306,821
Okegawa (★Tōkyō)	69,030
Okinawa	105,852
Ōme (★Tōkyō)	125,945
Ōmi-hachiman (★Ōsaka)	66,068
Ōmiya (★Tōkyō)	403,779
Ōmura	73,437
Ōmuta (★225,000)	150,461
Ōnojō (★Fukuoka)	75,217
Onomichi	97,104
Ōsaka (★16,900,000)	2,623,831
Ōta	139,801
Otaru (★Sapporo)	163,215
Ōtsu (★Ōsaka)	260,004
Owariashi (★Nagoya)	65,676
Oyama (▲142,263)	120,000
Sabae	62,284
Saga	169,964
Sagamihara (★Tōkyō)	531,562
Saijō	56,823
Saiki	52,325
Sakado (★Tōkyō)	95,736
Sakai (★Ōsaka)	807,859
Sakaide	63,878
Sakata	100,808
Saku (▲62,005)	50,000
Sakura (★Tōkyō)	144,688
Sakurai	60,261
Sanda (▲64,560 (★ Ōsaka)	54,500
Sanjō	85,824
Sano	83,484
Sapporo (★1,900,000)	1,671,765
Sasebo	244,693
Satte	54,339
Sayama (★Tōkyō)	157,307
Sayama (★Ōsaka)	54,323
Seki	68,386

Sendai, Kagoshima pref. (▲71,736)	58,000
Sendai, Miyagi pref. (★1,175,000)	918,378
Sennan (★Ōsaka)	60,054
Seto	126,343
Settsu (★Ōsaka)	87,465
Shibata (▲78,168)	63,600
Shibukawa	49,064
Shijōnawate (★Ōsaka)	50,036
Shiki (★Tōkyō)	63,492
Shimada (▲73,809)	64,500
Shimizu (★Shizuoka)	241,524
Shimodate (▲66,030)	54,100
Shimonoseki (★Kitakyūshū)	262,643
Shiogama (★Sendai)	62,025
Shizuoka (★975,000)	472,199
Sōka (★Tōkyō)	206,129
Suita (★Ōsaka)	345,187
Suwa	52,465
Suzuka	174,103
Tachikawa (★Tōkyō)	152,817
Tagajō (★Sendai)	58,456
Tagawa	57,701
Tajimi (★Nagoya)	94,036
Takaishi (★Ōsaka)	65,084
Takamatsu	329,695
Takaoka (★220,000)	175,469
Takarazuka (★Ōsaka)	201,863
Takasago (★Ōsaka)	93,267
Takasaki	236,463
Takatsuki (★Ōsaka)	359,867
Takayama	65,245
Takefu	70,188
Takikawa	49,591
Tama (★Tōkyō)	144,490
Tamano	73,240
Tanabe (▲69,861)	59,100
Tanashi (★Tōkyō)	75,141
Tatebayashi	76,223
Tenri	68,818
Tochigi	86,216
Toda (★Tōkyō)	87,600
Tōkai (★Nagoya)	97,359
Toki	64,946
Tokoname (★Nagoya)	51,784
Tokorozawa (★Tōkyō)	303,047
Tokushima	263,336
Tokuyama (★250,000)	110,900
• TŌKYŌ (★30,300,000)	8,163,127
Tomakomai	160,116
Tondabayashi (★Ōsaka)	110,444
Toride (★Tōkyō)	81,667
Tosu	55,878
Tottori	142,477
Toyama	321,459
Toyoake (★Nagoya)	62,156
Toyohashi	337,988
Toyokawa	111,731
Toyonaka (★Ōsaka)	409,843
Toyota	332,336
Tsu	157,178
Tsuchiura	127,470
Tsuruga	68,039
Tsuruoka	99,891
Tsushima (★Nagoya)	59,345
Tsuyama	89,405
Ube (★230,000)	175,052
Ueda	119,435
Ueno (▲60,239)	51,400
Uji (★Ōsaka)	177,018
Uozu	49,516
Urasoe	89,993
Urawa (★Tōkyō)	418,267
Urayasu (★Tōkyō)	115,675
Usa (▲50,830)	38,600
Ushiku	60,698
Utsunomiya	426,809
Wakayama (★495,000)	396,554
Wakkanai	48,232
Wakō (★Tōkyō)	56,891
Warabi (★Tōkyō)	73,620
Yachiyo (★Tōkyō)	148,615
Yaizu (★Shizuoka)	112,188
Yamagata	249,493
Yamaguchi	129,467
Yamato (★Tōkyō)	194,870
Yamato-kōriyama (★Ōsaka)	92,948
Yamato-takada (★Ōsaka)	68,236
Yame (▲39,817)	32,800
Yao (★Ōsaka)	277,724
Yashio (★Tōkyō)	72,474
Yatsushiro (▲108,135)	88,300
Yawata (★Ōsaka)	75,761
Yokkaichi	274,184
Yokohama (★Tōkyō)	3,220,350
Yokosuka (★Tōkyō)	433,361
Yonago	131,453
Yonezawa	94,763
Yono (★Tōkyō)	79,058
Yotsukaidō (★Tōkyō)	72,157
Yukuhashi	65,713
Zama (★Tōkyō)	112,100
Zushi (★Tōkyō)	56,705

JERSEY

1986 C	80,212
• SAINT HELIER (★46,500)	27,083

JORDAN / Al-Urdun

1989 E	3,111,000
Al-Baq'ah (★'Ammān)	63,985
• 'AMMĀN (★1,625,000)	936,300
Ar-Ruṣayfah (★'Ammān)	72,580
As-Salṭ	47,585
Az-Zarqā' (★'Ammān)	318,055
Irbid	167,785

KAZAKHSTAN

1991 E	16,793,100
Akt'ubinsk	266,600
• ALMA-ATA (★1,190,000)	1,156,200
Arkalyk	64,900
Balchaš	87,600
Čelinograd	286,000
Čimkent	438,800
Džambul	312,300
Džetygara	48,900
Džezkazgan	111,100
Ekibastuz	138,900
Gurjev	156,700
Karaganda	608,600
Kentau	65,100
Kokčetav	143,300
Kustanaj	233,900
Kzyl-Orda	158,200
Leninogorsk	69,500
Pavlodar	342,500
Petropavlovsk	248,300
Rudnyj	128,800
Šachtinsk	65,300
Saptajev	61,400
Saran'	62,600
Ščučinsk	56,000
Semipalatinsk	344,700
Ševčenko	169,000
Taldy-Kurgan	136,100
Turkestan	81,200
Ural'sk	214,000
Ust'-Kamenogorsk	332,900
Žanatas	53,000
Zyr'anovsk	53,800

KENYA

1990 E	24,870,000
Eldoret (1979C)	50,503
Kisumu (1984E)	167,100
Machakos (1983E)	92,300
Meru (1979C)	72,049
Mombasa	537,000
• NAIROBI	1,505,000
Nakuru (1984E)	101,700

KIRIBATI

1990 C	72,298
BAIRIKI	2,226
• Bikenibeu	5,055

KOREA, NORTH / Chosŏn-minjujuŭi-inmīn-konghwaguk

1981 E	18,317,000
Ch'ŏngjin	490,000
Haeju (1983E)	213,000
Hamhŭng (1970E)	150,000
Hŭngnam (1976E)	260,000
Kaesŏng	259,000
Kanggye (1967E)	130,000
Kimch'aek (Sŏngjin) (1967E)	265,000
Namp'o	241,000
• P'YŎNGYANG (★1,600,000)	1,283,000
Sinŭiju	305,000
Songnim (1944C)	53,035
Wŏnsan	398,000

KOREA, SOUTH / Taehan-min'guk

1990 C	43,520,199
Andong	116,932
Ansan (★Sŏul)	252,157
Anyang (★Sŏul)	480,668
Bucheon (★Sŏul)	667,777
Changsŭngp'o	48,614
Changwŏn (★Masan)	323,138
Chech'on	102,037
Cheju	232,687
Chinhae	120,207
Chinju	258,365
Chŏmch'on	47,802
Ch'ŏnan	211,382
Ch'ŏngju	497,429
Chŏnju	86,850
Chŏnju, Chŏlla Pukdo prov.	517,104
Ch'unch'ŏn	174,153
Ch'ungju	129,994
Ch'ungmu	92,159
Hanam (★Sŏul)	101,278
Inch'ŏn (★Sŏul)	1,818,293
Iri	203,401
Kangnŭng	152,605
Kimch'ŏn	81,349
Kimhae	106,166
Kimje	55,136
Kongju	65,195
Kumi	206,101
Kŭmsŏng (1985C)	58,897
Kunp'o (★Sŏul)	99,956
Kunsan	218,216
Kwachŏn (★Sŏul)	72,328
Kwangju	1,144,695
Kwangmyŏng (★Sŏul)	328,803
Kyŏngju	141,895
Masan (★625,000)	496,639
Mikŭm (★Sŏul)	74,688
Miryang	52,995
Mokp'o	253,423
Naju	55,306
Namwŏn	63,121
P'ohang	318,595
Pusan (★3,800,000)	3,797,566
P'yŏngt'aek	79,238
Samch'ŏnp'o	62,824
Sangju	51,875
Shihŭng (★Sŏul)	107,190
Sŏgwipo	88,292
Sŏkch'o	73,796
Sŏngnam (★Sŏul)	540,764
Songtan	77,460
Sŏsan	55,930
• SŎUL (★15,850,000)	10,627,790
Sunch'ŏn	167,209
Suwŏn (★Sŏul)	644,968
T'aebaek	89,770
Taech'ŏn	56,922
Taegu	2,228,834
Taejŏn	1,062,084
Tongduchŏn	71,448
Tonghae	89,162
Tongkwang	70,118
Ŭijŏngbu (★Sŏul)	212,368
Ŭiwang	96,892
Ulsan	682,978
Wŏnju	173,013
Yŏch'ŏn	63,802
Yŏngch'ŏn	48,890
Yŏngju	84,335
Yŏsu	173,164

KUWAIT / Al-Kuwayt

1985 C	1,697,301
Abraq Khīṭān (★Al-Kuwayt)	45,120
Al-Aḥmadī (★285,000)	26,899
Al-Farwānīyah (★Al-Kuwayt)	68,701
Al-Fuḥayḥīl (★Al-Aḥmadī)	50,081
Al-Jahrah (★Al-Kuwayt)	111,222
• AL-KUWAYT (★1,375,000)	44,335
As-Sālimīyah (★Al-Kuwayt)	153,359
Aṣ-Ṣulaybīyah (★Al-Kuwayt)	51,314
Ḥawallī (★Al-Kuwayt)	145,126
Qalīb ash-Shuyūkh (★Al-Kuwayt)	114,771
South Khīṭān (★Al-Kuwayt)	69,256
Subahiya (★Al-Aḥmadī)	60,787

KYRGYZSTAN

1991 E	4,422,200
• BIŠKEK	631,300
Džalal-Abad	79,900
Kara-Balta	55,000
Karakol (Prževal'sk)	64,300
Kyzyl-Kija	49,400
Oš	238,200
Tokmak	71,200

LAOS / Lao

1985 C	3,584,803
Savannakhét (1975E)	53,000
• VIANGCHAN (VIENTIANE)	377,409

LATVIA / Latvija

1991 E	2,680,500
Daugavpils	129,000
Jelgava	74,500
Jūrmala (★Rīga)	66,500
Liepāja	114,900
• RĪGA (★1,005,000)	910,200
Ventspils	50,400

LEBANON / Lubnān

1982 E	2,637,000
• BAYRŪT (★1,675,000)	509,000
Ṣaydā	105,000
Ṣūr (Tyre) (1970E)	12,500
Ṭarābulus (Tripoli) (★950,000)	198,000

LESOTHO

1986 C	1,577,536
• MASERU	109,382

LIBERIA

1986 E	2,221,000
• MONROVIA	465,000

LIBYA / Lībiyā

1988 E	3,772,500
Al-Bayḍā (Beida) (1984C)	67,120
Banghāzī	446,250
Darnah (1984C)	62,179
Miṣrātah	121,669
• ṬARĀBULUS (TRIPOLI)	591,062
Ṭubruq (Tobruk) (1984C)	75,282

LIECHTENSTEIN

1990 E	28,452
• VADUZ	4,874

LITHUANIA / Lietuva

1989 C	3,690,000
Alytus (1987E)	71,000
Kaunas	423,000
Klaipėda (Memel)	204,000
Panevėžys	126,000
Šiauliai	145,000
• VILNIUS	582,000

LUXEMBOURG

1991 C	385,317
Esch-sur-Alzette (★83,000)	23,914
• LUXEMBOURG (★136,000)	75,622

MACAU

1987 E	429,000
• MACAU	429,000

MACEDONIA / Makedonija

1987 E	2,064,581
Bitola (▲143,090)	76,200
• SKOPJE (▲547,214)	444,900

MADAGASCAR / Madagasikara

1988 E	11,238,000
• ANTANANARIVO	1,250,000
Antsirabe (▲100,000)	52,700
Antsiranana	220,000
Fianarantsoa	300,000
Mahajanga	200,000
Toamasina	230,000
Toliara	150,000

MALAWI / Malaŵi

1987 C	7,982,607
• Blantyre	331,588
LILONGWE	233,973

MALAYSIA

1980 C	13,136,109
Alor Setar	69,435
Batu Pahat	64,727
Butterworth (★George Town)	77,982
George Town (Pinang) (★495,000)	248,241
Ipoh	293,849
Johor Baharu (★Singapore)	246,395
Kelang	192,080
Keluang	50,315
Kota Baharu	167,872
Kota Kinabalu (Jesselton)	55,997
• KUALA LUMPUR (★1,475,000)	919,610
Kuala Terengganu	180,296
Kuantan	131,547
Kuching	72,555
Melaka	87,494
Miri	52,125

▲ Población de un municipio, comuna o distrito entero, incluyendo sus áreas rurales.
• Ciudad más grande de un país.
★ Población o designación de un área metropolitana, incluyendo los suburbios.
C Censo. **E** Estimado oficial. **U** Estimado no oficial.

▲ Population d'une municipalité, d'une commune ou d'un district, zone rurale incluse.
• Ville la plus peuplée du pays.
★ Population de l'agglomération (ou nom de la zone métropolitaine englobante).
C Recensement. **E** Estimation officielle. **U** Estimation non officielle.

▲ População de um municipio, comuna ou distrito, inclusive as respectivas áreas rurais.
• Maior cidade de um país.
★ População ou indicação de uma área metropolitana.
C Censo. **E** Estimativa oficial. **U** Estimativa não oficial.

Muar (Bandar Maharani) 65,151
Petaling Jaya (★Kuala Lumpur) 207,805
Sandakan 70,420
Seremban 132,911
Sibu 85,231
Taiping 146,000
Telok Anson 49,148

MALDIVES

1985 C 181,453
• MALE 46,334

MALI

1987 C 7,696,348
• BAMAKO 658,275
Gao 54,874
Kayes 48,216
Koutiala 48,010
Mopti 73,979
Ségou 88,877
Sikasso 73,050
Tombouctou (Timbuktu) 31,925

MALTA

1991 E 355,910
• VALLETTA (★215,000) 9,199

MARSHALL ISLANDS

1980 C 30,873
• Jarej-Uliga-Delap 8,583

MARTINIQUE

1982 C 328,566
• FORT-DE-FRANCE (★116,017) 99,844

MAURITANIA / Mauritanie / Mūrītāniyā

1987 E 2,007,000
• NOUAKCHOTT 285,000

MAURITIUS

1989 E 1,081,669
Beau Bassin-Rose Hill (★Port Louis) 94,236
Curepipe (★Port Louis) 66,704
• PORT LOUIS (★420,000) 141,870
Quatre Bornes (★Port Louis) 65,759
Vacoas-Phoenix (★Port Louis) 56,335

MAYOTTE

1985 E 67,205
• DZAOUDZI (★6,979) 5,865

MEXICO / México

1980 C 67,395,826
Acapulco [de Juárez] 301,902
Aguascalientes 293,152
Apatzingán de la Constitución 55,522
Atlixco 53,207
Campeche 128,434
Cancún 33,273
Celaya 141,675
Chetumal 56,709
Chihuahua 385,603
Chilpancingo de los Bravo 67,498
Ciudad del Carmen 72,489
• CIUDAD DE MÉXICO (★14,100,000) 8,831,079
Ciudad Guzmán 60,938
Ciudad Juárez (★El Paso, Tex., U.S.A.) 544,496
Ciudad Madero (★Tampico) 132,444
Ciudad Mante 70,647
Ciudad Obregón 165,572
Ciudad Valles 65,609
Ciudad Victoria 140,161
Coatzacoalcos 127,170
Colima 86,044
Córdoba 99,972
Cuernavaca 192,770
Culiacán 304,826
Delicias 65,504
Durango 257,915
Ecatepec (★Ciudad de México) 741,821
Ensenada 120,483
Fresnillo 56,066
Garza García (★Monterrey) 81,974
Gómez Palacio (★Torreón) 116,967
Guadalajara (★2,325,000) 1,626,152
Guadalupe (★Monterrey) 370,524
Guanajuato 48,981
Guaymas 54,826
Hermosillo 297,175
Heroica Zitácuaro 47,520
Hidalgo del Parral 75,590
Iguala 66,005
Irapuato 170,138
La Paz 91,453
La Piedad de Cabadas 47,441
Las Choapas 35,807
León 593,002
Los Mochis 122,531
Matamoros (★Brownsville, Tex., U.S.A.) 188,745
Mazatlán 199,830
Mérida 400,142
Mexicali (★365,000) 341,559
Minatitlán 106,765
Monclova 115,786
Monterrey (★2,015,000) 1,090,009
Morelia 297,544
Naucalpan de Juárez (★Ciudad de México) 723,723
Navojoa 62,901
Nezahualcóyotl (★Ciudad de México) 1,341,230
Nogales 65,603
Nuevo Laredo (★Laredo, Tex., U.S.A.) 201,731
Oaxaca [de Juárez] 154,223
Ocotlán 48,931
Orizaba (★215,000) 114,848
Pachuca 110,351
Piedras Negras 67,455
Poza Rica 166,799
Puebla (★1,055,000) 835,759
Puerto Vallarta 38,645
Querétaro 215,976
Reynosa 194,693
Río Bravo 55,236
Salamanca 96,703
Saltillo 284,937
San Luis Potosí (★470,000) 362,371
San Luis Río Colorado 76,684
San Nicolás de los Garza (★Monterrey) 280,696
Santa Catarina (★Monterrey) 87,673
Soledad Díez Gutiérrez (★San Luis Potosí) 49,173
Tampico (★435,000) 267,957
Tapachula 85,766
Tecomán 46,371
Tehuacán 79,547
Tepic 145,741
Tijuana (★San Diego, Calif., U.S.A.) 429,500
Tlalnepantla (★Ciudad de México) 778,173
Tlaquepaque (★Guadalajara) 133,500
Toluca [de Lerdo] 199,778
Torreón (★575,000) 328,086
Tulancingo 53,400
Tuxpan 56,037
Tuxtla Gutiérrez 131,096
Uruapan del Progreso 122,828
Veracruz [Llave] (★385,000) 284,822
Villahermosa 158,216
Xalapa 204,594
Zacatecas 80,088
Zamora de Hidalgo 86,998
Zapopan (★Guadalajara) 345,390

MICRONESIA, FEDERATED STATES OF

1985 E 94,534
• KOLONIA 6,306

MOLDOVA

1991 E 4,366,300
Bel'c' 164,900
Bendery 141,500
• KIŠIN'OV 676,700
Rybnica 62,900
Tiraspol' 186,000

MONACO

1990 C 29,972
• MONACO (★87,000) 29,972

MONGOLIA / Mongol Ard Uls

1989 E 2,040,000
Darchan (1985E) 69,800
• ULAANBAATAR 548,400

MONTSERRAT

1980 C 11,606
• PLYMOUTH 1,568

MOROCCO / Al-Magreb

1982 C 20,419,555
Agadir 110,479
Beni-Mellal 95,003
Berkane 60,490
• Casablanca (Dar-el-Beida) (★2,475,000) 2,139,204
El-Jadida (Mazagan) 81,455
Fès (★535,000) 448,823
Kenitra 188,194
Khemisset 58,925
Khouribga 127,181
Ksar-el-Kebir 73,541
Larache 63,893
Marrakech (★535,000) 439,728
Meknès (★375,000) 319,783
Mohammedia (Fedala) (★Casablanca) 105,120
Nador 62,040
Oued-Zem 58,744
Oujda 260,082
RABAT (★980,000) 518,616
Safi 197,309
Salé (★Rabat) 289,391
Settat 65,203
Sidi Kacem 55,833
Sidi Slimane 50,457
Tanger (Tangier) (★370,000) 266,346
Tan-Tan 41,451
Taza 77,216
Temera (★Rabat) 48,644
Tétouan 199,615

MOZAMBIQUE / Moçambique

1989 E 15,326,476
Beira 291,604
Chimoio (1986E) 86,928
Inhambane (1986E) 64,274
• MAPUTO 1,069,727
Nacala 101,615
Nampula 197,379
Pemba (1986E) 50,215
Quelimane 78,520
Tete (1986E) 56,178
Xai-Xai (1986E) 51,620

NAMIBIA

1988 E 1,760,000
• WINDHOEK 114,500

NAURU / Naoero

1987 E 8,000

NEPAL / Nepāl

1981 C 15,022,839
Bhaktapur 48,472
• KĀTHMĀNDAU (★320,000) 235,160
Wirāṭnagar 93,544

NETHERLANDS / Nederland

1991 E 15,010,000
Alkmaar (★124,000) 90,767
Almelo 62,664
Alphen aan den Rijn 62,404
Amersfoort 101,966
Amstelveen (★Amsterdam) 70,337
• AMSTERDAM (★1,875,000) 702,686
Apeldoorn 148,195
Arnhem (★305,000) 131,707
Assen 50,353
Bergen op Zoom 46,897
Breda (★163,000) 124,792
Delft (★'s-Gravenhage) 89,369
Den Helder 61,463
Deventer 67,473
Dordrecht (★209,000) 110,472
Ede (▲94,721) 50,000
Eindhoven (★384,000) 192,810
Emmen (▲92,896) 36,900
Enschede (★252,000) 146,509
Geleen (★179,000) 33,833
Gouda 65,918
Groningen (★208,000) 168,701
Haarlem (★Amsterdam) 149,464
Haarlemmermeer (▲98,070) (★ Amsterdam) 13,600
Heerlen (★267,500) 94,304
Helmond 69,968
Hengelo (★Enschede) 76,377
Hilversum (★Amsterdam) 84,602
Hoorn 58,202
IJmuiden (★Amsterdam) 60,129
Kerkrade (★Heerlen) 53,276
Leeuwarden 85,697
Leiden (★190,000) 111,927
Maastricht (★163,000) 117,398
Nieuwegein (★Utrecht) 58,912
Nijmegen (★242,000) 145,646
Oss 51,688
Purmerend (★Amsterdam) 61,056
Ridderkerk (★Rotterdam) 45,990
Rijswijk (★'s-Gravenhage) 47,709
Roosendaal 60,732
Rotterdam (★1,120,000) 582,238
Schiedam (★Rotterdam) 70,206
'S-GRAVENHAGE (THE HAGUE) (★772,000) 444,256
's-Hertogenbosch (★200,000) 92,052
Soest (★Amersfoort) 41,415
Spijkenisse (★Rotterdam) 69,103
Tilburg (★233,000) 158,839
Utrecht (★527,000) 231,232
Veenendaal 49,689
Venlo (★87,000) 64,386
Vlaardingen (★Rotterdam) 73,711
Vlissingen (Flushing) (▲43,799) 25,100
Zaanstad (★Amsterdam) 130,684
Zeist (★Utrecht) 59,363
Zoetermeer (★'s-Gravenhage) 99,094
Zwolle 95,574

NETHERLANDS ANTILLES / Nederlandse Antillen

1990 E 189,687
• WILLEMSTAD (★130,000) (1981C) 31,883

NEW CALEDONIA / Nouvelle-Calédonie

1989 C 164,173
• NOUMÉA (★97,581) 65,110

NEW ZEALAND

1986 C 3,307,084
• Auckland (★850,000) 149,046
Christchurch (★320,000) 168,200
Dunedin (★109,000) 76,964
Hamilton (★101,814) 94,511
Invercargill (★52,807) 48,197
Lower Hutt (★Wellington) 63,862
Manukau (★Auckland) 177,248
Napier (★107,060) 49,428
Palmerston North (★67,405) 60,503
Rotorua (★52,001) 40,597
Takapuna (★Auckland) 69,419
Tauranga (★59,435) 41,611
Waitemata (★Auckland) 96,365
WELLINGTON (★350,000) 137,495

NICARAGUA

1985 E 3,272,100
Chinandega 75,000
Granada (1981E) 64,642
León 101,000
• MANAGUA 682,000
Masaya 75,000
Matagalpa 68,000

NIGER

1988 C 7,250,383
Agadez 50,164
Maradi 112,965
• NIAMEY 398,265
Tahoua 51,607
Zinder 120,892

NIGERIA

1987 E 101,907,000
Aba 239,800
Abakaliki 56,800
Abeokuta 341,300
Ado-Ekiti 287,000
Afikpo 65,790
Agege 83,810
Akure 129,600
Amaigbo 53,690
Apomu 49,570
Aramoko 48,280
Asaba 47,410
Awka 88,800
Azare 50,020
Bauchi 68,840
Benin City 183,200
Bida 100,200
Calabar 139,800
Deba 110,600
Duku 52,880
Ede 245,200
Effon-Alaiye 122,300
Ejigbo 84,570
Emure-Ekiti 58,750
Enugu 252,500
Epe 80,560
Erin-Oshogbo 59,940
Eruwa 49,140
Fiditi 49,440
Gboko 49,390
Gbongan 53,990
Gombe 86,120
Gusau 126,200
Ibadan 1,144,000
Idah 50,550
Idanre 56,080
Ife 237,000
Ifon-Oshogbo 65,980
Igbasa-Odo 48,040
Igboho 85,230
Igbo-Ora 68,060
Igede-Ekiti 56,570
Ihiala 73,240
Ijebu-Igbo 78,680
Ijebu-Ode 124,900
Ijero-Ekiti 76,420
Ikare 112,500
Ikerre 195,400
Ikire 94,450
Ikirun 144,900
Ikole 71,860
Ikorodu 147,700
Ikot Ekpene 69,440
Ila 210,800
Ilawe-Ekiti 147,300
Ilesha 302,100
Ilobu 159,000
Ilorin 380,000
Inisa 95,630
Ipoti-Ekiti 53,220
Ise-Ekiti 82,580
Iseyin 173,500
Iwo 289,100
Jega (1985E) 47,000
Jimeta 66,130
Jos 164,700
Kaduna 273,200
Kano 538,300
Katsina 165,000
Kaura Namoda 52,910
Keffi 57,790
Kishi 77,210
Kumo 118,200
Lafia 97,810
Lafiagi 57,580
• LAGOS (★3,800,000) 1,213,000
Lalupon 56,130
Lere 49,670
Maiduguri 255,100
Makurdi 98,350
Minna 109,300
Mubi 51,190
Mushin (★Lagos) 266,100
Nguru 78,770
Nsukka 47,760
Ode-Ekiti 48,910
Offa 157,500
Ogbomosho 582,900
Oka 114,400
Oke-Mesi 55,040
Okwe 52,550
Olupona 65,720
Ondo 135,300
Onitsha 298,200
Opobo 64,620
Oron 62,260
Oshogbo 380,800
Owerri (1985E) 37,000
Owo 146,600
Oyan 50,930
Oyo 204,700
Pindiga 64,130
Port Harcourt 327,300
Potiskum 56,490
Sapele 111,200
Shagamu 93,610
Shaki 139,000
Shomolu (★Lagos) 120,700
Sokoto 163,700
Ugep 81,910
Umuahia 52,550
Uyo 60,500
Warri 100,700
Zaria 302,800

NIUE

1989 C 2,267
• ALOFI 706

NORTHERN MARIANA ISLANDS

1980 C 16,780
• Chalan Kanoa 2,678
Garapan 2,063

NORWAY / Norge

1987 E 4,190,000
Bærum (★Oslo) (1985E) 83,000
Bærum (★Oslo) (1985E) 83,000
Bergen (★239,000) 209,320
Drammen (★73,000) (1985E) 50,700
Fredrikstad (★52,000) (1983E) 27,618
Hammerfest (1983E) 7,208
Kristiansand (1985E) 62,200
Narvik (1983E) 19,080
• OSLO (★720,000) 452,415
Skien (★77,981) (1985E) 46,700
Stavanger (★132,000) (1985E) 94,200
Tromsø (1985E) 47,800
Trondheim 135,010
Louga (1988C) 52,763

OMAN / 'Umān

1983 E 1,131,000
• MASQAT (MUSCAT) 30,000
Maṭraḥ (1971E) 14,000
Ṣūr 30,000

PAKISTAN / Pākistān

1981 C 84,253,644
Abbottābād (★65,996) 32,188
Ahmadpur East 56,979
Attock (★39,986) 26,233
Bahāwalnagar 74,533
Bahāwalpur (★180,263) 152,009
Bannu (★43,210) 35,170
Bhakkar 41,934
Chārsadda 62,530
Chīchāwatni 50,241
Chiniot 105,559
Chishtiān Mandi 61,959
Daska 55,555
Dera Ghāzi Khān 102,007
Dera Ismāīl Khān (★68,145) 64,358
Drigh Road Cantonment (★Karāchi) 56,742

▲ Population of an entire municipality, commune, or district, including rural area.
• Largest city in country.
★ Population or designation of the metropolitan area, including suburbs.
C Census. **E** Official estimate. **U** Unofficial estimate.

▲ Bevölkerung eines ganzen städtischen Verwaltungsgebietes, eines Kommunalbezirkes oder eines Distrikts, einschliesslich ländlicher Gebiete.
• Grösste Stadt des Landes.
★ Bevölkerung oder Bezeichnung der Stadtregion einschliesslich Vororte.
C Volkszählung. **E** Offizielle Schätzung. **U** Inoffizielle Schätzung.

Faisalabad (Lyallpur)	1,104,209
Gojra	68,000
Gujrānwāla (★658,753)	600,993
Gujrānwāla Cantonment (★Gujrānwāla)	57,760
Gujrāt	155,058
Hāfizābād	83,464
Hyderābād (★800,000)	702,539
Hyderābād Cantonment (★Hyderābād)	48,990
ISLĀMĀBĀD (★Rāwalpindi)	204,364
Jacobābād	79,365
Jarānwāla	69,459
Jhang Sadar	195,558
Jhelum (★106,462)	92,646
Kamālia	61,107
Kāmoke	71,097
• Karāchi (★5,300,000)	4,901,627
Karāchi Cantonment (★Karāchi)	181,981
Kasūr	155,523
Khairpur	61,447
Khānewāl	89,090
Khānpur	70,589
Khāriān Cantonment (★51,506)	16,042
Khushāb	56,274
Kohāt (★77,604)	55,832
Lahore (★3,025,000)	2,707,215
Lahore Cantonment (★Lahore)	245,474
Lārkāna	123,890
Leiah	51,482
Malir Cantonment (★Karāchi)	47,588
Mandi Būrewāla	86,311
Mardān (★147,977)	141,842
Miānwāli	59,159
Mingāora	88,078
Mīrpur Khās	124,371
Multān (★732,070)	696,316
Muzaffargarh	53,000
Nawābshāh	102,139
Nowshera (★74,913)	38,875
Okāra (★153,483)	127,455
Pākpattan	69,820
Peshāwar (★566,248)	506,896
Peshāwar Cantonment (★Peshāwar)	59,352
Quetta (★285,719)	244,842
Rahīmyār Khān (★132,635)	119,036
Rāwalpindi (★1,040,000)	457,091
Rāwalpindi Cantonment (★Rāwalpindi)	337,752
Sādiqābād	63,935
Sāhīwal	150,954
Sargodha (★291,362)	231,895
Sargodha Cantonment (★Sargodha)	59,467
Shekhūpura	141,168
Shikārpur	88,138
Shorkot (★50,568)	18,533
Siālkot (★302,009)	258,147
Sukkur	190,551
Tando Ādam	62,744
Turbat	52,337
Vihāri	53,799
Wāh Cantonment	122,335
Wazīrābād	62,725

PALAU / Belau

1986 C	13,873
• KOROR	8,629

PANAMA / Panamá

1990 C	2,315,047
Balboa (★Panamá)	1,214
Colón (★96,000)	54,469
David	65,635
• PANAMÁ (★770,000)	411,549
San Miguelito (★Panamá)	242,529

PAPUA NEW GUINEA

1990 C	3,534,038
Lae	78,265
• PORT MORESBY	193,242
Rabaul	16,883

PARAGUAY

1985 E	3,279,000
• ASUNCIÓN (★700,000)	477,100
Ciudad del Este	64,000
Fernando de la Mora (★Asunción)	80,000
Lambaré (★Asunción)	84,000
San Lorenzo (★Asunción) (1982C)	74,632

PERU / Perú

1981 C	17,031,221
Arequipa (★446,942)	108,023
Ayacucho (★69,533)	57,432
Barranco (★Lima)	46,478
Breña (★Lima)	112,398
Cajamarca	62,259
Callao (★Lima)	264,133
Cerro de Pasco (★66,373)	55,597
Chiclayo (★279,527)	213,095
Chimbote	223,341
Chorrillos (★Lima)	141,881
Chosica	65,139
Cuzco (★184,550)	89,563
Huacho	43,398
Huancayo (★164,954)	84,845
Huánuco	61,812
Ica	114,786
Iquitos	178,738
Jesús María (★Lima)	83,179
Juliaca	87,651
La Victoria (★Lima)	270,778
• LIMA (★4,608,010)	371,122
Lince (★Lima)	80,456
Magdalena (★Lima)	55,535
Miraflores (★Lima)	103,453
Pisco	55,604
Piura (★207,934)	144,609
Pucallpa	112,263
Pueblo Libre (★Lima)	83,985
Puno	67,397
Rímac (★Lima)	184,484
San Isidro (★Lima)	71,203
San Martin de Porras (★Lima)	404,856
Santiago de Surco (★Lima)	146,636
Sullana	89,037
Surquillo (★Lima)	134,158
Tacna	97,173
Talara	57,351
Trujillo (★354,301)	202,469
Tumbes	47,936
Vitarte (★Lima)	145,504

PHILIPPINES / Pilipinas

1990 C	60,477,000
Angeles	236,000
Antipolo (▲68,912) (1980C)	54,117
Bacolod	364,000
Bacoor (★Manila) (1980C)	90,364
Baguio	183,000
Baliuag (1980C)	70,555
Biñan (★Manila) (1980C)	83,684
Binangonan (1980C)	80,980
Bislig (▲81,615) (1980C)	49,498
Bocaue (1980C)	49,693
Butuan (▲228,000)	99,000
Cabanatuan (▲173,000)	75,700
Cagayan de Oro (▲340,000)	255,000
Cainta (★Manila) (1980C)	59,025
Calamba (▲121,175) (1980C)	72,359
Caloocan (★Manila)	746,000
Carmona (★Manila) (1980C)	65,014
Cavite (★195,000)	92,000
Cebu (★825,000)	610,000
Cotabato	127,000
Dagupan	122,000
Davao (▲850,000)	569,300
Dumaguete	80,000
General Santos (Dadiangas) (▲250,000)	157,600
Guagua (1980C)	72,609
Iloilo	311,000
Isabela (Basilan) (▲49,891) (1980C)	11,491
Jolo (1980C)	52,429
Lapu-Lapu (Opon)	146,000
Las Piñas (★Manila) (1984E)	190,364
Legaspi (▲121,000)	63,000
Lucena	151,000
Mabalacat (▲80,966) (1980C)	54,988
Makati (★Manila) (1984E)	408,991
Malabon (★Manila) (1984E)	212,930
Malolos (1980C)	95,699
Mandaluyong (★Manila) (1984E)	226,670
Mandaue (★Cebu)	180,000
Mangaldan (1980C)	50,434
• MANILA (★9,650,000)	1,587,000
Marawi	92,000
Marikina (★Manila) (1984E)	248,183
Meycauayan (★Manila) (1980C)	83,579
Muntinglupa (★Manila) (1984E)	172,421
Naga	115,000
Navotas (★Manila) (1984E)	146,899
Olongapo	192,000
Pagadian (▲107,000)	52,400
Parañaque (★Manila) (1984E)	252,791
Pasay (★Manila)	354,000
Pasig (★Manila) (1984E)	318,853
Puerto Princesa (▲92,000)	52,000
Quezon City (★Manila)	1,632,000
San Fernando (1980C)	110,891
San Juan del Monte (★Manila) (1984E)	139,126
San Pablo (▲161,000)	83,900
San Pedro (1980C)	74,556
Santa Cruz (1980C)	60,620
Santa Rosa (★Manila) (1980C)	64,325
Tacloban	138,000
Tagbilaran	56,000
Tagig (★Manila) (1984E)	130,719
Taytay (★Manila) (1980C)	75,328
Valenzuela (★Manila) (1984E)	275,725
Zamboanga (▲444,000)	107,000

PITCAIRN

1988 C	59
• ADAMSTOWN	59

POLAND / Polska

1991 E	38,183,200
Będzin (★Katowice)	76,200
Bełchatów	57,400
Biała Podlaska	53,100
Białystok	270,600
Bielsko-Biała	181,300
Bydgoszcz	381,500
Bytom (Beuthen) (★Katowice)	231,200
Chełm	66,400
Chorzów (★Katowice)	131,900
Częstochowa	258,000
Dąbrowa Górnicza (★Katowice)	136,900
Dzierżoniów (Reichenbach) (★89,000)	38,000
Elbląg (Elbing)	126,100
Ełk	52,400
Gdańsk (Danzig) (★909,000)	465,100
Gdynia (★Gdańsk)	251,500
Gliwice (Gleiwitz) (★Katowice)	214,200
Głogów	73,300
Gniezno	70,400
Gorzów Wielkopolski (Landsberg an der Warthe)	124,300
Grudziądz	102,300
Inowrocław	77,700
Jastrzębie-Zdrój	103,700
Jaworzno (★Katowice)	99,500
Jelenia Góra (Hirschberg)	93,400
Kalisz	106,200
• Katowice (★2,778,000)	366,800
Kędzierzyn Kozle	71,700
Kielce	214,200
Konin	80,300
Koszalin (Köslin)	108,700
Kraków (★828,000)	750,500
Krosno	49,700
Kutno	50,400
Legionowo (★Warszawa)	50,800
Legnica (Liegnitz)	105,200
Leszno	58,300
Łódź (★1,061,000)	848,200
Łomża	59,300
Lubin	82,300
Lublin (★389,000)	351,400
Mielec	61,800
Mysłowice (★Katowice)	93,800
Nowy Sącz	78,200
Olsztyn (Allenstein)	162,900
Opole (Oppeln)	128,400
Ostrołęka	50,700
Ostrowiec Świętokrzyski	78,600
Ostrów Wielkopolski	73,300
Pabianice (★Łódź)	75,200
Piekary Śląskie (★Katowice)	68,500
Piła (Schneidemühl)	72,300
Piotrków Trybunalski	81,000
Płock	123,400
Poznań (★672,000)	590,100
Pruszków (★Warszawa)	53,700
Przemyśl	68,500
Puławy	85,700
Racibórz (Ratibor)	64,400
Radom	228,500
Radomsko	50,400
Ruda Śląska (★Katowice)	171,000
Rybnik	144,000
Rzeszów	153,000
Siedlce	72,000
Siemianowice Śląskie (★Katowice)	81,100
Skarżysko-Kamienna	50,900
Słupsk (Stolp)	101,200
Sopot (★Gdańsk)	46,700
Sosnowiec (★Katowice)	259,400
Stalowa Wola	70,000
Starachowice	56,600
Stargard Szczeciński (Stargard in Pommern)	71,000
Starogard Gdański	49,500
Suwałki	61,300
Świdnica (Schweidnitz)	63,300
Świętochłowice (★Katowice)	60,500
Świnoujście (Swinemünde)	43,300
Szczecin (Stettin) (★449,000)	413,400
Tarnów	121,200
Tarnowskie Góry (★Katowice)	74,100
Tczew	59,500
Tomaszów Mazowiecki	69,900
Toruń	202,300
Tychy (★Katowice)	191,700
Wałbrzych (Waldenburg) (★207,000)	141,000
WARSZAWA (★2,323,000)	1,655,700
Włocławek	122,200
Wodzisław Śląski	111,800
Wrocław (Breslau)	643,200
Zabrze (Hindenburg) (★Katowice)	205,000
Zamość	61,800
Zawiercie	56,600
Zgierz (★Łódź)	59,000
Zielona Góra (Grünberg)	114,100
Żory	67,000

PORTUGAL

1981 C	9,833,014
Amadora (★Lisboa)	95,518
Barreiro (★Lisboa)	50,863
Braga	63,033
Coimbra	74,616
• LISBOA (★2,250,000)	807,167
Ponta Delgada	21,187
Porto (★1,225,000)	327,368
Setúbal	77,885
Vila Nova de Gaia (★Porto)	62,469

PUERTO RICO

1990 C	3,522,037
Arecibo (★160,500)	49,545
Bayamón (▲220,262) (★ San Juan)	202,103
Caguas (▲133,447) (★ San Juan)	92,429
Carolina (▲177,806) (★ San Juan)	162,404
Guaynabo (▲92,886) (★ San Juan)	73,385
Mayagüez (★200,600)	83,010
Ponce (★232,700)	159,151
• SAN JUAN (★1,877,000)	426,832

QATAR / Qatar

1986 C	369,079
• AD-DAWḤAH (DOHA) (★310,000)	217,294
Ar-Rayyān (★Ad-Dawḥah)	91,996

REUNION / Réunion

1982 C	515,814
• SAINT-DENIS (▲109,072)	84,400

ROMANIA / România

1989 E	23,151,564
Alba Iulia	72,331
Alexandria	58,384
Arad	191,428
Bacău	193,269
Baia Mare	150,456
Bîrlad	75,843
Bistrița	79,544
Botoșani	119,563
Brăila	242,595
Brașov	352,640
• BUCUREȘTI (BUCHAREST) (★2,300,000)	2,036,894
Buzău	145,423
Călărași	76,240
Cluj-Napoca	317,914
Constanța	315,917
Craiova	300,030
Deva	77,336
Drobeta-Turnu Severin	107,420
Focșani	101,799
Galați	307,376
Gheorghe Gheorghiu-Dej	57,057
Giurgiu	72,275
Hunedoara	88,583
Iași	330,195
Lugoj	54,350
Mediaș	75,521
Miercurea-Ciuc	49,148
Oradea	225,416
Petroșani (★76,000)	53,324
Piatra Neamț	115,782
Pitești	162,395
Ploiești (★310,000)	247,502
Reșița	110,260
Rîmnicu Vîlcea	107,996
Roman	77,021
Satu Mare	136,881
Sfîntu-Gheorghe	72,092
Sibiu	184,036
Slatina	86,360
Slobozia	50,995
Suceava	105,921
Timișoara	333,365
Tîrgoviște	100,426
Tîrgu Jiu	93,252
Tîrgu-Mureș	164,781
Tulcea	94,935
Turda	64,374
Vaslui	73,666
Zalău	65,190

RUSSIA / Rossija

1991 E	148,542,700
Abakan	157,300
Achtubinsk	50,800
Ačinsk	122,000
Alapajevsk	50,300
Alatyr'	47,700
Aleksandrov	68,600
Aleksin	74,200
Al'metjevsk	132,700
Amursk	59,600
Anapa	55,900
Angarsk	268,500
Anžero-Sudžensk	107,000
Apatity	88,600
Archangel'sk	420,400
Armavir	162,200
Arsenjev	71,200
Art'om	70,100
Arzamas	111,800
Asbest	84,900
Astrachan'	511,900
Azov	80,700
Balakovo	201,300
Balašicha (★Moskva)	137,600
Balašov	97,300
Barnaul (★673,000)	606,800
Batajsk (★Rostov-na-Donu)	93,300
Belaja Kalitva	48,500
Belebej	54,500
Belgorod	311,400
Belogorsk	74,300
Belorečensk	51,900
Beloreck	73,100
Belovo	92,900
Berdsk (★Novosibirsk)	80,400
Berezniki	199,700
Berezovskiy	48,300
Ber'ozovskij	51,900
Bijsk	234,600
Birobidžan	86,300
Blagoveščensk	211,000
Bor (★Nižnij Novgorod)	64,500
Borisoglebsk	72,100
Boroviči	62,800
Br'ansk	458,900
Bratsk	259,400
Bud'onnovsk	57,500
Bugul'ma	91,100
Buguruslan	54,100
Buj	62,900
Bujnaksk	57,900
Buzuluk	85,100
Čajkovskij	88,300
Čapajevsk	96,000
Čebarkul'	50,700
Čeboksary	436,000
Čechov	60,200
Čel'abinsk (★1,325,000)	1,148,300
Čeremchovo	73,600
Čerepovec	315,900
Čerkessk	117,000
Černogorsk	79,700
Chabarovsk	613,300
Chasavjurt	72,800
Chimki (★Moskva)	135,500
Cholmsk	51,800
Čistopol'	66,600
Čita	376,300
Čusovoj	58,000
Derbent	81,500
Dimitrovgrad	127,000
Dmitrov	65,600
Dolgoprudnyj (★Moskva)	71,100
Domodedovo (★Moskva)	56,300
Doneck	48,900
Dubna	67,200
Dzeržinsk (★Nižnij Novgorod)	286,700
Elektrostal' (★Moskva)	153,000
Elista	92,700
Engel's (★Saratov)	183,600
Fr'azino (★Moskva)	54,000
Gatčina (★Sankt-Peterburg)	80,600
Gelendžik	48,600
Georgijevsk	63,700
Georgiu-Dež	54,600
Glazov	106,000
Gorno-Altajsk	47,500
Gr'azi	47,700
Groznyj	401,400
Gubkin	76,400
Gukovo	67,700
Gus'-Chrustal'nyj	77,000
Inta	60,900
Irbit	51,300
Irkutsk	640,500
Išim	65,900
Išimbaj	71,000
Iskitim	68,700
Ivanovo	482,200
Ivantejevka (★Moskva)	53,200
Iževsk	646,800
Jakutsk	193,300
Jarcevo	54,000
Jaroslavl'	638,100
Jefremov	56,600
Jegorjevsk	74,200
Jejsk	79,400
Jelabuga	60,500
Jelec	121,300
Jelizovo	48,700
Jermolajevo	65,600
Jessentuki	86,300
Joškar-Ola	247,800
Jurga	94,000

▲ Población de un municipio, comuna o distrito entero, incluyendo sus áreas rurales.
• Ciudad más grande de un país.
★ Población o designación de un área metropolitana, incluyendo los suburbios.
C Censo. **E** Estimado oficial. **U** Estimado no oficial.

▲ Population d'une municipalité, d'une commune ou d'un district, zone rurale incluse.
• Ville la plus peuplée du pays.
★ Population de l'agglomération (ou nom de la zone métropolitaine englobante).
C Recensement. **E** Estimation officielle. **U** Estimation non officielle.

▲ População de um municipio, comuna ou distrito, inclusive as respectivas áreas rurais.
• Maior cidade de um país.
★ População ou indicação de uma área metropolitana.
C Censo. **E** Estimativa oficial. **U** Estimativa não oficial.

Južno-Sachalinsk	164,000
Kačkanar	48,900
Kaliningrad (Königsberg)	408,100
Kaliningrad (★Moskva)	161,500
Kaluga	315,500
Kamensk-Šachtinskij	73,100
Kamensk-Ural'skij	208,700
Kamyšin	124,400
Kanaš	56,100
Kandalakša	54,300
Kansk	109,900
Kaspijsk	61,900
Kazan' (★1,165,000)	1,107,300
Kemerovo	520,700
Kimry	62,000
Kinel'	33,800
Kinešma	104,900
Kiriši	53,100
Kirov	491,200
Kirovo-Čepeck	95,600
Kisel'ovsk (★Prokopjevsk)	126,900
Kislovodsk	116,800
Kizel	36,600
Klimovsk (★Moskva)	57,600
Klin	95,100
Klincy	71,200
Kogalym	48,200
Kol'čugino	45,600
Kolomna	163,500
Kolpino (★Sankt-Peterburg)	144,500
Komsomol'sk-na-Amure	318,800
Kopejsk (★Čel'abinsk)	78,300
Korkino	44,800
Korsakov	45,300
Kostroma	281,800
Kotlas	68,900
Kovrov	161,900
Krasnodar	631,200
Krasnogorsk (★Moskva)	91,700
Krasnojarsk	924,400
Krasnokamensk	57,800
Krasnokamsk	67,000
Krasnoturjinsk	67,200
Krasnoufimsk	46,100
Krasnoural'sk	34,800
Krasnyj Sulin	43,200
Kropotkin	76,600
Krymsk	51,100
Kstovo (★Nižnij Novgord)	65,300
Kujbyšev	51,600
Kungur	81,800
Kurgan	363,833
Kursk	433,300
Kušva	43,300
Kuzneck	100,000
Kyzyl	88,000
Labinsk	58,600
Leninogorsk, Tatarskaja A. S. S. R.	63,300
Leninsk-Kuzneckij	133,400
Lipeck	460,100
Livny	52,600
Lobn'a (★Moskva)	61,000
L'ubercy (★Moskva)	164,900
Lys'va	77,800
Lytkarino (★Moskva)	51,700
Machačkala	333,500
Magadan	154,900
Magnitogorsk	443,900
Majkop	152,500
Mcensk	49,200
Meleuz	55,200
Meždurečensk	107,500
Miass	169,700
Michajlovka	58,700
Mičurinsk	109,400
Mineral'nyje Vody	72,500
Minusinsk	74,200
Mončegorsk	68,100
Moršansk	50,500
• MOSKVA (MOSCOW) (★13,150,000)	8,801,500
Murmansk	472,900
Murom	126,000
Mytišči (★Moskva)	153,900
Nabereżnyje Čelny	510,100
Nachodka	164,500
Nadym	52,200
Nal'čik	240,600
Naro-Fominsk (★Moskva)	58,800
Nazarovo	65,200
Neftejugansk	95,500
Ner'ungri	77,200
Nevinnomyssk	123,300
Nikolo-Berjozovka	110,500
Nižnekamsk	196,200
Nižnevartovsk	247,400
Nižnij Novgorod (Gorky) (★2,025,000)	1,445,000
Nižnij Tagil	439,200
Njagan	59,800
Noginsk (★Moskva)	122,700
Nojabr'sk	88,900
Noril'sk	169,000
Novgorod	233,800
Novoaltajsk (★Barnaul)	55,200
Novočeboksarsk	119,300
Novočerkassk	188,500
Novodvinsk	50,300
Novokujbyševsk (★Samara)	113,200
Novokuzneck	601,900
Novomoskovsk, Tula oblast' (★365,000)	145,800
Novorossijsk	188,600
Novošachtinsk	107,300
Novosibirsk (★1,600,000)	1,446,300
Novotroick	107,600
Novyj Urengoj	93,600
Obninsk	103,700
Odincovo (★Moskva)	128,400
Okt'abr'skij	106,700
Omsk (★1,190,000)	1,166,800
Orechovo-Zujevo (★205,000)	136,800
Orenburg	556,500
Or'ol	345,200
Orsk	272,200
Osinniki	63,200
Otradnyj	49,600
Partizansk	50,000
P'atigorsk	131,100
Pavlovo	72,200
Pavlovskij Posad	70,800
Pečora	65,500
Penza	551,100
Perm' (★1,180,000)	1,110,400
Pervoural'sk	143,700
Petrodvorec (★Sankt-Peterburg)	83,800
Petropavlovsk-Kamčatskij	272,900
Petrozavodsk	277,400
Podol'sk (★Moskva)	208,500
Polevskoj	71,900
Prochladnyj	58,500
Prokopjevsk (★410,000)	272,600
Pskov	207,500
Puškin (★Sankt-Peterburg)	95,300
Puškino	75,800
Ramenskoje	88,800
Rasskazovo	49,800
R'azan'	527,200
Reutov (★Moskva)	68,900
Revda	66,000
Roslavl'	60,700
Rossoš'	58,900
Rostov-na-Donu (★1,165,000)	1,027,600
Rubcovsk	172,500
Ruzajevka	52,100
Rybinsk	252,600
Ržev	70,900
Šachty	227,700
Šadrinsk	87,500
Safonovo	56,300
Salavat	151,400
Sal'sk	61,700
Samara (★1,505,000)	1,257,300
Sankt-Peterburg (Saint Petersburg) (★5,525,000)	4,466,800
Saransk	319,600
Sarapul	110,600
Saratov (★1,155,000)	911,100
Šatka	51,100
Ščelkovo (★Moskva)	109,600
Ščokino	68,800
Sergijev Posad (Zagorsk)	115,600
Serov	103,800
Serpuchov	141,200
Severodvinsk	251,500
Severomorsk	66,200
Slav'ansk-Na-Kubani	58,500
Smolensk	349,800
Soči	341,500
Sokol	46,700
Solikamsk	110,200
Solnečnogorsk (★Moskva)	56,700
Sosnovyj Bor	56,700
Spassk-Dal'nij	61,100
Staryj Oskol	181,900
Stavropol'	328,300
Sterlitamak	252,200
Stupino	74,600
Šuja	69,000
Surgut	261,100
Sverdlovsk, Sverdlovsk oblast' (★1,620,000)	1,375,400
Svetlogorsk	71,600
Svobodnyj	80,900
Syktyvkar	224,000
Syzran'	174,900
Taganrog	293,600
Talnach	65,600
Tambov	309,600
Temirtau	213,100
Tichoreck	67,600
Tichvin	71,800
Tobol'sk	96,800
Toljatti	654,700
Tomsk	505,600
Toržok	50,500
Troick	89,800
Tuapse	63,800
Tujmazy	59,800
Tula (★640,000)	543,600
Tulun	53,700
T'umen'	494,200
Tver'	455,300
Tyndinskij	64,700
Uchta	112,100
Ufa (★1,118,000)	1,097,000
Uglič	40,000
Ulan-Ude	362,400
Uljanovsk	648,300
Usolje-Sibirskoje	106,800
Ussurijsk	160,200
Ust'-Ilimsk	112,200
Ust'-Kut	61,800
Uzlovaja (★Novomoskovsk)	64,000
V'az'ma	59,900
Velikije Luki	115,400
Verchn'aja Pyšma (★Sverdlovsk)	53,500
Verchn'aja Salda	55,100
Vičuga	49,700
Vidnoje	56,900
Vladikavkaz	306,000
Vladimir	355,600
Vladivostok	648,000
Volchov	50,100
Volgodonsk	180,700
Volgograd (Stalingrad) (★1,360,000)	1,007,300
Vologda	289,200
Vol'sk	65,500
Volžsk	62,000
Volžskij (★Volgograd)	278,400
Vorkuta	117,400
Voronež	900,000
Voskresensk	81,400
Votkinsk	104,500
Vyborg	81,100
Vyksa	62,200
Vyšnij Voločok	64,600
Zarinsk	51,800
Zelenograd (★Moskva)	162,700
Železnodorožnyj (★Moskva)	99,300
Železnogorsk	89,200
Zel'onodol'sk	97,000
Žigulevsk	45,000
Zima	39,400
Zlatoust	208,200
Žukovskij	101,300

RWANDA

1983 E	5,762,000
• KIGALI	181,600

SAINT HELENA

1987 C	5,644
• JAMESTOWN	1,413

SAINT KITTS AND NEVIS

1980 C	44,404
• BASSETERRE	14,725
Charlestown	1,771

SAINT LUCIA

1987 E	142,342
• CASTRIES	53,933

SAINT PIERRE AND MIQUELON / Saint-Pierre-et-Miquelon

1982 C	6,041
• SAINT-PIERRE	5,371

SAINT VINCENT AND THE GRENADINES

1987 E	112,589
• KINGSTOWN (★28,936)	19,028

SAN MARINO

1988 E	22,304
• SAN MARINO	2,777

SAO TOME AND PRINCIPE / São Tomé e Príncipe

1970 C	73,631
• SÃO TOMÉ	17,380

SAUDI ARABIA / Al-'Arabīyah as-Su'ūdīyah

1980 E	9,229,000
Abhā (1974C)	30,150
Ad-Dammām	200,000
Al-Hufūf (1974C)	101,271
Al-Khubar (1974C)	48,817
Al-Madīnah (Medina)	290,000
Al-Mubarraz (1974C)	54,325
AR-RIYĀD (RIYADH)	1,250,000
At-Tā'if	300,000
Buraydah (1974C)	69,940
Hā'il (1974C)	40,502
• Jiddah	1,300,000
Khamīs Mushayt (1974C)	49,581
Makkah (Mecca)	550,000
Najran (1974C)	47,501
Tabūk (1974C)	74,825

SENEGAL / Sénégal

1988 C	6,892,720
• DAKAR	1,490,450
Diourbel	77,548
Kaolack	152,007
Saint-Louis	160,689
Thiès	184,902
Ziguinchor	124,283

SEYCHELLES

1984 E	64,718
• VICTORIA	23,000

SIERRA LEONE

1985 C	3,515,812
Bo	59,768
• FREETOWN (★525,000)	469,776
Kenema	52,473
Koidu	82,474
Makeni	49,038

SINGAPORE

1990 C	2,690,100
• SINGAPORE (★3,025,000)	2,690,100

SLOVENIA / Slovenija

1987 E	1,936,606
• LJUBLJANA (▲316,607)	233,200
Maribor (▲187,651)	107,400

SOLOMON ISLANDS

1986 C	285,176
• HONIARA	30,413

SOMALIA / Somaliya

1984 E	5,423,000
Berbera	65,000
Hargeysa	70,000
Kismaayo	70,000
Marka	60,000
• MUQDISHO	600,000

SOUTH AFRICA / Suid-Afrika

1985 C	23,385,645
Alberton (★Johannesburg)	66,155
Alexandra (★Johannesburg)	67,276
Atteridgeville (★Pretoria)	73,439
Bellville (★Cape Town)	68,915
Benoni (★Johannesburg)	94,926
Bloemfontein (★235,000)	104,381
Boksburg (★Johannesburg)	110,832
Botshabelo (★Bloemfontein)	95,625
Brakpan (★Johannesburg)	46,416
CAPE TOWN (KAAPSTAD) (★1,790,000)	776,617
Carletonville (★120,499)	97,874
Daveyton (★Johannesburg)	99,056
Diepmeadow (★Johannesburg)	192,682
Durban (★1,550,000)	634,301
East London (Oos-Londen) (★320,000)	85,699
Edendale (★Pietermaritzburg)	47,001
Elsies River (★Cape Town)	70,067
Empumalanga (★Durban)	47,938
Evaton (★Vereeniging)	52,559
Galeshewe (★Kimberley)	63,238
Germiston (★Johannesburg)	116,718
Grassy Park (★Cape Town)	50,193
Guguleto (★Cape Town)	63,893
• Johannesburg (★3,650,000)	632,369
Kagiso (★Johannesburg)	50,647
Katlehong (★Johannesburg)	137,745
Kayamnandi (★Port Elizabeth)	220,548
Kempton Park (★Johannesburg)	87,721
Kimberley (★145,000)	74,061
Klerksdorp (★205,000)	48,947
Krugersdorp (★Johannesburg)	73,767
Kwa Makuta (★Durban)	71,378
Kwa Mashu (★Durban)	111,593
Kwanobuhle (★Port Elizabeth)	52,376
Kwa-Thema (★Johannesburg)	78,640
Ladysmith (★31,670)	25,102
Lekoa (Shapeville) (★Vereeniging)	218,392
Madadeni (★Newcastle)	65,832
Mamelodi (★Pretoria)	127,033
Mangaung (★Bloemfontein)	79,851
Ntuzuma (★Durban)	61,834
Nyanga (★Cape Town)	148,882
Ozisweni (★Newcastle)	51,934
Paarl (★Cape Town)	63,671
Parow (★Cape Town)	60,294
Pietermaritzburg (★230,000)	133,809
Pinetown (★Durban)	55,770
Port Elizabeth (★690,000)	272,844
PRETORIA (★960,000)	443,059
Randburg (★Johannesburg)	74,347
Randfontein (★Johannesburg)	43,763
Roodepoort-Maraisburg (★Johannesburg)	141,764
Sandton (★Johannesburg)	86,089
Soshanguve (★Pretoria)	68,598
Soweto (★Johannesburg)	521,948
Springs (★Johannesburg)	68,235
Tembisa (★Johannesburg)	149,282
Thabong (★Welkom)	43,470
Uitenhage (★Port Elizabeth)	54,987
Umlazi (★Durban)	194,933
Vanderbijlpark (★Vereeniging)	59,865
Vereeniging (★525,000)	60,584
Verwoerdburg (★Pretoria)	49,891
Vosloosrus (★Johannesburg)	52,061
Walvisbaai (Walvis Bay) (★16,607)	9,687
Welkom (★215,000)	54,488
Westonaria (★Johannesburg)	46,523

SPAIN / España

1988 E	39,217,804
Alacant (Alicante)	261,051
Albacete	125,997
Alcalá de Guadaira	50,935
Alcalá de Henares (★Madrid)	150,021
Alcobendas (★Madrid)	73,455
Alcoi (Alcoy)	66,074
Alcorcón (★Madrid)	139,796
Algeciras	99,528
Almería	157,644
Avilés (★131,000)	87,811
Badajoz (▲122,407)	106,400
Badalona (★Barcelona)	225,229
Baracaldo (★Bilbao)	113,502
Barcelona (★4,040,000)	1,714,355
Bilbao (★985,000)	384,733
Burgos	160,561
Cáceres	71,598
Cádiz (★240,000)	156,591
Cartagena (▲172,710)	70,000
Castelló de la Plana	131,809
Ciudad Real	56,300
Córdoba	302,301
Cornellà de Llobregat (★Barcelona)	86,866
Coslada (★Madrid)	68,765
Donostia (San Sebastián) (★285,000)	177,622
Dos Hermanas (▲68,456)	60,600
Elda	56,756
El Ferrol del Caudillo (★129,000)	86,503
El Prat de Llobregat (★Barcelona)	64,193
El Puerto de Santa María (▲62,285)	49,900
Elx (Elche) (▲180,256)	158,300
Fuenlabrada (★Madrid)	128,872
Gernika-Lumo (Guernica y Luno) (▲17,836) (1981C)	12,214
Getafe (★Madrid)	135,367
Gijón	262,156
Granada	263,334
Granollers (★Barcelona)	49,045
Guadalajara	61,309
Huelva	137,826
Irún	54,886
Jaén	106,435
Jerez de la Frontera (▲183,007)	156,200
La Coruña	248,862
La Línea	60,956
Las Palmas de Gran Canaria (▲366,347)	319,000
Leganés (★Madrid)	168,403
León (★159,000)	136,558
L'Hospitalet de Llobregat (★Barcelona)	278,449
Linares	58,622
Lleida (Lérida) (▲109,795)	91,500
Logroño	119,038
Lugo (▲78,795)	68,700
• MADRID (★4,650,000)	3,102,846
Málaga	574,456
Manresa	65,607
Mataró	100,817
Mérida	52,368
Móstoles (★Madrid)	181,648
Murcia (▲314,124)	149,800
Orense	106,042
Oviedo (▲190,073)	168,900
Palencia	76,692
Palma (▲314,608)	249,000
Pamplona	180,598
Parla (★Madrid)	66,253
Portugalete (★Bilbao)	57,813
Puertollano	52,284
Reus	83,800
Rubí (★Barcelona)	48,807
Sabadell (★Barcelona)	189,489
Salamanca	159,342
San Baudilio de Llobrega (★Barcelona)	77,502
San Cristóbal de la Laguna (▲111,533)	25,900
San Fernando (★Cádiz)	81,975
San Sebastián de los Reyes (★Madrid)	51,653
Santa Coloma de Gramanet (★Barcelona)	136,042
Santa Cruz de Tenerife	215,228
Santander (▲190,795)	166,800
Santiago de Compostela (▲88,110)	68,800
Santurce-Antiguo (★Bilbao)	52,334
Segovia	54,402
Sevilla (★945,000)	663,132
Talavera de la Reina	68,158

▲ Population of an entire municipality, commune, or district, including rural area.
• Largest city in country.
★ Population or designation of the metropolitan area, including suburbs.
C Census. E Official estimate. U Unofficial estimate.

▲ Bevölkerung eines ganzen städtischen Verwaltungsgebietes, eines Kommunalbezirkes oder eines Distrikts, einschliesslich ländlicher Gebiete.
• Grösste Stadt des Landes.
★ Bevölkerung oder Bezeichnung der Stadtregion einschliesslich Vororte.
C Volkszählung. E Offizielle Schätzung. U Inoffizielle Schätzung.

Tarragona (▲109,586)	63,500
Tarrasa (★Barcelona)	161,410
Toledo	59,551
Torrejón de Ardoz (★Madrid)	83,267
Torrent (★València)	55,751
València (★1,270,000)	743,933
Valladolid	331,461
Vigo (▲271,128)	179,500
Vitoria (Gasteiz)	204,264
Zamora	62,047
Zaragoza	582,239

SPANISH NORTH AFRICA / Plazas de Soberanía en el Norte de África

1988 E	122,905
• Ceuta	67,188
Melilla	55,717

SRI LANKA

1986 E	16,117,000
Battaramulla (★Colombo) (1981C)	56,535
• COLOMBO (★2,050,000)	683,000
Dehiwala-Mount Lavinia (★Colombo)	191,000
Galle	109,000
Jaffna	143,000
Kandy	130,000
Matale (1985E)	57,000
Matara (1985E)	57,000
Moratuwa (★Colombo)	138,000
Negombo (1985E)	76,000
Ratnapura (1985E)	51,000
SRI JAYAWARDENEPURA (KOTTE) (★Colombo)	104,000
Trincomalee (1985E)	51,000

SUDAN / As-Sūdān

1983 C	20,564,364
Al-Fāshir (1973C)	51,932
• AL-KHARṬŪM (★1,450,000)	476,218
Al-Kharṭūm Baḥrī (★Al-Kharṭūm)	341,146
Al-Qaḍārif (1973C)	66,465
Al-Ubayyiḍ	140,000
'Atbarah	73,000
Būr Sūdān (Port Sudan)	206,727
Jūbā (1980E)	116,000
Kassalā	143,000
Kūstī (1973C)	65,257
Nyala (1973C)	59,852
Umm Durmān (Omdurman) (★Al-Kharṭūm)	526,287
Wad Madanī	141,000
Wāw (1980E)	116,000

SURINAME

1988 E	392,000
• PARAMARIBO (★296,000)	241,000
Wanica (★Paramaribo)	55,000

SWAZILAND

1986 C	712,131
LOBAMBA	
Manzini (★30,000)	18,084
• MBABANE	38,290

SWEDEN / Sverige

1991 E	8,590,630
Borås	101,766
Eskilstuna	89,765
Gävle (▲88,568)	67,900
Göteborg (★710,894)	433,042
Halmstad (▲80,061)	51,300
Helsingborg	109,267
Huddinge (★Stockholm)	73,829
Järfälla (★Stockholm)	56,359
Jönköping	111,486
Karlstad	76,467
Linköping	122,268
Luleå	68,412
Lund (★Malmö)	87,681
Malmö (★445,000)	233,887
Mölndal (★Göteborg)	52,028
Nacka (★Stockholm)	64,056
Norrköping	120,522
Örebro	120,944
Södertälje (★Stockholm)	81,786
Sollentuna (★Stockholm)	51,377
Solna (★Stockholm)	51,841
• STOCKHOLM (★1,449,972)	674,452
Sundsvall (▲93,808)	50,800
Täby (★Stockholm)	56,714
Trollhättan	51,047
Tumba (★Stockholm)	68,542
Umeå (▲91,258)	59,500
Uppsala	167,508
Västerås	119,761
Växjö (▲69,547)	46,000

SWITZERLAND / Schweiz / Suisse / Svizzera

1990 E	6,673,850
Aarau (★58,903)	15,881
Arbon (★41,639)	12,284
Baden (★71,769)	14,545
Basel (Bâle) (★575,000)	169,587
BERN (BERNE) (★298,363)	134,393
Biel (Bienne) (★83,133)	52,023
Fribourg (Freiburg) (★59,141)	33,962
Genève (Geneva) (★470,000)	165,404
Lausanne (★263,442)	122,600
Locarno (★42,350)	14,149
Lugano (★94,800)	26,055
Luzern (★163,026)	59,115
Neuchâtel (★66,457)	32,509
Sankt Gallen (★126,845)	73,191
Schaffhausen (★53,501)	33,956
Thun (★78,978)	37,707
Vevey (★65,074)	15,207
Winterthur (★110,000) (1991E)	86,496
Zug (★68,698)	21,467
• Zürich (★870,000) (1991E)	347,634

SYRIA / Sūrīyah

1988 E	11,338,000
Al-Ḥasakah (1981C)	73,426
Al-Lādhiqīyah (Latakia)	249,000
Al-Qāmishlī	126,236
Ar-Raqqah	113,000
Dar'ā (1981C)	49,534
Dārayyā (★Dimashq)	53,204
Dayr az-Zawr	112,000
• DIMASHQ (DAMASCUS) (★2,000,000)	1,326,000
Dūmā (★Dimashq)	66,130
Ḥalab (Aleppo) (★1,335,000)	1,261,000
Ḥamāh	222,000
Ḥimṣ	447,000
Idlib (1981C)	51,682
Jaramānah (★Dimashq)	96,681
Kābir aṣ Ṣaghīr	47,728
Madīnat ath Thawrah	58,151
Ṭarṭūs (1981C)	52,589

TAIWAN / T'aiwan

1991 E	20,352,966
Changhua (▲215,224)	165,000
Chiai	257,597
Chilung	352,919
Chungho (★T'aipei)	374,339
Chungli	269,804
Chutung (1988E)	104,797
Fangshan (★Kaohsiung)	290,777
Fengyüan (▲151,642)	121,100
Hsichih (★T'aipei) (1980C)	70,031
Hsinchu	324,426
Hsinchuang (★T'aipei)	299,174
Hsintien (★T'aipei)	225,517
Hualien	107,552
Ilan (▲81,751) (1980C)	70,900
Kangshan (1980C)	78,049
Kaohsiung (★1,845,000)	1,386,723
Lotung (1980C)	57,925
Lukang (1980C)	72,019
Miaoli (1980C)	81,500
Nant'ou (1980C)	84,038
P'ingchen (★T'aipei)	147,030
P'ingtung (▲210,801)	172,400
Sanchung (★T'aipei)	375,996
Shulin (★T'aipei)	111,993
Tach'i (1980C)	67,209
T'aichung	761,802
T'ainan	683,251
• T'AIPEI (★6,130,000)	2,719,659
T'aipeihsien (★T'aipei)	538,954
T'aitung (▲108,196)	79,100
Taoyüan	241,263
T'oufen (1980C)	66,536
T'uch'eng (▲136,928)(★T'aipei)	80,300
Yangmei (1980C)	84,353
Yüanlin (▲121,251)	53,200
Yungho (★T'aipei)	249,736
Yungkang (▲136,705)	70,900

TAJIKISTAN

1991 E	5,358,300
Chudžand (Leninabad)	164,500
• DUŠANBE	582,400
Kul'ab	79,300
Kurgan-T'ube	58,400

TANZANIA

1984 E	21,062,000
Arusha	69,000
• DAR ES SALAAM	1,300,000
Dodoma	54,000
Iringa	67,000
Kigoma (1978C)	50,044
Mbeya	93,000
Morogoro	72,000
Moshi	62,000
Mtwara (1978C)	48,510
Mwanza (1978C)	110,611
Tabora	87,000
Tanga	121,000
Ujiji (1967C)	21,369
Zanzibar (1985E)	133,000

THAILAND / Prathet Thai

1988 E	54,960,917
Chiang Mai	164,030
Chon Buri	47,286
Hat Yai	138,046
Khon Kaen	131,340
• KRUNG THEP (BANGKOK) (★7,025,000) (1989E)	5,845,152
Nakhon Ratchasima	204,982
Nakhon Sawan	105,220
Nakhon Si Thammarat	72,407
Nonthaburi (★Krung Thep)	218,354
Pattaya	56,402
Phitsanulok	77,675
Phra Nakhon Si Ayutthaya	60,847
Sakon Nakhon	25,110
Samut Prakan (★Krung Thep)	73,327
Samut Sakhon	53,984
Saraburi	61,206
Songkhla	84,433
Trang	48,042
Ubon Ratchathani	100,374
Udon Thani	81,202
Yala	67,383

TOGO

1987 E	3,148,000
• LOMÉ	500,000
Sokodé	55,000

TOKELAU

1986 C	1,690

TONGA

1986 C	94,535
• NUKU'ALOFA	21,265

TRANSKEI

1987 E	3,081,770
• UMTATA (1978E)	30,000

TRINIDAD AND TOBAGO

1990 C	1,234,388
• PORT OF SPAIN (★370,000)	50,878
San Fernando (★75,000)	30,092

TUNISIA / Tunis / Tunisie

1984 C	6,975,450
Ariana (★Tunis)	98,655
Bardo (★Tunis)	65,669
Ben Arous (★Tunis)	52,105
Bizerte	94,509
Gabès	92,258
Gafsa	60,970
Hammam Lif (★Tunis)	47,009
Houmt Essouk	92,269
Kairouan	72,254
Kasserine	47,606
La Goulette (★Tunis)	61,609
Menzel Bourguiba	51,399
Sfax (★310,000)	231,911
Sousse (★160,000)	83,509
• TUNIS (★1,225,000)	596,654
Zarzis	49,063

TURKEY / Türkiye

1990 C	56,473,035
Adana	916,150
Adapazarı	171,225
Adıyaman	100,045
Afyon	95,643
Ağrı	58,038
Akhisar	73,944
Aksaray	90,698
Akşehir	51,746
Alanya	52,460
Amasya	57,288
ANKARA (★2,650,000)	2,559,471
Antakya (Antioch)	123,871
Antalya	378,208
Aydın	107,011
Bafra	65,600
Balıkesir	170,589
Bandırma	77,444
Batman	147,347
Bilecik	23,273
Bolu	60,789
Burdur	56,432
Bursa	834,576
Çanakkale	53,995
Ceyhan	85,308
Cizre	50,023
Çorlu	74,681
Çorum	116,810
Denizli	204,118
Diyarbakır	381,144
Düzce	61,878
Edirne	102,345
Elazığ	204,603
Elbistan	54,741
Ereğli, Konya prov.	74,283
Ereğli, Zonguldak prov.	63,987
Erzincan	91,772
Erzurum	242,391
Esenyurt (★İstanbul)	70,280
Eskişehir	413,082
Gaziantep	603,434
Gebze (★İstanbul)	159,116
Gelibolu	18,670
Gemlik	50,237
Giresun	67,604
Gölcük	64,911
Gümüşhane	26,014
Hakkâri	30,407
İçel (Mersin)	422,357
İnegöl	71,120
İskenderun	154,807
Isparta	112,117
• İstanbul (★7,550,000)	6,620,241
İzmir (★1,900,000)	1,757,414
İzmit	256,882
Kadirli	55,061
Karabük	105,373
Karaman	76,525
Kars	78,455
Kastamonu	51,560
Kayseri	421,362
Kilis	82,882
Kırıkhan	68,601
Kırıkkale	185,431
Kırşehir	73,538
Kızıltepe	60,134
Konya	513,346
Körfez	65,786
Kozan	54,451
Kütahya	130,994
Lüleburgaz	52,384
Malatya	281,776
Manisa	158,928
Maraş	228,129
Mardin	53,005
Muş	44,019
Nazilli	80,277
Nevşehir	52,719
Niğde	55,035
Nizip	58,604
Nusaybin	49,671
Ödemiş	51,620
Ordu	102,107
Osmaniye	123,307
Polatlı	60,158
Rize	52,031
Salihli	70,861
Samsun	303,979
Siirt	68,320
Silvan (Miyafarkin)	59,865
Sinop	25,537
Sivas	221,512
Siverek	63,049
Söke	50,866
Soma	49,977
Sultanbeyli (★İstanbul)	82,298
Tarsus	187,508
Tatvan	54,071
Tekirdağ	80,442
Tokat	83,058
Trabzon	143,941
Tunceli	24,513
Turgutlu	73,634
Turhal	68,384
Urfa	276,528
Uşak	105,270
Van	153,111
Viranşehir	57,461
Yalova (★İstanbul)	65,823
Yozgat	50,335
Zonguldak (★220,000)	116,725

TURKMENISTAN

1991 E	3,714,100
• AŠCHABAD	412,200
Čardžou	166,400
Mary	94,900
Nebit-Dag	59,500
Nebit-Dag	89,100
Tašauz	117,000

TURKS AND CAICOS ISLANDS

1990 C	12,350
• GRAND TURK	3,761

TUVALU

1979 C	7,349
• FUNAFUTI	2,191

UGANDA

1991 C	16,582,700
Jinja	60,979
• KAMPALA	773,463
Masaka	49,070
Mbale	53,634

UKRAINE / Ukrayina

1991 E	51,944,400
Achtyrka	52,300
Aleksandrija	104,900
Antracit (★Krasnyj Luč)	72,800
Art'omovsk	90,800
Belaja Cerkov'	204,400
Belgorod-Dnestrovskij	56,800
Berd'ansk	138,700
Berdičev	93,400
Borispol' (★Kijev)	52,700
Br'anka (★Stachanov)	64,500
Brovary (★Kijev)	84,800
Čerkassy	302,200
Černigov	305,700
Černovcy	258,800
Červonograd	74,000
Charcyzsk (★Doneck)	69,300
Char'kov (★2,050,000)	1,622,800
Cherson	365,400
Chmel'nickij	244,500
Dimitrov (★Krasnoarmejsk)	65,500
Dneprodzeržinsk (★Dnepropetrovsk)	284,400
Dnepropetrovsk (★1,600,000)	1,189,300
Doneck (★2,125,000)	1,121,300
Drogobyč	79,200
Družkovka (★Kramatorsk)	74,400
Džankoj	54,500
Dzeržinsk (★Gorlovka)	50,500
Energodar	51,500
Fastov	54,400
Feodosija	85,600
Gorlovka (★700,000)	336,600
Iljičovsk (★Odessa)	56,000
Ivano-Frankovsk	241,000
Izmail	95,100
Iz'um	64,800
Jalta	89,300
Jenakijevo (★Gorlovka)	120,100
Jevpatorija	110,500
Kaluš	69,400
Kamenec-Podol'skij	104,900
Kerč'	178,300
• KIJEV (★3,250,000)	2,635,000
Kirovograd	277,900
Kolomyja	66,200
Kommunarsk (★Stachanov)	126,000
Komsomol'sk	56,000
Konotop	97,700
Konstantinovka	107,800
Korosten'	67,500
Kovel'	69,700
Kramatorsk (★515,000)	201,300
Krasnoarmejsk (★180,000)	73,300
Krasnodon (★165,000)	54,800
Krasnyj Luč (★320,000)	113,400
Kremenčug	240,600
Krivoj Rog	724,000
Lisičansk (★415,000)	126,400
Lozovaja	74,100
Lubny	60,300
Luck	209,500
Lugansk (Vorošilovgrad) (★650,000)	503,900
L'vov	802,200
Makejevka (★Doneck)	423,900
Marganec	54,700
Mariupol' (Ždanov)	521,800
Melitopol'	176,900
Mukačevo	88,000
Nežin	82,000
Nikolajev	511,600
Nikopol'	159,000
Novaja Kachovka	59,000
Novograd-Volynskij	56,100
Novomoskovsk, Dnepropetrovsk oblast'	76,600
Novovolynsk	56,400
Odessa (★1,185,000)	1,100,700
Pavlograd	134,300
Pervomajsk	83,800
Pervomajsk (★Stachanov)	52,000
Poltava	320,100
Priluki	72,900
Romny	57,700
Roven'ki	58,500
Rovno	239,300
Rubežnoje (★Lisičansk)	75,100
Šacht'orsk (★Torez)	73,100
Šepetovka	51,900
Sevastopol'	366,200
Severodoneck (★Lisičansk)	133,300
Simferopol'	352,600
Slav'ansk (★Kramatorsk)	137,100
Smela	81,200
Snežnoje (★Torez)	68,900
Šostka	95,200
Stachanov (★700,000)	112,700
Stryj	68,200
Sumy	303,300
Sverdlovsk, Vorosilovgrad oblast' (★145,000)	83,700
Svetlovodsk	57,900
Ternopol'	219,200
Torez (★320,000)	88,100
Uman'	97,700
Užgorod	122,600
Vinnica	380,900
Zaporožje	896,600

▲ Población de un municipio, comuna o distrito entero, incluyendo sus áreas rurales.
• Ciudad más grande de un país.
★ Población o designación de un área metropolitana, incluyendo los suburbios.
C Censo. **E** Estimado oficial. **U** Estimado no oficial.

▲ Population d'une municipalité, d'une commune ou d'un district, zone rurale incluse.
• Ville la plus peuplée du pays.
★ Population de l'agglomération (ou nom de la zone métropolitaine englobante).
C Recensement. **E** Estimation officielle. **U** Estimation non officielle.

▲ População de um municipio, comuna ou distrito, inclusive as respectivas áreas rurais.
• Maior cidade de um país.
★ População ou indicação de uma área metropolitana.
C Censo. **E** Estimativa oficial. **U** Estimativa não oficial.

Žitomir	297,500
Žoltyje Vody	64,900

UNITED ARAB EMIRATES / Al-Imārāt al-ʻArabīyah al-Muttaḥidah

1980 C	980,000
ABŪ ẒABY (ABU DHABI)	242,975
Al-ʻAyn	101,663
Ash-Shāriqah	125,149
• Dubayy	265,702
Ra's al-Khaymah	42,000

UNITED KINGDOM

1981 C	55,678,079

UNITED KINGDOM: ENGLAND

1981 C	46,220,955
Aldershot (★London)	53,665
Ashton-under-Lyne (★Manchester)	43,605
Aylesbury	51,999
Barnsley	76,783
Barrow-in-Furness	50,174
Basildon (★London)	94,800
Basingstoke	73,027
Bath	84,283
Bebington (★Liverpool)	62,618
Bedford	75,632
Beeston and Stapleford (★Nottingham)	64,785
Benfleet (★London)	50,783
Birkenhead (★Liverpool)	99,075
Birmingham (★2,675,000)	1,013,995
Blackburn (★221,900)	109,564
Blackpool (★280,000)	146,297
Bognor Regis	50,323
Bolton (★Manchester)	143,960
Bootle	70,860
Bournemouth (★315,000)	142,829
Bracknell (★London)	52,257
Bradford (★Leeds)	293,336
Brentwood (★London)	51,212
Brighton (★420,000)	134,581
Bristol (★630,000)	413,861
Burnley (★160,000)	76,365
Burton upon Trent	59,040
Bury (★Manchester)	61,785
Bury Saint Edmunds	30,563
Camberley see Frimley and Camberley	
Cambridge	87,111
Cannock (★Birmingham)	54,503
Canterbury	34,546
Carlisle	72,206
Carlton (★Nottingham)	46,053
Chatham (★London)	65,835
Cheadle and Gatley (★Manchester)	59,478
Chelmsford (★London)	91,109
Cheltenham	87,188
Cheshunt (★London)	49,616
Chester	80,154
Chesterfield (★127,000)	73,352
Clacton-on-Sea	39,618
Colchester	87,476
Corby	48,704
Coventry (★645,000)	318,718
Crawley (★London)	80,113
Crewe	59,097
Crosby (★Liverpool)	54,103
Darlington	85,519
Dartford (★London)	62,032
Derby (★275,000)	218,026
Dewsbury (★Leeds)	49,612
Doncaster	74,727
Dover	33,461
Dudley (★Birmingham)	186,513
Dunstable (★Luton)	48,436
Durham	38,105
Eastbourne	86,715
Eastleigh (★Southampton)	58,585
Ellesmere Port (★Liverpool)	65,829
Epsom and Ewell (★London)	65,830
Esher / Molesey (★London)	46,688
Exeter	88,235
Fareham / Portchester (★Portsmouth)	55,563
Farnborough (★London)	48,063
Folkestone	42,949
Frimley and Camberley (★London)	45,108
Gateshead (★Newcastle)	91,429
Gillingham (★London)	92,531
Gloucester (★115,000)	106,526
Gosport (★Portsmouth)	69,664
Gravesend (★London)	53,450
Grays (★London)	45,881
Greasby / Moreton (★Liverpool)	56,410
Great Yarmouth	54,777
Grimsby (★145,000)	91,532
Guildford (★London)	61,509
Halesowen (★Birmingham)	57,533
Halifax	76,675
Harlow (★London)	79,150
Harrogate	63,637
Hartlepool (★Middlesbrough)	91,749
Hastings	74,979
Havant (★Portsmouth)	50,098
Hemel Hempstead (★London)	80,110
Hereford	48,277
Hertford (★London)	21,350
High Wycombe (▲156,800)	69,575
Hove (★Brighton)	65,587
Huddersfield (▲377,400)	147,825
Huyton-with-Roby (★Liverpool)	62,011
Ipswich	129,661
Keighley (★Leeds)	49,188
Kidderminster	50,385
Kingston upon Hull (★350,000)	322,144
Kingswood (★Bristol)	54,736
Kirkby (★Liverpool)	52,825
Lancaster	43,902
Leeds (★1,540,000)	445,242
Leicester (★495,000)	324,394
Lincoln	79,980
Littlehampton	46,028
Liverpool (★1,525,000)	538,809
• LONDON (★11,100,000)	6,574,009
Loughborough	44,895
Lowestoft	59,430
Luton (★220,000)	163,209
Macclesfield	47,525
Maidenhead (★London)	59,809
Maidstone	86,067
Manchester (★2,775,000)	437,612
Mansfield (★198,000)	71,325
Margate	53,137
Middlesbrough (★580,000)	158,516
Middleton (★Manchester)	51,373
Milton Keynes	36,886
Newcastle-under-Lyme (★Stoke-on-Trent)	73,208
Newcastle upon Tyne (★1,300,000)	199,064
Northampton	154,172
Norwich (★230,000)	169,814
Nottingham (★655,000)	273,300
Nuneaton (★Coventry)	60,337
Oldbury / Smethwick (★Birmingham)	153,268
Oldham (★Manchester)	107,095
Oxford (★230,000)	113,847
Penzance	18,501
Peterborough	113,404
Plymouth (★290,000)	238,583
Poole (★Bournemouth)	122,815
Portsmouth (★485,000)	174,218
Preston (★250,000)	166,675
Ramsgate	36,678
Reading (★200,000)	194,727
Redditch (★Birmingham)	61,639
Reigate / Redhill (★London)	48,241
Rochdale (★Manchester)	97,292
Rotherham (★Sheffield)	122,374
Royal Leamington Spa (★Coventry)	56,552
Royal Tunbridge Wells	57,699
Rugby	59,039
Runcorn (★Liverpool)	63,995
Saint Albans (★London)	76,709
Saint Helens	114,397
Sale (★Manchester)	57,872
Salford (★Manchester)	96,525
Salisbury	36,890
Scarborough	36,665
Scunthorpe	79,043
Sheffield (★710,000)	470,685
Shrewsbury	57,731
Slough (★London)	106,341
Solihull (★Birmingham)	93,940
Southampton (★415,000)	211,321
Southend-on-Sea (★London)	155,720
Southport (★Liverpool)	88,596
South Shields (★Newcastle)	86,488
Stafford	60,915
Staines (★London)	51,949
Stapleford see Beeston and Stapleford	
Stevenage	74,757
Stockport (★Manchester)	135,489
Stockton-on-Tees (★Middlesbrough)	86,699
Stoke-on-Trent (★440,000)	272,446
Stourbridge (★Birmingham)	55,136
Stratford-upon-Avon	20,941
Stretford (★Manchester)	47,522
Sunderland (★Newcastle)	195,064
Sutton Coldfield (★Birmingham)	102,572
Swindon	127,348
Tanworth	63,260
Taunton	47,793
Torquay (★112,400)	54,430
Wakefield (★Leeds)	74,764
Wallasey (★Liverpool)	62,465
Walsall (★Birmingham)	177,923
Walton and Weybridge (★London)	50,031
Warrington	81,366
Washington (★Newcastle)	48,856
Waterlooville (★Portsmouth)	57,296
Watford (★London)	109,503
West Bromwich (★Birmingham)	153,725
Weston-super-Mare	60,821
Weybridge see Walton and Weybridge	
Widnes	55,973
Wigan (★Manchester)	88,725
Woking (★London)	92,667
Wolverhampton (★Birmingham)	263,501
Worcester	75,466
Worthing (★Brighton)	90,687
York (★145,000)	123,126

UNITED KINGDOM: NORTHERN IRELAND

1987 E	1,575,200
Bangor (★Belfast)	70,700
Belfast (★685,000)	303,800
Castlereagh (★Belfast)	57,900
Londonderry (★97,200)	97,500
Lurgan (★63,000) (1981C)	20,991
Newtownabbey (★Belfast)	72,300

UNITED KINGDOM: SCOTLAND

1989 E	5,090,700
Aberdeen	210,700
Ayr (★100,000) (1981C)	48,493
Clydebank (★Glasgow) (1981C)	51,832
Coatbridge (1981C)	50,831
Cumbernauld (★Glasgow)	50,300
Dundee	172,540
Dunfermline (★125,817) (1981C)	52,105
East Kilbride (★Glasgow)	69,500
Edinburgh (★630,000)	433,200
Falkirk (★148,171) (1981C)	36,372
Glasgow (★1,800,000)	695,630
Greenock (★101,000) (1981C)	58,436
Hamilton (★Glasgow) (1981C)	51,666
Irvine (★94,000)	55,900
Kilmarnock (★84,000) (1981C)	51,799
Kirkcaldy (★148,171) (1981C)	46,356
Motherwell (★Glasgow) (1981C)	30,616
Paisley (★Glasgow) (1981C)	84,330
Perth (1981C)	41,916
Stirling (★61,000) (1981C)	36,640

UNITED KINGDOM: WALES

1981 C	2,790,462
Cardiff (★625,000)	262,313
Cwmbran (★Newport)	44,592
Llanelli	45,336
Merthyr Tydfil	38,893
Neath (★Swansea)	48,687
Newport (★310,000)	115,896
Pontypool (★Newport)	36,064
Port Talbot (★130,000)	40,078
Rhondda (★Cardiff)	70,980
Swansea (★275,000)	172,433
Wrexham	39,929

UNITED STATES

1990 C	248,709,873

UNITED STATES: ALABAMA

1990 C	4,040,587
Anniston (★116,034)	26,623
Auburn	33,830
Birmingham (★907,810)	265,968
Decatur (★131,556)	48,761
Dothan (★130,964)	53,589
Florence (★131,327)	36,426
Gadsden (★99,840)	42,523
Huntsville (★238,912)	159,789
Mobile (★476,923)	196,278
Montgomery (★292,517)	187,106
Tuscaloosa (★150,522)	77,759

UNITED STATES: ALASKA

1990 C	550,043
Anchorage (★226,338)	226,338
Fairbanks	30,843
Juneau	26,751

UNITED STATES: ARIZONA

1990 C	3,665,228
Chandler (★Phoenix)	90,533
Glendale (★Phoenix)	148,134
Mesa (★Phoenix)	288,091
Nogales	19,489
Phoenix (★2,122,101)	900,013
Scottsdale (★Phoenix)	130,069
Sun City (★Phoenix)	38,126
Tempe (★Phoenix)	141,865
Tucson (★666,880)	405,390
Yuma (★106,895)	54,923

UNITED STATES: ARKANSAS

1990 C	2,350,725
Fayetteville (★113,409)	42,099
Fort Smith (★175,911)	72,798
Hot Springs National Park	32,462
Jonesboro	46,535
Little Rock (★513,117)	175,795
North Little Rock (★Little Rock)	61,741
Pine Bluff (★85,487)	57,140

UNITED STATES: CALIFORNIA

1990 C	29,760,021
Alameda (★Oakland)	76,459
Alhambra (★Los Angeles)	82,106
Anaheim (★2,410,556)(★ Los Angeles)	266,406
Antioch (★Oakland)	62,195
Arden (★Sacramento)	62,900
Bakersfield (★543,477)	174,820
Baldwin Park (★Los Angeles)	69,330
Bellflower (★Los Angeles)	61,815
Berkeley (★Oakland)	102,724
Buena Park (★Anaheim)	68,784
Burbank (★Los Angeles)	93,643
Calexico	18,633
Camarillo (★Oxnard)	52,303
Carlsbad (★San Diego)	63,126
Carmichael (★Sacramento)	48,702
Carson (★Los Angeles)	83,995
Cerritos (★Los Angeles)	53,240
Chico (★182,120)	40,079
Chino (★Riverside)	59,682
Chula Vista (★San Diego)	135,163
Citrus Heights (★Sacramento)	112,800
Clovis (★Fresno)	50,323
Compton (★Los Angeles)	90,454
Concord (★Oakland)	111,348
Corona (★Riverside)	76,095
Costa Mesa (★Anaheim)	96,357
Cucamonga (★Riverside)	101,409
Daly City (★San Francisco)	92,311
Diamond Bar (★Los Angeles)	53,672
Downey (★Los Angeles)	91,444
East Los Angeles (★Los Angeles)	126,379
El Cajon (★San Diego)	88,693
El Monte (★Los Angeles)	106,209
El Toro (★Anaheim)	62,685
Escondido (★San Diego)	108,635
Eureka	27,025
Fairfield (★Vallejo)	77,211
Fontana (★Riverside)	87,535
Fountain Valley (★Anaheim)	53,691
Fremont (★Oakland)	173,339
Fresno (★667,490)	354,202
Fullerton (★Anaheim)	114,144
Gardena (★Los Angeles)	49,847
Garden Grove (★Anaheim)	143,050
Glendale (★Los Angeles)	180,038
Hacienda Heights (★Los Angeles)	58,200
Hawthorne (★Los Angeles)	71,349
Hayward (★Oakland)	111,498
Hemet (★Riverside)	36,094
Huntington Beach (★Anaheim)	181,519
Huntington Park (★Los Angeles)	56,065
Inglewood (★Los Angeles)	109,602
Irvine (★Anaheim)	110,330
La Habra (★Anaheim)	51,266
Lakewood (★Los Angeles)	73,557
La Mesa (★San Diego)	52,931
Lancaster (★Los Angeles)	97,291
Livermore (★Oakland)	56,741
Lodi (★Stockton)	51,874
Lompoc (★Santa Barbara)	37,649
Long Beach (★Los Angeles)	429,433
Los Angeles (★14,531,529)	3,485,398
Lynwood (★Los Angeles)	61,945
Merced (★178,403)	56,216
Milpitas (★San Jose)	50,686
Mission Viejo (★Anaheim)	72,820
Modesto (★370,522)	164,730
Montebello (★Los Angeles)	59,564
Monterey (★Salinas)	31,954
Monterey Park (★Los Angeles)	60,738
Mountain View (★San Jose)	67,460
Napa (★Vallejo)	61,842
National City (★San Diego)	54,249
Newport Beach (★Anaheim)	66,643
Norwalk (★Los Angeles)	94,279
Oakland (★2,082,914)(★ San Francisco)	372,242
Oceanside (★San Diego)	128,398
Ontario (★Riverside)	133,179
Orange (★Anaheim)	110,658
Oxnard (★669,016)(★ Los Angeles)	142,216
Palm Springs (★Riverside)	40,181
Palo Alto (★San Jose)	55,900
Pasadena (★Los Angeles)	131,591
Pico Rivera (★Los Angeles)	59,177
Pleasanton (★Oakland)	50,553
Pomona (★Los Angeles)	131,723
Porterville (★Visalia)	29,563
Rancho Cordova (★Sacramento)	48,731
Redding (★147,036)	66,462
Redlands (★Riverside)	60,394
Redondo Beach (★Los Angeles)	60,167
Redwood City (★San Francisco)	66,072
Rialto (★Riverside)	72,388
Richmond (★Oakland)	87,425
Riverside (★2,588,793)(★ Los Angeles)	226,505
Rosemead (★Los Angeles)	51,638
Sacramento (★1,481,102)	369,365
Salinas (★355,660)	108,777
San Bernardino (★Riverside)	164,164
San Diego (★2,949,000)	1,110,549
San Francisco (★6,253,311)	723,959
San Jose (★1,497,577)(★ San Francisco)	782,248
San Leandro (★Oakland)	68,223
San Mateo (★San Francisco)	85,486
Santa Ana (★Anaheim)	293,742
Santa Barbara (★369,608)	85,571
Santa Clara (★San Jose)	93,613
Santa Cruz (★229,734)(★ San Francisco)	49,040
Santa Maria (★Santa Barbara)	61,284
Santa Monica (★Los Angeles)	86,905
Santa Rosa (★388,222)(★ San Francisco)	113,313
Santee (★San Diego)	52,902
Simi Valley (★Oxnard)	100,217
South Gate (★Los Angeles)	86,284
South San Francisco (★San Francisco)	54,312
South Whittier (★Los Angeles)	51,100
Spring Valley (★San Diego)	54,600
Stockton (★480,628)	210,943
Sunnyvale (★San Jose)	117,229
Thousand Oaks (★Oxnard)	104,352
Torrance (★Los Angeles)	133,107
Tustin (★Anaheim)	50,689
Union City (★Oakland)	53,762
Upland (★Riverside)	63,374
Vacaville (★Vallejo)	71,479
Vallejo (★451,186)(★ San Francisco)	109,199
Ventura (San Buenaventura)(★Oxnard)	92,575
Visalia (★311,921)	75,636
Vista (★San Diego)	71,872
Walnut Creek (★Oakland)	60,569
Watsonville (★Santa Cruz)	31,099
West Covina (★Los Angeles)	96,086
Westminster (★Anaheim)	78,118
Whittier (★Los Angeles)	77,671
Yorba Linda (★Anaheim)	52,422
Yuba City (★122,643)	27,437

UNITED STATES: COLORADO

1990 C	3,294,394
Arvada (★Denver)	89,235
Aurora (★Denver)	222,103
Boulder (★225,339)(★ Denver)	83,312
Colorado Springs (★397,014)	281,140
Denver (★1,848,319)	467,610
Fort Collins (★186,136)	87,758
Grand Junction	29,034
Greeley (★131,821)	60,536
Lakewood (★Denver)	126,481
Longmont (★Denver)	51,555
Loveland (★Fort Collins)	37,352
Pueblo (★123,051)	98,640
Thornton (★Denver)	55,031
Westminster (★Denver)	74,625

UNITED STATES: CONNECTICUT

1990 C	3,287,116
Bridgeport (★443,722)(★ New York, N.Y.)	141,686
Bristol (★79,488)(★ Hartford)	60,640
Danbury (★187,867)(★ New York, N.Y.)	65,585
East Hartford (★Hartford)	50,452
Fairfield (★Bridgeport)	53,418
Greenwich (★Stamford)	58,441
Hamden (★New Haven)	53,100
Hartford (★1,085,837)	139,739
Manchester (★Hartford)	51,000
Meriden (★New Haven)	59,479
Milford (★Bridgeport)	48,168
New Britain (★148,188)(★ Hartford)	75,491
New Haven (★530,180)	130,474
New London (★266,819)	28,540
Norwalk (★127,378)(★ New York, N.Y.)	78,331
Stamford (★202,557)(★ New York, N.Y.)	108,056
Stratford (★Bridgeport)	49,389
Torrington (★	33,687
Waterbury (★221,629)	108,961
West Hartford (★Hartford)	59,100
West Haven (★New Haven)	54,021

UNITED STATES: DELAWARE

1990 C	666,168
Dover	27,630
Wilmington (★Philadelphia, Pa.)	71,529

UNITED STATES: DISTRICT OF COLUMBIA

1990 C	606,900
WASHINGTON (★3,923,574)	606,900

UNITED STATES: FLORIDA

1990 C	12,937,926

▲ Population of an entire municipality, commune, or district, including rural area.
• Largest city in country.
★ Population or designation of the metropolitan area, including suburbs.
C Census. **E** Official estimate. **U** Unofficial estimate.

▲ Bevölkerung eines ganzen städtischen Verwaltungsgebietes, eines Kommunalbezirkes oder eines Distrikts, einschliesslich ländlicher Gebiete.
• Grösste Stadt des Landes.
★ Bevölkerung oder Bezeichnung der Stadtregion einschliesslich Vororte.
C Volkszählung. **E** Offizielle Schätzung. **U** Inoffizielle Schätzung.

Boca Raton (★West Palm Beach)	61,492
Brandon (★Tampa)	57,985
Cape Coral (★Fort Myers)	74,991
Carol City (★Miami)	52,800
City of Sunrise (★Fort Lauderdale)	64,407
Clearwater (★Tampa)	98,784
Daytona Beach (★370,712)	61,921
De Land (★Daytona Beach)	16,491
Fort Lauderdale (★1,255,488) (★ Miami)	149,377
Fort Myers (★335,113)	45,206
Fort Pierce (★251,071)	36,830
Fort Walton Beach (★143,776)	21,471
Gainesville (★204,111)	84,770
Hialeah (★Miami)	188,004
Hollywood (★Fort Lauderdale)	121,697
Jacksonville (★906,727)	635,230
Kendall (★Miami)	53,100
Lakeland (★405,382)	70,576
Largo (★Tampa)	65,674
Melbourne (★398,978)	59,646
Miami (★3,192,582)	358,548
Miami Beach (★Miami)	92,639
Naples (★152,099)	19,505
Ocala (★194,833)	42,045
Orlando (★1,072,748)	164,693
Panama City (★126,994)	34,378
Pembroke Pines (★Fort Lauderdale)	65,452
Pensacola (★344,406)	58,165
Plantation (★Fort Lauderdale)	66,692
Pompano Beach (★Fort Lauderdale)	72,411
Saint Petersburg (★Tampa)	238,629
Sarasota (★277,776)	50,961
Tallahassee (★233,598)	124,773
Tampa (★2,067,959)	280,015
Venice (★Sarasota)	16,922
West Palm Beach (★863,518)	67,643
Winter Haven (★Lakeland)	24,725

UNITED STATES: GEORGIA

1990 C	6,478,216
Albany (★112,561)	78,122
Athens (★156,267)	45,734
Atlanta (★2,833,511)	394,017
Augusta (★396,809)	44,639
Columbus (★243,072)	178,681
Macon (★281,103)	106,612
Rome	30,326
Savannah (★242,622)	137,560
Valdosta	39,806
Warner Robins (★Macon)	43,726

UNITED STATES: HAWAII

1990 C	1,108,229
Hilo	37,808
Honolulu (★836,231)	365,272

UNITED STATES: IDAHO

1990 C	1,006,749
Boise (★205,775)	125,738
Idaho Falls	43,929
Lewiston	28,082
Nampa	28,365
Pocatello	46,080

UNITED STATES: ILLINOIS

1990 C	11,430,602
Arlington Heights (★Chicago)	75,460
Aurora (★356,884) (★ Chicago)	99,581
Bloomington (★129,180)	51,972
Champaign (★173,025)	63,502
Chicago (★8,065,633)	2,783,726
Cicero (★Chicago)	67,436
Danville	33,828
Decatur (★117,206)	83,885
De Kalb	34,925
Des Plaines (★Chicago)	53,223
East Saint Louis (★Saint Louis, Mo.)	40,944
Elgin (★Aurora)	77,010
Evanston (★Chicago)	73,233
Galesburg	33,530
Joliet (★389,650) (★ Chicago)	76,836
Kankakee (★96,255)	27,575
Mount Prospect (★Chicago)	53,170
Naperville (★Chicago)	85,351
Oak Lawn (★Chicago)	56,182
Oak Park (★Chicago)	53,648
Peoria (★339,172)	113,504
Quincy	39,681
Rockford (★283,719)	139,426
Schaumburg (★Chicago)	68,586
Skokie (★Chicago)	59,432
Springfield (★189,550)	105,227
Waukegan (★Chicago)	69,392
Wheaton (★Chicago)	51,464

UNITED STATES: INDIANA

1990 C	5,544,159
Anderson (★130,669)	59,459
Bloomington (★108,978)	60,633
Columbus	31,802
Elkhart (★156,198)	43,627
Evansville (★278,990)	126,272
Fort Wayne (★363,811)	173,072
Gary (★ 604,526) (★ Chicago, Il.)	116,646
Hammond (★Gary)	84,236
Indianapolis (★1,249,822)	731,327
Kokomo (★96,946)	44,962
Lafayette (★130,598)	43,764
Marion	32,618
Michigan City	33,822
Muncie (★119,659)	71,035
Richmond	38,705
South Bend (★247,052)	105,511
Terre Haute (★130,812)	57,483

UNITED STATES: IOWA

1990 C	2,776,755
Ames	47,198
Cedar Rapids (★168,767)	108,751
Clinton	29,201
Council Bluffs (★Omaha, Ne.)	54,315
Davenport (★350,861)	95,333
Des Moines (★392,928)	193,187
Dubuque (★86,403)	57,546
Iowa City (★96,119)	59,738
Mason City	29,040
Sioux City (★115,018)	80,505
Waterloo (★146,611)	66,467

UNITED STATES: KANSAS

1990 C	2,477,574
Hutchinson	39,308
Kansas City (★Kansas City, Mo.)	149,767
Lawrence (★81,798)	65,608
Manhattan	37,712
Olathe (★Kansas City, Mo.)	63,352
Overland Park (★Kansas City, Mo.)	111,790
Salina	42,303
Topeka (★160,976)	119,883
Wichita (★485,270)	304,011

UNITED STATES: KENTUCKY

1990 C	3,685,296
Bowling Green	40,641
Covington (★Cincinnati, Oh.)	43,264
Frankfort	25,968
Lexington (★348,428)	225,366
Louisville (★952,662)	269,063
Owensboro (★87,189)	53,549
Paducah	27,256

UNITED STATES: LOUISIANA

1990 C	4,219,973
Alexandria (★131,556)	49,188
Baton Rouge (★528,264)	219,531
Bossier City (★Shreveport)	52,721
Houma (★182,842)	96,982
Kenner (★New Orleans)	72,033
Lafayette (★208,740)	94,440
Lake Charles (★168,134)	70,580
Metairie (★New Orleans)	149,428
Monroe (★142,191)	54,909
New Iberia	31,828
New Orleans (★1,238,816)	496,938
Shreveport (★334,341)	198,525

UNITED STATES: MAINE

1990 C	1,227,928
Augusta	21,325
Bangor (★88,745)	33,181
Lewiston (★88,141)	39,757
Portland (★215,281)	64,358

UNITED STATES: MARYLAND

1990 C	4,781,468
Annapolis (★Baltimore)	33,187
Baltimore (★2,382,172)	736,014
Bethesda (★Washington, D.C.)	62,936
Columbia (★Baltimore)	75,883
Cumberland (★101,643)	23,706
Dundalk (★Baltimore)	65,800
Hagerstown (★121,393)	35,445
Salisbury	20,592
Silver Spring (★Washington, D.C.)	76,046
Towson (★Baltimore)	49,445
Wheaton (★Washington, D.C.) (1989)	58,300

UNITED STATES: MASSACHUSETTS

1990 C	6,016,425
Amherst	17,773
Boston (★4,171,643)	574,283
Brockton (★189,478) (★ Boston)	92,788
Brookline (★Boston)	54,718
Cambridge (★Boston)	95,802
Chicopee (★Springfield)	56,632
Fall River (★157,272) (★ Providence)	92,703
Fitchburg (★102,797)	41,194
Framingham (★Boston)	64,989
Haverhill (★Lawrence)	51,418
Lawrence (★393,516) (★ Boston)	70,207
Lowell (★273,067) (★ Boston)	103,439
Lynn (★Salem)	81,245
Malden (★Boston)	53,884
Medford (★Boston)	57,407
New Bedford (★175,641)	99,922
Newton (★Boston)	82,585
Northampton (★Springfield)	29,289
Pittsfield (★79,250)	48,622
Quincy (★Boston)	84,985
Somerville (★Boston)	76,210
Springfield (★529,519)	156,983
Taunton	49,832
Waltham (★Boston)	57,878
Weymouth (★Boston)	54,063
Worcester (★436,905)	169,759

UNITED STATES: MICHIGAN

1990 C	9,295,297
Ann Arbor (★282,937) (★ Detroit)	109,592
Battle Creek (★135,982)	53,540
Benton Harbor (★161,378)	12,818
Clinton Township (★Detroit)	77,900
Dearborn (★Detroit)	89,286
Dearborn Heights (★Detroit)	60,838
Detroit (★4,665,236)	1,027,974
East Lansing (★Lansing)	50,677
Farmington Hills (★Detroit)	74,652
Flint (★430,459)	140,761
Grand Rapids (★688,399)	189,126
Holland (★Grand Rapids)	30,745
Jackson (★149,756)	37,446
Kalamazoo (★223,411)	80,277
Lansing (★432,674)	127,321
Livonia (★Detroit)	100,850
Monroe (★Detroit)	22,902
Muskegon (★158,983)	40,283
Pontiac (★Detroit)	71,166
Port Huron (★Detroit)	33,694
Redford Township (★Detroit)	54,387
Roseville (★Detroit)	51,412
Royal Oak (★Detroit)	65,410
Saginaw (★399,320)	69,512
Saint Clair Shores (★Detroit)	68,107
Sault Sainte Marie	14,689
Southfield (★Detroit)	75,728
Sterling Heights (★Detroit)	117,810
Taylor (★Detroit)	70,811
Troy (★Detroit)	72,884
Warren (★Detroit)	144,864
Westland (★Detroit)	84,724
Wyoming (★Grand Rapids)	63,891

UNITED STATES: MINNESOTA

1990 C	4,375,099
Bloomington (★Minneapolis)	86,335
Brooklyn Park (★Minneapolis)	56,381
Burnsville (★Minneapolis)	51,288
Coon Rapids (★Minneapolis)	52,978
Duluth (★239,971)	85,493
Mankato	31,477
Minneapolis (★2,464,124)	368,383
Plymouth (★Minneapolis)	50,889
Rochester (★106,470)	70,745
Saint Cloud (★190,921)	48,812
Saint Paul (★Minneapolis)	272,235

UNITED STATES: MISSISSIPPI

1990 C	2,573,216
Biloxi (★197,125)	46,319
Columbus	23,799
Greenville	45,226
Gulfport (★Biloxi)	40,775
Hattiesburg	41,882
Jackson (★395,396)	196,637
Laurel	18,827
Meridian	41,036
Natchez	19,460
Pascagoula (★115,243)	25,899
Vicksburg	20,908

UNITED STATES: MISSOURI

1990 C	5,117,073
Cape Girardeau	34,438
Columbia (★112,379)	69,101
Florissant (★Saint Louis)	51,206
Independence (★Kansas City)	112,301
Jefferson City	35,481
Joplin (★134,910)	40,961
Kansas City (★1,566,280)	435,146
Saint Charles (★Saint Louis)	54,555
Saint Joseph (★83,083)	71,852
Saint Louis (★2,444,099)	396,685
Springfield (★240,593)	140,494

UNITED STATES: MONTANA

1990 C	799,065
Billings (★113,419)	81,151
Butte	33,336
Great Falls (★77,691)	55,097
Helena	24,569
Missoula	42,918

UNITED STATES: NEBRASKA

1990 C	1,578,385
Grand Island	39,386
Lincoln (★213,641)	191,972
Omaha (★618,262)	335,795

UNITED STATES: NEVADA

1990 C	1,201,833
Carson City	40,443
Henderson (★Las Vegas)	64,942
Las Vegas (★741,459)	258,295
Paradise (★Las Vegas)	124,682
Reno (★254,667)	133,850
Sparks (★Reno)	53,367
Sunrise Manor (★Las Vegas)	95,362

UNITED STATES: NEW HAMPSHIRE

1990 C	1,109,252
Concord	36,006
Manchester (★147,809)	99,567
Nashua (★180,557) (★ Boston, Ma.)	79,662
Portsmouth (★223,578)	25,925

UNITED STATES: NEW JERSEY

1990 C	7,730,188
Atlantic City (★319,416)	37,986
Bayonne (★Jersey City)	61,444
Bloomfield (★Newark)	45,061
Brick Township (★New York, N.Y.)	66,473
Camden (★Philadelphia, Pa.)	87,492
Cherry Hill (★Philadelphia, Pa.)	69,319
Clifton (★New York, N.Y.)	71,742
East Orange (★Newark)	73,552
Edison (★New York, N.Y.)	88,680
Elizabeth (★Newark)	110,002
Irvington (★Newark)	59,774
Jersey City (★553,099) (★ New York, N.Y.)	228,537
Middletown (★New York, N.Y.)	62,298
Newark (★1,824,321) (★ New York, N.Y.)	275,221
Passaic (★New York, N.Y.)	58,041
Paterson (★New York, N.Y.)	140,891
Trenton (★325,824) (★ Philadelphia, Pa.)	88,675
Union (★Newark)	50,024
Union City (★Jersey City)	58,012
Vineland (★138,053) (★ Philadelphia, Pa.)	54,780
Woodbridge (★New York, N.Y.)	17,434

UNITED STATES: NEW MEXICO

1990 C	1,515,069
Albuquerque (★480,577)	384,736
Farmington	33,997
Las Cruces (★135,510)	62,126
Roswell	44,654
Santa Fe (★117,043)	55,859

UNITED STATES: NEW YORK

1990 C	17,990,455
Albany (★874,304)	101,082
Amherst (★Buffalo) (1989)	45,600
Auburn	31,258
Binghamton (★264,497)	53,008
Buffalo (★1,189,288)	328,123
Cheektowaga (★Buffalo)	84,387
Elmira (★95,195)	33,724
Glens Falls (★118,539)	15,023
Greece (★Rochester)	15,632
Hempstead (★New York)	49,453
Hicksville (★New York)	40,174
Irondequoit (★Rochester)	52,322
Ithaca	29,541
Jamestown (★141,895)	34,681
Kingston	23,095
Levittown (★New York)	53,286
Lockport (★Niagara Falls)	24,426
Middletown (★New York)	24,160
Mount Vernon (★New York)	67,153
Newburgh (★New York)	26,454
New Rochelle (★New York)	67,265
• New York (★18,087,251)	7,322,564
Niagara Falls (★220,756) (★ Buffalo)	61,840
Poughkeepsie (★259,462)	28,844
Rochester (★1,002,410)	231,636
Schenectady (★Albany)	65,566
Syracuse (★659,864)	163,860
Town of Tonawanda (★Buffalo)	17,284
Troy (★Albany)	54,269
Utica (★316,633)	68,637
West Seneca (★Buffalo)	47,866
Yonkers (★New York)	188,082

UNITED STATES: NORTH CAROLINA

1990 C	6,628,637
Asheville (★174,821)	61,607
Burlington (★108,213)	39,498
Charlotte (★1,162,093)	395,934
Durham (★Raleigh)	136,611
Fayetteville (★274,566)	75,695
Gastonia (★Charlotte)	54,732
Goldsboro	40,709
Greensboro (★942,091)	183,521
Hickory (★221,700)	28,301
High Point (★Greensboro)	69,496
Jacksonville (★149,838)	30,013
Kannapolis (★Charlotte)	29,696
Raleigh (★735,480)	207,951
Rocky Mount	48,997
Salisbury (★Charlotte)	23,087
Wilmington (★120,284)	55,530
Winston-Salem (★Greenboro)	143,485

UNITED STATES: NORTH DAKOTA

1990 C	638,800
Bismarck (★83,831)	49,256
Fargo (★153,296)	74,111
Grand Forks (★70,683)	49,425
Minot	34,544

UNITED STATES: OHIO

1990 C	10,347,115
Akron (★657,575) (★ Cleveland)	223,019
Alliance (★Canton)	23,376
Ashtabula	21,633
Brunswick (★Cleveland)	28,230
Canton (★394,106)	84,161
Cincinnati (★1,744,124)	364,040
Cleveland (★2,759,823)	505,616
Cleveland Heights (★Cleveland)	54,052
Columbus (★1,377,419)	632,910
Dayton (★951,270)	182,044
East Liverpool	13,654
Elyria (★Lorain)	56,746
Euclid (★Cleveland)	54,875
Hamilton (★291,479) (★ Cincinnati)	61,368
Kettering (★Dayton)	60,569
Lakewood (★Cleveland)	59,718
Lancaster (★Columbus)	34,507
Lima (★154,340)	45,549
Lorain (★271,126) (★ Cleveland)	71,245
Mansfield (★126,137)	50,627
Marion	34,075
Middletown (★Cincinnati)	46,022
Newark (★Columbus)	44,389
Parma (★Cleveland)	87,876
Portsmouth	22,676
Sandusky	29,764
Springfield (★Dayton)	70,487
Steubenville (★142,523)	22,125
Toledo (★614,128)	332,943
Warren (★Youngstown)	50,793
Youngstown (★492,619)	95,732
Zanesville	26,778

UNITED STATES: OKLAHOMA

1990 C	3,145,585
Broken Arrow (★Tulsa)	58,043
Edmond (★Oklahoma City)	52,315
Enid (★56,735)	45,309
Lawton (★111,486)	80,561
Midwest City (★Oklahoma City)	52,267
Muskogee	37,708
Norman (★Oklahoma City)	80,071
Oklahoma City (★958,839)	444,719
Tulsa (★708,954)	367,302

UNITED STATES: OREGON

1990 C	2,842,321
Beaverton (★Portland)	53,310
Corvallis	44,757
Eugene (★282,912)	112,669
Gresham (★Portland)	68,235
Medford (★146,389)	46,951
Portland (★1,477,895)	437,319
Salem (★278,024)	107,786

UNITED STATES: PENNSYLVANIA

1990 C	11,881,643
Abington (★Philadelphia)	59,300
Allentown (★686,688)	105,090
Altoona (★130,542)	51,881
Bensalem (★Philadelphia)	56,788
Bethlehem (★Allentown)	71,428
Bristol (★Philadelphia)	57,129
Butler	15,714
Coatesville (★Philadelphia)	11,038
Erie (★275,572)	108,718
Hanover (★York)	14,399
Harrisburg (★587,986)	52,376
Haverford (★Philadelphia)	49,848

▲ Población de un municipio, comuna o distrito entero, incluyendo sus áreas rurales.
• Ciudad más grande de un país.
★ Población o designación de un área metropolitana, incluyendo los suburbios.
C Censo. **E** Estimado oficial. **U** Estimado no oficial.

▲ Population d'une municipalité, d'une commune ou d'un district, zone rurale incluse.
• Ville la plus peuplée du pays.
★ Population de l'agglomération (ou nom de la zone métropolitaine englobante).
C Recensement. **E** Estimation officielle. **U** Estimation non officielle.

▲ População de um municipio, comuna ou distrito, inclusive as respectivas áreas rurais.
• Maior cidade de um país.
★ População ou indicação de uma área metropolitana.
C Censo. **E** Estimativa oficial. **U** Estimativa não oficial.

Hazleton (★Scranton)	24,730
Johnstown (★241,247)	28,134
Lancaster (★422,822)	55,551
Lebanon (★Harrisburg)	24,800
Lower Merion Township (★Philadelphia)	58,003
New Castle	28,334
Oil City	11,949
Penn Hills (★Pittsburgh)	51,430
Philadelphia (★5,899,345)	1,585,577
Pittsburgh (★2,242,798)	369,879
Pottstown (★Philadelphia)	21,831
Pottsville	16,603
Reading (★336,523)	78,380
Scranton (★734,175)	81,805
Sharon (★121,003)	17,493
State College (★123,786)	38,923
Uniontown (★Pittsburgh)	12,034
Upper Darby (★Philadelphia)	84,054
Washington (★Pittsburgh)	15,864
Wilkes-Barre (★Scranton)	47,523
Williamsport (★118,710)	31,933
York (★417,848)	42,192

UNITED STATES: RHODE ISLAND

1990 C	1,003,464
Cranston (★Providence)	76,060
East Providence (★Providence)	50,380
Newport	28,227
Pawtucket (★329,384) (★Providence)	72,644
Providence (★1,141,510)	160,728
Warwick (★Providence)	85,427

UNITED STATES: SOUTH CAROLINA

1990 C	3,486,703
Anderson (★145,196)	26,184
Charleston (★506,875)	80,414
Columbia (★453,331)	98,052
Florence (★114,344)	29,813
Greenville (★640,861)	58,282
North Charleston (★Charleston)	70,218
Rock Hill (★Charlotte, N.C.)	41,643
Spartanburg (★Greenville)	43,467
Sumter	41,943

UNITED STATES: SOUTH DAKOTA

1990 C	696,004
Pierre	12,906
Rapid City (★81,343)	54,523
Sioux Falls (★123,809)	100,814

UNITED STATES: TENNESSEE

1990 C	4,877,185
Bristol (★Johnson City)	23,421
Chattanooga (★433,210)	152,466
Clarksville (★169,439)	75,494
Jackson (★77,982)	48,949
Johnson City (★436,047)	49,381
Kingsport (★Johnson City)	36,365
Knoxville (★604,816)	165,121
Memphis (★981,747)	610,337
Murfreesboro (★Nashville)	44,922
Nashville (★985,026)	487,969

UNITED STATES: TEXAS

1990 C	16,986,510
Abilene (★119,655)	106,654
Amarillo (★187,547)	157,615
Arlington (★Fort Worth)	261,721
Austin (★781,572)	465,622
Baytown (★Houston)	63,850
Beaumont (★361,226)	114,323
Brownsville (★460,000)	98,962
Bryan (★121,862)	55,002
Carrollton (★Dallas)	82,169
College Station (★Bryan)	52,456
Corpus Christi (★349,894)	257,453
Dallas (★3,885,415)	1,006,877
Denton (★Dallas)	66,270
El Paso (★650,000)	515,342
Fort Worth (★1,332,053) (★ Dallas)	447,619
Freeport (★Houston)	11,389
Galveston (★217,399) (★ Houston)	59,070
Garland (★Dallas)	180,650
Grand Prairie (★Dallas)	99,616
Harlingen (★Brownsville)	48,735
Houston (★3,711,043)	1,630,553
Irving (★Dallas)	155,037
Killeen (★255,301)	63,535
Laredo (★354,000)	122,899
Longview (★162,431)	70,311
Lubbock (★222,636)	186,206
Lufkin	30,206
McAllen (★383,545)	84,021
Mesquite (★Dallas)	101,484
Midland (★106,611)	89,443
Odessa (★118,934)	89,699
Pasadena (★Houston)	119,363
Plano (★Dallas)	128,713
Port Arthur (★Beaumont)	58,724
Richardson (★Dallas)	74,840
San Angelo (★98,458)	84,474
San Antonio (★1,302,099)	935,933
Sherman (★95,021)	31,601
Temple (★Killeen)	46,109
Texarkana (★120,132)	31,656
Tyler (★151,309)	75,450
Victoria (★74,361)	55,076
Waco (★189,123)	103,590
Wichita Falls (★122,378)	96,259

UNITED STATES: UTAH

1990 C	1,722,850
Logan	32,762
Ogden (★Salt Lake City)	63,909
Orem (★Provo)	67,561
Provo (★263,590)	86,835
Salt Lake City (★1,072,227)	159,936
Sandy (★Salt Lake City)	75,058
West Valley City (★Salt Lake City)	86,976

UNITED STATES: VERMONT

1990 C	562,758
Burlington (★131,439)	39,127
Montpelier	8,247
Rutland	18,230

UNITED STATES: VIRGINIA

1990 C	6,187,358
Alexandria (★Washington, D.C.)	111,183
Annandale (★Washington, D.C.)	50,975
Arlington (★Washington, D.C.)	170,936
Charlottesville (★131,107)	40,341
Chesapeake (★Norfolk)	151,976
Danville (★108,711)	53,056
Hampton (★Norfolk)	133,793
Lynchburg (★142,199)	66,049
Martinsville	16,162
Newport News (★Norfolk)	170,045
Norfolk (★1,396,107)	261,229
Portsmouth (★Norfolk)	103,907
Richmond (★865,640)	203,056
Roanoke (★224,477)	96,397
Suffolk (★Norfolk)	52,141
Virginia Beach (★Norfolk)	393,069

UNITED STATES: WASHINGTON

1990 C	4,866,692
Bellevue (★Seattle)	86,874
Bellingham (★127,780)	52,179
Bremerton (★189,731)	38,142
Everett (★Seattle)	69,961
Lakes District (★Tacoma)	58,412
Longview	31,499
Olympia (★161,238)	33,840
Pasco (★Richland)	20,337
Seattle (★2,559,164)	516,259
Spokane (★361,364)	177,196
Tacoma (★586,203)(★Seattle)	176,664
Yakima (★188,823)	54,827

UNITED STATES: WEST VIRGINIA

1990 C	1,793,477
Beckley	18,296
Charleston (★250,454)	57,287
Clarksburg	18,059
Fairmont	20,210
Huntington (★312,529)	54,844
Morgantown	25,879
Parkersburg (★149,169)	33,862
Wheeling (★159,301)	34,882

UNITED STATES: WISCONSIN

1990 C	4,891,769
Appleton (★315,121)	65,695
Beloit (★Janesville)	35,573
Eau Claire (★137,543)	56,856
Fond du Lac	37,757
Green Bay (★194,594)	96,466
Janesville (★139,510)	52,133
Kenosha (★128,181) (★ Chicago, Il.)	80,352
La Crosse (★97,904)	51,003
Madison (★367,085)	191,262
Manitowoc	32,520
Milwaukee (★1,607,183)	628,088
Oshkosh (★Appleton)	55,006
Racine (★175,034) (★ Milwaukee)	84,298
Sheboygan (★103,877)	49,676
Waukesha (★Milwaukee)	56,958
Wausau (★115,400)	37,060
Wauwatosa (★Milwaukee)	49,366
West Allis (★Milwaukee)	63,221

UNITED STATES: WYOMING

1990 C	453,588
Casper (★61,226)	46,742
Cheyenne (★73,142)	50,008

URUGUAY

1985 C	2,955,241
Las Piedras (★Montevideo)	58,288
Melo	42,615
Mercedes	36,702
Minas	34,661
• MONTEVIDEO (★1,550,000)	1,251,647
Paysandú	76,191
Rivera	57,316
Salto	80,823

UZBEKISTAN

1991 E	20,708,200
Almalyk	116,400
Andižan	298,300
Angren	132,600
Bekabad	82,800
Buchara	249,600
Chodžejli	61,200
Čirčik (★Taškent)	158,400
Čust	48,700
Denau	49,300
Džizak	110,900
Fergana	226,500
Gulistan	56,900
Jangijul'	56,900
Kagan	49,800
Karši	168,000
Kattakurgan	59,600
Kokand	175,000
Margilan	124,900
Namangan	319,200
Navoi	111,600
Nukus	179,600
Šachrisabz	53,200
Samarkand	370,500
• TAŠKENT (★2,325,000)	2,113,300
Termez	90,400
Urgenč	130,400

VANUATU

1989 C	142,944
• PORT VILA (★23,000)	18,905

VATICAN CITY / Città del Vaticano

1988 E	766

VENDA

1985 C	459,819
Makwarela	3,712
• Shayandima	4,853
THOHOYANDOU	3,641

VENEZUELA

1981 C	14,516,735
Acarigua	91,662
Barcelona	156,461
Barinas	110,462
Barquisimeto	497,635
Baruta (★Caracas)	200,063
Cabimas	140,435
Cagua	53,704
Calabozo	61,995
• CARACAS (★3,600,000)	1,816,901
Carora	58,694
Carúpano	64,579
Catia La Mar (★Caracas)	87,916
Chacao (★Caracas)	72,703
Ciudad Bolívar	182,941
Ciudad Guayana	314,497
Ciudad Ojeda (Lagunillas)	83,565
Coro	96,339
Cumaná	179,814
El Limón	65,122
El Tigre	73,595
Guacara	72,727
Guanare	64,025
Guarenas (★Caracas)	101,742
La Victoria	70,828
Los Dos Caminos (★Caracas)	63,346
Los Teques (★Caracas)	112,857
Maiquetía (★Caracas)	66,056
Maracaibo	890,643
Maracay	322,560
Mariara	47,242
Maturín	154,976
Mérida	143,209
Petare (★Caracas)	395,715
Porlamar	51,079
Pozuelos	80,342
Puerto Cabello	71,759
Puerto la Cruz	53,881
Punto Fijo	71,114
San Cristóbal	198,793
San Felipe	57,526
San Fernando	57,308
San Juan de los Morros	57,219
Turmero	111,186
Valencia	616,224
Valera	102,068
Valle de la Pascua	55,761

VIETNAM / Viet Nam

1989 C	64,411,668
Bac Giang	50,879
Bac Lieu	83,483
Bien Hoa	273,879
Buon Me Thuot	97,044
Ca Mau	81,901
Cam Pha	105,336
Can Tho (1978C)	208,078
Chau Doc	50,935
Da Lat	102,583
Da Nang	369,734
Dong Hoi	22,254
Hai Duong	53,370
Hai Phong (▲1,447,523)	351,919
HA NOI (★1,275,000)	905,939
Hoa Binh	69,323
Hon Gai	123,102
Hue	211,718
Long Xuyen	128,814
Minh Hai (1979C)	72,517
My Tho	104,724
Nam Dinh	165,629
Nha Trang	213,460
Phan Rang	71,111
Phan Thiet	114,236
Play Cu	76,991
Qui Nhon	159,852
Rach Gia	137,784
Sa Dec	50,733
Soc Trang (1979C)	74,967
Soc Trang	87,899
Tan An	50,288
Thai Binh	57,640
Thai Nguyen	124,871
Thanh Hoa	84,951
• Thanh Pho Ho Chi Minh (Saigon) (★3,300,000)	2,796,229
Tra Vinh	47,785
Tuy Hoa	54,081
Uong Bi	49,595
Viet Tri	73,347
Vinh	110,793
Vinh Long	81,620
Vung Tau	123,528
Yen Bai	58,645

VIRGIN ISLANDS OF THE UNITED STATES

1990 C	101,809
• CHARLOTTE AMALIE (★32,000)	12,331

WALLIS AND FUTUNA / Wallis et Futuna

1983 E	12,408
• MATA-UTU	815
Ono (1976C)	624

WESTERN SAHARA

1982 E	142,000
• EL AAIÚN	93,875

WESTERN SAMOA / Samoa i Sisifo

1981 C	156,349
• APIA	33,170

YEMEN / Al-Yaman

1990 E	15,267,000
'Adan (★318,000) (1984E)	176,100
Al-Hudaydah (1986C)	155,110
Al-Mukallā (1984E)	58,000
• ṢAN'Ā' (1986C)	427,150
Ta'izz (1986C)	178,043

YUGOSLAVIA / Jugoslavija

1987 E	10,342,020
• BEOGRAD (★1,400,000)	1,130,000
Kragujevac (▲171,609)	94,800
Niš (▲240,219)	168,400
Novi Sad (▲266,772)	176,000
Pančevo (★Beograd)	62,700
Priština (▲244,830)	125,400
Subotica (▲153,306)	100,500
Titograd (▲145,163)	82,500
Zrenjanin (▲140,009)	65,400

ZAIRE / Zaïre

1984 C	29,671,407
Bandundu	63,189
Beni	73,319
Boma	88,556
Bukavu	171,064
Bumba	46,823
Bunia	46,224
Butembo	78,633
Gandajika	60,263
Gemena	62,641
Goma	76,745
Ilebo (Port-Francqui)	48,831
Isiro	78,871
Kabinda	81,752
Kalemie (Albertville)	70,694
Kananga (Luluabourg)	290,898
Kikwit	146,784
Kindu	68,044
• KINSHASA (LÉOPOLDVILLE) (1986E)	3,000,000
Kisangani (Stanleyville)	282,650
Kolwezi	201,382
Likasi (Jadotville)	194,465
Lisala	40,471
Lubumbashi (Élisabethville)	543,268
Manono	51,755
Matadi	144,742
Mbandaka (Coquilhatville)	125,263
Mbuji-Mayi (Bakwanga)	423,363
Mwene-Ditu	72,567
Tshikapa	105,484
Yangambi	53,726

ZAMBIA

1980 C	5,661,801
Chililabombwe (Bancroft) (★56,582)	25,900
Chingola	130,872
Kabwe (Broken Hill)	127,420
Kalulushi	53,383
Kitwe (★283,962)	207,500
Livingstone	61,296
Luanshya (★113,422)	61,600
• LUSAKA (1989E)	921,000
Mufulira (★138,824)	77,100
Ndola	250,490

ZIMBABWE

1983 E	7,740,000
Bulawayo	429,000
Chitungwiza (★Harare)	202,000
Gweru (1982C)	78,940
• HARARE (★890,000)	681,000
Mutare (1982C)	75,358

▲ Population of an entire municipality, commune, or district, including rural area.
• Largest city in country.
★ Population or designation of the metropolitan area, including suburbs.
C Census. E Official estimate.
U Unofficial estimate.

▲ Bevölkerung eines ganzen städtischen Verwaltungsgebietes, eines Kommunalbezirkes oder eines Distrikts, einschliesslich ländlicher Gebiete.
• Grösste Stadt des Landes.
★ Bevölkerung oder Bezeichnung der Stadtregion einschliess lich Vororte.
C Volkszählung. E Offizielle Schätzung.
U Inoffizielle Schätzung.

▲ Población de un municipio, comuna o distrito entero, incluyendo sus áreas rurales.
• Ciudad más grande de un país.
★ Población o designación de un área metropolitana, incluyendo los suburbios.
C Censo. E Estimado oficial.
U Estimado no oficial.

▲ Population d'une municipalité, d'une commune ou d'un district, zone rurale incluse.
• Ville la plus peuplée du pays.
★ Population de l'agglomération (ou nom de la zone métropolitaine englobante).
C Recensement. E Estimation officielle.
U Estimation non officielle.

▲ População de um municipio, comuna ou distrito, inclusive as respectivas áreas rurais.
• Maior cidade de um país.
★ População ou indicação de uma área metropolitana.
C Censo. E Estimativa oficial.
U Estimativa não oficial.

The index includes in a single alphabetical list some 170,000 names appearing on the maps. Each name is followed by a page reference to one or more maps and by the location of the feature on the map, in coordinates of latitude and longitude. If a page contains several maps, a lowercase letter identifies the particular map. The page reference for two-page maps is always to the left-hand page.

Most map features are indexed to the largest-scale map on which they appear. However, a feature usually is not indexed to a Metropolitan Area map if it is also shown on another map where it can be seen in a broader setting. Countries, mountain ranges, and other extensive features are generally indexed to the largest-scale map that shows them in their entirety.

The order in which index information is presented is shown in the English, German, Spanish, French, and Portuguese headings at the center of each two-page spread.

For example:

ENGLISH			
Name	Page	Lat.°′	Long.°′

The features indexed are of three types: *point, areal,* and *linear.* For *point* features (for example, cities, mountain peaks, dams), latitude and longitude coordinates give the location of the point on the map. For *areal* features (countries, mountain ranges, etc.), the coordinates generally indicate the approximate center of the feature. For *linear* features (rivers, canals, aqueducts), the coordinates locate a terminating point—for example, the mouth of a river, or the point at which a feature reaches the map margin.

Name Forms Names in the index, as on the maps, are generally in the local language and insofar as possible are spelled according to official practice. Diacritical marks are included, except that those used to indicate tone, as in Vietnamese, are usually not shown. Most features that extend beyond the boundaries of one country have no single official name, and these are usually named in English. Many English, German, Spanish, French, and Portuguese names, which may not be shown on the maps, appear in the index as cross references. All cross references are indicated by the symbol →. A name that appears in a shortened version on the map due to space limitations is given in full in the index, with the portion that is omitted on the map enclosed in brackets, for example, Acapulco [de Juárez].

Transliteration For names in languages not written in the Roman alphabet, the locally official transliteration system has been used where one exists. Thus, names in Russia and Bulgaria have been transliterated according to the systems adopted by the academies of science of these countries. Similarly, the transliteration for mainland Chinese names follows the Pinyin system, which has been officially adopted in mainland China. For languages with no one locally accepted transliteration system, notably Arabic, transliteration in general follows closely a system adopted by the United States Board on Geographic Names.

Alphabetization Names are alphabetized in the order of the letters of the English alphabet. Spanish *ll* and *ch*, for example, are not treated as distinct letters. Furthermore, diacritical marks are disregarded in alphabetization—German or Scandinavian *ä* or *ö* are treated as *a* or *o*.

The names of physical features may appear inverted, since they are always alphabetized under the proper, not the generic, part of the name, thus: "Gibraltar, Strait of Ʉ." Otherwise every entry, whether consisting of one word or more, is alphabetized as a single continuous entity. "Lakeland," for example, appears after "La Crosse" and before "La Salle." Names beginning with articles (Le Havre, Den Helder, Al-Qāhirah, As-Suways) are not inverted. Names beginning with "St." and "Sainte" are alphabetized as though spelled "Saint."

In the case of identical names, towns are listed first, then political divisions, then physical features. Entries that are completely identical (including symbols, discussed below) are distinguished by abbreviations of their official country names and are sequenced alphabetically by country name. The many duplicate names in Canada, the United Kingdom, and the United States are further distinguished by abbreviations of the names of their primary subdivisions. (See list of abbreviations on pages 319-320).

Abbreviation and Capitalization Abbreviation and styling have been standardized for all languages. A period is used after every abbreviation even when this may not be the local practice. The abbreviation "St." is used only for "Saint." "Sankt" and other forms of the term are spelled out.

All names are written with an initial capital letter except for a few Dutch names, such as 's-Gravenhage. Capitalization of noninitial words in a name generally follows local practice.

Symbols The symbols that appear in the index represent graphically the broad categories of the features named, for example, ∧ for mountain (Everest, Mount ∧). An abbreviated key to the symbols, in the five atlas languages, appears at the foot of each pair of index pages. Superior numbers following some symbols in the index indicate finer distinctions, for example, $\wedge^{1}$ for volcano (Fuji-san $\wedge^{1}$). A complete list of the symbols and superior numbers is given on page I•1.

Das Register umfasst in alphabetischer Anordnung etwa 170 000 in den Karten erscheinende Namen. Nach jedem Namen folgt die Seitenangabe zu einer oder mehreren Karten und die Lageangabe des Objektes in der Karte mit geographischer Länge und Breite. Enthält eine Seite mehrere Karten, so wird die betreffende Karte durch einen Kleinbuchstaben gekennzeichnet. Die Seitenangabe für Doppelseiten bezieht sich immer auf die linke Seite.

Die Verweise für die meisten Objekte in den Karten beziehen sich auf die Karte mit dem grössten Massstab. Normalerweise werden jedoch Verweise auf Objekte in den Karten der Stadtregionen nicht gegeben, wenn sie auf einer anderen Karte in grösserem Zusammenhang dargestellt sind. Die Lageangaben für Länder, Gebirgszüge und andere ausgedehnte Objekte beziehen sich allgemein auf die Karte grössten Massstabes, die sie in ihrer ganzen Ausdehnung zeigt.

Die Anordnung, in welcher die Lageangabe erfolgt, geht aus den englischen, deutschen, spanischen, französischen und portugiesischen Überschriften in der Mitte jeder Doppelseite hervor.

Zum Beispiel:

DEUTSCH			
Name	Seite	Breite°′	Länge°′ E = Ost

Die aufgeführten Objekte gliedern sich in drei Gruppen: *punkt-, flächen-* und *linienförmige* Objekte. Bei *punktförmigen* Objekten (z.B. Städte, Berge, Dämme) beziehen sich die Angaben nach Länge und Breite auf die Signatur in der Karte. Bei *flächenhaften* Objekten (Länder, Gebirgszüge usw.) verweisen die Koordinaten im allgemeinen auf das ungefähre Zentrum des Objektes. Bei *linienhaften* Objekten (Flüsse, Kanäle, Wasserleitungen) beziehen sich die Koordinaten auf einen bestimmten Punkt, z.B. die Mündung eines Flusses oder den Punkt, an dem das Objekt den Kartenrand schneidet.

Namengebung Wie in den Karten so sind auch im Register die Namen im allgemeinen in der örtlichen Namensform wiedergegeben und soweit als möglich in der amtlichen Schreibweise. Diakritische Zeichen wurden gesetzt; sie wurden nur dort weggelassen, wo sie, wie im Vietnamesischen, Tonhöhen kennzeichnen. Meist haben Objekte, die sich über die Grenzen eines Landes hinaus erstrecken, keinen einzelnen offiziellen Namen; normalerweise sind sie daher englisch beschriftet. Viele englische, deutsche, spanische, französische und portugiesische Namensformen, die nicht in den Karten enthalten sind, erscheinen im Register als Kreuzverweis. Alle Kreuzverweise werden durch das Symbol → gekennzeichnet. Namen, die aus Platzgründen in abgekürzter Form in der Karte erscheinen, werden im Register voll ausgeschrieben, wobei der auf der Karte weggelassene Teil in Klammern gesetzt ist, z.B. Acapulco [de Juárez].

Transkription Für die Transkription von Namen aus Sprachen, die nicht im lateinischen Alphabet geschrieben werden, wurde das offizielle Transkriptionssystem benutzt, sofern ein solches vorhanden ist. So wurden die Namen in Russland und in Bulgarien nach dem von den wissenschaftlichen Akademien dieser Länder angewandten System transkribiert. Entsprechend wurden die Namen auf dem chinesischen Festland nach dem Pinyin-System übertragen, das offiziell in der Volksrepublik China eingeführt wurde. Bei Sprachen, für die ein allgemein anerkanntes Transkriptionssystem nicht vorliegt, vor allem für Arabisch, erfolgte die Transkription in enger Anlehnung an das vom United States Board on Geographic Names angewandte System.

Alphabetische Ordnung Die alphabetische Ordnung der Namen entspricht der Reihenfolge der Buchstaben im englischen Alphabet. So werden z.B. das spanische *ll* und *ch* nicht als besondere Buchstaben behandelt. Ferner wurden diakritische Zeichen beim Alphabetisieren nicht berücksichtigt, das deutsche oder skandinavische *ä* oder *ö* als *a* oder *o* behandelt.

Physische Objekte können umgestellt erscheinen, da sie immer nach dem Eigennamen und nicht nach dem Gattungsbegriff eingeordnet wurden, z.B. "Gibraltar, Strait of Ʉ." Ansonsten wurde jeder Eintrag, ob er aus einem Wort oder aus mehreren besteht, als eine einzige Einheit behandelt. So ist z.B. "Lakeland" nach "La Crosse," aber vor "La Salle" aufgeführt. Namen, die mit einem Artikel beginnen, wurden nicht umgestellt (Le Havre, Den Helder, Al-Qāhirah, As-Suways). Namen, die mit "St." und "Sainte" beginnen, sind der Schreibweise "Saint" nach eingeordnet.

Wo Namensgleichheit besteht, werden zunächst die Städte aufgeführt, dann politische Einheiten und schliesslich physische Objekte. Eintragungen, die vollkommen identisch sind (einschliesslich der weiter unten erläuterten Symbole), werden durch Hinzufügung der Abkürzung des offiziellen Ländernamens unterschieden und sind den Ländernamen nach alphabetisch geordnet. Die zahlreichen identischen Namen in Kanada, dem Vereinigten Königreich und den Vereinigten Staaten sind darüber hinaus noch durch Abkürzungen der obersten Verwaltungseinheit unterschieden. (Siehe Verzeichnis der Abkürzungen, Seite 319-320).

Abkürzungen und Grossschreibung Abkürzung und Schreibweise wurden für alle Sprachen vereinheitlicht. Nach jeder Abkürzung steht ein Punkt, auch wenn dies nicht der jeweiligen Gepflogenheit entspricht. Die Abkürzung "St." wird ausschliesslich für "Saint" gebraucht. "Sankt" und andere Formen dieses Begriffes werden ausgeschrieben.

Der erste Buchstabe eines Namens wird gross geschrieben, ausgenommen einige holländische Namen wie 's-Gravenhage. Die Grossschreibung der weiteren Worte eines zusammengesetzten Namens folgt im allgemeinen der landesüblichen Schreibweise.

Symbole Die im Register verwendeten Symbole veranschaulichen graphisch die zahlreichen Kategorien der benannten Objekte, z.B. ∧ = Berg (Everest, Mount ∧). Eine kurzgefasste Erläuterung der Symbole erscheint in jeder der fünf Sprachen des Atlas am Fusse jeder Doppelseite des Registers. Hochgestellte Ziffern hinter Symbolen im Register bezeichnen feinere Unterscheidungen, z.B. $\wedge^{1}$ = Vulkan (Fuji-san $\wedge^{1}$). Eine vollständige Übersicht der Symbole und hochgestellten Ziffern findet sich auf Seite I•1.

El índice contiene en una sola lista alfabética, alrededor de 170 000 nombres que aparecen en los mapas. Después de cada nombre está indicada la página o las páginas de referencia, en los cuales se encuentran los mismos, y las coordinadas de la latitud y la longitud del lugar del rasgo. Si una página contiene various mapas, letras minúsculas identifican el mapa correspondiente. Para mapas que ocupan dos páginas, la página de referencia siempre es la de la izquierda.

La mayoría de los nombres que figuran en el índice, se efiere a los mapas en la escala más grande. Sin embargo, un nombre no se refiere en un mapa metropolitano si ya aparece en otro mapa, donde se muestra en un marco de mayor proporción. Los países, sierras y otros rasgos extensivos se refieren generalmente en el índice en los mapas de escalas mayores en que se muestran completos.

En orden en que la información del índice se presenta, aparece en un encabezamiento al centro de cada par de páginas, en inglés, alemán, español, francés y portugués.

Por ejemplo:

ESPAÑOL			
Nombre	Página	Lat.°′	Long.°′ W = Oeste

Los rasgos anotados en el índice son de tres tipos: *el punto, el área y la extensión linear.* Para rasgos que indican *el punto* (como por ejemplo, las ciudades, picos de montañas, presas), las coordinadas de latitud y longitud indican la posición exacta del punto sobre el mapa. Respecto a *las áreas* (como países, sierras, etc.), las coordinadas indican usualmente el centro aproximado del rasgo particular. En cuanto a *los rasgos lineares* (ríos, canales, acueductos) las coordinadas indican los puntos terminales, por ejemplo, la boca de un río, o el punto en que un rasgo físico alcanza el margen del mapa.

Las Formas de los Nombres Los nombres que aparecen en el índice, así como también en los mapas, se dan en general en el idioma local, y en tanto que es posible siguen la ortografía oficialmente aceptada. Incluímos también marcas diacríticas, excepto las que se usan para indicar tono, como en la lengua vietnamita. A causa de que la mayoría de los rasgos que se extienden más allá de las fronteras de un país no tienen un solo nombre oficial, éstos se denominan usualmente en inglés. Muchos nombres, en inglés, alemán, español, francés y portugués, que pueden no figurar en el mapa, se dan como referencia de una página a otra en el índice. Todas las referencias que pasan a otras páginas se indican con el símbolo →. Un nombre que aparece en el mapa en forma abreviada, debido a la limitación de espacio, en el índice figura en su forma completa, poniendo entre paréntesis angulares la parte omitida en el mapa, por ejemplo Acapulco [de Juárez].

"Trasliteración" Para los nombres escritos en los idiomas que no usan el alfabeto latino, el sistema oficial de trasliteración ha sido utilizado donde localmente existe. Así, los nombres de Rusia y de Bulgaria se trasliteran conforme a los sistemas aceptados por las academias de las ciencias de sus respectivos países. De la misma manera, la trasliteración de los nombres en chino continental siguen el sistema Pinyin que ha sido oficialmente adoptado en este país. Para idiomas sin ningún sistema localmente aceptado de trasliteración, particularmente para el árabe, éstos se trasliteran usando por lo general un sistema adoptado por el United States Board on Geographic Names.

Alfabetización Los nombres se han ordenado de acuerdo con el alfabeto inglés. Las letras del alfabeto en español *ll* y *ch* por ejemplo, no se han considerado letras separadas. Además, los signos diacríticos no se toman en cuenta en la alfabetización — en alemán o escadinavo letras *ä* u *ö* se tratan como *a* u *o*.

Los nombres de los rasgos físicos algunas veces se invierten, ya que se ordenan alfabéticamente según la parte propia y no genérica del nombre. Así por ejemplo, en el caso del Estrecho de Gibraltar aparece: Gibraltar, Strait of ʉ. Por lo demás, cada renglón, sea una palabra o una frase, se alfabetiza como una unidad. Por ejemplo, "Lakeland" aparece después de "La Crosse" y antes de "La Salle." Los nombres que comienzan con artículos (Le Havre, Den Helder, Al-Qāhirah, As-Suways) no están invertidos. Nombres que empiezan con "St." y "Sainte" se alfabetizan como "Saint".

En los casos de nombres idénticos, las poblaciones aparecen primero, las divisiones políticas después y finalmente los rasgos físicos. En caso de ser completamente idénticos (incluyendo los símbolos, discutidos más abajo) se distinguen por medio de abreviaciones de los nombres oficiales de los países a que pertenecen y son puestos en orden alfabético, de acuerdo al nombre de cada país. Hay muchos nombres duplicados en Canadá, el Reino Unido y los Estados Unidos de América, y éstos se distinguen además, por sus subdivisiones primarias. (Vease abajo, la lista de abreviaciones en las páginas 319-320).

Abreviaciones y Mayúsculas Las abreviaciones y el uso de las mayúsculas se han hecho uniformes para todos los idiomas. Se usa un punto al final de la abreviación, aun cuando en algunos casos no sea ésta la práctica local. La abreviación "St." se usa sólo para "Saint." Las otras formas del mismo término, como "Sankt," se escriben completas.

La mayúscula se usa al comienzo de todos los nombres a excepción de algunos holandeses, como 's-Gravenhage. Las palabras que no son iniciales, se dan con mayúscula o minúscula, según la práctica local.

Símbolos Los símbolos que aparecen en el índice representan gráficamente las grandes categorías do los rasgos que se han ido nombrando, por ejemplo, ʌ para montaña (Everest, Mount ʌ). Una clave abreviada para los símbolos aparece en los cinco idiomas del atlas al pie de cada par de páginas del índice. Los números que siguen más arriba del símbolo indican alguna diferencia más precisa, pro ejemplo, ʌ^1 para un volcán (Fuji- san ʌ^1). Una lista completa de símbolos y números superiores aparece en la página I•1.

L'index rassemble en une seule liste alphabétique, quelque 170 000 noms qui figurent sur les cartes. Chaque nom est suivi d'un renvoi à une ou plusieurs pages de cartes et de coordonnées géographiques qui permettent de localiser ce qu'il désigne. Si une page contient plusieurs cartes, une lettre minuscule permet d'identifier chaque carte. Pour les cartes en double page, la référence indiquée est toujours celle de la page de gauche.

En général, l'index renvoie aux cartes où l'information recherchée est reproduite à la plus grande échelle; cependant, les cartes de zones métropolitaines ne sont pas utilisées si le terme géographique figure sur une autre carte dans un contexte plus large. Pour les éléments de grande dimension comme les pays et les chaînes de montagnes, l'index renvoie généralement à la carte à grande échelle qui les représente en entier.

L'ordre des informations de l'index est rappelé en tête de chaque double page dans les cinq langues: anglais, allemand, espagnol, français et portugais.

Par exemple:

FRANÇAIS

Nom	Page	Lat.°'	Long.°' W = Ouest

Les termes de l'index désignent des réalités géographiques de type *ponctuel*, *spatial* ou *linéaire*. Leur position est déterminée par les coordonnées géographiques du lieu quand les données sont de type *ponctuel* (villes, sommets, barrages, etc.), quand elles sont de type *spatial* (pays, chaînes de montagnes, etc.) par les coordonnées du centre approximatif de la zone considérée, et, quand elles sont du type *linéaire* (aqueducs, canaux, etc.) par les coordonnées soit d'un point terminal comme l'embouchure d'un cours d'eau, soit du point où les limites de la carte les interrompent.

Forme des Toponymes Les noms de l'index comme ceux des cartes sont généralement reproduits dans la langue locale et, dans la mesure du possible, selon leur orthographe officielle. Les signes diacritiques sont conservés, à l'exclusion de ceux qui servent à indiquer le ton, comme en vietnamien. La plupart des données géographiques qui s'étendent au-delà des frontières d'un pays sont nommées souvent en anglais, car elles n'ont pas de nom officiel unique. Beaucoup de noms anglais, allemands, espagnols, français et portugais, qui ne se trouvent pas sur les cartes, sont cités dans l'index sous forme de renvois. Tous les renvois sont signalés par le symbole (⟶). Un nom écrit sur la carte sous forme abrégée, par manque de place, figure en entier dans l'index; la partie omise est entre crochets, par exemple: Acapulco [de Juárez].

Transcription des Noms Pour les noms qui viennent de langues n'utilisant pas l'alphabet romain, le système local et officiel de transcription a été utilisé là où il existait. Ainsi, les noms russes et bulgares ont été transcrits selon les systèmes adoptés par les académies des sciences de ces pays. De même, pour la transcription des noms de la Chine continentale, on a employé le système Pinyin, officiellement adopté en Chine continentale. Pour les langues qui n'ont pas de système officiel de transcription en alphabet romain, notamment l'arabe, la transcription suit généralement de près le système adopté par le United States Board on Geographic Names (Comité américain pour les noms géographiques).

Ordre Alphabétique Les noms sont classés dans l'ordre de l'alphabet anglais. Les *ll* et *ch* espagnols, par exemple, ne sont pas traités comme des lettres séparées. De plus, on ne tient pas compte des signes diacritiques: le *ä* et le *ö* allemand ou scandinave correspondent au *a* et *o* sans tréma.

Les noms des données physiques peuvent se trouver inversés car ils sont toujours classés suivant le nom propre. Exemple: "Gibraltar, Strait of ʉ." Par ailleurs, les noms composés d'un ou plusieurs mots sont considérés comme une seule entité. Exemple: "Lakeland" est inscrit après "La Crosse" et avant "La Salle." Les noms qui commencent par un article (Le Havre, Den Helder, Al-Qāhirah, As-Suways) ne sont pas inversés. Les noms qui commencent par "St." ou "Sainte" sont classés comme s'ils s'écrivaient "Saint."

Dans le cas de noms identiques, les villes sont inscrites d'abord, puis les divisions politiques, et ensuite les données physiques. Les noms qui sont tout à fait identiques (y compris les symboles qui s'y rapportent) se distinguent par leur pays d'origine, noté en abrégé dans l'ordre alphabétique. Les noms que l'on rencontre plusieurs fois, au Canada, au Royaume-Uni et aux Etats-Unis se distinguent grâce à l'abréviation de la première subdivision administrative de ce pays (voir la liste des abréviations de la page 319-320).

Abréviations et Majuscules L'usage des abréviations a été standardisé pour toutes les langues. Un point suit chaque abréviation, même quand ce n'est pas l'usage dans certaines langues. L'abréviation "St." sert uniquement pour le mot "Saint." "Sankt" et les autres formes du mot "Saint" sont écrites en entier.

Tous les noms commencent par une majuscule, sauf quelques noms des Pays-Bas comme 's-Gravenhage. Certains noms prennent une majuscule, même s'ils ne se trouvent pas au début du terme; on a adopté, en général, l'orthographe locale.

Symboles Les symboles utilisés dans l'index donnent une représentation graphique des réalités géographiques mentionnées. Par exemple, ʌ pour une montagne (Everest, Mount ʌ). Une explication abrégée des symboles dans les cinq langues de l'Atlas se trouve au bas de chaque double page de l'index. Les indices qui accompagnent certains symboles permettent une distinction plus précise. Par exemple, ʌ^1 pour volcan (Fujisan ʌ^1). Une liste complète des symboles et indices est donnée à la page I•1.

O Índice contém, numa só lista alfabética, cerca de 170,000 nomes que figuram nos mapas. Segue-se a cada nome a referência a um ou mais mapas e a localização do acidente geográfico no mapa pelas respectivas coordenadas de latitude e longitude. A referência a mapas que ocupam duas páginas fica sempre na página da esquerda. A maior parte dos acidentes geográficos estão indexados no mapa em que aparecem em escala maior. No entanto, um acidente geográfico não é geralmente indexado num mapa de Área Metropolitana se também figura em outro mapa em que aparece em contexto mais amplo. Os países, cordilheiras e outros acidentes geográficos de maior extensão estão geralmente indexados no mapa em escala maior que os apresente em seu todo.

A ordem em que as informações são apresentadas no Índice figura no cabeçalho, a cada duas páginas, em inglês, alemão, espanhol, francês e PORTUGUÊS.

Por exemplo:

PORTUGUÊS

Nome	Página	Lat.°'	Long.°' W = Oeste

Os acidentes indexados são de três tipos: *Ponto, espacial* (área) e *linear* (extensão). Para acidentes que indicam *pontos* (como, por exemplo, cidades, picos de montanhas, represas), as coordenadas de latitude e longitude indicam a posição exata do ponto no mapa. No que se refere aos *acidentes espaciais* (como países, cordilheiras etc.), as coordenadas geralmente indicam o centro aproximado do acidente específico. Quanto aos *acidentes lineares* (rios, canais, aquedutos), as coordenadas localizam os pontos terminais, como, por exemplo, a foz de um rio, ou o ponto em que um acidente físico atinge a margem do mapa.

Formas dos nomes Os nomes que aparecem no Índice, assim como também nos mapas, são geralmente apresentados na língua local, e tanto quanto possível, seguem a ortografia oficial. Usam-se, também, os sinais diacríticos, exceto os que indicam tom, como na língua vietnamita. A maioria dos acidentes geográficos que se estendem além das fronteiras de um só país não possuem um nome oficial único; nesses casos, estão geralmente indicados em inglês. Muitos nomes em inglês, alemão, espanhol, português e francês podem não figurar nos mapas, mas aparecem no Índice como referências remissivas. Todas essas referências são indicadas pelo símbolo (⟶). Um nome que aparece no mapa em forma abreviada devido a limitações de espaço, figura no Índice em sua forma completa, com a parte omitida no mapa entre chaves (por exemplo, Acapulco [de Juárez]).

Transliteração Para os nomes escritos em línguas que não usam o alfabeto latino, foi utilizado o sistema oficial de transliteração, sempre que este existia. Assim, os nomes da Rússia e da Bulgária foram transliterados de acordo com os sistemas adotados pelas academias de ciências desses países. Do mesmo modo, a transliteração dos nomes da China continental seguem o sistema Pinyin, que foi oficialmente adotado nesse país. Para as línguas que não possuem um sistema de transliteração adotado oficialmente, em especial o árabe, a transliteração geralmente segue de perto o sistema adotado pelo Conselho de Nomes Geográficos dos Estados Unidos (United States Board on Geographic Names).

Alfabetação Os nomes foram ordenados de acordo com o alfabeto inglês. Por exemplo, o espanhol *ll* e *ch* não foram considerados como letras separadas. Ademais, os sinais diacríticos não foram considerados na alfabetação. Por exemplo, em alemão ou escandinavo as letras *ä* ou *ö* foram tratradas como *a* ou *o*.

Os nomes dos acidentes físicos podem aparecer, às vezes, invertidos, já que foram sempre alfabetados pela parte específica e não genérica do nome, como, por exemplo, *Gibraltar, estreito de* ʉ. Por outro lado, cada entrada do Índice, quer constituída por uma só palavra ou mais de uma, foi alfabetada como uma unidade contínua. Por exemplo, "Lakeland" aparece depois de "La Grosse" e antes de "La Salle". Os nomes que começam por artigo (Le Havre, Den Helder, Al-Qāhirah, As-Suways) não são invertidos. Os nomes que começam por "St." e "Sainte" são alfabetados como se fossem soletrados "Saint".

Nos casos de nomes idênticos, as cidades estão relacionadas em primeiro lugar; depois as divisões políticas e em seguida os acidentes físicos. As entradas completamente idênticas (inclusive símbolos, mencionados mais abaixo), distinguem-se pelas abreviaturas dos nomes oficiais dos países a que pertencem e são arrolados na ordem alfabética do nome do país. Os muitos nomes repetidos no Canadá, no Reino Unido e nos Estados Unidos, são ainda diferenciados pelas abreviaturas dos nomes das respectivas subdivisões primárias (Ver a lista de abreviaturas, das páginas 319-320).

Abreviações e uso de maiúsculas As abreviaturas e o estilo foram normalizados em todas as línguas. Usa-se um ponto depois de cada abreviatura, mesmo que não seja essa a prática local. A abreviatura "St." só é usada para "Saint". As outras formas do termo, tal como "Sankt", são escritas por extenso.

Todos os nomes são escritos com a inicial maiúscula exceto em alguns nomes holandeses, como 's-Gravenhage. O uso de maiúsculas em palavras não iniciais de um nome segue geralmente a prática local.

Símbolos Os símbolos que aparecem no Índice representam graficamente as grandes categorias dos acidentes indicados, por exemplo, ʌ para montanha (Everest, Mount ʌ). Uma chave abreviada dos símbolos nas cinco línguas do Atlas figura no pé de cada par de páginas do Índice. Os números altos que acompanham certos símbolos do Índice indicam diferenças mais precisas, como, por examplo, ʌ^1 para vulcão (Fuji-san ʌ^1). Uma lista completa de símbolos e números altos aparece à pág. I•1.

	LOCAL NAME	ENGLISH	DEUTSCH	ESPAÑOL	FRANÇAIS	PORTUGUÊS
Ab., Can.	Alberta	Alberta	Alberta	Alberta	Alberta	Alberta
Afg.	Afghānestān	Afghanistan	Afghanistan	Afganistán	Afghanistan	Afeganistão
Afr.	. . .	Africa	Afrika	Africa	Afrique	África
Ak., U.S.	Alaska	Alaska	Alaska	Alaska	Alaska	Alasca
Al., U.S.	Alabama	Alabama	Alabama	Alabama	Alabama	Alabama
Alg.	Algérie / Djazaïr	Algeria	Algerien	Argelia	Algérie	Argélia
Am. Sam.	American Samoa / Amerika Samoa	American Samoa	Amerikanisch-Samoa	Samoa Americana	Samoa américaines	Samoa Americana
And.	Andorra	Andorra	Andorra	Andorra	Andorre	Andorra
Ang.	Angola	Angola	Angola	Angola	Angola	Angola
Anguilla	Anguilla	Anguilla	Anguilla	Anguilla	Anguilla	Anguilla
Ant.	. . .	Antarctica	Antarktis	Antártida	Antarctique	Antártida
Antig.	Antigua and Barbuda	Antigua and Barbuda	Antigua und Barbuda	Antigua y Barbuda	Antigua-et-Barbuda	Antígua e Barbuda
Ar., U.S.	Arkansas	Arkansas	Arkansas	Arkansas	Arkansas	Arkansas
Arg.	Argentina	Argentina	Argentinien	Argentina	Argentine	Argentina
Ar. Su.	Al-'Arabīyah as-Su'ūdīyah	Saudi Arabia	Saudi-Arabien	Arabia Saudita	Arabie saoudite	Arábia Saudita
Aruba	Aruba	Aruba	Aruba	Aruba	Aruba	Aruba
Asia	. . .	Asia	Asien	Asia	Asie	Ásia
Austl.	Australia	Australia	Australien	Australia	Australie	Austrália
Az., U.S.	Arizona	Arizona	Arizona	Arizona	Arizona	Arizona
Azer.	Azerbaijan	Azerbaijan	Aserbaidschan	Azerbaiján	Azerbaïdjan	Azerbaijão
Ba.	Bahamas	Bahamas	Bahamas	Bahamas	Bahamas	Bahamas
Bahr.	Al-Bahrayn	Bahrain	Bahrain	Bahrein	Bahreïn	Bahrein
Barb.	Barbados	Barbados	Barbados	Barbados	Barbade	Barbados
B.C., Can.	British Columbia / Colombie-Britannique	British Columbia	Britisch Kolumbien	Columbia Británica	Colombie britannique	Colúmbia Britânica
Bdi.	Burundi	Burundi	Burundi	Burundi	Burundi	Burundi
Bel.	Belgique / België	Belgium	Belgien	Bélgica	Belgique	Bélgica
Belize	Belize	Belize	Belize	Belice	Bélize	Belize
Bela.	Belarus	Belarus	Belorussland	Bielorrusia	Biélorussie	Bielorrússia
Bénin	Bénin	Benin	Benin	Benin	Bénin	Benin
Ber.	Bermuda	Bermuda	Bermuda	Bermudas	Bermudes	Bermudas
B.I.O.T.	British Indian Ocean Territory	British Indian Ocean Territory	Britisch-Indien Ozean-Territorium	Territorio Británico del Océano Indico	Territoire britannique de l'océan Indien	Território Britânico do Oceano Indico
Blg.	Bâlgarija	Bulgaria	Bulgarien	Bulgaria	Bulgarie	Bulgária
Bngl.	Bangladesh	Bangladesh	Bangladesch	Bangladesh	Bangladesh	Bangladesh
Bol.	Bolivia	Bolivia	Bolivien	Bolivia	Bolivie	Bolívia
Boph.	Bophuthatswana	Bophuthatswana	Bophuthatswana	Bophuthatswana	Bophuthatswana	Bophuthatswana
Bos.	Bosna i Hercegovina	Bosnia and Hercegovina	Bosnien und Herzegowina	Bosnia y Herzegovina	Bosnie et Herzégovine	Bósnia e Herzegovina
Bots.	Botswana	Botswana	Botswana	Botswana	Botswana	Botsuana
Bra.	Brasil	Brazil	Brasilien	Brasil	Brésil	Brasil
Bru.	Brunei	Brunei	Brunei	Brunei	Brunéi	Brunei
Br. Vir. Is.	British Virgin Islands	British Virgin Islands	Britische Jungferninseln	Islas Vírgenes Británicas	Îles Vierges britanniques	Virgens Británicas, Ilhas
Burkina	Burkina Faso	Burkina Faso	Burkina Faso	Burkina Faso	Burkina Faso	Burkina Faso
Ca., U.S.	California	California	Kalifornien	California	Californie	Califórnia
Cam.	Cameroun / Cameroon	Cameroon	Kamerun	Camerún	Cameroun	Camarão
Can.	Canada	Canada	Kanada	Canadá	Canada	Canadá
Cay. Is.	Cayman Islands	Cayman Islands	Caiman-Inseln	Islas Caimán	Îles Caïmanes	Cayman, Ilhas
Centraf.	République centrafricaine	Central African Republic	Zentralafrikanische Republik	República Centroafricana	République centrafricaine	Centro-Africana, República
Česko.	Československo	Czechoslovakia	Tschechoslowakei	Checoslovaquia	Tchécoslovaquie	Tchecoslováquia
Chile	Chile	Chile	Chile	Chile	Chili	Chile
Christ. I.	Christmas Island	Christmas Island	Weihnachtsinsel	Isla Christmas	Île Christmas	Christmas, Ilha
Ciskei	Ciskei	Ciskei	Ciskei	Ciskei	Ciskei	Ciskei
C. Iv.	Côte d'Ivoire	Ivory Coast	Elfenbeinküste	Costa de Marfil	Côte d'Ivoire	Costa do Marfim
C.M.I.K.	Chosŏn-minjujuŭi-inmīn-konghwaguk	Korea, North	Nordkorea	Corea del Norte	Corée du Nord	Coréia do Norte
Co., U.S.	Colorado	Colorado	Colorado	Colorado	Colorado	Colorado
Cocos Is.	Cocos (Keeling) Islands	Cocos (Keeling) Islands	Cokos-Inseln	Islas Cocos (Keeling)	Îles Cocos (Keeling)	Cocos (Keeling), Ilhas
Col.	Colombia	Colombia	Kolumbien	Colombia	Colombie	Colômbia
Comores	Comores / Al-Qumur	Comoros	Komoren	Comoras	Comores	Comores
Congo	Congo	Congo	Kongo	Congo	Congo	Congo
Cook Is.	Cook Islands	Cook Islands	Cook-Inseln	Islas Cook	Îles Cook	Cook, Ilhas
C.R.	Costa Rica	Costa Rica	Costa Rica	Costa Rica	Costa Rica	Costa Rica
Ct., U.S.	Connecticut	Connecticut	Connecticut	Connecticut	Connecticut	Connecticut
Cuba	Cuba	Cuba	Kuba	Cuba	Cuba	Cuba
C.V.	Cabo Verde	Cape Verde	Kap Verde	Cabo Verde	Cap-Vert	Cabo Verde
Dan.	Danmark	Denmark	Dänemark	Dinamarca	Danemark	Dinamarca
D.C., U.S.	District of Columbia	District of Columbia	District of Columbia	District of Columbia	District of Columbia	Distrito de Columbia
De., U.S.	Delaware	Delaware	Delaware	Delaware	Delaware	Delaware
Dji.	Djibouti	Djibouti	Djibouti	Djibouti	Djibouti	Djibouti
Dom.	Dominica	Dominica	Dominica	Dominica	Dominique	Dominica
Dtsch.	Deutschland	Germany	Deutschland	Alemania	Allemagne	Alemanha
D.Y.	Druk-Yul	Bhutan	Bhutan	Bhután	Bhoutan	Butã
Ec.	Ecuador	Ecuador	Ecuador	Ecuador	Équateur	Equador
Eesti	Eesti	Estonia	Estland	Estonia	Estonie	Estónia
Ellás	Ellás	Greece	Griechenland	Grecia	Grèce	Grécia
El Sal.	El Salvador	El Salvador	El Salvador	El Salvador	El Salvador	El Salvador
Eng., U.K.	England	England	England	Inglaterra	Angleterre	Inglaterra
Esp.	España	Spain	Spanien	España	Espagne	Espanha
Europe	. . .	Europe	Europa	Europa	Europe	Europa
Falk. Is.	Falkland Islands	Falkland Islands	Falkland-Inseln	Islas Malvinas	Îles Falkland	Falkland, Ilhas
Fiji	Fiji	Fiji	Fidschi	Fiji	Fidji	Fiji (Fidji)
Fl., U.S.	Florida	Florida	Florida	Florida	Floride	Flórida
Før.	Føroyar	Faeroe Islands	Färöer	Islas Feroe	Îles Féroé	Faeroe, Ilhas
Fr.	France	France	Frankreich	Francia	France	França
Ga., U.S.	Georgia	Georgia	Georgia	Georgia	Georgie	Geórgia
Gabon	Gabon	Gabon	Gabun	Gabón	Gabon	Gabão
Gam.	Gambia	Gambia	Gambia	Gambia	Gambie	Gâmbia
Ghana	Ghana	Ghana	Ghana	Ghana	Ghana	Gana
Gib.	Gibraltar	Gibraltar	Gibraltar	Gibraltar	Gibraltar	Gibraltar
Gren.	Grenada	Grenada	Grenada	Granada	Grenade	Grenada
Guad.	Guadeloupe	Guadeloupe	Guadeloupe	Guadalupe	Guadeloupe	Guadalupe
Guam	Guam	Guam	Guam	Guam	Guam	Guam
Guat.	Guatemala	Guatemala	Guatemala	Guatemala	Guatemala	Guatemala
Guernsey	Guernsey	Guernsey	Guernsey	Guernsey	Guernesey	Guernsey
Gui.-B.	Guiné-Bissau	Guinea-Bissau	Guinea-Bissau	Guinea-Bissau	Guinée-Bissau	Guiné-Bissau
Gui. Ecu.	Guinea Ecuatorial	Equatorial Guinea	Äquatorial-guinea	Guinea Ecuatorial	Guinée équatoriale	Guiné Equatorial
Guinée	Guinée	Guinea	Guinea	Guinea	Guinée	Guiné
Guy.	Guyana	Guyana	Guyana	Guyana	Guyane	Guiana
Guy. fr.	Guyane française	French Guiana	Französisch-Guayana	Guayana Francesa	Guyane française	Guiana Francesa
Haï.	Haïti	Haiti	Haiti	Haití	Haïti	Haiti
Haya.	Hayastan	Armenia	Armenien	Armenia	Arménie	Arménia
Hi., U.S.	Hawaii	Hawaii	Hawaii	Hawaii	Hawaii	Havaí
H.K.	Hong Kong	Hong Kong	Hongkong	Hong Kong	Hong-Kong	Hong Kong
Hond.	Honduras	Honduras	Honduras	Honduras	Honduras	Honduras
Hrv.	Hrvatska	Croatia	Kroatien	Croacia	Croatie	Croácia
Ia., U.S.	Iowa	Iowa	Iowa	Iowa	Iowa	Iowa
I.A.M.	Al-Imārāt al-'Arabīyah al-Muttaḥidah	United Arab Emirates	Vereinigte Arabische Emirate	Emiratos Arabes Unidos	Émirats arabes unis	Emirados Árabes Unidos
Id., U.S.	Idaho	Idaho	Idaho	Idaho	Idaho	Idaho

	LOCAL NAME	ENGLISH	DEUTSCH	ESPAÑOL	FRANÇAIS	PORTUGUÊS
Il., U.S.	Illinois	Illinois	Illinois	Illinois	Illinois	Illinois
In., U.S.	Indiana	Indiana	Indiana	Indiana	Indiana	Indiana
India	India / Bharat	India	Indien	India	Inde	Índia
Indon.	Indonesia	Indonesia	Indonesien	Indonesia	Indonésie	Indonésia
I. of Man	Isle of Man	Isle of Man	Insel Man	Isla de Man	Île de Man	Man, Ilha de
Īrān	Īrān	Iran	Iran	Irán	Iran	Irã
'Irāq	Al-'Irāq	Iraq	Irak	Iraq	Iraq	Iraque
Ire.	Ireland / Éire	Ireland	Irland	Irlanda	Irlande	Irlanda
Ísland	Ísland	Iceland	Island	Islandia	Islande	Islândia
Isr. Occ.	. . .	Israeli Occupied Areas	Von Israel besetztes Gebiet	Áreas ocupadas por Israel	Territoires occupés par Israël	Áreas occupadas por Israel
It.	Italia	Italy	Italien	Italia	Italie	Itália
Ityo.	Ityopiya	Ethiopia	Äthiopien	Etiopía	Éthiopie	Etiópia
Jam.	Jamaica	Jamaica	Jamaika	Jamaica	Jamaïque	Jamaica
Jersey	Jersey	Jersey	Jersey	Jersey	Jersey	Jersey
Jugo.	Jugoslavija	Yugoslavia	Jugoslawien	Yugoslavia	Yougoslavie	Iugoslávia
Kal. Nun.	Kalaallit Nunaat / Grønland	Greenland	Grönland	Groenlandia	Groenland	Groenlândia
Kâm.	Kâmpŭchéa	Cambodia	Kambodscha	Camboya	Cambodge	Camboja
Kaz.	Kazachstan	Kazakhstan	Kasachstan	Kazajstán	Kazakhstan	Cazaquistão
Kenya	Kenya	Kenya	Kenia	Kenya	Kenya	Quênia
Kıbrıs	Kuzey Kıbrıs	Cyprus, North	Türkische Republik Nordzypern	República Turca de Chipre del Norte	République turque du Nord de Chypre	República Turca do Norte de Chipre
Kípros	Kípros / Kıbrıs	Cyprus	Zypern	Chipre	Chypre	Chipre
Kiribati	Kiribati	Kiribati	Kiribati	Kiribati	Kiribati	Kiribati
Ks., U.S.	Kansas	Kansas	Kansas	Kansas	Kansas	Kansas
Kuwayt	Al-Kuwayt	Kuwait	Kuwait	Kuwait	Koweït	Kuwait
Ky., U.S.	Kentucky	Kentucky	Kentucky	Kentucky	Kentucky	Kentucky
Kyrg.	Kyrgyzstan	Kyrgyzstan	Kirgisistan	Kirguizia	Kirghizistan	Quirguistão
La., U.S.	Louisiana	Louisiana	Louisiana	Luisiana	Louisiane	Louisiana
Lao	Lao	Laos	Laos	Laos	Laos	Lao
Lat.	Latvija	Latvia	Lettland	Letonia	Lettonie	Letónia
Leso.	Lesotho	Lesotho	Lesotho	Lesotho	Lesotho	Lesoto
Liber.	Liberia	Liberia	Liberia	Liberia	Libéria	Libéria
Lībiyā	Lībiyā	Libya	Libyen	Libia	Libye	Líbia
Liech.	Liechtenstein	Liechtenstein	Liechtenstein	Liechtenstein	Liechtenstein	Liechtenstein
Liet.	Lietuva	Lithuania	Litauen	Lituania	Lithuanie	Lituânia
Lubnān	Lubnān	Lebanon	Libanon	Líbano	Liban	Líbano
Lux.	Luxembourg	Luxembourg	Luxemburg	Luxemburgo	Luxembourg	Luxemburgo
Ma., U.S.	Massachusetts	Massachusetts	Massachusetts	Massachusetts	Massachusetts	Massachusetts
Macau	Macau	Macau	Macao	Macao	Macao	Macau
Mac.	Makedonija	Macedonia	Makedonien	Macedonia	Macédoine	Macedonia
Madag.	Madagasikara / Madagascar	Madagascar	Madagaskar	Madagascar	Madagascar	Madagascar
Magreb	Al-Magreb	Morocco	Marokko	Marruecos	Maroc	Marrocos
Magy.	Magyarország	Hungary	Ungarn	Hungría	Hongrie	Hungria
Malaŵi	Malaŵi	Malawi	Malawi	Malawi	Malawi	Malaui
Malay.	Malaysia	Malaysia	Malaysia	Malasia	Malaisie	Malásia
Mald.	Maldives	Maldives	Malediven	Maldivas	Maldives	Maldivas
Mali	Mali	Mali	Mali	Malí	Mali	Mali
Malta	Malta	Malta	Malta	Malta	Malte	Malta
Marsh. Is.	Marshall Islands	Marshall Islands	Marshall Islands	Islas Marshall	Îles Marshall	Marshall Islands
Mart.	Martinique	Martinique	Martinique	Martinica	Martinique	Martinica
Maur.	Mauritanie / Mūrītāniyā	Mauritania	Mauretanien	Mauritania	Mauritanie	Mauritânia
Maus.	Mauritius	Mauritius	Mauritius	Mauricio	Maurice	Maurício
Mayotte	Mayotte	Mayotte	Mayotte	Mayotte	Mayotte	Mayotte
Mb., Can.	Manitoba	Manitoba	Manitoba	Manitoba	Manitoba	Manitoba
Md., U.S.	Maryland	Maryland	Maryland	Maryland	Maryland	Maryland
Me., U.S.	Maine	Maine	Maine	Maine	Maine	Maine
Méx.	México	Mexico	Mexiko	México	Mexique	México
Mi., U.S.	Michigan	Michigan	Michigan	Michigan	Michigan	Michigan
Micron.	Federated States of Micronesia	Micronesia, Federated States of	Federated States of Micronesia	Estado Federal de Micronesia	États fédérés de Micronésie	Federated States of Micronesia
Mid. Is.	Midway Islands	Midway Islands	Midway-Inseln	Islas Midway	Îles Midway	Midway, Ilhas
Miṣr	Miṣr	Egypt	Ägypten	Egipto	Égypte	Egito
Mn., U.S.	Minnesota	Minnesota	Minnesota	Minnesota	Minnesota	Minnesota
Mo., U.S.	Missouri	Missouri	Missouri	Misuri	Missouri	Missouri
Moç.	Moçambique	Mozambique	Mosambik	Mozambique	Mozambique	Moçambique
Mol.	Moldova	Moldova	Moldawien	Moldavia	Moldavie	Moldávia
Monaco	Monaco	Monaco	Monaco	Mónaco	Monaco	Mônaco
Mong.	Mongol Ard Uls	Mongolia	Mongolei	Mongolia	Mongolie	Mongólia
Monts.	Montserrat	Montserrat	Montserrat	Montserrat	Montserrat	Montserrat
Ms., U.S.	Mississippi	Mississippi	Mississippi	Misisipí	Mississippi	Mississippi
Mt., U.S.	Montana	Montana	Montana	Montana	Montana	Montana
Mya.	Myanmar	Burma	Birma	Birmania	Birmanie	Birmânia
N.A.	. . .	North America	Nordamerika	América del Norte	Amérique du Nord	América do Norte
Namibia	Namibia	Namibia	Namibia	Namibia	Namibie	Namíbia
Nauru	Nauru / Naoero	Nauru	Nauru	Nauru	Nauru	Nauru
N.B., Can.	New Brunswick / Nouveau-Brunswick	New Brunswick	Neubraunschweig	Nueva Brunswick	Nouveau-Brunswick	Nova Brunswick
N.C., U.S.	North Carolina	North Carolina	Nord Karolina	Carolina del Norte	Caroline du Nord	Carolina do Norte
N. Cal.	Nouvelle-Calédonie	New Caledonia	Neukaledonien	Nueva Caledonia	Nouvelle Calédonie	Nova Caledônia
N.D., U.S.	North Dakota	North Dakota	Nord Dakota	Dakota del Norte	Dakota du Nord	Dakota do Norte
Ne., U.S.	Nebraska	Nebraska	Nebraska	Nebraska	Nebraska	Nebraska
Ned.	Nederland	Netherlands	Niederlande	Países Bajos	Pays-Bas	Países Baixos
Ned. Ant.	Nederlandse Antillen	Netherlands Antilles	Niederländische Antillen	Antillas Neerlandesas	Antilles néerlandaises	Antilhas Holandesas
Nepāl	Nepāl	Nepal	Nepal	Nepal	Népal	Nepal
Nf., Can.	Newfoundland / Terre-Neuve	Newfoundland	Neufundland	Terranova	Terre-Neuve	Terra Nova
N.H., U.S.	New Hampshire	New Hampshire	New Hampshire	Nuevo Hampshire	New Hampshire	Nova Hampshire
Nic.	Nicaragua	Nicaragua	Nicaragua	Nicaragua	Nicaragua	Nicarágua
Nig.	Nigeria	Nigeria	Nigeria	Nigeria	Nigéria	Nigéria
Niger	Niger	Niger	Niger	Níger	Niger	Níger
Nihon	Nihon	Japan	Japan	Japón	Japon	Japão
N. Ire., U.K.	Northern Ireland	Northern Ireland	Nordirland	Irlanda del Norte	Irlande du Nord	Irlanda do Norte
Niue	Niue	Niue	Niue	Niue	Nioué	Niue
N.J., U.S.	New Jersey	New Jersey	New Jersey	Nueva Jersey	New Jersey	Nova Jersey
N.M., U.S.	New Mexico	New Mexico	New Mexico	Nuevo México	Nouveau-Mexique	Nova México
N. Mar. Is.	Northern Mariana Islands	Northern Mariana Islands	Northern Mariana Islands	Islas Marianas	Îles Mariannes du Nord	Northern Mariana Islands
Nor.	Norge	Norway	Norwegen	Noruega	Norvège	Noruega
Norf. I.	Norfolk Island	Norfolk Island	Norfolk-Insel	Isla Norfolk	Île Norfolk	Norfolk, Ilha
N.S., Can.	Nova Scotia / Nouvelle-Écosse	Nova Scotia	Neu Schottland	Nueva Escocia	Nouvelle-Écosse	Nova Scotia
N.T., Can.	Northwest Territories / Territoires du Nord-Ouest	Northwest Territories	Nord-West Territorien	Territorios del Noroeste	Territoires du Nord-Ouest	Territórios do Noroeste
Nv., U.S.	Nevada	Nevada	Nevada	Nevada	Nevada	Nevada
N.Y., U.S.	New York	New York	New York	Nueva York	New York	Nova York
N.Z.	New Zealand	New Zealand	Neuseeland	Nueva Zelanda	Nouvelle-Zélande	Nova Zelândia
Oc.	. . .	Oceania	Ozeanien	Oceanía	Océanie	Oceania
Oh., U.S.	Ohio	Ohio	Ohio	Ohio	Ohio	Ohio
Ok., U.S.	Oklahoma	Oklahoma	Oklahoma	Oklahoma	Oklahoma	Oklahoma

	LOCAL NAME	ENGLISH	DEUTSCH	ESPAÑOL	FRANÇAIS	PORTUGUÊS
On., Can.	Ontario	Ontario	Ontario	Ontario	Ontario	Ontário
Or., U.S.	Oregon	Oregon	Oregon	Oregón	Oregon	Oregon
Öst.	Österreich	Austria	Österreich	Austria	Autriche	Austria
Pa., U.S.	Pennsylvania	Pennsylvania	Pennsylvanien	Pensilvania	Pennsylvanie	Pennsylvania
Pāk.	Pākistān	Pakistan	Pakistan	Pakistán	Pakistan	Paquistão
Palau	Palau / Belau	Palau	Palau	Palau	Palau (Belau)	Palau
Pan.	Panamá	Panama	Panama	Panamá	Panama	Panamá
Pap. N. Gui.	Papua New Guinea	Papua New Guinea	Papua-Neuguinea	Papua Nueva Guinea	Papouasie-Nouvelle Guinée	Papua-Nova Guiné
Para.	Paraguay	Paraguay	Paraguay	Paraguay	Paraguay	Paraguai
P.E., Can.	Prince Edward Island / Île-du-Prince-Édouard	Prince Edward Island	Prinz Edward-Insel	Isla Príncipe Eduardo	Île-du-Prince Édouard	Príncipe Eduardo, Ilha do
Perú	Perú	Peru	Peru	Perú	Pérou	Peru
Pil.	Pilipinas / Philippines	Philippines	Philippinen	Filipinas	Philippines	Filipinas
Pit.	Pitcairn	Pitcairn	Pitcairn	Pitcairn	Pitcairn	Pitcairn
Pol.	Polska	Poland	Polen	Polonia	Pologne	Polônia
Poly. fr.	Polynésie française	French Polynesia	Französisch-Polynesien	Polinesia Francesa	Polynésie française	Polinésia Francesa
Port.	Portugal	Portugal	Portugal	Portugal	Portugal	Portugal
P.Q., Can.	Québec	Quebec	Quebec	Quebec	Québec	Québec
P.R.	Puerto Rico	Puerto Rico	Puerto Rico	Puerto Rico	Porto Rico	Porto Rico
P.S.N.Á.	Plazas de Soberanía en el Norte de África	Spanish North Africa	Spanisch-Nordafrika	Plazas de Soberanía en el Norte de África	Afrique du Nord espagnole	África do Norte Espanhola
Qaṭar	Qaṭar	Qatar	Katar	Qatar	Qatar	Qatar
Rep. Dom.	República Dominicana	Dominican Republic	Dominikanische Republik	República Dominicana	République dominicaine	Dominicana, República
Réu.	Réunion	Reunion	Réunion	Reunión	Réunion	Reunião
R.I., U.S.	Rhode Island	Rhode Island	Rhode Island	Rhode Island	Rhode Island	Rhode Island
Rom.	România	Romania	Rumänien	Rumanía	Roumanie	Romênia
Ross.	Rossija	Russia	Russland	Rusia	Russie	Rússia
Rw.	Rwanda	Rwanda	Ruanda	Rwanda	Rwanda	Ruanda
S.A.	. . .	South America	Südamerika	América del Sur	Amérique du Sud	América do Sul
S. Afr.	South Africa / Suid-Afrika	South Africa	Südafrika	Sudáfrica	Afrique du Sud	África do Sul
Sak.	Sakartvelo	Georgia	Georgien	Georgia	Géorgie	Geórgia
S.C., U.S.	South Carolina	South Carolina	Süd Karolina	Carolina del Sur	Caroline du Sud	Carolina do Sul
Schw.	Schweiz / Suisse / Svizzera	Switzerland	Schweiz	Suiza	Suisse	Suíça
Scot., U.K.	Scotland	Scotland	Schottland	Escocia	Écosse	Escócia
S.D., U.S.	South Dakota	South Dakota	Süd Dakota	Dakota del Sur	Dakota du Sud	Dakota do Sul
Sén.	Sénégal	Senegal	Senegal	Senegal	Sénégal	Senegal
Sey.	Seychelles	Seychelles	Seschellen	Seychelles	Seychelles	Seychelles
Shq.	Shqipëri	Albania	Albanien	Albania	Albanie	Albânia
Sing.	Singapore	Singapore	Singapur	Singapur	Singapour	Cingapura
Sk., Can.	Saskatchewan	Saskatchewan	Saskatchewan	Saskatchewan	Saskatchewan	Saskatchewan
S.L.	Sierra Leone	Sierra Leone	Sierra Leone	Sierra Leona	Sierra Leone	Serra Leoa
S. Lan.	Sri Lanka	Sri Lanka	Sri Lanka	Sri Lanka	Sri Lanka	Sri Lanka
Slo.	Slovenija	Slovenia	Slowenien	Eslovenia	Slovénie	Eslovênia
S. Mar.	San Marino	San Marino	San Marino	San Marino	Saint-Marin	San Marino
Sol. Is.	Solomon Islands	Solomon Islands	Salomonen	Islas Salomón	Îles Salomon	Salomão, Ilhas
Som.	Somaliya	Somalia	Somalia	Somalia	Somalie	Somália
St. Hel.	St. Helena	St. Helena	Sankt Helena	Santa Elena	Sainte-Hélène	Santa Helena
St. K./N.	St. Kitts and Nevis	St. Kitts and Nevis	Sankt Kitts und Nevis	San Kitts y Nevis	Saint-Kitts-et-Nevis	São Kitts e Nevis
St. Luc.	St. Lucia	St. Lucia	Sankt Lucia	Santa Lucía	Sainte-Lucie	Santa Lúcia
S. Tom./P.	São Tomé e Príncipe	Sao Tome and Principe	São Tomé und Principe	Santo Tomé y Princípe	Sao Tomé-et-Principe	São Tomé e Príncipe
St. P./M.	Saint-Pierre-et-Miquelon	St. Pierre and Miquelon	Saint-Pierre und Miquelon	San Pedro y Miquelón	Saint-Pierre-et-Miquelon	São Pedro e Miquelon
St. Vin.	St. Vincent and the Grenadines	St. Vincent and the Grenadines	Sankt Vincent und die Grenadinen	San Vicente y las Granadinas	Saint-Vincent-et-Grenadines	São Vicente e Granadinas
Sūd.	As-Sūdān	Sudan	Sudan	Sudán	Soudan	Sudão
Suomi	Suomi / Finland	Finland	Finnland	Finlandia	Finlande	Finlândia
Sur.	Suriname	Suriname	Suriname	Suriname	Suriname	Suriname

	LOCAL NAME	ENGLISH	DEUTSCH	ESPAÑOL	FRANÇAIS	PORTUGUÊS
Sūrīy.	Sūrīyah	Syria	Syrien	Siria	Syrie	Síria
Sve.	Sverige	Sweden	Schweden	Suecia	Suéde	Suécia
Swaz.	Swaziland	Swaziland	Swasiland	Swazilandia	Swaziland	Suazilândia
T.a.a.f.	Terres australes et antarctiques françaises	French Southern and Antarctic Territories	Französische Süd- und Antarktis-Gebiete	Tierras Australes y Antárticas Francesas	Terres australes et antarctiques françaises	Terras Austrais e Antárticas Francesas
Taehan	Taehan-min'guk	Korea, South	Südkorea	Corea del Sur	Corée du Sud	Coréia do Sul
T'aiwan	T'aiwan	Taiwan	Taiwan	Taiwán	Taïwan	Taiwan (Formosa)
Taj.	Tajikistan	Tajikistan	Tadschikistan	Tadjikistán	Tadjikistan	Tajiquistão
Tan.	Tanzania	Tanzania	Tansania	Tanzanía	Tanzanie	Tanzânia
Tchad	Tchad	Chad	Tschad	Chad	Tchad	Tchad
T./C. Is.	Turks and Caicos Islands	Turks and Caicos Islands	Turks- und Caicos-Inseln	Islas Turcas y Caicos	Îles Turques et Caïques	Turcas e Caicos, Ilhas
Thai	Prathet Thai	Thailand	Thailand	Tailandia	Thaïlande	Tailândia
Tn., U.S.	Tennessee	Tennessee	Tennessee	Tennessee	Tennessee	Tennessee
Togo	Togo	Togo	Togo	Togo	Togo	Togo
Tok.	Tokelau	Tokelau	Tokelau	Tokelau	Tokélaou	Tokelau
Tonga	Tonga	Tonga	Tonga	Tonga	Tonga	Tonga
Transkei	Transkei	Transkei	Transkei	Transkei	Transkei	Transkei
Trin.	Trinidad and Tobago	Trinidad and Tobago	Trinidad und Tobago	Trinidad y Tabago	Trinité-et-Tobago	Trinidad e Tobago
Tun.	Tunisie / Tunis	Tunisia	Tunesien	Túnez	Tunisie	Tunísia
Tür.	Türkiye	Turkey	Türkei	Turquía	Turquie	Turquia
Turk.	Turkmenistan	Turkmenistan	Turkmenistan	Turkmenia	Turkmenistan	Turquemenistão
Tuvalu	Tuvalu	Tuvalu	Tuvalu	Tuvalu	Tuvalu	Tuvalu
Tx., U.S.	Texas	Texas	Texas	Texas	Texas	Texas
Ug.	Uganda	Uganda	Uganda	Uganda	Ouganda	Uganda
U.K.	United Kingdom	United Kingdom	Vereinigtes Königreich	Reino Unido	Royaume-Uni	Reino Unido
Ukr.	Ukraina	Ukraine	Ukraine	Ucrania	Ukraine	Ucrânia
'Umān	'Umān	Oman	Oman	Omán	Oman	Omã
Ur.	Uruguay	Uruguay	Uruguay	Uruguay	Uruguay	Uruguai
Urd.	Al-Urdun	Jordan	Jordanien	Jordania	Jordanie	Jordânia
U.S.	United States	United States	Vereinigte Staaten	Estados Unidos	États-Unis	Estados Unidos
Ut., U.S.	Utah	Utah	Utah	Utah	Utah	Utah
Uzb.	Uzbekistan	Uzbekistan	Usbekistan	Uzbekistán	Ouzbekistan	Usbequistão
Va., U.S.	Virginia	Virginia	Virginia	Virginia	Virginie	Virgínia
Vanuatu	Vanuatu	Vanuatu	Vanuatu	Vanuatu	Vanuatu	Vanuatu
Vat.	Cittá del Vaticano	Vatican City	Vatikanstadt	Ciudad del Vaticano	Cité du Vatican	Vaticano
Ven.	Venezuela	Venezuela	Venezuela	Venezuela	Venezuela	Venezuela
Venda	Venda	Venda	Venda	Venda	Venda	Venda
Viet	Viet Nam	Vietnam	Vietnam	Viet Nam	Viet Nam	Vietnam
Vir. Is., U.S.	Virgin Islands (U.S.)	Virgin Islands (U.S.)	Amerikanische Jungferninseln	Islas Vírgenes (americanas)	Îles Vierges (américaines)	Virgens Americanas, Ilhas
Vt.	Vermont	Vermont	Vermont	Vermont	Vermont	Vermont
Wa., U.S.	Washington	Washington	Washington	Washington	Washington	Washington
Wake I.	Wake Island	Wake Island	Wake	Isla Wake	Île Wake	Wake
Wales, U.K.	Wales	Wales	Wales	Gales	Galles	Gales
Wal./F.	Wallis et Futuna	Wallis and Futuna	Wallis und Futuna	Wallis y Futuna	Wallis et Futuna	Wallis e Futuna
Wi., U.S.	Wisconsin	Wisconsin	Wisconsin	Wisconsin	Wisconsin	Wisconsin
W. Sah.	. . .	Western Sahara	Westliche Sahara	Sahara Occidental	Sahara occidental	Saara Ocidental
W. Sam.	Western Samoa / Samoa i Sisifo	Western Samoa	Westsamoa	Samoa Occidental	Samoa-Occidental	Samoa Ocidental
W.V., U.S.	West Virginia	West Virginia	West Virginia	Virginia Occidental	Virginie Occidentale	Virgínia Ocidental
Wy., U.S.	Wyoming	Wyoming	Wyoming	Wyoming	Wyoming	Wyoming
Yaman	Al-Yaman	Yemen	Jemen	Yemen	Yémen	Iêmen
Yis.	Yisra'el / Isrā'īl	Israel	Israel	Israel	Israël	Israel
Yk., Can.	Yukon Territory	Yukon Territory	Yukon	Yukón	Yukon	Yukon
Zaïre	Zaïre	Zaire	Zaire	Zaire	Zaïre	Zaire
Zam.	Zambia	Zambia	Sambia	Zambia	Zambie	Zâmbia
Zhg.	Zhongguo	China	China	China	Chine	China
Zimb.	Zimbabwe	Zimbabwe	Simbabwe	Zimbabwe	Zimbabwe	Zimbabwe

Key to Index Symbols

The symbols below represent the categories into which the physical and cultural features are classified in the Index. Broad categories appear in **boldface** type. Symbols with superior numbers identify subcategories.

Schlüssel zu den Symbolen des Registers

Die folgenden Symbole veranschaulichen die Kategorien, nach denen physische und kulturgeographische Objekte im Register geordnet sind. Die Oberbegriffe sind in **Fettdruck** hervorgehoben. Symbole mit hochgestellten Nummern kennzeichnen Unterbegriffe.

Clave de los Símbolos del Índice

Los símbolos abajo representan las categorías dentro de las cuales están clasificados los rasgos físicos y culturales que están incluídos en el Índice. Las grandes categorías aparecen en **negrilla**. Los símbolos que tienen números en su parte superior identifican las subcategorías.

Signification des Symboles de l'Index

Les symboles ci-dessous représentent les catégories sous lesquelles les données physiques et culturelles sont classées dans l'indes. Les symboles en caractèter **gras** correspondent aux catégories principales. Ceux suivis d'un indice désignent les subdivisions d'une même catégorie.

Chave dos Símbolos do Índice

Os símbolos abaixo representam as categorias em que estão classificados os acidentes físicos e culturais no Índice. As grandes categorias aparecem em **negrito**. Os símbolos acompanhados de números altos identificam as subcategorias.

ENGLISH	DEUTSCH	ESPANOL	FRANCAIS	PORTUGUES
∧ **Mountain**	∧ **Berg**	∧ **Montaña**	∧ **Montagne**	∧ **Montanha**
∧[1] Volcano	∧[1] Vulkan	∧[1] Volcán	∧[1] Volcan	∧[1] Vulcão
∧[2] Hill	∧[2] Hügel	∧[2] Colina	∧[2] Colline	∧[2] Colina
Mountains	**Gebirge**	**Montañas**	**Montagnes**	**Montanhas**
[1] Plateau	[1] Hochebene	[1] Meseta	[1] Plateau	[1] Planalto
[2] Hills	[2] Hügel	[2] Colinas	[2] Collines	[2] Colinas
Pass	**Paß**	**Paso**	**Col**	**Passo**
V **Valley, Canyon**	V **Tal, Cañon**	V **Valle, Cañón**	V **Vallée, Canyon**	V **Vale, Canhão**
Plain	**Ebene**	**Llano**	**Plaine**	**Planície**
[1] Basin	[1] Becken	[1] Cuenca	[1] Bassin	[1] Bacia
[2] Delta	[2] Delta	[2] Delta	[2] Delta	[2] Delta
› **Cape**	› **Kap**	› **Cabo**	› **Cap**	› **Cabo**
›[1] Peninsula	›[1] Halbinsel	›[1] Península	›[1] Péninsule	›[1] Península
›[2] Spit, Sand Bar	›[2] Landzunge, Sandbarre	›[2] Lengua de Tierra, Bajo	›[2] Flèche, Banc de sable	›[2] Ponta de Terra, Banco de Areia
I **Island**	I **Insel**	I **Isla**	I **Île**	I **Ilha**
I[1] Atoll	I[1] Atoll	I[1] Atolón	I[1] Atoll	I[1] Atol
I[2] Rock	I[2] Fels	I[2] Roca	I[2] Rocher	I[2] Rochedo
II **Islands**	II **Inseln**	II **Islas**	II **Îles**	II **Ilhas**
II[1] Rocks	II[1] Felsen	II[1] Rocas	II[1] Rochers	II[1] Rochedos
Other Topographic Features	**Andere Topographische Objekte**	**Otros Elementos Topográficos**	**Autres données topographiques**	**Outros Acidentes Topográficos**
[1] Continent	[1] Erdteil	[1] Continente	[1] Continent	[1] Continente
[2] Coast, Beach	[2] Küste, Strand	[2] Costa, Playa	[2] Côte, Plage	[2] Costa, Praia
[3] Isthmus	[3] Landenge	[3] Istmo	[3] Isthme	[3] Istmo
[4] Cliff	[4] Kliff	[4] Risco	[4] Falaise	[4] Falésia
[5] Cave, Caves	[5] Höhle, Höhlen	[5] Cueva, Cuevas	[5] Caverne, Cavernes	[5] Caverna, Cavernas
[6] Crater	[6] Krater	[6] Cráter	[6] Cratère	[6] Cratera
[7] Depression	[7] Senke	[7] Depresión	[7] Dépression	[7] Depressão
[8] Dunes	[8] Dünen	[8] Dunas	[8] Dunes	[8] Dunas
[9] Lava Flow	[9] Lavastrom	[9] Corriente de Lava	[9] Coulée de lave	[9] Corrente de Lava
≏ **River**	≏ **Fluß**	≏ **Río**	≏ **Rivière, Fleuve**	≏ **Rio**
≏[1] River Channel	≏[1] Flussarm	≏[1] Brazo de Río	≏[1] Bras de rivière	≏[1] Canal de Rio
Canal	**Kanal**	**Canal**	**Canal**	**Canal**
[1] Aqueduct	[1] Aquädukt	[1] Acueducto	[1] Aqueduc	[1] Aqueduto
Waterfall, Rapids	**Wasserfall, Stromschnellen**	**Cascada, Rápidos**	**Chute d'eau, Rapides**	**Quedas d'água, Rápidos**
Strait	**Meeresstrasse**	**Estrecho**	**Détroit**	**Estreito**
⊂ **Bay, Gulf**	⊂ **Bucht, Golf**	⊂ **Bahía, Golfo**	⊂ **Baie, Golfe**	⊂ **Baía, Golfo**
⊂[1] Estuary	⊂[1] Trichtermündung	⊂[1] Estuario	⊂[1] Estuaire	⊂[1] Estuário
⊂[2] Fjord	⊂[2] Fjord	⊂[2] Fiordo	⊂[2] Fjord	⊂[2] Fiorde
⊂[3] Bight	⊂[3] Bucht	⊂[3] Bahía	⊂[3] Baie	⊂[3] Enseada
Lake, Lakes	**See, Seen**	**Lago, Lagos**	**Lac, Lacs**	**Lago, Lagos**
[1] Reservoir	[1] Stausee	[1] Embalse	[1] Réservoir, Retenue	[1] Reservatório
Swamp	**Sumpf**	**Pantano**	**Marais**	**Pântano**
Ice Features, Glacier	**Eis- und Gletscherformen**	**Accidentes Glaciales, Glaciar**	**Formes glaciaires, Glacier**	**Acidentes Glaciares, Geleira**
Other Hydrographic Features	**Andere Hydrographische Objekte**	**Otros Elementos Hidrográficos**	**Autres données hydrographiques**	**Outros Acidentes Hidrográficos**
[1] Ocean	[1] Ozean	[1] Océano	[1] Océan	[1] Oceano
[2] Sea	[2] Meer	[2] Mar	[2] Mer	[2] Mar
[3] Anchorage	[3] Ankerplatz	[3] Ancladero	[3] Ancrage	[3] Ancoradouro
[4] Oasis, Well, Spring	[4] Oase, Brunnen, Quelle	[4] Oasis, Pozo, Manantial	[4] Oasis, Puits, Source	[4] Oásis, Poço, Fonte, Manancial

ENGLISH	DEUTSCH	ESPANOL	FRANCAIS	PORTUGUES
Submarine Features	**Untermeerische Objekte**	**Accidentes Submarinos**	**Formes de relief sous-marin**	**Acidentes Submarinos**
[1] Depression	[1] Senke	[1] Depresión	[1] Dépression	[1] Depressão
[2] Reef, Shoal	[2] Riff, Untiefe	[2] Arrecife, Bajo	[2] Récif, Haut-fond	[2] Recife, Baixio
[3] Mountain, Mountains	[3] Berg, Gebirge	[3] Montaña, Montañas	[3] Montagne, Montagnes	[3] Montanha, Montanhas
[4] Slope, Shelf	[4] Abhang, Schelf	[4] Talud, Plataforma	[4] Talus, Plateau continental	[4] Talude, Plataforma
□ **Political Unit**	□ **Politische Einheit**	□ **Unidad Política**	□ **Entité politique**	□ **Unidade Política**
□[1] Independent Nation	□[1] Unabhängiger Staat	□[1] Nación Independiente	□[1] État indépendant	□[1] País Independente
□[2] Dependency	□[2] Abhängiges Gebiet	□[2] Dependencia	□[2] Dépendance	□[2] Dependência
□[3] State, Canton, Republic	□[3] Land, Kanton, Republik	□[3] Estado, Cantón, República	□[3] État, Canton, République	□[3] Estado, Cantão, República
□[4] Province, Region, Oblast	□[4] Provinz, Landschaft, Oblast	□[4] Provincia, Región, Oblast	□[4] Province, Région, Oblast	□[4] Província, Região, Oblast
□[5] Department, District, Prefecture	□[5] Département, Distrikt, Präfektur	□[5] Departamento, Distrito, Prefectura	□[5] Département, District, Préfecture	□[5] Departamento, Distrito, Prefeitura
□[6] County	□[6] Grafschaft	□[6] Condado	□[6] Comté	□[6] Condado
□[7] City, Municipality	□[7] Stadt, Stadtkreis	□[7] Ciudad, Municipalidad	□[7] Ville, Municipalité	□[7] Cidade, Municipalidade
□[8] Miscellaneous	□[8] Verschiedenes	□[8] Misceláneo	□[8] Divers	□[8] Diversos
□[9] Historical	□[9] Historisch	□[9] Histórico	□[9] Historique	□[9] Sítio Histórico
Cultural Institution	**Kulturelle Institution**	**Institución Cultural**	**Institution culturelle**	**Instituição Cultural**
[1] Religious Institution	[1] Religiöse Institution	[1] Institución Religiosa	[1] Institution religieuse	[1] Instituição Religiosa
[2] Educational Institution	[2] Erziehungsinstitution	[2] Institución Educacional	[2] Établissement d'éducation	[2] Estabelecimento de Ensino
[3] Scientific, Industrial Facility	[3] Wissenschaftliche, Industrielle Anlage	[3] Institución Científica o Industrial	[3] Établissement scientifique ou industriel	[3] Estabelecimento Científico ou Industrial
⊥ **Historical Site**	⊥ **Historische Stätte**	⊥ **Sitio Histórico**	⊥ **Site historique**	⊥ **Sítio Histórico**
♠ **Recreational Site**	♠ **Erholungs- und Ferienort**	♠ **Sitio de Recreo**	♠ **Centre de loisirs**	♠ **Área de Lazer**
⊠ **Airport**	⊠ **Flughafen**	⊠ **Aeropuerto**	⊠ **Aéroport**	⊠ **Aeroporto**
■ **Military Installation**	■ **Militäranlage**	■ **Instalación Militar**	■ **Installation militaire**	■ **Instalação Militar**
Miscellaneous	**Verschiedenes**	**Misceláneo**	**Divers**	**Diversos**
[1] Region	[1] Region	[1] Región	[1] Région	[1] Região
[2] Desert	[2] Wüste	[2] Desierto	[2] Désert	[2] Deserto
[3] Forest, Moor	[3] Wald, Moor	[3] Bosque, Páramo	[3] Forêt, Lande	[3] Floresta, Pântano
[4] Reserve, Reservation	[4] Reservat	[4] Reserva, Reservación	[4] Réserve	[4] Reserva
[5] Transportation	[5] Verkehr	[5] Transporte	[5] Transport	[5] Transporte
[6] Dam	[6] Damm	[6] Presa	[6] Barrage	[6] Represa
[7] Mine, Quarry	[7] Bergwerk, Steinbruch	[7] Mina, Cantera	[7] Mine, Carrière	[7] Mina, Pedreira
[8] Neighborhood	[8] Nachbarschaft	[8] Barrio	[8] Quartier	[8] Arredores, Vizinhança
[9] Shopping Center	[9] Einkaufszentrum	[9] Mercado	[9] Centre commercial	[9] Shopping Center

A

Aa ≏	**50**	51.01 N	2.06 E
Aach	**58**	47.50 N	8.51 E
Aachen	**56**	50.47 N	6.05 E
Aach im Allgäu	**58**	47.31 N	9.58 E
Aach-Linz	**58**	47.54 N	9.11 E
Aadorf	**58**	47.30 N	8.54 E
Aaiun → El Aaiún	**148**	27.09 N	13.12 W
Aalen	**56**	48.50 N	10.05 E
Aʿālī an-Nīl □[4]	**140**	9.30 N	31.00 E
Aalsmeer	**52**	52.16 N	4.45 E
Aalst (Alost), Bel.	**50**	50.56 N	4.02 E
Aalst, Ned.	**52**	51.23 N	5.29 E
Aalten	**52**	51.56 N	6.35 E
Aalter	**50**	51.05 N	3.27 E
Aalwynsfontein	**158**	30.27 S	18.38 E
Äänekoski	**26**	62.36 N	25.44 E
Aansluit	**158**	26.44 S	22.28 E
Aar ≏	**56**	50.23 N	8.00 E
Aarau	**58**	47.23 N	8.03 E
Aarberg	**58**	47.03 N	7.16 E
Aarburg	**58**	47.19 N	7.54 E
Aardenburg	**52**	51.16 N	3.27 E
Aare ≏	**58**	47.37 N	8.13 E
Aareschlucht ♠	**58**	46.44 N	8.12 E
Aargau □[3]	**58**	47.30 N	8.10 E
Aarle-Rixtel	**52**	51.31 N	5.38 E
Aaronsburg	**210**	40.54 N	77.27 W
Aarschot	**56**	50.59 N	4.50 E
Aarwangen	**58**	47.15 N	7.46 E
Aazanèn	**34**	35.13 N	3.10 W
Aba, Nig.	**150**	5.06 N	7.21 E
Aba, Zaïre	**154**	3.52 N	30.14 E
Aba, Zhg.	**102**	33.06 N	101.59 E
Abā al-Bawl, Qurayn ∧[2]	**128**	24.56 N	51.13 E
Abā al-Waqf	**142**	28.35 N	30.46 E
Abā as-Suʿūd	**144**	17.29 N	44.08 E
Abacaxis ≏	**242**	3.54 S	58.47 W
Abaco I	**238**	26.28 N	77.05 W
Abacou, Pointe ›	**238**	18.03 N	73.47 W
Abadab, Jabal ∧	**140**	18.53 N	35.59 E
Ābādān	**128**	30.20 N	48.16 E
Ābādeh	**128**	31.10 N	52.37 E
Abadia dos Dourados	**255**	18.28 S	47.24 W
Abadiânia	**255**	16.06 S	48.48 W
Abadla	**148**	31.01 N	2.44 W
Abaeté	**255**	19.09 S	45.27 W
Abaeté ≏	**255**	18.02 S	45.12 W
Abaetetuba	**250**	1.42 S	48.54 W
Abagajtuj	**88**	49.35 N	117.49 E
Abagnar Qi	**102**	43.58 N	116.04 E
Abag Qi	**102**	43.53 N	114.33 E
Abaí	**252**	26.01 S	55.57 W
Abaj, Kaz.	**86**	49.38 N	72.52 E
Abaj, Ross.	**86**	50.27 N	85.05 E
Abaji	**150**	8.28 N	6.57 E
Abajo Mountains	**200**	37.50 N	109.25 W
Abajo Peak ∧	**200**	37.51 N	109.28 W
Abak	**150**	4.57 N	7.47 E
Abakaliki	**150**	6.21 N	8.06 E
Abakan	**86**	53.43 N	91.26 E
Abakan ≏	**86**	53.43 N	91.30 E
Abakanovo	**76**	59.18 N	37.39 E
Abakanskij chrebet	**86**	52.20 N	88.50 E
Abala, Congo	**152**	1.21 S	15.30 E
Abala, Niger	**150**	14.56 N	3.26 E
Abalak, Niger	**150**	15.27 N	6.17 E
Abalak, Ross.	**86**	58.08 N	68.36 E
Abalemma, Vallée d' V	**150**	15.34 N	6.23 E
Abalessa	**148**	22.54 N	4.50 E
Aban	**88**	56.41 N	96.04 E
Abancay	**248**	13.35 S	72.55 W
Abanga ≏	**152**	0.20 S	10.30 E
Abano Terme	**64**	45.21 N	11.47 E
Abaokoro	**174t**	1.29 N	173.02 E
Abar Irir	**144**	4.53 N	46.10 E
Abar Kūh	**128**	31.08 N	53.17 E
Abarra	**144**	5.23 N	39.58 E
Abarracamento	**256**	22.12 S	43.30 W
Abaša	**84**	42.12 N	42.13 E
Abascay, Arroyo ≏	**258**	35.17 S	58.07 W
Abashiri	**92a**	44.01 N	144.17 E
Abasolo, Méx.	**196**	25.57 N	100.24 W
Abasolo, Méx.	**196**	27.12 N	101.24 W
Abasolo, Méx.	**204**	32.39 N	115.21 W
Abasolo, Méx.	**232**	25.18 N	104.40 W
Abasolo, Méx.	**232**	24.04 N	98.22 W
Abasolo, Méx.	**234**	20.27 N	101.32 W
Abasolo del Valle	**234**	17.44 N	95.29 W
Abasto	**258**	34.58 S	58.06 W
Abastumani	**84**	41.46 N	42.50 E
Abate	**85**	39.03 N	77.36 E
Abate Alonia, Lago di ⊜	**68**	41.01 N	15.45 E
Abatimbo el Gumas	**144**	10.36 N	35.13 E
Abatskij	**86**	56.18 N	70.28 E
Abau	**164**	10.11 S	148.42 E
Abava ≏	**76**	57.06 N	21.54 E
Abaya, Lake ⊜	**144**	6.20 N	37.55 E
Abay → Blue Nile ≏	**140**	15.38 N	32.31 E
Abayuba	**258**	34.51 S	56.14 W
Abaza	**86**	52.39 N	90.06 E
Abba	**152**	5.20 N	15.11 E
Abbabach ≏	**263**	51.28 N	7.41 E
Abbadia San Salvatore	**66**	42.53 N	11.41 E
ʿAbbāsābād ◆[8]	**267d**	35.44 N	51.25 E
Abbasanta	**71**	40.08 N	8.49 E
Abbaye, Étang de l' ⊜	**261**	48.41 N	1.56 E
Abbé, Lac (Lake Abe) ⊜	**144**	11.06 N	41.50 E
Abbehausen	**52**	53.29 N	8.26 E
Abbekås	**41**	55.24 N	13.36 E
Abbensen	**52**	52.23 N	10.11 E
Abbert ≏	**48**	53.25 N	8.53 W
Abbess Roding	**260**	51.47 N	0.17 E
Abbeville, Fr.	**50**	50.06 N	1.50 E
Abbeville, Ga., U.S.	**192**	31.59 N	83.18 W
Abbeville, La., U.S.	**194**	29.58 N	92.08 W
Abbeville, Ms., U.S.	**194**	34.30 N	89.30 W
Abbeville, S.C., U.S.	**192**	34.10 N	82.22 W
Abbey	**184**	50.43 N	108.45 W
Abbeydorney	**48**	52.19 N	9.41 W
Abbeyfeale	**48**	52.24 N	9.18 W
Abbey Head ›	**44**	54.46 N	3.58 W
Abbeyleix	**48**	52.55 N	7.20 W
Abbey Peak ∧	**164**	14.18 S	144.29 E
Abbey Wood ◆[8]	**260**	51.29 N	0.08 E
Abbiategrasso	**62**	45.24 N	8.54 E
Abbot, Mount ∧	**166**	20.03 S	147.45 E
Abbots Bromley	**42**	52.48 N	1.52 W
Abbotsbury	**42**	50.40 N	2.36 W
Abbotsford, Austl.	**274a**	33.51 S	151.08 E
Abbotsford, B.C., Can.	**224**	49.03 N	122.17 W
Abbotsford, Wi., U.S.	**190**	44.56 N	90.18 W
Abbots Langley	**260**	51.43 N	0.25 W
Abbott, Arg.	**258**	35.17 S	58.48 W
Abbott, Tx., U.S.	**222**	31.53 N	97.04 W
Abbottābād	**123**	34.09 N	73.13 E
Abbott Butte ∧	**202**	42.57 N	122.33 W
Abbottstown	**208**	39.53 N	76.59 W
Abchazskaja Avtonomnaja Sovetskaja Socialističeskaja Respublika □[3]	**84**	43.10 N	41.00 E
Abcoude	**52**	52.16 N	4.58 E
ʿAbd al-ʿAzīz, Jabal	**130**	36.25 N	40.20 E
ʿAbd al-Ḥafiẓ, Qārat ∧[2]	**142**	28.53 N	30.08 E
ʿAbd al-Kūrī I	**118**	12.12 N	52.13 E
ʿAbd Allāh	**140**	13.30 N	23.02 E
ʿAbd Allāh, Khawr	**128**	29.50 N	48.20 E
ʿAbd al-Shāhīd	**273c**	29.55 N	31.13 E
Ābdānān	**128**	32.58 N	47.26 E
Ábdēra ⊥	**38**	40.59 N	24.58 E
Abdrachmanovo	**80**	54.46 N	52.30 E
Abdul Hakīm	**123**	30.33 N	72.07 E
Abdulino	**80**	53.42 N	53.40 E
Abdulovo	**80**	54.16 N	53.27 E
Abe ≏	**94**	34.56 N	138.24 E
Abe, Lake (Lac Abbé) ⊜	**144**	11.06 N	41.50 E
Abéché	**146**	13.49 N	20.49 E
Abéjar	**34**	41.48 N	2.47 W
Abejonal, Cerro ∧	**236**	11.39 N	86.10 W
Abejorral	**246**	5.47 N	75.26 W
Abekr	**140**	12.43 N	28.55 E
Abelek	**140**	7.23 N	28.46 E
Abel Tasman National Park ♠	**172**	40.55 S	173.00 E
Abelti	**144**	8.10 N	37.34 E
Abemama I[1]	**14**	0.21 N	173.51 E
Abenberg	**56**	49.14 N	10.57 E
Abengourou	**150**	6.44 N	3.29 W
Abeno ◆[8]	**270**	34.38 N	135.32 E
Abenójar	**34**	38.53 N	4.21 W
Åbenrå	**41**	55.02 N	9.26 E
Åbenrå Fjord ⊂	**41**	55.03 N	9.34 E
Abens ≏	**60**	48.51 N	11.46 E
Abensberg	**60**	48.49 N	11.51 E
Abeokuta	**150**	7.10 N	3.26 E
Aber	**154**	2.12 N	32.21 E
Aberaeron	**42**	52.15 N	4.15 W
Aberaman	**42**	51.42 N	3.25 W
Aberavon → Port Talbot	**42**	51.36 N	3.47 W
Abercarn	**42**	51.39 N	3.08 W
Aberchirder	**46**	57.33 N	2.38 W
Abercorn	**206**	45.02 N	72.40 W
Abercorn → Mbala	**154**	8.50 S	31.22 E
Abercrombie ≏	**170**	34.09 S	149.40 E
Aberdare	**42**	51.43 N	3.27 W
Aberdare National Park ♠	**154**	0.30 S	36.45 E
Aberdare Range	**154**	0.25 S	36.38 E
Aberdaron	**42**	52.49 N	4.43 W
Aberdeen, Sk., Can.	**184**	52.19 N	106.17 W
Aberdeen (Xianggangzi), H.K.	**271d**	22.15 N	114.09 E
Aberdeen, S. Afr.	**158**	32.29 S	24.05 E
Aberdeen, Scot., U.K.	**46**	57.10 N	2.04 W
Aberdeen, Id., U.S.	**202**	42.56 N	112.50 W
Aberdeen, Md., U.S.	**208**	39.30 N	76.09 W
Aberdeen, Ms., U.S.	**194**	33.49 N	88.32 W
Aberdeen, N.C., U.S.	**192**	35.07 N	79.25 W
Aberdeen, Oh., U.S.	**218**	38.39 N	83.45 W
Aberdeen, S.D., U.S.	**198**	45.27 N	98.29 W
Aberdeen, Wa., U.S.	**224**	46.58 N	123.48 W
Aberdeen Lake ⊜	**176**	64.27 N	99.00 W
Aberdeen Lake ⊜[1]	**194**	33.55 N	88.30 W
Aberdeen Proving Ground ■	**208**	39.25 N	76.10 W
Aberdour	**46**	56.03 N	3.19 W
Aberdulais	**42**	51.41 N	3.48 W
Aberdyfi	**42**	52.33 N	4.02 W
Aberfeldy	**46**	56.37 N	3.54 W
Aberfoyle	**46**	56.11 N	4.23 W
Abergavenny	**42**	51.50 N	3.00 W
Abergele	**44**	53.17 N	3.34 W
Abergwynfi	**42**	51.40 N	3.35 W
Abergynolwyn	**42**	52.40 N	3.58 W
Aberjona ≏	**283**	42.27 N	71.08 W
Abermain	**170**	32.49 S	151.25 E
Abernathy	**196**	33.50 N	101.51 W
Abernethy, Sk., Can.	**184**	50.45 N	103.25 W
Abernethy, Scot., U.K.	**46**	56.20 N	3.19 W
Aberporth	**42**	52.09 N	4.33 W
Abersoch	**42**	52.50 N	4.29 W
Abersychan	**42**	51.44 N	3.04 W
Abert, Lake ⊜	**202**	42.38 N	120.13 W
Abertillery	**42**	51.45 N	3.09 W
Aberuthven	**46**	56.19 N	3.39 W
Aberystwyth	**42**	52.25 N	4.05 W
Abessinien, Hochland von → Ethiopian Plateau [1]	**144**	9.00 N	38.00 E
Abetone	**66**	44.08 N	10.40 E
Abez'	**24**	66.32 N	61.42 E
Abhā	**144**	18.13 N	42.30 E
Abhar	**128**	36.09 N	49.13 E
Abharwat ∧	**123**	34.02 N	74.25 E
Abhayāpuri	**124**	26.20 N	90.40 E
Abhaynagar	**126**	23.01 N	89.28 E
Abiaca Creek ≏	**194**	33.20 N	90.15 W
Abid, Oued el ≏	**148**	32.18 N	7.03 W
Ābidīn	**140**	13.33 N	29.38 E
ʿAbīdīyah	**140**	18.14 N	33.57 E
Abidjan	**150**	5.19 N	4.02 W
ʿĀbid Mār, Tall ∧	**132**	32.26 N	36.42 E
Abiengama	**154**	2.35 N	27.46 E
Abiko	**94**	35.52 N	140.03 E
Abilene, Ks., U.S.	**198**	38.55 N	97.12 W
Abilene, Tx., U.S.	**196**	32.26 N	99.43 W

≏ River	Fluß	Río	Rivière	Rio
Canal	Kanal	Canal	Canal	Canal
Waterfall, Rapids	Wasserfall, Stromschnellen	Cascada, Rápidos	Chute d'eau, Rapides	Cascata, Rápidos
Strait	Meeresstraße	Estrecho	Détroit	Estreito
⊂ Bay, Gulf	Bucht, Golf	Bahía, Golfo	Baie, Golfe	Baía, Golfo
⊜ Lake, Lakes	See, Seen	Lago, Lagos	Lac, Lacs	Lago, Lagos
Swamp	Sumpf	Pantano	Marais	Pântano
Ice Features, Glacier	Eis- und Gletscherformen	Accidentes Glaciales	Formes glaciaires	Acidentes glaciares
Other Hydrographic Features	Andere Hydrographische Objekte	Otros Elementos Hidrográficos	Autres données hydrographiques	Outros acidentes hidrográficos
Submarine Features	Untermeerische Objekte	Accidentes Submarinos	Formes de relief sous-marin	Acidentes submarinos
□ Political Unit	Politische Einheit	Unidad Politica	Entité politique	Unidade política
Cultural Institution	Kulturelle Institution	Institución Cultural	Institution culturelle	Instituição cultural
⊥ Historical Site	Historische Stätte	Sitio Histórico	Site historique	Sitio histórico
♠ Recreational Site	Erholungs- und Ferienort	Sitio de Recreo	Centre de loisirs	Area de Lazer
⊠ Airport	Flughafen	Aeropuerto	Aéroport	Aeroporto
■ Military Installation	Militäranlage	Instalación Militar	Installation militaire	Instalação militar
◆ Miscellaneous	Verschiedenes	Misceláneo	Divers	Diversos

Name	Page	Lat.°′	Long.°′
Abingdon, Eng., U.K.	42	51.41 N	1.17 W
Abingdon, Il., U.S.	190	40.48 N	90.24 W
Abingdon, Il., U.S.	194	40.48 N	90.24 W
Abingdon, Va., U.S.	192	36.42 N	81.58 W
Abinger	260	51.12 N	0.24 W
Abington, Ct., U.S.	207	41.51 N	72.00 W
Abington, Ma., U.S.	207	42.06 N	70.56 W
Abington, Pa., U.S.	208	40.07 N	75.07 W
Abington Reefs ✧[2]	166	18.00 S	149.36 E
Abino, Point ➤	212	42.50 N	79.05 W
Abino Bay ⊂	284a	42.51 N	79.05 W
Abinsk	78	44.52 N	38.09 E
Abiod, Rmel el ≗[8]	148	31.30 N	9.30 E
Abiquiu	200	36.12 N	106.19 W
Abiquiu Reservoir ⊜[1]	200	36.18 N	106.32 W
Abiseo ≃	248	7.18 S	76.50 W
Abiseo, Parque Nacional ♠	248	7.35 S	77.10 W
Abisko	24	68.20 N	18.51 E
Abisko Nationalpark ♠	24	68.20 N	18.30 E
Abita Springs	194	30.28 N	90.02 W
Abitau ≃	176	59.53 N	109.03 W
Abitibi ≃	176	51.03 N	80.55 W
Abitibi, Lake ⊜	190	48.42 N	79.45 W
Abiy Adi	144	13.26 N	39.05 E
Abiyata, Lake ⊜	144	7.37 N	38.36 E
Abja-Paluoja	76	58.08 N	25.21 E
Ableiges	261	49.05 N	1.59 E
Ablis	50	48.31 N	1.50 E
Ablon-sur-Seine	261	48.43 N	2.25 E
Abnūb	142	27.16 N	31.09 E
Abóbada	266c	38.43 N	9.20 W
Abodom	150	5.32 N	0.49 W
Abohar	123	30.09 N	74.11 E
Aboisso	150	5.28 N	3.12 W
Abomey	150	7.11 N	1.59 E
Abondance	58	46.17 N	6.44 E
Abong	146	6.59 N	10.44 E
Abongabong, Gunung ∧	114	4.15 N	96.48 E
Abong Mbang	152	3.59 N	13.10 E
Abonnema	150	4.43 N	6.47 E
Abony	30	47.11 N	20.01 E
Aborigen, pik ∧	74	61.59 N	149.19 E
Aborlan	116	9.26 N	118.33 E
Aborrebjerg ∧[2]	41	54.59 N	12.32 E
Aboso	150	5.22 N	1.56 W
Abō-tōge)(	94	36.11 N	137.35 E
Åbo — Turku	26	60.27 N	22.17 E
Abou	144	4.21 N	43.03 E
Abou-Deïa	146	11.27 N	19.17 E
Abounamy ≃	250	4.24 N	54.26 W
Aboyne	46	57.05 N	2.50 W
Abra □[4]	116	17.35 N	120.50 E
Abra ≃	116	17.31 N	120.23 E
Abraão	256	23.08 S	44.10 W
Abraham Lake ⊜[1]	182	52.15 N	116.23 W
Abraham Lincoln Birthplace National Historic Site ⊥	194	37.32 N	85.44 W
Abrahamsdam	158	29.08 S	22.39 E
Abraka	150	5.50 N	6.05 E
Abram	262	53.31 N	2.35 W
Abramcevo	265b	55.50 N	37.50 E
Abramovka	78	51.12 N	41.01 E
Abramovskaja	24	65.11 N	51.43 E
Abram S. Hewitt State Forest ♠	276	41.11 N	74.22 W
Abrantes	34	39.28 N	8.12 W
Abra Pampa	252	22.43 S	65.42 W
Abraq, Wādī al- ∨	146	26.27 N	18.48 E
Abrau-D'urso	78	44.43 N	37.37 E
Abra Vieja, Arroyo ≃	288	34.26 S	58.34 W
Abre-Campo	255	20.18 S	42.29 W
Ábrego	246	8.05 N	73.13 W
Abreojos, Punta ➤	232	26.42 N	113.35 W
Abreschviller	58	48.38 N	7.06 E
Abreu e Lima	250	7.54 S	34.53 W
ʿAbrī, Sūd.	140	11.40 N	30.28 E
ʿAbrī, Sūd.	140	20.48 N	30.20 E
Abriachan	46	57.22 N	4.24 W
Abridge	260	51.39 N	0.07 E
Abriès	62	44.47 N	6.56 E
Abring	123	33.42 N	76.35 E
Abriola	68	40.30 N	15.49 E
Abrud	38	46.17 N	23.04 E
Abruka saar I	76	58.10 N	22.30 E
Abrunheira	266c	38.46 N	9.21 W
Abruzzi □[4]	66	42.20 N	13.45 E
Abruzzo, Parco Nazionale d' ♠	66	41.45 N	13.45 E
Absam	64	47.18 N	11.30 E
Absaroka Range ⋏	202	44.45 N	109.50 W
Absarokee	202	45.31 N	109.26 W
Abscon	50	50.20 N	3.18 E
Absdorf	61	48.24 N	15.59 E
Absecon	208	39.25 N	74.29 W
Absecon Bay ⊂	208	39.24 N	74.28 W
Abşeker	130	38.55 N	39.11 E
Abtenau	64	47.33 N	13.21 E
Abtsgmünd	56	48.54 N	10.00 E
Abtsteinach	56	49.33 N	8.47 E
Abu	96	34.30 N	131.28 E
Abu ≃	96	34.25 N	131.24 E
Abū Ahl ▾[4]	128	34.06 N	43.45 E
Abū ʿAlāwī, Wādī ∨	142	30.07 N	31.51 E
Abū al-Ghayṭ	273c	30.09 N	31.11 E
Abū al-Ḥamām, Jabal ∧	132	30.27 N	35.38 E
Abū al-Hawl (Sphinx) ⊥	142	29.59 N	31.08 E
Abū ʿAlī I	128	27.20 N	49.33 E
Abū al-Khaṣīb	128	30.27 N	47.59 E
Abū al-Maṭāmīr	142	30.55 N	30.11 E
Abū al-ʿUrūq, Bi'r ▾[4]	142	30.45 N	32.23 E
Abū an-Numrus	273c	29.57 N	31.12 E
Abū ʿAradeib, Wādī ∨	140	14.12 N	23.06 E
Abū ʿArīsh	144	16.57 N	42.50 E
Abū Ballās ∧[2]	140	24.26 N	27.39 E
Abū Daraj, Ra's ➤	142	29.23 N	32.34 E
Abū Dā'ūd, Ra's ➤	128	23.19 N	58.55 E
Abū Dā'ūd as-Sibākh	142	30.55 N	31.34 E
Abū Dawm	140	16.16 N	32.36 E
Abū Dawm, Wādī ∨	140	18.28 N	31.49 E
Abu Dhabi — Abū Ẓaby	128	24.28 N	54.22 E
Abū Dhi'ābah, Wādī ∨	142	29.37 N	32.06 E
Abū Dīs	140	19.08 N	33.34 E
Abū Dulayq	140	15.54 N	33.49 E
Abufari	248	5.25 S	62.59 W
Abū Gatta Hills ⋏[2]	140	6.06 N	27.44 E
Abū Gelba	140	13.11 N	31.52 E
Abū Ghālib	142	30.16 N	30.56 E
Abū Habl, Khawr ∨	140	12.49 N	31.15 E
Abū Ḥād, Wādī ∨	142	28.20 N	32.49 E
Abū Ḥadīmah, Bi'r ▾[4]	142	30.44 N	29.51 E
Abū Hamad	140	19.32 N	33.19 E
Abū Ḥammād al-Maḥaṭṭah	142	30.32 N	31.40 E
Abū Ḥarāz, Sūd.	140	12.58 N	29.52 E
Abū Ḥarāz, Sūd.	140	19.04 N	32.07 E
Abū Ḥasan, Jabal ∧	144	17.42 N	42.54 E
Abū Ḥummuṣ	142	31.06 N	30.19 E
Abū Ḥushsh, Bi'r ▾[4]	142	30.49 N	29.57 E
Abuja	150	9.12 N	7.11 E
Abū Jābirah	140	11.04 N	26.51 E
Abū Jandīr	142	29.14 N	30.41 E
Abū Jirj	142	28.32 N	30.47 E
Abū Jubayhah	140	11.27 N	31.14 E
Abū Kabīr	142	30.44 N	31.40 E
Abū Kamāl	130	34.27 N	40.55 E
Abū Kharjah, Wādī ∨	142	28.38 N	31.44 E
Abū Khashabah, Jabal ∧	142	28.08 N	32.52 E
Abūksāh	142	29.23 N	30.42 E
Abū Kulaywāt	140	12.20 N	26.00 E
Abukuma ≃	92	38.02 N	140.56 E
Abukuma-kōchi ⋏	92	37.30 N	140.45 E
Abū Latt I	144	19.58 N	40.08 E
Abulug	116	18.27 N	121.27 E
Abulug ≃	116	18.29 N	121.25 E
Abū Madd, Ra's ➤	128	24.50 N	37.07 E
Abū Makhlūf, Bi'r ▾[4]	142	30.45 N	29.42 E
Abū Maṭāriq	140	10.58 N	26.17 E
Abu Mendi	144	11.47 N	35.43 E
Abū Minqār, Bi'r ▾[4]	140	26.30 N	27.35 E
Abumombazi	152	3.42 N	22.10 E
Abū Muḥammad, Bi'r ▾[4]	132	29.43 N	34.13 E
Abū Muḥarrik, Ghurd ≗[8]	140	27.50 N	29.40 E
Abū Mūsā I	128	25.52 N	55.03 E
Abuna	248	9.42 S	65.23 W
Abuná (Abunã) ≃	248	9.41 S	65.23 W
Abū Naʿāmah	140	12.44 N	34.08 E
Abune Yosef ∧	144	12.10 N	39.12 E
Abū Qarḍī, Qāʿ ≍	132	32.08 N	37.11 E
Abū Qashsh	132	31.57 N	35.11 E
Abū Qīr ◆[8]	142	31.19 N	30.04 E
Abū Qīr, Khalīj (Abu Qir Bay) ⊂	142	31.23 N	30.13 E
Abū Qurqāṣ	142	27.56 N	30.50 E
Aburatsubo-kō ⊂	268	35.09 N	139.38 E
Abū Rimth, Wādī ∨, Miṣr	142	30.21 N	31.53 E
Abū Rimth, Wādī ∨, Miṣr	142	28.45 N	31.27 E
Abū Rīshat, Wādī ∨	142	28.54 N	31.37 E
Ābu Road	120	24.29 N	72.47 E
Abū Rubayq	128	23.44 N	39.42 E
Abū Rujmayn, Jabal ⋏	130	34.52 N	38.20 E
Abū Sanṭ, Wādī ∨	140	14.11 N	23.06 E
Abū Shajarah, Ra's ➤	140	21.04 N	37.14 E
Abū Shāmah, Jabal ∧	142	29.52 N	31.38 E
Abū Shanab, Sūd.	140	10.47 N	29.32 E
Abū Shanab, Sūd.	140	13.57 N	27.47 E
Abū Shaykhāt, Ḍahr ∧[2]	130	36.36 N	39.40 E
Abu Simbel — Abū Sunbul ⊥	140	22.22 N	31.38 E
Abū Ṣīr	273c	29.53 N	31.13 E
Abu Ṣīr al-Malaq	142	29.15 N	31.05 E
Abū Ṣīr-Banā	142	30.55 N	31.15 E
Abū Ṣīr Pyramids ⊥	273c	29.54 N	31.12 E
Abū Sulṭan	142	30.25 N	32.19 E
Abū Sunbul ⊥	140	22.22 N	31.38 E
Abū Ṣuwayr al-Maḥaṭṭah	142	30.34 N	32.07 E
Abū Ṣuwayr Military Base ■	142	30.34 N	32.06 E
Abuta	92a	42.33 N	140.46 E
Abū Ṭabarī ▾[4]	140	17.35 N	28.31 E
Abū Ṭarafah, Wādī ∨	132	30.12 N	36.13 E
Abut Head ➤	172	43.07 S	170.15 E
Abū Tīj	140	27.02 N	31.19 E
Abū Ṭunayṭin	140	14.24 N	31.01 E
Abū Ṭurayfīyah, Jabal ∧, Miṣr	142	29.58 N	32.06 E
Abū Ṭurayfīyah, Jabal ∧, Miṣr	142	29.42 N	31.49 E
Abū ʿUwayjilah ▾[4]	132	30.50 N	34.07 E
Abuye Meda ∧	144	10.28 N	39.44 E
Abuyog	116	10.45 N	125.01 E
Abū Zabad	140	12.21 N	29.15 E
Abū Zaʿbal	142	30.15 N	31.21 E
Abū Ẓaby (Abu Dhabi)	128	24.28 N	54.22 E
Abū Zanīmah	140	29.03 N	33.06 E
Abwong	140	9.07 N	32.12 E
Åby	40	58.40 N	16.11 E
Åby ◆[8]	41	56.09 N	10.10 E
Aby, Lagune ⊂	150	5.15 N	3.14 W
Abyaḍ	140	13.46 N	26.28 E
Abyaḍ, Al-Baḥr al- — White Nile ≃	140	15.38 N	32.31 E
Abyaḍ, Wādī al- ∨	142	29.38 N	32.13 E
Åbyälven ≃	26	65.01 N	21.24 E
Abyār	142	30.50 N	30.52 E
Abyār ʿAlī	128	24.25 N	39.32 E
Åbybro	26	57.09 N	9.45 E
Abydos	162	21.25 S	118.54 E
Abyei	140	9.36 N	28.26 E
Åbyggeby	40	60.44 N	17.07 E
Åbytorp	40	59.07 N	15.04 E
Abzanovo	86	53.50 N	58.36 E
Acacías	246	3.59 N	73.46 W
Academia	214	40.25 N	82.28 W
Academy Corners	208	41.57 N	77.23 W
Academy of Sciences ʋ[3]	282	37.46 N	122.28 W
Acadia National Park ♠	188	44.18 N	68.15 W
Acadia Valley	184	51.08 N	110.13 W
Acahay	252	25.55 S	57.09 W
Açailandia	250	4.57 S	47.29 W
Acajete	234	19.06 N	97.57 W
Acajutiba	250	11.40 S	38.01 W
Acajutla	236	13.36 N	89.50 W
Acala	234	16.34 N	92.48 W
Acalayong	152	1.05 N	9.40 E
Acámbaro	234	20.02 N	100.44 W
Acampo	226	38.10 N	121.13 W
Acandí	246	8.32 N	77.14 W
Acaponeta	234	22.30 N	105.22 W
Acaponeta ≃	234	22.20 N	105.37 W
Acapulco [de Juárez]	234	16.51 N	99.55 W
Acará	250	1.57 S	48.11 W
Acará ≃	250	1.40 S	48.25 W
Acará, Lago ⊜	246	3.39 S	62.40 W
Acaraí ≃	250	2.02 S	52.15 W
Acarai Mountains ⋏	246	1.30 N	58.15 W
Acará-Mirim ≃	250	1.58 S	48.12 W
Acaraú	250	2.53 S	40.07 W
Acaraú ≃	250	2.51 S	40.08 W
Acaray ≃	252	25.29 S	54.42 W
Acari, Bra.	250	6.31 S	36.38 W
Acarí, Perú	248	15.26 S	74.37 W
Acari ≃, Bra.	248	5.18 S	59.42 W
Acari ≃, Bra.	255	16.00 S	45.03 W
Acarí ≃, Perú	248	15.39 S	74.39 W
Acarigua	246	9.33 N	69.12 W
Acate	70	37.02 N	14.28 E
Acate ≃	70	37.00 N	14.20 E
Acatic	234	20.47 N	102.53 W
Acatlán ≃	234	18.04 N	98.19 W
Acatlán de Juárez	234	20.26 N	103.38 W
Acatlán de Osorio	234	18.12 N	98.03 W
Acatlán de Pérez Figueroa	234	18.32 N	96.37 W
Acatzingo [de Hidalgo]	234	18.59 N	97.47 W
Acay, Nevado de ∧	252	24.21 S	66.12 W
Acayucan	234	17.57 N	94.55 W
Accadia	68	41.10 N	15.20 E
Acceglio	62	44.28 N	7.00 E
Aččen, mys ➤	180	64.45 N	175.30 W
Accettura	68	40.29 N	16.09 E
Aččhoj-Martan	84	43.11 N	45.18 E
Ačči	85	39.57 N	68.14 E
Acciano	66	42.10 N	13.43 E
Accokeek	208	38.40 N	77.02 W
Accomac	208	37.43 N	75.39 W
Accomack □[6]	208	37.45 N	75.40 W
Accord, Ma., U.S.	283	42.10 N	70.53 W
Accord, N.Y., U.S.	210	41.47 N	74.13 W
Accord Brook ≃	283	42.10 N	70.53 W
Accord Pond ⊜	283	42.10 N	70.53 W
Accotink Creek ≃	284c	38.46 N	77.13 W
Accotink Creek, Bear Branch ≃	284c	38.52 N	77.15 W
Accotink Creek, Long Branch ≃	284c	38.48 N	77.13 W
Accoville	192	37.46 N	81.50 W
Accra	150	5.33 N	0.13 W
Accra □[4]	150	5.40 N	0.10 W
Accrington	262	53.46 N	2.21 W
Accumoli	66	42.42 N	13.15 E
Acebuches	232	28.15 N	102.43 W
Aceguá	252	31.52 S	54.09 W
Aceh □[4]	114	4.00 N	97.00 E
Aceh ≃	114	5.36 N	95.20 E
Acerentia ⊥	68	39.16 N	16.49 E
Acerenza	68	40.48 N	15.57 E
Acerno	68	40.44 N	15.03 E
Acerra	68	40.57 N	14.22 E
Acevedo	252	33.45 S	60.27 W
Achacachi	248	16.03 S	68.43 W
Achaguas	246	7.46 N	68.14 W
Achalciche	84	41.38 N	42.59 E
Achali-Kindgi	84	42.48 N	41.16 E
Achalkalaki	84	41.25 N	43.29 E
Achalpur	120	21.16 N	77.31 E
Achangaran	85	40.54 N	69.37 E
Achao	254	42.28 S	73.30 W
Achar	252	32.25 S	56.10 W
Acharacle	46	56.44 N	5.47 W
Achar uul ∧	102	45.10 N	103.45 E
Achau	264b	48.05 N	16.23 E
Achavanich	46	58.22 N	3.24 W
Achelouma, Enneri ∨	146	21.55 N	13.35 E
Achêne	56	50.16 N	5.03 E
Acheng	89	45.32 N	126.59 E
Achenkirch	64	47.31 N	11.42 E
Achénouma	146	19.08 N	12.55 E
Achen Pass)(	64	47.35 N	11.38 E
Achensee ⊜	64	47.28 N	11.42 E
Achères	261	48.58 N	2.04 E
Achern	56	48.37 N	8.04 E
Acheron ≃, Austl.	169	37.14 S	145.42 E
Acheron ≃, N.Z.	172	42.24 S	172.58 E
Acheux-en-Amiénois	50	50.04 N	2.32 E
Achhābal	123	33.41 N	75.14 E
Achhnera	124	27.11 N	77.46 E
Achí, Col.	246	8.34 N	74.33 W
Achi, Nihon	94	35.27 N	137.45 E
Achiasi	150	5.52 N	1.00 W
Achicourt	50	50.16 N	2.46 E
Achigan, Lac de l' ⊜	206	45.56 N	73.58 W
Achiguate ≃	236	13.55 N	90.55 W
Achill	28	53.56 N	9.54 W
Achilles	208	37.17 N	76.27 W
Achill Head ➤	48	53.59 N	10.13 W
Achill Island I	48	54.00 N	10.00 W
Achill Sound	48	53.55 N	9.58 W
Achim	52	53.00 N	9.02 E
Achīn	120	34.08 N	70.42 E
Achiras	252	33.10 S	65.00 W
Achir-Ula, gora ∧	88	50.21 N	94.31 E
Achmeta	84	42.02 N	45.13 E
Achnasaul	46	56.58 N	4.59 W
Achnasheen	46	57.35 N	5.06 W
Achol	140	6.34 N	31.31 E
Achosnich	46	56.45 N	6.06 W
Achsu	84	40.34 N	48.24 E
Achterwasser ⊂	54	54.00 N	13.57 E
Achterwehr	41	54.19 N	9.57 E
Achthuizen	52	51.42 N	4.16 E
Achtuba	80	51.37 N	44.22 E
Achtuba ≃	80	46.42 N	48.00 E
Achtubinsk	80	48.17 N	46.10 E
Achty	84	41.28 N	47.43 E
Achtyrka	78	50.19 N	34.55 E
Achtyrskij	78	44.52 N	38.20 E
Achuapa	236	13.03 N	86.35 W
Achur'an (Arpaçay) ≃	84	40.06 N	43.39 E
Achwa ≃	154	3.43 N	31.55 E
Ači	85	41.17 N	73.02 E
Aci Castello	70	37.33 N	15.08 E
Aci Catena	70	37.36 N	15.08 E
Acıgöl	130	38.35 N	34.31 E
Acı Göl ⊜	130	37.50 N	29.54 E
Acikak	88	54.11 N	106.18 E
Ačikulak	84	44.34 N	44.50 E
Acilia ◆[8]	267a	41.47 N	12.22 E
Ačimovy Vtoryje	86	60.04 N	75.12 E
Ačinsk	86	56.17 N	90.30 E
Acıpayam	130	37.25 N	29.22 E
Acireale	70	37.37 N	15.10 E
Acîş	38	47.33 N	22.47 E
Ačisaj	85	43.35 N	68.53 E
Aci Sant'Antonio	70	37.36 N	15.07 E
Ačisu	84	42.38 N	47.40 E
Ačit	86	56.48 N	57.54 E
Ačit nuur ⊜	86	49.30 N	90.30 E
Ackerly	196	32.32 N	101.43 W
Ackerman	194	33.18 N	89.10 W
Ackermanville	210	40.49 N	75.17 W
Ackerson Lake	216	42.11 N	84.20 W
Ackley	190	42.33 N	93.03 W
Acklins I	238	22.26 N	73.58 W
Acklins, Bight of ⊂[3]	238	22.30 N	74.15 W
Acland, Mount ∧	166	24.55 S	148.05 E
Acle	42	52.38 N	1.33 E
Aclimação ◆[8]	287b	23.34 S	46.37 W
Acme, Ab., Can.	182	51.30 N	113.30 W
Acme, Pa., U.S.	214	40.08 N	79.26 W
Acme, Wa., U.S.	224	48.43 N	122.12 W
Acmetonia	279b	40.32 N	79.49 W
Acobamba	248	12.48 S	74.34 W
Acolla	248	11.44 S	75.34 W
Acoma Indian Reservation ◆[4]	200	34.52 N	107.40 W
Acomayo, Perú	248	13.55 S	71.41 W
Acomayo, Perú	248	9.46 S	76.05 W
Aconcagua, Cerro ∧	252	32.39 S	70.01 W
Aconchi	232	29.50 N	110.12 W
Aconibe	152	1.18 N	10.56 E
Acopiara	250	6.06 S	39.27 W
Açores (Azores) II	148a	38.30 N	28.00 W
Acoria	248	12.37 S	74.53 W
Acorizal	248	15.12 S	56.22 W
Acornhoek	156	24.37 S	31.02 E
Acosta	214	40.07 N	79.04 W
Acoyapa	236	11.58 N	85.10 W
Acoyapa ≃	236	11.48 N	85.16 W
Acquabona, Passo di)(	68	39.02 N	16.20 E
Acquacalda	70	38.31 N	14.57 E
Acqualagna	66	43.37 N	12.40 E
Acquanegra sul Chiese	64	45.10 N	10.26 E
Acquapendente	66	42.44 N	11.52 E
Acquappesa	68	39.29 N	15.57 E
Acquarossa	58	46.28 N	8.57 E
Acquasanta Terme	66	42.46 N	13.24 E
Acquasparta	66	42.41 N	12.33 E
Acquaviva	66	43.57 N	12.25 E
Acquaviva delle Fonti	68	40.54 N	16.50 E
Acquaviva Platani	70	37.34 N	13.42 E
Acqui Terme	62	44.41 N	8.28 E
Acra	210	42.19 N	74.03 W
Acraman, Lake ⊜	162	32.02 S	135.26 E
Acre □[3]	248	9.00 S	70.00 W
Acre ≃	248	8.45 S	67.22 W
Acre — ʿAkko	132	32.55 N	35.05 E
Acre Homes	222	29.53 N	95.27 W
Acri	68	39.29 N	16.23 E
Acropolis ⊥	267c	37.58 N	23.43 E
Acrotambo, Cerro ∧	248	8.50 S	76.50 W
Acton, On., Can.	212	43.37 N	80.02 W
Acton, Ca., U.S.	228	34.28 N	118.11 W
Acton, Ma., U.S.	207	42.29 N	71.26 W
Acton, Tx., U.S.	222	32.27 N	97.41 W
Acton ◆[8]	260	51.30 N	0.16 W
Acton Bridge	262	53.16 N	2.36 W
Acton Homes	158	28.36 S	29.26 E
Acton Lake ⊜	218	39.34 N	84.45 W
Acton Turville	42	51.32 N	2.17 W
Acton-Vale	206	45.39 N	72.34 W
Actopan	234	20.16 N	98.56 W
Actopan ≃	234	19.25 N	96.20 W
Açu	250	5.34 S	36.54 W
Açuã ≃	248	7.12 S	64.11 W
Açucena	255	19.04 S	42.32 W
Acuitzio del Canje	234	19.29 N	101.20 W
Ačujevo	78	45.43 N	37.45 E
Acuña	252	29.55 S	57.58 W
Acurauá ≃	248	7.37 S	70.48 W
Acurenam	152	1.02 N	10.40 E
Acushnet	207	41.41 N	70.55 W
Acuto	66	41.47 N	13.10 E
Acvež	80	58.21 N	47.46 E
Acworth	192	34.03 N	84.40 W
Ada, Ghana	150	5.47 N	0.24 E
Ada, Jugo.	38	45.48 N	20.08 E
Ada, Nihon	174m	26.44 N	128.19 E
Ada, Mi., U.S.	216	42.57 N	85.29 W
Ada, Mn., U.S.	198	47.18 N	96.31 W
Ada, Oh., U.S.	216	40.46 N	83.49 W
Ada, Ok., U.S.	196	34.46 N	96.40 W
Ada, Mount ∧	180	56.41 N	134.41 W
Adaba	144	7.00 N	39.24 E
A-da-Beja	266c	38.47 N	9.14 W
ʿAdabīyah, Ra's ➤	142	29.52 N	32.30 E
Adachi ◆[8]	268	35.45 N	139.48 E
Adachi-yama ∧	96	33.51 N	130.55 E
Adado, Ras ➤	144	11.20 N	48.40 E
Adâfer el Abioḍ ◆[1]	150	19.30 N	10.00 W
Adai	272c	19.01 N	73.08 E
Adailo	144	14.29 N	40.52 E
Adainville	261	48.43 N	1.39 E
Adair, Ia., U.S.	198	41.22 N	94.19 W
Adair, Ok., U.S.	196	36.26 N	95.16 W
Adair □[6]	219	40.08 N	92.22 W
Adair, Bahía de ⊂	200	31.30 N	113.48 W
Adair, Cape ➤	176	71.24 N	71.13 W
Adairsville	192	34.22 N	84.56 W
Adairville	194	36.40 N	86.51 W
Adaja ≃	34	41.32 N	4.52 W
Adajevka	86	51.47 N	62.06 E
Adak, Ross.	24	66.30 N	59.38 E
Adak, Ak., U.S.	180	51.54 N	176.35 W
Adaka-shima I	174m	26.45 N	128.20 E
Adak Island I	180	51.45 N	176.40 W
Adaklı	130	39.14 N	40.30 E
Ådalen ∨	26	63.10 N	17.16 E
Ādam	118	22.24 N	57.32 E
Adam, Mount ∧	254	51.36 S	59.55 W
Adamantina	255	21.42 S	51.04 W
Adamaoua ⋏	152	7.00 N	12.00 E
Adamawa — Adamaoua ⋏	152	7.00 N	12.00 E
Adamclisi	38	44.05 N	27.57 E
Adamello ⋏	64	46.10 N	10.35 E
Adaminaby	171b	36.03 S	148.43 E
Adami Tulu	144	7.52 N	38.42 E
Adamovka	86	51.32 N	59.56 E
Adamovskoje	82	54.52 N	35.57 E
Adamów	30	51.45 N	22.17 E
Ādampur	123	31.26 N	75.43 E
Adams, In., U.S.	218	39.22 N	85.33 W
Adams, Ma., U.S.	207	42.37 N	73.07 W
Adams, Mn., U.S.	190	43.33 N	92.43 W
Adams, Ne., U.S.	198	40.27 N	96.30 W
Adams, N.Y., U.S.	212	43.48 N	76.01 W
Adams, N.D., U.S.	198	48.25 N	98.04 W
Adams, Tn., U.S.	194	36.34 N	87.03 W
Adams, Wi., U.S.	190	43.57 N	89.49 W
Adams □[6], Il., U.S.	219	39.56 N	91.23 W
Adams □[6], In., U.S.	216	40.50 N	84.56 W
Adams □[6], Oh., U.S.	218	38.48 N	83.32 W
Adams □[6], Pa., U.S.	208	39.48 N	77.15 W
Adams ≃	182	50.52 N	119.35 W
Adams, Mount ∧, N.Z.	172	41.19 S	175.46 E
Adams, Mount ∧, Wa., U.S.	224	46.12 N	121.28 W
Adams Bridge ✧[2]	122	9.04 N	79.37 E
Adamsburg	279b	40.19 N	79.40 W
Adams Center	212	43.51 N	76.00 W
Adams Creek ≃	224	46.18 N	121.40 W
Adams Lake ⊜	182	51.13 N	119.33 W
Adams Mills	214	40.09 N	81.57 W
Adams National Historic Site ⊥	283	42.15 N	71.01 W
Adams Park	216	42.08 N	85.29 W
Adams Park ♠	275b	43.48 N	79.09 W
Adams Peak ∧	122	6.48 N	80.30 E
Adams Rock I[2]	174e	25.04 S	130.05 W
Adamston	208	40.02 N	74.05 W
Adamstown, Austl.	170	32.56 S	151.44 E
Adamstown, Pit.	174e	25.04 S	130.05 W
Adamstown, Md., U.S.	208	39.18 N	77.28 W
Adamstown, Pa., U.S.	208	40.14 N	76.03 W
Adamsville, P.Q., Can.	206	45.17 N	72.47 W
Adamsville, Mi., U.S.	216	41.47 N	86.00 W
Adamsville, Oh., U.S.	214	40.04 N	81.53 W
Adamsville, Pa., U.S.	214	41.31 N	80.22 W
Adamsville, Tn., U.S.	194	35.14 N	88.23 W
ʿAdan (Aden)	144	12.45 N	45.12 E
Adana	130	37.01 N	35.18 E
Adana □[4]	130	37.20 N	35.45 E
Adanero	34	40.56 N	4.36 W
Adapazarı	130	40.46 N	30.24 E
Adarama	140	17.05 N	34.54 E
Adare	48	52.34 N	8.48 W
Adare, Cape ➤	9	71.17 S	170.14 E
Adar Gwagwa, Jabal ∧	140	22.15 N	35.20 E
Adarot	140	17.50 N	36.07 E
Adaševo	80	53.56 N	44.19 E
Adauli	272c	19.06 N	73.02 E
Adaut	164	8.08 S	131.07 E
Adavale	166	25.55 S	144.36 E
Adda ≃, It.	36	45.08 N	9.53 E
Adda ≃, Sūd.	140	9.51 N	24.50 E
Aḍ-Ḍabʿah	140	31.02 N	28.26 E
Ad-Dabbah	140	18.03 N	30.57 E
Ad-Dafīnah	128	23.18 N	41.58 E
Aḍ-Ḍafrah ◆[1]	128	23.25 N	53.25 E
Ad-Dahnā' ◆[2]	128	24.30 N	48.10 E
Ad-Daljamūn	142	30.48 N	30.50 E
Ad-Damazin	140	11.49 N	34.23 E
Ad-Dāmir	140	17.35 N	33.58 E
Ad-Dammām	128	26.26 N	50.07 E
Ad-Dāmūr	132	33.44 N	35.27 E
Ad-Dānā	130	36.13 N	36.46 E
Ad-Daqahlīyah □[4]	142	31.10 N	31.30 E
Ad-Darb	144	17.43 N	42.15 E
Ad-Dawādimī	128	24.28 N	44.18 E
Ad-Dawḥah (Doha)	128	25.17 N	51.32 E
Ad-Dayr, Miṣr	140	25.20 N	32.35 E
Ad-Dayr, Miṣr	142	30.20 N	31.16 E
Adderbury	42	52.00 N	1.17 W
Ad-Dibdibah ◆[1]	128	28.00 N	46.30 E
Addicks	222	29.47 N	95.39 W
Addicks Reservoir ⊜[1]	222	29.49 N	95.40 W
Addieville	219	38.23 N	89.29 W
Aḍ-Ḍiffah (Libyan Plateau) ⋏[1]	140	30.30 N	25.30 E
Ad-Dilam	128	23.59 N	47.12 E
Ad-Dilinjāt	142	30.50 N	30.30 E
Ad-Dīmās	132	33.35 N	36.05 E
Addingham	44	53.57 N	1.53 W
Addington	260	51.18 N	0.23 E
Addis	194	30.21 N	91.15 W
Addis Ababa — Adis Abeba	144	9.02 N	38.42 E
Addison, Il., U.S.	216	41.55 N	87.59 W
Addison, Mi., U.S.	216	41.59 N	84.21 W
Addison, N.Y., U.S.	210	42.06 N	77.14 W
Addison, Tx., U.S.	222	32.57 N	96.49 W
Addison Creek ≃	278	41.51 N	87.51 W
Ad-Dīwānīyah	128	31.59 N	44.56 E
Addlestone	260	51.22 N	0.30 W
Addo	158	33.32 S	25.45 E
Addo Elephant National Park ♠	158	33.29 S	25.46 E
Ad-Du'ayn	140	11.26 N	26.09 E
Aḍ-Ḍuhayr	132	31.11 N	34.08 E
Ad-Duqqī	273c	30.04 N	31.15 E
Ad-Duwayd	128	30.15 N	42.17 E
Ad-Duwaym	140	14.00 N	32.19 E
Ad-Duwayr	132	33.23 N	35.25 E
Adébour	146	13.20 N	11.54 E
Adegem	50	51.12 N	3.29 E
Adego	144	8.58 N	49.35 E
Adel, Ga., U.S.	192	31.08 N	83.25 W
Adel, Ia., U.S.	190	41.36 N	94.01 W
Adelaida — Adelaide	168b	34.55 S	138.35 E
Adelaide, Austl.	168b	34.55 S	138.35 E
Adelaide, Ba.	240b	25.00 N	77.31 W
Adelaide, S. Afr.	158	32.42 S	26.20 E
Adelaide Airport ⊠	168b	34.58 S	138.32 E
Adelaide Island I	9	67.15 S	68.30 W
Adelaide Peninsula ➤[1]	176	68.09 N	97.45 W
Adelaide River	164	13.15 S	131.06 E
Adelanto	228	34.34 N	117.24 W
Adelbert Range ⋏	164	4.35 S	145.10 E
Adelboden	58	46.30 N	7.33 E
Adelebsen	52	51.34 N	9.45 E
Adèle Island I	160	15.32 S	123.09 E
Adelfia	68	41.00 N	16.52 E
Adélie Coast ≗[2]	9	67.00 S	139.00 E
Adelong	171b	35.19 S	148.03 E
Adelong Creek ≃	171b	35.06 S	148.02 E
Adelphi	284c	39.00 N	76.58 W
Adelphia	208	40.13 N	74.15 W
Adelphi University ʋ[2]	276	40.43 N	73.36 W
Adelsheim	56	49.24 N	9.23 E
Adelsö I	40	59.23 N	17.30 E
Adelzhausen	60	48.21 N	11.08 E
Aden, Gulf of ⊂	136	12.30 N	48.00 E
Adena	214	40.13 N	80.52 W
Aden — ʿAdan	144	12.45 N	45.12 E
Adenau	56	50.23 N	6.55 E
Adendorf	52	53.17 N	10.26 E
Adendorp	158	32.20 S	24.33 E
Ader ⋏[1]	150	14.50 N	5.15 E
Aderklaa	264b	48.17 N	16.32 E
Adéta	150	7.08 N	0.44 E
Adhāta	272b	22.52 N	88.32 E
ʿĀdhirīyāt, Jibāl al- ⋏[2]	132	30.25 N	36.48 E
Adi	154	3.24 N	30.48 E
Adi, Pulau I	164	4.18 S	133.26 E
Adiaké	150	5.16 N	3.17 W
Adi Arkay	144	13.27 N	37.57 E
Adi Dairo	144	14.23 N	38.12 E
Adieu, Cape ➤	162	31.59 S	132.09 E
Adigala	144	10.25 N	42.14 E
Adige (Etsch) ≃	64	45.10 N	12.20 E
Adigeni	84	41.42 N	42.42 E
Adigrat	144	14.17 N	39.28 E
Adıgüzel Barajı ⊜[1]	130	38.10 N	29.15 E
Adi Keyih	144	14.51 N	39.22 E
Adi Kwala	144	14.38 N	38.50 E
Ādilābād	122	19.40 N	78.32 E
Adilang	154	2.44 N	33.29 E
Adilcevaz	84	38.44 N	42.44 E
Adimi	89	47.20 N	138.56 E
Adin	204	41.11 N	120.56 W
Adinkerke	50	51.04 N	2.36 E
Adirondack Mountains ⋏	188	44.00 N	74.00 W
Adirondack Park ♠	188	44.00 N	74.20 W
Adis Abeba (Addis Ababa)	144	9.02 N	38.42 E
Adis Zemen	144	12.07 N	37.47 E
Adi Ugri	144	14.53 N	38.49 E
Adiwerna	115a	6.56 S	109.07 E
Adıyaman	130	37.46 N	38.17 E
Adıyaman □[4]	130	37.45 N	38.30 E
Adjan	112	2.11 N	113.12 E
Adjelman, Oued ∨	148	22.09 N	3.47 E
Adjohon	150	6.42 N	2.28 E
Adjud	38	46.04 N	27.11 E
Adjumani	154	3.22 N	31.47 E
Adjuntas	240m	18.10 N	66.43 W
Adler	78	43.27 N	39.55 E
Adler Planetarium ʋ	278	41.52 N	87.37 W
Adlershof ◆[8]	264a	52.26 N	13.33 E
Adlington	262	53.37 N	2.36 W
Adlington Hall ⊥	262	53.19 N	2.09 W
Adliswil	58	47.19 N	8.32 E
Admer, Erg d' ◆[2]	148	24.00 N	9.15 E
Admiral	184	49.43 N	108.01 W
Admiralitäts-Inseln — Admiralty Islands II	164	2.10 S	147.00 E
Admiralty Bay ⊂, St. Vin.	241h	13.00 N	61.16 W
Admiralty Bay ⊂, Ak., U.S.	180	70.53 N	155.45 W
Admiralty Gulf ⊂	160	14.20 S	125.50 E
Admiralty Gulf Aboriginal Reserve ◆[4]	164	14.40 S	125.30 E
Admiralty Inlet ⊂, N.T., Can.	176	73.00 N	86.00 W
Admiralty Inlet ⊂, Wa., U.S.	224	48.05 N	122.39 W
Admiralty Island I, N.T., Can.	176	69.30 N	101.00 W
Admiralty Island I, Ak., U.S.	180	57.50 N	134.30 W
Admiralty Islands II	164	2.10 S	147.00 E
Admiralty Mountains ⋏	9	71.45 S	168.30 E
Admont	61	47.34 N	14.27 E
Adna	224	46.38 N	123.04 W
Ado ≃	94	35.19 N	136.05 E
Adobe Creek ≃, Ca., U.S.	282	37.26 N	122.06 W
Adobe Creek ≃, Co., U.S.	198	38.05 N	103.18 W
Ado-Ekiti	150	7.38 N	5.12 E
Adogawa	94	35.20 N	136.02 E
Adok	140	8.11 N	30.19 E
Adolfo López Mateos	232	28.28 N	107.20 W
Adolfo López Mateos, Presa ⊜[1]	232	25.13 N	107.25 W
Adolfsberg	40	59.15 N	15.10 E
Adolphus Reach ʉ	212	44.05 N	76.55 W
Adonara, Pulau I	112	8.20 S	123.10 E
Ādoni	122	15.38 N	77.17 E
Ado-Odo	150	6.36 N	2.56 E
Adorf	54	50.19 N	12.15 E
Adoua, Korén ∨	150	14.37 N	6.40 E
Adour ≃	32	43.32 N	1.32 W
Adowa — Adwa	144	14.10 N	38.55 E
Adra, Esp.	34	36.44 N	3.01 W
Ādra, India	126	23.30 N	86.40 E
ʿAdrā, Sūrīy.	132	33.37 N	36.30 E
Adranga	154	2.54 N	30.26 E
Adrano	70	37.40 N	14.50 E
Adrar	148	27.54 N	0.17 W
Adrar □[4]	150	20.05 N	11.00 W
Adrar □[5]	148	26.00 N	1.00 W
Adrâr ◆[1]	134	20.30 N	13.30 W
Adraskan	128	33.39 N	62.16 E
Adrasman	85	40.38 N	69.58 E
Adré	146	13.28 N	22.12 E
Adrī	146	27.32 N	13.14 E
Adria	64	45.03 N	12.03 E
Adrian, Ga., U.S.	192	32.31 N	82.35 W
Adrian, Mi., U.S.	216	41.53 N	84.02 W
Adrian, Mn., U.S.	198	43.38 N	95.55 W
Adrian, Mo., U.S.	194	38.23 N	94.21 W
Adrian, Oh., U.S.	214	41.03 N	83.20 W
Adrian, Or., U.S.	202	43.44 N	117.04 W
Adrian, Pa., U.S.	214	40.53 N	79.32 W
Adrian, Tx., U.S.	196	35.16 N	102.40 W
Adrian, W.V., U.S.	188	38.54 N	80.16 W
Adrianople — Edirne	130	41.40 N	26.34 E
Adrianópolis	287a	22.39 S	43.30 W
Adrianovka	88	51.34 N	114.30 E
Adriatico, Mar — Adriatic Sea ▾[2]	22	42.30 N	16.00 E
Adriatic Sea ▾[2]	22	42.30 N	16.00 E
Adriatique, Mer — Adriatic Sea ▾[2]	22	42.30 N	16.00 E
Adriatisches Meer — Adriatic Sea ▾[2]	22	42.30 N	16.00 E
Adrigole	48	51.40 N	9.42 W
Adro	64	45.37 N	9.57 E
Adrogué — Almirante Brown	258	34.48 S	58.23 W
Adstock, Mont ∧	206	46.02 N	71.12 W

Name	Seite	Breite°′	Länge°′ E = Ost
Adua	164	1.55 S	129.50 E
Aduard	52	53.15 N	6.26 E
Adujevo	82	54.59 N	35.59 E
Aduku	154	2.01 N	32.43 E
A Dun ≃	110	13.24 N	108.28 E
Adur ≃	42	50.49 N	0.16 W
Adusa	154	1.23 N	28.01 E
Adutiškis	76	55.09 N	26.36 E
Advance	194	37.06 N	89.54 W
Adventure, Bahía ʉ	254	44.50 S	74.45 W
Advie	46	57.23 N	3.27 W
Advocate Harbour	186	45.20 N	64.47 W
Adwa	144	14.10 N	38.55 E
Adwick le Street	44	53.34 N	1.11 W
Adyča ≃	74	68.13 N	134.41 E
Adyge	84	44.19 N	41.57 E
Adygejskaja Avtonomnaja Sovetskaja Socialističeskaja Respublika □[3]	78	45.00 N	40.00 E
Adyk	80	45.48 N	45.38 E
Adžarskaja Avtonomnaja Sovetskaja Socialističeskaja Respublika □[3]	84	41.40 N	42.00 E
Adž Bogd uul ⋏	102	44.52 N	95.10 E
Adžikend	84	40.31 N	46.21 E
Adžima	89	48.08 N	139.40 E
Adzopé	150	6.06 N	3.52 W
Adz'va ≃	24	66.36 N	59.28 E
Adz'vavom	24	66.36 N	59.12 E
Ae, Water of ≃	44	55.08 N	3.27 W
Æbelø I	41	55.38 N	10.12 E
Aegean Sea ▾[2]	38	38.30 N	25.00 E
Aegerisee ⊜	58	47.07 N	8.38 E
Aegina — Aíyina I	38	37.46 N	23.26 E
Aegviidu	76	59.17 N	25.37 E
Aek Humbang	114	1.59 N	99.11 E
Aeknabara	114	1.17 N	99.45 E
Aeon Point ➤	174o	1.46 N	157.11 W
Aerhuola	89	51.01 N	120.10 E
Aerku Hu ⊜	120	30.43 N	82.55 E
Ærø I	41	54.53 N	10.20 E
Aeroflotskij	78	45.03 N	34.01 E
Aeron ≃	42	52.14 N	4.16 W
Aeronáutica, Centro de Instrucción de ʋ[2]	286d	12.09 S	77.00 W
Ærøskøbing	41	54.53 N	10.25 E
Aerqi Shan ∧	89	48.35 N	121.07 E
Aershatu	102	44.11 N	113.36 E
Aerzen	52	52.03 N	9.16 E
Aesch	58	47.28 N	7.36 E
Aeschi	58	46.40 N	7.42 E
Aetna	182	49.08 N	113.15 W
Afaahiti	174s	17.43 S	149.19 W
Afadé	146	12.14 N	14.38 E
Afadjoto ∧[2]	150	7.05 N	0.35 E
ʿAfak	128	32.04 N	45.15 E
Afan ≃	42	51.35 N	3.48 W
Afanasjevka	78	50.47 N	38.36 E
Afanasjevo, Ross.	24	58.52 N	53.12 E
Afanasjevo, Ross.	82	54.20 N	37.01 E
Afanasjevo, Ross.	82	55.18 N	36.12 E
Afanasjevskoje	86	56.49 N	58.17 E
Afándou	38	36.17 N	28.10 E
Afar	148	25.30 N	8.22 E
Afareaitu	174s	17.33 S	149.47 W
Afars and Issas — Djibouti □[1]	144	11.30 N	43.00 E
Afaspida	272c	19.08 N	73.04 E
Afdem	144	9.28 N	41.00 E
Afferde, Dtsch.	52	52.06 N	9.25 E
Afferde, Dtsch.	263	51.34 N	7.39 E
Afféry	150	6.19 N	3.57 W
Affi	64	45.33 N	10.46 E
Affing	58	48.27 N	10.58 E
Afflisses, Oued ∨	148	28.29 N	1.09 E
Affoltern am Albis	58	47.17 N	8.27 E
Affori ◆[8]	266b	45.31 N	9.10 E
Affric ≃	46	57.19 N	4.50 W
Affric, Glen ∨	46	57.17 N	4.56 W
Affton	219	38.33 N	90.19 W
Afghānestān — Afghanistan □[1]	118	33.00 N	65.00 E
Afghanistan (Afghānestān) □[1]	118	33.00 N	65.00 E
Afgooye	144	2.09 N	45.07 E
Afia	114	1.23 N	97.32 E
ʿAfīf	128	23.55 N	42.56 E
Afikpo	150	5.53 N	7.56 E
Afipskij	78	44.55 N	38.50 E
Afiqim	132	32.40 N	35.35 E
Åfjord	26	63.58 N	10.12 E
Aflao	150	6.05 N	1.08 E
Aflenz Kurort	61	47.32 N	15.14 E
Aflou	148	34.07 N	2.06 E
Afmadow	144	0.31 N	42.04 E
Afodo	144	10.14 N	34.39 E
Afogados da Ingazeira	250	7.45 S	37.39 W
Afognak Island I	180	58.15 N	152.30 W
Afollé ⋏[2]	150	16.55 N	10.25 W
Afonicha	24	68.13 N	53.17 E
Afono Bay ⊂	174u	14.15 S	170.39 W
Afonso Arinos	256	22.00 S	43.20 W
Afonso Bezerra	250	5.30 S	36.30 W
Afonso Claudio	255	20.05 S	41.08 W
Afonsos, Campo dos ■	287a	22.53 S	43.23 W
Afragola	68	40.55 N	14.18 E
Afram ≃	150	7.00 N	0.52 W
Afrera YeChew Hayk ⊜	144	13.17 N	40.54 E
Africa ≗[1]	4	10.00 N	22.00 E
Africa ≗[1]	10	10.00 N	22.00 E
Africa del Sur — South Africa □[1]	156	30.00 S	26.00 E
Africo	68	38.04 N	15.59 E
Afrika — Africa ≗[1]	10	10.00 N	22.00 E
Afrikanda	24	67.25 N	32.43 E
ʿAfrīn	130	36.31 N	36.52 E
ʿAfrīn ≃	130	36.22 N	36.28 E
Afrique — Africa ≗[1]	10	10.00 N	22.00 E
Afrique du Sud (République d') — South Africa □[1]	156	30.00 S	26.00 E
Afritz	64	46.43 N	13.48 E
Afşin	130	38.15 N	36.55 E
Afsluitdijk ◆[5]	52	53.00 N	5.15 E
Afton, De., U.S.	285	39.49 N	75.29 W
Afton, Ia., U.S.	194	41.01 N	94.11 W
Afton, N.Y., U.S.	210	42.13 N	75.31 W
Afton, Ok., U.S.	196	36.41 N	94.57 W
Afton, Wi., U.S.	216	42.36 N	89.04 W
Afton, Wy., U.S.	200	42.43 N	110.55 W
Aftout ◆[1]	148	26.40 N	3.48 W
Afuá	250	0.10 S	50.23 W
ʿAfula	132	32.36 N	35.17 E
ʿAfula ʿIllit	132	32.38 N	35.20 E
Afulu	114	1.17 N	97.15 E
Afyon	130	38.45 N	30.33 E
Afyon □[4]	130	38.40 N	30.30 E
Afyonkarahisar — Afyon	130	38.45 N	30.33 E
Afzalgarh	124	29.24 N	78.41 E
Aga, Nor.	26	60.18 N	6.36 E
Aga, Ross.	88	51.12 N	115.10 E
Aga ≃	88	51.30 N	115.50 E
Agačag	85	44.03 N	71.58 E
Agačören	130	38.52 N	33.55 E
Agadez	150	16.58 N	7.59 E
Agadez □[5]	148	19.45 N	12.00 E
Agadez, Ighazer oua-n- ∨	150	17.28 N	6.26 E
Agadir	148	30.26 N	9.36 W
Agadir □[4]	148	30.40 N	8.55 W
Agâdîr, Râs ➤	148	20.34 N	16.32 W

Symbols in the index entries represent the broad categories identified in the key at the right. Symbols with superior numbers (⋏[1]) identify subcategories (see complete key on page *I · 1*).

Symbole im Register stellen die rechts im Schlüssel erklärten Kategorien dar. Symbole mit hochgestellten Ziffern (⋏[1]) bezeichnen Unterabteilungen einer Kategorie (vgl. vollständiger Schlüssel auf Seite *I · 1*).

Los símbolos incluídos en el texto del índice representan las grandes categorias identificadas con la clave a la derecha. Los símbolos con numeros en su parte superior (⋏[1]) identifican las subcategorias (véase la clave completa en la página *I · 1*).

Les symboles de l'index représentent les catégories indiquées dans la légende. Les symboles suivis d'un indice (⋏[1]) représentent des sous-catégories (voir légende complète à la page *I · 1*).

Os símbolos incluídos no texto do índice representam as grandes categorias identificadas com a chave à direita. Os símbolos com números em sua parte superior (⋏[1]) identificam as subcategorias (veja-se a chave completa na página *I · 1*).

∧ Mountain	Berg	Montaña	Montagne	Montanha
⋏ Mountains	Gebirge	Montañas	Montagnes	Montanhas
)(Pass	Paß	Paso	Col	Passo
∨ Valley, Canyon	Tal, Cañon	Valle, Cañón	Vallée, Canyon	Vale, Canhão
≍ Plain	Ebene	Llano	Plaine	Planície
➤ Cape	Kap	Cabo	Cap	Cabo
I Island	Insel	Isla	Île	Ilha
II Islands	Inseln	Islas	Îles	Ilhas
⊥ Other Topographic Features	Andere Topographische Objekte	Otros Elementos Topográficos	Autres données topographiques	Outros acidentes topográficos

ESPAÑOL

Nombre	Página	Lat.°′	Long.°′ W = Oeste
Agadyr'	86	48.17 N	72.53 E
Agafonovka	80	50.36 N	47.26 E
Agāhpur	272a	28.34 N	77.22 E
Agaie	150	9.03 N	6.18 E
Ägäisches Meer → Aegean Sea ⍑ 2	38	38.30 N	25.00 E
Agalak	140	11.01 N	32.42 E
Agalega Islands ɪɪ	138	10.24 S	56.37 E
Agal Terara ʌ	144	6.57 N	40.08 E
Agan ≃	72	61.23 N	74.35 E
Agana	174p	13.28 N	144.45 E
Agana Heights	174p	13.28 N	144.45 E
Agano ≃	92	37.57 N	139.08 E
Agapa	74	71.27 N	89.15 E
Aga Point ›	174p	13.15 N	144.43 E
Agapovka	86	53.18 N	59.28 E
Agar	120	23.42 N	76.01 E
Agara	84	42.03 N	43.49 E
Agâraktem ⍑ 4	148	23.11 N	6.20 W
Ågård	41	55.35 N	9.26 E
Agaro	144	7.50 N	36.40 E
Agartala	120	23.49 N	91.16 E
Agartu	80	49.49 N	47.06 E
Agaru	140	10.59 N	34.44 E
Agaruut	102	43.10 N	109.26 E
Agasan	272c	19.11 N	73.04 E
Agassiz	224	49.14 N	121.46 W
Agassiz, Cape ›	9	68.29 S	62.56 W
Agassiz Pool ⊜	198	48.20 N	95.58 W
Agat	174p	13.24 N	144.39 E
Agat Bay ᴄ	174p	13.24 N	144.39 E
Agate	198	39.27 N	103.56 W
Agate Beach	202	44.40 N	124.03 W
Agate Fossil Beds National Monument ♦	198	42.25 N	103.43 W
Agathonísion ɪ	38	37.28 N	27.00 E
Agats	164	5.33 S	138.08 E
Agatsuma	94	36.34 N	138.50 E
Agatsuma ≃	94	36.30 N	139.01 E
Agatti Island ɪ	122	10.50 N	72.12 E
Agattu Island ɪ	181a	52.25 N	173.35 E
Agattu Strait ʯ	181a	52.35 N	173.25 E
Agawa	96	33.34 N	133.10 E
Agawa ≃	190	47.21 N	84.38 W
Agawa Bay ᴄ	190	47.20 N	84.42 W
Agawa Canyon V	190	47.27 N	84.29 W
Agawam, Ma., U.S.	207	42.04 N	72.36 W
Agawam, Mt., U.S.	182	48.00 N	112.10 W
Agay	62	43.26 N	6.51 E
Agazzano	62	44.57 N	9.31 E
Agbaja	150	7.58 N	6.38 E
Agbede	273a	6.40 N	3.29 E
Agbélouvé	150	6.40 N	1.10 E
Agboju	273a	6.28 N	3.17 E
Agboville	150	5.56 N	4.13 W
Agboyi Creek ≃	273a	6.34 N	3.25 E
Agcawayan	116	13.46 N	120.16 E
Agdam	84	39.59 N	46.57 E
Agdaš	84	40.38 N	47.28 E
Agde	32	43.19 N	3.28 E
Agde, Cap d' ›	32	43.16 N	3.30 E
Agdžabedi	84	40.03 N	47.28 E
Agege	273a	6.37 N	3.20 E
Agejevo	82	54.10 N	36.29 E
Agematsu	94	35.47 N	137.42 E
Agen	32	44.12 N	0.37 E
Agency	190	40.59 N	92.18 W
Agency Lake ⊜	202	42.32 N	121.58 W
Ageo	94	35.58 N	139.36 E
Agepsta, gora ʌ	84	43.32 N	40.30 E
Ager ≃	60	48.05 N	13.51 E
Agerbæk	41	55.36 N	8.48 E
Agerskov	41	55.07 N	9.08 E
Agersø ɪ	41	55.12 N	11.12 E
Agery	168b	34.10 S	137.44 E
Ágfalva	61	47.41 N	16.31 E
Aggeneis	158	29.03 S	18.51 E
Agger ≃	56	50.48 N	7.11 E
Aggherar	144	4.03 N	42.40 E
Aggius	71	40.46 N	9.04 E
Aggstein ⊥	61	48.18 N	15.25 E
Aggteleki Nemzeti Park ♦	30	48.30 N	20.32 E
Āghā Jārī	128	30.42 N	49.50 E
Aghleam	48	54.08 N	10.07 W
Aghzoumal, Sabkhat ⊜	148	24.21 N	12.52 W
Agia	124	26.05 N	90.32 E
Agidingbi	273a	6.38 N	3.21 E
Agimont	56	50.10 N	4.48 E
Ağın	130	38.57 N	38.43 E
Agincourt ◆ 8	275b	43.48 N	79.17 W
Aginskij Burjatskij Avtonomnyj Okrug □ 8	88	51.00 N	114.00 E
Aginskoje, Ross.	86	55.15 N	94.55 E
Aginskoje, Ross.	88	51.06 N	114.32 E
Agira	70	37.39 N	14.31 E
Aglasterhausen	56	49.21 N	8.59 E
Ağlasun	130	37.40 N	30.32 E
Agliana	66	43.54 N	11.00 E
Agliano	62	44.47 N	8.15 E
Aglientu	71	41.05 N	9.07 E
Agly ≃	32	42.47 N	3.02 E
Agna	64	45.10 N	11.58 E
Agnadello	62	45.26 N	9.33 E
Agnes, Mount ʌ	162	26.51 S	128.59 E
Agnes Lake ⊜	190	48.13 N	91.21 W
Agnew	162	28.01 S	120.30 E
Agnew Lake ⊜ 1	190	46.22 N	81.45 W
Agnews Hill ʌ 2	48	54.51 N	5.56 W
Agnibilékrou	150	7.08 N	3.12 W
Agnije-Afanasjevskij	89	51.57 N	138.45 E
Agnita	38	45.59 N	24.38 E
Agno, Pil.	116	16.07 N	119.48 E
Agno, Schw.	58	46.00 N	8.54 E
Agno ≃, It.	64	45.15 N	11.28 E
Agno ≃, Pil.	116	16.02 N	120.08 E
Agnone	66	41.48 N	14.22 E
Agnone Bagni ◆ 8	70	37.18 N	15.06 E
Ago	92	34.20 N	136.51 E
Agogna ≃	62	45.04 N	8.54 E
Agogo, Ghana	150	6.47 N	1.04 W
Agogo, Sūd.	140	7.49 N	28.52 E
Agoo	116	16.20 N	120.22 E
Agordat → Akordat	144	15.33 N	37.53 E
Agordo	64	46.17 N	12.02 E
Agostinho Pôrto	287a	22.47 S	43.23 W
Agostitlán	234	19.33 N	100.41 W
Agou, Mont ʌ	150	6.52 N	0.46 E
Agouna	150	7.34 N	1.42 E
Agoura Hills	228	34.08 N	118.44 W
Agout ≃	32	43.47 N	1.41 E
Agoza ⊥	146	18.30 N	23.45 E
Āgra	124	27.11 N	78.01 E
Āgra Canal ≊	272a	28.34 N	77.18 E
Agrachanskij poluostrov › 1	84	43.42 N	47.36 E
Agraciada	258	33.48 S	58.15 W
Agrado	246	2.15 N	75.46 W
Agraf'novka	83	47.45 N	39.29 E
Agramonte	240p	22.41 N	81.07 W
Agram → Zagreb	36	45.48 N	15.58 E
Agrate Brianza	62	45.34 N	9.21 E
Ágreda	34	41.51 N	1.56 W
Ağrı	84	39.44 N	43.03 E
Ağrı □ 4	84	39.30 N	43.15 E
Agri ≃	68	40.13 N	16.44 E
Agri Bavnehøj ʌ 2	41	56.14 N	10.33 E
Ağrı Dağı (Mount Ararat) ʌ	84	39.42 N	44.18 E
Agrigento	70	37.18 N	13.35 E
Agrigento □ 4	70	37.27 N	13.30 E
Agrihan ɪ	108	18.46 N	145.40 E
Agrínion	38	38.37 N	21.24 E
Agrio ≃	252	38.21 S	69.43 W
Agropoli	68	40.21 N	15.00 E
Agro Pontino ◆ 1	66	41.25 N	12.55 E
Agryz	80	56.33 N	53.00 E

FRANÇAIS

Nom	Page	Lat.°′	Long.°′ W = Ouest
Agtuuganon, Mount ʌ	116	7.48 N	126.12 E
Agua, Ilha d' ɪ	287a	22.49 S	43.10 W
Agua, Volcán de ʌ 1	236	14.28 N	90.45 W
Água Branca, Bra.	250	9.17 S	37.55 W
Água Branca, Bra.	250	7.31 S	37.40 W
Água Branca, Bra.	250	5.53 S	42.38 W
Agua Brava, Laguna ᴄ	234	22.10 N	105.32 W
Agua Caliente, Méx.	232	27.27 N	108.32 W
Agua Caliente, Méx.	234	23.20 N	105.20 W
Agua Caliente Creek ≃	282	37.29 N	121.56 W
Agua Caliente Grande	232	26.31 N	108.22 W
Aguacate	240p	22.59 N	81.49 W
Aguachica	246	8.19 N	73.38 W
Água Clara	255	20.27 S	52.52 W
Aguada	240m	18.23 N	67.11 W
Aguada, Zanjón de la ≃	286e	33.30 S	70.47 W
Aguada Cecilio	254	40.51 S	65.51 W
Aguada de Guerra	254	41.04 S	68.25 W
Aguada de Pasajeros	240p	22.23 N	80.51 W
Aguadas	246	5.37 N	75.27 W
Aguadilla	240m	18.26 N	67.09 W
Água Doce	252	27.00 S	51.33 W
Agua Dulce, Méx.	234	18.08 N	94.08 W
Aguadulce, Pan.	236	8.15 N	80.33 W
Agua Dulce, Ca., U.S.	228	34.30 N	118.23 W
Agua Dulce, Tx., U.S.	196	27.47 N	97.54 W
Agua Fria ≃	200	33.23 N	112.21 W
Agua Fria Creek ≃	282	37.28 N	121.56 W
Aguaí	256	22.04 S	46.58 W
Agualeguas	232	26.18 N	99.34 W
Água Limpa	255	18.06 S	48.46 W
Agualva-Cacém	266c	38.46 N	9.18 W
Aguán ≃	236	15.57 N	85.44 W
Aguanaval ≃	232	25.28 N	102.53 W
Agua Negra	286c	10.28 N	67.01 W
Aguanish	186	50.13 N	62.05 W
Aguanus ≃	186	50.13 N	62.05 W
Aguapeí ≃, Bra.	248	15.53 S	58.25 W
Aguapeí ≃, Bra.	255	21.03 S	51.47 W
Aguapey ≃	252	29.07 S	56.36 W
Água Preta, Igarapé ≃	246	1.41 S	63.48 W
Agua Prieta	232	31.18 N	109.34 W
Aguaragüe, Serranía de ⋏	248	21.30 S	63.40 W
Aguaray	252	22.16 S	63.44 W
Aguaray-Guazú ≃, Para.	252	24.47 S	57.19 W
Aguaray-Guazú ≃, Para.	252	24.05 S	56.40 W
Aguarico ≃	246	0.59 S	75.11 W
Aguaro-Guariquito, Parque Nacional ♦	246	8.10 N	66.50 W
Aguaruto	232	24.47 N	107.29 W
Aguas ≃	34	37.09 N	1.49 W
Águas, Serra das ʌ	256	21.55 S	45.25 W
Aguasabon ≃	190	48.46 N	87.07 W
Águas Belas	250	9.07 S	37.07 W
Aguas Buenas	240m	18.15 N	66.06 W
Aguascalientes, Méx.	200	32.18 N	115.10 W
Aguascalientes, Méx.	234	21.53 N	102.18 W
Aguascalientes □ 3	234	22.00 N	102.30 W
Aguascalientes, Río de ≃	234	21.23 N	102.28 W
Aguas Corrientes	258	34.31 S	56.24 W
Águas da Prata	256	21.56 S	46.43 W
Águas de Contendas	256	21.54 S	45.01 W
Águas de Lindóia	256	22.29 S	46.39 W
Águas Formosas	255	17.05 S	40.57 W
Aguasvivas ≃	34	41.20 N	0.25 W
Agua Tibia ʌ	228	33.24 N	116.59 W
Água Vermelha, Reprêsa de ⊜ 1	255	20.00 S	50.00 W
Agua-Viva	256	21.41 S	42.33 W
Aguayo	252	31.40 S	65.54 W
Aguaytía ≃	248	8.08 S	74.37 W
Agua Zarca	200	31.10 N	110.59 W
Agu Bay ᴄ	176	70.18 N	86.30 W
Agudos	255	22.28 S	49.00 W
Águeda	34	40.34 N	8.27 W
Águeda ≃	34	41.02 N	6.56 W
Aguelhok	150	19.28 N	0.52 E
Aguema	152	12.03 S	21.49 E
Aguenier, Lac ⊜	186	50.43 N	68.13 W
Agugliano	66	43.32 N	13.23 E
Agui	94	34.55 N	136.55 E
Aguié	150	13.30 N	7.47 E
Aguijan ɪ	108	14.51 N	145.34 E
Aguila	200	33.56 N	113.10 W
Aguilar, Esp.	34	37.31 N	4.39 W
Aguilar, Co., U.S.	198	37.24 N	104.39 W
Aguilares, Arg.	252	27.26 S	65.37 W
Aguilares, El Sal.	236	13.58 N	89.12 W
Águilas	34	37.24 N	1.35 W
Aguililla	234	18.44 N	102.44 W
Aguirre ≃	246	8.28 N	61.02 W
Aguirre, Arroyo ≃	288	34.46 S	58.35 W
Aguirre, Bahía ᴄ	254	54.57 S	65.50 W
Aguit	102	41.52 N	112.56 E
Aguita Zarc	234	23.10 N	104.28 W
Aguja, Cerro ʌ	254	42.11 S	71.51 W
Aguja, Punta ›	248	5.48 S	81.06 W
Aguja Point ›	116	12.42 N	123.23 E
Agujas, Cabo de las → Agulhas, Cape ›	158	34.52 S	20.00 E
Agujereada, Punta ›	240m	18.31 N	67.08 W
Agujita	196	27.53 N	101.09 W
Agul ≃	88	55.44 N	95.41 E
Agulai	144	13.41 N	39.35 E
Agulhas	158	34.50 S	20.00 E
Agulhas, Cape ›	158	34.52 S	20.00 E
Agulhas Basin ✦ 1	8	47.00 S	27.00 E
Agulhas Negras	256	22.28 S	44.27 W
Agulhas Negras, Pico das ʌ	256	22.23 S	44.38 W
Agulhas Plateau ✦ 3	10	40.00 S	26.00 E
Agung, Gunung ʌ	115b	8.21 S	115.30 E
Aguni-jima ɪ	93b	26.35 N	127.14 E
Agusan ≃	116	9.00 N	125.31 E
Agusan del Norte □ 4	116	9.00 N	125.30 E
Agusan del Sur □ 4	116	8.30 N	125.40 E
Agustín Codazzi	246	10.02 N	73.14 W
Agutaya	116	11.09 N	120.56 E
Agutaya Island ɪ	116	11.09 N	120.58 E
Ağva	130	41.09 N	29.50 E
Agvali	84	42.33 N	46.06 E
Agwarra	150	10.42 N	4.35 E
Ägypten → Egypt □ 1	140	27.00 N	30.00 E
Aha	174m	26.43 N	128.17 E
Ahaggar (Hoggar) ⋏	148	23.00 N	6.30 E
Ahaggar, Tassili ta-n- ⋏ 1	148	21.00 N	6.00 E
Aha Hills ⋏ 2	156	19.45 S	21.10 E
Aha-kō ᴄ	174m	26.43 N	128.18 E
Aham	60	48.32 N	12.28 E
Ahar	128	38.28 N	47.04 E
Ahar ≃	128	38.32 N	47.31 E
Ahascragh	48	53.24 N	8.20 W
Ahaura	172	42.21 S	171.32 E
Ahaura ≃	172	42.21 S	171.31 E
Ahaus	52	52.04 N	7.00 E
Ahe ≃	263	51.13 N	7.43 E
Aheggar ʌ	148	24.43 N	5.39 E
Ahfir	148	34.57 N	2.17 W
Ahimanawa Range ⋏	172	39.00 S	176.27 E
Ahipara	172	35.10 S	173.10 E
Ahipara Bay ᴄ	172	35.10 S	173.07 E
'Āhirah	132	32.53 N	36.28 E
Ahırlı	130	37.14 N	32.08 E
Ahklun Mountains ⋏	180	59.15 N	161.00 W
Ahlat, Tür.	128	38.45 N	42.29 E
Ahlat, Tür.	130	38.45 N	42.29 E
Ahlbeck	54	53.40 N	14.11 E
Ahlem	52	52.23 N	9.40 E
Ahlen	52	51.46 N	7.53 E
Ahlenberg	263	51.25 N	7.28 E

PORTUGUÊS

Nome	Página	Lat.°′	Long.°′ W = Oeste
Ahlenmoor ◆ 3	52	53.40 N	8.45 E
Ahlhorn	52	52.54 N	8.14 E
Ahlsdorf	54	51.32 N	11.28 E
Ahmadābād	120	23.02 N	72.37 E
Aḥmadābād-e Sarjām	128	35.51 N	59.36 E
Aḥmad al-Bāqir, Jabal ʌ	132	29.36 N	35.08 E
Ahmadgarh	123	30.41 N	75.50 E
Ahmadnagar	122	19.05 N	74.44 E
Ahmadpur, India	124	23.31 N	77.13 E
Ahmadpur, India	126	23.50 N	87.42 E
Ahmadpur East	123	29.09 N	71.16 E
Ahmadpur Siāl	123	30.41 N	71.46 E
Ahmad Wāl	120	29.25 N	65.56 E
Aḥmar, Al-Baḥr al- → Red Sea ⍑ 2	136	20.00 N	38.00 E
Aḥmar, 'Erg el ◆ 2	148	23.30 N	4.54 W
Aḥmar, Jabal al- ʌ	132	29.40 N	35.09 E
Ahmar Mountains ⋏	144	9.15 N	41.00 E
Ahmedabad → Ahmadābād	120	23.02 N	72.37 E
Ahmetli	130	38.31 N	27.57 E
Ahmic Lake ⊜	190	45.37 N	79.42 W
Ahnet ⋏	148	24.58 N	2.57 E
Ahnet, Tanezrouft n- ◆ 2	148	22.15 N	1.30 E
Ahoada	150	5.05 N	6.38 E
Ahoghill	48	54.51 N	6.22 W
Ahome	232	25.55 N	109.11 W
Ahon, Tarso ʌ	146	20.23 N	18.18 E
Ahornspitz ʌ	64	47.08 N	11.56 E
Ahoskie	192	36.17 N	76.59 W
Ahousat	182	49.17 N	126.04 W
Ahr ≃	56	50.33 N	7.17 E
Ahram	128	28.52 N	51.16 E
Ahrāmāt Dahshūr (North and Bent Pyramids) ⊥	142	29.48 N	31.13 E
Ahrāmāt Maydūm (Maydūm Pyramid) ⊥	142	29.23 N	31.10 E
Ahraura	124	25.01 N	83.01 E
Ahrensbök	54	54.00 N	10.34 E
Ahrensburg	52	53.40 N	10.14 E
Ahrensdorf, Dtsch.	54	52.10 N	14.05 E
Ahrensdorf, Dtsch.	264a	52.19 N	13.12 E
Ahrensfelde	264a	52.35 N	13.35 E
Ahrgebirge ⋏	56	50.30 N	6.50 E
Ahtanum	224	46.34 N	120.37 W
Ahtanum Creek ≃	202	46.32 N	120.31 W
Ahtanum Ridge ʌ	224	46.30 N	120.50 W
Ähtäri	26	62.34 N	24.06 E
Ähtärinjärvi ⊜	26	62.40 N	24.03 E
Ähtävänjoki ≃	26	63.38 N	22.48 E
Ahtopol	38	42.06 N	27.57 E
Ahu	98	34.27 N	118.39 E
Ahuacatlán, Méx.	234	21.03 N	104.29 W
Ahuacatlán, Méx.	234	20.00 N	97.52 W
Ahuachapán	236	13.55 N	89.51 W
Ahuacuotzingo	234	17.42 N	98.56 W
Ahualulco de Mercado	234	20.42 N	103.59 W
Ahuijullo	234	19.05 N	103.05 W
Ahuijullo ≃	234	18.49 N	103.37 W
Ahumada, Méx.	204	32.30 N	115.30 W
Ahumada, Méx.	232	30.37 N	106.31 W
Ahun	32	46.05 N	2.05 E
Ahuntsic ◆ 8	275a	45.33 N	73.39 W
Ahunui ɪ 1	14	19.39 S	140.25 W
Ahuriri ≃	172	44.33 S	170.11 E
Åhus	26	55.55 N	14.17 E
Ahuzhen	98	34.27 N	118.39 E
Ahvāz	128	31.19 N	48.42 E
Ahvenanmaa □ 4	26	60.15 N	20.00 E
Ahwahnee	226	37.21 N	119.43 W
Aḥwar	144	13.31 N	46.42 E
Ahwa-ri	98	35.54 N	129.02 E
Ai ≃	98	40.13 N	124.30 E
Aialik Cape ›	180	59.42 N	149.31 W
Aiándion	267c	37.55 N	23.28 E
Aiapuá	246	4.29 S	62.04 W
Aiapuá, Lago ⊜	246	4.27 S	62.08 W
Aibag ≃	102	42.40 N	110.42 E
Aibonito	240m	18.08 N	66.16 W
Aich	64	47.25 N	13.49 E
Aichach	60	48.28 N	11.08 E
Aicha vorm Wald	60	48.41 N	13.18 E
Aichi □ 5	94	35.00 N	137.15 E
Aichi-kōgen-kokutei-kōen ♦	94	35.10 N	137.25 E
Aichi-yōsui ≊	94	34.42 N	136.57 E
Aichstetten	58	47.54 N	10.04 E
Aide ≃	42	52.10 N	1.27 E
Aidenbach	60	48.34 N	13.06 E
Aidomaggiore	71	40.10 N	8.51 E
Aidone	70	37.25 N	14.27 E
Aidong	102	24.46 N	107.21 E
Aiduma, Pulau ɪ	164	3.58 S	134.06 E
Aiea	229c	21.22 N	157.56 W
Aiello Calabro	68	39.07 N	16.10 E
Aigáleo Óros ʌ 2	267c	38.00 N	23.37 E
Aigburth ◆ 8	262	53.22 N	2.55 W
Aigen im Mühlkreis	60	48.39 N	13.58 E
Aigenmiao	89	43.36 N	120.50 E
Aigle	58	46.19 N	6.58 E
Aigle, Île à l' ɪ	275a	45.42 N	73.28 W
Aigle, Lac à l' ⊜	186	51.12 N	65.25 W
Aignay-le-Duc	58	47.40 N	4.44 E
Aigre	32	45.54 N	0.01 E
Aiguá	252	34.12 S	54.45 W
Aiguebelette, Lac d' ⊜	62	45.33 N	5.48 E
Aiguebelette-le-Lac	62	45.32 N	5.49 E
Aiguebelle	62	45.32 N	6.18 E
Aiguebelle, Réserve ♦	190	48.33 N	78.45 W
Aigueperse	32	46.01 N	3.12 E
Aigues ≃	62	44.07 N	4.43 E
Aigues-Mortes	62	43.34 N	4.11 E
Aigues-Mortes, Golfe d' ᴄ	62	43.31 N	4.03 E
Aigüestortes, Parc National d' ♦	34	42.30 N	1.01 E
Aigues-Vives	62	43.44 N	4.10 E
Aiguilles	62	44.47 N	6.52 E
Aiguines	62	43.46 N	6.15 E
Aigurande	32	46.26 N	1.50 E
Aihui (Heihe)	89	50.16 N	127.28 E
Aija	248	9.46 S	77.38 W
Aikawa, Nihon	92	38.02 N	138.15 E
Aikawa, Nihon	94	35.32 N	139.17 E
Aiken	192	33.33 N	81.43 W
Aikens Lake ⊜	184	51.12 N	95.20 W
Ailao Shan ⋏	102	24.08 N	101.25 E
Ailefroide	62	44.53 N	6.27 E
Aileron	162	22.39 S	133.20 E
Ailette ≃	50	49.35 N	3.10 E
Aileu	112	8.43 S	125.34 E
Ailimutou Shan ʌ	104	42.19 N	121.25 E
Ailingen	58	47.41 N	9.29 E
Ailinglapalap ɪ 1	14	7.23 N	168.46 E
Ailinzhuang	105	39.27 N	117.36 E
Aillant-sur-Tholon	50	47.52 N	3.21 E
Aille ≃	62	43.26 N	6.30 E
Ailly-le-Haut-Clocher	50	50.05 N	2.00 E
Ailly-sur-Noye	50	49.45 N	2.22 E
Ailly-sur-Somme	50	49.55 N	2.12 E
Ailo	164	4.50 S	151.40 E
Ailsa Craig	190	43.08 N	81.33 W
Ailsa Craig ɪ	44	55.16 N	5.07 W
Ailuk ɪ 1	14	10.20 N	169.56 E
Aim	74	58.50 N	134.12 E
Aimargues	62	43.41 N	4.12 E
Aime	62	45.33 N	6.39 E
Aimere	115b	8.50 S	120.52 E
Aimi	96	35.22 N	133.22 E
Aimogasta	252	28.33 S	66.49 W
Aimorés	255	19.30 S	41.04 W
Aimoto	270	34.59 N	135.10 E
Ain □ 5	32	46.10 N	5.20 E
Ain ≃	62	45.48 N	5.10 E
Aïn Arnat	34	36.11 N	5.19 E
Aïn Azel	34	35.49 N	5.31 E
Ainaži	76	57.52 N	24.21 E

'Aïn Belbela, Sebkha ≚	148	27.30 N	5.20 W
Aïn Benian	148	36.48 N	2.55 E
Aïn Ben Tili	148	26.00 N	9.32 W
Aïn Berda	36	36.39 N	7.35 E
Aïn Bessem	34	36.18 N	3.40 E
Aincourt	261	49.04 N	1.47 E
Aïn Defla	34	36.16 N	1.58 E
Aïn Deheb	148	34.51 N	1.33 E
Aïn Draham	148	36.47 N	8.42 E
Aine ≃	56	50.23 N	5.31 E
Aïn el Beïda	148	35.48 N	7.24 E
Aïn el Hadjel	34	35.40 N	3.53 E
Aïn el Kebira	34	36.22 N	5.30 E
Aïn Milia	148	36.02 N	6.34 E
Aino	270	34.57 N	135.10 E
Aino-shima ɪ, Nihon	96	33.59 N	130.50 E
Aino-shima ɪ, Nihon	96	33.45 N	130.23 E
Aïn Oulmène	34	35.55 N	5.18 E
Ainring	64	47.48 N	12.56 E
Ainsdale	262	53.36 N	3.02 W
Aïn Sefra	148	32.45 N	0.35 W
Ain Shams University ʊ 2	273c	30.03 N	31.17 E
Ainslie, Mount ʌ	171b	35.16 S	149.10 E
Ainslie Lake ⊜	186	46.08 N	61.12 W
Ainsworth, Eng., U.K.	262	53.35 N	2.22 W
Ainsworth, Ne., U.S.	198	42.33 N	99.51 W
Aïn Taghrout	34	36.08 N	5.05 E
Aïn Tedelès	148	36.00 N	0.18 E
Aïn Témouchent	148	35.18 N	1.08 W
Aïn Touta	148	35.23 N	5.54 E
Aintree	262	53.29 N	2.56 W
Aintree Race Course ♦	262	53.28 N	2.56 W
Aïn Wessara	148	35.27 N	2.54 E
Aïn Yagout	148	35.47 N	6.25 E
Aio	96	34.00 N	131.26 E
Aioi	96	34.48 N	134.28 E
Aiome	164	5.10 S	144.45 E
Aiora	34	39.04 N	1.03 W
Aipe	246	3.13 N	75.15 W
Aiquara	255	14.07 S	39.52 W
Aiquile	248	18.10 S	65.10 W
Aïr ⋏	150	18.00 N	8.30 E
Airabu, Pulau ɪ	112	2.46 N	106.14 E
Airai Airport ⊠	175b	7.22 N	134.33 E
Airaines	50	49.58 N	1.57 E
Airão	246	1.56 S	61.22 W
Airasca	62	44.55 N	7.29 E
Airbangis	110	0.12 N	99.23 E
Airdikit	112	2.40 S	101.15 E
Airdrie, Ab., Can.	182	51.18 N	114.02 W
Airdrie, Scot., U.K.	46	55.52 N	3.59 W
Aire	32	43.42 N	0.16 W
Aire ≃, Fr.	56	49.19 N	4.49 E
Aire ≃, Eng., U.K.	44	53.44 N	0.54 W
Aire-sur-la-Lys	50	50.38 N	2.24 E
Air Force Island ɪ	176	67.55 N	74.10 W
Airgegas	112	2.42 S	106.25 E
Airgin Sum	102	42.58 N	111.08 E
Airhaji	112	1.57 S	100.53 E
Airjamban	114	1.13 N	101.14 E
Airlie	166	20.16 S	148.43 E
Airmolek	112	0.22 S	102.17 E
Airmont	276	41.06 N	74.06 W
Airola	68	41.04 N	14.33 E
Airole	62	43.52 N	7.33 E
Airolo	58	46.32 N	8.37 E
Airor	46	57.04 N	5.46 W
Airport West	274b	37.44 S	144.53 E
Airtenang	112	3.08 S	101.43 E
Airterjun	114	1.20 N	100.27 E
Airuno	62	45.45 N	9.25 E
Airvault	32	46.50 N	0.08 W
Aisch ≃	60	49.46 N	11.01 E
Aisega	164	5.44 S	148.21 E
Aisén del General Carlos Ibáñez del Campo □ 4	254	46.30 S	73.30 W
Aisey-sur-Seine	58	47.45 N	4.35 E
Aishihik	180	61.35 N	137.30 W
Aishihik Lake ⊜	180	61.25 N	137.06 W
Ai-shima ɪ	96	34.30 N	131.17 E
Aisinaike	85	39.47 N	75.47 E
Aislingen	56	48.30 N	10.27 E
Aisne □ 5	50	49.30 N	3.30 E
Aisne ≃	50	49.26 N	2.50 E
Aisne à la Marne, Canal de l' ≊	50	49.24 N	3.55 E
Aïssa, Djebel ʌ	148	32.51 N	0.30 W
Aïssey	58	47.16 N	6.20 E
Aist ≃	61	48.14 N	14.35 E
Aisy-sur-Armançon	50	47.39 N	4.13 E
Aitana, Serra d' ʌ	34	38.44 N	0.16 W
Aitape	164	3.08 S	142.21 E
Aiterach ≃	60	48.54 N	12.38 E
Aiterhofen	60	48.51 N	12.37 E
Aith	46a	60.16 N	1.23 W
Aitkin	190	46.31 N	93.42 W
Aït-Melloul	148	30.21 N	9.31 W
Aitolikón	38	38.27 N	21.22 E
Aït-Ourir	148	31.38 N	7.42 W
Aitrach	58	47.56 N	10.05 E
Aitutaki ɪ 1	14	18.52 S	159.45 W
Ait Youssef ou Ali	34	35.13 N	3.55 W
Aiuaba	250	6.38 S	40.07 W
Aiud	38	46.19 N	23.44 E
Aiún → El Aaiún	148	27.09 N	13.12 W
Aiuruoca	256	21.58 S	44.36 W
Aiuruoca ≃, Bra.	256	21.32 S	44.26 W
Aiuruoca ≃, Bra.	256	21.42 S	44.22 W
Aiva	287a	22.42 S	43.28 W
Aiviekste ≃	76	56.37 N	25.45 E
Aix, Mount ʌ	224	46.47 N	121.15 W
Aix-en-Othe	50	48.13 N	3.44 E
Aix-en-Provence	62	43.32 N	5.26 E
Aix-la-Chapelle → Aachen	56	50.47 N	6.05 E
Aix-les-Bains	62	45.42 N	5.55 E
Aiyáleo	267c	37.59 N	23.41 E
Aiyang, Mount ʌ	164	5.05 S	141.19 E
Aiyansh	182	55.17 N	129.03 W
Aíyina	38	37.44 N	23.27 E
Aíyina ɪ	38	37.46 N	23.26 E
Aiyínion	38	40.30 N	22.33 E
Aíyion	38	38.15 N	22.05 E
Āīzawl	120	23.44 N	92.43 E
Aizhaipuzi	104	40.57 N	124.01 E
Aizpute	76	56.43 N	21.38 E
Aizu-bange	92	37.34 N	139.49 E
Aizu-wakamatsu	92	37.30 N	139.56 E
Aj ≃	86	56.08 N	57.40 E
Ajā	142	30.57 N	31.17 E
Ajā', Jabal ⋏	128	27.20 N	41.45 E
'Ajab Shīr	128	37.28 N	45.54 E
Ajaccio	36	41.55 N	8.44 E
Ajaguz	86	47.56 N	80.23 E
Ajaguz ≃	86	46.42 N	79.15 E
Ajajú ≃	246	0.59 N	72.20 W
Ajalpan	234	18.22 N	97.15 W
'Ajaltūn	132	33.58 N	35.41 E
Ajalvir	266a	40.32 N	3.29 W
'Ajamī	130	36.28 N	37.42 E
Ajan, Ross.	74	56.27 N	138.10 E
Ajan, Ross.	88	54.43 N	110.55 E
Ajan ≃	74	70.10 N	95.50 E
Ajana	162	27.57 S	114.38 E
Ajanta	122	20.32 N	75.45 E
Ajanta Range ⋏	122	20.30 N	76.00 E
Ajaokuta	150	7.28 N	6.39 E
Ajarani ≃	246	1.33 N	61.16 W
Ajasse	150	8.17 N	4.48 E
Ajasso	150	5.52 N	8.52 E
Ajat ≃	86	52.54 N	63.02 E
Ajax	212	43.51 N	79.02 W
Ajay ≃	126	23.39 N	88.08 E
Ajbas	80	47.51 N	49.37 E
Ajdābiyā	146	30.48 N	20.14 E
Ajdabul'	86	52.42 N	68.59 E
Ajdar	78	50.03 N	38.56 E
Ajdar ≃	83	48.42 N	39.13 E

Ajdarkul', ozero ⊜ 1	72	40.45 N	67.20 E
Ajdarly	86	44.32 N	65.50 E
Ajdar-Nikolajevka	83	48.58 N	38.58 E
Ajdovščina	64	45.53 N	13.53 E
Ajdyrlinskij	86	52.03 N	59.50 E
Ajegunle	273a	6.36 N	3.17 E
Ajgurka ≃	80	45.46 N	43.12 E
Ajgyrkol', ozero ⊜	80	48.15 N	52.50 E
Ajhūr al-Kubrā	142	30.18 N	31.09 E
Aji	96	34.23 N	134.08 E
Ajibar	144	10.52 N	38.40 E
Ajibarang	115a	7.25 S	109.04 E
Ajigasawa	92	40.47 N	140.12 E
'Ajīj, Wādī al- V	130	35.19 N	41.09 E
Ajijic	234	20.18 N	103.17 W
Ajil	114	5.05 N	103.05 E
Ājimganj	126	24.14 N	88.15 E
Ajimu	96	33.26 N	131.21 E
Ajipuzicun	104	42.16 N	123.33 E
Ajisu	96	34.00 N	131.22 E
Ajjer, Tassili-n- ⋏ 1	148	25.10 N	8.00 E
Ajka	30	47.07 N	17.34 E
Ajke, ozero ⊜	86	50.57 N	61.36 E
Ajkino	24	62.15 N	49.56 E
'Ajlūn	132	32.20 N	35.45 E
Ajlune	224	46.31 N	122.26 W
'Ajmah, Jabal al- ⋏	140	29.12 N	34.02 E
Ajmer	120	26.27 N	74.38 E
Ajnāla	123	31.51 N	74.48 E
Ajni	85	39.23 N	68.32 E
Ajo	200	32.22 N	112.51 W
Ajo, Cabo de ›	34	43.31 N	3.35 W
Ajok	140	9.15 N	28.27 E
Ajon, ostrov ɪ	74	69.50 N	168.40 E
Ajoya	232	24.04 N	106.22 W
Aj-Petri, gora ʌ	78	44.27 N	34.03 E
Ajrag nuur ⊜	88	48.54 N	93.28 E
'Ajramīyah, Bi'r al- ⍑ 4	142	29.39 N	31.50 E
Ajrum	84	41.13 N	44.53 E
Ajryk	86	50.30 N	76.48 E
Ajsary	86	53.18 N	71.52 E
Ajtos	38	42.42 N	27.15 E
Ajuchitlán del Progreso	234	18.09 N	100.29 W
Ajuda ◆ 8	266c	38.43 N	9.12 W
Ajusco	204	31.35 N	116.25 W
Ajusco ◆ 8	286a	19.14 N	99.12 W
Ajuta ≃	83	47.34 N	40.07 E
Ajuterique	236	14.20 N	87.43 W
Ajutinskij	83	47.46 N	40.08 E
Ajuy	116	11.10 N	123.01 E
Ajuy Bay ᴄ	116	11.10 N	123.02 E
Ajzkraukle	76	56.38 N	25.13 E
Aka ≃	92	38.54 N	139.50 E
Akaba	150	7.57 N	1.03 E
Akabane	94	34.37 N	137.12 E
Akabira	92a	43.34 N	142.03 E
Akabli	148	26.42 N	1.22 E
Akabori	94	36.22 N	139.14 E
Akademii, zaliv ᴄ	89	54.15 N	138.05 E
Akagera (Kagera) ≃	154	0.57 S	31.47 E
Akagera, Parc National de l' ♦	154	1.30 S	30.35 E
Akagi, Nihon	94	36.33 N	139.03 E
Akagi, Nihon	96	35.00 N	132.43 E
Akagi-san ʌ	94	36.33 N	139.11 E
Akaishi-dake ʌ	94	35.27 N	138.09 E
Akaishi-sammyaku ⋏	94	35.18 N	138.07 E
Akaka Falls State Park ♦	229d	19.52 N	155.09 W
Akaki Beseka	144	8.52 N	38.47 E
Akālgarh	123	32.16 N	73.49 E
Akalkot	122	17.32 N	76.13 E
Akamaruno-misaki ›	174m	26.44 N	128.09 E
Akámas, Akrotírion ›	130	35.06 N	32.17 E
Akan	92a	43.06 N	144.10 E
Akana-tōge)(	96	34.57 N	132.44 E
Akan-kokuritsu-kōen ♦	92a	43.30 N	144.15 E
Akaoka	96	33.32 N	133.43 E
Ak-Aral	86	49.10 N	90.57 E
Akaroa	172	43.48 S	172.58 E
Akaroa Harbour ᴄ	172	43.50 S	172.56 E
Åkarp	41	55.39 N	13.07 E
Akarsu, Tür.	130	37.14 N	41.04 E
Akarsu, Tür.	130	39.56 N	38.38 E
Akasaki	96	35.31 N	133.38 E
'Akasha East	140	21.05 N	30.43 E
Akashat	130	33.45 N	39.58 E
Akashi	96	34.38 N	134.59 E
Akashi ≃	270	34.38 N	134.59 E
Akashi-kaikyō ʯ	96	34.37 N	135.02 E
Akashina	94	36.21 N	137.56 E
Akatani-ko ⊜ 1	94	36.43 N	138.54 E
Akatjevo	82	54.59 N	38.45 E
Akatova	76	55.09 N	31.48 E
Akatsuka ◆ 8	268	35.46 N	139.39 E
Akatsutsumi ◆ 8	268	35.39 N	139.39 E
Akbaba ◆ 8	267b	41.09 N	29.06 E
Akbaba Dağı ʌ	130	40.12 N	40.51 E
Akbajtal	85	38.32 N	73.49 E
Akbajtal, pereval)(	85	38.32 N	73.40 E
Akbarpur, India	124	26.25 N	82.33 E
Akbarpur, India	124	24.39 N	83.58 E
Akbeit	86	51.38 N	70.02 E
Akbou	148	36.28 N	4.32 E
Akbulak, Kaz.	86	49.26 N	80.28 E
Akbulak, Ross.	86	51.01 N	55.37 E
Akbura ≃	85	40.39 N	72.36 E
Akçaabat	130	41.02 N	39.34 E
Akçadağ	130	38.21 N	37.59 E
Akçakale	130	36.41 N	38.56 E
Akcakışla	130	39.33 N	36.22 E
Akçakoca	130	41.05 N	31.09 E
Akçakoyunlu	130	36.46 N	37.38 E
Akçaova, Tür.	130	37.30 N	28.02 E
Akçaova, Tür.	130	41.03 N	29.57 E
Akçapınar	130	38.57 N	38.57 E
Akčatau	86	47.59 N	74.02 E
Akçay	130	36.36 N	29.45 E
Akçay ≃	130	37.50 N	28.15 E
Akchâr ◆ 1	150	20.00 N	14.30 W
Akči	85	44.00 N	76.20 E
Akdağ	130	40.43 N	36.00 E
Akdağ ʌ	130	39.29 N	41.54 E
Akdağmadeni	130	39.40 N	35.54 E
Akdala	86	45.02 N	74.35 E
Akdoğan	130	35.06 N	33.41 E
Ak-Dovurak	86	51.16 N	90.31 E
Akechi	94	35.18 N	137.23 E
Akehama	96	33.19 N	132.26 E
Akeley	190	47.00 N	94.43 W
Aken	54	51.51 N	12.02 E
Akeno, Nihon	94	36.15 N	140.02 E
Akeno, Nihon	94	35.46 N	138.26 E
Åker	40	59.15 N	17.05 E
Akera ≃	84	39.09 N	46.51 E
Åkerby	40	60.25 N	17.46 E
Åkersberga	40	59.29 N	18.18 E
Akershus □ 6	26	60.00 N	11.10 E
Akersloot	52	52.34 N	4.44 E
Akespe	86	46.48 N	60.31 E
Aketi	152	2.44 N	23.46 E
Aketilepa	85	39.57 N	74.03 E
Aketu-Oja	273a	6.41 N	3.23 E
Åkforsån ≃	40	58.54 N	16.28 E
Akgöl ⊜	130	38.58 N	31.48 E
Akharnaí	38	38.05 N	23.44 E
Akhḍar, Al-Jabal al- ⋏, Lībiyā	146	32.30 N	21.30 E
Akhḍar, Al-Jabal al- ⋏, 'Umān	128	23.15 N	57.20 E
Akhelóös ≃	38	38.36 N	21.14 E
Akh Gol ⊜	84	39.33 N	44.47 E
Akhiok	180	56.57 N	154.10 W
Akhisar	130	38.55 N	27.51 E
Akhmīm	140	26.34 N	31.44 E
Akhnūr	123	32.54 N	74.44 E
Akhtarīn	130	36.31 N	37.20 E
Aki, Nihon	96	33.30 N	133.54 E
Aki, Nihon	96	33.28 N	131.43 E
Aki ≃, Nihon	94	35.41 N	139.21 E

Aki ≃, Nihon	96	33.30 N	133.55 E
Akiachak	180	60.55 N	161.27 W
Akiak	180	60.55 N	161.12 W
Akiéni	152	1.11 S	13.53 E
Akima	88	53.06 N	115.44 E
Akimiski Island ɪ	176	53.00 N	81.20 W
Akimovka	78	46.42 N	35.09 E
Aki-nada ⍑ 2	96	34.05 N	132.48 E
Akıncı	130	37.10 N	40.52 E
Akıncı Burun ›	130	36.19 N	35.47 E
Akıncılar, Tür.	130	37.45 N	38.50 E
Akıncılar, Tür.	130	40.06 N	38.21 E
Akiode	273a	6.38 N	3.21 E
Åkirkeby	26	55.04 N	14.56 E
Akishima	94	35.41 N	139.22 E
Akišma ≃	89	52.08 N	132.40 E
Akita	92	39.43 N	140.07 E
Akita-heiya ≚	92	39.45 N	140.10 E
Akitan	273a	6.39 N	3.16 E
Akitipa	150	8.17 N	6.16 E
Akitkan, chrebet ⋏	88	57.05 N	109.05 E
Akitsu, Nihon	96	34.19 N	132.50 E
Akitsu, Nihon	270	34.56 N	135.06 E
Akiyama	94	35.34 N	139.05 E
Akiyoshi-dai ⋏ 1	96	34.15 N	131.15 E
Akiyoshi-dai-kokutei-kōen ♦	96	34.15 N	131.17 E
Akiyoshi-do ⩋ 5	96	34.14 N	131.19 E
Akjar	86	51.50 N	58.14 E
Akjoujt	150	19.45 N	14.23 W
Akka	148	29.22 N	8.14 W
Akkala	86	43.43 N	59.31 E
Akkani	180	65.30 N	171.10 W
Akkerman → Belgorod-Dnestrovskij	78	46.12 N	30.20 E
Akkermanovka	86	51.11 N	58.12 E
Akkerwoude	52	53.17 N	5.58 E
Akkeshi	92a	43.02 N	144.51 E
Akkışla	130	39.00 N	36.11 E
'Akko (Acre)	132	32.55 N	35.05 E
Akkol', Kaz.	85	43.25 N	70.47 E
Akkol', Kaz.	86	45.02 N	75.40 E
Akkol', ozero ⊜	85	43.24 N	70.40 E
Akkol'skij	86	52.12 N	75.05 E
Akköy	130	37.29 N	27.15 E
Akkra → Accra	150	5.33 N	0.13 W
Akkrum	52	53.03 N	5.50 E
Ak-Kul'	85	41.41 N	74.16 E
Akkuş	130	40.49 N	37.01 E
Aklan □ 4	116	11.40 N	122.20 E
Aklan ≃	116	11.44 N	122.20 E
Aklan Point ›	116	11.44 N	122.22 E
Aklavik	180	68.12 N	135.00 W
'Aklé 'Aouâna ◆ 1	150	18.00 N	5.30 W
Akmeņrags ›	76	56.51 N	21.03 E
Akmeqit	120	37.01 N	76.59 E
Akmeşe	130	40.51 N	30.12 E
Akmuz	85	41.16 N	76.09 E
Ākna	272b	22.59 N	88.21 E
Aknet, gora ʌ	86	50.51 N	75.40 E
Aknīste	76	56.10 N	25.45 E
Aknoul	148	34.43 N	3.49 W
Ako, Nig.	146	10.17 N	10.58 E
Akō, Nihon	96	34.45 N	134.24 E
Akoba	80	49.28 N	47.25 E
Akobo	140	7.47 N	33.01 E
Akobo (Akūbū) ≃	140	7.47 N	33.03 E
Akodiya	124	23.23 N	76.36 E
Akok, Cam.	152	2.46 N	10.18 E
Akok, Gabon	152	0.31 N	9.45 E
Akola	122	20.44 N	77.00 E
Akonolinga	152	3.47 N	12.15 E
Akop	140	8.21 N	29.05 E
Akor	150	14.53 N	6.58 W
Akora	123	34.00 N	72.08 E
Akordat	144	15.33 N	37.53 E
Akören	130	37.27 N	32.23 E
Akosombo Dam ◆ 6	150	6.16 N	0.03 E
Akot, India	120	21.11 N	77.04 E
Akot, Sūd.	140	6.33 N	30.03 E
Akoupé	150	6.23 N	3.54 W
Akowonjo	273a	6.37 N	3.19 E
Akpatok Island ɪ	176	60.25 N	68.00 W
Akpınar, Tür.	130	37.34 N	38.13 E
Akpınar, Tür.	130	39.17 N	33.40 E
Akqi	85	40.52 N	77.58 E
Åkrafjorden ᴄ 2	26	59.46 N	6.06 E
Akranes	24a	64.18 N	22.02 W
Åkrehamn	26	59.16 N	5.11 E
Akrítas, Ákra ›	38	36.43 N	21.54 E
Akrofuom	150	6.07 N	1.39 W
Akrokórinthos ⊥	38	37.54 N	22.56 E
Akron, Co., U.S.	198	40.09 N	103.12 W
Akron, In., U.S.	216	41.02 N	86.01 W
Akron, Ia., U.S.	198	42.49 N	96.33 W
Akron, N.Y., U.S.	210	43.01 N	78.29 W
Akron, Oh., U.S.	214	41.04 N	81.31 W
Akron, Pa., U.S.	208	40.09 N	76.12 W
Akron-Canton Regional Airport ⊠	214	40.55 N	81.27 W
Akron City Reservoir ⊜ 1	214	41.20 N	81.17 W
Akrotíri	130	34.36 N	32.57 E
Akša	88	50.16 N	113.17 E
Aksa ◆ 8	272c	19.10 N	72.48 E
Aksaj, Kaz.	80	51.09 N	53.00 E
Aksaj, Kaz.	85	43.22 N	70.12 E
Aksaj, Ross.	80	47.58 N	43.59 E
Aksaj, Ross.	83	47.15 N	39.52 E
Aksaj (Toxkan) ≃, Asia	85	40.55 N	78.16 E
Aksaj ≃, Ross.	83	47.15 N	39.53 E
Aksaj ≃, Ross.	84	43.32 N	46.51 E
Aksakovo	80	54.02 N	54.09 E
Aksaray	130	38.23 N	34.03 E
Aksarka	74	66.36 N	67.46 E
Akšatau	86	49.23 N	54.36 E
Aksaut ≃	84	43.55 N	41.42 E
Aksay	102	39.28 N	94.15 E
Aksayqin Hu ⊜	120	35.12 N	79.50 E
Akşehir	130	38.21 N	31.25 E
Akşehir Gölü ⊜	130	38.30 N	31.28 E
Akseki	130	37.02 N	31.48 E
Aksengir ≃	85	43.40 N	76.14 E
Aksenkino	80	53.59 N	53.06 E
Aksenovo	82	55.40 N	38.15 E
Aksentjevo	82	55.25 N	35.54 E
Akšij	86	47.37 N	55.56 E
Akšijrak, chrebet ⋏	85	41.20 N	74.15 E
Aksinjino, Ross.	82	55.44 N	36.59 E
Aksinjino, Ross.	82	56.02 N	38.12 E
Aks'onovo	88	58.51 N	101.43 E
Aks'onovo-Zilovskoje	88	53.04 N	117.32 E
Aksoran, gora ʌ	86	48.27 N	75.32 E
Akstafa	84	41.08 N	45.28 E
Akstafa ≃	84	41.15 N	45.26 E
Aksu, Kaz.	80	50.56 N	53.06 E
Aksu, Kaz.	86	52.28 N	71.59 E
Aksu, Kaz.	86	45.37 N	79.30 E
Aksu, Tür.	130	36.58 N	30.50 E
Aksu, Zhg.	90	41.10 N	80.20 E
Aksu ≃, Asia	85	43.22 N	73.54 E
Aksu ≃, Kaz.	86	46.20 N	78.15 E
Aksu ≃, Tür.	130	37.25 N	36.54 E
Aksu ≃, Tür.	130	36.51 N	30.54 E
Aksuart, ozero ⊜	86	51.24 N	64.28 E
Aksuat, Kaz.	86	51.32 N	64.34 E
Aksuat, Kaz.	86	47.45 N	82.40 E
Aksuat, Kaz.	86	48.16 N	83.50 E
Aksubajevo	80	54.52 N	50.50 E
Aksu-Džabaglinskij zapovednik ♦	85	42.20 N	70.35 E
Aksum	144	14.08 N	38.43 E
Aktag ʌ	120	36.45 N	84.40 E
Aktal	85	41.25 N	75.03 E
Aktanyš	80	55.43 N	54.05 E
Aktas, Kaz.	85	42.57 N	70.04 E
Aktas, Kaz.	86	48.02 N	66.21 E
Aktas, Kaz.	86	49.47 N	72.59 E
Aktas, Kaz.	86	50.06 N	76.40 E
Aktaš, Ross.	86	50.18 N	87.44 E

≃	River	Fluß	Río	Rivière	Rio	✦	Submarine Features	Untermeerische Objekte
≊	Canal	Kanal	Canal	Canal	Canal	□	Political Unit	Politische Einheit
ᒪ	Waterfall, Rapids	Wasserfall, Stromschnellen	Cascada, Rápidos	Chute d'eau, Rapides	Cascata, Rápidos	ʊ	Cultural Institution	Kulturelle Institution
ʯ	Strait	Meeresstraße	Estrecho	Détroit	Estreito	⊥	Historical Site	Historische Stätte
ᴄ	Bay, Gulf	Bucht, Golf	Bahía, Golfo	Baie, Golfe	Baía, Golfo	♦	Recreational Site	Erholungs- und Ferienort
⊜	Lake, Lakes	See, Seen	Lago, Lagos	Lac, Lacs	Lago, Lagos	⊠	Airport	Flughafen
⁝	Swamp	Sumpf	Pantano	Marais	Pântano	■	Military Installation	Militäranlage
⊓	Ice Features, Glacier	Eis- und Gletscherformen	Accidentes Glaciales	Formes glaciaires	Acidentes glaciares	◆	Miscellaneous	Verschiedenes
⍑	Other Hydrographic Features	Andere Hydrographische Objekte	Otros Elementos Hidrográficos	Autres données hydrographiques	Outros acidentes hidrográficos			

Accidentes Submarinos	Formes de relief sous-marin	Acidentes submarinos
Unidad Politica	Entité politique	Unidade política
Institución Cultural	Institution culturelle	Institução cultural
Sitio Histórico	Site historique	Sitio histórico
Sitio de Recreo	Centre de loisirs	Area de Lazer
Aeropuerto	Aéroport	Aeroporto
Instalación Militar	Installation militaire	Instalação militar
Misceláneo	Divers	Diversos

Aktaš, Uzb. 85 41.38 N 69.44 E
Aktaş Gölü ⊜ 84 41.15 N 43.12 E
Aktasty 86 50.44 N 61.43 E
Aktau 86 50.16 N 73.02 E
Aktau, gora ʌ 86 48.00 N 71.45 E
Aktepe 130 36.44 N 36.27 E
Akterek, Kaz. 85 43.22 N 75.18 E
Akterek, Kyrg. 85 42.14 N 77.45 E
Akto 85 39.08 N 75.57 E
Aktobe 85 43.13 N 67.46 E
Aktogaj, Kaz. 86 44.27 N 76.42 E
Aktogaj, Kaz. 86 48.18 N 74.58 E
Aktogaj, Kaz. 86 46.57 N 79.40 E
Aktubek 86 48.37 N 71.06 E
Akt'ubinsk 86 50.17 N 57.10 E
Akt'ubinskij 80 54.49 N 52.47 E
Aktuluk 130 39.03 N 39.32 E
Aktumsyk 86 46.40 N 57.19 E
Akt'uz 85 42.54 N 76.07 E
Aku 150 6.42 N 7.20 E
Akūbū (Akobo) ≐ 140 7.47 N 33.03 E
Akui ≐ 96 34.06 N 134.33 E
Akula 152 2.22 N 20.11 E
Akuliči Pervyje 76 53.11 N 33.13 E
Akulovo, Ross. 82 55.31 N 36.42 E
Akulovo, Ross. 82 56.05 N 38.59 E
Akumadan 150 7.24 N 1.57 W
Akune 92 32.01 N 130.11 E
Akun Island I 180 54.12 N 165.35 W
Akure 150 7.15 N 5.12 E
Akureyri 24a 65.44 N 18.08 W
Akurli 272c 19.01 N 73.08 E
Akuša 84 42.17 N 47.21 E
Akuse 150 6.06 N 0.08 E
Akuseki-jima I 93b 29.27 N 129.37 E
Akutan 180 54.08 N 165.46 W
Akutan Island I 180 54.10 N 165.55 W
Akutan Pass ⋓ 180 54.00 N 166.10 W
Akuticha 86 52.27 N 84.29 E
Akwa Ibom □3 150 4.50 N 7.50 E
Akwanga 150 8.55 N 8.23 E
Akwatia 150 6.04 N 0.49 W
Akwawa ʌ2 150 6.27 N 0.25 W
Akwaya 152 6.30 N 9.40 E
Akyab
— Sittwe 110 20.09 N 92.54 E
Akyazı 130 40.41 N 30.37 E
Akyel 144 12.33 N 37.04 E
Akyr-T'ube 85 42.59 N 72.07 E
Akyurt 130 40.08 N 33.06 E
Akžajkyn, ozero ⊜ 86 44.55 N 67.46 E
Akžal, Kaz. 86 49.13 N 81.25 E
Akžal, Kaz. 86 47.47 N 74.02 E
Akžar, Kaz. 85 43.08 N 71.38 E
Akžar, Kaz. 86 47.35 N 83.42 E
Akžaryk 86 48.34 N 75.30 E
Ål 26 60.38 N 8.34 E
Ala 64 45.45 N 11.00 E
Ala ≐ 86 42.42 N 89.12 E
Alà, Monti di ⋀ 71 40.40 N 9.14 E
Al-Ab'ādīyah 142 31.22 N 31.07 E
Alabama 210 43.06 N 78.23 W
Alabama □3, U.S. 178 32.50 N 87.00 W
Alabama □3, U.S. 194 32.50 N 87.00 W
Alabama ≐ 194 31.08 N 87.57 W
Alabama and Coushatta Indian Reservation ◆4 222 30.43 N 94.42 W
Alabaster 194 33.14 N 86.48 W
Alabat Island I 116 14.07 N 122.03 E
Al-'Abbāsah ash-Sharqīyah 142 30.32 N 31.43 E
Al-'Abbāsīyah 140 12.10 N 31.18 E
Al-'Abbāsīyah ◆8 273c 30.04 N 31.17 E
Alabino 82 55.31 N 37.01 E
Āl-'Ābis 144 18.04 N 43.10 E
Alabuga ≐ 85 41.26 N 74.41 E
Ala-Buka 85 41.23 N 71.30 E
Alaca 130 40.10 N 34.51 E
Alacahan 130 39.07 N 37.37 E
Alacalı 130 41.11 N 29.27 E
Alaçam 130 41.37 N 35.37 E
Alaçam Dağları ⋀ 130 39.20 N 28.32 E
Alacant 34 38.21 N 0.29 W
Alacant □4 34 38.30 N 0.45 W
Alaçatı 130 38.16 N 26.23 E
Alachadzy 84 43.14 N 40.18 E
Alachua 192 29.47 N 82.29 W
Alacrán, Arrecife ✦2 232 22.24 N 89.42 W
Alacranes, Presa ⊜1 240p 22.45 N 80.08 W
Aladağ 130 37.02 N 32.41 E
Aladağ ʌ, Tür. 84 40.11 N 42.49 E
Aladağ ʌ, Tür. 130 37.44 N 35.09 E
Aladağlar ⋀, Tür. 84 39.20 N 43.35 E
Ala Dağlar ⋀, Tür. 130 37.55 N 35.13 E
Al-'Adasīyah 132 32.40 N 35.37 E
Alà dei Sardi 71 40.39 N 9.20 E
Aladino 82 54.49 N 38.12 E
Aladinskij, porog ⌊ 86 58.24 N 95.29 E
Ala di Stura 62 45.19 N 7.19 E
Aladjino 82 56.21 N 37.04 E
Aladža manastir ❦1 38 43.17 N 28.01 E
Alafia ≐ 220 27.52 N 82.23 W
Alafia, South Prong ≐ 220 27.51 N 82.08 W
Alagbado 273a 6.41 N 3.18 E
Alagir 72 43.03 N 44.14 E
Alagna Valsesia 62 45.51 N 7.56 E
Alag nuur ⊜ 102 45.09 N 94.28 E
Alagoa 256 22.10 S 44.38 W
Alagoa Grande 250 7.03 S 35.38 W
Alagoa Nova 250 7.04 S 35.46 W
Alagoas □3 250 9.00 S 36.00 W
Alagoinhas 255 12.07 S 38.26 W
Alagón 34 41.46 N 1.07 W
Alagón ≐ 34 39.44 N 6.53 W
Alaguntan 273a 6.26 N 3.30 E
Alah ≐ 116 6.53 N 124.33 E
Alahanpanjang 112 1.05 S 100.47 E
Alahärmä 26 63.14 N 22.51 E
Alaior 34 39.56 N 4.08 E
Al-Ait 140 12.22 N 27.27 E
Al-'Ajamīyīn 142 29.20 N 30.43 E
Alajärvi 26 63.00 N 23.49 E
Alajku 85 40.18 N 74.25 E
Alajõe 76 59.01 N 27.26 E
Alajskaja dolina V 85 39.30 N 73.00 E
Alajskij chrebet ⋀ 85 39.45 N 72.00 E
Alajuela 236 10.01 N 84.13 W
Alajuela □4 236 10.30 N 84.30 W
Alajuela, Lago ⊜1 236 9.15 N 79.35 W
Ālājūjeh 84 38.57 N 46.41 E
Alakai Swamp ≡ 229b 22.08 N 159.35 W
Alakamisy 157b 21.19 S 47.14 E
Alakanuk 180 62.41 N 164.37 W
Alaknanda ≐ 124 30.08 N 78.36 E
Alakol', ozero ⊜ 86 46.10 N 81.45 E
Al-'Akrīshah 142 31.08 N 30.09 E
Alaktara 124 22.01 N 82.26 E
Alak'ul'a 265a 59.44 N 29.56 E
Alakurtti 24 66.57 N 30.18 E
Al-'Āl 132 32.48 N 35.44 E
Alalakeiki Channel ⋓ 229a 20.35 N 156.30 W
Al-'Alamayn 140 30.49 N 28.57 E
Al-'Alāqimah 142 30.37 N 31.38 E
Alalaú ≐ 246 0.30 S 61.09 W
Al-'Amādīyah 128 37.06 N 43.29 E
Alamagan I 108 17.36 N 145.50 E
Al-'Amārah 128 31.50 N 47.09 E
Al-'Amār al-Kubrā 142 30.21 N 31.08 E
Alamata 144 12.25 N 39.33 E
Alamdānga 124 23.46 N 88.57 E
Alameda, Esp. 34 37.12 N 4.39 W
Alameda, Ca., U.S. 226 37.45 N 122.14 W
Alameda, N.M., U.S. 200 35.11 N 106.37 W
Alameda □6 226 37.35 N 121.55 W
Alameda, Estación ◆5 286e 33.27 S 70.41 W
Alameda Creek ≐ 226 37.35 N 122.09 W
Alameda Naval Air Station ■ 226 37.47 N 122.18 W
Alamedin 85 42.54 N 74.37 E
Alamein
— Al-'Alamayn 140 30.49 N 28.57 E
Alamillo 200 31.02 N 110.35 W
Alaminos 116 16.10 N 119.59 E
Al-'Āmirīyah 142 31.01 N 29.48 E
'Alam Lek 128 37.02 N 65.57 E
Álamo, Méx. 234 20.55 N 97.41 W
Alamo, Ca., U.S. 226 37.51 N 122.02 W
Alamo, Ga., U.S. 192 32.08 N 82.46 W
Alamo, Mi., U.S. 216 42.22 N 85.43 W
Alamo, Nv., U.S. 204 37.21 N 115.09 W
Alamo, Tn., U.S. 194 35.47 N 89.07 W
Alamo ≐ 204 33.14 N 115.39 W
Alamo Creek ≐ 282 37.42 N 121.55 W
Alamo Creek, West Branch ≐ 282 37.45 N 121.55 W
Alamogordo 200 32.53 N 105.57 W
Alamogordo Creek ≐ 196 34.40 N 104.23 W
Alamo Heights 196 29.29 N 98.27 W
Alamo Indian Reservation ◆4 200 34.30 N 107.30 W
Alamo Lake ⊜1 200 34.20 N 113.30 W
Alamo Oaks 282 37.51 N 121.59 W
Alamor 246 4.02 S 80.02 W
Alamos, Méx. 196 26.25 N 100.25 W
Álamos, Méx. 232 27.01 N 108.56 W
Álamos, Río de los ≐ 196 27.53 N 101.12 W
Alamosa 200 37.28 N 105.52 W
Alamosa ≐ 200 37.22 N 105.46 W
Alamosa Creek ≐, N.M., U.S. 196 34.26 N 103.58 W
Alamosa Creek ≐, N.M., U.S. 200 33.20 N 107.21 W
Alamosa East 200 37.28 N 105.49 W
Álamos de Márquez 232 28.40 N 103.30 W
Ālampur, Bngl. 126 23.49 N 89.06 E
Alampur, India 272b 22.25 N 88.08 E
Alanäs 26 64.10 N 15.42 E
Al-'Ānāt 132 32.21 N 36.48 E
Al-Anbār □4 128 33.45 N 41.45 E
Aland 122 17.34 N 76.34 E
Åland (Ahvenanmaa) II 26 60.15 N 20.00 E
Aland ≐ 54 53.02 N 11.34 E
Åland-Inseln
— Åland II 26 60.15 N 20.00 E
Ålands hav ⊤2 26 60.00 N 19.30 E
Alandur 122 13.02 N 80.15 E
Alangalang 116 11.12 N 124.51 E
Alang-besar, Pulau I 114 2.12 N 100.39 E
Alanje 236 8.24 N 82.33 W
Alano di Piave 64 45.55 N 11.52 E
Alanson 190 45.26 N 84.47 W
Alanya 130 36.33 N 32.01 E
Al-'Anz 132 32.23 N 36.38 E
Alaotra, Lac ⊜ 157b 17.30 S 48.30 E
Alapaha 192 31.23 N 83.13 W
Alapaha ≐ 192 30.26 N 83.06 W
Alapajevsk 86 57.52 N 61.42 E
Alaplı 130 41.11 N 31.24 E
Al-'Aqabah 132 29.31 N 35.00 E
'Alaqah, Jabal ʌ 142 29.59 N 32.53 E
Alaquines 234 22.08 N 99.36 W
Al-'Arabīyah as-Su'ūdīyah
— Saudi Arabia □1 118 25.00 N 45.00 E
Alarcón 34 39.33 N 2.05 W
Alarcón, Embalse de ⊜1 34 39.36 N 2.10 W
Al-'Arīsh 132 31.08 N 33.48 E
Al-'Armah ⋀1 128 25.30 N 46.30 E
Alarobia Vohiposa 157b 20.59 S 47.09 E
Alas 115b 8.32 S 117.00 E
Alas ≐, Indon. 114 3.05 N 97.55 E
Alaš ≐, Ross. 86 51.15 N 90.54 E
Alas, Selat ⋓ 115b 8.40 S 116.40 E
Alasan 112 1.45 S 123.19 E
Alasdair, Sgurr ʌ 46 57.12 N 6.14 W
Alaşehir 130 38.21 N 28.32 E
Alashanyouqi 102 40.02 N 103.33 E
Al-'Ashārah 130 34.55 N 40.34 E
Al-Ashmūnayn 142 27.47 N 30.49 E
Alaska 216 42.50 N 85.29 W
Alaska □3 180 65.00 N 153.00 W
Alaska, Gulf of c 16 58.00 N 146.00 W
Alaska Peninsula ≻1 180 57.00 N 158.00 W
Alaska Range ⋀ 180 62.30 N 150.00 W
Al-'Assāfīyah 128 28.21 N 39.08 E
Alassio 62 44.00 N 8.10 E
Alastaro 26 60.56 N 22.55 E
Alastuey 258 34.25 S 59.13 W
Al'at, Azer. 84 39.57 N 49.25 E
Alat, Uzb. 128 39.26 N 63.48 E
Al-'Atāminah 142 27.20 N 30.50 E
Alatan'aola
— Xin Barag Youqi 88 48.41 N 116.53 E
Al-Atārib 130 36.08 N 36.49 E
Al-Aṭāwilah 142 27.14 N 31.13 E
Al-'Aṭf 142 29.39 N 31.16 E
Al-'Athāmīn ⋀ 128 30.22 N 43.40 E
Alatna ≐ 180 66.34 N 152.34 W
Alatri 66 41.43 N 13.21 E
Al-'Aṭrūn 140 18.11 N 26.36 E
Alatyr' 80 54.51 N 46.36 E
Alatyr' ≐ 80 54.52 N 46.36 E
Alausí 246 2.12 S 78.50 W
Alava, Cape ≻ 224 48.10 N 124.43 W
Alaverdi 84 41.08 N 44.39 E
Alavieska 26 64.10 N 24.18 E
Alavus 26 62.35 N 23.37 E
Alaw ≐ 44 53.18 N 4.32 W
Alaw, Llyn ⊜1 44 53.20 N 4.22 W
Alawa 150 10.20 N 6.39 E
Alāwalpur 123 31.26 N 75.39 E
Alawoona 168 34.45 S 140.30 E
Al-'Awjā' 142 30.58 N 30.32 E
Al-'Awsajīyah 128 26.49 N 41.41 E
'Ālayh 132 33.48 N 35.36 E
Al-'Ayn 128 24.13 N 55.46 E
Al-'Ayn ⊤4 140 16.36 N 29.19 E
Al-'Ayyāsh ash-Sharqī 142 31.33 N 31.13 E
Al-'Ayyāṭ 142 29.37 N 31.15 E
Alazani ≐ 84 41.05 N 46.40 E
Alazeja ≐ 74 70.51 N 153.34 E
Al-Azhar University ❦2 273c 30.03 N 31.16 E
Al'Azīzah 142 31.11 N 31.57 E
Al-'Azīzīyah, Lībiyā 146 32.32 N 13.01 E
Al-'Azīzīyah, Miṣr 142 30.29 N 31.18 E
Al-'Azīzīyah, Miṣr 273c 29.52 N 31.15 E
Al-Azraq ◆1 132 31.52 N 36.50 E
Alb ≐ 58 47.35 N 8.08 E
Alba, It. 62 44.42 N 8.02 E
Alba, Mi., U.S. 190 44.58 N 84.58 W
Alba, Pa., U.S. 210 41.42 N 76.50 W
Alba, Tx., U.S. 222 32.48 N 95.38 W
Alba □6 38 46.15 N 23.30 E
Alba, Foum de)(148 20.27 N 3.36 W
Al-Bāb 130 36.22 N 37.31 E
Albacete 34 38.59 N 1.51 W
Albacete □4 34 38.50 N 1.50 W
Albachten 52 51.55 N 7.31 E
Albacina 66 43.21 N 13.01 E
Al-Bad' 128 28.25 N 35.04 E
Al-Badārī 140 26.59 N 31.25 E
Alba de Tormes 34 40.49 N 5.31 W
Al-Badrashayn 142 29.51 N 31.16 E
Ålbæk 26 57.36 N 10.25 E
Al-Bahnasā 142 28.32 N 30.39 E
Al-Baḥr al-Abyaḍ □4 140 13.15 N 32.25 E
Al-Baḥr al-Aḥmar □4, Miṣr 142 28.45 N 32.00 E
Al-Baḥr al-Aḥmar □4, Sūd. 140 20.00 N 35.15 E
Al-Baḥrayn
— Bahrain □1 128 26.00 N 50.30 E
Albaida 34 38.51 N 0.31 W
Albairate 266b 45.25 N 8.56 E
Alba Iulia 38 46.04 N 23.35 E
Al-Bajalāt 142 31.10 N 31.37 E
Al-Bājūr 142 30.26 N 31.02 E
Al-Bakātūsh 142 31.03 N 30.48 E
Al-Balāmūn 142 30.49 N 31.26 E
Al-Balāshūn 142 30.26 N 31.26 E
Al-Ballaḥ 142 30.46 N 32.19 E
Al-Ballāṣ 140 26.01 N 32.46 E
Al-Balqā' □8 132 32.00 N 35.40 E
Al-Bālū'ah ⊜ 130 35.55 N 36.28 E
Al-Balyanā 140 26.14 N 32.00 E
Alban 32 43.54 N 2.28 E
Albanel, Lac ⊜ 176 50.55 N 73.12 W
Albanella 68 40.30 N 15.08 E
Albani, Colli ⋀2 66 41.45 N 12.45 E
Albania, Col. 246 11.01 N 72.40 W
Albania, Col. 246 1.21 N 75.57 W
Albania (Shqipëri) □1, Europe 22 41.00 N 20.00 E
Albania (Shqipëri) □1, Europe 38 41.00 N 20.00 E
Albanie
— Albania □1 38 41.00 N 20.00 E
Albanien
— Albania □1 38 41.00 N 20.00 E
Albano, Lago ⊜ 66 41.45 N 12.40 E
Albano, Monte ʌ 66 43.50 N 10.58 E
Albano di Lucania 68 40.35 N 16.02 E
Albano Laziale 66 41.44 N 12.39 E
Albany, Austl. 162 35.02 S 117.53 E
Albany, Ca., U.S. 226 37.53 N 122.17 W
Albany, Ga., U.S. 192 31.34 N 84.09 W
Albany, Il., U.S. 190 41.47 N 90.13 W
Albany, In., U.S. 216 40.18 N 85.14 W
Albany, Ky., U.S. 194 36.41 N 85.08 W
Albany, Mn., U.S. 190 45.37 N 94.34 W
Albany, Mo., U.S. 194 40.14 N 94.19 W
Albany, N.Y., U.S. 210 42.39 N 73.45 W
Albany, Oh., U.S. 188 39.13 N 82.12 W
Albany, Or., U.S. 202 44.38 N 123.06 W
Albany, Tx., U.S. 196 32.43 N 99.17 W
Albany, Wi., U.S. 190 42.42 N 89.26 W
Albany □6 210 42.39 N 73.45 W
Albany ≐ 176 52.17 N 81.31 W
Albany County Airport ⊠ 210 42.45 N 73.48 W
Albany Creek 171a 27.21 S 152.58 E
Albany Park ◆8 278 41.58 N 87.43 W
Al-Baq'ah 132 32.05 N 35.53 E
Al-Barājīl 273c 30.04 N 31.09 E
Al-Barāmūn 142 31.07 N 31.26 E
Albardón 252 31.26 S 68.32 W
Albaredo d'Adige 64 45.19 N 11.16 E
Al-Bāriḥah 132 32.34 N 35.50 E
Al-Barnūjī 142 30.56 N 30.23 E
Albaron 62 43.37 N 4.28 E
Albaron ʌ 62 45.20 N 7.07 E
Albarracín 34 40.25 N 1.26 W
Al-Barrah 128 24.55 N 45.52 E
Albarraque 266c 38.46 N 9.21 W
Al-Barshā 142 27.43 N 30.54 E
Al-Barun 140 11.44 N 33.30 E
Al-Basātīn ◆8 273c 29.59 N 31.16 E
Al-Baslaqūn 142 31.06 N 30.08 E
Al-Basqalūn 142 28.42 N 30.44 E
Al-Baṣrah (Basra) 128 30.30 N 47.47 E
Al-Baṣrah □4 128 30.20 N 47.35 E
Al-Batānūn 142 30.37 N 30.59 E
Al-Baṭḥā' 128 31.06 N 45.53 E
Al-Bāṭinah ◆1 128 23.45 N 57.20 E
Albatross Bay c 164 12.45 S 141.43 E
Albatross Point ≻ 172 38.06 S 174.41 E
Al-Batrūn 130 34.15 N 35.39 E
Al-Baṭrūnah 132 33.39 N 36.02 E
Al-Bauga 140 18.16 N 33.55 E
Al-Bawīṭī 140 28.21 N 28.52 E
Albay □4 116 13.00 N 123.40 E
Al-Bayahū 142 28.16 N 30.44 E
Al-Bayḍā (Beida), Lībiyā 146 28.22 N 18.55 E
Al-Bayḍā' (Beida), Lībiyā 146 32.46 N 21.43 E
Al-Bayḍā', Miṣr 142 31.10 N 30.05 E
Albay Gulf c 116 13.10 N 124.00 E
Albazino 89 53.23 N 124.05 E
Albbruck 58 47.35 N 8.07 E
Albegna ≐ 66 42.30 N 11.11 E
Albemarle 192 35.13 N 80.13 W
Albemarle and Chesapeake Canal ≊ 208 36.43 N 76.15 W
Albemarle Sound ⋓ 192 36.03 N 76.12 W
Albenga 62 44.03 N 8.13 E
Albens 62 45.47 N 5.57 E
Alberche ≐ 34 39.58 N 4.46 W
Alberdi 252 26.10 S 58.09 W
Alberene 192 37.53 N 78.37 W
Alberga, Austl. 162 27.12 S 135.28 E
Ålberga, Sve. 40 58.44 N 16.34 E
Alberga Creek ≐ 162 27.06 S 135.33 E
Albergaria-a-Velha 34 40.42 N 8.29 W
Alberhill 228 33.44 N 117.23 W
Alberic 34 39.07 N 0.31 W
Alberni Inlet c 182 49.07 N 124.50 W
Alberobello 68 40.47 N 17.15 E
Alberona 68 41.26 N 15.07 E
Albero Sole ʌ 70a 35.31 N 12.32 E
Albers 219 38.33 N 89.37 W
Alberschwende 58 47.27 N 9.49 E
Albersloh 52 51.52 N 7.43 E
Albert 50 50.00 N 2.39 E
Albert ≐ 171a 27.42 S 153.15 E
Albert, Lake ⊜, Afr. 154 1.40 N 31.00 E
Albert, Lake ⊜, Austl. 166 35.38 S 139.17 E
Alberta 194 32.13 N 87.24 W
Alberta □4, Can. 176 54.00 N 113.00 W
Alberta □4, Can. 182 54.00 N 113.00 W
Alberta, Mount ʌ 182 52.18 N 117.28 W
Albert Canyon 182 51.08 N 117.52 W
Albert City 198 42.46 N 94.56 W
Albert Edward, Mount ʌ 164 8.23 S 147.24 E
Albert Edward Bay c 176 69.32 N 103.00 W
Albert Falls 158 29.27 S 30.25 E
Albertfalva ◆8 264c 47.27 N 19.02 E
Alberti 252 35.02 S 60.16 W
Al'bertin 76 53.05 N 25.23 E
Albertina 256 22.12 S 46.37 W
Albertinia 158 34.13 S 21.36 E
Albertirsa 30 47.15 N 19.38 E
Albertkanaal ≊ 56 50.39 N 5.37 E
Albert Lea 190 43.38 N 93.22 W
Albert Markham, Mount ʌ 9 81.23 S 158.12 E
Albert Nile ≐ 154 3.36 N 32.02 E
Alberto, Lago
— Albert, Lake ⊜ 154 1.40 N 31.00 E
Alberto Eduardo
— Albert Edward, Mount ʌ 164 8.23 S 147.24 E
Alberton, P.E., Can. 186 46.49 N 64.04 W
Alberton, S. Afr. 273d 26.16 S 28.08 E
Alberton, Mt., U.S. 202 47.00 N 114.29 W
Albert Park ♠ 274b 37.51 S 144.57 E
Albert Peak ʌ 182 51.02 N 117.51 W
Albertshof 264a 52.42 N 13.40 E
Albertson 276 40.46 N 73.38 W
Albertson Brook ≐ 285 39.41 N 74.43 W
Albertson Brook, Blue Anchor Branch ≐ 285 39.42 N 74.49 W
Albertson Brook, Pump Branch ≐ 285 39.42 N 74.49 W
Albertville, Fr. 62 45.41 N 6.23 E
Albertville, Al., U.S. 194 34.16 N 86.12 W
Albertville
— Kalemie 154 5.56 S 29.12 E
Albestroff 56 48.56 N 6.51 E
Albettone 64 45.21 N 11.35 E
Albi 32 43.56 N 2.09 E
Albia, Ia., U.S. 190 41.01 N 92.48 W
Albia, N.Y., U.S. 210 42.43 N 73.39 W
Albiate 266b 45.39 N 9.15 E
Al Bidia 146 10.33 N 20.13 E
Albidona 68 39.55 N 16.28 E
Albignasego 64 45.21 N 11.52 E
Albin 198 41.25 N 104.05 W
Albina 250 5.30 N 54.03 W
Albina, Ponta ≻ 152 15.51 S 11.44 E
Albinea 64 44.37 N 10.36 E
Albino 62 45.46 N 9.47 E
Albion, Austl. 274b 37.47 S 144.49 E
Albion, B.C., Can. 224 49.11 N 122.33 W
Albion, Ca., U.S. 204 39.13 N 123.46 W
Albion, Id., U.S. 202 42.24 N 113.34 W
Albion, Il., U.S. 194 38.22 N 88.03 W
Albion, In., U.S. 216 41.23 N 85.25 W
Albion, Ia., U.S. 190 42.06 N 92.59 W
Albion, Mi., U.S. 216 42.14 N 84.45 W
Albion, Ne., U.S. 198 41.41 N 98.00 W
Albion, N.J., U.S. 285 39.47 N 74.56 W
Albion, N.Y., U.S. 210 43.14 N 78.11 W
Albion, Pa., U.S. 214 41.53 N 80.22 W
Albion, R.I., U.S. 207 41.57 N 71.27 W
Albion, Wa., U.S. 202 46.47 N 117.14 W
Albion, Wi., U.S. 216 42.52 N 89.04 W
Albion Airstrip ⊠ 285 39.46 N 74.58 W
Albion Park 170 34.34 S 150.47 E
Al-Biqā' □4 130 34.00 N 36.00 E
Al-Biqā' V 128 33.50 N 36.00 E
Al-Bi'r 128 28.50 N 36.19 E
Al-Bīrah 132 31.54 N 35.13 E
Al-Birīgāt 142 30.30 N 30.49 E
Al-Birk 144 18.13 N 41.33 E
Al-Birkah 146 24.54 N 10.11 E
Al-Birkah ⊤4 144 22.12 N 40.43 E
Albisola Marina 62 44.19 N 8.30 E
Albisola Superiore 62 44.20 N 8.31 E
Albizzate 62 45.43 N 8.44 E
Alblasserdam 52 51.52 N 4.40 E
Albo, Monte ʌ 71 40.32 N 9.35 E
Albocàsser 34 40.21 N 0.02 E
Albogas 266c 38.51 N 9.15 W
Alborán, Isla de I 34 35.58 N 3.02 W
Alborán Sea ⊤2 34 36.00 N 3.00 W
Ålborg 26 57.03 N 9.56 E
Ålborg Bugt c 26 56.45 N 10.30 E
Alborz, Reshteh-ye Kūhhā-ye (Elburz Mountains) ⋀ 128 36.00 N 53.00 E
Albreda 182 52.38 N 119.09 W
Albright-Knox Art Gallery ❦ 284a 42.56 N 78.53 W
Albrighton 42 52.38 N 2.16 W
Albuch ⋀ 56 48.15 N 9.50 E
Albuera 116 10.55 N 124.42 E
Albufeira 34 37.05 N 8.15 W
Ālbū Gharz, Sabkhat ⊜ 130 34.45 N 41.15 E
Al-Buḥayrah □4, Miṣr 142 30.59 N 30.12 E
Al-Buḥayrah □4, Sūd. 140 7.30 N 29.30 E
Albula ≐ 58 46.42 N 9.27 E
Al-Bunbah 146 32.24 N 23.08 E
Albuñol 34 36.47 N 3.12 W
Albuquerque, Bra. 248 19.23 S 57.26 W
Albuquerque, N.M., U.S. 200 35.05 N 106.39 W
Albuquerque, Cayos de II 236 12.10 N 81.50 W
Al-Buraymī 128 24.15 N 55.45 E
Alburg 206 44.58 N 73.18 W
Al-Burj 142 31.35 N 30.59 E
Al-Burjāyah 142 28.09 N 30.44 E
Alburno, Monte ʌ 68 40.33 N 15.17 E
Alburquerque 34 39.13 N 7.00 W
Alburtis 208 40.31 N 75.36 W
Al-Burumbul 142 29.19 N 31.14 E
Albury, Austl. 166 36.05 S 146.55 E
Albury, N.Z. 172 44.14 S 170.52 E
Albury, Eng., U.K. 260 51.13 N 0.30 W
Albury Park ♠ 260 51.13 N 0.29 W
Al-Buṣaylī 142 31.20 N 30.24 E
Al-Busayṭā' ≚ 128 29.30 N 38.45 E
Al-Buṭānah ◆1 140 15.00 N 34.40 E
Al-Buṭaynah 132 32.57 N 36.42 E
Al-Buwayḍah 132 32.28 N 36.04 E
Al-Buzūn 144 15.35 N 50.55 E
Albuzzano 62 45.11 N 9.16 E
Alby, Fr. 62 45.49 N 6.01 E
Alby, Sve. 26 62.30 N 15.28 E
Alca 248 15.08 S 72.46 W
Alcabideche 266c 38.44 N 9.24 W
Alcácer do Sal 34 38.22 N 8.30 W
Alcains 34 39.55 N 7.27 W
Alcala 116 17.54 N 121.39 E
Alcalá de Guadaira 34 37.20 N 5.50 W
Alcalá de Henares 34 40.29 N 3.22 W
Alcalá la Real 34 37.28 N 3.56 W
Alcalde 200 36.05 N 106.03 W
Alcamachi ≐ 248 16.08 S 66.50 W
Alcamo 70 37.59 N 12.58 E
Alčan ≐ 89 46.38 N 134.22 E
Alcanadre ≐ 34 41.37 N 0.12 E
Alcanar 34 40.33 N 0.29 E
Alcañices 34 41.42 N 6.21 W
Alcañiz 34 41.03 N 0.08 W
Alcântara, Bra. 250 2.24 S 44.24 W
Alcántara, Esp. 34 39.43 N 6.53 W
Alcantara, Pil. 116 12.16 N 122.03 E
Alcântara ◆8 266c 38.42 N 9.10 W
Alcantara ≐ 70 37.49 N 15.16 E
Alcántara, Embalse de ⊜1 34 39.45 N 6.25 W
Alcantarilla 34 37.58 N 1.13 W
Alcantilado 255 16.23 S 53.31 W
Alcara li Fusi 70 38.01 N 14.42 E
Alcaraz 34 38.40 N 2.29 W
Alcarrache ≐ 34 38.16 N 7.24 W
Alcatraz Island I 282 37.49 N 122.26 W
Alcaudete 34 37.36 N 4.05 W
Alcázar de San Juan 34 39.24 N 3.12 W
Alcazarquivir
— Er-Rachidia 148 31.58 N 4.25 W
Alcester, Eng., U.K. 42 52.13 N 1.52 W
Alcester, S.D., U.S. 198 43.01 N 96.37 W
Alcester Island I 164 9.35 S 152.25 E
Alcira (Gigena) 252 32.45 S 64.20 W
Alcoa 192 35.47 N 83.58 W
Alcoa Center 279b 40.33 N 79.39 W
Alcoa Lake ⊜1 222 30.34 N 97.03 W
Alcobaça, Bra. 255 17.30 S 39.13 W
Alcobaça, Port. 34 39.33 N 8.59 W
Alcobaça ≐ 255 17.32 S 39.12 W
Alcobendas 34 40.32 N 3.38 W
Alcochete 266c 38.45 N 8.58 W
Alcockspruit 158 27.55 S 30.01 E
Alcoi 34 38.42 N 0.28 W
Alcoi ≐ 34 38.59 N 0.09 W
Alcoitão 266c 38.44 N 9.24 W
Alcolea del Pinar 34 41.02 N 2.28 W
Alcolu 192 33.45 N 80.12 W
Alcomunga 234 18.25 N 97.02 W
Alconbury Brook ≐ 42 52.19 N 0.12 W
Alconchel 34 38.31 N 7.04 W
Alcony 218 40.01 N 84.04 W
Alcorcón 266a 40.21 N 3.50 W
Alcorn 194 31.52 N 91.09 W
Alcorta 252 33.32 S 61.07 W
Alcoutim 34 37.28 N 7.28 W
Alcova Reservoir ⊜1 200 42.32 N 106.45 W
Alcove 210 42.28 N 73.55 W
Alcove Reservoir ⊜1 210 42.29 N 73.57 W
Alcovy ≐ 192 33.26 N 83.50 W
Alcubierre 34 41.48 N 0.27 W
Alcúdia 34 39.52 N 3.07 E
Alcúdia, Badia d' c 34 39.48 N 3.13 E
Alcyon Lake ⊜ 285 39.44 N 75.08 W
Aldabra Island I 138 9.25 S 46.22 E
Aldama, Méx. 232 28.51 N 105.54 W
Aldama, Méx. 234 22.55 N 98.04 W
Aldama, Arroyo ≐ 286b 23.05 N 82.15 W
Aldan, Ross. 74 58.37 N 125.24 E
Aldan, Pa., U.S. 285 39.55 N 75.17 W
Aldan ≐ 74 63.28 N 129.35 E
Aldanskoje nagorje ⋀1 74 57.00 N 127.00 E
Aldbourne 42 51.31 N 1.37 W
Aldbrough 44 53.50 N 0.07 W
Aldbury 42 51.48 N 0.36 W
Alde ≐ 42 52.03 N 1.28 E
Aldea Apeleg 254 44.41 S 70.51 W

ENGLISH — Name | Page | Lat.°′ | Long.°′

Aldeburgh 42 52.09 N 1.35 E
Aldeia de Paio Pires 266c 38.38 N 9.05 W
Aldeia Nova de Santo Bento 34 37.55 N 7.25 W
Aldeia Velha 256 22.47 S 42.55 W
Aldemha 287b 23.45 S 46.53 W
Alden, Il., U.S. 216 42.27 N 88.31 W
Alden, Ia., U.S. 190 42.31 N 93.22 W
Alden, Mn., U.S. 190 43.40 N 93.34 W
Alden, N.Y., U.S. 210 42.54 N 78.29 W
Alden, Pa., U.S. 210 41.10 N 76.00 W
Alden Center 212 42.55 N 78.32 W
Aldenham 260 51.40 N 0.21 W
Aldenhoven 56 50.53 N 6.16 E
Aldenrade ◆8 263 51.31 N 6.44 E
Alder, Ben ʌ 46 56.48 N 4.28 W
Alder Creek ≐ 202 45.50 N 119.56 W
Aldergrove 224 49.04 N 122.28 W
Alder Lake ⊜1 224 46.45 N 122.15 W
Alderley Edge 262 53.18 N 2.15 W
Aldermaston 42 51.23 N 1.09 W
Alderney I 43b 49.43 N 2.12 W
Alder Peak ʌ 226 35.53 N 121.22 W
Aldersbach 60 48.36 N 13.05 E
Aldershot 42 51.15 N 0.47 W
Alderson 192 37.44 N 80.38 W
Alderton 224 47.10 N 122.14 W
Alderwood Manor 224 47.49 N 122.17 W
Aldine 222 29.54 N 95.24 W
Aldinga 168b 35.17 S 138.29 E
Aldinga Bay c 168b 35.20 S 138.25 E
Aldinga Beach 168b 35.18 S 138.27 E
Aldingen 58 48.05 N 8.41 E
Aldino 64 46.23 N 11.20 E
Aldo Bonzi 288 34.42 S 58.31 W
Aldridge 42 52.36 N 1.55 W
Aldwell, Lake ⊜1 224 48.05 N 123.34 W
Alechovščina 76 60.25 N 33.52 E
Aled ≐ 44 53.14 N 3.34 W
Aledo, Il., U.S. 190 41.11 N 90.44 W
Aledo, Tx., U.S. 222 32.42 N 97.36 W
Alefa 144 11.57 N 36.52 E
Aleg 150 17.03 N 13.55 W
Alegranza, Isla I 148 29.23 N 13.30 W
Alegre 255 20.46 S 41.32 W
Alegre ≐ 248 15.01 S 59.57 W
Alegres Mountain ʌ 200 34.09 N 108.11 W
Alegrete 252 29.46 S 55.46 W
Alej ≐ 86 52.52 N 83.36 E
Alejandría
— Al-Iskandarīyah 142 31.12 N 29.54 E
Alejandro, Isla
— Alexander Island I 9 71.00 S 70.00 W
Alejandro Roca 252 33.21 S 63.43 W
Alejandro Selkirk, Isla (Isla Más Afuera) I 244 33.45 S 80.46 W
Alejo Ledesma 252 33.37 S 62.37 W
Alejsk 86 52.28 N 82.45 E
Aleknagik 180 59.17 N 158.38 W
Aleknagik, Lake ⊜ 180 59.20 N 158.45 W
Aleksandrija 78 48.40 N 33.07 E
Aleksandrijskaja 84 43.54 N 47.08 E
Aleksandrinka 83 47.47 N 37.41 E
Aleksandro-Kalinovo 83 48.25 N 37.40 E
Aleksandro-Nevskaja 84 43.55 N 46.35 E
Aleksandro-Nevskij 80 53.28 N 40.13 E
Aleksandropol' 83 49.42 N 38.50 E
Aleksandrov 82 56.24 N 38.43 E
Aleksandrov Gaj 80 50.09 N 48.34 E
Aleksandrovka, Kaz. 80 50.47 N 52.59 E
Aleksandrovka, Kaz. 85 43.27 N 77.20 E
Aleksandrovka, Kaz. 86 53.07 N 69.50 E
Aleksandrovka, Ross. 78 46.47 N 39.01 E
Aleksandrovka, Ross. 80 52.36 N 50.37 E
Aleksandrovka, Ross. 83 47.26 N 39.13 E
Aleksandrovka, Ross. 86 56.32 N 90.47 E
Aleksandrovka, Ross. 86 52.43 N 54.17 E
Aleksandrovka, Ukr. 78 48.43 N 36.55 E
Aleksandrovka, Ukr. 78 48.57 N 32.14 E
Aleksandrovka, Ukr. 78 47.42 N 31.16 E
Aleksandrovka, Ukr. 78 46.32 N 35.29 E
Aleksandrovka, Ukr. 83 47.55 N 37.35 E
Aleksandrovka, Ukr. 83 48.05 N 37.27 E
Aleksandrovsk 83 48.35 N 39.12 E
Aleksandrovskaja, Ross. 265a 60.03 N 29.59 E
Aleksandrovskaja, Ross. 265a 59.44 N 30.21 E
Aleksandrovskij 78 51.03 N 36.44 E
Aleksandrovskij Šl'uz 86 59.26 N 89.20 E
Aleksandrovskij Zavod 88 50.55 N 117.57 E
Aleksandrovskoje, Ross. 84 44.42 N 43.00 E
Aleksandrovskoje, Ross. 86 56.44 N 85.23 E
Aleksandrovskoje, Ross. 86 60.26 N 77.50 E
Aleksandrovsk-Sachalinskij 89 50.54 N 142.10 E
Aleksandrów Kujawski 30 52.52 N 18.42 E
Aleksandrów Łódzki 30 51.49 N 19.19 E
Aleksaskino 80 50.57 N 47.42 E
Aleksejevka, Kaz. 80 50.58 N 52.25 E
Aleksejevka, Kaz. 86 53.31 N 69.30 E
Aleksejevka, Kaz. 86 51.59 N 70.59 E
Aleksejevka, Kaz. 86 47.16 N 81.34 E
Aleksejevka, Kaz. 86 48.25 N 85.40 E
Aleksejevka, Ross. 78 50.37 N 38.42 E
Aleksejevka, Ross. 80 52.35 N 51.17 E
Aleksejevka, Ross. 80 53.15 N 50.30 E
Aleksejevka, Ross. 80 53.02 N 42.46 E
Aleksejevka, Ross. 80 51.49 N 43.56 E
Aleksejevka, Ross. 80 52.18 N 48.01 E
Aleksejevka, Ross. 82 54.41 N 36.34 E
Aleksejevka, Ross. 83 47.41 N 39.54 E
Aleksejevka, Ross. 83 47.38 N 38.49 E
Aleksejevka, Ross. 86 52.30 N 79.33 E
Aleksejevka, Ross. 86 54.31 N 81.08 E
Aleksejevka, Ross. 86 55.22 N 72.03 E
Aleksejevka, Ukr. 78 47.14 N 36.32 E
Aleksejevka, Ukr. 83 49.25 N 38.46 E
Aleksejevka, Ukr. 83 49.01 N 39.11 E
Aleksejevo-Družkovka 83 48.34 N 37.36 E
Aleksejevo-Lozovskoje 78 49.24 N 40.39 E
Aleksejevo-Orlovka ◆8 83 48.04 N 38.25 E
Aleksejevo-Tuzlovka 83 47.50 N 39.24 E
Aleksejevsk 88 57.50 N 108.23 E
Aleksejevskaja 80 50.17 N 42.11 E
Aleksejevskoje 80 55.18 N 50.06 E
Aleksin 82 54.31 N 37.05 E
Aleksinac 38 43.32 N 21.43 E
Alella 266d 41.30 N 2.18 E
Alemanha
— Germany □1 30 51.00 N 10.00 E
Alemania 252 25.36 S 65.38 W
Alemania
— Germany □1 30 51.00 N 10.00 E
Alem Dağı ʌ 267b 41.04 N 29.12 E
Alemdar ◆8 267b 41.03 N 29.14 E
Além Paraíba 256 21.52 S 42.41 W
Alençon 50 48.26 N 0.05 E
Alenquer 250 1.56 S 54.46 W
Alentejo □9 34 38.00 N 8.00 W
Alenuihaha Channel ⋓ 229a 20.26 N 156.00 W
Aléoutiennes, Îles
— Aleutian Islands II 180 52.00 N 176.00 W
Alep
— Ḥalab 130 36.12 N 37.10 E
Aleppo
— Ḥalab 130 36.12 N 37.10 E
Aléria 36 42.05 N 9.30 E
Alert 16 82.29 N 62.22 W
Alert Bay 182 50.35 N 126.55 W
Alès, Fr. 62 44.08 N 4.05 E
Ales, It. 71 39.46 N 8.49 E

DEUTSCH — Name | Seite | Breite°′ | Länge°′ E = Ost

Aleşd 38 47.04 N 22.24 E
Alešino, Ross. 82 56.09 N 37.45 E
Alešino, Ross. 82 55.04 N 36.05 E
Aleški 80 51.38 N 41.46 E
Aleškovo 82 54.53 N 36.23 E
Alessandria 62 44.54 N 8.37 E
Alessandria □4 62 44.49 N 8.42 E
Alessandria del Carretto 68 39.57 N 16.23 E
Alessandria della Rocca 70 37.34 N 13.27 E
Alessano 68 39.53 N 18.20 E
Ålestrup 26 56.42 N 9.30 E
Ålesund 26 62.28 N 6.09 E
Aletschhorn ʌ 58 46.28 N 8.00 E
Alëuten
— Aleutian Islands II 180 52.00 N 176.00 W
Aleutianas, Islas
— Aleutian Islands II 180 52.00 N 176.00 W
Aleutian Basin ✦1 16 57.00 N 177.00 E
Aleutian Islands II 180 52.00 N 176.00 W
Aleutian Range ⋀ 180 59.00 N 155.00 W
Aleutian Trench ✦1 6 51.00 N 170.00 W
Aleutka 74 45.57 N 150.10 E
Alevina, mys ≻ 74 58.50 N 151.20 E
Ale Water ≐ 46 55.31 N 2.35 W
Alex 196 34.54 N 97.46 W
Alexander, Mb., Can. 184 49.50 N 100.17 W
Alexander, Il., U.S. 219 39.43 N 90.02 W
Alexander, N.Y., U.S. 210 42.54 N 78.16 W
Alexander, N.D., U.S. 198 47.50 N 103.38 W
Alexander ≐ 132 32.24 N 34.52 E
Alexander, Cape ≻ 175e 6.35 S 156.30 E
Alexander, Mount ʌ, Austl. 162 22.39 S 115.32 E
Alexander, Mount ʌ, Austl. 169 36.59 S 144.18 E
Alexander Archipelago II 180 56.30 N 134.00 W
Alexander Bay 156 28.40 S 16.30 E
Alexander City 194 32.56 N 85.57 W
Alexander Dam ⊜1 273d 26.13 S 28.25 E
Alexander Ditch ≊ 279a 41.20 N 82.05 W
Alexander Hamilton Airport ⊠ 241n 17.42 N 64.48 W
Alexander Indian Reserve ◆4 182 53.48 N 113.58 W
Alexander Island I 9 71.00 S 70.00 W
Alexander Nevsky Monastery ❦1 265a 59.55 N 30.24 E
Alexandra, Austl. 169 37.12 S 145.43 E
Alexandra, N.Z. 172 45.15 S 169.24 E
Alexandra, S. Afr. 273d 26.06 S 28.05 E
Alexandra ≐ 166 18.14 S 139.54 E
Alexandra Canal ≊ 274a 33.56 S 151.10 E
Alexandra Falls ⌊ 176 60.29 N 116.18 W
Alexandra Park ♠ 262 53.27 N 2.15 W
Alexandra Park Race Course ♠ 260 51.36 N 0.08 W
Alexandretta, Gulf of
— İskenderun Körfezi c 130 36.30 N 35.40 E
Alexandretta
— İskenderun 130 36.37 N 36.07 E
Alexandria, Austl. 166 19.05 S 136.40 E
Alexandria, Bra. 250 6.25 S 38.01 W
Alexandria, B.C., Can. 182 52.38 N 122.27 W
Alexandria, On., Can. 206 45.19 N 74.38 W
Alexandria, Rom. 38 43.58 N 25.20 E
Alexandria, S. Afr. 158 33.40 S 26.24 E
Alexandria, Scot., U.K. 46 55.59 N 4.36 W
Alexandria, In., U.S. 216 40.15 N 85.40 W
Alexandria, Ky., U.S. 218 38.57 N 84.23 W
Alexandria, La., U.S. 194 31.18 N 92.26 W
Alexandria, Mn., U.S. 198 45.53 N 95.22 W
Alexandria, Mo., U.S. 194 40.21 N 91.27 W
Alexandria, Ne., U.S. 198 40.14 N 97.23 W
Alexandria, Oh., U.S. 214 40.05 N 82.37 W
Alexandria, Pa., U.S. 214 40.34 N 78.06 W
Alexandria, S.D., U.S. 198 43.39 N 97.46 W
Alexandria, Tn., U.S. 194 36.04 N 86.02 W
Alexandria, Va., U.S. 208 38.48 N 77.02 W
Alexandria
— Al-Iskandarīyah 142 31.12 N 29.54 E
Alexandria Bay 212 44.20 N 75.55 W
Alexandrie
— Al-Iskandarīyah 142 31.12 N 29.54 E
Alexandrina, Lake ⊜ 168b 35.26 S 139.10 E
Alexandroúpolis 38 40.50 N 25.52 E
Alexis 190 41.03 N 90.33 W
Alexis Creek 182 52.05 N 123.17 W
Alexis Indian Reserve ◆4 182 53.46 N 114.30 W
Alezio 68 40.04 N 18.03 E
Alf 56 50.03 N 7.07 E
Ālfādānga 126 23.18 N 89.42 E
Al-Fahmīyīn 142 29.36 N 31.17 E
Al-Fallūjah 128 33.20 N 43.46 E
Alfambra 34 40.33 N 1.02 W
Alfambra ≐ 34 40.21 N 1.07 W
Al-Fant 142 28.46 N 30.53 E
Alfarata 208 40.39 N 77.27 W
Al-Farḍah 144 14.51 N 48.27 E
Alfaro 34 42.11 N 1.45 W
Alfarràs 34 41.49 N 0.35 E
Al-Fāshir 140 13.38 N 25.21 E
Al-Fashn 142 28.49 N 30.54 E
Alfatar 38 43.57 N 27.17 E
Alfavaca, Ilha I 287a 23.02 S 43.18 W
Al-Fāw 128 29.58 N 48.29 E
Al-Fayyūm 142 29.19 N 30.50 E
Al-Fayyūm □4 142 29.19 N 30.48 E
Al-Fāzah 144 14.08 N 43.05 E
Alfbach ≐ 56 50.03 N 7.08 E
Alfedena 66 41.44 N 14.02 E
Alfeld, Dtsch. 52 51.59 N 9.50 E
Alfeld, Dtsch. 60 49.26 N 11.33 E
Alfenas 256 21.25 S 45.57 W
Alfianello 64 45.16 N 10.10 E
Al-Fifi 140 10.03 N 25.01 E
Alfiós ≐ 38 37.40 N 21.33 E
Al-Firdān 142 30.41 N 32.20 E
Alföld ≚ 30 47.00 N 20.00 E
Alfonsine 66 44.30 N 12.03 E
Alford, Austl. 168b 33.49 S 137.49 E
Alford, Eng., U.K. 44 53.16 N 0.10 E
Alford, Scot., U.K. 46 57.13 N 2.42 W
Alfortville 261 48.49 N 2.25 E
Ålfotbreen ⊓ 26 61.45 N 5.40 E
Alfred, On., Can. 206 45.34 N 74.53 W
Alfred, Me., U.S. 188 43.28 N 70.43 W
Alfred, N.Y., U.S. 210 42.15 N 77.47 W
Alfred National Park ♠ 166 37.35 S 149.20 E
Alfredo M. Terrazas 234 21.28 N 98.51 W
Alfreton 44 53.06 N 1.23 W
Alfriston 42 50.48 N 0.10 E
Alfta 26 61.21 N 16.05 E
Al-Fujayrah 128 25.06 N 56.21 E
Al-Fuqahā' 146 27.50 N 16.22 E
Al-Furzul 132 33.52 N 35.56 E
Alga 86 49.46 N 57.20 E
Algabas, Kaz. 80 50.39 N 52.07 E
Algabas, Kaz. 86 44.41 N 78.06 E
Algabas, Kaz. 86 48.21 N 81.39 E
Algači 88 50.43 N 117.47 E
Ålgarås 40 58.48 N 14.14 E
Ålgård 26 58.46 N 5.51 E
Al-Garef 140 12.03 N 34.19 E
Algarrobal 252 28.08 S 70.39 W
Algarrobo, Arg. 252 38.53 S 63.08 W
Algarrobo, Arg. 252 31.44 S 68.18 W
Algarrobo, Chile 252 33.22 S 71.40 W
Algarrobo del Águila 252 36.26 S 67.09 W
Algarve □9 34 37.10 N 8.15 W
Algás ≐ 34 41.08 N 0.39 E
Algasovo 76 53.41 N 41.40 E
Al-Gebir 140 13.43 N 29.49 E
Algeciras, Col. 246 2.35 N 75.18 W

Symbols in the index entries represent the broad categories identified in the key at the right. Symbols with superior numbers (⋀1) identify subcategories (see complete key on page *I* · 1).

Symbole im Register stellen die rechts im Schlüssel erklärten Kategorien dar. Symbole mit hochgestellten Ziffern (⋀1) bezeichnen Unterabteilungen einer Kategorie (vgl. vollständiger Schlüssel auf Seite *I* · 1).

Los símbolos incluídos en el texto del índice representan las grandes categorias identificadas con la clave a la derecha. Los símbolos con numeros en su parte superior (⋀1) identifican las subcategorías (véase la clave completa en la página *I* · 1).

Les symboles de l'index représentent les catégories indiquées dans la légende à droite. Les symboles suivis d'un indice (⋀1) représentent des sous-catégories (voir légende complète à la page *I* · 1).

Os símbolos incluídos no texto do índice representam as grandes categorias identificadas com a chave à direita. Os símbolos com números em sua parte superior (⋀1) identificam as subcategorias (veja-se a chave completa à página *I* · 1).

	English	Deutsch	Español	Français	Português
ʌ	Mountain	Berg	Montaña	Montagne	Montanha
⋀	Mountains	Gebirge	Montañas	Montagnes	Montanhas
)(	Pass	Paß	Paso	Col	Passo
V	Valley, Canyon	Tal, Cañon	Valle, Cañón	Vallée, Canyon	Vale, Canhão
≚	Plain	Ebene	Llano	Plaine	Planície
≻	Cape	Kap	Cabo	Cap	Cabo
I	Island	Insel	Isla	Île	Ilha
II	Islands	Inseln	Islas	Îles	Ilhas
≗	Other Topographic Features	Andere Topographische Objekte	Otros Elementos Topográficos	Autres données topographiques	Outros acidentes topográficos

ESPAÑOL — Nombre · Página · Lat.°′ · Long.°′ W = Oeste
FRANÇAIS — Nom · Page · Lat.°′ · Long.°′ W = Ouest
PORTUGUÊS — Nome · Página · Lat.°′ · Long.°′ W = Oeste

Algeciras, Esp. 34 36.08 N 5.30 W
Algemesí 34 39.11 N 0.26 W
Algena 144 17.19 N 38.31 E
Alger 216 40.42 N 83.50 W
Alger, Baie d' c 34 36.50 N 3.15 E
Alger → El Djazaïr 148 36.47 N 3.03 E
Algeria (Algérie) □[1], Afr. 134 28.00 N 3.00 E
Algeria (Algérie) □[1], Afr. 148 28.00 N 3.00 E
Algérie → Algeria □[1] 148 28.00 N 3.00 E
Algerien → Algeria □[1] 148 28.00 N 3.00 E
Algermissen 52 52.15 N 9.58 E
Algés 266c 38.42 N 9.13 W
Al-Ghāb ⊜ 130 35.30 N 36.18 E
Al-Gharaq as-Sulṭānī 142 29.08 N 30.42 E
Al-Gharbīyah □[4] 142 30.45 N 31.00 E
Al-Ghāriyah 132 32.23 N 36.39 E
Al-Ghāṭ 128 26.00 N 45.03 E
Al-Ghawr V 132 31.50 N 35.30 E
Al-Ghayatah 142 30.57 N 30.06 E
Al-Ghayḍah 118 16.12 N 52.15 E
Al-Ghazālah 128 26.48 N 41.19 E
Al-Ghazālī 142 30.49 N 31.49 E
Al-Ghāzīyah 132 33.31 N 35.22 E
Alghero 71 40.34 N 8.19 E
Al-Ghurayfah 128 24.00 N 56.29 E
Al-Ghurdaqah 140 27.14 N 33.50 E
Algier → El Djazaïr 148 36.47 N 3.03 E
Algiers → El Djazaïr 148 36.47 N 3.03 E
Alginet 34 39.16 N 0.28 W
Algoa 222 29.24 N 95.11 W
Algoabaai c 158 33.50 S 25.50 E
Algodão, Ilha do I 256 23.13 S 44.36 W
Algodón ≃ 246 2.23 S 71.56 W
Algodones 200 35.22 N 106.28 W
Algodor ≃ 34 39.55 N 3.53 W
Algoma 190 44.36 N 87.25 W
Algoma Mills 190 46.10 N 82.50 W
Algona, Ia., U.S. 190 43.04 N 94.13 W
Algona, Wa., U.S. 224 47.16 N 122.15 W
Algonac 214 42.37 N 82.31 W
Algonquin 216 42.09 N 88.17 W
Algonquin Lake ⊜ 216 42.40 N 85.20 W
Algonquin Provincial Park ♠ 190 45.45 N 78.26 W
Algood 194 36.11 N 85.26 W
Algorta, Esp. 34 43.22 N 3.01 W
Algorta, Ur. 252 32.25 S 57.23 W
Alguierão-Mem Martins 266c 38.48 N 9.20 W
Al-Ḥaddādī 142 31.20 N 30.47 E
Al-Ḥaddayn 142 30.44 N 30.38 E
Al-Ḥadīthah 128 34.07 N 42.23 E
Al-Ḥadr 128 35.35 N 42.44 E
Al-Ḥaffah 130 35.35 N 36.02 E
Al-Ḥafīr Al-Fawqānī 132 33.42 N 36.28 E
Al-Ḥajālīj 140 14.36 N 31.54 E
Al-Ḥajarah ◆[1] 128 30.00 N 44.00 E
Al-Ḥajar al-Gharbī ⋏ 128 24.10 N 56.15 E
Al-Ḥajar ash-Sharqī ⋏ 128 22.45 N 59.00 E
Al Hajeb 148 33.43 N 5.13 W
Al-Ḥājir 142 30.41 N 31.49 E
Al-Ḥalfāyah 128 31.49 N 47.26 E
Al-Ḥamād ≡ 128 32.00 N 39.30 E
Alhama de Granada 34 37.00 N 3.59 W
Alhama de Murcia 34 37.51 N 1.25 W
Al-Ḥamal ◆[1] 128 23.30 N 49.45 E
Alhambra, Ca., U.S. 228 34.05 N 118.07 W
Alhambra, Il., U.S. 219 38.53 N 89.44 W
Al-Ḥamīdīyah 130 34.43 N 35.56 E
Al-Ḥammām 140 30.50 N 29.23 E
Al-Ḥamrā', Ar. Su. 128 23.57 N 38.52 E
'Al-Ḥamrā', Lubnān 132 33.42 N 35.27 E
Al-Ḥamrah 142 31.10 N 30.52 E
Al-Ḥāmūl 142 31.19 N 31.10 E
Alhandra 250 7.26 S 34.54 W
Alhandra, Mouchão de I 266c 38.54 N 9.00 W
Al-Ḥarāk 132 32.44 N 36.18 E
Al-Ḥarīq 128 23.37 N 46.31 E
Al-Ḥārrah 132 33.03 N 36.00 E
Al-Ḥarrah ⊥[9] 128 31.00 N 38.30 E
Al-Ḥarūj al-Aswad ⋏[2] 146 27.00 N 17.10 E
Al-Ḥasakah 130 36.29 N 40.45 E
Al-Ḥasakah □[8] 130 36.30 N 41.00 E
Al-Ḥasānī I 128 24.58 N 37.05 E
Alhaurín el Grande 34 36.38 N 4.41 W
Al-Ḥawāmidīyah 273c 29.54 N 31.15 E
Al-Ḥawātah 140 13.25 N 34.38 E
Al-Ḥawātikah 142 27.16 N 31.01 E
Al-Ḥawrah 144 13.49 N 47.37 E
Al-Ḥawṭah 144 15.50 N 48.27 E
Al-Ḥawwārīyah 142 30.58 N 29.41 E
Al-Ḥayy, 'Irāq 128 32.10 N 46.03 E
Al-Ḥayy, Miṣr 142 29.39 N 31.18 E
Al-Ḥayyānīyah 128 28.38 N 42.45 E
Al-Ḥayz 140 28.02 N 28.39 E
Al-Ḥībah 142 28.45 N 30.55 E
Al-Ḥijānah 132 33.21 N 36.33 E
Al-Ḥijāz ◆[1] 118 24.30 N 38.30 E
Al-Ḥillah, 'Irāq 128 32.29 N 44.25 E
Al-Ḥillah, Sūd. 140 13.27 N 27.08 E
Al-Ḥilmīyah ◆[8] 273c 30.07 N 31.19 E
Al-Hindīyah 128 32.33 N 44.13 E
Al-Hirmil 130 34.23 N 36.23 E
Al-Ḥiṣn 132 32.29 N 35.52 E
Al-Hoceïma 148 35.15 N 3.55 W
Al-Hoceïma □[4] 148 35.00 N 4.30 W
Al Hoceïma, Baie d' c 34 35.20 N 3.50 W
Alhos Vedros 266c 38.39 N 9.02 W
Alhucemas, Peñón de I 34 35.13 N 3.53 W
Al-Ḥudayb 140 13.00 N 32.50 E
Al-Ḥudaydah 144 14.48 N 42.57 E
Al-Ḥufrah 146 29.10 N 18.02 E
Al-Ḥufrah ◆[1] 128 28.40 N 38.30 E
Al-Hufūf 128 25.22 N 49.34 E
Al-Ḥulwah 128 23.27 N 46.47 E
Al-Ḥumayshah 144 13.41 N 45.52 E
Al-Ḥumrah ◆[1] 128 23.20 N 54.30 E
Al-Ḥuṣayḥiṣah 140 14.44 N 33.18 E
Al-Ḥusaynīyah 142 30.52 N 31.55 E
Al-Ḥusaynīyah ⊤[4] 144 17.48 N 44.27 E
Al-Ḥuwaylizah 132 33.02 N 35.51 E
Al-Ḥuwaymī 144 14.05 N 47.44 E
Al-Ḥuwayyiṭ 128 25.36 N 40.23 E
Alì 70 38.02 N 15.25 E
Ali ◆[8] 272a 28.31 N 77.18 E
'Alī, As-Sadd al- (Aswān High Dam) ◆[6] 140 23.58 N 32.52 E
Alía, Esp. 34 39.27 N 5.13 W
Alia, It. 70 37.47 N 13.43 E
Aliabad, Azer. 84 41.29 N 46.37 E
'Alīābād, Īrān 128 36.57 N 54.59 E
Alīābād, Pāk. 123 36.18 N 74.37 E
Aliade 150 7.16 N 8.28 E
Aliaga, Esp. 34 40.40 N 0.42 W
Aliağa, Tür. 130 38.48 N 26.59 E
Aliákmon ≃ 38 40.30 N 22.36 E
Aliákmonos, Tekhnití Límni ⊜[1] 38 40.15 N 22.00 E
Aliaksin, Cape › 180 55.30 N 160.43 W
'Alī al-Gharbī 128 32.27 N 46.41 E
Aliança 250 7.35 S 35.13 W
Aliano 68 40.19 N 16.14 E
Alībāg 122 18.39 N 72.54 E
Alibahadır ◆[8] 267b 41.11 N 29.12 E
Ali-Bajramly 84 39.56 N 48.56 E
Alibardak 130 38.06 N 40.25 E
Alibates Flint Quarries National Monument ♠ 196 35.35 N 101.39 W
Alibej, ozero ⊜ 78 45.48 N 30.02 E
Alibejli 84 41.23 N 46.49 E
Alibey ≃ 267b 41.03 N 28.56 E
Alibey Adası I 130 39.20 N 26.38 E
Alibey Barajı ⊜[1] 267b 41.07 N 28.55 E
Alibeyköy ◆[8] 267b 41.04 N 28.56 E
Alibijaban Island I 116 13.20 N 122.43 E
Alibori ≃ 150 11.56 N 3.17 E
Al-Ibrāhīmīyah 142 30.57 N 31.35 E
Alibunar 38 45.05 N 20.58 E
Alicante → Alacant 34 38.21 N 0.29 W
Alice, Ciskei 158 32.47 S 26.50 E
Alice, Tx., U.S. 196 27.45 N 98.04 W
Alice ≃, Austl. 164 15.22 S 141.58 E
Alice ≃, Austl. 166 24.02 S 144.50 E
Alice, Punta › 68 39.24 N 17.10 E
Alice Arm 182 55.29 N 129.29 W
Alicedale 158 33.19 S 26.05 E
Alice Downs 162 17.45 S 127.56 E
Alice Springs 162 23.42 S 133.53 E
Alice Superiore 62 45.28 N 7.47 E
Alice Town 238 25.44 N 79.17 W
Aliceville 194 33.07 N 88.09 W
Alicia, Pil. 116 16.45 N 121.42 E
Alicia, Pil. 116 7.30 N 122.55 E
Alıcık 130 40.49 N 35.21 E
Alick Creek ≃ 166 20.25 S 142.00 E
Alicudi, Isola I 70 38.32 N 14.21 E
Alicurá, Embalse de ⊜[1] 254 40.40 S 71.00 W
Al-'Idwah 142 29.21 N 30.55 E
Alief 222 29.43 N 95.35 W
Alife 68 41.20 N 14.20 E
Al-Ifranj 132 31.11 N 35.41 E
Alīganj, India 124 28.07 N 80.36 E
Alīganj, India 124 27.30 N 79.11 E
Alīgarh 124 27.53 N 78.05 E
Alignements de Carnac ⊥ 32 47.35 N 3.05 W
Alīgūdarz 128 33.24 N 49.41 E
Alijos, Islas II 232 24.57 N 115.44 W
'Alī Kheyl 120 33.57 N 69.43 E
Al-Ikhṣāṣ al-Qiblīyah 142 29.42 N 31.17 E
Al-Ikhwān II 118 12.08 N 53.10 E
Alikovo 80 55.45 N 46.45 E
Alima ≃ 152 1.36 S 16.36 E
Al-Imām ◆[8] 273c 30.01 N 31.10 E
Al-Imārāt al-'Arabīyah al-Muttaḥidah → United Arab Emirates □[1] 128 24.00 N 54.00 E
Al-'Imārīyah 142 27.37 N 30.53 E
Alimena 70 37.42 N 14.07 E
Alimini Grande ⊜ 68 40.12 N 18.27 E
Alimini Piccolo ⊜ 68 40.10 N 18.27 E
Aliminusa 70 37.52 N 13.47 E
Alim Island I 164 2.55 S 147.05 E
Alimkent 85 40.58 N 69.11 E
Alimodian 116 10.49 N 122.26 E
Alindao 152 5.02 N 21.13 E
Alingsås 26 57.56 N 12.31 E
Alipur, India 272b 22.43 N 88.12 E
Alipur, India 272b 22.55 N 88.11 E
Alīpur, Pāk. 123 29.23 N 70.55 E
Ālīpur ◆[8] 126 22.31 N 88.20 E
Ālīpur Duār 124 26.29 N 89.44 E
Alīpur Janūbi 123 30.13 N 71.18 E
Aliquippa 214 40.38 N 80.14 W
Aliquippa-Hopewell Airport ⊠ 279b 40.35 N 80.17 W
Alīrājpur 120 22.19 N 74.21 E
Al-'Irāq 132 31.05 N 35.39 E
Al-'Irāq → Iraq □[1] 128 33.00 N 44.00 E
Al-'Irqah 144 13.30 N 47.22 E
Ali-Sabieh 144 11.09 N 42.42 E
Al-'Īsāwīyah 128 30.38 N 37.53 E
Aliseda 34 39.26 N 6.41 W
Alise-Sainte-Reine 58 47.32 N 4.29 E
Alīshārī 84 39.02 N 47.15 E
Al-Iskandarīyah (Alexandria) 142 31.12 N 29.54 E
Al-Iskandarīyah □[4] 142 31.10 N 29.53 E
Al-Ismā'īlīyah (Ismailia) 142 30.35 N 32.16 E
Al-Ismā'īlīyah □[4] 142 30.30 N 32.15 E
Al-Ismā'īlīyah Military Base ■ 142 30.35 N 32.14 E
Aliso Canyon V, Ca., U.S. 280 34.18 N 118.33 W
Aliso Canyon V, Ca., U.S. 280 33.53 N 117.40 W
Aliso Creek ≃ 228 33.31 N 117.45 W
Al-Istiwā'īyah al-Gharbīyah □[4] 140 5.55 N 28.15 E
Al-Istiwā'īyah ash-Sharqīyah □[4] 154 4.30 N 33.00 E
Alistráti 38 41.04 N 23.57 E
Alitak, Cape › 180 56.51 N 154.21 W
Alitak Bay c 180 57.00 N 154.05 W
Alitanguo 120 35.10 N 83.30 E
Alì Terme 70 38.01 N 15.26 E
Alivérion 38 38.24 N 24.02 E
Aliwal North 158 30.45 S 26.45 E
Alix 182 52.24 N 113.11 W
Al-'Izzīyah 142 27.13 N 30.59 E
Al-Jabal al-Abyaḍ ∧[2] 142 28.46 N 31.00 E
Al-Jabal al-Aḥmar ∧[2] 142 28.19 N 31.07 E
Al-Jabalayn 140 12.36 N 32.48 E
Al-Jadīdah 140 25.34 N 28.51 E
Al-Jafādūn 142 28.50 N 30.48 E
Al-Jafr 132 30.18 N 36.13 E
Al-Jāfūrah ◆[2] 128 24.14 N 50.00 E
Al-Jaghbūb 146 29.45 N 24.31 E
Al-Jaghbūb ⊤[4] 146 29.40 N 24.43 E
Al-Jahrah 128 29.20 N 47.40 E
Al-Jamālīyah 142 31.11 N 31.51 E
Al-Jarnūs 142 28.36 N 30.43 E
Al-Jawf, Ar. Su. 128 29.50 N 39.52 E
Al-Jawf, Lībiyā 146 24.11 N 23.19 E
Al-Jawsh 146 32.00 N 11.40 E
Al-Jaylī 140 16.01 N 32.36 E
Al-Jazā'ir → Algeria □[1] 148 28.00 N 3.00 E
Al-Jazīrah □[4] 140 14.30 N 33.20 E
Al-Jazīrah ◆[1] 140 14.25 N 33.00 E
Aljezur, Bra. 287a 22.40 S 43.36 W
Aljezur, Port. 34 37.19 N 8.48 W
Al-Jibāb 132 33.06 N 36.15 E
Al-Jifārah 128 23.59 N 45.11 E
Al-Jifārah (Jeffara) ≡ 146 32.30 N 11.45 E
Al-Jīzah (Giza), Miṣr 142 30.01 N 31.13 E
Al-Jīzah, Urd. 132 31.43 N 35.58 E
Al-Jīzah □[4] 142 29.46 N 31.18 E
Al-Jubayl 128 27.01 N 49.40 E
Al-Jubayn 140 12.07 N 35.10 E
Aljucén ≃ 34 38.56 N 6.25 W
Al-Judaydah 132 33.54 N 35.34 E
Al-Judayyidah, Urd. 132 31.15 N 35.49 E
Al-Judayyidah, Urd. 132 31.32 N 35.39 E
Al-Jufrah ⊤[4] 146 29.10 N 16.00 E
Al-Julaydah ⊤[4] 128 29.03 N 45.38 E
Al-Junaynah, Miṣr 142 31.06 N 31.41 E
Al-Junaynah, Sūd. 140 13.27 N 22.27 E
Al-Junaynah, Sūrīy. 132 32.54 N 36.44 E
Al-Jundīyah 142 28.34 N 30.50 E
Aljustrel 34 37.52 N 8.10 W
Al-Kāb 142 30.57 N 32.18 E
Al-Kabrit Military Base ■ 142 30.15 N 32.29 E
Al-Kafr 132 32.38 N 36.38 E
Al-Kafr ash-Sharqī 142 37.17 N 31.10 E
Al-Kahfah 128 27.04 N 43.02 E
Alkali Creek ≃, Ab., Can. 184 50.52 N 110.30 W
Alkali Creek ≃, Wy., U.S. 202 43.16 N 107.40 W
Alkali Lake 182 51.47 N 122.14 W
Alkali Lake ⊜, Nv., U.S. 204 41.42 N 119.50 W
Alkali Lake ⊜, Or., U.S. 202 42.58 N 120.02 W
Alkamari 146 13.24 N 11.07 E
Al-Kāmilīn 140 15.05 N 33.11 E
Al-Karabah 140 18.33 N 33.42 E
Al-Karak 132 31.11 N 35.42 E
Al-Karak □[8] 132 31.10 N 35.45 E
Al-Karnak 140 25.43 N 32.39 E
Al-Kawah 140 13.44 N 32.30 E
Al-Kawd 144 13.05 N 45.22 E
Al-Kawm 130 35.11 N 38.52 E
Al-Kawm al-Akhḍar 142 30.58 N 30.17 E
Al-Kawm Aṭ-Ṭawīl 142 31.12 N 31.05 E
Alken 56 50.15 N 7.26 E
Al-Khabrā' 128 26.04 N 43.33 E
Al-Khābūrah 128 23.59 N 57.08 E
Al-Khafaqān ⊜ 128 23.24 N 40.24 E
Al-Khalīl (Hebron) 132 31.32 N 35.06 E
Al-Khālis 128 33.49 N 44.32 E
Al-Khandaq 140 18.36 N 30.34 E
Al-Khānkah 142 30.13 N 31.21 E
Al-Kharaqānīyah 273c 30.10 N 31.10 E
Al-Khārijah 140 25.26 N 30.33 E
Al-Kharṭūm (Khartoum) 140 15.36 N 32.32 E
Al-Kharṭūm □[4] 140 15.45 N 32.30 E
Al-Kharṭūm Baḥrī 140 15.38 N 32.33 E
Al-Khaṣab 128 26.12 N 56.15 E
Al-Khatam ◆[1] 128 24.00 N 55.10 E
Al-Khirbah as-Samrā' 132 32.11 N 36.10 E
Al-Khiyām 132 33.19 N 35.36 E
Al-Khubar 128 26.17 N 50.12 E
Al-Khums (Homs) 146 32.39 N 14.16 E
Al-Khuraybah, Urd. 132 32.40 N 35.52 E
Al-Khuraybah, Yaman 144 15.06 N 48.19 E
Al-Khurmah 144 21.54 N 42.03 E
Al-Khushnīyah 132 33.00 N 35.48 E
Al-Khuṣūṣ 273c 30.09 N 31.19 E
Al-Kifl 128 32.14 N 44.22 E
Al-Kiswah 132 33.21 N 36.14 E
Alkmaar 52 52.37 N 4.44 E
Alkoven 61 48.17 N 14.06 E
Al-Kūbrī 142 30.02 N 32.33 E
Al-Kūfah 128 32.02 N 44.24 E
Al-Kufrah (Cufra) ⊤[4] 146 24.20 N 23.15 E
Al-Kunayyisah 273c 29.59 N 31.11 E
Al-Kuntillah 140 30.00 N 34.41 E
Al-Kūt 128 32.25 N 45.49 E
Al-Kuwayt 128 29.20 N 47.59 E
Al-Kuwayt → Kuwait □[1] 128 29.30 N 47.45 E
Alkvettern ⊜ 40 59.25 N 14.21 E
Allaben 210 42.07 N 74.22 W
Al-Labwah 130 34.12 N 36.21 E
Allacapan 116 18.15 N 121.35 E
Allach-Jun' 74 61.08 N 138.03 E
Allada 150 6.39 N 2.09 E
Al-Lādhiqīyah (Latakia) 130 35.31 N 35.47 E
Al-Lādhiqīyah □[8] 130 35.30 N 36.00 E
Allagash ≃ 186 47.05 N 69.02 W
Allagen 56 51.28 N 8.14 E
Al-Lagowa 140 11.24 N 29.08 E
Allahābād, India 124 25.27 N 81.51 E
Allāhābād, Pāk. 123 28.57 N 70.53 E
Allāhbās 272a 28.31 N 77.25 E
Allahüekber Dağları ⋏ 130 40.35 N 42.32 E
Al-Lāhūn 142 29.13 N 30.59 E
Allāhwardipur 272a 28.33 N 77.26 E
Allaines 50 48.12 N 1.50 E
Allaire State Park ♠ 208 40.08 N 74.08 W
Allakaket 180 66.34 N 152.41 W
Allaman 58 46.28 N 6.24 E
Allamuchy 210 40.55 N 74.48 W
Allan 184 51.53 N 106.04 W
Allan, Pointe › 275a 45.26 N 73.45 W
Allanche 32 45.14 N 2.56 E
Alland 61 48.03 N 16.05 E
Allan Island I 224 48.28 N 122.42 W
Allanmyo 110 19.22 N 95.13 E
Allanridge 158 27.55 S 26.44 E
Allanson 168a 33.20 S 116.06 E
Allanton 46 55.47 N 3.51 W
Allan Water ≃ 46 56.08 N 3.56 W
Allapattah Flats ≡ 220 27.29 N 82.34 W
'Allāq, Bi'r ⊤[4] 146 31.05 N 11.42 E
'Allāqī, Wādī al- V 140 22.42 N 33.12 E
Allard, Lac ⊜ 186 50.32 N 63.31 W
Allardt 194 36.22 N 84.53 W
Allariz 34 42.11 N 7.48 W
Allatoona Lake ⊜[1] 192 34.08 N 84.38 W
Allauch 62 43.20 N 5.29 E
Al-Layyah 140 16.16 N 35.25 E
Alldays 156 22.44 S 29.04 E
Alle, Bel. 56 49.51 N 4.58 E
Alle, Schw. 58 47.26 N 7.08 E
Ålleberg ∧[2] 26 58.08 N 13.36 E
Allegan 216 42.31 N 85.51 W
Allegan □[6] 216 42.35 N 85.53 W
Allegan, Lake ⊜ 216 42.33 N 85.55 W
Allegany 210 42.05 N 78.29 W
Allegany □[6] 210 42.13 N 78.02 W
Allegany Indian Reservation ◆[4] 210 42.10 N 78.47 W
Allegany State Park ♠ 210 42.04 N 78.44 W
Alleghany 226 39.28 N 120.51 W
Alleghe 64 46.24 N 12.01 E
Allegheny □[6] 214 40.26 N 79.59 W
Allegheny ≃ 214 40.27 N 80.00 W
Allegheny Acres 279b 40.37 N 79.53 W
Allegheny Center ♥ 279b 40.27 N 80.01 W
Allegheny County Airport ⊠ 279b 40.21 N 79.56 W
Allegheny County Park ♠ 279b 40.34 N 79.55 W
Allegheny Mountains ⋏ 188 38.30 N 80.00 W
Allegheny Observatory ♥[3] 279b 40.29 N 80.01 W
Allegheny Plateau ⋏[1] 188 41.30 N 78.00 W
Allegheny Portage Railroad National Historic Site ⊥ 214 40.28 N 78.32 W
Allegheny Reservoir ⊜[1] 214 42.00 N 78.56 W
Allègre 62 45.12 N 3.42 E
Allègre, Pointe › 241o 16.22 N 61.45 W
Allemagne → Germany □[1] 30 51.00 N 10.00 E
Allemands, Lac Des ⊜ 194 29.55 N 90.35 W
Allemanskraaldam ⊜[1] 158 28.16 S 27.07 E
Allemant 261 48.45 N 1.37 E
Allemont 62 45.08 N 6.02 E
Allen, Arg. 252 38.58 S 67.50 W
Allen, Pil. 116 12.30 N 124.17 E
Allen, Md., U.S. 208 38.17 N 75.41 W
Allen, Mi., U.S. 216 41.57 N 84.46 W
Allen, Ne., U.S. 198 42.24 N 96.50 W
Allen, Ok., U.S. 196 34.52 N 96.24 W
Allen, Pa., U.S. 208 40.10 N 77.05 W
Allen, S.D., U.S. 198 43.16 N 101.55 W
Allen, Tx., U.S. 222 33.06 N 96.40 W
Allen, Wa., U.S. 224 48.31 N 122.23 W
Allen □[6], In., U.S. 216 41.04 N 85.09 W
Allen □[6], Oh., U.S. 216 40.46 N 84.06 W
Allen ≃ 44 54.58 N 2.19 W
Allen, Lough ⊜ 48 54.08 N 8.08 W
Allen, Mount ∧, N.Z. 172 47.05 S 167.48 E
Allen, Mount ∧, Ak., U.S. 180 62.14 N 142.13 W
Allenby Bridge ◆[5] 132 31.52 N 35.52 E
Allendale, Il., U.S. 194 38.32 N 87.43 W
Allendale, Mi., U.S. 216 42.58 N 85.57 W
Allendale, N.J., U.S. 276 41.02 N 74.07 W
Allendale, S.C., U.S. 192 33.00 N 81.18 W
Allendale Town 44 54.54 N 2.15 W
Allende, Méx. 232 28.20 N 100.51 W
Allende, Méx. 234 18.09 N 94.16 W
Allendorf 56 51.02 N 8.38 E
Allenfarm 222 30.24 N 96.14 W
All England Lawn Tennis Club ♠ 260 51.26 N 0.13 W
Allen Grove 216 42.35 N 88.41 W
Allen Park 216 42.15 N 83.12 W
Allenport, Pa., U.S. 214 40.20 N 77.53 W
Allenport, Pa., U.S. 214 40.06 N 79.51 W
Allensbach 58 47.43 N 9.03 E
Allenstein → Olsztyn 30 53.48 N 20.29 E
Allensville 214 40.32 N 77.49 W
Allenton, Mi., U.S. 214 42.55 N 82.57 W
Allenton, R.I., U.S. 207 41.32 N 71.28 W
Allentown, N.J., U.S. 208 40.10 N 74.35 W
Allentown, N.Y., U.S. 210 42.05 N 78.03 W
Allentown, Oh., U.S. 216 40.46 N 84.12 W
Allentown, Pa., U.S. 208 40.36 N 75.28 W
Allentsteig 61 48.42 N 15.20 E
Allenwood, N.J., U.S. 208 40.12 N 74.13 W
Allenwood, N.Y., U.S. 276 40.48 N 73.44 W
Allenwood, Pa., U.S. 210 41.07 N 76.54 W
Alleppey 122 9.29 N 76.19 E
Aller ≃ 30 52.57 N 9.11 E
Allerona 66 42.49 N 11.58 E
Allersberg 60 49.15 N 11.15 E
Allershausen 60 48.26 N 11.36 E
Allerslev 41 55.05 N 12.03 E
Allerton, Ia., U.S. 190 40.42 N 93.21 W
Allerton, Ma., U.S. 283 42.18 N 70.53 W
Allerton ◆[8] 262 53.22 N 2.53 W
Allerton, Point › 207 42.18 N 70.53 W
Allestree 42 52.57 N 1.29 W
Allevard 62 45.24 N 6.04 E
Alley Park ♠ 276 40.45 N 73.44 W
Alleyton 222 29.43 N 96.29 W
Allgäu ◆[1] 58 47.35 N 10.10 E
Allgäuer Alpen ⋏ 58 47.20 N 10.25 E
Allhallows 260 51.28 N 0.39 E
Alli ≃ 68 38.51 N 16.40 E
Alliance, Ab., Can. 182 52.26 N 111.47 W
Alliance, Ne., U.S. 198 42.12 N 102.58 W
Alliance, Oh., U.S. 214 40.54 N 81.06 W
Allibaudières 50 48.35 N 4.07 E
Al-Lidām 144 20.29 N 44.50 E
Allier □[5] 32 46.25 N 3.00 E
Allier ≃, Fr. 32 46.58 N 3.04 E
Allier ≃, Fr. 62 45.05 N 3.35 E
Alligator ≃ 192 35.58 N 75.58 W
Alligator Creek ≃, Ga., U.S. 192 31.58 N 82.22 W
Alligator Creek ≃, Tx., U.S. 222 30.42 N 97.07 W
Alligator Lake ⊜ 220 28.13 N 81.13 W
Alligator Pond 241q 17.52 N 77.34 W
Alligny-en-Morvan 50 47.12 N 4.10 E
Allihies 48 51.38 N 10.03 W
Allinagaram 122 10.02 N 77.30 E
Allinge 26 55.16 N 14.49 E
Allington Castle ⊥ 260 51.17 N 0.31 E
Al-Lisān ›[1] 132 31.17 N 35.28 E
Al-Lisht 142 29.34 N 31.14 E
Allison 190 42.45 N 92.47 W
Allison, Mount ∧ 282 37.30 N 121.52 W
Allison Gulch V 280 34.16 N 117.44 W
Allison Park 214 40.34 N 79.57 W
Alliste 68 39.57 N 18.05 E
Alliston 212 44.09 N 79.52 W
Al-Līth 144 20.09 N 40.16 E
Allmendingen 58 48.20 N 9.43 E
Alloa 46 56.07 N 3.49 W
Allochio, Galleria degli ◆[5] 66 44.03 N 11.30 E
Allogny 50 47.13 N 2.19 E
Allonby 44 54.46 N 3.25 W
Alloné Abba 132 32.44 N 35.10 E
Allonnes, Dtsch. 50 47.58 N 0.09 E
Allonnes, Fr. 50 48.20 N 1.40 E
Allora 171a 28.02 S 151.59 E
Allos 62 44.14 N 6.38 E
Allott, Mount ∧[2] 162 26.06 S 124.46 E
Allouez 190 44.28 N 88.00 W
Alloway 208 39.33 N 75.21 W
Alloway Creek ≃ 208 39.27 N 75.30 W
Allport 214 40.58 N 78.12 W
Allred Peak ∧ 200 40.32 N 108.33 W
All Saints 240c 17.03 N 61.48 W
Allschwil 58 47.33 N 7.33 E
Allstedt 54 51.24 N 11.23 E
Allston ◆[8] 283 42.22 N 71.08 W
Alluets, Forêt des ♠ 261 48.55 N 1.55 E
Al-Luḥayyah 144 15.42 N 42.42 E
Allumette Lake ⊜ 190 45.53 N 77.13 W
Allumettes, Île des I 190 45.50 N 77.05 W
Allumiere 66 42.09 N 11.54 E
Allview Estates 208 39.12 N 76.51 W
Allyn 224 47.23 N 122.49 W
Alm ≃ 60 48.05 N 13.55 E
Alma, N.B., Can. 186 45.36 N 64.57 W
Alma, P.Q., Can. 186 48.33 N 71.39 W
Alma, Ar., U.S. 194 35.28 N 94.13 W
Alma, Ga., U.S. 192 31.32 N 82.27 W
Alma, Il., U.S. 219 38.43 N 88.55 W
Alma, Ks., U.S. 198 39.01 N 96.17 W
Alma, Mi., U.S. 190 43.22 N 84.39 W
Alma, Ne., U.S. 198 40.05 N 99.21 W
Alma, N.Y., U.S. 210 42.01 N 78.03 W
Alma, Wi., U.S. 190 44.19 N 91.54 W
Al-Ma'ābidah 142 27.20 N 31.01 E
Al-Ma'ādī ◆[8] 142 29.58 N 31.15 E
Alma-Ata 85 43.15 N 76.57 E
Alma-Atinskij zapovednik ♠ 85 43.10 N 77.25 E
Alma Center 190 44.26 N 90.54 W
Almada 34 38.41 N 9.09 W
Almaden, Austl. 166 17.20 S 144.41 E
Almadén, Esp. 34 38.46 N 4.50 W
Almadén de la Plata 34 37.52 N 6.04 W
Al-Madīnah (Medina) 128 24.28 N 39.36 E
Al-Madīnah al-Fikrīyah 142 27.56 N 30.49 E
Al-Madwar 132 32.17 N 36.00 E
Al-Mafāzah 140 13.36 N 34.33 E
Al-Mafraq 132 32.21 N 36.12 E
Al-Mafraq □[8] 132 32.15 N 36.30 E
Almafuerte 252 32.12 S 64.15 W
Al-Maghārīm 144 15.01 N 47.51 E
Al-Maghrah ⊤[4] 140 30.14 N 28.56 E
Almagor 132 32.55 N 35.36 E
Almagre, Laguna c 234 23.48 N 97.48 W
Al-Magreb → Morocco □[1] 148 32.00 N 5.00 W
Almagro 34 38.53 N 3.43 W
Almagro Island I 116 11.56 N 124.18 E
Al-Maḥallah al-Kubrā 142 30.58 N 31.10 E
Al-Maḥārīq 140 25.37 N 30.39 E
Al Mahbas 148 27.13 N 9.44 W
Alma Hill ∧[2] 210 42.03 N 78.01 W
Al-Maḥmūdīyah 142 31.11 N 30.32 E
Al-Maḥraṣ 142 27.49 N 30.48 E
Al-Maḥsamah 142 30.34 N 32.01 E
Al-Majdal 132 32.47 N 36.30 E
Al-Majma'ah 128 25.54 N 45.20 E
Almăjului, Munţii ⋏ 38 44.43 N 22.12 E
Al-Maks ◆[8] 142 31.09 N 29.51 E
Al-Mālikīyah 130 37.10 N 42.08 E
Almalyk 85 40.50 N 69.35 E
Al-Ma'mūrah ◆[8] 142 31.18 N 30.03 E
Al-Manāmah 128 26.13 N 50.35 E
Al-Manāqil 140 14.15 N 32.59 E
Al-Manāṣif ◆[1] 130 35.17 N 40.50 E
Al-Manāwāt 273c 29.55 N 31.14 E
Almanor, Lake ⊜ 204 40.15 N 121.08 W
Almansa 34 38.52 N 1.05 W
Al-Manshāh 140 26.28 N 31.48 E
Al-Manṣūrah, Isr. Occ 132 33.08 N 35.48 E
Al-Manṣūrah, Miṣr 142 31.03 N 31.23 E
Al-Manṣūrīyah 142 30.08 N 31.05 E
Almanza 34 42.39 N 5.02 W
Al-Manzilah 142 31.09 N 31.56 E
Almanzor ∧ 34 40.15 N 5.18 W
Almanzora ≃ 34 37.14 N 1.46 W
Almar ≃ 34 40.54 N 5.29 W
Al-Marāghah 140 26.42 N 31.36 E
Almargem do Bispo 266c 38.51 N 9.16 W
Al-Marj 146 32.30 N 20.54 E
Al-Marj ◆[8] 273c 30.09 N 31.20 E
Almas 250 11.33 S 47.09 W
Almaș ≃ 38 47.14 N 23.19 E
Almas, Pico das ∧ 255 13.33 S 41.56 W
Al-Ma'ṣarah, Miṣr 142 27.42 N 30.52 E
Al-Ma'ṣarah, Miṣr 142 31.13 N 31.19 E
Al-Ma'sarah ◆[8] 142 29.54 N 31.17 E
Al-Mashqūq 132 32.24 N 36.43 E
Al-Mashrafah 130 34.50 N 36.52 E
Al-Masīd 140 15.15 N 32.57 E
Almassora 34 39.57 N 0.03 W
Al-Matammah 140 16.43 N 33.22 E
Al-Maṭarīyah 142 31.11 N 32.02 E
Al-Maṭarīyah ◆[8] 142 30.07 N 31.19 E
Al-Matnah 140 13.47 N 35.03 E
Al-Mawṣil (Mosul) 128 36.20 N 43.08 E
Al-Mayādīn 130 35.01 N 40.27 E
Al-Maymūn 142 29.14 N 31.12 E
Almazán 34 41.29 N 2.32 W
Al-Mazār, Urd. 132 31.04 N 35.42 E
Almazar, Uzb. 85 40.59 N 68.54 E
Almaznaja ◆[8] 83 48.31 N 38.35 E
Almaznyj 83 48.02 N 40.03 E
Almazovka ◆[8] 83 48.04 N 39.18 E
Almazovo 265b 55.51 N 38.02 E
Al-Mazra'ah 132 31.16 N 35.31 E
Al-Mazzah 132 33.30 N 36.15 E
Alme 56 51.28 N 8.37 E
Almeer 52 52.20 N 5.14 E
Almeida 34 40.43 N 6.54 W
Almeirim, Bra. 250 1.32 S 52.34 W
Almeirim, Port. 34 39.12 N 8.38 W
Almelo 52 52.21 N 6.39 E
Almelo-Nordhorn, Kanaal ≍ 52 52.20 N 6.40 E
Almena 198 39.53 N 99.42 W
Almenara 255 16.11 S 40.42 W
Almenar de Soria 34 41.41 N 2.12 W
Almendares ≃ 286b 23.08 N 82.25 W
Almendra, Embalse de ⊜[1] 34 41.15 N 6.10 W
Almendralejo 34 38.41 N 6.24 W
Almenêches 50 48.42 N 0.07 E
Al'menevo 86 54.57 N 63.34 E
Almenno San Salvatore 62 45.45 N 9.35 E
Almería 34 36.50 N 2.27 W
Almería □[4] 34 37.10 N 2.25 W
Almería, Golfo de c 34 36.46 N 2.30 W
Al'metjevsk 80 54.53 N 52.20 E
Al'mež 24 60.03 N 48.03 E
Älmhult 26 56.33 N 14.08 E
Al-Midhnab 128 25.54 N 44.14 E
Al-Mīnā' 130 34.27 N 35.49 E
Almina, Punta › 34 35.53 N 5.15 W
Almino Afonso 250 6.09 S 37.46 W
Al-Minshāt al-Kubrā 142 31.03 N 30.54 E
Al-Minūfīyah □[4] 142 30.30 N 31.00 E
Al-Minyā, Miṣr 142 28.06 N 30.45 E
Al-Minyā, Miṣr 142 29.45 N 31.18 E
Al-Minyā, Miṣr 142 29.14 N 30.45 E
Al-Minyā □[4] 142 28.26 N 30.42 E
Al-Miqdādīyah 128 33.59 N 44.56 E
Almira 202 47.42 N 118.56 W
Almirantazgo, Islas → Admiralty Islands II 164 2.10 S 147.00 E
Almirantazgo, Montes → Admiralty Mountains ⋏ 9 71.45 S 168.30 E
Almirante 236 9.18 N 82.24 W
Almirante, Bahía de c 236 9.20 N 82.18 W
Almirante Brown 258 34.48 S 58.23 W
Almirante Brown □[5] 288 34.50 S 58.20 W
Almirante Guillermo Brown, Parque ♠ 288 34.40 S 58.28 W
Almirante Latorre 252 29.38 S 70.58 W
Almirante Montt, Golfo ⊔ 254 51.55 S 72.45 W
Almirós 38 39.11 N 22.46 E
Almiroú, Kólpos c 38 35.23 N 24.20 E
Al-Mismīyah 132 33.08 N 36.23 E
Almo 202 42.06 N 113.37 W
Almoçageme 266c 38.48 N 9.28 W
Almodôvar 34 37.31 N 8.04 W
Almodóvar del Campo 34 38.43 N 4.10 W
Almolonga 236 14.49 N 91.30 W
Almond, N.Y., U.S. 210 42.19 N 77.44 W
Almond, Wi., U.S. 190 44.15 N 89.24 W
Almond ≃, Scot., U.K. 46 55.58 N 3.18 W
Almond ≃, Scot., U.K. 46 56.25 N 3.27 W
Almondbank 46 56.24 N 3.33 W
Almondsbury 42 51.34 N 2.34 W
Almonesson 208 39.49 N 75.06 W
Almont 214 42.55 N 83.02 W
Almont ≃ 261 48.32 N 2.40 E
Almonte, On., Can. 212 45.14 N 76.12 W
Almonte, Esp. 34 37.15 N 6.31 W
Almonte, Ca., U.S. 282 37.53 N 122.32 W
Almora 124 29.37 N 79.40 E
Almsee ⊜ 64 47.45 N 13.57 E
Älmsta 40 59.58 N 18.48 E
Al-Mu'aḍḍamīyah 132 33.45 N 36.39 E
Al-Mubarraz, Ar. Su. 128 25.25 N 49.35 E
Al-Mubarraz, Ar. Su. 144 22.17 N 46.44 E
Al-Mudawwarah 128 29.19 N 35.59 E
Almudébar 34 42.03 N 0.35 W
Al-Muglad 140 11.02 N 27.44 E
Al-Muḥarraq 128 26.16 N 50.37 E
Al-Mukallā 144 14.32 N 49.08 E
Al-Mukhā (Mocha) 144 13.19 N 43.15 E
Al-Munājāt al-Kubrā 142 30.50 N 32.01 E
Almuñécar 34 36.43 N 3.41 W
Almunge 40 59.53 N 18.03 E
Al-Muntazah ◆[8] 142 31.17 N 30.01 E
Almus 130 40.23 N 36.55 E
Al-Musallamīyah 140 14.34 N 33.21 E
Al-Musayfirah 132 32.37 N 36.20 E
Al-Musayjīd 128 24.05 N 39.06 E
Al-Musayyib 128 32.47 N 44.18 E
Almus Barajı ⊜[1] 130 40.20 N 37.00 E
Al-Mushannaf 132 32.44 N 36.46 E
Al-Musharrak Qiblī 142 29.23 N 30.34 E
Al-Mutā'iyah 132 32.29 N 36.17 E
Al-Mu'tamadīyah 142 31.02 N 31.05 E
Al-Mutayn 132 33.54 N 35.44 E
Al-Muthannā □[4] 128 30.30 N 45.15 E
Al-Muṭī'ah 142 27.08 N 31.18 E
Al-Muwaqqar ⊥ 132 31.49 N 36.06 E
Al-Muwassam 144 16.25 N 42.20 E
Al-Muwayh 144 22.45 N 41.36 E
Al-Muwayliḥ 128 27.41 N 35.27 E
Aln ≃ 44 55.23 N 1.37 W
Alnarp 41 55.39 N 13.05 E
Al-Narrānīyah 273c 29.58 N 31.10 E
Al'n'aš 80 56.44 N 54.43 E
Alnaši 80 56.11 N 52.28 E
Al-Nasser 140 24.32 N 32.55 E
Alne ≃ 42 52.13 N 1.52 W
Alness 46 57.41 N 4.15 W
Alnmouth 44 55.23 N 1.36 W
Alnön I 26 62.25 N 17.26 E
Alnor 41 54.55 N 9.36 E
Alnwick 44 55.25 N 1.42 W
Alnwick Indian Reserve ◆[4] 212 44.10 N 78.06 W
Alo 146 11.47 N 20.53 E
Aloândia 255 17.43 S 49.29 W
Alofau 174u 14.16 S 170.36 W
Alofi 174v 19.01 S 169.55 W
Alofi Bay c 174v 19.01 S 169.56 W
Aloha 224 45.29 N 122.51 W
Aloha, Lake ⊜ 226 38.52 N 120.09 W
Aloi 154 2.17 N 33.10 E
Aloja 76 57.46 N 24.53 E
Alondra 280 33.55 N 118.15 W
Along 120 28.18 N 94.39 E
Alónnisos 38 39.08 N 23.50 E
Alónnisos I 38 39.13 N 23.55 E
Alor, Kepulauan II 112 8.15 S 124.30 E
Alor, Pulau I 112 8.15 S 124.45 E
Alor, Selat ⊔ 112 8.20 S 123.48 E
Álora 34 36.48 N 4.42 W
Alor Gajah 114 2.23 N 102.13 E
Alor Setar 114 6.07 N 100.22 E
Alor Star → Alor Setar 114 6.07 N 100.22 E
Alorton 219 38.36 N 90.08 W
Al'oškino 88 58.35 N 100.32 E
Al'ošn'a, Ross. 76 53.38 N 33.29 E
Al'ošn'a, Ross. 82 54.14 N 37.16 E
Alosno 34 37.33 N 7.07 W
Alost → Aalst 50 50.56 N 4.02 E
Alotau 164 10.14 S 150.30 E
Alouette ≃ 224 49.16 N 122.42 W
Alouette Lake ⊜ 224 49.19 N 122.28 W
Alovo 80 54.38 N 46.27 E
Aloxe-Corton 58 47.04 N 4.52 E
Aloysius, Mount ∧ 162 26.01 S 128.34 E
Alpachiri 252 37.22 S 63.46 W
Alpaugh 226 35.53 N 119.29 W
Alpen 52 51.35 N 6.30 E
Alpena, Ar., U.S. 194 36.17 N 93.17 W
Alpena, Mi., U.S. 190 45.03 N 83.25 W
Alpena, S.D., U.S. 198 44.10 N 98.21 W
Alpen → Alps ⋏ 32 46.25 N 10.00 E
Alpercatas ≃ 250 6.02 S 44.19 W
Alpes → Alps ⋏ 32 46.25 N 10.00 E
Alpes-de-Haute-Provence □[5] 62 44.10 N 6.00 E
Alpes Dináricos → Dinara ⋏ 36 43.50 N 16.35 E
Alpes Maritimes □[5] 62 44.00 N 7.10 E
Alpes Marítimos → Maritime Alps ⋏ 62 44.15 N 7.10 E
Alpes Transilvanos → Carpaţii Meridionali ⋏ 38 45.30 N 24.15 E
Alpha, Austl. 166 23.39 S 146.38 E
Alpha, Il., U.S. 190 41.12 N 90.23 W
Alpha, Mi., U.S. 190 46.02 N 88.22 W
Alpha, N.J., U.S. 210 40.40 N 75.09 W
Alpharetta 192 34.04 N 84.17 W
Alphen aan den Rijn 52 52.07 N 4.40 E
Alphington 42 50.42 N 3.31 W
Alphin Pike ∧[2] 262 53.31 N 2.00 W
Alphonse Island I 138 7.00 S 52.45 E
Alpi, Monte ∧ 68 40.07 N 15.59 E
Alpi → Alps ⋏ 32 46.25 N 10.00 E
Alpiarça 34 39.15 N 8.35 W
Alpi Dinariche → Dinara ⋏ 36 43.50 N 16.35 E
Alpignano 62 45.06 N 7.31 E
Alpilles, Chaîne des ⋏[2] 62 43.45 N 4.50 E
Alpine, Az., U.S. 200 33.50 N 109.08 W
Alpine, Ca., U.S. 204 32.50 N 116.47 W
Alpine, N.J., U.S. 276 40.57 N 73.55 W
Alpine, N.Y., U.S. 210 42.19 N 76.44 W
Alpine, Tx., U.S. 196 30.21 N 103.39 W
Alpine □[6] 226 38.41 N 119.47 W
Alpine Creek ≃ 282 37.19 N 122.17 W
Alpine National Park ♠ 166 37.00 S 147.15 E
Alpinópolis 255 20.52 S 46.23 W
Alpi Retiche → Rhaetian Alps ⋏ 58 46.30 N 10.00 E
Alpirsbach 58 48.21 N 8.23 E
Alplaus Kill ≃ 210 42.51 N 73.54 W
Alpnachstad 58 46.57 N 8.17 E
Alps ⋏ 22 46.25 N 10.00 E
Alpsee ⊜ 58 47.34 N 10.10 E
Alpu 130 39.47 N 30.58 E
Al-Qābil 128 23.57 N 55.48 E
Al-Qābūn 132 33.33 N 36.20 E
Al-Qadam 132 33.28 N 36.17 E
Al-Qaḍārif 140 14.02 N 35.24 E
Al-Qaḍīmah 144 22.21 N 39.09 E
Al-Qādisīyah □[4] 128 31.55 N 45.00 E
Al-Qāhirah (Cairo), Miṣr 142 30.03 N 31.15 E
Al-Qāhirah (Cairo), Miṣr 273c 30.03 N 31.15 E
Al-Qāhirah □[4] 142 30.02 N 31.17 E
Al-Qāhirah West Military Base ■ 142 30.06 N 30.56 E
Al-Qaḥmah 144 18.00 N 41.41 E
Al-Qā'im 128 34.21 N 41.07 E
Al-Qā'īyah ⊤[4] 128 26.27 N 45.35 E
Al-Qāiyāt 142 28.40 N 30.41 E
Al-Qalaj 142 30.11 N 31.21 E
Al-Qalībah 128 28.32 N 37.42 E
Al-Qalyūbīyah □[4] 142 30.18 N 31.18 E
Al-Qāmishlī 130 37.02 N 41.14 E
Al-Qanāṭir al-Khayrīyah 142 30.12 N 31.08 E
Al-Qanāyāt 142 30.37 N 31.28 E
Al-Qanṭarah 142 30.52 N 32.19 E
Al-Qaryah ash-Sharqīyah 146 30.24 N 13.36 E
Al-Qaryatayn 130 34.14 N 37.14 E
Al-Qaṣabāt 146 32.35 N 14.03 E
Al-Qaṣābī 142 31.16 N 30.41 E
Al-Qaṣr, Miṣr 140 25.42 N 28.53 E
Al-Qaṣr, Urd. 132 31.19 N 35.45 E
Al-Qaṣṣāṣīn 142 30.34 N 31.56 E
Al-Qaṭīf 128 26.33 N 50.00 E
Al-Qaṭrānah 132 31.15 N 36.03 E
Al-Qaṭrūn 146 24.56 N 14.38 E
Al-Qaṭṭā 142 30.13 N 30.58 E
Al-Qaṭṭāwīyah 142 30.33 N 31.40 E
Al-Qays 142 28.29 N 30.47 E
Al-Qayṣūmah 128 28.16 N 46.03 E
Al-Qir'awn 132 33.34 N 35.43 E
Al-Qiṣfah 132 32.38 N 35.52 E
Al-Quds → Yerushalayim 132 31.46 N 35.14 E
Alquízar 240p 22.48 N 82.35 W
Al-Qun'abah 132 33.08 N 35.40 E
Al-Qunayṭirah 132 33.07 N 35.49 E
Al-Qunayṭirah □[8] 132 33.00 N 35.50 E
Al-Qunfudhah 144 19.08 N 41.05 E
Al-Qurayn 142 30.37 N 31.44 E
Al-Qurayyah 132 32.32 N 36.36 E
Al-Qurnah 128 31.00 N 47.26 E
Al-Quṣaymah 132 30.40 N 34.22 E
Al-Quṣayr, Miṣr 128 26.06 N 34.17 E
Al-Quṣayr, Miṣr 142 27.27 N 30.52 E
Al-Quṣayr, Sūrīy. 130 34.31 N 36.35 E
Al-Qūṣīyah 142 27.26 N 30.49 E
Al-Quṭayfah 132 33.44 N 36.36 E
Al-Quṭaynah 140 14.52 N 32.21 E
Al-Quway'īyah 128 24.03 N 45.15 E
Al-Quwaysī 140 13.20 N 34.05 E
Alrø I 41 55.51 N 10.05 E
Alroy Downs 162 19.18 S 136.04 E
Als I 41 54.59 N 9.55 E
Alsace □[9] 58 48.30 N 7.30 E
Alsace, Ballon d' ∧ 58 47.50 N 6.51 E
Alsager 44 53.06 N 2.17 W
Alsask 184 51.23 N 109.59 W
Alsasua 34 42.54 N 2.10 W
Alsdorf 56 50.53 N 6.10 E
Alsea 202 44.22 N 123.35 W
Alsea ≃ 202 44.26 N 124.05 W
Alsek ≃ 180 59.10 N 138.10 W
Alsen 198 48.37 N 98.42 W
Alseno 64 44.54 N 9.59 E
Alsenz 56 49.43 N 7.49 E
Alsenz ≃ 56 49.49 N 7.51 E
Alsey 219 39.34 N 90.25 W
Alsfeld 56 50.45 N 9.16 E
Als Fjord c[2] 41 55.02 N 9.38 E
Alsh, Loch c 46 57.15 N 5.39 W
Al-Shallūfa Military Base ■ 142 30.03 N 32.32 E
Alsike 40 59.45 N 17.45 E
Alsina 252 33.54 S 59.23 W
Alsip 216 41.40 N 87.44 W
Alsleben 54 51.42 N 11.41 E
Alsónémedi 264c 47.19 N 19.10 E
Alstaden ◆[8] 263 51.28 N 6.50 E
Älstäket 40 59.20 N 18.28 E
Alstätte 52 52.08 N 6.55 E

Symbol	English	Deutsch	Español	Français	Português
≃	River	Fluß	Río	Rivière	Rio
≍	Canal	Kanal	Canal	Canal	Canal
⌊	Waterfall, Rapids	Wasserfall, Stromschnellen	Cascada, Rápidos	Chute d'eau, Rapides	Cascata, Rápidos
⊔	Strait	Meeresstraße	Estrecho	Détroit	Estreito
c	Bay, Gulf	Bucht, Golf	Bahía, Golfo	Baie, Golfe	Baía, Golfo
⊜	Lake, Lakes	See, Seen	Lago, Lagos	Lac, Lacs	Lago, Lagos
≡	Swamp	Sumpf	Pantano	Marais	Pântano
⊼	Ice Features, Glacier	Eis- und Gletscherformen	Accidentes Glaciales	Formes glaciaires	Acidentes glaciares
⊤	Other Hydrographic Features	Andere Hydrographische Objekte	Otros Elementos Hidrográficos	Autres données hydrographiques	Outros acidentes hidrográficos
⇸	Submarine Features	Untermeerische Objekte	Accidentes Submarinos	Formes de relief sous-marin	Acidentes submarinos
□	Political Unit	Politische Einheit	Unidad Politica	Entité politique	Unidade política
♥	Cultural Institution	Kulturelle Institution	Institución Cultural	Institution culturelle	Instituição cultural
⊥	Historical Site	Historische Stätte	Sitio Histórico	Site historique	Sitio histórico
♠	Recreational Site	Erholungs- und Ferienort	Sitio de Recreo	Centre de loisirs	Area de Lazer
⊠	Airport	Flughafen	Aeropuerto	Aéroport	Aeroporto
■	Military Installation	Militäranlage	Instalación Militar	Installation militaire	Instalação militar
◆	Miscellaneous	Verschiedenes	Misceláneo	Divers	Diversos

ENGLISH: Name · Page · Lat.°′ · Long.°′ — DEUTSCH: Name · Seite · Breite°′ · Länge°′ E = Ost

Alstead ≃ 184 55.50 N 107.26 W
Alster 40 59.24 N 13.36 E
Alster ≃ 52 53.36 N 9.59 E
Alsterbro 26 56.57 N 15.55 E
Alstern ⊜ 40 59.40 N 13.55 E
Alston 44 54.49 N 2.26 W
Alsunga 76 56.59 N 21.34 E
Alswede 52 52.20 N 8.33 E
Alt ≃ 262 53.32 N 3.03 W
Alta, Nor. 24 69.55 N 23.12 E
Älta, Sve. 40 59.16 N 18.11 E
Alta, Ca., U.S. 226 39.12 N 120.49 W
Alta, Ia., U.S. 198 42.40 N 95.17 W
Alta, Cachoeira ⌊ 250 5.46 S 54.28 W
Alta, Mount ∧ 172 44.30 S 168.58 E
Altadena 228 34.11 N 118.07 W
Alta Floresta 250 9.57 S 56.06 W
Alta Gracia, Arg. 252 31.40 S 64.26 W
Altagracia, Nic. 236 11.34 N 85.35 W
Altagracia, Ven. 246 10.43 N 71.32 W
Altagracia de Orituco 246 9.52 N 66.23 W
Alta Hill 226 39.14 N 121.04 W
Al Tahoe 226 38.57 N 119.59 W
Altai ⩘ 90 48.00 N 90.00 E
Altair 222 29.34 N 96.28 W
Altaj, Mong. 86 48.18 N 89.35 E
Altaj (Jesönbulag), Mong. 90 46.20 N 96.18 E
Altaj, Ross. 86 53.27 N 91.48 E
Altajskij 86 51.58 N 85.22 E
Alta Loma, Ca., U.S. 228 34.07 N 117.36 W
Alta Loma, Tx., U.S. 222 29.22 N 95.04 W
Altamaha ≃ 192 31.19 N 81.17 W
Altamira, Arg. 258 34.40 S 59.22 W
Altamira, Bra. 250 3.12 S 52.12 W
Altamira, Chile 252 25.47 S 69.51 W
Altamira, C.R. 236 10.30 N 84.23 W
Altamira, Méx. 234 22.24 N 97.55 W
Altamira, Las Cuevas de ≛[5] 34 43.18 N 4.08 W
Altamirano, Arg. 258 35.21 S 58.09 W
Altamirano, Méx. 196 25.55 N 97.47 W
Altamont, Il., U.S. 219 39.03 N 88.44 W
Altamont, Ks., U.S. 198 37.11 N 95.17 W
Altamont, N.Y., U.S. 210 42.42 N 74.02 W
Altamont, Or., U.S. 202 42.12 N 121.44 W
Altamont, Tn., U.S. 194 35.25 N 85.43 W
Altamonte Springs 220 28.39 N 81.21 W
Altamura 68 40.50 N 16.33 E
Altamura, Isla I 232 25.00 N 108.10 W
Altan, Ross. 88 49.53 N 109.04 E
Altan, Ross. 88 49.31 N 111.32 E
Altanbulag, Mong. 88 50.19 N 106.30 E
Altanbulag, Mong. 88 47.41 N 106.22 E
Altan-Cögor 86 49.03 N 90.27 E
Altanširee 102 45.35 N 110.27 E
Altar 232 30.43 N 111.44 W
Altar ≃ 232 30.39 N 111.53 W
Altar, Desierto de ◆[2] 232 31.50 N 114.15 W
Altar de Los Sacrificios ⊥ 232 16.28 N 90.32 W
Altare 62 44.20 N 8.20 E
Altario 184 51.55 N 110.09 W
Altarnun 42 50.37 N 4.30 W
Altar of the Earth ʊ[1] 271a 39.57 N 116.24 E
Altar of the Moon ʊ[1] 271a 39.55 N 116.20 E
Altar of the Sun ʊ[1] 271a 39.54 N 116.27 E
Altar Wash V 200 32.05 N 111.19 W
Altaskij Kraj □[8] 86 52.30 N 83.00 E
Altastenberg 56 51.11 N 8.28 E
Altata, Méx. 232 24.38 N 107.55 W
Altata, Ross. 80 51.07 N 48.44 E
Alta Verapaz □[5] 236 15.40 N 90.00 W
Altavilla Irpina 68 41.00 N 14.47 E
Altavilla Milicia 70 38.02 N 13.32 E
Altavilla Silentina 68 40.32 N 15.08 E
Altaville 226 38.05 N 120.33 W
Alta Vista, Ks., U.S. 198 38.51 N 96.29 W
Altavista, Va., U.S. 192 37.06 N 79.17 W
Altay, Ross. 86 60.20 N 68.58 E
Altay, Zhg. 86 47.52 N 88.07 E
Alt Buchhorst 264a 52.26 N 13.51 E
Altdöbern 54 51.39 N 14.02 E
Altdorf, Dtsch. 60 48.34 N 12.07 E
Altdorf, Schw. 58 46.53 N 8.39 E
Altdorf bei Nürnberg 60 49.23 N 11.21 E
Alte Donau ⊜ 264b 48.14 N 16.26 E
Alteelva ≃ 24 69.58 N 23.23 E
Altefähr 54 54.20 N 13.07 E
Alteglofsheim 60 48.55 N 12.12 E
Alte Grund 264a 52.28 N 13.47 E
Altena 56 51.17 N 7.40 E
Altenahr 56 50.31 N 6.59 E
Altenau 52 51.48 N 10.26 E
Altenbeken 52 51.46 N 8.56 E
Altenberg 54 50.46 N 13.45 E
Altenberge 52 52.03 N 7.27 E
Altenbruch 52 53.49 N 8.46 E
Altenbüren 56 51.23 N 8.30 E
Altenburg, Dtsch. 54 50.59 N 12.26 E
Altenburg, Öst. 61 48.38 N 15.35 E
Altenderne Oberbecker ◆[8] 263 51.35 N 7.33 E
Altendorf 263 51.29 N 7.40 E
Altendorf ◆[8] 263 51.25 N 7.06 E
Altendorf-Ulfkotte 263 51.38 N 7.00 E
Altenesch 52 53.08 N 8.37 E
Altenessen ◆[8] 263 51.29 N 7.00 E
Altenfelden 60 48.29 N 13.58 E
Altengamme ◆[8] 52 53.25 N 10.16 E
Altenhagen, Dtsch. 52 52.03 N 8.38 E
Altenhagen, Dtsch. 54 53.45 N 13.06 E
Altenhagen ◆[8] 263 51.22 N 7.28 E
Altenhof 54 52.55 N 13.43 E
Altenholz 41 54.24 N 10.07 E
Altenkirchen, Dtsch. 54 54.38 N 13.20 E
Altenkirchen (Westerwald), Dtsch. 56 50.41 N 7.38 E
Altenkrempe 54 54.08 N 10.49 E
Altenkunstadt 54 50.07 N 11.14 E
Altenmarkt an der Alz 60 48.00 N 12.32 E
Altenoythe 52 53.02 N 7.52 E
Altenpleen 54 54.21 N 12.57 E
Altenstadt an der Waldnaab 60 49.48 N 12.10 E
Altensteig 56 48.35 N 8.37 E
Altentreptow 54 53.42 N 13.14 E
Altenvoerde 263 51.18 N 7.22 E
Altenwalde 52 53.49 N 8.40 E
Altenweddingen 54 52.00 N 11.31 E
Alte Oder ≃ 54 52.52 N 14.09 E
Alter do Chão 34 39.12 N 7.40 W
Alterosa 256 21.15 S 46.08 W
Alter Rhein ≃ 263 51.35 N 6.36 E
Altes Land ◆[1] 52 53.33 N 9.38 E
Altevatnet ⊜ 24 68.32 N 19.30 E
Altfraunhofen 60 48.27 N 12.10 E
Altfriedland 54 52.38 N 14.12 E
Altglashütten 58 47.51 N 8.06 E
Alt-Glienicke ◆[8] 264a 52.25 N 13.32 E
Altgruland 263 51.27 N 7.41 E
Altha 192 30.34 N 85.07 W
Altham 262 53.47 N 2.21 W
Alt-Hartmannsdorf 264a 52.21 N 13.50 E
Althea Lake ⊜ 283 42.40 N 71.23 W
Altheim 60 48.15 N 13.13 E
Altheimer 194 34.19 N 91.50 W
Althofen 61 46.54 N 14.27 E
Altınekin 130 38.19 N 32.53 E
Altinho 250 8.29 S 36.04 W
Altınoluk 130 39.34 N 26.44 E
Altinópolis 255 21.02 S 47.23 W
Altınova 130 39.13 N 26.47 E
Altınözü 130 36.08 N 36.12 E
Altıntaş 130 39.04 N 30.07 E
Altınyaka 130 36.34 N 30.21 E
Altiplano ⩘[1] 248 18.00 S 68.00 W
Alt Käbelich 54 53.29 N 13.29 E
Altkirch 58 47.37 N 7.15 E
Altlandsberg 54 52.33 N 13.43 E
Altlangerwisch 264a 52.19 N 13.04 E
Altlewin 54 52.42 N 14.16 E
Altlüdersdorf 54 53.02 N 13.11 E
Altlünen 52 51.38 N 7.31 E
Altmannsdorf ◆[8] 264b 48.10 N 16.20 E
Altmannstein 60 48.54 N 11.39 E
Altmar 212 43.31 N 76.00 W
Altmark □[9] 54 52.40 N 11.20 E
Altmittweida 54 50.58 N 12.57 E
Altmühl ≃ 60 48.54 N 11.54 E
Altmünster 64 47.54 N 13.45 E
Altnaharra 46 58.16 N 4.27 W
Alto, Mi., U.S. 216 42.51 N 85.22 W
Alto, Tx., U.S. 222 31.39 N 95.04 W
Alto, Cerro ∧, Méx. 234 20.50 N 100.22 W
Alto, Cerro ∧, Ca., U.S. 226 35.25 N 120.43 W
Alto Anapu ≃ 250 2.15 S 51.27 W
Alto Araguaia 255 17.19 S 53.12 W
Alto Cauale 152 7.34 S 16.16 E
Alto Cedro 240p 20.31 N 75.58 W
Alto Chicapa 152 10.53 S 19.14 E
Alto Coité 255 15.47 S 54.20 W
Alto Cuito 152 13.27 S 18.49 E
Alto da Moóca ◆[8] 287b 23.34 S 46.35 W
Alto da Serra 256 22.53 S 44.14 W
Alto de las Vizcachas, Cerro ∧ 286e 33.25 S 70.26 W
Alto del Carmen 252 28.46 S 70.30 W
Alto de Ña Paula 286c 10.24 N 66.48 W
Alto do Rio Doce 255 21.02 S 43.25 W
Altofonte 70 38.03 N 13.18 E
Alto Garças 255 16.56 S 53.32 W
Alto Ligonha 154 15.30 S 38.20 E
Alto Longá 250 5.15 S 42.12 W
Alto Lucero 234 19.37 N 96.43 W
Alto Molócuè 154 15.38 S 37.42 E
Altomonte 68 39.42 N 16.08 E
Altomünster 60 48.23 N 11.15 E
Alton, On., Can. 212 43.52 N 80.04 W
Alton, Eng., U.K. 42 51.09 N 0.59 W
Alton, Il., U.S. 219 38.53 N 90.11 W
Alton, Ia., U.S. 198 42.59 N 96.00 W
Alton, Ks., U.S. 198 39.28 N 98.56 W
Alton, Ky., U.S. 218 38.04 N 84.55 W
Alton, Mo., U.S. 194 36.41 N 91.23 W
Alton, N.H., U.S. 188 43.27 N 71.13 W
Alton, N.Y., U.S. 210 43.13 N 76.59 W
Alton, R.I., U.S. 207 41.26 N 71.43 W
Altona, Austl. 162 27.34 S 120.00 E
Altona, Austl. 169 37.52 S 144.50 E
Altona, Mb., Can. 184 49.06 N 97.33 W
Altona, In., U.S. 216 41.21 N 85.09 W
Altona ◆[8] 52 53.32 N 9.56 E
Altona Bay ⊂ 274b 37.53 S 144.51 E
Altona North 274b 37.50 S 144.51 E
Altona Sports Park ♦ 274b 37.52 S 144.52 E
Altoona, Al., U.S. 194 34.01 N 86.19 W
Altoona, Fl., U.S. 220 28.57 N 81.38 W
Altoona, Ia., U.S. 190 41.39 N 93.28 W
Altoona, Ks., U.S. 198 37.31 N 95.39 W
Altoona, Pa., U.S. 214 40.31 N 78.23 W
Altoona, Wa., U.S. 224 46.16 N 123.39 W
Altoona, Wi., U.S. 190 44.48 N 91.26 W
Alto Pacajá ≃ 250 3.07 S 50.20 W
Alto Paraguai 248 14.30 S 56.31 W
Alto Paraguay □[5] 248 21.00 S 58.45 W
Alto Paraíso de Goiás 255 14.07 S 47.31 W
Alto Paraná □[5] 252 25.00 S 54.50 W
Alto Parnaíba 250 9.06 S 45.57 W
Alto Purús ≃ 248 9.34 S 70.36 W
Alto Río Mayo 254 45.35 S 71.06 W
Alto Río Senguer 254 45.02 S 70.50 W
Altos 250 5.03 S 42.28 W
Alto Santo 250 5.31 S 38.15 W
Alto Sucuriú 255 19.19 S 52.47 W
Altotonga 234 19.46 N 97.14 W
Altötting 60 48.13 N 12.40 E
Alto Volta → Burkina Faso □[1] 150 13.00 N 1.30 W
Alto Yurua ≃ 248 9.24 S 72.43 W
Altrincham 262 53.24 N 2.21 W
Alt Rüdersdorf 264a 52.28 N 13.49 E
Altruppin 54 52.56 N 12.50 E
Altshausen 58 47.56 N 9.32 E
Alt Stahnsdorf 264a 52.17 N 13.53 E
Altstätten 58 47.23 N 9.33 E
Alt Töplitz 264a 52.26 N 12.55 E
Altuchovo 76 52.40 N 34.20 E
Āltūn Kūprī 128 35.45 N 44.09 E
Altun Shan ⩘ 90 38.00 N 88.00 E
Alturas 204 41.29 N 120.32 W
Altus, Ar., U.S. 194 35.26 N 93.45 W
Altus, Ok., U.S. 196 34.38 N 99.20 W
Altus, Lake ⊜[1] 196 34.56 N 99.18 W
Altus Air Force Base ■ 196 34.40 N 99.16 W
Altusried 58 47.48 N 10.13 E
Altyagač 84 40.50 N 48.54 E
Altyaryk 85 40.23 N 71.30 E
Altykarasu 86 49.12 N 55.52 E
Altynaj 86 57.04 N 62.00 E
Altynasar ⊥ 86 45.10 N 63.07 E
Altynkul' 85 40.48 N 72.10 E
Altynovka 78 51.27 N 33.10 E
Altyntau 86 44.08 N 68.03 E
Altyn-Topkan 85 40.38 N 69.35 E
Alu I 175e 7.02 S 155.47 E
Al-Ubayyiḍ 140 13.11 N 30.13 E
Alubijid 116 8.35 N 124.29 E
Alucra 130 40.20 N 38.46 E
Al-ʿUdaysāt 140 25.35 N 32.29 E
Al-Uḍayyah 140 12.03 N 28.17 E
Aluk 140 8.26 N 27.27 E
Alūksne 76 57.25 N 27.03 E
Al-ʿUlā 128 26.37 N 37.52 E
Alum Bank 214 40.14 N 78.34 W
Alum Creek ≃ 218 39.53 N 82.54 W
Alum Creek Lake ⊜[1] 214 40.15 N 82.58 W
Aluminé 254 39.13 S 70.57 W
Aluminé ≃ 254 39.50 S 70.53 W
Aluminé, Lago ⊜ 252 38.55 S 71.09 W
Alum Rock 226 37.21 N 121.49 W
Alum Rock Park ♦ 282 37.24 N 121.49 W
Alunda 40 60.04 N 18.05 E
Alunitdag 84 40.32 N 46.03 E
Alupka 78 44.26 N 34.03 E
Al-ʿUqaylah 146 30.16 N 19.12 E
Al-ʿUqayr 128 25.39 N 50.12 E
Al-Uqṣur (Luxor) 140 25.41 N 32.39 E
Al-ʿUrayq ≛[8] 128 29.10 N 39.15 E
Al-ʿUrayq ◆[1] 128 24.47 N 42.55 E
Al-Urdun → Jordan □[1] 128 31.00 N 36.00 E
Al-Urdunn → Jordan ≃ 132 31.46 N 35.33 E
Alušta 78 44.42 N 34.24 E
Al-ʿUṭayshān ⫧[4] 140 16.25 N 34.30 E
Al-ʿUwaynāt 146 25.46 N 10.34 E
Al-ʿUwaynidhīyah I 128 26.37 N 36.05 E
Al-ʿUyaynah 128 24.54 N 46.23 E
Alva, Scot., U.K. 46 56.09 N 3.48 W
Alva, Fl., U.S. 220 26.42 N 81.36 W
Alva, Ok., U.S. 196 36.48 N 98.39 W
Alva ≃ 34 40.18 N 8.15 W
Alvada 214 41.03 N 83.24 W
Alvaiázere 34 39.49 N 8.23 W
Alvaneu-Bad 58 46.40 N 9.39 E
Älvängen 26 57.58 N 12.07 E
Alvanley 262 53.16 N 2.45 W
Alvarado, Méx. 234 18.46 N 95.46 W
Alvarado, Tx., U.S. 222 32.24 N 97.12 W
Alvarado, Lake ⊜[1] 222 32.23 N 97.15 W
Alvarães 246 3.12 S 64.50 W
Álvarez Jonte 258 35.19 S 57.28 W
Alvarinhos 266c 38.54 N 9.22 W
Álvaro Obregón 234 19.50 N 101.05 W
Álvaro Obregón ◆[8] 286a 19.21 N 99.12 W
Álvaro Obregón, Presa ⊜[1] 232 27.55 N 109.52 W
Alvastra ⊥ 26 58.18 N 14.39 E
Alvdal 26 62.07 N 10.39 E
Älvdalen 26 61.14 N 14.02 E
Alvear 252 29.06 S 56.33 W
Alvechurch 42 52.21 N 1.57 W
Alverca 34 38.54 N 9.02 W
Alverda 214 40.38 N 78.52 W
Alvernia, Mount ∧[2] 238 24.15 N 75.24 W
Alverton 214 40.08 N 79.35 W
Alves 46 57.38 N 3.27 W
Alvesta 26 56.54 N 14.33 E
Alveston 42 51.36 N 2.32 W
Alviano, Lago di ⊜[1] 66 42.36 N 12.15 E
Ålvik, Nor. 26 60.26 N 6.26 E
Alvik, Sve. 26 62.25 N 17.24 E
Alvin, Il., U.S. 216 40.19 N 87.37 W
Alvin, Tx., U.S. 222 29.25 N 95.14 W
Alvinópolis 255 20.06 S 43.03 W
Alvinston 214 42.49 N 81.52 W
Alviso ◆[8] 282 37.26 N 121.58 W
Alviso Slough ≃ 282 37.27 N 122.02 W
Alvito, It. 66 41.41 N 13.45 E
Alvito, Port. 34 38.15 N 7.59 W
Älvkarleby 40 60.34 N 17.27 E
Älvkarleö bruk 40 60.32 N 17.24 E
Alvord 196 33.22 N 97.42 W
Alvord Desert ◆[2] 202 42.30 N 118.25 W
Alvord Lake ⊜ 202 42.23 N 118.36 W
Alvordton 216 41.40 N 84.26 W
Alvra, Pass d')(58 46.35 N 9.50 E
Älvros 26 62.03 N 14.39 E
Älvsborgs Län □[6] 26 58.00 N 12.30 E
Älvsbyn 24 65.39 N 20.59 E
Älvsnabben ⊥ 40 58.59 N 18.10 E
Al-Wafāʾīyah 142 30.46 N 30.36 E
Al-Wajh 128 26.15 N 36.26 E
Al-Wakrah 128 25.10 N 51.36 E
Al-Walīdīyah 142 27.12 N 31.10 E
Alwar 124 27.34 N 76.36 E
Alwar Hills ⩘[2] 124 27.20 N 76.15 E
Al-Wāṣifīyah 142 30.35 N 32.10 E
Al-Wāsiṭah 142 29.20 N 31.12 E
Alwaye 122 10.07 N 76.21 E
Al-Wazīrīyah 142 31.11 N 30.57 E
Al-Wazz 140 15.01 N 30.10 E
Alwen ≃ 42 52.58 N 3.24 W
Al-Widy 142 29.31 N 31.16 E
Alxa Zuoqi 102 38.50 N 105.32 E
Al-Yamāmah → As-Sulaymānīyah 128 24.09 N 47.19 E
Al-Yaman → Yemen □[1] 144 15.00 N 47.00 E
Al Yāmūn 132 32.29 N 35.14 E
Alygdžer 88 53.38 N 98.16 E
Alyn and Deeside □[8] 262 53.16 N 3.02 W
Alypsatar 86 48.03 N 80.21 E
Alyth 46 56.37 N 3.13 W
Alytus 76 54.24 N 24.03 E
Alz ≃ 60 48.16 N 12.49 E
Alzamaj 88 55.33 N 98.39 E
Alzano Lombardo 62 45.44 N 9.43 E
Al-Zarqa 142 31.13 N 31.38 E
Alzenau 56 50.05 N 9.04 E
Alzette ≃ 56 49.22 N 6.09 E
Alzey 56 49.45 N 8.07 E
Alzira (Alcira) 34 39.09 N 0.26 W
Amab, Khawr V 140 17.08 N 34.51 E
Amacayacu, Parque Nacional ♦ 246 3.45 S 70.10 W
Amacuro ≃ 246 8.32 N 60.28 W
Amacuzac ≃ 234 17.53 N 99.12 W
Amadeus, Lake ⊜ 162 24.50 S 130.45 E
Āmādi, Bngl. 126 22.28 N 89.19 E
Amadi, Zaïre 154 3.35 N 26.47 E
Amadjuak Lake ⊜ 176 65.00 N 71.00 W
Amador □[6] 226 38.21 N 120.46 W
Amadora 266c 38.45 N 9.14 W
Amador City 226 38.25 N 120.56 W
Amador Valley V 282 37.41 N 121.51 W
Amagansett 207 40.58 N 72.08 W
Amagasaki 96 34.43 N 135.25 E
Amagase 96 33.15 N 131.02 E
Amager I 41 55.37 N 12.37 E
Amagi 96 33.25 N 130.39 E
Amagi-san ∧ 94 34.51 N 139.00 E
Amagi-yugashima 94 34.53 N 138.56 E
Amagoi-dake ∧ 94 35.01 N 136.23 E
Amagunze 150 6.20 N 7.40 E
Amahai 164 3.20 S 128.55 E
Amaichá del Valle 252 26.36 S 65.55 W
Amaimon 164 5.10 S 145.25 E
Amajac ≃ 234 21.15 N 98.46 W
Amaka ≃ 236 14.14 N 85.07 W
Ama Keng 271c 1.24 N 103.42 E
Amak Island I 180 55.25 N 163.07 W
Amakusa-nada ⫧[2] 92 32.35 N 130.05 E
Amakusa-shotō II 92 32.20 N 130.15 E
Amakuso-Shimo-shima I 92 32.20 N 130.05 E
Amal, Lībiyā 146 29.25 N 21.10 E
Åmål, Sve. 26 59.03 N 12.42 E
Amalāpuram 122 16.35 N 82.01 E
Amalat ≃ 88 54.49 N 115.12 E
Amalfi, Col. 246 6.55 N 75.04 W
Amalfi, It. 68 40.38 N 14.36 E
Amalia 158 27.16 S 25.03 E
Amaliás 38 37.49 N 21.23 E
Amalner 120 21.03 N 75.04 E
Amamaki-zan ∧ 94 36.25 N 140.09 E
Amambaí 255 23.05 S 55.13 W
Amambaí ≃ 255 23.22 S 53.56 W
Amambay □[5] 252 23.00 S 56.00 W
Amami-Ō-shima I 93b 28.15 N 129.20 E
Amami-shotō II 93b 28.16 N 129.21 E
Amamula 154 0.18 S 27.50 E
Amana 190 41.48 N 91.52 W
Amanã ≃, Bra. 250 4.25 S 57.34 W
Amana ≃, Ven. 238 9.45 N 62.39 W
Amanã, Lago ⊜ 246 2.35 S 64.40 W
Amanab 164 3.35 S 141.13 E
Amanave 174u 14.19 S 170.49 W
Amance 58 47.48 N 6.04 E
Amancey 58 47.02 N 6.05 E
Amancio 240p 20.49 N 77.35 W
Amanda 188 39.38 N 82.44 W
Amanda Park 224 47.28 N 123.54 W
Amandola 66 42.59 N 13.21 E
Amānganj 124 24.26 N 80.02 E
Amangel'dy, Kaz. 85 43.43 N 71.07 E
Amangel'dy, Kaz. 86 50.10 N 65.13 E
Amangel'dy, Kaz. 86 49.52 N 59.00 E
Åmänningen ⊜ 40 59.57 N 15.56 E
Amano 270 34.26 N 135.33 E
Amanotkel' 86 46.07 N 61.34 E
Amantea 68 39.08 N 16.05 E
Amantogaj 86 50.22 N 65.33 E
Amanu I[1] 14 17.48 S 140.46 W
Amanzimtofi 158 30.03 S 30.53 E
Amapá 250 2.03 N 50.48 W
Amapá □[3] 250 1.00 N 52.00 W
Amapa ≃ 234 18.18 N 96.19 W
Amapala 236 13.17 N 87.40 W
Amapala, Punta de ≻ 236 13.10 N 87.54 W
Amapari ≃ 250 0.43 N 51.32 W
Amaraji 250 8.24 S 35.27 W
Amaral 287a 22.42 S 43.29 W
Amaramba, Lago ⊜ 154 14.30 S 35.55 E
Amarante 250 6.14 S 42.50 W
Amarante do Maranhão 250 5.36 S 46.45 W
Amaranth 184 50.36 N 98.43 W
Amarapura 110 21.54 N 96.03 E
Amărăştii-de-Jos 38 43.59 N 24.10 E
ʿAmārat Abū Sinn 140 15.21 N 35.45 E
Amarāvati ≃ 122 10.51 N 78.11 E
Amarda 126 21.47 N 87.08 E
Amareleja 34 38.12 N 7.14 W
Amares 34 41.38 N 8.21 W
Amargosa 255 13.02 S 39.36 W
Amargosa ≃ 204 36.13 N 116.48 W
Amargosa Range ⩘ 204 36.15 N 116.45 W
Amarillo 196 35.13 N 101.49 W
Amarillo, Mar → Yellow Sea ⫧[2] 90 36.00 N 123.00 E
ʿAmar Jadīd 140 14.28 N 25.14 E
Amarkantak 124 22.40 N 81.45 E
Amarnāth 122 19.11 N 73.10 E
Amarnāth Cave ≛[5] 123 34.13 N 75.31 E
Amaro, Monte ∧ 66 42.05 N 14.05 E
Amaroúsion 267c 38.03 N 23.49 E
Amarpātan 124 24.19 N 80.59 E
Amarube-saki ≻ 96 35.40 N 134.32 E
Amarume 92 38.50 N 139.55 E
Amarwāra 124 22.18 N 79.10 E
Amasa 190 46.13 N 88.26 W
Amaseno ≃ 66 41.34 N 13.13 E
Amasija 84 40.58 N 43.46 E
Amasra 130 41.45 N 32.24 E
Amasya 130 40.39 N 35.51 E
Amasya □[4] 130 40.45 N 35.30 E
Amataurá 246 3.29 S 68.06 W
Amatignak Island I 181a 51.15 N 179.08 W
Amatikulu 158 29.06 S 31.27 E
Amatique, Bahía de ⊂ 236 15.55 N 88.45 W
Amatitán 234 20.50 N 103.43 W
Amatitlán 236 14.29 N 90.37 W
Amatitlán, Lago de ⊜ 236 14.27 N 90.34 W
Amatlán de Cañas 234 20.52 N 104.27 W
Amatlán de los Reyes 234 18.50 N 96.55 W
Amatrice 66 42.38 N 13.17 E
Amatsu-kominato 94 35.07 N 140.10 E
Amau 164 10.02 S 148.34 E
Amausi 124 26.46 N 80.51 E
Amawalk 210 41.17 N 73.46 W
Amay 56 50.33 N 5.19 E
Ama-zaki ≻ 94 37.08 N 136.40 E
Amazar 89 53.54 N 120.53 E
Amazon (Solimões) (Amazonas) ≃ 242 0.10 S 49.00 W
Amazonas □[3] 242 5.00 S 63.00 W
Amazonas □[5], Col. 246 1.00 S 72.00 W
Amazonas □[5], Perú 248 5.30 S 78.00 W
Amazonas □[8] 246 3.30 N 66.00 W
Amazonas → Amazon ≃ 242 0.10 S 49.00 W
Amazônia, Parque Nacional da ♦, Bra. 250 4.30 S 56.30 W
Amb 123 34.19 N 72.51 E
Ambāh 124 26.43 N 78.14 E
Ambahikily 157b 21.36 S 43.41 E
Ambahita 157b 24.01 S 45.16 E
Ambaí 287a 22.43 S 43.28 W
Ambājogāi 122 18.44 N 76.23 E
Ambakaka 157b 24.10 S 46.17 E
Ambāla 124 30.21 N 76.50 E
Ambāla Airport ⊠ 123 30.22 N 76.50 E
Ambalabe 157b 18.24 S 49.10 E
Ambalafany 157b 22.32 S 47.36 E
Ambalangoda 122 6.14 N 80.03 E
Ambalanjanakomby 157b 16.42 S 47.05 E
Ambalavao 157b 21.50 S 46.56 E
Ambam 152 2.23 N 11.17 E
Amba Maryam 144 11.26 N 39.17 E
Ambanja 157b 13.41 S 48.27 E
Ambar 248 10.44 S 77.16 W
Ambararata 157b 15.03 S 48.33 E
Ambarawa 115a 7.15 S 110.24 E
Ambarčik, Ross. 74 69.39 N 162.20 E
Ambarčik, Ross. 88 55.09 N 95.46 E
Ambargasta, Salinas de ≚ 252 29.15 S 64.30 W
Ambarijeby 157b 14.56 S 47.41 E
Ambarnyj 24 65.56 N 33.43 E
Ambaro, Baie d' ⊂ 157b 13.23 S 48.38 E
Ambāsamudram 122 8.42 N 77.28 E
Ambassador Bridge ◆[5] 281 42.20 N 83.05 W
Ambato, Ec. 246 1.15 S 78.37 W
Ambato, Madag. 157b 13.24 S 48.29 E
Ambato Boeny 157b 16.28 S 46.43 E
Ambatofinandrahana 157b 20.33 S 46.48 E
Ambatolampy 157b 19.23 S 47.25 E
Ambatomainty 157b 17.41 S 45.40 E
Ambatomanoina 157b 18.18 S 47.37 E
Ambatondrazaka 157b 17.50 S 48.25 E
Ambatosoratra 157b 17.34 S 48.32 E
Ambeláki 267c 37.57 N 23.32 E
Ambelau, Pulau I 164 3.51 S 127.12 E
Ámbelos, Ákra ≻ 38 39.56 N 23.55 E
Ambenja 157b 15.17 S 46.58 E
Amber ≃ 44 53.04 N 1.29 W
Amberes → Antwerpen 50 51.13 N 4.25 E
Amberg, Dtsch. 60 49.27 N 11.52 E
Amberg, Wi., U.S. 190 45.30 N 87.59 W
Ambergris Cay I 232 18.03 N 87.56 W
Ambérieu-en-Bugey 58 45.57 N 5.21 E
Amberley 172 43.10 S 172.44 E
Amberley Royal Australian Air Force Base ■ 171a 27.37 S 152.41 E
Amberson 214 40.10 N 77.41 W
Ambert 62 45.33 N 3.45 E
Ambevongo 157b 15.27 S 47.27 E
Ambia 216 40.29 N 87.31 W
Ambidédi 150 14.35 N 11.47 W
Ambikānagar 126 22.57 N 86.46 E
Ambikāpur 124 23.07 N 83.12 E
Ambil 116 13.49 N 120.20 E
Ambil Island I 116 13.48 N 120.18 E
Ambilobe 157b 13.12 S 49.04 E
Ambinanindrano 157b 20.20 S 48.19 E
Ambinanitelo 157b 15.21 S 49.35 E
Ambinda 157b 16.25 S 45.52 E
Ambivy 157b 21.31 S 44.02 E
Ambjörby 26 60.30 N 13.10 E
Ambla 76 59.11 N 25.51 E
Amble 44 55.20 N 1.34 W
Amblecote 42 52.28 N 2.09 W
Ambler, Ak., U.S. 180 67.05 N 157.52 W
Ambler, Pa., U.S. 208 40.09 N 75.13 W
Ambleside 44 54.26 N 2.58 W
Ambleteuse 50 50.49 N 1.36 E
Amblève ≃ 56 50.28 N 5.36 E
Ambo 248 10.07 S 76.10 W
Amboahangy 157b 24.15 S 46.22 E
Amboasary, Madag. 157b 18.26 S 48.16 E
Amboasary, Madag. 157b 25.02 S 46.23 E
Ambodifototra 157b 16.59 S 49.52 E
Ambodilazana 157b 18.06 S 49.10 E
Ambodiriana 157b 17.55 S 49.18 E
Ambohibary 157b 19.20 S 46.17 E
Ambohidratrimo 157b 18.50 S 47.26 E
Ambohidray 157b 18.36 S 48.18 E
Ambohimahamasina 157b 21.56 S 47.11 E
Ambohimahasoa 157b 21.07 S 47.13 E
Ambohimanga du Sud 157b 20.52 S 47.36 E
Ambohimitombo 157b 20.43 S 47.26 E
Amboina → Ambon 164 3.43 S 128.12 E
Amboise 50 47.25 N 0.59 E
Amboíva 152 11.32 S 14.44 E
Ambon 164 3.43 S 128.12 E
Ambon, Pulau I 164 3.40 S 128.10 E
Ambondro 157b 25.13 S 45.44 E
Ambonnay 50 49.04 N 4.10 E
Amboseli, Lake ⊜ 154 2.37 S 37.08 E
Amboseli National Park ♦ 154 2.30 S 37.15 E
Amboshe 272c 19.09 N 73.08 E
Ambositra 157b 20.31 S 47.15 E
Ambovombe 157b 25.11 S 46.05 E
Amboy, Il., U.S. 190 41.42 N 89.19 W
Amboy, In., U.S. 216 40.36 N 85.55 W
Amboy, Mn., U.S. 190 43.53 N 94.09 W
Amboy, Wa., U.S. 224 45.54 N 122.26 W
Ambre, Cap d' ≻ 157b 11.57 S 49.17 E
Ambre, Montagne d' ∧ 157b 12.30 S 49.10 E
Ambridge 214 40.35 N 80.13 W
Ambridge Heights 214 40.36 N 80.13 W
Ambridge Reservoir ⊜[1] 214 40.34 N 80.21 W
Ambrières 32 48.24 N 0.38 W
Ambriz 152 7.50 S 13.06 E
Ambrolauri 84 42.31 N 43.09 E
Ambronay 58 46.00 N 5.21 E
Ambrose 198 48.57 N 103.28 W
Ambrose Brook ≃ 276 40.33 N 74.32 W
Ambrose Channel ⌇ 276 40.32 N 74.02 W
Ambrosia Lake 200 35.25 N 107.49 W
Ambrym □[8] 175f 16.15 S 168.12 E
Ambrym I 175f 16.15 S 168.10 E
Ambuklao Dam ◆[6] 116 16.28 N 120.45 E
Ambulong Island I 116 12.12 N 121.01 E
Ambulu 115a 8.21 S 113.36 E
Ambuntentimur 115a 6.54 S 113.45 E
Ambunti 164 4.14 S 142.50 E
Āmbūr 122 12.47 N 78.42 E
Amburambur 115b 8.15 S 116.18 E
Amburayan Nabunga ≃ 116 16.55 N 120.27 E
Amby 56 50.53 N 5.44 E
Amchitka Island I 181a 51.30 N 179.00 E
Amchitka Pass ⌇ 181a 51.30 N 179.30 W
ʿAmd 144 15.18 N 48.00 E
Am-Dam 146 12.46 N 20.29 E
Āmdānga 272b 22.49 N 88.31 E
Amded, Oued V 148 22.09 N 3.15 E
Amden 58 47.09 N 9.11 E
Amderma 72 69.45 N 61.39 E
Amdo 120 32.18 N 91.04 E
Ameagle 188 37.56 N 81.25 W
Ameca 234 20.33 N 104.02 W
Ameca ≃ 234 20.41 N 105.18 W
Amecameca [de Juárez] 234 19.07 N 98.46 W
Ameghino 252 34.50 S 62.27 W
Ameglia 64 44.04 N 9.57 E
Ameisberg ∧ 60 48.33 N 13.50 E
Ameixoeira ◆[8] 266c 38.47 N 9.10 W
Ameland I 52 53.25 N 5.45 E
Amele 164 5.16 S 145.42 E
Amelia, It. 66 42.33 N 12.25 E
Amelia, Oh., U.S. 218 39.01 N 84.13 W
Amelia, Passo d')(66 42.36 N 12.32 E
Amelia Court House 192 37.20 N 77.58 W
Amelia Earhart Peak ∧ 226 37.47 N 119.17 W
Amelia Island I 192 30.37 N 81.27 W
Amelinghausen 52 53.08 N 10.13 E
Amelsbüren 52 51.53 N 7.37 E
Amendolara 68 39.57 N 16.35 E
Ameng 102 23.50 N 104.32 E
Amenia 210 41.50 N 73.33 W
Amenucourt 261 49.06 N 1.39 E
Āmer 120 26.59 N 75.52 E
Amerang 60 48.00 N 12.18 E
Amerevo 265b 55.55 N 38.03 E
America 52 51.26 N 5.59 E
América del Norte → North America ≛[1] 16 45.00 N 100.00 W
América del Sur → South America ≛[1] 18 15.00 S 60.00 W
American ≃, Ca., U.S. 226 38.36 N 121.30 W
American ≃, Wa., U.S. 224 46.58 N 121.08 W
American, Middle Fork ≃ 226 38.55 N 121.02 W
American, North Fork ≃ 226 38.43 N 121.09 W
American, South Fork ≃ 226 38.43 N 121.09 W
Americana 255 22.45 S 47.20 W
American Canyon 226 38.10 N 122.15 W
American Cemetery and Memorial ◆ 269f 14.33 N 121.03 E
American Falls 202 42.47 N 112.51 W
American Falls ⌊ 284a 43.05 N 79.04 W
American Falls Reservoir ⊜[1] 202 42.45 N 112.45 W
American Fork 200 40.22 N 111.47 W
American Highland ⩘[1] 9 72.30 S 78.00 E
American Lake ⊜ 224 47.07 N 122.34 W
American Museum of Natural History ʊ 276 40.47 N 73.59 W
Americano 250 1.19 S 48.04 W
American River 168b 35.47 S 137.47 E
American Samoa □[2], Oc. 14 14.20 S 170.00 W
American Samoa □[2], Oc. 175a 14.20 S 170.00 W
American University ʊ[2] 284c 38.56 N 77.05 W
Américas, Hipódromo de las ♦ 286a 19.26 N 99.13 W
Americus, Ga., U.S. 192 32.04 N 84.13 W
Americus, Ks., U.S. 198 38.30 N 96.15 W
Amerikanisches Hochland → American Highland ⩘[1] 9 72.30 S 78.00 E
Ameringkogel ∧ 61 47.04 N 14.48 E
Amérique du Nord → North America ≛[1] 16 45.00 N 100.00 W
Amern 56 51.14 N 6.15 E
Amerongen 52 52.00 N 5.27 E
Amersfoort, Ned. 52 52.09 N 5.24 E
Amersfoort, S. Afr. 158 27.01 S 29.51 E
Amersham 260 51.40 N 0.38 W
Amery, Austl. 162 31.09 S 117.05 E
Amery, Mb., Can. 184 56.34 N 94.03 W
Amery, Wi., U.S. 190 45.18 N 92.21 W
Amery Ice Shelf ⊓ 9 69.30 S 72.00 E
Ames, Ia., U.S. 190 42.02 N 93.37 W
Ames, N.Y., U.S. 210 42.50 N 74.36 W
Ames, Tx., U.S. 222 30.03 N 94.46 W
Amesbury, Eng., U.K. 42 51.10 N 1.45 W
Amesbury, Ma., U.S. 207 42.51 N 70.55 W
Ames Long Pond ⊜ 283 42.05 N 71.07 W
Ames Nowell State Park ♦ 283 42.07 N 70.59 W
Ames Pond ⊜ 283 42.38 N 71.13 W
Ames Research Center ʊ[3] 282 37.25 N 122.04 W
Amet Sound ⌇ 186 45.47 N 63.13 W
Amfíklia 38 38.38 N 22.35 E
Amfilokhía 38 38.51 N 21.10 E
Ámfissa 38 38.31 N 22.24 E
Amfreville-la-Campagne 50 49.13 N 0.57 E
Amfreville-les-Champs 50 49.19 N 1.19 E
Amga 74 60.53 N 132.00 E
Amga ≃ 74 62.38 N 134.32 E
Am Géréda 146 12.52 N 21.10 E
Amguema 180 66.58 N 179.16 W
Amguema ≃ 180 68.10 N 177.40 W
Amguid 148 26.26 N 5.22 E
Amgun' ≃ 89 52.56 N 139.40 E
Amherst, N.S., Can. 186 45.49 N 64.14 W
Amherst, Ma., U.S. 207 42.22 N 72.31 W
Amherst, N.H., U.S. 207 42.51 N 71.37 W
Amherst, N.Y., U.S. 210 42.58 N 78.48 W
Amherst, Oh., U.S. 214 41.23 N 82.13 W
Amherst, Tx., U.S. 196 34.01 N 102.25 W
Amherst, Va., U.S. 192 37.35 N 79.03 W
Amherst, Wi., U.S. 190 44.27 N 89.17 W
Amherst, Mount ∧ 162 18.11 S 126.59 E
Amherstburg 214 42.06 N 83.06 W
Amherstdale 188 37.47 N 81.48 W
Amherst Island I 212 44.08 N 76.45 W
Amherstview 212 44.13 N 76.38 W
Ami 94 36.02 N 140.14 E
Amianan Island I 108 21.07 N 121.57 E
Amiata, Monte ∧ 66 42.53 N 11.37 E
Amicalola Falls State Park ♦ 192 34.33 N 84.15 W
Amidon 198 46.28 N 103.19 W
Amiens, Austl. 166 28.35 S 151.49 E
Amiens, Fr. 50 49.54 N 2.18 E
Amili, India 120 28.26 N 95.52 E
Amili, Zhg. 120 28.25 N 95.52 E
Amīn as-Samālūsī, Bi'r ⫧[4] 142 29.52 N 30.02 E
Amīndīvi Islands II 122 11.23 N 72.23 E
Aminga 252 28.50 S 66.54 W
Amini Island I 122 11.07 N 72.44 E
Amino, Ityo. 144 4.31 N 41.49 E
Amino, Nihon 96 35.41 N 135.02 E
Aminuis 156 23.43 S 19.21 E
Amīrābād 128 36.04 N 54.10 E
Amīrābād ◆[8] 267d 35.43 N 51.23 E
Amirante Islands II 138 6.00 S 53.10 E
Amirauté, Îles de l' → Admiralty Islands II 164 2.10 S 147.00 E
Amisk 182 52.33 N 111.04 W
Amisk Lake ⊜ 184 54.35 N 102.13 W
Amistad, Parque Internacional de la ♦ 236 9.25 N 83.10 W
Amistad, Presa de la (Amistad Reservoir) ⊜[1] 196 29.34 N 101.15 W
Amistad National Recreation Area ♦ 196 29.32 N 101.12 W
Amistad Reservoir (Presa de la Amistad) ⊜[1] 196 29.34 N 101.15 W
Amite 194 30.43 N 90.30 W
Amite ≃ 194 30.12 N 90.35 W
Amite, East Fork ≃ 194 30.58 N 90.51 W
Amiterno ⊥ 66 42.21 N 13.42 E
Amitori 175d 24.18 N 123.41 E
Amity, Ar., U.S. 194 34.15 N 93.27 W
Amity, Oh., U.S. 214 40.03 N 83.17 W
Amity, Or., U.S. 224 45.06 N 123.12 W
Amity Point ≻ 171a 27.24 S 153.27 E
Amityville 276 40.40 N 73.25 W
Amixtlán 234 20.03 N 97.48 W
Amizmiz 148 31.14 N 8.14 W
Āmjhori ∧ 126 21.51 N 86.19 E
Āmjhupi 126 23.45 N 88.42 E
Āmla, Bngl. 126 23.54 N 88.56 E
Amla, India 124 21.56 N 78.07 E
Āmlāgora 126 22.50 N 87.20 E
Amlekhgañj 124 27.17 N 84.59 E
Åmli 26 58.47 N 8.30 E
Amlia Island I 180 52.06 N 173.30 W
Amloh 124 30.37 N 76.14 E
Am Loubia 146 13.39 N 20.08 E
Amlwch 44 53.25 N 4.20 W
ʿAmm-Adām 140 16.22 N 36.06 E
Ammagan 85 38.56 N 67.15 E
ʿAmmān 132 31.57 N 35.56 E
ʿAmmān □[8] 132 31.45 N 36.15 E
Ammanford 42 51.48 N 3.59 W
Ämmänsaari 26 64.53 N 28.55 E
Ammansville 222 29.47 N 96.51 W
ʿAmmār, Tall ∧[2] 132 32.53 N 36.29 E
Ammarnäs 24 65.56 N 16.09 E
Ammaroo 162 21.45 S 135.15 E
Åmmeberg 40 58.52 N 15.00 E
Ammeloe 52 52.05 N 6.47 E
Ammendorf ◆[8] 54 51.25 N 11.59 E
Ammer ≃ 64 47.57 N 11.08 E
Ammerån ≃ 26 63.09 N 16.13 E
Ammerbuch 56 48.33 N 8.58 E
Ammer Gebirge ⩘ 64 47.35 N 10.55 E
Ammerland ◆[1] 52 53.15 N 8.00 E
Ammerman Mountain ∧ 180 68.21 N 141.03 W
Ammerschwihr 58 48.07 N 7.17 E
Ammersee ⊜ 60 48.00 N 11.08 E
Ammerthal 60 49.26 N 11.45 E
Ammon 202 43.28 N 111.57 W
Ammonoosuc ≃ 188 44.10 N 72.02 W
Amnān 272b 22.56 N 88.18 E
Amnat Charoen 110 15.51 N 104.38 E
Amnay ≃ 116 12.58 N 120.46 E
Amne Machin Shan → A'nyêmaqên Shan ⩘ 102 34.30 N 100.00 E
Amnicon ≃ 190 46.41 N 91.52 W
Amnok-kang (Yalu) ≃ 98 39.55 N 124.22 E
Amo ≃, Asia 124 26.16 N 89.36 E
Amo ≃, Zhg. 102 22.58 N 101.44 E
Āmol 128 36.23 N 52.20 E
Amolar 248 18.01 S 57.30 W
Amöneburg 56 50.48 N 8.55 E
Amorbach 56 49.39 N 9.13 E
Amorgós 38 36.50 N 25.54 E
Amorgós I 38 36.50 N 25.59 E
Amorim, Morro ∧[2] 287a 23.00 S 43.26 W
Amorinópolis 255 16.36 S 51.08 W
Amorosi 68 41.12 N 14.28 E
Amory 194 33.59 N 88.29 W
Amos 190 48.35 N 78.07 W
Åmose Å ≃ 41 55.35 N 11.18 E
Åmot, Nor. 26 59.54 N 9.54 E
Åmot, Nor. 26 59.35 N 8.00 E
Åmotfors 26 59.46 N 12.22 E
Amour, Djebel ⩘ 148 34.00 N 2.15 E
Amour → Amur ≃ 74 52.56 N 141.10 E
Amoy → Xiamen 100 24.28 N 118.07 E
Amozoc 234 19.02 N 98.03 W
Ampana 112 0.51 S 121.32 E
Ampanavoana 157b 15.41 S 50.22 E
Ampang 115b 8.47 S 118.00 E
Ampanihy 157b 24.42 S 44.45 E
Ampaoid, Mount ∧ 116 7.57 N 125.41 E
Amparafaravola 157b 17.35 S 48.13 E
Amparihy, Madag. 157b 16.40 S 44.49 E
Amparihy, Madag. 157b 23.57 S 47.20 E
Amparo 256 22.42 S 46.45 W
Ampasibe 157b 22.56 S 46.58 E
Ampasinambo 157b 20.31 S 48.00 E
Ampasindava, Baie d' ⊂ 157b 13.16 S 48.43 E
Ampasindava, Presq'île d' ≻[1] 157b 13.45 S 48.00 E
Ampato, Nevado ∧ 248 15.50 S 71.52 W
Ampel 115a 7.27 S 110.32 E
Amper 150 9.20 N 9.43 E
Amper ≃ 60 48.30 N 11.58 E
Ampezzo 64 46.25 N 12.48 E
Ampezzo, Valle d' V 64 46.30 N 12.10 E
Ampfing 60 48.16 N 12.25 E
Ampflwang 64 48.05 N 13.34 E
Amphion-les-Bains 58 46.23 N 6.32 E
Ampisikina 157b 12.57 S 49.49 E
Ampleforth 44 54.12 N 1.06 W
Ampollino, Lago ⊜ 68 39.12 N 16.37 E
Ampombiantambo 157b 12.42 S 48.57 E
Amposta 34 40.43 N 0.35 E
Ampotaka 157b 25.03 S 44.41 E
Ampoza 157b 22.20 S 44.44 E
Ampthill 42 52.02 N 0.30 W
Ampuis 62 45.29 N 4.49 E
Ampus 62 43.36 N 6.23 E
Amqui 186 48.28 N 67.26 W
Āmr, Jabal al- ⩘ 132 30.45 N 34.20 E
Amraoti → Amrāvati 120 20.56 N 77.45 E
Amrāvati 120 20.56 N 77.45 E
Am-Raya 146 14.00 N 16.35 E
Amreli 120 21.37 N 71.14 E
Āmreswar 272b 22.28 N 88.34 E
Amriswil 58 47.33 N 9.18 E
Amritsar 123 31.35 N 74.53 E
Amroha 124 28.55 N 78.28 E
Amrūka 123 30.19 N 73.53 E
Amrum I 30 54.39 N 8.21 E
Amsdell Heights 284a 42.45 N 78.54 W
Amsden 214 41.13 N 83.20 W
Amsel 148 22.37 N 5.26 E
Åmsele 26 64.32 N 19.20 E
Am Sigan 146 11.41 N 19.51 E
Amsoldingen 58 46.43 N 7.35 E
Amsteg 58 46.46 N 8.41 E
Amstel ≃ 52 52.22 N 4.54 E
Amstelmeer ⊜ 52 52.52 N 4.45 E
Amstelveen 52 52.18 N 4.51 E
Amsterdam, Ned. 52 52.22 N 4.54 E
Amsterdam, S. Afr. 158 26.35 S 30.45 E

Symbols in the index entries represent the broad categories identified in the key at the right. Symbols with superior numbers (⩘[1]) identify subcategories (see complete key on page *I · 1*).

Symbole im Register stellen die rechts im Schlüssel erklärten Kategorien dar. Symbole mit hochgestellten Ziffern (⩘[1]) bezeichnen Unterabteilungen einer Kategorie (vgl. vollständiger Schlüssel auf Seite *I · 1*).

Los símbolos incluídos en el texto del índice representan las grandes categorias identificadas con la clave a la derecha. Los símbolos con numeros en su parte superior (⩘[1]) identifican las subcategorias (véase la clave completa en la página *I · 1*).

Les symboles de l'index représentent les catégories indiquées dans la légende à droite. Les symboles suivis d'un indice (⩘[1]) représentent des sous-catégories (voir légende complète à la page *I · 1*).

Os símbolos incluídos no texto do índice representam as grandes categorias identificadas com a chave à direita. Os símbolos com números em sua parte superior (⩘[1]) identificam as subcategorias (veja-se a chave completa à página *I · 1*).

∧ Mountain	Berg	Montaña	Montagne	Montanha
⩘ Mountains	Gebirge	Montañas	Montagnes	Montanhas
)(Pass	Paß	Paso	Col	Passo
V Valley, Canyon	Tal, Cañon	Valle, Cañón	Vallée, Canyon	Vale, Canhão
≚ Plain	Ebene	Llano	Plaine	Planície
≻ Cape	Kap	Cabo	Cap	Cabo
I Island	Insel	Isla	Île	Ilha
II Islands	Inseln	Islas	Îles	Ilhas
≛ Other Topographic Features	Andere Topographische Objekte	Otros Elementos Topográficos	Autres données topographiques	Outros acidentes topográficos

ESPAÑOL

Nombre	Página	Lat.°′	Long.°′ W = Oeste
Amsterdam, N.Y., U.S.	210	42.56 N	74.11 W
Amsterdam, Oh., U.S.	214	40.28 N	80.55 W
Amsterdam, Île I	6	37.52 S	77.32 E
Amsterdam-Rijnkanaal ≊	52	51.57 N	5.20 E
Amstetten	61	48.07 N	14.53 E
Amston	207	41.37 N	72.20 W
Āmta	126	22.35 N	88.01 E
Amt'ae-do I	98	34.50 N	126.07 E
Āmtala	126	23.55 N	88.27 E
Amtāli	126	22.08 N	90.14 E
Am Timan	146	11.02 N	20.17 E
Amtrak Station ◆[5]	281	42.19 N	83.04 W
Amubri	236	9.31 N	82.56 W
ʿĀmūdah	130	37.05 N	40.54 E
Amu-Darja	128	37.53 N	65.15 E
Amu Darya (Amudarja) ≃	72	43.40 N	59.01 E
Amudat	154	1.57 N	34.57 E
Amugulang → Xin Barag Zuoqi	88	48.14 N	118.18 E
Amukta Island I	180	52.29 N	171.15 W
Amukta Pass ⊎	180	52.25 N	172.00 W
Amulree	46	56.30 N	3.47 W
Amun	175e	5.57 S	154.45 E
Amundsen Bay ⊂	9	66.55 S	50.00 E
Amundsen Gulf ⊂	176	71.00 N	124.00 W
Amundsen-Scott ⊍[3]	9	90.00 S	0.00
Amundsen Sea ⊤[2]	9	72.30 S	112.00 W
Amung, Mount ∧	164	7.26 S	146.36 E
Amungen ◎	26	61.09 N	15.39 E
Amuntai	112	2.26 S	115.15 E
Amur (Heilong) ≃	74	52.56 N	141.10 E
ʿAmūr, Wādī V	140	18.56 N	33.34 E
Amurang	112	1.11 N	124.35 E
Amuria	154	2.01 N	33.38 E
Amursk	89	50.13 N	136.52 E
Amurskaja Oblast' □[8]	89	53.00 N	129.00 E
Amurskij liman ⊂	89	52.45 N	141.40 E
Amursko-Zejskaja ravnina ⋏[1]	89	52.30 N	128.30 E
Amurzet	89	47.42 N	131.05 E
Amutag	116	12.23 N	123.16 E
Amuwo	273a	6.28 N	3.18 E
Amuyimusu	98	42.25 N	113.21 E
Amuzhong	120	30.33 N	84.28 E
Amvamg	152	1.45 N	10.29 E
Amvrakikós Kólpos ⊂	38	39.00 N	21.00 E
Amvrosijevka	83	47.47 N	38.29 E
Amwom, Khawr V	140	7.50 N	31.13 E
Amyl ≃	86	53.47 N	92.54 E
Amyūn	130	34.18 N	35.49 E
Amz'a	80	56.13 N	54.23 E
Amzi, Oued ti-n- V	148	20.30 N	4.35 E
An	110	19.47 N	94.02 E
Anaa I[1]	14	17.25 S	145.30 W
Anabanua	112	3.57 S	120.04 E
Anabar	174b	0.30 S	166.57 E
Anabar ≃	74	73.08 N	113.36 E
ʿAnabtā	132	32.19 N	35.07 E
Anabuki	96	34.02 N	134.11 E
Anacapri	68	40.33 N	14.13 E
Anaco	246	9.27 N	64.28 W
Anacoco	194	31.15 N	93.20 W
Anacoco, Bayou ≃	194	30.52 N	93.34 W
Anaconda	202	46.07 N	112.56 W
Anaconda Range ⋏	202	45.55 N	113.30 W
Anacortes	224	48.30 N	122.36 W
Anacostia ◆[8]	284c	38.52 N	76.59 W
Anacostia ≃	284c	38.52 N	77.01 W
Anacostia, Little Paint Branch ≃	284c	39.01 N	76.56 W
Anacostia, Northeast Branch ≃	284c	38.57 N	76.57 W
Anacostia, Paint Branch ≃	284c	38.58 N	76.55 W
Anacostia Park ♠	284c	38.54 N	76.58 W
Anacuao, Mount ∧	116	16.16 N	121.53 E
Anadarko	196	35.04 N	98.14 W
Anadia	250	9.42 S	36.18 W
Anadolufeneri ◆[8]	267b	41.12 N	29.09 E
Anadoluhisarı ⊥	267b	41.04 N	29.03 E
Anadyr'	180	64.45 N	177.29 E
Anadyr' ≃	74	64.55 N	176.05 E
Anadyrskaja nizmennost' ≡	180	65.30 N	176.00 E
Anadyrskij liman ⊂	180	64.30 N	177.45 E
Anadyrskij zaliv ⊂	180	64.00 N	179.00 W
Anadyrskoje ploskogorje ⋏[1]	180	67.00 N	174.00 E
Anáfi I	38	36.21 N	25.50 E
Anagni	66	41.44 N	13.09 E
ʿĀnah	128	34.28 N	41.56 E
Anaheim	228	33.50 N	117.54 W
Anaheim Shopping Center ◆[9]	280	33.51 N	117.56 W
Anaheim Stadium ♠	280	33.51 N	117.57 W
Anaheim Union Canal ≊	280	33.54 N	117.52 W
Anahi, Baie ⊂	174x	9.45 S	138.56 W
Anahim Lake	182	52.28 N	125.18 W
Anahola	229b	22.08 N	159.18 W
Anahola Bay ⊂	229b	22.09 N	159.18 W
Anáhuac, Méx.	196	25.48 N	97.45 W
Anáhuac, Méx.	232	27.14 N	100.09 W
Anáhuac, Méx.	232	28.25 N	106.40 W
Anahuac, Tx., U.S.	222	29.46 N	94.41 W
Anahuac, Lake ◎	222	29.48 N	94.41 W
Anaimala	122	10.35 N	76.56 E
Ānai Mudi ∧	122	10.10 N	77.04 E
Anajás	250	0.59 S	49.57 W
Anajás, Ilha I	250	0.20 S	50.30 W
Anajatuba	250	3.16 S	44.37 W
Anakāpalle	122	17.41 N	83.01 E
Anaklia	84	42.24 N	41.34 E
Anaktuvuk ≃	180	69.32 N	151.30 W
Anaktuvuk Pass	180	68.10 N	151.50 W
Analalava	157b	14.38 S	47.45 E
Analapatsy	157b	25.10 S	46.42 E
Analavoka	157b	22.33 S	46.30 E
Analomink	210	41.03 N	75.13 W
Anamã	246	3.35 S	61.22 W
Anamã, Lago ◎	246	3.32 S	61.35 W
Anama Bay	184	51.56 N	98.05 W
Ana María, Cayos de II	240p	21.29 N	78.46 W
Ana María, Golfo de ⊂	240p	21.25 N	78.40 W
Anambas, Kepulauan II	112	3.00 N	106.00 E
Anambra □[3]	150	6.30 N	7.20 E
Anambra ≃	150	6.11 N	6.46 E
Anamizu	94	37.14 N	136.54 E
Anamoose	198	47.52 N	100.14 W
Anamosa	190	42.06 N	91.17 W
Anamu ≃	250	0.56 N	57.03 W
Anamur	130	36.06 N	32.50 E
Anamur Burnu ›	130	36.03 N	32.48 E
Anan, Nihon	94	35.19 N	137.49 E
Anan, Nihon	96	33.55 N	134.39 E
Ānand	120	22.34 N	72.56 E
Ananda	150	7.17 N	4.16 W
Anandanagar	272b	22.51 N	88.16 E
Ānandapur, India	120	21.14 N	86.07 E
Anandapur, India	126	22.34 N	87.25 E
Anandpur Sahib	123	31.15 N	76.30 E
Ananea	248	14.42 S	69.33 W
Ananindeua	250	1.22 S	48.23 W
Ananjev	78	47.40 N	29.55 E
Ananjevo	85	42.45 N	77.40 E
Anantapur	122	14.41 N	77.36 E
Anantnāg (Islāmābād)	123	33.44 N	75.09 E
Anao-aon	116	9.47 N	125.25 E
Anapa	78	44.53 N	37.19 E
Anapo ≃	70	47.03 N	15.16 E
Anápolis	255	16.20 S	48.58 W
Anapu ≃	250	1.53 S	50.53 W
Anapurus	250	3.40 S	43.06 W
Anār, Īrān	128	30.53 N	55.18 E
Anar, Kaz.	86	50.38 N	72.27 E
Anāra	126	23.28 N	86.33 E

FRANÇAIS

Nom	Page	Lat.°′	Long.°′ W = Ouest
Anārak	128	33.20 N	53.42 E
Anarchaj	85	44.02 N	75.15 E
Anār Darreh	128	32.46 N	61.39 E
Anaš	86	54.52 N	91.00 E
Anasagasti	258	35.01 S	59.24 W
Añasco	240m	18.17 N	67.08 W
Ånäset	26	64.16 N	21.03 E
Anastácio	255	21.31 S	54.08 W
Anastasia Island I	192	29.48 N	81.16 W
Anastasijevka	83	47.34 N	38.31 E
Anastasijevskaja	78	45.13 N	37.53 E
ʿAnātā	132	31.49 N	35.16 E
Anatahan I	108	16.22 N	145.40 E
Anatoljevka	78	46.48 N	31.13 E
Anatom I	175f	20.12 S	169.45 E
Añatuya	252	28.28 S	62.50 W
Anauá ≃	246	0.58 N	61.21 W
Anaurilândia	255	22.03 S	52.45 W
Anavilhanas, Arquipélago das II	246	2.42 S	60.45 W
Anawalt	192	37.20 N	81.26 W
Anbanjing	102	23.57 N	100.55 E
Anbei, Zhg.	102	40.45 N	96.06 E
Anbei, Zhg.	102	40.49 N	108.56 E
Anbianbu	102	37.39 N	108.11 E
Anbo	98	39.51 N	122.19 E
Anbu	100	23.28 N	116.44 E
Anbyŏn	98	39.03 N	127.32 E
Ancarano	66	42.50 N	13.44 E
Ancash □[5]	248	9.30 S	77.45 W
Ancaster, On., Can.	212	43.12 N	80.00 W
Ancaster, Eng., U.K.	44	52.59 N	0.32 W
Ancasti	252	28.49 S	65.30 W
Ancasti, Sierra de ⋏	252	28.50 S	65.39 W
Ance ≃, Fr.	62	45.17 N	4.08 E
Ance ≃, Fr.	62	44.58 N	3.40 E
Ancenis	32	47.22 N	1.11 W
Ancerville	58	48.38 N	5.02 E
Anchang	100	30.09 N	120.30 E
Anchau	150	10.59 N	8.23 E
Anchieta ◆[8]	287a	22.49 S	43.24 W
Anchieta, Ilha I	256	23.33 S	45.04 W
Anch'ing → Anqing	100	30.31 N	117.02 E
Ancho, Canal ⊎	254	49.54 S	74.23 W
Ancholme ≃	44	53.41 N	0.32 W
Anchor	216	40.34 N	88.32 W
Anchorage	180	61.13 N	149.54 W
Anchor Bay ⊂	214	42.38 N	82.45 W
Anchor Bay Gardens	214	42.39 N	82.49 W
Anchorena	252	35.41 S	65.27 W
Anchor Point	180	59.46 N	151.52 W
Anchor Point ›	180	59.47 N	151.52 W
Anchorville	214	42.42 N	82.41 W
Anchuras	34	39.29 N	4.50 W
Anci (Langfang)	105	39.31 N	116.41 E
Ancien Ekalla	152	1.27 S	14.00 E
Ancien Goubéré	140	5.51 N	26.46 E
Ancienne-Lorette	206	46.48 N	71.21 W
Anciferovo, Ross.	76	58.58 N	34.01 E
Anciferovo, Ross.	82	55.33 N	38.49 E
Ancipa, Lago di ◎	70	37.50 N	14.34 E
Anclitas, Cayo I	240p	20.48 N	78.54 W
Anclote ≃	220	39.59 N	88.49 W
Anclote Keys II	220	28.12 N	82.51 W
Ancón, Méx.	234	22.35 N	101.11 W
Ancón, Perú	248	11.47 S	77.11 W
Ancona, It.	66	43.38 N	13.30 E
Ancona, S. Afr.	158	27.40 S	26.32 E
Ancona □[4]	66	43.33 N	13.10 E
Ancón de Sardinas, Bahía de ⊂	246	1.30 N	79.00 W
Ancoraimes	248	15.54 S	68.58 W
Ancram	210	42.03 N	73.38 W
Ancre ≃	50	49.54 N	2.28 E
Ancrum	46	55.31 N	2.35 W
Ancuabe	154	12.58 S	39.54 E
Ancud	254	41.52 S	73.50 W
Ancud, Golfo de ⊂	254	42.05 S	73.00 W
Ancy-le-Franc	50	47.46 N	4.10 E
Ancy-sur-Moselle	56	49.03 N	6.04 E
Anda, Pil.	116	16.17 N	119.57 E
Anda, Zhg.	89	46.24 N	125.19 E
Andacollo, Arg.	252	37.11 S	70.41 W
Andacollo, Chile	252	30.14 S	71.06 W
Andahuaylas	248	13.39 S	73.23 W
Andaingo	157b	18.12 S	48.17 E
Andāl	124	23.36 N	87.12 E
Andalgalá	252	27.36 S	66.19 W
Andalo	64	46.10 N	11.00 E
Åndalsnes	26	62.34 N	7.42 E
Andalucía □[4]	34	37.30 N	4.30 W
Andalucía □[9]	34	37.36 N	4.30 W
Andalusia, Al., U.S.	194	31.19 N	86.29 W
Andalusia, Pa., U.S.	285	40.04 N	74.58 W
Andaman and Nicobar Islands □[8]	110	11.00 N	93.00 E
Andaman Basin ✢[1]	12	10.00 N	94.00 E
Andamanen → Andaman Islands II	110	12.00 N	92.45 E
Andaman Islands II	110	12.00 N	92.45 E
Andaman Sea ⊤[2]	110	10.00 N	95.00 E
Andamarca, Bol.	248	18.49 S	67.31 W
Andamarca, Perú	248	11.46 S	74.44 W
Andamooka	166	30.27 S	137.12 E
Andance	62	45.14 N	4.47 E
Andapa	157b	14.39 S	49.39 E
Andara	152	18.03 S	21.27 E
Andaraí	255	12.48 S	41.20 W
Andaraí ◆[8]	287a	22.56 S	43.15 W
Andarax ≃	34	36.48 N	2.26 W
Andaray	248	15.49 S	72.50 W
Andau	61	47.46 N	17.02 E
Andechs, Kloster ⊍[1]	64	47.58 N	11.10 E
Andeer	58	46.36 N	9.26 E
Andelfingen	58	47.36 N	8.41 E
Andelle ≃	50	49.19 N	1.44 E
Andelot	58	48.15 N	5.18 E
Andelot-en-Montagne	58	46.51 N	5.56 E
Andelu	261	48.53 N	1.50 E
Anden → Andes ⋏	18	20.00 S	67.00 W
Andenes	24	69.16 N	16.08 E
Andenne	56	50.29 N	5.06 E
Andéranboukane	150	15.26 N	3.02 E
Ånderdalen Nasjonalpark ♠	24	69.14 N	17.17 E
Anderlecht	50	50.50 N	4.18 E
Anderlues	50	50.24 N	4.16 E
Andermatt	58	46.38 N	8.36 E
Andernach	56	50.26 N	7.24 E
Andersen Air Force Base ■	174p	13.35 N	144.56 E
Anderslöv	41	55.26 N	13.22 E
Anderson, Al., U.S.	194	34.55 N	87.15 W
Anderson, Ak., U.S.	180	64.21 N	149.10 W
Anderson, Ca., U.S.	204	40.26 N	122.17 W
Anderson, In., U.S.	218	40.06 N	85.40 W
Anderson, Mo., U.S.	194	36.39 N	94.26 W
Anderson, S.C., U.S.	192	34.30 N	82.39 W
Anderson, Tx., U.S.	222	30.29 N	95.59 W
Anderson □[6], Ky., U.S.	218	38.05 N	84.55 W
Anderson □[6], Tx., U.S.	222	31.47 N	95.40 W
Anderson ≃	180	69.43 N	128.58 W
Anderson, Mount ∧	224	47.43 N	123.20 W
Anderson Creek ≃	194	33.18 N	94.26 W
Anderson Dam	202	43.30 N	115.30 W
Anderson Inlet ⊂	169	38.39 S	145.48 E
Anderson Island I	224	47.10 N	122.42 W
Anderson Lake ◎	182	50.41 N	122.07 W
Anderson Lake ◎[1]	226	37.11 N	121.37 W
Anderson Peak ∧	228	34.08 N	116.53 W
Anderson Ranch Reservoir ◎[1]	202	43.25 N	115.20 W
Andersonville	218	39.30 N	85.17 W
Andersonville National Historical Site ⊥	192	32.12 N	84.07 W
Anderstorp	26	57.17 N	13.38 E
Anderten	52	52.21 N	9.51 E

PORTUGUÊS

Nome	Página	Lat.°′	Long.°′ W = Oeste
Anderton	262	53.17 N	2.32 W
Andes, Col.	246	5.40 N	75.53 W
Andes, N.Y., U.S.	210	42.12 N	74.47 W
Andes ⋏	18	20.00 S	67.00 W
Andes, Lake ◎	198	43.11 N	98.27 W
Andeville	50	49.15 N	2.10 E
Andevoranto	157b	18.57 S	49.06 E
Andfjorden ⊎	24	69.10 N	16.20 E
Andheri ◆[8]	272c	19.07 N	72.51 E
Andhra Lake ◎	122	18.54 N	73.32 E
Andhra Pradesh □[3]	122	16.00 N	79.00 E
Andijk	52	52.45 N	5.12 E
Andijskoje Kojsu ≃	84	42.47 N	46.48 E
Andikíthira I	38	35.52 N	23.18 E
Andilamena	157b	17.01 S	48.35 E
Andimákhia	38	36.48 N	27.07 E
Andīmeshk	128	32.27 N	48.21 E
Andingpu	102	37.58 N	107.02 E
Anding Zhan	105	39.38 N	116.29 E
Andinkerke	50	51.04 N	2.36 E
Andíparos I	38	37.00 N	25.03 E
Andirá ≃	250	2.45 S	56.49 W
Andirá, Riozinho do ≃	248	9.21 S	67.31 W
Andırın	130	37.34 N	36.20 E
Andirlang	120	37.36 N	83.50 E
Andisleben	54	51.04 N	10.56 E
Ándissa	38	39.14 N	25.59 E
Andižan	85	40.45 N	72.22 E
Andkhvoy	120	36.56 N	65.08 E
Andlau-au-Val	58	48.23 N	7.25 E
Ando	270	34.37 N	135.46 E
Andoam	164	12.40 S	141.55 E
Andoas	246	2.50 S	76.30 W
Andoga ≃	76	59.10 N	37.27 E
Andogskaja gr'ada ∧	76	59.25 N	37.30 E
Andolsheim	58	48.04 N	7.25 E
Andomskij Pogost	24	61.14 N	36.36 E
Andong, Taehan	98	36.35 N	128.44 E
Andong, Zhg.	100	30.16 N	121.13 E
Andong-chŏsuji ◎[1]	98	36.41 N	128.49 E
Andong-ni	98	39.28 N	127.27 E
Andora	62	43.59 N	8.08 E
Andorf	60	48.23 N	13.35 E
Andorno Micca	62	45.37 N	8.03 E
Andorra	34	42.30 N	1.31 E
Andorra □[1], Europe	22	42.30 N	1.30 E
Andorra □[1], Europe	34	42.30 N	1.30 E
Andorre → Andorra □[1]	34	42.30 N	1.30 E
Andover, Eng., U.K.	42	51.13 N	1.28 W
Andover, Ct., U.S.	207	41.44 N	72.22 W
Andover, Me., U.S.	188	44.38 N	70.45 W
Andover, Ma., U.S.	207	42.39 N	71.08 W
Andover, N.J., U.S.	210	40.59 N	74.44 W
Andover, N.Y., U.S.	210	42.09 N	77.47 W
Andover, Oh., U.S.	214	41.36 N	80.34 W
Andover, S.D., U.S.	198	45.24 N	97.54 W
Andowj	123	37.02 N	71.27 E
Andøya I	24	69.08 N	15.54 E
Andradas	256	22.04 S	46.34 W
Andrade Pinto	256	22.14 S	43.22 W
Andradina	255	20.54 S	51.23 W
Andramasina	157b	19.11 S	47.35 E
Andranopasy	157b	21.17 S	43.44 E
Andranovory	157b	23.08 S	44.10 E
Andrate	62	45.32 N	7.53 E
Andreafsky ≃	180	62.02 N	163.16 W
Andreafsky, East Fork ≃	180	62.03 N	163.07 W
Andreanof Islands II	180	52.00 N	176.00 W
Andreapol'	76	56.39 N	32.15 E
Andreas, I. of Man	44	54.22 N	4.26 W
Andreas, Pa., U.S.	208	40.45 N	75.48 W
André Félix, Parc National ♠	146	9.25 N	23.20 E
Andrejevka, Kaz.	86	52.59 N	67.23 E
Andrejevka, Kaz.	86	45.50 N	80.35 E
Andrejevka, Ross.	80	55.42 N	54.23 E
Andrejevka, Ross.	80	52.19 N	51.55 E
Andrejevka, Ross.	82	55.07 N	38.37 E
Andrejevka, Ross.	82	55.59 N	37.08 E
Andrejevka, Ukr.	78	49.32 N	36.38 E
Andrejevka, Ukr.	78	47.06 N	36.35 E
Andrejevka, Ukr.	83	48.49 N	37.33 E
Andrejevka, Ukr.	83	47.28 N	37.39 E
Andrejevo	80	55.56 N	41.08 E
Andrejevo-Ivanovka	78	47.28 N	30.28 E
Andrejevsk	88	58.06 N	114.08 E
Andrejevskaja	80	47.21 N	43.02 E
Andrejevskoje, Ross.	82	54.23 N	36.12 E
Andrejevskoje, Ross.	82	56.24 N	39.01 E
Andrejevskoje, Ross.	82	55.46 N	36.35 E
Andrejkoviči	76	52.25 N	33.00 E
Andrelândia	256	21.44 S	44.18 W
Andrésy	261	48.59 N	2.04 E
Andretta	68	40.56 N	15.19 E
Andrew	182	53.53 N	112.21 W
Andrew, Mount ∧	162	32.52 S	122.56 E
Andrews, In., U.S.	216	40.51 N	85.36 W
Andrews, Mi., U.S.	216	41.57 N	86.22 W
Andrews, N.C., U.S.	192	35.12 N	83.49 W
Andrews, S.C., U.S.	192	33.18 N	79.17 W
Andrews, Tx., U.S.	196	32.19 N	102.32 W
Andrews Air Force Base ■	208	38.48 N	76.52 W
Andrews Manor	284c	38.49 N	76.54 W
Andrezel	261	48.37 N	2.49 E
Andrézieux Bouthéon	62	45.32 N	4.16 E
Andria	68	41.13 N	16.18 E
Andriamena	157b	17.26 S	47.30 E
Andriandampy	157b	22.45 S	45.41 E
Andriba	157b	17.36 S	46.55 E
Andrija, Otok I	36	43.02 N	15.45 E
Andrijevica	38	42.44 N	19.46 E
Androka	157b	25.02 S	44.05 E
Andronovskoje	76	60.39 N	34.46 E
Andropov → Rybinsk	76	58.03 N	38.52 E
Ándros	38	37.50 N	24.57 E
Andros I, Ba.	238	24.26 N	77.57 W
Ándros I, Ellás	38	37.45 N	24.42 E
Androscoggin ≃	188	43.55 N	69.55 W
Androsovka	80	52.41 N	49.35 E
Andros Town	238	24.43 N	77.47 W
Āndrott Island I	122	10.50 N	73.41 E
Andrupene	76	56.11 N	27.23 E
Andr'ušino	86	59.12 N	62.59 E
Andrušovka	78	50.01 N	29.01 E
Andrychów	30	49.52 N	19.21 E
Andudu	154	2.29 N	28.41 E
Andújar	34	38.03 N	4.04 W
Andulo	152	11.30 S	16.45 E
Anduze	62	44.03 N	3.59 E
Andžijevskij	84	44.14 N	43.05 E
Âne, Dos d' ∧	241o	16.19 N	61.46 W
Aneby	26	57.50 N	14.48 E
Anécho	150	6.14 N	1.36 E
Anecón Grande, Cerro ∧	254	41.25 S	70.16 W
Anefis i-n-Darane	150	18.03 N	0.36 E
Anegada I	238	18.45 N	64.20 W
Anegada, Bahía ⊂	254	40.15 S	62.15 W
Anegada Passage ⊎	238	18.30 N	63.40 W
Anegam	200	32.22 N	112.01 W
Anegasaki	268	35.28 N	140.02 E
Anelngauhat	175f	20.14 S	169.44 E
Añelo	252	38.21 S	68.47 W
Anémata, Passe d' ⊎	175f	20.31 S	166.12 E
Anepahan Peak ∧	116	9.40 N	118.25 E
Aneroid	184	49.43 N	107.20 W
Anet	50	48.51 N	1.26 E
Aneta	198	47.40 N	97.59 W
Aneto, Pico de ∧	34	42.38 N	0.40 E
Aney	146	19.24 N	12.56 E
Anfeng, Zhg.	100	32.44 N	120.24 E
Anfeng, Zhg.	100	33.06 N	120.08 E
Anfengqiao	100	26.41 N	118.08 E
Anfo	64	45.46 N	10.29 E
Anfu	100	27.23 N	114.37 E
Anfuzhen, Zhg.	107	28.47 N	104.41 E
Anfuzhen, Zhg.	107	29.21 N	105.28 E
Anga	88	53.58 N	106.12 E

Angamacutiro [de la Unión]	234	20.10 N	101.41 W
Angamos, Punta ›	252	23.01 S	70.32 W
Angangueo	234	19.37 N	100.18 W
Ang'angxi	89	47.09 N	123.48 E
An'ganka	89	52.18 N	126.17 E
Angao	100	33.08 N	112.22 E
Angar	164	3.39 S	130.50 E
Angara ≃	88	58.06 N	93.00 E
Angara-Débou	150	11.19 N	3.03 E
Angarbaka	140	9.44 N	24.44 E
Āngāria	126	22.29 N	90.22 E
Angarsk	88	52.34 N	103.54 E
Angas ≃	168b	35.23 S	138.59 E
Angas Downs	162	24.49 S	132.14 E
Angas Hills ⋏[2]	162	22.55 S	128.00 E
Angastaco	252	25.38 S	66.11 W
Angaston	168b	34.30 S	139.02 E
Angat ≃	116	14.53 N	120.46 E
Angatuba	255	23.29 S	48.25 W
Angaul	88	53.49 N	100.18 E
Angaur I	175b	6.54 N	134.09 E
Angden Pass)(	124	29.43 N	86.17 E
Angduo	102	32.20 N	98.55 E
Ånge	26	62.31 N	15.37 E
Ángel, Salto (Angel Falls) ∟	246	5.57 N	62.30 W
Angel Albino Corzo	234	15.55 N	92.43 W
Angel City	220	28.20 N	80.40 W
Ángel de la Guarda, Isla I	232	29.20 N	113.25 W
Angeles	116	15.09 N	120.35 E
Angeles National Forest ♠	280	34.15 N	117.56 W
Angel Etcheverry	258	35.02 S	58.04 W
Angel Falls → Ángel, Salto ∟	246	5.57 N	62.30 W
Ängelholm	41	56.15 N	12.51 E
Ängelholm flygplats ⊠	41	56.20 N	12.51 E
Angelica	210	42.18 N	78.00 W
Angelina □[6]	222	31.17 N	94.42 W
Angelina ≃	194	30.53 N	94.12 W
Angelina, East Fork ≃	222	31.50 N	94.56 W
Angel Island I	282	37.52 N	122.26 W
Angellala Creek ≃	166	26.40 S	146.08 E
Angeln ◆[1]	41	54.39 N	9.44 E
Angelo ≃	162	23.43 S	117.45 E
Angel R. Cabada	234	18.35 N	95.26 W
Ängelsberg	40	59.58 N	16.00 E
Angels Camp	226	38.04 N	120.33 W
Angels Creek ≃	226	38.01 N	120.33 W
Angelus, Lake ◎	281	42.41 N	83.20 W
Angemuk ∧	164	3.30 S	138.34 E
Anger	61	47.16 N	15.42 E
Angera	62	45.46 N	8.35 E
Angerbach ≃	263	51.23 N	6.44 E
Angereb ≃	144	13.51 N	36.08 E
Angeren	52	51.55 N	5.58 E
Angerhausen ◆[8]	263	51.23 N	6.44 E
Ångermanälven ≃	26	62.48 N	17.56 E
Ångermanland □[9]	26	63.30 N	18.05 E
Angermund ◆[8]	263	51.20 N	6.47 E
Angermünde	54	53.01 N	14.00 E
Angern, Dtsch.	54	52.21 N	11.44 E
Angern, Öst.	61	48.22 N	16.50 E
Angers	32	47.28 N	0.33 W
Angerville	50	48.19 N	2.00 E
Angervilliers	261	48.36 N	2.04 E
Ängesön I	26	63.43 N	20.55 E
Angevillers	56	49.23 N	6.02 E
Anggowala, Bukit ∧	112	4.15 S	121.44 E
Anghelu Ruiu, Necropoli ⊥	71	40.38 N	8.20 E
Anghiari	66	43.32 N	12.03 E
Angical	255	12.00 S	44.42 W
Angical do Piauí	250	6.05 S	42.44 W
Angicos	250	5.40 S	36.36 W
Angier	192	35.30 N	78.44 W
Angijak Island I	176	65.40 N	62.15 W
Angikuni Lake ◎	176	62.13 N	99.50 W
Angke, Kali ≃	269e	6.06 S	106.46 E
Angkor Wat ⊥	110	13.26 N	103.52 E
Ângk Tasaôm	110	11.01 N	104.41 E
Anglais, Baie des ⊂	186	49.15 N	68.07 W
Anglais, Jardin ♠	261	48.38 N	1.49 E
Anglais, Rivière des (English) ≃	206	45.13 N	73.50 W
Angle	42	51.41 N	5.06 W
Angle Inlet	198	49.21 N	95.04 W
Anglem, Mount ∧	172	46.44 S	167.56 E
Anglesea	169	38.25 S	144.11 E
Anglesey I	44	53.17 N	4.22 W
Anglet	32	43.29 N	1.31 W
Angleterre → England □[8]	28	52.30 N	1.30 W
Angleton	222	29.10 N	95.25 W
Anglezarke Moor ◆[3]	262	53.40 N	2.33 W
Anglezarke Reservoir ◎[1]	262	53.39 N	2.35 W
Angling ≃	184	56.45 N	93.36 W
Angling Lake ◎	184	53.55 N	93.52 W
Anglona ◆[1]	71	40.50 N	8.45 E
Anglo-Normandes, Îles → Channel Islands II	28	49.20 N	2.20 W
Anglure	50	48.35 N	3.49 E
Angmagssalik	176	65.36 N	37.41 W
Angmering	42	50.48 N	0.28 W
Ang Mo Kio	271c	1.22 N	103.51 E
Ango	154	4.02 N	25.52 E
Angoche	154	16.15 S	39.54 E
Angoche, Ilha I	154	16.20 S	39.50 E
Angohrān	128	26.35 N	57.54 E
Angol	252	37.48 S	72.43 W
Angola, In., U.S.	216	41.38 N	84.59 W
Angola, N.Y., U.S.	210	42.38 N	79.01 W
Angola □[1], Afr.	138	12.30 S	18.30 E
Angola □[1], Afr.	152	12.30 S	18.30 E
Angola Basin ✢[1]	10	15.00 S	3.00 E
Angola Lake Shore	214	42.37 N	79.05 W
Angono	269f	14.31 N	121.09 E
Angoon	180	57.30 N	134.35 W
Angora → Ankara	130	39.56 N	32.52 E
Angoram	164	4.04 S	144.04 E
Angostura	232	25.22 N	108.11 W
Angostura, Presa de la ◎[1]	234	16.10 N	92.40 W
Angostura → Ciudad Bolívar	246	8.08 N	63.33 W
Angostura Reservoir ◎[1]	198	43.18 N	103.27 W
Angoulême	32	45.39 N	0.09 E
Angoumois □[9]	32	45.30 N	0.05 W
Angra, Meos I	164	2.42 S	134.50 E
Angra do Heroísmo	148a	38.39 N	27.13 W
Angra do Heroísmo □[5]	148a	38.50 N	27.30 W
Angra dos Reis	256	23.00 S	44.18 W
Angren	85	41.01 N	70.12 E
Angren ≃	85	40.48 N	68.53 E
Angri	68	40.44 N	14.34 E
Angrignon Zoological Park ♠	275a	45.26 N	73.36 W
Angrogna	62	44.50 N	7.13 E
Ängsö	40	59.32 N	16.51 E
Ängsö Nationalpark ♠	40	59.39 N	18.44 E
Ang Thong	110	14.35 N	100.27 E
Angu	154	3.33 N	24.28 E
Angu ≃	256	21.48 S	42.30 W
Angualasto	252	30.03 S	69.09 W
Anguang	89	45.31 N	123.45 E
Anguchang	107	29.30 N	103.39 E
Anguciana, Cerro ∧	236	8.50 N	83.07 W
Anguilas, Arroyo ≃	288	34.26 S	58.31 W
Anguilla	194	32.58 N	90.49 W
Anguilla □[2], N.A.	230	18.15 N	63.05 W
Anguilla □[2], N.A.	238	18.15 N	63.05 W
Anguilla Cays II	238	23.31 N	79.33 W
Anguillara Sabazia	66	42.05 N	12.16 E
Anguillara Veneta	64	45.08 N	11.53 E

Anguille, Cape ›	186	47.55 N	59.25 W
Anguli Nur ◎	98	41.13 N	114.32 E
Angumu	154	0.07 S	27.42 E
Anguo	98	38.25 N	115.19 E
Anguozhuang	105	39.44 N	117.59 E
Anguruga	164	14.00 S	136.29 E
Angus	212	44.19 N	79.53 W
Angus Place	170	33.20 S	150.06 E
Angustura	256	21.45 S	42.41 W
Angusville	184	50.44 N	101.01 W
Angwa ≃	154	15.51 S	30.35 E
Angwin	226	38.34 N	122.26 W
Angyalföld ◆[8]	264c	47.33 N	19.05 E
Angyō	268	35.51 N	139.46 E
An Hai, Viet	110	15.13 N	108.56 E
Anhai, Zhg.	100	24.45 N	118.27 E
Anhalt □[9]	54	52.00 N	11.30 E
Anholt	52	51.52 N	6.27 E
Anholt I	26	56.42 N	11.34 E
Anhovo	64	46.03 N	13.37 E
Anhua	102	28.18 N	111.14 E
Anhuai	100	33.04 N	117.50 E
Anhui (Anhwei) □[4]	100	32.00 N	117.00 E
Anhŭng	98	36.41 N	126.10 E
Anhwei → Anhui □[4]	100	32.00 N	117.00 E
Aniak	180	61.35 N	159.33 W
Aniak ≃	180	61.34 N	159.30 W
Aniakchak National Monument ♠	180	56.50 N	157.50 W
Anibare Bay ⊂	174b	0.32 S	166.57 E
Aniche	50	50.20 N	3.15 E
Anicuns	255	16.28 S	49.58 W
Anié	150	7.45 N	1.12 E
Anié ≃	150	7.40 N	1.18 E
Anie, Pic d' ∧	32	42.57 N	0.43 W
Aniene ≃	66	41.56 N	12.30 E
Anif	64	47.45 N	13.04 E
Anik ◆[8]	272c	19.02 N	72.53 E
Anikino, Ross.	86	56.32 N	73.56 E
Anikino, Ross.	88	53.26 N	120.20 E
Anikovo	76	59.23 N	43.45 E
Anil	250	2.32 S	44.14 W
Anil, Rio do ≃	287a	22.59 S	43.21 W
Animas	200	31.56 N	108.48 W
Animas ≃	200	36.43 N	108.13 W
Animas Peak ∧	200	31.35 N	108.47 W
Animas Valley V	200	31.45 N	108.50 W
Anin	110	15.40 N	97.46 E
Anina	38	45.05 N	21.51 E
Anipemza	84	40.27 N	43.37 E
Aniskino	82	55.54 N	38.06 E
Añisoc	152	1.51 N	10.46 E
Anita, Ia., U.S.	198	41.26 N	94.45 W
Anita, Pa., U.S.	214	41.00 N	78.58 W
Anıtkaya	130	38.57 N	30.18 E
Aniva	89	46.43 N	142.32 E
Aniva, mys ›	89	46.01 N	143.25 E
Aniva, zaliv ⊂	89	46.16 N	142.48 E
Anivorano	157b	18.44 S	48.58 E
Anivorano Nord	157b	12.44 S	49.13 E
Aniwa I	175f	19.17 S	169.35 E
Anizy-le-Château	50	49.30 N	3.27 E
Anjad	120	22.02 N	75.03 E
Anjan	26	63.41 N	12.49 E
Anjangaon	120	21.10 N	77.18 E
Anjār, India	120	23.08 N	70.01 E
ʿAnjar, Lubnān	132	33.42 N	35.54 E
ʿAnjarah	132	32.18 N	35.45 E
Anjavimihavana	157b	12.32 S	49.16 E
Anji	106	30.43 N	119.41 E
Anjiabe	157b	12.07 S	49.20 E
Anjiang	105	40.45 N	117.38 E
Anjigami Lake ◎	190	47.51 N	84.34 W
Anjō	94	34.57 N	137.05 E
Anjou	206	45.36 N	73.33 W
Anjou □[9]	32	47.20 N	0.30 W
Anjozorobe	157b	18.24 S	47.52 E
Anju, C.M.I.K.	98	39.36 N	125.40 E
Anju, Zhg.	100	31.45 N	113.11 E
Anju, Zhg.	107	30.21 N	105.27 E
Anjudin	24	62.33 N	58.12 E
Anjuzhen	107	29.59 N	106.02 E
Anka	150	12.07 N	5.55 E
Ankang	102	32.42 N	109.05 E
Ankara	130	39.56 N	32.52 E
Ankara □[4]	130	39.50 N	32.50 E
Ankara ≃	130	39.51 N	31.55 E
Ankaramena	157b	21.57 S	46.39 E
Ankaratra ⋏	157b	19.25 S	47.12 E
Ankarimbelo	157b	22.08 S	47.20 E
Ankaroaka ∧	157b	17.48 S	48.32 E
Ankarsrum	26	57.42 N	16.19 E
Ankasakasa	157b	16.21 S	44.52 E
Ankata	80	50.44 N	51.34 E
Ankavandra	157b	18.46 S	45.18 E
Ankazoabo	157b	22.18 S	44.31 E
Ankazobe	157b	18.21 S	47.07 E
Ankazomiriotra	157b	19.38 S	46.32 E
Ankeny	190	41.43 N	93.36 W
An Khe	110	13.57 N	108.39 E
Ankilimalinika	157b	22.58 S	43.45 E
Ankilizato	157b	20.25 S	45.01 E
Anking → Anqing	100	30.31 N	117.02 E
Ankisabe	157b	19.17 S	46.29 E
Anklam	54	53.51 N	13.41 E
Ankleshwar	120	21.36 N	73.00 E
Ankober	144	9.35 N	39.44 E
Ankoro	154	6.45 S	26.57 E
Ankororoka	157b	25.30 S	45.11 E
Ankou	100	25.03 N	113.24 E
An'kovo	80	56.57 N	39.57 E
Ankpa	150	7.23 N	7.37 E
Ankum	52	52.32 N	7.52 E
Ankwe ≃	150	8.03 N	9.26 E
Anlinnuoer	98	41.11 N	114.31 E
Anliu	100	23.42 N	115.42 E
Anloga	150	5.47 N	0.50 E
Anlong	102	25.02 N	105.31 E
Ânlóng Vêng	110	14.14 N	104.05 E
Anlu	100	31.17 N	113.40 E
Anma-do I	98	35.21 N	126.02 E
Anmyŏn-do I	98	36.30 N	126.22 E
Ånn ◎	26	63.16 N	12.34 E
Ann, Cape ›, Ant.	9	66.10 S	51.22 E
Ann, Cape ›, Ma., U.S.	283	42.39 N	70.38 W
Anna, Ross.	78	51.29 N	40.25 E
Anna, Il., U.S.	194	37.27 N	89.14 W
Anna, Oh., U.S.	216	40.23 N	84.10 W
Anna, Tx., U.S.	196	33.21 N	96.33 W
Anna, Lake ◎[1]	188	38.04 N	77.45 W
Annaba (Bône)	148	36.54 N	7.46 E
Annaba □[5]	148	36.50 N	8.00 E
An-Nabaṭīyah □[4]	132	33.20 N	35.30 E
An-Nabaṭīyah at-Taḥtā	132	33.23 N	35.29 E
Annaberg, Öst.	61	47.52 N	15.22 E
Annaberg, Öst.	64	47.31 N	13.26 E
Annaberg-Buchholz	54	50.35 N	13.00 E
An-Nabī Shīt	132	33.52 N	36.07 E
An-Nabk	130	34.01 N	36.44 E
An-Nabqīyah I	128	26.44 N	36.01 E
Annaburg	54	51.44 N	13.03 E
Annaburger Heide ◆[3]	54	51.40 N	13.05 E
An-Nafūd ◆[2]	128	28.30 N	41.00 E
Annagassan	48	53.53 N	6.20 W
Annahütte	54	51.34 N	13.53 E
An-Najaf	128	31.59 N	44.28 E
An-Najaf □[4]	128	31.00 N	44.00 E
Annaka	94	36.19 N	138.54 E
An-Nakhl, Miṣr	140	29.55 N	33.45 E
An-Nakhl, Sūrīy.	132	33.00 N	36.07 E
Annalee ≃	48	54.03 N	7.24 W
Annalee Heights	208	38.51 N	77.10 W
Annalong	48	54.06 N	5.53 W
Anna Maria	220	27.31 N	82.44 W
Anna Maria Island I	220	27.30 N	82.43 W
An-Nāmir	132	32.47 N	36.13 E
Annamitique, Chaîne ⋏	110	17.00 N	106.00 E

Annam → Trung Phan □[9]	110	15.00 N	108.00 E
Annan	44	54.59 N	3.16 W
Annan ≃	44	54.59 N	3.16 W
Annanberg	164	4.55 S	144.40 E
Annandale, Austl.	166	21.57 S	148.22 E
Annandale, Mn., U.S.	190	45.15 N	94.07 W
Annandale, N.J., U.S.	210	40.38 N	74.52 W
Annandale, Va., U.S.	208	38.49 N	77.11 W
Annandale V	44	55.10 N	3.25 W
Annandale-on-Hudson	210	42.01 N	73.54 W
Anna Pink, Bahía ⊂	254	45.50 S	74.50 W
Anna Plains	162	19.17 S	121.37 E
Anna Point ›	174b	0.30 S	166.56 E
Annapolis	208	38.58 N	76.29 W
Annapolis Basin ⊂	186	44.39 N	65.42 W
Annapolis Royal	186	44.45 N	65.31 W
Annapūrṇa ∧	124	28.34 N	83.50 E
Annapūrṇapratham ∧	124	28.31 N	84.08 E
An-Naqīrah ⊤[4]	128	27.53 N	48.15 E
Ann Arbor	216	42.16 N	83.43 W
Ann Arbor Municipal Airport ⊠	281	42.14 N	83.45 W
Anna Regina	246	7.16 N	58.30 W
Annaricken Brook ≃	285	40.03 N	74.42 W
An-Nāṣirīyah, ʿIrāq	128	31.02 N	46.16 E
An-Nāṣirīyah, Sūrīy.	130	33.52 N	36.49 E
Annaspan ◎	158	28.33 S	25.47 E
An-Nawfalāb	140	15.52 N	32.32 E
An-Nawfalīyah	146	30.47 N	17.50 E
An-Nazlah	132	31.32 N	34.29 E
An-Nazlat	142	29.19 N	30.39 E
Annbank	44	55.28 N	4.30 W
Annean, Lake ◎	162	26.54 S	118.14 E
Anne Arundel □[6]	208	38.59 N	76.30 W
Annebault	50	49.15 N	0.04 E
Annecy	58	45.54 N	6.07 E
Annecy, Lac d' ◎	58	45.51 N	6.11 E
Annecy-le-Vieux	58	45.55 N	6.09 E
Annemasse	58	46.12 N	6.15 E
Annen	263	51.27 N	7.22 E
Annenkov Island I	244	54.29 S	37.05 W
Annenskij Most	76	60.45 N	37.10 E
Annenskoje	86	53.08 N	60.26 E
Anner ≃	48	52.22 N	7.39 W
Annet I	42a	49.54 N	6.21 W
Annet-sur-Marne	261	48.56 N	2.43 E
Annette	182	55.03 N	131.34 W
Annette Island I	182	55.10 N	131.28 W
Annevoie-Rouillon	56	50.21 N	4.50 E
Annezin	50	50.32 N	2.37 E
Annfield Plain	44	54.51 N	1.45 W
An Nhon	110	13.53 N	109.06 E
Anniangniang	89	51.33 N	125.49 E
Annicco	62	45.14 N	9.52 E
An-Nīl □[4]	140	19.00 N	33.00 E
An-Nīl al-Azraq □[4]	140	12.00 N	34.00 E
Anning	102	24.59 N	102.18 E
Anningdu	102	36.56 N	104.31 E
Anninger ∧	264b	48.03 N	16.15 E
Annino	265a	59.46 N	30.03 E
Anninskije Mineral'nyje Vody	89	52.44 N	140.12 E
Annisquam	283	42.39 N	70.41 W
Annisquam ≃	283	42.39 N	70.41 W
Anniston	194	33.39 N	85.49 W
Annobón I	138	1.25 S	5.36 E
Annonay	62	45.14 N	4.40 E
Annopol	30	50.54 N	21.52 E
Anno-Rebrikovo	83	49.36 N	40.12 E
Annot	62	43.58 N	6.40 E
Annotto Bay	241q	18.16 N	76.46 W
Annsjön ◎	40	58.48 N	15.26 E
An-Nubayrah	142	30.54 N	30.35 E
An-Nuhūd	140	12.42 N	28.26 E
An-Nuʿmān I	128	27.08 N	35.46 E
An-Nuʿmānīyah	128	32.32 N	45.25 E
An-Nuwayrah	142	29.06 N	30.59 E
Annville, Ky., U.S.	192	37.19 N	83.58 W
Annville, Pa., U.S.	208	40.19 N	76.30 W
Annweiler am Trifels	56	49.12 N	7.58 E
Anō	94	34.46 N	136.27 E
Anoia	68	38.27 N	16.05 E
Anoia ≃	34	41.28 N	1.56 E
Anoka	190	45.11 N	93.23 W
Áno Liósia	267c	38.05 N	23.42 E
Año Nuevo Bay ⊂	226	37.07 N	122.19 W
Anopino	80	55.42 N	40.40 E
Anori, Bra.	246	3.47 S	61.38 W
Anorí, Col.	246	7.05 N	75.08 W
Anorotsangana	157b	13.56 S	47.55 E
Anosibe	157b	19.26 S	48.13 E
Anosyennes, Chaînes ⋏	157b	24.30 S	46.50 E
Anotaié ≃	250	3.29 N	52.04 W
Anpilogovo	78	51.47 N	36.01 E
Anping, Zhg.	98	38.16 N	115.30 E
Anping, Zhg.	98	34.01 N	115.07 E
Anping, Zhg.	100	26.33 N	113.22 E
Anping, Zhg.	104	41.11 N	123.26 E
Anping, Zhg.	105	39.43 N	116.53 E
Anpu	102	21.27 N	110.00 E
ʿAnqābīyah, Jabal al- ∧[2]	142	30.01 N	31.37 E
Anqing	100	30.31 N	117.02 E
Anqiu	98	36.25 N	119.10 E
Anrath	56	51.17 N	6.28 E
Anren, Zhg.	100	28.04 N	119.20 E
Anren, Zhg.	100	26.42 N	113.16 E
Anrenzhen	107	30.31 N	103.38 E
Anröchte	52	51.33 N	8.19 E
Ans, Bel.	56	50.39 N	5.32 E
Ans, Dan.	41	56.19 N	9.36 E
Ansager	41	55.42 N	8.45 E
Ansai	102	36.54 N	109.10 E
ʿAnṣār	132	33.23 N	35.21 E
Ansbach	56	49.17 N	10.34 E
Anschan → Anshan	104	41.08 N	122.59 E
Anschlag	263	51.10 N	7.29 E
Anse	58	45.56 N	4.43 E
Anseba ≃	144	17.03 N	37.24 E
Anse-Bertrand	241o	16.29 N	61.31 W
Anse-d'Hainault	238	18.30 N	74.27 W
Anse La Raye	241f	13.57 N	61.03 W
Anselmo	198	41.37 N	99.51 W
Anseremme	56	50.15 N	4.54 E
Anserma	246	5.13 N	75.48 W
Ansfelden	61	48.13 N	14.17 E
Anshan	104	41.08 N	122.59 E
Anshun	102	26.15 N	105.56 E
Ansina	252	31.54 S	55.28 W
Ansley	198	41.17 N	99.22 W
Anson	196	32.45 N	99.53 W
Anson Bay ⊂, Austl.	164	13.20 S	130.06 E
Anson Bay ⊂, Norf. I.	174c	29.01 S	167.55 E
Anson Creek ≃	212	44.53 N	79.03 W
Ansŏng	98	37.02 N	127.16 E
Ansongo	150	15.40 N	0.30 E
Ansonia, Ct., U.S.	207	41.20 N	73.04 W
Ansonia, Oh., U.S.	216	40.12 N	84.38 W
Ansonville, N.C., U.S.	192	35.06 N	80.06 W
Ansonville, Pa., U.S.	214	40.51 N	78.34 W
Ansouis	62	43.44 N	5.28 E
Ansted	188	38.08 N	81.05 W
Anstey	42	52.40 N	1.11 W
Anstruther	46	56.13 N	2.42 W
Anstruther Lake ◎	212	44.45 N	78.12 W
Ansudu	164	2.08 S	139.20 E
Ansus	164	1.44 S	135.49 E
Anta, Bra.	256	22.03 S	42.59 W
Anta, Perú	248	13.29 S	72.09 W
Antabamba	248	14.19 S	72.55 W
Antakya (Antioch)	130	36.14 N	36.07 E
Antalaha	157b	14.53 S	50.16 E
Antalieptė	76	55.40 N	25.51 E
Antalovcy	78	48.38 N	22.31 E
Antalya	130	36.53 N	30.42 E
Antalya □[4]	130	37.00 N	31.00 E
Antalya, Gulf of → Antalya Körfezi ⊂	130	36.30 N	31.00 E

≃	River	Fluß	Río	Rivière	Rio
≊	Canal	Kanal	Canal	Canal	Canal
∟	Waterfall, Rapids	Wasserfall, Stromschnellen	Cascada, Rápidos	Chute d'eau, Rapides	Cascata, Rápidos
⊎	Strait	Meeresstraße	Estrecho	Détroit	Estreito
⊂	Bay, Gulf	Bucht, Golf	Bahía, Golfo	Baie, Golfe	Baía, Golfo
◎	Lake, Lakes	See, Seen	Lago, Lagos	Lac, Lacs	Lago, Lagos
≡	Swamp	Sumpf	Pantano	Marais	Pântano
⊓	Ice Features, Glacier	Eis- und Gletscherformen	Accidentes Glaciales	Formes glaciaires	Acidentes glaciares
⊤	Other Hydrographic Features	Andere Hydrographische Objekte	Otros Elementos Hidrográficos	Autres données hydrographiques	Outros acidentes hidrográficos

✢	Submarine Features	Untermeerische Objekte	Accidentes Submarinos	Formes de relief sous-marin	Acidentes submarinos
□	Political Unit	Politische Einheit	Unidad Politica	Entité politique	Unidade política
⊍	Cultural Institution	Kulturelle Institution	Institución Cultural	Institution culturelle	Institução cultural
⊥	Historical Site	Historische Stätte	Sitio Histórico	Site historique	Sitio histórico
♠	Recreational Site	Erholungs- und Ferienort	Sitio de Recreo	Centre de loisirs	Area de Lazer
⊠	Airport	Flughafen	Aeropuerto	Aéroport	Aeroporto
■	Military Installation	Militäranlage	Instalación Militar	Installation militaire	Instalação militar
◆	Miscellaneous	Verschiedenes	Misceláneo	Divers	Diversos

Name	Page	Lat.°′	Long.°′
Antalya Körfezi ⊂	130	36.30 N	31.00 E
Antambohobe	157b	22.20 S	46.47 E
An Tan	110	15.26 N	108.39 E
Antanambao Manampotsy	157b	19.29 S	48.34 E
Antanambe	157b	16.26 S	49.52 E
Antananarivo	157b	18.55 S	47.31 E
Antananarivo □[4]	157b	19.00 S	47.00 E
Antanetibe	157b	18.27 S	46.42 E
Antanifotsy	157b	19.39 S	47.19 E
Antanimieva	157b	22.12 S	43.44 E
Antanimora	157b	24.49 S	45.40 E
Antar, Djebel ∧	148	31.57 N	1.56 W
Antarctica ⊥[1]	9	87.00 S	60.00 E
Antarctic Peninsula ≻[1]	9	69.30 S	65.00 W
Antarctique, Péninsule — Antarctic Peninsula ≻[1]	9	69.30 S	65.00 W
Antarctiques territoires britanniques — British Antarctic Territory □[2]	9	60.00 S	45.00 W
Antarktis — Antarctica ⊥[1]	9	87.00 S	60.00 E
Antártica, Península — Antarctic Peninsula ≻[1]	9	69.30 S	65.00 W
Antas	250	10.23 S	38.20 W
Antas, Ribeirão das ≃	256	21.47 S	46.36 W
Antas, Rio das ≃	252	29.04 S	51.21 W
An Teallach ∧	46	57.48 N	5.14 W
Antechamber Bay ⊂	168b	35.48 S	138.05 E
Antegnate	62	45.29 N	9.47 E
Antela, Laguna de ⊜	34	42.07 N	7.41 W
Antelope Acres	228	34.44 N	118.19 W
Antelope Creek ≃, Nv., U.S.	204	40.00 N	117.24 W
Antelope Creek ≃, S.D., U.S.	198	45.19 N	102.27 W
Antelope Creek ≃, Wy., U.S.	198	43.29 N	105.23 W
Antelope Island I	202	40.57 N	112.12 W
Antelope Mine	154	21.02 S	28.27 E
Antelope Peak ∧	204	41.19 N	114.58 W
Antelope Reservoir ⊜[1]	202	42.54 N	117.13 W
Antelope Valley V	228	34.45 N	118.20 W
Antelope Wash V	204	39.33 N	116.17 W
Antenor Navarro	250	6.44 S	38.27 W
Antequera, Esp.	34	37.01 N	4.33 W
Antequera, Para.	252	24.08 S	57.07 W
Antero Reservoir ⊜[1]	200	39.00 N	105.55 W
Anterselva, Lago d' ⊜	64	46.53 N	12.10 E
Anterselva di Sopra	64	46.52 N	12.08 E
Antes Fort	210	41.12 N	77.14 W
Antetikireja	157b	14.42 S	47.29 E
Antevamena	157b	21.02 S	44.08 E
Antey-Saint-André	62	45.48 N	7.36 E
Anthéor	62	43.26 N	6.53 E
Anthon	198	42.23 N	95.51 W
Anthony, Fl., U.S.	192	29.17 N	82.06 W
Anthony, Ks., U.S.	198	37.09 N	98.01 W
Anthony, N.M., U.S.	200	32.00 N	106.36 W
Anthony, R.I., U.S.	207	41.41 N	71.32 W
Anthony, Tx., U.S.	200	31.59 N	106.36 W
Anthony Chabot Regional Park ♦	282	37.45 N	122.06 W
Anthony Creek ≃	188	37.54 N	80.20 W
Anthony Lagoon	162	17.59 S	135.32 E
Anthony Peak ∧	204	39.51 N	122.58 W
Anti-Atlas ⋏	148	30.00 N	8.30 W
Antibes	62	43.35 N	7.07 E
Antibes, Cap d' ≻	62	43.32 N	7.07 E
Anticosti, Île d' I	186	49.30 N	63.00 W
Antiesen ≃	60	48.22 N	13.24 E
Antietam Creek, West Branch ≃	208	39.41 N	77.37 W
Antietam National Battlefield ♦	188	39.24 N	77.47 W
Antifer, Cap d' ≻	50	49.41 N	0.10 E
Antignano	66	43.30 N	10.19 E
Antigo	190	45.08 N	89.09 W
Antigonish	186	45.35 N	61.55 W
Antigorio, Valle V	58	46.18 N	8.20 E
Antigua I	240c	17.03 N	61.48 W
Antigua and Barbuda □[1], N.A.	230	17.03 N	61.48 W
Antigua and Barbuda □[1], N.A.	240c	17.03 N	61.48 W
Antigua Guatemala	236	14.34 N	90.44 W
Antigua International Airport ⊠	240c	17.09 N	61.47 W
Antigues, Pointe d' ≻	241o	16.26 N	61.33 W
Antiguo Morelos	234	22.33 N	99.05 W
Anti-Lebanon — Sharqī, Al-Jabal ash- ⋏	132	33.35 N	36.00 E
Antilla, Arg.	252	26.07 S	64.36 W
Antilla, Cuba	240p	20.50 N	75.45 W
Antillas, Archipiélago de las — West Indies II	230	19.00 N	70.00 W
Antillas Holandesas — Netherlands Antilles □[2]	241s	12.15 N	69.00 W
Antilles hollandaise — Netherlands Antilles □[2]	241s	12.15 N	69.00 W
Antilles néerlandaises — Netherlands Antilles □[2]	241s	12.15 N	69.00 W
Antillo	70	37.58 N	15.15 E
Antilyās	132	33.55 N	35.35 E
Antímano ◆[8]	286c	10.28 N	66.59 W
Antimony	200	38.07 N	111.59 W
Anting	106	31.18 N	121.09 E
Antioch, Ca., U.S.	226	38.00 N	121.48 W
Antioch, Il., U.S.	216	42.28 N	88.05 W
Antioch — Antakya	130	36.14 N	36.07 E
Antioquia	246	6.33 N	75.50 W
Antioquia □[5]	246	7.00 N	75.30 W
Antipino, Ross.	76	55.55 N	33.16 E
Antipino, Ross.	86	59.01 N	55.10 E
Antipino, Ross.	86	57.49 N	66.34 E
Antipodes Islands II	9	49.40 S	178.47 E
Antipolo	116	14.35 N	121.10 E
Antipovka	80	49.50 N	45.20 E
Antiquarian Museum ʊ	283	42.27 N	71.20 W
Antique □[4]	116	11.00 N	121.45 E
Antizana ∧[1]	246	0.30 S	78.08 W
Antler ≃	184	49.08 N	101.00 W
Antlers	196	34.13 N	95.37 W
Antoetra	157b	20.46 S	47.20 E
Antofagasta	252	23.39 S	70.24 W
Antofagasta □[4]	252	23.30 S	69.00 W
Antofagasta de la Sierra	252	26.04 S	67.25 W
Antofalla, Salar de ≅	252	25.44 S	67.45 W
Antofalla, Volcán ∧[1]	252	25.34 S	67.55 W
Antoing	50	50.34 N	3.27 E
Antolana ∧	157b	17.04 S	48.09 E
Antón, Pan.	236	8.24 N	80.16 W
Anton, Tx., U.S.	196	33.49 N	102.10 W
Anton Chico	200	35.12 N	105.08 W
Antongila, Helodrano ⊂	157b	15.45 S	49.50 E
Antonia	219	38.21 N	90.27 W
Antonibe	157b	15.07 S	47.24 E
Antonina	252	25.27 S	48.43 W
Antonina do Norte	250	6.43 S	39.58 W
Antoniny	78	49.49 N	26.52 E
Antonio Amaro	232	24.16 N	104.01 W
Antonio Carboni	258	35.12 S	59.20 W
Antônio Carlos	256	21.19 S	43.45 W
Antonio de Biedma	254	47.29 S	66.30 W
Antonio Escobedo	234	20.46 N	103.57 W
Antônio Lemos	250	1.22 S	50.50 W
Antônio Prado	252	28.51 S	51.17 W
Antonito	200	37.05 N	106.00 W
Antón Lizardo, Punta ≻	234	19.03 N	95.58 W
Antonov	78	49.37 N	29.47 E
Antonovka, Kaz.	86	53.19 N	68.26 E
Antonovka, Kaz.	86	45.38 N	80.15 E
Antonovka, Ross.	80	54.55 N	49.30 E
Antonovo	80	49.23 N	51.47 E
Antony	50	48.45 N	2.18 E
Antopol'	76	52.12 N	24.47 E
Antou	100	26.07 N	118.11 E
Antracit	83	48.06 N	39.06 E
Antraigues	62	44.43 N	4.21 E
Antrain	32	48.27 N	1.29 W
Antratsit — Antracit	83	48.06 N	39.06 E
Antrift ≃	56	50.54 N	9.15 E
Antrim, N. Ire., U.K.	48	54.43 N	6.13 W
Antrim, Oh., U.S.	214	40.06 N	81.23 W
Antrim, Pa., U.S.	210	41.37 N	77.18 W
Antrodoco	66	42.25 N	13.05 E
Antronapiana	58	46.03 N	8.07 E
Antropologia, Museo Nacional de ʊ	286a	19.25 N	99.11 W
Antropovo, Ross.	80	58.26 N	43.00 E
Antropovo, Ross.	82	55.15 N	37.39 E
Antsakabary	157b	15.03 S	48.56 E
Antsalova	157b	18.40 S	44.37 E
Antsenavolo	157b	21.24 S	48.03 E
Antsiafabositra	157b	17.18 S	46.57 E
Antsirabe, Madag.	157b	14.00 S	49.59 E
Antsirabe, Madag.	157b	15.57 S	48.58 E
Antsirabe, Madag.	157b	19.51 S	47.02 E
Antsiranana	157b	12.16 S	49.17 E
Antsiranana □[4]	157b	13.30 S	49.10 E
Antsla	76	57.50 N	26.32 E
Antsohihy	157b	14.52 S	47.59 E
Anttis	24	67.16 N	22.52 E
Antu (Songjiang)	98	42.32 N	128.18 E
Antufash, Jazīrat I	144	15.42 N	42.25 E
Antulai, Gunong ∧	112	4.40 N	116.21 E
Antun'	89	47.36 N	135.46 E
Antung — Dandong	98	40.08 N	124.20 E
Antuševo, Ross.	76	59.59 N	42.18 E
Antuševo, Ross.	76	59.54 N	37.40 E
Antwerp, N.Y., U.S.	212	44.11 N	75.36 W
Antwerp, Oh., U.S.	216	41.10 N	84.44 W
Antwerp — Antwerpen	50	51.13 N	4.25 E
Antwerpen (Anvers)	50	51.13 N	4.25 E
Antwerpen □[4]	56	51.10 N	4.50 E
Antykan	89	54.55 N	135.12 E
Anua	174u	14.16 S	170.40 W
Anučino, Ross.	80	52.58 N	43.52 E
Anučino, Ross.	89	43.58 N	133.02 E
Anugul	120	20.51 N	85.06 E
Anŭi	98	35.38 N	127.48 E
An'uj ≃	89	49.18 N	136.27 E
An'ujsk	74	68.18 N	161.38 E
An'ujskij chrebet ⋏, Ross.	74	67.30 N	166.00 E
Anujskij chrebet ⋏, Ross.	86	51.30 N	84.55 E
Anundshögen ⊥	40	59.38 N	16.37 E
Anūpgarh	123	29.11 N	73.13 E
Anūpshahr	124	28.22 N	78.16 E
Ānūr	126	22.55 N	87.39 E
Anuradhapura	122	8.21 N	80.23 E
Anversa degli Abruzzi	66	41.59 N	13.48 E
Anvers — Antwerpen	50	51.13 N	4.25 E
Anvers Island I	9	64.33 S	63.35 W
Anvik	180	62.40 N	160.12 W
Anvik ≃	180	62.39 N	160.14 W
Anvil Peak ∧	181a	52.00 N	179.35 E
Anvil Range ⋏	180	62.30 N	133.50 W
Anvin	50	50.27 N	2.15 E
Anxi, Zhg.	100	25.06 N	118.12 E
Anxi, Zhg.	100	25.15 N	115.06 E
Anxi, Zhg.	102	40.32 N	95.51 E
Anxi, Zhg.	106	30.25 N	120.01 E
Anxian	102	31.40 N	104.32 E
Anxiang	102	29.23 N	112.09 E
Anxin (Xin'anzhen)	105	38.55 N	115.55 E
Anxing	106	31.24 N	119.06 E
Anxious Bay ⊂	162	33.25 S	134.35 E
Anyama	150	5.30 N	4.03 W
Anyang, Taehan	98	37.23 N	126.55 E
Anyang, Zhg.	98	36.06 N	114.21 E
Anyang ≃	98	36.01 N	114.46 E
Anyeke	154	2.24 N	32.31 E
A'nyêmaqên Shan ⋏	102	34.30 N	100.00 E
Anyer Kidul	115a	6.04 S	105.53 E
Anyi	100	28.50 N	115.31 E
Anykščiai	76	55.32 N	25.06 E
Anyox	182	55.25 N	129.49 W
Anysberg	158	33.31 S	20.46 E
Anyuan, Zhg.	100	26.36 N	116.38 E
Anyuan, Zhg.	100	27.37 N	113.54 E
Anyuan, Zhg.	100	25.08 N	115.28 E
Anyuanyi — Tianzhu	102	37.14 N	102.59 E
Anyue	107	30.06 N	105.21 E
Anza ≃	58	46.00 N	8.17 E
Anza-Borrego Desert State Park ♦	204	33.00 N	116.26 W
Anzac	184	56.27 N	111.02 W
Anzaldo	248	17.50 S	65.55 W
Anzano di Puglia	68	41.07 N	15.17 E
Anzbari ∧	123	34.40 N	74.50 E
Anze	102	36.11 N	112.16 E
Anžero-Sudžensk	86	56.07 N	86.00 E
Anzhen	106	31.36 N	120.28 E
Anzhou	105	38.52 N	115.49 E
Anzhuang	106	31.04 N	121.01 E
Anzi, It.	68	40.31 N	15.55 E
Anzi, Zaïre	152	0.52 S	23.24 E
Anzicun	105	39.46 N	115.50 E
Anzin	50	50.22 N	3.30 E
Anzio	66	41.27 N	12.37 E
Anzoátegui □[3]	246	9.00 N	64.30 W
Anzob	85	39.10 N	68.48 E
Anzob, pereval)(	85	39.07 N	68.52 E
Anzola dell'Emilia	64	44.33 N	11.11 E
Anzon ≃	62	45.45 N	3.57 E
Anžu, ostrova II	74	75.30 N	143.00 E
Aoba I	175f	15.25 S	167.50 E
Aoba / Maewo □[8]	175f	15.05 S	168.00 E
Aogaki	96	35.14 N	135.00 E
Aoga-shima I	90	32.28 N	139.46 E
Aohaibolihu	104	42.01 N	121.32 E
Aohandaba	104	42.05 N	121.59 E
Aohan Qi (Xinhui)	98	42.19 N	119.59 E
Aoíz	34	42.47 N	1.22 W
Aoji	98	42.31 N	130.23 E
Aojiang	100	27.37 N	120.33 E
Aojiao	100	23.37 N	117.26 E
Aola	175e	9.32 S	160.29 E
Aoliyingzi	104	42.14 N	121.58 E
Ao Luk	110	8.23 N	98.43 E
Aomar	34	36.30 N	3.47 E
Aomen — Macau	100	22.14 N	113.35 E
Aomori	92	40.49 N	140.45 E
Aonla	124	28.17 N	79.09 E
Aono-yama ∧	96	34.27 N	131.48 E
Aóös (Vijosë) ≃	38	40.37 N	19.20 E
A'opo	175a	13.29 S	172.30 W
Aôral, Phnum ∧	110	12.02 N	104.10 E
Aorangi Mountains ⋏	172	41.26 S	175.20 E
Aore I	175f	15.35 S	167.10 E
Aorere ≃	172	40.41 S	172.40 E
Aoshang	100	25.42 N	113.00 E
Ao-shima I, Nihon	96	33.44 N	132.29 E
Ao-shima I, Nihon	96	33.55 N	134.44 E
Aosta	62	45.44 N	7.20 E
Aosta □[4]	58	45.45 N	7.20 E
Aosta, Valle d' V	62	45.46 N	7.25 E
Aoste	62	45.35 N	5.36 E
Aotou	100	22.44 N	114.33 E
Aoudaghost ⊥	150	17.25 N	10.40 W
Aouderas	150	17.37 N	8.26 E
Aoudour, Oued ≃	34	35.02 N	5.02 W
Aouk, Bahr ≃	146	8.51 N	18.53 E
Aoukalé ≃	146	9.17 N	22.42 E
Aouk-Aoukalé, Réserve de Faune de l' ◆[4]	146	10.00 N	21.15 E
Aoukâr ◆[1]	150	18.00 N	9.30 W
Aoulime, Jebel ∧	148	30.48 N	8.50 W
Aoumou	175f	21.24 S	165.50 E
Aourou	150	14.57 N	11.35 W
Aoya	96	35.31 N	133.59 E
Aoyama	94	34.40 N	136.11 E
Aoyama-tōge)(	94	34.40 N	136.16 E
Aozi	146	21.04 N	18.41 E
Aozou	146	21.49 N	17.25 E
Apa ≃	252	22.06 S	58.00 W
Apache	196	34.53 N	98.21 W
Apache Junction	200	33.24 N	111.32 W
Apache Lake ⊜[1]	200	33.36 N	111.16 W
Apache Peak ∧	200	31.49 N	110.25 W
Apalachee ≃	192	33.32 N	83.17 W
Apalachee Bay ⊂	192	30.00 N	84.13 W
Apalaches — Appalachian Mountains ⋏	178	41.00 N	77.00 W
Apalachicola	192	29.43 N	84.59 W
Apalachicola ≃	192	29.44 N	84.59 W
Apalachicola Bay ⊂	192	29.40 N	85.00 W
Apalachin	210	42.04 N	76.09 W
Apam	150	5.17 N	0.44 W
Apan	234	19.43 N	98.25 W
Apanas, Laguna de ⊜[1]	236	13.11 N	85.59 W
Apango	234	17.44 N	99.20 W
Apapa ◆[8]	273a	6.27 N	3.22 E
Apapa Wharf ◆[5]	273a	6.23 N	3.23 E
Apaporis ≃	246	1.23 S	69.25 W
Aparados da Serra, Parque Nacional de ♦	252	29.30 S	50.32 W
Aparan	84	40.36 N	44.23 E
Aparecida	256	22.50 S	45.14 W
Aparima ≃	172	46.20 S	168.01 E
Aparri	116	18.22 N	121.39 E
Apartadó	246	7.54 N	76.39 W
Apaseo El Grande	234	20.33 N	100.41 W
Apastovo	80	55.11 N	48.30 E
Apatin	38	45.40 N	18.59 E
Apatity	24	67.34 N	33.18 E
Apatou	250	5.09 N	54.20 W
Apatzingán de la Constitución	234	19.05 N	102.21 W
Apaxtla de Castrejón	234	18.09 N	99.52 W
Apayacu ≃	246	3.19 S	71.51 W
Ap Ba Tien	269c	10.44 N	106.36 E
Ap Binh Quoi	269c	10.48 N	106.36 E
Ap Binh Thanh	110	11.11 N	108.42 E
Apcheron, Péninsule de l' — Apšeronskij poluostrov ≻[1]	84	40.30 N	50.00 E
Ape	76	57.32 N	26.40 E
Apeadero Funke	258	35.28 S	58.59 W
Apecchio	66	43.33 N	12.25 E
Ape Dale V	42	52.30 N	2.45 W
Apeganau Lake ⊜	184	55.35 N	99.35 W
Apelação	266c	38.49 N	9.08 W
Apeldoorn	52	52.13 N	5.58 E
Apeleg, Arroyo ≃	254	44.58 S	70.07 W
Apen	52	53.13 N	7.48 E
Apenes	224	49.16 N	124.41 W
Apeninos — Appennino ⋏	36	43.00 N	13.00 E
Apenninen — Appennino ⋏	36	43.00 N	13.00 E
Apennines — Appennino ⋏	36	43.00 N	13.00 E
Apennins — Appennino ⋏	36	43.00 N	13.00 E
Apensen	52	53.26 N	9.37 E
Apese ◆[8]	273a	6.25 N	3.25 E
Apetlon	61	47.45 N	16.50 E
Apex	192	35.43 N	78.51 W
Apex Mountain ∧	180	62.28 N	138.04 W
Api	154	3.40 N	25.26 E
Api ∧	124	30.00 N	80.57 E
Api, Tanjung ≻	112	0.48 S	121.39 E
Apía, Col.	246	5.05 N	75.58 W
Apia, W. Sam.	175a	13.50 S	171.44 W
Apiacá ≃	250	9.16 S	57.03 W
Apiacás, Serra dos ⋏[1]	248	10.15 S	57.15 W
Apiaí	252	24.31 S	48.50 W
Apiaú ≃	246	2.39 N	61.12 W
Apice	68	41.07 N	14.56 E
Apipilulco	234	18.11 N	99.41 W
Apishapa ≃	198	38.08 N	103.57 W
Apiti	172	39.58 S	175.53 E
Apizaco	234	19.25 N	98.09 W
Apizolaya	232	24.50 N	102.15 W
Aplahoué	150	6.56 N	1.41 E
Aplao	248	16.05 S	72.31 W
Ap Lei Chau I	271d	22.15 N	114.09 E
Aplerbeck ◆[8]	263	51.29 N	7.33 E
Aplinskij, porog ∟	88	58.28 N	100.32 E
Apo	234	19.25 N	102.25 W
Apo, Mount ∧	116	6.59 N	125.16 E
Apodi	250	5.39 S	37.48 W
Apodi ≃	250	4.56 S	37.10 W
Apo East Pass ʯ	116	12.40 N	120.40 E
Apoera	250	5.12 N	57.10 W
Apolakkiá	38	36.06 N	27.50 E
Apolda	54	51.01 N	11.31 E
Apolima Strait ʯ	175a	13.50 S	172.10 W
Apolinario Saravia	252	24.25 S	64.02 W
Apollo	214	40.34 N	79.34 W
Apollo Bay	166	38.45 S	143.40 E
Apollo Beach	220	27.45 N	82.25 W
Apollonia ⊥	146	32.54 N	21.58 E
Apolo	248	14.43 S	68.31 W
Apón ≃	246	10.06 N	72.23 W
Aponguao ≃	246	4.48 N	61.36 W
Apopa	236	13.48 N	89.11 W
Apopka	220	28.40 N	81.30 W
Apopka, Lake ⊜	220	28.37 N	81.38 W
Apoquindo	286e	33.24 S	70.32 W
Aporá	250	11.39 S	38.05 W
Aporé	255	18.58 S	52.01 W
Aporé ≃	255	19.27 S	50.57 W
Apo Reef ✦[2]	116	12.40 N	120.29 E
Aporema	250	1.14 N	50.49 W
Aporo	234	19.41 N	100.25 W
Apostle Islands II	190	46.50 N	90.30 W
Apostle Islands National Lakeshore ♦	190	46.55 N	91.00 W
Apóstoles	252	27.55 S	55.46 W
Apostolovo	78	47.39 N	33.44 E
Appalachen — Appalachian Mountains ⋏	178	41.00 N	77.00 W
Appalaches, Monts — Appalachian Mountains ⋏	178	41.00 N	77.00 W
Appalachia	192	36.54 N	82.46 W
Appalachian Mountains ⋏	178	41.00 N	77.00 W
Äppelbo	40	60.30 N	14.00 E
Appelhülsen	52	51.54 N	7.25 E
Appen	52	53.40 N	9.44 E
Appennino (Apennines) ⋏	36	43.00 N	13.00 E
Appennino, Galleria dell' ◆[5]	66	44.10 N	11.10 E
Appennino Abruzzese ⋏	66	42.00 N	14.00 E
Appennino Calabrese ⋏	68	39.00 N	16.30 E
Appennino Campano ⋏	66	41.30 N	15.00 E
Appennino Ligure ⋏	62	44.30 N	9.00 E
Appennino Lucano ⋏	68	40.30 N	16.00 E
Appennino Tosco-Emiliano ⋏	36	44.00 N	11.30 E
Appennino Umbro-Marchigiano ⋏	66	43.00 N	13.00 E
Appenzell	58	47.20 N	9.25 E
Appenzell-Ausser Rhoden □[3]	58	47.22 N	9.28 E
Appenzell-Inner Rhoden □[3]	58	47.18 N	9.25 E
Appiano (Eppan)	64	46.28 N	11.15 E
Appiano Gentile	62	45.44 N	8.59 E
Appin	170	34.12 S	150.47 E
Appingedam	52	53.18 N	6.52 E
Apple ≃, U.S.	190	42.11 N	90.14 W
Apple ≃, Wi., U.S.	190	45.09 N	92.45 W
Appleby, S. Afr.	158	27.39 S	22.36 E
Appleby, Eng., U.K.	44	54.36 N	2.29 W
Appleby, Tx., U.S.	222	31.43 N	94.36 W
Apple Creek	214	40.45 N	81.50 W
Apple Creek ≃, Il., U.S.	219	39.22 N	90.37 W
Apple Creek ≃, Mo., U.S.	194	37.35 N	89.32 W
Apple Creek ≃, N.D., U.S.	198	46.40 N	100.46 W
Applecross	46	57.25 N	5.49 W
Appledore	42	51.03 N	4.10 W
Applegate	226	39.06 N	120.59 W
Applegate ≃	202	42.26 N	123.27 W
Apple Hill	206	45.13 N	74.46 W
Apple Orchard Mountain ∧	192	37.31 N	79.31 W
Apples	58	46.34 N	6.25 E
Apple Springs	222	31.13 N	94.58 W
Appleton, Eng., U.K.	262	53.21 N	2.33 W
Appleton, Mn., U.S.	198	45.11 N	96.01 W
Appleton, Wa., U.S.	224	45.48 N	121.16 W
Appleton, Wi., U.S.	190	44.15 N	88.24 W
Appleton City	194	38.11 N	94.01 W
Apple Valley	228	34.30 N	117.11 W
Applewold	214	40.47 N	79.36 W
Appley Bridge	262	53.35 N	2.43 W
Appling	192	33.32 N	82.18 W
Appoigny	50	47.53 N	3.32 E
Appomattox	192	37.21 N	78.49 W
Appomattox ≃	192	37.18 N	77.18 W
Appomattox Court House National Historical Park ♦	192	37.23 N	78.48 W
Approuague ≃	250	4.38 N	51.58 W
Apra Harbor ⊂	174p	13.27 N	144.38 E
Aprelevka	82	55.33 N	37.04 E
Aprel'sk	88	58.10 N	114.34 E
Aprel'skij	89	53.30 N	126.16 E
Apremont	58	46.13 N	5.40 E
Apremont-la-Forêt	56	48.51 N	5.38 E
Aprica, Passo d')(	64	46.09 N	10.09 E
Apricena	68	41.47 N	15.27 E
Aprigliano	68	39.14 N	16.20 E
April ≃	164	4.18 S	142.26 E
Aprilia	66	41.36 N	12.39 E
Apscheron — Apšeronskij poluostrov ≻[1]	84	40.30 N	50.00 E
Apšeronsk	84	44.28 N	39.44 E
Apšeronskij poluostrov ≻[1]	84	40.30 N	50.00 E
Apshawa	276	41.01 N	74.22 W
Apsley	212	44.45 N	78.06 W
Apt	62	43.53 N	5.24 E
Aptakisic	278	42.12 N	87.56 W
Ap Tan Hoa	269c	10.45 N	106.35 E
Ap Tan My	110	11.43 N	108.49 E
Aptos	226	36.58 N	121.53 W
Apuane, Alpi ⋏	64	44.09 N	10.15 E
Apuaú ≃	246	2.32 S	60.48 W
Apucarana	255	23.33 S	51.29 W
Apulia Station	210	42.49 N	76.05 W
Apure □[3]	246	7.10 N	68.50 W
Apure ≃	246	7.37 N	66.25 W
Apurímac □[5]	248	14.00 S	73.00 W
Apurímac ≃	248	11.48 S	74.03 W
Apurito	246	7.56 N	68.27 W
Āq ≃	84	38.59 N	45.27 E
Aqaba, Gulf of ⊂	128	29.00 N	34.40 E
Aqabah, Wādī al- V	132	30.14 N	33.53 E
Āqbolāgh	84	38.54 N	44.32 E
Āqchah	120	36.56 N	66.11 E
ʻAqīq	140	18.14 N	38.12 E
ʻAqīq, Khalīj ⊂	140	18.20 N	38.10 E
ʻAqīq, Wādī al- V	128	24.17 N	40.10 E
Aq Qalʻeh	128	37.01 N	54.30 E
Aqqikkol Hu ⊜	120	37.05 N	88.05 E
ʻAqrabah	132	33.06 N	36.00 E
ʻAqrah	128	36.45 N	43.54 E
Aquarius Plateau ⋏[1]	200	38.05 N	111.40 W
Aquasco	208	38.35 N	76.43 W
Aquashicola	210	40.49 N	75.35 W
Aquashicola Creek ≃	210	40.47 N	75.37 W
Äquatorial-Guinea — Equatorial Guinea □[1]	152	2.00 N	9.00 E
Aquebogue	207	40.56 N	72.37 W
Aqueduct Race Track ♦	276	40.40 N	73.50 W
Aquia Creek ≃	208	38.23 N	77.18 W
Aquiaulne ≃	50	47.37 N	2.30 E
Aquidabã	250	10.17 S	37.02 W
Aquidabã ≃	248	20.58 S	57.50 W
Aquidabán ≃	252	23.11 S	57.32 W
Aquidauana	248	20.28 S	55.48 W
Aquidauana ≃	248	19.44 S	56.50 W
Aquila, Méx.	234	18.36 N	103.30 W
Aquila, Schw.	58	46.31 N	8.57 E
Aquileia	64	45.46 N	13.22 E
Aquiles Serdán, Méx.	232	28.36 N	105.53 W
Aquiles Serdán, Méx.	232	25.38 N	97.50 W
Aquili, Cachoeira ∟	250	11.08 S	55.22 W
Aquilla, Oh., U.S.	214	41.34 N	81.09 W
Aquilla, Tx., U.S.	222	31.51 N	97.13 W
Aquilla Creek ≃	222	31.40 N	97.10 W
Aquilonia (S.M.)	68	41.00 N	15.29 E
Aquin	238	18.17 N	73.24 W
Aquincumi Museum ʊ	264c	47.34 N	19.03 E
Aquino	66	41.30 N	13.42 E
Aquio ≃	246	2.42 N	67.34 W
Ara	124	25.34 N	84.40 E
Ara ≃, Esp.	34	42.25 N	0.09 E
Ara ≃, Ire.	48	52.24 N	7.56 W
Ara ≃, Nihon	92	38.09 N	139.25 E
Ara ≃, Nihon	94	35.39 N	139.51 E
Arab	194	34.19 N	86.29 W
ʻArab, Baḥr al- ≃	140	9.02 N	29.28 E
ʻArab, Khalīj al- ⊂	140	30.55 N	29.05 E
Arab, Oued el V	148	34.41 N	6.31 E
Arab, Shatt al- ≃	128	29.57 N	48.34 E
ʻArab, Wādī al- V	132	32.35 N	35.35 E
ʻArabābād	128	33.02 N	57.41 E
ʻArabah, Wādī V	142	29.07 N	32.39 E
ʻArabah, Wādī al- (Haʻ Arava) V	132	30.10 N	35.10 E
Arabako □[4]	34	42.50 N	2.45 W
Araban	130	37.26 N	37.41 E
Arabatskaja strelka ≻[2]	78	45.40 N	35.00 E
Arabatskij zaliv ⊂	78	45.20 N	35.30 E
Arabba	64	46.30 N	11.52 E
Arabelo	246	4.55 N	64.13 W
Arabi	194	29.57 N	90.00 W
Arabian Basin ✦[1]	12	11.30 N	65.00 E
Arabian Desert — Sharqīyah, Aṣ-Ṣaḥrā' ash- ◆[2]	140	28.00 N	32.00 E
Arabian Gulf — Persian Gulf ⊂	128	27.00 N	51.00 E
Arabian Peninsula ≻[1]	12	25.00 N	45.00 E
Arabian Sea ⫪[2]	118	15.00 N	65.00 E
Arabia Saudita — Saudi Arabia □[1]	118	25.00 N	45.00 E
Arabie, Mer d' — Arabian Sea ⫪[2]	118	15.00 N	65.00 E
Arabie Saoudite — Saudi Arabia □[1]	118	25.00 N	45.00 E
Arabique, Péninsule — Arabian Peninsula ≻[1]	12	25.00 N	45.00 E
Arabisches Meer — Arabian Sea ⫪[2]	118	15.00 N	65.00 E
Arab-Jengidža	84	39.29 N	44.58 E
ʻArab Muṭayr	142	27.16 N	31.14 E
Ara-Bure, porog ∟	88	53.00 N	100.12 E
Araç	130	41.15 N	33.21 E
Araçá ≃	246	0.25 S	62.55 W
Aracaju	250	10.55 S	37.04 W
Araçariguama	256	23.26 S	47.04 W
Aracataca	246	10.36 N	74.12 W
Aracati	250	4.34 S	37.46 W
Araçatuba	255	21.12 S	50.25 W
Araceli	116	10.33 N	119.59 E
Aracena	34	37.53 N	6.33 W
Arâches-les-Carroz	58	46.02 N	6.39 E
Arachino-seki ⊥	94	35.33 N	136.05 E
Araci	250	11.20 S	38.57 W
Aracides, Cape ≻	175e	8.39 S	161.01 E
Aracitaba	256	21.20 S	43.23 W
Aracoiaba	250	4.23 S	38.49 W
Aracruz	255	19.49 S	40.16 W
Araçuaí	255	16.52 S	42.04 W
Araçuaí ≃	255	16.46 S	42.02 W
Arad, Rom.	38	46.11 N	21.20 E
ʻArad, Yis.	132	31.15 N	35.13 E
Arad □[6]	38	46.20 N	21.40 E
Arada, Hond.	236	14.48 N	88.18 W
Arada, Tchad	146	15.01 N	20.40 E
Aradeo	68	40.08 N	18.08 E
Aradhíppou	130	34.57 N	33.35 E
Arafali	144	15.05 N	39.45 E
Arafune-san ∧	94	36.12 N	138.38 E
Arafura Sea ⫪[2]	164	9.00 S	133.00 E
Arafura Shelf ✦[4]	14	10.00 S	137.00 E
Aragac, gora ∧	84	40.32 N	44.14 E
Aragarças	255	15.55 S	52.15 W
Arago, Cape ≻	202	43.18 N	124.25 W
Aragon	192	34.02 N	85.03 W
Aragón □[4]	34	41.30 N	0.30 W
Aragón ≃	34	42.13 N	1.44 W
Aragona	70	37.24 N	13.37 E
Aragua □[3]	246	10.00 N	67.10 W
Araguacema	250	8.50 S	49.34 W
Araguaçu	255	12.49 S	49.51 W
Aragua de Barcelona	246	9.28 N	64.49 W
Aragua de Maturín	246	9.58 N	63.29 W
Araguaia ≃	242	5.21 S	48.41 W
Araguaia, Braço Menor ≃	250	9.50 S	50.10 W
Araguaia, Parque Nacional do ♦	250	12.00 S	50.20 W
Araguaína	250	7.12 S	48.12 W
Araguainha	255	16.49 S	53.05 W
Araguao, Caño ≃[1]	246	9.15 N	60.50 W
Araguari	255	18.38 S	48.11 W
Araguari ≃, Bra.	250	1.15 N	49.55 W
Araguari ≃, Bra.	255	18.21 S	48.40 W
Araguatins	250	5.38 S	48.07 W
Aragvi ≃	84	41.50 N	44.43 E
ʻĀrah, Ra's al- ≻	144	12.36 N	43.56 E
Arai, Nihon	94	34.41 N	137.34 E
Arai, Nihon	94	37.01 N	138.15 E
Āraihāzar	126	23.47 N	90.40 E
Araioses	250	2.53 S	41.55 W
Ârak, Alg.	148	25.18 N	3.45 E
Arāk, Īrān	128	34.05 N	49.41 E
Araka	154	4.20 N	30.23 E
Arakamčečen, ostrov I	180	64.45 N	172.30 W
Arakan, porog ∟	88	57.35 N	96.36 E
Arakan Yoma ⋏	110	19.00 N	94.40 E
Arakawa, Nihon	94	35.57 N	139.02 E
Arakawa, Nihon	174m	26.39 N	128.15 E
Arakawa ◆[8]	268	35.47 N	139.47 E
Arakawa-dake ∧	94	35.30 N	138.10 E
Arákhova	38	38.29 N	22.35 E
Árakhthos ≃	38	39.01 N	21.03 E
Arakkonam	122	13.06 N	79.40 E
Araklı	130	40.57 N	40.03 E
Arakmeer, gora ∧	84	42.38 N	46.49 E
Arakpur ◆[8]	272a	28.35 N	77.10 E
Araks (Aras) ≃	84	39.56 N	48.28 E
Aral, Kyrg.	85	42.32 N	72.40 E
Aral, Kyrg.	85	41.50 N	73.03 E
Araldy	84	44.18 N	50.24 E
Aral Sea — Aral'skoje more ⫪[2]	86	45.00 N	60.00 E
Aral'sk	86	46.48 N	61.40 E
Aral'skoje more (Aral Sea) ⫪[2]	86	45.00 N	60.00 E
Aralsor, ozero ⊜, Kaz.	80	48.42 N	52.24 E
Aralsor, ozero ⊜, Kaz.	80	49.05 N	48.12 E
Aralsul'fat	86	46.50 N	61.58 E
Aramá ≃	250	1.06 S	50.40 W
Aramac	166	22.59 S	145.14 E
Aramac ≃	166	23.02 S	144.31 E
Aramari	255	12.04 S	38.30 W
Ārāmbāg	126	22.53 N	87.47 E
Aramberri	232	24.06 N	99.49 W
Aramia ≃	164	7.55 S	143.22 E
Aramon	62	43.53 N	4.41 E
Arampampa	248	17.55 S	66.04 W
Aramtalla	140	6.47 N	29.13 E
Ārān	128	34.04 N	51.29 E
Arana	258	35.00 S	57.54 W
Arancio, Lago ⊜	70	37.38 N	13.05 E
Aranda de Duero	34	41.41 N	3.41 W
Arandai	164	2.10 S	133.01 E
Arandas	234	20.42 N	102.21 W
Aranđelovac	38	44.18 N	20.35 E
Arandis	156	22.24 S	15.00 E
Aran Fawddwy ∧	42	52.47 N	3.41 W
Arang	120	21.12 N	81.58 E
Aranhegyi-patak ≃	264c	47.34 N	19.04 E
Ārāni, Bngl.	126	24.17 N	88.52 E
Arani, Bol.	248	17.34 S	65.46 W
Ārani, India	122	12.40 N	79.17 E
Aran Island I	48	54.58 N	8.33 W
Aran Islands II	48	53.07 N	9.43 W
Aranjuez	34	40.02 N	3.36 W
Aranos	156	24.09 S	19.09 E
Aransas ≃	196	28.04 N	97.14 W
Aransas Pass	196	27.54 N	97.08 W
Arantāngi	122	10.10 N	78.59 E
Arantina	256	21.56 S	44.15 W
Aranyaprathet	110	13.41 N	102.30 E
Arao	96	32.57 N	130.28 E
Araouane	150	18.54 N	3.33 W
Arapa, Laguna ⊜	248	15.10 S	70.01 W
Arapaho	196	35.34 N	98.57 W
Arapahoe	198	40.18 N	99.54 W
Arapaho National Recreation Area ♦	200	40.07 N	105.48 W
Arāpānja	272b	22.26 N	88.28 E
Arapawa Island I	172	41.11 S	174.19 E
Arapeí	256	22.41 S	44.27 W
Arapey	252	30.58 S	57.32 W
Arapey Chico ≃	252	30.57 S	57.30 W
Arapey Grande ≃	252	30.55 S	57.49 W
Arapiraca	250	9.45 S	36.39 W
Arapiri, Ilha I	250	2.04 S	54.56 W
Arápis	267c	37.59 N	23.32 E
Arapiuns ≃	250	2.18 S	55.00 W
Arapkir	130	39.03 N	38.30 E
Arapongas	255	23.23 S	51.27 W
Arapoti	255	24.08 S	49.50 W
Arapuni	172	38.04 S	175.39 E
Araquil ≃	34	42.48 N	1.45 W
ʻArʻar	128	30.59 N	41.02 E
ʻArʻar, Wādī V	128	31.23 N	42.26 E
Araracuara	246	0.38 S	72.15 W
Araranguá	252	28.56 S	49.29 W
Araraquara	255	21.47 S	48.10 W
Araras	255	22.22 S	47.23 W
Araras, Açude ⊜[1]	250	4.20 S	40.28 W
Araras, Ribeirão das ≃, Bra.	256	22.52 S	46.37 W
Araras, Ribeirão das ≃, Bra.	256	21.18 S	45.45 W
Ararat, Austl.	169	37.17 S	142.56 E
Ararat, Haya.	84	39.50 N	44.42 E
Ararat, Mount — Ağrı Dağı ∧	84	39.42 N	44.18 E
Arari	250	3.28 S	44.47 W
Arari, Lago ⊜	250	0.37 S	49.07 W
Arāria	124	26.08 N	87.24 E
Araripe	250	7.12 S	40.08 W
Araripe, Chapada do ⋏[1]	250	7.20 S	40.00 W
Araripina	250	7.33 S	40.34 W
Ararirá ≃	246	0.30 S	63.33 W
Arar Lugole	144	3.16 N	45.28 E
Araruama, Lagoa de ⊂	255	22.53 S	42.12 W
Araruna	250	6.32 S	35.44 W
Aras (Araks) ≃	84	39.56 N	48.28 E
ʻAras, Ḥawḍ al- ⫪[4]	142	30.51 N	32.32 E
Arashi-yama ∧[2]	270	35.01 N	135.40 E
Åråsviken ⊂	40	59.02 N	14.01 E
Ara Terra	144	6.38 N	40.57 E
Áratos	38	41.05 N	25.33 E
Aratuípe	255	13.05 S	39.00 W
Aratula	171a	27.59 S	152.32 E
Arau	114	6.26 N	100.16 E
Arauá ≃, Bra.	246	4.06 S	63.36 W
Arauã ≃, Bra.	248	7.59 S	65.14 W
Arauá ≃, Bra.	248	5.40 S	60.48 W
Arauca	246	7.05 N	70.45 W
Arauca □[5]	246	6.40 N	71.00 W
Arauca ≃	246	7.24 N	66.35 W
Araucária	252	25.35 S	49.25 W
Arauco	252	37.15 S	73.19 W
Arauco, Golfo de ⊂	252	37.11 S	73.25 W
Araújo, Ilha do I	256	23.09 S	44.42 W
Araújos	255	19.56 S	45.04 W
Arauquita	246	7.02 N	71.25 W
Araure	246	9.34 N	69.13 W
Aravaca ◆[8]	266a	40.28 N	3.46 W
Aravaipa Creek ≃	200	32.50 N	110.43 W
Arāvalli Range ⋏	120	25.00 N	73.30 E
Aravan	85	40.32 N	72.30 E
Arawata ≃	172	44.00 S	168.41 E
Araxá	255	19.35 S	46.55 W
Araya	246	10.34 N	64.15 W
Araya, Punta de ≻	246	10.38 N	64.18 W
Arayat	116	15.10 N	120.46 E
Arba	144	9.01 N	40.23 E
Arba ≃	34	41.52 N	1.18 W
Arbagar	88	51.56 N	116.15 E
Ārbālia	126	22.41 N	88.47 E
Arba Minch	144	6.02 N	37.33 E
Arbatax	71	39.56 N	9.42 E
Arbaž	80	57.41 N	48.18 E
Arbedo	58	46.12 N	9.03 E
Arbél	132	32.49 N	35.29 E
Arbesbach	61	48.29 N	14.57 E
Arbia ≃	66	43.08 N	11.28 E
Arboga	40	59.24 N	15.50 E
Arbogaån ≃	40	59.26 N	16.04 E
Arbois	58	46.54 N	5.46 E
Arboledas	252	36.53 S	61.29 W
Arboletes	246	8.51 N	76.26 W
Arbolito, Cerro ∧[2]	286d	12.10 S	76.57 W
Arbon	58	47.31 N	9.26 E
Arbonne	50	48.25 N	2.34 E
Arborea	71	39.46 N	8.35 E
Arborea ◆[1]	71	39.50 N	8.50 E
Arborfield	184	53.06 N	103.39 W
Arborg	184	50.55 N	97.15 W
Arbrå	26	61.29 N	16.23 E
Arbroath	46	56.34 N	2.35 W
Arbu, Monte ∧	71	39.15 N	9.27 E
Arbuckle	226	39.01 N	122.03 W
Arbuckle, Lake ⊜	220	27.41 N	81.24 W
Arbuckle Creek ≃	220	27.26 N	81.17 W
Arbuckle Mountains ⋏	196	34.25 N	97.20 W
Arbuckles, Lake of the ⊜[1]	196	34.25 N	97.00 W
Arbury Hills	216	41.33 N	87.51 W
Arbus	71	39.32 N	8.36 E
Arbutus Lake ⊜	276	40.31 N	74.10 W
Arbuzinka	78	47.53 N	31.19 E
Arbuzovo	76	56.21 N	32.27 E
Arc ≃, Fr.	62	43.31 N	5.07 E
Arc ≃, Fr.	62	45.34 N	6.12 E
Arc, Bayou des ≃	194	35.00 N	91.30 W
Arcachon	32	44.37 N	1.12 W
Arcachon, Bassin d' ⊂	32	44.40 N	1.10 W
Arcadas	256	22.42 S	46.52 W
Arcade, It.	64	45.47 N	12.13 E
Arcade, Ca., U.S.	226	34.02 N	118.15 W
Arcade, N.Y., U.S.	210	42.32 N	78.25 W
Arcadia, Ca., U.S.	228	34.08 N	118.02 W
Arcadia, Fl., U.S.	220	27.12 N	81.51 W
Arcadia, In., U.S.	218	40.10 N	86.01 W
Arcadia, Ia., U.S.	198	42.01 N	95.02 W
Arcadia, Ks., U.S.	198	37.38 N	94.37 W
Arcadia, La., U.S.	194	32.32 N	92.55 W
Arcadia, Mi., U.S.	190	44.29 N	86.13 W
Arcadia, Mo., U.S.	194	37.35 N	90.37 W
Arcadia, Ne., U.S.	198	41.25 N	99.07 W
Arcadia, Oh., U.S.	216	41.06 N	83.31 W
Arcadia, Pa., U.S.	214	40.47 N	78.51 W
Arcadia, S.C., U.S.	192	34.57 N	81.59 W
Arcadia, Tx., U.S.	222	29.23 N	95.07 W
Arcadia, Wi., U.S.	190	44.15 N	91.30 W
Arcângelo	256	21.18 S	44.19 W
Arcanum	218	39.59 N	84.33 W
Arcas, Cayos II	232	20.12 N	91.58 W
Arcata	204	40.52 N	124.04 W
Arcatao	236	14.05 N	88.45 W
Arc de Triomphe ⊥	261	48.53 N	2.17 E
Arc Dome ∧	204	38.50 N	117.21 W
Arce	66	41.35 N	13.34 E
Arceburgo	256	21.22 S	46.56 W
Arčeda ≃	80	49.52 N	43.10 E
Arčedinsko-Donskije peski ◆[2]	80	49.33 N	43.15 E
Arcelia	234	18.17 N	100.16 W
Arcen	52	51.29 N	6.11 E
Arc-en-Barrois	58	47.57 N	5.00 E
Arces	50	48.05 N	3.36 E
Arc-et-Senans	58	47.02 N	5.46 E
Arcevia	66	43.30 N	12.56 E
Archambault, Lac ⊜	206	46.18 N	74.15 W
Archangaj □[8]	88	48.00 N	101.30 E
Archangel — Archangel'sk	24	64.34 N	40.32 E
Archangel'sk	24	64.34 N	40.32 E
Archangel'skaja	78	45.41 N	40.15 E
Archangel'skoje, Ross.	76	53.16 N	37.42 E
Archangel'skoje, Ross.	78	51.27 N	40.55 E
Archangel'skoje, Ross.	80	55.13 N	44.05 E
Archangel'skoje, Ross.	80	54.26 N	48.40 E
Archangel'skoje, Ross.	82	55.19 N	35.58 E
Archangel'skoje, Ross.	84	44.37 N	44.05 E
Archangel'skoje, Ross.	265b	55.47 N	37.18 E
Archara	89	49.27 N	130.07 E
Archara ≃	89	49.13 N	129.53 E
Archbald	210	41.29 N	75.32 W
Archbold	216	41.31 N	84.18 W
Archdale	192	35.54 N	79.58 W
Archer	192	29.31 N	82.31 W
Archer ≃	164	13.28 S	141.41 E
Archer, Lake ⊜	283	42.04 N	71.20 W
Archer, Mount ∧	166	23.20 S	150.34 E
Archer Bay ⊂	164	13.25 S	141.43 E
Archer Bend National Park ♦	164	13.30 S	142.20 E
Archer City	196	33.35 N	98.37 W
Archer's Post	154	0.39 N	37.41 E

Symbols in the index entries represent the broad categories identified in the key at the right. Symbols with superior numbers (⋏[1]) identify subcategories (see complete key on page I · 1).

Symbole im Register stellen die rechts im Schlüssel erklärten Kategorien dar. Symbole mit hochgestellten Ziffern (⋏[1]) bezeichnen Unterabteilungen einer Kategorie (vgl. vollständiger Schlüssel auf Seite I · 1).

Los símbolos incluídos en el texto del índice representan las grandes categorias identificadas con la clave a la derecha. Los símbolos con numeros en su parte superior (⋏[1]) identifican las subcategorías (véase la clave completa en la página I · 1).

Les symboles de l'index représentent les catégories indiquées dans la légende à droite. Les symboles suivis d'un indice (⋏[1]) représentent des sous-catégories (voir légende complète à la page I · 1).

Os símbolos incluídos no texto do índice representam as grandes categorias identificadas com a chave à direita. Os símbolos com números em sua parte superior (⋏[1]) identificam as subcategorias (veja-se a chave completa à página I · 1).

∧	Mountain	Berg	Montaña	Montagne	Montanha
⋏	Mountains	Gebirge	Montañas	Montagnes	Montanhas
)(	Pass	Paß	Paso	Col	Passo
V	Valley, Canyon	Tal, Cañon	Valle, Cañón	Vallée, Canyon	Vale, Canhão
≅	Plain	Ebene	Llano	Plaine	Planície
≻	Cape	Kap	Cabo	Cap	Cabo
I	Island	Insel	Isla	Île	Ilha
II	Islands	Inseln	Islas	Îles	Ilhas
⊥	Other Topographic Features	Andere Topographische Objekte	Otros Elementos Topográficos	Autres données topographiques	Outros acidentes topográficos

ESPAÑOL — Nombre · Página · Lat.°' · Long.°' W = Oeste
FRANÇAIS — Nom · Page · Lat.°' · Long.°' W = Ouest
PORTUGUÊS — Nome · Página · Lat.°' · Long.°' W = Oeste

Nombre	Página	Lat.°'	Long.°' W = Oeste
Arches	58	48.07 N	6.32 E
Arches National Park ♠	200	38.42 N	109.45 W
Archi	66	42.05 N	14.23 E
Archiac	32	45.31 N	0.18 W
Archidona	34	37.05 N	4.23 W
Archipo-Osipovka	78	44.22 N	38.33 E
Archipovka	80	56.38 N	41.14 E
Archipovo	24	66.26 N	45.52 E
Archonskaja	84	43.07 N	44.30 E
Archshofen	56	49.27 N	10.04 E
Archville	276	41.07 N	73.52 W
Arci, Monte ∧	71	39.47 N	8.44 E
Arcidosso	66	42.52 N	11.33 E
Arcille	66	42.48 N	11.15 E
Arcinazzo Romano	66	41.48 N	13.12 E
Arcisate	62	45.54 N	8.52 E
Arcis-sur-Aube	50	48.32 N	4.08 E
Arciz	78	46.00 N	29.26 E
Arckaringa	162	27.56 S	134.45 E
Arckaringa Creek ≃	162	28.10 S	135.22 E
Arc-les-Gray	58	47.27 N	5.35 E
Arco, It.	64	45.55 N	10.53 E
Arco, Id., U.S.	202	43.38 N	113.17 W
Arco de Baúlhe	34	41.29 N	7.58 W
Arcola, Sk., Can.	184	49.37 N	102.30 W
Arcola, It.	64	44.07 N	9.54 E
Arcola, Il., U.S.	194	39.41 N	88.18 W
Arcola, In., U.S.	216	41.06 N	85.17 W
Arcola, Ms., U.S.	194	33.16 N	90.52 W
Arcola, Pa., U.S.	285	40.09 N	75.27 W
Arcola, Tx., U.S.	222	29.31 N	95.27 W
Arconate	266b	45.32 N	8.51 E
Arcore	266b	45.38 N	9.19 E
Arcos	255	20.17 S	45.32 W
Arcos de la Frontera	34	36.45 N	5.48 W
Arcot	122	12.54 N	79.20 E
Arcoverde	250	8.25 S	37.04 W
Arctic Bay	176	73.02 N	85.11 W
Arctic Ocean ⊤[1]	16	85.00 N	170.00 E
Arctic Red ≃	180	67.27 N	133.46 W
Arctic Red River	180	67.27 N	133.46 W
Arctic Village	180	68.08 N	145.19 W
Arctique, Océan Glacial → Arctic Ocean ⊤[1]	16	85.00 N	170.00 E
Arctowski ⊍[3]	9	62.09 S	58.28 W
Arcturus	154	17.47 S	31.20 E
Arcueil	261	48.48 N	2.20 E
Arcuentu, Monte ∧	71	39.35 N	8.33 E
Arcy-sur-Cure	50	47.36 N	3.45 E
Ard, Loch ⊜	46	56.11 N	4.28 W
Arḍ, Ra's al- ›	128	29.21 N	48.05 E
Arda ≃, Europe	38	41.39 N	26.29 E
Arda ≃, It.	64	45.02 N	10.02 E
Ardabīl	128	38.15 N	48.18 E
Ardagger	61	48.11 N	14.50 E
Ardagh	48	52.28 N	9.04 W
Ardahan	130	41.07 N	42.41 E
Ardakān, Īrān	128	30.16 N	52.01 E
Ardakān, Īrān	128	32.19 N	53.59 E
Ardal	128	31.59 N	50.39 E
Ardalanish, Rubh' ›	46	56.17 N	6.18 W
Årdalsfjorden ⊂[2]	26	61.12 N	7.30 E
Årdalstangen	26	61.14 N	7.43 E
Ardanuç	130	41.08 N	42.04 E
Ardara, Ire.	48	54.46 N	8.25 W
Árdara, It.	71	40.37 N	8.48 E
Ardara, Pa., U.S.	279b	40.22 N	79.44 W
Ardarroch	46	57.25 N	5.38 W
Ardatov, Ross.	80	55.15 N	43.06 E
Ardatov, Ross.	80	54.51 N	46.13 E
Ardbeg	46	55.39 N	6.05 W
Ardcharnich	46	57.51 N	5.05 W
Ardea	66	41.36 N	12.33 E
Ardèche □[5]	62	44.40 N	4.20 E
Ardèche ≃	62	44.16 N	4.39 E
Ardee	48	53.52 N	6.33 W
Ardélik	146	12.26 N	21.25 E
Arden, Mb., Can.	184	50.17 N	99.14 W
Arden, Ca., U.S.	226	38.36 N	121.23 W
Arden, De., U.S.	208	39.48 N	75.29 W
Arden, Forest of ◆[3]	42	52.23 N	1.42 W
Arden, Mount ∧	166	32.09 S	137.59 E
Ardenay-sur-Mérize	50	48.00 N	0.25 E
Arden Mines	279b	40.12 N	80.17 W
Ardennes □[5]	50	49.40 N	4.40 E
Ardennes ◆[1]	56	50.10 N	5.45 E
Ardennes, Canal des ≍	50	49.26 N	4.02 E
Ardenno	58	46.10 N	9.39 E
Ardentinny	46	56.03 N	4.55 W
Ardenza	66	43.31 N	10.19 E
Arderin ∧[2]	48	53.02 N	7.40 W
Ardersier	46	57.34 N	4.02 W
Ardeşen	130	41.12 N	41.00 E
Ardestān	128	33.22 N	52.23 E
Ardey	263	51.28 N	7.43 E
Ardeygebirge ⋏[2]	263	51.25 N	7.20 E
Ardez	58	46.46 N	10.11 E
Ardfern	46	56.10 N	5.32 W
Ardglass	48	54.16 N	5.37 W
Ardgroom	48	51.42 N	9.52 W
Ardıçlı	130	40.40 N	37.00 E
Ardila ≃	34	38.12 N	7.28 W
Ardill	184	49.53 N	105.49 W
Ardino	38	41.35 N	25.08 E
Ardlethan	166	34.21 S	146.54 E
Ardlui	46	56.18 N	4.43 W
Ardlussa	46	56.02 N	5.47 W
Ardmolich	46	56.49 N	5.41 W
Ardmore, Ire.	48	51.57 N	7.43 W
Ardmore, Al., U.S.	194	34.59 N	86.50 W
Ardmore, In., U.S.	216	41.41 N	86.19 W
Ardmore, Md., U.S.	284c	38.56 N	76.51 W
Ardmore, Ok., U.S.	196	34.10 N	97.08 W
Ardmore, Pa., U.S.	208	40.01 N	75.18 W
Ardmore Point ›, Scot., U.K.	46	55.42 N	6.01 W
Ardmore Point ›, Scot., U.K.	46	56.39 N	6.07 W
Ardnamurchan ›[1]	46	56.43 N	6.00 W
Ardnamurchan, Point of ›	46	56.44 N	6.13 W
Ardnaree	48	54.06 N	9.08 W
Ardnave Point ›	46	55.54 N	6.20 W
Ardoch	166	27.26 S	144.08 E
Ardon, Ross.	84	43.12 N	44.18 E
Ardon, Schw.	58	46.13 N	7.15 E
Ardon ≃	84	43.17 N	44.18 E
Ardon, Har ∧	132	30.38 N	34.57 E
Ardooie	50	50.59 N	3.12 E
Ardore	68	38.11 N	16.10 E
Ardoux ≃	50	47.42 N	1.35 E
Ardoz, Arroyo de ≃	266a	40.26 N	3.27 W
Ardres	50	50.51 N	1.59 E
Ardres ≃	50	49.18 N	3.40 E
Ardrishaig	46	56.01 N	5.27 W
Ardrossan, Austl.	168b	34.25 S	137.55 E
Ardrossan, Scot., U.K.	46	55.39 N	4.49 W
Ardsley, Eng., U.K.	44	53.32 N	1.28 W
Ardsley, N.Y., U.S.	276	41.00 N	73.50 W
Ardtalnaig	46	56.31 N	4.06 W
Arduan Island I	140	19.55 N	30.22 E
Ardusson ≃	50	48.30 N	3.32 E
Ardvasar	46	57.04 N	5.54 W
Are	26	63.24 N	13.04 E
Areado	256	21.21 S	46.09 W
Areal	256	22.14 S	43.07 W
Arèches	62	45.41 N	6.34 E
Arecibo	240m	18.28 N	66.43 W
Arecibo, Observatorio de ⊍[3]	240m	18.20 N	66.46 W
Areco ≃	258	33.56 S	59.16 W
Areeiro	266c	38.39 N	9.12 W
Arefjevo	86	57.01 N	90.40 E
Areguá	252	25.18 S	57.25 W
Areia, Bra.	250	6.58 S	35.42 W
Areia, Port.	266c	38.43 N	9.08 W
Areia, Ribeirão da ≃	255	16.07 S	45.52 W
Areia Branca, Bra.	250	4.56 S	37.07 W
Areia Branca, Bra.	287a	22.44 S	43.25 W
Areias	256	22.35 S	44.42 W
Arena	68	38.34 N	16.13 E
Arena, Point ›	204	38.57 N	123.44 W
Arena, Punta ›	232	23.33 N	109.28 W
Arena de la Ventana, Punta ›	232	24.04 N	109.52 W
Arena Island I	116	9.14 N	120.46 E
Arenal, C.R.	236	10.29 N	84.53 W
Arenal, P.R.	240m	17.59 N	66.19 W
Arenal, Laguna de ⊜	236	10.32 N	84.56 W
Arenal, Volcán ∧[1]	236	10.28 N	84.44 W
Arenápolis	248	14.26 S	56.49 W
Arenas, Cayo I	232	22.08 N	91.24 W
Arenas, Punta ›	240m	18.07 N	65.35 W
Arenas, Punta de ›	254	53.09 S	68.13 W
Arenas de San Pedro	34	40.12 N	5.05 W
Arendal	26	58.27 N	8.48 E
Arendonk	56	51.19 N	5.05 E
Arendsee	54	52.53 N	11.30 E
Arendsee ⊜	54	52.53 N	11.30 E
Arendtsville	208	39.55 N	77.18 W
Arenes ≃	266d	41.29 N	2.02 E
Arenig Fawr ∧	42	52.55 N	3.45 W
Arenillas	246	3.33 S	80.04 W
Arenosa Creek ≃	196	28.52 N	96.44 W
Arenys de Mar	34	41.35 N	2.33 E
Arenzano	62	44.24 N	8.41 E
Arenzville	219	39.53 N	90.22 W
Arequipa	248	16.24 S	71.33 W
Arequipa □[5]	248	16.00 S	72.15 W
Arequito	252	33.09 S	61.28 W
Arero	144	4.45 N	38.49 E
Arês, Bra.	250	6.11 S	35.09 W
Arès, Fr.	32	44.46 N	1.08 W
Arese	266b	45.33 N	9.05 E
Aresing	60	48.32 N	11.18 E
Åreskutan ∧	26	63.26 N	13.06 E
Areuse ≃	58	46.56 N	6.53 E
Arévalo	34	41.04 N	4.43 W
Arezzo	66	43.25 N	11.53 E
Arezzo □[4]	66	43.32 N	11.50 E
Arfa', Jabal ∧	132	29.51 N	35.27 E
'Arfā', Wādī al- V	132	30.16 N	36.34 E
Arga ≃	34	42.18 N	1.47 W
Argada	88	54.14 N	110.41 E
Argadargada	166	21.40 S	136.40 E
Argajaš	86	55.29 N	60.52 E
Argamasilla de Alba	34	39.07 N	3.06 W
Arganda	34	40.18 N	3.26 W
Argao	116	9.52 N	123.36 E
Arga-Sala ≃	74	68.30 N	112.12 E
Argedeb	144	6.10 N	41.10 E
Argegno	58	45.56 N	9.08 E
Argel → El Djazaïr	148	36.47 N	3.03 E
Argelès-Gazost	32	43.01 N	0.06 E
Argelès-sur-Mer	32	42.33 N	3.01 E
Argelia → Algeria □[1]	148	28.00 N	3.00 E
Argen ≃	58	47.35 N	9.33 E
Argens ≃	62	43.24 N	6.44 E
Argent	158	26.04 S	28.50 E
Argent, Côte d' ≛[2]	32	43.30 N	1.30 W
Argenta, It.	66	44.37 N	11.50 E
Argenta, Il., U.S.	219	39.58 N	88.49 W
Argentan	32	48.45 N	0.01 W
Argentario, Monte ∧	66	42.24 N	11.09 E
Argentat	32	45.06 N	1.56 E
Argentera	62	44.24 N	6.57 E
Argentera ∧	62	44.10 N	7.18 E
Argenteuil	50	48.57 N	2.15 E
Argenteuil □[6]	206	45.45 N	74.30 W
Argentia	186	47.18 N	53.59 W
Argentiera	71	40.44 N	8.09 E
Argentière	58	45.59 N	6.56 E
Argentières	261	48.39 N	2.52 E
Argentina □[1]	244	34.00 S	64.00 W
Argentina ≃	62	43.50 N	7.51 E
Argentine	216	42.47 N	83.51 W
Argentine → Argentina □[1]	244	34.00 S	64.00 W
Argentine Basin ⊹[1]	18	45.00 S	45.00 W
Argentinien → Argentina □[1]	244	34.00 S	64.00 W
Argentino, Hipódromo ♠	288	34.34 S	58.26 W
Argentino, Lago ⊜	254	50.13 S	72.25 W
Argentona	266d	41.33 N	2.24 E
Argentona, Riera d' ≃	266d	41.31 N	2.26 E
Argenton-Château	32	46.59 N	0.27 W
Argenton-sur-Creuse	32	46.35 N	1.31 E
Argent-sur-Sauldre	50	47.33 N	2.27 E
Argeș □[6]	38	45.00 N	24.45 E
Argeș ≃	38	44.04 N	26.37 E
Arghandāb ≃	128	31.27 N	64.23 E
Arghastān ≃	120	31.23 N	65.45 E
Argirita	256	21.37 S	42.50 W
Argıthanı	130	38.17 N	31.43 E
Argo	140	19.31 N	30.25 E
Ārgoal	126	21.58 N	87.38 E
Argo Island I	140	19.25 N	30.27 E
Argolikós Kólpos ⊂	38	37.33 N	22.45 E
Argonia	198	37.15 N	97.45 W
Argonne	190	45.39 N	88.52 W
Argonne ◆[1]	56	49.30 N	5.00 E
Argonne National Laboratory ⊍[3]	216	41.43 N	87.58 W
Argopuro, Gunung ∧	115a	7.57 S	113.33 E
Árgos, Ellás	38	37.39 N	22.44 E
Argos, In., U.S.	216	41.14 N	86.15 W
Árgos Orestikón	38	40.28 N	21.16 E
Argostólion	38	38.10 N	20.30 E
Argoules	50	50.21 N	1.50 E
Argueil	50	49.32 N	1.31 E
Arguello, Point ›	204	34.35 N	120.39 W
Argun	84	43.16 N	45.52 E
Argun ≃	84	43.22 N	45.55 E
Argun' (Ergun) ≃, Asia	74	53.20 N	121.28 E
Argungu	150	12.45 N	4.31 E
Arguni, Teluk ⊂	164	3.06 S	133.42 E
Ārgur	272b	22.48 N	88.13 E
Argut	86	49.51 N	87.03 E
Argut ≃	86	50.16 N	86.43 E
Arguvan	130	38.47 N	38.17 E
Argyle, Austl.	162	33.32 S	115.46 E
Argyle, Mn., U.S.	198	48.19 N	96.49 W
Argyle, Mo., U.S.	219	38.18 N	92.02 W
Argyle, N.Y., U.S.	210	43.14 N	73.30 W
Argyle, Tx., U.S.	222	33.07 N	97.11 W
Argyle, Lake ⊜[1]	164	16.15 S	128.45 E
'Arhāb, Wādī V	142	28.55 N	31.09 E
Arhavi	130	41.22 N	41.16 E
Arhéa Epídavros ⊥	38	37.37 N	23.02 E
Århus	41	56.09 N	10.13 E
Århus □[6]	41	56.15 N	10.05 E
Århus Bugt ⊂	41	56.09 N	10.18 E
Aria	172	38.33 S	174.59 E
Aria ≃	164	5.45 S	149.15 E
Ariadnoje	89	45.08 N	134.25 E
Ariah	126	23.33 N	86.20 E
Ariake-kai ⊂	92	33.00 N	130.20 E
Ariāl Khān ≃	126	23.56 N	90.46 E
Ariamácina, Lago di ⊜[1]	68	39.20 N	16.32 E
Ariamsvlei	156	28.07 S	19.49 E
Ariana	36	36.52 N	10.12 E
Ariano, Isola d' I	64	45.10 N	12.10 E
Ariano Irpino	68	41.09 N	15.05 E
Ariano nel Polesine	64	44.56 N	12.07 E
Ariari ≃	246	2.35 N	72.47 W
Arias	252	33.38 S	62.25 W
Arias, Arroyo de ≃	258	34.17 S	56.06 W
Arias, Cañada ≃	258	34.39 S	58.59 W
Ariaú	250	3.11 S	57.14 W
Aribinda	150	14.14 N	0.52 W
Arica, Chile	248	18.29 S	70.20 W
Arica, Col.	246	2.08 S	71.47 W
Arıcak	130	38.33 N	39.48 E
Aricanduva, Ribeirão ≃	287b	23.32 S	46.33 W
Ariccia	66	41.43 N	12.40 E
Arichat	186	45.31 N	61.01 W
Arichuna	246	7.42 N	67.08 W
Arid, Cape ›	162	34.00 S	123.09 E
Arida, Nig.	273a	6.34 N	3.16 E
Arida, Nihon	96	34.05 N	135.07 E
Arida ≃	96	34.05 N	135.06 E
Aridal, Sabkhat ⊜	148	26.12 N	14.05 W
Aridhaía	38	40.59 N	22.03 E
Ariège □[5]	32	43.00 N	1.30 E
Ariège ≃	32	43.31 N	1.25 E
Ari'el, Isr. Occ	132	32.06 N	35.06 E
Ariel, Wa., U.S.	224	45.57 N	122.34 W
Arienzo	68	41.01 N	14.30 E
Arieș ≃	38	46.26 N	23.59 E
'Arif, Har ∧	132	30.26 N	34.44 E
Ārifwāla	123	30.17 N	73.04 E
Ariguanabo, Laguna de ⊜	286b	22.56 N	82.33 W
Ariguaní ≃	246	9.35 N	73.46 W
Arīḥā (Jericho), Isr. Occ	132	31.52 N	35.27 E
Arīḥā, Sūrīy.	130	35.48 N	36.36 E
Arīḥā, Urd.	132	31.25 N	35.47 E
Arikaree ≃	198	40.01 N	101.56 W
Arikaree, North Fork ≃	198	39.39 N	102.57 W
Arikawa	92	32.59 N	129.07 E
Arikha, Har ∧[2]	132	30.39 N	34.47 E
Arild	41	56.16 N	12.34 E
Arima	241r	10.38 N	61.17 W
Arima ◆[8]	270	34.48 N	135.15 E
Arima ≃	270	34.52 N	135.15 E
Arima-fuji ∧[2]	270	34.55 N	135.14 E
Arimine-dam ◆[6]	94	36.29 N	137.27 E
Arinagour	46	56.37 N	6.31 W
Aringay	116	16.26 N	120.21 E
Arino ◆[8]	270	34.50 N	135.14 E
Arinos ≃	248	10.25 S	58.20 W
Arinthod	58	46.23 N	5.34 E
Ario de Rosales	234	19.12 N	101.43 W
Ariogala	76	55.16 N	23.30 E
Aripeka	220	28.25 N	82.39 W
Ariporo ≃	246	6.03 N	69.54 W
Aripuanã	248	9.10 S	60.38 W
Aripuanã ≃	248	5.07 S	60.24 W
Ariquemes	248	9.56 S	63.04 W
Arisa ≃	246	7.32 N	64.00 W
Arisaig	46	56.51 N	5.51 W
Arisaig, Sound of ⊂	46	56.51 N	5.51 W
'Arīsh, Wādī al- V	140	31.09 N	33.49 E
Arismendi	246	8.29 N	68.22 W
Aristazabal Island I	182	52.30 N	129.05 W
Aristes	210	40.49 N	76.20 W
Aristizábal, Cabo ›	254	45.13 S	66.31 W
Aristovo	82	54.37 N	36.40 E
Arıt	130	41.41 N	32.39 E
Aritao	116	16.18 N	121.02 E
Ariton	194	31.36 N	85.43 W
Aritzo	71	39.57 N	9.12 E
Arivonimamo	157b	19.01 S	47.15 E
Ariyalūr	122	11.08 N	79.05 E
Arizaro, Salar de ≋	252	24.42 S	67.45 W
Arizgoiti	34	43.13 N	2.54 W
Arizona	252	35.43 S	65.18 W
Arizona □[3], U.S.	178	34.00 N	112.00 W
Arizona □[3], U.S.	200	34.00 N	112.00 W
Arizpe	232	30.20 N	110.10 W
Arja	80	57.30 N	46.00 E
Årjäng	26	59.23 N	12.08 E
Arjasa	112	6.51 S	115.16 E
Arjawinangun	115a	6.39 S	108.24 E
Arjay	192	36.48 N	83.38 W
Arjeplog	24	66.00 N	17.58 E
Arjona, Col.	246	10.15 N	75.21 W
Arjona, Esp.	34	37.56 N	4.03 W
Arka	74	60.03 N	142.12 E
Arkabutla Lake ⊜[1]	194	34.45 N	90.06 W
Arkadak	80	51.58 N	43.28 E
Arkadelphia	194	34.07 N	93.03 W
Arkaig, Loch ⊜	46	56.58 N	5.08 W
Arkalyk	86	50.13 N	66.50 E
Arkansas □[3], U.S.	178	34.50 N	92.30 W
Arkansas □[3], U.S.	194	34.50 N	92.30 W
Arkansas ≃	178	33.48 N	91.04 W
Arkansas, Salt Fork ≃	196	36.36 N	97.03 W
Arkansas City, Ar., U.S.	194	33.36 N	91.12 W
Arkansas City, Ks., U.S.	198	37.03 N	97.02 W
Arkansas Post National Memorial ⊥	194	33.55 N	91.26 W
Arkanū, Jabal ∧	146	22.13 N	24.41 E
Arkatag Shan ⋏	120	36.48 N	89.10 E
Arken-Ahon ∧	146	20.05 N	18.25 E
Arkhangélos	38	36.12 N	28.08 E
Arkhangel'sk → Archangel'sk, Ross.	24	64.34 N	40.32 E
Arki	123	31.09 N	76.58 E
Árki I	38	37.22 N	26.45 E
Arkit	85	41.47 N	71.58 E
Arklow	48	52.48 N	6.09 W
Arkoma	194	35.21 N	94.26 W
Arkona, Kap ›	54	54.41 N	13.26 E
Arkösund	26	58.30 N	16.56 E
Arkport	210	42.23 N	77.41 W
Arktičeskij, mys ›	74	81.15 N	95.45 E
Arktičeskogo Instituta, ostrova II	74	75.20 N	81.55 E
Arkul'	80	57.17 N	50.03 E
Arkville	210	42.08 N	74.37 W
Arkwright	207	41.43 N	71.33 W
Ärla	40	59.17 N	16.40 E
Arlan	80	55.58 N	54.15 E
Arlan, gora ∧	128	39.40 N	54.33 E
Arlanc	62	45.25 N	3.44 E
Arlanda flygplats ⊠	40	59.37 N	17.55 E
Arlanza ≃	34	42.06 N	4.09 W
Arlanzón ≃	34	42.03 N	4.17 W
Arlbergpass)(	64	47.08 N	10.12 E
Arlberg-Tunnel ◆[5]	58	47.08 N	10.12 E
Arlee	202	47.09 N	114.05 W
Arles	62	43.40 N	4.38 E
Arles à Port de Bouc, Canal d' ≍	62	43.40 N	4.37 E
Arlesey	42	52.01 N	0.14 W
Arlesheim	58	47.30 N	7.37 E
Arleta ◆[8]	280	34.15 N	118.26 W
Arleux	50	50.17 N	3.06 E
Arley	262	53.19 N	2.30 W
Arli	150	11.35 N	1.28 E
Arli, Parc National de l' ♠	150	11.35 N	1.30 E
Arlington, S. Afr.	158	28.06 S	27.54 E
Arlington, Ga., U.S.	192	31.26 N	84.43 W
Arlington, In., U.S.	218	39.38 N	85.34 W
Arlington, Ia., U.S.	190	42.44 N	91.40 W
Arlington, Ks., U.S.	198	37.53 N	98.10 W
Arlington, Ky., U.S.	194	36.47 N	89.00 W
Arlington, Ma., U.S.	207	42.24 N	71.09 W
Arlington, Mn., U.S.	190	44.36 N	94.04 W
Arlington, Ne., U.S.	198	41.27 N	96.21 W
Arlington, N.Y., U.S.	210	41.41 N	73.53 W
Arlington, Oh., U.S.	216	40.53 N	83.39 W
Arlington, Or., U.S.	202	45.43 N	120.11 W
Arlington, S.D., U.S.	198	44.21 N	97.07 W
Arlington, Tn., U.S.	194	35.18 N	89.40 W
Arlington, Tx., U.S.	222	32.44 N	97.06 W
Arlington, Vt., U.S.	210	43.04 N	73.09 W
Arlington, Va., U.S.	208	38.52 N	77.06 W
Arlington, Wa., U.S.	224	48.11 N	122.07 W
Arlington □[6]	284c	38.50 N	77.10 W
Arlington, Lake ⊜[1]	222	32.42 N	97.13 W
Arlington Heights, Il., U.S.	216	42.05 N	87.58 W
Arlington Heights, Ma., U.S.	283	42.25 N	71.11 W
Arlington Memorial Bridge ◆[5]	284c	38.53 N	77.03 W
Arlington Mill Reservoir ⊜[1]	283	42.48 N	71.13 W
Arlington National Cemetery ◆	284c	38.53 N	77.04 W
Arlit	150	19.00 N	7.38 E
Arlod	58	46.06 N	5.49 E
Arlon	56	49.41 N	5.49 E
Arlöv	41	55.39 N	13.05 E
Arltunga	162	23.26 S	134.41 E
Arl'uk	86	55.26 N	84.50 E
Arluno	62	45.30 N	8.56 E
Arly ≃	62	45.40 N	6.23 E
Arlyn Oaks	276	40.40 N	73.27 W
Arm ≃	184	50.46 N	105.00 W
Arma	198	37.32 N	94.42 W
Armação, Ponta da ›	287a	22.53 S	43.08 W
Armada	214	42.50 N	82.53 W
Armadale, Austl.	168a	32.09 S	116.00 E
Armadale, On., Can.	275b	43.50 N	79.15 W
Armadale, S. Afr.	273d	26.17 S	27.57 E
Armadale, Scot., U.K.	46	55.54 N	3.42 W
Arma di Taggia	62	43.50 N	7.51 E
Armageddon → Tel Megiddo ⊥	132	32.35 N	35.11 E
Armagh, N. Ire., U.K.	48	54.21 N	6.39 W
Armagh, Pa., U.S.	214	40.27 N	79.02 W
Armagnac □[9]	32	43.45 N	0.10 E
Armah, Wādī V	144	18.12 N	51.02 E
Armainvilliers, Étang d' ⊜	261	48.45 N	2.44 E
Armainvilliers, Forêt d' ♠	261	48.45 N	2.45 E
Armance ≃	50	47.26 N	3.33 E
Armançon ≃, Fr.	50	47.57 N	3.30 E
Armançon ≃, Fr.	58	47.33 N	4.17 E
Arm'ansk	78	46.07 N	33.41 E
Armant	140	25.37 N	32.32 E
Armavir	72	45.00 N	41.08 E
Armazém	252	28.16 S	49.01 W
Armbrust	214	40.13 N	79.33 W
Armells Creek ≃	202	47.37 N	108.40 W
Armenia	246	4.31 N	75.41 W
Armenia □[9]	84	40.30 N	43.30 E
Armenia □[1], Asia	72	40.00 N	45.00 E
Armenia (Hayastan) □[1], Asia	84	40.00 N	45.00 E
Armenija → Armenia □[1]	72	40.00 N	45.00 E
Armeniș	38	45.12 N	22.19 E
Armenistís	38	37.36 N	26.08 E
Armeniya → Armenia □[1]	72	40.00 N	45.00 E
Armeno	62	45.49 N	8.26 E
Armenonville-les-Gâtineaux	261	48.33 N	1.39 E
Armentières	50	50.41 N	2.53 E
Armento	68	40.18 N	16.04 E
Armería	234	18.56 N	103.58 W
Armería ≃	234	18.52 N	103.59 W
Armero	246	4.58 N	74.54 W
Armidale	166	30.31 S	151.39 E
Armijo	200	35.03 N	106.40 W
Armitage	42	52.44 N	1.53 W
Armit Lake ⊜	176	64.10 N	91.32 W
Armizonskoje	86	55.57 N	67.42 E
Armona	226	36.19 N	119.42 W
Armonk	276	41.07 N	73.42 W
Armor	210	42.44 N	78.48 W
Armori	122	20.28 N	79.59 E
Armour	198	43.19 N	98.20 W
Armoy	58	46.21 N	6.31 E
Armstrong, Arg.	252	32.47 S	61.36 W
Armstrong, B.C., Can.	182	50.27 N	119.12 W
Armstrong, Il., U.S.	216	40.18 N	87.53 W
Armstrong, Ia., U.S.	198	43.23 N	94.28 W
Armstrong, Mo., U.S.	194	39.16 N	92.42 W
Armstrong □[6]	214	40.49 N	79.32 W
Armstrong ≃	164	16.46 S	131.12 E
Armstrong, Mount ∧	180	63.12 N	133.16 W
Armstrong Station	176	50.18 N	89.02 W
Armthorpe	44	53.32 N	1.03 W
Ārmūr	122	18.48 N	78.17 E
Armutlu	130	40.31 N	28.50 E
Arnå ≃	41	54.57 N	8.53 E
Arnaccio	66	43.40 N	10.17 E
Arnaía	38	40.29 N	23.35 E
Arnarfjörður ⊂[2]	24a	65.45 N	23.40 W
Ärnäs	40	58.41 N	13.35 E
Arnaud ≃	176	59.59 N	69.46 W
Arnaudville	194	30.24 N	91.56 W
Arnavad, gora ∧	85	38.33 N	71.31 E
Arnavutköy ≃	267b	41.13 N	29.12 E
Arnay-le-Duc	58	47.08 N	4.29 E
Arnaz	62	45.38 N	7.43 E
Arnborg	41	56.01 N	8.59 E
Arnbruck	60	49.08 N	13.00 E
Arncliffe	274a	33.56 S	151.09 E
Arneburg	54	52.40 N	12.00 E
Arnedo	34	42.13 N	2.06 W
Arneiro dos Marinheiros	266c	38.51 N	9.25 W
Arneiroz	250	6.20 S	40.08 W
Arnejevo	82	54.58 N	37.35 E
Arnemuiden	52	51.30 N	3.41 E
Årnes	26	60.09 N	11.28 E
Arnett	196	36.08 N	99.46 W
Arney ≃	48	54.16 N	7.37 W
Arnhem	52	51.59 N	5.55 E
Arnhem, Cape ›	164	12.21 S	136.21 E
Arnhem Bay ⊂	164	12.20 S	136.12 E
Arnhem Land ◆[1]	164	13.10 S	134.30 E
Arnhem Land Aboriginal Reserve ◆[4]	164	13.10 S	134.30 E
Arni	64	44.04 N	10.15 E
Arnis	41	54.38 N	9.56 E
Árnissa	38	40.48 N	21.50 E
Arno I[1]	14	7.05 N	171.41 E
Arno ≃	66	43.41 N	10.17 E
Arno, Torrente ≃	266b	45.42 N	8.48 E
Arno Bay	166	33.54 S	136.34 E
Arnold, B.C., Can.	224	49.08 N	122.03 W
Arnold, Eng., U.K.	44	53.00 N	1.08 W
Arnold, Ca., U.S.	204	38.15 N	120.21 W
Arnold, Md., U.S.	208	39.01 N	76.30 W
Arnold, Mn., U.S.	190	46.52 N	92.05 W
Arnold, Mo., U.S.	219	38.25 N	90.22 W
Arnold, Ne., U.S.	198	41.25 N	100.11 W
Arnold, Pa., U.S.	214	40.34 N	79.46 W
Arnold ≃	164	15.19 S	134.06 E
Arnold Arboretum ♠	283	42.18 N	71.08 W
Arnold Mills	283	41.58 N	71.23 W
Arnold Mills Reservoir ⊜[1]	283	41.59 N	71.25 W
Arnolds Park	198	43.22 N	95.08 W
Arnoldstein	64	46.33 N	13.43 E
Arnon ≃	50	48.16 N	0.38 E
Arnos Vale Airport ⊠	241h	13.09 N	61.13 W
Arnot	210	41.39 N	77.07 W
Arnouville-lès-Gonesse	261	49.00 N	2.25 E
Arnouville-lès-Mantes	261	48.55 N	1.44 E
Arnoya ≃	34	42.15 N	8.09 W
Arnprior	212	45.26 N	76.21 W
Arnsberg	56	51.24 N	8.03 E
Arnsberg □[5]	52	51.20 N	8.00 E
Arnschwang	60	49.16 N	12.49 E
Arnsdorf	54	51.05 N	13.59 E
Arnside	44	54.12 N	2.50 W
Arnstadt	54	50.50 N	10.57 E
Arnstein	56	49.58 N	9.58 E
Arnstorf	60	48.34 N	12.49 E
Arnum	41	55.15 N	8.59 E
Ärø I	41	55.15 N	9.45 E
Aro ≃	246	8.01 N	64.11 W
Aroa	246	10.26 N	68.54 W
Aroa ≃	246	10.40 N	68.19 W
Aroa, Pointe ›	174s	17.28 S	149.46 W
Aroab	156	26.47 S	19.40 E
Aroali	126	24.03 N	87.56 E
Arochukwu	150	5.23 N	7.55 E
Aroeiras	250	7.31 S	35.41 W
Ar'ofino	80	58.16 N	39.15 E
Arolla	58	46.02 N	7.29 E
Arolsen	56	51.23 N	9.01 E
Aroma	140	15.49 N	36.08 E
Aroma Park	216	41.04 N	87.48 W
Aromas	226	36.53 N	121.39 W
Aromaševo	86	56.52 N	68.39 E
Aron ≃	50	47.15 N	2.02 E
Arona, It.	62	45.46 N	8.34 E
Arona, Pap. N. Gui.	164	6.20 S	146.00 E
Arona, Pa., U.S.	279b	40.16 N	79.39 W
Aroostook ≃	186	46.48 N	67.45 W
Arop Island I	164	5.20 S	147.05 E
Aropuk Lake ⊜	180	61.12 N	163.50 W
Arorae I	14	2.38 S	176.49 E
Arorangi	174k	21.13 S	159.49 W
Aroroy	116	12.31 N	123.24 E
Aros ≃	232	29.09 N	109.40 W
Arosa	58	46.47 N	9.41 E
Arosa, Ría de ⊂[1]	34	42.28 N	8.57 W
Arosbaya	115a	6.56 S	112.51 E
Årøsund	41	55.16 N	9.45 E
Aro Usu, Tanjung ›	164	8.20 S	130.45 E
Arowhana ∧	172	38.07 S	177.52 E
Arp	222	32.13 N	95.03 W
Arpa ≃	84	39.28 N	44.57 E
Arpaçay	84	40.52 N	43.20 E
Arpaçay (Achur'an) ≃	84	40.06 N	43.39 E
Arpačin	83	47.14 N	40.11 E
Arpaia	68	41.02 N	14.33 E
Arpajon	50	48.35 N	2.15 E
Ārpāra	126	23.23 N	89.23 E
Arpino	66	41.39 N	13.36 E
Arpoador, Ponta do ›	287a	22.59 S	43.12 W
Arquà Petrarca	64	45.16 N	11.43 E
Arquà Polesine	64	45.01 N	11.45 E
Arquata del Tronto	66	42.46 N	13.18 E
Arquata Scrivia	62	44.41 N	8.53 E
Arque	248	17.48 S	66.23 W
Arques	50	50.44 N	2.17 E
Arques-la-Bataille	50	49.53 N	1.08 E
Ar-Rabad	128	23.11 N	39.32 E
Ar-Rabbah	132	31.16 N	35.44 E
Arracourt	58	48.44 N	6.32 E
Ar-Radīsīyah Baḥrī	140	24.57 N	32.53 E
Ar-Rafīd	132	32.57 N	35.53 E
Arraga	252	28.04 S	64.14 W
Arrah	150	6.40 N	3.58 W
Ar-Rahad	140	12.43 N	30.39 E
Ar-Raḥāminah	142	31.18 N	31.45 E
Ar-Raḥmānīyah	142	31.06 N	30.38 E
Arraial do Cabo	255	22.58 S	42.01 W
Arraias	255	12.56 S	46.57 W
Arraias ≃, Bra.	250	11.10 S	53.35 W
Arraias ≃, Bra.	255	12.28 S	47.18 W
'Arrām, Wādī V	132	32.55 N	36.10 E
Ar-Ramādī	128	33.25 N	43.17 E
Ar-Ramthā	132	32.34 N	36.00 E
Arran, Island of I	46	55.35 N	5.15 W
Ar-Rank	140	11.45 N	32.48 E
Arran Lake ⊜	212	44.29 N	81.16 W
Ar-Raqqah	130	35.56 N	39.01 E
Ar-Raqqah □[8]	130	36.00 N	39.00 E
Arras	50	50.17 N	2.47 E
Arras, Nuraghe ⊥	71	39.40 N	9.25 E
Ar-Rāshidah	140	25.35 N	28.56 E
Ar-Rass	128	25.52 N	43.28 E
Ar-Rastan	130	34.55 N	36.44 E
Arrats ≃	32	44.06 N	0.52 E
Ar-Rawḍah, Ar. Su.	128	26.05 N	40.37 E
Ar-Rawḍah, Miṣr	142	27.48 N	30.52 E
Ar-Rawḍah, Miṣr	142	29.27 N	31.00 E
Ar-Rawḍah, Yaman	144	14.28 N	47.17 E
Ar-Rāwuk	144	15.45 N	48.54 E
Ar-Rayramūn	142	27.45 N	30.52 E
Ar-Rayyāḥ ar-Minūfīya ≍	142	30.20 N	31.00 E
Ar-Rayyāḥ at-Tawfīqī ≍	142	30.11 N	31.07 E
Ar-Rayyān	128	25.18 N	51.27 E
Arrecife	148	28.57 N	13.32 W
Arrecifes	252	34.03 S	60.07 W
Arrée, Montagnes d' ⋏	32	48.26 N	3.55 W
Arregui, Laguna ⊜	258	35.05 S	57.33 W
Arrentela	266c	38.38 N	9.06 W
Arresø ⊜	41	55.58 N	12.08 E
Arrey	200	32.50 N	107.19 W
Arriaga	234	16.14 N	93.54 W
Arriba	198	39.17 N	103.16 W
Arrild	41	55.09 N	8.58 E
Ar-Riyāḍ (Riyadh)	128	24.38 N	46.43 E
Arrochar	46	56.12 N	4.44 W
Arroio Grande	252	32.14 S	53.05 W
Arrojado ≃	255	13.24 S	44.20 W
Arronches	34	39.07 N	7.17 W
Arrone ≃, It.	66	41.52 N	12.11 E
Arrone ≃, It.	66	42.18 N	11.38 E
Arros ≃	32	43.40 N	0.02 W
Arroscia ≃	62	44.03 N	8.11 E
Arroux ≃	32	46.29 N	3.58 E
Arrow ≃, Eng., U.K.	42	52.12 N	2.43 W
Arrow ≃, Eng., U.K.	42	52.09 N	1.53 W
Arrow, Lough ⊜	48	54.04 N	8.21 W
Arrow Creek ≃	202	47.43 N	109.50 W
Arrowhead, Lake ⊜[1], Ca., U.S.	228	34.15 N	117.11 W
Arrowhead, Lake ⊜[1], Tx., U.S.	196	33.40 N	98.20 W
Arrowhead Peak ∧	228	34.13 N	117.16 W
Arrowhead Provincial Park ♠	212	45.24 N	79.13 W
Arrowhead Village	208	40.04 N	74.07 W
Arrow Lake ⊜	190	48.08 N	90.18 W
Arrowrock Reservoir ⊜[1]	202	43.36 N	115.51 W
Arrowsmith	216	40.27 N	88.38 W
Arrowsmith, Mount ∧, Austl.	166	30.09 S	141.50 E
Arrowsmith, Mount ∧, B.C., Can.	224	49.13 N	124.36 W
Arrowsmith, Mount ∧, N.Z.	172	43.21 S	170.59 E
Arrowtown	172	44.56 S	168.50 E
Arrowwood	182	50.44 N	113.09 W
Arroyan, Arroyo ≃[1]	288	34.24 S	58.32 W
Arroyito	252	31.25 S	63.03 W
Arroyo	240m	17.58 N	66.04 W
Arroyo de la Luz	34	39.29 N	6.35 W
Arroyo Grande	204	35.07 N	120.35 W
Arroyo Grande → Ismael Cortinas	258	33.58 S	57.06 W
Arroyo Hondo	200	36.32 N	105.40 W
Arroyo Naranjo ◆[8]	286b	23.02 N	82.23 W
Arroyo Seco	252	33.14 S	60.50 W
Arroyo Seco Park ♠	280	34.06 N	118.12 W
Arroyos y Esteros	252	25.04 S	57.06 W
Arrozal	256	22.37 S	44.03 W
Ar-Ru'at	140	12.21 N	32.17 E
Ar-Rub' al-Khālī ◆[2]	118	20.00 N	51.00 E
Ar-Rubayqī	142	30.10 N	31.46 E
Ar-Ruḥaybah	132	33.45 N	36.42 E
Ar-Rukhaymīyah ⊤[4]	128	29.14 N	45.35 E
Ar-Rumaythah	128	31.32 N	45.12 E
Ar-Rummān	132	32.10 N	35.50 E
Ar-Ruqayyah ⊥	132	32.47 N	37.05 E
Ar-Ruṣāfah ⊥	130	35.37 N	38.45 E
Ar-Ruṣayfah	132	32.01 N	36.03 E
Ar-Ruṣayriṣ	140	11.51 N	34.23 E
Ar-Rushaydah	132	32.40 N	36.50 E
Ar-Ruṭbah	128	33.02 N	40.17 E
Ar-Ru'ūs	142	29.21 N	31.04 E
Ar-Ruways	128	26.08 N	51.13 E
Års	26	56.48 N	9.32 E
Aršan, Ross.	88	51.54 N	102.27 E
Aršan, Ross.	88	53.54 N	99.54 E
Arsanjān	128	29.56 N	53.18 E
Aršan'-Zel'men'	80	47.36 N	44.36 E
Ārsāpota	272b	22.55 N	88.18 E
Arsbeck	56	51.08 N	6.12 E
Arsenal de Marinha ■	266c	38.39 N	9.09 W
Arsenal Football Club ♠	260	51.33 N	0.06 W
Arsenault Lake ⊜	184	55.06 N	108.30 W
Arsenjev	89	44.10 N	133.15 E
Arsenjevka ≃	89	44.54 N	133.35 E
Arsenjevo	76	53.44 N	36.40 E
Ars-en-Ré	32	46.12 N	1.31 W
Arsi □[4]	144	8.00 N	39.40 E
Arsiè	64	45.59 N	11.45 E
Arsiero	64	45.48 N	11.21 E
Arsikere	122	13.20 N	76.15 E
Arsin	130	40.58 N	39.56 E
Aršincevo	78	45.17 N	36.25 E
Arsk	80	56.06 N	49.54 E
Arslanbob	85	41.21 N	72.56 E
Årslev	41	55.18 N	10.29 E
Arso	164	2.56 S	140.47 E
Arsoli	66	42.02 N	13.01 E
Ársos	130	34.50 N	32.46 E
Ars-sur-Formans	58	45.59 N	4.49 E
Ars-sur-Moselle	56	49.05 N	6.04 E
Årsta havsbad	40	59.05 N	18.10 E
Arsufhsa ≃	84	39.08 N	46.50 E
Årsunda	40	60.32 N	16.44 E
Art, Île I	175f	19.43 S	163.38 E
Árta, Ellás	38	39.09 N	20.59 E
Artà, Esp.	34	39.42 N	3.21 E
Artarmon	274a	33.49 S	151.11 E
Artašat	84	39.59 N	44.33 E
Arta Terme	64	46.28 N	13.01 E
Arteaga	234	18.28 N	102.25 W
Arteche	116	12.17 N	125.22 E
Arte Contemporânea, Museu de ⊍	287b	23.32 S	46.38 W
Artegna	64	46.14 N	13.09 E
Artemare	62	45.52 N	5.42 E
Artemisa	240p	22.49 N	82.46 W
Artemón	38	36.59 N	24.43 E
Artémou	150	15.31 N	12.16 W
Artemovsk → Art'omovsk	83	48.35 N	38.00 E
Artèn	64	46.00 N	11.50 E
Artenay	50	48.05 N	1.53 E
Artern	54	51.22 N	11.17 E
Artesia, Ca., U.S.	280	33.51 N	118.04 W
Artesia, Ms., U.S.	194	33.24 N	88.38 W
Artesia, N.M., U.S.	196	32.50 N	104.24 W
Artesia Lake ⊜	226	38.57 N	119.22 W
Artesia → Mosomane	156	24.04 S	26.15 E
Artesian	198	44.00 N	97.55 W
Arth	58	47.04 N	8.31 E
Arthabaska	206	46.02 N	71.55 W
Arthabaska □[6]	206	46.05 N	72.00 W
Arthal	123	33.16 N	76.11 E
Arthala	272a	28.40 N	77.24 E
Arthies	261	49.06 N	1.48 E
Arthonnay	50	47.56 N	4.13 E
Arthur, On., Can.	212	43.50 N	80.32 W
Arthur, Il., U.S.	194	39.43 N	88.28 W
Arthur, Ne., U.S.	198	41.34 N	101.41 W
Arthur, N.D., U.S.	198	47.06 N	97.19 W
Arthur, Tn., U.S.	192	36.32 N	83.40 W
Arthur ≃, Austl.	166	41.03 S	144.40 E
Arthur ≃, Austl.	168a	33.31 S	116.50 E
Arthur, Lake ⊜[1]	214	40.57 N	80.05 W
Arthur Creek ≃	162	22.55 S	136.45 E
Arthur Kill ⋓	276	40.30 N	74.15 W
Arthurs Pass	172	42.57 S	171.34 E
Arthurs Pass)(	172	42.54 S	171.34 E
Arthur's Pass National Park ♠	172	42.50 S	171.40 E
Arthurs Seat ∧[2]	169	38.21 S	144.57 E
Arthur's Town	238	24.38 N	75.42 W
Arthurton	168b	34.16 S	137.45 E
Arti	86	56.26 N	58.32 E
Artibonite ≃	238	19.15 N	72.47 W
Artico, Océano → Arctic Ocean ⊤[1]	16	85.00 N	170.00 E
Artigas	252	30.24 S	56.28 W
Artigas ◆[8]	286c	10.30 N	66.56 W
Artigas, Casa de ⊥	258	34.39 S	56.03 W
Artik	84	40.37 N	43.59 E
Artilleros	258	34.22 S	57.34 W
Artilleros, Punta ›	258	34.28 S	57.32 W
Artillery Lake ⊜	176	63.09 N	107.52 W
Artlenburg	52	53.22 N	10.29 E
Artney, Glen V	46	56.20 N	4.04 W
Artois □[9]	50	50.30 N	2.30 E
Artois, Collines de l' ⋏[2]	50	50.25 N	2.10 E
Art'om	89	43.22 N	132.13 E
Art'om-Ostrov	84	40.28 N	50.20 E
Art'omovka, Ukr.	78	49.46 N	35.04 E
Art'omovka, Ukr.	83	48.29 N	37.23 E
Art'omovka, Ukr.	83	47.53 N	38.38 E
Art'omovo	83	48.22 N	37.53 E
Art'omovsk, Ross.	86	54.21 N	93.26 E
Art'omovsk, Ukr.	83	48.27 N	38.42 E
Art'omovsk, Ukr.	83	48.35 N	38.00 E
Art'omovskij, Ross.	86	57.21 N	61.54 E
Art'omovskij, Ross.	88	58.12 N	114.45 E
Art'omovskij, Ross.	89	43.27 N	132.22 E
Artova	130	40.03 N	36.19 E
Artpark ♠	284a	43.10 N	79.03 W
Artrutx, Cap d' ›	34	39.56 N	3.48 E
Artuby ≃	62	43.44 N	6.22 E
Artur Nogueira	256	22.35 S	47.09 W
Arturo Merino Benítez, Aeropuerto ⊠	286e	33.23 S	70.49 W
Arturo Segui ◆[8]	258	34.51 S	58.09 W
Artvin	130	41.11 N	41.49 E
Artvin □[4]	130	41.05 N	42.00 E
Artybaš	86	51.48 N	87.16 E
Artyk	74	64.12 N	145.06 E
Aru, Kepulauan II	164	6.00 S	134.30 E
Aru, Tanjung ›	112	2.10 S	116.34 E
Aru, Teluk ⊂	114	4.09 N	98.12 E
Arua	154	3.01 N	30.55 E
Aruã ≃	250	2.39 S	55.38 W
Aruaddin	144	16.15 N	38.43 E
Aruanã	255	14.54 S	51.05 W
Aruângua (Luangwa) ≃	154	15.36 S	30.25 E
Aruba □[2]	241s	12.30 N	69.58 W
Aru Basin ⊹[1]	14	5.00 S	134.00 E
Arucas	148	28.07 N	15.31 W
Arue	174s	17.32 S	149.32 W
Arufu	150	7.50 N	9.14 E
Arujá	256	23.24 S	46.20 W
Arujá □[7]	287b	23.24 S	46.20 W
Arumanduba	250	1.29 S	52.29 W
Arume	174m	26.36 N	128.07 E
Arume-wan ⊂	174m	26.35 N	128.08 E
Aruṇ (Pong) ≃, Asia	124	26.49 N	87.09 E
Arun ≃, Eng., U.K.	42	50.48 N	0.33 W
Arunāchal Pradesh □[3]	120	28.30 N	95.00 E
Arundel, P.Q., Can.	206	45.58 N	74.37 W
Arundel, Eng., U.K.	42	50.51 N	0.34 W
Arun Qi	89	48.07 N	123.28 E
Årup	41	55.23 N	10.04 E
Aruppukkottai	122	9.31 N	78.06 E
Arurandeua ≃	250	3.43 S	48.50 W
Arusha	154	3.22 S	36.41 E
Arusha □[4]	154	4.00 S	36.15 E
Arusha Chini	154	3.35 S	37.20 E
Arusha National Park ♠	154	3.17 S	36.56 E
Arut ≃	112	2.42 S	111.34 E
Aruvi ≃	122	8.49 N	79.55 E
Aruwimi ≃	138	1.13 N	23.36 E
Arvada	200	39.48 N	105.05 W
Arvagh	48	53.55 N	7.34 W
Arvajcheer	90	46.15 N	102.48 E
Arve ≃	58	46.12 N	6.08 E
Arverne ◆[8]	276	40.35 N	73.48 W
Arves, Les Aiguilles d' ∧	62	45.08 N	6.21 E
Arvi	120	20.59 N	78.14 E
Arvida	186	48.25 N	71.11 W
Arvidsjaur	24	65.35 N	19.07 E
Arvier	62	45.42 N	7.11 E

≃	River	Fluß	Río	Rivière	Rio
≍	Canal	Kanal	Canal	Canal	Canal
⌞	Waterfall, Rapids	Wasserfall, Stromschnellen	Cascada, Rápidos	Chute d'eau, Rapides	Cascata, Rápidos
⋓	Strait	Meeresstraße	Estrecho	Détroit	Estreito
⊂	Bay, Gulf	Bucht, Golf	Bahía, Golfo	Baie, Golfe	Baía, Golfo
⊜	Lake, Lakes	See, Seen	Lago, Lagos	Lac, Lacs	Lago, Lagos
≋	Swamp	Sumpf	Pantano	Marais	Pântano
⊼	Ice Features, Glacier	Eis- und Gletscherformen	Accidentes Glaciales	Formes glaciaires	Acidentes glaciares
⊤	Other Hydrographic Features	Andere Hydrographische Objekte	Otros Elementos Hidrográficos	Autres données hydrographiques	Outros acidentes hidrográficos

⊹	Submarine Features	Untermeerische Objekte	Accidentes Submarinos	Formes de relief sous-marin	Acidentes submarinos
□	Political Unit	Politische Einheit	Unidad Politica	Entité politique	Unidade política
⊍	Cultural Institution	Kulturelle Institution	Institución Cultural	Institution culturelle	Instituição cultural
⊥	Historical Site	Historische Stätte	Sitio Histórico	Site historique	Sitio histórico
♠	Recreational Site	Erholungs- und Ferienort	Sitio de Recreo	Centre de loisirs	Area de Lazer
⊠	Airport	Flughafen	Aeropuerto	Aéroport	Aeroporto
■	Military Installation	Militäranlage	Instalación Militar	Installation militaire	Instalação militar
◆	Miscellaneous	Verschiedenes	Misceláneo	Divers	Diversos

Arvieux 62 44.46 N 6.44 E
Arvika 26 59.39 N 12.36 E
Arvillard 62 45.27 N 6.07 E
Arvin 228 35.12 N 118.49 W
Arvo, Lago ⊜ 68 39.14 N 16.29 E
Arvon, Mount ∧ 190 46.45 N 88.09 W
Arvonia 192 37.40 N 78.20 W
Arvorezinha 252 28.53 S 52.10 W
Arwal 124 25.15 N 84.41 E
Arwala 112 7.41 S 126.49 E
Arxan 89 47.11 N 119.57 E
Aryamūn 142 31.11 N 30.54 E
Aryiroúpolis 267c 37.54 N 23.45 E
Arys' 85 42.26 N 68.48 E
Arys' ≐ 85 42.48 N 68.12 E
Arys, ozero ⊜ 86 45.50 N 66.20 E
Arzachena 71 41.05 N 9.23 E
Arzamas 80 55.23 N 43.50 E
Arzana 71 39.55 N 9.31 E
Arzano 68 40.55 N 14.16 E
Arzberg 60 50.04 N 12.12 E
Arzew, Golfe d' ⊂ 34 35.50 N 0.10 W
Arzew, Salines d' ⊜ 34 35.40 N 0.15 W
Arzfeld 56 50.05 N 6.16 E
Arzignano 64 45.31 N 11.20 E
Arziw 148 35.51 N 0.19 W
Arz Lubnān ◈[3] 130 34.14 N 36.03 E
Arzni 84 40.19 N 44.36 E
Arzon ≐ 62 45.11 N 3.54 E
Arzúa 34 42.56 N 8.09 W
As, Bel. 56 51.01 N 5.35 E
Aš, Česko. 54 50.10 N 12.10 E
Ås, Nor. 26 59.40 N 10.48 E
Asa, Nihon 96 34.33 N 132.26 E
Aša, Ross. 86 55.00 N 57.16 E
Asa ≐, Nihon 94 35.39 N 139.26 E
Asa ≐, Nihon 96 34.01 N 131.09 E
Asa ≐, Ven. 246 6.50 N 63.18 W
Asab 156 25.29 S 17.59 E
Asaba, Nig. 150 6.12 N 6.44 E
Asaba, Nihon 94 34.42 N 137.56 E
Asad, Buḥayrat al- ⊜[1] 130 36.00 N 38.10 E
Asadābād, Afg. 120 34.52 N 71.09 E
Asadābād, Īrān 128 34.47 N 48.07 E
Asafo 150 6.11 N 0.28 W
Asaga Strait)(174y 14.11 S 169.40 W
Asagaya ◈[8] 268 35.42 N 139.38 E
Aşağıbostancı 130 35.10 N 33.00 E
Aşağıçiğil 130 38.03 N 31.52 E
Aşağı Dağ ∧ 84 40.01 N 43.11 E
Aşağı Kuluşağı 130 38.39 N 38.39 E
Aşağılahan 130 38.50 N 39.59 E
Aşağı Mestikân 130 38.25 N 38.46 E
Ašagy-G'ojn'uk 84 41.18 N 47.00 E
Asahan 114 2.23 N 102.33 E
Asahan ≐ 114 3.02 N 99.52 E
Asahi, Nihon 94 35.14 N 137.22 E
Asahi, Nihon 94 35.43 N 140.39 E
Asahi, Nihon 94 36.14 N 140.31 E
Asahi, Nihon 94 35.02 N 136.40 E
Asahi, Nihon 94 36.07 N 137.52 E
Asahi, Nihon 94 36.05 N 137.21 E
Asahi, Nihon 94 35.59 N 136.07 E
Asahi, Nihon 94 36.57 N 137.34 E
Asahi, Nihon 96 34.59 N 133.50 E
Asahi, Nihon 96 34.51 N 132.16 E
Asahi, Nihon 96 34.17 N 131.28 E
Asahi ◈[8], Nihon 268 35.29 N 139.33 E
Asahi ◈[8], Nihon 270 34.44 N 135.34 E
Asahi ≐ 96 34.36 N 133.58 E
Asahi-dake ∧, Nihon 92a 43.40 N 142.51 E
Asahi-dake ∧, Nihon 94 37.14 N 139.21 E
Asahigawa — Asahikawa 92a 43.46 N 142.22 E
Asahi-gawa-daiichi-dam ◈[6] 96 34.53 N 133.22 E
Asahikawa 92a 43.46 N 142.22 E
Asahikawa-chūtonchi, Rikujō-Jieitai- ■ 92a 43.49 N 142.25 E
Asahi-ko ⊜[1] 96 34.56 N 133.51 E
Asahi-sanchi ⩓ 92 38.25 N 139.50 E
Asaka 94 35.48 N 139.36 E
Asaka, Camp ■ 268 35.47 N 139.36 E
Asakanskij Golec, gora ∧ 88 50.18 N 109.55 E
Asakawa 94 37.05 N 140.25 E
Asake ≐ 94 35.00 N 136.41 E
Asako 96 35.14 N 134.48 E
Asakura 96 33.23 N 130.44 E
Asakusa ◈[8] 268 35.43 N 139.49 E
Asālafpur ◈[8] 272a 28.38 N 77.05 E
Asale 144 14.22 N 40.32 E
Asale, Lake ⊜ 144 14.19 N 40.18 E
Asamankese 150 5.52 N 0.42 W
Asama-yama ∧ 94 36.24 N 138.31 E
Asanbani, India 126 22.43 N 86.20 E
Asanbāni, India 126 24.07 N 87.27 E
Asani 154 4.25 S 29.05 E
Asankrangwa 150 5.48 N 2.26 W
Asan-man ⊂ 98 36.56 N 126.51 E
Āsānsol, India 126 24.14 N 87.17 E
Āsānsol, India 126 23.41 N 86.59 E
Ašap 86 57.07 N 56.30 E
Asar 88 47.56 N 117.38 E
Åsarna 26 62.39 N 14.21 E
Asarum 26 56.12 N 14.50 E
Asashina 94 36.16 N 138.25 E
Āsāsuni 126 22.32 N 89.10 E
Asati 272b 22.29 N 88.14 E
Asa-yama ∧ 96 34.47 N 132.23 E
Asayita 144 11.33 N 41.30 E
Asbach 56 50.40 N 7.25 E
Asbeck 263 51.21 N 7.18 E
Asberg 263 51.26 N 6.40 E
Asbesberg ⩓ 158 28.55 S 23.15 E
Asbest 86 57.00 N 61.30 E
Asbestos 206 45.46 N 71.57 W
Asbestos Range National Park ♦ 166 41.08 S 146.39 E
Asbe Teferi 144 9.02 N 40.58 E
Åsbro 40 59.00 N 15.03 E
Asbury 210 40.41 N 75.00 W
Asbury Park 208 40.13 N 74.01 W
Ascea 68 40.08 N 15.11 E
Ascensión 232 31.06 N 107.59 W
Ascension I 10 7.57 S 14.22 W
Ascent 158 27.12 S 29.03 E
Aščerino 265b 55.36 N 37.46 E
Asch 58 47.57 N 10.49 E
Aschabad 128 37.57 N 58.23 E
Aschabad □[8] 128 38.30 N 58.25 E
Aschach an der Donau 61 48.22 N 14.02 E
Aschaffenburg 56 49.59 N 9.09 E
Aschbach Markt 61 48.04 N 14.45 E
Ascheberg, Dtsch. 52 51.47 N 7.37 E
Ascheberg, Dtsch. 54 54.08 N 10.20 E
Aschendorf 52 53.04 N 7.22 E
Aschersleben 54 51.45 N 11.27 E
Asciano 66 43.14 N 11.33 E
Aščikol', ozero ⊜ 86 45.05 N 67.15 E
Aščiozek ≐ 80 49.12 N 48.06 E
Aščitastysor, ozero ⊜ 86 49.19 N 63.59 E
Ascoli Piceno 66 42.51 N 13.34 E
Ascoli Piceno □[4] 66 43.01 N 13.34 E
Ascoli Satriano 68 41.12 N 15.34 E
Ascona 58 46.09 N 8.46 E
Ascope 248 7.43 S 79.07 W
Ascot, Austl. 171a 27.26 S 153.04 E
Ascot, Eng., U.K. 42 51.25 N 0.41 W
Ascot ≐ 206 45.21 N 71.51 W
Ascotán 252 21.44 S 68.18 W
Ascros 62 43.55 N 7.01 E
Aščykol', ozero ⊜ 85 43.32 N 70.35 E
Aščysu ≐ 86 49.54 N 78.58 E
Aseb 144 13.00 N 42.45 E
Åseda 26 57.10 N 15.20 E
Asedjrad ⩓[1] 148 24.28 N 1.52 E
Asekejevo 80 53.36 N 52.49 E
Asela 144 7.59 N 39.08 E
Åsele 26 64.10 N 17.20 E
Asem ≐ 115a 6.14 S 107.42 E
Asembagus 115a 7.45 S 114.14 E
Asembourg 56 49.43 N 6.02 E
Åsen 26 63.36 N 11.03 E
Asendabo 144 9.50 N 37.33 E
Asendorf 52 52.46 N 9.00 E
Asenovgrad 38 42.01 N 24.52 E
Åsensbruk 26 58.48 N 12.25 E
Aseri 76 59.27 N 26.52 E
Aşfar, Jabal al- ∧ 132 32.12 N 36.54 E
Asfordby 42 52.46 N 0.57 W
Aşfūn al-Maṭā'inah 140 25.23 N 32.32 E
Åsgårdstrand 26 59.21 N 10.28 E
Ash, Eng., U.K. 42 51.17 N 1.16 E
Ash, Eng., U.K. 42 51.15 N 0.44 W
Ashalim 132 30.58 N 34.40 E
Åshammar 40 60.39 N 16.32 E
Ashanti □[4] 150 6.45 N 1.30 W
'Asharah, Wādī al- ∨ 142 30.21 N 32.15 E
Asharoken 276 40.56 N 73.22 W
Ashaway 207 41.25 N 71.47 W
Ashbourne, Ire. 48 53.31 N 6.24 W
Ashbourne, Eng., U.K. 44 53.02 N 1.44 W
Ash Brook Swamp Reservation ♦ 276 40.37 N 74.21 W
Ashburn, Ga., U.S. 192 31.42 N 83.39 W
Ashburn, Mo., U.S. 219 39.33 N 91.10 W
Ashburn, Va., U.S. 208 39.02 N 77.29 W
Ashburnham 207 42.38 N 71.54 W
Ashburton, Austl. 274b 37.52 S 145.05 E
Ashburton, N.Z. 172 43.55 S 171.45 E
Ashburton, Eng., U.K. 42 50.31 N 3.45 W
Ashburton ≐, Austl. 162 21.40 S 114.56 E
Ashburton ≐, N.Z. 172 44.04 S 171.48 E
Ashburton, North Branch ≐ 172 43.54 S 171.44 E
Ashburton, South Branch ≐ 172 43.44 S 171.32 E
Ashburton Downs 162 23.24 S 117.04 E
Ashby 207 42.40 N 71.49 W
Ashby, Lake ⊜ 220 28.56 N 81.07 W
Ashby-de-la-Zouch 42 52.46 N 1.28 W
Ashchurch 42 52.00 N 2.07 W
Ash Creek ≐, Ca., U.S. 204 41.05 N 121.08 W
Ash Creek ≐, Ct., U.S. 276 41.08 N 73.14 W
Ashcroft 182 50.43 N 121.17 W
Ashdod, Ma., U.S. 283 42.04 N 70.45 W
Ashdod, Yis. 132 31.49 N 34.40 E
Ashdod, Tel ⊥ 132 31.45 N 34.40 E
Ashdot Ya'aqov 132 32.40 N 35.35 E
Ashdown 194 33.40 N 94.07 W
Asheboro 192 35.42 N 79.48 W
Ashern 184 51.11 N 98.21 W
Asherton 196 28.26 N 99.45 W
Asheville 192 35.36 N 82.33 W
Ashewat Ziārat 120 31.22 N 68.32 E
Asheweig ≐ 176 54.17 N 87.12 W
Ashfield, Austl. 274a 33.53 S 151.08 E
Ashfield, Ma., U.S. 207 42.31 N 72.47 W
Ash Flat 194 36.13 N 91.36 W
Ashford, Austl. 166 29.20 S 151.06 E
Ashford, Eng., U.K. 42 51.08 N 0.53 E
Ashford, Eng., U.K. 260 51.26 N 0.27 W
Ashford, Al., U.S. 194 31.10 N 85.14 W
Ashford, Wa., U.S. 224 46.46 N 122.02 W
Ashford Airport ⊠ 42 51.04 N 1.01 E
Ash Fork 200 35.13 N 112.28 W
Ash Grove 194 37.18 N 93.35 W
Ashhurst 172 40.18 S 175.45 E
Ashibe 92 33.48 N 129.46 E
Ashibetsu 92a 43.31 N 142.11 E
Ashida ≐ 96 34.26 N 133.25 E
Ashikaga 94 36.20 N 139.27 E
Ashikagga-gakkō ⊥ 94 36.22 N 139.30 E
Ashingdon 260 51.36 N 0.42 E
Ashington 44 55.12 N 1.35 W
Ashino-ko ⊜ 94 35.13 N 139.00 E
Ashio 94 36.38 N 139.27 E
Ashio-sanchi ⩓ 94 36.35 N 139.30 E
Ashippun 216 43.14 N 88.31 W
Ashippun ≐ 216 43.10 N 88.33 W
Ashitaka-yama ∧ 94 35.12 N 138.49 E
Ashiya, Nihon 96 33.53 N 130.40 E
Ashiya, Nihon 96 34.43 N 135.17 E
Ashiya ≐ 270 34.43 N 135.18 E
Ashiyasu 94 35.38 N 138.23 E
Ashiyoro 92a 43.15 N 143.30 E
Ashizuri-misaki ➤ 92 32.44 N 133.01 E
Ashizuri-Uwakai-kokuritsu-kōen ♦, Nihon 92 32.45 N 132.45 E
Ashizuri-Uwakai-kokuritsu-kōen ♦, Nihon 96 33.07 N 132.27 E
Ashkhabad — Aschabad 128 37.57 N 58.23 E
Ashkum 216 40.53 N 87.57 W
Ashland, Al., U.S. 194 33.16 N 85.50 W
Ashland, Ca., U.S. 226 37.41 N 122.06 W
Ashland, Il., U.S. 219 39.53 N 90.00 W
Ashland, Ks., U.S. 198 37.11 N 99.45 W
Ashland, Ky., U.S. 188 38.28 N 82.38 W
Ashland, Me., U.S. 186 46.37 N 68.24 W
Ashland, Ma., U.S. 207 42.15 N 71.27 W
Ashland, Ms., U.S. 194 34.49 N 89.10 W
Ashland, Mo., U.S. 219 38.46 N 92.15 W
Ashland, Mt., U.S. 202 45.35 N 106.16 W
Ashland, Ne., U.S. 198 41.02 N 96.22 W
Ashland, N.H., U.S. 188 43.41 N 71.37 W
Ashland, N.J., U.S. 285 39.51 N 75.00 W
Ashland, N.Y., U.S. 210 42.18 N 74.20 W
Ashland, Oh., U.S. 214 40.52 N 82.19 W
Ashland, Or., U.S. 202 42.11 N 122.42 W
Ashland, Pa., U.S. 210 40.46 N 76.20 W
Ashland, Va., U.S. 208 37.45 N 77.28 W
Ashland, Wi., U.S. 190 46.35 N 90.53 W
Ashland □[6] 214 40.52 N 82.19 W
Ashland, Mount ∧ 202 42.05 N 122.43 W
Ashland City 194 36.16 N 87.03 W
Ashley, Austl. 166 29.19 S 149.49 E
Ashley, Eng., U.K. 262 53.21 N 2.20 W
Ashley, Il., U.S. 219 38.20 N 89.11 W
Ashley, In., U.S. 216 41.32 N 85.04 W
Ashley, Mi., U.S. 190 43.11 N 84.28 W
Ashley, Mo., U.S. 219 39.15 N 91.14 W
Ashley, N.D., U.S. 198 46.01 N 99.22 W
Ashley, Oh., U.S. 214 40.24 N 82.57 W
Ashley, Pa., U.S. 210 41.12 N 75.53 W
Ashley ≐ 172 43.16 S 172.43 E
Ashley Creek ≐ 200 40.21 N 109.22 W
Ashley Falls 207 42.03 N 73.20 W
Ashley Green 260 51.44 N 0.35 W
Ashmore 194 39.32 N 88.01 W
Ashmore Islands II 160 12.14 S 123.05 E
Ashmūn 142 30.18 N 30.58 E
Ashokan Reservoir ⊜[1] 210 41.58 N 74.10 W
Ashoknagar 120 24.34 N 77.43 E
Ashqelon 132 31.40 N 34.35 E
Ashridge Park ♦ 260 51.48 N 0.34 W
Ash-Shabakah 128 30.49 N 43.39 E
Ash-Shabb ⫪[4] 140 22.19 N 29.46 E
Ash-Shaddādah 130 36.02 N 40.45 E
Ash-Shāgūr 132 31.50 N 35.39 E
Ash-Shā'ib ∧[2] 142 29.50 N 30.56 E
Ash-Shajarah 132 32.39 N 35.56 E
Ash-Shallūfah 142 30.07 N 32.34 E
Ash-Shamāl □[4] 130 34.30 N 36.00 E
Ash-Shamālīyah □[4] 140 19.15 N 29.00 E
Ash-Shāmīyah 128 31.57 N 44.36 E
Ash-Shanāwīyah 142 29.08 N 31.08 E
Ash-Sharāh ◈[1] 132 30.20 N 35.30 E
Ash-Shāriqah 128 25.22 N 55.23 E
Ash-Sharmah 128 28.01 N 35.18 E
Ash-Sharqāṭ 128 35.27 N 43.16 E
Ash-Sharqīyah □[4] 142 30.48 N 31.48 E
Ash-Sharqīyah ◈[1] 128 27.00 N 49.00 E
Ash-Shaṭrah 128 31.25 N 46.10 E
Ash-Shawāshinah 142 29.22 N 30.36 E
Ash-Shawbak 132 30.32 N 35.34 E
Ash-Shawmarah 132 33.07 N 35.08 E
Ash-Shaykh Faḍl 142 28.29 N 30.50 E
Ash-Shaykh 'Ibādah 142 27.48 N 30.52 E
Ash-Shaykh Sa'd 132 32.50 N 36.02 E
Ash-Shaykh Timay 142 27.53 N 30.51 E
Ash-Shiḥr 144 14.44 N 49.35 E
Ash-Shīn 142 31.01 N 30.53 E
Ash-Shināfīyah 128 31.35 N 44.39 E
Ash-Shīyāḥ 132 33.51 N 35.30 E
Ash-Shufayyah 128 23.50 N 39.08 E
Ash-Shuhadā' 142 30.36 N 30.54 E
Ash-Shumlul 128 26.31 N 47.19 E
Ash-Shuqayq 144 17.43 N 42.01 E
Ash-Shurayf 128 25.43 N 39.14 E
Ash-Shurayk 140 18.48 N 33.34 E
Ash-Shuwayfāt 132 33.49 N 35.31 E
Ash Slough ≐ 226 37.02 N 120.32 W
Ashta, India 122 16.57 N 74.24 E
Ashta, India 124 23.01 N 76.43 E
Ashtabula 214 41.51 N 80.47 W
Ashtabula □[6] 214 41.44 N 80.46 W
Ashtabula ≐ 214 41.55 N 80.47 W
Ashtabula, East Branch ≐ 214 41.48 N 80.37 W
Ashtabula, Lake ⊜[1] 198 47.11 N 97.58 W
Ashtabula, West Branch ≐ 214 41.48 N 80.37 W
Ashtead 260 51.19 N 0.18 W
Ashton, S. Afr. 158 33.50 S 20.05 E
Ashton, Eng., U.K. 262 53.13 N 2.45 W
Ashton, Id., U.S. 202 44.04 N 111.26 W
Ashton, Il., U.S. 190 41.51 N 89.13 W
Ashton, Ia., U.S. 198 43.18 N 95.47 W
Ashton, Md., U.S. 208 39.08 N 77.00 W
Ashton, Ne., U.S. 198 41.14 N 98.47 W
Ashton, R.I., U.S. 207 41.46 N 71.25 W
Ashton-in-Makerfield 262 53.29 N 2.39 W
Ashton-under-Lyne 262 53.29 N 2.06 W
Ashton upon Mersey 262 53.26 N 2.19 W
Ashuanipi Lake ⊜ 176 52.35 N 66.10 W
Ashuelot ≐ 188 42.46 N 72.29 W
Ashurst's Beacon ∧[2] 262 53.34 N 2.45 W
Ashville, Al., U.S. 194 33.52 N 86.17 W
Ashville, N.Y., U.S. 214 42.06 N 79.23 W
Ashville, Oh., U.S. 218 39.42 N 82.57 W
Ashville, Pa., U.S. 214 40.34 N 78.33 W
Ashwater 42 50.44 N 4.16 W
Ashwaubenon 190 44.30 N 88.06 W
Ashworth Moor Reservoir ⊜[1] 262 53.38 N 2.16 W
Asi (Nahr al-'Āṣī) ≐ 130 36.02 N 35.58 E
Asia ⊥[1] 4 50.00 N 100.00 E
Asia ⊥[1] 12 50.00 N 100.00 E
Asia, Kepulauan II 108 1.03 N 131.18 E
Asiago 64 45.52 N 11.30 E
Asia Menor — Asia Minor □[9] 22 39.00 N 32.00 E
Asia Minor □[9] 22 39.00 N 32.00 E
Asid Gulf ⊂ 116 12.07 N 123.30 E
Asie — Asia ⊥[1] 12 50.00 N 100.00 E
Asie Mineure — Asia Minor □[9] 22 39.00 N 32.00 E
Asien — Asia ⊥[1] 12 50.00 N 100.00 E
āsika 120 19.36 N 84.39 E
Asikuma 150 5.35 N 1.00 W
Asilah 148 35.32 N 6.00 W
Asinara, Golfo dell' ⊂ 71 41.00 N 8.32 E
Asinara, Isola I 71 41.04 N 8.16 E
Asinaro ≐ 70 36.53 N 15.08 E
Asino 86 57.00 N 86.09 E
Asipoquobah Lake ⊜ 184 53.40 N 91.15 W
'Asīr ◈[1] 144 19.00 N 42.00 E
Ašitkovo 82 55.26 N 38.36 E
Aşkale 130 39.55 N 40.42 E
Askam in Furness 44 54.11 N 3.13 W
Askanija-Nova 78 46.27 N 33.52 E
Askanija-nova zapovednik ♦ 78 46.37 N 33.54 E
Askarovo 86 53.21 N 58.30 E
Askeaton 48 52.36 N 8.58 W
Asker 26 59.50 N 10.26 E
Askern 44 53.37 N 1.09 W
Askersund 40 58.53 N 14.54 E
Askham 158 26.59 S 20.47 E
Askim 26 59.35 N 11.10 E
Askino 86 56.05 N 56.34 E
Askira 146 10.39 N 12.55 E
Askival ∧ 46 56.59 N 6.17 W
Askiz 86 53.08 N 90.32 E
Askja ∧[1] 24a 65.00 N 16.48 W
Askø I 41 54.54 N 11.30 E
Äsköping 40 59.09 N 16.04 E
Askov 41 55.28 N 9.06 E
Askraal 158 34.09 S 20.52 E
Askrigg 44 54.19 N 2.04 W
Askvoll 26 61.21 N 5.04 E
Aslanapa 130 39.13 N 29.52 E
Aslan-Sara 84 39.02 N 48.16 E
Aslantaş Barajı ⊜[1] 130 37.20 N 36.15 E
Asleigh 284c 39.01 N 77.10 W
Åsljunga 41 56.19 N 13.22 E
Ašlyk 86 57.33 N 68.40 E
Ašlyk ≐ 86 57.50 N 69.12 E
Asmār 120 35.02 N 71.22 E
Asmara — Asmera 144 15.20 N 38.53 E
Asmera 144 15.20 N 38.53 E
Asmundtorp 41 55.53 N 12.56 E
Asnæs 41 55.49 N 11.31 E
Asnæs ➤[1] 41 55.40 N 11.00 E
Asnebumskit Hill ∧[2] 207 42.18 N 71.54 W
Åsnen ⊜ 26 56.38 N 14.42 E
Asni 148 31.14 N 7.55 W
Asnières [-sur-Seine] 50 48.55 N 2.17 E
Asō, Nihon 94 35.59 N 140.29 E
Aso, Nihon 96 32.58 N 131.02 E
Aso ≐ 66 43.06 N 13.51 E
Asoc 152 1.26 N 11.18 E
Aso-kokuritsu-kōen ♦ 92 33.00 N 131.07 E
Asola 64 45.13 N 10.24 E
Asolo 64 45.48 N 11.54 E
Asomante 240m 18.23 N 66.36 W
Ason 273a 6.34 N 3.31 E
Asosa 144 10.03 N 34.32 E
Aso-san ∧ 92 32.53 N 131.06 E
Asoteriba, Jabal ∧ 140 21.51 N 36.30 E
Asotin 202 46.20 N 117.02 W
Asouf, Oued ∨ 148 25.51 N 1.33 E
Asowsches Meer — Azovskoje more ⫪[2] 78 46.00 N 36.00 E
Asp 34 38.21 N 0.46 W
Aspach 60 48.11 N 13.18 E
Aspach-le-Bas 58 47.46 N 7.09 E
Aspang Markt 61 47.33 N 16.06 E
Aspara ≐ 85 43.17 N 73.28 E
Aspatria 44 54.46 N 3.20 W
Aspe, Gave d' ≐ 32 43.12 N 0.36 W
Aspen 200 39.11 N 106.49 W
Aspen Butte ∧ 202 42.19 N 122.05 W
Aspendale 274b 38.02 S 145.07 E
Aspendos ⊥ 130 37.00 N 31.10 E
Aspen Hill 284c 39.04 N 77.04 W
Aspen Knolls 284c 39.05 N 77.05 W
Aspen Lake ⊜ 202 42.18 N 122.00 W
Asperg 56 48.54 N 9.07 E
Aspermont 196 33.08 N 100.13 W
Aspern ◈[8] 264b 48.13 N 16.29 E
Aspers 208 39.59 N 77.13 W
Asperup 41 55.29 N 9.55 E
Aspid, Mount ∧ 180 53.30 N 167.33 W
Aspindza 84 41.36 N 43.15 E
Aspinwall 279b 40.29 N 79.54 W
Aspinwall — Colón 236 9.22 N 79.54 W
Aspiring, Mount ∧ 172 44.23 S 168.44 E
Aspö 40 59.29 N 17.02 E
Aspres-sur-Buëch 62 44.31 N 5.45 E
Aspromonte ⩓ 68 38.10 N 15.55 E
Asprópirgos 267c 38.04 N 23.35 E
Aspull 262 53.34 N 2.35 W
Aspy Bay ⊂ 186 46.55 N 60.25 W
Asquins 50 47.29 N 3.45 E
Asquith, Austl. 274a 33.41 S 151.06 E
Asquith, Sk., Can. 184 52.08 N 107.13 W
Asralt chajrchan ∧ 88 48.29 N 107.24 E
Asrāni 123 29.31 N 72.07 E
Assa, Kaz. 85 43.02 N 71.10 E
Assa, Magreb 148 28.34 N 9.27 W
Assa ≐, Kaz. 85 43.55 N 70.25 E
Assa ≐, Ross. 84 43.13 N 45.25 E
As-Sa'ata 140 13.37 N 29.59 E
Assab — Aseb 144 13.00 N 42.45 E
Assabet ≐ 283 42.28 N 71.21 W
As-Sabkhah 130 35.48 N 39.15 E
Aṣ-Ṣadārah 144 14.30 N 48.04 E
As-Sa'dīyah 128 34.11 N 45.07 E
Aṣ-Ṣaff 140 29.34 N 31.17 E
As-Saffānīyah 128 27.58 N 48.47 E
Aṣ-Ṣāfī 132 31.02 N 35.28 E
As-Safīrah 130 36.04 N 37.22 E
Aṣ-Ṣāfiyah 140 15.31 N 30.07 E
Assago 266b 45.24 N 9.08 E
Assaí 255 23.22 S 50.49 W
Aṣ-Ṣa'īd □[9] 140 26.00 N 32.00 E
Assaikwatamo ≐ 184 56.52 N 95.50 W
Assal, Lac ⊜ 144 11.41 N 42.25 E
'Assāl al-Ward 132 33.52 N 36.24 E
Aṣ-Ṣāliḥīyah 142 30.47 N 31.59 E
As-Salīmah 144 14.02 N 45.46 E
As-Sallūm 140 31.34 N 25.09 E
As-Salmān 128 30.30 N 44.32 E
As-Salṭ 132 32.03 N 35.44 E
Assam □[3] 120 26.00 N 93.00 E
As-Samāwah 128 31.18 N 45.17 E
As-Samū' 132 31.24 N 35.04 E
Assam Valley ∨ 124 26.30 N 90.30 E
'Assān 130 36.05 N 37.14 E
Aṣ-Ṣanāfīn Al-Qiblīyah 142 30.27 N 31.18 E
Aṣ-Ṣanamayn 132 33.05 N 36.10 E
As-Santah 142 30.45 N 31.08 E
Assaq, Oued ∨ 148 25.41 N 14.40 W
Aṣ-Ṣaqlabiyah 130 35.22 N 36.23 E
Aṣ-Ṣarafand 132 33.27 N 35.18 E
Assaré 250 6.52 S 39.52 W
Aṣ-Ṣarīḥ 132 32.30 N 35.54 E
As-Sarīrīyah 142 28.20 N 30.45 E
Assateague Island I 208 38.05 N 75.10 W
Assateague Island National Seashore ♦ 208 38.00 N 75.15 W
Assawoman Bay ⊂ 208 38.25 N 75.05 W
Assawoman Canal ≍ 208 38.31 N 75.04 W
Assawompset Pond ⊜ 207 41.50 N 70.55 W
Asse 50 50.55 N 4.12 E
Asse ≐ 62 43.53 N 5.53 E
Assean Lake ⊜ 184 56.13 N 96.30 W
Assebroek 50 51.12 N 3.16 E
Assekaifaf 148 27.08 N 8.50 E
Assel 52 53.41 N 9.25 E
Asseln ◈[8] 263 51.32 N 7.35 E
Assembleia Nacional, Palacio da ◈ 266c 38.43 N 9.09 W
Assemini 71 39.17 N 9.00 E
Assen 52 52.59 N 6.34 E
Assendelft 52 52.27 N 4.45 E
Assenede 50 51.14 N 3.45 E
Assens 41 55.16 N 9.55 E
Asserbo 41 56.01 N 12.01 E
Assergi 66 42.25 N 13.30 E
Asseria ⊥ 36 44.02 N 15.39 E
As-Sīb 128 23.41 N 58.11 E
As-Sidr 128 23.27 N 39.45 E
As-Sijn 132 32.47 N 36.28 E
As-Simākīyah 132 31.18 N 35.48 E
As-Sinbillāwayn 142 30.53 N 31.27 E
Assíni ⊥ 38 37.36 N 22.48 E
Assiniboia 184 49.38 N 105.59 W
Assiniboine ≐ 184 49.53 N 97.08 W
Assiniboine, Mount ∧ 182 50.52 N 115.39 W
Assiniboine Indian Reserve ◈[4] 184 50.21 N 103.28 W
Assinika ≐ 184 52.37 N 96.10 W
Assinippi 283 42.09 N 70.51 W
Assis 255 22.40 S 50.25 W
Assis Chataaubriand 252 24.29 S 53.32 W
Assiscunk Creek ≐ 208 40.05 N 74.51 W
Assisi 66 43.04 N 12.37 E
Asslar 56 50.35 N 8.28 E
Assling 60 48.00 N 12.00 E
Asso 62 45.52 N 9.16 E
Assodé ⫪[4] 150 18.26 N 8.28 E
Assomada 150a 15.06 N 23.41 W
Assonet 207 41.47 N 71.04 W
Assoro 70 37.37 N 14.25 E
As-Subū' ⊥ 140 22.45 N 32.34 E
As-Sūdān — Sudan □[1] 140 15.00 N 30.00 E
As-Sudd ◈[1] 140 8.00 N 31.00 E
As-Sufāl 144 14.06 N 48.42 E
Aṣ-Ṣufayyah 140 15.30 N 34.42 E
Aṣ-Ṣūfīyah 142 30.55 N 31.46 E
As-Sukhnah, Sūrīy. 130 34.52 N 38.52 E
As-Sukhnah, Urd. 132 32.08 N 36.04 E
As-Sulaymānīyah, Ar. Su. 128 24.09 N 47.19 E
As-Sulaymānīyah, 'Irāq 128 35.33 N 45.26 E
As-Sulaymānīyah □[4] 128 35.30 N 45.25 E
As-Sulaymī 128 26.17 N 41.21 E
As-Sulayyil 144 20.27 N 45.34 E
As-Sulṭān 146 31.07 N 17.10 E
As-Sumayḥ 140 9.49 N 27.39 E
Aṣ-Ṣummān ◈[1] 128 25.00 N 47.00 E
As-Summāqīyāt 132 32.26 N 36.24 E
Assumption, Il., U.S. 219 39.31 N 89.02 W
Assumption, Oh., U.S. 216 41.40 N 83.54 W
Assumption Island I 138 9.45 S 46.30 E
Assunpink Creek ≐ 285 40.13 N 74.46 W
As-Su'ūdīyah 142 29.33 N 31.14 E
Aṣ-Ṣuwār 130 35.30 N 40.39 E
As-Suwaydā' 132 32.42 N 36.34 E
As-Suwaydā' □[8] 132 32.45 N 36.45 E
As-Suways (Suez) 142 29.58 N 32.33 E
As-Suways □[4] 142 30.12 N 32.30 E
Assynt, Loch ⊜ 46 58.11 N 5.06 W
Ašt 85 40.41 N 70.20 E
Asta, Cima d' ∧ 64 46.10 N 11.36 E
Astachovo 83 47.52 N 39.37 E
Astaffort 32 44.04 N 0.40 E
Astakós 38 38.32 N 21.05 E
Āstāneh, Īrān 128 37.17 N 49.59 E
Āstāneh, Īrān 128 33.53 N 49.22 E
Astara, Azer. 84 38.28 N 48.52 E
Āstārā, Īrān 128 38.26 N 48.52 E
Aštarak 84 40.18 N 44.22 E
Astaškovo 82 55.32 N 38.38 E
Astatula 220 28.43 N 81.44 W
Asten, Ned. 52 51.24 N 5.45 E
Asten, Öst. 61 48.13 N 14.25 E
Asti 62 44.54 N 8.12 E
Asti □[4] 62 44.55 N 8.10 E
Astica 252 30.56 S 67.23 W
Astico ≐ 64 45.37 N 11.37 E
Astillero 34 43.24 N 3.49 W
Astipálaia 38 36.30 N 26.30 E
Astipálaia I 38 36.35 N 26.25 E
Astley Bridge 262 53.36 N 2.26 W
Astley Green 262 53.29 N 2.27 W
Astley Hall ⊥ 262 53.39 N 2.38 W
Astola Island I 128 25.07 N 63.51 E
Astolfo Dutra 256 21.19 S 42.52 W
Aston, Eng., U.K. 262 53.18 N 2.40 W
Aston, Pa., U.S. 285 39.52 N 75.26 W
Aston Clinton 42 51.48 N 0.44 W
Aston-on-Trent 42 52.52 N 1.23 W
Astor 123 35.22 N 74.51 E
Astor ≐ 123 35.34 N 74.41 E
Astorga, Bra. 255 23.13 S 51.40 W
Astorga, Esp. 34 42.27 N 6.03 W

ENGLISH

Name Page Lat.°' Long.°'
Astorga, Pil. 116 6.54 N 125.27 E
Astoria, Il., U.S. 219 40.13 N 90.21 W
Astoria, Or., U.S. 224 46.11 N 123.49 W
Astoria ◈[8] 276 40.46 N 73.55 W
Astoria Bridge ◈[5] 224 46.13 N 123.52 W
Astoria Column ⊥ 224 46.11 N 123.50 W
Åstorp 41 56.08 N 12.57 E
Astove Island I 138 10.06 S 47.45 E
Astra 254 45.44 S 67.30 W
Astrachan' 80 46.21 N 48.03 E
Astrachanka 86 51.33 N 69.47 E
Astrachanskij 80 46.12 N 47.16 E
Astrachanskij zapovednik ◈[4] 80 46.00 N 48.32 E
Astrakhan — Astrachan' 80 46.21 N 48.03 E
Astrodome ♦ 222 29.41 N 95.25 W
Astrolabe, Cape ➤ 175e 8.20 S 160.34 E
Astrolabe Bay ⊂ 164 5.20 S 145.50 E
Astrolabe Reefs ✣[2] 175f 19.48 S 165.37 E
Astudillo 34 42.12 N 4.18 W
Astura, Torre ⊥ 66 41.24 N 12.46 E
Asturias 116 10.34 N 123.43 E
Asturias □[4], Esp. 34 43.20 N 6.00 W
Asturias □[4], Esp. 34 43.20 N 6.00 W
Astwood Bank 42 52.15 N 1.56 W
Asubulak 86 49.31 N 83.03 E
Asuisui, Cape ➤ 175a 13.47 S 172.29 W
Asuka 96 34.28 N 135.50 E
Asuka ◈[3] 9 71.32 S 24.08 E
Asuke 94 35.08 N 137.19 E
Asunción 252 25.16 S 57.40 W
Asunción, Bahía ⊂ 232 27.06 N 114.11 W
Asuncion Island I 108 19.40 N 145.24 E
Asunción Ixtaltepec 234 16.30 N 95.03 W
Asunción Mita 236 14.20 N 89.43 W
Asunción Nochixtlán 234 17.28 N 97.14 W
Åsunden ⊜, Sve. 26 57.58 N 15.50 E
Åsunden ⊜, Sve. 26 57.44 N 13.22 E
Asunga, Wādī ∨ 146 13.21 N 22.17 E
Asuni 71 39.52 N 8.56 E
'Āṣūr, Tall ∧ 132 31.59 N 35.17 E
Asuwa 94 36.01 N 136.16 E
Asuwa ≐ 94 36.04 N 136.11 E
Aswad, Ar-Ra's al- ➤ 144 21.22 N 39.08 E
Aswān 140 24.05 N 32.53 E
Aswān High Dam — 'Ālī, As-Sadd al- ◈[6] 140 23.58 N 32.52 E
Aswatthaberia 272b 22.26 N 88.32 E
Asy ≐ 85 43.31 N 78.20 E
Asyūṭ 142 27.11 N 31.11 E
Asyūṭ □[4] 142 27.20 N 30.50 E
Asyūṭī, Wādī al- ∨ 142 27.11 N 31.16 E
Aszód 30 47.39 N 19.31 E
'Ata I, Tonga 14 22.20 S 176.12 W
Ata I, Tonga 174w 21.03 S 175.00 W
Atabaj 85 43.30 N 68.20 E
Atabapo ≐ 246 4.03 N 67.42 W
Atabasca, Lago — Athabasca, Lake ⊜ 176 59.07 N 110.00 W
Atabasca — Athabasca ≐ 176 58.40 N 110.50 W
Atabey 130 37.57 N 30.39 E
Atacama □[4] 252 27.30 S 70.00 W
Atacama, Desierto de ◈[2] 18 24.30 S 69.15 W
Atacama, Puna de ⩓[1] 252 24.30 S 67.30 W
Atacama, Salar de ≚ 252 23.30 S 68.15 W
Ataco 246 3.35 N 75.23 W
Atacora, Chaîne de l' ⩓ 150 10.45 N 1.30 E
Atacuari ≐ 246 3.47 S 70.44 W
Atafu I[1] 14 8.33 S 172.30 W
Atagaj 88 55.06 N 99.23 E
Atago-yama ∧, Nihon 94 35.07 N 139.59 E
Atago-yama ∧, Nihon 96 35.03 N 135.37 E
Ātāi ≐[1] 126 22.51 N 89.33 E
'Aṭā'iṭah, Jabal al- ∧ 132 30.40 N 35.39 E
Atakakup Indian Reserve ◈[4] 184 53.24 N 106.55 W
Atakano-seki ⊥ 94 36.24 N 136.25 E
Ataki 78 48.25 N 27.47 E
Atakora □[5] 150 10.00 N 1.35 E
Atakora, Réserve d' ◈[4] 150 11.30 N 2.10 E
Atakpamé 150 7.32 N 1.08 E
Atalaia, Bra. 250 9.31 S 36.02 W
Atalaia, Port. 266c 38.42 N 8.55 W
Atalándi 38 38.39 N 23.00 E
Atalanka 88 54.50 N 103.05 E
Atalaya, Arg. 258 35.02 S 57.32 W
Atalaya, Pan. 236 8.03 N 80.56 W
Atalaya, Perú 248 10.44 S 73.45 W
Atalaya, Cerro ∧, Chile 254 52.45 S 72.42 W
Atalaya, Cerro ∧, Perú 248 12.38 S 71.56 W
Atalaya, Punta ➤ 258 35.01 S 57.31 W
Atamanovka 88 51.56 N 113.37 E
Atamanovo 86 56.24 N 93.36 E
Atambua 112 9.07 S 124.54 E
Atami 94 35.05 N 139.04 E
Atapupu 112 9.00 S 124.51 E
'Atāq 144 14.33 N 46.48 E
'Atāqah, Jabal ⩓ 142 29.58 N 32.20 E
Atâr 150 20.31 N 13.03 W
Ataram, 'Erg n- ◈[2] 148 23.46 N 1.44 E
Atarés, Castillo de ⊥ 286b 23.08 N 82.21 W
Atāri 123 31.36 N 74.35 E
Atary 80 57.32 N 49.18 E
Atascadero 226 35.29 N 120.40 W
Atascosa ≐ 196 28.26 N 98.12 W
At'aševo 80 54.36 N 46.06 E
Atasu 86 48.42 N 71.38 E
Atas uul ∧ 102 43.18 N 96.36 E
Atata I 174w 21.03 S 175.15 W
Atatürk Barajı ⊜[1] 130 37.30 N 38.30 E
Ataturk Tower ⊥ 267b 41.00 N 28.59 E
Ataur 272a 28.43 N 77.24 E
Atauro, Pulau I 112 8.13 S 125.35 E
Atbara ('Aṭbarah) ≐ 140 17.40 N 33.56 E
'Aṭbarah 140 17.42 N 33.59 E
'Aṭbarah (Atbara) ≐ 140 17.40 N 33.56 E
Atbasar 86 51.48 N 68.20 E
At-Baši 85 41.10 N 75.48 E
Atbaši ≐ 85 41.24 N 75.38 E
Atbaši, chrebet ⩓ 85 40.55 N 75.40 E
Atchafalaya ≐ 194 29.53 N 91.28 W
Atchafalaya Bay ⊂ 194 29.25 N 91.20 W
Atchison 198 39.33 N 95.07 W
Atco 208 39.46 N 74.53 W
Ate 286d 12.03 S 76.58 W
Atebubu 150 7.45 N 0.59 W
Ateca 34 41.20 N 1.47 W
Atelchu ≐ 255 12.05 S 53.46 W
Ateleta 66 41.51 N 14.12 E
Ateli 124 28.06 N 76.17 E
Atella 68 40.52 N 15.39 E
Atemajac de Brizuela 234 20.11 N 103.42 W
Atemar 80 54.11 N 45.24 E
Atemble 164 5.05 S 144.45 E
Atena Lucana 68 40.27 N 15.33 E
Atenango del Río 234 18.05 N 99.06 W
Atenas — Athínai 38 37.58 N 23.43 E
Atencingo 234 18.30 N 98.36 W
Atengo ≐ 234 21.50 N 104.43 W
Atenguillo 234 20.25 N 104.31 W
Atenguillo ≐ 234 20.55 N 104.38 W
Atenquique 234 19.31 N 103.30 W
Atepcevo 82 55.20 N 36.46 E
Aterno ≐ 66 42.11 N 13.51 E
Aterrado, Ribeirão do ≐ 256 22.09 S 45.03 W
Atessa 66 42.04 N 14.27 E
Aṭfīḥ 142 29.24 N 31.15 E
Aṭfīḥī, Wādī al- ∨ 142 29.23 N 31.16 E
Ātgharia 126 24.06 N 89.14 E
Atglen 208 39.57 N 75.58 W
Ath 50 50.38 N 3.47 E
Athabasca 182 54.43 N 113.17 W

DEUTSCH

Name Seite Breite°' Länge°' E = Ost
Athabasca ≐ 176 58.40 N 110.50 W
Athabasca, Lake ⊜ 176 59.07 N 110.00 W
Athalmer 182 50.32 N 116.02 W
Athapapuskow Lake ⊜ 184 54.33 N 101.40 W
Athārabānki ≐[1] 126 22.49 N 89.39 E
Athārān Hazāri 123 31.11 N 72.06 E
Athboy 48 53.37 N 6.55 W
Athea 48 52.28 N 9.17 W
Athena 202 45.48 N 118.29 W
Athen — Athínai 38 37.58 N 23.43 E
Athènes — Athínai 38 37.58 N 23.43 E
Athenry 48 53.18 N 8.45 W
Athens, On., Can. 212 44.38 N 75.57 W
Athens, Al., U.S. 194 34.48 N 86.58 W
Athens, Ga., U.S. 192 33.57 N 83.22 W
Athens, Il., U.S. 219 39.57 N 89.43 W
Athens, La., U.S. 194 32.39 N 93.01 W
Athens, Mi., U.S. 216 42.05 N 85.14 W
Athens, N.Y., U.S. 210 42.15 N 73.48 W
Athens, Oh., U.S. 188 39.19 N 82.06 W
Athens, Pa., U.S. 210 41.57 N 76.31 W
Athens, Tn., U.S. 192 35.26 N 84.35 W
Athens, Tx., U.S. 222 32.12 N 95.51 W
Athens, W.V., U.S. 192 37.25 N 81.00 W
Athens, Wi., U.S. 190 45.01 N 90.04 W
Athens — Athínai 38 37.58 N 23.43 E
Athenstedt 54 51.56 N 10.55 E
Athens University ◈[2] 267c 37.59 N 23.44 E
Atherley 212 44.36 N 79.22 W
Atherstone 42 52.35 N 1.31 W
Atherton, Austl. 166 17.16 S 145.29 E
Atherton, Eng., U.K. 262 53.31 N 2.31 W
Atherton, Ca., U.S. 226 37.27 N 122.11 W
Athi ≐ 154 2.59 S 38.31 E
Athiaínou 130 35.04 N 33.32 E
Athiémé 150 6.35 N 1.40 E
Athies-sous-Laon 50 49.34 N 3.41 E
Athínai (Athens), Ellás 38 37.58 N 23.43 E
Athínai (Athens), Ellás 267c 37.58 N 23.43 E
Äthiopien — Ethiopia □[1] 144 9.00 N 39.00 E
Athi River 154 1.27 S 36.59 E
Athis-Mons 261 48.43 N 2.24 E
Athlat al-Bāshā ∧[2] 142 27.31 N 32.20 E
Athleague 48 53.34 N 8.15 W
Athlone 48 53.25 N 7.56 W
Athni 122 16.44 N 75.04 E
Athok 110 17.12 N 95.05 E
Athol, N.Z. 172 45.31 S 168.35 E
Athol, Ma., U.S. 207 42.35 N 72.13 W
Athol Bay ⊂ 212 43.53 N 77.15 W
Athol Island I 240b 25.05 N 77.16 W
Atholl, Forest of ◈[3] 46 56.50 N 4.00 W
Athol Springs 210 42.46 N 78.52 W
Áthos ∧ 38 40.09 N 24.19 E
Ath-Tha'lah 132 32.42 N 36.26 E
Ath-Thamad 140 29.41 N 34.18 E
Ath-Thanīyah 132 31.10 N 35.43 E
Athus 56 49.34 N 5.50 E
Athy 48 53.00 N 7.00 W
Ati 146 13.13 N 18.20 E
Atiak 154 3.15 N 32.07 E
Atibaia 256 23.07 S 46.33 W
Atibainha ≐ 256 22.42 S 47.17 W
Atibainha, Reservatório ⊜[1] 256 23.10 S 46.20 W
Atico 248 16.14 S 73.39 W
Aticonipi, Lac ⊜ 186 51.52 N 59.22 W
Atienza 34 41.12 N 2.52 W
Atigun Pass)(180 68.08 N 149.29 W
Atik Lake ⊜ 184 55.16 N 96.00 W
Atikokan 190 48.45 N 91.37 W
Atikonak Lake ⊜ 176 52.40 N 64.30 W
Atil 200 30.50 N 111.35 W
Atimari ≐ 248 9.04 S 67.23 W
Atimonan 116 14.00 N 121.55 E
Atina 66 41.37 N 13.48 E
Atiparaná ≐[1] 246 1.51 S 65.37 W
Atiquizaya 236 13.58 N 89.46 W
Atirāmpattinam 122 10.21 N 79.24 E
Atitlán, Lago de ⊜ 236 14.42 N 91.12 W
Atitlán, Volcán ∧[1] 236 14.35 N 91.11 W
Atiu I 14 20.02 S 158.07 W
Atka, Ross. 74 60.50 N 151.48 E
Atka, Ak., U.S. 180 52.12 N 174.12 W
Atka Island I 180 52.15 N 174.30 W
Atkaracalar 130 40.50 N 33.04 E
Atkarsk 80 51.52 N 45.00 E
Atkins 194 35.14 N 92.56 W
Atkinson, Il., U.S. 190 41.25 N 90.00 W
Atkinson, Ne., U.S. 198 42.31 N 98.58 W
Atkinson, N.H., U.S. 207 42.50 N 71.08 W
Atkinson, N.C., U.S. 192 34.31 N 78.10 W
Atkinson Island I 222 29.40 N 94.58 W
Atkinson Lake ⊜ 184 55.59 N 94.48 W
Atkri 164 1.44 S 130.04 E
Atlacomulco 234 19.48 N 99.53 W
Atlanta, Ga., U.S. 192 33.44 N 84.23 W
Atlanta, Il., U.S. 194 40.15 N 89.14 W
Atlanta, Mi., U.S. 190 45.00 N 84.08 W
Atlanta, Mo., U.S. 194 39.53 N 92.28 W
Atlanta, N.Y., U.S. 210 42.33 N 77.28 W
Atlanta, Oh., U.S. 218 39.34 N 83.11 W
Atlanta, Tx., U.S. 194 33.06 N 94.09 W
Atlantic, Ia., U.S. 198 41.24 N 95.00 W
Atlantic, N.C., U.S. 192 34.53 N 76.20 W
Atlantic, Pa., U.S. 214 41.30 N 80.21 W
Atlantic, Va., U.S. 208 37.54 N 75.30 W
Atlantic □[6] 208 39.27 N 74.44 W
Atlantic Beach, Fl., U.S. 192 30.20 N 81.23 W
Atlantic Beach, N.Y., U.S. 276 40.35 N 73.44 W
Atlantic City 208 39.21 N 74.25 W
Atlantic Highlands 208 40.24 N 74.02 W
Atlantic-Indian Basin ✣[1] 6 60.00 S 15.00 E
Atlantic-Indian Ridge ✣[3] 4 53.00 S 15.00 E
Atlántico □[5] 246 10.45 N 75.00 W
Atlántico, Océano — Atlantic Ocean ⫪[1] 8 5.00 S 25.00 W
Atlantic Ocean ⫪[1] 4 5.00 S 25.00 W
Atlantic Ocean ⫪[1] 8 5.00 S 25.00 W
Atlantic Peak ∧ 200 42.37 N 109.00 W
Atlántida 252 34.46 S 55.45 W
Atlántida □[5] 236 15.40 N 87.00 W
Atlantique 276 40.39 N 73.10 W
Atlantique □[5] 150 6.35 N 2.15 E
Atlantique, Océan — Atlantic Ocean ⫪[1] 8 5.00 S 25.00 W
Atlantischer Ozean — Atlantic Ocean ⫪[1] 8 5.00 S 25.00 W
Atlas, Mi., U.S. 216 42.56 N 83.32 W
Atlas, Pa., U.S. 208 40.48 N 76.26 W
Atlasburg 214 40.20 N 80.23 W
Atlas Mountains ⩓ 148 33.00 N 2.00 W
Atlasova, ostrov I 74 50.53 N 155.27 E
Atlasovo 92a 46.01 N 142.09 E
Atlas Saharien ⩓ 148 33.25 N 1.20 E
Atlas Tellien ⩓ 148 36.00 N 3.00 E
Atlin 180 59.35 N 133.42 W
Atlin Lake ⊜ 180 59.20 N 133.45 W
'Atlit 132 32.41 N 34.56 E
Atlixco 234 18.54 N 98.26 W
Ātmakūr 122 15.53 N 78.35 E
Atmanov Ugol 80 53.07 N 41.23 E
Atmis 80 53.28 N 43.57 E
Atmore 194 31.01 N 87.29 W
Atna ≐ 26 61.44 N 10.49 E
Ätna — Etna, Monte ∧[1] 70 37.46 N 15.00 E
Atna Peak ∧ 182 53.57 N 128.03 W
Atnarko ≐ 182 52.22 N 126.04 W
Atnis 86 58.48 N 69.38 E
Atnosen 26 61.44 N 10.49 E

Symbols in the index entries represent the broad categories identified in the key at the right. Symbols with superior numbers (⩓[1]) identify subcategories (see complete key on page *I · 1).*

Symbole im Register stellen die rechts im Schlüssel erklärten Kategorien dar. Symbole mit hochgestellten Ziffern (⩓[1]) bezeichnen Unterabteilungen einer Kategorie (vgl. vollständiger Schlüssel auf Seite *I · 1).*

Los símbolos incluídos en el texto del índice representan las grandes categorías identificadas con la clave a la derecha. Los símbolos con numeros en su parte superior (⩓[1]) identifican las subcategorías (véase la clave completa en la página *I · 1).*

Les symboles de l'index représentent les catégories indiquées dans la légende à droite. Les symboles suivis d'un indice (⩓[1]) représentent des sous-catégories (voir légende complète à la page *I · 1).*

Os símbolos incluídos no texto do índice representam as grandes categorias identificadas com a chave à direita. Os símbolos com números em sua parte superior (⩓[1]) identificam as subcategorias (veja-se a chave completa à página *I · 1).*

∧	Mountain	Berg	Montaña	Montagne	Montanha
⩓	Mountains	Gebirge	Montañas	Montagnes	Montanhas
)(	Pass	Paß	Paso	Col	Passo
∨	Valley, Canyon	Tal, Cañon	Valle, Cañón	Vallée, Canyon	Vale, Canhão
≚	Plain	Ebene	Llano	Plaine	Planície
➤	Cape	Kap	Cabo	Cap	Cabo
I	Island	Insel	Isla	Île	Ilha
II	Islands	Inseln	Islas	Îles	Ilhas
⊥	Other Topographic Features	Andere Topographische Objekte	Otros Elementos Topográficos	Autres données topographiques	Outros acidentes topográficos

ESPAÑOL

Nombre	Página	Lat.°′	Long.°′ W = Oeste
Atō	96	34.24 N	131.43 E
Atocha	248	20.56 S	66.14 W
Atocha, Estación de ◆[5]	266a	40.24 N	3.41 W
Atocongo	286d	12.08 S	76.56 W
Atocongo ⊥	286d	12.12 S	76.55 W
Atoka	196	34.23 N	96.07 W
Atotonilco	232	24.15 N	102.45 W
Atotonilco, Cerro ∧	196	26.08 N	104.43 W
Atotonilco, Lago ⊜	234	20.22 N	103.39 W
Atotonilco de Tula	234	20.00 N	99.13 W
Atotonilco El Alto	234	20.33 N	102.31 W
Atoui, Khaṭṭ ∨	150	20.04 N	15.59 W
Atoyac	234	20.01 N	103.32 W
Atoyac ≃, Méx.	234	17.05 N	100.29 W
Atoyac ≃, Méx.	234	19.02 N	96.08 W
Atoyac ≃, Méx.	234	18.10 N	98.31 W
Atoyac ≃, Méx.	234	16.30 N	97.31 W
Atoyac de Álvarez	234	17.12 N	100.26 W
Atoyaquillo ≃	234	16.37 N	97.41 W
Atpur	272b	22.50 N	88.23 E
Atrå	26	59.59 N	8.45 E
ʿAṭrah, Jabal ∧	132	29.40 N	35.34 E
Atrai ≃	124	24.29 N	89.03 E
Atrak (Atrek) ≃	128	37.28 N	53.57 E
Ätran ≃	26	56.53 N	12.30 E
Atrato ≃	246	8.17 N	76.58 W
Atrauli	124	28.02 N	78.17 E
Atrek (Atrak) ≃	128	37.28 N	53.57 E
Atri	66	42.35 N	13.58 E
Atripalda	68	40.55 N	14.50 E
Atrisco	200	34.59 N	106.41 W
Atrop ◆[8]	263	51.24 N	6.43 E
Atsion Lake ⊜	285	39.44 N	74.44 W
Atsugi	94	35.27 N	139.22 E
Atsugi-hikōjō ■	94	35.28 N	139.27 E
Atsumi, Nihon	92	38.37 N	139.35 E
Atsumi, Nihon	94	34.37 N	137.07 E
Atsumi-hantō ≻[1]	94	34.39 N	137.15 E
Atta	272a	28.34 N	77.20 E
At-Tabbīn	142	29.47 N	31.18 E
Aṭ-Ṭafīlah	132	30.50 N	35.36 E
Aṭ-Ṭafīlah ▫[8]	132	30.45 N	35.45 E
At-Taḥrīr ▫[4]	142	30.40 N	30.15 E
Aṭ-Ṭā'if	144	21.16 N	40.24 E
Attainville	261	49.03 N	2.21 E
At-Tāj	146	24.13 N	23.18 E
Aṭ-Ṭalibīyah	273c	30.00 N	31.11 E
At-Tall	132	33.36 N	36.18 E
Attalla	194	34.01 N	86.05 W
At-Tall al-Kabīr	142	30.34 N	31.47 E
At-Ta'mīm ▫[4]	128	35.25 N	44.20 E
At-Tamīmī	146	32.20 N	23.04 E
Attapu	110	14.48 N	106.50 E
Attar, Oued el ∨	148	33.27 N	5.26 E
At-Taṭālīyah	142	27.20 N	30.50 E
Attáviros ∧	38	36.12 N	27.52 E
Attawapiskat	176	52.55 N	82.26 W
Attawapiskat ≃	176	52.57 N	82.18 W
Attawapiskat Lake ⊜	176	52.18 N	87.54 W
Attawaugan	207	41.52 N	71.52 W
At-Ṭawd	142	30.47 N	30.37 E
At-Ṭawīl ⋏	128	29.20 N	39.35 E
At-Ṭayrīyah	142	30.39 N	30.46 E
At-Taysīyah ≚	128	28.00 N	44.00 E
Aṭ-Ṭayyibah, Miṣr	142	28.16 N	30.39 E
Aṭ-Ṭayyibah, Sūrīy.	132	32.33 N	36.14 E
Aṭ-Ṭayyibah, Sūrīy.	132	32.48 N	36.46 E
Aṭ-Ṭayyibah, Urd.	132	32.33 N	35.43 E
Attel ≃	64	48.01 N	12.11 E
Attendorn	56	51.07 N	7.54 E
Attenhausen	58	47.59 N	10.20 E
Attenkirchen	60	48.30 N	11.46 E
Atterbury	219	40.04 N	89.55 W
Attersee	64	47.55 N	13.33 E
Attersee ⊜	64	47.52 N	13.33 E
Attert ≃	56	49.52 N	6.05 E
Attica, In., U.S.	216	40.17 N	87.14 W
Attica, Ks., U.S.	198	37.14 N	98.13 W
Attica, N.Y., U.S.	210	42.51 N	78.16 W
Attica, Oh., U.S.	214	41.03 N	82.53 W
Attichy	50	49.25 N	3.03 E
Attigliano	66	42.31 N	12.17 E
Attigny	56	49.29 N	4.35 E
Attikí ▫[5]	267c	38.00 N	23.40 E
Attikí ▫[9]	38	38.00 N	23.30 E
ʿAttīl	132	32.22 N	35.04 E
Attimis	64	46.11 N	13.16 E
At-Tīnah	142	31.03 N	32.18 E
Attingal	122	8.41 N	76.50 E
Attir	140	6.04 N	30.50 E
Attleboro	207	41.56 N	71.17 W
Attleborough	42	52.31 N	1.01 E
Attnang	60	48.01 N	13.43 E
Attock	123	33.54 N	72.15 E
Attoyac ≃	194	31.29 N	94.18 W
Attu	181a	52.56 N	173.14 E
At-Tubah	144	12.40 N	43.30 E
Attu Island I	181a	52.55 N	173.00 E
Aṭ-Ṭunayb	132	31.48 N	35.57 E
Āttūr, India	122	11.36 N	78.37 E
Aṭ-Ṭūr, Miṣr	140	28.14 N	33.37 E
Aṭ-Ṭuwayshah	140	12.21 N	26.32 E
Aṭ-Ṭuwayyah	128	27.36 N	41.13 E
Attymon	48	53.19 N	8.35 W
Atucatiquini ≃	248	7.44 S	67.57 W
Atucha	258	33.58 S	59.18 W
Atuel ≃	252	36.17 S	66.50 W
Atuel, Bañados del ≡	252	36.30 S	66.55 W
Atuntaqui	246	0.20 N	78.13 W
Atuona	174x	9.48 S	139.02 W
At'urjevo	80	54.21 N	43.19 E
Atushi	85	39.43 N	76.08 E
Åtvidaberg	26	58.12 N	16.00 E
Atwater, Sk., Can.	184	50.47 N	102.10 W
Atwater, Ca., U.S.	226	37.20 N	120.36 W
Atwater, Il., U.S.	219	39.20 N	89.44 W
Atwater, Mn., U.S.	198	45.08 N	94.46 W
Atwater, Oh., U.S.	214	41.01 N	81.10 W
Atwood, On., Can.	212	43.40 N	81.01 W
Atwood, Ca., U.S.	280	33.52 N	117.50 W
Atwood, Il., U.S.	194	39.48 N	88.28 W
Atwood, In., U.S.	216	41.15 N	85.58 W
Atwood, Ks., U.S.	198	39.48 N	101.02 W
Atwood, Tn., U.S.	194	35.58 N	88.40 W
Atwood Lake ⊜[1]	214	40.33 N	81.13 W
Atzalpur	272a	28.43 N	77.21 E
Atzendorf	54	51.55 N	11.35 E
Atzgersdorf ◆[8]	264b	48.09 N	16.18 E
Au	58	47.19 N	9.59 E
Auagrām	126	23.31 N	87.41 E
Auaiá-Miçu ≃	250	10.51 S	53.08 W
Aua Island I	164	1.27 S	143.04 E
Aual Edo	144	4.14 N	40.37 E
Auari ≃	246	3.33 N	63.48 W
Auau Channel ɰ	229a	20.51 N	156.45 W
Aub	56	49.33 N	10.04 E
Aubá	112	9.02 S	125.22 E
Aubagne	62	43.17 N	5.34 E
Aubange	56	49.35 N	5.48 E
Aube ▫[5]	50	48.15 N	4.05 E
Aube ≃	50	48.34 N	3.43 E
Aubenas	62	44.37 N	4.23 E
Aubenton	50	49.50 N	4.12 E
Aubepierre	261	48.38 N	2.53 E
Aubergenville	261	48.58 N	1.51 E
Auberive	58	47.47 N	5.03 E
Auberry	226	37.04 N	119.29 W
Aubervilliers	50	48.55 N	2.23 E
Aubetin ≃	50	48.49 N	3.01 E
Aubette ≃	261	49.00 N	1.54 E
Aubigny-en-Artois	50	50.21 N	2.35 E
Aubigny-sur-Nère	50	47.29 N	2.26 E
Aubin	32	44.32 N	2.14 E
Aubinadong ≃	190	46.51 N	83.22 W
Aubonne	58	46.28 N	6.24 E
Auboué	56	49.13 N	5.59 E
Aubrac ⋏	32	44.40 N	3.00 E
Aubrey Cliffs ⫠[4]	200	35.45 N	113.00 W
Aubrey Lake ⊜[1]	190	46.54 N	83.11 W
Aubrives	56	50.06 N	4.46 E
Aubry Lake ⊜	180	67.23 N	126.30 W
Auburn, Austl.	168b	34.01 S	138.41 E

FRANÇAIS

Nom	Page	Lat.°′	Long.°′ W = Ouest
Auburn, Austl.	274a	33.51 S	151.02 E
Auburn, Al., U.S.	194	32.36 N	85.28 W
Auburn, Ca., U.S.	226	38.53 N	121.04 W
Auburn, Il., U.S.	219	39.35 N	89.44 W
Auburn, In., U.S.	216	41.22 N	85.03 W
Auburn, Ky., U.S.	194	37.02 N	86.54 W
Auburn, Me., U.S.	188	44.05 N	70.13 W
Auburn, Ma., U.S.	207	42.11 N	71.50 W
Auburn, Mi., U.S.	190	43.36 N	84.04 W
Auburn, Ne., U.S.	198	40.23 N	95.50 W
Auburn, N.J., U.S.	285	39.42 N	75.22 W
Auburn, N.Y., U.S.	210	42.55 N	76.33 W
Auburn, Pa., U.S.	208	40.35 N	76.05 W
Auburn, Wa., U.S.	224	47.18 N	122.13 W
Auburn ≃	166	25.38 S	151.12 E
Auburndale, Fl., U.S.	220	28.03 N	81.47 W
Auburndale, Ma., U.S.	283	42.21 N	71.22 W
Auburn Heights	216	42.38 N	83.13 W
Auburn Range ⋏	166	25.10 S	150.30 E
Auburn Ravine ∨	226	38.51 N	121.31 W
Auburn Southeast	210	42.54 N	76.32 W
Aubusson	32	45.57 N	2.11 E
Auby-sur-Semois	56	49.49 N	5.10 E
Auca Mahuida	252	37.53 S	68.31 W
Auca Mahuida, Cerro ∧	252	37.45 S	68.56 W
Aucará	248	14.15 S	74.05 W
Auce	76	56.28 N	22.53 E
Auch	32	43.39 N	0.35 E
Auchel	50	50.30 N	2.28 E
Auchenblae	46	56.54 N	2.26 W
Auchencairn	44	54.51 N	3.53 W
Auchi	150	7.02 N	6.14 E
Auchinleck	44	55.28 N	4.17 W
Auchterarder	46	56.18 N	3.43 W
Auchterderran	46	56.09 N	3.16 W
Auchtermuchty	46	56.17 N	3.15 W
Aucilla ≃	192	30.05 N	83.59 W
Auckland	172	36.52 S	174.46 E
Auckland Islands II	9	50.40 S	166.30 E
Auckland Park ◆[8]	273d	26.11 S	28.00 E
Auckland Park Race Course ✦	273d	26.11 S	28.00 E
Aude ▫[5]	32	43.05 N	2.30 E
Aude ≃	32	43.13 N	3.14 E
Audenge	32	44.41 N	1.00 W
Audenshaw	262	53.28 N	2.08 W
Audenshaw Reservoirs ⊜[1]	262	53.28 N	2.08 W
Auderghem	50	50.49 N	4.26 E
Audeux	58	47.16 N	5.53 E
Audierne	32	48.01 N	4.32 W
Audincourt	58	47.29 N	6.50 E
Audley	44	53.03 N	2.18 W
Audobon Park	285	39.54 N	75.05 W
Audo Range ⋏	144	6.30 N	41.30 E
Audrain ▫[6]	219	39.12 N	91.50 W
Audresselles	50	50.49 N	1.36 E
Audruicq	50	50.53 N	2.05 E
Audubon, Ia., U.S.	198	41.43 N	94.55 W
Audubon, N.J., U.S.	208	39.53 N	75.04 W
Audubon, Pa., U.S.	285	40.07 N	75.27 W
Audubon Lake ⊜[1]	198	47.35 N	101.10 W
Audubon Park	218	38.12 N	85.43 W
Audun-le-Roman	56	49.22 N	5.53 E
Aue	54	50.35 N	12.42 E
Aue ≃	52	53.05 N	8.04 E
Auerbach, Dtsch.	54	50.41 N	12.54 E
Auerbach, Dtsch.	54	50.30 N	12.23 E
Auerbach, Dtsch.	60	48.48 N	13.06 E
Auerbach in der Oberpfalz	60	49.42 N	11.38 E
Auer → Ora	64	46.21 N	11.18 E
Auersberg ∧	54	50.27 N	12.39 E
Auerswalde	54	50.54 N	12.55 E
Auezov	86	49.46 N	81.38 E
Auf dem Kreinberge	263	51.27 N	7.36 E
Auffargis	261	48.42 N	1.53 E
Auffay	50	49.43 N	1.06 E
Aufsess	60	49.54 N	11.13 E
Augarten ✦	264b	48.14 N	16.23 E
Augathella	166	25.48 S	146.35 E
Augher	48	54.26 N	7.09 W
Aughnacloy	48	54.25 N	6.58 W
Aughrim	48	52.51 N	6.17 W
Aughton, Eng., U.K.	44	53.22 N	1.18 W
Aughton, Eng., U.K.	262	53.32 N	2.56 W
Aughton Park	262	53.33 N	2.53 W
Aughwick Creek ≃	214	40.22 N	77.50 W
Auglaize ▫[6]	216	40.34 N	84.12 W
Auglaize ≃	216	41.17 N	84.21 W
Augrabies	158	28.37 S	20.20 E
Augrabies Falls National Park ✦	158	28.35 S	20.19 E
Augrabiesvalle ∟	158	28.35 S	20.19 E
Au Gres	190	44.02 N	83.41 W
Au Gres ≃	190	44.02 N	83.40 W
Au Gres, East Branch ≃	190	44.05 N	83.41 W
Augsburg	58	48.23 N	10.53 E
Augusta, Austl.	162	34.19 S	115.10 E
Augusta, It.	70	37.13 N	15.13 E
Augusta, Ar., U.S.	194	35.16 N	91.21 W
Augusta, Ga., U.S.	192	33.28 N	82.01 W
Augusta, Il., U.S.	194	40.13 N	90.57 W
Augusta, Ks., U.S.	198	37.41 N	97.58 W
Augusta, Ky., U.S.	218	38.46 N	84.00 W
Augusta, Me., U.S.	188	44.18 N	69.46 W
Augusta, Mi., U.S.	216	42.20 N	85.21 W
Augusta, Mo., U.S.	219	38.34 N	90.53 W
Augusta, Mt., U.S.	202	47.29 N	112.23 W
Augusta, N.J., U.S.	210	41.07 N	74.43 W
Augusta, Oh., U.S.	214	40.41 N	81.01 W
Augusta, Wi., U.S.	190	44.40 N	91.07 W
Augusta, Golfo di ⊂	70	37.12 N	15.13 E
Augustdorf	52	51.53 N	8.43 E
Augustenborg	41	54.57 N	9.53 E
Augustine Island I	180	59.22 N	153.28 W
Augusto Severo	250	5.52 S	37.19 W
Augustów	30	53.51 N	22.59 E
Augustowski, Kanał ≊	76	53.54 N	23.26 E
Augustus, Mount ∧	162	24.20 S	116.50 E
Augustusburg	54	50.49 N	13.06 E
Augustus Downs	166	18.33 S	139.52 E
Augustus Island I	164	15.20 S	124.30 E
Auila, Ribeirão ≃	255	12.09 S	53.20 W
Au in der Hallertau	60	48.33 N	11.45 E
Aujon ≃	58	48.09 N	4.48 E
Auki	175e	8.46 S	160.42 E
Aulander	192	36.13 N	77.06 W
Aulanko	26	61.02 N	24.27 E
Auld, Lake ⊜	162	22.32 S	123.44 E
Auldearn	46	57.34 N	3.49 W
Aulendorf	58	47.57 N	9.38 E
Aulestad	26	61.13 N	10.17 E
Auletta	68	40.34 N	15.25 E
Aulla	64	44.12 N	9.58 E
Aulnay	32	46.01 N	0.21 W
Aulnay-sous-Bois	50	48.57 N	2.31 E
Aulnay-sur-Mauldre	261	48.56 N	1.51 E
Aulne ≃	32	48.17 N	4.16 W
Aulneau Peninsula ≻[1]	184	49.23 N	94.29 W
Aulnois-sur-Seille	56	48.52 N	6.19 E
Aulnoye-Aymeries	50	50.12 N	3.50 E
Ault, Fr.	50	50.06 N	1.27 E
Ault, Co., U.S.	200	40.34 N	104.43 W
Ault, Ky., U.S.	218	38.12 N	83.14 W
Aultbea	46	57.50 N	5.35 W
Aultman	214	40.34 N	79.16 W
Aultshire	216	40.13 N	85.19 W
Auma	54	50.42 N	11.54 E
Aumale	50	49.46 N	1.45 E
Auma Point ≻	164	7.55 S	145.25 E
Aumetz	56	49.25 N	5.56 E
Aumont-Aubrac	32	44.43 N	3.17 E
Aumühle	52	53.31 N	10.19 E
Auna	150	10.12 N	4.45 E
Auneau	50	48.27 N	1.46 E
Auneuil	50	49.22 N	2.00 E
Auning	26	56.26 N	10.23 E

PORTUGUÊS

Nome	Página	Lat.°′	Long.°′ W = Oeste
Auno	146	11.50 N	12.53 E
Aunuu I	174u	14.17 S	170.33 W
Auob ≃	156	26.25 S	20.35 E
Auponhia	112	1.56 S	125.29 E
Aups	62	43.37 N	6.14 E
Aur, Pulau I	112	2.27 N	104.31 E
Aura	26	60.36 N	22.34 E
Aurach	56	49.15 N	10.25 E
Aurach ≃	56	49.34 N	10.59 E
Aurachmat	85	41.34 N	70.07 E
Auraiya	124	26.28 N	79.31 E
Aurangābād, India	122	19.53 N	75.20 E
Aurangābād, India	124	24.45 N	84.22 E
Auray	32	47.40 N	2.59 W
Aurdal	26	60.56 N	9.24 E
Aure	26	63.16 N	8.32 E
Aurelia	198	42.42 N	95.26 W
Aurelius	216	42.31 N	84.31 W
Aurès, Massif de l' ⋏	148	35.08 N	6.30 E
Auri, Kepulauan II	164	1.59 S	134.42 E
Aurich	52	53.28 N	7.29 E
Auriesville Shrine ⊍[1]	210	42.54 N	74.19 W
Auriflama	255	20.41 S	50.34 W
Aurigny → Alderney I	43b	49.43 N	2.12 W
Aurilândia	255	16.44 S	50.28 W
Aurillac	32	44.56 N	2.26 E
Aurina, Valle ∨	64	47.00 N	12.00 E
Aurine, Alpi (Zillertaler Alpen) ⋏	64	47.00 N	11.55 E
Aurino ≃	64	46.48 N	11.55 E
Auriol	62	43.23 N	5.38 E
Aurisina	64	45.45 N	13.41 E
Aurlandsfjorden ⊂[2]	26	61.05 N	7.02 E
Aurlandsvangen	26	60.54 N	7.11 E
Aurolzmünster	60	48.15 N	13.27 E
Auron	62	44.14 N	6.56 E
Auronzo di Cadore	64	46.33 N	12.26 E
Aurora, Bra.	250	6.57 S	38.58 W
Aurora, Bra.	287a	22.46 S	43.24 W
Aurora, On., Can.	212	44.00 N	79.28 W
Aurora, S. Afr.	158	32.42 S	18.29 E
Aurora, Co., U.S.	200	39.43 N	104.49 W
Aurora, Il., U.S.	216	41.45 N	88.19 W
Aurora, In., U.S.	218	39.03 N	84.54 W
Aurora, Me., U.S.	188	44.51 N	68.19 W
Aurora, Mn., U.S.	190	47.31 N	92.14 W
Aurora, Mo., U.S.	194	36.58 N	93.43 W
Aurora, Ne., U.S.	198	40.52 N	98.00 W
Aurora, N.Y., U.S.	210	42.45 N	76.42 W
Aurora, N.C., U.S.	192	35.18 N	76.47 W
Aurora, Oh., U.S.	214	41.19 N	81.20 W
Aurora, Or., U.S.	224	45.13 N	122.45 W
Aurora, Ut,. U.S.	200	38.55 N	111.56 W
Aurora, W.V., U.S.	188	39.19 N	79.33 W
Aurora ▫[4]	116	16.00 N	121.40 E
Aurora ⊍	265a	59.57 N	30.21 E
Aurora do Norte	255	12.43 S	46.24 W
Aurora Pond ⊜	279a	41.20 N	81.23 W
Auroux	62	44.45 N	3.44 E
Aursunden ⊜	26	62.40 N	11.40 E
Aurukun	164	13.19 S	141.45 E
Aurukun Aboriginal Land Trust ◆[4]	164	13.45 S	141.45 E
Aurunci, Monti ⋏	66	41.22 N	13.40 E
Aus	156	26.40 S	16.15 E
Ausable ≃, On., Can.	190	43.19 N	81.46 W
Au Sable ≃, Mi., U.S.	190	44.25 N	83.20 W
Au Sable, North Branch ≃	190	44.40 N	84.23 W
Au Sable, South Branch ≃	190	44.40 N	84.23 W
Au Sable Forks	188	44.26 N	73.40 W
Au Sable Point ≻	190	44.20 N	83.20 W
Auschwitz → Oświęcim	30	50.03 N	19.12 E
Ausevik ⊥	26	61.32 N	5.16 E
Auskerry I	46	59.02 N	2.34 W
Ausoni, Monti ⋏	66	41.25 N	13.20 E
Ausserferrera	58	46.33 N	9.26 E
Ausserfragant	64	46.56 N	13.06 E
Aussig → Ústí nad Labem	54	50.40 N	14.02 E
Aussois	62	45.14 N	6.45 E
Aust-Agder ▫[6]	26	58.50 N	8.00 E
Austerlitz, Ned.	52	52.05 N	5.19 E
Austerlitz, N.Y., U.S.	210	42.19 N	73.28 W
Austerlitz, Gare ◆[5]	261	48.50 N	2.22 E
Austerlitz → Slavkov u Brna	61	49.09 N	16.52 E
Austin, Bra.	287a	22.43 S	43.32 W
Austin, Mb., Can.	184	49.57 N	98.56 W
Austin, In., U.S.	218	38.45 N	85.48 W
Austin, Mn., U.S.	190	43.40 N	92.58 W
Austin, Nv., U.S.	204	39.29 N	117.04 W
Austin, Pa., U.S.	214	41.37 N	78.05 W
Austin, Tx., U.S.	222	30.16 N	97.44 W
Austin ▫[6]	222	29.53 N	96.15 W
Austin ◆[8]	278	41.54 N	87.45 W
Austin, Lake ⊜	162	27.40 S	118.00 E
Austin, Lake ⊜[1]	222	30.19 N	97.46 W
Austin Bayou ≃	222	29.07 N	95.18 W
Austinburg	214	41.46 N	80.51 W
Austin Channel ɰ	176	75.35 N	103.25 W
Austin Lake ⊜	216	42.11 N	85.33 W
Austinmer	170	34.18 S	150.56 E
Austin's Post	158	29.32 S	25.49 E
Austintown	214	41.06 N	80.45 W
Austinville	192	36.51 N	80.54 W
Austnes	26	62.38 N	6.16 E
Austonio	222	31.11 N	95.38 W
Austonley	262	53.34 N	1.50 W
Austral	274a	33.56 S	150.48 E
Australes, Îles II	14	23.00 S	150.00 W
Australia ▫[1]	160	25.00 S	135.00 E
Australia Mountain ∧	180	63.36 N	138.08 W
Australian Capital Territory ▫[8]	171b	35.30 S	149.00 E
Australian War Memorial ⊥	171b	35.17 S	149.09 E
Australia Plains	168b	34.06 S	139.09 E
Australie → Australia ▫[1]	160	25.00 S	135.00 E
Australien → Australia ▫[1]	160	25.00 S	135.00 E
Australind	168a	33.16 S	115.44 E
Austral Seamounts ⊹[3]	14	22.40 S	152.45 W
Austrått	26	63.43 N	9.45 E
Austria (Österreich) ▫[1], Europe	22	47.20 N	13.20 E
Austria (Österreich) ▫[1], Europe	30	47.20 N	13.20 E
Austvågøya I	24	68.20 N	14.36 E
Autazes	246	3.35 S	59.08 W
Auteuil, Fr.	50	49.21 N	2.05 E
Auteuil, Fr.	261	48.50 N	1.49 E
Autheuil	50	49.06 N	1.17 E
Authie ≃	50	50.21 N	1.38 E
Authon	62	44.14 N	6.08 E
Authon-du-Perche	50	48.12 N	0.55 E
Authon-la-Plaine	50	48.27 N	1.57 E
Auth Village	284c	38.49 N	76.55 W
Autlán de Navarro	234	19.46 N	104.22 W
Autore, Monte ∧	66	41.58 N	13.12 E
Autrey-lès-Gray	58	47.29 N	5.30 E
Autriche → Austria ▫[1]	30	47.20 N	13.20 E
Autumn Hill	284b	39.16 N	76.48 W
Autun	32	46.57 N	4.18 E
Auve	56	49.02 N	4.42 E
Auvergne	164	15.41 S	130.01 E
Auvergne ▫[9]	32	45.25 N	2.30 E
Auvernaux	261	48.32 N	2.30 E
Auvers-sur-Oise	50	49.04 N	2.10 E
Auvézère ≃	32	45.12 N	0.51 E
Aux Cayes → Les Cayes	238	18.12 N	73.45 W
Auxerre	50	47.48 N	3.34 E
Auxier	192	37.44 N	82.45 W
Auxi-le-Château	50	50.14 N	2.07 E
Auxon	50	48.06 N	3.55 E
Auxonne	58	47.12 N	5.23 E
Aux Sable Creek ≃	216	41.23 N	88.20 W
Auxvasse	219	39.01 N	91.53 W
Auxvasse Creek ≃	219	38.41 N	91.49 W
Auxy	58	46.57 N	4.24 E
Auyamita, Quebrada ≃	286c	10.30 N	66.46 W
Auyán Tepuy ∧	246	5.55 N	62.32 W
Auzances	32	46.02 N	2.30 E
Auzangate, Nevado ∧	248	13.48 S	71.14 W
Auzon ≃, Fr.	58	48.00 N	4.20 E
Auzon ≃, Fr.	62	44.02 N	4.54 E
Ava, Il., U.S.	194	37.53 N	89.29 W
Ava, Mo., U.S.	194	36.57 N	92.39 W
Avadchara	84	43.31 N	40.39 E
Avadh Plains ≚	124	26.20 N	82.00 E
Avaí	255	22.08 S	49.22 W
Āvaj	128	35.34 N	49.13 E
Avakubi	154	1.20 N	27.34 E
Aval'	85	40.19 N	71.50 E
Aval, Falaise d' ⫠[4]	50	49.45 N	0.10 E
Avala ⊥	38	44.45 N	20.35 E
Avaldsnes	26	59.21 N	5.16 E
Avallon	50	47.29 N	3.54 E
Avaloirs, Les ∧[2]	32	48.28 N	0.07 W
Avalon, Ca., U.S.	228	33.20 N	118.19 W
Avalon, N.J., U.S.	208	39.06 N	74.43 W
Avalon, Pa., U.S.	214	40.30 N	80.04 W
Avalon, Tx., U.S.	222	32.12 N	96.48 W
Avalon, Wi., U.S.	216	42.38 N	88.52 W
Avalon Peninsula ≻[1]	186	47.30 N	53.30 W
Ávalos	232	28.35 N	106.00 W
Avana ≃	174k	21.14 S	159.43 W
Avanley	262	53.16 N	2.45 W
Avanos	130	38.43 N	34.51 E
Avant	196	36.29 N	96.03 W
Avaré	255	23.05 S	48.55 W
Avarskoje Kojsu ≃	84	42.47 N	46.48 E
Avarua	174k	21.12 S	159.46 W
Avarua Harbour ⊂	174k	21.11 S	159.46 W
Avatanak Island I	180	54.03 N	165.19 W
Avatele	174v	19.06 S	169.55 W
Avatele Bay ⊂	174v	19.05 S	169.56 W
Avatiu	174k	21.12 S	159.47 W
Avatiu Harbour ⊂	174k	21.11 S	159.47 W
Avčala	84	41.48 N	44.48 E
Avdejevka	83	48.08 N	37.46 E
Avdotjino	83	47.55 N	37.51 E
Ave ≃	34	41.20 N	8.45 W
Avebury	42	51.27 N	1.51 W
Avebury Stone Circle ⊥	42	51.28 N	1.51 W
ʿAvedat, Ḥorvot ⊥	132	30.48 N	34.46 E
Avegbadje ∧	150	7.14 N	0.38 E
Aveiro, Bra.	250	3.15 S	55.10 W
Aveiro, Port.	34	40.38 N	8.39 W
Aveiro, Ria de ≃[1]	34	40.38 N	8.44 W
Avelar	256	22.20 S	43.25 W
Avelengo	64	46.38 N	11.13 E
Aveley	260	51.30 N	0.16 E
Avelgem	50	50.46 N	3.26 E
Avella, It.	68	40.58 N	14.36 E
Avella, Pa., U.S.	214	40.16 N	80.27 W
Avellaneda, Arg.	252	29.07 S	59.40 W
Avellaneda, Arg.	258	34.39 S	58.23 W
Avellaneda ▫[5]	288	34.40 S	58.20 W
Avellaneda, Estacion ◆[5]	288	34.41 S	58.22 W
Avelle, Île I	275a	45.24 N	74.00 W
Avellino	68	40.54 N	14.47 E
Avellino ▫[4], It.	68	41.00 N	15.10 E
Avellino ▫[4], It.	68	40.57 N	15.00 E
Avenal	226	36.00 N	120.07 W
Avenal Creek ≃	226	35.47 N	120.04 W
Aven Armand ⫠[5]	32	44.15 N	3.22 E
Avenas	58	46.12 N	4.37 E
Avenches	58	46.53 N	7.02 E
Avenel	276	40.34 N	74.17 W
Aventureiro, Rio do ≃	256	21.52 S	42.39 W
Avenue	208	38.15 N	76.46 W
Avenwedde	52	51.55 N	8.27 E
Averbode	56	51.02 N	4.59 E
Averbode, Abbaye d' ⊍[1]	56	51.02 N	4.59 E
Averill Lake ⊜	206	44.59 N	71.44 W
Averill Park	210	42.38 N	73.33 W
Avern ⊜	40	58.54 N	15.32 E
Avernakø I	41	55.01 N	10.17 E
Avernes	261	49.05 N	1.52 E
Avernes, Ru des ≃	261	49.04 N	2.51 E
Averøya I	26	63.01 N	7.34 E
Aversa	68	40.58 N	14.12 E
Avery, Ca., U.S.	226	38.13 N	120.22 W
Avery, Id., U.S.	202	47.15 N	115.48 W
Avery, Tx., U.S.	194	33.33 N	94.47 W
Avery Island	194	29.54 N	91.54 W
Avesnelles	50	50.07 N	3.57 E
Avesnes	32	50.07 N	3.56 E
Avesnes-le-Comte	50	50.17 N	2.32 E
Avesnes-lès-Aubert	50	50.12 N	3.23 E
Avesnes-sur-Helpe	50	50.07 N	3.56 E
Avesta	40	60.09 N	16.12 E
Aveto ≃	62	44.42 N	9.23 E
Avetrana	68	40.21 N	17.43 E
Aveyron ▫[5]	32	44.15 N	2.40 E
Aveyron ≃	32	44.05 N	1.16 E
Avezzano	66	42.02 N	13.25 E
Avgustovka	80	52.16 N	50.44 E
Aviano	64	46.04 N	12.36 E
Avich, Loch ⊜	46	56.16 N	5.20 W
Aviemore	46	57.12 N	3.50 W
Avigliana	62	45.05 N	7.23 E
Avigliano	68	40.44 N	15.44 E
Avignon	62	43.57 N	4.49 E
Ávila	34	40.39 N	4.42 W
Ávila ▫[4]	34	40.35 N	5.00 W
Ávila, Sierra de ⋏	34	40.35 N	5.08 W
Avila Beach	226	35.10 N	120.43 W
Avilés	34	43.33 N	5.55 W
Avilla	216	41.22 N	85.14 W
Avilley	58	47.26 N	6.16 E
Avinger	222	32.54 N	94.33 W
Avinurme	76	58.59 N	26.51 E
Avio	64	45.44 N	10.56 E
Avion	50	50.24 N	2.50 E
Avioth	56	49.34 N	5.24 E
Avis	210	41.11 N	77.18 W
Avisio ≃	64	46.07 N	11.05 E
Avispa, Cerro ∧	246	1.16 N	65.51 W
Aviston	219	38.36 N	89.36 W
Aviz	34	39.03 N	7.53 W
Avize	50	48.58 N	4.01 E
Avlan Gölü ⊜	130	36.34 N	29.57 E
Avlum	41	56.16 N	8.48 E
Avnbøl	41	54.58 N	9.39 E
Avnik	130	38.39 N	40.20 E
Avoca, Austl.	169	37.05 S	143.28 E
Avoca, Ia., U.S.	198	41.28 N	95.20 W
Avoca, N.Y., U.S.	210	42.24 N	77.25 W
Avoca, Pa., U.S.	210	41.20 N	75.44 W
Avoca ≃, Austl.	166	35.42 S	143.44 E
Avoca ≃, Ire.	48	52.48 N	6.09 W
Avoca, Mount ∧	169	37.07 S	143.21 E
Avoca Beach	170	33.29 S	151.29 E
Avocado Heights	280	34.08 N	117.54 W
Avola, B.C., Can.	182	51.47 N	119.19 W
Avola, It.	70	36.54 N	15.08 E
Avon, Austl.	168b	34.17 S	138.20 E
Avon, Fr.	50	48.24 N	2.43 E
Avon, Ct., U.S.	207	41.48 N	72.49 W
Avon, Il., U.S.	190	40.39 N	90.26 W
Avon, Ma., U.S.	207	42.07 N	71.02 W
Avon, Mn., U.S.	190	45.36 N	94.27 W
Avon, Mt., U.S.	202	46.35 N	112.36 W
Avon, N.Y., U.S.	210	42.54 N	77.44 W
Avon, N.C., U.S.	192	35.21 N	75.30 W
Avon, Oh., U.S.	214	41.27 N	82.02 W
Avon, Pa., U.S.	208	40.22 N	76.23 W
Avon, S.D., U.S.	198	43.00 N	98.03 W
Avon ▫[6]	42	51.30 N	2.40 W
Avon ≃, Austl.	168a	31.40 S	116.07 E
Avon ≃, N.S., Can.	186	45.10 N	64.15 W
Avon ≃, On., Can.	212	43.18 N	81.11 W
Avon ≃, Eng., U.K.	42	51.30 N	2.43 W
Avon ≃, Eng., U.K.	42	50.17 N	3.52 W
Avon ≃, Eng., U.K.	42	50.43 N	1.46 W
Avon ≃, Eng., U.K.	42	52.25 N	1.31 W
Avon ≃, Eng., U.K.	42	51.59 N	2.10 W
Avon ≃, Scot., U.K.	46	56.01 N	3.40 W
Avon ≃, Scot., U.K.	46	57.25 N	3.23 W
Avon, Ben ∧	46	57.05 N	3.27 W
Avon, Ru d' ≃	261	48.39 N	2.46 E
Avon Basin ⊂	279a	41.30 N	82.03 W
Avon by the Sea	208	40.11 N	74.00 W
Avondale, Az., U.S.	200	33.26 N	112.20 W
Avondale, Co., U.S.	198	38.14 N	104.21 W
Avondale, Md., U.S.	284c	38.56 N	76.59 W
Avondale, Oh., U.S.	214	39.47 N	84.08 W
Avondale Heights	274b	37.46 S	144.51 E
Avon Downs	166	20.05 S	137.30 E
Avondrust	158	34.21 S	21.51 E
Avon Lake	214	41.30 N	82.01 W
Avonlea	184	50.00 N	105.04 W
Avonmore, On., Can.	206	45.10 N	74.58 W
Avonmore, Pa., U.S.	214	40.31 N	79.27 W
Avonmore ≃	48	52.50 N	6.13 W
Avonmouth	42	51.31 N	2.42 W
Avon Park	220	27.35 N	81.30 W
Avon Reservoir ⊜[1]	170	34.24 S	150.40 E
Avontuur	158	33.44 S	23.11 E
Avon Valley National Park ✦	168a	31.41 S	116.06 E
Avon Water ≃	46	55.47 N	4.01 W
Avoudrey	58	47.08 N	6.26 E
Avrainville	261	48.34 N	2.15 E
Avranches	32	48.41 N	1.22 W
Avranlo	84	41.39 N	43.52 E
Avre ≃, Fr.	50	49.53 N	2.20 E
Avre ≃, Fr.	50	48.47 N	1.22 E
Avrieux	62	45.13 N	6.43 E
Avroult	50	50.38 N	2.09 E
Avtatkuul' ≃	180	64.06 N	178.10 E
Avtovo ◆[8]	265a	59.52 N	30.15 E
Avu Avu	175e	9.50 S	160.23 E
Awa, Nihon	96	34.04 N	134.12 E
Awa, Nihon	174m	26.36 N	127.56 E
Awaba	170	33.01 S	151.33 E
Aʿwaj, Nahr al- ≃	132	33.20 N	36.34 E
Awaji	96	34.35 N	135.01 E
Awaji-shima I	96	34.21 N	134.51 E
Awakino	172	38.39 S	174.38 E
ʿAwālī	128	26.05 N	50.33 E
Awang	115b	8.54 S	116.24 E
Awano	94	36.31 N	139.41 E
Awanui	172	35.03 S	173.15 E
Awar	164	4.09 S	144.51 E
Awara	94	36.13 N	136.12 E
Awarawar, Tanjung ≻	115a	6.45 S	111.56 E
Aware	144	8.15 N	44.10 E
Awarua Point ≻	172	44.15 S	168.03 E
Awasa	144	6.45 N	38.15 E
Awasa, Lake ⊜	144	7.05 N	38.25 E
Awasan Bay ⊂	116	9.56 N	125.36 E
Awash	144	8.59 N	40.10 E
Awash ≃	144	11.45 N	41.05 E
Awa-shima I, Nihon	92	38.27 N	139.14 E
Awa-shima I, Nihon	96	34.16 N	133.38 E
Awash National Park ✦	144	9.05 N	40.00 E
Awaso	150	6.14 N	2.16 W
Awatere ≃	172	41.37 S	174.10 E
Awbārī	146	26.35 N	12.46 E
Awbārī, Ṣaḥrā' ⫠[8]	146	28.00 N	11.30 E
Awdheegle	144	1.59 N	44.50 E
Awe	150	8.09 N	9.07 E
Awe, Loch ⊜	46	56.15 N	5.17 W
Awegyun	110	12.44 N	98.44 E
Awgu	150	6.04 N	7.29 E
Awīsh al-Ḥajar	142	31.01 N	31.19 E
ʿAwjā', Wādī al- ∨	132	31.56 N	35.31 E
Awjilah	146	29.09 N	21.15 E
Awka	150	6.12 N	7.05 E
Awlād Mūsā	142	30.48 N	31.44 E
Awled Djellal	148	34.28 N	5.02 E
Awlef	148	26.58 N	1.05 E
Aworo Kit	140	10.59 N	32.38 E
Aworro	164	7.45 S	143.10 E
Awosting	276	41.09 N	74.20 W
Awsīm	273c	30.07 N	31.08 E
Awul	164	6.00 S	151.00 E
Awuna ≃	180	69.04 N	155.30 W
Awwal, Ash-Shallāl al- (First Cataract) ∟	140	24.01 N	32.52 E
Awwalī, Nahr al- ≃	132	33.35 N	35.23 E
Axamilpa ≃	234	18.35 N	98.11 W
Axams	64	47.14 N	11.18 E
Axat	32	42.48 N	2.14 E
Axbridge	42	51.18 N	2.49 W
Axe ≃, Eng., U.K.	42	51.19 N	2.59 W
Axe ≃, Eng., U.K.	42	50.42 N	3.03 W
Axe Creek ≃	169	36.46 S	144.30 E
Axedale	169	36.47 S	144.30 E
Axe Edge ⋏[2]	262	53.14 N	1.57 W
Axel	52	51.16 N	3.55 E
Axel Heiberg Island I	16	79.45 N	91.00 W
Axim	150	4.52 N	2.14 W
Axinim	246	4.02 S	59.22 W
Axiós (Vardar) ≃	38	40.35 N	22.50 E
Axis	194	30.55 N	88.01 W
Axixá	250	2.51 S	44.04 W
Ax-les-Thermes	32	42.43 N	1.50 E
Axminster	42	50.47 N	3.00 W
Axmouth	42	50.42 N	3.02 W
Axochiapan	234	18.30 N	98.46 W
Axtell, Ks., U.S.	198	39.52 N	96.15 W
Axtell, Ne., U.S.	198	40.28 N	99.07 W
Axtell, Tx., U.S.	222	31.39 N	96.58 W
Aÿ	50	49.03 N	4.00 E
Ayabaca	246	4.38 S	79.43 W
Ayabe	96	35.18 N	135.15 E
Ayachi, Ari n' ∧	148	32.29 N	4.57 W
Ayacucho, Arg.	252	37.09 S	58.29 W
Ayacucho, Bol.	248	17.51 S	63.20 W
Ayacucho, Perú	248	13.07 S	74.13 W
Ayacucho ▫[5]	248	14.00 S	74.00 W
Ayakkum Hu ⊜	120	37.30 N	89.20 E
Ayamé	150	5.37 N	3.11 W
Ayamiken	152	2.07 N	10.01 E
Ayamonte	34	37.13 N	7.24 W
Āyān	272b	22.43 N	88.09 E
Ayancık	130	41.57 N	34.36 E
Ayangba	150	7.30 N	7.08 E
Ayapel	246	8.19 N	75.09 W
Ayarza, Laguna de ⊜	236	14.25 N	90.08 W
Ayas, It.	62	45.50 N	7.41 E
Ayaş, Tür.	130	40.01 N	32.21 E
Ayase	94	35.26 N	139.26 E
Ayase ≃	268	35.45 N	139.49 E
Ayauta	96	34.13 N	133.53 E
Ayaviri	248	14.52 S	70.35 W
Ayaviri ≃	248	15.01 S	70.22 W
ʿAybāl, Jabal ∧	132	32.14 N	35.16 E
Aybastı, Tür.	130	39.42 N	39.02 E
Aybastı, Tür.	130	40.41 N	37.24 E
Ayden	192	35.28 N	77.24 W
Aydere	128	38.24 N	56.45 E
Aydın	130	37.51 N	27.51 E
Aydın ▫[4]	130	37.45 N	28.00 E
Aydıncık, Tür.	130	36.08 N	33.19 E
Aydıncık, Tür.	130	40.08 N	35.18 E
Aydın Dağları ⋏	130	38.00 N	28.00 E
Aydınkent	130	37.06 N	31.36 E
Aydıntepe	130	40.24 N	40.09 E
Aydin Ula ∧	86	42.55 N	87.35 E
Aydosdağı ∧	267b	40.56 N	29.15 E
Ayelu ∧	144	10.04 N	40.46 E
Ayer, Schw.	58	46.11 N	7.36 E
Ayer, Ma., U.S.	207	42.33 N	71.35 W
Ayer Baloi	114	1.35 N	103.20 E
Ayer Chawan, Pulau I	271c	1.17 N	103.42 E
Ayer Hitam, Malay.	114	1.55 N	103.11 E
Ayer Hitam, Malay.	114	2.56 N	102.24 E
Ayer Jerneh	114	4.24 N	103.24 E
Ayer Kuning Selatan	114	2.30 N	102.28 E
Ayer Merbau, Pulau I	271c	1.16 N	103.43 E
Ayers Cliff	206	45.10 N	72.03 W
Ayers Rock ∧	162	25.23 S	131.05 E
Ayersville	216	41.14 N	84.17 W
Ayeyarwady ▫[8]	110	17.00 N	95.00 E
Ayeyarwady (Irrawaddy) ≃	110	15.50 N	95.06 E
Aygün	130	38.26 N	41.17 E
Ayía Marína	38	37.09 N	26.52 E
Ayía Paraskeví, Ellás	38	39.15 N	26.16 E
Ayía Paraskeví, Ellás	267c	38.01 N	23.50 E
Ayiássos	38	39.05 N	26.23 E
Ayía Varvára	267c	37.59 N	23.39 E
Ayina ≃	152	1.48 N	13.10 E
Áyioi Anáryiroi	267c	38.02 N	23.43 E
Áyion Óros ≻[1]	38	40.15 N	24.15 E
Áyios Dhimítrios	267c	37.56 N	23.44 E
Áyios Evstrátios I	38	39.31 N	25.00 E
Áyios Ioánnis Réndis	267c	37.58 N	23.40 E
Áyios Kírikos	38	37.37 N	26.14 E
Áyios Nikólaos	38	35.11 N	25.42 E
Ayiou Nikolaou Monastery ⊍[1]	267c	37.53 N	23.27 E
Ayíou Órous, Kólpos ⊂	38	40.12 N	24.03 E
Ayl	132	30.13 N	35.32 E
Aylesbury	42	51.50 N	0.50 W
Aylesford	260	51.18 N	0.29 E
Aylesham	42	51.13 N	1.13 E
Aylmer	188	45.26 N	75.50 W
Aylmer, Lake ⊜	206	45.50 N	71.22 W
Aylmer, Mount ∧	182	51.19 N	115.26 W
Aylmer-East	212	45.26 N	75.50 W
Aylmer Lake ⊜	176	64.05 N	108.30 W
Aylmer West	212	42.46 N	80.59 W
Aylsham, Sk., Can.	184	53.11 N	103.49 W
Aylsham, Eng., U.K.	42	52.49 N	1.15 E
ʿAyn al-ʿArab	130	36.54 N	38.21 E
ʿAyn Dār	128	25.59 N	49.23 E
ʿAyn Dīwār	130	37.17 N	42.11 E
ʿAynīn ⊤[4]	144	20.48 N	41.39 E
Aynor	192	33.59 N	79.11 W
ʿAynūnah	128	28.05 N	35.08 E
Ayo	248	15.41 S	72.16 W
Ayo Ayo	248	17.05 S	68.00 W
Ayod	140	8.07 N	31.26 E
Ayodhya	124	26.48 N	82.12 E
Ayo El Chico	234	20.32 N	102.21 W
Ayom	140	7.52 N	28.23 E
Ayorou	150	14.44 N	0.55 E
Ayos	152	3.54 N	12.31 E
'Ayoûn el 'Atroûs	150	16.40 N	9.37 W
Ayr, Austl.	166	19.35 S	147.24 E
Ayr, On., Can.	212	43.17 N	80.27 W
Ayr, Scot., U.K.	44	55.28 N	4.38 W
Ayr ≃	44	55.29 N	4.28 W
ʿAyrah	132	32.37 N	36.32 E
Ayrancı	130	37.22 N	33.42 E
Ayre, Point of ≻	44	54.26 N	4.22 W
Aysgarth	44	54.17 N	2.00 W
Aysha	144	10.46 N	42.37 E
ʿAytā al-Fakhkhār	132	33.38 N	35.54 E
ʿAytanīt	132	33.34 N	35.40 E
Ayton, Austl.	164	15.56 S	145.22 E
Ayton, On., Can.	212	44.03 N	80.56 W
Ayton, Eng., U.K.	44	54.14 N	0.29 W
Ayu, Kepulauan II	108	0.28 N	131.03 E
Ayubnagar	126	23.46 N	90.23 E
Ayulhai	102	44.36 N	115.36 E
Ayuñgon	116	9.51 N	123.08 E
Ayuquila ≃	234	19.23 N	103.51 W
Ayutla	234	20.07 N	104.22 W
Ayutla de los Libres	234	16.54 N	99.13 W
Ayvacık, Tür.	130	39.36 N	26.24 E
Ayvacık, Tür.	130	41.00 N	36.39 E
Ayvalı	130	38.44 N	37.38 E
Ayvalık	130	39.18 N	26.41 E
Aywaille	56	50.28 N	5.40 E
Azabarabān, Ra's ≻	142	28.51 N	32.43 E
Azacualpa, Hond.	236	14.27 N	86.09 W
Azacualpa, Hond.	236	15.19 N	88.33 W
Azādpur ◆[8]	272a	28.43 N	77.11 E
Azai	94	35.26 N	136.18 E
Azaila	34	41.17 N	0.29 W
Azalea Park	220	28.32 N	81.18 W
Azama	174m	26.11 N	127.49 E
Azamatovo	80	53.18 N	53.28 E
Azambuja	34	39.04 N	8.52 W
Āzamgarh	124	26.04 N	83.11 E
Azamiga-dake ∧	96	34.20 N	131.47 E
Azángaro	248	14.55 S	70.13 W
Azángaro ≃	248	15.17 S	70.10 W
Azanka	86	58.02 N	64.48 E
Azao ∧	148	25.12 N	8.08 E
Azaouâd ◆[1]	150	19.00 N	3.00 W
Azaouagh, Vallée de l' ∨	150	15.30 N	3.18 E
Azapa, Quebrada de ≃	248	18.30 S	70.17 W
Azar ∨	150	16.02 N	4.04 E
Azara	150	8.21 N	9.12 E
Āzārbāyjān-e Gharbī ▫[4]	128	37.40 N	45.00 E
Āzārbāyjān-e Sharqī ▫[4]	128	38.00 N	47.00 E
Azare	150	11.40 N	10.11 E
Āzar Shahr	128	37.45 N	45.59 E
Azas ≃	88	52.26 N	96.15 E
Azat, gora ∧[2]	86	46.55 N	69.00 E
Azay-le-Rideau	50	47.16 N	0.28 E
Azay-sur-Cher	50	47.21 N	0.51 E
Azay-sur-Indre	50	47.12 N	0.57 E
Aʿzāz	130	36.35 N	37.03 E
Azazga	148	36.44 N	4.22 E
Azcuénaga	258	34.23 S	59.21 W
Aždaak, gora ∧	84	40.13 N	44.56 E
Azdavay	130	41.39 N	33.18 E
Azeffâl ⫠[8]	148	21.00 N	14.45 W
Azeffoun	148	36.53 N	4.25 E
Azejevo	80	54.41 N	42.02 E
Azemmour	148	33.20 N	8.25 W
Azenhas do Mar	266c	38.50 N	9.28 W
Azennezal, 'Erg ∨	148	22.50 N	0.25 E
Azerbaidzhan → Azerbaijan ▫[1]	22	40.30 N	47.30 E
Azerbaijan ▫[1], Asia	72	40.30 N	47.30 E
Azerbaijan ▫[1], Asia	84	40.30 N	47.30 E
Azerbajdžan → Azerbaijan ▫[1]	72	40.30 N	47.30 E
Azerbaydzan → Azerbaijan ▫[1]	72	40.30 N	47.30 E
Azergues ≃	58	45.56 N	4.44 E
Azezo	144	12.35 N	37.28 E
Azgir	80	47.50 N	47.54 E
Azhikode	122	11.59 N	75.21 E
Azilal	148	31.58 N	6.34 W
Azilal ▫[4]	148	31.55 N	6.30 W
Azile	154	3.32 N	29.52 E
Azincourt	50	50.28 N	2.08 E
Azizbekov	84	39.40 N	45.30 E
Azle	222	32.53 N	97.32 W
Aznakajevo	80	54.53 N	53.04 E
Aznapuquio	286d	11.59 S	77.04 W
Azogues	246	2.44 S	78.50 W
Azoia	266c	38.46 N	9.29 W
Azor	132	32.01 N	34.48 E
Azores → Açores II	148a	38.30 N	28.00 W
Azores-Gibraltar Ridge ⊹[3]	10	37.00 N	16.00 W
Azores Plateau ⊹[3]	10	39.00 N	30.00 W
Azoum, Bahr (Wādī ʿAẓūm) ∨	146	10.53 N	20.15 E
Azov	83	47.07 N	39.25 E
Azov, Sea of → Azovskoje more ⊤[2]	78	46.00 N	36.00 E
Azovo-Sivašskij zapovednik ◆[4]	78	46.08 N	35.08 E
Azovskij kanal ≊	83	47.07 N	39.27 E
Azovskoje	78	45.34 N	34.34 E
Azovskoje more (Sea of Azov) ⊤[2]	78	46.00 N	36.00 E
Azoyú	234	16.43 N	98.44 W

≃ River	Fluß	Río	Rivière	Rio	⊹ Submarine Features	Untermeerische Objekte	Accidentes Submarinos	Formes de relief sous-marin	Acidentes submarinos
≊ Canal	Kanal	Canal	Canal	Canal	▫ Political Unit	Politische Einheit	Unidad Política	Entité politique	Unidade política
∟ Waterfall, Rapids	Wasserfall, Stromschnellen	Cascada, Rápidos	Chute d'eau, Rapides	Cascata, Rápidos	⊍ Cultural Institution	Kulturelle Institution	Institución Cultural	Institution culturelle	Instituição cultural
ɰ Strait	Meeresstraße	Estrecho	Détroit	Estreito	⊥ Historical Site	Historische Stätte	Sitio Histórico	Site historique	Sitio histórico
⊂ Bay, Gulf	Bucht, Golf	Bahía, Golfo	Baie, Golfe	Baía, Golfo	✦ Recreational Site	Erholungs- und Ferienort	Sitio de Recreo	Centre de loisirs	Area de Lazer
⊜ Lake, Lakes	See, Seen	Lago, Lagos	Lac, Lacs	Lago, Lagos	⊠ Airport	Flughafen	Aeropuerto	Aéroport	Aeroporto
≡ Swamp	Sumpf	Pantano	Marais	Pântano	■ Military Installation	Militäranlage	Instalación Militar	Installation militaire	Instalação militar
⊓ Ice Features, Glacier	Eis- und Gletscherformen	Accidentes Glaciales	Formes glaciaires	Acidentes glaciares	◆ Miscellaneous	Verschiedenes	Misceláneo	Divers	Diversos
⊤ Other Hydrographic Features	Andere Hydrographische Objekte	Otros Elementos Hidrográficos	Autres données hydrographiques	Outros acidentes hidrográficos					

ESPAÑOL

Nombre	Página	Lat.°′	Long.°′ W = Oeste
Blackville	**192**	33.21 N	81.16 W
Black Volta (Volta Noire) ≃	**150**	8.41 N	1.33 W
Blackwall Tunnel ◆[5]	**260**	51.30 N	0.01 E
Blackwalnut Point ›	**208**	38.40 N	76.20 W
Black Warrior ≃	**194**	32.32 N	87.51 W
Blackwatch Hills	**210**	43.05 N	77.27 W
Blackwater, Austl.	**166**	23.35 S	148.53 E
Blackwater, Ire.	**48**	52.26 N	6.21 W
Blackwater ≃, Europe	**44**	54.31 N	6.34 W
Blackwater ≃, Ire.	**48**	51.51 N	7.50 W
Blackwater ≃, Ire.	**48**	53.39 N	6.43 W
Blackwater ≃, Eng., U.K.	**260**	51.45 N	1.00 E
Blackwater ≃, U.S.	**194**	30.36 N	87.02 W
Blackwater ≃, Md., U.S.	**208**	38.21 N	76.01 W
Blackwater ≃, Mo., U.S.	**194**	38.56 N	92.51 W
Blackwater ≃, Va., U.S.	**208**	36.33 N	76.55 W
Blackwater Creek ≃, Austl.	**166**	25.56 S	144.20 E
Black Water Creek ≃, Fl., U.S.	**220**	28.51 N	81.24 W
Blackwater Draw V	**196**	33.35 N	101.50 W
Blackwaterfoot	**46**	55.30 N	5.19 W
Blackwater Lake ⊜	**180**	64.00 N	123.05 W
Blackwater Reservoir ⊜[1], Scot., U.K.	**46**	56.41 N	4.46 W
Blackwater Reservoir ⊜[1], Scot., U.K.	**46**	56.44 N	3.14 W
Blackwater Sound ⊔	**220**	25.10 N	80.25 W
Blackwell, Ok., U.S.	**196**	36.48 N	97.16 W
Blackwell, Tx., U.S.	**196**	32.05 N	100.19 W
Blackwood, Austl.	**168b**	35.02 S	138.37 E
Blackwood, Austl.	**169**	37.29 S	144.19 E
Blackwood, N.J., U.S.	**285**	39.48 N	75.03 W
Blackwood ≃	**162**	34.19 S	115.11 E
Blackwood, Cape ›	**164**	7.50 S	144.30 E
Blackwood Terrace	**285**	39.48 N	75.05 W
Bladel	**52**	51.23 N	5.13 E
Bladenboro	**192**	34.32 N	78.47 W
Bladensburg, Md., U.S.	**284c**	38.56 N	76.56 W
Bladensburg, Oh., U.S.	**214**	40.17 N	82.17 W
Blades	**208**	38.38 N	75.36 W
Bladgrond	**158**	28.52 S	19.57 E
Bladnoch ≃	**44**	54.51 N	4.25 W
Bladworth	**184**	51.18 N	106.09 W
Blaenau Ffestiniog	**42**	52.59 N	3.56 W
Blaenavon	**42**	51.48 N	3.05 W
Bláfell ∧	**24a**	64.32 N	19.53 W
Blagaj	**36**	43.15 N	17.50 E
Blagdon	**42**	51.20 N	2.43 W
Blagodarnoje	**86**	47.03 N	82.10 E
Blagodarnyj	**72**	45.06 N	43.27 E
Blagodatnoje, Kaz.	**86**	51.18 N	72.49 E
Blagodatnoje, Ross.	**78**	51.32 N	34.54 E
Blagodatnoje, Ukr.	**83**	47.42 N	37.25 E
Blagodatnoje, Ukr.	**83**	47.53 N	38.29 E
Blagodatovka	**80**	52.14 N	50.27 E
Blagoevgrad	**38**	42.01 N	23.06 E
Blagoveščenka, Kaz.	**86**	54.22 N	66.58 E
Blagoveščenka, Ross.	**80**	51.19 N	44.03 E
Blagoveščenka, Ross.	**86**	52.50 N	79.52 E
Blagoveščensk, Ross.	**86**	55.01 N	55.59 E
Blagoveščensk, Ross.	**89**	50.17 N	127.32 E
Blagoveščenskoje, Kaz.	**85**	43.18 N	74.12 E
Blagoveščenskoje, Ross.	**86**	58.08 N	62.58 E
Blåhø ∧	**26**	62.45 N	9.19 E
Blåhøj	**41**	55.51 N	9.01 E
Blaichach	**58**	47.34 N	10.15 E
Blaikfjället ∧	**26**	64.33 N	16.12 E
Blain, Fr.	**32**	47.29 N	1.46 W
Blain, Pa., U.S.	**208**	40.20 N	77.31 W
Blaina	**42**	51.46 N	3.10 W
Blain City	**214**	40.45 N	78.34 W
Blaine, Mn., U.S.	**190**	45.09 N	93.14 W
Blaine, Wa., U.S.	**224**	48.59 N	122.44 W
Blaine Creek ≃	**188**	38.11 N	82.37 W
Blaine Hill	**279b**	40.16 N	79.53 W
Blaine Lake	**184**	52.50 N	106.54 W
Blaineys	**224**	48.53 N	123.47 W
Blainville	**206**	45.40 N	73.52 W
Blainville-sur-l'Eau	**58**	48.33 N	6.24 E
Blair, On., Can.	**212**	43.23 N	80.23 W
Blair, Ne., U.S.	**198**	41.32 N	96.07 W
Blair, Ok., U.S.	**196**	34.46 N	99.20 W
Blair, Wi., U.S.	**190**	44.18 N	91.14 W
Blair □[6]	**214**	40.30 N	78.25 W
Blair Athol	**166**	22.42 S	147.33 E
Blair Atholl	**46**	56.46 N	3.51 W
Blairgowrie	**46**	56.36 N	3.21 W
Blairs Mills	**214**	40.17 N	77.43 W
Blairstown, Ia., U.S.	**190**	41.54 N	92.05 W
Blairstown, N.J., U.S.	**210**	40.59 N	74.57 W
Blairsville, Ga., U.S.	**192**	34.52 N	83.57 W
Blairsville, Pa., U.S.	**214**	40.25 N	79.15 W
Blaise ≃, Fr.	**50**	48.46 N	1.25 E
Blaise ≃, Fr.	**58**	48.38 N	4.43 E
Blaisy-Bas	**58**	47.22 N	4.44 E
Blaj	**38**	46.11 N	23.55 E
Blakehurst	**274a**	33.59 S	151.07 E
Blakeley Canal ≋	**226**	36.09 N	119.48 W
Blakely, Ga., U.S.	**192**	31.22 N	84.56 W
Blakely, Pa., U.S.	**210**	41.28 N	75.35 W
Blakely Island I	**224**	48.33 N	122.50 W
Blakeney, Eng., U.K.	**42**	51.46 N	2.29 W
Blakeney, Eng., U.K.	**42**	52.58 N	1.00 E
Blake Plateau ✣[4]	**16**	31.00 N	79.00 W
Blake Point ›	**190**	48.12 N	88.25 W
Blake Ridge ✣[3]	**16**	29.00 N	73.30 W
Blakes	**208**	37.30 N	76.22 W
Blakesburg	**190**	40.57 N	92.38 W
Blakeslee, Oh., U.S.	**216**	41.31 N	84.44 W
Blakeslee, Pa., U.S.	**210**	41.06 N	75.36 W
Blalock Island I	**202**	45.53 N	119.41 W
Blâmont, Fr.	**58**	48.35 N	6.51 E
Blamont, Fr.	**58**	47.23 N	6.51 E
Blanc, Cap ›	**36**	37.20 N	9.51 E
Blanc, Cap → Nouâdhibou, Râs ›	**148**	20.46 N	17.03 W
Blanc, Mont ∧, P.Q., Can.	**186**	48.47 N	66.52 W
Blanc, Mont (Monte Bianco) ∧, Europe	**62**	45.50 N	6.52 E
Blanca	**200**	37.27 N	105.31 W
Blanca, Bahía ⊂	**252**	38.55 S	62.10 W
Blanca, Isla I	**248**	9.06 S	78.38 W
Blanca, Laguna ⊜	**254**	52.25 S	71.10 W
Blanca, Punta ›, Arg.	**258**	34.57 S	57.40 W
Blanca, Punta ›, Chile	**252**	25.06 S	70.30 W
Blanca, Sierra ∧	**200**	31.15 N	105.26 W
Blanca Lake ⊜	**224**	47.53 N	121.21 W
Blanca Peak ∧	**200**	37.35 N	105.29 W
Blancas, Peñas ⋏	**236**	13.15 N	85.41 W
Blanc du Cheilon, Mont ∧	**58**	45.59 N	7.25 E
Blanchard, Ok., U.S.	**196**	35.08 N	97.39 W
Blanchard, Pa., U.S.	**210**	41.04 N	77.36 W
Blanchard, Wa., U.S.	**224**	48.35 N	122.24 W
Blanchard ≃	**216**	41.02 N	84.18 W
Blanchardville	**190**	42.48 N	89.51 W
Blanche ≃, On., Can.	**190**	47.34 N	79.32 W
Blanche ≃, P.Q., Can.	**206**	46.40 N	72.08 W
Blanche, Cape ›	**162**	33.01 S	134.09 E
Blanche, Dent ∧	**58**	46.03 N	7.36 E
Blanche, Lake ⊜, Austl.	**162**	22.25 S	123.17 E

FRANÇAIS

Nom	Page	Lat.°′	Long.°′ W = Ouest
Blanche, Lake ⊜, Austl.	**166**	29.15 S	139.39 E
Blanche, Mer → Beloje more ⊤[2]	**24**	65.30 N	38.00 E
Blanche Channel ⊔	**175e**	8.30 S	157.30 E
Blancheface	**261**	48.32 N	2.06 E
Blanche Marie Val ∟	**250**	4.44 N	56.53 W
Blanchester	**218**	39.17 N	83.59 W
Blanchisseuse	**241r**	10.47 N	61.18 W
Blanco, S. Afr.	**158**	33.57 S	22.24 E
Blanco, Tx., U.S.	**196**	30.06 N	98.25 W
Blanco ≃, Arg.	**252**	30.12 S	69.05 W
Blanco ≃, Arg.	**254**	47.22 S	71.12 W
Blanco ≃, Bol.	**248**	13.09 S	63.46 W
Blanco ≃, Ec.	**246**	0.28 N	79.25 W
Blanco ≃, Tx., U.S.	**196**	29.51 N	97.55 W
Blanco, Cabo ›	**236**	9.34 N	85.07 W
Blanco, Cabo → Nouâdhibou, Râs ›	**148**	20.46 N	17.03 W
Blanco, Cañon V	**200**	35.20 N	105.05 W
Blanco, Cape ›	**202**	42.50 N	124.34 W
Blanco, Lago ⊜	**254**	54.03 S	69.00 W
Blanco, Mar → Beloje more ⊤[2]	**24**	65.30 N	38.00 E
Blanco, Monte → Blanc, Mont ∧	**62**	45.50 N	6.52 E
Blanco, Rio ≃	**200**	37.07 N	107.03 W
Blanco Creek ≃	**196**	28.19 N	97.19 W
Blanc-Sablon	**186**	51.25 N	57.07 W
Bland, Mo., U.S.	**219**	38.18 N	91.37 W
Bland, Va., U.S.	**192**	37.06 N	81.06 W
Blanda ≃	**24a**	65.39 N	20.18 W
Blandburg	**214**	40.41 N	78.24 W
Blandford	**207**	42.10 N	72.55 W
Blandford Forum	**42**	50.52 N	2.11 W
Blanding	**200**	37.37 N	109.28 W
Blandinsville	**190**	40.33 N	90.51 W
Blandon	**208**	40.26 N	75.53 W
Blandy	**261**	48.34 N	2.47 E
Blanes	**34**	41.41 N	2.48 E
Blangkejeren	**114**	3.59 N	97.20 E
Blangpidie	**114**	3.45 N	96.51 E
Blangy-le-Château	**50**	49.14 N	0.17 E
Blangy-sur-Bresle	**50**	49.56 N	1.38 E
Blanice ≃	**61**	49.05 N	14.03 E
Blankenberg	**56**	50.45 N	7.22 E
Blankenberge	**50**	51.19 N	3.08 E
Blankenburg	**54**	51.48 N	10.58 E
Blankenburg ◆[8]	**264a**	52.35 N	13.28 E
Blankenese ◆[8]	**52**	53.33 N	9.48 E
Blankenfelde	**54**	52.20 N	13.23 E
Blankenfelde ◆[8]	**264a**	52.37 N	13.23 E
Blankenhain	**54**	50.51 N	11.21 E
Blankenheim, Dtsch.	**54**	51.31 N	11.25 E
Blankenheim, Dtsch.	**56**	50.26 N	6.39 E
Blankensee	**54**	52.14 N	13.08 E
Blankenstein	**263**	51.24 N	7.14 E
Blanket	**196**	31.49 N	98.47 W
Blanquilla, Isla I	**246**	11.51 N	64.37 W
Blansko	**30**	49.22 N	16.39 E
Blanský Les ◆[3]	**61**	48.52 N	14.16 E
Blantyre	**154**	15.47 S	35.00 E
Blanzac	**62**	45.07 N	3.51 E
Blanzy	**58**	46.42 N	4.23 E
Blaricum	**52**	52.16 N	5.15 E
Blarney	**48**	51.56 N	8.34 W
Blarney Castle ⊥	**48**	51.56 N	8.34 W
Blasdell	**210**	42.47 N	78.49 W
Blasheim	**52**	52.18 N	8.34 E
Błaszki	**30**	51.39 N	18.27 E
Blatná	**60**	49.26 N	13.53 E
Blatnica	**38**	43.42 N	28.31 E
Blatten	**58**	46.25 N	7.50 E
Blatzheim	**56**	50.51 N	6.38 E
Blau ≃	**58**	48.23 N	9.49 E
Blaubeuren	**58**	48.24 N	9.47 E
Blauen ∧	**58**	47.47 N	7.42 E
Blauer Nil → Blue Nile ≃	**140**	15.38 N	32.31 E
Blaufelden	**56**	49.18 N	9.58 E
Blaustein	**58**	48.25 N	9.53 E
Blauvelt	**276**	41.03 N	73.57 W
Blauvelt State Park ♠	**276**	41.04 N	73.56 W
Blåvands Huk ›	**26**	55.33 N	8.05 E
Blawenburg	**276**	40.24 N	74.42 W
Blawnox	**279b**	40.29 N	79.51 W
Blaxland	**170**	33.45 S	150.36 E
Blaxland Creek ≃	**274a**	33.48 S	150.46 E
Blaydon	**44**	54.58 N	1.42 W
Blaye-et-Sainte-Luce	**32**	45.08 N	0.39 W
Blayney	**166**	33.32 S	149.15 E
Blaze, Point ›	**164**	12.56 S	130.12 E
Błażowa	**30**	49.54 N	22.05 E
Bleaker Island I	**254**	52.13 S	58.53 W
Bleaklow Head ∧	**262**	53.28 N	1.50 W
Blean	**42**	51.19 N	1.02 E
Bleckede	**54**	53.17 N	10.44 E
Bled	**36**	46.22 N	14.06 E
Bledsoe	**196**	33.38 N	103.01 W
Bleecker	**210**	43.07 N	74.22 W
Blefjell ∧	**26**	59.48 N	9.10 E
Blega	**115a**	7.08 S	113.03 E
Bleibach	**58**	48.07 N	8.01 E
Bleiberg ob Villach	**64**	46.37 N	13.41 E
Bleiburg	**61**	46.35 N	14.48 E
Bleicherode	**54**	51.26 N	10.34 E
Blekendorf	**54**	54.16 N	10.38 E
Blekinge □[9]	**26**	56.20 N	15.05 E
Blekinge Län □[6]	**26**	56.20 N	15.20 E
Blendecques	**50**	50.43 N	2.16 E
Bléneau	**50**	47.42 N	2.57 E
Blenheim, Austl.	**171a**	27.39 S	152.20 E
Blenheim, On., Can.	**214**	42.20 N	82.00 W
Blenheim, N.Z.	**172**	41.31 S	173.57 E
Blenheim, N.J., U.S.	**285**	39.48 N	75.05 W
Blenheim Palace ʊ	**42**	51.47 N	1.21 W
Blenio, Val V	**58**	46.27 N	8.58 E
Blénod-lès-Pont-à-Mousson	**56**	48.53 N	6.03 E
Blénod-lès-Toul	**58**	48.36 N	5.50 E
Bléone ≃	**62**	44.03 N	6.00 E
Blérancourt	**50**	49.31 N	3.09 E
Bléré	**50**	47.20 N	1.00 E
Blerick	**52**	51.23 N	6.10 E
Blériot-Plage	**50**	50.57 N	1.50 E
Blesbokspruit ≃	**273d**	26.14 S	28.29 E
Blessing	**222**	28.52 N	96.13 W
Blessington	**48**	53.10 N	6.32 W
Bletchingley	**260**	51.14 N	0.06 W
Bletchley	**42**	52.00 N	0.46 W
Bletterans	**58**	46.45 N	5.27 E
Bleu → Chang ≃	**90**	31.48 N	121.10 E
Bleue, Mer ≡	**212**	45.24 N	75.30 W
Bleury	**261**	48.31 N	1.45 E
Bleus, Monts ⋏	**154**	1.30 N	30.30 E
Blevio	**62**	45.50 N	9.05 E
Blewett Falls Lake ⊜[1]	**192**	35.03 N	79.54 W
Blexen	**52**	53.32 N	8.32 E
Blidö I	**40**	59.37 N	18.54 E
Blidworth	**44**	53.06 N	1.07 W
Bliedinghausen ◆[8]	**263**	51.09 N	7.12 E
Bliersheim ◆[8]	**263**	51.23 N	6.43 E
Blies ≃	**56**	49.07 N	7.04 E
Blieskastel	**56**	49.14 N	7.16 E
Bligh Sound ⊔	**172**	44.50 S	167.32 E
Bligh Water ⊔	**175g**	17.00 S	178.00 E
Bligny	**50**	49.11 N	3.52 E
Bligny-sur-Ouche	**58**	47.06 N	4.40 E
Blik, Mount ∧	**116**	6.58 N	124.15 E
Blina	**162**	17.46 S	124.32 E
Blind ≃	**276**	40.57 N	73.42 W
Blind Creek ≃	**274b**	37.54 S	145.12 E
Blindley Heath	**260**	51.12 N	0.04 W
Blind River	**190**	46.10 N	82.58 W
Blinman	**166**	31.06 S	138.41 E
Blinnenhorn ∧	**58**	46.26 N	8.19 E
Blinovskij	**80**	49.23 N	42.19 E
Bliss	**210**	42.34 N	78.15 W
Blissfield, Mi., U.S.	**216**	41.49 N	83.51 W
Blissfield, Oh., U.S.	**214**	40.24 N	81.58 W

PORTUGUÊS

Nome	Página	Lat.°′	Long.°′ W = Oeste
Blitar	**115a**	8.06 S	112.09 E
Blithe ≃	**42**	52.45 N	1.50 W
Blithfield Reservoir ⊜[1]	**42**	52.48 N	1.53 W
Blitta	**150**	8.19 N	0.59 E
Blizn'uki	**78**	48.52 N	36.33 E
Blocher	**218**	38.43 N	85.39 W
Block Dam ◆[6]	**212**	45.12 N	76.54 W
Block Island	**207**	41.10 N	71.33 W
Block Island I	**207**	41.11 N	71.35 W
Block Island Sound ⊔	**207**	41.10 N	71.45 W
Blockley	**42**	52.01 N	1.45 W
Blockton	**198**	40.36 N	94.28 W
Blodgett Mills	**210**	42.34 N	76.08 W
Bloed ≃	**158**	28.15 S	30.30 E
Bloedel	**182**	50.07 N	125.23 W
Bloedrivier, S. Afr.	**158**	28.06 S	30.33 E
Bloedrivier, S. Afr.	**158**	27.53 S	30.30 E
Bloekomspruit	**158**	26.45 S	28.21 E
Bloemendaal	**52**	52.24 N	4.37 E
Bloemfontein	**158**	29.12 S	26.07 E
Bloemhof	**158**	27.38 S	25.32 E
Bloemhofdam ⊜[1]	**158**	27.40 S	25.40 E
Blois	**50**	47.35 N	1.20 E
Blokhus	**26**	57.15 N	9.35 E
Blokzijl	**52**	52.44 N	5.57 E
Blombacher Bach ◆[8]	**263**	51.15 N	7.14 E
Blombacka	**40**	59.37 N	13.47 E
Blomberg	**52**	51.56 N	9.05 E
Blomstermåla	**26**	56.59 N	16.20 E
Blonay	**58**	46.28 N	6.54 E
Blönduós	**24a**	65.39 N	20.15 W
Blongas	**115b**	8.53 S	116.02 E
Blonville-sur-Mer	**50**	49.19 N	0.02 E
Blood Indian Creek ≃	**184**	50.55 N	111.03 W
Blood Indian Reserve ◆[4]	**182**	49.30 N	113.10 W
Blood Mountain ∧	**192**	34.44 N	83.56 W
Blood River ⊥	**158**	28.20 S	30.35 E
Bloodsworth Island I	**208**	38.10 N	76.03 W
Bloodvein ≃	**184**	51.45 N	96.44 W
Bloody Foreland ›	**48**	55.09 N	8.17 W
Bloomdale	**216**	41.10 N	83.33 W
Bloomer	**190**	45.06 N	91.29 W
Bloomfield, On., Can.	**212**	43.59 N	77.14 W
Bloomfield, Ct., U.S.	**207**	41.49 N	72.43 W
Bloomfield, In., U.S.	**194**	39.01 N	86.56 W
Bloomfield, Ia., U.S.	**190**	40.45 N	92.24 W
Bloomfield, Ky., U.S.	**194**	37.54 N	85.19 W
Bloomfield, Mo., U.S.	**194**	36.53 N	89.55 W
Bloomfield, Ne., U.S.	**198**	42.35 N	97.38 W
Bloomfield, N.J., U.S.	**210**	40.48 N	74.11 W
Bloomfield, N.M., U.S.	**200**	36.42 N	107.59 W
Bloomfield, Oh., U.S.	**214**	40.03 N	81.44 W
Bloomfield ◆[8]	**279b**	40.27 N	79.56 W
Bloomfield Glens	**281**	42.33 N	83.20 W
Bloomfield Highlands	**281**	42.36 N	83.16 W
Bloomfield Hills	**216**	42.35 N	83.14 W
Bloomfield Village	**216**	42.33 N	83.15 W
Bloomingburg, N.Y., U.S.	**210**	41.33 N	74.26 W
Bloomingburg, Oh., U.S.	**218**	39.36 N	83.23 W
Bloomingdale, Il., U.S.	**216**	41.57 N	88.04 W
Bloomingdale, Mi., U.S.	**216**	42.22 N	85.57 W
Bloomingdale, N.J., U.S.	**210**	41.00 N	74.19 W
Bloomingdale, Oh., U.S.	**214**	40.21 N	80.49 W
Blooming Glen	**208**	40.22 N	75.15 W
Blooming Grove, In., U.S.	**218**	39.30 N	85.04 W
Blooming Grove, N.Y., U.S.	**210**	41.25 N	74.11 W
Blooming Grove, Pa., U.S.	**210**	41.21 N	75.09 W
Blooming Grove, Tx., U.S.	**222**	32.06 N	96.43 W
Blooming Prairie	**190**	43.52 N	93.03 W
Bloomington, Ca., U.S.	**228**	34.04 N	117.23 W
Bloomington, Il., U.S.	**216**	40.29 N	88.59 W
Bloomington, In., U.S.	**218**	39.09 N	86.31 W
Bloomington, Mn., U.S.	**190**	44.50 N	93.17 W
Bloomington, N.Y., U.S.	**210**	41.53 N	74.03 W
Bloomington, Tx., U.S.	**196**	28.38 N	96.53 W
Bloomington, Wi., U.S.	**190**	42.53 N	90.55 W
Bloomington, Lake ⊜[1]	**216**	40.37 N	88.55 W
Blooming Valley	**214**	41.40 N	80.03 W
Bloomsburg	**210**	41.00 N	76.27 W
Bloomsbury, Austl.	**166**	20.43 S	148.35 E
Bloomsbury, N.J., U.S.	**210**	40.39 N	75.05 W
Bloomsdale Gardens	**285**	40.07 N	74.52 W
Bloomville, N.Y., U.S.	**210**	42.20 N	74.48 W
Bloomville, Oh., U.S.	**214**	41.03 N	83.00 W
Blora	**115a**	6.57 S	111.25 E
Bloserville	**208**	40.12 N	77.24 W
Blossburg	**210**	41.40 N	77.03 W
Blossom	**196**	33.39 N	95.23 W
Blossom Hill	**208**	40.05 N	76.19 W
Blötberget	**40**	60.07 N	15.04 E
Blotzheim	**58**	47.36 N	7.29 E
Blouberg	**156**	23.08 S	28.56 E
Blouberg ∧	**156**	23.01 S	28.59 E
Bloubergstrand	**158**	33.47 S	18.28 E
Blouin, Lac ⊜	**190**	48.10 N	77.44 W
Bloumet	**148**	23.27 N	6.06 E
Blountstown	**192**	30.26 N	85.02 W
Blountsville	**194**	34.04 N	86.35 W
Blountville	**192**	36.31 N	82.19 W
Blovice	**60**	49.35 N	13.33 E
Blovstrød	**41**	55.52 N	12.24 E
Blowering Reservoir ⊜[1]	**171b**	35.30 S	148.15 E
Blowing Rock	**192**	36.08 N	81.40 W
Bloxham	**42**	52.02 N	1.22 W
Bloxom	**208**	37.49 N	75.37 W
Blšanka ≃	**54**	50.10 N	13.34 E
Blšany	**54**	50.10 N	13.29 E
Bludenz	**58**	47.09 N	9.49 E
Bludnaja ≃	**88**	51.24 N	110.39 E
Blue ≃, Az., U.S.	**200**	33.13 N	109.11 W
Blue ≃, Co., U.S.	**200**	40.03 N	106.24 W
Blue ≃, In., U.S.	**216**	41.07 N	85.30 W
Blue ≃, In., U.S.	**218**	38.11 N	86.19 W
Blue ≃, Ok., U.S.	**196**	33.53 N	95.56 W
Blue, Middle Fork ≃	**218**	38.33 N	86.07 W
Blue, South Fork ≃	**218**	38.26 N	86.11 W
Blue, West Fork ≃	**218**	38.33 N	86.07 W
Blue Anchor	**285**	39.41 N	74.52 W
Blue Anchor Brook ≃	**285**	39.42 N	74.49 W
Blue Ash	**218**	39.13 N	84.22 W
Blue Ball	**218**	39.29 N	84.21 W
Blue Bell	**208**	40.09 N	75.16 W
Bluebell Hill	**260**	51.20 N	0.30 E
Blue Bonnets, Champ de Course ♠	**275a**	45.29 N	73.39 W
Blue Brook ≃	**276**	40.40 N	74.25 W
Blue Buck Knob ∧[2]	**194**	36.57 N	92.07 W
Bluebush Swamp ≡	**162**	20.30 S	137.25 E
Blue Creek, Oh., U.S.	**218**	38.47 N	83.20 W
Blue Creek, Wa., U.S.	**182**	48.19 N	117.49 W
Blue Creek, Wa., U.S.	**202**	48.19 N	117.49 W
Blue Creek ≃, Ca., U.S.	**226**	38.28 N	120.22 W
Blue Creek ≃, Id., U.S.	**202**	42.02 N	116.08 W
Blue Creek ≃, Ne., U.S.	**198**	41.19 N	102.10 W
Blue Creek ≃, Oh., U.S.	**216**	41.07 N	84.26 W
Blue Creek ≃, Ut,. U.S.	**200**	41.31 N	112.24 W
Blue Cypress Lake ⊜	**220**	27.44 N	80.45 W
Blue Earth	**190**	43.38 N	94.06 W
Blue Earth ≃	**190**	44.09 N	94.02 W
Bluefield, Va., U.S.	**192**	37.15 N	81.16 W
Bluefield, W.V., U.S.	**192**	37.16 N	81.13 W
Bluefields	**236**	12.00 N	83.45 W
Bluefields, Bahía de ⊂	**236**	12.02 N	83.44 W
Bluefields Bay ⊂	**241q**	18.10 N	78.03 W
Blue Grass Airport ⊠	**218**	38.02 N	84.36 W
Blue Grotto → Azzurra, Grotta ⚲[5]	**68**	40.35 N	14.14 E
Blue Hill, Me., U.S.	**188**	44.24 N	68.35 W
Blue Hill, Ne., U.S.	**198**	40.19 N	98.26 W
Blue Hill Bay ⊂	**188**	44.15 N	68.30 W
Blue Hills	**207**	41.40 N	72.56 W
Blue Hills of Couteau ⋏[2]	**186**	47.59 N	57.43 W
Blue Hills Reservation ♠	**283**	42.13 N	71.05 W
Blue Island	**216**	41.39 N	87.40 W
Blue Jay	**228**	34.15 N	117.13 W
Bluejoint Lake ⊜	**202**	42.35 N	119.40 W
Blue Knob ∧	**214**	40.17 N	78.34 W
Blue Knob State Park ♠	**214**	40.16 N	78.35 W
Blue Lagoon National Park ♠	**154**	15.30 S	27.25 E
Blue Lake National Park ♠	**171a**	27.31 S	153.29 E
Blue Licks Battlefield State Park ♠	**218**	38.26 N	84.00 W
Blue Marsh Lake ⊜[1]	**208**	40.25 N	76.05 W
Blue Mesa Reservoir ⊜[1]	**200**	38.27 N	107.10 W
Blue Mosque ʊ[1]	**273c**	30.02 N	31.15 E
Blue Mound, Il., U.S.	**219**	39.42 N	89.07 W
Blue Mound, Ks., U.S.	**198**	38.05 N	95.00 W
Blue Mound, Tx., U.S.	**222**	32.51 N	97.19 W
Blue Mountain, Ms., U.S.	**194**	34.40 N	89.01 W
Blue Mountain, N.Y., U.S.	**210**	42.07 N	74.01 W
Blue Mountain ∧, N.B., Can.	**186**	47.49 N	66.19 W
Blue Mountain ∧, Nf., Can.	**186**	50.24 N	57.10 W
Blue Mountain ∧, Ar., U.S.	**194**	34.41 N	94.03 W
Blue Mountain ∧, Mt., U.S.	**198**	47.16 N	104.10 W
Blue Mountain ∧, N.H., U.S.	**188**	44.47 N	71.28 W
Blue Mountain ∧, Pa., U.S.	**188**	40.15 N	77.30 W
Blue Mountain ∧[2], On., Can.	**190**	48.15 N	80.07 W
Blue Mountain ∧[2], On., Can.	**212**	44.40 N	77.58 W
Blue Mountain Peak ∧	**241q**	18.03 N	76.35 W
Blue Mountains ⋏, Austl.	**170**	33.37 S	150.17 E
Blue Mountains ⋏, Jam.	**241q**	18.06 N	76.40 W
Blue Mountains ⋏, U.S.	**202**	45.30 N	118.15 W
Blue Mountains ⋏, Me., U.S.	**188**	44.50 N	70.35 W
Blue Mountains National Park ♠	**170**	33.40 S	150.25 E
Blue Mud Bay ⊂	**164**	13.26 S	135.56 E
Blue Nile (Al-Baḥr al-Azraq) (Abay) ≃	**140**	15.38 N	32.31 E
Bluenose Lake ⊜	**180**	68.25 N	119.45 W
Blue Point	**276**	40.45 N	73.02 W
Blue Point ›	**276**	40.44 N	73.02 W
Blue Rapids	**198**	39.40 N	96.39 W
Blue Ridge, Ab., Can.	**182**	54.08 N	115.22 W
Blue Ridge, Ga., U.S.	**192**	34.51 N	84.19 W
Blue Ridge, Il., U.S.	**216**	40.17 N	88.29 W
Blue Ridge ⋏	**178**	37.00 N	82.00 W
Blue Ridge Summit	**208**	39.43 N	77.28 W
Blue River	**182**	52.05 N	119.17 W
Blue Rock Springs Park ♠	**282**	38.08 N	122.12 W
Bluesky	**182**	56.04 N	118.14 W
Blue Springs	**198**	40.08 N	96.39 W
Blue Stack Mountains ⋏	**48**	54.45 N	8.05 W
Bluestone ≃	**192**	37.34 N	80.59 W
Bluestone Dam ◆[6]	**192**	37.36 N	80.53 W
Bluestone Lake ⊜[1]	**192**	37.30 N	80.50 W
Bluestone State Park ♠	**192**	37.37 N	80.56 W
Bluewater	**200**	35.15 N	107.59 W
Blue Water Bridge ◆[5]	**214**	43.00 N	82.25 W
Bluff, N.Z.	**172**	46.36 S	168.20 E
Bluff, Ut,. U.S.	**200**	37.17 N	109.33 W
Bluff Cape ›	**110**	18.00 N	94.26 E
Bluff City, Il., U.S.	**219**	38.57 N	89.02 W
Bluff City, Tn., U.S.	**192**	36.28 N	82.15 W
Bluff Cove ⊂	**280**	33.48 N	118.24 W
Bluff Creek ≃, U.S.	**196**	36.58 N	97.26 W
Bluff Creek ≃, Ks., U.S.	**198**	37.02 N	99.29 W
Bluff Dale	**196**	32.21 N	98.01 W
Bluff Head ›	**271d**	22.11 N	114.12 E
Bluff Island I	**271d**	22.19 N	114.21 E
Bluff Knoll ∧	**162**	34.23 S	118.20 E
Bluff Park	**194**	33.24 N	86.51 W
Bluff Point ›	**162**	27.50 S	114.06 E
Bluffs	**219**	39.45 N	90.32 W
Bluff Springs	**219**	39.59 N	90.21 W
Bluffton, In., U.S.	**216**	40.44 N	85.10 W
Bluffton, Oh., U.S.	**216**	40.53 N	83.53 W
Bluffton, S.C., U.S.	**192**	32.14 N	80.51 W
Bluffy Lake ⊜	**184**	50.47 N	92.55 W
Bluford	**219**	38.20 N	88.45 W
Blum	**222**	32.09 N	97.24 W
Blumberg, Dtsch.	**54**	52.36 N	13.37 E
Blumberg, Dtsch.	**58**	47.50 N	8.31 E
Blumenau	**252**	26.56 S	49.03 W
Blumenhof	**184**	50.01 N	107.41 W
Blümlisalp ∧	**58**	46.30 N	7.47 E
Blunt	**198**	44.30 N	99.59 W
Blup Blup Island I	**164**	3.30 S	144.37 E
Bly	**202**	42.23 N	121.02 W
Blying Sound ⊔	**180**	59.50 N	149.15 W
Blyth, Austl.	**168b**	33.51 S	138.29 E
Blyth, On., Can.	**190**	43.44 N	81.26 W
Blyth, Eng., U.K.	**44**	55.07 N	1.30 W
Blyth ≃, Austl.	**164**	12.04 S	134.35 E
Blyth ≃, Eng., U.K.	**42**	52.18 N	1.40 E
Blyth ≃, Eng., U.K.	**44**	55.08 N	1.31 W
Blyth Bridge	**46**	55.42 N	3.24 W
Blythe	**204**	33.36 N	114.35 W
Blythedale	**214**	40.15 N	79.48 W
Blytheswood	**214**	42.07 N	82.36 W
Blytheville	**194**	35.55 N	89.55 W
Blytheville Air Force Base ■	**194**	35.57 N	89.57 W
Blyth Range ⋏	**162**	26.50 S	129.00 E
Bnei Braq → Bene Beraq	**132**	32.05 N	34.50 E
Bø, Nor.	**24**	68.37 N	14.33 E
Bø, Nor.	**26**	59.25 N	9.04 E
Bo, S.L.	**150**	7.56 N	11.21 W
Boa	**154**	10.32 S	28.06 E
Boac	**116**	13.27 N	121.50 E
Boaco	**236**	12.28 N	85.40 W
Boaco □[5]	**236**	12.30 N	85.30 W
Boadilla del Monte	**266a**	40.24 N	3.53 W
Boa Esperança, Bra.	**255**	21.05 S	45.34 W
Boa Esperança, Bra.	**256**	22.48 S	42.34 W
Boa Esperança, Bra.	**256**	22.24 S	43.05 W
Boa Esperança, Represa ⊜[1]	**250**	6.50 S	44.00 W
Bo'ai	**102**	35.10 N	113.04 E
Boali	**152**	4.48 N	18.07 E
Boalia	**126**	23.35 N	88.57 E
Boalsburg	**214**	40.46 N	77.48 W
Boane	**156**	26.06 S	32.19 E
Boano, Pulau I	**164**	2.56 S	127.56 E
Boa Nova	**255**	14.22 S	40.10 W
Bo'ao	**110**	19.14 N	110.34 E
Boara Pisani	**64**	45.08 N	11.47 E
Boara Polesine	**64**	45.07 N	11.48 E
Board Camp Mountain ∧	**204**	40.42 N	123.43 W
Boardman	**214**	41.01 N	80.39 W
Boardman ≃	**190**	44.46 N	85.38 W
Boarhills	**46**	56.19 N	2.42 W
Boario Terme	**64**	45.54 N	10.10 E
Boat Basin	**182**	49.29 N	126.25 W
Boat Channel ⊔	**212**	44.10 N	76.31 W
Boath	**46**	57.44 N	4.23 W
Boat Lake ⊜	**212**	44.44 N	81.13 W
Boatman	**166**	27.16 S	146.55 E
Boat of Garten	**46**	57.20 N	3.44 W
Boa Viagem	**250**	5.07 S	39.44 W
Boa Vista, Bra.	**246**	2.49 N	60.40 W
Boa Vista, Bra.	**256**	21.25 S	45.35 W
Boa Vista I	**150a**	16.05 N	22.50 W
Boa Vista, Morro ∧[2]	**287a**	22.53 S	43.06 W
Boavita	**246**	6.20 N	72.35 W
Boawai	**115b**	8.46 S	121.10 E
Boayan Island I	**116**	10.34 N	119.09 E
Boaz	**194**	34.12 N	86.09 W
Boba	**115b**	8.57 S	121.04 E
Bobai	**102**	22.12 N	109.52 E
Bobbau	**54**	51.41 N	12.16 E
Bobbili	**122**	18.34 N	83.22 E
Bobbing	**260**	51.21 N	0.43 E
Bobbingworth	**260**	51.44 N	0.13 E
Bobbin Head	**274a**	33.39 S	151.08 E
Bobbio	**62**	44.46 N	9.23 E
Bobbio Pellice	**62**	44.48 N	7.07 E
Bobbys Run ≃	**285**	39.58 N	74.48 W
Bobcaygeon	**212**	44.33 N	78.33 W
Bobenheim-Roxheim	**56**	49.35 N	8.21 E
Bobigny	**50**	48.54 N	2.27 E
Böbingen, Dtsch.	**56**	48.49 N	9.54 E
Bobingen, Dtsch.	**58**	48.16 N	10.50 E
Bobitz	**54**	53.47 N	11.20 E
Bob Lake ⊜	**212**	44.55 N	78.47 W
Böblingen	**56**	48.41 N	9.01 E
Boblo Island Amusement Park ♠	**281**	42.06 N	83.07 W
Bobo Dioulasso	**150**	11.12 N	4.18 W
Boboiob, gora ∧	**85**	40.52 N	70.21 E
Bobo Island I	**164**	9.08 S	143.14 E
Bobolice	**30**	53.57 N	16.36 E
Bobonaza ≃	**246**	2.36 S	76.38 W
Bobonong	**156**	21.58 S	28.17 E
Bobos ≃	**234**	20.15 N	96.47 W
Bobotsari	**115a**	7.18 S	109.22 E
Bobr	**76**	54.20 N	29.16 E
Bobr ≃, Bela.	**76**	54.03 N	28.51 E
Bóbr ≃, Pol.	**30**	52.04 N	15.04 E
Bobrik ≃	**76**	52.08 N	26.46 E
Bobrikovo	**83**	47.56 N	39.13 E
Bobrinec	**78**	48.03 N	32.09 E
Bobrka	**78**	49.38 N	24.18 E
Bobrov	**78**	51.06 N	40.02 E
Bobrovica	**78**	50.44 N	31.22 E
Bobrujsk	**76**	53.09 N	29.14 E
Bobs Creek ≃	**219**	38.57 N	90.42 W
Bobs Lake ⊜	**212**	44.40 N	76.35 W
Bobtown	**188**	39.45 N	79.58 W
Bobuk	**140**	11.30 N	34.05 E
Bobures	**246**	9.15 N	71.11 W
Boby, Pic ∧	**157b**	22.12 S	46.55 E
Boca ◆[8]	**288**	34.38 S	58.21 W
Bôca, Cachoeira da ∟	**250**	5.27 S	54.24 W
Boca Brava, Isla I	**236**	8.13 N	82.16 W
Boca Chica	**240m**	17.59 N	66.32 W
Boca Chica Key I	**220**	24.34 N	81.42 W
Bôca da Mata	**250**	9.41 S	36.11 W
Boca del Monte	**236**	8.21 N	82.07 W
Boca del Río	**234**	19.06 N	96.06 W
Boca del Rosario	**258**	34.26 S	57.17 W
Boca de Pozo	**246**	11.00 N	64.23 W
Boca de Quadra ⊔	**182**	55.08 N	130.50 W
Boca do Acre	**248**	8.45 S	67.23 W
Bôca do Jari	**250**	1.07 S	51.58 W
Bocage, Cap ›	**175f**	21.12 S	165.35 E
Boca Grande	**220**	26.44 N	82.15 W
Boca Grande Channel ⊔	**220**	24.34 N	82.03 W
Boca Grande Key I	**220**	24.32 N	82.00 W
Bocaina ≃	**256**	22.40 S	45.00 W
Bocaina, Parque Nacional de ♠	**256**	23.00 S	44.15 W
Bocaina, Serra da ⋏	**256**	22.43 S	44.40 W
Bocaina de Minas	**256**	22.10 S	44.24 W
Bocaiúva	**255**	17.07 S	43.49 W
Bocanda	**150**	7.04 N	4.30 W
Bocanegra	**286d**	12.01 S	77.07 W
Bocaranga	**152**	6.59 N	15.39 E
Boca Raton	**220**	26.21 N	80.05 W
Boca Reservoir ⊜[1]	**226**	39.24 N	120.06 W
Bocas del Toro	**236**	9.20 N	82.15 W
Bocas del Toro □[4]	**236**	8.50 N	82.10 W
Bocas del Toro, Archipiélago de II	**236**	9.20 N	82.10 W
Bocaue	**116**	14.48 N	120.55 E
Bocay	**236**	14.19 N	85.10 W
Bocay ≃	**236**	14.20 N	85.10 W
Boccaleone	**66**	44.39 N	11.48 E
Boccea ◆[8]	**267a**	41.58 N	12.19 E
Bocchigliero	**68**	39.25 N	16.45 E
Boccon	**64**	45.19 N	11.39 E
Bocconi	**64**	44.01 N	11.46 E
Bočejkovo	**76**	55.01 N	29.09 E
Bochan	**88**	53.09 N	103.48 E
Bochil	**234**	16.59 N	92.55 W
Böch Möron	**86**	49.40 N	90.20 E
Bochnia	**30**	49.58 N	20.26 E
Bocholt, Bel.	**56**	51.10 N	5.35 E
Bocholt, Dtsch.	**52**	51.50 N	6.36 E
Bocholtz	**56**	50.49 N	6.00 E
Bochov	**54**	50.06 N	13.02 E
Bochum, Dtsch.	**56**	51.28 N	7.13 E
Bochum, Dtsch.	**263**	51.28 N	7.13 E
Bochum, S. Afr.	**156**	23.17 S	29.07 E
Bockel	**52**	53.12 N	9.17 E
Böckel ◆[8]	**263**	51.13 N	7.12 E
Bockenem	**52**	52.00 N	10.07 E
Bockhorn	**52**	53.23 N	8.01 E
Böckstein	**64**	47.05 N	13.07 E
Bockum ◆[8], Dtsch.	**263**	51.21 N	6.38 E
Bockum ◆[8], Dtsch.	**263**	51.20 N	6.44 E
Bockum-Hövel	**52**	51.42 N	7.46 E
Bocognano	**36**	42.05 N	9.03 E
Bocón, Caño ≃	**246**	3.42 N	67.53 W
Boconó	**246**	9.15 N	70.16 W
Bocq ≃	**56**	50.20 N	4.53 E
Bocșa	**38**	45.23 N	21.47 E
Boczów	**54**	52.19 N	14.58 E
Boda, Centraf.	**152**	4.19 N	17.28 E
Böda, Sve.	**26**	57.15 N	17.03 E
Boda, Sve.	**26**	61.01 N	15.13 E
Bodafors	**26**	57.30 N	14.42 E
Boda Glasbruk	**26**	56.44 N	15.40 E
Bodāi	**272b**	22.48 N	88.29 E
Bodajbo	**88**	57.51 N	114.10 E
Bodalangi	**152**	3.14 N	22.14 E
Bodalla	**166**	36.05 S	150.03 E
Bodallin	**162**	31.22 S	118.52 E
Bodåsgruvan	**40**	60.25 N	16.26 E
Bodcau Creek ≃	**194**	33.01 N	93.31 W
Boddam, Scot., U.K.	**46**	57.28 N	1.47 W
Boddam, Scot., U.K.	**46a**	59.55 N	1.17 W
Boddington	**168a**	32.48 S	116.28 E
Bode	**198**	42.52 N	94.17 W
Bode ≃	**54**	52.01 N	11.12 E
Bodega Bay ⊂	**204**	38.15 N	123.00 W
Bodegraven	**52**	52.05 N	4.45 E
Bodélé ◆[1]	**146**	16.30 N	16.30 E
Bodelschwingh ◆[8]	**263**	51.33 N	7.22 E
Boden	**26**	65.50 N	21.42 E
Bodenburg	**52**	52.01 N	10.01 E
Bodenfelde	**52**	51.38 N	9.33 E
Boden → Fleres	**64**	46.58 N	11.21 E
Bodenheim	**56**	49.56 N	8.18 E
Bodenmais	**60**	49.04 N	13.06 E
Bodensee (Lake Constance) ⊜	**58**	47.35 N	9.25 E
Bodenteich	**54**	52.50 N	10.41 E
Bodenwerder	**52**	51.59 N	9.31 E
Bodenwies ∧	**61**	47.45 N	14.34 E
Bodenwöhr	**60**	49.16 N	12.19 E
Boderg, Lough ⊜	**48**	53.52 N	7.58 W
Bode Sadu	**150**	9.00 N	4.47 E
Bodhan	**122**	18.40 N	77.54 E
Bodh Gaya	**124**	24.42 N	84.59 E
Bodiam	**42**	51.00 N	0.33 E
Bodināyakkanūr	**122**	10.01 N	77.21 E
Bodine, Mount ∧	**182**	55.37 N	125.49 W
Bodjoki	**152**	2.59 N	22.18 E
Bodjokola	**152**	3.54 N	20.17 E
Bodmin	**42**	50.29 N	4.43 W
Bodmin Moor ◆[3]	**42**	50.33 N	4.33 W
Bodø	**24**	67.17 N	14.23 E
Bodocó	**250**	7.47 S	39.55 W
Bodoquena, Serra da ⋏[1]	**248**	21.00 S	56.50 W
Bodoukpa	**152**	5.43 N	17.36 E
Bodri ≃	**115a**	6.52 S	110.10 E
Bodrog ≃	**38**	48.07 N	21.25 E
Bodrum	**130**	37.02 N	27.26 E
Bodstedt	**54**	54.22 N	12.37 E
Bo Duc	**110**	11.58 N	106.48 E
Bodzentyn	**30**	50.56 N	20.57 E
Boè, Piz ∧	**64**	46.31 N	11.48 E
Boëge	**58**	46.13 N	6.25 E
Boekelo	**52**	52.13 N	6.47 E
Boele ◆[8]	**263**	51.24 N	7.28 E
Boémbé	**152**	2.54 S	15.39 E
Boende	**152**	0.13 S	20.52 E
Bœng Lvea	**110**	12.36 N	105.34 E
Boeni	**157a**	12.55 S	45.06 E
Boën-sur-Lignon	**62**	45.44 N	3.59 E
Boeo, Capo ›	**70**	37.48 N	12.25 E
Boerboonfontein	**158**	33.43 S	20.32 E
Boerne	**196**	29.47 N	98.43 W
Boeslunde	**41**	55.18 N	11.17 E
Boesmanland □[5]	**156**	19.30 S	20.00 E
Boesmans ≃, S. Afr.	**158**	28.46 S	30.09 E
Boesmans ≃, S. Afr.	**158**	33.42 S	26.39 E
Boesmansriviermond	**158**	33.42 S	26.39 E
Boetsap	**158**	27.59 S	24.30 E
Boeuf ≃	**194**	31.52 N	91.47 W
Boeuf Creek ≃	**219**	38.36 N	91.09 W
Boffa	**150**	10.10 N	14.02 W
Boffalora	**266b**	45.28 N	8.50 E
Boffzen	**52**	51.45 N	9.23 E
Bofoku	**152**	0.57 S	20.53 E
Bofors	**40**	59.20 N	14.32 E
Bofosso	**150**	8.40 N	9.42 W
Bōfu → Hōfu	**96**	34.03 N	131.34 E
Boga	**154**	1.03 N	29.56 E
Bogachiel ≃	**224**	47.55 N	124.28 W
Bogadjim	**164**	5.25 S	145.45 E
Bogal, Lagh ≃	**154**	0.45 N	40.50 E
Bogale	**110**	16.17 N	95.24 E
Bogalusa	**194**	30.47 N	89.50 W
Bogan ≃	**166**	29.57 S	146.21 E
Bogandé	**150**	12.59 N	0.08 W
Bog and Vly Meadows ≡	**276**	40.56 N	74.19 W
Bogan Gate	**166**	33.07 S	147.48 E
Bogangolo	**152**	5.34 N	18.15 E
Bogantungan	**166**	23.39 S	147.18 E
Bogart, Mount ∧	**182**	50.55 N	115.14 W
Bogastow Brook ≃	**283**	42.12 N	71.22 W
Bogata	**196**	33.28 N	95.13 W
Bogataja Černeščina	**78**	48.59 N	35.35 E
Bogatiščevo-Jepišino	**82**	54.47 N	38.25 E
Bogatoje	**80**	53.04 N	51.24 E
Bogatyje Saby	**80**	56.01 N	50.27 E
Bogatynia	**54**	50.53 N	15.00 E
Bogatyr'	**80**	53.25 N	50.02 E
Bogatyrevo	**80**	50.22 N	48.46 E
Boğazkale	**130**	40.02 N	34.37 E
Boğazkaya	**130**	41.27 N	35.54 E
Boğazköy ◆[8]	**267b**	41.11 N	28.46 E
Boğazköy ≃	**267b**	41.10 N	28.49 E
Boğazlıyan	**130**	39.12 N	35.15 E
Bogbonga	**152**	1.35 N	19.25 E
Bogcang ≃	**120**	31.56 N	87.24 E
Bogd	**102**	45.11 N	100.43 E
Bogdanovič	**86**	56.47 N	62.01 E
Bogdanovka, Ross.	**80**	52.42 N	50.46 E
Bogdanovka, Ross.	**80**	52.10 N	52.37 E
Bogdanovka, Sak.	**84**	41.18 N	43.35 E
Bogda Shan ⋏	**90**	43.30 N	89.45 E
Bogdo Ula ∧	**86**	43.50 N	88.20 E
Bogel	**56**	50.11 N	7.48 E
Bogembaj	**86**	52.29 N	72.20 E
Bogen	**60**	48.55 N	12.43 E
Bogense	**41**	55.34 N	10.06 E
Boger City	**192**	35.29 N	81.12 W
Boges	**56**	50.11 N	7.48 E
Bogess Creek ≃	**282**	37.18 N	122.19 W
Boget	**80**	49.40 N	47.59 E
Boggabilla	**166**	28.37 S	150.21 E
Boggabri	**166**	30.42 S	150.02 E
Boggeragh Mountains ⋏	**48**	52.03 N	8.55 W
Boggola, Mount ∧	**162**	23.48 S	117.40 E
Boggs Run ≃	**279b**	40.32 N	80.14 W
Boggstown	**218**	39.34 N	85.55 W
Boggy Creek ≃	**222**	31.07 N	95.46 W
Boggy Peak ∧	**240c**	17.03 N	61.51 W
Bogia	**164**	4.15 S	144.55 E
Bogie Lake ⊜	**281**	42.37 N	83.31 W
Bogilima	**152**	3.34 N	19.16 E
Bogliasco	**62**	44.23 N	9.04 E
Bognanco Fonti	**58**	46.07 N	8.12 E
Bognes	**24**	68.10 N	16.00 E
Bognor Regis	**42**	50.47 N	0.41 W
Bogny-sur-Meuse	**56**	49.51 N	4.46 E
Bogo, Cam.	**146**	10.44 N	14.36 E
Bogo, Pil.	**116**	11.03 N	124.00 E
Bogø I	**41**	54.56 N	12.04 E
Bogo Bay ⊂	**116**	11.05 N	124.01 E
Bogoduchov	**78**	50.10 N	35.30 E
Bogol Manyo	**144**	4.31 N	41.32 E
Bogol'ubovo, Ross.	**76**	55.32 N	32.57 E
Bogol'ubovo, Ross.	**80**	56.13 N	40.31 E
Bogomila	**38**	41.36 N	21.28 E
Bogong, Mount ∧	**166**	36.45 S	147.18 E
Bogong Peaks ⋏	**171b**	35.34 S	148.28 E
Bogor	**115a**	6.35 S	106.47 E
Bogoria, Lake ⊜	**154**	0.15 N	36.06 E
Bogoro	**154**	1.24 N	30.17 E
Bogorodčany	**78**	48.48 N	24.32 E
Bogorodick	**76**	53.46 N	38.08 E
Bogorodickoje	**80**	46.20 N	41.10 E
Bogorodičnoje	**83**	49.01 N	37.30 E
Bogorodsk, Ross.	**24**	62.16 N	52.28 E
Bogorodsk, Ross.	**80**	56.06 N	43.31 E
Bogorodskoje, Ross.	**80**	57.51 N	50.45 E
Bogorodskoje, Ross.	**80**	46.20 N	43.53 E
Bogorodskoje, Ross.	**82**	55.02 N	38.29 E
Bogorodskoje, Ross.	**82**	55.26 N	36.14 E
Bogorodskoje, Ross.	**89**	52.22 N	140.30 E
Bogorodskoje ◆[8]	**265b**	55.49 N	37.44 E
Bogoso	**150**	5.34 N	2.01 W
Bogosskij chrebet ⋏	**84**	42.15 N	46.05 E
Bogota	**276**	40.52 N	74.01 W
Bogotá → Santa Fe de Bogotá	**246**	4.36 N	74.05 W
Bogotol	**86**	56.12 N	89.33 E
Bogou	**150**	10.39 N	0.11 E
Bogovarovo	**24**	58.59 N	47.01 E

≃	River	Fluß	Río	Rivière	Rio
≋	Canal	Kanal	Canal	Canal	Canal
∟	Waterfall, Rapids	Wasserfall, Stromschnellen	Cascada, Rápidos	Chute d'eau, Rapides	Cascata, Rápidos
⊔	Strait	Meeresstraße	Estrecho	Détroit	Estreito
⊂	Bay, Gulf	Bucht, Golf	Bahía, Golfo	Baie, Golfe	Baía, Golfo
⊜	Lake, Lakes	See, Seen	Lago, Lagos	Lac, Lacs	Lago, Lagos
≡	Swamp	Sumpf	Pantano	Marais	Pântano
⊓	Ice Features, Glacier	Eis- und Gletscherformen	Accidentes Glaciales	Formes glaciaires	Acidentes glaciares
⊤	Other Hydrographic Features	Andere Hydrographische Objekte	Otros Elementos Hidrográficos	Autres données hydrographiques	Outros acidentes hidrográficos

✣	Submarine Features	Untermeerische Objekte	Accidentes Submarinos	Formes de relief sous-marin	Acidentes submarinos
□	Political Unit	Politische Einheit	Unidad Política	Entité politique	Unidade política
ʊ	Cultural Institution	Kulturelle Institution	Institución Cultural	Institution culturelle	Instituição cultural
⊥	Historical Site	Historische Stätte	Sitio Histórico	Site historique	Sítio histórico
♠	Recreational Site	Erholungs- und Ferienort	Sitio de Recreo	Centre de loisirs	Area de Lazer
⊠	Airport	Flughafen	Aeropuerto	Aéroport	Aeroporto
■	Military Installation	Militäranlage	Instalación Militar	Installation militaire	Instalação militar
◆	Miscellaneous	Verschiedenes	Misceláneo	Divers	Diversos

Bogra 124 24.51 N 89.22 E
Bograd 86 54.13 N 90.51 E
Bogrie Hill ∧[2] 44 55.08 N 3.55 W
Bogučany 88 58.23 N 97.29 E
Bogučar 78 49.57 N 40.33 E
Bogučar ≃ 78 49.57 N 40.39 E
Bogué 150 16.35 N 14.16 W
Bogue Chitto 194 31.26 N 90.27 W
Bogue Chitto ≃ 194 30.35 N 89.49 W
Bogue Chitto Creek ≃ 194 32.10 N 87.14 W
Bogue Phalia ≃ 194 33.15 N 90.44 W
Bogues Bay ⊂ 208 37.52 N 75.29 W
Böğürtlen 130 37.10 N 38.04 E
Boguševsk 76 54.51 N 30.13 E
Boguslav 78 49.33 N 30.53 E
Bogustan 85 41.41 N 70.05 E
Bo Hai (Gulf of Chihli) ⊂ 98 38.30 N 120.00 E
Bohai Haixia Ʉ 98 38.15 N 121.00 E
Bohain-en-Vermandois 50 49.59 N 3.27 E
Bohai Wan ⊂ 98 38.40 N 118.20 E
Bohan 56 49.52 N 4.53 E
Bohannon 208 37.24 N 76.22 W
Böheimkirchen 61 48.12 N 15.46 E
Bohemia 210 40.46 N 73.06 W
Bohemia ≃ 208 39.29 N 75.55 W
Bohemia → Čechy □[9] 30 49.50 N 14.00 E
Bohemia Downs 162 18.53 S 126.14 E
Bohemian Forest ⋏ 30 49.15 N 12.45 E
Bohetai 104 42.01 N 123.13 E
Bohicon 150 7.12 N 2.04 E
Bohin 144 11.44 N 51.15 E
Bohinjska Bistrica 36 46.17 N 13.57 E
Böhlen 54 51.12 N 12.23 E
Böhlitz-Ehrenberg ◆[8] 54 51.21 N 12.17 E
Böhme ≃ 52 52.46 N 9.28 E
Böhmen → Čechy □[9] 30 49.50 N 14.00 E
Böhmenkirch 56 48.41 N 9.55 E
Böhmerwald → Bohemian Forest ⋏ 30 49.15 N 12.45 E
Bohmte 52 52.22 N 8.19 E
Bohners Lake 216 42.37 N 88.17 W
Böhnsdorf ◆[8] 264a 52.24 N 13.33 E
Bohodou 150 9.46 N 9.04 W
Bohol 144 5.45 N 46.09 E
Bohol □[4] 116 9.50 N 124.10 E
Bohol I 116 9.50 N 124.10 E
Bohol Sea ⫪[2] 116 9.10 N 124.25 E
Bohon 116 18.30 N 120.35 E
Bohongou 150 12.30 N 0.42 E
Bohorg 152 6.23 N 15.37 E
Bohorok 114 3.30 N 98.12 E
Bohsdorf 54 51.38 N 14.32 E
Bohuslän □[9] 26 58.15 N 11.50 E
Bohušovice nad Ohří 54 50.29 N 14.07 E
Bohutín 60 49.40 N 13.55 E
Boi 150 9.34 N 9.27 E
Boi, Ponta do ≻ 256 23.58 S 45.15 W
Boiaçu 246 0.27 S 61.46 W
Boiano 66 41.29 N 14.29 E
Boiceville 210 41.59 N 74.15 W
Boiestown 186 46.27 N 66.25 W
Boigu Island I 164 9.16 S 142.12 E
Boila 154 16.10 S 39.50 E
Boiling Springs, N.C., U.S. 192 35.30 N 81.37 W
Boiling Springs, Pa., U.S. 208 40.08 N 77.07 W
Boim 250 2.49 S 55.10 W
Boinville-en-Mantois 261 48.56 N 1.46 E
Boinvilliers 261 48.55 N 1.40 E
Boipeba, Ilha de I 255 13.39 S 38.55 W
Boiro 34 42.39 N 8.54 W
Bois, Lac des ⊜ 180 66.40 N 125.15 W
Bois, Lac des → Woods, Lake of the ⊜ 184 49.15 N 94.45 W
Bois, Rio dos ≃ 255 18.35 S 50.02 W
Bois Blanc Island I 190 45.45 N 84.28 W
Boisbriand 275a 45.37 N 73.51 W
Bois Brule ≃ 190 46.45 N 91.37 W
Boischâtel 206 46.54 N 71.08 W
Bois-Colombes 261 48.55 N 2.16 E
Boisdale, Loch ⊂ 46 57.08 N 7.19 W
Bois d'Arc Creek ≃ 196 33.50 N 95.50 W
Bois-d'Arcy 261 48.48 N 2.01 E
Bois-des-Filion 206 45.40 N 73.45 W
Bois de Sioux ≃ 198 46.16 N 96.36 W
Boise 202 43.36 N 116.12 W
Boise ≃ 202 43.49 N 117.01 W
Boise, Middle Fork ≃ 202 43.42 N 115.38 W
Boise, North Fork ≃ 202 43.42 N 115.38 W
Boise, South Fork ≃ 202 43.36 N 115.51 W
Boise City 196 36.43 N 102.30 W
Boisemont 261 49.01 N 2.00 E
Bois-Guillaume 50 49.28 N 1.08 E
Bois-le-Roi 50 48.28 N 2.42 E
Boissettes 261 48.31 N 2.37 E
Boissevain 184 49.14 N 100.03 W
Boissise-la-Bertrand 261 48.32 N 2.35 E
Boissy-l'Aillerie 261 49.05 N 2.02 E
Boissy-Saint-Léger 50 48.45 N 2.31 E
Boissy-sous-Saint-Yon 261 48.34 N 2.13 E
Boistfort Peak ∧ 224 46.29 N 123.12 W
Boitzenburg 54 53.15 N 13.37 E
Boizenburg 54 53.22 N 10.43 E
Boja 115a 7.06 S 110.16 E
Bojadła 30 51.57 N 15.50 E
Bojarka 78 50.19 N 30.19 E
Bojarkino 82 54.57 N 38.31 E
Bojarsk 88 56.19 N 106.04 E
Bojayá ≃ 246 6.35 N 76.54 W
Bojeador, Cape ≻ 116 18.30 N 120.34 E
Bojelebung 116 6.31 N 122.11 E
Bojevo 78 51.24 N 39.19 E
Boji Plain ≚ 154 1.30 N 39.45 E
Bojizhang 98 41.49 N 117.46 E
Bojnūrd 128 37.28 N 57.19 E
Bojonegoro 115a 7.09 S 111.52 E
Boju 150 7.25 N 7.52 E
Boju Ega 150 7.24 N 8.04 E
B'ojuk-Kirs, gora ∧ 84 39.41 N 46.44 E
Bojuru 252 31.38 S 51.26 W
Bokad 272c 18.53 N 72.58 E
Bokada 152 4.08 N 19.23 E
Bokal 168a 33.29 S 116.54 E
Bokala, Zaïre 152 3.07 S 17.02 E
Bokala, Zaïre 152 2.03 N 18.59 E
Bokani 150 9.26 N 5.13 E
Bokāro Steel City 124 23.45 N 86.07 E
Bokatola 152 0.38 S 18.46 E
Bokchito 196 34.01 N 96.08 W
Boké 150 10.56 N 14.18 W
Bokeelia 220 26.42 N 82.09 W
Bokel 52 53.23 N 8.46 E
Bokela 152 1.08 S 21.56 E
Bokes Creek ≃ 188 40.19 N 83.10 W
Bokfontein 158 32.48 S 19.16 E
Bokhara 158 27.57 S 20.30 E
Bokhara ≃ 166 29.55 S 146.42 E
Boki 146 8.48 N 13.32 E
Bokino 80 52.38 N 41.26 E
Bokkol ∧ 154 1.50 N 37.02 E
Bok Koŭ 110 10.37 N 104.03 E
Böklund 41 54.36 N 9.34 E
Boknafjorden ⊂[2] 26 59.10 N 5.35 E
Boko, Congo 152 4.47 S 14.38 E
Boko, Kaz. 86 49.05 N 81.38 E
Bokod 116 16.30 N 120.50 E
Bokode 152 3.58 N 19.29 E
Bokolako 150 13.36 N 12.33 W
Bokonbajevskoje 85 42.07 N 77.00 E
Bokondji 152 2.22 N 18.42 E
Bokondo 152 0.15 N 22.32 E
Bokong 112 9.58 S 124.04 E
Bokoro 146 12.23 N 17.03 E
Boko Songo 152 4.26 S 13.37 E
Bokota 152 0.51 S 22.18 E
Bokote 152 0.05 S 20.08 E
Bokovo-Antratsit → Antracit 83 48.06 N 39.06 E
Bokovo Platovo 83 48.07 N 39.01 E
Bokovskaja 80 49.15 N 41.49 E
Bokpunt ≻ 158 33.34 S 18.19 E
Bokpyin 110 11.16 N 98.46 E
Boksburg 158 26.12 S 28.14 E
Boksburg □[5] 273d 26.12 S 28.14 E
Boksburg-Noord 273d 26.12 S 28.15 E
Boksburg South 273d 26.14 S 28.15 E
Boksburg-West 273d 26.13 S 28.14 E
Boksitogorsk 76 59.28 N 33.51 E
Bokungu 152 0.41 S 22.19 E
Bol, Cro. 36 43.16 N 16.40 E
Bol, Tchad 146 13.28 N 14.43 E
Bolaang Mongondow 112 0.56 N 124.10 E
Bolama, Gui.-B. 150 11.35 N 15.28 W
Bolama, Zaïre 152 1.57 N 22.58 E
Bolaman 130 41.03 N 37.37 E
Bolān ≃ 120 28.38 N 67.42 E
Bolanda, Jabal ∧ 140 7.44 N 25.28 E
Bol'andkiik ≃ 85 39.11 N 72.17 E
Bolangum 166 36.46 S 142.53 E
Bolaños 234 21.41 N 103.47 W
Bolaños ≃ 234 21.14 N 104.08 W
Bolaños de Calatrava 34 38.54 N 3.40 W
Bolān Pass)(120 29.45 N 67.35 E
Bolans 240c 17.02 N 61.53 W
Bolay I 152 4.20 N 17.21 E
Bolayır 130 40.31 N 26.45 E
Bolbec 50 49.34 N 0.29 E
Bolčary 86 59.49 N 68.48 E
Bolchov 76 53.27 N 36.01 E
Bolchuny 80 47.59 N 46.25 E
Bolda ≃ 80 46.10 N 48.14 E
Boldasevo 80 54.43 N 45.33 E
Boldekow 54 53.43 N 13.35 E
Bolderslev 41 54.59 N 9.18 E
Bold Heath 262 53.24 N 2.42 W
Boldon 44 54.57 N 1.27 W
Bol'džuan 85 38.19 N 69.40 E
Bole, Ghana 150 9.02 N 2.29 W
Bole, Zhg. 86 44.53 N 82.05 E
Bolechov 78 49.04 N 23.52 E
Boleko 152 1.31 S 19.53 E
Bolero 154 10.59 S 33.45 E
Boles 194 34.46 N 94.02 W
Bolesławiec 30 51.16 N 15.34 E
Boleszkowice 30 52.44 N 14.36 E
Boletice nad Labem 54 50.45 N 14.13 E
Boley 196 35.29 N 96.29 W
Bolgarčaj ≃ 84 39.28 N 48.36 E
Bolgart 162 31.16 S 116.30 E
Bolgatanga 150 10.46 N 0.52 W
Bolgrad 78 45.41 N 28.36 E
Boli, Sūd. 140 6.01 N 28.43 E
Boli, Tchad 146 10.50 N 18.43 E
Boli, Zhg. 89 45.46 N 130.31 E
Bolia 152 1.36 S 18.23 E
Boliden 26 64.52 N 20.23 E
Boligee 194 32.45 N 88.01 W
Boligeqiu 104 42.14 N 121.40 E
Bolíkov 61 49.02 N 15.22 E
Bolinao 116 16.23 N 119.54 E
Bolinas 226 37.54 N 122.42 W
Boling 222 29.15 N 95.56 W
Bolingbrook 216 41.41 N 88.04 W
Bolinger Creek ≃ 282 37.47 N 122.00 W
Bolingo 152 3.30 S 21.43 E
Bolishan 89 43.50 N 123.31 E
Bolivar, Austl. 168b 34.46 S 138.36 E
Bolívar, Col. 246 5.50 N 76.01 W
Bolívar, Col. 246 1.50 N 76.58 W
Bolívar, Col. 246 4.21 N 76.10 W
Bolívar, Perú 248 7.18 S 77.48 W
Bolivar, Mo., U.S. 194 37.36 N 93.24 W
Bolivar, N.Y., U.S. 210 42.04 N 78.10 W
Bolivar, Oh., U.S. 214 40.39 N 81.27 W
Bolivar, Pa., U.S. 214 40.23 N 79.09 W
Bolivar, Tn., U.S. 194 35.15 N 88.59 W
Bolívar □[3] 246 6.20 N 63.30 W
Bolívar □[4] 246 1.35 S 79.00 W
Bolívar □[5] 246 9.00 N 74.40 W
Bolívar, Cerro ∧ 246 7.28 N 63.25 W
Bolívar, Pico ∧ 246 8.30 N 71.02 W
Bolivar Peninsula ≻[1] 196 29.27 N 94.39 W
Bolivar Run 214 41.59 N 78.39 W
Bolivia □[1], S.A. 242 17.00 S 65.00 W
Bolivia □[1], S.A. 248 17.00 S 65.00 W
Bolivie → Bolivia □[1] 248 17.00 S 65.00 W
Bolivien → Bolivia □[1] 248 17.00 S 65.00 W
Boljarovo 38 42.09 N 26.49 E
Boljoon 116 9.38 N 123.29 E
Bolkar Dağları ⋏ 130 37.15 N 34.20 E
Bölkenbusch 263 51.21 N 7.06 E
Boll 56 48.38 N 9.37 E
Bolladello 266b 45.41 N 8.50 E
Bollate 62 45.33 N 9.07 E
Böllberg ∧[2] 263 51.23 N 7.19 E
Bollendorf 56 49.51 N 6.22 E
Bollène 62 44.17 N 4.45 E
Bollensdorf 264a 52.31 N 13.43 E
Bolles Canal ≅ 220 26.38 N 80.34 W
Bolles Harbor 216 41.51 N 83.24 W
Bollin ≃ 262 53.23 N 2.28 W
Bolling Air Force Base ■ 284c 38.51 N 77.02 W
Bollington, Eng., U.K. 262 53.22 N 2.25 W
Bollington, Eng., U.K. 262 53.18 N 2.06 W
Bollnäs 26 61.21 N 16.25 E
Bollon 166 28.05 S 147.15 E
Bollstabruk 26 63.00 N 17.39 E
Bollstanäs 40 59.30 N 17.56 E
Bollullos par del Condado 34 37.20 N 6.32 W
Bollwerk 263 51.10 N 7.35 E
Bolmen ⊜ 26 56.55 N 13.40 E
Bolnisi 84 41.28 N 44.33 E
Bolo 144 8.50 N 39.22 E
Bolobo 152 2.10 S 16.14 E
Bolochovo 82 54.05 N 37.50 E
Bologna 64 44.29 N 11.20 E
Bologna □[4] 64 44.28 N 11.26 E
Bologne 58 48.12 N 5.08 E
Bologne → Bologna 64 44.29 N 11.20 E
Bolognesi 248 6.35 S 73.10 W
Bolognetta 70 37.58 N 13.27 E
Bolognola 66 42.59 N 13.14 E
Bologoje 76 57.54 N 34.02 E
Bologovo 76 56.54 N 31.42 E
Bololo 152 3.50 S 21.08 E
Bolomba 152 0.29 N 19.12 E
Bolombo 152 3.59 S 21.22 E
Bolombo ≃ 152 1.32 N 21.14 E
Bolon' 89 49.55 N 136.07 E
Bolon', ozero ⊜ 89 49.51 N 136.22 E
Bolonchén de Rejón 232 20.00 N 89.49 W
Bolondo 152 0.27 N 20.01 E
Bolondrón 240p 22.46 N 81.27 W
Bolong ≃ 170 34.15 S 149.36 E
Bolonia → Bologna 64 44.29 N 11.20 E
Bolótana 71 40.20 N 8.57 E
Bolotino 78 47.42 N 27.21 E
Bolotnoje 86 55.41 N 84.23 E
Boloto 82 54.10 N 36.20 E
Bolotovskoje 86 58.33 N 62.28 E
Bolovens, Plateau des ⋏[1] 110 15.20 N 106.20 E
Bolpur 126 23.40 N 87.43 E
Bol'šaja 76 59.36 N 41.48 E
Bol'šaja ≃ 80 48.36 N 41.00 E
Bol'šaja Atn'a 80 56.15 N 49.27 E
Bol'šaja Balachn'a ≃ 74 73.37 N 107.05 E
Bol'šaja Ber'ostovica 76 53.11 N 24.01 E
Bol'šaja Blagoveščenka 78 46.51 N 34.03 E
Bol'šaja Brembola 82 56.45 N 38.55 E
Bol'šaja Bukon' 86 48.53 N 82.43 E
Bol'šaja Čalykla ≃ 80 51.51 N 49.34 E
Bol'šaja Černigovka 80 52.07 N 50.52 E
Bol'šaja Chalan' 78 50.56 N 37.26 E
Bol'šaja Cheta ≃ 74 69.33 N 84.15 E
Bol'šaja Chobda ≃ 86 50.56 N 54.34 E
Bol'šaja Chundala 76 60.04 N 34.18 E
Bol'šaja Čuja ≃ 88 58.56 N 112.13 E
Bol'šaja Čurakovka 86 53.03 N 64.20 E
Bol'šaja Damba 80 46.57 N 51.47 E
Bol'šaja Dmitrijevka 80 51.21 N 45.15 E
Bol'šaja Dora 76 59.05 N 37.38 E
Bol'šaja Džalga 80 45.59 N 42.41 E
Bol'šaja Glušica 80 52.24 N 50.28 E
Bol'šaja Ižora 76 59.56 N 29.34 E
Bol'šaja Ižorka ≃ 265a 59.48 N 30.36 E
Bol'šaja Kakša ≃ 80 57.53 N 45.28 E
Bol'šaja Kamenka 80 53.39 N 50.31 E
Bol'šaja Kamenka ≃ 83 48.22 N 40.04 E
Bol'šaja Kandala 80 54.32 N 49.22 E
Bol'šaja Kaskara 86 57.11 N 65.58 E
Bol'šaja Ket' 86 57.39 N 91.45 E
Bol'šaja Kinel' ≃ 80 53.14 N 50.30 E
Bol'šaja Kirsanovka 83 47.40 N 38.54 E
Bol'šaja Kokšaga ≃ 80 56.08 N 47.47 E
Bol'šaja Konkudera ≃ 88 57.34 N 112.30 E
Bol'šaja Kugul'ta ≃ 80 45.45 N 41.57 E
Bol'šaja Kuonamka ≃ 74 70.45 N 113.24 E
Bol'šaja Laba ≃ 84 44.16 N 40.53 E
Bol'šaja Lipovica 80 52.33 N 41.20 E
Bol'šaja Martynovka 80 47.17 N 41.40 E
Bol'šaja Mošanica 76 53.58 N 29.37 E
Bol'šaja Murta 86 56.55 N 93.07 E
Bol'šaja Neva ≃ 265a 59.58 N 30.13 E
Bol'šaja Norja 80 56.41 N 52.43 E
Bol'šaja Ochta ◆[8] 265a 59.57 N 30.25 E
Bol'šaja Ol'šanka 80 51.32 N 44.17 E
Bol'šaja Orlovka 80 47.20 N 41.16 E
Bol'šaja Osinovaja ≃ 180 66.30 N 174.00 E
Bol'šaja Pas'ma 80 58.38 N 43.53 E
Bol'šaja Rečka 88 51.57 N 104.44 E
Bol'šaja Ržaksa 80 52.08 N 42.13 E
Bol'šaja Sestra ≃ 82 56.16 N 35.56 E
Bol'šaja Smedva ≃ 82 54.50 N 38.34 E
Bol'šaja Sosnova 80 57.40 N 54.36 E
Bol'šaja Talovaja 78 46.58 N 40.37 E
Bol'šaja Tarel' 88 53.45 N 106.40 E
Bol'šaja Tavoložka 80 52.07 N 49.04 E
Bol'šaja Uča 80 56.37 N 52.05 E
Bol'šaja Usa 86 56.44 N 55.06 E
Bol'šaja Ussurka ≃ 89 45.57 N 133.42 E
Bol'šaja Višera 76 58.55 N 32.08 E
Bol'šaja Vladimirovka 86 50.53 N 79.31 E
Bol'šaja Vys' ≃ 78 48.45 N 30.54 E
Bolsa Knolls 226 36.44 N 121.38 W
Bol'šakovo, Ross. 76 54.53 N 21.40 E
Bol'šakovo, Ross. 265b 55.54 N 37.17 E
Bol'šečernigovka 83 48.57 N 39.25 E
Bol'šekrepinskaja 83 47.36 N 39.22 E
Bol'šelig 24 62.07 N 52.25 E
Bolsena 66 42.39 N 11.59 E
Bolsena, Lago di ⊜ 66 42.36 N 11.56 E
Bol'šenarymskoje 86 49.16 N 84.32 E
Bol'šerečje 86 56.06 N 74.38 E
Bol'šereck 74 52.25 N 156.24 E
Bol'šetroickoje 78 50.33 N 37.17 E
Bol'šeustjikinskoje 86 55.57 N 58.16 E
Bol'ševik, Bela. 76 52.34 N 30.53 E
Bol'ševik, Ross. 74 62.44 N 147.30 E
Bol'ševik, Ross. 265a 59.49 N 30.30 E
Bol'ševik, ostrov I 74 78.40 N 102.30 E
Bol'šezemel'skaja Tundra ◆[1] 72 67.30 N 56.00 E
Bolshoi Theatre ♁ 265b 55.46 N 37.37 E
Bol'šije Algaši 80 55.22 N 46.29 E
Bol'šije Avt'uki 78 52.04 N 29.32 E
Bol'šije Belyniči 82 54.38 N 38.50 E
Bol'šije Berezniki 80 54.11 N 45.58 E
Bol'šije Gorki, Ross. 82 56.28 N 35.51 E
Bol'šije Gorki, Ross. 265a 59.42 N 29.51 E
Bol'šije Kajbicy 80 55.25 N 48.13 E
Bol'šije Kizi, ozero ⊜ 89 51.38 N 140.20 E
Bol'šije Kl'uči 80 55.59 N 48.47 E
Bol'šije Kl'učišči 80 54.08 N 48.14 E
Bol'šije Liachvi ≃ 84 41.58 N 44.06 E
Bol'šije Michalicyny 80 58.29 N 48.14 E
Bol'šije Ozerki 80 52.36 N 46.33 E
Bol'šije Pom'aly 80 56.42 N 46.40 E
Bol'šije Ručji 82 56.36 N 36.58 E
Bol'šije Saly 83 47.24 N 39.41 E
Bol'šije Tarchany 80 54.42 N 48.34 E
Bol'šije Ugli 88 57.47 N 112.51 E
Bol'šije Uki 86 56.57 N 72.37 E
Bol'šije Ždanovy 80 58.40 N 49.05 E
Bol'šoj 80 50.13 N 43.26 E
Bol'šoj An'uj ≃ 74 68.30 N 160.49 E
Bol'šoj Ažbulat, ozero ⊜ 86 53.17 N 77.25 E
Bol'šoj Begičev, ostrov I 74 74.20 N 112.30 E
Bol'šoj Bogdo, gora ∧[2] 80 48.08 N 46.52 E
Bol'šoj Boktybaj, gora ∧ 86 48.27 N 58.30 E
Bol'šoj Čeremšan ≃ 80 54.11 N 49.39 E
Bol'šoj Civil' ≃ 80 55.54 N 47.28 E
Bol'šoje, ozero ⊜ 265a 60.04 N 30.39 E
Bol'šoje Aksu 86 43.20 N 79.35 E
Bol'šoje Aleksejevskoje 82 55.14 N 38.12 E
Bol'šoje Boldino 80 54.59 N 45.19 E
Bol'šoje Bun'kovo 82 55.51 N 38.37 E
Bol'šoje Goloustnoje 88 52.01 N 105.25 E
Bol'šoje Gorodišče, Ross. 76 57.17 N 30.31 E
Bol'šoje Gorodišče, Ross. 78 50.37 N 37.06 E
Bol'šoje Ignatovo 80 55.02 N 45.34 E
Bol'šoje Jarovoje, ozero ⊜ 86 52.53 N 78.36 E
Bol'šoje Jašaltinskoje, ozero ⊜ 80 46.17 N 42.27 E
Bol'šoje Kibejevo 80 56.55 N 47.05 E
Bol'šoje Korovino 82 54.30 N 39.02 E
Bol'šoje Manuškino 265a 59.53 N 30.49 E
Bol'šoje Michajlovskoje 82 56.47 N 38.04 E
Bol'šoje Mikuškino 80 53.56 N 51.42 E
Bol'šoje Muraškino 80 55.47 N 44.46 E
Bol'šoje Nagatkino 80 54.31 N 47.58 E
Bol'šoje Nurkejevo 80 55.22 N 52.40 E
Bol'šoje Nyrsy 80 55.44 N 50.19 E
Bol'šoje Ogar'ovo 76 53.33 N 37.43 E
Bol'šoje Pikino 80 56.25 N 44.22 E
Bol'šoje Polpino 76 53.14 N 34.30 E
Bol'šoje Ramenje 76 58.21 N 36.40 E
Bol'šoje Rybuškino 80 55.25 N 45.48 E
Bol'šoje Sazonovo 80 58.06 N 53.21 E
Bol'šoje Selo 76 57.43 N 38.56 E
Bol'šoje Šem'akino 80 55.03 N 48.38 E
Bol'šoje Soldatskoje 78 51.21 N 35.31 E
Bol'šoje Sudačje 80 50.49 N 44.05 E
Bol'šoje Topol'noje, ozero ⊜ 86 53.20 N 78.00 E
Bol'šoje Uro 88 53.32 N 109.48 E
Bol'šoje Zagorje 76 57.51 N 28.57 E
Bol'šoje Žokovo 82 54.35 N 38.57 E
Bol'šoj Gašun ≃ 80 47.22 N 42.43 E
Bol'šoj Ginaldag, gora ∧ 84 40.20 N 45.57 E
Bol'šoj Golec, gora ∧ 88 51.52 N 119.24 E
Bol'šoj Irgiz ≃ 80 52.01 N 47.24 E
Bol'šoj Jenisej (Bij-Chem) ≃ 88 51.43 N 94.26 E
Bol'šoj Jugan ≃ 86 60.55 N 73.40 E
Bol'šoj Kamen' 89 43.06 N 132.21 E
Bol'šoj Kandarat' 80 54.25 N 47.00 E
Bol'šoj Kanym, gora ∧ 86 54.13 N 88.20 E
Bol'šoj Karagaj 86 57.57 N 70.15 E
Bol'šoj Karaman ≃ 80 51.40 N 46.38 E
Bol'šoj Kavkaz (Caucasus) ⋏ 84 42.30 N 45.00 E
Bol'šoj Ketmen' 86 43.27 N 80.24 E
Bol'šoj Kujal'nik ≃ 78 46.46 N 30.36 E
Bol'šoj Kujaš 86 55.50 N 61.06 E
Bol'šoj Kundyš ≃ 80 56.32 N 47.23 E
Bol'šoj Kuvaj 80 54.37 N 47.05 E
Bol'šoj Kymynej, gora ∧ 180 66.34 N 172.32 W
Bol'šoj L'achovskij, ostrov I 74 73.35 N 142.00 E
Bol'šoj Lug 88 52.07 N 104.10 E
Bol'šoj Matačynaj, gora ∧ 180 66.28 N 179.25 W
Bol'šoj Melik 80 51.38 N 43.18 E
Bol'šoj Nesvetaj ≃ 83 47.27 N 39.54 E
Bol'šoj Onguren 88 53.38 N 107.36 E
Bol'šoj Patom ≃ 88 59.15 N 113.56 E
Bol'šoj Pit ≃ 86 59.01 N 91.44 E
Bol'šoj Porog 86 52.35 N 92.18 E
Bol'šoj Šagan 80 50.57 N 51.08 E
Bol'šoj Sajan ⋏ 88 52.00 N 99.30 E
Bol'šoj Salym ≃ 86 60.55 N 70.25 E
Bol'šoj Šantar, ostrov I 89 55.00 N 137.42 E
Bol'šoj Šatan, gora ∧ 86 53.41 N 57.36 E
Bol'šoj Simonogont 265a 59.50 N 29.49 E
Bol'šoj Sorokino 86 56.38 N 69.53 E
Bol'šoj Suchodol 83 48.25 N 39.53 E
Bol'šoj Sundyr' 80 56.07 N 46.46 E
Bol'šoj Tal'cy 76 59.13 N 33.00 E
Bol'šoj Tolkaj 80 53.30 N 51.57 E
Bol'šoj T'uters, ostrov I 76 59.51 N 27.13 E
Bol'šoj Uluj 86 56.39 N 90.36 E
Bol'šoj Uran ≃ 80 52.24 N 53.15 E
Bol'šoj Uvat, ozero ⊜ 86 57.35 N 70.30 E
Bol'šoj Uzen' ≃ 80 48.50 N 49.40 E
Bol'šoj Uzigont 265a 59.48 N 29.53 E
Bol'šoj Vjass 80 53.48 N 45.30 E
Bol'šoj Vlasjevo 89 53.24 N 140.55 E
Bol'šoj Zelenčuk ≃ 84 44.36 N 41.56 E
Bol'šovcy 78 49.12 N 24.44 E
Bolsover 44 53.14 N 1.18 W
Bolsward 52 53.03 N 5.31 E
Boltaña 34 42.27 N 0.04 E
Boltigen 58 46.38 N 7.24 E
Boltino 265b 55.58 N 37.41 E
Bolton, On., Can. 212 43.53 N 79.44 W
Bolton, Eng., U.K. 262 53.35 N 2.26 W
Bolton, Ct., U.S. 207 41.46 N 72.26 W
Bolton, Ms., U.S. 194 32.20 N 90.27 W
Bolton, N.C., U.S. 192 34.19 N 78.24 W
Bolton □[8] 262 53.34 N 2.28 W
Bolton Abbey 44 53.59 N 1.53 W
Bolton Abbey ♁[1] 44 53.59 N 1.54 W
Bolton Bridge 44 53.58 N 1.57 W
Bolton Center 207 41.47 N 72.26 W
Bolton Creek ≃ 212 44.58 N 76.23 W
Bolton Lake ⊜ 184 54.16 N 95.47 W
Bolton-le-Sands 44 54.06 N 2.47 W
Bolton upon Dearne 44 53.31 N 1.19 W
Bolton Wanderers Football Ground ♦ 262 53.34 N 2.25 W
Bolu 130 40.44 N 31.37 E
Bolu □[4] 130 40.40 N 31.30 E
Bölükyazı 130 38.18 N 42.10 E
Boluntay 120 36.34 N 92.38 E
Boluo, Zhg. 100 24.27 N 113.03 E
Boluo, Zhg. 100 23.11 N 114.17 E
Boluochi 98 41.24 N 119.56 E
Boluokeng 100 24.05 N 113.22 E
Bolus Head ≻ 48 51.46 N 10.21 W
Bolva ≃ 76 53.17 N 34.20 E
Bolvadin 130 38.42 N 31.04 E
Bolwarra 166 17.24 S 144.11 E
Bóly 30 45.58 N 18.32 E
Bolyčevo 82 55.46 N 35.43 E
Bolzaneto 62 44.27 N 8.54 E
Bolzano (Bozen) 64 46.31 N 11.22 E
Bolzano □[4] 64 46.43 N 11.30 E
Boma 152 5.51 S 13.03 E
Bomaderry 170 34.51 S 150.37 E
Bomal 56 50.23 N 5.32 E
Bomandjokou 152 0.34 N 14.23 E
Bomaneh 152 1.18 N 23.47 E
Bomarsund 26 60.13 N 20.15 E
Bomate 152 1.10 S 19.41 E
Bomba 66 42.02 N 14.22 E
Bombakabo 152 3.04 N 19.42 E
Bombala 166 36.54 S 149.14 E
Bombarral 34 39.16 N 9.09 W
Bombat 130 38.08 N 42.14 E
Bombay, India 122 18.58 N 72.50 E
Bombay, India 272c 18.58 N 72.50 E
Bombay, N.Y., U.S. 206 44.56 N 74.34 W
Bombay, University of ♁[2] 272c 18.57 N 72.50 E
Bombay Harbour ⊂ 272c 18.57 N 72.53 E
Bomberai, Semenanjung ≻[1] 164 3.00 S 133.00 E
Bombetoka, Baie de ⊂ 157b 15.50 S 46.17 E
Bombimba 152 0.31 N 19.24 E
Bombo 154 0.35 N 32.32 E
Bombo ≃ 152 3.58 S 15.59 E
Bombo-Kasanji 152 5.54 S 21.51 E
Bomboma 152 2.25 N 18.54 E
Bombo-Makuka 152 5.26 S 16.19 E
Bombombwa 154 1.21 N 25.30 E
Bombon 261 48.34 N 2.52 E
Bomboyo 146 12.01 N 15.28 E
Bom Conselho 250 9.10 S 36.41 W
Bom Despacho 255 19.43 S 45.15 W
Bomdila 120 27.27 N 92.17 E
Bomei 100 22.57 N 115.46 E
Bömenzien 54 52.59 N 11.31 E
Bom Fim do Bom Jesus 256 23.17 S 47.02 W
Bomhus 40 60.41 N 17.13 E
Bomili 154 1.40 N 27.01 E
Bom Jardim, Ilha do I 287a 23.02 S 43.35 W
Bom Jardim de Goiás 255 16.17 S 52.07 W
Bom Jardim de Minas 256 21.57 S 44.11 W
Bom Jesus, Ang. 152 9.09 S 13.34 E
Bom Jesus, Bra. 250 9.04 S 44.22 W
Bom Jesus da Lapa 255 13.15 S 43.25 W
Bom Jesus de Goiás 255 18.12 S 49.44 W
Bom Jesus dos Perdões 256 23.08 S 46.28 W
Bømlafjorden ⊂[2] 26 59.39 N 5.20 E
Bomlitz 52 52.54 N 9.37 E
Bømlo I 26 59.46 N 5.12 E
Bommerholz 263 51.23 N 7.18 E
Bommern 263 51.25 N 7.20 E
Bomnak 89 54.46 N 128.51 E
Bomokandi ≃ 154 3.39 N 26.08 E
Bomongiri 152 1.57 S 21.13 E
Bomongo 152 1.22 N 18.21 E
Bompata 150 6.38 N 1.04 W
Bompensiere 70 37.28 N 13.47 E
Bompietro 70 37.44 N 14.06 E
Bomputu 152 0.20 S 20.06 E
Bom Repouso 256 22.28 S 46.09 W
Bom Retiro 252 27.48 S 49.31 W
Bom Retiro ◆[8] 287b 23.32 S 46.38 W
Bom Sucesso, Bra. 248 15.43 S 56.07 W
Bom Sucesso, Bra. 255 23.42 S 51.45 W
Bom Sucesso, Bra. 256 22.17 S 42.49 W
Bom Sucesso, Bra. 287b 23.25 S 46.24 W
Bomu (Mbomou) ≃ 136 4.08 N 22.26 E
Bon, Cap ≻ 36 37.05 N 11.03 E
Bona 40 58.34 N 15.03 E
Bona Bona Island I 164 10.30 S 149.50 E
Bon Accord 158 25.38 S 28.11 E
Bonaduz 58 46.49 N 9.25 E
Bonaero Park 273d 26.07 S 28.16 E
Bonai 114 1.16 N 100.52 E
Bonaigarh 120 21.50 N 84.57 E
Bonair, In., U.S. 278 41.31 N 87.22 W

ENGLISH Name	Page	Lat.°′	Long.°′

Bon Air, Va., U.S. 208 37.31 N 77.33 W
Bon Aire 214 40.54 N 79.55 W
Bonaire I 241s 12.10 N 68.15 W
Bonampak ⊥ 232 16.44 N 91.05 W
Bönan 40 60.44 N 17.18 E
Bonandolok 114 1.47 N 98.48 E
Bonanza, Nic. 236 14.01 N 84.35 W
Bonanza, Or., U.S. 202 42.11 N 121.24 W
Bonanza, Ut,. U.S. 200 40.01 N 109.10 W
Bonanza Peak ∧ 224 48.14 N 120.52 W
Bonao 238 18.56 N 70.25 W
Bonaparte 190 40.41 N 91.48 W
Bonaparte ≃ 182 50.46 N 121.17 W
Bonaparte, Lake ⊜ 212 44.09 N 75.23 W
Bonaparte, Mount ∧ 202 48.45 N 119.08 W
Bonaparte Archipelago II 160 14.17 S 125.18 E
Bonaparte Lake ⊜ 182 51.16 N 120.35 W
Bonar Bridge 46 57.53 N 4.21 W
Bonarcado 71 40.04 N 8.38 E
Bonasila Dome ∧ 180 62.19 N 160.30 W
Bonasse 241r 10.05 N 61.52 W
Bonassola 62 44.11 N 9.35 E
Bonaventure 186 48.03 N 65.29 W
Bonaventure ≃ 186 48.02 N 65.28 W
Bonaventure, Île I 186 48.30 N 64.10 W
Bonavista 186 48.39 N 53.07 W
Bonavista, Cape ≻ 186 48.42 N 53.05 W
Bonavista Bay ⊂ 186 48.45 N 53.20 W
Bonawe 46 56.26 N 5.13 W
Bonawon 116 9.08 N 122.55 E
Bonbeach 274b 38.04 S 145.08 E
Bonboillon 58 47.20 N 5.42 E
Bon Bon 162 30.26 S 135.28 E
Bonbonon Point ≻ 116 9.03 N 123.08 E
Bonchester Bridge 44 55.24 N 2.40 W
Boncourt 58 47.30 N 6.56 E
Boncuk Dağı ∧ 130 36.53 N 29.17 E
Bond 194 30.54 N 89.10 W
Bond □[6] 219 38.53 N 89.25 W
Bondari 80 52.57 N 42.04 E
Bondar'ov 83 49.22 N 39.10 E
Bondar'ovka 83 49.23 N 39.37 E
Bondeno 64 44.53 N 11.25 E
Bondi 274a 33.53 S 151.17 E
Bondo, Zaïre 152 1.22 S 23.53 E
Bondo, Zaïre 152 3.49 N 23.40 E
Bondoc Peninsula ≻[1] 116 13.30 N 122.30 E
Bondoc Point ≻ 116 13.10 N 122.36 E
Bondorf 58 48.31 N 8.49 E
Bondoufle 261 48.37 N 2.23 E
Bondoukou 150 8.02 N 2.48 W
Bondowoso 115a 7.55 S 113.49 E
Bondsville 207 42.12 N 72.20 W
Bonduel 190 44.44 N 88.26 W
Bondues 50 50.42 N 3.06 E
Bondy 261 48.54 N 2.28 E
Bondy, Forêt de ♦ 261 48.55 N 2.35 E
Bone, Indon. 112 4.46 S 122.52 E
Bone, Indon. 112 5.09 S 122.37 E
Bone, Teluk ⊂ 112 4.00 S 120.40 E
Bône → Annaba 148 36.54 N 7.46 E
Bonebone 112 2.36 S 120.33 E
Bon Echo Provincial Park ♦ 212 44.52 N 77.15 W
Bonefro 66 41.42 N 14.56 E
Bone Island I 212 44.56 N 79.51 W
Bonelipu 112 4.50 S 123.11 E
Bonelohe 112 5.48 S 120.27 E
Bönen 52 51.36 N 7.44 E
Boneogeh 112 7.16 S 120.48 E
Bonerate, Pulau I 112 7.22 S 121.08 E
Bon Espérance, Cap de → Good Hope, Cape of ≻ 158 34.24 S 18.30 E
Bo'ness 46 56.01 N 3.37 W
Bonesteel 198 43.04 N 98.56 W
Bonete, Cerro ∧ 252 27.51 S 68.47 W
Bonete Chico, Cerro ∧ 252 28.01 S 68.45 W
Bonětice 60 49.41 N 12.49 E
Bone → Watampone 112 4.32 S 120.20 E
Bonfield 216 41.09 N 88.03 W
Bonfinópolis de Minas 255 16.28 S 45.59 W
Bonfol 58 47.29 N 7.09 E
Bonga 144 7.17 N 36.15 E
Bongabon 116 15.38 N 121.08 E
Bongabon ≃ 116 12.40 N 121.33 E
Bongabong 116 12.45 N 121.29 E
Bongaigaon 124 26.28 N 90.34 E
Bongak 140 7.27 N 33.14 E
Bongandanga 152 1.30 N 21.03 E
Bongao Island I 116 5.01 N 119.46 E
Bongaree 171a 27.05 S 153.10 E
Bonggaw 116 5.02 N 119.46 E
Bongka 112 0.58 S 121.27 E
Bongka ≃ 112 0.59 S 121.05 E
Bong Mieu 110 15.25 N 108.24 E
Bongo, Ang. 152 8.48 S 17.49 E
Bongo, Gabon 152 2.10 S 10.12 E
Bongo, Massif des ⋏ 146 8.40 N 22.25 E
Bongo I 152 3.01 N 20.06 E
Bongo II 152 1.47 S 17.41 E
Bongo Island I 116 7.20 N 124.02 E
Bongolu 152 2.48 N 22.29 E
Bongon 112 6.35 N 116.52 E
Bongor 146 10.17 N 15.22 E
Bongou ≃ 140 6.42 N 22.04 E
Bongouanou 150 6.39 N 4.12 W
Bong Range ⋏ 150 6.50 N 10.00 W
Bong Son 110 14.26 N 109.01 E
Bonham 196 33.34 N 96.10 W
Bonheiden 56 51.02 N 4.32 E
Bonhomme, Col du)(58 48.10 N 7.06 E
Bonhomme, Morne ∧ 238 19.05 N 72.18 W
Bonhomme Island I 219 38.42 N 90.36 W
Bonifacio, Fr. 36 41.23 N 9.10 E
Bonifacio, Pil. 116 8.03 N 123.37 E
Bonifacio, Strait of Ʉ 36 41.20 N 9.15 E
Bonifacio Monument ⊥ 269f 14.39 N 120.59 E
Bonifati 68 39.35 N 15.54 E
Bonifati, Capo ≻ 68 39.35 N 15.52 E
Bonifay 194 30.47 N 85.40 W
Bonifica del Volturno ≚ 68 41.01 N 14.00 E
Bonilla Island I 182 53.29 N 130.36 W
Bonin Islands → Ogasawara-guntō II 14 27.00 N 142.10 E
Bonita 194 32.55 N 91.40 W
Bonita, Point ≻ 282 37.49 N 122.32 W
Bonita Springs 220 26.20 N 81.46 W
Bonito, Bra. 248 21.08 S 56.28 W
Bonito, Bra. 250 8.29 S 35.44 W
Bonito, It. 68 41.06 N 15.00 E
Bonito ≃, Bra. 255 16.31 S 51.23 W
Bonito ≃, Bra. 256 22.12 S 43.02 W
Bonito ≃, Bra. 256 22.09 S 43.40 W
Bonito, Pico ∧ 236 15.38 N 86.55 W
Bonito, Rio ≃ 200 33.23 N 105.16 W
Bonito de Santa Fé 250 7.19 S 38.31 W
Bonjol 112 0.01 S 100.13 E
Bonkoukou 150 14.01 N 3.13 E
Bon Meade 279b 40.33 N 80.14 W
Bonn 56 50.44 N 7.05 E
Bonnanaro 71 40.32 N 8.45 E
Bonndorf im Schwarzwald 58 47.49 N 8.20 E
Bonneauville 208 39.46 N 77.10 W
Bonne Bay (Woody Point) 186 49.30 N 57.56 W
Bonne Bay ⊂ 186 49.33 N 57.55 W
Bonnebosq 50 49.12 N 0.05 E
Bonnechere ≃ 190 45.31 N 76.33 W
Bonneia 144 5.41 N 37.45 E
Bonnelles 261 48.37 N 2.02 E
Bonner 202 46.52 N 113.51 W
Bonners Ferry 202 48.41 N 116.18 W

DEUTSCH Name	Seite	Breite°′	Länge°′ E = Ost

Bonne-sur-Ménoge 58 46.10 N 6.20 E
Bonnet, Lac du ⊜ 184 50.22 N 95.55 W
Bonnétable 50 48.11 N 0.26 E
Bonne Terre 194 37.55 N 90.33 W
Bonnet Plume ≃ 180 65.55 N 134.58 W
Bonneuil-sur-Marne 261 48.46 N 2.29 E
Bonneval 50 48.11 N 1.24 E
Bonneval-sur-Arc 62 45.22 N 7.03 E
Bonnevaux 58 46.18 N 6.40 E
Bonneville, Fr. 58 46.05 N 6.25 E
Bonneville, Or., U.S. 224 45.38 N 121.57 W
Bonneville Dam ◆[6] 224 45.39 N 121.56 W
Bonneville Peak ∧ 202 42.46 N 112.08 W
Bonneville Salt Flats ≚ 200 40.45 N 113.52 W
Bonney, Lake ⊜ 166 37.48 S 140.22 E
Bonney Lake 224 47.10 N 122.11 W
Bonnie Doone 192 35.05 N 78.57 W
Bonnières 50 49.02 N 1.35 E
Bonnie Rock 162 30.32 S 118.21 E
Bonnieux 62 43.49 N 5.18 E
Bonnievale 158 33.57 S 20.06 E
Bönninghardt 263 51.35 N 6.28 E
Bönninghardt ⋏[2] 263 51.34 N 6.27 E
Bonnots Mill 219 38.34 N 91.58 W
Bonny 150 4.27 N 7.10 E
Bonny ≃[1] 150 4.20 N 7.10 E
Bonnyrigg, Austl. 274a 33.54 S 150.54 E
Bonnyrigg, Scot., U.K. 46 55.52 N 3.08 W
Bonny-sur-Loire 50 47.34 N 2.50 E
Bonnyville 182 54.16 N 110.44 W
Bono, It. 71 40.25 N 9.02 E
Bono, Ar., U.S. 194 35.54 N 90.48 W
Bono, Oh., U.S. 214 41.38 N 83.16 W
Bonoi 164 1.51 S 137.48 E
Bonorva 71 40.25 N 8.46 E
Bonoua 150 5.16 N 3.36 W
Bonpas Creek ≃ 194 38.16 N 87.59 W
Bonriki 174t 1.23 N 173.09 E
Bonriki Airport ⊠ 174t 1.22 N 173.10 E
Bons 58 46.16 N 6.23 E
Bonsall 228 33.17 N 117.13 W
Bonsari 272c 19.04 N 73.02 E
Bon Secour 194 30.18 N 87.43 W
Bon-Secours, Bel. 50 50.30 N 3.36 E
Bonsecours, Fr. 50 49.26 N 1.08 E
Bonshaw 186 46.12 N 63.21 W
Bonsucesso ◆[8] 287a 22.52 S 43.15 W
Bontang 112 0.08 N 117.30 E
Bontberg ∧ 158 32.21 S 21.04 E
Bontebok National Park ♦ 158 34.07 S 20.23 E
Bonthe 150 7.32 N 12.30 W
Bontoc 116 17.05 N 120.58 E
Bon Wier 194 30.44 N 93.39 W
Bonyhád 30 46.19 N 18.32 E
Boo, Kepulauan II 164 1.12 S 129.24 E
Booby Point ≻ 284b 39.17 N 76.23 W
Boock 54 53.29 N 14.15 E
Boody 219 39.46 N 89.03 W
Boogardie 162 28.02 S 117.47 E
Booischot 56 51.03 N 4.46 E
Bookabie 162 31.50 S 132.41 E
Bookaloo 166 31.55 S 137.22 E
Book Cliffs ⊥[4] 200 39.20 N 109.00 W
Booke 152 2.33 S 22.00 E
Booker 196 36.27 N 100.32 W
Booker T. Washington National Monument ♦ 192 37.01 N 79.45 W
Bookwalter 218 39.42 N 83.32 W
Boola 150 8.22 N 8.43 W
Boolaloo 162 22.35 S 115.51 E
Booleroo Centre 166 32.53 S 138.21 E
Booligal 166 33.52 S 144.53 E
Boologooro 162 24.21 S 114.02 E
Boom 50 51.05 N 4.22 E
Boomarra 166 19.33 S 140.20 E
Boomer 188 38.09 N 81.17 W
Boomi 166 28.44 S 149.35 E
Boomrivier 158 29.33 S 20.27 E
Boonah 171a 28.00 S 152.41 E
Böön cagaan nuur ⊜ 102 45.35 N 99.09 E
Boone, Ia., U.S. 190 42.03 N 93.52 W
Boone, N.C., U.S. 192 36.13 N 81.40 W
Boone □[6], Il., U.S. 216 42.15 N 88.50 W
Boone □[6], In., U.S. 218 40.03 N 86.28 W
Boone □[6], Ky., U.S. 218 38.57 N 84.45 W
Boone □[6], Mo., U.S. 219 38.55 N 92.15 W
Boone ≃ 190 42.19 N 93.56 W
Boone Draw V 196 33.51 N 103.42 W
Boone Grove 216 41.21 N 87.08 W
Boone Lake ⊜[1] 192 36.25 N 82.25 W
Boone Reservoir ⊜[1] 279b 40.15 N 80.08 W
Boones Mill 192 37.06 N 79.57 W
Booneville, Ar., U.S. 194 35.08 N 93.55 W
Booneville, Ky., U.S. 192 37.28 N 83.40 W
Booneville, Ms., U.S. 194 34.39 N 88.34 W
Boon Point ≻ 240c 17.10 N 61.50 W
Boons 158 25.59 S 27.13 E
Boonsboro 208 39.30 N 77.39 W
Boonsville 222 33.04 N 97.52 W
Boonton 210 40.54 N 74.24 W
Boonton Reservoir ⊜[1] 276 40.53 N 74.25 W
Boonville, Ca., U.S. 204 39.00 N 123.21 W
Boonville, In., U.S. 194 38.02 N 87.16 W
Boonville, Mo., U.S. 194 38.58 N 92.44 W
Boonville, N.Y., U.S. 212 43.29 N 75.20 W
Boopi ≃ 248 15.41 S 67.15 W
Boorabbin National Park ♦ 162 31.13 S 120.10 E
Boorama 144 9.56 N 43.11 E
Boorindal 166 30.21 S 146.08 E
Booroorban 166 34.56 S 144.46 E
Boorowa 166 34.26 S 148.43 E
Boos 50 49.23 N 1.12 E
Boosaaso 144 11.17 N 49.11 E
Boossen 54 52.22 N 14.29 E
Boot 44 54.24 N 3.17 W
Bootahnie Indian Reserve ◆[4] 182 50.24 N 121.31 W
Booth 194 32.30 N 86.34 W
Booth, Lac ⊜ 190 46.45 N 78.34 W
Boothbay Harbor 188 43.51 N 69.37 W
Boothby, Cape ≻ 9 66.34 S 57.16 E
Booth Corner 285 39.51 N 75.29 W
Boothia, Gulf of ⊂ 176 71.00 N 91.00 W
Boothia Peninsula ≻[1] 176 70.30 N 95.00 W
Boothstown 262 53.30 N 2.25 W
Boothville 194 29.20 N 89.25 W
Booth Wood Reservoir ⊜[1] 262 53.38 N 1.58 W
Boothwyn 285 39.49 N 75.26 W
Bootle 262 53.28 N 3.00 W
Boot Reefs ✣[2] 164 10.00 S 144.40 E
Booué 152 0.06 S 11.56 E
Booysens ◆[8] 273d 26.14 S 28.01 E
Booze Creek ≃ 284c 38.59 N 77.07 W
Bopfingen 56 48.51 N 10.21 E
Bo Phloi 110 14.19 N 99.31 E
Bophuthatswana □[1], Afr. 138 26.00 S 25.35 E
Bophuthatswana □[1], Afr. 156 26.00 S 25.35 E
Boping 98 36.36 N 116.07 E
Boping Ling ⋏ 100 25.00 N 117.00 E
Bopo 150 7.37 N 7.52 E
Bopolu 150 7.03 N 10.32 W
Boppard 56 50.14 N 7.35 E
Boqér, Har ∧ 132 30.52 N 34.43 E
Boqueirão, Ilha do I 287a 22.46 S 43.09 W
Boqueirão, Serra do ⋏[2] 250 11.30 S 43.45 W
Boquerón 236 8.30 N 82.34 W
Boquerón □[5] 252 21.30 S 60.00 W
Boquerón, Bahía de ⊂ 240m 18.01 N 67.12 W
Boquerón, Túnel ◆[5] 286c 10.34 N 67.00 W
Boquet 279b 40.23 N 79.36 W

Symbols in the index entries represent the broad categories identified in the key at the right. Symbols with superior numbers (⋏[1]) identify subcategories (see complete key on page *I · 1)*.

Symbole im Register stellen die rechts im Schlüssel erklärten Kategorien dar. Symbole mit hochgestellten Ziffern (⋏[1]) bezeichnen Unterabteilungen einer Kategorie (vgl. vollständiger Schlüssel auf Seite *I · 1)*.

Los símbolos incluídos en el texto del índice representan las grandes categorias identificadas con la clave a la derecha. Los símbolos con numeros en su parte superior (⋏[1]) identifican las subcategorías (véase la clave completa en la página *I · 1)*.

Les symboles de l'index représentent les catégories indiquées dans la légende à droite. Les symboles suivis d'un indice (⋏[1]) représentent des sous-catégories (voir légende complète à la page *I · 1)*.

Os símbolos incluídos no texto do índice representam as grandes categorias identificadas com a chave à direita. Os símbolos com números em sua parte superior (⋏[1]) identificam as subcategorias (veja-se a chave completa à página *I · 1)*.

	English	Deutsch	Español	Français	Português
∧	Mountain	Berg	Montaña	Montagne	Montanha
⋏	Mountains	Gebirge	Montañas	Montagnes	Montanhas
)(	Pass	Paß	Paso	Col	Passo
V	Valley, Canyon	Tal, Cañon	Valle, Cañón	Vallée, Canyon	Vale, Canhão
≚	Plain	Ebene	Llano	Plaine	Planície
≻	Cape	Kap	Cabo	Cap	Cabo
I	Island	Insel	Isla	Île	Ilha
II	Islands	Inseln	Islas	Îles	Ilhas
⊥	Other Topographic Features	Andere Topographische Objekte	Otros Elementos Topográficos	Autres données topographiques	Outros acidentes topográficos

ESPAÑOL Nombre	Página	Lat.°′	Long.°′ W = Oeste

Boquilla, Presa de la ⊜[1] 232 27.30 N 105.30 W
Boquilla del Refugio 196 25.33 N 102.28 W
Boquillas del Carmen 232 29.17 N 102.53 W
Boquim 250 11.09 S 37.37 W
Bor, Česko. 60 49.43 N 12.47 E
Bor, Jugo. 38 44.05 N 22.07 E
Bor, Ross. 24 63.00 N 42.38 E
Bor, Ross. 80 56.22 N 44.05 E
Bor, Sūd. 140 6.12 N 31.33 E
Bor, Tür. 130 37.54 N 34.34 E
Bor, Lak ≃ 154 1.18 N 40.40 E
Bora-Bora I 14 16.30 S 151.45 W
Borabu 110 16.02 N 103.07 E
Boracay Island I 116 11.59 N 121.55 E
Boraha, Nosy I 157b 16.50 S 49.55 E
Borah Peak ∧ 202 44.08 N 113.48 W
Boraldaj ≃ 85 42.33 N 69.07 E
Borale 144 9.10 N 42.35 E
Borambola 171b 35.12 S 147.41 E
Borang, Tanjung > 164 5.16 S 133.07 E
Borås 26 57.43 N 12.55 E
Borāzjān 128 29.16 N 51.12 E
Borba, Bra. 246 4.24 S 59.35 W
Borba, Port. 34 38.48 N 7.27 W
Borbeck ➜[8] 263 51.29 N 6.57 E
Borbera ≃ 62 44.42 N 8.52 E
Borca di Cadore 64 46.26 N 12.13 E
Borcea, Brațul ≃ 38 44.40 N 27.53 E
Borchen 52 51.39 N 8.44 E
Borçka 130 41.22 N 41.40 E
Borculo, Ned. 52 52.07 N 6.31 E
Borculo, Mi., U.S. 216 42.53 N 86.01 W
Borda, Cape > 166 35.45 S 136.34 E
Borda da Mata 256 22.16 S 46.10 W
Bordeaux, Fr. 32 44.50 N 0.34 W
Bordeaux, S. Afr. 273d 26.06 S 28.01 E
Bordeaux ➜[8] 275a 45.33 N 73.41 W
Bordeaux Mountain ∧[2] 240m 18.20 N 64.44 W
Borden, Austl. 162 34.05 S 118.16 E
Borden, Sk., Can. 184 52.25 N 107.13 W
Borden, Eng., U.K. 260 51.20 N 0.42 E
Borden, In., U.S. 218 38.28 N 85.57 W
Borden, Canadian Forces Base ■ 212 44.17 N 79.55 W
Borden Lake ⊜ 190 47.50 N 83.18 W
Borden Peninsula >[1] 176 73.00 N 83.00 W
Bordentown 208 40.08 N 74.42 W
Border Mountains ⋀ 164 3.40 S 141.05 E
Borders □[4] 46 55.37 N 3.15 W
Bordertown 166 36.19 S 140.47 E
Bordesholm 30 54.11 N 10.01 E
Borðeyri 24a 65.15 N 21.10 W
Bordighera 62 43.46 N 7.39 E
Bording 41 56.12 N 9.17 E
Bording Kirkeby 41 56.10 N 9.15 E
Bordino, Fiume di ≃ 70 37.53 N 12.37 E
Bordj Bou Arreridj 148 36.04 N 4.46 E
Bordj Bounaama 34 35.51 N 1.36 E
Bordj Menaïel 148 36.44 N 3.43 E
Bordj Omar Idriss 148 28.09 N 6.43 E
Bordj Sidi Toui 148 32.44 N 11.22 E
Bordunskij 85 42.40 N 75.37 E
Bore, It. 62 44.43 N 9.47 E
Bore, Ityo. 144 4.40 N 37.40 E
Boré, Mali 150 15.08 N 3.29 W
Boreda 144 6.32 N 37.48 E
Boreham 260 51.46 N 0.33 E
Borehamwood 260 51.40 N 0.16 W
Borel Hill ∧ 282 37.19 N 122.12 W
Borello, It. 64 41.55 N 14.18 E
Borello, It. 66 44.03 N 12.11 E
Borensberg 26 58.34 N 15.17 E
Boreray I 46 57.42 N 7.18 W
Boretto 64 44.54 N 10.33 E
Borgallo, Galleria del ➜[5] 62 44.25 N 9.53 E
Borgå → Porvoo 26 60.24 N 25.40 E
Borgarnes 24a 64.35 N 21.53 W
Borgata Costiera 70 37.43 N 12.39 E
Børgefjell Nasjonalpark ♠ 24 65.10 N 14.00 E
Borgentreich 52 51.34 N 9.14 E
Börger, Dtsch. 52 52.54 N 7.32 E
Borger, Ned. 52 52.55 N 6.46 E
Borger, Tx., U.S. 196 35.40 N 101.23 W
Borgerhout 50 51.13 N 4.26 E
Borgetto 70 38.03 N 13.08 E
Borggård 40 58.44 N 15.32 E
Borghetto 64 45.41 N 10.56 E
Borghetto di Vara 62 44.13 N 9.43 E
Borghetto Lodigiano 62 45.13 N 9.30 E
Borghetto Santo Spirito 62 44.06 N 8.14 E
Borgholm 26 56.53 N 16.39 E
Borghorst 52 52.07 N 7.23 E
Borgia 68 38.49 N 16.30 E
Borgio-Verezzi 62 44.10 N 8.18 E
Borgloon 56 50.48 N 5.20 E
Borg Mountain ∧ 9 72.42 S 3.30 W
Borgne, Lake c 194 30.05 N 89.40 W
Borgnesse, Pointe > 240e 14.27 N 60.54 W
Borgo 64 46.03 N 11.27 E
Borgo alla Collina 66 43.45 N 11.43 E
Borgo a Mozzano 66 43.59 N 10.33 E
Borgo Cerreto 66 42.49 N 12.54 E
Borgo d'Ale 62 45.21 N 8.03 E
Borgoforte 64 45.03 N 10.45 E
Borgofranco d'Ivrea 62 45.30 N 7.51 E
Borgolavezzaro 62 45.19 N 8.42 E
Borgomanero 62 45.42 N 8.28 E
Borgomaro 62 43.58 N 7.56 E
Borgonovo Val Tidone 62 45.01 N 9.26 E
Borgo Pace 66 43.39 N 12.17 E
Borgoricco 64 45.32 N 11.58 E
Borgorose 66 42.11 N 13.13 E
Borgo San Dalmazzo 62 44.20 N 7.30 E
Borgo San Giacomo 64 45.21 N 9.58 E
Borgo San Lorenzo 66 43.57 N 11.23 E
Borgosatollo 64 45.28 N 10.14 E
Borgosesia 62 45.43 N 8.16 E
Borgo Ticino 266b 45.41 N 8.36 E
Borgo Tossignano 66 44.16 N 11.35 E
Borgou □[5] 150 10.30 N 2.50 E
Borgo Val di Taro 62 44.29 N 9.46 E
Borgo Vercelli 62 45.21 N 8.28 E
Borgsdorf 54 52.42 N 13.14 E
Borgsdorf, Forst ➜[3] 264a 52.42 N 13.19 E
Borgu Game Reserve ➜[4] 150 10.15 N 4.10 E
Borgund ᵾ[1] 26 61.03 N 7.49 E
Bori 150 4.42 N 7.21 E
Borig Delijn els ➜[2] 88 50.00 N 94.00 E
Borikhan 110 18.33 N 103.43 E
Borilovo 76 53.22 N 35.58 E
Borinage □[9] 50 50.30 N 4.00 E
Boring, Md., U.S. 208 39.31 N 76.49 W
Boring, Or., U.S. 224 45.25 N 122.22 W
Borinskoje 76 52.27 N 39.22 E
Borislav 78 49.16 N 23.27 E
Borisoglebsk 80 51.23 N 42.06 E
Borisoglebskij 80 57.16 N 39.09 E
Borisov, Bela. 76 54.15 N 28.30 E
Borisov, Ukr. 78 50.11 N 26.31 E
Borisovka, Ross. 76 52.50 N 39.58 E
Borisovka, Ross. 78 50.36 N 36.01 E
Borisovo 82 55.25 N 36.03 E
Borisovo ➜[8] 265b 55.38 N 37.45 E
Borisovo-Sudskoje 76 59.54 N 36.01 E
Borisovskaja 76 60.12 N 39.48 E
Borispol' 78 50.21 N 30.57 E
Borja, Esp. 34 41.50 N 1.32 W
Borja, Perú 246 4.26 S 77.33 W
Bork 52 51.40 N 7.30 E
Borken, Dtsch. 52 51.51 N 6.51 E
Borken, Dtsch. 56 51.03 N 9.16 E
Borkenwirthe 52 51.53 N 6.50 E
Borki, Ross. 86 59.08 N 82.15 E
Borki, Ukr. 78 49.42 N 36.02 E
Borkoldoj, chrebet ⋀ 85 41.25 N 77.50 E

FRANÇAIS Nom	Page	Lat.°′	Long.°′ W = Ouest

Børkop 41 55.39 N 9.39 E
Borkou ➜[1] 146 18.15 N 18.50 E
Borkou-Ennedi-Tibesti □[5] 146 18.15 N 18.50 E
Borkoviči 76 55.40 N 28.20 E
Borkum 52 53.35 N 6.40 E
Borkum I 52 53.35 N 6.41 E
Borland Manor 279b 40.15 N 80.09 W
Borlänge 40 60.29 N 15.25 E
Borle ➜[8] 272c 19.02 N 72.55 E
Borlu 130 38.44 N 28.27 E
Bormes-les-Mimosas 62 43.09 N 6.20 E
Bormida ≃ 62 44.23 N 8.13 E
Bormida di Millesimo ≃ 62 44.40 N 8.20 E
Bormida di Spigno ≃ 62 44.40 N 8.20 E
Bormio 64 46.28 N 10.22 E
Born, Dtsch. 41 54.23 N 12.31 E
Born, Dtsch. 54 52.22 N 11.28 E
Born, Dtsch. 54 45.22 N 12.31 E
Borna, Dtsch. 54 51.19 N 13.11 E
Borna, Dtsch. 54 51.07 N 12.30 E
Borndiep c 52 53.25 N 5.35 E
Borne 52 52.18 N 6.45 E
Borne ≃ 62 45.03 N 3.54 E
Borneo (Kalimantan) I 112 0.30 N 114.00 E
Bornheim 56 50.46 N 6.59 E
Bornholm I 26 55.10 N 15.00 E
Bornholte 52 51.52 N 8.29 E
Bornhöved 54 54.04 N 10.16 E
Börnicke, Dtsch. 54 52.41 N 12.56 E
Börnicke, Dtsch. 264a 52.40 N 13.38 E
Börnig ➜[8] 263 51.33 N 7.16 E
Bornim ➜[8] 264a 52.26 N 13.00 E
Borno 64 45.56 N 10.12 E
Bornos, Embalse de ⊜[1] 34 36.50 N 5.30 W
Bornsdorf 54 51.46 N 13.41 E
Bornstedt ➜[8] 264a 52.25 N 13.02 E
Bornu □[3] 146 12.00 N 12.45 E
Boro ≃ 140 8.52 N 26.11 E
Borobudur ⊥ 115a 7.36 S 110.12 E
Borod'anka 78 50.39 N 29.56 E
Borodarou 150 10.59 N 2.53 E
Borodino, Ross. 82 55.32 N 35.50 E
Borodino, Ross. 82 56.53 N 37.00 E
Borodino, Ross. 88 55.55 N 94.55 E
Borodino, Ukr. 78 46.18 N 29.13 E
Borodulicha 86 50.43 N 80.55 E
Borodulino 80 57.59 N 54.20 E
Borogoncy 74 62.42 N 131.08 E
Borohoro Shan ⋀ 86 44.06 N 83.10 E
Boroko 112 0.55 N 123.16 E
Boroml'a 78 50.37 N 34.59 E
Boromo 150 11.45 N 2.56 W
Boron, Mali 150 14.01 N 7.30 W
Boron, Ca., U.S. 228 34.59 N 117.38 W
Boronga Islands II 110 19.58 N 93.06 E
Borongan 116 11.37 N 125.26 E
Boronia 274b 37.52 S 145.17 E
Boron'ki 76 53.09 N 32.08 E
Borore 71 40.13 N 8.48 E
Borotou 150 8.44 N 7.30 W
Boroughbridge 44 54.06 N 1.23 W
Borough Green 260 51.17 N 0.19 E
Borough Park ➜[8] 276 40.38 N 74.00 W
Borovaja, Ukr. 78 50.12 N 30.07 E
Borovaja, Ukr. 83 49.24 N 37.40 E
Borovaja ≃ 83 48.58 N 38.24 E
Borovan 38 43.26 N 23.45 E
Borovany 61 48.54 N 14.39 E
Boroviči 76 58.24 N 33.55 E
Borovik ≃ 83 49.11 N 38.33 E
Borovka ≃ 80 52.54 N 52.00 E
Borovl'anka 86 52.38 N 84.29 E
Borovoj 24 59.55 N 51.38 E
Borovoje, Kaz. 86 53.04 N 70.19 E
Borovoje, Ukr. 78 51.06 N 27.13 E
Borovsk 82 55.12 N 36.30 E
Borovskaja 24 60.46 N 41.06 E
Borovskij 86 57.03 N 65.44 E
Borovskoj 86 53.48 N 64.12 E
Borovskoje, Ross. 86 52.39 N 82.08 E
Borovskoje, Ukr. 83 48.51 N 38.34 E
Borovucha 76 55.36 N 28.37 E
Borovy 60 49.33 N 13.18 E
Borozdino 82 54.07 N 38.22 E
Borraan 144 10.14 N 48.44 E
Borrachudo ≃ 255 18.12 S 45.16 W
Borrazópolis 255 23.56 S 51.36 W
Borrby 26 55.27 N 14.10 E
Borre 41 55.00 N 12.28 E
Borre ⊥ 26 59.23 N 10.28 E
Borreby 41 55.14 N 11.19 E
Borriana, Esp. 34 39.53 N 0.05 W
Borriana, It. 62 45.30 N 8.02 E
Borris 48 52.35 N 6.06 W
Borrisokane 48 52.59 N 8.07 W
Borrisoleigh 48 52.45 N 7.57 W
Borroloola 164 16.04 S 136.17 E
Borroloola Aboriginal Reserve ➜[4] 164 16.00 S 136.15 E
Borrowdale 44 54.31 N 3.10 W
Börry 52 52.01 N 9.27 E
Borș 38 47.07 N 21.49 E
Borșa, Rom. 38 46.56 N 23.40 E
Borșa, Rom. 38 47.39 N 24.40 E
Borsad 120 22.25 N 72.54 E
Borsano 266b 45.35 N 8.51 E
Borschemich 263 51.04 N 6.25 E
Borščov 78 48.48 N 26.03 E
Borščovo 82 56.30 N 36.51 E
Borščovočnyj chrebet ⋀ 88 52.00 N 117.00 E
Borsdorf 54 51.21 N 12.32 E
Borskoje 80 53.02 N 51.43 E
Borsod-Abaúj-Zemplén □[6] 30 48.15 N 21.00 E
Börssum 54 52.04 N 10.35 E
Borstendorf 54 50.46 N 13.10 E
Bortala ≃ 86 44.50 N 82.45 E
Borth, Dtsch. 52 51.36 N 6.33 E
Borth, Wales, U.K. 42 52.29 N 4.03 W
Borthwick Water ≃ 44 55.24 N 2.50 W
Bortigali 71 40.17 N 8.50 E
Bortigiadas 71 40.53 N 9.02 E
Bort-les-Orgues, Fr. 32 45.24 N 2.30 E
Bort-les-Orgues, Fr. 32 43.49 N 2.53 E
Bortniči 78 50.22 N 30.41 E
Borto 88 53.35 N 111.53 E
Bortondale 285 39.54 N 79.24 W
Boru 164 10.14 S 148.50 E
Boruca 236 9.00 N 83.20 W
Borūjen 128 31.59 N 51.18 E
Borūjerd 128 33.54 N 48.46 E
Bor Ul Shan ⋀ 102 41.20 N 98.55 E
Borve 46 56.58 N 7.32 W
Borz'a 88 50.24 N 116.31 E
Borz'a ≃ 88 50.38 N 115.38 E
Borzna 78 51.15 N 32.25 E
Boržomi 84 41.50 N 43.21 E
Boržomskij zapovednik ♠ 84 41.50 N 43.10 E
Borzonasca 62 44.25 N 9.23 E
Borzyszkowy 30 54.03 N 17.22 E
Bosa 71 40.18 N 8.30 E
Bosaga 86 47.55 N 72.58 E
Bosambi 152 2.24 N 22.39 E
Bosanska Dubica 36 45.11 N 16.49 E
Bosanska Gradiška 36 45.09 N 17.15 E
Bosanska Krupa 36 44.53 N 16.10 E
Bosanski Novi 36 45.03 N 16.23 E
Bosanski Petrovac 36 44.33 N 16.22 E
Bosanski Šamac 38 45.03 N 18.28 E
Bosansko Grahovo 36 44.11 N 16.22 E
Bősárkány 61 47.41 N 17.14 E
Bosau 54 54.06 N 10.25 E
Bosavi, Mount ∧ 164 6.35 S 142.50 E
Boscastle 42 50.41 N 4.42 W
Bosco, It. 66 44.53 N 12.14 E
Bosco, It. 66 43.08 N 12.28 E
Boscobel 190 43.08 N 90.42 W
Bosco Chiesanuova 64 45.37 N 11.02 E

PORTUGUÊS Nome	Página	Lat.°′	Long.°′ W = Oeste

Bosco Marengo 62 44.49 N 8.41 E
Boscoreale 68 40.46 N 14.28 E
Bose 102 23.54 N 106.37 E
Bösel 52 53.00 N 7.58 E
Bosencheve, Parque Nacional ♠ 234 19.36 N 100.15 W
Bosenge 152 1.18 N 22.19 E
Bósforo, Estrecho del → İstanbul Boğazı ᵫ 130 41.06 N 29.04 E
Bosham 42 50.49 N 0.52 W
Boshan 98 36.29 N 117.50 E
Boshkung Lake ⊜ 212 45.04 N 78.44 W
Boshoek 156 25.30 S 27.09 E
Boshof 158 28.34 S 25.04 E
Boshrūyeh 128 33.53 N 57.26 E
Bosilegrad 38 42.29 N 22.28 E
Bösingen 58 48.14 N 8.34 E
Bosjökloster 41 55.54 N 13.31 E
Boškajnar 85 38.13 N 68.51 E
Boskoop 52 52.04 N 4.35 E
Boskop 158 26.34 S 27.08 E
Boskop ∧ 273d 26.05 S 27.57 E
Boskovice 30 49.29 N 16.40 E
Boskuil 158 27.23 S 25.51 E
Bosman 164 4.10 S 144.40 E
Bosna 272b 22.37 N 88.30 E
Bosna ≃ 38 45.04 N 18.29 E
Bosna-Hercegovina → Bosnia and Hercegovina □[1] 36 44.15 N 17.30 E
Bošn'akovo 89 49.38 N 142.10 E
Bosnia and Hercegovina (Bosna-Hercegovina) □[1] 36 44.15 N 17.30 E
Bosnik 164 1.10 S 136.14 E
Boso 272b 22.58 N 88.08 E
Bosobolo 152 4.11 N 19.54 E
Boso-Djafo 152 1.06 N 19.14 E
Bosogo 85 41.09 N 76.25 E
Bōsō-hantō >[1] 94 35.18 N 140.10 E
Bōsō-kyūryō ⋀[2] 268 35.08 N 139.56 E
Bososama 152 4.18 N 20.00 E
Bösperde 263 51.28 N 7.46 E
Bosphore, Détroit du → İstanbul Boğazı ᵫ 130 41.06 N 29.04 E
Bosporus → İstanbul Boğazı ᵫ 130 41.06 N 29.04 E
Bosque □[6] 222 31.55 N 97.35 W
Bosque, Paseo del ♠ 288 34.55 S 57.56 W
Bosque Farms 200 34.53 N 106.40 W
Bosques 288 34.49 S 58.14 W
Bosques Petrificados, Monumento Natural ♠ 254 47.39 S 68.07 W
Bosqueville 222 31.38 N 97.13 W
Bossangoa 152 6.29 N 17.27 E
Bossdorf 54 51.59 N 12.40 E
Bossé Bangou 150 13.21 N 1.18 E
Bossembélé 152 5.16 N 17.39 E
Bossentele 152 5.41 N 16.38 E
Bossert Estates 285 40.09 N 74.44 W
Bossier City 194 32.30 N 93.43 W
Bossley Park 274a 33.52 S 150.54 E
Bosso 146 13.42 N 13.19 E
Bosso, Dallol V 150 12.25 N 2.50 E
Bossolasco 62 44.32 N 8.02 E
Bossut, Cape > 162 18.43 S 121.38 E
Bostān, Īrān 128 31.43 N 48.00 E
Bostān, Pāk. 120 30.26 N 67.02 E
Bostancı ➜[8] 267b 40.57 N 29.05 E
Bostandyk 80 49.38 N 48.54 E
Bosten Hu ⊜ 90 42.00 N 87.00 E
Bostock Green 262 53.13 N 2.30 W
Boston, Pil. 116 7.52 N 126.22 E
Boston, Eng., U.K. 44 52.59 N 0.01 W
Boston, Ga., U.S. 192 30.47 N 83.47 W
Boston, In., U.S. 218 39.44 N 84.51 W
Boston, Ma., U.S. 207 42.21 N 71.03 W
Boston, Ma., U.S. 283 42.21 N 71.03 W
Boston, N.Y., U.S. 210 42.38 N 78.44 W
Boston, Pa., U.S. 279b 40.18 N 79.49 W
Boston Bar 182 49.52 N 121.26 W
Boston Bay c 283 42.22 N 70.54 W
Boston Brook ≃ 283 42.37 N 71.00 W
Boston College ᵾ[2] 283 42.20 N 71.10 W
Boston Common ♠ 283 42.21 N 71.05 W
Boston Corners 210 42.03 N 73.31 W
Boston Creek ≃ 212 43.02 N 79.56 W
Boston Harbor 224 47.08 N 122.54 W
Boston Harbor c 283 42.20 N 70.58 W
Boston Heights 214 41.15 N 81.30 W
Boston Mill 214 41.16 N 81.34 W
Boston Mountains ⋀ 194 35.50 N 93.20 W
Boston Spa 44 53.54 N 1.21 W
Boston University ᵾ[2] 283 42.21 N 71.07 W
Bosumtwi, Lake ⊜ 150 6.30 N 1.25 W
Bosut ≃ 38 44.57 N 19.22 E
Boswell, In., U.S. 216 40.31 N 87.22 W
Boswell, Ok., U.S. 196 34.01 N 95.52 W
Boswell, Pa., U.S. 214 40.09 N 79.01 W
Boswell Bay 180 60.24 N 146.08 W
Bosworth 194 39.28 N 93.20 W
Bosworth Airport ⊠ 279a 41.26 N 82.00 W
Bosworth Field ⊥ 42 52.36 N 1.25 W
Botād 120 22.10 N 71.40 E
Botafogo ➜[8] 287a 22.57 S 43.11 W
Botafogo, Enseada de c 287a 22.57 S 43.10 W
Botany 274a 33.57 S 151.12 E
Botany Bay ➜[8] 260 51.41 N 0.07 W
Botany Bay c 170 33.59 S 151.12 E
Botejevo 78 46.41 N 35.52 E
Botelhos 256 21.39 S 46.24 W
Botera 152 11.37 S 14.17 E
Botersleegte 158 30.35 S 21.22 E
Botesdale 42 52.20 N 1.01 E
Boteti ≃ 156 20.08 S 23.23 E
Botev ∧ 38 42.43 N 24.55 E
Botevgrad 38 42.54 N 23.47 E
Botha's Hill 158 29.45 S 30.45 E
Bothaville 158 27.27 S 26.36 E
Bothell 224 47.45 N 122.12 W
Bothe-Napa Valley State Park ♠ 226 38.32 N 122.32 W
Bothnia, Gulf of c 26 63.00 N 20.00 E
Bothwell, Austl. 166 42.23 S 147.00 E
Bothwell, On., Can. 214 42.38 N 81.52 W
Boticas 34 41.41 N 7.40 W
Botija, Ilha da I 246 3.58 S 62.53 W
Botija, Isla I 258 33.52 S 59.02 W
Botkins 216 40.28 N 84.10 W
Botkul', ozero ⊜ 80 48.46 N 46.40 E
Botkyrka 40 59.14 N 17.49 E
Botlich 84 42.39 N 46.14 E
Bot Makak 152 4.00 N 10.55 E
Botna ≃ 78 46.45 N 29.34 E
Botnia, Golfo de → Bothnia, Gulf of c 26 63.00 N 20.00 E
Botola 152 1.17 S 18.13 E
Botolan 116 15.17 N 120.01 E
Botoșani 38 47.45 N 26.40 E
Botoșani □[6] 38 48.00 N 26.45 E
Botoșanița 38 47.53 N 26.07 E
Botou 150 12.40 N 2.03 E
Botovo 82 56.03 N 38.26 E
Bo Trach 110 17.35 N 106.32 E
Botrange ∧ 56 50.30 N 6.08 E
Botricello 68 38.56 N 16.51 E
Botro 150 7.51 N 5.19 W
Botsford 210 41.21 N 73.15 W
Botswana □[1], Afr. 138 22.00 S 24.00 E
Botswana □[1], Afr. 156 22.00 S 24.00 E
Botte Donato, Monte ∧ 68 39.17 N 16.26 E
Bottenhavet (Selkämeri) c 26 62.00 N 20.00 E
Bottenviken (Perämeri) c 26 65.00 N 23.00 E
Bottesford 42 52.56 N 0.48 W
Bottineau 198 48.49 N 100.26 W
Bottisham 42 52.13 N 0.16 E
Bottnischer Meerbusen → Bothnia, Gulf of c 26 63.00 N 20.00 E
Bottoms Reservoir ⊜[1] 262 53.28 N 1.58 W
Bottrop 52 51.31 N 6.55 E
Botucatu 255 22.52 S 48.26 W
Botwood 186 49.09 N 55.21 W
Boty 88 52.24 N 118.32 E
Bötzingen 58 48.04 N 7.44 E
Bötzow 54 52.39 N 13.08 E
Bötzsee ⊜ 264a 52.34 N 13.50 E
Bouaflé, C. Iv. 150 6.59 N 5.45 W
Bouafle, Fr. 261 48.58 N 1.54 E
Bou Ahmed 148 35.25 N 5.00 W
Bouaké 150 7.41 N 5.02 W
Bou Ali, Oued V 148 31.14 N 4.16 E
Bouânane 148 32.03 N 3.03 W
Bouandougou 150 8.13 N 5.40 W
Bouar 152 5.57 N 15.36 E
Bou Arada 36 36.20 N 9.38 E
Bou Areg, Sebkha c 34 35.10 N 2.45 W
Bouârfa 148 32.30 N 1.59 W
Bouaye 32 47.09 N 1.42 W
Boubandjidah, Parc National de ♠ 146 8.45 N 14.45 E
Bou Bernous 148 27.18 N 2.59 W
Boubín ∧ 60 48.59 N 13.51 E
Bouca 152 6.30 N 18.17 E
Bouchain 50 50.17 N 3.19 E
Bouchegouf 36 36.28 N 7.44 E
Boucher ≃ 186 49.10 N 69.06 W
Boucher, Lac ⊜ 186 51.07 N 59.35 W
Boucherville 206 45.36 N 73.27 W
Boucherville, Îles de II 275a 45.37 N 73.28 W
Bouches-du-Rhône □[5] 62 43.30 N 5.00 E
Bouchoir 50 49.45 N 2.41 E
Bouclans 58 47.14 N 6.15 E
Boucle du Baoulé, Parc National de la ♠ 150 13.50 N 9.00 W
Bouddi National Park ♠ 170 33.31 S 131.24 E
Boudjellil 34 36.20 N 4.21 E
Boudnib 148 31.57 N 4.38 W
Boudouaou 34 36.43 N 3.25 E
Boudry 58 46.57 N 6.50 E
Boué 50 50.01 N 3.42 E
Bouenza □[5] 152 4.00 S 13.45 E
Boufarik 148 36.34 N 2.55 E
Bouffémont 261 49.03 N 2.18 E
Bou Ficha 36 36.18 N 10.29 E
Bougaa 34 36.20 N 5.05 E
Bougainville □[5] 175e 6.00 S 155.00 E
Bougainville I 175e 6.00 S 155.00 E
Bougainville, Cape > 164 13.54 S 126.06 E
Bougainville, Détroit de ᵫ 175f 15.50 S 167.10 E
Bougainville Reef ✥[2] 164 15.30 S 147.06 E
Bougainville Strait ᵫ 175e 6.40 S 156.10 E
Bougar'oûn, Cap > 34 37.06 N 6.28 E
Bough Beech Reservoir ⊜[1] 260 51.13 N 0.08 E
Boughton 44 53.12 N 1.00 W
Boughton Green 260 51.14 N 0.32 E
Boughton Malherbe 260 51.13 N 0.42 E
Boughton Place ᵾ 260 51.13 N 0.32 E
Bougie → Bejaïa 148 36.45 N 5.05 E
Bougou 152 3.45 S 11.12 E
Bougouni 150 11.25 N 7.29 W
Bougouriba ≃ 150 10.42 N 2.56 W
Bougzoul 34 35.42 N 2.51 E
Bou Hadjar 36 36.30 N 8.06 E
Bou Hajar 36 35.42 N 10.48 E
Bouillante 241o 16.06 N 61.45 W
Bouillon 56 49.48 N 5.04 E
Bouilly 50 48.12 N 4.00 E
Bouïra 148 36.23 N 3.54 E
Bouïra □[5] 148 36.00 N 4.00 E
Bouisy, Ru de ≃ 261 48.34 N 2.45 E
Bou Izakarn 148 29.09 N 9.44 W
Boujad 148 32.48 N 6.26 W
Boujailles 58 46.53 N 6.05 E
Boujdour, Cap > 148 26.08 N 14.30 W
Bouka ≃ 150 11.00 N 10.50 W
Bou Kadir 148 36.04 N 1.07 E
Bou Khadra 36 35.45 N 8.02 E
Boukiéro 273b 4.12 S 15.18 E
Boukiéro, Mont ∧[2] 273b 4.11 S 15.17 E
Boukombé 150 10.11 N 1.06 E
Boula Ibib 146 9.34 N 13.46 E
Boulaide 56 49.54 N 5.49 E
Boularderie Island I 186 46.15 N 60.30 W
Boulay-Moselle 56 49.11 N 6.30 E
Boulbon 62 43.52 N 4.41 E
Boulder, Austl. 162 30.47 S 121.29 E
Boulder, Co., U.S. 200 40.00 N 105.16 W
Boulder, Mt., U.S. 202 46.14 N 112.07 W
Boulder ≃ 202 45.52 N 111.57 W
Boulder City 204 35.58 N 114.49 W
Boulder Creek 226 37.07 N 122.07 W
Boulder Creek ≃ 200 37.47 N 111.22 W
Boulder Hill 216 41.41 N 88.25 W
Bouleaux, Lac des ⊜ 275a 45.33 N 73.19 W
Bouli ≃ 150 13.15 N 0.03 E
Boulia 166 22.54 S 139.54 E
Bouligny 56 49.17 N 5.45 E
Boullay-les-Troux 261 48.41 N 2.03 E
Boulmane 148 33.22 N 4.45 W
Boulmane □[4] 148 33.00 N 4.00 W
Boulogne ➜[8] 258 34.31 S 58.34 W
Boulogne, Bois de ♠ 261 48.50 N 2.15 E
Boulogne-Billancourt 50 48.50 N 2.15 E
Boulogne-sur-Gesse 32 43.18 N 0.39 E
Boulogne-sur-Mer 50 50.43 N 1.37 E
Bouloire 50 47.58 N 0.33 E
Boulouli 150 15.34 N 9.21 W
Bouloupari 175f 21.52 S 166.04 E
Boulouris-sur-Mer 62 43.25 N 6.48 E
Boulsa 150 12.39 N 0.34 W
Boulsworth Hill ∧ 262 53.48 N 2.06 W
Bouly 150 15.19 N 11.48 W
Bou Maad, Djebel ∧ 34 36.26 N 2.08 E
Boumalne 148 31.32 N 5.27 W
Boumba ≃ 152 2.02 N 15.12 E
Boumbé I ≃ 152 4.04 N 15.23 E
Boumbé II ≃ 152 4.08 N 15.08 E
Boumboum 150 15.01 N 1.42 W
Boûmdeïd 150 17.26 N 9.50 W
Bou Medfaa 34 36.22 N 2.28 E
Boumentana 152 6.59 N 16.56 E
Boumnyebe 152 3.52 N 10.49 E
Boumou 146 9.02 N 16.26 E
Bouna 150 9.16 N 3.00 W
Boundary 180 64.04 N 141.06 W
Boundary Bay c 224 49.00 N 122.58 W
Boundary Peak ∧ 204 37.51 N 118.21 W
Boundary Ranges ⋀ 180 59.00 N 134.00 W
Bound Brook 210 40.34 N 74.32 W
Bound Brook ≃, Ma., U.S. 283 42.13 N 70.47 W
Bound Brook ≃, N.J., U.S. 276 40.35 N 74.30 W
Boundiali 150 9.31 N 6.29 W
Boun Nua 110 21.38 N 101.54 E
Bountiful 200 40.53 N 111.52 W
Bounty Bay c 174e 25.04 S 130.05 W
Bounty Islands II 14 47.42 S 179.04 E
Bounty Trough ✥[1] 14 46.00 S 178.00 E
Bouqteb 148 34.02 N 0.05 E
Bouquet Reservoir ⊜[1] 228 34.35 N 118.24 W
Bouqueval 261 49.01 N 2.26 E
Boura 150 12.25 N 4.33 W
Bouradière 62 43.58 N 5.19 E
Bourail 175f 21.34 S 165.30 E
Bouray-sur-Juine 261 48.31 N 2.18 E
Bourbeuse ≃ 194 38.24 N 90.53 W
Bourbeuse, Dry Fork ≃ 194 38.16 N 91.26 W
Bourbon, In., U.S. 216 41.17 N 86.06 W
Bourbon, Mo., U.S. 194 38.09 N 91.14 W
Bourbon □[6] 218 38.14 N 84.14 W
Bourbon ≃ 206 46.17 N 71.55 W
Bourbon-Lancy 32 46.38 N 3.46 E
Bourbonnais 216 41.08 N 87.52 W
Bourbonnais □[9] 32 46.20 N 3.00 E
Bourbonne-les-Bains 58 47.57 N 5.45 E
Bourbourg 50 50.57 N 2.12 E
Bourbre ≃ 62 45.47 N 5.11 E
Bourdeaux 62 44.35 N 5.08 E
Bourdon, Île I 275a 45.43 N 73.29 W
Bourdon, Réservoir du ⊜[1] 50 47.36 N 3.07 E
Bourdonné 261 48.45 N 1.40 E
Bou Regreg, Oued ≃ 148 34.03 N 6.50 W
Bourem 150 16.57 N 0.21 W
Bourg 194 29.33 N 90.36 W
Bourg-Achard 50 49.21 N 0.49 E
Bourganeuf 32 45.57 N 1.46 E
Bourg-Argental 62 45.18 N 4.33 E
Bourg-de-Péage 62 45.02 N 5.03 E
Bourg-en-Bresse 58 46.12 N 5.13 E
Bourges 32 47.05 N 2.24 E
Bourget 206 45.26 N 75.09 W
Bourget, Lac du ⊜ 62 45.44 N 5.52 E
Bourg-la-Reine 261 48.47 N 2.19 E
Bourg-Lastic 32 45.39 N 2.33 E
Bourg-lés-Valence 62 44.57 N 4.53 E
Bourgneuf 261 48.36 N 2.00 E
Bourgneuf-en-Retz 32 47.02 N 1.57 W
Bourgogne 50 49.21 N 4.04 E
Bourgogne (Burgundy) □[9] 32 47.00 N 4.30 E
Bourgogne, Canal de ≊ 50 47.58 N 3.30 E
Bourgoin-Jallieu 62 45.35 N 5.17 E
Bourg-Saint-Andéol 62 44.22 N 4.39 E
Bourg-Saint-Maurice 62 45.37 N 6.46 E
Bourg-Saint-Pierre 58 45.57 N 7.12 E
Bourgtheroulde 50 49.18 N 0.53 E
Bourgueil 50 47.17 N 0.10 E
Bou Rjeïmât ⏚[4] 150 19.04 N 15.08 W
Bourke 166 30.05 S 145.56 E
Bourmont 58 48.12 N 5.35 E
Bourne 42 52.46 N 0.23 W
Bourne ≃, Fr. 62 45.04 N 5.15 E
Bourne ≃, Eng., U.K. 42 51.02 N 1.47 W
Bournebridge 260 51.38 N 0.11 E
Bourne End 260 51.45 N 0.32 W
Bournemouth 42 50.43 N 1.54 W
Bourneville, Fr. 50 49.23 N 0.37 E
Bourneville, Oh., U.S. 218 39.17 N 83.09 W
Bourn Vincent Memorial Park ♠ 48 52.01 N 9.30 W
Bouroum 150 13.37 N 0.39 W
Bourron-Marlotte 50 48.20 N 2.42 E
Bourscheid 56 49.55 N 6.04 E
Bourtange 52 53.00 N 7.11 E
Bourtanger Moor ➜[3] 52 53.00 N 7.15 E
Bourton-on-the-Water 42 51.53 N 1.45 W
Bourzanga 150 13.41 N 1.33 W
Bou Saâda 148 35.12 N 4.11 E
Bou Salem 36 36.36 N 8.59 E
Bousbecque 50 50.46 N 3.05 E
Bouse 200 33.55 N 114.00 W
Bou Sellam, Oued ≃ 34 36.26 N 4.34 E
Bouse Wash V 200 34.02 N 114.20 W
Bou Smail 148 36.38 N 2.41 E
Boussac 32 46.21 N 2.13 E
Boussé, Burkina 150 12.39 N 1.53 W
Bousse, Fr. 56 49.17 N 6.12 E
Boussières 58 47.09 N 5.54 E
Bousso 146 10.29 N 16.43 E
Boussois 50 50.17 N 4.03 E
Boussouma 150 12.55 N 1.05 W
Boussu 50 50.26 N 3.48 E
Boussy-Saint-Antoine 261 48.41 N 2.32 E
Bout, Pointe du > 240e 14.34 N 61.03 W
Bouteille, Lac de la ⊜ 206 46.42 N 73.41 W
Bouteldja 36 36.47 N 8.12 E
Bou Temezguida ∧ 148 29.21 N 9.55 W
Boutilimit 150 17.33 N 14.42 W
Bouttencourt 50 49.56 N 1.38 E
Bouvard, Cape > 168a 32.41 S 115.37 E
Bouvetøya I 9 54.26 S 3.24 E
Bouvier Bay c 281 42.39 N 82.38 W
Bouvières 62 44.30 N 5.13 E
Bouxières-aux-Dames 56 48.45 N 6.10 E
Bouxwiller 56 48.49 N 7.29 E
Bouyon 62 43.50 N 7.07 E
Bouza 150 14.25 N 6.02 E
Bou Zadjar 34 35.35 N 1.09 W
Bouzonville 56 49.18 N 6.32 E
Bov 41 54.50 N 9.23 E
Bova 68 38.00 N 15.56 E
Bøvågen 26 60.40 N 4.58 E
Bovalino Marina 68 38.10 N 16.11 E
Bova Marina 68 37.56 N 15.55 E
Bovard 279b 40.19 N 79.30 W
Bovec 36 46.20 N 13.33 E
Bovegno 64 45.48 N 10.16 E
Bovenden 52 51.35 N 9.55 E
Bovenkarspel 52 52.42 N 5.15 E
Bøverdal 26 61.43 N 8.21 E
Boves, Fr. 50 49.51 N 2.23 E
Boves, It. 62 44.19 N 7.33 E
Bovey 190 47.17 N 93.25 W
Bovey ≃ 42 50.34 N 3.37 W
Bovey Tracey 42 50.36 N 3.40 W
Bovill 202 46.51 N 116.23 W
Boville Ernica 66 41.38 N 13.28 E
Bovina 196 34.31 N 102.53 W
Bovina Center 210 42.16 N 74.47 W
Bovingdon 260 51.44 N 0.32 W
Bövinghausen ➜[8] 263 51.31 N 7.19 E
Bovington Camp 42 50.42 N 2.14 W
Bovino 68 41.15 N 15.20 E
Bovisio Masciago 266b 45.37 N 9.09 E
Bovolenta 64 45.16 N 11.56 E
Bovolone 64 45.15 N 11.07 E
Bovril 252 31.21 S 59.26 W
Bovrup 41 54.59 N 9.36 E
Bow 224 48.33 N 122.23 W
Bow ≃, Austl. 162 16.32 S 128.39 E
Bow ≃, Ab., Can. 182 49.56 N 111.42 W
Bow ≃, Sk., Can. 184 54.56 N 105.13 W
Bo-Wadrif 158 32.26 S 20.07 E
Bowang 106 31.34 N 118.50 E
Bowbells 198 48.48 N 102.14 W
Bow Brook ≃ 42 52.04 N 2.07 W
Bowburn 44 54.43 N 1.31 W
Bow Creek ≃ 198 39.35 N 99.14 W
Bowden 182 51.55 N 114.02 W
Bowdle 198 45.27 N 99.39 W
Bowdoin, Lake ⊜ 202 48.24 N 107.41 W
Bowdon, Eng., U.K. 262 53.23 N 2.22 W
Bowdon, Ga., U.S. 192 33.32 N 85.15 W
Bowdon, N.D., U.S. 198 47.28 N 99.42 W
Bowelling 168a 33.25 S 116.29 E
Bowen, Arg. 252 35.00 S 67.31 W
Bowen, Austl. 166 20.01 S 148.15 E
Bowen, Il., U.S. 194 40.14 N 91.04 W
Bowen ≃ 166 20.24 S 147.21 E
Bowenfels 170 33.31 S 150.07 E
Bowens Creek ≃ 170 33.21 S 150.35 E
Bowers 208 39.15 N 75.36 W
Bowers Gifford 260 51.34 N 0.32 E
Bowers Mansion ⊥ 226 39.17 N 119.50 W
Bowers Marshes ≋ 260 51.33 N 0.32 E
Bowers Ridge ✥[3] 16 54.00 N 179.00 E
Bowerston 214 40.25 N 81.11 W
Bowersville 218 39.34 N 83.43 W
Bowgreave 44 53.52 N 2.45 W
Bowie, Az., U.S. 200 32.19 N 109.29 W
Bowie, Md., U.S. 208 39.00 N 76.46 W
Bowie, Tx., U.S. 196 33.33 N 97.50 W
Bowie Creek ≃ 194 31.26 N 89.24 W
Bow Island 184 49.52 N 111.22 W
Bowland, Forest of ➜[3] 44 53.58 N 2.32 W
Bowles Creek ≃ 222 32.02 N 94.59 W
Bowley Bar >[2] 284b 39.18 N 76.23 W
Bowleys Quarters 284b 39.19 N 76.24 W
Bowling Green, Fl., U.S. 220 27.38 N 81.49 W
Bowling Green, Ky., U.S. 194 36.59 N 86.26 W
Bowling Green, Mo., U.S. 219 39.20 N 91.11 W
Bowling Green, Oh., U.S. 216 41.22 N 83.39 W
Bowling Green, Pa., U.S. 285 39.55 N 75.23 W
Bowling Green, Va., U.S. 208 38.02 N 77.20 W
Bowling Green, Cape > 166 19.19 S 147.25 E
Bowling Green Bay National Park ♠ 166 19.28 S 147.14 E
Bowman, Ca., U.S. 226 38.57 N 121.03 W
Bowman, Ga., U.S. 192 34.12 N 83.01 W
Bowman, N.D., U.S. 198 46.10 N 103.23 W
Bowman, S.C., U.S. 192 33.20 N 80.40 W
Bowman, Mount ∧ 182 51.10 N 121.55 W
Bowman Creek ≃, Pa., U.S. 210 41.31 N 75.58 W
Bowman Creek ≃, Wa., U.S. 224 45.50 N 121.03 W
Bowman-Haley Lake ⊜[1] 198 46.00 N 103.20 W
Bowman Island I 9 65.17 S 103.08 E
Bowman Lake ⊜[1] 226 39.27 N 120.38 W
Bowmans 168b 34.09 S 138.16 E
Bowmansdale 208 40.10 N 76.59 W
Bowmanstown 208 40.48 N 75.40 W
Bowmansville, N.Y., U.S. 212 42.56 N 78.41 W
Bowmansville, Pa., U.S. 208 40.10 N 76.04 W
Bowmanville 212 43.55 N 78.41 W
Bowmanville Creek ≃ 212 43.53 N 78.40 W
Bowmont Water ≃ 44 55.34 N 2.09 W
Bowmore 46 55.45 N 6.17 W
Bowness-on-Windermere 44 54.22 N 2.55 W
Bowokan, Kepulauan II 112 2.05 S 123.35 E
Bowral 170 34.28 S 150.25 E
Bowraville 166 30.39 S 152.51 E
Bowron ≃ 182 54.04 N 121.48 W
Bowron Lake Provincial Park ♠ 182 53.10 N 121.06 W
Bowsman 184 52.14 N 101.14 W
Bowwood 154 17.07 S 26.17 E
Box 42 51.26 N 2.15 W
Boxberg 56 49.29 N 9.38 E
Box Butte Creek ≃ 198 42.28 N 102.37 W
Box Creek ≃, Tx., U.S. 222 31.33 N 95.43 W
Box Creek ≃, Tx., U.S. 222 31.35 N 95.10 W
Box Elder 202 48.19 N 110.00 W
Boxelder Creek ≃, U.S. 198 45.59 N 103.57 W
Boxelder Creek ≃, Co., U.S. 198 40.33 N 105.00 W
Box Elder Creek ≃, Co., U.S. 198 40.23 N 104.28 W
Box Elder Creek ≃, Mt., U.S. 202 46.57 N 108.04 W
Boxelder Creek ≃, S.D., U.S. 198 44.01 N 102.27 W
Boxey 186 47.25 N 55.34 W
Boxey Point > 186 47.24 N 55.35 W
Boxford 207 42.39 N 70.59 W
Boxford State Forest ♠ 283 42.39 N 71.02 W
Box Grove 275b 43.51 N 79.14 W
Box Hill 169 37.49 S 145.08 E
Boxholm 26 58.12 N 15.03 E
Boxian 100 33.53 N 115.45 E
Boxing 98 37.08 N 118.07 E
Boxley 260 51.18 N 0.33 E
Boxmeer 52 51.39 N 5.57 E
Boxmoor 260 51.45 N 0.29 W
Boxodoi 98 42.34 N 115.18 E
Boxtel 52 51.35 N 5.20 E
Boyabat 130 41.28 N 34.47 E
Boyabo 152 3.43 N 18.46 E
Boyacá □[5] 246 5.30 N 73.30 W
Boyacıköy ➜[8] 267b 41.06 N 29.02 E
Boyalı 130 41.02 N 33.19 E
Boyalık 130 41.15 N 28.37 E
Boyang 100 28.59 N 116.40 E
Boyanup 168a 33.29 S 115.44 E
Boyasengese 152 3.29 N 20.33 E
Boyce 194 31.23 N 92.40 W
Boyceville 190 45.02 N 92.02 W
Boyd, Mn., U.S. 198 44.50 N 95.54 W
Boyd, Tx., U.S. 222 33.05 N 97.34 W
Boyd ≃ 166 29.51 S 152.35 E
Boyd's Cove 186 49.27 N 54.39 W
Boydton 192 36.40 N 78.23 W
Boyenge 152 0.25 N 18.51 E
Boyer ≃ 198 41.28 N 95.55 W
Boyera 152 0.38 S 19.25 E
Boyer Aḥmadī va Kohkīlūyeh □[4] 128 30.40 N 50.40 E
Boyer Run ≃ 279b 40.13 N 79.32 W
Boyers 214 41.06 N 79.54 W
Boyer's Creek ≃ 284a 43.00 N 79.02 W
Boyertown 208 40.20 N 75.38 W
Boyes Hot Springs 226 38.19 N 122.29 W
Boykins 208 36.34 N 77.12 W
Boyle, Ab., Can. 182 54.35 N 112.49 W
Boyle, Ire. 48 53.58 N 8.18 W
Boyle, Ms., U.S. 194 33.42 N 90.50 W
Boyle Drain ≃ 212 43.42 N 81.06 W
Boyle Heights ➜[8] 280 34.02 N 118.13 W
Boylston, Al., U.S. 194 32.26 N 86.17 W
Boylston, Ma., U.S. 207 42.23 N 71.42 W
Boyne 275b 43.29 N 79.50 W
Boyne ≃, Austl. 166 23.56 S 151.21 E
Boyne ≃, Mb., Can. 184 49.34 N 97.52 W
Boyne ≃, On., Can. 212 44.10 N 79.49 W
Boyne ≃, Ire. 48 53.43 N 6.15 W
Boyne Battlesite ⊥ 48 53.42 N 6.23 W
Boyne City 190 45.12 N 85.00 W
Boynton 196 35.38 N 95.39 W
Boynton Beach 220 26.31 N 80.04 W
Boyo 152 5.43 N 21.33 E
Boyolali 115a 7.32 S 110.35 E
Boysen Reservoir ⊜[1] 202 43.19 N 108.11 W
Boysen State Park ♠ 202 43.23 N 108.07 W
Boys Ranch 196 35.32 N 102.15 W
Boyuibe 248 20.25 S 63.17 W
Boyup Brook 162 33.50 S 116.24 E
Bozburun 130 36.41 N 28.04 E
Boz Burun > 130 40.32 N 28.46 E
Bozburun Yarımadası >[1] 130 36.40 N 28.10 E
Bozcaada 130 39.50 N 26.04 E
Boz Dağ ∧, Tür. 130 37.18 N 29.12 E
Boz Dağ ∧, Tür. 130 38.19 N 28.08 E
Bozdağ ∧, Tür. 130 36.50 N 36.22 E
Boz Dağlar ⋀ 130 38.20 N 27.45 E
Bozdoğan 130 37.40 N 28.19 E
Bozel 62 45.27 N 6.39 E
Bozeman 202 45.40 N 111.02 W
Bozen → Bolzano 64 46.31 N 11.22 E
Bozene 152 2.56 N 19.12 E
Bozhen 98 38.07 N 116.32 E
Boží Dar 54 50.24 N 12.55 E
Bozkır 130 37.11 N 32.15 E
Bozkurt, Tür. 130 37.49 N 29.37 E
Bozkurt, Tür. 130 41.57 N 34.01 E
Bozman 208 38.46 N 76.16 W
Bozoğlak 130 39.38 N 38.49 E
Bozok 130 37.18 N 40.22 E
Bozoum 152 6.19 N 16.23 E

≃ River	Fluß	Río	Rivière	Rio
≊ Canal	Kanal	Canal	Canal	Canal
⌐ Waterfall, Rapids	Wasserfall, Stromschnellen	Cascada, Rápidos	Chute d'eau, Rapides	Cascata, Rápidos
ᵫ Strait	Meeresstraße	Estrecho	Détroit	Estreito
c Bay, Gulf	Bucht, Golf	Bahía, Golfo	Baie, Golfe	Baía, Golfo
⊜ Lake, Lakes	See, Seen	Lago, Lagos	Lac, Lacs	Lago, Lagos
≋ Swamp	Sumpf	Pantano	Marais	Pântano
⍓ Ice Features, Glacier	Eis- und Gletscherformen	Accidentes Glaciales	Formes glaciaires	Acidentes glaciares
⏚ Other Hydrographic Features	Andere Hydrographische Objekte	Otros Elementos Hidrográficos	Autres données hydrographiques	Outros acidentes hidrográficos

✥ Submarine Features	Untermeerische Objekte	Accidentes Submarinos	Formes de relief sous-marin	Acidentes submarinos
□ Political Unit	Politische Einheit	Unidad Politica	Entité politique	Unidade política
ᵾ Cultural Institution	Kulturelle Institution	Institución Cultural	Institution culturelle	Institução cultural
⊥ Historical Site	Historische Stätte	Sitio Histórico	Site historique	Sitio histórico
♠ Recreational Site	Erholungs- und Ferienort	Sitio de Recreo	Centre de loisirs	Area de Lazer
⊠ Airport	Flughafen	Aeropuerto	Aéroport	Aeroporto
■ Military Installation	Militäranlage	Instalación Militar	Installation militaire	Instalação militar
➜ Miscellaneous	Verschiedenes	Misceláneo	Divers	Diversos

ENGLISH — Name | Page | Lat.°′ | Long.°′
DEUTSCH — Name | Seite | Breite°′ | Länge°′ E = Ost

Bozova, Tür. **130** 37.22 N 38.31 E
Bozova, Tür. **130** 37.13 N 30.18 E
Bozovici **38** 44.55 N 21.59 E
Bozšakol' **86** 51.50 N 74.20 E
Bozum **52** 53.05 N 5.42 E
Bozüyük **130** 39.54 N 30.03 E
Bozzolo **64** 45.06 N 10.29 E
Bra **62** 44.42 N 7.51 E
Braan ≃ **46** 56.33 N 3.35 W
Braås **26** 57.04 N 15.03 E
Brabant □[4] **56** 50.45 N 4.30 E
Brabante, Isla de → Brabant Island I **9** 64.15 S 62.20 W
Brabant Island I **9** 64.15 S 62.20 W
Brabant Lake ◎ **184** 56.00 N 103.43 W
Brabrand **41** 56.09 N 10.07 E
Brač, Otok I **36** 43.20 N 16.40 E
Bracadale, Loch c **46** 57.19 N 6.30 W
Bracciano **66** 42.06 N 12.10 E
Bracciano, Lago di ◎ **66** 42.07 N 12.14 E
Bracco, Passo del)(**62** 44.15 N 9.34 E
Bracebridge **212** 45.02 N 79.19 W
Bracebridge Heath **44** 53.13 N 0.33 W
Braceville, Il., U.S. **216** 41.14 N 88.16 W
Braceville, Oh., U.S. **214** 41.14 N 80.58 W
Brachfield **222** 32.03 N 94.39 W
Bracieux **50** 47.33 N 1.33 E
Bracigliano **68** 40.49 N 14.42 E
Bracigovo **38** 42.01 N 24.22 E
Bräcke **26** 62.43 N 15.27 E
Brackel ✦[8] **263** 51.32 N 7.33 E
Bracken □[6] **218** 38.40 N 84.06 W
Brackendale **182** 49.46 N 123.09 W
Brackenheim **56** 49.05 N 9.03 E
Brackenhurst **273d** 26.19 S 28.06 E
Bracken Lake ◎ **184** 53.37 N 99.50 W
Brackenridge **214** 40.36 N 79.44 W
Brackett Field ⊠ **280** 34.05 N 117.47 W
Brackettville **196** 29.18 N 100.25 W
Brački Kanal ʉ **36** 43.24 N 16.40 E
Brackley **42** 52.02 N 1.09 W
Bracknell **42** 51.26 N 0.45 W
Bracktown **218** 38.04 N 84.31 W
Brackwede **52** 51.59 N 8.31 E
Braclav **78** 48.50 N 28.55 E
Braco **46** 56.15 N 3.53 W
Braço do Norte **252** 28.17 S 49.11 W
Bracuí ≃ **256** 22.57 S 44.24 W
Brad **38** 46.08 N 22.47 E
Bradano ≃ **68** 40.23 N 16.51 E
Bradbury **280** 34.08 N 117.59 W
Bradbury Heights **284c** 38.52 N 76.56 W
Braddock, N.J., U.S. **285** 39.42 N 74.53 W
Braddock, Pa., U.S. **214** 40.24 N 79.52 W
Braddock Acres **284c** 38.49 N 77.10 W
Braddock Heights, Md., U.S. **208** 39.25 N 77.30 W
Braddock Heights, N.Y., U.S. **210** 43.19 N 77.42 W
Braddock Hills **279b** 40.25 N 79.51 W
Braddock Point > **210** 43.19 N 77.43 W
Braddocks Millpond ◎ **285** 39.49 N 74.51 W
Braden ≃ **220** 27.30 N 82.32 W
Bradenton **220** 27.29 N 82.34 W
Bradenton Beach **220** 27.28 N 82.42 W
Bradenville **214** 40.19 N 79.20 W
Braderup **41** 54.50 N 8.53 E
Bradford, On., Can. **212** 44.07 N 79.34 W
Bradford, Eng., U.K. **44** 53.48 N 1.45 W
Bradford, Ar., U.S. **194** 35.25 N 91.27 W
Bradford, Il., U.S. **190** 41.10 N 89.39 W
Bradford, N.Y., U.S. **210** 42.22 N 77.07 W
Bradford, Oh., U.S. **218** 40.08 N 84.26 W
Bradford, Pa., U.S. **214** 41.57 N 78.38 W
Bradford, R.I., U.S. **207** 41.23 N 71.44 W
Bradford, Tn., U.S. **194** 36.04 N 88.48 W
Bradford, Vt., U.S. **188** 43.59 N 72.09 W
Bradford □[6] **210** 41.56 N 78.40 W
Bradford □[8] **262** 53.47 N 1.52 W
Bradford Hills **285** 40.01 N 75.39 W
Bradford Mountain ∧ **207** 41.59 N 73.18 W
Bradford-on-Avon **42** 51.20 N 2.15 W
Bradford Regional Airport ⊠ **214** 41.48 N 78.38 W
Bradfordwoods **214** 40.38 N 80.05 W
Brading **42** 50.41 N 1.09 W
Bradley, Ar., U.S. **194** 33.05 N 93.39 W
Bradley, Ca., U.S. **226** 35.51 N 120.47 W
Bradley, Fl., U.S. **220** 27.48 N 81.59 W
Bradley, Il., U.S. **216** 41.08 N 87.51 W
Bradley, Mi., U.S. **216** 42.38 N 85.39 W
Bradley, S.D., U.S. **198** 45.05 N 97.38 W
Bradley Beach **208** 40.12 N 74.01 W
Bradley Farms **284c** 39.00 N 77.11 W
Bradley Gardens **276** 40.34 N 74.39 W
Bradley Institute **154** 17.02 S 31.27 E
Bradley International Airport ⊠ **207** 41.55 N 72.40 W
Bradley Reefs ✢[2] **175e** 6.52 S 160.48 E
Bradley Woods Reservation ♦ **279a** 41.25 N 81.58 W
Bradley W. Palmer State Park ♦ **283** 42.39 N 70.54 W
Bradner, B.C., Can. **224** 49.06 N 122.25 W
Bradner, Oh., U.S. **214** 41.19 N 83.26 W
Bradninch **42** 50.50 N 3.25 W
Bradore-Bay **186** 51.28 N 57.14 W
Bradshaw, Eng., U.K. **262** 53.36 N 2.24 W
Bradshaw, Md., U.S. **208** 39.25 N 76.22 W
Bradshaw, Ne., U.S. **198** 40.53 N 97.44 W
Bradshaw, W.V., U.S. **192** 37.21 N 81.47 W
Bradwell-on-Sea **42** 51.44 N 0.54 E
Bradworthy **42** 50.54 N 4.22 W
Brady, Mt., U.S. **202** 48.02 N 111.50 W
Brady, Ne., U.S. **198** 41.01 N 100.22 W
Brady, Tx., U.S. **196** 31.08 N 99.20 W
Brady Creek ≃ **196** 31.07 N 98.59 W
Brady Lake **214** 41.09 N 81.19 W
Brady Mountains ⋏[2] **196** 31.20 N 99.40 W
Brae **46a** 60.23 N 1.21 W
Brædstrup **41** 55.58 N 9.37 E
Braemar **46** 57.01 N 3.23 W
Braeside, Austl. **162** 21.12 S 121.01 E
Braeside, Austl. **274b** 37.59 S 145.07 E
Braeside, On., Can. **212** 45.28 N 76.24 W
Braga **34** 41.33 N 8.26 W
Bragado **252** 35.08 S 60.30 W
Bragança, Bra. **250** 1.03 S 46.46 W
Bragança, Bra. **256** 23.18 S 45.38 W
Bragança, Port. **34** 41.49 N 6.45 W
Bragança Paulista **256** 22.57 S 46.34 W
Bragar **46** 58.24 N 6.40 W
Bragin **78** 51.47 N 30.14 E
Braginka ≃ **78** 51.22 N 30.24 E
Braginovka **78** 48.29 N 36.21 E
Braham **190** 45.43 N 93.10 W
Brahetrolleborg ⊥ **41** 55.09 N 10.22 E
Brahma Island I **220** 27.52 N 81.15 W
Brāhmanbāria **120** 23.59 N 91.07 E
Brāhmani ≃, India **120** 20.39 N 86.46 E
Brāhmani ≃, India **126** 24.09 N 88.01 E
Brahmapur, India **122** 19.19 N 84.47 E
Brahmapur, India **272b** 22.28 N 88.22 E
Brahmaputra (Yarlung) ≃ **120** 24.02 N 90.59 E
Brāhmaur **123** 32.27 N 76.32 E
Braich y Pwll > **42** 52.48 N 4.36 W
Braidwood, Austl. **166** 35.27 S 149.48 E
Braidwood, Il., U.S. **216** 41.15 N 88.12 W
Braies (Prags) **64** 46.42 N 12.08 E
Brăila **38** 45.16 N 27.58 E
Brăila □[6] **38** 45.00 N 27.40 E
Brailov **78** 49.06 N 28.09 E
Brain ≃ **42** 51.48 N 0.39 E
Brainard, Ne., U.S. **198** 41.11 N 97.00 W
Brainard, N.Y., U.S. **210** 42.30 N 73.31 W
Braine **50** 49.20 N 3.32 E
Braine-l'Alleud **50** 50.41 N 4.22 E
Braine-le-Château **50** 50.41 N 4.16 E
Braine-le-Comte **50** 50.36 N 4.08 E
Brainerd **190** 46.21 N 94.12 W
Braint ≃ **44** 53.08 N 4.19 W
Braintree, Eng., U.K. **42** 51.53 N 0.32 E
Braintree, Ma., U.S. **207** 42.13 N 71.00 W
Braintree □[8] **260** 51.47 N 0.36 E
Brak ≃, S. Afr. **158** 29.35 S 22.55 E
Brak ≃, S. Afr. **158** 31.32 S 21.33 E
Brake, Dtsch. **52** 53.19 N 8.28 E
Brake, Dtsch. **52** 52.01 N 8.55 E
Brake, Dtsch. **52** 52.04 N 8.35 E
Brakel, Bel. **50** 50.48 N 3.46 E
Brakel, Dtsch. **52** 51.43 N 9.10 E
Brakna □[4] **150** 17.30 N 13.30 W
Brakpan **158** 26.14 S 28.22 E
Brakpan □[5] **273d** 26.16 S 28.21 E
Brakpoort **158** 31.20 S 23.22 E
Brakputs **158** 29.29 S 18.24 E
Brakwater **156** 22.24 S 17.06 E
Brålanda **26** 58.34 N 12.22 E
Bralorne **182** 50.47 N 122.49 W
Bramalea **212** 43.44 N 79.43 W
Bramall Hall ⊥ **262** 53.23 N 2.09 W
Braman **196** 36.55 N 97.20 W
Brambauer **263** 51.35 N 7.27 E
Bramberg am Wildkogel **64** 47.16 N 12.21 E
Bramble Bay c **171a** 27.17 S 153.05 E
Bramble Cay I **164** 9.08 S 143.52 E
Bramdrupdam **41** 55.31 N 9.28 E
Bramey-Lenningsen **263** 51.34 N 7.46 E
Bramfeld ✦[8] **52** 53.37 N 10.04 E
Bramford **42** 52.04 N 1.06 E
Bramhall **262** 53.22 N 2.10 W
Bramhope **44** 53.53 N 1.37 W
Bramley **260** 51.12 N 0.34 W
Bramley ✦[8] **273d** 26.08 S 28.05 E
Bramley Mountain ∧ **210** 42.18 N 74.49 W
Bramming **41** 55.28 N 8.42 E
Brampton, On., Can. **212** 43.41 N 79.46 W
Brampton, Eng., U.K. **42** 52.19 N 0.14 W
Brampton, Eng., U.K. **44** 54.57 N 2.43 W
Brampton Airfield ⊠ **275b** 43.40 N 79.47 W
Bramsche **52** 52.24 N 7.58 E
Bramsöfjärden ◎ **40** 60.20 N 17.10 E
Bramstedt **52** 53.22 N 8.41 E
Brancaleone Marina **68** 37.58 N 16.06 E
Brancaster **42** 52.58 N 0.39 E
Brancaster Roads ⩦[3] **42** 53.00 N 0.41 E
Branch **186** 46.53 N 53.57 W
Branch □[6] **216** 41.55 N 85.03 W
Branch Brook Park ♦ **276** 40.46 N 74.10 W
Branch Dale **208** 40.41 N 76.20 W
Branchport **210** 42.36 N 77.09 W
Branchville, Ct., U.S. **207** 41.16 N 73.26 W
Branchville, N.J., U.S. **210** 41.08 N 74.45 W
Branchville, S.C., U.S. **192** 33.15 N 80.48 W
Branchville, Va., U.S. **208** 36.34 N 77.14 W
Branco **152** 12.30 S 20.32 E
Branco ≃, Bra. **246** 1.24 S 61.51 W
Branco ≃, Bra. **248** 10.03 S 67.51 W
Branco ≃, Bra. **248** 21.00 S 57.48 W
Branco ≃, Bra. **248** 7.44 S 61.46 W
Branco ≃, Bra. **248** 9.12 S 64.22 W
Branco ≃, Bra. **248** 9.37 S 60.33 W
Branco ≃, Bra. **250** 7.01 S 51.42 W
Branco ≃, Bra. **250** 12.00 S 44.56 W
Branco, Ilhéu I **150a** 16.39 N 24.41 W
Brand, Dtsch. **56** 50.43 N 6.09 E
Brand, Öst. **58** 47.06 N 9.44 E
Brandamore **208** 40.03 N 75.50 W
Brandaris ∧[2] **241s** 12.17 N 68.24 W
Brandberg ∧ **156** 21.10 S 14.33 E
Brandbu **26** 60.28 N 10.30 E
Brande **41** 55.57 N 9.07 E
Brandebourg → Brandenburg **54** 52.24 N 12.32 E
Brandeis University ʊ[2] **283** 42.22 N 71.16 W
Brandenberg **64** 47.29 N 11.53 E
Brandenberg ∧[2] **263** 51.20 N 7.37 E
Brandenburg, Dtsch. **54** 52.24 N 12.32 E
Brandenburg, Ky., U.S. **194** 38.00 N 86.10 W
Brandenburg □[3] **30** 52.30 N 13.30 E
Brandenburger Tor ⊥ **264a** 52.31 N 13.23 E
Brand-Erbisdorf **54** 50.52 N 13.19 E
Brandfort **158** 28.47 S 26.30 E
Br'andino **80** 54.23 N 49.23 E
Brandis, Dtsch. **54** 51.48 N 13.10 E
Brandis, Dtsch. **54** 51.20 N 12.36 E
Brandizzo **62** 45.11 N 7.51 E
Brandkop **158** 31.13 S 19.13 E
Brandon, Mb., Can. **184** 49.50 N 99.57 W
Brandon, Eng., U.K. **42** 52.27 N 0.37 E
Brandon, Eng., U.K. **44** 54.46 N 1.39 W
Brandon, Fl., U.S. **220** 27.56 N 82.17 W
Brandon, Ms., U.S. **194** 32.16 N 89.59 W
Brandon, S.D., U.S. **198** 43.35 N 96.34 W
Brandon, Tx., U.S. **222** 32.03 N 96.58 W
Brandon, Vt., U.S. **188** 43.47 N 73.05 W
Brandon, Wi., U.S. **190** 43.44 N 88.46 W
Brandon Bay c **48** 52.15 N 10.05 W
Brandon Head > **48** 52.16 N 10.14 W
Brandon Mountain ∧ **48** 52.14 N 10.15 W
Brandon Road Lock and Dam ✦[5] **278** 41.30 N 88.06 W
Brandonville **210** 40.52 N 76.10 W
Brand Park ♦ **280** 34.11 N 118.16 W
Brandsen **258** 35.10 S 58.14 W
Brands Hatch Motor Race Circuit ♦ **260** 51.22 N 0.16 E
Brandsø I **41** 55.21 N 9.43 E
Brandt **218** 39.54 N 84.05 W
Brandvlei **158** 30.25 S 20.30 E
Brandy Camp **214** 41.19 N 78.41 W
Brandy Peak ∧ **202** 42.36 N 123.53 W
Brandýsek **54** 50.10 N 14.10 E
Brandýs nad Labem **54** 50.10 N 14.41 E
Brandywine Battlefield ⊥ **208** 39.53 N 75.35 W
Brandywine Creek ≃, U.S. **285** 39.44 N 75.32 W
Brandywine Creek ≃, In., U.S. **218** 39.31 N 85.52 W
Brandywine Creek ≃, Oh., U.S. **279a** 41.17 N 81.34 W
Brandywine Creek, East Branch ≃ **208** 39.55 N 75.39 W
Brandywine Creek, West Branch ≃ **208** 39.55 N 75.39 W
Brandywine Creek State Park ♦ **285** 39.48 N 75.35 W
Brandywine Park ♦ **285** 39.45 N 75.33 W
Brandywine Raceway ♦ **285** 39.50 N 75.32 W
Brandywine Springs Park ♦ **285** 39.45 N 75.38 W
Branford, Ct., U.S. **207** 41.16 N 72.48 W
Branford, Fl., U.S. **192** 29.57 N 82.55 W
Brani, Pulau I **271c** 1.15 N 103.50 E
Braniewo **30** 54.24 N 19.50 E
Branka, Česko. **60** 49.50 N 12.33 E
Br'anka, Ross. **86** 59.08 N 93.27 E
Br'anka, Ukr. **83** 48.29 N 38.39 E
Branlin ≃ **50** 47.51 N 3.06 E
Brannenburg **64** 47.44 N 12.05 E
Branquinho ≃ **248** 5.45 S 71.27 W
Bransby **166** 28.14 S 142.04 E
Bransfield Strait ʉ **9** 63.00 S 59.00 W
Bransgore **42** 50.47 N 1.44 W
Brańsk, Pol. **30** 52.45 N 22.51 E
Br'ansk, Ross. **76** 53.15 N 34.22 E
Br'ansk, □[4] **76** 53.00 N 34.00 E
Br'anskaja Kosa, mys > **84** 44.22 N 47.00 E
Branson **194** 36.38 N 93.13 W
Brant **210** 42.35 N 79.01 W
Brant □[6] **212** 43.10 N 80.20 W
Brant ≃ **44** 53.09 N 0.35 W
Br'anta ≃ **89** 54.27 N 127.42 E
Brantas ≃ **115a** 7.28 S 112.25 E
Brantford **212** 43.08 N 80.16 W
Brantingham Lake ◎ **212** 43.42 N 75.17 W
Brant Lake **188** 43.40 N 73.45 W
Brantley **194** 31.34 N 86.15 W
Brantôme **32** 45.22 N 0.39 E
Brant Rock **283** 42.05 N 70.38 W
Brantville **186** 47.22 N 64.58 W
Branxholme **166** 37.51 S 141.47 E
Branxton **170** 32.39 S 151.22 E
Branzi **64** 46.00 N 9.46 E
Brás ✦[8] **287b** 23.32 S 46.36 W
Brás Cubas **256** 23.32 S 46.13 W
Bras d'Or Lake ◎ **186** 45.52 N 60.50 W
Brashear **222** 33.07 N 95.44 W
Brasilândia ✦[8] **287b** 23.28 S 46.41 W
Brasil → Brazil □[1] **242** 10.00 S 55.00 W
Brasiléia **248** 11.00 S 68.44 W
Brasília **255** 15.47 S 47.55 W
Brasília, Parque Nacional de ♦ **255** 15.36 S 48.08 W
Brasília de Minas **255** 16.12 S 44.26 W
Brasília Legal **250** 3.49 S 55.36 W
Brasilien → Brazil □[1] **242** 10.00 S 55.00 W
Braslav **76** 55.38 N 27.02 E
Brasopolis **256** 22.28 S 45.37 W
Brașov **38** 45.39 N 25.37 E
Brașov □[6] **38** 45.45 N 25.15 E
Brass **150** 4.19 N 6.14 E
Brass Castle **210** 40.47 N 74.58 W
Brasschaat **50** 51.17 N 4.27 E
Brassert **263** 51.40 N 7.05 E
Brassey, Banjaran ⋏ **112** 4.54 N 117.30 E
Brassey, Mount ∧ **162** 23.05 S 134.38 E
Brass Islands II **240m** 18.24 N 64.58 W
Brassó → Brașov **38** 45.39 N 25.37 E
Brasstown Bald ∧ **192** 34.52 N 83.48 W
Brastad **26** 58.23 N 11.29 E
Brasted **260** 51.16 N 0.17 E
Brasted Chart **260** 51.16 N 0.06 E
Břasy **60** 49.50 N 13.35 E
Bratca **38** 46.56 N 22.37 E
Bratcevo ✦[8] **265b** 55.51 N 37.24 E
Bratejevo ✦[8] **265b** 55.38 N 37.45 E
Bratenahl **279a** 41.32 N 81.37 W
Brateș, Lacul ◎ **38** 45.30 N 28.05 E
Bratislava **30** 48.09 N 17.07 E
Bratol'ubovka **86** 51.13 N 66.46 E
Bratsk **88** 56.05 N 101.48 E
Bratskaja Kada **88** 55.02 N 102.06 E
Bratskoje **78** 47.52 N 31.34 E
Bratskoje vodochranilišče ◎[1] **88** 56.10 N 102.10 E
Brattfors **40** 59.40 N 14.01 E
Brattleboro **207** 42.51 N 72.33 W
Bratto **64** 45.55 N 10.04 E
Brattvåg **26** 62.36 N 6.27 E
Braubach **56** 50.16 N 7.40 E
Braulio Carrillo, Parque Nacional ♦ **236** 10.10 N 84.00 W
Braúnas **255** 19.04 S 42.43 W
Braunau am Inn **60** 48.15 N 13.02 E
Braunfels **56** 50.31 N 8.23 E
Braunlage **54** 51.44 N 10.37 E
Bräunlingen **58** 47.55 N 8.26 E
Braunsbedra **54** 51.15 N 11.49 E
Braunschweig, Dtsch. **52** 52.16 N 10.31 E
Braunschweig, S. Afr. **158** 32.48 S 27.22 E
Braunschweig □[6] **54** 52.10 N 10.30 E
Braunston **42** 52.17 N 1.12 W
Braunton **42** 51.07 N 4.10 W
Braunwald **58** 46.56 N 9.00 E
Brava I **150a** 14.52 N 24.43 W
Brava, Costa ⊥[2] **34** 41.45 N 3.04 E
Brava, Laguna ◎ **252** 28.22 S 68.50 W
Brava, Punta > **258** 34.56 S 56.10 W
Brave **188** 39.44 N 80.16 W
Bravičа **78** 47.22 N 28.26 E
Bråviken c **40** 58.38 N 16.32 E
Bravo, Cerro ∧, Bol. **248** 17.40 S 64.35 W
Bravo, Cerro ∧, Perú **248** 5.32 S 79.15 W
Bravo del Norte (Rio Grande) ≃ **178** 25.55 N 97.09 W
Brawley **204** 32.58 N 115.31 W
Brawley Peaks ⋏ **204** 38.15 N 118.55 W
Brawley Wash V **200** 32.34 N 111.26 W
Bray, Bel. **50** 50.26 N 4.06 E
Bray, Ire. **48** 53.12 N 6.06 W
Bray ≃ **42** 50.59 N 3.53 W
Bray, Pays de ✦[1] **50** 49.46 N 1.26 E
Braybrook **274b** 37.47 S 144.51 E
Bray-Dunes **50** 51.05 N 2.31 E
Braye ≃ **50** 47.45 N 0.42 E
Bray Head > **48** 51.53 N 10.26 W
Bray Island I **176** 69.20 N 76.45 W
Braymer **194** 39.35 N 93.47 W
Braysur-Seine **50** 48.25 N 3.14 E
Bray-sur-Somme **50** 49.56 N 2.43 E
Brayton **44** 53.46 N 1.05 W
Brazeau ≃ **182** 52.55 N 115.15 W
Brazeau, Mount ∧ **182** 52.33 N 117.21 W
Brazeau Dam ✦[6] **182** 52.45 N 115.30 W
Brazen Head > **158** 31.43 S 29.25 E
Brazey-en-Plaine **58** 47.08 N 5.13 E
Brazil **194** 39.31 N 87.07 W
Brazil (Brasil) □[1] **242** 10.00 S 55.00 W
Brazil Basin ✢[1] **8** 15.00 S 25.00 W
Brazo Chico, Arroyo ≃ **258** 33.45 S 58.32 W
Brazo Largo, Arroyo ≃ **258** 33.47 S 58.36 W
Brazoria **222** 29.02 N 95.34 W
Brazoria □[6] **222** 29.12 N 95.25 W
Brazoria Reservoir ◎[1] **222** 29.05 N 95.01 W
Brazos □[6] **222** 30.40 N 96.18 W
Brazos ≃ **196** 28.53 N 95.23 W
Brazos, Clear Fork ≃ **196** 33.01 N 98.40 W
Brazos, Double Mountain Fork ≃ **196** 33.15 N 100.00 W
Brazos, Salt Fork ≃ **196** 33.15 N 100.00 W
Brazo Sur [del Rio Coig] ≃ **254** 51.32 S 70.04 W
Brazzaville, Congo **152** 4.16 S 15.17 E
Brazzaville, Congo **273b** 4.16 S 15.17 E
Brazzaville (Maya Maya) Airport ⊠ **273b** 4.15 S 15.15 E
Brčko **38** 44.53 N 18.48 E
Brda ≃ **30** 53.07 N 18.08 E
Brdy ⋏ **60** 49.40 N 13.50 E
Brea **228** 33.55 N 117.53 W
Brea, Punta > **240m** 17.56 N 66.55 W
Brea Canyon V **280** 33.55 N 117.55 W
Brea Creek ≃ **280** 33.53 N 117.59 W
Breadalbane **166** 23.49 S 139.35 E
Brea Dam ✦[6] **280** 33.54 N 117.56 W
Breaden Bluff ∧[2] **162** 26.56 S 124.32 E
Breadysville **285** 40.13 N 75.04 W
Breakenridge, Mount ∧ **182** 49.43 N 121.56 W
Breakheart Reservation ♦ **283** 42.29 N 71.02 W
Breaksea Sound ʉ **172** 45.35 S 166.40 E
Breaks Interstate Park ♦ **192** 37.17 N 82.18 W
Bream **42** 51.45 N 2.34 W
Bream Bay c **172** 35.55 S 174.30 E
Bream Head > **172** 35.51 S 174.35 E
Breamish ≃ **44** 55.31 N 1.56 W
Bream Tail > **172** 36.03 S 174.35 E
Brea Pozo **252** 28.15 S 63.57 W
Breaston **44** 52.54 N 1.19 W
Bréau **261** 48.34 N 2.53 E
Breaux Bridge **194** 30.16 N 91.53 W
Breaza **38** 45.11 N 25.40 E
Brebes **115a** 6.53 S 109.03 E
Bré → Bray **48** 53.12 N 6.06 W
Brécey **32** 48.44 N 1.10 W
Brechen **56** 50.20 N 8.14 E
Brechfa **42** 51.54 N 4.36 W
Brechin **46** 56.44 N 2.40 W
Brecht **56** 51.21 N 4.38 E
Brechten ✦[8] **263** 51.35 N 7.28 E
Breckenridge, Co., U.S. **200** 39.28 N 106.02 W
Breckenridge, Mi., U.S. **190** 43.24 N 84.28 W
Breckenridge, Mn., U.S. **198** 46.15 N 96.35 W
Breckenridge, Mo., U.S. **194** 39.45 N 93.48 W
Breckenridge, Tx., U.S. **196** 32.45 N 98.54 W
Breckerfeld **56** 51.16 N 7.28 E
Breckland ✦[1] **42** 52.28 N 0.37 E
Brecknock, Península >[1] **254** 54.35 S 71.50 W
Brecknock → Brecon **42** 51.57 N 3.24 W
Brecksville **214** 41.19 N 81.37 W
Břeclav **30** 48.46 N 16.53 E
Brecon **42** 51.57 N 3.24 W
Brecon Beacons ∧ **42** 51.53 N 3.31 W
Brecon Beacons National Park ♦ **42** 51.52 N 3.25 W
Bred **41** 55.22 N 10.07 E
Breda, Ned. **52** 51.35 N 4.46 E
Breda, Ia., U.S. **198** 42.10 N 94.58 W
Bredaryd **26** 57.10 N 13.44 E
Bredasdorp **158** 34.32 S 20.02 E
Bredbo **171b** 35.57 S 149.10 E
Bredbo ≃ **171b** 35.58 S 149.08 E
Bredbury **262** 53.25 N 2.06 W
Bredbyn **26** 63.27 N 18.06 E
Breddin **54** 52.52 N 12.13 E
Brede Å ≃ **41** 55.09 N 8.42 E
Bredebro **41** 55.03 N 8.49 E
Bredell **273d** 26.05 S 28.17 E
Bredenbeck **52** 52.15 N 9.37 E
Bredenbruch **263** 51.21 N 7.45 E
Bredenbury **184** 50.57 N 102.03 W
Bredene **50** 51.14 N 2.58 E
Bredeney ✦[8] **263** 51.24 N 6.59 E
Bredenscheid-Stüter **263** 51.22 N 7.11 E
Bredereiche **54** 53.08 N 13.14 E
Bredgar **260** 51.18 N 0.42 E
Bredhurst **260** 51.20 N 0.35 E
Bredon Hill ∧[2] **42** 52.06 N 2.03 W
Bredsjö **40** 59.50 N 14.44 E
Bredsjön ◎ **40** 60.13 N 13.55 E
Bredstedt **41** 54.37 N 8.59 E
Bredsten **41** 55.42 N 9.24 E
Bredy **86** 52.26 N 60.21 E
Bree **56** 51.08 N 5.36 E
Breë ≃ **158** 34.24 S 20.50 E
Breeches, Lac ◎ **206** 45.54 N 71.28 W
Breedoge ≃ **48** 53.55 N 8.27 W
Breeds Pond ◎ **283** 42.28 N 70.59 W
Breedsville **216** 42.21 N 86.08 W
Breese **219** 38.36 N 89.31 W
Breesport **210** 42.10 N 76.44 W
Breeza Plains **164** 14.50 S 144.07 E
Breezewood **279b** 40.34 N 80.03 W
Breg ≃ **58** 47.57 N 8.31 E
Bregalnica ≃ **38** 41.43 N 22.09 E
Breganze **64** 45.42 N 11.34 E
Bregenz **58** 47.30 N 9.46 E
Bregenzer Wald ⋏ **58** 47.20 N 10.00 E
Bregninge, Dan. **41** 55.41 N 11.19 E
Bregninge, Dan. **41** 55.01 N 10.37 E
Bregovo **38** 44.09 N 22.39 E
Breguzzo **64** 46.00 N 10.42 E
Brégy **261** 49.05 N 2.52 E
Bréhal **32** 48.54 N 1.31 W
Brehna **54** 51.33 N 12.12 E
Breiðafjörður c **24a** 65.15 N 23.15 W
Breidbach **158** 32.54 S 27.27 E
Breid Bay c **9** 70.15 S 24.15 E
Breidenbach **56** 49.08 N 7.25 E
Breidenstein **56** 50.55 N 8.28 E
Breil-sur-Roya **62** 43.56 N 7.30 E
Breinizer **214** 40.24 N 79.16 W
Breisach **58** 48.01 N 7.40 E
Breisgau □[9] **58** 47.45 N 7.45 E
Breitenbrunn **54** 50.29 N 12.46 E
Breitenfelde **52** 53.36 N 10.38 E
Breitenfurt bei Wien **61** 48.08 N 16.08 E
Breitengüssbach **56** 49.58 N 10.53 E
Breitenlee ✦[8] **264b** 48.15 N 16.30 E
Breitenstein **54** 51.37 N 10.56 E
Breitenworbis **54** 51.24 N 10.25 E
Breithorn ∧ **58** 45.56 N 7.45 E
Breitlingsee ◎ **54** 52.23 N 12.28 E
Breitscheid, Dtsch. **56** 50.41 N 8.11 E
Breitscheid, Dtsch. **56** 51.22 N 6.52 E
Breitsetten **61** 48.12 N 16.42 E
Breitungen **54** 50.45 N 10.20 E
Brejinho de Nazaré **250** 11.01 S 48.34 W
Brejo **250** 3.41 S 42.47 W
Brejões **255** 13.06 S 39.48 W
Brejo Grande **250** 10.26 S 36.28 W
Brejo Santo **250** 7.29 S 39.00 W
Brejtovo **76** 58.18 N 37.52 E
Brekken **26** 62.39 N 11.53 E
Brekstad **26** 63.41 N 9.41 E
Breloh **52** 53.01 N 10.04 E
Bremangerlandet I **26** 61.51 N 5.02 E
Brembio **62** 45.13 N 9.34 E
Brembo ≃ **62** 45.35 N 9.32 E
Brême → Bremen **52** 53.04 N 8.49 E
Bremelau **58** 48.20 N 9.32 E
Bremen, Dtsch. **52** 53.04 N 8.49 E
Bremen, Ga., U.S. **192** 33.43 N 85.08 W
Bremen, In., U.S. **216** 41.26 N 86.08 W
Bremen, Oh., U.S. **188** 39.42 N 82.25 W
Bremen □[3] **52** 53.05 N 8.50 E
Bremen, Flughafen ⊠ **52** 53.03 N 8.46 E
Bremer ≃, Austl. **168b** 35.23 S 139.02 E
Bremer ≃, Austl. **171a** 27.39 S 152.45 E
Bremer Bay **162** 34.24 S 119.22 E
Bremer Bay c **162** 34.23 S 119.25 E
Bremerhaven **52** 53.33 N 8.34 E
Bremerton **224** 47.34 N 122.37 W
Bremerton East **224** 47.35 N 122.38 W
Bremervörde **52** 53.29 N 9.08 E
Bremgarten **58** 47.21 N 8.21 E
Bremke, Dtsch. **52** 52.07 N 9.06 E
Bremke, Dtsch. **56** 51.15 N 8.12 E
Bremke, Dtsch. **263** 51.23 N 7.41 E
Bremner ≃ **190** 48.41 N 85.31 W
Bremond **222** 31.09 N 96.40 W
Brem River **182** 50.26 N 124.39 W
Breña **286d** 12.04 S 77.04 W
Brendel Lake ◎ **281** 42.38 N 83.30 W
Brenderup **41** 55.29 N 9.59 E
Brendlorenzen **56** 50.20 N 10.13 E
Brendon Hills ⋏[2] **42** 51.07 N 3.25 W
Brenham **222** 30.10 N 96.23 W
Brenig, Llyn ◎[1] **44** 53.05 N 3.32 W
Brenish **46** 58.08 N 7.08 W
Brenish, Aird > **46** 58.08 N 7.08 W
Bren Mar Park **284c** 38.48 N 77.09 W
Brenne ≃ **50** 47.38 N 4.16 E
Brennero (Brenner) **64** 47.00 N 11.30 E
Brennero, Passo del → Brenner Pass)(**64** 47.00 N 11.30 E
Brenner Pass)(**64** 47.00 N 11.30 E
Breno, It. **64** 45.57 N 10.18 E
Breno, Schw. **58** 46.02 N 8.53 E
Brénod **58** 46.04 N 5.36 E
Brent, Al., U.S. **194** 32.56 N 87.09 W
Brent, Fl., U.S. **194** 30.28 N 87.14 W
Brent ✦[8] **260** 51.34 N 0.17 W
Brent ≃ **260** 51.28 N 0.18 W
Brenta ≃ **64** 45.11 N 12.18 E
Brenta, Gruppo di ⋏ **64** 46.11 N 10.54 E
Brentford ✦[8] **260** 51.29 N 0.18 W
Brenthurst **273d** 26.16 S 28.23 E
Brentino **64** 45.40 N 10.55 E
Brentonico **64** 45.49 N 10.57 E
Brent Reservoir ◎[1] **260** 51.35 N 0.15 W
Brentwood, Eng., U.K. **260** 51.38 N 0.18 E
Brentwood, Ca., U.S. **226** 37.55 N 121.41 W
Brentwood, Md., U.S. **208** 38.56 N 76.57 W
Brentwood, N.Y., U.S. **210** 40.46 N 73.14 W
Brentwood, Oh., U.S. **218** 39.13 N 84.31 W
Brentwood, Pa., U.S. **214** 40.22 N 79.58 W
Brentwood, Tn., U.S. **194** 36.01 N 86.46 W
Brentwood □[8] **260** 51.37 N 0.20 E
Brentwood Bay **224** 48.35 N 123.28 W
Brentwood Estates **214** 40.25 N 80.45 W
Brentwood Heights ✦[8] **280** 34.04 N 118.30 W
Brentwood Lake **214** 41.19 N 82.05 W
Brentwood Park **273d** 26.08 S 28.18 E
Brenz ≃ **56** 48.34 N 10.24 E
Breo **62** 44.23 N 7.49 E
Bréon, Ruisseu du ≃ **261** 48.40 N 2.49 E
Brera, Palazzo di ʊ **266b** 45.28 N 9.11 E
Brereton Park **158** 26.55 S 30.30 E
Brescello **64** 44.54 N 10.31 E
Brescia **64** 45.33 N 13.15 E
Brescia □[4] **64** 45.38 N 10.18 E
Bresewitz **54** 54.24 N 12.40 E
Brésil → Brazil □[1] **242** 10.00 S 55.00 W
Breskens **52** 51.24 N 3.34 E
Breslau, On., Can. **212** 43.28 N 80.25 W
Breslau, Tx., U.S. **222** 29.31 N 97.00 W
Breslau → Wrocław **30** 51.06 N 17.00 E
Bresle ≃ **50** 50.04 N 1.22 E
Bresles **50** 49.25 N 2.15 E
Bresnahan, Mount ∧ **162** 23.50 S 117.55 E
Bressanone (Brixen) **64** 46.43 N 11.39 E
Bressay I **46a** 60.08 N 1.05 W
Bressay Sound ʉ **46a** 60.07 N 1.09 W
Bresse ✦[1] **58** 46.30 N 5.15 E
Bresso **266b** 45.32 N 9.11 E
Bressuire **32** 46.51 N 0.30 W
Brest, Blg. **38** 43.38 N 24.35 E
Brest, Bela. **76** 52.06 N 23.42 E
Brest, Fr. **32** 48.24 N 4.29 W
Brest □[8] **78** 52.00 N 26.00 E
Brestanica **36** 45.59 N 15.29 E
Bretagne (Brittany) □[9] **32** 48.00 N 3.00 W
Bretenoux **32** 44.55 N 1.50 E
Breteuil **50** 49.38 N 2.18 E
Breteuil-sur-Iton **50** 48.50 N 0.55 E
Bréthencourt **261** 48.30 N 1.55 E
Bretherton **262** 53.41 N 2.48 W
Brétigny ■ **261** 48.35 N 2.20 E
Brétigny-sur-Orge **50** 48.37 N 2.19 E
Bretnig **54** 51.08 N 14.04 E
Breton **182** 53.07 N 114.28 W
Bretón, Canal de ʉ **240p** 21.10 N 79.30 W
Breton, Pertuis ʉ **32** 46.25 N 1.20 W
Breton Bay c **208** 38.16 N 76.39 W
Breton Islands II **194** 29.28 N 89.11 W
Breton Sound ʉ **194** 29.30 N 89.30 W
Breton Woods **208** 40.02 N 74.06 W
Brett ≃ **42** 51.58 N 0.58 E
Brett, Cape > **172** 35.10 S 174.20 E
Bretten **56** 49.02 N 8.42 E
Breu, Rio do ≃ **246** 3.29 S 66.20 W
Breueh, Pulau I **110** 5.41 N 95.05 E
Breuil-Bois-Robert **261** 48.57 N 1.43 E
Breuil-Cervinia **58** 45.56 N 7.38 E
Breuillet **261** 48.34 N 2.10 E
Breuilpont **50** 48.58 N 1.26 E
Breukelen **52** 52.10 N 5.00 E
Breux **261** 48.34 N 2.11 E
Brevard **192** 35.14 N 82.44 W
Brevard □[6] **220** 28.18 N 80.42 W
Brévenne ≃ **62** 45.51 N 4.40 E
Brevens bruk **40** 59.01 N 15.35 E
Breves **250** 1.40 S 50.29 W
Brevig Mission **180** 65.20 N 166.29 W
Brevik, Nor. **26** 59.04 N 9.42 E
Brevik, Sve. **40** 59.21 N 18.12 E
Brevoort Island I **176** 63.30 N 64.20 W
Brewarrina **166** 29.57 S 146.52 E
Brewer **188** 44.47 N 68.45 W
Brewer Island I **282** 37.33 N 122.16 W
Brewersville **218** 39.05 N 85.37 W
Brewerton **210** 43.14 N 76.08 W
Brewerville **150** 6.26 N 10.47 W
Brewongle **170** 33.29 S 149.43 E
Brewood **42** 52.41 N 2.10 W
Brewster, Ks., U.S. **198** 39.22 N 101.22 W
Brewster, Ma., U.S. **207** 41.45 N 70.05 W
Brewster, Mn., U.S. **198** 43.41 N 95.28 W
Brewster, Ne., U.S. **198** 41.56 N 99.51 W
Brewster, N.Y., U.S. **210** 41.23 N 73.37 W
Brewster, Oh., U.S. **214** 40.42 N 81.35 W
Brewster, Wa., U.S. **202** 48.05 N 119.46 W
Brewster, Kap > **16** 70.19 N 22.05 W
Brewster, Lake ◎ **166** 33.28 S 146.00 E
Brewster, Mount ∧ **172** 44.04 S 169.27 E
Brewton **194** 31.06 N 87.04 W
Breyten **158** 26.16 S 30.00 E
Březany **61** 48.52 N 16.20 E
Brežice **36** 45.54 N 15.36 E
Brézina **148** 33.04 N 1.14 E
Brézins **62** 45.21 N 5.19 E
Březnice **60** 49.33 N 13.57 E
Breznik **38** 42.44 N 22.54 E
Brezno, Česko. **30** 48.50 N 19.39 E
Březno, Česko. **54** 50.24 N 13.26 E
Brézolles **50** 48.41 N 1.04 E
Březová **54** 50.06 N 12.39 E
Březové Hory **60** 49.41 N 13.58 E
Bria **152** 6.32 N 21.59 E
Brian Boru Peak ∧ **182** 55.05 N 127.35 W
Briançon **62** 44.54 N 6.39 E
Brian Head ∧ **200** 37.41 N 112.50 W
Brianza □[9] **62** 45.40 N 9.10 E
Briar **222** 33.00 N 97.34 W
Briarcliff Manor **210** 41.08 N 73.49 W
Briar Creek **210** 40.10 N 76.46 W
Briar Creek ≃ **222** 32.06 N 96.22 W
Briare **50** 47.38 N 2.44 E
Briare, Canal de ≍ **50** 48.02 N 2.43 E
Briarres-sur-Essonne **50** 48.14 N 2.25 E
Briarwood Beach **214** 41.06 N 81.54 W
Briarwood Center ✦[9] **281** 42.14 N 83.45 W
Briatico **68** 38.43 N 16.02 E
Bribano **64** 46.06 N 12.05 E
Bribie Island I **171a** 27.00 S 153.07 E
Bričany **78** 48.22 N 27.04 E
Bricelyn **190** 43.33 N 93.48 W
Brice Run ≃ **284b** 39.19 N 76.50 W
Brices Cross Roads National Battlefield Site ⊥ **194** 34.31 N 88.41 W
Briceville **192** 36.10 N 84.11 W
Bricherasio **62** 44.49 N 7.18 E
Bricht **263** 51.41 N 6.51 E
Brickebacken **40** 59.15 N 15.15 E
Brick Lake ◎ **220** 28.10 N 81.12 W
Brick Township **208** 40.04 N 74.08 W
Briçonnet, Lac ◎ **186** 51.27 N 60.11 W
Bricquebec **32** 49.28 N 1.38 W
Bridal Veil **224** 45.33 N 122.10 W
Bridalveil Fall L **226** 37.43 N 119.39 W
Bride **44** 54.22 N 4.22 W
Bride ≃ **48** 52.04 N 7.52 W
Bridesburg ✦[8] **285** 40.00 N 75.04 W
Bridge **42** 51.14 N 1.07 E
Bridge ≃ **182** 50.45 N 121.55 W
Bridge City **194** 30.01 N 93.50 W
Bridge Creek ≃ **224** 48.26 N 120.52 W
Bridgehampton **207** 40.56 N 72.18 W
Bridge Lake **182** 51.29 N 120.43 W
Bridgend, Scot., U.K. **46** 56.48 N 2.45 W
Bridgend, Scot., U.K. **46** 55.48 N 6.16 W
Bridgend, Wales, U.K. **42** 51.31 N 3.35 W
Bridgenorth **212** 44.23 N 78.23 W
Bridge of Allan **46** 56.09 N 3.57 W
Bridge of Gaur **46** 56.41 N 4.27 W
Bridge of Orchy **46** 56.30 N 4.46 W
Bridge of Weir **46** 55.52 N 4.35 W
Bridgeport, On., Can. **212** 43.29 N 80.29 W
Bridgeport, Al., U.S. **194** 34.56 N 85.42 W
Bridgeport, Ca., U.S. **226** 38.10 N 119.13 W
Bridgeport, Ct., U.S. **207** 41.10 N 73.12 W
Bridgeport, Il., U.S. **194** 38.42 N 87.45 W
Bridgeport, Mi., U.S. **190** 43.21 N 83.52 W
Bridgeport, Ne., U.S. **198** 41.39 N 103.05 W
Bridgeport, N.J., U.S. **285** 39.48 N 75.20 W
Bridgeport, N.Y., U.S. **210** 43.09 N 75.58 W
Bridgeport, Oh., U.S. **214** 40.04 N 80.44 W
Bridgeport, Pa., U.S. **285** 40.06 N 75.21 W
Bridgeport, Tx., U.S. **222** 33.12 N 97.45 W
Bridgeport, Wa., U.S. **202** 48.00 N 119.40 W
Bridgeport, W.V., U.S. **188** 39.17 N 80.15 W
Bridgeport ✦[8] **278** 41.51 N 87.39 W
Bridgeport, Lake ◎[1] **222** 33.13 N 97.48 W
Bridgeport, University of ʊ[2] **276** 41.10 N 73.12 W
Bridgeport Airport ⊠ **285** 39.47 N 75.20 W
Bridgeport Harbor c **276** 41.10 N 73.11 W
Bridgeport Municipal Airport ⊠ **276** 41.10 N 73.08 W
Bridgeport Reservoir ◎[1] **226** 38.22 N 119.14 W
Bridger **202** 45.17 N 108.54 W
Bridge River Indian Reserve ✦[4] **182** 50.45 N 122.00 W
Bridger Peak ∧ **200** 41.12 N 107.02 W
Bridges Point > **174o** 1.58 N 157.28 W
Bridgeton, Mo., U.S. **219** 38.44 N 90.24 W
Bridgeton, N.J., U.S. **208** 39.25 N 75.14 W
Bridgetown, Austl. **162** 33.57 S 116.08 E
Bridgetown, Barb. **241g** 13.06 N 59.37 W
Bridgetown, N.S., Can. **186** 44.51 N 65.18 W
Bridgetown, Oh., U.S. **218** 39.09 N 84.38 W
Bridge Trafford **262** 53.14 N 2.49 W
Bridgeview **278** 41.45 N 87.48 W
Bridgeville, De., U.S. **208** 38.44 N 75.36 W
Bridgeville, Pa., U.S. **214** 40.21 N 80.06 W
Bridgewater, Austl. **166** 42.44 S 147.14 E
Bridgewater, Austl. **168b** 35.02 S 138.47 E
Bridgewater, N.S., Can. **186** 44.23 N 64.31 W
Bridgewater, Ct., U.S. **210** 41.32 N 73.22 W
Bridgewater, Me., U.S. **186** 46.25 N 67.50 W
Bridgewater, Ma., U.S. **207** 41.59 N 70.58 W
Bridgewater, N.Y., U.S. **210** 42.58 N 75.15 W
Bridgewater, Pa., U.S. **285** 40.05 N 74.55 W
Bridgewater, S.D., U.S. **198** 43.33 N 97.30 W
Bridgewater, Va., U.S. **188** 38.22 N 78.58 W
Bridgewater Canal ≍ **262** 53.20 N 2.45 W
Bridgewater State College ʊ[2] **283** 41.59 N 70.58 W
Bridgman **216** 41.57 N 86.33 W
Bridgnorth **42** 52.33 N 2.25 W
Bridgton **188** 44.03 N 70.42 W
Bridgwater **42** 51.08 N 3.00 W
Bridgwater Bay c **42** 51.16 N 3.12 W
Bridlington **44** 54.05 N 0.12 W
Bridlington Bay c **44** 54.04 N 0.08 W
Bridport **42** 50.44 N 2.46 W
Brie ✦[1] **50** 48.40 N 3.20 E
Briec **32** 48.06 N 4.00 W
Brie-Comte-Robert **50** 48.41 N 2.37 E
Brie Française ✦[1] **261** 48.40 N 2.50 E
Brieg → Brzeg **30** 50.52 N 17.27 E
Brielle, Ned. **52** 51.54 N 4.10 E
Brielle, N.J., U.S. **208** 40.06 N 74.03 W
Brienne-le-Château **58** 48.24 N 4.32 E
Brienne-sur-Aisne **50** 49.26 N 4.03 E
Brienno **58** 45.55 N 9.07 E
Brienon-sur-Armançon **50** 48.00 N 3.37 E
Brien Run ≃ **284b** 39.20 N 76.28 W
Brienz **58** 46.46 N 8.03 E
Brienza **68** 40.29 N 15.37 E
Brienzer Rothorn ∧ **58** 46.48 N 8.04 E
Brienzersee ◎ **58** 46.43 N 7.57 E
Brier Creek ≃ **192** 32.47 N 81.26 W
Brierfield **44** 53.50 N 2.14 W
Brier Hill **212** 44.32 N 75.40 W
Brier Island I **186** 44.16 N 66.22 W
Brierley Hill **42** 52.29 N 2.07 W
Brier Mountain ∧ **210** 41.37 N 77.02 W
Briese **264a** 52.42 N 13.18 E
Briese ≃ **264a** 52.41 N 13.15 E
Brieselang **54** 52.35 N 13.00 E
Briesen **54** 52.20 N 14.16 E
Brieske **54** 51.29 N 13.57 E
Brieskow-Finkenheerd **54** 52.16 N 14.35 E
Briest **54** 52.31 N 12.08 E
Briey **56** 49.15 N 5.56 E
Brig **58** 46.19 N 8.00 E
Brigach ≃ **58** 47.58 N 8.30 E
Brigantine **208** 39.24 N 74.21 W
Brig Bay **186** 51.04 N 56.55 W
Brigden **214** 42.49 N 82.17 W
Brigg **44** 53.34 N 0.30 W
Briggs **196** 30.53 N 97.56 W
Brigham City **200** 41.30 N 112.00 W
Brighouse **44** 53.42 N 1.47 W
Brighstone **42** 50.38 N 1.24 W
Bright **166** 36.44 S 146.58 E
Brightlingsea **42** 51.49 N 1.02 E
Brightmoor ✦[8] **281** 42.24 N 83.14 W
Brighton, Austl. **168b** 35.01 S 138.31 E
Brighton, Austl. **169** 37.55 S 145.00 E
Brighton, On., Can. **212** 44.02 N 77.44 W
Brighton, N.Z. **172** 45.57 S 170.20 E
Brighton, Eng., U.K. **42** 50.50 N 0.08 W
Brighton, Co., U.S. **200** 39.59 N 104.49 W
Brighton, Fl., U.S. **220** 27.14 N 81.06 W
Brighton, Il., U.S. **219** 39.02 N 90.08 W
Brighton, Ia., U.S. **190** 41.10 N 91.49 W
Brighton, Md., U.S. **284b** 39.21 N 76.43 W
Brighton, Mi., U.S. **216** 42.31 N 83.46 W
Brighton, N.Y., U.S. **210** 43.08 N 77.33 W
Brighton ✦[8] **283** 42.21 N 71.08 W
Brighton Downs **166** 23.22 S 141.34 E
Brighton Indian Reservation ✦[4] **220** 27.04 N 81.05 W
Brighton-Le-Sands **274a** 33.58 S 151.09 E
Brighton Park ✦[8] **278** 41.49 N 87.42 W
Brighton State Recreation Area ♦ **216** 42.30 N 83.48 W
Brightsand Lake ◎ **184** 53.36 N 108.52 W
Brightwater **172** 41.23 S 173.07 E
Brightwaters **276** 40.43 N 73.16 W
Brightwood **224** 45.23 N 122.01 W
Brightwood ✦[8] **284c** 38.58 N 77.02 W
Brigittenau ✦[8] **264b** 48.14 N 16.22 E
Brignoles **62** 43.24 N 6.04 E
Brignoud **62** 45.15 N 5.54 E
Brig o'Turk **46** 56.13 N 4.22 W
Brigstock **42** 52.27 N 0.36 W
Brigus **186** 47.32 N 53.13 W
Brihuega **34** 40.45 N 2.52 W
Briis-sous-Forges **261** 48.38 N 2.07 E
Brijuni (Brioni) **64** 44.55 N 13.46 E
Brijuni I **64** 44.55 N 13.46 E
Brikama **150** 13.15 N 16.39 W
Brilhante ≃ **255** 21.58 S 54.18 W
Brill **42** 51.49 N 1.03 W
Brilliant, B.C., Can. **182** 49.19 N 117.38 W
Brilliant, Al., U.S. **194** 34.01 N 87.45 W
Brilliant, Oh., U.S. **214** 40.15 N 80.37 W
Brillion **190** 44.10 N 88.03 W
Brilon **56** 51.24 N 8.34 E
Brilyn Park **284c** 38.54 N 77.10 W
Brimfield, Eng., U.K. **42** 52.18 N 2.42 W

Symbols in the index entries represent the broad categories identified in the key at the right. Symbols with superior numbers (⋏[1]) identify subcategories (see complete key on page *I* · *1*).

Symbole im Register stellen die rechts im Schlüssel erklärten Kategorien dar. Symbole mit hochgestellten Ziffern (⋏[1]) bezeichnen Unterabteilungen einer Kategorie (vgl. vollständiger Schlüssel auf Seite *I* · *1*).

Los símbolos incluídos en el texto del índice representan las grandes categorias identificadas con la clave a la derecha. Los símbolos con numeros en su parte superior (⋏[1]) identifican las subcategorías (véase la clave completa en la página *I* · *1*).

Les symboles de l'index représentent les catégories indiquées dans la légende à droite. Les symboles suivis d'un indice (⋏[1]) représentent des sous-catégories (voir légende complète à la page *I* · *1*).

Os símbolos incluídos no texto do índice representam as grandes categorias identificadas com a chave à direita. Os símbolos com números em sua parte superior (⋏[1]) identificam as subcategorias (veja-se a chave completa à página *I* · *1*).

	English	Deutsch	Español	Français	Português
∧	Mountain	Berg	Montaña	Montagne	Montanha
⋏	Mountains	Gebirge	Montañas	Montagnes	Montanhas
)(	Pass	Paß	Paso	Col	Passo
V	Valley, Canyon	Tal, Cañon	Valle, Cañón	Vallée, Canyon	Vale, Canhão
≚	Plain	Ebene	Llano	Plaine	Planície
>	Cape	Kap	Cabo	Cap	Cabo
I	Island	Insel	Isla	Île	Ilha
II	Islands	Inseln	Islas	Îles	Ilhas
⊥	Other Topographic Features	Andere Topographische Objekte	Otros Elementos Topográficos	Autres données topographiques	Outros acidentes topográficos

ESPAÑOL / FRANÇAIS / PORTUGUÊS

Nombre / Nom / Nome	Página / Page / Página	Lat.°′	Long.°′ W = Oeste / W = Ouest / W = Oeste
Brimfield, In., U.S.	216	41.27 N	85.24 W
Brimfield, Ma., U.S.	207	42.07 N	72.12 W
Brimfield, Oh., U.S.	214	41.06 N	81.21 W
Brimington	44	53.16 N	1.23 W
Brindabella	171b	35.23 S	148.45 E
Brindisi	68	40.38 N	17.56 E
Brindisi □[4]	68	40.35 N	17.40 E
Brindisi Montagna	68	40.37 N	15.57 E
Brindle	262	53.43 N	2.36 W
Brindley Heath	260	51.12 N	0.03 W
Bringelly	170	33.56 S	150.44 E
Bringelly Creek ≃	274a	33.58 S	150.38 E
Brinje	36	45.00 N	15.08 E
Brinkerton	279b	40.13 N	79.32 W
Brinkhaven	214	40.28 N	82.12 W
Brinkleigh	284b	39.18 N	76.50 W
Brinkley, Austl.	168b	35.14 S	139.13 E
Brinkley, Ar., U.S.	194	34.53 N	91.11 W
Brinkum	52	53.00 N	8.47 E
Brinkworth	166	33.42 S	138.24 E
Brinnon	224	47.40 N	122.53 W
Brinon-sur-Beuvron	50	47.17 N	3.30 E
Brins, Ābār al- ⫪[4]	142	30.29 N	30.05 E
Brinscall	262	53.41 N	2.34 W
Brinyan	46	59.07 N	2.59 W
Brion, Île I	186	47.48 N	61.28 W
Brione	58	46.18 N	8.47 E
Briones Hills ⋏[2]	282	37.56 N	122.08 W
Briones Regional Park ♦	282	37.56 N	122.08 W
Briones Reservoir ⊜[1]	282	37.55 N	122.12 W
Brionne	50	49.12 N	0.43 E
Brion-sur-Ource	58	47.55 N	4.39 E
Brioude	32	45.18 N	3.23 E
Briouze	32	48.42 N	0.22 W
Brisbane, Austl.	171a	27.28 S	153.02 E
Brisbane, Ca., U.S.	226	37.41 N	122.24 W
Brisbane ≃	171a	27.24 S	153.09 E
Brisbane, Mount ∧	171a	27.05 S	152.32 E
Brisbane International Airport ⊠	171a	27.27 S	153.11 E
Brisbane Ranges National Park ♦	169	37.52 S	144.14 E
Brisbane Water ⊂	170	33.28 S	151.20 E
Brisbane Water National Park ♦	170	33.30 S	151.15 E
Brisben	210	42.22 N	75.41 W
Brisbin	214	40.50 N	78.21 W
Briseñas	234	20.16 N	102.33 W
Brisighella	66	44.13 N	11.46 E
Brissac	62	43.52 N	3.42 E
Brissago	58	46.07 N	8.43 E
Bristol, Eng., U.K.	42	51.27 N	2.35 W
Bristol, Ct., U.S.	207	41.41 N	72.57 W
Bristol, Fl., U.S.	192	30.25 N	84.58 W
Bristol, Il., U.S.	216	41.39 N	88.27 W
Bristol, In., U.S.	216	41.43 N	85.49 W
Bristol, N.H., U.S.	188	43.35 N	71.44 W
Bristol, Pa., U.S.	208	40.06 N	74.51 W
Bristol, R.I., U.S.	207	41.40 N	71.16 W
Bristol, S.D., U.S.	198	45.20 N	97.44 W
Bristol, Tn., U.S.	192	36.35 N	82.11 W
Bristol, Vt., U.S.	188	44.08 N	73.04 W
Bristol, Va., U.S.	192	36.35 N	82.11 W
Bristol, Wi., U.S.	216	42.33 N	88.02 W
Bristol □[6], Ma., U.S.	207	41.54 N	71.06 W
Bristol □[6], R.I., U.S.	207	41.42 N	71.18 W
Bristol (Lulsgate) Airport ⊠	42	51.23 N	2.43 W
Bristol Bay ⊂	180	58.00 N	159.00 W
Bristol-Blake Reservation ♦	283	42.06 N	71.19 W
Bristol Center	210	42.49 N	77.23 W
Bristol Channel ⩌	42	51.20 N	4.00 W
Bristol Lake ⊜	204	34.28 N	115.41 W
Bristolville	214	41.23 N	80.52 W
Bristow	196	35.49 N	96.23 W
Britânia	255	15.14 S	51.09 W
Británicas, Islas → British Isles II	4	54.00 N	4.00 W
Britannia	275b	43.37 N	79.41 W
Britannia Beach	182	49.38 N	123.12 W
Britische Jungfern-Inseln → British Virgin Islands □[2]	240m	18.30 N	64.30 W
Britisches Antarktis-Territorium → British Antarctic Territory □[2]	9	60.00 S	45.00 W
British Antarctic Territory □[2]	9	60.00 S	45.00 W
British Columbia □[4], Can.	176	54.00 N	125.00 W
British Columbia □[4], Can.	182	54.00 N	125.00 W
British Honduras → Belize □[1]	232	17.15 N	88.45 W
British Indian Ocean Territory □[2]	12	7.00 S	72.00 E
British Isles II	4	54.00 N	4.00 W
British Mountains ⋏	180	69.00 N	140.20 W
British Museum ʊ	260	51.31 N	0.08 W
British Solomon Islands → Solomon Islands □[1]	175e	8.00 S	159.00 E
British Virgin Islands □[2], N.A.	230	18.30 N	64.30 W
British Virgin Islands □[2], N.A.	240m	18.30 N	64.30 W
Britland Edge Hill ∧[2]	262	53.31 N	1.50 W
Briton Ferry	42	51.38 N	3.49 W
Brits	158	25.42 S	27.45 E
Britstown	158	30.37 S	23.30 E
Britt	190	43.05 N	93.48 W
Brittany → Bretagne □[9]	32	48.00 N	3.00 W
Brittas	48	53.14 N	6.27 W
Britten	158	27.42 S	25.17 E
Brittingham	196	25.45 N	103.24 W
Britton, Mi., U.S.	216	41.59 N	83.49 W
Britton, S.D., U.S.	198	45.47 N	97.45 W
Britton, Tx., U.S.	222	32.33 N	97.04 W
Britton, Mount ∧[2]	162	26.31 S	134.43 E
Britz	54	52.53 N	13.49 E
Britz ⊸[8]	264a	52.27 N	13.26 E
Brive-la-Gaillarde	32	45.10 N	1.32 E
Brives-Charensac	62	45.03 N	3.56 E
Briviesca	34	42.33 N	3.19 W
Brivio	62	45.44 N	9.27 E
Brixen im Thale	64	47.27 N	12.15 E
Brixham	42	50.24 N	3.30 W
Brixlegg	64	47.25 N	11.53 E
Brixton	166	23.32 S	144.57 E
Brixworth	42	52.20 N	0.54 W
Brlik	85	43.40 N	73.49 E
Brloh	61	48.56 N	14.13 E
Brno	30	49.12 N	16.37 E
Bro	40	59.31 N	17.38 E
Broa, Ensenada de la ⊂	240p	22.35 N	82.00 W
Broad ≃, U.S.	192	34.00 N	81.04 W
Broad ≃, Fl., U.S.	220	25.28 N	81.09 W
Broad ≃, Ga., U.S.	192	33.59 N	82.39 W
Broadalbin	210	43.03 N	74.11 W
Broad Arrow	162	30.20 S	121.27 E
Broad Axe	285	40.10 N	75.15 W
Broadback ≃	176	51.21 N	78.52 W
Broad Bay ⊂	46	58.15 N	6.15 W
Broadbottom	262	53.26 N	2.01 W
Broad Brook	207	41.54 N	72.32 W
Broad Chalke	42	51.02 N	1.57 W
Broadclyst	42	50.46 N	3.26 W
Broad Creek ⊂	208	38.45 N	76.15 W
Broad Creek ≃	208	39.42 N	76.14 W
Broadford, Austl.	169	37.13 S	145.03 E
Broadford, Scot., U.K.	46	57.14 N	5.54 W
Broad Haven ⊂	48	54.18 N	9.55 W
Broadheath	262	53.24 N	2.21 W
Broadhurst Range ⋏	162	22.23 S	122.09 E
Broadkill ≃	208	38.47 N	75.10 W
Broad Law ∧	46	55.30 N	3.22 W
Broadley Common	260	51.45 N	0.04 E
Broadmeadows	169	37.40 S	144.54 E
Broadmoor	226	37.41 N	122.29 W
Broad Neck ≻[1]	208	39.03 N	76.27 W
Broad Oak	42	50.57 N	0.36 E
Broad Pass)(	180	63.18 N	149.09 W
Broad Run ≃, Pa., U.S.	285	39.56 N	75.41 W
Broad Run ≃, Pa., U.S.	285	39.59 N	75.40 W
Broad Run ≃, Va., U.S.	208	38.41 N	77.29 W
Broad Sound ⩌, Austl.	166	22.10 S	149.45 E
Broad Sound ⩌, Ma., U.S.	283	42.25 N	70.58 W
Broad Sound Channel ⩌	166	22.05 S	150.20 E
Broadstairs	42	51.22 N	1.27 E
Broad Street	260	51.17 N	0.38 E
Broad Top	214	40.12 N	78.08 W
Broadus	198	45.26 N	105.24 W
Broadview, Sk., Can.	184	50.20 N	102.30 W
Broadview, Il., U.S.	216	41.51 N	87.51 W
Broadview, In., U.S.	218	39.10 N	87.33 W
Broadview Heights	214	41.18 N	81.41 W
Broadwater	198	41.35 N	102.51 W
Broadway, Eng., U.K.	42	52.02 N	1.51 W
Broadway, Oh., U.S.	214	40.20 N	83.24 W
Broadway, Va., U.S.	188	38.38 N	78.46 W
Broadwell	219	40.04 N	89.27 W
Broadwindsor	42	50.49 N	2.48 W
Broadwood	172	35.16 S	173.23 E
Broager	41	54.53 N	9.41 E
Brobo	150	7.43 N	4.42 W
Broby	26	56.15 N	14.05 E
Brobyværk	41	55.14 N	10.15 E
Broc	58	46.36 N	7.06 E
Brocēni	76	56.42 N	22.35 E
Brochel	46	57.26 N	6.01 W
Brochet	176	57.53 N	101.40 W
Brochet, Lac au ⊜	186	49.40 N	69.37 W
Brochterbeck	52	52.13 N	7.44 E
Brock	184	51.27 N	108.42 W
Brock ≃	44	53.52 N	2.47 W
Brock Creek ≃	285	40.15 N	74.50 W
Brocken ∧	54	51.48 N	10.36 E
Brockenhurst	42	50.49 N	1.34 W
Brockenscheidt	263	51.38 N	7.25 E
Brockhagen	52	51.59 N	8.20 E
Brockham	260	51.14 N	0.17 W
Brockman ≃	168a	31.41 S	116.07 E
Brockman, Mount ∧	162	22.28 S	117.18 E
Brock Monument ⊥	284a	43.09 N	79.04 W
Brockport, N.Y., U.S.	210	43.12 N	77.56 W
Brockport, Pa., U.S.	214	41.16 N	78.44 W
Brocks Beach	212	44.27 N	80.06 W
Brocks Creek	164	13.28 S	131.25 E
Brockton, Ma., U.S.	207	42.05 N	71.01 W
Brockton, Mt., U.S.	198	48.09 N	104.54 W
Brockton, Pa., U.S.	208	40.45 N	76.04 W
Brockton Reservoir ⊜[1]	283	42.07 N	71.03 W
Brock University ʊ[2]	284a	43.07 N	79.15 W
Brockville	212	44.35 N	75.41 W
Brockway	214	41.15 N	78.47 W
Brockworth	42	51.51 N	2.09 W
Brocoió, Ilha de I	287a	22.45 S	43.07 W
Brocton	214	42.23 N	79.26 W
Brod, Česko.	60	49.51 N	12.45 E
Brod, Mac.	38	41.31 N	21.12 E
Broddbo	40	59.59 N	16.28 E
Brodenbach	56	50.14 N	7.26 E
Broderick	226	38.35 N	121.30 W
Brodeur Peninsula ≻[1]	176	73.00 N	88.00 W
Brodhead, Ky., U.S.	192	37.24 N	84.24 W
Brodhead, Wi., U.S.	190	42.37 N	89.22 W
Brodhead Creek ≃	210	40.59 N	75.08 W
Brodheadsville	210	40.55 N	75.24 W
Brodick	46	55.35 N	5.09 W
Brodnax	192	36.42 N	78.01 W
Brodnica	30	53.16 N	19.23 E
Brodokalmak	86	55.35 N	62.06 E
Brody, Pol.	30	51.45 N	14.45 E
Brody, Ukr.	78	50.06 N	25.10 E
Broedersput	158	26.49 S	25.08 E
Broek [op Langendijk]	52	52.40 N	4.48 E
Brogan	202	44.14 N	117.30 W
Broglie	50	49.01 N	0.32 E
Brohlbach ≃	56	50.29 N	7.20 E
Broich ⊸[8]	263	51.25 N	6.51 E
Broichweiden	56	50.49 N	6.09 E
Brok	30	52.43 N	21.52 E
Brok ∧	123	34.32 N	76.35 E
Brokdorf	52	53.52 N	9.19 E
Broke	170	32.45 S	151.06 E
Broke Inlet ⊂	162	34.55 S	116.25 E
Broken ≃	169	36.41 S	146.00 E
Broken Arrow	196	36.03 N	95.47 W
Broken Bay ⊂	170	33.34 S	151.18 E
Broken Bow, Ne., U.S.	198	41.24 N	99.38 W
Broken Bow, Ok., U.S.	194	34.01 N	94.44 W
Broken Bow Lake ⊜[1]	194	34.10 N	94.40 W
Broken Cross, Eng., U.K.	262	53.15 N	2.29 W
Broken Cross, Eng., U.K.	262	53.15 N	2.10 W
Brokenhead ≃	184	50.25 N	96.40 W
Broken Hill	166	31.57 S	141.27 E
Broken Hill → Kabwe	154	14.27 S	28.27 E
Broken Ridge ✣[3]	12	31.30 S	95.00 E
Brokenstraw Creek ≃	214	41.51 N	79.09 W
Broken Sword Creek ≃	214	40.46 N	83.11 W
Brokopondo	250	5.04 N	54.58 W
Brokopondo □[5]	250	4.40 N	55.00 W
Brokopondo Stuwmeer ⊜[1]	250	4.45 N	55.00 W
Brölbach ≃	56	50.47 N	7.18 E
Brolo	70	38.09 N	14.50 E
Bromberg → Bydgoszcz	30	53.08 N	18.00 E
Bromborough	262	53.19 N	2.59 W
Brome, P.Q., Can.	206	45.12 N	72.34 W
Brome, Dtsch.	54	52.36 N	10.56 E
Brome □[6]	206	45.10 N	72.30 W
Brome, Lac ⊜	206	45.15 N	72.30 W
Brome, Mont ∧	206	45.17 N	72.38 W
Bromham	42	52.09 N	0.31 W
Bromley ⊸[8]	260	51.24 N	0.02 E
Bromley Common ⊸[8]	260	51.22 N	0.03 E
Bromley Plateau ✣[3]	18	32.00 S	35.00 W
Bromma ⊸[8]	40	59.21 N	17.55 E
Bromma flygplats ⊠	40	59.21 N	17.55 E
Brommö I	40	58.50 N	13.41 E
Bromo, Gunung ∧	115a	7.57 S	112.57 E
Bromölla	26	56.04 N	14.28 E
Brompton, Eng., U.K.	44	54.22 N	1.25 W
Brompton, Eng., U.K.	260	51.23 N	0.33 E
Brompton, Lac ⊜	206	45.27 N	72.09 W
Bromptonville	206	45.28 N	71.57 W
Bromsgrove	42	52.20 N	2.03 W
Bromyard	42	52.11 N	2.30 W
Bron	62	45.44 N	4.55 E
Bron, Aéroport de ⊠	62	45.43 N	4.56 E
Brønderslev	26	57.16 N	9.58 E
Bronevskaja	24	61.43 N	39.10 E
Brong-Ahafo □[4]	150	7.45 N	1.30 W
Broni	62	45.04 N	9.16 E
Bronickaja Guta	78	50.56 N	27.19 E
Bronkhorstspruit	158	25.48 S	28.44 E
Bronkhorstspruitdam ⊜[1]	158	25.55 S	28.42 E
Bronkow	54	51.40 N	13.55 E
Bronllys	42	52.01 N	3.16 W
Bronlund Peak ∧	176	57.26 N	126.38 W
Bronn	60	49.44 N	11.28 E
Bronnicy	82	55.25 N	38.16 E
Bronnikovo	86	58.32 N	68.25 E
Bronnoje	76	52.19 N	30.29 E
Brønnøysund	24	65.30 N	12.10 E
Bronnzell	56	50.31 N	9.41 E
Brøns	41	55.11 N	8.44 E
Bronson, Fl., U.S.	192	29.26 N	82.38 W
Bronson, Ks., U.S.	198	37.54 N	95.04 W
Bronson, Mi., U.S.	216	41.52 N	85.11 W
Bronson, Tx., U.S.	194	31.21 N	94.01 W
Bronson Lake ⊜	184	53.52 N	109.43 W
Bronte, It.	70	37.47 N	14.50 E
Bronte, Tx., U.S.	196	31.53 N	100.18 W
Bronte Creek ≃	212	43.23 N	79.43 W
Bronwood	192	31.49 N	84.21 W
Bronx □[6]	210	40.49 N	73.56 W
Bronx ⊸[8]	276	40.49 N	73.56 W
Bronx ≃	276	40.49 N	73.52 W
Bronx Park ♦	276	40.52 N	73.53 W
Bronxville	276	40.56 N	73.49 W
Bronx-Whitestone Bridge ⊸[5]	276	40.48 N	73.50 W
Bronx Zoo ♦	276	40.51 N	73.53 W
Bronzolo (Branzoll)	64	46.24 N	11.19 E
Brooch, Lac ⊜	186	50.44 N	67.58 W
Broodsnyersplaas	158	26.03 S	29.29 E
Brook	216	40.51 N	87.21 W
Brookdale	226	37.06 N	122.06 W
Brooke	208	38.23 N	77.22 W
Brooke □[6]	214	40.18 N	80.33 W
Brookeborough	48	54.19 N	7.24 W
Brookeland	194	31.09 N	94.00 W
Brooker	192	29.53 N	82.19 W
Brooke's Point	116	8.47 N	117.50 E
Brookfield, N.S., Can.	186	45.15 N	63.17 W
Brookfield, Ct., U.S.	207	41.28 N	73.24 W
Brookfield, Il., U.S.	216	41.49 N	87.51 W
Brookfield, Ma., U.S.	207	42.12 N	72.06 W
Brookfield, Mi., U.S.	216	42.27 N	84.47 W
Brookfield, Mo., U.S.	194	39.47 N	93.04 W
Brookfield, N.Y., U.S.	210	42.48 N	75.19 W
Brookfield, Oh., U.S.	214	41.14 N	80.34 W
Brookfield, Wi., U.S.	216	43.03 N	88.06 W
Brookfield Center	207	41.27 N	73.23 W
Brookfield Zoo ♦	278	41.50 N	87.50 W
Brookford	192	35.42 N	81.20 W
Brookhaven, De., U.S.	285	39.42 N	75.41 W
Brookhaven, Ms., U.S.	194	31.34 N	90.26 W
Brookhaven, Pa., U.S.	285	39.52 N	75.22 W
Brookhaven Manor	278	41.44 N	87.58 W
Brookhaven National Laboratory ʊ[3]	207	40.54 N	72.52 W
Brookings, Or., U.S.	202	42.03 N	124.16 W
Brookings, S.D., U.S.	198	44.18 N	96.47 W
Brookland, Eng., U.K.	42	50.59 N	0.50 E
Brookland, Ar., U.S.	194	35.54 N	90.34 W
Brookland ⊸[8]	284c	38.56 N	76.59 W
Brooklands	214	42.38 N	83.06 W
Brookland Terrace	285	39.44 N	75.37 W
Brooklandville	284b	39.25 N	76.40 W
Brooklawn	285	39.52 N	75.07 W
Brooklet	192	32.22 N	81.39 W
Brooklin	212	43.57 N	78.57 W
Brookline, Ma., U.S.	207	42.21 N	71.07 W
Brookline, N.H., U.S.	207	42.44 N	71.39 W
Brooklyn, N.S., Can.	186	44.03 N	64.42 W
Brooklyn, Ct., U.S.	207	41.47 N	71.57 W
Brooklyn, Il., U.S.	219	40.14 N	90.46 W
Brooklyn, In., U.S.	218	39.32 N	86.22 W
Brooklyn, Ia., U.S.	190	41.44 N	92.26 W
Brooklyn, Md., U.S.	284b	39.14 N	76.37 W
Brooklyn, Mi., U.S.	216	42.06 N	84.14 W
Brooklyn, Ms., U.S.	194	31.03 N	89.11 W
Brooklyn, Oh., U.S.	214	41.26 N	81.44 W
Brooklyn, Pa., U.S.	210	41.45 N	75.48 W
Brooklyn, Wa., U.S.	224	46.47 N	123.31 W
Brooklyn, Wi., U.S.	216	42.51 N	89.22 W
Brooklyn ⊸[8], Md., U.S.	284b	39.14 N	76.36 W
Brooklyn ⊸[8], N.Y., U.S.	210	40.42 N	74.00 W
Brooklyn Battery Tunnel ⊸[5]	276	40.42 N	74.01 W
Brooklyn Bridge ⊸[5]	276	40.42 N	74.00 W
Brooklyn Center	190	45.04 N	93.19 W
Brooklyn Heights	279a	41.24 N	81.40 W
Brooklyn Marine Park ♦	276	40.35 N	73.55 W
Brooklyn Museum ʊ	276	40.40 N	73.58 W
Brookmans Park	260	51.43 N	0.12 W
Brookmere	182	49.49 N	120.53 W
Brookmont	284c	38.57 N	77.07 W
Brookneal	192	37.03 N	78.56 W
Brook Park	214	41.23 N	81.48 W
Brookport	194	37.07 N	88.37 W
Brooks, Ab., Can.	182	50.35 N	111.53 W
Brooks, Ca., U.S.	226	38.45 N	122.09 W
Brooks, Me., U.S.	188	44.33 N	69.07 W
Brooks, Or., U.S.	224	45.02 N	122.57 W
Brooks, Mount ∧	180	63.11 N	150.40 W
Brooks Air Force Base ■	196	29.21 N	98.25 W
Brooks Bay ⊂	182	50.13 N	127.55 W
Brooksburg	218	38.44 N	85.15 W
Brookshire	222	29.47 N	95.57 W
Brookside, De., U.S.	285	39.40 N	75.43 W
Brookside, N.J., U.S.	276	40.48 N	74.34 W
Brookside, Pa., U.S.	214	42.08 N	80.00 W
Brookside, Tx., U.S.	222	29.35 N	95.18 W
Brookside Park ♦	279a	41.27 N	81.43 W
Brooks Island I	282	37.54 N	122.21 W
Brooks Mountain ∧	180	65.33 N	167.09 W
Brooks Place	283	42.02 N	71.01 W
Brooks Range ⋏	180	68.00 N	154.00 W
Brookston	216	40.36 N	86.52 W
Brook Street	260	51.37 N	0.17 E
Brooksville, Fl., U.S.	220	28.33 N	82.23 W
Brooksville, Ky., U.S.	218	38.40 N	84.03 W
Brooksville, Ms., U.S.	194	33.14 N	88.34 W
Brookton	162	32.22 S	117.01 E
Brooktondale	210	42.23 N	76.24 W
Brookvale	274a	33.46 S	151.17 E
Brookview	210	42.32 N	73.43 W
Brookville, In., U.S.	218	39.25 N	85.00 W
Brookville, Ma., U.S.	207	42.07 N	71.00 W
Brookville, N.Y., U.S.	276	40.48 N	73.34 W
Brookville, Oh., U.S.	218	39.50 N	84.24 W
Brookville, Pa., U.S.	214	41.09 N	79.05 W
Brookville Lake ⊜[1]	218	39.30 N	85.00 W
Brookwood, Eng., U.K.	260	51.18 N	0.38 W
Brookwood, In., U.S.	278	40.30 N	87.22 W
Brooloo	166	26.29 S	152.42 E
Broom, Little Loch ⊂	46	57.54 N	5.22 W
Broom, Loch ⊂	46	57.52 N	5.08 W
Broomall	285	39.58 N	75.21 W
Broome	162	17.58 S	122.14 E
Broome □[6]	210	42.08 N	75.54 W
Broome County Airport ⊠	210	42.13 N	75.59 W
Broomes Island	208	38.25 N	76.32 W
Broomfield, Eng., U.K.	260	51.14 N	0.38 E
Broomfield, Eng., U.K.	260	51.46 N	0.28 E
Broomfield, Co., U.S.	200	39.55 N	105.05 W
Broons	32	48.19 N	2.16 W
Brooten	198	45.30 N	95.07 W
Brophy, Mount ∧[2]	162	19.11 S	128.51 E
Brora	46	58.01 N	3.51 W
Brora ≃	46	58.01 N	3.52 W
Brørup	41	55.29 N	9.01 E
Broseley	42	52.37 N	2.29 W
Brosewere Bay ⊂	276	40.37 N	73.42 W
Brosna ≃	48	53.13 N	7.58 W
Brošnev-Osada	78	49.00 N	24.13 E
Brossac	32	45.20 N	0.03 W
Brossard	206	45.26 N	73.29 W
Brossasco	62	44.34 N	7.21 E
Brosso	62	45.30 N	7.48 E
Brotas de Macaúbas	255	12.00 S	42.38 W
Brothers Brook ≃	276	41.02 N	73.36 W
Brötjärna	40	60.30 N	15.01 E
Broto	34	42.36 N	0.06 W
Brotterode	54	50.49 N	10.26 E
Brotton	44	54.34 N	0.56 W
Brou	50	48.13 N	1.11 E
Brough, Eng., U.K.	44	54.32 N	2.19 W
Brough, Eng., U.K.	44	53.44 N	0.35 W
Brough, Scot., U.K.	46	58.39 N	3.20 W
Brougham	212	43.55 N	79.06 W
Brough Head ≻	46	59.08 N	3.17 W
Broughshane	48	54.54 N	6.12 W
Broughton, Eng., U.K.	42	52.23 N	0.46 W
Broughton, Eng., U.K.	44	53.34 N	0.33 W
Broughton, Eng., U.K.	44	53.49 N	2.44 W
Broughton, Eng., U.K.	262	53.49 N	2.43 W
Broughton, Scot., U.K.	46	55.37 N	3.25 W
Broughton, Wales, U.K.	44	53.10 N	2.59 W
Broughton, Pa., U.S.	214	40.21 N	79.59 W
Broughton in Furness	44	54.17 N	3.12 W
Broughton Island I	176	67.35 N	63.50 W
Broughtown	46	59.15 N	2.36 W
Broughty Ferry	46	56.28 N	2.53 W
Broumov	30	50.35 N	16.20 E
Brousseval	58	48.29 N	4.58 E
Brou-sur-Chantereine	261	48.53 N	2.38 E
Brouvelieures	58	48.14 N	6.44 E
Brouwersdam ⊸[6]	52	51.46 N	3.51 E
Brouwershaven	52	51.44 N	3.54 E
Brovary	78	50.31 N	30.46 E
Brovst	26	57.06 N	9.32 E
Broward □[6]	220	26.09 N	80.29 W
Browerville	198	46.05 N	94.51 W
Brown □[6], Il., U.S.	219	39.59 N	90.45 W
Brown □[6], In., U.S.	218	39.12 N	86.15 W
Brown □[6], Oh., U.S.	218	38.52 N	83.54 W
Brown, Mount ∧	202	48.52 N	111.09 W
Brown, Point ≻	224	46.56 N	124.10 W
Brownbacks	285	40.11 N	75.37 W
Brown City	190	43.12 N	82.59 W
Brown Clee Hill ∧[2]	42	52.28 N	2.35 W
Brown County State Park ♦	218	39.09 N	86.14 W
Brown Creek ≃	276	40.43 N	73.04 W
Browndale	210	41.40 N	75.27 W
Brown Deer	216	43.09 N	87.57 W
Browne Bay ⊂	176	73.08 N	97.30 W
Brownfield	196	33.10 N	102.16 W
Brown Gelly ∧[2]	42	50.32 N	4.32 W
Brownhills	42	52.39 N	1.55 W
Browning, Il., U.S.	219	40.08 N	90.22 W
Browning, Mo., U.S.	194	40.02 N	93.09 W
Browning, Mt., U.S.	202	48.33 N	113.00 W
Browning Entrance ⊂	182	53.41 N	130.30 W
Browning Island I	212	45.00 N	79.25 W
Brown Lake ⊜	176	65.55 N	91.15 W
Brownlee Park	216	42.18 N	85.05 W
Brownlee Reservoir ⊜[1]	202	44.40 N	117.05 W
Brown Mountain ∧, Ca., U.S.	204	35.41 N	117.01 W
Brown Mountain ∧, Ca., U.S.	280	34.14 N	118.08 W
Brown Mountain ∧[2]	222	31.51 N	97.39 W
Brown Point ≻	276	40.43 N	73.04 W
Brownsberg, Natuurpark ♦	250	4.50 N	55.10 W
Brownsboro	222	32.18 N	95.37 W
Browns Brook ≃	276	41.09 N	73.17 W
Brownsburg, P.Q., Can.	206	45.41 N	74.25 W
Brownsburg, In., U.S.	218	39.50 N	86.23 W
Browns Canyon V	280	34.18 N	118.35 W
Brownsdale	190	43.44 N	92.52 W
Browns Island I	282	38.02 N	121.52 W
Browns Lake	216	42.42 N	88.14 W
Brownsmead	224	46.13 N	123.32 W
Browns Mills	208	39.58 N	74.35 W
Browns Point	224	47.18 N	122.21 W
Browns Town, Jam.	241q	18.24 N	77.22 W
Brownstown, Il., U.S.	219	38.59 N	88.57 W
Brownstown, In., U.S.	218	38.52 N	86.02 W
Brownstown, Pa., U.S.	208	40.08 N	76.13 W
Brownstown Creek ≃	281	42.06 N	83.13 W
Browns Valley, Ca., U.S.	226	39.15 N	121.23 W
Browns Valley, Mn., U.S.	198	45.35 N	96.49 W
Brownsville, On., Can.	212	42.52 N	80.50 W
Brownsville, Ca., U.S.	226	39.28 N	121.16 W
Brownsville, Fl., U.S.	220	25.50 N	80.17 W
Brownsville, In., U.S.	218	39.39 N	85.00 W
Brownsville, Ky., U.S.	194	37.11 N	86.16 W
Brownsville, La., U.S.	194	32.30 N	92.10 W
Brownsville, Or., U.S.	202	44.23 N	122.59 W
Brownsville, Pa., U.S.	188	40.01 N	79.53 W
Brownsville, Tn., U.S.	194	35.35 N	89.15 W
Brownsville, Tx., U.S.	196	25.54 N	97.29 W
Brownton	190	44.43 N	94.21 W
Browntown	276	40.24 N	74.19 W
Brownvale	182	56.08 N	117.53 W
Brownville, Al., U.S.	194	33.23 N	87.45 W
Brownville, Me., U.S.	188	45.18 N	69.02 W
Brownville, Ne., U.S.	198	40.23 N	95.39 W
Brownville, N.Y., U.S.	212	44.00 N	75.59 W
Brownville Junction	188	45.21 N	69.03 W
Brown Willy ∧[2]	42	50.35 N	4.36 W
Brownwood	196	31.42 N	98.59 W
Brownwood, Lake ⊜[1]	196	31.51 N	99.02 W
Browse Island I	160	14.07 S	123.33 E
Broxbourne	260	51.45 N	0.01 W
Broxbourne □[8]	260	51.44 N	0.04 W
Broxton	192	31.37 N	82.53 W
Broye ≃	58	46.55 N	7.02 E
Broyhill Park	284c	38.51 N	77.11 W
Broža	76	52.57 N	29.07 E
Brozas	34	39.37 N	6.46 W
Brozzo	64	45.43 N	10.14 E
Brtonigla	64	45.23 N	13.38 E
Brû	58	48.21 N	6.41 E
Bruay-en-Artois	50	50.29 N	2.33 E
Bruay-sur-l'Escaut	50	50.23 N	3.32 E
Bruce, Ms., U.S.	194	33.59 N	89.20 W
Bruce, S.D., U.S.	198	44.26 N	96.53 W
Bruce, Wi., U.S.	190	45.27 N	91.16 W
Bruce □[6]	212	44.30 N	81.15 W
Bruce, Mount ∧	162	22.36 S	118.08 E
Bruce Bay	172	43.35 S	169.41 E
Bruce Creek ≃	275b	43.52 N	79.18 W
Bruce Lake	184	50.48 N	93.24 W
Bruce Lake ⊜	184	50.49 N	93.20 W
Bruce Mines	190	46.18 N	83.48 W
Bruce Museum ʊ	276	41.01 N	73.37 W
Bruce Peninsula ≻[1]	190	44.50 N	81.20 W
Bruce Peninsula National Park ♦	190	45.12 N	81.40 W
Bruce Rock	162	31.53 S	118.09 E
Bruceville	222	31.19 N	97.14 W
Bruchberg ∧	54	51.47 N	10.29 E
Bruchhausen	56	51.26 N	8.01 E
Bruchhausen-Vilsen	52	52.50 N	9.00 E
Bruchmühlbach-Miesau	56	49.24 N	7.26 E
Bruchmühle	264a	52.33 N	13.47 E
Br'uchoveckaja	78	45.48 N	38.59 E
Bruchsal	56	49.07 N	8.35 E
Brück, Dtsch.	54	52.12 N	12.46 E
Bruck, Öst.	64	47.17 N	12.49 E
Bruck an der Leitha	61	47.57 N	16.44 E
Bruck an der Mur	61	47.25 N	15.16 E
Bruckhausen ⊸[8]	263	51.29 N	6.44 E
Bruck in der Oberpfalz	60	49.15 N	12.18 E
Brückl	61	46.45 N	14.32 E
Bruckmühl	64	47.53 N	11.54 E
Brucoli ⊸[8]	70	37.17 N	15.11 E
Brudager	41	55.07 N	10.41 E
Bruderheim	182	53.47 N	112.56 W
Brue ≃	42	51.13 N	3.00 W
Brue-Auriac	62	43.32 N	5.57 E
Brueil-en-Vexin	261	49.02 N	1.49 E
Brüel	54	53.44 N	11.43 E
Bruff	48	52.29 N	8.33 W
Bruges → Brugge	50	51.13 N	3.14 E
Brugg	58	47.29 N	8.12 E
Brugge (Bruges), Bel.	50	51.13 N	3.14 E
Brügge, Dtsch.	263	51.13 N	7.34 E
Brüggen	56	51.14 N	6.11 E
Brugherio	62	45.33 N	9.18 E
Brugnato	62	44.14 N	9.43 E
Brühl	56	50.48 N	6.54 E
Bruin, Ky., U.S.	218	38.11 N	83.01 W
Bruin, Pa., U.S.	214	41.04 N	79.44 W
Bruinisse	52	51.40 N	4.06 E
Bruin Point ∧	200	39.39 N	110.22 W
Bruit, Pulau I	112	2.35 N	111.20 E
Bruja, Cerro ∧	236	9.29 N	79.34 W
Brule	198	41.05 N	101.53 W
Brule ≃	190	45.57 N	88.12 W
Brûlé, Lac ⊜, Can.	176	52.17 N	63.52 W
Brûlé, Lac ⊜, P.Q., Can.	190	46.57 N	77.12 W
Brule Lake ⊜	212	45.03 N	77.04 W
Brûly	50	49.58 N	4.31 E
Brumadinho	255	20.08 S	44.13 W
Brumado	255	14.13 S	41.40 W
Brumath	56	48.44 N	7.43 E
Brumby Creek ≃	162	24.09 S	118.39 E
Brummen	52	52.05 N	6.09 E
Brumunddal	26	60.53 N	10.56 E
Bruna ≃	66	42.45 N	10.53 E
Brunate	62	45.49 N	9.06 E
Brunau	54	52.45 N	11.28 E
Brundall	42	52.37 N	1.26 E
Brundby	41	55.49 N	10.37 E
Brundidge	194	31.43 N	85.48 W
Brune ≃	50	49.45 N	3.47 E
Bruneau	202	42.52 N	115.47 W
Bruneau ≃	202	42.57 N	115.58 W
Brunei □[1], Asia	108	4.30 N	114.40 E
Brunei □[1], Asia	112	4.30 N	114.40 E
Brunei, Teluk ⊂	112	5.05 N	115.18 E
Brunei → Bandar Seri Begawan	112	4.56 N	114.55 E
Brünen	52	51.43 N	6.39 E
Brunette Creek ≃	162	18.47 S	135.41 E
Brunette Downs	162	18.38 S	135.57 E
Brunette Island I	186	47.16 N	55.54 W
Brunflo	26	63.05 N	14.49 E
Brungle	171b	35.10 S	148.14 E
Brunico (Bruneck)	64	46.48 N	11.56 E
Brünigpass)(	58	46.46 N	8.09 E
Brüninghausen	263	51.13 N	7.41 E
Brunkeberg	26	59.26 N	8.29 E
Brünn, Dtsch.	54	50.27 N	10.51 E
Brunn, Dtsch.	54	53.40 N	13.22 E
Brunna	40	59.51 N	17.26 E
Brunn am Gebirge	61	48.07 N	16.17 E
Brünn → Brno	30	49.12 N	16.37 E
Brunnen, Dtsch.	60	48.38 N	11.18 E
Brunnen, Schw.	58	47.00 N	8.36 E
Brunner, Lake ⊜	172	42.37 S	171.27 E
Brunnerville	208	40.11 N	76.17 W
Brunni	58	47.03 N	8.42 E
Brunnsvik	40	60.12 N	15.08 E
Bruno	184	52.15 N	105.30 W
Brunot Island I	279b	40.28 N	80.03 W
Brunow	264a	52.44 N	13.52 E
Brunoy	50	48.42 N	2.30 E
Brunsbüttel	52	53.54 N	9.07 E
Brunsbüttelkoog	52	53.54 N	9.08 E
Brunson	192	32.55 N	81.11 W
Brunssum	56	50.56 N	5.59 E
Brunswick, Austl.	274b	37.46 S	144.58 E
Brunswick, Ga., U.S.	192	31.08 N	81.29 W
Brunswick, Me., U.S.	188	43.54 N	69.57 W
Brunswick, Md., U.S.	208	39.18 N	77.37 W
Brunswick, Mo., U.S.	194	39.25 N	93.07 W
Brunswick, Oh., U.S.	214	41.14 N	81.50 W
Brunswick ≃	168a	33.15 S	115.45 E
Brunswick, Península ≻[1]	254	53.30 S	71.25 W
Brunswick → Braunschweig	52	52.16 N	10.31 E
Brunswick Junction	168a	33.15 S	115.51 E
Brunswick Lake ⊜	190	49.00 N	83.23 W
Brunswick Naval Air Station ■	188	43.54 N	69.56 W
Brunswick Square ⊸[9]	276	40.25 N	74.23 W
Bruntál	30	49.59 N	17.28 E
Bruree	48	52.26 N	8.36 W
Brus, Laguna de ⊂	236	15.50 N	84.35 W
Brus'any	80	53.13 N	49.24 E
Brusasco	62	45.09 N	8.04 E
Bruselas → Bruxelles	50	50.50 N	4.20 E
Brusendorf	264a	52.19 N	13.31 E
Brush	198	40.15 N	103.37 W
Brush Creek ≃, Oh., U.S.	216	41.26 N	84.24 W
Brush Creek ≃, Pa., U.S.	279b	40.23 N	79.46 W
Brush Run ≃, Pa., U.S.	279b	40.18 N	80.07 W
Brush Run ≃, Pa., U.S.	279b	40.16 N	80.10 W
Brush Valley	214	40.32 N	79.04 W
Brushy Creek ≃, Austl.	274b	37.43 S	145.17 E
Brushy Creek ≃, Ok., U.S.	196	34.55 N	95.34 W
Brushy Creek ≃, Tx., U.S.	222	32.59 N	96.12 W
Brushy Creek ≃, Tx., U.S.	222	30.48 N	95.09 W
Brushy Creek ≃, Tx., U.S.	222	31.55 N	95.26 W
Brushy Creek ≃, Tx., U.S.	222	30.43 N	97.03 W
Brushy Creek ≃, Tx., U.S.	222	29.04 N	96.34 W
Brusilov	78	50.17 N	29.32 E
Brusio	58	46.14 N	10.07 E
Brus Laguna	236	15.47 N	84.35 W
Brusovo	76	57.51 N	35.24 E
Brusque	252	27.06 S	48.56 W
Brussel → Bruxelles	50	50.50 N	4.20 E
Brussels, On., Can.	212	43.44 N	81.15 W
Brussels, Il., U.S.	219	38.57 N	90.36 W
Brussels → Bruxelles	50	50.50 N	4.20 E
Brusson	62	45.45 N	7.44 E
Brüssow	54	53.24 N	14.07 E
Brusy	30	53.53 N	17.45 E
Brutelles	50	50.08 N	1.31 E
Bruthen	166	37.43 S	147.48 E
Bruton	42	51.07 N	2.27 W
Bruxelles (Brussels) (Brussel)	56	50.50 N	4.20 E
Bruxelles National, Aéroport ⊠	50	50.54 N	4.30 E
Brüx → Most	54	50.32 N	13.39 E
Bruyères	58	48.12 N	6.43 E
Bruyères-le-Châtel	261	48.36 N	2.11 E
Bruzual	246	8.03 N	69.19 W
Bruzzano Zeffirio	68	38.02 N	16.05 E
Brwinów	30	52.09 N	20.43 E
Bryan, Oh., U.S.	216	41.28 N	84.33 W
Bryan, Tx., U.S.	222	30.40 N	96.22 W
Bryan, Mount ∧	166	33.26 S	138.59 E
Bryan Coast ⫠[2]	9	73.45 S	82.00 W
Bryansk → Br'ansk	76	53.15 N	34.22 E
Bryans Road	208	38.37 N	77.04 W
Bryant, Ar., U.S.	194	34.35 N	92.29 W
Bryant, In., U.S.	216	40.32 N	84.58 W
Bryant, S.D., U.S.	198	44.35 N	97.28 W
Bryant Creek ≃	194	36.36 N	92.17 W
Bryant Mountain ∧	207	42.28 N	72.58 W
Bryantville	207	42.02 N	70.50 W
Bryas, Lac ⊜	206	46.44 N	73.05 W
Bryce Canyon National Park ♦	200	37.29 N	112.12 W
Bryher I	42a	49.57 N	6.20 W
Brykalansk	24	65.30 N	54.12 E
Brykovka	80	52.32 N	48.35 E
Bryli	76	53.54 N	30.33 E
Brymbo	44	53.06 N	3.04 W
Bryn	262	53.30 N	2.39 W
Brynamman	42	51.49 N	3.52 W
Bryn Athyn	285	40.08 N	75.04 W
Bryn Brawd ∧[2]	42	52.09 N	3.54 W
Bryncethin	42	51.33 N	3.34 W
Bryne	26	58.44 N	5.39 E
Brynford	262	53.16 N	3.14 W
Bryn Gates	262	53.30 N	2.37 W
Bryn'kovskaja	78	46.02 N	38.35 E
Brynmawr, Wales, U.K.	42	51.49 N	3.11 W
Bryn Mawr, Ca., U.S.	228	34.03 N	117.14 W
Bryn Mawr, Pa., U.S.	208	40.01 N	75.18 W
Bryn Mawr College ʊ[2]	285	40.02 N	75.19 W
Bryrup	41	56.01 N	9.31 E
Bryson, P.Q., Can.	188	45.41 N	76.37 W
Bryson, Tx., U.S.	196	33.10 N	98.23 W
Bryson City	192	35.25 N	83.26 W
Bryte	226	38.36 N	121.33 W
Brza Palanka	38	44.28 N	22.27 E
Brzeg	30	50.52 N	17.27 E
Brześć Kujawski	30	52.37 N	18.55 E
Brześć nad Bugiem → Brest	76	52.06 N	23.42 E
Brzesko	30	49.59 N	20.36 E
Brzeszcze	30	49.59 N	19.08 E
Brzeziny	30	51.48 N	19.46 E
Brzozów	30	49.42 N	22.02 E
Bsharrī	130	34.15 N	36.01 E
Bua ≃	154	12.42 S	34.13 E
Bu'aale	144	1.05 N	42.35 E
Buada Lagoon ⊂	174b	0.31 S	166.55 E
Buad Island I	116	11.40 N	124.51 E
Buagan ≃	269e	6.17 S	106.55 E
Buala	175e	8.08 S	159.35 E
Bū al-Ḥīdān, Wādī V	146	27.25 N	19.22 E
Buangor, Mount ∧	169	37.18 S	143.13 E
Buapinang	112	4.46 S	121.34 E
Buariki	174t	1.36 N	172.58 E
Buatan	114	0.44 N	101.51 E
Bua Yai	110	15.35 N	102.25 E
Buayan ≃	116	6.06 N	125.14 E
Bu'ayrāt al-Ḥasūn	146	31.24 N	15.44 E
Buba	150	11.36 N	14.55 W
Bubai	268	35.40 N	139.29 E
Bū Bānī, Jabal ∧	140	22.38 N	25.00 E
Bubanza	154	3.06 S	29.23 E
Bubaque	150	11.17 N	15.50 W
Bubendorf	58	47.27 N	7.44 E
Bubia	164	6.40 S	146.55 E
Būbiyān I	128	29.45 N	48.15 E
Bubu ≃	154	6.03 S	35.19 E
Bubu, Gunong ∧	114	4.42 N	100.47 E
Bubuan Island I, Pil.	116	6.21 N	121.58 E
Bubuan Island I, Pil.	116	6.11 N	120.58 E
Bubuduo	120	30.06 N	84.38 E
Buburu	152	1.26 N	18.03 E
Bubye ≃	154	22.20 S	31.07 E
Buc	261	48.46 N	2.08 E
Bučač	78	49.04 N	25.23 E
Bucak	130	37.28 N	30.36 E
Bucakkışla	130	36.57 N	33.02 E
Bucaramanga	246	7.08 N	73.09 W
Bucarest → București	38	44.26 N	26.06 E
Bucas Grande Island I	116	9.40 N	125.57 E
Buccaneer Archipelago II	160	16.17 S	123.20 E
Buccheri	70	37.08 N	14.51 E
Bucchianico	66	42.18 N	14.11 E
Buccinasco	266b	45.24 N	9.07 E
Buccino	68	40.37 N	15.23 E
Buccurale	144	4.31 N	42.01 E
Bucelas	266c	38.54 N	9.07 W
Bucelas ∧[2]	266c	38.53 N	9.07 W
Buch ⊸[8]	264a	52.38 N	13.30 E
Buchanan, Arg.	258	34.58 S	58.13 W
Buchanan, Sk., Can.	184	51.43 N	102.45 W
Buchanan, Liber.	150	5.57 N	10.02 W
Buchanan, Ga., U.S.	192	33.48 N	85.11 W
Buchanan, Mi., U.S.	216	41.49 N	86.21 W
Buchanan, N.Y., U.S.	210	41.16 N	73.56 W
Buchanan, Va., U.S.	192	37.31 N	79.40 W
Buchanan, Lake ⊜	166	21.28 S	145.52 E
Buchanan, Lake ⊜[1]	196	30.48 N	98.25 W
Buchanan Creek ≃	162	19.11 S	136.16 E
Buchanan Field ⊠	282	37.59 N	122.03 W
Buchanan Hills ⋏[2]	162	18.53 S	131.02 E
Buchan Ness ≻	46	57.28 N	1.45 W
Buchans	186	48.49 N	56.52 W
Buchara	128	39.48 N	64.25 E
Buchara □[8]	128	40.00 N	64.00 E
Bucharest → București	38	44.26 N	26.06 E
Buchbach	60	48.19 N	12.17 E
Buchelay	261	48.59 N	1.40 E
Büchen, Dtsch.	52	53.29 N	10.36 E
Buchen, Dtsch.	56	49.32 N	9.17 E
Buchenberg	58	47.42 N	10.14 E
Büchenbeuren	56	49.55 N	7.16 E
Buchenwald-Denkmal ⊥	54	51.01 N	11.15 E
Buchholz, Dtsch.	54	52.10 N	12.55 E
Buchholz, Dtsch.	56	50.41 N	7.23 E
Buchholz, Dtsch.	263	51.23 N	7.15 E
Buchholz, Dtsch.	264a	52.35 N	13.47 E
Buchholz ⊸[8], Dtsch.	263	51.23 N	6.46 E
Buchholz ⊸[8], Dtsch.	264a	52.36 N	13.26 E
Buchholz in der Nordheide	52	53.20 N	9.52 E
Büchlberg	60	48.40 N	13.30 E
Buchloe	58	48.02 N	10.44 E
Bucholt	263	51.39 N	6.43 E
Buchon, Point ≻	226	35.15 N	120.54 W
Buchow-Karpzow	264a	52.31 N	12.57 E
Buchs, Schw.	58	47.23 N	8.04 E
Buchs, Schw.	58	47.10 N	9.28 E
Buchufontein	158	30.18 S	19.36 E
Buchy	50	49.35 N	1.22 E
Bučina	60	48.58 N	13.36 E
Bucine	66	43.29 N	11.37 E
Buck, Lake ⊜	162	19.38 S	130.21 E
Buckatunna	194	31.32 N	88.31 W
Buckatunna Creek ≃	194	31.30 N	88.32 W
Buck Branch ≃	284b	39.01 N	77.10 W
Buck Creek	216	40.29 N	86.46 W
Buck Creek ≃, U.S.	196	34.35 N	99.58 W
Buck Creek ≃, In., U.S.	218	39.37 N	85.56 W
Buck Creek ≃, In., U.S.	218	40.11 N	85.30 W
Buck Creek ≃, Ky., U.S.	192	36.59 N	84.29 W
Buck Creek ≃, Oh., U.S.	218	39.56 N	83.51 W
Buck Creek ≃, Pa., U.S.	285	40.15 N	74.50 W
Buckden, Eng., U.K.	42	52.17 N	0.16 W
Buckden, Eng., U.K.	44	54.12 N	2.05 W
Bückeburg	52	52.16 N	9.02 E
Bücken	52	52.46 N	9.07 E

	English	Deutsch	Español	Français	Português
≃	River	Fluß	Río	Rivière	Rio
	Canal	Kanal	Canal	Canal	Canal
	Waterfall, Rapids	Wasserfall, Stromschnellen	Cascada, Rápidos	Chute d'eau, Rapides	Cascata, Rápidos
⩌	Strait	Meeresstraße	Estrecho	Détroit	Estreito
⊂	Bay, Gulf	Bucht, Golf	Bahía, Golfo	Baie, Golfe	Baía, Golfo
⊜	Lake, Lakes	See, Seen	Lago, Lagos	Lac, Lacs	Lago, Lagos
	Swamp	Sumpf	Pantano	Marais	Pântano
⫠	Ice Features, Glacier	Eis- und Gletscherformen	Accidentes Glaciales	Formes glaciaires	Acidentes glaciares
⫪	Other Hydrographic Features	Andere Hydrographische Objekte	Otros Elementos Hidrográficos	Autres données hydrographiques	Outros acidentes hidrográficos
✣	Submarine Features	Untermeerische Objekte	Accidentes Submarinos	Formes de relief sous-marin	Acidentes submarinos
□	Political Unit	Politische Einheit	Unidad Política	Entité politique	Unidade política
ʊ	Cultural Institution	Kulturelle Institution	Institución Cultural	Institution culturelle	Instituição cultural
⊥	Historical Site	Historische Stätte	Sitio Histórico	Site historique	Sítio histórico
♦	Recreational Site	Erholungs- und Ferienort	Sitio de Recreo	Centre de loisirs	Área de Lazer
⊠	Airport	Flughafen	Aeropuerto	Aéroport	Aeroporto
■	Military Installation	Militäranlage	Instalación Militar	Installation militaire	Instalação militar
⊸	Miscellaneous	Verschiedenes	Misceláneo	Divers	Diversos

ENGLISH / DEUTSCH

Name	Page / Seite	Lat.°′ / Breite°′	Long.°′ / Länge°′ E = Ost
Buckeye	200	33.22 N	112.34 W
Buckeye Creek ≃	226	38.54 N	121.55 W
Buckeye Lake	188	39.56 N	82.28 W
Buckeystown	208	39.20 N	77.25 W
Buckfastleigh	42	50.29 N	3.46 W
Buckhannon	188	38.59 N	80.13 W
Buckhaven	46	56.11 N	3.03 W
Buck Hill Falls	210	41.11 N	75.15 W
Buck Hollow ≃	224	45.10 N	120.50 W
Buckholts	222	30.52 N	97.08 W
Buckhorn ≃	180	66.13 N	161.10 W
Buckhorn Draw V	196	30.39 N	100.52 W
Buckhorn Island State Park ♠	284a	43.03 N	78.59 W
Buckhorn Lake ⊜, On., Can.	212	44.28 N	78.23 W
Buckhorn Lake ⊜, Ca., U.S.	228	34.50 N	117.59 W
Buckie	46	57.40 N	2.58 W
Buckingham, Austl.	168a	33.24 S	116.19 E
Buckingham, P.Q., Can.	188	45.35 N	75.25 W
Buckingham, Eng., U.K.	42	52.00 N	1.00 W
Buckingham, Pa., U.S.	208	40.18 N	75.01 W
Buckingham, Va., U.S.	192	37.32 N	78.37 W
Buckingham Bay ⊂	164	12.10 S	135.46 E
Buckingham Palace Ʊ	260	51.30 N	0.08 W
Buckinghamshire □[6]	42	51.45 N	0.48 W
Buck Island I	241n	17.48 N	64.37 W
Buck Island Reef National Monument ♠	241n	17.48 N	64.37 W
Buck Lake ⊜, Ab., Can.	182	53.00 N	114.45 W
Buck Lake ⊜, On., Can.	212	45.25 N	79.24 W
Buckland, Austl.	166	42.37 S	147.43 E
Buckland, Eng., U.K.	260	51.15 N	0.15 W
Buckland, Ak., U.S.	180	65.59 N	161.07 W
Buckland, Ma., U.S.	207	42.35 N	72.47 W
Buckland, Oh., U.S.	216	40.37 N	84.16 W
Buckland Brewer	42	50.57 N	4.14 W
Buckland Common	260	51.45 N	0.39 W
Bucklands	158	29.03 S	23.44 E
Buckleboo	166	32.55 S	136.12 E
Buckley, Wales, U.K.	44	53.09 N	3.04 W
Buckley, Il., U.S.	216	40.36 N	88.02 W
Buckley, Wa., U.S.	224	47.09 N	122.01 W
Buckley ≃	166	20.22 S	137.57 E
Buckley Bay ⊂	9	68.16 S	148.12 E
Bucklin, Ks., U.S.	198	37.32 N	99.38 W
Bucklin, Mo., U.S.	194	39.46 N	92.53 W
Buck Lodge	284c	39.01 N	76.58 W
Buck Mountain ∧, Va., U.S.	192	36.40 N	81.15 W
Buck Mountain ∧, Wa., U.S.	202	48.26 N	119.50 W
Bucknell Heights	284c	38.46 N	77.04 W
Bucknell Manor	208	38.46 N	77.04 W
Buckner	218	38.23 N	85.26 W
Buckner Creek ≃	198	38.11 N	99.34 W
Buckners Creek ≃	222	29.53 N	96.53 W
Buckow	54	52.34 N	14.04 E
Buckow ◆[8]	264a	52.25 N	13.26 E
Bucks □[6]	208	40.19 N	75.08 W
Bucksburn	46	57.12 N	2.18 W
Buckshot Lake ⊜	212	45.00 N	77.04 W
Buckskin Creek ≃	218	39.14 N	83.17 W
Buckskin Gulch V	200	37.01 N	111.52 W
Bucks Knob ∧	224	46.41 N	123.20 W
Bucksport	188	44.34 N	68.47 W
Bucktown	285	40.10 N	75.43 W
Bückwitz	54	52.52 N	12.29 E
Buc-Louis-Blériot, Aérodrome de ⊠	261	48.45 N	2.05 E
Bučmany	78	51.04 N	28.04 E
Bucoda	224	46.47 N	122.52 W
Buco Zau	152	4.46 S	12.33 E
Bucquoy	50	50.08 N	2.42 E
Buctouche	186	46.28 N	64.43 W
Bucun	98	36.37 N	117.27 E
București (Bucharest)	38	44.26 N	26.06 E
Bucutua Island I	116	6.09 N	121.49 E
Bucy-lès-Pierrepont	50	49.39 N	3.54 E
Bucyrus	214	40.48 N	82.58 W
Bud	26	62.55 N	6.55 E
Buda, Il., U.S.	190	41.19 N	89.40 W
Buda, Tx., U.S.	196	30.05 N	97.51 W
Buda ◆[8]	264c	47.30 N	19.02 E
Buda Castle ⊥	264c	47.30 N	19.02 E
Budafok ◆[8]	264c	47.26 N	19.02 E
Budagovo	88	54.38 N	100.08 E
Budai-hegység ⋏	264c	47.31 N	18.58 E
Budakalász	264c	47.37 N	19.03 E
Budakeszi	264c	47.31 N	18.56 E
Buda-Kosel'ovo	76	52.43 N	30.34 E
Budalin	110	22.22 N	95.08 E
Budaörs	264c	47.27 N	18.58 E
Budapest, Magy.	30	47.30 N	19.05 E
Budapest, Magy.	264c	47.30 N	19.05 E
Budapest □[7]	264c	47.30 N	19.05 E
Búđardalur	24a	65.10 N	21.42 W
Budarin	80	47.54 N	42.36 E
Budarino	80	50.31 N	51.04 E
Budatétény ◆[8]	264c	47.25 N	19.01 E
Budaun	124	28.03 N	79.07 E
Budawang National Park ♠	170	35.26 S	150.02 E
Budawang Range ⋏	170	35.20 S	150.03 E
Budayuan	98	40.56 N	125.19 E
Budberg	263	51.32 N	6.38 E
Budbud	144	4.11 N	46.28 E
Budd Coast ±[2]	9	66.30 S	113.00 E
Buddh Gaya → Bodh Gaya	124	24.42 N	84.59 E
Budd Inlet ⊂	224	47.06 N	122.54 W
Budd Lake	210	40.52 N	74.44 W
Buddtown	285	39.56 N	74.42 W
Buddu	140	11.54 N	24.08 E
Buddusò	71	40.35 N	9.15 E
Bude, Eng., U.K.	42	50.50 N	4.33 W
Bude, Ms., U.S.	194	31.27 N	90.51 W
Bude Bay ⊂	42	50.50 N	4.37 W
Budel	52	51.17 N	5.35 E
Budelli, Isola I	71	41.17 N	9.21 E
Büdelsdorf	41	54.18 N	9.40 E
Büderich	52	51.37 N	6.34 E
Buderus	263	51.33 N	7.38 E
Budești	38	44.14 N	26.28 E
Budge Budge	126	22.27 N	88.10 E
Budhāthum	124	28.04 N	84.50 E
Budhhāta	126	22.36 N	89.10 E
Budhī Gandakī ≃	124	27.48 N	84.45 E
Budhlāda	123	29.56 N	75.34 E
Budi	152	3.04 S	23.56 E
Büdingen	56	50.17 N	9.07 E
Búđir	24a	64.56 N	13.58 W
Budišov nad Budišovkou	30	49.47 N	17.38 E
Budjala	152	2.39 N	19.42 E
Budkov	61	49.03 N	15.39 E
Budleigh Salterton	42	50.38 N	3.20 W
Budogošč'	76	59.17 N	32.27 E
Budogovišči	76	53.36 N	36.18 E
Budoni	71	40.43 N	9.42 E
Bud'onnovka	80	50.52 N	52.48 E
Bud'onnovsk	84	44.46 N	44.09 E
Bud'onnovskaja	80	46.56 N	41.33 E
Bud'onnyj, Kyrg.	85	42.30 N	72.35 E
Bud'onnyj, Ross.	83	47.27 N	39.46 E
Budrio	64	44.32 N	11.32 E
Budslav	76	54.47 N	27.27 E
Budweis → České Budějovice	30	48.59 N	14.28 E
Budworth Mere ⊜	262	53.17 N	2.31 W
Budy	78	49.53 N	36.02 E
Budylka	78	50.30 N	34.26 E
Budyně nad Ohří	54	50.22 N	14.09 E
Budžak ⋏[1]	78	46.10 N	29.00 E
Buea	152	4.09 N	9.14 E
Buëch ≃	62	44.12 N	5.57 E
Buechel	218	38.11 N	85.39 W
Buehl Airport ⊠	285	40.11 N	74.54 W
Bueil	50	48.56 N	1.27 E
Buela	152	5.55 S	14.33 E
Buell	219	39.02 N	91.27 W
Bue Marino, Grotta del ±[5]	71	40.15 N	9.38 E
Buena	208	39.30 N	74.55 W
Buena Esperanza	252	34.45 S	65.15 W
Buena Esperanza, Cabo de → Good Hope, Cape of >	158	34.24 S	18.30 E
Buena Park, Ca., U.S.	228	33.52 N	117.59 W
Buena Park, Wi., U.S.	216	42.48 N	88.14 W
Buenaventura, Col.	246	3.53 N	77.04 W
Buenaventura, Méx.	232	29.51 N	107.29 W
Buena Vista, Bol.	248	17.27 S	63.40 W
Buena Vista, Méx.	204	32.32 N	116.44 W
Buenavista, Méx.	234	22.36 N	100.09 W
Buena Vista, Para.	252	26.08 S	56.03 W
Buenavista, Pil.	116	8.59 N	125.24 E
Buenavista, Pil.	116	13.15 N	121.57 E
Buenavista, Pil.	116	10.04 N	118.49 E
Buenavista, Pil.	116	7.15 N	122.16 E
Buena Vista, Co., U.S.	200	38.50 N	106.07 W
Buena Vista, Fl., U.S.	220	28.11 N	82.44 W
Buena Vista, Ga., U.S.	192	32.19 N	84.31 W
Buena Vista, Md., U.S.	284c	38.57 N	76.50 W
Buena Vista, Ms., U.S.	194	33.53 N	88.50 W
Buena Vista, Pa., U.S.	279b	40.17 N	79.48 W
Buena Vista, Va., U.S.	192	37.44 N	79.21 W
Buena Vista, Bahía de ⊂	240p	22.30 N	79.08 W
Buena Vista Canal ≅	228	35.21 N	119.06 W
Buenavista de Cuéllar	234	18.27 N	99.25 W
Buena Vista Lake Bed ⊜	204	35.11 N	119.17 W
Buenavista Tomatlán	234	19.12 N	102.36 W
Buen Día	196	26.21 N	104.32 W
Buendia, Embalse de ⊜[1]	34	40.25 N	2.43 W
Buenga ≃	152	6.07 S	15.58 E
Bueno ≃	254	40.13 S	73.43 W
Bueno Brandão	256	22.27 S	46.21 W
Buenópolis	255	17.54 S	44.11 W
Buenos Aires, Arg.	258	34.36 S	58.27 W
Buenos Aires, Arg.	288	34.36 S	58.27 W
Buenos Aires, Col.	246	3.02 N	76.38 W
Buenos Aires, C.R.	236	9.10 N	83.20 W
Buenos Aires □[4]	252	36.00 S	60.00 W
Buenos Aires, Lago (Lago General Carrera) ⊜	254	46.35 S	72.00 W
Buen Pasto	254	45.05 S	69.28 W
Buer ◆[8]	263	51.36 N	7.03 E
Buerarema	255	14.57 S	39.19 W
Buerāt, Bi'r ⊤[4]	142	28.59 N	32.10 E
Buertuokai	85	39.35 N	74.58 E
Buesaco	246	1.23 N	77.09 W
Buescher State Park ♠	222	30.02 N	97.09 W
Buet, Le ∧	58	46.02 N	6.52 E
Buey ≃	240p	20.28 N	77.05 W
Bufalotta, Fosso della ≃	267a	41.59 N	12.30 E
Buffalo, Il., U.S.	219	39.51 N	89.25 W
Buffalo, In., U.S.	216	40.53 N	86.45 W
Buffalo, Ks., U.S.	198	37.42 N	95.41 W
Buffalo, Mn., U.S.	190	45.10 N	93.52 W
Buffalo, Mo., U.S.	194	37.38 N	93.05 W
Buffalo, N.Y., U.S.	210	42.53 N	78.52 W
Buffalo, N.Y., U.S.	284a	42.53 N	78.52 W
Buffalo, Oh., U.S.	188	39.54 N	81.31 W
Buffalo, Ok., U.S.	196	36.50 N	99.37 W
Buffalo, S.C., U.S.	192	34.43 N	81.41 W
Buffalo, S.D., U.S.	198	45.35 N	103.32 W
Buffalo, Tx., U.S.	222	31.28 N	96.04 W
Buffalo, Wy., U.S.	202	44.20 N	106.41 W
Buffalo ≃, Can.	176	60.55 N	115.00 W
Buffalo ≃, S. Afr.	158	28.43 S	30.37 E
Buffalo ≃, Ar., U.S.	194	36.10 N	92.26 W
Buffalo ≃, Mn., U.S.	198	47.06 N	96.49 W
Buffalo ≃, Ms., U.S.	194	31.04 N	91.34 W
Buffalo ≃, N.Y., U.S.	284a	42.53 N	78.53 W
Buffalo ≃, Tn., U.S.	194	36.00 N	87.50 W
Buffalo ≃, Wi., U.S.	190	44.22 N	91.55 W
Buffalo, State University College at Ʊ[2]	284a	42.56 N	78.53 W
Buffalo Airpark ⊠	284a	42.52 N	78.43 W
Buffalo Bayou ≃	222	29.46 N	95.05 W
Buffalo Bill Ranch State Historical Park ♠	198	41.10 N	100.48 W
Buffalo Bill Reservoir ⊜[1]	202	44.29 N	109.13 W
Buffalo Bill State Park ♠	202	44.30 N	109.14 W
Buffalo Center	190	43.23 N	93.56 W
Buffalo Coast Guard Base ■	284a	42.52 N	78.54 W
Buffalo Creek ≃, U.S.	198	45.57 N	102.56 W
Buffalo Creek ≃, U.S.	214	40.16 N	80.37 W
Buffalo Creek ≃, Il., U.S.	278	42.08 N	87.55 W
Buffalo Creek ≃, Ia., U.S.	190	42.06 N	91.18 W
Buffalo Creek ≃, Ks., U.S.	198	39.35 N	97.43 W
Buffalo Creek ≃, Ky., U.S.	218	38.28 N	83.03 W
Buffalo Creek ≃, Mn., U.S.	198	44.51 N	94.00 W
Buffalo Creek ≃, N.Y., U.S.	210	42.52 N	78.47 W
Buffalo Creek ≃, Ok., U.S.	196	36.47 N	99.15 W
Buffalo Creek ≃, Pa., U.S.	208	40.29 N	77.08 W
Buffalo Creek ≃, Pa., U.S.	210	40.58 N	76.53 W
Buffalo Creek ≃, Pa., U.S.	214	40.40 N	79.41 W
Buffalo Grove	216	42.09 N	87.57 W
Buffalo Harbor ⊂	284a	42.51 N	78.52 W
Buffalo Lake	198	44.44 N	94.37 W
Buffalo Lake ⊜, Ab., Can.	182	52.27 N	112.54 W
Buffalo Lake ⊜, N.T., Can.	176	60.10 N	115.30 W
Buffalo Lake ⊜[1]	196	34.54 N	102.07 W
Buffalo Museum of Science Ʊ	284a	42.54 N	78.51 W
Buffalo Narrows	184	55.51 N	108.30 W
Buffalo National River ♠	194	35.58 N	92.53 W
Buffalo Pound Lake ⊜	184	50.39 N	105.30 W
Buffalo Pound Provincial Park ♠	184	50.36 N	105.30 W
Buffalo Run ≃	279b	40.12 N	79.37 W
Buffalo Zoo ♠	284a	42.56 N	78.51 W
Buffels ≃, S. Afr.	156	29.41 S	17.03 E
Buffels ≃, S. Afr.	158	33.45 S	21.11 E
Buffington Harbor ⊂	278	41.38 N	87.25 W
Buffum, Lake ⊜	220	27.48 N	81.40 W
Buford, Ga., U.S.	192	34.07 N	84.00 W
Buford, Oh., U.S.	218	39.04 N	83.50 W
Buford Dam ◆[6]	192	34.11 N	84.03 W
Buftea	38	44.34 N	25.57 E
Bug ≃	22	52.31 N	21.05 E
Buga, Col.	246	3.54 N	76.17 W
Buga, Nig.	150	8.30 N	7.21 E
Bugajevka, Ross.	83	49.39 N	39.42 E
Bugajevka, Ukr.	83	48.25 N	38.53 E
Bugajevka, Ukr.	83	49.28 N	37.23 E
Bugalagrande	246	4.11 N	76.09 W
Bugala Island I	154	0.40 S	32.20 E
Bugallon	116	15.57 N	120.13 E
Buganga	154	0.03 S	31.59 E
Bugasong	116	11.03 N	122.04 E
Bugat, Mong.	86	48.59 N	90.10 E
Bugat, Mong.	88	47.55 N	101.16 E
Bugbrooke	42	52.12 N	1.01 W
Bug Catooti	144	10.44 N	50.35 E
Buğdaylı	130	40.13 N	27.46 E
Bugeat	32	45.35 N	1.59 E
Bugel, Ujung >	115a	6.26 S	111.03 E
Bugene	154	1.35 S	31.08 E
Bugey ◆[1]	58	45.55 N	5.30 E
Buggenhout	50	51.01 N	4.12 E
Buggerru	71	39.24 N	8.24 E
Bugio I	266c	38.39 N	9.18 W
Bugiri	154	0.34 N	33.45 E
Bugle	42	50.24 N	4.47 W
Bug Méridional → Južnyj Bug ≃	78	46.59 N	31.58 E
Bugojno	36	44.03 N	17.27 E
Bugøynes	24	69.58 N	29.39 E
Bugrino	24	68.48 N	49.09 E
Bugry, Ross.	76	58.46 N	35.15 E
Bugry, Ross.	265a	60.04 N	30.24 E
Bugsanga ≃	116	12.26 N	120.59 E
Bugsuk Island I	116	8.15 N	117.18 E
Bugt, Zhg.	89	48.46 N	121.57 E
Bugt, Zhg.	98	42.20 N	120.43 E
Buguba	164	3.41 S	137.30 E
Buguey	116	18.17 N	121.50 E
Bugui Point >	116	12.36 N	123.14 E
Bugul'dejka	88	52.33 N	106.05 E
Bugul'ma	80	54.33 N	52.48 E
Bugul'minsko-Belebejevskaja vozvyšennost' ⋏[1]	80	54.54 N	52.42 E
Bugun' ≃	85	42.58 N	68.35 E
Bugun'skoje vodochranilišče ⊜[1]	85	42.45 N	69.05 E
Buguruslan	80	53.39 N	52.26 E
Buh ≃	102	36.58 N	99.48 E
Buhanhua	104	42.39 N	122.46 E
Bū Hashīshah, Thamad ⊤[4]	146	26.23 N	18.47 E
Buhayrah, Rayyāh al- ≅	142	30.43 N	30.45 E
Buhaythān, Jabal al- ∧	132	30.55 N	35.53 E
Buhera	154	19.18 S	31.29 E
Buhi	116	13.26 N	123.31 E
Buhi, Lake ⊜	116	13.26 N	123.31 E
Bühl, Dtsch.	56	48.42 N	8.08 E
Buhl, Fr.	58	47.56 N	7.11 E
Buhl, Id., U.S.	202	42.35 N	114.45 W
Buhl, Mn., U.S.	190	47.29 N	92.46 W
Buhler	198	38.08 N	97.46 W
Bühler ≃	56	49.10 N	9.47 E
Bühlertal	56	48.41 N	8.10 E
Buhuai	120	33.22 N	80.36 E
Buhuși	38	46.43 N	26.41 E
Bui Dam ◆[6]	150	8.22 N	2.10 W
Buie, Loch ⊂	46	56.20 N	5.52 W
Buile Hill Park ♠	262	53.29 N	2.18 W
Builth Wells	42	52.09 N	3.24 W
Buin, Chile	252	33.44 S	70.45 W
Buin, Pap. N. Gui.	175e	6.50 S	155.44 E
Buin, Piz ∧	58	46.50 N	10.08 E
Buinen	52	52.55 N	6.50 E
Buinsk, Ross.	80	55.12 N	47.03 E
Buinsk, Ross.	80	54.57 N	48.17 E
Buíque	250	8.37 S	37.09 W
Buis-les-Baronnies	62	44.16 N	5.16 E
Buitenpost	52	53.15 N	6.09 E
Buj	80	58.30 N	41.30 E
Buj ≃	80	56.13 N	54.12 E
Bujaki	24	59.03 N	48.40 E
Bujalance	34	37.54 N	4.22 W
Bujant, Mong.	86	48.33 N	89.34 E
Bujant, Mong.	86	48.10 N	91.55 E
Bujant ≃	88	47.08 N	97.38 E
Bujant-Ovoo	102	44.58 N	107.05 E
Bujaraloz	34	41.30 N	0.09 W
Buje	36	45.24 N	13.40 E
Buji	102	33.58 N	95.22 E
Bujnaksk	84	42.49 N	47.07 E
Bujnoviči	78	51.52 N	28.33 E
Bujr nuur ⊜	88	47.48 N	117.42 E
Bujukly	89	49.30 N	142.47 E
Bujumbura	154	3.23 S	29.22 E
Bük, Magy.	61	47.23 N	16.45 E
Buk, Pol.	30	52.22 N	16.31 E
Buka	85	40.48 N	69.11 E
Bukačača	88	52.59 N	116.55 E
Bukačevcy	78	49.15 N	24.29 E
Buka Island I	175e	5.15 S	154.35 E
Bukama	154	9.12 S	25.51 E
Būkān, Īrān	128	36.31 N	46.12 E
Bukan', Ross.	76	53.55 N	34.42 E
Bukanovskaja	80	49.42 N	42.18 E
Buka Passage)(	175e	5.25 S	154.41 E
Bukarest → București	38	44.26 N	26.06 E
Bukarevo	82	55.57 N	36.44 E
Bukavu	154	2.30 S	28.52 E
Bukene	154	4.14 S	32.53 E
Bukhara → Buchara	128	39.48 N	64.25 E
Bukhayt, Bi'r ⊤[4]	142	29.13 N	32.17 E
Bukide, Pulau I	112	3.47 N	125.36 E
Bukidnon □[4]	116	8.00 N	125.00 E
Bukima	154	1.48 S	33.25 E
Bukit Baharu	114	2.13 N	102.16 E
Bukitbatu	114	1.27 N	102.00 E
Bukit Betong	114	4.15 N	101.56 E
Bukit Fraser	114	3.43 N	101.45 E
Bukit Kachi	114	6.24 N	100.32 E
Bukit Mandai	271c	1.25 N	103.45 E
Bukit Mertajam	114	5.22 N	100.28 E
Bukit Panjang	271c	1.23 N	103.46 E
Bukit Serok	114	2.55 N	102.50 E
Bukit Timah	271c	1.20 N	103.47 E
Bukit Timah Race Course ♠	271c	1.20 N	103.48 E
Bukittinggi	112	0.19 S	100.22 E
Bükk ⋏	30	48.05 N	20.30 E
Bukoba	154	1.20 S	31.49 E
Bukombe	154	3.31 S	32.03 E
Bukovica ◆[1]	36	44.10 N	15.40 E
Bukovina □[9]	78	48.00 N	25.30 E
Bukrino	82	54.48 N	36.14 E
Bukuka	88	51.11 N	116.39 E
Bukukun	88	49.27 N	111.08 E
Bukum, Pulau I	271c	1.14 N	103.47 E
Bukumbirwa	154	0.46 S	28.44 E
Bukum Kechil, Pulau I	271c	1.14 N	103.46 E
Bukunga	154	7.41 S	25.56 E
Bukuru	150	9.48 N	8.51 E
Bukuya	154	0.41 N	31.50 E
Bula	164	3.06 S	130.30 E
Bula ≃	80	55.12 N	48.23 E
Bula Atumba	152	8.40 S	14.48 E
Bulacan □[4]	116	15.00 N	121.05 E
Bulacaue Point >	116	11.36 N	123.09 E
Bülach	58	47.31 N	8.32 E
Bulajevo	86	54.54 N	70.26 E
Bulak	88	51.02 N	115.21 E
Bulaka ≃	164	8.06 S	139.12 E
Bulak Gölü ⊜	130	38.32 N	32.55 E
Bulalacao	116	12.20 N	121.20 E
Bulalacao Island I	116	11.45 N	120.10 E
Bulalaqui Point >	116	11.17 N	124.03 E
Bulan, Pil.	116	12.40 N	123.52 E
Bulan, Pil.	116	6.44 N	124.47 E
Bulan, Ky., U.S.	192	37.18 N	83.09 W
Bulanaš	86	57.16 N	62.00 E
Bulancak	130	40.57 N	38.14 E
Bulandshahr	124	28.24 N	77.51 E
Bulanicha	86	52.48 N	84.57 E
Bulanık	130	39.05 N	42.15 E
Bulan Island I	116	6.08 N	121.50 E
Bulanovo	86	52.27 N	55.10 E
Būlāq	140	25.12 N	30.32 E
Būlāq ◆[8]	273c	30.04 N	31.14 E
Būlāq ad-Dakrūr	273c	30.02 N	31.11 E
Bulava	89	51.55 N	140.25 E
Bulavinovka	83	49.25 N	38.58 E
Bulawa, Gunung ∧	112	0.30 N	123.34 E
Bulawayo	154	20.09 S	28.36 E
Bulbjerg ∧[2]	26	57.09 N	9.02 E
Bulbul	130	36.46 N	36.49 E
Bulbul, Wādī V	140	10.59 N	24.33 E
Bulcherry Island I	126	21.33 N	88.31 E
Buldan	130	38.03 N	28.51 E
Buldāna	122	20.32 N	76.11 E
Buldern	52	51.52 N	7.22 E
Buldibuyo	248	8.07 S	77.22 W
Buldir Island I	181a	52.21 N	175.54 E
Buldon	116	7.33 N	124.25 E
Buldurtinskij	80	50.05 N	53.11 E
Buldyrty ≃	80	49.48 N	52.34 E
Bulembu	158	25.56 S	31.06 E
Bulga	170	32.39 S	151.01 E
Bulgakovka	83	49.11 N	38.33 E
Bulgakovo	76	55.14 N	32.08 E
Bulgan, Mong.	86	46.53 N	91.05 E
Bulgan, Mong.	88	48.45 N	103.34 E
Bulgan, Mong.	102	44.05 N	103.32 E
Bulgan □[4]	88	49.00 N	103.30 E
Bulgar	80	54.57 N	49.05 E
Bulgaria (Bâlgarija) □[1], Europe	22	43.00 N	25.00 E
Bulgaria (Bâlgarija) □[1], Europe	38	43.00 N	25.00 E
Bulgarie → Bulgaria □[1]	38	43.00 N	25.00 E
Bulgarien → Bulgaria □[1]	38	43.00 N	25.00 E
Bulger	214	40.23 N	80.20 W
Bulgnéville	58	48.13 N	5.50 E
Bulgroo	166	25.48 S	143.59 E
Bulhale	144	5.20 N	46.29 E
Buliluyan	116	8.20 N	117.12 E
Buliluyan, Cape >	116	8.20 N	117.11 E
Bulim	271c	1.22 N	103.43 E
Bulimba	171a	27.25 S	153.04 E
Bulki	144	6.10 N	36.40 E
Bulkington	42	52.29 N	1.25 W
Bulkley ≃	182	55.13 N	127.40 W
Bulkley Ranges ⋏	182	54.30 N	127.30 W
Bull ≃	182	49.28 N	115.26 W
Bullabulling	162	31.01 S	120.32 E
Bullaque ≃	34	38.59 N	4.17 W
Bullara	162	22.40 S	114.03 E
Bullard	222	32.08 N	95.19 W
Bulla Regia ⊥	36	36.34 N	8.46 E
Bullas	34	38.03 N	1.40 W
Bullaxaar	144	10.23 N	44.25 E
Bullay	56	50.03 N	7.08 E
Bull Creek ≃, Nv., U.S.	204	38.43 N	115.34 W
Bull Creek ≃, N.Y., U.S.	284a	43.03 N	78.50 W
Bull Creek ≃, Oh., U.S.	214	40.42 N	80.32 W
Bull Creek ≃, S.D., U.S.	198	43.41 N	99.28 W
Bull Creek ≃, S.D., U.S.	198	45.40 N	103.18 W
Bull Creek ≃, Tx., U.S.	196	32.36 N	101.10 W
Bulldog	164	7.45 S	146.25 E
Bulle	58	46.37 N	7.04 E
Buller ≃	172	41.44 S	171.35 E
Buller, Mount ∧	169	37.09 S	146.26 E
Bullfinch	162	30.59 S	119.06 E
Bullfrog Creek ≃	200	37.19 N	110.44 W
Bull Harbour	182	50.54 N	127.55 W
Bullhead	198	45.45 N	101.04 W
Bullhead City	204	35.08 N	114.34 W
Bull Hide Creek ≃	222	31.23 N	97.01 W
Bull Hill ∧[2]	262	53.40 N	2.21 W
Bulli	170	34.20 S	150.55 E
Bullicame ♠	66	42.22 N	12.04 E
Büllingen	56	50.25 N	6.16 E
Bullioh	171b	36.12 S	147.20 E
Bullion	261	48.37 N	2.00 E
Bull Lake ⊜[1]	202	43.11 N	109.07 W
Bull Lake Creek ≃	202	43.14 N	109.02 W
Bull Mountain ∧	202	46.05 N	112.04 W
Bullock	192	36.30 N	78.33 W
Bullock Creek	166	17.43 S	144.31 E
Bullock Creek ≃	166	21.40 S	145.09 E
Bulloo ≃	166	28.43 S	142.30 E
Bulloo Downs	166	28.31 S	142.57 E
Bulloo Lake ⊜	166	28.43 S	142.25 E
Bulloo River Overflow ≚	166	28.50 S	142.40 E
Bullpound Creek ≃	182	51.05 N	111.58 W
Bull Run ≃, Or., U.S.	224	45.26 N	122.15 W
Bull Run ≃, Va., U.S.	208	38.43 N	77.23 W
Bull Run Lake ⊜	224	45.27 N	121.50 W
Bull Run Reservoir Number 2 ⊜[1], Or., U.S.	224	45.28 N	122.10 W
Bull Run Reservoir Number 1 ⊜[1], Or., U.S.	224	45.30 N	122.04 W
Bullrun Rock ∧	202	44.21 N	118.17 W
Bulls	172	40.10 S	175.23 E
Bulls Bay ⊂	192	32.59 N	79.33 W
Bullsbrook	168a	31.40 S	116.01 E
Bulls Gap	192	36.15 N	83.05 W
Bull Shoals	194	36.23 N	92.34 W
Bull Shoals Lake ⊜[1]	194	36.30 N	92.50 W
Bullskin Creek ≃	218	38.10 N	85.19 W
Bullville	210	41.33 N	74.22 W
Bully Creek ≃	202	43.58 N	117.15 W
Bully Hill	214	41.22 N	79.50 W
Bully-les-Mines	50	50.26 N	2.43 E
Bulmke-Hüllen ◆[8]	263	51.31 N	7.06 E
Bulnaj nuruu ⋏	88	49.05 N	98.30 E
Bulnes	252	36.44 S	72.18 W
Bulo Ghedudo	144	2.52 N	43.01 E
Bulolo	164	7.10 S	146.40 E
Bulpham	260	51.33 N	0.22 E
Bulpitt	219	39.35 N	89.26 W
Bulsār	122	20.38 N	72.56 E
Bulstrode ≃	206	46.02 N	72.15 W
Bultei	71	40.27 N	9.03 E
Bultfontein	158	28.20 S	26.05 E
Buluan	116	6.44 N	124.47 E
Buluan ≃	116	6.47 N	124.47 E
Buluan, Lake ⊜	116	6.40 N	124.49 E
Buluduku	114	2.20 N	98.14 E
Bulugansk	88	52.24 N	110.23 E
Bulukumba	112	5.33 S	120.11 E
Bulukuto	152	0.12 S	21.42 E
Bululawang	115a	8.05 S	112.38 E
Bulungu, Zaïre	152	6.04 S	21.54 E
Bulungu, Zaïre	152	4.33 S	18.36 E
Bulupayung	114	1.38 N	99.11 E
Bulusan	116	12.45 N	124.08 E
Bulusan Volcano ∧	116	12.46 N	124.03 E
Bulwater	158	32.29 S	21.48 E
Bulwer	158	29.46 S	29.47 E
Bulyčevo	82	55.06 N	37.15 E
Bulyee	162	32.22 S	117.31 E
Bumba	152	2.11 N	22.28 E
Bumbah, Khalīj al- ⊂	146	32.20 N	23.10 E
Bumbire Island I	154	1.40 S	31.53 E
Bumbles Green	260	51.44 N	0.02 E
Bumbo	152	6.55 S	19.16 E
Bumbu ≃	273b	4.23 S	15.18 E
Bumbulan	112	0.29 N	122.04 E
Bumbun, Pulau I	112	4.27 N	118.40 E
Bumbuna	150	9.03 N	11.44 W
Bumbunga Lake ⊜	168b	33.54 S	138.11 E
Bumiayu	115a	7.15 S	109.00 E
Bumijawa	115a	7.10 S	109.07 E
Bumkin Island I	283	42.17 N	70.54 W
Bumping ≃	224	46.59 N	121.06 W
Bumping Lake ⊜	224	46.52 N	121.19 W
Bumpus, Mount ∧[2]	176	69.33 N	112.40 W
Bumtang ≃	124	26.56 N	90.51 E
Bumu Hu ⊜	120	31.15 N	91.10 E
Buna, Kenya	154	2.47 N	39.31 E
Buna, Pap. N. Gui.	164	8.40 S	148.25 E
Buna, Tx., U.S.	194	30.26 N	93.58 W
Buna, Zaïre	152	3.15 S	18.59 E
Bunagāti	126	23.19 N	89.25 E
Bunai	164	2.11 S	147.14 E
Bunaj	85	38.26 N	71.32 E
Bun'atino	82	56.24 N	37.15 E
Bunavista	196	35.39 N	101.28 W
Bunawan	116	8.12 N	125.57 E
Bunazi	154	1.13 S	31.24 E
Bunbeg	48	55.03 N	8.18 W
Bunbury	168a	33.19 S	115.38 E
Bunceton	194	38.47 N	92.47 W
Bunclody	48	52.38 N	6.40 W
Buncrana	48	55.08 N	7.27 W
Bundaberg	166	24.52 S	152.21 E
Bundanoon	170	34.39 S	150.18 E
Bundarra	166	30.10 S	151.05 E
Bunde, Dtsch.	52	53.11 N	7.16 E
Bünde, Dtsch.	52	52.12 N	8.35 E
Bunde, Ned.	56	50.54 N	5.45 E
Bundeena	274a	34.05 S	151.09 E
Bundenthal	56	49.06 N	7.48 E
Bundey ≃	162	21.46 S	135.37 E
Bündheim	54	51.53 N	10.32 E
Būndi, India	120	25.27 N	75.39 E
Bundi, Pap. N. Gui.	164	5.40 S	145.15 E
Bundick Creek ≃	194	30.36 N	92.57 W
Bundoora	274b	37.42 S	145.04 E
Bundoran	48	54.28 N	8.17 W
Būndu, India	124	23.11 N	85.35 E
Bundu, S. Afr.	158	29.45 S	22.02 E
Bunduqiyah	154	5.06 N	30.53 E
Bund'ur	86	57.32 N	82.01 E
Buner □[9]	123	34.35 N	72.35 E
Bunessan	46	56.19 N	6.14 W
Bunga	150	11.04 N	9.38 E
Bunga ≃	150	11.23 N	9.56 E
Bungamas	112	3.42 S	102.23 E
Bungay	42	52.28 N	1.26 E
Bungbulang	115a	7.27 S	107.35 E
Bunge	26	57.51 N	19.01 E
Bungegep	164	7.48 S	139.52 E
Bungendore	171b	35.15 S	149.27 E
Bunger Hills ⋏[2]	9	66.17 S	100.47 E
Bung Kan	110	18.23 N	103.37 E
Bungku	112	2.33 S	121.58 E
Bungo	152	7.26 S	15.23 E
Bungoma	154	0.34 N	34.34 E
Bungonia	170	34.51 S	149.57 E
Bungo-suidō)(	92	33.00 N	132.13 E
Bungo-takada	96	33.33 N	131.27 E
Bungsberg ∧[2]	54	54.12 N	10.43 E
Bungtlang	120	22.20 N	92.46 E
Bungu	154	7.38 S	39.03 E
Buni ≃	115a	7.26 S	106.47 E
Bunia	154	1.34 N	30.15 E
Bunianga	152	3.34 S	20.06 E
Būnīken, Kūh-e ∧	128	26.46 N	58.12 E
Buninyong	169	37.39 S	143.53 E
Buninyong, Mount ∧	169	37.39 S	143.56 E
Bunji	123	35.40 N	74.36 E
Bunkeflo strand	41	55.33 N	12.57 E
Bunker	194	37.27 N	91.12 W
Bunker Group II	166	23.48 S	152.20 E
Bunker Hill, Il., U.S.	219	39.02 N	89.57 W
Bunker Hill, In., U.S.	216	40.40 N	86.06 W
Bunker Hill, Or., U.S.	202	43.21 N	124.12 W
Bunker Hill, Tx., U.S.	222	29.46 N	95.32 W
Bunker Hill ∧	204	39.15 N	117.08 W
Bunker Hill Monument ⊥	283	42.22 N	71.04 W
Bunkeya	154	10.07 S	27.17 E
Bunkie	194	30.57 N	92.10 W
Bunkyō ◆[8]	268	35.43 N	139.45 E
Bunnahowen	48	54.11 N	9.54 W
Bunnell	192	29.27 N	81.15 W
Bunnik	52	52.04 N	5.12 E
Bünningstedt	52	53.41 N	10.13 E
Bunola	214	40.14 N	79.56 W
Bun Plains ≚	154	0.44 N	40.42 E
Bunratty Castle ⊥	48	52.42 N	8.48 W
Bunschoten	52	52.14 N	5.22 E
Bunsuru ≃	150	13.21 N	6.23 E
Bunta	112	0.48 S	122.10 E
Buntine	162	29.59 S	116.34 E
Buntingford	42	51.57 N	0.01 W
Buntok	112	1.42 S	114.48 E
Bununu Dass	150	10.00 N	9.31 E
Bunut	112	0.46 N	112.30 E
Bunyambili	154	2.21 S	29.25 E
Bünyan	130	38.51 N	35.52 E
Bunyip	169	38.06 S	145.43 E
Bunyip ≃	169	38.13 S	145.27 E
Bunyolo	34	39.25 N	0.47 W
Bunyrevo	82	54.34 N	37.09 E
Bunyu, Pulau I	112	3.30 N	117.50 E
Bunza	150	12.08 N	4.00 E
Buochs	58	46.58 N	8.22 E
Buol	112	1.10 N	121.26 E
Buolkalach	74	72.56 N	119.50 E
Buonalbergo	68	41.13 N	14.59 E
Buona Vista	271c	1.16 N	103.47 E
Buon Bu N'jang	110	12.06 N	107.40 E
Buonconvento	66	43.08 N	11.29 E
Buon Me Thuot	110	12.40 N	108.03 E
Buon Mrong	110	12.48 N	108.28 E
Buon Ngo	110	12.30 N	108.28 E
Buon Thach Hom	110	12.17 N	108.48 E
Buon Ya Soup	110	13.05 N	107.52 E
Buor-Chaja, guba ⊂	74	71.30 N	131.00 E
Buor-Chaja, mys >	74	71.56 N	132.40 E
Bupul	164	7.31 S	140.52 E
Buqay'āwīyah, Qā' al- ≚	132	32.03 N	37.07 E
Buqayq	128	25.56 N	49.40 E
Buqda Koosaar	144	4.31 N	44.49 E
Buqde Caqable	144	4.04 N	45.15 E
Buquira ≃	256	23.10 S	45.54 W
Buquirivu ≃	287b	23.28 S	46.28 W
Buqūm, Harrat al- ±[9]	144	20.54 N	42.00 E
Bur	88	58.47 N	107.01 E
Bura, Kenya	154	3.30 S	38.18 E
Bura, Kenya	154	1.06 S	39.57 E
Bura Gaurānga ≃[1]	126	22.00 N	90.33 E
Burakin	162	30.31 S	117.10 E
Buraly	80	55.04 N	52.52 E
Buram	140	10.49 N	25.10 E
Buran	86	48.04 N	85.15 E
Burang	120	30.16 N	81.14 E
Burangulovo	86	53.26 N	58.23 E
Buranhém ≃	255	16.27 S	39.04 W
Burankol'	86	46.14 N	54.12 E
Burannoje	86	50.59 N	54.28 E
Burano ≃	66	43.37 N	12.40 E
Burao Kibir	144	8.42 N	45.29 E
Burāq	132	33.10 N	36.29 E
Burāri ◆[8]	272a	28.46 N	77.12 E
Buras	194	29.21 N	89.31 W
Buraševo	82	56.44 N	35.52 E
Burauen	116	10.58 N	124.53 E
Burayd, Bi'r ⊤[4]	142	29.08 N	32.07 E
Buraydah	128	26.20 N	43.59 E
Burayk	146	26.33 N	13.08 E
Buraykah	132	32.50 N	36.34 E
Burbach	56	50.45 N	8.05 E
Burbage, Eng., U.K.	42	51.20 N	1.40 W
Burbage, Eng., U.K.	262	53.15 N	1.56 W
Burbank, Ca., U.S.	226	37.19 N	121.55 W
Burbank, Ca., U.S.	228	34.10 N	118.18 W
Burbank, Il., U.S.	216	41.45 N	87.45 W
Burbank, Oh., U.S.	214	40.59 N	81.59 W
Burbank, Wa., U.S.	202	46.12 N	119.00 W
Burbank Studios Ʊ[3]	280	34.09 N	118.21 W
Burbure	50	50.32 N	2.28 E
Burç	130	37.02 N	37.10 E
Burcei	71	39.21 N	9.21 E
Burcevo	82	55.02 N	38.09 E
Burcher	166	33.32 S	147.18 E
Burcin	62	45.26 N	5.26 E
Burco	144	9.31 N	45.34 E
Burda	124	25.50 N	77.35 E
Burdalyk	128	38.25 N	64.20 E
Burdekin ≃	166	19.39 S	147.30 E
Burdekin Falls L	166	20.39 S	147.09 E
Burden	198	37.18 N	96.45 W
Burdeos	116	14.51 N	121.58 E
Burdeos Bay ⊂	116	14.44 N	122.06 E
Burdeos → Bordeaux	32	44.50 N	0.34 W
Burdett, Ab., Can.	182	49.50 N	111.32 W
Burdett, Ks., U.S.	198	38.11 N	99.31 W
Burdett, N.Y., U.S.	210	42.25 N	76.50 W
Burdul	272c	19.07 N	73.07 E
Burdur	130	37.43 N	30.17 E
Burdur □[4]	130	37.30 N	30.00 E
Burdur Gölü ⊜	130	37.44 N	30.12 E
Burdwood Bank ✦[3]	18	54.15 S	59.00 W
Bure, Ityo.	144	8.15 N	35.09 E
Bure, Ityo.	144	10.47 N	37.06 E
Bure ≃	42	52.37 N	1.43 E
Bure, Pic de ∧	62	44.38 N	5.56 E
Bureå	26	64.37 N	21.12 E
Bureälven ≃	26	64.37 N	21.13 E
Bureg Changaj	88	48.14 N	103.57 E
Bureinskij chrebet ⋏	89	50.35 N	133.35 E
Bureja	89	49.52 N	129.48 E
Bureja ≃	89	49.25 N	129.35 E
Burekup	168a	33.19 S	115.49 E
Büren, Dtsch.	52	51.33 N	8.33 E
Büren, Mong.	88	47.13 N	95.54 E
Büren an der Aare	58	47.08 N	7.23 E
Büren Chaan	88	49.29 N	99.14 E
Bürengijn nuruu ⋏	88	49.15 N	104.30 E
Bures	261	48.57 N	1.58 E
Bures-sur-Yvette	261	48.42 N	2.10 E
Burey-en-Vaux	58	48.34 N	5.40 E
Burfjord	24	69.56 N	22.00 E
Burford, On., Can.	212	43.06 N	80.26 W
Burford, Eng., U.K.	42	51.49 N	1.38 W
Būr Fu'ād ◆[8]	142	31.15 N	32.19 E
Burg, Dtsch.	54	51.49 N	14.08 E
Burg, Dtsch.	54	52.16 N	11.51 E
Burg, Dtsch.	56	50.42 N	8.19 E
Burg ◆[8]	263	51.08 N	7.09 E
Burg, Schloss ⊥	263	51.08 N	7.10 E
Burga	76	58.45 N	32.29 E
Burgas	38	42.30 N	27.28 E
Burgas □[4]	130	42.10 N	27.00 E
Burgaski zaliv ⊂	38	42.30 N	27.33 E
Burgau	58	48.26 N	10.25 E
Burg [auf Fehmarn]	54	54.26 N	11.12 E
Burgaw	192	34.33 N	77.55 W
Burgaz ◆[8]	267b	40.53 N	29.03 E
Burgaz Adası I	267b	40.53 N	29.04 E
Burgbernheim	56	49.27 N	10.19 E
Burgdorf, Dtsch.	52	52.27 N	10.00 E
Burgdorf, Schw.	58	47.04 N	7.37 E
Burgebrach	56	49.50 N	10.44 E
Bürgel	54	50.56 N	11.45 E
Burgenland □[3]	61	47.30 N	16.20 E
Burgeo	186	47.37 N	57.37 W
Burgersdorp	158	31.00 S	26.20 E
Burger Township	273d	26.05 S	27.46 E
Burges, Mount ∧[2]	162	30.50 S	121.06 E
Burgess	208	37.53 N	76.21 W
Burgess Hill	42	50.57 N	0.07 W
Burgessville	212	43.01 N	80.39 W
Burgettstown	214	40.22 N	80.23 W
Burggrafenberg ∧[2]	263	51.13 N	7.07 E
Burghausen	60	48.09 N	12.49 E
Burghead	46	57.42 N	3.30 W
Burgheim	60	48.42 N	11.01 E
Burgh Heath	260	51.18 N	0.13 W
Burghill	214	41.22 N	80.34 W
Burgh le Marsh	44	53.09 N	0.15 E
Burghūth, Sabkhat al- ⊜	130	34.58 N	41.06 E
Burgin	194	37.45 N	84.46 W
Burgio	70	37.36 N	13.17 E
Burgjoss	56	50.12 N	9.29 E
Burgkirchen	60	48.12 N	13.06 E
Burgkunstadt	54	50.08 N	11.14 E
Bürglen, Schw.	58	46.53 N	8.40 E
Bürglen, Schw.	58	47.33 N	9.09 E
Burglengenfeld	60	49.13 N	12.03 E
Burgoon	214	41.16 N	83.15 W
Burgos, Esp.	34	42.21 N	3.42 W
Burgos, It.	71	40.23 N	8.59 E
Burgos, Méx.	232	24.57 N	98.47 W
Burgos, Pil.	116	16.04 N	119.52 E
Burgos, Pil.	116	15.30 N	120.24 E
Burgos □[4]	34	42.20 N	3.40 W
Burgsinn	56	50.09 N	9.38 E
Burgstädt	54	50.55 N	12.49 E
Burgstall	54	52.24 N	11.41 E
Burgstall → Postal	64	46.36 N	11.11 E
Burg Stargard	54	53.29 N	13.18 E
Burgsvik	26	57.03 N	18.16 E
Burgueño, Arroyo ≃	288	34.24 S	58.47 W
Burgund → Bourgogne □[9]	32	47.00 N	4.30 E
Burgundy → Bourgogne □[9]	32	47.00 N	4.30 E
Burgusio (Burgeis)	64	46.42 N	10.31 E
Burgwedel	52	52.29 N	9.51 E
Burgwindheim	56	49.49 N	10.35 E
Burhābalang ≃	126	21.28 N	87.04 E
Burham	260	51.20 N	0.29 E
Burhan Budai Shan ⋏	102	36.00 N	96.00 E
Burhaniye, Tür.	130	37.57 N	28.45 E
Burhaniye, Tür.	130	39.30 N	26.58 E
Burhānpur	120	21.18 N	76.14 E
Burhar	124	23.13 N	81.32 E
Burhave	52	53.34 N	8.21 E
Burholme ◆[8]	285	40.03 N	75.05 W
Buri	255	23.48 S	48.35 W
Burias Island I	116	12.57 N	123.08 E
Burias Pass)(	116	13.00 N	123.15 E
Buribaj	86	51.57 N	58.11 E
Būr Ibrāhīm ◆[8]	142	29.57 N	32.34 E
Burica, Punta >	236	8.03 N	82.53 W
Burien	224	47.28 N	122.20 W
Burigi, Lake ⊜	154	2.05 S	31.15 E
Burila Mare	38	44.27 N	22.34 E
Burin	186	47.02 N	55.10 W
Burin Peninsula >[1]	186	47.00 N	55.40 W
Buri Ram	110	15.00 N	103.07 E
Buriswar ≃[1]	126	21.58 N	90.02 E
Buritama	255	21.03 S	50.08 W
Buriti, Bra.	250	3.55 S	42.57 W
Buriti, Bra.	255	16.27 S	53.27 W
Buriti ≃	248	12.50 S	58.28 W
Buriti Alegre	255	18.09 S	49.03 W
Buriti Bravo	250	5.50 S	43.50 W
Buriticupu ≃	250	4.13 S	46.33 W
Buriti dos Lopes	250	3.10 S	41.52 W
Buritizeiro	255	17.21 S	44.58 W
Būriya	124	30.09 N	77.21 E
Burj al-'Arab	140	30.55 N	29.32 E
Burjassot	34	39.31 N	0.25 W
Burjatskaja Avtonomnaja Sovetskaja Socialističeskaja Respublika □[3]	88	53.00 N	109.00 E
Burji	144	5.20 N	37.57 E
Burj Islām	130	35.41 N	35.48 E
Burj Mughayzil	142	31.27 N	30.23 E
Burkan ≃	85	41.43 N	76.46 E
Burkau	54	51.10 N	14.10 E
Burkburnett	196	34.05 N	98.34 W
Burke, S.D., U.S.	198	43.10 N	99.17 W
Burke, Tx., U.S.	222	31.14 N	94.46 W
Burke, Va., U.S.	284c	38.47 N	77.16 W
Burke ≃	166	23.12 S	139.33 E

Symbols in the index entries represent the broad categories identified in the key at the right. Symbols with superior numbers (⋏[1]) identify subcategories (see complete key on page I · 1).

Symbole im Register stellen die rechts im Schlüssel erklärten Kategorien dar. Symbole mit hochgestellten Ziffern (⋏[1]) bezeichnen Unterabteilungen einer Kategorie (vgl. vollständiger Schlüssel auf Seite I · 1).

Los símbolos incluídos en el texto del índice representan las grandes categorias identificadas con la clave a la derecha. Los símbolos con numeros en su parte superior (⋏[1]) identifican las subcategorías (véase la clave completa en la página I · 1).

Les symboles de l'index représentent les catégories indiquées dans la légende à droite. Les symboles suivis d'un indice (⋏[1]) représentent des sous-catégories (voir légende complète à la page I · 1).

Os símbolos incluídos no texto do índice representam as grandes categorias identificadas com a chave à direita. Os símbolos com números em sua parte superior (⋏[1]) identificam as subcategorias (veja-se a chave completa à página I · 1).

∧	Mountain	Berg	Montaña	Montagne	Montanha
⋏	Mountains	Gebirge	Montañas	Montagnes	Montanhas
)(	Pass	Paß	Paso	Col	Passo
V	Valley, Canyon	Tal, Cañon	Valle, Cañón	Vallée, Canyon	Vale, Canhão
≚	Plain	Ebene	Llano	Plaine	Planície
>	Cape	Kap	Cabo	Cap	Cabo
I	Island	Insel	Isla	Île	Ilha
II	Islands	Inseln	Islas	Îles	Ilhas
±	Other Topographic Features	Andere Topographische Objekte	Otros Elementos Topográficos	Autres données topographiques	Outros acidentes topográficos

ESPAÑOL / FRANÇAIS / PORTUGUÊS

Nombre / Nom / Nome	Página / Page	Lat.°′	Long.°′ W = Oeste / W = Ouest
Burke Channel Ʊ	182	52.07 N	127.38 W
Burke Island I	9	73.15 S	104.35 W
Burke Lake County Park ♠	284c	38.45 N	77.18 W
Burke Lakefront Airport ⊠	279a	41.31 N	81.41 W
Burkesville	194	36.47 N	85.22 W
Burket	216	41.09 N	85.58 W
Burketown	166	17.43 S	139.34 E
Burkett Gardens	226	37.57 N	121.15 W
Burkettsville	216	40.21 N	84.39 W
Burkhardtsdorf	54	50.44 N	12.55 E
Burkina Faso □[1], Afr.	134	13.00 N	1.30 W
Burkina Faso □[1], Afr.	150	13.00 N	1.30 W
Burkit	80	47.03 N	50.42 E
Burksville	219	38.16 N	90.09 W
Burla	86	53.19 N	78.21 E
Burla ≃	86	53.20 N	78.02 E
Burladingen	58	48.17 N	9.07 E
Burleigh	208	39.02 N	74.51 W
Burleigh Falls	212	44.34 N	78.13 W
Burleigh Heads	171a	28.06 S	153.27 E
Burleson	222	32.32 N	97.19 W
Burleson □[6]	222	30.30 N	96.43 W
Burley, Id., U.S.	202	42.32 N	113.47 W
Burley, Wa., U.S.	224	47.25 N	122.37 W
Burley Griffin, Lake ⊜	171b	35.13 S	149.05 E
Burli, Kaz.	80	51.25 N	52.44 E
Burli, Kaz.	86	53.36 N	61.55 E
Burlingame, Ca., U.S.	226	37.35 N	122.21 W
Burlingame, Ks., U.S.	198	38.45 N	95.00 W
Burlingame State Park ♠	207	41.22 N	71.43 W
Burlington, Nf., Can.	186	49.45 N	56.02 W
Burlington, On., Can.	212	43.19 N	79.47 W
Burlington, Co., U.S.	198	39.18 N	102.16 W
Burlington, Ct., U.S.	207	41.46 N	72.57 W
Burlington, Il., U.S.	216	42.03 N	88.33 W
Burlington, In., U.S.	216	40.29 N	86.24 W
Burlington, Ia., U.S.	190	40.48 N	91.06 W
Burlington, Ks., U.S.	198	38.11 N	95.44 W
Burlington, Ky., U.S.	218	39.01 N	84.43 W
Burlington, Ma., U.S.	207	42.30 N	71.11 W
Burlington, Mi., U.S.	216	42.06 N	85.05 W
Burlington, N.J., U.S.	208	40.04 N	74.51 W
Burlington, N.C., U.S.	192	36.05 N	79.26 W
Burlington, N.D., U.S.	198	48.16 N	101.25 W
Burlington, Pa., U.S.	210	41.47 N	76.37 W
Burlington, Tx., U.S.	222	31.01 N	96.60 W
Burlington, Vt., U.S.	188	44.28 N	73.12 W
Burlington, Wa., U.S.	224	48.28 N	122.19 W
Burlington, Wi., U.S.	216	42.40 N	88.16 W
Burlington, Wy., U.S.	202	44.26 N	108.25 W
Burlington □[6]	208	39.50 N	74.47 W
Burlington Beach	216	41.30 N	87.03 W
Burlington County Airpark ⊠	285	39.56 N	74.50 W
Burlington Island I	285	40.05 N	74.51 W
Burlington Junction	194	40.26 N	95.03 W
Burlington Mall ◆[9]	283	42.29 N	71.13 W
Burlit	89	46.33 N	134.14 E
Burluk	80	50.34 N	44.33 E
Burma (Myanmar) □[1]	110	22.00 N	98.00 E
Burmā, Tall ∧	132	30.38 N	35.50 E
Burmakino	80	57.27 N	40.20 E
Burn ≃	44	54.12 N	1.38 W
Burnaby	224	49.15 N	122.57 W
Burnaby Island I	182	52.24 N	131.20 W
Burnage	262	53.26 N	2.12 W
Burnas, ozero ⊜	78	45.52 N	30.08 E
Burnet	196	30.45 N	98.13 W
Burnett ≃	166	24.46 S	152.25 E
Burnett Bay c	176	73.53 N	124.00 W
Burnett Brook ≃	276	40.46 N	74.38 W
Burnett Heads	166	24.46 S	152.25 E
Burnettsville	216	40.46 N	86.36 W
Burney, Ca., U.S.	204	40.52 N	121.39 W
Burney, In., U.S.	218	39.19 N	85.38 W
Burnham, Eng., U.K.	260	51.33 N	0.39 W
Burnham, Il., U.S.	278	41.39 N	87.34 W
Burnham, Pa., U.S.	208	40.38 N	77.34 W
Burnham Beeches ◆[3]	260	51.34 N	0.38 W
Burnham Market	42	52.57 N	0.44 E
Burnham-on-Crouch	42	51.38 N	0.49 E
Burnham-on-Sea	42	51.15 N	3.00 W
Burnhamthorpe	275b	43.37 N	79.36 W
Burnhaven	46	57.29 N	1.47 W
Burnie	166	41.04 S	145.54 E
Burning Tree Estates	284c	39.01 N	77.12 W
Burnips	216	42.44 N	85.50 W
Burniston	44	54.19 N	0.26 W
Burnley	44	53.48 N	2.14 W
Burnley □[8]	262	53.46 N	2.15 W
Burnley Creek ≃	212	44.13 N	77.51 W
Burnley Football Ground ♠	262	53.48 N	2.14 W
Burnmouth	46	55.50 N	2.04 W
Burnoje	85	42.37 N	70.46 E
Burno-Okt'abr'skoje	85	42.42 N	70.49 E
Burnpur	126	23.40 N	86.57 E
Burns, Ks., U.S.	198	38.05 N	96.53 W
Burns, Or., U.S.	202	43.35 N	119.03 W
Burns, Tn., U.S.	194	36.03 N	87.18 W
Burns, Wy., U.S.	198	41.11 N	104.21 W
Burns Creek ≃	198	47.22 N	104.25 W
Burns Flat	196	35.20 N	99.10 W
Burns Harbor	216	41.37 N	87.10 W
Burnside, Austl.	168b	34.57 S	138.40 E
Burnside, Ky., U.S.	192	36.59 N	84.36 W
Burnside, Pa., U.S.	214	40.49 N	78.47 W
Burnside ≃	176	66.51 N	108.04 W
Burnside, Lake ⊜	162	25.33 S	123.02 E
Burns Lake	182	54.14 N	125.46 W
Burnsville, Al., U.S.	194	32.28 N	86.53 W
Burnsville, Ms., U.S.	194	34.50 N	88.18 W
Burnsville, N.C., U.S.	192	35.55 N	82.18 W
Burnsville, W.V., U.S.	188	38.51 N	80.39 W
Burnt ≃, On., Can.	212	44.35 N	78.46 W
Burnt ≃, Or., U.S.	202	44.22 N	117.14 W
Burnt Cabins	214	40.05 N	77.54 W
Burnt Corn Creek ≃	194	31.06 N	87.04 W
Burnt Hills	210	42.54 N	73.53 W
Burnt Island, Nf., Can.	186	47.36 N	58.53 W
Burntisland, Scot., U.K.	46	56.03 N	3.15 W
Burnt Meadow Brook ≃	276	41.05 N	74.18 W
Burnt Mills, Lake ⊜	208	36.50 N	76.38 W
Burnt Mills Hills	284c	39.02 N	77.00 W
Burnt Mills Manor	284c	39.02 N	77.00 W
Burnt Mountain ∧	228	33.12 N	117.04 W
Burntop	158	26.49 S	30.54 E
Burnt Pine	174c	29.02 S	167.56 E
Burnt Pond ⊜	186	48.11 N	57.24 W
Burntwick Island I	260	51.25 N	0.41 E
Burntwood	42	52.41 N	1.56 W
Burntwood ≃	184	56.08 N	96.30 W
Burntwood Lake ⊜	184	55.29 N	100.07 W
Burnyj, porog ᒪ	86	57.43 N	95.18 E
Buro	144	11.28 N	49.41 E
Buron	84	42.48 N	44.03 E
Buronzo	62	45.29 N	8.16 E
Burow	54	53.46 N	13.16 E
Burpengary	171a	27.10 S	152.57 E
Burpham	260	51.15 N	0.33 W
Burqin	86	47.43 N	86.53 E
Burqin ≃	86	47.40 N	86.55 E
Burra	166	33.40 S	138.56 E
Burra Burra Creek ≃	170	34.10 S	149.38 E
Burracoppin	162	31.23 S	118.29 E
Burra Creek ≃	168b	33.51 S	139.18 E
Burrage	283	42.02 N	70.51 W
Burrage Pond ⊜	283	42.01 N	70.52 W
Burragorang, Lake ⊜[1]	170	33.57 S	150.26 E
Burramurra	166	20.30 S	137.20 E
Burravoe	46a	60.32 N	1.28 W
Burrawang	170	34.36 S	150.31 E
Burray I	46	58.51 N	2.54 W
Burrel, Shq.	38	41.37 N	20.00 E
Burrel, Ca., U.S.	226	36.30 N	119.59 W
Burrendong Reservoir ⊜[1]	166	32.39 S	149.15 E
Burren Junction	166	30.06 S	148.58 E
Burrill Lake c	170	35.23 S	150.27 E
Burrinjuck Reservoir ⊜[1]	166	35.00 S	148.45 E
Burro, Serranías del ⋏	196	29.10 N	102.05 W
Burr Oak, In., U.S.	216	41.15 N	86.25 W
Burr Oak, Ks., U.S.	198	39.51 N	98.18 W
Burr Oak, Mi., U.S.	216	41.50 N	85.19 W
Burro Burro ≃	246	4.48 N	58.51 W
Burro Creek ≃	200	34.32 N	113.35 W
Burro Peak ∧	200	32.35 N	108.26 W
Burrowa, Mount ∧	171b	36.05 S	147.42 E
Burrowa-Pine Mountain National Park ♠	171b	36.06 S	147.44 E
Burrow Head ›	44	54.41 N	4.24 W
Burrowhill	260	51.21 N	0.36 W
Burrows	216	40.40 N	86.30 W
Burrows Island I	224	48.29 N	122.42 W
Burr Ridge	278	41.46 N	87.55 W
Burrs Mill Brook ≃	285	39.53 N	74.42 W
Burrton	198	38.01 N	97.40 W
Burrumbeet, Lake ⊜	169	37.30 S	143.39 E
Burrundie	164	13.32 S	131.42 E
Burruyacú	252	26.30 S	64.45 W
Burrwood	194	28.58 N	89.22 W
Burry Holms I	42	51.37 N	4.18 W
Burry Port	42	51.42 N	4.15 W
Bürs	58	47.09 N	9.48 E
Bursa	130	40.11 N	29.04 E
Bursa □[4]	130	40.10 N	29.00 E
Būr Safājah	140	26.44 N	33.56 E
Būr Saʿīd (Port Said)	142	31.16 N	32.18 E
Būr Saʿīd □[4]	142	30.36 N	32.15 E
Burscheid	56	51.05 N	7.06 E
Burscough	262	53.35 N	2.51 W
Burscough Bridge, Eng., U.K.	44	53.36 N	2.52 W
Burscough Bridge, Eng., U.K.	262	53.36 N	2.51 W
Bursey, Mount ∧	9	76.00 S	132.40 W
Bursol'	86	53.11 N	78.27 E
Bürstadt	56	49.38 N	8.27 E
Burstall	184	50.40 N	109.54 W
Burštyn	78	49.17 N	24.37 E
Būr Sūdān (Port Sudan)	140	19.37 N	37.14 E
Burt, Ia., U.S.	190	43.11 N	94.13 W
Burt, N.Y., U.S.	210	43.19 N	78.43 W
Būr Tawfīq ◆[8]	128	29.57 N	32.34 E
Burtenbach	58	48.20 N	10.26 E
Burt Lake ⊜	190	45.27 N	84.40 W
Burtnieku ezers ⊜	76	57.45 N	25.16 E
Burton, B.C., Can.	182	49.59 N	117.54 W
Burton, Eng., U.K.	42	50.44 N	1.45 W
Burton, Eng., U.K.	262	53.16 N	3.01 W
Burton, Il., U.S.	219	39.55 N	91.15 W
Burton, Mi., U.S.	216	43.02 N	83.36 W
Burton, Mi., U.S.	216	43.01 N	84.16 W
Burton, Oh., U.S.	214	41.28 N	81.08 W
Burton, Tx., U.S.	222	30.11 N	96.36 W
Burton, Wa., U.S.	224	47.23 N	122.27 W
Burton, Lake ⊜[1]	192	34.50 N	83.33 W
Burton Fleming	44	54.08 N	0.20 W
Burton Latimer	42	52.23 N	0.41 W
Burtons Bridge	216	42.17 N	88.14 W
Burton Seamount ✦[3]	14	32.00 S	171.45 W
Burtonsville	208	39.07 N	76.56 W
Burton upon Stather	44	53.39 N	0.41 W
Burton upon Trent	42	52.49 N	1.36 W
Burtonwood	262	53.26 N	2.39 W
Burtonwood Airfield ⊠	262	53.24 N	2.39 W
Burträsk	26	64.31 N	20.39 E
Burtundy	166	33.44 S	142.16 E
Burṭus	142	30.09 N	31.08 E
Buru I	108	3.24 S	126.40 E
Buruanga	116	11.51 N	121.53 E
Burukan	89	53.02 N	136.03 E
Buruldaj	85	42.48 N	75.52 E
Burullus, Buḥayrat al- ⊜	142	31.30 N	30.50 E
Burūm	144	14.22 N	48.57 E
Burundaj	85	43.23 N	76.51 E
Burundi □[1], Afr.	138	3.15 S	30.00 E
Burundi □[1], Afr.	154	3.15 S	30.00 E
Burundučicha	80	58.21 N	46.07 E
Burun-Šibertuj, gora ∧	88	49.42 N	109.59 E
Bururi	154	3.57 S	29.37 E
Burutu	150	5.21 N	5.31 E
Buruz Bāgān	126	23.03 N	89.00 E
Burwash	190	46.19 N	80.48 W
Burwash Landing	180	61.21 N	139.00 W
Burwell, Eng., U.K.	42	52.16 N	0.19 E
Burwell, Ne., U.S.	198	41.46 N	99.07 W
Burwell Bay c	208	37.04 N	76.38 W
Burwick	46	58.44 N	2.57 W
Burwood, Austl.	274a	33.53 S	151.06 E
Burwood, Austl.	274b	37.51 S	145.06 E
Bury, P.Q., Can.	206	45.28 N	71.30 W
Bury, Eng., U.K.	42	50.54 N	0.34 W
Bury, Eng., U.K.	262	53.36 N	2.17 W
Bury □[8]	262	53.35 N	2.19 W
Buryn'	78	51.13 N	33.49 E
Bury Saint Edmunds	42	52.15 N	0.43 E
Burzaco	258	34.49 S	58.24 W
Burzet	62	44.44 N	4.15 E
Burzil	123	34.52 N	75.07 E
Burzil Pass)(	123	34.54 N	75.06 E
Būṣ, Ghubbat al- c	142	29.36 N	32.22 E
Busa, Mount ∧	116	6.08 N	124.39 E
Busachi	71	40.02 N	8.54 E
Busalla	62	44.34 N	8.57 E
Busambra, Rocca ∧	70	37.51 N	13.24 E
Busana	64	44.22 N	10.19 E
Busanga	152	0.51 S	22.04 E
Busanga Swamp ☷	154	14.10 S	25.50 E
Busangu	154	8.32 S	25.31 E
Busan → Pusan	98	35.06 N	129.03 E
Buṣayrah	130	35.09 N	40.26 E
Busby, Austl.	274a	33.54 S	150.53 E
Busby, Mt., U.S.	202	45.32 N	106.57 W
Busca	62	44.31 N	7.29 E
Buscate	266b	45.32 N	8.49 E
Buscbusc ≃	144	1.08 S	41.49 E
Buschberg ∧[2]	61	48.34 N	16.23 E
Busche	64	46.02 N	11.59 E
Busch Gardens ♠	280	34.13 N	118.28 W
Buschhausen ◆[8]	263	51.30 N	6.51 E
Busdorf	41	54.29 N	9.32 E
Buseck	56	50.36 N	8.47 E
Buseto Palizzolo	70	38.01 N	12.43 E
Būsh	142	29.09 N	31.08 E
Bush ≃, N. Ire., U.K.	44	55.13 N	6.32 W
Bush ≃, S.C., U.S.	192	34.08 N	81.36 W
Būshehr □[4]	128	28.50 N	51.20 E
Bushenyi	154	0.32 S	30.11 E
Bushey	260	51.39 N	0.22 W
Bushey Heath	260	51.38 N	0.20 W
Bushi	268	35.50 N	139.22 E
Bushimaie ≃	152	6.02 S	23.45 E
Bushiribana	241s	12.33 N	69.58 W
Bushkill	210	41.06 N	75.00 W
Bush Kill ≃	210	41.05 N	74.59 W
Bushkill Falls ᒪ	210	41.09 N	75.01 W
Bushland	196	35.11 N	102.04 W
Bush Lot	246	6.12 N	57.16 W
Bushman Land □[9]	158	29.15 S	20.00 E
Bushmills	48	55.12 N	6.32 W
Bushnell, Fl., U.S.	220	28.39 N	82.06 W
Bushnell, Il., U.S.	190	40.33 N	90.30 W
Bush River ≃	208	39.21 N	76.14 W
Bushton	198	38.30 N	98.23 W
Bū Shubayrim, Wādī V	146	27.07 N	19.30 E
Bushwick ◆[8]	276	40.42 N	73.55 W
Bushy Park	166	21.16 S	139.43 E
Bushy Park ♠	260	51.25 N	0.20 W
Bushy Run ≃	279b	40.20 N	79.40 W
Bushy Run Battlefield ⊥	279b	40.21 N	79.38 W
Busia	154	0.28 N	34.05 E
Busigny	50	50.02 N	3.28 E
Busing, Pulau I	271c	1.14 N	103.45 E
Businga	152	3.20 N	20.53 E
Büsingen	58	47.42 N	8.41 E
Busira ≃	152	0.15 S	18.59 E
Busjön ⊜, Sve.	40	60.06 N	13.28 E
Busjön ⊜, Sve.	40	60.31 N	13.58 E
Busk	78	49.58 N	24.37 E
Buskerud □[6]	26	60.25 N	9.12 E
Buskhyttan	40	58.40 N	16.56 E
Busko Zdrój	30	50.28 N	20.44 E
Buskul'	86	53.45 N	61.12 E
Busle	144	5.28 N	44.25 E
Busoga □[5]	154	0.40 N	33.30 E
Busovača	36	44.06 N	17.53 E
Buṣrā al-Ḥarīrī (Bosor)	132	32.50 N	36.20 E
Buṣrá ash-Shām	132	32.31 N	36.29 E
Bussana	62	43.49 N	7.51 E
Bussang	58	47.53 N	6.51 E
Bussang, Col de)(	58	47.54 N	6.54 E
Busselton	162	33.39 S	115.20 E
Busseri ≃	140	7.41 N	28.03 E
Busseto	64	44.59 N	10.02 E
Bussey	190	41.12 N	92.52 W
Bussières	62	45.50 N	4.16 E
Bussi sul Tirino	66	42.12 N	13.49 E
Busskoje	84	43.50 N	44.37 E
Bussolengo	64	45.28 N	10.51 E
Bussoleno	62	45.08 N	7.09 E
Bussum	52	52.16 N	5.10 E
Bussy-Rabutin, Château de ⊥	58	47.35 N	4.31 E
Bussy-Saint-Georges	261	48.51 N	2.42 E
Bustamante, Méx.	232	26.33 N	100.30 W
Bustamante, Méx.	234	23.26 N	99.47 W
Bustān, Wādī al- V	142	28.24 N	30.49 E
Buštěhrad	54	50.09 N	14.10 E
Buşteni	38	45.25 N	25.32 E
Busti	214	42.02 N	79.17 W
Bustleton ◆[8]	285	40.05 N	75.02 W
Busto Arsizio	62	45.37 N	8.51 E
Busto Garolfo	62	45.33 N	8.53 E
Buston, Taj.	85	40.31 N	69.19 E
Buston, Uzb.	128	40.04 N	64.49 E
Buštyna	78	48.04 N	23.27 E
Busu-Adula	152	2.05 N	21.40 E
Busuanga	116	12.10 N	119.55 E
Busuanga Island I	116	12.05 N	120.05 E
Busu-Djanoa	152	1.43 N	21.23 E
Bušuicha	76	59.02 N	40.26 E
Bušulej	88	52.45 N	117.13 E
Büsum	30	54.08 N	8.51 E
Busu-Melo	152	1.48 N	20.15 E
Bū Sunbul, Jabal ⋏[2]	146	23.10 N	22.21 E
Buta, Ross.	80	55.02 N	51.57 E
Buta, Zaïre	154	2.48 N	24.44 E
Butag	116	12.38 N	123.56 E
Butajira	144	8.07 N	38.22 E
Butala	164	6.42 S	147.37 E
Butan	38	43.39 N	23.45 E
Bután → Bhutan □[1]	120	27.30 N	90.30 E
Butand State Park ♠	226	37.13 N	122.20 W
Butantã ◆[8]	287b	23.34 S	46.43 W
Butantã, Instituto ʊ[3]	287b	23.34 S	46.43 W
Buta Ranquil	252	37.03 S	69.50 W
Butare	154	2.36 S	29.44 E
Butaritari I[1]	14	3.07 N	172.48 E
Butarque, Arroyo de ≃	266a	40.19 N	3.39 W
Butauanan Island I	116	14.07 N	123.17 E
Butchart Gardens ♠	224	48.33 N	123.28 W
Butcher Island (Dia Deva) I	272c	18.58 N	72.54 E
Bute	168b	33.52 S	138.01 E
Bute, Island of I	46	55.50 N	5.06 W
Bute, Kyles of Ʊ	46	55.53 N	5.13 W
Bute, Sound of Ʊ	46	55.44 N	5.12 W
Büteelijn nuruu ⋏	88	50.00 N	104.50 E
Bute Giarti	144	4.33 N	37.45 E
Bute Inlet c	182	50.37 N	124.53 W
Butemba	154	1.09 N	31.36 E
Butembo	154	0.09 N	29.17 E
Butendorf ◆[8]	263	51.33 N	6.59 E
Butera	70	37.11 N	14.11 E
Butere	154	0.13 N	34.30 E
Bütgenbach	56	50.26 N	6.12 E
Butha Buthe	158	28.45 S	28.15 E
Butha Qi (Zalantun)	89	48.02 N	122.43 E
Buthidaung	110	20.52 N	92.32 E
Buthier ≃	62	45.44 N	7.22 E
Buthroton ⊥	38	39.46 N	20.00 E
Buti	66	43.44 N	10.35 E
Butiá	252	30.07 S	51.58 W
Butiaba	154	1.49 N	31.19 E
Butig Mountains ⋏	116	7.39 N	124.20 E
Butka	86	56.47 N	63.47 E
Butler, Al., U.S.	194	32.05 N	88.13 W
Butler, Ga., U.S.	192	32.33 N	84.14 W
Butler, Il., U.S.	219	39.12 N	89.32 W
Butler, In., U.S.	216	41.25 N	84.52 W
Butler, Ky., U.S.	218	38.47 N	84.22 W
Butler, Mo., U.S.	194	38.15 N	94.19 W
Butler, N.J., U.S.	210	41.00 N	74.20 W
Butler, Oh., U.S.	214	40.35 N	82.25 W
Butler, Ok., U.S.	196	35.38 N	99.11 W
Butler, Pa., U.S.	214	40.51 N	79.53 W
Butler, Tx., U.S.	222	30.19 N	97.18 W
Butler, Wi., U.S.	216	43.06 N	88.04 W
Butler □[6], Oh., U.S.	218	39.26 N	84.30 W
Butler □[6], Pa., U.S.	214	40.52 N	79.54 W
Butler, Lake ⊜	220	28.28 N	81.33 W
Butler Lake ⊜	278	42.17 N	87.58 W
Butler Point ›	207	41.40 N	70.43 W
Butler Reservoir ⊜[1]	276	40.59 N	74.23 W
Butlers Bridge	48	54.02 N	7.22 W
Butlerville	218	39.02 N	85.30 W
Butmīyah	132	32.56 N	35.53 E
Butnau Lake ⊜	184	56.13 N	95.20 W
Butner	192	36.07 N	78.45 W
Buto	152	15.46 S	15.09 E
Buton, Pulau I	112	5.00 S	122.55 E
Butong	112	1.06 S	114.50 E
Butru	166	21.30 S	139.43 E
Butsha	154	0.57 N	29.13 E
Buttapietra	64	45.20 N	11.00 E
Butte, Mt., U.S.	202	46.00 N	112.32 W
Butte, Ne., U.S.	198	42.54 N	98.50 W
Butte □[6]	226	39.27 N	121.30 W
Butte City	226	39.28 N	121.59 W
Butte Creek ≃, Ca., U.S.	204	39.12 N	121.56 W
Butte Creek ≃, Or., U.S.	224	45.09 N	122.46 W
Butte du Lion ♠	50	50.40 N	4.24 E
Butte Falls	202	42.32 N	122.33 W
Buttelstedt	54	51.05 N	11.20 E
Butte Mountains ⋏	204	39.50 N	115.05 W
Butten	56	48.58 N	7.13 E
Butter Brook ≃	283	42.31 N	71.24 W
Butter Creek ≃	202	45.52 N	119.19 W
Butterfield, Il., U.S.	278	41.50 N	88.02 W
Butterfield, Mn., U.S.	198	43.57 N	94.47 W
Butterfield Creek ≃	278	41.33 N	87.37 W
Butterfield Lake ⊜	212	44.19 N	75.46 W
Butterley Reservoir ⊜[1]	262	53.35 N	1.56 W
Buttermere	44	54.33 N	3.17 W
Butternut	190	46.00 N	90.29 W
Butternut Creek ≃, N.Y., U.S.	210	42.25 N	75.22 W
Butternut Creek ≃, N.Y., U.S.	210	43.06 N	76.00 W
Butterwick	44	52.59 N	0.05 E
Butterworth, Malay.	114	5.25 N	100.24 E
Butterworth, Transkei	158	32.23 S	28.04 E
Buttevant	48	52.14 N	8.40 W
Büttgen	56	51.12 N	6.36 E
Buttlar	56	50.45 N	9.57 E
Buttle Lake ⊜	182	49.46 N	125.36 W
Button Islands II	176	60.35 N	64.45 W
Buttonville	275b	43.52 N	79.22 W
Buttonville Airfield ⊠	275b	43.52 N	79.23 W
Buttonwillow	226	35.24 N	119.28 W
Buttrio	64	46.01 N	13.20 E
Buttstädt	54	51.07 N	11.25 E
Butty Head ›	162	33.54 S	121.38 E
Buttzville	210	40.49 N	75.00 W
Butuan	116	8.57 N	125.33 E
Butuan Bay c	116	9.06 N	125.20 E
Butuj	88	53.27 N	112.22 E
Bū Tumayyim, Wādī V	146	26.56 N	19.13 E
Buṭūris	142	31.00 N	30.15 E
Buturlino, Ross.	80	55.34 N	44.55 E
Buturlino, Ross.	82	54.55 N	37.29 E
Buturlinovka	78	50.50 N	40.36 E
Buṭwal	124	27.42 N	83.27 E
Butylicy	80	55.32 N	41.31 E
Butzbach	56	50.26 N	8.40 E
Bützfleth	52	53.39 N	9.28 E
Bützow	54	53.50 N	11.59 E
Bützsee ⊜	54	52.49 N	12.53 E
Butztown	208	40.39 N	75.22 W
Buuhoodle	144	8.15 N	46.20 E
Buulo Berde	144	3.51 N	45.34 E
Buur Gaabo	144	1.12 S	41.51 E
Buurgplaatz ∧	56	50.10 N	6.01 E
Buur Hakaba	144	2.47 N	44.05 E
Buur Haybe	144	3.57 N	45.07 E
Buwarah, Sabkhat al- ☷	130	35.09 N	41.12 E
Buwaydān	132	33.12 N	36.26 E
Buxar	124	25.35 N	83.59 E
Buxtehude	52	53.28 N	9.41 E
Buxton, Boph.	158	27.38 S	24.42 E
Buxton, Guy.	246	6.47 N	58.02 W
Buxton, Eng., U.K.	262	53.15 N	1.55 W
Buxton, N.C., U.S.	192	35.16 N	75.32 W
Buxton, N.D., U.S.	198	47.36 N	97.05 W
Buxton, Or., U.S.	224	45.41 N	123.11 W
Buxton, Mount ∧	182	51.35 N	127.55 W
Buxy	58	46.43 N	4.41 E
Buye	154	4.38 N	27.30 E
Buyiqiao	106	31.47 N	119.48 E
Buyo	150	6.16 N	7.03 W
Buyo, Barrage de ◆[6]	150	6.15 N	7.05 W
Buyuan ≃	102	21.51 N	101.13 E
Büyükada	130	40.52 N	29.07 E
Büyükada I	267b	40.52 N	29.07 E
Büyükarmutlu	130	39.35 N	38.26 E
Büyükbakkal ◆[8]	267b	40.59 N	29.11 E
Büyükçeçeli	130	39.43 N	33.52 E
Büyükçekmece	130	41.01 N	28.34 E
Büyükdere ◆[8]	267b	41.09 N	29.02 E
Büyükeceli	130	36.11 N	33.40 E
Büyükkale	130	38.01 N	27.34 E
Büyükkarıştıran	130	41.18 N	27.32 E
Büyükkemikli Burnu ›	130	40.18 N	26.14 E
Büyükmenderes ≃	130	37.28 N	27.11 E
Büyükzap → Great Zab ≃	128	36.00 N	43.21 E
Buyun Shan ∧	98	40.06 N	122.42 E
Buyun Uzun	128	39.13 N	63.19 E
Buzan ≃	80	46.18 N	49.06 E
Buzanaj, peski ◆[2]	80	47.30 N	49.50 E
Buzançais	32	46.53 N	1.25 E
Buzancy	56	49.25 N	4.57 E
Bužaninovo	82	56.23 N	38.18 E
Bužarovo	82	55.59 N	36.47 E
Buzău	38	45.09 N	26.49 E
Buzău □[6]	38	45.15 N	26.45 E
Buzău ≃	38	45.26 N	27.44 E
Buzen	96	33.37 N	131.08 E
Búzi ≃	156	19.50 S	34.43 E
Buziaș	38	45.39 N	21.36 E
Buziji	100	33.49 N	118.14 E
Buzinovka	80	48.32 N	43.53 E
Búzios, Ilha dos I	256	23.48 S	45.08 W
Búzios, Ponta dos ›	255	22.44 S	41.53 W
Buzlanovo	265b	55.46 N	37.13 E
Buzovna	84	40.31 N	50.04 E
Buzuluk, Kaz.	86	51.55 N	66.16 E
Buzuluk, Ross.	80	52.47 N	52.15 E
Buzuluk ≃, Ross.	80	50.13 N	42.12 E
Buzuluk ≃, Ross.	80	52.47 N	52.16 E
Buzzards Bay	207	41.44 N	70.37 W
Buzzards Bay c	207	41.33 N	70.47 W
Bwana Mkubwa	154	13.01 S	28.42 E
Bwasa	152	3.53 S	18.25 E
Bwendi	154	4.01 N	26.41 E
Bwlch	42	51.54 N	3.15 W
By	40	60.12 N	16.28 E
Byādgi	122	14.41 N	75.29 E
Byam Channel Ʊ	176	75.20 N	105.20 W
Byam Martin Channel Ʊ	176	75.45 N	104.00 W
Byam Martin Island I	176	75.15 N	104.00 W
Byberry Creek ≃	285	40.04 N	74.59 W
Byblos → Jubayl	130	34.07 N	35.39 E
Byček ≃	83	48.26 N	37.47 E
Bychawa	30	51.01 N	22.32 E
Bychov	76	53.32 N	30.12 E
Byčicha	76	55.41 N	29.58 E
Byčki, Ross.	76	54.15 N	34.39 E
Byčki, Ross.	80	53.38 N	40.54 E
Byculla ◆[8]	272c	18.58 N	72.49 E
Byczyna	30	51.07 N	18.11 E
Bydalen	26	63.06 N	13.47 E
Bydgoszcz	30	53.08 N	18.00 E
Bydgoszcz □[4]	30	53.15 N	18.00 E
Byelorussia → Belarus □[1], Europe	72	53.50 N	28.00 E
Byelorussian Station ◆[5]	265b	55.47 N	37.35 E
Byers, Pa., U.S.	285	40.05 N	75.41 W
Byers, Tx., U.S.	196	34.04 N	98.11 W
Byersdale	279b	40.37 N	80.13 W
Byers Run ≃	279b	40.24 N	79.42 W
Byesville	188	39.58 N	81.32 W
Byfang ◆[8]	263	51.24 N	7.06 E
Byfield, Eng., U.K.	42	52.11 N	1.14 W
Byfield, Ma., U.S.	207	42.45 N	70.56 W
Byfleet	260	51.20 N	0.29 W
Byford	168a	32.13 S	116.00 E
Byforde	284c	39.01 N	77.05 W
Bygdeå	26	64.04 N	20.51 E
Bygdeträsket ⊜	26	64.26 N	20.32 E
Bygdin	26	61.20 N	8.48 E
Bygdin ⊜	26	61.21 N	8.36 E
Bygi	80	57.13 N	53.44 E
Byglandsfjord	26	58.41 N	7.48 E
Byglandsfjorden ⊜	26	58.48 N	7.50 E
Byhalia	194	34.52 N	89.41 W
Byk ≃	78	46.55 N	29.28 E
Bykle	26	59.21 N	7.20 E
Bykov	89	47.21 N	142.32 E
Bykovec	78	47.13 N	28.27 E
Bykovka, Ross.	82	55.29 N	37.40 E
Bykovka, Ukr.	78	50.17 N	27.58 E
Bykovo, Ross.	80	49.47 N	45.22 E
Bykovo, Ross.	82	54.01 N	37.54 E
Bykovo, Ross.	82	55.37 N	38.04 E
Bykovo Airport ⊠	265b	55.36 N	38.05 E
Bylas	200	33.08 N	110.07 W
Bylbasovka	83	48.51 N	37.30 E
Bylderup	41	54.57 N	9.07 E
Byley	262	53.13 N	2.25 W
Bylkyldak	86	48.38 N	75.16 E
Bylnice	30	49.04 N	18.01 E
Bylot Island I	176	73.13 N	78.34 W
Byng Inlet	190	45.46 N	80.33 W
Bynum, Mt., U.S.	182	47.58 N	112.18 W
Bynum, N.C., U.S.	192	35.46 N	79.08 W
Bynum, Tx., U.S.	222	31.58 N	97.00 W
Byōdōin Temple ʊ[1]	270	34.53 N	135.48 E
Byram ≃	276	40.59 N	73.39 W
Byramgore Reef ✦[2]	122	11.54 N	71.49 E
Byram Lake Reservoir ⊜[1]	276	41.10 N	73.41 W
Byrd, Lac ⊜	190	47.01 N	76.56 W
Byrdstown	194	36.34 N	85.07 W
Byrka	88	50.39 N	118.31 E
Byrnedale	214	41.17 N	78.30 W
Byro	162	26.05 S	116.09 E
Byrock	166	30.40 S	146.24 E
Byron, Ca., U.S.	226	37.52 N	121.38 W
Byron, Ga., U.S.	192	32.39 N	83.45 W
Byron, Il., U.S.	190	42.07 N	89.15 W
Byron, Mi., U.S.	216	42.49 N	83.57 W
Byron, N.Y., U.S.	210	43.04 N	78.03 W
Byron, Wy., U.S.	202	44.47 N	108.30 W
Byron, Cape ›	166	28.39 S	153.38 E
Byron, Isla I	254	47.47 S	75.12 W
Byron Bay	166	28.39 S	153.37 E
Byron Center	216	42.49 N	85.42 W
Byrranga, gory ⋏	74	75.00 N	104.00 E
Byšice-Liblice	54	50.19 N	14.38 E
Bysjön ⊜	40	60.23 N	14.30 E
Byske	26	64.57 N	21.12 E
Byskeälven ≃	26	64.57 N	21.13 E
Bystraja ≃	80	47.58 N	41.00 E
Bystřany	54	50.38 N	13.51 E
Bystrica ≃	80	58.38 N	49.05 E
Bystřice	30	49.45 N	14.41 E
Bystřice pod Hostýnem	30	49.24 N	17.40 E
Bystrij Tanyp ≃	86	55.46 N	54.35 E
Bystrovka	85	42.47 N	75.43 E
Bystryj	86	57.50 N	73.58 E
Bystryj Istok	86	52.23 N	84.24 E
Bystrzyca Kłodzka	30	50.18 N	16.38 E
Bytantaj ≃	74	68.46 N	134.20 E
Bytča, Bela.	76	54.18 N	28.24 E
Bytča, Česko.	30	49.14 N	18.36 E
Byten'	76	52.54 N	25.29 E
Bytkov	78	48.38 N	24.26 E
Bytom (Beuthen)	30	50.22 N	18.54 E
Bytoš'	76	53.50 N	34.06 E
Bytów	30	54.11 N	17.30 E
Byumba	154	1.35 S	30.04 E
Byvalki	78	51.51 N	30.37 E
Byxelkrok	26	57.20 N	17.00 E
Bzyb' ≃	84	43.12 N	40.18 E
Bzybskij chrebet ⋏	84	43.18 N	40.41 E
C			
Ça ≃	110	18.46 N	105.47 E
Čaa-Chol'	86	51.32 N	92.23 E
Caacupé	252	25.23 S	57.09 W
Čaadajevka	80	53.09 N	45.56 E
Čaadajevo	80	55.40 N	42.02 E
Caaguazú	252	25.26 S	56.02 W
Caaguazú □[5]	252	25.00 S	55.45 W
Caála	152	12.51 S	15.33 E
Caamaño Sound Ʊ	182	52.49 N	129.28 W
Caapiranga	246	3.18 S	61.13 W
Caapucú	252	26.13 S	57.12 W
Caarapó	255	22.38 S	54.48 W
Caatinga	255	17.10 S	45.53 W
Caazapá	252	26.09 S	56.24 W
Caazapá □[5]	252	26.10 S	56.00 W
Cabaçal ≃	248	16.00 S	57.42 W
Cabadbaran	116	9.10 N	125.38 E
Cabadiangan Plateau ⋏[1]	116	9.50 N	122.36 E
Cabagan	116	17.26 N	121.46 E
Cabaiguán	240p	22.05 N	79.30 W
Cabalete Island I	116	14.17 N	121.50 E
Cabalian	116	10.16 N	125.10 E
Cabaliana, Lago ⊜	246	3.20 S	60.50 W
Cabalian Bay c	116	10.13 N	125.10 E
Cabalian Point ›	116	12.06 N	122.01 E
Caballero Creek ≃	280	34.11 N	118.32 W
Caballito ◆[8]	288	34.37 S	58.27 W
Caballones, Cayo I	240p	20.52 N	79.00 W
Caballo Reservoir ⊜[1]	200	32.58 N	107.18 W
Cabana	248	8.24 S	78.02 W
Cabanaconde	248	15.37 S	71.59 W
Cabañas	240p	22.58 N	82.55 W
Cabanatuan	116	15.29 N	120.58 E
Cabangan	116	15.10 N	120.03 E
Çabano	186	47.41 N	68.53 W
Čabanovka	83	49.02 N	38.46 E
Cabarroguis	116	16.33 N	121.32 E
Cabarruyan Island I	116	16.18 N	119.59 E
Cabaun Island I	116	12.34 N	124.30 E
Cabeceiras	255	15.48 S	46.59 W
Cabeço de Montachique	266c	38.54 N	9.11 W
Cabellera, Sierra de la ⋏	200	30.55 N	109.07 W
Cabery	216	41.00 N	88.12 W
Cabeza del Buey	34	38.43 N	5.13 W
Cabeza de Tigre	286c	10.28 N	66.46 W
Cabezas	248	18.46 S	63.24 W
Cabiao	116	15.15 N	120.51 E
Cabiate	266b	45.40 N	9.10 E
Cabildo, Arg.	252	38.29 S	61.54 W
Cabildo, Chile	252	32.26 S	71.05 W
Cabimas	246	10.23 N	71.28 W
Cabin Branch ≃, Md., U.S.	284b	39.13 N	76.35 W
Cabin Branch ≃, Md., U.S.	284c	38.51 N	76.48 W
Cabin Creek ≃	198	46.55 N	104.52 W
Cabinda	152	5.33 S	12.12 E
Cabinda □[5]	152	5.00 S	12.30 E
Cabinet Mountains ⋏	202	48.20 N	116.00 W
Cabingaan Island I	116	5.41 N	121.03 E
Cabin John	208	38.58 N	77.09 W
Cabin John Creek ≃	284b	38.58 N	77.09 W
Cabin John Creek Park ♠	284c	38.59 N	77.09 W
Cabin John Regional Park ♠	284c	39.02 N	77.09 W
Cabiri	152	8.52 S	13.39 E
Cabixi ≃	248	13.41 S	60.44 W
Cable	190	46.12 N	91.17 W
Cable Airport ⊠	280	34.08 N	117.41 W
Cables	162	27.59 S	123.23 E
Cabo	250	8.17 S	35.02 W
Cabo Blanco	254	47.12 S	65.45 W
Cabo de Hornos, Parque Nacional ♠	250	55.45 S	67.25 W
Cabo Delgado □[5]	154	12.35 S	39.00 E
Cabo Frio	255	22.53 S	42.01 W
Cabo Gracias a Dios	236	14.59 N	83.10 W
Cabo Ledo	152	9.39 S	13.17 E
Cabonga, Réservoir ⊜[1]	190	47.20 N	76.35 W
Cabool	194	37.07 N	92.06 W
Caboolture	166	27.05 S	152.57 E
Cabo Orange, Parque Nacional do ♠	250	3.00 N	51.00 W
Cabora Bassa	154	15.35 S	32.48 E
Cabora Bassa Dam ◆[6]	154	15.35 S	32.42 E
Cabo Raso	254	44.21 S	65.14 W
Caborca	232	30.37 N	112.06 W
Cabo Rojo	240m	18.05 N	67.09 W
Cabot, Ar., U.S.	194	34.58 N	92.00 W
Cabot, Pa., U.S.	214	40.46 N	79.46 W
Cabot, Mount ∧	188	44.31 N	71.24 W
Cabot Head ›	212	45.14 N	81.17 W
Cabot Strait Ʊ	186	47.20 N	59.30 W
Cabo Verde	256	21.28 S	46.24 W
Cabo Verde ≃	256	21.28 S	46.17 W
Cabo Verde → Cape Verde □[1]	150a	16.00 N	24.00 W
Cabra	34	37.28 N	4.27 W
Cabra Corral, Embalse ⊜[1]	252	25.15 S	65.25 W
Cabra Island I	116	13.53 N	120.02 E
Cabramatta	274a	33.54 S	150.56 E
Cabramatta Creek ≃	274a	33.54 S	150.57 E
Cabramurra	171b	35.58 S	148.23 E
Cabras	71	39.56 N	8.32 E
Cabras, Stagno di ⊜	71	39.57 N	8.29 E
Cabras Island I	174p	13.27 N	144.40 E
Cabrel	234	20.06 N	105.14 W
Cabrera ≃, Col.	246	3.26 N	75.07 W
Cabrera ≃, Esp.	34	42.25 N	6.49 W
Cabrera, Illa de I	34	39.09 N	2.56 E
Cabrera, Sierra de la ⋏	34	42.12 N	6.40 W
Cabrera de Mar	266d	41.32 N	2.24 E
Cabreúva	256	23.18 S	47.08 W
Cabri	184	50.37 N	108.28 W
Cabriel ≃	34	39.14 N	1.03 W
Cabrillo National Monument ♠	228	32.41 N	117.15 W
Cabrils	266d	41.32 N	2.22 E
Cabrobó	250	8.31 S	39.19 W
Cabruta	246	7.38 N	66.15 W
Cabucgayan	116	11.29 N	124.34 E
Cabuçu	256	22.50 S	42.55 W
Cabuçu ≃, Bra.	287a	22.59 S	43.37 W
Cabuçu ≃, Bra.	287a	22.48 S	43.37 W
Cabuçu de Cima ≃	287b	23.31 S	46.33 W
Cabugao	116	17.48 N	120.27 E
Cabulauan Island I	116	11.23 N	120.06 E
Cabullónes, Punta ›	240m	17.58 N	66.35 W
Cabulo	152	10.15 S	16.40 E
Cabure	246	11.08 N	69.38 W
Cabuta	152	9.50 S	14.48 E
Cabuya	236	9.36 N	85.06 W
Cabuyal	236	10.40 N	85.40 W
Cabuyaro	246	4.18 N	72.49 W
Caca	80	48.11 N	44.40 E
Çaçador	252	26.47 S	51.00 W
Čačak	38	43.53 N	20.21 E
Cacaohatán	236	14.59 N	92.10 W
Cacaoui, Lac ⊜	186	50.53 N	66.58 W
Caçapava	256	23.06 S	45.42 W
Caçapava do Sul	252	30.30 S	53.30 W
Caçapava Velha	256	23.07 S	45.39 W
Cacapon ≃	188	39.37 N	78.16 W
Cacapon State Park ♠	188	39.32 N	78.23 W
Cacas	130	38.23 N	41.17 E
Caccamo	70	37.56 N	13.40 E
Caccia, Capo ›	71	40.34 N	8.09 E
Çaccuri	68	39.14 N	16.47 E
Čačenka ≃	265b	55.46 N	37.18 E
Cacequi	252	29.53 S	54.49 W
Cáceres, Bra.	248	16.04 S	57.41 W
Cáceres, Col.	246	7.35 N	75.20 W
Cáceres, Esp.	34	39.29 N	6.22 W
Cáceres □[4]	34	39.40 N	6.05 E
Cachan	261	48.48 N	2.20 E
Cacharí	252	36.24 S	59.32 W
Cache	196	34.37 N	98.37 W
Cache ≃, Ar., U.S.	194	34.42 N	91.20 W
Cache ≃, Il., U.S.	194	37.04 N	89.10 W
Caché, Lac ⊜	206	46.21 N	74.39 W
Cache Creek	182	50.48 N	121.19 W
Cache Creek ≃, Ca., U.S.	226	38.42 N	121.42 W
Cache Creek ≃, Ca., U.S.	228	35.06 N	117.58 W
Cache Creek, North Fork ≃	226	38.59 N	122.30 W
Cache la Poudre ≃	200	40.25 N	104.36 W
Cache la Poudre, North Fork ≃	198	40.54 N	105.22 W
Cache Mountain ∧	180	65.31 N	147.20 W
Cache Peak ∧, Ca., U.S.	228	35.13 N	118.15 W
Cache Peak ∧, Id., U.S.	202	42.11 N	113.40 W
Cache Slough ≃	226	38.11 N	121.40 W
Cacheu	150	12.16 N	16.10 W
Cacheu c[1]	150	12.10 N	16.21 W
Cachí	252	25.06 S	66.11 W
Cachimbo	250	9.24 S	54.56 W
Cachimbo, Serra do ⋏	250	8.30 S	55.50 W
Cachimo	152	8.21 S	21.20 E
Cachingues	152	13.05 S	16.43 E
Cachir	88	48.06 N	98.52 E
Cachkadzor	84	40.33 N	44.43 E
Cachoeira ≃	256	23.06 S	46.29 W
Cachoeira, Reservatório ⊜[1]	256	23.03 S	46.15 W
Cachoeira, Rio da ≃	287a	23.00 S	43.18 W
Cachoeira Alta	255	18.48 S	50.58 W
Cachoeira de Goiás	255	16.44 S	50.38 W
Cachoeira de Manteiga	255	16.39 S	45.16 W
Cachoeira de Minas	256	22.21 S	45.47 W
Cachoeira do Arari	250	1.01 S	48.58 W
Cachoeira do Sul	252	30.02 S	52.54 W
Cachoeira Grande, Alto da ∧	256	21.54 S	44.06 W
Cachoeira Paulista	256	22.40 S	45.01 W
Cachoeiras	287a	22.39 S	43.28 W
Cachoeiras de Macacu	256	22.28 S	42.39 W
Cachoeirinha	250	8.29 S	36.14 W
Cachoeiro de Itapemirim	255	20.51 S	41.06 W
Cachos, Punta ›	252	27.39 S	71.02 W
Çachos, Rio dos ≃	287b	23.36 S	46.26 W
Čachrov	60	49.16 N	13.18 E
Cachuela Esperanza	248	10.32 S	65.38 W
Cachuma, Lake ⊜[1]	204	34.35 N	119.55 W
Cacilhas	266c	38.41 N	9.09 W
Cacine	150	11.08 N	14.57 W
Caciporé ≃	250	3.51 N	51.08 W
Caciporé, Cabo ›	250	3.55 N	51.07 W
Căciulați	38	44.38 N	26.10 E
Cacnipa Island I	116	10.30 N	119.04 E
Cacocum	240p	20.44 N	76.23 W
Cacólo	152	10.07 S	19.17 E
Caconda	152	13.43 S	15.06 E
Caconde	256	21.33 S	46.38 W
Cacra	248	12.48 S	75.48 W
Cactus	196	36.04 N	102.00 W
Cactus Flat ☷	204	37.45 N	116.45 W
Cactus Peak ∧	204	37.47 N	116.53 W
Caçu	255	18.37 S	51.04 W
Cacuaco	152	8.47 S	13.22 E
Cacula	152	14.29 S	14.10 E
Caculé	255	14.30 S	42.13 W
Caculuvar ≃	152	16.46 S	14.36 E
Cacuri, Ang.	152	8.14 S	18.20 E
Cacuri, Ven.	246	4.48 N	65.21 W
Cacuso	152	9.26 S	15.43 E
Çadale	144	2.45 N	46.19 E
Čadan	86	51.17 N	91.35 E
Cadaqués	34	42.17 N	3.17 E
Çadariri ≃	248	6.20 S	57.46 W
Čadca	30	49.26 N	18.48 E
Caddington	42	51.51 N	0.27 W
Caddo, Ok., U.S.	196	34.07 N	96.15 W
Caddo, Tx., U.S.	196	32.38 N	98.40 W
Caddo ≃	194	34.10 N	93.03 W
Caddo Creek ≃	196	34.14 N	96.59 W
Caddo Lake ⊜[1]	194	32.42 N	94.01 W
Caddo Mills	222	33.04 N	96.14 W
Caddo Peak ∧	222	32.29 N	97.24 W
Caddy Vista	216	42.50 N	87.54 W
Cadell ≃	166	22.51 S	141.55 E
Cadena, Arroyo de la ≃	196	26.17 N	104.00 W
Cadena, Cerro ∧	196	25.50 N	104.04 W
Cadena, Punta ›	240m	18.18 N	67.14 W
Cadenberge	52	53.46 N	9.04 E
Cadenet	62	43.44 N	5.22 E
Cadeo	62	44.58 N	9.48 E
Cader Bronwyn ∧	42	52.54 N	3.22 W
Cadereyta de Jiménez	232	25.36 N	100.00 W
Cader Idris ∧	42	52.42 N	3.54 W
Cadibarrawirracanna, Lake ⊜	162	28.52 S	135.27 E
Cadig, Mount ∧	116	14.09 N	122.27 E
Cadillac, Sk., Can.	184	49.44 N	107.43 W

	English	Deutsch	Español	Français	Português
≃	River	Fluß	Río	Rivière	Rio
≅	Canal	Kanal	Canal	Canal	Canal
ᒪ	Waterfall, Rapids	Wasserfall, Stromschnellen	Cascada, Rápidos	Chute d'eau, Rapides	Cascata, Rápidos
Ʊ	Strait	Meeresstraße	Estrecho	Détroit	Estreito
c	Bay, Gulf	Bucht, Golf	Bahía, Golfo	Baie, Golfe	Baía, Golfo
⊜	Lake, Lakes	See, Seen	Lago, Lagos	Lac, Lacs	Lago, Lagos
☷	Swamp	Sumpf	Pantano	Marais	Pântano
⍓	Ice Features, Glacier	Eis- und Gletscherformen	Accidentes Glaciales	Formes glaciaires	Acidentes glaciares
⍑	Other Hydrographic Features	Andere Hydrographische Objekte	Otros Elementos Hidrográficos	Autres données hydrographiques	Outros acidentes hidrográficos

	English	Deutsch	Español	Français	Português
✦	Submarine Features	Untermeerische Objekte	Accidentes Submarinos	Formes de relief sous-marin	Acidentes submarinos
□	Political Unit	Politische Einheit	Unidad Politica	Entité politique	Unidade política
ʊ	Cultural Institution	Kulturelle Institution	Institución Cultural	Institution culturelle	Institução cultural
⊥	Historical Site	Historische Stätte	Sitio Histórico	Site historique	Sitio histórico
♠	Recreational Site	Erholungs- und Ferienort	Sitio de Recreo	Centre de loisirs	Area de Lazer
⊠	Airport	Flughafen	Aeropuerto	Aéroport	Aeroporto
■	Military Installation	Militäranlage	Instalación Militar	Installation militaire	Instalação militar
◆	Miscellaneous	Verschiedenes	Misceláneo	Divers	Diversos

ENGLISH: Name | Page | Lat.°′ | Long.°′ — DEUTSCH: Name | Seite | Breite°′ | Länge°′ E = Ost

Name	Page	Lat.°′	Long.°′
Cadillac, Fr.	32	44.38 N	0.19 W
Cadillac, Mi., U.S.	190	44.15 N	85.24 W
Cadipietra (Steinhaus)	64	46.59 N	11.59 E
Cadishead	262	53.25 N	2.26 W
Cadix → Cádiz	34	36.32 N	6.18 W
Cádiz, Esp.	34	36.32 N	6.18 W
Cadiz, Pil.	116	10.57 N	123.18 E
Cadiz, In., U.S.	218	39.57 N	85.30 W
Cadiz, Ky., U.S.	194	36.51 N	87.50 W
Cadiz, Oh., U.S.	214	40.16 N	80.59 W
Cádiz □[4]	34	36.35 N	5.50 W
Cádiz, Bahía de ⊂	34	36.32 N	6.16 W
Cádiz, Golfo de ⊂	34	36.50 N	7.10 W
Cadiz Lake ⊜	204	34.18 N	115.24 W
Cadlao Island I	116	11.13 N	119.21 E
Cadnam	42	50.55 N	1.35 W
Čadobec	88	58.40 N	98.51 E
Čadobec ≃	88	58.40 N	98.50 E
Cadogan	214	40.45 N	79.34 W
Cadomin	182	53.02 N	117.20 W
Cadoneghe	64	45.26 N	11.55 E
Cadore ⊕[1]	64	46.30 N	12.20 E
Cadosia	210	41.58 N	75.16 W
Cadott	190	44.56 N	91.09 W
Cadoux	162	30.47 S	117.08 E
Caduruan Point >	116	11.45 N	124.05 E
Caduta, Fosso delle ≃	267a	41.56 N	12.12 E
Cadwell	192	32.20 N	83.02 W
Cady Marsh Ditch ≊	278	41.33 N	87.29 W
Cady Mountain ∧[2]	224	48.33 N	123.07 W
Čadyr-Lunga	78	46.03 N	28.47 E
Cadzand	52	51.22 N	3.25 E
Caen	32	49.11 N	0.21 W
Caengo (Kwenge) ≃	152	4.50 S	18.42 E
Caerano di San Marco	64	45.47 N	12.00 E
Caere ⊥	66	42.02 N	12.07 E
Caergwrle	44	53.07 N	3.03 W
Caerleon	42	51.37 N	2.57 W
Caernarfon	44	53.08 N	4.16 W
Caernarfon Bay ⊂	44	53.05 N	4.30 W
Caernarfon Castle ⊥	44	53.08 N	4.16 W
Caerphilly	42	51.35 N	3.14 W
Caerphilly Castle ⊥	42	51.34 N	3.14 W
Caersws	42	52.31 N	3.25 W
Caesar Creek ≃	218	39.29 N	84.06 W
Caesar Creek, Anderson Fork ≃	218	39.33 N	83.58 W
Caesar Creek Lake ⊜[1]	218	39.30 N	84.00 W
Cæsarea → Qesari, Ḥorbat ⊥	132	32.30 N	34.53 E
Caetanópolis	255	19.18 S	44.24 W
Caeté	255	19.54 S	43.40 W
Caeté ≃	248	9.03 S	68.39 W
Caeté, Morro ∧[2]	287a	23.03 S	43.31 W
Caetité	255	14.04 S	42.29 W
Cafayate	252	26.05 S	65.58 W
Cafelândia do Leste	255	16.40 S	53.25 W
Cafima	152	16.39 S	16.27 E
Cafu	152	16.27 S	15.14 E
Cafuini ≃	246	1.17 N	57.11 W
Cagaan Chajrchan	88	49.25 N	94.15 E
Cagaan Gol	86	48.57 N	89.07 E
Cagaan Nuur, Mong.	86	49.32 N	89.42 E
Cagaannuur, Mong.	88	50.20 N	105.03 E
Cagaan-Ovoo	102	45.51 N	105.17 E
Cagaan Uul	88	49.28 N	98.30 E
Cagaan-Üür	88	50.32 N	101.30 E
Cágado ≃	256	22.02 S	43.09 W
Čagan ≃	80	51.12 N	51.20 E
Cagan-Aman	80	47.34 N	46.43 E
Cagan-Churtej, chrebet ⩙	88	51.32 N	110.00 E
Cagarras, Ilhas II	287a	23.02 S	43.12 W
Cagayan □[4]	116	18.00 N	121.50 E
Cagayan ≃	116	18.22 N	121.37 E
Cagayancillo	116	9.34 N	121.12 E
Cagayan de Oro	116	8.29 N	124.39 E
Cagayan de Tawi-Tawi	116	7.01 N	118.30 E
Cagayan Island I	116	9.36 N	121.14 E
Cagayan Islands II	116	9.40 N	121.16 E
Cagayan Sulu Island I	116	7.01 N	118.30 E
Čagda	74	58.45 N	130.37 E
Cageri	84	42.39 N	42.45 E
Caggiano	68	40.34 N	15.29 E
Çağış	130	39.30 N	28.01 E
Çağlarca	130	39.05 N	39.10 E
Cagli	66	43.33 N	12.39 E
Cagliari	71	39.13 N	9.07 E
Cagliari □[4]	71	39.30 N	8.45 E
Cagliari, Golfo di ⊂	71	39.08 N	9.11 E
Cagliari, Stagno di ⊜	71	39.13 N	9.02 E
Čaglinka ≃	86	53.59 N	69.47 E
Cagnano Varano	68	41.49 N	15.47 E
Cagnes-sur-Mer	62	43.40 N	7.09 E
Čagoda	76	59.10 N	35.17 E
Čagoda ≃	76	59.05 N	35.18 E
Čagodošča ≃	76	58.57 N	36.35 E
Čagojan	89	52.08 N	128.15 E
Čagra ≃	80	52.37 N	48.15 E
Cagraray Island I	116	13.18 N	123.52 E
Cagua	246	10.11 N	67.27 W
Caguán ≃	246	0.08 S	74.18 W
Caguas	240m	18.14 N	66.02 W
Cagveri	84	41.48 N	43.29 E
Cagwait	116	8.55 N	126.18 E
Cahaba ≃	194	32.20 N	87.05 W
Cahabón	236	15.34 N	89.49 W
Cahabón ≃	236	15.25 N	89.36 W
Cahama	152	16.17 S	14.19 E
Caha Mountains ⩙	48	51.45 N	9.45 W
Caher	48	52.21 N	7.56 W
Caherdaniel	48	51.45 N	10.05 W
Cahersiveen	48	51.57 N	10.13 W
Cahokia	219	38.34 N	90.11 W
Cahokia Creek ≃	219	38.47 N	90.01 W
Cahokia Mounds State Park ◆	219	38.39 N	90.03 W
Cahoon Creek ≃	279a	41.29 N	81.55 W
Cahoon Park ◆	279a	41.29 N	81.56 W
Cahoonzie	210	41.26 N	74.43 W
Cahore Point >	48	52.34 N	6.11 W
Cahors	32	44.27 N	1.26 E
Cahto Peak ∧	204	39.41 N	123.35 W
Cahuilla Indian Reservation ⊕[4]	204	33.30 N	116.43 W
Cahuinari ≃	246	1.21 S	70.44 W
Cahuita, Punta >	236	9.45 N	82.49 W
Caí ≃	252	29.56 S	51.16 W
Caia ≃	34	38.50 N	7.05 W
Caianda	152	11.02 S	23.31 E
Caiapó ≃, Bra.	250	8.52 S	49.36 W
Caiapó ≃, Bra.	255	15.49 S	51.53 W
Caiapó, Serra do ⩙	255	17.00 S	52.00 W
Caiapônia	255	16.57 S	51.49 W
Caiazzo	68	41.11 N	14.22 E
Caibarién	240p	22.31 N	79.28 W
Cai Bau, Dao I	110	21.10 N	107.27 E
Caibiran	116	11.34 N	124.35 E
Caiçara, Bra.	250	6.36 S	35.29 W
Caiçara, Bra.	255	15.34 S	50.12 W
Caicara, Caño ≃	246	7.44 N	69.04 W
Caicara de Maturín	246	9.49 N	63.36 W
Caicara de Orinoco	246	7.37 N	66.10 W
Caicedonia	246	4.20 N	75.50 W
Caicó	250	6.27 S	37.06 W
Caicos Bank ✢[4]	238	21.35 N	71.55 W
Caicos Islands II	238	21.56 N	71.58 W
Caicos Passage ⊔	238	22.00 N	72.30 W
Caieiras	256	23.22 S	46.44 W
Caieiras □[7]	287b	23.23 S	46.41 W
Caigou	100	33.16 N	114.32 E
Caiguna	162	32.17 S	125.25 E
Caihuaping	100	26.54 N	113.23 E
Caijiachang	107	29.44 N	106.29 E
Caijiagang	107	28.55 N	106.21 E
Caijialou	104	41.24 N	121.06 E
Caijiapo	102	34.17 N	107.39 E
Caijiazhuang	105	40.48 N	114.44 E
Caille	62	43.46 N	6.44 E
Cailloma	248	15.12 S	71.46 W
Caillou Bay ⊂	194	29.06 N	90.56 W
Caima Bay ⊂	116	13.42 N	122.48 E
Caimán, Islas → Cayman Islands □[2]	238	19.30 N	80.40 W
Caimanera	240p	19.59 N	75.09 W
Caïmanes → Cayman Islands □[2]	238	19.30 N	80.40 W
Caiman Point >	116	15.55 N	119.46 E
Caimbambo	152	12.58 S	14.01 E
Cain ≃	42	52.46 N	3.08 W
Cain Creek ≃	198	44.17 N	98.10 W
Cainde	152	15.42 S	13.12 E
Caine ≃	248	18.23 S	65.21 W
Caino	64	45.38 N	10.18 E
Cains ≃	186	46.40 N	65.47 W
Cainsdorf	54	50.41 N	12.29 E
Cainsville	194	40.28 N	93.59 W
Cainta	269f	14.35 N	121.07 E
Cai Nuoc	110	8.56 N	105.01 E
Cairano	68	40.54 N	15.22 E
Cairari	250	2.33 S	49.07 W
Caird Coast ⍊[2]	9	76.00 S	24.30 W
Caire, Le → Al-Qāhirah	142	30.03 N	31.15 E
Cairnbrook	214	40.07 N	78.49 W
Cairn Curran Reservoir ⊜[1]	169	37.04 S	143.59 E
Cairndow	46	56.15 N	4.56 W
Cairngorm Mountains ⩙	46	57.04 N	3.50 W
Cairn Mountain ∧	180	61.10 N	155.20 W
Cairnryan	44	54.58 N	5.02 W
Cairns	166	16.55 S	145.46 E
Cairns Lake ⊜	184	51.42 N	94.30 W
Cairnsmore of Carsphairn ∧	44	55.15 N	4.12 W
Cairnsmore of Fleet ∧	44	54.59 N	4.20 W
Cairn Table ∧	44	55.29 N	4.02 W
Cairn Water ≃	44	55.07 N	3.45 W
Cairo, Ga., U.S.	192	30.52 N	84.12 W
Cairo, Il., U.S.	194	37.00 N	89.10 W
Cairo, Ne., U.S.	198	41.00 N	98.36 W
Cairo, N.Y., U.S.	210	42.17 N	73.59 W
Cairo, Oh., U.S.	216	40.49 N	84.05 W
Cairo, W.V., U.S.	188	39.12 N	81.09 W
Cairo (Almaza) Airport ⊠, Miṣr	273c	30.06 N	31.22 E
Cairo (Imbābah) Airport ⊠, Miṣr	273c	30.04 N	31.12 E
Cairo, University of ʊ[2]	273c	30.02 N	31.12 E
Cairo → Al-Qāhirah	142	30.03 N	31.15 E
Cairoçu, Pico do ∧	256	23.18 S	44.36 W
Cairofa	152	14.05 S	12.54 E
Cairo International Airport ⊠	142	30.08 N	31.24 E
Cairo Main Station ⊕[5]	273c	30.04 N	31.15 E
Cairo Montenotte	62	44.24 N	8.16 E
Cairu	255	13.30 S	39.03 W
Caister-on-Sea	42	52.39 N	1.44 E
Caistor	44	53.30 N	0.20 W
Caitingqiao	105	39.54 N	117.39 E
Caitou	152	14.28 S	13.06 E
Caiundo	152	15.46 S	17.28 E
Caivano	68	40.57 N	14.18 E
Caiwan	102	25.50 N	110.50 E
Caixi	100	25.15 N	116.28 E
Caiyu	105	39.39 N	116.37 E
Caizhuang	98	34.17 N	114.08 E
Caizi Hu ⊜	100	30.48 N	117.05 E
Čaja ≃, Ross.	86	58.08 N	82.57 E
Čaja ≃, Ross.	88	58.15 N	109.35 E
Cajabamba, Ec.	246	1.42 S	78.45 W
Cajabamba, Perú	248	7.37 S	78.03 W
Cajacay	248	10.10 S	77.26 W
Caja de Muertos, Isla I	240m	17.54 N	66.32 W
Cajamar	256	23.21 S	46.53 W
Cajamarca	248	7.10 S	78.31 W
Cajamarca □[5]	248	6.15 S	78.50 W
Čajan	85	43.02 N	69.23 E
Čajan ≃	85	42.52 N	68.56 E
Cajapió	250	2.58 S	44.48 W
Cajarc	32	44.29 N	1.50 E
Cajari	250	3.20 S	45.01 W
Cajari ≃	250	0.48 S	51.43 W
Cajatambo	248	10.29 S	77.02 W
Čajatyn, chrebet ⩙	89	52.25 N	138.25 E
Cajàzeiras	250	6.54 S	38.34 W
Čajek	85	41.56 N	74.30 E
Čajkovskij	80	56.47 N	54.09 E
Čajniče	38	43.33 N	19.04 E
Cajones ≃	234	17.45 N	95.55 W
Cajones, Cayos ✢[2]	236	16.05 N	83.12 W
Cajon Mountain ∧	228	34.16 N	117.25 W
Cajon Pass)(	228	34.19 N	117.26 W
Cajon Summit)(	228	34.21 N	117.27 W
Caju ⊕[8]	287a	22.53 S	43.13 W
Cajuru	255	21.17 S	47.18 W
Caka	102	36.48 N	99.19 E
Caka Yanhu ⊜	102	36.40 N	99.20 E
Čakčar, chrebet ⩙	85	38.35 N	67.28 E
Cakeni	152	17.48 S	19.27 E
Cakir	88	50.27 N	103.35 E
Çakıralan	130	41.10 N	35.47 E
Çakırgöl Dağı ∧	130	40.34 N	39.42 E
Çakırhüyük	130	37.34 N	37.50 E
Çakmak	130	37.37 N	34.19 E
Çakmak Dağı ∧	130	39.46 N	42.12 E
Čakovec	61	46.23 N	16.26 E
Čakovice ⊕[8]	54	50.08 N	14.31 E
Cakung ≃	269e	6.06 S	106.56 E
Çal	130	38.05 N	29.24 E
Cala, Transkei	158	31.30 S	27.37 E
Cala, Tür.	84	41.05 N	43.21 E
Cala, Embalse de ⊜[1]	34	37.50 N	6.00 W
Calabacillas	234	23.13 N	99.45 W
Calabanga	116	13.42 N	123.12 E
Calabar	150	4.57 N	8.19 E
Calabasas, Arroyo ≃	280	34.12 N	118.36 W
Calabazar ⊕[8]	286b	23.01 N	82.22 W
Calabazas Creek ≃	282	37.25 N	121.58 W
Calabernardo	70	36.52 N	15.08 E
Calabogie	212	45.18 N	76.43 W
Calabogie Lake ⊜	212	45.16 N	76.45 W
Calabozo	246	8.56 N	67.26 W
Calabozo, Ensenada de ⊂	246	11.30 N	71.45 W
Calabria □[4]	68	39.00 N	16.30 E
Calabria, Parco Nazionale di ◆	68	38.09 N	15.54 E
Calabritto	68	40.47 N	15.13 E
Calabro ≃	70	37.53 N	14.11 E
Calabugdong Island I	116	11.06 N	119.41 E
Calaca	116	13.56 N	120.49 E
Calacuccia	36	42.20 N	9.03 E
Caladang, Mount ∧	116	14.49 N	121.21 E
Caladesi Island I	220	28.02 N	82.49 W
Caladesi Island State Park ◆	220	28.02 N	82.48 W
Cala d'Oliva	71	41.05 N	8.20 E
Calafat	38	43.59 N	22.56 E
Calafquén, Lago ⊜	254	39.31 S	72.10 W
Calagnaan Island I	116	11.29 N	123.13 E
Cala Gonone	71	40.18 N	9.38 E
Calagua Islands II	116	14.27 N	122.55 E
Calahorra	34	42.18 N	1.58 W
Calais, Fr.	50	50.57 N	1.50 E
Calais, Me., U.S.	188	45.11 N	67.16 W
Calais, Canal de ≊	50	50.57 N	1.51 E
Calais, Pas de (Strait of Dover) ⊔	50	51.00 N	1.30 E
Calala	152	12.59 S	23.30 E
Calalaste, Sierra de ⩙	252	25.30 S	67.30 W
Calalzo di Cadore	64	46.27 N	12.23 E
Calama	252	22.28 S	68.56 W
Calamar, Col.	246	10.15 N	74.55 W
Calamar, Col.	246	1.58 N	72.41 W
Calamarca	248	16.55 S	68.09 W
Calamba, Pil.	116	14.13 N	121.10 E
Calamba, Pil.	116	8.35 N	123.39 E
Calamian Group II	116	12.00 N	120.00 E
Calamity Creek ≃	196	29.41 N	103.42 W
Calamocha	34	40.55 N	1.18 W
Calamonaci	70	37.31 N	13.17 E
Calamus ≃	198	41.48 N	99.09 W
Calañas	34	37.39 N	6.53 W
Calanca, Val ∨	58	46.22 N	9.07 E
Calanda	34	40.56 N	0.14 W
Calandagan Island I	116	10.39 N	120.15 E
Calang	114	4.38 N	95.34 E
Calangianus	71	40.56 N	9.11 E
Calanna	68	38.11 N	15.43 E
Calapan	116	13.25 N	121.10 E
Calape	116	9.54 N	123.52 E
Calapooia ≃	202	44.38 N	123.08 W
Calapooya Mountains ⩙	202	43.30 N	122.50 W
Călărași	38	44.11 N	27.20 E
Călărași □[6]	38	44.20 N	27.10 E
Calarcá	246	4.31 N	75.38 W
Calascibetta	70	37.35 N	14.16 E
Calasetta	71	39.07 N	8.22 E
Calatabiano	70	37.49 N	15.14 E
Calatafimi	70	37.55 N	12.52 E
Calatagan	116	13.50 N	120.38 E
Calatayud	34	41.21 N	1.38 W
Calau	54	51.45 N	13.56 E
Calauag Bay ≃	116	14.02 N	122.13 E
Calavá, Capo >	70	38.11 N	14.55 E
Calaveras □[6]	226	38.12 N	120.41 W
Calaveras ≃	226	37.58 N	121.22 W
Calaveras, North Fork ≃	226	38.12 N	120.43 W
Calaveras Big Trees State Park ◆	226	38.16 N	120.19 W
Calaveras Point >	282	37.28 N	122.03 W
Calaveras Reservoir ⊜[1]	226	37.28 N	121.49 W
Calaveritas Creek ≃	226	38.10 N	120.40 W
Calavino	64	46.03 N	10.59 E
Calavite, Cape >	116	13.27 N	120.18 E
Calavite, Mount ∧	116	13.29 N	120.24 E
Calavite Passage ⊔	116	13.36 N	120.25 E
Calavon ≃	62	43.51 N	5.00 E
Calawah ≃	224	47.56 N	124.27 W
Calawah, North Fork ≃	224	47.58 N	124.20 W
Calawah, South Fork ≃	224	47.58 N	124.20 W
Calayan	116	19.16 N	121.28 E
Calayan Island I	116	19.20 N	121.27 E
Čalba	89	52.43 N	131.27 E
Calbayog	116	12.04 N	124.36 E
Calbe	54	51.54 N	11.46 E
Calbiga	116	11.38 N	125.01 E
Calbuco	254	41.46 S	73.08 W
Calca	248	13.20 S	71.57 W
Calçado ≃	256	22.05 S	43.04 W
Calcasieu ≃	194	30.05 N	93.20 W
Calcasieu Lake ⊜	194	29.50 N	93.17 W
Calceta	246	0.51 S	80.10 W
Calcha	248	21.06 S	67.31 W
Calchaquí	252	29.54 S	60.18 W
Calchaquí ≃	252	26.03 S	65.50 W
Calciano	68	40.35 N	16.11 E
Calcinaia	66	43.41 N	10.37 E
Calcinato	64	45.27 N	10.24 E
Calcio	62	45.30 N	9.50 E
Calcium	212	44.01 N	75.51 W
Calçoene	250	2.30 N	50.57 W
Calçoene ≃	250	2.30 N	50.50 W
Calcutta, India	126	22.32 N	88.22 E
Calcutta, India	272b	22.32 N	88.22 E
Calcutta, Oh., U.S.	214	40.40 N	80.34 W
Calcutta University ʊ[2]	272b	22.35 N	88.22 E
Caldaro (Kaltern)	64	46.25 N	11.14 E
Caldarola	66	43.08 N	13.13 E
Caldas, Bra.	256	21.56 S	46.23 W
Caldas, Col.	246	6.05 N	75.38 W
Caldas □[5]	246	5.15 N	75.30 W
Caldas da Rainha	34	39.24 N	9.08 W
Caldas de Reyes	34	42.36 N	8.38 W
Caldas Novas	255	17.45 S	48.38 W
Caldè	58	45.57 N	8.38 E
Caldecott Tunnel ⊕[5]	282	37.52 N	122.12 W
Calder ≃, Eng., U.K.	44	53.44 N	1.21 W
Calder ≃, Eng., U.K.	262	53.49 N	2.24 W
Calder, Loch ⊜	46	58.31 N	3.36 W
Caldera	252	27.04 S	70.50 W
Caldera de Taburiente, Parque Nacional de la ◆	148	28.48 N	17.52 W
Calder and Hebble Navigation Canal ≊	262	53.43 N	1.54 W
Calder Bridge	44	54.27 N	3.29 W
Calderbrook	262	53.39 N	2.05 W
Calderdale □[8]	262	53.44 N	2.00 W
Calderstones Park ◆	262	53.23 N	2.54 W
Caldes	64	46.22 N	10.56 E
Caldes ≃	266d	41.31 N	2.13 E
Caldew ≃	44	54.54 N	2.56 W
Caldey Island I	42	51.38 N	4.41 W
Caldicot	42	51.36 N	2.45 W
Caldiero	64	45.22 N	11.11 E
Çaldıran	84	39.09 N	43.55 E
Caldonazzo	64	45.59 N	11.16 E
Caldonazzo, Lago di ⊜	64	46.01 N	11.15 E
Čaldonka	88	53.47 N	119.12 E
Caldwell, Id., U.S.	202	43.39 N	116.41 W
Caldwell, Ks., U.S.	198	37.01 N	97.36 W
Caldwell, N.J., U.S.	276	40.51 N	74.17 W
Caldwell, Oh., U.S.	188	39.44 N	81.31 W
Caldwell, Tx., U.S.	222	30.31 N	96.41 W
Caldwell □[6]	222	29.50 N	97.40 W
Caldwell Creek ≃	214	41.37 N	79.37 W
Caldwell-Wright Airport ⊠	276	40.53 N	74.17 W
Caldy	262	53.21 N	3.10 W
Cale ≃	42	50.59 N	2.20 W
Caledon, On., Can.	212	43.52 N	80.00 W
Caledon, S. Afr.	158	34.12 S	19.23 E
Caledon (Mohokare) ≃	158	30.31 S	26.05 E
Caledon East	212	43.52 N	79.52 W
Caledonia, Belize	232	18.14 N	88.29 W
Caledonia, N.S., Can.	186	44.22 N	65.02 W
Caledonia, On., Can.	212	43.04 N	79.56 W
Caledonia, Il., U.S.	216	42.22 N	88.53 W
Caledonia, Mi., U.S.	216	42.47 N	85.31 W
Caledonia, Mn., U.S.	190	43.38 N	91.29 W
Caledonia, Ms., U.S.	194	33.40 N	88.19 W
Caledonia, N.Y., U.S.	210	42.58 N	77.51 W
Caledonia, Oh., U.S.	214	40.38 N	82.58 W
Caledonia, Pa., U.S.	214	41.17 N	78.27 W
Caledonian Canal ≊	46	56.50 N	5.06 W
Caledonia State Park ◆	208	39.56 N	77.29 W
Calego	152	12.10 S	23.36 E
Calella	34	41.37 N	2.40 E
Calemba	152	16.04 S	15.44 E
Calen	166	20.54 S	148.46 E
Calendžicha	84	42.37 N	42.04 E
Calenzano	66	43.51 N	11.09 E
Calera, Al., U.S.	194	33.06 N	86.45 W
Calera, Ok., U.S.	196	33.56 N	96.25 W
Calera Creek ≃	282	37.27 N	121.54 W
Caleta, Punta >	240p	20.04 N	74.18 W
Caleta Olivia	254	46.26 S	67.32 W
Caleufú	252	35.35 S	64.33 W
Calexico	204	32.40 N	115.29 W
Calf Island I	283	42.20 N	70.54 W
Calf Islands II	276	40.59 N	73.38 W
Calfkiller ≃	194	35.49 N	85.29 W
Calf of Man I	44	54.03 N	4.48 W
Calfpasture ≃	188	37.58 N	79.28 W
Calf Pasture Point >	276	41.05 N	73.24 W
Calgary	182	51.03 N	114.05 W
Calhan	198	39.02 N	104.17 W
Calhariz ⊕[8]	266c	38.44 N	9.12 W
Calhoun, Al., U.S.	194	32.03 N	86.32 W
Calhoun, Ga., U.S.	192	34.30 N	84.57 W
Calhoun, Ky., U.S.	194	37.32 N	87.15 W
Calhoun, Mo., U.S.	194	38.28 N	93.37 W
Calhoun, Tn., U.S.	192	35.17 N	84.44 W
Calhoun □[6], Il., U.S.	219	39.09 N	90.37 W
Calhoun □[6], Mi., U.S.	216	42.14 N	85.00 W
Calhoun City	194	33.51 N	89.18 W
Calhoun Falls	192	34.05 N	82.35 W
Cali, Col.	246	3.27 N	76.31 W
Çalı, Tür.	130	40.10 N	28.54 E
Calian Point >	116	6.07 N	125.42 E
Calicoan Island I	116	10.59 N	125.48 E
Calico Ghost Town ⊥	228	34.57 N	116.52 W
Calico Rock	194	36.07 N	92.08 W
Calicut	122	11.15 N	75.46 E
Caliente, Ca., U.S.	228	35.17 N	118.37 W
Caliente, Nv., U.S.	204	37.36 N	114.30 W
Caliente Creek ≃	228	35.17 N	118.48 W
Califon	210	40.43 N	74.50 W
California, Mo., U.S.	194	38.37 N	92.33 W
California, Pa., U.S.	214	40.03 N	79.53 W
California □[3], U.S.	178	37.30 N	119.30 W
California □[3], U.S.	204	37.30 N	119.30 W
California, Golfo de ⊂	232	28.00 N	112.00 W
California, University of ʊ[2]	282	37.52 N	122.15 W
California Aqueduct ≊[1]	204	33.52 N	117.12 W
California City	228	35.08 N	117.58 W
California Creek ≃	196	33.05 N	99.33 W
California Institute of Technology ʊ[2]	280	34.08 N	118.08 W
California Institution for Men ʊ	280	33.59 N	117.40 W
California Institution for Women ʊ	280	33.57 N	117.38 W
California-Los Angeles, University of (U.C.L.A.) ʊ[2]	280	34.04 N	118.26 W
California State Polytechnic University ʊ[2]	280	34.04 N	117.49 W
California State University (Los Angeles) ʊ[2], Ca., U.S.	280	34.04 N	118.10 W
California State University (Northridge) ʊ[2], Ca., U.S.	280	34.14 N	118.32 W
California State University (Dominguez Hills) ʊ[2], Ca., U.S.	280	33.52 N	118.17 W
California State University (Fullerton) ʊ[2], Ca., U.S.	280	33.53 N	117.53 W
California State University (Long Beach) ʊ[2], Ca., U.S.	280	33.47 N	118.06 W
California State University (Hayward) ʊ[2], Ca., U.S.	282	37.39 N	122.04 W
Calihualá	234	17.35 N	98.10 W
Calilegua	252	23.47 S	64.47 W
Calilegua, Parque Nacional ◆	252	23.40 S	64.50 W
Călimănești	38	45.14 N	24.20 E
Călimani, Munții ⩙	38	47.07 N	25.03 E
Calimera	68	40.15 N	18.17 E
Calimere, Point >	122	10.18 N	79.52 E
Calimesa	228	34.00 N	117.03 W
Calindó ≃	255	14.26 S	43.51 W
Calingasta	252	31.19 S	69.25 W
Calingiri	162	31.06 S	116.27 E
Calinog	116	11.07 N	122.32 E
Calintaan	116	12.35 N	120.56 E
Calion	194	33.19 N	92.32 W
Calipatria	204	33.07 N	115.30 W
Calispell Peak ∧	202	48.26 N	117.30 W
Calistoga	226	38.34 N	122.34 W
Calitri	68	40.54 N	15.27 E
Calitzdorp	158	33.33 S	21.42 E
Calizzano	62	44.14 N	8.07 E
Calka	84	41.37 N	44.05 E
Calkinskoje vodochranilišče ⊜[1]	84	41.38 N	44.03 E
Čalkojdy	85	40.44 N	73.39 E
Calla	226	37.46 N	121.11 W
Callabonna, Lake ⊜	166	29.45 S	140.04 E
Callabonna Creek ≃	166	29.38 S	140.08 E
Callac	32	48.24 N	3.26 W
Callaghan, Mount ∧	204	39.42 N	116.57 W
Callahan	192	30.33 N	81.49 W
Callahan, Mount ∧	200	39.26 N	108.07 W
Callahans	276	40.58 N	74.37 W
Callan	48	52.33 N	7.23 W
Callander, On., Can.	190	46.13 N	79.23 W
Callander, Scot., U.K.	46	56.15 N	4.14 W
Callang	116	17.02 N	121.38 E
Callanish	46	58.12 N	6.43 W
Callanmarca	248	12.52 S	74.38 W
Callanna	166	29.38 S	137.55 E
Callantsoog	52	52.49 N	4.41 E
Callao, Perú	248	12.04 S	77.09 W
Callao, Va., U.S.	208	37.58 N	76.33 W
Callao □[4]	286d	12.04 S	77.09 W
Callaquén, Volcán ∧[1]	252	37.54 S	71.26 W
Callas	62	43.35 N	6.32 E
Callaway	198	41.17 N	99.55 W
Callaway □[6]	219	38.50 N	91.52 W
Callaway Gardens ◆	192	32.51 N	84.52 W
Calle	56	51.20 N	8.13 E
Callensburg	214	41.08 N	79.33 W
Callery	214	40.45 N	80.02 W
Call Hill ∧[2]	210	42.13 N	77.40 W
Calliano, It.	62	45.00 N	8.15 E
Calliano, It.	64	45.56 N	11.05 E
Calliaqua	241h	13.08 N	61.12 W
Callicoon	210	41.46 N	75.03 W
Callicoon Center	210	41.50 N	74.57 W
Calliham	196	28.29 N	98.21 W
Calling Lake	182	55.15 N	113.12 W
Calling Lake ⊜	182	55.13 N	113.15 W
Callington, Austl.	168b	35.07 S	139.02 E
Callington, Eng., U.K.	42	50.30 N	4.18 W
Calliope	166	24.00 S	151.12 E
Callosa d'En Sarrià	34	38.39 N	0.07 W
Callosa de Segura	34	38.08 N	0.52 W
Calloway Canal ≊	226	35.24 N	119.01 W
Calmar, Ab., Can.	182	53.16 N	113.49 W
Calmar, Ia., U.S.	190	43.11 N	91.51 W
Calmar → Kalmar	26	56.40 N	16.22 E
Călmățui ≃	38	44.50 N	27.50 E
Calmazzo	66	43.40 N	12.46 E
Calmbach	56	48.46 N	8.35 E
Calm Lake ⊜	190	48.46 N	92.04 W
Čal'mny-Varre	24	67.10 N	37.33 E
Čalna	24	61.55 N	34.01 E
Calnali	234	20.55 N	98.35 W
Calne	42	51.27 N	2.00 W
Calobre	236	8.19 N	80.51 W
Calola	152	16.30 S	17.51 E
Calolbon	116	13.36 N	124.06 E
Calólo	152	10.00 S	14.53 E
Calolziocorte	62	45.48 N	9.26 E
Calonne-Ricouart	50	50.29 N	2.29 E
Caloocan	116	14.39 N	120.58 E
Caloosahatchee ≃	220	26.31 N	82.01 W
Caloosahatchee Canal ≊	220	26.46 N	81.27 W
Caloote	168b	34.58 S	139.16 E
Calore ≃, It.	68	41.11 N	14.28 E
Calore ≃, It.	68	40.31 N	15.01 E
Caloundra	166	26.48 S	153.09 E
Calouste-Gulbenkian, Museu de ʊ	266c	38.44 N	9.08 W
Caloveto	68	39.30 N	16.45 E
Calp	34	38.39 N	0.03 E
Calpulalpan	234	19.35 N	98.35 W
Čalpy	80	55.05 N	53.06 E
Calshot	42	50.49 N	1.19 W
Calstock	42	50.30 N	4.12 W
Caltabellotta	70	37.34 N	13.13 E
Caltagirone	70	37.14 N	14.31 E
Caltagirone ≃	70	37.21 N	14.42 E
Caltanissetta	70	37.29 N	14.04 E
Caltanissetta □[4]	70	37.29 N	14.04 E
Caltavuturo	70	37.49 N	13.53 E
Çaltılıbük	130	39.57 N	28.36 E
Caltra	48	53.26 N	8.25 W
Čaltyr'	83	47.17 N	39.30 E
Caluango	152	8.21 S	19.40 E
Calubian	116	11.27 N	124.26 E
Calucinga	152	11.18 S	16.12 E
Călugăreni	38	44.07 N	26.01 E
Caluire-et-Cuire	62	45.48 N	4.51 E
Calumbolaca	152	9.09 S	13.48 E
Calumet, Mi., U.S.	190	47.14 N	88.27 W
Calumet, Mn., U.S.	190	47.19 N	93.16 W
Calumet, Pa., U.S.	214	40.13 N	79.28 W
Calumet ≃	278	41.44 N	87.32 W
Calumet, Lake ⊜	216	41.41 N	87.35 W
Calumet City	216	41.36 N	87.31 W
Calumet Harbor ⊂	278	41.44 N	87.32 W
Calumet Park	278	41.39 N	87.39 W
Calumet Park ◆	278	41.43 N	87.32 W
Calumet Sag Channel ≊	278	41.42 N	87.57 W
Calumpit	116	14.55 N	120.46 E
Calunda	152	12.06 S	23.23 E
Caluquembe	152	13.47 S	14.44 E
Calusa Island I	116	9.37 N	121.01 E
Caluso	62	45.18 N	7.53 E
Caluula	144	11.58 N	50.45 E
Caluula, Raasiga >	144	11.59 N	50.47 E
Caluya Island I	116	11.55 N	121.34 E
Calvados □[5]	32	49.10 N	0.30 W
Calvello	68	40.28 N	15.51 E
Calver	44	53.16 N	1.38 W
Calvera	68	40.09 N	16.09 E
Calvert, Al., U.S.	194	31.09 N	88.01 W
Calvert, Tx., U.S.	222	30.58 N	96.40 W
Calvert □[6]	208	38.33 N	76.35 W
Calvert ≃	164	16.17 S	137.44 E
Calvert, Lough ⊜	169	38.11 S	143.42 E
Calvert City	194	37.02 N	88.21 W
Calvert Hills	166	17.15 S	137.20 E
Calvert Island I	182	51.35 N	128.00 W
Calverton, Eng., U.K.	44	53.02 N	1.05 W
Calverton, Md., U.S.	284c	39.03 N	76.56 W
Calverton, N.Y., U.S.	207	40.55 N	72.45 W
Calvi	32	42.34 N	8.45 E
Calvi, Monte ∧	66	43.05 N	10.37 E
Calvia	34	39.34 N	2.31 E
Calvi dell'Umbria	66	42.24 N	12.34 E
Calvillo	234	21.51 N	102.43 W
Calvin, Ok., U.S.	196	34.58 N	96.14 W
Calvin, Pa., U.S.	214	40.20 N	78.02 W
Calvinia	158	31.25 S	19.45 E
Calvisano	64	45.20 N	10.20 E
Calvo, Monte ∧	68	41.44 N	15.46 E
Calvörde	54	52.23 N	11.17 E
Calw	56	48.43 N	8.44 E
Calwa	226	36.42 N	119.45 W
Calypso	192	35.09 N	78.06 W
Calzada	248	6.02 S	77.02 W
Cam ≃	42	52.21 N	0.15 E
Camabatela	152	8.11 S	15.22 E
Camaçã ≃	248	6.35 S	66.27 W
Camaçari	255	12.41 S	38.18 W
Camachigama, Lac ⊜	190	47.50 N	76.19 W
Camacupa	152	12.03 S	17.30 E
Camaguán	246	8.06 N	67.36 W
Camagüey	240p	21.23 N	77.55 W
Camagüey □[4]	240p	21.30 N	78.00 W
Camagüey, Archipiélago de II	240p	22.30 N	78.10 W
Camaiore	64	43.56 N	10.18 E
Camaiú ≃	248	5.30 S	59.42 W
Camajuaní	240p	22.28 N	79.44 W
Camaldoli, Eremo di ʊ[1]	66	43.46 N	11.47 E
Camamu	255	13.57 S	39.07 W
Camaná	248	16.37 S	72.42 W
Camaná ≃	248	16.39 S	72.46 W
Camanaú ≃	246	1.51 S	61.14 W
Camanche	190	41.47 N	90.15 W
Camanche Reservoir ⊜[1]	226	38.13 N	120.58 W
Camandag Island I	116	11.59 N	124.25 E
Camanducaia	256	22.46 S	46.09 W
Camanducaia ≃, Bra.	256	22.39 S	46.58 W
Camanducaia ≃, Bra.	256	22.55 S	46.25 W
Camano Island I	224	48.10 N	122.30 W
Camaoí ≃	250	3.12 S	48.04 W
Camapuã	255	19.30 S	54.05 W
Camaquã	252	30.51 S	51.49 W
Camaquã ≃	252	31.17 S	51.47 W
Camará	246	3.55 S	62.44 W
Camarajibe	250	8.01 S	34.58 W
Camararé ≃	248	12.15 S	58.55 W
Camarat, Cap >	62	43.12 N	6.41 E
Camarda	66	42.23 N	13.29 E
Çamardı	130	37.50 N	35.00 E
Camarès	32	43.49 N	2.53 E
Camargo, Bol.	248	20.39 S	65.13 W
Camargo, Méx.	232	27.40 N	105.10 W
Camargos, Reprêsa de ⊜[1]	256	21.25 S	44.30 W
Camargue ⊕[1]	62	43.34 N	4.34 E
Camargue, Parc Naturel Regional de ◆	62	43.30 N	4.28 E
Camarillo	228	34.12 N	119.02 W
Camarillo Heights	228	34.14 N	119.02 W
Camarina ⊥	70	36.52 N	14.27 E
Camariñas	34	43.07 N	9.10 W
Camarines Norte □[4]	116	14.10 N	122.40 E
Camarines Sur □[4]	116	13.35 N	123.20 E
Camarón, Arroyo ≃	196	27.08 N	100.00 W
Camarón, Cabo >	236	16.00 N	85.05 W
Camarones	254	44.48 S	65.42 W
Camarones, Bahía ⊂	254	44.45 S	65.34 W
Camas, Esp.	34	37.24 N	6.02 W
Çamaş, Tür.	130	40.55 N	37.32 E
Camas, Wa., U.S.	224	45.35 N	122.23 W
Camas Creek ≃, Id., U.S.	202	43.20 N	114.24 W
Camas Creek ≃, Id., U.S.	202	44.53 N	114.44 W
Camas Creek ≃, Id., U.S.	202	43.53 N	112.21 W
Camas Creek ≃, Or., U.S.	202	45.01 N	118.59 W
Camastra	70	37.15 N	13.47 E
Camatagua, Embalse de ⊜[1]	246	9.50 N	67.00 W
Camatambo	152	6.30 S	15.18 E
Ca Mau	110	9.11 N	105.08 E
Ca Mau, Mui >	110	8.38 N	104.44 E
Camaxilo	152	8.21 S	18.56 E
Camba	112	4.54 S	119.50 E
Camba Cassai	152	9.40 S	19.18 E
Cambados	34	42.30 N	8.48 W
Cambará	255	23.03 S	50.05 W
Camberley	42	51.21 N	0.45 W
Camberwell	169	37.50 S	145.04 E
Camberwell ⊕[8]	260	51.28 N	0.05 W
Cambiano	62	44.58 N	7.47 E
Cambo	44	55.10 N	1.57 W
Cambo ≃	152	7.40 S	17.17 E
Cambodia □[1], Asia	108	13.00 N	105.00 E
Cambodia (Kâmpŭchéa) □[1], Asia	110	13.00 N	105.00 E
Cambois	44	55.10 N	1.31 W
Cambonda, Serra ⩙	152	12.06 S	14.00 E
Camboon	166	25.03 S	150.26 E
Cambooya	171a	27.42 S	151.52 E
Camboriú	252	27.01 S	48.38 W
Camborne	42	50.12 N	5.19 W
Cambra	210	41.11 N	76.18 W
Cambrai, Austl.	168b	34.39 S	139.17 E
Cambrai, Fr.	50	50.10 N	3.14 E
Cambremer	50	49.09 N	0.03 E
Cambria, Ca., U.S.	226	35.33 N	121.04 W
Cambria, In., U.S.	216	40.22 N	86.33 W
Cambria, Mi., U.S.	216	41.49 N	84.39 W
Cambria, Wi., U.S.	190	43.32 N	89.06 W
Cambria □[6]	214	40.29 N	79.16 W
Cambria Ice Field ⍓	182	55.55 N	129.30 W
Cambrian Mountains ⩙	42	52.35 N	3.35 W
Cambrian Park	226	37.15 N	121.55 W
Cambridge (Galt), On., Can.	212	43.22 N	80.19 W
Cambridge, N.Z.	172	37.53 S	175.28 E
Cambridge, Eng., U.K.	42	52.13 N	0.08 E
Cambridge, Id., U.S.	202	44.34 N	116.41 W
Cambridge, Il., U.S.	190	41.18 N	90.11 W
Cambridge, Ia., U.S.	190	41.53 N	93.31 W
Cambridge, Md., U.S.	208	38.33 N	76.04 W
Cambridge, Ma., U.S.	207	42.22 N	71.06 W
Cambridge, Mn., U.S.	190	45.34 N	93.13 W
Cambridge, Ne., U.S.	198	40.16 N	100.09 W
Cambridge, N.Y., U.S.	210	43.01 N	73.22 W
Cambridge, Oh., U.S.	188	40.02 N	81.35 W
Cambridge, Wi., U.S.	216	43.00 N	89.01 W
Cambridge Bay	176	69.03 N	105.05 W
Cambridge City	218	39.48 N	85.10 W
Cambridge Fiord ⊂[2]	176	71.20 N	74.44 W
Cambridge Gulf ⊂	164	14.55 S	128.15 E
Cambridge Park	274a	33.45 S	150.43 E
Cambridge Reservoir ⊜[1]	283	42.24 N	71.16 W
Cambridgeshire □[6]	42	52.20 N	0.05 E
Cambridge Springs	214	41.48 N	80.03 W
Cambrils	34	41.04 N	1.03 E
Cambriú, Ponta de >	252	25.10 S	47.55 W
Cambuci ⊕[8]	287b	23.34 S	46.37 W
Cambuí	256	22.37 S	46.04 W
Cambulo	152	7.48 S	21.14 E
Cambundi-Catembo	152	10.09 S	17.31 E
Cambuquira	256	21.51 S	45.18 W
Cambural	286c	10.26 N	66.59 W
Camburg	54	51.03 N	11.42 E
Camburú ≃	256	23.41 S	45.28 W
Camby	218	39.40 N	86.19 W
Čamčakly	128	37.56 N	63.06 E
Camden, Austl.	170	34.03 S	150.42 E
Camden, S. Afr.	158	26.38 S	30.07 E
Camden, Al., U.S.	194	31.59 N	87.17 W
Camden, Ar., U.S.	194	33.35 N	92.50 W
Camden, De., U.S.	208	39.06 N	75.32 W
Camden, Il., U.S.	219	40.09 N	90.46 W
Camden, In., U.S.	216	40.36 N	86.32 W
Camden, Me., U.S.	188	44.12 N	69.03 W
Camden, Mi., U.S.	216	41.45 N	84.45 W
Camden, Ms., U.S.	194	32.46 N	89.50 W
Camden, N.J., U.S.	208	39.55 N	75.07 W
Camden, N.Y., U.S.	210	43.20 N	75.44 W
Camden, N.C., U.S.	192	36.19 N	76.10 W
Camden, Oh., U.S.	218	39.37 N	84.38 W
Camden, S.C., U.S.	192	34.14 N	80.36 W
Camden, Tn., U.S.	194	36.03 N	88.05 W
Camden, Tx., U.S.	222	30.55 N	94.44 W
Camden □[6], N.J., U.S.	208	39.57 N	75.07 W
Camden □[6], N.C., U.S.	208	36.28 N	76.21 W
Camden ⊕[8]	260	51.33 N	0.10 W
Camden, Grupo II	254	54.40 S	71.58 W
Camden Aerodrome ⊠	274a	34.03 S	150.41 E
Camden Bay ⊂	180	70.00 N	145.00 W
Camden Hills State Park ◆	188	44.17 N	69.05 W
Camden Lake ⊜	212	44.25 N	76.52 W
Camden Station ⊕[5]	284b	39.17 N	76.37 W
Camdenton	194	38.00 N	92.44 W
Camedo	58	46.09 N	8.37 E
Cameia, Parque Nacional da ◆	152	11.45 S	21.20 E
Camel ≃	42	50.33 N	4.55 W
Camel, Mount ∧[2]	169	36.45 S	144.43 E
Camelback Mountain ∧, Ak., U.S.	180	62.33 N	157.20 W
Camelback Mountain ∧, Pa., U.S.	210	41.03 N	75.21 W
Camelford	42	50.37 N	4.41 W
Çameli	130	37.05 N	29.20 E
Camels Hump ∧	188	44.19 N	72.53 W
Cameo Acres	282	37.51 N	121.58 W
Camerano	66	43.32 N	13.33 E
Cameri	62	45.30 N	8.39 E
Cameri, Aeroporto di ⊠	266b	45.32 N	8.40 E
Camerino	66	43.08 N	13.04 E
Cameron, Ca., U.S.	226	38.39 N	120.56 W
Cameron, La., U.S.	194	29.47 N	93.19 W
Cameron, Mo., U.S.	194	39.44 N	94.14 W
Cameron, N.Y., U.S.	210	42.12 N	77.24 W
Cameron, Pa., U.S.	214	41.27 N	78.10 W
Cameron, S.C., U.S.	192	33.33 N	80.42 W
Cameron, Tx., U.S.	222	30.51 N	96.58 W
Cameron, W.V., U.S.	188	39.49 N	80.34 W
Cameron, Wi., U.S.	190	45.24 N	91.44 W
Cameron □[6]	214	41.31 N	78.14 W
Cameron ≃	224	49.17 N	124.38 W
Cameron, Lac ⊜	206	46.06 N	74.50 W
Cameron Highlands	114	4.29 N	101.27 E
Cameron Hills ⩙[2]	176	59.48 N	118.00 W
Cameron Lake ⊜, B.C., Can.	224	49.17 N	124.37 W
Cameron Lake ⊜, On., Can.	212	44.34 N	78.45 W
Cameron Mills	210	42.11 N	77.22 W
Cameron Mountains ⩙	172	46.00 S	167.00 E
Cameron Run ≃	284c	38.48 N	77.04 W
Cameroon (Cameroun) □[1]	134	6.00 N	12.00 E
Cameroon Mountain ∧	152	4.12 N	9.11 E
Camerota	68	40.02 N	15.23 E
Cameroun → Cameroon □[1]	134	6.00 N	12.00 E
Camerún → Cameroon □[1]	134	6.00 N	12.00 E
Cametá	250	2.15 S	49.30 W
Camfield	164	17.09 S	131.21 E
Çamiçi Gölü ⊜	130	37.30 N	27.25 E
Camiguin □[4]	116	9.15 N	124.40 E
Camiguin Island I, Pil.	116	18.56 N	121.55 E
Camiguin Island I, Pil.	116	9.11 N	124.42 E
Camiling	116	15.42 N	120.24 E
Camilla	192	31.13 N	84.12 W
Camillus	210	43.02 N	76.19 W
Camin	54	53.27 N	10.58 E
Camiña	248	19.18 S	69.26 W
Caminha	34	41.52 N	8.50 W
Camino	226	38.44 N	120.40 W
Camiranga	250	1.48 S	46.17 W
Camiri	248	20.03 S	63.31 W
Camisano Vicentino	64	45.31 N	11.43 E
Camisea ≃	248	11.35 S	72.58 W
Camissombo	152	8.10 S	20.39 E
Camlad ≃	42	52.36 N	3.10 W
Çamlıbel	130	40.05 N	36.29 E
Çamlıdere, Tür.	130	37.08 N	39.03 E
Çamlıdere, Tür.	130	40.30 N	32.29 E
Çamlıyayla	130	37.09 N	34.36 E
Cam Lo	110	16.49 N	106.59 E
Čamlyk ≃	84	44.45 N	40.45 E
Cammal	210	41.24 N	77.28 W
Cammarata	70	37.38 N	13.38 E
Cammarta, Monte ∧	70	37.37 N	13.36 E

Symbols in the index entries represent the broad categories identified in the key at the right. Symbols with superior numbers (⩙[1]) identify subcategories (see complete key on page *I · 1).*

Symbole im Register stellen die rechts im Schlüssel erklärten Kategorien dar. Symbole mit hochgestellten Ziffern (⩙[1]) bezeichnen Unterabteilungen einer Kategorie (vgl. vollständiger Schlüssel auf Seite *I · 1).*

Los símbolos incluídos en el texto del índice representan las grandes categorias identificadas con la clave a la derecha. Los símbolos con numeros en su parte superior (⩙[1]) identifican las subcategorías (véase la clave completa en la página *I · 1).*

Les symboles de l'index représentent les catégories indiquées dans la légende à droite. Les symboles suivis d'un indice (⩙[1]) représentent des sous-catégories (voir légende complète à la page *I · 1).*

Os símbolos incluídos no texto do índice representam as grandes categorias identificadas com a chave à direita. Os símbolos com números em sua parte superior (⩙[1]) identificam as subcategorias (veja-se a chave completa à página *I · 1).*

Symbol	English	Deutsch	Español	Français	Português
∧	Mountain	Berg	Montaña	Montagne	Montanha
⩙	Mountains	Gebirge	Montañas	Montagnes	Montanhas
)(	Pass	Paß	Paso	Col	Passo
∨	Valley, Canyon	Tal, Cañon	Valle, Cañón	Vallée, Canyon	Vale, Canhão
≃	Plain	Ebene	Llano	Plaine	Planície
>	Cape	Kap	Cabo	Cap	Cabo
I	Island	Insel	Isla	Île	Ilha
II	Islands	Inseln	Islas	Îles	Ilhas
⍊	Other Topographic Features	Andere Topographische Objekte	Otros Elementos Topográficos	Autres données topographiques	Outros acidentes topográficos

ESPAÑOL

Nombre	Página	Lat.°'	Long.°' W = Oeste
Camoapa	236	12.23 N	85.31 W
Camocim	250	2.54 S	40.50 W
Camogli	62	44.21 N	9.09 E
Çamoluk	130	40.08 N	38.45 E
Camonica, Val V	64	46.00 N	10.20 E
Camooweal	166	19.55 S	138.07 E
Camopi ≃	250	3.11 N	52.20 W
Camorim ≃	287a	22.59 S	43.25 W
Camorim, Reprêsa do ⊜[1]	287a	22.58 S	43.27 W
Camorta Island I	110	8.08 N	93.30 E
Camote, Cerro ∧	286d	11.57 S	77.06 W
Camotes Islands II	116	10.40 N	124.24 E
Camotes Sea ⍑[2]	116	10.30 N	124.15 E
Camotlán ≃	234	22.01 N	104.15 W
Camowen ≃	48	54.36 N	7.18 W
Camp □[6]	222	33.00 N	94.58 W
Campagna	68	40.40 N	15.08 E
Campagna di Roma ➔[1]	66	41.50 N	12.35 E
Campagna Lupia	64	45.21 N	12.06 E
Campagnano di Roma	66	42.08 N	12.23 E
Campagnatico	66	42.53 N	11.16 E
Campagne-lès-Hesdin	50	50.24 N	1.52 E
Campaign	194	35.46 N	85.37 W
Campamento	236	14.33 N	86.42 W
Campana, Arg.	258	34.10 S	58.57 W
Campana, It.	68	39.24 N	16.50 E
Campana, Isla I	254	48.20 S	75.15 W
Campanario	34	38.52 N	5.37 W
Campanario, Cerro de ∧	248	5.57 S	77.31 W
Campanella, Punta ›	68	40.34 N	14.19 E
Campanero, Cerro ∧	246	5.54 N	65.12 W
Campanha	256	21.50 S	45.24 W
Campania □[4]	68	40.55 N	14.50 E
Campania Island I	182	53.05 N	129.30 W
Camparada	266b	45.39 N	9.19 E
Campaspe ≃, Austl.	166	21.00 S	146.24 E
Campaspe ≃, Austl.	169	36.41 S	144.31 E
Campbell, S. Afr.	158	28.48 S	23.44 E
Campbell, Ca., U.S.	226	37.17 N	121.56 W
Campbell, Mn., U.S.	198	46.05 N	96.24 W
Campbell, Mo., U.S.	194	36.29 N	90.04 W
Campbell, Ne., U.S.	198	40.18 N	98.44 W
Campbell, N.Y., U.S.	210	42.13 N	77.11 W
Campbell, Oh., U.S.	214	41.04 N	80.35 W
Campbell, Tx., U.S.	222	33.09 N	95.57 W
Campbell □[6]	218	38.55 N	84.20 W
Campbell, Cape ›	172	41.44 S	174.17 E
Campbell Airport ⊠	279b	40.21 N	80.11 W
Campbellfield	274b	37.41 S	144.57 E
Campbellford	212	44.18 N	77.48 W
Campbell Hall	210	41.27 N	74.16 W
Campbell Hill ∧[2]	216	40.22 N	83.43 W
Campbell Island	182	52.10 N	128.09 W
Campbell Island I	9	52.30 S	169.05 E
Campbell Lake ⊜	182	50.01 N	125.27 W
Campbell Plateau ✤[3]	9	51.00 S	170.00 E
Campbell Point ›	171a	27.22 S	153.55 E
Campbellpore	123	33.46 N	72.22 E
Campbell Range ⩘	180	61.08 N	129.45 W
Campbell River	182	50.01 N	125.15 W
Campbells ≃	170	33.42 S	149.37 E
Campbell's Airport ⊠	278	42.20 N	88.04 W
Campbell's-Bay	188	45.44 N	76.36 W
Campbellsburg, In., U.S.	218	38.39 N	86.15 W
Campbellsburg, Ky., U.S.	218	38.31 N	85.12 W
Campbell Slough ≃	226	39.22 N	121.51 W
Campbellsport	190	43.35 N	88.16 W
Campbells River	170	33.54 S	149.37 E
Campbells Run ≃	279b	40.24 N	80.05 W
Campbellsville	194	37.20 N	85.20 W
Campbellton, N.B., Can.	186	48.00 N	66.40 W
Campbellton, Nf., Can.	186	49.17 N	54.56 W
Campbellton, P.E., Can.	186	46.47 N	64.18 W
Campbellton, Fl., U.S.	192	30.56 N	85.24 W
Campbell Town, Austl.	166	41.56 S	147.29 E
Campbelltown, Austl.	168b	34.53 S	138.40 E
Campbelltown, Austl.	170	34.04 S	150.49 E
Campbelltown, Pa., U.S.	208	40.17 N	76.35 W
Campbellville	212	43.29 N	79.59 W
Campbeltown	44	55.26 N	5.36 W
Camp Creek ≃, Ca., U.S.	226	38.38 N	120.40 W
Camp Creek ≃, Mo., U.S.	219	39.02 N	91.12 W
Camp Creek Lake ⊜[1]	222	31.03 N	96.19 W
Camp David ᵾ	208	39.38 N	77.28 W
Camp de Frileuse ■	261	48.52 N	1.55 E
Camp de Satory ■	261	48.47 N	2.06 E
Camp Dix	218	38.29 N	83.17 W
Camp Douglas	190	43.55 N	90.16 W
Campeche	232	19.51 N	90.32 W
Campeche □[3]	232	19.00 N	90.30 W
Campeche, Bahía de ⊂	232	20.00 N	94.00 W
Campeche Bank ✤[4]	16	22.00 N	90.00 W
Campechuela	240p	20.14 N	77.17 W
Campegine	64	44.45 N	10.32 E
Campello Monti	58	45.56 N	8.15 E
Camperdown, Austl.	169	38.14 S	143.09 E
Camperdown, S. Afr.	158	29.42 S	30.33 E
Camperville	184	51.59 N	100.09 W
Campestre	256	21.43 S	46.15 W
Cam Pha	110	21.01 N	107.19 E
Camp Hill, Al., U.S.	194	32.48 N	85.39 W
Camp Hill, Pa., U.S.	208	40.14 N	76.55 W
Campi Bisenzio	66	43.49 N	11.08 E
Campidano ➔[1]	71	39.30 N	8.47 E
Campiglia dei Fosci	66	43.27 N	11.03 E
Campiglia Marittima	66	43.03 N	10.37 E
Campillo de Llerena	34	38.30 N	5.50 W
Campillos	34	37.03 N	4.51 W
Campina ➔[1]	34	37.45 N	4.45 W
Campina Grande	250	7.13 S	35.53 W
Campinas	256	22.54 S	47.05 W
Campina Verde	255	19.31 S	49.28 W
Campinho, Rio do ≃	287a	22.52 S	43.37 W
Campione del Garda	64	45.45 N	10.45 E
Campi Salentina	68	40.24 N	18.01 E
Campitello	64	46.28 N	11.44 E
Camp King	150	4.55 N	7.58 W
Camp Lake	216	42.32 N	88.09 W
Camp Lake ⊜	212	45.27 N	78.54 W
Camp Leger ■	261	48.34 N	2.34 E
Camp Lejeune Marine Corps Base ■	192	34.40 N	77.21 W
Campli	66	42.43 N	13.41 E
Camplong	112	10.02 S	123.55 E
Campo, Cam.	152	2.22 N	9.49 E
Campo, Moç.	156	17.44 S	36.21 E
Campo, Co., U.S.	198	37.06 N	102.34 W
Campo, Réserve de ➔[4]	152	2.35 N	9.57 E
Campoalegre	246	2.41 N	75.20 W
Campo Alegre ≃	250	9.19 S	50.06 W
Campo Alegre de Goiás	255	17.39 S	47.45 W
Campobasso	66	41.34 N	14.39 E
Campobasso □[4]	66	41.38 N	14.35 E
Campobello di Licata	70	37.15 N	13.55 E
Campobello di Mazara	70	37.38 N	12.45 E
Campobello Island I	186	44.53 N	66.55 W
Campo Belo	255	20.53 S	45.16 W
Campo Blenio	58	46.34 N	8.56 E
Campo Catino	66	41.48 N	13.20 E
Campocologno	58	46.13 N	10.08 E
Campodarsego	64	45.30 N	11.54 E
Campo de Criptana	34	39.24 N	3.07 W
Campo de la Cruz	246	10.23 N	74.53 W
Campo de Marte ♠	286d	12.04 S	77.03 W

FRANÇAIS

Nom	Page	Lat.°'	Long.°' W = Ouest
Campo de Marte ■	287b	23.30 S	46.37 W
Campo de Mayo ■	288	34.32 S	58.38 W
Campo di Giove	66	42.01 N	14.03 E
Campo di Trens (Trens)	64	46.52 N	11.29 E
Campo do Coelho	256	22.15 S	42.39 W
Campodolcino	58	46.24 N	9.21 E
Campo Erê	252	26.23 S	53.03 W
Campofelice di Fitalia	70	37.50 N	13.29 E
Campofelice di Roccella	70	37.59 N	13.53 E
Campofiorito	70	37.45 N	13.16 E
Campo Florido	255	19.47 S	48.35 W
Campoformido	64	46.01 N	13.09 E
Campo Formoso	250	10.31 S	40.20 W
Campofranco	70	37.30 N	13.43 E
Campogalliano	64	44.41 N	10.50 E
Campo Gallo	252	26.35 S	62.51 W
Campo Grande, Arg.	252	27.13 S	54.58 W
Campo Grande, Bra.	255	20.27 S	54.37 W
Campo Grande ➔[8], Bra.	256	22.54 S	43.34 W
Campo Grande ➔[8], Port.	266c	38.45 N	9.09 W
Campo Indian Reservation ➔[4]	204	32.40 N	116.20 W
Campo Largo, Arg.	252	26.48 S	60.50 W
Campo Largo, Bra.	252	25.26 S	49.32 W
Campolaro	64	45.55 N	10.20 E
Campolasta (Astfeld)	64	46.40 N	11.22 E
Campolato, Capo ›	70	37.17 N	15.12 E
Campo Libertad ■	286b	23.05 N	82.26 W
Campolide	256	21.36 S	43.53 W
Campolieto	66	41.38 N	14.46 E
Campo Ligure	62	44.32 N	8.42 E
Campo Limpo Paulista	256	23.12 S	46.48 W
Campo Maior, Bra.	250	4.49 S	42.10 W
Campo Maior, Port.	34	39.01 N	7.04 W
Campomarino	66	41.57 N	15.02 E
Campo Militar Número Uno ■	286a	19.27 N	99.14 W
Campomorone	62	44.30 N	8.53 E
Campo Mourão	255	24.03 S	52.22 W
Campo Novo	252	27.42 S	53.48 W
Campo Pequeno ♠	266c	38.44 N	9.08 W
Campo Quijano	252	24.55 S	65.39 W
Campora	68	40.19 N	15.17 E
Camporeale	70	37.54 N	13.06 E
Camporgiano	64	44.09 N	10.20 E
Camporredondo	248	6.07 S	78.21 W
Campos	255	21.45 S	41.18 W
Campos Altos	255	19.41 S	46.10 W
Camposampiero	64	45.34 N	11.56 E
Campo Santo, Arg.	252	24.40 S	65.06 W
Camposanto, It.	64	44.47 N	11.08 E
Campos Belos	255	13.03 S	46.53 W
Campos de Cunha	256	22.55 S	44.49 W
Campos do Jordão	256	22.44 S	45.35 W
Campos Elisios	256	22.42 S	43.17 W
Campos Gerais	256	21.14 S	45.46 W
Campos Novos	252	27.24 S	51.12 W
Campos Sales	250	7.04 S	40.23 W
Campo Tencia, Pizzo ∧	58	46.26 N	8.43 E
Campotosto	66	42.33 N	13.22 E
Campotosto, Lago di ⊜	66	42.32 N	13.22 E
Campo Tures (Sand in Taufers)	64	46.55 N	11.57 E
Campovalano	66	42.44 N	13.40 E
Camp Parks Communications Annex ■	282	37.44 N	121.54 W
Camp Pendleton Marine Corps Base ■	228	33.19 N	117.18 W
Camp Point	219	40.02 N	91.04 W
Camp Ruby	222	30.42 N	94.45 W
Campsie	274a	33.55 S	151.06 E
Campsie Fells ⩘[2]	46	56.02 N	4.12 W
Camp Springs	208	38.48 N	76.54 W
Campti	194	31.53 N	93.07 W
Campton	192	37.44 N	83.32 W
Camptonville	226	39.27 N	121.03 W
Camptown	210	41.43 N	76.14 W
Campus	216	41.01 N	88.18 W
Campuya ≃	246	1.43 S	73.30 W
Camp Verde	200	34.33 N	111.51 W
Campville	210	42.06 N	76.09 W
Camp Wood	196	29.40 N	100.01 W
Cam Ranh	110	11.54 N	109.09 E
Cam Ranh, Vinh ⊂	110	11.53 N	109.10 E
Camrose, Ab., Can.	182	53.01 N	112.50 W
Camrose, Wales, U.K.	42	51.51 N	5.01 W
Camsell ≃	176	65.40 N	118.07 W
Camu ≃	250	1.15 N	57.09 W
Camucia	66	43.16 N	11.58 E
Camucuio	152	14.12 S	13.20 E
Camurí Chiquito, Quebrada ≃	286c	10.37 N	66.52 W
Çamurlu Dağ ∧	130	40.21 N	42.26 E
Camuy	240m	18.29 N	66.51 W
Cam Xuyen	110	18.15 N	106.00 E
Čamyndy	85	41.37 N	74.20 E
Čamzinka	80	54.24 N	45.47 E
Çan, Tür.	130	40.02 N	27.03 E
Çan, Tür.	130	39.09 N	40.13 E
Čan ≃	260	51.48 N	0.25 E
Čaňa	30	48.37 N	21.18 E
Canaan, Ct., U.S.	207	42.01 N	73.19 W
Canaan, Fl., U.S.	220	28.48 N	81.14 W
Canaan, In., U.S.	218	38.52 N	85.25 W
Canaan, N.Y., U.S.	210	42.25 N	73.27 W
Canaan, Vt., U.S.	206	44.59 N	71.32 W
Canaan ≃	186	45.55 N	65.47 W
Canaan Lake ⊜	276	40.47 N	73.01 W
Canaan Valley State Park ♠	188	39.02 N	79.32 W
Cana-brava ≃, Bra.	255	13.11 S	48.11 W
Cana-brava ≃, Bra.	255	12.12 S	48.40 W
Cañacao Bay ⊂	269f	14.29 N	120.55 E
Canaçarí, Lago ⊜	250	2.57 S	58.15 W
Canada □[1]	176	60.00 N	95.00 W
Cañada, Loma la ∧[2]	240p	21.41 N	82.57 W
Canada Bay ⊂	186	50.43 N	56.10 W
Cañada de Caracheo	234	20.22 N	100.57 W
Cañada de Gómez	252	32.49 S	61.24 W
Cañada Honda	252	31.59 S	68.33 W
Canada Lake ⊜	210	43.10 N	74.32 W
Cañada Nieto	258	33.43 S	58.05 W
Canadarago Lake ⊜	210	42.48 N	75.01 W
Canada's Wonderland ♠	275b	43.51 N	79.33 W
Cañada Verde → Villa Huidobro	252	34.50 S	64.35 W
Canadaway Creek ≃	214	42.28 N	79.22 W
Canadensis	210	41.11 N	75.15 W
Canadian	196	35.54 N	100.22 W
Canadian ≃, U.S.	196	35.27 N	95.03 W
Canadian ≃, Co., U.S.	200	40.53 N	106.20 W
Canadian, Deep Fork ≃	196	35.28 N	95.50 W
Canadian Forces Base Trenton ■	212	44.07 N	77.33 W
Canadice Lake ⊜	210	42.43 N	77.34 W
Cañadón Seco	254	46.33 S	67.35 W
Canaguá ≃	246	7.57 N	69.36 W
Canaima	246	6.14 N	62.52 W
Canaima, Parque Nacional ♠	246	4.27 N	62.00 W
Canajoharie	210	42.54 N	74.34 W
Çanakkale	130	40.09 N	26.24 E
Çanakkale □[4]	130	40.10 N	26.45 E
Çanakkale Boğazı (Dardanelles) ʮ	130	40.15 N	26.25 E
Canal, Islas del → Channel Islands II	28	49.20 N	2.20 W
Canala	175f	21.32 S	165.57 E
Canale	62	44.48 N	8.00 E

PORTUGUÊS

Nome	Página	Lat.°'	Long.°' W = Oeste
Canale, Val V	64	46.29 N	13.30 E
Canale del Ferro ≃	64	46.21 N	13.07 E
Canalejas	234	19.57 N	99.39 W
Canal Flats	182	50.09 N	115.48 W
Canal Fulton	214	40.53 N	81.35 W
Canal Lake ⊜	212	44.34 N	79.03 W
Canal Lewisville	214	40.18 N	81.50 W
Canal Point	220	26.51 N	80.38 W
Canals	252	33.33 S	62.53 W
Canal Winchester	188	39.51 N	82.48 W
Canamã ≃	248	8.45 S	59.15 W
Canandaigua	210	42.52 N	77.20 W
Canandaigua Lake ⊜	210	42.49 N	77.16 W
Canandaigua Outlet ≃	210	43.04 N	77.00 W
Cananea	232	30.57 N	110.18 W
Cananéia	252	25.01 S	47.57 W
Canan Station	214	40.28 N	78.26 W
Canapine, Forca)(	66	42.45 N	13.12 E
Canápolis	255	18.44 S	49.13 W
Canapville	50	49.19 N	0.08 E
Cañar	246	2.33 S	78.56 W
Cañar □[4]	246	2.30 S	79.00 W
Canard ≃	214	42.09 N	83.06 W
Canard, Lac au ⊜	206	45.48 N	71.31 W
Canarias, Islas (Canary Islands) II	148	28.00 N	15.30 W
Canaries	241f	13.55 N	61.04 W
Canaro	64	44.56 N	11.40 E
Canarreos, Archipiélago de los II	240p	21.50 N	82.30 W
Canarsie ➔[8]	276	40.38 N	73.53 W
Canarsie Park ♠	276	40.38 N	73.53 W
Canarsie Pol I	276	40.37 N	73.52 W
Canary Basin ✤[1]	10	30.00 N	25.00 W
Canary Islands → Canarias, Islas II	148	28.00 N	15.30 W
Cañas	236	10.25 N	85.07 W
Canaseraga	210	42.27 N	77.46 W
Canaseraga Creek ≃	210	42.45 N	77.50 W
Cañasgordas	246	6.45 N	76.01 W
Canastota	210	43.04 N	75.45 W
Canatlán	232	24.31 N	104.47 W
Canaveral, Cape ›	220	28.27 N	80.32 W
Canaveral Bight ⊂[3]	220	28.26 N	80.33 W
Canaveral National Seashore ♠	220	28.45 N	80.45 W
Canaveral Peninsula ›[1]	220	28.28 N	80.34 W
Cañaveras	34	40.22 N	2.24 W
Canavese □[9]	62	45.20 N	7.40 E
Canavieiras	255	15.39 S	38.57 W
Cañazas	236	8.19 N	81.13 W
Canazei	64	46.28 N	11.46 E
Canbelego	166	31.33 S	146.19 E
Canberra	171b	35.17 S	149.08 E
Canberra Wildlife Gardens ♠	171b	35.20 S	149.09 E
Canby, Ca., U.S.	204	41.26 N	120.52 W
Canby, Mn., U.S.	198	44.42 N	96.16 W
Canby, Or., U.S.	224	45.15 N	122.41 W
Cancajanang, Mount ∧	116	11.04 N	124.47 E
Cancale	32	48.41 N	1.51 W
Cancano, Lago di ⊜	64	46.31 N	10.18 E
Cance ≃	62	45.12 N	4.48 E
Cancellara	68	40.44 N	15.56 E
Cancello e Arnone	68	41.04 N	14.03 E
Canchaque	248	5.24 S	79.36 W
Canche ≃	50	50.31 N	1.39 E
Cancon	32	44.32 N	0.38 E
Çancún	232	21.05 N	86.46 W
Čančur	88	53.49 N	106.59 E
Canda	64	45.03 N	11.30 E
Candala → Qandala	144	11.28 N	49.52 E
Candarave	248	17.16 S	70.15 W
Çandarlı	130	38.56 N	26.56 E
Çandarlı Körfezi ⊂	130	38.52 N	26.55 E
Čandás	34	43.35 N	5.46 W
Candé	32	47.34 N	1.02 W
Candeias, Bra.	255	12.40 S	38.33 W
Candeias, Bra.	255	20.47 S	45.16 W
Candeias ≃	248	8.39 S	63.31 W
Candela, It.	68	41.08 N	15.31 E
Candela, Méx.	232	26.50 N	100.40 W
Candela, Río de ≃	196	27.16 N	100.18 W
Candelaria, Arg.	252	27.28 S	55.44 W
Candelaria, Arg.	252	32.04 S	65.49 W
Candelária, Bra.	252	29.40 S	52.48 W
Candelaria, Col.	246	3.25 N	76.20 W
Candelaria, Cuba	240p	22.44 N	82.58 W
Candelaria, Pil.	116	15.38 N	119.56 E
Candelaria ≃	232	18.37 N	91.14 W
Candelaria Loxicha	234	15.54 N	96.31 W
Candelaro ≃	68	41.34 N	15.53 E
Candeleda	34	40.09 N	5.14 W
Candelo, Austl.	166	36.46 S	149.42 E
Candelo, It.	62	45.33 N	8.07 E
Candiac	206	45.23 N	73.31 W
Candia Canavese	62	45.20 N	7.53 E
Candia → Iráklion	38	35.20 N	25.09 E
Candia Lomellina	62	45.11 N	8.36 E
Cándido Aguilar	232	25.30 N	98.02 W
Cândido de Abreu	252	24.35 S	51.20 W
Cândido Mendes	250	1.27 S	45.43 W
Candies Creek ≃	192	35.18 N	84.51 W
Candijay	116	9.49 N	124.30 E
Çandır, Tür.	130	40.16 N	33.29 E
Çandır, Tür.	130	39.15 N	35.32 E
Čandle	180	65.55 N	161.56 W
Candle Lake ⊜	184	53.50 N	105.18 W
Candlemas Islands II	18	57.03 S	26.40 W
Candlestick	194	32.15 N	90.20 W
Candlestick Park ♠	282	37.43 N	122.23 W
Candlewood, Lake ⊜	207	41.32 N	73.27 W
Candlewood Isle	207	41.28 N	73.27 W
Candlewood Knolls	207	41.28 N	73.27 W
Candlewood Shores	207	41.28 N	73.26 W
Çandman', Mong.	86	50.02 N	92.03 E
Čandman', Mong.	102	45.20 N	97.59 E
Cando, Ang.	152	16.30 S	18.19 E
Cando, Sk., Can.	184	52.23 N	108.14 W
Cando, N.D., U.S.	198	48.29 N	99.12 W
Candombé ≃	152	16.54 S	21.52 E
Candon	116	17.12 N	120.27 E
Candon Point ›	116	17.13 N	120.24 E
Candor, N.Y., U.S.	210	42.13 N	76.20 W
Candor, N.C., U.S.	192	35.17 N	79.44 W
Candover	158	27.28 S	31.57 E
Cane ≃, Austl.	162	21.33 S	115.23 E
Cane ≃, La., U.S.	194	31.31 N	92.43 W
Cane ≃, N.C., U.S.	192	36.00 N	82.16 W
Caneadea	210	42.23 N	78.09 W
Canea → Khaniá	38	35.31 N	24.02 E
Caneças	266c	38.49 N	9.14 W
Cane Creek ≃	194	36.29 N	90.28 W
Canegrate	266b	45.34 N	8.56 E
Canela	252	29.22 S	50.50 W
Canelas	232	25.06 N	106.34 W
Canelles, Embalse de ⊜[1]	34	42.10 N	0.30 E
Canelli	62	44.43 N	8.17 E
Canelones	258	34.32 S	56.17 W
Canelones □[5]	258	34.35 S	56.15 W
Canelón Grande, Arroyo ≃	258	34.30 S	56.24 W
Cane Run ≃	218	38.13 N	84.37 W
Cañete, Chile	252	37.48 S	73.24 W
Cañete, Esp.	34	40.03 N	1.35 W
Caneva	64	45.58 N	12.26 E
Caney	198	37.00 N	95.56 W
Caney ≃	196	36.20 N	95.42 W
Caney Brook ≃	276	41.07 N	73.50 W
Caney Creek ≃, Ar., U.S.	194	33.46 N	93.07 W
Caney Creek ≃, Tx., U.S.	196	28.46 N	95.39 W
Caney Creek ≃, Tx., U.S.	222	32.48 N	95.33 W
Caney Creek ≃, Tx., U.S.	222	30.28 N	95.38 W
Caney Creek ≃, Tx., U.S.	222	30.04 N	96.08 W
Caney Creek ≃, Tx., U.S.	222	31.52 N	96.13 W
Caney Creek ≃, Tx., U.S.	222	31.03 N	94.33 W
Caney Creek ≃, Tx., U.S.	222	30.53 N	95.48 W
Caney Creek ≃, Tx., U.S.	222	30.07 N	95.10 W
Canfield	214	41.01 N	80.45 W
Canfield Island I	276	41.06 N	73.23 W
Canfranc	34	42.43 N	0.31 W
Cangaíba ➔[8]	287b	23.30 S	46.31 W
Cangallo	248	13.33 S	74.12 W
Cangamba	152	13.40 S	19.54 E
Cangandala	152	9.45 S	16.33 E
Cangandala, Parque Nacional da ♠	152	9.45 S	16.50 E
Cangas, Bra.	248	16.05 S	56.33 W
Cangas, Esp.	34	42.16 N	8.47 W
Cangas de Narcea	34	43.11 N	6.33 W
Cangas de Onís	34	43.21 N	5.07 W
Cangbu	100	30.49 N	114.35 E
Can Gioc ≃	269c	10.42 N	106.37 E
Cangkuang, Tanjung ›	115a	6.51 S	105.15 E
Cangniutun	105	39.23 N	115.54 E
Cango Caves ⊥[5]	158	33.23 S	22.14 E
Cangola	152	7.58 S	15.52 E
Cangombe	152	14.24 S	19.59 E
Cangongo	152	9.24 S	17.30 E
Cangqian, Zhg.	106	30.18 N	120.00 E
Cangqian, Zhg.	106	30.17 N	120.25 E
Cangshangtun	105	40.03 N	117.32 E
Canguaretama	250	6.24 S	35.08 W
Canguçu	252	31.24 S	52.41 W
Canguera	256	23.36 S	47.09 W
Cangumbe	152	12.00 S	19.17 E
Cangwu	102	23.22 N	111.13 E
Çangxi	102	31.48 N	105.57 E
Čangyrtas	85	40.53 N	72.50 E
Cangyuan	102	23.12 N	99.16 E
Cangzhou	98	38.19 N	116.51 E
Canhoca	152	9.15 S	14.41 E
Canhotinho	250	8.53 S	36.12 W
Caniapiscau ≃	176	57.40 N	69.30 W
Caniapiscau, Lac ⊜	176	54.10 N	69.55 W
Canicanian	116	14.46 N	122.01 E
Canicattì	70	37.21 N	13.51 E
Canicattini Bagni	70	37.02 N	15.04 E
Canigao Channel ʮ	116	10.15 N	124.42 E
Canigou, Pic du ∧	32	42.31 N	2.27 E
Canillas ➔[8]	266a	40.28 N	3.38 W
Canillejas ➔[8]	266a	40.27 N	3.37 W
Canim Lake	182	51.46 N	120.54 W
Canim Lake ⊜	182	51.52 N	120.45 W
Canim Lake Indian Reserve ➔[4]	182	51.47 N	121.00 W
Canindé	250	4.22 S	39.19 W
Canindé ≃	250	6.15 S	42.52 W
Canindeyú □[5]	252	24.15 S	55.15 W
Canino	66	42.28 N	11.45 E
Canipaan	116	8.35 N	117.16 E
Canipo Island I	116	10.59 N	120.57 E
Canisius College ᵾ[2]	284a	42.55 N	78.52 W
Canisp ∧	46	58.07 N	5.03 W
Canistear Reservoir ⊜[1]	276	41.08 N	74.29 W
Canisteo	210	42.16 N	77.36 W
Canisteo ≃	210	42.07 N	77.08 W
Canistota	198	43.35 N	97.17 W
Cañitas de Felipe Pescador	234	23.36 N	102.43 W
Canjáyar	34	37.00 N	2.44 W
Canjinge	152	10.12 S	21.17 E
Cankhor	144	10.46 N	46.13 E
Çankırı	130	40.36 N	33.37 E
Çankırı □[4]	130	40.45 N	33.25 E
Čanlaon	116	10.22 N	123.12 E
Canlaon Volcano ∧[1]	116	10.25 N	123.08 E
Canley Vale	274a	33.53 S	150.57 E
Canmore	182	51.05 N	115.21 W
Canna	68	40.05 N	16.30 E
Canna I	46	57.04 N	6.34 W
Canna, Sound of ʮ	46	57.03 N	6.25 W
Cannanore	122	11.51 N	75.22 E
Cannara	66	43.00 N	12.35 E
Canne ⊥	68	41.18 N	16.09 E
Cannel City	192	37.47 N	83.16 W
Cannelton	194	37.54 N	86.44 W
Canner ≃	56	49.24 N	6.16 E
Cannero-Riviera	58	46.01 N	8.41 E
Cannes	62	43.33 N	7.01 E
Cannes, Bayou des ≃	194	30.12 N	92.35 W
Canneto, It.	66	43.12 N	10.44 E
Canneto, It.	70	38.29 N	14.58 E
Canneto sull'Oglio	64	45.09 N	10.25 E
Cannich	46	57.21 N	4.46 W
Cannich ≃	46	57.21 N	4.44 W
Cannifton	212	44.12 N	77.23 W
Canning, Arg.	288	34.53 S	58.30 W
Canning, Austl.	168a	32.02 S	115.56 E
Canning, N.S., Can.	186	45.09 N	64.25 W
Canning ≃, Austl.	168a	32.01 S	115.51 E
Canning ≃, Ak., U.S.	180	70.05 N	145.30 W
Canning Hill ∧[2]	162	28.50 S	117.49 E
Canning Lake ⊜	212	44.56 N	78.38 W
Canning Reservoir ⊜[1]	168a	32.10 S	116.09 E
Cannington, On., Can.	212	44.21 N	79.02 W
Cannington, Eng., U.K.	42	51.09 N	3.04 W
Cannobio	58	46.04 N	8.42 E
Cannock	42	52.42 N	2.09 W
Cannock Chase ➔[4]	42	52.43 N	2.00 W
Cannon ≃	190	44.35 N	92.33 W
Cannon Air Force Base ■	196	34.23 N	103.18 W
Cannon Ball	198	46.23 N	100.35 W
Cannonball ≃	198	46.26 N	100.38 W
Cannon Beach	224	45.53 N	123.57 W
Cannondale	207	41.12 N	73.25 W
Cannon Falls	190	44.30 N	92.54 W
Cannonsburg	216	43.03 N	85.28 W
Cannonsville Reservoir ⊜[1]	210	42.08 N	75.19 W
Cannonvale	166	20.17 S	148.42 E
Cann River	166	37.34 S	149.10 E
Caño, Isla del I	236	8.44 N	83.53 W
Canoas	252	29.56 S	51.11 W
Canoas ≃, Bra.	252	27.36 S	51.25 W
Canoas ≃, Bra.	256	21.30 S	47.09 W
Canobie Lake	283	42.48 N	71.14 W
Canobie Lake ⊜	283	42.49 N	71.15 W
Canobie Lake Park ♠	283	42.48 N	71.15 W
Canoe	182	50.45 N	119.13 W
Canoe ≃, B.C., Can.	182	52.09 N	118.27 W
Canoe ≃, Ma., U.S.	283	41.58 N	71.08 W
Canoe Brook ≃	276	40.45 N	74.22 W
Canoe Brook Reservoirs ⊜[1]	276	40.45 N	74.21 W
Canoe Creek Indian Reserve ➔[4]	182	51.32 N	122.15 W
Canoe Lake ⊜	184	55.11 N	108.15 W
Canoe Lake Indian Reserve ➔[4]	184	55.08 N	108.12 W
Canoga Park ➔[8]	280	34.12 N	118.35 W
Canoinhas	252	26.10 S	50.24 W
Canol	180	65.14 N	126.56 W
Canon	192	34.21 N	83.07 W
Canon ≃	224	46.36 N	123.53 W
Canonbie	44	55.05 N	2.57 W
Canon City	200	38.24 N	105.13 W
Cañón del Sumidero, Parque Nacional ♠	234	16.45 N	93.05 W
Caño Negro	236	10.54 N	84.44 W
Canonsburg	214	40.15 N	80.11 W
Canonsburg Lake ⊜	279b	40.16 N	80.07 W
Canoochee ≃	192	31.59 N	81.18 W
Canoole Cise	144	2.02 N	42.19 E
Canopus ⊥	142	31.18 N	30.03 E
Canora	184	51.37 N	102.26 W
Canosa di Puglia	68	41.13 N	16.04 E
Canossa ⊥	64	44.35 N	10.27 E
Canot, Pointe ›	241o	16.12 N	61.28 W
Canouan I	238	12.43 N	61.20 W
Canova	198	43.52 N	97.30 W
Canova Beach	220	28.08 N	80.34 W
Cañovanas	240m	18.23 N	65.54 W
Cánoves ≃	266d	41.37 N	2.22 E
Canow	54	53.12 N	12.54 E
Canowindra	166	33.34 S	148.38 E
Can Quer, Torrente de ≃	266d	41.31 N	2.11 E
Cansado	148	20.51 N	17.02 W
Cansanção	250	10.41 S	39.31 W
Canso	186	45.20 N	61.00 W
Canso, Strait of ʮ	186	45.37 N	61.25 W
Canta	248	11.25 S	76.38 W
Cantabria	234	19.50 N	101.44 W
Cantabria (Santander) □[4], Esp.	34	43.15 N	4.00 W
Cantabria □[4], Esp.	34	43.15 N	4.00 W
Cantábrica, Cordillera ⩘	34	43.00 N	5.00 W
Cantabriques → Cantábrica, Cordillera ⩘	34	43.00 N	5.00 W
Cantagalo	255	21.58 S	42.22 W
Cantagalo, Cachoeira ʟ	250	7.18 S	54.52 W
Cantal □[5]	32	45.05 N	2.45 E
Cantalejo	34	41.15 N	3.55 W
Cantalupo in Sabina	66	42.18 N	12.39 E
Çantalupo nel Sannio	66	41.31 N	14.24 E
Čantal'vejergyn ≃	180	67.38 N	179.22 W
Cantanhede, Bra.	250	3.39 S	44.24 W
Cantanhede, Port.	34	40.21 N	8.36 W
Cantareira ➔[8]	287b	23.27 S	46.37 W
Cantareira, Serra da ∧	287b	23.25 S	46.39 W
Cantaura	246	9.19 N	64.21 W
Cant Clough Reservoir ⊜[1]	262	53.46 N	2.09 W
Canteleu	50	49.27 N	1.02 E
Canterbury, Austl.	274a	33.55 S	151.07 E
Canterbury, Austl.	274b	37.49 S	145.05 E
Canterbury, N.B., Can.	186	45.53 N	67.29 W
Canterbury, Eng., U.K.	42	51.17 N	1.05 E
Canterbury Bight ⊂[3]	172	44.15 S	171.38 E
Canterbury Cathedral ᵾ[1]	42	51.17 N	1.05 E
Canterbury Park Racecourse ♠	274a	33.54 S	151.07 E
Canterbury Plains ≚	172	44.00 S	171.45 E
Canterbury Woods	284c	38.49 N	77.15 W
Can Tho	110	10.02 N	105.47 E
Cantiano	66	43.28 N	12.38 E
Cantil	228	35.18 N	117.58 W
Cantiles, Cayo I	240p	21.36 N	82.02 W
Cantin Lake ⊜	184	53.27 N	95.10 W
Canto do Buriti	250	8.07 S	42.58 W
Canto do Pontes	287a	22.58 S	43.04 W
Canto Grande, Quebrada V	286d	11.59 S	77.01 W
Cantoira	62	45.21 N	7.23 E
Canton, Ct., U.S.	207	41.49 N	72.53 W
Canton, Ga., U.S.	192	34.14 N	84.29 W
Canton, Il., U.S.	190	40.33 N	90.02 W
Canton, Ks., U.S.	198	38.23 N	97.25 W
Canton, Ma., U.S.	207	42.09 N	71.08 W
Canton, Mn., U.S.	190	43.31 N	91.55 W
Canton, Ms., U.S.	194	32.36 N	90.02 W
Canton, Mo., U.S.	219	40.07 N	91.37 W
Canton, N.J., U.S.	208	39.28 N	75.24 W
Canton, N.Y., U.S.	188	44.35 N	75.10 W
Canton, N.C., U.S.	192	35.31 N	82.50 W
Canton, Oh., U.S.	214	40.47 N	81.22 W
Canton, Ok., U.S.	196	36.03 N	98.35 W
Canton, Pa., U.S.	210	41.39 N	76.51 W
Canton, S.D., U.S.	198	43.18 N	96.35 W
Canton, Tx., U.S.	222	32.33 N	95.51 W
Canton Airport ⊠	174h	2.46 S	171.43 W
Canton → Guangzhou	100	23.06 N	113.16 E
Canton → Kanton I	174h	2.50 S	171.40 W
Canton Lake ⊜[1]	196	36.08 N	98.36 W
Canton Lake State Recreational Area ♠	196	36.08 N	98.39 W
Cantonment	194	30.36 N	87.20 W
Cantorbéry → Canterbury	42	51.17 N	1.05 E
Cantrall	219	39.56 N	89.41 W
Cantribana	266c	38.53 N	9.25 W
Cantù	62	45.44 N	9.08 E
Cantu ≃	252	24.46 S	52.54 W
Cantua Creek	226	36.30 N	120.19 W
Cantua Creek ≃	226	36.28 N	120.17 W
Cantwell	180	63.23 N	148.57 W
Cañuelas	258	35.03 S	58.44 W
Cañuelas □[5]	288	34.56 S	58.41 W
Cañuelas, Arroyo ≃	258	34.55 S	58.38 W
Canumã	246	4.02 S	59.04 W
Canumã ≃	246	3.55 S	59.10 W
Canungra	171a	28.01 S	153.10 E
Canungra Creek ≃	171a	27.55 S	153.06 E
Canungra Jungle Training Ground ■	171a	28.02 S	153.10 E
Canutama	248	6.32 S	64.20 W
Canutillo	200	31.54 N	106.35 W
Canvastown	172	41.18 S	173.40 E
Canvey Island	260	51.32 N	0.36 E
Çanvey Island I	260	51.33 N	0.34 E
Čany	86	55.19 N	76.46 E
Čany, ozero ⊜	86	54.50 N	77.30 E
Cany-Barville	50	49.47 N	0.38 E
Canyon, Yk., Can.	180	60.52 N	137.02 W
Canyon, Ca., U.S.	282	37.49 N	122.09 W
Canyon, Tx., U.S.	196	34.58 N	101.55 W
Canyon City	202	44.23 N	118.56 W
Canyon Country	228	34.25 N	118.28 W
Canyon Creek	182	55.22 N	115.05 W
Canyon Creek ≃, Az., U.S.	200	33.49 N	110.40 W
Canyon Creek ≃, Ca., U.S.	226	39.22 N	120.45 W
Canyon Creek ≃, Id., U.S.	202	42.59 N	115.59 W
Canyon Creek ≃, Wa., U.S.	224	45.57 N	122.22 W
Canyon Creek ≃, Wa., U.S.	224	48.43 N	120.55 W
Canyon de Chelly National Monument ♠	200	36.01 N	109.26 W
Canyon Ferry Lake ⊜[1]	202	46.33 N	111.37 W
Canyon Lake ⊜[1]	196	29.52 N	98.16 W
Canyonlands National Park ♠	200	38.10 N	110.00 W
Canyonville	202	42.55 N	123.16 W
Canzar	152	7.38 S	21.32 E
Canzo	62	45.51 N	9.16 E
Cao ≃, Zhg.	98	40.29 N	124.08 E
Cao ≃, Zhg.	105	38.52 N	115.46 E
Cao Bang	110	22.40 N	106.15 E
Caochi	107	30.19 N	104.24 E
Caocun	106	31.42 N	118.56 E
Caodian, Zhg.	100	28.39 N	120.23 E
Caodian, Zhg.	100	33.21 N	112.39 E
Caodian, Zhg.	102	32.32 N	111.11 E
Cao'e	100	30.01 N	120.52 E
Cao'e ≃	100	30.06 N	120.46 E
Caofang	100	26.04 N	116.35 E
Caogezhai	105	40.09 N	117.50 E
Caohe, Zhg.	105	38.57 N	115.32 E
Caohe, Zhg.	269b	31.09 N	121.25 E
Caohecheng	104	40.46 N	124.02 E
Caohekou	104	40.54 N	123.53 E
Caohezhang	104	41.04 N	124.03 E
Caojian	102	25.38 N	99.07 E
Caojiawopeng	104	42.00 N	122.20 E
Caojiawopu	104	42.37 N	122.19 E
Caojiawu	105	39.24 N	116.31 E
Caojiazhen	106	31.55 N	121.38 E
Caojiezi	107	29.53 N	106.24 E
Caojing	106	30.47 N	121.24 E
Caojun	100	29.41 N	116.17 E
Cao Lanh	110	10.27 N	105.38 E
Caolaoji	100	33.06 N	117.22 E
Caolisport, Loch ⊂	46	55.54 N	5.37 W
Caomaji	98	34.52 N	116.17 E
Caombo	152	8.43 S	16.51 E
Caonao ≃	240p	22.05 N	78.05 W
Caonian	100	32.56 N	120.20 E
Caonillas, Lago ⊜	240m	18.16 N	66.39 W
Caopeng	106	31.44 N	121.17 E
Caoping	100	28.48 N	118.22 E
Caopu	98	34.34 N	118.52 E
Caoqiao	106	31.32 N	119.59 E
Caorle	64	45.36 N	12.53 E
Caorso	62	45.03 N	9.52 E
Caoshi, Zhg.	98	42.17 N	125.16 E
Caoshi, Zhg.	100	33.32 N	116.29 E
Caota	100	29.42 N	120.08 E
Caotang	106	31.16 N	118.59 E
Caoxi	100	28.42 N	117.18 E
Caoxian	98	34.53 N	115.33 E
Caoyangxi	100	26.34 N	118.47 E
Cap, Le → Cape Town	158	33.55 S	18.22 E
Cap, Pointe du ›	241f	14.07 N	60.57 W
Capac	190	43.00 N	82.55 W
Capaccio	68	40.25 N	15.05 E
Capacciotti, Lago di ⊜[1]	68	41.10 N	15.47 E
Capaci	70	38.10 N	13.14 E
Çapage	152	13.21 S	21.05 E
Çapajev	80	50.12 N	51.10 E
Çapajevka, Ross.	82	54.38 N	35.50 E
Çapajevka, Ukr.	78	49.33 N	32.06 E
Çapajevka, Ukr.	78	49.23 N	30.26 E
Çapajevka, Ukr.	78	47.29 N	36.20 E
Çapajevka ≃	80	53.08 N	49.37 E
Çapajevo	78	49.21 N	35.54 E
Čapajevsk	80	52.58 N	49.41 E
Capala	152	13.37 S	14.45 E
Capalbio	66	42.27 N	11.25 E
Capalonga	116	14.20 N	122.30 E
Capanaparo ≃	246	7.01 N	67.07 W
Capanema, Bra.	250	1.12 S	47.11 W
Capanema, Bra.	252	25.40 S	53.48 W
Capangombe	152	15.05 S	13.08 E
Capanne, Monte ∧	66	42.46 N	10.10 E
Capannoli	66	43.35 N	10.41 E
Capannori	66	43.50 N	10.34 E
Capão Bonito	255	24.01 S	48.20 W
Capão Doce, Morro do ∧	252	26.43 S	51.25 W
Capão Redondo ➔[8]	287b	23.40 S	46.46 W
Capaotigamau, Lac ⊜	186	50.18 N	68.14 W
Caparaó, Parque Nacional do ♠	255	20.33 S	41.45 W
Caparica	266c	38.40 N	9.12 W
Caparo Viejo ≃	246	7.46 N	70.23 W
Capas	116	15.20 N	120.35 E
Capatárida	246	11.11 N	70.37 W
Cap-aux-Meules (Grindstone Island)	186	47.23 N	61.52 W
Cap aux Meules, Île du I	186	47.23 N	61.54 W
Capay	226	38.32 N	122.03 W
Cap-Chat	186	49.06 N	66.42 W
Cap-de-la-Madeleine	206	46.22 N	72.31 W
Cape (Kaap) □[4]	156	31.00 S	23.00 E
Cape ≃	166	20.49 S	146.51 E
Cape Arid National Park ♠	162	33.40 S	123.25 E
Cape Barren Island I	166	40.25 S	148.12 E
Cape Basin ✤[1]	8	37.00 S	7.00 E
Cape Bougainville Aboriginal Reserve ➔[4]	164	14.10 S	126.30 E
Cape Breton Highlands National Park ♠	186	46.45 N	60.45 W
Cape Breton Island I	186	46.00 N	60.30 W
Cape Broyle	186	47.06 N	52.57 W
Cape Canaveral	220	28.24 N	80.36 W
Cape Canaveral Air Force Station ■	220	28.29 N	80.35 W
Cape Charles	208	37.16 N	76.01 W
Cape Coast	150	5.05 N	1.15 W
Cape Cod Bay ⊂	207	41.52 N	70.22 W
Cape Cod Canal ≅	207	41.47 N	70.30 W
Cape Cod National Seashore ♠	207	41.56 N	70.00 W
Cape Comorin → Kanniyākumari	122	8.05 N	77.34 E
Cape Coral	220	26.33 N	81.56 W
Cape Croker Indian Reserve ➔[4]	212	44.55 N	81.01 W
Cape Dorset	176	64.14 N	76.32 W
Cape Elizabeth	188	43.33 N	70.12 W
Cape Fear ≃	192	33.53 N	78.00 W
Cape Girardeau	194	37.18 N	89.31 W
Cape Hatteras National Seashore ♠	192	35.30 N	76.35 W
Cape Henlopen State Park ♠	208	38.45 N	75.06 W
Cape Jervis	168b	35.36 S	138.06 E
Cape Johnson Tablemount ✤[3]	14	17.08 N	177.15 W
Cape Krusenstern National Monument ♠	180	67.30 N	163.40 W
Capela	250	10.30 S	37.04 W
Cape LaHave Island I	186	44.12 N	64.22 W
Cape la Hune	186	47.33 N	56.52 W
Capel Curig	44	53.06 N	3.54 W
Capelengue	152	9.12 S	19.43 E
Capelinha	255	17.42 S	42.31 W
Capelinha do Embirazal	256	22.02 S	45.26 W
Cape Lisburne	180	68.52 N	166.05 W
Capel'ka	76	58.03 N	28.59 E
Capella	166	23.05 S	148.02 E
Capella ∧	164	5.00 S	141.05 E
Capelle [aan de IJssel]	52	51.55 N	4.35 E
Capellen	56	49.38 N	5.59 E
Capelongo	152	14.54 S	15.08 E
Cape Lookout National Seashore ♠	192	34.40 N	76.23 W
Cape Lookout State Park ♠	224	45.21 N	123.59 W
Capel Saint Mary	42	52.00 N	1.04 E
Cape May	208	38.56 N	74.54 W
Cape May □[6]	208	38.56 N	74.55 W
Cape May Coast Guard Air Station ■	208	38.57 N	74.53 W
Cape May Court House	208	39.04 N	74.49 W
Cape May Point	208	39.09 N	74.46 W
Capembé ≃	152	16.10 S	21.00 E
Cape Melville National Park ♠	164	14.20 S	144.30 E
Capenda Camulemba	152	9.24 S	18.27 E
Capenga ≃	287a	22.49 S	43.37 W
Capenhurst	262	53.15 N	2.57 W
Cape of Good Hope Nature Reserve ➔[4]	158	34.18 S	18.26 E
Cape Pole	180	55.58 N	133.48 W
Cape Pond ⊜	283	42.38 N	70.38 W
Cape Porpoise	188	43.22 N	70.26 W
Cape Range National Park ♠	162	22.10 S	113.55 E

	English	Deutsch	Español	Français	Português
≃	River	Fluß	Río	Rivière	Rio
≅	Canal	Kanal	Canal	Canal	Canal
ʟ	Waterfall, Rapids	Wasserfall, Stromschnellen	Cascada, Rápidos	Chute d'eau, Rapides	Cascata, Rápidos
ʮ	Strait	Meeresstraße	Estrecho	Détroit	Estreito
⊂	Bay, Gulf	Bucht, Golf	Bahía, Golfo	Baie, Golfe	Baía, Golfo
⊜	Lake, Lakes	See, Seen	Lago, Lagos	Lac, Lacs	Lago, Lagos
⁝	Swamp	Sumpf	Pantano	Marais	Pântano
⍓	Ice Features, Glacier	Eis- und Gletscherformen	Accidentes Glaciales	Formes glaciaires	Acidentes glaciares
⍑	Other Hydrographic Features	Andere Hydrographische Objekte	Otros Elementos Hidrográficos	Autres données hydrographiques	Outros acidentes hidrográficos
✤	Submarine Features	Untermeerische Objekte	Accidentes Submarinos	Formes de relief sous-marin	Acidentes submarinos
□	Political Unit	Politische Einheit	Unidad Politica	Entité politique	Unidade política
ᵾ	Cultural Institution	Kulturelle Institution	Institución Cultural	Institution culturelle	Institução cultural
⊥	Historical Site	Historische Stätte	Sitio Histórico	Site historique	Sitio histórico
♠	Recreational Site	Erholungs- und Ferienort	Sitio de Recreo	Centre de loisirs	Area de Lazer
⊠	Airport	Flughafen	Aeropuerto	Aéroport	Aeroporto
■	Military Installation	Militäranlage	Instalación Militar	Installation militaire	Instalação militar
➔	Miscellaneous	Verschiedenes	Misceláneo	Divers	Diversos

Name	Page	Lat.°′	Long.°′
Cape Rise ✢[3]	8	42.00 S	15.00 E
Capernaum → Kefar Naḥum ⊥	132	32.53 N	35.34 E
Cape Romanzof	180	61.49 N	165.56 W
Capertee	170	33.09 S	149.59 E
Capertee ≃	170	33.12 S	150.28 E
Cape Sable Island I	186	43.25 N	65.37 W
Cape Scott Provincial Park ♦	182	50.45 N	128.20 W
Capesterre	241o	15.54 N	61.13 W
Capesterre, Pointe de la >	241o	16.03 N	61.33 W
Capesterre-Belle-Eau	241o	16.03 N	61.34 W
Capesthorne Hall ⊥	262	53.15 N	2.14 W
Capestrano	66	42.16 N	13.46 E
Capetinga ≃	256	22.04 S	47.14 W
Cape Tormentine	186	46.08 N	63.47 W
Cape Town (Kaapstad)	158	33.55 S	18.22 E
Cape Verde (Cabo Verde) □[1], Afr.	134	16.00 N	24.00 W
Cape Verde (Cabo Verde) □[1], Afr.	150a	16.00 N	24.00 W
Cape Verde Basin ✢[1]	8	15.00 N	30.00 W
Cape Verde Islands → Cape Verde □[1]	150a	16.00 N	24.00 W
Cape Verde Terrace ✢[3]	10	18.00 N	20.00 W
Capeville	208	37.12 N	75.57 W
Cape Vincent	212	44.07 N	76.19 W
Cape Yakataga	180	60.04 N	142.26 W
Cape York Peninsula >[1]	164	14.00 S	142.30 E
Cap-Haïtien	238	19.45 N	72.12 W
Capilla de Farruco	252	32.53 S	55.25 W
Capilla del Monte	252	30.51 S	64.31 W
Capilla del Señor	258	34.18 S	59.06 W
Capim ≃	250	1.40 S	47.47 W
Capim Melado, Morro do ʌ	287a	22.50 S	43.29 W
Capinas Point >	116	11.05 N	125.14 E
Capinópolis	255	18.41 S	49.35 W
Capinota	248	17.43 S	66.14 W
Capinzal	252	27.20 S	51.36 W
Capira	236	8.45 N	79.53 W
Cap Island I	116	5.57 N	120.06 E
Capistrano, Bra.	250	4.28 S	38.55 W
Capistrano, It.	68	38.41 N	16.17 E
Capistrano Beach	228	33.27 N	117.40 W
Capistrello	66	41.57 N	13.23 E
Capitachouane ≃	190	47.36 N	76.54 W
Capitachouane, Lac ⊜	190	48.05 N	75.55 W
Capital Airport ⊠	219	39.51 N	89.41 W
Capital Centre Arena ♦	284c	38.54 N	76.51 W
Capital City Airport ⊠	216	42.47 N	84.35 W
Capitan	200	33.32 N	105.34 W
Capitán Aracena, Isla I	254	54.10 S	71.20 W
Capitán Arturo Prat ʊ[3]	9	62.30 S	59.41 W
Capitán Bado	255	23.16 S	55.32 W
Capitán Bermúdez	252	32.49 S	60.43 W
Capitán Meza	252	26.55 S	55.15 W
Capitan Peak ʌ	200	33.36 N	105.16 W
Capitán Sarmiento	252	34.10 S	59.48 W
Capitão de Campos	250	4.28 S	41.57 W
Capitão Enéas	255	16.21 S	43.43 W
Capitola	226	36.58 N	121.57 W
Capitol Heights	208	38.53 N	76.54 W
Capitol Park	208	39.08 N	75.30 W
Capitol Peak ʌ	204	41.50 N	117.18 W
Capitol Reef National Park ♦	200	38.11 N	111.20 W
Capitol View	192	33.57 N	80.56 W
Capivari	255	23.00 S	47.31 W
Capivari ≃, Bra.	248	19.16 S	57.10 W
Capivari ≃, Bra.	255	12.30 S	39.55 W
Capivari ≃, Bra.	256	22.14 S	44.57 W
Capivari ≃, Bra.	256	24.09 S	46.48 W
Capivari ≃, Bra.	256	21.53 S	46.15 W
Capivari ≃, Bra.	256	22.26 S	45.47 W
Capivari ≃, Bra.	256	22.56 S	47.16 W
Capivari ≃, Bra.	256	21.30 S	44.20 W
Capivari ≃, Bra.	256	21.12 S	44.52 W
Capivari, Canal ≖	287a	22.42 S	43.21 W
Capiz □[4]	116	11.30 N	122.30 E
Capiz → Roxas	116	11.35 N	122.45 E
Capizzi	70	37.51 N	14.29 E
Caplan	186	48.06 N	65.41 W
Čaplejevka	78	51.43 N	33.12 E
Caplen	222	29.29 N	94.33 W
Caples Lake ⊜[1]	226	38.42 N	120.03 W
Caplina ≃	248	18.14 S	70.33 W
Čaplinka	78	46.23 N	33.32 E
Čaplino, Ross.	180	64.25 N	172.15 W
Čaplino, Ukr.	78	48.09 N	36.14 E
Čapljina	36	43.07 N	17.42 E
Caplone, Monte ʌ	64	45.48 N	10.38 E
Čaplygin	76	53.14 N	39.58 E
Cap Mountain ʌ	180	63.25 N	123.29 W
Capnoyan Island I	116	10.44 N	120.54 E
Capoche ≃	154	15.23 S	32.53 E
Capodichino, Aeroporto di ⊠	68	40.50 N	14.17 E
Capodimonte	66	42.33 N	11.55 E
Capo di Ponte	64	46.02 N	10.21 E
Capo d'Orlando	70	38.10 N	14.53 E
Capoeira, Corredeira ʟ	250	6.48 S	58.21 W
Capolago	58	45.55 N	8.59 E
Capoliveri	66	42.45 N	10.22 E
Caporolo ≃	152	12.56 S	13.00 E
Caposele	68	40.49 N	15.13 E
Capostrada	66	43.57 N	10.54 E
Capot ≃	240e	14.51 N	61.05 W
Capoterra	71	39.11 N	8.58 E
Capoti-an, Mount ʌ	116	11.45 N	125.15 E
Capotoan, Mount ʌ	116	12.09 N	124.57 E
Cappadocia □[9]	130	38.30 N	36.00 E
Cappamore	48	52.37 N	8.20 W
Cap-Pelé	186	46.13 N	64.18 W
Cappella Islands II	240m	18.17 N	64.54 W
Cappelle	66	42.03 N	13.22 E
Cappelle sul Tavo	66	42.28 N	14.06 E
Cappeln	52	52.48 N	8.07 E
Cappenberg	263	51.39 N	7.32 E
Cappenberg, Schloss ⊥	263	51.39 N	7.32 E
Cappercleuch	44	55.29 N	3.12 W
Cappoquin	48	52.08 N	7.50 W
Capracotta	66	41.50 N	14.16 E
Capraia	66	43.03 N	9.50 E
Capraia, Isola I	66	42.08 N	15.31 E
Capraia, Isola di I	66	43.02 N	9.49 E
Capranica	66	42.15 N	12.11 E
Caprara, Punta >	71	41.07 N	8.19 E
Caprarola	66	42.19 N	12.14 E
Capreol	190	46.43 N	80.56 W
Caprera, Isola I	71	41.12 N	9.28 E
Caprese Michelangelo	66	43.39 N	11.59 E
Capri	68	40.33 N	14.14 E
Capri, Isola di I	68	40.33 N	14.13 E
Capriati a Volturno	68	41.28 N	14.08 E
Capricorn, Cape >	166	23.30 S	151.13 E
Capricorn Channel ʯ	166	23.00 S	152.20 E
Capricorn Group II	166	23.28 S	152.00 E
Capri Leone	70	38.05 N	14.44 E
Caprino Veronese	64	45.36 N	10.47 E
Caprivi Oss □[5]	156	17.45 S	24.00 E
Caprivi Zipfel (Caprivi Strip) □[9]	156	17.59 S	23.00 E
Caprolace, Lago di ⊜	66	41.21 N	12.58 E
Capron, Il., U.S.	216	42.24 N	88.44 W
Capron, Va., U.S.	208	36.42 N	77.12 W
Cap Saint Jacques → Vung Tau	110	10.21 N	107.04 E
Cap-Santé	206	46.40 N	71.47 W
Capstone	260	51.21 N	0.34 E
Captain Anthony Meldahl Dam ◆[6]	218	38.48 N	84.11 W
Captain Cook	229d	19.29 N	155.55 W
Captain Cook Bridge ◆[5]	274a	34.00 S	151.08 E
Captain Cook Landing Place Park ⊥	274a	34.00 S	151.14 E
Captain Cook Monument ⊥	174c	29.00 S	167.56 E
Captain Daniel Wright Woods ♦	278	42.13 N	87.56 W
Captain Harbor ⊂	276	41.00 N	73.36 W
Captain Pond ⊜	283	42.48 N	71.10 W
Captains Flat	171b	35.35 S	149.27 E
Captieux	32	44.18 N	0.16 W
Captina Creek ≃	188	39.52 N	80.48 W
Captiva	220	26.31 N	82.11 W
Captiva Island I	220	26.31 N	82.11 W
Captree Island I	276	40.39 N	73.16 W
Captree State Park ♦	276	40.39 N	73.16 W
Capua	68	41.06 N	14.12 E
Capual Island I	116	6.02 N	121.24 E
Capuáva	287b	23.39 S	46.29 W
Capuça I	152	17.22 S	21.18 E
Capucapu ≃	246	1.45 S	58.35 W
Capucin >	240d	15.38 N	61.28 W
Capul	116	12.25 N	124.11 E
Capulín, Río del ≃	196	27.31 N	101.33 W
Capulin Mountain National Monument ♦	196	36.48 N	103.55 W
Capul Island I	116	12.26 N	124.10 E
Capuna	152	15.38 S	19.43 E
Capunda	152	14.57 S	14.03 E
Capurro	258	34.25 S	56.28 W
Capurso	68	41.03 N	16.55 E
Caputh	54	52.21 N	13.00 E
Cap-Vert → Cape Verde □[1]	150a	16.00 N	24.00 W
Caquende	256	21.20 S	44.33 W
Caquetá □[8]	246	1.00 N	74.00 W
Caquetá (Japurá) ≃	246	3.08 S	64.46 W
Caquiaviri	248	17.03 S	68.38 W
Čar ≃	86	50.22 N	80.55 E
Čara, Ityo.	144	5.52 N	37.12 E
Čara, Ross.	88	56.54 N	118.12 E
Čara ≃	74	60.22 N	120.50 E
Cará, Ilha do I	250	0.01 S	50.50 W
Caraballeda	286c	10.37 N	66.50 W
Caraballeda, Punta >	286c	10.37 N	66.50 W
Carabanchel Alto ◆[8]	266a	40.22 N	3.45 W
Carabanchel Bajo ◆[8]	266a	40.23 N	3.47 W
Carabao Island I	116	12.04 N	121.56 E
Carabaya ≃	248	14.43 S	70.17 W
Carabaya, Cordillera de ⋏	248	13.50 S	70.45 W
Carabayllo	286d	11.52 S	77.02 W
Carabelas Grande ≃	258	34.15 S	58.43 W
Carabinani ≃	246	1.58 S	61.31 W
Carabobo □[3]	246	10.10 N	68.05 W
Carabost	171b	35.36 S	147.44 E
Caracal	38	44.07 N	24.21 E
Caracalla, Terme di ⊥	267a	41.53 N	12.29 E
Caracaraí	246	1.50 N	61.08 W
Caracas, Ven.	246	10.30 N	66.56 W
Caracas, Ven.	286c	10.30 N	66.56 W
Čarach	86	59.03 N	62.15 E
Carache	246	9.38 N	70.14 W
Caracol, Bra.	250	9.17 S	43.20 W
Caracol, Bra.	252	22.01 S	57.02 W
Caracollo	248	17.39 S	67.10 W
Caracorum → Karakoram Range ⋏	120	35.30 N	77.00 E
Carácuaro de Morelos	234	18.46 N	101.02 W
Caradoc Indian Reserve ◆[4]	214	42.48 N	81.29 W
Caraffa di Catanzaro	68	38.53 N	16.29 E
Caraga	116	7.20 N	126.34 E
Caraga ≃	116	7.20 N	126.34 E
Caragh, Lough ⊜	48	52.03 N	9.52 W
Caraghnan Mountain ʌ	166	31.20 S	149.03 E
Caraglio	62	44.25 N	7.26 E
Caraguata, Arroyo ≃	288	34.24 S	58.38 W
Caraguatatuba	256	23.37 S	45.25 W
Caraguatatuba, Enseada de ⊂	256	23.40 S	45.20 W
Caraguatay	252	25.14 S	56.52 W
Caraí	255	17.12 S	41.42 W
Caraibamba	248	14.24 S	73.09 W
Caraïbes, Îles des → West Indies II	230	19.00 N	70.00 W
Caraïbes, Mer des → Caribbean Sea ⍑[2]	230	15.00 N	73.00 W
Caraigres, Cerro ʌ	236	9.43 N	84.05 W
Caraíva ≃	255	16.48 S	39.08 W
Carajari ≃	250	4.45 S	54.20 W
Carajás	250	6.06 S	50.23 W
Carajás, Serra dos ⋏	250	5.50 S	51.20 W
Caralue Bluff ʌ[2]	166	33.26 S	136.16 E
Caramagna-Piemonte	62	44.46 N	7.44 E
Caramanico Terme	66	42.09 N	14.00 E
Caramay	116	10.11 N	119.14 E
Caramoan	116	13.46 N	123.52 E
Caramoan Peninsula >[1]	116	13.48 N	123.40 E
Caramoran	116	13.59 N	124.08 E
Caramy ≃	62	43.26 N	6.12 E
Caranavi	248	15.46 S	67.36 W
Carandaí	255	20.57 S	43.48 W
Carandayti	248	20.45 S	63.04 W
Carangola	255	20.44 S	42.02 W
Carano	64	46.16 N	11.27 E
Caransebeș	38	45.25 N	22.13 E
Carapá ≃	252	24.30 S	54.20 W
Carapachay ≃[1]	288	34.25 S	58.35 W
Carapajó	250	2.16 S	49.22 W
Cara-Paraná ≃	246	1.45 S	73.13 W
Carapeguá	252	25.48 S	57.14 W
Carapelle ≃	68	41.30 N	15.55 E
Carapicuíba	256	23.31 S	46.50 W
Carapicuíba □[7]	287b	23.31 S	46.53 W
Carapo ≃	246	7.30 N	64.02 W
Caraquet	186	47.48 N	64.57 W
Caráquez	246	0.36 S	80.25 W
Carare ≃	246	6.48 N	74.06 W
Carasco	62	44.21 N	9.21 E
Caraș-Severin □[6]	38	45.00 N	22.00 E
Caratasca, Laguna de ⊂	236	15.23 N	83.55 W
Carate Brianza	62	45.41 N	9.14 E
Caratinga	255	19.47 S	42.08 W
Carauari	246	4.52 S	66.54 W
Caraúbas	250	5.47 S	37.34 W
Caravaca	34	38.06 N	1.51 W
Caravaggio	62	45.30 N	9.38 E
Caravela, Ilha I	150	11.30 N	16.20 W
Caravelas	255	17.45 S	39.15 W
Caravelí	248	15.46 S	73.22 W
Caravelle, Presqu'île de la >[1]	240e	14.45 N	60.55 W
Caravius, Monte is ʌ	71	39.09 N	8.49 E
Caraway	194	35.45 N	90.19 W
Carayaó	252	25.10 S	56.26 W
Caraz	248	9.03 S	77.45 W
Caraza ◆[8]	288	34.42 S	58.26 W
Carazinho	252	28.18 S	52.48 W
Carazo □[5]	236	11.45 N	86.15 W
Carballiño	34	42.26 N	8.04 W
Carballo	34	43.13 N	8.41 W
Carberry	184	49.52 N	99.20 W
Carbet, Pitons du ⋏	240e	14.42 N	61.07 W
Carbo	232	29.42 N	110.58 W
Carbol ≃	70	37.32 N	12.59 E
Carbon, Ab., Can.	182	51.29 N	113.09 W
Carbon, Pa., U.S.	279b	40.17 N	79.34 W
Carbon, Tx., U.S.	196	32.16 N	98.50 W
Carbon □[6]	210	40.52 N	75.45 W
Carbon ≃	224	47.07 N	122.13 W
Carbon, Cap >	34	36.47 N	5.06 E
Carbonado	224	47.04 N	122.03 W
Carbonara, Capo >	71	39.06 N	9.31 E
Carbonara, Pizzo ʌ	70	37.54 N	14.02 E
Carbonare	64	45.56 N	11.13 E
Carbonate	266b	45.41 N	8.56 E
Carbon-Blanc	32	44.53 N	0.31 W
Carbon Canyon Dam ◆[6]	280	33.55 N	117.50 W
Carbon Creek ≃	280	33.49 N	118.04 W
Carbondale, Co., U.S.	200	39.24 N	107.12 W
Carbondale, Il., U.S.	194	37.43 N	89.13 W
Carbondale, Ks., U.S.	198	38.49 N	95.41 W
Carbondale, Pa., U.S.	210	41.34 N	75.30 W
Carbone	68	40.09 N	16.05 E
Carbonear	186	47.45 N	53.13 W
Carboneras de Guadazaon	34	39.53 N	1.48 W
Carbon Hill	194	33.53 N	87.31 W
Carbonia	71	39.10 N	8.31 E
Carbonin	64	46.37 N	12.13 E
Carbost	46	57.18 N	6.22 W
Carcaixent	34	39.08 N	0.27 W
Carcajou ≃	180	65.37 N	128.43 W
Carcalgong Hill ʌ	170	32.52 S	149.41 E
Carcans, Lac de ⊂	32	45.08 N	1.08 W
Carcar	116	10.06 N	123.38 E
Carcarañá	252	32.51 S	61.09 W
Carcarañá ≃	252	32.27 S	60.48 W
Carcare	62	44.21 N	8.18 E
Carcar Point >	116	10.05 N	123.41 E
Carcassonne	32	43.13 N	2.21 E
Carcastillo	34	42.23 N	1.26 W
Carcavelos, Port.	266c	38.41 N	9.20 W
Carcavelos, Port.	266c	38.53 N	9.14 W
Carceri, Eremo delle ʊ[1]	66	43.05 N	12.42 E
Carcès	62	43.28 N	6.11 E
Carchi □[4]	246	0.45 N	78.00 W
Carcroft	44	53.34 N	1.11 W
Carcross	180	60.10 N	134.42 W
Cardabia	162	23.06 S	113.48 E
Çardak, Tür.	130	38.06 N	36.49 E
Čardak, Uzb.	85	41.37 N	69.56 E
Cardal	258	34.18 S	56.24 W
Cardano al Campo	266b	45.39 N	8.47 E
Čardara	85	41.17 N	67.55 E
Čardara, step' ⋏[1]	85	42.00 N	68.00 E
Čardarinskoje vodochranilišče ⊜[1]	85	41.10 N	68.15 E
Cardeña	34	38.13 N	4.19 W
Cárdenas, Cuba	240p	23.02 N	81.12 W
Cárdenas, Méx.	234	22.00 N	99.40 W
Cárdenas, Méx.	234	17.59 N	93.22 W
Cárdenas, Nic.	236	11.12 N	85.31 W
Cárdenas, Bahía de ⊂	240p	23.05 N	81.10 W
Cardener ≃	34	41.41 N	1.51 E
Carderock Springs	284c	38.59 N	77.10 W
Cardiel, Lago ⊜	254	48.55 S	71.15 W
Cardiff, Austl.	170	32.57 S	151.41 E
Cardiff, Wales, U.K.	42	51.29 N	3.13 W
Cardiff, Md., U.S.	208	39.43 N	76.20 W
Cardiff, N.J., U.S.	208	39.24 N	74.35 W
Cardiff by the Sea	228	33.01 N	117.16 W
Cardigan, P.E., Can.	186	46.14 N	62.37 W
Cardigan, Wales, U.K.	42	52.06 N	4.40 W
Cardigan Bay ⊂, P.E., Can.	186	46.10 N	62.30 W
Cardigan Bay ⊂, Wales, U.K.	42	52.30 N	4.20 W
Cardigan Island I	42	52.08 N	4.41 W
Cardigan State Park ♦	188	43.38 N	71.54 W
Cardinal	212	44.47 N	75.23 W
Cardinale	68	38.38 N	16.23 E
Cardinal Heights	212	45.27 N	75.37 W
Cardinal Lake ⊜	182	56.14 N	117.44 W
Cardington, Boph.	158	27.11 S	23.30 E
Cardington, Oh., U.S.	214	40.30 N	82.53 W
Cardinia Creek ≃	274b	38.12 S	145.23 E
Cardinia Reservoir ⊜[1]	169	37.58 S	145.25 E
Cardona	258	33.53 S	57.23 W
Cardonal, Punta >	232	28.28 N	111.45 W
Cardoso	255	20.04 S	49.54 W
Cardozo	252	32.38 S	56.21 W
Card Sound ʯ	220	25.20 N	80.18 W
Cardston	182	49.12 N	113.18 W
Cardwell, Austl.	166	18.16 S	146.02 E
Cardwell, Mo., U.S.	194	36.02 N	90.17 W
Cardwell Mountain ʌ	194	35.41 N	85.41 W
Čardžou	128	39.06 N	63.34 E
Čardžou □[8]	128	38.51 N	63.34 E
Careaçu	256	22.02 S	45.42 W
Careen Lake ⊜	184	57.00 N	108.10 W
Carega, Cima ʌ	64	45.44 N	11.08 E
Carei	38	47.42 N	22.28 E
Careiro	246	3.12 S	59.45 W
Careiro, Ilha do I	246	3.10 S	59.44 W
Carén	252	30.51 S	70.47 W
Čarencavan	84	40.24 N	44.38 E
Carencro	194	30.19 N	92.02 W
Carentan	32	49.18 N	1.14 W
Careri	68	38.10 N	16.07 E
Cares ≃	34	43.19 N	4.36 W
Caresana	62	45.13 N	8.30 E
Caretta	192	37.20 N	81.40 W
Carevščina	80	52.27 N	46.43 E
Carey	214	40.57 N	83.22 W
Carey, Lake ⊜	162	29.05 S	122.15 E
Carey Downs	162	25.38 S	115.27 E
Careysburg	150	6.30 N	10.32 W
Cargados Carajos Shoals II	12	16.38 S	59.38 E
Cargill	46	56.30 N	3.22 W
Carhaix-Plouguer	32	48.17 N	3.35 W
Carhuamayo	248	10.55 S	76.02 W
Carhuanca	248	13.45 S	73.48 W
Carhuaz	248	9.16 S	77.38 W
Carhué	252	37.11 S	62.44 W
Caria □[9]	130	37.30 N	28.00 E
Cariacica	255	20.16 S	40.25 W
Cariaco	246	10.29 N	63.33 W
Cariaco, Golfo de ⊂	246	10.30 N	64.00 W
Cariamanga	246	4.20 S	79.35 W
Cariango	152	10.37 S	15.20 E
Cariati	68	39.30 N	16.56 E
Caribana, Punta >	246	8.37 N	76.52 W
Caribbean Sea ⍑[2]	230	15.00 N	73.00 W
Caribe, Mar → Caribbean Sea ⍑[2]	230	15.00 N	73.00 W
Cariboo ≃	182	52.40 N	121.40 W
Cariboo Mountains ⋏	182	53.00 N	121.00 W
Caribou, N.S., Can.	186	45.44 N	62.42 W
Caribou, Me., U.S.	186	46.51 N	68.00 W
Caribou ≃	176	59.20 N	94.44 W
Caribou, Lac du ⊜	206	46.56 N	72.50 W
Caribou Island I	190	47.22 N	85.49 W
Caribou Mountain ʌ, Id., U.S.	202	43.06 N	111.18 W
Caribou Mountain ʌ, Me., U.S.	188	45.26 N	70.38 W
Caribou Mountains ⋏	176	59.12 N	115.40 W
Caribou Range ⋏	202	43.05 N	111.15 W
Caričanka	78	48.57 N	34.29 E
Carichic	232	27.56 N	107.03 W
Caricuao	286c	10.27 N	66.59 W
Caricuao, Quebrada ≃	286c	10.26 N	66.59 W
Caricyn → Volgograd	80	48.44 N	44.25 E
Caridad, Pil.	116	10.50 N	124.45 E
Caridad, Pil.	269f	14.29 N	120.53 E
Caridade	250	4.13 S	39.12 W
Carife	68	41.01 N	15.12 E
Carigara	116	11.18 N	124.41 E
Carigara Bay ⊂	116	11.24 N	124.40 E
Carignan, P.Q., Can.	275a	45.27 N	73.18 W
Carignan, Fr.	56	49.38 N	5.10 E
Carignano, It.	62	44.55 N	7.40 E
Carignano, It.	66	43.49 N	12.56 E
Cari Laufquen Grande, Lago ⊜	254	41.07 S	69.30 W
Carinda	166	30.28 S	147.41 E
Cariñena	34	41.20 N	1.13 W
Caringbah	274a	34.03 S	151.08 E
Carinhanha	255	14.18 S	43.47 W
Carinhanha ≃	255	14.20 S	43.47 W
Carini	70	38.08 N	13.11 E
Carini, Golfo di ⊂	70	38.12 N	13.22 E
Carinish	46	57.31 N	7.18 W
Carinola	68	41.11 N	13.58 E
Carioca, Serra da ʌ	256	22.47 S	44.18 W
Caripe	246	10.12 N	63.29 W
Caripi ≃	250	3.56 N	51.27 W
Caripito	246	10.08 N	63.06 W
Carira	250	10.21 S	37.42 W
Cariré	250	3.57 S	40.27 W
Caririaçu	250	7.02 S	39.17 W
Carisbrook	169	37.02 S	143.49 E
Carisbrooke	42	50.41 N	1.19 W
Carisolo	64	46.10 N	10.45 E
Carite	286c	10.24 N	67.01 W
Carite, Lago ⊜	240m	18.04 N	66.06 W
Cariús	250	6.32 S	39.30 W
Čarkesar	85	41.02 N	70.53 E
Carlentini	70	37.16 N	15.01 E
Carle Place	276	40.45 N	73.36 W
Carles	116	11.34 N	123.08 E
Carlet	34	39.14 N	0.31 W
Carleton, Mi., U.S.	216	42.03 N	83.23 W
Carleton, Ne., U.S.	198	40.18 N	97.40 W
Carleton, Mount ʌ	186	47.23 N	66.53 W
Carleton Place	212	45.08 N	76.09 W
Carletonville	158	26.23 S	27.22 E
Carlin	204	40.42 N	116.06 W
Carling	56	49.10 N	6.43 E
Carlingford	274a	33.47 S	151.03 E
Carlingford Lough ⊂	44	54.04 N	6.10 W
Carlinville	219	39.16 N	89.52 W
Carlinville, Lake ⊜[1]	219	39.14 N	89.51 W
Carlisle, On., Can.	212	43.23 N	79.59 W
Carlisle, Eng., U.K.	44	54.54 N	2.55 W
Carlisle, Ar., U.S.	194	34.46 N	91.44 W
Carlisle, In., U.S.	194	38.58 N	87.24 W
Carlisle, Ia., U.S.	190	41.30 N	93.29 W
Carlisle, Ky., U.S.	218	38.18 N	84.01 W
Carlisle, Ma., U.S.	283	42.31 N	. 0 W
Carlisle, N.Y., U.S.	210	42.45 N	74.27 W
Carlisle, Oh., U.S.	218	39.35 N	84.20 W
Carlisle, Pa., U.S.	208	40.12 N	77.11 W
Carlisle Barracks ■	208	40.13 N	77.11 W
Carlisle Bay ⊂	241g	13.05 N	59.37 W
Carlisle Gardens	210	43.11 N	78.39 W
Carlisle Island I	180	52.52 N	170.02 W
Carlisle Springs	208	40.16 N	77.10 W
Carl Junction	194	37.10 N	94.33 W
Carlls ≃	276	40.41 N	73.20 W
Carloforte	71	39.08 N	8.18 E
Carlopoli	68	39.03 N	16.27 E
Carlópolis	255	23.25 S	49.41 W
Carlos, Isla I	254	54.03 S	73.20 W
Carlos Alves	256	21.37 S	43.07 W
Carlos Barbosa	252	29.18 S	51.30 W
Carlos Beguerie	258	35.29 S	59.06 W
Carlos Casares	252	35.38 S	61.21 W
Carlos Chagas	255	17.43 S	40.45 W
Carlos City	218	40.02 N	85.02 W
Carlos Forseca Amador	236	11.59 N	86.31 W
Carlos Keen	258	34.29 S	59.14 W
Carlos Manuel de Céspedes	240p	21.35 N	78.17 W
Carlos Pellegrini	252	32.03 S	61.48 W
Carlos Reyles	252	33.03 S	56.29 W
Carlos Sampaio	287a	22.42 S	43.31 W
Carlos Tejedor	252	35.23 S	62.25 W
Carlow	48	52.50 N	6.55 W
Carlow □[6]	48	53.40 N	6.50 W
Carloway	46	58.17 N	6.48 W
Carl Sandburg Home National Historic Site ⊥	192	35.16 N	82.27 W
Carlsbad, Ca., U.S.	228	33.09 N	117.20 W
Carlsbad, N.M., U.S.	196	32.25 N	104.13 W
Carlsbad, Tx., U.S.	196	31.36 N	100.38 W
Carlsbad Caverns National Park ♦	196	32.08 N	104.35 W
Carlsbad → Karlovy Vary	54	50.11 N	12.52 E
Carlsberg Ridge ✢[3]	12	6.00 N	61.00 E
Carlsborg	224	48.05 N	123.10 W
Carlsfeld	54	50.26 N	12.35 E
Carlstadt	276	40.50 N	74.05 W
Carlton, Austl.	274a	33.58 S	151.08 E
Carlton, Eng., U.K.	42	52.58 N	1.05 W
Carlton, Eng., U.K.	44	53.42 N	1.01 W
Carlton, Mn., U.S.	190	46.39 N	92.25 W
Carlton, Or., U.S.	224	45.18 N	123.11 W
Carlton, Tx., U.S.	196	31.55 N	98.10 W
Carlton Gardens ♦	274b	37.48 S	144.59 E
Carlton Lake ⊜	224	45.18 N	123.11 W
Carluke	46	55.45 N	3.51 W
Carlyle, Sk., Can.	184	49.38 N	102.16 W
Carlyle, Il., U.S.	219	38.36 N	89.22 W
Carlyle Lake ⊜[1]	219	38.40 N	89.18 W
Carmacks	180	62.05 N	136.18 W
Carmagnola	62	44.51 N	7.43 E
Carman	184	49.32 N	98.00 W
Carmanah Creek ≃	224	48.37 N	124.44 W
Carmangay	182	50.08 N	113.07 W
Carmanville	186	49.24 N	54.17 W
Carmarthen	42	51.52 N	4.19 W
Carmarthen Bay ⊂	42	51.40 N	4.30 W
Carmaux	32	44.03 N	2.09 E
Carmel, Wales, U.K.	262	53.17 N	3.15 W
Carmel, Ca., U.S.	226	36.33 N	121.55 W
Carmel, In., U.S.	218	39.58 N	86.07 W
Carmel, N.J., U.S.	208	39.26 N	75.07 W
Carmel, N.Y., U.S.	210	41.26 N	73.41 W
Carmel ≃	226	36.32 N	121.56 W
Carmel, Mount ʌ	226	36.23 N	121.47 W
Carmel, Mount → Karmel, Har ʌ	132	32.44 N	35.02 E
Carmel Bay ⊂	226	36.33 N	121.57 W
Carmel Head >	44	53.24 N	4.34 W
Carmel Highlands	226	36.30 N	121.56 W
Carmel Hills	226	36.32 N	121.53 W
Carmel Mountain ʌ[2]	228	32.55 N	117.13 W
Carmelo	258	34.00 S	58.17 W
Carmel Point	226	36.31 N	122.55 W
Carmel Valley	226	36.29 N	121.43 W
Carmel Woods	226	36.34 N	121.54 W
Carmen, Pil.	116	8.59 N	125.17 E
Carmen, Pil.	116	9.50 N	124.12 E
Carmen, Pil.	116	10.35 N	124.01 E
Carmen, Pil.	116	12.37 N	122.07 E
Carmen, Ok., U.S.	196	36.34 N	98.27 W
Carmen, Ur.	252	33.15 S	56.01 W
Carmen, Isla I	232	25.57 N	111.12 W
Carmen, Isla del I	232	18.42 N	91.40 W
Carmen, Río del ≃	252	28.45 S	70.30 W
Carmen Alto	252	23.11 S	69.40 W
Carmen → Ciudad del Carmen	232	18.38 N	91.50 W
Carmen de Apicalá	246	4.09 N	74.44 W
Carmen de Areco	252	34.22 S	59.49 W
Carmen de Huechuraba	286e	33.21 S	70.40 W
Carmen de Patagones	254	40.48 S	62.59 W
Carmer Hill ʌ[2]	214	41.54 N	77.58 W
Carmi	194	38.05 N	88.09 W
Carmi, Lake ⊜	206	44.58 N	72.53 W
Carmiano	68	40.21 N	18.03 E
Carmichael	226	38.37 N	121.19 W
Carmignano di Brenta	64	45.38 N	11.42 E
Carmila	166	21.55 S	149.25 E
Carmine	222	30.09 N	96.41 W
Carmo	256	21.56 S	42.37 W
Carmo, Monte ʌ	62	44.11 N	8.11 E

ENGLISH

Name	Page	Lat.°′	Long.°′
Carmo, Ribeirão do ≃	256	21.20 S	45.10 W
Carmo, Rio do ≃	250	5.02 S	37.12 W
Carmo da Cachoeira	256	21.28 S	45.13 W
Carmo de Minas	256	22.07 S	45.08 W
Carmo do Paranaíba	255	18.59 S	46.21 W
Carmo do Rio Verde	255	15.21 S	49.42 W
Carmody Hills	284c	38.54 N	76.54 W
Carmona, Esp.	34	37.28 N	5.38 W
Carmona, Pil.	116	14.19 N	121.03 E
Carmópolis de Minas	255	20.33 S	44.38 W
Carmzow	54	53.23 N	14.02 E
Carnaíba	250	7.48 S	37.49 W
Carnamah	162	29.42 S	115.53 E
Carnarvon, Austl.	162	24.53 S	113.40 E
Carnarvon, S. Afr.	158	30.56 S	22.08 E
Carnarvon → Caernarfon	44	53.08 N	4.16 W
Carnarvon National Park ♦	166	25.00 S	148.00 E
Carnatic □[9]	118	12.30 N	78.15 E
Carnation	224	47.38 N	121.54 W
Carnaval, Arroyo ≃	288	34.52 S	58.02 W
Carnaxide	266c	38.43 N	9.15 W
Carncastle	48	54.54 N	5.53 W
Carndonagh	48	55.15 N	7.15 W
Carnduff	184	49.10 N	101.50 W
Carnedd Llewelyn ʌ	44	53.10 N	3.58 W
Carnedd Wen ʌ	42	52.41 N	3.35 W
Carnegie, Austl.	162	25.43 S	122.59 E
Carnegie, N.Y., U.S.	210	42.45 N	78.51 W
Carnegie, Ok., U.S.	196	35.06 N	98.36 W
Carnegie, Pa., U.S.	214	40.24 N	80.05 W
Carnegie, Lake ⊜	162	26.10 S	122.30 E
Carnegie Institute ʊ[2]	279b	40.27 N	79.57 W
Carnegie-Mellon University ʊ[2]	279b	40.27 N	79.57 W
Carnegie Ridge ✢[3]	18	1.00 S	85.00 W
Carnelian Bay	226	39.14 N	120.05 W
Carnetin	261	48.54 N	2.42 E
Carnew	48	52.43 N	6.30 W
Carneys Point	208	39.42 N	75.28 W
Carnforth	44	54.08 N	2.46 W
Carnia	64	46.22 N	13.08 E
Carnia ◆[1]	64	46.25 N	13.00 E
Carniche, Alpi (Karnische Alpen) ⋏	64	46.40 N	13.00 E
Car Nicobar Island I	110	9.10 N	92.47 E
Carnide ◆[8]	266c	38.46 N	9.11 W
Carnières	50	50.10 N	3.21 E
Carniques → Karnische Alpen ⋏	64	46.40 N	13.00 E
Carnlough	48	54.59 N	6.00 W
Carno	42	52.33 N	3.31 W
Carnon-Plage	62	43.32 N	3.59 E
Carnot, Centraf.	152	4.56 N	15.52 E
Carnot, Pa., U.S.	214	40.31 N	80.13 W
Carnot, Cape >	166	34.57 S	135.38 E
Carnoules	62	43.18 N	6.11 E
Carnoustie	46	56.30 N	2.44 W
Carnsore Point >	48	52.10 N	6.22 W
Carnwath	46	55.43 N	3.38 W
Carnwath ≃	180	68.26 N	128.50 W
Caro	190	43.29 N	83.23 W
Caroga Creek ≃	210	42.58 N	74.38 W
Caroga Lake	210	43.08 N	74.29 W
Carol Beach Estates	216	42.31 N	87.49 W
Carol City	220	25.56 N	80.14 W
Carole Acres	284c	39.04 N	77.00 W
Caroleen	192	35.16 N	81.47 W
Carole Highlands	284c	38.58 N	76.59 W
Carolei	68	39.15 N	16.13 E
Carolina, Bra.	250	7.20 S	47.28 W
Carolina, Col.	246	6.43 N	75.17 W
Carolina, El Sal.	236	13.51 N	88.19 W
Carolina, P.R.	240m	18.23 N	65.57 W
Carolina, S. Afr.	158	26.05 S	30.06 E
Carolina, R.I., U.S.	207	41.27 N	71.39 W
Carolina Beach	192	34.02 N	77.53 W
Carolinas, Puntan >	174n	14.55 N	145.38 E
Caroline □[6], Md., U.S.	208	38.53 N	75.50 W
Caroline □[6], Va., U.S.	208	38.00 N	77.20 W
Caroline I[1]	14	9.58 S	150.13 W
Caroline du Nord → North Carolina □[3]	192	35.30 N	80.00 W
Caroline du Sud → South Carolina □[3]	192	34.00 N	81.00 W
Caroline Islands II	14	8.00 N	147.00 E
Caroline Livermore, Mount ʌ[2]	282	37.52 N	122.26 W
Caroline Peak ʌ	172	45.56 S	167.13 E
Carol Stream	278	41.54 N	88.08 W
Caron	184	50.28 N	105.52 W
Caron, Lac ⊜	190	48.00 N	78.53 W
Carona	64	46.01 N	9.47 E
Čaronda	76	60.34 N	38.59 E
Caroní ≃	246	8.21 N	62.43 W
Caronia	70	38.01 N	14.26 E
Caronia ≃	70	38.03 N	14.26 E
Caronno Pertusella	266b	45.36 N	9.03 E
Carora	246	10.11 N	70.05 W
Carosino	68	40.27 N	17.23 E
Carouge	58	46.11 N	6.09 E
Car'ov	80	48.40 N	45.22 E
Carovigno	68	40.42 N	17.39 E
Carovilli	66	41.43 N	14.17 E
Car'ovščina	80	53.37 N	44.45 E
Čarozero	76	60.28 N	38.39 E
Carp	212	45.21 N	76.02 W
Carp ≃, On., Can.	212	45.29 N	76.14 W
Carp ≃, Mi., U.S.	190	46.02 N	84.42 W
Carpaneto Piacentino	62	44.55 N	9.47 E
Carpanzano	68	39.09 N	16.18 E
Carpates → Carpathian Mountains ⋏	22	48.00 N	24.00 E
Carpathian Mountains ⋏	22	48.00 N	24.00 E
Carpații Meridionali ⋏	38	45.30 N	24.15 E
Cárpatos → Carpathian Mountains ⋏	22	48.00 N	24.00 E
Carpegna	66	43.47 N	12.20 E
Carpenedolo	64	45.22 N	10.26 E
Carpentaria, Gulf of ⊂	164	14.00 S	139.00 E
Carpenter	198	41.02 N	104.21 W
Carpenter Creek ≃	216	40.54 N	87.12 W
Carpenter Lake ⊜	182	50.50 N	122.30 W
Carpentersville	216	42.07 N	88.15 W
Carpentertown	279b	40.11 N	79.31 W
Carpentras	62	44.03 N	5.03 E
Carpet Museum ʊ	267d	35.43 N	51.24 E
Carpi	64	44.47 N	10.53 E
Carpignano Sesia	62	45.32 N	8.25 E
Carpina	250	7.51 S	35.15 W
Carpineti	64	44.28 N	10.31 E
Carpineto Romano	66	41.36 N	13.05 E
Carpino	68	41.51 N	15.51 E
Carpinone	66	41.35 N	14.19 E
Carpinteria	204	34.23 N	119.31 W
Carpio	198	48.26 N	101.42 W
Carp Lake ⊜	182	54.45 N	123.20 W
Carpolac	166	36.44 S	141.19 E
Carquefou	32	47.18 N	1.30 W
Carqueiranne	62	43.05 N	6.05 E
Carquinez Bridge ◆[5]	282	38.04 N	122.14 W
Carquinez Strait ʯ	282	38.02 N	122.12 W
Carra, Lough ⊜	48	53.42 N	9.16 W
Carrabelle	192	29.51 N	84.39 W
Carradale	46	55.35 N	5.28 W
Carramar	274a	33.53 S	150.58 E
Carrancas	256	21.30 S	44.39 W
Carr and Craggs Moor ◆[3]	262	53.43 N	2.09 W
Carranglan	116	15.58 N	121.04 E
Carranza, Cabo >	252	35.36 S	72.38 W
Carrao ≃	246	6.17 N	62.51 W
Carrara	64	44.05 N	10.06 E

DEUTSCH

Name	Seite	Breite°′	Länge°′ E = Ost
Carrascal	116	9.22 N	125.56 E
Carrasco ◆[8]	258	34.54 S	56.05 W
Carrasco, Aeropuerto Nacional de ⊠	258	34.52 S	56.02 W
Carrathool	166	34.24 S	145.26 E
Carrauntoohil ʌ	48	51.59 N	9.45 W
Carrazedo	250	1.36 S	51.54 W
Carrboro	192	35.54 N	79.04 W
Carr Bridge	46	57.17 N	3.49 W
Carrcroft	285	39.47 N	75.30 W
Carrcroft Crest	285	39.47 N	75.30 W
Carrefour Pompadour ♦	261	48.46 N	2.26 E
Carregueira, Serra da ⋏[2]	266c	38.48 N	9.15 W
Carreria	252	21.59 S	58.35 W
Carreta, Punta >	248	14.13 S	76.18 W
Carreta Quemada, Arroyo ≃	258	34.21 S	56.41 W
Carriacou I	238	12.30 N	61.27 W
Carrick ◆[8]	279b	40.23 N	79.59 W
Carrick ◆[1]	44	55.12 N	4.38 W
Carrickart	48	55.10 N	7.47 W
Carrickfergus	48	54.43 N	5.49 W
Carrickmacross	48	53.58 N	6.43 W
Carrick on Shannon	48	53.57 N	8.05 W
Carrick on Suir	48	52.21 N	7.25 W
Carrie, Mount ʌ	224	47.53 N	123.39 W
Carriere	194	30.37 N	89.39 W
Carrière, Lac ⊜	190	47.14 N	77.12 W
Carrières, Pointe aux >	275a	45.31 N	73.54 W
Carrières-sous-Bois	261	48.57 N	2.07 E
Carrières-sous-Poissy	261	48.57 N	2.03 E
Carrières-sur-Seine	261	48.55 N	2.11 E
Carriers Mills	194	37.41 N	88.38 W
Carrieton	166	32.26 S	138.32 E
Carrigahorig	48	53.04 N	8.09 W
Carrigaline	48	51.48 N	8.24 W
Carrigallen	48	53.59 N	7.39 W
Carrillo, C.R.	236	9.52 N	85.30 W
Carrillo, Méx.	232	26.54 N	103.55 W
Carrington, Eng., U.K.	262	53.26 N	2.24 W
Carrington, N.D., U.S.	198	47.26 N	99.07 W
Carrington Island I	202	41.00 N	112.37 W
Carrington Moss ◆[3]	262	53.25 N	2.23 W
Carr Inlet ⊂	224	47.17 N	122.42 W
Carrión ≃	34	41.53 N	4.32 W
Carrión de los Condes	34	42.20 N	4.36 W
Carrizal ≃	234	23.03 N	97.46 W
Carrizal, Cerro ʌ	196	26.43 N	100.36 W
Carrizal Bajo	252	28.05 S	71.10 W
Carrizo	34	42.35 N	5.50 W
Carrizo Creek ≃, U.S.	196	36.05 N	102.36 W
Carrizo Creek ≃, N.M., U.S.	196	35.40 N	103.43 W
Carrizo Mountain ʌ	200	33.41 N	105.42 W
Carrizo Mountains ⋏	200	36.45 N	109.10 W
Carrizo Plain ≚	226	35.25 N	120.00 W
Carrizo Springs	196	28.31 N	99.51 W
Carrizo Wash V, U.S.	200	34.36 N	109.26 W
Carrizo Wash V, Ca., U.S.	204	33.05 N	115.56 W
Carrizozo	200	33.38 N	105.52 W
Carro	62	43.20 N	5.02 E
Carrodano	62	44.14 N	9.39 E
Carroll, Ia., U.S.	198	42.03 N	94.52 W
Carroll, Ne., U.S.	198	42.16 N	97.11 W
Carroll □[6], In., U.S.	216	40.36 N	86.41 W
Carroll □[6], Ky., U.S.	218	38.39 N	85.06 W
Carroll □[6], Md., U.S.	208	39.35 N	77.00 W
Carroll □[6], Oh., U.S.	214	40.34 N	81.05 W
Carroll Lake ⊜	184	51.07 N	95.05 W
Carroll Park ♦	284b	39.17 N	76.39 W
Carrolls	224	46.05 N	122.52 W
Carrollton, Al., U.S.	194	33.10 N	88.06 W
Carrollton, Ga., U.S.	192	33.35 N	85.05 W
Carrollton, Il., U.S.	219	39.18 N	90.24 W
Carrollton, Ky., U.S.	218	38.40 N	85.10 W
Carrollton, Mi., U.S.	190	43.27 N	83.55 W
Carrollton, Ms., U.S.	194	33.30 N	89.55 W
Carrollton, Mo., U.S.	194	39.21 N	93.29 W
Carrollton, Oh., U.S.	214	40.34 N	81.05 W
Carrollton, Tx., U.S.	222	32.57 N	96.53 W
Carrollton Manor	208	39.05 N	76.35 W
Carrolltown	214	40.36 N	78.43 W
Carrollwood	284b	39.20 N	76.23 W
Carron ≃, Austl.	166	17.42 S	141.06 E
Carron ≃, Scot., U.K.	46	57.25 N	5.27 W
Carron ≃, Scot., U.K.	46	56.02 N	3.44 W
Carron ≃, Scot., U.K.	46	57.53 N	4.21 W
Carron, Loch ⊂	46	57.22 N	5.31 W
Carronbridge	44	55.16 N	3.48 W
Carron Valley Reservoir ⊜[1]	46	56.02 N	4.05 W
Carros	62	43.48 N	7.11 E
Carrot ≃	184	53.50 N	101.17 W
Carrot River	184	53.17 N	103.35 W
Carrouges	28	48.34 N	0.09 W
Carrowmore Lake ⊜	48	54.12 N	9.47 W
Carrsville	208	36.43 N	76.50 W
Carrù	62	44.29 N	7.52 E
Carrum	169	38.05 S	145.08 E
Carrum Downs	274b	38.06 S	145.11 E
Carrum North	274b	38.03 S	145.09 E
Carrville	194	32.32 N	85.52 W
Carryduff	48	54.31 N	5.53 W
Carry Falls Reservoir ⊜[1]	188	44.25 N	74.45 W
Carry-le-Rouet	62	43.20 N	5.09 E
Carsaig	46	56.17 N	6.00 W
Çarşamba	130	41.12 N	36.44 E
Čaršanga	128	37.30 N	66.01 E
Carseland	182	50.51 N	113.28 W
Carshalton ◆[8]	260	51.22 N	0.10 W
Čarsk	86	49.35 N	81.05 E
Carsoli	66	42.06 N	13.05 E
Carson, Ca., U.S.	228	33.49 N	118.16 W
Carson, N.D., U.S.	198	46.25 N	101.33 W
Carson, Va., U.S.	208	37.02 N	77.23 W
Carson, Wa., U.S.	224	45.43 N	121.49 W
Carson ≃	204	39.45 N	118.40 W
Carson, East Fork ≃	226	38.59 N	119.49 W
Carson, West Fork ≃	226	38.59 N	119.49 W
Carson City, Mi., U.S.	190	43.10 N	84.50 W
Carson City, Nv., U.S.	226	39.10 N	119.46 W
Carsondale	284c	38.57 N	76.50 W
Carson Lake ⊜, On., Can.	212	45.31 N	77.46 W
Carson Lake ⊜, Nv., U.S.	204	39.19 N	118.43 W
Carson Range ⋏	226	39.15 N	119.50 W
Carson Sink ⊜	204	39.45 N	118.30 W
Carson Valley V	226	39.00 N	119.48 W
Carstairs, Ab., Can.	182	51.34 N	114.06 W
Carstairs, Scot., U.K.	46	55.42 N	3.42 W
Carstensz-Toppen → Jaya, Puncak ʌ	164	4.05 S	137.11 E
Carswell Air Force Base ■	222	32.47 N	97.26 W
Cartagena, Chile	252	33.33 S	71.37 W
Cartagena, Col.	246	10.25 N	75.32 W
Cartagena, Esp.	34	37.36 N	0.59 W
Cartago, Col.	246	4.45 N	75.55 W
Cartago, C.R.	236	9.52 N	83.55 W
Cartago □[4]	236	9.50 N	83.45 W
Čartak	85	41.05 N	71.50 E
Cartaxo	34	39.09 N	8.47 W
Cartaxos ʌ[2]	266c	38.54 N	9.20 W
Cartaya	34	37.17 N	7.09 W
Carter	196	35.13 N	99.30 W
Carter □[6]	218	38.20 N	83.05 W
Carter Bridge ◆[5]	273a	6.28 N	3.23 E
Carter Caves State Resort Park ♦	218	38.22 N	83.10 W
Carteret	210	40.34 N	74.13 W

Symbols in the index entries represent the broad categories identified in the key at the right. Symbols with superior numbers (⋏[1]) identify subcategories (see complete key on page *I · 1*).

Symbole im Register stellen die rechts im Schlüssel erklärten Kategorien dar. Symbole mit hochgestellten Ziffern (⋏[1]) bezeichnen Unterabteilungen einer Kategorie (vgl. vollständiger Schlüssel auf Seite *I · 1*).

Los símbolos incluídos en el texto del índice representan las grandes categorias identificadas con la clave a la derecha. Los símbolos con numeros en su parte superior (⋏[1]) identifican las subcategorías (véase la clave completa en la página *I · 1*).

Les symboles de l'index représentent les catégories indiquées dans la légende à droite. Les symboles suivis d'un indice (⋏[1]) représentent des sous-catégories (voir légende complète à la page *I · 1*).

Os símbolos incluídos no texto do índice representam as grandes categorias identificadas com a chave à direita. Os símbolos com números em sua parte superior (⋏[1]) identificam as subcategorias (veja-se a chave completa à página *I · 1*).

	English	Deutsch	Español	Français	Português
ʌ	Mountain	Berg	Montaña	Montagne	Montanha
⋏	Mountains	Gebirge	Montañas	Montagnes	Montanhas
)(	Pass	Paß	Paso	Col	Passo
V	Valley, Canyon	Tal, Cañon	Valle, Cañón	Vallée, Canyon	Vale, Canhão
≚	Plain	Ebene	Llano	Plaine	Planície
>	Cape	Kap	Cabo	Cap	Cabo
I	Island	Insel	Isla	Île	Ilha
II	Islands	Inseln	Islas	Îles	Ilhas
⊥	Other Topographic Features	Andere Topographische Objekte	Otros Elementos Topográficos	Autres données topographiques	Outros acidentes topográficos

ESPAÑOL — Nombre / Página / Lat.°′ / Long.°′ W = Oeste

FRANÇAIS — Nom / Page / Lat.°′ / Long.°′ W = Ouest

PORTUGUÊS — Nome / Página / Lat.°′ / Long.°′ W = Oeste

Nombre	Página	Lat.°′	Long.°′ W = Oeste
Carter Lake	198	41.17 N	95.55 W
Carter Mountain ∧	202	44.12 N	109.25 W
Carters Lake ⊜[1]	192	34.35 N	84.35 W
Cartersville	192	34.09 N	84.48 W
Carterton, N.Z.	172	41.02 S	175.31 E
Carterton, Eng., U.K.	42	51.45 N	1.35 W
Carterville	194	37.45 N	89.04 W
Carthage, Tun.	148	36.51 N	10.21 E
Carthage, Ar., U.S.	194	34.04 N	92.33 W
Carthage, Il., U.S.	190	40.24 N	91.08 W
Carthage, In., U.S.	218	39.44 N	85.34 W
Carthage, Ms., U.S.	194	32.43 N	89.32 W
Carthage, Mo., U.S.	194	37.10 N	94.18 W
Carthage, N.Y., U.S.	212	43.58 N	75.36 W
Carthage, N.C., U.S.	192	35.20 N	79.25 W
Carthage, S.D., U.S.	198	44.10 N	97.42 W
Carthage, Tn., U.S.	194	36.15 N	85.57 W
Carthage, Tx., U.S.	194	32.09 N	94.20 W
Carthage ⊥	36	36.52 N	10.20 E
Cartier Islands ıı	160	12.32 S	123.32 E
Cartierville ◆[8]	275a	45.32 N	73.42 W
Cartierville, Aéroport de ⊠	275a	45.31 N	73.43 W
Cartridge Hill ∧[2]	262	53.41 N	2.30 W
Cartura	64	45.16 N	11.50 E
Cartwright, Mb., Can.	184	49.06 N	99.20 W
Cartwright, Nf., Can.	176	53.42 N	57.01 W
Caruaru	250	8.17 S	35.58 W
Caruban	115a	7.33 S	111.39 E
Çarumas	248	16.49 S	70.43 W
Čarüngol	88	49.14 N	106.29 E
Carunjamba ≃	152	13.57 S	12.25 E
Carúpano	246	10.40 N	63.14 W
Caruray	116	10.20 N	119.00 E
Carutapera	250	1.13 S	46.01 W
Caruthers	226	36.32 N	119.50 W
Caruthersville	194	36.11 N	89.39 W
Carutu ≃	246	5.05 N	63.28 W
Carvalhopolis	256	21.47 S	46.51 W
Carvalhos	256	22.00 S	44.28 W
Carver	207	41.53 N	70.45 W
Carversville	208	40.23 N	75.04 W
Carvin	50	50.29 N	2.58 E
Carvoeiro	246	1.24 S	61.59 W
Carvoeiro, Cabo ≻	34	39.21 N	9.24 W
Cary, Il., U.S.	216	42.12 N	88.14 W
Cary, Ms., U.S.	194	32.48 N	90.55 W
Cary, N.C., U.S.	192	35.47 N	78.46 W
Cary ≃	42	51.09 N	2.59 W
Caryčelekskij zapovednik ♠	85	41.50 N	71.55 E
Çaryk, ozero ⊜	80	46.13 N	42.43 E
Čarymovo	86	58.31 N	77.42 E
Čaryn	86	43.46 N	79.24 E
Čaryš ≃	86	52.22 N	83.45 E
Čaryšskoje	86	51.24 N	83.35 E
Caryville, Fl., U.S.	194	30.46 N	85.48 W
Caryville, Tn., U.S.	192	36.17 N	84.13 W
Casablanca (Dar-el-Beida)	148	33.39 N	7.35 W
Casablanca □[4]	148	33.35 N	7.30 W
Casablanca ◆[8]	286b	23.09 N	82.20 W
Casabona	68	39.15 N	16.57 E
Casa Branca	256	21.46 S	47.04 W
Casacalenda	66	41.44 N	14.51 E
Casa de la Torrecilla	266a	40.19 N	3.37 W
Casa del Campo ♠	266a	40.32 N	3.47 W
Casa de Piedra, Embalse ⊜[1]	252	38.15 S	67.20 W
Casa Grande	200	32.52 N	111.45 W
Casa Grande National Monument ♠	200	32.59 N	111.32 W
Casainhos	266c	38.53 N	9.10 W
Casalanguida	66	42.03 N	14.30 E
Casalattico	66	41.37 N	13.43 E
Casalbordino	66	42.09 N	14.35 E
Casalbuono	68	40.13 N	15.41 E
Casalbuttano	64	45.15 N	9.58 E
Casal di Principe	68	41.00 N	14.08 E
Casale Abbruciato ◆[8]	267a	41.44 N	12.33 E
Casalecchio di Reno	64	44.28 N	11.16 E
Casale Monferrato	62	45.08 N	8.27 E
Casale sul Sile	64	45.36 N	12.19 E
Casaletto Spartano	68	40.09 N	15.37 E
Casalmaggiore	64	44.59 N	10.26 E
Casalmorano	62	45.17 N	9.54 E
Casalnuovo Monterotaro	68	41.37 N	15.06 E
Casa Loma ⋎	275b	43.41 N	79.25 W
Casalone ◆[8]	267a	41.56 N	12.41 E
Casalotti ◆[8]	267a	41.55 N	12.22 E
Casalpusterlengo	62	45.11 N	9.39 E
Casal Velino	68	40.11 N	15.06 E
Casalvieri	66	41.38 N	13.43 E
Casamance ≃	150	12.33 N	16.46 W
Casamari, Abbazia di ⋎[1]	66	41.41 N	13.29 E
Casamassima	68	40.57 N	16.55 E
Casamicciola Terme	68	40.45 N	13.54 E
Casanare □[3]	246	5.45 N	72.00 W
Casanare ≃	246	6.02 N	69.51 W
Casanay	246	10.30 N	63.25 W
Casa Nova	250	9.07 S	40.58 W
Casarano	68	40.00 N	18.10 E
Casar de Cáceres	34	39.34 N	6.25 W
Casarsa della Delizia	64	45.57 N	12.50 E
Casas	234	23.44 N	98.45 W
Casas Adobes	200	32.19 N	110.59 W
Casas Grandes ≃	232	31.22 N	107.31 W
Casas Ibáñez	34	39.17 N	1.28 W
Casasimarro	34	39.22 N	2.02 W
Casauman ≃	116	7.16 N	126.31 E
Casa Verde ◆[8]	287b	23.30 S	46.39 W
Casavieja	34	40.17 N	4.46 W
Casbas	252	36.45 S	62.30 W
Casca	252	28.34 S	51.59 W
Casca, Rio da ≃	248	14.52 S	55.52 W
Cascadas Basaseachic, Parque Nacional ♠	232	28.10 N	108.22 W
Cascade, B.C., Can.	182	49.01 N	118.13 W
Cascade, Id., U.S.	202	44.30 N	116.02 W
Cascade, Ia., U.S.	190	42.17 N	91.00 W
Cascade, Mi., U.S.	216	42.55 N	85.30 W
Cascade, Mt., U.S.	202	47.16 N	111.41 W
Cascade, Wi., U.S.	190	43.39 N	88.00 W
Cascade ≃, N.Z.	172	44.02 S	168.22 E
Cascade ≃, Wa., U.S.	224	48.32 N	121.26 W
Cascade Bay ⊂	174c	29.01 S	167.58 E
Cascade Locks	224	45.40 N	121.53 W
Cascade Mountains (Cascade Range) ⋀	202	45.00 N	121.30 W
Cascade Park ♠	279a	41.23 N	82.06 W
Cascade Point ≻	172	44.00 S	168.22 E
Cascade Range ⋀	178	45.00 N	121.30 W
Cascade Reservoir ⊜[1]	202	44.35 N	116.06 W
Cascade Tunnel ◆[5]	224	47.40 N	121.03 W
Cascadura ◆[8]	287a	22.53 S	43.20 W
Cascais	34	38.42 N	9.25 W
Cascalho Rico	255	18.34 S	47.52 W
Cascapédia ≃	186	48.11 N	65.54 W
Cascatinha	256	22.29 S	43.09 W
Cascavel, Bra.	250	4.07 S	38.14 W
Cascavel, Bra.	252	24.57 S	53.28 W
Cascia	66	42.43 N	13.01 E
Casciana Terme	66	43.31 N	10.32 E
Cascina	66	43.41 N	10.33 E
Casco Bay ⊂	188	43.40 N	70.00 W
Çascumpec Bay ⊂	186	46.45 N	64.03 W
Čascy	82	55.37 N	36.52 E
Casei Gerola	62	45.00 N	8.55 E
Case Inlet ⊂	224	47.19 N	122.53 W
Casekow	54	53.12 N	14.12 E
Casella	62	44.32 N	9.00 E
Caselle, Aeroporto di ⊠	62	45.13 N	7.40 E
Caselle in Pittari	68	40.10 N	15.33 E
Caselle Torinese	62	45.10 N	7.39 E
Cà Selva, Lago di ⊜[1]	64	46.16 N	12.40 E
Casenove	66	42.58 N	12.50 E
Casentino ∨	66	43.40 N	11.50 E
Casenuove	266b	45.38 N	8.42 E
Case-Pilote	240e	14.38 N	61.08 W
Caseros	258	34.36 S	58.33 W
Caserta	68	41.04 N	14.20 E
Caserta □[4]	68	41.14 N	14.10 E
Caseville	190	43.56 N	83.16 W
Case Western Reserve University ⋎[2]	279a	41.30 N	81.36 W
Casey, Il., U.S.	194	39.17 N	87.59 W
Casey, Ia., U.S.	198	41.30 N	94.31 W
Casey ⋎[3]	9	66.17 S	110.32 E
Casey, Mount ∧	202	48.26 N	116.42 W
Casey Bay ⊂	9	67.20 S	48.00 E
Casey Key ı	220	27.10 N	82.29 W
Caseyr ≻	144	11.49 N	51.15 E
Caseyville	219	38.38 N	90.02 W
Cash	222	32.59 N	96.07 W
Cashel, Ire.	48	53.25 N	9.48 W
Cashel, Ire.	48	52.31 N	7.53 W
Cashie ≃	192	35.53 N	76.49 W
Cashiers	192	35.06 N	83.05 W
Cashmere	202	47.31 N	120.28 W
Cashmere Downs	162	28.58 S	119.35 E
Cashton	190	43.44 N	90.46 W
Cashtown	208	39.53 N	77.22 W
Casigua	246	8.46 N	72.30 W
Casiguran, Pil.	116	16.17 N	122.07 E
Casiguran, Pil.	116	12.52 N	124.00 E
Casiguran Sound ⊔	116	16.06 N	121.58 E
Casilda, Arg.	252	33.03 S	61.10 W
Casilda, Cuba	240p	21.46 N	79.59 W
Casimcea	38	44.43 N	28.23 E
Casimiro Castillo	234	19.38 N	104.28 W
Casina	64	44.30 N	10.30 E
Casino	166	28.52 S	153.03 E
Casiquiare ≃	246	2.01 N	67.07 W
Casita	200	31.00 N	110.53 W
Çasitas Springs	228	34.22 N	119.18 W
Čáslav	30	49.54 N	15.23 E
Çasma	248	9.28 S	78.19 W
Čašniki	76	54.52 N	29.08 E
Čašnikovo	265b	55.59 N	37.25 E
Časnočor, gora ∧	24	67.45 N	33.25 E
Casola in Lunigiana	64	44.14 N	10.10 E
Casola Valsenio	66	44.13 N	11.37 E
Casole d'Elsa	66	43.20 N	11.02 E
Casoli	66	42.07 N	14.18 E
Cason	222	33.02 N	94.49 W
Casorate Primo	62	45.19 N	9.01 E
Casorate Sempione	62	45.40 N	8.44 E
Casorezzo	266b	45.31 N	8.54 E
Çasoria	68	40.54 N	14.17 E
Časov Jar	83	48.35 N	37.50 E
Časovo	24	62.01 N	50.36 E
Caspe	34	41.14 N	0.02 W
Casper	200	42.52 N	106.18 W
Casper Creek, Middle Fork ≃	200	43.01 N	106.29 W
Caspian	190	46.03 N	88.37 W
Caspian Sea ⊤[2]	72	42.00 N	50.30 E
Caspienne, Mer → Caspian Sea ⊤[2]	72	42.00 N	50.30 E
Caspio, Depresión del → Prikaspijskaja nizmennost' ≚	80	48.00 N	52.00 E
Caspio, Mar → Caspian Sea ⊤[2]	72	42.00 N	50.30 E
Caspoggio	64	46.16 N	9.52 E
Cass □[6], Il., U.S.	219	39.57 N	90.13 W
Cass □[6], In., U.S.	216	40.45 N	86.21 W
Cass □[6], Mi., U.S.	216	41.55 N	86.01 W
Cass □[6], Tx., U.S.	222	33.05 N	94.32 W
Cass ≃	190	43.23 N	83.59 W
Cassadaga	214	42.20 N	79.18 W
Cassadaga Creek ≃	214	42.05 N	79.08 W
Cassadaga Lakes ⊜	214	42.21 N	79.19 W
Cassaday Point ≻	284a	42.52 N	79.13 W
Cassagnas	62	44.16 N	3.45 E
Cassai	152	10.33 S	21.59 E
Cassai (Kasai) ≃	152	3.02 S	16.57 E
Cassamba	152	13.06 S	20.18 E
Cassandra	214	40.24 N	78.38 W
Cassanje ≃	248	17.06 S	57.23 W
Cassano allo Ionio	68	39.47 N	16.20 E
Cassano d'Adda	62	45.32 N	9.31 E
Cassano delle Murge	68	40.53 N	16.46 E
Cassano Magnago	62	45.41 N	8.50 E
Cassaro	70	37.07 N	14.56 E
Cass Benton Parkway ♠	281	42.25 N	83.28 W
Cass City	190	43.36 N	83.10 W
Cassel	50	50.48 N	2.29 E
Casselberry	220	28.40 N	81.19 W
Cassella	216	40.25 N	84.34 W
Casselman	206	45.19 N	75.05 W
Casselton	198	46.54 N	97.12 W
Cássia, Bra.	255	20.36 S	46.56 W
Cassia, Fl., U.S.	220	28.53 N	81.28 W
Cássia dos Coqueiros	256	21.17 S	47.10 W
Cassiar	180	59.16 N	129.40 W
Cassiar Mountains ⋀	176	59.00 N	129.00 W
Cassibile ≃	70	36.57 N	15.11 E
Cassidy	224	49.04 N	123.53 W
Cassidy Airfield ⊠	174o	1.57 N	157.18 W
Cassilândia	255	19.09 S	51.45 W
Cassimbazar	126	24.07 N	88.16 E
Cassine	62	44.45 N	8.31 E
Cassinetta di Lugagnano	266b	45.25 N	8.54 E
Cassinga	152	15.08 S	16.05 E
Cassino, Bra.	252	32.11 S	52.10 W
Cassino, It.	66	41.30 N	13.49 E
Cassio	64	44.35 N	10.02 E
Cassipore ◆[8]	272b	22.37 N	88.22 E
Cassis	62	43.13 N	5.32 E
Cass Lake	190	47.22 N	94.36 W
Cass Lake ⊜, Mi., U.S.	281	42.36 N	83.22 W
Cass Lake ⊜, Mn., U.S.	190	47.25 N	94.32 W
Cassley ≃	46	57.58 N	4.35 W
Cassoalala	152	9.30 S	14.22 E
Cassoango	152	13.42 S	20.56 E
Cassolnovo	62	45.22 N	8.48 E
Cassone	64	45.44 N	10.46 E
Cassongue	152	11.51 S	15.03 E
Cassopolis	216	41.54 N	86.00 W
Casstown	218	40.03 N	84.07 W
Cassumba, Ilha ı	255	17.46 S	39.17 W
Cassunda	152	10.57 S	21.03 E
Cassununga	255	16.03 S	53.38 W
Cassville, In., U.S.	216	40.33 N	86.08 W
Cassville, Mo., U.S.	194	36.40 N	93.52 W
Cassville, N.Y., U.S.	210	42.57 N	75.15 W
Cassville, Pa., U.S.	214	40.18 N	78.02 W
Cassville, Wi., U.S.	190	42.42 N	90.59 W
Castac Lake ⊜	228	34.50 N	118.51 W
Castagnaro	64	45.07 N	11.24 E
Castagneto Carducci	66	43.10 N	10.36 E
Castaic	228	34.30 N	118.37 W
Castaic Creek ≃	228	34.25 N	118.37 W
Castaic Lake ⊜[1]	228	34.32 N	118.37 W
Castalia	214	41.24 N	82.48 W
Castanea	210	41.07 N	77.25 W
Castanhal	250	1.18 S	47.55 W
Castanheira de Pêra	34	40.00 N	8.13 W
Castaños	196	26.47 N	101.25 W
Castañones, Punta ≻	236	12.28 N	87.11 W
Castano Primo	62	45.33 N	8.47 E
Casteggio	62	45.00 N	9.07 E
Castel	43b	49.28 N	2.34 W
Castelar	258	34.40 S	58.40 W
Castel Baronia	68	41.03 N	15.11 E
Castel Bolognese	66	44.19 N	11.48 E
Castelbuono	70	37.56 N	14.05 E
Castelcivita	68	40.30 N	15.15 E
Casteldaccia	70	38.03 N	13.32 E
Castel d'Ario	64	45.11 N	10.58 E
Casteldarne (Ehrenburg)	64	46.48 N	11.50 E
Casteldelfino	62	44.35 N	7.04 E
Castel del Monte	66	42.22 N	13.43 E
Castel del Piano	66	42.53 N	11.32 E
Castel del Rio	66	44.12 N	11.30 E
Castel di Decima ◆[8]	267a	41.45 N	12.26 E
Castel di Guido ◆[8]	267a	41.54 N	12.17 E
Castel di Ieri	66	42.06 N	13.44 E
Castel di Iudica	70	37.30 N	14.38 E
Castel di Leva ◆[8]	267a	41.47 N	12.32 E
Castel di Lucio	70	37.53 N	14.19 E
Castel di Sangro	66	41.47 N	14.06 E
Castel di Tora	66	42.13 N	12.58 E
Castelfidardo	66	43.28 N	13.33 E
Castelfiorentino	66	43.36 N	10.58 E
Castelfondo	64	46.27 N	11.07 E
Castelforte	66	41.18 N	13.49 E
Castelfranco Emilia	64	44.37 N	11.03 E
Castelfranco in Miscano	68	41.18 N	15.05 E
Castelfranco Veneto	64	45.40 N	11.55 E
Castel Frentano	66	42.12 N	14.22 E
Castel Fusano ◆[8]	267a	41.44 N	12.19 E
Castel Gandolfo	66	41.45 N	12.39 E
Castel Giorgio	66	42.42 N	11.59 E
Castelgrande	68	40.47 N	15.26 E
Castelhanos, Baía de ⊂	256	23.51 S	45.15 W
Castelhanos, Ponta dos ≻	256	23.10 S	44.06 W
Casteljaloux	32	44.19 N	0.05 E
Castellabate	68	40.17 N	14.57 E
Castell'Alfero	62	44.59 N	8.13 E
Castellalto	66	42.40 N	13.49 E
Castellammare, Golfo di ⊂	70	38.08 N	12.54 E
Castellammare del Golfo	70	38.01 N	12.53 E
Castellammare di Stabia	68	40.42 N	14.29 E
Castellamonte	62	45.23 N	7.42 E
Castellana, Grotte di ⩡[5]	68	40.53 N	17.07 E
Castellana Grotte	68	40.53 N	17.11 E
Castellana Sicula	70	37.47 N	14.02 E
Castellane	62	43.51 N	6.31 E
Castellaneta	68	40.37 N	16.57 E
Castellanza	62	45.37 N	8.54 E
Castellarano	64	44.30 N	10.44 E
Castell'Arquato	62	44.51 N	9.52 E
Castell'Azzara	66	42.46 N	11.42 E
Castellazzo Bormida	62	44.51 N	8.34 E
Castellbisbal	266d	41.29 N	1.59 E
Castelldefels	266d	41.17 N	1.59 E
Castelleone	62	45.18 N	9.46 E
Castelletto	266b	45.30 N	8.48 E
Castelletto di Brenzone	64	45.41 N	10.45 E
Castelli, Arg.	252	36.06 S	57.47 W
Castelli, It.	66	42.29 N	13.43 E
Castellina in Chianti	66	43.28 N	11.17 E
Castellina Marittima	66	43.25 N	10.35 E
Castelli Romani ◆[1]	267a	41.46 N	12.42 E
Castelló □[4]	34	40.10 N	0.10 W
Castello, Monte ∧	66	43.03 N	9.49 E
Castello d'Annone	62	44.53 N	8.19 E
Castelló de la Plana	34	39.59 N	0.02 W
Castello di Fiemme	64	46.17 N	11.26 E
Castello Lavazzo	64	46.17 N	12.18 E
Castellote	34	40.48 N	0.19 W
Castello Tesino	64	46.04 N	11.38 E
Castellucchio	64	45.09 N	10.39 E
Castelluccio	68	40.00 N	15.58 E
Castell'Umberto	70	38.05 N	14.48 E
Castelluzzo	70	38.06 N	12.44 E
Castel Madama	66	41.58 N	12.52 E
Castel Maggiore	64	44.34 N	11.22 E
Castelmagno	62	44.24 N	7.13 E
Castelmassa	64	45.01 N	11.18 E
Castelmauro	66	41.50 N	14.43 E
Castelmezzano	68	40.32 N	16.03 E
Castelmoron-sur-Lot	32	44.24 N	0.30 E
Castelnaudary	32	43.19 N	1.57 E
Castelnau-Montratier	32	44.16 N	1.21 E
Castelnovo di Sotto	64	44.49 N	10.34 E
Castelnovo ne'Monti	64	44.26 N	10.24 E
Castelnuovo	64	45.26 N	10.47 E
Castelnuovo Berardenga	66	43.21 N	11.30 E
Castelnuovo dell'Abate	66	43.00 N	11.31 E
Castelnuovo della Daunia	68	41.35 N	15.07 E
Castelnuovo di Garfagnana	64	44.06 N	10.24 E
Castelnuovo di Porto	66	42.07 N	12.30 E
Castelnuovo di Val di Cecina	66	43.12 N	10.59 E
Castelnuovo Don Bosco	62	45.03 N	7.58 E
Castelnuovo Nigra	62	45.26 N	7.41 E
Castelnuovo Rangone	64	44.33 N	10.56 E
Castelnuovo Scrivia	62	44.59 N	8.53 E
Castelo	255	20.36 S	41.12 W
Castelo Branco	34	39.49 N	7.30 W
Castelo do Piauí	250	5.20 S	41.33 W
Castel Pagano	68	41.24 N	14.48 E
Castel Porziano ◆[8]	267a	41.44 N	12.24 E
Castelraimondo	66	43.12 N	13.04 E
Castel Romano ◆[8]	267a	41.44 N	12.27 E
Castel San Gimignano	66	43.24 N	11.00 E
Castel San Giorgio	68	40.47 N	14.42 E
Castel San Giovanni	62	45.04 N	9.26 E
Castel San Lorenzo	68	40.25 N	15.14 E
Castel San Pietro Terme	66	44.24 N	11.35 E
Castel Sant'Elia	66	42.15 N	12.22 E
Castelsaraceno	68	40.10 N	16.00 E
Castelsardo	71	40.55 N	8.43 E
Castelsarrasin	32	44.02 N	1.06 E
Castelsilano	68	39.16 N	16.46 E
Casteltermini	70	37.32 N	13.39 E
Castelvecchio Subequo	66	42.08 N	13.44 E
Castelvetere in Val Fortore	68	41.27 N	14.56 E
Castelvetrano	70	37.41 N	12.47 E
Castelvetro di Modena	64	44.30 N	10.57 E
Castelvetro Piacentino	64	45.05 N	9.59 E
Castel Viscardo	66	42.45 N	12.00 E
Castel Volturno, It.	66	44.13 N	11.37 E
Castel Volturno, It.	68	41.02 N	13.56 E
Castenaso	64	44.30 N	11.28 E
Castenedolo	64	45.28 N	10.18 E
Casterton	166	37.35 S	141.24 E
Castets	32	43.53 N	1.09 W
Castiglioncello	66	43.24 N	10.24 E
Castiglione Chiavarese	62	44.16 N	9.31 E
Castiglione d'Adda	62	45.13 N	9.41 E
Castiglione dei Pepoli	64	44.08 N	11.09 E
Castiglione del Lago	66	43.07 N	12.03 E
Castiglione della Pescaia	66	42.46 N	10.53 E
Castiglione delle Stiviere	64	45.23 N	10.29 E
Castiglione del Pepoli	66	44.08 N	11.09 E
Castiglione di Sicilia	70	37.53 N	15.07 E
Castiglione d'Orcia	66	43.00 N	11.37 E
Castiglione d'Ossola	58	46.03 N	8.13 E
Castiglione Messer Marino	66	41.52 N	14.27 E
Castiglione Olona	62	45.46 N	8.52 E
Castiglion Fibocchi	66	43.32 N	11.46 E
Castiglion Fiorentino	66	43.20 N	11.55 E
Castile	210	42.37 N	78.03 W
Castilho	255	20.52 S	51.29 W
Castilla	248	5.12 S	80.38 W
Castilla, Playa de ⩡[2]	34	37.00 N	6.33 W
Castilla-La Mancha □[4]	34	39.30 N	3.00 W
Castilla la Nueva □[9]	34	40.00 N	3.45 W
Castilla la Vieja □[9]	34	41.30 N	4.00 W
Castilla-León □[4]	34	41.30 N	5.00 W
Castillo	258	33.53 S	57.40 W
Castillo, Cerro ∧	254	43.03 S	71.57 W
Castillo, Pampa del ≚	254	45.58 S	68.24 W
Castillo de San Marcos National Monument ♠	192	29.44 N	81.20 W
Castillo Incaico de Ingapirca ⊥	246	2.34 S	78.50 W
Castillon-la-Bataille	32	44.51 N	0.03 W
Castillos	252	34.12 S	53.50 W
Castillos, Laguna de ⊜	252	34.20 S	53.54 W
Castine	188	44.23 N	68.48 W
Castione della Presolana	64	45.54 N	10.04 E
Castions di Strada	64	45.54 N	13.11 E
Castle Acre	42	52.42 N	0.41 E
Castle Air Force Base ■	226	37.22 N	120.34 W
Castlebar	48	53.52 N	9.17 W
Castlebay	46	56.57 N	7.28 W
Castlebellingham	48	53.54 N	6.23 W
Castleberry	194	31.17 N	87.01 W
Castleblayney	48	54.07 N	6.44 W
Castle Bruce	240d	15.26 N	61.16 W
Castle Cape ≻	180	56.15 N	158.06 W
Castle Cary	42	51.06 N	2.31 W
Castlecliff	172	39.57 S	174.59 E
Castlecomer	48	52.48 N	7.12 W
Castleconnell	48	52.43 N	8.30 W
Castlecrag	274a	33.48 S	151.13 E
Castle Crags State Park ♠	204	41.10 N	122.20 W
Castle Creek	210	42.14 N	75.55 W
Castle Creek ≃, Austl.	169	36.41 S	145.29 E
Castle Creek ≃, Id., U.S.	202	43.06 N	116.16 W
Castle Dale	200	39.23 N	110.27 W
Castledawson	44	54.47 N	6.33 W
Castlederg	48	54.42 N	7.36 W
Castledermot	48	52.55 N	6.50 W
Castle Dome Peak ∧	200	33.05 N	114.08 W
Castle Donington	42	52.51 N	1.19 W
Castle Douglas	44	54.57 N	3.56 W
Castlefinn	48	54.47 N	7.35 W
Castleford	44	53.44 N	1.21 W
Castlegar	182	49.19 N	117.40 W
Castle Harbour ⊂	240a	32.21 N	64.40 W
Castle Hill	274a	33.44 S	151.00 E
Castle Hills, De., U.S.	208	39.41 N	75.33 W
Castle Hills, Tx., U.S.	196	29.32 N	98.31 W
Castleisland	48	52.14 N	9.27 W
Castlemaine, Austl.	169	37.04 S	144.13 E
Castlemaine, Ire.	48	52.09 N	9.43 W
Castlemartyr	48	51.55 N	8.03 W
Castlemore	275b	43.47 N	79.41 W
Castle Mountain ∧, Ab., Can.	182	51.18 N	115.55 W
Castle Mountain ∧, Yk., Can.	180	64.32 N	135.25 W
Castle Mountain ∧, Ca., U.S.	226	35.56 N	120.20 W
Castle Neck ≻[1]	283	42.41 N	70.45 W
Castle Neck ≃	283	42.40 N	70.44 W
Castle Park	228	32.36 N	117.04 W
Castle Peak ∧, Co., U.S.	200	39.01 N	106.52 W
Castle Peak ∧, Id., U.S.	202	44.02 N	114.35 W
Castle Peak ∧, Wa., U.S.	224	48.58 N	120.51 W
Castlepoint	172	40.54 S	176.13 E
Castle Point □[8]	260	51.33 N	0.35 E
Castlepollard	48	53.40 N	7.17 W
Castlerea	48	53.46 N	8.29 W
Castlereagh ≃	166	30.12 S	147.32 E
Castle Rock, Co., U.S.	200	39.22 N	104.51 W
Castle Rock, Pa., U.S.	285	39.58 N	75.26 W
Castle Rock, Wa., U.S.	224	46.16 N	122.54 W
Castle Rock ∧, Or., U.S.	202	44.02 N	118.11 W
Castle Rock ∧, Va., U.S.	192	37.57 N	78.44 W
Castle Rock Butte ∧	198	45.00 N	103.27 W
Castle Rock Lake ⊜[1]	190	43.56 N	89.58 W
Castle Shannon	279b	40.21 N	80.01 W
Castleshaw Moor ◆[3]	262	53.36 N	2.00 W
Castleside	44	54.50 N	1.52 W
Castleton, Eng., U.K.	44	53.21 N	1.46 W
Castleton, Eng., U.K.	44	54.28 N	0.56 W
Castleton, Eng., U.K.	262	53.35 N	2.11 W
Castleton, In., U.S.	218	39.54 N	86.03 W
Castleton, Vt., U.S.	188	43.36 N	73.10 W
Castleton on Hudson	210	42.32 N	73.45 W
Castletown, I. of Man	44	54.04 N	4.40 W
Castletown, Scot., U.K.	46	58.35 N	3.23 W
Castletown Bearhaven (Castletown Bere)	48	51.39 N	9.55 W
Castletown Bere → Castletown Bearhaven	48	51.39 N	9.55 W
Castletown Geoghegan	48	53.26 N	7.38 W
Castletownroche	48	52.10 N	8.28 W
Castletownshend	48	51.32 N	9.11 W
Castlewellan	48	54.16 N	5.57 W
Castlewood, Ky., U.S.	218	38.04 N	84.27 W
Castlewood, S.D., U.S.	198	44.43 N	97.01 W
Castlewood, Va., U.S.	192	36.53 N	82.16 W
Častoje	82	54.11 N	37.47 E
Častooz'ornoje	86	55.34 N	67.53 E
Castor	182	52.13 N	111.53 W
Castor ≃, On., Can.	212	45.18 N	75.10 W
Castor ≃, Mo., U.S.	194	36.51 N	89.44 W
Castorano	66	42.54 N	13.43 E
Castor Creek ≃	194	31.47 N	92.22 W
Castorland	212	43.53 N	75.30 W
Castra Vetera ⊥	263	51.39 N	6.28 E
Castres	32	43.36 N	2.15 E
Castricum	52	52.33 N	4.39 E
Castries, Fr.	62	43.40 N	3.59 E
Castries, St. Luc.	241f	14.01 N	61.00 W
Castries, Port ⊂	241f	14.01 N	61.01 W
Castro, Bra.	252	24.47 S	50.00 W
Castro, Chile	254	42.29 S	73.46 W
Castro, It.	64	45.48 N	10.04 E
Castro, Arroyo de ≃	258	33.37 S	56.10 W
Castro, Punta ≻	254	43.22 S	65.03 W
Castro Barros	252	30.35 S	65.44 W
Castrocaro Terme	66	44.10 N	11.57 E
Castrocielo	66	41.32 N	13.42 E
Castro Daire	34	40.54 N	7.56 W
Castro dei Volsci	66	41.30 N	13.24 E
Castro del Río	34	37.41 N	4.28 W
Castrofilippo	70	37.21 N	13.46 E
Castrojeriz	34	42.17 N	4.08 W
Castro Marim	34	37.13 N	7.26 W
Castronuño	34	41.23 N	5.16 W
Castronuovo di Sant'Andrea	68	40.11 N	16.11 E
Castronuovo di Sicilia	70	37.41 N	13.36 E
Castropignano	66	41.37 N	14.33 E
Castropol	34	43.32 N	7.02 W
Castrop-Rauxel	52	51.34 N	7.18 E
Castroreale	70	38.06 N	15.12 E
Castro-Urdiales	34	43.23 N	3.13 W
Castro Valley	226	37.41 N	122.05 W
Castro Verde	34	37.42 N	8.05 W
Castrovillari	68	39.49 N	16.13 E
Castroville, Ca., U.S.	226	36.45 N	121.45 W
Castroville, Tx., U.S.	196	29.21 N	98.52 W
Castrovirreyna	248	13.16 S	75.19 W
Castuera	34	38.43 N	5.33 W
Çast uul ∧	86	48.40 N	90.45 E
Častyje	80	57.19 N	54.59 E
Casummit Lake	184	51.28 N	92.24 W
Casupá	252	34.07 S	55.39 W
Caswell Sound ⊔	172	45.00 S	167.10 E
Çat	130	39.40 N	41.00 E
Čat ≃	184	51.07 N	91.25 W
Catabola	152	12.09 S	17.16 E
Cataby	162	30.43 S	115.31 E
Catacamas	236	14.48 N	85.54 W
Catacaos	248	5.16 S	80.41 W
Catacocha	246	4.04 S	79.38 W
Cataguarino	256	21.18 S	42.43 W
Cataguases	256	21.24 S	42.41 W
Catahoula Lake ⊜	194	31.30 N	92.06 W
Çatak	128	38.01 N	43.07 E
Çatakköprü	130	38.09 N	41.12 E
Catalaban Island ı	116	11.51 N	125.28 E
Çatalan	130	37.14 N	35.16 E
Catalão	255	18.10 S	47.57 W
Catalão, Ponta do ≻	287a	22.51 S	43.13 W
Çatalca	130	41.09 N	28.27 E
Çatalçam	130	40.00 N	38.51 E
Catalfaro ≃	70	37.22 N	14.43 E
Catalina, Nf., Can.	186	48.31 N	53.05 W
Catalina, Chile	252	25.13 S	69.43 W
Catalina, Punta ≻	254	52.32 S	68.47 W
Catalina → Santa Catalina Island ı	228	33.23 N	118.24 W
Catalonia → Catalunya □[4]	34	41.40 N	1.30 E
Catalunya □[4]	34	41.40 N	1.30 E
Catalzeytin	130	41.57 N	34.13 E
Catamarca □[4]	252	27.00 S	67.00 W
Catamare	286c	10.36 N	67.02 W
Catamayo	246	3.59 S	79.21 W
Catamayo ≃	246	4.18 S	80.09 W
Catanauan	116	13.36 N	122.19 E
Catanduanes □[4]	116	13.47 N	124.16 E
Catanduanes Island ı	116	13.45 N	124.15 E
Catanduva	255	21.08 S	48.58 W
Catane → Catania	70	37.30 N	15.06 E
Catania	70	37.30 N	15.06 E
Catania □[4]	70	37.23 N	14.40 E
Catania, Golfo di ⊂	70	37.24 N	15.09 E
Catania, Piana di ≚	70	37.25 N	14.51 E
Cataño	240m	18.27 N	66.07 W
Catanzaro	68	38.54 N	16.36 E
Catanzaro □[4]	68	38.54 N	16.36 E
Catanzaro Lido	68	38.49 N	16.36 E
Cataonia □[9]	130	38.00 N	35.00 E
Catára ≃	152	13.34 S	12.35 E
Cataract Canyon ∨	200	36.03 N	112.35 W
Cataract Reservoir ⊜[1]	170	34.16 S	150.48 E
Catarama	246	1.35 S	79.28 W
Cataraqui	212	44.16 N	76.32 W
Cataraqui ≃	212	44.13 N	76.28 W
Catarina	250	6.12 S	39.54 W
Catarman, Pil.	116	9.08 N	124.40 E
Catarman, Pil.	116	12.30 N	124.38 E
Catarroja	34	39.24 N	0.24 W
Catasauqua	208	40.39 N	75.29 W
Catatumbo ≃	246	9.22 N	71.45 W
Catawba	218	40.00 N	83.37 W
Catawba ≃	192	34.36 N	80.54 W
Catawba Island	214	41.35 N	82.50 W
Catawissa, Mo., U.S.	219	38.25 N	90.47 W
Catawissa, Pa., U.S.	210	40.57 N	76.27 W
Catawissa Creek ≃	210	40.57 N	76.28 W
Cataxa	154	15.58 S	33.12 E
Cat Ba, Dao ı	110	20.50 N	107.00 E
Catbalogan	116	11.46 N	124.53 E
Catchabutan, Punta ≻	236	15.50 N	86.32 W
Catchacoma Lake ⊜	212	44.45 N	78.20 W
Cateco Cangola	152	8.27 S	15.48 E
Catedral, Cerro ∧[2]	252	34.23 S	54.40 W
Cateel	116	7.48 N	126.27 E
Cateel ≃	116	7.47 N	126.27 E
Cateel Bay ⊂	116	7.54 N	126.25 E
Catemaco	234	18.25 N	95.07 W
Catemaco, Laguna ⊜	234	18.25 N	95.05 W
Catembe	156	26.00 S	32.33 E
Catenanuova	70	37.34 N	14.41 E
Caterham	260	51.17 N	0.04 W
Caterino Rodriguez	232	24.51 N	100.19 W
Catete	152	9.06 S	13.43 E
Catete ◆[8]	287a	22.55 S	43.10 W
Catete ≃	250	6.04 S	54.09 W
Catfish Creek ≃, On., Can.	212	42.39 N	81.01 W
Catfish Creek ≃, N.Y., U.S.	212	43.31 N	76.19 W
Catfish Creek ≃, Tx., U.S.	222	31.47 N	95.56 W
Catford ◆[8]	260	51.27 N	0.01 W
Catharine Creek ≃	210	42.21 N	76.51 W
Cathcart	158	32.18 S	27.09 E
Cathead Mountain ∧	210	43.17 N	74.17 W
Cathedral City	204	33.46 N	116.27 W
Cathedral Gorge State Park ♠	204	37.50 N	114.30 W
Cathedral Mountain ∧	196	30.10 N	103.40 W
Cathedral of the Pines ⋎[1]	207	42.47 N	71.58 W
Cathedral Provincial Park ♠	202	49.05 N	120.10 W
Cathedral Range ⋀	226	37.47 N	119.21 W
Catherines Peak ∧	241q	18.04 N	76.42 W
Catheys Valley	226	37.25 N	120.06 W
Cathlamet	224	46.12 N	123.22 W
Catholic University ⋎[2]	284c	38.56 N	77.00 W
Catia ◆[8]	286c	10.31 N	66.57 W
Catia La Mar	286c	10.36 N	67.02 W
Ca' Tiepolo	66	44.56 N	12.22 E
Catignano	66	42.21 N	13.57 E
Catió	150	11.13 N	15.10 W
Catirina, Punta ≻	71	40.29 N	9.32 E
Cat Island ı, Ba.	238	24.27 N	75.30 W
Cat Island ı, Ma., U.S.	283	42.31 N	70.49 W
Cat Island ı, Ms., U.S.	194	30.13 N	89.06 W
Čatkal ≃	85	41.38 N	70.01 E
Čatkal'skij chrebet ⋀	85	41.40 N	71.05 E
Cat Lake ⊜	184	51.40 N	91.50 W
Catlettsburg	188	38.24 N	82.36 W
Catlin	194	40.03 N	87.42 W
Catlins ≃	172	46.29 S	169.43 E
Catlodge	46	57.00 N	4.15 W
Catnip Mountain ∧	204	41.52 N	119.23 W
Cato	210	43.10 N	76.34 W
Catoche, Cabo ≻	232	21.35 N	87.05 W
Catoctin Creek ≃	208	39.18 N	77.33 W
Catoctin Mountain ∧	208	39.26 N	77.31 W
Cato Island ı	166	23.15 S	155.32 E
Catolé do Rocha	250	6.21 S	37.45 W
Católica, Universidad ⋎[2], Chile	286e	33.27 S	70.39 W
Católica, Universidad ⋎[2], Perú	286d	12.04 S	77.05 W
Caton	44	54.04 N	2.43 W
Catonsville	208	39.16 N	76.43 W
Catonsville Manor	284b	39.18 N	76.44 W
Catoosa	196	36.11 N	95.44 W
Catorce	234	23.42 N	100.54 W
Catorce, Sierra de ⋀	234	23.36 N	100.52 W
Catota	152	13.52 S	17.15 E
Catria, Monte ∧	66	43.28 N	12.42 E
Catriló	252	36.26 S	63.24 W
Catrimani ≃	246	0.28 N	61.44 W
Catrine	46	55.30 N	4.20 W
Cats, Mont des ∧[2]	50	50.47 N	2.40 E
Catshill	42	52.22 N	2.03 W
Catskill	210	42.13 N	73.51 W
Catskill Aqueduct ≃	276	41.11 N	73.48 W
Catskill Creek ≃	210	42.12 N	73.51 W
Catskill Game Farm ♠	210	42.15 N	74.01 W
Catskill Mountains ⋀	210	42.10 N	74.30 W
Catskill Park ♠	210	42.00 N	74.30 W
Cat Spring	222	29.51 N	96.20 W
Catt, Mount ∧	182	54.21 N	128.47 W
Cattai Creek ≃	274a	33.40 S	150.56 E
Cattaraugus	210	42.19 N	78.52 W
Cattaraugus □[6]	214	42.15 N	78.45 W
Cattaraugus Creek ≃	214	42.35 N	79.10 W
Cattaraugus Creek, South Branch ≃	214	42.26 N	78.53 W
Cattaraugus Indian Reservation ◆[4]	210	42.33 N	78.56 W
Cattenom	56	49.25 N	6.15 E
Catterick	44	54.22 N	1.38 W
Catterick Garrison	44	54.22 N	1.43 W
Cattle Canyon ∨	280	34.14 N	117.46 W
Cattolica	66	43.58 N	12.44 E
Cattolica del Sacro Cuore, Università ⋎[2]	266b	45.27 N	9.11 E
Cattolica Eraclea	70	37.26 N	13.24 E
Catton	44	54.55 N	2.15 W
Catu	255	12.21 S	38.23 W
Catuala	152	16.29 S	19.03 E
Catuane	156	26.48 S	32.18 E
Catubig	116	12.24 N	125.03 E
Catubig ≃	116	12.34 N	125.01 E
Catuçaba	256	23.15 S	45.12 W
Catumbela	152	12.25 S	13.34 E
Catumbela ≃	152	12.27 S	13.29 E
Catur	154	13.45 S	35.30 E
Catus	32	44.34 N	1.20 E
Çatwick, Îles ıı	110	10.00 N	109.00 E
Çatyrk'ol', ozero ⊜	85	40.38 N	75.17 E
Čatyrtaš	85	40.55 N	76.26 E
Cau ≃	110	21.07 N	106.18 E
Cau, Rach ≃	269c	10.51 N	106.49 E
Cauaburi ≃	246	0.17 S	65.56 W
Cauayan, Pil.	116	16.56 N	121.46 E
Cauayan, Pil.	116	9.58 N	122.37 E
Caubvick, Mount (Mont d'Iberville) ∧	176	58.53 N	63.43 W
Cauca □[5]	246	2.30 N	76.50 W
Cauca ≃	246	8.54 N	74.28 W
Caucaia	250	3.42 S	38.39 W
Caucaia do Alto	256	23.41 S	47.02 W
Caucase, Monts du → Bol'šoj Kavkaz ⋀	84	42.30 N	45.00 E
Caucasia	246	8.00 N	75.12 W
Caucaso → Bol'šoj Kavkaz ⋀	84	42.30 N	45.00 E
Caucasus → Bol'šoj Kavkaz ⋀	84	42.30 N	45.00 E
Caucete	252	31.39 S	68.17 W
Cauchari, Salar de ≚	252	23.50 S	66.50 W
Cauchon Lake ⊜	184	55.25 N	96.30 W
Caudebec-en-Caux	50	49.32 N	0.44 E
Caudebec-lés-Elbeuf	50	49.17 N	1.02 E
Caudry	50	50.08 N	3.25 E
Caughdenoy	210	43.16 N	76.12 W
Caughnawaga	275a	45.25 N	73.41 W
Caughnawaga Indian Reserve ◆[4]	206	45.23 N	73.41 W
Cauitan, Mount ∧	116	17.16 N	121.00 E
Cauit Point ≻, Pil.	116	12.16 N	122.38 E
Cauit Point ≻, Pil.	116	9.18 N	126.12 E
Cauldcleuch Head ∧	44	55.18 N	2.51 W
Caulfield	169	37.53 S	145.03 E
Caulfield Racecourse ♠	274b	37.53 S	145.02 E
Caulkerbush	44	54.54 N	3.40 W
Caulonia	68	38.23 N	16.25 E
Caumont-sur-Durance	62	43.54 N	4.57 E
Caumsett State Park ♠	276	40.55 N	73.28 W
Çaúngula	152	8.25 S	18.40 E
Čaunskaja guba ⊂	74	69.20 N	170.00 E
Cauquenes	252	35.58 S	72.21 W
Caura ≃	246	7.38 N	64.53 W
Caurés ≃	246	1.21 S	62.20 W
Caurimare ≃	286c	10.28 N	66.48 W
Çausapscal	186	48.22 N	67.14 W
Čausovo	82	54.49 N	36.55 E
Çaussade	32	44.10 N	1.32 E
Čausy	76	53.48 N	30.58 E
Cautário ≃	248	12.13 S	64.34 W
Caution, Cape ≻	182	51.10 N	127.47 W
Çauto ≃	240p	20.33 N	77.14 W
Čauvaj	85	40.08 N	72.13 E
Caux, Pays de ◆[1]	50	49.40 N	0.40 E
Cava	256	22.41 S	43.26 W
Cava de' Tirreni	68	40.42 N	14.42 E
Cávado ≃	34	41.32 N	8.48 W
Cavaglià	62	45.24 N	8.05 E
Cavaillon	62	43.50 N	5.02 E
Cavalaire-sur-Mer	62	43.10 N	6.32 E
Cavalcante	255	13.48 S	47.30 W
Cavalese	64	46.17 N	11.27 E
Cavalheiro	255	17.15 S	48.02 W
Cavalier	198	48.47 N	97.37 W
Cavalière	62	43.09 N	6.26 E
Cavalla (Cavally) ≃	150	4.22 N	7.32 W
Cavalleria, Cap de ≻	34	40.05 N	4.05 E
Cavallermaggiore	62	44.43 N	7.41 E
Cavalli Islands ıı	172	35.02 S	173.58 E
Cavallino, Litorale di ⩡[2]	64	45.27 N	12.30 E
Cavallo, Île ı	71	41.21 N	9.16 E
Cavallo, Monte ∧	64	46.08 N	12.30 E
Cavally (Cavalla) ≃	150	4.22 N	7.32 W
Cavalos, Ribeirão dos ≃	256	21.29 S	44.13 W
Cava Manara	62	45.08 N	9.07 E
Cavan	48	54.00 N	7.21 W
Cavan □[6]	48	53.55 N	7.15 W
Çavanaugh, Lake ⊜	224	48.23 N	122.00 W
Čavan'ga	24	66.06 N	37.47 E
Cavarzere	64	45.08 N	12.05 E
Cavaso del Tomba	64	45.51 N	11.52 E
Çavdır	130	37.09 N	29.42 E
Cave, It.	66	41.49 N	12.56 E
Cave, N.Z.	172	44.19 S	170.57 E
Cave City, Ar., U.S.	194	35.56 N	91.32 W
Cave City, Ky., U.S.	194	37.08 N	85.57 W
Cave Creek ≃	200	33.34 N	112.07 W
Cave del Predil	64	46.26 N	13.34 E
Cavedine	64	45.59 N	10.59 E
Cave In Rock	194	37.29 N	88.10 W
Caveiras ≃	252	27.35 S	50.56 W
Cavelo	152	17.33 S	19.21 E
Cavendish	166	37.31 S	142.02 E
Cavernago	62	45.38 N	9.46 E
Cavertitz	54	51.23 N	13.08 E
Cave Run Lake ⊜[1]	188	38.03 N	83.30 W
Cave Spring	192	34.14 N	85.20 W
Cavettsville	279b	40.22 N	79.46 W
Cavezzo	64	44.50 N	11.02 E
Cavi	62	44.17 N	9.22 E
Caviana de Fora, Ilha ı	250	0.10 N	50.10 W
Cavili Island ı	116	9.17 N	120.50 E
Cavinzas, Isla ı	286d	12.07 S	77.13 W
Cavite	116	14.29 N	120.55 E
Çavite □[4]	116	14.15 N	120.50 E
Čavka	84	41.44 N	41.45 E
Čavlisaj	85	41.08 N	69.44 E
Cavo, Monte ∧	267a	41.45 N	12.42 E
Cavoli, Isola dei ı	71	39.05 N	9.33 E
Cavonne ≃	68	40.17 N	16.47 E
Cavour	62	44.47 N	7.22 E
Cavour, Canale ≅	62	45.11 N	7.54 E
Cavriago	64	44.42 N	10.31 E
Cavriana	64	45.21 N	10.36 E
Cavtat	38	42.35 N	18.13 E
Çavuş	130	37.36 N	31.56 E
Çavuşbaşı ≃	267b	40.58 N	28.51 E
Çavuşçu Gölü ⊜	130	38.25 N	31.53 E

Symbol	English	Deutsch	Español	Français	Português
≃	River	Fluß	Río	Rivière	Rio
≅	Canal	Kanal	Canal	Canal	Canal
∟	Waterfall, Rapids	Wasserfall, Stromschnellen	Cascada, Rápidos	Chute d'eau, Rapides	Cascata, Rápidos
⊔	Strait	Meeresstraße	Estrecho	Détroit	Estreito
⊂	Bay, Gulf	Bucht, Golf	Bahía, Golfo	Baie, Golfe	Baía, Golfo
⊜	Lake, Lakes	See, Seen	Lago, Lagos	Lac, Lacs	Lago, Lagos
⊞	Swamp	Sumpf	Pantano	Marais	Pântano
⊓	Ice Features, Glacier	Eis- und Gletscherformen	Accidentes Glaciales	Formes glaciaires	Acidentes glaciares
⊤	Other Hydrographic Features	Andere Hydrographische Objekte	Otros Elementos Hidrográficos	Autres données hydrographiques	Outros acidentes hidrográficos
✣	Submarine Features	Untermeerische Objekte	Accidentes Submarinos	Formes de relief sous-marin	Acidentes submarinos
□	Political Unit	Politische Einheit	Unidad Politica	Entité politique	Unidade política
⋎	Cultural Institution	Kulturelle Institution	Institución Cultural	Institution culturelle	Instituição cultural
⊥	Historical Site	Historische Stätte	Sitio Histórico	Site historique	Sitio histórico
♠	Recreational Site	Erholungs- und Ferienort	Sitio de Recreo	Centre de loisirs	Area de Lazer
⊠	Airport	Flughafen	Aeropuerto	Aéroport	Aeroporto
■	Military Installation	Militäranlage	Instalación Militar	Installation militaire	Instalação militar
◆	Miscellaneous	Verschiedenes	Misceláneo	Divers	Diversos

ENGLISH / DEUTSCH

Name	Page	Lat.°′	Long.°′
Cawatose, Lac ⊜	190	47.20 N	77.07 W
Cawayan	116	11.56 N	123.46 E
Cawdor	46	57.31 N	3.56 W
Cawker City	198	39.30 N	98.26 W
Cawnpore → Kānpur	124	26.28 N	80.21 E
Cawood, Eng., U.K.	44	53.50 N	1.07 W
Cawood, Ky., U.S.	192	36.47 N	83.13 W
Cawston, B.C., Can.	182	49.11 N	119.45 W
Cawston, Eng., U.K.	42	52.46 N	1.10 E
Cawthon	222	30.25 N	96.14 W
Caxambu	256	21.59 S	44.56 W
Caxias, Bra.	250	4.50 S	43.21 W
Caxias, Port.	266c	38.42 N	9.16 W
Caxias do Sul	252	29.10 S	51.11 W
Caxinas, Punta ›	236	16.01 N	86.02 W
Caxito	152	8.33 S	13.36 E
Caxiuana, Baía de c	250	1.45 S	51.20 W
Caxopa	152	11.52 S	20.52 E
Çay	130	38.35 N	31.02 E
Çayacal, Punta ›	234	17.56 N	102.11 W
Çayağzı ◆[8]	267b	41.13 N	29.12 E
Çayağzı ≃	267b	41.14 N	29.12 E
Cayambe	246	0.03 N	78.08 W
Cayambe ∧[1]	246	0.00	77.59 W
Cayapoñga	116	5.48 N	125.33 E
Çaybaşı	130	41.02 N	37.06 E
Cayce	192	33.57 N	81.04 W
Çaycuma	130	41.25 N	32.05 E
Caycuse	224	48.53 N	124.22 W
Caycuse ≃	224	48.48 N	124.41 W
Cay Duong, Vinh c	110	10.10 N	104.45 E
Cayenne	250	4.56 N	52.20 W
Cayenne □[8]	250	4.00 N	52.30 W
Cayes → Les Cayes	238	18.12 N	73.45 W
Cayeux-sur-Mer	50	50.11 N	1.29 E
Cayey	240m	18.07 N	66.10 W
Cayey, Sierra de ⋏	240m	18.07 N	66.02 W
Çayıralan	130	39.18 N	35.40 E
Çayırbaşı	130	40.53 N	42.36 E
Çayırhan	130	40.06 N	31.37 E
Çayırlı	130	39.48 N	40.01 E
Çaylarbası	130	37.41 N	39.00 E
Caylus	32	44.14 N	1.46 E
Cayman Brac I	238	19.43 N	79.49 W
Cayman Islands □[2], N.A.	230	19.30 N	80.40 W
Cayman Islands □[2], N.A.	238	19.30 N	80.40 W
Cayman Trench ✦[1]	16	19.00 N	80.00 W
Cayna	248	10.11 S	76.20 W
Caynabo	144	8.57 N	46.26 E
Cayo Agua, Isla I	236	9.09 N	82.02 W
Çayözü	130	39.36 N	38.11 E
Çay Point ›	240b	24.59 N	77.25 W
Çayra	130	40.41 N	39.06 E
Cayres	62	44.55 N	3.48 E
Cay Sal Bank ✦[2]	238	23.45 N	80.00 W
Çaytepe	130	38.48 N	40.41 E
Cayucos	226	35.27 N	120.54 W
Cayuga, In., U.S.	194	39.56 N	87.27 W
Cayuga, N.Y., U.S.	210	42.55 N	76.44 W
Cayuga, N.D., U.S.	198	46.04 N	97.23 W
Cayuga, Tx., U.S.	222	31.57 N	95.57 W
Cayuga □[6]	210	42.56 N	76.34 W
Cayuga and Seneca Canal ≍	210	42.56 N	76.44 W
Cayuga Creek ≃, N.Y., U.S.	210	42.52 N	78.47 W
Cayuga Creek ≃, N.Y., U.S.	284a	43.04 N	78.57 W
Cayuga Heights	210	42.27 N	76.29 W
Cayuga Lake ⊜	210	42.45 N	76.45 W
Cayuta	210	42.17 N	76.42 W
Cayuta Creek ≃	210	41.59 N	76.30 W
Cazage	152	11.02 S	20.45 E
Cazalla de la Sierra	34	37.56 N	5.45 W
Căzănești	38	44.37 N	27.01 E
Cazaux et de Sanguinet, Lac de c	32	44.30 N	1.10 W
Cazenovia	210	42.55 N	75.51 W
Cazenovia Creek ≃	210	42.52 N	78.50 W
Cazenovia Creek, East Branch ≃	210	42.46 N	78.38 W
Cazenovia Creek, West Branch ≃	210	42.46 N	78.39 W
Cazenovia Lake ⊜	210	42.57 N	75.53 W
Cazenovia Park ♦	284a	42.51 N	78.48 W
Cazères	32	43.13 N	1.05 E
Cazhai	269b	31.12 N	121.34 E
Cazin	36	44.58 N	15.57 E
Çazis	58	46.43 N	9.25 E
Čazma	36	45.45 N	16.37 E
Cazombo	152	11.54 S	22.52 E
Cazones ≃	234	20.44 N	97.12 W
Cazones, Golfo de c	240p	21.55 N	81.20 W
Cazorla, Esp.	34	37.55 N	3.00 W
Cazorla, Ven.	246	8.01 N	67.00 W
Cazula	154	15.25 S	33.40 E
Ccapi	248	13.52 S	72.05 W
Cchaltubo	84	42.20 N	42.35 E
Cchenisckali ≃	84	42.07 N	42.18 E
Cchinvali	84	42.13 N	43.56 E
Cchorocku	84	42.32 N	42.07 E
Cchunkuri	84	42.23 N	42.34 E
Cea ≃	34	42.00 N	5.36 W
Ceanannus Mór	48	53.44 N	6.53 W
Ceará □[3]	250	5.00 S	40.00 W
Ceará → Fortaleza	250	3.43 S	38.30 W
Ceará-Mirim	250	5.38 S	35.26 W
Ceará-Mirim ≃	250	5.40 S	35.13 W
Ceatharlach → Carlow	48	52.50 N	6.55 W
Cebaco, Isla De I	246	7.32 N	81.09 W
Çeballos	232	26.32 N	104.09 W
Čebarkul'	86	54.58 N	60.25 E
Çebeci ◆[8]	267b	41.07 N	28.52 E
Čeboksarskoje vodochranilišče ⊜[1]	24	56.10 N	46.00 E
Čeboksary	80	56.09 N	47.15 E
Cebolla Creek ≃	200	38.29 N	107.13 W
Cebollar	252	29.06 S	66.33 W
Cebollas	234	23.23 N	104.50 W
Cebollatí	252	33.16 S	53.47 W
Cebollatí ≃	252	33.09 S	53.38 W
Cebollita Peak ∧	200	34.43 N	107.51 W
Céboruco, Volcán ∧[1]	234	21.09 N	104.30 W
Čebotovka, Ross.	83	48.42 N	39.51 E
Čebotovka, Ross.	83	48.41 N	40.00 E
Cebreros	34	40.27 N	4.28 W
Čebrikovo	78	47.09 N	30.06 E
Čebsara	76	59.12 N	38.50 E
Cebu	116	10.18 N	123.54 E
Cebu □[4]	116	10.20 N	123.45 E
Cebu I	116	10.20 N	123.45 E
Čeburgol'	78	45.34 N	38.07 E
Cebu Strait ⋓	116	9.45 N	123.40 E
Ceccano	66	41.34 N	13.20 E
Cecchignola ◆[8]	267a	41.49 N	12.29 E
Çeceda	196	26.04 N	103.25 W
Čečel'nik	78	48.14 N	29.21 E
Čečen', ostrov I	84	43.58 N	47.45 E
Čečeno-Ingušskaja Avtonomnaja Sovetskaja Socialističeskaja Respublika □[3]	84	43.15 N	45.40 E
Cecer Chaan → Öndörchaan	88	47.19 N	110.39 E
Cecerleg, Mong.	88	48.52 N	101.14 E
Cecerleg, Mong.	88	47.30 N	101.27 E
Çecerleg, Mong.	88	49.30 N	97.36 E
Čečersk	76	52.55 N	30.55 E
Čečeviči	76	53.31 N	29.51 E
Çecheng	105	39.06 N	116.48 E
Čechov, Ross.	82	55.09 N	37.27 E
Čechov, Ross.	89	47.28 N	141.59 E
Čechova, gora ∧	89	47.03 N	142.50 E
Čechtice	30	49.37 N	15.03 E
Čechy □[9]	30	49.50 N	14.00 E
Cecil, Ga., U.S.	192	31.02 N	83.23 W
Cecil, Oh., U.S.	216	41.13 N	84.35 W
Cecil, Pa., U.S.	214	40.19 N	80.10 W
Cecil □[6]	208	39.36 N	75.50 W
Cecil Field Naval Air Station ■	192	30.12 N	81.52 W
Cecilia	194	37.39 N	85.57 W
Cecilia, Mount ∧[2]	162	20.45 S	120.55 E
Cecil Park	274a	33.52 S	150.51 E
Cecil Plains	166	27.32 S	151.12 E
Cecil Rhodes, Mount ∧	162	25.26 S	121.26 E
Cecilton	208	39.24 N	75.52 W
Cecina	66	43.19 N	10.31 E
Cecina ≃	66	43.18 N	10.29 E
Çecita, Lago di ⊜	68	39.24 N	16.30 E
Čečuj ≃	88	58.12 N	109.18 E
Čečujsk	88	58.05 N	108.42 E
Cedar ≃, U.S.	190	41.17 N	91.21 W
Cedar ≃, Mi., U.S.	190	43.53 N	84.29 W
Cedar ≃, Mi., U.S.	190	45.25 N	87.21 W
Cedar ≃, Ne., U.S.	198	41.22 N	97.57 W
Cedar ≃, N.Y., U.S.	188	43.51 N	74.11 W
Cedar ≃, Wa., U.S.	224	47.30 N	122.12 W
Cedar, Middle Branch ≃	216	42.38 N	84.05 W
Cedar, West Branch ≃	216	42.41 N	84.09 W
Cedar, West Fork ≃	190	42.37 N	92.29 W
Cedar Bayou ≃	222	29.41 N	94.56 W
Cedar Beach	284b	39.17 N	76.25 W
Cedar Bluff Reservoir ⊜[1]	198	38.47 N	99.47 W
Cedar Bluffs	198	41.23 N	96.36 W
Cedar Breaks National Monument ♦	200	37.29 N	112.53 W
Cedar Brook	208	39.42 N	74.54 W
Cedar Brook ≃, N.J., U.S.	276	40.19 N	74.33 W
Cedar Brook ≃, N.J., U.S.	276	40.23 N	74.23 W
Cedar Brook ≃, N.J., U.S.	285	39.40 N	74.43 W
Cedar Brook Park ♦	275b	43.45 N	79.14 W
Cedarburg	190	43.17 N	87.59 W
Cedar City, Mo., U.S.	219	38.35 N	92.10 W
Cedar City, Ut,. U.S.	200	37.40 N	113.03 W
Cedar Creek	222	30.05 N	97.30 W
Cedar Creek ≃, Al., U.S.	194	32.13 N	87.06 W
Cedar Creek ≃, Az., U.S.	200	33.48 N	110.18 W
Cedar Creek ≃, Ct., U.S.	276	41.09 N	73.13 W
Cedar Creek ≃, De., U.S.	208	38.55 N	75.20 W
Cedar Creek ≃, Ga., U.S.	194	34.08 N	85.19 W
Cedar Creek ≃, Id., U.S.	202	42.24 N	114.49 W
Cedar Creek ≃, In., U.S.	216	41.12 N	85.02 W
Cedar Creek ≃, Ia., U.S.	190	40.58 N	91.40 W
Cedar Creek ≃, Ia., U.S.	198	42.24 N	94.59 W
Cedar Creek ≃, Ky., U.S.	218	38.25 N	84.53 W
Cedar Creek ≃, Mo., U.S.	219	38.38 N	92.13 W
Cedar Creek ≃, N.D., U.S.	198	46.07 N	101.18 W
Cedar Creek ≃, Oh., U.S.	214	41.38 N	83.17 W
Cedar Creek ≃, Pa., U.S.	279b	40.10 N	79.47 W
Cedar Creek ≃, Tx., U.S.	196	32.53 N	98.37 W
Cedar Creek ≃, Tx., U.S.	222	30.51 N	96.12 W
Cedar Creek ≃, Tx., U.S.	222	32.04 N	96.05 W
Cedar Creek ≃, Tx., U.S.	222	30.02 N	97.17 W
Cedar Creek ≃, Wa., U.S.	224	45.56 N	122.37 W
Cedar Creek Reservoir ⊜[1]	222	32.20 N	96.10 W
Cedar Crest Manor	285	39.41 N	75.28 W
Cedaredge	200	38.54 N	107.55 W
Cedar Falls	190	42.31 N	92.26 W
Cedar Grove, On., Can.	275b	43.52 N	79.12 W
Cedar Grove, In., U.S.	218	39.21 N	84.56 W
Cedar Grove, N.J., U.S.	276	40.51 N	74.13 W
Cedar Grove, W.V., U.S.	188	38.13 N	81.25 W
Cedar Grove, Wi., U.S.	190	43.34 N	87.49 W
Cedar Grove Reservoir ⊜[1]	276	40.52 N	74.13 W
Cedar Heights, Md., U.S.	284c	38.54 N	76.54 W
Cedar Heights, Pa., U.S.	285	40.05 N	75.17 W
Cedar Hill, Mo., U.S.	219	38.21 N	90.39 W
Cedar Hill, N.Y., U.S.	210	42.33 N	73.47 W
Cedar Hill, Tn., U.S.	194	36.33 N	86.59 W
Cedar Hill, Tx., U.S.	222	32.35 N	96.57 W
Cedar Hills	224	45.30 N	122.47 W
Cedar Hollow	285	40.04 N	75.31 W
Cedarhurst, Md., U.S.	208	39.07 N	76.41 W
Cedarhurst, N.Y., U.S.	276	40.37 N	73.43 W
Cedar Island I, Md., U.S.	208	37.56 N	75.52 W
Cedar Island I, N.Y., U.S.	276	40.38 N	73.21 W
Cedar Island I, Va., U.S.	208	37.39 N	75.36 W
Cedar Island Lake ⊜	281	42.38 N	83.28 W
Cedar Key	192	29.08 N	83.02 W
Cedar Knolls	276	40.49 N	74.26 W
Cedar Lake, In., U.S.	216	41.21 N	87.26 W
Cedar Lake, Tx., U.S.	222	28.54 N	95.35 W
Cedar Lake ⊜, On., Can.	190	46.02 N	78.30 W
Cedar Lake ⊜, In., U.S.	216	41.22 N	87.26 W
Cedar Lake ⊜, N.J., U.S.	276	40.55 N	74.28 W
Cedar Lake ⊜, Tx., U.S.	196	32.49 N	102.17 W
Cedar Lake ⊜[1]	184	53.15 N	100.10 W
Cedar Lake Creek ≃	222	28.50 N	95.35 W
Cedar Lane	222	28.54 N	95.38 W
Cedar Mill	224	45.32 N	122.51 W
Cedarmont	158	26.50 S	29.01 E
Cedar Mountain ∧	204	41.36 N	120.16 W
Cedar Point	216	41.16 N	89.08 W
Cedar Point ›, Ct., U.S.	276	41.06 N	73.22 W
Cedar Point ›, Oh., U.S.	214	41.42 N	83.20 W
Cedar Point ›, Oh., U.S.	214	41.30 N	82.41 W
Cedar Pond ⊜	276	41.07 N	74.06 W
Cedar Rapids, Ia., U.S.	190	41.59 N	91.40 W
Cedar Rapids, Ne., U.S.	198	41.34 N	98.09 W
Cedar Ridge	226	39.12 N	121.01 W
Cedar Run ≃	208	38.41 N	77.29 W
Cedars	285	40.13 N	75.22 W
Cedars of Lebanon → Arz Lubnān ◆[3]	130	34.14 N	36.03 E
Cedar Springs, On., Can.	214	42.17 N	82.02 W
Cedar Springs, Mi., U.S.	190	43.13 N	85.33 W
Cedar Swamp ≡, Ma., U.S.	283	42.33 N	71.05 W
Cedar Swamp ≡, N.J., U.S.	285	39.48 N	75.20 W
Cedartown	192	34.03 N	85.15 W
Cedarvale, B.C., Can.	182	55.01 N	128.20 W
Cedar Vale, Ks., U.S.	198	37.06 N	96.30 W
Cedarville, S. Afr.	158	30.23 S	29.03 E
Cedarville, Ca., U.S.	204	41.31 N	120.10 W
Cedarville, In., U.S.	216	41.12 N	85.01 W
Cedarville, Ma., U.S.	207	41.48 N	70.33 W
Cedarville, Mi., U.S.	190	46.00 N	84.22 W
Cedarville, N.J., U.S.	208	39.19 N	75.12 W
Cedarville, N.Y., U.S.	210	42.56 N	75.07 W
Cedarville, Oh., U.S.	218	39.44 N	83.48 W
Cedarville, Pa., U.S.	285	40.14 N	75.40 W
Cedarville Reservoir ⊜[1]	216	41.12 N	85.01 W
Cedar Wash V	200	35.53 N	111.25 W
Cedarwood Park	208	40.03 N	74.08 W
Cedegolo	64	46.05 N	10.21 E
Çedeira	34	43.39 N	8.03 W
Čeder	88	51.25 N	94.45 E
Cedillo, Embalse de ⊜[1]	34	39.40 N	7.25 W
Cedral	234	23.48 N	100.44 W
Cedrino ≃	71	40.23 N	9.44 E
Cedro	250	6.36 S	39.03 W
Cedro, Cerro ∧	234	18.35 N	99.42 W
Cedros, Hond.	236	14.35 N	87.08 W
Cedros, Méx.	232	24.41 N	101.47 W
Cedros, Isla I	232	28.12 N	115.15 W
Ceduna	162	32.07 S	133.40 E
Cedynia	30	52.50 N	14.14 E
Ceel	102	45.36 N	95.51 E
Ceelaayo	144	11.15 N	48.54 E
Ceel Afweyne	144	9.55 N	47.15 E
Ceel Berdaale	144	3.14 N	43.11 E
Ceel Berde	144	4.50 N	43.39 E
Ceel Buur	144	4.40 N	46.37 E
Ceel Dhaab	144	8.56 N	46.30 E
Ceel Dheere, Som.	144	3.51 N	47.12 E
Ceeldheere, Som.	144	5.22 N	46.11 E
Ceel Doofaar	144	10.38 N	49.02 E
Ceel Waaq	144	2.44 N	41.01 E
Ceel Xamurre	144	7.13 N	48.54 E
Ceemadle	144	5.14 N	46.56 E
Ceepeecee	182	49.52 N	126.43 W
Ceerigaabo	144	10.37 N	47.22 E
Cefalà Diana	70	37.54 N	13.28 E
Cefalonia → Kefallinía I	38	38.15 N	20.35 E
Cefalù	70	38.02 N	14.01 E
Cefni ≃	44	53.12 N	4.23 W
Cefn-mawr	42	52.58 N	3.04 W
Ceg	144	8.58 N	45.20 E
Çega ≃	34	41.33 N	4.46 W
Čeganly	80	53.54 N	53.34 E
Čegdomyn	89	51.07 N	133.05 E
Čegem ≃	84	43.38 N	43.48 E
Čegem Pervyj	84	43.34 N	43.35 E
Čegitun'	180	66.34 N	171.06 W
Cegléd	30	47.10 N	19.48 E
Ceglie Messapico	68	40.39 N	17.31 E
Cehegín	34	38.06 N	1.48 W
Ceheng	102	25.10 N	105.48 E
Cehnice	60	49.12 N	14.02 E
Cehu-Silvaniei	38	47.25 N	23.11 E
Ceiba	240m	18.16 N	65.39 W
Ceibo ≃	258	33.57 S	58.27 W
Ceilán → Sri Lanka □[1]	122	7.00 N	81.00 E
Čeil'dag	84	40.17 N	49.18 E
Ceiriog ≃	42	52.57 N	3.02 W
Çeirw ≃	42	52.59 N	3.27 W
Čejč	61	48.57 N	16.57 E
Čekalin	82	54.06 N	36.15 E
Čekan	80	54.51 N	53.34 E
Čekanovskij	88	56.13 N	101.25 E
Çekerek	130	40.04 N	35.31 E
Çekerek ≃	130	40.34 N	35.46 E
Čekmaguš	86	55.08 N	54.40 E
Çekme ◆[8]	267b	41.03 N	29.10 E
Čekšino	76	59.39 N	40.33 E
Čekujevo	24	63.34 N	38.56 E
Čekunda	89	50.48 N	132.10 E
Čel'abinsk	86	55.10 N	61.24 E
Čelákovice	54	50.10 N	14.46 E
Celâlli	130	39.42 N	37.26 E
Celano	66	42.05 N	13.33 E
Celanova	34	42.09 N	7.58 W
Çelaya	234	20.31 N	100.49 W
Čelbas ≃	78	46.06 N	38.59 E
Čelbasskaja	78	45.59 N	39.22 E
Celbridge	48	53.20 N	6.33 W
Celebes Basin ✦[1]	14	4.00 N	122.00 E
Celebes Sea ▾[2]	112	3.00 N	122.00 E
Celebes → Sulawesi I	112	2.00 S	121.00 E
Čeleken	128	39.26 N	53.07 E
Celendín	248	6.52 S	78.09 W
Celenza sul Trigno	66	41.52 N	14.35 E
Celenza Valfortore	68	41.34 N	14.58 E
Celerina	58	46.31 N	9.51 E
Celeryville	214	41.02 N	82.45 W
Celeste	196	33.18 N	96.12 W
Celestún	232	20.52 N	90.24 W
Celica	246	4.07 S	79.59 W
Celico	68	39.19 N	16.20 E
Çelikhan	130	38.02 N	38.15 E
Čelina, Ross.	80	46.32 N	41.02 E
Celina, Oh., U.S.	216	40.32 N	84.34 W
Celina, Tn., U.S.	194	36.33 N	85.30 W
Celina, Tx., U.S.	196	33.19 N	96.47 W
Celinnoje, Ross.	86	53.04 N	85.40 E
Celinnoje, Ross.	86	54.31 N	63.39 E
Celinnyj	80	46.40 N	44.32 E
Celinograd	86	51.10 N	71.30 E
Çelje	36	46.14 N	15.16 E
Čelkar	86	47.50 N	59.36 E
Cellar Head ›	46	58.26 N	6.10 W
Celldömölk	30	47.16 N	17.09 E
Celle	52	52.37 N	10.05 E
Celle, Ruisseau la ≃	261	48.35 N	2.01 E
Celle Ligure	62	44.20 N	8.33 E
Celles	56	50.14 N	5.01 E
Celles-sur-Plaine	58	48.28 N	6.57 E
Cellettes	50	47.32 N	1.23 E
Cellina ≃	64	46.02 N	12.47 E
Cellino Attanasio	66	42.36 N	13.52 E
Çellino San Marco	68	40.28 N	17.58 E
Čelmozero	24	64.18 N	31.48 E
Čelno-Veršiny	80	54.26 N	51.06 E
Čelobitjevo	265b	55.55 N	37.40 E
Celone ≃	68	41.36 N	15.41 E
Celorico da Beira	34	40.38 N	7.23 W
Celoron	214	42.06 N	79.17 W
Celtic Sea ▾[2]	28	51.00 N	6.30 W
Celtic Shelf ✦[4]	10	49.15 N	7.00 W
Çeltikçi, Tür.	130	40.20 N	32.28 E
Çeltikçi, Tür.	130	37.32 N	30.29 E
Čel'uš	86	51.32 N	87.46 E
Čel'uskin, mys ›	74	77.45 N	104.20 E
Čel'uskincev park ♦	265a	60.01 N	30.19 E
Cemaes Head ›	42	52.07 N	4.44 W
Çemal	86	51.25 N	86.01 E
Čembilej	80	55.19 N	45.43 E
Cembra	64	46.10 N	11.13 E
Cembra, Val di V	64	46.10 N	11.13 E
Cement	196	34.55 N	98.08 W
Cement City	216	42.04 N	84.19 W
Cementon, N.Y., U.S.	210	42.09 N	73.55 W
Çementon, Pa., U.S.	208	40.41 N	75.30 W
Čemer	78	51.07 N	31.13 E
Čemerisy	78	51.42 N	30.24 E
Čemerno	36	43.11 N	18.37 E
Čemerno)(	38	43.14 N	18.37 E
Čemerovcy	78	49.01 N	26.21 E
Cemesskaja buchta c	78	44.40 N	37.50 E
Cemilbey	130	40.21 N	35.04 E
Çemişkezek	130	39.04 N	38.55 E
Çemmaes	42	52.37 N	3.42 W
Čemolgan	85	43.23 N	76.37 E
Çempi, Teluk c	115b	8.44 S	118.25 E
Čenča	88	55.57 N	110.59 E
Cencenighe	64	46.21 N	11.58 E
Çenchermandal	88	47.37 N	109.05 E
Čency	82	56.03 N	36.01 E
Cenderawasih, Teluk c	164	2.30 S	135.20 E
Cendras	62	44.09 N	4.04 E
Cene	62	45.47 N	9.49 E
Cenepa ≃	246	4.35 S	78.12 W
Ceneri, Monte)(	58	46.08 N	8.55 E
Çengel	86	48.56 N	89.10 E
Čengel'dy, Kaz.	85	41.51 N	68.59 E
Čengel'dy, Kaz.	85	43.59 N	77.26 E
Çengelköy ◆[8]	267b	41.03 N	29.03 E
Čengerli	130	39.48 N	38.52 E
Cengles, Croda di ∧	64	46.34 N	10.38 E
Ceno ≃	36	44.41 N	10.05 E
Cenovo	38	43.32 N	25.39 E
Cenrana	112	3.18 S	118.50 E
Censeau	58	46.49 N	6.04 E
Centallo	62	44.30 N	7.35 E
Centenario	252	38.48 S	68.08 W
Centenário do Sul	255	22.48 S	51.37 W
Centennial Lake ⊜	285	39.50 N	74.51 W
Centennial Lake ⊜[1]	212	45.10 N	72.05 W
Centennial Mountains ⋏	202	44.35 N	111.55 W
Centennial Park ♦, Austl.	274a	33.54 S	151.14 E
Centennial Park ♦, On., Can.	275b	43.39 N	79.35 W
Centennial Wash V	200	33.14 N	112.46 W
Centeno	66	42.48 N	11.49 E
Center, Co., U.S.	200	37.45 N	106.06 W
Center, In., U.S.	216	40.26 N	86.04 W
Center, Mo., U.S.	219	39.30 N	91.31 W
Center, Ne., U.S.	198	42.36 N	97.52 W
Center, N.D., U.S.	198	47.06 N	101.17 W
Center, Tx., U.S.	194	31.47 N	94.10 W
Centerbrook	207	41.21 N	72.24 W
Center Brunswick	210	42.45 N	73.37 W
Centerburg	214	40.18 N	82.41 W
Center City	190	45.23 N	92.48 W
Center Cross	208	37.48 N	76.46 W
Centereach	210	40.51 N	73.06 W
Centerfield	218	38.21 N	83.24 W
Center Hill	220	28.38 N	81.59 W
Center Hill Lake ⊜[1]	194	36.00 N	85.45 W
Center Line	214	42.29 N	83.01 W
Center Moriches	188	40.48 N	72.47 W
Center Mountain ∧	202	45.06 N	115.13 W
Center Point, Al., U.S.	194	33.37 N	86.41 W
Center Point, Ia., U.S.	190	42.11 N	91.47 W
Center Point, Tx., U.S.	196	29.57 N	99.02 W
Centerport, N.Y., U.S.	210	40.54 N	73.22 W
Centerport, Pa., U.S.	208	40.29 N	76.01 W
Center Square, N.J., U.S.	285	39.46 N	75.23 W
Center Square, Pa., U.S.	208	40.10 N	75.18 W
Centerton, In., U.S.	218	39.30 N	86.23 W
Centerton, N.J., U.S.	285	39.31 N	75.10 W
Center Valley	208	40.32 N	75.24 W
Centerville, De., U.S.	285	39.49 N	75.37 W
Centerville, In., U.S.	218	39.49 N	84.59 W
Centerville, Ia., U.S.	190	40.43 N	92.52 W
Centerville, Ma., U.S.	207	41.38 N	70.20 W
Centerville, Mo., U.S.	194	37.26 N	90.57 W
Centerville, N.Y., U.S.	210	42.29 N	78.15 W
Centerville, Oh., U.S.	218	39.37 N	84.09 W
Centerville, Pa., U.S.	188	40.02 N	79.58 W
Centerville, S.D., U.S.	198	43.07 N	96.57 W
Centerville, Tn., U.S.	194	35.46 N	87.28 W
Centerville, Tx., U.S.	222	31.15 N	95.58 W
Centerville, Ut,. U.S.	200	40.55 N	111.52 W
Centerville, Wa., U.S.	224	45.45 N	120.54 W
Centinela	196	28.47 N	100.34 W
Cento	64	44.43 N	11.17 E
Centocelle ◆[8]	267a	41.53 N	12.34 E
Cento Croci, Passo di)(	62	44.25 N	9.37 E
Centola	68	40.04 N	15.19 E
Central, Bra.	250	11.08 S	42.08 W
Central, Ak., U.S.	180	65.34 N	144.48 W
Central, Az., U.S.	200	32.52 N	109.47 W
Central, N.M., U.S.	200	32.46 N	108.08 W
Central, S.C., U.S.	192	34.43 N	82.46 W
Central, Tx., U.S.	222	31.26 N	94.49 W
Central □[4], Ghana	150	5.30 N	1.00 W
Central □[4], Kenya	154	0.45 S	37.00 E
Central □[4], Malaŵi	154	13.00 S	34.00 E
Central □[4], Sol.Is.	175e	9.10 S	159.50 E
Central □[4], Scot., U.K.	46	56.05 N	4.20 W
Central □[4], Zam.	154	14.30 S	29.00 E
Central □[5], Bots.	156	21.30 S	26.00 E
Central □[5], Pap. N. Gui.	164	9.00 S	147.00 E
Central □[5], Para.	252	25.30 S	57.30 W
Central □[5], Ug.	154	0.10 N	32.00 E
Central, Cordillera ⋏, Col.	246	5.00 N	75.00 W
Central, Cordillera ⋏, C.R.	236	10.10 N	84.05 W
Central, Cordillera ⋏, Pan.	236	8.30 N	81.30 W
Central, Cordillera ⋏, Perú	248	8.00 S	77.00 W
Central, Cordillera ⋏, Pil.	116	17.20 N	120.57 E
Central, Cordillera ⋏, P.R.	240m	18.10 N	66.35 W
Central, Macizo → Central, Massif ⋏	32	45.00 N	3.10 E
Central, Massif ⋏	32	45.00 N	3.10 E
Central, Planalto ⋏[1]	242	18.00 S	47.00 W
Central, Sistema ⋏	34	40.30 N	5.00 W
Central African Republic □[1]	136	7.00 N	21.00 E
Central Aguirre	240m	17.57 N	66.13 W
Central Barren	218	38.22 N	86.06 W
Central Brāhui Range ⋏	120	29.20 N	66.55 E
Central Bridge	210	42.42 N	74.20 W
Central Butte	184	50.47 N	106.30 W
Central City, Il., U.S.	219	38.32 N	89.07 W
Central City, Ia., U.S.	190	42.12 N	91.31 W
Central City, Ky., U.S.	194	37.17 N	87.07 W
Central City, Ne., U.S.	198	41.06 N	98.00 W
Central City, Pa., U.S.	214	40.06 N	78.48 W
Central Division □[5]	175g	18.05 S	178.30 E
Central Falls	207	41.53 N	71.23 W
Central Heights	200	33.24 N	110.48 W
Central Highlands	279b	40.16 N	79.50 W
Centralia, Il., U.S.	219	38.31 N	89.08 W
Centralia, Ks., U.S.	198	39.43 N	96.07 W
Centralia, Mo., U.S.	219	39.12 N	92.08 W
Centralia, Tx., U.S.	222	31.16 N	95.02 W
Centralia, Wa., U.S.	224	46.42 N	122.57 W
Centralia, Lake ⊜	219	38.32 N	88.59 W
Centralia Draw V	196	31.27 N	101.16 W
Centralia Reservoir ⊜[1]	219	38.32 N	89.08 W
Centralina	255	18.34 S	49.13 W
Central Intelligence Agency ♁	284c	38.57 N	77.09 W
Central Island I	154	3.30 N	36.03 E
Central Islip	210	40.47 N	73.12 W
Central Kalahari Game Reserve ◆[4]	156	22.15 S	23.45 E
Central Lake	190	45.04 N	85.15 W
Central Makrān Range ⋏	128	26.40 N	64.30 E
Central'no-Bokovskoj ◆[8]	83	48.11 N	39.03 E
Central'nolesnoj Zapovednik ◆[4]	76	56.32 N	32.50 E
Central Nyack	276	41.06 N	73.57 W
Central'nyj, Ross.	76	53.41 N	39.38 E
Central'nyj, Ross.	86	55.12 N	87.40 E
Central'nyj, Ross.	86	58.45 N	84.28 E
Central'nyj, Ross.	86	57.41 N	80.57 E
Central'nyj, Ross.	265b	55.53 N	37.52 E
Central'nyje Karakumy ◆[2]	128	39.00 N	60.00 E
Central Pacific Basin ✦[1]	14	5.00 N	175.00 W
Central Park, N.J., U.S.	276	40.26 N	74.18 W
Central Park, Wa., U.S.	224	46.58 N	123.41 W
Central Park ♦	276	40.47 N	73.58 W
Central Point	202	42.22 N	122.54 W
Central Railroad Station ◆[5]	272c	18.58 N	72.50 E
Central Range ⋏, Leso.	158	29.35 S	28.35 E
Central Range ⋏, Pap. N. Gui.	164	5.00 S	142.30 E
Central Square	210	43.17 N	76.08 W
Central Utah Canal ≍	200	39.35 N	112.12 W
Central Valley, Ca., U.S.	204	40.40 N	122.22 W
Central Valley, N.Y., U.S.	210	41.19 N	74.07 W
Central Village	207	41.43 N	71.54 W
Centre	194	34.09 N	85.40 W
Centre □[6]	210	40.55 N	77.47 W
Centre, Canal du ≍	32	46.27 N	4.07 E
Centre Atomique de Marcoule ♁[3]	62	44.08 N	4.42 E
Centre City	285	39.46 N	75.10 W
Centre d'Énergie de Pierrelatte ♁[3]	62	44.21 N	4.44 E
Centre Hall	214	40.50 N	77.41 W
Centre Island	276	40.54 N	73.32 W
Centre Island I	172	46.28 S	167.51 E
Centre Island Park ♦	275b	43.37 N	79.23 W
Centre Lake ⊜	212	44.36 N	75.51 W
Centre Peak ∧	182	55.41 N	126.26 W
Centre-Sud □[4]	152	4.10 N	12.00 E
Centreville, Al., U.S.	194	32.56 N	87.08 W
Centreville, Il., U.S.	219	38.35 N	90.07 W
Centreville, Ky., U.S.	218	38.13 N	84.24 W
Centreville, Md., U.S.	208	39.02 N	76.04 W
Centreville, Mi., U.S.	216	41.55 N	85.31 W
Centreville, Ms., U.S.	194	31.05 N	91.04 W
Centreville, Va., U.S.	208	38.50 N	77.25 W
Centro Puntas	240m	18.22 N	67.16 W
Centro Simón Bolívar ◆[9]	286c	10.30 N	66.55 W
Centuripe	70	37.37 N	14.44 E
Century, Fl., U.S.	194	30.58 N	87.15 W
Century, W.V., U.S.	188	39.05 N	80.11 W
Century City ◆[8]	280	34.03 N	118.26 W
Century III Mall ◆[9]	279b	40.21 N	79.57 W
Century Village	220	26.42 N	80.05 W
Çenxi	102	22.59 N	111.00 E
Čepca	80	57.54 N	53.25 E
Čepca ≃	80	58.36 N	50.04 E
Čepeckij	80	58.29 N	51.12 E
Čepel'	78	49.19 N	36.55 E
Čepelare	38	41.44 N	24.41 E
Čepel'ovo	82	55.11 N	37.30 E
Čepovan	64	46.03 N	13.47 E
Cepoy	50	48.03 N	2.44 E
Çeprano	66	41.33 N	13.31 E
Čepřovice	60	49.10 N	13.59 E
Ceptia	152	12.56 S	17.35 E
Cepu	115a	7.09 S	111.35 E
Ceraino	64	45.35 N	10.50 E
Cerami	70	37.49 N	14.30 E
Cerami ≃	70	37.42 N	14.29 E
Ceram Sea → Seram, Laut ▾[2]	108	2.30 S	128.00 E
Ceram → Seram I	164	3.00 S	129.00 E
Cerano, It.	62	45.25 N	8.47 E
Cerano, Méx.	234	20.07 N	101.23 W
Ceraso	68	40.11 N	15.15 E
Çerbicale, Îles II	71	41.34 N	9.24 E
Čerčany	30	49.51 N	14.43 E
Çerchiara di Calabria	68	39.51 N	16.23 E
Čerchov ∧	60	49.23 N	12.47 E
Cercié	58	46.07 N	4.40 E
Cerco, Alto do ∧	256	22.38 S	45.22 W
Cercola	66	40.51 N	14.21 E
Çerda	70	37.54 N	13.49 E
Čerdakly	80	54.23 N	48.51 E
Cerdanyola del Vallès	266d	41.30 N	2.09 E
Cerdas	248	20.48 S	66.29 W
Cerdeña, Isla de → Sardegna I	71	40.00 N	9.00 E
Čerdojak	86	48.48 N	84.00 E
Cerdon, Fr.	50	47.38 N	2.22 E
Çerdon, Fr.	58	46.05 N	5.28 E
Čerdyn'	24	60.23 N	56.24 E
Cère ≃	32	44.55 N	1.53 E
Cerea	64	45.12 N	11.13 E
Cereal	184	51.25 N	110.48 W
Çereales	252	36.49 S	63.51 W
Čerecha ≃	76	57.46 N	28.21 E
Çereglio	64	44.18 N	11.04 E
Čereja	76	54.37 N	29.17 E
Čerek ≃	84	43.42 N	44.03 E
Čeremchovo	88	53.09 N	103.05 E
Čeremisinovo	78	51.54 N	37.15 E
Čeremoš ≃	78	48.23 N	25.37 E
Čeremšan, Ross.	80	55.15 N	48.07 E
Čeremšan, Ross.	80	54.40 N	51.30 E
Čeremšanka, Ross.	86	56.07 N	60.19 E
Čeremšanka, Ross.	86	59.10 N	76.51 E
Čeremšany	89	44.42 N	135.43 E
Çerenti	112	0.30 S	101.52 E
Čerepanovka	80	57.07 N	54.10 E
Čerepanovo	86	54.13 N	83.22 E
Čerepaška, ostrov I	83	47.11 N	38.59 E
Čerepet'	82	54.07 N	36.23 E
Čerepkovo ◆[8]	265b	55.46 N	37.23 E
Čerepovec	76	59.08 N	37.54 E
Ceres, Arg.	252	29.53 S	61.57 W
Ceres, Bra.	255	15.17 S	49.35 W
Ceres, It.	62	45.19 N	7.23 E
Ceres, S. Afr.	158	33.21 S	19.18 E
Ceres, Ca., U.S.	226	37.35 N	120.57 W
Ceres, N.Y., U.S.	210	42.00 N	78.16 W
Ceresco, Mi., U.S.	216	42.16 N	85.04 W
Ceresco, Ne., U.S.	198	41.03 N	96.38 W
Ceresole Reale	62	45.26 N	7.15 E
Céreste	62	43.51 N	5.35 E
Céret	32	42.29 N	2.45 E
Çereté	246	8.53 N	75.48 W
Čerevkovka	78	48.50 N	37.40 E
Čerevkovka ◆[8]	83	48.50 N	37.40 E
Čerevkovo	24	61.46 N	45.12 E
Cereweh	115b	8.52 S	116.51 E
Çerf Island I	138	9.32 S	50.59 E
Čerga	86	51.35 N	85.38 E
Cergy	261	49.02 N	2.04 E
Ceri ≃	42	52.03 N	4.29 W
Ceriale	62	44.06 N	8.14 E
Ceriana	62	43.53 N	7.46 E
Ceriano	266b	45.38 N	9.05 E
Çerignola	68	41.16 N	15.54 E
Čerikov	76	53.34 N	31.23 E
Cérilly	32	46.37 N	2.49 E
Cerisano	68	39.16 N	16.11 E
Çerisiers	50	48.08 N	3.29 E
Čerkašina	88	58.37 N	108.30 E
Čerkasovo	82	54.33 N	36.48 E
Čerkasskoje, Ross.	80	52.26 N	47.13 E
Čerkasskoje, Ukr.	78	48.44 N	35.22 E
Čerkasskoje, Ukr.	83	48.50 N	37.23 E
Čerkassy, Ross.	76	52.41 N	38.43 E
Čerkassy, Ukr.	78	49.26 N	32.04 E
Çerkeş	130	40.50 N	32.54 E
Čerkesovskij	80	50.41 N	42.34 E
Čerkessk	84	44.14 N	42.04 E
Çerkezköy	130	41.17 N	28.00 E
Čerkizovo, Ross.	82	55.12 N	38.45 E
Čerkizovo, Ross.	265b	55.58 N	37.48 E
Čerkizovo, Ross.	265b	55.57 N	37.22 E
Cerknica	36	45.48 N	14.22 E
Čerkovišče	76	55.54 N	30.51 E
Čerlak	86	54.09 N	74.48 E
Čerlakskij	86	53.47 N	74.31 E
Çermei	38	46.33 N	21.51 E
Čermen	84	43.11 N	44.42 E
Cermignano	66	42.35 N	13.47 E
Çermik	130	38.09 N	39.27 E
Čermoz	86	58.53 N	56.08 E
Čern'	76	53.27 N	36.55 E
Cerna, Cro.	38	45.11 N	18.42 E
Çerna, Rom.	38	45.04 N	28.18 E
Čern'achov	78	50.27 N	28.39 E
Čern'achovsk (Insterburg)	76	54.38 N	21.49 E
Černá hora ∧	60	48.58 N	13.48 E
Čern'ajevo	89	52.45 N	126.00 E
Černak	85	43.24 N	68.02 E
Čern'anka	78	50.55 N	37.49 E
Cernăuți → Černovcy	78	48.18 N	25.56 E
Černava	76	53.37 N	39.09 E
Černavčicy	76	52.13 N	23.44 E
Černavka, Ross.	80	52.18 N	47.14 E
Černavka, Ross.	80	52.11 N	42.25 E
Cernavodă	38	44.21 N	28.01 E
Černá v Pošumaví	61	48.44 N	14.07 E
Cernay	58	47.49 N	7.10 E
Cernay-la-Ville	50	48.40 N	1.58 E
Çerne Abbas	42	50.49 N	2.29 W
Černeckoje	82	55.15 N	37.20 E
Cernei, Munții ⋏	38	45.02 N	22.31 E
Černelica	78	48.48 N	25.26 E
Černevcy	78	48.33 N	28.09 E
Černigov	78	51.30 N	31.18 E
Černigovka, Kaz.	86	50.28 N	71.27 E
Černigovka, Ross.	89	49.37 N	129.57 E
Černigovka, Ross.	89	44.21 N	132.33 E
Černigovka, Ukr.	78	47.13 N	36.14 E
Černigovskaja	78	44.41 N	39.40 E
Černi vrăh ∧	38	42.34 N	23.17 E
Černobaj	78	49.41 N	32.19 E
Cernobbio	62	45.50 N	9.04 E
Černobyl'	78	51.16 N	30.14 E
Černogolovka	82	56.00 N	38.22 E
Černogorsk	86	53.49 N	91.18 E
Černokol'skaja	86	56.42 N	72.49 E
Černomorskij zapovednik ◆[4]	78	46.10 N	32.00 E
Černorečenskoje	85	43.00 N	74.55 E
Černorečje	84	43.15 N	45.41 E
Černošín	60	49.49 N	12.53 E
Černovcy	78	48.18 N	25.56 E
Čerňovice	60	49.49 N	13.06 E
Černovka, Ross.	86	56.47 N	76.28 E
Černovka, Ross.	89	51.43 N	128.12 E
Čern'ovo, Ross.	76	58.39 N	28.14 E
Čern'ovo, Ross.	82	54.43 N	38.36 E
Čern'ovo, Ross.	265b	55.50 N	37.18 E
Černovskije Kopi	88	52.00 N	113.15 E
Černovskoje, Ross.	80	58.42 N	47.23 E
Černovskoje, Ross.	80	57.29 N	54.36 E
Černucha	80	55.36 N	43.46 E
Černuchi	78	50.16 N	32.57 E
Černuchino	83	48.19 N	38.30 E
Cernusco sul Naviglio	62	45.31 N	9.19 E
Černuška, Ross.	86	56.29 N	56.03 E
Černuška, Ross.	88	52.58 N	101.55 E
Cerny-en-Laonnois	50	49.27 N	3.40 E
Černyševsk	88	52.35 N	117.00 E
Černyševskij	74	63.00 N	112.15 E
Černyškovskij	80	48.27 N	42.14 E
Černyšova, gr'ada ⋏	24	66.30 N	59.00 E
Čer'omuchova	80	54.57 N	51.09 E
Čer'omuski ◆[8]	265b	55.41 N	37.35 E
Cerralvo	232	26.06 N	99.37 W
Cerralvo, Isla I	232	24.15 N	109.55 W
Cerreto, Passo del)(	64	44.18 N	10.13 E
Cerreto d'Esi	66	43.19 N	12.59 E
Cerreto Guidi	66	43.45 N	10.53 E
Cerreto Sannita	68	41.17 N	14.33 E
Cerrigydrudion	44	53.02 N	3.33 W
Cërrik	38	41.02 N	19.57 E
Cerrillos, Arg.	252	24.54 S	65.29 W
Cerrillos, Chile	286e	33.30 S	70.43 W
Cerrillos, N.M., U.S.	200	35.26 N	106.07 W
Cerrina	62	45.07 N	8.13 E
Cerritos, Méx.	234	22.26 N	100.17 W
Cerritos, Ca., U.S.	280	33.52 N	118.05 W
Cerro	58	45.54 N	8.36 E
Cerro, Forca di)(	66	42.45 N	12.47 E
Cerro Azul, Arg.	252	27.38 S	55.29 W
Cerro Azul, Bra.	252	24.50 S	49.15 W
Cerro Azul, Méx.	234	21.12 N	97.44 W
Cerro Azul, Perú	248	13.02 S	76.30 W
Cerro Chato	252	33.06 S	55.08 W
Cerro Colorado	252	33.52 S	55.33 W
Cerro Corá	250	6.03 S	36.21 W
Cerro de las Mesas ⊥	234	18.47 N	96.05 W
Cerro de los Angeles ♁[1]	266a	40.19 N	3.41 W
Cerro de Pasco	248	10.41 S	76.16 W
Cerro Gordo	219	39.53 N	88.43 W
Cerro Grande ≃	286c	10.37 N	66.49 W
Cerro Largo	252	28.09 S	54.45 W
Cerro Maggiore	266b	45.36 N	8.58 E
Cerro Moreno	252	23.28 S	70.25 W
Cerrón, Cerro ∧	246	10.19 N	70.39 W
Cerro Navia	286e	33.25 S	70.43 W
Cerrón Grande, Embalse ⊜[1]	236	14.00 N	89.00 W
Cerro Prieto	204	32.27 N	115.17 W
Cerros Colorados, Embalse ⊜[1]	252	38.35 S	68.40 W
Cerros de Amotape, Parque Nacional ♦	246	4.10 S	80.30 W
Cerro Vera	252	33.11 S	57.28 W
Čerskij	74	68.45 N	161.45 E
Čerskogo, chrebet ⋏, Ross.	74	65.00 N	144.00 E
Čerskogo, chrebet ⋏, Ross.	88	52.00 N	114.00 E
Čerskogo, gora ∧	88	55.05 N	108.40 E
Cersosimo	68	40.03 N	16.21 E
Certaldo	66	43.33 N	11.02 E
Čertanovka ≃	265b	55.38 N	37.47 E
Čertanovo ◆[8]	265b	55.38 N	37.37 E
Čertkovo	83	49.23 N	40.10 E
Čertolino	76	56.12 N	33.54 E
Čertomlyk	78	47.37 N	34.09 E
Certosa (Karthaus)	64	46.42 N	10.54 E
Certosa di Pavia	62	45.15 N	9.09 E
Čerusti	76	55.33 N	40.01 E
Červ'anka	88	57.41 N	99.33 E
Cervantes, Austl.	162	30.30 S	115.04 E
Cervantes, Pil.	116	16.59 N	120.44 E
Cervarezza	64	44.23 N	10.20 E
Cervaro	66	41.29 N	13.54 E
Cervaro ≃	68	41.30 N	15.52 E
Cervati, Monte ∧	68	40.17 N	15.29 E
Cervelló	266d	41.24 N	1.57 E
Cervello, Cozzo ∧	68	39.24 N	16.05 E
Cervelló, Riera de ≃	266d	41.24 N	2.01 E
Červen'	76	53.42 N	28.26 E
Červen Brjag	38	43.16 N	24.06 E
Červený Kostelec	30	50.29 N	16.06 E
Cervera	34	41.40 N	1.17 E
Cervera del Río Alhama	34	42.01 N	1.57 W
Cervera de Pisuerga	34	42.52 N	4.30 W
Cerveteri	66	42.00 N	12.06 E
Cervi, Monte dei ∧	70	37.53 N	13.58 E
Cervia	66	44.15 N	12.22 E
Cervialto, Monte ∧	68	40.47 N	15.08 E
Cervignano del Friuli	64	45.49 N	13.20 E

Symbols in the index entries represent the broad categories identified in the key at the right. Symbols with superior numbers (⋏[1]) identify subcategories (see complete key on page *I · 1).*

Symbole im Register stellen die rechts im Schlüssel erklärten Kategorien dar. Symbole mit hochgestellten Ziffern (⋏[1]) bezeichnen Unterabteilungen einer Kategorie (vgl. vollständiger Schlüssel auf Seite *I · 1).*

Los símbolos incluídos en el texto del índice representan las grandes categorias identificadas con la clave a la derecha. Los símbolos con numeros en su parte superior (⋏[1]) identifican las subcategorías (véase la clave completa en la página *I · 1).*

Les symboles de l'index représentent les catégories indiquées dans la légende à droite. Les symboles suivis d'un indice (⋏[1]) représentent des sous-catégories (voir légende complète à la page *I · 1).*

Os símbolos incluídos no texto do índice representam as grandes categorias identificadas com a chave à direita. Os símbolos com números em sua parte superior (⋏[1]) identificam as subcategorias (veja-se a chave completa à página *I · 1).*

English	Deutsch	Español	Français	Português
∧ Mountain	Berg	Montaña	Montagne	Montanha
⋏ Mountains	Gebirge	Montañas	Montagnes	Montanhas
)(Pass	Paß	Paso	Col	Passo
V Valley, Canyon	Tal, Cañon	Valle, Cañón	Vallée, Canyon	Vale, Canhão
≚ Plain	Ebene	Llano	Plaine	Planície
› Cape	Kap	Cabo	Cap	Cabo
I Island	Insel	Isla	Île	Ilha
II Islands	Inseln	Islas	Îles	Ilhas
⊥ Other Topographic Features	Andere Topographische Objekte	Otros Elementos Topográficos	Autres données topographiques	Outros acidentes topográficos

ESPAÑOL · FRANÇAIS · PORTUGUÊS

Nombre / Nom / Nome	Página / Page	Lat.°′	Long.°′ W = Oeste / Ouest
Cervin, Mont → Matterhorn ∧	58	45.59 N	7.43 E
Cervinara	68	41.01 N	14.37 E
Cervino (Matterhorn) ∧	58	45.59 N	7.43 E
Cervione	36	42.20 N	9.31 E
Červl'onnaja	84	43.30 N	45.54 E
Cervo, Esp.	34	43.40 N	7.25 W
Cervo, It.	62	43.55 N	8.07 E
Cervo ≃	62	45.22 N	8.24 E
Cervo, Capo ›	62	43.55 N	8.08 E
Cervo, Rio do ≃, Bra.	256	22.07 S	45.49 W
Cervo, Rio do ≃, Bra.	256	21.12 S	45.10 W
Cervo, Serra do ∧	256	22.06 S	46.07 W
Červonaja Kamenka	78	48.38 N	33.26 E
Červonoarmejsk, Ukr.	78	50.08 N	25.16 E
Červonoarmejsk, Ukr.	78	50.28 N	28.14 E
Červonoarmejskoje, Ukr.	78	45.47 N	28.44 E
Červonoarmejskoje, Ukr.	78	47.57 N	35.27 E
Červonograd	78	50.24 N	24.14 E
Červonogranitnoje	78	50.34 N	28.33 E
Červonoje, Ukr.	78	51.46 N	34.04 E
Červonoje, Ukr.	78	49.57 N	28.53 E
Červonoje, ozero ⊜	76	52.24 N	27.57 E
Červonopartizansk	83	48.04 N	39.50 E
Červonyj Donec	78	49.29 N	36.34 E
Cesana Torinese	62	44.57 N	6.47 E
Cesano, It.	66	43.45 N	13.10 E
Cesano, It.	66	42.07 N	12.21 E
Cesano ≃	66	43.45 N	13.10 E
Cesano Boscone	266b	45.27 N	9.06 E
Cesano Maderno	62	45.38 N	9.08 E
Cesar □ 5	246	9.20 N	73.30 W
Cesar ≃	246	9.00 N	73.58 W
Cesaró	70	37.50 N	14.43 E
Cesate	266b	45.36 N	9.05 E
Cesena	66	44.08 N	12.15 E
Cesenatico	66	44.12 N	12.24 E
Cesi, Poggio ∧ 2	267a	42.02 N	12.44 E
Cesiomaggiore	64	46.05 N	11.59 E
Cēsis	76	57.18 N	25.15 E
Česká Kamenice	54	50.47 N	14.26 E
Česká Kublice	60	49.22 N	12.52 E
Česká Lípa	54	50.42 N	14.32 E
Česká Republika □ 3	30	49.40 N	15.10 E
Česká Třebová	30	49.54 N	16.27 E
České Budějovice	61	48.59 N	14.28 E
České středohoří ⩘	54	50.35 N	14.09 E
Českomoravská vrchovina ⩘ 1	30	49.20 N	15.30 E
Československo → Czechoslovakia □ 1	30	49.30 N	17.00 E
Český Brod	54	50.02 N	14.58 E
Český Krumlov	61	48.49 N	14.19 E
Česma	86	53.50 N	60.40 E
Çeşme	130	38.18 N	26.19 E
Cessalto	64	45.42 N	12.36 E
Češskaja guba c	24	67.30 N	46.30 E
Cessnock	170	32.50 S	151.21 E
Cesson	261	48.34 N	2.36 E
Cestos ≃	150	5.40 N	9.10 W
Cesvaine	76	56.58 N	26.19 E
Čet' ≃	86	56.51 N	86.48 E
Cetara	68	40.39 N	14.42 E
Cetate	38	44.06 N	23.03 E
Cetatea Albă → Belgorod-Dnestrovskij	78	46.12 N	30.20 E
Četbulak	85	41.17 N	73.58 E
Cetian	100	25.44 N	116.22 E
Cetina ≃	36	43.26 N	16.42 E
Cetinje	38	42.23 N	18.55 E
Çetinkaya	130	39.15 N	37.38 E
Cetona	66	42.58 N	11.54 E
Cetona, Monte ∧	66	42.56 N	11.52 E
Cetraro	68	39.31 N	15.56 E
Cetronia	208	40.35 N	75.31 W
Četyrboki	78	50.02 N	27.01 E
Céüse, Montagne de ∧	62	44.31 N	5.57 E
Ceuta	34	35.53 N	5.19 W
Ceva	62	44.23 N	8.02 E
Cevedale, Monte (Zufallspitze) ∧	64	46.27 N	10.37 E
Cevennen → Cévennes ⬥ 1	32	44.00 N	3.30 E
Cévennes ⬥ 1	32	44.00 N	3.30 E
Cévennes, Parc National des ♦	32	44.15 N	3.40 E
Cevins	62	45.35 N	6.28 E
Cevio	58	46.19 N	8.36 E
Cevizli	130	37.12 N	31.45 E
Ceyhan	130	37.04 N	35.47 E
Ceyhan ≃	130	36.45 N	35.41 E
Ceylanpınar	130	36.51 N	40.02 E
Ceylon, Sk., Can.	184	49.28 N	104.36 W
Ceylon, Mn., U.S.	198	43.32 N	94.37 W
Ceylon → Sri Lanka □ 1	122	7.00 N	81.00 E
Ceyzériat	58	46.10 N	5.19 E
Cèze ≃	62	44.06 N	4.42 E
Chaam, Ned.	52	51.31 N	4.52 E
Cha-am, Thai	110	12.48 N	99.58 E
Chaanling	100	29.39 N	113.49 E
Chaatl Island I	182	53.00 N	132.25 W
Chabanais	32	45.52 N	0.43 E
Chabang Tiga	114	5.19 N	103.08 E
Chabaricha	24	65.50 N	52.16 E
Chabařovice	54	50.40 N	13.56 E
Chabarovo	72	69.39 N	60.24 E
Chabarovsk	89	48.27 N	135.06 E
Chabarovsk □ 8	89	54.00 N	136.00 E
Chabarowsk → Chabarovsk	89	48.27 N	135.06 E
Chabary	86	53.37 N	79.33 E
Chabás	252	33.15 S	61.22 W
Chabeuil	62	44.54 N	5.01 E
Chabez	84	44.02 N	41.47 E
Chābi	124	22.49 N	80.41 E
Chabjuwardoo Bay c	162	22.57 S	113.48 E
Chablais ⬥ 1	58	46.18 N	6.39 E
Chablis	50	47.49 N	3.48 E
Chabogongba	120	31.47 N	81.14 E
Chaboje	265a	59.53 N	30.46 E
Chabot, Lake ⊜, Ca., U.S.	282	38.08 N	122.14 W
Chabot, Lake ⊜, Ca., U.S.	282	37.43 N	122.07 W
Chabris	50	47.15 N	1.39 E
Chabuchaer	86	43.42 N	81.04 E
Chabu-Rabot, pereval)(	85	38.40 N	70.43 E
Chacabuco	252	34.38 S	60.29 W
Chacaito, Quebrada ≃	286c	10.29 N	66.52 W
Chacaltianguis	234	18.20 N	95.50 W
Chacao	286c	10.30 N	66.51 W
Chácara	256	21.41 S	43.13 W
Chacarita, Cementerio de la ⬥	288	34.33 S	58.28 W
Chacarrão, Cachoeira do ∟	250	6.32 S	58.12 W
Chacayán	248	10.24 S	76.25 W
Chachani, Nevado ∧	248	16.12 S	71.33 W
Chachapoyas, Perú	242	6.13 S	77.51 W
Chachapoyas, Perú	248	6.13 S	77.51 W
Chachas	248	15.30 S	72.16 W
Chachoengsao	110	13.42 N	101.05 E
Chāchora	124	24.10 N	76.59 E
Chāchro	120	25.07 N	70.15 E
Chachu	120	33.16 N	81.41 E
Chačinčaj ≃	84	40.13 N	47.18 E
Chaclacyo	248	11.59 S	76.46 W
Chačmas	84	41.28 N	48.48 E
Chaco □ 4	252	26.25 S	60.30 W
Chaco □ 5	248	20.00 S	60.30 W
Chaco ≃	200	36.46 N	108.39 W
Chaco Austral ⬥ 1	252	26.30 S	61.30 W
Chaco Boreal ⬥ 1	252	23.00 S	60.00 W
Chaco Central ⬥ 1	252	25.00 S	59.45 W
Chaco Culture National Historical Park ♦	200	36.06 N	108.00 W
Chaco Mesa ∧	200	35.47 N	107.35 W
Chacón, Arroyo ≃	288	34.53 S	58.39 W
Chacon, Cape ›	182	54.42 N	132.00 W
Chacra Cerro	286d	11.55 S	77.04 W
Chacuaco Creek ≃	196	37.34 N	103.38 W
Chad (Tchad) □ 1, Afr.	136	15.00 N	19.00 E
Chad (Tchad) □ 1, Afr.	146	15.00 N	19.00 E
Chad, Lake (Lac Tchad) ⊜	146	13.20 N	14.00 E
Chada-Bulak	88	50.38 N	116.18 E
Chadbourn	192	34.19 N	78.49 W
Chadderton	262	53.33 N	2.08 W
Chadds Ford	285	39.52 N	75.35 W
Chādegān	128	32.46 N	50.39 E
Chadian, Zhg.	102	26.48 N	105.48 E
Chadian, Zhg.	105	39.14 N	117.45 E
Chadian, Zhg.	107	30.14 N	105.56 E
Chadianzi	107	30.31 N	104.22 E
Chadiza	154	14.05 S	32.28 E
Chadron	198	42.49 N	103.00 W
Chadstone	274b	37.53 S	145.05 E
Chadwell Saint Mary	260	51.29 N	0.22 E
Chadwick	190	42.01 N	89.53 W
Chadwick Manor	284b	39.19 N	76.46 W
Chadwick Pond ⊜	283	42.44 N	71.05 W
Chadwicks	210	43.01 N	75.16 W
Chadyženskk	78	44.25 N	39.33 E
Chadžalmachi	84	42.26 N	47.13 E
Chadžibejskij liman ⊜	78	46.39 N	30.33 E
Chae Hom	110	18.43 N	99.35 E
Chaem ≃	110	18.11 N	98.38 E
Chaersen	89	46.19 N	121.54 E
Chaeryŏng	98	38.24 N	125.36 E
Chafarinas, Islas II	34	35.11 N	2.26 W
Chafe	150	11.56 N	6.55 E
Chaffee	194	37.10 N	89.39 W
Chaffins	207	42.21 N	71.51 W
Chāgai	128	29.18 N	64.42 E
Chāgai Hills ⩘ 2	128	29.30 N	64.15 E
Chagandianlisu	102	41.47 N	103.29 E
Chagang Do □ 4	98	40.50 N	126.30 E
'Chaghcharān	120	34.32 N	65.15 E
Chagny	58	46.55 N	4.45 E
Chagos Archipelago II	12	6.00 S	72.00 E
Chagos-Laccadive Plateau ✣ 3	12	3.00 N	73.00 E
Chagrin ≃	214	41.40 N	81.27 W
Chagrin, Aurora Branch ≃	279a	41.25 N	81.25 W
Chagrin Falls	214	41.26 N	81.24 W
Chagrin Falls Park	214	41.21 N	81.32 W
Chagrin Valley Parkway ♦	279a	41.26 N	81.25 W
Chaguanas	241r	10.31 N	61.25 W
Chaguaramas	246	9.20 N	66.16 W
Chahaignes	50	47.44 N	0.31 E
Chāhak	128	33.17 N	58.54 E
Chahal	236	15.45 N	89.34 W
Chahancheluo	98	41.39 N	114.22 E
Chahanwusu → Dulan	102	36.16 N	98.28 E
Chahār Borjak	128	30.17 N	62.03 E
Chahār Deh-ye Ghowrband	120	34.59 N	68.44 E
Chahār Maḥāl va Bakhtīārī □ 4	128	32.00 N	51.00 E
Chahayang	89	48.24 N	124.15 E
Chahe, Zhg.	100	33.16 N	119.02 E
Chahe, Zhg.	102	33.48 N	97.22 E
Chahe, Zhg.	105	39.50 N	115.21 E
Chāh Gheybī, Hāmūn-e ≡	128	28.06 N	60.50 E
Chahuamiao	100	33.00 N	115.56 E
Chahuites	234	16.17 N	94.11 W
Chai ≃	104	42.20 N	123.52 E
Chai Badan	110	15.04 N	101.05 E
Chāībāsa	124	22.34 N	85.49 E
Chaigou	98	36.15 N	119.36 E
Chaihe	89	44.47 N	129.42 E
Chaijiawan	100	29.10 N	113.06 E
Chaillé-les-Marais	32	46.24 N	1.01 W
Chailley	50	48.05 N	3.42 E
Chailly-en-Bière	50	48.28 N	2.35 E
Chai Nat	110	15.11 N	100.08 E
Chainhurst	260	51.12 N	0.29 E
Chain O'Lakes State Park ♦, Il., U.S.	216	42.27 N	88.11 W
Chain O'Lakes State Park ♦, In., U.S.	216	41.20 N	85.26 W
Chainpur	124	23.08 N	84.15 E
Chaipudyrskaja guba c	24	68.30 N	59.30 E
Chaiqiao	100	29.51 N	121.56 E
Chairel, Laguna de c	234	22.17 N	97.57 W
Chaishudian	105	40.46 N	116.30 E
Chaiši	84	42.57 N	42.12 E
Chait	85	39.11 N	70.53 E
Chaital	126	22.31 N	88.47 E
Chaitén	254	42.55 S	72.43 W
Chaiwopu	86	43.33 N	87.59 E
Chaiya	110	9.23 N	99.14 E
Chaiyaphum	110	15.48 N	102.02 E
Chajarí	252	30.46 S	57.59 W
Chajdarken	85	39.57 N	71.21 E
Chajia	107	29.37 N	104.27 E
Chajian	100	32.40 N	118.46 E
Chajianling	98	39.14 N	114.36 E
Chajiaqiao	100	34.00 N	120.07 E
Chajrchan	88	48.35 N	101.56 E
Chajrchandulaan	102	45.57 N	102.03 E
Chajul	236	15.30 N	91.02 W
Chaka	154	4.49 N	31.14 E
Chakachamna Lake ⊜	180	61.13 N	152.35 W
Chakāltor	126	23.14 N	86.22 E
Chak Amru	123	32.22 N	75.11 E
Chakari	154	18.05 S	29.51 E
Chakaria	120	21.45 N	92.05 E
Chakarnaba	146	14.13 N	20.51 E
Chakasskaja Avtonomnaja Sovetskaja Socialističeskaja Respublika □ 3	86	53.00 N	90.00 E
Chākdaha, India	126	23.05 N	88.31 E
Chakdaha, India	272b	22.20 N	88.20 E
Chake Chake	154	5.15 S	39.46 E
Chakhānsūr	128	31.10 N	62.04 E
Chākia	124	26.25 N	85.03 E
Chakkarat	110	15.00 N	102.16 E
Chakou, Zhg.	98	38.03 N	113.36 E
Chakou, Zhg.	105	38.53 N	116.41 E
Chakradharpur	124	22.42 N	85.38 E
Chakrāta	120	30.42 N	77.51 E
Chāksu	120	26.36 N	75.57 E
Chākulia	126	22.29 N	86.43 E
Chakwadām	102	27.29 N	98.31 E
Chakwāl	123	32.56 N	72.52 E
Chal	272c	19.06 N	73.08 E
Chala	248	15.52 S	74.16 W
Chalabesa	154	11.22 S	31.01 E
Chalais	32	45.16 N	0.02 E
Chālakuda	122	10.18 N	76.20 E
Chalamont	58	46.00 N	5.10 E
Chalampé	58	47.49 N	7.33 E
Chalan Kanoa	174n	15.08 N	145.43 E
Chalatenango	236	14.03 N	88.56 W
Chalaua	154	16.06 S	39.11 E
Chalaux ≃	50	47.23 N	3.54 E
Chalaxung	102	34.10 N	97.44 E
Chalbi Desert ⬥ 2	154	3.00 N	37.20 E
Chalchgol	88	48.11 N	114.54 E
Chalchihuites	234	23.29 N	103.53 W
Chalchis Terara ∧	144	9.08 N	36.44 E
Chalchuapa	236	13.59 N	89.41 W
Chalchyn ≃	88	47.55 N	117.47 E
Chalcis → Khalkís	38	38.28 N	23.36 E
Chalco ≃	286a	19.19 N	99.08 W
Chaldan	84	40.43 N	47.15 E
Chaldon	260	51.17 N	0.07 W
Chaleine	261	48.36 N	1.43 E
Chalengkou	120	38.02 N	93.54 E
Châlette-sur-Loing	50	48.01 N	2.44 E
Chaleur Bay c	186	48.00 N	65.45 W
Chalfant	279b	40.25 N	79.52 W
Chalfant Run ≃	279b	40.25 N	79.48 W
Chalfont	208	40.17 N	75.13 W
Chalfont Common	260	51.38 N	0.33 W
Chalfonte	285	39.49 N	75.32 W
Chalfont Saint Giles	260	51.38 N	0.34 W
Chalfont Saint Peter	260	51.37 N	0.33 W
Chalford	42	51.45 N	2.09 W
Chalhuanca	248	14.17 S	73.15 W
Chalía ≃	254	49.35 S	69.34 W
Chalifert	261	48.53 N	2.46 E
Chalilovo	86	51.24 N	58.04 E
Chalindrey	58	47.48 N	5.26 E
Chaling	100	26.47 N	113.33 E
Chālisgaon	122	20.28 N	75.01 E
Chalisi	102	32.55 N	102.04 E
Chaliun	88	48.50 N	103.59 E
Chalk	260	51.26 N	0.25 E
Chalkabad	86	42.42 N	59.43 E
Chalk Draw ∨	196	29.36 N	103.15 W
Chalk River	190	46.01 N	77.27 W
Chalkyitsik	180	66.39 N	143.43 W
Challakere	122	14.19 N	76.39 E
Challans	32	46.51 N	1.53 W
Challapata	248	18.54 S	66.47 W
Challenge	226	39.29 N	121.13 W
Challenger, Mount ∧	224	48.50 N	121.20 W
Challenger Deep ✣ 1	14	11.21 N	142.12 E
Challes-les-Eaux	62	45.33 N	5.59 E
Challis	202	44.30 N	114.13 W
Challviri, Salar de ≡	248	22.32 S	67.34 W
Chal'mer-Ju	24	67.58 N	64.50 E
Chalmers	216	40.39 N	86.52 W
Chalmette	194	29.56 N	89.57 W
Chalone Creek ≃	226	36.21 N	121.14 W
Chalonnes-sur-Loire	32	47.21 N	0.46 W
Châlons-sur-Marne	50	48.57 N	4.22 E
Chalon-sur-Saône	58	46.47 N	4.51 E
Chalosse ⬥ 1	32	43.45 N	0.30 W
Chalt	123	36.15 N	74.20 E
Chaltel, Cerro (Monte Fitzroy) ∧	254	49.17 S	73.05 W
Chalturin	80	58.33 N	48.50 E
Chalturino	78	49.31 N	35.17 E
Chaluhe	89	43.43 N	126.00 E
Châlus, Fr.	32	45.39 N	0.59 E
Chālūs, Īrān	128	36.38 N	51.26 E
Cham, Dtsch.	60	49.13 N	12.41 E
Cham, Schw.	58	47.11 N	8.28 E
Chama	200	36.54 N	106.34 W
Chama ≃	246	9.03 N	71.40 W
Chama, Rio ≃	200	36.03 N	106.05 W
Chamah, Gunong ∧	114	5.13 N	101.33 E
Chamaicó	252	35.03 S	64.58 W
Chamama	154	12.55 S	33.43 E
Chamamat'urt	84	43.36 N	46.30 E
Chaman	120	30.55 N	66.27 E
Chamangonge	152	11.16 S	20.24 E
Chamao, Khao ∧	110	12.57 N	101.45 E
Chamarande	261	48.31 N	2.13 E
Chamar-Daban, chrebet ⩘	88	51.15 N	105.00 E
Chāmārpāra	272b	22.35 N	88.08 E
Chamaya ≃	248	5.44 S	78.39 W
Chamb ≃	60	49.13 N	12.42 E
Chamba, India	123	32.34 N	76.08 E
Chamba, Moç.	154	12.07 S	36.57 E
Chamba, Tan.	154	11.35 S	36.58 E
Chambal ≃	120	26.30 N	79.15 E
Chambaran, Plateau de ⩘ 1	62	45.15 N	5.15 E
Chambas	240p	22.12 N	78.55 W
Chamberlain, Sk., Can.	184	50.50 N	105.34 W
Chamberlain, S.D., U.S.	198	43.48 N	99.19 W
Chamberlain ≃	164	15.08 S	128.06 E
Chamberlain Lake ⊜	186	46.17 N	69.20 W
Chamberlin, Mount ∧	180	69.16 N	144.55 W
Chamberry, Ruisseau ≃	275a	45.20 N	73.58 W
Chambers, Az., U.S.	200	35.11 N	109.25 W
Chambers, Ne., U.S.	198	42.12 N	98.44 W
Chambers, N.Y., U.S.	210	42.16 N	76.57 W
Chambers □ 6	222	29.42 N	94.40 W
Chambers Brook ≃	276	40.35 N	74.41 W
Chambersburg, Il., U.S.	219	39.49 N	90.39 W
Chambersburg, In., U.S.	218	38.31 N	86.24 W
Chambersburg, Pa., U.S.	208	39.56 N	77.39 W
Chambers Corner	285	40.01 N	74.44 W
Chambers Creek ≃	222	31.58 N	96.10 W
Chambers Creek, North Fork ≃	222	32.16 N	96.58 W
Chambers Creek, South Fork ≃	222	32.16 N	96.58 W
Chambers Island I	190	45.11 N	87.21 W
Chambéry	62	45.34 N	5.56 E
Chambeshi ≃	154	11.21 S	30.37 E
Chambi, Jebel ∧	148	35.11 N	8.42 E
Chambira ≃, Perú	246	3.55 S	73.45 W
Chambira ≃, Perú	246	4.28 S	74.50 W
Chamblee	192	33.53 N	84.17 W
Chambley-Bussières	56	49.03 N	5.54 E
Chambly, P.Q., Can.	206	45.27 N	73.17 W
Chambly, Fr.	50	49.10 N	2.15 E
Chambly □ 6	206	45.30 N	73.20 W
Chambly, Bassin de ⊜	206	45.27 N	73.17 W
Chambly, Canal de ≅	275a	45.25 N	73.15 W
Chambois	50	48.48 N	0.07 E
Chambon-sur-Dolore	62	45.30 N	3.37 E
Chambon-sur-Voueize	32	46.11 N	2.25 E
Chambord, Château de ⊥	50	47.37 N	1.31 E
Chambourcy	261	48.54 N	2.03 E
Chambri Lake ⊜	164	4.16 S	143.08 E
Chambry	261	49.00 N	2.54 E
Chamburi Kalāt	128	26.09 N	64.43 E
Chamdo → Qamdo	102	31.11 N	97.15 E
Chāme, Nepāl	124	28.33 N	84.15 E
Chame, Pan.	236	8.35 N	79.53 W
Chame, Punta ›	236	8.39 N	79.42 W
Chamela	234	19.32 N	105.05 W
Chamelecón	236	15.24 N	88.01 W
Chamelecón ≃	236	15.51 N	87.49 W
Chamical	252	30.21 S	66.19 W
Chamizo	258	34.10 S	56.41 W
Chamizo, Arroyo ≃	258	34.15 S	56.44 W
Chamkanī	120	33.48 N	69.49 E
Chāmlūjā ≃	124	29.38 N	80.24 E
Chamo, Lake ⊜	144	5.50 N	37.33 E
Chamois, It.	62	45.50 N	7.37 E
Chamois, Mo., U.S.	219	38.40 N	91.46 W
Chamojie	89	49.25 N	124.45 E
Chamoli	124	30.24 N	79.21 E
Chamonix-Mont-Blanc	58	45.55 N	6.52 E
Chamousset	62	45.33 N	6.12 E
Chamoux-sur-Gelon	62	45.32 N	6.13 E
Chāmpa	124	22.03 N	82.39 E
Champagne, Yk., Can.	180	60.47 N	136.29 W
Champagne, Fr.	62	45.16 N	4.48 E
Champagne □ 9	32	49.00 N	4.30 E
Champagne Castle ∧	158	29.06 S	29.20 E
Champagne-en-Valromay	58	45.54 N	5.41 E
Champagner-Berg ∧ 2	264a	52.31 N	13.05 E
Champagne-sur-Seine	50	48.24 N	2.48 E
Champagney	58	47.42 N	6.41 E
Champagnole	58	46.45 N	5.55 E
Champagny	62	45.27 N	6.42 E
Chāmpāhāti	126	22.23 N	88.29 E
Champaign	194	40.06 N	88.14 W
Champaign □ 6, Il., U.S.	216	40.07 N	88.12 W
Champaign □ 6, Oh., U.S.	218	40.07 N	83.45 W
Champapur	126	24.02 N	86.31 E
Champaquí, Cerro ∧	252	31.59 S	64.56 W
Champasak	110	14.53 N	105.52 E
Champāwat	124	29.20 N	80.06 E
Champcueil	261	48.31 N	2.27 E
Champdāni	126	22.48 N	88.21 E
Champdeniers	32	46.29 N	0.24 W
Champdepraz	62	45.41 N	7.39 E
Champdeuil	261	48.37 N	2.44 E
Champdor	58	46.01 N	5.36 E
Champdoré, Lac ⊜	176	55.55 N	65.49 W
Champeaux	50	48.35 N	2.48 E
Champeix	32	45.36 N	3.08 E
Champerico	236	14.18 N	91.55 W
Champéry	58	46.10 N	6.52 E
Champex	58	46.02 N	7.07 E
Champier	62	45.27 N	5.17 E
Champigneulles	56	48.44 N	6.10 E
Champigny-sur-Marne	261	48.49 N	2.31 E
Champion, Ab., Can.	182	50.14 N	113.09 W
Champion, Mi., U.S.	190	46.30 N	87.57 W
Champion, Oh., U.S.	214	41.17 N	80.51 W
Champion, Pa., U.S.	214	40.05 N	79.21 W
Champions	222	29.59 N	95.31 W
Champlain	206	44.59 N	73.26 W
Champlain □ 6	206	46.45 N	72.35 W
Champlain ≃	206	46.27 N	72.17 W
Champlain, Lake ⊜	188	44.45 N	73.15 W
Champlain, Pont ⬥ 5	206	45.28 N	73.32 W
Champlain Canal ≅	210	43.20 N	73.34 W
Champlan	261	48.43 N	2.16 E
Champlin Creek ≃	276	40.43 N	73.12 W
Champlitte-et-le-Prélot	58	47.37 N	5.31 E
Champlon	56	50.07 N	5.28 E
Champoluc	62	45.50 N	7.44 E
Champotón	232	19.21 N	90.43 W
Champrond-en-Gâtine	50	48.24 N	1.05 E
Champs	50	47.44 N	3.36 E
Champs-sur-Marne	261	48.51 N	2.36 E
Chāmpua	124	22.05 N	85.40 E
Champvans	58	47.06 N	5.26 E
Chāmrāil	272b	22.38 N	88.18 E
Chāmrājnagar Rāmasamudram	122	11.55 N	76.57 E
Chamrousse	62	45.08 N	5.52 E
Chamsara ≃	88	52.42 N	95.46 E
Chamusca	34	39.21 N	8.29 W
Chamza Chakimzada	85	40.26 N	71.30 E
Chana	110	6.55 N	100.44 E
Chanabadskij	85	40.49 N	72.58 E
Chanakyapuri □ 9	272a	28.36 N	77.11 E
Chañar	252	30.32 S	65.58 W
Chañaral	252	26.21 S	70.37 W
Chañaral, Isla I	252	29.02 S	71.35 W
Chanas	62	45.18 N	4.49 E
Chānasma	120	23.43 N	72.07 E
Chanbogd	102	43.12 N	107.10 E
Chancay	248	11.35 S	77.16 W
Chancay ≃	248	11.37 S	77.15 W
Chance	208	38.10 N	75.56 W
Chanceaux	58	47.31 N	4.42 E
Chanceaux-sur-Choisille	50	47.28 N	0.42 E
Chanch	88	51.30 N	100.40 E
Chanchelulla Peak ∧	204	40.28 N	122.59 W
Chanchiang → Zhanjiang	102	21.16 N	110.28 E
Chanchöchij uul ⩘	88	49.30 N	94.30 E
Chanchongor	102	43.50 N	104.25 E
Chanco	252	35.44 S	72.32 W
Chancy	58	46.08 N	6.00 E
Chanda	88	55.00 N	107.14 E
Chanda ≃	88	55.00 N	107.14 E
Chāndābila	126	22.05 N	87.00 E
Chanda → Chandrapur	122	19.57 N	79.18 E
Chandagajty	86	50.44 N	92.03 E
Chandalar	180	67.30 N	148.30 W
Chandalar ≃	180	66.36 N	145.48 W
Chandalar, East Fork ≃	180	67.05 N	147.16 W
Chandalar, Middle Fork ≃	180	67.10 N	148.19 W
Chandalar, North Fork ≃	180	67.10 N	148.19 W
Chandan Chauki	124	28.33 N	80.47 E
Chandankiāri	126	23.34 N	86.22 E
Chandannagar	126	22.51 N	88.21 E
Chandanpratāp	126	23.33 N	89.24 E
Chāndar	126	23.54 N	89.58 E
Chandausi	124	28.27 N	78.46 E
Chāndbāli	120	20.47 N	86.46 E
Chandeleur Islands II	194	29.48 N	88.51 W
Chandeleur Sound Ʉ	194	29.55 N	89.10 W
Chanderi	124	24.43 N	78.08 E
Chandernagore → Chandannagar	126	22.51 N	88.21 E
Chandīgarh	123	30.44 N	76.55 E
Chandīgarh □ 8	123	30.45 N	76.50 E
Chāndil	124	22.58 N	86.03 E
Chandīpur	126	23.59 N	89.01 E
Chanditala	272b	22.41 N	88.16 E
Chandla	124	25.05 N	80.12 E
Chandler, P.Q., Can.	186	48.21 N	64.41 W
Chandler, Az., U.S.	200	33.18 N	111.50 W
Chandler, In., U.S.	194	38.02 N	87.22 W
Chandler, Ok., U.S.	196	35.42 N	96.52 W
Chandler, Tx., U.S.	222	32.18 N	95.29 W
Chandler ≃	180	69.27 N	151.30 W
Chandler, Mount ∧ 2	162	27.00 S	133.20 E
Chandler Lake ⊜	180	68.15 N	152.43 W
Chandler Park ♦	281	42.24 N	82.58 W
Chandler's Cross	260	51.40 N	0.27 W
Chandler's Ford	42	50.59 N	1.23 W
Chandlers Valley	214	41.56 N	79.18 W
Chandlerville	219	40.02 N	90.09 W
Chandless ≃	248	9.08 S	69.51 W
Chāndor Hills ⩘ 2	122	20.30 N	74.00 E
Chandos Lake ⊜	212	44.49 N	78.00 W
Chāndpara	126	22.58 N	88.47 E
Chāndpur, Bngl.	120	22.08 N	91.55 E
Chāndpur, Bngl.	124	23.13 N	90.39 E
Chāndpur, India	124	29.09 N	78.16 E
Chāndpur ⬥ 8	272a	28.45 N	77.01 E
Chāndra	126	22.28 N	87.09 E
Chandrabhāga ≃	123	32.59 N	76.25 E
Chandra Dighalia	126	23.04 N	89.46 E
Chandrakona	126	22.44 N	87.31 E
Chandrakona Road	126	22.44 N	87.21 E
Chandrapur	122	19.57 N	79.18 E
Chāndvad	122	20.20 N	74.15 E
Chandyga	74	62.40 N	135.36 E
Chanfang	105	39.56 N	115.55 E
Chang (Yangtze) ≃, Zhg.	90	31.48 N	121.10 E
Chang ≃, Zhg.	100	26.53 N	119.41 E
Chang ≃, Zhg.	100	28.59 N	116.42 E
Chang, Ko I	110	12.05 N	102.20 E
Changa	84	44.27 N	50.36 E
Changaj	88	47.52 N	99.28 E
Changajn nuruu ⩘	90	47.30 N	100.00 E
Changal	88	49.19 N	104.24 E
Changalane	156	26.17 S	32.11 E
Chang'an	102	26.00 N	109.34 E
Changanācheri	122	9.28 N	76.33 E
Changane ≃	156	24.43 S	33.32 E
Changan → Xi'an	102	34.15 N	108.52 E
Chang'anzhen	106	30.28 N	120.27 E
Changara	154	16.54 S	33.14 E
Changarul'skij chrebet ⩘	88	51.10 N	103.00 E
Changbai	98	41.26 N	128.11 E
Changbai Shan ⩘	98	41.40 N	128.00 E
Changbu	100	23.48 N	115.26 E
Changcaocun	105	39.49 N	115.47 E
Changchaoling	106	31.00 N	119.40 E
Changcheng, Zhg.	100	31.49 N	116.54 E
Changcheng, Zhg.	110	19.24 N	108.42 E
Chang Cheng (Great Wall) ⊥	98	40.30 N	116.30 E
Chang Chenmo ≃	120	34.17 N	78.19 E
Changchiak'ou → Zhangjiakou	105	40.50 N	114.53 E
Ch'angchih → Changzhi	102	36.11 N	113.08 E
Changchou → Zhangzhou	100	24.33 N	117.39 E
Changchow → Changzhou	106	31.47 N	119.57 E
Changchun	89	43.53 N	125.19 E
Changchunling	89	45.22 N	125.28 E
Changdan	98	37.56 N	126.45 E
Changdang Hu ⊜	106	31.35 N	119.35 E
Changdao (Sihou)	98	37.56 N	120.42 E
Changde	102	29.02 N	111.41 E
Changdian	105	40.01 N	116.32 E
Ch'angdo	98	38.30 N	127.40 E
Ch'ang-dong	98	39.03 N	126.34 E
Change Islands	186	49.40 N	54.25 W
Changeon ≃	50	47.16 N	0.05 E
Changfeng	100	32.27 N	117.09 E
Changgang	100	24.38 N	113.05 E
Changgangzi	104	41.26 N	122.41 E
Changge	100	34.15 N	113.50 E
Changgi-ap ›	98	36.05 N	129.34 E
Changgi-li	271b	37.35 N	126.44 E
Changgi-ri	271b	37.38 N	126.41 E
Changgou	105	39.34 N	115.53 E
Changgouyu	105	39.44 N	115.52 E
Changguandian	100	32.58 N	115.16 E
Changguowei	100	29.15 N	121.56 E
Changgye-ri	98	34.33 N	126.49 E
Changgyong Palace ʋ	271b	37.36 N	127.00 E
Changhai	98	39.18 N	122.35 E
Chang-hai → Shanghai	106	31.14 N	121.28 E
Changhang	98	36.01 N	126.40 E
Changhe	106	30.11 N	120.11 E
Changhowŏn	98	37.08 N	127.39 E
Chang Hu ⊜	100	30.15 N	112.35 E
Changhua, T'aiwan	100	24.05 N	120.32 E
Changhua, Zhg.	100	30.11 N	119.13 E
Changhŭng	98	34.41 N	126.52 E
Changhŭng-ni	98	40.24 N	128.19 E
Changi	271c	1.23 N	103.59 E
Changi, Tanjong ›	271c	1.23 N	104.00 E
Changi International Airport ⊠	271c	1.22 N	103.59 E
Changi Prison ʋ	271c	1.22 N	103.58 E
Changji	86	44.01 N	87.19 E
Changjiang, Zhg.	100	25.19 N	113.56 E
Changjiang, Zhg.	110	19.17 N	109.02 E
Changjiangbu	100	30.52 N	113.43 E
Changjiapuzi	104	40.51 N	123.43 E
Changjiazhuang	105	40.35 N	115.24 E
Changjie	100	29.16 N	121.40 E
Changjing	106	31.45 N	120.29 E
Changjin-gang ≃	98	41.24 N	127.45 E
Changjin-ŭp	98	40.23 N	127.15 E
Changkai	100	28.04 N	116.18 E
Changkalajier	85	40.09 N	76.59 E
Changkeng	106	30.19 N	121.57 E
Changkiakow → Zhangjiakou	105	40.50 N	114.53 E
Changlapod Pass)(	124	30.08 N	87.06 E
Changle, Zhg.	98	36.42 N	118.49 E
Changle, Zhg.	100	29.25 N	120.37 E
Changle, Zhg.	100	26.00 N	119.31 E
Changlejie	100	28.52 N	113.19 E
Changleqiao	106	30.21 N	119.51 E
Changlezhen	106	31.56 N	121.15 E
Changli, Zhg.	98	36.57 N	119.45 E
Changli, Zhg.	98	39.43 N	119.11 E
Changling	89	44.15 N	123.58 E
Changlingfeng	105	40.11 N	118.24 E
Changlingji	100	32.30 N	114.54 E
Changlingzi, Zhg.	98	39.47 N	122.43 E
Changlingzi, Zhg.	98	39.33 N	121.19 E
Changlinhe	100	31.40 N	117.29 E
Changlun	114	6.26 N	100.26 E
Changmar	120	34.15 N	79.45 E
Changmong-ni	98	34.58 N	128.41 E
Changning, Zhg.	102	26.19 N	112.21 E
Changning, Zhg.	102	24.55 N	99.35 E
Changning (Anningqiao), Zhg.	102	28.21 N	104.53 E
Changning, Zhg.	105	39.59 N	114.55 E
Ch'angnyŏng	98	35.33 N	128.29 E
Changnyŏn-ni	98	38.37 N	125.16 E
Changokurt	72	61.58 N	64.18 E
Ch'angpin	100	23.19 N	121.27 E
Changping	105	40.14 N	116.14 E
Changputong	102	28.05 N	98.29 E
Ch'angp'yŏng-dong	98	41.27 N	127.31 E
Changqiao, Zhg.	100	24.15 N	117.39 E
Changqiao, Zhg.	100	26.49 N	118.50 E
Changqing	98	36.34 N	116.43 E
Changsa	102	19.51 N	110.53 E
Changsan-got ›	98	38.08 N	124.39 E
Changsha, Zhg.	100	28.12 N	112.58 E
Changsha, Zhg.	100	24.13 N	116.07 E
Changshaba Shuiku ⊜ 1	107	29.42 N	104.40 E
Changshageng	107	30.00 N	104.35 E
Changshan, Zhg.	98	36.54 N	117.50 E
Changshan, Zhg.	100	28.55 N	118.30 E
Changshan, Zhg.	107	29.30 N	104.13 E
Changshan ≃	100	28.57 N	118.50 E
Changshan Qundao II	98	39.00 N	122.45 E
Changsheng	100	26.16 N	116.01 E
Changshengqiao	107	29.31 N	106.39 E
Changshitai	104	42.33 N	120.43 E
Changshitou	102	35.03 N	99.11 E
Changshou	102	29.51 N	107.06 E
Changshoudian	100	31.26 N	112.35 E
Changshoujie	100	28.44 N	113.57 E
Changshu	106	31.39 N	120.45 E
Changshui	102	34.21 N	111.29 E
Changsŏng	98	35.20 N	126.49 E
Changsŏng-ni	98	40.58 N	127.04 E
Changsu	98	35.40 N	127.32 E
Changtai, Zhg.	100	24.40 N	117.46 E
Changtai, Zhg.	100	28.34 N	118.37 E
Changtai, Zhg.	104	41.34 N	122.00 E
Changtancun	104	41.33 N	123.02 E
Ch'angte → Changde	102	29.02 N	111.41 E
Changteh → Anyang	98	36.06 N	114.21 E
Changting, Zhg.	89	44.32 N	128.47 E
Changting, Zhg.	100	25.52 N	116.20 E
Changtumiao	102	43.30 N	114.34 E
Changuinola	236	9.25 N	82.32 W
Changuinola ≃	236	9.28 N	82.27 W
Changwu, Zhg.	89	46.00 N	125.36 E
Changwu, Zhg.	102	35.09 N	107.42 E
Changxindianzhen	105	39.49 N	116.12 E
Changxing	106	31.01 N	119.54 E
Changxing Dao I, Zhg.	98	39.34 N	121.23 E
Changxing Dao I, Zhg.	106	31.24 N	121.42 E
Changxingdian, Zhg.	104	41.27 N	121.44 E
Changxingdian, Zhg.	104	41.33 N	123.23 E
Changxingzhen	104	41.40 N	122.14 E
Changxuanling	100	31.08 N	114.20 E
Changyi	98	36.51 N	119.23 E
Changyŏn	98	38.15 N	125.06 E
Changyuan	98	35.13 N	114.39 E
Changyukou	105	40.46 N	115.08 E
Changzhi	102	36.11 N	113.08 E
Changzhou (Changchow)	106	31.47 N	119.57 E
Chanhanga	152	16.04 S	14.07 E
Chanh Hung	269c	10.44 N	106.41 E
Chani	88	57.05 N	120.58 E
Chani ≃	88	57.02 N	120.59 E
Chanino	76	54.13 N	36.37 E
Chanka, ozero (Xingkai Hu) ⊜	89	45.00 N	132.24 E
Chankiang → Zhanjiang	102	21.16 N	110.28 E
Chankou	102	35.52 N	104.27 E
Chanlar	84	40.34 N	46.20 E
Channagiri	122	14.02 N	75.56 E
Channahon	216	41.26 N	88.14 W
Channapatna	122	12.39 N	77.13 E
Channel Country ⬥ 1	166	24.45 S	141.00 E
Channel Islands II, Europe	43b	49.20 N	2.20 W
Channel Islands II, Ca., U.S.	204	33.30 N	119.15 W
Channel Islands National Park ♦	204	33.28 N	119.02 W
Channel Lake	216	42.29 N	88.08 W
Channel-Port-aux-Basques	186	47.34 N	59.09 W
Channelview	222	29.46 N	95.06 W
Channing, Mi., U.S.	190	46.08 N	88.05 W
Channing, Tx., U.S.	196	35.41 N	102.20 W
Chānpādānga	126	22.50 N	87.58 E
Chantada	34	42.37 N	7.46 W
Chantajskoje, ozero ⊜	74	68.20 N	91.00 E
Chantajskoje vodochranilišče ⊜ 1	72	68.00 N	88.00 E
Chantang	100	33.41 N	117.37 E
Chantau	86	44.13 N	73.51 E
Chanteloup	261	48.51 N	2.44 E
Chanteloup-les-Vignes	261	48.59 N	2.02 E
Chanthaburi	110	12.36 N	102.09 E
Chantilly	50	49.12 N	2.28 E
Chantonnay	32	46.41 N	1.03 W
Chantraine	58	48.10 N	6.26 E
Chantrans	58	47.03 N	6.09 E
Chantrey Inlet c	176	67.48 N	96.20 W
Chanty-Mansijsk	74	61.00 N	69.06 E
Chanty-Mansijskij Avtonomnyj Okrug □ 8	86	60.15 N	70.45 E
Chanujn ≃	88	49.22 N	102.22 E
Chanumla	110	8.19 N	93.05 E
Chanute	198	37.40 N	95.27 W
Chanute Air Force Base ■	216	40.18 N	88.09 W
Chanuwāla	123	32.44 N	73.08 E
Chanžonkovo	83	48.06 N	38.06 E
Chao ≃	105	40.36 N	117.08 E
Chao, Isla I	248	8.45 S	78.47 W
Chao'an	100	23.41 N	116.38 E
Chaobai ≃	105	39.48 N	117.08 E
Chaobai Xinhe ≃	105	39.37 N	117.26 E
Chaocheng	98	36.05 N	115.35 E
Ch'aochou	100	22.33 N	120.32 E
Ch'aochou → Chao'an	100	23.41 N	116.38 E
Chao Hu ⊜	100	31.31 N	117.33 E
Chaomidian	105	39.04 N	117.01 E
Chao Phraya ≃	110	13.32 N	100.36 E
Chaor ≃	89	46.48 N	123.37 E
Chaoshui, Zhg.	89	49.44 N	127.21 E
Chaoshui, Zhg.	98	37.42 N	120.55 E
Chaouen	148	35.10 N	5.16 W
Chaouen □ 4	148	35.15 N	5.00 W
Chaource	50	48.04 N	4.08 E
Chaoxian	100	31.36 N	117.52 E
Chaoyang, Zhg.	89	44.34 N	126.20 E
Chaoyang, Zhg.	100	23.17 N	116.37 E
Chaoyang, Zhg.	104	41.35 N	120.28 E
Chaoyangchuan	98	42.54 N	129.21 E
Chaoyangcun	89	50.02 N	124.16 E
Chaoyanggou	104	42.07 N	121.04 E
Chaoyangpo	89	43.37 N	124.42 E
Chaoyangshan	89	43.02 N	125.40 E
Chaozhuang	98	34.18 N	114.56 E
Chapada dos Guimarães	248	15.26 S	55.45 W
Chapada dos Veadeiros, Parque Nacional da ♦	255	13.58 S	47.30 W
Chapadinha	250	3.44 S	43.21 W
Chapala	234	20.18 N	103.12 W
Chapala, Laguna de ⊜	234	20.15 N	103.00 W
Chapare ≃, Bol.	248	15.58 S	64.42 W
Chapare ≃, Bol.	248	16.25 S	64.35 W
Chapareillan	62	45.28 N	5.58 E
Chāparmukh	120	26.12 N	92.32 E
Chaparra, Bahía de c	240p	21.13 N	76.31 W
Chaparral	246	3.43 N	75.28 W
Chapčeranga	88	49.42 N	112.24 E
Chapeauroux	62	44.50 N	3.44 E
Chapecó	252	27.06 S	52.36 W
Chapel-en-le-Frith	262	53.20 N	1.54 W
Chapelfell Top ∧	44	54.41 N	2.13 W
Chapelhall	46	55.50 N	3.56 W
Chapel Hill, De., U.S.	285	39.42 N	75.44 W
Chapel Hill, N.C., U.S.	192	35.54 N	79.03 W
Chapel Hill, Tn., U.S.	194	35.37 N	86.41 W
Chapel Hill Channel Ʉ	276	40.32 N	74.02 W
Chapelle Creek ≃	198	44.16 N	99.55 W
Chapellerie	261	49.02 N	2.26 E
Chapel Oaks	284c	38.54 N	76.55 W
Chapel Point ›	42	50.16 N	4.46 W
Chapel Saint Leonards	44	53.13 N	0.19 E
Chapelton	241q	18.05 N	77.16 W
Chapeltown, Eng., U.K.	44	53.28 N	1.28 W
Chapeltown, Eng., U.K.	262	53.38 N	2.24 W
Chapet	261	48.58 N	1.56 E
Chapéu, Morro do ∧	255	14.55 S	42.31 W
Chapéu, Ribeirão do ≃	256	23.14 S	45.18 W
Chapicuy	252	31.39 S	57.54 W
Chapimarca	248	13.58 S	73.04 W
Chapin	219	39.46 N	90.24 W
Chapin, Lake ⊜	216	41.56 N	86.21 W
Chaplain, Lake ⊜ 1	224	47.57 N	121.51 W
Chapleau	190	47.50 N	83.24 W
Chapleau ≃	190	48.29 N	82.57 W
Chapleau, Lac ⊜	206	46.14 N	74.57 W
Chaplin, Sk., Can.	184	50.28 N	106.40 W
Chaplin, Ct., U.S.	207	41.47 N	72.07 W
Chaplin ≃	194	37.50 N	85.11 W
Chaplin Lake ⊜	184	50.18 N	106.35 W
Chapman, Ks., U.S.	198	38.58 N	97.01 W
Chapman, Ne., U.S.	198	41.01 N	98.09 W
Chapman, Pa., U.S.	208	40.46 N	75.24 W
Chapman, Cape ›	176	69.12 N	88.59 W
Chapman, Mount ∧	182	51.50 N	118.20 W
Chapman College ʋ 2	280	33.47 N	117.51 W
Chapman Creek ≃	198	38.58 N	97.00 W
Chapman Lake ⊜	184	56.58 N	98.12 W
Chapman's (Okwa) ≃	156	22.30 S	23.00 E
Chapmanville	188	37.58 N	82.01 W
Chapman Woods	280	34.08 N	118.05 W
Chapo	196	29.17 N	104.20 W
Chaponval	261	49.04 N	2.09 E
Chappaqua	210	41.09 N	73.45 W
Chappell	198	41.05 N	102.28 W
Chappell Hill	222	30.09 N	96.16 W
Chāpra	126	23.32 N	88.33 E
Chapry	83	47.14 N	39.31 E
Chaptico Bay c	208	38.21 N	76.49 W
Chapultepec, Méx.	204	31.50 N	116.38 W
Chapultepec, Méx.	204	32.22 N	115.05 W
Chapultepec, Bosque de ♦	286a	19.25 N	99.12 W
Chapultepec, Castillo de ⊥	286a	19.25 N	99.11 W

≃	River	Fluß	Río	Rivière	Rio
≅	Canal	Kanal	Canal	Canal	Canal
∟	Waterfall, Rapids	Wasserfall, Stromschnellen	Cascada, Rápidos	Chute d'eau, Rapides	Cascata, Rápidos
Ʉ	Strait	Meeresstraße	Estrecho	Détroit	Estreito
c	Bay, Gulf	Bucht, Golf	Bahía, Golfo	Baie, Golfe	Baía, Golfo
⊜	Lake, Lakes	See, Seen	Lago, Lagos	Lac, Lacs	Lago, Lagos
≡	Swamp	Sumpf	Pantano	Marais	Pântano
⍓	Ice Features, Glacier	Eis- und Gletscherformen	Accidentes Glaciales	Formes glaciaires	Acidentes glaciares
⍑	Other Hydrographic Features	Andere Hydrographische Objekte	Otros Elementos Hidrográficos	Autres données hydrographiques	Outros acidentes hidrográficos

✣	Submarine Features	Untermeerische Objekte	Accidentes Submarinos	Formes de relief sous-marin	Acidentes submarinos
□	Political Unit	Politische Einheit	Unidad Politica	Entité politique	Unidade política
ʋ	Cultural Institution	Kulturelle Institution	Institución Cultural	Institution culturelle	Instituição cultural
⊥	Historical Site	Historische Stätte	Sitio Histórico	Site historique	Sitio histórico
♦	Recreational Site	Erholungs- und Ferienort	Sitio de Recreo	Centre de loisirs	Area de Lazer
⊠	Airport	Flughafen	Aeropuerto	Aéroport	Aeroporto
■	Military Installation	Militäranlage	Instalación Militar	Installation militaire	Instalação militar
⬥	Miscellaneous	Verschiedenes	Misceláneo	Divers	Diversos

Name	Page	Lat. °′	Long. °′
Chá Pungana	152	13.44 S	18.39 E
Chaqui	248	19.36 S	65.32 W
Chaquiago	252	27.32 S	66.21 W
Char ≃	42	50.44 N	2.53 W
Char ⩒[4]	148	21.31 N	12.51 W
Charaa ≃	88	49.38 N	105.49 E
Charabali	80	47.24 N	47.16 E
Chara-Chužar	88	52.30 N	99.39 E
Charadai	252	27.38 S	59.54 W
Charagua	248	19.48 S	63.13 W
Charagun	88	51.36 N	111.05 E
Char-Ajrag	102	45.49 N	109.17 E
Charal	88	51.58 N	96.39 E
Charalá	246	6.17 N	73.10 W
Charām	128	30.45 N	50.44 E
Charaña	248	17.36 S	69.28 W
Charanor	88	50.05 N	116.40 E
Charanpur	126	23.45 N	87.02 E
Charapán	234	19.41 N	102.06 W
Charapucu, Ilha I	250	0.18 S	50.48 W
Charata	252	27.13 S	61.12 W
Charauz	88	52.16 N	106.17 E
Charavines-les-Bains	62	45.26 N	5.31 E
Charazani → Amarete	248	15.14 S	68.58 W
Charazargaj	88	52.57 N	104.41 E
Charbala	74	64.07 N	120.19 E
Char Bansi	126	22.59 N	90.43 E
Charbatovo	88	53.46 N	106.00 E
Charbon	170	32.54 S	149.58 E
Charcana	248	15.15 S	73.04 W
Charcas	234	23.08 N	101.07 W
Charco Azul, Bahía de ⊂	236	8.15 N	82.45 W
Charco Hondo	240m	18.25 N	66.43 W
Charcos de Figueroa	232	27.45 N	102.11 W
Charcos de Risa	232	26.15 N	103.10 W
Charcot Island I	9	69.45 S	75.15 W
Charcyzsk	83	48.02 N	38.09 E
Chard	42	50.53 N	2.58 W
Chardon	214	41.36 N	81.08 W
Charduār	120	26.52 N	92.46 E
Chardzhou → Čardžou	128	39.06 N	63.34 E
Charef, Oued V	148	34.07 N	2.05 W
Charente □[5]	32	45.40 N	0.10 E
Charente ≃	32	45.57 N	1.05 W
Charente-Maritime □[5]	32	45.30 N	0.45 W
Charenton-du-Cher	32	46.44 N	2.38 E
Charenton-le-Pont	261	48.49 N	2.25 E
Charentonne ≃	50	49.07 N	0.44 E
Charest ≃	206	46.36 N	72.14 W
Chārghāt	126	24.17 N	88.45 E
Char Hāim	126	23.04 N	90.38 E
Chari ≃	146	12.58 N	14.31 E
Chariāl Canal ≍	272b	22.28 N	88.11 E
Chari-Baguirmi □[5]	146	11.30 N	16.30 E
Charik	88	54.15 N	101.39 E
Chārīkār	120	35.01 N	69.11 E
Charing	42	51.13 N	0.48 E
Charing Cross	214	42.20 N	82.06 W
Charino, Ross.	76	59.57 N	43.44 E
Charino, Ross.	82	54.33 N	37.52 E
Charistvala	84	42.26 N	43.02 E
Chariton	190	41.00 N	93.18 W
Chariton ≃	194	39.19 N	92.57 W
Chariton, Mussel Fork ≃	194	39.24 N	92.55 W
Charitonovo, Ross.	24	61.27 N	47.28 E
Charitonovo, Ross.	82	56.52 N	36.44 E
Charity	246	7.24 N	58.36 W
Charkhāri	124	25.24 N	79.45 E
Charkhi Dādri	124	28.37 N	76.16 E
Char'kin	80	48.46 N	51.49 E
Charkop ◆[8]	272c	19.13 N	72.49 E
Char'kov (Kharkov)	78	50.00 N	36.15 E
Char'kov □[8]	83	49.42 N	37.10 E
Charkow → Char'kov	78	50.00 N	36.15 E
Char Lākhpur	126	24.04 N	90.40 E
Charland, Lac ⊜	206	46.52 N	74.11 W
Charlbury	42	51.53 N	1.29 W
Charl Cilliers	158	26.39 S	29.12 E
Charlemagne	206	45.43 N	73.29 W
Charlemont	207	42.37 N	72.52 W
Charleroi, Bel.	50	50.25 N	4.26 E
Charleroi, Pa., U.S.	214	40.08 N	79.53 W
Charleroi à Bruxelles, Canal de ≍	50	50.51 N	4.19 E
Charles □[6]	208	38.32 N	76.59 W
Charles ≃	207	42.22 N	71.03 W
Charles, Cape ›	208	37.08 N	75.58 W
Charles, Lake ⊜	278	42.15 N	87.58 W
Charles, Peak ∧	162	32.52 S	121.11 E
Charlesbourg	206	46.51 N	71.16 W
Charles Branch ≃	284c	38.47 N	76.48 W
Charles City, Ia., U.S.	190	43.03 N	92.40 W
Charles City, Va., U.S.	208	37.20 N	77.04 W
Charles City □[6]	208	37.20 N	77.02 W
Charles de Gaulle, Aéroport ⊠	50	49.01 N	2.33 E
Charles Island I	176	62.40 N	74.15 W
Charles Lee Tilden Regional Park ♦	282	37.54 N	122.15 W
Charles Mill Lake ⊜[1]	214	40.45 N	82.22 W
Charles Mound ∧[2]	190	42.30 N	90.14 W
Charles Point ›	164	12.23 S	130.36 E
Charles Sound ⊔	172	45.02 S	167.04 E
Charleston, Austl.	168b	34.55 S	138.54 E
Charleston, N.Z.	172	41.54 S	171.26 E
Charleston, Ar., U.S.	194	35.17 N	94.02 W
Charleston, Il., U.S.	194	39.29 N	88.10 W
Charleston, Ms., U.S.	194	34.00 N	90.03 W
Charleston, Mo., U.S.	194	36.55 N	89.21 W
Charleston, S.C., U.S.	192	32.46 N	79.55 W
Charleston, W.V., U.S.	188	38.20 N	81.37 W
Charleston Air Force Base ■	192	32.55 N	80.03 W
Charleston Lake ⊜	212	44.32 N	76.00 W
Charleston Peak ∧	204	36.16 N	115.42 W
Charlestown, Austl.	170	32.58 S	151.42 E
Charlestown, Ire.	48	53.57 N	8.49 W
Charlestown, St. K.-N.	238	17.08 N	62.37 W
Charlestown, S. Afr.	158	27.30 S	29.55 E
Charlestown, In., U.S.	218	38.27 N	85.40 W
Charlestown, Md., U.S.	208	39.34 N	75.58 W
Charlestown, N.H., U.S.	188	43.14 N	72.25 W
Charlestown, Pa., U.S.	285	40.06 N	75.33 W
Charlestown, R.I., U.S.	207	41.22 N	71.38 W
Charles Town, W.V., U.S.	188	39.17 N	77.51 W
Charlestown ◆[8]	283	42.23 N	71.04 W
Charlestown of Aberlour	46	57.28 N	3.14 W
Charlesworth	262	53.26 N	1.59 W
Charleville	166	26.24 S	146.15 E
Charleville-Mézières	56	49.46 N	4.43 E
Charleville → Ráth Luirc	48	52.21 N	8.41 W
Charlevoix	190	45.19 N	85.15 W
Charlevoix, Lake ⊜	190	45.15 N	85.08 W
Charley ≃	180	65.20 N	142.49 W
Charlie Bluff	216	42.50 N	88.58 W
Charlie Creek ≃	220	27.21 N	81.49 W
Charlie Lake	182	56.16 N	120.57 W
Charlieu	32	46.10 N	4.10 E
Charlotte, Mi., U.S.	216	42.33 N	84.50 W
Charlotte, N.C., U.S.	192	35.13 N	80.50 W
Charlotte, Tn., U.S.	194	36.10 N	87.20 W
Charlotte, Tx., U.S.	196	28.51 N	98.42 W
Charlotte □[6]	220	26.54 N	81.58 W
Charlotte Amalie	240m	18.21 N	64.56 W
Charlotte Court House	192	37.03 N	78.39 W
Charlotte Creek ≃	210	42.27 N	75.01 W
Charlotte Harbor	220	26.57 N	82.04 W
Charlotte Harbor ⊂	220	26.45 N	82.12 W
Charlotte Lake ⊜	182	52.11 N	125.20 W
Charlottenberg	26	59.53 N	12.17 E
Charlottenburg ◆[8]	264a	52.31 N	13.16 E
Charlottenburg, Schloss ⊥	264a	52.31 N	13.14 E
Charlottesburg Reservoir ⊜[1]	276	41.02 N	74.26 W
Charlottes Pass ♦	171b	36.25 S	145.20 E
Charlottesville, In., U.S.	218	39.47 N	85.36 W
Charlottesville, Va., U.S.	192	38.01 N	78.28 W
Charlottetown	186	46.14 N	63.08 W
Charlotteville	210	42.33 N	74.40 W
Charlovka	24	68.47 N	37.15 E
Charlton, Austl.	166	36.16 S	143.21 E
Charlton, Ma., U.S.	207	42.08 N	71.58 W
Charlton ◆[8]	260	51.29 N	0.02 E
Charlton City	207	42.08 N	71.59 W
Charlton Island I	176	52.00 N	79.30 W
Charlton Kings	42	51.53 N	2.03 W
Charlu	24	61.48 N	30.52 E
Charly-sur-Marne	50	48.58 N	3.17 E
Charm	214	40.30 N	81.47 W
Charmentray	261	48.57 N	2.47 E
Charmes	58	48.22 N	6.17 E
Charmes-sur-Rhône	62	44.52 N	4.50 E
Charmey	58	46.38 N	7.10 E
Charminster	42	50.43 N	2.28 W
Charmois-l'Orgueilleux	58	48.06 N	6.16 E
Charmont-en-Beauce	50	48.14 N	2.06 E
Charmouth	42	50.45 N	2.55 W
Charnay-lès-Mâcon	58	46.18 N	4.47 E
Charneca	266c	38.44 N	9.27 W
Charneca ◆[8]	266c	38.47 N	9.08 W
Charnley ≃	164	16.25 S	124.57 E
Charnock Richard	262	53.38 N	2.41 W
Char nuur ⊜, Mong.	88	48.20 N	96.05 E
Char nuur ⊜, Mong.	88	48.06 N	93.12 E
Charnwood Forest ◆[3]	42	52.43 N	1.15 W
Charny, P.Q., Can.	206	46.43 N	71.16 W
Charny, Fr.	50	47.53 N	3.06 E
Charny, Fr.	261	48.58 N	2.46 E
Charny-sur-Meuse	56	49.12 N	5.22 E
Charo	234	19.45 N	101.03 W
Charolles	32	46.26 N	4.17 E
Charouine	148	29.01 N	0.16 W
Charovsk	76	59.59 N	40.11 E
Charpi ≃	89	49.40 N	136.10 E
Charquemont	58	47.13 N	6.49 E
Charred Oak Estates	284c	39.00 N	77.10 W
Charrette Creek ≃	219	38.37 N	91.03 W
Charron Lake ⊜	184	52.45 N	95.15 W
Charroux	32	46.09 N	0.24 E
Chars	50	49.10 N	1.56 E
Chārsadda	123	34.09 N	71.44 E
Charter Oak, Ca., U.S.	280	34.06 N	117.52 W
Charter Oak, Ia., U.S.	198	42.04 N	95.35 W
Charters Towers	166	20.05 S	146.16 E
Charterwood	279b	40.33 N	80.00 W
Chartiers Creek ≃	214	40.28 N	80.03 W
Chartiers Run ≃, Pa., U.S.	279b	40.36 N	79.43 W
Chartiers Run ≃, Pa., U.S.	279b	40.15 N	80.12 W
Chartley	207	41.56 N	71.13 W
Chartres	50	48.27 N	1.30 E
Chartrettes	50	48.29 N	2.42 E
Chartridge	260	51.44 N	0.39 W
Chart Sutton	260	51.13 N	0.35 E
Chartwell ⊥	260	51.14 N	0.05 E
Char Us nuur ⊜	90	48.00 N	92.10 E
Charutajuvom	24	66.49 N	59.30 E
Chās	126	23.38 N	86.10 E
Chasav'urt	84	43.15 N	46.37 E
Chascomús	258	35.34 S	58.01 W
Chascomús, Laguna ⊜	258	35.36 S	58.01 W
Chašdala	85	39.42 N	67.07 E
Chase, B.C., Can.	182	50.49 N	119.41 W
Chase, Ak., U.S.	180	62.27 N	150.07 W
Chase, Ks., U.S.	198	38.21 N	98.20 W
Chase, Md., U.S.	208	39.21 N	76.22 W
Chase, Mount ∧	188	46.07 N	68.29 W
Chase Brook ≃	283	42.48 N	71.27 W
Chase City	192	36.47 N	78.27 W
Chase Field Naval Air Station ■	196	28.21 N	97.40 W
Chasefu	154	11.55 S	33.08 E
Chase Lake	212	43.46 N	75.19 W
Chase River	224	49.08 N	123.55 W
Chashma Barrage ◆[6]	123	32.26 N	71.23 E
Chasicó	254	40.18 S	68.58 W
Chasidaba	104	42.19 N	121.19 E
Chaska	190	44.47 N	93.36 W
Chaslands Mistake ›	172	46.38 S	169.22 E
Chasŏng	98	41.27 N	126.37 E
Chasŏngganggu	98	41.34 N	126.36 E
Chassahowitzka	220	28.43 N	82.34 W
Chassahowitzka Bay ⊂	220	28.41 N	82.40 W
Chassahowitzka Swamp ≡	220	28.38 N	82.37 W
Chasseron, Mont ∧	58	46.51 N	6.33 E
Chasse-sur-Rhône	62	45.34 N	4.49 E
Chassezac ≃	62	44.26 N	4.19 E
Chašuri	84	42.00 N	43.36 E
Chasurta	88	52.17 N	108.52 E
Chasuta	248	6.35 S	76.11 W
Chāt	128	37.59 N	55.16 E
Chatanbulag	102	43.09 N	109.08 E
Chatanga	74	71.58 N	102.30 E
Chatanga ≃	74	72.55 N	106.00 E
Chatangskij zaliv ⊂	74	73.30 N	109.00 E
Chatanika	180	65.07 N	147.31 W
Chatanika ≃	180	65.04 N	149.18 W
Château-Arnoux	62	44.06 N	6.00 E
Chateaubelair	241h	13.17 N	61.15 W
Châteaubriant	32	47.43 N	1.23 W
Château-Chinon	32	47.04 N	3.56 E
Château d'Oex	58	46.28 N	7.08 E
Château-du-Loir	50	47.42 N	0.25 E
Châteaudun	50	48.05 N	1.20 E
Châteaufort	261	48.44 N	2.06 E
Chateaugay	206	44.55 N	74.04 W
Château-Gontier	32	47.50 N	0.42 W
Châteauguay	206	45.23 N	73.45 W
Châteauguay □[6]	206	45.15 N	73.45 W
Châteauguay ≃	188	45.24 N	73.45 W
Châteauguay-Centre	206	45.21 N	73.45 W
Châteauguay Heights	275a	45.23 N	73.44 W
Château-Landon	50	48.09 N	2.42 E
Château-la-Vallière	50	47.33 N	0.19 E
Châteaulin	32	48.12 N	4.05 W
Châteaumeillant	32	46.34 N	2.12 E
Châteauneuf	62	43.23 N	5.10 E
Châteauneuf-de-Randon	62	44.39 N	3.40 E
Châteauneuf-du-Pape	62	44.03 N	4.50 E
Châteauneuf-du-Rhône	62	44.29 N	4.43 E
Châteauneuf-en-Thymerais	50	48.35 N	1.15 E
Châteauneuf-sur-Charente	32	45.36 N	0.03 W
Châteauneuf-sur-Loire	50	47.52 N	2.14 E
Châteauneuf-sur-Sarthe	32	47.41 N	0.30 W
Châteauneuf-Val-de-Bargis	50	47.17 N	3.14 E
Château-Porcien	50	49.32 N	4.15 E
Château-Queyras	62	44.45 N	6.47 E
Châteauredon	62	44.01 N	6.13 E
Châteaurenard, Fr.	50	47.56 N	2.56 E
Châteaurenard, Fr.	62	43.53 N	4.51 E
Château-Renault	50	47.35 N	0.55 E
Château-Richer	186	46.58 N	71.01 W
Châteauroux	32	46.49 N	1.42 E
Château-Salins	56	48.49 N	6.30 E
Château-Thierry	50	49.03 N	3.24 E
Châteauvillain	58	48.02 N	4.55 E
Châtel	58	46.17 N	6.50 E
Châtel-Censoir	50	47.31 N	3.38 E
Châtelet	50	50.24 N	4.31 E
Châtelineau	56	50.25 N	4.31 E
Châtellerault	32	46.49 N	0.33 E
Châtel-Saint-Denis	58	46.32 N	6.54 E
Châtel-sur-Moselle	58	48.18 N	6.24 E
Châtelus-Malvaleix	32	46.18 N	2.01 E
Châtenay-en-France	261	49.04 N	2.27 E
Châtenay-Malabry	261	48.46 N	2.17 E
Châtenois, Fr.	58	48.18 N	5.50 E
Châtenois, Fr.	58	48.16 N	7.24 E
Châtenois-les-Forges	58	47.34 N	6.51 E
Chatfield, Mn., U.S.	190	43.50 N	92.11 W
Chatfield, Oh., U.S.	214	40.57 N	82.56 W
Chatgal	88	50.26 N	100.09 E
Chatham, N.B., Can.	186	47.02 N	65.28 W
Chatham, On., Can.	214	42.24 N	82.11 W
Chatham, Eng., U.K.	42	51.23 N	0.32 E
Chatham, Il., U.S.	219	39.40 N	89.42 W
Chatham, La., U.S.	194	32.18 N	92.27 W
Chatham, Ma., U.S.	207	41.40 N	69.57 W
Chatham, N.J., U.S.	210	40.44 N	74.23 W
Chatham, N.Y., U.S.	210	42.21 N	73.35 W
Chatham, Oh., U.S.	214	41.06 N	82.01 W
Chatham, Pa., U.S.	208	39.51 N	75.49 W
Chatham, Va., U.S.	192	36.49 N	79.23 W
Chatham ◆[8]	278	41.45 N	87.37 W
Chatham ≃	220	25.42 N	81.17 W
Chatham, Isla I	254	50.40 S	74.20 W
Chatham Head	186	47.00 N	65.33 W
Chatham Islands II	14	43.55 S	176.30 W
Chatham Rise ✦[3]	14	43.30 S	178.00 W
Chatham Sound ⊔	182	54.32 N	130.35 W
Chatham Strait ⊔	180	57.30 N	134.45 W
Chatian	100	27.54 N	118.58 E
Châtillon, Fr.	261	48.48 N	2.17 E
Châtillon, It.	62	45.45 N	7.37 E
Châtillon-Coligny	50	47.50 N	2.51 E
Châtillon-en-Bazois	32	47.03 N	3.40 E
Châtillon-en-Diois	62	44.41 N	5.28 E
Châtillon-la-Borde	261	48.33 N	2.49 E
Châtillon-sur-Chalaronne	58	46.07 N	4.58 E
Châtillon-sur-Indre	32	46.59 N	1.11 E
Châtillon-sur-Loire	50	47.35 N	2.45 E
Châtillon-sur-Marne	50	49.06 N	3.45 E
Châtillon-sur-Seine	58	47.51 N	4.33 E
Chating	106	31.21 N	119.25 E
Chātmohar	126	24.13 N	89.15 E
Chat Moss ◆[3]	262	53.27 N	2.27 W
Chato, Cerro ∧	254	42.29 S	72.01 W
Chatom	194	31.27 N	88.15 W
Chatonville	261	48.33 N	1.52 E
Chatou	261	48.54 N	2.09 E
Chatpur ◆[8]	272b	22.36 N	88.22 E
Chatra, India	124	24.13 N	84.52 E
Chatra, India	272b	22.46 N	88.20 E
Châtres	261	48.43 N	2.49 E
Chats, Lac des ⊜	212	45.28 N	76.23 W
Chatsquot Mountain ∧	182	53.08 N	127.30 W
Chatswood	274a	33.48 S	151.12 E
Chatsworth, Austl.	166	21.58 S	140.19 E
Chatsworth, On., Can.	212	44.27 N	80.54 W
Chatsworth, Ga., U.S.	192	34.45 N	84.46 W
Chatsworth, Il., U.S.	216	40.45 N	88.17 W
Chatsworth, N.J., U.S.	208	39.49 N	74.32 W
Chatsworth, Zimb.	154	19.38 S	31.13 E
Chatsworth ◆[8]	280	34.15 N	118.36 W
Chatsworth Reservoir ⊜[1]	228	34.14 N	118.37 W
Chattahoochee	192	30.42 N	84.50 W
Chattahoochee ≃	192	30.52 N	84.57 W
Chattanooga, Oh., U.S.	216	40.38 N	84.47 W
Chattanooga, Tn., U.S.	194	35.02 N	85.18 W
Chattaroy	192	37.42 N	82.16 W
Chattenden	260	51.25 N	0.32 E
Chatteris	42	52.27 N	0.03 E
Châttillon-de-Michaille	58	46.08 N	5.47 E
Chattolanee	284b	39.24 N	76.45 W
Chatton	44	55.33 N	1.55 W
Chatun'	82	55.00 N	37.50 E
Chaturat	110	15.34 N	101.51 E
Chatwood	208	39.58 N	75.35 W
Chatyrka	74	62.03 N	175.15 E
Chaubaria	126	22.59 N	88.40 E
Chaubourg, Mount ∧[2]	241f	14.02 N	60.57 W
Chauconin	261	48.58 N	2.51 E
Chaudes-Aigues	32	44.51 N	3.00 E
Chaudfontaine	56	50.35 N	5.38 E
Chaudière ≃	186	46.45 N	71.17 W
Chau Doc	110	10.42 N	105.07 E
Chauekuktuli, Lake ⊜	180	60.03 N	158.45 W
Chauffayer	62	44.45 N	6.01 E
Chaugācha, Bngl.	126	23.16 N	89.01 E
Chaugācha, Bngl.	126	23.16 N	89.01 E
Chauhtan	120	25.29 N	71.04 E
Chauk	110	20.54 N	94.50 E
Chaukhandi	272a	28.37 N	77.24 E
Chaullay	248	12.57 S	72.39 W
Chaulnes	50	49.49 N	2.48 E
Chaumergy	58	46.51 N	5.29 E
Chaumes-en-Brie	261	48.40 N	2.51 E
Chaumont, Fr.	58	48.07 N	5.08 E
Chaumont, N.Y., U.S.	212	44.04 N	76.07 W
Chaumont ≃	212	44.04 N	76.08 W
Chaumont Bay ⊂	212	44.02 N	76.13 W
Chaumont-en-Vexin	50	49.16 N	1.53 E
Chaumont-Porcien	50	49.39 N	4.15 E
Chaumont-sur-Aire	56	48.56 N	5.15 E
Chaumont-sur-Loire	50	47.29 N	1.11 E
Chaumont-sur-Tharonne	50	47.37 N	1.54 E
Chaumua	272b	22.39 N	88.33 E
Chauncey	188	39.23 N	82.07 W
Chaŭn-do I	98	34.53 N	126.03 E
Chaungwabyin	110	13.41 N	98.22 E
Chaungzon	110	16.22 N	97.32 E
Chauny	50	49.37 N	3.13 E
Chaupāran	124	24.23 N	85.15 E
Chaussin	58	46.58 N	5.25 E
Chausu-yama ∧	94	35.14 N	137.39 E
Chausuyama-kofun ⊥	94	36.25 N	139.50 E
Chautārā	124	27.46 N	85.42 E
Chautauqua	214	42.12 N	79.28 W
Chautauqua □[6]	214	42.15 N	79.30 W
Chautauqua Creek ≃	214	42.20 N	79.36 W
Chautauqua Lake ⊜	214	42.12 N	79.27 W
Chautengo, Laguna ⊂	234	16.37 N	99.07 W
Chauvigny	32	46.34 N	0.39 E
Chauvin, Ab., Can.	184	52.42 N	110.07 W
Chauvin, La., U.S.	194	29.26 N	90.35 W
Chauvirey-le-Châtel	58	47.47 N	5.45 E
Chauvry	261	49.03 N	2.16 E
Chavakkad	122	10.32 N	76.06 E
Chaval	250	3.02 S	41.15 W
Chavanges	58	48.31 N	4.34 E
Chavannes, Lac ⊜	190	46.51 N	77.10 W
Chavarría, Arg.	252	28.57 S	58.35 W
Chavarría, Perú	286d	12.01 S	77.05 W
Chavast	85	40.13 N	68.50 E
Chavenay	261	48.51 N	1.59 E
Chavenay-Villepreux, Aérodrome de ⊠	261	48.51 N	1.58 E
Chavertovo	82	54.17 N	39.12 E
Chaves, Bra.	250	0.10 S	49.55 W
Chaves, Port.	34	41.44 N	7.28 W
Chaville	261	48.48 N	2.10 E
Chaviña	248	14.59 S	73.50 W
Cháviva	246	4.22 N	72.20 W
Chavki	82	54.20 N	38.13 E
Chavornay	58	46.43 N	6.34 E
Chavuma	152	13.05 S	22.40 E
Chawa'nanake	120	31.36 N	89.41 E
Chawang	110	8.25 N	99.30 E
Chawinda	123	32.21 N	74.42 E
Chay ≃	110	21.39 N	105.12 E
Chayanta	248	18.27 S	66.30 W
Chayuan, Zhg.	100	29.20 N	121.34 E
Chayuan, Zhg.	100	27.40 N	112.57 E
Chayue	106	30.49 N	119.21 E
Chazay-d'Azergues	62	45.53 N	4.37 E
Chazelles-sur-Lyon	62	45.38 N	4.23 E
Chazratišoch, chrebet ∧∧	85	38.30 N	70.15 E
Chazy	188	44.53 N	73.26 W
Chbar ≃	110	13.19 N	107.05 E
Cheadle, Eng., U.K.	42	52.59 N	1.59 W
Cheadle, Eng., U.K.	262	53.24 N	2.13 W
Cheadle Hulme	262	53.22 N	2.12 W
Cheaha Mountain ∧	194	33.30 N	85.47 W
Cheakamus Indian Reserve ◆[4]	182	49.48 N	123.11 W
Cheam ◆[8]	260	51.21 N	0.13 W
Cheam View	224	49.15 N	121.41 W
Cheapside	222	29.17 N	97.24 W
Cheat ≃	188	39.45 N	79.54 W
Cheat, Shavers Fork ≃	188	39.06 N	79.33 W
Cheb	54	50.01 N	12.25 E
Chebacco Lake ⊜	283	42.37 N	70.48 W
Chebanse	216	41.00 N	87.54 W
Chebba	148	35.14 N	10.02 E
Chebeigou	89	43.28 N	127.04 E
Chebogue Point ›	186	43.45 N	66.07 W
Cheboksary → Čeboksary	80	56.09 N	47.15 E
Cheboygan	190	45.38 N	84.28 W
Chech, Erg ◆[2]	148	25.00 N	2.15 W
Ch'ech'eng	100	22.05 N	120.42 E
Chech'on	98	37.08 N	128.12 E
Chęciny	30	50.48 N	20.28 E
Checleset Bay ⊂	182	50.03 N	127.40 W
Checoslovaquia → Czechoslovakia □[1]	30	49.30 N	17.00 E
Checotah	196	35.28 N	95.31 W
Chedabucto Bay ⊂	186	45.23 N	61.10 W
Chedaoyu	105	40.22 N	117.57 E
Cheddar	42	51.17 N	2.46 W
Cheddleton	44	53.04 N	2.02 W
Cheduba Island I	110	18.48 N	93.38 E
Cheduba Strait ⊔	110	18.56 N	93.45 E
Chedun	100	24.09 N	117.19 E
Chée ≃	56	48.45 N	4.39 E
Cheektowaga	210	42.55 N	78.46 W
Cheepie	166	26.39 S	145.01 E
Cheesequake	276	40.25 N	74.17 W
Cheesequake Creek ≃	276	40.28 N	74.16 W
Cheesequake State Park ♦	276	40.26 N	74.16 W
Cheetham Hill ◆[8]	262	53.31 N	2.15 W
Chefang, Zhg.	104	41.35 N	121.26 E
Chefang, Zhg.	106	31.15 N	120.45 E
Chef-Boutonne	32	46.07 N	0.04 W
Chefoo → Yantai	98	37.33 N	121.20 E
Chefornak	180	60.13 N	164.12 W
Chefumage ≃	152	12.15 S	22.19 E
Chefuzwe	156	17.38 S	24.30 E
Chegar Perah	114	4.25 N	101.56 E
Chegga ⩒[4]	148	25.30 N	5.46 W
Chegutu	154	18.10 S	30.14 E
Chehalis	224	46.39 N	122.57 W
Chehalis ≃	224	46.57 N	123.50 W
Chehalis, South Fork ≃	224	46.40 N	123.15 W
Chehalis Indian Reservation ◆[4]	224	46.49 N	123.13 W
Chehe	102	25.00 N	107.38 E
Chehel Dokhtarān	128	35.06 N	62.19 E
Cheheqiao	105	40.21 N	118.16 E
Cheil, Ras el ›	144	7.44 N	49.50 E
Cheine	54	52.52 N	11.04 E
Cheiron, Cime du ∧	62	43.49 N	6.58 E
Chejiatun	104	41.57 N	123.01 E
Chejiawopeng	104	42.29 N	123.07 E
Cheju	90	33.31 N	126.32 E
Cheju-do I	90	33.20 N	126.30 E
Chekiang → Zhejiang □[4]	100	29.00 N	120.00 E
Chek Jawa, Tanjong ›	271c	1.24 N	104.00 E
Chek Kang	271d	22.26 N	114.21 E
Chela, Serra da ∧	152	16.00 S	13.10 E
Chelan	202	47.50 N	120.00 W
Chelan □[6]	224	47.56 N	120.52 W
Chelan, Lake ⊜	202	48.05 N	120.30 W
Chelas ◆[8]	266c	38.45 N	9.07 W
Cheleiros	266c	38.53 N	9.20 W
Cheleiros, Ribeira de ≃	266c	38.54 N	9.22 W
Chelelektu	144	6.00 N	38.09 E
Chelford	262	53.16 N	2.16 W
Chelforó	252	39.04 S	66.32 W
Chelghoum el Aïd	148	36.10 N	6.10 E
Chéliff, Oued ≃	148	36.01 N	0.07 E
Chelīk-e Yās Khān	120	37.05 N	66.14 E
Chellaston	42	52.53 N	1.27 W
Chelles	50	48.53 N	2.36 E
Chelles-le-Pin, Aérodrome de ⊠	261	48.55 N	2.35 E
Chełm	30	51.10 N	23.28 E
Chełm □[4]	30	51.20 N	23.20 E
Chelmer ≃	260	51.48 N	0.40 E
Chelmer and Blackwater Navigation ≍	260	51.44 N	0.43 E
Chełmno	30	53.22 N	18.26 E
Chelmorton	262	53.13 N	1.50 W
Chelmsford, On., Can.	190	46.35 N	81.12 W
Chelmsford, Eng., U.K.	260	51.44 N	0.28 E
Chelmsford, Ma., U.S.	207	42.35 N	71.21 W
Chelmsford □[8]	260	51.44 N	0.30 E
Chelmsford Dam ⊜[1]	158	28.02 S	29.52 E
Chełmża	30	53.12 N	18.37 E
Chelsea, Austl.	169	38.03 S	145.07 E
Chelsea, Ia., U.S.	190	41.55 N	92.23 W
Chelsea, Ma., U.S.	207	42.23 N	71.02 W
Chelsea, Mi., U.S.	216	42.19 N	84.01 W
Chelsea, Ok., U.S.	196	36.32 N	95.25 W
Chelsea, Pa., U.S.	285	39.52 N	75.28 W
Chelsea, Vt., U.S.	188	43.59 N	72.26 W
Chelsea Estates	208	39.41 N	75.36 W
Chelsea Park	224	47.28 N	122.21 W
Chelsfield ◆[8]	260	51.21 N	0.08 E
Cheltenham, Austl.	274a	33.46 S	151.05 E
Cheltenham, Austl.	274b	37.58 S	145.03 E
Cheltenham, Eng., U.K.	42	51.54 N	2.04 W
Cheltenham, Md., U.S.	208	38.44 N	76.49 W
Cheltenham, Pa., U.S.	208	40.03 N	75.05 W
Chel'ul'ja	26	61.44 N	30.41 E
Chelvand	128	38.18 N	48.50 E
Chelyabinsk → Čel'abinsk	86	55.10 N	61.24 E
Chelyāma	126	23.37 N	86.33 E
Chelyan	188	38.11 N	81.29 W
Chelyuskintsy Ice Tongue ⊓	9	66.20 S	82.00 E
Chemaïa	148	32.05 N	8.37 W
Chemainus	224	48.55 N	123.43 W
Chemainus ⊜	224	48.53 N	123.41 W
Chemaogang	106	31.33 N	121.52 E
Chemax	232	20.39 N	87.56 W
Chemba	154	17.08 S	34.52 E
Chembūr ◆[8]	272c	19.04 N	72.54 E
Chemchâm, Sebkhet ⊜	148	21.05 N	12.05 W
Chemčik ≃	86	51.47 N	92.00 E
Chemehuevi Indian Reservation ◆[4]	204	34.30 N	114.23 W
Chemillé	32	47.13 N	0.44 W
Chemin	58	46.59 N	5.19 E
Cheminis, Colline ∧[2]	190	48.08 N	79.31 W
Chemnitz	54	50.50 N	12.55 E
Chemnitz ≃	54	50.59 N	12.47 E
Chemor	114	4.43 N	101.07 E
Chemulpo → Inch'ŏn	98	37.28 N	126.38 E
Chemult	202	43.13 N	121.46 W
Chemung, Il., U.S.	216	42.25 N	88.40 W
Chemung, N.Y., U.S.	210	42.01 N	76.37 W
Chemung □[6]	210	42.06 N	76.49 W
Chemung ≃	210	41.55 N	76.31 W
Chemung County Airport ⊠	210	42.10 N	76.53 W
Chemung Lake ⊜	212	44.25 N	78.22 W
Chena, Cerro ∧	286e	33.36 N	70.45 W
Chenāb ≃	123	29.23 N	71.02 E
Chenachane	148	26.00 N	4.15 W
Chenail Ecarté ≃[1]	214	42.28 N	82.29 W
Chenango □[6]	210	42.32 N	75.31 W
Chenango ≃	210	42.05 N	75.55 W
Chenango Bridge	210	42.10 N	75.51 W
Chenango Forks	210	42.14 N	75.50 W
Chenango Valley State Park ♦	210	42.14 N	75.50 W
Chenārān	128	36.39 N	59.06 E
Chenaut	258	34.15 S	59.13 W
Chen Barag Qi	89	49.21 N	119.31 E
Chenbofang	98	37.27 N	115.18 E
Chencai	100	29.37 N	120.22 E
Chenchiang → Zhenjiang	106	32.13 N	119.26 E
Chencun	100	22.58 N	113.13 E
Chendai	100	23.48 N	117.24 E
Chendauli ◆[8]	272c	19.07 N	72.54 E
Chenderiang	114	4.16 N	101.14 E
Chenderoh, Tasek ⊜	114	4.58 N	100.57 E
Chêne, Rivière du ≃, P.Q., Can.	206	46.34 N	72.00 W
Chêne, Rivière du ≃, P.Q., Can.	206	45.33 N	73.54 W
Chenele	152	12.54 S	23.54 E
Chenequa	216	43.06 N	88.23 W
Chénéville	206	45.53 N	75.03 W
Cheney, Ks., U.S.	198	37.37 N	97.46 W
Cheney, Wa., U.S.	202	47.29 N	117.34 W
Cheney Reservoir ⊜[1]	198	37.45 N	97.50 W
Cheneys Point	214	42.08 N	79.24 W
Cheneyville	194	31.00 N	92.17 W
Chenfang	100	28.01 N	117.32 E
Cheng'an	98	36.27 N	114.41 E
Chengannūr	122	9.20 N	76.38 E
Chengbu	102	26.18 N	110.13 E
Chengchow → Zhengzhou	102	34.48 N	113.39 E
Chengde, Zhg.	105	40.58 N	117.53 E
Chengde (Xiabancheng), Zhg.	105	40.47 N	118.08 E
Chengdu (Chengtu)	107	30.39 N	104.04 E
Chengele	120	28.47 N	96.16 E
Chenggang	100	26.32 N	115.26 E
Chenggu	102	33.10 N	107.22 E
Chenghai	100	23.30 N	116.46 E
Cheng Hu ⊜	106	31.13 N	120.49 E
Chenghuang	102	22.32 N	109.39 E
Chengjia	100	24.50 N	112.50 E
Chengjiahe	100	32.18 N	112.27 E
Chengjiang	102	24.45 N	102.54 E
Chengjiangzhen	107	29.52 N	106.23 E
Chengjiazhen	107	29.24 N	104.36 E
Chengkou	102	31.54 N	108.41 E
Chenglingji	100	29.26 N	113.09 E
Chenglong	100	24.51 N	114.41 E
Chengmai	110	19.48 N	110.02 E
Chengmao	106	31.10 N	120.53 E
Chengpu	100	25.46 N	118.48 E
Chengqian	98	35.21 N	117.21 E
Chengqianwei	100	28.09 N	116.13 E
Chengshan Jiao ›	98	37.24 N	122.42 E
Chengteh → Chengde	105	40.58 N	117.53 E
Chengtu → Chengdu	107	30.39 N	104.04 E
Ch'engtzuliao	269d	25.06 N	121.27 E
Chengwu	98	34.58 N	115.52 E
Chengxian	102	33.43 N	105.41 E
Chengxi Hu ⊜	100	32.24 N	116.15 E
Chengyang, Zhg.	98	36.18 N	120.22 E
Chengyang, Zhg.	100	29.59 N	119.44 E
Chengzi, Zhg.	98	41.57 N	117.16 E
Chengzi, Zhg.	105	39.58 N	116.02 E
Chengzitan	98	39.30 N	122.30 E
Ch'enhsien → Chenxian	100	25.48 N	112.59 E
Chen Hu ⊜	100	30.29 N	113.22 E
Chenies	260	51.41 N	0.32 W
Chenil, Lac ⊜	186	51.51 N	59.41 W
Cheniménil	58	48.08 N	6.36 E
Chenji	100	33.50 N	119.11 E
Chenjiachang, Zhg.	107	29.35 N	104.52 E
Chenjiachang, Zhg.	107	30.04 N	105.15 E
Chenjiagang	98	34.25 N	119.49 E
Chenjiahe	102	29.28 N	109.59 E
Chenjiaji	100	30.42 N	114.21 E
Chenjiapang	106	31.14 N	119.42 E
Chenjiapu	105	40.31 N	115.37 E
Chenjiaqiao	106	31.27 N	121.16 E
Chenjiatun, Zhg.	104	42.20 N	124.06 E
Chenjiatun, Zhg.	104	40.57 N	121.01 E
Chenjiawan	106	31.02 N	120.35 E
Chenjiaxiang	100	31.29 N	113.45 E
Chenjiazhen	106	31.30 N	121.48 E
Chenjiazui	105	39.17 N	116.59 E
Chenkeng	100	25.06 N	116.15 E
Chenlingjiao	106	30.23 N	118.47 E
Chenliu	98	34.43 N	114.31 E
Chenlong	269b	31.17 N	121.25 E
Chennevières	261	49.00 N	2.07 E
Chennevières-lès-Lovres	261	49.03 N	2.33 E
Chenoa	216	40.44 N	88.43 W
Chenonceaux	50	47.20 N	1.04 E
Chenonceaux, Château de ⊥	50	47.20 N	1.04 E
Chenôve	58	47.17 N	5.00 E
Chenoweth	224	45.37 N	121.13 W
Chenqiao	98	34.58 N	114.32 E
Chenquingqiao	89	49.08 N	127.16 E
Chenshanzhuang	105	39.43 N	117.30 E
Chenshichang	107	29.17 N	106.00 E
Chens-sur-Léman	58	46.20 N	6.16 E
Chentang	102	23.54 N	110.39 E
Chentejn nuruu ∧∧	88	48.30 N	108.30 E
Chentij	88	48.05 N	109.45 E
Chentij □[4]	88	48.00 N	110.30 E
Chenxi	102	27.51 N	109.59 E
Chenxian	100	25.48 N	112.59 E
Chenxiangtun	104	41.36 N	123.30 E
Chenyang	100	33.47 N	120.10 E
Chenyang → Shenyang	104	41.48 N	123.27 E
Cheonan → Ch'ŏnan	98	36.48 N	127.09 E
Cheongju → Ch'ŏngju	98	36.39 N	127.31 E
Cheo Reo	110	13.24 N	108.27 E
Chepachet	207	41.54 N	71.40 W
Chepaúa	152	12.58 S	22.43 E
Chepén	248	7.13 S	79.27 W
Chépénéhé	175f	20.47 S	167.09 E
Chepes	252	31.21 S	66.36 W
Chepkotet ∧	154	1.15 N	35.26 E
Chepo	246	9.10 N	79.06 W
Chepstow	42	51.39 N	2.41 W
Cheptainville	261	48.33 N	2.16 E
Cher □[5]	32	47.05 N	2.30 E
Cher ≃	32	47.21 N	0.29 E
Cheradi, Isole II	68	40.27 N	17.10 E
Cherain	56	50.11 N	5.52 E
Cherán	234	19.41 N	101.57 W
Chéran ≃	62	45.53 N	5.56 E
Cheranchi	150	12.40 N	7.42 E
Cherangany Hills ∧∧[2]	154	1.15 N	35.27 E
Cherasco	62	44.39 N	7.51 E
Cherāt	123	33.49 N	71.53 E
Cheraw	192	34.41 N	79.53 W
Cheraw State Park ♦	192	34.36 N	79.55 W
Cherbaniani Reef ✦[2]	122	12.18 N	71.53 E
Cherbourg	32	49.39 N	1.39 W
Cherchell	148	36.36 N	2.12 E
Cheremkhovo → Čeremchovo	88	53.09 N	103.05 E
Chérence	261	49.05 N	1.41 E
Chereponi	150	10.09 N	0.17 E
Cherepovets → Čerepovec	76	59.08 N	37.54 E
Chergui, Chott ech ⊜	148	34.21 N	0.30 E
Chergui, Île I	148	34.44 N	11.14 E
Chergui, Zahrez ⊜	148	35.12 N	3.32 E
Cheribon → Cirebon	115a	6.44 S	108.34 E
Cherio ≃	64	45.46 N	9.55 E
Cherita, Sebkhet ⊜	36	35.21 N	10.19 E
Cheriton	208	37.17 N	75.58 W
Cheriyam Island I	122	10.09 N	73.40 E
Cherkassy → Čerkassy	78	49.26 N	32.04 E
Cherkessk → Čerkessk	84	44.14 N	42.04 E
Cherlen → Kerulen ≃	90	48.48 N	117.00 E
Chermside	171a	27.23 S	153.02 E
Chernigov → Černigov	78	51.30 N	31.18 E
Chernobyl → Černobyl'	78	51.16 N	30.14 E
Chernofski	180	53.24 N	167.33 W
Chernogorsk → Černogorsk	86	53.49 N	91.18 E
Chernovtsy → Černovcy	78	48.18 N	25.56 E
Chero ≃	62	44.58 N	9.51 E
Cherokee, Al., U.S.	194	34.45 N	87.58 W
Cherokee, Ia., U.S.	198	42.44 N	95.33 W
Cherokee, Ks., U.S.	198	37.20 N	94.48 W
Cherokee, Ok., U.S.	196	36.45 N	98.21 W
Cherokee, Tx., U.S.	196	30.59 N	98.43 W
Cherokee □[6]	222	31.48 N	95.10 W
Cherokee, Lake ⊜[1]	222	32.21 N	94.39 W
Cherokee Canal ≍	226	39.18 N	121.55 W
Cherokee Lake ⊜[1]	192	36.16 N	83.20 W
Cherokee Point ›	192	26.16 N	77.03 W
Cherokee Ranch	208	40.25 N	75.55 W
Cherokees, Lake O' The ⊜[1]	194	36.39 N	94.49 W
Cherokee Village	194	36.17 N	91.30 W
Chéroy	50	48.12 N	3.00 E
Cherpuči	89	53.01 N	138.52 E
Cherquenco	252	38.41 S	72.00 W
Cherrabun	162	18.29 S	125.19 E
Cherrapunji	120	25.18 N	91.42 E
Cherry Brook ≃, Ma., U.S.	283	42.23 N	71.17 W
Cherry Brook ≃, N.J., U.S.	276	41.01 N	74.00 W
Cherry City	279b	40.29 N	79.58 W
Cherry Creek, B.C., Can.	224	49.17 N	124.47 W
Cherry Creek, N.Y., U.S.	214	42.17 N	79.06 W
Cherry Creek ≃, Az., U.S.	200	33.41 N	110.49 W
Cherry Creek ≃, Ca., U.S.	226	37.53 N	119.58 W
Cherry Creek ≃, Co., U.S.	198	39.45 N	105.01 W
Cherry Creek ≃, Mt., U.S.	198	46.48 N	105.15 W
Cherry Creek ≃, N.D., U.S.	198	47.41 N	103.02 W
Cherry Creek ≃, S.D., U.S.	198	44.36 N	101.30 W
Cherry Creek ≃, Tx., U.S.	196	31.13 N	103.34 W
Cherry Creek, East Fork ≃	226	38.06 N	119.47 W
Cherry Creek, West Fork ≃	226	38.04 N	119.54 W
Cherry Fork	218	38.53 N	83.37 W
Cherry Grove, N.Y., U.S.	210	40.39 N	73.06 W
Cherry Grove, Or., U.S.	224	45.26 N	123.14 W
Cherry Hill, Il., U.S.	278	41.32 N	88.02 W
Cherry Hill, N.J., U.S.	208	39.56 N	75.01 W
Cherry Hill ◆[8]	284b	39.15 N	76.38 W
Cherry Hill Mall ◆[9]	285	39.56 N	75.02 W
Cherry Island I	285	39.43 N	75.31 W
Cherry Lake ⊜[1]	226	38.00 N	119.54 W
Cherryland	226	37.41 N	122.06 W
Cherry Lane	279b	40.34 N	79.33 W
Cherryplain	210	42.38 N	73.22 W
Cherry Point Marine Corps Air Station ■	192	34.54 N	76.54 W
Cherryvale	198	37.16 N	95.33 W
Cherry Valley, Ar., U.S.	194	35.24 N	90.45 W
Cherry Valley, Ca., U.S.	228	33.57 N	116.53 W
Cherry Valley, Il., U.S.	216	42.14 N	88.56 W
Cherry Valley, Ma., U.S.	207	42.14 N	71.52 W
Cherry Valley, N.Y., U.S.	210	42.47 N	74.45 W
Cherry Valley, Pa., U.S.	214	41.10 N	79.48 W
Cherry Valley Creek ≃	210	42.35 N	74.56 W
Cherryville, N.C., U.S.	192	35.22 N	81.22 W
Cherryville, Pa., U.S.	208	40.45 N	75.33 W
Cherrywood	275b	43.52 N	79.08 W
Cherson	78	46.38 N	32.35 E
Chersonesskij, mys ›	78	44.35 N	33.23 E
Chertsey	260	51.24 N	0.30 W
Cherwell ≃	42	51.44 N	1.15 W
Chesaco Park	284b	39.19 N	76.30 W
Chesaning	190	43.11 N	84.06 W
Chesapeake	208	36.49 N	76.16 W
Chesapeake and Delaware Canal ≍	208	39.32 N	75.51 W
Chesapeake and Ohio Canal National Historical Park ♦	208	39.03 N	77.16 W
Chesapeake Bay ⊂	208	38.40 N	76.25 W
Chesapeake Bay Bridge-Tunnel ◆[5]	208	37.00 N	76.02 W
Chesapeake Beach	208	38.41 N	76.32 W
Chesaw	182	48.56 N	119.03 W
Chesdin, Lake ⊜[1]	208	37.15 N	77.33 W
Cheseaux	58	46.35 N	6.36 E
Chesham	260	51.43 N	0.38 W
Chesham Bois	260	51.41 N	0.37 W
Cheshire, Ct., U.S.	207	41.29 N	72.54 W
Cheshire, Ma., U.S.	207	42.33 N	73.09 W
Cheshire, N.Y., U.S.	210	42.49 N	77.20 W
Cheshire □[6], Eng., U.K.	44	53.23 N	2.30 W
Cheshire □[6], N.H., U.S.	207	42.50 N	72.15 W
Cheshire Plain ≚	44	53.17 N	2.40 W
Cheshire Reservoir ⊜[1]	207	42.32 N	73.11 W
Chesht-e Sharīf	128	34.21 N	63.44 E
Cheshunt	42	51.43 N	0.02 W
Chesil Beach ≗[2]	42	50.38 N	2.33 W
Chesilhurst	285	39.43 N	74.52 W
Cheslatta Lake ⊜	182	53.44 N	125.18 W

Symbols in the index entries represent the broad categories identified in the key at the right. Symbols with superior numbers (∧∧[1]) identify subcategories (see complete key on page *I · 1).*

Symbole im Register stellen die rechts im Schlüssel erklärten Kategorien dar. Symbole mit hochgestellten Ziffern (∧∧[1]) bezeichnen Unterabteilungen einer Kategorie (vgl. vollständiger Schlüssel auf Seite *I · 1).*

Los símbolos incluídos en el texto del índice representan las grandes categorías identificadas con la clave a la derecha. Los símbolos con numeros en su parte superior (∧∧[1]) identifican las subcategorías (véase la clave completa en la página *I · 1).*

Les symboles de l'index représentent les catégories indiquées dans la légende à droite. Les symboles suivis d'un indice (∧∧[1]) représentent des sous-catégories (voir légende complète à la page *I · 1).*

Os símbolos incluídos no texto do índice representam as grandes categorias identificadas com a chave à direita. Os símbolos com números em sua parte superior (∧∧[1]) identificam as subcategorias (veja-se a chave completa à página *I · 1).*

Symbol	English	Deutsch	Español	Français	Português
∧	Mountain	Berg	Montaña	Montagne	Montanha
∧∧	Mountains	Gebirge	Montañas	Montagnes	Montanhas
⋈	Pass	Paß	Paso	Col	Passo
V	Valley, Canyon	Tal, Cañon	Valle, Cañón	Vallée, Canyon	Vale, Canhão
≚	Plain	Ebene	Llano	Plaine	Planície
›	Cape	Kap	Cabo	Cap	Cabo
I	Island	Insel	Isla	Île	Ilha
II	Islands	Inseln	Islas	Îles	Ilhas
≗	Other Topographic Features	Andere Topographische Objekte	Otros Elementos Topográficos	Autres données topographiques	Outros acidentes topográficos

ESPAÑOL Nombre	Página	Lat.°'	Long.°' W = Oeste
Chesley	212	44.17 N	81.05 W
Chesnee	192	35.08 N	81.51 W
Chess ≃	260	51.38 N	0.27 W
Chessington ◆[8]	260	51.21 N	0.18 W
Chessy	261	48.53 N	2.46 E
Chest Creek ≃	214	40.53 N	78.44 W
Chester, Eng., U.K.	262	53.12 N	2.54 W
Chester, Ca., U.S.	204	40.18 N	121.13 W
Chester, Ct., U.S.	207	41.24 N	72.27 W
Chester, Il., U.S.	194	37.54 N	89.49 W
Chester, Md., U.S.	208	38.58 N	76.17 W
Chester, Ma., U.S.	207	42.16 N	72.58 W
Chester, Mt., U.S.	202	48.30 N	110.58 W
Chester, Ne., U.S.	198	40.00 N	97.37 W
Chester, N.J., U.S.	210	40.47 N	74.41 W
Chester, Ok., U.S.	196	36.12 N	98.55 W
Chester, Pa., U.S.	208	39.50 N	75.21 W
Chester, S.C., U.S.	192	34.42 N	81.12 W
Chester, Tx., U.S.	222	30.55 N	94.36 W
Chester, Vt., U.S.	188	43.15 N	72.35 W
Chester, Va., U.S.	208	37.21 N	77.26 W
Chester, W.V., U.S.	214	40.36 N	80.33 W
Chester □[6]	208	39.58 N	75.36 W
Chester □[8]	262	53.16 N	2.52 W
Chester ≃	208	39.00 N	76.10 W
Chester Basin	186	44.34 N	64.19 W
Chesterbrook	284c	38.55 N	77.09 W
Chester Brook ≃	283	42.23 N	71.14 W
Chesterbrook Woods	284c	38.56 N	77.08 W
Chester Creek ≃	208	39.50 N	75.22 W
Chester Creek, East Branch ≃	285	39.56 N	75.32 W
Chester Creek, West Branch ≃	285	39.54 N	75.27 W
Chesterfield, Eng., U.K.	44	53.15 N	1.25 W
Chesterfield, Ct., U.S.	207	41.24 N	72.11 W
Chesterfield, Il., U.S.	219	39.15 N	90.04 W
Chesterfield, In., U.S.	218	40.06 N	85.35 W
Chesterfield, Ma., U.S.	207	42.23 N	72.50 W
Chesterfield, S.C., U.S.	192	34.44 N	80.05 W
Chesterfield, Va., U.S.	192	37.22 N	77.30 W
Chesterfield □[6]	208	37.20 N	77.25 W
Chesterfield, Île I	157b	16.20 S	43.58 E
Chesterfield, Îles II	160	19.30 S	158.00 E
Chesterfield Inlet	176	63.21 N	90.42 W
Chesterfield Inlet c	176	63.25 N	90.45 W
Chester Heights	285	39.53 N	75.28 W
Chester Hill, Austl.	274a	33.53 S	151.00 E
Chesterhill, Oh., U.S.	188	39.29 N	81.51 W
Chester Hill, Pa., U.S.	214	40.53 N	78.14 W
Chester Island I	285	39.50 N	75.21 W
Chesterland	214	41.31 N	81.21 W
Chester-le-Street	44	54.52 N	1.34 W
Chester Morse Lake ◎[1]	224	47.23 N	121.42 W
Chesters	44	55.23 N	2.36 W
Chester Springs	285	40.06 N	75.37 W
Chesterton	216	41.36 N	87.03 W
Chesterton Range ⋏	166	25.30 S	147.27 E
Chestertown	208	39.12 N	76.04 W
Chesterville, On., Can.	212	45.06 N	75.14 W
Chesterville, Oh., U.S.	214	40.29 N	82.41 W
Chestnut	219	40.03 N	89.11 W
Chestnut Hill, Ma., U.S.	283	42.20 N	71.10 W
Chestnut Hill, Pa., U.S.	210	40.04 N	75.12 W
Chestnut Hill ◆[8]	285	40.04 N	75.13 W
Chestnut Hill ∧[2]	285	40.13 N	75.45 W
Chestnut Hill Estates	285	39.41 N	75.42 W
Chestnut Hill Reservoir ◎[1]	283	42.20 N	71.10 W
Chestnut Ridge ∧	214	40.09 N	79.24 W
Chestnut Ridge Park ♦	284a	42.43 N	78.46 W
Chest Peak ∧	172	43.06 S	172.01 E
Chesuncook Lake ◎	188	46.00 N	69.20 W
Cheswick	214	40.32 N	79.47 W
Cheswold	208	39.13 N	75.35 W
Chet ≃	42	52.33 N	1.32 E
Cheta ≃	74	71.54 N	102.06 E
Chetaibi	36	37.04 N	7.23 E
Chetco ≃	202	42.03 N	124.16 W
Chetek	190	45.18 N	91.39 W
Chéticamp	186	46.38 N	61.01 W
Chet Iter, Oued V	148	21.39 N	2.30 E
Chetopa	198	37.02 N	95.05 W
Chettlatt Island I	122	11.42 N	72.42 E
Chetumal	232	18.30 N	88.18 W
Chetumal, Bahía c	232	18.20 N	88.05 W
Chetwynd	182	55.42 N	121.40 W
Cheung Chau I	271d	22.12 N	114.01 E
Cheung Shue Tan	271d	22.26 N	114.12 E
Chevak	180	61.39 N	165.17 W
Cheval-Blanc, Montagne du ⋏	62	44.07 N	6.26 E
Chevannes	261	48.32 N	2.27 E
Chevelon Creek ≃	200	34.57 N	110.31 W
Chevening	260	51.18 N	0.08 E
Chevenoz	58	46.20 N	6.39 E
Cheverly	284c	38.55 N	76.54 W
Cheverny	50	47.30 N	1.28 E
Chevillon	58	48.32 N	5.08 E
Chevilly-Larue	261	48.46 N	2.21 E
Cheviot, N.Z.	172	42.49 S	173.16 E
Cheviot, Oh., U.S.	218	39.09 N	84.36 W
Cheviot Hills ⋏[2]	44	55.22 N	2.22 W
Chevreuse	50	48.42 N	2.03 E
Chèvreville	261	49.07 N	2.51 E
Chevril, Lac du ◎	62	45.29 N	6.56 E
Chevry-Cossigny	261	48.43 N	2.40 E
Chevy Chase	284c	38.58 N	77.04 W
Chevy Chase Heights	214	40.36 N	79.08 W
Chevy Chase View	284c	39.01 N	77.05 W
Chewaucan ≃	202	42.30 N	120.18 W
Chew Bahir (Lake Stefanie) ◎	144	4.40 N	36.50 E
Chewelah	202	48.16 N	117.42 W
Chew Magna	42	51.22 N	2.35 W
Chew Reservoir ◎[1]	262	53.31 N	1.56 W
Chews Landing	285	39.50 N	75.04 W
Chewton, Austl.	169	37.05 S	144.16 E
Chewton, Pa., U.S.	214	40.53 N	80.20 W
Chexbres	58	46.29 N	6.47 E
Cheyenne, Ok., U.S.	196	35.36 N	99.40 W
Cheyenne, Wy., U.S.	200	41.08 N	104.49 W
Cheyenne ≃	198	44.40 N	101.15 W
Cheyenne, Dry Fork ≃	198	43.25 N	105.23 W
Cheyenne River Indian Reservation ◆[4]	198	45.00 N	100.40 W
Cheyenne Wells	198	38.49 N	102.21 W
Cheyne Bay c	162	34.35 S	118.50 E
Cheyne Point ›	162	33.58 S	122.34 E
Cheyney	285	39.56 N	75.31 W
Cheyney University of Pennsylvania ᵾ[2]	285	39.56 N	75.32 W
Chezhen	98	37.54 N	117.37 E
Chhabra	124	24.40 N	76.50 E
Chhachhrauli	124	30.15 N	77.22 E
Chhajārsi	272a	28.38 N	77.23 E
Chhalera Bāngar	272a	28.33 N	77.20 E
Chhanka	126	23.59 N	89.55 E
Chhapra	124	25.46 N	84.45 E
Chhātak	120	25.02 N	91.40 E
Chhatarpur, India	124	24.23 N	84.11 E
Chhatarpur, India	124	24.55 N	79.36 E
Chhātna	126	23.18 N	86.58 E
Chhatrapur	122	19.21 N	84.59 E
Chhattīsgarh ≅	122	21.15 N	82.00 E
Chhay Arêng ≃	110	11.31 N	103.25 E
Chhêb Kândal	110	13.45 N	105.24 E
Chhibrāmau	124	27.09 N	79.31 E
Chhināmor	272b	22.48 N	88.18 E
Chhindwāra	124	22.04 N	78.56 E

FRANÇAIS Nom	Page	Lat.°'	Long.°' W = Ouest
Chhiruti	126	24.01 N	88.11 E
Chhitauni	124	27.09 N	83.58 E
Chhlong ≃	110	12.15 N	105.58 E
Chhota Bāisdia	126	22.00 N	90.27 E
Chhota-Chhindwāra	124	23.03 N	79.29 E
Chhota Udepur	120	22.19 N	74.01 E
Chhukha Dzong	124	27.09 N	89.36 E
Chi ≃, Thai	110	15.11 N	104.43 E
Chi ≃, Thai	110	15.18 N	103.31 E
Chi ≃, Zhg.	100	32.51 N	117.59 E
Chía	246	4.52 N	74.04 W
Chia, Laguna ◎	234	22.10 N	98.02 W
Chiador	256	22.01 S	43.03 W
Chiahsien	100	23.05 N	120.35 E
Chiahsing → Jiaxing	106	30.46 N	120.45 E
Chiai	100	23.29 N	120.27 E
Chialamberto	62	45.22 N	7.21 E
Chiali	100	23.10 N	120.10 E
Chiambala ≃	152	16.22 S	11.49 E
Chiampo	64	45.33 N	11.17 E
Chiampo ≃	64	45.20 N	11.16 E
Chiamussu → Jiamusi	89	46.50 N	130.21 E
Chiana, Val di V	66	43.15 N	11.50 E
Chianciano Terme	66	43.03 N	11.50 E
Chiang Dao	110	19.22 N	98.58 E
Chiange	152	15.45 S	13.48 E
Chiang Kham	110	19.32 N	100.18 E
Chiang Khan	110	17.52 N	101.36 E
Chiang Khian	110	19.37 N	100.00 E
Chiang Mai	110	18.47 N	98.59 E
Chiangmen → Jiangmen	100	22.35 N	113.05 E
Chiang Rai	110	19.54 N	99.50 E
Chiang Saen	110	20.16 N	100.05 E
Chiangtu → Yangzhou	100	32.24 N	119.26 E
Chiangyin → Jiangyin	106	31.55 N	120.16 E
Chiani ≃	66	42.52 N	12.14 E
Chian → Ji'an	100	27.07 N	114.58 E
Chianni	66	43.29 N	10.38 E
Chianti □[4]	66	43.22 N	11.23 E
Chianti ⋏[1]	66	43.25 N	11.20 E
Chianti, Monti del ⋏	66	43.32 N	11.25 E
Chiaohsi	100	24.49 N	121.46 E
Chiaohsien → Jiaoxian	98	36.18 N	119.58 E
Chiaopan	100	24.50 N	121.21 E
Chiaotso → Jiaozuo	102	35.15 N	113.13 E
Chiao-Tung Normal University ᵾ[2]	269b	31.14 N	121.24 E
Chiapa	248	19.32 S	69.13 W
Chiapa de Corzo	234	16.42 N	93.00 W
Chiapaot'ai	100	24.11 N	121.00 E
Chiapas □[3]	232	16.30 N	92.30 W
Chiaramonte Gulfi	70	37.02 N	14.42 E
Chiaramonti	71	40.45 N	8.49 E
Chiaravalle	66	43.36 N	13.19 E
Chiaravalle Centrale	68	38.41 N	16.25 E
Chiareggio	64	46.19 N	9.47 E
Chiari	62	45.32 N	9.56 E
Chiaromonte	68	40.07 N	16.13 E
Chiasso	58	45.50 N	9.01 E
Chiautla de Tapia	234	18.17 N	98.36 W
Chiautzingo	234	19.12 N	98.28 W
Chiavari	62	44.19 N	9.19 E
Chiavenna	58	46.19 N	9.24 E
Chiawelo	273d	26.17 S	27.52 E
Chiba	94	35.36 N	140.07 E
Chiba □[5]	94	35.30 N	140.20 E
Chibabava	156	20.19 S	33.39 E
Chiba-kō c	268	35.35 N	140.06 E
Chibakou	100	29.36 N	113.01 E
Chibango	152	13.38 S	21.56 E
Chiba University ᵾ[2]	268	35.38 N	140.06 E
Chibemba	152	15.45 S	14.05 E
Chibi	154	20.19 S	30.30 E
Chibia	152	15.11 S	13.41 E
Chibouet ≃	206	45.47 N	72.52 W
Chibougamau	176	49.55 N	74.22 W
Chibuto	156	24.44 S	33.33 E
Chibuzhangchu Hu ◎	120	33.25 N	90.15 E
Chibwe	154	14.12 S	28.31 E
Chicago, Il., U.S.	216	41.51 N	87.39 W
Chicago, Il., U.S.	278	41.51 N	87.39 W
Chicago, North Branch ≃	216	41.53 N	87.38 W
Chicago, North Branch, West Fork ≃	278	42.03 N	87.54 W
Chicago, South Branch ≃	278	41.53 N	87.38 W
Chicago, University of ᵾ[2]	278	41.47 N	87.36 W
Chicago Botanic Garden ♦	278	42.09 N	87.47 W
Chicago Harbor c	278	41.53 N	87.37 W
Chicago Heights	216	41.30 N	87.38 W
Chicago-Hinsdale Airport ⊠	278	41.46 N	87.56 W
Chicago Lawn ◆[8]	278	41.47 N	87.41 W
Chicago-Midway Airport ⊠	216	41.47 N	87.45 W
Chicago-O'Hare International Airport ⊠	278	41.59 N	87.54 W
Chicago Park	226	39.09 N	120.58 W
Chicago Portage National Historic Site ⊥	278	41.48 N	87.49 W
Chicago Ridge	216	41.42 N	87.46 W
Chicago Sanitary and Ship Canal ≅	216	41.32 N	88.05 W
Chicago Stadium ♦	278	41.53 N	87.40 W
Chicama ≃	248	7.56 S	79.17 W
Chicamacomico ≃	208	38.26 N	75.59 W
Chicamba, Barragem de ◆[6]	156	19.08 S	33.00 E
Chicapa ≃	152	6.26 S	20.47 E
Chicayán ≃	234	21.59 N	94.06 W
Chic-Chocs, Monts ⋏	186	48.55 N	66.00 W
Chichagof Island I	180	57.30 N	135.30 W
Chichas, Cordillera de ⋏	248	21.00 S	66.20 W
Chīchāwatni	123	30.32 N	72.42 E
Chiché ≃	250	8.15 S	53.30 W
Chicheng	98	40.54 N	115.46 E
Chichén Itzá ⊥	232	20.40 N	88.35 W
Chichester, Eng., U.K.	42	50.50 N	0.48 W
Chichester, N.Y., U.S.	210	42.06 N	74.19 W
Chichester Range ⋏	162	22.00 S	118.50 E
Chichi	100	23.50 N	120.47 E
Chichibu	94	35.59 N	139.05 E
Chichibu-Tama-kokuritsu-kōen ♦	94	35.52 N	139.00 E
Chichica	236	8.22 N	81.40 W
Chichicastenango	236	14.56 N	91.07 W
Chichigalpa	236	12.34 N	87.02 W
Chichigapa	234	17.47 N	94.25 W
Ch'ich'ihaerh → Qiqihar	89	47.19 N	123.55 E
Chichihualco	234	17.41 N	99.39 W
Chichijima-rettō II	14	27.06 N	142.12 E
Chichimilá	232	20.37 N	88.13 W
Chichiriviche	246	10.56 N	68.16 W
Chicholi	124	22.01 N	77.40 E
Chichra	126	22.19 N	86.53 E
Chickahominy ≃	208	37.14 N	76.53 W
Chickaloon	180	61.48 N	148.28 W
Chickamauga	192	34.52 N	85.17 W
Chickamauga Lake ◎[1]	192	35.22 N	85.02 W
Chickamin ≃	182	55.47 N	130.58 W
Chickasaw, Al., U.S.	194	30.45 N	88.04 W
Chickasaw, Oh., U.S.	216	40.26 N	84.30 W
Chickasaw Bogue ≃	194	32.17 N	87.55 W

PORTUGUÊS Nome	Página	Lat.°'	Long.°' W = Oeste
Chickasawhatchie Creek ≃	192	31.19 N	84.29 W
Chickasawhay ≃	194	31.00 N	88.45 W
Chickasaw National Recreation Area ♦	196	34.25 N	96.59 W
Chickasha	196	35.03 N	97.56 W
Chicken	180	64.04 N	141.56 W
Chicken Brook ≃	283	42.08 N	71.25 W
Chickerell	42	50.37 N	2.30 W
Chickies Creek ≃	208	40.03 N	76.32 W
Chiclana de la Frontera	34	36.25 N	6.08 W
Chiclayo	248	6.46 S	79.51 W
Chico, Ca., U.S.	204	39.43 N	121.50 W
Chico, Tx., U.S.	196	33.17 N	97.47 W
Chico, Wa., U.S.	224	47.36 N	122.42 W
Chico ≃, Arg.	254	43.48 S	66.25 W
Chico ≃, Arg.	254	42.25 S	70.30 W
Chico ≃, Arg.	254	49.56 S	68.32 W
Chico ≃, Cuba	286b	23.02 N	82.17 W
Chico ≃, Pan.	236	8.20 N	80.28 W
Chico ≃, Pil.	116	17.58 N	121.36 E
Chico ≃, S.A.	254	51.40 S	69.09 W
Chicoasén, Presa ◎[1]	234	16.55 N	93.05 W
Chicobi, Lac ◎	190	48.53 N	78.30 W
Chico Creek ≃	198	38.15 N	104.20 W
Chicolete Creek ≃	222	29.05 N	96.49 W
Chicomba	152	14.09 S	14.57 E
Chicomo	156	24.31 S	34.17 E
Chicomuselo	232	15.46 N	92.16 W
Chiconautla, Cerro ∧	286a	19.39 N	98.58 W
Chiconono	154	12.56 S	35.43 E
Chicontepec de Tejeda	234	20.58 N	98.10 W
Chicopee, Ga., U.S.	192	34.15 N	83.50 W
Chicopee, Ma., U.S.	207	42.08 N	72.36 W
Chicopee ≃	207	42.09 N	72.37 W
Chicora	214	40.56 N	79.44 W
Chicot, Lake ◎	194	33.20 N	91.14 W
Chicot, Rivière du ≃	275a	45.35 N	73.51 W
Chicot State Park ♦	194	30.47 N	92.19 W
Chicoutimi	186	48.26 N	71.04 W
Chicoutimi ≃	186	48.26 N	71.05 W
Chicoutimi, Réserve ♦	186	48.30 N	70.15 W
Chicú, Cerro ∧	236	8.35 N	80.51 W
Chicualoque	234	20.23 N	97.39 W
Chicuma	152	13.23 S	14.51 E
Chicxulub	232	21.08 N	89.31 W
Chidambaram	122	11.24 N	79.42 E
Chiddingfold	42	51.06 N	0.37 W
Chiddingstone Causeway	260	51.12 N	0.10 E
Chidenguele	156	24.54 S	34.13 E
Chidlow	168a	31.52 S	116.14 E
Chi-do I	98	35.04 N	126.13 E
Chidralada Palace ᵾ	269a	13.46 N	100.32 E
Chief	222	32.33 N	96.10 W
Chief Justice William Cushing Memorial State Park ♦	283	42.10 N	70.45 W
Chiefland	192	29.28 N	82.51 W
Chiefs Point ›	212	44.42 N	81.18 W
Chief's Point Indian Reserve ◆[4]	212	44.41 N	81.17 W
Chiehyang → Jieyang	100	23.35 N	116.21 E
Chiemgauer Alpen ⋏	64	47.40 N	12.30 E
Chiemsee ◎	64	47.54 N	12.29 E
Chien, Bayou de ≃	194	36.35 N	89.11 W
Chienes (Kiens)	64	46.48 N	11.50 E
Chiengi	154	8.39 S	29.10 E
Chiengo	152	13.20 S	21.55 E
Chiens, Rivière aux ≃	275a	45.39 N	73.46 W
Chienti ≃	66	43.18 N	13.45 E
Chieo Lan Reservoir ◎[1]	110	9.00 N	98.45 E
Chieri	62	45.01 N	7.49 E
Chiers ≃	56	49.39 N	5.00 E
Chiesa in Valmalenco	64	46.16 N	9.51 E
Chiese ≃	64	45.08 N	10.25 E
Chieti	66	42.21 N	14.10 E
Chieti □[4]	66	42.07 N	14.21 E
Chietla	234	18.31 N	98.35 W
Chieuti	68	41.51 N	15.10 E
Chieveley	42	51.27 N	1.19 W
Chièvres	50	50.35 N	3.48 E
Chifeng (Ulanhad)	98	42.18 N	119.00 E
Chigasaki	94	35.19 N	139.24 E
Chiginagak, Mount ∧	180	57.08 N	156.59 W
Chigmit Mountains ⋏	180	60.00 N	153.00 W
Chignahuapan	234	19.50 N	98.02 W
Chignall Saint James	260	51.46 N	0.25 E
Chignall Smealy	260	51.47 N	0.25 E
Chignecto, Cape ›	186	45.20 N	64.57 W
Chignecto Bay c	186	45.35 N	64.45 W
Chignik	180	56.18 N	158.23 W
Chignik Bay c	180	56.22 N	158.15 W
Chignik Lagoon	180	56.21 N	158.31 W
Chignik Lake	180	56.15 N	158.45 W
Chignolo Po	62	45.09 N	9.29 E
Chigombe ≃	156	23.26 S	33.19 E
Chigorodó	246	7.41 N	76.42 W
Chigu	100	27.34 N	114.40 E
Chigubo	156	22.50 S	33.34 E
Chigu Co ◎	120	28.40 N	91.45 E
Chigwell	260	51.38 N	0.05 E
Chigwell Row	260	51.37 N	0.07 E
Chigyŏng	98	39.51 N	127.26 E
Chihaya-akasaka	270	34.24 N	135.38 E
Chihaya Castle ⊥	270	34.24 N	135.40 E
Chihe	100	32.32 N	117.58 E
Ch'ihfeng → Chifeng	98	42.18 N	119.00 E
Chihli, Gulf of → Bo Hai c	98	38.30 N	120.00 E
Chihpen	100	22.42 N	121.02 E
Ch'ihshang	100	23.07 N	121.12 E
Chihsi → Jixi	89	45.17 N	130.59 E
Ch'ihsing Shan ∧, T'aiwan	100	25.10 N	121.33 E
Ch'ihsing Shan ∧, T'aiwan	269d	25.10 N	121.33 E
Ch'ihsing Yen I	100	21.46 N	120.49 E
Chihtungtsun	100	22.44 N	120.14 E
Chihu	100	24.07 N	117.51 E
Chihuahua	232	28.38 N	106.05 W
Chihuahua □[3]	232	28.30 N	106.00 W
Chihuahuan Desert ◆[2]	16	35.00 N	106.00 W
Chii-san ∧	98	35.20 N	127.44 E
Chii-san Kukrip Kongwŏn ♦	98	35.20 N	127.39 E
Chiitola	26	61.16 N	29.38 E
Chikaskia ≃	196	36.37 N	97.15 W
Chik Ballāpur	122	13.28 N	77.44 E
Chikhli	122	20.21 N	76.15 E
Chikindzonot	232	20.20 N	88.29 W
Chikmagalūr	122	13.19 N	75.47 E
Chiknai ≃	126	24.06 N	89.17 E
Chiknāyakanhalli	122	13.26 N	76.37 E
Chikoa	154	13.24 S	32.07 E
Chikodi	122	16.26 N	74.36 E
Chikou	100	30.44 N	117.32 E
Chikrêng ≃	110	12.51 N	104.14 E
Ch'iku	100	23.08 N	120.07 E
Chikugo	96	33.12 N	130.30 E
Chikugo ≃	92	33.09 N	130.21 E
Chikujō-kichi, Kōkū-jieitai- ■	96	33.41 N	131.03 E
Chikuma ≃	94	36.59 N	138.35 E
Chikuminuk Lake ◎	180	60.14 N	159.00 W
Chikura	94	34.57 N	139.57 E
Chikusa	96	35.09 N	134.26 E
Chikusa ≃	96	34.44 N	134.24 E
Chikushino	96	33.29 N	130.31 E
Chikwawa	154	16.03 S	34.48 E
Chi-kyaw	110	20.17 N	93.54 E
Chikyu-misaki ›	92a	42.18 N	141.00 E
Chila	152	12.04 S	14.29 E
Chilacachapa	234	18.17 N	99.43 W
Chilakalūrupet	122	16.05 N	80.10 E

Nome	Página	Lat.°'	Long.°'
Chilako ≃	182	53.54 N	122.59 W
Chilam Chauki	123	35.03 N	75.07 E
Chilanga	154	15.34 S	28.17 E
Chilanko Forks	182	52.06 N	124.10 W
Chilapa de Álvarez	234	17.36 N	99.10 W
Chilās	123	35.26 N	74.05 E
Chilaw	122	7.34 N	79.47 E
Chilca, Perú	248	12.32 S	76.44 W
Chilca, Perú	248	12.09 S	75.11 W
Chilca, Punta ›	248	12.27 S	76.48 W
Chilchota	234	19.51 N	102.08 W
Chilcotin ≃	182	51.45 N	122.24 W
Chilcott Island I	166	16.58 S	149.58 E
Childers	166	25.14 S	152.17 E
Childersburg	194	33.16 N	86.21 W
Childer Thornton	262	53.17 N	2.57 W
Childress	196	34.25 N	100.12 W
Childs	210	41.34 N	75.32 W
Chile □[1]	244	30.00 S	71.00 W
Chile, Hipódromo ♦	286e	33.24 S	70.41 W
Chile, Universidad de ᵾ[2]	286e	33.27 S	70.40 W
Chile Basin ✢[1]	18	33.00 S	80.00 W
Chile Chico	254	46.33 S	71.44 W
Chilecito, Arg.	252	29.10 S	67.30 W
Chilecito, Arg.	252	33.53 S	69.03 W
Chilengue, Serra do ⋏	152	13.10 S	15.18 E
Chileno, Arroyo ≃, Ur.	258	33.55 S	58.08 W
Chileno, Arroyo ≃, Ur.	288	34.22 S	57.54 W
Chile Rise ✢[3]	18	40.00 S	90.00 W
Chilete	248	7.14 S	78.51 W
Chilham	42	51.15 N	0.57 E
Chilhowie	192	36.47 N	81.40 W
Chili	216	40.52 N	86.02 W
Chili ≃	248	16.23 S	71.46 W
Chili, Ouadi V	146	16.44 N	20.53 E
Chilia, Brațul ≃[1]	78	45.18 N	29.40 E
Chili Center	210	43.06 N	77.44 W
Chili → Chile □[1]	244	30.00 S	71.00 W
Chilika Lake ◎	122	19.45 N	85.25 E
Chililabombwe (Bancroft)	154	12.18 S	27.43 E
Chilingchang	107	28.58 N	105.31 E
Chilin → Jilin	89	43.51 N	126.33 E
Chilivani	71	40.36 N	8.56 E
Chilkat Pass)(	180	59.43 N	136.35 W
Chilko ≃	182	52.08 N	123.30 W
Chilko Lake ◎	182	51.20 N	124.05 W
Chilko Lake Indian Reserve ◆[4]	182	51.25 N	124.07 W
Chillagoe	166	17.09 S	144.32 E
Chillán	252	36.36 S	72.07 W
Chillar	252	37.18 S	59.59 W
Chilla Saroda ◆[8]	272a	28.36 N	77.18 E
Chillicothe, Il., U.S.	190	40.55 N	89.29 W
Chillicothe, Mo., U.S.	194	39.47 N	93.33 W
Chillicothe, Oh., U.S.	218	39.19 N	82.58 W
Chillicothe, Tx., U.S.	196	34.15 N	99.30 W
Chilliwack	224	49.10 N	121.57 W
Chilliwack ≃	224	49.05 N	121.57 W
Chilliwack Lake ◎	224	49.03 N	121.25 W
Chillón	286d	11.55 S	77.05 W
Chillón ≃	248	11.57 S	77.09 W
Chillon, Château de ⊥	58	46.25 N	6.56 E
Chillum	284c	38.58 N	76.59 W
Chilly	84	39.25 N	49.05 E
Chilly-Mazarin	261	48.42 N	2.19 E
Chilmāri	124	25.33 N	89.43 E
Chilmark	207	41.20 N	70.44 W
Chilo	218	38.48 N	84.08 W
Chiloane, Ilha I	156	20.40 S	34.55 E
Chiloé, Isla Grande de I	254	42.30 S	73.55 W
Chilok	88	51.21 N	110.28 E
Chilok ≃	88	51.19 N	106.59 E
Chilón	232	17.14 N	92.25 W
Chilonga	154	12.03 S	31.21 E
Chilongo	152	13.55 S	16.35 E
Chiloquin	202	42.34 N	121.51 W
Chilovo	76	57.46 N	29.23 E
Chilpancingo de los Bravo	234	17.33 N	99.30 W
Chilpi	124	22.15 N	81.33 E
Chilston Park ♦	260	51.12 N	0.42 E
Chiltern □[8]	260	51.40 N	0.37 W
Chiltern Hills ⋏[2]	42	51.42 N	0.48 W
Chilton, Eng., U.K.	44	54.39 N	1.33 W
Chilton, Tx., U.S.	222	31.16 N	97.03 W
Chilton, Wi., U.S.	190	44.01 N	88.09 W
Chiluage	152	9.30 S	21.47 E
Chilubula Mission	154	10.09 S	31.00 E
Chilumba	154	10.28 S	34.12 E
Chilung	100	25.08 N	121.44 E
Chilung ≃	269d	25.07 N	121.27 E
Chilung Kang c	269d	25.09 N	121.45 E
Chilung Shih □[7]	269d	25.08 N	121.45 E
Chiluvya	154	12.18 S	34.01 E
Chilwa, Lake ◎	154	15.12 S	35.50 E
Chilwell	169	38.10 S	144.21 E
Chimaco	152	15.12 S	21.56 E
Chimacum	224	48.00 N	122.46 W
Chimacum Creek ≃	224	48.03 N	122.45 W
Chimakela	152	15.24 S	16.58 E
Chimaltenango	236	14.40 N	90.49 W
Chimaltenango □[5]	236	14.40 N	90.55 W
Chimaltitán	234	21.46 N	103.50 W
Chimán	246	8.42 N	78.37 W
Chimanimani National Park ♦	154	19.48 S	33.56 E
Chimay	50	50.03 N	4.19 E
Chimayo	200	36.00 N	105.55 W
Chimbarongo	252	34.42 S	71.03 W
Chimbas	252	31.29 S	68.32 W
Chimborazo □[4]	246	2.00 S	78.40 W
Chimborazo ∧	236	13.05 N	85.58 W
Chimborazo ∧[1]	246	1.28 S	78.48 W
Chimbote	248	9.05 S	78.36 W
Chimbu □[5]	164	6.05 S	145.00 E
Chimbua	152	16.32 S	15.08 E
Ch'imei Yü I	100	23.13 N	119.26 E
Chimichagua	246	9.15 N	73.49 W
Chimkent → Čimkent	85	42.18 N	69.36 E
Chimki	82	55.54 N	37.26 E
Chimki-Chovrino ◆[8]	265b	55.51 N	37.30 E
Chimkinskoje vodochranilišče ◎[1]	265b	55.51 N	37.28 E
Chimney Reservoir ◎[1]	204	41.25 N	117.10 W
Chimney Rock National Historic Site ♦	198	41.39 N	103.20 W
Chimoio	156	19.08 S	33.29 E
Chimon Island I	276	41.04 N	73.23 W
Chimpay	252	39.10 S	66.09 W
Chimpembe	154	9.31 S	29.33 E
Chimpôro ≃	152	17.20 S	17.17 E
Chin □[8]	110	22.00 N	93.30 E
China, Méx.	232	25.42 N	99.14 W
Chinā, Nihon	174m	26.24 N	127.46 E
China (Zhongguo) □[1]	90	35.00 N	105.00 E
China, Tanjong ›	271c	1.14 N	103.51 E
Chinácota	246	7.37 N	72.36 W
China Grove	192	35.34 N	80.34 W
China Lake ◎	204	35.46 N	117.39 W
China Lake Naval Weapons Center ■	204	35.35 N	117.10 W
Chinameca	236	13.30 N	88.21 W
China Meridional, Mar de → South China Sea ∓[2]	108	10.00 N	113.00 E
Chinan	98	35.48 N	127.25 E
Chinandega	236	12.37 N	87.09 W
Chinandega □[5]	236	12.45 N	87.05 W
Chinan → Jinan	98	36.40 N	116.57 E
China Spring	222	31.39 N	97.18 W

Nome	Página	Lat.°'	Long.°'
Chinati Peak ∧	196	29.57 N	104.29 W
Chinatown ◆[8]	282	37.48 N	122.26 W
Chincha Alta	248	13.27 S	76.08 W
Chinchaga ≃	176	58.50 N	118.20 W
Chincheros	248	13.27 S	73.44 W
Chinchiang → Quanzhou	100	24.54 N	118.35 E
Chinchilla, Austl.	166	26.45 S	150.38 E
Chinchilla, Pa., U.S.	210	41.28 N	75.41 W
Chinchiná	246	4.58 N	75.36 W
Chincholi	272c	19.10 N	73.08 E
Chinchón, Esp.	34	40.08 N	3.25 W
Chinch'ŏn, Taehan	98	36.52 N	127.26 E
Chinchorro, Banco ✢[4]	232	18.35 N	87.22 W
Chinchou → Jinzhou	104	41.07 N	121.08 E
Chincilla de Monte Aragón	34	38.55 N	1.43 W
Chincolco	252	32.13 S	70.50 W
Chincoteague	208	37.55 N	75.22 W
Chincoteague Bay c	208	38.06 N	75.15 W
Chincoteague Inlet c	208	37.53 N	75.25 W
Chinde	156	18.37 S	36.24 E
Chindo	98	34.28 N	126.15 E
Chin-do I	98	34.25 N	126.15 E
Chindong	98	35.07 N	128.29 E
Chindwinn ≃	110	21.26 N	95.15 E
Chine (la République populaire de) → China □[1], Asia	90	35.00 N	105.00 E
Chine (nationaliste) → Taiwan □[1], Asia	100	23.30 N	121.00 E
Chinen	174m	26.09 N	127.49 E
Chineni	123	33.02 N	75.17 E
Chine Orientale, Mer de → East China Sea ∓[2]	90	30.00 N	126.00 E
Chinese Camp	226	37.52 N	120.26 W
Chinese Cemetery ◆	269f	14.38 N	120.59 E
Chinese University ᵾ[2]	271d	22.26 N	114.12 E
Chingamba	152	12.49 S	18.20 E
Chingansk	89	49.07 N	131.11 E
Chingarora Creek ≃	276	40.27 N	74.12 W
Ch'ingchiang → Qingjiang	100	33.35 N	119.02 E
Chingford ◆[8]	260	51.38 N	0.01 E
Chingleput	122	12.42 N	79.59 E
Chingmei ◆[8]	269d	24.59 N	121.32 E
Chingola	154	12.32 S	27.52 E
Chingoni	157a	12.48 S	45.08 E
Chingoroi	152	13.37 S	14.01 E
Chingshih → Jinshi	102	29.39 N	111.52 E
Ch'ingtao → Qingdao	98	36.06 N	120.19 E
Chingtechen → Jingdezhen	100	29.16 N	117.11 E
Ch'ingt'ung	269d	25.02 N	121.43 E
Chinguar	152	12.36 S	16.20 E
Chinguetti	150	20.27 N	12.22 W
Chingune	156	20.38 S	34.55 E
Chinhae	98	35.09 N	128.40 E
Chinhae-man c	98	35.01 N	128.34 E
Chin Hills ⋏[2]	110	22.30 N	93.30 E
Chinhoyi	154	17.22 S	30.12 E
Chinhsien → Jinxian	98	39.04 N	121.40 E
Chinhua → Jinhua	100	29.07 N	119.39 E
Ch'inhuangtao → Qinhuangdao	98	39.56 N	119.36 E
Chīni	120	31.32 N	78.15 E
Chiniak, Cape ›	180	57.36 N	152.08 W
Chining → Jining, Zhg.	98	35.25 N	116.36 E
Chining → Jining, Zhg.	102	40.57 N	113.02 E
Chiniot	123	31.43 N	72.59 E
Chinĭt ≃	110	12.55 N	105.35 E
Chinitna Point ›	180	59.43 N	153.02 W
Chinizíua	156	19.00 S	35.09 E
Chinjan	120	30.34 N	67.58 E
Chinju	98	35.11 N	128.05 E
Chinkiang → Zhenjiang	106	32.13 N	119.26 E
Chinko ≃	136	4.50 N	23.53 E
Chinkuashih	100	25.07 N	121.51 E
Chin Lakes ◎	182	49.37 N	112.13 W
Chinle	200	36.09 N	109.33 W
Chinle Creek ≃	200	37.12 N	109.43 W
Chinle Wash V	200	36.54 N	109.45 W
Chinley	262	53.20 N	1.56 W
Chinley Churn ∧[2]	262	53.21 N	1.57 W
Chinmen	100	24.27 N	118.21 E
Chinmen Tao I	100	24.27 N	118.23 E
Chinnampo → Namp'o	98	38.45 N	125.23 E
Chinnor	42	51.43 N	0.56 W
Chino, Nihon	94	35.59 N	138.09 E
Chino, Ca., U.S.	228	34.00 N	117.41 W
Chino Airport ⊠	280	33.59 N	117.38 W
Chino Creek ≃	280	33.53 N	117.38 W
Chino Hills ⋏[2]	280	33.56 N	117.45 W
Chinon	50	47.10 N	0.15 E
Chinook, Ab., Can.	184	51.27 N	110.56 W
Chinook, Mt., U.S.	202	48.35 N	109.13 W
Chinook, Wa., U.S.	224	46.16 N	123.56 W
Chinook Cove	182	51.14 N	120.10 W
Chino Valley	200	34.45 N	112.27 W
Chinowths Corner	226	36.20 N	119.19 W
Chinpāi	126	23.50 N	87.28 E
Chinquapin	192	34.49 N	77.49 W
Chinsali	154	10.34 S	32.03 E
Chinshan	100	25.13 N	121.38 E
Chinshui	100	24.36 N	120.53 E
Chintāmani	122	13.24 N	78.04 E
Chintembwe	154	13.25 S	33.59 E
Chintheche	154	11.52 S	34.09 E
Chinú	246	9.06 N	75.24 W
Chinunje	154	11.19 S	37.19 E
Chinwangtao → Qinhuangdao	98	39.56 N	119.36 E
Chiny	56	49.44 N	5.20 E
Chinyama Litapi	152	13.31 S	22.21 E
Chioco	154	16.25 S	32.50 E
Chioggia	64	45.13 N	12.17 E
Chiomonte	62	45.07 N	6.59 E
Chios → Khíos	38	38.22 N	26.08 E
Chios → Khíos I	38	38.22 N	26.00 E
Chipamanu (Xipamanu) ≃	248	10.43 S	67.50 W
Chipao	248	14.15 S	73.57 W
Chipata (Fort Jameson)	154	13.39 S	32.40 E
Chipei Tao I	100	23.45 N	119.37 E
Chipera	154	15.28 S	32.30 E
Chiperone ∧	154	16.28 S	35.12 E
Chipili	154	10.44 S	29.04 E
Chiping	98	36.37 N	116.16 E
Chipinge	154	20.12 S	32.38 E
Chip Lake ◎	182	53.40 N	115.20 W
Chipley	194	30.46 N	85.32 W
Chiplūn	122	17.32 N	73.31 E
Chipman	186	46.11 N	65.53 W
Chipogolo	154	6.52 S	36.02 E
Chipoka	154	14.00 S	34.31 E
Chipola ≃	192	30.01 N	85.05 W
Chippawa ◆[8]	284a	43.04 N	79.03 W
Chippawa Channel ≃[1]	284a	43.04 N	79.01 W
Chippego Lake ◎	212	44.34 N	76.49 W
Chippenham	42	51.28 N	2.07 W
Chipperfield	260	51.42 N	0.29 W
Chippewa ≃, Mi., U.S.	190	43.35 N	84.17 W
Chippewa ≃, Mn., U.S.	198	44.56 N	95.44 W
Chippewa ≃, Wi., U.S.	190	44.25 N	92.10 W

Nome	Página	Lat.°'	Long.°'
Chippewa, East Branch ≃	198	45.20 N	95.36 W
Chippewa, East Fork ≃	190	45.53 N	91.05 W
Chippewa, Lake ◎	190	45.56 N	91.13 W
Chippewa Bay c	212	44.27 N	75.47 W
Chippewa Creek ≃	212	44.27 N	75.46 W
Chippewa Falls	190	44.56 N	91.23 W
Chippewa Lake	214	41.04 N	81.54 W
Chippewanuck Creek ≃	216	41.07 N	86.12 W
Chipping Campden	42	52.03 N	1.46 W
Chipping Norton	42	51.56 N	1.32 W
Chipping Ongar	260	51.43 N	0.15 E
Chipping Sodbury	42	51.33 N	2.24 W
Chippis	58	46.17 N	7.33 E
Chippokes Plantation State Park ♦	208	37.08 N	76.44 W
Chipps Island I	282	38.03 N	121.55 W
Chipre → Cyprus □[1]	130	35.00 N	33.00 E
Chipstead, Eng., U.K.	260	51.17 N	0.09 E
Chipstead, Eng., U.K.	260	51.18 N	0.10 W
Chipuriro	154	16.39 S	30.42 E
Chiquelequele	152	16.40 S	19.06 E
Chiquián	248	10.09 S	77.11 W
Chiquihuitlán	234	17.59 N	96.48 W
Chiquimula	236	14.48 N	89.33 W
Chiquimula □[5]	236	14.40 N	89.25 W
Chiquimulilla	236	14.05 N	90.23 W
Chiquinquirá	246	5.37 N	73.50 W
Chiquintirca	248	13.09 S	73.41 W
Chiquita	152	8.38 S	17.05 E
Chiquito ≃	234	18.29 N	101.07 W
Chiquito Creek ≃	226	37.20 N	119.20 W
Chira ≃	246	4.54 S	81.08 W
Chira, Isla I	236	10.06 N	85.09 W
Chirad	272c	19.09 N	73.07 E
Chiradzulu	154	15.42 S	35.10 E
Chirāgh Delhi ◆[8]	272a	28.32 N	77.14 E
Chīrāla	122	15.49 N	80.21 E
Chiramba	154	16.55 S	34.39 E
Chirape	156	21.18 S	33.33 E
Chirāwa	120	28.15 N	75.38 E
Chirchik → Čirčik	85	41.29 N	69.35 E
Chire (Shire) ≃	154	17.42 S	35.19 E
Chiredzi	154	21.03 S	31.45 E
Chireno	194	31.30 N	94.21 W
Chirens	62	45.25 N	5.33 E
Chirfa	146	20.57 N	12.21 E
Chīrgaon	124	25.35 N	78.49 E
Chiriaco ≃	248	5.05 S	78.19 W
Chiricahua Mountains ⋏	200	31.50 N	109.15 W
Chiricahua National Monument ♦	200	32.02 N	109.19 W
Chiricahua Peak ∧	200	31.52 N	109.20 W
Chiriguaná	246	9.22 N	73.36 W
Chirikof Island I	180	55.50 N	155.35 W
Chirilagua	236	13.13 N	88.08 W
Chirinos	248	5.16 S	78.52 W
Chiriquí	236	8.24 N	82.19 W
Chiriquí □[4]	236	8.30 N	82.00 W
Chiriquí, Golfo de c	246	8.00 N	82.20 W
Chiriquí, Laguna de c	236	9.03 N	82.00 W
Chiriquí Grande	236	8.57 N	82.07 W
Chiriquí Viejo ≃	236	8.20 N	82.41 W
Chirk	42	52.56 N	3.03 W
Chirki	126	24.03 N	86.09 E
Chirle	272c	18.56 N	73.02 E
Chirmiri	124	23.12 N	82.21 E
Chirnside	46	55.48 N	2.13 W
Chiromo	154	16.33 S	35.08 E
Chirovo	76	58.56 N	33.24 E
Chirripó ≃	236	10.41 N	83.41 W
Chirripó, Cerro ∧	236	9.29 N	83.30 W
Chirripó, Parque Nacional ♦	236	9.30 N	83.30 W
Chirsa	84	41.31 N	46.06 E
Chirundu	154	15.59 S	28.54 E
Chirvosti	265a	59.57 N	30.37 E
Chiryū	94	35.00 N	137.02 E
Chisago City	190	45.22 N	92.53 W
Chisamba	154	14.58 S	28.23 E
Chisana	180	62.09 N	142.10 W
Chisasibi	176	53.50 N	79.00 W
Chiscas	246	6.33 N	72.29 W
Chisec	236	15.49 N	90.17 W
Chiseldon	42	51.31 N	1.44 W
Chisenga	154	9.56 S	33.26 E
Chisep'o	98	34.50 N	128.42 E
Ch'ishan	100	22.53 N	120.28 E
Chishanji	98	36.56 N	122.23 E
Chishi	100	27.42 N	117.58 E
Chishisi	100	25.32 N	113.11 E
Chisholm, Al., U.S.	194	32.25 N	86.15 W
Chisholm, Me., U.S.	188	44.28 N	70.12 W
Chisholm, Mn., U.S.	190	47.29 N	92.53 W
Chisholm, Tx., U.S.	222	32.51 N	96.22 W
Chisholm Mills	182	54.55 N	114.08 W
Chishtiān Mandi	123	29.48 N	72.52 E
Chishui	102	28.29 N	105.38 E
Chishui ≃, Zhg.	102	28.53 N	105.48 E
Chishui ≃, Zhg.	107	28.49 N	105.50 E
Chishuihe	102	27.50 N	105.32 E
Chišig-Öndör	88	48.19 N	103.25 E
Chisimaio → Kismaayo	144	0.22 N	42.32 E
Chișinău → Kišin'ov	78	47.00 N	28.50 E
Chișineu-Criș	38	46.31 N	21.31 E
Chislaviči	76	54.11 N	32.10 E
Chislehurst ◆[8]	260	51.25 N	0.04 E
Chisone ≃	62	44.49 N	7.25 E
Chisone, Valle del V	62	45.01 N	7.07 E
Chisos Mountains ⋏	196	29.15 N	103.20 W
Chisseaux	50	47.20 N	1.05 E
Chissengue	152	9.14 S	20.42 E
Chissilo	152	13.34 S	16.30 E
Chistochina	180	62.34 N	144.40 W
Chistopol → Čistopol'	80	55.21 N	50.37 E
Chiswellgreen	260	51.44 N	0.22 W
Chiswick ◆[8]	260	51.29 N	0.16 W
Chita, Bol.	248	20.06 S	66.57 W
Chita, Col.	246	6.11 N	72.28 W
Chita, Nihon	94	35.00 N	136.51 E
Chita → Čita	88	52.03 N	113.30 E
Chitado	152	17.20 S	13.54 E
Chitagá	246	7.09 N	72.40 W
Chita-hantō ›[1]	94	34.50 N	136.53 E
Chitambo	154	12.55 S	30.39 E
Chitanda ≃	152	16.01 S	15.12 E
Chitarda	126	21.50 N	86.57 E
Chitata	152	13.47 S	15.43 E
Chitato	152	7.20 S	20.47 E
Chita-wan c	94	34.47 N	136.58 E
Chitek ≃	184	54.06 N	108.16 W
Chitek Lake ◎, Mb., Can.	184	52.26 N	99.25 W
Chitek Lake ◎, Sk., Can.	184	53.44 N	107.47 W
Chitembo	152	13.34 S	16.40 E
Chitina	180	61.31 N	144.27 W
Chitina ≃	180	61.30 N	144.28 W
Chitipa	154	9.43 S	33.16 E
Chitokoloki	152	13.50 S	23.13 E
Chitose	92a	42.49 N	141.39 E
Chitose-chūtonchi, Rikujō-jieitai- ■	92a	42.46 N	141.40 E
Chitou Shan I	100	27.40 N	120.50 E
Chitra ≃[1]	126	22.53 N	89.40 E
Chitradurga	122	14.14 N	76.24 E
Chitrakūt Dham	124	25.11 N	80.52 E
Chitrāl	123	35.51 N	71.47 E
Chitrasāli	272b	22.52 N	88.09 E
Chitrāvati ≃	122	14.48 N	78.14 E
Chitré	236	7.58 N	80.26 W
Chittagong	120	22.20 N	91.50 E
Chittagong □[5]	120	23.00 N	91.00 E
Chittāpur	122	17.07 N	77.05 E

≃	River	Fluß	Río	Rivière	Rio
≅	Canal	Kanal	Canal	Canal	Canal
⌐	Waterfall, Rapids	Wasserfall, Stromschnellen	Cascada, Rápidos	Chute d'eau, Rapides	Cascata, Rápidos
)(	Strait	Meeresstraße	Estrecho	Détroit	Estreito
c	Bay, Gulf	Bucht, Golf	Bahía, Golfo	Baie, Golfe	Baía, Golfo
◎	Lake, Lakes	See, Seen	Lago, Lagos	Lac, Lacs	Lago, Lagos
≛	Swamp	Sumpf	Pantano	Marais	Pântano
⌆	Ice Features, Glacier	Eis- und Gletscherformen	Accidentes Glaciales	Formes glaciaires	Acidentes glaciares
∓	Other Hydrographic Features	Andere Hydrographische Objekte	Otros Elementos Hidrográficos	Autres données hydrographiques	Outros acidentes hidrográficos

✢	Submarine Features	Untermeerische Objekte	Accidentes Submarinos	Formes de relief sous-marin	Acidentes submarinos
□	Political Unit	Politische Einheit	Unidad Politica	Entité politique	Unidade política
ᵾ	Cultural Institution	Kulturelle Institution	Institución Cultural	Institution culturelle	Instituição cultural
⊥	Historical Site	Historische Stätte	Sitio Histórico	Site historique	Sitio histórico
♦	Recreational Site	Erholungs- und Ferienort	Sitio de Recreo	Centre de loisirs	Area de Lazer
⊠	Airport	Flughafen	Aeropuerto	Aéroport	Aeroporto
■	Military Installation	Militäranlage	Instalación Militar	Installation militaire	Instalação militar
◆	Miscellaneous	Verschiedenes	Misceláneo	Divers	Diversos

ENGLISH: Name / Page / Lat.°′ / Long.°′
DEUTSCH: Name / Seite / Breite°′ / Länge°′ E = Ost

Chittaranjan 126 23.52 N 86.52 E
Chittaurgarh 120 24.53 N 74.38 E
Chittenango 210 43.02 N 75.52 W
Chittenango Creek ≃ 210 43.11 N 76.00 W
Chittenango Falls 210 42.59 N 75.50 W
Chittering 162 31.29 S 116.06 E
Chittoor 122 13.12 N 79.07 E
Chittūr 122 10.42 N 76.45 E
Chitu, Ityo. 144 8.36 N 37.59 E
Ch'itu, T'aiwan 269d 25.06 N 121.43 E
Chitungwiza 154 17.45 S 31.16 E
Chiuchiang → Jiujiang 100 29.44 N 115.59 E
Chíuchíu 252 22.21 S 68.39 W
Chiuduno 62 45.40 N 9.51 E
Chiumbe 152 12.29 S 16.08 E
Chiumbe ≃ 152 7.00 S 21.12 E
Chiúme 152 15.03 S 21.14 E
Chiuppano 64 45.46 N 11.28 E
Chiuro 64 46.10 N 9.59 E
Chiusa (Klausen) 64 46.38 N 11.34 E
Chiusa di Pesio 62 44.19 N 7.40 E
Chiusa di San Michele 62 45.06 N 7.19 E
Chiusaforte 64 46.24 N 13.18 E
Chiusa Sclafani 70 37.41 N 13.16 E
Chiusella ≃ 62 45.24 N 7.55 E
Chiusi 66 43.01 N 11.57 E
Chiusi, Lago di ⊜ 66 43.03 N 11.58 E
Chiúta 154 15.34 S 33.17 E
Chiuta, Lake ⊜ 154 14.55 S 35.50 E
Chiv 84 41.46 N 47.54 E
Chiva 72 41.24 N 60.22 E
Chivacoa 246 10.10 N 68.54 W
Chivasso 62 45.11 N 7.53 E
Chivato, Punta › 232 27.05 N 111.59 W
Chivay 248 15.40 S 71.35 W
Chivhu 154 19.01 S 30.53 E
Chivilcoy 252 34.53 S 60.01 W
Chivirira Falls ↳ 154 21.14 S 32.20 E
Chiwanda 154 11.22 S 34.54 E
Chiwawa ≃ 224 47.47 N 120.40 W
Chixi 100 28.22 N 116.22 E
Chixoy (Salinas) ≃ 232 16.28 N 90.33 W
Chixoy, Embalse ⊜[1] 236 15.15 N 90.30 W
Chiyoda, Nihon 94 36.12 N 139.26 E
Chiyoda, Nihon 94 36.11 N 140.14 E
Chiyoda, Nihon 96 34.41 N 132.32 E
Chiyoda ◆[8] 268 35.41 N 139.44 E
Chizarira National Park ♦ 154 17.45 S 28.00 E
Chizhen 100 31.55 N 118.12 E
Chizizhen 100 32.22 N 115.11 E
Chizu 96 35.16 N 134.14 E
Chjargas 88 49.32 N 93.48 E
Chjargas nuur ⊜ 88 49.12 N 93.24 E
Chkalov → Orenburg 86 51.54 N 55.06 E
Chlebnikovo, Ross. 80 56.38 N 49.56 E
Chlebnikovo, Ross. 265b 55.58 N 37.31 E
Chlebodarnyj 80 46.41 N 40.50 E
Chlebodarovka 83 47.29 N 37.23 E
Chlevnoje 76 52.12 N 39.05 E
Chloride 200 35.24 N 114.11 W
Chlum 60 48.52 N 13.55 E
Chlum ∧ 61 48.42 N 14.04 E
Chmelevicy 80 57.45 N 46.22 E
Chmelevo 82 56.09 N 39.08 E
Chmelevoje 78 48.34 N 31.24 E
Chmelita 76 55.25 N 33.53 E
Chmel'nickij 78 49.25 N 27.00 E
Chmel'nik 78 49.33 N 27.57 E
Chmel'niki, Ross. 82 56.52 N 38.13 E
Chmel'niki, Ross. 82 56.53 N 38.39 E
Chmielnik 30 50.37 N 20.46 E
Chmost' ≃ 76 54.45 N 32.34 E
Choa Chu Kang 271c 1.22 N 103.41 E
Choāli 272b 22.24 N 88.24 E
Chŏâm Khsant 110 14.13 N 104.56 E
Choba 154 2.26 N 38.03 E
Chobe □[5] 156 18.30 S 25.00 E
Chobe ≃ 156 17.50 S 25.05 E
Chobeju 24 64.53 N 60.10 E
Chobe National Park ♦ 156 18.45 S 24.15 E
Chobham 260 51.21 N 0.36 W
Chobham Common ♦ 260 51.23 N 0.37 W
Chobi 84 42.21 N 41.53 E
Chocamán 234 18.59 N 97.01 W
Choccolocco Creek ≃ 194 33.33 N 86.11 W
Choceň 30 50.00 N 16.13 E
Chocenice 60 49.33 N 13.31 E
Chochis, Cerro ∧ 248 18.04 S 60.03 W
Choch'iwŏn 98 36.37 N 127.18 E
Chochloma 80 56.58 N 43.54 E
Chöchmor't 88 47.21 N 94.33 E
Chochol'skij 78 51.34 N 38.45 E
Cho Chu 110 21.54 N 105.39 E
Chocianów 30 51.25 N 15.55 E
Chociwel 30 53.28 N 15.19 E
Chocó □[5] 246 6.00 N 77.00 W
Chocolate Bay c 222 29.11 N 95.09 W
Chocolate Bayou ≃ 222 29.13 N 95.13 W
Chocolate Mountains ⋏ 204 33.20 N 115.15 W
Chocontá 246 5.09 N 73.41 W
Chocope 248 7.47 S 79.13 W
Choctawhatchee, East Fork ≃ 194 31.21 N 85.33 W
Choctawhatchee, West Fork ≃ 194 31.21 N 85.33 W
Choctawhatchee Bay c 194 30.25 N 86.21 W
Choctaw Lake ⊜[1] 218 39.58 N 83.29 W
Chodarus 88 52.36 N 99.19 E
Chodavaram 122 17.50 N 82.57 E
Chodecz 30 52.24 N 19.01 E
Ch'o-do I, C.M.I.K. 98 38.32 N 124.50 E
Ch'o-do I, Taehan 98 34.14 N 127.15 E
Chodoi 114 2.50 N 101.27 E
Chodorov 78 49.24 N 24.17 E
Chodosy 76 53.56 N 31.29 E
Chodov 54 50.11 N 12.43 E
Chodovaja Griva 80 57.08 N 50.16 E
Chodovaricha 24 68.57 N 53.40 E
Chodz' ≃ 84 44.43 N 40.45 E
Chodžaimetk 85 39.37 N 69.14 E
Chodžakala 128 38.43 N 56.20 E
Chodžejli 72 42.48 N 59.25 E
Chodzież 30 52.59 N 16.56 E
Choele-Choel 252 39.16 S 65.41 W
Chofombo 154 14.35 S 31.50 E
Chōfu 94 35.39 N 139.33 E
Chofu Airport ⊠ 268 35.40 N 139.32 E
Chogo Lungma Glacier ⊓ 123 35.52 N 75.19 E
Chogot 88 53.15 N 105.52 E
Choiceland 184 53.27 N 104.25 W
Choichuff, Laga ≃ 154 1.34 N 39.24 E
Choire, Loch ⊜ 46 58.13 N 4.21 W
Choisel 261 48.41 N 2.01 E
Choiseul 241f 13.47 N 61.03 W
Choiseul I 175e 7.05 S 157.00 E
Choiseul Sound ⊔ 254 51.57 S 58.35 W
Choisy 58 45.59 N 6.03 E
Choisy-le-Roi 261 48.46 N 2.25 E
Choix 232 26.43 N 108.17 W
Chojna 30 52.58 N 14.28 E
Chojnice 30 53.42 N 17.34 E
Chojniki 78 51.53 N 29.56 E
Chojnów 30 51.17 N 15.56 E
Chōkai-san ∧ 92 39.06 N 140.03 E
Choke ⋏ 144 10.45 N 37.35 E
Choke Canyon Lake ⊜[1] 196 28.30 N 98.20 W
Chokio 198 45.34 N 96.10 W
Chokoloskee 220 25.48 N 81.21 W
Chokwé 156 24.36 S 33.00 E
Cholame 226 35.43 N 120.17 W
Cholame Creek ≃ 226 35.39 N 120.22 W
Cholame Hills ⋏[2] 226 35.45 N 120.30 W
Cholbon 88 51.53 N 116.15 E
Choldarkipčak 85 39.51 N 68.52 E
Cholet 32 47.04 N 0.53 W
Cholila 254 42.31 S 71.27 W
Chŏlla Namdo □[4] 98 34.45 N 127.00 E
Chŏlla Pukdo □[4] 98 35.45 N 127.15 E
Cholm 76 57.09 N 31.11 E
Cholmeč', Bela. 78 52.09 N 30.37 E
Cholmec, Ross. 76 56.21 N 33.21 E
Cholmogorovka 86 44.25 N 78.31 E
Cholmogorskaja 24 63.49 N 40.39 E
Cholmogory 24 64.15 N 41.40 E
Cholmsk 89 47.03 N 142.03 E
Cholmskij 78 44.52 N 38.24 E
Cholmy, Ross. 82 54.56 N 38.33 E
Cholmy, Ukr. 78 51.52 N 32.36 E
Cholm-Žirkovskij 76 55.31 N 33.29 E
Cholodnaja Balka 83 48.02 N 38.04 E
Choloj ≃ 88 53.12 N 112.47 E
Choloma 236 15.34 N 87.56 W
Chölönbujr 88 47.55 N 112.57 E
Cholopeniči 76 54.31 N 28.58 E
Ch'ŏlsan 98 39.46 N 124.40 E
Cholsey 42 51.34 N 1.10 W
Choltobino 82 54.11 N 38.28 E
Choltoson 88 50.20 N 103.20 E
Choluj, Ross. 80 56.34 N 41.53 E
Choluj, Ross. 80 56.04 N 42.08 E
Cholula [de Rivadabia] 234 19.04 N 98.18 W
Choluteca 236 13.18 N 87.12 W
Choluteca □[5] 236 13.20 N 87.10 W
Choluteca ≃ 236 13.07 N 87.19 W
Choma 154 16.48 S 26.59 E
Chomedey ◆[8] 275a 45.32 N 73.44 W
Chomen Swamp ⩸ 144 9.25 N 37.20 E
Chomérac 62 44.42 N 4.39 E
Chomičev 80 48.11 N 45.01 E
Chomiomo ∧ 124 28.01 N 88.31 E
Cho Moi, Viet 110 10.33 N 105.24 E
Cho Moi, Viet 269c 10.51 N 106.38 E
Chomo Lhāri ∧ 124 27.50 N 89.15 E
Chom Thong 110 18.25 N 98.41 E
Chomūm 120 27.10 N 75.44 E
Chomutec 78 50.06 N 33.44 E
Chomutov 54 50.28 N 13.26 E
Chomutovka 78 51.56 N 34.33 E
Chomutovka ≃ 54 50.11 N 13.37 E
Chomutovo, Ross. 76 52.51 N 37.27 E
Chomutovo, Ross. 88 52.28 N 104.25 E
Chomutovskaja 83 47.03 N 40.04 E
Chomutovskaja Step', zapovednik ♦ 83 47.17 N 38.11 E
Chōnan, Nihon 94 35.24 N 140.14 E
Ch'ŏnan, Taehan 98 36.48 N 127.09 E
Chon'atino 82 55.11 N 38.07 E
Chon Buri 110 13.22 N 100.59 E
Chonchi 254 42.38 S 73.47 W
Choncholoj 88 51.08 N 108.14 E
Chon Daen 110 16.11 N 100.51 E
Chone 246 0.41 S 80.06 W
Chone ≃ 246 0.35 S 80.25 W
Chong'an 100 27.45 N 118.02 E
Ch'ŏngch'ŏn-gang ≃ 98 39.35 N 125.28 E
Ch'ŏngdan 98 37.58 N 125.56 E
Chongde 106 30.32 N 120.26 E
Ch'ŏngdo 98 35.38 N 128.43 E
Chonggu 106 31.12 N 121.10 E
Ch'ŏngha 98 36.13 N 129.20 E
Ch'onghak-ni 271b 37.43 N 127.05 E
Chonghe 89 44.43 N 127.45 E
Ch'ŏngjin 98 41.47 N 129.50 E
Chŏngju, C.M.I.K. 98 39.41 N 125.13 E
Ch'ŏngju, Taehan 98 36.39 N 127.31 E
Chŏng Kal 110 13.57 N 103.35 E
Chongkanzhen 107 30.09 N 105.37 E
Chongli (Xiwanzi) 98 40.54 N 115.16 E
Chongming 106 31.37 N 121.24 E
Chongming Dao I 106 31.36 N 121.33 E
Chongoene 156 25.00 S 33.47 E
Chongor 102 45.59 N 112.45 E
Chongos Bajo 248 12.07 S 75.16 W
Chongoyape 248 6.39 S 79.24 W
Chong Pang 271c 1.26 N 103.50 E
Chŏngp'yŏng-chŏsuji ⊜[1] 98 37.40 N 127.30 E
Chongqing, Zhg. 107 30.39 N 103.41 E
Chongqing (Chungking), Zhg. 107 29.34 N 106.35 E
Chongren, Zhg. 100 29.37 N 120.43 E
Chongren, Zhg. 100 27.46 N 116.01 E
Chongru 100 27.01 N 120.10 E
Ch'ŏngsan 98 36.22 N 127.46 E
Ch'ŏngsan-do I 98 34.11 N 126.54 E
Chongshi 100 25.24 N 115.28 E
Chŏngsŏn 98 37.22 N 128.38 E
Ch'ŏngsong 98 41.47 N 129.48 E
Chŏngŭp 98 35.36 N 126.51 E
Chongwe ≃ 154 15.43 S 29.20 E
Chongwu 100 24.53 N 118.55 E
Chongxi 98 42.07 N 128.59 E
Chongxin 102 35.13 N 107.29 E
Ch'ŏngyang, Taehan 98 36.27 N 126.48 E
Chongyang, Zhg. 100 29.33 N 114.00 E
Chongyang ≃ 100 27.18 N 118.08 E
Chongyi 100 25.44 N 114.18 E
Chongzuo 102 22.21 N 107.26 E
Choni 84 42.20 N 42.25 E
Chŏnju 98 35.49 N 127.08 E
Chonkham 120 27.48 N 96.02 E
Ch'ŏnma 98 40.03 N 125.01 E
Chonos, Archipiélago de los II 254 45.00 S 74.00 W
Ch'ŏnsu-ri 98 41.43 N 128.45 E
Chontaleña, Cordillera ⋏ 236 11.50 N 84.50 W
Chontales □[5] 236 12.05 N 85.10 W
Chon Thanh 110 11.24 N 106.36 E
Chŏnŭi 98 36.42 N 127.11 E
Chonuu 74 66.27 N 143.06 E
Chonzie, Ben ∧ 46 56.27 N 3.59 W
Cho Oyu → Chopu ∧ 124 28.06 N 86.39 E
Chopda 120 21.15 N 75.18 E
Cho Phuoc Hai 110 10.26 N 107.18 E
Chopim ≃ 252 25.35 S 53.05 W
Chopinzinho 252 25.51 S 52.30 W
Chopon 124 24.31 N 83.02 E
Chop'or ≃ 80 49.36 N 42.19 E
Chop'orskij zapovednik ◆[4] 80 51.15 N 41.48 E
Choptank ≃ 208 38.38 N 76.13 W
Chopu ∧ 124 28.06 N 86.39 E
Chopwell 44 54.55 N 1.49 W
Chor 89 47.53 N 134.58 E
Chor ≃ 89 47.48 N 134.43 E
Chora Saādatpur 272a 28.36 N 77.21 E
Chordil sar'dag ⋏ 88 50.50 N 99.40 E
Chorejver 24 67.25 N 58.03 E
Chorges 62 44.33 N 6.17 E
Chori 84 41.37 N 45.59 E
Chorin ⊥ 54 52.54 N 13.52 E
Chorina ≃ 83 49.23 N 38.13 E
Chorinsk 88 52.10 N 109.46 E
Chorley 262 53.39 N 2.39 W
Chorley □[8] 262 53.38 N 2.38 W
Chorleywood 260 51.39 N 0.31 W
Chorlovo 82 55.20 N 38.49 E
Chorlton-cum-Hardy ◆[8] 262 53.27 N 2.17 W
Chorog 120 37.31 N 71.33 E
Chorol', Ross. 89 44.25 N 132.04 E
Chorol, Ukr. 78 49.47 N 33.17 E
Chorol ≃ 78 49.28 N 33.47 E
Chorolque, Cerro ∧ 248 20.56 S 66.01 W
Choros, Isla I 252 29.16 S 71.33 W
Chorošovo 82 55.08 N 38.47 E
Chorošovo ◆[8] 265b 55.47 N 37.28 E
Chorostkov 78 49.13 N 25.55 E
Choroszcz 30 53.09 N 22.59 E
Chorreras 232 28.50 N 105.18 W
Chorrillos 286d 12.10 S 77.02 W
Chorrochó 250 8.59 S 39.06 W
Chorro Creek ≃ 226 35.20 N 120.50 W
Chort'ak, gora ∧ 88 53.15 N 110.45 E
Ch'ŏrwŏn 98 38.16 N 127.12 E
Chorzele 30 53.16 N 20.55 E
Ch'osan 98 40.50 N 125.47 E
Chosanch'am 98 40.22 N 126.11 E
Chosedachard 24 67.02 N 59.22 E
Chosen 220 26.42 N 80.41 W
Chošeutovo 80 47.02 N 47.50 E
Chōshi 94 35.44 N 140.50 E
Choshi-ōhashi ◆[5] 94 35.44 N 140.50 E
Chōshi-zuka-kofun ⊥ 94 34.42 N 137.50 E
Choshui ≃ 100 24.03 N 120.24 E
Chosica 248 11.54 S 76.42 W
Chos Malal 252 37.23 S 70.16 W
Chosŏn Minjujuŭi In'min Konghwaguk → Korea, North □[1] 98 40.00 N 127.00 E
Chosrech 84 41.59 N 47.18 E
Chosta 84 43.33 N 39.53 E
Choszczno 30 53.10 N 15.26 E
Chota 248 6.33 S 78.39 W
Chotanāgpur Plateau ⋏[1] 124 23.30 N 84.30 E
Chotča ≃ 82 56.54 N 37.35 E
Choteau 202 47.48 N 112.10 W
Choteau Creek ≃ 198 42.51 N 98.09 W
Chotěboř 30 49.43 N 15.40 E
Choten' 78 51.07 N 34.46 E
Chotěšov, Česko. 60 49.39 N 13.12 E
Chotešov, Ukr. 78 51.43 N 24.47 E
Chotila 120 22.25 N 71.11 E
Chotilovo 76 57.44 N 34.05 E
Chotimsk 76 53.26 N 32.35 E
Chotin 78 48.29 N 26.30 E
Chotisino 82 54.24 N 36.33 E
Chot'kovo, Ross. 76 52.56 N 35.23 E
Chot'kovo, Ross. 76 53.46 N 35.14 E
Chot'kovo, Ross. 82 56.15 N 38.00 E
Chotovn'a 76 53.17 N 30.32 E
Chotuš' 82 54.32 N 37.44 E
Chotynec 76 53.08 N 35.24 E
Chotyniči 76 52.38 N 26.18 E
Chouchiak'ou → Shangshui 100 33.33 N 114.34 E
Chouk'ou → Shangshui 100 33.33 N 114.34 E
Choûm 148 21.18 N 13.01 W
Chouteau 196 36.11 N 95.20 W
Chovaling 85 38.21 N 69.58 E
Chovd, Mong. 86 49.16 N 90.55 E
Chovd, Mong. 86 48.08 N 91.23 E
Chovd, Mong. 86 48.01 N 91.38 E
Chovd, Mong. 102 44.42 N 102.24 E
Chovd □[4] 86 48.00 N 91.30 E
Chovd ≃ 90 48.06 N 92.11 E
Chövsgöl 102 43.36 N 109.39 E
Chövsgöl □[4] 88 50.00 N 100.00 E
Chövsgöl nuur ⊜ 88 51.00 N 100.30 E
Chovu-Aksy 88 51.11 N 93.53 E
Chowan ≃ 192 36.00 N 76.40 W
Chowchilla 226 37.07 N 120.15 W
Chowchilla ≃ 226 37.07 N 120.32 W
Chowchilla, East Fork ≃ 226 37.20 N 119.50 W
Chowchilla, West Fork ≃ 226 37.20 N 119.50 W
Chowkay 123 34.41 N 70.56 E
Chown, Mount ∧ 182 53.24 N 119.22 W
Ch'owŏn-ni 98 39.40 N 127.17 E
Choya 252 28.30 S 64.52 W
Choyak-to I 98 34.22 N 126.54 E
Chrapun' 78 51.42 N 27.29 E
Chr'aščevka 80 53.48 N 49.06 E
Chrást 60 49.48 N 13.29 E
Chrebtovo 82 56.35 N 38.16 E
Chrenovoje 80 51.07 N 40.17 E
Chreščatij 83 49.37 N 39.42 E
Chřibská 54 50.50 N 14.29 E
Chříč 60 49.57 N 13.39 E
Chriesman 222 30.36 N 96.46 W
Chrisman 194 39.48 N 87.40 W
Chrissiesmeer 158 26.16 S 30.13 E
Chrissiesmeer ⊜ 158 26.19 S 30.13 E
Christanshåb (Qasigiannguit) 176 68.50 N 51.12 W
Christchurch, N.Z. 172 43.32 S 172.38 E
Christchurch, Eng., U.K. 42 50.44 N 1.45 W
Christ Church Cathedral ◆[1] 273a 6.27 N 3.23 E
Christian □[6] 219 39.33 N 89.18 W
Christian ≃ 180 66.36 N 145.49 W
Christian, Cape › 176 70.31 N 68.18 W
Christian, Point › 174e 25.04 S 130.07 W
Christiana, Jam. 241q 18.10 N 77.29 W
Christiana, S. Afr. 158 27.52 S 25.08 E
Christiana, De., U.S. 285 39.39 N 75.39 W
Christiana, Pa., U.S. 208 39.57 N 75.59 W
Christiana Creek ≃ 216 41.41 N 85.59 W
Christianburg 218 38.17 N 85.06 W
Christian Channel ⊔ 212 44.47 N 80.08 W
Christian Island I 212 44.50 N 80.13 W
Christian Island Indian Reserve ◆[4] 212 44.50 N 80.10 W
Christiansburg, Oh., U.S. 218 40.03 N 84.01 W
Christiansburg, Va., U.S. 192 37.07 N 80.24 W
Christiansfeld 41 55.21 N 9.29 E
Christiansø I 26 55.19 N 15.12 E
Christian Sound ⊔ 180 55.56 N 134.40 W
Christiansted 241n 17.45 N 64.42 W
Christie, Mount ∧ 180 63.01 N 129.40 W
Christie, Mount ∧[2] 216 42.53 N 83.20 W
Christie Bay c 176 62.32 N 111.10 W
Christie Lake ⊜, Mb., Can. 184 56.54 N 96.56 W
Christie Lake ⊜, On., Can. 212 44.48 N 76.26 W
Christina ≃, Ab., Can. 184 56.40 N 111.03 W
Christina ≃, De., U.S. 285 39.43 N 75.31 W
Christina Lake ⊜, Ab., Can. 182 55.38 N 110.55 W
Christina Lake ⊜, B.C., Can. 182 49.05 N 118.14 W
Christinovka 78 48.49 N 29.58 E
Christišče 83 48.55 N 37.30 E
Christmas 220 28.32 N 81.01 W
Christmas Bay c 222 29.03 N 95.11 W
Christmas Creek 162 18.53 S 125.55 E
Christmas Creek ≃ 162 18.29 S 125.23 E
Christmas Island □[2], Oc. 108 10.30 S 105.40 E
Christmas Island □[2], Oc. 112 10.30 S 105.40 E
Christmas Island → Kiritimati I[1] 174o 1.52 N 157.20 W
Christmas Mountain ∧ 180 64.34 N 160.34 W
Christmas Ridge ◆[3] 14 5.00 N 160.00 W
Christoforovka 78 47.59 N 33.05 E
Christoforovo 24 60.53 N 47.13 E
Christ of the Andes → Cristo Redentor ⊥ 252 32.50 S 70.05 W
Christoph Columbus-Spitze → Cristóbal Colón, Pico ∧ 246 10.50 N 73.41 W
Christopher 194 37.58 N 89.03 W
Christopher, Lake ⊜ 162 24.49 S 127.42 E
Christoval 196 31.12 N 100.30 W
Chroma ≃ 74 71.36 N 144.49 E
Chromtau 86 50.17 N 58.27 E
Chrudim 30 49.57 N 15.48 E
Chrustal'nyj 89 44.24 N 135.06 E
Chrzanów 30 50.09 N 19.24 E
Chu (Xam) ≃, Asia 110 19.53 N 105.45 E
Chu ≃, Zhg. 100 32.08 N 118.43 E
Chu ≃, Zhg. 106 32.15 N 119.03 E
Chuādanga 124 23.38 N 88.51 E
Chualar 226 36.34 N 121.31 W
Chuanbu 106 31.17 N 119.49 E
Chuanchang ⩸ 100 33.46 N 119.51 E
Chuanergu 105 39.20 N 117.43 E
Chuan'gang 106 31.57 N 121.04 E
Chuangjiapuzi 104 40.50 N 124.06 E
Chuanliao 100 28.17 N 120.13 E
Chuansha 106 31.12 N 121.42 E
Chuanshan 100 29.53 N 121.57 E
Chuanxindian 104 41.25 N 120.30 E
Chuanyao Gang c 106 32.12 N 121.25 E
Chuathbaluk 180 61.40 N 159.15 W
Chubbuck 202 42.55 N 112.27 W
Chūbu-Sangaku-kokuritsu-kōen ♦ 94 36.30 N 137.41 E
Chubut □[4] 254 44.00 S 69.00 W
Chubut ≃ 254 43.20 S 65.03 W
Ch'üchiang → Shaoguan 100 24.50 N 113.37 E
Chuchi Lake ⊜ 182 55.10 N 124.33 W
Chuchou → Zhuzhou 100 27.50 N 113.09 E
Chuchra 78 50.13 N 34.49 E
Chu Chua 182 51.21 N 120.10 W
Chuchuwayha Indian Reserve ◆[4] 182 49.21 N 120.06 W
Chuckatuck 208 36.52 N 76.35 W
Chučni 84 41.57 N 47.55 E
Chucuito 248 15.53 S 69.53 W
Chucun 100 33.04 N 116.32 E
Chucunaque ≃ 246 8.09 N 77.44 W
Chudan ≃ 88 52.08 N 109.40 E
Chudanskij chrebet ⋏ 88 52.00 N 110.00 E
Chudat 84 41.38 N 48.42 E
Chudeč 60 49.58 N 13.05 E
Chudleigh 42 50.36 N 3.38 W
Chudojelan' 88 54.42 N 99.37 E
Chudžand (Leninabad) 85 40.17 N 69.37 E
Chudzirt 86 47.05 N 91.10 E
Chuen Lung 271d 22.24 N 114.06 E
Chugach Islands II 180 59.06 N 151.42 W
Chugach Mountains ⋏ 180 61.00 N 145.00 W
Chuginadak Island I 180 52.49 N 169.50 W
Chūgoku-sanchi ⋏ 96 34.58 N 132.57 E
Chugwater 200 41.45 N 104.49 W
Chugwater Creek ≃ 198 42.07 N 104.51 W
Chugyn-ri 271b 37.39 N 126.50 E
Chūhar Kāna 123 31.45 N 73.48 E
Chuhe 100 34.03 N 113.35 E
Chuhuichupa 232 29.38 N 108.22 W
Chuí 252 33.41 S 53.27 W
Chuius Mountain ∧ 182 54.51 N 124.30 W
Chukai 114 4.15 N 103.25 E
Chukchi Sea ⊤[2] 16 69.00 N 171.00 W
Chuke Hu ⊜ 120 31.40 N 88.00 E
Chukou 100 25.44 N 113.22 E
Chulalongkorn University ◆[2] 269a 13.44 N 100.33 E
Chula Vista 228 32.38 N 117.05 W
Chuld 102 45.04 N 105.35 E
Chulga ≃ 24 64.20 N 61.00 E
Chullora 274a 33.54 S 151.04 E
Chulmleigh 42 50.55 N 3.52 W
Chulo 84 41.41 N 42.18 E
Chulp'o 98 35.37 N 126.40 E
Chulucanas 248 5.06 S 80.10 W
Chulumani 248 16.24 S 67.31 W
Chuluota 220 28.38 N 81.10 W
Chuma 248 15.24 S 68.56 W
Chumalag 84 43.14 N 44.28 E
Chumbicha 252 28.52 S 66.14 W
Chummi, ozero ⊜ 89 50.18 N 137.17 E
Chum Phae 110 16.32 N 102.06 E
Chumphon 110 10.30 N 99.10 E
Chumphon Buri 110 15.21 N 103.24 E
Chumpi 248 15.06 S 73.46 W
Chum Saeng 110 15.54 N 100.19 E
Chumunjin 98 37.54 N 128.49 E
Chunal 262 53.25 N 1.57 W
Chunan, T'aiwan 100 24.41 N 120.52 E
Chun'an, Zhg. 100 29.35 N 118.58 E
Chunār 124 25.08 N 82.54 E
Chuncheon → Ch'unch'ŏn 98 37.52 N 127.43 E
Chunchi, Ec. 246 2.17 S 78.55 W
Chunchi, Zhg. 100 27.22 N 119.20 E
Ch'unch'ŏn 98 37.52 N 127.43 E
Chunchula 194 30.55 N 88.12 W
Chūnd 123 31.26 N 72.16 E
Chung-ang University ◆[2] 271b 37.30 N 126.58 E
Chungari ≃ 89 50.04 N 136.55 E
Ch'ungch'ŏng Namdo □[4] 98 36.30 N 127.00 E
Ch'ungch'ŏng Pukdo □[4] 98 36.45 N 128.00 E
Chunggang-ni 98 40.52 N 127.20 E
Chung Hau 271d 22.16 N 114.00 E
Chungho 269d 25.00 N 121.30 E
Chung Hsing Bridge ◆[5] 269d 25.03 N 121.29 E
Chunghwa 98 38.52 N 125.47 E
Ch'ungju 98 36.58 N 127.58 E
Chungking → Chongqing 107 29.34 N 106.35 E
Chungli 100 24.57 N 121.13 E
Chungliao 100 22.41 N 121.28 E
Ch'ungmu 98 34.51 N 128.25 E
Chungp'u 100 23.25 N 120.31 E
Chungp'yŏngjang 98 41.11 N 128.03 E
Chungsam-ni 98 38.34 N 127.09 E
Chŭngsan 98 39.06 N 125.22 E
Chŭngsanha-ri ◆[8] 271b 37.35 N 126.54 E
Chungshan Bridge ◆[5] 269d 25.05 N 121.31 E
Chungshan → Zhongshan 100 22.31 N 113.22 E
Chunguj ≃ 88 48.51 N 93.32 E
Chungyang Shanmo ⋏ 100 23.30 N 121.00 E
Chunheji 100 32.12 N 115.22 E
Chunhua, Zhg. 102 34.50 N 108.31 E
Chunhua, Zhg. 106 31.56 N 118.56 E
Chunhuhux 232 19.12 N 88.55 W
Chūniān 123 30.58 N 73.59 E
Chuntuquí 232 17.31 N 90.09 W
Chünüj ≃ 88 48.48 N 102.00 E
Chunya 154 8.32 S 33.25 E
Ch'unyang, Taehan 98 36.56 N 128.54 E
Chunyang, Zhg. 89 43.43 N 129.28 E
Chunzach 84 42.33 N 46.43 E
Chūō 96 35.00 N 133.58 E
Chūō ◆[8], Nihon 268 35.40 N 139.47 E
Chūō ◆[8], Nihon 270 34.42 N 135.11 E
Chuŏr Phnum Krâvanh ⋏ 110 12.00 N 103.15 E
Chuosijia 102 31.53 N 101.59 E
Chupaca 248 12.04 S 75.19 W
Chupadera Arroyo V 200 33.47 N 106.37 W
Chupadero, Cerro ∧ 200 31.01 N 111.37 W
Chupara Point › 241r 10.48 N 61.22 W
Chuquibamba 248 15.50 S 72.39 W
Chuquibambilla 248 14.07 S 72.43 W
Chuquicamata 252 22.19 S 68.56 W
Chuquisaca □[5] 248 20.00 S 64.20 W
Chuquitanta 286d 11.58 S 77.06 W
Chur 58 46.51 N 9.32 E
Churach ≃ 88 48.37 N 110.42 E
Churāchāndpur 120 24.20 N 93.40 E
Churāmankāti 126 23.14 N 89.09 E
Churcampa 248 12.42 S 74.24 W
Church 262 53.45 N 2.24 W
Churchdown 42 51.53 N 2.10 W
Church Hill 192 36.31 N 82.42 W
Churchill, Mb., Can. 176 58.46 N 94.10 W
Churchill, Oh., U.S. 214 41.09 N 80.39 W
Churchill, Pa., U.S. 279b 40.27 N 79.51 W
Churchill, Va., U.S. 284c 38.54 N 77.10 W
Churchill ≃, Can. 176 58.47 N 94.12 W
Churchill ≃, Nf., Can. 176 53.30 N 60.10 W
Churchill, Cape › 176 58.46 N 93.12 W
Churchill, Mount ∧, B.C., Can. 182 49.58 N 123.51 W
Churchill, Mount ∧, Ak., U.S. 180 61.25 N 141.43 W
Churchill Downs ♦ 218 38.12 N 85.46 W
Churchill Falls ↳ 176 53.35 N 64.27 W
Churchill Lake ⊜ 184 55.55 N 108.20 W
Churchill National Park ♦ 169 37.58 S 145.17 E
Church Point 194 30.24 N 92.12 W
Church Rock 200 35.32 N 108.35 W
Church Street 260 51.26 N 0.28 E
Church Stretton 42 52.32 N 2.49 W
Churchton 208 38.48 N 76.32 W
Churchtown, Eng., U.K. 262 53.40 N 2.58 W
Churchtown, Pa., U.S. 208 40.08 N 75.58 W
Church View 208 37.41 N 76.41 W
Churchville, On., Can. 275b 43.38 N 79.45 W
Churchville, Md., U.S. 208 39.33 N 76.14 W
Churchville, N.Y., U.S. 210 43.06 N 77.53 W
Churchville, Pa., U.S. 285 40.11 N 75.01 W
Churdan 198 42.09 N 94.28 W
Churen Himāl ∧ 124 28.44 N 83.12 E
Chure Śringklā ⋏ 124 27.40 N 83.40 E
Churfirsten ⋏ 58 47.08 N 9.17 E
Chürmen 102 43.20 N 104.05 E
Churmuli 89 51.00 N 136.50 E
Churn ≃ 42 51.38 N 1.53 W
Churn Creek ≃ 182 51.30 N 122.17 W
Churnet ≃ 42 52.55 N 1.50 W
Churni ≃[1] 126 23.08 N 88.30 E
Chursdorf 54 50.46 N 12.15 E
Chūru 120 28.18 N 74.57 E
Churubusco, In., U.S. 216 41.13 N 85.19 W
Churubusco, N.Y., U.S. 206 44.57 N 73.56 W
Churuguara 246 10.49 N 69.32 W
Churumuco de Morelos 234 18.37 N 101.38 W
Churwalden 58 46.47 N 9.33 E
Chušenga 88 51.27 N 110.55 E
Chushan 100 23.45 N 120.40 E
Chushul 120 33.36 N 78.39 E
Chuska Mountains ⋏ 200 36.15 N 108.50 W
Chuska Peak ∧ 200 35.53 N 108.50 W
Chusovoy → Čusovoj 86 58.17 N 57.49 E
Chust 78 48.10 N 23.18 E
Chusuut uul ∧ 88 47.45 N 105.45 E
Chūta 174m 26.32 N 127.58 E
Chutag 88 49.23 N 102.43 E
Chutag Uul 102 43.23 N 110.13 E
Chute-à-Blondeau 206 45.35 N 74.29 W
Chute-Panet 206 46.51 N 71.51 W
Chutorskoj 80 46.52 N 42.59 E
Chutu ≃ 89 49.27 N 140.02 E
Chutung 100 24.44 N 121.05 E
Chuŭl 98 41.33 N 129.34 E
Chuwang 98 36.02 N 114.52 E
Chuwang-san Kukrip Kongwŏn ♦ 98 36.26 N 129.10 E
Chuwei 269d 25.08 N 121.27 E
Chuxian 100 32.19 N 118.17 E
Chuxiong 102 25.02 N 101.30 E
Chuy 252 33.41 S 53.27 W
Chuzenji-ko ⊜ 94 36.44 N 139.29 E
Chuzhai 100 33.22 N 113.37 E
Chužir 88 53.11 N 107.20 E
Chūzu 94 35.06 N 136.00 E
Chvalynsk 80 52.30 N 48.07 E
Chvančkara 84 42.34 N 43.01 E
Chvastoviči 76 53.28 N 35.06 E
Chvatovka 80 52.21 N 46.34 E
Chvojnaja 76 58.54 N 34.32 E
Chvorost'anka 80 52.36 N 48.59 E
Chvostovo 92a 46.08 N 142.14 E
Chwefru ≃ 42 52.09 N 3.25 W
Ch'wiya-ri 98 38.03 N 125.32 E
Chynčešt' 78 46.49 N 28.34 E
Chypre → Cyprus □[1] 130 35.00 N 33.00 E
Chyrov 78 49.33 N 22.49 E
Ci ≃, Zhg. 98 38.19 N 115.23 E
Ci ≃, Zhg. 100 33.27 N 115.31 E
Ciago 64 46.12 N 12.46 E
Ciagola, Monte ∧ 68 39.54 N 15.53 E
Ciales 240m 18.20 N 66.28 W
Ciamis 115a 7.20 S 108.21 E
Ciampino 66 41.48 N 12.36 E
Ciampino, Aeroporto di ⊠ 267a 41.48 N 12.36 E
Cianciana 70 37.31 N 13.26 E
Ciandur 115a 6.24 S 105.59 E
Cianjur 115a 6.49 S 107.08 E
Ciano d'Enza 64 44.36 N 10.24 E
Cianorte 255 23.37 S 52.37 W
Çians, Gorges du V 62 43.57 N 6.59 E
Čiatura 84 42.17 N 43.17 E
Ciavolo 70 37.46 N 12.33 E
Ciawi, Indon. 115a 7.10 S 108.09 E
Ciawi, Indon. 115a 6.40 S 106.50 E
Ciawigebang 115a 6.58 S 108.34 E
Ciba 107 29.07 N 105.55 E
Cibadak 115a 6.53 S 106.46 E
Cibaliung 115a 6.46 S 105.51 E
Čibargata 85 41.08 N 69.48 E
Cibatu 115a 7.06 S 107.59 E
Cibeber 115a 6.56 S 107.07 E
Cibecue 200 34.02 N 110.29 W
Cibiana 64 46.23 N 12.17 E
Cibinong 115a 6.27 S 106.51 E
Čibisovka 78 50.47 N 40.05 E
Čibižek 86 54.27 N 93.40 E
Cibolo Creek ≃, Tx., U.S. 196 28.27 N 98.54 W
Cibolo Creek ≃, Tx., U.S. 196 28.57 N 97.53 W
Cibolo Creek ≃, Tx., U.S. 196 29.34 N 104.24 W
Cibuta 200 31.04 N 110.54 W
Cicagna 62 44.25 N 9.14 E
Cicala 68 39.01 N 16.29 E
Cicalengka 115a 6.59 S 107.50 E
Ćićarija ⋏ 36 45.30 N 13.54 E
Čičatka 89 54.03 N 121.18 E
Cicciano 68 40.58 N 14.32 E
Cicero, Il., U.S. 216 41.50 N 87.45 W
Cicero, In., U.S. 218 40.07 N 86.00 W
Cicero, N.Y., U.S. 210 43.10 N 76.07 W
Cicero Creek ≃ 194 40.01 N 86.01 W
Cícero Dantas 250 10.36 S 38.23 W
Čichačovo, Ross. 76 57.17 N 29.54 E
Čichačovo, Ross. 89 51.50 N 141.07 E
Čichareši 84 42.48 N 43.03 E
Ciche, Sgurr na ∧ 46 57.01 N 5.27 W
Cicheng 100 30.00 N 121.22 E
Čičikleja ≃ 78 47.23 N 31.34 E
Čičkajul ≃ 86 57.34 N 85.44 E
Cicladas, Islas → Kikládhes II 38 37.30 N 25.00 E
Cicolano ◆[1] 66 42.12 N 13.12 E
Cicurug 115a 6.47 S 106.47 E
Cidacos ≃ 34 42.19 N 1.55 W
Cidade, Rio da ≃ 256 22.25 S 43.09 W
Cidade Universitária ◆[2], Bra. 287a 22.52 S 43.14 W
Cidade Universitária ◆[2], Bra. 287b 23.33 S 46.43 W
Cide 130 41.54 N 33.00 E
Cidra 240m 18.11 N 66.10 W
Cidra, Lago de ⊜[1] 240m 18.12 N 66.08 W
Ciechanów 30 52.53 N 20.38 E
Ciechanów □[4] 30 53.00 N 20.20 E
Ciechanowiec 30 52.42 N 22.31 E
Ciechocinek 30 52.52 N 18.49 E
Ciego de Ávila 240p 21.51 N 78.46 W
Ciego de Ávila □[4] 240p 22.00 N 78.40 W
Ciempozuelos 34 40.10 N 3.37 W
Ciénaga 246 11.01 N 74.15 W
Ciénaga de Oro 246 8.53 N 75.37 W
Ciénega de Flores 196 25.57 N 100.11 W
Cienfuegos 240p 22.09 N 80.27 W
Cienfuegos □[4] 240p 22.10 N 80.25 W
Cienfuegos, Bahía de c 240p 22.07 N 80.29 W
Čierna [nad Tisou] 30 48.25 N 22.05 E
Čierny Balog 30 48.45 N 19.40 E
Cíes, Islas II 34 42.13 N 8.54 W
Cieszanów 30 50.16 N 23.08 E
Cieszyn 30 49.45 N 18.38 E
Cieza 34 38.14 N 1.25 W
Çiftalan ◆[8] 267b 41.15 N 28.54 E
Çiftehan 130 37.31 N 34.46 E
Çifteler 130 39.22 N 31.03 E
Çiftlik 130 38.11 N 34.30 E
Čifuentes, Cuba 240p 22.39 N 80.03 W
Cifuentes, Esp. 34 40.47 N 2.37 W
Čiganak, Kaz. 86 45.06 N 73.58 E
Čiganak, Ross. 80 51.47 N 43.18 E
Čiganaki 80 47.57 N 43.05 E
Čigirin 78 49.04 N 32.40 E
Cigliano 62 45.18 N 8.01 E
Čigorak 80 51.26 N 42.09 E
Cigou 100 33.51 N 113.35 E
Cigüela ≃ 34 39.08 N 3.44 W
Cihanbeyli 130 38.40 N 32.56 E
Cihara 115a 6.52 S 106.06 E
Cihuatlán 234 19.14 N 104.35 W
Čiili 86 44.10 N 66.45 E
Cijara, Embalse de ⊜[1] 34 39.18 N 4.52 W
Čijen 85 43.08 N 75.55 E
Cijiawu 105 39.48 N 115.59 E
Čijirčik, pereval ⟩⟨ 85 40.15 N 73.20 E
Čijli ≃ 85 40.17 N 72.38 E
Cijulang 115a 7.44 S 108.27 E
Čik 86 55.01 N 82.27 E
Cikajang 115a 7.22 S 107.47 E
Cikalong-kulon 115a 6.42 S 107.12 E
Cikampek 115a 6.24 S 107.27 E
Čikan 88 54.54 N 105.39 E
Cikarang 115a 6.15 S 107.09 E
Cikatomas 115a 7.37 S 108.15 E
Čikišl'ar 128 37.34 N 53.55 E
Čikoj 88 50.16 N 106.54 E
Čikoj ≃ 88 51.02 N 106.39 E
Čikola 84 43.12 N 43.55 E
Cikou 100 29.42 N 114.46 E
Cıksı 130 38.30 N 40.55 E
Cilacap 115a 7.44 S 109.00 E
Cilamaya 115a 6.15 S 107.35 E
Cilavegna 62 45.19 N 8.44 E
Çıldır 84 41.08 N 43.07 E
Çıldır Gölü ⊜ 84 41.04 N 43.15 E
Ciledug 115a 6.54 S 108.44 E
Cilegon 115a 6.01 S 106.03 E
Čilekovo 80 47.50 N 43.30 E
Cilento ⋏ 68 40.17 N 15.19 E
Cilento ◆[1] 36 40.15 N 15.10 E
Čil'gazi 85 40.10 N 70.39 E
Cili 102 29.17 N 111.00 E
Cilicia □[9] 130 36.40 N 34.20 E
Čilik, Kaz. 85 43.36 N 78.15 E
Čilik, Kaz. 86 51.07 N 54.07 E
Čilik ≃ 85 43.05 N 78.28 E
Cililin 115a 6.56 S 107.26 E
Cilimus 115a 6.52 S 108.29 E
Cilincing ◆[8] 269e 6.06 S 106.56 E
Cill Airne → Killarney 48 52.03 N 9.30 W
Cill Chainnigh → Kilkenny 48 52.39 N 7.15 W
Cilleruelo de Bezana 34 42.58 N 3.51 W
Cil'ma ≃ 24 65.27 N 52.06 E
Cimabanche (Schluderbach) 64 46.37 N 12.11 E
Cima Gogna 64 46.31 N 12.28 E
Cimahi 115a 6.53 S 107.32 E
Cimalaka 115a 6.49 S 107.56 E
Cimalmotto 58 46.17 N 8.29 E
Cimarron, Ks., U.S. 198 37.48 N 100.20 W
Cimarron, N.M., U.S. 200 36.30 N 104.54 W
Cimarron ≃, U.S. 196 36.10 N 96.17 W
Cimarron ≃, N.M., U.S. 196 36.20 N 104.31 W
Cimarron, North Fork ≃ 196 37.25 N 101.13 W
Čimbaj 86 42.57 N 59.47 E
Čimčinej, gora ∧[2] 180 63.37 N 178.04 E
Cimini, Monti ⋏ 66 42.20 N 12.10 E
Ciminna 70 37.54 N 13.34 E
Cimino, Monte ∧ 66 42.24 N 12.12 E
Čimion 85 40.16 N 71.31 E
Čimišlija 78 46.32 N 28.44 E
Cimitile 68 40.56 N 14.31 E
Čimkent 85 42.18 N 69.36 E
Čimkorgon 85 42.50 N 75.30 E
Cimla ≃ 80 48.01 N 42.24 E
Ciml'ansk 80 47.38 N 42.04 E
Ciml'anskoje vodochranilišče ⊜[1] 80 48.00 N 43.00 E
Cimolais 64 46.17 N 12.26 E
Cimone, Monte ∧ 64 44.12 N 10.42 E
Cîmpeni 38 46.22 N 23.03 E
Cîmpia Turzii 38 46.33 N 23.54 E
Cîmpina 38 45.08 N 25.44 E
Cimpu 112 3.25 S 120.22 E
Cîmpulung 38 45.16 N 25.03 E
Cîmpulung Moldovenesc 38 47.31 N 25.34 E
Čimtarga, gora ∧ 85 39.12 N 68.10 E
Čina ≃ 88 54.20 N 112.24 E
Cina, Tanjung › 112 5.56 S 104.45 E
Činabad 85 40.52 N 71.58 E
Činadijevo 78 48.30 N 22.50 E
Cinandali 84 41.53 N 45.34 E
Çınar 130 37.44 N 40.25 E
Çınarcık 130 40.39 N 29.06 E
Cinaruco ≃ 246 6.41 N 67.07 W
Činaz 85 40.56 N 68.45 E
Cinca ≃ 34 41.26 N 0.21 E
Cincar ∧ 36 43.54 N 17.04 E
Cincinnati, Ia., U.S. 190 40.37 N 92.55 W
Cincinnati, Oh., U.S. 218 39.09 N 84.27 W
Cincinnatus 210 42.32 N 75.53 W
Cinco, Canal Numero ⩸ 252 37.35 S 57.20 W
Cinco Balas, Cayos II 240p 21.06 N 79.20 W
Cinco de Mayo 196 25.46 N 104.19 W
Cinco Pinos 236 13.14 N 86.52 W
Cinco Saltos 252 38.49 S 68.04 W
Cinderella 273d 26.15 S 28.16 E
Cinderella Dam ⊜[1] 273d 26.15 S 28.14 E
Cinderford 42 51.50 N 2.29 W
Cinder Island I 276 40.36 N 73.36 W
Çine 130 37.36 N 28.04 E
Činebar 224 46.36 N 122.32 W
Cinecittà ◆[3] 267a 41.51 N 12.34 E
Cinema 182 53.14 N 122.27 W
Ciney 56 50.18 N 5.06 E
Cinfães 34 41.04 N 8.05 W
Čingaly 86 60.13 N 69.45 E
Čingis 86 54.08 N 81.41 E
Čingistaj 86 49.13 N 85.55 E
Cingoli 66 43.22 N 13.13 E
Cinigiano 66 42.53 N 11.24 E
Cinisello Balsamo 62 45.33 N 9.13 E
Činišeucy 78 47.42 N 28.52 E
Cinisi 70 38.09 N 13.06 E
Činja-Voryk 24 63.13 N 52.38 E
Cinkota ◆[8] 264c 47.31 N 19.14 E
Cinnaminson 285 40.00 N 74.59 W
Cínovec 54 50.43 N 13.45 E
Cinq, Lac des ⊜ 206 46.51 N 72.59 W
Cinq Doigts, Lac ⊜ 206 46.36 N 74.32 W
Cinquefrondi 68 38.25 N 16.06 E
Cinquemiglia, Piano delle ⩸ 66 41.50 N 14.00 E
Cinqueterre □[9] 62 44.10 N 9.45 E
Cintalapa 234 16.44 N 93.43 W
Cinto, Monte ∧ 36 42.23 N 8.56 E
Cinto Euganeo 64 45.16 N 11.40 E

Symbols in the index entries represent the broad categories identified in the key at the right. Symbols with superior numbers (⋏[1]) identify subcategories (see complete key on page *I · 1*).

Symbole im Register stellen die rechts im Schlüssel erklärten Kategorien dar. Symbole mit hochgestellten Ziffern (⋏[1]) bezeichnen Unterabteilungen einer Kategorie (vgl. vollständiger Schlüssel auf Seite *I · 1*).

Los símbolos incluídos en el texto del índice representan las grandes categorias identificadas con la clave a la derecha. Los símbolos con numeros en su parte superior (⋏[1]) identifican las subcategorías (véase la clave completa en la página *I · 1*).

Les symboles de l'index représentent les catégories indiquées dans la légende à droite. Les symboles suivis d'un indice (⋏[1]) représentent des sous-catégories (voir légende complète à la page *I · 1*).

Os símbolos incluídos no texto do índice representam as grandes categorias identificadas com a chave à direita. Os símbolos com números em sua parte superior (⋏[1]) identificam as subcategorias (veja-se a chave completa à página *I · 1*).

English	Deutsch	Español	Français	Português
∧ Mountain	Berg	Montaña	Montagne	Montanha
⋏ Mountains	Gebirge	Montañas	Montagnes	Montanhas
⟩⟨ Pass	Paß	Paso	Col	Passo
V Valley, Canyon	Tal, Cañon	Valle, Cañón	Vallée, Canyon	Vale, Canhão
⩸ Plain	Ebene	Llano	Plaine	Planície
› Cape	Kap	Cabo	Cap	Cabo
I Island	Insel	Isla	Île	Ilha
II Islands	Inseln	Islas	Îles	Ilhas
⊥ Other Topographic Features	Andere Topographische Objekte	Otros Elementos Topográficos	Autres données topographiques	Outros acidentes topográficos

ESPAÑOL

Nombre	Página	Lat.°′	Long.°′ W = Oeste
Cintra, Golfe de ⊂	148	23.00 N	16.20 W
Cintra → Sintra	34	38.48 N	9.23 W
Ciocănești	38	44.12 N	27.04 E
Ciociaria ◈[1]	66	41.45 N	13.15 E
Ciomas	115a	6.12 S	106.01 E
Čiovo, Otok I	36	43.30 N	16.20 E
Cipa ≃	88	55.23 N	115.55 E
Ciparay	115a	7.03 S	107.43 E
Cipatujah	115a	7.45 S	108.00 E
Cipikan	88	54.55 N	113.21 E
Cipikan ≃	88	55.14 N	113.05 E
Cipó	250	11.06 S	38.31 W
Cipó ≃	255	18.40 S	43.59 W
Cipolândia	255	20.08 S	55.24 W
Cipolletti	252	38.56 S	67.59 W
Ciqikou	107	29.35 N	106.26 E
Čir	80	48.29 N	43.10 E
Čir ≃	80	48.35 N	42.51 E
Ciraadhame	144	10.30 N	49.22 E
Čirachčaj ≃	84	41.40 N	48.11 E
Čiragidzor	84	40.27 N	46.19 E
Ciranjang	115a	6.49 S	107.14 E
Circeo, Monte ʌ	66	41.14 N	13.03 E
Circeo, Parco Nazionale del ♠	66	41.17 N	13.05 E
Čirčik	85	41.29 N	69.35 E
Čirčik ≃	85	40.54 N	68.41 E
Çırçır	130	40.04 N	36.48 E
Circle, Ak., U.S.	180	65.50 N	144.04 W
Circle, Mt., U.S.	202	47.20 N	105.35 W
Circle Hot Springs	180	65.28 N	144.39 W
Circleville, N.Y., U.S.	210	41.31 N	75.23 W
Circleville, Oh., U.S.	218	39.36 N	82.56 W
Circleville, Pa., U.S.	279b	40.20 N	79.44 W
Circleville, Ut,. U.S.	200	38.10 N	112.16 W
Circleville Mountain ʌ	200	38.12 N	112.24 W
Circular Reef ✢[2]	164	3.25 S	147.47 E
Circus World ♠	220	28.14 N	81.38 W
Cirebon	115a	6.44 S	108.34 E
Cireglio	66	43.59 N	10.51 E
Ciremay, Gunung ʌ	115a	6.54 S	108.24 E
Cirencester	42	51.44 N	1.59 W
Cirey-sur-Vezouze	58	48.35 N	6.57 E
Čirgalandy	88	50.36 N	97.20 E
Ciriè	62	45.14 N	7.36 E
Cirigliano	68	40.24 N	16.10 E
Čirikovo	82	55.23 N	37.14 E
Ciriquiri ≃	248	8.05 S	65.18 W
Cirk, gora ʌ	180	64.33 N	175.25 E
Cîrlibaba	38	47.35 N	25.07 E
Ciró	68	39.23 N	17.04 E
Ciró Marina	68	39.22 N	17.08 E
Ciro Redondo	240p	22.01 N	78.43 W
Čirpan	38	42.12 N	25.20 E
Ciruas	115a	6.06 S	106.13 E
Cisa, Passo della)(	64	44.28 N	9.55 E
Cisano	64	45.32 N	10.43 E
Cisarua	115a	6.40 S	106.59 E
Cisco, Il., U.S.	219	40.01 N	88.43 W
Cisco, Tx., U.S.	196	32.23 N	98.58 W
Cishan	98	36.37 N	114.07 E
Cishangang	106	30.55 N	119.31 E
Ciskei □[1], Afr.	138	32.50 S	27.00 E
Ciskei □[1], Afr.	158	32.50 S	27.00 E
Cislago	62	45.39 N	8.58 E
Cisliano	266b	45.27 N	8.59 E
Cismar	54	54.11 N	10.59 E
Čismena	82	56.02 N	36.13 E
Cismon ≃	64	46.55 N	11.43 E
Cismon del Grappa	64	45.55 N	11.44 E
Čišmy	86	54.35 N	55.20 E
Cisnădie	38	45.43 N	24.09 E
Cisne	194	38.31 N	88.26 W
Cisneros	246	6.33 N	75.04 W
Cisnes ≃	254	44.45 S	72.42 W
Cisolok	115a	6.57 S	106.26 E
Cison di Valmarino	64	45.58 N	12.10 E
Cispus ≃	224	46.25 N	122.10 W
Cisse ≃	50	47.25 N	0.47 E
Cissna Park	216	40.33 N	87.53 W
Čistá, Česko.	54	50.06 N	12.44 E
Čistá, Česko.	60	50.02 N	13.35 E
Cisterna di Latina	66	41.35 N	12.49 E
Cisternino	68	40.44 N	17.25 E
Cistern Point ≻	238	23.43 N	77.35 W
Cistierna	34	42.48 N	5.07 W
Čistoje	80	56.32 N	43.02 E
Čistooz'ornoje	86	54.43 N	76.33 E
Čistopol'	80	55.21 N	50.37 E
Čistopolje, Kaz.	86	52.34 N	67.15 E
Čistopolje, Ross.	83	47.31 N	39.27 E
Čistovodovka	83	49.24 N	37.20 E
Čita	88	52.03 N	113.30 E
Čita □[8]	88	52.00 N	117.00 E
Čita ≃	88	52.00 N	113.30 E
Citac, Nevado ʌ	248	12.48 S	75.14 W
Citaré ≃	250	1.11 N	54.41 W
Cité Universitaire ʊ[2]	261	48.49 N	2.20 E
Citra	192	29.24 N	82.06 W
Citronelle	194	31.05 N	88.13 W
Citrus □[6]	220	28.52 N	82.28 W
Citrusdal	158	32.36 S	19.00 E
Citrus Heights	226	38.42 N	121.16 W
Citrus Springs	220	29.00 N	82.27 W
Citrus Tower ʊ	220	28.33 N	81.44 W
Cittadella	64	45.39 N	11.47 E
Città della Pieve	66	42.57 N	12.00 E
Città del Vaticano → Vatican City □[1]	66	41.54 N	12.27 E
Città di Castello	66	43.27 N	12.14 E
Cittaducale	66	42.23 N	12.57 E
Cittanova	68	38.21 N	16.05 E
Cittareale	66	42.37 N	13.10 E
Città Sant'Angelo	66	42.31 N	14.03 E
Città Universitaria ʊ[2]	267a	41.55 N	12.31 E
City Beach	168a	31.56 S	115.45 E
City Bell ◈[8]	258	34.52 S	58.05 W
City Island ◈[8]	276	40.51 N	73.47 W
City Mills	283	42.06 N	71.21 W
City of Hope National Medical Center ʊ	280	34.08 N	117.58 W
City Of Industry	280	34.01 N	117.57 W
City of London ◈[8]	260	51.31 N	0.05 W
City of Refuge → Pu'uhonua o Honaunau National Historic Site ♠	229d	19.25 N	155.54 W
City of Sunrise	220	26.08 N	80.14 W
City of Westminster ◈[8]	260	51.30 N	0.09 W
City Point	220	28.24 N	80.45 W
City University of New York Brooklyn College ʊ[2]	276	40.38 N	73.57 W
City University of New York City College ʊ[2]	276	40.49 N	73.57 W
City University of New York Queens College ʊ[2]	276	40.44 N	73.49 W
City University of New York York College ʊ[2]	276	40.42 N	73.48 W
Ciucaș, Vîrful ʌ	38	45.31 N	25.55 E
Ciudad Acuña	232	29.18 N	100.55 W
Ciudad Altamirano	234	18.20 N	100.40 W
Ciudad Barrios	236	13.46 N	88.16 W
Ciudad Bolívar	246	8.08 N	63.33 W
Ciudad Bolivia	246	8.21 N	70.34 W
Ciudad Camargo	232	26.19 N	98.50 W
Ciudad Constitución	232	24.59 N	111.39 W
Ciudad Cortés	236	8.58 N	83.32 W
Ciudad Cuauhtémoc	234	22.28 N	102.20 W
Ciudad Darío	236	12.43 N	86.08 W
Ciudad de Carangas	248	17.53 S	66.11 W
Ciudad de Guayana → Ciudad Guayana	246	8.22 N	62.40 W
Ciudad de la Habana □[4]	240p	23.08 N	82.22 W
Ciudad del Cabo → Cape Town	158	33.55 S	18.22 E
Ciudad del Carmen	232	18.38 N	91.50 W

FRANÇAIS

Nom	Page	Lat.°′	Long.°′ W = Ouest
Ciudad del Este	252	25.30 S	54.36 W
Ciudad del Maíz	234	22.24 N	99.36 W
Ciudad de los Deportes ♠	286a	19.23 N	99.11 W
Ciudad del Vaticano → Vatican City □[1]	66	41.54 N	12.27 E
Ciudad de México (Mexico City), Méx.	234	19.24 N	99.09 W
Ciudad de México (Mexico City), Méx.	286a	19.24 N	99.09 W
Ciudad de Nutrias	246	8.05 N	69.18 W
Ciudad Deportiva ♠, Cuba	286b	23.07 N	82.22 W
Ciudad Deportiva ♠, Méx.	286a	19.24 N	99.06 W
Ciudadela, Parque de la ♠	266d	41.23 N	2.11 E
Ciudad General Belgrano	288	34.43 S	58.32 W
Ciudad Guayana	246	8.22 N	62.40 W
Ciudad Guzmán	234	19.41 N	103.29 W
Ciudad Hidalgo, Méx.	234	19.41 N	100.34 W
Ciudad Hidalgo, Méx.	236	14.41 N	92.09 W
Ciudad Juárez	232	31.44 N	106.29 W
Ciudad Lerdo	196	25.32 N	103.32 W
Ciudad Lerdo de Tejada	234	18.37 N	95.31 W
Ciudad Lineal ◈[8]	266a	40.27 N	3.40 W
Ciudad López Mateos	286a	19.33 N	99.15 W
Ciudad Madero	234	22.16 N	97.50 W
Ciudad Mante	234	22.44 N	98.57 W
Ciudad Manuel Doblado	234	20.44 N	101.56 W
Ciudad Mendoza	234	18.48 N	97.11 W
Ciudad Miguel Alemán	232	26.23 N	99.01 W
Ciudad Morelos	232	32.38 N	114.52 W
Ciudad Obregón	232	27.29 N	109.56 W
Ciudad Ojeda (Lagunillas)	246	10.12 N	71.19 W
Ciudad Piar	246	7.27 N	63.19 W
Ciudad Real	34	38.59 N	3.56 W
Ciudad Real □[4]	34	38.50 N	3.45 W
Ciudad Rodrigo	34	40.36 N	6.32 W
Ciudad Sahagún	234	19.47 N	98.33 W
Ciudad Sandino	236	13.43 N	86.08 W
Ciudad Serdán	234	18.59 N	97.27 W
Ciudad Tecún Umán	236	14.40 N	92.09 W
Ciudad Trujillo → Santo Domingo	238	18.28 N	69.54 W
Ciudad Universitaria ◈[8]	266a	40.27 N	3.44 W
Ciudad Universitaria ʊ[2], Esp.	266a	40.27 N	3.43 W
Ciudad Universitaria ʊ[2], Méx.	286a	19.20 N	99.11 W
Ciudad Universitaria ʊ[2], Ven.	286c	10.29 N	66.53 W
Ciudad Valles	234	21.59 N	99.01 W
Ciudad Victoria, Méx.	204	32.20 N	115.06 W
Ciudad Victoria, Méx.	234	23.44 N	99.08 W
Ciudad Vieja	236	14.31 N	90.46 W
Ciuma	152	13.14 S	15.40 E
Ciutadella	34	40.02 N	3.50 E
Civa Burnu ≻	130	41.22 N	36.35 E
Civate	62	45.50 N	9.21 E
Civenna	58	45.56 N	9.16 E
Civetta, Monte ʌ	64	46.23 N	12.03 E
Civezzano	64	46.05 N	11.11 E
Cividale del Friuli	64	46.06 N	13.25 E
Cividate al Piano	62	45.33 N	9.50 E
Cividate Camuno	64	45.57 N	10.17 E
Civil' ≃	80	56.08 N	47.35 E
Civil'sk	80	55.53 N	47.29 E
Civita	68	39.49 N	16.18 E
Civitacampomarano	66	41.47 N	14.41 E
Civita Castellana	66	42.17 N	12.25 E
Civita di Bagno	66	42.18 N	13.26 E
Civitanova Alta	66	43.19 N	13.40 E
Civitanova del Sannio	66	41.40 N	14.24 E
Civitanova Marche	66	43.18 N	13.44 E
Civitaquana	66	42.19 N	13.54 E
Civitavecchia	66	42.06 N	11.48 E
Civitella del Tronto	66	42.46 N	13.40 E
Civitella di Romagna	66	44.00 N	11.56 E
Civitella in Val di Chiana	66	43.25 N	11.43 E
Civitella Marittima	66	43.00 N	11.17 E
Civitella Roveto	66	41.54 N	13.25 E
Civray	32	46.09 N	0.18 E
Çivril	130	38.18 N	29.45 E
Ciwidey	115a	7.06 S	107.27 E
Cixerri ≃	71	39.17 N	8.59 E
Cixi	100	30.11 N	121.15 E
Cixian	98	36.22 N	114.23 E
Ciyutuo	104	41.31 N	122.53 E
Čiža	24	67.06 N	44.19 E
Čižapka ≃	86	59.01 N	79.36 E
Čiža Vtoraja	80	50.52 N	49.40 E
Cize	58	46.12 N	5.26 E
Cizhuping	107	29.11 N	103.36 E
Čižinskije razlivy ≋	80	50.25 N	49.40 E
Cizre	130	37.20 N	42.12 E
C.J. Strike Reservoir ⊜[1]	202	42.57 N	115.53 W
Čkalovo, Kaz.	86	53.38 N	70.24 E
Čkalovo, Ukr.	78	46.28 N	34.11 E
Čkalov → Orenburg	86	51.54 N	55.06 E
Čkalovsk, Kaz.	85	41.15 N	68.00 E
Čkalovsk, Ross.	80	56.46 N	43.16 E
Čkalovsk, Taj.	85	40.13 N	69.50 E
Čkalovskij	265b	55.54 N	38.04 E
C K Creek ≃	202	47.36 N	108.29 W
Čkyně	60	49.07 N	13.49 E
Čl'a, ozero ⊜	89	53.27 N	140.03 E
Clachan	46	55.45 N	5.34 W
Clackamas	224	45.24 N	122.34 W
Clackamas □[6]	224	45.10 N	122.16 W
Clackamas ≃	224	45.22 N	122.36 W
Clackamas, Oak Grove Fork ≃	224	45.05 N	122.03 W
Clackamas Heights	224	45.23 N	122.34 W
Clackline	168a	31.43 S	116.31 E
Clackmannan	46	56.06 N	3.46 W
Clacton-on-Sea	42	51.48 N	1.09 E
Cladich	46	56.21 N	5.05 W
Claerwen ≃	42	52.16 N	3.35 W
Claerwen Reservoir ⊜[1]	42	52.17 N	3.43 W
Claflin	198	38.31 N	98.32 W
Claiborne	194	31.32 N	87.31 W
Clain ≃	32	46.47 N	0.32 E
Claire, Lake ⊜	176	58.35 N	112.05 W
Claire, Pointe ≻	275a	45.25 N	73.50 W
Clairefontaine-en-Yvelines	50	48.37 N	1.55 E
Clair Engle Lake ⊜[1]	204	40.52 N	122.43 W
Claireville	275b	43.45 N	79.38 W
Claireville Reservoir ⊜[1]	275b	43.44 N	79.39 W
Clairis ≃	50	48.07 N	2.45 E
Clairmarais	50	50.46 N	2.18 E
Clairmont	182	55.16 N	118.47 W
Clairton	214	40.17 N	79.52 W
Clairvaux-les-Lacs	58	46.34 N	5.45 E
Claix	62	45.07 N	5.40 E
Clallam □[6]	224	48.10 N	123.49 W
Clallam Bay	224	48.15 N	124.15 W
Clam ≃, Mi., U.S.	190	44.05 N	85.00 W
Clam ≃, Wi., U.S.	190	45.57 N	92.33 W
Clam, North Fork ≃	190	45.46 N	92.18 W
Clamart	261	48.48 N	2.16 E
Clamecy	50	47.27 N	3.31 E
Clam Gulch	180	60.15 N	151.22 W
Clam Lake ⊜	184	55.19 N	105.43 W
Clampton	162	29.56 S	119.06 E
Clan Alpine Mountains ⩘	204	39.40 N	117.55 W
Clandonald	182	53.34 N	110.44 W
Clandon Park ♠	260	51.15 N	0.30 W
Clandulla	170	32.55 S	149.57 E

PORTUGUÊS

Nome	Página	Lat.°′	Long.°′ W = Oeste
Clane	48	53.18 N	6.41 W
Clans	62	44.00 N	7.09 E
Clanton	194	32.50 N	86.37 W
Clanwilliam	158	32.11 S	18.54 E
Claonaig	46	55.46 N	5.22 W
Clapham	42	52.09 N	0.29 W
Clapier, Mont ʌ	62	44.07 N	7.25 E
Clapperton Island I	190	46.02 N	82.13 W
Clapp Farm	214	41.24 N	79.32 W
Clàr, Loch nan ⊜	46	58.17 N	4.08 W
Clara, Arg.	252	31.50 S	58.49 W
Clara, Ire.	48	53.20 N	7.36 W
Clara, Ms., U.S.	194	31.34 N	88.41 W
Clara ≃	166	18.30 S	141.18 E
Clara City	198	44.57 N	95.21 W
Clara Island I	110	10.54 N	97.55 E
Claraz	252	37.54 S	59.17 W
Clare, Austl.	166	33.25 S	143.55 E
Clare, Austl.	168b	33.50 S	138.36 E
Clare, Eng., U.K.	42	52.25 N	0.35 E
Clare, Mi., U.S.	190	43.49 N	84.46 W
Clare □[6]	48	52.50 N	9.00 W
Clare ≃, On., Can.	212	44.28 N	77.17 W
Clare ≃, Ire.	48	53.20 N	9.03 W
Clarecastle	48	52.49 N	8.57 W
Claregalway	48	53.21 N	8.57 W
Clare Island I	48	53.48 N	10.00 W
Claremont, On., Can.	212	43.58 N	79.07 W
Claremont, Eng., U.K.	260	51.21 N	0.22 W
Claremont, Ca., U.S.	228	34.05 N	117.43 W
Claremont, N.H., U.S.	188	43.22 N	72.20 W
Claremont, S.D., U.S.	198	45.40 N	98.00 W
Claremont, Va., U.S.	208	37.13 N	76.57 W
Claremont ʌ	204	39.53 N	120.57 W
Claremore	196	36.18 N	95.36 W
Claremorris	48	53.44 N	9.00 W
Clarence, N.Z.	172	42.10 S	173.56 E
Clarence, Il., U.S.	216	40.28 N	87.58 W
Clarence, Ia., U.S.	190	41.53 N	91.03 W
Clarence, Mo., U.S.	219	39.44 N	92.15 W
Clarence, N.Y., U.S.	210	42.59 N	78.35 W
Clarence, Pa., U.S.	214	41.03 N	77.56 W
Clarence ≃, Austl.	166	29.25 S	153.22 E
Clarence ≃, N.Z.	172	42.10 S	173.57 E
Clarence, Isla I	254	54.10 S	71.50 W
Clarence, Port ⊂	180	65.15 N	166.40 W
Clarence Cannon Dam ◈[6]	219	39.31 N	91.39 W
Clarence Center	210	43.00 N	78.35 W
Clarence Creek	206	45.30 N	75.13 W
Clarence Fahnestock Memorial State Park ♠	210	41.26 N	73.50 W
Clarence Island I	9	61.09 S	54.06 W
Clarence J. Brown Reservoir ⊜[1]	218	39.58 N	83.44 W
Clarence Strait ʯ, Austl.	164	12.00 S	131.00 E
Clarence Strait ʯ, Ak., U.S.	180	55.25 N	132.00 W
Clarence Town, Austl.	170	32.35 S	151.47 E
Clarence Town, Ba.	238	23.06 N	74.59 W
Clarenceville, P.Q., Can.	206	45.04 N	73.15 W
Clarenceville, Mi., U.S.	281	42.27 N	83.19 W
Clarendon, Austl.	168b	35.07 S	138.38 E
Clarendon, Ar., U.S.	194	34.41 N	91.18 W
Clarendon, N.Y., U.S.	210	43.11 N	78.04 W
Clarendon, Pa., U.S.	214	41.46 N	79.05 W
Clarendon, Tx., U.S.	196	34.56 N	100.53 W
Clarendon Hills	278	41.47 N	87.57 W
Clarens	158	28.30 S	28.29 E
Clarenville	186	48.10 N	53.58 W
Claresholm	182	50.02 N	113.35 W
Claret	62	43.52 N	3.54 E
Clarholz	52	51.54 N	8.11 E
Claridge	214	40.21 N	79.37 W
Clarie Coast ⍓[2]	9	66.30 S	133.00 E
Clarin	116	9.58 N	124.01 E
Clarinda	198	40.44 N	95.02 W
Clarines	246	9.56 N	65.10 W
Clarington	214	41.20 N	79.07 W
Clarion, Ia., U.S.	190	42.43 N	93.43 W
Clarion, Pa., U.S.	214	41.12 N	79.23 W
Clarion □[6]	214	41.13 N	79.24 W
Clarion ≃	214	41.07 N	79.41 W
Clarión, Isla I	232	18.22 N	114.44 W
Clarion, West Branch ≃	214	41.29 N	78.41 W
Clarion Fracture Zone ✢	16	18.00 N	122.00 W
Clarissa	198	46.07 N	94.56 W
Clark, N.J., U.S.	276	40.38 N	74.18 W
Clark, Oh., U.S.	214	40.27 N	81.54 W
Clark, S.D., U.S.	198	44.52 N	97.43 W
Clark, Tx., U.S.	222	30.23 N	94.46 W
Clark □[6], In., U.S.	218	38.17 N	85.44 W
Clark □[6], Oh., U.S.	218	39.56 N	83.49 W
Clark □[6], Wa., U.S.	224	45.48 N	122.31 W
Clark, Lake ⊜	180	60.15 N	154.15 W
Clark, Mount ʌ	180	64.25 N	124.12 W
Clark, Point ≻	190	44.04 N	81.45 W
Clark Air Base (U.S.) ■	116	15.11 N	120.32 E
Clark Branch ≃	285	39.43 N	74.45 W
Clark Canyon Reservoir ⊜[1]	202	44.58 N	112.51 W
Clark Creek ≃	208	40.22 N	76.58 W
Clarkdale	200	34.46 N	112.03 W
Clarke ≃	166	19.12 S	145.30 E
Clarke City	186	50.12 N	66.38 W
Clarke Island I	166	40.33 S	148.10 E
Clarke Lake ⊜	184	54.25 N	106.51 W
Clarke Range ⩘	166	20.50 S	148.33 E
Clarkesville	192	34.36 N	83.31 W
Clarkfield	198	44.47 N	95.48 W
Clark Fork	202	48.08 N	116.10 W
Clark Fork ≃	202	48.09 N	116.15 W
Clark Hill	218	38.18 N	83.12 W
Clarklake	216	42.04 N	84.21 W
Clark Lake ⊜	216	42.07 N	84.19 W
Clark Mills	210	43.06 N	75.22 W
Clark Mountain ʌ, Ca., U.S.	204	35.32 N	115.35 W
Clark Mountain ʌ, Wa., U.S.	224	48.03 N	120.57 W
Clarks, La., U.S.	194	32.01 N	92.08 W
Clarks, Ne., U.S.	198	41.12 N	97.50 W
Clarks ≃	194	37.03 N	88.33 W
Clarks, West Fork ≃	194	36.59 N	88.31 W
Clarksboro	285	39.47 N	75.13 W
Clarksburg, On., Can.	212	44.43 N	80.27 W
Clarksburg, Ca., U.S.	226	38.25 N	121.32 W
Clarksburg, Il., U.S.	219	39.20 N	88.44 W
Clarksburg, In., U.S.	218	39.26 N	85.20 W
Clarksburg, Md., U.S.	208	39.14 N	77.16 W
Clarksburg, N.J., U.S.	208	40.11 N	74.26 W
Clarksburg, Oh., U.S.	218	39.30 N	83.09 W
Clarksburg, W.V., U.S.	188	39.16 N	80.20 W
Clarksburg State Park ♠	207	42.43 N	73.06 W
Clarks Creek ≃, Ks., U.S.	198	39.05 N	96.42 W
Clarks Creek ≃, Ky., U.S.	218	38.40 N	84.44 W
Clarksdale	194	34.12 N	90.34 W
Clarks Green	210	41.30 N	75.42 W
Clark's Harbour	186	43.26 N	65.38 W
Clarks Hill	216	40.14 N	86.43 W
Clarks Hill Lake ⊜[1]	192	33.50 N	82.20 W
Clarks Island I	283	42.01 N	70.38 W
Clarks Mills	214	41.24 N	80.11 W
Clarkson, On., Can.	275b	43.31 N	79.37 W
Clarkson, Ky., U.S.	194	37.29 N	86.13 W
Clarkson, Ne., U.S.	198	41.43 N	97.07 W
Clarkson, N.Y., U.S.	210	43.14 N	77.56 W
Clarks Point	180	58.51 N	158.30 W
Clarks Summit	210	41.29 N	75.42 W
Clarkston, Mi., U.S.	216	42.44 N	83.25 W
Clarkston, Wa., U.S.	202	46.24 N	117.02 W
Clark's Town	241q	18.25 N	77.34 W
Clarksville, Ar., U.S.	194	35.28 N	93.27 W
Clarksville, De., U.S.	208	38.32 N	75.08 W
Clarksville, In., U.S.	218	38.15 N	85.47 W
Clarksville, Ia., U.S.	190	42.47 N	92.40 W
Clarksville, Md., U.S.	208	39.12 N	76.56 W
Clarksville, Mi., U.S.	216	42.50 N	85.14 W
Clarksville, Mo., U.S.	219	39.22 N	90.54 W
Clarksville, N.Y., U.S.	210	42.35 N	73.58 W
Clarksville, Oh., U.S.	218	39.24 N	83.58 W
Clarksville, Tn., U.S.	194	36.31 N	87.21 W
Clarksville, Tx., U.S.	196	33.36 N	95.03 W
Clarksville, Va., U.S.	192	36.37 N	78.33 W
Clarksville City	222	32.32 N	94.34 W
Clarkton, Mo., U.S.	194	36.27 N	89.58 W
Clarkton, N.C., U.S.	192	34.29 N	78.39 W
Claro ≃, Bra.	248	13.25 S	56.35 W
Claro ≃, Bra.	255	15.28 S	51.43 W
Claro ≃, Bra.	255	19.06 S	47.52 W
Claro ≃, Bra.	255	19.08 S	50.40 W
Claro, Arroyo ≃	288	34.25 S	58.41 W
Claro, Ribeirão ≃	287b	23.40 S	46.17 W
Clary	50	50.05 N	3.24 E
Claryville	210	41.55 N	74.34 W
Clashmore	48	52.00 N	7.48 W
Clatskanie	224	46.06 N	123.12 W
Clatskanie ≃	224	46.08 N	123.14 W
Clatsop □[6]	224	46.01 N	123.41 W
Clatsop Spit ≻[2]	224	46.13 N	124.01 W
Clatteringshaws Lake ⊜	44	55.05 N	4.17 W
Claude	196	35.07 N	101.22 W
Claudy	48	54.54 N	7.09 W
Claughton	44	54.06 N	2.40 W
Claussnitz	54	50.56 N	12.53 E
Clausthal-Zellerfeld	52	51.48 N	10.20 E
Claver	116	9.35 N	125.44 E
Claverack	210	42.13 N	73.44 W
Claveria, Pil.	116	18.37 N	121.05 E
Claveria, Pil.	116	8.38 N	124.55 E
Clavet	184	52.00 N	106.23 W
Clavey ≃	226	37.52 N	120.07 W
Clawit, Mount ʌ	116	16.58 N	120.58 E
Clawson, Mi., U.S.	281	42.32 N	83.08 W
Clawson, Tx., U.S.	222	31.24 N	94.47 W
Claxton	192	32.09 N	81.54 W
Clay, Ky., U.S.	194	37.28 N	87.49 W
Clay, Tx., U.S.	222	30.23 N	96.21 W
Clay, W.V., U.S.	188	38.27 N	81.05 W
Clay □[6]	219	38.45 N	88.40 W
Claybank Creek ≃	194	31.10 N	85.44 W
Clay Center, Ks., U.S.	198	39.22 N	97.07 W
Clay Center, Ne., U.S.	198	40.31 N	98.03 W
Clay Center, Oh., U.S.	214	41.33 N	83.21 W
Clay City, Il., U.S.	194	38.41 N	88.21 W
Clay City, In., U.S.	194	39.16 N	87.06 W
Clay City, Ky., U.S.	192	37.51 N	83.55 W
Clay Creek ≃	198	38.06 N	102.31 W
Clay Cross	44	53.10 N	1.24 W
Claydon	42	52.06 N	1.07 E
Claye-Souilly	50	48.57 N	2.42 E
Claygate	260	51.22 N	0.20 W
Claygate Cross	260	51.16 N	0.19 E
Clayhole Wash ⋁	200	36.59 N	113.17 W
Clayhurst	182	56.15 N	120.01 W
Claymont	208	39.48 N	75.27 W
Clayoquot Sound ʯ	182	49.11 N	126.08 W
Claypole	288	34.48 S	58.20 W
Claypool, Az., U.S.	200	33.24 N	110.50 W
Claypool, In., U.S.	216	41.07 N	85.52 W
Claysburg	214	40.17 N	78.27 W
Clay Springs	200	34.21 N	110.17 W
Claysville	214	40.07 N	80.24 W
Clayton, Austl.	274b	37.56 S	145.07 E
Clayton, Eng., U.K.	262	53.47 N	1.52 W
Clayton, Al., U.S.	194	31.52 N	85.26 W
Clayton, Ca., U.S.	282	37.57 N	121.56 W
Clayton, De., U.S.	208	39.17 N	75.38 W
Clayton, Ga., U.S.	192	34.52 N	83.24 W
Clayton, Il., U.S.	219	40.01 N	90.57 W
Clayton, In., U.S.	218	39.41 N	86.31 W
Clayton, La., U.S.	194	31.43 N	91.32 W
Clayton, Mi., U.S.	216	41.52 N	84.14 W
Clayton, Mo., U.S.	219	38.38 N	90.19 W
Clayton, N.J., U.S.	208	39.39 N	75.05 W
Clayton, N.M., U.S.	196	36.27 N	103.11 W
Clayton, N.Y., U.S.	212	44.14 N	76.05 W
Clayton, N.C., U.S.	192	35.39 N	78.27 W
Clayton, Ok., U.S.	196	34.35 N	95.21 W
Clayton, Tx., U.S.	222	32.06 N	94.28 W
Clayton, Wa., U.S.	182	48.00 N	117.33 W
Clayton ≃	166	29.06 S	138.05 E
Claytonia	214	41.00 N	79.58 W
Clayton-le-Moors	262	53.47 N	2.23 W
Clayton-le-Woods	262	53.41 N	2.38 W
Clayton Park ♠	285	39.52 N	75.29 W
Clayton Valley ⋁	282	37.58 N	121.58 W
Claytonville	216	40.34 N	87.49 W
Clay Village	218	38.11 N	85.07 W
Clayville	210	42.59 N	75.15 W
Clear ≃	182	56.11 N	119.42 W
Clear, Cape ≻, Ire.	48	51.24 N	9.30 W
Clear, Cape ≻, Ak., U.S.	180	59.48 N	147.54 W
Clear, Lake ⊜	212	45.26 N	77.12 W
Clear, Mount ʌ	171b	35.52 S	149.04 E
Clear Boggy Creek ≃	196	34.03 N	95.47 W
Clearbrook, B.C., Can.	224	49.08 N	122.26 W
Clearbrook, Mn., U.S.	198	47.41 N	95.25 W
Clear Creek	218	39.07 N	86.32 W
Clear Creek ≃, Al., U.S.	194	34.00 N	87.19 W
Clear Creek ≃, Az., U.S.	200	34.59 N	110.38 W
Clear Creek ≃, Ca., U.S.	204	40.31 N	122.22 W
Clear Creek ≃, Ca., U.S.	280	34.17 N	118.12 W
Clear Creek ≃, Ca., U.S.	282	37.20 N	122.21 W
Clear Creek ≃, Ky., U.S.	218	38.10 N	85.17 W
Clear Creek ≃, Mo., U.S.	194	38.00 N	93.56 W
Clear Creek ≃, Mt., U.S.	202	48.46 N	109.25 W
Clear Creek ≃, Ne., U.S.	198	41.08 N	99.06 W
Clear Creek ≃, Oh., U.S.	218	39.33 N	84.20 W
Clear Creek ≃, Or., U.S.	224	45.23 N	122.29 W
Clear Creek ≃, Or., U.S.	224	45.09 N	121.31 W
Clear Creek ≃, Tn., U.S.	192	36.05 N	84.42 W
Clear Creek ≃, Tx., U.S.	196	33.16 N	97.03 W
Clear Creek ≃, Tx., U.S.	222	29.33 N	95.05 W
Clear Creek ≃, Tx., U.S.	222	29.09 N	97.23 W
Clear Creek ≃, Wa., U.S.	224	46.07 N	122.00 W
Clear Creek ≃, Wy., U.S.	202	44.53 N	106.04 W
Clear Creek State Park ♠	214	41.20 N	79.05 W
Clearfield, Ia., U.S.	198	40.48 N	94.28 W
Clearfield, Ky., U.S.	218	38.09 N	83.25 W
Clearfield, Pa., U.S.	214	41.01 N	78.26 W
Clearfield, Ut,. U.S.	200	41.06 N	112.01 W
Clearfield □[6]	214	41.02 N	78.27 W
Clearfield Creek ≃	214	41.02 N	78.24 W
Clear Fork Reservoir ⊜[1]	214	40.42 N	82.38 W
Clearing ◈[8]	278	41.47 N	87.47 W
Clear Island I	48	51.26 N	9.30 W
Clearlake, Ca., U.S.	226	38.57 N	122.38 W
Clear Lake, Ia., U.S.	190	43.08 N	93.22 W
Clear Lake, S.D., U.S.	198	44.44 N	96.40 W
Clearlake, Wa., U.S.	224	48.28 N	122.14 W
Clear Lake, Wi., U.S.	190	45.15 N	92.16 W
Clear Lake ⊜, Mb., Can.	184	50.42 N	100.00 W
Clear Lake ⊜, On., Can.	212	44.59 N	79.33 W
Clear Lake ⊜, On., Can.	212	45.14 N	79.57 W
Clear Lake ⊜, On., Can.	212	44.30 N	78.13 W
Clear Lake ⊜, In., U.S.	216	41.44 N	84.50 W
Clear Lake ⊜[1], Ca., U.S.	204	39.02 N	122.50 W
Clear Lake ⊜[1], La., U.S.	194	31.55 N	93.05 W
Clearlake Oaks	226	39.07 N	122.40 W
Clearlake Park	226	38.58 N	122.39 W
Clear Lake Reservoir ⊜[1]	204	41.52 N	121.08 W
Clear Lake Shores	222	29.33 N	95.02 W
Clearmont	202	44.38 N	106.22 W
Clear Run	214	41.08 N	78.45 W
Clear Site	180	64.19 N	149.11 W
Clearview, Oh., U.S.	214	41.25 N	82.10 W
Clearview, Wa., U.S.	224	47.45 N	122.06 W
Clearview, W.V., U.S.	214	40.09 N	80.41 W
Clearview Estates	279b	40.34 N	80.16 W
Clearwater, B.C., Can.	182	51.38 N	120.02 W
Clearwater, Mb., Can.	184	49.08 N	99.01 W
Clearwater, Fl., U.S.	220	27.57 N	82.48 W
Clearwater, Ks., U.S.	198	37.30 N	97.30 W
Clearwater, Ne., U.S.	198	42.10 N	98.11 W
Clearwater, S.C., U.S.	192	33.29 N	81.53 W
Clearwater, Wa., U.S.	224	47.34 N	124.17 W
Clearwater ≃, Can.	184	56.44 N	111.23 W
Clearwater ≃, Ab., Can.	182	52.23 N	114.50 W
Clearwater ≃, B.C., Can.	182	51.42 N	120.00 W
Clearwater ≃, Id., U.S.	202	46.25 N	117.02 W
Clearwater ≃, Mn., U.S.	198	47.54 N	96.16 W
Clearwater ≃, Mt., U.S.	202	46.58 N	113.23 W
Clearwater ≃, Wa., U.S.	224	47.33 N	124.21 W
Clearwater, Middle Fork ≃	202	46.09 N	115.59 W
Clearwater, North Fork ≃	202	46.30 N	116.19 W
Clearwater, South Fork ≃	202	46.09 N	115.59 W
Clear Water Bay ⊂	271d	22.17 N	114.18 E
Clearwater Beach Island I	220	27.59 N	82.49 W
Clearwater Lake ⊜, B.C., Can.	182	52.15 N	120.13 W
Clearwater Lake ⊜, Mb., Can.	184	54.05 N	101.00 W
Clearwater Lake Provincial Park ♠	184	54.03 N	101.10 W
Clearwater Mountains ⩘	202	46.00 N	115.30 W
Cleator Moor	44	54.31 N	3.30 W
Clebit	196	34.21 N	94.52 W
Cleburne	222	32.20 N	97.23 W
Cleckheaton	44	53.43 N	1.43 W
Cle Elum	224	47.11 N	120.56 W
Cle Elum ≃	224	47.11 N	121.01 W
Cle Elum Lake ⊜[1]	224	47.18 N	121.06 W
Cleethorpes	44	53.34 N	0.02 W
Cleeve Cloud ʌ[2]	42	51.34 N	2.00 W
Clefmont	58	48.06 N	5.31 E
Cleggan	48	53.33 N	10.09 W
Cleland Conservation Park ♠	168b	34.59 S	138.44 E
Cleland Heights	285	39.44 N	75.34 W
Clelles	62	44.50 N	5.37 E
Clementon	285	39.48 N	74.59 W
Clementsport	186	44.40 N	65.37 W
Clemson	192	34.41 N	82.50 W
Clemville	222	29.00 N	96.08 W
Clendenin	188	38.29 N	81.20 W
Clendening Lake ⊜[1]	214	40.16 N	81.13 W
Clenze	54	52.56 N	10.58 E
Cleobury Mortimer	42	52.23 N	2.29 W
Cleona	208	40.20 N	76.28 W
Cléon-d'Andran	62	44.37 N	4.56 E
Cleopatra Needle ʌ	116	10.07 N	118.58 E
Clères	50	49.36 N	1.07 E
Clerke Rocks II[1]	244	55.01 S	34.41 W
Clermont, Austl.	166	22.49 S	147.39 E
Clermont, P.Q., Can.	186	47.41 N	70.14 W
Clermont, Fr.	50	49.23 N	2.24 E
Clermont, Fl., U.S.	220	28.32 N	81.46 W
Clermont, N.J., U.S.	285	39.59 N	74.48 W
Clermont, Pa., U.S.	214	41.41 N	78.29 W
Clermont □[6]	218	39.05 N	84.11 W
Clermont-en-Argonne	56	49.06 N	5.04 E
Clermont-Ferrand	32	45.47 N	3.05 E
Clermont State Park ♠	210	42.05 N	73.55 W
Clerval	58	47.24 N	6.30 E
Clervaux	56	50.04 N	6.01 E
Cléry-Saint-André	50	47.49 N	1.45 E
Cles	64	46.22 N	11.02 E
Cleve	166	33.42 S	136.30 E
Clevedon	42	51.27 N	2.51 W
Cleveland, Austl.	171a	27.32 S	153.17 E
Cleveland, Al., U.S.	194	33.59 N	86.34 W
Cleveland, Fl., U.S.	220	26.57 N	82.00 W
Cleveland, Ga., U.S.	192	34.35 N	83.45 W
Cleveland, Ms., U.S.	194	33.44 N	90.43 W
Cleveland, N.Y., U.S.	210	43.14 N	75.53 W
Cleveland, N.C., U.S.	192	35.43 N	80.40 W
Cleveland, Oh., U.S.	214	41.29 N	81.41 W
Cleveland, Oh., U.S.	279a	41.29 N	81.41 W
Cleveland, Ok., U.S.	196	36.18 N	96.27 W
Cleveland, Tn., U.S.	194	35.09 N	84.52 W
Cleveland, Tx., U.S.	222	30.20 N	95.05 W
Cleveland, Va., U.S.	192	36.56 N	82.09 W
Cleveland □[6]	44	54.35 N	1.15 W
Cleveland, Cape ≻	166	19.11 S	147.01 E
Cleveland, Mount ʌ, Austl.	166	41.25 S	145.23 E
Cleveland, Mount ʌ, Mt., U.S.	202	48.56 N	113.51 W
Cleveland Heights	214	41.31 N	81.33 W
Cleveland Hills ⩘[2]	44	54.23 N	1.05 W
Cleveland-Hopkins International Airport ⊠	279a	41.25 N	81.51 W
Clevelândia	252	26.24 S	52.21 W
Clevelândia do Norte	250	3.49 N	51.52 W
Cleveland Museum of Art ʊ	279a	41.31 N	81.37 W
Cleveland National Forest ♠	280	33.47 N	117.38 W
Cleveland Park ◈[8]	284c	38.56 N	77.04 W
Cleveland Peninsula ≻[1]	182	55.45 N	132.00 W
Cleveland Pond ⊜	283	42.07 N	70.58 W
Cleveland State University ʊ[2]	279a	41.30 N	81.40 W
Cleveland Zoo ♠	279a	41.27 N	81.43 W
Cleveleys	44	53.53 N	3.03 W
Cleversburg	208	40.02 N	77.28 W
Cleves	218	39.10 N	84.45 W
Cleves → Kleve	52	51.48 N	6.09 E
Clew Bay ⊂	48	53.50 N	9.50 W
Clewer	158	25.55 S	29.07 E
Clewiston	220	26.45 N	80.56 W
Cley next the Sea	42	52.58 N	1.03 E
Clichy	50	48.54 N	2.18 E
Clichy-sous-Bois	261	48.55 N	2.33 E
Clifden	48	53.29 N	10.01 W
Clifden Bay ⊂	48	53.28 N	10.05 W
Cliffdale Creek ≃	166	16.56 S	138.48 E
Cliffdell	224	46.44 N	120.42 W
Cliffe	260	51.28 N	0.30 E
Cliffe Marshes ≋	260	51.28 N	0.30 E
Cliffe Woods	260	51.26 N	0.30 E
Clifford, On., Can.	212	43.58 N	80.58 W
Clifford, S. Afr.	158	31.04 S	27.28 E
Clifford, In., U.S.	218	39.16 N	85.52 W
Clifford, Pa., U.S.	210	41.39 N	75.36 W
Clifford Park ♠	274b	37.43 S	145.16 E
Cliffside	210	42.31 N	74.59 W
Cliffside Park	276	40.58 N	73.57 W
Cliffwood	276	40.26 N	74.14 W
Cliffwood Beach	276	40.26 N	74.13 W
Clifton, Austl.	171a	27.56 S	151.54 E
Clifton, Eng., U.K.	262	53.46 N	2.49 W
Clifton, Az., U.S.	200	33.03 N	109.17 W
Clifton, Il., U.S.	216	40.56 N	87.56 W
Clifton, Ks., U.S.	198	39.34 N	97.16 W
Clifton, N.J., U.S.	210	40.51 N	74.09 W
Clifton, N.Y., U.S.	210	43.03 N	77.49 W
Clifton, Or., U.S.	224	46.12 N	123.27 W
Clifton, Tn., U.S.	194	35.23 N	87.59 W
Clifton, Tx., U.S.	222	31.46 N	97.34 W
Clifton, Lake ⊜	168a	32.49 S	115.41 E
Clifton Court Forebay ⊜[1]	226	37.50 N	121.35 W
Clifton Forge	192	37.48 N	79.49 W
Clifton Gorge ⋁	42	51.28 N	2.37 W
Clifton Heights, N.Y., U.S.	284a	42.44 N	78.56 W
Clifton Heights, Pa., U.S.	285	39.55 N	75.17 W
Clifton Hills	166	26.52 S	138.50 E
Clifton Knolls	210	42.52 N	73.46 W
Clifton Park ♠	284b	39.19 N	76.35 W
Clifton Point ≻	240b	25.01 N	77.34 W
Clifton Springs	210	42.57 N	77.08 W
Clifty, Mount ʌ	224	47.07 N	121.10 W
Clifty Creek ≃	218	39.09 N	85.54 W
Clifty Falls State Park ♠	218	38.45 N	85.26 W
Clignon ≃	50	49.07 N	3.04 E
Climax, Sk., Can.	184	49.13 N	108.23 W
Climax, Co., U.S.	200	39.22 N	106.10 W
Climax, Ga., U.S.	192	30.52 N	84.25 W
Climax, Mi., U.S.	216	42.14 N	85.20 W
Climax, Pa., U.S.	214	40.59 N	79.23 W
Clinch ≃	192	35.53 N	84.29 W
Clinchco	192	37.09 N	82.21 W
Clingen	54	51.14 N	10.55 E
Clingmans Dome ʌ	192	35.35 N	83.30 W
Clinton, B.C., Can.	182	51.05 N	121.35 W
Clinton, On., Can.	190	43.37 N	81.32 W
Clinton, N.Z.	172	46.12 S	169.22 E
Clinton, Al., U.S.	194	32.55 N	88.00 W
Clinton, Ar., U.S.	194	35.35 N	92.27 W
Clinton, Ct., U.S.	207	41.16 N	72.31 W
Clinton, Il., U.S.	219	40.09 N	88.57 W
Clinton, In., U.S.	194	39.39 N	87.23 W
Clinton, Ia., U.S.	190	41.50 N	90.11 W
Clinton, Ky., U.S.	194	36.40 N	88.59 W
Clinton, La., U.S.	194	30.51 N	91.00 W
Clinton, Me., U.S.	188	44.38 N	69.30 W
Clinton, Md., U.S.	208	38.45 N	76.53 W
Clinton, Ma., U.S.	207	42.25 N	71.41 W
Clinton, Mi., U.S.	216	42.04 N	83.58 W
Clinton, Mn., U.S.	198	45.27 N	96.26 W
Clinton, Ms., U.S.	194	32.20 N	90.19 W
Clinton, Mo., U.S.	194	38.22 N	93.46 W
Clinton, N.J., U.S.	210	40.38 N	74.54 W
Clinton, N.Y., U.S.	210	43.02 N	75.22 W
Clinton, N.C., U.S.	192	34.59 N	78.19 W
Clinton, Oh., U.S.	214	40.56 N	81.42 W
Clinton, Ok., U.S.	196	35.30 N	98.58 W
Clinton, Pa., U.S.	214	40.29 N	80.18 W
Clinton, S.C., U.S.	192	34.28 N	81.52 W
Clinton, Tn., U.S.	192	36.06 N	84.07 W
Clinton, Tx., U.S.	222	33.06 N	96.14 W
Clinton, Wa., U.S.	224	47.58 N	122.21 W
Clinton, Wi., U.S.	216	42.33 N	88.51 W
Clinton □[6], Il., U.S.	219	38.37 N	89.22 W
Clinton □[6], In., U.S.	216	40.17 N	86.31 W
Clinton □[6], Mi., U.S.	216	42.56 N	84.36 W
Clinton □[6], N.Y., U.S.	206	44.57 N	73.42 W
Clinton □[6], Oh., U.S.	218	39.27 N	83.50 W
Clinton □[6], Pa., U.S.	210	41.08 N	71.26 W
Clinton ≃	214	42.36 N	82.48 W
Clinton, Cape ≻	166	22.32 S	150.47 E
Clinton, Lake ⊜[1]	194	40.10 N	88.50 W
Clinton, Middle Branch ≃	281	42.36 N	82.54 W
Clinton, North Branch ≃	214	42.36 N	82.54 W
Clinton-Colden Lake ⊜	176	63.58 N	107.27 W
Clintondale	210	41.01 N	77.29 W
Clinton Lake ⊜[1]	198	38.55 N	95.25 W
Clinton Park	210	42.36 N	73.43 W
Clinton Reservoir ⊜[1]	276	41.05 N	74.27 W
Clinton Township	214	42.33 N	82.53 W
Clintonville, Mi., U.S.	281	42.43 N	83.22 W
Clintonville, Pa., U.S.	214	41.12 N	79.53 W
Clintonville, Wi., U.S.	190	44.37 N	88.45 W
Clintwood	192	37.09 N	82.27 W
Clio, Al., U.S.	194	31.42 N	85.36 W
Clio, Mi., U.S.	190	43.10 N	83.44 W
Clio, S.C., U.S.	192	34.34 N	79.32 W
Clipperton, Île I[1]	230	10.17 N	109.13 W
Clipperton Fracture Zone ✢	16	10.00 N	115.00 W
Clisham ʌ	46	57.57 N	6.49 W
Clisson	32	47.05 N	1.17 W
Clitheroe	44	53.53 N	2.23 W
Clitunno ≃	66	42.56 N	12.37 E
Clive	172	39.35 S	176.55 E
Cloates, Point ≻	162	22.43 S	113.40 E
Clock Face	262	53.25 N	2.43 W
Clocolan	158	29.00 S	27.30 E
Clodomira	252	27.35 S	64.08 W
Cloe	214	40.56 N	78.56 W
Cloete	196	27.55 N	101.10 W
Cloghan, Ire.	48	54.51 N	7.56 W
Cloghan, Ire.	48	53.13 N	7.53 W
Cloghane	48	52.13 N	10.12 W
Clogheen	48	52.16 N	8.00 W
Clogher	48	54.25 N	7.12 W
Clogher Head ≻	48	53.48 N	6.12 W
Cloghjordan	48	52.57 N	8.02 W
Clonakilty	48	51.37 N	8.54 W
Clonakilty Bay ⊂	48	51.35 N	8.50 W
Cloncurry	166	20.42 S	140.30 E
Cloncurry ≃	166	18.37 S	140.40 E
Clondalkin	48	53.19 N	6.24 W
Clonee	48	53.25 N	6.26 W
Clones	48	54.11 N	7.15 W
Clonfert	48	53.14 N	8.05 W
Clonmacnois ⊥	48	53.20 N	7.59 W
Clonmany	48	55.14 N	7.25 W
Clonmel	48	52.21 N	7.42 W
Clonroche	48	52.27 N	6.43 W
Clontarf	274a	33.48 S	151.16 E
Cloone	48	53.57 N	7.46 W
Clo-oose	224	48.40 N	124.49 W
Cloppenburg	52	52.50 N	8.02 E
Cloquallum Creek ≃	224	46.58 N	123.24 W
Cloquet	190	46.43 N	92.27 W
Cloquet ≃	190	46.52 N	92.35 W
Clorinda	252	25.17 S	57.43 W
Closter	276	40.58 N	73.57 W
Cloudcroft	200	32.57 N	105.44 W
Cloud Peak ʌ, Ak., U.S.	180	68.24 N	148.26 W
Cloud Peak ʌ, Wy., U.S.	202	44.25 N	107.10 W
Cloudy Bay ⊂	172	41.27 S	174.10 E
Cloudy Mountain ʌ	180	63.11 N	156.05 W
Clough	48	54.18 N	5.50 W
Clough Foot	262	53.43 N	2.08 W

Symbol	English	Deutsch	Español	Français	Português
≃	River	Fluß	Río	Rivière	Rio
⌶	Canal	Kanal	Canal	Canal	Canal
ᒐ	Waterfall, Rapids	Wasserfall, Stromschnellen	Cascada, Rápidos	Chute d'eau, Rapides	Cascata, Rápidos
ʯ	Strait	Meeresstraße	Estrecho	Détroit	Estreito
⊂	Bay, Gulf	Bucht, Golf	Bahía, Golfo	Baie, Golfe	Baía, Golfo
⊜	Lake, Lakes	See, Seen	Lago, Lagos	Lac, Lacs	Lago, Lagos
≋	Swamp	Sumpf	Pantano	Marais	Pântano
⍓	Ice Features, Glacier	Eis- und Gletscherformen	Accidentes Glaciales	Formes glaciaires	Acidentes glaciares
⏚	Other Hydrographic Features	Andere Hydrographische Objekte	Otros Elementos Hidrográficos	Autres données hydrographiques	Outros acidentes hidrográficos

Symbol	English	Deutsch	Español	Français	Português
✢	Submarine Features	Untermeerische Objekte	Accidentes Submarinos	Formes de relief sous-marin	Acidentes submarinos
□	Political Unit	Politische Einheit	Unidad Politica	Entité politique	Unidade política
ʊ	Cultural Institution	Kulturelle Institution	Institución Cultural	Institution culturelle	Institução cultural
⊥	Historical Site	Historische Stätte	Sitio Histórico	Site historique	Sitio histórico
♠	Recreational Site	Erholungs- und Ferienort	Sitio de Recreo	Centre de loisirs	Area de Lazer
⊠	Airport	Flughafen	Aeropuerto	Aéroport	Aeroporto
■	Military Installation	Militäranlage	Instalación Militar	Installation militaire	Instalação militar
◈	Miscellaneous	Verschiedenes	Misceláneo	Divers	Diversos

Clova 46 56.50 N 3.06 W
Clova, Glen V 46 56.49 N 3.04 W
Clove Lakes Park ♠ 276 40.37 N 74.07 W
Clovelly, Austl. 274a 33.55 S 151.16 E
Clovelly, Eng., U.K. 42 51.00 N 4.24 W
Clover 192 35.06 N 81.13 W
Clover Bank 210 42.45 N 78.53 W
Clover Creek ≃, Id., U.S. 202 42.34 N 115.38 W
Clover Creek ≃, Id., U.S. 202 43.00 N 115.11 W
Cloverdale, B.C., Can. 224 49.06 N 122.44 W
Cloverdale, Al., U.S. 194 34.56 N 87.46 W
Cloverdale, Ca., U.S. 204 38.48 N 123.00 W
Cloverdale, Il., U.S. 278 41.56 N 88.07 W
Cloverdale, In., U.S. 194 39.30 N 86.47 W
Cloverdale, Ky., U.S. 218 38.10 N 84.53 W
Cloverdale, Mi., U.S. 216 42.32 N 85.23 W
Cloverdale, Oh., U.S. 216 41.01 N 84.18 W
Cloverdale, Or., U.S. 224 45.12 N 123.53 W
Cloverdale Mall ◆[9] 275b 43.38 N 79.34 W
Cloverdene 273d 26.09 S 28.22 E
Cloverleaf 222 29.46 N 95.10 W
Clover Pass 182 55.28 N 131.47 W
Cloverport 194 37.50 N 86.37 W
Cloverville 216 43.11 N 86.10 W
Clovis, Ca., U.S. 226 36.49 N 119.42 W
Clovis, N.M., U.S. 196 34.24 N 103.12 W
Clowbridge Reservoir ⊜[1] 262 53.45 N 2.16 W
Clowne 44 53.18 N 1.16 W
Cloyes-sur-le-Loir 50 48.00 N 1.14 E
Cloyne 48 51.51 N 8.08 W
Cluain Meala → Clonmel 48 52.21 N 7.42 W
Cluanie, Loch ⊜ 46 57.07 N 5.05 W
Cluj-Napoca 38 46.47 N 23.36 E
Cluj-Napoca □[6] 38 46.45 N 23.45 E
Clun 42 52.26 N 3.00 W
Clun ≃ 42 52.22 N 2.53 W
Clune 214 40.34 N 79.18 W
Clunes 169 37.18 S 143.47 E
Clun Forest ◆[3] 42 52.28 N 3.07 W
Clunie Water ≃ 46 57.00 N 3.24 W
Cluny, Austl. 166 24.31 S 139.35 E
Cluny, Fr. 58 46.26 N 4.39 E
Cluses 58 46.04 N 6.36 E
Clusone 64 45.53 N 9.57 E
Clute 222 29.01 N 95.23 W
Clutha ≃ 172 46.21 S 169.48 E
Clwyd □[6] 44 53.05 N 3.20 W
Clwyd ≃ 44 53.20 N 3.30 W
Clwyd, Vale of V 44 53.12 N 3.24 W
Clwydian Range ⩘ 44 53.10 N 3.20 W
Clydach 42 51.43 N 3.50 W
Clyde, Austl. 274a 33.50 S 151.00 E
Clyde, Ab., Can. 182 54.09 N 113.39 W
Clyde, N.Z. 172 45.11 S 169.19 E
Clyde, Ca., U.S. 226 38.02 N 122.02 W
Clyde, Ks., U.S. 198 39.35 N 97.23 W
Clyde, Mi., U.S. 281 42.41 N 83.37 W
Clyde, N.Y., U.S. 210 43.05 N 76.52 W
Clyde, N.C., U.S. 192 35.32 N 82.54 W
Clyde, Oh., U.S. 214 41.18 N 82.58 W
Clyde, Tx., U.S. 196 32.24 N 99.30 W
Clyde ≃, Austl. 170 35.23 S 150.15 E
Clyde ≃, N.S., Can. 186 43.35 N 65.25 W
Clyde ≃, On., Can. 212 44.58 N 76.22 W
Clyde ≃, Scot., U.K. 46 55.56 N 4.29 W
Clyde ≃, N.Y., U.S. 210 43.04 N 77.00 W
Clyde ≃, Vt., U.S. 188 44.56 N 72.12 W
Clyde, Firth of ⊂[1] 46 55.42 N 5.00 W
Clydebank 46 55.54 N 4.24 W
Clydegale Lake ⊜ 212 45.25 N 78.23 W
Clyde Lake ⊜ 182 55.18 N 111.28 W
Clyde No.03 214 39.59 N 80.03 W
Clyde Park 202 45.53 N 110.36 W
Clyde Potts Reservoir ⊜[1] 276 40.48 N 74.35 W
Clyde River 176 70.25 N 68.30 W
Clydesdale 158 26.54 S 27.55 E
Clydesdale V 46 55.42 N 3.50 W
Clymer, N.Y., U.S. 214 42.01 N 79.37 W
Clymer, Pa., U.S. 214 40.40 N 79.00 W
Clynnog-fawr 44 53.01 N 4.23 W
Clywedog ≃ 42 52.27 N 3.32 W
Ćmielów 30 50.53 N 21.31 E
Cna ≃, Bela. 76 52.10 N 27.03 E
Cna ≃, Ross. 76 57.33 N 34.36 E
Cna ≃, Ross. 80 54.32 N 42.05 E
Cna ≃, Ross. 82 55.03 N 39.09 E
Côa ≃ 34 41.05 N 7.06 W
Coacalco 286a 19.37 N 9.05 W
Coachella 204 33.40 N 116.10 W
Coachella Canal ≋ 204 33.34 N 116.00 W
Coachford 48 51.53 N 8.48 W
Coacoyole 232 24.31 N 106.34 W
Coacuilco 234 21.07 N 98.35 W
Coahoma 196 32.18 N 101.18 W
Coahuayana 234 18.44 N 103.41 W
Coahuayutla de Guerrero 234 18.19 N 101.49 W
Coahuila 200 32.12 N 114.59 W
Coahuila □[3] 232 27.20 N 102.00 W
Coal ≃ 180 59.39 N 126.57 W
Coalbrook 158 26.51 S 27.53 E
Coalbrookdale 42 52.38 N 2.30 W
Coalburg 214 41.11 N 80.36 W
Coalburn 46 55.36 N 3.54 W
Coal City 216 41.17 N 88.17 W
Coalcomán ≃ 234 18.11 N 103.08 W
Coalcomán de Matamoros 234 18.47 N 103.09 W
Coal Creek 180 65.22 N 143.10 W
Coal Creek ≃, Co., U.S. 198 40.30 N 104.26 W
Coal Creek ≃, In., U.S. 194 39.57 N 87.25 W
Coal Creek ≃, Wa., U.S. 202 47.19 N 118.36 W
Coal Creek Flat 172 45.29 S 169.18 E
Coaldale, Ab., Can. 182 49.43 N 112.37 W
Coaldale, Pa., U.S. 210 40.49 N 75.54 W
Coal Fire Creek ≃ 194 33.15 N 88.18 W
Coal Fork 188 38.19 N 81.32 W
Coalgate, N.Z. 172 43.29 S 171.58 E
Coalgate, Ok., U.S. 196 34.32 N 96.13 W
Coal Grove 188 38.30 N 82.38 W
Coal Harbour 182 50.36 N 127.35 W
Coal Hill 194 35.26 N 93.40 W
Coal Hill Park ♠ 271a 39.56 N 116.23 E
Coalhurst 182 49.45 N 112.56 W
Coalinga 226 36.08 N 120.21 W
Coalisland 48 54.33 N 6.42 W
Coal Island I 172 46.07 S 166.38 E
Coalmont 182 49.31 N 120.41 W
Coalpit Heath 42 51.32 N 2.28 W
Coalport 214 40.44 N 78.32 W
Coal River 180 59.45 N 126.55 W
Coal Run ≃ 279b 40.21 N 80.07 W
Coalspur 182 53.11 N 117.01 W
Coalton 219 39.17 N 89.19 W
Coaltown 214 41.02 N 80.20 W
Coal Valley V 204 38.00 N 115.05 W
Coalville, S. Afr. 158 26.01 S 29.10 E
Coalville, Eng., U.K. 42 52.44 N 1.20 W
Coalville, Ut,. U.S. 200 40.55 N 111.23 W
Coamo 240m 18.05 N 66.22 W
Coamo, Lago ⊜[1] 240m 18.01 N 66.23 W
Coapilla 234 17.08 N 93.10 W
Coaraci 255 14.38 S 39.32 W
Coari 246 4.05 S 63.08 W
Coari ≃ 246 4.30 S 63.33 W
Coari, Lago de ⊜ 246 4.15 S 63.22 W
Coarsegold 226 37.16 N 119.42 W
Coast □[4] 154 3.00 S 39.30 E
Coast Mountains ⩘ 176 55.00 N 129.00 W
Coast Ranges ⩘ 178 41.00 N 123.30 W
Coatán ≃ 236 14.48 N 92.31 W
Coatbridge 46 55.52 N 4.01 W
Coatepec 234 19.27 N 96.58 W
Coatepec Harinas 234 18.54 N 99.43 W
Coatepeque 236 14.42 N 91.52 W
Coatepeque, Lago de ⊜ 236 13.52 N 89.33 W
Coates Creek ≃ 212 44.24 N 79.54 W
Coatesville 208 39.58 N 75.49 W
Coaticook 206 45.08 N 71.48 W
Coaticook ≃ 206 45.20 N 71.53 W
Coatsburg 219 40.02 N 91.10 W
Coats Island I 176 62.30 N 83.00 W
Coats Land ◆[1] 9 77.00 S 28.00 W
Coatzacoalcos 234 18.09 N 94.25 W
Coatzacoalcos ≃ 234 18.10 N 94.27 W
Coatzintla 234 20.29 N 97.27 W
Coayllo 248 12.44 S 76.28 W
Coazze 62 45.03 N 7.18 E
Cobá ⊥ 232 20.36 N 87.35 W
Cobadin 38 44.04 N 28.13 E
Coballo Cocha 246 3.54 S 70.32 W
Cobalt, On., Can. 190 47.24 N 79.41 W
Cobalt, Ct., U.S. 207 41.33 N 72.33 W
Cobán 236 15.29 N 90.19 W
Çobanlar 130 38.41 N 30.47 E
Čobar 166 31.30 S 145.49 E
Cobargo 166 36.23 S 149.53 E
Cobb 226 38.49 N 122.43 W
Cobb Creek ≃ 196 35.05 N 98.25 W
Cobberas, Mount ∧ 166 36.52 S 148.10 E
Cobbetts Pond ⊜ 283 42.48 N 71.17 W
Cobbin's Brook ≃ 260 51.41 N 0.01 W
Cobb Island 208 38.16 N 76.51 W
Cobb Island I, Md., U.S. 208 38.16 N 76.51 W
Cobb Island I, Va., U.S. 208 37.20 N 75.44 W
Cobbitty 274a 34.01 S 150.41 E
Cobbitty ∧[2] 274a 33.59 S 150.42 E
Cobble Hill 224 48.41 N 123.36 W
Cobble Mountain Reservoir ⊜[1] 207 42.08 N 72.55 W
Cobblestone Mountain ∧ 228 34.37 N 118.52 W
Cobb Neck ≻[1] 208 38.20 N 76.55 W
Cobbs Creek ≃ 285 39.54 N 75.15 W
Cobbs Creek Park ♠ 285 39.58 N 75.16 W
Cobb Seamount ✣[3] 16 46.46 N 130.49 W
Cobden, Austl. 169 38.20 S 143.05 E
Cobden, On., Can. 190 45.38 N 76.53 W
Cobden, Il., U.S. 194 37.31 N 89.15 W
Cobeña 266a 40.34 N 3.30 W
Cobequid Bay ⊂ 186 45.21 N 63.45 W
Cobequid Mountains ⩘ 186 45.31 N 64.05 W
Cobh 48 51.51 N 8.17 W
Cobham, Eng., U.K. 260 51.23 N 0.24 E
Cobham, Eng., U.K. 260 51.20 N 0.25 W
Cobham ≃ 184 53.15 N 93.58 W
Cobham Hall ⊥ 260 51.23 N 0.25 E
Cobija, Bol. 248 11.02 S 68.44 W
Cobija, Chile 252 22.33 S 70.16 W
Coblenz → Koblenz 56 50.21 N 7.35 E
Cobleskill 210 42.40 N 74.29 W
Cobleskill Creek ≃ 210 42.43 N 74.20 W
Coboconk 212 44.39 N 78.48 W
Cobo Hall ʋ 281 42.19 N 83.03 W
Cobolgo, gora ∧ 84 42.50 N 46.23 E
Çoboto, Cerro ∧ 200 31.29 N 112.05 W
Čoboty 265b 55.39 N 37.21 E
Cobourg 212 43.58 N 78.10 W
Cobourg Peninsula ≻[1] 164 11.20 S 132.15 E
Cobquecura 252 36.08 S 72.47 W
Cobram 166 35.55 S 145.39 E
Cobras, Ilha das I 287a 22.54 S 43.10 W
Cobras, Ribeirão das ≃ 256 23.08 S 46.05 W
Cobre ≃ 236 8.01 N 81.18 W
Cobre, Barranca del V 232 27.28 N 107.50 W
Cóbuè 154 12.04 S 34.50 E
Coburg, Austl. 169 37.45 S 144.58 E
Coburg, Dtsch. 56 50.15 N 10.58 E
Coburg Island I 176 76.00 N 79.25 W
Coburn 210 40.52 N 77.28 W
Coburn Mountain ∧ 188 45.28 N 70.06 W
Coca ≃ 246 0.29 S 76.58 W
Coca, Laguna ⊜ 286b 22.57 N 82.27 W
Coca, Pizzo di ∧ 64 46.04 N 10.01 E
Cocachacra 248 17.06 S 71.46 W
Cocais, Ribeirão dos ≃ 256 21.59 S 47.15 W
Cocal 250 3.28 S 41.34 W
Cocalico Creek ≃ 208 40.07 N 76.14 W
Coccaglio 64 45.34 N 9.58 E
Cocconato 62 45.05 N 8.02 E
Cocentaina 34 38.45 N 0.26 W
Cochabamba 248 17.24 S 66.09 W
Çochabamba □[5] 248 17.30 S 65.40 W
Čochatauri 84 42.01 N 42.15 E
Cochato ≃ 283 42.10 N 71.01 W
Coche, Isla I 246 10.45 N 63.55 W
Cochem 56 50.11 N 7.09 E
Cochesett 283 42.01 N 71.02 W
Cochetopa Creek ≃ 200 38.31 N 106.47 W
Cochichewick, Lake ⊜ 283 42.42 N 71.06 W
Cochin 122 9.58 N 76.14 E
Cochin China → Nam Phan □[9] 110 11.00 N 107.00 E
Cochinos, Bahía de (Bay of Pigs) ⊂ 240p 22.07 N 81.10 W
Cochinos, Cayos II 236 15.57 N 86.33 W
Cochise Head ∧ 200 32.03 N 109.18 W
Cochiti Indian Reservation ◆[4] 200 35.37 N 106.20 W
Cochituate 207 42.19 N 71.21 W
Cochituate, Lake ⊜ 283 42.17 N 71.22 W
Cochituate State Park ♠ 207 42.20 N 71.22 W
Cochran 192 32.23 N 83.21 W
Cochrane, Ab., Can. 182 51.11 N 114.28 W
Cochrane, On., Can. 176 49.04 N 81.01 W
Cochrane, Chile 254 47.16 S 72.33 W
Cochrane, Wi., U.S. 190 44.13 N 91.50 W
Cochrane ≃ 176 57.52 N 101.38 W
Cochrane, Cerro (Monte San Lorenzo) ∧ 254 47.37 S 72.19 W
Cochrane, Lago (Lago Pueyrredón) ⊜ 254 47.20 S 72.00 W
Cochranton 214 41.31 N 80.02 W
Cochranville 208 39.53 N 75.55 W
Cochstedt 54 51.53 N 11.24 E
Cockatoo-Inseln → Buccaneer Archipelago II 160 16.17 S 123.20 E
Cock Bridge 46 57.09 N 3.14 W
Cockburn 166 32.05 S 141.00 E
Cockburn, Canal ʊ 254 54.20 S 71.30 W
Cockburn, Cape ≻ 164 11.20 S 132.52 E
Cockburn, Mount ∧ 162 22.46 S 130.36 E
Cockburn Island I 190 45.55 N 83.22 W
Cockburn Sound ʊ 168a 32.12 S 115.42 E
Cockburnspath 46 55.56 N 2.21 W
Cock Clarks 260 51.42 N 0.37 E
Cockenoe Island I 276 41.05 N 73.21 W
Cockenzie 46 55.58 N 2.58 W
Cocker ≃ 44 54.39 N 3.22 W
Cockerham 44 53.59 N 2.50 W
Cockermouth 44 54.40 N 3.21 W
Cockeysville 208 39.28 N 76.38 W
Cockfield 44 54.37 N 1.48 W
Cockfosters ◆[8] 260 51.39 N 0.09 W
Cocklebiddy 162 32.02 S 126.06 E
Cockpit Country ◆[1] 241q 18.18 N 77.43 W
Cockrell Hill 222 32.44 N 96.53 W
Cockroach Island I 240m 18.24 N 65.04 W
Cockscomb Point ≻ 174u 14.14 S 170.40 W
Coclé □[4] 236 8.30 N 80.15 W
Coclé del Norte ≃ 236 9.05 N 80.35 W
Coclois 50 48.28 N 4.20 E
Coco ≃ 236 15.00 N 83.10 W
Coco, Cayo I 240p 22.30 N 78.28 W
Coco, Isla del I 230 5.32 N 87.04 W
Côco, Rio do ≃ 250 9.27 S 50.02 W
Cocoa 220 28.23 N 80.44 W
Cocoa Beach 220 28.19 N 80.36 W
Cocobeach 152 0.59 N 9.36 E
Coco Channel ʊ 110 13.45 N 93.00 E
Cococi 250 6.25 S 40.30 W
Cocodrie Lake ⊜[1] 194 30.58 N 92.25 W
Coco Islands II 110 14.05 N 93.18 E
Coconino Plateau ⩘[1] 200 35.50 N 112.30 W
Cocorocuma, Cayos ✣[2] 236 15.45 N 83.00 W
Cocos 255 14.10 S 44.33 W
Cocos (Keeling) Islands □[2] 14 12.10 S 96.55 E
Cocos Bay ⊂ 241r 10.27 N 61.00 W
Cocos Island I 174p 13.14 N 144.39 E
Cocos Lagoon ⊂ 174p 13.14 N 144.38 E
Cocos Ridge ✣[3] 16 5.30 N 86.00 W
Cocotá ◆[8] 287a 22.49 S 43.11 W
Cocuiza ≃ 246 10.59 N 71.17 W
Cocula, Méx. 234 18.14 N 99.40 W
Cocula, Méx. 234 20.23 N 103.50 W
Cod ≃ 44 54.10 N 1.22 W
Cod, Cape ≻[1] 207 41.42 N 70.15 W
Codăești 38 46.52 N 27.46 E
Codajás 246 3.50 S 62.05 W
Codaruina 71 40.56 N 8.49 E
Coddenham 42 52.09 N 1.07 E
Codera, Cabo ≻ 246 10.35 N 66.05 W
Coderre 184 50.10 N 106.23 W
Coderre, Ruisseau ≃ 275a 45.43 N 73.19 W
Codesa 182 55.45 N 118.04 W
Codfish Island I 172 46.47 S 167.38 E
Codigoro 66 44.49 N 12.08 E
Cod Island I 176 57.45 N 61.50 W
Codlea 38 45.42 N 25.27 E
Codnor 44 53.03 N 1.23 W
Codó 250 4.29 S 43.53 W
Codogno 62 45.09 N 9.42 E
Codorus 208 39.48 N 76.52 W
Codorus Creek ≃ 208 40.03 N 76.38 W
Codorus State Park ♠ 208 39.48 N 76.54 W
Codòzinho 250 4.46 S 44.10 W
Çodpa 248 18.50 S 69.44 W
Čodro 86 50.50 N 88.34 E
Codroipo 64 45.58 N 12.59 E
Codrongianos 71 40.39 N 8.41 E
Codroy 186 47.53 N 59.24 W
Codroy Pond 186 48.04 N 58.52 W
Codru-Moma, Munții ⩘ 38 46.30 N 22.20 E
Codsall 42 52.38 N 2.12 W
Cody, Ne., U.S. 198 42.56 N 101.14 W
Cody, Wy., U.S. 202 44.31 N 109.03 W
Coeburn 192 36.56 N 82.27 W
Coelemu 252 36.29 S 72.42 W
Coelho da Rocha 256 22.47 S 43.23 W
Coelho Neto 250 4.15 S 43.00 W
Coemba 152 12.08 S 18.05 E
Coen 164 13.56 S 143.12 E
Coen ≃, Austl. 164 13.56 S 142.02 E
Coén ≃, C.R. 236 9.34 N 82.58 W
Coeneo [de la Libertad] 234 19.49 N 101.35 W
Coeroeni ≃ 250 3.21 N 57.31 W
Coesfeld 52 51.56 N 7.10 E
Coetivy Island I 138 7.08 S 56.16 E
Coeur d'Alene 202 47.40 N 116.46 W
Coeur d'Alene ≃ 202 47.28 N 116.48 W
Coeur d'Alene Indian Reservation ◆[4] 202 47.18 N 116.45 W
Coeur d'Alene Lake ⊜ 202 47.32 N 116.48 W
Coeur d'Alene Mountains ⩘ 202 47.50 N 116.05 W
Coevorden 52 52.40 N 6.45 E
Coeymans 210 42.28 N 73.48 W
Coffeen 219 39.05 N 89.24 W
Coffeen Lake ⊜[1] 219 39.03 N 89.20 W
Coffeeville 194 33.58 N 89.40 W
Coffeyville 198 37.02 N 95.36 W
Coffin Bay 162 34.37 S 135.29 E
Coffin Bay ⊂ 162 34.27 S 135.19 E
Coffin Bay Peninsula ≻[1] 162 34.32 S 135.15 E
Coffs Harbour 166 30.18 S 153.08 E
Cofimvaba 158 32.00 S 27.35 E
Cofradía 236 15.24 N 88.09 W
Cofre de Perote, Cerro ∧ 234 19.29 N 97.08 W
Cofre de Perote, Parque Nacional ♠ 234 19.32 N 97.10 W
Cofrents 34 39.14 N 1.04 W
Coggeshall 42 51.52 N 0.41 E
Coggiola 62 45.41 N 8.11 E
Coggon 190 42.16 N 91.31 W
Coghill, Mount ∧ 170 35.10 S 149.44 E
Coghinas ≃ 71 40.56 N 8.48 E
Coghinas, Lago del ⊜ 71 40.45 N 9.02 E
Coglians, Monte (Hohe Warte) ∧ 64 46.37 N 12.53 E
Cogliate 266b 45.39 N 9.05 E
Cognac 32 45.42 N 0.20 W
Cogne 62 45.37 N 7.21 E
Cognin 62 45.34 N 5.54 E
Cogo 152 1.05 N 9.42 E
Cogoleto 62 44.23 N 8.39 E
Cogolin 62 43.15 N 6.32 E
Cogollo del Cengio 64 45.47 N 11.25 E
Cogolludo 34 40.57 N 3.05 W
Cogolo 64 46.21 N 10.41 E
Çogoon ≃ 166 27.19 S 148.50 E
Čograjuskoje vodochranilišče ⊜[1] 80 45.30 N 44.25 E
Cogswell 198 46.06 N 97.46 W
Cogswell Reservoir ⊜[1] 280 34.14 N 117.58 W
Cogt 102 45.20 N 96.38 E
Cogtoandman' 102 45.50 N 104.28 E
Cogton Bay ⊂ 116 9.51 N 124.33 E
Cogt-Ovoo 102 44.25 N 105.20 E
Çoğun 130 39.20 N 34.08 E
Čohansey ≃ 208 39.21 N 75.22 W
Cohasset 207 42.14 N 70.48 W
Cohasset Harbor ⊂ 283 42.15 N 70.47 W
Cohengu ≃ 248 10.17 S 73.57 W
Cohoctah 216 42.46 N 83.57 W
Cohocton 210 42.30 N 77.30 W
Cohocton ≃ 210 42.09 N 77.05 W
Cohoe 180 60.23 N 151.18 W
Cohoes 210 42.46 N 73.42 W
Cohoon, Lake ⊜[1] 208 36.45 N 76.38 W
Cohuna 166 35.49 S 144.13 E
Coiba, Isla de I 246 7.27 N 81.45 W
Coig ≃ 254 50.58 S 69.11 W
Coigeach, Rubha ≻ 46 58.06 N 5.26 W
Coignières 261 48.45 N 1.55 E
Coihaique 254 45.34 S 72.04 W
Coils Creek ≃ 204 39.32 N 116.16 W
Coimbatore 122 11.00 N 76.58 E
Coimbra, Bra. 248 19.55 S 57.47 W
Coimbra, Bra. 255 20.52 S 42.48 W
Coimbra, Port. 34 40.12 N 8.25 W
Coín, Esp. 34 36.40 N 4.45 W
Coin, Ia., U.S. 198 40.39 N 95.13 W
Coina ≃ 266c 38.38 N 9.03 W
Coipasa, Lago ⊜ 248 19.12 S 68.07 W
Coipasa, Salar de ≚ 248 19.26 S 68.09 W
Coire → Chur 58 46.51 N 9.32 E
Čojbalsan, Mong. 88 48.25 N 114.52 E
Čojbalsan, Mong. 88 48.04 N 114.30 E
Čojbalsan uul ∧ 88 47.49 N 107.00 E
Cojedes 246 9.37 N 68.55 W
Cojedes □[3] 246 9.20 N 68.20 W
Cojímar ◆[8] 286b 23.10 N 82.18 W
Cojímar ≃ 286b 23.10 N 82.17 W
Cojudo Blanco, Cerro ∧ 254 47.05 S 69.20 W
Cojumatlán de Régules 234 20.07 N 102.50 W
Cojutepeque 236 13.43 N 88.56 W
Çokak 130 37.45 N 36.19 E
Čokato 190 45.04 N 94.11 W
Cokeburg 214 40.06 N 80.04 W
Coker 273a 6.29 N 3.20 E
Çokeville 200 42.04 N 110.57 W
Čoktal 85 42.36 N 76.44 E
Čokurdach 74 70.38 N 147.55 E
Colāba ◆[8] 272c 18.54 N 72.48 E
Colāba Point ≻ 272c 18.53 N 72.48 E
Colac 169 38.20 S 143.35 E
Colac, Lake ⊜ 169 38.18 S 143.35 E
Çolaklı 130 38.22 N 38.33 E
Čolalao del Valle 252 26.22 S 65.57 W
Colapsin Point ≻ 116 6.38 N 125.25 E
Colares, Bra. 250 0.56 S 48.17 W
Colares, Port. 266c 38.48 N 9.27 W
Colares, Ribeira de ≃ 266c 38.49 N 9.28 W
Colatina 255 19.32 S 40.37 W
Cölbe 56 50.51 N 8.48 E
Colbeck, Cape ≻ 9 77.06 S 157.48 W
Colberry Park 281 42.36 N 83.16 W
Colbert 196 33.51 N 96.30 W
Colbinabbin 166 36.35 S 144.49 E
Colbitz 54 52.19 N 11.36 E
Colbitz-Letzlinger Heide ◆[3] 54 52.27 N 11.35 E
Colborne, On., Can. 212 42.51 N 80.19 W
Colborne, On., Can. 212 44.00 N 77.53 W
Colbún 252 35.42 S 71.25 W
Colbún, Embalse ⊜[1] 252 35.40 S 71.20 W
Colburn, Eng., U.K. 44 54.23 N 1.41 W
Colburn, In., U.S. 216 40.31 N 86.42 W
Colby, Ks., U.S. 198 39.23 N 101.03 W
Colby, Wi., U.S. 190 44.54 N 90.18 W
Colca 248 12.18 S 75.13 W
Colca ≃ 248 15.51 S 72.26 W
Colcamar 248 6.16 S 77.55 W
Colchester, On., Can. 214 41.59 N 82.56 W
Colchester, Eng., U.K. 42 51.54 N 0.54 E
Colchester, Ct., U.S. 207 41.34 N 72.19 W
Colchester, Il., U.S. 190 40.25 N 90.47 W
Coldbackie 46 58.31 N 4.23 W
Cold Bay 180 55.11 N 162.30 W
Cold Bay ⊂ 180 55.13 N 162.33 W
Coldblow ◆[8] 260 51.26 N 0.10 E
Cold Brook 210 43.15 N 75.03 W
Cold Creek ≃ 212 44.12 N 77.36 W
Colden 210 42.39 N 78.41 W
Cold Fell ∧ 44 54.54 N 2.36 W
Cold Harbor Battlefield ⊥ 208 37.36 N 77.20 W
Coldingham 46 55.53 N 2.10 W
Colditz 54 51.07 N 12.48 E
Cold Lake 184 54.27 N 110.10 W
Cold Lake ⊜ 184 54.33 N 110.05 W
Cold Lake, Canadian Forces Base ■ 184 54.25 N 110.17 W
Cold Lake Indian Reserve ◆[4] 184 54.33 N 110.10 W
Cold Norton 260 51.40 N 0.40 E
Coldrano 64 46.38 N 10.50 E
Cold Spring, Ky., U.S. 218 39.01 N 84.26 W
Cold Spring, Mn., U.S. 190 45.27 N 94.25 W
Cold Spring, N.J., U.S. 208 38.58 N 74.55 W
Cold Spring, N.Y., U.S. 210 41.25 N 73.57 W
Coldspring, Tx., U.S. 222 30.36 N 95.08 W
Cold Spring Harbor 276 40.52 N 73.27 W
Cold Spring Harbor ⊂ 276 40.53 N 73.28 W
Coldsprings, On., Can. 212 44.17 N 78.18 W
Cold Springs, N.Y., U.S. 210 43.08 N 76.15 W
Cold Spring Terrace 276 40.50 N 73.26 W
Coldstream, Austl. 169 37.44 S 145.23 E
Coldstream, Scot., U.K. 46 55.39 N 2.15 W
Cold Stream ≃ 226 39.35 N 120.22 W
Coldwater, On., Can. 212 44.42 N 79.40 W
Coldwater, Ks., U.S. 198 37.16 N 99.19 W
Coldwater, Mi., U.S. 216 41.56 N 85.00 W
Coldwater, Ms., U.S. 194 34.41 N 89.58 W
Coldwater, Oh., U.S. 216 40.28 N 84.37 W
Coldwater ≃, On., Can. 212 44.44 N 79.39 W
Coldwater ≃, Mi., U.S. 216 42.04 N 85.08 W
Coldwater ≃, Ms., U.S. 194 34.11 N 90.13 W
Coldwater Canyon V 280 34.14 N 117.44 W
Coldwater Creek ≃ 196 36.40 N 101.08 W
Coldwater Indian Reserve ◆[4] 182 50.04 N 120.48 W
Coldwater Lake ⊜ 216 41.49 N 84.58 W
Cole □[6] 219 38.30 N 92.13 W
Cole ≃, Ang. 152 9.07 S 15.50 E
Cole ≃, Eng., U.K. 42 51.42 N 1.42 W
Coleambally 166 34.49 S 145.52 E
Colebrook, N.H., U.S. 188 44.53 N 71.29 W
Colebrook, Oh., U.S. 214 41.32 N 80.46 W
Colebrook River Lake ⊜[1] 207 42.03 N 73.04 W
Cole Camp 194 38.27 N 93.12 W
Coledale 170 34.17 S 150.57 E
Coleen ≃ 180 67.05 N 142.31 W
Coleford, Eng., U.K. 42 51.14 N 2.27 W
Coleford, Eng., U.K. 42 51.48 N 2.36 W
Colégio, Morro do ∧ 287b 23.38 S 46.21 W
Coleman, Ab., Can. 182 49.38 N 114.30 W
Coleman, Fl., U.S. 220 28.47 N 82.04 W
Coleman, Md., U.S. 208 39.20 N 76.04 W
Coleman, Mi., U.S. 190 43.45 N 84.35 W
Coleman, Tx., U.S. 196 31.49 N 99.25 W
Coleman, Wi., U.S. 190 45.03 N 88.02 W
Coleman ≃ 164 15.06 S 141.38 E
Coleman, Lake ⊜[1] 196 32.02 N 99.30 W
Colembert 50 50.45 N 1.50 E
Colen Lakes ⊜ 184 54.33 N 95.25 W
Colenso 158 28.50 S 29.44 E
Colerain 214 40.07 N 80.49 W
Coleraine, Austl. 166 37.36 S 141.42 E
Coleraine, N. Ire., U.K. 48 55.08 N 6.40 W
Coleraine, Mn., U.S. 190 47.17 N 93.25 W
Coleridge 198 42.30 N 97.12 W
Coleridge, Lake ⊜ 172 43.17 S 171.30 E
Coles 194 31.16 N 91.01 W
Coles, Punta ≻ 248 17.42 S 71.23 W
Colesberg 158 30.45 S 25.05 E
Coles Brook ≃ 276 40.55 N 74.02 W
Coleshill, Eng., U.K. 42 52.30 N 1.42 W
Coleshill, Eng., U.K. 260 51.39 N 0.38 W
Coles Point 208 38.09 N 76.38 W
Colesville, Md., U.S. 284c 39.05 N 77.00 W
Colesville, N.J., U.S. 210 41.15 N 74.39 W
Coleto Creek ≃ 196 28.41 N 97.01 W
Coleville, Sk., Can. 184 51.43 N 109.16 W
Coleville, Ca., U.S. 226 38.33 N 119.30 W
Colfax, Ca., U.S. 226 39.06 N 120.57 W
Colfax, Il., U.S. 216 40.34 N 88.36 W
Colfax, In., U.S. 194 40.11 N 86.40 W
Colfax, Ia., U.S. 190 41.40 N 93.14 W
Colfax, La., U.S. 194 31.31 N 92.42 W
Colfax, Wa., U.S. 202 46.52 N 117.21 W
Colfax, Wi., U.S. 190 44.59 N 91.43 W
Colfiorito 66 43.02 N 12.55 E
Colgate 216 43.12 N 88.12 W
Colgate Creek ≃ 284b 39.15 N 76.32 W
Colgong 124 25.16 N 87.13 E
Colgrave Sound ʊ 46a 60.37 N 0.58 W
Colhué Huapi, Lago ⊜ 254 45.30 S 68.48 W
Coliban ≃ 169 36.56 S 144.33 E
Colibris, Pointe des ≻, Guad. 241o 16.15 N 61.11 W
Colibris, Pointe des ≻, Guad. 241o 16.17 N 61.06 W
Colico 58 46.08 N 9.22 E

ENGLISH Name	Page	Lat.°′	Long.°′

Coligny, Fr. 58 46.23 N 5.21 E
Coligny, S. Afr. 158 26.17 S 26.15 E
Colijnsplaat 52 51.46 N 3.51 E
Colima, Méx. 200 32.25 N 115.05 W
Colima, Méx. 234 19.14 N 103.43 W
Colima □[3] 234 19.10 N 104.00 W
Colima, Nevado de ∧ 234 19.33 N 103.38 W
Colimes ≃ 246 1.32 S 80.00 W
Colin ≃ 50 47.08 N 2.32 E
Colina 252 33.12 S 70.41 W
Colinas, Bra. 250 6.02 S 44.14 W
Colinas, Bra. 255 14.12 S 48.03 W
Colinet 186 47.13 N 53.33 W
Colinton, Austl. 171b 35.51 S 149.09 E
Colinton, Ab., Can. 182 54.37 N 113.15 W
Coll I 46 56.38 N 6.34 W
Colla 258 34.04 S 57.21 W
Colla, Arroyo ≃ 258 34.19 S 57.20 W
Collagna 64 44.21 N 10.16 E
Collalbo (Klobenstein) 64 46.32 N 11.28 E
Collalto Sabino 66 42.08 N 13.02 E
Collamer 210 43.06 N 76.04 W
Collarenebri 166 29.33 S 148.35 E
Collarmele 66 42.03 N 13.38 E
Collaroy 274a 33.44 S 151.18 E
Collazzone 66 42.54 N 12.26 E
Collbran 200 39.14 N 107.57 W
Collecchio 64 44.45 N 10.13 E
Collecorvino 66 42.27 N 14.01 E
Colle di Tora 66 42.13 N 12.57 E
Colle di Val d'Elsa 66 43.25 N 11.07 E
Colleen Bawn 154 21.00 S 29.13 E
Colleferro 66 41.44 N 12.59 E
College 180 64.51 N 147.47 W
College City 226 39.00 N 122.00 W
College Corner 218 39.30 N 84.36 W
Collegedale 194 35.04 N 85.03 W
College Meadows 218 39.56 N 86.07 W
College Park, Ga., U.S. 192 33.39 N 84.26 W
College Park, Md., U.S. 208 38.58 N 76.56 W
College Park Airport ⊠ 284c 38.58 N 76.55 W
College Place 202 46.02 N 118.23 W
College Point ◆[8] 276 40.47 N 73.51 W
College Station, Ar., U.S. 194 34.43 N 92.13 W
College Station, Tx., U.S. 222 30.37 N 96.20 W
Collegeville, In., U.S. 216 40.54 N 87.09 W
Collegeville, Pa., U.S. 208 40.11 N 75.27 W
Collégien 261 48.50 N 2.40 E
Collegno 62 45.05 N 7.34 E
Colle Isarco (Gossensass) 64 46.56 N 11.26 E
Collepardo 66 41.46 N 13.22 E
Collepasso 68 40.04 N 18.10 E
Collepietro 66 42.13 N 13.46 E
Collerina 166 29.41 S 146.38 E
Collesalvetti 66 43.35 N 10.28 E
Colle Sannita 68 41.22 N 14.50 E
Collesano 70 37.55 N 13.56 E
Colletorto 66 41.40 N 14.58 E
Colleymount 182 54.01 N 126.09 W
Colleyville 222 32.52 N 97.09 W
Colliano 68 40.43 N 15.17 E
Colli a Volturno 66 41.36 N 14.06 E
Colli del Tronto 66 42.52 N 13.44 E
Colli di Monte Bove 66 42.06 N 13.09 E
Collie 168a 33.21 S 116.09 E
Collie ≃ 168a 33.18 S 115.44 E
Collie East ≃ 168a 33.18 S 116.10 E
Collier □[6] 220 26.10 N 81.22 W
Collier Bay ⊂ 160 16.10 S 124.15 E
Collier Bridge ◆[5] 220 26.57 N 82.04 W
Collier City 220 26.14 N 80.09 W
Collier Law ∧[2] 44 54.46 N 1.58 W
Collier Range ⩘ 162 24.43 S 119.12 E
Collier Range National Park ♠ 162 24.40 S 119.15 E
Collier Row ◆[8] 260 51.36 N 0.10 E
Colliers 214 40.22 N 80.32 W
Collier-Seminole State Park ♠ 220 25.59 N 81.36 W
Colliersville 210 42.29 N 74.59 W
Collierville 194 35.02 N 89.39 W
Collie South ≃ 168a 33.18 S 116.10 E
Collieston 46 57.21 N 1.56 W
Colliford Lake Reservoir ⊜[1] 42 50.32 N 4.33 W
Colligan ≃ 48 52.06 N 7.38 W
Collin □[6] 222 33.07 N 96.35 W
Collina, Passo della)(66 44.01 N 10.56 E
Collingbourne Kingston 42 51.18 N 1.13 W
Collingdale 208 39.54 N 75.16 W
Collingham 44 53.54 N 1.24 W
Collingswood 285 39.55 N 75.04 W
Collingwood, Austl. 274b 37.48 S 145.00 E
Collingwood, On., Can. 212 44.29 N 80.13 W
Collingwood, N.Z. 172 40.40 S 172.41 E
Collingwood Bay ⊂ 164 9.20 S 149.30 E
Collins, Ga., U.S. 192 32.10 N 82.06 W
Collins, Ia., U.S. 190 41.54 N 93.18 W
Collins, Ms., U.S. 194 31.38 N 89.33 W
Collins, N.Y., U.S. 210 42.30 N 78.55 W
Collins, Oh., U.S. 214 41.16 N 82.30 W
Collins ≃ 194 35.48 N 85.37 W
Collins, Mount ∧[2] 190 47.51 N 80.59 W
Collins Bay 212 44.15 N 76.36 W
Collinsburg 214 40.13 N 79.46 W
Collins Center 210 42.30 N 78.51 W
Collins Lake ⊜ 212 44.22 N 76.27 W
Collins Park 208 39.41 N 75.33 W
Collinston 194 32.41 N 91.52 W
Collinsville, Austl. 166 20.34 S 147.51 E
Collinsville, Al., U.S. 194 34.15 N 85.51 W
Collinsville, Ca., U.S. 282 38.05 N 121.51 W
Collinsville, Ct., U.S. 207 41.48 N 72.55 W
Collinsville, Il., U.S. 219 38.40 N 89.59 W
Collinsville, Ms., U.S. 194 32.29 N 88.50 W
Collinsville, N.J., U.S. 276 40.49 N 74.28 W
Collinsville, Ok., U.S. 196 36.21 N 95.50 W
Collinsville, Tx., U.S. 196 33.32 N 96.54 W
Collinwood 194 35.10 N 87.44 W
Collio 64 45.48 N 10.20 E
Collipulli 252 37.57 S 72.26 W
Collister 202 43.38 N 116.15 W
Collobrières 62 43.14 N 6.18 E
Collombey 58 46.16 N 6.57 E
Collomsville 210 41.09 N 77.09 W
Collon 48 53.47 N 6.29 W
Collonges 58 46.08 N 5.54 E
Collooney 48 54.11 N 8.29 W
Collserola, Serra de ⩘ 266d 41.26 N 2.07 E
Colma 226 37.41 N 122.28 W
Colma Creek ≃ 282 37.38 N 122.23 W
Colman 198 43.58 N 96.48 W
Colmar 58 48.05 N 7.22 E
Colmar Manor 284c 38.55 N 76.56 W
Colmars 62 44.11 N 6.38 E
Colmenar 34 36.54 N 4.20 W
Colmenar de Oreja 34 40.06 N 3.23 W
Colmenar Viejo 34 40.40 N 3.46 W
Colmeneros 234 18.06 N 101.40 W
Colmesneil 194 30.54 N 94.25 W
Colmnitz 54 50.54 N 13.31 E
Colmonell 44 55.08 N 4.55 W
Coln ≃ 42 51.42 N 1.42 W
Colnbrook 260 51.29 N 0.31 W
Colne 44 53.52 N 2.09 W
Colne ≃, Eng., U.K. 42 51.48 N 1.01 E
Colne ≃, Eng., U.K. 260 51.26 N 0.30 W
Colney Heath 260 51.44 N 0.15 W
Colney Street 260 51.42 N 0.20 W
Colo 190 42.01 N 93.18 W
Colo ≃ 170 33.26 S 150.53 E
Colobraro 68 40.11 N 16.25 E
Cologna Veneta 64 45.18 N 11.23 E
Cologne, Mn., U.S. 190 44.46 N 93.46 W
Cologne, N.J., U.S. 208 39.30 N 74.36 W

DEUTSCH Name	Seite	Breite°′	Länge°′ E = Ost

Cologne → Köln 56 50.56 N 6.59 E
Cologno al Serio 62 45.37 N 9.42 E
Cologno Monzese 266b 45.32 N 9.17 E
Cololo, Nevado ∧ 248 14.53 S 69.06 W
Coloma, Ca., U.S. 226 38.48 N 120.53 W
Coloma, Mi., U.S. 216 42.11 N 86.18 W
Coloma, Wi., U.S. 190 44.02 N 89.31 W
Colomb-Béchar → Béchar 148 31.37 N 2.13 W
Colombes 50 48.55 N 2.15 E
Colombey-les-Belles 58 48.32 N 5.54 E
Colombey-les-Deux-Eglises 58 48.13 N 4.53 E
Colômbia, Bra. 255 20.30 S 48.37 W
Colombia, Col. 246 3.24 N 74.49 W
Colombia, Cuba 240p 20.59 N 77.25 W
Colombia, Méx. 196 27.42 N 99.45 W
Colombia □[1], S.A. 242 4.00 N 72.00 W
Colombia □[1], S.A. 246 4.00 N 72.00 W
Colombian Basin ✣[1] 16 13.00 N 76.00 W
Colombie-Britannique → British Columbia □[4] 182 54.00 N 125.00 W
Colombie → Colombia □[1] 246 4.00 N 72.00 W
Colombier 58 46.58 N 6.52 E
Colombo, Bra. 252 25.17 S 49.14 W
Colombo, S. Lan. 122 6.56 N 79.51 E
Colome 198 43.15 N 99.42 W
Colomiers 32 43.37 N 1.20 E
Colón, Arg. 252 33.53 S 61.07 W
Colón, Arg. 252 32.13 S 58.08 W
Colón, Cuba 240p 22.43 N 80.54 W
Colón, Méx. 234 20.48 N 100.03 W
Colón, Pan. 236 9.22 N 79.54 W
Colon, Mi., U.S. 216 41.57 N 85.19 W
Colón, Ur. 252 33.53 S 54.43 W
Colón, Ur. 258 34.48 S 56.14 W
Colón □[4] 236 9.00 N 80.20 W
Colón □[5] 236 15.40 N 85.30 W
Colón, Archipiélago de (Galapagos Islands) II 246a 0.30 S 90.30 W
Colón, Cementerio ◆ 286b 23.08 N 82.23 W
Colón, Isla I 236 9.24 N 82.17 W
Colón, Montañas de ⩘ 236 14.55 N 84.45 W
Colón, Teatro ♠ 288 34.36 S 58.23 W
Colona 162 31.38 S 132.05 E
Colonard-Corubert 50 48.25 N 0.39 E
Colonarie ≃ 241h 13.14 N 61.06 W
Colonel Danforth Park ♠ 275b 43.47 N 79.10 W
Colonelganj 124 27.08 N 81.42 E
Colonești 38 46.34 N 27.18 E
Colonet 204 31.05 N 116.10 W
Colonet, Cabo ≻ 204 30.58 N 116.19 W
Colongulac, Lake ⊜ 169 38.10 S 143.11 E
Colonia, Micron. 174q 9.31 N 138.08 E
Colonia, N.J., U.S. 210 40.34 N 74.18 W
Colonia □[5] 258 34.10 S 57.30 W
Colônia ≃ 255 15.11 S 39.45 W
Colonia, Aeropuerto ⊠ 258 34.28 S 57.49 W
Colonia, Cuchilla de la ⩘[2] 258 34.15 S 57.35 W
Colonia Alvear 252 35.00 S 67.40 W
Colonia Caroya 252 31.02 S 64.05 W
Colonia del Sacramento 258 34.28 S 57.51 W
Colonia Dora 252 28.36 S 62.57 W
Colonia Elisa 252 26.56 S 59.32 W
Colonia Guadalupe 204 32.04 N 116.37 W
Colonia Hogar Ricardo Gutiérrez 288 34.51 S 58.51 W
Colonia José Mármol 252 26.59 S 60.44 W
Colonia → Köln 56 50.56 N 6.59 E
Colonial Acres 208 39.31 N 76.20 W
Colonia Lavalleja 252 31.06 S 57.01 W
Colonial Beach 208 38.15 N 76.57 W
Colonial Crest 208 40.20 N 76.50 W
Colônia Leopoldina 250 8.57 S 35.39 W
Colonial Heights, Il., U.S. 278 41.05 N 88.01 W
Colonial Heights, Va., U.S. 208 37.14 N 77.24 W
Colonial Manor 285 39.51 N 75.09 W
Colonial National Historical Park ♠ 208 37.12 N 76.45 W
Colonial Park 208 40.18 N 76.48 W
Colonial Village, N.Y., U.S. 210 43.08 N 78.58 W
Colonial Village, Pa., U.S. 285 40.04 N 75.24 W
Colonial Village Airport ⊠ 284a 43.08 N 78.58 W
Colonial Williamsburg ⊥ 208 37.16 N 76.42 W
Colonia Morelos 200 30.50 N 109.10 W
Colonia Nicolich 258 34.50 S 56.02 W
Colonia Progreso 204 32.35 N 115.37 W
Colonia Providencia 240m 17.59 N 66.00 W
Colonias Unidas 252 26.42 S 59.38 W
Colonia Valdense 258 34.20 S 57.14 W
Colonia Vicente Guerrero 232 30.45 N 116.00 W
Colonia Villafañe 252 26.12 S 59.05 W
Colonie 210 42.43 N 73.50 W
Colon Koret 152 0.34 N 23.28 E
Colonna 267a 41.50 N 12.45 E
Colonna, Capo ≻ 68 39.02 N 17.11 E
Colonnata 64 44.05 N 10.10 E
Colón Ridge ✣[3] 18 2.00 N 96.00 W
Colonsay 184 51.59 N 105.53 W
Colonsay I 46 56.04 N 6.13 W
Colony 198 38.04 N 95.21 W
Colora 208 39.40 N 76.06 W
Colorada, Laguna ⩸ 254 44.50 S 68.15 W
Colorada, Punta ≻ 288 34.45 S 58.06 W
Coloradas, Lomas ⩘[2] 254 43.24 S 67.24 W
Colorado, C.R. 236 10.46 N 83.35 W
Colorado, Hond. 236 15.47 N 87.19 W
Colorado, Ak., U.S. 180 63.09 N 149.26 W
Colorado □[6] 222 29.40 N 96.30 W
Colorado □[3] 178 39.00 N 105.30 W
Colorado ≃, Arg. 244 39.50 S 62.08 W
Colorado ≃, Bra. 248 13.03 S 62.20 W
Colorado ≃, Méx. 234 16.30 N 97.31 W
Colorado ≃, N.A. 200 31.54 N 114.57 W
Colorado ≃, Tx., U.S. 196 28.36 N 95.58 W
Colorado, Canal do ≋ 287a 23.00 S 43.25 W
Colorado, Cerro ∧, Arg. 254 45.02 S 69.38 W
Colorado, Cerro ∧, Chile 286e 33.24 S 70.45 W
Colorado, Cerro ∧, Perú 286d 12.07 S 76.55 W
Colorado, Williams Fork ≃ 200 40.03 N 106.11 W
Colorado City, Az., U.S. 200 36.59 N 112.58 W
Colorado City, Co., U.S. 200 37.56 N 104.50 W
Colorado City, Tx., U.S. 196 32.23 N 100.51 W
Colorado de Abajo 196 26.28 N 99.54 W
Colorado Grande, Salina ≚ 252 38.15 S 63.47 W
Colorado National Monument ♠ 200 39.04 N 108.25 W
Colorado Plateau ⩘[1] 200 36.30 N 108.00 W
Colorado River Aqueduct ≋[1] 204 33.50 N 117.23 W
Colorado River Indian Reservation ◆[4] 200 34.00 N 114.25 W
Colorados, Archipiélago de los II 240p 22.36 N 84.20 W
Colorado Springs 200 38.50 N 104.49 W
Colorines 234 19.07 N 100.12 W
Colorno 64 44.56 N 10.23 E

Symbols in the index entries represent the broad categories identified in the key at the right. Symbols with superior numbers (⩘[1]) identify subcategories (see complete key on page *I · 1*).

Symbole im Register stellen die rechts im Schlüssel erklärten Kategorien dar. Symbole mit hochgestellten Ziffern (⩘[1]) bezeichnen Unterabteilungen einer Kategorie (vgl. vollständiger Schlüssel auf Seite *I · 1*).

Los símbolos incluídos en el texto del índice representan las grandes categorías identificadas con la clave a la derecha. Los símbolos con numeros en su parte superior (⩘[1]) identifican las subcategorías (véase la clave completa en la página *I · 1*).

Les symboles de l'index représentent les catégories indiquées dans la légende à droite. Les symboles suivis d'un indice (⩘[1]) représentent des sous-catégories (voir légende complète à la page *I · 1*).

Os símbolos incluídos no texto do índice representam as grandes categorias identificadas com a chave à direita. Os símbolos com números em sua parte superior (⩘[1]) identificam as subcategorias (veja-se a chave completa à página *I · 1*).

∧ Mountain	Berg	Montaña	Montagne	Montanha
⩘ Mountains	Gebirge	Montañas	Montagnes	Montanhas
)(Pass	Paß	Paso	Col	Passo
V Valley, Canyon	Tal, Cañon	Valle, Cañón	Vallée, Canyon	Vale, Canhão
≚ Plain	Ebene	Llano	Plaine	Planície
≻ Cape	Kap	Cabo	Cap	Cabo
I Island	Insel	Isla	Île	Ilha
II Islands	Inseln	Islas	Îles	Ilhas
⊥ Other Topographic Features	Andere Topographische Objekte	Otros Elementos Topográficos	Autres données topographiques	Outros acidentes topográficos

ESPAÑOL
Nombre | Página | Lat.°′ | Long.°′ W = Oeste

Colosimi 68 39.07 N 16.24 E
Colosseo ⊥ 267a 41.54 N 12.29 E
Colotepec ≏ 234 15.47 N 97.03 W
Colotlán 234 22.06 N 103.16 W
Colotlán ≏ 234 22.06 N 103.42 W
Colotlipa 234 17.25 N 99.09 W
Colo Vale 170 34.24 S 150.29 E
Čolpon 85 42.12 N 75.28 E
Čolpon-Ata 85 42.40 N 77.06 E
Colpoys Bay c 212 44.47 N 81.05 W
Colquechaca 248 18.40 S 66.01 W
Colquencha 248 17.00 S 68.17 W
Colquiri 248 17.25 S 67.08 W
Colquitt 192 31.10 N 84.44 W
Colsterworth 42 52.48 N 0.37 W
Colstrip 202 45.53 N 106.37 W
Colt 194 35.07 N 90.48 W
Colta 248 15.10 S 73.18 W
Coltauco 252 34.18 S 71.06 W
Coltishall 42 52.44 N 1.22 E
Colton, Austl. 162 33.29 S 134.56 E
Colton, Ca., U.S. 228 34.04 N 117.18 W
Colton, Oh., U.S. 216 41.28 N 83.57 W
Colton, Or., U.S. 224 45.10 N 122.26 W
Colton, S.D., U.S. 198 43.47 N 96.55 W
Coltons Point 208 38.13 N 76.45 W
Colts Neck 208 40.17 N 74.10 W
Coltsville Center 214 41.05 N 80.34 W
Columbia, Al., U.S. 192 31.17 N 85.06 W
Columbia, Ca., U.S. 226 38.02 N 120.24 W
Columbia, Ct., U.S. 207 41.42 N 72.18 W
Columbia, Il., U.S. 219 38.26 N 90.12 W
Columbia, In., U.S. 218 39.35 N 85.12 W
Columbia, Ky., U.S. 194 37.06 N 85.18 W
Columbia, La., U.S. 194 32.06 N 92.04 W
Columbia, Md., U.S. 208 39.14 N 76.50 W
Columbia, Ms., U.S. 194 31.15 N 89.50 W
Columbia, Mo., U.S. 219 38.57 N 92.20 W
Columbia, N.J., U.S. 210 40.55 N 75.05 W
Columbia, N.C., U.S. 192 35.55 N 76.15 W
Columbia, Pa., U.S. 208 40.02 N 76.30 W
Columbia, S.C., U.S. 192 34.00 N 81.02 W
Columbia, Tn., U.S. 194 35.36 N 87.02 W
Columbia □[6], N.Y., U.S. 210 42.15 N 73.47 W
Columbia □[6], Or., U.S. 224 45.57 N 123.03 W
Columbia □[6], Pa., U.S. 210 41.00 N 76.28 W
Columbia ≏ 176 46.15 N 124.05 W
Columbia, Cape › 16 83.08 N 70.35 W
Columbia, Lake ⊜[1] 216 42.05 N 84.18 W
Columbia, Mount ʌ 182 52.09 N 117.25 W
Columbia Airport ⊠ 279a 41.19 N 81.58 W
Columbia Basin ≚[1] 202 46.45 N 119.05 W
Columbia Center 279a 41.19 N 81.56 W
Columbia City, In., U.S. 216 41.09 N 85.29 W
Columbia City, Or., U.S. 224 45.53 N 122.48 W
Columbia Cross Roads 210 41.50 N 76.48 W
Columbia Falls, Me., U.S. 188 44.39 N 67.43 W
Columbia Falls, Mt., U.S. 202 48.22 N 114.10 W
Columbia Heights 224 46.09 N 122.58 W
Columbia Hills 284b 39.15 N 76.50 W
Columbia Icefield ⍌ 182 52.10 N 117.30 W
Columbia Lake ⊜ 182 50.15 N 115.57 W
Columbia Lake Indian Reserve ◆[4] 182 50.25 N 115.57 W
Columbia Mountains ⋏ 182 52.00 N 119.00 W
Columbiana, Al., U.S. 194 33.10 N 86.36 W
Columbiana, Oh., U.S. 214 40.53 N 80.41 W
Columbiana □[6] 214 40.47 N 80.46 W
Columbia Plateau ⋏[1] 202 44.00 N 117.30 W
Columbia Regional Airport ⊠ 219 38.50 N 92.13 W
Columbia Road Reservoir ⊜[1] 198 45.45 N 98.15 W
Columbia State Historical Park ♠ 226 38.02 N 120.25 W
Columbia Station 214 41.20 N 81.57 W
Columbia University ♁[2] 276 40.48 N 73.58 W
Columbiaville, Mi., U.S. 190 43.09 N 83.24 W
Columbiaville, N.Y., U.S. 210 42.19 N 73.45 W
Columbine, Cape › 158 32.47 S 17.52 E
Columbrets, Illes II 34 39.52 N 0.40 E
Columbus, Ga., U.S. 192 32.29 N 84.59 W
Columbus, In., U.S. 218 39.12 N 85.55 W
Columbus, Ks., U.S. 198 37.10 N 94.50 W
Columbus, Ms., U.S. 194 33.29 N 88.25 W
Columbus, Mt., U.S. 202 45.38 N 109.15 W
Columbus, Ne., U.S. 198 41.25 N 97.22 W
Columbus, N.J., U.S. 208 40.04 N 74.43 W
Columbus, N.M., U.S. 200 31.49 N 107.38 W
Columbus, N.C., U.S. 192 35.15 N 82.11 W
Columbus, N.D., U.S. 198 48.54 N 102.46 W
Columbus, Oh., U.S. 214 39.57 N 82.59 W
Columbus, Pa., U.S. 214 41.56 N 79.35 W
Columbus, Tx., U.S. 222 29.42 N 96.32 W
Columbus, Wi., U.S. 190 43.20 N 89.00 W
Columbus Air Force Base ■ 194 33.38 N 88.26 W
Columbus Grove 216 40.55 N 84.03 W
Columbus Junction 190 41.16 N 91.21 W
Columbus Lake ⊜[1] 194 33.35 N 88.30 W
Columbus Park ♠ 278 41.53 N 87.47 W
Columbus Point ›, Ba. 238 24.08 N 75.16 W
Columbus Point ›, Trin. 241r 11.08 N 60.48 W
Columbus Salt Marsh ≚ 204 38.04 N 117.58 W
Coluna 255 18.14 S 42.50 W
Colusa 226 39.12 N 122.00 W
Colusa □[6] 226 39.13 N 122.01 W
Colusa Trough ≊ 226 39.02 N 121.59 W
Colver 214 40.32 N 78.47 W
Colville, N.Z. 172 36.38 S 175.28 E
Colville, Wa., U.S. 202 48.32 N 117.54 W
Colville ≏, Ak., U.S. 180 70.25 N 150.30 W
Colville ≏, Wa., U.S. 202 48.37 N 118.05 W
Colville, Cape › 172 36.28 S 175.21 E
Colville Channel ʮ 172 36.23 S 175.24 E
Colville Indian Reservation ◆[4] 202 48.15 N 119.00 W
Colville Lake ⊜ 180 67.10 N 126.00 W
Colvin Run 284c 38.58 N 77.18 W
Colwell 44 55.04 N 2.04 W
Colwood 224 48.26 N 123.29 W
Colwyn 285 39.55 N 75.15 W
Colwyn Bay 44 53.18 N 3.43 W
Colyton, Austl. 274a 33.47 S 150.48 E
Colyton, Eng., U.K. 42 50.44 N 3.04 W
Comacchio 66 44.42 N 12.11 E
Comacchio, Valli di c 66 44.38 N 12.06 E
Comal 115a 6.55 S 109.31 E
Comala 234 19.19 N 103.45 W
Comalapa, Guat. 236 14.44 N 90.53 W
Comalapa, Nic. 236 12.17 N 85.31 W
Comalcalco 234 18.16 N 93.13 W
Comallo, Arroyo ≏ 254 40.29 S 70.12 W
Coman, Mount ʌ 9 74.02 S 65.04 W
Comana 38 43.54 N 28.19 E
Comanche, Ok., U.S. 196 34.22 N 97.57 W
Comanche, Tx., U.S. 196 31.53 N 98.36 W
Comanche Creek ≏, Co., U.S. 198 39.53 N 104.19 W
Comanche Creek ≏, Tx., U.S. 196 31.06 N 102.24 W
Comandante Ferraz ♁[3] 9 62.05 S 58.23 W
Comandante Fontana 252 25.20 S 59.41 W
Comandante Leal 252 30.53 S 65.47 W
Comandante Luis Piedrabuena 254 49.59 S 68.54 W

FRANÇAIS
Nom | Page | Lat.°′ | Long.°′ W = Ouest

Comandante Nicanor Otamendi 252 38.07 S 57.51 W
Comănești 38 46.25 N 26.26 E
Comanjá de Corona 234 21.19 N 101.42 W
Comarapa 248 17.54 S 64.29 W
Comar Gambon 144 3.10 N 45.47 E
Comas, Perú 248 11.46 S 75.02 W
Comas, Perú 286d 11.57 S 77.04 W
Comayagua 236 14.25 N 87.37 W
Comayagua □[5] 236 14.30 N 87.40 W
Comayagua, Montañas de ⋏ 236 14.23 N 87.26 W
Combahee ≏ 192 32.30 N 80.31 W
Combarbalá 252 31.11 S 71.02 W
Combeaufontaine 58 47.43 N 5.53 E
Combe Martin 42 51.13 N 4.02 W
Comber, On., Can. 214 42.14 N 82.33 W
Comber, N. Ire., U.K. 48 54.33 N 5.45 W
Comberbach 262 53.17 N 2.32 W
Combermere Bay c 110 19.37 N 93.34 E
Comberton 42 52.11 N 0.02 E
Combe Seamount ✢[3] 14 12.32 S 177.35 W
Combie, Lake ⊜[1] 226 39.01 N 121.02 W
Comblain-au-Pont 56 50.28 N 5.35 E
Combles 50 50.01 N 2.52 E
Combloux 62 45.54 N 6.39 E
Combourg 32 48.25 N 1.45 W
Comboyne 166 31.36 S 152.29 E
Comboyuro Point › 171a 27.04 S 153.24 E
Combres 50 48.19 N 1.04 E
Combronde 32 45.59 N 3.05 E
Combs 262 53.18 N 1.57 W
Combs-la-Ville 50 48.40 N 2.34 E
Combs Reservoir ⊜[1] 262 53.19 N 1.57 W
Comburg ♁[1] 56 49.06 N 9.44 E
Comb Wash V 200 37.13 N 109.42 W
Come by Chance 186 47.51 N 53.58 W
Comeglians 64 46.31 N 12.52 E
Comelico Superiore 64 46.35 N 12.30 E
Comendado Levy Gasparain 256 22.01 S 43.12 W
Comendador 238 18.53 N 71.42 W
Comendador Gomes 255 19.41 S 49.05 W
Comer 192 34.03 N 83.07 W
Comercinho 255 16.19 S 41.47 W
Comerío 240m 18.13 N 66.14 W
Comet 166 23.37 S 148.33 E
Comet ≏ 166 23.34 S 148.32 E
Cometela 156 21.51 S 34.29 E
Comfort, N.C., U.S. 192 35.00 N 77.30 W
Comfort, Tx., U.S. 196 29.58 N 98.54 W
Comfort, Cape › 176 65.08 N 83.21 W
Comfort, Point › 276 40.27 N 74.08 W
Comfrey 198 44.06 N 94.54 W
Comilla 124 23.27 N 91.12 E
Comines 50 50.46 N 3.01 E
Comino, Capo › 71 40.32 N 9.49 E
Comino → Kemmuna I 36 36.00 N 14.20 E
Comiskey Park ♠ 278 41.50 N 87.38 W
Comiso 70 36.56 N 14.36 E
Comitan de Dominguez 232 16.15 N 92.08 W
Comitini 70 37.24 N 13.39 E
Comloșu Mare 38 45.54 N 20.38 E
Commack 210 40.50 N 73.17 W
Commagene □[9] 130 37.50 N 38.00 E
Commencement Bay c 224 47.17 N 122.28 W
Commentry 32 46.17 N 2.44 E
Commerce, Ga., U.S. 192 34.12 N 83.27 W
Commerce, Mi., U.S. 216 42.34 N 83.30 W
Commerce, Ok., U.S. 196 36.56 N 94.52 W
Commerce, Tx., U.S. 196 33.14 N 95.53 W
Commerce City 198 39.49 N 104.56 W
Commerciale Luigi Bocconi, Università ♁[2] 266b 45.26 N 9.11 E
Commercial Point 218 39.46 N 83.04 W
Commercy 56 48.45 N 5.35 E
Commewijne □[5] 250 5.50 N 55.00 W
Comminges ◆[1] 32 43.15 N 0.45 E
Committee Bay c 176 68.30 N 86.30 W
Commodore 214 40.43 N 78.57 W
Commodore Barry Bridge ◆[5] 285 39.49 N 75.22 W
Commondale 158 27.20 S 30.56 E
Common Edge 262 53.47 N 3.02 W
Commonwealth Bay c 9 66.54 S 142.40 E
Commonwealth Range ⋏ 9 84.15 S 172.20 E
Commoron Creek ≏ 166 28.22 S 150.08 E
Community Center 228 34.16 N 118.44 W
Como, Austl. 274a 34.00 S 151.04 E
Como, It. 62 45.47 N 9.05 E
Como, Ms., U.S. 194 34.30 N 89.56 W
Como, N.C., U.S. 208 36.30 N 77.00 W
Como, Tx., U.S. 222 33.03 N 95.28 W
Como, Wi., U.S. 216 42.37 N 88.28 W
Como □[4] 58 45.59 N 9.13 E
Como, Lago di ⊜ 58 46.00 N 9.20 E
Como, Lake ⊜ 216 42.36 N 88.29 W
Como, Mount ʌ 226 39.02 N 119.28 W
Comodoro Rivadavia 254 45.52 S 67.30 W
Como Lake ⊜ 190 47.55 N 83.30 W
Comologno 58 46.12 N 8.34 E
Comonfort 234 20.43 N 100.46 W
Comoras → Comoros □[1] 157a 12.10 S 44.15 E
Comores, Archipel des II 157a 12.10 S 44.15 E
Comores → Comoros □[1] 157a 12.10 S 44.15 E
Comorin, Cape › 122 8.06 N 77.33 E
Comoros (Comores) □[1], Afr. 138 12.10 S 44.15 E
Comoros (Comores) □[1], Afr. 157a 12.10 S 44.15 E
Comox 182 49.40 N 124.55 W
Comox, Canadian Forces Base ■ 182 49.43 N 124.54 W
Companhia Siderúrgica Nacional ♁[3] 256 22.31 S 44.07 W
Compans 261 49.00 N 2.40 E
Compatsch 58 46.58 N 10.25 E
Compiègne 50 49.25 N 2.50 E
Compo Cove c 276 41.07 N 73.21 W
Compostela, Méx. 234 21.15 N 104.53 W
Compostela, Pil. 116 7.40 N 126.02 E
Comprida, Ilha I, Bra. 252 24.50 S 47.42 W
Comprida, Ilha I, Bra. 287a 23.02 S 43.12 W
Comps-sur-Artuby 62 43.43 N 6.30 E
Compstall 262 53.25 N 2.03 W
Compton, Eng., U.K. 260 51.13 N 0.38 W
Compton, Ca., U.S. 228 33.53 N 118.13 W
Compton, Il., U.S. 216 41.42 N 89.05 W
Compton □[6] 206 45.20 N 71.25 W
Compton Airport ⊠ 280 33.53 N 118.15 W
Compton Creek ≏, Ca., U.S. 280 33.50 N 118.12 W
Compton Creek ≏, N.J., U.S. 276 40.26 N 74.05 W
Comptonville 273d 26.17 S 27.58 E
Comrie 46 56.22 N 4.00 W
Comstock, Mi., U.S. 216 42.17 N 85.30 W
Comstock, Ne., U.S. 198 41.33 N 99.15 W
Comstock, Tx., U.S. 196 29.41 N 101.11 W
Comstock Park 216 43.02 N 85.40 W
Comunanza 66 42.57 N 13.25 E
Con ≏, Ross. 76 52.54 N 36.00 E
Çon ≏, Viet 110 19.02 N 104.58 E
Čona ≏, Ross. 74 62.54 N 111.06 E
Cona ≏, Scot., U.K. 46 56.46 N 5.14 W
Co Nag ⊜ 120 32.00 N 91.15 E
Conakry 150 9.31 N 13.43 W
Conambo ≏ 246 2.07 S 76.03 W
Conanicut Island I 207 41.32 N 71.21 W
Cona Niyeo 254 41.53 S 67.00 W
Conara Junction 166 41.50 S 147.26 E
Conasauga ≏ 192 34.33 N 84.55 W

PORTUGUÊS
Nome | Página | Lat.°′ | Long.°′ W = Oeste

Conaskonk Point › 276 40.27 N 74.11 W
Conca ≏ 66 43.58 N 12.43 E
Concarán 252 32.34 S 65.15 W
Concarneau 32 47.52 N 3.55 W
Conceição, Bra. 248 7.24 S 58.05 W
Conceição, Bra. 250 7.33 S 38.31 W
Conceição, Moç. 156 18.45 S 36.10 E
Conceição, Cachoeira ʟ 248 9.34 S 64.22 W
Conceição, Ilha da I 287a 22.52 S 43.07 W
Conceição da Barra 255 18.35 S 39.45 W
Conceição da Pedra 256 22.09 S 45.27 W
Conceição das Alagoas 255 19.55 S 48.23 W
Conceição de Ipanema 255 19.55 S 41.41 W
Conceição de Jacareí 256 23.02 S 44.09 W
Conceição do Almeida 255 12.48 S 39.12 W
Conceição do Araguaia 250 8.15 S 49.17 W
Conceição do Canindé 250 7.54 S 41.34 W
Conceição do Coité 250 11.33 S 39.16 W
Conceição do Formoso 256 21.25 S 43.21 W
Conceição do Mato Dentro 255 19.01 S 43.25 W
Conceição do Maú 246 3.35 N 59.53 W
Conceição do Norte 255 12.13 S 47.18 W
Conceição do Rio Verde 256 21.53 S 45.05 W
Conceição dos Ouros 256 22.25 S 45.47 W
Concepción, Arg. 252 28.23 S 57.53 W
Concepción, Arg. 252 27.20 S 65.35 W
Concepción, Bol. 248 11.29 S 66.31 W
Concepción, Bol. 248 16.15 S 62.04 W
Concepción, Chile 252 36.50 S 73.03 W
Concepción, Col. 246 6.46 N 72.42 W
Concepción, Para. 252 23.25 S 57.17 W
Concepción, Perú 248 11.55 S 75.17 W
Concepcion, Pil. 116 11.13 N 123.06 E
Concepcion, Pil. 116 10.42 N 123.03 E
Concepcion, Pil. 116 12.24 N 122.06 E
Concepcion, Pil. 116 15.19 N 120.39 E
Concepción □[5] 252 23.00 S 57.00 W
Concepción, Bahía c 232 26.39 N 111.48 W
Concepción, Canal ʮ 254 50.30 S 74.55 W
Concepción, Laguna ⊜ 248 17.29 S 61.25 W
Concepción, Volcán ʌ[1] 236 11.34 N 85.37 W
Concepcion Bay c 116 11.15 N 123.07 E
Concepción de Ataco 236 13.52 N 89.51 W
Concepción de Buenos Aires 234 19.58 N 103.16 W
Concepción de la Sierra 252 27.59 S 55.31 W
Concepcíon del Oro 232 24.38 N 101.25 W
Concepción del Uruguay 252 32.29 S 58.14 W
Concepcion Huista 236 15.37 N 91.41 W
Concepción Quezaltepeque 236 14.06 N 88.58 W
Conception, Point › 204 34.27 N 120.27 W
Conception Bay c, Nf., Can. 186 47.45 N 53.00 W
Conception Bay c, Namibia 156 23.53 S 14.28 E
Concession 154 17.22 S 30.57 E
Conchagua 236 13.19 N 87.52 W
Conchagua, Volcán ʌ[1] 236 13.14 N 87.46 W
Conchal 256 22.20 S 47.10 W
Conchalí 286e 33.24 S 70.39 W
Conchalí, Cerros de ⋏ 286e 33.20 S 70.38 W
Conchas ≏ 196 35.23 N 104.18 W
Conchas Dam 196 35.22 N 104.11 W
Conchas Lake ⊜[1] 196 35.25 N 104.14 W
Conche 186 50.53 N 55.54 W
Conches-en-Ouche 50 48.58 N 0.56 E
Conchi 252 22.02 S 68.38 W
Conchillas 258 34.15 S 58.04 W
Conchitas, Arroyo ≏ 288 34.45 S 58.09 W
Concho 200 34.28 N 109.36 W
Concho ≏ 196 31.34 N 99.43 W
Conchos ≏, Méx. 232 29.35 N 104.25 W
Conchos ≏, Méx. 232 24.55 N 97.40 W
Concise 58 46.51 N 6.43 E
Conco 64 45.48 N 11.36 E
Concón 252 32.55 S 71.31 W
Concononongon Point › 116 12.14 N 120.13 E
Conconully 182 48.33 N 119.44 W
Concord, Austl. 274a 33.52 S 151.06 E
Concord, On., Can. 275b 43.48 N 79.29 W
Concord, Ca., U.S. 226 37.58 N 122.01 W
Concord, Ga., U.S. 192 33.05 N 84.26 W
Concord, Il., U.S. 219 39.49 N 90.22 W
Concord, Ky., U.S. 218 38.41 N 83.29 W
Concord, Ma., U.S. 207 42.27 N 71.20 W
Concord, Mi., U.S. 216 42.10 N 84.38 W
Concord, Mo., U.S. 219 38.31 N 90.23 W
Concord, N.H., U.S. 188 43.12 N 71.32 W
Concord, N.C., U.S. 192 35.24 N 80.34 W
Concord, Pa., U.S. 214 40.15 N 77.42 W
Concord, Tx., U.S. 222 31.16 N 96.09 W
Concord ≏ 283 42.39 N 71.18 W
Concord Battleground ⊥ 283 42.28 N 71.21 W
Concordia, Arg. 252 31.24 S 58.02 W
Concórdia, Bra. 246 4.35 S 66.35 W
Concórdia, Bra. 252 27.14 S 52.01 W
Concordia, Méx. 234 23.17 N 106.04 W
Concordia, Perú 246 4.30 S 74.55 W
Concordia, Ks., U.S. 198 39.34 N 97.39 W
Concordia, Mo., U.S. 194 38.59 N 93.34 W
Concordia Gardens 216 41.09 N 85.08 W
Concordia Sagittaria ⊥ 64 45.45 N 12.51 E
Concordia sulla Secchia 64 44.55 N 10.59 E
Concord Naval Weapons Station ■ 282 38.03 N 122.02 W
Concordville 285 39.53 N 75.31 W
Concord West 274a 33.51 S 151.05 E
Concorezzo 62 45.35 N 9.20 E
Concrete 224 48.32 N 121.44 W
Con Cuong 110 19.02 N 104.54 E
Conda 152 11.06 S 14.20 E
Condamine 166 26.56 S 150.08 E
Condamine ≏ 166 27.07 S 149.48 E
Condat-en-Féniers 32 45.21 N 2.46 E
Condé, Ang. 152 10.50 S 14.37 E
Conde, Bra. 255 11.49 S 37.37 W
Condé, Fr. 32 48.51 N 0.33 W
Conde, S.D., U.S. 198 45.09 N 98.05 W
Condécourt 261 49.02 N 1.57 E
Condé-en-Brie 50 49.00 N 3.33 E
Condega 236 13.21 N 86.24 W
Condeixa 250 0.54 S 48.36 W
Condé-sur-l'Escaut 50 50.27 N 3.35 E
Condè-sur-Vesgre 261 48.45 N 1.40 E
Condeúba 255 14.53 S 41.59 W
Condevilla 286d 12.02 S 77.05 W
Condino 64 45.53 N 10.36 E
Condobolin 166 33.05 S 147.09 E
Condom 32 43.58 N 0.22 E
Condon 202 45.14 N 120.11 W
Condoto 246 5.06 N 76.37 W
Condove 62 45.07 N 7.18 E
Condrieu 62 45.27 N 4.46 E
Condroz □[9] 56 50.25 N 5.00 E
Cone 196 33.48 N 101.23 W
Conecuh ≏ 194 30.58 N 87.14 W
Conegliano 64 45.53 N 12.18 E
Conejos 200 37.05 N 106.01 W
Conejos ≏ 200 37.18 N 105.44 W
Conemaugh 214 40.24 N 78.52 W
Conemaugh ≏ 214 40.28 N 79.27 W
Conemaugh River Lake ⊜[1] 214 40.28 N 79.17 W
Conembaro, Cerro ʌ 234 18.40 N 102.06 W

Cone Mountain ʌ 180 66.12 N 156.03 W
Conero, Monte ʌ 66 43.33 N 13.36 E
Conestoga 208 39.57 N 76.21 W
Conestoga Creek ≏ 208 39.56 N 76.23 W
Conestogo 212 43.32 N 80.30 W
Conestogo ≏ 212 43.32 N 80.29 W
Conestogo Lake ⊜ 212 43.44 N 80.44 W
Conesus 210 42.43 N 77.41 W
Conesus Lake ⊜ 210 42.47 N 77.43 W
Conesville 214 40.11 N 81.53 W
Conewago Creek ≏ 208 40.07 N 76.42 W
Conewago Lake ⊜ 208 40.06 N 76.52 W
Conewango Creek ≏ 214 41.50 N 79.09 W
Coney Island ◆[8] 276 40.34 N 74.00 W
Confederation Lake ⊜ 184 51.05 N 92.44 W
Configni 66 42.25 N 12.38 E
Conflans-en-Jarnisy 56 49.10 N 5.51 E
Conflans-Sainte-Honorine 50 48.59 N 2.06 E
Conflenti 68 39.04 N 16.17 E
Conflict Group II 164 10.45 S 151.45 E
Confluence 188 39.48 N 79.21 W
Confolens 32 46.01 N 0.41 E
Confraternidad, Parque ♠ 286d 12.09 S 77.02 W
Confusion Bay c 186 49.58 N 55.47 W
Confuso ≏ 252 25.09 S 57.34 W
Cong 48 53.32 N 9.19 W
Congamond 207 42.01 N 72.46 W
Congaree ≏ 192 33.45 N 80.37 W
Congelin 168a 32.50 S 116.54 E
Congers 210 41.09 N 73.56 W
Congers Lake ⊜ 276 41.09 N 73.57 W
Cong Hoa Stadium ♠ 269c 10.45 N 106.40 E
Conghua 100 23.32 N 113.32 E
Congjiang 102 25.41 N 108.47 E
Congleton 44 53.10 N 2.13 W
Congo □[1], Afr. 138 1.00 S 15.00 E
Congo □[1], Afr. 152 1.00 S 15.00 E
Congo (Zaire) (Zaïre) ≏ 138 6.04 S 12.24 E
Congo, Democratic Republic of the → Zaire □[1] 138 4.00 S 25.00 E
Congo, République démocratique du → Zaire □[1] 138 4.00 S 25.00 E
Congo, république du → Congo □[1] 152 1.00 S 15.00 E
Congo, Serra do ⋏ 152 6.30 S 13.43 E
Congo Basin ≚[1] 10 0.00 20.00 E
Congonhal 256 22.09 S 46.02 W
Congonhas, Aeroporto de ⊠ 256 23.38 S 46.38 W
Congost ≏ 266d 41.33 N 2.15 E
Congresbury 42 51.23 N 2.48 W
Congress, Sk., Can. 184 49.46 N 106.00 W
Congress, Oh., U.S. 214 40.55 N 82.03 W
Conie ≏ 50 48.06 N 1.30 E
Conigli, Isola dei I 70a 35.30 N 12.33 E
Coningsby 44 53.07 N 0.10 W
Conisbrough 44 53.29 N 1.13 W
Coniston, On., Can. 190 46.29 N 80.51 W
Coniston, Eng., U.K. 44 54.22 N 3.05 W
Coniston Water ⊜ 44 54.20 N 3.04 W
Conitaca 232 24.10 N 106.43 W
Conjeeveram → Kānchipuram 122 12.50 N 79.43 E
Conjola 170 35.13 S 150.27 E
Çonjola Lake c 170 35.16 S 150.27 E
Čon-Kemin ≏ 85 42.42 N 75.54 E
Conklin, Ab., Can. 182 55.38 N 111.05 W
Conklin, N.Y., U.S. 210 42.02 N 75.48 W
Conklingville Dam ◆[6] 210 43.17 N 74.02 W
Conklin Point › 276 40.41 N 73.17 W
Conkouati 152 4.00 S 11.13 E
Conliège 58 46.39 N 5.36 E
Conlin, Lake ⊜ 220 28.14 N 81.07 W
Conn, Lough ⊜ 48 54.04 N 9.20 W
Connah's Quay 44 53.13 N 3.03 W
Connaught □[9] 48 53.45 N 9.00 W
Connaughton 285 40.05 N 75.19 W
Connaughton, Mount ʌ[2] 162 22.42 S 122.40 E
Connaught Place ♠ 272a 28.38 N 77.12 E
Connaux 62 44.05 N 4.36 E
Conneaut 214 41.56 N 80.33 W
Conneaut Creek ≏ 214 41.58 N 80.33 W
Conneaut Lake 214 41.36 N 80.19 W
Conneaut Lake ⊜ 214 41.37 N 80.18 W
Conneaut Outlet ≏ 214 41.33 N 80.06 W
Conneautville 214 41.45 N 80.22 W
Connecticut □[3], U.S. 178 41.45 N 72.45 W
Connecticut □[3], U.S. 207 41.45 N 72.45 W
Connecticut ≏ 188 41.17 N 72.21 W
Connell 202 46.39 N 118.51 W
Connell, Mount ʌ 182 49.18 N 115.38 W
Connellsville 188 40.01 N 79.35 W
Connelly 210 41.55 N 73.59 W
Connel Park 44 55.23 N 4.12 W
Connemara 166 24.13 S 142.17 E
Connemara ◆[1] 48 53.25 N 9.45 W
Conner 116 17.48 N 121.19 E
Conner, Mount ʌ 162 25.23 S 131.54 E
Connerré 50 48.03 N 0.30 E
Connersville, Fl., U.S. 220 27.54 N 81.47 W
Connersville, In., U.S. 218 39.38 N 85.08 W
Connetquot ≏ 276 40.43 N 73.08 W
Connetquot Brook ≏ 276 40.45 N 73.09 W
Connetquot River State Park ♠ 210 40.46 N 73.09 W
Connewarre, Lake ⊜ 169 38.14 S 144.27 E
Conn Island I 284c 39.00 N 77.16 W
Conn Lake ⊜ 176 70.34 N 73.30 W
Connoquenessing 214 40.49 N 80.59 W
Connoquenessing Creek ≏ 214 40.51 N 80.19 W
Connors Range ⋏ 166 21.40 S 149.10 E
Conodoguinet Creek ≏ 208 40.17 N 76.55 W
Conon ≏ 46 57.34 N 4.26 W
Cononaco ≏ 246 1.32 S 75.35 W
Cononbridge 46 57.34 N 4.26 W
Conorochite ≏ 246 2.41 N 67.29 W
Conotton Creek ≏ 214 40.34 N 81.23 W
Conover 192 35.42 N 81.13 W
Conowingo 208 39.40 N 76.09 W
Conowingo ◆[6] 208 39.33 N 76.04 W
Conowingo Creek ≏ 208 39.41 N 76.12 W
Conowingo Dam ◆[6] 208 39.39 N 76.10 W
Conquest 184 51.32 N 107.17 W
Conquista 255 19.56 S 47.33 W
Conrad, Ia., U.S. 190 42.13 N 92.52 W
Conrad, Mt., U.S. 202 48.10 N 111.56 W
Conrado 256 22.32 S 43.33 W
Conroe 222 30.18 N 95.27 W
Conroe, Lake ⊜[1] 222 30.25 N 95.37 W
Çonsandolo 66 44.39 N 11.46 E
Čon-Saryoj 85 42.37 N 76.53 E
Conscience Bay c 276 40.57 N 73.07 W
Consdorf 56 49.46 N 6.20 E
Consecon 212 44.00 N 77.31 W
Conselheiro Lafaiete 255 20.40 S 43.48 W
Conselheiro Paulino 256 22.13 S 42.31 W
Conselheiro Pena 255 19.10 S 41.30 W
Conselice 66 44.31 N 11.49 E
Conselve 64 45.14 N 11.52 E
Conservatória 256 22.18 S 43.57 W
Consett 44 54.51 N 1.49 W
Conshohocken 208 40.04 N 75.18 W
Consolação 256 22.33 S 45.55 W
Consolação ◆[8] 287b 23.33 S 46.39 W
Consolación del Sur 240p 22.30 N 83.31 W
Consolidated Main Reef Mines ◆[7] 273d 26.11 S 27.56 E
Con Son II 110 8.43 N 106.36 E
Consort 184 52.01 N 110.46 W
Constable 206 44.56 N 74.18 W
Constableville 212 43.34 N 75.25 W
Constance, Lake → Bodensee ⊜ 58 47.35 N 9.25 E

Constance → Konstanz 58 47.40 N 9.10 E
Constance Lake ⊜ 212 45.25 N 75.58 W
Constância 34 39.28 N 8.20 W
Constanța 38 44.11 N 28.39 E
Constanța □[6] 38 44.20 N 28.20 E
Constant Creek ≏ 212 45.17 N 76.46 W
Constantia 210 43.14 N 76.00 W
Constantina 34 37.52 N 5.37 W
Constantine 216 41.50 N 85.40 W
Constantine, Cape › 180 58.25 N 158.50 W
Constantine → Qacentina 148 36.22 N 6.37 E
Constantinople → İstanbul 130 41.01 N 28.58 E
Constant Lake ⊜ 212 45.24 N 77.00 W
Constitución, Chile 252 35.20 S 72.25 W
Constitución, Ur. 252 31.05 S 57.50 W
Constitución ◆[8] 288 34.37 S 58.23 W
Constitución de 01080507, Parque Nacional ♠ 204 32.05 N 115.55 W
Constitution, Mount ʌ 224 48.40 N 122.50 W
Consuegra 34 39.28 N 3.36 W
Consul 184 49.21 N 109.30 W
Consuma 66 43.47 N 11.35 E
Consuma, Passo della)(66 43.47 N 11.36 E
Contai 126 21.47 N 87.45 E
Contamana 248 7.15 S 74.54 W
Contarina 64 45.00 N 12.13 E
Contas, Rio de ≏ 255 14.17 S 39.01 W
Contee 208 39.05 N 76.52 W
Contendas do Sincorá 255 13.45 S 41.02 W
Contentnea Creek ≏ 192 35.21 N 77.23 W
Contes 62 43.49 N 7.19 E
Contessa Entellina 70 37.44 N 13.11 E
Contigliano 66 42.24 N 12.46 E
Continental 216 41.06 N 84.15 W
Continental Peak ʌ 200 42.16 N 108.43 W
Contoocook Lake ⊜ 207 42.47 N 72.01 W
Contraalmirante Cordero 252 38.44 S 68.10 W
Contra Costa □[6] 226 37.55 N 121.55 W
Contra Costa Canal ≊ 282 38.02 N 121.58 W
Contra Loma Reservoir ⊜[1] 282 37.58 N 121.49 W
Contramaestre 240p 20.18 N 76.15 W
Contramaestre ≏ 240p 20.31 N 76.18 W
Contratación 246 6.18 N 73.29 W
Contrecoeur 206 45.51 N 73.14 W
Contre Island ›[1] 276 40.54 N 73.32 W
Contreras, Embalse de ⊜[1] 34 39.32 N 1.30 W
Contreras, Isla I 254 51.55 S 74.55 W
Contres 50 47.25 N 1.26 E
Contrexéville 58 48.11 N 5.54 E
Contrisson 56 48.48 N 4.57 E
Controller Bay c 180 60.07 N 144.15 W
Contumazá 248 7.22 S 78.49 W
Contursi 68 40.39 N 15.14 E
Contwoyto Lake ⊜ 176 65.42 N 110.50 W
Conty 50 49.44 N 2.09 E
Contz-les-Bains 56 49.27 N 6.21 E
Convención 246 8.28 N 73.21 W
Convent 194 30.01 N 90.49 W
Convento 236 9.21 N 83.30 W
Convent Station 276 40.47 N 74.26 W
Conversano 68 40.58 N 17.08 E
Converse 216 40.34 N 85.52 W
Converse Lake ⊜ 276 41.08 N 73.39 W
Converse Pond Brook ≏ 276 41.03 N 73.40 W
Convoy 216 40.55 N 84.42 W
Conway, P.E., Can. 186 46.40 N 63.59 W
Conway, S. Afr. 158 31.43 S 25.16 E
Conway, Ar., U.S. 194 35.05 N 92.26 W
Conway, Fl., U.S. 220 28.30 N 81.19 W
Conway, Ma., U.S. 207 42.30 N 72.42 W
Conway, Mo., U.S. 194 37.30 N 92.49 W
Conway, N.H., U.S. 188 43.58 N 71.07 W
Conway, N.C., U.S. 192 36.26 N 77.13 W
Conway, Pa., U.S. 214 40.39 N 80.14 W
Conway, S.C., U.S. 192 33.50 N 79.02 W
Conway, Wa., U.S. 224 48.21 N 122.21 W
Conway, Cape › 166 20.32 S 148.56 E
Conway, Lake ⊜ 162 28.17 S 135.35 E
Conway, Lake ⊜[1] 194 35.00 N 92.25 W
Conway, Mount ʌ 162 23.45 S 133.25 E
Conway National Park ♠ 166 20.22 S 148.51 E
Conway Springs 198 37.23 N 97.38 W
Conwy 44 53.17 N 3.50 W
Conwy ≏ 44 53.17 N 3.50 W
Conwy, Vale of V 44 53.12 N 3.48 W
Conwy Bay c 44 53.18 N 3.55 W
Conyers 192 33.40 N 84.01 W
Conyngham 210 40.59 N 76.03 W
Coo 56 50.24 N 5.52 E
Coober Pedy 162 29.01 S 134.43 E
Coogee, Austl. 168a 32.07 S 115.46 E
Coogee, Austl. 274a 33.55 S 151.16 E
Coogee Bay c 274a 33.55 S 151.16 E
Cook, Austl. 162 30.37 S 130.25 E
Cook, In., U.S. 216 41.22 N 87.26 W
Cook, Mn., U.S. 190 47.51 N 92.41 W
Cook, Ne., U.S. 198 40.30 N 96.09 W
Cook, Wa., U.S. 224 45.43 N 121.40 W
Cook □[6] 216 41.53 N 87.45 W
Cook, Bahía c 254 55.10 S 70.10 W
Cook, Baie de c 174s 17.29 S 149.49 W
Cook, Cape › 182 50.08 N 127.55 W
Cook, Mount ʌ 172 43.36 S 170.10 E
Cook, Point › 274b 37.55 S 144.48 E
Cook, Récif de ✢[2] 175f 19.25 S 163.50 E
Cookardinia 171b 35.34 S 147.14 E
Cook Bay c 212 44.15 N 79.30 W
Cook Creek ≏ 224 47.17 N 124.05 W
Cooke, Mount ʌ 168a 32.25 S 116.18 E
Cookernup 168a 33.00 S 115.54 E
Cookes Peak ʌ 200 32.32 N 107.44 W
Cookeville 194 36.09 N 85.30 W
Cook Forest State Park ♠ 214 41.22 N 79.12 W
Cookham 42 51.34 N 0.43 W
Cookhouse 158 32.45 S 25.49 E
Cook Ice Shelf ⍌ 9 68.40 S 152.30 E
Cooking Lake ⊜ 182 53.25 N 113.02 W
Cook Inlet c 180 60.30 N 152.00 W
Cook-Inseln → Cook Islands □[2] 14 20.00 S 158.00 W
Cook Island I 174o 1.57 N 157.28 W
Cook Islands □[2] 14 20.00 S 158.00 W
Cooks 274a 33.56 S 151.10 E
Cooksburg 214 41.20 N 79.12 W
Cooks Falls 210 41.57 N 74.59 W
Cook's Harbour 186 51.36 N 55.52 W
Cookshire 206 45.25 N 71.38 W
Cooksmill Green 260 51.44 N 0.22 E
Cooks Mills 284a 43.00 N 79.11 W
Cookstown, On., Can. 212 44.11 N 79.42 W
Cookstown, N. Ire., U.K. 48 54.39 N 6.45 W
Cook Strait ʮ 172 41.15 S 174.30 E
Cooksville, Il., U.S. 216 40.33 N 88.43 W
Cooksville, Md., U.S. 208 39.19 N 77.01 W
Cooksville, Wi., U.S. 216 42.50 N 89.14 W
Cooksville Creek ≏ 275b 43.34 N 79.34 W
Cooktown 164 15.28 S 145.15 E
Cookville 222 33.11 N 94.51 W
Coolabah 166 31.02 S 146.43 E
Cooladdi 166 26.39 S 145.28 E
Coolah 166 31.50 S 149.42 E
Coolamon 166 34.49 S 147.12 E
Coolaney 48 54.11 N 8.29 W
Coolangatta 171a 28.10 S 153.32 E
Coolawanyah 162 21.47 S 117.48 E
Coole ≏ 50 48.56 N 4.21 E
Cooleemee 192 35.48 N 80.33 W

Cooley Lake ⊜ 281 42.37 N 83.27 W
Coolgardie 162 30.57 S 121.10 E
Coolidge, Az., U.S. 200 32.58 N 111.31 W
Coolidge, Ga., U.S. 192 31.00 N 83.51 W
Coolidge, Tx., U.S. 222 31.45 N 96.38 W
Coolidge, Mount ʌ 198 43.44 N 103.29 W
Coolidge Dam ◆[6] 200 33.00 N 110.20 W
Coolidge Point › 283 42.34 N 70.44 W
Coolin 202 48.28 N 116.50 W
Cooling 260 51.27 N 0.32 E
Cooloola National Park ♠ 166 26.05 S 153.00 E
Cooloongup, Lake ⊜ 168a 32.18 S 115.47 E
Coolspring 214 41.02 N 79.05 W
Coolumburra Hill ʌ 170 35.01 S 150.10 E
Coolup 168a 32.44 S 115.53 E
Cooma 171b 36.14 S 149.08 E
Cooma Creek ≏ 171b 36.07 S 149.11 E
Coombe Cottage ⊥ 274b 37.43 S 145.23 E
Coomberdale 162 30.28 S 116.02 E
Coomera 171a 27.52 S 153.19 E
Coomera ≏ 171a 27.53 S 153.24 E
Coominya 171a 27.23 S 152.30 E
Coonabarabran 166 31.16 S 149.17 E
Coonalpyn 166 35.42 S 139.51 E
Coonamble 166 30.57 S 148.23 E
Coonana 162 31.01 S 123.07 E
Coon Creek ≏, Ca., U.S. 226 38.51 N 121.34 W
Coon Creek ≏, Il., U.S. 216 42.15 N 88.48 W
Coon Creek ≏, Tx., U.S. 222 31.59 N 95.52 W
Coon Creek Lake ⊜[1] 222 32.04 N 95.52 W
Coondambo 166 31.04 S 135.52 E
Coongan ≏ 162 20.53 S 119.47 E
Coonoor 122 11.21 N 76.49 E
Coon Rapids, Ia., U.S. 198 41.52 N 94.41 W
Coon Rapids, Mn., U.S. 190 45.10 N 93.19 W
Coontown 276 40.37 N 74.31 W
Coon Valley 190 43.42 N 91.00 W
Cooper 196 33.22 N 95.41 W
Cooper ≏, N.J., U.S. 285 39.57 N 75.07 W
Cooper ≏, Wa., U.S. 224 47.23 N 121.23 W
Cooper, Mount ʌ, Austl. 162 26.11 S 127.56 E
Cooper, Mount ʌ, B.C., Can. 182 50.11 N 117.12 W
Cooper, North Branch ≏ 285 39.55 N 75.02 W
Cooper Center 216 42.23 N 85.37 W
Cooper Creek ≏ 166 28.29 S 137.46 E
Cooper Island I 240m 18.22 N 64.30 W
Cooper Landing 180 60.29 N 149.51 W
Cooper Mountain ʌ 180 60.23 N 149.51 W
Cooper River Parkway ♠ 285 39.55 N 75.03 W
Cooper Road 194 32.26 N 93.48 W
Coopers 194 32.46 N 86.33 W
Coopersale Common 260 51.42 N 0.08 E
Coopersburg 208 40.30 N 75.23 W
Coopers Plains, Austl. 171a 27.34 S 153.02 E
Coopers Plains, N.Y., U.S. 210 42.11 N 77.08 W
Cooperstown, N.Y., U.S. 210 42.42 N 74.55 W
Cooperstown, N.D., U.S. 198 47.26 N 98.07 W
Cooperstown, Pa., U.S. 214 41.30 N 79.52 W
Cooperstown, Pa., U.S. 214 40.43 N 79.57 W
Coopersville 216 43.03 N 85.56 W
Coorabie 162 31.54 S 132.18 E
Cooranbong 170 33.04 S 151.27 E
Coorong National Park ♠ 166 36.01 S 139.32 E
Coorow 162 29.53 S 116.01 E
Cooroy 166 26.25 S 152.55 E
Coorparoo 171a 27.30 S 153.03 E
Coos □[6] 206 45.04 N 71.20 W
Coosa ≏ 194 32.30 N 86.16 W
Coosawhatchie ≏ 192 32.32 N 80.52 W
Coos Bay 202 43.22 N 124.12 W
Coos Bay c 202 43.23 N 124.16 W
Cootamundra 166 34.39 S 148.02 E
Cootehill 48 54.04 N 7.05 W
Cooyar 171a 26.59 S 151.50 E
Cooyar Creek ≏ 171a 26.50 S 152.04 E
Çooyar Mountain ʌ 171a 26.57 S 151.47 E
Čop 78 48.26 N 22.10 E
Copacabana, Arg. 252 28.12 S 67.29 W
Copacabana, Bol. 248 16.10 S 69.05 W
Copacabana, Col. 246 6.20 N 75.30 W
Copacabana ◆[8] 287a 22.58 S 43.11 W
Copacabana, Forte de ⊥ 287a 22.59 S 43.11 W
Copainalá 234 17.05 N 93.12 W
Copake 210 42.06 N 73.33 W
Copake Falls 210 42.07 N 73.31 W
Copala 234 16.37 N 98.58 W
Copalillo 234 18.02 N 99.07 W
Copalis ≏ 224 47.07 N 124.13 W
Copalis Beach 224 47.06 N 124.10 W
Copalita ≏ 234 15.46 N 96.03 W
Copán, Hond. 236 14.50 N 89.09 W
Copan, Ok., U.S. 196 36.53 N 95.55 W
Copán □[5] 236 14.50 N 89.00 W
Copán ⊥ 236 14.50 N 89.09 W
Copanatoyac 234 17.15 N 98.45 W
Copándaro 234 19.53 N 101.13 W
Copan Lake ⊜[1] 196 36.55 N 95.56 W
Copano Bay c 196 28.05 N 97.05 W
Copatana 246 2.48 S 67.04 W
Cope 198 39.39 N 102.51 W
Copeá, Paraná ≏[1] 246 3.52 S 63.20 W
Copeau ≏ 184 52.45 N 103.00 W
Copeland 220 25.57 N 81.21 W
Copeland Island I 48 54.41 N 5.32 W
Copenhagen 212 43.53 N 75.40 W
Copenhagen → København 41 55.40 N 12.35 E
Copenhague → København 41 55.40 N 12.35 E
Copenhaver 284c 39.04 N 77.11 W
Copertino 68 40.16 N 18.03 E
Copetonas 252 38.43 S 60.27 W
Copeville 222 33.05 N 96.25 W
Copiague 210 40.40 N 73.24 W
Copiague Neck ›[1] 276 40.40 N 73.22 W
Copiapó 252 27.22 S 70.20 W
Copiapó ≏ 252 27.19 S 70.56 W
Copinsay I 46 58.54 N 2.40 W
Coplay 208 40.40 N 75.29 W
Copley, Austl. 166 30.32 S 138.25 E
Copley, Oh., U.S. 214 41.06 N 81.39 W
Copmanthorpe 44 53.55 N 1.08 W
Copoas, Mount ʌ 116 10.48 N 119.17 E
Çopolo 152 10.22 S 14.07 E
Čopoviči 78 50.49 N 27.58 E
Copparo 64 44.54 N 11.49 E
Coppell 222 32.57 N 97.01 W
Coppename ≏ 250 5.48 N 55.55 W
Coppenbrügge 52 52.07 N 9.32 E
Copper ≏ 180 60.30 N 144.50 W
Copperas Cove 196 31.07 N 97.54 W
Copperas Mountain ʌ 276 41.02 N 74.28 W
Copperbelt □[4] 154 13.00 S 28.00 E
Copper Butte ʌ 202 48.42 N 118.28 W
Copper Canyon → Cobre, Barranca del V 232 27.28 N 107.50 W
Copper Center 180 61.58 N 145.19 W
Copper Cliff 190 46.28 N 81.04 W
Copper Creek ≏ 192 36.40 N 82.45 W
Copper Harbor 190 47.27 N 87.53 W
Coppermine 176 67.50 N 115.05 W
Coppermine ≏ 176 67.49 N 115.04 W
Copper Mine Point ›, Br. Vir. Is. 240m 18.26 N 64.25 W

Symbol	English	Deutsch	Español	Français	Português
≏	River	Fluß	Río	Rivière	Rio
≊	Canal	Kanal	Canal	Canal	Canal
ʟ	Waterfall, Rapids	Wasserfall, Stromschnellen	Cascada, Rápidos	Chute d'eau, Rapides	Cascata, Rápidos
ʮ	Strait	Meeresstraße	Estrecho	Détroit	Estreito
c	Bay, Gulf	Bucht, Golf	Bahía, Golfo	Baie, Golfe	Baía, Golfo
⊜	Lake, Lakes	See, Seen	Lago, Lagos	Lac, Lacs	Lago, Lagos
≚	Swamp	Sumpf	Pantano	Marais	Pântano
⍌	Ice Features, Glacier	Eis- und Gletscherformen	Accidentes Glaciales	Formes glaciaires	Acidentes glaciares
⍑	Other Hydrographic Features	Andere Hydrographische Objekte	Otros Elementos Hidrográficos	Autres données hydrographiques	Outros acidentes hidrográficos
✢	Submarine Features	Untermeerische Objekte	Accidentes Submarinos	Formes de relief sous-marin	Acidentes submarinos
□	Political Unit	Politische Einheit	Unidad Politica	Entité politique	Unidade política
♁	Cultural Institution	Kulturelle Institution	Institución Cultural	Institution culturelle	Institução cultural
⊥	Historical Site	Historische Stätte	Sitio Histórico	Site historique	Sitio histórico
♠	Recreational Site	Erholungs- und Ferienort	Sitio de Recreo	Centre de loisirs	Area de Lazer
⊠	Airport	Flughafen	Aeropuerto	Aéroport	Aeroporto
■	Military Installation	Militäranlage	Instalación Militar	Installation militaire	Instalação militar
◆	Miscellaneous	Verschiedenes	Misceláneo	Divers	Diversos

ESPAÑOL — Nombre · Página · Lat.°′ · Long.°′ W = Oeste
FRANÇAIS — Nom · Page · Lat.°′ · Long.°′ W = Ouest
PORTUGUÊS — Nome · Página · Lat.°′ · Long.°′ W = Oeste

Nombre / Nom / Nome	Página / Page / Página	Lat.°′	Long.°′ W = Oeste / Ouest
Eging	60	48.43 N	13.16 E
Egipto → Egypt □[1]	140	27.00 N	30.00 E
Égletons	32	45.24 N	2.03 E
Eglin Air Force Base ■	194	30.29 N	86.30 W
Eglinton	48	55.02 N	7.11 W
Eglisau	58	47.34 N	8.32 E
Egloskerry	42	50.39 N	4.27 W
Égly	261	48.35 N	2.13 E
Egmond aan Zee	52	52.36 N	4.37 E
Egmond-Binnen	52	52.35 N	4.39 E
Egmont, Cape ≻	172	39.17 S	173.45 E
Egmont, Mount → Taranaki, Mount ∧	172	39.18 S	174.04 E
Egmont Bay ⊂	186	46.35 N	64.12 W
Egmont Channel ʮ	220	27.36 N	82.45 W
Egmont Key I	220	27.35 N	82.46 W
Egmont National Park ♦	172	39.15 S	174.05 E
Egna (Neumarkt)	64	46.19 N	11.16 E
Egnach	58	47.33 N	9.23 E
Egnazia ⊥	68	40.53 N	17.24 E
Egoryevsk → Jegorjevsk	82	55.23 N	39.02 E
Egota ◆[8]	268	35.43 N	139.40 E
Egra	126	21.54 N	87.32 E
Egremont, Ab., Can.	182	54.02 N	113.08 W
Egremont, Eng., U.K.	44	54.29 N	3.33 W
Égreville	50	48.10 N	2.52 E
Eğridir	130	37.52 N	30.51 E
Eğridir Gölü ⊜	130	38.02 N	30.53 E
Eğriköy	130	38.44 N	27.21 E
Egrisskij chrebet ⋀	84	42.49 N	42.24 E
Egton	44	54.26 N	0.45 W
Egtved	41	55.37 N	9.18 E
Éguas, Rio das ≃	255	13.26 S	44.14 W
Éguilles	62	43.34 N	5.22 E
Eguisheim	58	48.03 N	7.18 E
Egum Atoll I[1]	164	9.25 S	151.55 E
Egvekinot	180	66.19 N	179.10 W
Egyházasrádóc	61	47.05 N	16.37 E
Egypt, Ma., U.S.	207	42.12 N	70.45 W
Egypt, Pa., U.S.	208	40.41 N	75.32 W
Egypt, Tx., U.S.	222	29.24 N	96.14 W
Egypt (Mişr) □[1], Afr.	136	27.00 N	30.00 E
Egypt (Mişr) □[1], Afr.	140	27.00 N	30.00 E
Egypt, Lake of ⊜[1]	194	37.35 N	88.55 W
Égypte → Egypt □[1]	140	27.00 N	30.00 E
Egyptian Museum ʊ	273c	30.03 N	31.14 E
Eha-Amufu	150	6.40 N	7.46 E
Ehekirchen	60	48.38 N	11.06 E
Ehen ≃	44	54.25 N	3.30 W
Ehime □[5]	96	33.40 N	132.50 E
Ehingen	58	48.17 N	9.43 E
Ehingen ◆[8]	263	51.22 N	6.42 E
Ehle ≃	54	52.12 N	11.44 E
Ehmen	54	52.24 N	10.41 E
Ehra-Lessien	54	52.34 N	10.46 E
Ehrang	56	49.49 N	6.41 E
Ehrenberg	200	33.36 N	114.31 W
Ehrenberg Range ⋀	162	23.18 S	130.20 E
Ehrenbreitstein, Feste ⊥	56	50.21 N	7.37 E
Ehrenburg ⊥	56	50.12 N	7.27 E
Ehrenfeld	214	40.22 N	78.46 W
Ehrenfriedersdorf	54	50.38 N	12.58 E
Ehrenhausen	61	46.43 N	15.35 E
Ehreshoven	56	50.58 N	7.20 E
Ehrhardt	192	33.05 N	81.00 W
Ehrhorn	52	53.10 N	9.53 E
Ehringhausen	263	51.11 N	7.33 E
Ehringhausen ◆[8]	263	51.09 N	7.11 E
Ehrwald	58	47.24 N	10.55 E
Ehwa Women's University ʊ[2]	271b	37.34 N	126.56 E
Ei	92	31.12 N	130.30 E
Eibar	34	43.11 N	2.28 W
Eibau	54	50.58 N	14.40 E
Eibelstadt	56	49.43 N	10.00 E
Eibenstock	54	50.29 N	12.35 E
Eibergen	52	52.06 N	6.39 E
Eibiswald	61	46.41 N	15.15 E
Eibsee ⊜	64	47.27 N	10.58 E
Eicha	54	50.21 N	10.34 E
Eich-Berg ∧[2]	264a	52.39 N	13.50 E
Eiche, Dtsch.	264a	52.25 N	12.58 E
Eiche, Dtsch.	264a	52.34 N	13.36 E
Eichenbarleben	54	52.10 N	11.24 E
Eichenbrandt	264a	52.38 N	13.51 E
Eichendorf	60	48.38 N	12.51 E
Eichgraben	61	48.10 N	15.59 E
Eichlinghofen ◆[8]	263	51.29 N	7.24 E
Eichsfeld ◆[1]	56	51.25 N	10.20 E
Eichstädt	264a	52.42 N	13.07 E
Eichstätt	60	48.54 N	11.12 E
Eichstetten	58	48.05 N	7.44 E
Eichtersheim	56	49.14 N	8.46 E
Eichwalde	54	52.22 N	13.37 E
Eickelborn	52	51.39 N	8.13 E
Eicken ◆[8]	263	51.13 N	6.26 E
Eickerend	263	51.13 N	6.34 E
Eickerkopf ∧[2]	263	51.21 N	7.42 E
Eicklingen	52	52.33 N	10.10 E
Eide	26	62.55 N	7.26 E
Eidelstedt ◆[8]	52	53.36 N	9.53 E
Eider ≃	41	54.19 N	8.58 E
Eiderstedt ≻[1]	41	54.22 N	8.50 E
Eidfjord	26	60.28 N	7.05 E
Eidsvåg, Nor.	26	60.27 N	5.21 E
Eidsvåg, Nor.	26	62.47 N	8.03 E
Eidsvold	166	25.22 S	151.07 E
Eidsvoll	26	60.19 N	11.14 E
Eifa	56	50.58 N	8.34 E
Eifel ⋀	56	50.15 N	6.45 E
Eiffel, Tour ⊥	261	48.51 N	2.18 E
Eiffel Flats	154	18.15 S	29.59 E
Eifgenbach ≃	263	51.05 N	7.09 E
Eige, Carn ∧	46	57.17 N	5.07 W
Eigen ◆[8]	263	51.33 N	6.57 E
Eigenji	94	35.04 N	136.18 E
Eigenrieden	54	51.11 N	10.22 E
Eiger ∧	58	46.35 N	8.00 E
Eigg I	46	56.54 N	6.10 W
Eigg, Sound of ʮ	46	56.51 N	6.13 W
Eight Degree Channel ʮ	122	8.00 N	73.00 E
Eighteenmile Creek ≃, N.Y., U.S.	210	42.43 N	78.58 W
Eighteenmile Creek ≃, N.Y., U.S.	210	43.21 N	78.43 W
Eight Mile Creek ≃, On., Can.	284a	43.14 N	79.11 W
Eightmile Creek ≃, In., U.S.	216	40.57 N	85.22 W
Eightmile Creek ≃, Or., U.S.	224	45.36 N	121.05 W
Eights Coast ⫫[2]	9	73.30 S	93.00 W
Eighty Four	279b	40.11 N	80.08 W
Eighty Mile Beach ⫫[2]	162	19.45 S	121.00 E
Eiheiji	94	36.05 N	136.20 E
Eijerlandsche Gat ⊂	52	53.12 N	4.50 E
Eijsden	56	50.47 N	5.43 E
Eikeren ⊜	26	59.38 N	9.58 E
Eikisdalsvatnet ⊜	26	62.34 N	8.11 E
Eildon	169	37.14 S	145.56 E
Eildon, Lake ⊜[1]	169	37.11 S	145.55 E
Eilean Gowan Island I	212	45.02 N	79.25 W
Eileen	216	41.17 N	88.15 W
Eilenburg	54	51.27 N	12.37 E
Eil Malk I	175b	7.09 N	134.22 E
Eilpe ◆[8]	263	51.21 N	7.29 E
Eilsleben	54	52.09 N	11.13 E
Eimbeckhausen	52	52.14 N	9.25 E
Eimke	52	52.58 N	10.19 E
Eina	26	60.38 N	10.36 E
Einasleigh	166	18.31 S	144.05 E
Einasleigh ≃	166	17.30 S	142.17 E
Einbeck	52	51.49 N	9.52 E
Eindhoven	52	51.26 N	5.28 E
Eine	50	50.52 N	3.37 E
Einme	110	16.54 N	95.11 E
Einöd	56	49.16 N	7.19 E
Einödriegel ∧	60	48.56 N	13.02 E
Einruhr	56	50.35 N	6.22 E
Einsiedel	54	50.46 N	12.58 E
Einsiedeln	58	47.08 N	8.45 E
Einville-au-Jard	58	48.39 N	6.30 E
Eirauli	272c	19.10 N	72.59 E
Éire → Ireland □[1]	48	53.00 N	8.00 W
Eiru ≃	248	6.42 S	69.52 W
Eirunepé	248	6.40 S	69.52 W
Eisbach ≃	56	49.38 N	8.22 E
Eisch ≃	56	49.45 N	6.07 E
Eiseb ≃	156	20.33 S	20.59 E
Eisenach	54	50.59 N	10.19 E
Eisenberg, Dtsch.	54	50.58 N	11.53 E
Eisenberg, Dtsch.	56	49.38 N	8.05 E
Eisenberg ∧[2]	61	47.12 N	16.24 E
Eisenerz	61	47.33 N	14.53 E
Eisenerzer Alpen ⋀	61	47.28 N	14.45 E
Eisenhower Center ʊ	198	38.54 N	97.12 W
Eisenhower Memorial Park ♦	276	40.44 N	73.34 W
Eisenhüttenstadt	54	52.10 N	14.39 E
Eisenkappel	61	46.29 N	14.35 E
Eisenschmitt	56	50.03 N	6.43 E
Eisenstadt	61	47.51 N	16.32 E
Eisfeld	54	50.26 N	10.54 E
Eisgarn	61	48.54 N	15.06 E
Eishken	46	58.01 N	6.32 W
Eishort, Loch ⊂	46	57.10 N	5.59 W
Eišiškės	76	54.10 N	25.00 E
Eisk → Jejsk	78	46.42 N	38.16 E
Eisleben	54	51.31 N	11.32 E
Eislingen	56	48.42 N	9.42 E
Eisriesenwelt ⫫[5]	64	47.32 N	13.10 E
Eita	174t	1.21 N	173.05 E
Eitorf	56	50.46 N	7.26 E
Eivissa	34	38.54 N	1.26 E
Eivissa (Ibiza) I	34	39.00 N	1.25 E
Ejasi → Eyasi, Lake ⊜	154	3.40 S	35.05 E
Ejby, Dan.	41	55.30 N	12.07 E
Ejby, Dan.	41	55.26 N	9.57 E
Ejea de los Caballeros	34	42.08 N	1.08 W
Ejeda	157b	24.20 S	44.31 E
Ejército Rebelde, Presa ⊜[1]	286b	23.01 N	82.20 W
Ejido	246	8.33 N	71.14 W
Ejido Jaboncillos	232	28.57 N	102.39 W
Ejigbo	273a	6.33 N	3.18 E
Ejin Horo Qi	102	39.27 N	109.40 E
Ejin Qi	102	41.50 N	100.50 E
Ejstrup	41	55.59 N	9.17 E
Ejura	150	7.23 N	1.22 W
Ejutla de Crespo	234	16.34 N	96.44 W
Ekalaka	198	45.53 N	104.33 W
Ekáli	267c	38.07 N	23.50 E
Ekanga	152	2.23 S	23.14 E
Ekas	115b	8.53 S	116.27 E
Ekaterinburg → Jekaterinburg	86	56.51 N	60.36 E
Ekaterinodar → Krasnodar	78	45.02 N	39.00 E
Ekaterinoslav → Dnepropetrovsk	78	48.27 N	34.59 E
Ekeby	41	56.00 N	12.58 E
Ekenäs (Taamisaari)	26	59.58 N	23.26 E
Ekenässjön	26	57.30 N	15.00 E
Ekerö I	40	59.18 N	17.43 E
Eket, Nig.	150	4.39 N	7.56 E
Eket, Sve.	41	56.15 N	13.11 E
Eketahuna	172	40.39 S	175.42 E
Ekhínos	38	41.17 N	24.59 E
Ekiatapskij chrebet ⋀	74	68.30 N	179.00 E
Ekibastuz	86	51.42 N	75.22 E
Ekimčan	89	53.04 N	132.58 E
Ekitykskij chrebet ⋀	180	67.45 N	179.00 E
Eko → Lagos	150	6.27 N	3.24 E
Ekoli	152	0.23 S	24.16 E
Ekoln ⊜	40	59.45 N	17.37 E
Ekolsund	40	59.37 N	17.22 E
Ekolsundsviken ⊂	40	59.35 N	17.24 E
Ekombe	152	1.16 N	21.36 E
Ekonda	74	65.47 N	105.17 E
Ekoungounou	152	0.33 S	15.38 E
Ekovamou	152	0.07 N	16.31 E
Ekpoma	150	6.46 N	6.08 E
Eksāra	272b	22.38 N	88.17 E
Eksel	56	51.09 N	5.23 E
Eksjö	26	57.40 N	14.57 E
Ekuk	180	58.49 N	158.34 W
Ekuku	152	0.42 S	21.38 E
Ekuta	152	2.59 N	18.42 E
Ekwan ≃	176	53.14 N	82.13 W
Ekwata	152	0.13 S	9.18 E
Ekwendeni	154	11.23 S	33.50 E
Ekwok	180	59.22 N	157.30 W
Ela	110	19.37 N	96.13 E
El Aaiún (La'youn)	148	27.09 N	13.12 W
El Abiadh Sidi Cheikh	148	32.56 N	0.42 E
El 'Açâba □[4]	150	16.10 N	11.30 W
El 'Açâba ⋀[1]	150	16.00 N	12.00 W
El- → Ad-, Al-, An-, Ar-, As-, Ash-, At-, Az-			
El-Adde	144	2.35 N	46.09 E
El Adeb Larache	148	27.22 N	8.52 E
El Adelanto	236	14.10 N	89.50 W
El Affroun	34	36.30 N	2.38 E
El Agreb	148	30.48 N	5.30 E
El Aguacate	286c	10.28 N	66.59 W
El Aguacate ≃	234	18.16 N	100.40 W
El Aguilar	252	23.12 S	65.42 W
El Agustino	286d	12.03 S	76.59 W
El Agustino, Cerro ∧[2]	286d	12.04 S	77.00 W
Elaía	38	39.35 N	20.20 E
Elaine	194	34.18 N	90.51 W
El Alamein → Al-'Alamayn	140	30.49 N	28.57 E
El Álamo, Méx.	196	27.32 N	100.52 W
El Álamo, Méx.	196	26.29 N	99.46 W
El Álamo, Méx.	204	31.34 N	116.02 W
El Alia	36	37.10 N	10.03 E
El Alto, Arg.	252	28.18 S	65.22 W
El Alto, Perú	246	4.18 S	81.07 W
Elam	285	39.51 N	75.32 W
Elamanchili	122	17.33 N	82.52 E
El Amparo de Apure	246	7.06 N	70.45 W
Elan ≃	38	46.07 N	28.04 E
Élancourt	261	48.47 N	1.58 E
Elands ≃, S. Afr.	156	25.10 S	29.10 E
Elands ≃, S. Afr.	158	25.31 S	26.39 E
Elandsbaai	158	32.19 S	18.21 E
Elandsfontein	273d	26.10 S	28.12 E
Elandsvlei	158	32.19 S	19.33 E
El Angel	246	0.37 N	77.56 W
Elanora Heights	274a	33.42 S	151.17 E
El Aouinet	36	35.52 N	7.54 E
El Arahal	34	37.16 N	5.33 W
El Arba	34	36.37 N	3.13 E
El Arco	232	28.00 N	113.25 W
El Arenal	234	20.47 N	103.42 W
El Aricha	148	34.09 N	1.10 W
El Aroussa	36	36.22 N	9.28 E
El Arrayán	286e	33.21 S	70.28 W
Elassón	38	39.54 N	22.11 E
Elat	132	29.33 N	34.57 E
Elat, Gulf of → Aqaba, Gulf of ⊂	128	29.00 N	34.40 E
Elat, Sede Te'Ufa ⊠	132	29.34 N	34.55 E
El Avagi	144	3.36 N	46.57 E
El Ávila, Cerro ∧	286c	10.33 N	66.52 W
El Ávila, Parque Nacional ♦	246	10.35 N	66.48 W
Elazığ	130	38.41 N	39.14 E
Elazığ □[4]	130	38.35 N	39.30 E
El Azúcar, Presa de ⊜[1]	196	26.10 N	99.00 W
El Azul, Sierra ⋀	234	23.25 N	100.30 W
Elba, Al., U.S.	194	31.24 N	86.04 W
Elba, Mi., U.S.	216	43.02 N	83.26 W
Elba, N.Y., U.S.	210	43.04 N	78.11 W
Elba, Isola d' I	66	42.46 N	10.17 E
Elba → Elbe ≃	30	53.50 N	9.00 E
El'ban	89	50.06 N	136.31 E
El Banco	246	9.00 N	73.58 W
El Barco de Avila	34	40.21 N	5.31 W
El Barco de Valdeorras	34	42.25 N	6.59 W
El Barreal	200	31.17 N	107.10 W
El Barril	234	23.02 N	102.08 W
Elbasan	38	41.06 N	20.05 E
Elbaşı	130	38.41 N	35.59 E
El Baúl	246	8.57 N	68.17 W
El Baúl, Cerro ∧, Méx.	234	17.38 N	100.19 W
El Baúl, Cerro ∧, Méx.	234	16.36 N	94.13 W
Elbe	224	46.45 N	121.49 W
Elbe (Labe) ≃	30	53.50 N	9.00 E
Elbe, Île d' → Elba, Isola di I	66	42.46 N	10.17 E
Elbe-Havel-Kanal ≊	54	52.24 N	12.23 E
El Beïd (Ebeji) ≃	146	12.32 N	14.11 E
El-Beida → Al-Bayḍā'	146	32.46 N	21.43 E
Elbe-Lübeck-Kanal ≊	54	53.50 N	10.36 E
Elberfeld ◆[8]	263	51.16 N	7.08 E
Elbert	198	39.13 N	104.32 W
Elbert, Mount ∧	200	39.07 N	106.27 W
Elberta	190	44.37 N	86.13 W
Elberton	192	34.06 N	82.52 W
Elbeuf	50	49.17 N	1.00 E
Elbeyli	130	36.41 N	37.26 E
El Beyyadh	148	33.40 N	1.01 E
Elbing → Elbląg	30	54.10 N	19.25 E
Elbingerode	54	51.45 N	10.46 E
Elbistan	130	38.13 N	37.12 E
Elbląg (Elbing)	30	54.10 N	19.25 E
Elbląg □[4]	30	54.00 N	19.30 E
El Bluff	236	11.59 N	83.40 W
El Bolsón	254	41.58 S	71.31 W
El Bonillo	34	38.57 N	2.32 W
El-Borj	34	35.43 N	5.40 W
El-Borouj	148	32.30 N	7.10 W
El Bosque, Chile	286e	33.34 S	70.41 W
El Bosque, Méx.	234	17.04 N	92.44 W
El Boulaïda	148	36.28 N	2.50 E
El Boulaïda □[5]	148	36.20 N	2.20 E
Elbow	184	51.07 N	106.35 W
Elbow ≃	182	51.03 N	114.02 W
Elbow Cay I	238	23.57 N	80.29 W
Elbow Lake	198	45.59 N	95.58 W
Elbow Lake ⊜	184	54.50 N	100.53 W
Elbridge	210	43.02 N	76.27 W
El'brus, gora (Mount Elbrus) ∧	84	43.21 N	42.26 E
Elbrus, Mount → El'brus, gora ∧	84	43.21 N	42.26 E
El'brusskij	84	43.38 N	42.10 E
Elbsandsteingebirge ⋀	54	50.50 N	14.20 E
Elburg	52	52.26 N	5.50 E
El Burgo de Osma	34	41.35 N	3.04 W
Elburn	216	41.53 N	88.28 W
Elburz Mountains → Alborz, Reshteh-ye Kūhhā-ye ⋀	128	36.00 N	53.00 E
El'buzd	83	46.53 N	39.41 E
El'buzd ≃	83	46.53 N	39.43 E
El Cabezo, Arrecife ✣[2]	234	19.04 N	95.51 W
El Caburé	252	26.01 S	62.22 W
El Caimanero, Laguna ⊂	234	23.00 N	106.07 W
El Cajon	228	32.47 N	116.57 W
El Cajón, Embalse ⊜[1]	236	15.00 N	87.35 W
El Calafate	254	50.20 S	72.18 W
El Callao	246	7.21 N	61.49 W
El Calvario, Col.	246	4.22 N	73.40 W
El Calvario, Ven.	246	8.59 N	67.00 W
El Calvario ◆[8]	286b	23.05 N	82.20 W
El Campamento	240m	18.22 N	66.28 W
El Campamento ◆[8]	266a	40.24 N	3.46 W
El Campo	222	29.11 N	96.16 W
El Capitan ∧, Ca., U.S.	226	37.43 N	119.38 W
El Capitan ∧, Mt., U.S.	202	46.01 N	114.23 W
El Caracol Depósito de Evaporación Solar ʊ[3]	286a	19.35 N	99.00 W
El Caribe	286c	10.37 N	66.50 W
El Carmen, Arg.	252	24.23 S	65.16 W
El Cármen, Bol.	248	18.49 S	58.33 W
El Carmen, Chile	286e	33.21 S	70.43 W
El Carmen, Col.	246	8.30 N	73.27 W
El Carmen, Méx.	234	15.35 N	93.05 W
El Carmen, Perú	248	13.30 S	76.04 W
El Carmen, Ven.	286c	10.24 N	67.01 W
El Carmen, Ven.	286c	10.24 N	66.50 W
El Carmen ≃	232	30.42 N	106.29 W
El Carmen, Canal ≊	286e	33.18 S	70.41 W
El Carmen, Laguna ⊂	234	18.17 N	93.48 W
El Carmen de Bolívar	246	9.43 N	75.08 W
El Carricito	232	28.24 N	103.23 W
El Carril	252	25.05 S	65.28 W
El Casco	196	25.34 N	104.35 W
El Castillo de La Concepción	236	11.01 N	84.24 W
El Cedral	236	16.26 N	90.03 W
El Cedrito	232	29.11 N	101.59 W
El Cenajo, Embalse de ⊜[1]	34	38.25 N	2.00 W
El Centinela	204	32.38 N	115.40 W
El Centinela, Cerro ∧	234	19.13 N	104.17 W
El Centro	204	32.47 N	115.33 W
El Cerrito, Col.	246	3.42 N	76.19 W
El Cerrito, Ca., U.S.	226	37.54 N	122.18 W
El Cerrito, Ca., U.S.	228	37.54 N	122.18 W
El Cerro, Bol.	248	17.31 S	61.34 W
El Cerro, Ur.	258	34.00 S	58.15 W
El Cerro Del Aripo ∧	241r	10.43 N	61.15 W
El Chamal	234	23.56 N	97.54 W
El Chante	234	19.41 N	104.10 W
Elche de la Sierra	34	38.27 N	2.03 W
Elche → Elx	34	38.15 N	0.42 W
El Chichonal, Volcán ∧[1]	234	17.22 N	93.14 W
El Chile, Montaña ∧	236	14.22 N	86.51 W
El'chkakvun ≃	180	68.42 N	171.00 E
Elcho	190	45.26 N	89.11 W
Elcho Island I	164	11.55 S	135.45 E
El Chorrillo	252	33.18 S	66.16 W
El Ciprés	204	31.50 N	116.38 W
El Cobre	240p	20.03 N	75.57 W
El Cocuy	246	6.25 N	72.27 W
El Cojo	286c	10.37 N	66.53 W
El Cojo, Quebrada ≃	286c	10.37 N	66.53 W
El Colorado	252	26.18 S	59.22 W
El Cóndor, Cerro ∧	252	26.38 S	68.22 W
El Congo	236	13.54 N	89.30 W
El Corazón	246	1.12 S	79.06 W
El Corcovado	254	43.32 S	71.36 W
El Corozo	286c	10.35 N	66.58 W
El Corpus	236	13.16 N	87.03 W
El Corte ≃	234	17.03 N	94.54 W
El Corte de Madera Creek ≃	282	37.19 N	122.20 W
El Cortijo	286e	33.22 S	70.42 W
El Coto	240m	18.28 N	66.44 W
El Coyote	200	30.50 N	112.40 W
El Coyote ≃	232	30.32 N	113.02 W
El Coyote, Laguna ⊜	196	27.14 N	103.18 W
El Cozón	232	31.18 N	112.29 W
El Cristo	240p	20.07 N	75.45 W
El Cubo → Casigua	246	8.46 N	72.30 W
El Cuco	236	13.10 N	88.07 W
El Cuervo, Laguna ⊜	232	29.17 N	105.57 W
El Cuidado	234	22.20 N	103.07 W
El Cuy	254	39.56 S	68.20 W
Elda	34	38.29 N	0.47 W
Eldagsen	52	52.10 N	9.40 E
El Dambahaddo	144	3.17 N	46.40 E
El Dátil	232	30.07 N	112.15 W
Elde ≃	54	53.14 N	11.27 E
Eldekanal ≊	54	53.24 N	11.36 E
Eldena, Dtsch.	54	53.13 N	11.25 E
Eldena, Dtsch.	54	54.05 N	13.26 E
El Der ∨	144	8.49 N	47.28 E
El Dere	144	5.07 N	43.10 E
Elder Island I	276	40.38 N	73.23 W
Elder Mills	275b	43.49 N	79.38 W
Eldersville	214	40.21 N	80.29 W
Elderton	214	40.42 N	79.21 W
El Descanso	204	32.12 N	116.55 W
El Desemboque, Méx.	232	29.30 N	112.27 W
El Desemboque, Méx.	232	30.30 N	112.59 W
Eldforsen	40	60.26 N	14.13 E
El'dikan	74	60.48 N	135.11 E
Eldingen	52	52.41 N	10.21 E
Eld Inlet ⊂	224	47.04 N	123.01 W
Eldivan	130	40.32 N	33.31 E
El Diviso	246	1.22 N	78.14 W
El Djazaïr (Algiers)	148	36.47 N	3.03 E
El Djazaïr □[5]	148	36.50 N	3.00 E
El Djelfa	148	34.40 N	3.15 E
El Djelfa □[5]	148	35.20 N	3.50 E
El Doce	234	17.13 N	94.03 W
Eldon, Ia., U.S.	190	40.55 N	92.13 W
Eldon, Mo., U.S.	194	38.20 N	92.34 W
Eldon Hazlet State Park ♦	219	38.39 N	89.22 W
Eldora, Ia., U.S.	190	42.21 N	93.05 W
Eldora, Pa., U.S.	279b	40.10 N	79.53 W
Eldorado, Arg.	252	26.24 S	54.38 W
Eldorado, Bra.	252	24.32 S	48.06 W
El Dorado, Méx.	232	24.17 N	107.21 W
El Dorado, Ar., U.S.	194	33.12 N	92.39 W
El Dorado, Ca., U.S.	226	38.41 N	120.51 W
Eldorado, Il., U.S.	194	37.48 N	88.26 W
El Dorado, Ks., U.S.	198	37.49 N	96.51 W
Eldorado, Oh., U.S.	218	39.54 N	84.40 W
Eldorado, Ok., U.S.	196	34.28 N	99.38 W
Eldorado, Tx., U.S.	196	30.51 N	100.36 W
El Dorado, Ven.	246	6.44 N	61.38 W
El Dorado □[6]	226	38.43 N	120.48 W
Eldorado Hills	226	38.37 N	120.27 W
Eldoradopark	273d	26.18 S	27.53 E
El Dorado Park ♦	280	33.49 N	118.05 W
Eldorado Peak ∧	224	48.32 N	121.08 W
El Dorado Springs	194	37.52 N	94.01 W
Eldoret	154	0.31 N	35.17 E
Eldred, Il., U.S.	219	39.17 N	90.33 W
Eldred, N.Y., U.S.	210	41.32 N	74.53 W
Eldred, Pa., U.S.	214	41.57 N	78.23 W
Eldridge	190	41.39 N	90.35 W
Eldridge, Mount ∧	180	64.46 N	141.48 W
Eldridges Hill	285	39.40 N	75.18 W
El Dudu	144	2.37 N	41.46 E
El Durazno, Arroyo ≃	258	34.41 S	58.52 W
Eleanor	188	38.32 N	81.55 W
Eleanor, Lake ⊜[1]	226	37.59 N	119.51 W
Eleasar	158	26.40 S	26.53 E
Electra	196	34.01 N	98.55 W
Electric City	202	47.56 N	119.02 W
Eleele	229b	21.55 N	159.35 W
Elefante, Isla del → Elephant Island I	9	61.10 S	55.14 W
Elefantes, Estero ⊂[2]	254	46.10 S	73.41 W
Elefantes, Rio dos (Olifants) ≃	156	24.10 S	32.40 E
Elegest ≃	88	51.32 N	94.05 E
El Eglab ◆[2]	148	26.25 N	5.00 W
Elei, Wādī ∨	140	22.04 N	34.27 E
Eleja	76	56.26 N	23.42 E
Elektrogorsk	82	55.53 N	38.47 E
Elektrostal'	82	55.47 N	38.28 E
Elektrougli	82	55.43 N	38.13 E
Elektrozavod	80	52.34 N	54.01 E
Elele	150	5.07 N	6.48 E
Elena	38	42.56 N	25.53 E
El Encantado	286c	10.27 N	66.47 W
El Encanto, Col.	246	1.37 S	73.14 W
El Encanto, Guat.	232	17.17 N	89.34 W
Elend	54	51.44 N	10.41 E
Elepete	273a	6.41 N	3.28 E
Elephant, Mount ∧[2]	169	37.58 S	143.12 E
Elephanta Caves ⫫[5]	272c	18.58 N	72.56 E
Elephanta Island (Ghārāpuri) I	272c	18.57 N	72.55 E
Elephant Butte Lake State Park ♦	200	33.11 N	107.14 W
Elephant Butte Reservoir ⊜[1]	200	33.19 N	107.10 W
Elephant Island I	9	61.10 S	55.14 W
Elephant Lake ⊜	212	45.08 N	78.07 W
Elephant Mountain ∧	188	44.46 N	70.46 W
Elesbão Veloso	250	6.13 S	42.08 W
Eleşkirt	130	39.48 N	42.42 E
El Espinal	234	16.29 N	95.03 W
El Estor	236	15.32 N	89.21 W
Elets → Jelec	76	52.37 N	38.30 E
El Eulma	148	36.08 N	5.40 E
Eleusis → Elevsís	38	38.02 N	23.32 E
Eleutério	256	22.19 S	46.43 W
Eleutero ≃	70	38.06 N	13.29 E
Eleuthera I	238	25.10 N	76.14 W
Eleuthera Point ≻	238	24.40 N	76.11 W
Eleva	190	44.34 N	91.28 W
Eleven Point ≃	194	36.09 N	91.05 W
Elevsínos, Kólpos ⊂	267c	38.02 N	23.34 E
Elevsís	38	38.02 N	23.32 E
Elevtheroúpolis	38	40.55 N	24.16 E
El Fahs	36	36.22 N	9.55 E
El Faro, It.	71	40.36 N	8.13 E
El Faro, P.R.	240m	18.00 N	66.47 W
Elfenbeinküste → Ivory Coast □[1]	150	8.00 N	5.00 W
El Ferrol del Caudillo	34	43.29 N	8.14 W
Elfers	220	28.13 N	82.43 W
Elfgen	263	51.05 N	6.32 E
Elfin Cove	180	58.12 N	136.20 W
Elfrida	200	31.41 N	109.41 W
Elfros	184	51.43 N	103.52 W
El Fud	144	7.20 N	42.50 E
El Fuerte	232	26.25 N	108.39 W
El Galpón	252	25.23 S	64.38 W
Elgershausen	56	51.16 N	9.22 E
El Ghazawet	148	35.06 N	1.51 W
Elgin, Austl.	168a	33.31 S	115.37 E
Elgin, On., Can.	212	44.36 N	76.13 W
Elgin, Scot., U.K.	46	57.39 N	3.20 W
Elgin, Il., U.S.	216	42.02 N	88.16 W
Elgin, Ia., U.S.	190	42.57 N	91.37 W
Elgin, Mn., U.S.	190	44.07 N	92.15 W
Elgin, Ne., U.S.	198	41.59 N	98.05 W
Elgin, N.D., U.S.	198	46.24 N	101.50 W
Elgin, Oh., U.S.	216	40.44 N	84.28 W
Elgin, Ok., U.S.	196	34.46 N	98.17 W
Elgin, Or., U.S.	202	45.33 N	117.54 W
Elgin, Pa., U.S.	214	41.54 N	79.45 W
Elgin, Tx., U.S.	222	30.20 N	97.22 W
Elgin □[6]	214	42.42 N	81.15 W
Elgin, Lake ⊜	206	45.45 N	71.20 W
Elgol	46	57.09 N	6.06 W
El Golfete ⊜	236	15.44 N	88.53 W
El Goloso ◆[8]	266a	40.33 N	3.42 W
Elgon, Mount ∧	154	1.08 N	34.33 E
Elgoras, gora ∧	24	68.06 N	31.30 E
El Granada	226	37.30 N	122.28 W
El Grara	148	32.46 N	4.34 E
El Grove	34	42.30 N	8.52 W
El Grullo	234	19.48 N	104.13 W
El Guaje	232	27.52 N	103.18 W
El Guaje, Laguna ⊜	232	28.00 N	103.13 W
El Guamo	246	10.02 N	74.59 W
El Guanábano	286c	10.24 N	67.01 W
El Guapo	246	10.09 N	65.58 W
El Guarapo	286c	10.36 N	66.58 W
El Guayabo de Abajo	232	26.00 N	107.26 W
El Guayaneco, Parque Nacional ♦	254	48.15 S	75.30 W
El'gygytgyn, ozero ⊜	180	67.30 N	172.00 E
El Hadjar	36	36.48 N	7.45 E
Elham	42	51.10 N	1.07 E
El Ḥammâmi ◆[1]	148	23.03 N	11.30 W
El Hank ⫫[4]	148	24.30 N	7.00 W
El Haouaria	36	37.03 N	11.02 E
El Hatillo	286c	10.26 N	66.49 W
El Hatillo, Quebrada ≃	286c	10.27 N	66.47 W
El Havre → Le Havre	50	49.30 N	0.08 E
El Higo	234	21.46 N	98.28 W
Elhovo	38	42.10 N	26.34 E
El Huecú	252	37.37 S	70.36 W
El Huisache	234	22.55 N	100.25 W
Eliase	164	8.21 S	130.47 E
Elías Romero	258	34.46 S	58.52 W
Eliasville	196	32.57 N	98.46 W
Elida, N.M., U.S.	196	33.56 N	103.39 W
Elida, Oh., U.S.	216	40.47 N	84.12 W
El Ídolo, Isla I	234	21.25 N	97.27 W
El Idrissia	148	34.30 N	2.37 E
Elila	154	2.43 S	25.53 E
Elila ≃	154	2.45 S	25.53 E
Elim, Namibia	156	17.48 S	15.31 E
Elim, S. Afr.	158	34.35 S	19.45 E
Elim, Ak., U.S.	180	64.37 N	162.15 W
Elimsport	210	41.08 N	77.02 W
El Infiernillo, Canal ʮ	232	29.09 N	112.15 W
Elingampangu	152	2.03 S	24.02 E
Elin Pelin	38	42.40 N	23.36 E
Eliot	188	43.09 N	70.48 W
Elipa	152	0.53 S	24.34 E
Elisabeth-Sophien-Koog	41	54.30 N	8.53 E
Élisabethville	261	48.58 N	1.51 E
Élisabethville → Lubumbashi	154	11.40 S	27.28 E
Elisenvaara	24	61.25 N	29.46 E
Eliseu Martins	250	8.13 S	43.42 W
Elista	80	46.16 N	44.14 E
Elizabeth, Austl.	168b	34.43 S	138.40 E
Elizabeth, Co., U.S.	200	39.21 N	104.35 W
Elizabeth, Il., U.S.	190	42.19 N	90.13 W
Elizabeth, La., U.S.	194	30.52 N	92.47 W
Elizabeth, N.J., U.S.	210	40.39 N	74.12 W
Elizabeth, Pa., U.S.	214	40.16 N	79.53 W
Elizabeth, W.V., U.S.	188	39.03 N	81.23 W
Elizabeth ≃, N.J., U.S.	276	40.38 N	74.12 W
Elizabeth ≃, Va., U.S.	208	36.54 N	76.20 W
Elizabeth, Bahía ⊂	246a	0.38 S	91.27 W
Elizabeth, Cape ≻	224	47.22 N	124.22 W
Elizabeth, Lake ⊜[1]	282	37.33 N	121.58 W
Elizabeth, West Branch ≃	276	40.42 N	74.14 W
Elizabeth Bay ⊂	156	27.04 S	15.11 E
Elizabeth City	192	36.18 N	76.13 W
Elizabeth Creek ≃	222	33.02 N	97.14 W
Elizabeth Islands II	207	41.27 N	70.47 W
Elizabeth Lake ⊜	281	42.38 N	83.23 W
Elizabeth Lake Estates	281	42.38 N	83.22 W
Elizabeth Park ♦	281	42.07 N	83.11 W
Elizabeth Reef I[1]	160	29.56 S	159.04 E
Elizabethton	192	36.20 N	82.12 W
Elizabethtown, Il., U.S.	194	37.26 N	88.18 W
Elizabethtown, In., U.S.	218	39.08 N	85.48 W
Elizabethtown, Ky., U.S.	194	37.41 N	85.51 W
Elizabethtown, N.Y., U.S.	188	44.12 N	73.35 W
Elizabethtown, N.C., U.S.	192	34.37 N	78.36 W
Elizabethtown, Pa., U.S.	208	40.09 N	76.36 W
Elizabethville	208	40.32 N	76.48 W
Eliza Howell Park ♦	281	42.24 N	83.16 W
Elizaville, In., U.S.	218	40.08 N	86.24 W
Elizaville, N.Y., U.S.	210	42.03 N	73.48 W
El-Jadida (Mazagan)	148	33.16 N	8.30 W
El-Jadida □[4]	148	33.00 N	8.40 W
El Jaralito	232	26.07 N	104.10 W
El Jebel	200	39.23 N	107.05 W
El-Jebha	34	35.13 N	4.38 W
El Jem	148	35.18 N	10.43 E
El Jícaro ≃	236	13.31 N	86.00 W
El Jobean	220	26.58 N	82.13 W
El Juile	234	17.45 N	94.59 W
Ełk	30	53.50 N	22.22 E
Elk □[6]	214	41.26 N	78.43 W
Elk ≃, Ab., Can.	182	52.55 N	115.40 W
Elk ≃, B.C., Can.	182	49.10 N	115.14 W
Ełk ≃, Pol.	30	53.31 N	22.47 E
Elk ≃, U.S.	194	34.46 N	87.16 W
Elk ≃, Co., U.S.	200	40.29 N	106.58 W
Elk ≃, Ks., U.S.	198	37.15 N	95.41 W
Elk ≃, Mn., U.S.	190	45.18 N	93.34 W
Elk ≃, Mo., U.S.	194	36.38 N	94.38 W
Elk ≃, W.V., U.S.	188	38.21 N	81.38 W
Elk ≃, Wi., U.S.	190	45.42 N	90.37 W
Elkader	190	42.51 N	91.24 W
El Kantara	148	33.41 N	10.55 E
El-Karafab	140	18.10 N	31.36 E
Elk Bayou ≃	226	36.06 N	119.24 W
Elk City	196	35.24 N	99.24 W
Elk City Lake ⊜[1]	198	37.15 N	95.55 W
Elk Creek	204	39.36 N	122.32 W
Elk Creek ≃, Ok., U.S.	196	34.48 N	99.09 W
Elk Creek ≃, Or., U.S.	202	43.38 N	123.34 W
Elk Creek ≃, Pa., U.S.	214	42.01 N	80.22 W
Elk Creek ≃, S.D., U.S.	198	44.15 N	102.22 W
Elk Creek ≃, Wa., U.S.	224	46.38 N	123.17 W
Elkedra ≃	162	21.08 S	136.22 E
El Kef	148	36.11 N	8.43 E
El Kef □[8]	148	36.00 N	9.00 E
El-Kelâa-des-Srarhna	148	32.02 N	7.23 W
El-Kelâa-des-Srarhna □[4]	148	32.05 N	7.30 W
El Kere	144	5.51 N	42.06 E
El Kerma	34	35.36 N	0.35 W
Elk Grove	226	38.24 N	121.22 W
Elk Grove Village	278	42.00 N	87.58 W
Elkhart, Il., U.S.	219	40.01 N	89.29 W
Elkhart, In., U.S.	216	41.40 N	85.58 W
Elkhart, Ks., U.S.	198	37.00 N	101.53 W
Elkhart, Tx., U.S.	222	31.38 N	95.35 W
Elkhart □[6]	216	41.35 N	85.50 W
Elkhart ≃	216	41.41 N	85.58 W
Elkhart Lake	190	43.50 N	88.01 W
El Khaṭṭ ⫫[4]	148	22.40 N	10.05 W
Elkhead Creek ≃	200	40.31 N	107.26 W
Elkhead Mountains ⋀	200	40.50 N	107.05 W
Elk Hills ⋀[2]	226	35.15 N	119.25 W
El Khnâchîch ⫫[4]	148	21.50 N	3.45 W
Elkhorn, Mb., Can.	184	49.58 N	101.14 W
Elk Horn, Ia., U.S.	198	41.35 N	95.03 W
Elkhorn, Wi., U.S.	216	42.40 N	88.32 W
Elkhorn ≃	198	41.07 N	96.19 W
Elkhorn City	192	37.18 N	82.21 W
Elkhorn Creek ≃, Ky., U.S.	218	38.19 N	84.52 W
Elkhorn Creek ≃, Mo., U.S.	219	39.05 N	91.20 W
Elkhorn Mountain ∧	182	49.48 N	125.50 W
Elkin	192	36.14 N	80.50 W
Elkins	188	38.55 N	79.50 W
Elkins Park	208	40.04 N	75.07 W
Elk Island I	184	50.45 N	96.32 W
Elk Island National Park ♦	182	53.37 N	112.45 W
Elkland	210	41.59 N	77.18 W
Elk Mills	208	39.39 N	75.49 W
Elk Mountain	200	41.41 N	106.24 W
Elk Mountain ∧, Wa., U.S.	224	46.08 N	122.28 W
Elk Mountain ∧, Wy., U.S.	200	41.38 N	106.32 W
Elk Neck ≻[1]	208	39.35 N	75.55 W
Elk Neck State Park ♦	208	39.30 N	75.58 W
Elko, B.C., Can.	182	49.18 N	115.07 W
Elko, Nv., U.S.	204	40.49 N	115.45 W
El Kouif	36	35.29 N	8.19 E
Elk Peak ∧	202	46.27 N	110.46 W
Elk Plain	224	47.04 N	122.24 W
Elk Point, Ab., Can.	182	53.54 N	110.54 W
Elk Point, S.D., U.S.	198	42.41 N	96.41 W
Elk Rapids	190	44.53 N	85.24 W
El Krib	36	36.19 N	9.09 E
Elkridge	284b	39.12 N	76.42 W
Elk River, Id., U.S.	202	46.47 N	116.10 W
Elk River, Mn., U.S.	190	45.18 N	93.35 W
Elk River ⊂	208	39.31 N	75.55 W
El Kseur	34	36.46 N	4.49 E
Elk State Park ♦	214	41.38 N	78.34 W
Elkton, Ky., U.S.	194	36.48 N	87.09 W
Elkton, Md., U.S.	208	39.36 N	75.50 W
Elkton, Mi., U.S.	190	43.49 N	83.10 W
Elkton, Oh., U.S.	214	40.46 N	80.42 W
Elkton, S.D., U.S.	198	44.14 N	96.28 W
Elkton, Va., U.S.	188	38.24 N	78.37 W
El Kure	144	5.41 N	42.21 E
Elkville	194	37.54 N	89.14 W
Ell, Lake ⊜	162	29.13 S	127.46 E
Ellamar	180	60.54 N	146.42 W
Elland	262	53.41 N	1.50 W
Ellard Lake ⊜	184	54.33 N	91.55 W
Ellás → Greece □[1]	38	39.00 N	22.00 E
Ellavalla	162	25.05 S	114.22 E
Ellaville	192	32.14 N	84.18 W
Ellefeld	54	50.29 N	12.23 E
Ellef Ringnes Island I	16	78.30 N	104.00 W
El Leh	144	3.48 N	39.48 E
Elleker	162	35.00 S	117.43 E
Ellemandsbjerg ∧[2]	41	56.07 N	10.32 E
Ellen ≃	44	54.43 N	3.30 W
Ellen, Mount ∧	200	38.07 N	110.49 W
Ellen Brook ≃	168a	31.48 S	116.00 E
Ellendale, Austl.	162	17.56 S	124.48 E
Ellendale, De., U.S.	208	38.48 N	75.25 W
Ellendale, Mn., U.S.	190	43.52 N	93.18 W
Ellendale, N.D., U.S.	198	46.00 N	98.31 W
Ellensburg	202	46.59 N	120.32 W
Ellenton, Fl., U.S.	220	27.31 N	82.31 W
Ellenton, Ga., U.S.	192	31.10 N	83.35 W
Ellenville	210	41.43 N	74.23 W
Eller ◆[8]	263	51.12 N	6.51 E
Ellerbe	192	35.04 N	79.46 W
Ellero ≃	62	44.27 N	7.54 E
Ellerspring ∧[2]	56	49.55 N	7.37 E
Ellès	36	35.57 N	9.06 E
Ellesmere	42	52.54 N	2.54 W
Ellesmere, Lake ⊂	172	43.48 S	172.25 E
Ellesmere Island I	16	81.00 N	80.00 W
Ellesmere Park	262	53.29 N	2.20 W
Ellesmere Port	262	53.17 N	2.54 W
Ellesmere Port □[8]	262	53.18 N	2.47 W
Ellettsville	194	39.14 N	86.37 W
Ellewoutsdijk	52	51.24 N	3.49 E
Ellezelles	50	50.44 N	3.41 E
Ellice ≃	176	68.02 N	103.26 W
Ellice Islands → Tuvalu □[1]	14	8.00 S	178.00 E
Ellichpur → Achalpur	120	21.16 N	77.31 E
Ellicott City	208	39.16 N	76.47 W
Ellicott Creek ≃	210	43.01 N	78.53 W
Ellicott Creek Park ♦	284a	43.01 N	78.50 W
Ellicottville	210	42.16 N	78.40 W
Ellijay	192	34.41 N	84.28 W
El Limón, Méx.	234	18.05 N	101.59 W
El Limón, Méx.	234	19.49 N	104.11 W
El Limoncito	286c	10.29 N	66.47 W
El Limón de Teachi	232	24.43 N	107.08 W
Ellingen	56	49.04 N	10.58 E
Ellinger	222	29.50 N	96.44 W
Ellinghorst ◆[8]	263	51.34 N	6.57 E
Ellington, Eng., U.K.	44	55.13 N	1.34 W
Ellington, Ct., U.S.	207	41.54 N	72.28 W
Ellington, Mo., U.S.	194	37.14 N	90.58 W
Ellington, N.Y., U.S.	214	42.13 N	79.07 W
Elliniko International Airport ⊠	267c	37.54 N	23.44 E
Ellinikón	267c	37.53 N	23.44 E
Ellinwood	198	38.21 N	98.34 W
Elliot	158	31.18 S	27.50 E
Elliot, Mount ∧	166	19.29 S	146.58 E
Elliotdale	158	31.55 S	28.38 E
Elliotganj	126	23.31 N	90.52 E
Elliot Lake	190	46.23 N	82.39 W
Elliot Lake ⊜	184	52.55 N	95.20 W
Elliott, Austl.	162	17.33 S	133.32 E
Elliott, Il., U.S.	216	40.28 N	88.16 W
Elliott, Ia., U.S.	198	41.09 N	95.10 W
Elliott, Ms., U.S.	194	33.36 N	89.45 W
Elliott □[6]	218	38.13 N	83.10 W
Elliott, Mount ∧	162	20.29 S	126.37 E
Elliott Bay ⊂	224	47.36 N	122.22 W
Elliott Key I	220	25.27 N	80.11 W
Elliottville	218	38.11 N	83.16 W
Ellis	198	38.56 N	99.33 W
Ellis □[6]	222	32.20 N	96.48 W
Ellisburg	212	43.44 N	76.08 W
Ellis Island I	276	40.42 N	74.02 W
Ellis Mountain ∧	224	48.10 N	124.19 W
Ellison Creek Reservoir ⊜[1]	222	32.56 N	94.43 W
Ellisport	224	47.25 N	122.26 W
Ellisras	156	23.40 S	27.46 E
Elliston, Austl.	162	33.39 S	134.55 E
Elliston, Nf., Can.	186	48.38 N	53.03 W
Elliston, Mt., U.S.	202	46.33 N	112.25 W
Ellisville, Ms., U.S.	194	31.36 N	89.11 W
Ellisville, Mo., U.S.	219	38.35 N	90.35 W
Ellmau	64	47.31 N	12.18 E
Ellmauer Halt ∧	64	47.34 N	12.18 E
Ellon	46	57.22 N	2.05 W
Ellora	122	20.01 N	75.10 E
Elloree	192	33.31 N	80.34 W
Ellore → Elūru	122	16.42 N	81.06 E
Ellport	214	40.51 N	80.15 W
Ellrich	54	51.35 N	10.40 E
Ellsworth, Il., U.S.	216	40.27 N	88.43 W
Ellsworth, Ks., U.S.	198	38.43 N	98.13 W
Ellsworth, Me., U.S.	188	44.32 N	68.25 W
Ellsworth, Mi., U.S.	190	45.09 N	85.14 W
Ellsworth, Mn., U.S.	198	43.31 N	96.01 W
Ellsworth, Oh., U.S.	214	41.01 N	80.52 W
Ellsworth, Pa., U.S.	214	40.06 N	80.01 W
Ellsworth, Wa., U.S.	224	45.37 N	122.36 W
Ellsworth, Wi., U.S.	190	44.43 N	92.29 W
Ellsworth Air Force Base ■	198	44.08 N	103.05 W
Ellsworth Land ◆[1]	9	75.30 S	80.00 W
Ellsworth Mountains ⋀	9	79.00 S	85.00 W
El Lucero	196	25.53 N	103.25 W
Ellwangen	56	48.57 N	10.07 E
Ellwanger Berge ⋀[2]	56	49.00 N	10.15 E
Ellwood City	214	40.51 N	80.17 W
Elm, Dtsch.	52	53.31 N	9.12 E
Elm, Schw.	58	46.55 N	9.11 E

Symbol	English	Deutsch	Español	Français	Português
≃	River	Fluß	Río	Rivière	Rio
≊	Canal	Kanal	Canal	Canal	Canal
⌞	Waterfall, Rapids	Wasserfall, Stromschnellen	Cascada, Rápidos	Chute d'eau, Rapides	Cascata, Rápidos
ʮ	Strait	Meeresstraße	Estrecho	Détroit	Estreito
⊂	Bay, Gulf	Bucht, Golf	Bahía, Golfo	Baie, Golfe	Baía, Golfo
⊜	Lake, Lakes	See, Seen	Lago, Lagos	Lac, Lacs	Lago, Lagos
☷	Swamp	Sumpf	Pantano	Marais	Pântano
⊡	Ice Features, Glacier	Eis- und Gletscherformen	Accidentes Glaciales	Formes glaciaires	Acidentes glaciares
⊤	Other Hydrographic Features	Andere Hydrographische Objekte	Otros Elementos Hidrográficos	Autres données hydrographiques	Outros acidentes hidrográficos
✣	Submarine Features	Untermeerische Objekte	Accidentes Submarinos	Formes de relief sous-marin	Acidentes submarinos
□	Political Unit	Politische Einheit	Unidad Politica	Entité politique	Unidade política
ʊ	Cultural Institution	Kulturelle Institution	Institución Cultural	Institution culturelle	Instituição cultural
⊥	Historical Site	Historische Stätte	Sitio Histórico	Site historique	Sitio histórico
♦	Recreational Site	Erholungs- und Ferienort	Sitio de Recreo	Centre de loisirs	Area de Lazer
⊠	Airport	Flughafen	Aeropuerto	Aéroport	Aeroporto
■	Military Installation	Militäranlage	Instalación Militar	Installation militaire	Instalação militar
◆	Miscellaneous	Verschiedenes	Misceláneo	Divers	Diversos

Elm, Eng., U.K. 42 52.38 N 0.10 E
Elm ∧ 64 47.40 N 13.57 E
Elm ⋏[2] 54 52.09 N 10.53 E
Elm ≃, U.S. 198 45.36 N 98.19 W
Elm ≃, Il., U.S. 194 38.24 N 88.14 W
Elm ≃, N.D., U.S. 198 47.15 N 96.50 W
Elma, Ia., U.S. 190 43.14 N 92.26 W
Elma, N.Y., U.S. 210 42.51 N 78.38 W
Elma, Wa., U.S. 224 47.00 N 123.24 W
El Macero 226 38.33 N 121.41 W
El Machorro, Punta › 200 31.03 N 114.51 W
Elmadağ (Küçükyozgat) 130 39.55 N 33.15 E
Elmadağ ∧ 130 39.49 N 33.00 E
El Mahia ◆[1] 148 22.30 N 2.30 W
El Maitén 254 42.03 S 71.10 W
El Malah 34 35.24 N 1.05 W
Elmalı 130 36.44 N 29.56 E
Elmalı Bendi ◆[6] 267b 41.04 N 29.06 E
El Maneadero 232 31.45 N 116.35 W
El Manteco 246 7.27 N 62.32 W
El Marsa el Kebir 148 35.45 N 0.43 W
Elmas 71 39.16 N 9.03 E
Elmas, Aeroporto di ✈ 71 39.14 N 9.03 E
Elmas Burnu › 267b 41.13 N 29.13 E
El Masnou 266d 41.29 N 2.19 E
Elmaton 222 28.53 N 96.09 W
El Mayoco 254 42.39 S 70.59 W
Elmbridge ▫[8] 260 51.22 N 0.23 W
Elm Brook ≃ 283 42.29 N 71.16 W
Elm City 192 35.48 N 77.51 W
Elm Creek, Mb., Can. 184 49.41 N 98.00 W
Elm Creek, Ne., U.S. 198 40.43 N 99.22 W
Elm Creek ≃, Mn., U.S. 198 43.45 N 94.11 W
Elm Creek ≃, S.D., U.S. 198 44.21 N 102.42 W
Elm Creek ≃, Tx., U.S. 196 28.54 N 100.12 W
Elm Creek ≃, Tx., U.S. 196 32.40 N 99.41 W
Elm Creek ≃, Tx., U.S. 196 33.12 N 98.50 W
Elm Creek ≃, Tx., U.S. 222 29.15 N 97.32 W
El Meco 234 22.35 N 99.20 W
El Médano 232 24.25 N 111.30 W
Elmen 58 47.20 N 10.32 E
El Menia 148 30.30 N 2.50 E
Elmer 208 39.35 N 75.10 W
El Mghayyar 148 33.55 N 5.58 E
Elm Grove 216 43.02 N 88.04 W
Elmhurst, Austl. 169 37.11 S 143.15 E
Elmhurst, Il., U.S. 216 41.53 N 87.56 W
Elmhurst, Pa., U.S. 210 41.22 N 75.32 W
Elmhurst ◆[8] 276 40.44 N 73.53 W
El Mijao 286c 10.23 N 66.48 W
El Milagro 252 31.01 S 65.59 W
El Miliyya 148 36.48 N 6.14 E
El Mimbre 196 25.40 N 102.20 W
Elmina 150 5.05 N 1.21 W
El Minao 240m 18.22 N 66.05 W
Elmira, On., Can. 212 43.36 N 80.33 W
Elmira, P.E., Can. 186 46.27 N 62.04 W
Elmira, Ca., U.S. 226 38.21 N 121.55 W
Elmira, N.Y., U.S. 210 42.05 N 76.48 W
El Mirador ∧ 234 19.25 N 98.42 W
El Mirage 200 33.36 N 112.19 W
El Mirage Lake ⊜ 228 34.38 N 117.35 W
Elmira Heights 210 42.07 N 76.49 W
Elm Mott 222 31.40 N 97.06 W
Elmo, Mt., U.S. 182 47.49 N 114.20 W
Elmo, Tx., U.S. 222 32.43 N 96.10 W
El Mochito 236 14.49 N 88.06 W
El Mohammadia 148 35.33 N 0.03 E
El Molinillo 34 39.28 N 4.13 W
Elmont, N.Y., U.S. 276 40.42 N 73.42 W
Elmont, Va., U.S. 208 37.42 N 77.29 W
El Monte, Chile 252 33.41 S 71.01 W
El Monte, Ca., U.S. 228 34.04 N 118.01 W
El Monte Airport ✈ 280 34.06 N 118.02 W
Elmora 214 40.36 N 78.45 W
El Moral 196 28.51 N 100.39 W
Elmore, Austl. 166 36.30 S 144.37 E
Elmore, Mn., U.S. 190 43.30 N 94.05 W
Elmore, Oh., U.S. 214 41.28 N 83.17 W
Elmore City 196 34.37 N 97.23 W
El Morro I 240m 18.28 N 66.07 W
El Morro National Monument ♦ 200 35.05 N 108.22 W
Elm Point › 276 40.49 N 73.46 W
Elmpt 56 51.13 N 6.10 E
El Mreïti ⊽[4] 148 23.29 N 7.52 W
El Mreyyé ◆[1] 150 19.30 N 7.00 W
Elmschenhagen ◆[8] 54 54.18 N 10.12 E
Elmsdale 186 44.58 N 63.30 W
Elmsford 210 41.03 N 73.49 W
Elmshorn 52 53.45 N 9.39 E
Elm Springs 194 36.12 N 94.14 W
Elmsta 26 59.58 N 18.48 E
Elmstein 56 49.21 N 7.56 E
Elmswell 42 52.15 N 0.53 E
El Mulato 196 29.22 N 104.10 W
El Multe 232 17.41 N 91.24 W
Elmvale 212 44.35 N 79.52 W
Elmville 218 38.20 N 84.46 W
Elmwood, On., Can. 212 44.14 N 81.03 W
Elmwood, Il., U.S. 190 40.46 N 89.57 W
Elmwood, Md., U.S. 284b 39.21 N 76.32 W
Elmwood, Ma., U.S. 283 42.00 N 70.57 W
Elmwood, Ne., U.S. 198 40.50 N 96.17 W
Elmwood, Wi., U.S. 190 44.46 N 92.08 W
Elmwood ◆[8] 285 39.56 N 75.14 W
Elmwood Park, Il., U.S. 216 41.55 N 87.48 W
Elmwood Park, N.J., U.S. 276 40.54 N 74.07 W
Elmwood Park, Wi., U.S. 216 42.41 N 87.50 W
Elmwood Park ♦ 285 40.08 N 75.21 W
El Naranjo ≃ 234 18.41 N 103.45 W
El Naranjo de Chila 234 18.55 N 102.28 W
Elne 32 42.36 N 2.58 E
El Negralejo 266a 40.24 N 3.31 W
El Negrito 236 15.19 N 87.41 W
El Nido, Pil. 116 11.11 N 119.23 E
El Nido, Ca., U.S. 226 37.08 N 120.29 W
El Nihuil 252 35.02 S 68.40 W
El Niybo 144 4.32 N 39.59 E
El Nopal, Cerro ∧ 232 28.15 N 107.36 W
Elnora, Ab., Can. 182 51.59 N 113.12 W
Elnora, In., U.S. 194 38.52 N 87.05 W
El Oasis 286c 10.35 N 66.59 W
El-Obeid → Al-Ubayyid 140 13.11 N 30.13 E
Elobey, Islas II 152 0.59 N 9.30 E
El Ocote, Cerro ∧ 232 25.58 N 106.08 W
Elogbatindi 152 3.27 N 10.08 E
Eloida, Lake ⊜ 212 44.40 N 75.58 W
Elói Mendes 256 21.37 S 45.34 W
Eloise 220 27.59 N 81.44 W
Elora, On., Can. 212 43.41 N 80.26 W
Elora, Tn., U.S. 194 35.00 N 86.21 W
El Oro ▫[4] 246 3.30 S 79.50 W
Elortondo 252 33.42 S 61.37 W
Elorza 246 7.03 N 69.31 W
El Otro Lado 286c 10.24 N 66.49 W
Eloy 200 32.45 N 111.33 W
Eloy Alfaro 246 2.12 S 79.50 W
Éloyes 58 48.06 N 6.37 E
El Pacayal 232 15.37 N 92.02 W
El Palmar, Bol. 248 21.54 S 63.39 W
El Palmar, Ven. 246 7.58 N 61.53 W
El Palmar, Ven. 286c 10.38 N 66.52 W
El Palomar 288 34.36 S 58.36 W
El Palomar, Base Aérea Militar ■ 288 34.37 S 58.37 W
El Palqui 252 30.45 S 70.59 W
El Pantanoso, Arroyo ≃ 288 34.47 S 58.40 W
El Pao, Ven. 246 8.01 N 62.38 W
El Pao, Ven. 246 9.38 N 68.08 W
El Papiol 266d 41.26 N 2.01 E
El Paraíso, Hond. 236 13.51 N 86.34 W
El Paraíso, Méx. 234 17.25 N 100.15 W
El Paraíso ▫[5] 236 14.10 N 86.30 W
El Pardo ◆[8] 266a 40.31 N 3.47 W
El Pardo, Embalse de ⊜[1] 266a 40.33 N 3.48 W
El Pardo, Monte de ⋏[2] 266a 40.33 N 3.48 W
El Paso, Il., U.S. 216 40.44 N 89.00 W
El Paso, Tx., U.S. 200 31.45 N 106.29 W
El Paso Creek ≃ 228 35.02 N 118.51 W
El Paso de Robles → Paso Robles 226 35.38 N 120.41 W
El Paso Peaks ⋏ 204 35.28 N 117.43 W
El Pauji 286c 10.26 N 66.49 W
El Pedregal ◆[8] 286c 10.30 N 66.51 W
El Peñón Blanco, Cerro ∧ 234 22.31 N 101.40 W
El Peñuelo 232 24.34 N 100.46 W
El Peral 286e 33.35 S 70.34 W
El Perú 246 7.19 N 61.49 W
El Pescadero, Laguna ⊂ 234 22.12 N 105.20 W
El Pescado, Arroyo ≃ 258 34.54 S 57.47 W
Elphin 48 53.51 N 8.12 W
Elphinstone 184 50.33 N 100.19 W
El Picacho, Cerro ∧ 234 20.40 N 100.43 W
El Pilar 246 10.32 N 63.09 W
El Pinar, Parque Nacional ♦ 286c 10.29 N 66.56 W
El Piñón 246 10.24 N 74.50 W
El Pintado 252 24.38 S 61.27 W
El Piojo, Arroyo ≃ 288 34.50 S 58.45 W
El Piquete 252 24.13 S 64.39 W
El Pital, Cerro ∧ 236 14.23 N 89.08 W
El Placer 234 23.33 N 106.10 W
El Planchón, Volcán ∧[1] 252 35.13 S 70.34 W
El Plantío ◆[8] 266a 40.28 N 3.49 W
El Plomo 200 31.15 N 112.04 W
El Polvorín 240m 18.26 N 66.17 W
El Pont de Segur 34 42.24 N 0.45 E
El Porcal 266a 40.18 N 3.32 W
El Portal, Ca., U.S. 226 37.40 N 119.46 W
El Portal, Fl., U.S. 220 25.51 N 80.11 W
El Port de Pollença 34 39.55 N 3.05 E
El Porvenir, Méx. 196 27.33 N 104.57 W
El Porvenir, Méx. 234 15.44 N 93.22 W
El Porvenir, Perú 248 8.05 S 79.00 W
El Potosí, Punta › 234 17.32 N 101.28 W
El Potrero 196 26.23 N 100.27 W
El Prat de Llobregat 34 41.20 N 2.06 E
El Progreso, Ec. 246a 0.54 S 89.33 W
El Progreso, Guat. 236 14.21 N 89.51 W
El Progreso, Hond. 236 15.21 N 87.49 W
El Progreso ▫[5] 236 14.50 N 90.00 W
El Puente del Arzobispo 34 39.48 N 5.10 W
El Puerto de Santa María 34 36.36 N 6.13 W
El Puesto 252 27.57 S 67.38 W
El Qala 148 36.50 N 8.30 E
El Qoll 148 37.00 N 6.34 E
El Quebrachal 252 25.17 S 64.04 W
El Quelite 232 23.32 N 106.28 W
Elquera Bushland ♦ 274a 33.42 S 151.04 E
Elqui ≃ 252 29.54 S 71.17 W
Elrama 214 40.15 N 79.55 W
El Ranchito 234 18.40 N 103.41 W
El Rastro 246 9.03 N 67.27 W
El Real de Santa María 246 8.08 N 77.43 W
El Recreo ◆[8] 286c 10.30 N 66.53 W
El Refugio 234 21.57 N 100.02 W
El Remolino 196 28.44 N 101.07 W
El Reno 196 35.31 N 97.57 W
El Rey, Parque Nacional ♦ 252 25.00 S 64.40 W
El Rio 228 34.13 N 119.10 W
El Rito 200 36.20 N 106.11 W
El Rito ≃ 200 36.12 N 106.14 W
El Roba 154 3.57 N 40.01 E
El Roble, Mesa ∧ 232 31.31 N 115.31 W
El Rom 132 33.11 N 35.46 E
El Rosario, Laguna ⊜ 234 17.52 N 93.48 W
El Rosarito 232 28.38 N 114.04 W
Elrose 184 51.13 N 108.01 W
Elroy 190 43.44 N 90.16 W
El Rucio 234 23.21 N 102.05 W
Elsa, Yk., Can. 180 63.55 N 135.28 W
Elsa, Tx., U.S. 196 26.17 N 97.59 W
Elsa ≃ 66 43.43 N 10.52 E
Elsah 219 38.57 N 90.22 W
El Sahuaro 200 31.05 N 112.55 W
El Salado 252 26.25 S 70.19 W
El Salado, Parque Nacional ♦ 246 2.12 S 80.00 W
El Salitre 246 1.50 S 79.48 W
El Salto, Méx. 234 23.47 N 105.22 W
El Salto, Méx. 234 20.32 N 103.11 W
El Salvador, Chile 252 26.17 S 69.43 W
El Salvador, Pil. 116 8.34 N 124.32 E
El Salvador ▫[1], N.A. 230 13.50 N 88.55 W
El Salvador ▫[1], N.A. 236 13.50 N 88.55 W
El Samán de Apure 246 7.55 N 68.44 W
El Sauce 240p 22.42 N 79.41 W
Elsass → Alsace ▫[9] 32 48.30 N 7.30 E
El Sauce, Laguna ⊜ 258 35.20 S 58.16 W
El Sauz 232 29.02 N 106.16 W
El Sauzal 232 31.54 N 116.41 W
Elsberry 219 39.10 N 91.32 W
Elsbethen 64 47.45 N 13.05 E
Elsburg 273d 26.15 S 28.12 E
Elsdorf, Dtsch. 52 53.14 N 9.20 E
Elsdorf, Dtsch. 56 50.54 N 6.34 E
El Seco, Laguna ⊜ 258 35.31 S 58.42 W
El Segundo 228 33.55 N 118.24 W
El Seibo 238 18.46 N 69.02 W
Elsen 52 51.44 N 8.39 E
Elsenham 42 51.55 N 0.14 E
Elsen Nur ⊜ 120 35.11 N 92.15 E
Elsenz ≃ 56 49.24 N 8.48 E
Elsey 166 15.02 S 133.07 E
Elsfleth 52 53.14 N 8.28 E
El Siasgo, Arroyo ≃ 258 35.33 S 58.33 W
Elsie, Mi., U.S. 216 43.05 N 84.23 W
Elsie, Or., U.S. 224 45.52 N 123.35 W
Elsinore 200 38.40 N 112.08 W
Elsinore, Lake ⊜[1] 228 33.39 N 117.21 W
Elsinore → Helsingør 41 56.02 N 12.37 E
El Sitio 286c 10.28 N 66.46 W
Elsmere, De., U.S. 208 39.44 N 75.35 W
Elsmere, Ky., U.S. 218 39.00 N 84.36 W
Elsmere, N.Y., U.S. 210 42.37 N 73.49 W
El Sobrante 226 37.58 N 122.17 W
El Socorro 246 8.59 N 65.44 W
El Sombrero 246 9.23 N 67.03 W
Elspark 273d 26.16 S 28.14 E
Elspeet 52 52.17 N 5.46 E
Elst 52 51.55 N 5.50 E
Elstal 54 52.32 N 12.59 E
Elstead 42 51.11 N 0.43 W
Elster 54 51.50 N 12.49 E
Elsterberg 54 50.36 N 12.10 E
Elstergebirge ⋏ 54 50.15 N 12.20 E
Elsterwerda 54 51.28 N 13.31 E
Elston, In., U.S. 216 40.22 N 86.55 W
Elston, Mo., U.S. 219 38.37 N 92.19 W
Elstra 54 51.13 N 14.08 E
Elstree 42 51.39 N 0.16 W
Elstree Aerodrome ✈ 260 51.39 N 0.19 W
El Sueco 232 29.54 N 106.24 W
El Tagarete, Cerro ∧ 232 26.31 N 105.56 W
El Tajín ⊥ 234 20.27 N 97.23 W
El Tala 252 26.07 S 65.17 W
El Talar 258 34.27 S 58.39 W
El Tamarindo 236 13.11 N 87.54 W
El Tambo, Col. 246 1.26 N 77.23 W
El Tambo, Perú 248 12.04 S 75.13 W
El Tanque 196 26.28 N 99.38 W
El Tapexcle 234 23.52 N 105.33 W
El Tarf 36 36.45 N 8.20 E
El Tecuán 232 25.29 N 107.00 W
El Tejocote, Cerro ∧ 234 18.48 N 103.03 W
Elten 52 51.52 N 6.10 E
El Terrero 234 18.58 N 102.28 W
Eltham, Austl. 169 37.44 S 145.09 E
Eltham, N.Z. 172 39.26 S 174.18 E
Eltham ◆[8] 260 51.27 N 0.04 E
Eltham Palace ♦ 260 51.27 N 0.03 E
El Tigre 246 8.55 N 64.15 W
El Tigre, Isla I 236 13.16 N 87.38 W
El Tigrito → San José de Guanipa 246 8.54 N 64.09 W
El Timbiriche 234 18.38 N 101.31 W
Eltmann 56 49.58 N 10.40 E
El Tocuyo 246 9.47 N 69.48 W
El Tofo 252 29.27 S 71.15 W
El'ton, Ross. 80 49.08 N 46.50 E
Elton, Eng., U.K. 262 53.16 N 2.49 W
Elton, La., U.S. 194 30.28 N 92.41 W
Elton, Pa., U.S. 214 40.17 N 78.48 W
El'ton, ozero ⊜ 80 49.16 N 46.35 E
El Toreo ♦ 286a 19.27 N 99.13 W
El Toro 228 33.37 N 117.41 W
El Toro ∧ 240m 18.16 N 65.49 W
El Toro, Isla I 234 21.26 N 97.31 W
El Toro Marine Corps Air Station ■ 228 33.41 N 117.44 W
El Tranco, Embalse de ⊜[1] 34 38.10 N 2.45 W
El Tránsito, Chile 252 28.52 S 70.17 W
El Tránsito, El Sal. 236 13.22 N 88.21 W
El Trébol 252 32.12 S 61.42 W
El Triunfo, Hond. 236 13.06 N 87.00 W
El Triunfo, Méx. 232 23.47 N 110.08 W
El Triunfo, Cerro ∧ 236 15.40 N 92.49 W
El Triunfo de la Cruz 236 15.46 N 87.26 W
El Tuito 234 20.19 N 105.22 W
El Tulillo 234 22.30 N 104.05 W
El Tunal 252 25.15 S 64.27 W
El Turbio 254 51.41 S 72.05 W
Eltville 56 50.02 N 8.07 E
Eltz, Burg ⊥ 56 50.12 N 7.20 E
El-Uarre 144 3.41 N 45.20 E
Elura → Ellora 122 20.01 N 75.10 E
Elūru 122 16.42 N 81.06 E
Elva 76 58.13 N 26.25 E
El Valle 236 8.36 N 80.08 W
El Valle ◆[8] 286c 10.27 N 66.55 W
Elvas 34 38.53 N 7.10 W
Elvas ≃ 256 21.12 S 44.08 W
Elven 32 47.44 N 2.35 W
El Vendrell 34 41.13 N 1.32 E
El Verano 226 38.18 N 122.29 W
El Verde 234 23.21 N 106.09 W
Elverdissen 52 52.05 N 8.38 E
Elverlingsen 263 51.17 N 7.42 E
Elverta 226 38.43 N 121.28 W
Elverum 26 60.53 N 11.34 E
El Viejo 236 12.40 N 87.10 W
El Vigia 246 8.38 N 71.39 W
El Vigía, Cerro ∧ 234 21.19 N 104.03 W
Elvins 194 37.50 N 90.31 W
Elvira 258 35.14 S 59.29 W
Elvo ≃ 62 45.23 N 8.21 E
El Volcán 252 33.49 S 70.11 W
El Wad 148 33.20 N 6.58 E
El Wak 154 2.49 N 40.56 E
El Walamo 234 23.07 N 106.15 W
El Wanza 148 35.57 N 8.04 E
Elwell, Lake ⊜[1] 202 48.22 N 111.17 W
Elwha ≃ 224 48.10 N 123.35 W
Elwood, Austl. 274b 37.53 S 144.59 E
Elwood, Il., U.S. 216 41.24 N 88.07 W
Elwood, In., U.S. 216 40.16 N 85.50 W
Elwood, Ks., U.S. 198 39.45 N 94.52 W
Elwood, Ne., U.S. 198 40.35 N 99.51 W
Elwood, N.J., U.S. 208 39.35 N 74.43 W
Elwood, N.Y., U.S. 207 40.50 N 73.20 W
Elwood Park, Fl., U.S. 220 27.28 N 82.30 W
Elwood Park, Pa., U.S. 279b 40.10 N 80.17 W
Elwy ≃ 44 53.16 N 3.26 W
Elwyn 285 39.54 N 75.24 W
Elx 34 38.15 N 0.42 W
Elxleben 54 51.02 N 10.56 E
Ely, Eng., U.K. 42 52.24 N 0.16 E
Ely, Mn., U.S. 190 47.54 N 91.52 W
Ely, Mo., U.S. 219 39.41 N 91.39 W
Ely, Nv., U.S. 204 39.14 N 114.53 W
Ely, Isle of ◆[1] 42 52.25 N 0.10 E
El Yagual 246 7.29 N 68.25 W
Ely Cathedral ♦[1] 42 52.24 N 0.16 E
Elyria 214 41.22 N 82.06 W
Elyria Airport ✈ 279a 41.20 N 82.06 W
Elysburg 210 40.51 N 76.33 W
Elysian Park ♦ 280 34.05 N 118.14 W
El Yunque ∧ 240m 18.19 N 65.48 W
Elywood Park ♦ 279a 41.23 N 82.06 W
Elz 56 50.25 N 8.02 E
Elz ≃ 58 48.21 N 7.45 E
Elzach 58 48.10 N 8.04 E
El Zamural 286c 10.27 N 67.00 W
El Zapotal 234 15.27 N 93.10 W
Elzbach ≃ 56 50.12 N 7.22 E
Elze, Dtsch. 52 52.35 N 9.44 E
Elze, Dtsch. 52 52.07 N 9.44 E
El Zig-Zag 286c 10.33 N 66.58 W
Émaé I 175f 17.04 S 168.24 E
Emajõgi ≃ 76 58.26 N 27.15 E
Emali 154 2.05 S 37.38 E
Emam Khomeyni Mosque ♦[1] 267d 35.40 N 51.25 E
Emāmshahr (Shāhrūd) 128 36.25 N 55.01 E
Emån ≃ 26 57.08 N 16.30 E
Émancé 261 48.35 N 1.44 E
Emas, Parque Nacional das ♦ 255 18.08 S 52.48 W
Emba 86 48.50 N 58.08 E
Emba ≃ 80 46.38 N 53.14 E
Embarcación 252 23.13 S 64.06 W
Embarras ≃, Ab., Can. 182 53.27 N 116.37 W
Embarras ≃, Il., U.S. 194 38.39 N 87.37 W
Embarras, North Fork ≃ 194 38.55 N 87.59 W
Embarrass 190 44.39 N 88.42 W
Embarrass ≃, Mn., U.S. 190 47.24 N 92.25 W
Embarrass ≃, Wi., U.S. 190 44.23 N 88.45 W
Embetsu 92a 44.44 N 141.47 E
Embid 34 40.58 N 1.43 W
Embleton 44 55.30 N 1.37 W
Embo 46 57.54 N 3.59 W
Emboabas 256 21.18 S 44.08 W
Embondo 152 0.15 N 19.38 E
Emborcação, Reprêsa ⊜[1] 255 18.30 S 47.50 W
Embrach 58 47.30 N 8.36 E
Embreeville, Pa., U.S. 285 39.56 N 75.44 W
Embreeville, Tn., U.S. 192 36.10 N 82.27 W
Embro 212 43.09 N 80.54 W
Embrun, On., Can. 212 45.16 N 75.17 W
Embrun, Fr. 62 44.34 N 6.30 E
Embry 50 50.29 N 1.58 E
Embsay 44 53.58 N 1.59 W
Embu, Bra. 256 23.39 S 46.51 W
Embu, Kenya 154 0.32 S 37.27 E
Embu ▫[7] 287b 23.40 S 46.50 W
Embu-Guaçu 256 23.49 S 46.48 W
Embu-Guaçu ▫[7] 287b 23.48 S 46.48 W
Embu-mirim ≃ 287b 23.39 S 46.51 W
Emden, Dtsch. 52 53.22 N 7.12 E
Emden, Il., U.S. 194 40.18 N 89.29 W
Emden, Mo., U.S. 219 39.48 N 91.52 W
Emei 107 29.36 N 103.31 E
Emeigh 214 40.42 N 78.47 W
Emel' (Emin) ≃ 86 46.20 N 81.46 E
Emelle 194 32.43 N 88.18 W
Emerado 198 47.55 N 97.21 W
Émerainville 261 48.49 N 2.37 E
Emerald, Austl. 166 23.32 S 148.10 E
Emerald, Austl. 169 37.56 S 145.26 E
Emerald Bay State Park ♦ 226 38.57 N 120.05 W
Emerald Lake 226 37.28 N 122.16 W
Emerson, Mb., Can. 184 49.00 N 97.12 W
Emerson, Ar., U.S. 194 33.05 N 93.11 W
Emerson, Ga., U.S. 192 34.07 N 84.45 W
Emerson, Ia., U.S. 198 41.01 N 95.24 W
Emerson, Mo., U.S. 219 39.53 N 91.42 W
Emerson, Ne., U.S. 198 42.17 N 96.44 W
Emerson, N.J., U.S. 276 40.58 N 74.01 W
Emery, S.D., U.S. 198 43.36 N 97.37 W
Emery, Ut,. U.S. 200 38.55 N 111.14 W
Emeryville, On., Can. 214 42.18 N 82.45 W
Emeryville, Ca., U.S. 226 37.50 N 122.17 W
Emet 130 39.20 N 29.15 E
Emgayet 146 29.04 N 12.58 E
Emhouse 222 32.09 N 96.35 W
Emi 88 50.36 N 97.49 E
Emigrant Gap 226 39.17 N 120.40 W
Emigrant Gap)(226 39.18 N 120.40 W
Emigsville 208 40.01 N 76.44 W
Emiliano Mitre, Canal ⩌ 288 34.36 S 58.18 W
Emiliano Zapata, Méx. 232 17.45 N 91.46 W
Emiliano Zapata, Méx. 234 16.10 N 94.01 W
Emiliano Zapata, Bahía ⊂ 232 19.40 N 87.30 W
Emilia-Romagna ▫[4] 66 44.35 N 11.00 E
Emílio de Carvalho 152 5.55 S 12.57 E
Emily Provincial Park ♦ 212 44.21 N 78.31 W
Emin 86 46.32 N 83.39 E
Emin (Emel') ≃ 86 46.20 N 81.46 E
Eminābād 123 32.02 N 74.16 E
Emine, nos › 38 42.42 N 27.51 E
Eminence, Ky., U.S. 218 38.22 N 85.10 W
Eminence, Mo., U.S. 194 37.09 N 91.21 W
Emiralem 130 38.36 N 27.09 E
Emiratos Arabes Unidos → United Arab Emirates ▫[1] 128 24.00 N 54.00 E
Emirau Island I 164 1.40 S 150.00 E
Emirdağ 130 39.01 N 31.10 E
Emır Dağları ⋏ 130 38.50 N 31.15 E
Emirhan 130 39.42 N 37.46 E
Emir Pasha Gulf ⊂ 154 2.32 S 31.52 E
Emissi, Tarso ∧ 146 21.13 N 18.32 E
Emita 166 40.00 S 147.54 E
Emlembe ∧ 158 25.57 S 31.11 E
Emlenton 214 41.11 N 79.43 W
Emlichheim 52 52.36 N 6.50 E
Emmaån ≃ 40 58.44 N 15.35 E
Emmaboda 26 56.38 N 15.32 E
Emmaste 76 58.42 N 22.36 E
Emmaus, Ross. 82 56.47 N 36.07 E
Emmaus, Pa., U.S. 208 40.32 N 75.29 W
Emmaville 166 29.26 S 151.36 E
Emme ≃ 58 47.13 N 7.34 E
Emmeline Lake ⊜ 184 55.00 N 106.22 W
Emmeloord 52 52.43 N 5.45 E
Emmen 52 52.47 N 6.54 E
Emmenbrücke 58 47.04 N 8.17 E
Emmendingen 58 48.07 N 7.50 E
Emmental V 58 46.56 N 7.45 E
Emmer ≃ 52 52.03 N 9.23 E
Emmer-Compascuum 52 52.48 N 7.02 E
Emmer-Erfscheidenveen 52 52.48 N 7.01 E
Emmerich 52 51.50 N 6.15 E
Emmerstedt 54 52.15 N 10.58 E
Emmerthal 52 52.03 N 9.23 E
Emmet, Austl. 166 24.40 S 144.28 E
Emmet, Ar., U.S. 194 33.43 N 93.28 W
Emmetsburg 198 43.06 N 94.40 W
Emmett, Id., U.S. 202 43.52 N 116.29 W
Emmett, Mi., U.S. 214 42.59 N 82.45 W
Emmiganūru 122 15.44 N 77.29 E
Emmitsburg 208 39.42 N 77.20 W
Emmonak 180 62.46 N 164.30 W
Emneth 42 52.38 N 0.11 E
Emo 190 48.38 N 93.50 W
Emőd 30 47.56 N 20.49 E
Emory 222 32.52 N 95.46 W
Emory ≃ 192 35.56 N 84.29 W
Emory Peak ∧ 196 29.13 N 103.17 W
Empalme 232 27.58 N 110.51 W
Empalme Escobedo 234 20.41 N 100.44 W
Empalme Purísima 234 23.55 N 105.05 W
Empalme San Vicente 258 34.58 S 58.22 W
Empangeni 158 28.50 S 31.48 E
Empedrado, Arg. 252 27.57 S 58.48 W
Empedrado, Chile 252 35.36 S 72.17 W
Emperor Jimmu, Tomb of ⊥ 270 34.29 N 135.47 E
Emperor Nintoku, Tomb of ⊥ 270 34.34 N 135.29 E
Emperor Range ⋏ 175e 5.45 S 154.55 E
Emperor Seamounts ✦[3] 6 42.00 N 170.00 E
Emperor Tenchi, Tomb of ⊥ 270 34.59 N 135.48 E
Empfingen 58 48.24 N 8.42 E
Empire, Ca., U.S. 226 37.38 N 120.54 W
Empire, La., U.S. 194 29.23 N 89.35 W
Empire, Nv., U.S. 204 40.34 N 119.20 W
Empire, Oh., U.S. 214 40.30 N 80.37 W
Empoli 66 43.43 N 10.57 E
Emporia, Ks., U.S. 198 38.24 N 96.10 W
Emporia, Va., U.S. 208 36.41 N 77.32 W
Emporium 214 41.30 N 78.14 W
Empress 184 50.57 N 110.00 W
Empress Augusta Bay ⊂ 175e 6.25 S 155.05 E
Emptinne 56 50.19 N 5.07 E
Empty Quarter → Ar-Rub' al-Khālī ◆[2] 118 20.00 N 51.00 E
Ems ≃ 52 53.30 N 7.00 E
Emscher ≃ 263 51.34 N 6.42 E
Emscherbruch ◆[1] 263 51.34 N 7.09 E
Emsdetten 52 52.10 N 7.31 E
Ems-Jade-Kanal ≅ 52 53.19 N 7.10 E
Emskirchen 56 49.33 N 10.43 E
Emsland ◆[1] 52 52.50 N 7.20 E
Emst ◆[8] 263 51.21 N 7.30 E
Emstek 52 52.50 N 8.09 E
Emsworth, Eng., U.K. 42 50.51 N 0.56 W
Emsworth, Pa., U.S. 214 40.30 N 80.05 W
Emu 89 43.45 N 128.10 E
Emu, Mount ∧[2] 169 37.35 S 143.27 E
Emu Creek ≃ 171a 26.56 S 152.19 E
Emu Downs 168b 33.54 S 138.59 E
Emukae 92 33.18 N 129.38 E
Emu Park 166 23.15 S 150.50 E
Emu Plains 274a 33.45 S 150.41 E
Emur ≃ 89 53.24 N 124.00 E
Emuren 273a 6.40 N 3.31 E
Emyvale 48 54.20 N 6.59 W
En (Inn) ≃, Europe 32 48.35 N 13.28 E
En ≃, Zhg. 100 27.12 N 115.08 E
Ena 94 35.27 N 137.25 E
Enana 156 17.29 S 16.19 E
Enånger 26 61.32 N 17.00 E
Enard Bay ⊂ 46 58.05 N 5.20 W
Enarotali 164 3.55 S 136.21 E
Ena-san ∧ 94 35.26 N 137.36 E
Ena-san Tunnel ◆[5] 94 35.30 N 137.40 E
Enbacka 40 60.25 N 15.36 E
Enborne ≃ 42 51.24 N 1.06 W
Encampment 200 41.12 N 106.47 W
Encampment ≃ 200 41.18 N 106.43 W
Encantado 252 29.15 S 51.53 W
Encantado ◆[8] 287a 22.54 S 43.18 W

ENGLISH

Name | Page | Lat.°′ | Long.°′

Encanto, Cape › 116 15.44 N 121.37 E
Encarnação ◆[8] 266c 38.47 N 9.06 W
Encarnación 252 27.20 S 55.54 W
Encarnación de Díaz 234 21.31 N 102.14 W
Encha 98 37.25 N 115.42 E
Enchenberg 56 49.01 N 7.20 E
Enchi 150 5.49 N 2.49 W
Enchilayas 200 30.50 N 112.50 W
Enchovas, Enseada das ⊂ 256 23.57 S 45.18 W
Enciastraia, Monte ∧ 62 44.22 N 6.53 E
Encinal 196 28.02 N 99.21 W
Encinitas 228 33.02 N 117.17 W
Encino, N.M., U.S. 200 34.39 N 105.27 W
Encino, Tx., U.S. 196 26.57 N 98.08 W
Encino ◆[8] 280 34.09 N 118.30 W
Encino Reservoir ⊜[1] 280 34.05 N 118.31 W
Encontrados 246 9.03 N 72.14 W
Encounter Bay ⊂ 168b 35.35 S 138.44 E
Encrucijada, Cuba 240p 22.37 N 79.52 W
Encrucijada, Méx. 234 18.18 N 93.29 W
Encruzilhada 255 15.31 S 40.54 W
Encruzilhada do Sul 252 30.32 S 52.31 W
Encs 30 48.20 N 21.08 E
Endako 182 54.05 N 125.02 W
Endako ≃ 182 54.05 N 124.55 W
Endau ≃ 114 2.39 N 103.38 E
Ende 115b 8.50 S 121.39 E
Ende, Pulau I 115b 8.53 S 121.32 E
Ende, Teluk ⊂ 115b 8.52 S 121.30 E
Endeavor, Pa., U.S. 214 41.35 N 79.23 W
Endeavor, Wi., U.S. 190 43.42 N 89.27 W
Endeavour 184 52.08 N 102.40 W
Endeavour Strait ⩌ 164 10.50 S 142.15 E
Endelave I 41 55.46 N 10.17 E
Enderbury I[1] 14 3.08 S 171.05 W
Enderby, B.C., Can. 182 50.33 N 119.08 W
Enderby, Eng., U.K. 42 52.36 N 1.12 W
Enderby Land ◆[1] 9 67.30 S 53.00 E
Enderlin 198 46.37 N 97.36 W
Endicott, N.Y., U.S. 210 42.05 N 76.02 W
Endicott, Wa., U.S. 202 46.55 N 117.40 W
Endicott Mountains ⋏ 180 67.50 N 152.00 W
Endimari ≃ 248 8.46 S 66.07 W
Endine 64 45.46 N 9.59 E
Endine Gaiano 64 45.48 N 9.59 E
Endingen 58 48.09 N 7.42 E
Endja, Oued ≃ 34 36.31 N 6.15 E
Endō 268 35.23 N 139.27 E
Endola 156 17.37 S 15.50 E
'En Dor 132 32.39 N 35.25 E
Endorf in Oberbayern 64 47.54 N 12.18 E
Endre ≃ 62 43.28 N 6.36 E
Endrick ∧ 170 35.12 S 150.12 E
Endrick ≃ 170 35.01 S 150.03 E
Endwell 210 42.06 N 76.01 W
Ene ≃ 248 11.09 S 74.19 W
Eneabba 162 29.50 S 115.20 E
Enemonzo 64 46.25 N 12.53 E
Enewetak I[1] 14 11.30 N 162.15 E
Enez 130 40.44 N 26.04 E
Enfida 36 36.07 N 10.23 E
Enfield, Austl. 168b 34.53 S 138.35 E
Enfield, Austl. 274a 33.53 S 151.06 E
Enfield, N.Z. 172 45.03 S 170.52 E
Enfield, Ct., U.S. 207 41.58 N 72.35 W
Enfield, N.H., U.S. 188 43.38 N 72.08 W
Enfield, N.C., U.S. 192 36.10 N 77.40 W
Enfield, Va., U.S. 208 37.43 N 77.12 W
Enfield ◆[8] 260 51.40 N 0.05 W
Enga ▫[5] 164 5.30 S 143.30 E
Engadine 170 34.04 S 151.01 E
Engaño, Cabo › 238 18.37 N 68.20 W
Engaru 92a 44.03 N 143.31 E
Engažimo 88 57.51 N 114.56 E
Engcobo 158 31.37 S 28.00 E
'En Gedi 132 31.27 N 35.23 E
Engelberg 58 46.49 N 8.25 E
Engelhard 192 35.30 N 75.59 W
Engelhartszell 60 48.31 N 13.44 E
Engel's 80 51.30 N 46.07 E
Engelsdorf 54 51.20 N 12.29 E
Engelskirchen 56 50.59 N 7.24 E
Engelsmanplaat I 52 53.28 N 6.02 E
Engel's'ovo 83 48.22 N 39.23 E
Engen, B.C., Can. 182 54.02 N 124.18 W
Engen, Dtsch. 58 47.51 N 8.46 E
Engenheiro Navarro 255 17.17 S 43.57 W
Engenheiro Passos 256 22.30 S 44.41 W
Engenheiro Paulo de Frontin 256 22.33 S 43.41 W
Engenho 248 15.10 S 56.25 W
Engenho, Ilha do I 287a 22.50 S 43.07 W
Engenho de Dentro ◆[8] 287a 22.54 S 43.18 W
Engenho do Mato 287a 22.52 S 43.01 W
Éngenho Novo 256 21.49 S 43.00 W
Engenho Nôvo ◆[8] 287a 22.55 S 43.17 W
Enger 52 52.08 N 8.34 E
Engestofte 41 54.46 N 11.34 E
Engesvang 41 56.10 N 9.21 E
'En Gev 132 32.47 N 35.38 E
Enggano, Pulau I 112 5.24 S 102.16 E
Enghershatu ∧ 144 16.40 N 38.20 E
Enghien (Edingen) 50 50.42 N 4.02 E
Enghien-les-Bains 261 48.58 N 2.19 E
Enghien-Moisselles, Aéroport d' ✈ 261 49.02 N 2.21 E
Engiadina Bassa V 58 46.50 N 10.20 E
Engis 56 50.35 N 5.25 E
Engizek Dağı ∧ 130 37.50 N 37.10 E
Engjan 26 63.09 N 8.32 E
England 194 34.32 N 91.58 W
England ▫[8] 28 52.30 N 1.30 W
England Air Force Base ■ 194 31.20 N 92.33 W
Englebright Lake ⊜[1] 226 39.15 N 121.15 W
Englee 186 50.44 N 56.06 W
Englefield, Cape › 176 69.51 N 85.39 W
Englefield Green 260 51.26 N 0.35 W
Englefontaine 50 50.11 N 3.39 E
Englehart 190 47.49 N 79.52 W
Englehart ≃ 190 47.51 N 79.50 W
Engleside 208 38.43 N 77.05 W
Englewood, B.C., Can. 182 50.33 N 126.53 W
Englewood, Co., U.S. 200 39.38 N 104.59 W
Englewood, Fl., U.S. 220 26.57 N 82.21 W
Englewood, In., U.S. 218 38.50 N 86.31 W
Englewood, Ks., U.S. 198 37.02 N 99.58 W
Englewood, N.J., U.S. 210 40.53 N 73.58 W
Englewood, Oh., U.S. 218 39.52 N 84.18 W
Englewood, Tn., U.S. 192 35.25 N 84.29 W
Englewood ◆[8] 278 41.47 N 87.39 W
Englewood Cliffs 276 40.53 N 73.57 W
Englewood Dam ◆[6] 218 39.52 N 84.17 W
English, In., U.S. 218 38.20 N 86.27 W
English, Ky., U.S. 218 38.37 N 85.08 W
English ≃, On., Can. 176 50.12 N 95.00 W
English (Rivière des Anglais) ≃, N.A. 206 45.13 N 73.50 W
English ≃, Ia., U.S. 190 41.29 N 91.30 W
English Bay 180 59.22 N 151.55 W
English Bāzār → Ingrāj Bāzār 124 25.00 N 88.09 E
English Center 210 41.26 N 77.17 W
English Channel (La Manche) ⩌ 28 50.20 N 1.00 W
English Coast ⊥[2] 9 73.45 S 73.00 W
English Harbour West 186 47.28 N 55.29 W
Englishman ≃ 224 49.22 N 124.18 W
Englishtown 208 40.17 N 74.21 W
Engong 152 0.36 N 10.06 E
Engter 52 52.23 N 8.04 E
Énguera 34 38.59 N 0.41 W
Engum 41 55.44 N 9.40 E
Engure 76 57.10 N 23.13 E
Engures ezers ⊜ 76 57.16 N 23.06 E
Engwilen 58 47.37 N 9.05 E
'En Harod 132 32.33 N 35.23 E
'En HaShofét 132 32.35 N 35.06 E

DEUTSCH

Name | Seite | Breite°′ | Länge°′ E = Ost

Enid 196 36.23 N 97.52 W
Enid Lake ⊜[1] 194 34.10 N 89.50 W
Enilda 182 55.25 N 116.18 W
Eningen unter Achalm 58 48.29 N 9.16 E
Eniwa 92a 42.45 N 141.33 E
Eniwetok → Enewetak I[1] 14 11.30 N 162.15 E
eNjesuthi ∧ 158 29.09 S 29.23 E
Enka 192 35.32 N 82.39 W
Enkenbach 56 49.29 N 7.54 E
Enkhuizen 52 52.42 N 5.17 E
Enkirch 56 49.59 N 7.07 E
Enköping 40 59.38 N 17.04 E
Enle 102 24.00 N 101.07 E
Enmedio 196 29.04 N 103.29 W
Enmedio, Cerro de ∧ 234 19.48 N 100.36 W
Enmelen 180 65.01 N 175.54 W
Enna 70 37.34 N 14.16 E
Enna ▫[4] 70 37.35 N 14.26 E
Ennadai Lake ⊜ 176 60.53 N 101.15 W
Enné, Ouadi V 146 14.24 N 18.45 E
Ennedi ⋏[1] 146 17.15 N 22.00 E
Ennell, Lough ⊜ 48 53.28 N 7.24 W
Ennenda 58 47.01 N 9.05 E
Ennepe ≃ 263 51.22 N 7.27 E
Ennepestausee ⊜[1] 263 51.14 N 7.25 E
Ennepetal 56 51.18 N 7.22 E
Ennerdale Water ⊜ 44 54.31 N 3.23 W
Ennery 261 49.05 N 2.06 E
Enngonia 166 29.19 S 145.51 E
Enniger 52 51.50 N 7.56 E
Ennigerloh 52 51.50 N 8.02 E
Ennigloh 52 52.12 N 8.34 E
Ennis, Ire. 48 52.50 N 8.59 W
Ennis, Mt., U.S. 202 45.20 N 111.43 W
Ennis, Tx., U.S. 222 32.19 N 96.37 W
Enniscorthy 48 52.30 N 6.34 W
Enniskillen 48 54.21 N 7.38 W
Ennis Lake ⊜[1] 202 45.26 N 111.41 W
Ennistimon 48 52.57 N 9.15 W
Enns 61 48.13 N 14.29 E
Enns ≃ 30 48.14 N 14.32 E
Ennstaler Alpen ⋏ 61 47.37 N 14.35 E
Eno 26 62.48 N 30.09 E
Enø I 41 55.10 N 11.40 E
Eno ≃ 96 34.53 N 132.41 E
Enochs 196 33.52 N 102.46 W
Enogera Military Camp ■ 171a 27.25 S 152.58 E
Enola 208 40.17 N 76.56 W
Enon 218 39.53 N 83.56 W
Enontekiö 24 68.23 N 23.38 E
Enon Valley 214 40.51 N 80.28 W
Enoree ≃ 192 34.26 N 81.25 W
Enosburg Falls 188 44.54 N 72.48 W
Eno-shima I 94 35.18 N 139.29 E
Enping 102 22.11 N 112.17 E
Enrekang 112 3.34 S 119.47 E
Enrile 116 17.34 N 121.42 E
Enrique Fynn 258 34.50 S 59.08 W
Enrique Urien 252 27.34 S 60.32 W
Enriquillo 238 17.54 N 71.14 W
Enriquillo, Lago ⊜ 238 18.27 N 71.39 W
Ens 52 52.38 N 5.50 E
Ensay I 46 57.46 N 7.05 W
Enschede 52 52.12 N 6.53 E
Ensdorf 60 49.21 N 11.56 E
Ensenada, Arg. 258 34.51 S 57.55 W
Ensenada, Méx. 232 31.52 N 116.37 W
Ensenada, P.R. 240m 17.58 N 66.56 W
Ensenada ▫[5] 288 34.50 S 58.00 W
Enshi 102 30.17 N 109.19 E
Enshū-nada ⊤[2] 92 34.27 N 137.38 E
Ensisheim 58 47.52 N 7.21 E
Enstaberga 40 58.45 N 16.51 E
Entebbe 154 0.04 N 32.28 E
Entenbühl ∧ 60 49.46 N 12.24 E
Enter 52 52.18 N 6.34 E
Enterprise, Guy. 246 6.56 N 58.24 W
Enterprise, Al., U.S. 194 31.18 N 85.51 W
Enterprise, Ca., U.S. 204 39.32 N 121.22 W
Enterprise, Ks., U.S. 198 38.54 N 97.07 W
Enterprise, Ms., U.S. 194 32.10 N 88.49 W
Enterprise, Or., U.S. 202 45.25 N 117.16 W
Enterprise, Ut,. U.S. 200 37.34 N 113.43 W
Entiat ≃ 202 47.40 N 120.14 W
Entiat, Lake ⊜[1] 202 47.40 N 120.12 W
Entiat Mountains ⋏ 224 48.00 N 120.42 W
Entinas, Punta de las › 34 36.41 N 2.46 W
Entlebuch 58 47.00 N 8.04 E
Entlebuch V 58 46.58 N 8.00 E
Entracque 62 44.14 N 7.24 E
Entraigues-sur-Sorgue 62 44.00 N 4.55 E
Entrains-sur-Nohain 50 47.27 N 3.15 E
Entrance, Cape › 164 2.21 S 150.12 E
Entraunes 62 44.11 N 6.45 E
Entraygues 32 44.39 N 2.34 E
Entrechaux 62 44.13 N 5.08 E
Entrée, Île d' I 186 47.17 N 61.42 W
Entremont-le-Vieux 62 45.26 N 5.53 E
Entrepeñas, Embalse de ⊜[1] 34 40.34 N 2.42 W
Entre Rios, Bol. 248 21.32 S 64.12 W
Entre Rios, Bra. 255 11.56 S 38.05 W
Entre Ríos ▫[4] 252 32.00 S 59.00 W
Entre Ríos, Cordillera ⋏ 236 14.05 N 85.37 W
Entre-Rios de Minas 255 20.41 S 44.04 W
Entrevaux 62 43.57 N 6.49 E
Entrèves 62 45.49 N 6.57 E
Entriken 214 40.20 N 78.12 W
Entroncamento 34 39.28 N 8.28 W
Entupido 256 22.30 S 44.51 W
Entwistle 182 53.36 N 115.00 W
Enu, Pulau I 164 7.05 S 134.30 E
Enugu 150 6.27 N 7.27 E
Enumclaw 224 47.12 N 121.59 W
Enurmino 180 66.57 N 171.49 W
Envalira, Port d')(34 42.35 N 1.45 E
Envermeu 50 49.54 N 1.16 E
Envies, Rivière des ≃ 206 46.37 N 72.24 W
Envigado 246 6.10 N 75.35 W
Envira 248 7.18 S 70.13 W
Envira ≃ 248 6.42 S 69.46 W
'En Yahav 132 30.38 N 35.11 E
Enyamba 154 3.40 S 24.58 E
Enyang 102 31.48 N 106.31 E
Enyellé 152 2.49 N 18.06 E
Enys, Mount ∧ 172 43.14 S 171.38 E
Enz ≃ 56 49.01 N 9.07 E
Enza ≃ 64 44.54 N 10.31 E
Enzan 94 35.42 N 138.44 E
Enzbach ≃ 56 49.54 N 6.25 E
Enzenkirchen 60 48.23 N 13.39 E
Enzesfeld 61 47.55 N 16.10 E
Enzklösterle 56 48.40 N 8.28 E
Eo ≃ 34 43.28 N 7.03 W
Eolia 219 39.14 N 91.00 W
Eolie o Lipari, Isole II 70 38.30 N 14.50 E
Epanomí 38 40.26 N 22.56 E
Épars, Bois de l' ♦ 261 48.45 N 1.45 E
Epe, Dtsch. 52 52.11 N 7.02 E
Epe, Ned. 52 52.21 N 6.00 E
Epe, Nig. 150 6.37 N 3.59 E
Epecuén, Lago ⊜ 252 37.10 S 62.54 W
Épéhy 50 50.02 N 3.10 E
Epéna 152 1.22 N 17.29 E
Épernay 50 49.03 N 3.57 E
Épernon 50 48.37 N 1.41 E
Epes 194 32.41 N 88.07 W
Ephesus → Efes ⊥ 130 37.55 N 27.17 E
Ephraim 200 39.21 N 111.35 W
Ephrata, Pa., U.S. 208 40.10 N 76.10 W
Ephrata, Wa., U.S. 202 47.19 N 119.33 W
Ephrata Cloister ⊥ 208 40.12 N 76.09 W
Ephratah 210 43.00 N 74.32 W
Epi ▫[8] 175f 16.42 S 168.15 E
Épi I 175f 16.43 S 168.15 E
Épiais-lès-Louvres 261 49.02 N 2.33 E

Symbols in the index entries represent the broad categories identified in the key at the right. Symbols with superior numbers (⋏[1]) identify subcategories (see complete key on page *I · 1).*

Symbole im Register stellen die rechts im Schlüssel erklärten Kategorien dar. Symbole mit hochgestellten Ziffern (⋏[1]) bezeichnen Unterabteilungen einer Kategorie (vgl. vollständiger Schlüssel auf Seite *I · 1).*

Los símbolos incluídos en el texto del índice representan las grandes categorias identificadas con la clave a la derecha. Los símbolos con numeros en su parte superior (⋏[1]) identifican las subcategorías (véase la clave completa en la página *I · 1).*

Les symboles de l'index représentent les catégories indiquées dans la légende à droite. Les symboles suivis d'un indice (⋏[1]) représentent des sous-catégories (voir légende complète à la page *I · 1).*

Os símbolos incluídos no texto do índice representam as grandes categorias identificadas com a chave à direita. Os símbolos com números em sua parte superior (⋏[1]) identificam as subcategorias (veja-se a chave completa à página *I · 1).*

∧ Mountain	Berg	Montaña	Montagne	Montanha
⋏ Mountains	Gebirge	Montañas	Montagnes	Montanhas
)(Pass	Paß	Paso	Col	Passo
V Valley, Canyon	Tal, Cañon	Valle, Cañón	Vallée, Canyon	Vale, Canhão
≚ Plain	Ebene	Llano	Plaine	Planície
› Cape	Kap	Cabo	Cap	Cabo
I Island	Insel	Isla	Île	Ilha
II Islands	Inseln	Islas	Îles	Ilhas
⊥ Other Topographic Features	Andere Topographische Objekte	Otros Elementos Topográficos	Autres données topographiques	Outros acidentes topográficos

ESPAÑOL

Nombre	Página	Lat.°′	Long.°′ W = Oeste
Épila	34	41.36 N	1.17 W
Épinac-Les-Mines	58	46.59 N	4.31 E
Épinal	58	48.11 N	6.27 E
Épinay-sous-Sénart	261	48.42 N	2.31 E
Épinay-sur-Orge	261	48.40 N	2.20 E
Épinay-sur-Seine	261	48.57 N	2.19 E
Epirus — Ípeiros □[9]	38	39.40 N	20.50 E
Episcopia	68	40.04 N	16.06 E
Episkopí	130	34.40 N	32.54 E
Époisses	50	47.30 N	4.10 E
Epokiro	156	21.41 S	19.08 E
Epomeo, Monte ∧	68	40.44 N	13.54 E
Épône	261	48.57 N	1.49 E
Eport, Loch ⊂	46	57.33 N	7.11 W
Eppalock, Lake ◎[1]	169	36.52 S	144.31 E
Eppelborn	56	49.24 N	6.58 E
Eppendorf ◆[8]	263	51.27 N	7.11 E
Eppenhausen ◆[8]	263	51.21 N	7.31 E
Eppeville	50	49.44 N	3.03 E
Epping, Austl.	169	37.39 S	145.02 E
Epping, Austl.	274a	33.46 S	151.05 E
Epping, Eng., U.K.	260	51.43 N	0.07 E
Epping, N.H., U.S.	188	43.02 N	71.04 W
Eppingen	56	49.08 N	8.54 E
Epping Forest □[8]	260	51.43 N	0.10 E
Epping Forest ◆[3]	260	51.40 N	0.03 E
Epping Green, Eng., U.K.	260	51.44 N	0.05 E
Epping Green, Eng., U.K.	260	51.45 N	0.07 W
Epping Upland	260	51.43 N	0.06 E
Epsom	260	51.20 N	0.16 W
Epsom and Ewell □[8]	260	51.20 N	0.16 W
Epsom Downs Race Course ♠	260	51.19 N	0.15 W
Epte ≃	50	49.04 N	1.37 E
Épuisay	50	47.54 N	0.56 E
Epukiro ≃	156	20.45 S	21.05 E
Epupa Falls ⌞	152	16.55 S	13.10 E
Epuyén	254	42.14 S	71.21 W
Epworth	44	53.32 N	0.49 W
Eqlīd	128	30.55 N	52.39 E
Equality	194	37.44 N	88.20 W
Équateur □[4]	152	1.00 N	20.30 E
Équateur — Ecuador □[1]	246	2.00 S	77.30 W
Equatorial Guinea (Guinea Ecuatorial) □[1]	152	2.00 N	9.00 E
Équihen-Plage	50	50.41 N	1.34 E
Equimina ≃	152	13.11 S	12.47 E
Equinox Mountain ∧	210	43.10 N	73.08 W
Equinunk	210	41.51 N	75.14 W
Equi Terme	64	44.09 N	10.10 E
Era ≃, It.	66	43.40 N	10.38 E
Era ≃, Pap. N. Gui.	164	7.35 S	144.41 E
Erac Creek ≃	166	26.56 S	145.48 E
Eraclea	64	45.35 N	12.40 E
Eraclea ⊥	68	40.13 N	16.40 E
Eraclea Minoa ⊥	70	37.23 N	13.17 E
Eradu	162	28.41 S	115.02 E
Éragny	261	49.01 N	2.06 E
Eramosa ≃	212	43.32 N	80.14 W
Eran Bay ⊂	116	9.06 N	117.43 E
Eranga	152	1.52 S	18.56 E
Erangal ◆[8]	272c	19.10 N	72.47 E
Erap	164	6.35 S	146.40 E
Erath	194	29.57 N	92.02 W
Erave	164	6.40 S	143.50 E
Erave ≃	164	6.40 S	143.55 E
Erba	62	45.48 N	9.15 E
Erba, Jabal ∧, Sūd.	140	19.04 N	36.46 E
Erba, Jabal ∧, Sūd.	140	20.45 N	36.50 E
Erbaa	130	40.42 N	36.36 E
Erbach, Dtsch.	56	49.40 N	8.59 E
Erbach, Dtsch.	58	48.20 N	9.53 E
Erbendorf	60	49.50 N	12.03 E
Erbeskopf ∧	56	49.44 N	7.05 E
Erchie	68	40.26 N	17.44 E
Erciş	84	39.02 N	43.22 E
Erciyes Dağı ∧	130	38.32 N	35.28 E
Ercolano	68	40.48 N	14.21 E
Ercolano (Herculaneum) ⊥	68	40.46 N	14.20 E
Érd	30	47.23 N	18.56 E
Erdao ≃, Zhg.	98	42.39 N	127.35 E
Erdao ≃, Zhg.	104	42.16 N	122.20 E
Erdao Bai ≃	98	42.34 N	128.08 E
Erdaobaihe	98	42.22 N	128.07 E
Erdaofang, Zhg.	104	41.54 N	123.57 E
Erdaofang, Zhg.	104	41.37 N	122.34 E
Erdaofangshen	104	42.09 N	123.17 E
Erdaogangzi, Zhg.	104	41.57 N	122.09 E
Erdaogangzi, Zhg.	104	42.04 N	123.06 E
Erdaohe	89	43.37 N	127.35 E
Erdaohezi, Zhg.	89	45.07 N	127.16 E
Erdaohezi, Zhg.	89	45.08 N	129.39 E
Erdaojingzi	104	41.49 N	122.20 E
Erdaoliangzi, Zhg.	98	40.50 N	119.04 E
Erdaoliangzi, Zhg.	105	40.31 N	118.03 E
Erdaowan	89	47.58 N	124.33 E
Erdek	130	40.24 N	27.48 E
Erdemli	130	36.37 N	34.18 E
Erdene, Mong.	88	47.48 N	107.55 E
Erdene, Mong.	102	44.15 N	111.14 E
Erdene, Mong.	102	45.08 N	97.45 E
Erdene Bulgan	88	50.07 N	101.35 E
Erdene-Büren	86	48.26 N	91.27 E
Erdenedalaj	102	46.02 N	104.55 E
Erdene Mandal	88	48.30 N	101.21 E
Erdenheim	285	40.05 N	75.12 W
Erdevik	38	45.07 N	19.25 E
Erdiao	106	32.12 N	121.12 E
Erding	60	48.18 N	11.54 E
Erdinger Moos ≡	60	48.22 N	11.52 E
Erdnijevskij	80	46.52 N	46.17 E
Erebato ≃	246	5.54 N	64.16 W
Erebus, Mount ∧	9	77.32 S	167.09 E
Ereğli, Tür.	130	37.31 N	34.04 E
Ereğli, Tür.	130	41.17 N	31.25 E
Eregun	273a	6.36 N	3.22 E
Erei, Monti ⋏	70	37.27 N	14.19 E
Erenas	116	12.25 N	124.19 E
Erenhot	102	43.46 N	112.05 E
Erenköy ◆[8]	267b	40.58 N	29.04 E
Erepecuru, Lago do ◎	250	1.20 S	56.35 W
Eresma ≃	34	41.26 N	4.45 W
Eressós	38	39.18 N	25.51 E
Erétria	38	38.24 N	23.48 E
Erexim	252	27.38 S	52.17 W
Erez	132	31.34 N	34.34 E
Érezée	56	50.18 N	5.33 E
Erfa ≃	56	49.40 N	9.23 E
Erfde	41	54.19 N	9.19 E
Erfelek	130	41.53 N	34.55 E
Erfenisdam ◎[1]	158	28.33 S	26.50 E
Erfoud	148	31.28 N	4.10 W
Erft ≃	56	51.11 N	6.44 E
Erftstadt	56	50.48 N	6.46 E
Erfurt	54	50.58 N	11.01 E
Ergak-Targak-Tajga, chrebet ⋏	88	53.25 N	95.30 E
Ergani	130	38.17 N	39.46 E
Ergene ≃	130	41.01 N	26.22 E
Ergenzingen	58	48.29 N	8.48 E
Erges (Erjas) ≃	34	39.40 N	7.01 W
Ērgļi	76	56.54 N	25.38 E
Ergolding	60	48.35 N	12.10 E
Ergoldsbach	60	48.41 N	12.12 E
Ergste	56	51.25 N	7.34 E
Erguig, Bahr ≃	146	11.22 N	15.24 E
Ergun (Argun') ≃	74	53.20 N	121.28 E
Ergun Youqi	89	50.14 N	120.10 E
Ergun Zuoqi	89	50.47 N	121.31 E
Erguvejem ≃	180	65.20 N	176.00 W
Er Hai ◎	102	25.48 N	100.11 E
Erhlin	100	23.54 N	120.22 E
Erhshui	100	23.49 N	120.36 E
Erhulai	98	41.23 N	125.08 E
Eria ≃	34	42.03 N	5.44 W
Erial	208	39.46 N	75.00 W

FRANÇAIS

Nom	Page	Lat.°′	Long.°′ W = Ouest
Eriba	140	16.37 N	36.04 E
Eriboll	46	58.28 N	4.41 W
Eriboll, Loch ⊂	46	58.31 N	4.41 W
Erica, Austl.	169	37.59 S	146.22 E
Erica, Ned.	52	52.43 N	6.55 E
Erice	70	38.02 N	12.35 E
Ericeira	34	38.59 N	9.25 W
Erichsen Lake ◎	176	70.38 N	80.21 W
Erichshagen	52	52.40 N	9.14 E
Ericht, Loch ◎	46	56.48 N	4.24 W
Erick	196	35.12 N	99.51 W
Erickson, B.C., Can.	182	49.05 N	116.28 W
Erickson, Mb., Can.	184	50.30 N	99.55 W
Ericson	198	41.46 N	98.40 W
Erie, Co., U.S.	200	40.03 N	105.03 W
Erie, Il., U.S.	190	41.39 N	90.04 W
Erie, Ks., U.S.	198	37.34 N	95.14 W
Erie, Mi., U.S.	216	41.47 N	83.29 W
Erie, Pa., U.S.	214	42.07 N	80.05 W
Erie □[6], N.Y., U.S.	210	42.54 N	78.53 W
Erie □[6], Oh., U.S.	214	41.27 N	82.42 W
Erie □[6], Pa., U.S.	214	42.08 N	80.04 W
Erie, Lake ◎	214	42.15 N	81.00 W
Erieau	214	42.16 N	81.56 W
Erie Basin ⊂	276	40.40 N	74.01 W
Erie Beach, On., Can.	214	42.16 N	82.00 W
Erie Beach, On., Can.	284a	42.53 N	78.57 W
Erie Canal — New York State Barge Canal ≍	210	43.05 N	78.43 W
Erie County Fairgrounds ♠	284a	42.45 N	78.49 W
Erie International Airport ⊠	214	42.05 N	80.11 W
Eriksberg ⊥	40	58.56 N	16.22 E
Eriksdale	184	50.52 N	98.06 W
Erímanthos ∧	38	37.59 N	21.51 E
Erimo	92a	42.01 N	143.09 E
Erimo-misaki ›	92a	41.55 N	143.15 E
Erin, On., Can.	212	43.45 N	80.07 W
Erin, N.Y., U.S.	210	42.11 N	76.40 W
Erin, Tn., U.S.	194	36.19 N	87.41 W
Erindale	275b	43.32 N	79.39 W
Ering	60	48.18 N	13.09 E
Eriskay I	46	57.04 N	7.18 W
Erisort, Loch ⊂	46	58.07 N	6.24 W
Eriswil	58	47.05 N	7.51 E
Erith ◆[8]	260	51.29 N	0.10 E
Erithraí	38	38.13 N	23.19 E
Eritrea □[9]	144	15.20 N	39.00 E
Erivan — Jerevan	84	40.11 N	44.30 E
Erjas (Erges) ≃	34	39.40 N	7.01 W
Erjiazhen	106	32.02 N	121.13 E
Erkelenz	56	51.05 N	6.19 E
Erken ◎	40	59.51 N	18.34 E
Erken-Jurt	84	44.27 N	41.54 E
Erkheim	58	48.02 N	10.20 E
Erkilet	130	38.49 N	35.27 E
Erkina ≃	48	52.51 N	7.23 W
Erkner	54	52.25 N	13.45 E
Erkner, Forst ◆[3]	264a	52.22 N	13.47 E
Erkowit	140	18.46 N	37.07 E
Erkrath	56	51.13 N	6.55 E
Erl	64	47.41 N	12.11 E
Erlach, Öst.	61	47.43 N	16.13 E
Erlach, Schw.	58	47.03 N	7.06 E
Erlands Point	224	47.36 N	122.42 W
Erlangen	60	49.36 N	11.01 E
Erlanger	218	39.01 N	84.36 W
Erlanghe	100	30.19 N	116.04 E
Erlangmiao	100	33.46 N	112.23 E
Erlau ≃	60	48.34 N	13.36 E
Erlauf ≃	61	48.12 N	15.11 E
Erlbach	54	50.18 N	12.22 E
Erldunda	162	25.14 S	133.12 E
Erle ◆[8]	263	51.33 N	7.05 E
Erli	62	44.08 N	8.06 E
Erling	106	31.53 N	119.36 E
Erling, Lake ◎[1]	194	33.05 N	93.35 W
Erlistoun	162	28.20 S	122.08 E
Erlongshan, Zhg.	89	47.20 N	132.28 E
Erlongshan, Zhg.	89	50.04 N	126.47 E
Erlongshantun	89	48.28 N	126.31 E
Erlsbach	64	46.55 N	12.15 E
Erma	208	38.58 N	74.54 W
Ermana, chrebet ⋏	88	50.00 N	113.30 E
Ermatingen	58	47.41 N	9.06 E
Erme ≃	42	50.18 N	3.56 W
Ermelindo Matarazo ◆[8]	287b	23.29 S	46.29 W
Ermelo, Ned.	52	52.17 N	5.37 E
Ermelo, S. Afr.	158	26.34 S	29.58 E
Ermendegou	104	42.02 N	121.56 E
Ermenek	130	36.38 N	32.54 E
Ermenek ≃	130	36.35 N	33.23 E
Ermenonville	50	49.08 N	2.42 E
Ermidas	34	38.00 N	8.23 W
Ermil Post	140	13.37 N	27.36 E
Ermineskin Indian Reserve ◆[4]	182	52.52 N	113.30 W
Ermington	274a	33.48 S	151.04 E
Ermita de Guadalupe	234	22.36 N	103.03 W
Ermita de los Correas	234	22.54 N	103.01 W
Ermont	50	48.59 N	2.16 E
Ermoúpolis	38	37.26 N	24.56 E
Ermsleben	54	51.44 N	11.21 E
Ernaballa	162	26.17 S	132.07 E
Erndtebrück	56	50.59 N	8.15 E
Erne ≃	48	54.30 N	8.16 W
Erne, Lower Lough ◎	48	54.26 N	7.46 W
Erne, Upper Lough ◎	48	54.14 N	7.32 W
Ernée	32	48.18 N	0.56 W
Ernest	214	40.41 N	79.10 W
Ernestina	258	35.16 S	59.34 W
Ernest Sound ⊔	182	55.52 N	132.10 W
Ernici, Monti ⋏	66	41.48 N	13.22 E
Ernstbrunn	61	48.32 N	16.22 E
Ernst Thälmann, Pioneerpark ♠	264a	52.28 N	13.33 E
Ernst-Thälmann-Stadion ♠	264a	52.23 N	13.05 E
Erode	122	11.21 N	77.44 E
Eromanga	166	26.40 S	143.16 E
Erongo	156	21.44 S	15.53 E
Erongo ⋏	156	21.45 S	15.37 E
Erota	144	16.14 N	37.55 E
Erp	56	50.46 N	6.43 E
Erpuzi	105	40.29 N	115.33 E
Erquelinnes	50	50.18 N	4.07 E
Err, Piz d' ∧	58	46.33 N	9.41 E
Errabiddy	162	25.28 S	117.07 E
Er-Rachidia	148	31.58 N	4.25 W
Er-Rachidia □[4]	148	31.15 N	4.05 W
Errego	154	16.02 S	37.14 E
Errer ≃	144	7.32 N	42.05 E
Er-Riad — Ar-Riyāḍ	128	24.38 N	46.43 E
Errigal Mountain ∧	48	55.02 N	8.07 W
Errington	224	49.17 N	124.22 W
Erris Head ›	48	54.19 N	10.00 W
Errochty, Loch ◎	46	56.45 N	4.12 W
Errogie	46	57.16 N	4.22 W
Errol Heights	224	45.28 N	122.36 W
Erromango I	175f	18.45 S	169.05 E
Ersekë	38	40.20 N	20.41 E
Ershijiazi	104	41.17 N	120.32 E
Ershilipu	105	40.07 N	117.24 E
Ershiqizhan	89	53.23 N	123.16 E
Ershiwuzhan	89	53.22 N	123.55 E
Erskine	198	47.40 N	96.00 W
Erskine, Lake ◎	276	41.06 N	74.15 W
Erskine Inlet ⊂	176	76.15 N	102.20 W
Erskine Park	274a	33.49 S	150.47 E
Erstein	58	48.26 N	7.40 E
Erste Wiener Hochquellenleitung ≍[1]	61	48.10 N	16.17 E
Erstfeld	58	46.49 N	8.39 E
Ertai, Zhg.	86	46.07 N	90.06 E
Ertai, Zhg.	86	44.14 N	80.52 E
Ertaizi, Zhg.	104	41.52 N	121.56 E

PORTUGUÊS

Nome	Página	Lat.°′	Long.°′ W = Oeste
Ertaizi, Zhg.	104	42.05 N	123.35 E
Ertaizi, Zhg.	104	42.35 N	124.00 E
Ertaizi, Zhg.	104	40.47 N	120.54 E
Ertil'	78	51.51 N	40.49 E
Ertingen	58	48.06 N	9.28 E
Ertix (Irtyš) ≃	74	61.04 N	68.52 E
Erto	64	46.16 N	12.22 E
Ertra □[4]	144	15.20 N	39.00 E
Ertuğrul	130	39.34 N	27.43 E
Ertvelde	50	51.11 N	3.45 E
Eruar	126	23.28 N	87.52 E
Erudina	166	31.28 S	139.23 E
Eruh	130	37.46 N	42.11 E
Erundu	156	20.36 S	16.25 E
Erunkan	273a	6.37 N	3.24 E
Erva, Ponta da ›	266c	38.50 N	8.58 W
Erval	252	32.02 S	53.24 W
Erval d'Oeste	252	27.13 S	51.34 W
Ervalla	40	59.22 N	15.15 E
Erving	207	42.36 N	72.23 W
Ervy-le-Châtel	50	48.02 N	3.55 E
Erwin, N.C., U.S.	192	35.19 N	78.40 W
Erwin, Tn., U.S.	192	36.08 N	82.25 W
Erwitte	52	51.37 N	8.20 E
Erwood	184	52.50 N	102.10 W
Erxleben	54	52.13 N	11.14 E
Érythrée — Eritrea □[9]	144	15.20 N	39.00 E
Eryuan	102	26.06 N	99.55 E
Erzaohang	106	31.05 N	121.49 E
Erzberg ◆[7]	61	47.32 N	14.54 E
Erzgebirge (Krušné hory) ⋏	54	50.30 N	13.10 E
Erzhan	89	43.58 N	128.44 E
Erzhuang	105	39.24 N	117.22 E
Erzin	88	50.15 N	95.10 E
Erzincan	130	39.44 N	39.29 E
Erzincan □[4]	130	39.40 N	39.30 E
Erzingen	58	47.39 N	8.25 E
Erzurum	130	39.55 N	41.17 E
Erzurum □[4]	130	40.00 N	41.30 E
Esa'ala	164	9.44 S	150.49 E
Esambo	152	3.40 S	23.24 E
Esan-misaki ›	92a	41.49 N	141.11 E
Esashi, Nihon	92	39.12 N	141.09 E
Esashi, Nihon	92	41.52 N	140.07 E
Esashi, Nihon	92a	44.56 N	142.35 E
Esbiye	130	40.57 N	38.44 E
Esbjerg	26	55.28 N	8.27 E
Esbly	261	48.54 N	2.49 E
Esbo — Espoo	26	60.13 N	24.40 E
Esborn	263	51.23 N	7.20 E
Esca ≃	34	42.37 N	1.03 W
Escada	250	8.22 S	35.14 W
Escalada	258	34.10 S	59.07 W
Escalante, Pil.	116	10.50 N	123.33 E
Escalante, Ut,. U.S.	200	37.46 N	111.36 W
Escalante ≃, Ut,. U.S.	200	37.17 N	110.53 W
Escalante ≃, Ven.	246	9.15 N	71.50 W
Escalante Desert ◆[2]	200	37.50 N	113.30 W
Escalaplano	71	39.37 N	9.21 E
Escalón, Méx.	232	26.45 N	104.20 W
Escalon, Ca., U.S.	226	37.47 N	120.59 W
Escalona	34	40.10 N	4.24 W
Escambia ≃	194	30.32 N	87.11 W
Escanaba	190	45.44 N	87.04 W
Escanaba ≃	190	45.47 N	87.04 W
Escandón, Puerto)(	34	40.17 N	1.00 W
Escárcega	232	18.37 N	90.43 W
Escarpada Point ›	116	18.31 N	122.13 E
Escarpado Peak ∧	116	8.36 N	117.22 E
Escarpment	284a	43.10 N	79.00 W
Escatawpa ≃	194	30.25 N	88.35 W
Escaudain	50	50.20 N	3.21 E
Escaut (Schelde) ≃	50	51.22 N	4.15 E
Esch ≃	56	48.54 N	6.04 E
Eschach	58	47.44 N	9.36 E
Eschau	58	48.29 N	7.43 E
Eschebrügge	52	52.37 N	6.46 E
Eschede	52	52.44 N	10.14 E
Eschen	58	47.13 N	9.31 E
Eschenau	60	49.34 N	11.12 E
Eschenbach	60	49.45 N	11.49 E
Eschenburg	56	50.49 N	8.20 E
Eschenlohe	64	47.36 N	11.11 E
Eschershausen	52	51.56 N	9.38 E
Eschlkam	60	49.18 N	12.55 E
Escholzmatt	58	46.55 N	7.56 E
Eschscholtz Bay ⊂	180	66.18 N	161.25 W
Esch-sur-Alzette	56	49.30 N	5.59 E
Esch-sur-Sûre	56	49.55 N	5.55 E
Eschwege	56	51.11 N	10.04 E
Eschweiler	56	50.49 N	6.16 E
Esclave, Grand Lac de l' — Great Slave Lake ◎	176	61.30 N	114.00 W
Esclavo, Gran Lago del — Great Slave Lake ◎	176	61.30 N	114.00 W
Escobal	236	9.09 N	79.58 W
Escobar □[5]	288	34.23 S	58.46 W
Escobar, Arroyo ≃	288	34.21 S	58.44 W
Escobedo, Méx.	196	27.13 N	101.21 W
Escobedo, Méx.	232	29.05 N	102.19 W
Escocesa, Bahía ⊂	238	19.25 N	69.45 W
Escoheag	207	41.36 N	71.45 W
Escondido	228	33.07 N	117.05 W
Escondido ≃, Méx.	196	28.39 N	100.34 W
Escondido ≃, Nic.	236	12.04 N	83.45 W
Escondido Creek ≃	228	33.01 N	117.15 W
Escorial — San Lorenzo de El Escorial	34	40.35 N	4.09 W
Escoutay ≃	62	44.29 N	4.42 E
Escravos ≃[1]	150	5.35 N	5.10 E
Escrick	44	53.53 N	1.02 W
Escuadrón 201 ◆[8]	286a	19.22 N	99.06 W
Escudero, Arroyo ≃	258	34.20 S	57.05 W
Escudo de Veraguas, Isla I	236	9.06 N	81.33 W
Escuinapa de Hidalgo	234	22.51 N	105.48 W
Escuintla, Guat.	236	14.18 N	90.47 W
Escuintla, Méx.	232	15.20 N	92.38 W
Escuintla □[5]	236	14.10 N	91.00 W
Escuminac, Point ›	186	47.04 N	64.46 W
Esebi	154	2.57 N	30.39 E
Eséka	152	3.39 N	10.46 E
Eşen	130	36.27 N	29.16 E
Eşen ≃	130	36.16 N	29.15 E
Esenler ◆[8]	267b	41.02 N	28.51 E
Esens	52	53.39 N	7.37 E
Esera ≃	34	42.06 N	0.15 E
Esesi	130	39.49 N	39.19 E
Eşfahān (Isfahan)	128	32.40 N	51.38 E
Eşfahān □[4]	128	33.00 N	52.00 E
Esfandaqeh	128	28.38 N	57.12 E
Esfarāyen	128	37.02 N	57.27 E
Esgueva ≃	34	41.40 N	4.43 W
Eshan	102	24.11 N	102.22 E
Esher ◆[8]	260	51.23 N	0.22 W
Eshkāshem	123	36.42 N	71.34 E
Eshowe	158	28.58 S	31.29 E
Esh-Sham — Dimashq	132	33.30 N	36.18 E
Eshta'ol	132	31.47 N	35.00 E
Esh Winning	44	54.47 N	1.43 W
Esiama	150	4.56 N	2.21 W
Esigodini	154	20.18 S	28.56 E
Esine	64	45.55 N	10.15 E
Esino ≃	66	43.39 N	13.22 E
Esira	157b	24.20 S	46.42 E
Esk	171a	27.15 S	152.25 E
Esk ≃, N.Z.	172	43.06 S	171.57 E
Esk ≃, U.K.	44	54.58 N	3.04 W
Esk ≃, Eng., U.K.	44	54.29 N	0.37 W
Esk ≃, Eng., U.K.	44	54.21 N	3.23 W
Esk ≃, Scot., U.K.	46	55.57 N	3.03 W
Eskdale, N.Z.	172	39.24 S	176.50 E
Eskdale, W.V., U.S.	188	38.05 N	81.26 W

Eskdale V	44	55.10 N	3.00 W
Eske, Lough ◎	48	54.41 N	8.03 W
Eski Dzhumaya — Târgovište	38	43.15 N	26.34 E
Eskifjörður	24a	65.04 N	13.59 W
Eskiikan	85	43.12 N	68.31 E
Eskilstrup	41	54.51 N	11.54 E
Eskilstuna	40	59.22 N	16.30 E
Eskimalatya	130	38.26 N	38.23 E
Eskimo Lakes ◎	180	69.15 N	132.17 W
Eskimo Point	176	61.07 N	94.03 W
Eskipazar	130	40.58 N	32.33 E
Eskişehir	130	39.46 N	30.32 E
Eskişehir □[4]	130	39.35 N	31.10 E
Eskridge	198	38.51 N	96.06 W
Esla ≃	34	41.29 N	6.03 W
Eslāmābād	128	34.06 N	46.31 E
Eslām Qal'eh	128	34.40 N	61.04 E
Eslāmshahr	128	35.40 N	51.10 E
Eslarn	60	49.35 N	12.32 E
Eslohe	56	51.15 N	8.09 E
Eslöv	41	55.50 N	13.20 E
Eşme	130	38.24 N	28.59 E
Esmeralda, Austl.	166	18.50 S	142.34 E
Esmeralda, Cuba	240p	21.51 N	78.07 W
Esmeralda, Méx.	196	25.40 N	103.30 W
Esmeralda, Isla I	254	48.57 S	75.25 W
Esmeraldas	246	0.59 N	79.42 W
Esmeraldas □[4]	246	0.40 N	79.30 W
Esmeraldas ≃	246	0.58 N	79.38 W
Esmirna — İzmir	130	38.25 N	27.09 E
Esmond, N.D., U.S.	198	48.02 N	99.45 W
Esmond, R.I., U.S.	207	41.52 N	71.29 W
Esnagi Lake ◎	190	48.38 N	84.32 W
Esneux	56	50.32 N	5.34 E
Esong	152	2.09 N	10.58 E
Esopus Creek ≃	210	42.04 N	73.56 W
Espada, Punta ›	246	12.05 N	71.07 W
Espagne — Spain □[1]	34	40.00 N	4.00 W
Espalion	32	44.31 N	2.46 E
Espaly-Saint-Marcel	62	45.03 N	3.52 E
España — Spain □[1]	34	40.00 N	4.00 W
Espanola, On., Can.	190	46.15 N	81.46 W
Espanola, N.M., U.S.	200	35.59 N	106.04 W
Española, Isla I	246a	1.25 S	89.42 W
Esparto	226	38.41 N	122.00 W
Esparza	236	9.59 N	84.40 W
Espasingen	58	47.49 N	9.00 E
Espe, Dan.	41	55.12 N	10.25 E
Espe, Kaz.	85	43.52 N	74.10 E
Espejo	34	37.41 N	4.33 W
Espelkamp	52	52.25 N	8.36 E
Espenberg, Cape ›	180	66.33 N	163.36 W
Espenhain	54	51.11 N	12.29 E
Espera, Arroyo ≃[1]	288	34.24 S	58.36 W
Espera Feliz	255	20.39 S	41.55 W
Esperança, Bra.	246	4.24 S	69.52 W
Esperança, Bra.	250	7.01 S	35.51 W
Esperance, Austl.	162	33.51 S	121.53 E
Esperance, N.Y., U.S.	210	42.46 N	74.15 W
Esperance Bay ⊂	162	33.51 S	121.53 E
Esperantina	250	3.54 S	42.14 W
Esperantinópolis	250	4.53 S	44.53 W
Esperanza, Arg.	252	31.27 S	60.56 W
Esperanza, Cuba	240p	22.27 N	80.06 W
Esperanza, Méx.	232	27.35 N	109.56 W
Esperanza, Méx.	234	18.52 N	97.24 W
Esperanza, Pil.	116	8.43 N	125.36 E
Esperanza, Pil.	116	11.44 N	124.03 E
Esperanza, P.R.	240m	18.06 N	65.28 W
Esperanza, S. Afr.	158	30.21 S	30.40 E
Esperanza ʊ[3]	9	63.24 S	56.59 W
Esperanza Inlet ⊂	182	49.48 N	126.50 W
Espergærde	41	56.00 N	12.34 E
Esperia	66	41.23 N	13.41 E
Esperito, Arroyo ≃[1]	288	34.23 S	58.36 W
Espevær	26	59.36 N	5.10 E
Espichel, Cabo ›	34	38.25 N	9.13 W
Espinal	246	4.09 N	74.53 W
Espinazo	196	26.16 N	101.06 W
Espinazo, Sierra del — Espinhaço, Serra do ⋏[3]	255	17.30 S	43.30 W
Espingarda ≃	250	10.03 S	47.13 W
Espinhaço, Serra do ⋏	255	17.30 S	43.30 W
Espinho	34	41.00 N	8.39 W
Espinillo	252	24.58 S	58.34 W
Espinillo, Arroyo ≃	258	34.59 S	57.36 W
Espinillo, Punta del ›	258	34.50 S	56.26 W
Espino	246	8.34 N	66.01 W
Espinosa	255	14.56 S	42.50 W
Espírito Santo □[3]	255	19.30 S	40.30 W
Espírito Santo do Dourado	256	22.03 S	45.58 W
Espírito Santo — Vila Velha	250	3.13 N	51.13 W
Espiritu Santo I	175f	15.15 S	166.50 E
Espíritu Santo, Isla I	232	24.30 N	110.22 W
Espita	232	21.01 N	88.19 W
Espoir, Bay d' ⊂	186	47.50 N	55.51 W
Espoo (Esbo)	26	60.13 N	24.40 E
Esposende	34	41.32 N	8.47 W
Esposizione Universale di Roma ♠	267a	41.50 N	12.28 E
Espugues de Llobregat	266d	41.22 N	2.05 E
Espumoso	252	28.44 S	52.51 W
Espungabera	156	20.29 S	32.48 E
Espy	210	41.00 N	76.24 W
Espyville Station	214	41.36 N	80.29 W
Esquatzel Coulee V	202	46.17 N	119.07 W
Esquel	254	42.54 S	71.19 W
Esquimalt	224	48.26 N	123.24 W
Esquina	252	30.01 S	59.32 W
Esquina Negra	258	35.02 S	58.03 W
Esquipulas, Guat.	236	14.34 N	89.21 W
Esquipulas, Nic.	236	12.40 N	85.47 W
Esquiú	252	29.23 S	65.17 W
Esrum Sø ◎	41	56.00 N	12.24 E
Essa ≃	76	54.53 N	28.40 E
Essaoui Mellene, Oued V	148	27.26 N	6.40 E
Essaouira (Mogador)	148	31.30 N	9.47 W
Essaouira □[4]	148	31.25 N	9.30 W
Essarts	261	48.30 N	1.46 E
Essé	152	4.05 N	11.53 E
Esse ≃	66	43.16 N	11.54 E
Esseg — Osijek	38	45.33 N	18.41 E
Es-Sekhira	148	34.17 N	10.06 E
Essen, Bel.	50	51.28 N	4.28 E
Essen, Dtsch.	52	52.43 N	7.57 E
Essen, Dtsch.	56	51.28 N	7.01 E
Essen, Dtsch.	263	51.28 N	7.01 E
Essenbach	60	48.37 N	12.13 E
Essenberg ◆[8]	263	51.26 N	6.42 E
Essendon, Austl.	169	37.46 S	144.55 E
Essendon, Eng., U.K.	260	51.46 N	0.09 W
Essendon, Mount ∧	162	24.59 S	120.28 E
Essendon Airport ⊠	169	37.43 S	144.53 E
Essen-Mülheim, Flughafen ⊠	263	51.24 N	6.58 E
Essentuki — Jessentuki	84	44.03 N	42.51 E
Essequibo ≃	246	6.59 N	58.23 W
Essequibo Islands-West Demerara □[4]	246	6.40 N	58.30 W
Es Sers	36	36.04 N	9.02 E
Essex, On., Can.	214	42.10 N	82.49 W
Essex, Ct., U.S.	207	41.21 N	72.23 W
Essex, Il., U.S.	216	41.11 N	88.11 W
Essex, Ia., U.S.	198	40.50 N	95.18 W
Essex, Md., U.S.	208	39.18 N	76.28 W
Essex, Ma., U.S.	207	42.37 N	70.47 W
Essex, Mo., U.S.	194	36.48 N	89.51 W
Essex, Mt., U.S.	182	48.16 N	113.36 W
Essex □[6], On., Can.	214	42.10 N	82.50 W

Essex □[6], Eng., U.K.	42	51.48 N	0.40 E
Essex □[6], Ma., U.S.	207	42.40 N	70.55 W
Essex □[6], N.J., U.S.	210	40.48 N	74.12 W
Essex □[6], Vt., U.S.	206	44.57 N	71.43 W
Essex □[6], Va., U.S.	208	37.55 N	76.55 W
Essex ≃	283	42.39 N	70.46 W
Essex Bay ⊂	283	42.39 N	70.44 W
Essex Fells	276	40.49 N	74.17 W
Essex Junction	188	44.29 N	73.06 W
Essex Skypark ⊠	284b	39.18 N	76.28 W
Essexville	190	43.36 N	83.50 W
Essing	60	48.56 N	11.47 E
Essington	285	39.52 N	75.18 W
Essling ◆[8]	264b	48.13 N	16.32 E
Esslingen	56	48.45 N	9.16 E
Es Smala es Souassi	36	35.21 N	10.33 E
Esson Lake ◎	212	45.02 N	78.16 W
Essonne □[5]	50	48.36 N	2.20 E
Essonne ≃	50	48.37 N	2.29 E
Essoyes	58	48.04 N	4.32 E
Es-Suki	140	13.20 N	33.54 E
Essvik	26	62.19 N	17.24 E
Est □[4]	152	4.00 N	14.00 E
Est, Canal de l' ≍	58	48.45 N	5.35 E
Est, Cap ›	157b	15.16 S	50.29 E
Est, Gare ◆[5]	261	48.53 N	2.22 E
Est, Île de l' I	186	47.37 N	61.26 W
Est, Pointe de l' ›	186	49.08 N	61.41 W
Estacada	224	45.17 N	122.19 W
Estaca de Bares, Punta de la ›	34	43.46 N	7.42 W
Estacado, Llano ≡	196	33.30 N	102.40 W
Estación La Colorado	234	23.52 N	102.26 W
Estado, Parque do ♠	287b	23.39 S	46.37 W
Estados, Isla de los (Staten Island) I	254	54.47 S	64.15 W
Estados Unidos — United States □[1]	178	38.00 N	97.00 W
Eṣṭahbān	128	29.08 N	54.04 E
Estaires	50	50.38 N	2.43 E
Estambul — İstanbul	130	41.01 N	28.58 E
Estância, Bra.	250	11.16 S	37.26 W
Estancia, Pil.	116	11.28 N	123.09 E
Estancia, S. Afr.	158	26.17 S	29.52 E
Estancia, N.M., U.S.	200	34.45 N	106.03 W
Estancia Los López	234	20.53 N	104.31 W
Estanislao del Campo	252	25.03 S	60.06 W
Estanzuelas	236	13.38 N	88.30 W
Estarreja	34	40.45 N	8.34 W
Estats, Pique d' ∧	34	42.40 N	1.24 E
Estavayer-le-Lac	58	46.51 N	6.50 E
Estcourt	158	29.01 S	29.52 E
Este	64	45.14 N	11.39 E
Este ≃	52	53.32 N	9.47 E
Este, Parque Nacional del ♠	286c	10.30 N	66.50 W
Este, Punta ›	240m	18.08 N	65.16 W
Esteban Echeverría	258	34.50 S	58.28 W
Esteban Echeverría □[5]	288	34.51 S	58.32 W
Estefanía, Lago — Stefanie, Lake ◎	144	4.40 N	36.50 E
Esteio	252	29.51 S	51.10 W
Estelí	236	13.05 N	86.23 W
Estelí □[5]	236	13.10 N	86.20 W
Estella	34	42.40 N	2.02 W
Estelline, S.D., U.S.	198	44.34 N	96.54 W
Estelline, Tx., U.S.	196	34.33 N	100.26 W
Estell Manor	208	39.24 N	74.44 W
Estèng	62	44.14 N	6.45 E
Estepa	34	37.18 N	4.54 W
Estepas de Kirguises — Kirgizskij chrebet ⋏	85	42.30 N	74.00 E
Estepona	34	36.26 N	5.08 W
Ester	180	64.51 N	148.01 W
Esterel ⋏	62	43.30 N	6.50 E
Esterhazy	184	50.40 N	102.08 W
Esterhazy, Schloss ⊥	61	47.51 N	16.32 E
Estérias, Cap ›	152	0.37 N	9.20 E
Esternay	50	48.44 N	3.34 E
Estero	220	26.26 N	81.49 W
Estero Bay ⊂, Ca., U.S.	226	35.24 N	120.53 W
Estero Bay ⊂, Fl., U.S.	220	26.25 N	81.52 W
Estero Island I	220	26.26 N	81.56 W
Estéron ≃	62	43.49 N	7.11 E
Esteros	252	26.37 S	63.39 W
Esterwegen	52	52.59 N	7.38 E
Estes Park	200	40.22 N	105.31 W
Este Sudeste, Cayos del II	236	12.26 N	81.27 W
Estevan	184	49.08 N	102.59 W
Estevan Group II	182	53.05 N	129.40 W
Estevan Point	182	49.23 N	126.33 W
Esther Island I	180	60.50 N	148.05 W
Estherville	198	43.24 N	94.49 W
Estill	192	32.45 N	81.14 W
Estissac	50	48.16 N	3.49 E
Estiva	256	22.28 S	46.02 W
Estiva, Ribeirão da ≃	287b	23.44 S	46.23 W
Estiva, Rio da ≃	255	12.23 S	45.05 W
Estling, Lake ◎	276	40.53 N	74.30 W
Estocolmo — Stockholm	40	59.20 N	18.03 E
Eston, Sk., Can.	184	51.10 N	108.46 W
Eston, Eng., U.K.	44	54.34 N	1.07 W
Estonia (Eesti) □[1], Europe	22	59.00 N	26.00 E
Estonia (Eesti) □[1], Europe	76	59.00 N	26.00 E
Estoril	34	38.42 N	9.23 W
Estrasburgo — Strasbourg	58	48.35 N	7.45 E
Estrées-Saint-Denis	50	49.26 N	2.39 E
Estrela	252	29.29 S	51.58 W
Estrela ∧	34	40.19 N	7.37 W
Estrela ≃	287a	22.43 S	43.13 W
Estrela, Serra da ⋏	34	40.20 N	7.38 W
Estrela do Norte	255	13.49 S	49.04 W
Estrela do Sul	255	18.46 S	47.42 W
Estrella ≃	226	35.45 N	120.41 W
Estremadura □[9]	34	39.15 N	9.10 W
Estremoz	34	38.51 N	7.35 W
Estribo	234	22.26 N	99.17 W
Estrondo, Serra do ⋏[1]	250	9.00 S	48.45 W
Estuaire □[4]	152	0.15 N	10.00 E
Estuary	184	50.56 N	109.46 W
Esumba, Île I	152	2.00 N	21.12 E
Eszék — Osijek	38	45.33 N	18.41 E
Esztergom	30	47.48 N	18.45 E
Étables	32	48.38 N	2.50 W
Etadunna	166	28.43 S	138.38 E
Etah, India	124	27.38 N	78.40 E
Etah, Kal. Nun.	16	78.19 N	72.38 W
Étain	56	49.13 N	5.38 E
Etajima	96	34.15 N	132.30 E
Eta-jima I	96	34.15 N	132.28 E
Étalle	56	49.41 N	5.36 E
Étamaniou ≃	186	50.17 N	59.58 W
Étampes	50	48.26 N	2.09 E
Etamunbanie, Lake ◎	166	26.15 S	139.44 E
Étaples	50	50.31 N	1.39 E
États-Unis — United States □[1]	178	38.00 N	97.00 W
Etāwah	124	26.46 N	79.02 E
Etchemin ≃	186	46.46 N	71.14 W
Etchojoa	232	26.55 N	109.38 W
Etéké	152	1.29 S	11.35 E
Etembue	152	1.17 N	9.25 E
Etendard, Pic de l' ∧	62	45.09 N	6.09 E
Ethan	198	43.32 N	97.59 W
Ethel	194	33.07 N	89.27 W
Ethel ≃	162	24.09 S	118.26 E
Ethel, Mount ∧	200	40.39 N	106.41 W
Ethelbert	184	51.31 N	100.22 W

Ethel Creek	162	22.54 S	120.09 E
Ethel Lake ◎	180	63.21 N	136.00 W
Etherow ≃	262	53.24 N	2.03 W
Ethiopia (Ityopiya) □[1], Afr.	136	9.00 N	39.00 E
Ethiopia (Ityopiya) □[1], Afr.	144	9.00 N	39.00 E
Ethiopian Plateau ⋏[1]	144	9.00 N	38.00 E
Ethiopie — Ethiopia □[1]	144	9.00 N	39.00 E
Ethridge, Mt., U.S.	202	48.33 N	112.07 W
Ethridge, Tn., U.S.	194	35.19 N	87.18 W
Eticoga	150	11.09 N	16.08 W
Eticuera Creek ≃	226	38.41 N	122.16 W
Etigo-heiya ≡	92	37.45 N	139.00 E
Etili	130	39.59 N	26.54 E
Étiolles	261	48.38 N	2.29 E
Etiopía — Ethiopia □[1]	144	9.00 N	39.00 E
Etive, Loch ◎	46	56.29 N	5.09 W
Etiwanda	228	34.08 N	117.31 W
Etjo ∧	156	21.09 S	16.30 E
Etna, Ca., U.S.	204	41.27 N	122.53 W
Etna, N.Y., U.S.	210	42.29 N	76.23 W
Etna, Pa., U.S.	214	40.30 N	79.56 W
Etna, Wy., U.S.	200	43.02 N	111.00 W
Etna, Monte (Mongibello) ∧[1]	70	37.46 N	15.00 E
Etna Green	216	41.17 N	86.03 W
Etne	26	59.40 N	5.56 E
Etobicoke	212	43.42 N	79.32 W
Etobicoke Creek ≃	212	43.35 N	79.32 W
Etoile	154	11.38 S	27.34 E
Étoile, Chaîne de l' ⋏	62	43.22 N	5.30 E
Etoka	152	0.10 N	23.23 E
Etolin Island I	180	56.08 N	132.26 W
Etolin Strait ⊔	180	60.20 N	165.15 W
Etomami ≃	184	52.48 N	102.33 W
Eton, Austl.	166	21.16 S	148.58 E
Eton, Eng., U.K.	260	51.31 N	0.37 W
Eton College ʊ[2]	260	51.30 N	0.36 W
Etondo	152	7.46 S	23.36 E
Etorofu-tō — Iturup, ostrov I	92a	44.54 N	147.30 E
Etosha National Park ♠	156	19.00 S	15.50 E
Etosha Pan ≡	156	18.45 S	16.15 E
Etoumbi	152	0.01 S	14.57 E
Etowah	192	35.19 N	84.31 W
Etowah ≃	192	34.15 N	85.11 W
Étréchy	50	48.30 N	2.12 E
Étrépagny	50	49.18 N	1.37 E
Étretat	50	49.42 N	0.12 E
Etrotroka	157b	22.53 S	47.36 E
Etroubles	62	45.49 N	7.14 E
Etrusca, Necropoli ⊥	66	42.15 N	11.47 E
Etsch — Adige ≃	64	45.10 N	12.20 E
Ettal	64	47.34 N	11.05 E
Ettalong	170	33.31 S	151.21 E
Ettelbruck	56	49.52 N	6.05 E
Ettenheim	58	48.15 N	7.49 E
Etten-Leur	52	51.34 N	4.38 E
Etterbeek	56	50.50 N	4.23 E
Etters	208	40.09 N	76.45 W
Et Tîdra I	150	19.44 N	16.24 W
Ettington	42	52.09 N	1.36 W
Ettlingen	56	48.56 N	8.24 E
Ettrema Creek ≃	170	34.50 S	150.22 E
Ettrick	208	37.14 N	77.25 W
Ettrick Forest ◆[3]	46	55.30 N	3.00 W
Ettrick Pen ∧	44	55.22 N	3.16 W
Ettrick Water ≃	46	55.31 N	2.55 W
Ettringen, Dtsch.	56	50.21 N	7.13 E
Ettringen, Dtsch.	58	48.06 N	10.39 E
Etuku	154	3.43 S	25.44 E
Etyka	88	51.00 N	116.50 E
Etzatlán	234	20.46 N	104.05 W
Etzikom Coulee ≃	184	49.25 N	111.10 W
Etzná ⊥	232	19.35 N	90.15 W
Eu	50	50.03 N	1.25 E
Eua I	14	21.22 S	174.56 W
Eua Iki I	174w	21.07 S	174.59 W
Eubank Acres	222	30.23 N	97.42 W
Euboea — Évvoia I	38	38.34 N	23.50 E
Eucalyptus Hills	228	32.56 N	116.56 W
Euchiniko ≃	182	53.14 N	123.30 W
Eucla	162	31.43 S	128.52 E
Euclid, Oh., U.S.	214	41.35 N	81.31 W
Euclid, Pa., U.S.	214	41.00 N	79.56 W
Euclid Center	216	42.08 N	86.24 W
Euclid Creek ≃	279a	41.35 N	81.35 W
Euclid Creek Reservation ♠	279a	41.33 N	81.32 W
Euclides da Cunha	250	10.31 S	39.01 W
Eucumbene	171b	36.07 S	148.38 E
Eucumbene ≃	171b	36.21 S	148.38 E
Eucumbene, Lake ◎[1]	171b	36.05 S	148.45 E
Eudistes, Lac des ◎	186	50.30 N	65.15 W
Eudora, Ar., U.S.	194	33.06 N	91.15 W
Eudora, Ks., U.S.	198	38.56 N	95.05 W
Eudunda	168b	34.11 S	139.04 E
Eufaula, Al., U.S.	194	31.53 N	85.08 W
Eufaula, Ok., U.S.	196	35.17 N	95.34 W
Eufaula Lake ◎[1]	196	35.17 N	95.31 W
Eufrates — Euphrates ≃	128	31.00 N	47.25 E
Euganei, Colli ⋏[2]	64	45.19 N	11.40 E
Eugendorf	64	47.52 N	13.07 E
Eugene	202	44.03 N	123.05 W
Eugenia, Punta ›	232	27.50 N	115.05 W
Eugenia Lake ◎	212	44.20 N	80.30 W
Eugenio Bustos	252	33.46 S	69.04 W
Eugênio de Melo	256	23.09 S	45.47 W
Eugmo I	26	63.49 N	22.45 E
Eugowra	166	33.26 S	148.23 E
Euijeongbu — Ŭijŏngbu	98	37.44 N	127.03 E
Euless	222	32.50 N	97.04 W
Eulo	166	28.10 S	145.03 E
Eume ≃	34	43.25 N	8.08 W
Eumemmerring Creek ≃	274b	38.03 S	145.10 E
Eumungerie	166	31.57 S	148.37 E
Eunápolis	255	16.22 S	39.35 W
Eungella National Park ♠	166	21.00 S	148.30 E
Eunice, La., U.S.	194	30.29 N	92.25 W
Eunice, N.M., U.S.	196	32.26 N	103.09 W
Eupen	56	50.38 N	6.02 E
Euphrates (Firat) (Nahr al-Furāt) ≃	128	31.00 N	47.25 E
Euphrat — Euphrates ≃	128	31.00 N	47.25 E
Eupora	194	33.32 N	89.16 W
Eure	208	36.25 N	76.51 W
Eure □[5]	50	49.10 N	1.00 E
Eure ≃	50	49.18 N	1.12 E
Eure-et-Loir □[5]	50	48.30 N	1.30 E
Eureka, Ak., U.S.	180	61.56 N	147.10 W
Eureka, Ca., U.S.	204	40.48 N	124.09 W
Eureka, Il., U.S.	190	40.43 N	89.16 W
Eureka, Ks., U.S.	198	37.49 N	96.17 W
Eureka, Mo., U.S.	219	38.30 N	90.37 W
Eureka, Mt., U.S.	202	48.52 N	115.03 W
Eureka, Nv., U.S.	204	39.30 N	115.57 W
Eureka, Pa., U.S.	214	40.15 N	78.46 W
Eureka, S.C., U.S.	192	34.42 N	81.11 W
Eureka, S.D., U.S.	198	45.46 N	99.37 W
Eureka, Tx., U.S.	222	32.01 N	96.18 W
Eureka, Ut,. U.S.	200	39.57 N	112.07 W
Eureka, Mount ∧	162	26.34 S	121.32 E
Eureka Springs	194	36.24 N	93.44 W
Eurialo, Castello ⊥	70	37.06 N	15.14 E
Eurinilla Creek ≃	166	30.50 S	140.01 E
Euroa	169	36.45 S	145.35 E
Euro Disney, Parc ♠	261	48.51 N	2.47 E
Europa, Île I	138	22.20 S	40.22 E
Europa, Picos de ⋏	34	43.12 N	4.48 W
Europabrücke ◆[5]	64	47.11 N	11.23 E
Europa Point ›	34	36.10 N	5.22 W
Europe ⊥[1]	4	50.00 N	28.00 E

Symbol	English	Deutsch	Español	Français	Português
≃	River	Fluß	Río	Rivière	Rio
≍	Canal	Kanal	Canal	Canal	Canal
⌞	Waterfall, Rapids	Wasserfall, Stromschnellen	Cascada, Rápidos	Chute d'eau, Rapides	Cascata, Rápidos
⊔	Strait	Meeresstraße	Estrecho	Détroit	Estreito
⊂	Bay, Gulf	Bucht, Golf	Bahía, Golfo	Baie, Golfe	Baía, Golfo
◎	Lake, Lakes	See, Seen	Lago, Lagos	Lac, Lacs	Lago, Lagos
≡	Swamp	Sumpf	Pantano	Marais	Pântano
⊓	Ice Features, Glacier	Eis- und Gletscherformen	Accidentes Glaciales	Formes glaciaires	Acidentes glaciares
⊤	Other Hydrographic Features	Andere Hydrographische Objekte	Otros Elementos Hidrográficos	Autres données hydrographiques	Outros acidentes hidrográficos
V	Submarine Features	Untermeerische Objekte	Accidentes Submarinos	Formes de relief sous-marin	Acidentes submarinos
□	Political Unit	Politische Einheit	Unidad Politica	Entité politique	Unidade política
ʊ	Cultural Institution	Kulturelle Institution	Institución Cultural	Institution culturelle	Instituição cultural
⊥	Historical Site	Historische Stätte	Sitio Histórico	Site historique	Sitio histórico
♠	Recreational Site	Erholungs- und Ferienort	Sitio de Recreo	Centre de loisirs	Area de Lazer
⊠	Airport	Flughafen	Aeropuerto	Aéroport	Aeroporto
■	Military Installation	Militäranlage	Instalación Militar	Installation militaire	Instalação militar
◆	Miscellaneous	Verschiedenes	Misceláneo	Divers	Diversos

Name	Page	Lat.°′	Long.°′
Europe ± [1]	10	50.00 N	28.00 E
Europoort ◆ [5]	52	51.58 N	4.00 E
Eursinge	52	52.46 N	6.28 E
Eurville	58	48.35 N	5.02 E
Euseigne	58	46.10 N	7.25 E
Euskal Herriko □ [4]	34	43.00 N	2.30 W
Euskirchen	56	50.39 N	6.47 E
Eustace	222	32.18 N	96.01 W
Eustis, Fl., U.S.	220	28.51 N	81.41 W
Eustis, Ne., U.S.	198	40.39 N	100.09 W
Eustis, Lake ⊜	220	28.50 N	81.44 W
Euston	166	34.35 S	142.44 E
Euston Station ◆ [5]	260	51.32 N	0.08 W
Eutaw	194	32.50 N	87.53 W
Eutin	54	54.08 N	10.37 E
Eutingen	56	48.28 N	8.44 E
Eutsuk Lake ⊜	182	53.20 N	126.44 W
Eutzsch	54	51.49 N	12.38 E
Euxton, Eng., U.K.	44	53.39 N	2.40 W
Euxton, Eng., U.K.	262	53.40 N	2.41 W
Euzet-les-Bains	62	44.04 N	4.14 E
Eva	194	34.20 N	86.46 W
Evadale	194	30.21 N	94.04 W
Eva Downs	162	18.01 S	134.52 E
Evale	152	16.33 S	15.44 E
Evällen ⊜	40	60.03 N	18.20 E
Evançon ≃	62	45.40 N	7.41 E
Evandale	166	41.34 S	147.14 E
Evans	200	40.22 N	104.41 W
Evans, Lac ⊜	176	50.55 N	77.00 W
Evans, Mount ∧	200	39.35 N	105.38 W
Evansburg, Ab., Can.	182	53.36 N	115.01 W
Evansburg, Pa., U.S.	285	40.11 N	75.26 W
Evans Center	210	42.39 N	79.02 W
Evans City	214	40.46 N	80.03 W
Evans Creek ≃	202	42.25 N	123.11 W
Evansdale	190	42.28 N	92.16 W
Evans Head >	166	29.07 S	153.26 E
Evans Mills	212	44.05 N	75.48 W
Evansport	216	41.25 N	84.24 W
Evans Strait ⊍	176	63.15 N	82.00 W
Evanston, Il., U.S.	216	42.02 N	87.41 W
Evanston, Pa., U.S.	279b	40.16 N	79.41 W
Evanston, Wy., U.S.	200	41.16 N	110.57 W
Evansville, Il., U.S.	194	38.05 N	89.56 W
Evansville, In., U.S.	194	37.58 N	87.33 W
Evansville, Mn., U.S.	198	46.00 N	95.40 W
Evansville, Wi., U.S.	216	42.46 N	89.17 W
Evansville, Wy., U.S.	200	42.51 N	106.16 W
Evant	196	31.29 N	98.09 W
Evanton	46	57.40 N	4.20 W
Eva Perón → La Plata	258	34.55 S	57.57 W
Evart	190	43.54 N	85.15 W
Evarts	192	36.51 N	83.11 W
Evaz	128	27.46 N	53.59 E
Ève	261	49.05 N	2.42 E
Evecquemont	261	49.02 N	1.57 E
Eveking	263	51.14 N	7.44 E
Eveleth	190	47.27 N	92.32 W
Evelyn, Mount ∧ [2]	164	13.36 S	132.53 E
Evening Shade	194	36.04 N	91.37 W
Evenkamp	263	51.40 N	7.39 E
Evenkijskij Avtonomiyj Okrug □ [8]	88	59.15 N	104.00 E
Evenlode ≃	42	51.47 N	1.21 W
Evensk	74	61.57 N	159.14 E
Evenwood	44	54.37 N	1.46 W
Even Yehuda	132	32.16 N	34.53 E
Everard, Lake ⊜	162	31.25 S	135.05 E
Everard, Mount ∧, Austl.	162	26.16 S	132.04 E
Everard, Mount ∧, B.C., Can.	182	51.05 N	125.45 W
Everard Ranges ⋏	162	27.05 S	132.28 E
Evercreech	42	51.09 N	2.30 W
Evere	56	50.52 N	4.24 E
Everest	198	39.40 N	95.25 W
Everest, Mount (Qomolangma Feng) ∧	124	27.59 N	86.56 E
Everett, On., Can.	212	44.11 N	79.57 W
Everett, Ma., U.S.	207	42.24 N	71.03 W
Everett, N.J., U.S.	276	40.21 N	74.09 W
Everett, Pa., U.S.	188	40.00 N	78.22 W
Everett, Wa., U.S.	224	47.58 N	122.12 W
Everett, Mount ∧	207	42.06 N	73.25 W
Evergem	50	51.07 N	3.42 E
Everglades City	220	25.52 N	81.23 W
Everglades National Park ♠	220	25.27 N	80.53 W
Evergreen, Al., U.S.	194	31.26 N	86.57 W
Evergreen, Ca., U.S.	204	35.54 N	120.26 W
Evergreen, Mt., U.S.	202	48.13 N	114.18 W
Evergreen, Tx., U.S.	222	30.33 N	95.14 W
Evergreen Lake ⊜ [1]	216	40.40 N	89.02 W
Evergreen Park	216	41.43 N	87.42 W
Evergreen Plaza ◆ [9]	278	41.43 N	87.41 W
Everly	198	43.09 N	95.19 W
Everman	222	32.37 N	97.17 W
Everman, Volcán ∧ [1]	232	18.48 N	110.59 W
Everöd	26	55.54 N	14.06 E
Eversael	263	51.33 N	6.39 E
Eversberg	56	51.21 N	8.20 E
Eversen	52	52.45 N	10.02 E
Everson, Pa., U.S.	214	40.05 N	79.35 W
Everson, Wa., U.S.	224	48.55 N	122.20 W
Everswinkel	52	51.55 N	7.50 E
Everton	218	39.34 N	85.05 W
Everton ◆ [8]	262	53.25 N	2.58 W
Everton Football Ground ♠	262	53.26 N	2.58 W
Evesen	52	52.17 N	8.59 E
Evesham, Sk., Can.	184	52.24 N	109.50 W
Evesham, Eng., U.K.	42	52.06 N	1.56 W
Evesham, Vale of V	42	52.06 N	1.50 W
Évian-les-Bains	58	46.23 N	6.35 E
Evijärvi	26	63.22 N	23.29 E
Evinayong	152	1.27 N	10.34 E
Eving ◆ [8]	263	51.33 N	7.29 E
Evingsen	263	51.18 N	7.44 E
Evionnaz	58	46.11 N	7.01 E
Evisa	36	42.15 N	8.47 E
Evje	26	58.36 N	7.51 E
Evolène	58	46.07 N	7.30 E
Évora	34	38.34 N	7.54 W
Evoron, ozero ⊜	89	51.28 N	136.30 E
Evpatoria → Jevpatorija	78	45.12 N	33.22 E
Évrange	56	49.30 N	6.12 E
Évreux	50	49.01 N	1.09 E
Evrieu	62	45.35 N	5.34 E
ʻEvron	132	32.59 N	35.06 E
Évros (Marica) (Meriç) ≃	38	40.52 N	26.12 E
Evrótas ≃	38	36.48 N	22.40 E
Évry	50	48.38 N	2.27 E
Évry-les-Châteaux	261	48.39 N	2.38 E
E. V. Spence Reservoir ⊜ [1]	196	31.55 N	100.35 W
Evungu	154	4.27 S	25.12 E
Évvoia I	38	38.34 N	23.50 E
Évzonos ∧	267c	37.57 N	23.49 E
Ewa	229c	21.20 N	158.02 W
Ewa Beach	229c	21.18 N	158.00 W
Ewan	285	39.42 N	75.11 W
Ewaninga	162	23.58 S	133.58 E
Ewan Lake ⊜	285	39.42 N	75.11 W
Ewansville	285	39.59 N	74.44 W
Ewbank	158	26.14 S	23.35 E
Ewbank da Câmara	256	21.31 S	43.33 W
Ewe, Loch c	46	57.48 N	5.40 W
Ewell, Eng., U.K.	260	51.21 N	0.15 W
Ewell, Md., U.S.	208	37.59 N	76.02 W
Ewen	190	46.32 N	89.16 W
Ewenkiku Zizhiqi	89	49.07 N	119.40 E
Ewes Water ≃	44	55.08 N	3.00 W
Ewing, Ky., U.S.	218	38.25 N	83.51 W
Ewing, Mo., U.S.	219	40.00 N	91.42 W
Ewing, Ne., U.S.	198	42.15 N	98.20 W
Ewing, Va., U.S.	192	36.38 N	83.25 W
Ewingsville	279b	40.24 N	80.06 W
Ewing Township	208	40.16 N	74.46 W
Ewo	152	0.53 S	14.49 E
Ewu	273a	6.33 N	3.19 E
Exaltación	248	13.16 S	65.15 W
Excelda	158	32.16 S	22.08 E
Excello	218	39.29 N	84.25 W
Excelsior	158	28.56 S	27.06 E
Excelsior Mountain ∧	226	38.02 N	119.18 W
Excelsior Park ♠	274a	33.45 S	151.01 E
Excelsior Springs	194	39.20 N	94.13 W
Excenevex	58	46.21 N	6.21 E
Exchange	210	41.07 N	76.41 W
Exchange Station ◆ [5]	262	53.29 N	2.15 W
Excursion Inlet	180	58.25 N	135.27 W
Exe ≃	42	50.37 N	3.25 W
Executive Committee Range ⋏	9	76.50 S	126.00 W
Exeter, Austl.	170	34.38 S	150.19 E
Exeter, On., Can.	190	43.21 N	81.29 W
Exeter, Eng., U.K.	42	50.43 N	3.31 W
Exeter, Ca., U.S.	226	36.17 N	119.08 W
Exeter, Ne., U.S.	198	40.38 N	97.27 W
Exeter, N.H., U.S.	188	42.58 N	70.56 W
Exeter, Pa., U.S.	210	41.19 N	75.49 W
Exeter, R.I., U.S.	207	41.34 N	71.32 W
Exeter ≃	188	43.02 N	70.55 W
Exeter Sound ⊍	176	66.14 N	62.00 W
Exford	42	51.08 N	3.38 W
Exhibition of Economic Achievements ʊ	265b	55.50 N	37.37 E
Exhibition Park ♠	275b	43.38 N	79.25 W
Exhibition Stadium ♠	275b	43.38 N	79.25 W
Exincourt	58	47.30 N	6.50 E
Exira	198	41.35 N	94.52 W
Exline Slough ≃	216	41.05 N	87.47 W
Exloërmond	52	52.54 N	6.57 E
Exmes	50	48.46 N	0.11 E
Exminster	42	50.41 N	3.29 W
Exmoor ⋏ [1]	42	51.10 N	3.45 W
Exmoor National Park ♠	42	51.12 N	3.46 W
Exmore	208	37.31 N	75.49 W
Exmouth, Austl.	162	21.56 S	114.07 E
Exmouth, Eng., U.K.	42	50.37 N	3.25 W
Exmouth Gulf c	162	22.00 S	114.20 E
Exmouth Plateau ✣ [3]	14	19.00 S	114.00 E
Exning	42	52.16 N	0.21 E
Expedition Range ⋏	166	24.30 S	149.05 E
Experiment	192	33.15 N	84.16 W
Exploits ≃	186	49.05 N	55.20 W
Exploits, Bay of c	186	49.24 N	55.00 W
Exploits Dam ◆ [6]	186	48.45 N	56.30 W
Expo Memorial Park ♠	270	34.48 N	135.32 E
Export	214	40.25 N	79.37 W
Exposition Park ♠	280	34.01 N	118.17 W
Exshaw	182	51.03 N	115.09 W
Extension	224	49.06 N	123.57 W
Exter	52	52.08 N	8.46 E
Externsteine ⊥	52	51.52 N	8.55 E
Extertal	52	52.04 N	9.07 E
Exton	208	40.02 N	75.37 W
Extoraz ≃	234	21.06 N	99.23 W
Extrema	256	22.51 S	46.19 W
Extremadura □ [4]	34	39.15 N	6.15 W
Exu	250	7.31 S	39.43 W
Exuma Cays II	238	24.15 N	76.30 W
Exuma Sound ⊍	238	24.15 N	76.00 W
Eyak	180	60.32 N	145.36 W
Eyam	44	53.17 N	1.41 W
Eyasi, Lake ⊜	154	3.40 S	35.05 E
Eydehavn	26	58.31 N	8.53 E
Eye, Eng., U.K.	42	52.19 N	1.09 E
Eye, Eng., U.K.	42	52.35 N	0.10 W
Eyebrow	184	50.47 N	106.09 W
Eyehill Creek ≃	184	52.40 N	109.39 W
Eyemouth	46	55.52 N	2.06 W
Eye Peninsula > [1]	46	58.13 N	6.13 W
Eyers Grove	210	41.05 N	76.31 W
Eye Water ≃	46	55.53 N	2.06 W
Eygalières	62	43.45 N	4.57 E
Eyguières	62	43.42 N	5.02 E
Eyhorne Street	260	51.16 N	0.38 E
Eyjafjörður c [2]	24a	65.54 N	18.15 W
Eyl	144	7.59 N	49.49 E
Eylar Mountain ∧	204	37.28 N	121.33 W
Eymet	32	44.40 N	0.24 E
Eymir	130	40.02 N	35.14 E
Eymoutiers	32	45.44 N	1.44 E
Eynesil	130	41.03 N	39.08 E
Eynhallow Sound ⊍	46	59.08 N	3.06 W
Eynort, Loch c	46	57.13 N	7.18 W
Eynsford	260	51.22 N	0.13 E
Eynsham	42	51.48 N	1.22 W
Eyota	190	43.59 N	92.13 W
Eyrarbakki	24a	63.53 N	21.05 W
Eyre	162	32.15 S	126.18 E
Eyrecourt	48	53.11 N	8.07 W
Eyre Creek ≃	166	26.40 S	139.00 E
Eyre Mountains ⋏	172	45.20 S	168.30 E
Eyre North, Lake ⊜	166	28.40 S	137.10 E
Eyre Peninsula > [1]	162	34.00 S	135.45 E
Eyre South, Lake ⊜	166	29.30 S	137.20 E
Eyrieux ≃	62	44.48 N	4.48 E
Eystrup	52	52.46 N	9.13 E
Eythorne	42	51.11 N	1.17 E
Eythra	54	51.14 N	12.17 E
Eyüp ◆ [8]	267b	41.03 N	28.55 E
Eyvānekey	128	35.20 N	52.04 E
Eyzaguirre, Canal ≊	286e	33.36 S	70.41 W
Ézanville	261	49.02 N	2.22 E
Ezbekīyah ◆ [8]	273c	30.03 N	31.15 E
Ezeiza, Aeropuerto Internacional de ⊠	288	34.49 S	58.32 W
Ezequiel Ramos Mexía, Embalse ⊜ [1]	254	39.30 S	69.00 W
Ezere	76	56.26 N	22.22 E
Ežerėlis	76	54.53 N	23.37 E
Ezeriș	38	45.24 N	21.53 E
Ezine	130	39.47 N	26.20 E
Ezinepazarı	130	40.34 N	36.09 E
Ezop, chrebet ⋏	89	52.36 N	133.37 E
Ežva	24	61.47 N	50.40 E
Ézy-sur-Eure	50	48.52 N	1.25 E
Ezzell	222	29.17 N	96.58 W
F			
Faaa Airport ⊠	174s	17.33 S	149.36 W
Faafaxdhuun	144	2.13 N	41.37 E
Faal	174q	9.37 N	138.10 E
Faaone	174s	17.40 S	149.18 W
Fabala	150	9.44 N	9.05 W
Fabbrico	64	44.52 N	10.50 E
Fabens	200	31.30 N	106.09 W
Fåberg	26	61.10 N	10.24 E
Faber Lake ⊜	176	63.56 N	117.15 W
Fabert Seamount ✣ [3]	14	24.07 S	158.33 W
Fabius	210	42.50 N	75.59 W
Fåborg	41	55.06 N	10.15 E
Fábrega, Cerro ∧	236	9.07 N	82.52 W
Fabrègues	62	43.33 N	3.46 E
Fabreville ◆ [8]	275a	45.34 N	73.50 W
Fabriano	66	43.20 N	12.54 E
Fabrica di Roma	66	42.20 N	12.18 E
Fabričnyj	85	43.11 N	76.24 E
Fabrizia	68	38.29 N	16.18 E
Facatativá	246	4.49 N	74.22 W
Facha	146	29.27 N	17.18 E
Faches-Thumesnil	50	50.35 N	3.04 E
Fachi	146	18.06 N	11.34 E
Facpi Point >	174p	13.20 N	144.38 E
Factoryville	210	41.34 N	75.47 W
Facundo	254	45.18 S	69.58 W
Fada	146	17.14 N	21.33 E
Fada, Lochan ⊜	46	57.41 N	5.18 W
Fadalto	64	46.05 N	12.20 E
Fada Ngourma	150	12.04 N	0.21 E
Fadd	30	46.28 N	18.50 E
Faddeja, zaliv c	74	76.40 N	107.20 E
Faddejevskij, ostrov I	74	75.30 N	144.00 E
Faddoi	140	8.07 N	32.07 E
Fadian Point >	174p	13.26 N	144.49 E
Fadiffolu Atoll I [1]	122	5.25 N	73.30 E
Fadit	140	9.58 N	32.13 E
Faedis	64	46.10 N	13.20 E
Fænø I	41	55.29 N	9.42 E
Faenza	66	44.17 N	11.53 E
Faeroe Islands □ [2]	22	62.00 N	7.00 W
Faeröerne → Faeroe Islands □ [2]	22	62.00 N	7.00 W
Faete, Monte ∧	267a	41.45 N	12.44 E
Fafa	150	15.20 N	0.43 E
Fafa ≃	152	7.18 N	18.16 E
Fafakourou	150	13.04 N	14.34 W
Fafe	34	41.27 N	8.10 W
Fafen ≃	144	5.59 N	44.25 E
Faga ≃	150	13.15 N	0.55 E
Fagaitua	174u	14.16 S	170.37 W
Fagamalo	175a	13.25 S	172.21 W
Făgăraș	38	45.51 N	24.58 E
Făgărașului, Munții ⋏	38	45.35 N	25.00 E
Fagasa	174u	14.17 S	170.43 W
Fagatogo	174u	14.17 S	170.41 W
Fagel	41	54.27 N	9.31 E
Fagernes	26	60.59 N	9.15 E
Fagersta	40	60.00 N	15.47 E
Fagertärn ◆ [4]	40	58.46 N	14.42 E
Fagerviken	40	60.33 N	17.45 E
Făget	38	45.51 N	22.10 E
Faggen Bach ≃	64	47.05 N	10.40 E
Faggo	150	11.23 N	9.57 E
Fagnano, Lago ⊜	254	54.35 S	68.00 W
Fagnano Castello	68	39.34 N	16.03 E
Fagnano Olona	62	45.40 N	8.52 E
Fagnières	50	48.58 N	4.19 E
Faguibine, Lac ⊜	150	16.45 N	3.54 W
Fagundes, Rio do ≃	256	22.12 S	43.11 W
Fagurhólsmýri	24a	63.54 N	16.38 W
Fagwir	140	9.33 N	30.25 E
Fahan	48	55.05 N	7.28 W
Fahl, Oued el V	148	31.15 N	4.41 E
Fahraj	128	28.58 N	58.52 E
Fährdorf	54	53.58 N	11.28 E
Fahrland	54	52.28 N	13.01 E
Fahrlander See ⊜	264a	52.27 N	13.01 E
Fahrnau	58	47.39 N	7.50 E
Fahrn → Varna	64	46.44 N	11.38 E
Fahuaqiao	106	30.52 N	121.25 E
Faial I	148a	38.34 N	28.42 W
Faichuk II	175c	7.23 N	151.40 E
Fā'id	142	30.19 N	32.19 E
Fā'id Military Base ■	142	30.20 N	32.16 E
Faido	58	46.29 N	8.48 E
Faillon, Lac ⊜	190	48.21 N	76.38 W
Failsworth	262	53.31 N	2.09 W
Fains-les-Sources	56	48.47 N	5.08 E
Fairbairn Airport ⊠	171b	35.18 S	149.15 E
Fairbairn Park ♠	274b	37.47 S	144.55 E
Fairbairn Reservoir ⊜ [1]	166	23.45 S	148.00 E
Fairbank	190	42.38 N	92.02 W
Fairbanks, Ak., U.S.	180	64.51 N	147.43 W
Fairbanks, La., U.S.	194	30.00 N	92.02 W
Fair Bluff	192	34.18 N	79.02 W
Fairborn	218	39.49 N	84.01 W
Fairbourne	42	52.41 N	4.03 W
Fairburn	192	33.34 N	84.34 W
Fairbury, Il., U.S.	216	40.44 N	88.30 W
Fairbury, Ne., U.S.	198	40.08 N	97.10 W
Fairchance	188	39.49 N	79.45 W
Fairchild	190	44.36 N	90.57 W
Fairchild Air Force Base ■	202	47.38 N	117.38 W
Fairchild Creek ≃	212	43.07 N	80.07 W
Fairdale	216	42.06 N	88.56 W
Faire	116	17.53 N	121.34 E
Fairfax, Al., U.S.	194	32.47 N	85.11 W
Fairfax, Ca., U.S.	226	37.59 N	122.35 W
Fairfax, De., U.S.	285	39.47 N	75.32 W
Fairfax, Mn., U.S.	198	44.31 N	94.43 W
Fairfax, Mo., U.S.	194	40.20 N	95.23 W
Fairfax, Ok., U.S.	196	36.34 N	96.42 W
Fairfax, S.C., U.S.	192	32.57 N	81.14 W
Fairfax, S.D., U.S.	198	43.01 N	98.53 W
Fairfax, Vt., U.S.	188	44.39 N	73.00 W
Fairfax, Va., U.S.	208	38.50 N	77.18 W
Fairfax □ [6]	208	38.45 N	77.15 W
Fairfax Forest	284c	38.52 N	77.15 W
Fairfax Park	284c	38.47 N	77.14 W
Fairfax State Recreation Area ♠	218	39.02 N	86.29 W
Fairfax Station	284c	38.48 N	77.19 W
Fairfield, Austl.	170	33.52 S	150.57 E
Fairfield, Al., U.S.	194	33.33 N	86.47 W
Fairfield, Ca., U.S.	226	38.14 N	122.02 W
Fairfield, Ct., U.S.	210	41.08 N	73.15 W
Fairfield, Id., U.S.	202	43.20 N	114.47 W
Fairfield, Il., U.S.	194	38.22 N	88.21 W
Fairfield, Ia., U.S.	190	41.00 N	91.57 W
Fairfield, Me., U.S.	188	44.35 N	69.35 W
Fairfield, Mt., U.S.	202	47.36 N	111.58 W
Fairfield, Ne., U.S.	198	40.25 N	98.06 W
Fairfield, N.J., U.S.	276	40.53 N	74.16 W
Fairfield, N.Y., U.S.	210	43.08 N	74.55 W
Fairfield, Oh., U.S.	218	39.20 N	84.33 W
Fairfield, Pa., U.S.	214	39.47 N	77.22 W
Fairfield, Tx., U.S.	222	31.43 N	96.09 W
Fairfield □ [6]	207	41.15 N	73.20 W
Fairfield Lake ⊜ [1]	222	31.50 N	96.05 W
Fairfield University ʊ [2]	276	41.09 N	73.15 W
Fairford	42	51.44 N	1.47 W
Fairgrove	190	43.31 N	83.32 W
Fair Harbor	210	40.38 N	73.11 W
Fairhaven, Ma., U.S.	207	41.38 N	70.54 W
Fair Haven, Mi., U.S.	214	42.40 N	82.39 W
Fair Haven, N.J., U.S.	208	40.21 N	74.02 W
Fair Haven, N.Y., U.S.	210	43.18 N	76.42 W
Fairhaven, Oh., U.S.	218	39.38 N	84.47 W
Fair Haven, Vt., U.S.	188	43.35 N	73.15 W
Fair Haven, Va., U.S.	284c	38.47 N	77.05 W
Fairhaven Bay ⊜	283	42.26 N	71.21 W
Fair Haven Beach State Park ♠, N.Y., U.S.	210	43.21 N	76.41 W
Fair Haven Beach State Park ♠, N.Y., U.S.	212	43.21 N	76.41 W
Fair Head >	48	55.13 N	6.09 W
Fairhope, Al., U.S.	194	30.31 N	87.54 W
Fairhope, Oh., U.S.	214	40.51 N	81.19 W
Fairhope, Pa., U.S.	214	40.07 N	79.50 W
Fair Isle I	46	59.32 N	1.39 W
Fairknoll	284c	39.05 N	76.59 W
Fairland, In., U.S.	218	39.35 N	85.51 W
Fairland, Md., U.S.	284c	39.05 N	76.58 W
Fairland, Ok., U.S.	196	36.45 N	94.50 W
Fairlane Town Center ◆ [9]	281	42.19 N	83.13 W
Fair Lawn, N.J., U.S.	210	40.56 N	74.07 W
Fairlawn, Oh., U.S.	214	41.07 N	81.36 W
Fairlee	284c	38.52 N	77.16 W
Fairleigh Dickinson University ʊ [2], N.J., U.S.	276	40.50 N	74.07 W
Fairleigh Dickinson University (Teaneck) ʊ [2], N.J., U.S.	276	40.53 N	74.02 W
Fairleigh Dickinson University (Florham-Madison) ʊ [2], N.J., U.S.	276	40.46 N	74.26 W
Fairless Hills	208	40.10 N	74.51 W
Fairlie, N.Z.	172	44.06 S	170.50 E
Fairlie, Scot., U.K.	46	55.46 N	4.51 W
Fairlight	42	50.53 N	0.40 E
Fairmont, Il., U.S.	216	41.33 N	88.03 W
Fairmont, Mn., U.S.	198	43.39 N	94.27 W
Fairmont, Ne., U.S.	198	40.38 N	97.35 W
Fairmont, N.C., U.S.	192	34.29 N	79.06 W
Fairmont, Pa., U.S.	279b	40.19 N	79.43 W
Fairmont, Wa., U.S.	224	48.54 N	122.16 W
Fairmont, W.V., U.S.	188	39.29 N	80.08 W
Fairmont City	219	38.40 N	90.06 W
Fairmont Hot Springs	182	50.19 N	115.53 W
Fairmont Reservoir ⊜ [1]	228	34.43 N	118.26 W
Fairmont Terrace	282	37.43 N	122.07 W
Fairmount, Ga., U.S.	192	34.26 N	84.42 W
Fairmount, Il., U.S.	194	40.03 N	87.56 W
Fairmount, In., U.S.	216	40.24 N	85.39 W
Fairmount, N.Y., U.S.	210	43.02 N	76.14 W
Fairmount, N.D., U.S.	198	46.03 N	96.36 W
Fairmount City	214	41.01 N	79.19 W
Fairmount Heights	208	38.54 N	76.54 W
Fairmount Park ♠	285	40.00 N	75.12 W
Fair Ness >	176	63.24 N	72.05 W
Fair Oaks, Ca., U.S.	226	38.38 N	121.16 W
Fair Oaks, Ga., U.S.	192	33.54 N	84.32 W
Fair Oaks, In., U.S.	216	41.05 N	87.16 W
Fairoaks, Pa., U.S.	279b	40.34 N	80.13 W
Fairoaks Airport ⊠	260	51.21 N	0.32 W
Fair Plain	216	42.05 N	86.27 W
Fairplains	192	36.13 N	81.10 W
Fairplay	200	39.13 N	106.00 W
Fairpoint	214	40.07 N	80.55 W
Fairport, On., Can.	275b	43.49 N	79.05 W
Fairport, N.Y., U.S.	210	43.05 N	77.26 W
Fairport Beach	275b	43.48 N	79.06 W
Fairport Harbor	214	41.44 N	81.16 W
Fairseat	260	51.20 N	0.20 E
Fairton	208	39.22 N	75.13 W
Fairview, Austl.	164	15.33 S	144.19 E
Fairview, Ab., Can.	182	56.04 N	118.23 W
Fairview, Ga., U.S.	192	34.56 N	85.17 W
Fairview, Il., U.S.	190	40.38 N	90.10 W
Fairview, In., U.S.	216	40.18 N	85.11 W
Fairview, Ks., U.S.	198	39.50 N	95.43 W
Fairview, Md., U.S.	208	39.09 N	76.29 W
Fairview, Mi., U.S.	190	44.43 N	84.03 W
Fairview, Mt., U.S.	198	47.51 N	104.02 W
Fairview, N.J., U.S.	276	40.51 N	73.58 W
Fairview, N.Y., U.S.	210	41.43 N	73.55 W
Fairview, Oh., U.S.	214	40.03 N	81.14 W
Fairview, Ok., U.S.	196	36.16 N	98.28 W
Fairview, Pa., U.S.	214	42.01 N	80.15 W
Fairview, Tn., U.S.	194	35.58 N	87.07 W
Fairview, Ut,. U.S.	200	39.37 N	111.26 W
Fairview, W.V., U.S.	188	39.35 N	80.14 W
Fairview Heights	219	38.10 N	90.00 W
Fairview Lanes	214	41.23 N	82.40 W
Fairview Mall ◆ [9]	275b	43.47 N	79.21 W
Fairview Park, In., U.S.	194	39.40 N	87.25 W
Fairview Park, Oh., U.S.	214	41.26 N	81.51 W
Fairview Park, Pa., U.S.	210	41.10 N	75.53 W
Fairview Peak ∧, Nv., U.S.	204	39.14 N	118.08 W
Fairview Peak ∧, Or., U.S.	202	43.35 N	122.39 W
Fairview Pointe Claire Centre ◆ [9]	275a	45.28 N	73.50 W
Fairview Shores	220	28.35 N	81.23 W
Fairview Village	285	40.10 N	75.23 W
Fairvilla	220	28.35 N	81.24 W
Fairville	285	39.51 N	75.38 W
Fairweather Mountain ∧	180	58.54 N	137.32 W
Fairy Lake ⊜	212	45.20 N	79.11 W
Fairy Meadow	170	34.23 S	150.54 E
Fairy Stone State Park ♠	192	36.48 N	80.06 W
Fairy Water ≃	48	54.37 N	7.20 W
Fais I	108	9.46 N	140.31 E
Faisalabad (Lyallpur)	123	31.25 N	73.05 E
Faison	192	35.06 N	78.08 W
Faistós ⊥	38	35.01 N	24.48 E
Faith	198	45.01 N	102.02 W
Faiyum → Al-Fayyūm	142	29.19 N	30.50 E
Faizābād	124	26.47 N	82.08 E
Fajansovyj	76	54.04 N	34.24 E
Fajardo	240m	18.20 N	65.39 W
Fajou, Îlet à I	241o	16.21 N	61.35 W
Fajr, Wādī V	128	30.06 N	38.18 E
Fajzabad	85	38.34 N	69.19 E
Fakahatchee Strand ≡	220	39.35 N	89.25 W
Fakaofo I [1]	14	9.22 S	171.14 W
Fakarava I [1]	14	16.20 S	145.37 W
Fakejev	80	48.57 N	49.56 E
Fakel	80	57.38 N	53.02 E
Fakenham	42	52.50 N	0.51 E
Fakfak	164	2.55 S	132.18 E
Fakılı	130	39.13 N	35.00 E
Fakīrganj	124	25.58 N	90.02 E
Fakī Ṣādiq	140	12.08 N	23.55 E
Fakrinkotti	140	18.01 N	31.20 E
Fakse	41	55.15 N	12.08 E
Fakse Bugt c	41	55.10 N	12.15 E
Fakse Ladeplads	41	55.13 N	12.11 E
Faku	104	42.30 N	123.24 E
Fal ≃	42	50.08 N	5.02 W
Falaba	150	9.51 N	11.19 W
Faladyé	150	13.08 N	8.20 W
Falaise	32	48.54 N	0.12 W
Fālākāta	124	26.32 N	89.12 E
Falam	110	22.55 N	93.40 E
Falāvarjān	128	32.33 N	51.30 E
Falcade	64	46.21 N	11.51 E
Falcão	256	22.17 S	44.16 W
Fălciu	38	46.18 N	28.08 E
Falck	56	49.14 N	6.38 E
Falcognana di Sotto ◆ [8]	267a	41.45 N	12.33 E
Falcón □ [3]	246	11.00 N	69.50 W
Falcon, Cap >	34	35.46 N	0.48 W
Falcon, Cape >	224	45.46 N	123.59 W
Falcón, Presa (Falcon Reservoir) ⊜ [1]	196	26.37 N	99.11 W
Falconara Albanese	68	39.16 N	16.05 E
Falconara Alta	66	43.37 N	13.24 E
Falconara Marittima	66	43.37 N	13.24 E
Falconbridge	190	46.35 N	80.48 W
Falconcrest	285	39.58 N	75.33 W
Falcone	70	38.07 N	15.05 E
Falcone, Capo del >	71	40.58 N	8.12 E
Falconer	214	42.07 N	79.11 W
Falcon Heights	202	42.08 N	121.45 W
Falcon Reservoir (Presa Falcón) ⊜ [1]	196	26.37 N	99.11 W
Falconwood	210	43.00 N	78.57 W
Faldsled	41	55.09 N	10.09 E
Faléa	150	12.16 N	11.17 W
Faleasao	174y	14.13 S	169.32 W
Falelatai	175a	13.55 S	171.59 W
Falelima	175a	13.32 S	172.41 W
Falémé ≃	150	14.46 N	12.14 W
Falenki	80	58.22 N	51.35 E
Falerii Novi ⊥	66	42.16 N	12.20 E
Falerna	68	39.00 N	16.10 E
Falerone	66	43.06 N	13.28 E
Falešty	78	47.34 N	27.43 E
Falfurrias	196	27.13 N	98.08 W
Falher	182	55.44 N	117.12 W
Falicon	62	43.45 N	7.17 E
Fálirou, Órmos c	267c	37.56 N	23.40 E
Falkenberg, Dtsch.	54	52.48 N	13.58 E
Falkenberg, Dtsch.	54	51.35 N	13.14 E
Falkenberg, Dtsch.	60	49.52 N	12.14 E
Falkenberg, Dtsch.	60	48.28 N	12.43 E
Falkenberg, Sve.	26	56.54 N	12.28 E
Falkenberg ◆ [8]	264a	52.34 N	13.33 E
Falkenhagen, Dtsch.	54	53.12 N	12.12 E
Falkenhagen, Dtsch.	54	52.26 N	14.19 E
Falkenhagener See ⊜	264a	52.34 N	13.08 E
Falkenrehde	264a	52.30 N	12.56 E
Falkensee	54	52.33 N	13.04 E
Falkenstein	54	50.29 N	12.22 E
Falkenthal	54	52.54 N	13.17 E

ENGLISH

Name	Page	Lat.°′	Long.°′
Falkirk	46	56.00 N	3.48 W
Falkland, B.C., Can.	182	50.30 N	119.33 W
Falkland, Scot., U.K.	46	56.15 N	3.12 W
Falkland-Inseln → Falkland Islands □ [2]	254	51.45 S	59.00 W
Falkland Islands □ [2], S.A.	244	51.45 S	59.00 W
Falkland Islands □ [2], S.A.	254	51.45 S	59.00 W
Falkland Plateau ✣ [3]	18	51.00 S	50.00 W
Falkland Sound ⊍	254	51.45 S	59.25 W
Falköping	26	58.10 N	13.31 E
Falkville	194	34.22 N	86.54 W
Fall ≃, On., Can.	212	44.59 N	76.22 W
Fall ≃, Ks., U.S.	198	37.24 N	95.40 W
Fall ≃, Wa., U.S.	224	46.47 N	123.30 W
Falla	40	58.41 N	15.45 E
Fallais	56	50.37 N	5.10 E
Fallbach	61	48.39 N	16.25 E
Fallbrook	228	33.22 N	117.15 W
Fallbrook Square ◆ [9]	280	34.12 N	118.38 W
Fall City	224	47.34 N	121.53 W
Fall Creek	190	44.45 N	91.16 W
Fall Creek ≃, In., U.S.	218	39.47 N	86.11 W
Fall Creek ≃, N.Y., U.S.	210	42.28 N	76.31 W
Fall Creek Falls State Park ♠, Tn., U.S.	192	35.39 N	85.25 W
Fall Creek Falls State Park ♠, Tn., U.S.	194	35.39 N	85.25 W
Fallen Jerusalem I	240m	18.25 N	64.27 W
Fallen Leaf	226	38.53 N	120.04 W
Fallen Leaf Reservoir ⊜ [1]	226	38.54 N	120.03 W
Fallentimber	214	40.41 N	78.30 W
Fallentimber Creek ≃	182	51.45 N	114.39 W
Fallen Timbers State Memorial ⊥	216	41.33 N	83.42 W
Fallersleben	54	52.25 N	10.43 E
Fallin	46	56.06 N	3.52 W
Falling ≃	192	37.01 N	78.55 W
Fallingbostel	52	52.52 N	9.41 E
Falling Creek ≃	208	37.26 N	77.26 W
Fallon, Mt., U.S.	198	46.50 N	105.07 W
Fallon, Nv., U.S.	204	39.28 N	118.46 W
Fall River, Ks., U.S.	198	37.36 N	96.01 W
Fall River, Ma., U.S.	207	41.42 N	71.09 W
Fall River, Wi., U.S.	190	43.23 N	89.02 W
Fall River Lake ⊜ [1]	198	37.42 N	96.08 W
Fall River Mills	204	41.00 N	121.26 W
Falls	210	41.28 N	75.51 W
Falls □ [6]	222	31.17 N	96.55 W
Fallsburg	210	41.44 N	74.36 W
Falls Church	208	38.53 N	77.11 W
Falls City, Ne., U.S.	198	40.03 N	95.36 W
Falls City, Or., U.S.	202	44.51 N	123.26 W
Falls Creek, Austl.	170	34.59 S	150.36 E
Falls Creek, Pa., U.S.	214	41.09 N	78.48 W
Falls Creek ≃	226	37.57 N	119.46 W
Fallsington	208	40.12 N	74.48 W
Falls Lake ⊜ [1]	192	36.00 N	78.45 W
Falls Pond ⊜	283	41.58 N	71.20 W
Falls Run ≃	284b	39.22 N	76.52 W
Fallston	208	39.31 N	76.25 W
Falls Village	207	41.57 N	73.21 W
Falmer	42	50.51 N	0.04 W
Falmey	150	12.36 N	2.51 E
Falmouth, Jam.	241q	18.30 N	77.39 W
Falmouth, Eng., U.K.	42	50.08 N	5.04 W
Falmouth, Ky., U.S.	218	38.40 N	84.19 W
Falmouth, Me., U.S.	188	43.43 N	70.14 W
Falmouth, Ma., U.S.	207	41.33 N	70.36 W
Falmouth, Va., U.S.	208	38.19 N	77.28 W
Falmouth Bay c	42	50.05 N	5.01 W
Falmouth Heights	207	41.33 N	70.36 W
False Cape >, Fl., U.S.	220	28.35 N	80.34 W
False Cape >, Va., U.S.	208	36.39 N	76.51 W
False Divi Point >	122	15.43 N	80.49 E
False Ducks Islands II	212	43.57 N	76.49 W
False Pass	180	54.52 N	163.24 W
Falset	34	41.08 N	0.49 E
Falsino ≃	250	0.56 N	51.35 W
Fal'šivyj Gelendžik	78	44.31 N	38.09 E
Falso, Cabo >, Hond.	236	15.12 N	83.20 W
Falso, Cabo >, Rep. Dom.	238	17.47 N	71.41 W
Falso Cabo de Hornos >	254	55.43 S	68.05 W
Falster I	41	54.48 N	11.58 E
Falsterbo	41	55.24 N	12.50 E
Falstone	44	55.11 N	2.25 W
Falterona, Monte ∧	66	43.52 N	11.42 E
Fălticeni	38	47.28 N	26.18 E
Falun, Sve.	40	60.36 N	15.38 E
Falun, Zhg.	107	29.58 N	104.29 E
Falzarego, Passo di)(	64	46.31 N	12.00 E
Fam, Kepulauan II	164	0.40 S	130.15 E
Fama	256	21.25 S	46.51 W
Fama, Ouadi V	146	15.22 N	20.34 E
Famagusta → Gazimağusa	130	35.07 N	33.57 E
Famaillá	252	27.03 S	65.24 W
Famatina	252	28.55 S	67.31 W
Famatina, Sierra de ⋏	252	29.00 S	67.51 W
Fambach	54	50.44 N	10.22 E
Fameck	56	49.18 N	6.07 E
Famenne ◆ [1]	56	50.10 N	5.15 E
Familleureux	50	50.31 N	4.12 E
Family Lake ⊜	184	51.54 N	95.30 W
Fan ≃	104	42.16 N	123.40 E
Fana	150	12.47 N	6.57 W
Fanaco, Lago ⊜	70	37.39 N	13.33 E
Fanad Head >	48	55.16 N	7.38 W
Fanado ≃	255	17.10 S	42.40 W
Fanambana	157b	13.34 S	50.00 E
Fanan I	175c	7.11 N	151.59 E
Fanano	64	44.12 N	10.47 E
Fanārah	142	30.17 N	32.21 E
Fanchang	100	31.07 N	118.12 E
Fanch'eng → Xiangfan	102	32.03 N	112.01 E
Fancher, Il., U.S.	219	39.16 N	88.47 W
Fancher, N.Y., U.S.	210	43.15 N	66.06 W
Fanchon, Pointe >	238	18.26 N	74.29 W
Fanchuan	100	32.40 N	119.42 E
Fancy	241h	13.22 N	61.11 W
Fancy Creek ≃	198	39.28 N	96.45 W
Fancy Prairie	219	39.59 N	89.36 W
Fandriana	157b	20.14 S	47.23 E
Fane ≃	48	53.57 N	6.22 W
Fanepura	123	31.29 N	72.54 E
Faneromenis Monastery ʊ [1]	267c	37.59 N	23.26 E
Fang	110	19.55 N	99.13 E
Fangaga ∧	144	17.30 N	38.01 E
Fangak	140	9.04 N	30.53 E
Fangbian	106	31.42 N	119.06 E
Fangcheng, Zhg.	100	33.16 N	112.59 E
Fangcheng, Zhg.	102	21.49 N	108.22 E
Fangcheng, Zhg.	105	39.16 N	115.28 E
Fangcun, Zhg.	100	29.04 N	118.36 E
Fangcun, Zhg.	100	26.50 N	118.15 E
Fangdao	100	27.01 N	118.06 E
Fängersee ⊜	264a	52.35 N	13.50 E
Fangguan	105	39.20 N	115.58 E
Fangji	100	31.54 N	115.35 E
Fangjiachang	107	30.05 N	104.16 E
Fangjiazhuang	106	30.45 N	119.53 E
Fangliao	100	22.22 N	120.35 E
Fangmutun	98	42.34 N	124.34 E
Fangniu	102	27.40 N	100.25 E
Fangshan, T'aiwan	100	22.16 N	120.39 E
Fangshan, Zhg.	98	39.42 N	115.58 E
Fang Shan ∧	106	31.40 N	119.16 E
Fang Shan ∧ [2]	106	31.29 N	119.09 E
Fangshanzhen	104	41.54 N	122.05 E
Fangshen	104	42.02 N	124.04 E
Fangshengpu	107	30.20 N	104.54 E

DEUTSCH

Name	Seite	Breite°′	Länge°′ E = Ost
Fangsi	98	36.56 N	116.29 E
Fangtai	106	31.19 N	121.12 E
Fangxi	100	28.23 N	114.38 E
Fangxian	102	32.02 N	110.45 E
Fangxianzhen	106	32.00 N	119.44 E
Fangzheng	89	45.50 N	128.50 E
Fangzi	98	36.36 N	119.07 E
Fanhões	266c	38.53 N	9.09 W
Fanipol'	76	53.45 N	27.20 E
Fanjakana	157b	21.10 S	46.53 E
Fanjiadai	106	32.04 N	120.15 E
Fanjiadian	104	41.41 N	121.50 E
Fanjiatun	89	43.43 N	125.06 E
Fanjiazhuang	105	39.12 N	117.20 E
Fannaråki ∧	26	61.31 N	7.55 E
Fannettsburg	214	40.04 N	77.50 W
Fannich, Loch ⊜	46	57.38 N	5.00 W
Fannrem	26	63.16 N	9.50 E
Fanny, Mount ∧	202	45.20 N	117.41 W
Fanny Bay	182	49.30 N	124.50 W
Fano	66	43.50 N	13.01 E
Fanø I	26	55.25 N	8.25 E
Fanqiao	100	28.48 N	121.10 E
Fans, Col des)(	62	44.56 N	4.47 E
Fanshan, Zhg.	100	27.21 N	120.24 E
Fanshan, Zhg.	105	40.13 N	115.25 E
Fanshang	106	31.40 N	120.01 E
Fanshawe Lake ⊜	212	43.05 N	81.10 W
Fansher Creek ≃	214	42.37 N	82.01 W
Fanshui	100	33.07 N	119.25 E
Fan Si Pan ∧	110	22.15 N	103.46 E
Fantasy Island ♠	284a	43.02 N	78.58 W
Fanthyttan	40	59.40 N	15.06 E
Fanwood	276	40.38 N	74.23 W
Fanxian	98	35.57 N	115.38 E
Fanzhen	98	36.14 N	117.21 E
Faoileann, Bàgh nam c	46	57.23 N	7.17 W
Faqīrah, Wādī V	142	28.52 N	30.57 E
Faqqūʻah	132	32.30 N	35.24 E
Fāqūs	142	30.44 N	31.48 E
Farab	85	39.14 N	67.28 E
Faraday ʊ [3]	9	65.15 S	64.16 W
Faraday, Mount ∧	172	42.02 S	171.34 E
Faradje	154	3.44 N	29.43 E
Faradofay	157b	25.02 S	47.00 E
Farafangana	157b	22.49 S	47.50 E
Farāfirah, Al-Wāḥat al- ⍑ [4]	140	27.15 N	28.10 E
Farāh	128	32.22 N	62.07 E
Farāh □ [4]	128	33.00 N	62.30 E
Farāh ≃	128	31.29 N	61.24 E
Farahābād	267d	35.42 N	51.30 E
Farahalana	157b	14.26 S	50.10 E
Farā'id, Jabal al- ∧	140	23.31 N	35.20 E
Fara in Sabina	66	42.12 N	12.43 E
Farallón, Paso del ⊍	288	34.41 S	57.57 W
Farallon de Medinilla I	108	16.01 N	146.04 E
Farallon de Pajaros I	108	20.32 N	144.54 E
Farallon Islands II	204	37.43 N	123.03 W
Faramana	150	12.03 N	4.40 W
Faranah	150	10.02 N	10.44 W
Farángi Samariás (Samaria Gorge) V	38	35.18 N	24.00 E
Fara Novarese	62	45.33 N	8.27 E
Farasān, Jazā'ir II	144	16.48 N	41.54 E
Farasān al-Kabīr I	144	16.42 N	42.00 E
Faratsiho	157b	19.24 S	46.57 E
Faraulep I [1]	108	8.36 N	144.33 E
Farber	219	39.16 N	91.34 W
Farbovano	78	50.09 N	31.51 E
Farcău, Vîrful ∧	38	47.56 N	24.27 E
Farchant	64	47.32 N	11.06 E
Farcy	261	48.31 N	2.37 E
Fardes ≃	34	37.35 N	3.00 W
Fare ≃	50	47.39 N	0.14 E
Fareara, Pointe >	174s	17.52 S	149.39 W
Fareham	42	50.51 N	1.10 W
Fårevejle	41	55.48 N	11.27 E
Farewell	180	62.31 N	153.53 W
Farewell, Cape >	172	40.30 S	172.41 E
Farewell Spit > [2]	172	40.31 S	172.52 E
Färgelanda	26	58.34 N	11.59 E
Fargniers	50	49.39 N	3.19 E
Fargo	198	46.52 N	96.47 W
Far Hills	276	40.41 N	74.38 W
Faria ≃	287a	22.53 S	43.15 W
Fāriʻah, Wādī al- V	132	32.06 N	35.31 E
Faribault	190	44.17 N	93.16 W
Faribault, Lac ⊜	176	59.00 N	72.00 W
Farīdābad	124	28.26 N	77.19 E
Farīdganj	126	23.08 N	90.45 E
Farīdkot	123	30.40 N	74.45 E
Farīdnagar	124	28.46 N	77.37 E
Farīdpur, Bngl.	126	24.10 N	89.26 E
Farīdpur, Bngl.	126	23.36 N	89.50 E
Farīdpur, India	124	28.13 N	79.33 E
Farié Haoussa	150	13.48 N	1.38 E
Fārigh, Wādī al- V	146	29.59 N	19.25 E
Färila	26	61.48 N	15.51 E
Farilhões II	34	39.28 N	9.34 W
Farim	150	12.27 N	15.17 W
Farīmān	128	35.43 N	59.53 E
Farina	219	38.50 N	88.46 W
Faringdon	42	51.40 N	1.35 W
Farington	262	53.43 N	2.42 W
Farinha ≃	250	6.51 S	47.30 W
Farini d'Olmo	62	44.43 N	9.34 E
Fariš	85	40.35 N	66.52 E
Fariske	130	36.37 N	32.38 E
Fāriskūr	142	31.20 N	31.43 E
Farit, Amba ∧	144	10.56 N	38.58 E
Färjestaden	26	56.39 N	16.27 E
Farkwa	154	5.24 S	35.36 E
Farleigh	260	51.19 N	0.02 W
Farley	190	42.26 N	91.00 W
Farley Green	260	51.12 N	0.29 W
Farmahīn	128	34.30 N	49.41 E
Farmer City	216	40.14 N	88.38 W
Farmers Branch	222	32.55 N	96.53 W
Farmersburg	194	39.14 N	87.22 W
Farmers Fork	208	38.02 N	76.45 W
Farmer's Museum ʊ	210	42.42 N	74.57 W
Farmers Retreat	218	38.58 N	85.06 W
Farmersville, Ca., U.S.	226	36.17 N	119.12 W
Farmersville, Il., U.S.	219	39.26 N	89.39 W
Farmersville, Pa., U.S.	208	40.08 N	76.10 W
Farmersville, Tx., U.S.	222	33.09 N	96.21 W
Farmersville Station	210	42.26 N	78.22 W
Farmerville	194	32.46 N	92.24 W
Farmingdale, N.J., U.S.	208	40.11 N	74.10 W
Farmingdale, N.Y., U.S.	276	40.43 N	73.26 W
Farmington, Ca., U.S.	226	37.56 N	120.59 W
Farmington, Ct., U.S.	207	41.43 N	72.49 W
Farmington, De., U.S.	208	38.52 N	75.34 W
Farmington, Il., U.S.	190	40.41 N	90.00 W
Farmington, Ia., U.S.	190	40.38 N	91.44 W
Farmington, Me., U.S.	188	44.40 N	70.09 W
Farmington, Mi., U.S.	216	42.27 N	83.22 W
Farmington, Mn., U.S.	190	44.38 N	93.08 W
Farmington, Mo., U.S.	194	37.47 N	90.25 W
Farmington, Mt., U.S.	182	47.54 N	112.11 W
Farmington, N.H., U.S.	188	43.23 N	71.03 W
Farmington, N.M., U.S.	200	36.43 N	108.13 W
Farmington, Ut,. U.S.	200	40.58 N	111.53 W
Farmington ≃	207	41.51 N	72.38 W
Farmington, West Branch ≃	207	41.52 N	72.57 W
Farmington Flood Control Basin ⊜ [1]	226	37.55 N	120.55 W
Farmington Hills	281	42.28 N	83.23 W
Farmingville	210	40.49 N	73.01 W
Farmland	218	40.11 N	85.07 W

Symbols in the index entries represent the broad categories identified in the key at the right. Symbols with superior numbers (⋏ [1]) identify subcategories (see complete key on page I · 1).

Symbole im Register stellen die rechts im Schlüssel erklärten Kategorien dar. Symbole mit hochgestellten Ziffern (⋏ [1]) bezeichnen Unterabteilungen einer Kategorie (vgl. vollständiger Schlüssel auf Seite I · 1).

Los símbolos incluídos en el texto del índice representan las grandes categorias identificadas con la clave a la derecha. Los símbolos con numeros en su parte superior (⋏ [1]) identifican las subcategorías (véase la clave completa en la página I · 1).

Les symboles de l'index représentent les catégories indiquées dans la légende à droite. Les symboles suivis d'un indice (⋏ [1]) représentent des sous-catégories (voir légende complète à la page I · 1).

Os símbolos incluídos no texto do índice representam as grandes categorias identificadas com a chave à direita. Os símbolos com números em sua parte superior (⋏ [1]) identificam as subcategorias (veja-se a chave completa à página I · 1).

∧	Mountain	Berg	Montaña	Montagne	Montanha
⋏	Mountains	Gebirge	Montañas	Montagnes	Montanhas
)(	Pass	Paß	Paso	Col	Passo
V	Valley, Canyon	Tal, Cañon	Valle, Cañón	Vallée, Canyon	Vale, Canhão
≚	Plain	Ebene	Llano	Plaine	Planície
>	Cape	Kap	Cabo	Cap	Cabo
I	Island	Insel	Isla	Île	Ilha
II	Islands	Inseln	Islas	Îles	Ilhas
±	Other Topographic Features	Andere Topographische Objekte	Otros Elementos Topográficos	Autres données topographiques	Outros acidentes topográficos

ESPAÑOL — Nombre | Página | Lat.°' | Long.°' W = Oeste
FRANÇAIS — Nom | Page | Lat.°' | Long.°' W = Ouest
PORTUGUÊS — Nome | Página | Lat.°' | Long.°' W = Oeste

Far Mountain ∧ 182 52.46 N 125.17 W
Farm Pond ⊜, Ma., U.S. 283 42.17 N 71.26 W
Farm Pond ⊜, Ma., U.S. 283 42.14 N 71.21 W
Farmville, N.C., U.S. 192 35.35 N 77.35 W
Farmville, Va., U.S. 192 37.18 N 78.23 W
Färna 40 59.47 N 15.51 E
Farnam 198 40.42 N 100.12 W
Farnawā 142 30.59 N 30.39 E
Farnborough 42 51.17 N 0.46 W
Farnborough ◆[8] 260 51.21 N 0.04 E
Farncombe 260 51.12 N 0.36 W
Farndon 44 53.05 N 0.51 W
Färnebofjärden ⊜ 40 60.14 N 16.47 E
Farne Islands II 44 55.38 N 1.38 W
Farnham, P.Q., Can. 206 45.17 N 72.59 W
Farnham, Eng., U.K. 42 51.13 N 0.49 W
Farnham, N.Y., U.S. 214 42.36 N 79.05 W
Farnham, Va., U.S. 208 37.53 N 76.37 W
Farnham, Mount ∧ 182 50.29 N 116.30 W
Farnham Common 260 51.33 N 0.37 W
Farnham Royal 260 51.32 N 0.37 W
Farnhamville 198 42.16 N 94.24 W
Farningham 260 51.23 N 0.13 E
Farnroda 54 50.56 N 10.23 E
Farnworth 262 53.33 N 2.24 W
Faro, Bra. 250 2.11 S 56.44 W
Faro, Port. 34 37.01 N 7.56 W
Faro □[5] 34 37.15 N 8.00 W
Faro ≃ 146 9.21 N 12.55 E
Faro, Punta del ≻ 70 38.16 N 15.39 E
Faro, Réserve du ◆[4] 146 8.10 N 12.35 E
Färöer → Faeroe Islands □[2] 22 62.00 N 7.00 W
Fårön I 26 57.56 N 19.08 E
Fårösund 26 57.52 N 19.03 E
Farquhar, Cape ≻ 162 23.37 S 113.37 E
Farquhar Group II 138 10.10 S 51.10 E
Farr 46 57.21 N 4.12 W
Farra d'Isonzo 64 45.56 N 12.31 E
Farragut 198 40.43 N 95.28 W
Farragut State Recreation Area ♠ 202 47.55 N 116.35 W
Farrandsville 210 41.10 N 77.31 W
Farrar ≃ 46 57.24 N 4.50 W
Farrar Pond ⊜ 283 42.25 N 71.21 W
Farrars Creek ≃ 166 25.35 S 140.43 E
Farrāshband 128 28.53 N 52.06 E
Farrell 214 41.12 N 80.29 W
Farrell Flat 168b 33.50 S 138.47 E
Farrer Park ♠ 271c 1.19 N 103.51 E
Farrington Lake ⊜ 276 40.26 N 74.28 W
Farrington Lake Heights 276 40.26 N 74.27 W
Far Rockaway ◆[8] 276 40.36 N 73.45 W
Farrukhābād 124 27.24 N 79.34 E
Farrukhnagar, India 124 28.27 N 76.49 E
Farrukhnagar, India 272a 28.43 N 77.23 E
Fārs □[4] 128 29.00 N 53.00 E
Fársala 38 39.18 N 22.23 E
Farschviller 56 49.06 N 6.54 E
Fārsī 128 33.47 N 63.15 E
Fārsī, Jazīreh-ye I 128 27.58 N 50.11 E
Farsīs 142 30.40 N 31.14 E
Farsø 26 56.47 N 9.21 E
Farsta 40 59.14 N 18.04 E
Farsund 26 58.05 N 6.48 E
Fartak, Ra's ≻ 118 15.38 N 52.15 E
Farukolu I 122 6.12 N 73.16 E
Farum 41 55.48 N 12.22 E
Fårvang 41 56.16 N 9.44 E
Farvel, Kap ≻ 176 59.45 N 44.00 W
Farwell, Mi., U.S. 190 43.50 N 84.52 W
Farwell, Tx., U.S. 196 30.15 N 103.15 W
Fāryāb □[4] 128 36.00 N 65.00 E
Fasā 128 28.56 N 53.42 E
Fasano 68 40.50 N 17.22 E
Faščovka 83 48.16 N 38.37 E
Fashkhah, 'Ayn ∓[4] 132 31.43 N 35.27 E
Fåsjön ⊜ 40 59.36 N 14.58 E
Fasmund ≻[1] 41 54.32 N 13.35 E
Fassa 150 13.26 N 8.15 W
Fassberg 52 52.54 N 10.10 E
Fasterholt 41 56.01 N 9.07 E
Fastnet Rock I[2] 48 51.24 N 9.35 W
Fastov 78 50.06 N 29.55 E
Fastoveckaja 78 45.56 N 40.09 E
Fatagar Tuting, Tanjung ≻ 164 2.46 S 131.57 E
Fataki 154 4.46 S 28.11 E
Fatala ≃ 150 10.13 N 14.00 W
Fat Deer Key I 220 24.44 N 81.00 W
Fate 222 32.56 N 96.23 W
Fatehābād, India 123 29.31 N 75.27 E
Fatehābād, India 124 27.01 N 78.19 E
Fatehgarh, India 124 27.22 N 79.38 E
Fatehgarh, India 124 24.48 N 76.58 E
Fatehgarh Chūriān 123 31.52 N 74.58 E
Fatehjang 123 33.34 N 72.39 E
Fatehpur, India 120 27.59 N 74.57 E
Fatehpur, India 124 27.10 N 81.13 E
Fatehpur, India 124 25.56 N 80.48 E
Fatehpur, India 126 22.17 N 88.14 E
Fatehpur, India 126 24.05 N 87.44 E
Fatehpur, Pāk. 123 31.09 N 71.13 E
Fatehpur Sīkri 124 27.06 N 77.40 E
Fathai 140 8.05 N 31.48 E
Fathom Five National Marine Park ♠ 190 45.15 N 81.40 W
Fatick 150 14.20 N 16.25 W
Fatick □[4] 150 14.00 N 16.30 W
Fatigue, Mount ∧ 169 38.34 S 146.18 E
Fatima, Arg. 258 34.26 S 59.00 W
Fátima, Port. 34 39.37 N 8.39 W
Fatima do Sol 255 22.16 S 54.25 W
Fatima do Sul 252 22.16 S 54.22 W
Fāṭimah, Wādī V 144 21.27 N 39.09 E
Fatoto 150 13.26 N 13.52 W
Fat'ož 78 52.07 N 35.52 E
Fatsa 130 41.02 N 37.31 E
Fatshan → Foshan 100 23.03 N 113.09 E
Fat Tong Point ≻ 271d 22.16 N 114.15 E
Fatu-Berlio 112 8.56 S 125.52 E
Fatulla 126 23.38 N 90.29 E
Fatumu 174w 21.13 S 175.07 W
Fatunda 152 4.08 S 17.13 E
Fatwā 124 25.31 N 85.19 E
Fauabu 175e 8.34 S 160.43 E
Faucigny 58 46.07 N 6.22 E
Faucille, Col de la)(58 46.22 N 6.02 E
Faucilles, Monts ⋏ 58 48.07 N 6.16 E
Faucogney 58 47.51 N 6.34 E
Faucon-de-Barcelonnette 62 44.24 N 6.41 E
Fauglia 66 43.34 N 10.31 E
Fauldhouse 46 55.50 N 3.37 W
Faulkton 198 45.02 N 99.07 W
Faulquemont 56 49.03 N 6.36 E
Fauquembergues 50 50.36 N 2.05 E
Fauquier 182 49.53 N 118.05 W
Fauquier □[6] 208 38.35 N 77.35 W
Făurei 38 45.06 N 27.14 E
Faure Island I 162 25.51 S 113.52 E
Fauresmith 158 29.42 S 25.21 E
Fauro Island I 175e 6.55 S 156.04 E
Fauske 24 67.15 N 15.24 E
Faust 182 55.19 N 115.38 W
Faustovo 82 55.26 N 38.29 E
Fauville-en-Caux 50 49.39 N 0.35 E
Fauvillers 56 49.51 N 5.40 E
Faux-Cap 157b 25.33 S 45.32 E
Fåvang 26 61.27 N 10.11 E
Favara 70 37.19 N 13.39 E
Faverges 62 45.45 N 6.18 E
Faverney 58 47.46 N 6.06 E
Faversham 42 51.20 N 0.53 E
Favières 261 48.46 N 2.47 E
Favignana 70 37.56 N 12.20 E
Favignana, Isola I 70 37.56 N 12.19 E
Favoriten ◆[8] 264b 48.11 N 16.23 E
Favourable Lake ⊜ 184 52.53 N 93.56 W
Favrieux 261 48.57 N 1.39 E
Fawcett 182 54.32 N 114.05 W
Fawcett Lake ⊜ 182 55.19 N 113.57 W
Fawkham Green 260 51.22 N 0.17 E
Fawkner 274b 37.43 S 144.58 E
Fawkner Park ♠ 274b 37.50 S 144.59 E
Fawley 42 50.49 N 1.20 W
Fawn ≃, On., Can. 176 55.22 N 88.20 W
Fawn ≃, U.S. 216 41.51 N 85.40 W
Fawn Grove 208 39.44 N 76.27 W
Fawnie Nose ∧ 182 53.16 N 125.08 W
Fawnie Range ⋏ 182 53.10 N 125.00 W
Fawsett Farms 284c 38.59 N 77.14 W
Faxaflói ⊂ 24a 64.25 N 23.00 W
Faxälven ≃ 26 63.13 N 17.13 E
Faxinal 255 23.59 S 51.22 W
Faxinal do Soturno 252 29.37 S 53.26 W
Faxon 210 41.15 N 76.58 W
Faya 146 17.55 N 19.07 E
Fayd 128 27.07 N 42.27 E
Fayence 62 43.37 N 6.41 E
Fayerweather Island I 276 41.08 N 73.13 W
Fayette, Al., U.S. 194 33.41 N 87.49 W
Fayette, Ia., U.S. 190 42.50 N 91.48 W
Fayette, Ms., U.S. 194 31.42 N 91.03 W
Fayette, Mo., U.S. 194 39.08 N 92.41 W
Fayette, N.Y., U.S. 210 42.49 N 76.49 W
Fayette, Oh., U.S. 216 41.40 N 84.19 W
Fayette □[6], Il., U.S. 219 38.58 N 89.06 W
Fayette □[6], In., U.S. 218 39.39 N 85.08 W
Fayette □[6], Ky., U.S. 218 38.07 N 84.30 W
Fayette □[6], Oh., U.S. 218 39.32 N 83.26 W
Fayette □[6], Pa., U.S. 214 40.05 N 79.39 W
Fayette □[6], Tx., U.S. 222 29.50 N 96.57 W
Fayette, Lake ⊜[1] 222 29.56 N 96.44 W
Fayette City 214 40.06 N 79.50 W
Fayetteville, Ar., U.S. 194 36.03 N 94.09 W
Fayetteville, Ga., U.S. 192 33.26 N 84.27 W
Fayetteville, Il., U.S. 219 38.22 N 89.48 W
Fayetteville, N.Y., U.S. 210 43.02 N 76.00 W
Fayetteville, N.C., U.S. 192 35.03 N 78.52 W
Fayetteville, Oh., U.S. 218 39.11 N 83.55 W
Fayetteville, Pa., U.S. 208 39.54 N 77.33 W
Fayetteville, Tn., U.S. 194 35.09 N 86.34 W
Fayetteville, Tx., U.S. 222 29.54 N 96.41 W
Fayetteville, W.V., U.S. 188 38.03 N 81.06 W
Faylakah I 128 29.27 N 48.20 E
Fayl-Billot 58 47.47 N 5.36 E
Fayrā 144 13.17 N 43.25 E
Fay-sur-Lignon 62 44.59 N 4.14 E
Fayville 207 42.17 N 71.30 W
Fayyum → Al-Fayyūm 142 29.19 N 30.50 E
Fažana 64 44.55 N 13.49 E
Fazao 150 8.42 N 0.46 E
Fazao, Parc National du ♠ 150 8.40 N 0.42 E
Fazeley 42 52.37 N 1.42 W
Fazenda de Cima 248 15.56 S 56.37 W
Fazenda Libongo 152 8.24 S 13.24 E
Fazenda Nova 255 16.11 S 50.48 W
Fāzilka 123 30.24 N 74.02 E
Fāzilpur 120 29.18 N 70.27 E
Fazzān (Fezzan) □[9] 146 26.00 N 14.00 E
Fdérik 148 22.41 N 12.43 W
Feale ≃ 48 52.28 N 9.40 W
Fear, Cape ≻ 192 33.50 N 77.58 W
Fearnhead 262 53.25 N 2.33 W
Feasterville 208 40.08 N 75.00 W
Feather ≃ 204 38.47 N 121.36 W
Feather, Middle Fork ≃ 204 39.34 N 121.26 W
Feather, North Fork ≃ 204 39.34 N 121.28 W
Feather, North Fork, East Branch ≃ 204 40.01 N 121.13 W
Feather, South Fork ≃ 204 39.33 N 121.28 W
Featherbed Top ∧ 262 53.26 N 1.52 W
Featherly Regional Park ♠ 280 33.52 N 117.42 W
Featherston 172 41.07 S 175.20 E
Featherstone, Eng., U.K. 44 53.41 N 1.21 W
Featherstone, Zimb. 154 18.42 S 30.49 E
Feathertop, Mount ∧ 166 36.54 S 147.08 E
Fécamp 50 49.45 N 0.22 E
Fedala → Mohammedia 148 33.44 N 7.24 W
Fedderwardergroden 52 53.35 N 8.05 E
Feddet ≻[1] 41 55.09 N 12.07 E
Federación 252 31.00 S 57.54 W
Federal, Arg. 252 30.57 S 58.48 W
Federal, Pa., U.S. 279b 40.23 N 80.09 W
Federal Capital Territory □[3] 150 9.00 N 7.15 E
Federalsburg 208 38.41 N 75.46 W
Federal Territory □[8] 273a 6.29 N 3.25 E
Federal Way 224 47.19 N 122.18 W
Federation Forest State Park ♠ 224 47.09 N 121.40 W
Federsee ⊜ 58 48.05 N 9.38 E
Fedeshk 128 32.45 N 58.50 E
Fedje 26 60.47 N 4.42 E
Fedorino 82 55.08 N 36.06 E
Fedosejevka 80 46.53 N 44.00 E
Fedosejevskaja 24 62.07 N 40.42 E
Fedosicha 86 54.47 N 81.54 E
Fedosjino 82 55.08 N 38.30 E
Fedotovo 82 55.41 N 39.12 E
Feeagh, Lough ⊜ 48 53.55 N 9.36 W
Feeding Hills 207 42.04 N 72.40 W
Feehanville 278 42.05 N 87.54 W
Feerfeer 144 8.30 N 47.55 E
Feesburg 218 38.52 N 83.58 W
Fefan I 175c 7.21 N 151.51 E
Fehérgyarmat 30 47.58 N 22.32 E
Fehmarn I 54 54.28 N 11.08 E
Fehmarnbelt (Femer Bælt) μ 41 54.35 N 11.15 E
Fehmarnsund μ 54 54.24 N 11.07 E
Fehrbellin 54 52.49 N 12.46 E
Fehring 61 46.56 N 16.01 E
Feia, Lagoa ⊂ 255 22.00 S 41.20 W
Feicheng 98 36.15 N 116.46 E
Feichten 58 47.02 N 10.44 E
Feidong 100 31.52 N 117.29 E
Feignies 50 50.18 N 3.55 E
Feigumfossen ∟ 26 61.23 N 7.26 E
Feiheji 100 33.36 N 115.36 E
Fei Huang ≃ 100 33.35 N 119.02 E
Feijó 248 8.09 S 70.21 W
Feiketu 89 45.46 N 127.09 E
Feilding 172 40.13 S 175.34 E
Feiler ∧ 58 47.07 N 10.52 E
Feiliqiao 106 31.05 N 119.05 E
Feilitzsch 54 50.22 N 11.56 E
Feilong, Zhg. 107 30.25 N 106.20 E
Feilong, Zhg. 107 30.36 N 105.54 E
Feilongguan 107 28.57 N 105.05 E
Feiluan 100 26.35 N 119.35 E
Feira 154 15.37 S 30.25 E
Feira de Santana 255 12.15 S 38.57 W
Feistritz ≃ 61 47.01 N 16.08 E
Feistritz an der Gail 64 46.34 N 13.36 E
Feistritzer Spitze ∧ 61 46.31 N 14.45 E
Feixi 100 31.42 N 117.10 E
Feixian 98 35.18 N 117.57 E
Feixiang 98 36.34 N 114.49 E
Feiyun ≃ 100 27.48 N 120.36 E
Fejaj, Chott ☷ 148 33.55 N 9.10 E
Fejér □[6] 30 47.10 N 18.35 E
Fejø I 41 54.57 N 11.26 E
Feke 130 37.53 N 35.58 E
Feklistova, ostrov I 89 55.02 N 136.55 E
Felâhiye 130 39.06 N 35.35 E
Felanitx 34 39.28 N 3.08 E
Felbertauren-Tunnel ◆[5] 64 47.08 N 12.31 E
Felda 220 26.33 N 81.26 W
Felda ≃, Dtsch. 56 50.51 N 10.05 E
Felda ≃, Dtsch. 56 50.42 N 9.03 E
Feldafing 64 47.57 N 11.17 E
Feldaist ≃ 61 48.19 N 14.34 E
Feld am See 64 46.47 N 13.45 E
Feldbach 61 46.57 N 15.54 E
Feldberg, Dtsch. 54 53.20 N 13.26 E
Feldberg, Dtsch. 58 47.51 N 8.02 E
Feldberg ∧ 58 47.52 N 8.00 E
Felderbach ≃ 263 51.22 N 7.08 E
Feldhausen ◆[8] 263 51.37 N 6.59 E
Feldis 58 46.48 N 9.26 E
Feldkirch 58 47.14 N 9.36 E
Feldkirchen an der Donau 61 48.21 N 14.03 E
Feldkirchen bei Graz 61 47.01 N 15.27 E
Feldkirchen in Kärnten 61 46.43 N 14.05 E
Feldmark 263 51.41 N 6.38 E
Feldstetten 58 48.28 N 9.37 E
Felhit 144 16.43 N 38.02 E
Feliciano, Méx. 234 18.01 N 101.58 W
Feliciano, P.R. 240m 18.28 N 67.08 W
Feliciano, Arroyo ≃ 252 31.06 S 59.54 W
Felicity 218 38.50 N 84.05 W
Felino 64 44.42 N 10.15 E
Felipe Carrillo Puerto, Méx. 234 21.09 N 104.52 W
Felipe Carrillo Puerto, Méx. 234 19.08 N 102.42 W
Felix, Cape ≻ 176 69.54 N 97.50 W
Felix, Rio ≃ 196 33.08 N 104.19 W
Felixburg 154 19.29 S 30.51 E
Felixdorf 61 47.53 N 16.15 E
Felixlândia 255 18.47 S 44.55 W
Felixstowe 42 51.58 N 1.20 E
Felixton 158 28.50 S 31.53 E
Félix U. Gómez 232 29.50 N 111.30 W
Felizzano 62 44.54 N 8.26 E
Fella ≃ 64 46.21 N 13.07 E
Fellbach 56 48.48 N 9.15 E
Felletin 32 45.53 N 2.10 E
Felling 44 54.57 N 1.33 W
Fellingsbro 40 59.26 N 15.35 E
Fellows 226 35.11 N 119.32 W
Fellows Creek ≃ 281 42.17 N 83.26 W
Fellowship 285 39.55 N 74.58 W
Fellsburg 214 40.11 N 79.49 W
Fellsmere 220 27.46 N 80.36 W
Fellwick 285 40.08 N 75.11 W
Felpham 42 50.47 N 0.39 W
Felsberg 56 51.08 N 9.25 E
Felső-Válicka ≃ 61 46.52 N 16.53 E
Feltham ◆[8] 260 51.27 N 0.24 W
Felt Lake ⊜ 282 37.23 N 122.11 W
Felton, Ca., U.S. 226 37.03 N 122.04 W
Felton, De., U.S. 208 39.00 N 75.34 W
Felton, Pa., U.S. 208 39.51 N 76.34 W
Feltre 64 46.01 N 11.54 E
Felts Mills 212 44.01 N 75.46 W
Feltwell 42 52.29 N 0.32 E
Femer Bælt (Fehmarnbelt) μ 41 54.35 N 11.15 E
Femme Osage Creek ≃ 219 38.39 N 90.44 W
Femmøller 41 56.14 N 10.35 E
Femø I 41 54.58 N 11.33 E
Femund ⊜ 26 62.12 N 11.52 E
Femundsenden 26 61.55 N 11.55 E
Femundsmarka Nasjonalpark ♠ 26 62.20 N 12.07 E
Fen ≃ 102 35.36 N 110.42 E
Fena Valley Reservoir ⊜[1] 174p 13.21 N 144.42 E
Fendaozi 104 41.35 N 120.51 E
Fenelon Falls 212 44.32 N 78.45 W
Fenelton 214 40.52 N 79.44 W
Fener ◆[8] 267b 41.02 N 28.56 E
Fenerbahce Stadium ♠ 267b 40.59 N 29.02 E
Fener Burnu ≻ 130 41.07 N 39.25 E
Fener Tepesi ∧[2] 267b 41.09 N 28.47 E
Fenestrelle 62 45.02 N 7.03 E
Fénétrange 56 48.51 N 7.01 E
Feng ≃ 105 39.25 N 116.57 E
Fengcheng, Zhg. 98 40.27 N 124.02 E
Fengcheng, Zhg. 100 28.10 N 115.46 E
Fengcheng, Zhg. 102 38.32 N 101.50 E
Fengcheng, Zhg. 106 30.55 N 121.38 E
Fengdengwu 105 39.42 N 117.55 E
Fengdian 107 30.41 N 104.51 E
Fengdu 102 29.58 N 107.41 E
Fengfeng 98 36.28 N 114.14 E
Fenggang, Zhg. 100 28.34 N 116.34 E
Fenggang, Zhg. 102 27.58 N 107.47 E
Fenggaopu 107 29.24 N 105.41 E
Fenghua 100 29.40 N 121.24 E
Fenghuang, Zhg. 100 23.58 N 116.44 E
Fenghuang, Zhg. 102 24.25 N 107.17 E
Fenghuang, Zhg. 102 27.58 N 109.19 E
Fenghuang, Zhg. 106 31.21 N 121.44 E
Fenghuangchang 107 29.44 N 106.19 E
Fenghuang Shan ∧ 107 28.54 N 106.35 E
Fenghuanjing 100 31.11 N 117.49 E
Fenghui 100 29.56 N 120.58 E
Fengjia, Zhg. 98 37.03 N 121.42 E
Fengjia, Zhg. 104 42.35 N 122.30 E
Fengjiabao 102 36.12 N 104.49 E
Fengjiakou 98 38.11 N 116.44 E
Fengjianjiao 106 30.41 N 120.51 E
Fengjiatun 104 41.14 N 122.00 E
Fengjiawopeng 104 42.19 N 123.40 E
Fengjiaxiang 106 30.56 N 121.06 E
Fengjie 102 31.03 N 109.31 E
Fengjing 106 30.53 N 121.01 E
Fengkou 100 30.05 N 113.18 E
Fengle, Zhg. 89 45.47 N 125.26 E
Fengle, Zhg. 100 27.13 N 118.11 E
Fenglezhen 98 36.14 N 114.18 E
Fengliang 100 23.59 N 116.14 E
Fenglin, T'aiwan 100 23.45 N 121.26 E
Fenglin, Zhg. 100 28.19 N 120.46 E
Fengling Guan)(100 28.14 N 118.29 E
Fenglingtou 100 28.26 N 117.50 E
Fengman 89 43.46 N 126.41 E
Fengnan (Xugezhuang) 105 39.34 N 118.06 E
Fengning (Dagezhen) 98 41.12 N 116.32 E
Fengpin 100 23.36 N 121.31 E
Fengpingzi 102 32.46 N 105.12 E
Fengqiao, Zhg. 100 29.46 N 120.26 E
Fengqiao, Zhg. 106 31.19 N 120.33 E
Fengqing 102 24.46 N 99.52 E
Fengqiu 98 35.05 N 114.25 E
Fengrun 105 39.50 N 118.07 E
Fengshan, Zhg. 89 46.22 N 128.30 E
Fengshan, Zhg. 98 41.14 N 117.05 E
Fengshan, Zhg. 102 22.01 N 109.59 E
Fengshi 100 24.42 N 116.34 E
Fengshun 100 23.48 N 116.11 E
Fengtai, Zhg. 100 32.44 N 116.43 E
Fengtai, Zhg. 105 39.51 N 116.16 E
Fengtian, Zhg. 100 27.24 N 114.43 E
Fengtian, Zhg. 100 25.46 N 115.30 E
Fengtien → Shenyang 104 41.48 N 123.27 E
Fengting 100 25.16 N 118.54 E
Fengwan 100 24.48 N 113.50 E
Fengxi 102 31.48 N 109.50 E
Fengxian, Zhg. 98 34.42 N 116.34 E
Fengxian, Zhg. 102 33.57 N 106.44 E
Fengxian, Zhg. 106 30.55 N 121.27 E
Fengxiang 102 34.29 N 107.29 E
Fengxin 100 28.43 N 115.23 E
Fengyang, Zhg. 100 32.52 N 117.34 E
Fengyang, Zhg. 100 24.49 N 117.53 E
Fengyi 102 31.44 N 103.53 E
Fengyu 100 26.31 N 119.18 E
Fengyüan 100 24.15 N 120.43 E
Fengzhen 102 40.24 N 113.09 E
Fengzhou 100 25.41 N 113.52 E
Fengzhuangtou 106 31.00 N 118.39 E
Fenholloway ≃ 192 29.59 N 83.47 W
Fen Hu ⊜ 106 31.00 N 120.47 E
Feni 124 23.00 N 91.24 E
Fenicia Moncata ⊥ 70 37.33 N 14.57 E
Feni Islands II 14 4.05 S 153.42 E
Fenimore Pass μ 180 52.00 N 175.35 W
Fenino 265b 55.44 N 37.57 E
Fenis 62 45.44 N 7.29 E
Feniscowles 262 53.43 N 2.32 W
Fenjie 106 32.17 N 120.20 E
Fennimore 190 42.59 N 90.39 W
Fennville 216 42.35 N 86.06 W
Fenny Compton 42 52.09 N 1.20 W
Fenny Stratford 42 52.00 N 0.43 W
Feno, Capo di ≻, Fr. 36 41.57 N 8.36 E
Feno, Capo di ≻, Fr. 71 41.23 N 9.06 E
Fenoarivo, Madag. 157b 18.26 S 46.34 E
Fenoarivo, Madag. 157b 21.43 S 46.24 E
Fenoarivo, Madag. 157b 20.52 S 46.53 E
Fenoarivo Atsinanana 157b 17.22 S 49.25 E
Fensfjorden ⊂[2] 26 60.51 N 4.50 E
Fenshui 104 40.41 N 122.32 E
Fenshui ≃ 100 29.49 N 119.41 E
Fenshui'ao 100 25.20 N 114.43 E
Fenshuidunshen 106 31.30 N 120.01 E
Fenshuiling, Zhg. 107 28.51 N 105.35 E
Fenshuiling, Zhg. 107 30.20 N 105.15 E
Fenshuipu 107 30.05 N 104.05 E
Fenshuizhen 107 29.44 N 103.55 E
Fenshuizui 100 30.35 N 113.38 E
Fensmark 41 55.17 N 11.49 E
Fenstanton 42 52.18 N 0.04 W
Fenton, Mi., U.S. 216 42.47 N 83.42 W
Fenton, Mo., U.S. 219 38.32 N 90.22 W
Fenton, Lake ⊜ 216 42.50 N 83.43 W
Fentou 105 38.53 N 116.32 E
Fentress 222 29.45 N 97.47 W
Fenway Park ♠ 283 42.21 N 71.06 W
Fenwick 188 38.13 N 80.34 W
Fenwick Island ≻[1] 208 38.25 N 75.03 W
Fenyang 102 37.17 N 111.48 E
Fenyi 100 27.47 N 114.42 E
Feodosija 78 45.02 N 35.23 E
Feodosijskij zaliv ⊂ 78 45.05 N 35.35 E
Fépin 56 50.01 N 4.44 E
Fer, Cap de ≻ 148 37.05 N 7.10 E
Ferbane 48 53.15 N 7.49 W
Ferbitz 264a 52.30 N 13.01 E
Ferch 264a 52.19 N 12.56 E
Fercher Berge ∧[2] 264a 52.19 N 12.57 E
Ferchland 54 52.26 N 12.00 E
Ferdig 182 48.45 N 111.46 W
Ferdinand 194 38.13 N 86.51 W
Ferdinandshof 54 53.39 N 13.53 E
Ferdows 128 34.00 N 58.09 E
Fère-Champenoise 50 48.45 N 3.59 E
Fère-en-Tardenois 50 49.12 N 3.31 E
Ferencváros ◆[8] 264c 47.28 N 19.06 E
Ferentillo 66 42.37 N 12.47 E
Ferentino 66 41.42 N 13.15 E
Fergana 85 40.23 N 71.46 E
Ferganskaja dolina V 85 40.50 N 71.30 E
Ferganskij chrebet ⋏ 85 41.00 N 74.00 E
Fergus 212 43.42 N 80.22 W
Fergus Falls 198 46.16 N 96.04 W
Ferguson, Austl. 168a 33.26 S 115.51 E
Ferguson, B.C., Can. 182 50.41 N 117.28 W
Ferguson, Ky., U.S. 192 37.04 N 84.36 W
Ferguson, Mo., U.S. 219 38.44 N 90.18 W
Ferguson ≃ 168a 33.21 S 115.40 E
Fergusonville 285 40.07 N 74.54 W
Fergusson Island I 164 9.30 S 150.40 E
Fériana 148 34.57 N 8.34 E
Ferihegyi Airport ⊠ 264c 47.26 N 19.15 E
Ferkéssédougou 150 9.36 N 5.12 W
Ferla 70 37.07 N 14.56 E
Ferlach 61 46.31 N 14.18 E
Ferleiten 64 47.10 N 12.49 E
Ferlo ◆[1] 150 0.15 N 0.14 W
Ferlo, Vallée du V 150 15.42 N 15.30 W
Fermiers, Île aux I 275a 45.40 N 73.27 W
Fermignano 66 43.40 N 12.39 E
Fermin, Point ≻ 228 33.42 N 118.18 W
Fermi National Accelerator Laboratory ʊ[3] 216 41.50 N 88.15 W
Fermo 66 43.09 N 13.43 E
Fermont 176 52.47 N 67.05 W
Fermoselle 34 41.19 N 6.23 W
Fermoy 48 52.08 N 8.16 W
Fernández 252 27.55 S 63.54 W
Fernández Leal 200 30.51 N 108.17 W
Fernandina, Isla I 246a 0.25 S 91.30 W
Fernandina Beach 192 30.40 N 81.27 W
Fernando de la Mora 252 25.19 S 57.36 W
Fernando de Noronha, Ilha I 250 3.51 S 32.25 W
Fernandópolis 255 20.16 S 50.14 W
Fernando Póo → Bioko I 152 3.30 N 8.40 E
Fernán-Núñez 34 37.40 N 4.43 W
Fernão Veloso, Baía de ⊂ 154 14.20 S 40.45 E
Ferndale, S. Afr. 273d 26.05 S 27.59 E
Ferndale, Ca., U.S. 204 40.34 N 124.15 W
Ferndale, Fl., U.S. 220 28.37 N 81.42 W
Ferndale, Md., U.S. 208 39.10 N 76.38 W
Ferndale, Mi., U.S. 216 42.27 N 83.08 W
Ferndale, N.Y., U.S. 210 41.46 N 74.44 W
Ferndale, Pa., U.S. 214 40.17 N 78.54 W
Ferndale, Wa., U.S. 202 48.50 N 122.35 W
Ferndale Lake ⊜ 222 32.57 N 95.05 W
Ferndown 42 50.48 N 1.55 W
Ferney-Voltaire 58 46.15 N 6.07 E
Fern Glen 210 40.57 N 76.10 W
Fernhatten ⋏[2] 41 56.15 N 10.48 E
Fernhill Heath 42 52.14 N 2.12 W
Fernie 182 49.30 N 115.03 W
Fernilee 262 53.18 N 1.58 W
Fernilee Reservoir ⊜[1] 262 53.17 N 1.59 W
Fernley 204 39.36 N 119.15 W
Ferno 62 45.37 N 8.45 E
Fernow, Mount ∧ 224 47.45 N 121.14 W
Fern Park 220 28.41 N 81.20 W
Fernpass)(58 47.22 N 10.50 E
Fern Ridge Lake ⊜[1] 202 44.05 N 123.18 W
Ferns 48 52.35 N 6.31 W
Fernvale 171a 27.27 S 152.39 E
Fernway, Il., U.S. 278 41.36 N 87.50 W
Fernway, Pa., U.S. 214 40.41 N 80.07 W
Fernwood, Id., U.S. 202 47.06 N 116.23 W
Fernwood, N.Y., U.S. 210 43.16 N 73.40 W
Fernwood, Pa., U.S. 285 39.57 N 75.15 W
Ferny Creek 274b 37.53 S 145.21 E
Feroé, Islas → Faeroe Islands □[2] 22 62.00 N 7.00 W
Feroës → Faeroe Islands □[2] 22 62.00 N 7.00 W
Ferokh 122 11.11 N 75.51 E
Feroleto Antico 68 38.58 N 16.23 E
Feroleto della Chiesa 68 38.28 N 16.04 E
Ferolle Point ≻ 186 51.05 N 57.07 W
Ferozepore → Fīrozpur 123 30.55 N 74.36 E
Ferrandina 68 40.29 N 16.28 E
Ferrara 64 44.50 N 11.35 E
Ferrara □[4] 64 44.48 N 11.50 E
Ferrat, Cap ≻ 34 35.54 N 0.23 W
Ferrato, Capo ≻ 71 39.18 N 9.38 E
Ferraz de Vasconcelos 256 23.32 S 46.22 W
Ferraz de Vasconcelos □[7] 287b 23.33 S 46.21 W
Ferrazzano 66 41.32 N 14.40 E
Ferré, Cap ≻ 240e 14.28 N 60.49 W
Ferreira, Ang. 152 12.53 S 22.48 E
Ferreira, S. Afr. 158 29.13 S 26.10 E
Ferreira do Alentejo 34 38.03 N 8.07 W
Ferreira Gomes 250 0.48 N 51.08 W
Ferreiros 256 22.25 S 43.34 W
Ferrell 285 39.41 N 75.12 W
Ferrell's Bridge Dam ◆[6] 222 32.45 N 94.30 W
Ferreñafe 248 6.38 S 79.45 W
Ferrera Erbognone 62 45.07 N 8.52 E
Ferret 58 45.55 N 7.06 E
Ferret, Cap ≻ 32 44.37 N 1.15 W
Ferreyra 252 31.28 S 64.08 W
Ferriday 194 31.37 N 91.33 W
Ferriere 62 44.38 N 9.30 E
Ferrière-la-Grande 50 50.15 N 4.00 E
Ferrières 50 48.05 N 2.47 E
Ferrières-en-Brie 50 48.49 N 2.43 E
Ferris 222 32.32 N 96.39 W
Ferritslev 41 55.18 N 10.36 E
Ferro ≃ 255 12.27 S 54.31 W
Ferrol, Península de ≻[1] 248 9.10 S 78.37 W
Ferrol → El Ferrol del Caudillo 34 43.29 N 8.14 W
Ferron 200 39.05 N 111.08 W
Ferron Creek ≃ 200 39.09 N 110.55 W
Ferros 255 19.14 S 43.02 W
Ferru, Monte ∧ 71 39.44 N 9.38 E
Ferruzzano 68 38.02 N 16.05 E
Ferry, Pointe ≻ 241o 16.17 N 61.49 W
Ferryhill 44 54.41 N 1.33 W
Ferryland 186 47.02 N 52.53 W
Ferry Point Park ♠ 276 40.49 N 73.50 W
Ferrysburg 216 43.05 N 86.13 W
Ferry Village 284a 43.58 N 78.57 W
Ferryville → Menzel Bourguiba 148 37.10 N 9.48 E
Feršampenuaz 86 53.32 N 59.51 E
Fertile 198 47.32 N 96.16 W
Fertilia, Aeroporto di ⊠ 71 40.37 N 8.15 E
Fertő (Neusiedler See) ⊜ 61 47.50 N 16.45 E
Fertőd ⊥ 61 47.37 N 16.53 E
Fertőrákos 61 47.43 N 16.39 E
Fertőújlak 61 47.40 N 16.51 E
Ferulargiu, Monte ∧ 71 40.31 N 9.34 E
Ferzikovo 82 54.32 N 36.45 E
Fès 148 34.05 N 4.57 W
Fès □[4] 148 33.55 N 4.57 W
Feshi 152 6.07 S 18.10 E
Feshie ≃ 46 57.08 N 3.55 W
Fessenden 198 47.38 N 99.37 W
Festus 219 38.13 N 90.23 W
Fetcham 260 51.17 N 0.22 W
Fet Dom, Tanjung ≻ 164 1.53 S 129.43 E
Fété Bowé 150 14.56 N 13.30 W
Fetești 38 44.23 N 27.50 E
Fethaland, Point of ≻ 46a 60.38 N 1.18 W
Fethard 48 52.27 N 7.41 W
Fethiye 130 36.37 N 29.07 E
Fethiye Körfezi ⊂ 130 36.40 N 29.00 E
Fetisovo 72 42.46 N 52.38 E
Fetlar I 46a 60.37 N 0.52 W
Fetsund 26 59.56 N 11.10 E
Fetterangus 46 57.33 N 2.01 W
Fettercairn 46 56.51 N 2.34 W
Feucherolles 261 48.52 N 1.58 E
Feucht 60 49.22 N 11.13 E
Feuchtwangen 56 49.10 N 10.20 E
Feudingen 56 50.56 N 8.19 E
Feuerland → Tierra del Fuego, Isla Grande de I 254 54.00 S 69.00 W
Feuet 146 24.57 N 10.04 E
Feuilles, Baie aux ⊂ 176 58.55 N 69.20 W
Feuilles, Rivière aux ≃ 176 58.47 N 70.04 W
Feuquières-en-Vimeu 50 50.04 N 1.36 E
Feura Bush 210 42.35 N 73.53 W
Feurs 62 45.45 N 4.14 E
Fevik 26 58.23 N 8.42 E
Fevzipaşa 130 37.07 N 36.37 E
Féy 56 49.02 N 6.06 E
Feyẕābād, Afg. 120 37.06 N 70.34 E
Feyẕābād, Īrān 128 35.01 N 58.46 E
Feyzin 62 45.40 N 4.51 E
Fez → Fès 148 34.05 N 4.57 W
Fezzan → Fazzān □[9] 146 26.00 N 14.00 E
Ffestiniog 42 52.58 N 3.55 W
Fforest Fawr ◆[1] 42 51.52 N 3.36 W
F. Gilbert Hills State Forest ♠ 283 42.03 N 71.17 W
Fhada, Beinn ∧ 46 57.13 N 5.18 W
Fiambalá 252 27.41 S 67.38 W
Fiamignano 66 42.16 N 13.07 E
Fian 150 10.23 N 2.29 W
Fianarantsoa 157b 21.26 S 47.05 E
Fianarantsoa □[4] 157b 22.00 S 47.00 E
Fianga 146 9.55 N 15.09 E
Fiano 62 45.13 N 7.31 E
Fiantsonana 157b 19.09 S 46.12 E
Fiastra, Abbazia di ʊ[1] 66 43.13 N 13.25 E
Fiavè 64 46.00 N 10.50 E
Ficarazzi 70 38.05 N 13.28 E
Ficarolo 64 44.57 N 11.26 E
Ficarra 70 38.06 N 14.50 E
Fiche 144 9.52 N 38.46 E
Fichtelberg 60 50.01 N 11.51 E
Fichtelberg ∧ 54 50.26 N 12.57 E
Fichtelgebirge ⋏ 30 50.00 N 11.55 E
Fichtenau 264a 52.27 N 13.42 E
Ficksburg 158 28.57 S 27.50 E
Ficulle 66 42.50 N 12.04 E
Ficuzza ≃ 70 37.00 N 14.20 E
Fidalgo ≃ 250 7.28 S 42.32 W
Fidalgo Island I 224 48.25 N 122.35 W
Fidān, Wādī al- V 132 30.46 N 35.18 E
Fiddlers Hamlet 260 51.41 N 0.08 E
Fiddletown 226 38.30 N 120.46 W
Fiddyment Creek ≃ 278 41.36 N 88.03 W
Fidelity 219 39.09 N 90.10 W
Fidenza 64 44.52 N 10.03 E
Fidīmīn 142 29.23 N 30.46 E
Fiditi 150 7.45 N 3.53 E
Fidji → Fiji □[1] 175g 18.00 S 178.00 E
Fidler Lake ⊜ 184 57.11 N 96.57 W
Fidschi → Fiji □[1] 175g 18.00 S 178.00 E
Fiè (Völs) 64 46.31 N 11.30 E
Fieberbrunn 64 47.29 N 12.33 E
Field 182 51.24 N 116.29 W
Fieldale 192 36.42 N 79.56 W
Field Museum ʊ 278 41.53 N 87.37 W
Fieldon 219 39.07 N 90.30 W
Fieldsboro 285 40.08 N 74.43 W
Fieldstone 276 40.44 N 74.33 W
Fiemme, Val di V 64 46.24 N 11.25 E
Fiener Bruch ☷ 54 52.19 N 12.10 E
Fienvillers 50 50.07 N 2.14 E
Fier 38 40.43 N 19.34 E
Fier ≃ 58 45.56 N 5.50 E
Fiéra Campionaria ♠ 266b 45.28 N 9.09 E
Fiera di Primiero 64 46.10 N 11.49 E
Fierenana 157b 18.29 S 48.24 E
Fiery Creek ≃, Austl. 166 18.23 S 139.52 E
Fiery Creek ≃, Austl. 169 37.44 S 142.56 E
Fiery Range ⋏ 171b 35.30 S 148.40 E
Fierzës, Liqeni i ⊜[1] 38 42.10 N 20.15 E
Fiesch 58 46.20 N 8.10 E
Fiesole 66 43.48 N 11.17 E
Fiesso d'Artico 64 45.24 N 12.02 E
Fiesso Umbertiano 64 44.56 N 11.36 E
Fife 224 47.14 N 122.22 W
Fife □[4] 46 56.13 N 3.02 W
Fife Lake, Sk., Can. 184 49.12 N 105.43 W
Fife Lake, Mi., U.S. 190 44.34 N 85.21 W
Fife Lake ⊜ 184 49.14 N 105.53 W
Fife Ness ≻ 46 56.17 N 2.36 W
Fifield 190 45.52 N 90.25 W
Fifteenmile Creek ≃, Or., U.S. 224 45.37 N 121.07 W
Fifteenmile Creek ≃, Wy., U.S. 202 44.01 N 108.01 W
Fifth Cataract → Khāmis, Ash-Shallāl al- ∟ 140 18.23 N 33.47 E
Fifth Depot Lake ⊜ 212 44.36 N 76.52 W
Figeac 32 44.37 N 2.02 E
Figeholm 26 57.22 N 16.33 E
Fig Garden 226 36.48 N 119.47 W
Fighting Island I 281 42.13 N 83.07 W
Figline Valdarno 66 43.37 N 11.28 E
Figtree 154 20.24 S 28.21 E
Figueira 287a 22.42 S 43.27 W
Figueira, Cachoeira ∟ 250 9.49 S 58.13 W
Figueira da Foz 34 40.09 N 8.52 W
Figueira → Governador Valadares 255 18.51 S 41.56 W
Figueres 34 42.16 N 2.58 E
Figuig 148 32.10 N 1.15 W
Figuig □[4] 148 32.40 N 2.15 W
Fihaonana 157b 18.36 S 47.12 E
Fiherenana ≃ 157b 23.19 S 43.37 E
Fiji □[1], Oc. 14 18.00 S 178.00 E
Fiji □[1], Oc. 175g 18.00 S 178.00 E
Fiji Islands II 14 18.00 S 178.00 E
Fijnaart 52 51.37 N 4.31 E
Fik 144 8.10 N 42.18 E
Fika 146 11.17 N 11.18 E
Fiktūriyā, Bi'r ∓[4] 142 30.24 N 30.36 E
Filabusi 154 20.34 S 29.20 E
Filadélfia, Bra. 250 7.21 S 47.30 W
Filadelfia, C.R. 236 10.26 N 85.34 W
Filadelfia, It. 68 38.48 N 16.18 E
Filadelfia → Philadelphia 208 39.57 N 75.07 W
Fil'akovo 30 48.17 N 19.51 E
Filandari 68 38.37 N 16.02 E
Filatova Gora 76 57.40 N 28.10 E
Filchner Ice Shelf ⊓ 9 79.00 S 40.00 W
Filderstadt 56 48.41 N 9.13 E
File Lake ⊜ 184 54.53 N 100.20 W
Filettino 66 41.53 N 13.19 E
Filey 44 54.12 N 0.17 W
Filey Bay ⊂ 44 54.12 N 0.16 W
Fili ◆[8] 265b 55.45 N 37.31 E
Filí ⊥ 38 38.10 N 23.40 E
Filiano 68 40.49 N 15.42 E
Filiași 38 44.33 N 23.31 E
Filiatrá 38 37.10 N 21.35 E
Filicudi, Isola I 70 38.34 N 14.34 E
Filimonovo 86 56.12 N 95.28 E
Filingué 150 14.21 N 3.19 E
Filipinas, Mar de → Philippine Sea ∓[2] 14 20.00 N 135.00 E
Filipinas → Philippines □[1] 116 13.00 N 122.00 E
Filipino Cemetery and Memorial ◆ 269f 14.31 N 121.02 E
Fílippoi ⊥ 38 41.00 N 24.16 E
Filippovka 80 53.59 N 49.46 E
Filippovo 80 58.18 N 50.30 E
Filippovskoje, Ross. 82 56.06 N 38.37 E
Filippovskoje, Ross. 82 56.48 N 39.07 E
Filipstad 40 59.43 N 14.10 E
Filisola 234 17.50 N 94.19 W
Fillmore, Sk., Can. 184 49.50 N 103.25 W
Fillmore, Ca., U.S. 228 34.23 N 118.55 W
Fillmore, Il., U.S. 219 39.07 N 89.17 W
Fillmore, N.Y., U.S. 210 42.27 N 78.06 W
Fillmore, Ut,. U.S. 200 38.58 N 112.19 W
Fillmore Glen State Park ♠ 210 42.42 N 76.20 W
Filogaso 68 38.41 N 16.14 E
Filomeno Mata 234 20.12 N 97.42 W
Filonovskaja 80 50.34 N 42.46 E
Filottrano 66 43.26 N 13.21 E
Fils ≃ 56 48.42 N 9.25 E
Filskov 41 55.48 N 9.02 E
Filton 42 51.31 N 2.35 W
Filtu 144 5.07 N 40.39 E
Filzbach 58 47.07 N 9.08 E
Fimi ≃ 152 3.01 S 16.58 E
Fina, Réserve de ◆[4] 150 12.50 N 8.30 W
Finale Emilia 64 44.50 N 11.17 E
Finale Ligure 62 44.10 N 8.20 E
Finarwa 144 13.06 N 39.01 E
Fincastle 192 37.29 N 79.52 W
Finch 206 45.11 N 75.07 W
Fincham 42 52.37 N 0.30 E
Finchley ◆[8] 260 51.36 N 0.10 W
Finderne 276 40.34 N 74.35 W
Findhorn 46 57.39 N 3.36 W
Findhorn ≃ 46 57.38 N 3.38 W
Fındık 130 37.31 N 41.58 E
Findlay, Il., U.S. 219 39.31 N 88.45 W
Findlay, Oh., U.S. 216 41.02 N 83.39 W
Findlay, Mount ∧ 182 50.04 N 116.28 W
Findley Lake 214 42.07 N 79.44 W
Findley Lake ⊜ 214 42.06 N 79.43 W
Findochty 46 57.41 N 2.54 W
Fine Arts, Museum of ʊ 283 42.20 N 71.06 W
Finedon 42 52.20 N 0.39 W
Finejevo 82 56.02 N 38.53 E
Finesville 210 40.36 N 75.10 W
Fingal, On., Can. 214 42.43 N 81.19 W
Fingal, N.D., U.S. 198 46.45 N 97.47 W
Finger Lake ⊜ 184 53.09 N 93.30 W
Fíngoè 154 15.12 S 31.50 E
Finike 130 36.18 N 30.09 E
Finike Körfezi ⊂ 130 36.17 N 30.16 E
Finisk ≃ 48 52.07 N 7.50 W
Finistère □[5] 32 48.20 N 4.00 W
Finisterre 196 25.59 N 103.15 W
Finisterre, Cabo de ≻ 34 42.53 N 9.16 W
Finisterre → Land's End ≻ 42 50.03 N 5.44 W
Finisterre Range ⋏ 164 5.50 S 146.05 E
Finja 41 56.10 N 13.41 E
Finjasjön ⊜ 41 56.08 N 13.42 E
Finke 162 25.34 S 134.35 E
Finke ≃ 162 26.20 S 136.00 E
Finke, Mount ∧[2] 162 30.55 S 134.02 E
Finke Gorge National Park ♠ 162 24.15 S 132.50 E
Finkenkrug 264a 52.34 N 13.03 E
Finkenwerder ◆[8] 52 53.31 N 9.52 E
Finksburg 208 39.29 N 76.53 W
Finland (Suomi) □[1], Europe 22 64.00 N 26.00 E
Finland (Suomi) □[1], Europe 24 64.00 N 26.00 E
Finland, Gulf of (Suomenlahti) (Finskij zaliv) ⊂ 26 60.00 N 27.00 E
Finlande → Finland □[1] 24 64.00 N 26.00 E
Finlandia, Golfo de → Finland, Gulf of ⊂ 26 60.00 N 27.00 E
Finlandia → Finland □[1] 24 64.00 N 26.00 E
Finland Station ◆[5] 265a 59.57 N 30.22 E
Finlas, Loch ⊜ 44 55.15 N 4.25 W
Finlay ≃ 176 56.54 N 124.57 W
Finley, Austl. 166 35.39 S 145.35 E
Finley, N.D., U.S. 198 47.30 N 97.50 W
Finley Creek ≃ 194 36.58 N 93.22 W
Finleyville, Pa., U.S. 214 40.09 N 78.11 W
Finleyville, Pa., U.S. 214 40.15 N 80.00 W
Finleyville Airport ⊠ 279b 40.15 N 80.01 W
Finmoore 182 53.59 N 123.37 W
Finn ≃ 48 54.50 N 7.29 W
Finne ◆[1] 54 51.13 N 11.19 E
Finnegan 182 51.07 N 112.04 W
Finnentrop 56 51.09 N 7.58 E
Finnerödja 40 58.56 N 14.26 E
Finney Creek ≃ 224 48.31 N 121.51 W
Finnhamn 40 59.28 N 18.50 E

Symbol	English	Deutsch	Español	Français	Português
≃	River	Fluß	Río	Rivière	Rio
≊	Canal	Kanal	Canal	Canal	Canal
∟	Waterfall, Rapids	Wasserfall, Stromschnellen	Cascada, Rápidos	Chute d'eau, Rapides	Cascata, Rápidos
μ	Strait	Meeresstraße	Estrecho	Détroit	Estreito
⊂	Bay, Gulf	Bucht, Golf	Bahía, Golfo	Baie, Golfe	Baía, Golfo
⊜	Lake, Lakes	See, Seen	Lago, Lagos	Lac, Lacs	Lago, Lagos
☷	Swamp	Sumpf	Pantano	Marais	Pântano
⊓	Ice Features, Glacier	Eis- und Gletscherformen	Accidentes Glaciales	Formes glaciaires	Acidentes glaciares
∓	Other Hydrographic Features	Andere Hydrographische Objekte	Otros Elementos Hidrográficos	Autres données hydrographiques	Outros acidentes hidrográficos
✤	Submarine Features	Untermeerische Objekte	Accidentes Submarinos	Formes de relief sous-marin	Acidentes submarinos
□	Political Unit	Politische Einheit	Unidad Politica	Entité politique	Unidade política
ʊ	Cultural Institution	Kulturelle Institution	Institución Cultural	Institution culturelle	Instituição cultural
⊥	Historical Site	Historische Stätte	Sitio Histórico	Site historique	Sitio histórico
♠	Recreational Site	Erholungs- und Ferienort	Sitio de Recreo	Centre de loisirs	Area de Lazer
⊠	Airport	Flughafen	Aeropuerto	Aéroport	Aeroporto
■	Military Installation	Militäranlage	Instalación Militar	Installation militaire	Instalação militar
◆	Miscellaneous	Verschiedenes	Misceláneo	Divers	Diversos

ENGLISH Name	Page	Lat.°′	Long.°′
Finnigan, Mount ∧	164	15.49 S	145.17 E
Finnis, Cape ➤	162	33.38 S	134.51 E
Finnischer Meerbusen → Finland, Gulf of c	26	60.00 N	27.00 E
Finniss	168b	35.24 S	138.49 E
Finniss ≃	168b	35.30 S	138.53 E
Finnland → Finland □[1]	24	64.00 N	26.00 E
Finnmark □[6]	24	70.00 N	25.00 E
Finn Mountain ∧	180	60.37 N	157.11 W
Finno ∧[2]	154	3.27 N	41.32 E
Finnskogen ✦[3]	26	60.40 N	12.40 E
Finnsnes	24	69.14 N	17.59 E
Finocchio ✦[8]	267a	41.53 N	12.41 E
Finow	54	52.50 N	13.43 E
Finowfurt	54	52.51 N	13.41 E
Finowkanal ≋	54	52.51 N	13.24 E
Fins, Fr.	50	50.02 N	3.03 E
Fins, 'Umān	128	22.56 N	59.13 E
Finsbury	273d	26.13 S	27.39 E
Finschhafen	164	6.35 S	147.50 E
Finse	26	60.36 N	7.30 E
Finskij zaliv → Finland, Gulf of c	26	60.00 N	27.00 E
Finspång	40	58.43 N	15.47 E
Finsta	40	59.44 N	18.30 E
Finsteraarhorn ∧	58	46.32 N	8.08 E
Finsterwalde	54	51.38 N	13.42 E
Finsterwolde	52	53.12 N	7.04 E
Fintel	52	53.10 N	9.40 E
Fintona	48	54.30 N	7.19 W
Fintown	48	54.52 N	8.08 W
Finvoy	48	55.00 N	6.30 W
Fionn Loch ◎	46	57.46 N	5.29 W
Fiora ≃	66	42.20 N	11.34 E
Fiorano Modenese	64	44.32 N	10.49 E
Fiordland National Park ♦	172	45.30 S	167.20 E
Fiorenzuola d'Arda	62	44.56 N	9.55 E
Fiorenzuola di Focara	66	43.57 N	12.48 E
Fiorito ✦[8]	288	34.42 S	58.27 W
Fīq	132	32.47 N	35.42 E
Fırat → Euphrates ≃	128	31.00 N	47.25 E
Firavitoba	246	5.40 N	73.00 W
Fircrest	224	47.14 N	122.30 W
Fire ≃	190	48.52 N	83.21 W
Firebaugh	226	36.51 N	120.27 W
Firebrick	218	38.41 N	83.03 W
Fire Island I	210	40.42 N	73.00 W
Fire Island Inlet c	276	40.38 N	73.16 W
Fire Island National Seashore ♦	188	40.38 N	73.08 W
Fire Island Pines	276	40.40 N	73.04 W
Fire Islands II	276	40.40 N	73.11 W
Firenze (Florence)	66	43.46 N	11.15 E
Firenze □[4]	66	43.50 N	11.20 E
Firenzuola	66	44.07 N	11.23 E
Firesteel Creek ≃	198	43.43 N	97.58 W
Firgrove	262	53.37 N	2.08 W
Firmat	252	33.27 S	61.29 W
Firminópolis	255	16.40 S	50.19 W
Firminy	62	45.23 N	4.18 E
Firmo	68	39.43 N	16.10 E
Firovo	76	57.29 N	33.40 E
Fīrozābād	124	27.09 N	78.25 E
Fīrozpur	123	30.55 N	74.36 E
Fīrozpur Jhirka	124	27.48 N	76.57 E
Firsanovka	265b	55.57 N	37.15 E
Firsovo	88	52.20 N	118.06 E
First Broad ≃	192	35.11 N	81.37 W
First Cataract → Awwal, Ash-Shallāl al- ⌞	140	24.01 N	32.52 E
First Cliff ⊥[4]	283	42.12 N	70.43 W
First Connecticut Lake ◎	206	45.05 N	71.15 W
First Han-gang Bridge ✦[5]	271b	37.32 N	126.56 E
First Herring Brook ≃	283	42.11 N	70.45 W
First Watchung Mountain ∧	276	40.55 N	74.10 W
Firth	198	40.31 N	96.36 W
Firth ≃	180	69.32 N	139.22 W
Fir'uza	128	37.56 N	58.04 E
Fīrūzābād	128	28.50 N	52.36 E
Fīrūz Kūh	128	35.45 N	52.47 E
Fischa ≃	264b	48.04 N	16.35 E
Fischamend	61	48.07 N	16.37 E
Fischbach, Dtsch.	56	49.44 N	7.23 E
Fischbach, Dtsch.	60	49.25 N	11.12 E
Fischbachau	64	47.43 N	11.57 E
Fischbacher Alpen ⩘	61	47.28 N	15.30 E
Fischbeck, Dtsch.	52	52.09 N	9.17 E
Fischbeck, Dtsch.	54	52.32 N	12.01 E
Fischeln ✦[8]	263	51.18 N	6.35 E
Fischen	58	47.28 N	10.16 E
Fischhausen → Primorsk	76	54.44 N	20.01 E
Fischland ⊥[2]	54	54.22 N	12.25 E
Fish ≃, Austl.	170	33.29 S	149.37 E
Fish (Vis) ≃, Namibia	156	28.07 S	17.45 E
Fish ≃, Al., U.S.	194	30.25 N	87.50 W
Fish ≃, Me., U.S.	186	47.15 N	68.36 W
Fishbourne	42	50.44 N	1.12 W
Fish Brook ≃, Ma., U.S.	283	42.38 N	70.58 W
Fish Brook ≃, Ma., U.S.	283	42.42 N	71.13 W
Fish Camp	226	37.29 N	119.38 W
Fish Canyon V	280	34.11 N	117.55 W
Fish Creek ≃, On., Can.	212	43.13 N	81.13 W
Fish Creek ≃, U.S.	216	41.28 N	84.45 W
Fish Creek ≃, Mi., U.S.	190	43.04 N	84.51 W
Fish Creek ≃, Mt., U.S.	202	46.17 N	109.13 W
Fish Creek ≃, N.Y., U.S.	212	43.12 N	75.43 W
Fish Creek ≃, Or., U.S.	224	45.09 N	122.09 W
Fish Creek, East Branch ≃	212	43.16 N	75.38 W
Fish Creek, West Branch ≃	212	43.16 N	75.38 W
Fish Creek Mountain ∧	224	45.05 N	122.08 W
Fisheating Creek ≃	220	26.57 N	81.07 W
Fisher, Austl.	162	30.33 S	130.58 E
Fisher, Ar., U.S.	194	35.29 N	90.58 W
Fisher, Il., U.S.	216	40.18 N	88.21 W
Fisher, La., U.S.	194	31.29 N	93.27 W
Fisher, Pa., U.S.	214	41.16 N	79.15 W
Fisher ≃, Mb., Can.	184	51.26 N	97.18 W
Fisher ≃, Mt., U.S.	202	48.22 N	115.19 W
Fisher Bay c, Mb., Can.	184	51.30 N	97.16 W
Fisher Bay c, Mi., U.S.	281	42.36 N	82.39 W
Fisher Branch	184	51.05 N	97.37 W
Fisher Channel ʉ	182	52.10 N	127.42 W
Fisher Heights	279b	40.10 N	79.54 W
Fishermans Island I	208	37.06 N	75.58 W
Fisherman's Wharf ✦	282	37.48 N	122.25 W
Fisher Peak ∧	192	36.33 N	80.50 W
Fisher River Indian Reserve ✦[4]	184	51.26 N	97.20 W
Fishers, In., U.S.	218	39.57 N	86.00 W
Fishers, N.Y., U.S.	210	43.00 N	77.28 W
Fishers Island I	207	41.16 N	72.02 W
Fishers Peak ∧	196	37.06 N	104.28 W
Fisher Strait ʉ	176	63.15 N	83.30 W
Fishertown	214	40.08 N	78.35 W
Fisherville	275b	43.47 N	79.28 W
Fishguard	42	51.59 N	4.59 W
Fishhook	219	39.48 N	90.53 W
Fish House	210	43.08 N	74.08 W
Fishing Bay c	208	38.18 N	76.01 W
Fishing Creek	208	38.20 N	76.14 W
Fishing Creek ≃, Ky., U.S.	192	37.06 N	84.41 W
Fishing Creek ≃, N.C., U.S.	192	35.57 N	77.31 W
Fishing Creek ≃, Pa., U.S.	210	41.07 N	77.29 W
Fishing Creek ≃, Pa., U.S.	210	40.58 N	76.28 W
Fishing Creek ≃, S.C., U.S.	192	34.36 N	80.54 W
Fishing Islands II	212	44.45 N	81.20 W
Fishing Lake ◎, Mb., Can.	184	52.07 N	95.25 W
Fishing Lake ◎, Sk., Can.	184	51.50 N	103.32 W
Fishkill	210	41.32 N	73.53 W
Fishkill Creek ≃	210	41.29 N	73.59 W
Fish Lake	216	41.34 N	86.33 W
Fish Lake ◎, On., Can.	212	44.06 N	77.11 W
Fish Lake ◎, Mi., U.S.	216	42.03 N	85.52 W
Fish Lake ◎, Wa., U.S.	224	47.50 N	120.42 W
Fishmoor Reservoir ◎[1]	262	53.44 N	2.28 W
Fish Point ➤	214	41.43 N	82.40 W
Fishpool	262	53.35 N	2.17 W
Fish River	166	17.55 S	137.45 E
Fishs Eddy	210	41.58 N	75.10 W
Fisk	194	36.46 N	90.12 W
Fiskárdhon	38	38.27 N	20.35 E
Fiskdale	207	42.06 N	72.06 W
Fiskebäckskil	26	58.15 N	11.27 E
Fismes	50	49.18 N	3.41 E
Fišt, gora ∧	84	43.58 N	39.54 E
Fitchburg, Ma., U.S.	207	42.35 N	71.48 W
Fitchburg, Wi., U.S.	216	42.57 N	89.28 W
Fitchville, Ct., U.S.	207	41.33 N	72.09 W
Fitchville, Oh., U.S.	214	41.06 N	82.29 W
Fitful Head ➤	46a	59.54 N	1.23 W
Fitiuta	174y	14.13 S	169.27 W
Fito, Mount ∧	175a	13.55 S	171.44 W
Fitri, Lac ◎	146	12.50 N	17.28 E
Fittja	40	59.15 N	17.52 E
Fittleworth	42	50.58 N	0.35 W
Fitzgerald	192	31.42 N	83.15 W
Fitzgerald River National Park ♦	162	34.00 S	119.30 E
Fitz Henry	279b	40.10 N	79.45 W
Fitz Hugh Sound ʉ	182	51.40 N	127.57 W
Fitzmaurice ≃	164	14.50 S	129.44 E
Fitz Roy, Arg.	254	47.02 S	67.15 W
Fitzroy, Austl.	274b	37.48 S	144.59 E
Fitzroy ≃, Austl.	162	17.31 S	123.35 E
Fitzroy ≃, Austl.	166	23.32 S	150.52 E
Fitzroy, Monte (Cerro Chaltel) ∧	254	49.17 S	73.05 W
Fitzroy Crossing	162	18.11 S	125.35 E
Fitzroy Falls Reservoir ◎[1]	170	34.38 S	150.30 E
Fitzwilliam	207	42.46 N	72.08 W
Fitzwilliam Island I	190	45.30 N	81.45 W
Fiuggi	66	41.48 N	13.13 E
Fiumalbo	64	44.11 N	10.39 E
Fiumedinisi	70	38.02 N	15.23 E
Fiumefreddo Bruzio	68	39.14 N	16.04 E
Fiumefreddo di Sicilia	70	37.47 N	15.12 E
Fiume → Rijeka	36	45.20 N	14.27 E
Fiumesino	66	43.38 N	13.22 E
Fiume Veneto	64	45.56 N	12.44 E
Fiumicino	36	41.46 N	12.14 E
Fiumicino ✦[8]	66	41.46 N	12.14 E
Five Corners	283	42.01 N	71.07 W
Five Cowrie Creek ≃[1]	273a	6.27 N	3.27 E
Five Dock	274a	33.52 S	151.08 E
Five Forks	284c	38.47 N	77.16 W
Five Islands	186	45.25 N	64.02 W
Five Islands Harbour c	240c	17.06 N	61.54 W
Fivemile ≃	276	41.03 N	73.27 W
Fivemile Creek ≃, N.Y., U.S.	210	42.22 N	77.22 W
Fivemile Creek ≃, Or., U.S.	224	45.36 N	121.05 W
Fivemile Creek ≃, Wy., U.S.	202	43.14 N	108.12 W
Fivemile Point	210	42.06 N	75.48 W
Fivemiletown	48	54.23 N	7.18 W
Five Penny Borve	46	58.25 N	6.25 W
Five Points, Ca., U.S.	226	36.26 N	120.06 W
Five Points, In., U.S.	218	39.35 N	86.20 W
Five Points, N.M., U.S.	200	35.03 N	106.39 W
Five Points, Oh., U.S.	218	39.41 N	83.12 W
Five Points, Pa., U.S.	214	40.34 N	80.15 W
Five Points, Pa., U.S.	285	39.50 N	75.42 W
Fivizzano	64	44.14 N	10.08 E
Fiwila Mission	154	13.58 S	29.36 E
Fixin	58	47.15 N	4.58 E
Fix-Saint-Geneys	62	45.08 N	3.40 E
Fizi	154	4.18 S	28.57 E
Fizuli	84	39.37 N	47.08 E
Fjællebroen	41	55.03 N	10.24 E
Fjærlandsfjorden c[2]	26	61.17 N	6.40 E
Fjällåsen	24	67.29 N	20.10 E
Fjällbacka	26	58.36 N	11.17 E
Fjällsjöälven ≃	26	63.29 N	16.50 E
Fjärdhundra	40	59.47 N	16.56 E
Fjärdhundra □[9]	40	59.47 N	16.55 E
Fjenneslev	41	55.26 N	11.40 E
Fjerritslev	26	57.05 N	9.16 E
Fjugesta	40	59.10 N	14.52 E
Fkih-Ben-Salah	148	32.32 N	6.40 W
Flacksta	40	59.23 N	16.27 E
Fladnitz im Raabtal	61	46.59 N	15.47 E
Fladså ≃	41	55.19 N	8.54 E
Fladungen	56	50.31 N	10.08 E
Flag Creek ≃	278	41.43 N	87.55 W
Flagler	198	39.17 N	103.04 W
Flagler Beach	192	29.28 N	81.07 W
Flagstaff, Transkei	158	31.05 S	29.29 E
Flagstaff, Az., U.S.	200	35.11 N	111.39 W
Flagstaff Lake ◎[1]	188	45.10 N	70.15 W
Flagtown	276	40.31 N	74.41 W
Flaken-See ◎	264a	52.25 N	13.46 E
Flåm	26	60.50 N	7.07 E
Flambeau ≃	190	45.18 N	91.15 W
Flambeau, South Fork ≃	190	45.39 N	90.48 W
Flamborough, On., Can.	212	43.20 N	79.53 W
Flamborough, Eng., U.K.	44	54.06 N	0.07 W
Flamborough Head ➤	44	54.07 N	0.04 W
Fläming ✦[1]	54	52.00 N	12.30 E
Flaming Gorge National Recreation Area ♦	200	41.30 N	109.30 W
Flaming Gorge Reservoir ◎[1]	200	41.15 N	109.30 W
Flamingo	220	25.09 N	80.56 W
Flamingo, Teluk c	164	5.33 S	138.00 E
Flanagan	216	40.52 N	88.51 W
Flanagan ≃	184	52.50 N	93.28 W
Flanagan Passage ʉ	240m	18.18 N	64.39 W
Flanders, On., Can.	190	48.44 N	92.05 W
Flanders, N.J., U.S.	276	40.50 N	74.41 W
Flanders, N.Y., U.S.	207	40.49 N	72.36 W
Flanders (Flandre) (Vlaanderen) □[9]	50	51.00 N	3.00 E
Flanders Airport ⊠	276	40.50 N	74.41 W
Flandes	246	4.18 N	74.49 W
Flandorf	264b	48.21 N	16.23 E
Flandreau	198	44.02 N	96.35 W
Flandre → Flanders □[9]	50	51.00 N	3.00 E
Flannan Islands II	46	58.18 N	7.36 W
Flåren ◎	26	57.02 N	14.06 E
Flasher	198	46.27 N	101.13 W
Fläsjön ◎	26	64.06 N	15.51 E
Flat, Ak., U.S.	180	62.27 N	158.01 W
Flat, Tx., U.S.	222	31.19 N	97.38 W
Flat ≃, N.T., Can.	180	61.33 N	125.18 W
Flat ≃, Mi., U.S.	190	42.56 N	85.20 W
Flat ≃, N.C., U.S.	192	36.05 N	78.49 W
Flat Bay	186	48.24 N	58.36 W
Flat Branch ≃	219	39.33 N	89.16 W
Flatbush ✦[8]	276	40.39 N	73.56 W
Flat Creek ≃, Ky., U.S.	218	38.17 N	83.48 W
Flat Creek ≃, Mo., U.S.	194	36.45 N	93.31 W
Flat Creek ≃, Mt., U.S.	202	47.43 N	109.50 W
Flat Creek ≃, N.J., U.S.	276	40.27 N	74.10 W
Flat Creek Reservoir ◎[1]	222	32.14 N	95.45 W
Flatey	24a	65.19 N	23.07 W
Flateyri	24a	65.59 N	23.42 W
Flathead ≃	202	47.22 N	114.47 W
Flathead, Middle Fork ≃	202	48.28 N	114.04 W
Flathead, North Fork ≃	202	48.28 N	114.04 W
Flathead, South Fork ≃	202	48.23 N	114.04 W
Flathead Indian Reservation ✦[4]	202	47.30 N	114.25 W
Flathead Lake ◎	202	47.52 N	114.08 W
Flat Holm I	42	51.23 N	3.08 W
Flat Lake ◎	182	54.39 N	112.55 W
Flat Lick	192	36.49 N	83.46 W
Flatonia	222	29.41 N	97.06 W
Flatow	264a	52.44 N	12.57 E
Flat River, P.E., Can.	186	46.01 N	62.52 W
Flat River, Mo., U.S.	194	37.51 N	90.31 W
Flat River Reservoir ◎[1]	207	41.42 N	71.37 W
Flat Rock, Al., U.S.	194	34.46 N	85.42 W
Flat Rock, Il., U.S.	194	38.54 N	87.40 W
Flat Rock, In., U.S.	218	39.22 N	85.50 W
Flat Rock, Mi., U.S.	216	42.05 N	83.17 W
Flat Rock, Oh., U.S.	214	41.14 N	82.51 W
Flatrock ≃	218	39.12 N	85.56 W
Flatrock Creek ≃	216	41.10 N	84.27 W
Flatrock Lake ◎	184	55.37 N	100.47 W
Flatruet ⩘[2]	26	62.45 N	12.50 E
Flats	222	32.50 N	95.53 W
Flattery, Cape ➤, Austl.	164	14.58 S	145.21 E
Flattery, Cape ➤, Wa., U.S.	224	48.23 N	124.43 W
Flatts	240a	32.19 N	64.44 W
Flatwillow Creek ≃	202	46.56 N	107.55 W
Flatwood	194	32.27 N	86.15 W
Flatwoods	188	38.31 N	82.43 W
Flaugherty Run ≃	279b	40.33 N	80.13 W
Flaunden	260	51.42 N	0.32 W
Flavigny-sur-Moselle	58	48.34 N	6.11 E
Flavigny-sur-Ozerain	58	47.30 N	4.32 E
Flavy-le-Martel	50	49.43 N	3.12 E
Flawil	58	47.24 N	9.12 E
Flaxcombe	184	51.29 N	109.36 W
Flaxman Island I	180	70.13 N	146.00 W
Flax Pond ◎, Ma., U.S.	283	42.29 N	70.57 W
Flax Pond ◎, N.Y., U.S.	276	40.58 N	73.08 W
Flaxton	198	48.53 N	102.23 W
Flaxville	198	48.48 N	105.10 W
Flechas Point ➤	116	10.22 N	119.34 E
Flechtingen	54	52.20 N	11.14 E
Fleckeby	41	54.29 N	9.41 E
Flecken Zechlin	54	53.09 N	12.46 E
Fleesensee ◎	54	53.30 N	12.29 E
Fleet	42	51.16 N	0.50 W
Fleet ≃	46	57.57 N	4.05 W
Fleets Bay c	208	37.40 N	76.19 W
Fleetville	210	41.36 N	75.43 W
Fleetwing Estates	285	40.07 N	74.51 W
Fleetwood, Eng., U.K.	44	53.56 N	3.01 W
Fleetwood, Pa., U.S.	208	40.27 N	75.49 W
Flehe ✦[8]	263	51.12 N	6.47 E
Flehingen	56	49.05 N	8.46 E
Fleischmanns	210	42.09 N	74.31 W
Fleischman Village	284c	38.51 N	76.57 W
Flekkefjord	26	58.17 N	6.41 E
Fleming, Co., U.S.	198	40.40 N	102.50 W
Fleming, Pa., U.S.	214	40.55 N	77.52 W
Fleming □[6]	218	38.21 N	83.42 W
Fleming Creek ≃, On., Can.	214	42.38 N	81.47 W
Fleming Creek ≃, Ky., U.S.	218	38.22 N	83.57 W
Fleming Creek ≃, Mi., U.S.	281	42.16 N	83.40 W
Fleming-Neon	192	37.11 N	82.42 W
Flemingsburg	218	38.25 N	83.44 W
Flemington, N.J., U.S.	210	40.30 N	74.51 W
Flemington, Pa., U.S.	210	41.07 N	77.28 W
Flemington Racecourse ♦	274b	37.47 S	144.55 E
Flemish Cap ✧[4]	16	47.00 N	45.00 W
Flemsdorf	54	53.02 N	14.10 E
Flen	40	59.04 N	16.35 E
Flensburg	41	54.47 N	9.26 E
Flensburger Förde c	41	54.49 N	9.45 E
Fleres (Boden)	64	46.58 N	11.21 E
Flers	32	48.45 N	0.34 W
Flers-sur-Noye	50	49.44 N	2.15 E
Flesherton	212	44.16 N	80.33 W
Flesko, Tanjung ➤	112	0.29 N	124.30 E
Fletcher, On., Can.	214	42.18 N	82.18 W
Fletcher, N.C., U.S.	192	35.25 N	82.30 W
Fletcher, Oh., U.S.	218	40.08 N	84.06 W
Fletcher, Ok., U.S.	196	34.49 N	98.14 W
Fletcher Islands II	9	72.40 S	94.10 W
Fletcher Moss Museum ʊ	262	53.25 N	2.14 W
Fletcher Pond ◎[1]	190	44.58 N	83.52 W
Fletchers Creek ≃	275b	43.38 N	79.42 W
Fleurance	32	43.50 N	0.40 E
Fleur-de-Lys	186	50.07 N	56.08 W
Fleurier	58	46.54 N	6.35 E
Fleurieu Peninsula ➤[1]	168b	35.30 S	138.30 E
Fleurus	56	50.29 N	4.33 E
Fleurville	58	46.27 N	4.53 E
Fleury-les-Aubrais	50	47.56 N	1.55 E
Fleury-Mérogis	261	48.38 N	2.22 E
Fleury-sur-Andelle	50	49.22 N	1.22 E
Fleuth ≃	263	51.32 N	6.26 E
Flevoland □[4]	52	52.30 N	5.30 E
Flexanville	261	48.51 N	1.44 E
Flexenpass)(	58	47.09 N	10.10 E
Fley ✦[8]	263	51.23 N	7.30 E
Flieden	56	50.25 N	9.33 E
Flierich	263	51.35 N	7.48 E
Flight Locks ʊ[3]	284a	43.08 N	79.12 W
Flimby	44	54.41 N	3.31 W
Flims	58	46.50 N	9.17 E
Flinders	169	38.28 S	145.01 E
Flinders ≃	166	17.36 S	140.36 E
Flinders Bay c	162	34.23 S	115.19 E
Flinders Chase National Park ♦	166	36.00 S	136.45 E
Flinders Island I, Austl.	162	33.44 S	134.31 E
Flinders Island I, Austl.	166	40.00 S	148.00 E
Flinders Peak ∧	171a	27.49 S	152.49 E
Flinders Peak ∧[2]	169	37.51 S	144.24 E
Flinders Ranges National Park ♦	166	31.20 S	138.45 E
Flinders Reefs ✧[2]	166	17.37 S	148.31 E
Flinders Street Station ✦[5]	274b	37.49 S	144.58 E
Flinesjön ◎	40	60.23 N	16.06 E
Flines-lèz-Râches	50	50.25 N	3.11 E
Flin Flon	184	54.46 N	101.53 W
Flingern ✦[8]	263	51.14 N	6.49 E
Flins-sur-Seine	261	48.58 N	1.52 E
Flint, Wales, U.K.	44	53.15 N	3.07 W
Flint, Mi., U.S.	216	43.00 N	83.41 W
Flint, Tx., U.S.	222	32.12 N	95.21 W
Flint I	14	11.26 S	151.48 W
Flint ≃, U.S.	194	34.30 N	86.31 W
Flint ≃, Ga., U.S.	192	30.52 N	84.38 W
Flint ≃, Mi., U.S.	190	43.21 N	84.03 W
Flint, South Branch ≃	216	43.10 N	83.23 W
Flint Castle ⊥	262	53.16 N	3.07 W
Flint Creek ≃, Al., U.S.	194	34.30 N	86.57 W
Flint Creek ≃, Mt., U.S.	202	46.39 N	113.08 W
Flint Creek ≃, N.Y., U.S.	210	42.57 N	77.03 W
Flint Creek Range ⩘	202	46.20 N	113.05 W
Flinthill	219	38.53 N	90.52 W
Flint Hills ⩘[2]	198	37.50 N	96.40 W
Flint Lake ◎, N.T., Can.	176	69.10 N	74.20 W
Flint Lake ◎, In., U.S.	216	41.31 N	87.03 W
Flinton, Austl.	166	27.54 S	149.34 E
Flinton, Pa., U.S.	214	40.43 N	78.31 W
Flint Peak ∧	280	34.10 N	118.12 W
Flint Pond ◎	283	42.40 N	71.26 W
Flinträinnan ʉ	41	55.34 N	12.50 E
Flintridge	228	34.11 N	118.11 W
Flintville	194	35.03 N	86.25 W
Flipper Point ➤	174a	19.18 N	166.35 E
Flippin	194	36.16 N	92.35 W
Flirey	56	48.53 N	5.50 E
Flirsch	58	47.09 N	10.24 E
Flisa	26	60.34 N	12.06 E
Flitwick	42	52.00 N	0.29 W
Flix, Pantà de ◎[1]	34	41.15 N	0.25 E
Flixecourt	50	50.01 N	2.05 E
Flize	56	49.42 N	4.46 E
Flobecq (Vloesberg)	50	50.44 N	3.44 E
Floby	26	58.08 N	13.20 E
Floda, Sve.	26	57.48 N	12.22 E
Floda, Sve.	40	59.04 N	16.21 E
Flodden	44	55.38 N	2.10 W
Flodden Field Battlesite ⊥	44	55.38 N	2.13 W
Flogny	50	47.57 N	3.52 E
Flöha	54	50.51 N	13.04 E
Flöha ≃	54	50.51 N	13.04 E
Floing	56	49.43 N	4.56 E
Flomaton	194	31.00 N	87.15 W
Flomborn	56	49.41 N	8.08 E
Flomot	196	34.14 N	100.59 W
Floodwood	190	46.55 N	92.55 W
Flora, Il., U.S.	194	38.40 N	88.29 W
Flora, In., U.S.	216	40.32 N	86.31 W
Flora, Ms., U.S.	194	32.32 N	90.18 W
Florac	32	44.19 N	3.36 E
Florala	194	31.00 N	86.19 W
Floral City	220	28.45 N	82.17 W
Floral Park, Mt., U.S.	202	45.57 N	112.26 W
Floral Park, N.Y., U.S.	210	40.43 N	73.42 W
Florange	56	49.20 N	6.07 E
Florânia	250	6.08 S	36.49 W
Flora Vista	200	36.47 N	108.04 W
Flore, Piton ∧	241f	13.58 N	60.57 W
Floreffe	56	50.26 N	4.45 E
Florence, Al., U.S.	194	34.47 N	87.40 W
Florence, Az., U.S.	200	33.02 N	111.23 W
Florence, Ca., U.S.	228	33.58 N	118.14 W
Florence, Co., U.S.	200	38.23 N	105.07 W
Florence, Ks., U.S.	198	38.14 N	96.55 W
Florence, Ky., U.S.	218	38.59 N	84.37 W
Florence, N.J., U.S.	285	40.07 N	74.49 W
Florence, Or., U.S.	202	43.58 N	124.05 W
Florence, Pa., U.S.	214	40.26 N	80.26 W
Florence, S.C., U.S.	192	34.11 N	79.45 W
Florence, Tx., U.S.	222	30.51 N	97.48 W
Florence, Wi., U.S.	190	45.55 N	88.15 W
Florence → Firenze	66	43.46 N	11.15 E
Florencia	246	1.36 N	75.36 W
Florencia → Firenze	66	43.46 N	11.15 E
Florencio Sánchez	258	33.53 S	57.24 W
Florencio Varela	258	34.49 S	58.17 W
Florencio Varela □[5]	288	34.52 S	58.15 W
Florennes	56	50.15 N	4.37 E
Florentia	273d	26.16 S	28.08 E
Florentino Ameghino, Embalse ◎[1]	254	43.55 S	66.20 W
Florenville	56	49.42 N	5.18 E
Florenz → Firenze	66	43.46 N	11.15 E
Flores	250	7.51 S	37.59 W
Flores □[5]	258	33.48 S	56.50 W
Flores ✦[8]	288	34.38 S	58.28 W
Flores I, Indon.	115b	8.30 S	121.00 E
Flores I, Port.	148a	39.26 N	31.13 W
Flores, Laut (Flores Sea) ▾[2]	112	8.00 S	120.00 E
Flores, Rio das ≃	256	22.05 S	43.34 W
Flores, Selat ʉ	115b	8.25 S	122.55 E
Flores da Cunha	252	29.02 S	51.11 W
Flores de Goiás	255	14.34 S	47.04 W
Flores Island I	182	49.20 N	126.10 W
Flores Sea → Flores, Laut ▾[2]	112	8.00 S	120.00 E
Floresta, Bra.	250	8.36 S	38.34 W
Floresta, It.	70	37.59 N	14.55 E
Floresta ✦[8]	288	34.38 S	58.29 W
Floresta Azul	255	14.51 S	39.41 W
Florestal de Monsanto, Parque ♦	266c	38.43 N	9.11 W
Floreşty	78	47.53 N	28.17 E
Floresville	196	29.08 N	98.09 W
Florham Park	210	40.47 N	74.23 W
Floriano, Bra.	250	6.47 S	43.01 W
Floriano, Bra.	256	22.27 S	44.18 W
Floriano Peixoto	248	9.03 S	67.24 W
Florianópolis	252	27.35 S	48.34 W
Florida, Col.	246	3.21 N	76.15 W
Florida, Cuba	240p	21.32 N	78.14 W
Florida, Hond.	236	15.01 N	88.50 W
Florida, Perú	248	5.50 S	77.55 W
Florida, P.R.	240m	18.22 N	66.34 W
Florida, P.R.	240m	18.14 N	65.47 W
Florida, S. Afr.	273d	26.11 S	27.55 E
Florida, In., U.S.	218	40.10 N	85.42 W
Florida, N.Y., U.S.	210	41.19 N	74.21 W
Florida, Oh., U.S.	216	41.20 N	84.12 W
Florida, Ur.	258	34.06 S	56.13 W
Florida □[5]	258	34.00 S	56.15 W
Florida ✦[8]	288	34.31 S	58.30 W
Florida □[3], U.S.	178	28.00 N	82.00 W
Florida □[3], U.S.	192	28.00 N	82.00 W
Florida ≃	200	37.03 N	107.52 W
Florida, Cape ➤	220	25.40 N	80.09 W
Florida, Straits of ʉ	238	25.00 N	79.45 W
Florida Bay c	220	25.00 N	80.45 W
Floridablanca	246	7.04 N	73.06 W
Florida Caverns State Park ♦	192	30.50 N	85.18 W
Florida City	220	25.26 N	80.28 W
Florida Islands II	175e	9.00 S	160.10 E
Florida Keys II	220	24.45 N	81.00 W
Florida Lake ◎[1]	273d	26.11 S	27.54 E
Florida Ridge	220	27.35 N	80.23 W
Floridia	70	37.05 N	15.09 E
Florido ≃	232	27.43 N	105.10 W
Floridsdorf ✦[8]	264b	48.16 N	16.24 E
Floridsdorfer Brücke ✦[5]	264b	48.14 N	16.23 E
Florien	194	31.26 N	93.27 W
Florin	226	38.29 N	121.24 W
Flórina	38	40.47 N	21.24 E
Florisbad	158	28.46 S	26.06 E
Florissant	219	38.47 N	90.19 W
Florissant Fossil Beds National Monument ♦	200	38.54 N	105.16 W
Floriston	226	39.24 N	120.01 W
Florø	26	61.36 N	5.00 E
Flörsheim	56	50.01 N	8.26 E
Florvåg	26	60.25 N	5.14 E
Flosaille	62	45.39 N	5.18 E
Floss	60	49.44 N	12.17 E
Flossach ≃, Dtsch.	58	48.24 N	10.25 E
Flossach ≃, Dtsch.	64	48.13 N	10.30 E
Flossenbürg	60	49.44 N	12.21 E
Flossmoor	216	41.32 N	87.41 W
Flotantes, Jardínes ♦	286a	19.16 N	99.06 W
Flöthbach ≃	263	51.17 N	6.26 E
Flotta I	46	58.50 N	3.07 W
Flotte, Cap de ➤	175f	21.10 S	167.25 E
Flotten Lake ◎	184	54.38 N	108.30 W
Flourtown	285	40.06 N	75.12 W
Flowerfield	278	41.52 N	88.02 W
Flower Hill	276	40.48 N	73.40 W
Flower Mound	222	33.02 N	97.04 W
Flower's Cove	186	51.18 N	56.44 W
Flowery Branch	192	34.11 N	83.55 W
Floyd, N.M., U.S.	196	34.13 N	103.35 W
Floyd, Tx., U.S.	222	33.09 N	96.15 W
Floyd, Va., U.S.	192	36.54 N	80.19 W
Floyd □[6]	218	38.18 N	85.49 W
Floyd ≃	198	42.29 N	96.23 W
Floydada	196	33.59 N	101.20 W
Floyds Fork ≃	194	38.00 N	85.41 W
Fluchthorn ∧	58	46.53 N	10.13 E
Flüela Pass)(	58	46.45 N	9.57 E
Flüelen	58	46.54 N	8.38 E
Fluessen ◎	52	52.57 N	5.30 E
Flughafen Wien-Schwechat ⊠	61	48.07 N	16.33 E
Flühli	58	46.53 N	8.01 E
Flumen ≃	34	41.43 N	0.09 W
Flumendosa ≃	71	39.26 N	9.37 E
Flumendosa, Lago Alto del ◎	71	39.56 N	9.26 E
Flumeri	68	41.05 N	15.09 E
Flumet	62	45.49 N	6.30 E
Fluminimaggiore	71	39.26 N	8.30 E
Flums	58	47.05 N	9.20 E
Flüren	263	51.41 N	6.33 E
Flushing, Mi., U.S.	216	43.03 N	83.51 W
Flushing, Oh., U.S.	214	40.08 N	81.03 W
Flushing ✦[8]	276	40.45 N	73.49 W
Flushing Airport ⊠	276	40.47 N	73.50 W
Flushing Bay c	276	40.47 N	73.51 W
Flushing Meadow-Corona Park ♦	276	40.45 N	73.51 W
Flushing → Vlissingen	52	51.26 N	3.35 E
Fluvanna, N.Y., U.S.	214	42.07 N	79.18 W
Fluvanna, Tx., U.S.	196	32.53 N	101.09 W
Fluvià ≃	34	42.12 N	3.07 E
Fly ≃	164	8.30 S	143.41 E
Fly Creek	210	42.43 N	74.59 W
Fly Creek ≃	202	45.59 N	107.59 W
Flyinge	41	55.45 N	13.21 E
Flying Fish Cove	112	10.25 S	105.43 E
Flynn	222	31.09 N	96.08 W
Foam Lake	184	51.39 N	103.33 W
Fobbing	260	51.32 N	0.29 E
Fobello	62	45.53 N	8.10 E
Foča, Bos.	38	43.31 N	18.46 E
Foça, Tür.	130	38.39 N	26.46 E
Focene ✦[8]	267a	41.48 N	12.14 E
Fochabers	46	57.37 N	3.05 W
Fochville	158	26.30 S	27.30 E
Fockbek	41	54.18 N	9.36 E
Focşani	38	45.41 N	27.11 E
Fodda, Oued ≃	34	35.14 N	1.28 E
Fodé	152	5.29 N	23.18 E
Fodécontea	150	10.50 N	14.22 W
Foding Shan ∧	102	27.08 N	108.02 E
F'odorovka, Kaz.	80	51.09 N	51.59 E
F'odorovka, Kaz.	86	53.22 N	76.18 E
F'odorovka, Kaz.	86	53.38 N	62.42 E
F'odorovka, Ross.	80	53.28 N	49.38 E
F'odorovka, Ross.	80	52.21 N	52.55 E
F'odorovka, Ross.	82	56.15 N	37.14 E
F'odorovka, Ross.	83	47.20 N	38.23 E
F'odorovka, Ross.	86	53.11 N	55.11 E
F'odorovka, Ross.	86	56.05 N	78.49 E
F'odorovka, Ukr.	78	49.23 N	35.07 E
F'odorovka, Ukr.	78	47.33 N	36.33 E
F'odorovskoje, Ross.	82	56.44 N	36.58 E
F'odorovskoje, Ross.	82	56.08 N	38.04 E
F'odorovskoje, Ross.	82	56.07 N	38.52 E
Foëcy	50	47.10 N	2.10 E
Foelsche ≃	164	16.03 S	136.50 E
Foeni	38	45.30 N	20.53 E
Fogang (Shijiao)	100	23.52 N	113.32 E
Fogdön ➤[1]	40	59.25 N	16.52 E
Fogelevo	85	42.03 N	69.32 E
Fogelsville	208	40.35 N	75.38 W
Foggaret el Arab	148	27.03 N	2.59 E
Foggaret ez Zoua	148	27.20 N	3.00 E
Foggia	68	41.27 N	15.34 E
Foggia □[4]	68	41.30 N	15.30 E
Foggy Island Bay c	180	70.15 N	147.30 W
Foglia ≃	66	43.55 N	12.54 E
Foglianise	68	41.10 N	14.40 E
Fogliano, Lago di c	66	41.24 N	12.54 E
Foglizzo	62	45.16 N	7.49 E
Fogo	186	49.43 N	54.17 W
Fogo I	150a	14.55 N	24.25 W
Fogo, Cape ➤	186	49.39 N	54.00 W
Fogo Island I	186	49.40 N	54.13 W
Fogolawa	150	12.19 N	8.41 E
Fogueteiro	266c	38.37 N	9.07 W
Fohnsdorf	61	47.13 N	14.41 E
Föhr I	30	54.43 N	8.30 E
Foia ∧	34	37.19 N	8.36 W
Foiano della Chiana	66	43.15 N	11.49 E
Foiano di Val Fortore	68	41.21 N	14.59 E
Foinaven ∧	46	58.25 N	4.53 W
Foins, Lac aux ◎	190	47.05 N	78.11 W
Foivre ≃	56	49.30 N	4.32 E
Foix	32	42.58 N	1.36 E
Foix □[9]	32	43.00 N	1.40 E
Fojnica	36	43.58 N	17.54 E
Foki	80	56.42 N	54.21 E
Fokino	76	53.27 N	34.24 E
Fokku	150	11.40 N	4.31 E
Folakara	157b	18.20 S	45.02 E
Folamasi	104	41.56 N	121.27 E
Folarskardnuten ∧	26	60.37 N	7.45 E
Folcroft	208	39.53 N	75.17 W
Folda c[2]	24	67.36 N	14.50 E
Foldingbro	41	55.26 N	9.01 E
Folembray	50	49.33 N	3.17 E
Foley, Al., U.S.	194	30.24 N	87.41 W
Foley, Mn., U.S.	190	45.39 N	93.54 W
Foley, Mo., U.S.	219	39.02 N	90.44 W
Foleyet	190	48.15 N	82.27 W
Foley Island I	176	68.35 N	75.10 W
Folgaria	64	45.55 N	11.10 E
Folgefonni ⊓	26	60.00 N	6.20 E
Folger Hill ∧[2]	207	41.17 N	70.01 W
Foligno	66	42.57 N	12.42 E
Folk	219	38.26 N	92.06 W
Folkärna	40	60.09 N	16.19 E
Folkestone	42	51.05 N	1.11 E
Folkingham	42	52.54 N	0.24 W
Folkston	192	30.49 N	82.00 W
Folkwangmuseum ʊ	263	51.27 N	7.00 E
Follafoss	26	63.59 N	11.06 E
Follainville-Dennemont	261	49.01 N	1.43 E
Follansbee	214	40.19 N	80.35 W
Folldal	26	62.08 N	10.03 E
Folle Anse, Pointe de ➤	241o	15.57 N	61.20 W
Follebu	26	61.14 N	10.17 E
Follets Island I	222	29.02 N	95.10 W
Follett	196	36.26 N	100.08 W
Follina	64	45.57 N	12.07 E
Föllinge	26	63.40 N	14.37 E
Follonica	66	42.55 N	10.45 E
Follonica, Golfo di c	66	42.54 N	10.43 E
Folly Branch ≃	284b	38.56 N	76.49 W
Folmhusen	52	53.10 N	7.28 E
Folschviller	56	49.04 N	6.41 E
Folsom, Ca., U.S.	226	38.40 N	121.10 W
Folsom, N.J., U.S.	208	39.36 N	74.50 W
Folsom, Pa., U.S.	285	39.53 N	75.19 W
Folsom Lake ◎[1]	226	38.43 N	121.08 W
Folsom Lake State Recreation Area ♦	226	38.46 N	121.06 W
Fomboni	157a	12.16 S	43.45 E
Fomento, Cuba	240p	22.06 N	79.43 W
Fomento, Ur.	258	34.26 S	57.14 W
Fomin	80	46.58 N	43.38 E
Fominiči	76	54.07 N	34.41 E
Fominki	80	55.57 N	42.22 E
Fominskaja	24	61.17 N	48.40 E
Fominskoje, Ross.	24	59.43 N	42.05 E
Fominskoje, Ross.	76	58.59 N	39.06 E
Fomkino	80	54.25 N	50.30 E
Foncine-le-Bas	58	46.38 N	6.03 E
Fonda, Ia., U.S.	198	42.34 N	94.50 W
Fonda, N.Y., U.S.	210	42.57 N	74.22 W
Fondachelli	70	37.58 N	15.11 E
Fond du Lac, Sk., Can.	176	59.19 N	107.10 W
Fond du Lac, Wi., U.S.	190	43.46 N	88.26 W
Fond du Lac ≃	176	59.17 N	106.00 W
Fond du Lac Indian Reservation ✦[4]	190	46.45 N	92.37 W
Fondi	66	41.21 N	13.25 E
Fondi, Lago di c	66	41.19 N	13.20 E
Fondo	64	46.26 N	11.08 E
Fondouk el Aouareb	36	35.34 N	9.46 E
Fongfong	140	12.56 N	23.14 E
Fonni	71	40.07 N	9.15 E
Fonsagrada	34	43.08 N	7.04 W
Fonseca	246	10.54 N	72.51 W
Fonseca, Golfo de c	236	13.10 N	87.40 W
Fons-Outre-Gardon	62	43.54 N	4.11 E
Font ≃	44	55.10 N	1.44 W
Fontaine, Fr.	58	47.40 N	7.00 E
Fontaine, Fr.	62	45.11 N	5.40 E
Fontainebleau, Fr.	50	48.24 N	2.42 E
Fontainebleau, S. Afr.	273d	26.07 S	27.59 E
Fontaine-Française	58	47.31 N	5.22 E
Fontaine-le-Dun	50	49.49 N	0.51 E
Fontaine-lès-Dijon	58	47.21 N	5.01 E
Fontaine-lès-Grès	50	48.25 N	3.54 E
Fontaine-lès-Luxeuil	58	47.51 N	6.20 E
Fontaines	58	46.51 N	4.46 E
Fontaines-sur-Saône	62	45.50 N	4.51 E
Fontan	62	44.00 N	7.33 E
Fontana, Arg.	252	27.25 S	59.02 W
Fontana, Ca., U.S.	228	34.05 N	117.26 W
Fontana, Wi., U.S.	216	42.33 N	88.34 W
Fontana, Lago ◎	254	44.56 S	71.30 W
Fontanafredda	64	45.58 N	12.34 E
Fontana Lake ◎[1]	192	35.26 N	83.38 W
Fontanarosa	68	41.01 N	15.01 E
Fontanarossa, Aeroporto di ⊠	70	37.29 N	15.03 E
Fontanelas	266c	38.51 N	9.26 W
Fontanelice	66	44.15 N	11.33 E
Fontanella	64	45.27 N	9.48 E
Fontanellato	64	44.53 N	10.10 E
Fontanelle	198	41.17 N	94.33 W
Fontanetto Po	62	45.12 N	8.11 E
Fontanigorda	62	44.33 N	9.19 E
Fontarabie, Lac ◎	186	51.10 N	66.25 W
Fontas ≃	176	58.20 N	121.50 W
Fonte, Bra.	287b	23.25 S	46.21 W
Fonte, It.	64	45.47 N	11.53 E
Fonte, It.	66	41.46 N	13.13 E
Fonte Avellana, Monastero di ʊ[1]	66	43.29 N	12.45 E
Fonte Blanda	66	42.34 N	11.10 E
Fonte Boa	246	2.32 S	66.01 W
Fonte Colombo, Convento di ʊ[1]	66	42.23 N	12.50 E
Fontenay, Abbaye de ʊ[1]	50	47.39 N	4.24 E
Fontenay-aux-Roses	261	48.47 N	2.17 E
Fontenay-en-Parisis	261	49.03 N	2.27 E
Fontenay-le-Comte	32	46.28 N	0.48 W
Fontenay-le-Fleury	261	48.49 N	2.03 E
Fontenay-lès-Briis	261	48.37 N	2.09 E
Fontenay-le-Vicomte	261	48.33 N	2.24 E
Fontenay-Saint-Père	261	49.02 N	1.45 E
Fontenay-sous-Bois	261	48.51 N	2.29 E
Fontenay-Trésigny	50	48.42 N	2.52 E
Fonteneau, Lac ◎	186	51.55 N	61.30 W
Fontenelle	186	48.53 N	64.33 W
Fontenelle Creek ≃	200	42.05 N	110.08 W
Fontenelle Reservoir ◎[1]	200	42.05 N	110.06 W
Fontespina	66	43.17 N	13.45 E
Fontevivo	64	44.51 N	10.10 E
Font Hill Manor	284b	39.17 N	76.52 W
Fonti del Clitunno ▾[4]	66	42.49 N	12.46 E
Fontoy	56	49.21 N	6.00 E
Fontur ➤	24a	66.23 N	14.30 W
Fontvieille	62	43.43 N	4.43 E
Fonyód	30	46.44 N	17.34 E
Fonzaso	64	46.01 N	11.48 E
Foochow → Fuzhou	100	26.06 N	119.17 E
Foot Creek ≃	198	45.26 N	98.29 W
Foothill Farms	226	38.40 N	121.20 W
Foothills	182	53.04 N	116.48 W
Footprint Lake ◎	184	55.47 N	98.53 W
Footscray	169	37.48 S	144.54 E
Footville	216	42.40 N	89.12 W
Foping	102	33.21 N	107.59 E
Foppolo	64	46.03 N	9.45 E
Fora, Ponta de ➤	287a	22.57 S	43.07 W
Foraker, Mount ∧	180	62.56 N	151.26 W
Forari	175f	17.39 S	168.32 E
Forbach, Dtsch.	56	48.41 N	8.21 E
Forbach, Fr.	56	49.11 N	6.54 E
Forbes	166	33.23 S	148.01 E
Forbes, Lac ◎	206	46.31 N	74.12 W
Forbes, Mount ∧	182	51.52 N	116.56 W
Forbes Field ♦	279b	40.27 N	79.57 W
Forbesganj	124	26.18 N	87.15 E
Forbes Reef	158	26.10 S	31.05 E
Forbes Road	214	40.21 N	79.32 W
Forbestown	226	39.31 N	121.16 W
Forcados	150	5.22 N	5.24 E
Forcados ≃[1]	150	5.25 N	5.19 E
Forcalquier	62	43.58 N	5.47 E
Force	214	41.15 N	78.30 W
Forchheim, Dtsch.	54	50.43 N	13.16 E
Forchheim, Dtsch.	60	49.43 N	11.04 E
Forclaz, Col de la)(	58	46.04 N	7.00 E
Ford, Scot., U.K.	46	56.10 N	5.26 W
Ford, Ks., U.S.	198	37.38 N	99.45 W
Ford □[6]	216	40.27 N	88.06 W
Ford ≃	190	45.40 N	87.09 W
Ford, Cape ➤	164	13.26 S	129.52 E
Ford City, Ca., U.S.	226	35.09 N	119.27 W
Ford City, Pa., U.S.	214	40.46 N	79.31 W
Ford City ✦[9]	278	41.46 N	87.44 W
Ford Cliff	214	40.45 N	79.32 W
Ford Dam ✦[6]	281	42.13 N	83.33 W
Ford Dry Lake ◎	204	33.38 N	115.00 W
Førde, Nor.	26	59.36 N	5.29 E
Førde, Nor.	26	61.27 N	5.52 E
Førdefjorden c[2]	26	61.28 N	5.39 E
Forden	42	52.36 N	3.08 W
Förderstedt	54	51.54 N	11.38 E
Fordham University ʊ[2]	276	40.51 N	73.53 W
Fordingbridge	42	50.56 N	1.47 W
Ford Lake ◎	281	42.13 N	83.36 W
Ford Mansion ⊥	276	40.48 N	74.28 W
Ford Motor Company (River Rouge Plant) ʊ[3]	281	42.18 N	83.10 W
Ford Museum ʊ	281	42.18 N	83.14 W
Fordongianus	71	39.59 N	8.48 E
Ford Ranges ⩘	9	77.00 S	145.00 W
Fords	276	40.31 N	74.18 W
Fords Bridge	166	29.45 S	145.26 E

Symbols in the index entries represent the broad categories identified in the key at the right. Symbols with superior numbers (⩘[1]) identify subcategories (see complete key on page I · 1).

Symbole im Register stellen die rechts im Schlüssel erklärten Kategorien dar. Symbole mit hochgestellten Ziffern (⩘[1]) bezeichnen Unterabteilungen einer Kategorie (vgl. vollständiger Schlüssel auf Seite I · 1).

Los símbolos incluídos en el texto del índice representan las grandes categorías identificadas con la clave a la derecha. Los símbolos con numeros en su parte superior (⩘[1]) identifican las subcategorías (véase la clave completa en la página I · 1).

Les symboles de l'index représentent les catégories indiquées dans la légende à droite. Les symboles suivis d'un indice (⩘[1]) représentent des sous-catégories (voir légende complète à la page I · 1).

Os símbolos incluídos no texto do índice representam as grandes categorias identificadas com a chave à direita. Os símbolos com números em sua parte superior (⩘[1]) identificam as subcategorias (veja-se a chave completa à página I · 1).

∧ Mountain	Berg	Montaña	Montagne	Montanha
⩘ Mountains	Gebirge	Montañas	Montagnes	Montanhas
)(Pass	Paß	Paso	Col	Passo
V Valley, Canyon	Tal, Cañon	Valle, Cañón	Vallée, Canyon	Vale, Canhão
⊒ Plain	Ebene	Llano	Plaine	Planície
➤ Cape	Kap	Cabo	Cap	Cabo
I Island	Insel	Isla	Île	Ilha
II Islands	Inseln	Islas	Îles	Ilhas
✦ Other Topographic Features	Andere Topographische Objekte	Otros Elementos Topográficos	Autres données topographiques	Outros acidentes topográficos

ESPAÑOL

Nombre	Página	Lat.°′	Long.°′ W = Oeste
Fordsburg ✦[8]	273d	26.13 S	28.02 E
Fords Prairie	224	46.44 N	122.59 W
Fordsville	194	37.38 N	86.43 W
Fordville	198	48.13 N	97.47 W
Fordyce	194	33.48 N	92.24 W
Fordyce Lake ◎[1]	226	39.23 N	120.28 W
Foré	150	13.08 N	10.42 W
Forécariah	150	9.26 N	13.06 W
Forel, Mont ∧	176	67.00 N	37.00 W
Foreland Point ›	42	51.16 N	3.47 W
Foreman	194	33.43 N	94.23 W
Foremost	184	49.29 N	111.25 W
Forenza	68	40.51 N	15.51 E
Forepaugh Airport ⊠	279a	41.21 N	81.30 W
Foresman	216	40.52 N	87.18 W
Forest, Bel.	50	50.48 N	4.19 E
Forest, On., Can.	190	43.06 N	82.00 W
Forest, In., U.S.	216	40.22 N	86.19 W
Forest, Ms., U.S.	194	32.21 N	89.28 W
Forest, Oh., U.S.	216	40.48 N	83.30 W
Forest □[6]	214	41.29 N	79.27 W
Forest, Middle Branch ≃	198	48.13 N	97.48 W
Forest Acres	192	34.01 N	80.59 W
Forestburg	182	52.35 N	112.04 W
Forest City, Ia., U.S.	190	43.15 N	93.38 W
Forest City, N.C., U.S.	192	35.20 N	81.51 W
Forest City, Pa., U.S.	210	41.39 N	75.28 W
Forest Creek ≃	226	38.23 N	120.28 W
Forest Gate ✦[8]	260	51.33 N	0.02 E
Forest Glade	222	31.39 N	96.31 W
Forest Grove, B.C., Can.	182	51.46 N	121.06 W
Forest Grove, Or., U.S.	224	45.31 N	123.06 W
Forest Grove, Pa., U.S.	279b	40.18 N	75.04 W
Forest Heights	284c	38.49 N	77.00 W
Forest Hill, Austl.	171a	27.35 S	152.22 E
Forest Hill, Austl.	171b	35.09 S	147.27 E
Forest Hill, Austl.	274b	37.50 S	145.11 E
Foresthill, Ca., U.S.	226	39.01 N	120.49 W
Forest Hill, Md., U.S.	208	39.35 N	76.23 W
Forest Hill, Tx., U.S.	222	32.40 N	97.16 W
Forest Hill ✦[8]	275b	43.42 N	79.24 W
Forest Hill Park ♠	279a	41.31 N	81.35 W
Forest Hill Parkway ♠	279a	41.33 N	81.36 W
Forest Hills	279b	40.25 N	79.51 W
Forest Hills ✦[8]	276	40.42 N	73.51 W
Forest Home	194	31.52 N	86.50 W
Forestier Peninsula ›[1]	166	42.57 S	147.55 E
Forest Knolls	284c	39.02 N	77.01 W
Forest Lake, Il., U.S.	216	42.13 N	88.03 W
Forest Lake, Mn., U.S.	190	45.16 N	92.59 W
Forest Lake ◎, Il., U.S.	278	42.13 N	88.03 W
Forest Lake ◎, Ma., U.S.	283	42.43 N	71.15 W
Forest Lawn Memorial Park ✦	280	34.09 N	118.19 W
Forest Manor	284c	38.50 N	76.53 W
Forest Park, Ga., U.S.	192	33.37 N	84.22 W
Forest Park, Il., U.S.	278	41.52 N	87.48 W
Forest Park, Oh., U.S.	218	39.16 N	84.34 W
Forest Park ✦[8]	284b	39.19 N	76.41 W
Forest Park ♠	276	40.42 N	73.51 W
Forest River	278	42.05 N	87.54 W
Forest Row	42	51.06 N	0.02 E
Forest View	278	41.49 N	87.47 W
Forestville, Austl.	274a	33.46 S	151.13 E
Forestville, P.Q., Can.	186	48.45 N	69.06 W
Forestville, Md., U.S.	284c	38.50 N	76.52 W
Forestville, N.Y., U.S.	214	42.28 N	79.10 W
Forestville, Pa., U.S.	214	41.06 N	80.00 W
Forestville, Wi., U.S.	190	44.41 N	87.28 W
Forêt l'Orient, Lac de la ◎[1]	50	48.17 N	4.20 E
Forêt-Noire → Schwarzwald ⋏	58	48.00 N	8.15 E
Forez, Monts du ⋏	32	45.35 N	3.48 E
Forfar	46	56.38 N	2.54 W
Forfry	261	49.03 N	2.51 E
Forgan	196	36.54 N	100.32 W
Forgaria	64	46.13 N	12.58 E
Forge Acres	284b	39.25 N	76.27 W
Forge Heights	284b	39.25 N	76.25 W
Forges-les-Bains	261	48.38 N	2.06 E
Forges-les-Eaux	50	49.37 N	1.33 E
Forget, Pointe ›	275a	45.27 N	73.58 W
Forge Village	207	42.34 N	71.29 W
Forggensee ◎	58	47.36 N	10.44 E
Forillon, Parc National de ♠	186	48.55 N	64.12 W
Forino	68	40.52 N	14.44 E
Foristell	219	38.49 N	90.57 W
Fork	208	39.28 N	76.27 W
Forked Creek ≃	216	41.19 N	88.09 W
Forked Deer ≃	194	35.56 N	89.35 W
Forked Deer, Middle Fork ≃	194	36.01 N	89.13 W
Forked Deer, North Fork ≃	194	36.00 N	89.26 W
Forked Deer, South Fork ≃	194	36.00 N	89.26 W
Forked River	208	39.50 N	74.11 W
Forks	224	47.57 N	124.23 W
Forkston	210	41.31 N	76.07 W
Forksville	210	41.29 N	76.36 W
Forleti, Arroyo ≃	288	34.35 S	58.41 W
Forlì	66	44.13 N	12.03 E
Forlì □[4]	64	44.05 N	12.02 E
Forlimpopoli	66	44.11 N	12.07 E
Forman	198	46.06 N	97.38 W
Formazza	58	46.22 N	8.26 E
Formby	262	53.34 N	3.05 W
Formby Hills ⋏[2]	262	53.34 N	3.06 W
Formby Point ›	262	53.33 N	3.06 W
Formentera I	34	38.42 N	1.28 E
Formentor, Cap de ›	34	39.58 N	3.12 E
Formerie	50	49.39 N	1.44 E
Formia	66	41.15 N	13.37 E
Formiga	255	20.27 S	45.25 W
Formiga ≃	250	11.15 S	48.27 W
Formigine	64	44.34 N	10.51 E
Formignana	64	44.50 N	11.51 E
Formosa, Arg.	252	26.11 S	58.11 W
Formosa, Bra.	255	15.32 S	47.20 W
Formosa □[4]	252	25.00 S	60.00 W
Formosa, Ilha I	150	11.29 N	15.58 W
Formosa, Serra ⋏[1]	250	12.00 S	55.00 W
Formosa Strait → Taiwan Strait ʯ	100	24.00 N	119.00 E
Formosa → Taiwan □[1]	100	23.30 N	121.00 E
Formoso ≃, Bra.	250	10.34 S	49.56 W
Formoso ≃, Bra.	255	13.26 S	44.14 W
Formoso ≃, Bra.	255	18.25 S	52.28 W
Formoso ≃, Bra.	256	21.20 S	43.10 W
Forncelle	66	43.55 N	11.06 E
Fornelli	71	41.00 N	8.14 E
Forney	222	32.44 N	96.28 W
Forni Avoltri	64	46.35 N	12.46 E
Forni di sopra	64	46.25 N	12.35 E
Forni di sotto	64	46.23 N	12.40 E
Forni di Val d'Astico	64	45.51 N	11.22 E
Forno	64	46.21 N	11.37 E
Forno Alpi Graie	62	45.22 N	7.13 E
Forno di Zoldo	64	46.21 N	12.11 E
Fornosovo	76	59.35 N	30.35 E
Fornovo di Taro	64	44.42 N	10.06 E
Foro Romano ⊥	267a	41.54 N	12.29 E
Føroyar → Faeroe Islands □[2]	22	62.00 N	7.00 W
Forpost	86	56.47 N	72.10 E
Forres, Arg.	252	27.53 S	63.58 W
Forres, Scot., U.K.	46	57.37 N	3.38 W
Forrest, Austl.	162	30.51 S	128.06 E

FRANÇAIS

Nom	Page	Lat.°′	Long.°′ W = Ouest
Forrest, Austl.	169	38.31 S	143.43 E
Forrest, Il., U.S.	216	40.45 N	88.24 W
Forrest ≃	164	15.18 S	128.04 E
Forrest, Mount ∧	162	24.48 S	127.45 E
Forrestal Research Center ʋ[3]	276	40.21 N	74.37 W
Forrest City	194	35.00 N	90.47 W
Forrester Island I	182	54.48 N	133.32 W
Forrest Lakes ◎	162	29.12 S	128.46 E
Forreston, Il., U.S.	190	42.07 N	89.34 W
Forreston, Tx., U.S.	222	32.16 N	96.52 W
Forrest River Aboriginal Reserve ✦[4]	164	15.00 S	127.40 E
Fors	40	60.13 N	16.18 E
Forsan	196	32.07 N	101.22 W
Forsayth	166	18.35 S	143.36 E
Forsbacka	40	60.37 N	16.53 E
Forsby	26	60.30 N	25.56 E
Forserum	26	57.42 N	14.28 E
Forshaga	40	59.32 N	13.28 E
Forsmark	40	60.22 N	18.09 E
Forssa	26	60.49 N	23.38 E
Forst	54	51.44 N	14.39 E
Förste	52	51.44 N	10.10 E
Forster	166	32.11 S	152.31 E
Forstwald ✦[8]	263	51.18 N	6.30 E
Forsyth, Ga., U.S.	192	33.02 N	83.56 W
Forsyth, Il., U.S.	219	39.56 N	88.57 W
Forsyth, Mo., U.S.	194	36.41 N	93.07 W
Forsyth, Mt., U.S.	202	46.15 N	106.40 W
Forsyth Island I	164	16.50 S	139.06 E
Forsyth Range ⋏	166	22.45 S	143.15 E
Fort ✦[8]	272c	18.56 N	72.50 E
Fort Abbās	123	29.12 N	72.52 E
Fort Adams	194	31.05 N	91.32 W
Fort Albany	176	52.15 N	81.37 W
Fort Alexander Indian Reserve ✦[4]	184	50.27 N	96.15 W
Fortaleza	250	3.43 S	38.30 W
Fortaleza ≃	248	10.40 S	77.52 W
Fortaleza de Santa Teresa ♠	252	33.59 S	53.32 W
Fortaleza do Ituxi	248	7.29 S	66.20 W
Fortaleza dos Nogueiras	250	6.54 S	46.09 W
Fort Amherst National Historic Park ♠	186	46.12 N	63.09 W
Fort Ancient State Memorial ⊥	218	39.24 N	84.06 W
Fort Anne National Historic Park ♠	186	44.44 N	65.26 W
Fort Apache Indian Reservation ✦[4]	200	34.01 N	110.28 W
Fort-Archambault → Sarh	146	9.09 N	18.23 E
Fort Assiniboine	182	54.20 N	114.46 W
Fort Atkinson	216	42.55 N	88.50 W
Fort Augusta ⊥	210	40.53 N	76.46 W
Fort Augustus	46	57.09 N	4.41 W
Fort Baker ■	282	37.50 N	122.29 W
Fort Battleford National Historic Park ♠	184	52.42 N	108.15 W
Fort Bayard → Zhanjiang	102	21.16 N	110.28 E
Fort Beaufort	158	32.46 S	26.40 E
Fort Beauséjour National Historic Park ♠	186	45.51 N	64.18 W
Fort Belknap Agency	202	48.28 N	108.45 W
Fort Belknap Indian Reservation ✦[4]	202	48.16 N	108.38 W
Fort Belvoir ■	208	38.44 N	77.10 W
Fort Bend □[6]	222	29.32 N	95.47 W
Fort Benjamin Harrison ■	218	39.52 N	86.01 W
Fort Benning ■	192	32.22 N	84.50 W
Fort Benton	202	47.49 N	110.40 W
Fort Berthold Indian Reservation ✦[4]	198	47.40 N	102.25 W
Fort Bidwell	204	41.51 N	120.09 W
Fort Bliss ■	200	32.15 N	106.00 W
Fort Bowie National Historic Site ⊥	200	32.09 N	109.24 W
Fort Bragg	204	39.26 N	123.48 W
Fort Bragg ■	192	35.09 N	78.59 W
Fort Branch	194	38.15 N	87.34 W
Fort Bridger	200	41.19 N	110.23 W
Fort Calhoun	198	41.27 N	96.01 W
Fort Campbell ■	194	36.39 N	87.29 W
Fort Canby State Park ♠	224	46.17 N	124.04 W
Fort-Carnot	157b	21.53 S	47.28 E
Fort Caroline National Memorial ⊥	192	30.20 N	81.30 W
Fort Carson ■	200	38.44 N	104.48 W
Fort Casey Historical State Park ♠	224	48.10 N	122.40 W
Fort Chambly National Historic Park ♠	206	45.27 N	73.17 W
Fort Chipewyan	176	58.42 N	111.08 W
Fort Churchill Historic State Monument ⊥	226	39.18 N	119.17 W
Fort Clatsop National Memorial ⊥	224	46.08 N	123.54 W
Fort Cobb	196	35.05 N	98.26 W
Fort Cobb Reservoir ◎[1]	196	35.12 N	98.29 W
Fort Collins	200	40.35 N	105.05 W
Fort Columbia Historical State Park ♠	224	46.15 N	123.56 W
Fort Constantine	166	20.28 S	140.37 E
Fort-Coulonge	188	45.51 N	76.44 W
Fort Covington	206	44.59 N	74.29 W
Fort Custer State Recreation Area ♠	216	42.18 N	85.20 W
Fort Davis, Al., U.S.	194	32.14 N	85.42 W
Fort Davis, Tx., U.S.	196	30.35 N	103.53 W
Fort Davis National Historic Site ⊥	196	30.33 N	103.53 W
Fort de Douaumont ⊥	56	49.13 N	5.25 E
Fort Defiance	200	35.44 N	109.04 W
Fort-de-France	240e	14.36 N	61.05 W
Fort-de-France, Baie de ⊂	240e	14.34 N	61.04 W
Fort-de-France-Lamentin, Aérodrome de ⊠	240e	14.35 N	61.00 W
Fort Deposit	194	31.59 N	86.34 W
Fort Detrick ■	208	39.27 N	77.26 W
Fort de Vaux ⊥	56	49.12 N	5.28 E
Fort Devens ■	207	42.32 N	71.37 W
Fort Dix ■	208	40.00 N	74.33 W
Fort Dodge	190	42.29 N	94.10 W
Fort Donelson National Military Park ♠	194	36.26 N	87.49 W
Fort Duchesne	200	40.17 N	109.51 W
Fort Dupont Park ♠	284c	38.53 N	76.57 W
Forte, Monte ∧	71	40.43 N	8.15 E
Forteau	186	51.28 N	56.58 W
Forte dei Marmi	64	43.57 N	10.10 E
Forte de Magoito	266c	38.52 N	9.27 W
Fort Edward	210	43.16 N	73.35 W
Forte República	152	7.45 S	16.23 E
Fort Erie	212	42.54 N	78.56 W
Fort Erie Race Track ♠	284a	42.55 N	78.56 W
Fortescue ≃	162	21.00 S	116.06 E
Fort Eustis ■	208	37.09 N	76.35 W
Fortevoit	46	56.20 N	3.32 W
Fortezza (Franzensfeste)	64	46.47 N	11.37 E
Fort Fairfield	186	46.46 N	67.50 W
Fort Fitzgerald	176	59.53 N	111.37 W
Fort Foote Village	284c	38.46 N	77.01 W
Fort-Foureau	146	12.05 N	15.02 E
Fort Frances	190	48.36 N	93.24 W
Fort Franklin	180	65.11 N	123.46 W

PORTUGUÊS

Nome	Página	Lat.°′	Long.°′ W = Oeste
Fort Fraser	182	54.04 N	124.33 W
Fort Frederica National Monument ♠	192	31.12 N	81.26 W
Fort Gaines	192	31.36 N	85.02 W
Fort Garland	200	37.25 N	105.26 W
Fort Gay	188	38.06 N	82.35 W
Fort George ⊥	284a	43.15 N	79.04 W
Fort George G. Meade ■	208	39.05 N	76.50 W
Fort Gibson	196	35.47 N	95.15 W
Fort Gibson Lake ◎[1]	196	36.00 N	95.18 W
Fort Good Hope	180	66.15 N	128.38 W
Fort Gordon ■	192	33.25 N	82.11 W
Fort-Gouraud → Fdérik	148	22.41 N	12.43 W
Fort Green	220	27.36 N	81.56 W
Forth	46	55.47 N	3.41 W
Forth ≃	46	56.03 N	3.44 W
Forth, Carse of V	46	56.08 N	4.05 W
Forth, Firth of ⊂	46	56.10 N	2.45 W
Förtha	56	50.56 N	10.14 E
Fort Hall	202	43.02 N	112.26 W
Fort Hall Indian Reservation ✦[4]	202	43.10 N	112.10 W
Fort Hamilton ■	276	40.37 N	74.02 W
Forth Bridge ✦[5]	46	56.00 N	3.25 W
Fort Hertz → Putao	102	27.21 N	97.24 E
Fort Hill ■	188	38.04 N	77.19 W
Fort Hill → Chitipa	154	9.43 S	33.16 E
Fort Hill State Memorial ⊥	218	39.07 N	83.25 W
Fort Hood ■	222	31.08 N	97.46 W
Fort Howard	208	39.12 N	76.27 W
Fort Huachuca ■	200	31.33 N	110.20 W
Fort Hunter	210	42.57 N	74.17 W
Fort Hunter Liggett ■	226	35.55 N	121.15 W
Fortierville	206	46.29 N	72.02 W
Fortín	234	18.54 N	97.00 W
Fortin, Lac ◎	186	50.50 N	67.46 W
Fortín Ayacucho	248	19.58 S	59.47 W
Fortín Coroneles Sanchez	248	19.20 S	59.58 W
Fortine	182	48.45 N	114.54 W
Fortín Florida	248	20.45 S	59.17 W
Fortín Garrapatal	248	21.27 S	61.30 W
Fortín Teniente Montanía	252	22.04 S	59.57 W
Fortín Uno	252	38.51 S	65.17 W
Fort Jackson ■	192	34.01 N	80.57 W
Fort Jameson → Chipata	154	13.39 S	32.40 E
Fort Jefferson National Monument ♠	220	24.37 N	82.54 W
Fort Jennings	216	40.54 N	84.17 W
Fort Jeudy, Point of ›	241k	12.00 N	61.42 W
Fort Johnson	210	42.57 N	74.14 W
Fort Johnston → Mangochi	154	14.28 S	35.16 E
Fort Jones	204	41.36 N	122.50 W
Fort Kent	186	47.15 N	68.35 W
Fort Klamath	202	42.42 N	121.59 W
Fort Knox ■	194	37.54 N	85.57 W
Fort-Lamy → N'Djamena	146	12.07 N	15.03 E
Fort Langley	224	49.10 N	122.35 W
Fort Langley National Historic Park ♠	224	49.10 N	122.35 W
Fort Laramie	200	42.12 N	104.31 W
Fort Laramie National Historic Site ♠	198	42.09 N	104.41 W
Fort Larned National Historic Site ⊥	198	38.10 N	99.12 W
Fort Lauderdale	220	26.07 N	80.08 W
Fort Lauderdale-Hollywood International Airport ⊠	220	26.04 N	80.09 W
Fort Laurens State Memorial ⊥	214	40.38 N	81.27 W
Fort Leavenworth ■	198	39.21 N	94.55 W
Fort Le Boeuf ⊥	214	41.56 N	79.59 W
Fort Lee	210	40.51 N	73.58 W
Fort Lee ■	208	37.14 N	77.20 W
Fort Lennox National Historic Park ♠	206	45.06 N	73.16 W
Fort Leonard Wood ■	194	37.45 N	92.07 W
Fort Lewis ■	224	47.05 N	122.37 W
Fort Liard	176	60.15 N	123.28 W
Fort-Liberté	238	19.39 N	71.49 W
Fort Lincoln State Park ♠	198	46.45 N	100.52 W
Fort Littleton	214	40.04 N	77.58 W
Fort Loramie	216	40.21 N	84.22 W
Fort Loudoun Lake ◎[1]	192	35.45 N	84.10 W
Fort Lupton	200	40.05 N	104.48 W
Fort Lyon Canal ≅	198	38.11 N	102.31 W
Fort Macleod	182	49.43 N	113.25 W
Fort Madison	190	40.37 N	91.18 W
Fort-Mahon-Plage	50	50.21 N	1.34 E
Fort Malden National Historic Park ♠	281	42.06 N	83.07 W
Fort Matanzas National Monument ♠	192	29.40 N	81.18 W
Fort McClellan ■	194	33.43 N	85.47 W
Fort McDermitt Indian Reservation ✦[4]	202	42.00 N	117.32 W
Fort McDowell Indian Reservation ✦[4]	200	33.38 N	111.41 W
Fort McHenry National Monument and Historic Shrine ♠	208	39.16 N	76.35 W
Fort Mckinley	218	39.47 N	84.15 W
Fort McMurray	184	56.44 N	111.23 W
Fort McNair ■	284c	38.52 N	77.04 W
Fort McPherson	180	67.27 N	134.53 W
Fort Meade	220	27.45 N	81.48 W
Fort Mill	192	35.00 N	80.56 W
Fort Miller	210	43.10 N	73.35 W
Fort Mitchell, Al., U.S.	192	32.21 N	85.01 W
Fort Mitchell, Ky., U.S.	218	39.03 N	84.32 W
Fort Mojave Indian Reservation ✦[4]	200	34.55 N	114.35 W
Fort Monmouth ■	208	40.19 N	74.02 W
Fort Monroe ■	208	37.00 N	76.18 W
Fort Montgomery	210	41.20 N	73.59 W
Fort Morgan	198	40.15 N	103.47 W
Fort Myer ■	284c	38.53 N	77.05 W
Fort Myers	220	26.38 N	81.52 W
Fort Myers Beach	220	26.27 N	81.56 W
Fort Myers Shores	220	26.43 N	81.45 W
Fort Myers Villas	220	26.34 N	81.52 W
Fort Necessity National Battlefield ⊥	188	39.47 N	79.39 W
Fort Neck ›[1]	276	40.39 N	73.28 W
Fort Nelson	176	58.49 N	122.43 W
Fort Nelson ≃	176	59.30 N	124.00 W
Fort Niagara Beach	284a	43.16 N	79.03 W
Fort Niagara State Park ♠, N.Y., U.S.	210	43.16 N	79.03 W
Fort Niagara State Park ♠, N.Y., U.S.	284a	43.16 N	79.03 W
Fort Nonsense ⊥	276	40.48 N	74.29 W
Fort Norman	180	64.54 N	125.34 W
Fort Nottingham	158	29.25 S	29.55 E
Fort Ogden	220	27.05 N	81.57 W
Fort Ord ■	226	36.40 N	121.48 W
Fortore ≃	68	41.55 N	15.17 E
Fort Parker State Park ♠	222	31.36 N	96.33 W
Fort Payne	194	34.26 N	85.43 W
Fort Peck	202	48.00 N	106.26 W
Fort Peck Dam ✦[6]	202	47.52 N	106.38 W
Fort Peck Indian Reservation ✦[4]	202	48.22 N	105.40 W
Fort Peck Lake ◎[1]	202	47.45 N	106.50 W
Fort Pierce	220	27.26 N	80.19 W
Fort Pierce Inlet ⊂	220	27.28 N	80.18 W
Fort Pierre	198	44.21 N	100.22 W
Fort Pitt Tunnels ✦[5]	279b	40.25 N	80.00 W
Fort Plain	210	42.55 N	74.37 W
Fort Point National Historical Site ⊥	282	37.48 N	122.28 W
Fort Polk ■	194	31.04 N	93.11 W
Fort Portal	154	0.40 N	30.17 E
Fort Providence	176	61.21 N	117.39 W
Fort Pulaski National Monument ♠	192	32.01 N	80.59 W
Fort Qu'Appelle	184	50.46 N	103.48 W
Fort Raleigh National Historic Site ⊥	192	35.55 N	75.40 W
Fort Randall Dam ✦[6]	198	42.48 N	98.35 W
Fort Recovery	216	40.24 N	84.46 W
Fort Resolution	176	61.10 N	113.40 W
Fortress Mountain ∧	202	44.20 N	109.47 W
Fortress of Louisbourg National Historic Park ♠	186	45.56 N	59.57 W
Fort Riley ■	198	39.04 N	96.47 W
Fort Ritchie ■	208	39.43 N	77.30 W
Fort Rixon	154	20.01 S	29.18 E
Fort Robinson State Park ♠	198	42.41 N	103.30 W
Fort Rodd Hill National Historic Park ♠	224	48.26 N	123.28 W
Fortrose, N.Z.	172	46.34 S	168.48 E
Fortrose, Scot., U.K.	46	57.34 N	4.09 W
Fort Rosebery → Mansa	154	11.12 S	28.53 E
Fort Rucker ■	194	31.20 N	85.42 W
Fort Saint James	182	54.26 N	124.15 W
Fort Saint John	182	56.15 N	120.51 W
Fort Salonga	276	40.55 N	73.18 W
Fort Sam Houston ■	196	29.27 N	98.27 W
Fort Saskatchewan	182	53.43 N	113.13 W
Fort Scott	198	37.50 N	94.42 W
Fort Şeneca	214	41.13 N	83.10 W
Fort-Ševčenko	84	44.31 N	50.16 E
Fort Severn	176	56.00 N	87.38 W
Fort Shawnee	216	40.41 N	84.08 W
Fort Sheridan ■	216	42.13 N	87.48 W
Fort Sill ■	196	34.40 N	98.25 W
Fort Simcoe Historical State Park ♠	224	46.21 N	120.50 W
Fort Simpson	176	61.52 N	121.23 W
Fort Sisseton State Park ♠	198	45.39 N	97.32 W
Fort Smith, N.T., Can.	176	60.00 N	111.53 W
Fort Smith, Ar., U.S.	194	35.23 N	94.23 W
Fort Steele	182	49.37 N	115.38 W
Fort Stevens State Park ♠	224	46.10 N	124.00 W
Fort Stewart ■	192	31.52 N	81.37 W
Fort Stockton	196	30.53 N	102.52 W
Fort Sumner	196	34.28 N	104.14 W
Fort Sumter National Monument ♠	192	32.44 N	79.46 W
Fort Supply	196	36.34 N	99.34 W
Fort Tejon State Historical Park ♠	228	34.52 N	118.53 W
Fort Thomas, Az., U.S.	200	33.02 N	109.57 W
Fort Thomas, Ky., U.S.	218	39.04 N	84.26 W
Fort Thompson	198	44.04 N	99.26 W
Fort Tilden ■	276	40.33 N	73.53 W
Fort Totten	198	47.58 N	98.59 W
Fort Totten Indian Reservation ✦[4]	198	47.53 N	98.50 W
Fort Totten Park ♠	284c	38.57 N	77.00 W
Fort Towson	196	34.01 N	95.15 W
Fort-Trinquet → Bîr Mogreïn	148	25.14 N	11.35 W
Fortuna, Arg.	252	35.07 S	65.23 W
Fortuna, C.R.	236	10.30 N	84.35 W
Fortuna, Ca., U.S.	204	40.35 N	124.09 W
Fortuna, Río de la ≃	248	16.36 S	58.46 W
Fortuna Ledge (Marshall)	180	61.53 N	162.05 W
Fortune	186	47.04 N	55.50 W
Fortune Bay ⊂	186	47.25 N	55.25 W
Fortune Ditch ≅	279a	41.20 N	82.03 W
Fortune Harbour	186	49.31 N	55.15 W
Fortuneswell	42	50.34 N	2.27 W
Fort Union National Monument ♠	200	35.55 N	105.01 W
Fort Union Trading Post National Historical Site ⊥	198	48.00 N	104.03 W
Fort Valley	192	32.33 N	83.53 W
Fort Vancouver National Historic Site ⊥	224	45.38 N	122.37 W
Fort Vermilion	176	58.24 N	116.00 W
Fortville	218	39.55 N	85.50 W
Fort Wadsworth ■	276	40.36 N	74.04 W
Fort Walton Beach	194	30.24 N	86.37 W
Fort Washakie	200	43.00 N	108.52 W
Fort Washington	208	40.08 N	75.12 W
Fort Washington Forest	208	38.43 N	76.59 W
Fort Washington State Park ♠	285	40.07 N	75.14 W
Fort Wayne	216	41.07 N	85.07 W
Fort Wayne Military Museum ʋ	281	42.18 N	83.06 W
Fort Wellington	246	6.24 N	57.36 W
Fort Wellington National Historic Park ♠	212	44.44 N	75.31 W
Fort White	192	29.55 N	82.42 W
Fort William	46	56.49 N	5.07 W
Fort William → Thunder Bay	190	48.23 N	89.15 W
Fort Worth	222	32.43 N	97.19 W
Fort Yates	198	46.05 N	100.37 W
Forty Foot Drain ≅	42	52.28 N	0.05 W
Forty Fort	210	41.16 N	75.52 W
Fortymile ≃	180	64.26 N	140.32 W
Fort Yukon	180	66.34 N	145.17 W
Fort Yuma Indian Reservation ✦[4]	204	32.48 N	114.34 W
Forum ♠, P.Q., Can.	275a	45.29 N	73.35 W
Forum ♠, Ca., U.S.	280	33.57 N	118.20 W
Forūr, Jazīreh-ye I	128	26.17 N	54.32 E
Forza d'Agrò	70	37.55 N	15.20 E
Foscagno, Passo di)(	64	46.30 N	10.08 E
Fosdinovo	64	44.08 N	10.01 E
Fosforescente, Bahía ⊂	240m	17.59 N	67.01 W
Fosforitnyj	82	55.19 N	38.54 E
Foshan	100	23.03 N	113.09 E
Fosna ›[1]	24	64.00 N	10.30 E
Fosnavåg	26	62.21 N	5.39 E
Foso	150	5.42 N	1.17 W
Foss	46	56.41 N	3.58 W
Foss ≃, Eng., U.K.	44	53.57 N	1.06 W
Foss ≃, Wa., U.S.	224	47.43 N	121.18 W
Fossacesia	66	42.15 N	14.29 E
Fossacesia Marina	66	42.15 N	14.30 E
Fossa Eugeniana ≅	263	51.33 N	6.36 E
Fossano	62	44.33 N	7.43 E
Fossanova, Abbazia di ʋ[1]	66	41.29 N	13.13 E
Fossato, Colle di)(	66	43.19 N	12.47 E
Fossato di Vico	66	43.18 N	12.46 E
Fossé	56	49.27 N	5.00 E
Fosse-Martin	261	49.05 N	2.54 E
Fosses	261	49.06 N	2.29 E
Fosses-la-Ville	56	50.24 N	4.42 E
Fossil	202	44.59 N	120.12 W
Fossil Butte National Monument ♠	202	41.50 N	110.40 W
Fossil Downs	162	18.08 S	125.38 E
Fossil Lake ◎	202	43.18 N	120.15 W
Fossombrone	66	43.41 N	12.48 E
Fosston	198	47.34 N	95.45 W
Fos-sur-Mer	62	43.26 N	4.57 E
Foster, Austl.	169	38.39 S	146.12 E
Foster, Ky., U.S.	218	38.47 N	84.12 W
Foster, R.I., U.S.	207	41.51 N	71.45 W
Foster ≃	184	55.47 N	105.49 W
Foster, Mount ∧	180	59.48 N	135.29 W
Foster Brook	214	41.59 N	78.37 W
Foster City	226	37.33 N	122.16 W
Foster Creek ≃	198	44.34 N	98.12 W
Fosterdale	210	41.42 N	74.58 W
Foster Joseph Sayers Reservoir ◎[1]	214	41.02 N	77.40 W
Foster Park	228	34.21 N	119.18 W
Fosters	194	33.05 N	87.41 W
Fosters Pond ◎	283	42.37 N	71.08 W
Foster Street	260	51.46 N	0.09 E
Foster Village	229c	21.21 N	157.55 W
Fostoria	214	41.09 N	83.25 W
Fót	264c	47.37 N	19.12 E
Fotadrevo	157b	24.03 S	45.01 E
Fotan	100	24.12 N	117.53 E
Fóti-Somlyó ∧[2]	264c	47.38 N	19.13 E
Foucarmont	50	49.51 N	1.34 E
Fou-Chouen → Fushun	104	41.52 N	123.53 E
Fouesnant	32	47.54 N	4.01 W
Foug	56	48.41 N	5.47 E
Fougamou	152	1.13 S	10.36 E
Fougères	32	48.21 N	1.12 W
Fougères-sur-Bièvre	50	47.27 N	1.21 E
Fougerolles	58	47.53 N	6.24 E
Fouhsin → Fuxin	104	42.03 N	121.46 E
Fouju	261	48.35 N	2.47 E
Fouke	194	33.16 N	93.53 W
Foula I	46a	60.08 N	2.05 W
Foulain	58	48.02 N	5.13 E
Foulalaba	150	10.41 N	7.22 W
Foula Mori	150	12.10 N	13.51 W
Foulatari	146	13.41 N	12.03 E
Foul Bay ⊂	140	23.30 N	35.39 E
Fouling → Fuling	102	29.42 N	107.21 E
Foulness ≃	44	53.47 N	0.43 W
Foulness Island I	42	51.36 N	0.55 E
Foulness Point ›	42	51.38 N	0.57 E
Foulpointe	157b	17.41 S	49.31 E
Foulsham	42	52.48 N	1.01 E
Foulwind, Cape ›	172	41.45 S	171.28 E
Foumban	152	5.43 N	10.55 E
Foumbot	152	5.30 N	10.38 E
Foumbouni	157a	11.50 S	43.30 E
Foum-el-Hisn	148	28.59 N	8.55 W
Foum-Zguid	148	30.04 N	6.54 W
Foundiougne	150	14.08 N	16.28 W
Fountain, Co., U.S.	198	38.40 N	104.42 W
Fountain, Fl., U.S.	192	30.09 N	85.38 W
Fountain □[6]	216	40.17 N	87.13 W
Fountain City, In., U.S.	218	39.57 N	84.55 W
Fountain City, Wi., U.S.	190	44.07 N	91.43 W
Fountain Creek ≃, Co., U.S.	198	38.15 N	104.35 W
Fountain Creek ≃, Il., U.S.	219	38.20 N	90.22 W
Fountain Green	200	39.37 N	111.38 W
Fountain Hill	208	40.36 N	75.23 W
Fountain Inn	192	34.41 N	82.11 W
Fountain Park	216	41.50 N	84.32 W
Fountain Peak ∧	204	34.57 N	115.32 W
Fountain Place	194	30.31 N	91.09 W
Fountains Abbey ʋ[1]	44	54.07 N	1.34 W
Fountains Creek ≃	208	36.33 N	77.21 W
Fountaintown	218	39.41 N	85.46 W
Fountain Valley	228	33.42 N	117.57 W
Fourche LaFave ≃	194	34.58 N	92.35 W
Fourche Maline ≃	194	34.55 N	94.55 W
Fourchu	186	45.43 N	60.15 W
Four Corners	202	44.55 N	122.58 W
Four Elms	260	51.13 N	0.06 E
Four Hole Swamp ≃	192	33.03 N	80.24 W
Fouriesburg	158	28.38 S	28.14 E
Fourmies	50	50.00 N	4.03 E
Four Mile Creek ≃, On., Can.	284a	43.15 N	79.08 W
Fourmile Creek ≃, N.Y., U.S.	284a	43.17 N	79.00 W
Four Mile Creek ≃, Oh., U.S.	218	39.26 N	84.32 W
Four Mile Creek State Park ♠	284a	43.16 N	79.00 W
Fourmile Draw V	196	32.40 N	104.18 W
Four Mile Lake ◎	212	44.40 N	78.44 W
Four Mile Run ≃	284c	38.50 N	77.02 W
Four Mountains, Islands of II	180	52.50 N	170.00 W
Fournaise, Piton de la ∧	157c	21.14 S	55.43 E
Fourneau, Pointe à ›	275a	45.22 N	73.51 W
Fourneaux, Fr.	50	47.53 N	1.48 E
Fourneaux, Fr.	62	45.11 N	6.39 E
Fournier, Lac ◎	186	51.33 N	65.25 W
Fournière, Lac ◎	190	48.04 N	78.03 W
Foúrnoi I	38	37.34 N	26.30 E
Four Oaks	192	35.26 N	78.25 W
Fourqueux	261	48.53 N	2.04 E
Fours	32	46.49 N	3.43 E
Fourteenmile Creek ≃	218	38.26 N	85.37 W
Fourth Cataract → Rābi', Ash-Shallāl ar- ∟	140	18.47 N	32.03 E
Fourth Cliff ⊥[4]	283	42.09 N	70.42 W
Four Towns	281	42.37 N	83.25 W
Fous, Pointe des ›	240d	15.12 N	61.20 W
Foussard ≃	50	48.16 N	1.17 E
Fouta Djalon ✦[1]	150	11.30 N	12.30 W
Fou-Tcheou → Fuzhou	100	26.06 N	119.17 E
Foux, Cap à ›	238	19.41 N	73.27 W
Fouyang → Fuyang	100	32.54 N	115.49 E
Fouzon ≃	50	47.16 N	1.27 E
Foveaux Strait ʯ	172	46.35 S	168.00 E
Foveran	46	57.18 N	2.02 W
Fowey	42	50.20 N	4.38 W
Fowler, Ca., U.S.	226	36.37 N	119.40 W
Fowler, Co., U.S.	198	38.07 N	104.01 W
Fowler, In., U.S.	216	40.37 N	87.19 W
Fowler, Ks., U.S.	198	37.23 N	100.11 W
Fowler, Mi., U.S.	216	43.00 N	84.44 W
Fowler, Oh., U.S.	214	41.19 N	80.40 W
Fowler, Lake ◎	168b	35.06 S	137.37 E
Fowler, Point ›	162	32.02 S	132.29 E
Fowler Creek ≃	281	42.17 N	83.30 W
Fowlers Bay	162	31.59 S	132.27 E
Fowlerton	196	28.28 N	98.48 W
Fowlerville	216	42.39 N	84.04 W
Fowliang → Jingdezhen	100	29.16 N	117.11 E
Fowman	128	37.13 N	49.19 E
Fox	180	64.51 N	147.46 W
Fox ≃, Mb., Can.	184	56.03 N	93.18 W
Fox ≃, U.S.	194	40.18 N	91.30 W
Fox ≃, U.S.	216	41.21 N	88.50 W
Fox ≃, Il., U.S.	194	38.32 N	88.08 W
Fox ≃, Wi., U.S.	190	44.32 N	88.01 W
Fox, Cape ›	182	54.47 N	130.51 W
Foxboro, On., Can.	212	44.15 N	77.26 W
Foxboro, Ma., U.S.	207	42.03 N	71.15 W
Foxboro Raceway ♠	283	42.06 N	71.16 W
Fox Brook ≃	276	41.03 N	74.13 W
Foxburg	214	41.09 N	79.41 W
Fox Chapel	279b	40.30 N	79.55 W
Fox Chase ✦[8]	285	40.04 N	75.05 W
Fox Chase Manor	285	40.05 N	75.06 W
Fox Creek ≃, Ky., U.S.	218	38.16 N	83.41 W
Fox Creek ≃, N.Y., U.S.	210	42.41 N	74.18 W
Foxe Basin ⊂	176	68.25 N	77.00 W
Foxe-Becken → Foxe Basin ⊂	176	68.25 N	77.00 W
Foxe Channel ʯ	176	64.30 N	80.00 W
Foxen ◎	26	59.23 N	11.52 E
Foxe Peninsula ›[1]	176	65.00 N	76.00 W
Foxford	48	53.58 N	9.08 W
Fox Glacier	172	43.28 S	170.00 E
Foxhall	284c	39.04 N	77.03 W
Fox Harbour	186	47.19 N	53.55 W
Fox Hills	284c	39.02 N	77.11 W
Foxhole	42	50.21 N	4.52 W
Foxholes	44	54.08 N	0.28 W
Fox Hollow Lake ◎	276	41.02 N	74.40 W
Fox Island I, On., Can.	212	44.28 N	78.24 W
Fox Island I, Wa., U.S.	224	47.16 N	122.37 W
Fox Islands II	180	53.30 N	168.00 W
Fox Lake, Il., U.S.	216	42.23 N	88.11 W
Fox Lake, Wi., U.S.	190	43.33 N	88.54 W
Fox Lake ◎	216	42.25 N	88.09 W
Fox Mountain ∧	180	61.55 N	133.22 W
Foxpark	200	41.05 N	106.09 W
Fox Point	216	43.09 N	87.54 W
Fox Point ›	276	40.54 N	73.35 W
Fox River Estates	216	41.58 N	88.20 W
Fox River Grove	216	42.12 N	88.12 W
Foxton	172	40.28 S	175.18 E
Foxton Beach	172	40.28 S	175.13 E
Foxvale	283	42.02 N	71.14 W
Fox Valley, Austl.	274a	33.45 S	151.06 E
Fox Valley, Sk., Can.	184	50.29 N	109.28 W
Foxwells	208	37.38 N	76.18 W
Foxwist Green	262	53.12 N	2.34 W
Foxworth	194	31.14 N	89.52 W
Foyedong	98	40.41 N	119.12 E
Foyers	46	57.14 N	4.29 W
Foyle ≃	48	54.59 N	7.18 W
Foyle, Lough ⊂	48	55.06 N	7.08 W
Foynes	48	52.37 N	9.06 W
Foza	64	45.54 N	11.38 E
Foz do Areia, Represa de ◎[1]	252	26.00 S	51.35 W
Foz do Cunene	152	17.16 S	11.50 E
Foz do Iguaçu	252	25.33 S	54.35 W
Foz do Jordão	248	9.23 S	71.56 W
Foz Giraldo	34	40.00 N	7.43 W
Foziling	100	31.20 N	116.17 E
Frabosa Soprana	62	44.17 N	7.48 E
Frackville	208	40.47 N	76.13 W
Fraction Run ≃	278	41.34 N	88.04 W
Fraga, Arg.	252	33.30 S	65.48 W
Fraga, Esp.	34	41.31 N	0.21 E
Fragagnano	68	40.26 N	17.28 E
Fragneto Monforte	68	41.15 N	14.46 E
Fragoso, Cayo I	240p	22.44 N	79.30 W
Fragrant Hills Park ♠	271a	39.59 N	116.11 E
Fragua, Sierra de la ⋏	196	26.41 N	102.13 W
Fraile Muerto	252	32.31 S	54.32 W
Fraïn, Chott el ◎	34	35.57 N	5.38 E
Fraire	50	50.16 N	4.30 E
Fraisans	58	47.09 N	5.46 E
Fraisse	62	45.23 N	4.15 E
Fraize	58	48.11 N	7.00 E
Fram	61	46.27 N	15.38 E
Frameries	50	50.24 N	3.54 E
Framingham	207	42.16 N	71.25 W
Framingham State College ʋ[2]	283	42.18 N	71.26 W
Framlingham	42	52.13 N	1.21 E
Frammersbach	56	50.04 N	9.28 E
Framnes Mountains ⋏	9	67.50 S	62.35 E
Frampol	30	50.41 N	22.40 E
Frampton Cotterell	42	51.32 N	2.29 W
Frampton on Severn	42	51.46 N	2.22 W
França, Bra.	250	11.34 S	40.36 W
Franca, Bra.	255	20.32 S	47.24 W
Franca-Iosifa, Zeml'a (Franz Josef Land) II	12	81.00 N	55.00 E
Français, Récif des ✧[2]	175f	19.40 S	163.20 E
Francavilla al Mare	66	42.25 N	14.17 E
Francavilla Angitola	68	38.46 N	16.16 E
Francavilla d'Ete	66	43.11 N	13.32 E
Francavilla di Sicilia	70	37.54 N	15.08 E
Francavilla Fontana	68	40.31 N	17.35 E
Francavilla in Sinni	68	40.05 N	16.12 E
Francavilla Marittima	68	39.49 N	16.23 E
France □[1], Europe	22	46.00 N	2.00 E
France □[1], Europe	32	46.00 N	2.00 E
Frances ≃	180	60.12 N	129.02 W
Francés, Cabo ›, Cuba	240p	21.38 N	83.12 W
Francés, Cabo ›, Cuba	240p	21.54 N	84.02 W
Frances Creek	164	13.35 S	131.52 E
Francês dos Carvalhos	256	22.05 S	44.29 W
Frances Lake ◎	180	61.25 N	129.30 W
Francés Viejo, Cabo ›	238	19.39 N	69.55 W
Francesville	216	40.59 N	86.52 W
Franceville	152	1.38 S	13.35 E
Francfort-sur-Main → Frankfurt am Main	56	50.07 N	8.40 E
Franche-Comté □[9]	58	47.00 N	6.00 E
Franchère, Lac ◎	206	46.47 N	74.58 W
Franches-Montagnes ⋏	58	47.12 N	7.00 E
Francia	252	32.33 S	56.37 W
Francia, Estación de ✦[5]	266d	41.23 N	2.11 E
Francia, Peña de ∧	34	42.35 N	8.02 W
Francia → France □[1]	32	46.00 N	2.00 E
Francis	184	50.05 N	103.55 W
Francis, Lake ◎	206	45.02 N	71.20 W
Francis Case, Lake ◎[1]	198	43.15 N	99.00 W
Francisco A. Berra	258	35.23 S	58.51 W
Francisco Álvarez	258	34.38 S	58.52 W
Francisco Beltrão	252	26.05 S	53.04 W
Francisco I. Madero, Méx.	232	25.45 N	103.21 W
Francisco I. Madero, Méx.	232	24.32 N	104.22 W
Francisco I. Madero, Méx.	234	21.36 N	104.49 W
Francisco José, Tierra → Franca-Iosifa, Zeml'a II	12	81.00 N	55.00 E
Francisco Morato	256	23.16 S	46.45 W
Francisco Morazán □[5]	236	14.15 N	87.15 W
Francisco Murguía	234	24.00 N	103.01 W
Francisco Perito Moreno, Parque Nacional ♠	254	47.50 S	72.08 W
Francisco Sá	255	16.28 S	43.30 W
Francisco Zarco	204	32.06 N	116.30 W
Francis E. Warren Air Force Base ■	198	41.09 N	104.52 W
Francistown	156	21.11 S	27.32 E
Francitas	222	28.52 N	96.20 W
Franco da Rocha	256	23.20 S	46.43 W
Francofonte	70	37.14 N	14.53 E
François	186	47.35 N	56.45 W
François, Lacs à ◎	186	51.40 N	65.49 W
François-Joseph, Îles du → Frnca-Iosifa, Zeml'a II	12	81.00 N	55.00 E
François Lake	182	54.04 N	125.44 W

≃ River	Fluß	Río	Rivière	Rio	
≅ Canal	Kanal	Canal	Canal	Canal	
∟ Waterfall, Rapids	Wasserfall, Stromschnellen	Cascada, Rápidos	Chute d'eau, Rapides	Cascata, Rápidos	
ʯ Strait	Meeresstraße	Estrecho	Détroit	Estreito	
⊂ Bay, Gulf	Bucht, Golf	Bahía, Golfo	Baie, Golfe	Baía, Golfo	
◎ Lake, Lakes	See, Seen	Lago, Lagos	Lac, Lacs	Lago, Lagos	
⩩ Swamp	Sumpf	Pantano	Marais	Pântano	
⍓ Ice Features, Glacier	Eis- und Gletscherformen	Accidentes Glaciales	Formes glaciaires	Acidentes glaciares	
⍑ Other Hydrographic Features	Andere Hydrographische Objekte	Otros Elementos Hidrográficos	Autres données hydrographiques	Outros acidentes hidrográficos	

✧ Submarine Features	Untermeerische Objekte	Accidentes Submarinos	Formes de relief sous-marin	Acidentes submarinos
□ Political Unit	Politische Einheit	Unidad Politica	Entité politique	Unidade política
ʋ Cultural Institution	Kulturelle Institution	Institución Cultural	Institution culturelle	Institução cultural
⊥ Historical Site	Historische Stätte	Sitio Histórico	Site historique	Sitio histórico
♠ Recreational Site	Erholungs- und Ferienort	Sitio de Recreo	Centre de loisirs	Area de Lazer
⊠ Airport	Flughafen	Aeropuerto	Aéroport	Aeroporto
■ Military Installation	Militäranlage	Instalación Militar	Installation militaire	Instalação militar
✦ Miscellaneous	Verschiedenes	Misceláneo	Divers	Diversos

ENGLISH: Name · Page · Lat.°′ · Long.°′
DEUTSCH: Name · Seite · Breite°′ · Länge°′ E = Ost

Name	Page	Lat.°′	Long.°′
François Lake ⊜	182	54.00 N	125.40 W
Francolise	68	41.11 N	14.03 E
Franconia Notch State Park ♦	188	44.06 N	71.43 W
Franconville	261	48.59 N	2.14 E
Francs Peak ∧	202	43.58 N	109.20 W
Francueil	50	47.19 N	1.05 E
Franeker	52	53.11 N	5.32 E
Frangy	58	46.01 N	5.56 E
Frank	279b	40.16 N	79.48 W
Frank and Poet Drain ≊	281	42.06 N	83.12 W
Frankby	262	53.22 N	3.08 W
Frankel City	196	32.23 N	102.47 W
Franken □[9]	30	50.00 N	10.00 E
Frankenau	56	51.05 N	8.56 E
Frankenbach	56	50.40 N	8.34 E
Frankenberg	54	50.54 N	13.01 E
Frankenberg-Eder	56	51.03 N	8.48 E
Frankenburg	60	48.05 N	13.30 E
Frankenheim	56	50.32 N	10.04 E
Frankenhöhe ⋏	56	49.15 N	10.15 E
Frankenmarkt	64	47.59 N	13.25 E
Frankenmuth	190	43.19 N	83.44 W
Frankenstein	56	49.26 N	7.58 E
Frankenthal	56	49.32 N	8.21 E
Frankenwald ⋏	54	50.18 N	11.36 E
Frankfield	241q	18.09 N	77.22 W
Frankford, On., Can.	212	44.12 N	77.36 W
Frankford, De., U.S.	208	38.31 N	75.14 W
Frankford, Mo., U.S.	219	39.29 N	91.19 W
Frankford ◆[8]	285	40.01 N	75.05 W
Frankford Arsenal ■	285	40.00 N	75.04 W
Frankfort, S. Afr.	158	32.44 S	27.28 E
Frankfort, S. Afr.	158	27.17 S	28.30 E
Frankfort, Il., U.S.	216	41.29 N	87.50 W
Frankfort, In., U.S.	216	40.16 N	86.30 W
Frankfort, Ks., U.S.	198	39.42 N	96.25 W
Frankfort, Ky., U.S.	218	38.12 N	84.52 W
Frankfort, Mi., U.S.	190	44.38 N	86.14 W
Frankfort, N.Y., U.S.	210	43.02 N	75.04 W
Frankfort, Oh., U.S.	218	39.24 N	83.10 W
Frankfort, S.D., U.S.	198	44.52 N	98.18 W
Frankfort Springs	214	40.30 N	80.25 W
Frankfurt am Main	56	50.07 N	8.40 E
Frankfurt am Main, Flughafen ⊠	56	50.02 N	8.33 E
Frankfurt an der Oder	54	52.20 N	14.33 E
Frank G. Bonelli Regional County Park ♦	280	34.05 N	117.49 W
Frank Hann National Park ♦	162	32.50 S	120.25 E
Fränkische Alb ⋏[2]	60	49.20 N	11.30 E
Fränkische Rezat ≃	56	49.11 N	11.01 E
Fränkische Saale ≃	56	50.03 N	9.42 E
Fränkische Schweiz ◆[1]	60	49.45 N	11.25 E
Frank Key I	220	25.07 N	80.54 W
Frankland ≃	162	34.58 S	116.49 E
Frankleben	54	51.18 N	11.56 E
Franklin, S. Afr.	158	30.18 S	29.30 E
Franklin, Az., U.S.	200	32.40 N	109.04 W
Franklin, Ga., U.S.	192	33.16 N	85.05 W
Franklin, Id., U.S.	202	42.00 N	111.48 W
Franklin, Il., U.S.	219	39.37 N	90.03 W
Franklin, In., U.S.	218	39.28 N	86.03 W
Franklin, Ky., U.S.	194	36.43 N	86.34 W
Franklin, La., U.S.	194	29.47 N	91.30 W
Franklin, Me., U.S.	188	44.35 N	68.13 W
Franklin, Ma., U.S.	207	42.05 N	71.23 W
Franklin, Mi., U.S.	281	42.31 N	83.18 W
Franklin, Mn., U.S.	198	44.31 N	94.52 W
Franklin, Ne., U.S.	198	40.05 N	98.57 W
Franklin, N.H., U.S.	188	43.26 N	71.38 W
Franklin, N.J., U.S.	210	41.07 N	74.34 W
Franklin, N.Y., U.S.	210	42.20 N	75.09 W
Franklin, N.C., U.S.	192	35.10 N	83.22 W
Franklin, Oh., U.S.	218	39.33 N	84.18 W
Franklin, Pa., U.S.	214	41.24 N	79.50 W
Franklin, Tn., U.S.	194	35.55 N	86.52 W
Franklin, Tx., U.S.	222	31.01 N	96.29 W
Franklin, Vt., U.S.	206	44.58 N	72.55 W
Franklin, Va., U.S.	208	36.40 N	76.55 W
Franklin, W.V., U.S.	188	38.39 N	79.20 W
Franklin, Wi., U.S.	216	42.54 N	88.03 W
Franklin □[6], In., U.S.	218	39.25 N	85.01 W
Franklin □[6], Ky., U.S.	218	38.14 N	84.52 W
Franklin □[6], Ma., U.S.	207	42.36 N	72.36 W
Franklin □[6], Mo., U.S.	219	38.25 N	91.03 W
Franklin □[6], N.Y., U.S.	206	44.57 N	74.18 W
Franklin □[6], Oh., U.S.	218	39.57 N	83.00 W
Franklin □[6], Pa., U.S.	208	39.56 N	77.40 W
Franklin □[6], Tx., U.S.	222	33.07 N	95.13 W
Franklin □[6], Vt., U.S.	206	44.57 N	72.52 W
Franklin, Mount ∧	171b	35.29 S	148.47 E
Franklin, Point ›	180	70.54 N	158.48 W
Franklin Bay ⊂	176	69.45 N	126.00 W
Franklin Canyon Reservoir ⊜[1]	280	34.06 N	118.25 W
Franklin Delano Roosevelt National Historic Site ⊥	210	41.46 N	73.56 W
Franklin Delano Roosevelt Park ♦	285	39.54 N	75.11 W
Franklin D. Roosevelt Lake ⊜[1]	202	48.20 N	118.10 W
Franklin Farms	279b	40.10 N	80.16 W
Franklin Grove	190	41.50 N	89.18 W
Franklin Harbor ⊂	166	33.42 S	136.56 E
Franklin Institute ʊ	285	39.57 N	75.11 W
Franklin Island I	212	45.24 N	80.20 W
Franklin Lake ⊜, N.T., Can.	176	66.56 N	96.03 W
Franklin Lake ⊜, Nv., U.S.	204	40.24 N	115.12 W
Franklin Lake ⊜, N.J., U.S.	276	40.59 N	74.13 W
Franklin Lakes	276	41.01 N	74.12 W
Franklin-Lower Gordon Wild Rivers National Park ♦	166	42.46 S	145.45 E
Franklin Mountains ⋏, N.T., Can.	180	63.00 N	123.50 W
Franklin Mountains ⋏, N.Z.	172	44.55 S	167.45 E
Franklin Park, Il., U.S.	216	41.56 N	87.51 W
Franklin Park, Md., U.S.	284c	39.03 N	77.06 W
Franklin Park, N.J., U.S.	276	40.26 N	74.32 W
Franklin Park, N.Y., U.S.	210	43.05 N	76.05 W
Franklin Park, Pa., U.S.	279b	40.35 N	80.06 W
Franklin Park, Va., U.S.	284c	38.55 N	77.09 W
Franklin Park ♦	283	42.18 N	71.06 W
Franklin Pond ⊜	276	41.06 N	74.35 W
Franklin Ridge ∧	282	38.00 N	122.10 W
Franklin River	224	49.06 N	124.49 W
Franklin Roosevelt Park ◆[8]	273d	26.09 S	27.59 E
Franklin Springs	210	43.02 N	75.24 W
Franklin Square	210	40.42 N	73.40 W
Franklin State Forest ♦	283	42.04 N	71.26 W
Franklin Strait ʯ	176	72.00 N	96.00 W
Franklinton, La., U.S.	194	30.50 N	90.09 W
Franklinton, N.C., U.S.	192	36.06 N	78.27 W
Franklintown	208	40.05 N	77.02 W
Franklinville, N.J., U.S.	208	39.37 N	75.04 W
Franklinville, N.Y., U.S.	210	42.20 N	78.27 W
Frankreich → France □[1]	32	46.00 N	2.00 E
Frankston, Austl.	169	38.08 S	145.07 E
Frankston, Tx., U.S.	222	32.03 N	95.30 W
Franksville	216	42.45 N	87.54 W
Frankton	216	40.13 N	85.46 W
Frankville	194	31.38 N	88.08 W
Frånö	26	62.54 N	17.50 E
Fr'anovo	82	56.08 N	38.27 E
Franschhoek	158	33.55 S	19.09 E
Fransfontein	156	20.12 S	15.01 E
Fränsta	26	62.30 N	16.09 E
Františkovy Lázně	54	50.04 N	12.21 E
Franvillers	50	49.58 N	2.30 E
Franzburg	54	54.11 N	12.52 E
Franzensburg ⊥	264b	48.04 N	16.22 E
Franzensfeste → Fortezza	64	46.47 N	11.37 E
Franz Josef	172	43.24 S	170.11 E
Franz Josef Land → Franca Iosifa, Zeml'a II	12	81.00 N	55.00 E
Franz-Josefs-Bahnhof ◆[5]	264b	48.13 N	16.21 E
Franz-Josefs-Höhe ♦	64	47.04 N	12.45 E
Französische Süd- und Antarktis-Gebiete → French Southern and Antarctic Territories □[2]	6	49.30 S	69.30 E
Französisch-Polynesien → French Polynesia □[2]	14	15.00 S	140.00 W
Frasca, Capo della ›	71	39.46 N	8.27 E
Frascati	66	41.48 N	12.41 E
Frascineto	68	39.50 N	16.16 E
Frasdorf	64	47.48 N	12.16 E
Fraser, Co., U.S.	200	39.56 N	105.49 W
Fraser, Mi., U.S.	281	42.32 N	82.56 W
Fraser ≃, B.C., Can.	182	49.09 N	123.12 W
Fraser ≃, Nf., Can.	176	56.35 N	61.55 W
Fraser ≃, Co., U.S.	200	40.06 N	105.58 W
Fraser, Mount ∧	162	25.39 S	118.23 E
Fraserburg	158	31.55 S	21.30 E
Fraserburgh	46	57.42 N	2.00 W
Fraser Island I	166	25.15 S	153.10 E
Fraser Lake	182	54.04 N	124.51 W
Fraser Lake ⊜	182	54.05 N	124.35 W
Fraser Mills	224	49.14 N	122.52 W
Fraser National Park ♦	169	37.10 S	145.50 E
Fraser Plateau ⋏[1]	182	52.00 N	123.00 W
Fraser Range	162	32.03 S	122.48 E
Frasertown	172	38.58 S	177.24 E
Frasne	58	46.51 N	6.10 E
Frasnes-lez-Anvaing	50	50.40 N	3.36 E
Frassine ≃	64	45.18 N	11.37 E
Frassinoro	64	44.18 N	10.34 E
Frati, Monte dei ∧	66	43.40 N	12.10 E
Fratres	61	48.59 N	15.21 E
Frattamaggiore	68	40.57 N	14.16 E
Frattócchie	267a	41.46 N	12.37 E
Frauenfeld	58	47.34 N	8.54 E
Frauenkirchen	61	47.50 N	16.56 E
Frauenstein	54	50.48 N	13.32 E
Frauental an der Lassnitz	61	46.48 N	15.14 E
Frauenwald	54	50.35 N	10.51 E
Fray Bentos	252	33.08 S	58.18 W
Fray Jorge, Parque Nacional ♦	252	30.40 S	71.45 W
Fray Luis Beltrán	252	39.19 S	65.46 W
Fray Marcos	252	34.11 S	55.44 W
Frazee	198	46.43 N	95.42 W
Frazer, Mt., U.S.	202	48.03 N	106.02 W
Frazer, Pa., U.S.	208	40.02 N	75.33 W
Frazeysburg	214	40.07 N	82.07 W
Frazier Mountain ∧	228	34.47 N	118.58 W
Frazier Park	228	34.49 N	118.56 W
Fr'azino	82	55.58 N	38.04 E
Frazzanò	70	38.04 N	14.44 E
Frechen	56	50.54 N	6.49 E
Frechilla	34	42.08 N	4.50 W
Freckenhorst	52	51.55 N	7.58 E
Freckleton	262	53.45 N	2.52 W
Freddo ≃	70	38.01 N	12.54 E
Fredeburg	56	51.11 N	8.18 E
Freden	52	51.56 N	9.54 E
Fredensborg	41	55.58 N	12.24 E
Fredensborg ⊥	41	55.58 N	12.23 E
Frederic	190	45.39 N	92.28 W
Frederica	208	39.00 N	75.27 W
Fredericia	41	55.35 N	9.46 E
Frederick, Il., U.S.	219	40.04 N	90.26 W
Frederick, Md., U.S.	208	39.24 N	77.24 W
Frederick, Ok., U.S.	196	34.23 N	99.01 W
Frederick, S.D., U.S.	198	45.49 N	98.30 W
Frederick □[6]	208	39.25 N	77.25 W
Frederick Hills ⋏[2]	164	12.41 S	136.00 E
Frederick House ≃	190	49.06 N	81.10 W
Frederick House Lake ⊜	190	48.40 N	80.55 W
Frederick Island I	162	34.04 S	122.00 E
Frederick Reef ✦[2]	166	20.58 S	154.23 E
Fredericksburg, In., U.S.	218	38.26 N	86.11 W
Fredericksburg, Ia., U.S.	190	42.57 N	92.11 W
Fredericksburg, Oh., U.S.	214	40.40 N	81.52 W
Fredericksburg, Pa., U.S.	214	40.27 N	76.26 W
Fredericksburg, Tx., U.S.	196	30.16 N	98.52 W
Fredericksburg, Va., U.S.	208	38.18 N	77.27 W
Fredericksburg Battlefield ⊥	208	38.17 N	77.28 W
Frederick Sound ʯ	180	57.00 N	133.00 W
Fredericktown, Mo., U.S.	194	37.33 N	90.17 W
Fredericktown, Oh., U.S.	214	40.28 N	82.32 W
Frederico Westphalen	252	27.22 S	53.24 W
Fredericton	186	45.58 N	66.39 W
Fredericton Junction	186	45.40 N	66.37 W
Frederik Hendrikeiland → Yos Sudarso, Pulau I	164	7.50 S	138.30 E
Frederiksberg, Dan.	41	55.25 N	11.34 E
Frederiksberg, Dan.	41	55.41 N	12.32 E
Frederiksborg □[6]	41	55.56 N	12.18 E
Frederiksborg Slot ⊥	41	55.56 N	12.19 E
Frederikshåb (Paamiut)	176	62.00 N	49.43 W
Frederikshavn	26	57.26 N	10.32 E
Frederikssund	41	55.50 N	12.04 E
Frederiksted	241n	17.43 N	64.53 W
Frederiksværk	41	55.58 N	12.02 E
Frederik Willem IV Vallen ∟	250	3.28 N	57.37 W
Fredersdorf bei Berlin	54	52.31 N	13.44 E
Fredonia, Col.	246	5.55 N	75.41 W
Fredonia, Az., U.S.	200	36.03 N	112.08 W
Fredonia, Ks., U.S.	198	37.32 N	95.49 W
Fredonia, N.Y., U.S.	214	42.26 N	79.19 W
Fredonia, N.D., U.S.	198	46.19 N	99.05 W
Fredonia, Pa., U.S.	214	41.20 N	80.14 W
Fredrika	26	64.05 N	18.24 E
Fredriksberg	40	60.08 N	14.23 E
Fredrikstad	26	59.13 N	10.57 E
Freeburg, Il., U.S.	219	38.25 N	89.54 W
Freeburg, Mo., U.S.	219	38.18 N	91.55 W
Freeburg, Pa., U.S.	208	40.46 N	76.57 W
Freedom, Ca., U.S.	226	36.56 N	121.46 W
Freedom, Pa., U.S.	214	40.40 N	80.14 W
Freehold, N.J., U.S.	208	40.15 N	74.16 W
Freehold, N.Y., U.S.	210	42.22 N	74.03 W
Freeland, Mi., U.S.	190	43.31 N	84.07 W
Freeland, Pa., U.S.	210	41.01 N	75.53 W
Freeland, Wa., U.S.	224	48.01 N	122.32 W
Freeland Park	216	40.37 N	87.30 W
Freeling, Mount ∧	162	22.35 S	133.06 E
Freel Peak ∧	226	38.52 N	119.54 W
Freels, Cape ›, Nf., Can.	186	49.15 N	53.28 W
Freels, Cape ›, Nf., Can.	186	46.37 N	53.33 W
Freeman	198	43.21 N	97.26 W
Freeman ≃	182	54.20 N	114.47 W
Freeman, Lake ⊜	216	40.42 N	86.45 W
Freemansburg	210	40.37 N	75.20 W
Freemount	48	52.16 N	8.53 W
Freeport, Ba.	238	26.30 N	78.45 W
Freeport, N.S., Can.	186	44.17 N	66.19 W
Freeport, On., Can.	212	43.25 N	80.25 W
Freeport, Fl., U.S.	194	30.29 N	86.08 W
Freeport, Il., U.S.	190	42.17 N	89.37 W
Freeport, Me., U.S.	188	43.51 N	70.06 W
Freeport, Mi., U.S.	216	42.45 N	85.18 W
Freeport, N.Y., U.S.	210	40.39 N	73.35 W
Freeport, Oh., U.S.	214	40.12 N	81.15 W
Freeport, Pa., U.S.	210	40.40 N	79.41 W
Freeport, Tx., U.S.	222	28.57 N	95.21 W
Freer	196	27.52 N	98.37 W
Freest	54	54.08 N	13.43 E
Freeston	222	31.32 N	96.15 W
Freestone	171a	28.08 S	152.08 E
Freestone □[6]	222	31.44 N	96.10 W
Freetown, Antig.	240c	17.03 N	61.42 W
Freetown, S.L.	150	8.30 N	13.15 W
Freetown, In., U.S.	218	38.58 N	86.07 W
Freetown, N.Y., U.S.	207	40.58 N	72.11 W
Freeville	210	42.30 N	76.20 W
Freewood Acres	208	40.10 N	74.15 W
Freezeout Lake ⊜	202	47.40 N	112.03 W
Fregenal de la Sierra	34	38.10 N	6.39 W
Fregene ◆[8]	66	41.51 N	12.12 E
Freiberg	54	50.54 N	13.20 E
Freiberger Mulde ≃	54	51.10 N	12.48 E
Freiburg □[5]	58	48.00 N	8.25 E
Freiburg an der Elbe	52	53.49 N	9.17 E
Freiburg → Fribourg	58	46.48 N	7.09 E
Freiburg im Breisgau	58	47.59 N	7.51 E
Freienbach	58	47.12 N	8.45 E
Freienhufen	54	51.35 N	13.58 E
Freie Universität ʊ[2]	264a	52.26 N	13.16 E
Freigericht	56	50.08 N	9.07 E
Freihung	60	49.37 N	11.55 E
Freiland	61	47.58 N	15.34 E
Freilassing	64	47.50 N	12.59 E
Freilingen	56	50.33 N	7.50 E
Freinberg	60	48.34 N	13.31 E
Freinsheim	56	49.30 N	8.13 E
Freirina	252	28.30 S	71.06 W
Freisen	56	49.33 N	7.14 E
Freisenbruch ◆[8]	263	51.27 N	7.06 E
Freising	60	48.23 N	11.44 E
Freistadt	61	48.31 N	14.31 E
Freital	54	51.00 N	13.39 E
Freiwalde	54	51.58 N	13.44 E
Freixial	266c	38.54 N	9.09 W
Fréjus	62	43.26 N	6.44 E
Fréjus, Tunnel du ◆[5]	62	45.08 N	6.40 E
Frémainville	261	49.04 N	1.52 E
Fremantle	168a	32.03 S	115.45 E
Fremdingen	56	48.58 N	10.27 E
Fremington	42	51.04 N	4.07 W
Fremont, Ca., U.S.	226	37.32 N	121.59 W
Fremont, In., U.S.	216	41.43 N	84.55 W
Fremont, Ia., U.S.	190	41.12 N	92.26 W
Fremont, Mi., U.S.	190	43.28 N	85.56 W
Fremont, Ne., U.S.	198	41.26 N	96.29 W
Fremont, N.C., U.S.	192	35.32 N	77.58 W
Fremont, Oh., U.S.	214	41.21 N	83.07 W
Fremont, Wi., U.S.	190	44.15 N	88.51 W
Fremont ≃	200	38.24 N	110.42 W
Fremont Canyon V	280	33.48 N	117.42 W
Fremont Island I	200	41.09 N	112.20 W
Fremont Lake ⊜	202	42.57 N	109.49 W
Fremont Peak ∧, Ca., U.S.	226	36.46 N	121.30 W
Fremont Peak ∧, Ca., U.S.	228	35.12 N	117.27 W
Fremont Valley V	228	35.10 N	118.00 W
French ≃	190	45.56 N	80.54 W
French Broad ≃	192	35.57 N	83.51 W
Frenchburg	192	37.57 N	83.37 W
French Camp	226	37.53 N	121.16 W
Frenchcap Cay I	240m	18.14 N	64.51 W
French Creek ≃, Mb., Can.	184	57.02 N	92.12 W
French Creek ≃, U.S.	214	41.25 N	79.50 W
French Creek ≃, Oh., U.S.	279a	41.27 N	82.07 W
French Creek ≃, Pa., U.S.	208	40.08 N	75.31 W
French Creek ≃, S.D., U.S.	198	43.38 N	102.55 W
French Creek, South Branch ≃, Pa., U.S.	214	41.54 N	79.54 W
French Creek, South Branch ≃, Pa., U.S.	285	40.10 N	75.42 W
French Creek, West Branch ≃	214	41.58 N	79.52 W
French Creek State Park ♦	208	40.13 N	75.47 W
French Frigate Shoals ✦[2]	14	23.45 N	166.10 W
French Guiana (Guyane français) □[2], S.A.	242	4.00 N	53.00 W
French Guiana (Guyane français) □[2], S.A.	250	4.00 N	53.00 W
French Island I	169	38.21 S	145.21 E
French Lick	194	38.32 N	86.37 W
Frenchman (Frenchman Creek) ≃	202	48.24 N	107.05 W
Frenchman Bay ⊂	188	44.25 N	68.10 W
Frenchman Butte	184	53.35 N	109.38 W
Frenchman Creek (Frenchman) ≃, N.A.	202	48.24 N	107.05 W
Frenchman Creek ≃, U.S.	198	40.13 N	100.50 W
Frenchman Lake ⊜	204	36.48 N	116.56 W
Frenchman Point ›	212	44.35 N	81.18 W
Frenchman's Bay ⊂	275b	43.49 N	79.05 W
Frenchmans Cap ∧	166	42.16 S	145.50 E
Frenchman's Creek ≃, On., Can.	284a	42.56 N	78.56 W
Frenchmans Creek ≃, Ca., U.S.	282	37.29 N	122.27 W
French Meadows Reservoir ⊜[1]	226	39.07 N	120.25 W
Frenchpark	48	53.52 N	8.26 W
French Pass	172	40.56 S	173.50 E
French Polynesia □[2]	14	15.00 S	140.00 W
Frenchs Forest	274a	33.45 S	151.14 E
French Southern and Antarctic Territories □[2]	6	49.30 S	69.30 E
French Stream ≃	283	42.07 N	70.53 W
Frenchtown	210	40.31 N	75.03 W
Frenda	148	35.02 N	1.01 E
Freneuse	261	49.03 N	1.36 E
Frensdorferhaar	52	52.25 N	7.03 E
Frenštát pod Radhoštěm	30	49.33 N	18.14 E
Frentani, Monti dei ⋏	66	41.54 N	14.37 E
Frépillon	261	49.03 N	2.12 E
Frere	158	28.52 S	29.47 E
Freren	52	52.29 N	7.32 E
Fresco	150	5.05 N	5.34 W
Fresco ≃	250	6.39 S	51.59 W
Freshfield	262	53.34 N	3.04 W
Freshfield, Mount ∧	182	51.44 N	116.57 W
Freshford	48	52.43 N	7.24 W
Fresh Meadows ◆[8]	276	40.44 N	73.48 W
Fresh Pond ⊜, Ma., U.S.	283	42.23 N	71.09 W
Fresh Pond ⊜, N.Y., U.S.	276	40.55 N	73.18 W
Freshwater	42	50.40 N	1.30 W
Freshwater Creek ≃	226	39.12 N	122.04 W
Fresia	254	41.09 S	73.27 W
Fresnes	261	48.45 N	2.19 E
Fresne-Saint-Mamès	58	47.33 N	5.52 E
Fresnes-en-Woëvre	56	49.08 N	5.39 E
Fresnes-sur-Escaut	50	50.26 N	3.35 E
Fresnes-sur-Marne	261	48.56 N	2.45 E
Fresnillo	234	23.10 N	102.53 W
Fresno, Col.	246	5.09 N	75.01 W
Fresno, Ca., U.S.	226	36.44 N	119.46 W
Fresno, Oh., U.S.	214	40.20 N	81.44 W
Fresno, Tx., U.S.	222	29.32 N	95.27 W
Fresno □[6]	226	36.38 N	119.45 W
Fresno ≃	226	37.05 N	120.33 W
Fresno, Lewis Fork ≃	226	37.20 N	119.39 W
Fresno Air Terminal ⊠	226	36.46 N	119.43 W
Fresno Reservoir ⊜[1]	202	48.41 N	109.57 W
Fresno Slough ≃	226	36.47 N	120.22 W
Fresnoy-Folny	50	49.53 N	1.26 E
Fresnoy-le-Grand	50	49.57 N	3.25 E
Fressenneville	50	50.04 N	1.34 E
Fressin	50	50.27 N	2.03 E
Freswick	46	58.35 N	3.05 W
Fréteval	50	47.53 N	1.13 E
Frétigney-et-Velloreille	58	47.29 N	5.56 E
Fretin	50	50.33 N	3.08 E
Frettes	58	47.41 N	5.34 E
Freu, Cap des ›	34	39.45 N	3.27 E
Freudenberg, Dtsch.	56	49.44 N	9.19 E
Freudenberg, Dtsch.	56	50.54 N	7.52 E
Freudenberg, Dtsch.	264a	52.42 N	13.49 E
Freudenstadt	58	48.28 N	8.25 E
Frévent	50	50.16 N	2.17 E
Frew ≃	162	20.00 S	135.38 E
Frewena	162	19.25 S	135.25 E
Frewsburg	214	42.03 N	79.09 W
Freyburg	54	51.13 N	11.46 E
Freycinet, Cape ›	162	34.06 S	114.59 E
Freycinet Estuary ⊂[1]	162	26.25 S	113.45 E
Freycinet National Park ♦	166	42.10 S	148.20 E
Freycinet Peninsula ›[1]	166	42.13 S	148.18 E
Freyenstein	54	53.17 N	12.20 E
Freyming-Merlebach	56	49.09 N	6.48 E
Freyre	252	31.10 S	62.06 W
Freystadt	60	49.12 N	11.20 E
Freyung	60	48.48 N	13.33 E
Fria	150	10.05 N	13.32 W
Fria, Cape ›	152	18.30 S	12.01 E
Friant	226	36.59 N	119.42 W
Friant Dam ◆[6]	226	37.00 N	119.43 W
Friant-Kern Canal ≊	226	35.22 N	119.06 W
Friars Point	194	34.22 N	90.38 W
Frías, Arg.	252	28.39 S	65.09 W
Frías, Perú	248	4.52 S	79.57 W
Fribourg (Freiburg)	58	46.48 N	7.09 E
Fribourg (Freiburg) □[3]	58	46.45 N	7.05 E
Frick	58	47.31 N	8.01 E
Frick Park ♦	279b	40.26 N	79.54 W
Friday	222	31.07 N	95.15 W
Friday Harbor	224	48.32 N	123.00 W
Fridaythorpe	44	54.01 N	0.40 W
Fridingen an der Donau	58	48.01 N	8.56 E
Fridley	190	45.05 N	93.15 W
Fridolfing	60	48.00 N	12.49 E
Fridtjof Nansen, Mount ∧	9	85.21 S	167.33 W
Friedberg, Dtsch.	56	50.20 N	8.45 E
Friedberg, Dtsch.	58	48.21 N	10.58 E
Friedberg, Öst.	61	47.27 N	16.03 E
Friedeburg [/Saale]	54	51.37 N	11.44 E
Friedenau ◆[8]	264a	52.28 N	13.20 E
Friedens	214	40.03 N	79.00 W
Friedensburg	208	40.36 N	76.14 W
Friedersdorf, Dtsch.	54	52.17 N	13.47 E
Friedersdorf, Dtsch.	54	51.01 N	14.34 E
Friedersdorf, Dtsch.	54	51.39 N	12.21 E
Friedesheim	158	27.55 S	26.43 E
Friedland, Dtsch.	54	52.06 N	14.16 E
Friedland, Dtsch.	54	53.40 N	13.33 E
Friedland, Dtsch.	56	51.25 N	9.55 E
Friedrich-Ebert-Brücke ◆[5]	263	51.28 N	6.43 E
Friedrich Krupp-Aktiengesellschaft ʊ[3]	263	51.28 N	7.00 E
Friedrichroda	54	50.52 N	10.34 E
Friedrichsbrunn	54	51.41 N	11.02 E
Friedrichsdorf	56	50.15 N	8.38 E
Friedrichsfeld	263	51.38 N	6.39 E
Friedrichsfelde ◆[8]	264a	52.31 N	13.31 E
Friedrichshafen	58	47.39 N	9.28 E
Friedrichshagen ◆[8]	264a	52.27 N	13.38 E
Friedrichshof	264a	52.19 N	13.46 E
Friedrichsort ◆[8]	54	54.24 N	10.11 E
Friedrichsruh, Schloss ⊥	52	53.32 N	10.20 E
Friedrichsruhe	54	53.31 N	11.45 E
Friedrichstadt	41	54.22 N	9.05 E
Friedrichsthal, Dtsch.	54	52.48 N	13.16 E
Friedrichsthal, Dtsch.	56	49.19 N	7.06 E
Friedrichstrasse, Bahnhof ◆[5]	264a	52.31 N	13.24 E
Friedrichswalde	54	53.02 N	13.42 E
Frielas	266c	38.49 N	9.09 W
Frielendorf	56	50.58 N	9.19 E
Friemersheim ◆[8]	263	51.23 N	6.42 E
Friend, Ne., U.S.	198	40.39 N	97.17 W
Friend, Or., U.S.	224	45.21 N	121.16 W
Friends Colony ◆[8]	272a	28.34 N	77.16 E
Friendship, N.Y., U.S.	210	42.12 N	78.08 W
Friendship, Tn., U.S.	194	35.54 N	89.14 W
Friendship, Wi., U.S.	190	43.58 N	89.49 W
Friendship Creek ≃	285	39.55 N	74.43 W
Friendship Shoal ✦[2]	112	5.58 N	112.31 E
Friends Meeting House State Memorial ⊥	214	40.09 N	80.47 W
Friendswood	222	29.31 N	95.12 W
Friern Barnet ◆[8]	260	51.37 N	0.10 W
Fries	192	36.42 N	80.58 W
Friesach	61	46.57 N	14.24 E
Friesack	54	52.44 N	12.34 E
Friesenheim	58	48.22 N	7.53 E
Friesenhofen	58	47.45 N	10.04 E
Friesenried	58	47.52 N	10.31 E
Friesland □[4]	52	53.03 N	5.45 E
Friesland □[9]	30	53.00 N	5.40 E
Fries Mills	285	39.39 N	75.03 W
Friesoythe	52	53.01 N	7.51 E
Frigate Point ›	174g	28.11 N	177.24 W
Frigento	68	41.01 N	15.06 E
Frignano	68	41.00 N	14.10 E
Frignano ◆[1]	64	44.20 N	10.51 E
Friguia	150	12.03 N	10.56 W
Friitala	26	61.26 N	21.52 E
Frillendorf ◆[8]	263	51.28 N	7.05 E
Frindsbury	260	51.24 N	0.30 E
Frinsted	260	51.17 N	0.43 E
Frinton-on-Sea	42	51.50 N	1.14 E
Frintrop ◆[8]	263	51.29 N	6.55 E
Frío ≃, N.A.	236	11.08 N	84.46 W
Frio ≃, Tx., U.S.	196	28.30 N	98.10 W
Frio, Cabo ›	255	22.53 S	42.00 W
Friockheim	46	56.38 N	2.38 W
Frio Draw V	196	34.50 N	102.19 W
Friona	196	34.38 N	102.43 W
Frisa, Loch ⊜	46	56.34 N	6.05 W
Frisange	56	49.32 N	6.12 E
Frisches Haff → Vislinskij zaliv ⊂	30	54.27 N	19.40 E
Frisco, Pa., U.S.	214	40.51 N	80.16 W
Frisco, Tx., U.S.	222	33.09 N	96.49 W
Frisco City	194	31.26 N	87.24 W
Frisco Creek ≃	196	36.34 N	101.23 W
Frisian Islands II	30	53.35 N	6.40 E
Friskney	44	53.04 N	0.11 E
Fristad	26	57.50 N	13.01 E
Fritch	196	35.38 N	101.36 W
Fritsla	26	57.33 N	12.47 E
Fritzlar	56	51.08 N	9.16 E
Friuli □[9]	64	46.00 N	13.00 E
Friuli-Venezia Giulia □[4]	64	46.00 N	13.00 E
Friza, proliv ʯ	74	45.30 N	149.10 E
Frizington	44	54.32 N	3.30 W
Frobisher	184	49.12 N	102.26 W
Frobisher Bay ⊂	176	62.30 N	66.00 W
Frobisher Lake ⊜	184	56.25 N	108.20 W
Frodsham	262	53.18 N	2.44 W
Frog Lake ⊜	184	53.55 N	110.18 W
Frohavet ʯ	24	63.52 N	9.26 E
Frohburg	54	51.03 N	12.33 E
Frohlinde ◆[8]	263	51.32 N	7.21 E
Frohnau ◆[8]	264a	52.38 N	13.18 E
Frohnhausen	263	51.29 N	7.48 E
Frohnhausen ◆[8]	263	51.27 N	6.58 E
Frohnleiten	61	47.16 N	15.20 E
Frohse	54	52.02 N	11.43 E
Froid	198	48.20 N	104.30 W
Froid, Lac ⊜	206	46.40 N	74.32 W
Froid, Ruisseau ≃	206	46.23 N	74.46 W
Froidmont-Cohartille	50	49.41 N	3.42 E
Froidos	56	49.03 N	5.07 E
Froissy	50	49.34 N	2.13 E
Froitzheim	56	50.42 N	6.34 E
Frolišči, Ross.	80	56.25 N	42.39 E
Frolišči, Ross.	82	56.18 N	39.13 E
Frolovo	80	49.47 N	43.39 E
Froman Run ≃	279b	40.12 N	80.00 W
Fromberg	202	45.23 N	108.54 W
Frombork	30	54.22 N	19.41 E
Frome	42	51.14 N	2.20 W
Frome ≃, Austl.	166	29.06 S	137.52 E
Frome ≃, Eng., U.K.	42	52.03 N	2.38 W
Frome ≃, Eng., U.K.	42	50.41 N	2.04 W
Frome, Lake ⊜	166	30.48 S	139.48 E
Frome Downs	166	31.13 S	139.46 E
Fromelennes	56	50.08 N	4.52 E
Fromentières	50	48.54 N	3.43 E
Frömern	263	51.30 N	7.44 E
Frommern	58	48.15 N	8.52 E
Fröndenberg	56	51.28 N	7.46 E
Frönsberg	263	51.21 N	7.46 E
Fronteiras	250	7.05 S	40.37 W
Frontenac, Fl., U.S.	220	28.27 N	80.46 W
Frontenac, Ks., U.S.	198	37.27 N	94.41 W
Frontenac □[6], On., Can.	212	44.40 N	76.45 W
Frontenac □[6], P.Q., Can.	206	45.42 N	71.15 W
Frontenard	58	46.55 N	5.10 E
Frontenex-Villard-Rosset	62	45.38 N	6.19 E
Frontera, Méx.	232	26.56 N	101.27 W
Frontera, Méx.	234	18.32 N	92.38 W
Fronteras	200	30.56 N	109.31 W
Frontier, Sk., Can.	184	49.12 N	108.34 W
Frontier, Mi., U.S.	216	41.47 N	84.36 W
Frontier, Wy., U.S.	200	41.48 N	110.32 W
Frontignan	62	43.27 N	3.45 E
Frontino	246	6.46 N	76.08 W
Frontino, Páramo ∧	246	6.28 N	76.04 W
Frontón, Isla I	286d	12.07 S	77.11 W
Front Range ⋏, Leso.	158	29.05 S	28.20 E
Front Range ⋏, Co., U.S.	200	39.45 N	105.45 W
Front Royal	188	38.55 N	78.11 W
Frose	54	51.48 N	11.23 E
Frosinone	66	41.38 N	13.19 E
Frosinone □[4]	66	41.37 N	13.27 E
Frosna ›[1]	26	63.45 N	10.25 E
Frosolone	66	41.36 N	14.27 E
Frösön	26	63.11 N	14.32 E
Frost	222	32.05 N	96.48 W
Frostavallen	41	55.58 N	13.30 E
Frostburg	188	39.39 N	78.55 W
Frost Creek ≃	276	40.54 N	73.37 W
Frostproof	220	27.44 N	81.31 W
Frotheim	52	52.21 N	8.40 E
Frouard	56	48.46 N	6.08 E
Frövi	40	59.28 N	15.22 E
Frøya I	24	63.43 N	8.42 E
Fruges	50	50.31 N	2.08 E
Fruita	200	39.09 N	108.43 W
Fruitdale, Al., U.S.	194	31.20 N	88.24 W
Fruitdale, Or., U.S.	202	42.24 N	123.20 W
Fruithurst	194	33.43 N	85.26 W
Fruitland, Id., U.S.	202	44.00 N	116.54 W
Fruitland, Md., U.S.	208	38.19 N	75.37 W
Fruitland Park	220	28.51 N	81.54 W
Fruitport	216	43.07 N	86.09 W
Fruitvale, B.C., Can.	182	49.07 N	117.33 W
Fruitvale, Tx., U.S.	222	32.41 N	95.48 W
Fruitvale, Wa., U.S.	202	46.37 N	120.33 W
Fruitville	192	27.19 N	82.27 W
Frumușița	38	45.40 N	28.04 E
Frunze, Kyrg.	85	40.07 N	71.44 E
Frunze, Ukr.	78	46.16 N	34.52 E
Frunze, Ukr.	83	48.40 N	38.45 E
Frunze → Biškek	85	42.54 N	74.36 E
Frunzovka	78	47.20 N	29.44 E
Frutal	255	20.02 S	48.55 W
Frutigen	58	46.35 N	7.39 E
Frutillar	254	41.07 S	73.03 W
Fryburg	214	41.21 N	79.26 W
Frýdek-Místek	30	49.41 N	18.22 E
Frýdlant	30	50.56 N	15.05 E
Frye	279b	40.11 N	79.56 W
Fryeburg	188	44.00 N	70.58 W
Fryerning	260	51.41 N	0.22 E
Fryingpan ≃	200	39.22 N	107.02 W
Fu ≃, Zhg.	100	28.36 N	116.04 E
Fu ≃, Zhg.	100	29.52 N	115.28 E
Fu ≃, Zhg.	102	29.59 N	106.16 E
Fua'amotu	174w	21.16 S	175.08 W
Fua'amotu International Airport ⊠	174w	21.17 S	175.08 W
Fu'an, Zhg.	100	27.08 N	119.40 E
Fu'an, Zhg.	100	32.41 N	120.41 E
Fuanjie	100	25.29 N	117.53 E
Fubao	107	28.47 N	106.05 E
Fubine	62	44.58 N	8.26 E
Fucecchio	66	43.44 N	10.48 E
Fuchang	100	30.06 N	113.08 E
Fucheng	98	37.52 N	116.07 E
Fuchikou	100	29.51 N	115.27 E
Fuchow → Fuzhou	100	28.01 N	116.20 E
Fuchs-Berg ∧[2]	264a	52.27 N	13.51 E
Fuchskaute ∧	56	50.27 N	7.52 E
Füchtorf	52	52.03 N	8.02 E
Fuchū, Nihon	94	35.40 N	139.29 E
Fuchū, Nihon	94	36.39 N	137.10 E
Fuchū, Nihon	96	34.24 N	132.30 E
Fuchū, Nihon	96	34.34 N	133.14 E
Fuchun ≃	106	30.10 N	120.09 E
Fucine	64	46.18 N	10.44 E
Fucino, Conca del ≚	66	42.01 N	13.31 E
Fudan University ʊ[2]	269b	31.17 N	121.29 E
Fuday I	46	57.03 N	7.23 W
Fuding	100	27.21 N	120.12 E
Fudu ≃	107	29.52 N	106.10 E
Fuefuki ≃	94	35.33 N	138.28 E
Fuego, Volcán de ∧[1]	236	14.29 N	90.53 W
Fuelbeckestausee ⊜[1]	263	51.15 N	7.40 E
Fuencaliente	34	38.24 N	4.18 W
Fuencarral ◆[8]	266a	40.30 N	3.41 W
Fuenlabrada	266a	40.17 N	3.48 W
Fuensalida	34	40.03 N	4.12 W
Fuensanta, Embalse de ⊜[1]	34	38.23 N	2.13 W
Fuente	196	28.40 N	100.32 W
Fuente de Cantos	34	38.15 N	6.18 W
Fuente de Oro	246	3.28 N	73.37 W
Fuenteobejuna	34	38.16 N	5.25 W
Fuentesaúco	34	41.14 N	5.30 W
Fuentes de Ebro	34	41.31 N	0.38 W
Fuerli	105	39.40 N	116.41 E
Fuerte ≃	232	25.54 N	109.22 W
Fuerte Olimpo	248	21.02 S	57.54 W
Fuerteventura I	148	28.20 N	14.00 W
Fuerza, Castillo de la ⊥	286b	23.09 N	82.21 W
Fufeng	102	34.20 N	107.51 E
Fuga Island I	116	18.52 N	121.22 E
Fugama, Wādī V	140	14.43 N	24.36 E
Fügen	64	47.21 N	11.51 E
Fuglebjerg	41	55.18 N	11.34 E
Fugløysund ʯ	24	70.12 N	20.20 E
Fugong	102	27.09 N	98.52 E
Fugou	98	34.04 N	114.24 E
Fuhai	86	47.06 N	87.23 E
Fuhe	100	23.22 N	113.37 E
Fuhlenbrock ◆[8]	263	51.32 N	6.54 E
Fuhrberg	52	52.34 N	9.50 E
Fuhse ≃	52	52.37 N	10.03 E
Fuhsien → Fuxian	98	39.37 N	122.01 E
Fuhu	100	29.11 N	118.04 E
Fuji, Nihon	94	35.09 N	138.39 E
Fuji, Zhg.	98	34.24 N	114.48 E
Fuji, Zhg.	107	29.09 N	105.23 E
Fuji ≃	94	35.07 N	138.39 E
Fuji, Mount → Fuji-san ∧[1]	94	35.22 N	138.44 E
Fujiafeng	105	39.11 N	117.32 E
Fujian (Fukien) □[4]	100	26.00 N	118.00 E
Fujiatun	104	41.42 N	123.44 E
Fujiawopu	104	40.58 N	122.14 E
Fujiazhen	107	29.57 N	104.18 E
Fujiazhuangcun	104	41.15 N	122.20 E
Fujie	106	31.09 N	119.27 E
Fujieda	94	34.52 N	138.16 E
Fuji-Hakone-Izu-kokuritsu-kōen ♦	94	35.21 N	138.44 E
Fujiidera	96	34.34 N	135.36 E
Fujikawa	94	35.08 N	138.37 E
Fujikubo	268	35.50 N	139.32 E
Fujimi, Nihon	94	36.27 N	139.05 E
Fujimi, Nihon	94	35.55 N	138.15 E
Fujimi, Nihon	94	35.51 N	139.33 E
Fujin	89	47.14 N	132.00 E
Fujino	94	35.37 N	139.10 E
Fujinomiya	94	35.12 N	138.38 E
Fujioka, Nihon	94	35.12 N	137.12 E
Fujioka, Nihon	94	36.15 N	139.05 E
Fujioka, Nihon	94	36.15 N	139.39 E
Fuji-san ∧[1]	94	35.22 N	138.44 E
Fujisawa	94	35.21 N	139.29 E
Fujishiro	94	35.55 N	140.07 E
Fujiwara, Nihon	94	35.09 N	136.30 E
Fujiwara, Nihon	94	36.51 N	139.44 E
Fujiwara-dam ◆[6]	94	36.49 N	139.02 E
Fujiyama → Fuji-san ∧[1]	94	35.22 N	138.44 E
Fuji-yoshida	94	35.29 N	138.48 E
Fukagawa	92a	43.43 N	142.03 E
Fukagawa ◆[8]	268	35.40 N	139.48 E
Fukami	268	35.28 N	139.28 E
Fukane I	174w	21.05 S	175.02 W
Fukang	86	44.10 N	87.59 E
Fukasaka-tunnel ◆[5]	94	35.35 N	136.10 E
Fuka Shan ∧	89	47.55 N	120.53 E
Fukaya	94	36.12 N	139.17 E
Fukiage	94	36.06 N	139.27 E
Fukiai ◆[8]	270	34.42 N	135.12 E
Fukien → Fujian □[4]	100	26.00 N	118.00 E
Fukou, Zhg.	100	25.45 N	118.28 E
Fukou, Zhg.	100	26.28 N	117.40 E
Fukube	96	35.33 N	134.18 E
Fukuchiyama	96	35.18 N	135.07 E
Fukude	94	34.40 N	137.53 E
Fukue	92	32.41 N	128.50 E
Fukuei Chiao ›	100	25.18 N	121.32 E
Fukue-jima I	92	32.40 N	128.45 E
Fukui, Nihon	94	36.04 N	136.13 E
Fukui, Nihon	270	34.51 N	135.34 E
Fukui □[5]	92	36.00 N	136.15 E
Fukuma	96	33.46 N	130.28 E
Fukumitsu	94	36.33 N	136.52 E
Fukuno	94	36.35 N	136.55 E
Fukuoka, Nihon	94	35.34 N	137.27 E
Fukuoka, Nihon	94	36.42 N	136.56 E
Fukuoka, Nihon	96	33.35 N	130.24 E
Fukuoka □[5]	96	33.45 N	130.30 E
Fukuoka-chūtonchi, Rikujō-jieitai- ■	96	33.32 N	130.28 E
Fukuroda-no-taki ∟	94	36.46 N	140.25 E
Fukuroi	94	34.45 N	137.55 E
Fukushima, Nihon	92	37.45 N	140.28 E
Fukushima, Nihon	92a	41.29 N	140.15 E
Fukushima □[5]	94	37.08 N	140.00 E
Fukushima ◆[8]	270	34.42 N	135.29 E
Fukusumi	270	34.37 N	135.56 E
Fukutani ◆[8]	270	34.43 N	135.02 E
Fukuyama	96	34.29 N	133.22 E
Fukuzaki	96	34.57 N	134.45 E
Fulacunda	150	11.44 N	15.03 W
Fūlādī, Kūh-e ∧	120	34.38 N	67.32 E
Fūlād Maḩalleh	128	36.02 N	53.44 E
Fulanga Island I	175g	19.08 S	178.34 W
Fulanga Passage ʯ	175g	19.00 S	178.40 W
Fulbourn	42	52.11 N	0.13 E
Fulda, Dtsch.	56	50.33 N	9.41 E
Fulda, Mn., U.S.	198	43.52 N	95.36 W
Fulda ≃	30	51.25 N	9.39 E
Fuldatal	56	51.22 N	9.31 E
Fuldera	58	46.37 N	10.22 E
Fule	102	25.27 N	104.19 E
Fulerum ◆[8]	263	51.26 N	6.57 E
Fulford Harbour	224	48.46 N	123.27 W
Fulgatore	70	37.57 N	12.42 E
Fulham ◆[8]	260	51.29 N	0.12 W
Fuli	100	23.11 N	121.14 E
Fuliji	100	33.46 N	116.58 E
Fuling	102	29.42 N	107.21 E
Fulitun	89	46.42 N	131.10 E
Fullarton ≃	166	20.15 S	141.10 E
Fullen ⊜	40	60.31 N	16.09 E
Fuller Springs	222	31.18 N	94.41 W
Fullerton, Ca., U.S.	228	33.52 N	117.55 W
Fullerton, Ky., U.S.	218	38.43 N	82.58 W
Fullerton, Md., U.S.	284b	39.22 N	76.31 W
Fullerton, Ne., U.S.	198	41.21 N	97.58 W
Fullerton, Pa., U.S.	208	40.38 N	75.28 W
Fullerton Municipal Airport ⊠	280	33.52 N	117.59 W
Fullerton Point ›	240c	17.06 N	61.54 W
Fulmer	260	51.33 N	0.34 W
Fulong	102	22.57 N	107.41 E
Fulongchang	107	30.03 N	103.38 E
Fulongquan	89	44.22 N	124.36 E
Fulpmes	64	47.10 N	11.21 E
Fulshear	222	29.41 N	95.54 W
Fulton, Al., U.S.	194	31.47 N	87.43 W
Fulton, Ar., U.S.	194	33.36 N	93.48 W
Fulton, Il., U.S.	190	41.52 N	90.09 W
Fulton, In., U.S.	216	40.56 N	86.15 W
Fulton, Ks., U.S.	198	38.00 N	94.43 W
Fulton, Ky., U.S.	194	36.30 N	88.52 W
Fulton, Md., U.S.	208	39.09 N	76.55 W
Fulton, Mi., U.S.	216	47.17 N	88.21 W
Fulton, Ms., U.S.	194	34.16 N	88.24 W
Fulton, Mo., U.S.	219	38.50 N	91.56 W
Fulton, N.Y., U.S.	210	43.19 N	76.25 W
Fulton, Oh., U.S.	214	40.27 N	82.49 W
Fulton, Tx., U.S.	196	28.04 N	97.02 W
Fulton □[6], Il., U.S.	219	40.13 N	90.17 W
Fulton □[6], In., U.S.	216	41.04 N	86.13 W
Fulton □[6], N.Y., U.S.	210	43.00 N	74.22 W
Fulton □[6], Oh., U.S.	216	41.33 N	84.09 W
Fulton □[6], Pa., U.S.	214	40.06 N	78.04 W
Fulton ≃	182	54.48 N	126.07 W
Fultondale	194	33.36 N	86.47 W
Fultonham	210	42.31 N	75.03 W
Fultonville	210	42.57 N	74.22 W
Fuluchang	107	29.38 N	106.08 E
Fulufjället ∧	26	61.33 N	12.43 E

Symbols in the index entries represent the broad categories identified in the key at the right. Symbols with superior numbers (⋏[1]) identify subcategories (see complete key on page *I · 1).*

Symbole im Register stellen die rechts im Schlüssel erklärten Kategorien dar. Symbole mit hochgestellten Ziffern (⋏[1]) bezeichnen Unterabteilungen einer Kategorie (vgl. vollständiger Schlüssel auf Seite *I · 1).*

Los símbolos incluídos en el texto del índice representan las grandes categorias identificadas con la clave a la derecha. Los símbolos con numeros en su parte superior (⋏[1]) identifican las subcategorías (véase la clave completa en la página *I · 1).*

Les symboles de l'index représentent les catégories indiquées dans la légende à droite. Les symboles suivis d'un indice (⋏[1]) représentent des sous-catégories (voir légende complète à la page *I · 1).*

Os símbolos incluídos no texto do índice representam as grandes categorias identificadas com a chave à direita. Os símbolos com números em sua parte superior (⋏[1]) identificam as subcategorias (veja-se a chave completa à página *I · 1).*

∧ Mountain	Berg	Montaña	Montagne	Montanha
⋏ Mountains	Gebirge	Montañas	Montagnes	Montanhas
)(Pass	Paß	Paso	Col	Passo
V Valley, Canyon	Tal, Cañon	Valle, Cañón	Vallée, Canyon	Vale, Canhão
≚ Plain	Ebene	Llano	Plaine	Planície
› Cape	Kap	Cabo	Cap	Cabo
I Island	Insel	Isla	Île	Ilha
II Islands	Inseln	Islas	Îles	Ilhas
⊥ Other Topographic Features	Andere Topographische Objekte	Otros Elementos Topográficos	Autres données topographiques	Outros acidentes topográficos

ESPAÑOL Nombre	Página	Lat.°′	Long.°′ W = Oeste

FRANÇAIS Nom	Page	Lat.°′	Long.°′ W = Ouest

PORTUGUÊS Nome	Página	Lat.°′	Long.°′ W = Oeste

Fuluzhen 107 29.18 N 103.40 E
Fulwood 262 53.47 N 2.41 W
Fumaça 256 22.17 S 44.19 W
Fumahashi 94 36.42 N 137.19 E
Fumane 156 24.29 S 33.58 E
Fumay 56 49.59 N 4.42 E
Fumel 32 44.29 N 0.57 E
Fumin, Zhg. 102 25.16 N 102.26 E
Fumin, Zhg. 106 31.54 N 121.10 E
Fumintun 98 42.29 N 126.22 E
Fuminzhen 106 31.37 N 121.39 E
Funa ≃ 273b 4.23 S 15.19 E
Funabashi 94 35.42 N 139.59 E
Funafuti I 14 8.31 S 179.13 E
Funagawa
→ Oga 92 39.53 N 139.51 E
Funakuyā 175d 24.30 N 124.17 E
Funan 100 32.39 N 115.32 E
Funan Gaba 144 4.25 N 37.57 E
Funaoka 96 35.23 N 134.14 E
Funasaka 270 34.48 N 135.17 E
Funäsdalen 26 62.32 N 12.33 E
Funchal 148 32.38 N 16.54 W
Funchal □[5] 148 32.40 N 16.55 W
Fundación 246 10.31 N 74.11 W
Fundão 34 40.08 N 7.30 W
Fundão, Ilha do I 287a 22.51 S 43.14 W
Funde 272c 18.54 N 72.58 E
Fundo ≃ 250 10.12 S 44.39 W
Fundo, Arroio ≃ 287a 22.58 S 43.22 W
Fundy, Bay of ⊂ 186 45.00 N 66.00 W
Fundy National Park ♠ 186 45.38 N 65.00 W
Fünfkirchen
→ Pécs 30 46.05 N 18.13 E
Funhalouro 156 23.03 S 34.25 E
Funil, Reprêsa do ⊜[1] 256 22.33 S 44.35 W
Funil, Ribeirão do ≃ 256 22.02 S 43.46 W
Funil, Rio do ≃ 256 22.58 S 44.34 W
Funing, Zhg. 98 39.54 N 119.14 E
Funing, Zhg. 100 33.47 N 119.48 E
Funing, Zhg. 102 23.33 N 105.35 E
Funiuchang 107 29.03 N 106.33 E
Funiu Shan ⋏ 100 33.40 N 112.30 E
Funk Island I 186 49.46 N 53.10 W
Funks Creek ≃ 226 39.19 N 122.11 W
Funkturm ʋ 264a 52.31 N 13.16 E
Funne ≃ 263 51.42 N 7.36 E
Funnel Creek ≃ 166 22.18 S 148.57 E
Funnel Hill ∧[2] 272c 18.54 N 73.07 E
Funo 96 34.53 N 132.47 E
Funshinagh, Lough ⊜ 48 53.31 N 8.07 W
Funsi 150 10.17 N 1.58 W
Funtana Coberta ⊥ 71 39.34 N 9.21 E
Funtua 150 11.31 N 7.17 E
Funza 246 4.40 N 74.09 W
Fuorn, Pass dal (Ofenpass))(58 46.37 N 10.15 E
Fuping 102 34.47 N 109.07 E
Fuqiao 106 31.36 N 121.12 E
Fuqikou 100 29.44 N 117.48 E
Fuqing 100 25.44 N 119.22 E
Fuquay-Varina 192 35.35 N 78.48 W
Füramoos 58 48.00 N 9.53 E
Furancungo 154 14.55 S 33.35 E
Furano 92a 43.21 N 142.24 E
Furāt, Nahr al-
→ Euphrates ≃ 128 31.00 N 47.25 E
Furci Siculo 70 37.57 N 15.23 E
Furculești 38 43.52 N 25.09 E
Fures 62 45.19 N 5.30 E
Fūrg 128 28.18 N 55.13 E
Furkapass)(58 46.34 N 8.25 E
Furka-Tunnel ◆[5] 58 46.33 N 8.26 E
Furlong 208 40.18 N 75.05 W
Furmanov 80 57.15 N 41.07 E
Furmanovka 86 44.17 N 72.57 E
Furmanovo 80 49.42 N 49.28 E
Furn, Wādī al- V 142 30.13 N 31.40 E
Furnace 46 56.09 N 5.10 W
Furnace Brook ≃ 283 42.06 N 70.43 W
Furnace Creek ≃ 284b 39.11 N 76.35 W
Furnace Pond ⊜ 283 42.03 N 70.49 W
Furnari 70 38.07 N 15.08 E
Furnas, Reprêsa de ⊜[1] 255 20.45 S 46.00 W
Furn ash-Shubbāk 132 33.52 N 35.31 E
Furneaux Group II 166 40.10 S 148.05 E
Furness Abbey ʋ[1] 44 54.07 N 3.12 W
Furness Fells ⋏[2] 44 54.18 N 3.07 W
Furnes
→ Veurne 50 51.04 N 2.40 E
Furong Shan ∧ 100 27.30 N 115.52 E
Furqlus 130 34.36 N 37.05 E
Fürstenau, Dtsch. 52 51.50 N 9.19 E
Fürstenau, Dtsch. 52 52.31 N 7.40 E
Fürstenberg, Dtsch. 52 51.44 N 9.24 E
Fürstenberg, Dtsch. 54 52.09 N 14.40 E
Fürstenberg/Havel 54 53.11 N 13.08 E
Fürstenfeld 61 47.03 N 16.05 E
Fürstenfeldbruck 60 48.10 N 11.15 E
Fürstenhagen 56 51.12 N 9.41 E
Fürstenstein 60 48.43 N 13.20 E
Fürstenwalde 54 52.21 N 14.04 E
Fürstenwerder 54 53.24 N 13.34 E
Fürstenzell 60 48.32 N 13.19 E
Furtei 71 39.34 N 8.57 E
Fürth, Dtsch. 56 49.28 N 10.59 E
Fürth, Dtsch. 56 49.39 N 8.47 E
Furth im Wald 60 49.18 N 12.51 E
Furtwangen 58 48.03 N 8.12 E
Furuba ≃ 256 23.21 S 44.57 W
Furubō-san ∧[2] 270 34.53 N 135.19 E
Furudal 26 61.10 N 15.08 E
Furudono 94 37.05 N 140.34 E
Furukawa, Nihon 92 38.34 N 140.58 E
Furukawa, Nihon 94 36.14 N 137.11 E
Furulund 41 55.46 N 13.04 E
Furusund 40 59.40 N 18.55 E
Furu-tone ≃ 94 35.48 N 139.51 E
Furuvik 40 60.39 N 17.20 E
Furuyakami 268 35.55 N 139.32 E
Fürwiggestausee ⊜[1] 263 51.09 N 7.41 E
Fury and Hecla Strait ʊ 176 69.56 N 84.00 W
Fusagasugá 246 4.21 N 74.22 W
Fusain ≃ 50 48.09 N 2.45 E
Fusan
→ Pusan 98 35.06 N 129.03 E
Fuscaldo 68 39.25 N 16.02 E
Fusch 64 47.13 N 12.49 E
Fuschl am See 64 47.48 N 13.18 E
Fuschun
→ Fushun 104 41.52 N 123.53 E
Fuse 268 35.53 N 140.00 E
Fuse
→ Higashiōsaka 96 34.39 N 135.35 E
Fushan, Zhg. 98 37.29 N 121.16 E
Fushan, Zhg. 102 35.58 N 111.51 E
Fushan, Zhg. 106 31.49 N 120.46 E
Fushimi ◆[8] 270 34.55 N 135.46 E
Fushino ≃ 96 34.03 N 131.24 E
Fushuigang 100 31.21 N 113.40 E
Fushun (Funan), Zhg. 104 41.52 N 123.53 E
Fushun, Zhg. 107 29.11 N 105.00 E
Fushuncheng 104 41.53 N 123.51 E
Fusignano 66 44.28 N 11.57 E
Fusilier 184 51.51 N 109.46 W
Fusine in Valromana 64 46.30 N 13.39 E
Fusin
→ Fuxin 104 42.03 N 121.46 E
Fusio 58 46.27 N 8.40 E
Fusō 94 35.21 N 136.55 E
Fusong 98 42.18 N 127.20 E
Fussa 94 35.45 N 139.20 E
Füssen 64 47.34 N 10.42 E
Fuste, Picacho del ∧ 196 27.35 N 102.47 W
Fusui 102 22.32 N 107.56 E
Futa, Passo della)(66 44.05 N 11.17 E
Futaba 94 35.41 N 138.30 E
Futago-san ∧ 96 33.35 N 131.36 E
Futamatagawa ◆[8] 268 35.28 N 139.33 E
Futamata
→ Tenryū 94 34.52 N 137.49 E
Futami, Nihon 94 34.30 N 136.47 E
Futami, Nihon 96 33.41 N 132.38 E
Futang, Zhg. 102 24.26 N 112.09 E
Futang, Zhg. 106 30.40 N 119.35 E
Futaoi-jima I 96 34.06 N 130.47 E
Futatabi-yama ∧ 270 34.43 N 135.11 E
Futatsubashi ◆[8] 268 35.28 N 139.30 E
Futatsu-ne I[2] 174f 24.46 N 141.18 E
Fu Tau Pun Chau I 271d 22.21 N 114.22 E
Futian 100 27.26 N 114.56 E
Futianhe 100 31.30 N 115.05 E
Futianpu 100 27.22 N 112.47 E
Futjāni ≃ 126 24.06 N 90.09 E
Futschou
→ Fuzhou 100 26.06 N 119.17 E
Futtsu, Nihon 94 35.19 N 139.49 E
Futtsu, Nihon 94 35.13 N 139.52 E
Futtsu-misaki › 268 35.19 N 139.46 E
Futun ≃ 100 26.51 N 117.46 E
Futuna I 175f 19.32 S 170.14 E
Futuna, Île I 14 14.15 S 178.09 W
Futuyu 105 39.18 N 114.50 E
Fuveau 62 43.27 N 5.34 E
Fuwah 142 31.12 N 30.33 E
Fuwen 86 47.13 N 89.39 E
Fuxi, Zhg. 100 27.14 N 119.50 E
Fuxi, Zhg. 100 25.14 N 113.52 E
Fuxi ≃ 107 29.09 N 104.57 E
Fuxian (Wafangdian), Zhg. 98 39.37 N 122.01 E
Fuxian, Zhg. 102 36.02 N 109.13 E
Fuxian Hu ⊜ 102 24.30 N 102.55 E
Fuxin, Zhg. 104 42.08 N 121.45 E
Fuxin, Zhg. 104 42.03 N 121.46 E
Fuxing, Zhg. 107 30.24 N 104.53 E
Fuxing, Zhg. 107 29.54 N 105.43 E
Fuxing, Zhg. 107 30.27 N 106.04 E
Fuxingchang 107 29.40 N 105.13 E
Fuxing Dao I 269b 31.17 N 121.23 E
Fuxinghao 104 42.35 N 120.32 E
Fuyang, Zhg. 100 32.54 N 115.49 E
Fuyang, Zhg. 100 30.03 N 119.57 E
Fuyang, Zhg. 100 23.36 N 116.37 E
Fuyang ≃ 98 38.14 N 116.05 E
Fuyouertuo Shan ∧ 89 45.52 N 119.48 E
Fuyu, Zhg. 89 47.49 N 124.27 E
Fuyu, Zhg. 89 45.10 N 124.50 E
Fuyuan, Zhg. 89 48.21 N 134.18 E
Fuyuan, Zhg. 102 25.39 N 104.12 E
Fuzhai 100 29.32 N 120.02 E
Fuzhong 102 24.28 N 111.22 E
Fuzhou, Zhg. 100 28.01 N 116.20 E
Fuzhou (Foochow), Zhg. 100 26.06 N 119.17 E
Fuzhoucheng 98 39.45 N 121.47 E
Fuzhuang 98 34.57 N 118.17 E
Fuzhuangyi 98 38.02 N 116.08 E
Fyfield 260 51.45 N 0.16 E
Fylde □[8] 262 53.46 N 2.53 W
Fylde ›[1] 262 53.47 N 2.56 W
Fylland ›[1] 41 56.00 N 9.15 E
Fyn □[6] 41 55.20 N 10.25 E
Fyn I 41 55.20 N 10.30 E
Fyne, Loch ⊂ 46 56.00 N 5.24 W
Fyns Hoved › 41 55.37 N 10.36 E
Fyresvatn ⊜ 26 59.06 N 8.12 E
Fyrisån ≃ 40 59.47 N 17.39 E
Fysingen ⊜ 40 59.34 N 17.55 E
Fyvie 46 57.25 N 2.23 W
Fzâra, Gara'et ⊜ 36 36.47 N 7.30 E

G

Ga 150 9.47 N 2.30 W
Gaaden 264b 48.03 N 16.12 E
Gaalkacyo 144 6.47 N 47.26 E
Gaanderen 52 51.56 N 6.21 E
Gabah 144 8.08 N 50.02 E
Gabai 146 11.05 N 11.39 E
Gabaldon 116 15.28 N 121.19 E
Gabare 38 43.19 N 23.55 E
Gabarus 186 45.50 N 60.09 W
Gabarus Bay ⊂ 186 45.51 N 60.07 W
Gabas ≃ 32 43.46 N 0.42 W
Gabbs 204 38.52 N 117.55 W
Gabby Heights 214 40.09 N 80.15 W
Gabela 152 10.48 S 14.20 E
Gaberones
→ Gaborone 156 24.45 S 25.55 E
Gabès 148 33.53 N 10.07 E
Gabès □[8] 148 33.15 N 9.00 E
Gabès, Golfe de ⊂ 148 34.00 N 10.25 E
Gabia 152 4.34 S 17.07 E
Gabiarra 255 16.15 S 39.41 W
Gabicce Mare 66 43.58 N 12.46 E
Gabii ⊥ 267a 41.54 N 12.43 E
Gabil 146 11.09 N 18.12 E
Gabilan Creek ≃ 226 36.41 N 121.38 W
Gabilan Range ⋏ 226 36.30 N 121.15 W
Gąbin 30 52.25 N 19.44 E
Gabir 140 8.35 N 24.40 E
Gable Mountain ∧ 182 54.30 N 121.40 W
Gablenz 54 51.41 N 14.31 E
Gablingen 58 48.27 N 10.49 E
Gablitz 61 48.14 N 16.09 E
Gablonz
→ Jablonec nad Nisou 30 50.44 N 15.10 E
Gabon □[1], Afr. 138 1.00 S 11.45 E
Gabon □[1], Afr. 152 1.00 S 11.45 E
Gabon, Estuaire du ⊂[1] 152 0.25 N 9.20 E
Gaborone 156 24.45 S 25.55 E
Gabras 140 10.16 N 26.14 E
Gabria 64 45.52 N 13.34 E
Gabriel 250 11.14 S 41.53 W
Gabriel Strait ʊ 176 61.45 N 65.30 W
Gabriel y Galan, Embalse de ⊜[1] 34 40.15 N 6.15 W
Gabriel Zamora 234 19.05 N 102.05 W
Gābrīk 128 25.44 N 58.28 E
Gabriola 224 49.12 N 123.50 W
Gabriola Island I 224 49.10 N 123.47 W
Gabrovo 38 42.52 N 25.19 E
Gabun
→ Gabon □[1] 152 1.00 S 11.45 E
Gaby 62 45.43 N 7.53 E
Gacé 50 48.48 N 0.18 E
Gachetá 246 4.49 N 73.36 W
Gachpar 174q 9.33 N 138.10 E
Gachsārān 128 30.12 N 50.47 E
Gackle 198 46.37 N 99.08 W
Gacko 38 43.10 N 18.32 E
Gad'ač 78 50.22 N 34.00 E
Gadag 122 15.25 N 75.37 E
Gadamai 140 17.09 N 36.06 E
Gādarwāra 124 22.55 N 78.47 E
Gadbjerg 41 55.46 N 9.20 E
Gäddede 26 64.30 N 14.09 E
Gadderbaum 52 52.00 N 8.31 E
Gade ≃ 260 51.38 N 0.28 W
Gadebusch 54 53.42 N 11.07 E
Gadein 140 8.11 N 28.44 E
Gadera ≃ 64 46.47 N 11.54 E
Gadevang 41 55.58 N 12.18 E
Gadilovići 76 53.05 N 30.16 E
Gadis ≃ 114 1.03 N 98.55 E
Gadmen 58 46.44 N 8.21 E
Gado Bravo, Ilha do I 250 10.54 S 42.52 W
Gádor 34 36.57 N 2.29 W
Gadra 120 25.40 N 70.37 E
Gadrut 84 39.32 N 47.02 E
Gadsden, Al., U.S. 194 34.00 N 86.00 W
Gadsden, Az., U.S. 200 32.33 N 114.47 W
Gadwāl 122 16.14 N 77.48 E
Gadzi 152 4.47 N 16.42 E
Gaerwen 44 53.13 N 4.16 W
Găești 38 44.43 N 25.19 E
Gaeta 66 41.12 N 13.35 E
Gaeta, Golfo di ⊂ 66 41.06 N 13.30 E
Gaferut I 108 9.14 N 145.23 E
Gaffney 192 35.04 N 81.39 W
Gafour 36 36.18 N 9.19 E
Gafsa 148 34.25 N 8.48 E
Gafsa □[8] 148 34.15 N 8.25 E
Gafurov 85 40.14 N 69.44 E
Gag, Pulau I 164 0.27 S 129.52 E
Gagal 146 9.01 N 15.08 E
Gagarawa 150 12.25 N 9.32 E
Gagarin 76 55.33 N 35.00 E
Gage 196 36.18 N 99.45 W
Gagere ≃ 150 13.21 N 6.23 E
Gages Lake 278 42.21 N 87.59 W
Gages Lake ⊜ 278 42.21 N 88.00 W
Gagetown 186 45.47 N 66.09 W
Gagetown, Canadian Forces Base ■ 186 45.43 N 66.15 W
Gaggenau 56 48.48 N 8.19 E
Gaggi 70 37.51 N 15.13 E
Gaggiano 62 45.24 N 9.02 E
Gaghamni 140 11.41 N 28.19 E
Gagil Tamil I 174q 9.32 N 138.10 E
Gagino 80 55.14 N 45.02 E
Gagliano Castelferrato 70 37.43 N 14.32 E
Gagliano del Capo 68 39.50 N 18.22 E
Gagnef 40 60.35 N 15.04 E
Gagnia 152 1.28 S 16.02 E
Gagnoa 150 6.08 N 5.56 W
Gagnon 176 51.53 N 68.10 W
Gagnon, Lac ⊜ 206 46.07 N 75.07 W
Gagny 261 48.53 N 2.32 E
Gagra 84 43.20 N 40.15 E
Gagret 123 31.40 N 76.04 E
Gahanna 218 40.01 N 82.52 W
Gahlen 52 51.40 N 6.52 E
Gaiarine 64 45.52 N 12.29 E
Gaibandha 124 25.19 N 89.33 E
Gaichtpass)(58 47.27 N 10.37 E
Gaigalava 76 56.40 N 27.18 E
Gaighāta 126 22.56 N 88.44 E
Gaijiatun 104 40.50 N 122.37 E
Gail 196 32.46 N 101.27 W
Gail ≃ 64 46.36 N 13.53 E
Gailberg Sattel)(64 46.43 N 12.58 E
Gail Creek ≃ 222 31.07 N 95.23 W
Gaildorf 56 49.00 N 9.46 E
Gaillac 32 43.54 N 1.55 E
Gaillard, Château ⊥ 50 48.09 N 1.54 E
Gaillard, Lac ⊜ 186 50.06 N 68.47 W
Gaillard, Lake ⊜ 207 41.21 N 72.46 W
Gaillefontaine 50 49.39 N 1.37 E
Gaillimh
→ Galway 48 53.16 N 9.03 W
Gaillon, Fr. 50 49.10 N 1.20 E
Gaillon, Fr. 261 49.02 N 1.54 E
Gailtaler Alpen ⋏ 64 46.42 N 13.00 E
Gaima 164 8.20 S 142.55 E
Gaimán 254 43.17 S 65.29 W
Gaimersheim 60 48.49 N 11.22 E
Gaines, Mi., U.S. 216 42.52 N 83.54 W
Gaines, Pa., U.S. 210 41.45 N 77.34 W
Gainesboro 194 36.21 N 85.39 W
Gainesville, Fl., U.S. 192 29.39 N 82.19 W
Gainesville, Ga., U.S. 192 34.17 N 83.49 W
Gainesville, Mo., U.S. 194 36.36 N 92.25 W
Gainesville, N.Y., U.S. 210 42.38 N 78.08 W
Gainesville, Tx., U.S. 196 33.37 N 97.07 W
Gainford 44 54.32 N 1.44 W
Gainsborough, Sk., Can. 184 49.10 N 101.26 W
Gainsborough, Eng., U.K. 44 53.24 N 0.46 W
Gainsborough Creek ≃ 184 49.10 N 101.02 W
Gaiole in Chianti 66 43.28 N 11.26 E
Gairatganj 124 23.24 N 78.13 E
Gairdner ≃ 162 34.17 S 119.28 E
Gairdner, Lake ⊜ 162 31.35 S 136.00 E
Gairloch 46 57.42 N 5.40 W
Gairloch, Loch ⊂ 46 57.44 N 5.44 W
Gairn ≃ 46 57.03 N 3.05 W
Gais, It. 64 46.50 N 11.57 E
Gais, Schw. 58 47.22 N 9.27 E
Gaisberg ∧ 64 47.48 N 13.07 E
Gaisbeuren 58 47.54 N 9.43 E
Gaital, Cerro ∧ 236 8.37 N 80.07 W
Gaither 208 39.21 N 76.59 W
Gaithersburg 208 39.08 N 77.12 W
Gaixian 98 40.24 N 122.22 E
Gaizina Kalns ∧[2] 76 56.52 N 25.57 E
Gaj, Cro. 36 45.29 N 17.02 E
Gaj, Ross. 86 51.27 N 58.27 E
Gajā 272b 22.52 N 88.10 E
Gajahmungkur, Waduk ⊜[1] 115a 7.55 S 110.55 E
Gajčur ≃ 78 47.57 N 36.11 E
Gajendragarh 122 15.44 N 75.59 E
Gajiram 146 12.30 N 13.12 E
Gajny 24 60.15 N 54.15 E
Gājol 124 25.13 N 88.12 E
Gajsin 78 48.48 N 29.24 E
Gajsinghpur 123 29.40 N 73.27 E
Gajuapara ≃ 250 4.17 S 47.25 W
Gajutino 76 58.42 N 38.32 E
Gajvoron 78 48.22 N 29.52 E
Gakarosa ∧ 158 27.54 S 23.33 E
Gakona 180 62.18 N 145.18 W
Gākuch 123 36.10 N 73.45 E
Gakugsa 24 61.34 N 36.26 E
Gāla, Bngl. 126 24.18 N 89.54 E
Gala, Zhg. 124 28.16 N 89.23 E
Galaassija 128 39.52 N 64.27 E
Galāchipa 126 22.10 N 90.25 E
Galahad 182 52.31 N 111.56 W
Galamares 266c 38.48 N 9.25 W
Galán, Cerro ∧ 252 25.55 S 66.52 W
Galana ≃ 154 3.09 S 40.08 E
Galangue 152 13.48 S 16.09 E
Galanovo 80 56.09 N 54.07 E
Galanta 30 48.12 N 17.43 E
Galápagos □[4] 246a 0.30 S 90.30 W
Galápagos, Parque Nacional de ♠ 246a 0.15 S 90.15 W
Galapagos Islands
→ Colón, Archipiélago de II 246a 0.30 S 90.30 W
Galaroza 34 37.55 N 6.42 W
Galas ≃ 114 5.31 N 102.12 E
Galashiels 46 55.37 N 2.49 W
Galata ◆[8] 267b 41.01 N 28.58 E
Galata Köprüsü ◆[5] 267b 41.00 N 28.57 E
Galata Tower ʋ 267b 41.01 N 28.58 E
Galatea 172 38.25 S 176.45 E
Galați 38 45.26 N 28.03 E
Galați □[6] 38 45.45 N 27.45 E
Galatia 194 37.50 N 88.36 W
Galatia □[9] 130 39.30 N 32.40 E
Galatina 68 40.10 N 18.10 E
Galatone 68 40.09 N 18.04 E
Galatro 68 38.28 N 16.06 E
Galátsion 267c 38.01 N 23.45 E
Galatz
→ Galați 38 45.26 N 28.03 E
Galaure ≃ 62 45.11 N 4.49 E
Gala Water ≃ 46 55.37 N 2.48 W
Galax 192 36.39 N 80.55 W
Galaxídhion 38 38.22 N 22.23 E
Galbyn gov' ◆[2] 102 42.30 N 107.00 E
Galdhøpiggen ∧ 26 61.37 N 8.17 E
Gale, Lac ⊜ 190 46.46 N 76.51 W
Galeairy Lake ⊜ 212 45.29 N 78.17 W
Galeana, Méx. 232 30.07 N 107.38 W
Galeana, Méx. 232 24.50 N 100.04 W
Galeão, Aeroporto do ⊠ 256 22.50 S 43.15 W
Galeata 66 44.00 N 11.55 E
Galegu 140 12.36 N 35.02 E
Galeh Dār 128 27.38 N 52.42 E
Galela 108 1.50 N 127.50 E
Galena, Austl. 162 27.50 S 114.41 E
Galena, Ak., U.S. 180 64.44 N 156.57 W
Galena, Il., U.S. 190 42.25 N 90.25 W
Galena, In., U.S. 218 38.21 N 85.56 W
Galena, Ks., U.S. 198 37.04 N 94.38 W
Galena, Md., U.S. 208 39.20 N 75.52 W
Galena, Mo., U.S. 194 36.48 N 93.27 W
Galena, Oh., U.S. 214 40.12 N 82.52 W
Galena Park 222 29.43 N 95.13 W
Galenbecker See ⊜ 54 53.38 N 13.43 E
Galeota Point › 241r 10.08 N 60.59 W
Galera ≃ 248 14.25 S 60.07 W
Galera, Punta ›, Chile 254 39.59 S 73.43 W
Galera, Punta ›, Ec. 246 0.49 N 80.03 W
Galera, Punta de › 34 39.10 N 1.05 E
Galera Point › 241r 10.49 N 60.55 W
Galeras, Volcán ∧[1] 246 1.13 N 77.22 W
Galeria ⊥ 267a 42.02 N 12.18 E
Galeria, Fosso la ≃ 267a 41.48 N 12.21 E
Galesburg, Il., U.S. 190 40.56 N 90.22 W
Galesburg, Mi., U.S. 216 42.17 N 85.25 W
Gales Creek 224 45.35 N 123.12 W
Gales Creek ≃ 224 45.29 N 123.06 W
Gales Ferry 207 41.25 N 72.04 W
Gales Point › 283 42.33 N 70.47 W
Galesville, Md., U.S. 208 38.50 N 76.32 W
Galesville, Wi., U.S. 190 44.04 N 91.20 W
Galeton 214 41.43 N 77.38 W
Galeville 210 43.05 N 76.10 W
Galgasc 144 0.11 N 41.38 E
Galgate 44 54.00 N 2.47 W
Galguduud □[4] 144 5.00 N 46.30 E
Galheiros 255 13.18 S 46.25 W
Gali 84 42.38 N 41.44 E
Gali, Torrente de ≃ 266d 41.28 N 2.00 E
Galiano 224 48.52 N 123.21 W
Galiano Island I 224 48.56 N 123.29 W
Galibier, Col du)(62 45.04 N 6.24 E
Galič, Ross. 80 58.23 N 42.21 E
Galič, Ukr. 78 49.08 N 24.43 E
Galicia □[4] 34 42.45 N 8.00 W
Galicia □[9] 22 49.00 N 22.00 E
Galičskaja vozvyšennost' ⋏[2] 24 58.25 N 42.20 E
Galičskoje, ozero ⊜ 80 58.24 N 42.18 E
Galien 216 41.47 N 86.29 W
Galien ≃ 216 41.48 N 86.45 W
Galilee 207 41.22 N 71.30 W
Galilee, Lake ⊜ 166 22.21 S 145.48 E
Galilee, Sea of
→ Kinneret, Yam ⊜ 132 32.48 N 35.35 E
Galilee
→ HaGalil □[9] 132 32.54 N 35.20 E
Galiléia 255 19.00 S 41.33 W
Galim 152 7.06 N 12.29 E
Galina Point › 241q 18.24 N 76.53 W
Galindo Creek ≃ 282 37.58 N 122.02 W
Galion 214 40.44 N 82.47 W
Galion, Baie du ⊂ 240e 14.44 N 60.57 W
Galis 115a 7.08 S 113.33 E
Galisteo Creek ≃ 200 35.31 N 106.22 W
Galite, Canal de la ʊ 36 37.20 N 9.00 E
Galiuro Mountains ⋏ 200 32.40 N 110.20 W
Galiwinku 164 12.02 S 135.34 E
Galižana 64 44.56 N 13.52 E
Galka'yo 144 6.47 N 47.26 E
Galkhausen 263 51.05 N 6.58 E
Galkino, Kaz. 86 52.14 N 78.20 E
Galkino, Ross. 82 54.46 N 35.49 E
Galkino, Ross. 86 55.36 N 62.55 E
Gall'aaral 85 40.02 N 67.35 E
Gallan Head › 46 58.14 N 7.03 W
Gallarate 62 45.40 N 8.47 E
Gallardon 50 48.32 N 1.42 E
Gallatin, Mo., U.S. 194 39.54 N 93.57 W
Gallatin, Pa., U.S. 279b 40.12 N 79.53 W
Gallatin, Tn., U.S. 194 36.23 N 86.26 W
Gallatin, Tx., U.S. 222 31.54 N 95.09 W
Gallatin □[6] 218 38.45 N 84.51 W
Gallatin ≃ 202 45.56 N 111.29 W
Gallatin Range ⋏ 202 45.15 N 111.05 W
Galle 122 6.02 N 80.13 E
Gállego ≃ 34 41.39 N 0.51 W
Gallegos ≃ 254 51.36 S 68.59 W
Galles
→ Wales □[8] 28 52.30 N 3.30 W
Galleyend 260 51.42 N 0.29 E
Galley Head › 48 51.30 N 8.57 W
Galleywood 260 51.42 N 0.28 E
Galliano 194 29.26 N 90.17 W
Galliate 62 45.29 N 8.42 E
Gallicano 64 44.04 N 10.26 E
Gallicano nel Lazio 267a 41.52 N 12.49 E
Gallicchio 68 40.17 N 16.08 E
Gallico 68 38.10 N 15.41 E
Galliera Veneta 64 45.39 N 11.49 E
Gallinara I 62 44.02 N 8.14 E
Gallinas ≃ 196 35.10 N 104.55 W
Gallinas, Punta › 246 12.28 N 71.40 W
Gallinas Creek ≃ 282 38.01 N 122.30 W
Gallinas Peak ∧ 200 34.13 N 105.45 W
Gallio 64 45.53 N 11.33 E
Gallipoli, Austl. 166 19.10 S 137.55 E
Gallipoli, It. 68 40.03 N 17.58 E
Gallipoli
→ Gelibolu 130 40.24 N 26.40 E
Gallipoli Peninsula
→ Gelibolu Yarımadası ›[1] 130 40.20 N 26.30 E
Gallipolis 188 38.48 N 82.12 W
Gallitzin 214 40.28 N 78.33 W
Gallivaggio 58 46.21 N 9.21 E
Gällivare 24 67.07 N 20.45 E
Gallneukirchen 61 48.21 N 14.25 E
Gällö 26 62.55 N 15.14 E
Gallo, Capo › 70 38.13 N 13.19 E
Gallo, Lago del ⊜[1] 64 46.07 N 10.10 E
Gallo, Lago di ⊜[1] 58 46.37 N 10.10 E
Gallo, Laguna ⊜ 258 35.30 S 58.28 W
Gallo Arroyo V 200 33.55 N 105.00 W
Galloo Island I 212 43.54 N 76.25 W
Galloupes Point › 283 42.28 N 70.53 W
Galloway □[9] 44 55.00 N 4.25 W
Galloway, Mull of › 44 54.38 N 4.50 W
Galloway Creek ≃, Md., U.S. 284b 39.18 N 76.23 W
Galloway Creek ≃, Mi., U.S. 281 42.39 N 83.12 W
Galluis 261 48.48 N 1.48 E
Gallup 200 35.31 N 108.44 W
Gallupville 210 42.40 N 74.14 W
Gallur 34 41.52 N 1.19 W
Gallura ◆[1] 71 41.00 N 9.13 E
Gally, Ru de ≃ 261 48.53 N 1.53 E
Gälnan ʊ 40 59.31 N 18.45 E
Gålö I 40 59.05 N 18.17 E
Galop Island I 212 44.46 N 75.24 W
Galoppo, Ippodromo del ♠ 266b 45.28 N 9.07 E
Galougo 150 13.50 N 11.04 W
Galsi 126 23.20 N 87.42 E
Galston 46 55.36 N 4.24 W
Galt, Mong. 88 48.46 N 99.53 E
Galt, Ca., U.S. 226 38.15 N 121.17 W
Gal Tardo 144 3.34 N 45.58 E
Galtat Zemmour 148 25.15 N 12.20 W
Galtelli 71 40.23 N 9.37 E
Galten 41 56.09 N 9.55 E
Galten ⊂ 40 59.27 N 16.09 E
Galtür 58 46.58 N 10.11 E
Galtymore Mountain ∧ 48 52.22 N 8.10 W
Galty Mountains ⋏ 48 52.25 N 8.10 W
Galūgāh-e Āsīyeh 128 34.01 N 59.55 E
Galugur 114 2.34 N 99.39 E
Galula 154 8.36 S 33.02 E
Galunggung, Gunung ∧ 115a 7.15 S 108.03 E
Galuut 88 48.33 N 113.12 E
Galva, Il., U.S. 190 41.10 N 90.02 W
Galva, Ia., U.S. 198 42.30 N 95.25 W
Galva, Ks., U.S. 198 38.22 N 97.32 W
Galvarino 252 38.24 S 72.47 W
Galveston, In., U.S. 216 40.34 N 86.11 W
Galveston, Tx., U.S. 222 29.17 N 94.47 W
Galveston □[6] 222 29.20 N 94.53 W
Galveston Bay ⊂ 222 29.36 N 94.57 W
Galveston Island I 222 29.13 N 94.55 W
Gálvez 252 32.02 S 61.13 W
Gálvez ≃ 248 5.12 S 72.53 W
Galvin, Austl. 274b 37.51 S 144.49 E
Galvin, Wa., U.S. 224 46.44 N 123.01 W
Galway (Gaillimh), Ire. 48 53.16 N 9.03 W
Galway, N.Y., U.S. 210 43.01 N 74.02 W
Galway □[6] 48 53.20 N 9.00 W
Galway Bay ⊂ 48 53.10 N 9.15 W
Gam (Jin) ≃ 110 21.55 N 105.12 E
Gam, Pulau I 164 0.27 S 130.36 E
Gama, Isla I 254 40.29 S 62.12 W
Gamaches 50 49.59 N 1.33 E
Gamagōri 94 34.50 N 137.14 E
Gamalejevka 80 52.16 N 53.26 E
Gamaliel 194 36.38 N 85.47 W
Ga-Mankoeng 156 23.57 S 29.42 E
Gamare, Lake ⊜ 144 11.30 N 41.40 E
Gamarra 246 8.20 N 73.45 W
Gamawa 146 12.08 N 10.32 E
Gamay 116 12.23 N 125.18 E
Gamay Bay ⊂ 116 12.21 N 125.21 E
Gamba 120 28.17 N 88.32 E
Gambach 56 50.28 N 8.44 E
Gambaga 150 10.32 N 0.26 W
Gambais 261 48.46 N 1.40 E
Gambaiseuil 261 48.45 N 1.44 E
Gambang 114 3.43 N 103.06 E
Gambara, It. 64 45.15 N 10.18 E
Gámbara, Méx. 234 18.55 N 102.05 W
Gambarie 68 38.10 N 15.50 E
Gambassi 66 43.32 N 10.57 E
Gambatesa 66 41.30 N 14.54 E
Gambela 144 8.18 N 34.37 E
Gambell 180 63.46 N 171.46 W
Gambellara 64 45.28 N 11.20 E
Gamber 208 39.27 N 76.56 W
Gambia □[1], Afr. 134 13.30 N 15.30 W
Gambia □[1], Afr. 150 13.30 N 15.30 W
Gambia (Gambie) ≃ 150 13.28 N 16.34 W
Gambi Atrash 140 10.03 N 33.47 E
Gambie (Gambia) ≃ 150 13.28 N 16.34 W
Gambie
→ Gambia □[1] 150 13.30 N 15.30 W
Gambier 214 40.22 N 82.23 W
Gambier, Îles II 6 21.20 S 136.30 W
Gamble Mansion State Historic Site ⊥ 220 27.32 N 82.32 W
Gambo, Nf., Can. 186 48.46 N 54.14 W
Gambo, Centraf. 152 4.39 N 22.16 E
Gamboa 236 9.07 N 79.42 W
Gamboli 120 29.50 N 68.26 E
Gambolò 62 45.15 N 8.51 E
Gamboma 152 1.53 S 15.51 E
Gamboula 152 4.08 N 15.09 E
Gambrill State Park ♠ 208 39.30 N 77.30 W
Gamchab ≃ 156 28.15 S 17.26 E
Gamé 150 6.44 N 1.11 E
Game Creek ≃ 285 39.41 N 75.28 W
Gamen-See ⊜ 264a 52.40 N 13.51 E
Gaming 61 47.56 N 15.06 E
Gamka ≃ 158 33.18 S 21.39 E
Gamlakarleby
→ Kokkola 26 63.50 N 23.07 E
Gamla Uppsala 40 59.54 N 17.38 E
Gamleby 26 57.54 N 16.24 E
Gamlitz 61 46.43 N 15.33 E
Gammel Estrup ⊥ 26 56.26 N 10.21 E
Gammelstad ʋ[1] 26 65.38 N 22.01 E
Gammertingen 58 48.15 N 9.13 E
Gammon ≃ 184 51.07 N 95.09 W
Gammon, Point › 207 41.36 N 70.16 W
Gammon Ranges National Park ♠ 166 30.29 S 139.10 E
Gamō, Nihon 94 35.03 N 136.11 E
Gamō, Nihon 268 35.52 N 139.48 E
Gamoep 158 29.55 S 18.25 E
Ga-Mogara ≃ 158 27.07 S 22.57 E
Gamo Gofa □[4] 144 5.45 N 37.00 E
Gamon 150 13.20 N 12.55 W
Gamova, mys › 89 42.35 N 131.12 E
Gamph, Slieve ⋏ 48 54.05 N 9.00 W
Gampoko 273b 4.16 S 15.10 E
Gampola 122 7.10 N 80.34 E
Gampongbatak 114 4.48 N 97.39 E
Gampoui 273b 4.08 S 15.22 E
Gams 58 47.12 N 9.28 E
Gamsfeld ∧ 64 47.37 N 13.29 E
Gamtoos ≃ 158 33.58 S 25.01 E
Gamud ∧ 144 4.05 N 38.03 E
G'amyš, gora ∧ 84 40.18 N 46.23 E
Gan ≃, Zhg. 89 49.12 N 125.14 E
Gan ≃, Zhg. 100 29.12 N 116.00 E
Ganado, Az., U.S. 200 35.42 N 109.32 W
Ganado, Tx., U.S. 222 29.02 N 96.31 W
Ganano ≃ 116 16.45 N 121.44 E
Gananoque 212 44.20 N 76.10 W
Gananoque ≃ 212 44.19 N 76.09 W
Gananoque Lake ⊜ 212 44.27 N 76.09 W
Ganaraska ≃ 212 43.57 N 78.18 W
Ganargua Creek ≃ 210 43.04 N 77.00 W
Ganassi 116 7.49 N 124.06 E
Ganāveh 128 29.34 N 50.31 E
Gancevići 76 52.45 N 26.26 E
Ganchangba 107 28.52 N 103.41 E
Ganči 85 39.58 N 69.08 E
Ganda, Ang. 152 13.02 S 14.40 E
Ganda, Zaïre 152 4.05 N 23.32 E
Gandadiwata, Bulu ∧ 112 2.42 S 119.27 E
Gandajika 152 6.45 S 23.57 E
Gandak (Nārāyaṇi) ≃ 124 25.39 N 85.13 E
Gaṇḍakī □[8] 124 28.15 N 84.15 E
Gandara 258 35.26 S 58.06 W
Ganda Singhwāla 123 31.02 N 74.31 E
Gandāva 120 28.37 N 67.29 E
Gandavaroyi Falls ᒐ 154 17.17 S 29.07 E
Gānde 126 24.10 N 86.26 E
Gander 186 48.57 N 54.37 W
Gander ≃ 186 49.15 N 54.30 W
Gander Bay 186 49.18 N 54.29 W
Gander Bay ⊂ 186 49.25 N 54.28 W
Ganderkesee 52 53.02 N 8.32 E
Gander Lake ⊜ 186 48.55 N 54.40 W
Gandesa 34 41.03 N 0.26 E
Gandevi 120 20.49 N 72.59 E
Gand
→ Gent 50 51.03 N 3.43 E
Gāndhinagar 120 23.12 N 72.40 E
Gāndhi Sāgar ⊜[1] 120 24.18 N 75.21 E
Gandi 150 12.55 N 5.49 E
Gandi, Wādī V 140 11.23 N 24.31 E
Gandia 34 38.58 N 0.11 W
Gandino 62 45.49 N 9.54 E
Gando 152 12.30 S 17.25 E
Gandole 146 8.26 N 11.34 E
Gandou 152 2.24 N 17.27 E
Gandrange 56 49.16 N 6.08 E
Gandria 58 46.01 N 9.00 E
Gandu 255 13.45 S 39.30 W
Gandy Bridge ◆[5] 220 27.53 N 82.34 W
G'andžačaj ≃ 84 40.54 N 46.28 E
Ganfang 100 28.40 N 114.51 E
Ganfosi 107 29.36 N 104.03 E
Gangādharpur 272b 22.36 N 88.11 E
Gangafani 150 14.23 N 2.24 W
Ganga
→ Ganges ≃ 124 23.22 N 90.32 E
Gangājalghāti 126 23.25 N 87.07 E
Gangala-Na-Bodio 154 3.41 N 29.08 E
Gangalingolo 273b 4.20 S 15.09 E
Gan Gan 254 42.30 S 68.16 W
Gangānagar 123 29.55 N 73.53 E
Gangāpur, India 120 25.13 N 74.16 E
Gangāpur, India 122 19.41 N 75.01 E
Gangāpur, India 124 26.29 N 76.43 E
Gangara, Niger 150 14.36 N 8.30 E
Gangara, Niger 150 13.33 N 7.14 E
Gangārāmpur 124 25.24 N 88.31 E
Ganga Sāgar 126 21.38 N 88.05 E
Gangaw 110 22.11 N 94.07 E
Gangāwati 122 15.26 N 76.32 E
Gangaw Range ⋏ 110 24.50 N 96.40 E
Ganga-Yamuna Doāb ⋏[1] 124 26.40 N 79.30 E
Gangcheng 98 35.52 N 116.52 E
Gangdaba, Tchabal ∧ 152 7.44 N 12.45 E
Gangdhār 120 23.57 N 75.37 E
Gangdisê Shan ⋏ 120 31.00 N 82.00 E
Gangelt 56 50.59 N 5.59 E
Ganges, B.C., Can. 224 48.51 N 123.30 W
Ganges, Fr. 62 43.56 N 3.42 E
Ganges (Ganga) (Padma) ≃ 124 23.22 N 90.32 E
Ganges, Mouths of the ≃[1] 120 22.00 N 89.00 E
Ganges Delta ≚[2] 124 23.00 N 89.00 E
Ganghu 120 32.05 N 86.45 E
Gangi 70 37.49 N 14.13 E
Gangkofen 60 48.26 N 12.34 E
Gangkou, Zhg. 100 29.45 N 115.44 E
Gangkou, Zhg. 100 29.21 N 117.58 E
Gangkou, Zhg. 100 22.38 N 113.22 E
Gangkou, Zhg. 100 22.36 N 114.54 E
Gangkou, Zhg. 100 29.12 N 113.19 E
Gangkou, Zhg. 106 30.44 N 118.54 E
Gangkouzhen 106 31.45 N 120.40 E
Gangmar Co ⊜ 120 33.46 N 84.15 E
Gang Mills 210 42.08 N 77.06 W
Gāngnāpur 126 23.09 N 88.38 E
Gangneung
→ Kangnŭng 98 37.45 N 128.54 E
Gango ≃ 152 9.48 S 15.40 E
Gangoa 102 37.15 N 100.28 E
Gangoh 124 29.46 N 77.15 E
Gangotri, India 120 30.56 N 79.02 E
Gangotri, India 120 31.01 N 78.27 E
Gangou 98 40.30 N 119.27 E
Gangoumen 98 41.40 N 116.35 E
Gangouyi 102 36.01 N 105.03 E
Gangqiao 107 30.13 N 105.22 E
Gang Ranch 182 51.33 N 122.20 W
Gangshangji 100 28.06 N 116.30 E
Gangtok 124 27.20 N 88.37 E
Gangtou 98 38.04 N 113.56 E
Gangtouli 106 31.42 N 119.02 E
Gangu 102 34.45 N 105.20 E
Gangwa, Zaïre 152 3.30 S 20.55 E
Gangwa, Zhg. 105 39.48 N 116.10 E
Gangwei 100 24.20 N 118.01 E
Ganhezi 86 44.08 N 88.32 E
Ganhu 102 44.33 N 94.09 E
Gani 164 0.47 S 128.13 E
Ganišob 85 39.03 N 70.47 E
Ganj Dundwara 124 27.44 N 78.57 E
Ganjiang 107 29.42 N 103.38 E
Ganlan Shan ∧ 124 29.54 N 90.02 E
Ganlu 106 31.32 N 120.35 E
Ganluchang 107 29.54 N 104.47 E
Ganluo 102 29.03 N 102.59 E
Gannahoek 158 26.44 S 24.08 E
Gannan 89 47.54 N 123.30 E
Gannano, Lago di ⊜ 68 40.19 N 16.26 E
Gannapan 158 30.23 S 22.12 E
Gannat 32 46.06 N 3.12 E
Gannett Peak ∧ 200 43.11 N 109.39 W
Gannovka 83 48.33 N 38.35 E
Gannvalley 198 44.02 N 98.59 W
Ganpingsi 102 35.13 N 102.30 E
Ganpu 106 30.24 N 120.53 E
Ganq 120 37.25 N 92.15 E
Ganquan 102 36.25 N 109.16 E
Gansbaai 158 34.35 S 19.22 E
Gänsbrunnen 58 47.16 N 7.28 E
Gänserndorf 61 48.20 N 16.43 E
Gansevoort 210 43.12 N 73.39 W
Ganspan 158 27.57 S 24.47 E
Gansu (Kansu) □[4] 102 37.00 N 103.00 E
Ganta 150 7.15 N 8.59 W
Gantan 100 29.37 N 119.34 E
Gantang, Zhg. 100 26.56 N 119.40 E
Gantang, Zhg. 102 22.58 N 109.00 E
Gantao ≃ 98 38.01 N 114.07 E
Gante
→ Gent 50 51.03 N 3.43 E
Gantheaume, Cape › 166 36.05 S 137.27 E
Gantheaume Bay ⊂ 162 27.44 S 114.07 E
Gantheaume Point › 162 17.59 S 122.10 E
Gantiadi 84 43.24 N 40.06 E
Gantian 100 27.30 N 113.10 E
Gantt 194 31.24 N 86.29 W
Gantung 112 2.58 S 108.09 E
Gantung, Mount ∧ 116 8.57 N 117.48 E
Gan'uškino 80 46.36 N 49.16 E
Ganwo 150 11.13 N 4.42 E
Ganxi, Zhg. 100 28.08 N 118.06 E
Ganxi, Zhg. 102 29.02 N 109.32 E
Ganyanchi 102 36.39 N 105.18 E
Ganyesa 158 26.35 S 24.10 E
Ganyu (Qing Kou) 98 34.52 N 119.10 E
Ganzê 102 31.40 N 100.01 E
Ganzhenyi 100 30.33 N 113.21 E
Ganzhou, Zhg. 100 25.54 N 114.55 E
Ganzhou, Zhg. 100 28.49 N 115.25 E
Ganzhou
→ Zhangye 102 38.56 N 100.27 E
Ganzhuermiao 88 48.24 N 118.08 E
Ganzlin 54 53.23 N 12.15 E
Ganzo Azul 248 8.51 S 74.44 W
Gao 150 16.16 N 0.03 W
Gao □[4] 150 18.00 N 1.30 E
Gao'an 100 28.25 N 115.22 E
Gaobaita 271a 39.53 N 116.30 E
Gaobei 100 26.37 N 114.38 E
Gaobeidian 271a 39.54 N 116.33 E
Gaobu 100 27.48 N 117.01 E
Gaochang 107 28.49 N 104.24 E
Gaocheng, Zhg. 98 38.04 N 114.49 E
Gaocheng, Zhg. 100 31.57 N 113.25 E
Gaocheng, Zhg. 106 31.28 N 119.48 E
Gaochengzhai 104 41.24 N 123.43 E
Gaochun 106 31.20 N 118.52 E
Gaocun 98 37.05 N 122.12 E
Gaodianzi 102 30.40 N 110.01 E
Gao Feng ∧ 106 30.34 N 118.40 E
Gaogongmiao 100 33.25 N 115.53 E
Gaogou 100 34.03 N 119.15 E
Gaohe 100 22.47 N 112.57 E
Gaohebu 100 30.44 N 116.50 E
Gaoil, Sliabh ∧ 46 55.55 N 5.28 W
Gaojiabu 102 38.30 N 110.11 E
Gaojiadi 98 41.33 N 114.58 E
Gaojiadian 98 42.40 N 124.28 E
Gaojian 100 29.04 N 121.14 E
Gaojiapuzi 104 41.22 N 123.36 E
Gaojiaqiao 106 30.43 N 120.38 E
Gaojiatun 104 41.06 N 121.19 E
Gaojiawopeng 104 41.28 N 122.10 E
Gaojiawopu 104 41.50 N 122.47 E
Gaojiazhai 269b 31.23 N 121.33 E
Gaojiazhen 102 30.05 N 107.51 E
Gaokan 104 40.46 N 122.23 E
Gaokeng 100 27.40 N 113.58 E
Gaolan 102 36.25 N 103.56 E
Gaolan Dao I 100 21.55 N 113.15 E
Gaolao 104 41.54 N 120.59 E
Gaoli 105 39.17 N 115.38 E
Gaoliang 107 29.45 N 105.15 E
Gaoliban 104 41.39 N 121.58 E

	English	Deutsch	Español	Français	Português
≃	River	Fluß	Río	Rivière	Rio
≅	Canal	Kanal	Canal	Canal	Canal
ᒐ	Waterfall, Rapids	Wasserfall, Stromschnellen	Cascada, Rápidos	Chute d'eau, Rapides	Cascata, Rápidos
ʊ	Strait	Meeresstraße	Estrecho	Détroit	Estreito
⊂	Bay, Gulf	Bucht, Golf	Bahía, Golfo	Baie, Golfe	Baía, Golfo
⊜	Lake, Lakes	See, Seen	Lago, Lagos	Lac, Lacs	Lago, Lagos
≡	Swamp	Sumpf	Pantano	Marais	Pântano
⊓	Ice Features, Glacier	Eis- und Gletscherformen	Accidentes Glaciales	Formes glaciaires	Acidentes glaciares
⫪	Other Hydrographic Features	Andere Hydrographische Objekte	Otros Elementos Hidrográficos	Autres données hydrographiques	Outros acidentes hidrográficos
✣	Submarine Features	Untermeerische Objekte	Accidentes Submarinos	Formes de relief sous-marin	Acidentes submarinos
□	Political Unit	Politische Einheit	Unidad Politica	Entité politique	Unidade política
ʋ	Cultural Institution	Kulturelle Institution	Institución Cultural	Institution culturelle	Institução cultural
⊥	Historical Site	Historische Stätte	Sitio Histórico	Site historique	Sitio histórico
♠	Recreational Site	Erholungs- und Ferienort	Sitio de Recreo	Centre de loisirs	Area de Lazer
⊠	Airport	Flughafen	Aeropuerto	Aéroport	Aeroporto
■	Military Installation	Militäranlage	Instalación Militar	Installation militaire	Instalação militar
◆	Miscellaneous	Verschiedenes	Misceláneo	Divers	Diversos

Gaolifangshen 104 42.27 N 123.21 E
Gaolimen 98 40.22 N 124.02 E
Gaoling 105 40.32 N 117.01 E
Gaolinying 105 39.06 N 115.38 E
Gaoliying 105 40.10 N 116.29 E
Gaoliyingzi 104 41.56 N 124.17 E
Gaolong 100 26.56 N 113.45 E
Gaolou 105 39.59 N 116.50 E
Gaolouchang, Zhg. 107 29.51 N 104.41 E
Gaolouchang, Zhg. 107 30.03 N 105.58 E
Gaoluo 98 37.27 N 113.55 E
Gaomi 98 36.23 N 119.44 E
Gaona 252 25.12 S 64.05 W
Gaopi 100 24.14 N 116.39 E
Gaoping, Zhg. 102 35.48 N 112.52 E
Gaoping, Zhg. 107 30.28 N 105.45 E
Gaopingba 107 30.47 N 106.06 E
Gaoqiao, Zhg. 100 30.08 N 119.56 E
Gaoqiao, Zhg. 100 26.36 N 117.46 E
Gaoqiao, Zhg. 102 28.06 N 106.36 E
Gaoqiao, Zhg. 106 32.14 N 119.38 E
Gaoqiao, Zhg. 106 31.21 N 121.34 E
Gaoqiaomen 106 32.01 N 118.51 E
Gaoqiaozhen 104 40.55 N 121.00 E
Gaoqing (Tianzhen) 98 37.11 N 117.47 E
Gaoqipu 104 41.32 N 121.40 E
Gaosha 100 26.27 N 117.56 E
Gaoshaling 105 38.51 N 117.36 E
Gaoshan, Zhg. 100 25.29 N 119.34 E
Gaoshan, Zhg. 107 29.26 N 104.28 E
Gaoshanbao 105 40.40 N 117.29 E
Gaoshangbao 98 39.11 N 118.30 E
Gaoshanpu 102 27.10 N 105.14 E
Gaoshantai 104 42.22 N 122.28 E
Gaoshanzi 104 41.34 N 122.02 E
Gaoshengchang 107 29.59 N 105.31 E
Gaoshengzhen 104 41.20 N 122.12 E
Gaoshi 107 29.36 N 104.44 E
Gaoshikan 107 29.12 N 105.04 E
Gaosichang 107 30.17 N 104.52 E
Gaotai 102 39.20 N 99.58 E
Gaotaishan 104 42.02 N 122.52 E
Gaotan, Zhg. 100 30.23 N 117.23 E
Gaotan, Zhg. 100 23.12 N 115.12 E
Gaotan, Zhg. 102 32.22 N 108.36 E
Gaotang 98 36.54 N 116.14 E
Gaotangji 100 32.24 N 116.01 E
Gaotingsi 100 26.05 N 112.53 E
Gaotuozi 104 41.08 N 122.40 E
Gaoua 150 10.20 N 3.11 W
Gaoual 150 11.45 N 13.12 W
Gaoxian 102 28.20 N 104.38 E
Gaoxingru 100 26.28 N 115.14 E
Gaoxinji 98 34.11 N 115.33 E
Gaoya 98 36.22 N 118.49 E
Gaoyang 98 34.30 N 114.40 E
Gaoyapu 107 29.14 N 106.19 E
Gaoyi 98 37.36 N 114.36 E
Gaoyou, Zhg. 100 32.47 N 119.27 E
Gaoyou, Zhg. 100 28.25 N 115.31 E
Gaoyou Hu ⊜ 100 32.50 N 119.20 E
Gaozhangjia 102 36.06 N 107.18 E
Gaozhou 102 21.55 N 110.50 E
Gaozi 106 32.11 N 119.18 E
Gaoziba 107 29.01 N 106.00 E
Gaozuo 100 33.57 N 118.03 E
Gap, Fr. 62 44.34 N 6.05 E
Gap, Pa., U.S. 208 39.59 N 76.01 W
Gapālinagar 272b 22.49 N 88.08 E
Gapan 116 15.19 N 120.57 E
Gapeau ≃ 62 43.07 N 6.11 E
Gapern ⊜ 40 59.31 N 13.40 E
Gar 120 32.11 N 79.59 E
Gar ≃ 120 32.28 N 79.44 E
Gara, Lough ⊜ 48 53.55 N 8.25 W
Garacad 144 6.57 N 49.19 E
Garachiné 246 8.04 N 78.22 W
Garadag 144 9.26 N 46.52 E
Garādāha 126 24.14 N 89.34 E
Garagoa 246 5.05 N 73.21 W
Garaguso 68 40.33 N 16.14 E
Garah 166 29.04 S 149.38 E
Garai ≃ [1] 126 23.32 N 89.31 E
Garaina 164 7.50 S 147.10 E
Garākhola
— Madhukhāli 126 23.33 N 89.38 E
Garamba ≃ 154 3.53 N 29.12 E
Garamba, Parc National de la ✦ 154 4.10 N 29.30 E
Gara Muleta ∧ 144 9.17 N 41.47 E
Garānberia 272b 22.24 N 88.34 E
Garancières 261 48.49 N 1.46 E
Garango 150 11.48 N 0.34 W
Garanhuns 250 8.54 S 36.29 W
Garapan 174n 15.12 N 145.43 E
Garara 164 8.37 S 148.17 E
Garautha 124 25.34 N 79.18 E
Garba 146 9.12 N 20.30 E
Garbagna 266b 45.23 N 8.39 E
Garbagnate Milanese 266b 45.35 N 9.05 E
Garbahaarey 144 3.19 N 42.13 E
Garbatella ✦ [8] 267a 41.52 N 12.29 E
Garba Tula 154 0.32 N 38.31 E
Garber 196 36.26 N 97.35 W
Garberville 204 40.06 N 123.47 W
Garbokaraj 88 54.09 N 99.52 E
Garboldisham 42 52.24 N 0.56 E
Garbsen 52 52.25 N 9.34 E
Garça 255 22.13 S 49.37 W
Garças, Rio das ≃ 255 15.54 S 52.16 W
Garcevo 76 52.45 N 32.59 E
Garches 261 48.51 N 2.11 E
Garching 60 48.15 N 11.39 E
Garching an der Alz 60 48.08 N 12.34 E
Garchitorena 116 13.52 N 123.40 E
Garcia 232 29.59 N 108.20 W
García, Laguna ⊜ 288 34.58 S 58.09 W
García de la Cadena 234 21.09 N 103.28 W
García de Sola, Embalse de ⊜ [1] 34 39.15 N 5.05 W
Garcia Hernandez 116 9.37 N 124.18 E
Garcias 255 20.34 S 52.13 W
Garcitas Creek ≃ 222 28.51 N 96.46 W
Gard □ [5] 62 44.00 N 4.00 E
Gard ≃ 62 43.51 N 4.37 E
Gard, Pont du ✦ [5] 62 43.56 N 4.36 E
Garda 64 45.34 N 10.42 E
Garda, Lago di ⊜ 64 45.40 N 10.41 E
Gardabani 84 41.28 N 45.06 E
Gardanne 62 43.27 N 5.28 E
Garde, Lac la ⊜ 190 46.46 N 78.14 W
Gardelegen 54 52.31 N 11.23 E
Garden 190 46.32 N 84.09 W
Gardena 228 33.53 N 118.18 W
Gardena, Val V 64 46.35 N 11.35 E
Garden Acres 226 37.58 N 121.13 W
Garden City, Ga., U.S. 192 32.06 N 81.09 W
Garden City, Ks., U.S. 198 37.58 N 100.52 W
Garden City, Mi., U.S. 216 42.19 N 83.19 W
Garden City, Mo., U.S. 194 38.33 N 94.11 W
Garden City, N.Y., U.S. 210 40.43 N 73.38 W
Garden City, Tx., U.S. 196 31.52 N 101.29 W
Garden City Park 276 40.44 N 73.39 W
Garden City
— Qasr al-Dubārā ✦ [8] 273c 30.02 N 31.14 E
Garden City Raceway ✦ 284a 43.09 N 79.11 W
Gardendale 194 33.39 N 86.48 W
Garden Farms 226 35.24 N 120.07 W
Garden Gate Village 282 37.20 N 122.02 W
Garden Grove, Ca., U.S. 228 33.46 N 117.56 W
Garden Grove, Ia., U.S. 190 40.50 N 93.36 W
Garden Home 224 45.27 N 122.45 W
Garden Island I, Austl. 168a 32.13 S 115.41 E
Garden Island I, Mi., U.S. 190 45.49 N 85.30 W
Garden Lakes 192 34.17 N 85.16 W
Garden Peninsula ≻ [1] 190 45.45 N 86.35 W
Garden Plain 198 37.39 N 97.41 W
Garden Prairie 216 42.15 N 88.44 W
Garden Reach 126 22.33 N 88.17 E
Gardenside 218 38.03 N 84.33 W
Garden State Arts Center ✦ 276 40.24 N 74.11 W
Garden State Plaza ✦ [9] 276 40.55 N 74.05 W
Gardenton 184 49.05 N 96.40 W
Garden Valley 226 38.51 N 120.51 W
Garden View 210 41.16 N 77.03 W
Gardenville 208 40.22 N 75.07 W
Gardermoen 26 60.13 N 11.06 E
Gardey 252 37.17 S 59.21 W
Gardeyz 120 33.37 N 69.07 E
Gardinas
— Grodno 76 53.41 N 23.50 E
Gardiner, Me., U.S. 188 44.13 N 69.46 W
Gardiner, Mt., U.S. 202 45.01 N 110.42 W
Gardiner, N.Y., U.S. 210 41.41 N 74.09 W
Gardiner, Or., U.S. 202 43.43 N 124.06 W
Gardiner, Wa., U.S. 224 48.03 N 122.55 W
Gardiner Dam ✦ [6] 184 51.17 N 106.51 W
Gardiner Range ∧ 162 23.50 S 131.46 E
Gardiners Bay c 207 41.08 N 72.10 W
Gardiners Creek ≃ 274b 37.50 S 145.02 E
Gardiners Island I 207 41.05 N 72.07 W
Garding 52 54.19 N 8.46 E
Gardner, Il., U.S. 216 41.11 N 88.18 W
Gardner, Ks., U.S. 198 38.48 N 94.55 W
Gardner, Ma., U.S. 207 42.34 N 71.59 W
Gardner Canal c 182 53.28 N 128.15 W
Gardner Lake ⊜ 207 41.31 N 72.13 W
Gardner Pinnacles II [1] 14 25.00 N 167.55 W
Gardnersville 218 38.46 N 84.30 W
Gardnertown 210 41.32 N 74.04 W
Gardnerville 226 38.56 N 119.44 W
Gardno 54 53.15 N 14.38 E
Gardolo 64 46.07 N 11.05 E
Gardon d'Alès ≃ 62 44.02 N 4.08 E
Gardon d'Anduze ≃ 62 44.02 N 4.08 E
Gardone Riviera 64 45.37 N 10.34 E
Gardone Val Trompia 64 45.41 N 10.11 E
Gårdsjö 40 58.52 N 14.19 E
Gårdskär 40 60.37 N 17.35 E
Gare Loch c 46 56.01 N 4.48 W
Garelochhead 46 56.05 N 4.50 W
Gareloi Island I 181a 51.47 N 178.48 W
Garenfeld ✦ [8] 263 51.24 N 7.31 E
Garenin 46 58.21 N 6.50 W
Gare Simon 273b 4.15 S 15.11 E
Garešnica 36 45.35 N 16.56 E
Garessio 62 44.12 N 8.02 E
Garet, Mont ∧ [1] 175f 14.16 S 167.30 E
Garfield, Ks., U.S. 198 38.04 N 99.14 W
Garfield, N.J., U.S. 210 40.52 N 74.06 W
Garfield, N.M., U.S. 200 32.45 N 107.15 W
Garfield, Wa., U.S. 202 47.00 N 117.08 W
Garfield Heights 214 41.25 N 81.36 W
Garfield Mountain ∧ 202 44.31 N 112.37 W
Garfield Park 284b 39.42 N 75.33 W
Garfield Park ✦, Il., U.S. 278 41.53 N 87.43 W
Garfield Park ✦, Oh., U.S. 279a 41.26 N 81.36 W
Garfield Peak ∧ 200 42.47 N 107.18 W
Garforth 44 53.48 N 1.22 W
Garga 88 54.26 N 110.33 E
Gargaliánoi 38 37.04 N 21.39 E
Gargano, Promontorio del ≻ 68 41.50 N 16.00 E
Gargano, Testa del ≻ 68 41.49 N 16.12 E
Gargantua, Cape ≻ 190 47.36 N 85.02 W
Garga Sarali 152 5.11 N 14.00 E
Gargazzone (Gargazon) 64 46.35 N 11.12 E
Gargellen 58 46.58 N 9.56 E
Gargenville 261 49.00 N 1.49 E
Garges-lès-Gonesse 261 48.58 N 2.25 E
Gargnano 64 45.41 N 10.40 E
Gargouna 150 15.56 N 0.13 E
Gargrave 44 53.59 N 2.06 W
Gargždai 76 55.43 N 21.24 E
Garhākota 124 23.46 N 79.09 E
Garhbeta 126 22.51 N 87.19 E
Garhdīwāla 123 31.44 N 75.45 E
Garhi Habībullāh Khān 123 34.24 N 73.23 E
Garhi Jasaya 272a 28.46 N 77.16 E
Garhi Katiya 272a 28.45 N 77.16 E
Garhi Khairo 120 28.04 N 67.59 E
Garhi Malehra 124 25.02 N 79.19 E
Garhjāt Hills ∧ [2] 126 21.47 N 86.20 E
Garhmuktesar 124 28.48 N 78.06 E
Garhshankar 123 31.13 N 76.08 E
Garhwa 124 24.11 N 83.49 E
Gari 86 59.26 N 62.21 E
Garibaldi, Bra. 252 29.15 S 51.32 W
Garibaldi, B.C., Can. 182 49.58 N 123.09 W
Garibaldi, Or., U.S. 224 45.34 N 123.55 W
Garibaldi, Casa di ⊥ 71 41.13 N 9.27 E
Garibaldi, Mount ∧ 182 49.51 N 123.01 W
Garibaldi Provincial Park ✦ 182 50.00 N 122.50 W
Garies 158 30.30 S 18.00 E
Garigliano ≃ 68 41.13 N 13.45 E
Gariglione, Monte ∧ 68 39.09 N 16.41 E
Garin 258 34.26 S 58.44 W
Garin, Arroyo ≃ 288 34.23 S 58.43 W
Garin Regional Park ✦ 282 37.38 N 122.03 W
Garipçe Burnu ≻ 267b 41.13 N 29.07 E
Garissa 154 0.28 S 39.38 E
Garita Palmera 236 13.44 N 90.05 W
Gariya 272b 22.28 N 88.23 E
Gārji 272b 22.51 N 88.19 E
Garkida 146 10.25 N 12.36 E
Garko 150 11.38 N 8.48 E
Garland, Al., U.S. 194 31.33 N 86.49 W
Garland, Md., U.S. 284b 39.11 N 76.39 W
Garland, Pa., U.S. 214 41.49 N 79.27 W
Garland, Tx., U.S. 222 32.54 N 96.38 W
Garland, Ut., U.S. 200 41.44 N 112.09 W
Garland Park ✦ 275b 43.44 N 79.35 W
Garland Peak ∧ 224 48.01 N 120.52 W
Garlasco 62 45.12 N 8.55 E
Garlate 62 45.49 N 9.23 E
Garlate, Lago di ⊜ 62 45.49 N 9.24 E
Garliava 76 54.49 N 23.52 E
Garlieston 44 54.48 N 4.22 W
Garlin 32 43.34 N 0.15 W
Garm 120 39.00 N 70.22 E
Garm Āb 120 32.14 N 65.01 E
Garmal 144 8.35 N 50.19 E
Garmersdorf 60 49.26 N 11.54 E
Garmī 128 39.01 N 48.03 E
Garmisch-Partenkirchen 64 47.29 N 11.05 E
Garmo 26 61.51 N 8.45 E
Garmsar 128 35.20 N 52.13 E
Garnavillo 190 42.52 N 91.14 W
Garne 261 48.41 N 1.58 E
Garner, Ia., U.S. 190 43.06 N 93.36 W
Garner, N.C., U.S. 192 35.42 N 78.36 W
Garnet Range ∧ 202 46.45 N 113.15 W
Garnett 198 38.16 N 95.14 W
Garnijskij zapovednik ✦ 84 40.00 N 44.55 E
Garnish 186 47.14 N 55.22 W
Garnock ≃ 46 55.38 N 4.42 W
Garnpung, Lake ⊜ 166 33.30 S 143.12 E
Garo Hills ∧ [2] 124 25.30 N 90.30 E
Garona
— Garonne ≃ 32 45.02 N 0.36 W
Garonne ≃ 32 45.02 N 0.36 W
Garoowe 144 8.24 N 48.29 E
Garou, Lac ⊜ 150 16.04 N 2.45 W
Garoua, Cam. 146 9.18 N 13.24 E
Garoua, Niger 146 13.53 N 13.11 E
Garoua Boulaï 152 5.53 N 14.33 E
Garove Island I 164 4.40 S 149.30 E
Garpenberg 40 60.19 N 16.12 E
Garphyttan 40 59.19 N 14.56 E
Garphyttans Nationalpark ✦ 40 59.17 N 14.51 E
Garqu Yan, Zhg. 118 34.29 N 92.35 E
Garqu Yan, Zhg. 120 33.50 N 92.28 E
Garraf, Costa de ≐ [2] 266d 41.16 N 2.02 E
Garrattsville 210 42.39 N 75.10 W
Garrel 52 52.57 N 8.01 E
Garret Mountain Reservation ✦ 276 40.54 N 74.11 W
Garretson 198 43.43 N 96.30 W
Garrett, In., U.S. 216 41.20 N 85.08 W
Garrett, Ky., U.S. 192 37.28 N 82.49 W
Garrett Creek ≃ 222 32.57 N 95.44 W
Garrett Park 208 39.02 N 77.05 W
Garrett Park Estates 284c 39.02 N 77.06 W
Garrettsville 214 41.17 N 81.06 W
Garrison, N. Ire., U.K. 48 54.25 N 8.05 W
Garrison, Ky., U.S. 218 38.36 N 83.10 W
Garrison, Md., U.S. 208 39.24 N 76.45 W
Garrison, Mt., U.S. 202 46.31 N 112.48 W
Garrison, N.Y., U.S. 210 41.23 N 73.56 W
Garrison, N.D., U.S. 198 47.39 N 101.24 W
Garrison, Tx., U.S. 222 31.49 N 94.30 W
Garrison Dam ✦ [6] 198 47.22 N 101.25 W
Garron Point ≻ 48 55.03 N 5.57 W
Garros 46 57.37 N 6.11 W
Garrovillas 34 39.43 N 6.33 W
Garry ≃ 46 56.43 N 3.47 W
Garry, Loch ⊜ 206 45.15 N 74.43 W
Garry Bay c 176 68.55 N 85.05 W
Garry Lake ⊜ 176 66.00 N 100.00 W
Gars am Kamp 61 48.36 N 15.40 E
Garsdale Head 44 54.19 N 2.20 W
Garsen 154 2.16 S 40.07 E
Garskolk 158 30.41 S 22.02 E
Gårslev 41 55.38 N 9.43 E
Garson 190 46.34 N 80.52 W
Garson Lake ⊜ 184 56.19 N 110.02 W
Garstang 44 53.55 N 2.47 W
Garstedt 52 53.41 N 9.58 E
Garsten 61 48.01 N 14.24 E
Garston 260 51.41 N 0.23 W
Garston ✦ [8] 262 53.21 N 2.53 W
Garswood 262 53.29 N 2.40 W
Gartempe ≃ 32 46.48 N 0.50 E
Gartenstadt ✦ [8] 263 51.30 N 7.26 E
Garthby Station (Beaulac) 206 45.50 N 71.23 W
Gartow 54 53.02 N 11.29 E
Gartrop-Bühl 263 51.40 N 6.49 E
Gartz 54 53.12 N 14.23 E
Garu 150 10.51 N 0.11 W
Garub 156 26.33 S 16.00 E
Garubhāsa 124 26.33 N 90.22 E
Gārulia 126 22.49 N 88.22 E
Garut 115a 7.13 S 107.54 E
Garve 46 57.37 N 4.42 W
Garvellachs II 46 56.14 N 5.47 W
Garvey Reservoir ⊜ [1] 280 34.13 N 118.07 W
Garvie Mountains ∧ 172 45.30 S 168.50 E
Garwin 190 42.05 N 92.40 W
Garwolin 30 51.54 N 21.37 E
Garwood, N.J., U.S. 276 40.39 N 74.19 W
Garwood, Tx., U.S. 222 29.27 N 96.24 W
Gary, In., U.S. 216 41.35 N 87.20 W
Gary, S.D., U.S. 198 44.47 N 96.27 W
Gary, Tx., U.S. 194 32.07 N 94.22 W
Gary, W.V., U.S. 192 37.21 N 81.33 W
Garyarsa 120 31.44 N 80.21 E
Gary Harbor c 278 41.38 N 87.20 W
Garyi 102 30.54 N 98.56 E
Gary Municipal Airport ✦ 278 41.37 N 87.25 W
Garysburg 208 36.27 N 77.33 W
Garz 54 54.19 N 13.20 E
Garza 252 28.09 S 63.32 W
Garza Ayala 196 26.29 N 100.02 W
Garza García 196 25.40 N 100.24 W
Garzas Creek ≃ 226 37.13 N 120.57 W
Garzeno 58 46.08 N 9.15 E
Garzón, Col. 246 2.12 N 75.38 W
Garzón, Ur. 252 34.36 S 54.33 W
Gas 261 48.34 N 1.40 E
Gasan 116 13.19 N 121.51 E
Gasan-Kuli 128 37.27 N 53.59 E
Gas City 216 40.29 N 85.36 W
Gascogne □ [9] 32 44.00 N 0.05 E
Gascogne, Golfe de
— Biscay, Bay of c 32 44.00 N 4.00 W
Gasconade 219 38.40 N 91.33 W
Gasconade ≃ 219 38.27 N 91.30 W
Gasconade □ [6] 194 38.40 N 91.33 W
Gasconade, Osage Fork ≃ 194 37.45 N 92.26 W
Gascoyne ≃ 162 24.52 S 113.37 E
Gascoyne, Mount ∧ 162 24.58 S 116.38 E
Gascoyne Junction 162 25.03 S 115.12 E
Gash (Nahr al-Qāsh) ≃ 140 16.48 N 35.51 E
Gashaka 146 7.21 N 11.27 E
Gasherbrum I ∧ 123 35.43 N 76.43 E
Gas Hu ⊜ 120 38.10 N 90.42 E
Gashua 146 12.54 N 11.00 E
Gasline 284a 42.53 N 79.11 W
Gasny 50 49.05 N 1.36 E
Gaspar 252 26.56 S 48.58 W
Gaspard Creek ≃ 182 51.34 N 122.17 W
Gasparilla Island I 220 26.46 N 82.16 W
Gasparilla Sound c 220 26.48 N 82.15 W
Gaspé 186 48.50 N 64.29 W
Gaspé, Baie de c 186 48.46 N 64.17 W
Gaspé, Cap ≻ 186 48.45 N 64.10 W
Gaspé Peninsula
— Gaspésie, Péninsule de la ≻ [1] 186 48.30 N 65.00 W
Gaspereau Lake ⊜ 186 44.57 N 64.34 W
Gasperina 68 38.44 N 16.30 E
Gaspésie, Parc Provincial de la ✦ 186 48.55 N 66.00 W
Gaspésie, Péninsule de la ≻ [1] 186 48.30 N 65.00 W
Gaspoltshofen 60 48.08 N 13.46 E
Gasport 210 43.11 N 78.34 W
Gaspra 78 44.27 N 34.07 E
Gassan 150 12.49 N 3.12 W
Gas-san ∧ 92 38.32 N 140.01 E
Gassaway 188 38.40 N 80.46 W
Gasse 64 47.23 N 11.09 E
Gasselte 52 52.58 N 6.47 E
Gassin 62 43.13 N 6.35 E
Gassino Torinese 62 45.08 N 7.49 E
Gassol 146 8.32 N 10.28 E
Gastein
— Badgastein 64 47.07 N 13.08 E
Gasteiner Tal V 64 47.11 N 13.06 E
Gasteiz
— Vitoria 34 42.51 N 2.40 W
Gastello 89 49.07 N 142.58 E
Gaston, In., U.S. 216 40.18 N 85.30 W
Gaston, N.C., U.S. 192 36.30 N 77.38 W
Gaston, Or., U.S. 224 45.26 N 123.08 W
Gaston, S.C., U.S. 192 33.49 N 81.05 W
Gaston, Lake ⊜ [1] 192 36.35 N 78.00 W
Gastonia, N.C., U.S. 192 35.15 N 81.11 W
Gastonia, Tx., U.S. 222 32.37 N 96.24 W
Gastonville 279b 40.15 N 79.59 W
Gastouní 38 37.51 N 21.16 E
Gastre 254 42.17 S 69.14 W
Gästrikland □ [9] 40 60.30 N 16.27 E
Gat 132 31.37 N 34.47 E
Gata, Cabo de ≻ 34 36.43 N 2.12 W
Gata, Sierra de ∧ 34 40.14 N 6.45 W
Gătaia 38 45.26 N 21.26 E
Gátas, Akrotírion ≻ 130 34.34 N 33.02 E
Gatčina 76 59.34 N 30.08 E
Gate 196 36.51 N 100.03 W
Gateacre ✦ [8] 262 53.23 N 2.51 W
Gate City 192 36.38 N 82.34 W
Gatehouse of Fleet 44 54.53 N 4.11 W
Gatersleben 54 51.49 N 11.17 E
Gates, N.Y., U.S. 210 43.09 N 77.41 W
Gates, N.C., U.S. 208 36.30 N 76.46 W
Gates □ [6] 208 36.28 N 76.43 W
Gateshead 44 54.58 N 1.37 W
Gateshead Island I 176 70.22 N 100.27 W
Gates Mills 279a 41.31 N 81.24 W
Gates of the Arctic National Park ✦ 180 67.45 N 153.30 W
Gatesville, N.C., U.S. 192 36.24 N 76.45 W
Gatesville, Tx., U.S. 222 31.26 N 97.44 W
Gateway 200 38.40 N 108.58 W
Gateway Arch ✦ 219 38.37 N 90.12 W
Gateway National Recreation Area ✦ 276 40.34 N 74.06 W
Gateway of India ⊥ 272c 18.55 N 72.50 E
Gaths Mine 154 20.00 S 30.31 E
Gathurst 262 53.34 N 2.42 W
Gatid Loumo 150 15.28 N 4.37 W
Gâtine, Hauteurs de ∧ [2] 32 46.40 N 0.50 W
Gatineau 212 45.29 N 75.38 W
Gatineau □ [6] 212 45.25 N 75.45 W
Gatineau ≃ 176 45.27 N 75.40 W
Gatineau, Parc de la ✦ 188 45.30 N 76.05 W
Gatley 262 53.23 N 2.14 W
Gatlinburg 192 35.42 N 83.30 W
Gato, Arroyo del ≃, Arg. 288 34.51 S 57.56 W
Gato, Arroyo del ≃, Arg. 288 34.55 S 58.37 W
Ga'ton 132 33.00 N 35.13 E
Gato Negro 286c 10.33 N 66.57 W
Gatow ✦ [8] 264a 52.29 N 13.11 E
Gatow, Flugplatz ✈ 264a 52.28 N 13.08 E
Gattendorf 61 48.01 N 16.59 E
Gattières 62 43.46 N 7.11 E
Gattinara 62 45.37 N 8.22 E
Gatton 171a 27.33 S 152.17 E
Gattorna 62 44.26 N 9.11 E
Gatún, Esclusas de ✦ [5] 236 9.16 N 79.55 W
Gatún, Lago ⊜ [1] 236 9.12 N 79.55 W
Gatvand 128 32.15 N 48.50 E
Gau-Algesheim 56 49.57 N 8.01 E
Gauchy 50 49.49 N 3.16 E
Gaucín 34 36.31 N 5.19 W
Gauer Lake ⊜ 184 57.00 N 97.50 W
Gauguin, Musée ✦ 174s 17.45 S 149.23 W
Gauja ≃ 76 57.09 N 24.16 E
Gaujiena 76 57.30 N 26.40 E
Gaukler Point ≻ 281 42.27 N 82.52 W
Gaula ≃ 26 63.21 N 10.14 E
Gauley ≃ 188 38.10 N 81.12 W
Gauley Bridge 188 38.10 N 81.11 W
Gaultois 186 47.36 N 55.54 W
Gaunless ≃ 44 54.40 N 1.41 W
Gau-Odernheim 56 49.47 N 8.11 E
Gaur 124 26.46 N 85.17 E
Gaurain-Ramecroix 50 50.35 N 3.29 E
Gaurambha 126 22.39 N 89.34 E
Gaurela 124 22.45 N 81.54 E
Gaurhāti 126 22.46 N 87.48 E
Gauribaradia 126 23.45 N 89.52 E
Gauribidanūr 122 13.37 N 77.31 E
Gauri Phānta 124 28.41 N 80.33 E
Gauripur 124 26.05 N 89.58 E
Gaurīśaṅgkar ∧ 124 27.57 N 86.21 E
Gaurnadi 126 22.58 N 90.14 E
Gause 222 30.47 N 96.43 W
Gausta ∧ 26 59.50 N 8.35 E
Gauthiot, Chutes ⌞ 146 9.43 N 14.34 E
Gauting 60 48.04 N 11.23 E
Gavà 34 41.18 N 2.01 E
Gāvanpāda 272c 18.57 N 73.01 E
Gavardo 64 45.35 N 10.26 E
Gávdhos I 38 34.50 N 24.06 E
Gávea ✦ [8] 287a 22.58 S 43.14 W
Gávea, Hipódromo da ✦ 287a 22.58 S 43.13 W
Gávea, Pedra da ∧ 287a 23.00 S 43.17 W
Gavel-Långsjön ⊜ 40 59.50 N 18.18 E
Gavello 64 45.01 N 11.55 E
Gavet 62 45.04 N 5.52 E
Gavi 62 44.41 N 8.49 E
Gavia, Arroyo de la ≃ 266a 40.21 N 3.40 W
Gavião ≃ 255 14.06 S 41.01 W
Gavião, Pico do ∧ 256 21.37 S 44.50 W
Gavien 164 3.54 S 144.07 E
Gavilán 286c 10.24 N 66.51 W
Gavinana 66 44.05 N 10.45 E
Gavins Point Dam ✦ [6] 198 42.48 N 97.40 W
Gaviões 256 22.34 S 42.33 W
Gavirate 62 45.50 N 8.43 E
Gavja ≃ 76 53.49 N 25.35 E
Gāv Khūnī, Bātlāq-e ≐ 128 32.10 N 52.50 E
Gävle 40 60.40 N 17.10 E
Gävleborgs Län □ [6] 26 61.30 N 16.15 E
Gävlebukten c 40 60.42 N 17.20 E
Gavnø 41 55.11 N 11.44 E
Gavoi 71 40.10 N 9.12 E
Gavorrano 66 42.55 N 10.54 E
Gavrilov-Jam 80 57.18 N 39.51 E
Gavrilovka 83 48.37 N 37.31 E
Gavrilovka Vtoraja 80 52.53 N 42.46 E
Gavrilov Posad 80 56.33 N 40.07 E
Gávrion 38 37.52 N 24.46 E
Gavry 76 56.55 N 27.52 E
Gawachab 156 27.03 S 17.50 E
Gawān 124 24.37 N 85.55 E
Gaweinstal 61 48.28 N 16.35 E
Gāwilgarh Hills ∧ [2] 122 21.20 N 77.00 E
Gawler 168b 34.37 S 138.44 E
Gawler ≃ 168b 34.41 S 138.27 E
Gawler Ranges ∧ 162 32.30 S 136.00 E
Gawso 150 6.48 N 2.31 W
Gawsworth 262 53.13 N 2.10 W
Gawthorpe Hall ⊥ 262 53.48 N 2.18 W
Gaxun Nur (Juyanhai) ⊜ 102 42.22 N 100.34 E
Gaya, India 124 24.47 N 85.00 E
Gaya, Niger 150 11.53 N 3.27 E
Gaya, Nig. 150 11.53 N 9.02 E
Gay City State Park ✦ 207 41.42 N 72.28 W
Gayéri 150 12.39 N 0.29 E
Gay Head 207 41.20 N 70.48 W
Gay Hill 222 30.16 N 96.30 W
Gaylord, Mi., U.S. 190 45.01 N 84.40 W
Gaylord, Mn., U.S. 190 44.33 N 94.13 W
Gaylordsville 207 41.38 N 73.29 W
Gayndah 166 25.37 S 151.36 E
Gays Mills 190 43.19 N 90.50 W
Gayton, Eng., U.K. 42 52.45 N 0.34 E
Gayton, Eng., U.K. 262 53.19 N 3.06 W
Gayt on Sands ✦ [4] 262 53.17 N 3.07 W
Gaza □ [5] 156 23.30 S 32.45 E
Gaza
— Ghazzah 128 31.30 N 34.28 E
Gazalkent 85 41.33 N 69.47 E
Gazaoua 150 13.32 N 7.55 E
Gaza Strip □ [9] 132 31.25 N 34.20 E
Gazelle Channel ⊻ 164 2.50 S 150.55 E
Gazelle Peninsula ≻ [1] 164 4.40 S 152.00 E
Gazeran 261 48.38 N 1.46 E
Gazeran, Bois de ✦ 261 48.40 N 1.45 E
Gazi, Kenya 154 4.25 S 39.30 E
Gazi, Zaire 154 1.03 N 24.30 E
Gaziantep 130 37.05 N 37.22 E
Gaziantep □ [4] 130 37.00 N 37.20 E

ENGLISH Name	Page	Lat.°′	Long.°′

Gazimağusa (Famagusta) 130 35.07 N 33.57 E
Gazimağusa Körfezi c 130 35.15 N 34.10 E
Gazimur ≃ 88 52.57 N 120.22 E
Gazimurskij Zavod 88 51.33 N 118.22 E
Gazipaşa 130 36.17 N 32.20 E
Gazira Sporting Club ✦ 273c 30.04 N 31.13 E
Gazivoda Jezero ⊜ [1] 38 42.55 N 20.40 E
Gaznau 85 40.10 N 71.02 E
Gazoldo degli Ippoliti 64 45.12 N 10.35 E
Gazos Creek ≃ 226 37.10 N 122.22 W
Gazzada 62 45.47 N 8.51 E
Gazzaniga 62 45.48 N 9.50 E
Gazzuolo 64 45.04 N 10.35 E
Gbangbatok 150 7.48 N 12.23 W
Gbanhala ≃ 150 10.14 N 8.38 W
Gbaoui Bodanga 152 5.33 N 16.45 E
Gbarnga 150 7.00 N 9.29 W
Gbogbo 273a 6.36 N 3.31 E
Gboko 150 7.20 N 8.57 E
Gbon 150 9.50 N 6.27 W
Gbwado 152 3.54 N 20.46 E
Gcoverega 156 19.08 S 24.15 E
Gdańsk (Danzig) 30 54.23 N 18.40 E
Gdańsk □ [4] 30 54.15 N 18.25 E
Gdańsk, Gulf of c 30 54.40 N 19.15 E
Gden' 78 51.20 N 30.25 E
Gdov 76 58.44 N 27.48 E
Gdyel 34 35.48 N 0.26 W
Gdynia 30 54.32 N 18.33 E
Gearhart 224 46.01 N 123.54 W
Gearhart Mountain ∧ 202 42.30 N 120.53 W
Gearhartville 214 40.53 N 78.15 W
Geary, N.B., Can. 186 45.46 N 66.29 W
Geary, Ok., U.S. 196 35.43 N 98.22 W
Geauga □ [6] 214 41.35 N 81.12 W
Geauga Lake Park ✦ 279a 41.21 N 81.23 W
Geba ≃ 150 11.46 N 15.36 W
Gebaberg ∧ 56 50.36 N 10.16 E
Gebe, Pulau I 164 0.05 S 129.20 E
Gebeit Mine 140 21.03 N 36.19 E
Gebenbach 60 49.32 N 11.53 E
Gebesee 54 51.07 N 10.56 E
Gebi 84 42.46 N 43.30 E
Gebilu 144 10.35 N 41.28 E
Gebiz 130 37.06 N 30.56 E
Gebra 54 51.24 N 10.35 E
Gebweiler
— Guebwiller 58 47.55 N 7.12 E
Gebze 130 40.48 N 29.25 E
Gecha 144 7.31 N 35.25 E
Gechang 98 31.05 N 119.27 E
Geçitkale 130 35.15 N 33.45 E
Gecun 106 32.10 N 119.37 E
Geddes, Mi., U.S. 281 42.16 N 83.40 W
Geddes, S.D., U.S. 198 43.15 N 98.41 W
Gede, Gunung ∧ 115a 6.47 S 106.59 E
Gedera 132 31.49 N 34.46 E
Gedern 56 50.25 N 9.12 E
Gedian 100 30.32 N 114.38 E
Gedikler 130 39.06 N 38.49 E
Gediksaray 130 40.27 N 35.38 E
Gedi National Monument ✦ 154 3.19 S 40.03 E
Gedinne 56 49.59 N 4.56 E
Gediz 130 39.02 N 29.25 E
Gediz ≃ 130 38.35 N 26.48 E
Gedlegube 144 6.52 N 45.02 E
Gedo 144 8.58 N 37.27 E
Gedo □ [4] 144 3.00 N 42.00 E
Gedongdalem 112 5.04 S 105.25 E
Gedongtataan 115a 5.23 S 105.10 E
Gedser 41 54.35 N 11.57 E
Gedser Odde ≻ 41 54.34 N 11.59 E
Geduld 273d 26.15 S 28.25 E
Gedun 100 27.39 N 118.26 E
Geebung 171a 27.22 S 153.03 E
Gee Cross 262 53.26 N 2.04 W
Geehi 171b 36.24 S 148.11 E
Geehi ≃ 171b 36.11 S 148.02 E
Geel 56 51.10 N 5.00 E
Geelong 169 38.08 S 144.21 E
Geelong West 169 38.08 S 144.20 E
Geelvink Channel ⊻ 162 28.30 S 114.10 E
Geer ≃ 56 50.51 N 5.42 E
Geeste ≃ 52 53.32 N 8.35 E
Geesthacht 52 53.26 N 10.22 E
Geeveston 166 43.10 S 146.55 E
Gefell 54 50.26 N 11.52 E
Gefle
— Gävle 40 60.40 N 17.10 E
Gefrees 54 50.06 N 11.44 E
Gegang 100 30.04 N 117.38 E
Gegenmiao 89 45.58 N 122.15 E
Gegong 100 30.05 N 117.11 E
Gegou 98 35.24 N 118.32 E
Gegu 106 31.23 N 119.46 E
Gehackte Berge ∧ [2] 264a 52.41 N 13.30 E
Gehrden 52 52.18 N 9.36 E
Gehren 54 50.39 N 10.59 E
Gehu 100 27.46 N 119.16 E
Ge Hu ⊜ 106 31.36 N 119.51 E
Gehua 164 10.20 S 150.25 E
Geidam 146 12.53 N 11.57 E
Geigertown 208 40.13 N 75.50 W
Geihoku 96 34.44 N 132.17 E
Geikie ≃ 176 57.45 N 103.52 W
Geilenkirchen 56 50.57 N 6.07 E
Geilo 26 60.31 N 8.12 E
Geinō 94 34.48 N 136.25 E
Geiranger 26 62.06 N 7.12 E
Geisa 56 50.43 N 9.57 E
Geisberg ∧ 60 49.53 N 11.03 E
Geisecke 263 51.27 N 7.37 E
Geisei 96 33.31 N 133.49 E
Geiselhöring 60 48.50 N 12.23 E
Geisenfeld 60 48.41 N 11.37 E
Geisenhausen 60 48.28 N 12.15 E
Geisenheim 56 49.59 N 7.58 E
Geisingen 58 47.55 N 8.38 E
Geislingen an der Steige 56 48.36 N 9.50 E
Geismar 56 51.31 N 9.57 E
Geispolsheim 58 48.31 N 7.39 E
Geisstein ∧ 64 47.20 N 12.30 E
Geistenbeck ✦ [8] 263 51.09 N 6.27 E
Geistown 214 40.17 N 78.52 W
Geist Reservoir ⊜ [1], In., U.S. 218 39.56 N 85.56 W
Geist Reservoir ⊜ [1], Pa., U.S. 285 39.57 N 75.24 W
Geisweid 56 50.55 N 8.01 E
Geita 154 2.52 S 32.10 E
Geithain 54 51.03 N 12.41 E
Geiyō-shotō II 96 34.10 N 132.45 E
Gejah 272a 28.31 N 77.23 E
Gejiatun 98 40.27 N 119.55 E
Gejiu (Kokiu) 102 23.22 N 103.06 E
Geka, mys ≻ 180 64.26 N 178.10 E
Gela 70 37.04 N 14.15 E
Gela ≃ 70 37.03 N 14.15 E
Gela, Golfo di c 70 37.03 N 14.10 E
Geladandong ∧ 120 33.16 N 91.27 E
Geladi 144 6.57 N 46.25 E
Gelai ∧ [1] 154 2.33 S 36.05 E
Gelan 102 30.03 N 107.04 E
Gelang, Tanjong ≻ 114 3.58 N 103.26 E
Gelaochang 107 29.36 N 103.39 E
Gelasa, Selat ⊻ 112 2.40 S 107.15 E
Gelber Fluss
— Huang ≃ 90 37.32 N 118.19 E
Gelbes Meer
— Yellow Sea ⊤ [2] 90 36.00 N 123.00 E
Gelderland □ [4] 52 52.10 N 5.50 E
Geldermalsen 52 51.53 N 5.17 E
Geldern 52 51.31 N 6.20 E
Geldrop 52 51.25 N 5.33 E
Geleen 56 50.58 N 5.52 E

DEUTSCH Name	Seite	Breite°′	Länge°′ E = Ost

Gelembe 130 39.10 N 27.50 E
Gelemso 144 8.48 N 40.35 E
Gelenau 54 50.42 N 12.58 E
Gelendost 130 38.07 N 31.01 E
Gelendžik 78 44.33 N 38.06 E
Gelfingen 58 47.13 N 8.16 E
Gelgaudiškis 76 55.05 N 23.00 E
Gelib
— Jilib 144 0.29 N 42.46 E
Gelibolu 130 40.24 N 26.40 E
Gelibolu Yarımadası (Gallipoli Peninsula) ≻ [1] 130 40.20 N 26.30 E
Gelibolu Yarımadası Milli Parkı ✦ 130 40.05 N 26.10 E
Gelinden 56 50.46 N 5.15 E
Gélise ≃ 32 44.11 N 0.17 E
Geliting 115b 8.39 S 122.18 E
Geliting, Teluk c 115b 8.36 S 122.17 E
Gellénháza 61 46.46 N 16.47 E
Gellenstrom ⊻ 54 54.28 N 13.03 E
Gellep-Stratum ✦ [8] 263 51.20 N 6.41 E
Gellibrand ≃ 169 38.41 S 143.09 E
Gellibrand, Mount ∧ [2] 169 38.14 S 143.48 E
Gellibrand, Point ≻ 274b 37.52 S 144.54 E
Gellibrand River 169 38.32 S 143.32 E
Gellingen
— Ghislenghien 50 50.39 N 3.52 E
Gellinsoor 144 6.26 N 46.42 E
Gel'm'azov 78 49.49 N 31.49 E
Gelnhausen 56 50.11 N 9.11 E
Gelså ≃ 41 55.19 N 8.54 E
Gelsdorf 56 50.35 N 7.02 E
Gelsenkirchen 52 51.31 N 7.07 E
Gelsenkirchen-Horst, Galopprennbahn ✦ 263 51.32 N 7.02 E
Gelsted 41 55.24 N 9.59 E
Gelt ≃ 44 54.56 N 2.47 W
Geltendorf 60 48.07 N 11.01 E
Gelterkinden 58 47.28 N 7.51 E
Gelting 41 54.45 N 9.53 E
Geltow 54 52.22 N 12.58 E
Geltsa 144 6.14 N 37.05 E
Geluji 98 37.08 N 121.50 E
Geluksburg 158 28.30 S 29.33 E
Geluwe 50 50.48 N 3.04 E
Gemas 114 2.35 N 102.37 E
Gembloux 56 50.34 N 4.41 E
Gembrook 169 37.57 S 145.33 E
Gemen 52 51.51 N 6.52 E
Gemena 152 3.15 N 19.46 E
Gémenos 62 43.18 N 5.38 E
Gemerek 130 39.11 N 36.05 E
Gemert 52 51.34 N 5.40 E
Gemla 26 56.52 N 14.38 E
Gemlik 130 40.26 N 29.09 E
Gemlik Körfezi c 130 40.25 N 28.55 E
Gemolong 115a 7.24 S 110.50 E
Gemona del Friuli 64 46.16 N 13.09 E
Gemonio 62 45.53 N 8.40 E
Gemsbok National Park ✦ 156 25.15 S 21.10 E
Gemünd 56 50.34 N 6.30 E
Gemünden, Dtsch. 56 50.03 N 9.41 E
Gemünden, Dtsch. 56 50.58 N 8.58 E
Gemünden, Dtsch. 56 49.54 N 7.28 E
Gen ≃ 89 50.16 N 119.22 E
Genadendal 158 34.02 S 19.33 E
Genaibashi 268 35.21 N 140.04 E
Genale (Jubba) ≃ 144 0.15 S 42.38 E
Genappe 50 50.36 N 4.27 E
Genarp 41 55.36 N 13.23 E
Genazzano 66 41.50 N 12.58 E
Genç 130 38.46 N 40.35 E
Gençay 32 46.23 N 0.24 E
Gencek 130 37.27 N 31.33 E
Gencsapáti 61 47.17 N 16.36 E
Gending 115a 7.48 S 113.18 E
Gendrey 58 47.12 N 5.41 E
Gendringen 52 51.52 N 6.22 E
Gendt 52 51.53 N 5.59 E
Genegantslet Creek ≃ 210 42.18 N 75.48 W
Genemuiden 52 52.37 N 6.07 E
General ≃ 236 8.59 N 83.11 W
General Acha 252 37.23 S 64.36 W
General Alvear, Arg. 252 36.03 S 60.01 W
General Alvear, Arg. 252 34.58 S 67.42 W
General Aquino 252 24.26 S 56.42 W
General Arenales 252 34.18 S 61.18 W
General Belgrano 252 35.46 S 58.30 W
General Bernardo O'Higgins ✦ [3] 9 63.19 S 57.54 W
General Bravo 232 25.48 N 99.10 W
General Butler State Resort Park ✦ 218 38.40 N 85.10 W
General Cabrera 252 32.48 S 63.52 W
General Campos 252 31.32 S 58.24 W
General Carneiro 255 15.42 S 52.45 W
General Carrera, Lago (Lago Buenos Aires) ⊜ 254 46.35 S 72.00 W
General Cepeda 232 25.23 N 101.27 W
General Conesa, Arg. 252 36.30 S 57.20 W
General Conesa, Arg. 254 40.06 S 64.26 W
General Daniel Cerri 252 38.42 S 62.24 W
General del Sur, Cementerio ✦ 286c 10.28 N 66.55 W
General Elizardo Aquino 252 26.53 S 56.17 W
General Enrique Martínez 252 33.12 S 53.48 W
General Enrique Mosconi 252 22.36 S 63.49 W
General Escobedo, Méx. 196 25.49 N 100.20 W
General Escobedo, Méx. 232 25.30 N 105.15 W
General Eugenio A. Garay, Para. 248 20.31 S 62.08 W
General Eugenio A. Garay, Para. 252 25.55 S 56.11 W
General Galarza 252 32.43 S 59.24 W
General Güemes 252 24.40 S 65.03 W
General Guido 252 36.40 S 57.46 W
General Hornos 258 34.53 S 58.56 W
General Island I 116 9.25 N 126.00 E
General José de San Martín 252 26.33 S 59.21 W
General Juan José Ríos 232 25.40 N 108.40 W
General Juan Madariaga 252 37.00 S 57.09 W
General La Madrid 252 37.16 S 61.17 W
General Las Heras 258 34.56 S 58.57 W
General Las Heras □ [5] 288 34.56 S 58.51 W
General Lavalle 252 36.24 S 56.58 W
General Leonidas Plaza Gutiérrez 246 2.58 S 78.25 W
General Levalle 252 34.01 S 63.56 W
General Lorenzo Vintter 254 40.44 S 64.29 W
General Luna 116 9.47 N 126.09 E
General MacArthur (Pambuhan Sur) 116 11.15 N 125.32 E
General Mansilla (Bartolomé Bavio) 258 35.05 S 57.45 W
General Manuel Belgrano, Cerro ∧ 252 29.01 S 67.49 W
General Mitchell Field ✈ 216 42.57 N 87.54 W
General Motors Corporation (Pontiac Division) ✦ [3] 281 42.49 N 83.17 W
General Motors Proving Grounds ✦ [3] 281 42.35 N 83.41 W
General Motors Technical Center ✦ [3] 281 42.31 N 83.02 W

Symbols in the index entries represent the broad categories identified in the key at the right. Symbols with superior numbers (∧[1]) identify subcategories (see complete key on page I · 1).

Symbole im Register stellen die rechts im Schlüssel erklärten Kategorien dar. Symbole mit hochgestellten Ziffern (∧[1]) bezeichnen Unterabteilungen einer Kategorie (vgl. vollständiger Schlüssel auf Seite I · 1).

Los símbolos incluídos en el texto del índice representan las grandes categorías identificadas con la clave a la derecha. Los símbolos con numeros en su parte superior (∧[1]) identifican las subcategorías (véase la clave completa en la página I · 1).

Les symboles de l'index représentent les catégories indiquées dans la légende à droite. Les symboles suivis d'un indice (∧[1]) représentent des sous-catégories (voir légende complète à la page I · 1).

Os símbolos incluídos no texto do índice representam as grandes categorias identificadas com a chave à direita. Os símbolos com números em sua parte superior (∧[1]) identificam as subcategorias (veja-se a chave completa à página I · 1).

∧ Mountain	Berg	Montaña	Montagne	Montanha
∧∧ Mountains	Gebirge	Montañas	Montagnes	Montanhas
✕ Pass	Paß	Paso	Col	Passo
V Valley, Canyon	Tal, Cañon	Valle, Cañón	Vallée, Canyon	Vale, Canhão
≐ Plain	Ebene	Llano	Plaine	Planície
≻ Cape	Kap	Cabo	Cap	Cabo
I Island	Insel	Isla	Île	Ilha
II Islands	Inseln	Islas	Îles	Ilhas
± Other Topographic Features	Andere Topographische Objekte	Otros Elementos Topográficos	Autres données topographiques	Outros acidentes topográficos

ESPAÑOL Nombre / FRANÇAIS Nom / PORTUGUÊS Nome	Página / Page / Página	Lat.°'	Long.°' W = Oeste / W = Ouest / W = Oeste
General'nyj ≃	265a	60.00 N	30.32 E
General O'Brien	252	34.54 S	60.45 W
General Pacheco	288	34.28 S	58.38 W
General Pânfilo Natera	234	22.40 N	102.06 W
General Paz	258	35.31 S	58.19 W
General Pico	252	35.40 S	63.44 W
General Pinedo	252	27.19 S	61.17 W
General Pinto	252	34.46 S	61.53 W
General Pizarro	252	24.13 S	64.01 W
General Roca	252	39.02 S	67.35 W
General Rodríguez	258	34.36 S	58.57 W
General San Martín, Arg.	252	37.59 S	63.34 W
General San Martín, Arg.	258	34.34 S	58.32 W
General San Martín □5	288	34.34 S	58.34 W
General Santos (Dadiangas)	116	6.07 N	125.11 E
General Sarmiento	258	34.33 S	58.43 W
General Sarmiento □5	288	34.32 S	58.43 W
General'skoje	83	47.28 N	39.35 E
General Terán	232	25.16 N	99.41 W
General Tinio	116	15.21 N	121.03 E
General Toševo	38	43.42 N	28.02 E
General Treviño	196	26.14 N	99.29 W
General Viamonte (Los Toldos)	252	35.01 S	61.01 W
General Villegas	252	35.02 S	63.01 W
General Vintter, Lago (Lago Palena) ⊘	254	43.55 S	71.40 W
General Warren Village	285	40.02 N	75.32 W
General Zuazua	196	25.54 N	100.07 W
Genesee, Id., U.S.	202	46.33 N	116.55 W
Genesee, Pa., U.S.	214	41.59 N	77.52 W
Genesee, Wi., U.S.	216	42.58 N	88.21 W
Genesee □6, Mi., U.S.	216	42.56 N	83.41 W
Genesee □6, N.Y., U.S.	210	43.00 N	78.11 W
Genesee ≃	210	43.16 N	77.36 W
Geneseo, Il., U.S.	190	41.26 N	90.09 W
Geneseo, Ks., U.S.	198	38.30 N	98.09 W
Geneseo, N.Y., U.S.	210	42.47 N	77.49 W
Gênes → Genova	62	44.25 N	8.57 E
Geneva, S. Afr.	158	27.50 S	27.08 E
Geneva, Al., U.S.	194	31.01 N	85.51 W
Geneva, Fl., U.S.	220	28.44 N	81.07 W
Geneva, Il., U.S.	216	41.53 N	88.18 W
Geneva, In., U.S.	216	40.35 N	84.57 W
Geneva, Ne., U.S.	198	40.31 N	97.35 W
Geneva, N.Y., U.S.	210	42.52 N	77.00 W
Geneva, Oh., U.S.	214	41.48 N	80.56 W
Geneva, Pa., U.S.	214	41.35 N	80.14 W
Geneva, Wa., U.S.	224	48.45 N	122.24 W
Geneva, Lake (Lac Léman) (Lac de Genève) ⊘, Europe	58	46.25 N	6.30 E
Geneva, Lake ⊘, Wi., U.S.	216	42.34 N	88.30 W
Geneva → Genève	58	46.12 N	6.09 E
Geneva-on-the-Lake	214	41.52 N	80.57 W
Genève (Geneva)	58	46.12 N	6.09 E
Genève □3	58	46.15 N	6.10 E
Genève, Lac de → Geneva, Lake ⊘	58	46.25 N	6.30 E
Genève-Cointrin, Aéroport ⊠	58	46.14 N	6.06 E
Genevois ◆1	58	46.03 N	6.14 E
Genevriers, Île des I	186	51.15 N	58.26 W
Genf → Genève	58	46.12 N	6.09 E
Genga	66	43.26 N	12.56 E
Gengenbach	58	48.24 N	8.01 E
Genghis Khan, Wall of ⊥, Asia	88	49.00 N	115.00 E
Genghis Khan, Wall of ⊥, Mong.	88	49.00 N	116.00 E
Gengji	100	33.47 N	112.47 E
Gengma	102	23.34 N	99.06 E
Gengputou	106	31.12 N	119.55 E
Gengzhuang	104	40.59 N	122.42 E
Geničesk	78	46.11 N	34.48 E
Génicourt	261	49.05 N	2.04 E
Génicourt-sur-Meuse	56	49.02 N	5.26 E
Genil ≃	34	37.42 N	5.19 W
Génissiat	58	46.03 N	5.47 E
Genk	56	50.58 N	5.30 E
Genkai	96	33.51 N	130.30 E
Genkai-kokutei-kōen ♦	96	33.54 N	130.31 E
Genkai-nada ⊤2	92	34.00 N	130.00 E
Genkanyj, chrebet ⋏	180	66.15 N	172.20 W
Genlis	58	47.14 N	5.13 E
Gennach ≃	58	48.10 N	10.43 E
Gennargentu, Monti del ⋏	71	40.01 N	9.19 E
Gennebreck	263	51.19 N	7.12 E
Gennep	52	51.42 N	5.58 E
Genner	41	55.07 N	9.26 E
Gennes	32	47.20 N	0.14 W
Gennevilliers	261	48.56 N	2.18 E
Genoa, Austl.	166	37.29 S	149.35 E
Genoa, Il., U.S.	216	42.05 N	88.41 W
Genoa, Ne., U.S.	198	41.26 N	97.43 W
Genoa, Nv., U.S.	226	39.00 N	119.50 W
Genoa, N.Y., U.S.	210	42.40 N	76.32 W
Genoa, Oh., U.S.	214	41.31 N	83.21 W
Genoa, Wi., U.S.	190	43.34 N	91.13 W
Genoa, Arroyo ≃	254	44.58 S	70.06 W
Genoa City	216	42.29 N	88.19 W
Genoa → Genova	62	44.25 N	8.57 E
Genoa Peak ∧	226	39.03 N	119.53 W
Genola	62	44.35 N	7.39 E
Génolhac	62	44.21 N	3.57 E
Genova (Genoa)	62	44.25 N	8.57 E
Genova □4	62	44.30 N	9.04 E
Genova, Golfo di c	62	44.10 N	8.55 E
Genova, Val V	64	46.11 N	10.40 E
Genovesa, Isla I	246a	0.20 N	89.58 W
Genrijetty, ostrov I	74	77.06 N	156.30 E
Gensan → Wŏnsan	98	39.09 N	127.25 E
Gens de Terre ≃	190	46.53 N	76.00 W
Genshagen	264a	52.19 N	13.19 E
Genshagener Heide ◆	264a	52.20 N	13.18 E
Genshiryoku-kenkyūsho ʋ3	94	36.27 N	140.36 E
Gensingen	56	49.53 N	7.55 E
Gensungen	56	51.08 N	9.26 E
Gent (Gand)	50	51.03 N	3.43 E
Gentbrugge	50	51.03 N	3.45 E
Gent-Brugge, Kanaal ≡	50	51.03 N	3.43 E
Genteng	115a	8.22 S	114.09 E
Genteng, Gili I	115a	7.12 S	113.54 E
Genteng, Tanjung >	115a	7.23 S	106.24 E
Genthin	54	52.24 N	12.09 E
Gentilly	261	48.49 N	2.21 E
Gentilly ≃	206	46.24 N	72.21 W
Genting	114	3.42 N	98.10 E
Gentio do Ouro	250	11.25 S	42.30 W
Gentioux	32	45.47 N	1.59 E
Gentofte	41	55.45 N	12.33 E
Gentry	194	36.16 N	94.29 W
Gentry, Lake ⊘	220	28.08 N	81.15 W
Genua → Genova	62	44.25 N	8.57 E
Genuang	114	2.29 N	102.53 E
Genval	50	50.43 N	4.29 E
Genyem	164	2.46 S	140.12 E
Genzano di Lucania	68	40.51 N	16.02 E
Genzano di Roma	66	41.42 N	12.41 E
Geographe Bay c	162	33.35 S	115.15 E
Geographe Channel ʊ	162	24.40 S	113.20 E
Geokčaj	84	40.39 N	47.44 E
Geokčaj ≃	84	40.39 N	47.45 E
Geok-Tepe	128	38.09 N	57.58 E
Geonkhāli	126	22.12 N	88.03 E
George, S. Afr.	158	33.58 S	22.24 E
George, Ia., U.S.	198	43.20 N	96.00 W
George, Tx., U.S.	222	30.59 N	96.07 W
George ≃, Austl.	162	20.50 S	117.28 E
George ≃, P.Q., Can.	176	58.49 N	66.10 W
George, Cape >	186	45.53 N	61.53 W
George, Lake ⊘, Austl.	162	22.37 S	123.38 E
George, Lake ⊘, Austl.	166	35.05 S	149.25 E
George, Lake ⊘, N.A.	190	46.28 N	84.10 W
George, Lake ⊘, Ug.	154	0.02 N	30.12 E
George, Lake ⊘, U.S.	216	41.45 N	85.00 W
George, Lake ⊘, Fl., U.S.	192	29.17 N	81.36 W
George, Lake ⊘, In., U.S.	216	41.40 N	87.30 W
George, Lake ⊘, N.Y., U.S.	188	43.35 N	73.35 W
George Air Force Base ■	228	34.35 N	117.22 W
George B. Stevenson Dam ◆6	214	41.25 N	78.01 W
George Gill Range ⋏	162	24.15 S	131.36 E
George H. Crosby Manitou State Park ♦	190	47.29 N	91.10 W
George Island I	254	52.19 S	59.45 W
George Mason University ʋ2	284c	38.50 N	77.17 W
Georgensgmünd	56	49.11 N	11.00 E
Georgenthal	54	50.49 N	10.40 E
Georges ≃	170	33.57 S	150.58 E
Georges Bank ✣4	16	41.15 N	67.30 W
Georges Island I	283	42.19 N	70.56 W
Georges Sound ʊ	172	44.50 S	167.23 E
Georges River Bridge ◆5	274a	34.00 S	151.07 E
Georges Run	214	40.21 N	80.37 W
Georges Run ≃	279b	40.23 N	80.06 W
Georgetown, Austl.	166	18.18 S	143.33 E
Georgetown, Austl.	166	41.06 S	146.50 E
Georgetown, P.E., Can.	186	46.11 N	62.32 W
George Town, Cay. Is.	238	19.18 N	81.23 W
Georgetown, Gam.	150	13.30 N	14.47 W
Georgetown, Guy.	246	6.48 N	58.10 W
George Town (Pinang), Malay.	114	5.25 N	100.20 E
Georgetown, St. Vin.	241h	13.16 N	61.08 W
Georgetown, Ca., U.S.	226	38.54 N	120.50 W
Georgetown, Co., U.S.	200	39.42 N	105.41 W
Georgetown, Ct., U.S.	207	41.15 N	73.26 W
Georgetown, De., U.S.	208	38.41 N	75.23 W
Georgetown, Fl., U.S.	192	29.23 N	81.38 W
Georgetown, Ga., U.S.	192	31.53 N	85.06 W
Georgetown, Id., U.S.	202	42.29 N	111.22 W
Georgetown, Il., U.S.	194	39.58 N	87.38 W
Georgetown, In., U.S.	218	38.17 N	85.58 W
Georgetown, Ky., U.S.	218	38.12 N	84.33 W
Georgetown, Ma., U.S.	207	42.43 N	70.59 W
Georgetown, Ms., U.S.	194	31.52 N	90.09 W
Georgetown, N.J., U.S.	285	40.04 N	74.39 W
Georgetown, N.Y., U.S.	210	42.46 N	75.44 W
Georgetown, Oh., U.S.	218	38.51 N	83.54 W
Georgetown, Pa., U.S.	214	40.39 N	80.30 W
Georgetown, S.C., U.S.	192	33.22 N	79.17 W
Georgetown, Tx., U.S.	222	30.37 N	97.40 W
Georgetown ◆8	284c	38.54 N	77.03 W
Georgetown, Lake ⊘1	222	30.40 N	97.45 W
Georgetown → Halton Hills	212	43.37 N	79.56 W
Georgetown Lake ⊘1	202	46.11 N	113.17 W
Georgetown Rowley State Forest ♦	283	42.42 N	70.58 W
Georgetown University ʋ2	284c	38.54 N	77.04 W
George V Coast ∧2	9	68.30 S	147.30 E
George VI Sound ʊ	9	71.00 S	68.00 W
George Washington Birthplace National Monument ♦	208	38.11 N	76.56 W
George Washington Bridge ◆5	276	40.51 N	73.57 W
George Washington Carver National Monument ♦	194	37.00 N	94.19 W
George West	196	28.19 N	98.07 W
Georg Forster ʋ3	9	70.47 S	11.51 E
Georgia □1, Asia	84	42.00 N	44.00 E
Georgia □1, Asia	84	42.00 N	44.00 E
Georgia □3, U.S.	178	32.50 N	83.15 W
Georgia □3, U.S.	192	32.50 N	83.15 W
Georgia, Strait of ʊ	182	49.20 N	124.00 W
Georgia del Sur, Isla de → South Georgia I	244	54.15 S	36.45 W
Georgia Heights	274	41.32 N	87.20 W
Georgiana	194	31.38 N	86.44 W
Georgian Bay c	190	45.15 N	80.50 W
Georgian Bay Islands National Park ♦	190	44.54 N	79.52 W
Géorgie du Sud → South Georgia I	244	54.15 S	36.45 W
Georgijevka, Kaz.	85	42.11 N	70.00 E
Georgijevka, Kaz.	85	43.03 N	74.43 E
Georgijevka, Kaz.	86	49.19 N	81.35 E
Georgijevka, Ross.	80	53.18 N	51.01 E
Georgijevka, Ukr.	83	48.26 N	39.17 E
Georgijevsk	84	44.09 N	43.28 E
Georgina ≃	166	23.30 S	139.47 E
Georgina Island I	212	44.23 N	79.17 W
Georgina Island Indian Reserve ◆4	212	44.22 N	79.19 W
Georgsmarienhütte	52	52.12 N	8.02 E
Georg von Neumayer ʋ3	9	70.37 S	8.22 W
Gera	54	50.52 N	12.04 E
Gera ≃	54	51.08 N	10.56 E
Geraardsbergen	50	50.46 N	3.52 E
Geraberg	54	50.43 N	10.50 E
Gerabronn	56	49.15 N	9.55 E
Gerace	68	38.16 N	16.13 E
Geraci Siculo	70	37.51 N	14.09 E
Geral, Serra ∧4, Bra.	250	11.15 S	46.30 W
Geral, Serra ∧4, Bra.	252	26.30 S	50.30 W
Gerald	219	38.23 N	91.19 W
Geral de Goiás, Serra ∧4	242	13.00 S	46.15 W
Geraldine, N.Z.	172	44.05 S	171.14 E
Geraldine, Mt., U.S.	202	47.36 N	110.15 W
Geraldton, Austl.	162	28.46 S	114.36 E
Geraldton, On., Can.	176	49.44 N	86.57 W
Gerar, Naḥal V	132	31.24 N	34.26 E
Gerard, Lake ⊘	276	41.06 N	74.33 W
Gerard, Mount ∧	162	27.13 S	122.41 E
Gérardmer	58	48.04 N	6.53 E
Geras	61	48.48 N	15.40 E
Gerasa ⊥	132	32.17 N	35.53 E
Gerasdorf	61	48.18 N	16.28 E
Gerasimovka	86	58.37 N	71.53 E
Gerber	204	40.03 N	122.08 W
Gerber Reservoir ⊘1	202	42.12 N	121.06 W
Gerbéviller	58	48.30 N	6.31 E
Gerblingerode	52	51.29 N	10.15 E
Gerbstedt	54	51.38 N	11.37 E
Gerca	78	48.09 N	26.16 E
Gerchsheim	56	49.42 N	9.47 E
Gercüş	130	37.34 N	41.23 E
Gerdau	158	26.28 S	26.06 E
Gerdine, Mount ∧	180	61.35 N	152.26 W
Gerdview	273d	26.10 S	28.11 E
Gère ≃	62	45.32 N	4.54 E
Gerede	130	40.48 N	32.12 E
Gereja Cathedral ʋ1	269e	6.10 S	106.49 E
Gerenzano	266b	45.38 N	9.00 E
Gereshk	120	31.48 N	64.34 E
Geretsried	64	47.51 N	11.28 E
Gérgal	34	37.07 N	2.33 W
Gerge'bil	84	42.31 N	47.05 E
Gerger	130	37.57 N	39.01 E
Geria Nij	126	23.56 N	86.55 E
Gerik	114	5.25 N	101.08 E
Gering	198	41.49 N	103.39 W
Geringswalde	54	51.04 N	12.54 E
Geriş	130	36.58 N	31.44 E
Gerlachovský štít ∧	30	49.12 N	20.08 E
Gerlafingen	58	47.10 N	7.34 E
Gerli ◆8	288	34.41 S	58.23 W
Gerlingen	56	48.48 N	9.03 E
Gerlos	64	47.14 N	12.02 E
Gerlospass)(	64	47.14 N	12.08 E
Gerlova Hut'	60	49.10 N	13.17 E
Germa (Jarmah) ⊥	146	26.33 N	13.04 E
Germagnano	62	45.15 N	7.28 E
Germain, Grand lac ⊘	186	51.12 N	66.41 W
Germania	214	41.39 N	77.40 W
Germano	214	40.25 N	80.57 W
Germanoviči	76	55.25 N	27.44 E
Germansen, Mount ∧	182	55.37 N	124.50 W
Germansen Lake ⊘	182	55.41 N	124.53 W
Germansen Landing	182	55.47 N	124.43 W
Germansville	208	40.42 N	75.42 W
Germantown, Il., U.S.	219	38.33 N	89.32 W
Germantown, Ky., U.S.	218	38.39 N	83.57 W
Germantown, N.Y., U.S.	210	42.08 N	73.54 W
Germantown, Oh., U.S.	218	39.37 N	84.22 W
Germantown, Tn., U.S.	194	35.05 N	89.48 W
Germantown, Wi., U.S.	216	43.13 N	88.06 W
Germantown ◆8	285	40.03 N	75.11 W
Germantown Dam ◆6	218	39.38 N	84.24 W
Germany □1, Europe	22	51.00 N	10.00 E
Germany (Deutschland) □1, Europe	30	51.00 N	10.00 E
Germany Flats ≚	276	41.05 N	74.39 W
Germay	58	48.25 N	5.21 E
Germencik	130	37.51 N	27.37 E
Germendorf	54	52.45 N	13.10 E
Germering	60	48.08 N	11.22 E
Germersheim	56	49.13 N	8.22 E
Germfask	190	46.14 N	85.55 W
Germiston	158	26.13 S	28.11 E
Germiston □5	273d	26.15 S	28.10 E
Germiston South	273d	26.15 S	28.10 E
Gernika-Lumo (Guernica y Luno)	34	43.19 N	2.41 W
Gernrode	54	51.43 N	11.08 E
Gernsbach	56	48.46 N	8.19 E
Gernsheim	56	49.44 N	8.29 E
Gero	94	35.48 N	137.14 E
Geroda	56	50.17 N	9.53 E
Gerola Alta	58	46.03 N	9.32 E
Geroldsgrün	54	50.20 N	11.35 E
Geroldstein	56	50.06 N	7.56 E
Gerolsbach	60	48.30 N	11.22 E
Gerolstein	56	50.13 N	6.40 E
Gerolzhofen	56	49.54 N	10.21 E
Gerona	116	15.36 N	120.36 E
Gerona → Girona	34	41.59 N	2.49 E
Geronimo	196	34.28 N	98.22 W
Gerpinnes	50	50.20 N	4.31 E
Gerrards Cross	260	51.35 N	0.34 W
Gerrei ◆1	71	39.28 N	9.17 E
Gerresheim ◆8	263	51.14 N	6.52 E
Gerringong	170	34.45 S	150.50 E
Gerry	214	42.12 N	79.15 W
Gers □5	32	43.40 N	0.30 E
Gers ≃	32	44.09 N	0.39 E
Gersau	58	47.00 N	8.32 E
Gersdorf	54	50.45 N	12.42 E
Gersfeld	56	50.27 N	9.55 E
Gershøj	41	55.43 N	11.59 E
Gersprenz ≃	56	49.59 N	9.04 E
Gerstetten	56	48.37 N	10.01 E
Gersthofen	58	48.25 N	10.53 E
Gerstungen	56	50.58 N	10.04 E
Gertak Sanggul, Tanjong >	114	5.15 N	100.11 E
Gerthe ◆8	263	51.31 N	7.17 E
Gerufa	156	19.17 S	26.02 E
Gervais	224	45.06 N	122.53 W
Gerwisch	54	52.10 N	11.44 E
Gerza	142	29.26 N	31.11 E
Gerze, Tür.	130	41.48 N	35.12 E
Gêrzê, Zhg.	120	32.16 N	84.12 E
Gerzen	60	48.31 N	12.25 E
Gerzensee	58	46.51 N	7.33 E
Gescher	52	51.57 N	6.59 E
Geschriebenstein (Írottkő) ∧	61	47.21 N	16.26 E
Geschwenda	54	50.44 N	10.49 E
Gesees	60	49.54 N	11.32 E
Geseke	52	51.38 N	8.31 E
Geser	164	3.53 S	130.54 E
Gesher HaZiw	132	33.02 N	35.06 E
Gesi	115a	7.20 S	111.01 E
Gesoa	164	8.25 S	143.35 E
Gespunsart	56	49.49 N	4.50 E
Gessertshausen	58	48.20 N	10.44 E
Gesso ≃	62	44.24 N	7.33 E
Gessopalena	66	42.03 N	14.16 E
Gesten	41	55.32 N	9.12 E
Gesualdo	68	41.00 N	15.04 E
Geta	26	60.23 N	19.50 E
Getafe	34	40.18 N	3.43 W
Getafe, Aeropuerto ⊠	266a	40.18 N	3.43 W
Gete ≃	56	50.57 N	5.07 E
Gethaoli	272c	19.08 N	73.01 E
Getiil	154	1.13 N	30.12 E
Getinge	26	56.49 N	12.44 E
Gettorf	41	54.24 N	9.58 E
Gettysburg, Oh., U.S.	218	40.06 N	84.29 W
Gettysburg, Pa., U.S.	208	39.49 N	77.13 W
Gettysburg, S.D., U.S.	198	45.00 N	99.57 W
Gettysburg National Military Park ♦	208	39.49 N	77.15 W
Getulândia	256	22.40 S	44.06 W
Getulina	255	21.49 S	49.55 W
Getulio	116	10.45 N	122.40 E
Getúlio Vargas	252	27.50 S	52.16 W
Getz Ice Shelf ⁑	9	75.00 S	129.00 W
Getzville	210	43.01 N	78.46 W
Geumpang	114	4.48 N	96.09 E
Geureudong, Gunung ∧	114	4.48 N	96.48 E
Gevān	128	26.03 N	57.17 E
Gevaş	128	38.16 N	43.07 E
Gevelsberg	56	51.19 N	7.20 E
Gevgelija	38	41.08 N	22.30 E
Gévora ≃	34	38.53 N	6.57 W
Gevrey-Chambertin	58	47.14 N	4.57 E
Gewane	144	10.10 N	40.39 E
Geweke ◆8	263	51.22 N	7.25 E
Gex	58	46.20 N	6.04 E
Geyer	54	50.37 N	12.55 E
Geyer Ditch ≡	216	41.36 N	86.25 W
Geyikli	130	39.48 N	26.12 E
Geysdorp	158	26.32 S	25.18 E
Geyser	202	47.15 N	110.29 W
Geyserville	204	38.42 N	122.54 W
Geyshtasar, Kūh-e ∧	84	38.51 N	47.14 E
Geyuan	100	28.31 N	117.44 E
Geyve	130	40.30 N	30.18 E
Gézenti	146	21.41 N	18.18 E
Gezer	132	31.52 N	34.55 E
Gföhl	61	48.31 N	15.30 E
Ghaapplato ⋏1	158	27.30 S	24.00 E
Ghabāghib	132	33.10 N	36.13 E
Ghābat al-'Arab	140	9.02 N	29.29 E
Ghadaf, Wādī al- V	132	31.46 N	36.50 E
Ghadāmis	146	30.08 N	9.30 E
Ghaddūwah	146	26.26 N	14.18 E
Ghafe	272c	19.05 N	73.07 E
Ghagghar ≃	123	29.30 N	74.53 E
Ghāghara ≃	124	25.47 N	84.37 E
Ghaghar Reservoir ⊘1	124	24.38 N	83.11 E
Ghāghra	124	23.17 N	84.33 E
Ghakhar	123	32.18 N	74.09 E
Ghallah, Wādī al- V	140	10.25 N	27.32 E
Ghammāzah al-Kubrā	142	29.43 N	31.18 E
Ghamrīn	142	30.30 N	30.55 E
Ghana □1, Afr.	134	8.00 N	1.00 W
Ghana □1, Afr.	150	8.00 N	1.00 W
Ghansoli	272c	19.08 N	72.59 E
Ghanzi	156	21.38 S	21.45 E
Ghanzi □5	158	22.00 S	23.00 E
Gharāpuri	272c	18.54 N	72.56 E
Gharaunda	124	29.33 N	76.58 E
Gharbah, Wādī V	142	29.40 N	31.58 E
Gharbi, Chott ⊘	148	33.50 N	1.30 W
Gharbi, Oued el V	148	31.50 N	0.51 E
Gharbīyah, As-Ṣaḥrā' al- (Western Desert) ◆2	140	27.00 N	27.00 E
Ghardaïa	148	32.31 N	3.37 E
Ghardimaou	36	36.26 N	8.27 E
Gharghoda	124	22.10 N	83.21 E
Gharībwāl	123	32.41 N	73.10 E
Gharīfah	132	33.38 N	35.31 E
Gharig	140	10.47 N	27.33 E
Ghārīyat al-Gharbīyah	132	32.41 N	36.13 E
Ghārīyat ash-Sharqīyah	132	32.40 N	36.16 E
Gharo	120	24.44 N	67.35 E
Gharrāf, Shaṭṭ al- ≃	128	32.30 N	45.48 E
Gharroli ◆8	272a	28.37 N	77.20 E
Gharsa, Chott el ⊘	148	34.06 N	7.50 E
Gharw, Jazīrat I	142	31.21 N	30.06 E
Gharyān	146	32.10 N	13.01 E
Ghaṣm	132	32.33 N	36.22 E
Ghāt	146	24.58 N	10.11 E
Ghātāl	126	22.40 N	87.43 E
Ghatampur	272b	22.54 N	88.10 E
Ghatere, Mount ∧	175e	7.49 S	158.54 E
Ghates Occidentales → Western Ghāts ⋏	122	14.00 N	75.00 E
Ghates Orientales → Eastern Ghāts ⋏	122	14.00 N	78.50 E
Ghātkopar ◆8	272c	19.05 N	72.54 E
Ghātprabha ≃	122	16.20 N	75.48 E
Ghātsīla	126	22.36 N	86.29 E
Għawdex (Gozo) I	36	36.03 N	14.15 E
Ghawr ash-Sharqīyah, Qanāt al- (East Ghor Canal) ≡	132	32.41 N	35.38 E
Ghaylah ∧1	132	33.11 N	37.05 E
Ghayl Bā Wazīr	144	14.48 N	49.21 E
Ghayl Bin Yumayn ⊤4	144	15.33 N	49.23 E
Ghayth, Wādī V	132	30.59 N	36.00 E
Ghazāl, Baḥr al- ≃	140	9.31 N	30.25 E
Ghazāl, Baḥr el V	146	13.11 N	15.28 E
Ghazālat al-Khīs	142	30.34 N	31.34 E
Ghāziābād	128	28.40 N	77.26 E
Ghāzīpur, India	124	25.35 N	83.34 E
Ghāzīpur, India	272b	22.36 N	88.34 E
Ghāzīpur ◆8	272a	28.38 N	77.19 E
Ghazīr	130	34.01 N	35.40 E
Ghazlūna	120	31.24 N	67.42 E
Ghaznī	120	33.33 N	68.26 E
Ghaznī □4	120	33.15 N	67.45 E
Ghaznī ≃	120	32.35 N	67.58 E
Ghazni Khel	123	32.33 N	70.44 E
Ghazzah (Gaza), Isr. Occ	132	31.30 N	34.28 E
Ghazzah, Lubnān	132	33.40 N	35.49 E
Gheā ≃	272b	22.52 N	88.19 E
Ghedi	64	45.24 N	10.16 E
Ghemme	62	45.37 N	8.25 E
Ghennes Heights	279b	40.09 N	79.56 W
Ghent, Ky., U.S.	218	38.44 N	85.03 W
Ghent, N.Y., U.S.	210	42.19 N	73.36 W
Ghent, Oh., U.S.	214	41.09 N	81.38 W
Ghent → Gent	50	51.03 N	3.43 E
Gheora ◆8	272a	28.42 N	77.01 E
Gheorghe Gheorghiu-Dej	38	46.14 N	26.44 E
Gheorgheni	38	46.43 N	25.36 E
Gherla	38	47.02 N	23.55 E
Ghesar	272c	19.09 N	73.05 E
Ghigo	62	44.53 N	7.03 E
Ghilarza	71	40.07 N	8.50 E
Ghilizane	148	35.44 N	0.30 E
Ghīn, Tall ∧	132	32.39 N	36.43 E
Ghior	126	23.54 N	89.53 E
Ghislenghien, Bel.	50	50.39 N	3.52 E
Ghislenghien (Gellingen), Bel.	50	50.39 N	3.52 E
Ghisonaccia	36	42.00 N	9.25 E
Ghizar ≃	123	36.15 N	73.25 E
Ghizunabeana Islands II	175e	7.31 S	158.42 E
Ghlin	50	50.28 N	3.53 E
Ghlò, Beinn a' ∧	46	56.50 N	3.43 W
Ghogha	120	21.41 N	72.17 E
Gholson	222	31.43 N	97.12 W
Ghonda ◆8	272a	28.41 N	77.16 E
Ghondi ◆8	272a	28.42 N	77.16 E
Ghorāsahan	124	26.50 N	85.08 E
Ghoshpur, Bngl.	126	23.27 N	89.39 E
Ghoshpur, India	272b	22.23 N	88.29 E
Ghotki	120	28.01 N	69.19 E
Ghowr □4	128	34.00 N	65.00 E
Ghubaysh	140	12.09 N	27.21 E
Ghudāf, Wādī al- V	128	32.56 N	43.30 E
Ghulayfiqah	144	14.27 N	43.02 E
Ghunthur	130	34.23 N	37.09 E
Ghurāb, Jabal ∧2	142	28.58 N	31.16 E
Ghurayrah	144	18.37 N	42.41 E
Ghūrīān	128	34.21 N	61.30 E
Ghushuri	272b	22.37 N	88.22 E
Ghuwaybah, Wādī V	142	29.36 N	32.20 E
Ghuwayr, 'Ayn al- ⊤4	132	31.37 N	35.25 E
Ghuzzayil, Sabkhat ⊘	146	29.50 N	19.35 E
Giaginskaja	78	44.53 N	40.05 E
Gianh ≃	110	17.40 N	106.30 E
Giannutri, Isola di I	66	42.15 N	11.06 E
Giano, Monte ∧	66	42.25 N	13.06 E
Giano dell'Umbria	66	42.50 N	12.35 E
Giant City State Park ♦	194	37.39 N	89.12 W
Giant Mountain ∧	188	44.10 N	73.44 W
Giant's Castle ∧	158	29.21 S	29.27 E
Giant's Castle Game Reserve ◆4	158	29.16 S	29.30 E
Giant's Causeway ♦	48	55.14 N	6.30 W
Giants Neck	207	41.18 N	72.13 W
Giants Tomb Island I	212	44.55 N	80.00 W
Gianyar	115b	8.32 S	115.20 E
Gia Rai	110	9.14 N	105.28 E
Giardinello	70	38.05 N	13.09 E
Giardinetto	68	41.19 N	15.24 E
Giardini	70	37.50 N	15.17 E
Giarratana	70	37.03 N	14.48 E
Giarre	70	37.43 N	15.11 E
Giaveno	62	45.02 N	7.21 E
Giazza	64	45.39 N	11.07 E
Giba	71	39.04 N	8.38 E
Gibara	240p	21.07 N	76.08 W
Gibbon, Mn., U.S.	190	44.32 N	94.31 W
Gibbon, Ne., U.S.	198	40.44 N	98.50 W
Gibbons	182	53.50 N	113.20 W
Gibbonsville	202	45.33 N	113.55 W
Gibb River	164	16.25 S	126.22 E
Gibbs, Mount ∧	162	32.55 S	120.00 E
Gibbsboro	285	39.50 N	74.58 W
Gibbstown	208	39.49 N	75.17 W
Gibellina	70	37.47 N	12.58 E
Gibeon	156	25.09 S	17.43 E
Gibilmanna, Santuario di ʋ1	70	37.59 N	14.02 E
Gibraleón	34	37.23 N	6.58 W
Gibraltar, Gib.	34	36.08 N	5.21 W
Gibraltar, Mi., U.S.	216	42.06 N	83.12 W
Gibraltar, Pa., U.S.	208	40.17 N	75.52 W
Gibraltar □2, Europe	22	36.08 N	5.21 W
Gibraltar □2, Europe	34	36.08 N	5.21 W
Gibraltar, Strait of (Estrecho de Gibraltar) ʊ	34	35.57 N	5.36 W
Gibraltar Point >, On., Can.	275b	43.36 N	79.23 W
Gibraltar Point >, Eng., U.K.	44	53.05 N	0.19 E
Gibsland	194	32.32 N	93.03 W
Gibson, Austl.	162	33.39 S	121.48 E
Gibson, Ga., U.S.	192	33.14 N	82.35 W
Gibson, N.Y., U.S.	210	42.08 N	76.59 W
Gibson, Pa., U.S.	210	41.44 N	75.38 W
Gibson ≃	212	44.58 N	79.51 W
Gibson, Lake ⊘1	284a	43.06 N	79.14 W
Gibsonburg	214	41.23 N	83.19 W
Gibson City	216	40.27 N	88.22 W
Gibson Desert ◆2	162	24.30 S	126.00 E
Gibson Hill ∧2	214	41.51 N	80.10 W
Gibsonia, Fl., U.S.	220	28.06 N	81.58 W
Gibsonia, Pa., U.S.	214	40.38 N	79.59 W
Gibson Indian Reserve ◆4	212	45.01 N	79.44 W
Gibson Island I	208	39.05 N	76.26 W
Gibsons	182	49.24 N	123.30 W
Gibsonton	220	27.51 N	82.22 W
Gidajevo	24	59.57 N	52.22 E
Gidami	144	9.58 N	34.37 E
Gidda	144	9.34 N	35.23 E
Giddalūr	122	15.21 N	78.55 E
Giddarbāha	123	30.12 N	74.40 E
Giddings	222	30.10 N	96.56 W
Gideälven ≃	26	63.20 N	19.08 E
Gidea Park ◆8	260	51.35 N	0.12 E
Gideåvallen	26	63.29 N	18.58 E
Gideon	194	36.27 N	89.55 W
Gidgee	162	27.16 S	119.22 E
Gidgi, Lake ⊘	162	29.16 S	126.03 E
Gidhni	126	22.29 N	86.51 E
Gidole	144	5.38 N	37.30 E
Gidrotorf	80	56.28 N	43.33 E
Gidžaki, gora ∧	84	40.25 N	49.01 E
Giebelstadt	56	49.39 N	9.56 E
Gieboldehausen	52	51.36 N	10.13 E
Giedraičiai	76	55.05 N	25.15 E
Gielow	54	53.42 N	12.44 E
Gielsdorf	264a	52.36 N	13.52 E
Gien	50	47.42 N	2.38 E
Giengen	56	48.37 N	10.14 E
Giens	62	43.02 N	6.08 E
Gier ≃	62	45.35 N	4.46 E
Gierath	263	51.07 N	6.33 E
Gierle	56	51.16 N	4.51 E
Gieselwerder	52	51.36 N	9.33 E
Giesenkirchen ◆8	263	51.09 N	6.30 E
Giesing ◆8	64	48.06 N	11.35 E
Giessbachfälle ʟ	58	46.42 N	8.03 E
Giessen	56	50.35 N	8.40 E
Giessen □5	56	50.40 N	8.40 E
Gieten	52	53.00 N	6.46 E
Giethoorn	52	52.43 N	6.05 E
Gièvres	50	47.16 N	1.40 E
Giez	62	45.45 N	6.15 E
Giffone	68	38.27 N	16.10 E
Giffoni Valle Piana	68	40.44 N	14.56 E
Gifford, Scot., U.K.	46	55.54 N	2.45 W
Gifford, Fl., U.S.	220	27.40 N	80.24 W
Gifford, Il., U.S.	216	40.18 N	88.01 W
Gifford, In., U.S.	216	41.06 N	87.01 W
Gifford, Pa., U.S.	214	41.51 N	78.36 W
Gifford ≃	176	70.21 N	83.05 W
Gifford Creek	162	24.05 S	116.11 E
Gifford Pinchot State Park ♦	208	40.04 N	76.53 W
Giffre ≃	58	46.05 N	6.30 E
Gifhorn	52	52.29 N	10.33 E
Giflitz	56	51.09 N	9.07 E
Gif-sur-Yvette	261	48.42 N	2.08 E
Gifu	94	35.25 N	136.45 E
Gifu □5	94	35.45 N	137.00 E
Gigant	80	46.30 N	41.20 E
Giganta, Sierra de la ⋏	232	26.00 N	111.30 W
Gigante	246	2.23 N	75.33 W
Gigante Islands II	116	11.36 N	123.20 E
Gigen	38	43.42 N	24.29 E
Gigena → Alcira	252	32.45 S	64.20 W
Giggleswick	44	54.04 N	2.17 W
Gigha, Sound of ʊ	46	55.41 N	5.42 W
Gigha Island I	46	55.41 N	5.46 W
Gig Harbor	224	47.19 N	122.34 W
Giglio, Isola del I	66	42.21 N	10.54 E
Giglio Castello	66	42.22 N	10.54 E
Gigliola	66	44.51 N	12.14 E
Giglio Porto	66	42.22 N	10.55 E
Gigmoto	116	13.47 N	124.23 E
Gignod	62	45.46 N	7.17 E
Gihu → Gifu	94	35.25 N	136.45 E
Gijón	34	43.32 N	5.40 W
Gikongoro	154	2.29 S	29.34 E
Gila ≃	200	32.43 N	114.33 W
Gila, Middle Fork ≃	200	33.14 N	108.14 W
Gila Bend	200	32.56 N	112.42 W
Gila Bend Indian Reservation ◆4	200	33.00 N	112.46 W
Gila Bend Mountains ⋏	200	33.10 N	113.10 W
Gila Cliff Dwellings National Monument ♦	200	33.02 N	108.16 W
Gila Mountains ⋏	200	33.05 N	109.50 W
Gīlān □4	128	37.15 N	49.30 E
Gīlān-e Gharb	128	34.08 N	45.55 E
Gila River Indian Reservation ◆4	200	33.12 N	112.00 W
Gilātala	126	22.36 N	89.41 E
Gilberdyke	44	53.45 N	0.44 W
Gilbert, La., U.S.	194	32.02 N	91.39 W
Gilbert, Mn., U.S.	190	47.29 N	92.27 W
Gilbert ≃, Austl.	166	16.35 S	141.15 E
Gilbert ≃, Austl.	168b	34.22 S	138.40 E
Gilbert, Mount ∧	182	50.51 N	124.20 W
Gilbert Airport ⊠	279a	41.22 N	81.58 W
Gilbert Island I	219	39.35 N	91.11 W
Gilbert Islands → Kiribati □1	14	5.00 S	170.00 W
Gilbert Lake ⊘	281	42.34 N	83.17 W
Gilbert Lake State Park ♦	210	42.36 N	75.08 W
Gilberton	210	40.48 N	76.13 W
Gilbertown	194	31.52 N	88.19 W
Gilbert Peak ∧	224	46.30 N	121.25 W
Gilbert Plains	184	51.09 N	100.29 W
Gilbert River	166	18.09 S	142.52 E
Gilberts	216	42.06 N	88.23 W
Gilbert Seamount ✣3	16	52.50 N	150.10 W
Gilbertsville, N.Y., U.S.	210	42.28 N	75.19 W
Gilbertsville, Pa., U.S.	208	40.19 N	75.37 W
Gilbertville	207	42.18 N	72.12 W
Gilbjerg Hoved >	41	56.08 N	12.17 E
Gilboa	216	41.01 N	83.55 W
Gilboa', Haré ⋏2	132	32.30 N	35.23 E
Gilbués	250	9.50 S	45.21 W
Gilching	60	48.07 N	11.17 E
Gildehaus	52	52.18 N	7.06 E
Gildford	202	48.34 N	110.17 W
Gilead	216	41.48 N	85.09 W
Giles, Arroyo de ≃	258	34.20 S	59.23 W
Giles Meteorological Station ʋ3	162	25.02 S	128.18 E
Giles Point >	168b	35.03 S	137.45 E
Gilette	62	43.51 N	7.10 E
Gilford	48	54.23 N	6.22 W
Gilford Island I	182	50.45 N	126.25 W
Gilford Park	208	39.58 N	74.08 W
Gilgai	162	31.15 S	119.56 E
Gilgandra	166	31.42 S	148.39 E
Gilgil	154	0.30 S	36.19 E
Gil Gil Creek ≃	166	29.10 S	148.51 E
Gilgit	123	35.55 N	74.18 E
Gilgit ≃	123	35.44 N	74.38 E
Gilgo Island I	276	40.38 N	73.25 W
Gilgo State Park ♦	276	40.38 N	73.22 W
Gilima	154	3.55 N	28.22 E
Gilimanuk	115a	8.10 S	114.26 E
Gilirang	112	3.55 S	120.09 E
Gil Island I	182	53.13 N	129.15 W
Gill, Lough ⊘	48	54.16 N	8.24 W
Gillam	184	56.21 N	94.43 W
Gilleland Creek ≃	222	30.13 N	97.32 W
Gilleleje	41	56.07 N	12.19 E
Gillen, Lake ⊘	162	26.11 S	124.38 E
Gilles, Lake ⊘	166	32.50 S	136.45 E
Gillespie	219	39.07 N	89.49 W
Gillespies Point >	172	43.24 S	169.50 E
Gillett, Ar., U.S.	194	34.07 N	91.22 W
Gillett, Pa., U.S.	210	41.57 N	76.48 W
Gillett, Wi., U.S.	190	44.53 N	88.18 W
Gillette, N.J., U.S.	276	40.41 N	74.28 W
Gillette, Wy., U.S.	198	44.17 N	105.30 W
Gillette Castle State Park ♦	207	41.26 N	72.25 W
Gillian, Lake ⊘	176	69.32 N	75.23 W
Gillingham, Eng., U.K.	42	51.02 N	2.17 W
Gillingham, Eng., U.K.	260	51.24 N	0.33 E
Gillingham □8	260	51.22 N	0.35 E
Gills Rock	190	45.17 N	87.01 W
Gilman, Ct., U.S.	207	41.34 N	72.11 W
Gilman, Il., U.S.	216	40.46 N	87.59 W
Gilman, Ia., U.S.	190	41.52 N	92.47 W
Gilman, Wi., U.S.	190	45.10 N	90.48 W
Gilman Hot Springs	228	33.50 N	116.59 W
Gilman Lake	285	39.41 N	75.11 W
Gilmer, Il., U.S.	278	42.14 N	88.02 W
Gilmer, Tx., U.S.	222	32.43 N	94.56 W
Gilmer Park	216	41.36 N	86.15 W
Gilmore	171b	35.20 S	148.11 E
Gilmore City	198	42.44 N	94.27 W
Gilmore Creek ≃	171b	35.18 S	148.13 E
Gilo ≃	144	8.10 N	33.15 E
Gilroy	226	37.00 N	121.34 W
Gilserberg	56	50.57 N	9.04 E
Gilsizer Slough ≃	226	38.58 N	121.44 W
Gilston Park ♦	260	51.48 N	0.04 E
Giltner	198	40.46 N	98.09 W
Gil'uj ≃	89	53.58 N	127.30 E
Giluwe, Mount ∧	164	6.05 S	143.50 E
Gilwern	42	51.51 N	3.06 W
Gilze	52	51.33 N	4.57 E
Gimån ≃	26	62.28 N	16.20 E
Gimbi	144	9.10 N	35.42 E
Gimcheon → Kimch'ŏn	98	36.07 N	128.05 E
Gimie, Mount ∧	241f	13.52 N	61.01 W
Gimigliano	68	38.58 N	16.32 E
Gimlet	218	38.13 N	83.09 W
Gimli	184	50.38 N	96.59 W
Gimo	40	60.11 N	18.11 E
Gimoly	24	63.03 N	32.19 E
Gimone ≃	32	44.00 N	1.06 E
Gimont	32	43.38 N	0.53 E
Gimpu	112	1.36 S	120.02 E
Ginderich	263	51.39 N	6.32 E
Ginebra → Genève	58	46.12 N	6.09 E
Gineste, Col de la)(	62	43.15 N	5.27 E
Gingell	216	42.43 N	83.17 W
Gingera, Mount ∧	171b	35.35 S	148.47 E
Ginger Hill	279b	40.12 N	80.00 W
Ginger Island I	240m	18.24 N	64.28 W
Gingin, Austl.	162	31.21 S	115.42 E
Gin Gin, Austl.	166	25.00 S	151.58 E
Gingindlovu	158	29.02 S	31.30 E
Gingoog	116	8.50 N	125.07 E
Gingoog Bay c	116	8.59 N	125.05 E
Gingst	54	54.27 N	13.16 E
Ginir	144	7.07 N	40.46 E
Ginkakuji Temple ʋ1	270	35.03 N	135.47 E
Ginkgo State Park ♦	202	46.59 N	120.01 W
Ginnosar	132	32.51 N	35.31 E
Ginosa	68	40.35 N	16.46 E
Ginostra	70	38.47 N	15.11 E
Ginowan	174m	26.17 N	127.46 E
Ginoza	174m	26.28 N	127.57 E
Ginter	214	40.46 N	78.23 W
Ginza ◆8	268	35.40 N	139.47 E
Gioi	68	40.17 N	15.13 E
Gioia, Golfo di c	68	38.30 N	15.45 E
Gioia dei Marsi	66	41.57 N	13.42 E
Gioia del Colle	68	40.48 N	16.56 E
Gioia Tauro	68	38.26 N	15.54 E
Gioia Vecchio	66	41.54 N	13.44 E
Gioiosa Ionica	68	38.20 N	16.18 E
Gioiosa Marea	70	38.10 N	14.54 E
Giong Rieng	110	9.55 N	105.19 E
Giornico	58	46.24 N	8.52 E
Giovi, Passo dei)(	62	44.33 N	8.57 E
Giovinazzo	68	41.11 N	16.40 E
Giporlos	116	11.07 N	125.27 E
Gipping ≃	42	52.04 N	1.10 E
Gipsy	214	40.48 N	78.53 W
Gipuzkoako □4	34	43.10 N	2.10 W
Giraglia, Île de la I	62	43.02 N	9.24 E
Giralia	162	22.41 S	114.21 E
Giraltovce	30	49.07 N	21.31 E
Girard, Il., U.S.	219	39.26 N	89.46 W
Girard, Ks., U.S.	198	37.30 N	94.50 W
Girard, Mi., U.S.	216	42.02 N	85.00 W
Girard, Oh., U.S.	214	41.09 N	80.42 W
Girard, Pa., U.S.	214	42.00 N	80.19 W
Girard, Tx., U.S.	196	33.22 N	100.40 W
Girardot	246	4.18 N	74.48 W
Girardville	208	40.47 N	76.17 W
Giraud, Pointe >	240d	15.19 N	61.15 W
Giraul ≃	152	15.04 S	12.08 E
Giraumont	56	49.10 N	5.55 E
Girbovu	38	44.44 N	23.21 E
Girdletree	208	38.05 N	75.23 W
Giresun	130	40.55 N	38.24 E
Giresun □4	130	40.30 N	38.30 E
Giresun Dağları ⋏	130	40.30 N	39.00 E
Girgarre	166	36.24 S	144.59 E
Girgaum ◆8	272c	18.57 N	72.48 E

Symbol	English	Deutsch	Español	Français	Português
≃	River	Fluß	Río	Rivière	Rio
≡	Canal	Kanal	Canal	Canal	Canal
ʟ	Waterfall, Rapids	Wasserfall, Stromschnellen	Cascada, Rápidos	Chute d'eau, Rapides	Cascata, Rápidos
ʊ	Strait	Meeresstraße	Estrecho	Détroit	Estreito
c	Bay, Gulf	Bucht, Golf	Bahía, Golfo	Baie, Golfe	Baía, Golfo
⊘	Lake, Lakes	See, Seen	Lago, Lagos	Lac, Lacs	Lago, Lagos
≚	Swamp	Sumpf	Pantano	Marais	Pântano
⁑	Ice Features, Glacier	Eis- und Gletscherformen	Accidentes Glaciales	Formes glaciaires	Acidentes glaciares
⊤	Other Hydrographic Features	Andere Hydrographische Objekte	Otros Elementos Hidrográficos	Autres données hydrographiques	Outros acidentes hidrográficos
✣	Submarine Features	Untermeerische Objekte	Accidentes Submarinos	Formes de relief sous-marin	Acidentes submarinos
□	Political Unit	Politische Einheit	Unidad Politica	Entité politique	Unidade política
ʋ	Cultural Institution	Kulturelle Institution	Institución Cultural	Institution culturelle	Instituição cultural
⊥	Historical Site	Historische Stätte	Sitio Histórico	Site historique	Sitio histórico
♦	Recreational Site	Erholungs- und Ferienort	Sitio de Recreo	Centre de loisirs	Area de Lazer
⊠	Airport	Flughafen	Aeropuerto	Aéroport	Aeroporto
■	Military Installation	Militäranlage	Instalación Militar	Installation militaire	Instalação militar
◆	Miscellaneous	Verschiedenes	Misceláneo	Divers	Diversos

ESPAÑOL | FRANÇAIS | PORTUGUÊS

Nombre / Nom	Página / Page	Lat.°′	Long.°′ W = Oeste / W = Ouest
Hennersdorf	264b	48.07 N	16.22 E
Hennessey	196	36.06 N	97.53 W
Hennessey, Lake ⊜[1]	226	38.29 N	122.22 W
Hennickendorf	54	52.30 N	13.51 E
Henniez	58	46.44 N	6.54 E
Hennigsdorf	54	52.38 N	13.12 E
Henniker	188	43.10 N	71.49 W
Henning, Il., U.S.	216	40.18 N	87.42 W
Henning, Mn., U.S.	198	46.19 N	95.26 W
Henning, Tn., U.S.	194	35.40 N	89.34 W
Henri ≃	206	46.30 N	71.47 W
Henri, Cap ≻	186	49.48 N	64.23 W
Henri-Chapelle	56	50.40 N	5.56 E
Henrichemont	50	47.18 N	2.32 E
Henrichenburg	263	51.35 N	7.19 E
Henrico □[6]	208	37.30 N	77.20 W
Henrietta, N.Y., U.S.	210	43.03 N	77.36 W
Henrietta, N.C., U.S.	192	35.15 N	81.47 W
Henrietta, Tx., U.S.	196	33.49 N	98.11 W
Henrietta Maria, Cape ≻	176	55.09 N	82.20 W
Henri Pittier, Parque Nacional ♦	246	10.25 N	67.43 W
Henry, Il., U.S.	190	41.06 N	89.21 W
Henry, S.D., U.S.	198	44.52 N	97.27 W
Henry □[6], In., U.S.	218	39.55 N	85.22 W
Henry □[6], Ky., U.S.	218	38.26 N	85.09 W
Henry □[6], Oh., U.S.	216	41.20 N	84.04 W
Henry ≃	162	22.40 S	115.40 E
Henry, Cape ≻	208	36.55 N	76.01 W
Henry, Mount ∧	202	48.53 N	115.31 W
Henry, Mount ∧[2]	274a	33.50 S	150.38 E
Henry, Point ≻	162	34.29 S	119.23 E
Henry Cowell Redwoods State Park ♦	226	37.02 N	122.03 W
Henryetta	196	35.26 N	95.58 W
Henry Island I	224	48.35 N	123.11 W
Henry Kater, Cape ≻	176	69.05 N	66.44 W
Henry Mountains ⋏	200	38.00 N	110.50 W
Henrys Bend	214	41.28 N	79.37 W
Henrys Fork ≃, U.S.	200	41.00 N	109.39 W
Henrys Fork ≃, Id., U.S.	202	43.45 N	111.56 W
Henryville, P.Q., Can.	206	45.08 N	73.11 W
Henryville, In., U.S.	218	38.32 N	85.46 W
Henry W. Coe State Park ♦	226	37.12 N	121.30 W
Hensall	190	43.26 N	81.30 W
Henshaw, Lake ⊜[1]	204	33.15 N	116.45 W
Hensley	194	34.30 N	92.12 W
Hensley Lake ⊜[1]	226	37.07 N	119.53 W
Henslow, Cape ≻	175e	9.56 S	160.38 E
Henson Creek ≃	284b	38.46 N	77.00 W
Hensonville	210	42.17 N	74.13 W
Henstedt-Ulzburg	52	53.47 N	9.58 E
Henstridge	42	50.59 N	2.24 W
Hentiesbaai	156	22.08 S	14.18 E
Henty	166	35.31 S	147.02 E
Henzada	110	17.38 N	95.28 E
Hepburn	184	52.31 N	106.43 W
Hepburn Springs	169	37.19 S	144.09 E
Hephzibah	192	33.18 N	82.05 W
Heping, Zhg.	100	27.10 N	117.18 E
Heping, Zhg.	100	22.01 N	112.59 E
Heping, Zhg.	100	23.17 N	116.29 E
Heping, Zhg.	100	24.28 N	114.58 E
Heping, Zhg.	106	30.50 N	119.54 E
Heppenheim	56	49.39 N	8.38 E
Heppner	202	45.21 N	119.33 W
Heptonstall	262	53.45 N	2.01 W
Heptonstall Moor ≃	262	53.46 N	2.05 W
Hepu (Lianzhou)	102	21.39 N	109.11 E
Hepworth	212	44.37 N	81.09 W
Heqiao, Zhg.	100	32.55 N	118.22 E
Heqiao, Zhg.	106	31.30 N	119.53 E
Heqing	102	26.34 N	100.12 E
Hequ	102	39.26 N	111.08 E
Héraðsflói c	24a	65.45 N	14.10 W
Hera Lacinia, Tempio di ⊥	68	39.01 N	17.13 E
Herāt	128	34.20 N	62.12 E
Herāt □[4]	128	34.30 N	62.00 E
Hérault □[5]	32	43.40 N	3.30 E
Hérault ≃	32	43.17 N	3.26 E
Herbasse ≃	62	45.02 N	4.57 E
Herbault	50	47.36 N	1.08 E
Herbede	56	51.25 N	7.16 E
Herbern	52	51.44 N	7.39 E
Herbert, Sk., Can.	184	50.26 N	107.12 W
Herbert, N.Z.	172	45.14 S	170.47 E
Herbert ≃	166	18.32 S	146.17 E
Herbert, Mount ∧	172	43.41 S	172.44 E
Herbertabad	110	11.43 N	92.37 E
Herbert Hoover National Historic Site ⊥	190	41.38 N	91.23 W
Herbertingen	58	48.04 N	9.26 E
Herbert Island I	180	52.45 N	170.10 W
Herberton	166	17.23 S	145.23 E
Herbertsdale	158	34.01 S	21.46 E
Herbeumont	56	49.47 N	5.14 E
Herbignac	32	47.27 N	2.19 W
Herb Lake	184	54.47 N	99.47 W
Herblay	50	49.00 N	2.10 E
Herblet Lake ⊜	184	54.56 N	99.54 W
Herbolzheim	58	48.13 N	7.47 E
Herborn	56	50.40 N	8.17 E
Herbrechtingen	56	48.37 N	10.10 E
Herbringhauser-Stausee ⊜[1]	263	51.14 N	7.16 E
Herbsleben	54	51.07 N	10.50 E
Herbstein	56	50.34 N	9.20 E
Herceg-Novi	38	42.27 N	18.32 E
Herculaneum	219	38.16 N	90.22 W
Hércules, Méx.	232	28.02 N	103.48 W
Hercules, Ca., U.S.	282	38.01 N	122.17 W
Herdecke	56	51.24 N	7.26 E
Herdorf	56	50.46 N	7.56 E
Herðubreið ∧	24a	65.13 N	16.18 W
Heredia	236	10.00 N	84.07 W
Heredia □[4]	236	10.30 N	84.00 W
Hereford, Eng., U.K.	42	52.04 N	2.43 W
Hereford, Az., U.S.	200	31.26 N	110.05 W
Hereford, Md., U.S.	208	39.35 N	76.39 W
Hereford, Tx., U.S.	196	34.48 N	102.23 W
Hereford and Worcester □[6]	42	52.10 N	2.30 W
Hereford Cathedral ᵾ[1]	42	52.04 N	2.43 W
Hereford Mountain ∧	206	45.05 N	71.36 W
Hereke	130	40.48 N	29.39 E
Herekino	172	35.15 S	173.13 E
Herencia	34	39.21 N	3.22 W
Herent	56	50.54 N	4.40 E
Herentals	56	51.11 N	4.50 E
Hereroland Oos □[5]	156	21.00 S	20.00 E
Hereroland Wes □[5]	156	20.30 S	18.15 E
Herfølge	41	55.25 N	12.10 E
Herford	52	52.06 N	8.40 E
Hergatz	58	47.39 N	9.50 E
Hergisdorf	54	51.32 N	11.28 E
Hergla	36	36.02 N	10.31 E
Herhahn	56	50.33 N	6.26 E
Héricourt	58	47.35 N	6.45 E
Hérimoncourt	58	47.26 N	6.53 E
Heringen	54	51.27 N	10.52 E
Heringsdorf	54	54.18 N	11.00 E
Herington	198	38.40 N	96.56 W
Heriot	172	45.50 S	169.16 E
Herisau	58	47.23 N	9.17 E
Heritage Range ⋏	9	79.30 S	84.00 W
Herk ≃	56	50.58 N	5.07 E
Herk-de-Stad	56	50.56 N	5.10 E
Herkimer	210	43.01 N	74.59 W
Herkimer □[6]	210	43.02 N	74.59 W
Herlen — Kerulen ≃	90	48.48 N	117.00 E
Herleshausen	56	51.00 N	10.09 E
Herlev	41	55.43 N	12.27 E
Herlong	204	40.09 N	120.08 W
Herlufmagle	41	55.19 N	11.46 E
Herlufsholm	41	55.15 N	11.46 E
Hermagor	64	46.37 N	13.22 E
Herman, Mn., U.S.	198	45.48 N	96.08 W
Herman, Ne., U.S.	198	41.40 N	96.12 W
Herman, Pa., U.S.	214	40.50 N	79.49 W
Herman, Lake ⊜	282	38.05 N	122.09 W
Hermana Mayor Island I	116	15.48 N	119.48 E
Hermanas	196	27.13 N	101.14 W
Herman Eksteen Park ♦	273d	26.10 S	28.02 E
Herma Ness ≻	46a	60.50 N	0.55 W
Hermann	219	38.42 N	91.26 W
Hermannsburg, Austl.	162	23.57 S	132.45 E
Hermannsburg, Dtsch.	52	52.50 N	10.05 E
Hermannsburg Aboriginal Reserve ◆[4]	162	24.00 S	132.45 E
Hermanns-Denkmal ⊥	52	51.55 N	8.50 E
Hermannskogel ∧	264b	48.16 N	16.18 E
Hermannstadt — Sibiu	38	45.48 N	24.09 E
Hermano Peak ∧	200	37.13 N	108.48 W
Hermansverk	26	61.11 N	6.51 E
Hermansville	190	45.42 N	87.36 W
Hermanus	158	34.25 S	19.16 E
Hermanville	194	31.57 N	90.50 W
Hermeray	261	48.38 N	1.41 E
Hermes	50	49.22 N	2.15 E
Hermeskeil	56	49.39 N	6.56 E
Hermidale	166	31.33 S	146.43 E
Hermies	50	50.07 N	3.02 E
Herminie	214	40.15 N	79.43 W
Hermiston	202	45.50 N	119.17 W
Hermitage, Nf., Can.	186	47.33 N	55.56 W
Hermitage, Eng., U.K.	42	51.27 N	1.16 W
Hermitage, Ar., U.S.	194	33.26 N	92.10 W
Hermitage, Mo., U.S.	194	37.56 N	93.18 W
Hermitage Bay c	186	47.35 N	56.05 W
Hermitage Park	284c	39.05 N	77.04 W
Hermite, Isla I	254	55.52 S	67.20 W
Hermit Islands II	164	1.30 S	145.05 E
Hermleigh	196	32.38 N	100.46 W
Hermon, S. Afr.	158	33.27 S	18.59 E
Hermon, N.Y., U.S.	212	44.28 N	75.13 W
Hermon, Mount — Shaykh, Jabal ash- ∧	132	33.26 N	35.51 E
Hermosa Beach	280	33.51 N	118.23 W
Hermosillo, Méx.	200	32.30 N	114.59 W
Hermosillo, Méx.	232	29.04 N	110.58 W
Hermoso, Cerro ∧	246	1.10 S	78.12 W
Hermsdorf	54	50.54 N	11.52 E
Hermsdorf ◆[8]	264a	52.37 N	13.18 E
Hermyingyi	110	14.15 N	98.21 E
Hernád ≃	30	47.56 N	21.08 E
Hernals ◆[8]	264b	48.13 N	16.20 E
Hernandarias	252	25.22 S	54.45 W
Hernández	234	23.01 N	102.01 W
Hernandez Reservoir ⊜[1]	226	36.22 N	120.49 W
Hernando, Arg.	252	32.25 S	63.44 W
Hernando, Fl., U.S.	220	28.54 N	82.22 W
Hernando, Ms., U.S.	194	34.49 N	89.59 W
Hernando □[6]	220	28.34 N	82.22 W
Hernando de Magallanes, Parque Nacional ♦	254	54.15 S	72.00 W
Hernani	116	11.20 N	125.37 E
Herndon, Ca., U.S.	226	36.49 N	119.54 W
Herndon, Ks., U.S.	198	39.54 N	100.47 W
Herndon, Pa., U.S.	210	40.42 N	76.50 W
Herndon, Va., U.S.	208	38.58 N	77.23 W
Herndon Canal ≅	226	36.46 N	119.46 W
Herne	52	51.32 N	7.13 E
Herne Bay	42	51.23 N	1.08 E
Herne Hill	168a	31.50 S	116.01 E
Herning	41	56.08 N	8.59 E
Hernwood Heights	284b	39.22 N	77.50 W
Heroica Zitácuaro	234	19.24 N	100.22 W
Herongate	260	51.36 N	0.21 E
Herongen	56	51.24 N	6.15 E
Heron Island I	166	23.26 S	151.55 E
Heron Lake	198	43.47 N	95.19 W
Hérons, Île aux I	275a	45.25 N	73.35 W
Heronsgate	260	51.38 N	0.31 W
Hérouville	261	49.06 N	2.08 E
Hérouville-Saint-Clair	32	49.12 N	0.21 W
Herpf	54	50.34 N	10.20 E
Herradura	252	26.29 S	58.18 W
Herräng	40	60.08 N	18.39 E
Herreid	198	45.50 N	100.04 W
Herrenalb	56	48.48 N	8.26 E
Herrenberg	56	48.35 N	8.52 E
Herrenchiemsee, Schloss ⊥	64	47.52 N	12.23 E
Herrera	252	28.29 S	63.04 W
Herrera □[4]	236	7.54 N	80.38 W
Herrera del Duque	34	39.10 N	5.03 W
Herrera de Pisuerga	34	42.36 N	4.20 W
Herrick, Austl.	166	41.06 S	147.52 E
Herrick, Il., U.S.	219	39.13 N	88.59 W
Herrick Creek ≃	182	54.20 N	121.30 W
Herrick Grove	212	44.04 N	76.12 W
Herricks	276	40.45 N	73.40 W
Herrieden	56	49.14 N	10.30 E
Herrin	194	37.48 N	89.01 W
Herring Bay c	208	38.44 N	76.33 W
Herring Brook ≃	283	42.10 N	70.44 W
Herring Cove, N.S., Can.	186	44.34 N	63.34 W
Herring Cove, Ak., U.S.	182	55.21 N	131.41 W
Herring Creek ≃	208	37.49 N	77.07 W
Herringen	52	51.40 N	7.44 E
Herring Run ≃	284b	39.18 N	76.31 W
Herring Run Park ♦	284b	39.19 N	76.33 W
Herritslev	41	54.42 N	11.41 E
Herrljunga	26	58.05 N	13.02 E
Herrnburg	54	53.47 N	10.45 E
Herrnhut	54	51.01 N	14.44 E
Herrsching am Ammersee	60	48.00 N	11.10 E
Herrs Island I	279b	40.28 N	79.58 W
Herrskogen	40	59.32 N	16.15 E
Herry	50	47.13 N	2.57 E
Hersbruck	60	49.30 N	11.26 E
Herschbach	56	50.34 N	7.44 E
Herscheid	56	51.10 N	7.44 E
Herschel, Sk., Can.	184	51.38 N	108.21 W
Herschel, Transkei	158	30.37 S	27.12 E
Herschel Island I	180	69.35 N	139.05 W
Herscher	216	41.03 N	88.06 W
Herselt	56	51.03 N	4.53 E
Herserange	56	49.31 N	5.47 E
Hersham	260	51.22 N	0.23 W
Hershey, Ne., U.S.	198	41.09 N	101.00 W
Hershey, Pa., U.S.	208	40.17 N	76.39 W
Hersman	219	39.57 N	90.44 W
Herstadberg	40	58.38 N	16.10 E
Herstal	56	50.40 N	5.38 E
Herstmonceux	42	50.53 N	0.20 E
Herten	52	51.35 N	7.07 E
Hertford, Eng., U.K.	260	51.48 N	0.05 W
Hertford, N.C., U.S.	192	36.11 N	76.27 W
Hertford □[6]	208	36.28 N	77.01 W
Hertfordshire □[6]	42	51.50 N	0.10 W
Hertingfordbury	260	51.48 N	0.06 W
Hertsmere □[8]	260	51.41 N	0.17 W
Hertzogville	158	28.08 S	25.33 E
Heruncun	104	40.58 N	123.27 E
Hervás	34	40.16 N	5.51 W
Herve	56	50.38 N	5.48 E
Hervest	263	51.40 N	7.01 E
Hervey Bay c	166	25.00 S	153.00 E
Herxheim	56	49.09 N	8.13 E
Héry, Fr.	50	47.54 N	3.38 E
Héry, Fr.	62	45.46 N	6.28 E
Herzberg, Dtsch.	54	52.54 N	12.58 E
Herzberg, Dtsch.	54	51.41 N	13.14 E
Herzberg am Harz	52	51.39 N	10.20 E
Herzebrock	52	51.53 N	8.14 E
Herzfelde	54	52.29 N	13.50 E
Herzhausen	56	51.11 N	8.53 E
Herzliyya	132	32.10 N	34.51 E
Herznach	58	47.28 N	8.03 E
Herzogenaurach	56	49.34 N	10.53 E
Herzogenbuchsee	58	47.12 N	7.41 E
Herzogenburg	61	48.17 N	15.42 E
Herzogenrath	56	50.52 N	6.06 E
Herzsprung	54	53.04 N	12.28 E
Heṣār, Kūh-e ⋏	120	34.50 N	66.30 E
Hesarak	267d	35.47 N	51.19 E
Hesdin	50	50.22 N	2.02 E
Hesel	52	53.18 N	7.35 E
Hesepe	52	52.26 N	7.58 E
Heshachang	107	30.37 N	105.40 E
Heshan	110	23.52 N	108.52 E
Heshangqiao	100	34.15 N	113.47 E
Heshengqiao	100	30.00 N	114.22 E
Heshi, Zhg.	100	25.04 N	118.37 E
Heshi, Zhg.	107	29.10 N	104.22 E
Heshui, Zhg.	100	24.24 N	114.56 E
Heshui, Zhg.	102	22.48 N	112.29 E
Heshuijian	100	30.33 N	116.05 E
Heshun, Zhg.	100	27.30 N	117.24 E
Heshun, Zhg.	102	37.21 N	113.35 E
Heshuo	86	42.15 N	86.53 E
Hesketh Bank	262	53.42 N	2.51 W
Hesketh Out Marsh ≋	262	53.43 N	2.55 W
Heskin Green	262	53.38 N	2.42 W
Hesler	218	38.28 N	84.47 W
Hesperange	56	49.34 N	6.09 E
Hesperia, Ca., U.S.	228	34.25 N	117.18 W
Hesperia, Mi., U.S.	190	43.34 N	86.02 W
Hesperus Mountain ∧	200	37.27 N	108.05 W
Hess ≃	180	63.34 N	133.57 W
Hesselager	41	55.10 N	10.45 E
Hesselberg ∧	56	49.04 N	10.32 E
Hesselø I	41	56.12 N	11.43 E
Hesselte	52	52.25 N	7.22 E
Hessen	54	52.02 N	10.15 E
Hessen □[3]	30	50.30 N	9.15 E
Hessen Cassal	216	41.00 N	85.05 W
Hessenthal	56	49.55 N	9.17 E
Hessisch Lichtenau	56	51.12 N	9.43 E
Hessisch Oldendorf	52	52.10 N	9.15 E
Hessle	44	53.44 N	0.26 W
Hesso	166	32.08 S	137.27 E
Hess Tablemount ✧[3]	14	17.50 N	174.15 W
Hesston, Ks., U.S.	198	38.08 N	97.25 W
Hesston, Pa., U.S.	214	40.26 N	78.07 W
Heston ◆[8]	260	51.29 N	0.22 W
Heswall	262	53.20 N	3.06 W
Het ≃	110	20.49 N	104.01 E
Hetai	102	23.22 N	112.19 E
Hetanbu	100	28.21 N	117.11 E
Hetang, Zhg.	100	26.40 N	119.09 E
Hetang, Zhg.	106	31.43 N	120.27 E
Hetang, Zhg.	107	28.58 N	106.03 E
Heṭauḍā	124	85.02 N	27.26 E
Hetch Hetchy Aqueduct ≅[1]	226	37.29 N	122.19 W
Hetch Hetchy Reservoir ⊜[1]	226	37.57 N	119.43 W
Hethersett	42	52.36 N	1.11 E
Hetian, Zhg.	100	25.41 N	116.26 E
Hetian, Zhg.	100	23.19 N	115.38 E
Het Loo, Paleis ᵾ	52	52.14 N	5.56 E
Hetou	100	24.18 N	113.29 E
Hetoudian	98	37.02 N	120.35 E
Hettange-Grande	56	49.24 N	6.09 E
Hettenleidelheim	56	49.32 N	8.04 E
Hettick	219	39.21 N	90.02 W
Hettingen	58	48.13 N	9.14 E
Hettinger	198	46.00 N	102.38 W
Hetton-le-Hole	44	54.50 N	1.27 W
Hettstedt	54	51.38 N	11.30 E
Hetupu	100	30.50 N	116.03 E
Hetzendorf ◆[8]	264b	48.10 N	16.18 E
Hetzerath	56	49.52 N	6.49 E
Het Zoute	50	51.21 N	3.18 E
Heuchin	50	50.28 N	2.16 E
Heudeber	54	51.54 N	10.50 E
Heule	50	50.50 N	3.14 E
Heuningspruit	158	27.26 S	27.28 E
Heusden	50	51.02 N	5.16 E
Heustreu	56	50.21 N	10.15 E
Heusweiler	56	49.20 N	6.55 E
Heuvelton	212	44.37 N	75.24 W
Hève, Cap de la ≻	50	49.31 N	0.04 E
Heven	263	51.26 N	7.17 E
Heverlee	56	50.52 N	4.42 E
Heves	30	47.36 N	20.17 E
Heves □[6]	30	47.50 N	20.15 E
Hevlín	61	48.45 N	16.23 E
Ḥevron, Naḥal V	132	31.15 N	34.50 E
Hewanorra International Airport ⊠	241f	13.45 N	60.56 W
Hewitt, N.J., U.S.	210	41.08 N	74.18 W
Hewitt, Tx., U.S.	222	31.27 N	97.11 W
Hewittsville	219	39.32 N	89.19 W
Hewlett, N.Y., U.S.	276	40.38 N	73.41 W
Hewlett, Va., U.S.	208	37.55 N	77.35 W
Hewlett Bay Park	276	40.38 N	73.42 W
Hewlett Harbor	276	40.38 N	73.41 W
Hewlett Neck	276	40.37 N	73.42 W
Hewlett Point ≻	276	40.50 N	73.45 W
Hewopu	104	41.14 N	122.24 E
Hewu	100	26.41 N	113.40 E
Hexen Kopf ∧	58	47.01 N	10.28 E
Hexham	44	54.58 N	2.06 W
Hexi, Zhg.	100	24.52 N	117.15 E
Hexi, Zhg.	102	24.09 N	102.39 E
Hexi, Zhg.	106	31.03 N	119.49 E
Hexian, Zhg.	100	31.43 N	118.22 E
Hexian, Zhg.	102	24.15 N	111.43 E
Hexibao	102	38.34 N	102.11 E
Hexingchang	107	30.05 N	104.35 E
Hexingjie	106	31.55 N	120.36 E
Hexiwu	105	39.38 N	116.58 E
Hex Rivierberge ⋏	158	33.25 S	19.37 E
Hextable	260	51.25 N	0.11 E
Hexton	172	38.37 S	177.58 E
Heyan	104	42.30 N	120.29 E
Heyang, Zhg.	98	35.27 N	118.33 E
Heyang, Zhg.	102	35.15 N	110.06 E
Heybeli ◆[8]	267b	40.53 N	29.05 E
Heybeli Ada I	267b	40.53 N	29.05 E
Heybridge	260	51.44 N	0.41 E
Heyburn	202	42.33 N	113.45 W
Heyerode	54	51.10 N	10.25 E
Heyrieux	62	45.38 N	5.03 E
Heysham	44	54.02 N	2.54 W
Heyuan	100	23.44 N	114.41 E
Heywood, Austl.	166	38.08 S	141.38 E
Heywood, Eng., U.K.	262	53.36 N	2.13 W
Heyworth	216	40.18 N	88.58 W
Heze (Caozhou)	98	35.17 N	115.27 E
Hezhang	102	27.00 N	104.37 E
Hezhao	98	37.08 N	115.17 E
Hezhen	100	29.56 N	120.10 E
Hezheng	102	35.25 N	103.10 E
Hezijian	105	40.13 N	116.03 E
Hezixu	100	24.54 N	115.14 E
Hezuo	102	34.58 N	102.57 E
Hiale	110	15.55 N	107.34 E
Hialeah	220	25.51 N	80.16 W
Hialeah Park Race Track ♦	220	25.51 N	80.17 W
Hiaohexi	100	31.21 N	114.02 E
Hiawassee	192	34.56 N	83.45 W
Hiawatha, Ks., U.S.	198	39.51 N	95.32 W
Hiawatha, Ut,. U.S.	200	39.29 N	111.00 W
Hiba-Dōgo-Taishaku-kokutei-kōen ♦	96	35.07 N	133.08 E
Hibaldstow	44	53.31 N	0.32 W
Hibbing	190	47.25 N	92.56 W
Hibbs, Point ≻	166	42.38 S	145.15 E
Hibernia	276	40.57 N	74.30 W
Hibernia Reef ✧[2]	160	12.00 S	123.23 E
Hibiki-nada ⊤[2]	96	34.00 N	130.30 E
Hiburi-shima I	96	33.10 N	132.17 E
Hibuson Island I	116	10.27 N	125.29 E
Hickam Air Force Base ■	229c	21.20 N	157.57 W
Hickey, Mount ∧	169	37.22 S	145.19 E
Hickman, Ca., U.S.	226	37.37 N	120.45 W
Hickman, Ky., U.S.	194	36.34 N	89.11 W
Hickman, Ne., U.S.	198	40.37 N	96.37 W
Hickman, Pa., U.S.	279b	40.23 N	80.09 W
Hickman's Harbour	186	48.06 N	53.44 W
Hickory, Ms., U.S.	194	32.19 N	89.01 W
Hickory, N.C., U.S.	192	35.43 N	81.20 W
Hickory, Pa., U.S.	214	40.18 N	80.18 W
Hickory Corners	216	42.26 N	85.22 W
Hickory Creek ≃, Il., U.S.	278	41.30 N	88.06 W
Hickory Creek ≃, Mi., U.S.	216	42.05 N	86.29 W
Hickory Creek ≃, Tx., U.S.	222	31.29 N	95.07 W
Hickory Flat	194	34.36 N	89.11 W
Hickory Hills	216	41.43 N	87.49 W
Hickory Run State Park ♦	210	41.02 N	75.41 W
Hickory Township	214	41.15 N	80.27 W
Hicks, Point ≻	166	37.48 S	149.17 E
Hicks Bay	172	37.36 S	178.18 E
Hickson Lake ⊜	184	56.17 N	104.25 W
Hicksville, N.Y., U.S.	210	40.46 N	73.31 W
Hicksville, Oh., U.S.	216	41.17 N	84.45 W
Hico	196	31.58 N	98.02 W
Hicpochee, Lake ⊜	220	26.50 N	81.10 W
Hida ≃	94	35.26 N	137.03 E
Hida — Hita	96	33.19 N	130.56 E
Hidaka, Nihon	94	35.54 N	139.21 E
Hidaka, Nihon	96	35.28 N	134.47 E
Hidaka, Nihon	96	33.55 N	135.09 E
Hidaka ≃	96	33.52 N	135.09 E
Hidaka-sammyaku ⋏	92a	42.35 N	142.45 E
Hida-Kiso-gawa-kokutei-kōen ♦	94	35.37 N	137.15 E
Hida-kōchi ⋏[1]	94	36.16 N	137.05 E
Hidalgo, Méx.	232	27.47 N	99.52 W
Hidalgo, Méx.	232	25.59 N	100.27 W
Hidalgo, Méx.	232	24.15 N	99.26 W
Hidalgo □[3]	234	20.30 N	99.00 W
Hidalgo del Parral	232	26.56 N	105.40 W
Hida-sammyaku ⋏	94	36.25 N	137.40 E
Hiddenhausen	52	52.08 N	8.38 E
Hidden Hills	228	34.09 N	118.43 W
Hiddensee I	54	54.33 N	13.07 E
Hidden Valley, Ca., U.S.	226	38.46 N	121.09 W
Hidden Valley, Tx., U.S.	222	29.54 N	95.25 W
Hiddesen	52	51.55 N	8.50 E
Hiddinghausen	263	51.22 N	7.17 E
Hıdırbaba	130	38.47 N	39.00 E
Hidrolândia	255	16.58 S	49.14 W
Hidrolina	255	14.37 S	49.25 W
Hieflau	61	47.36 N	14.44 E
Hienghène	175f	20.41 S	164.56 E
Hierapolis — Pamukkale ⊥	130	37.58 N	29.19 E
Hierges	56	50.06 N	4.44 E
Hierro (Ferro) I	148	27.45 N	18.00 W
Hiesfeld	263	51.33 N	6.46 E
Hietzing ◆[8]	264b	48.11 N	16.18 E
Higashi	174m	26.38 N	128.09 E
Higashi ◆[8]	270	34.41 N	135.31 E
Higashibetsuin	270	34.56 N	135.34 E
Higashifuji-enshūjō ■	94	35.17 N	138.51 E
Higashihiroshima	96	34.26 N	132.42 E
Higashiichiki	92	31.40 N	130.20 E
Higashiiyayama	96	33.52 N	133.54 E
Higashiizu	94	34.48 N	139.04 E
Higashi-jima I	174f	24.47 N	141.23 E
Higashikurume	268	35.45 N	139.32 E
Higashimatsuyama	94	36.02 N	139.24 E
Higashimonzen	268	35.56 N	139.40 E
Higashimurayama	94	35.46 N	139.29 E
Higashinada ◆[8]	270	34.43 N	135.16 E
Higashinakano	268	35.38 N	139.25 E
Higashinari ◆[8]	270	34.40 N	135.33 E
Higashine	92	38.26 N	140.24 E
Higashinose	270	34.55 N	135.30 E
Higashiōizumi ◆[8]	268	35.45 N	139.36 E
Higashiōsaka	96	34.39 N	135.35 E
Higashishirakawa	94	35.39 N	137.19 E
Higashisumiyoshi ◆[8]	270	34.37 N	135.32 E
Higashitokonoo-san ∧	96	35.25 N	134.55 E
Higashitsuno	96	33.23 N	133.02 E
Higashiura, Nihon	94	34.59 N	136.58 E
Higashiura, Nihon	270	34.33 N	135.00 E
Higashiyama ◆[8]	270	35.00 N	135.48 E
Higashiyamato	268	35.44 N	139.26 E
Higashiyodogawa ◆[8]	270	34.44 N	135.31 E
Higashiyoshino	94	34.24 N	135.58 E
Higbee	194	39.18 N	92.30 W
Higganum	207	41.29 N	72.33 W
Higgins	196	36.07 N	100.02 W
Higgins, Mount ∧	224	48.19 N	121.45 W
Higgins Lake ⊜	190	44.30 N	84.45 W
Higginsport	218	38.47 N	83.58 W
Higginsville, Austl.	162	31.45 S	121.43 E
Higginsville, Mo., U.S.	194	39.04 N	93.43 W
Higgs' Hope	158	29.19 S	23.16 E
Higham Ferrers	42	52.18 N	0.36 W
Higham Upshire	260	51.26 N	0.28 E
Highbank	222	31.10 N	96.50 W
High Bank Creek ≃	216	42.37 N	85.11 W
High Bar Indian Reserve ◆[4]	182	51.06 N	122.00 W
High Beach	260	51.39 N	0.02 E
High Bentham	44	54.08 N	2.30 W
High Bluff Island I	212	43.58 N	77.45 W
Highbridge, Eng., U.K.	42	51.13 N	2.49 W
High Bridge, N.J., U.S.	210	40.40 N	74.53 W
Highbury	164	16.25 S	143.09 E
Highcliff	279b	40.32 N	80.03 W
Higher Ballam	262	53.46 N	2.59 W
Higher Broughton ◆[8]	262	53.30 N	2.15 W
Higher Hogshead ∧[2]	262	53.42 N	2.09 W
Higher Penwortham	262	53.45 N	2.44 W
Higher Walton, Eng., U.K.	44	53.44 N	2.39 W
Higher Walton, Eng., U.K.	262	53.22 N	2.37 W
Higher Walton, Eng., U.K.	262	53.45 N	2.38 W
Higher Whitley	262	53.19 N	2.35 W
Highett	274b	37.57 S	145.03 E
High Falls	210	41.50 N	74.08 W
High Falls ∟	212	43.56 N	75.23 W
High Force ∟	44	54.38 N	2.13 W
Highgate	214	42.30 N	81.49 W
Highgate Center	206	44.56 N	73.02 W
Highgate Springs	206	44.58 N	73.06 W
Highgrove	228	34.01 N	117.20 W
High Halstow	260	51.27 N	0.34 E
High Hesket	44	54.48 N	2.48 W
High Hill	219	38.52 N	91.23 W
High Hill ∧[2]	276	40.49 N	73.25 W
High Hill ≃, Can.	184	56.45 N	110.30 W
High Hill ≃, Mb., Can.	184	55.52 N	94.42 W
High Hill Lake ⊜	184	55.34 N	95.40 W
High Island I, H.K.	271d	22.22 N	114.21 E
High Island I, Mi., U.S.	190	45.42 N	85.40 W
High Island Creek ≃	190	44.35 N	93.54 W
High Island Reservoir ⊜[1]	271d	22.23 N	114.21 W
Highland, Ca., U.S.	228	34.07 N	117.12 W
Highland, Il., U.S.	219	38.44 N	89.40 W
Highland, In., U.S.	216	41.33 N	87.27 W
Highland, Ks., U.S.	198	39.51 N	95.16 W
Highland, Md., U.S.	208	39.11 N	76.57 W
Highland, Mi., U.S.	281	42.38 N	83.37 W
Highland, N.Y., U.S.	210	41.43 N	73.57 W
Highland, Oh., U.S.	218	39.21 N	83.36 W
Highland, Pa., U.S.	279b	40.33 N	80.04 W
Highland □[4]	46	57.40 N	5.00 W
Highland □[6]	218	39.12 N	83.37 W
Highland Beach	220	26.25 N	80.04 W
Highland City	220	27.58 N	81.53 W
Highland Creek ≃, On., Can.	275b	43.46 N	79.08 W
Highland Creek ≃, Ca., U.S.	226	38.24 N	121.14 W
Highland Falls	210	41.22 N	73.58 W
Highland Heights, Ky., U.S.	218	39.04 N	84.27 W
Highland Heights, Oh., U.S.	214	41.33 N	81.28 W
Highland Hills	278	41.52 N	88.01 W
Highland Home	194	31.57 N	86.18 W
Highland Lake, Il., U.S.	278	42.21 N	88.04 W
Highland Lake, Ma., U.S.	283	42.41 N	72.37 W
Highland Lake, N.Y., U.S.	210	41.32 N	74.51 W
Highland Lake ⊜, Ct., U.S.	207	41.54 N	73.06 W
Highland Lake ⊜, Il., U.S.	278	42.22 N	88.04 W
Highland Lake ⊜, N.J., U.S.	276	41.10 N	74.28 W
Highland Lakes	210	41.10 N	74.28 W
Highland-on-the-Lake	284a	42.42 N	79.59 W
Highland Park, Il., U.S.	216	42.10 N	87.48 W
Highland Park, Md., U.S.	284c	38.54 N	76.54 W
Highland Park, Mi., U.S.	216	42.24 N	83.05 W
Highland Park, N.J., U.S.	210	40.29 N	74.25 W
Highland Park, Pa., U.S.	210	40.38 N	77.35 W
Highland Park, Tx., U.S.	222	32.50 N	96.48 W
Highland Park ◆[8]	280	34.07 N	118.13 W
Highland Park ♦, Ma., U.S.	283	42.30 N	70.55 W
Highland Park ♦, Pa., U.S.	279b	40.29 N	79.55 W
Highland Peak ∧	226	38.33 N	119.45 W
Highland Point ≻	220	25.30 N	81.12 W
Highlands, N.J., U.S.	208	40.24 N	73.59 W
Highlands, N.C., U.S.	192	35.03 N	83.11 W
Highlands, Tx., U.S.	222	29.49 N	95.03 W
Highlands □[6]	220	27.20 N	81.16 W
Highlands Hammock State Park ♦	220	27.28 N	81.33 W
Highland Silver Lake ⊜[1]	219	38.47 N	89.39 W
Highlands North ◆[8]	273d	26.09 S	28.05 E
Highland Springs	208	37.32 N	77.19 W
Highlands Reservoir ⊜[1]	222	29.50 N	95.02 W
Highland State Recreation Area ♦	216	42.39 N	83.33 W
Highlandtown ◆[8]	284b	39.17 N	76.33 W
High Laver	260	51.45 N	0.13 E
High Legh	262	53.21 N	2.27 W
Highley	42	52.27 N	2.23 W
Highmore	198	44.31 N	99.26 W
High Ongar	260	51.43 N	0.16 E
High Park ♦	275b	43.39 N	79.28 W
High Peak □[8]	262	53.23 N	1.55 W
High Peak ∧, Pil.	116	15.29 N	120.07 E
High Peak ∧, N.Y., U.S.	210	42.09 N	74.05 W
High Peak ◆[1]	44	53.22 N	1.50 W
High Point, Fl., U.S.	220	27.55 N	82.42 W
High Point, N.C., U.S.	192	35.57 N	80.00 W
Highpoint, Oh., U.S.	218	39.14 N	84.24 W
High Point ∧, N.J., U.S.	210	41.19 N	74.40 W
High Point ∧, Wy., U.S.	202	41.37 N	107.47 W
High Point State Park ♦	210	41.18 N	74.41 W
High Prairie	182	55.26 N	116.29 W
High Ridge	219	38.27 N	90.32 W
High River	182	50.35 N	113.52 W
High Rock	192	26.36 N	76.18 W
High Rock ∧	188	39.33 N	79.06 W
Highrock Indian Reserve ◆[4]	184	55.54 N	100.30 W
Highrock Lake ⊜, Mb., Can.	184	55.45 N	100.30 W
Highrock Lake ⊜, Sk., Can.	184	57.04 N	105.30 W
High Rock Lake ⊜[1]	192	35.40 N	80.17 W
High Seat ∧	44	54.24 N	2.18 W
High Spire	208	40.12 N	76.47 W
High Springs	192	29.49 N	82.35 W
High Street ∧	44	54.29 N	2.52 W
Hightown, Eng., U.K.	44	53.31 N	3.03 W
Hightown, Eng., U.K.	262	53.32 N	3.04 W
Hightstown	208	40.16 N	74.31 W
High View	210	41.33 N	74.27 W
Highwater	206	45.01 N	72.26 W
Highway City	226	36.49 N	119.54 W
High Willhays ∧	42	50.41 N	3.59 W
Highwood, Il., U.S.	216	42.11 N	87.48 W
Highwood, Mt., U.S.	202	47.35 N	110.47 W
Highwood ≃	182	50.49 N	113.47 W
Highwood Baldy ∧	202	47.27 N	110.37 W
Highwood Creek ≃	202	47.40 N	111.00 W
Highwood Mountains ⋏	202	47.25 N	110.30 W
Highworth	42	51.38 N	1.43 W
High Wycombe	42	51.38 N	0.46 W
Higlet	154	1.04 S	40.19 E
Higuera Blanca	234	19.42 N	105.10 W
Higuera de Abuya	232	24.16 N	107.04 W
Higuera de Zaragoza	232	25.59 N	109.16 W
Higueras	196	25.58 N	100.01 W
Higüero, Punta ≻	240m	18.22 N	67.16 W
Higüey	238	18.37 N	68.42 W
Higuito ≃	236	14.43 N	88.40 W
Hihétro	150	7.32 N	1.06 E
Hihyā	142	30.40 N	31.36 E
Hii ≃	96	35.26 N	132.54 E
Hiidenportin kansallispuisto ♦	26	63.50 N	28.59 E
Hiiraan □[4]	144	4.00 N	45.30 E
Hiiumaa I	76	58.52 N	22.40 E
Hījānah, Buḥayrat al- ⊜	132	33.18 N	36.36 E
Híjar	34	41.10 N	0.27 W
Hiji	96	33.22 N	131.32 E
Hiji ≃	96	33.36 N	132.29 E
Hijikawa	96	33.27 N	132.41 E
Hijiri-dake ∧	94	35.26 N	138.10 E
Hikami	96	35.10 N	135.02 E
Hikari, Nihon	94	35.39 N	140.30 E
Hikari, Nihon	96	33.58 N	131.56 E
Hikarigaoka	268	35.50 N	139.58 E
Hikawa	96	35.25 N	132.50 E
Hikawa Shrine ᵾ[1]	268	35.54 N	139.38 E
Hiketa	96	34.13 N	134.24 E
Hiki ≃	96	33.33 N	135.27 E
Hikigawa	96	33.34 N	135.27 E
Hikimi	96	34.34 N	132.01 E
Hikimi ≃	96	34.37 N	131.48 E
Hikiura	270	34.33 N	134.58 E
Hikone	94	35.15 N	136.15 E
Hikone-jō ⊥	94	35.15 N	136.14 E
Hiko-san ∧	96	33.27 N	130.54 E
Hikueru I[1]	14	17.36 S	142.37 W
Hikurangi	172	35.36 S	174.18 E
Hikurangi ∧	172	37.55 S	178.04 E
Hikutaia	172	37.17 S	175.39 E
Hikutivake	174v	18.56 S	169.53 W
Hila	112	7.35 S	127.24 E
Hilaban Island I	116	12.03 N	125.34 E
Hilāl, Jabal ⋏	132	30.40 N	34.00 E
Hilāl, Ra's al- ≻	146	32.57 N	22.10 E
Hilbersdorf	54	50.55 N	13.23 E
Hilbert	190	44.08 N	88.09 W
Hilbre Islands II	262	53.23 N	3.13 W
Hilbre Point ≻	262	53.23 N	3.12 W
Hilchenbach	56	51.00 N	8.06 E
Hilda	184	50.28 N	110.03 W
Hildburghausen	54	50.25 N	10.44 E
Hilden	56	51.10 N	6.56 E
Hildenborough	260	51.13 N	0.15 E
Hilders	56	50.34 N	10.00 E
Hildesheim	52	52.09 N	9.57 E
Hildreth	198	40.20 N	99.02 W
Hilgen	263	51.06 N	7.09 E
Hilialawa	114	0.41 N	97.53 E
Hiligeo	114	1.22 N	97.10 E
Hiliotaluwa	114	0.44 N	97.53 E
Hill □[6]	222	32.02 N	97.10 W
Hillaby, Mount ∧	241g	13.12 N	59.35 W
Hill Air Force Base ■	202	41.05 N	111.58 W
Hillandale, S. Afr.	158	33.06 S	20.36 E
Hillandale, Md., U.S.	284c	39.01 N	76.58 W
Hillandale Heights	284c	39.01 N	76.59 W
Hill Bank	232	17.35 N	88.42 W
Hillburn	210	41.08 N	74.10 W
Hill City, Ks., U.S.	198	39.21 N	99.50 W
Hill City, Mn., U.S.	190	46.59 N	93.35 W
Hill City, S.D., U.S.	198	43.55 N	103.34 W
Hill Creek ≃	200	39.55 N	109.40 W
Hillcrest, Il., U.S.	216	41.57 N	89.04 W
Hillcrest, N.Y., U.S.	210	41.07 N	74.02 W
Hillcrest, N.Y., U.S.	210	42.09 N	75.53 W
Hillcrest Center	228	35.23 N	118.57 W
Hillcrest Heights	284c	38.49 N	76.57 W
Hillcrest Mines	182	49.34 N	114.23 W
Hillcrest Orchard	216	41.51 N	83.29 W
Hillcrest Park	226	38.07 N	122.16 W
Hill Cumorah ⊥	210	43.01 N	77.15 W
Hille, Dtsch.	52	52.20 N	8.44 E
Hille, Sve.	40	60.44 N	17.11 E
Hillegom	52	52.18 N	4.35 E
Hillegossen	52	51.59 N	8.37 E
Hillerød	41	55.56 N	12.19 E
Hillers Creek ≃	219	38.38 N	91.54 W
Hillesheim	56	50.18 N	6.38 E
Hilli	124	25.17 N	89.01 E
Hilliard, Fl., U.S.	192	30.41 N	81.55 W
Hilliard, Oh., U.S.	218	40.02 N	83.09 W
Hilliards	214	41.05 N	79.50 W
Hillingdon ◆[8]	260	51.32 N	0.27 W
Hillisburg	216	40.17 N	86.20 W
Hill Island Lake ⊜	176	60.29 N	109.50 W
Hillister	194	30.40 N	94.23 W
Hillman	190	45.03 N	83.54 W
Hillman ≃	168a	33.26 S	116.48 E
Hillmersdorf	54	51.42 N	13.29 E
Hill of Fearn	46	57.45 N	3.56 W
Hills	198	43.31 N	96.21 W
Hills and Dales	214	39.42 N	84.13 W
Hillsboro, Il., U.S.	219	39.09 N	89.29 W
Hillsboro, Ks., U.S.	198	38.21 N	97.12 W
Hillsboro, Ky., U.S.	218	38.18 N	83.40 W
Hillsboro, Md., U.S.	208	38.55 N	75.56 W
Hillsboro, Mo., U.S.	219	38.13 N	90.33 W
Hillsboro, N.H., U.S.	188	43.06 N	71.53 W
Hillsboro, N.M., U.S.	200	32.55 N	107.33 W
Hillsboro, N.D., U.S.	198	47.24 N	97.03 W
Hillsboro, Oh., U.S.	218	39.12 N	83.36 W
Hillsboro, Or., U.S.	224	45.31 N	122.59 W
Hillsboro, Tx., U.S.	222	32.00 N	97.07 W
Hillsboro, Wi., U.S.	190	43.39 N	90.20 W
Hillsboro Beach	220	26.18 N	80.05 W
Hillsboro Canal ≅	220	26.19 N	80.05 W
Hillsborough, N.B., Can.	186	45.56 N	64.39 W
Hillsborough, N. Ire., U.K.	48	54.28 N	6.05 W
Hillsborough, Ca., U.S.	226	37.34 N	122.22 W
Hillsborough, N.C., U.S.	192	36.04 N	79.06 W
Hillsborough □[6], Fl., U.S.	220	27.55 N	82.15 W
Hillsborough □[6], N.H., U.S.	207	42.49 N	71.41 W
Hillsborough ≃	220	27.56 N	82.27 W
Hillsborough, Cape ≻	166	20.54 S	149.03 E
Hillsborough Bay c, P.E., Can.	186	46.10 N	63.05 W
Hillsborough Bay c, Fl., U.S.	220	27.52 N	82.27 W
Hillsborough River State Park ♦	220	28.09 N	82.14 W
Hillsburgh	212	43.47 N	80.09 W
Hills Creek Lake ⊜[1]	202	43.40 N	122.26 W
Hillsdale, Mi., U.S.	216	41.55 N	84.37 W
Hillsdale, N.J., U.S.	276	41.00 N	74.02 W
Hillsdale, N.Y., U.S.	210	42.10 N	73.31 W
Hillsdale, Pa., U.S.	214	40.45 N	78.53 W
Hillsdale □[6]	216	41.53 N	84.36 W
Hillsdale ◆[9]	282	37.32 N	122.18 W
Hillsdale Lake ⊜[1]	198	38.40 N	94.55 W
Hills Flat	226	39.14 N	121.03 W
Hillsgrove	210	41.27 N	76.42 W
Hillside, Austl.	162	21.44 S	119.23 E
Hillside, Scot., U.K.	46	56.44 N	2.29 W
Hillside, Il., U.S.	278	41.52 N	87.54 W
Hillside, Md., U.S.	284c	38.52 N	76.55 W
Hillside, N.J., U.S.	276	40.42 N	74.13 W
Hillside ◆[8]	276	40.42 N	73.47 W
Hillside Gardens	216	42.16 N	84.27 W
Hillside Heights	285	39.41 N	75.41 W
Hillside Lake	210	41.36 N	73.50 W
Hillston	166	33.29 S	145.32 E
Hillsville, Pa., U.S.	214	41.00 N	80.29 W
Hillsville, Va., U.S.	192	36.45 N	80.44 W
Hillswick	46a	60.28 N	1.30 W
Hilltop	208	39.49 N	75.04 W
Hilltop Center ◆[9]	282	37.59 N	122.19 W
Hilltown, N. Ire., U.K.	48	54.12 N	6.09 W
Hilltown, Pa., U.S.	208	40.20 N	75.14 W
Hillview	219	39.27 N	90.33 W
Hillview Reservoir ⊜[1]	276	40.55 N	73.52 W
Hillwood	284c	38.52 N	77.10 W
Hilmar	226	37.25 N	120.51 W
Hilo	229d	19.43 N	155.05 W
Hilo Bay c	229d	19.44 N	155.05 W
Hilonghilong, Mount ∧	116	9.06 N	125.44 E
Hilongos	116	10.23 N	124.45 E
Hilpotstein	60	49.12 N	11.12 E
Hilpsford Point ≻	44	54.03 N	3.12 W
Hils ∧	52	51.55 N	9.40 E
Hilshire Village	222	29.49 N	95.26 W
Hiltaba, Mount ∧	162	32.09 S	135.03 E
Hilter	52	52.08 N	8.08 E
Hilton, N.Y., U.S.	210	43.17 N	77.47 W
Hilton, Pa., U.S.	208	40.00 N	76.49 W
Hilton Head Island I	192	32.12 N	80.45 W
Hiltpoltstein	60	49.40 N	11.19 E
Hiltrop ◆[8]	263	51.30 N	7.15 E
Hiltrup	52	51.54 N	7.38 E
Hilvan	130	37.35 N	38.57 E
Hilvarenbeek	52	51.29 N	5.09 E
Hilversum	52	52.14 N	5.10 E
Hima	192	37.07 N	83.46 W

Symbol	English	Deutsch	Español	Français	Português
≃	River	Fluß	Río	Rivière	Rio
≅	Canal	Kanal	Canal	Canal	Canal
∟	Waterfall, Rapids	Wasserfall, Stromschnellen	Cascada, Rápidos	Chute d'eau, Rapides	Cascata, Rápidos
⊔	Strait	Meeresstraße	Estrecho	Détroit	Estreito
c	Bay, Gulf	Bucht, Golf	Bahía, Golfo	Baie, Golfe	Baía, Golfo
⊜	Lake, Lakes	See, Seen	Lago, Lagos	Lac, Lacs	Lago, Lagos
≋	Swamp	Sumpf	Pantano	Marais	Pântano
⊞	Ice Features, Glacier	Eis- und Gletscherformen	Accidentes Glaciales	Formes glaciaires	Acidentes glaciares
⊤	Other Hydrographic Features	Andere Hydrographische Objekte	Otros Elementos Hidrográficos	Autres données hydrographiques	Outros acidentes hidrográficos
✧	Submarine Features	Untermeerische Objekte	Accidentes Submarinos	Formes de relief sous-marin	Acidentes submarinos
□	Political Unit	Politische Einheit	Unidad Politica	Entité politique	Unidade política
ᵾ	Cultural Institution	Kulturelle Institution	Institución Cultural	Institution culturelle	Instituição cultural
⊥	Historical Site	Historische Stätte	Sitio Histórico	Site historique	Sitio histórico
♦	Recreational Site	Erholungs- und Ferienort	Sitio de Recreo	Centre de loisirs	Area de Lazer
⊠	Airport	Flughafen	Aeropuerto	Aéroport	Aeroporto
■	Military Installation	Militäranlage	Instalación Militar	Installation militaire	Instalação militar
◆	Miscellaneous	Verschiedenes	Misceláneo	Divers	Diversos

ENGLISH | DEUTSCH

Name / Name	Page / Seite	Lat.°′ / Breite°′	Long.°′ / Länge°′ E = Ost
Himāchal Pradesh □[3]	120	32.00 N	77.00 E
Himalayas ⋀	120	28.00 N	84.00 E
Himāl Chulī ∧	124	28.25 N	84.39 E
Himamaylan	116	10.06 N	122.52 E
Himanka	26	64.04 N	23.39 E
Himarë	38	40.07 N	19.44 E
Himatnagar	120	23.36 N	72.57 E
Himberg	61	48.05 N	16.26 E
Hime ≃	94	37.02 N	137.49 E
Himeji	96	34.49 N	134.42 E
Hime-shima I	96	33.43 N	131.40 E
Himeville	158	29.44 S	29.31 E
Himi	94	36.51 N	136.59 E
Himmelbjerget ⋀[2]	41	56.06 N	9.42 E
Himmelgeist ⊷[8]	263	51.10 N	6.49 E
Himmelpforten	52	53.36 N	9.18 E
Himmelsthür	52	52.09 N	9.55 E
Himmerfjärden c[2]	40	59.00 N	17.43 E
Himmerland ⊷[1]	26	56.50 N	9.45 E
Himmetdede	130	38.55 N	35.07 E
Himrod	210	42.35 N	76.57 W
Ḥimṣ (Homs)	130	34.44 N	36.43 E
Ḥimṣ □[8]	130	34.15 N	38.00 E
Hinabangan	116	11.42 N	125.04 E
Hīnah	132	33.21 N	35.56 E
Hinako, Kepulauan II	114	0.52 N	97.21 E
Hinase	96	34.44 N	134.16 E
Hinatuan	116	8.23 N	126.20 E
Hinatuan Island I	116	9.47 N	125.43 E
Hinatuan Passage ɥ	116	9.45 N	125.47 E
Hinche	238	19.09 N	72.01 W
Hinchinbrook Entrance ɥ	180	60.25 N	146.50 W
Hinchinbrook Island I, Austl.	166	18.23 S	146.17 E
Hinchinbrook Island I, Ak., U.S.	180	60.22 N	146.30 W
Hinchinbrook Island National Park ♦	166	18.20 S	146.20 E
Hinckley, Eng., U.K.	42	52.33 N	1.21 W
Hinckley, Il., U.S.	216	41.46 N	88.38 W
Hinckley, Mn., U.S.	190	46.00 N	92.56 W
Hinckley, Oh., U.S.	214	41.14 N	81.45 W
Hinckley, Ut,. U.S.	200	39.19 N	112.40 W
Hinckley Reservoir ⊜[1]	210	43.20 N	75.05 W
Hindan ≃	272a	28.30 N	77.27 E
Hindang	116	10.26 N	124.44 E
Hindaun	124	26.43 N	77.01 E
Hindelang	58	47.30 N	10.22 E
Hindelbank	58	47.03 N	7.32 E
Hindeloopen	52	52.56 N	5.24 E
Hindenburg → Zabrze	30	50.18 N	18.46 E
Hindhead	42	51.07 N	0.44 W
Hindley	262	53.32 N	2.35 W
Hindley Green	262	53.31 N	2.32 W
Hindman	192	37.20 N	82.58 W
Hindmarsh, Lake ⊜	166	36.03 S	141.55 E
Hindmarsh Island I	168b	35.32 S	138.52 E
Hindmarsh Valley	168b	35.30 S	138.38 E
Hindon	42	51.06 N	2.08 W
Hinds	172	44.00 S	171.34 E
Hindsholm ›[1]	41	55.33 N	10.40 E
Hinds Lake ⊜	186	48.57 N	57.00 W
Hindu Kush ⋀	120	36.00 N	71.30 E
Hindūmalkot	123	30.09 N	73.55 E
Hindupur	122	13.49 N	77.29 E
Hi-Nella	285	39.50 N	75.01 W
Hines	202	43.33 N	119.04 W
Hines Creek	182	56.15 N	118.36 W
Hines Creek ≃	182	55.54 N	118.37 W
Hines Peak ∧	228	34.31 N	119.05 W
Hinesville	192	31.50 N	81.35 W
Hinganghāt	122	20.34 N	78.50 E
Hingatungan	116	10.35 N	125.11 E
Hingham, Eng., U.K.	42	52.35 N	0.59 E
Hingham, Ma., U.S.	207	42.14 N	70.53 W
Hingham Bay c	207	42.17 N	70.55 W
Hingham Harbor c	283	42.15 N	70.53 W
Hingol ≃	128	25.23 N	65.28 E
Hingoli	122	19.43 N	77.09 E
Hinigaran	116	10.17 N	122.51 E
Hınıs	130	39.22 N	41.44 E
Hınıs ≃	130	39.18 N	42.12 E
Hinkley	228	34.56 N	117.11 W
Hinkson Creek ≃	219	38.56 N	92.23 W
Hinkston Creek ≃	188	38.18 N	84.14 W
Hinnerjoki	26	61.00 N	22.00 E
Hinnerup	41	56.16 N	10.04 E
Hinnøya I	24	68.30 N	16.00 E
Hino, Nihon	94	35.00 N	136.15 E
Hino, Nihon	94	35.41 N	139.24 E
Hino, Nihon	96	35.14 N	133.27 E
Hino ≃, Nihon	94	35.09 N	136.02 E
Hino ≃, Nihon	94	36.04 N	136.11 E
Hino ≃, Nihon	96	35.27 N	133.23 E
Hinoba-an	116	9.35 N	122.28 E
Hinode	94	35.45 N	139.14 E
Hinoemata	94	37.01 N	139.23 E
Hinohara	94	35.43 N	139.09 E
Hinojosa del Duque	34	38.30 N	5.09 W
Hinokage	92	32.39 N	131.24 E
Hinomi-saki ›, Nihon	96	33.53 N	135.04 E
Hinomi-saki ›, Nihon	96	35.26 N	132.38 E
Hinsbeck	56	51.21 N	6.17 E
Hinsdale, Il., U.S.	216	41.48 N	87.56 W
Hinsdale, Ma., U.S.	207	42.26 N	73.07 W
Hinsdale, Mt., U.S.	202	48.23 N	107.05 W
Hinsdale, N.H., U.S.	207	42.47 N	72.29 W
Hinsdale, N.Y., U.S.	210	42.10 N	78.23 W
Hinsel ⊷[8]	263	51.26 N	7.05 E
Hinsen ⊜	40	60.39 N	16.05 E
Hinte	52	53.25 N	7.11 E
Hinterbichl	64	47.01 N	12.20 E
Hinterbrühl	61	48.05 N	16.15 E
Hinterhermsdorf	54	50.55 N	14.22 E
Hinterrhein	58	46.32 N	9.12 E
Hinterrhein ≃	58	46.49 N	9.25 E
Hintersdorf	264b	48.18 N	16.13 E
Hintersee	54	53.37 N	14.16 E
Hinterstoder	61	47.41 N	14.09 E
Hintertux	64	47.07 N	11.41 E
Hinterweidenthal	56	49.12 N	7.45 E
Hinterzarten	58	47.54 N	8.06 E
Hinton, Ab., Can.	182	53.25 N	117.34 W
Hinton, Mo., U.S.	219	39.03 N	92.21 W
Hinton, Ok., U.S.	196	35.28 N	98.21 W
Hinton, W.V., U.S.	192	37.40 N	80.53 W
Hi-numa ⊜	94	36.16 N	140.30 E
Hinuma ≃	94	36.16 N	140.28 E
Hinundayan	116	10.21 N	125.15 E
Hinwil	58	47.18 N	8.51 E
Hinzik	84	40.08 N	40.58 E
Hípico, Club ♦	286e	33.28 S	70.41 W
Hipólito	232	25.41 N	101.26 W
Hipólito Yrigoyen	252	32.55 S	66.20 W
Hippolytushoef	52	52.54 N	4.57 E
Hirado	92	33.22 N	129.33 E
Hirado-shima I	92	33.20 N	129.30 E
Hiraiwa-hana ›	174f	24.48 N	141.18 E
Hiraizumi	92	38.59 N	141.07 E
Hirakata, Nihon	96	34.48 N	135.38 E
Hirakata, Nihon	268	35.56 N	139.33 E
Hirakawa	270	34.52 N	135.47 E
Hīrākud	122	21.31 N	83.57 E
Hīrākud Reservoir ⊜[1]	120	21.35 N	83.50 E
Hiram, Me., U.S.	188	43.52 N	70.48 W
Hiram, Oh., U.S.	214	41.18 N	81.08 W
Hiraman ≃	154	1.07 S	39.55 E
Hirano	175d	24.35 N	124.19 E
Hirano ⊷[8]	270	34.36 N	135.34 E
Hirao	96	33.56 N	132.04 E
Hirao-dai ♦	96	33.45 N	130.52 E
Hiraoka → Higashiōsaka	96	34.39 N	135.35 E
Hīrāpur	124	24.22 N	79.13 E
Hirara	175d	24.48 N	125.17 E
Hirata, Nihon	94	35.15 N	136.38 E
Hirata, Nihon	96	35.26 N	132.49 E
Hiratsuka	94	35.19 N	139.21 E
Hiraya	94	35.19 N	137.37 E
Hirfanlı Barajı ⊜[1]	130	39.10 N	33.35 E
Hirhafok	148	23.49 N	5.45 E
Hiriyūr	122	13.58 N	76.36 E
Ḥirjillah	132	33.22 N	36.18 E
Hîrlău	38	47.25 N	26.54 E
Hirokawa, Nihon	96	33.15 N	130.32 E
Hirokawa, Nihon	96	34.01 N	135.11 E
Hirok Sāmi	128	26.02 N	63.25 E
Hiromi	96	33.15 N	132.41 E
Hiroo	92a	42.17 N	143.19 E
Hirooka	268	35.15 N	140.04 E
Hirosaki	92	40.35 N	140.28 E
Hiroschima → Hiroshima	96	34.24 N	132.27 E
Hirose	96	35.22 N	133.10 E
Hiroshima	96	34.24 N	132.27 E
Hiroshima □[5]	96	34.30 N	133.00 E
Hiro-shima I	96	34.22 N	133.43 E
Hiroshima-wan c	96	34.06 N	132.20 E
Hirosima → Hiroshima	96	34.24 N	132.27 E
Hirota	270	34.45 N	135.21 E
Hirsau	56	48.44 N	8.44 E
Hirschaid	56	49.49 N	10.59 E
Hirschau	60	49.33 N	11.57 E
Hirschbach	54	50.33 N	10.44 E
Hirschberg	54	50.24 N	11.49 E
Hirschberg → Jelenia Góra	30	50.55 N	15.46 E
Hirschfeld	54	51.23 N	13.37 E
Hirschfelde, Dtsch.	54	50.57 N	14.53 E
Hirschfelde, Dtsch.	264a	52.38 N	13.48 E
Hirschhorn	56	49.27 N	8.53 E
Hirschstetten ⊷[8]	264b	48.14 N	16.29 E
Hirshfeld Brook ≃	276	40.57 N	74.02 W
Hirsingue	58	47.35 N	7.15 E
Hirson	50	49.55 N	4.05 E
Hîrşova	38	44.41 N	27.57 E
Hirsts Hill ∧	171a	27.13 S	152.06 E
Hirtshals	26	57.35 N	9.58 E
Hirtzfelden	58	47.55 N	7.27 E
Hirukawa	94	35.31 N	137.23 E
Hiru-zen ∧	96	35.19 N	133.40 E
Hirwaun	42	51.45 N	3.30 W
Hisābpur	272b	22.51 N	88.32 E
Hisai, Nihon	94	34.40 N	136.28 E
Hisai, Nihon	270	34.25 N	135.28 E
Hisār	123	29.10 N	75.43 E
Hisarönü	130	41.33 N	32.02 E
Ḥisbān	132	31.48 N	35.48 E
Hisiu	164	9.05 S	146.45 E
Hisn al-ʿAbr	144	16.05 N	47.22 E
Ḥiṣn al-Qarn	144	15.11 N	49.05 E
Hispaniola I	238	19.00 N	71.00 W
Hispar Glacier ⊓	123	36.05 N	75.20 E
Histon	42	52.15 N	0.06 E
Hisua	124	24.50 N	85.25 E
Ḥisyah	130	34.24 N	36.45 E
Hīt	128	33.38 N	42.49 E
Hita	96	33.19 N	130.56 E
Hitachi	94	36.36 N	140.39 E
Hitachi-ōta	94	36.32 N	140.31 E
Hitati → Hitachi	94	36.36 N	140.39 E
Hitchcock	222	29.20 N	95.00 W
Hitchin	42	51.57 N	0.17 W
Hitchins	218	38.16 N	82.55 W
Hither Green ⊷[8]	260	51.27 N	0.01 W
Hither Hills State Park ♦	207	41.01 N	72.01 W
Hitiaa	174s	17.36 S	149.18 W
Hitokura	270	34.55 N	135.25 E
Hitotsubashi University Ʊ[2]	268	35.42 N	139.27 E
Hitoyoshi	92	32.13 N	130.45 E
Hitra I	26	63.33 N	8.45 E
Hittarp	41	56.06 N	12.38 E
Hittisau	58	47.27 N	9.57 E
Hitzacker	54	53.09 N	11.02 E
Hitze-Berge ⋀[2]	264a	52.35 N	13.07 E
Hiu I	175f	13.10 S	166.35 E
Hiuchiga-take ∧	94	36.57 N	139.17 E
Hiuchi-nada ▾[2]	96	34.05 N	133.20 E
Hiūnchuli Pātan ∧	124	28.50 N	82.37 E
Hiva Oa I	174x	9.45 S	139.00 W
Hi Vista	228	34.44 N	117.47 W
Hiwa	96	34.59 N	132.59 E
Hiwannee	194	31.48 N	88.41 W
Hiwasa	96	33.44 N	134.32 E
Hiwassee ≃	192	35.19 N	84.47 W
Hiwassee Lake ⊜[1]	192	35.10 N	84.05 W
Hixon	182	53.27 N	122.36 W
Hixson	192	35.09 N	85.14 W
Hiyoshi, Nihon	94	35.53 N	137.45 E
Hiyoshi, Nihon	96	33.20 N	132.48 E
Hiyoshi, Nihon	96	35.09 N	135.31 E
Hiyoshi ⊷[8]	268	35.33 N	139.39 E
Ḥiyyon, Naḥal V	132	30.12 N	35.07 E
Hizaonna	174m	26.24 N	127.50 E
Hjälmare kanal ≍	40	59.24 N	15.56 E
Hjälmaren ⊜	40	59.15 N	15.45 E
Hjälmaresund ɥ	40	59.15 N	16.06 E
Hjarnø I	41	55.50 N	10.05 E
Hjelm I	41	56.08 N	10.48 E
Hjelmelandsvågen	26	59.14 N	6.11 E
Hjeltefjorden c[2]	26	60.40 N	4.55 E
Hjembæk	41	55.42 N	11.25 E
Hjo	26	58.18 N	14.17 E
Hjøllund	41	56.05 N	9.25 E
Hjordkær	41	55.01 N	9.19 E
Hjørring	26	57.28 N	9.59 E
Hjortkvarn	40	58.53 N	15.25 E
Hjørundfjorden c[2]	26	62.21 N	6.23 E
Hkakabo Razi ∧	102	28.20 N	97.32 E
Hkok (Kok) ≃	110	20.14 N	100.09 E
Hlabisa	158	28.08 S	31.52 E
Hlaingbwe	110	17.08 N	97.50 E
Hlatikulu	158	27.00 S	31.25 E
Hlegu	110	17.06 N	96.14 E
Hlinsko	30	49.45 N	15.55 E
Hlobane	158	27.42 S	31.00 E
Hlohovec	30	48.25 N	17.47 E
Hluboká ⊥	61	49.05 N	14.25 E
Hluboká nad Vltavou	61	49.03 N	14.27 E
Hluboš	60	49.45 N	14.02 E
Hlučín	30	49.54 N	18.12 E
Hluhluwe	158	28.01 S	32.15 E
Hluhluwe Game Reserve ⊷[4]	158	28.05 S	32.04 E
Hluti	158	27.13 S	31.35 E
Hmawbi	110	17.06 N	96.02 E
H. Neely Henry Lake ⊜[1]	194	33.55 N	86.05 W
Ho	150	6.35 N	0.30 E
Hoa Binh	110	20.50 N	105.20 E
Hoa Da	110	11.11 N	108.33 E
Hoagland	216	40.56 N	84.59 W
Hoagland Ditch ≍	216	40.48 N	86.48 W
Hoanib ≃	156	19.27 S	12.46 E
Hoare Bay c	176	65.20 N	62.30 W
Hoarusib ≃	156	19.03 S	12.36 E
Hoa Thoi	269c	10.44 N	106.35 E
Hoback ≃	202	43.19 N	110.44 W
Hobart, Austl.	166	42.53 S	147.19 E
Hobart, In., U.S.	216	41.31 N	87.15 W
Hobart, N.Y., U.S.	210	42.22 N	74.40 W
Hobart, Ok., U.S.	196	35.01 N	99.05 W
Hobart, Wa., U.S.	224	47.25 N	121.58 W
Hobbs, In., U.S.	216	40.17 N	85.57 W
Hobbs, N.M., U.S.	196	32.42 N	103.08 W
Hobbs Coast ⩡[2]	9	74.45 S	131.00 W
Hobe Sound	220	27.03 N	80.08 W
Hobgood	192	36.01 N	77.23 W
Hobhole Drain ≍	44	52.59 N	0.02 E
Hobhouse	158	29.31 S	27.08 E
Hobo	246	2.35 N	75.27 W
Hoboken, Bel.	50	51.10 N	4.21 E
Hoboken, N.J., U.S.	210	40.44 N	74.01 W
Hoboksar	86	46.47 N	85.43 E
Hobq Shamo ⊷[2]	102	40.30 N	107.55 E
Hobro	26	56.38 N	9.48 E
Hobson	202	47.00 N	109.52 W
Hobson Lake ⊜	182	52.30 N	120.20 W
Hobsons Bay c	274b	37.51 S	144.56 E
Hoburgen ›	26	56.55 N	18.07 E
Hobyo	144	5.21 N	48.32 E
Hocaköy	130	41.03 N	30.17 E
Hocalar	130	38.34 N	30.00 E
Hocalı	130	38.41 N	27.41 E
Hochalmspitze ∧	64	47.01 N	13.19 E
Hochandochtla Mountain ∧	180	65.32 N	154.50 W
Höchberg	56	49.49 N	9.51 E
Hochburg	60	48.07 N	12.52 E
Hochdahl	56	51.13 N	6.56 E
Hochdorf	58	47.10 N	8.17 E
Höchenschwand	58	47.44 N	8.10 E
Hochfeiler (Gran Pilastro) ∧	64	46.58 N	11.44 E
Hochfeld	156	21.28 S	17.58 E
Hochfeld ⊷[8]	263	51.25 N	6.46 E
Hochfelden	56	48.45 N	7.34 E
Hochfilzen	64	47.28 N	12.37 E
Hochfinstermünz	58	46.56 N	10.29 E
Hochgern ∧	64	47.45 N	12.30 E
Hochgolling ∧	64	47.16 N	13.45 E
Hochheide ⊷[8]	263	51.27 N	6.41 E
Hochheim, Dtsch.	56	50.01 N	8.20 E
Hochheim, Tx., U.S.	222	29.19 N	97.17 W
Hochiss ∧	64	47.27 N	11.46 E
Hochkirch	54	51.09 N	14.34 E
Hochkönig ∧	64	47.25 N	13.04 E
Hochkreuz ∧	64	46.49 N	13.04 E
Hochlantsch ∧	61	47.21 N	15.25 E
Hochlar	263	51.36 N	7.10 E
Hochneukirch	56	51.06 N	6.26 E
Hochobir ∧	61	46.30 N	14.29 E
Hochreichhart ∧	61	47.22 N	14.41 E
Hochries ∧	64	47.45 N	12.14 E
Hochschwab ∧	61	47.37 N	15.09 E
Hochschwab ⋀	61	47.36 N	15.05 E
Hochsimmer ∧	56	50.21 N	7.12 E
Hochspeyer	56	49.26 N	7.54 E
Höchst, Dtsch.	56	49.48 N	8.59 E
Höchst, Öst.	58	47.28 N	9.38 E
Höchst ⊷[8]	56	50.07 N	8.33 E
Höchstadt an der Aisch	56	49.42 N	10.44 E
Höchstädt an der Donau	56	48.36 N	10.34 E
Höchsten ⊷[8]	263	51.27 N	7.29 E
Höchstenbach	56	50.38 N	7.44 E
Hochstuhl (Veliki Stol) ∧	61	46.26 N	14.10 E
Hochtor)(	64	47.05 N	12.51 E
Hoch'uan → Hechuan	107	30.00 N	106.16 E
Ho Chung	271d	22.22 N	114.14 E
Hochvogel ∧	58	47.23 N	10.26 E
Hochwildstelle ∧	64	47.20 N	13.50 E
Hockenheim	56	49.19 N	8.33 E
Hockeroda	54	50.35 N	11.26 E
Hockessin	285	39.47 N	75.41 W
Hocking ≃	188	39.12 N	81.45 W
Hocking Hills State Park ♦	188	39.30 N	82.32 W
Hockley, Eng., U.K.	260	51.37 N	0.40 E
Hockley, Tx., U.S.	222	30.02 N	95.51 W
Hockomock Swamp ≋	283	41.59 N	71.05 W
Ḥôḍ ⊷[1]	150	16.10 N	8.40 W
Hodal	124	27.54 N	77.22 E
Hōdatsu-zan ∧	94	36.47 N	136.49 E
Hodder ≃	44	53.50 N	2.25 W
Hoddesdon	260	51.46 N	0.01 W
Hoddlesden	262	53.42 N	2.26 W
Hodeida → Al-Ḥudaydah	144	14.48 N	42.57 E
Hodenhagen	52	52.46 N	9.35 E
Hodge	194	32.16 N	92.43 W
Hodgenville	194	37.34 N	85.44 W
Hodges, Lake ⊜[1]	228	33.03 N	117.05 W
Hodges Brook ≃	283	41.58 N	71.14 W
Hodges Hill ∧[2]	186	49.04 N	55.53 W
Hodgeville	184	50.08 N	106.58 W
Hodgkins	278	41.46 N	87.51 W
Hodgson	184	51.13 N	97.34 W
Hodgson ≃	164	14.48 S	134.35 E
Hodgson, Mount ∧[2]	162	22.26 S	121.10 E
Hod HaSharon	132	32.09 N	34.53 E
Hodh ech Chargui □[4]	150	18.10 N	7.15 W
Hodh el Gharbi □[4]	150	16.30 N	10.00 W
Hódmezővásárhely	30	46.25 N	20.20 E
Hodmo V	144	10.41 N	46.13 E
Hodna, Chott el ⊜	148	35.25 N	4.45 E
Hodna, Monts du ⋀	34	35.50 N	4.50 E
Hodna, Plaine du ≚	34	35.38 N	4.30 E
Hodnet	42	52.51 N	2.35 W
Hodogaya ⊷[8]	268	35.27 N	139.36 E
Hodogaya Baseball Ground ♦	268	35.27 N	139.35 E
Hodonín	30	48.51 N	17.08 E
Hodoš	61	46.50 N	16.20 E
Hodzana ≃	180	66.15 N	147.48 W
Hoed	41	56.19 N	10.49 E
Hoedekenskerke	52	51.25 N	3.55 E
Hoehne	198	37.16 N	104.22 W
Hoeksche Waard I	52	51.45 N	4.30 E
Hoek van Holland	52	51.59 N	4.09 E
Hoeningen	263	51.05 N	6.41 E
Hoensbroek	56	50.55 N	5.55 E
Hœrdt	58	48.42 N	7.47 E
Hoerstgen	263	51.30 N	6.27 E
Hoeryŏng	98	42.27 N	129.44 E
Hoeyang	98	38.43 N	127.36 E
Hof, Dtsch.	54	50.18 N	11.55 E
Hof, Ísland	24a	64.34 N	14.39 W
Hofburg Ʊ	264b	48.12 N	16.22 E
Höfđakaupstađur	24a	65.50 N	20.19 W
Hofei → Hefei	100	31.51 N	117.17 E
Höfen	56	50.32 N	6.15 E
Hoffman, Il., U.S.	219	38.32 N	89.16 W
Hoffman, Mn., U.S.	198	45.49 N	95.47 W
Hoffman Estates	216	42.02 N	88.04 W
Hoffman Island I	276	40.35 N	74.03 W
Hoffmans	210	42.54 N	74.05 W
Hoffman Station	284a	43.04 N	78.50 W
Hoffnung	263	51.07 N	7.13 E
Hofgeismar	52	51.30 N	9.22 E
Hofheim	56	50.07 N	8.26 E
Hofheim in Unterfranken	56	50.08 N	10.31 E
Hofkirchen an der Trattnac	60	48.13 N	13.44 E
Höflein an der Donau	264b	48.21 N	16.17 E
Hofmeyr	158	31.39 S	25.50 E
Höfn	24a	64.17 N	15.10 W
Hofors	40	60.33 N	16.17 E
Hofsjökull ⊓	24a	64.48 N	18.50 W
Hofstade	50	50.58 N	4.02 E
Hofstede ⊷[8]	263	51.30 N	7.12 E
Hofstra University Ʊ[2]	276	40.43 N	73.36 W
Hōfu	96	34.03 N	131.34 E
Hofuf → Al-Hufūf	128	25.22 N	49.34 E
Hofweier	58	48.25 N	7.55 E
Hog, Tanjong ›	116	5.18 N	119.16 E
Hogalbāria	126	23.53 N	88.51 E
Höganäs	41	56.12 N	12.33 E
Hogan Lake ⊜	190	45.52 N	78.30 W
Hogansburg	206	44.58 N	74.39 W
Hogansville	192	33.10 N	84.54 W
Hogatza ≃	180	66.00 N	155.29 W
Hogback Mountain ∧, U.S.	207	42.43 N	72.25 W
Hogback Mountain ∧, Mt., U.S.	202	44.54 N	112.07 W
Hogback Mountain ∧, Ne., U.S.	198	41.40 N	103.44 W
Hogback Mountain ∧, S.C., U.S.	192	35.10 N	82.17 W
Högbo	40	60.40 N	16.48 E
Hog Canyon V	226	35.42 N	120.35 W
Hog Creek ≃	222	31.32 N	97.18 W
Hoge Veluwe, Nationale Park de ♦	52	52.02 N	5.55 E
Högfors	40	59.59 N	15.01 E
Hoggar → Ahaggar ⋀	148	23.00 N	6.30 E
Hoghton	262	53.44 N	2.35 W
Hoghton Tower ⊥	262	53.44 N	2.34 W
Hog Island I, Ma., U.S.	283	42.40 N	70.46 W
Hog Island I, Mi., U.S.	190	45.48 N	85.22 W
Hog Island I, Vt., U.S.	206	44.57 N	73.13 W
Hog Island I, Va., U.S.	208	37.25 N	75.41 W
Hog Island Bay c	208	37.27 N	75.46 W
Hogoro	154	5.57 S	36.27 E
Hog Point ›	208	37.12 N	76.41 W
Hogs Back ⩡[4]	42	51.13 N	0.40 W
Högsby	26	57.10 N	16.02 E
Högsjö	40	59.02 N	15.41 E
Hoh ≃	224	47.45 N	124.29 W
Hoh, South Fork ≃	224	47.46 N	124.01 W
Hohe Acht ∧	56	50.23 N	7.00 E
Hohebach	56	49.22 N	9.44 E
Hohegeiss	54	51.40 N	10.40 E
Hohenau	252	27.05 S	55.45 W
Hohenau an der March	61	48.36 N	16.55 E
Höhenberg	61	48.46 N	14.53 E
Hohenbrunn	60	48.03 N	11.42 E
Hohenbucko	54	51.46 N	13.28 E
Hohenbudberg ⊷[8]	263	51.23 N	6.40 E
Hohenburg	60	49.16 N	11.30 E
Hohendorf	54	54.01 N	13.44 E
Hohenebra	54	51.18 N	10.49 E
Hohenems	58	47.22 N	9.41 E
Hohenfels	60	49.12 N	11.51 E
Hohenfurch	58	47.51 N	10.54 E
Hohengüstow	54	53.14 N	13.59 E
Hohenhameln	52	52.15 N	10.03 E
Hohenheide	263	51.29 N	7.47 E
Hohenkammer	60	48.25 N	11.32 E
Hohenkirchen, Dtsch.	52	53.39 N	7.55 E
Hohenkirchen, Dtsch.	54	50.51 N	10.41 E
Hohenkirchen, Dtsch.	54	53.51 N	11.17 E
Hohenkirchen, Dtsch.	56	51.23 N	9.29 E
Hohenleipisch	54	51.30 N	13.34 E
Hohenleuben	54	50.43 N	12.03 E
Hohenlimburg	56	51.21 N	7.35 E
Hohenlimburg, Schloss ⊥	263	51.21 N	7.34 E
Hohenlinden	60	48.09 N	12.00 E
Hohenmölsen	54	51.09 N	12.06 E
Hohen Neuendorf	54	52.40 N	13.16 E
Hohenpolding	60	48.23 N	12.08 E
Hohensalza → Inowrocław	30	52.48 N	18.15 E
Hohenschönhausen ⊷[8]	264a	52.33 N	13.30 E
Hohenseeden	54	52.19 N	12.01 E
Hohenseefeld	54	51.53 N	13.18 E
Hohenstaufen	56	48.44 N	9.43 E
Hohenstein-Ernstthal	54	50.48 N	12.42 E
Hohensyburg ⊥	56	51.25 N	7.29 E
Hohentauern	61	47.26 N	14.29 E
Hohenthurm	54	51.31 N	12.05 E
Hohenthurn	64	46.33 N	13.40 E
Hohentwiel ∧	58	47.46 N	8.49 E
Hohenwald	194	35.32 N	87.33 W
Hohenwart	60	48.36 N	11.23 E
Hohenwarte-Stausee ⊜[1]	54	50.32 N	11.30 E
Hohenwarthe	54	52.13 N	11.42 E
Hohenwutzen	54	52.51 N	14.07 E
Hohenzethen	54	53.03 N	10.49 E
Hohenzollern, Burg ⊥	58	48.19 N	8.58 E
Hohenzollernkanal ≍	264a	52.32 N	13.20 E
Hoher Bogen ∧	60	49.15 N	12.55 E
Hoher Dachstein ∧	64	47.28 N	13.35 E
Hoher Freschen ∧	58	47.18 N	9.46 E
Hohe Rhön ⋀	56	50.30 N	10.00 E
Hoher Ifen ∧	58	47.21 N	10.05 E
Hoherlehme	264a	52.19 N	13.37 E
Hoher Mechtin ∧[2]	54	53.03 N	10.55 E
Hoher Riffler ∧	58	47.07 N	10.22 E
Hoher Sonnblick ∧	64	47.03 N	12.57 E
Hoher Zinken ∧	64	47.40 N	13.20 E
Hohe Tauern ⋀	64	47.10 N	12.45 E
Hohe Warte (Monte Coglians) ∧	64	46.37 N	12.53 E
Hoh Head ›	224	47.46 N	124.29 W
Hohhot	102	40.51 N	111.40 E
Höhn	56	50.37 N	8.00 E
Hohndorf	54	50.45 N	12.40 E
Hohne	52	52.35 N	10.22 E
Hohneck, Le ∧	58	48.02 N	7.01 E
Hohnstein	54	50.59 N	14.10 E
Hohoe	150	7.09 N	0.28 E
Hōhoku	96	34.17 N	130.57 E
Ho-Ho-Kus	276	40.59 N	74.06 W
Hohokus Brook ≃	276	40.57 N	74.06 W
Hoholitna ≃	180	61.31 N	157.00 W
Hoh Sai Hu ⊜	120	35.43 N	92.45 E
Höhscheid ⊷[8]	263	51.09 N	7.04 E
Hohultslätt	26	56.58 N	15.39 E
Hohwacht	54	54.19 N	10.41 E
Hohwachter Bucht c	41	54.20 N	10.45 E
Hoh Xil Hu ⊜	120	35.35 N	91.06 E
Hoh Xil Shan ⋀	120	35.20 N	90.00 E
Hoi An	110	15.52 N	108.19 E
Hoihow → Haikou	102	20.03 N	110.19 E
Hoima	154	1.26 N	31.21 E
Hoisdorf	52	53.39 N	10.20 E
Hoisington	198	38.31 N	98.46 W
Hoisten	263	51.08 N	6.42 E
Hoi Xuan	110	20.22 N	105.07 E
Hojāi	120	26.00 N	92.51 E
Højby, Dan.	41	55.55 N	11.37 E
Højby, Dan.	41	55.20 N	10.27 E
Höje	40	59.54 N	13.33 E
Højer	26	54.58 N	8.43 E
Højerup	41	55.17 N	12.27 E
Hōjō, Nihon	96	33.58 N	132.46 E
Hōjō, Nihon	96	34.54 N	134.56 E
Hōjō → Kasai	96	34.56 N	134.50 E
Hokah	190	43.45 N	91.20 W
Hokang → Hegang	89	47.24 N	130.17 E
Hökåsen	40	59.40 N	16.35 E
Hokendauqua	208	40.39 N	75.29 W
Hökensås ⋀[2]	26	58.11 N	14.08 E
Hokes Bluff	194	33.59 N	85.51 W
Hōki ≃	94	36.47 N	140.08 E
Hokianga Harbour c	172	35.32 S	173.22 E
Hokitika	172	42.43 S	170.58 E
Hokkaidō □[5]	92a	44.00 N	143.00 E
Hokkaidō I	92a	44.00 N	143.00 E
Hokksund	26	59.47 N	9.59 E
Hoko ≃	224	48.17 N	124.22 W
Hōkōji	270	34.52 N	135.07 E
Hököpinge	41	55.30 N	13.00 E
Hokota	94	36.09 N	140.31 E
Hok So Wan	271d	22.13 N	114.14 E
Hokubo	96	34.57 N	133.38 E
Hokudan	96	34.32 N	134.56 E
Hokura ≃	94	37.10 N	138.16 E
Hokuriku-tunnel ⊷[5]	94	35.42 N	136.10 E
Hokusei	94	35.09 N	136.31 E
Hola	154	1.29 S	40.02 E
Holalkere	122	14.02 N	76.11 E
Holanda → Netherlands □[1]	30	52.15 N	5.30 E
Holbæk	41	55.43 N	11.43 E
Holbeach	42	52.49 N	0.01 E
Holbeach Marsh ≋	42	52.52 N	0.05 E
Holberg	182	50.39 N	128.00 W
Holborn ⊷[8]	260	51.31 N	0.07 W
Holbrook, Austl.	171b	35.44 S	147.19 E
Holbrook, Az., U.S.	200	34.54 N	110.09 W
Holbrook, Il., U.S.	278	41.32 N	87.38 W
Holbrook, Md., U.S.	284b	39.24 N	76.51 W
Holbrook, Ma., U.S.	207	42.09 N	71.00 W
Holbrook, Ne., U.S.	198	40.18 N	100.00 W
Holbrook, N.Y., U.S.	210	40.48 N	73.04 W
Holbrook, Lake ⊜[1]	222	32.42 N	95.33 W
Holbrook Mountain ∧[2]	212	44.25 N	77.51 W
Holckenhavn	41	55.17 N	10.47 E
Holcomb, Il., U.S.	216	42.04 N	89.06 W
Holcomb, N.Y., U.S.	210	42.54 N	77.25 W
Holcomb Creek ≃	228	34.17 N	117.08 W
Holden, Ab., Can.	182	53.14 N	112.14 W
Holden, Ma., U.S.	207	42.21 N	71.51 W
Holden, Mo., U.S.	194	38.42 N	93.59 W
Holden, Ut,. U.S.	200	39.05 N	112.16 W
Holden, W.V., U.S.	188	37.49 N	82.03 W
Holden, Mount ∧[2]	216	41.40 N	87.03 W
Holdenstedt	52	52.55 N	10.31 E
Holden Village	224	48.12 N	120.47 W
Holdenville	196	35.04 N	96.23 W
Holder	220	28.58 N	82.25 W
Holderness ›[1]	44	53.47 N	0.10 W
Holdfast	184	50.58 N	105.25 W
Holdich	254	45.57 S	68.13 W
Holdingford	190	45.43 N	94.28 W
Holdorf	52	52.35 N	8.07 E
Holdrege	198	40.26 N	99.22 W
Holeby	41	54.43 N	11.28 E
Hole in the Mountain Peak ∧	204	40.55 N	115.05 W
Hole Narsipur	122	12.47 N	76.15 E
Holešov	30	49.20 N	17.35 E
Holetown	241g	13.11 N	59.39 W
Holgate, S. Afr.	158	33.59 S	22.21 E
Holgate, Oh., U.S.	216	41.14 N	84.07 W
Holguín	240p	20.53 N	76.15 W
Holguín □[4]	240p	20.55 N	75.50 W
Hol-Hol	144	11.19 N	42.57 E
Holíč	30	48.49 N	17.10 E
Holice	30	50.04 N	15.59 E
Holiday Beach Provincial Park ♦	214	42.02 N	83.05 W
Holiday Hills	216	42.18 N	88.13 W
Holiday Lake Amusement Park ♦	285	40.02 N	74.56 W
Holiday Shores	219	38.55 N	89.56 W
Holitna ≃	180	61.40 N	157.12 W
Höljes	26	60.54 N	12.36 E
Hollabrunn	61	48.34 N	16.05 E
Holladay	200	40.40 N	111.49 W
Holland, Mb., Can.	184	49.36 N	98.53 W
Holland, Mi., U.S.	216	42.47 N	86.06 W
Holland, N.Y., U.S.	210	42.38 N	78.32 W
Holland, Oh., U.S.	216	41.37 N	83.42 W
Holland, Pa., U.S.	285	40.10 N	74.59 W
Holland, Tx., U.S.	222	30.53 N	97.24 W
Holland, Va., U.S.	208	36.41 N	76.47 W
Holland □[9]	52	52.20 N	4.45 E
Holland ≃	212	44.12 N	79.31 W
Holland, Mount ∧[2]	162	32.12 S	119.44 E
Hollandale	194	33.10 N	90.51 W
Holland Creek ≃	169	36.43 S	146.06 E
Hollande, Étangs de ⊜	261	48.44 N	1.48 E
Holland Fen ≋	42	53.00 N	0.10 W
Hollandia → Jayapura	164	2.32 S	140.42 E
Holland Landing	212	44.06 N	79.29 W
Holland → Netherlands □[1]	30	52.15 N	5.30 E
Holland Park	171a	27.31 S	153.03 E
Holland Patent	210	43.14 N	75.15 W
Holland Point ›	208	38.43 N	76.32 W
Holland Pond State Park ♦	207	42.04 N	72.09 W
Hollandsbird Island I	156	24.45 S	14.34 E
Hollandsch Diep ɥ	52	51.42 N	4.30 E
Hollandstoun	46	59.21 N	2.16 W
Holland Straits ɥ	208	38.08 N	76.02 W
Holland Tunnel ⊷[5]	276	40.44 N	74.02 W
Hollansburg	218	39.59 N	84.47 W
Holleben	54	51.26 N	11.53 E
Hollenfels, Château ⊥	56	49.43 N	6.03 E
Höllengebirge ⋀	64	47.48 N	13.39 E
Hollenstedt	52	53.22 N	9.43 E
Hollenstein an der Ybbs	61	47.48 N	14.46 E
Höllensteinberg ∧	264b	48.06 N	16.11 E
Höllental V	61	47.45 N	15.47 E
Hollern	52	53.36 N	9.32 E
Holleton	162	31.57 S	119.02 E
Holley	210	43.13 N	78.01 W
Hollfeld	60	49.56 N	11.18 E
Hollick-Kenyon Plateau ⋀[1]	9	79.00 S	97.00 W
Holliday, Mo., U.S.	219	39.29 N	92.07 W
Holliday, Tx., U.S.	196	33.49 N	98.42 W
Holliday Creek ≃	196	33.55 N	98.28 W
Holliday Park ♦	281	42.21 N	83.24 W
Hollidaysburg	214	40.25 N	78.23 W
Hollingbourne	260	51.16 N	0.38 E
Hollingstedt	41	54.27 N	9.19 E
Hollingworth	262	53.28 N	1.59 W
Hollingworth Lake ⊜	262	53.38 N	2.06 W
Hollins, Eng., U.K.	262	53.34 N	2.17 W
Hollins, Va., U.S.	192	37.20 N	79.56 W
Hollins Green	262	53.25 N	2.27 W
Hollinswood	284c	38.55 N	77.13 W
Hollis, N.H., U.S.	207	42.44 N	71.35 W
Hollis, Ok., U.S.	196	34.41 N	99.54 W
Hollis ⊷[8]	276	40.43 N	73.46 W
Hollister	226	36.51 N	121.24 W
Hollister, Mount ∧[2]	162	22.08 S	114.01 E
Holliston	207	42.12 N	71.25 W
Hollman, Cape ›	164	4.59 S	150.06 E
Holloman Air Force Base ■	200	32.51 N	106.05 W
Holloway	214	40.10 N	81.08 W
Holloway Terrace	285	39.42 N	75.32 W
Hollow Rock	194	36.02 N	88.16 W
Hollowville	210	42.12 N	73.42 W
Hollsopple	214	40.13 N	78.56 W
Hollum	52	53.26 N	5.37 E
Höllviken c	41	55.26 N	12.54 E
Höllviksnäs	41	55.25 N	12.57 E
Holly, Co., U.S.	198	38.03 N	102.07 W
Holly, Mi., U.S.	216	42.47 N	83.37 W
Holly, Wa., U.S.	224	47.34 N	122.58 W
Holly, Mount ∧[2]	285	40.00 N	74.47 W
Holly Brook	285	39.59 N	74.48 W
Holly Grove	194	34.35 N	91.11 W
Holly Hill, Fl., U.S.	192	29.14 N	81.02 W
Holly Hill, S.C., U.S.	192	33.19 N	80.24 W
Holly Park, N.J., U.S.	208	39.53 N	74.10 W
Holly Park, Va., U.S.	284c	38.50 N	77.17 W
Holly Pond ⊜	276	41.03 N	73.30 W
Holly River State Park ♦	188	38.40 N	80.21 W
Holly Run ≃	285	39.47 N	75.03 W
Holly Springs	194	34.46 N	89.26 W
Holly State Recreation Area ♦	216	42.49 N	83.32 W
Hollywood, Ire.	48	53.06 N	6.35 W
Hollywood, Fl., U.S.	220	26.00 N	80.08 W
Hollywood, Md., U.S.	208	38.20 N	76.34 W
Hollywood, Pa., U.S.	285	40.05 N	75.06 W
Hollywood ⊷[8]	228	34.06 N	118.21 W
Hollywood, Mount ∧	280	34.08 N	118.18 W
Hollywood Bowl ♦	280	34.07 N	118.20 W
Hollywood-Burbank Airport ⊠	228	34.12 N	118.21 W
Hollywood Heights	219	38.39 N	89.59 W
Hollywood Indian Reservation ⊷[4]	220	26.02 N	80.13 W
Hollywood Park Race Track ♦	280	33.57 N	118.20 W
Hollywood Reservoir ⊜[1]	280	34.07 N	118.20 W
Holman	176	70.43 N	117.43 W
Hólmavík	24a	65.43 N	21.43 W
Holmdel	208	40.20 N	74.11 W
Holme, Dan.	41	56.07 N	10.11 E
Holme, Eng., U.K.	262	53.33 N	1.50 W
Holme ≃	44	53.41 N	1.43 W
Holme Chapel	262	53.45 N	2.11 W
Holmen, Nor.	26	60.40 N	10.22 E
Holmen, Wi., U.S.	190	43.57 N	91.15 W
Holme-on-Spaulding-Moor	44	53.50 N	0.46 W
Holmes, N.Y., U.S.	210	41.31 N	73.39 W
Holmes, Pa., U.S.	285	39.54 N	75.19 W
Holmes □[6]	214	40.33 N	81.55 W
Holmes, Mount ∧	202	44.49 N	110.51 W
Holmes Beach	220	27.31 N	82.43 W
Holmesburg ⊷[8]	285	40.02 N	75.03 W
Holmes Chapel	44	53.12 N	2.22 W
Holmes Creek ≃	194	30.30 N	85.47 W
Holmesglen	274b	37.53 S	145.06 E
Holmes Harbor c	224	48.04 N	122.32 W
Holmes Lake ⊜	184	57.05 N	96.45 W
Holmes Reef ✢[2]	164	16.27 S	148.00 E
Holmes Run ≃	284c	38.48 N	77.07 W
Holmes Run Acres	284c	38.51 N	77.13 W
Holmestrand	26	59.29 N	10.18 E
Holmesville, N.Y., U.S.	210	42.31 N	75.24 W
Holmesville, Oh., U.S.	214	40.37 N	81.55 W
Holmeswood	262	53.39 N	2.52 W
Holmfirth	44	53.35 N	1.46 W
Holmia	246	4.58 N	59.35 W
Holmön I	26	63.47 N	20.53 E
Holmsbu	26	59.33 N	10.27 E
Holmsjön ⊜, Sve.	26	62.41 N	16.33 E
Holmsjön ⊜, Sve.	26	62.25 N	15.20 E
Holmsund	26	63.42 N	20.21 E
Hölö	40	59.01 N	17.35 E
Holod	38	46.47 N	22.08 E
Holoit, Punta ›	232	21.37 N	88.08 W
Ḥolon	132	32.01 N	34.46 E
Holoog	156	27.22 S	17.55 E
Holopaw	220	28.08 N	81.04 W
Holroyd	274a	33.50 S	150.58 E
Holroyd ≃	164	14.10 S	141.36 E
Holsloot	52	52.44 N	6.48 E
Holstebro	26	56.21 N	8.38 E
Holsted	41	55.30 N	8.55 E
Holstein	198	42.29 N	95.32 W
Holsteinborg ⊥	41	55.13 N	11.28 E
Holsteinische Schweiz ⊷[1]	54	54.11 N	10.36 E
Holsteinsborg (Sisimiut)	176	66.55 N	53.40 W
Holsterhausen	263	51.41 N	6.57 E
Holston ≃	192	35.57 N	83.51 W
Holston, North Fork ≃	192	36.33 N	82.36 W
Holston High Knob ∧	192	36.27 N	82.05 W
Holsworthy	42	50.49 N	4.21 W
Holt, Eng., U.K.	42	52.55 N	1.05 E
Holt, Wales, U.K.	44	53.05 N	2.53 W
Holt, Al., U.S.	194	33.14 N	87.29 W
Holt, Ca., U.S.	226	37.56 N	121.26 W
Holt, Fl., U.S.	194	30.42 N	86.44 W
Holt, Mi., U.S.	216	42.38 N	84.30 W
Holt Creek ≃	198	42.28 N	98.50 W
Holte	41	55.49 N	12.28 E
Holtemme ≃	54	51.57 N	11.10 E
Holten	52	52.17 N	6.25 E
Holten ⊷[8]	263	51.31 N	6.48 E
Holtenau ⊷[8]	54	54.22 N	10.08 E
Holter Lake ⊜[1]	202	46.55 N	111.57 W
Holthausen, Dtsch.	52	52.33 N	7.17 E
Holthausen, Dtsch.	263	51.23 N	7.13 E
Holthausen ⊷[8]	263	51.34 N	7.26 E
Holthusen	52	53.08 N	7.18 E
Holton, In., U.S.	218	39.04 N	85.23 W
Holton, Ks., U.S.	198	39.27 N	95.44 W
Holtorf	52	52.40 N	9.13 E
Holts Summit	219	38.39 N	92.07 W
Holtsville	210	40.49 N	73.02 W
Holtug	41	55.21 N	12.25 E
Holtville	204	32.48 N	115.22 W
Holtwick	52	52.00 N	7.05 E
Holtwood	208	39.50 N	76.19 W
Holwerd	52	53.22 N	5.54 E
Holycross, Ire.	48	52.38 N	7.52 W
Holy Cross, Ak., U.S.	180	62.12 N	159.47 W
Holy Cross Mountain ∧	182	53.47 N	120.47 W
Holyhead	44	53.19 N	4.38 W
Holyhead Bay c	44	53.23 N	4.37 W
Holy Island I, Eng., U.K.	44	55.41 N	1.48 W
Holy Island I, Scot., U.K.	46	55.32 N	5.04 W
Holy Island I, Wales, U.K.	44	53.18 N	4.37 W
Holy Island I, Ma., U.S.	283	42.43 N	70.50 W
Holyoke, Co., U.S.	198	40.35 N	102.18 W
Holyoke, Ma., U.S.	207	42.12 N	72.37 W
Holyrood	198	38.35 N	98.24 W
Holyrood Palace Ʊ	46	55.56 N	3.12 W
Holýšov	60	49.36 N	13.05 E
Holywell	44	53.17 N	3.13 W
Holywell Green	262	53.41 N	1.52 W
Holywood	48	54.38 N	5.50 W
Holzbüttgen	263	51.12 N	6.37 E
Holzen	56	51.26 N	7.31 E
Holzgau	58	47.16 N	10.21 E
Holzgerlingen	56	48.38 N	9.00 E
Holzhausen, Dtsch.	52	52.17 N	8.32 E
Holzhausen, Dtsch.	52	52.13 N	8.01 E
Holzhausen, Dtsch.	52	52.01 N	8.44 E
Holzhausen, Dtsch.	54	51.18 N	12.28 E
Holzhausen an der Haide	56	50.13 N	7.55 E
Holzheim	56	51.09 N	6.39 E
Holzkirchen	64	47.52 N	11.42 E
Holzminden	52	51.50 N	9.27 E
Holzweissig	54	51.36 N	12.18 E
Holzwickede	52	51.30 N	7.36 E
Hom ≃	158	28.51 S	18.37 E
Homa Bay	154	0.31 S	34.27 E
Homalin	110	24.52 N	94.55 E
Homathko ≃	182	50.55 N	124.50 W
Homathko Icefield ⊓	182	51.05 N	124.30 W
Homberg, Dtsch.	56	50.43 N	8.59 E
Homberg, Dtsch.	56	51.02 N	9.24 E
Homberg, Dtsch.	56	51.28 N	6.43 E
Homberg, Dtsch.	263	51.18 N	6.56 E
Hombori	150	15.17 N	1.42 W
Hombori Tondo ∧	150	15.16 N	1.40 W
Hombourg-Haut	56	49.08 N	6.46 E
Hombre Muerto, Salar del ≚	252	25.23 S	67.06 W
Hombruch ⊷[8]	263	51.29 N	7.26 E
Homburg	56	49.19 N	7.20 E
Homburg → Bad Homburg vor der Höhe	56	50.13 N	8.37 E
Home, Pa., U.S.	214	40.44 N	79.06 W
Home, Wa., U.S.	224	47.17 N	122.46 W
Homeacre	214	40.51 N	79.55 W
Home Bay c, N.T., Can.	176	68.45 N	67.10 W
Home Bay c, Kiribati	174d	0.53 S	169.35 E
Homebush Bay c	274a	33.50 S	151.05 E
Home Corner	216	40.31 N	85.38 W
Homécourt	56	49.14 N	5.59 E
Home Creek ≃	196	31.29 N	99.14 W
Homedale, Id., U.S.	202	43.37 N	116.55 W
Homedale, Oh., U.S.	214	40.04 N	83.02 W

Symbols in the index entries represent the broad categories identified in the key at the right. Symbols with superior numbers (⋀[1]) identify subcategories (see complete key on page *I · 1).*

Symbole im Register stellen die rechts im Schlüssel erklärten Kategorien dar. Symbole mit hochgestellten Ziffern (⋀[1]) bezeichnen Unterabteilungen einer Kategorie (vgl. vollständiger Schlüssel auf Seite *I · 1).*

Los símbolos incluídos en el texto del índice representan las grandes categorias identificadas con la clave a la derecha. Los símbolos con numeros en su parte superior (⋀[1]) identifican las subcategorías (véase la clave completa en la página *I · 1).*

Les symboles de l'index représentent les catégories indiquées dans la légende à droite. Les symboles suivis d'un indice (⋀[1]) représentent des sous-catégories (voir légende complète à la page *I · 1).*

Os símbolos incluídos no texto do índice representam as grandes categorias identificadas com a chave à direita. Os símbolos com números em sua parte superior (⋀[1]) identificam as subcategorias (veja-se a chave completa à página *I · 1).*

	English	Deutsch	Español	Français	Português
∧	Mountain	Berg	Montaña	Montagne	Montanha
⋀	Mountains	Gebirge	Montañas	Montagnes	Montanhas
)(	Pass	Paß	Paso	Col	Passo
V	Valley, Canyon	Tal, Cañon	Valle, Cañón	Vallée, Canyon	Vale, Canhão
≚	Plain	Ebene	Llano	Plaine	Planície
›	Cape	Kap	Cabo	Cap	Cabo
I	Island	Insel	Isla	Île	Ilha
II	Islands	Inseln	Islas	Îles	Ilhas
⩡	Other Topographic Features	Andere Topographische Objekte	Otros Elementos Topográficos	Autres données topographiques	Outros acidentes topográficos

Home Gardens 228 33.52 N 117.31 W
Home Hill 166 19.40 S 147.25 E
Homeland, Ca., U.S. 228 33.44 N 117.07 W
Homeland, Fl., U.S. 220 27.49 N 81.49 W
Homeland Canal ≅ 226 35.57 N 119.27 W
Homeland Park 192 34.27 N 82.41 W
Home Place 218 39.56 N 86.08 W
Homer, Ak., U.S. 180 59.39 N 151.33 W
Homer, Ga., U.S. 192 34.20 N 83.29 W
Homer, La., U.S. 194 32.47 N 93.03 W
Homer, Mi., U.S. 216 42.08 N 84.48 W
Homer, Ne., U.S. 198 42.19 N 96.29 W
Homer, N.Y., U.S. 210 42.38 N 76.10 W
Homer, Oh., U.S. 214 40.15 N 82.31 W
Homer, Tx., U.S. 222 31.18 N 94.36 W
Homer City 214 40.32 N 79.09 W
Homert ∧ [2] 263 51.11 N 7.39 E
Homer Tunnel ◆ [5] 172 44.45 S 168.00 E
Homerville, Ga., U.S. 192 31.02 N 82.44 W
Homerville, Oh., U.S. 214 41.02 N 82.08 W
Home Wash V 204 34.20 N 115.02 W
Homer Youngs Peak ∧ 202 45.19 N 113.41 W
Home Seamount ✣ [3] 14 12.55 S 175.37 W
Homestead, Austl. 166 20.22 S 145.39 E
Homestead, Fl., U.S. 220 25.28 N 80.28 W
Homestead, Pa., U.S. 279b 40.24 N 79.54 W
Homestead Air Force Base ▪ 220 25.29 N 80.23 W
Homestead National Monument of America ♦ 198 40.14 N 96.54 W
Homestead Valley 282 37.54 N 122.32 W
Hometown, Il., U.S. 278 41.44 N 87.43 W
Hometown, Pa., U.S. 210 40.49 N 75.59 W
Homewood, Al., U.S. 194 33.28 N 86.48 W
Homewood, Ca., U.S. 226 39.05 N 120.09 W
Homewood, Il., U.S. 216 41.33 N 87.39 W
Homewood, Oh., U.S. 218 39.23 N 84.33 W
Homewood ◆ [8] 279b 40.27 N 79.54 W
Homewood Acres 278 41.34 N 87.43 W
Homeworth 214 40.50 N 81.03 W
Hominy 196 36.24 N 96.23 W
Hominy Creek ≃ 196 36.20 N 96.00 W
Hommersåk 26 58.58 N 5.42 E
Hommura 92 34.22 N 139.15 E
Homnābād 122 17.46 N 77.08 E
Homochitto ≃ 194 31.09 N 91.31 W
Homoine 156 23.52 S 35.09 E
Homonhon Island I 116 10.44 N 125.43 E
Homosassa 220 28.46 N 82.36 W
Homosassa Bay c 220 28.45 N 82.43 W
Homosassa Springs 220 28.48 N 82.35 W
Homs
— Al-Khums 146 32.39 N 14.16 E
Homs
— Ḥimṣ 130 34.44 N 36.43 E
Honai 96 33.30 N 132.25 E
Honaker 192 37.00 N 81.58 W
Honami 96 33.36 N 130.42 E
Honan
— Henan □ [4] 90 34.00 N 114.00 E
Honan
— Luoyang 102 34.41 N 112.28 E
Honāvar 122 14.17 N 74.27 E
Honaz 130 37.45 N 29.17 E
Honbetsu 92a 43.07 N 143.37 E
Hon Chong 110 10.10 N 104.37 E
Honda 246 5.12 N 74.45 W
Honda, Bahía c, Col. 246 12.21 N 71.47 W
Honda, Bahía c, Cuba 240p 22.57 N 83.10 W
Honda, Cañada ≃ 258 33.57 S 59.21 W
Honda Bay c 116 9.53 N 118.49 E
Honddu ≃, U.K. 42 51.54 N 2.58 W
Honddu ≃, Wales, U.K. 42 51.57 N 3.23 W
Hondeklipbaai 156 30.20 S 17.18 E
Honderfontein 158 32.12 S 21.22 E
Hon Dien, Nui ∧ 110 11.33 N 108.38 E
Hondo, Ab., Can. 182 55.04 N 114.02 W
Hondo, Nihon 92 32.27 N 130.12 E
Hondo, N.M., U.S. 200 33.23 N 105.16 W
Hondo, Tx., U.S. 196 29.20 N 99.08 W
Hondo ≃, Méx. 286a 19.26 N 99.15 W
Hondo ≃, N.A. 232 18.29 N 88.19 W
Hondo, Arroyo ≃ 226 37.28 N 121.47 W
Hondo, Rio ≃, Ca., U.S. 280 33.55 N 118.10 W
Hondo, Rio ≃, N.M., U.S. 196 33.22 N 104.24 W
Hondo Creek ≃ 196 28.45 N 99.11 W
Hondoji Temple ✠ [1] 268 35.51 N 139.56 E
Hondschoote 50 50.59 N 2.35 E
Hondsrug ∧ [2] 52 52.55 N 6.50 E
Honduras □ [1], N.A. 230 15.00 N 86.30 W
Honduras □ [1], N.A. 236 15.00 N 86.30 W
Honduras, Cabo de ≻ 236 16.01 N 86.02 W
Honduras, Gulf of c 230 16.10 N 87.50 W
Honduras, Port c 236 16.13 N 88.41 W
Honea Path 192 34.26 N 82.23 W
Hönebach 56 50.56 N 9.56 E
Hønefoss 26 60.10 N 10.18 E
Honeoye 210 42.47 N 77.31 W
Honeoye Creek ≃ 210 42.58 N 77.43 W
Honeoye Falls 210 42.57 N 77.35 W
Honeoye Lake ⊜ 210 42.45 N 77.31 W
Honesdale 210 41.34 N 75.15 W
Honey Brook 208 40.05 N 75.54 W
Honey Creek 216 42.44 N 88.18 W
Honey Creek ≃, Ia., U.S. 190 42.09 N 93.03 W
Honey Creek ≃, Mo., U.S. 194 39.53 N 93.34 W
Honey Creek ≃, Oh., U.S. 214 41.05 N 83.12 W
Honey Creek ≃, Pa., U.S. 208 40.36 N 77.35 W
Honey Creek ≃, Wi., U.S. 216 42.41 N 88.17 W
Honeydew 273d 26.05 S 27.55 E
Honeygo Run ≃ 284b 39.22 N 76.25 W
Honey Grove 196 33.35 N 95.54 W
Honey Lake ⊜ 204 40.16 N 120.19 W
Honeymoon Bay 224 48.49 N 124.10 W
Honeyville 200 41.38 N 112.04 W
Honfleur 50 49.25 N 0.14 E
Høng 41 55.31 N 11.18 E
Hong ≃ 100 32.25 N 115.35 E
Honga 152 15.09 S 15.12 E
Hon Gai 110 20.57 N 107.05 E
Hong'an 100 31.18 N 114.37 E
Honga River c 208 38.19 N 76.10 W
Hongawa 96 33.43 N 133.19 E
Hongchang 100 34.05 N 113.20 E
Hongch'ŏn 98 37.42 N 127.52 E
Hongchoudai 100 29.03 N 121.11 E
Hongcun, Zhg. 100 27.10 N 116.48 E
Hongcun, Zhg. 106 31.01 N 119.15 E
Höngen 56 51.02 N 5.56 E
Honggun 98 40.46 N 128.27 E
Honghai Wan c 100 22.40 N 115.10 E
Honghe 102 23.23 N 102.35 E
Honghu 100 29.48 N 113.27 E
Hong Hu ⊜ 100 29.52 N 113.23 E
Honghuaerji 89 48.15 N 120.01 E
Honghuaji 100 33.52 N 114.26 E
Honghualiangzi 89 48.06 N 123.12 E
Honghuanu 89 48.33 N 125.39 E
Hongjiang, Zhg. 100 26.49 N 120.03 E
Hongjiang, Zhg. 102 27.07 N 109.56 E
Hong Kong □ [2], Asia 90 22.15 N 114.10 E
Hong Kong □ [2], Asia 100 22.15 N 114.10 E
Hong Kong I 271d 22.15 N 114.11 E
Hong Kong, University of ✠ [2] 271d 22.17 N 114.08 E
Hong Kong
— Victoria 271d 22.17 N 114.09 E
Hongkong Park ♦ 269b 31.16 N 121.28 E
Honglai 100 25.08 N 118.32 E
Honglanbu 106 31.37 N 118.57 E
Honglingiao 106 30.59 N 118.59 E
Hongliutai 85 39.48 N 77.26 E
Hongliuyuan 102 41.04 N 95.26 E
Honglongdian 106 30.30 N 119.00 E
Honglongtang 105 40.41 N 117.37 E
Honglu 100 25.44 N 119.20 E
Hongluan 100 28.31 N 117.01 E
Hongluo Shan ∧ 104 40.56 N 120.42 E
Hongluoxian 104 41.01 N 120.53 E
Hongmeichang 105 39.50 N 115.51 E
Hongmendu 102 26.10 N 102.37 E
Hongmenkou 102 27.22 N 100.23 E
Hongmenpu 107 30.37 N 104.08 E
Hongmiaozi 107 28.47 N 104.02 E
Hong Ngu 110 10.48 N 105.21 E
Hongō, Nihon 96 34.24 N 132.59 E
Hongō, Nihon 96 34.17 N 132.02 E
Hongō ◆ [8] 268 35.42 N 139.47 E
Hongpailou 107 30.38 N 104.01 E
Hongqi 89 44.23 N 126.32 E
Hongqiao, Zhg. 100 28.14 N 121.01 E
Hongqiao, Zhg. 105 39.50 N 117.44 E
Hongqiao, Zhg. 106 31.29 N 121.49 E
Hongqiao, Zhg. 269b 31.12 N 121.22 E
Hongqiao Ji Chang ≋ 106 31.12 N 121.20 E
Hong
— Red ≃ 110 20.17 N 106.34 E
Hongrie
— Hungary □ [1] 30 47.00 N 20.00 E
Hongshan, Zhg. 89 48.02 N 129.00 E
Hongshan, Zhg. 98 36.37 N 118.00 E
Hongshanzi 98 42.34 N 117.14 E
Hongshi, Zhg. 89 43.00 N 127.04 E
Hongshi, Zhg. 98 41.21 N 119.32 E
Hongshidou 104 41.52 N 122.11 E
Hongshili 98 40.41 N 125.03 E
Hongshui 102 37.24 N 104.00 E
Hongshui ≃ 102 23.45 N 109.30 E
Hongshuichuan 105 40.06 N 117.55 E
Hongshuyangzi 105 40.36 N 116.36 E
Hongsŏng 98 36.36 N 126.39 E
Hongtang 100 26.06 N 119.14 E
Hongtian 100 25.52 N 117.15 E
Hongtong 102 36.19 N 111.39 E
Hongtuwan 98 41.03 N 113.39 E
Hongtu Zhang ∧ 100 23.46 N 115.56 E
Honguedo, Détroit d' 𝕦 186 49.15 N 64.00 W
Hongwŏn 98 40.02 N 127.57 E
Hongxin 100 32.43 N 117.47 E
Hongxing 105 39.48 N 116.27 E
Hongxingqiao 106 30.55 N 119.52 E
Hongyang, Zhg. 100 26.32 N 119.27 E
Hongyang, Zhg. 100 23.28 N 116.13 E
Hongyanzi 104 40.38 N 120.31 E
Hongyōtoku 268 35.41 N 139.55 E
Hongze 100 33.19 N 118.53 E
Hongze Hu ⊜ 100 33.16 N 118.34 E
Honiara 175e 9.26 S 159.57 E
Honiton 42 50.48 N 3.13 W
Hon-jima I 96 34.23 N 133.47 E
Honjō, Nihon 92 39.23 N 140.03 E
Honjō, Nihon 94 36.24 N 138.01 E
Honjō, Nihon 94 36.14 N 139.11 E
Honkamäki ∧ [2] 26 62.58 N 27.05 E
Hon-kawane 94 35.07 N 138.09 E
Honker Bay c 282 38.04 N 121.56 W
Hönne ≃ 263 51.28 N 7.46 E
Honnecourt-sur-Escaut 50 50.02 N 3.12 E
Honningsvåg 24 70.59 N 25.59 E
Hönö 26 57.42 N 11.39 E
Honokaa 229d 20.04 N 155.28 W
Honokahua 229a 21.00 N 156.39 W
Honokawai 229a 20.57 N 156.41 W
Honolulu 229c 21.18 N 157.51 W
Honolulu □ [6] 229c 21.19 N 157.52 W
Honolulu International Airport ≋ 229c 21.20 N 157.55 W
Honomu 229d 19.52 N 155.07 W
Honouliuli 229c 21.22 N 158.02 W
Hönow 54 52.32 N 13.38 E
Hon Quan 110 11.39 N 106.36 E
Honshū I 92 36.00 N 138.00 E
Hontoon Island State Park ♦ 220 28.59 N 81.22 W
Höntrop ◆ [8] 263 51.27 N 7.08 E
Honuapo Bay c 229d 19.05 N 155.33 W
Hoo 260 51.25 N 0.34 E
Hood 226 38.22 N 121.31 W
Hood □ [6] 222 32.25 N 97.45 W
Hood ≃, N.T., Can. 176 67.26 N 108.53 W
Hood ≃, Or., U.S. 224 45.42 N 121.30 W
Hood, East Fork ≃ 224 45.36 N 121.38 W
Hood, Mount ∧ 224 45.23 N 121.41 W
Hood, West Fork ≃ 224 45.36 N 121.38 W
Hood Canal c 224 47.35 N 123.00 W
Hood Canal Floating Bridge ◆ [5] 224 47.52 N 122.38 W
Hoodoo Peak ∧ 202 48.15 N 120.19 W
Hood Point ≻, Austl. 162 34.23 S 119.34 E
Hood Point ≻, Pap. N. Gui. 164 10.05 S 147.45 E
Hood Pond ⊜ 283 42.40 N 70.57 W
Hood River 224 45.42 N 121.31 W
Hoodsport 224 47.24 N 123.08 W
Hoods Range ∧ 166 28.35 S 144.30 E
Hoof 56 51.17 N 9.20 E
Hoogerheide 52 51.25 N 4.20 E
Hoogeveen 52 52.43 N 6.29 E
Hoogeveense Vaart ≅ 52 52.42 N 6.11 E
Hoogezand-Sappemeer 52 53.09 N 6.47 E
Hoogkerk 52 53.13 N 6.30 E
Hoogledе 50 50.59 N 3.05 E
Hoogstede 52 52.34 N 6.56 E
Hoogstraten 52 51.24 N 4.46 E
Hoogte 158 27.28 S 28.03 E
Hoogvliet 52 51.52 N 4.21 E
Hook 42 51.17 N 0.58 W
Hook ◆ [8] 260 51.22 N 0.18 W
Hooker 196 36.51 N 101.12 W
Hooker, Bi'r ⊤ [4] 142 30.23 N 30.20 E
Hooker Creek 162 18.20 S 130.40 E
Hooker Creek Aboriginal Reserve ◆ [4] 162 18.10 S 130.25 E
Hook Head ≻ 48 52.07 N 6.55 W
Hookina 166 31.45 S 138.20 E
Hook Island I 166 20.08 S 148.55 E
Hook Mountain State Park ♦ 276 41.09 N 73.55 W
Hook Norton 42 51.59 N 1.29 W
Hook Point ≻ 166 25.48 S 153.05 E
Hooks 194 33.28 N 94.15 W
Hooksiel 52 53.38 N 8.01 E
Hoolehua 229a 21.10 N 157.04 W
Hoonah 180 58.07 N 135.26 W
Hoopa 204 41.03 N 123.40 W
Hoopa Valley Indian Reservation ◆ [4] 204 41.08 N 123.40 W
Hooper 198 41.36 N 96.32 W
Hooper Bay 180 61.31 N 166.06 W
Hooper Islands II 208 38.20 N 76.13 W
Hooper Strait 𝕦 208 38.12 N 76.03 W
Hoopersville 208 38.15 N 76.10 W
Hoopes Reservoir ⊜ [1] 285 39.47 N 75.38 W
Hoopeston 216 40.28 N 87.40 W
Hooping Harbour 186 50.37 N 56.17 W
Hoople 198 48.32 N 97.38 W
Hoopstad 158 27.54 S 25.58 E
Hoopstick Brook ≃ 276 40.39 N 74.41 W
Höör 41 55.56 N 13.32 E
Hoorn 52 52.38 N 5.04 E
Hoorn, Kap
— Hornos, Cabo de ≻ 254 55.59 S 67.16 W
Hoosac Range ∧ 207 42.45 N 73.02 W
Hoosac Tunnel ◆ [5] 207 42.41 N 73.03 W
Hoosic ≃ 210 42.54 N 73.39 W
Hoosick 210 42.51 N 73.21 W
Hoosick Falls 210 42.54 N 73.21 W
Hooton 262 53.18 N 2.57 W
Hoot Owl Estates 285 39.53 N 74.50 W
Hoover Dam ◆ [6] 200 36.00 N 114.27 W
Hoover Reservoir ⊜ [1] 214 40.08 N 82.53 W
Hooversville 214 40.08 N 78.54 W
Hopa 130 41.25 N 41.24 E
Hopatcong 210 40.55 N 74.39 W
Hopatcong, Lake ⊜ 210 40.57 N 74.38 W
Hopatcong State Park ♦ 276 40.55 N 74.40 W
Hop Bottom 210 41.42 N 75.46 W
Hop Brook ≃ 276 40.19 N 74.08 W
Hope, B.C., Can. 182 49.23 N 121.26 W
Hope, Ak., U.S. 180 60.55 N 149.38 W
Hope, Ar., U.S. 194 33.40 N 93.35 W
Hope, In., U.S. 218 39.18 N 85.46 W
Hope, N.J., U.S. 210 40.54 N 74.58 W
Hope, N.D., U.S. 198 47.19 N 97.43 W
Hope, R.I., U.S. 207 41.44 N 71.33 W
Hope, Ben ∧ 46 58.24 N 4.37 W
Hope, Loch ⊜ 46 58.27 N 4.39 W
Hope, Point ≻ 180 68.21 N 166.50 W
Hope Bay c 212 44.55 N 81.08 W
Hopedale, Nf., Can. 176 55.28 N 60.13 W
Hopedale, Il., U.S. 194 40.25 N 89.24 W
Hopedale, La., U.S. 194 29.49 N 89.39 W
Hopedale, Ma., U.S. 207 42.07 N 71.32 W
Hopedale, Oh., U.S. 214 40.19 N 80.54 W
Hope Farm 210 41.44 N 73.40 W
Hopefield 158 33.04 S 18.22 E
Hopeh
— Hebei □ [4] 98 38.00 N 116.00 E
Hope Island I, B.C., Can. 182 50.55 N 127.53 W
Hope Island I, On., Can. 212 44.55 N 80.12 W
Hopeland 208 40.14 N 76.16 W
Hopelawn 276 40.31 N 74.17 W
Hopelchén 232 19.46 N 89.51 W
Hopeman 46 57.42 N 3.25 W
Hope Mills 192 34.58 N 78.56 W
Hopes Advance, Cap ≻ 176 61.04 N 69.34 W
Hopetoun, Austl. 162 33.57 S 120.07 E
Hopetoun, Austl. 166 35.44 S 142.22 E
Hopetown 158 29.34 S 24.03 E
Hope Vale Aboriginal Reserve ◆ [4] 164 15.10 S 145.15 E
Hope Valley, Austl. 168b 34.50 S 138.44 E
Hope Valley, R.I., U.S. 207 41.30 N 71.43 W
Hopewell, N.J., U.S. 208 40.23 N 74.45 W
Hopewell, Pa., U.S. 214 40.08 N 78.16 W
Hopewell, Va., U.S. 208 37.18 N 77.17 W
Hopewell Islands II 176 58.25 N 78.00 W
Hopewell Junction 210 41.35 N 73.48 W
Hopewell Village National Historic Site ⊥ 208 40.12 N 75.46 W
Hopfgarten 64 47.27 N 12.10 E
Hopfgarten in Defereggen 64 46.55 N 12.31 E
Hopi Buttes ∧ 200 35.20 N 110.15 W
Hopi
— Hebi 98 35.59 N 114.11 E
Hopi Indian Reservation ◆ [4] 200 35.45 N 110.35 W
Hopkins, Mi., U.S. 216 42.37 N 85.45 W
Hopkins, Mo., U.S. 190 40.33 N 94.49 W
Hopkins □ [6] 222 33.07 N 95.35 W
Hopkins ≃ 166 38.24 S 142.31 E
Hopkins, Lake ⊜ 162 24.15 S 128.50 E
Hopkins Creek ≃ 284a 43.17 N 78.46 W
Hopkinsville 194 36.51 N 87.29 W
Hopkinton, Ia., U.S. 190 42.20 N 91.14 W
Hopkinton, Ma., U.S. 207 42.13 N 71.31 W
Hopkinton, R.I., U.S. 207 41.27 N 71.46 W
Hopland 204 38.58 N 123.06 W
Hopolo Bouchard 252 34.43 S 63.31 W
Hoppegarten 264a 52.31 N 13.40 E
Hoppenrade 264a 52.32 N 12.56 E
Hoppo
— Hepu 102 21.39 N 109.11 E
Hopsten 52 52.23 N 7.36 E
Hoptrup 41 55.11 N 9.28 E
Ho Pui 271d 22.25 N 114.03 E
Hopwood, Mount ∧ 166 21.49 S 144.26 E
Hoque 152 14.39 S 13.54 E
Hoquiam 224 46.58 N 123.53 W
Hoquiam, East Fork ≃ 224 46.58 N 123.54 W
Hora Califo 144 8.49 N 43.07 E
Horace Mountain ∧ 180 67.40 N 149.06 W
Horado 94 35.36 N 136.50 E
Hōrai 94 34.56 N 137.34 E
Horana 124 6.43 N 80.04 E
Horancia 144 6.31 N 38.44 E
Horasan 130 40.03 N 42.11 E
Horatio 194 33.56 N 94.21 W
Horatio Gardens 278 42.10 N 87.57 W
Horažďovice 60 49.20 N 13.43 E
Horb am Neckar 58 48.26 N 8.41 E
Horbelev 41 54.49 N 12.04 E
Horbourg 58 48.05 N 7.23 E
Hörby 41 55.51 N 13.39 E
Horconcitos 236 8.19 N 82.10 W
Hordaland □ [6] 26 60.15 N 6.30 E
Hörde ◆ [8] 263 51.29 N 7.30 E
Horden 44 54.46 N 1.18 W
Horden ≃ 164 3.50 S 141.25 E
Horezu 38 45.08 N 23.59 E
Horgen 58 47.15 N 8.36 E
Horgoš 30 46.09 N 19.58 E
Hořice 50 50.22 N 15.38 E
Horicon 190 43.27 N 88.37 W
Horigane 268 35.50 N 139.27 E
Horine 219 38.16 N 90.25 W
Horinger 102 40.23 N 111.53 E
Horinouchi 94 37.14 N 138.56 E
Horinouchi ◆ [8] 268 35.41 N 139.40 E
Horizon Tablemount ✣ [3] 14 19.40 N 168.30 W
Horizontina 252 27.37 S 54.19 W
Horka 54 51.16 N 14.56 E
Hörken 40 60.02 N 14.56 E
Horley 44 51.11 N 0.11 W
Horlick Mountains ∧ 9 85.23 S 121.00 W
Horloff ≃ 56 50.20 N 8.52 E
Hormigueros 240m 18.09 N 67.08 W
Hormoz, Jazīreh-ye I 128 27.04 N 56.28 E
Hormozgān □ [4] 128 27.30 N 56.00 E
Hormuz, Strait of 𝕦 128 26.34 N 56.15 E
Horn, Öst. 61 48.40 N 15.40 E
Horn ≃ 52 51.51 N 8.56 E
Horn ◆ [8] 52 53.38 N 10.05 E
Horn ≃ 24a 66.28 N 22.28 W
Horn ≃, N.T., Can. 176 61.30 N 118.01 W
Horn ≃, Europe 56 49.15 N 7.20 E
Horn, Ben ∧ 46 58.01 N 4.02 W
Horn, Cape
— Hornos, Cabo de ≻ 254 55.59 S 67.16 W
Hornaday ≃ 180 69.22 N 123.50 W
Hornafjördur c 24a 64.17 N 15.16 W
Hornavan ⊜ 24 66.10 N 17.30 E
Hornbach 56 49.11 N 7.22 E
Hornbæk 41 56.05 N 12.28 E
Hornbeak 194 36.19 N 89.17 W
Hornbeck 194 31.19 N 93.23 W
Hornberg 58 48.13 N 8.13 E
Hornbrook 204 41.55 N 122.33 W
Hornburg 54 52.01 N 10.36 E
Hornby, On., Can. 275b 43.34 N 79.50 W
Hornby, N.Z. 172 43.33 S 172.32 E
Hornby Bay c 176 66.35 N 117.50 W
Horncastle 44 53.13 N 0.07 W
Hornchurch ◆ [8] 260 51.34 N 0.12 E
Horndal 40 60.18 N 16.25 E
Horndean 42 50.55 N 1.00 W
Horndon on the Hill 260 51.31 N 0.25 E
Horne 41 55.06 N 10.11 E
Horne, Îles de II 14 14.16 S 178.05 W
Hornebach ≃ 263 51.39 N 7.38 E
Horneburg, Dtsch. 52 53.30 N 9.34 E
Horneburg, Dtsch. 263 51.38 N 7.18 E
Hörnefors 26 63.38 N 19.54 E
Hornell 210 42.19 N 77.39 W
Hornepayne 176 49.13 N 84.47 W
Hornerstown 208 40.06 N 74.30 W
Hornhausen 54 52.02 N 11.10 E
Horn Head ≻ 48 55.14 N 7.59 W
Horn Hill 260 51.37 N 0.32 W
Horní Jiřetín 54 50.35 N 13.32 E
Hornindal 26 61.58 N 6.31 E
Hornindalsvatnet ⊜ 26 61.56 N 6.22 E
Horning 44 52.42 N 1.28 E
Hörningsholm 40 59.03 N 17.40 E
Horní Počernice 54 50.06 N 14.38 E
Hornisgrinde ∧ 56 48.36 N 8.12 E
Horn Island I, Austl. 164 10.37 S 142.17 E
Horn Island I, Ms., U.S. 194 30.13 N 88.38 W
Horní Slavkov 54 50.07 N 12.46 E
Horní Stropnice 61 48.46 N 14.44 E
Hornito, Cerro ∧ 236 8.39 N 82.09 W
Hornitos 226 37.30 N 120.14 W
Horní Vltavice 60 48.57 N 13.46 E
Horn Lake 194 34.58 N 90.02 W
Horn Lake ⊜ 212 45.24 N 79.36 W
Hornos, Cabo de (Cape Horn) ≻ 254 55.59 S 67.16 W
Hornos, Isla I 254 55.57 S 67.17 W
Hornos, Islas de II 288 34.25 S 57.55 W
Hornow 54 51.38 N 14.31 E
Hornoy 50 49.51 N 1.54 E
Horn Plateau ∧ [1] 176 62.15 N 119.15 W
Horn Pond ⊜ 283 42.28 N 71.09 W
Hornsby, Austl. 170 33.42 S 151.06 E
Hornsby, Il., U.S. 219 39.10 N 89.45 W
Hornsbyville 208 37.11 N 76.28 W
Hornsea 44 53.55 N 0.10 W
Hornsey ◆ [8] 260 51.35 N 0.07 W
Hornslet 41 56.19 N 10.20 E
Hornstorf 54 53.54 N 11.32 E
Hornsyld 41 55.45 N 9.51 E
Horntown 208 37.58 N 75.28 W
Hornu 50 50.26 N 3.49 E
Horoshiri-dake ∧ 92a 42.43 N 142.41 E
Horotiu 172 37.43 S 175.12 E
Hořovice 60 49.50 N 13.54 E
Horqin Youyi Qianqi (Ulan Hot) 89 46.05 N 122.05 E
Horqin Youyi Zhongqi 89 45.09 N 121.24 E
Horqin Zuoyi Houqi 89 42.58 N 122.20 E
Horqin Zuoyi Zhongqi 89 44.07 N 123.18 E
Horqueta 252 23.24 S 56.53 W
Horrabridge 42 50.31 N 4.05 W
Horrelville 172 43.20 S 172.20 E
Horrem 263 51.06 N 6.48 E
Hörsching 61 48.14 N 14.11 E
Horse ≃ 184 56.43 N 111.23 W
Horse Back Knob ∧ [2] 218 39.14 N 83.06 W
Horse Cave 194 37.10 N 85.54 W
Horse Creek 200 41.25 N 105.11 W
Horse Creek ≃, U.S. 198 41.57 N 103.58 W
Horse Creek ≃, Co., U.S. 198 38.05 N 103.19 W
Horse Creek ≃, Fl., U.S. 220 27.06 N 81.58 W
Horse Creek ≃, Il., U.S. 219 39.45 N 89.34 W
Horse Creek ≃, Mo., U.S. 194 37.46 N 93.53 W
Horsefly 182 52.20 N 121.24 W
Horsefly Lake ⊜ 182 52.25 N 121.00 W
Horsehead Creek ≃ 198 43.17 N 103.22 W
Horsehead Lake ⊜ 198 47.02 N 99.47 W
Horseheads 210 42.10 N 76.49 W
Horse Islands II 186 50.13 N 55.45 W
Horsell 260 51.19 N 0.34 W
Horseneck Brook ≃ 276 41.01 N 73.38 W
Horsens 41 55.52 N 9.52 E
Horsens Fjord c 41 55.50 N 10.05 E
Horseshoe Bend, Ar., U.S. 194 36.15 N 91.43 W
Horseshoe Bend, Id., U.S. 202 43.55 N 116.12 W
Horseshoe Bend National Military Park ♦ 194 33.00 N 85.46 W
Horseshoe Cove c 276 40.27 N 74.00 W
Horseshoe Creek ≃ 198 42.27 N 104.58 W
Horseshoe Falls ⊾ 284a 43.05 N 79.04 W
Horseshoe Lake ⊜, Mb., Can. 184 52.12 N 95.50 W
Horseshoe Lake ⊜, Mi., U.S. 281 42.24 N 83.45 W
Horseshoe Lake ⊜, N.J., U.S. 276 40.52 N 74.38 W
Horse Shoe Reef ✣ [2] 240m 18.40 N 64.12 W
Horsfjärden c 40 59.04 N 18.09 E
Horsforth 44 53.51 N 1.39 W
Horsham, Austl. 166 36.43 S 142.13 E
Horsham, Eng., U.K. 42 51.04 N 0.21 W
Horsham, Pa., U.S. 208 40.10 N 75.08 W
Hørsholm 41 55.53 N 12.30 E
Hörsingen 54 52.16 N 11.09 E
Horsley, Austl. 274a 33.51 S 150.51 E
Horsley, Eng., U.K. 260 51.16 N 0.26 W
Horslunde 41 54.54 N 11.14 E
Horšovský Týn 60 49.32 N 12.56 E
Horst, Dtsch. 52 53.48 N 9.37 E
Horst, Dtsch. 54 53.22 N 10.37 E
Horst, Ned. 52 51.27 N 6.04 E
Horst ◆ [8] 263 51.32 N 7.02 E
Horsted Keynes 42 51.02 N 0.01 W
Hörstel 52 52.18 N 7.35 E
Horstmar, Dtsch. 52 52.05 N 7.17 E
Horstmar, Dtsch. 263 51.36 N 7.33 E
Horsunlu 130 37.55 N 28.36 E
Horta 148a 38.32 N 28.38 W
Horta □ [5] 148a 38.30 N 29.00 W
Horta ◆ [8] 266d 41.26 N 2.00 E
Hortaleza ◆ [8] 266a 40.28 N 3.39 W
Horten 26 59.25 N 10.30 E
Hortobágy ≃ 30 47.35 N 21.00 E
Hortobágyi Nemzeti Park ♦ 30 47.30 N 21.10 E
Horton, Eng., U.K. 260 51.28 N 0.32 W
Horton, In., U.S. 218 40.05 N 86.09 W
Horton, Ks., U.S. 198 39.39 N 95.31 W
Horton, Mi., U.S. 216 42.09 N 84.31 W
Horton ≃ 180 70.00 N 126.53 W
Horton in Ribblesdale 44 54.09 N 2.17 W
Horton Kirby 260 51.23 N 0.15 E
Horton Lake ⊜ 180 67.29 N 122.31 W
Hortonville, N.Y., U.S. 210 41.46 N 75.02 W
Hortonville, Wi., U.S. 190 44.20 N 88.38 W
Horumersiel 52 53.41 N 8.00 E
Hørup 41 54.56 N 9.54 E
Hørve 41 55.45 N 11.28 E
Horw 58 47.01 N 8.18 E
Horwich 262 53.37 N 2.33 W
Horwood Lake ⊜ 190 48.03 N 82.20 W
Hory Matky Boží 60 49.14 N 13.27 E
Hōryūji Temple ✠ [1] 270 34.36 N 135.44 E
Hosaina 144 7.38 N 37.52 E
Hösbach 56 50.00 N 9.12 E
Hosei University ✠ [2] 268 35.42 N 139.44 E
Hösel 263 51.19 N 6.54 E
Hosena 54 51.27 N 14.01 E
Hoseré Vokré ∧ 146 8.20 N 13.15 E
Hoseynābād 128 35.33 N 47.08 E
Hoseynīyeh-ye Khodā-Dād 128 32.42 N 48.14 E
Hosford 192 30.23 N 84.47 W
Hoshāb 128 26.01 N 63.56 E
Hoshangābād 124 22.45 N 77.43 E
Hoshangābād Plain ≅ 124 22.35 N 77.25 E
Hoshiārpur, India 123 31.32 N 75.54 E
Hoshiārpur, India 272a 28.35 N 77.22 E
Hoshigajō ∧ 96 34.31 N 134.19 E
Hosingen 56 50.01 N 6.05 E
Hosjö 40 60.35 N 15.46 E
Hoskins 164 5.27 S 150.30 E
Hosmer, B.C., Can. 182 49.35 N 114.57 W
Hosmer, S.D., U.S. 198 45.34 N 99.28 W
Hosoe 94 34.49 N 137.39 E
Hospental 58 46.37 N 8.34 E
Hospers 198 43.04 N 95.54 W
Hospet 122 15.16 N 76.24 E
Hospital 48 52.29 N 8.25 W
Hospital de Orbigo 34 42.28 N 5.53 W
Hossegor 32 43.40 N 1.27 W
Hosston 194 32.53 N 93.52 W
Hosta Butte ∧ 200 35.35 N 108.12 W
Hoste, Isla I 254 55.15 S 69.00 W
Hostěradice 61 48.57 N 16.15 E
Hostetter 214 40.16 N 79.24 W
Hostigrām 272b 22.26 N 88.31 E
Hostivař ◆ [8] 54 50.01 N 14.32 E
Hostivice 54 50.04 N 14.15 E
Hošťka 54 50.30 N 14.20 E
Hostomice 54 50.35 N 13.46 E
Hostotipaquillo 234 21.04 N 104.04 W
Hostouň 60 49.34 N 12.46 E
Hosūr 122 12.43 N 77.49 E
Hot 110 18.06 N 98.36 E
Hota 268 35.08 N 139.51 E
Hotagen 26 63.59 N 14.15 E
Hotagen ⊜ 26 63.53 N 14.29 E
Hotagsfjällen ∧ 26 64.20 N 14.30 E
Hotaka 94 36.20 N 137.53 E
Hotaka-dake ∧ 94 36.17 N 137.39 E
Hotamış 130 37.36 N 33.13 E
Hotan 120 37.08 N 79.54 E
Hotan ≃ 90 40.30 N 80.45 E
Hotarele 38 44.10 N 26.22 E
Hotazel 158 27.15 S 23.00 E
Hotchkiss 200 38.47 N 107.43 W
Hotchkissville 207 41.34 N 73.13 W
Hot Creek Range ∧ 204 38.30 N 116.25 W
Hötensleben 54 52.08 N 11.01 E
Hotevilla 200 35.55 N 110.40 W
Hotham ≃ 168a 32.58 S 116.22 E
Hotham Inlet c 180 66.45 N 162.00 W
Hotham Peak ∧ 180 66.48 N 160.42 W
Hoting 26 64.07 N 16.10 E
Hot Springs, Mt., U.S. 202 47.36 N 114.40 W
Hot Springs, N.C., U.S. 192 35.53 N 82.49 W
Hot Springs, S.D., U.S. 198 43.25 N 103.28 W
Hot Springs, Va., U.S. 192 37.59 N 79.49 W
Hot Springs National Park 194 34.30 N 93.04 W
Hot Springs Peak ∧, Ca., U.S. 204 40.22 N 120.07 W
Hot Springs Peak ∧, Nv., U.S. 204 41.22 N 117.26 W
Hot Springs State Park ♦ 202 43.40 N 108.10 W
Hot Springs
— Truth or Consequences 200 33.08 N 107.15 W
Hot Sulphur Springs 200 40.04 N 106.06 W
Hottah Lake ⊜ 176 65.04 N 118.29 W
Hottentotbaai c 156 26.05 S 14.58 E
Hottentotskloof 158 33.15 S 19.40 E
Hotton 56 50.16 N 5.27 E
Hötzum 54 52.13 N 10.37 E
Houaïlou 175f 21.17 S 165.38 E
Houamuang 110 20.09 N 103.38 E
Houaphan □ [4] 110 20.15 N 104.00 E
Houbaishu 106 31.49 N 119.10 E
Houbao 98 41.54 N 125.14 E
Houcheng 106 31.55 N 120.26 E
Houdahepao 104 41.49 N 123.01 E
Houdain 50 50.27 N 2.32 E
Houdan 50 48.47 N 1.36 E
Houdelaincourt 58 48.33 N 5.28 E
Houdeng-Aimeries 50 50.29 N 4.08 E
Houeillès 32 44.12 N 0.02 E
Houffalize 56 50.08 N 5.47 E
Hougang 271c 1.22 N 103.54 E
Hough Green 262 53.23 N 2.47 W
Houghton, Mi., U.S. 190 47.07 N 88.34 W
Houghton, N.Y., U.S. 210 42.25 N 78.09 W
Houghton, Wa., U.S. 224 47.40 N 122.12 W
Houghton Estates ◆ [8] 273d 26.10 S 28.04 E
Houghton Green 262 53.25 N 2.34 W
Houghton Lake 190 44.18 N 84.45 W
Houghton Lake ⊜, Sk., Can. 184 52.23 N 105.08 W
Houghton Lake ⊜, Mi., U.S. 190 44.20 N 84.45 W
Houghton-le-Spring 44 54.51 N 1.28 W
Houghton Regis 42 51.55 N 0.31 W
Houguangzhengtai 104 41.13 N 122.07 E
Houguijiazi 104 42.21 N 123.22 E
Houhuangtukan 104 41.02 N 122.29 E
Houille ≃ 50 50.08 N 4.49 E
Houillères de la Sarre, Canal des ≅ 56 48.42 N 6.55 E
Houilles 261 48.56 N 2.11 E
Houjiangfushan 105 40.03 N 117.09 E
Houjiaping 107 30.02 N 104.38 E
Houjiaying 105 39.51 N 117.15 E
Houjie 100 22.58 N 113.39 E
Houjiumen 104 42.38 N 123.18 E
Houkou 98 37.34 N 115.09 E
Houliujia 104 40.47 N 122.19 E
Houlka 194 34.02 N 89.01 W
Houlton 188 46.07 N 67.50 W
Houluan 105 39.13 N 116.32 E
Houma, Tonga 174w 21.09 S 175.18 W
Houma, La., U.S. 194 29.35 N 90.43 W
Houma, Zhg. 102 35.36 N 111.21 E
Houmanzhoutun 104 42.29 N 123.14 E
Houmen 100 22.51 N 115.09 E
Houmet Essouq 148 33.59 N 10.51 E
Houmont Park 222 29.50 N 95.13 W
Houn Creek ≃ 222 47.13 N 11.23 W
Houndé 150 11.30 N 3.31 W
Hounslow ◆ [8] 260 51.29 N 0.22 W
Houplines 50 50.42 N 2.55 E
Houqianjiayu 104 40.50 N 120.41 E
Houqiao 105 40.04 N 116.39 E
Hourn, Loch c 46 57.08 N 5.36 W
Hourtin 32 45.11 N 1.04 W
Housatonic 207 42.15 N 73.22 W
Housatonic ≃ 207 41.10 N 73.07 W
House 196 34.38 N 103.54 W
House, Mount ∧ 184 56.13 N 112.31 W
House of Seven Gables ⊥ 283 42.32 N 70.53 W
Houserville 214 40.50 N 77.50 W
House Springs 219 38.24 N 90.34 W
Houshan 106 31.03 N 120.21 E
Houston, B.C., Can. 182 54.24 N 126.38 W
Houston, De., U.S. 208 38.55 N 75.30 W
Houston, Mn., U.S. 190 43.45 N 91.34 W
Houston, Ms., U.S. 194 33.53 N 88.59 W
Houston, Mo., U.S. 194 37.19 N 91.57 W
Houston, Oh., U.S. 216 40.15 N 84.20 W
Houston, Pa., U.S. 214 40.14 N 80.12 W
Houston, Tx., U.S. 222 29.45 N 95.21 W
Houston □ [6] 222 31.20 N 95.20 W
Houston ≃ 194 30.16 N 93.13 W
Houston, Lake ⊜ [1] 222 29.58 N 95.07 W
Houston County Lake ⊜ [1] 222 31.25 N 95.35 W
Houston Creek ≃ 218 38.13 N 84.15 W
Houston Intercontinental Airport ≋ 222 29.59 N 95.27 W
Houston Ship Channel ≅ 222 29.21 N 94.47 W
Hout ≃ 156 23.04 S 29.36 E
Houtbaai 158 34.03 S 18.21 E
Houthalen 56 51.02 N 5.22 E
Houthulst 50 50.59 N 2.57 E
Houtkop 158 26.36 S 27.52 E
Houtkraal 158 30.23 S 24.05 E
Houtman Abrolhos II 162 28.43 S 113.48 E
Houtskär I 26 60.12 N 21.22 E
Houtzdale 214 40.49 N 78.21 W
Houwuliangdian 104 41.31 N 121.55 E
Houwutaigou 104 41.46 N 121.42 E
Houx 261 48.34 N 1.37 E
Houxijie 100 28.46 N 118.49 E
Houxinlitun 104 41.05 N 122.33 E
Houxinqiu 104 42.34 N 122.43 E
Houyatai 104 41.26 N 121.49 E
Houying 105 39.42 N 118.18 E
Houyingzi 98 40.24 N 123.50 E
Houzhangcun 105 40.08 N 116.11 E
Houzhou 106 31.35 N 119.22 E
Houzitun 104 41.04 N 121.18 E
Hov 41 55.55 N 10.16 E
Hova 40 58.52 N 14.13 E
Hovborg 41 55.36 N 8.57 E
Høve, Dan. 41 55.50 N 11.30 E
Hove, Eng., U.K. 42 50.49 N 0.10 W
Hovedgård 41 55.57 N 9.58 E
Hövelhof 52 51.49 N 8.40 E
Hoven, Dan. 41 55.51 N 8.46 E
Hoven, S.D., U.S. 198 45.14 N 99.46 W
Hovenweep National Monument ♦ 200 37.25 N 109.04 W
Hovmantorp 26 56.47 N 15.08 E
Hovran ⊜ 40 60.16 N 16.03 E
Hovsta 40 59.21 N 15.13 E
Howa, Ouadi (Wādī Howar) V 140 17.30 N 27.08 E
Howakil I 144 15.10 N 40.16 E
Howar, Wādī (Ouadi Howa) V 140 17.30 N 27.08 E
Howard, Austl. 166 25.19 S 152.34 E
Howard, Ks., U.S. 198 37.28 N 96.15 W
Howard, Oh., U.S. 214 40.24 N 82.19 W
Howard, Pa., U.S. 214 41.00 N 77.39 W
Howard, S.D., U.S. 198 44.00 N 97.31 W
Howard, Wi., U.S. 190 44.32 N 88.05 W
Howard □ [6], In., U.S. 216 40.29 N 86.08 W
Howard □ [6], Md., U.S. 208 39.16 N 76.48 W
Howard Beach ◆ [8] 276 40.40 N 73.51 W
Howard City 190 43.23 N 85.28 W
Howard Draw V 196 30.08 N 101.35 W
Howard Hanson Reservoir ⊜ [1] 224 47.15 N 121.45 W
Howard Heights 284b 39.17 N 76.50 W
Howardian Hills ∧ [2] 44 54.07 N 1.00 W
Howard Island I 164 12.10 S 135.24 E
Howard Lake 190 45.03 N 94.04 W
Howard Prairie Lake ⊜ [1] 202 42.15 N 122.20 W
Howard University ✠ [2] 284c 38.55 N 77.01 W
Howden 44 53.45 N 0.52 W
Howe, In., U.S. 216 41.43 N 85.25 W
Howe, Tx., U.S. 196 33.30 N 96.37 W
Howe, Cape ≻ 166 37.31 S 149.59 E
Howe Caverns ⊾ [5] 210 42.42 N 74.25 W
Howe Green 260 51.42 N 0.32 E
Howe Island I 212 44.17 N 76.15 W
Howeke 150 4.50 N 7.45 W
Howell 216 42.36 N 83.55 W
Howell Airport ≋ 278 41.39 N 87.45 W
Howell Island I 219 38.40 N 90.42 W
Howells 198 41.43 N 97.00 W
Howells Pond ⊜ 276 41.03 N 74.42 W
Howes Cave 210 42.41 N 74.23 W
Howe Sound 𝕦 182 49.22 N 123.18 W
Howe's Range ∧ 170 33.08 S 150.47 E
Howes Valley 170 32.50 S 150.51 E
Howey In The Hills 220 28.43 N 81.47 W
Howick, P.Q., Can. 206 45.11 N 73.51 W
Howick, S. Afr. 158 29.28 S 30.14 E
Howitt, Mount ∧ 166 37.10 S 146.40 E
Howland 188 45.14 N 68.39 W
Howland Island I 14 0.48 N 176.38 W
Howley 186 49.10 N 57.07 W
Howley, Mount ∧ 186 48.17 N 58.26 W
Howmore 46 57.18 N 7.23 W
Howqua ≃ 169 37.14 S 146.08 E
Howrah
— Hāora 126 22.35 N 88.20 E
Howse Peak ∧ 182 51.49 N 116.41 W
Howser 182 50.18 N 116.57 W
Howson Peak ∧ 182 54.25 N 127.44 W
Howth 48 53.23 N 6.04 W
Howth Head ≻ 48 53.22 N 6.03 W
Ho Xa 110 17.04 N 107.02 E
Hoxie, Ar., U.S. 194 36.03 N 90.58 W
Hoxie, Ks., U.S. 198 39.21 N 100.26 W
Höxter 52 51.46 N 9.23 E
Hoxtolgay 86 46.35 N 86.01 E
Hoxton Park 274a 33.55 S 150.51 E
Hoxton Park Aerodrome ≋ 274a 33.54 S 150.50 E
Hoy I 46 58.51 N 3.18 W
Hoya, Dtsch. 52 52.48 N 9.08 E
Hōya, Nihon 94 35.43 N 139.34 E
Høyanger 26 61.13 N 6.05 E
Hoyerswerda 54 51.26 N 14.14 E
Hoylake 262 53.23 N 3.11 W
Hoyleton, Austl. 168b 34.01 S 138.33 E
Hoyleton, Il., U.S. 219 38.27 N 89.16 W
Hoym 54 51.47 N 11.19 E
Hoyos 34 40.10 N 6.43 W
Hōyo-shotō II 96 33.52 N 132.18 E
Höytiäinen ⊜ 26 62.48 N 29.39 E
Hoyt Lakes 190 47.31 N 92.08 W
Hoytville, Mi., U.S. 216 42.45 N 84.53 W
Hoytville, Oh., U.S. 216 41.11 N 83.47 W
Hozain ≃ 50 48.16 N 4.06 E
Hozat 130 39.07 N 39.14 E
Hozumi 94 35.24 N 136.41 E
Hpru-so 110 19.25 N 97.08 E
Hracholusky, údolní nádrž ⊜ [1] 60 49.47 N 13.07 E
Hradec Králové 30 50.12 N 15.50 E
Hrádek 61 48.46 N 16.16 E
Hrádek nad Nisou 54 50.48 N 14.51 E
Hradiště ∧ 54 50.13 N 13.08 E
Hranice, Česko. 30 49.33 N 17.44 E
Hranice, Česko. 54 50.15 N 12.10 E
Hrdlovka 54 50.36 N 13.40 E
Hřensko 54 50.50 N 14.14 E
Hriňová 30 48.36 N 19.31 E
Hrob 54 50.39 N 13.44 E
Hron ≃ 30 47.49 N 18.45 E
Hronov 30 50.29 N 16.12 E
Hrotovice 61 49.06 N 16.07 E
Hrubieszów 30 50.49 N 23.55 E
Hrubý Jeseník ∧ 30 50.00 N 17.20 E
Hrušovany 61 48.50 N 16.23 E
Hrvatska
— Croatia □ [1] 36 45.10 N 15.30 E
Hsenwi 110 23.18 N 97.58 E
Hsiakuan
— Xiaguan 102 25.34 N 100.14 E
Hsiamen
— Xiamen 100 24.28 N 118.07 E
Hsiang't'an
— Xiangtan 100 27.51 N 112.54 E
Hsiangyang
— Xiangfan 102 32.03 N 112.01 E
Hsian
— Xi'an 102 34.15 N 108.52 E
Hsiaohungt'ou Yü I 100 21.57 N 121.36 E
Hsichih 269d 25.04 N 121.39 E

≃ River | Fluß | Río | Rivière | Rio
≅ Canal | Kanal | Canal | Canal | Canal
⊾ Waterfall, Rapids | Wasserfall, Stromschnellen | Cascada, Rápidos | Chute d'eau, Rapides | Cascata, Rápidos
𝕦 Strait | Meeresstraße | Estrecho | Détroit | Estreito
c Bay, Gulf | Bucht, Golf | Bahía, Golfo | Baie, Golfe | Baía, Golfo
⊜ Lake, Lakes | See, Seen | Lago, Lagos | Lac, Lacs | Lago, Lagos
≡ Swamp | Sumpf | Pantano | Marais | Pântano
⊓ Ice Features, Glacier | Eis- und Gletscherformen | Accidentes Glaciales | Formes glaciaires | Acidentes glaciares
⊤ Other Hydrographic Features | Andere Hydrographische Objekte | Otros Elementos Hidrográficos | Autres données hydrographiques | Outros acidentes hidrográficos

✣ Submarine Features | Untermeerische Objekte | Accidentes Submarinos | Formes de relief sous-marin | Acidentes submarinos
□ Political Unit | Politische Einheit | Unidad Política | Entité politique | Unidade política
✠ Cultural Institution | Kulturelle Institution | Institución Cultural | Institution culturelle | Instituição cultural
⊥ Historical Site | Historische Stätte | Sitio Histórico | Site historique | Sítio histórico
♦ Recreational Site | Erholungs- und Ferienort | Sitio de Recreo | Centre de loisirs | Área de Lazer
≋ Airport | Flughafen | Aeropuerto | Aéroport | Aeroporto
▪ Military Installation | Militäranlage | Instalación Militar | Installation militaire | Instalação militar
◆ Miscellaneous | Verschiedenes | Misceláneo | Divers | Diversos

Name	Page	Lat.°′	Long.°′
Hsichi Yü I	100	23.15 N	119.37 E
Hsich'üan Tao I	100	25.59 N	119.56 E
Hsientung	269d	25.09 N	121.44 E
Hsienyang → Xianyang	102	34.22 N	108.42 E
Hsi-hseng	110	20.09 N	97.15 E
Hsihu	100	23.58 N	120.28 E
Hsilo	100	23.48 N	120.27 E
Hsilo ≃	100	23.50 N	120.15 E
Hsim ≃	110	20.48 N	98.31 E
Hsinch'eng	100	24.08 N	121.39 E
Hsinchu	100	24.48 N	120.58 E
Hsinchuang	100	25.02 N	121.27 E
Hsinghua → Xinghua	100	32.57 N	119.50 E
Hsingt'ai → Xingtai	98	37.04 N	114.29 E
Hsinhailien → Lianyungang	98	34.39 N	119.16 E
Hsinhsiang → Xinxiang	98	35.20 N	113.51 E
Hsinhua	100	23.02 N	120.18 E
Hsining → Xining	102	36.38 N	101.55 E
Hsinking → Changchun	89	43.53 N	125.19 E
Hsinpeit'ou •[8]	269d	25.09 N	121.30 E
Hsinp'u → Lianyungang	98	34.39 N	119.16 E
Hsinshih	100	23.05 N	120.17 E
Hsintien	100	24.57 N	121.32 E
Hsintien ≃	269d	25.02 N	121.29 E
Hsinyang → Xinyang	100	32.08 N	114.04 E
Hsipaw	110	22.37 N	97.18 E
Hsiukuluan ≃	100	23.28 N	121.30 E
Hsiyü	100	23.36 N	119.30 E
Hsüanhua → Xuanhua	105	40.37 N	115.03 E
Hsüch'ang → Xuchang	100	34.03 N	113.49 E
Hsüchou → Xuzhou	98	34.16 N	117.11 E
Hsüehchia	100	23.14 N	120.10 E
Hsüeh Shan ∧	100	24.23 N	121.13 E
Hsuphāng	110	20.18 N	98.42 E
Hua'an	100	25.02 N	117.34 E
Huab ≃	156	20.52 S	13.25 E
Huabu	100	29.00 N	118.20 E
Huacaña	248	14.02 S	74.02 W
Huacao	269b	31.14 N	121.19 E
Huacaraje	248	13.33 S	63.45 W
Huachacalla	248	18.45 S	68.17 W
Huacheng	100	24.04 N	115.38 E
Huachi	102	36.43 N	107.52 E
Huachi, Laguna ⊜	248	14.11 S	63.30 W
Huachipa	286d	12.00 S	76.56 W
Huacho	248	11.07 S	77.37 W
Huachón	248	10.40 S	75.57 W
Huachos	248	13.12 S	75.31 W
Huachuca City	200	31.37 N	110.20 W
Huaco	252	30.09 S	68.31 W
Huacrachuco	248	8.39 S	77.05 W
Huade	98	41.46 N	114.16 E
Huadian	89	42.58 N	126.43 E
Huading Shan ∧	100	29.15 N	121.05 E
Huafeng	106	32.14 N	121.16 E
Huagutang	106	30.55 N	119.18 E
Hua Hin	110	12.34 N	99.58 E
Huai ≃, Zhg.	98	37.28 N	114.55 E
Huai ≃, Zhg.	100	32.58 N	118.17 E
Huaiá-Miçu ≃	250	10.52 S	53.15 W
Huai'an (Chaigoubu), Zhg.	98	40.39 N	114.27 E
Huai'an, Zhg.	100	33.32 N	119.10 E
Huaibin	100	32.28 N	115.24 E
Huaide	89	43.32 N	124.50 E
Huaidezhen, Zhg.	89	43.54 N	124.47 E
Huaidezhen, Zhg.	107	28.59 N	105.15 E
Huaihuazhenshi	106	31.05 N	119.41 E
Huaiji	102	24.01 N	112.18 E
Huailai (Shacheng)	105	40.23 N	115.33 E
Huailin	100	31.26 N	117.36 E
Huaillati	248	14.05 S	72.31 W
Huainan	100	32.40 N	117.00 E
Huaining	100	30.25 N	116.38 E
Huairou	105	40.19 N	116.37 E
Huaite → Huaide	89	43.32 N	124.50 E
Huaitunas, Lagunas ⊜	248	13.06 S	66.00 W
Huaiyang	100	33.44 N	114.53 E
Huai Yot	110	7.45 N	99.37 E
Huaiyuan	100	32.57 N	117.12 E
Huaiyu Shan ⋏	100	28.50 N	117.50 E
Huaji	100	32.46 N	115.20 E
Huajiang	102	25.50 N	110.21 E
Huajianzi	104	40.48 N	122.12 E
Huajiapuzi	104	40.52 N	123.14 E
Huajiayingzi	104	42.20 N	121.00 E
Huajimic	234	21.42 N	104.20 W
Huajintepec	234	16.36 N	98.14 W
Huajuapan de León	234	17.48 N	97.46 W
Huakou	100	25.13 N	117.35 E
Hualahuises	232	24.53 N	99.41 W
Hualalai ∧[1]	229d	19.42 N	155.52 W
Hualañé	252	34.59 S	71.49 W
Hualapai Indian Reservation •[4]	200	35.38 N	113.30 W
Hualapai Mountains ⋏	200	34.50 N	113.55 W
Hualapai Peak ∧	200	35.04 N	113.54 W
Hualfín	252	27.14 S	66.50 W
Hualgayoc	248	6.46 S	78.37 W
Hualien	100	23.59 N	121.36 E
Hualien ≃	100	23.57 N	121.36 E
Hualingpuzi	104	41.31 N	123.54 E
Huallaga ≃	248	5.10 S	75.32 W
Huallamarca, Museo ⊽	286d	12.05 S	77.02 W
Huallanca, Perú	248	8.49 S	77.52 W
Huallanca, Perú	248	9.51 S	76.56 W
Huallayabamba ≃	248	7.04 S	77.10 W
Hualmay	248	11.06 S	77.38 W
Hualong	102	36.05 N	102.36 E
Huamanquiquia	248	13.44 S	74.15 W
Huamantla	234	19.19 N	97.56 W
Huambo (Nova Lisboa)	152	12.44 S	15.47 E
Huambo □[5]	152	12.30 S	15.40 E
Huambos	248	6.28 S	78.58 W
Huameiao	100	26.32 N	115.47 E
Huamei Shan ∧	100	25.28 N	113.58 E
Huamuxtitlán	234	17.49 N	98.34 W
Huan ≃	100	30.40 N	114.05 E
Huanan	89	46.13 N	130.32 E
Huancabamba, Perú	248	10.21 S	75.32 W
Huancabamba, Perú	248	5.14 S	79.28 W
Huancané	248	15.12 S	69.46 W
Huancapi	248	13.41 S	74.04 W
Huancarama	248	13.39 S	73.05 W
Huancarqui	248	16.06 S	72.29 W
Huancavelica	248	12.46 S	75.02 W
Huancavelica □[5]	248	13.00 S	75.00 W
Huancaybamba	248	9.05 S	76.50 W
Huancayo	248	12.04 S	75.14 W
Huanchaca	248	20.20 S	66.39 W
Huanchaca, Serranía de ⋏	248	14.30 S	60.39 W
Huandacareo	234	19.59 N	101.17 W
Huando	248	12.29 S	74.58 W
Huang ≃, Asia	110	17.49 N	101.33 E
Huang ≃, T'aiwan	269d	25.14 N	121.37 E
Huang (Yellow) ≃, Zhg.	90	37.32 N	118.19 E
Huang'aicun	106	31.43 N	118.40 E
Huang'an	98	35.28 N	115.42 E
Huang'anshi	100	29.06 N	113.34 E
Huangbai	98	41.17 N	126.21 E
Huangbaozi	102	39.54 N	99.26 E
Huangbeipu	104	42.21 N	123.25 E
Huangcaoping	100	25.42 N	113.27 E
Huangchong	100	22.18 N	113.03 E
Huangchuan	100	32.09 N	115.03 E
Huangcun	105	39.56 N	116.11 E
Huangdaizhen	106	31.26 N	120.33 E
Huangdan	107	29.10 N	103.44 E
Huangda Yang ⋓	100	30.03 N	122.26 E
Huangdi, Zhg.	98	40.14 N	120.15 E
Huangdi, Zhg.	105	40.57 N	118.24 E
Huangdu, Zhg.	106	30.47 N	118.51 E
Huangdu, Zhg.	106	31.16 N	121.13 E
Huangduqiao	100	29.18 N	120.55 E
Huanggai Hu ⊜	100	29.44 N	113.23 E
Huanggang	100	30.27 N	114.52 E
Huanggangji	98	34.39 N	116.03 E
Huanggangkou	100	28.32 N	114.33 E
Huanggang Shan ∧	100	27.50 N	117.45 E
Huanggangshi	100	33.09 N	115.55 E
Huangguayingzi	104	41.46 N	120.46 E
Huangguoshu	102	26.02 N	105.32 E
Huang Hai → Yellow Sea ⊤[2]	90	36.00 N	123.00 E
Huanghe Kou ≃[1]	98	37.54 N	118.48 E
Huangho → Huang ≃	90	37.32 N	118.19 E
Huanghu	106	30.27 N	119.48 E
Huanghua	98	38.22 N	117.21 E
Huanghuadianzi	104	41.44 N	122.48 E
Huanghuashi	100	28.14 N	113.14 E
Huangjialing	104	42.12 N	122.55 E
Huangjialu	106	31.00 N	121.45 E
Huangjiatun	104	41.11 N	122.54 E
Huangjiazhai	106	32.01 N	121.36 E
Huangjinbu	100	28.27 N	116.47 E
Huangjing	106	31.39 N	121.06 E
Huangjinggou	107	29.37 N	104.35 E
Huangjinjing	107	29.44 N	104.38 E
Huangjinzi	89	50.02 N	127.20 E
Huangjuezhen	107	29.50 N	106.27 E
Huangkan	105	40.22 N	116.28 E
Huangkeng	100	27.35 N	117.39 E
Huangkou	102	42.46 N	93.58 E
Huanglaomen	100	29.30 N	115.49 E
Huangli	106	31.39 N	119.42 E
Huanglian	107	29.17 N	106.18 E
Huangling	102	35.41 N	109.09 E
Huanglingji	100	30.25 N	114.03 E
Huanglong, Zhg.	100	31.58 N	112.28 E
Huanglong, Zhg.	102	35.45 N	109.42 E
Huanglongxi	107	30.19 N	103.58 E
Huangmao	100	28.07 N	114.04 E
Huangmapi	100	23.30 N	114.33 E
Huangmei	100	30.04 N	115.56 E
Huangnihe, Zhg.	89	43.32 N	127.59 E
Huangnihe, Zhg.	100	31.06 N	117.22 E
Huangpi, Zhg.	100	30.53 N	114.22 E
Huangpi, Zhg.	100	26.39 N	115.51 E
Huangpu ≃	106	31.24 N	121.31 E
Huangqi	100	26.21 N	119.54 E
Huangqiao	106	32.15 N	120.13 E
Huangqiao ≃	106	32.00 N	120.20 E
Huangshahe	102	26.03 N	110.58 E
Huangshajie	100	29.03 N	113.08 E
Huangshan	98	36.57 N	122.18 E
Huangshanguan	98	37.32 N	120.16 E
Huangshapu, Zhg.	100	25.08 N	112.44 E
Huangshapu, Zhg.	100	26.50 N	113.26 E
Huangshaqiao	100	28.56 N	114.40 E
Huangshatuo	104	41.12 N	122.31 E
Huangshi, Zhg.	100	25.23 N	119.04 E
Huangshi, Zhg.	100	30.13 N	115.05 E
Huangshi, Zhg.	102	29.00 N	111.02 E
Huangshidu	100	27.44 N	116.44 E
Huangshiguan	100	26.15 N	115.54 E
Huangshui	107	30.32 N	103.55 E
Huangtan, Zhg.	100	27.44 N	119.58 E
Huangtan, Zhg.	100	26.41 N	117.17 E
Huangtan ≃	100	24.48 N	116.31 E
Huangtang, Zhg.	100	23.44 N	114.58 E
Huangtang, Zhg.	106	31.46 N	120.21 E
Huangtang, Zhg.	106	31.47 N	119.40 E
Huangtang Hu ⊜	100	30.00 N	114.12 E
Huangtankou	100	28.50 N	118.53 E
Huangtantuan	100	30.53 N	113.33 E
Huangtian	100	23.52 N	114.58 E
Huangtianfan	100	29.10 N	120.08 E
Huangtu, Zhg.	100	27.36 N	118.00 E
Huangtu, Zhg.	106	31.52 N	120.03 E
Huangtuchang	107	30.41 N	104.18 E
Huangtugang	100	31.25 N	115.05 E
Huangtukan	104	41.21 N	122.45 E
Huangtuliangzi	98	41.14 N	118.39 E
Huangtuling	100	27.18 N	113.30 E
Huangtupo	105	39.47 N	116.16 E
Huanguelén	252	37.02 S	61.57 W
Huangwan	106	30.22 N	120.48 E
Huangxian	98	37.38 N	120.29 E
Huangxu	106	32.06 N	119.37 E
Huangyaguan	105	40.14 N	117.26 E
Huangyan	100	28.39 N	121.15 E
Huangyang Shan ⋏	105	40.20 N	115.00 E
Huangyanzhuang	105	40.01 N	118.21 E
Huangyuan	102	36.40 N	101.12 E
Huangyuzeng	104	42.05 N	124.11 E
Huangze	100	29.35 N	120.55 E
Huangze Yang ⋓	100	30.36 N	122.28 E
Huangzhai	100	29.27 N	120.00 E
Huangzhong	102	36.31 N	101.40 E
Huangzhu	110	19.29 N	110.24 E
Huangzhuang, Zhg.	100	34.05 N	112.15 E
Huangzhuang, Zhg.	105	39.29 N	117.31 E
Huangzhuang, Zhg.	105	39.53 N	117.05 E
Huangzhuang Wa ⊜	105	39.33 N	117.33 E
Huaning	102	24.14 N	102.56 E
Huaniugouzi	104	41.34 N	122.35 E
Huaniupuzi	104	41.23 N	123.31 E
Huanjiang	102	24.54 N	108.21 E
Huanren	98	41.14 N	125.21 E
Huanta	248	12.56 S	74.15 W
Huantai (Suozhen)	98	36.59 N	118.06 E
Huantan	100	31.49 N	113.04 E
Huántar	248	9.26 S	77.15 W
Huánuco	248	9.55 S	76.14 W
Huánuco □[5]	248	9.30 S	75.50 W
Huanuni	248	18.16 S	66.51 W
Huanxi	100	26.34 N	113.36 E
Huanxian	102	36.39 N	107.18 E
Huanxiang ≃	105	39.34 N	117.45 E
Huanxiling	104	41.17 N	123.54 E
Huanzo, Cordillera de ⋏	248	14.30 S	73.20 W
Huapango, Presa ⊜[1]	234	20.00 N	99.40 W
Huapí, Serranías ⋏	236	12.30 N	85.00 W
Huap'ing Yü I	100	25.26 N	121.56 E
Huaqiao, Zhg.	100	28.56 N	121.27 E
Huaqiao, Zhg.	100	29.32 N	117.11 E
Huaqiao, Zhg.	102	27.28 N	110.02 E
Huaqiao, Zhg.	107	30.28 N	103.52 E
Huaqiaozhen	107	30.47 N	106.41 E
Huaqiying	106	32.10 N	118.38 E
Huara	248	19.59 S	69.47 W
Huaral	248	11.30 S	77.12 W
Huaráz	248	9.32 S	77.32 W
Huari	248	9.20 S	77.14 W
Huariaca	248	10.27 S	76.07 W
Huaribamba	248	12.16 S	74.57 W
Huarina	248	16.12 S	68.38 W
Huarmey	248	10.04 S	78.10 W
Huarochirí	248	12.09 S	76.14 W
Huarocondo	248	13.25 S	72.13 W
Huarong	100	29.30 N	112.34 E
Huasaga ≃	246	3.42 S	76.26 W
Hua Sai	110	8.02 N	100.18 E
Huascarán, Nevado ∧	248	9.07 S	77.37 W
Huasco	252	28.28 S	71.14 W
Huasco ≃	252	28.27 S	71.13 W
Huashan	98	34.39 N	116.44 E
Huashaoying	98	40.12 N	114.36 E
Huashi	106	31.50 N	120.28 E
Huatabampo	232	26.50 N	109.38 W
Huatangpu	100	25.48 N	112.52 E
Huating	102	35.09 N	106.38 E
Huatong, Zhg.	98	40.03 N	121.56 E
Huatong, Zhg.	102	23.01 N	106.36 E
Huatusco	234	19.09 N	96.57 W
Huauchinango	234	20.11 N	98.03 W
Huaura	248	11.04 S	77.36 W
Huaura ≃	248	11.06 S	77.39 W
Huautla, Méx.	234	21.02 N	98.17 W
Huautla, Méx.	234	18.08 N	96.51 W
Huaxian (Daokou), Zhg.	98	35.37 N	114.32 E
Huaxian, Zhg.	100	23.22 N	113.12 E
Huaxian, Zhg.	102	34.30 N	109.40 E
Huayan	107	30.01 N	105.02 E
Huayang	107	30.32 N	104.04 E
Huayangzhen	102	33.25 N	107.44 E
Huaying Shan ∧	107	30.10 N	106.42 E
Huayingtai	104	40.43 N	122.19 E
Huayllay	248	11.01 S	76.21 W
Huayna Potosí, Nevado ∧	248	16.16 S	68.11 W
Huaytará	248	13.36 S	75.22 W
Hua Yü I	100	23.24 N	119.19 E
Huayuan, Zhg.	98	42.17 N	127.07 E
Huayuan, Zhg.	100	31.16 N	113.58 E
Huayuan, Zhg.	102	28.34 N	109.13 E
Huayuanzui	100	33.00 N	118.16 E
Huayunca, Nevado ∧	248	14.39 S	72.28 W
Huayuri, Pampa de ≚	248	14.30 S	75.30 W
Huazhou	102	21.40 N	110.33 E
Huazi	104	41.25 N	123.29 E
Huazigou	104	41.50 N	121.01 E
Huazikou	106	32.13 N	118.57 E
Ḥubārah, Wādī ∨	142	27.21 N	31.39 E
Ḥubayṭah, Bi'r ⊤[4]	142	30.27 N	32.27 E
Hubbard, Ia., U.S.	190	42.18 N	93.18 W
Hubbard, Oh., U.S.	214	41.09 N	80.34 W
Hubbard, Or., U.S.	224	45.10 N	122.48 W
Hubbard, Tx., U.S.	222	31.50 N	96.47 W
Hubbard Creek ≃	196	32.54 N	98.53 W
Hubbard Creek Reservoir ⊜[1]	196	32.45 N	99.00 W
Hubbard Lake ⊜	190	44.49 N	83.34 W
Hubbards	186	44.38 N	64.04 W
Hubbardston	207	42.28 N	72.00 W
Hubbard Woods	278	42.06 N	87.44 W
Hubbell	190	47.10 N	88.25 W
Hubbell Trading Post National Historical Site ⊥	200	35.43 N	109.33 W
Hubbelrath •[8]	263	51.16 N	6.55 E
Hubei (Hupeh) □[4]	90	31.00 N	112.00 E
Huben, Öst.	64	47.03 N	10.58 E
Huben, Öst.	64	46.56 N	12.34 E
Huberdeau	206	45.58 N	74.38 W
Huber Heights	218	39.50 N	84.07 W
Hublersburg	210	40.58 N	77.37 W
Hubli-Dhārwār	122	15.21 N	75.10 E
Hubuleng	102	41.19 N	111.08 E
Hucaogang	106	32.00 N	120.29 E
Hucclecote	42	51.51 N	2.11 W
Huch'ang	98	41.25 N	127.03 E
Hucheng	100	25.26 N	118.27 E
Huchi	100	31.08 N	117.40 E
Huchow → Huzhou	106	30.52 N	120.06 E
Huckarde •[8]	263	51.32 N	7.24 E
Hückelhoven	56	51.04 N	6.10 E
Hückeswagen	56	51.08 N	7.20 E
Hucking	260	51.18 N	0.39 E
Huckingen •[8]	263	51.22 N	6.43 E
Huckitta Creek ≃	162	22.38 S	135.30 E
Huckleberry Island I	276	40.53 N	73.45 W
Huckleberry Mountain ∧	202	43.51 N	122.19 W
Huckleberry Mountain ∧[2]	212	44.28 N	75.28 W
Hucknall	42	53.02 N	1.11 W
Hucqueliers	50	50.34 N	1.54 E
Hucun	105	39.02 N	115.56 E
Hudangtou	106	30.48 N	121.22 E
Huddart Park ◆	282	37.26 N	122.19 W
Hudderfield Narrow Canal ≍	262	53.29 N	2.06 W
Huddersfield	262	53.39 N	1.47 W
Huddinge	40	59.14 N	17.59 E
Huddle Park Municipal Golf Course ◆	273d	26.09 S	28.07 E
Huddunge	40	60.03 N	16.59 E
Hude	52	53.07 N	8.27 E
Huder	89	50.00 N	121.37 E
Hudgin Creek ≃	194	33.40 N	91.59 W
Hūdī	140	17.42 N	34.17 E
Hudiksvall	26	61.44 N	17.07 E
Hudong	100	22.51 N	115.56 E
Hudson, P.Q., Can.	206	45.27 N	74.09 W
Hudson, Il., U.S.	216	40.36 N	88.59 W
Hudson, In., U.S.	216	41.31 N	85.04 W
Hudson, Ia., U.S.	190	42.24 N	92.27 W
Hudson, Md., U.S.	208	38.35 N	76.15 W
Hudson, Ma., U.S.	207	42.23 N	71.34 W
Hudson, Mi., U.S.	216	41.51 N	84.21 W
Hudson, N.H., U.S.	207	42.45 N	71.26 W
Hudson, N.Y., U.S.	210	42.15 N	73.47 W
Hudson, N.C., U.S.	192	35.50 N	81.29 W
Hudson, Oh., U.S.	214	41.14 N	81.26 W
Hudson, S.D., U.S.	198	43.07 N	96.27 W
Hudson, Tx., U.S.	222	31.19 N	94.50 W
Hudson, Wi., U.S.	190	44.58 N	92.45 W
Hudson, Wy., U.S.	200	42.54 N	108.34 W
Hudson □[6]	276	40.44 N	74.02 W
Hudson ≃, U.S.	188	40.42 N	74.02 W
Hudson ≃, Ga., U.S.	192	34.14 N	83.10 W
Hudson, Cerro ∧	254	46.04 S	73.10 W
Hudson, Lake ⊜[1]	194	36.20 N	95.05 W
Hudson Bay	184	52.52 N	102.25 W
Hudson Bay c	176	60.00 N	86.00 W
Hudson-Bayonet Point	220	28.21 N	82.41 W
Hudson Falls	210	43.18 N	73.35 W
Hudson Highlands State Park ◆	210	41.26 N	73.58 W
Hudson Hope	182	56.02 N	121.55 W
Hudson Lake	216	41.42 N	86.32 W
Hudson Mountains ⋏	9	74.32 S	99.20 W
Hudsons Peak ∧	171b	36.26 S	149.10 E
Hudson Strait ⋓	176	62.30 N	72.00 W
Hudsonville	216	42.52 N	85.51 W
Hudwin Lake ⊜	184	53.12 N	95.42 W
Hue	110	16.28 N	107.36 E
Huebra ≃	34	41.02 N	6.48 W
Huechucuicui, Punta ≻	254	41.47 S	74.02 W
Huechulafquen, Lago ⊜	254	39.46 S	71.28 W
Huechuraba	286e	33.21 S	70.40 W
Huedin	38	46.52 N	23.02 E
Huehuetán	236	15.01 N	92.22 W
Huehuetenango	236	15.20 N	91.28 W
Huehuetenango □[5]	236	15.40 N	91.35 W
Huehuetlán El Chico	234	18.21 N	98.42 W
Huejúcar	234	22.21 N	103.13 W
Huejuquilla El Alto	234	22.36 N	103.52 W
Huejutla de Reyes	234	21.08 N	98.25 W
Huelgoat	32	48.22 N	3.45 W
Huelma	34	37.39 N	3.27 W
Huelva	34	37.16 N	6.57 W
Huelva □[4]	34	37.30 N	6.55 W
Huelva, Río de ≃	34	37.27 N	6.00 W
Huenque ≃	248	16.12 S	69.44 W
Huentelauquén	252	31.35 S	71.32 W
Huércal-Overa	34	37.23 N	1.57 W
Huerfano ≃	198	38.14 N	104.15 W
Huerfano Mountain ∧	200	36.26 N	107.51 W
Huerhuero Creek ≃	226	35.40 N	120.42 W
Huerlumada	120	32.45 N	90.00 E
Huerva ≃	34	41.39 N	0.52 W
Huesca	34	42.08 N	0.25 W
Huesca □[4]	34	42.05 N	0.10 W
Huéscar	34	37.49 N	2.32 W
Hueston Woods State Park ◆	218	39.34 N	84.44 W
Huetamo de Núñez	234	18.35 N	100.53 W
Huete	34	40.08 N	2.41 W
Huey	219	38.36 N	89.17 W
Hueyapan de Ocampo	234	18.07 N	95.09 W
Hueytown	194	33.27 N	86.59 W
Hufengzhen	107	29.43 N	106.07 E
Hüffenhardt	56	49.18 N	9.04 E
Huffman	222	30.01 N	95.05 W
Huffman Dam •[6]	218	39.48 N	84.05 W
Hüfingen	58	47.55 N	8.29 E
Ḥufrat an-Naḥās	140	9.45 N	24.19 E
Hufu	106	31.16 N	119.47 E
Hügel, Villa ⊽	263	51.25 N	7.01 E
Huggins, Mount ∧	9	78.17 S	162.28 E
Hugh ≃	162	25.01 S	134.01 E
Hugh Butler Lake ⊜[1]	198	40.22 N	100.42 W
Hughenden	166	20.51 S	144.12 E
Hughes, Austl.	162	30.42 S	129.31 E
Hughes, Ak., U.S.	180	66.03 N	154.16 W
Hughes, Ar., U.S.	194	34.56 N	90.28 W
Hughes ≃	184	56.46 N	100.01 W
Hughes, South Fork ≃	188	39.08 N	81.20 W
Hughes Airport ⊠	280	33.58 N	118.25 W
Hughes Creek ≃	169	36.53 S	145.08 E
Hughes Springs	222	33.05 N	94.38 W
Hughesville, Md., U.S.	208	38.31 N	76.47 W
Hughesville, Pa., U.S.	210	41.14 N	76.43 W
Hugh Keenleyside Dam •[6]	182	49.20 N	117.49 W
Hughson	226	37.36 N	120.52 W
Hughsonville	210	41.35 N	73.56 W
Hugh Town	42a	49.55 N	6.17 W
Hugli ≃	126	21.55 N	88.05 E
Hugli-Chinsurah	126	22.54 N	88.24 E
Hugo, Co., U.S.	198	39.08 N	103.28 W
Hugo, Ok., U.S.	196	34.00 N	95.30 W
Hugo Lake ⊜[1]	196	34.05 N	95.25 W
Hugoton	198	37.10 N	101.20 W
Hugou	100	33.23 N	117.08 E
Huguenot	210	41.25 N	74.38 W
Huguenot Lake ⊜	276	40.56 N	73.47 W
Huhehot → Hohhot	102	40.51 N	111.40 E
Huhsi	100	23.35 N	119.39 E
Hui'an, Zhg.	100	25.04 N	118.47 E
Huian, Zhg.	106	31.47 N	121.45 E
Huiarau Range ⋏	172	38.45 S	177.00 E
Huib-Hoch Plateau ⋏[1]	156	27.00 S	16.45 E
Huibie Yang ⋓	100	30.08 N	121.44 E
Huibu	100	28.18 N	115.15 E
Huichang, Zhg.	100	25.34 N	115.49 E
Huichang, Zhg.	105	39.04 N	115.04 E
Huichapan	234	20.23 N	99.39 W
Hŭich'ŏn	98	40.10 N	126.17 E
Huichou → Huizhou	100	23.05 N	114.24 E
Huichuan	102	35.11 N	104.02 E
Huicungo	248	7.17 S	76.48 W
Huidong	102	26.41 N	102.36 E
Huidui	105	39.04 N	117.16 E
Huihe, Zhg.	89	48.12 N	119.17 E
Huihe, Zhg.	106	31.45 N	121.43 E
Huiji ≃	100	33.53 N	115.36 E
Huíla	152	15.04 S	13.32 E
Huíla □[5], Ang.	152	15.00 S	15.00 E
Huila □[5], Col.	246	2.30 N	75.45 W
Huila, Nevado del ∧	246	3.00 N	76.00 W
Huilai	100	23.04 N	116.18 E
Huili	102	26.43 N	102.10 E
Huiliuji	100	32.50 N	115.58 E
Huillapima	252	28.44 S	65.59 W
Huilong, Zhg.	100	27.30 N	118.24 E
Huilong, Zhg.	100	25.22 N	116.24 E
Huilong, Zhg.	100	24.09 N	113.58 E
Huilong, Zhg.	107	30.28 N	105.26 E
Huilong, Zhg.	107	30.35 N	105.49 E
Huilongchang, Zhg.	107	29.41 N	104.17 E
Huilongchang, Zhg.	107	30.18 N	103.39 E
Huilongchang, Zhg.	107	30.41 N	106.34 E
Huilongchang, Zhg.	107	29.17 N	105.01 E
Huimanguillo	234	17.51 N	93.23 W
Huimin	98	37.29 N	117.29 E
Huinan (Chaoyang)	98	42.40 N	126.00 E
Huínaymarca, Lago ⊜	248	16.20 S	68.50 W
Huinca Renancó	252	34.50 S	64.23 W
Hüinghausen	263	51.11 N	7.48 E
Huining	102	35.41 N	105.08 E
Huisachal	196	26.47 N	101.07 W
Huisduinen	52	52.56 N	4.44 E
Huishan	106	31.35 N	120.16 E
Huishui	102	26.07 N	106.24 E
Huismes	50	47.14 N	0.15 E
Huisne ≃	50	47.59 N	0.11 E
Huissen	52	51.57 N	5.56 E
Huistepec	234	16.39 N	98.20 W
Huiten Nur ⊜	120	35.30 N	92.00 E
Huiting	98	34.05 N	116.04 E
Huitiupan	234	17.13 N	92.39 W
Huitong	102	26.54 N	109.31 E
Huitongqiao	102	24.43 N	98.56 E
Huittinen (Lauttakylä)	26	61.11 N	22.42 E
Huitzilán	234	19.58 N	97.41 W
Huitzo	234	17.15 N	96.52 W
Huitzuco de los Figueroa	234	18.18 N	99.21 W
Huixian	102	33.47 N	106.16 E
Huixtla	232	15.09 N	92.28 W
Huiyang → Huizhou	100	23.05 N	114.24 E
Huiyao	100	27.16 N	118.05 E
Huize	102	26.27 N	103.09 E
Huizen	52	52.17 N	5.14 E
Huizhou	100	23.05 N	114.24 E
Hujia, Zhg.	104	41.20 N	121.52 E
Hujia, Zhg.	106	31.25 N	121.37 E
Hujiadian	107	29.41 N	104.07 E
Hujiajie	104	41.06 N	122.10 E
Hujiasi	107	29.16 N	105.13 E
Hujiawopu	104	42.34 N	122.11 E
Hujiayu	105	39.28 N	115.27 E
Hujiazhuang, Zhg.	105	39.51 N	117.07 E
Hujiazhuang, Zhg.	269b	31.21 N	121.25 E
Hujie	102	24.56 N	100.32 E
Hukeng	100	27.29 N	114.18 E
Hukou	100	29.45 N	116.13 E
Hŭksan-chedo II	98	34.30 N	125.20 E
Hukui → Fukui	94	36.04 N	136.13 E
Ḥukūmah	140	13.52 N	36.07 E
Hukuntsi	156	24.02 S	21.48 E
Hukuoka → Fukuoka	96	33.35 N	130.24 E
Hukusima → Fukushima	92	37.45 N	140.28 E
Hukuyama → Fukuyama	96	34.29 N	133.22 E
Ḥula, 'Émeq ≚[1]	132	33.08 N	35.37 E
Hulahula ≃	180	70.00 N	144.01 W
Hulan	89	46.00 N	126.38 E
Hulan ≃	89	45.55 N	126.41 E
Hulan Ergi	89	47.13 N	123.39 E
Hulbert, Mi., U.S.	190	46.21 N	85.09 W
Hulbert, Ok., U.S.	194	35.55 N	95.08 W
Hulberton	210	43.15 N	78.04 W
Ḥulda	132	31.50 N	34.53 E
Huldrefossen ⌊	26	61.28 N	5.58 E
Hulei	100	24.50 N	116.48 E
Huleia Stream ≃	229b	21.57 N	159.22 W
Hulett	198	44.40 N	104.36 W
Hulín, Česko.	30	49.19 N	17.28 E
Hulin, Zhg.	89	45.46 N	132.59 E
Hulin ≃, Zhg.	89	44.55 N	122.35 E
Hulin ≃, Zhg.	89	45.19 N	124.06 E
Huliu ≃	98	40.10 N	114.33 E
Hull, P.Q., Can.	212	45.26 N	75.43 W
Hull, Il., U.S.	219	39.43 N	91.13 W
Hull, Ia., U.S.	198	43.11 N	96.08 W
Hull, Ma., U.S.	207	42.18 N	70.54 W
Hull, Tx., U.S.	222	30.09 N	94.39 W
Hull □[6]	212	45.40 N	75.35 W
Hull ≃	44	53.44 N	0.19 W
Hullavington	42	51.33 N	2.09 W
Hull Bay c	283	42.18 N	70.53 W
Hullbridge	260	51.37 N	0.38 E
Hull → Kingston upon Hull	44	53.45 N	0.20 W
Hullo	76	59.00 N	23.14 E
Hulmeville	285	40.08 N	74.55 W
Hüls, Dtsch.	56	51.22 N	6.30 E
Hüls, Dtsch.	263	51.40 N	7.08 E
Hülscheid	56	51.16 N	7.34 E
Hülser Berg •[8]	263	51.24 N	6.31 E
Hülser Berg ∧[2]	263	51.23 N	6.33 E
Hulst	52	51.17 N	4.03 E
Hult	40	58.40 N	16.07 E
Hultsfred	26	57.29 N	15.50 E
Huludao	104	40.43 N	121.00 E
Hulufa	105	39.42 N	116.12 E
Hulun → Hailar	89	49.12 N	119.42 E
Hulun Nur ⊜	88	49.01 N	117.32 E
Huluyu	105	40.14 N	116.53 E
Ḥulwān	142	29.51 N	31.20 E
Ḥulwān Observatory ⊽[3]	142	29.52 N	31.21 E
Huma, Tonga	174w	21.19 S	174.57 E
Huma, Zhg.	89	51.43 N	126.38 E
Huma ≃	89	51.40 N	126.44 E
Humacao	240m	18.09 N	65.50 W
Humahuaca	252	23.12 S	65.21 W
Humaitá, Bra.	248	7.31 S	63.02 W
Humaitá, Para.	252	27.03 S	58.33 W
Humaitá ≃	248	8.16 S	72.44 W
Humansdorp	158	34.02 S	24.46 E
Humansville	194	37.47 N	93.34 W
Humara, Jabal al- ∧	140	16.16 N	30.59 E
Humarock	283	42.08 N	70.41 W
Ḥumaydah	140	14.22 N	22.31 E
Humayingzi	98	41.06 N	116.48 E
Humayun's Tomb ⊥	272a	28.36 N	77.15 E
Humbe	152	16.40 S	14.55 E
Humbe, Serra do ⋏	152	12.13 S	15.25 E
Humbeek	50	50.58 N	4.23 E
Humber ≃, On., Can.	212	43.38 N	79.28 W
Humber ≃, Eng., U.K.	44	53.40 N	0.10 W
Humber, Mouth of the ≃[1]	44	53.32 N	0.08 E
Humber Bay c	275b	43.38 N	79.29 W
Humber Bridge •[5]	44	53.42 N	0.27 W
Humberside □[6]	44	53.55 N	0.40 W
Humberston	44	53.32 N	0.02 W
Humberto de Campos	250	2.37 S	43.27 W
Humber Valley Park ◆	275b	43.39 N	79.30 W
Humbird	190	44.31 N	90.53 W
Humble, Dan.	41	54.50 N	10.42 E
Humble, Tx., U.S.	222	29.59 N	95.15 W
Humboldt, Sk., Can.	184	52.12 N	105.07 W
Humboldt, Az., U.S.	200	34.30 N	112.14 W
Humboldt, Il., U.S.	194	39.36 N	88.19 W
Humboldt, Ia., U.S.	198	42.43 N	94.12 W
Humboldt, Ks., U.S.	198	37.48 N	95.26 W
Humboldt, Ne., U.S.	198	40.09 N	95.56 W
Humboldt, S.D., U.S.	198	43.38 N	97.04 W
Humboldt, Tn., U.S.	194	35.49 N	88.54 W
Humboldt ∧	175f	21.53 S	166.25 E
Humboldt ≃	204	40.02 N	118.31 W
Humboldt, North Fork ≃	204	40.56 N	115.32 W
Humboldt, Planetario ⊽	286c	10.30 N	66.50 W
Humboldt, South Fork ≃	204	40.47 N	115.53 W
Humboldt Bay c	204	40.47 N	124.11 W
Humboldt Lake ⊜	204	39.58 N	118.38 W
Humboldt Mountains ⋏	9	71.45 S	11.30 E
Humboldt Park ◆	278	41.54 N	87.42 W
Humboldt Redwoods State Park ◆	204	40.19 N	124.00 W
Humboldt Salt Marsh ≡	204	39.50 N	117.55 W
Hume, Ca., U.S.	204	36.47 N	118.55 W
Hume, N.Y., U.S.	210	42.29 N	78.08 W
Hume, Lake ⊜[1]	166	36.06 S	147.05 E
Hume and Hovell Lookout ◆	169	37.15 S	144.59 E
Humeburn	166	27.24 S	145.14 E
Hūmedān	128	25.24 N	59.39 E
Hu Men c[1]	100	22.44 N	113.40 E
Humenné	30	48.56 N	21.55 E
Húmera	266a	40.26 N	3.47 W
Humeston	190	40.51 N	93.29 W
Humlā Karṇālī ≃	124	29.38 N	81.52 E
Humlebæk	41	55.58 N	12.33 E
Hummelo	52	52.00 N	6.14 E
Hummelstown	208	40.16 N	76.43 W
Hummels Wharf	210	40.49 N	76.50 W
Hümmling ⋏	52	52.52 N	7.31 E
Humos, Isla I	254	45.38 S	73.59 W
Humpata	152	15.02 S	13.24 E
Hümpfershausen	56	50.40 N	10.13 E
Humphrey, Ar., U.S.	194	34.25 N	91.42 W
Humphrey, Ne., U.S.	198	41.41 N	97.29 W
Humphreys, Mount ∧	204	37.17 N	118.40 W
Humphreys Peak ∧	200	35.20 N	111.40 W
Humpolec	30	49.32 N	15.22 E
Humppila	26	60.56 N	23.22 E
Humptulips	224	47.13 N	123.57 W
Humptulips ≃	224	47.03 N	124.03 W
Humptulips, East Fork ≃	224	47.15 N	123.54 W
Humptulips, West Fork ≃	224	47.15 N	123.54 W
Humptulips Ridge ∧	224	47.20 N	123.45 W
Humpty Doo	164	12.38 S	131.15 E
Humula	171b	35.29 S	147.45 E
Humuya ≃	236	15.01 N	87.44 W
Hūn	146	29.07 N	15.56 E
Hun ≃, Zhg.	98	41.01 N	122.27 E
Hun ≃, Zhg.	98	40.52 N	125.42 E
Hunabasi → Funabashi	94	35.42 N	139.59 E
Húnaflói c	24a	65.50 N	20.50 W
Hunan □[4]	102	28.00 N	111.00 E
Ḥunayshāt, Ghurd al- ⊥[8]	142	30.07 N	29.47 E
Hunchun	98	42.54 N	130.22 E
Huncoat	262	53.46 N	2.20 W
Hundeluft	54	51.58 N	12.20 E
Hundested	41	55.58 N	11.52 E
Hundewāli	123	31.55 N	72.38 E
Hundorp	26	61.33 N	9.54 E
Hundred	188	39.41 N	80.27 W
Hundred End	262	53.42 N	2.53 W
Hundslund	41	55.55 N	10.04 E
Hundstein ∧	64	47.20 N	12.54 E
Hundwil	58	47.22 N	9.19 E
Hunedoara	38	45.45 N	22.54 E
Hunedoara □[6]	38	45.45 N	23.00 E
Hünfeld	56	50.40 N	9.46 E
Hungary (Magyarország) □[1], Europe	22	47.00 N	20.00 E
Hungary (Magyarország) □[1], Europe	30	47.00 N	20.00 E
Hungchiang → Hongjiang	102	27.07 N	109.56 E
Hungen	56	50.28 N	8.54 E
Hungerford, Austl.	166	29.00 S	144.25 E
Hungerford, Eng., U.K.	42	51.26 N	1.30 W
Hungerford, Tx., U.S.	222	29.24 N	96.05 W
Hŭngho-ri	98	37.14 N	127.44 E
Hŭngin-ni	98	39.03 N	126.26 E
Hung Long	269c	10.40 N	106.39 E
Hungmao	100	24.55 N	120.58 E
Hŭngnam	98	39.50 N	127.38 E
Hungría → Hungary □[1]	30	47.00 N	20.00 E
Hungry Hill ∧	48	51.41 N	9.48 W
Hungry Horse	202	48.23 N	114.03 W
Hungry Horse Dam •[6]	202	48.14 N	114.04 W
Hungry Horse Reservoir ⊜[1]	202	48.15 N	113.50 W
Hungry Lake ⊜	212	44.48 N	76.53 W
Hungry Law ∧[2]	44	55.21 N	2.24 W
Hung Yen	110	20.39 N	106.04 E
Hunhe	104	41.43 N	123.22 E
Huningue	58	47.36 N	7.35 E
Hunish, Rubha ≻	46	57.41 N	6.21 W
Huni Valley	150	5.28 N	1.55 W
Hunjiang (Badaojiang)	98	41.56 N	126.29 E
Hunker	279b	40.12 N	79.38 W
Hunkurāb, Ra's ≻	140	24.34 N	35.10 E
Hunlen Falls ⌊	182	52.17 N	125.47 W
Hunmanby	44	54.10 N	0.19 W
Hunn ⊜	40	58.51 N	15.57 E
Hunneberg ∧[2]	26	58.20 N	12.27 E
Hunnebostrand	26	58.27 N	11.18 E
Hunnewell	219	39.40 N	91.51 W
Hunnewell Lake ⊜	219	39.42 N	91.52 W
Hunsberge ⋏	156	27.45 S	17.12 E
Hunseby	41	54.48 N	11.32 E
Hunspach	56	48.57 N	7.57 E
Hunsrück ⋏	56	49.50 N	6.40 E
Hunstanton	42	52.57 N	0.30 E
Hunstein Range ⋏	164	4.30 S	142.40 E
Hunsūr	122	12.18 N	76.17 E
Hunswinkel	263	51.05 N	7.48 E
Hunt □[6]	222	33.03 N	96.05 W
Hunte ≃	52	52.30 N	8.19 E
Hunter, N.Y., U.S.	210	42.13 N	74.13 W
Hunter, N.D., U.S.	198	47.11 N	97.13 W
Hunter ≃, Austl.	170	32.50 S	151.42 E
Hunter ≃, N.Z.	172	44.22 S	169.25 E
Hunter, Île I	14	22.24 S	172.03 E
Hunter, Mount ∧	180	62.57 N	151.05 W
Hunter, Port c	170	32.55 S	151.48 E
Hunterdon □[6]	208	40.31 N	74.52 W
Hunter Island I, Austl.	166	40.32 S	144.45 E
Hunter Island I, B.C., Can.	182	51.55 N	128.05 W
Hunter Island I, N.Y., U.S.	276	40.53 N	73.47 W
Hunter Mountain ∧	210	42.10 N	74.14 W
Hunter Mountains ⋏	172	45.42 S	167.25 E
Hunter Range ⋏	170	32.50 S	150.50 E
Hunter Ridge ⊹[3]	14	21.30 S	174.30 E
Hunter River	186	46.21 N	63.21 W
Hunters	182	48.07 N	118.12 W
Hunters Bay c	110	19.57 N	93.19 E
Hunters Creek Village	222	29.46 N	95.24 W
Huntersfield Mountain ∧	210	42.21 N	74.21 W
Hunters Hill	274a	33.50 S	151.09 E
Hunters Point ≻	282	37.43 N	122.22 W
Hunter's Quay	46	55.58 N	4.55 W
Hunters Road	154	19.09 S	29.48 E
Hunters Run	208	40.05 N	77.11 W
Huntersville	192	35.25 N	80.50 W
Huntertown	216	41.13 N	85.10 W
Hunterville	172	39.56 S	175.34 E
Hunter Wash ∨	200	36.17 N	108.34 W
Huntingburg	194	38.17 N	86.57 W
Huntingdon, B.C., Can.	224	49.00 N	122.16 W
Huntingdon, P.Q., Can.	206	45.05 N	74.10 W
Huntingdon, Eng., U.K.	42	52.20 N	0.12 W
Huntingdon, Pa., U.S.	214	40.29 N	78.00 W
Huntingdon, Tn., U.S.	194	36.00 N	88.25 W
Huntingdon □[6], P.Q., Can.	206	45.05 N	74.00 W
Huntingdon □[6], Pa., U.S.	214	40.29 N	78.01 W
Huntingdon Valley	285	40.07 N	75.03 W
Huntingdon Valley Creek ≃	285	40.07 N	75.04 W
Hunting Island State Park ◆	192	32.20 N	80.30 W
Hunting Ridge	284c	38.55 N	77.12 W
Huntington, Eng., U.K.	44	54.01 N	1.04 W
Huntington, In., U.S.	216	40.52 N	85.29 W
Huntington, Ma., U.S.	207	42.14 N	72.52 W
Huntington, N.Y., U.S.	210	40.51 N	73.25 W
Huntington, Or., U.S.	202	44.21 N	117.15 W
Huntington, Tx., U.S.	222	31.16 N	94.34 W
Huntington, Ut,. U.S.	200	39.19 N	110.57 W
Huntington, Va., U.S.	284c	38.48 N	77.15 W
Huntington, W.V., U.S.	188	38.25 N	82.26 W
Huntington □[6]	216	40.53 N	85.30 W
Huntington Bay	276	40.53 N	73.24 W
Huntington Bay c	276	40.55 N	73.25 W
Huntington Beach, Ca., U.S.	228	33.39 N	117.59 W
Huntington Beach, N.Y., U.S.	276	40.54 N	73.23 W
Huntington Creek ≃, Nv., U.S.	204	40.37 N	115.43 W
Huntington Creek ≃, Pa., U.S.	210	41.06 N	76.22 W
Huntington Creek ≃, Ut,. U.S.	200	39.09 N	110.55 W
Huntington Harbor c	276	40.54 N	73.26 W
Huntington Lake	226	37.15 N	119.14 W
Huntington Lake ⊜[1], Ca., U.S.	226	37.14 N	119.12 W
Huntington Lake ⊜[1], In., U.S.	216	40.50 N	85.25 W
Huntington Library ⊽[3]	280	34.08 N	118.07 W
Huntington Mills	210	41.11 N	76.14 W
Huntington Park	228	33.58 N	118.13 W
Huntington Park ◆	279a	41.29 N	81.56 W
Huntington Station	210	40.51 N	73.24 W
Huntington Woods	281	42.28 N	83.10 W
Huntingtown	208	38.36 N	76.36 W
Hunting Valley	279a	41.31 N	81.23 W
Huntingville	206	45.20 N	71.51 W
Huntland	194	35.03 N	86.16 W
Huntley, Il., U.S.	216	42.10 N	88.25 W
Huntley, Mt., U.S.	202	45.53 N	108.18 W
Huntly, N.Z.	172	37.33 S	175.10 E
Huntly, Scot., U.K.	46	57.27 N	2.47 W
Hunt Mountain ∧	202	44.44 N	107.45 W
Hunton	260	51.13 N	0.28 E
Huntsburg	214	41.32 N	81.03 W
Hunt's Cross •[8]	262	53.21 N	2.51 W
Hunts Point	224	47.39 N	122.14 W
Huntsville, On., Can.	212	45.20 N	79.13 W
Huntsville, Al., U.S.	194	34.43 N	86.35 W
Huntsville, Ar., U.S.	194	36.05 N	93.44 W
Huntsville, Il., U.S.	219	40.11 N	90.52 W
Huntsville, In., U.S.	218	40.00 N	85.43 W
Huntsville, Mo., U.S.	194	39.26 N	92.33 W
Huntsville, Oh., U.S.	216	40.26 N	83.49 W
Huntsville, Tn., U.S.	192	36.24 N	84.29 W
Huntsville, Tx., U.S.	222	30.43 N	95.33 W
Huntsville, Ut,. U.S.	200	41.15 N	111.46 W
Huntsville State Park ◆	222	30.37 N	95.32 W
Hunū, Kathīb al- ⊥[8]	142	30.37 N	32.49 E
Hunucmá	232	21.01 N	89.52 W
Hunut	130	40.39 N	41.09 E
Hünxe	52	51.38 N	6.46 E
Hünxerwald ◆	263	51.40 N	6.50 E
Hunyani ≃	154	15.37 S	30.39 E
Hunyuan	98	39.48 N	113.41 E
Hun-yung	98	42.53 N	130.12 E

ENGLISH — Name, Page, Lat.°′, Long.°′ · DEUTSCH — Name, Seite, Breite°′, Länge°′ E = Ost

Symbols in the index entries represent the broad categories identified in the key at the right. Symbols with superior numbers (⋏[1]) identify subcategories (see complete key on page *I · 1).*

Symbole im Register stellen die rechts im Schlüssel erklärten Kategorien dar. Symbole mit hochgestellten Ziffern (⋏[1]) bezeichnen Unterabteilungen einer Kategorie (vgl. vollständiger Schlüssel auf Seite *I · 1).*

Los símbolos incluídos en el texto del índice representan las grandes categorías identificadas con la clave a la derecha. Los símbolos con numeros en su parte superior (⋏[1]) identifican las subcategorías (véase la clave completa en la página *I · 1).*

Les symboles de l'index représentent les catégories indiquées dans la légende à droite. Les symboles suivis d'un indice (⋏[1]) représentent des sous-catégories (voir légende complète à la page *I · 1).*

Os símbolos incluídos no texto do índice representam as grandes categorias identificadas com a chave à direita. Os símbolos com números em sua parte superior (⋏[1]) identificam as subcategorias (veja-se a chave completa à página *I · 1).*

∧ Mountain	Berg	Montaña	Montagne	Montanha
⋏ Mountains	Gebirge	Montañas	Montagnes	Montanhas
)(Pass	Paß	Paso	Col	Passo
∨ Valley, Canyon	Tal, Cañon	Valle, Cañón	Vallée, Canyon	Vale, Canhão
≚ Plain	Ebene	Llano	Plaine	Planície
≻ Cape	Kap	Cabo	Cap	Cabo
I Island	Insel	Isla	Île	Ilha
II Islands	Inseln	Islas	Îles	Ilhas
⊥ Other Topographic Features	Andere Topographische Objekte	Otros Elementos Topográficos	Autres données topographiques	Outros acidentes topográficos

ESPAÑOL | FRANÇAIS | PORTUGUÊS

Nombre / Nom / Nome	Página / Page	Lat.°′	Long.°′ W = Oeste / Ouest
Hunza □ 9	123	36.30 N	75.00 E
Hunza ≃	123	35.55 N	74.22 E
Huocheng	86	44.12 N	80.26 E
Huoergeluo	89	45.35 N	120.56 E
Huokou	100	26.28 N	119.16 E
Huolong	106	32.04 N	121.17 E
Huolongmen	89	49.48 N	125.47 E
Huolu	98	38.05 N	114.18 E
Huong Hoa	110	16.37 N	106.45 E
Huong Khe	110	18.13 N	105.41 E
Huong Thuy	110	16.25 N	107.40 E
Huon Gulf ⊂	164	7.10 S	147.25 E
Huon Peninsula > 1	164	6.25 S	147.25 E
Huonville	166	43.01 S	147.02 E
Huoqiu	100	32.20 N	116.16 E
Huorili	89	49.00 N	124.41 E
Huoshan	100	31.25 N	116.20 E
Huo Shan ∧	100	31.06 N	116.12 E
Huoshaoliao	100	25.00 N	121.45 E
Huotong	100	26.53 N	119.25 E
Huotong ≃	100	26.50 N	119.32 E
Huotuolaihuduke	102	40.19 N	104.18 E
Huoxian, Zhg.	102	36.37 N	111.40 E
Huoxian, Zhg.	105	39.46 N	116.46 E
Huoyan	100	33.42 N	113.40 E
Hupeh → Hubei □ 4	90	31.00 N	112.00 E
Huqiao	106	31.25 N	119.24 E
Hura	126	23.18 N	86.39 E
Hūrand	84	38.51 N	47.22 E
Hurāsāgar ≃	126	24.04 N	89.40 E
Ḥuraydīn, Wādī V	132	30.59 N	33.53 E
Ḥuraymilā	128	25.08 N	46.08 E
Hūrayn	142	30.39 N	31.08 E
Hurd, Cape >	190	45.13 N	81.44 W
Hurdalssjøen ⊜	26	60.20 N	11.05 E
Hurdiyo	144	10.33 N	51.08 E
Hurdland	219	40.09 N	92.18 W
Hurdsfield	262	53.16 N	2.06 W
Hurepoix ◆ 1	261	48.40 N	2.10 E
Hure Qi	98	42.44 N	121.40 E
Hurffville	285	39.46 N	75.07 W
Huri ∧ 2	154	3.41 N	37.51 E
Huriel	32	46.23 N	2.29 E
Hurleg Hu ⊜	102	37.20 N	96.54 E
Hurley, Ms., U.S.	194	30.39 N	88.29 W
Hurley, N.M., U.S.	200	32.41 N	108.07 W
Hurley, N.Y., U.S.	210	41.55 N	74.03 W
Hurley, S.D., U.S.	198	43.16 N	97.05 W
Hurley, Wi., U.S.	190	46.26 N	90.11 W
Hurleyville	210	41.44 N	74.40 W
Hurlford	46	55.36 N	4.28 W
Hurliness	46	58.47 N	3.15 W
Hurlingham	258	34.36 S	58.38 W
Hurlock	208	38.37 N	75.51 W
Hurmāgai	128	28.18 N	64.26 E
Huron, Ca., U.S.	226	36.12 N	120.06 W
Huron, Oh., U.S.	214	41.22 N	82.33 W
Huron, S.D., U.S.	198	44.21 N	98.12 W
Huron □ 6, On., Can.	212	43.45 N	81.10 W
Huron □ 6, Oh., U.S.	214	41.15 N	82.37 W
Huron ≃, Mi., U.S.	216	42.03 N	83.14 W
Huron ≃, Oh., U.S.	214	41.23 N	82.33 W
Huron, East Branch ≃	214	41.17 N	82.38 W
Huron, Lake ⊜	190	44.30 N	82.15 W
Huron, Point >	214	42.34 N	82.47 W
Huron, West Branch ≃	214	41.17 N	82.38 W
Huron Gardens	216	42.38 N	83.20 W
Huron Mountains ⋏ 2	190	46.50 N	87.55 W
Hurons, Rivière des ≃	206	45.28 N	73.16 W
Hurricane, Ak., U.S.	180	62.59 N	149.38 W
Hurricane, Ut,. U.S.	200	37.10 N	113.17 W
Hurricane, W.V., U.S.	188	38.25 N	82.01 W
Hurricane Bayou ≃	222	31.21 N	95.35 W
Hurricane Cliffs ≐ 4	200	37.20 N	113.10 W
Hurricane Creek ≃, Ar., U.S.	194	34.05 N	92.23 W
Hurricane Creek ≃, Ga., U.S.	192	31.23 N	82.19 W
Hurricane Creek ≃, Il., U.S.	219	38.53 N	89.13 W
Hurricane Lake ⊜	198	48.25 N	99.30 W
Hurricane Wash V	200	37.00 N	113.23 W
Hurshi	126	24.17 N	88.28 E
Hursley	42	51.02 N	1.24 W
Hurso	144	9.38 N	41.38 E
Hurst	222	32.49 N	97.10 W
Hurstbourne Tarrant	42	51.17 N	1.23 W
Hurstbridge	169	37.38 S	145.12 E
Hurstpierpoint	42	50.56 N	0.11 W
Hurstville	170	33.58 S	151.06 E
Hurstwood Reservoir ⊜ 1	262	53.47 N	2.10 W
Hurt	192	37.05 N	79.17 W
Hurtado ≃	252	30.35 S	71.11 W
Hurtaut ≃	50	49.42 N	4.01 E
Hürth	56	50.52 N	6.51 E
Hurtsboro	194	32.14 N	85.24 W
Hurunui ≃	172	42.55 S	173.17 E
Hurup	26	56.45 N	8.25 E
Hurworth-on-Tees	44	54.29 N	1.31 W
Husainābād	124	24.32 N	84.01 E
Husainīwāla	123	30.59 N	74.34 E
Husainpur	124	24.25 N	90.40 E
Húsavík	24a	66.04 N	17.18 W
Husby-Långhundra	40	59.45 N	18.01 E
Huse → Higashiōsaka	96	34.39 N	135.35 E
Husen ◆ 8	263	51.33 N	7.36 E
Hushan, Zhg.	89	45.35 N	130.35 E
Hushan, Zhg.	100	28.36 N	118.59 E
Hushan, Zhg.	100	22.09 N	113.10 E
Husheib	140	14.54 N	35.07 E
Hushi	107	28.57 N	105.22 E
Hushiha	98	40.52 N	116.59 E
Hushitai	104	41.57 N	123.30 E
Hushu, Zhg.	106	31.52 N	118.59 E
Hushu, Zhg.	106	30.18 N	120.08 E
Huși	38	46.40 N	28.04 E
Husinec	60	49.03 N	13.58 E
Huskisson	170	35.02 S	150.40 E
Huskvarna	26	57.48 N	14.16 E
Huslia	180	65.42 N	156.25 W
Hussar	182	51.03 N	112.41 W
Hussigny-Godbrange	56	49.29 N	5.52 E
Hustisford	190	43.21 N	88.36 W
Huston ≃	220	25.42 N	81.17 W
Hustontown	214	40.03 N	78.02 W
Hustopeče	61	48.57 N	16.44 E
Husum, Dtsch.	41	54.28 N	9.03 E
Husum, Sve.	26	63.20 N	19.10 E
Husum, Wa., U.S.	224	45.47 N	121.29 W
Hutaimbaru	114	1.34 N	99.44 E
Hutangqiao	106	31.46 N	119.57 E
Hutan Melintang	114	3.53 N	100.56 E
Hutanopan	114	0.41 N	99.42 E
Hutaym, Ḩarrat ≐ 9	128	26.15 N	40.20 E
Hutberg ∧ 2	54	52.09 N	14.33 E
Hutchins	222	32.39 N	96.43 W
Hutchinson, S. Afr.	158	31.30 S	23.09 E
Hutchinson, Ks., U.S.	198	38.03 N	97.55 W
Hutchinson, Mn., U.S.	190	44.53 N	94.22 W
Hutchinson, Pa., U.S.	214	40.13 N	79.44 W
Hutchinson ≃	276	40.52 N	73.50 W
Hutchinson Island I	220	27.25 N	80.17 W
Hutch Mountain ∧	200	34.47 N	111.22 W
Huthwaite	44	53.09 N	1.17 W
Hutou, Zhg.	100	25.15 N	118.03 E
Hutou, Zhg.	100	26.04 N	118.46 E
Hutou, Zhg.	106	31.37 N	119.37 E
Hutou, Zhg.	106	32.14 N	120.17 E
Hutouya	98	37.13 N	119.46 E
Hutsonville	194	39.06 N	87.39 W
Hüttau	64	47.25 N	13.18 E
Hütteldorf ◆ 8	264b	48.12 N	16.16 E
Hüttener Berge ⋏ 2	41	54.26 N	9.40 E
Hüttenheim ◆ 8	263	51.22 N	6.43 E
Hüttental	56	50.54 N	8.02 E
Hutte Sauvage, Lac de la ⊜	176	56.15 N	64.45 W
Huttig	194	33.02 N	92.10 W
Hütting	60	48.48 N	11.07 E
Hutto	222	30.33 N	97.33 W
Hutton, Eng., U.K.	260	51.38 N	0.22 E
Hutton, Eng., U.K.	262	53.44 N	2.46 W
Hutton, Mount ∧	166	25.51 S	148.20 E
Hutton Rudby	44	54.27 N	1.17 W
Huttonsville	212	43.38 N	79.48 W
Huttrop ◆ 8	263	51.27 N	7.03 E
Hüttschlag	64	47.10 N	13.14 E
Huttwil	58	47.07 N	7.51 E
Hutubi	86	44.07 N	86.57 E
Hutuo ≃	98	38.14 N	116.05 E
Hutwisch ∧	61	47.28 N	16.13 E
Huu	115b	8.48 S	118.25 E
Huvalu Forest ◆ 3	174v	19.03 S	169.51 W
Huveaune ≃	62	43.15 N	5.23 E
Huvudskär I	40	58.57 N	18.34 E
Huwan	100	31.41 N	114.53 E
Huwei	100	23.43 N	120.26 E
Huwun	144	4.23 N	40.08 E
Ḥuwwārah	132	32.09 N	35.15 E
Huxford	194	31.13 N	87.28 W
Huxi	100	26.12 N	114.44 E
Huxian	102	34.09 N	108.32 E
Huxley	182	51.56 N	113.14 W
Huy	56	50.31 N	5.14 E
Huy ∧	54	51.57 N	10.57 E
Huyangzhen	100	32.25 N	112.45 E
Huyton-with-Roby	262	53.25 N	2.52 W
Huyuesi	106	30.23 N	118.45 E
Hüyük	130	37.57 N	31.37 E
Huyutou	100	26.44 N	119.49 E
Hūzgān	128	31.27 N	48.04 E
Huzhen	100	28.50 N	120.15 E
Huzhou	106	30.52 N	120.06 E
Huzhu	102	37.00 N	102.00 E
Huzhuangtun	104	40.43 N	122.33 E
Huzi	100	30.56 N	113.42 E
Huzisawa → Fujisawa	94	35.21 N	139.29 E
Hvalsø	41	55.36 N	11.50 E
Hvannadalshnúkur ∧	24a	64.01 N	16.41 W
Hvar	36	43.10 N	16.27 E
Hvar, Otok I	36	43.09 N	16.45 E
Hvarski Kanal ɥ	36	43.15 N	16.37 E
Hveragerđi	24a	64.03 N	21.10 W
Hvide Sande	26	55.59 N	8.08 E
Hvidovre	41	55.39 N	12.29 E
Hvittingfoss	26	59.29 N	10.01 E
Hvolsvöllur	24a	63.45 N	20.10 W
Hwach'ŏn	98	38.06 N	127.41 E
Hwach'ŏn-chŏsuji ⊜ 1	98	38.07 N	127.52 E
Hwach'ŏn-ni	98	39.01 N	126.02 E
Hwainan → Huainan	100	32.40 N	117.00 E
Hwaining → Anqing	100	30.31 N	117.02 E
Hwange	154	18.22 S	26.29 E
Hwange National Park ♠	154	19.00 S	26.35 E
Hwanggong-ni	98	40.03 N	129.27 E
Hwanghae Namdo □ 4	98	38.15 N	125.30 E
Hwanghae Pukdo □ 4	98	38.30 N	126.25 E
Hwang Ho → Huang ≃	90	37.32 N	118.19 E
Hwangju	98	38.42 N	125.46 E
Hwangshih → Huangshi	100	30.13 N	115.05 E
Hyak	224	47.23 N	121.23 W
Hyakuna	174m	26.08 N	127.48 E
Hyakuri-ga-dake ∧	94	35.23 N	135.49 E
Hyakuri-kichi, Kōkū-jieitai- ■	94	36.11 N	140.25 E
Hyannis, Ma., U.S.	207	41.39 N	70.17 W
Hyannis, Ne., U.S.	198	42.00 N	101.45 W
Hyannis Port	207	41.38 N	70.18 W
Hyattsville	208	38.57 N	76.56 W
Hyattville	202	44.14 N	107.36 W
Hybla Valley	208	38.44 N	77.05 W
Hyco ≃	192	36.40 N	78.45 W
Hyco Lake ⊜ 1	192	36.30 N	79.05 W
Hydaburg	182	55.12 N	132.49 W
Hyde, N.Z.	172	45.18 S	170.15 E
Hyde, Eng., U.K.	262	53.27 N	2.04 W
Hyde, Pa., U.S.	214	41.00 N	78.28 W
Hyden, Austl.	162	32.27 S	118.53 E
Hyden, Ky., U.S.	192	37.10 N	83.22 W
Hyde Park, Guy.	246	6.30 N	58.16 W
Hyde Park, N.Y., U.S.	210	41.47 N	73.56 W
Hyde Park, Vt., U.S.	188	44.35 N	72.37 W
Hyde Park ◆ 8, Il., U.S.	278	41.48 N	87.36 W
Hyde Park ◆ 8, Ma., U.S.	283	42.15 N	71.08 W
Hyde Park ♠, Austl.	274a	33.53 S	151.13 E
Hyde Park ♠, Eng., U.K.	260	51.20 N	0.10 W
Hyde Park ♠, N.Y., U.S.	284a	43.06 N	79.01 W
Hyder	182	55.55 N	130.01 W
Hyderābād, India	122	17.23 N	78.29 E
Hyderābād, Pāk.	120	25.22 N	68.22 E
Hydetown	214	41.40 N	79.44 W
Hydra → Ídhra I	38	37.20 N	23.32 E
Hydraulic	182	52.36 N	121.42 W
Hydro	196	35.21 N	98.22 W
Hydrographers Passage ɥ	166	20.45 S	150.15 E
Hyen ⊜	40	60.36 N	16.12 E
Hyères	62	43.07 N	6.07 E
Hyères, Îles d' II	62	43.00 N	6.20 E
Hyères-Plage	62	43.06 N	6.10 E
Hyesan	98	41.23 N	128.12 E
Hyland ≃	180	59.50 N	128.10 W
Hylestad	26	59.05 N	7.32 E
Hyllekrog I	41	54.36 N	11.30 E
Hyllinge, Dan.	41	55.16 N	11.37 E
Hyllinge, Sve.	41	56.06 N	12.51 E
Hyllstofta	41	56.08 N	13.16 E
Hyltebruk	26	57.00 N	13.14 E
Hymaya ≃	232	24.31 N	107.41 W
Hymera	194	39.11 N	87.18 W
Hyndburn □ 8	262	53.45 N	2.23 W
Hyndman	188	39.49 N	78.43 W
Hyndman Peak ∧	202	43.45 N	114.08 W
Hyne Field ⊠	281	42.34 N	83.47 W
Hynish Bay ⊂	46	56.28 N	6.50 W
Hyōgo □ 5	96	35.00 N	135.00 E
Hyōgo ◆ 8	270	34.39 N	135.10 E
Hyŏn-ni	98	37.57 N	128.20 E
Hyōno-sen ∧	96	35.21 N	134.31 E
Hyōnosen-Ushiroyama-Nagisan-kokutei-kōen ♠	96	35.15 N	134.30 E
Hyŏpch'ŏn	98	35.35 N	128.08 E
Hyrum	200	41.38 N	111.51 W
Hyrynsalmi	26	64.40 N	28.32 E
Hysham	202	46.17 N	107.14 W
Hythe, Ab., Can.	182	55.20 N	119.33 W
Hythe, Eng., U.K.	42	51.05 N	1.05 E
Hythe, Eng., U.K.	42	50.51 N	1.24 W
Hythe End	260	51.27 N	0.32 W
Hyūga	92	32.25 N	131.38 E
Hyūga-nada ⊤ 2	92	32.00 N	131.35 E
Hyvinge → Hyvinkää	26	60.38 N	24.52 E
Hyvinkää	26	60.38 N	24.52 E
I			
Iacanga	255	21.54 S	49.01 W
Iaciara	255	14.09 S	46.40 W
Iaco (Yaco) ≃	248	9.03 S	68.34 W
Iaçu	255	12.45 S	40.13 W
Iaeger	192	37.27 N	81.48 W
Iago	222	29.17 N	95.58 W
Iakora	157b	23.06 S	46.40 E
Ialomița □ 6	38	44.40 N	27.20 E
Ialomița ≃	38	44.42 N	27.51 E
Ialomiței, Balta ≋	38	44.30 N	28.00 E
Iamonia, Lake ⊜	192	30.38 N	84.14 W
Ianaivo ≃	157b	22.56 S	46.54 E
Ianakafy	157b	23.21 S	45.28 E
Ianga	146	9.07 N	18.11 E
Iango	152	9.11 S	17.39 E
Iano, Monte ∧	267a	41.46 N	12.44 E
Iapó ≃	252	24.30 S	50.24 W
Iapu	255	19.26 S	42.13 W
Iași	38	47.10 N	27.35 E
Iași □ 6	38	47.15 N	27.15 E
Iato	70	37.58 N	13.07 E
Iatt, Lake ⊜ 1	194	31.35 N	92.40 W
Iauaretê	246	0.36 N	69.12 W
Iazu	38	44.44 N	27.25 E
Ib ≃	120	21.34 N	83.48 E
Iba, Pil.	116	15.20 N	119.58 E
Iba, Zaïre	152	3.05 S	17.38 E
'Ibādah, Wādī V	142	27.49 N	30.54 E
Ibadan	150	7.17 N	3.30 E
Ibagué	246	4.27 N	75.14 W
Ibaiti	255	23.50 S	50.10 W
Ibajay	116	11.49 N	122.10 E
Ibajay ≃	116	11.49 N	122.10 E
Ibaka	152	4.16 S	23.12 E
Ibambi	154	2.22 N	27.37 E
Ibanda	154	0.08 S	30.29 E
Ibănești	38	48.04 N	26.22 E
Ibans, Laguna de ⊂	236	15.53 N	84.52 W
Ibanshe	152	4.58 S	21.30 E
Ibapah Peak ∧	200	39.50 N	113.55 W
Ibar ≃	38	43.44 N	20.45 E
Ibara	96	34.36 N	133.28 E
Ibaraki, Nihon	94	36.17 N	140.26 E
Ibaraki, Nihon	96	34.49 N	135.34 E
Ibaraki □ 5	94	36.30 N	140.30 E
Ibarra	246	0.21 N	78.07 W
Ibarreta	252	25.13 S	59.51 W
Ibb	144	14.01 N	44.10 E
Ibba	154	4.48 N	29.06 E
Ibba ≃	140	7.09 N	28.41 E
Ibbenbüren	52	52.16 N	7.43 E
Ibeke Gembo	152	1.24 S	18.51 E
Ibembo	152	2.38 N	23.37 E
Ibenga ≃	152	2.20 N	18.08 E
Iberá, Esteros del ≋	252	28.05 S	57.05 W
Iberia, Mo., U.S.	194	38.05 N	92.17 W
Iberia, Oh., U.S.	214	40.40 N	82.51 W
Ibérica, Peninsula > 1	4	40.00 N	5.00 W
Ibérico, Sistema ⋏	34	41.00 N	2.30 W
Ibertioga	256	21.25 S	43.58 W
Iberville	206	45.18 N	73.14 W
Iberville □ 6	206	45.15 N	73.10 W
Iberville, Mont d' (Mount Caubvick) ∧	176	58.53 N	63.43 W
Ibese	273a	6.33 N	3.29 E
Ibeto	150	10.29 N	5.09 E
Ibi	150	8.12 N	9.45 E
Ibi ≃	94	35.03 N	136.42 E
Ibiá	255	19.29 S	46.32 W
Ibiapina	250	3.55 S	40.54 W
Ibicaraí	255	14.51 S	39.36 W
Ibicuí	255	14.51 S	39.59 W
Ibicuí ≃	252	29.25 S	56.47 W
Ibicuicito, Arroyo ≃	258	33.49 S	58.49 W
Ibicuy	258	33.44 S	59.10 W
Ibicuy ≃ 1	258	33.48 S	59.10 W
Ibigawa	94	35.29 N	136.34 E
Ibipira	250	6.31 S	44.38 W
Ibiquera	255	12.38 S	40.57 W
Ibiraci	255	20.28 S	47.08 W
Ibiraçu	255	19.50 S	40.22 W
Ibirama	252	27.04 S	49.31 W
Ibirapuã	255	17.39 S	40.07 W
Ibirapuera ◆ 8	287b	23.37 S	46.40 W
Ibirapuera, Parque ♠	287b	23.35 S	46.39 W
Ibirapuitã ≃	252	29.22 S	55.57 W
Ibirataia	255	14.04 S	39.38 W
Ibiri	154	4.56 S	32.33 E
Ibirubá	252	28.38 S	53.06 W
Ibitiara	255	12.39 S	42.13 W
Ibitinga	255	21.45 S	48.49 W
Ibitiúra De Minas	256	22.04 S	46.26 W
Ibiúna	256	23.39 S	47.13 W
Ibiza → Eivissa I	34	39.00 N	1.25 E
Iblei, Monti ⋏	70	37.10 N	14.50 E
Ibnahs	142	30.34 N	31.07 E
Ibn Hāni', Ra's >	130	35.35 N	35.43 E
Ibn Sarrār, Bi'r ⊤ 4	144	19.30 N	42.41 E
Ibo	154	12.20 S	40.35 E
Ibo ≃	96	34.46 N	134.35 E
Ibondo	154	2.38 S	32.40 E
Ibonma	164	3.28 S	133.28 E
Ibor ≃	34	39.49 N	5.33 W
Ibotirama	255	12.11 S	43.13 W
Iboundji, Mont ∧	152	1.08 S	11.48 E
Ibrah, Wādī V	140	10.36 N	24.58 E
Ibrāhīmīyah, Qārah al- ≊	142	29.10 N	31.10 E
Ibresi	80	55.18 N	47.03 E
'Ibrī	128	23.14 N	56.30 E
İbriktepe	130	41.00 N	26.30 E
Ibshān	142	31.10 N	31.10 E
Ibshawāy	142	29.22 N	30.41 E
Ibstock	42	52.42 N	1.23 W
Ibta'	132	32.47 N	36.09 E
Ibu	174m	26.45 N	128.19 E
Ibuki	94	35.24 N	136.23 E
Ibuki-jima I	96	34.08 N	133.32 E
Ibuki-sanchi ⋏	94	35.35 N	136.18 E
Ibuki-yama ∧	94	35.25 N	136.24 E
Iburg	52	52.09 N	8.02 E
Ibusuki	92	31.16 N	130.39 E
Ibwe Munyama	154	16.09 S	28.34 E
Ibychen, gora ∧	88	51.36 N	109.45 E
Ica	248	14.04 S	75.42 W
Ica □ 5	248	14.20 S	75.30 W
Ičа ≃, Lat.	76	56.52 N	26.59 E
Ica ≃, Perú	248	14.54 S	75.34 W
Ičа ≃, Ross.	86	55.30 N	77.13 E
Içá (Putumayo) ≃, S.A.	246	3.07 S	67.58 W
Icabarú ≃	246	4.45 N	62.15 W
Icacos Point >	241r	10.03 N	61.56 W
Icadambanauan Island I	116	10.49 N	119.38 E
Icamaquã ≃	252	28.34 S	56.00 W
Icamole	196	25.55 N	100.43 W
Içana	246	0.21 N	67.19 W
Içana (Isana) ≃	246	0.26 N	67.19 W
Icaño, Arg.	252	28.54 S	65.19 W
Icaño, Arg.	252	28.41 S	62.54 W
Icatu	250	2.46 S	44.04 W
Iceberg Pass)(	200	40.25 N	105.45 W
Ice House Reservoir ⊜ 1	226	38.49 N	120.23 W
İçel (Mersin)	130	36.48 N	34.38 E
İçel □ 4	130	36.45 N	34.00 E
Iceland (Ísland) □ 1, Europe	22	65.00 N	18.00 W
Iceland (Ísland) □ 1, Europe	24a	65.00 N	18.00 W
Iceland Basin ✢ 1	10	59.00 N	23.00 W
Icém	255	20.21 S	49.12 W
Ice Mountain ∧	182	54.25 N	121.08 W
Ičera	88	58.32 N	109.47 E
Ichaikaronji	122	16.42 N	74.28 E
Ichāmati ≃, Asia	126	22.35 N	88.57 E
Ichāmati ≃, Bngl.	126	24.00 N	89.15 E
Ichang → Yichang	102	30.42 N	111.17 E
Ichawaynochaway Creek ≃	192	31.10 N	84.28 W
Ich Bajan Ajrag uul ∧	88	47.55 N	95.02 E
Ichbulag	102	45.21 N	113.10 E
Ich Buural uul ∧	88	48.00 N	94.30 E
Ichchāpuram	122	19.07 N	84.42 E
Ichdžargalan	102	45.31 N	108.48 E
Ichenhausen	58	48.22 N	10.18 E
Ichenheim	58	48.26 N	7.49 E
Ichhapur	126	22.50 N	88.24 E
Ichhāwar	124	23.01 N	77.01 E
Ichi ≃	96	34.46 N	134.41 E
Ichiba	96	34.05 N	134.17 E
Ichihara	94	35.31 N	140.05 E
Ichikai	94	36.32 N	140.06 E
Ichikawa, Nihon	94	35.44 N	139.55 E
Ichikawa, Nihon	96	34.59 N	134.46 E
Ichikawa-daimon	94	35.34 N	138.30 E
Ichilo ≃	248	15.57 S	64.42 W
Ichinohe	92	40.13 N	141.17 E
Ichinomiya, Nihon	94	35.18 N	136.48 E
Ichinomiya, Nihon	94	35.22 N	140.22 E
Ichinomiya, Nihon	94	35.39 N	138.41 E
Ichinomiya, Nihon	94	34.41 N	137.26 E
Ichinomiya, Nihon	96	34.28 N	134.51 E
Ichinomiya, Nihon	96	32.57 N	131.07 E
Ichinomiya, Nihon	96	35.07 N	134.34 E
Ichinomoto	270	34.37 N	135.50 E
Ichinose	270	34.53 N	135.10 E
Ichinoseki	92	38.55 N	141.08 E
Ichino-tani ⊥	96	34.39 N	135.07 E
Ichiu	96	33.57 N	134.04 E
Ichkeul, Lac ⊜	36	37.10 N	9.40 E
Ichoa ≃	248	15.44 S	65.15 W
Ichoca	248	17.12 S	67.17 W
Ich'on, C.M.I.K.	98	38.30 N	126.50 E
Ich'ŏn, Taehan	98	37.17 N	127.27 E
Ich Ovoo uul ∧	90	44.40 N	95.08 E
Ichtamir	88	47.30 N	100.52 E
Ichtegem	50	51.06 N	3.00 E
Ichtershausen	54	50.52 N	10.58 E
Ich'un → Yichun	90	47.42 N	128.55 E
Ich Uul, Mong.	88	48.33 N	98.40 E
Ich Uul, Mong.	88	49.27 N	101.27 E
Icicle Creek ≃	224	47.34 N	120.40 W
Ičinskaja Sopka, vulkan ∧ 1	74	55.42 N	157.35 E
Ička, gora ∧ 2	80	51.13 N	50.15 E
Ickenham ◆ 8	260	51.34 N	0.27 W
Ickern	263	51.36 N	7.21 E
Ickesburg	208	40.27 N	77.21 W
Icking	64	47.57 N	11.25 E
İçme	130	38.37 N	39.34 E
Ičn'a	78	50.52 N	32.24 E
Icó	250	6.24 S	38.51 W
Icoca	152	6.11 S	16.19 E
Iconha	255	20.48 S	40.48 W
Icy Bay ⊂	180	60.00 N	141.15 W
Icy Cape >	180	70.20 N	161.52 W
Icy Strait ɥ	180	58.18 N	135.30 W
Ida	216	41.54 N	83.34 W
Ida, Mount ∧, Austl.	162	29.14 S	120.25 E
Ida, Mount ∧, Jam.	241q	17.58 N	77.43 W
Idabel	194	33.53 N	94.49 W
Idaga Hamus	144	14.12 N	39.48 E
Ida Grove	198	42.20 N	95.28 W
Idah	150	7.07 N	6.43 E
Idaho □ 3, U.S.	178	45.00 N	115.00 W
Idaho □ 3, U.S.	202	45.00 N	115.00 W
Idaho City	202	43.49 N	115.50 W
Idaho Falls	202	43.28 N	112.02 W
Idaho National Engineering Laboratory υ 3	202	43.40 N	112.45 W
Idaho Springs	200	39.44 N	105.00 W
Idalou	196	33.39 N	101.40 W
Idanha-a-Nova	34	39.55 N	7.14 W
Idāppādi	122	11.35 N	77.51 E
Idar	120	23.50 N	73.00 E
Idarkopf ∧	56	49.51 N	7.16 E
Idar-Oberstein	56	49.42 N	7.19 E
Idarwald ◆ 3	56	49.20 N	7.15 E
Idaville, In., U.S.	216	40.45 N	86.38 W
Idaville, Or., U.S.	224	45.30 N	123.51 W
Iddo ◆ 8	273a	6.28 N	3.23 E
Ide	96	34.47 N	135.49 E
Idel'	24	64.08 N	34.14 E
Idelès	148	23.58 N	5.53 E
Idemba	152	2.38 S	11.38 E
Iden	54	52.46 N	11.55 E
Ider	88	48.13 N	97.23 E
Iderijn ≃	88	49.16 N	100.41 E
Idermeg	88	47.40 N	111.05 E
Idfīnā	142	31.18 N	30.31 E
Idfū	140	24.58 N	32.52 E
Ídhi Óros ∧	38	35.18 N	24.43 E
Ídhra	38	37.20 N	23.29 E
Ídhra I	38	37.20 N	23.32 E
Idi	114	4.57 N	97.46 E
Idice ≃	64	44.35 N	11.49 E
Idi-cut	114	4.59 N	97.42 E
Ididole	144	5.53 N	43.36 E
Idifina Barrage ◆ 6	142	31.17 N	30.31 E
İdil	130	37.21 N	41.54 E
Idimu	273a	6.35 N	3.17 E
Idio	116	11.37 N	122.06 E
Idiofa	152	5.02 S	19.36 E
Iditarod ≃	180	63.02 N	158.58 W
Idjwi, Île I	154	2.09 S	29.04 E
Idkerberget	40	60.23 N	15.14 E
Idkū	142	31.18 N	30.18 E
Idkū, Buḥayrat ⊜	142	31.16 N	30.17 E
Idle Hill	260	51.15 N	0.08 E
Idlib	130	35.55 N	36.38 E
Idlib □ 8	130	35.50 N	36.40 E
Idmū	142	28.09 N	30.41 E
Idnah	132	31.34 N	34.59 E
Idodi	154	7.47 S	35.11 E
Idomogu	273a	6.43 N	3.30 E
Idracowra	162	25.00 S	133.47 E
Idre	26	61.52 N	12.43 E
Idria	226	36.25 N	120.40 W
Idrica	76	56.21 N	28.53 E
Idrigill Point >	46	57.20 N	6.35 W
Idrija	36	46.00 N	14.01 E
Idrijca ≃	64	46.09 N	13.45 E
Idrinskoje	86	54.21 N	92.07 E
Idro	64	45.44 N	10.29 E
Idro, Lago d' ⊜	64	45.47 N	10.30 E
Idroscalo ⊜	266b	45.28 N	9.18 E
Idstedt	41	54.35 N	9.31 E
Idstein	56	50.13 N	8.16 E
Idutywa	158	32.02 S	28.16 E
Idyllwild	204	33.45 N	116.43 W
Idylside	216	41.31 N	88.07 W
Idylwood	284c	38.54 N	77.12 W
Idževan	84	40.53 N	45.07 E
Ie	174m	26.42 N	127.48 E
Iecava	76	56.36 N	24.12 E
Iecava ≃	76	56.41 N	23.42 E
Ielsi	66	41.30 N	14.48 E
Ienne	66	41.53 N	13.10 E
Iepê	255	22.40 S	51.05 W
Ieper (Ypres)	50	50.51 N	2.53 E
Ierápetra	38	35.00 N	25.45 E
Ierisós	38	40.24 N	23.52 E
Ierzu	71	39.47 N	9.31 E
Ieshima	96	34.40 N	134.32 E
Ie-shima I	174m	26.43 N	127.47 E
Ieshima-shotō II	96	34.40 N	134.32 E
Iesolo	64	45.32 N	12.38 E
Ie-suidō ɥ	174m	26.42 N	127.51 E
If, Château d' ⊥	62	43.17 N	5.19 E
Ifakara	154	8.08 S	36.41 E
Ifako	273a	6.39 N	3.20 E
Ifalik I 1	108	7.15 N	144.27 E
Ifanadiana	157b	21.19 S	47.39 E
Ife	150	7.30 N	4.30 E
Iferouâne	150	19.04 N	8.24 E
Iferten → Yverdon	58	46.47 N	6.39 E
Iffezheim	56	48.49 N	8.08 E
Ifni □ 9	148	29.15 N	10.08 W
Ifôghas, Adrar des ⋏	150	20.00 N	2.00 E
Ifon	150	6.58 N	5.45 E
Ifould Lake ⊜	162	30.53 S	132.09 E
Ifrane	148	33.32 N	5.06 W
Ifrane □ 4	148	33.15 N	5.05 W
Ifta	56	51.04 N	10.11 E
Ifugao □ 4	116	16.45 N	121.15 E
Iga	94	34.49 N	136.13 E
Iga ≃	94	34.45 N	136.01 E
Igal	30	46.31 N	17.55 E
Igalula, Tan.	154	5.14 S	33.00 E
Igalula, Tan.	154	5.38 S	32.38 E
Igan	112	2.49 N	111.43 E
Igan ≃	112	2.51 N	111.39 E
Iganga	154	0.37 N	33.29 E
Iganmu ◆ 8	273a	6.29 N	3.22 E
Iganna	150	7.59 N	3.14 E
Igaporã	255	13.46 S	42.43 W
Igara	250	10.24 S	40.07 W
Igaraí	256	21.25 S	46.49 W
Igara Paraná ≃	246	2.09 S	71.47 W
Igarapé-Açu	250	1.07 S	47.37 W
Igarapé Grande	250	4.41 S	44.58 W
Igarapé-Miri	250	1.59 S	48.58 W
Igaratá	256	23.12 S	46.07 W
Igarka	74	67.28 N	86.35 E
Igarra	150	7.18 N	6.07 E
Igarukiro	154	3.08 S	33.31 E
Igatpuri	122	19.42 N	73.33 E
Igaun	273a	6.42 N	3.23 E
Igawa	154	8.35 S	34.28 E
Igbaja	150	8.23 N	4.52 E
Igbobi	273a	6.32 N	3.22 E
Igboho	150	8.51 N	3.45 E
Igbologun	273a	6.25 N	3.20 E
Igbo-Ora	150	7.26 N	3.17 E
Igbor	150	7.27 N	8.34 E
Igdir, Īrān	84	39.20 N	47.30 E
Iğdır, Tür.	84	39.55 N	44.02 E
Iğdır, Tür.	130	41.14 N	33.07 E
Iğdır, Tür.	130	40.16 N	35.38 E
Igdy	128	39.54 N	56.54 E
Igea Marina	66	44.08 N	12.29 E
Igel	56	49.42 N	6.32 E
Igelfors	40	58.51 N	15.41 E
Igelsberg	58	48.32 N	8.26 E
Igel'vejem ≃	180	65.40 N	172.50 W
Igersheim	56	49.29 N	9.49 E
Iggensbach	60	48.44 N	13.08 E
Iggesund	26	61.38 N	17.04 E
Igharghar, Oued V, Afr.	148	20.25 N	6.10 E
Igharghar, Oued V, Alg.	148	28.03 N	6.15 E
Ightham	260	51.17 N	0.17 E
Ightham Mote ⊥	260	51.15 N	0.16 E
Igikpak, Mount ∧	180	67.25 N	154.58 W
Igirma	88	56.59 N	103.37 E
Igiugig	180	59.20 N	155.55 W
Iglau → Jihlava	30	49.24 N	15.36 E
Iglesia	252	30.24 S	69.13 W
Iglesias	71	39.19 N	8.32 E
Iglesiente ◆ 1	71	39.18 N	8.40 E
Igli	148	30.25 N	2.12 W
Iglino	86	54.50 N	56.26 E
Igloolik	176	69.24 N	81.49 W
Iglovo	82	55.47 N	36.40 E
Igls	64	47.14 N	11.25 E
Ignacej	78	47.41 N	28.40 E
Ignacio, Ca., U.S.	226	38.05 N	122.32 W
Ignacio, Co., U.S.	200	37.06 N	107.37 W
Ignacio de la Llave	234	18.43 N	95.59 W
Ignacio Zaragoza, Méx.	232	29.35 N	107.30 W
Ignacio Zaragoza, Méx.	234	23.55 N	103.42 W
Ignacio Zaragoza, Méx.	234	23.15 N	98.50 W
Ignalina	76	55.21 N	26.10 E
Ignatjevcy	80	57.32 N	51.39 E
Ignatovka	80	53.57 N	47.38 E
Ignatovo	82	56.10 N	37.32 E
İğneada	130	41.52 N	27.58 E
İğneada Burnu >	130	41.54 N	28.03 E
Igney	58	48.17 N	6.24 E
Ignon ≃	58	47.31 N	5.10 E
Igny	261	48.45 N	2.14 E
Igodovo	80	58.01 N	42.21 E
Igombe ≃	154	4.38 S	31.40 E
Igoumenítsa	38	39.30 N	20.16 E
Igra	80	57.33 N	53.04 E
Igreja Nova	250	10.07 S	36.39 W
Iguaçu ≃, Bra.	256	22.45 S	43.14 W
Iguaçu ≃, S.A.	252	25.36 S	54.36 W
Iguaçu, Cataratas do (Iguassu Falls) ∟	252	25.41 S	54.26 W
Iguaí	255	14.45 S	40.04 W
Iguala	234	18.21 N	99.32 W
Igualada	34	41.35 N	1.38 E
Iguana ≃	246	7.54 N	65.46 W
Iguape	252	24.43 S	47.33 W
Iguará ≃	250	3.28 S	43.55 W
Iguassu Falls → Iguaçu, Cataratas 99do ∟	252	25.41 S	54.26 W
Iguatemi	255	23.40 S	54.34 W
Iguatemi ≃	255	23.55 S	54.10 W
Iguatu	250	6.22 S	39.18 W
Iguazú, Parque Nacional ♠	252	25.35 S	54.20 W
Iguéla	152	1.55 S	9.19 E
Iguéla, Lagune ⊂	152	1.55 S	9.25 E
Iguetti, Sebkhet ≋	148	25.05 N	9.50 W
Iguîdi, 'Erg ≐ 8	148	26.35 N	5.40 W
Iguig	116	17.45 N	121.44 E
Igumale	150	6.49 N	7.59 E
Igumnovo	82	55.37 N	38.18 E
Igvak, Cape >	180	57.26 N	156.00 W
Igžej	88	53.59 N	103.10 E
Ihavandiffulu Atoll I 1	122	7.00 N	72.55 E
Iheya-shima I	93b	27.04 N	127.58 E
Ihiala	150	5.51 N	6.51 E
Ihirène, Oued V	148	20.25 N	4.35 E
Ihle ≃	54	52.17 N	11.52 E
Ihlienworth	52	53.44 N	8.55 E
Ihlow	52	53.25 N	7.27 E
Ihmert	56	51.20 N	7.44 E
Ihnāsiyat al-Madīnah	142	29.05 N	30.56 E
Ihorombe	157b	23.00 S	47.33 E
Ihosy	157b	22.24 S	46.08 E
Ihosy ≃	157b	21.44 S	45.53 E
Ihotry, Lac ⊜	157b	21.56 S	43.41 E
Ihringen	58	48.02 N	7.39 E
Ihrlerstein	60	48.56 N	11.52 E
İhsangazi	130	41.11 N	33.33 E
Ih Tal	89	43.13 N	122.15 E
Ihtiman	38	42.26 N	23.49 E
Ihu	164	7.55 S	145.25 E
Ihugh	150	7.02 N	9.00 E
Ihwah	142	29.03 N	31.00 E
Ii	26	65.19 N	25.22 E
Iida	94	35.31 N	137.50 E
Iidaan	144	6.06 N	48.59 E
Iijima	94	35.40 N	137.56 E
Iijoki ≃	24	65.20 N	25.17 E
Iiktu, gora ∧	86	49.51 N	87.40 E
Iinan	94	34.27 N	136.24 E
Iinashi ≃	96	35.27 N	133.13 E
Iioka	94	35.42 N	140.43 E
Iisaku	76	59.06 N	27.19 E
Iisalmi	26	63.34 N	27.11 E
Iisvesi	26	62.40 N	27.02 E
Iitaka	94	34.26 N	136.21 E
Iittala	26	61.04 N	24.10 E
Iivaara ∧ 2	26	65.47 N	29.40 E
Iiyama	94	36.51 N	138.22 E
Iizuka	96	33.38 N	130.41 E
Ij ≃	88	52.34 N	96.10 E
Ija ≃	88	55.05 N	101.05 E
Ijâfene ◆ 2	134	20.30 N	8.00 W
Ijaiye	273a	6.40 N	3.18 E
Ijaji	144	8.59 N	37.13 E
Ijara	154	1.36 S	40.31 E
Ijebu-Igbo	150	6.56 N	4.01 E
Ijebu-Ode	150	6.50 N	3.56 E
Ijesa-Tedo	273a	6.30 N	3.19 E
Ijin	98	42.05 N	130.08 E
Ijira	94	35.31 N	136.44 E
IJmuiden	52	52.27 N	4.36 E
IJssel ≃	52	52.35 N	5.50 E
IJsselmeer (Zuiderzee) ⊤ 2	52	52.45 N	5.25 E
IJsselmuiden	52	52.34 N	5.56 E
IJsselstein	52	52.02 N	5.03 E
Ijuí	252	28.23 S	53.55 W
Ijuí ≃	252	27.58 S	55.20 W
Iju Junction	273a	6.40 N	3.19 E
Ijuw	174b	0.30 S	166.57 E
Iju Water Works υ 3	273a	6.40 N	3.20 E
IJzendijke	52	51.19 N	3.38 E
IJzer (Yser) ≃	50	51.09 N	2.43 E
Ik ≃	80	55.55 N	52.36 E
Ika	88	59.18 N	106.12 E
Ikaalinen	26	61.46 N	23.03 E
Ikaho	94	36.30 N	138.55 E
Ikalamavony	157b	21.09 S	46.35 E
Ikali	152	2.02 S	21.02 E
Ikalou	152	4.03 S	11.48 E
Ikamatua	172	42.16 S	171.41 E
Ikamba	273b	4.22 S	15.16 E
Ikang	150	4.50 N	8.32 E
Ikara	150	11.12 N	8.15 E
Ikare	150	7.32 N	5.45 E
Ikaría I	38	37.41 N	26.20 E
Ikari-dam ◆ 6	94	36.52 N	139.42 E
Ikari-ko ⊜	94	36.56 N	139.41 E
Ikaruga	96	34.36 N	135.44 E
Ikast	41	56.08 N	9.10 E
Ikatan	180	54.45 N	163.19 W
Ikatskij chrebet ⋏	88	54.00 N	111.00 E
Ikawa	94	35.13 N	138.15 E
Ikawa-dam ◆ 6	94	35.12 N	138.13 E
Ikawhenua Range ⋏	172	38.20 S	176.56 E
Ikazaki	96	33.32 N	132.39 E
Ikeda, Nihon	92a	42.55 N	143.27 E
Ikeda, Nihon	94	35.53 N	136.21 E
Ikeda, Nihon	94	35.26 N	136.34 E
Ikeda, Nihon	94	36.25 N	137.53 E
Ikeda, Nihon	96	34.49 N	135.25 E
Ikeda, Nihon	96	34.01 N	133.48 E
Ikegawa	96	33.36 N	133.11 E
Ikej	88	54.12 N	100.04 E
Ikeja	150	6.36 N	3.21 E
Ikeja □ 8	273a	6.30 N	3.25 E
Ikela	152	1.11 S	23.16 E
Ikélemba	152	1.14 N	16.31 E
Ikelemba ≃	152	0.07 N	18.17 E
Ikema-jima I	175d	24.56 N	125.16 E
Ikerre	150	7.31 N	5.14 E
Ike-shima I	174m	26.23 N	128.00 E
Ikeura	270	34.30 N	135.25 E
Iki I	92	33.47 N	129.43 E
Iki-Burul	80	45.49 N	44.39 E
Ikimba, Lake ⊜	154	1.28 S	31.30 E
Īkinjī Maryūt	142	31.00 N	29.45 E
Ikire	150	7.23 N	4.12 E
Ikirun	150	7.55 N	4.41 E
İkizce	130	39.36 N	32.40 E
İkizdere, Tür.	84	40.47 N	40.33 E
İkizdere, Tür.	130	40.47 N	40.33 E
Iko	152	0.35 S	16.01 E
Ikole	150	7.49 N	5.30 E
Ikolik, Cape >	180	57.17 N	154.48 W
Ikom	150	5.58 N	8.42 E
Ikoma, Nihon	96	34.41 N	135.42 E
Ikoma, Tan.	154	2.04 S	34.37 E
Ikoma-sanchi ⋏	270	34.40 N	135.40 E
Ikoma-tunnel ◆ 5	270	34.41 N	135.41 E
Ikoma-yama ∧	270	34.40 N	135.41 E
Ikon-Chal'	84	44.18 N	41.55 E
Ikopa ≃	157b	17.01 S	46.45 E
Ikorec ≃	78	50.58 N	39.45 E
Ikorodu	150	6.37 N	3.31 E
Ikot Ekpene	150	5.12 N	7.40 E
Ikoy ≃	152	0.53 S	10.36 E
Ikoyi ◆ 8	273a	6.27 N	3.26 E
Ikoyi Island I	273a	6.27 N	3.26 E
Ikoyi Prison υ	273a	6.25 N	3.25 E
Ikozi	154	2.32 S	27.37 E
Ikpikpuk ≃	180	70.50 N	154.25 W
Ikra	126	23.42 N	87.07 E
Ikr'anoje	80	46.06 N	47.45 E
Ikrāsh	142	30.45 N	31.30 E
Ikša	82	56.10 N	37.31 E
Iksa ≃	86	57.48 N	82.36 E
Ikti, Cape >	180	56.00 N	158.30 W
Ikuata	273a	6.25 N	3.22 E
Ikuchi-shima I	96	34.17 N	133.07 E
Ikuji-hana >	94	36.54 N	137.25 E
Ikuktlitlig Mountain ∧	180	59.16 N	161.27 W
Ikungu	154	1.34 S	33.40 E
Ikuno	96	35.10 N	134.48 E
Ikuno ◆ 8	270	34.39 N	135.34 E
Ikurangi, Mount ∧ 2	174k	21.13 S	159.45 W
Ikusaka	94	36.25 N	137.56 E
Ikusu ≃	273b	4.24 S	15.14 E
Ikuta	268	35.36 N	139.32 E
Ikva ≃, Magy.	61	47.42 N	16.58 E
Ikva ≃, Ukr.	78	50.33 N	25.24 E
Ikwah	142	30.41 N	31.28 E
Ila, Nig.	150	8.01 N	4.55 E
Ila, Zaïre	152	2.53 S	21.05 E
Ilabaya	248	17.25 S	70.31 W
Ilacaon Point >	116	11.00 N	123.12 E
Ilagala	154	5.12 S	29.50 E
Ilagan	116	17.10 N	121.54 E
Ilagan ≃	116	17.09 N	121.54 E
Ilaiyānkudi	122	9.38 N	78.38 E
Ilaka, Madag.	157b	19.33 S	48.52 E
Ilaka, Madag.	157b	20.20 S	47.09 E
Īlām, Īrān	128	33.38 N	46.26 E
Ilām, Nepāl	124	26.55 N	87.56 E
Īlām □ 4	128	33.15 N	46.45 E
Ilām Bāzār	126	23.38 N	87.32 E
Ilam → Sri Lanka □ 1	122	7.00 N	81.00 E
Ilan	100	24.46 N	121.45 E
Ilan ≃	100	24.43 N	121.49 E
Ilanskij	88	56.14 N	96.03 E
Ilanz	58	46.46 N	9.12 E
Ilara	273a	6.42 N	3.27 E
Ilaro	150	6.53 N	3.03 E
Ilasco	219	39.40 N	91.18 W
Ilave	248	16.06 S	69.41 W
Iława	30	53.37 N	19.33 E
Ilawe-Ekiti	150	7.37 N	5.06 E
Ilay	58	46.37 N	5.53 E
Ilbenge	74	62.49 N	124.24 E
Ilberstedt	54	51.48 N	11.40 E
Il Catalano	71	39.53 N	8.17 E
Ilchester, Eng., U.K.	42	51.01 N	2.41 W
Ilchester, Md., U.S.	284b	39.15 N	76.45 W
Ildefonso, Islas II	254	55.44 S	69.26 W
Île-à-la-Crosse	184	55.27 N	107.53 W
Île-à-la-Crosse, Lac ⊜	184	55.40 N	107.45 W
Ilebo (Port-Francqui)	152	4.19 S	20.35 E
Île-Cadieux	275a	45.25 N	74.01 W
Île-de-France □ 9	50	49.00 N	2.20 E
Île-de-Montréal □ 6	206	45.30 N	73.40 W
Île-Jésus □ 6	206	45.35 N	73.45 W

Symbol					
≃	River	Fluß	Río	Rivière	Rio
≊	Canal	Kanal	Canal	Canal	Canal
∟	Waterfall, Rapids	Wasserfall, Stromschnellen	Cascada, Rápidos	Chute d'eau, Rapides	Cascata, Rápidos
ɥ	Strait	Meeresstraße	Estrecho	Détroit	Estreito
⊂	Bay, Gulf	Bucht, Golf	Bahía, Golfo	Baie, Golfe	Baía, Golfo
⊜	Lake, Lakes	See, Seen	Lago, Lagos	Lac, Lacs	Lago, Lagos
≋	Swamp	Sumpf	Pantano	Marais	Pântano
⊡	Ice Features, Glacier	Eis- und Gletscherformen	Accidentes Glaciales	Formes glaciaires	Acidentes glaciares
⊤	Other Hydrographic Features	Andere Hydrographische Objekte	Otros Elementos Hidrográficos	Autres données hydrographiques	Outros acidentes hidrográficos
✢	Submarine Features	Untermeerische Objekte	Accidentes Submarinos	Formes de relief sous-marin	Acidentes submarinos
□	Political Unit	Politische Einheit	Unidad Politica	Entité politique	Unidade política
υ	Cultural Institution	Kulturelle Institution	Institución Cultural	Institution culturelle	Instituição cultural
⊥	Historical Site	Historische Stätte	Sitio Histórico	Site historique	Sitio histórico
♠	Recreational Site	Erholungs- und Ferienort	Sitio de Recreo	Centre de loisirs	Area de Lazer
⊠	Airport	Flughafen	Aeropuerto	Aéroport	Aeroporto
■	Military Installation	Militäranlage	Instalación Militar	Installation militaire	Instalação militar
◆	Miscellaneous	Verschiedenes	Misceláneo	Divers	Diversos

Ilek 80 51.30 N 53.22 E
Ilek ≃ 72 51.30 N 53.20 E
Ilen ≃ 48 51.33 N 9.19 W
Île-Perrot 206 45.23 N 73.57 W
Ileret 154 4.19 N 36.13 E
Îles, Grand lac des ⊜ 206 46.43 N 73.30 W
Îles, Lac des ⊜, P.Q., Can. 206 46.06 N 74.02 W
Îles, Lac des ⊜, Sk., Can. 184 54.26 N 109.25 W
Ilesha 150 7.38 N 4.45 E
Ilesha Ibarida 150 8.56 N 3.25 E
Ilet' ≃ 80 55.56 N 48.14 E
Ilevskij Pogost 24 60.41 N 43.46 E
Ileza 24 60.43 N 43.54 E
Ilfeld 54 51.34 N 10.47 E
Ilford, Austl. 170 32.58 S 149.51 E
Ilford, Mb., Can. 184 56.04 N 95.35 W
Ilford ◆8 260 51.33 N 0.05 E
Ilfov □6 38 44.30 N 26.15 E
Ilfracombe, Austl. 166 23.30 S 144.30 E
Ilfracombe, Eng., U.K. 42 51.13 N 4.08 W
Il Fuorn 58 46.40 N 10.12 E
Ilga ≃ 88 55.00 N 105.04 E
Ilgaz 130 40.56 N 33.38 E
Ilgaz Dağları ∧ 130 41.00 N 33.35 E
Ilgın 130 38.17 N 31.55 E
Ilha ◆8 256 23.00 S 43.33 W
Ilhabela 256 23.47 S 45.21 W
Ilha das Flores 250 10.27 S 36.33 W
Ilha Grande, Baía da ⊂ 256 23.09 S 44.30 W
Ilhas, Cachoeira das ⌞ 250 1.03 S 57.33 W
Ilha Solteira, Represa de ⊜1 255 20.25 S 51.20 W
Ilhavo 34 40.36 N 8.40 W
Ilhea Point ⟩ 156 23.25 S 14.27 E
Ilhéos — Ilhéus 255 14.49 S 39.02 W
Ilhéus 255 14.49 S 39.02 W
Ili ≃ 86 45.24 N 74.02 E
Ilia 38 45.56 N 22.39 E
Iliamna 180 59.45 N 154.54 W
Iliamna Lake ⊜ 180 59.30 N 155.00 W
Ilian, Mount ∧ 116 10.26 N 119.33 E
Iliatenco 234 16.58 N 98.40 W
Iliç 130 39.28 N 38.34 E
Ilica, Tür. 130 39.52 N 27.46 E
Ilica, Tür. 130 39.57 N 41.07 E
Ilicínia 255 20.56 S 45.50 W
Iliff 198 40.45 N 103.03 W
Iliff, Lake ⊜ 276 41.02 N 74.43 W
Iligan 116 8.14 N 124.14 E
Iligan Bay ⊂ 116 8.25 N 124.05 E
Ilijan 116 13.38 N 121.04 E
Ilijsk 85 43.53 N 77.10 E
Ilim ≃ 88 57.38 N 102.34 E
Ilimsk 88 56.46 N 103.52 E
Ilin 116 12.15 N 121.02 E
Ilinge 158 31.59 S 27.02 E
Ilin Island I 116 12.14 N 121.05 E
Ilinka 82 54.04 N 38.12 E
Ilinza ∧ 246 0.40 S 78.42 W
Ilion 210 43.00 N 75.02 W
Ilio Point ⟩ 229a 21.13 N 157.15 W
Ilioúpolis 267c 37.56 N 23.45 E
Ilir 88 55.13 N 100.40 E
Ilirska Bistrica 36 45.34 N 14.15 E
Ilisós ≃ 267c 37.57 N 23.41 E
Ilizi 148 26.29 N 8.28 E
Ilja 76 54.25 N 27.18 E
Iljak 86 60.11 N 77.59 E
Iljič 85 40.50 N 68.27 E
Iljičevsk 84 39.33 N 44.58 E
Iljičovsk 78 46.18 N 30.39 E
Iljincy 78 49.07 N 29.12 E
Iljinka 80 48.32 N 41.05 E
Iljino 76 55.57 N 31.40 E
Iljinskij, Ross. 24 61.02 N 32.41 E
Iljinskij, Ross. 86 58.35 N 55.41 E
Iljinskij, Ross. 88 52.05 N 114.10 E
Iljinskij, Ross. 89 47.58 N 142.12 E
Iljinskij, Ross. 265b 55.37 N 38.06 E
Iljinskij Pogost 82 55.28 N 38.54 E
Iljinskoje, Ross. 76 56.58 N 37.11 E
Iljinskoje, Ross. 76 58.47 N 44.36 E
Iljinskoje, Ross. 76 53.14 N 35.26 E
Iljinskoje, Ross. 76 57.19 N 38.32 E
Iljinskoje, Ross. 80 56.29 N 52.49 E
Iljinskoje, Ross. 82 54.59 N 36.11 E
Iljinskoje, Ross. 82 56.34 N 35.57 E
Iljinskoje, Ross. 265b 55.46 N 37.15 E
Iljinskoje-Chovanskoje 80 56.58 N 39.46 E
Iljinsko-Podomskoje 24 61.08 N 47.56 E
Iljinsko-Zaborskoje 80 57.16 N 44.23 E
Iljiny gory ∧2 76 56.34 N 34.12 E
Il'ka 88 51.43 N 108.32 E
Ilkal 122 15.58 N 76.08 E
Ilkeston 42 52.59 N 1.18 W
Il'kino 80 55.13 N 41.36 E
Ilkley 44 53.55 N 1.50 W
Ill ≃, Fr. 58 48.40 N 7.53 E
Ill ≃, Öst. 58 47.17 N 9.33 E
Illabot Creek ≃ 224 48.29 N 121.30 W
Illampu, Nevado ∧ 248 15.50 S 68.34 W
Illana Bay ⊂ 116 7.25 N 123.45 E
Illapel 252 31.38 S 71.10 W
Illarionovo 78 48.25 N 35.16 E
Illasi 64 45.28 N 11.10 E
Illawarra, Lake ⊂ 170 34.32 S 150.50 E
Illbillee, Mount ∧ 162 27.02 S 132.30 E
Ille-et-Vilaine □5 32 48.10 N 1.30 W
Illéla 150 14.28 N 5.15 E
Iller ≃ 58 48.23 N 9.58 E
Illertissen 58 48.13 N 10.06 E
Illescas, Esp. 34 40.07 N 3.50 W
Illescas, Méx. 234 23.13 N 102.07 W
Illfurth 58 47.40 N 7.16 E
Illhaeusern 58 48.11 N 7.26 E
Illi, Ba ≃ 146 10.44 S 15.21 E
Illiers 50 48.18 N 1.15 E
Illimani, Nevado ∧ 248 16.50 S 67.54 W
Illimo 248 6.28 S 79.51 W
Illingen 56 48.57 N 8.55 E
Illingworth 262 53.45 N 1.54 W
Illinois □3, U.S. 178 40.00 N 89.00 W
Illinois □3, U.S. 194 40.00 N 89.00 W
Illinois ≃, U.S. 194 35.30 N 95.06 W
Illinois ≃, Co., U.S. 200 40.45 N 106.18 W
Illinois ≃, Il., U.S. 194 38.58 N 90.27 W
Illinois ≃, Or., U.S. 202 42.33 N 124.03 W
Illinois and Michigan Canal ≡ 278 41.32 N 88.05 W
Illinois at Chicago, University of ◆2 278 41.52 N 87.39 W
Illinois Beach State Park ◆ 216 42.26 N 87.48 W
Illinois Institute of Technology ◆2 278 41.50 N 87.38 W
Illinois Peak ∧ 202 47.02 N 115.04 W
Illiopolis 219 39.51 N 89.14 W
Illkirch-Graffenstaden 58 48.32 N 7.43 E
Illminster 42 50.56 N 2.55 W
Illo 150 11.33 N 3.42 E
Illovo, S. Afr. 158 30.05 S 30.50 E
Illovo, S. Afr. 273d 26.08 S 28.03 E
Illzach 58 47.47 N 7.20 E
Ilm ≃, Dtsch. 54 51.07 N 11.40 E
Ilm ≃, Dtsch. 60 48.49 N 11.45 E
Ilmajoki 26 62.44 N 22.34 E
Il'men', ozero ⊜ 76 58.17 N 31.20 E
Ilmenau 54 50.41 N 10.55 E
Ilmenau ≃ 54 53.23 N 10.10 E
Il'menskij zapovednik ◆ 86 55.16 N 60.17 E
Il'mino 80 53.47 N 45.40 E
Ilo 248 17.38 S 71.20 W
Ilobasco 236 13.51 N 88.51 W
Ilobu 150 7.51 N 4.30 E
Iloc Island I 116 11.18 N 119.41 E
Ilocos Norte □4 116 18.10 N 120.45 E
Ilocos Sur □4 116 17.05 N 120.35 E
Iloilo 116 10.42 N 122.34 E
Iloilo □4 116 11.00 N 122.35 E
Iloilo Strait ⊻ 116 10.43 N 122.36 E
Ilomantsi 26 62.40 N 30.55 E
Ilondola Mission 154 10.42 S 31.47 E
Ilongero 154 4.40 S 34.52 E
Ilop 164 2.54 S 141.13 E
Ilopango, Lago de ⊜ 236 13.40 N 89.03 W
Ilora 150 7.45 N 3.50 E
Ilorin 150 8.30 N 4.32 E
Ilovajsk 83 47.56 N 38.13 E
Ilovatka 80 50.31 N 45.55 E
Ilovka 78 50.43 N 38.38 E
Ilovl'a 80 49.18 N 43.59 E
Ilovl'a ≃ 80 49.14 N 43.54 E
Ilowa 30 51.30 N 15.12 E
Il Palone ∧ 64 46.02 N 11.04 E
Il'pyrskij 74 59.56 N 164.10 E
Ilsan-ni 271b 37.41 N 126.46 E
Ilse ≃ 54 52.06 N 10.35 E
Ilshofen 56 49.10 N 9.55 E
Il'skij 78 44.51 N 38.35 E
Ilskov 41 56.14 N 9.06 E
Il Telegrafo ∧ 66 42.22 N 11.10 E
Ilten 52 52.21 N 9.55 E
Ilu 152 4.12 N 23.02 E
Ilubabor □4 144 7.50 N 35.00 E
Iluhār 126 22.48 N 90.06 E
Ilūkste 76 55.58 N 26.18 E
Ilverich 263 51.17 N 6.42 E
Ilwaco 224 46.19 N 124.03 W
Ilwaki 112 7.56 S 126.26 E
Ilwŏl-san ∧ 98 36.50 N 129.06 E
Ilyasbey 130 40.13 N 29.52 E
Ilz 61 47.05 N 15.55 E
Ilz ≃ 60 48.35 N 13.29 E
Iłża 30 51.11 N 21.14 E
Ima 88 55.13 N 115.55 E
Ima ≃ 96 33.45 N 131.01 E
Imabari 96 34.03 N 133.00 E
Imabu ≃ 250 0.44 S 57.22 W
Imadomi 268 35.28 N 140.06 E
Imaichi 94 36.43 N 139.41 E
Imajō 94 35.46 N 136.12 E
Imajuku 268 35.58 N 139.21 E
Imajuku ◆8 268 35.29 N 139.32 E
Imaki 270 34.24 N 135.46 E
Imaloto ≃ 157b 23.27 S 45.13 E
Imambara ◆1 272b 22.54 N 88.25 E
Imanbaj I 86 43.13 N 60.25 E
Imandan-Makit, gora ∧, Ross. 88 54.15 N 117.38 E
Imandan-Makit, gora ∧, Ross. 89 54.06 N 117.50 E
Imandra, ozero ⊜ 24 67.30 N 33.00 E
Imanombo 157b 24.26 S 45.49 E
Imantau 86 52.58 N 68.22 E
Imari 92 33.16 N 129.53 E
Imarui 252 28.21 S 48.49 W
Imaruí, Lagoa do ⊂ 252 28.21 S 48.52 W
Imasa 140 18.01 N 36.12 E
Imatra 26 61.10 N 28.46 E
Imavere 76 58.44 N 25.48 E
Imazu 94 35.24 N 136.02 E
Imbābah ◆8 142 30.04 N 31.13 E
Imbabura □4 246 0.22 N 78.25 W
Imba-numa ⊜ 94 35.45 N 140.12 E
Imbariê 256 22.39 S 43.13 W
Imbituba 252 28.14 S 48.40 W
Imbituva 252 25.12 S 50.35 W
Imboaçu, Canal ≡ 287a 22.48 S 43.04 W
Imboden 194 36.12 N 91.10 W
Imbonga 152 0.43 S 19.46 E
Imbundi 152 5.44 S 16.16 E
Ime, Beinn ∧ 46 56.14 N 4.49 W
Imeni Abaja 86 50.44 N 69.30 E
Imeni Babuškina 76 59.45 N 43.07 E
Imeni Bakinskich Komissarov 84 39.19 N 49.12 E
Imeni Čapajeva 85 43.28 N 76.50 E
Imeni C'urupy 82 55.30 N 38.39 E
Imeni Džambula, Kaz. 86 45.26 N 74.24 E
Imeni Džambula, Kaz. 86 47.43 N 74.09 E
Imeni Frunze 86 46.23 N 77.20 E
Imeni Il-Go Okt'abr'a 88 55.54 N 119.36 E
Imeni Kalinina, Kaz. 85 43.16 N 74.03 E
Imeni Kalinina, Kyrg. 85 41.28 N 76.22 E
Imeni Kalinina, Ross. 80 51.51 N 52.43 E
Imeni Kalinina, Uzb. 86 43.40 N 59.07 E
Imeni Karla Libknechta 78 51.37 N 35.27 E
Imeni Kirova, Kaz. 86 46.27 N 77.13 E
Imeni Kirova, Ross. 74 59.42 N 128.12 E
Imeni Leninskogo Komsomola 86 50.45 N 66.44 E
Imeni Marta 86 46.57 N 58.58 E
Imeni Michajla Ivanoviča Kalinina 80 57.59 N 45.07 E
Imeni Molodogvardejcev 86 54.03 N 70.44 E
Imeni Panfilova 85 43.23 N 77.07 E
Imeni Poliny Osipenko 89 52.25 N 136.28 E
Imeni Sardarova Karachana 85 38.26 N 68.46 E
Imeni Šeredy 83 46.52 N 40.03 E
Imeni Ševčenko 80 45.58 N 61.04 E
Imeni Stepana Razina 80 54.54 N 44.18 E
Imeni Tel'mana 89 48.36 N 134.59 E
Imeni Timir'azeva 86 53.39 N 65.31 E
Imeni Vladimira Iljiča Lenina 80 53.36 N 46.58 E
Imeni Vorovskogo, Ross. 80 55.43 N 41.06 E
Imeni Vorovskogo, Ross. 82 55.43 N 38.20 E
Imeni XXI Partsjezda 86 50.43 N 67.50 E
Imeni Žel'abova 76 58.57 N 36.36 E
Imera ⊥ 70 37.59 N 13.49 E
Imerimandroso 157b 17.23 S 48.38 E
Imese 152 2.07 N 18.06 E
Imgenbroich 56 50.34 N 6.16 E
Imi 144 6.28 N 42.18 E
Imias 240p 20.04 N 74.38 W
Imilac 252 24.14 S 68.53 W
Imilili ▽4 148 23.18 N 15.54 W
Imi-n'Tanout 148 31.10 N 8.51 W
Imishli 84 39.52 N 48.04 E
Imittós 267c 37.57 N 23.45 E
Imittós Óros ∧ 267c 37.55 N 23.47 E
Imja-do I 98 35.05 N 126.05 E
Imjin-gang ≃ 98 37.47 N 126.40 E
Imlay 204 40.39 N 118.08 W
Imlay City 190 43.01 N 83.04 W
Imlaystown 208 40.10 N 74.31 W
Imler 214 40.12 N 78.31 W
Immarna 162 30.30 S 132.09 E
Immendingen 58 47.56 N 8.44 E
Immenhausen 56 51.25 N 9.28 E
Immensen 52 52.23 N 10.04 E
Immenstaad 58 47.40 N 9.22 E
Immenstadt 58 47.33 N 10.13 E
Immigrath 263 51.06 N 6.57 E
Immingham 44 53.36 N 0.13 W
Immokalee 220 26.25 N 81.25 W
Imnaha ≃ 202 45.49 N 116.46 W
Imo □3 150 5.30 N 7.25 E
Imo ≃ 150 4.36 N 7.35 E
Imogiri 115a 7.55 S 110.23 E
Imokt'an 98 38.50 N 126.41 E
Imola 66 44.21 N 11.42 E
Imonda 164 3.20 S 141.10 E
Imore 273a 6.26 N 3.17 E
Imoro 273a 6.43 N 3.30 E
Im Ostholz ◆8 263 51.26 N 7.12 E
Imotski 36 43.27 N 17.13 E
Imp'a 98 35.59 N 126.49 E
Impasugong 116 8.19 N 125.00 E
Impe 152 2.44 S 15.17 E
Impendle 158 29.37 S 29.55 E
Imperatore, Campo ≡ 66 42.25 N 13.40 E
Imperatriz 250 5.32 S 47.29 W
Imperia 62 43.53 N 8.03 E
Imperia □4 62 43.58 N 7.47 E
Imperial, Sk., Can. 184 51.22 N 105.27 W
Imperial, Perú 248 13.04 S 76.21 W
Imperial, Ca., U.S. 204 32.50 N 115.34 W
Imperial, Mo., U.S. 219 38.22 N 90.22 W
Imperial, Ne., U.S. 198 40.31 N 101.38 W
Imperial, Pa., U.S. 214 40.26 N 80.14 W
Imperial, Tx., U.S. 196 31.16 N 102.41 W
Imperial ≃ 254 38.48 S 73.24 W
Imperial Beach 228 32.35 N 117.06 W
Imperial Dam ◆6 204 32.55 N 114.30 W
Imperial de Aragón, Canal ≡ 34 42.02 N 1.33 W
Imperiale 68 40.07 N 16.35 E
Imperial Mills 182 55.00 N 111.44 W
Imperial Palace ◆ 268 35.41 N 139.45 E
Imperial Valley V 204 32.50 N 115.30 W
Impflingen 56 49.10 N 8.07 E
Impfondo 152 1.37 N 18.04 E
Imphāl 120 24.49 N 93.57 E
Impilachti 24 61.40 N 31.04 E
Impruneta 66 43.41 N 11.15 E
Impulo 152 13.53 S 13.39 E
Imralı Adası I 130 40.32 N 28.32 E
Imranlı 130 39.54 N 38.07 E
Imroz 130 40.11 N 25.55 E
Imsil 98 35.37 N 127.15 E
Imst 58 47.14 N 10.44 E
Imtān 132 32.24 N 36.49 E
Imuris 232 30.47 N 110.52 W
Imuruan Bay ⊂ 116 10.40 N 119.16 E
Imuruk Basin ⊜ 180 65.06 N 165.36 W
Imuruk Lake ⊜ 180 65.36 N 163.10 W
Imute 273a 6.42 N 3.29 E
Imwŏn-ni 98 37.15 N 129.20 E
Ina, Nihon 94 37.10 N 139.32 E
Ina, Nihon 94 35.59 N 140.03 E
Ina, Nihon 94 35.50 N 137.57 E
Ina, Nihon 268 35.59 N 139.38 E
In'a, Ross. 74 59.24 N 144.48 E
In'a, Ross. 86 53.31 N 82.40 E
In'a, Ross. 86 50.48 N 86.37 E
Ina, Il., U.S. 194 38.09 N 88.54 W
Ina ≃, Nihon 94 37.16 N 139.33 E
Ina ≃, Nihon 96 34.43 N 135.28 E
Ina ≃, Pol. 54 53.32 N 14.38 E
In'a ≃, Ross. 74 59.23 N 144.54 E
In'a ≃, Ross. 86 54.59 N 82.59 E
Inaba 270 34.26 N 135.27 E
Inabe 94 35.07 N 136.33 E
Ina-bonchi ≡1 94 35.45 N 137.57 E
Inabu 94 35.13 N 137.30 E
Inaccessible Island I 10 37.17 S 12.45 W
Inada 270 34.54 N 135.08 E
Inagawa 96 34.53 N 135.22 E
Inagawan 116 9.33 N 118.39 E
Inage 268 35.38 N 140.05 E
Inagi 94 35.38 N 139.30 E
Inajá 250 8.54 S 37.49 W
Inajá ≃ 250 8.53 S 49.44 W
In'akino 94 54.26 N 41.07 E
Inakona 175e 9.49 S 160.02 E
Inala 171a 27.35 S 152.58 E
Inamangando ≃ 152 14.03 S 12.23 E
Inambari ≃ 248 12.41 S 69.44 W
In Amguel 148 23.40 N 5.10 E
Inami, Nihon 94 36.33 N 136.58 E
Inami, Nihon 96 34.45 N 134.54 E
Inami, Nihon 96 33.48 N 135.13 E
In Amnas 148 28.05 N 9.30 E
Inampulugan Island I 116 10.28 N 122.42 E
Inamuragasaki Point ⊥ 268 35.18 N 139.32 E
Inanda 273d 26.07 S 28.03 E
Inangahua Junction 172 41.51 S 171.57 E
Inanwatan 164 2.08 S 132.10 E
Iñapari 248 10.57 S 69.35 W
Inaporok 164 8.15 S 141.55 E
In'aptuk, gora ∧ 88 56.22 N 110.11 E
Inari 24 68.54 N 27.01 E
Inarigda 74 63.14 N 107.27 E
Inarijärvi ⊜ 24 69.00 N 28.00 E
Inas, Gunong ∧ 114 5.15 N 100.56 E
Inasa 94 34.50 N 137.40 E
Inatsuki 96 33.36 N 130.43 E
Inauini ≃ 248 8.30 S 67.24 W
Inawaia 164 8.40 S 146.35 E
Inawashiro-ko ⊜ 92 37.29 N 140.06 E
I-n-Azaoua ▽4 148 20.49 N 7.30 E
Inazawa 94 35.15 N 136.47 E
Inba 94 35.46 N 140.14 E
Inba-numa ⊜ 94 35.46 N 140.12 E
In Belbel 148 27.54 N 1.10 E
Inca 34 39.43 N 2.54 E
Inca de Oro 252 26.45 S 69.54 W
Incaguasi 252 29.13 S 71.03 W
Incahuasi, Nevado de ∧ 252 27.02 S 68.18 W
Ince 262 53.17 N 2.49 W
Ince Blundell 262 53.31 N 3.02 W
İnce Burun ⟩ 130 42.06 N 34.56 E
Ince-in-Makerfield 262 53.32 N 2.37 W
İncekum Burnu ⟩ 130 36.13 N 33.58 E
Incesu 130 38.38 N 35.11 E
Inch 48 52.08 N 9.59 W
I-n-Chaouâg ≃ 150 16.23 N 0.10 E
Inchard, Loch ⊂ 46 58.27 N 5.04 W
Inchas Military Base ■ 142 30.20 N 31.27 E
Inchbare 46 56.47 N 2.38 W
Inchcape I2 46 56.26 N 2.23 W
Inchelium 182 48.17 N 118.11 W
Inchiri □4 150 19.50 N 15.00 W
Inchmarnock I 46 55.47 N 5.09 W
Inchnadamph 46 58.09 N 4.59 W
Inch'ŏn 98 37.28 N 126.38 E
Inch'ŏn □4 98 37.28 N 126.38 E
Inchture 46 56.26 N 3.10 W
Inchwagh Lake ⊜ 281 42.27 N 83.41 W
İncirliova 130 37.50 N 27.43 E
Incisa in Val d'Arno 66 43.40 N 11.27 E
Incline Village 226 39.16 N 119.56 W
Incomáti (Komati) ≃ 156 25.46 S 32.43 E
Inconfidência 256 21.16 S 43.13 W
Inconfidentes 256 22.20 S 46.20 W
Inčoun 180 66.18 N 170.17 W
Incudine 64 46.14 N 10.22 E
Incudine, Monte ∧ 36 41.51 N 9.12 E
Incy 24 65.48 N 40.26 E
Indaal, Loch ⊂ 46 55.45 N 6.21 W
Indaiá ≃ 255 18.51 S 45.20 W
Indaiatuba 256 23.05 S 47.14 W
Indalsälven ≃ 26 62.31 N 17.27 E
Indanan 116 5.58 N 120.59 E
Indaparapeo 234 19.47 N 100.58 W
Inda Silase 144 14.05 N 38.20 E
Indaw 120 23.40 N 94.46 E
Indawgyi Lake ⊜ 110 25.10 N 96.19 E
Indé 232 25.54 N 105.13 W
Inde ≃ 56 50.54 N 6.21 E
Inde — India □1 118 20.00 N 77.00 E
Indemini 58 46.06 N 8.50 E
Independence, Ca., U.S. 204 36.48 N 118.11 W
Independence, In., U.S. 216 40.20 N 87.10 W
Independence, Ia., U.S. 190 42.28 N 91.53 W
Independence, Ks., U.S. 198 37.13 N 95.42 W
Independence, Ky., U.S. 218 38.56 N 84.32 W
Independence, La., U.S. 194 30.38 N 90.30 W
Independence, Mo., U.S. 194 39.05 N 94.24 W
Independence, Oh., U.S. 279a 41.23 N 81.38 W
Independence, Or., U.S. 202 44.51 N 123.11 W
Independence, Pa., U.S. 214 40.15 N 80.31 W
Independence, Tx., U.S. 222 30.19 N 96.21 W
Independence, Va., U.S. 192 36.37 N 81.09 W
Independence, Wi., U.S. 190 44.21 N 91.25 W
Independence ≃ 188 43.45 N 75.20 W
Independence Creek ≃ 196 30.27 N 101.44 W
Independence Hall ⊥ 285 39.57 N 75.09 W
Independence Lake ⊜1 226 39.26 N 120.18 W
Independence Mountains ∧ 204 41.15 N 115.55 W
Independencia, Bol. 248 17.05 S 66.53 W
Independência, Bra. 250 5.23 S 40.19 W
Independencia, Chile 286e 33.23 S 70.40 W
Independencia, Perú 286d 11.59 S 77.02 W
Independencia, Isla I 248 14.15 S 76.12 W
Independența 38 43.58 N 28.05 E
Inder, ozero ⊜ 80 48.27 N 51.54 E
Inderborskij 80 48.33 N 51.44 E
In der Bredde 263 51.20 N 7.23 E
Inderesi 130 37.50 N 35.42 E
Index 224 47.49 N 121.33 W
Index, Mount ∧ 224 47.46 N 121.35 W
Indi 122 17.10 N 75.58 E
India (Bhārat) □1 118 20.00 N 77.00 E
India Brook ≃ 276 40.47 N 74.37 W
India Gate ⊥ 272a 28.37 N 77.18 E
Indialantic 220 28.05 N 80.34 W
Indian ≃, On., Can. 212 45.16 N 76.14 W
Indian ≃, On., Can. 212 44.13 N 78.08 W
Indian ≃, De., U.S. 208 38.36 N 75.10 W
Indian ≃, Ma., U.S. 283 42.47 N 70.58 W
Indian ≃, Mi., U.S. 190 45.59 N 86.15 W
Indian ≃, N.Y., U.S. 212 44.24 N 75.39 W
Indiana 214 40.37 N 79.09 W
Indiana □6 214 40.37 N 79.09 W
Indiana □3, U.S. 178 40.00 N 86.15 W
Indiana □3, U.S. 194 40.00 N 86.15 W
Indiana Dunes National Lakeshore ◆ 216 41.40 N 87.00 W
Indiana Dunes State Park ◆ 216 41.40 N 87.02 W
Indian Agricultural Research Institute ◆3 272a 28.38 N 77.10 E
Indiana Harbor ⊂ 278 41.40 N 87.27 W
Indiana Harbor Canal ≡ 278 41.40 N 87.27 W
Indianapolis 218 39.46 N 86.09 W
Indianapolis International Airport ⊠ 218 39.43 N 86.16 W
Indianapolis Motor Speedway ◆ 218 39.48 N 86.14 W
Indian Bayou ≃ 194 34.14 N 91.52 W
Indian Brook 186 46.23 N 60.32 W
Indian Caverns ⊥5 214 40.38 N 78.05 W
Indian Church 232 17.45 N 88.40 W
Indian Creek 278 42.14 N 87.59 W
Indian Creek ≃, U.S. 218 39.19 N 84.38 W
Indian Creek ≃, Ca., U.S. 228 35.18 N 118.26 W
Indian Creek ≃, Il., U.S. 216 41.26 N 88.46 W
Indian Creek ≃, Il., U.S. 219 39.56 N 90.32 W
Indian Creek ≃, Il., U.S. 278 42.11 N 87.55 W
Indian Creek ≃, In., U.S. 216 40.55 N 86.42 W
Indian Creek ≃, In., U.S. 218 38.43 N 85.06 W
Indian Creek ≃, In., U.S. 218 38.10 N 86.14 W
Indian Creek ≃, In., U.S. 218 39.23 N 86.29 W
Indian Creek ≃, Md., U.S. 284c 38.59 N 76.55 W
Indian Creek ≃, Mo., U.S. 194 36.33 N 94.29 W
Indian Creek ≃, Mo., U.S. 219 39.10 N 91.11 W
Indian Creek ≃, N.M., U.S. 200 36.11 N 108.23 W
Indian Creek ≃, N.Y., U.S. 276 40.43 N 73.06 W
Indian Creek ≃, Oh., U.S. 218 39.19 N 84.38 W
Indian Creek ≃, Oh., U.S. 279a 41.17 N 81.31 W
Indian Creek ≃, S.D., U.S. 198 44.39 N 103.19 W
Indian Creek ≃, Tn., U.S. 194 35.13 N 88.08 W
Indian Creek Lake ⊜1 222 31.44 N 95.58 W
Indianford 216 42.49 N 88.35 W
Indian Grave Mountain ∧2 192 32.59 N 84.21 W
Indian Harbor Beach 220 28.08 N 80.35 W
Indian Head, Sk., Can. 184 50.32 N 103.40 W
Indian Head, Md., U.S. 208 38.36 N 77.09 W
Indian Head ⟩ 283 42.04 N 70.52 W
Indian Head Park 278 41.47 N 87.54 W
Indian Head Pond ⊜ 283 42.03 N 70.51 W
Indian Heights 216 40.25 N 86.07 W
Indian Island I 224 48.04 N 122.43 W
Indian Kentuck Creek ≃ 218 38.43 N 85.16 W
Indian Lake, Mi., U.S. 216 41.59 N 86.12 W
Indian Lake, N.Y., U.S. 188 43.46 N 74.16 W
Indian Lake ⊜, On., Can. 190 47.08 N 82.08 W
Indian Lake ⊜, Mi., U.S. 190 45.59 N 86.20 W
Indian Lake ⊜, Mi., U.S. 216 42.09 N 85.29 W
Indian Lake ⊜, Mi., U.S. 216 42.00 N 86.13 W
Indian Lake ⊜, N.J., U.S. 276 40.53 N 74.29 W
Indian Lake ⊜, Oh., U.S. 216 40.29 N 83.53 W
Indian Lake Estates 220 27.48 N 81.19 W
Indian Lakes ⊜ 216 41.33 N 85.25 W
Indian Lake State Park ◆ 216 40.29 N 83.52 W
Indian Mills Brook ≃ 285 39.47 N 74.44 W
Indian Mills Lake ⊜ 285 39.48 N 74.44 W
Indian Neck 283 41.15 N 72.48 W
Indian Ocean ▽1 6 10.00 S 70.00 E
Indian Ocean ▽1 6 10.00 S 70.00 E
Indianola, Ia., U.S. 190 41.21 N 93.33 W
Indianola, Ms., U.S. 194 33.27 N 90.39 W
Indianola, Ne., U.S. 198 40.14 N 100.25 W
Indianola, Pa., U.S. 279b 40.34 N 79.51 W
Indianola, Wa., U.S. 224 47.45 N 122.31 W
Indianópolis 255 19.02 S 47.55 W
Indianópolis ◆8 287b 23.36 S 46.38 W
Indian Peak ∧, Ut., U.S. 200 38.16 N 113.53 W
Indian Peak ∧, Wy., U.S. 202 44.47 N 109.51 W
Indian Point ⟩ 212 44.37 N 78.49 W
Indian Prairie Canal ≡ 220 27.02 N 80.57 W

ENGLISH Name	Page	Lat.°′	Long.°′

Indian Queen Estates 284c 38.46 N 77.02 W
Indian River 190 45.24 N 84.36 W
Indian River □6 220 27.43 N 80.36 W
Indian River ⊂ 220 28.00 N 80.30 W
Indian River Bay ⊂ 208 38.36 N 75.05 W
Indian River Inlet ⊂ 208 38.37 N 75.03 W
Indian Rock ∧ 224 45.59 N 120.49 W
Indian Rock Dam ◆6 208 39.57 N 76.45 W
Indian Rock Paintings ⊥ 224 46.38 N 120.31 W
Indian Rocks Beach 220 27.52 N 82.51 W
Indian Springs, Nv., U.S. 204 36.34 N 115.40 W
Indian Springs, Va., U.S. 284c 38.49 N 77.10 W
Indian Stream ≃ 206 45.03 N 71.26 W
Indiantown 220 27.01 N 80.29 W
Indian Town Point ⟩ 240c 17.06 N 61.40 W
Indian Valley Reservoir ⊜1 226 39.07 N 122.32 W
Indian Village, In., U.S. 218 40.10 N 85.22 W
Indian Village, N.Y., U.S. 210 42.57 N 76.10 W
Indiaporã 255 19.57 S 50.17 W
Indiaroba 250 11.32 S 37.31 W
Indibir 144 8.05 N 37.58 E
Indico, Océano — Indian Ocean ▽1 6 10.00 S 70.00 E
Indien, Océan — Indian Ocean ▽1 6 10.00 S 70.00 E
Indien, territoires britanniques de l'Ocean — British Indian Ocean Territory □2 12 7.00 S 72.00 E
Indien — India □1 118 20.00 N 77.00 E
Indiera Alta 240m 18.09 N 66.53 W
Indiga 24 67.41 N 49.00 E
Indigirka ≃ 74 70.48 N 148.54 E
Indija 38 45.03 N 20.05 E
Indin 120 20.16 N 92.57 E
Indio 204 33.43 N 116.12 W
Indio ≃, Nic. 236 10.57 N 83.44 W
Indio ≃, Pan. 236 9.12 N 80.11 W
Indio, Punta ⟩ 258 35.16 S 57.13 W
Indios, Canal de los ⊻ 240p 21.56 N 83.16 W
Indira Gandhi Canal ≡ 120 31.10 N 75.00 E
Indira Gandhi International Airport ⊠ 272a 28.35 N 77.07 E
Indischer Ozean — Indian Ocean ▽1 6 10.00 S 70.00 E
Indispensable Reefs ◆2 160 12.40 S 160.25 E
Indispensable Strait ⊻ 175e 9.00 S 160.30 E
Indochina ◆1 12 16.00 N 107.00 E
Indo — Indus ≃ 120 24.20 N 67.47 E
Indom 24 64.36 N 55.22 E
Indonesia □1 108 5.00 S 120.00 E
Indonesia, University of ◆2 269e 6.12 S 106.51 E
Indonesia in Miniature ◆ 269e 6.08 S 106.49 E
Indonesian Culture, Museum of ◆3 269e 6.09 S 106.49 E
Indonésie — Indonesia □1 108 5.00 S 120.00 E
Indonesien — Indonesia □1 108 5.00 S 120.00 E
Indooroopilly 171a 27.30 S 152.58 E
Indore 120 22.43 N 75.50 E
Indpur 126 23.10 N 86.56 E
Indragiri ≃ 112 0.22 S 103.26 E
Indramayu 115a 6.20 S 108.19 E
Indramayu, Ujung ⟩ 115a 6.14 S 108.17 E
Indrapuri 114 5.26 N 95.27 E
Indrāvati ≃ 122 18.44 N 80.16 E
Indre □5 32 46.45 N 1.30 E
Indre ≃ 32 47.16 N 0.19 E
Indre-et-Loire □5 32 47.15 N 0.45 E
Indrois ≃ 50 47.13 N 0.56 E
Indungo 152 14.48 S 16.17 E
Induno Olona 62 45.52 N 8.51 E
Indura 76 53.27 N 23.53 E
Indur — Indore 120 22.43 N 75.50 E
Indus ≃ 120 24.20 N 67.47 E
Industry, Il., U.S. 194 40.20 N 90.36 W
Industry, Pa., U.S. 214 40.39 N 80.25 W
Industry, Tx., U.S. 222 29.58 N 96.30 W
Indwe 158 31.27 S 27.23 E
Indwe ≃ 158 32.01 S 27.21 E
Ine 96 35.39 N 135.17 E
İnebolu 130 41.58 N 33.46 E
İnece 130 41.41 N 27.04 E
İnecik 130 40.56 N 27.16 E
In Ecker 148 24.09 N 5.03 E
İnegöl 130 40.05 N 29.31 E
Inerie, Gunung ∧ 115b 8.52 S 120.56 E
Inés, Monte ∧ 254 48.29 S 69.40 W
Ineu 38 46.26 N 21.49 E
Inez, Ky., U.S. 192 37.51 N 82.32 W
Inez, Tx., U.S. 222 28.54 N 96.47 W
Inez, Lake ⊜ 276 41.01 N 74.17 W
Infanta, Pil. 116 15.50 N 119.55 E
Infanta, Pil. 116 14.45 N 121.39 E
Infante, Kaap ⟩ 158 34.29 S 20.51 E
Inferior, Laguna ⊂ 234 16.20 N 94.40 W
Inferno, Cachoeira do ⌞ 250 1.00 S 56.04 W
Infiernillo, Presa del ⊜1 234 18.35 N 101.45 W
Infiesto 34 43.21 N 5.22 W
Infreschi, Ponta degli ⟩ 68 39.59 N 15.25 E
Ing ≃ 110 20.13 N 100.27 E
Ingá 250 7.17 S 35.36 W
Ingabu 110 17.49 N 95.16 E
Ingaí 256 21.24 S 44.55 W
Ingaí ≃ 256 21.23 S 44.52 W
Ingal 150 16.47 N 6.56 E
Ingalls 218 39.57 N 85.48 W
Ingalls Creek ≃ 224 47.28 N 120.39 W
Ingalls Park 278 41.31 N 88.02 W
Inganda 152 0.05 S 20.57 E
Inganno ≃ 70 38.04 N 14.37 E
Ingarö I 40 59.16 N 18.28 E
Ingatestone 42 51.41 N 0.22 E
Ingatestone Hall ⊥ 260 51.39 N 0.23 E
Ingelfingen 56 49.18 N 9.39 E
Ingelheim 56 49.58 N 8.03 E
Ingelmunster 50 50.55 N 3.15 E
Ingelstad 26 56.45 N 14.55 E
Ingende 152 0.15 S 18.57 E
Ingeniería, Universidad Nacional de ◆2 286d 12.02 S 77.02 W
Ingeniero Budge ◆8 288 34.43 S 58.28 W
Ingeniero Jacobacci 254 41.18 S 69.35 W
Ingeniero Juan Allan 258 34.53 S 58.11 W
Ingeniero Luiggi 252 35.25 S 64.29 W
Ingeniero Luis A. Huergo 252 39.05 S 67.14 W
Ingeniero Maschwitz 258 34.23 S 58.44 W
Ingeniero Romulo Otamendi 258 34.13 S 58.54 W
Ingeniero White 258 38.47 S 62.16 W
Ingeniero Williams 258 34.54 S 59.22 W
Ingenio La Esperanza 252 24.13 S 64.51 W
Ingenio Santa Ana 252 27.28 S 65.41 W
Ingeringbach ≃ 61 47.12 N 14.49 E
Ingersheim 58 48.06 N 7.18 E
Ingersoll 212 43.02 N 80.53 W

DEUTSCH Name	Seite	Breite°′	Länge°′ E = Ost

Ingham 166 18.39 S 146.10 E
Ingham □6 216 42.37 N 84.22 W
Ingička 85 39.52 N 67.20 E
Ingleborough ∧ 44 54.11 N 2.23 W
Ingleburn 170 34.00 S 150.52 E
Inglesa, Costa — English Coast ⊥2 9 73.45 S 73.00 W
Ingleside, Austl. 274a 33.41 S 151.13 E
Ingleside, On., Can. 206 45.00 N 75.00 W
Ingleside, Il., U.S. 216 42.23 N 88.09 W
Ingleside, Tx., U.S. 196 27.52 N 97.12 W
Ingleside ◆8 282 37.43 N 122.28 W
Ingleton 44 54.10 N 2.27 W
Inglewood, Austl. 166 28.25 S 151.05 E
Inglewood, Austl. 166 36.34 S 143.52 E
Inglewood, On., Can. 212 43.47 N 79.56 W
Inglewood, N.Z. 172 39.09 S 174.12 E
Inglewood, Ca., U.S. 228 33.57 N 118.21 W
Inglewood, Wa., U.S. 224 47.44 N 122.15 W
Inglewood Forest ◆3 44 54.45 N 2.50 W
Inglis, Mb., Can. 184 50.57 N 101.15 W
Inglis, Fl., U.S. 220 29.02 N 82.40 W
Inglis Lock ◆5 220 29.02 N 82.37 W
Ingoda ≃ 88 51.42 N 115.48 E
Ingogo 158 27.32 S 29.56 E
Ingoldmells 44 53.11 N 0.20 E
Ingolstadt 60 48.46 N 11.27 E
Ingomar 279b 40.35 N 80.05 W
Ingonish 186 46.42 N 60.22 W
Ingornachoix Bay ⊂ 186 50.38 N 57.20 W
Ingraham, Lake ⊜ 220 25.09 N 81.08 W
Ingrāj Bāzār 124 25.00 N 88.09 E
Ingram, Pa., U.S. 279b 40.26 N 80.04 W
Ingram, Tx., U.S. 196 30.04 N 99.14 W
Ingram Bay ⊂ 208 37.48 N 76.17 W
Ingrave 260 51.36 N 0.21 E
Ingrid Christensen Coast ⊥2 9 69.30 S 76.00 E
In Guezzam 150 19.32 N 5.42 E
Ingul ≃ 78 47.00 N 31.59 E
Ingulec 78 47.43 N 33.14 E
Ingulec ≃ 78 46.41 N 32.48 E
Ingulo-Kamenka 78 48.17 N 32.30 E
Inguri ≃ 84 42.24 N 41.33 E
Inguzet 86 58.50 N 83.52 E
Ingvallsbenning 40 60.15 N 15.53 E
Ingwavuma 158 27.09 S 32.00 E
Ingwe 154 13.02 S 26.25 E
Ingwiller 56 48.52 N 7.29 E
Inhaca, Ilha da I 158 26.03 S 32.57 E
Inhafenga 156 20.35 S 33.53 E
Inhambane 156 23.51 S 35.29 E
Inhambane □5 156 23.00 S 34.30 E
Inhambane, Baía de ⊂ 156 23.58 S 35.51 E
Inhambupe 255 11.47 S 38.21 W
Inhaminga 156 18.24 S 35.00 E
Inhanduí ≃ 255 21.37 S 52.59 W
Inhapim 255 19.33 S 42.07 W
Inharrime 156 24.29 S 35.01 E
Inharrime ≃ 156 24.29 S 35.01 E
Inhassoro 156 21.33 S 35.11 E
Inhaúma 255 19.29 S 44.22 W
Inhaúma ◆8 287a 22.52 S 43.17 W
Inhisar 130 40.03 N 30.23 E
Inhoaíba ◆8 256 22.54 S 43.36 W
Inhomirim 256 22.35 S 43.10 W
Inhomirim ≃ 287a 22.41 S 43.13 W
Inhuma 250 6.40 S 41.42 W
Inhumas 255 16.22 S 49.30 W
Ini ≃ 146 9.30 N 12.20 E
Iniesta 34 39.26 N 1.45 W
Inimutaba 255 18.45 S 44.22 W
Ining — Yining 86 43.54 N 81.21 E
Inirida ≃ 246 3.55 N 67.52 W
Inisa 150 7.52 N 4.20 E
Inishbofin I, Ire. 48 55.09 N 8.11 W
Inishbofin I, Ire. 48 53.37 N 10.15 W
Inishcrone 48 54.12 N 9.06 W
Inisheer I 48 53.02 N 9.26 W
Inishkea North I 48 54.08 N 10.12 W
Inishkea South I 48 54.07 N 10.13 W
Inishmaan I 48 53.05 N 9.32 W
Inishmore I 48 53.07 N 9.45 W
Inishmurray I 48 54.26 N 8.40 W
Inishowen ⟩1 48 55.12 N 7.20 W
Inishowen Head ⟩ 48 55.14 N 6.56 W
Inishshark I 48 53.37 N 10.18 W
Inishtrahull I 48 55.26 N 7.14 W
Inishturk I 48 53.43 N 10.08 W
Inistioge 48 52.29 N 7.04 W
Initao 116 8.30 N 124.18 E
Inje 98 38.05 N 128.09 E
Injibara 144 11.00 N 36.59 E
Injune 166 25.51 S 148.34 E
Inkeroinen 26 60.42 N 26.51 E
Inketete 152 2.37 S 21.53 E
Inkisi (Zadi) ≃ 152 4.46 S 14.52 E
Inkom 202 42.47 N 112.15 W
Inkster, Mi., U.S. 216 42.17 N 83.18 W
Inkster, N.D., U.S. 198 48.09 N 97.38 W
Inland Kaikoura Range ∧ 172 42.00 S 173.40 E
Inland Lake ⊜, Mb., Can. 184 52.17 N 99.42 W
Inland Lake ⊜, Ak., U.S. 180 66.20 N 159.47 W
Inland Sea — Seto-naikai ▽2 96 34.20 N 133.30 E
Inle Lake ⊜ 110 20.30 N 96.55 E
Inman, Ks., U.S. 198 38.13 N 97.46 W
Inman, S.C., U.S. 192 35.02 N 82.05 W
Inman Mills 192 35.02 N 82.06 W
Inman Valley 168b 35.30 S 138.28 E
Inn (En) ≃ 32 48.35 N 13.28 E
Innamincka 166 27.45 S 140.44 E
Innbach ≃ 61 48.18 N 14.07 E
Innellan 46 55.54 N 4.57 W
Inner Bay ⊂ 214 42.37 N 80.24 W
Innerbraz 58 47.09 N 9.55 E
Inner Channel ⊻ 232 16.35 N 88.17 W
Innerferrera 58 46.31 N 9.28 E
Innerfragant 64 46.59 N 13.02 E
Inner Harbor ⊂ 276 40.52 N 73.28 W
Inner Hebrides II 46 56.30 N 6.00 W
Innerkip 212 43.13 N 80.42 W
Innerleithen 46 55.38 N 3.05 W
Inner Mongolia — Nei Monggol Zizhiqu □4 90 43.00 N 115.00 E
Inner Sister Island I 166 39.42 S 147.55 E
Inner Sound ⊻ 46 57.25 N 5.56 W
Innerste ≃ 52 52.15 N 9.50 E
Innerstetalsperre ◆6 52 51.55 N 10.17 E
Innerthal 58 47.06 N 8.56 E
Innertkirchen 58 46.42 N 8.14 E
Innervillgraten 64 46.48 N 12.23 E
Innichen — San Candido 64 46.44 N 12.17 E
Inning 60 48.05 N 11.09 E
Innisfail, Austl. 166 17.32 S 146.02 E
Innisfail, Ab., Can. 182 52.02 N 113.57 W
Innisfil Creek ≃ 212 44.08 N 79.49 W
Innisfree 182 53.22 N 111.32 W
Innisplain 171a 28.10 S 152.55 E
Innokentjevka 89 49.42 N 136.57 E
Innokentjevskij 89 48.37 N 140.10 E
Innoko ≃ 180 62.14 N 159.45 W
Innolovo 265a 59.47 N 29.59 E
Innoshima 96 34.17 N 133.11 E
Inno-shima I 96 34.19 N 133.10 E
Innsbruck 64 47.16 N 11.24 E
Innviertel ◆1 60 48.10 N 13.15 E
Inny ≃ 48 53.33 N 7.48 W
Inny ≃, Eng., U.K. 42 50.35 N 4.17 W
Ino, Nihon 96 33.33 N 133.26 E
Ino, Va., U.S. 208 37.46 N 76.48 W
Inoã 256 22.55 S 42.57 W
Inobonto 112 0.52 N 123.57 E

Symbols in the index entries represent the broad categories identified in the key at the right. Symbols with superior numbers (∧1) identify subcategories (see complete key on page I · 1).

Symbole im Register stellen die rechts im Schlüssel erklärten Kategorien dar. Symbole mit hochgestellten Ziffern (∧1) bezeichnen Unterabteilungen einer Kategorie (vgl. vollständiger Schlüssel auf Seite I · 1).

Los símbolos incluídos en el texto del índice representan las grandes categorías identificadas con la clave a la derecha. Los símbolos con numeros en su parte superior (∧1) identifican las subcategorías (véase la clave completa en la página I · 1).

Les symboles de l'index représentent les catégories indiquées dans la légende à droite. Les symboles suivis d'un indice (∧1) représentent des sous-catégories (voir légende complète à la page I · 1).

Os símbolos incluídos no texto do índice representam as grandes categorias identificadas com a chave à direita. Os símbolos com números em sua parte superior (∧1) identificam as subcategorias (veja-se a chave completa à página I · 1).

	English	Deutsch	Español	Français	Português
∧	Mountain	Berg	Montaña	Montagne	Montanha
∧	Mountains	Gebirge	Montañas	Montagnes	Montanhas
✕	Pass	Paß	Paso	Col	Passo
V	Valley, Canyon	Tal, Cañon	Valle, Cañón	Vallée, Canyon	Vale, Canhão
≡	Plain	Ebene	Llano	Plaine	Planície
⟩	Cape	Kap	Cabo	Cap	Cabo
I	Island	Insel	Isla	Île	Ilha
II	Islands	Inseln	Islas	Îles	Ilhas
⊥	Other Topographic Features	Andere Topographische Objekte	Otros Elementos Topográficos	Autres données topographiques	Outros acidentes topográficos

ESPAÑOL

Nombre	Página	Lat.°′	Long.°′ W = Oeste
Inocência	255	19.47 S	51.48 W
Inokashira Park ♠	268	35.42 N	139.34 E
Inokovka	80	52.33 N	42.34 E
Inola	196	36.09 N	95.30 W
Ino-misaki ›	96	33.01 N	133.06 E
Inongo	152	1.57 S	18.16 E
Inoni	152	3.04 S	15.39 E
İnönü	130	39.48 N	30.09 E
Inoue	270	34.48 N	135.03 E
Inowrocław	30	52.48 N	18.15 E
Inozemcevo	84	44.06 N	43.06 E
Inp'ung-dong	98	41.25 N	126.34 E
Inrath ◆[8]	263	51.21 N	6.32 E
In Rhar	148	27.10 N	1.59 E
Ins	58	47.00 N	7.06 E
In Salah	148	27.12 N	2.28 E
Insan-ni	98	41.01 N	127.21 E
Insar	80	53.52 N	44.21 E
Insar ≏	80	54.43 N	45.18 E
Insch	46	57.21 N	2.37 W
Inscription, Cape ›	162	25.29 S	112.59 E
Inscription Point ›	274a	34.00 S	151.13 E
Insel Man → Isle of Man □[2]	44	54.15 N	4.30 W
Inshar	150	8.49 N	9.40 E
Inshāṣ ar-Raml	142	30.23 N	31.27 E
Insjön	26	60.41 N	15.05 E
Ińsko	30	53.27 N	15.33 E
In Sokki, Oued V	148	29.37 N	4.13 E
Inspiration	200	33.24 N	110.52 W
Insterburg → Čern'achovsk	76	54.38 N	21.49 E
Instow	184	49.44 N	108.16 W
Insurgente José María Morelos, Parque Nacional ♠	234	19.35 N	100.55 W
Inta	24	66.02 N	60.08 E
Intendente Alvear	252	35.14 S	63.35 W
İntepe	130	40.00 N	26.20 E
Intercession City	220	28.15 N	81.30 W
Intercourse	208	40.02 N	76.06 W
Interlagos ◆[8]	287b	23.42 S	46.42 W
Interlaken, Schw.	58	46.41 N	7.51 E
Interlaken, Ma., U.S.	210	42.18 N	73.19 W
Interlaken, N.J., U.S.	208	40.14 N	74.01 W
Interlaken, N.Y., U.S.	210	42.37 N	76.43 W
Interlândia	255	16.12 S	49.02 W
Internacional (Guarulhos), Aeroporto ⊠	287b	23.29 S	46.28 W
International Amphitheatre ♁	278	41.49 N	87.39 W
International Falls	190	48.36 N	93.24 W
International Peace Garden ♠	198	49.00 N	100.04 W
International Trade Fair ♠	267d	35.47 N	51.24 E
Interstate State Park ♠	190	45.23 N	92.40 W
Inthanon, Doi ∧	110	18.35 N	98.29 E
Intibucá	236	14.16 N	88.10 W
Intibucá □[5]	236	14.20 N	88.15 W
Intipucá	236	13.12 N	88.04 W
Intiyaco	252	28.39 S	60.05 W
Intracoastal Waterway ≊, U.S.	192	24.33 N	81.46 W
Intracoastal Waterway ≊, U.S.	196	26.04 N	97.12 W
Intragna	58	46.10 N	8.42 E
Intrånget	40	60.20 N	16.09 E
Introbio	58	45.57 N	9.27 E
Introdacqua	66	42.00 N	13.54 E
Intschön → Inch'ŏn	98	37.28 N	126.38 E
Intu	112	0.15 S	115.21 E
Intuto	246	3.39 S	74.44 W
Inubō-saki ›	94	35.42 N	140.53 E
Inukai	96	33.04 N	131.38 E
Inukjuak	176	58.27 N	78.06 W
Inútil, Bahía ⊂	254	53.30 S	69.50 W
Inuvik	180	68.25 N	133.30 W
Inuya ≏	248	10.41 S	73.30 W
Inuyama	94	35.23 N	136.56 E
In'va ≏	86	58.59 N	55.40 E
Inver	46	57.49 N	3.55 W
Inverallochy	46	57.40 N	1.55 W
Inveralochy	170	34.57 S	149.39 E
Inveraray	46	56.13 N	5.05 W
Inverarish	46	57.21 N	6.04 W
Inverarity	46	56.35 N	2.53 W
Inverbervie	46	56.51 N	2.17 W
Invercargill	172	46.24 S	168.21 E
Inverdruie	46	57.10 N	3.48 W
Inverell	166	29.47 S	151.07 E
Invergarry	46	57.02 N	4.47 W
Invergordon	46	57.42 N	4.10 W
Inverkeilor	46	56.38 N	2.32 W
Inverkeithing	46	56.02 N	3.25 W
Inverkeithny	46	57.30 N	2.37 W
Inverleigh	169	38.06 S	144.03 E
Inverloch	169	38.38 S	145.43 E
Invermay	184	51.48 N	103.09 W
Invermere	182	50.30 N	116.02 W
Invermoriston	46	57.13 N	4.38 W
Inverness, N.S., Can.	186	46.14 N	61.18 W
Inverness, P.Q., Can.	206	46.15 N	71.31 W
Inverness, Scot., U.K.	46	57.27 N	4.15 W
Inverness, Ca., U.S.	204	38.06 N	122.51 W
Inverness, Fl., U.S.	220	28.50 N	82.19 W
Inverness, Il., U.S.	216	42.07 N	88.05 W
Inverness, Ms., U.S.	194	33.21 N	90.35 W
Inveruglas	46	56.15 N	4.43 W
Inveruno	62	45.31 N	8.51 E
Inverurie	46	57.17 N	2.23 W
Inverway	162	17.50 S	129.38 E
Investigator Group II	162	33.45 S	134.30 E
Investigator Shoal ✣[2]	108	8.09 N	114.44 E
Investigator Strait ɥ	166	35.25 S	137.10 E
Inwood, Mb., Can.	184	50.30 N	97.30 W
Inwood, On., Can.	214	42.49 N	81.59 W
Inwood, Fl., U.S.	220	28.02 N	81.45 W
Inwood, In., U.S.	216	41.19 N	86.12 W
Inwood, Ia., U.S.	198	43.18 N	96.25 W
Inwood, N.Y., U.S.	276	40.37 N	73.44 W
Inwood Hill Park ♠	276	40.52 N	73.56 W
Inyanga	154	18.13 S	32.46 E
Inyanga Mountains ⩚	154	18.00 S	33.00 E
Inyangani ∧	154	18.20 S	32.50 E
Inyan Kara Mountain ∧	198	44.13 N	104.21 W
Inyantue	154	18.32 S	26.41 E
Inyati	154	19.39 S	28.54 E
Inyo, Mount ∧	204	36.44 N	117.59 W
Inyokern	204	35.38 N	117.48 W
Inyo Mountains ⩚	204	36.40 N	118.10 W
Inyonga	154	6.43 S	32.04 E
Inywa	110	23.56 N	96.17 E
Inza	80	53.51 N	46.21 E
Inza ≏	80	53.54 N	45.44 E
Inzago	62	45.32 N	9.29 E
Inzai	94	35.50 N	140.09 E
Inzana Lake ⊜	182	54.58 N	124.40 W
Inžavino	80	52.19 N	42.30 E
Inzell	64	47.46 N	12.44 E
Inzer	86	54.14 N	57.34 E
Inzer ≏	86	54.30 N	56.28 E
Inzersdorf ◆[8]	264b	48.09 N	16.21 E
Inzia ≏	152	3.45 S	17.57 E
Ioanna, gora ∧	180	64.50 N	178.08 E
Ioánnina	38	39.40 N	20.50 E
Ioco	224	49.18 N	122.52 W
Iō-jima (Iwo Jima) I	174f	24.47 N	141.20 E
Iokanga ≏	24	68.00 N	39.43 E
Iola, Ks., U.S.	198	37.55 N	95.23 W
Iola, Pa., U.S.	210	45.08 N	76.32 W
Iola, Tx., U.S.	222	30.46 N	96.05 W
Iola, Wi., U.S.	190	44.30 N	89.07 W
Iolgo, chrebet ⩚	86	51.30 N	86.25 E
Iolotan'	72	37.18 N	62.21 E

FRANÇAIS

Nom	Page	Lat.°′	Long.°′ W = Ouest
Ioma	164	8.20 S	147.50 E
Iôna, Ang.	152	16.50 S	12.20 E
Iona, N.S., Can.	186	45.58 N	60.48 W
Iona, Id., U.S.	202	43.31 N	111.55 W
Iona I	46	56.19 N	6.25 W
Iôna, Parque Nacional do ♠	152	16.30 S	12.00 E
Iona, Sound of ɥ	46	56.19 N	6.24 W
Iona College ♁[2]	276	40.56 N	73.47 W
Ione, Ca., U.S.	226	38.21 N	120.55 W
Ione, Or., U.S.	202	45.30 N	119.50 W
Ione, Wa., U.S.	202	48.44 N	117.24 W
Ionia, Mi., U.S.	216	42.59 N	85.04 W
Ionia, N.Y., U.S.	210	42.56 N	77.30 W
Ionia □[6]	216	42.56 N	85.04 W
Ionian Sea ⊤[2]	22	39.00 N	19.00 E
Ionia State Recreation Area ♠	216	42.58 N	85.36 W
Ionico, Mare → Ionian Sea ⊤[2]	22	39.00 N	19.00 E
Ionienne, Mer → Ionian Sea ⊤[2]	22	39.00 N	19.00 E
Iónioi Nísoi II	38	38.30 N	20.30 E
Ionisches Meer → Ionian Sea ⊤[2]	22	39.00 N	19.00 E
Ionivejem ≏	180	66.12 N	174.00 W
Iony, ostrov I	74	56.26 N	143.25 E
Ioppolo	68	38.35 N	15.53 E
Ioppolo Giancaxio	70	37.23 N	13.33 E
Iordan	85	39.58 N	71.46 E
Iori ≏	84	41.03 N	46.17 E
Iorskoje ploskogorje ⩚[1]	84	41.20 N	46.00 E
Iory	85	39.30 N	67.53 E
Íos	38	36.44 N	25.17 E
Íos I	38	36.42 N	25.24 E
Ioscoe, Lake ⊜	276	41.02 N	74.19 W
Iosegun ≏	182	54.44 N	117.11 W
Iosegun Lake	182	54.29 N	116.50 W
Iō-shima I	93b	30.48 N	130.18 E
Iota	194	30.19 N	92.29 W
Iovlevo	82	56.10 N	38.20 E
Iowa	194	30.14 N	93.00 W
Iowa □[3]	178	42.15 N	93.15 W
Iowa ≏	190	41.10 N	91.02 W
Iowa, South Fork ≏	190	42.18 N	93.04 W
Iowa City	190	41.39 N	91.31 W
Iowa Falls	190	42.31 N	93.15 W
Iowa Park	196	33.57 N	98.40 W
Iō-zen ∧	94	36.31 N	136.48 E
Ipa ≏	76	52.13 N	29.08 E
Ipala	154	4.30 S	32.53 E
Ipameri	255	17.43 S	48.09 W
Ipanema ◆[8]	256	22.59 S	43.12 W
Ipanema ≏	250	9.53 S	37.15 W
Ipanguaçu	250	5.30 S	36.52 W
Ipat	24	66.13 N	56.33 E
Ipatinga	255	19.30 S	42.32 W
Ipatovo	80	45.43 N	42.53 E
Ipaumirim	250	6.47 S	38.43 W
Ipava	194	40.21 N	90.19 W
Ípeiros □[9]	38	39.40 N	20.50 E
Ipel' (Ipoly) ≏	30	47.49 N	18.52 E
Iperu	150	6.52 N	3.38 E
Iphigenia Bay ⊂	180	55.40 N	133.55 W
Iphofen	56	49.42 N	10.15 E
Ipiabas	256	22.23 S	43.53 W
Ipiales	246	0.50 N	77.37 W
Ipiaú	255	14.08 S	39.44 W
Ipiíba	256	22.52 S	42.57 W
Ipil	116	7.47 N	122.35 E
Ipin → Yibin	107	28.47 N	104.38 E
Ipirá	255	12.10 S	39.44 W
Ipiranga, Bra.	252	25.01 S	50.35 W
Ipiranga, Bra.	287a	22.43 S	43.12 W
Ipiranga ◆[8]	287b	23.36 S	46.35 W
Ipiranga ≏, Bra.	256	23.21 S	45.10 W
Ipiranga ≏, Bra.	287a	22.48 S	43.37 W
Ipiranga, Canal ≊	287a	22.46 S	43.37 W
Ipiranga, Museu do ♁	287b	23.35 S	46.36 W
Ipita	248	19.20 S	63.32 W
Ipitinga ≏	250	0.02 N	53.01 W
Ipixuna	250	4.22 S	44.34 W
Ipixuna ≏, Bra.	248	7.11 S	71.51 W
Ipixuna ≏, Bra.	248	5.45 S	63.02 W
Ipixuna ≏, Bra.	248	6.16 S	61.52 W
Ipixuna, Igarapé ≏	250	4.32 S	52.40 W
Ipoh	114	4.35 N	101.05 E
Ipojuca ≏	250	8.25 S	34.58 W
Ipokera	154	8.03 S	35.41 E
Ipole	154	5.47 S	32.44 E
Ipoly (Ipel') ≏	30	47.49 N	18.52 E
Iporá, Bra.	255	16.28 S	51.07 W
Iporã, Bra.	255	23.59 S	53.37 W
Ipota	175f	18.48 S	169.16 E
Ippari ≏	70	36.52 N	14.26 E
Ippinghausen	56	51.17 N	9.08 E
Ipplepen	42	50.29 N	3.38 W
Ippy	152	6.15 N	21.12 E
İpsala	130	40.55 N	26.23 E
Ipswich, Austl.	171a	27.36 S	152.46 E
Ipswich, Eng., U.K.	42	52.04 N	1.10 E
Ipswich, Ma., U.S.	207	42.40 N	70.50 W
Ipswich, S.D., U.S.	198	45.26 N	99.01 W
Ipswich ≏	207	42.42 N	70.48 W
Ipswich Bay ⊂	207	42.41 N	70.42 W
Ipu	250	4.20 S	40.42 W
Ipubi	250	7.39 S	40.07 W
Ipueiras	250	4.33 S	40.43 W
Ipuh	112	3.00 S	101.30 E
Ipuiúna	256	22.06 S	46.11 W
Ipun, Isla I	254	44.37 S	74.46 W
Ipupiara	255	11.49 S	42.37 W
Iput' ≏	76	52.26 N	31.02 E
Iqaluit	176	63.44 N	68.28 W
Iqe ≏	102	38.14 N	94.18 E
Iqfahş	142	28.47 N	30.49 E
Iquaçu, Parque Nacional do ♠	252	25.30 S	53.50 W
Iquique	248	20.13 S	70.10 W
Iquitos	246	3.46 S	73.15 W
Ira	196	32.35 N	101.00 W
Iraan, Pil.	116	9.04 N	117.42 E
Iraan, Tx., U.S.	196	30.54 N	101.53 W
Ira Banda	152	5.57 N	22.04 E
Irabu	175d	24.50 N	125.09 E
Irabu-jima I	175d	24.50 N	125.10 E
Iracajá, Cachoeira do ∟	248	10.29 S	64.05 W
Iracema	250	5.48 S	38.18 W
Iracoubo	250	5.29 N	53.13 W
Irago-misaki ›	94	34.35 N	137.01 E
Irago-suidō ɥ	94	34.35 N	137.00 E
Iraí	252	27.11 S	53.15 W
Irajá ◆[8]	287a	22.51 S	43.19 W
Irajá ≏	287a	22.49 S	43.17 W
Irajol'	24	64.27 N	55.08 E
Irak → Iraq □[1]	128	33.00 N	44.00 E
Iráklion, Ellás	38	35.20 N	25.09 E
Iráklion, Ellás	267c	38.04 N	23.46 E
Iran (Īrān) □[1], Asia	118	32.00 N	53.00 E
Iran (Īrān) □[1], Asia	128	32.00 N	53.00 E
Iran, Pegunungan ⩚	112	2.05 N	114.55 E
Iran National Arts Museum ♁	267d	35.41 N	51.27 E
Īrānshahr	128	27.13 N	60.41 E
Irapa	246	10.34 N	62.35 W
Irapuato	234	20.41 N	101.21 W
Iraq (Al-ʿĪrāq) □[1], Asia	118	33.00 N	44.00 E
Iraq (Al-ʿĪrāq) □[1], Asia	128	33.00 N	44.00 E
Irará	255	12.02 S	38.46 W
Iratapuru ≏	250	0.36 S	52.35 W
Irati	252	25.27 S	50.39 W
Irati ≏	34	42.35 N	1.16 W
Irauçuba	250	3.45 S	39.47 W
Irazú, Volcán ∧[1]	236	9.58 N	83.53 W

PORTUGUÊS

Nome	Página	Lat.°′	Long.°′ W = Oeste
Irba	88	58.07 N	99.00 E
Irbejskoje	88	55.39 N	95.28 E
Irbeni väin (Irves šaurums) ɥ	76	57.48 N	22.05 E
Irbid	132	32.33 N	35.51 E
Irbid □[8]	132	32.30 N	35.45 E
Irbīl	128	36.11 N	44.01 E
Irbīl □[4]	128	36.10 N	44.00 E
Irbit	86	57.41 N	63.03 E
Irby	262	53.21 N	3.07 W
Irchester	42	52.16 N	0.38 W
Irdning	61	47.33 N	14.01 E
Irdyn'	78	49.23 N	31.44 E
Ire, Mount ∧	175e	9.10 S	161.05 E
Irebu	152	0.37 S	17.45 E
Irecê	250	11.18 S	41.52 W
Iregua ≏	34	42.27 N	2.24 W
Ireland (Eire) □[1], Europe	22	53.00 N	8.00 W
Ireland (Eire) □[1], Europe	48	53.00 N	8.00 W
Ireland Brook ≏	276	40.25 N	74.29 W
Iren' ≏	86	57.27 N	56.56 E
Irene, S. Afr.	158	25.53 S	28.13 E
Irene, S.D., U.S.	198	43.05 N	97.10 W
Irene, Tx., U.S.	222	31.59 N	96.52 W
Irene, Mount ∧	172	45.10 S	167.22 E
Ireng (Maú) ≏	246	3.33 N	59.51 W
Iresick Brook ≏	276	40.24 N	74.22 W
Ireton	198	42.58 N	96.19 W
Irfon ≏	42	52.09 N	3.24 W
Irgakly	84	44.22 N	44.45 E
Irgiz	86	48.37 N	61.16 E
Irgiz ≏	86	48.13 N	62.08 E
Iri	98	35.56 N	126.57 E
Irian Jaya □[4]	164	5.00 S	138.00 E
Iriba	146	15.07 N	22.15 E
Irié	150	8.17 N	9.11 W
Iriga	116	13.25 N	123.25 E
Irigny	62	45.40 N	4.49 E
Irîgui ◆[1]	150	16.43 N	5.30 W
Iriklinskij	86	51.39 N	58.38 E
Iringa	154	7.46 S	35.42 E
Iringa □[4]	154	9.00 S	35.00 E
Irinjālakuda	122	10.20 N	76.14 E
Iriomote-jima I	175d	24.20 N	123.50 E
Iriona	236	15.57 N	85.11 W
Iriri ≏, Bra.	250	3.52 S	52.37 W
Iriri ≏, Bra.	287a	22.41 S	43.05 W
Iriri Novo ≏	250	8.46 S	53.22 W
Irische See → Irish Sea ⊤[2]	28	53.30 N	5.20 W
Irish, Mount ∧	204	37.38 N	115.24 W
Irish Sea ⊤[2]	28	53.30 N	5.20 W
Irishtown	166	40.55 S	145.08 E
Irituia	250	1.46 S	47.26 W
Iriyamazu	268	35.16 N	139.39 E
Irkās, Wādī V	142	28.57 N	32.00 E
Irkeštam	85	39.41 N	73.55 E
Irkinejeva ≏	88	58.30 N	96.48 E
Irkinejevo	88	58.30 N	96.49 E
Irklijev	78	49.32 N	32.18 E
Irklijevskaja	78	45.51 N	39.39 E
Irkoutsk → Irkutsk	88	52.16 N	104.20 E
Irkut ≏	88	52.18 N	104.15 E
Irkutsk	88	52.16 N	104.20 E
Irkutsk □[8]	88	56.00 N	106.00 E
Irlam	44	53.28 N	2.25 W
Irlanda, Mar de → Irish Sea ⊤[2]	28	53.30 N	5.20 W
Irlande, Mer d' → Irish Sea ⊤[2]	28	53.30 N	5.20 W
Irlande → Ireland □[1]	48	53.00 N	8.00 W
Irland → Ireland □[1]	48	53.00 N	8.00 W
Irma	182	52.55 N	111.14 W
Irmauw	164	7.25 S	131.42 E
Irminger Basin ✣[1]	10	61.00 N	35.00 W
Irminio ≏	70	36.46 N	14.36 E
Irmino ◆[8]	83	48.36 N	38.36 E
Irnijärvi ⊜	26	65.36 N	29.05 E
Irnsum	52	53.05 N	5.47 E
Iro, Lac ⊜	146	10.06 N	19.25 E
Iroise ⊂	32	48.15 N	4.55 W
Iron Baron	166	32.59 S	137.09 E
Iron Belt	190	46.24 N	90.19 W
Iron Bottom Sound ɥ	175e	9.15 S	160.00 E
Iron Bridge, On., Can.	190	46.17 N	83.14 W
Iron Bridge, Eng., U.K.	42	52.38 N	2.29 W
Iron Bridge Dam ◆[6]	222	32.50 N	95.54 W
Iron City	194	35.01 N	87.34 W
Iron Cove ⊂	274a	33.52 S	151.10 E
Iron Creek ≏	182	52.43 N	111.14 W
Irondale, Al., U.S.	194	33.32 N	86.42 W
Irondale, Mo., U.S.	194	37.49 N	90.40 W
Irondale, Oh., U.S.	214	40.34 N	80.43 W
Irondale ≏	212	44.49 N	78.37 W
Irondequoit	210	43.12 N	77.36 W
Irondequoit Bay ⊂	210	43.12 N	77.32 W
Iron Gate V	38	44.41 N	22.31 E
Iron Gate Reservoir ⊜[1]	38	44.30 N	22.00 E
Ironia	276	40.49 N	74.37 W
Iron Knob	166	32.44 S	137.08 E
Iron Mountain	190	45.49 N	88.03 W
Iron Mountain ∧, Az., U.S.	200	33.27 N	111.10 W
Iron Mountain ∧, Ca., U.S.	280	34.17 N	117.43 W
Iron Mountains ⩚	192	36.30 N	81.50 W
Iron Range	164	12.42 S	143.18 E
Iron Range National Park ♠	164	12.44 S	143.16 E
Iron River, Mi., U.S.	190	46.05 N	88.38 W
Iron River, Wi., U.S.	190	46.33 N	91.24 W
Iron Springs	208	39.46 N	77.25 W
Ironton, Mn., U.S.	190	46.28 N	93.58 W
Ironton, Mo., U.S.	194	37.35 N	90.37 W
Ironton, Oh., U.S.	188	38.32 N	82.40 W
Ironwood	190	46.27 N	90.10 W
Ironworks Creek ≏	285	40.10 N	74.59 W
Iroquois, On., Can.	212	44.51 N	75.19 W
Iroquois, Il., U.S.	216	40.50 N	87.35 W
Iroquois, S.D., U.S.	198	44.22 N	97.51 W
Iroquois □[6]	216	40.47 N	87.44 W
Iroquois ≏	216	41.05 N	87.49 W
Iroquois Falls	190	48.46 N	80.41 W
Iroquois Lock and Dam ◆[5]	212	44.45 N	75.23 W
Irosin	116	12.42 N	124.02 E
Írottko (Geschriebenstein) ∧	61	47.21 N	16.26 E
Irō-zaki ›	94	34.36 N	138.51 E
Irpen'	78	50.31 N	30.15 E
Irpen' ≏	78	50.34 N	30.16 E
Irrawaddy, Mouths of the ≏[1]	110	15.45 N	94.50 E
Irrawaddy → Ayeyarwady ≏	110	20.32 N	96.55 E
Irregully Creek ≏	162	23.06 S	116.21 E
Irrel	56	49.51 N	6.28 E
Irricana	182	51.19 N	113.37 W
Irrigon	202	45.53 N	119.29 W
Irša ≏	78	50.45 N	29.30 E
Iršava	78	48.20 N	23.03 E
Irschenberg	64	47.50 N	11.55 E
Irsee	58	47.54 N	10.34 E
Irsina	68	40.45 N	16.15 E
Irt ≏	44	54.22 N	3.26 W
Irtek ≏	80	51.28 N	52.39 E
Irthing ≏	44	54.55 N	2.50 W
Irthlingborough	42	52.20 N	0.37 W
Irtyš	86	54.29 N	74.22 E
Irtyš (Ertix) ≏	74	61.04 N	68.52 E
Irtysch → Irtyš ≏	72	61.04 N	68.52 E
Irtysh → Irtyš ≏	72	61.04 N	68.52 E
Irtyšsk	86	53.21 N	75.27 E
Irubaj	80	50.11 N	51.21 E
Iruma	94	35.50 N	139.24 E
Iruma ≏	94	35.57 N	139.30 E
Iruma Air Base ■	268	35.50 N	139.24 E
Iruma-kichi, Kaijō-jieitai- ■	94	35.50 N	139.24 E
Irumu	154	1.27 N	29.52 E
Irún	34	43.21 N	1.47 W
Irupana	248	16.28 S	67.28 W
Irurzun	34	42.55 N	1.50 W
Irú Tepuy ∧	246	5.25 N	61.02 W
Irves šaurums (Irbeni väin) ɥ	76	57.48 N	22.05 E
Irvine, Ab., Can.	184	49.57 N	110.16 W
Irvine, Scot., U.K.	46	55.37 N	4.40 W
Irvine, Ca., U.S.	228	33.40 N	117.49 W
Irvine, Ky., U.S.	192	37.42 N	83.58 W
Irvine, Pa., U.S.	214	41.50 N	79.17 W
Irvine ≏	46	55.37 N	4.41 W
Irvine, Mount ∧	210	42.03 N	78.40 W
Irvine Creek ≏	212	43.41 N	80.25 W
Irvine Park ♠	280	33.48 N	117.45 W
Irvines Landing	182	49.38 N	124.03 W
Irvinestown	48	54.28 N	7.38 W
Irving, Il., U.S.	219	39.12 N	89.24 W
Irving, N.Y., U.S.	214	42.34 N	79.07 W
Irving, Tx., U.S.	222	32.48 N	96.56 W
Irving Park ◆[8]	278	41.57 N	87.43 W
Irvington, Il., U.S.	219	38.26 N	89.10 W
Irvington, Ky., U.S.	194	37.52 N	86.17 W
Irvington, N.J., U.S.	210	40.43 N	74.13 W
Irvington, N.Y., U.S.	210	41.02 N	73.51 W
Irvington, Oh., U.S.	218	39.51 N	84.15 W
Irvington, Va., U.S.	208	37.39 N	76.25 W
Irvington ◆[8]	284b	39.17 N	76.41 W
Irvona	214	40.46 N	78.33 W
Irwell ≏	44	53.27 N	2.17 W
Irwin, Austl.	162	29.12 S	115.04 E
Irwin, Oh., U.S.	218	40.07 N	83.29 W
Irwin, Pa., U.S.	279b	40.19 N	79.42 W
Irwin ≏	162	29.15 S	114.56 E
Irwin, Point ›	162	35.04 S	116.56 E
Irwindale	280	34.06 N	117.56 W
Irwinton	192	32.48 N	83.10 W
Is	86	58.48 N	59.43 E
Is, Jabal ∧	140	21.49 N	35.39 E
Isa	150	13.14 N	6.24 E
ʿĪsā, Ra's ›	144	15.11 N	42.39 E
Isaac ≏	166	22.52 S	149.20 E
Isaac Lake ⊜, B.C., Can.	182	53.10 N	120.50 W
Isaac Lake ⊜, On., Can.	212	44.47 N	81.14 W
Isaba	34	42.52 N	0.55 W
Isabel, Pil.	116	10.56 N	124.26 E
Isabel, S.D., U.S.	198	45.23 N	101.25 W
Isabel □[4]	175e	7.55 S	159.10 E
Isabela, Pil.	116	10.12 N	122.59 E
Isabela (Basilan), Pil.	116	6.42 N	121.58 E
Isabela, P.R.	240m	18.30 N	67.01 W
Isabela □[4]	116	17.00 N	122.00 E
Isabela, Cabo ›	238	19.56 N	71.01 W
Isabela, Canal ɥ	246a	0.20 S	90.55 W
Isabela, Isla I, Ec.	246a	0.30 S	91.06 W
Isabela, Isla I, Méx.	234	21.51 N	105.55 W
Isabela de Sagua	240p	22.57 N	80.01 W
Isabelia, Cordillera ⩚	236	13.45 N	85.15 W
Isabella Indian Reservation ◆[4]	190	43.41 N	84.48 W
Isabella Lake ⊜	212	45.24 N	79.49 W
Isabella Lake ⊜[1]	204	35.40 N	118.26 W
Isabelle ≏	190	47.50 N	91.41 W
Isábena ≏	34	42.11 N	0.21 E
Isaccea	38	45.16 N	28.28 E
Ísafjarðardjúp ⊂[2]	24a	66.10 N	23.00 W
Ísafjörður	24a	66.08 N	23.13 W
Isāgarh	124	24.50 N	77.53 E
Isagatedo	273a	6.32 N	3.20 E
Isahaya	92	32.50 N	130.03 E
Isak	114	4.28 N	96.55 E
Isaka, Tan.	154	3.54 S	32.56 E
Isaka, Zaïre	152	2.35 S	18.48 E
Isaka-Buku	152	3.55 S	22.03 E
Īsa Khel	123	32.41 N	71.17 E
Isakly	80	54.08 N	51.32 E
Isakovka	86	55.45 N	74.24 E
Isakovo, Ross.	76	60.30 N	41.13 E
Isakovo, Ross.	76	55.11 N	34.40 E
Isakovo, Ross.	82	54.36 N	37.02 E
Isakovo, Ross.	265b	55.59 N	37.23 E
Işalniţa	38	44.24 N	23.44 E
Isalo, Massif de l' ⩚	157b	22.45 S	45.15 E
Isalo, Parc National de l' ♠	157b	22.45 S	45.15 E
Isana (Içana) ≏	246	0.26 N	67.19 W
Īsānagar	124	27.54 N	81.13 E
Isandhlwana ⊥	158	28.21 S	30.39 E
Isandja Etat	152	2.59 S	22.00 E
Isando	273d	26.09 S	28.12 E
Isanga	152	1.26 S	22.18 E
Isangano National Park ♠	154	11.10 S	30.40 E
Isangel	175f	19.32 S	169.16 E
Isangi	152	0.46 N	24.15 E
Is'angulovo	86	52.12 N	56.36 E
Isanlu Makutu	150	8.17 N	5.46 E
Isan-ni	98	40.46 N	128.55 E
Isanti	190	45.29 N	93.14 W
Isar ≏	30	48.49 N	12.58 E
Isara	150	6.59 N	3.41 E
Isarco (Eisack) ≏	64	46.27 N	11.18 E
Isarco, Valle V	64	46.45 N	11.37 E
Isarog, Mount ∧	116	13.39 N	123.23 E
Isasi	273a	6.40 N	3.23 E
Isawa	94	35.39 N	138.38 E
Isbergues	50	50.37 N	2.27 E
Isbister	46a	60.36 N	1.19 W
İscehisar	130	38.51 N	30.45 E
Iščeino	76	52.57 N	38.50 E
Iščerskaja	84	43.43 N	45.08 E
Ischgl	58	47.01 N	10.17 E
Ischia	68	40.44 N	13.57 E
Ischia, Isola d' I	68	40.43 N	13.54 E
Ischia di Castro	66	42.33 N	11.45 E
Ischim → Išim ≏	86	57.45 N	71.12 E
Ischitella	68	41.54 N	15.54 E
Ischma → Ižma ≏	24	65.19 N	52.54 E
Ischodnaja, gora ∧	180	64.50 N	173.26 W
Ischua	210	42.15 N	78.24 W
Ischua Creek ≏	210	42.10 N	78.23 W
Iscuandé ≏	246	2.38 N	78.04 W
Isdell ≏	162	16.27 S	124.51 E
Isdes	50	47.40 N	2.15 E
Ise (Uji-yamada)	94	34.29 N	136.42 E
Ise ≏	54	52.30 N	10.33 E
Isefjord ⊂	41	55.52 N	11.49 E
Isehara	94	35.24 N	139.18 E
Išejevka	80	54.25 N	48.16 E
Iseke	154	6.25 S	35.01 E
Isel ≏	64	46.50 N	12.47 E
Iselin, N.J., U.S.	210	40.34 N	74.19 W
Iselin, Pa., U.S.	214	40.33 N	79.23 W
Iselle	58	46.12 N	8.12 E
Iseltwald	58	46.43 N	7.58 E
Isen	60	48.13 N	12.04 E
Isen ≏	60	48.15 N	12.40 E
Isenbajevo	80	56.03 N	53.25 E
Isenbüttel	52	52.26 N	10.34 E
Isenyela	154	8.36 S	33.30 E
Iseo	64	45.39 N	10.03 E
Iseo, Lago d' ⊜	64	45.43 N	10.04 E
Iseramagazi	154	4.40 S	32.09 E
Iseran, Col de l')(	62	45.25 N	7.02 E
Isère □[5]	62	45.10 N	5.50 E
Isère ≏	62	44.59 N	4.51 E
Iseri	273a	6.39 N	3.23 E
Iseri-Oke	273a	6.38 N	3.23 E
Iseri-Osun	273a	6.31 N	3.17 E
Iserlohn	56	51.22 N	7.41 E
Isernhagen	52	52.26 N	9.51 E
Isernia	66	41.36 N	14.14 E
Isernia □[4]	66	41.40 N	14.15 E
Isesaki	94	36.19 N	139.12 E
Ise-Shima-kokuritsu-kōen ♠	92	34.23 N	136.48 E
Iset' ≏	86	56.36 N	66.24 E
Isetskoje	86	56.29 N	65.21 E
Ise-wan ⊂	94	34.43 N	136.43 E
Iseyin	150	7.58 N	3.36 E
Isezaki → Isesaki	92	36.19 N	139.12 E
Isfahan → Eşfahān	128	32.40 N	51.38 E
Isfana	85	39.50 N	69.31 E
Isfana ≏	85	40.13 N	69.26 E
Isfara	85	40.07 N	70.38 E
ʿIsfiyā	132	32.43 N	35.04 E
Ishenga Oswe	152	3.46 S	22.34 E
Isheri-Olofin	273a	6.35 N	3.17 E
Isherton	246	2.19 N	59.22 W
Ishi ≏	270	34.35 N	135.38 E
Ishibashi	94	36.26 N	139.52 E
Ishibe	94	35.00 N	136.04 E
Ishigaki	175d	24.20 N	124.09 E
Ishigaki-shima I	175d	24.24 N	124.12 E
Ishige	94	36.07 N	139.58 E
Ishii	96	34.04 N	134.26 E
Ishikari ≏	92a	43.15 N	141.23 E
Ishikari-dake ∧	92a	43.33 N	143.02 E
Ishikari-heiya ≚	92a	43.15 N	141.23 E
Ishikari-sanchi ⩚	92a	43.35 N	143.00 E
Ishikari-wan ⊂	92a	43.25 N	141.01 E
Ishikawa, Nihon	94	37.09 N	140.27 E
Ishikawa, Nihon	174m	26.25 N	127.50 E
Ishikawa □[5]	94	36.45 N	136.45 E
Ishiki	94	34.48 N	137.01 E
Ishikiri	270	34.41 N	135.39 E
I-shima I	96	33.51 N	134.49 E
Ishinomaki	92	38.25 N	141.18 E
Ishinomaki-wan ⊂	92	38.18 N	141.18 E
Ishioka	94	36.11 N	140.16 E
Ishiyama	270	34.58 N	135.55 E
Ishizuchi-san ∧	96	33.46 N	133.07 E
Ishkumān	123	36.32 N	73.49 E
Ishmant	142	29.12 N	31.11 E
Ishpeming	190	46.29 N	87.40 W
Ishuizu ≏	270	34.33 N	135.27 E
Ishurdi	124	24.08 N	89.05 E
Isidro Casanova	288	34.42 S	58.35 W
Isigny	32	49.19 N	1.06 W
Işık Dağı ∧	130	38.21 N	36.32 E
Işıklı	130	38.19 N	29.51 E
Işıkli Burnu ›	267b	41.14 N	29.15 E
Isili	71	39.44 N	9.06 E
Isil'kul'	86	54.55 N	71.16 E
Išim	86	56.09 N	69.27 E
Išim ≏	86	57.45 N	71.12 E
Išimbaj	86	53.28 N	56.02 E
Išimka	86	51.24 N	67.08 E
Išimskaja step' ≚	86	55.00 N	70.00 E
Isimu	112	0.40 N	122.51 E
Isinga	88	52.55 N	112.00 E
Isiolo	154	0.21 N	37.35 E
Isiolo Game Reserve ◆[4]	154	0.32 N	37.34 E
Isipingo	158	29.59 S	30.56 E
Isipingo Beach	158	29.59 S	30.57 E
Isiro (Paulis)	154	2.47 N	27.37 E
Isis	166	25.12 S	152.13 E
Isisford	166	24.16 S	144.26 E
Iskandar	85	41.36 N	69.43 E
Iskâr ≏	38	43.44 N	24.27 E
Iskâr, jazovir ⊜[1]	38	42.28 N	23.35 E
Iškašim	123	36.44 N	71.37 E
Iskaten', chrebet ⩚	180	66.30 N	179.00 W
Iškejevo	80	55.51 N	50.56 E
İskele	130	35.17 N	33.52 E
İskenderun	130	36.37 N	36.07 E
İskenderun Körfezi (Gulf of Alexandretta) ⊂	130	36.30 N	35.40 E
Iske-R'az'ap	80	54.36 N	49.42 E
İskilip	130	40.45 N	34.29 E
Iski-Naukat	85	40.16 N	72.36 E
Iskininskij	80	47.13 N	52.41 E
Iskitim	86	54.38 N	83.18 E
Iskona ≏	82	55.34 N	36.05 E
Iskushuban	144	10.17 N	50.14 E
Iskut ≏	180	56.42 N	131.45 W
Isla	234	18.01 N	95.30 W
Isla ≏	46	57.30 N	2.47 W
Isla, Salar de la ≚	252	25.49 S	68.53 W
Isla Cristina	34	37.12 N	7.19 W
Isla de Maipo	252	33.45 S	70.54 W
İslâhiye	130	37.03 N	36.36 E
Islāmābād	123	33.42 N	73.10 E
Islāmābād → Anantnāg	123	33.44 N	75.09 E
Isla Mala	258	34.12 S	56.21 W
Islāmkot	120	24.42 N	70.11 E
Islamorada	220	24.55 N	80.37 W
Islāmpur, India	122	17.03 N	74.16 E
Islāmpur, India	124	25.09 N	85.12 E
Islāmpur, India	124	26.16 N	88.12 E
Islāmpur, India	126	21.43 N	87.39 E
Islāmpur, India	126	24.09 N	88.28 E
Isla Mujeres	232	21.12 N	86.43 W
Island	194	37.26 N	87.08 W
Island □[6]	224	48.07 N	122.36 W
Island ≏	262	53.44 N	2.51 W
Island Bay ⊂	116	9.06 N	118.10 E
Island Beach State Park ♠	208	39.50 N	74.06 W
Island Bend	171b	36.19 S	148.29 E
Island Creek	283	42.00 N	70.43 W
Island Falls, Sk., Can.	184	55.32 N	102.21 W
Island Falls, Me., U.S.	188	46.00 N	68.16 W
Island Heights	208	39.56 N	74.09 W
Islandia → Iceland □[1]	24a	65.00 N	18.00 W
Island → Iceland □[1]	24a	65.00 N	18.00 W
Island Lagoon ⊜	166	31.30 S	136.40 E
Island Lake, Mb., Can.	184	53.58 N	94.47 W
Island Lake, Il., U.S.	216	42.17 N	88.12 W
Island Lake, Mi., U.S.	281	42.31 N	83.44 W
Island Lake ⊜	184	53.47 N	94.25 W
Island Lake State Recreation Area ♠	216	42.30 N	83.43 W
Island Park, Id., U.S.	202	44.24 N	111.19 W
Island Park, N.Y., U.S.	276	40.36 N	73.39 W
Island Park, R.I., U.S.	207	41.37 N	71.13 W
Island Park Reservoir ⊜[1]	202	44.25 N	111.29 W
Island Point ›	162	30.20 S	115.02 E
Island Pond	188	44.48 N	71.52 W
Island Pond ⊜	186	48.25 N	56.23 W
Islands, Bay of ⊂, Nf., Can.	186	49.10 N	58.15 W
Islands, Bay of ⊂, N.Z.	172	35.12 S	174.10 E
Island View	216	40.31 N	83.53 W
Isla Patrulla	252	32.59 S	54.35 W
Islas de la Bahía □[5]	236	16.20 N	86.30 W
Islas Malvinas → Falkland Islands □[2]	254	51.45 S	59.00 W
Isla Verde	252	33.14 S	62.24 W
Isla Vista	204	34.25 N	119.50 W
Islay I	46	55.46 N	6.10 W
Islay, Punta ›	248	17.01 S	72.07 W
Islay, Rhinns of ›[1]	46	55.45 N	6.25 W
Islay, Sound of ɥ	46	55.50 N	6.01 W
Isle	190	46.08 N	93.28 W
Isle ≏, Fr.	32	44.55 N	0.15 W
Isle ≏, Eng., U.K.	42	50.59 N	2.53 W
Isle-Adam, Forêt de l' ♠	261	49.05 N	2.15 E
Isle-aux-Morts	186	47.35 N	58.59 W
Isle of Hope	192	31.58 N	81.05 W
Isle of Man □[2], Europe	22	54.15 N	4.30 W
Isle of Man □[2], Europe	44	54.15 N	4.30 W
Isle of Man (Ronaldsway) Airport ⊠	44	54.06 N	4.36 W
Isle of Palms	192	32.47 N	79.48 W
Isle of Wight	208	36.54 N	76.42 W
Isle of Wight □[6], Eng., U.K.	42	50.40 N	1.20 W
Isle of Wight □[6], Va., U.S.	208	36.50 N	76.42 W
Isle of Wight Bay ⊂	208	38.22 N	75.06 W
Isle Royale National Park ♠	190	48.00 N	89.00 W
Isles, Lake of the ⊜	212	44.19 N	75.59 W
Isle Saint George	214	41.43 N	82.49 W
Islesboro Island I	188	44.20 N	68.53 W
Isleta	200	34.54 N	106.41 W
Isleta Indian Reservation ◆[4]	200	34.55 N	106.45 W
Isleton	226	38.09 N	121.36 W
Islets-Caribou	186	49.30 N	67.14 W
Isleworth ◆[8]	260	51.28 N	0.20 W
Islington	207	42.13 N	71.11 W
Islington ◆[8], On., Can.	275b	43.39 N	79.32 W
Islington ◆[8], Eng., U.K.	42	51.34 N	0.06 W
Islip, Eng., U.K.	42	51.50 N	1.14 W
Islip, N.Y., U.S.	276	40.43 N	73.12 W
Islip Terrace	276	40.44 N	73.11 W
Islivig	46	58.05 N	7.11 W
Isloč' ≏	76	53.55 N	26.13 E
Islón	252	29.54 S	71.12 W
Isluga, Volcán ∧[1]	248	19.10 S	68.51 W
Ismael Cortinas (Arroyo Grande)	258	33.58 S	57.06 W
Ismailia → Al-Ismāʿīlīyah	142	30.35 N	32.16 E
Ismāʿīlīyah ◆[8]	273c	30.03 N	31.14 E
Ismāʿīlīyah, Turʿat al- ≊	142	30.04 N	31.16 E
İsmailli	130	38.56 N	27.13 E
Ismailly	84	40.47 N	48.09 E
Ismailovo	80	55.34 N	54.39 E
Ismaning	60	48.14 N	11.41 E
Isnā	140	25.18 N	32.33 E
Isny	58	47.41 N	10.02 E
Isoanala	157b	23.50 S	45.44 E
Isobe	94	34.22 N	136.49 E
Isogo ◆[8]	268	35.23 N	139.37 E
Isojoki	26	62.07 N	21.58 E
Isoka	154	10.10 S	32.35 E
Isokyrö	26	63.00 N	22.19 E
Isola, Fr.	62	44.11 N	7.03 E
Isola, Ms., U.S.	194	33.15 N	90.35 W
Isola, Monte ∧	64	45.42 N	10.05 E
Isola d'Asti	62	44.50 N	8.11 E
Isola del Cantone	62	44.39 N	8.57 E
Isola del Gran Sasso d'Italia	66	42.30 N	13.40 E
Isola della Scala	64	45.16 N	11.00 E
Isola del Liri	66	41.41 N	13.34 E
Isola di Capo Rizzuto	68	38.58 N	17.06 E
Isola Dovarese	64	45.10 N	10.18 E
Isola Farnese ◆[8]	66	42.01 N	12.23 E
Isola Vicentina	64	45.38 N	11.25 E
Isoletta	66	41.30 N	13.34 E
Isolillock Peak ∧	224	49.18 N	121.27 W
Isolo	273a	6.32 N	3.19 E
Isone	58	46.08 N	8.59 E
Isonzo (Soča) ≏	64	45.47 N	13.32 E
Isorella	64	45.18 N	10.19 E
Iso-Syöte ∧[2]	26	65.37 N	27.35 E
Iso-zaki ›	94	36.23 N	140.38 E
Ispani	68	40.08 N	15.34 E
Isparta	130	37.46 N	30.33 E
Isparta □[4]	130	38.00 N	31.00 E
Isperih	38	43.43 N	26.50 E
Ispica	70	36.47 N	14.55 E
Ispica, Cava d' ⊥[5]	70	36.51 N	14.51 E
Ispikān	128	26.14 N	62.12 E
İspir	130	40.29 N	41.00 E
Ispra	62	45.49 N	8.37 E
Ispringen	56	48.55 N	8.40 E
Israel (Yisra'el) □[1], Asia	118	31.30 N	35.00 E
Israel (Yisra'el) □[1], Asia	132	31.30 N	35.00 E
Israel ≏	188	44.29 N	71.35 W
Issa	80	53.52 N	44.51 E
Issa ≏	76	56.58 N	28.47 E
Issano	246	5.49 N	59.25 W
Issaquah	224	47.31 N	122.01 W
Issaran, Ra's ›	142	28.48 N	32.47 E
Issel (Oude IJssel) ≏	52	52.00 N	6.10 E
Isselburg	52	51.51 N	6.28 E
Isselhorst	52	51.57 N	8.24 E
Isser, Oued ≏, Alg.	34	36.52 N	3.48 E
Isser, Oued ≏, Alg.	34	35.08 N	1.28 W
Issia	150	6.29 N	6.35 W
Issigeac	32	44.44 N	0.36 E
Issime	62	45.41 N	7.51 E
Issogne	62	45.39 N	7.41 E
Issoire	32	45.33 N	3.15 E
Issole ≏	62	43.27 N	6.12 E
Issou	261	48.59 N	1.48 E
Issoudun	32	46.57 N	2.00 E
Issum	52	51.32 N	6.25 E
Issuna	154	5.23 S	34.46 E
Is-sur-Tille	58	47.31 N	5.06 E
Issy	50	48.49 N	2.17 E
Issyk	85	43.22 N	77.28 E
Issyk-Kul' (Rybačje)	85	42.26 N	76.12 E
Issyk-Kul', ozero ⊜	85	42.25 N	77.15 E
Issy-les-Moulineaux	261	48.49 N	2.17 E
Īstādeh-ye Moqor, Āb-e ⊜	120	32.32 N	67.57 E
Istana Presidential Palace ♁	269e	6.10 S	106.49 E
İstanbul, Tür.	130	41.01 N	28.58 E
İstanbul, Tür.	267b	41.01 N	28.58 E
İstanbul □[4]	130	41.10 N	28.45 E
Istanbul (Yeşilköy) International Airport ⊠	267b	40.58 N	28.49 E
İstanbul Boğazı (Bosporus) ɥ	130	41.06 N	29.04 E
Istanbul University ♁[2]	267b	41.00 N	28.58 E
Isṭanhā	142	30.28 N	31.07 E
Istead Rise	260	51.24 N	0.22 E
Isteren ⊜	26	61.58 N	11.48 E
Isthmus Bay ⊂	212	45.00 N	81.15 W
Istiaía	38	38.57 N	23.09 E
İstinye ◆[8]	267b	41.06 N	29.03 E
Istisu	84	39.57 N	45.59 E
Istmina	246	5.10 N	76.39 W
Isto, Mount ∧	180	69.12 N	143.48 W
Istobensk	80	58.25 N	48.48 E
Istobnoje, Ross.	78	51.08 N	37.21 E
Istobnoje, Ross.	78	51.16 N	38.39 E
Istok	38	42.47 N	20.29 E
Istokpoga, Lake ⊜	220	27.22 N	81.17 W
Istra	82	55.55 N	36.52 E
Istra ›[1]	36	45.15 N	14.00 E
Istra ≏	82	55.44 N	37.08 E
Istrana	64	45.41 N	12.07 E
Istres	62	43.31 N	4.59 E

≏ River	Fluß	Río	Rivière	Rio
≊ Canal	Kanal	Canal	Canal	Canal
∟ Waterfall, Rapids	Wasserfall, Stromschnellen	Cascada, Rápidos	Chute d'eau, Rapides	Cascata, Rápidos
ɥ Strait	Meeresstraße	Estrecho	Détroit	Estreito
⊂ Bay, Gulf	Bucht, Golf	Bahía, Golfo	Baie, Golfe	Baía, Golfo
⊜ Lake, Lakes	See, Seen	Lago, Lagos	Lac, Lacs	Lago, Lagos
≡ Swamp	Sumpf	Pantano	Marais	Pântano
⊓ Ice Features, Glacier	Eis- und Gletscherformen	Accidentes Glaciales	Formes glaciaires	Acidentes glaciares
⊤ Other Hydrographic Features	Andere Hydrographische Objekte	Otros Elementos Hidrográficos	Autres données hydrographiques	Outros acidentes hidrográficos

✣ Submarine Features	Untermeerische Objekte	Accidentes Submarinos	Formes de relief sous-marin	Acidentes submarinos
□ Political Unit	Politische Einheit	Unidad Politica	Entité politique	Unidade política
♁ Cultural Institution	Kulturelle Institution	Institución Cultural	Institution culturelle	Instituição cultural
⊥ Historical Site	Historische Stätte	Sitio Histórico	Site historique	Sitio histórico
♠ Recreational Site	Erholungs- und Ferienort	Sitio de Recreo	Centre de loisirs	Area de Lazer
⊠ Airport	Flughafen	Aeropuerto	Aéroport	Aeroporto
■ Military Installation	Militäranlage	Instalación Militar	Installation militaire	Instalação militar
◆ Miscellaneous	Verschiedenes	Misceláneo	Divers	Diversos

ENGLISH — Name, Page, Lat.°′, Long.°′
DEUTSCH — Name, Seite, Breite°′, Länge°′ E = Ost

Name	Page	Lat.°′	Long.°′
Istria — Istra ≻[1]	36	45.15 N	14.00 E
Istrinskoje vodochranilišče ⊜[1]	82	56.04 N	36.49 E
Isulan	116	6.34 N	124.37 E
Isumi	94	35.17 N	140.19 E
Isumi ≐	94	35.18 N	140.25 E
Isumrud Strait ʊ	164	4.45 S	145.50 E
Isunba	273a	6.27 N	3.17 E
Iswarīpur	126	22.19 N	89.07 E
Iswepe	158	26.50 S	30.31 E
Itá	252	25.29 S	57.21 W
Itabaiana, Bra.	250	7.20 S	35.20 W
Itabaiana, Bra.	250	10.41 S	37.26 W
Itabaiana, Bra.	250	11.16 S	37.47 W
Itabapoana	255	21.18 S	40.58 W
Itabashi ◆[8]	268	35.45 N	139.43 E
Itaberá	255	23.51 S	49.09 W
Itaberaba	255	12.32 S	40.18 W
Itaberaí	255	16.02 S	49.48 W
Itabi	250	10.08 S	37.06 W
Itabira	255	19.37 S	43.13 W
Itaboca	256	22.03 S	44.05 W
Itaboraí	256	22.45 S	42.52 W
Itaboraí □[7]	287a	22.43 S	43.00 W
Itabuna	255	14.48 S	39.16 W
Itacaiuna ≐	250	5.21 S	49.08 W
Itacajá	250	8.19 S	47.46 W
Itacambiruçu ≐	255	16.44 S	42.45 W
Itacaré	255	14.18 S	39.00 W
Itacoatiara	250	3.08 S	58.25 W
Itacoatiara, Ponta de ≻	287a	22.59 S	43.02 W
Itacurubí del Rosario	252	24.29 S	56.41 W
Itacurussá	256	22.55 S	43.55 W
Itacurussá, Ilha de I	256	22.56 S	43.53 W
Itaeté	255	12.59 S	40.58 W
Itagacaba ≐	256	22.34 S	44.56 W
Itagi	255	14.10 S	40.01 W
Itaguaçu	255	19.48 S	40.51 W
Itaguaí	256	22.52 S	43.47 W
Itaguajé	255	22.37 S	51.59 W
Itaguara	255	20.23 S	44.29 W
Itaguaré, Pico do ∧	256	22.30 S	45.10 W
Itaguari ≐	255	14.11 S	44.40 W
Itaguaru	255	15.44 S	49.37 W
Itaguatins	250	5.47 S	47.29 W
Itagüí	246	6.10 N	75.36 W
Itaí	255	23.24 S	49.06 W
Itá-Ibaté	252	27.26 S	57.20 W
Itaiçaba	250	4.40 S	37.51 W
Itaim	256	22.24 S	45.53 W
Itaim ≐, Bra.	250	7.02 S	42.02 W
Itaim ≐, Bra.	256	23.07 S	45.08 W
Itaim ≐, Bra.	256	22.19 S	45.51 W
Itainópolis	250	7.24 S	41.31 W
Itaiópolis	252	26.20 S	49.56 W
Itaipava	256	22.23 S	43.08 W
Itaipu, Bra.	256	22.58 S	43.02 W
Itaipu, Bra.	287a	22.44 S	43.26 W
Itaipu, Lagoa de c	287a	22.58 S	43.02 W
Itaipu, Ponta de ≻	287a	22.59 S	43.03 W
Itaipu, Reprêsa de ⊜[1]	252	25.00 S	54.30 W
Itäisen Suomenlahden kansallispuisto ♠	26	60.15 N	27.00 E
Itaituba	250	4.17 S	55.59 W
Itajá	255	19.07 S	51.37 W
Itajaí	252	26.53 S	48.39 W
Itajaí do Sul ≐	252	27.12 S	49.39 W
Itajipora	256	22.19 S	46.28 W
Itajubá	256	22.26 S	45.27 W
Itaju do Colônia	255	15.09 S	39.44 W
Itajuípe	255	14.41 S	39.22 W
Itaka, Ross.	88	53.53 N	118.42 E
Itaka, Tan.	154	8.52 S	32.47 E
Itaki	273a	6.43 N	3.17 E
Itako	94	35.56 N	140.33 E
Itakura, Nihon	94	36.13 N	139.36 E
Itakura, Nihon	94	37.03 N	138.18 E
Itala Game Reserve ◆[4]	158	27.31 S	31.19 E
Italia — Italy □[1]	36	42.50 N	12.50 E
Itálica ⊥	34	37.30 N	6.05 W
Italie — Italy □[1]	36	42.50 N	12.50 E
Italien — Italy □[1]	36	42.50 N	12.50 E
Italy	222	32.11 N	96.53 W
Italy (Italia) □[1], Europe	22	42.50 N	12.50 E
Italy (Italia) □[1], Europe	36	42.50 N	12.50 E
Itamaraju	255	17.05 S	39.31 W
Itamarandiba	255	17.51 S	42.51 W
Itamarandiba ≐	255	17.18 S	42.48 W
Itamarati de Minas	256	21.25 S	42.49 W
Itamari	255	13.47 S	39.37 W
Itamataré	250	2.16 S	46.24 W
Itambacuri	255	18.01 S	41.42 W
Itambé	255	15.15 S	40.37 W
Itambi	256	22.44 S	42.58 W
Itami	96	34.46 N	135.25 E
Itami, Camp ■	270	34.47 N	135.24 E
Itamonte	256	22.17 S	44.53 W
Itampolo	157b	24.41 S	43.57 E
Itānagar	120	27.09 N	93.33 E
Itandéua, Lago ⊜	250	2.01 S	55.10 W
Itandrano	157b	21.47 S	45.17 E
Itanhaém	255	24.11 S	46.47 W
Itanhandu	256	22.18 S	44.57 W
Itanhauã ≐	248	4.45 S	63.48 W
Itanhém	255	17.09 S	40.20 W
Itanhomi	255	19.10 S	41.52 W
Itano	96	34.07 N	134.28 E
Itaobim	255	16.34 S	41.30 W
Itaocaia	287a	22.58 S	43.01 W
Itapaci	255	14.57 S	49.34 W
Itapagipe	255	19.54 S	49.22 W
Itapajé	250	3.41 S	39.34 W
Itapanhaú ≐	256	23.51 S	46.10 W
Itaparaná ≐	248	5.47 S	63.03 W
Itaparica, Ilha de I	255	13.00 S	38.42 W
Itaparica, Reprêsa de ⊜[1]	250	8.50 S	38.40 W
Itapaya	248	17.34 S	66.21 W
Itapé	255	14.54 S	39.26 W
Itapebi	255	15.56 S	39.32 W
Itapecerica	255	20.28 S	45.07 W
Itapecerica da Serra	256	23.43 S	46.50 W
Itapecerica da Serra □[7]	287b	23.44 S	46.52 W
Itapecuru-Mirim	250	3.24 S	44.20 W
Itapemirim	255	21.01 S	40.50 W
Itapera	250	2.32 S	43.47 W
Itaperina, Pointe ≻	157b	24.59 S	47.06 E
Itaperuna	255	21.12 S	41.54 W
Itapetim	250	7.22 S	37.11 W
Itapetinga	255	15.15 S	40.15 W
Itapetininga	255	23.36 S	48.03 W
Itapetininga ≐	255	23.35 S	48.27 W
Itapeva, Bra.	255	23.58 S	48.52 W
Itapeva, Bra.	256	22.46 S	46.13 W
Itapevi	256	23.33 S	46.56 W
Itapevi □[7]	287b	23.31 S	46.55 W
Itapicuru	250	11.19 S	38.15 W
Itapicuru ≐, Bra.	250	2.52 S	44.12 W
Itapicuru ≐, Bra.	250	11.47 S	37.32 W
Itapipoca	250	3.30 S	39.35 W
Itapira	256	22.26 S	46.50 W
Itapiranga, Bra.	250	2.45 S	58.01 W
Itapiranga, Bra.	252	27.08 S	53.43 W
Itapirapuã	255	15.52 S	50.36 W
Itapitanga	255	14.26 S	39.34 W
Itapiúna	250	4.33 S	38.57 W
Itápolis	255	21.35 S	48.46 W
Itaporã	255	22.01 S	54.54 W
Itaporã de Goiás	250	8.02 S	48.39 W
Itaporanga, Bra.	250	7.18 S	38.10 W
Itaporanga, Bra.	255	23.42 S	49.29 W
Itaporanga d'Ajuda	250	10.59 S	37.18 W
Itapúa □[5]	252	26.50 S	55.50 W
Itapuranga	255	15.35 S	49.59 W
Itaquaí ≐	246	4.20 S	70.12 W
Itaquaquecetuba	256	23.29 S	46.21 W
Itaquaquecetuba □[7]	287b	23.28 S	46.20 W
Itaquara	255	13.27 S	39.57 W
Itaquari	255	20.20 S	40.22 W
Itaquaxiara	287b	23.47 S	46.51 W
Itaquaxiara, Ribeirão ≐	287b	23.44 S	46.47 W
Itaquera ◆[8]	256	23.32 S	46.27 W
Itaquera, Ribeirão ≐	287b	23.28 S	46.26 W
Itaqui	252	29.08 S	56.33 W
Itaquyry	252	24.56 S	55.13 W
Itarantim	255	15.39 S	40.03 W
Itararé	255	24.07 S	49.20 W
Itārsi	124	22.37 N	77.45 E
Itarumã	255	18.42 S	51.25 W
Itasca, Il., U.S.	278	41.58 N	88.00 W
Itasca, Tx., U.S.	222	32.09 N	97.08 W
Itasca, Lake ⊜	198	47.11 N	95.12 W
Itasca State Park ♠	198	47.18 N	95.18 W
Itata ≐	252	36.23 S	72.52 W
Itatí	252	27.16 S	58.15 W
Itatiaia	256	22.30 S	44.34 W
Itatiaia, Parque Nacional do ♠	256	22.28 S	44.37 W
Itatiba	256	23.00 S	46.51 W
Itatinga	255	23.07 S	48.36 W
Itatira	250	4.30 S	39.37 W
Itatka	86	56.49 N	85.37 E
Itatolo	273b	4.09 S	15.15 E
Itatskij	86	56.04 N	89.05 E
Itatupã	250	0.37 S	51.12 W
Itaú	250	5.50 S	37.59 W
Itaueira	250	7.36 S	43.02 W
Itaueira ≐	250	6.41 S	42.55 W
Itaúna	255	20.04 S	44.34 W
Itaúna, Morro do ∧[2]	287a	22.46 S	43.02 W
Itāwa	124	25.32 N	76.22 E
Itazuke-kūkō ⊠	96	33.35 N	130.28 E
Itbayat Island I	108	20.46 N	121.50 E
Itéa	38	38.26 N	22.24 E
Itenes (Guaporé) ≐	248	11.54 S	65.01 W
Ith ∧	52	52.05 N	9.35 E
Ithaca, Mi., U.S.	190	43.17 N	84.36 W
Ithaca, N.Y., U.S.	210	42.26 N	76.29 W
Itháki	38	38.23 N	20.42 E
Itháki I	38	38.24 N	20.42 E
Ithan Creek ≐	285	40.00 N	75.21 W
Ithnayn	142	30.41 N	32.21 E
Ithon ≐	42	52.12 N	3.27 W
Itigi	154	5.42 S	34.29 E
Itikawa — Ichikawa	94	35.44 N	139.55 E
Itimādpur	124	27.15 N	78.12 E
Itimbiri ≐	152	2.02 N	22.44 E
Itinga	255	16.36 S	41.47 W
Itinga ≐	255	16.35 S	41.45 W
Itinomiya — Ichinomiya	94	35.18 N	136.48 E
Itipo	152	0.50 S	18.35 E
Itiquira	255	17.12 S	54.07 W
Itiquira ≐	248	17.21 S	55.37 W
Itirapina	255	22.15 S	47.49 W
Itire	273a	6.31 N	3.21 E
Itiruçu	255	13.31 S	40.09 W
Itiúba	250	10.43 S	39.51 W
Itkillik ≐	180	70.08 N	150.57 W
Itlar'	82	56.51 N	39.17 E
Itlīdim	142	27.52 N	30.48 E
Itmīdah	142	30.46 N	31.20 E
Itmuryn, ozero ⊜	80	49.30 N	52.22 E
Itō	94	34.58 N	139.05 E
Itobi	256	21.44 S	46.58 W
Itobo	154	4.10 S	33.01 E
Itoculo	154	14.42 S	40.18 E
Itoigawa	94	37.02 N	137.51 E
Itoko	152	1.00 S	21.45 E
Itomamo, Lac ⊜	186	49.11 N	70.28 W
Itoman	174m	26.08 N	127.40 E
Iton ≐	50	49.09 N	1.12 E
Itonamas ≐	248	12.28 S	64.24 W
Itororó	255	15.07 S	40.06 W
Itri	66	41.17 N	13.32 E
Iṭsā	142	29.15 N	30.48 E
Itsukaichi, Nihon	94	35.44 N	139.13 E
Itsukaichi, Nihon	96	34.24 N	132.22 E
Itsuki	92	32.24 N	130.50 E
Itsuku-shima I	96	34.16 N	132.19 E
Itsuwa	92	32.30 N	130.10 E
Itta Bena	194	33.29 N	90.19 W
Ittel, Oued V	148	34.19 N	6.01 E
Itter ≐	263	51.09 N	6.52 E
Ittersum	52	52.28 N	6.07 E
Itteville	261	48.31 N	2.21 E
Ittiri	71	40.36 N	8.34 E
Itú	255	23.16 S	47.19 W
Itu ≐	252	29.25 S	55.51 W
Ituaçu	255	13.49 S	41.18 W
Ituango	246	7.04 N	75.45 W
Ituberá	255	13.44 S	39.09 W
Itucumã ≐	248	6.59 S	69.48 W
Itueta	255	19.23 S	41.11 W
Ituí	256	21.32 S	42.55 W
Ituí ≐	246	4.38 S	70.19 W
Ituim ≐	252	28.35 S	51.20 W
Ituiutaba	255	18.58 S	49.28 W
Itula	154	3.29 S	27.52 E
Itumbiara	255	18.25 S	49.13 W
Itumirim	256	21.19 S	44.53 W
Itum-Kale	84	42.43 N	45.35 E
Ituna	184	51.10 N	103.30 W
Itungi Port	154	9.35 S	33.56 E
Ituni	246	5.30 N	58.14 W
Itupararanga, Reprêsa de ⊜[1]	256	23.37 S	47.16 W
Itupeva	256	23.09 S	47.04 W
Itupeva, Rio da ≐	256	22.03 S	47.15 W
Itupiranga	250	5.09 S	49.20 W
Ituporanga	252	27.25 S	49.36 W
Iturama	255	19.44 S	50.11 W
Iturbe	252	26.01 S	56.30 W
Iturbide	232	19.40 N	89.37 W
Ituri ≐	154	1.40 N	27.01 E
Iturup, ostrov (Etorofu-tō) I	92a	44.35 N	147.10 E
Itutinga	256	21.18 S	44.40 W
Ituverava	255	20.20 S	47.47 W
Ituxi ≐	248	7.18 S	64.51 W
Ituzaingó, Arg.	252	27.36 S	56.41 W
Ituzaingó, Arg.	258	34.40 S	58.40 W
Ituzaingó, Ur.	258	34.25 S	56.26 W
Itwa	124	27.20 N	82.42 E
Ityāy al-Bārūd	142	30.53 N	30.40 E
Ityopiya — Ethiopia □[1]	144	9.00 N	39.00 E
Itz ≐	56	49.58 N	10.52 E
Itzehoe	52	53.55 N	9.31 E
Iubundha ≐	126	24.06 N	90.20 E
Iuka, Il., U.S.	219	38.37 N	88.47 W
Iuka, Ms., U.S.	194	34.48 N	88.11 W
Iul'tin	180	67.50 N	178.48 W
Iul'tin, gora ∧	180	67.50 N	178.25 W
Iúna	255	20.21 S	41.32 W
Iupeba	256	23.41 S	46.22 W
Iva	192	34.18 N	82.39 W
Ivacevīči	76	52.43 N	25.21 E
Ivačovo	76	60.32 N	36.22 E
Ivahona	157b	23.27 S	46.10 E
Ivaí ≐	255	23.18 S	53.42 W
Ivaiporã	252	24.15 S	51.45 W
Ivajlovgrad	38	41.32 N	26.08 E
Ivakoany, Massif de l' ⋏	157b	23.50 S	46.25 E
Ivalo	24	68.42 N	27.30 E
Ivalojoki ≐	24	68.43 N	27.36 E
Ivancevo	82	55.58 N	36.07 E
Ivančice	61	49.06 N	16.23 E
Ivancovo	82	56.39 N	35.50 E
Ivanec	36	46.13 N	16.08 E
Ivane-Puste	78	48.39 N	26.11 E
Ivangorod	76	59.24 N	28.10 E
Ivangrad	38	42.50 N	19.52 E
Ivanhoe, Austl.	166	32.54 S	144.18 E
Ivanhoe, Austl.	274b	37.46 S	145.03 E
Ivanhoe, Ca., U.S.	226	36.23 N	119.13 W
Ivanhoe, Il., U.S.	278	42.17 N	88.02 W
Ivanhoe, Mn., U.S.	198	44.27 N	96.14 W
Ivanhoe, Va., U.S.	192	36.50 N	80.58 W
Ivanhoe ≐	190	48.40 N	82.11 W
Ivanhoe Lake ⊜	190	48.05 N	82.38 W
Ivanica	78	50.47 N	32.36 E
Ivanić Grad	36	45.42 N	16.24 E
Ivaniči	78	50.39 N	24.20 E
Ivanišči, Ross.	76	56.36 N	35.13 E
Ivanišči, Ross.	80	55.46 N	40.26 E
Ivanjci	61	46.38 N	15.54 E
Ivanjica	38	43.35 N	20.14 E
Ivankov	78	50.56 N	29.54 E
Ivankovcy	89	49.06 N	134.28 E
Ivan'kovo	82	54.44 N	37.57 E
Ivan'kovskij	80	56.39 N	40.05 E
Ivan'kovskoje vodochranilišče ⊜[1]	82	56.37 N	36.32 E
Ivanof Bay	180	55.54 N	159.29 W
Ivano-Frankovo	78	49.55 N	23.43 E
Ivano-Frankovsk	78	48.55 N	24.43 E
Ivano-Frankovsk □[8]	38	48.30 N	24.30 E
Ivanopol'	78	49.52 N	28.12 E
Ivanopolje	83	48.28 N	37.46 E
Ivano-Šamševo	83	46.52 N	39.54 E
Ivanov	78	49.28 N	28.21 E
Ivanovka, Kyrg.	85	42.54 N	75.05 E
Ivanovka, Ross.	80	52.51 N	53.48 E
Ivanovka, Ross.	80	51.54 N	43.46 E
Ivanovka, Ross.	80	52.15 N	41.35 E
Ivanovka, Ross.	89	50.22 N	128.02 E
Ivanovka, Ross.	89	43.58 N	132.30 E
Ivanovka, Ukr.	78	46.43 N	34.33 E
Ivanovka, Ukr.	78	46.58 N	30.28 E
Ivanovka, Ukr.	83	47.35 N	37.19 E
Ivanovka, Ukr.	83	48.14 N	38.58 E
Ivanovo, Bela.	78	52.09 N	25.32 E
Ivanovo, Ross.	80	57.00 N	40.59 E
Ivanovo-Voznesensk — Ivanovo	80	57.00 N	40.59 E
Ivanovskaja, Ross.	24	60.48 N	55.52 E
Ivanovskaja, Ross.	78	45.17 N	38.29 E
Ivanovskoje, Ross.	76	59.17 N	28.49 E
Ivanovskoje, Ross.	78	51.37 N	34.57 E
Ivanovskoje, Ross.	82	55.05 N	37.50 E
Ivanovskoje, Ross.	82	54.55 N	36.50 E
Ivanovskoje, Ross.	82	55.52 N	36.55 E
Ivanovskoje, Ross.	82	56.23 N	37.07 E
Ivanovskoje, Ross.	265a	59.46 N	30.47 E
Ivan-Ozero	82	54.04 N	38.20 E
Ivan-Ozero, ozero ⊜	82	54.07 N	38.17 E
Ivanpah Lake ⊜	204	35.35 N	115.25 W
Ivantejevka, Ross.	80	52.16 N	49.07 E
Ivantejevka, Ross.	82	55.58 N	37.55 E
Ivantejevo	76	57.48 N	33.09 E
Ivato	157b	20.37 S	47.12 E
Ivatuba	255	23.37 S	52.13 W
Ivdel'	72	60.42 N	60.24 E
Ivenec	76	53.53 N	26.45 E
Iver	260	51.31 N	0.30 W
Iver Heath	260	51.32 N	0.31 W
Iverny	261	49.00 N	2.47 E
Ivigtut	176	61.12 N	48.10 W
Ivindo ≐	152	0.09 S	12.09 E
Ivinghoe	42	51.50 N	0.37 W
Ivinheima ≐	255	23.14 S	53.42 W
Ivje	76	53.56 N	25.46 E
Ivn'a	78	51.04 N	36.08 E
Ivnica	78	50.09 N	29.03 E
Ivohibe	157b	22.29 S	46.52 E
Ivolginsk	88	51.45 N	107.14 E
Ivón ≐	248	11.06 S	66.08 W
Ivondro	157b	24.47 S	46.52 E
Ivor	208	36.54 N	76.54 W
Ivorogbo	150	5.30 N	6.21 E
Ivory Coast (Côte d'Ivoire) □[1], Afr.	134	8.00 N	5.00 W
Ivory Coast (Côte d'Ivoire) □[1], Afr.	150	8.00 N	5.00 W
Ivory Coast ⊥[2]	150	5.10 N	5.00 W
Ivoryton	207	41.20 N	72.26 W
Ivösjön ⊜	26	56.06 N	14.27 E
Ivot, Ross.	76	53.42 N	34.12 E
Ivot, Ukr.	78	51.58 N	33.28 E
Ivotka ≐	78	51.57 N	33.22 E
Ivrea	62	45.28 N	7.52 E
İvrindi	130	39.34 N	27.29 E
Ivry-la-Bataille	50	48.53 N	1.28 E
Ivry [-sur-Seine]	50	48.49 N	2.23 E
Ivujivik	176	62.24 N	77.55 W
Ivybridge	42	50.23 N	3.56 W
Ivy Hatch	260	51.16 N	0.16 E
Ivyland	285	40.12 N	75.04 W
Iwade	96	34.15 N	135.19 E
Iwafune, Nihon	94	36.19 N	139.40 E
Iwafune, Nihon	270	34.44 N	135.54 E
Iwagi	96	34.15 N	133.09 E
Iwai	94	36.03 N	139.54 E
Iwai-shima I	96	33.47 N	131.58 E
Iwaizumi	92	39.50 N	141.48 E
Iwaki (Taira)	94	37.03 N	140.55 E
Iwaki ≐	92	41.01 N	140.22 E
Iwaki-san ∧	92	40.39 N	140.18 E
Iwakuni	96	34.09 N	132.11 E
Iwakuni Marine Corps Air Station ■	96	34.08 N	132.14 E
Iwakura	94	35.17 N	136.52 E
Iwama	94	36.18 N	140.16 E
Iwami, Nihon	96	34.53 N	132.26 E
Iwami, Nihon	96	35.35 N	134.20 E
Iwami-kōgen ⋏[1]	96	35.00 N	132.30 E
Iwami-kokubun-ji ⛩[1]	96	34.56 N	132.08 E
Iwamizawa	92a	43.12 N	141.46 E
Iwamura	94	35.22 N	137.26 E
Iwanai	92a	42.58 N	140.30 E
Iwanowo — Ivanovo	80	57.00 N	40.59 E
Iwanuma	92	38.06 N	140.52 E
Iwaoka ◆[8]	270	34.44 N	134.58 E
Iwase, Nihon	94	36.21 N	140.06 E
Iwase, Nihon	268	35.17 N	139.52 E
Iwata	94	34.42 N	137.48 E
Iwataki	96	35.34 N	135.09 E
Iwate □[5]	92	39.37 N	141.22 E
Iwate-san ∧	92	39.51 N	141.00 E
Iwatsuki	94	35.57 N	139.42 E
Iwaya	270	34.35 N	135.02 E
Iwaya — Awaji	96	34.35 N	135.01 E
Iwayama	270	34.52 N	135.52 E
Iwazono	270	34.45 N	135.19 E
Iwo	150	7.38 N	4.11 E
Iwo Jima — Iō-jima I	174f	24.47 N	141.20 E
Iwŏn	98	40.19 N	128.39 E
Iwuy	50	50.14 N	3.19 E
Ixcán ≐	236	16.07 N	91.05 W
Ixchiguán	236	15.12 N	91.53 W
Ixelles	50	50.50 N	4.22 E
Ixhuatlán	234	19.04 N	96.59 W
Ixiamas	248	13.45 S	68.09 W
Iximché ⊥	236	14.44 N	90.59 W
Ixmiquilpan	234	20.29 N	99.14 W
Ixonia	216	43.09 N	88.36 W
Ixopo	158	30.08 S	30.00 E
Ixtahuacán	236	15.25 N	91.46 W
Ixtapa	234	17.39 N	101.36 W
Ixtapa, Punta ≻	234	17.39 N	101.40 W
Ixtapan de la Sal	234	18.50 N	99.41 W
Ixtepec	234	16.34 N	95.06 W
Ixtlahuacán del Río	234	20.52 N	103.15 W
Ixtlán	234	20.11 N	102.24 W
Ixtlán de Juárez	234	17.20 N	96.29 W
Ixtlán del Río	234	21.02 N	104.22 W
Ixworth	42	52.18 N	0.50 E
Iya ≐	96	33.58 N	133.47 E
ʻIyādh	144	14.59 N	46.51 E
ʻIyāl Bakhīt	140	13.25 N	28.41 E
Iyang	98	34.53 N	127.01 E
Iyang, Gili I	115a	6.59 S	114.10 E
Iyang — Yiyang	102	28.36 N	112.20 E
Iyo	96	33.46 N	132.42 E
Iyo-mishima	96	33.58 N	133.33 E
Iyo-nada ⊤[2]	96	33.40 N	132.20 E
Iž ≐	80	55.58 N	52.38 E
Izabal	236	15.24 N	89.08 W
Izabal □[5]	236	15.30 N	89.00 W
Izabal, Lago de ⊜	236	15.30 N	89.10 W
ʻIzab al-Başāriţah	142	31.23 N	31.47 E
Īzad Khvāst	128	31.31 N	52.07 E
Izalco	236	13.45 N	89.40 W
ʻIzam, Jabal al- ∧	132	30.51 N	35.46 E
Izamal	232	20.56 N	89.01 W
Izapa ⊥	232	14.55 N	92.10 W
Iz'aslav	78	50.07 N	26.51 E
ʻIzbat Abū Şuql	132	31.09 N	33.49 E
Izberbaš	84	42.33 N	47.52 E
Izbica, Pol.	30	50.54 N	23.09 E
Izbica, Pol.	30	54.42 N	17.26 E
Izd'oškovo	76	55.08 N	33.37 E
Izegem	50	50.55 N	3.12 E
Īzeh	128	31.50 N	49.50 E
Izena-shima I	174m	26.56 N	127.56 E
Izendy	86	45.48 N	59.28 E
Izernore	58	46.13 N	5.33 E
Iževsk	80	56.51 N	53.14 E
Iževskoje	80	54.34 N	40.53 E
Izkī	128	22.56 N	57.46 E
Ižma	24	65.02 N	53.55 E
Ižma ≐	24	65.19 N	52.54 E
Izmail	78	45.21 N	28.50 E
Izmajlovo	80	53.43 N	47.14 E
Izmajlovo ◆[8]	265b	55.48 N	37.46 E
Izmajlovo Park ♠	265b	55.46 N	37.47 E
Izmalkovo	76	52.41 N	37.58 E
İzmir	130	38.25 N	27.09 E
İzmir □[4]	130	38.30 N	27.15 E
İzmir Körfezi c	130	38.30 N	26.50 E
İzmit (Kocaeli)	130	40.46 N	29.55 E
İzmit Körfezi c	130	40.45 N	29.35 E
Ižmorskij	86	56.11 N	86.38 E
Iznajar, Embalse de ⊜[1]	34	37.15 N	4.30 W
Iznalloz	34	37.23 N	3.31 W
İznik	130	40.26 N	29.43 E
İznik Gölü ⊜	130	40.26 N	29.30 E
Iznoski	76	54.59 N	35.19 E
Izola	64	45.32 N	13.40 E
Izoplit	82	56.38 N	36.12 E
Izopo, Punta ≻	236	15.48 N	87.23 W
Ižora ≐	265a	59.48 N	30.36 E
Izozog, Bañados del ≡	248	18.48 S	62.10 W
Izraʻ	132	32.51 N	36.15 E
Izsák	30	46.48 N	19.22 E
Iztacalco ◆[8]	286a	19.23 N	99.07 W
Iztaccíhuatl, Volcán ∧[1]	234	19.11 N	98.39 W
Iztaccíhuatl y Popocatéptl, Parques Nacionales ♠	234	19.10 N	98.38 W
Iztapa	236	13.56 N	90.43 W
Iztapalapa ◆[8]	286a	19.21 N	99.06 W
Izucar de Matamoros	234	18.36 N	98.28 W
Izu-hantō ≻[1]	94	34.45 N	139.00 E
Izuhara	92	34.12 N	129.17 E
Iz'um	83	49.12 N	37.19 E
Izumi, Nihon	92	32.05 N	130.22 E
Izumi, Nihon	92	38.20 N	140.53 E
Izumi, Nihon	94	35.54 N	136.40 E
Izumi, Nihon	96	34.29 N	135.26 E
Izumi, Nihon	96	34.55 N	134.55 E
Izumi ◆[8]	268	35.25 N	139.30 E
Izumi-ōtsu	96	34.30 N	135.24 E
Izumi-sano	96	34.25 N	135.19 E
Izumizaki	94	37.09 N	140.17 E
Izumo	96	35.22 N	132.46 E
Izumo ≐	94	34.38 N	136.33 E
Izumo-kokubun-ji ⛩[1]	96	35.26 N	133.06 E
Izumrud	86	57.05 N	61.23 E
Izu-nagaoka	94	35.02 N	138.56 E
Izushi	96	35.28 N	134.52 E
Izu-shotō II	6	32.00 N	140.00 E
Izu Trench ✦[1]	6	31.00 N	142.00 E
Izuwara	270	34.53 N	135.32 E
Izvarino	83	48.17 N	39.52 E
Izvestij CIK, ostrova II	74	75.55 N	82.30 E
Izvestkovyj	89	48.59 N	131.33 E
Izvorul Muntelui, Lacul ⊜[1]	38	47.00 N	26.00 E
Izynžul'	86	52.24 N	90.13 E
J			
Jaʻār, Birkat al- ⊜	142	30.28 N	30.10 E
Jääsjärvi ⊜	26	61.36 N	26.07 E
Jaba, Ityo.	144	6.17 N	35.12 E
Jaba, Pap. N. Gui.	175e	6.32 S	155.12 E
Jabā, Sūrīy.	132	33.10 N	35.56 E
Jabal, Bahr al- — Mountain Nile ≐	136	9.30 N	30.30 E
Jabal Abyad Plateau ⋏[1]	140	19.00 N	29.00 E
Jabal al-Awliyā'	140	15.14 N	32.30 E
Jabal al-Awliyā', Khazzān (White Nile Dam) ◆[6]	140	15.14 N	32.29 E
Jabalambre ∧	34	40.06 N	1.03 W
Jabal an-Nūr	142	28.57 N	31.02 E
Jabal Aṭ-Ṭayr	142	28.14 N	30.45 E
Jabal Dūd	140	13.25 N	33.09 E
Jabal Lubnān □[4]	132	33.50 N	35.40 E
Jabalón ≐	34	38.53 N	4.05 W
Jabal os Sarāj	120	35.07 N	69.14 E
Jabalpur	124	23.10 N	79.57 E
Jabal Qerri	140	16.15 N	32.48 E
Jabal ʻUwaybid	142	30.09 N	32.12 E
Jabālyah	132	31.32 N	34.29 E
Jabal Zuqar, Jazīrat I	144	14.00 N	42.45 E
Jabbān, Arḍ al- ◆[1]	132	32.08 N	36.35 E
Jabbeke	50	51.11 N	3.05 E
Jabbi	123	32.24 N	72.06 E
Jabbū, Qāʻ ≚	132	29.35 N	36.13 E
Jabbūl, Sabkhat al- ⊜	130	36.03 N	37.39 E
Jabel	54	53.32 N	12.32 E
Jabi	114	2.32 N	102.48 E
Jabiru	164	12.40 S	132.53 E
Jabjabah, Wādī V	140	22.37 N	33.17 E
Jablah	130	35.21 N	35.55 E
Jablanac	36	44.42 N	14.54 E
Jablanica	36	43.39 N	17.45 E
Jablanica ≐	38	43.07 N	21.57 E
Jablaničko Jezero ⊜[1]	36	43.40 N	17.50 E
Jablines	261	48.55 N	2.46 E
Jabločnoje	78	50.18 N	35.14 E
Jabločnyj	89	47.10 N	142.04 E
Jablonec nad Nisou	30	50.44 N	15.10 E
Jablonica	30	48.37 N	17.25 E
Jabłonka	30	49.29 N	19.41 E
Jablonné v Podještědí	54	50.48 N	14.47 E
Jablonoj — Jablonovyj chrebet ⋏	88	53.30 N	115.00 E
Jablonov	78	48.24 N	24.57 E
Jablonovo	88	51.51 N	112.49 E
Jablonovyj chrebet ⋏	88	53.30 N	115.00 E
Jabłonowo	30	53.24 N	19.09 E
Jablonowy-Gebirge — Jablonovyj chrebet ⋏	88	53.30 N	115.00 E
Jablunkov	30	49.35 N	18.47 E
Jaboatão	250	8.07 S	35.01 W
Jaboncillos Creek ≐	196	27.23 N	97.45 W
Jabonga	116	9.20 N	125.32 E
Jaborandi	255	20.40 S	48.25 W
Jaboticabal	255	21.16 S	48.19 W
Jabrat Saʻīd ⊤[4]	140	16.06 N	31.50 E
Jabron ≐	62	44.33 N	4.45 E
Jabron, Torrent le ≐	62	44.09 N	5.57 E
Jabung	115a	5.29 S	105.40 E
Jabung, Tanjung ≻	112	1.01 S	104.22 E
Jaca	34	42.34 N	0.33 W
Jacala	234	21.01 N	99.11 W
Jacaleapa	236	14.00 N	86.40 W
Jacaltenango	236	15.40 N	91.44 W
Jacana	274b	37.42 S	144.55 E
Jacaraci	255	14.51 S	42.26 W
Jacaré ≐, Bra.	248	5.49 S	63.35 W
Jacaré ≐, Bra.	250	10.10 S	41.58 W
Jacaré ≐, Bra.	255	13.50 S	40.42 W
Jacareí	256	23.19 S	45.58 W
Jacareí ≐	256	22.54 S	46.28 W
Jacarepaguá ◆[8]	256	22.56 S	43.20 W
Jacarepaguá, Lagoa de c	256	22.59 S	43.24 W
Jacarezinho	255	23.09 S	49.59 W
Jaceel V	144	10.25 N	51.01 E
Jaceruba	256	22.35 S	43.34 W
Jáchal ≐	252	30.44 S	68.08 W
Jachenau	64	47.36 N	11.25 E
Jachniki	78	50.26 N	33.10 E
Jachroma	82	56.17 N	37.30 E
Jachroma ≐	82	56.31 N	37.07 E
Jáchymov	54	50.20 N	12.55 E
Jaciara	255	15.59 S	54.57 W
Jacinto	255	16.10 S	40.17 W
Jacinto Aráuz	252	38.04 S	63.26 W
Jacinto City	222	29.46 N	95.14 W
Jacinto Machado	252	29.00 S	49.46 W
Jaciparaná	248	9.15 S	64.23 W
Jaciparaná ≐	248	9.22 S	64.22 W
Jackass Creek ≐	226	37.22 N	119.23 W
Jack Creek ≐	202	42.59 N	121.32 W
Jackfish Lake ⊜	184	53.05 N	108.25 W
Jackhead Harbour	184	51.52 N	97.16 W
Jack Lake ⊜	212	44.42 N	78.03 W
Jack London State Historical Park ♠	226	38.21 N	122.32 W
Jackman	188	45.38 N	70.15 W
Jackman Creek ≐	224	48.30 N	121.43 W
Jack Mountain ∧, Mt., U.S.	202	46.21 N	112.18 W
Jack Mountain ∧, Wa., U.S.	224	48.47 N	120.57 W
Jackpot	204	41.59 N	114.40 W
Jacksboro, Tn., U.S.	192	36.19 N	84.11 W
Jacksboro, Tx., U.S.	196	33.13 N	98.09 W
Jacks Creek ≐	208	40.35 N	77.33 W
Jacks Fork ≐	194	37.12 N	91.17 W
Jacks Island I	279b	40.37 N	79.43 W
Jacks Mountain ∧	210	40.45 N	77.30 W
Jackson, Al., U.S.	194	31.30 N	87.53 W
Jackson, Ca., U.S.	226	38.20 N	120.46 W
Jackson, Ga., U.S.	192	33.17 N	83.57 W
Jackson, Ky., U.S.	192	37.33 N	83.23 W
Jackson, La., U.S.	194	30.50 N	91.13 W
Jackson, Mi., U.S.	216	42.14 N	84.24 W
Jackson, Mn., U.S.	198	43.37 N	94.59 W
Jackson, Ms., U.S.	194	32.17 N	90.11 W
Jackson, Mo., U.S.	194	37.22 N	89.39 W
Jackson, N.J., U.S.	208	40.08 N	74.19 W
Jackson, N.C., U.S.	192	36.23 N	77.25 W
Jackson, Oh., U.S.	188	39.03 N	82.38 W
Jackson, Pa., U.S.	210	41.50 N	75.36 W
Jackson, S.C., U.S.	192	33.19 N	81.47 W
Jackson, Tn., U.S.	194	35.36 N	88.48 W
Jackson, Wy., U.S.	200	43.28 N	110.45 W
Jackson □[6], In., U.S.	218	38.53 N	86.03 W
Jackson □[6], Mi., U.S.	216	42.15 N	84.24 W
Jackson □[6], Tx., U.S.	222	29.00 N	96.35 W
Jackson ≐	188	37.47 N	79.46 W
Jackson, Cape ≻	172	41.00 S	174.18 E
Jackson, Lake ⊜, Fl., U.S.	192	30.30 N	84.17 W
Jackson, Lake ⊜, Fl., U.S.	220	27.29 N	81.28 W
Jackson, Lake ⊜, Fl., U.S.	220	27.55 N	81.10 W
Jackson, Mount ∧, Ant.	9	71.23 S	63.22 W
Jackson, Mount ∧, Austl.	162	30.15 S	119.16 E
Jackson, Port c	170	33.50 S	151.16 E
Jackson Bay c	172	43.58 S	168.42 E
Jackson Brook ≐	276	40.53 N	74.34 W
Jackson Butte ∧	226	38.20 N	120.43 W
Jackson Center, Oh., U.S.	216	40.27 N	84.02 W
Jackson Center, Pa., U.S.	214	41.16 N	80.09 W
Jackson Creek ≐, Can.	184	49.18 N	100.50 W
Jackson Creek ≐, Ca., U.S.	226	38.18 N	121.01 W
Jackson Creek ≐, Il., U.S.	216	41.26 N	88.10 W
Jackson Head ≻	172	43.58 S	168.37 E
Jackson Heights ◆[8]	276	40.45 N	73.53 W
Jackson Lake ⊜	202	43.55 N	110.40 W
Jackson Lake ⊜[1]	192	33.22 N	83.52 W
Jackson Meadows Reservoir ⊜[1]	226	39.29 N	120.32 W
Jackson Mountain ∧	188	44.46 N	70.32 W
Jackson Park ♠, On., Can.	281	42.17 N	83.01 W
Jackson Park ♠, Il., U.S.	278	41.47 N	87.35 W
Jackson's Arm	186	49.52 N	56.47 W
Jacksons Creek ≐	169	37.40 S	144.48 E
Jacksonville, Al., U.S.	194	33.48 N	85.45 W
Jacksonville, Ar., U.S.	194	34.51 N	92.06 W
Jacksonville, Fl., U.S.	192	30.19 N	81.39 W
Jacksonville, Il., U.S.	219	39.44 N	90.13 W
Jacksonville, N.J., U.S.	285	40.03 N	74.46 W
Jacksonville, N.Y., U.S.	210	42.31 N	76.37 W
Jacksonville, N.C., U.S.	192	34.45 N	77.25 W
Jacksonville, Or., U.S.	202	42.18 N	122.57 W
Jacksonville, Tx., U.S.	222	31.57 N	95.16 W
Jacksonville, Vt., U.S.	207	42.47 N	72.49 W
Jacksonville, Lake ⊜[1]	222	31.55 N	95.17 W
Jacksonville Beach	192	30.17 N	81.23 W
Jacksonville Naval Air Station ■	192	30.14 N	81.41 W
Jacks Reef	210	43.06 N	76.25 W
Jacks Run ≐	279b	40.13 N	79.35 W
Jacktown Acres	279b	40.19 N	79.45 W
Jacmel	238	18.14 N	72.32 W
Jaco	232	27.50 N	104.00 W
Jacob, Morne ∧	240e	14.46 N	61.06 W
Jacobābād	120	28.17 N	68.26 E
Jacobina	250	11.11 S	40.31 W
Jacob Island I	212	44.28 N	78.28 W
Jacob Riis Park ♠	276	40.34 N	73.52 W
Jacobs Creek ≐	214	40.07 N	79.44 W
Jacobsdal	158	29.13 S	24.41 E
Jacobus	208	39.53 N	76.43 W
Jacona de Plancarte	234	19.57 N	102.16 W
Jacques, Lac à ⊜	180	66.10 N	127.25 W
Jacques-Cartier	275a	45.31 N	73.29 W
Jacques-Cartier ≐	206	46.40 N	71.45 W
Jacques-Cartier, Détroit de ʊ	186	50.00 N	63.30 W
Jacques-Cartier, Mont ∧	186	48.59 N	65.57 W
Jacques-Cartier, Pont ◆[5]	275a	45.31 N	73.32 W
Jacquet River	186	47.55 N	66.00 W
Jacqueville	150	5.12 N	4.25 W
Jacquinot Bay c	164	5.35 S	151.30 E
Jacu ≐, Bra.	250	6.13 S	35.09 W
Jacú ≐, Bra.	256	23.05 S	45.08 W
Jacu, Rio do ≐	287b	23.29 S	46.27 W
Jacuba ≐	255	18.25 S	52.28 W
Jacuecanga	256	23.01 S	44.13 W
Jacuí ≐	252	30.02 S	51.15 W
Jacuípe ≐	255	12.30 S	39.05 W
Jacumba	204	32.37 N	116.11 W
Jacundá	250	4.33 S	49.28 W
Jacundá ≐	250	1.57 S	50.26 W
Jacupiranga	252	24.42 S	48.00 W
Jacuriaí ≐	250	10.57 S	39.35 W
Jacutinga	256	22.17 S	46.37 W
Jada	146	8.46 N	12.09 E
Jadaʻah, Jabal ∧[2]	142	29.58 N	30.40 E
Jādabpur	126	22.29 N	88.23 E
Jaddi, Rās ≻	128	25.14 N	63.31 E
Jade	52	53.20 N	8.14 E
Jade Buddha, Temple of the ⛩[1]	269b	31.14 N	121.26 E
Jadebusen c	52	53.30 N	8.10 E
Jäder	40	59.25 N	16.41 E
Jäderfors	40	60.41 N	16.40 E
Jade Run ≐	285	39.56 N	74.45 W
Jadīdah	128	34.01 N	42.28 E
Jadito Wash V	200	35.22 N	110.50 W
J.A.D. Jensens Nunatakker ∧	176	62.45 N	48.00 W
Jadotville — Likasi	154	10.59 S	26.44 E
Jadraque	34	40.55 N	2.55 W
Jadrin	80	55.56 N	46.12 E
Jadromino	82	55.57 N	36.36 E
Jādū	146	31.57 N	12.01 E
Jaduty	78	51.22 N	32.19 E
Jægerspris	41	55.51 N	11.59 E
Jaeger Summit ∧	154	2.52 S	35.47 E
Jaén, Esp.	34	37.46 N	3.47 W
Jaén, Perú	248	5.42 S	78.47 W
Jaén □[4]	34	38.00 N	3.30 E
Jæren ◆[1]	26	58.45 N	5.45 E
Jāfarābād, India	120	20.52 N	71.22 E
Jaʻfarābād, Īrān	128	35.43 N	50.43 E
Jāfarpur	126	22.29 N	89.06 E
Jāfarpur ◆[8]	272a	28.40 N	77.01 E
Jaffa, Cape ≻	166	36.58 S	139.40 E
Jaffa, Tel Aviv- — Tel Aviv-Yafo	132	32.04 N	34.46 E
Jaffna	122	9.40 N	80.00 E
Jaffna Lagoon c	122	9.35 N	80.15 E
Jaffrey	207	42.48 N	72.01 W
Jafr, Qāʻ al- ⊥[7]	132	30.17 N	36.20 E
Jagādhri	124	30.10 N	77.18 E
Jägala ≐	76	59.29 N	25.09 E
Jagalūr	122	14.32 N	76.21 E
Jāgan	120	28.05 N	68.30 E
Jagannāthganj Ghāt	124	24.45 N	89.49 E
Jagannāthpūr	272b	22.43 N	88.19 E
Jagati	126	23.54 N	89.06 E
Jagatnagar	272b	22.47 N	88.13 E
Jagatpur ◆[8]	272a	28.44 N	77.14 E
Jagatsingpur	120	20.16 N	86.10 E
Jagdalpur	122	19.04 N	82.02 E
Jagdīspur	124	25.29 N	84.25 E
Jagel	41	54.27 N	9.32 E
Jagel'urta, gora ∧[2]	24	67.33 N	38.02 E
Jagenbach	61	48.38 N	15.02 E
Jägerndorf — Krnov	30	50.05 N	17.41 E
Jagersfontein	158	29.44 S	25.29 E
Jaggayyapeta	122	16.54 N	80.06 E
Jagged Mountain ∧	180	58.38 N	162.02 W
Jagīn ≐	128	25.35 N	58.18 E
Jagnob ≐	85	39.15 N	68.35 E
Jagny-sous-Bois	261	49.05 N	2.27 E
Jagodnoje, Ross.	74	62.33 N	149.40 E
Jagodnoje, Ross.	80	53.36 N	49.04 E
Jagodnyj	86	59.44 N	65.04 E
Jagorlyckij zaliv c	78	46.24 N	31.50 E
Jagotin	78	50.17 N	31.46 E
Jagraon	123	30.47 N	75.29 E
Jagst ≐	56	49.14 N	9.11 E
Jagsthausen	56	49.19 N	9.28 E
Jagstzell	56	49.02 N	10.05 E
Jagtiāl	122	18.48 N	78.56 E
Jaguaquara	255	13.32 S	39.58 W
Jaguarão	252	32.34 S	53.23 W
Jaguarão (Yaguarón) ≐	252	32.39 S	53.12 W
Jaguarari	250	10.16 S	40.12 W
Jaguaretama	250	5.37 S	38.46 W
Jaguari	252	29.30 S	54.41 W
Jaguari ≐, Bra.	256	22.41 S	47.17 W
Jaguari ≐, Bra.	256	23.10 S	45.55 W
Jaguariaíva	252	24.15 S	49.42 W
Jaguaribara	250	5.40 S	38.37 W
Jaguaribe	250	5.53 S	38.37 W
Jaguaribe ≐	250	4.25 S	37.45 W
Jaguari-Mirim ≐	256	21.59 S	47.17 W
Jaguaripe	255	13.06 S	38.53 W
Jaguariúna	256	22.41 S	46.59 W
Jaguaruna	252	28.36 S	49.02 W
Jagüé	252	28.38 S	68.24 W
Jagüey Grande	240p	22.32 N	81.08 W
Jāguli	126	22.56 N	88.32 E
Jāgulia	272b	22.44 N	88.32 E
Jagungal, Mount ∧	171b	36.09 S	148.23 E
Jagunovskij	86	55.17 N	85.59 E
Jahānābād, India	124	25.13 N	84.59 E
Jahānābād, Pāk.	123	32.11 N	72.29 E
Jahāngīra	123	33.58 N	72.13 E
Jahāngīrābād	124	28.25 N	78.06 E
Jahangirpur ◆[8]	272a	28.44 N	77.13 E
Jahānia	123	30.02 N	71.49 E
Jahannam, Qārat ∧[2]	142	29.19 N	30.09 E
Jahdānīyah, Wādī al- V	132	30.12 N	36.22 E
Jahnsdorf	54	50.44 N	12.51 E
Jahrom	128	28.31 N	53.33 E
Jahú — Jaú	255	22.18 S	48.33 W
Jaicós	250	7.21 S	41.08 W
Jaidak	120	31.58 N	66.43 E
Jaihti ≐	126	24.08 N	86.48 E
Jaijon	123	31.21 N	76.09 E
Jailolo	108	1.05 N	127.30 E
Jaimanitas ≐	286b	23.05 N	82.29 W
Jainca	102	35.59 N	102.02 E
Jainti	124	26.42 N	89.36 E
Jaintiāpur	120	25.08 N	92.07 E
Jaipur	120	26.55 N	75.49 E
Jaipur Hāt	124	25.06 N	89.01 E
Jais	124	26.15 N	81.32 E
Jaisalmer	120	26.55 N	70.54 E
Jaito	123	30.28 N	74.53 E
Jaja	86	56.12 N	86.26 E
Jaja ≐	86	56.58 N	86.23 E
Jājapur	120	20.51 N	86.20 E
Jājarkoṭ	124	28.42 N	82.12 E
Jājarm	128	36.58 N	56.27 E
Jajce	36	44.21 N	17.16 E
Jajichi	174m	26.47 N	128.13 E
Jajjha	123	28.45 N	70.34 E
Jajl'u	86	51.48 N	87.36 E
Jajpan	85	40.23 N	70.48 E
Jajsan	86	50.51 N	56.14 E
Jajva	86	59.20 N	57.15 E
Jajva ≐	86	59.13 N	56.40 E
Ják	61	47.08 N	16.35 E
Jakarta, Indon.	115a	6.10 S	106.48 E
Jakarta, Indon.	269e	6.10 S	106.48 E
Jakarta, Teluk c	115a	6.05 S	106.48 E
Jakarta Kota Station ◆[5]	269e	6.08 S	106.49 E

Symbols in the index entries represent the broad categories identified in the key at the right. Symbols with superior numbers (⋏[1]) identify subcategories (see complete key on page *I · 1).*

Symbole im Register stellen die rechts im Schlüssel erklärten Kategorien dar. Symbole mit hochgestellten Ziffern (⋏[1]) bezeichnen Unterabteilungen einer Kategorie (vgl. vollständiger Schlüssel auf Seite *I · 1).*

Los símbolos incluídos en el texto del índice representan las grandes categorias identificadas con la clave a la derecha. Los símbolos con numeros en su parte superior (⋏[1]) identifican las subcategorías (véase la clave completa en la página *I · 1).*

Les symboles de l'index représentent les catégories indiquées dans la légende à droite. Les symboles suivis d'un indice (⋏[1]) représentent des sous-catégories (voir légende complète à la page *I · 1).*

Os símbolos incluídos no texto do índice representam as grandes categorias identificadas com a chave à direita. Os símbolos com números em sua parte superior (⋏[1]) identificam as subcategorias (veja-se a chave completa à página *I · 1).*

∧ Mountain	Berg	Montaña	Montagne	Montanha
⋏ Mountains	Gebirge	Montañas	Montagnes	Montanhas
)(Pass	Paß	Paso	Col	Passo
V Valley, Canyon	Tal, Cañon	Valle, Cañón	Vallée, Canyon	Vale, Canhão
≚ Plain	Ebene	Llano	Plaine	Planície
≻ Cape	Kap	Cabo	Cap	Cabo
I Island	Insel	Isla	Île	Ilha
II Islands	Inseln	Islas	Îles	Ilhas
⊥ Other Topographic Features	Andere Topographische Objekte	Otros Elementos Topográficos	Autres données topographiques	Outros acidentes topográficos

ESPAÑOL

Nombre	Página	Lat.°'	Long.°' W = Oeste
Jakarta Raya □[4]	115a	6.10 S	106.45 E
Jakdūl ⊜	140	17.39 N	32.59 E
Jake Creek Mountain ∧	204	41.13 N	116.54 W
Jakenan	115a	6.45 S	111.11 E
Jākhal	123	29.48 N	75.50 E
Jakhāu	120	23.13 N	68.43 E
Jakkonen	24	66.33 N	29.52 E
Jakobsberg	40	59.26 N	17.50 E
Jakobsdalsberget ∧[2]	40	58.41 N	16.07 E
Jakobshavn (Ilulissat)	176	69.13 N	51.06 W
Jakobstad (Pietarsaari)	26	63.40 N	22.42 E
Jakovleviči	76	54.20 N	30.31 E
Jakovlevka	89	44.26 N	133.28 E
Jakovlevo, Ross.	78	50.51 N	36.27 E
Jakovlevo, Ross.	82	54.48 N	37.26 E
Jakša	24	61.48 N	56.49 E
Jakšanga	80	58.23 N	45.56 E
Jakšur-Bodja	80	57.11 N	53.09 E
Jakupica ⩘	38	41.43 N	21.26 E
Jakutsk	74	62.00 N	129.40 E
Jakutskaja Avtonomnaja Sovetskaja Socialističeskaja Respublika □[3]	88	58.00 N	121.00 E
Jal	196	32.06 N	103.11 W
Jalacingo	234	19.48 N	97.18 W
Jalaid Qi	89	46.40 N	122.55 E
Jalājil	128	25.41 N	45.28 E
Jalālābād, Afg.	120	34.26 N	70.28 E
Jalālābād, India	123	30.37 N	74.15 E
Jalālābād, India	124	27.43 N	79.40 E
Jalālah al-Baḥrīyah, Jabal ⩘[1]	142	29.20 N	32.00 E
Jalālat al-Qiblīyah, Jabal al- ⩘	142	28.42 N	32.22 E
Jalālpur, India	124	26.19 N	82.44 E
Jalālpur, Pāk.	123	32.38 N	74.12 E
Jalālpur Pīrwāla	123	29.30 N	71.13 E
Jalama	84	41.44 N	48.34 E
Jalan'	86	58.21 N	91.53 E
Jalán ≃	236	14.39 N	86.12 W
Jalan Besar Stadium ♠	271c	1.18 N	103.52 E
Jalandhar	123	31.19 N	75.34 E
Jalangi	126	24.08 N	88.42 E
Jalangi ≃	126	23.25 N	88.22 E
Jalan Kayu	271c	1.24 N	103.52 E
Jalapa, Guat.	236	14.38 N	89.59 W
Jalapa, Méx.	234	17.43 N	92.49 W
Jalapa, Nic.	236	13.55 N	86.08 W
Jalapa □[5]	236	14.35 N	89.55 W
Jalasjärvi	26	62.30 N	22.45 E
Jalaud ≃	116	10.45 N	122.40 E
Jālaun	124	26.09 N	79.21 E
Jal'čiki	80	55.09 N	48.01 E
Jalcocotán	234	21.28 N	105.07 W
Jalda	126	21.56 N	87.30 E
Jaleaca de Catalán	234	17.26 N	99.51 W
Jalesar	124	27.29 N	78.19 E
Jaleshwar	126	21.49 N	87.13 E
Jaleśwar	124	26.38 N	85.48 E
Jālgaon, India	122	21.01 N	75.34 E
Jālgaon, India	122	21.03 N	76.32 E
Jal'gelevo	265a	59.44 N	29.57 E
Jalhay	56	50.34 N	5.58 E
Jalingo	146	8.53 N	11.22 E
Jalirpār	126	23.13 N	89.58 E
Jalisco □[3]	234	20.20 N	103.40 W
Jallas ≃	34	42.54 N	9.08 W
Jallieu	62	45.35 N	5.16 E
Jālna	122	19.50 N	75.53 E
Jalón ≃	34	41.47 N	1.04 W
Jālor	120	25.21 N	72.37 E
Jalostotitlán	234	21.12 N	102.28 W
Jalpa	234	21.38 N	102.58 W
Jalpa de Méndez	234	18.08 N	93.05 W
Jalpāiguri	124	26.31 N	88.44 E
Jalpan de Serra	234	21.14 N	99.29 W
Jalpug ≃	78	45.41 N	28.35 E
Jalpug, ozero ⊜	78	45.25 N	28.37 E
Jalta (Yalta), Ukr.	78	44.30 N	34.10 E
Jalta, Ukr.	83	46.58 N	37.16 E
Jaltepec ≃	234	17.26 N	94.59 W
Játipan de Morelos	234	17.58 N	94.42 W
Jaltuškov	78	48.58 N	27.30 E
Jaluit I[1]	14	6.00 N	169.35 E
Jalūlā'	128	34.16 N	45.10 E
Jalutorovsk	86	56.40 N	66.18 E
Jam, Ross.	82	55.29 N	37.45 E
Jam, Uzb.	85	40.07 N	68.11 E
Jām ≃	128	35.10 N	61.06 E
Jama	83	48.52 N	38.06 E
Jamaame (Margherita)	144	0.04 N	42.45 E
Jamaare ≃	146	12.06 N	10.14 E
Jāmāibāti	272b	22.51 N	88.08 E
Jamaica	240p	20.12 N	75.09 W
Jamaica ◆[8]	276	40.42 N	73.47 W
Jamaica □[1], N.A.	230	18.15 N	77.30 W
Jamaica □[1], N.A.	241q	18.15 N	77.30 W
Jamaica Bay c	210	40.36 N	73.51 W
Jamaica Channel ʉ	238	18.00 N	75.30 W
Jamaica Plain ◆[8]	283	42.19 N	71.06 W
Jamaika → Jamaica □[1]	241q	18.15 N	77.30 W
Jamaïque → Jamaica □[1]	241q	18.15 N	77.30 W
Jamal, poluostrov ≻[1]	74	70.00 N	70.00 E
Jam-Alin', chrebet ⩘	89	53.00 N	134.36 E
Jamālīyah ◆[8]	273c	30.03 N	31.16 E
Jamalo-Neneckij Avtonomyij Okrug □[8]	24	66.30 N	64.00 E
Jamālpur, Bngl.	124	24.55 N	89.56 E
Jamālpur, India	124	25.18 N	86.30 E
Jamālpurganj	126	23.04 N	87.59 E
Jamanchalinka	80	47.40 N	51.35 E
Jamanota ∧[2]	241s	12.29 N	69.57 W
Jamantau, gora ∧	86	54.15 N	58.06 E
Jamanxim ≃	250	4.43 S	56.18 W
Jamapará	256	21.55 S	42.43 W
Jamari ≃	248	8.27 S	63.30 W
Jamarovka	88	50.38 N	110.16 E
Jamašurma	80	55.58 N	49.36 E
Jamay	234	20.18 N	102.43 W
Jamba	152	13.50 S	15.30 E
Jāmbād	126	22.42 N	86.35 E
Jambeiro	256	23.16 S	45.41 W
Jambeiro, Serra do ⩘[2]	256	23.13 S	45.38 W
Jambelí, Canal de ʉ	246	3.00 S	80.00 W
Jamberoo	170	34.39 S	150.47 E
Jambes	56	50.28 N	4.52 E
Jambi	112	1.36 S	103.37 E
Jambi □[4]	112	1.30 S	103.00 E
Jambin	166	24.12 S	150.22 E
Jamboaye ≃	114	5.16 N	97.29 E
Jambol	38	42.29 N	26.30 E
Jambongan, Pulau I	116	6.40 N	117.27 E
Jambuair, Tanjung ≻	114	5.16 N	97.30 E
Jambusar	120	22.03 N	72.48 E
James ≃, Austl.	166	20.36 S	137.41 E
James ≃, Ab., Can.	182	51.55 N	114.34 W
James ≃, U.S.	198	42.52 N	97.18 W
James ≃, Mo., U.S.	194	36.45 N	93.30 W
James ≃, Va., U.S.	192	36.57 N	76.26 W
James, Isla I	254	44.57 S	74.07 W
James, Lake ⊜	216	41.42 N	85.02 W
James, Lake ⊜[1]	192	35.45 N	81.55 W
James Bay c	176	53.30 N	80.30 W
Jamesburg	208	40.21 N	74.26 W
James Bypass ≡	226	36.41 N	120.16 W
James City, N.C., U.S.	192	35.05 N	77.02 W
James City, Pa., U.S.	214	41.37 N	78.50 W
James City □[6]	208	37.17 N	76.48 W
James Craik	252	32.09 S	63.28 W

FRANÇAIS

Nom	Page	Lat.°'	Long.°' W = Ouest
James Creek	214	40.23 N	78.10 W
James Gardens ♠	275b	43.40 N	79.31 W
James Island, B.C., Can.	224	48.37 N	123.22 W
James Island, S.C., U.S.	192	32.44 N	79.57 W
James Island I	208	38.31 N	76.20 W
Jameson Raid Memorial ⊥	273d	26.11 S	27.49 E
James Point ≻	192	25.21 N	76.24 W
Jamesport	194	39.58 N	93.48 W
James Price Point ≻	162	17.30 S	122.08 E
James Ranges ⩘	162	24.06 S	132.30 E
James River Bridge ◆[5]	208	37.00 N	76.30 W
James Ross, Cape ≻	176	74.40 N	114.25 W
James Ross Island I	9	64.15 S	57.45 W
James Ross Strait ʉ	176	69.40 N	95.30 W
James Smith Indian Reserve ◆[4]	184	53.08 N	104.52 W
Jamestown, Austl.	166	33.12 S	138.36 E
Jamestown, Ire.	48	53.55 N	8.02 W
Jamestown, S. Afr.	158	31.06 S	26.45 E
Jamestown, Ca., U.S.	226	37.57 N	120.25 W
Jamestown, Ks., U.S.	198	39.35 N	97.51 W
Jamestown, Ky., U.S.	194	36.59 N	85.03 W
Jamestown, Mi., U.S.	216	42.50 N	85.51 W
Jamestown, N.Y., U.S.	214	42.05 N	79.14 W
Jamestown, N.C., U.S.	192	35.59 N	79.56 W
Jamestown, N.D., U.S.	198	46.54 N	98.42 W
Jamestown, Oh., U.S.	218	39.39 N	83.44 W
Jamestown, Pa., U.S.	214	41.29 N	80.26 W
Jamestown, R.I., U.S.	207	41.29 N	71.22 W
Jamestown, Tn., U.S.	194	36.25 N	84.55 W
Jamestown ⊥	208	37.12 N	76.46 W
Jamestown Festival Park ♠	208	37.14 N	76.48 W
Jamestown Island I	208	37.12 N	76.46 W
Jamestown Reservoir ⊜[1]	198	47.15 N	98.40 W
Jamesville, N.Y., U.S.	210	42.59 N	76.04 W
Jamesville, Va., U.S.	208	37.30 N	75.55 W
Jamet, Lac ⊜	206	46.34 N	74.30 W
Jametz	56	49.26 N	5.23 E
Jamieson ≃	169	37.18 S	146.08 E
Jaminauá ≃	248	9.20 S	70.59 W
Jaminsk	76	52.46 N	28.16 E
Jaminskij	80	50.21 N	42.14 E
Jāmira ≃	126	21.45 N	87.02 E
Jamira ≃[1]	126	21.35 N	88.28 E
Jamison	208	40.16 N	75.05 W
Jamison City	210	41.18 N	76.22 W
Jamison Town	274a	33.46 S	150.41 E
Jam-Ižora	265a	59.42 N	30.36 E
Jām Jodhpur	120	21.54 N	70.01 E
Jamkhandi	122	16.31 N	75.18 E
Jamki	86	59.33 N	66.47 E
Jamkino	82	55.55 N	38.24 E
Jamm	76	58.26 N	28.03 E
Jammalamadugu	122	14.50 N	78.24 E
Jammerbugten c	26	57.20 N	9.30 E
Jammerland Bugt c	41	55.35 N	11.05 E
Jammu	123	32.42 N	74.52 E
Jammu Airport ⊠	123	32.42 N	74.51 E
Jammu and Kashmīr □[2]	120	34.00 N	76.00 E
Jamnagar	120	22.28 N	70.04 E
Jamoigne	56	49.42 N	5.25 E
Jamor ≃	266c	38.42 N	9.15 W
Jampang-kulon	115a	7.16 S	106.37 E
Jampol', Ukr.	78	51.57 N	33.46 E
Jampol', Ukr.	78	48.16 N	28.17 E
Jampol', Ukr.	78	49.58 N	26.14 E
Jampol', Ukr.	83	48.56 N	37.58 E
Jāmpur, India	272b	22.56 N	88.12 E
Jāmpur, Pāk.	123	29.39 N	70.36 E
Jämsä	26	61.52 N	25.12 E
Jamsah	140	27.38 N	33.35 E
Jämsänkoski	26	61.55 N	25.11 E
Jamshedpur	126	22.48 N	86.11 E
Jamsk	74	59.35 N	154.10 E
Jamskaja Sloboda	82	55.29 N	36.01 E
Jāmtāra	126	23.57 N	86.48 E
Jämtland □[9]	26	63.30 N	14.00 E
Jämtlands Län □[6]	24	63.00 N	14.40 E
Jamuāni	126	21.57 N	86.14 E
Jamuga	82	56.24 N	36.40 E
Jamūi	124	24.55 N	86.13 E
Jamuna ≃, Bngl.	124	23.51 N	89.45 E
Jamuna ≃, India	272b	22.57 N	88.35 E
Jamundí	246	3.15 N	76.32 W
Jāmuria	126	23.44 N	87.02 E
Jāmurki	126	24.09 N	90.02 E
Jana ≃	74	71.31 N	136.32 E
Janāi	272b	22.43 N	88.16 E
Janāj	142	31.00 N	30.46 E
Janajkino	80	50.43 N	51.06 E
Janakpur	124	26.39 N	85.55 E
Janakpur □[8]	124	27.15 N	86.00 E
Janas	266c	38.49 N	9.26 W
Janauacá, Lago ⊜	246	3.28 S	60.17 W
Janaúba	255	15.48 S	43.19 W
Janaucu, Ilha I	250	0.30 N	50.10 W
Janaul	86	56.16 N	54.56 E
Jand	123	33.26 N	72.01 E
Janda, Laguna de la ⊜	34	36.15 N	5.51 W
Jandaia	255	17.06 S	50.07 W
Jandaia do Sul	255	23.36 S	51.39 W
Jandaíra	250	11.34 S	37.47 W
Jandalī, Wādī al- V	142	30.05 N	31.52 E
Jandaq	128	34.02 N	54.26 E
Jandelsbrunn	60	48.44 N	13.42 E
Jandiāla	123	31.36 N	75.03 E
Jandiatuba ≃	246	3.28 S	68.42 W
Jandira	256	23.31 S	46.54 W
Jandira □[7]	287b	23.32 S	46.54 W
Jandowae	166	26.47 S	151.06 E
Jandrakinot	180	64.54 N	172.32 W
Jándula ≃	34	38.03 N	4.06 W
Jándula, Embalse de ⊜[1]	34	38.30 N	4.00 W
Janeiro, Rio de ≃	250	11.51 S	45.09 W
Jane Peak ∧	172	45.20 S	168.19 E
Janes Island I	208	38.00 N	75.52 W
Janes Island State Park ♠	208	38.00 N	75.52 W
Janesville, Ca., U.S.	204	40.17 N	120.31 W
Janesville, Mn., U.S.	190	44.06 N	93.42 W
Janesville, Wi., U.S.	216	42.40 N	89.01 W
Jangal Bādhāl	126	23.07 N	89.21 E
Jangamo	156	24.06 S	35.21 E
Jangany	157b	23.14 S	45.27 E
Jangarej	24	68.46 N	61.25 E
Jangel'skij	86	53.08 N	58.59 E
Jangeru	112	2.20 S	116.29 E
Jangiabad	85	41.08 N	70.05 E
Jangi-Bazar	85	41.40 N	70.53 E
Jangijer	85	40.17 N	68.50 E
Jangijul'	85	41.07 N	69.03 E
Jangikišlak	85	40.25 N	67.10 E
Jangikurgan, Uzb.	85	40.34 N	71.09 E
Jangikurgan, Uzb.	85	41.12 N	71.44 E
Jangipāra	126	22.45 N	88.04 E
Jangīpur	124	24.28 N	88.04 E
Jangong	114	4.23 N	96.48 E
Jangoon	122	17.43 N	79.11 E
Jangulovo	80	56.26 N	50.25 E
Janikowo	30	52.45 N	18.07 E
Janīn	132	32.28 N	35.18 E
Janina → Ioánnina	38	39.40 N	20.50 E
Janino	265a	59.56 N	30.36 E
Janisjarvi, ozero ⊜	24	61.59 N	30.57 E

PORTUGUÊS

Nome	Página	Lat.°'	Long.°' W = Oeste
Janiuay	116	10.58 N	122.30 E
Janja	38	44.40 N	19.15 E
Janjina, Cro.	36	42.56 N	17.26 E
Janjina, Madag.	157b	20.30 S	45.50 E
Janka	126	21.52 N	87.56 E
Jankan, chrebet ⩘	88	55.45 N	118.00 E
Jankāpur	126	21.54 N	87.23 E
Jan Kempdorp (Andalusia)	158	27.55 S	24.51 E
Jan Lake ⊜	184	54.55 N	102.55 W
Janlohong	112	2.15 N	117.03 E
Jan Mayen I	12	71.00 N	8.20 W
Jan Mayen Ridge ✢[3]	10	69.00 N	8.00 W
Jannaale	144	1.48 N	44.42 E
Jannali	274a	34.01 S	151.04 E
Jannali Park ♠	274a	34.01 S	151.03 E
Janos	232	30.54 N	108.10 W
Jánoshalma	30	46.18 N	19.20 E
Jánosháza	30	47.08 N	17.10 E
János-hegy ∧	264c	47.31 N	18.58 E
Jánossomorja	61	47.47 N	17.08 E
Janoviči	76	55.17 N	30.42 E
Janowiec Wielkopolski	30	52.46 N	17.31 E
Janów Lubelski	30	50.43 N	22.24 E
Jānsath	124	29.20 N	77.51 E
Jansen	184	51.47 N	104.43 W
Jansenville	158	32.56 S	24.40 E
Janskij	74	68.28 N	134.48 E
Janskij zaliv c	74	71.50 N	136.00 E
Jantarnyj	76	54.52 N	19.57 E
Jantetelco	234	18.42 N	98.46 W
Jantikovo	80	55.32 N	47.48 E
Jantra ≃	38	43.38 N	25.34 E
Januária	255	15.29 S	44.22 W
Januário Cicco	250	6.09 S	35.35 W
Jan Van Riebeeck Park ♠	273d	26.10 S	27.59 E
Janvarcevo	80	51.26 N	52.15 E
Janville	50	48.12 N	1.53 E
Janville-sur-Juine	261	48.31 N	2.16 E
Janvry	261	48.39 N	2.09 E
Jany-Kurgan	85	43.55 N	67.15 E
Janzé	32	47.58 N	1.30 W
Janzūr	142	30.41 N	31.02 E
Jaora	120	23.38 N	75.08 E
Japan (Nihon) □[1], Asia	90	36.00 N	138.00 E
Japan (Nihon) □[1], Asia	92	36.00 N	138.00 E
Japan, Sea of ⊤[2]	90	40.00 N	135.00 E
Japan Basin ✢[1]	12	40.00 N	135.00 E
Japanisches Meer → Japan, Sea of ⊤[2]	90	40.00 N	135.00 E
Japan Trench ✢[1]	6	37.00 N	143.00 E
Japaratinga	250	9.05 S	35.15 W
Japaratuba	250	10.35 S	36.57 W
Japeri	256	22.39 S	43.40 W
Japi	250	6.27 S	35.56 W
Japim	248	7.37 S	72.54 W
Japla	124	24.33 N	84.01 E
Japoatã	250	10.20 S	36.48 W
Japón, Mar del → Japan, Sea of ⊤[2]	90	40.00 N	135.00 E
Japon → Japan □[1]	92	36.00 N	138.00 E
Japtiksal'a	74	69.21 N	72.32 E
Japuíba	256	22.35 S	42.42 W
Japurá	246	1.48 S	66.30 W
Japurá (Caquetá) ≃	246	3.08 S	64.46 W
Jaqué	246	7.31 N	78.10 W
Jaqueri-mirim ≃	287b	23.31 S	46.51 W
Jaquí	248	15.30 S	74.26 W
Jar	80	58.15 N	52.06 E
Jār, Jabal ∧	128	24.34 N	38.18 E
Jarābulus	130	36.49 N	38.01 E
Jarad	144	18.59 N	41.24 E
Jaradū	142	29.18 N	30.42 E
Jaraguá	255	15.45 S	49.20 W
Jaraguá ◆[8]	287b	23.27 S	46.44 W
Jaraguá, Pico do ∧	287b	23.26 S	46.46 W
Jaraguá do Sul	252	26.29 S	49.04 W
Jaraicejo	34	39.40 N	5.49 W
Jaraiz de la Vera	34	40.04 N	5.45 W
Jaral del Progreso	234	20.22 N	101.04 W
Jarales	200	34.36 N	106.45 W
Jarama ≃	34	40.02 N	3.39 W
Jarama, Canal del ≡	266a	40.18 N	3.32 W
Jaramānah	132	33.29 N	36.21 E
Jaramillo	254	47.11 S	67.09 W
Jaramor	80	56.07 N	48.44 E
Jaran' ≃	80	57.35 N	48.14 E
Jarandilla	34	40.08 N	5.39 W
Jaransk	80	57.19 N	47.54 E
Jarānwāla	123	31.20 N	73.26 E
Jarash	132	32.17 N	35.54 E
Jaraucu ≃	250	1.48 S	52.22 W
Jarawī, Wādī V	142	29.47 N	31.19 E
Jarbah, Jabal al- ∧	142	30.16 N	32.03 E
Jarbah, Wāḥat ⊤[4]	140	29.21 N	25.20 E
Jarbidge ≃	202	42.19 N	115.39 W
Järbo	40	60.43 N	16.36 E
Jarcevo	76	55.04 N	32.41 E
Jardas al-'Abīd	146	32.19 N	20.56 E
Jardim, Bra.	248	21.28 S	56.09 W
Jardim, Bra.	250	7.35 S	39.16 W
Jardim América ◆[8]	287b	23.34 S	46.41 W
Jardim de Piranhas	250	6.22 S	37.20 W
Jardim do Seridó	250	6.35 S	36.46 W
Jardim Paraiso	256	22.48 S	43.35 W
Jardim Paulista ◆[8]	287b	23.35 S	46.40 W
Jardín América	252	27.03 S	55.14 W
Jardine ≃	164	10.55 S	142.13 E
Jardine River National Park ♠	164	11.20 S	142.40 E
Jardines de la Reina, Archipiélago de los II	240p	20.50 N	78.55 W
Jardinópolis	255	21.02 S	47.46 W
Jardymly	84	38.55 N	48.15 E
Jaredi	150	12.46 N	5.05 E
Jaremča	78	48.27 N	24.33 E
Jaren'ga, Ross.	24	63.27 N	53.26 E
Jarenga, Ross.	24	62.43 N	49.30 E
Jarensk	24	62.11 N	49.02 E
Järfälla	40	59.24 N	17.50 E
Jargalang	89	43.06 N	122.54 E
Jargara	78	46.27 N	28.27 E
Jargeau	50	47.52 N	2.07 E
Jari ≃, Bra.	248	5.07 S	62.21 W
Jari ≃, Bra.	250	1.09 S	51.54 W
Jari, Lago ⊜	246	5.00 S	62.19 W
Jāria Jhānjail	124	25.02 N	90.39 E
Jaridih	124	23.38 N	86.04 E
Jarinu	256	23.06 S	46.44 W
Jarīr, Wādī al- V	128	25.38 N	42.30 E
Jarkino	88	59.08 N	99.23 E
Jarkovo	86	57.24 N	67.05 E
Jarkul'-Mat'uškino	86	55.51 N	76.06 E
Järlåsa	40	59.53 N	17.12 E
Jarmen	54	53.55 N	13.20 E
Jarmolincy	78	49.12 N	26.50 E
Järna	40	59.06 N	17.34 E
Jarnac	32	45.41 N	0.10 W
Jarny	56	49.09 N	5.53 E
Jaro	116	11.11 N	124.47 E
Jarochta	88	58.58 N	98.58 E
Jarocin	30	51.59 N	17.31 E
Jaroměř	30	50.21 N	15.55 E
Jaroměřice	61	49.05 N	15.53 E
Jaropolec	82	56.08 N	35.49 E
Jaroslavec	78	51.33 N	33.40 E
Jaroslavl'	80	57.37 N	39.52 E
Jaroslavl' □[8]	82	56.45 N	38.45 E
Jaroslavl' Station ◆[5]	265b	55.47 N	37.39 E
Jaroslavskaja	84	44.36 N	40.27 E
Jaroslavskij	89	44.10 N	132.13 E
Jarosław	30	50.02 N	22.42 E
Jarovaja	83	49.03 N	37.37 E
Järpen	26	63.21 N	13.29 E
Jarrahdale	168a	32.21 S	116.04 E
Jarratt	208	36.48 N	77.28 W
Jarreau	194	30.39 N	91.29 W
Jarrell	222	30.49 N	97.36 W
Jarrettsville	208	39.36 N	76.28 W
Jarrīs	142	27.55 N	30.46 E
Jarrow	44	54.59 N	1.29 W
Jarry, Parc ♠	275a	45.32 N	73.38 W
Jar-Sale	74	66.50 N	70.50 E
Jarsomovy	86	60.15 N	73.38 E
Jartai Yanchi ⊜	102	39.43 N	105.41 E
Jaru	248	10.26 S	62.27 W
Jaru ≃	248	10.05 S	61.59 W
Jarud Qi	89	44.37 N	120.58 E
Jaruu	88	48.08 N	96.45 E
Järva-Jaani	76	59.02 N	25.53 E
Järvakandi	76	58.47 N	24.49 E
Järvelä	26	60.52 N	25.17 E
Järvenpää	26	60.28 N	25.06 E
Jarvie	182	54.27 N	113.59 W
Jarville-la-Malgrange	58	48.40 N	6.13 E
Jarvis	212	42.53 N	80.06 W
Jarvisburg	192	36.12 N	75.52 W
Jarvis Island I	14	0.23 S	160.02 W
Järvsö	26	61.43 N	16.10 E
Jarwa	124	27.39 N	82.31 E
Jasaan	116	8.39 N	124.45 E
Jasai	272c	18.56 N	73.01 E
Jašalta	80	46.20 N	42.17 E
Jasašnaja Tašla	80	53.55 N	48.16 E
Jaša Tomić	38	45.27 N	20.51 E
Jasdan	120	22.02 N	71.12 E
Jasel'da ≃	76	52.07 N	26.28 E
Jasenevo ◆[8]	265b	55.36 N	37.33 E
Jasenki	78	51.32 N	38.12 E
Jasenovoje	82	54.10 N	36.47 E
Jasenovskij	83	48.10 N	39.10 E
Jasenskaja	78	46.22 N	38.16 E
Jashpurnagar	124	22.54 N	84.09 E
Jāshpur Pāts ◆[1]	124	22.55 N	84.00 E
Jasidih	124	24.31 N	86.39 E
Jasień	30	51.46 N	15.01 E
Jasienica	54	53.37 N	14.32 E
Jasikan	150	7.24 N	0.28 E
Jašil'kul', ozero ⊜	120	37.45 N	72.55 E
Jasin	114	2.19 N	102.26 E
Jasin'a	78	48.16 N	24.20 E
Jasinga	115a	6.29 S	106.27 E
Jasinovataja	83	48.08 N	37.51 E
Jasinovka	83	48.08 N	37.57 E
Jāsk	128	25.38 N	57.46 E
Jaskhar	272c	18.54 N	72.59 E
Jaškino, Ross.	80	52.41 N	53.26 E
Jaškino, Ross.	86	55.54 N	85.26 E
Jaskino, Ross.	265b	55.40 N	37.16 E
Jaškul'	80	46.11 N	45.21 E
Jaškul' ≃	80	46.15 N	45.05 E
Jasło	30	49.45 N	21.29 E
Jasmine Estates	220	28.17 N	82.42 W
Jasmund ≻[1]	54	54.32 N	13.35 E
Jasnaja Pol'ana ⊥	82	54.05 N	37.32 E
Jasnogorka	83	48.47 N	37.33 E
Jasnogorsk	82	54.29 N	37.42 E
Jasnomorskij	89	46.45 N	141.54 E
Jasnyj, Ross.	86	51.04 N	59.58 E
Jasnyj, Ross.	89	53.17 N	127.59 E
Jason Islands II	254	51.05 S	61.00 W
Jason Peninsula ≻[1]	9	66.10 S	61.00 W
Jasonville	194	39.09 N	87.11 W
Jasper, Ab., Can.	182	52.53 N	118.05 W
Jasper, Al., U.S.	194	33.49 N	87.16 W
Jasper, Ar., U.S.	194	36.00 N	93.11 W
Jasper, Fl., U.S.	192	30.31 N	82.56 W
Jasper, Ga., U.S.	192	34.28 N	84.25 W
Jasper, In., U.S.	194	38.23 N	86.55 W
Jasper, Mi., U.S.	216	41.48 N	84.02 W
Jasper, Mn., U.S.	198	43.51 N	96.23 W
Jasper, Mo., U.S.	194	37.20 N	94.18 W
Jasper, N.Y., U.S.	210	42.07 N	77.30 W
Jasper, Tn., U.S.	194	35.04 N	85.37 W
Jasper, Tx., U.S.	194	30.55 N	93.59 W
Jasper □[6]	216	40.57 N	87.09 W
Jasper Lake ⊜	182	53.07 N	118.00 W
Jasper National Park ♠	182	52.53 N	118.03 W
Jaspur	124	29.17 N	78.49 E
Jasra	124	25.17 N	81.48 E
Jassans-Riottier	58	45.59 N	4.45 E
Jassar	123	32.06 N	74.57 E
Jassy ≃	85	40.46 N	73.05 E
Jassy → Iaşi	38	47.10 N	27.35 E
Jastarnia	30	54.43 N	18.40 E
Jastrebarsko	36	45.40 N	15.39 E
Jastrebovka, Ross.	78	51.27 N	37.32 E
Jastrebovka, Ross.	82	54.36 N	36.24 E
Jastrowie	30	53.26 N	16.49 E
Jaswantnagar	124	26.53 N	78.55 E
Jászapáti	30	47.31 N	20.09 E
Jászberény	30	47.30 N	19.55 E
Jász-Nagykun-Szolnok □[6]	30	47.12 N	20.11 E
Jataí	255	17.53 S	51.43 W
Jatapu ≃	246	2.13 S	58.17 W
Jataté ≃	232	16.15 N	91.17 W
Jati, Bra.	250	7.41 S	39.01 W
Jāti, Pāk.	120	24.21 N	68.16 E
Jatibarang	115a	6.28 S	108.17 E
Jatibonico	240p	21.56 N	79.10 W
Jatibonico del Sur ≃	240p	21.33 N	79.09 W
Jatilawang	115a	7.32 S	109.06 E
Jatiluhur, Waduk ⊜[1]	115a	6.35 S	107.20 E
Jatinegara ◆[8]	269e	6.13 S	106.52 E
Jatiroto	115a	8.07 S	113.21 E
Jatisrono	115a	7.49 S	111.07 E
Jatiwangi	115a	6.44 S	108.15 E
Jatni	120	20.10 N	85.42 E
Jatniel	273d	26.07 S	28.19 E
Jatobá ≃	255	12.23 S	54.07 W
Jatobá, Ribeirão ≃	256	21.28 S	42.49 W
Jatoi Janūbi	123	29.31 N	70.51 E
Jātrāpur	126	22.44 N	89.45 E
Jatt (Tel Gat)	132	32.24 N	35.02 E
Jatznick	54	53.35 N	13.56 E
Jáu, Ang.	152	15.12 S	13.31 E
Jaú, Bra.	255	22.18 S	48.33 W
Jaú ≃	246	1.54 S	61.26 W
Jaú, Parque Nacional do ♠	246	2.30 S	63.00 W
Jauaperi ≃	246	1.26 S	61.35 W
Jauerling ∧	61	48.20 N	15.20 E
Jaugrām	126	23.06 N	88.05 E
Jauja	248	11.48 S	75.30 W
Jauli	272a	28.44 N	77.21 E
Jaumave	234	23.25 N	99.23 W
Jaunde → Yaoundé	152	3.52 N	11.31 E
Jaune, Mer → Yellow Sea ⊤[2]	90	36.00 N	123.00 E
Jaungulbene	76	57.04 N	26.36 E
Jaunjelgava	76	56.37 N	25.05 E
Jaunpass)(	58	46.36 N	7.20 E
Jaunpiebalga	76	57.11 N	26.03 E
Jaunpils	76	56.44 N	23.01 E
Jaunpur	124	25.44 N	82.41 E
Jaupaci	255	16.18 S	50.54 W
Jauquara ≃	248	15.06 S	57.06 W
Jáuregui	258	34.36 S	59.10 W
Jauru	250	11.06 S	57.30 W
Jauru ≃, Bra.	248	16.22 S	57.46 W
Jauru ≃, Bra.	255	18.40 S	54.36 W
Jausiers	62	44.25 N	6.44 E
Jauza ≃, Ross.	82	56.25 N	36.05 E
Jauza ≃, Ross.	265b	55.45 N	37.38 E
Java	198	45.30 N	99.53 W
Java Center	210	42.39 N	78.23 W
Javādi Hills ⩘[2]	122	12.35 N	78.50 E
Java → Jawa I	115a	7.30 S	110.00 E
Javan	85	38.19 N	69.02 E
Javari (Yavarí) ≃	242	4.21 S	70.02 W
Javas	80	54.26 N	42.51 E
Java Sea → Jawa, Laut ⊤[2]	112	5.00 S	110.00 E
Java Trench ✢[1]	12	10.30 S	110.00 E
Java Village	210	42.40 N	78.26 W
Jävenitz	54	52.31 N	11.30 E
Javier, Isla I	254	47.06 S	74.24 W
Javkino	78	47.16 N	32.37 E
Javlenka	86	54.21 N	68.27 E
Javor ⩘	38	44.05 N	18.55 E
Javořice ∧	61	49.14 N	15.20 E
Javorie ∧	30	48.27 N	19.18 E
Javorná	60	49.13 N	13.18 E
Javorník	30	50.23 N	17.00 E
Javorov	78	49.56 N	23.23 E
Javorová skála ∧	30	49.31 N	14.30 E
Javr ≃	24	68.09 N	30.06 E
Jävre	26	65.09 N	21.59 E
Jawa (Java) I	115a	7.30 S	110.00 E
Jawa, Laut (Java Sea) ⊤[2]	112	5.00 S	110.00 E
Jawa Barat □[4]	115a	7.00 S	107.00 E
Jaw'āliyāt, Jabal al- ∧	132	31.26 N	36.26 E
Jawāla Mukhi	123	31.53 N	76.19 E
Jawa Tengah □[4]	115a	7.30 S	110.00 E
Jawa Timur □[4]	115a	8.00 S	113.00 E
Jawbar	132	33.31 N	36.19 E
Jawf, Wādī V	144	15.50 N	45.30 E
Jawi	112	0.48 S	109.16 E
Jawor	30	51.03 N	16.11 E
Jaworzno	30	50.13 N	19.15 E
Jay, Fl., U.S.	194	30.57 N	87.09 W
Jay, Ok., U.S.	196	36.25 N	94.47 W
Jay □[6]	216	40.26 N	84.59 W
Jaya, Puncak ∧	164	4.05 S	137.11 E
Jayanca	248	6.24 S	79.50 W
Jayapura (Sukarnapura)	164	2.32 S	140.42 E
Jayb, Wādī al- (Ha'Arava) V	132	30.58 N	35.24 E
Jay Cooke State Park ♠	190	46.41 N	92.23 W
Jay Creek Aboriginal Reserve ◆[4]	162	23.45 S	133.35 E
Jaydebpur	124	24.00 N	90.26 E
Jaynagar	126	22.36 N	90.42 E
Jaynagar Majilpur	126	22.11 N	88.25 E
Jaynes	200	32.16 N	111.01 W
Jay Peak ∧	188	44.55 N	72.32 W
Jaypur, India	122	18.51 N	82.35 E
Jaypur, India	126	23.03 N	87.27 E
Jayrūd	130	33.49 N	36.44 E
Jayton	196	33.15 N	100.34 W
Jayuya	240m	18.13 N	66.36 W
Jaywick	42	51.47 N	1.08 E
Jaz	80	54.54 N	45.13 E
Jažełbicy	76	58.02 N	32.58 E
Jazevec	24	65.43 N	46.30 E
Jazgulem ≃	85	38.12 N	71.21 E
Jazīrat Muḥammad	273c	30.07 N	31.12 E
Jazjavan	85	40.39 N	71.44 E
Jažma	24	66.56 N	44.29 E
Jaz Mūrīān, Hāmūn-e ⊜	128	27.20 N	58.55 E
Jazovaja	86	49.27 N	85.20 E
Jazykovo	80	54.18 N	47.24 E
Jazzīn	132	33.32 N	35.34 E
Jbā'	132	33.29 N	35.31 E
J.B. Thomas, Lake ⊜[1]	196	32.35 N	101.10 W
J. C. Murphey Lake ⊜	216	40.58 N	87.30 W
Jdiouia	34	35.57 N	0.50 E
Jeanerette	194	29.54 N	91.39 W
Jeanesville	210	40.56 N	75.58 W
Jeannette	214	40.19 N	79.36 W
Jebba	150	9.08 N	4.50 E
Jebel	38	45.33 N	21.14 E
Jebeniana	148	35.02 N	10.55 E
Jeber-Bergfrieden	54	51.59 N	12.20 E
Jeberos	248	5.17 S	76.13 W
Jebri	120	27.18 N	65.44 E
Jebus	112	1.44 S	105.29 E
Jechegnadzor	84	39.46 N	45.21 E
Jéci, Serra ∧	154	12.48 S	35.12 E
Jedane, Oued ti-n- V	148	24.55 N	6.30 E
Jedarma	88	58.44 N	102.36 E
Jedburgh	44	55.29 N	2.34 W
Jedburgh Abbey ʊ[1]	44	55.27 N	2.34 W
Jeddore Lake ⊜[1]	186	48.03 N	55.55 W
Jedelevo	80	53.24 N	47.45 E
Jedepo	150	5.16 N	8.20 W
Jedincy	78	48.10 N	27.19 E
Jedisa	84	42.31 N	44.16 E
Jedlesee ◆[8]	264b	48.16 N	16.23 E
Jednevo	82	56.06 N	36.14 E
Jedogon	88	54.15 N	100.15 E
Jedrovo	76	57.55 N	33.38 E
Jędrzejów	30	50.39 N	20.18 E
Jedwabne	30	53.17 N	22.19 E
Jed Water ≃	46	55.32 N	2.33 W
Jeetzel (Jeetze) ≃	54	53.09 N	11.04 E
Jefawa	140	10.57 N	23.48 E
Jeffara (Al-Jifārah) ≚	146	32.30 N	11.45 E
Jeffers	198	44.03 N	95.11 W
Jefferson, Ga., U.S.	192	34.07 N	83.34 W
Jefferson, In., U.S.	216	40.17 N	86.36 W
Jefferson, Ia., U.S.	198	42.00 N	94.22 W
Jefferson, Md., U.S.	208	39.21 N	77.31 W
Jefferson, Ma., U.S.	207	42.21 N	71.52 W
Jefferson, N.J., U.S.	285	39.45 N	75.13 W
Jefferson, N.Y., U.S.	210	42.14 N	73.54 W
Jefferson, N.Y., U.S.	210	42.29 N	74.37 W
Jefferson, N.C., U.S.	192	36.25 N	81.28 W
Jefferson, Oh., U.S.	214	41.44 N	80.46 W
Jefferson, Or., U.S.	202	44.43 N	123.00 W
Jefferson, Pa., U.S.	279b	40.18 N	80.03 W
Jefferson, S.C., U.S.	192	34.39 N	80.23 W
Jefferson, S.D., U.S.	198	42.36 N	96.33 W
Jefferson, Tx., U.S.	194	32.45 N	94.20 W
Jefferson, Wi., U.S.	216	43.00 N	88.48 W
Jefferson □[6], Il., U.S.	219	38.19 N	88.55 W
Jefferson □[6], In., U.S.	218	38.44 N	85.23 W
Jefferson □[6], Ky., U.S.	218	38.14 N	85.10 W
Jefferson □[6], Mo., U.S.	219	38.20 N	90.34 W
Jefferson □[6], N.Y., U.S.	212	43.59 N	75.55 W
Jefferson □[6], Oh., U.S.	214	40.22 N	80.37 W
Jefferson □[6], Pa., U.S.	214	41.09 N	79.05 W
Jefferson □[6], Wa., U.S.	224	47.50 N	122.36 W
Jefferson □[6], Wi., U.S.	216	43.02 N	88.46 W
Jefferson ≃	202	45.56 N	111.30 W
Jefferson, Mount ∧, U.S.	202	44.34 N	111.30 W
Jefferson, Mount ∧, Nv., U.S.	204	38.46 N	116.55 W
Jefferson, Mount ∧, Or., U.S.	202	44.40 N	121.47 W
Jefferson City, Mo., U.S.	219	38.34 N	92.10 W
Jefferson City, Tn., U.S.	192	36.07 N	83.29 W
Jefferson Farms	285	39.40 N	75.34 W
Jefferson Manor	284c	38.47 N	77.04 W
Jefferson Park ◆[8]	278	41.59 N	87.46 W
Jefferson Proving Ground ■	218	38.50 N	85.25 W
Jeffersonton	188	38.38 N	77.55 W
Jeffersontown	218	38.11 N	85.33 W
Jefferson Village	284c	38.52 N	77.10 W
Jeffersonville, Ga., U.S.	192	32.41 N	83.20 W
Jeffersonville, In., U.S.	218	38.16 N	85.44 W
Jeffersonville, N.Y., U.S.	210	41.46 N	74.56 W
Jeffersonville, Oh., U.S.	218	39.39 N	83.33 W
Jeffrey City	200	42.29 N	107.49 W
Jeffreys Bay	158	34.02 S	24.54 E
Jeffries Creek ≃	192	34.05 N	79.32 W
Jefimovka	80	52.13 N	52.03 E
Jefimovskij	76	59.30 N	35.02 E
Jefremov	76	53.09 N	38.07 E
Jefremova	82	56.13 N	38.59 E
Jefremovka	83	47.19 N	38.29 E
Jefremovo-Stepanovka	78	48.43 N	40.50 E
Jefremovskaja	82	55.25 N	38.59 E
Jega	150	12.15 N	4.23 E
Jegenstorf	58	47.03 N	7.30 E
Jegindybulak, Kaz.	86	49.45 N	76.23 E
Jegindybulak, Kaz.	86	48.42 N	81.48 E
Jegizkara, gora ∧	86	46.24 N	64.09 E
Jegorjevka	89	50.42 N	127.42 E
Jegorjevsk	82	55.23 N	39.02 E
Jegorlyk ≃	80	46.33 N	41.52 E
Jehol → Chengde	105	40.58 N	117.53 E
Jeja ≃	78	46.41 N	38.36 E
Jejsk	78	46.42 N	38.16 E
Jejskij liman c	78	46.42 N	38.25 E
Jeju → Cheju	90	33.31 N	126.32 E
Jejur	272b	22.53 N	88.08 E
Jēkabpils	76	56.29 N	25.51 E
Jekaterinburg (Sverdlovsk)	86	56.51 N	60.36 E
Jekaterinino	76	55.49 N	33.58 E
Jekaterininskoje	86	56.53 N	74.34 E
Jekaterinoslav → Dnepropetrovsk	78	48.27 N	34.59 E
Jekaterinoslavka	89	50.23 N	129.08 E
Jekaterinovka, Kaz.	86	54.36 N	70.58 E
Jekaterinovka, Ross.	78	46.42 N	38.46 E
Jekaterinovka, Ross.	80	53.04 N	49.28 E
Jekaterinovka, Ross.	80	46.32 N	41.42 E
Jekaterinovka, Ross.	80	52.03 N	44.21 E
Jekaterinovka, Ross.	83	47.33 N	38.23 E
Jekaterinovka ◆[8]	265b	55.46 N	37.23 E
Jekaterinovskaja	78	46.20 N	39.58 E
Jekateriny, proliv ʉ, Ross.	74	44.30 N	146.45 E
Jekateriny, proliv ʉ, Ross.	92a	44.25 N	146.40 E
Jekimoviči	76	54.07 N	33.18 E
Jekpindykurylys	80	47.49 N	47.17 E
Jekyll Island I	192	31.04 N	81.25 W
Jekyll Island State Park ♠	192	31.02 N	81.25 W
Jelabuga	80	55.47 N	52.04 E
Jelai ≃, Indon.	112	2.59 S	110.45 E
Jelai ≃, Malay.	114	4.04 N	102.20 E
Jelan', Ross.	80	52.13 N	44.11 E
Jelan', Ross.	80	50.57 N	43.44 E
Jelan', Ross.	83	48.41 N	39.47 E
Jelan', Ross.	86	57.39 N	63.42 E
Jelan' ≃, Ross.	78	51.07 N	41.25 E
Jelan' ≃, Ross.	80	50.57 N	43.44 E
Jelan' ≃, Ross.	80	51.07 N	41.26 E
Jelancy	88	52.49 N	106.25 E
Jelanec	78	47.42 N	31.51 E
Jelanka	86	55.37 N	75.18 E
Jelan'-Koleno	78	51.09 N	41.14 E
Jelan'-Kolenovskij	78	51.10 N	41.10 E
Jelat'ma	80	54.58 N	41.45 E
Jelaur, Ross.	80	54.34 N	50.21 E
Jelaur, Ross.	80	53.50 N	48.48 E
Jelchovka	80	53.51 N	50.18 E
Jel'covka	86	53.15 N	86.15 E
Jel'cy, Ross.	76	56.40 N	33.51 E
Jel'cy, Ross.	82	56.11 N	38.46 E
Jelec	76	52.37 N	38.30 E
Jeleckij	24	67.03 N	64.10 E
Jelenia Góra (Hirschberg)	30	50.55 N	15.46 E
Jelenia Góra □[4]	30	51.10 N	15.30 E
Jelenskij	76	53.29 N	35.23 E
Jelep La Pass)(	124	27.23 N	88.51 E
Jelgava	76	56.39 N	23.42 E
Jelgavkrasti	76	57.28 N	24.26 E
Jelisejevka	78	47.02 N	36.24 E
Jelizarovo, Ross.	80	58.33 N	44.50 E
Jelizarovo, Ukr.	78	48.12 N	34.33 E
Jelizavetgradka	78	48.48 N	32.24 E
Jelizavetinka	86	51.28 N	71.12 E
Jelizavetopol'skoje	86	52.51 N	60.36 E
Jelizavetovka	78	46.39 N	38.53 E
Jelizavety, mys ≻	89	54.26 N	142.42 E
Jelizovo	76	53.24 N	29.01 E
Jelli	154	5.22 N	31.48 E
Jellico	192	36.35 N	84.07 W
Jelling	41	55.45 N	9.26 E
Jelloway	214	40.33 N	82.18 W
Jelm Mountain ∧	200	41.06 N	105.58 W
Jel'n'a	76	54.35 N	33.11 E
Jelnat'	80	57.20 N	42.49 E
Jel'niki	80	54.37 N	43.53 E
Jeloguj ≃	74	63.13 N	87.45 E
Jel'onovka, Ukr.	83	47.50 N	37.40 E
Jel'onovka, Ukr.	83	48.39 N	38.01 E
Jelošnoje	86	55.27 N	66.44 E
Jelovo	80	57.03 N	54.54 E
Jels	41	55.21 N	9.12 E
Jelšanka, Ross.	80	51.49 N	46.23 E
Jelšanka, Ross.	80	52.35 N	47.59 E
Jelšanka Pervaja	80	52.53 N	52.02 E
Jelšava	30	48.39 N	20.14 E
Jel'sk	78	51.48 N	29.09 E
Jema ≃	144	10.09 N	38.20 E
Jemaa	150	9.27 N	8.23 E
Jemaja, Pulau I	112	2.55 N	105.45 E
Jemaluang	114	2.17 N	103.52 E
Jemantajevo	80	53.34 N	53.50 E
Jemanželinsk	86	54.45 N	61.20 E
Jemappes	50	50.27 N	3.53 E
Jember	115a	8.10 S	113.42 E
Jemca	24	63.04 N	40.20 E
Jemca ≃	24	63.15 N	41.20 E
Jemeljanovka	78	45.32 N	34.53 E
Jemeljanovo	86	56.11 N	92.40 E
Jemel'stan	24	61.13 N	52.29 E
Jemen, Volksrepublik → Yemen □[1]	144	15.00 N	47.00 E
Jemen → Yemen □[1]	144	15.00 N	47.00 E
Jemez ≃	200	35.22 N	106.31 W
Jemez Canyon Reservoir ⊜[1]	200	35.28 N	106.39 W
Jemez Indian Reservation ◆[4]	200	35.35 N	106.45 W
Jemez Springs	200	35.46 N	106.41 W
Jemgum	52	53.16 N	7.23 E
Jemil'čino	78	50.52 N	27.48 E
Jeminary	86	47.32 N	85.38 E
Jemmal	148	35.38 N	10.46 E
Jemnice	61	49.01 N	15.35 E
Jempang, Kenohan ⊜	112	0.26 S	116.12 E
Jena, Dtsch.	54	50.56 N	11.35 E
Jena, La., U.S.	194	31.40 N	92.08 W
Jenakijevo	83	48.14 N	38.13 E
Jenašimskij Polkan, gora ∧	74	59.50 N	92.52 E
Jenaz	58	46.55 N	9.45 E
Jenbach	64	47.24 N	11.47 E
Jenbek	86	48.53 N	77.12 E
Jendarata	114	3.55 N	100.57 E
Jendongin	88	53.27 N	113.01 E

Symbol	English	Deutsch	Español	Français	Português
≃	River	Fluß	Río	Rivière	Rio
≡	Canal	Kanal	Canal	Canal	Canal
⌞	Waterfall, Rapids	Wasserfall, Stromschnellen	Cascada, Rápidos	Chute d'eau, Rapides	Cascata, Rápidos
ʉ	Strait	Meeresstraße	Estrecho	Détroit	Estreito
c	Bay, Gulf	Bucht, Golf	Bahía, Golfo	Baie, Golfe	Baía, Golfo
⊜	Lake, Lakes	See, Seen	Lago, Lagos	Lac, Lacs	Lago, Lagos
⁝	Swamp	Sumpf	Pantano	Marais	Pântano
⊡	Ice Features, Glacier	Eis- und Gletscherformen	Accidentes Glaciales	Formes glaciaires	Acidentes glaciares
✝	Other Hydrographic Features	Andere Hydrographische Objekte	Otros Elementos Hidrográficos	Autres données hydrographiques	Outros acidentes hidrográficos
✢	Submarine Features	Untermeerische Objekte	Accidentes Submarinos	Formes de relief sous-marin	Acidentes submarinos
□	Political Unit	Politische Einheit	Unidad Politica	Entité politique	Unidade política
ʊ	Cultural Institution	Kulturelle Institution	Institución Cultural	Institution culturelle	Instituição cultural
⊥	Historical Site	Historische Stätte	Sitio Histórico	Site historique	Sitio histórico
♠	Recreational Site	Erholungs- und Ferienort	Sitio de Recreo	Centre de loisirs	Area de Lazer
⊠	Airport	Flughafen	Aeropuerto	Aéroport	Aeroporto
■	Military Installation	Militäranlage	Instalación Militar	Installation militaire	Instalação militar
◆	Miscellaneous	Verschiedenes	Misceláneo	Divers	Diversos

Name (ENGLISH) / Name (DEUTSCH)	Page / Seite	Lat.°′ / Breite°′	Long.°′ / Länge°′ E = Ost
Jendouba (Souk el Arba)	148	36.30 N	8.47 E
Jendouba □[8]	148	36.30 N	8.45 E
Jeneponto	112	5.41 S	119.42 E
Jenera	216	40.54 N	83.44 W
Jeniang	114	5.49 N	100.38 E
Jenisej (Yenisey) ≃	72	71.50 N	82.40 E
Jenisejsk	86	58.27 N	92.10 E
Jenisejskij kr'až ⋏	74	59.00 N	93.00 E
Jenisejskij zaliv ⊂	74	72.30 N	80.00 E
Jenison	216	42.54 N	85.47 W
Jenkins, Ky., U.S.	192	37.10 N	82.37 W
Jenkins, Tx., U.S.	222	32.59 N	94.44 W
Jenkins, Mount ∧	162	25.36 S	129.41 E
Jenkinson Lake ⊜[1]	226	38.44 N	120.33 W
Jenkinsville	192	34.16 N	81.17 W
Jenkintown	208	40.05 N	75.07 W
Jenks	196	36.01 N	95.58 W
Jenli	100	23.15 N	120.08 E
Jenners	214	40.08 N	79.02 W
Jennersdorf	61	46.57 N	16.08 E
Jennerstown	214	40.10 N	79.04 W
Jennifer Branch ≃	284b	39.25 N	76.30 W
Jennings, Fl., U.S.	192	30.36 N	83.05 W
Jennings, La., U.S.	194	30.13 N	92.39 W
Jennings, Mo., U.S.	219	38.43 N	90.15 W
Jennings □[6]	218	38.59 N	85.36 W
Jennings Creek ≃	216	40.53 N	84.17 W
Jennings Lodge	224	45.23 N	122.36 W
Jenotajevka	80	47.15 N	47.03 E
Jenpeg Dam ◆[6]	184	54.33 N	98.02 W
Jensen	200	40.22 N	109.20 W
Jensen Beach	220	27.15 N	80.13 W
Jens Munk Island I	176	69.42 N	79.30 W
Jens Munks Ø I	176	64.40 N	40.30 W
Jenu	112	0.36 S	109.52 E
Jen'uka	88	57.58 N	121.42 E
Jeonju → Chŏnju	98	35.49 N	127.08 E
Jepač	24	66.58 N	61.22 E
Jepara	115a	6.35 S	110.39 E
Jeparit	166	36.09 S	141.59 E
Jepelacio	248	6.07 S	76.57 W
Jepichin	80	48.16 N	45.14 E
Jepifan'	76	53.49 N	38.33 E
Jeppener	258	35.17 S	58.12 W
Jeptha Knob ∧[2]	218	38.11 N	85.07 W
Jepua (Jeppo)	26	63.24 N	22.37 E
Jequeri	255	20.27 S	42.40 W
Jequetepeque ≃	248	7.21 S	79.36 W
Jequié	255	13.51 S	40.05 W
Jequitaí	255	17.15 S	44.28 W
Jequitinhonha	255	16.26 S	41.00 W
Jequitinhonha ≃	255	15.51 S	38.53 W
Jerachtur	80	54.43 N	41.09 E
Jerada	148	34.17 N	2.13 W
Jeradou	36	36.15 N	10.23 E
Jerangle	171b	35.52 S	149.22 E
Jeransang	114	3.52 N	102.22 E
Jerantut	114	3.56 N	102.22 E
Jerba, Île de I	148	33.48 N	10.54 E
Jerbar	140	5.39 N	31.05 E
Jerbent	128	39.19 N	58.36 E
Jerbogačon	74	61.16 N	108.00 E
Jercevo	24	60.48 N	40.05 E
Jerdenevo	82	54.55 N	36.27 E
Jerécuaro	234	20.09 N	100.31 W
Jeremejevka	83	46.58 N	39.33 E
Jeremejevo	82	55.57 N	37.01 E
Jérémie	238	18.39 N	74.07 W
Jeremino	82	56.27 N	37.58 E
Jeremoabo	250	10.04 S	38.21 W
Jeremy Hill ∧[2]	207	42.45 N	71.21 W
Jeremy Point ›	207	41.53 N	70.04 W
Jerevan	84	40.11 N	44.30 E
Jerez ≃	234	22.15 N	103.11 W
Jerez de García Salinas	234	22.39 N	103.00 W
Jerez de la Frontera	34	36.41 N	6.08 W
Jerez de los Caballeros	34	38.19 N	6.46 W
Jergač	86	57.28 N	56.39 E
Jergeni ⋏[2]	80	47.00 N	44.00 E
Jergeninskij	80	47.07 N	44.28 E
Jericho, Austl.	166	23.36 S	146.08 E
Jericho, N.J., U.S.	285	39.48 N	75.09 W
Jericho, N.Y., U.S.	210	40.47 N	73.32 W
Jericho → Arīḥā	132	31.52 N	35.27 E
Jericho Dam ⊜[1]	158	26.39 S	30.28 E
Jerichow	54	52.30 N	12.01 E
Jericó, Bra.	250	6.33 S	37.48 W
Jericó, Col.	246	5.47 N	75.47 W
Jericoacoara, Ponta de ›	250	2.48 S	40.29 W
Jerid, Chott ≡	148	33.42 N	8.26 E
Jerik ≃	83	48.59 N	38.30 E
Jerilderie	166	35.22 S	145.44 E
Jerimoth Hill ∧[2]	207	41.52 N	71.47 W
Jerki	78	48.59 N	31.00 E
Jermak	86	52.02 N	76.55 E
Jermakovo	80	53.11 N	49.38 E
Jermakovskaja	80	48.03 N	41.17 E
Jermakovskoje	86	53.16 N	92.24 E
Jermekejevo	80	54.05 N	53.40 E
Jermentau	86	51.38 N	73.10 E
Jermentau ⋏	86	51.10 N	73.10 E
Jermica	24	66.56 N	52.15 E
Jermilovka	86	57.40 N	72.55 E
Jermiš'	80	54.46 N	42.16 E
Jermolajevo, Ross.	86	55.13 N	92.10 E
Jermolajevo, Ross.	86	52.46 N	55.47 E
Jermolino, Ross.	82	55.12 N	36.36 E
Jermolino, Ross.	82	55.57 N	36.54 E
Jermolino, Ross.	82	56.48 N	37.49 E
Jermolino, Ross.	86	57.20 N	64.43 E
Jermyn	210	41.31 N	75.32 W
Jernhatten ∧[2]	41	56.15 N	10.48 E
Jernih	114	4.25 N	97.43 E
Jeroaquara	255	15.23 S	50.25 W
Jerofej Pavlovič	89	53.58 N	122.01 E
Jerome, Az., U.S.	200	34.44 N	112.06 W
Jerome, Id., U.S.	202	42.43 N	114.31 W
Jerome, Il., U.S.	219	39.46 N	89.41 W
Jerome, Mi., U.S.	216	42.01 N	84.28 W
Jerome, Pa., U.S.	214	40.12 N	78.59 W
Jeromesville	214	40.48 N	82.11 W
Jer'omino	86	58.35 N	79.25 E
Jerónimos, Mosteiro dos ʋ[1]	266c	38.42 N	9.12 W
Jeröö	88	49.45 N	106.40 E
Jeröö ≃	88	49.54 N	106.08 E
Jeropol	74	65.15 N	168.40 E
Jerpoint Abbey ⊥	48	53.29 N	7.08 W
Jerry City	216	41.15 N	83.36 W
Jerry Slough ≃	226	35.33 N	119.31 W
Jersey	214	40.03 N	82.46 W
Jersey □[6]	219	39.07 N	90.20 W
Jersey □[2], Europe	22	49.15 N	2.10 W
Jersey □[2], Europe	43b	49.15 N	2.10 W
Jersey City	210	40.43 N	74.04 W
Jersey City State College ʋ[2]	276	40.43 N	74.05 W
Jersey Mountain ∧	202	45.29 N	115.34 W
Jersey Shore	210	41.12 N	77.16 W
Jersey Village	222	29.52 N	95.35 W
Jerseyville	219	39.07 N	90.19 W
Jerši	76	54.24 N	34.12 E
Jeršiči	76	53.40 N	32.44 E
Jeršov	80	51.20 N	48.17 E
Jeršovka	86	54.07 N	64.59 E
Jeršovo	82	55.46 N	36.52 E
Jeršovskij	86	52.29 N	59.08 E
Jertarskij	86	56.47 N	64.18 E
Jerte ≃	34	39.58 N	6.17 W
Jerteh	114	5.45 N	102.30 E
Jertoma	24	63.32 N	47.48 E
Jerumenha	250	7.05 S	43.30 W
Jerusalem Airport ⊠	132	31.52 N	35.12 E
Jerusalem → Yerushalayim	132	31.46 N	35.14 E
Jerusalim (Talusan)	116	7.26 N	122.49 E
Jeruslan ≃	80	50.15 N	45.42 E
Jervaulx Abbey ʋ[1]	44	54.16 N	1.43 W
Jervis, Cape ›	168b	35.38 S	138.06 E
Jervis Bay	170	35.08 S	150.42 E
Jervis Bay ⊂	170	35.05 S	150.44 E
Jervis Inlet ⊂	182	49.46 N	124.10 W
Jervois Range ⋏	162	22.38 S	136.05 E
Jerxheim	54	52.05 N	10.54 E
Jerykly	80	55.11 N	51.26 E
Jerzens	58	47.10 N	10.45 E
Jesaulovka	83	48.03 N	39.02 E
Jesenankaty ≃	80	50.32 N	51.47 E
Jesenice, Česko.	54	50.04 N	13.29 E
Jesenice, Slo.	61	46.27 N	14.04 E
Jesenice, údolní nádrž ⊜[1]	60	50.04 N	12.27 E
Jeseník	30	50.14 N	17.13 E
Jesenoviči	76	57.17 N	34.14 E
Jesensaj	80	49.54 N	51.28 E
Ješera	84	43.04 N	40.55 E
Jeserig bei Wiesenburg	54	52.05 N	12.27 E
Jesi	66	43.31 N	13.14 E
Jesil'	86	51.58 N	66.24 E
Jes'ki	76	57.56 N	36.23 E
Jesönbulag → Altaj	90	46.20 N	96.18 E
Jessej	74	68.29 N	102.10 E
Jesselton → Kota Kinabalu	112	5.59 N	116.04 E
Jessen	54	51.47 N	12.58 E
Jessentuki	84	44.03 N	42.51 E
Jesser Point ›	158	27.32 S	32.40 E
Jessheim	26	60.09 N	11.11 E
Jessnitz	54	51.41 N	12.17 E
Jessore	124	23.10 N	89.13 E
Jessup, Md., U.S.	208	39.08 N	76.46 W
Jessup, Pa., U.S.	210	41.28 N	75.33 W
Jessup Park ♠	280	34.15 N	118.24 W
Jestetten	58	47.39 N	8.34 E
Jestřebí	54	50.38 N	14.36 E
Jésuite, Lac du ⊜	206	46.53 N	72.36 W
Jesup, Ga., U.S.	192	31.36 N	81.53 W
Jesup, Ia., U.S.	190	42.28 N	92.03 W
Jesup, Lake ⊜	220	28.43 N	81.14 W
Jesús	252	27.03 S	55.47 W
Jésus, Île I	206	45.35 N	73.45 W
Jesús Carranza	234	17.26 N	95.02 W
Jesús de Otoro	236	14.26 N	87.59 W
Jesús María, Arg.	252	30.59 S	64.06 W
Jesús María, Méx.	232	25.06 N	107.28 W
Jesús María, Méx.	234	21.58 N	102.21 W
Jesús María, Perú	286d	12.04 S	77.04 W
Jesús María ≃	234	21.51 N	104.42 W
Jesús María, Punta ›	258	34.39 S	56.55 W
Jesús Menéndez	240p	21.10 N	76.29 W
Jet	196	36.39 N	98.10 W
Jeta, Ilha de I	150	11.53 N	16.15 W
Jetafe	116	10.09 N	124.09 E
Jetmore	198	38.05 N	99.53 W
Jet Propulsion Laboratory ʋ[3]	280	34.12 N	118.11 W
Jetpur	120	21.44 N	70.37 E
Jetřichovice	54	50.49 N	14.25 E
Jett	218	38.11 N	84.49 W
Jette	50	50.52 N	4.20 E
Jettingen	58	48.23 N	10.26 E
Jeumont	50	50.18 N	4.06 E
Jeune Landing	182	50.27 N	127.30 W
Jeunieb	114	5.10 N	96.29 E
Jeuram	114	4.14 N	96.18 E
Jever	52	53.34 N	7.54 E
Jeverland ◆[1]	52	53.35 N	8.00 E
Jevgaščino	86	56.26 N	74.41 E
Jevgenjevka	85	43.31 N	77.40 E
Jevičko	30	49.38 N	16.43 E
Jevišovice	61	48.59 N	16.00 E
Jevišovka ≃	61	48.49 N	16.28 E
Jevlach	84	40.36 N	47.09 E
Jevlaš'ovo	80	53.07 N	46.51 E
Jevnaker	26	60.15 N	10.28 E
Jevpatorija	78	45.12 N	33.22 E
Jevra	86	59.56 N	64.27 E
Jevrejskaja Avtonomnaja Oblast' □[8]	89	48.30 N	132.00 E
Jevsug	83	49.13 N	39.18 E
Jevsug ≃	83	48.47 N	39.19 E
Jewel Cave National Monument ♠	198	43.42 N	103.50 W
Jewell, Ia., U.S.	190	42.18 N	93.38 W
Jewell, Ks., U.S.	198	39.40 N	98.09 W
Jewell, N.Y., U.S.	210	43.13 N	75.48 W
Jewell, Oh., U.S.	216	41.20 N	84.17 W
Jewell, Or., U.S.	224	45.56 N	123.30 W
Jewell Ridge	192	37.11 N	81.47 W
Jewell Village	218	39.10 N	85.51 W
Jewett, Il., U.S.	194	39.13 N	88.15 W
Jewett, Oh., U.S.	214	40.22 N	81.00 W
Jewett, Tx., U.S.	222	31.22 N	96.09 W
Jewett City	207	41.36 N	71.58 W
Jewett Creek ≃	212	44.22 N	75.45 W
Jewett Lake ⊜	184	56.09 N	104.40 W
Jewettville	284a	42.43 N	78.52 W
Jey ◆[8]	267d	35.41 N	51.21 E
Jeyretān	120	37.10 N	67.20 E
Jezerce ∧	38	42.26 N	19.49 E
Jezerišče	76	55.50 N	29.59 E
Jezerní hora ∧	60	49.10 N	13.11 E
Ježicha	80	58.06 N	47.40 E
Jeziorany	30	53.58 N	20.46 E
Ježovo	80	58.02 N	52.14 E
Jezreel, Valley of → Yizre'el, 'Émeq ≚	132	32.36 N	35.14 E
J. G. Strijdomdam ⊜[1]	158	27.25 S	32.05 E
Jhābua	120	22.46 N	74.36 E
Jhāhtipahāri	126	23.22 N	86.54 E
Jha Jha	124	24.46 N	86.22 E
Jhajjar	124	28.37 N	76.39 E
Jhal	120	28.17 N	67.27 E
Jhālakāti	124	22.39 N	90.12 E
Jhālarāpātan	124	24.33 N	76.10 E
Jhālāwār	124	24.36 N	76.09 E
Jhalida	124	23.22 N	85.58 E
Jhal Jhao	120	26.18 N	65.35 E
Jhālod	120	23.06 N	74.09 E
Jhang Sadar	123	31.16 N	72.19 E
Jhānsi	124	25.26 N	78.35 E
Jhānsi Post	123	33.52 N	71.24 E
Jhāpā	124	26.29 N	87.51 E
Jhārgrām	126	22.27 N	86.59 E
Jharia	126	23.45 N	86.24 E
Jhārpokhariā	126	22.10 N	86.38 E
Jhārsuguda	120	21.51 N	84.02 E
Jhawāriān	123	32.22 N	72.38 E
Jhelum	123	32.56 N	73.44 E
Jhelum ≃	123	31.12 N	72.08 E
Jhenida	124	23.33 N	89.10 E
Jhenkāri	272b	22.46 N	88.18 E
Jhikergacha	126	23.07 N	89.07 E
Jhikra	126	22.37 N	87.55 E
Jhilimili	126	22.49 N	86.37 E
Jhil Kuranga ◆[8]	272a	28.40 N	77.17 E
Jhilla ≃[1]	126	21.58 N	88.56 E
Jhinkpāni	124	22.25 N	85.47 E
Jhok Rind	120	31.27 N	70.26 E
Jhumra	123	31.34 N	73.11 E
Jhunjhunūn	120	28.08 N	75.24 E
Jiaban, Zhg.	102	25.10 N	107.03 E
Jiaban, Zhg.	102	25.38 N	107.07 E
Jiabong	116	11.46 N	124.57 E
Jiacha	120	29.11 N	92.44 E
Jiading	106	31.23 N	121.15 E
Jiāganj	126	24.14 N	88.16 E
Jiagedan	89	51.35 N	120.55 E
Jiahashitai	89	46.25 N	122.17 E
Jiahe	102	25.43 N	112.05 E
Jiajiachang, Zhg.	107	29.44 N	105.06 E
Jiajiachang, Zhg.	107	30.26 N	104.21 E
Jiajiagou, Zhg.	104	41.44 N	120.58 E
Jiajiagou, Zhg.	104	42.20 N	121.46 E
Jiajiang	107	29.45 N	103.34 E
Jiajiayuan	106	32.18 N	120.55 E
Jiakou	100	30.10 N	119.03 E
Jiakou Wa ≡	105	38.58 N	116.50 E
Jiali	120	30.47 N	93.24 E
Jialing ≃	102	29.34 N	106.35 E
Jialou	100	32.54 N	113.26 E
Jialu	106	30.26 N	118.50 E
Jialu ≃	100	33.38 N	114.36 E
Jiamingzhen	107	29.16 N	105.20 E
Jiamusi (Kiamusze)	89	46.50 N	130.21 E
Jiamuyingzi	104	41.56 N	121.43 E
Ji'an, Zhg.	98	41.06 N	126.08 E
Ji'an, Zhg.	100	27.07 N	114.58 E
Jian ≃, Zhg.	100	26.38 N	118.12 E
Jian ≃, Zhg.	104	40.59 N	121.51 E
Jian'an	89	43.04 N	125.03 E
Jianba	106	31.59 N	120.35 E
Jianbi	106	32.11 N	119.35 E
Jianchang, Zhg.	98	40.51 N	119.46 E
Jianchang, Zhg.	98	39.58 N	122.35 E
Jianchang, Zhg.	98	41.16 N	124.29 E
Ji'anchang, Zhg.	107	30.31 N	106.02 E
Jianchangying	98	40.06 N	118.49 E
Jianchapu	105	39.06 N	116.31 E
Jianchaxi, Zhg.	102	28.08 N	108.04 E
Jianchaxi, Zhg.	107	30.22 N	104.03 E
Jianchuan	102	26.34 N	99.53 E
Jiande	100	29.29 N	119.16 E
Jiang'an	107	28.44 N	105.05 E
Jiangba	100	33.08 N	118.45 E
Jiangbei (Lianglukou)	107	29.44 N	106.38 E
Jiangbeixu	100	26.20 N	115.26 E
Jiangbian	102	24.03 N	103.37 E
Jiangbianzhai	102	23.49 N	100.11 E
Jiangcheng, Zhg.	102	22.40 N	101.48 E
Jiangcheng, Zhg.	105	38.52 N	115.22 E
Jiangcun	100	28.17 N	117.49 E
Jiangdi	102	25.08 N	104.45 E
Jiangdihe	102	25.55 N	101.31 E
Jiangdu	100	32.26 N	119.34 E
Jiangduo	100	32.22 N	120.15 E
Jiange	102	32.06 N	105.29 E
Jianggezhuang	98	39.27 N	119.09 E
Jianghua (Shuikou)	102	24.58 N	111.38 E
Jianghuaqiao	106	32.05 N	120.00 E
Jiangji	100	32.19 N	115.44 E
Jiangjia, Zhg.	106	31.58 N	121.28 E
Jiangjia, Zhg.	106	31.40 N	121.09 E
Jiangjiadian	104	41.41 N	121.03 E
Jiangjiagou	104	41.44 N	121.44 E
Jiangjiaji	100	31.59 N	115.16 E
Jiangjiatun, Zhg.	104	41.42 N	122.02 E
Jiangjiatun, Zhg.	104	41.42 N	122.25 E
Jiangjin	107	29.17 N	106.15 E
Jiangjing	100	25.34 N	119.25 E
Jiangjunmiao	86	44.43 N	90.05 E
Jiangjunqiao	102	31.18 N	100.55 E
Jiangkou, Zhg.	100	29.43 N	121.25 E
Jiangkou, Zhg.	100	27.44 N	114.49 E
Jiangkou, Zhg.	100	27.27 N	118.03 E
Jiangkou, Zhg.	100	25.29 N	119.12 E
Jiangkou, Zhg.	100	27.21 N	115.31 E
Jiangkou, Zhg.	102	29.38 N	110.20 E
Jiangkou, Zhg.	102	23.31 N	110.17 E
Jiangkou, Zhg.	102	33.39 N	107.12 E
Jiangkou, Zhg.	102	27.37 N	108.48 E
Jiangkou, Zhg.	102	30.26 N	111.42 E
Jiangkou, Zhg.	107	30.14 N	103.55 E
Jiangkouji	100	32.50 N	116.16 E
Jiangkoutang	100	27.30 N	112.44 E
Jiangle	100	26.42 N	117.25 E
Jiangliadian	98	42.33 N	117.27 E
Jiangling	102	30.20 N	112.06 E
Jianglingxi	102	31.28 N	107.13 E
Jiangmen	100	22.35 N	113.05 E
Jiangmifeng	89	43.58 N	126.45 E
Jiangning	106	31.58 N	118.50 E
Jiangpu	100	32.04 N	118.37 E
Jiangqiao	89	46.48 N	123.45 E
Jiangqiaotou	106	30.37 N	120.38 E
Jiangshan	100	28.45 N	118.37 E
Jiangshan ≃	100	28.57 N	118.50 E
Jiangshe	106	31.34 N	120.08 E
Jiangshui	98	37.13 N	113.59 E
Jiangsu (Kiangsu) □[4]	90	33.00 N	120.00 E
Jiangtian	100	25.52 N	119.34 E
Jiangtun, Zhg.	102	23.41 N	112.37 E
Jiangtun, Zhg.	104	41.37 N	122.22 E
Jiangwakou	105	39.31 N	117.42 E
Jiangwan, Zhg.	100	29.25 N	118.02 E
Jiangwan, Zhg.	106	31.18 N	121.29 E
Jiangwan Airport ⊠	269b	31.20 N	121.30 E
Jiangxi	102	22.51 N	101.50 E
Jiangxi (Kiangsi) □[4]	100	28.00 N	116.00 E
Jiangxiacun	106	31.44 N	121.50 E
Jiangxiang	100	32.16 N	117.37 E
Jiangxikou	100	27.36 N	118.23 E
Jiangya	102	29.17 N	110.39 E
Jiangyi	100	29.12 N	115.46 E
Jiangyin	106	31.55 N	120.16 E
Jiangyou	102	31.47 N	104.45 E
Jiangyu, Zhg.	98	36.16 N	118.40 E
Jiangyu, Zhg.	100	27.50 N	112.46 E
Jiangyuanzhen	107	30.35 N	103.48 E
Jiangzaogang	106	32.01 N	121.03 E
Jiangzhasiji	120	30.28 N	88.55 E
Jiangzhong	120	29.10 N	93.32 E
Jianhe, Zhg.	102	26.27 N	108.33 E
Jianhe, Zhg.	105	39.14 N	118.03 E
Jianhu	100	33.28 N	119.50 E
Jianli	100	29.49 N	112.53 E
Jianling	100	32.45 N	113.12 E
Jianning	100	26.50 N	116.49 E
Jian'ou	100	27.03 N	118.19 E
Jianping (Yebaishou)	98	41.24 N	119.37 E
Jianqiao	106	30.20 N	120.12 E
Jianqigou	104	40.54 N	123.17 E
Jianshan, Zhg.	100	29.14 N	120.44 E
Jianshan, Zhg.	100	29.58 N	120.16 E
Jian Shan ∧	104	41.49 N	121.44 E
Jianshi	102	30.36 N	109.38 E
Jianshui	102	23.38 N	102.49 E
Jiantiao	100	29.04 N	121.36 E
Jiantou	105	39.26 N	115.41 E
Jiantouji	98	34.35 N	117.34 E
Jianyang, Zhg.	100	27.22 N	118.04 E
Jianyang, Zhg.	100	33.27 N	119.40 E
Jianyang, Zhg.	107	30.24 N	104.32 E
Jiao ≃	100	26.48 N	119.42 E
Jiaocheng	102	37.33 N	112.02 E
Jiaodao	105	39.39 N	116.06 E
Jiaodianzi	104	41.32 N	121.49 E
Jiaodonggou	104	40.50 N	123.58 E
Jiaohe, Zhg.	89	43.42 N	127.19 E
Jiaohe, Zhg.	98	38.01 N	116.17 E
Jiaojiapuzi	104	40.47 N	123.48 E
Jiaolai ≃, Zhg.	89	43.43 N	123.05 E
Jiaolai ≃, Zhg.	98	42.47 N	120.44 E
Jiaolai ≃, Zhg.	98	37.07 N	119.35 E
Jiaoling	100	24.41 N	116.10 E
Jiaomei	100	24.32 N	117.54 E
Jiaonan (Wanggezhuang)	98	35.51 N	119.59 E
Jiao Shan I	106	31.21 N	120.06 E
Jiaoshanhe	100	29.38 N	112.33 E
Jiaoxi	106	31.49 N	120.10 E
Jiaoxian	98	36.18 N	119.58 E
Jiaoyang	100	27.56 N	119.16 E
Jiaozhou Wan ⊂	98	36.10 N	120.15 E
Jiaozhuang	100	33.14 N	114.02 E
Jiaozuo	102	35.15 N	113.13 E
Jiapu	106	31.06 N	119.56 E
Jiashan, Zhg.	100	32.47 N	118.00 E
Jiashan, Zhg.	106	30.51 N	120.54 E
Jiashi	85	39.28 N	76.45 E
Jiashun Hu ⊜	120	34.35 N	86.05 E
Jiasi	107	29.06 N	106.24 E
Jiatan	107	30.12 N	106.29 E
Jiatanchang	107	29.09 N	106.16 E
Jiawang	98	34.27 N	117.27 E
Jiaxian, Zhg.	100	33.58 N	113.13 E
Jiaxian, Zhg.	102	38.01 N	110.31 E
Jiaxiang	98	35.25 N	116.21 E
Jiaxing	106	30.46 N	120.45 E
Jiayin	89	48.53 N	130.24 E
Jiayu	100	29.58 N	113.55 E
Jiayun Hu ⊜	120	35.02 N	85.40 E
Jiaze	106	31.42 N	119.47 E
Jiazhai	98	34.33 N	115.48 E
Jiazhuang	105	39.19 N	117.22 E
Jiazi	100	22.55 N	116.04 E
Jiazier	85	38.40 N	76.33 E
Jibacoa ≃	240p	20.15 N	77.12 W
Jibagalle	144	8.04 N	48.39 E
Jibalei	144	10.09 N	50.53 E
Jibannagar	126	23.25 N	88.50 E
Jíbaro ≃	286b	23.03 N	82.23 W
Jibat ∧	144	8.45 N	37.29 E
Jibiya	150	13.05 N	7.12 E
Jiboa ≃	236	13.22 N	89.04 W
Jibóia, Ilha da I	256	23.03 S	44.22 W
Jibuti → Djibouti	144	11.36 N	43.09 E
Jicamarca, Quebrada V	286d	12.02 S	76.57 W
Jicarilla Apache Indian Reservation ◆[4]	200	36.40 N	107.00 W
Jicarón, Isla I	246	7.16 N	81.47 W
Jicatuyo ≃	236	14.59 N	88.16 W
Jicheng	105	39.23 N	116.17 E
Jičín	30	50.26 N	15.21 E
Jicotea ≃	286b	23.01 N	82.14 W
Jidād	140	11.05 N	24.44 E
Jiddah	144	21.30 N	39.12 E
Jidingxilin	120	32.52 N	92.21 E
Jidy, Wādī al- V	142	30.13 N	32.46 E
Jiebu	100	28.15 N	115.02 E
Jiedong	100	26.02 N	113.00 E
Jiegou	100	33.21 N	117.55 E
Jiehe	98	35.16 N	117.04 E
Jieji	100	33.33 N	118.24 E
Jiejiang	106	31.58 N	120.43 E
Jiejinkou	89	47.57 N	132.50 E
Jielingkou	98	40.09 N	119.15 E
Jielongchang	107	29.13 N	106.32 E
Jiemian	100	25.56 N	118.02 E
Jiepai, Zhg.	100	26.41 N	112.46 E
Jiepai, Zhg.	100	29.34 N	115.06 E
Jiepai, Zhg.	106	30.55 N	119.32 E
Jiepai, Zhg.	107	29.28 N	104.43 E
Jiepaiji	100	32.15 N	117.50 E
Jiesheng	100	22.45 N	115.25 E
Jieshi, Zhg.	100	22.51 N	115.49 E
Jieshi, Zhg.	107	29.27 N	105.17 E
Jieshi Wan ⊂	100	22.46 N	115.40 E
Jieshou, Zhg.	100	33.18 N	115.20 E
Jieshou, Zhg.	100	27.22 N	117.40 E
Jieshou, Zhg.	100	33.00 N	119.27 E
Jiexi	100	23.28 N	115.56 E
Jiexiu	102	37.05 N	111.51 E
Jieyang	100	23.35 N	116.21 E
Jiezhongdian	100	32.41 N	112.29 E
Jieznas	76	54.36 N	24.10 E
Jifjāfah, Bi'r ⊤[4]	140	30.27 N	33.11 E
Jiftūn, Jazā'ir II	140	27.13 N	33.56 E
Jiggalong	162	23.25 S	120.47 E
Jiggalong Creek ≃	162	22.53 S	120.14 E
Jigongying	102	26.18 N	104.48 E
Jigongzhen	98	34.02 N	115.32 E
Jiguaní	240p	20.22 N	76.26 W
Jiguanshan, Zhg.	98	40.32 N	123.55 E
Jiguanshan, Zhg.	104	42.08 N	124.15 E
Jiguanshan, Zhg.	104	41.18 N	123.36 E
Jigüey, Bahía de ⊂	240p	22.08 N	78.05 W
Jigzhi	102	33.28 N	101.29 E
Jihe	100	32.15 N	112.48 E
Jiheier	85	38.11 N	75.46 E
Jihlava	30	49.24 N	15.36 E
Jihlava ≃	61	48.55 N	16.37 E
Jihočeský Kraj □[4]	30	49.05 N	14.30 E
Jihomoravský Kraj □[4]	30	49.10 N	16.40 E
Jiiqley	144	4.25 N	45.22 E
Jijel	148	36.48 N	5.46 E
Jijel □[5]	148	36.45 N	6.00 E
Jijia ≃	38	46.54 N	28.05 E
Jijiadianzi	98	35.31 N	118.59 E
Jijiamiao	107	29.18 N	104.06 E
Jijiapuzi	104	41.16 N	124.12 E
Jijiashi	106	32.08 N	120.18 E
Jijiaying	105	40.20 N	115.24 E
Jijiga	144	9.22 N	42.47 E
Jikawo	144	8.22 N	33.46 E
Jikawo ≃	144	8.22 N	33.47 E
Jike	102	31.00 N	99.41 E
Jilalin	89	51.19 N	119.55 E
Jilantai	102	39.47 N	105.45 E
Jilbānah, Bi'r al- ⊤[4]	142	30.55 N	32.29 E
Jilemutu	89	52.14 N	120.47 E
Jilib	144	0.29 N	42.46 E
Jilibulake	120	33.05 N	93.10 E
Jili Hu ⊜	86	46.57 N	87.27 E
Jilin (Kirin)	89	43.51 N	126.33 E
Jilin (Kirin) □[4]	90	44.00 N	126.00 E
Jiliu ≃	89	52.04 N	120.48 E
Jill, Kediet ej ∧	148	22.38 N	12.33 W
Jill, Sebkhet ej ⊜	148	22.47 N	12.53 W
Jiloca ≃	34	41.21 N	1.39 W
Jilotepec de Abasolo	234	19.58 N	99.32 W
Jilotlán de los Dolores	234	19.14 N	102.59 W
Jílové	54	50.46 N	14.07 E
Jima	144	7.36 N	36.50 E
Jimbaran	115b	8.46 S	115.11 E
Jimbolia	38	45.47 N	20.43 E
Jimboomba	171a	27.50 S	153.02 E
Jimei	100	24.37 N	118.07 E
Jimena de la Frontera	34	36.26 N	5.27 W
Jiménez, Méx.	232	29.02 N	100.41 W
Jiménez, Méx.	232	27.08 N	104.55 W
Jimenez, Pil.	116	8.20 N	123.50 E
Jiménez, Arroyo ≃	288	34.44 S	58.13 W
Jiménez, Laguna de ⊜	258	35.26 S	59.01 W
Jiménez del Téul	234	23.10 N	104.05 W
Jimeta	146	9.16 N	12.27 E
Jimi ≃	164	5.20 S	144.20 E
Jimingcun	105	39.19 N	116.09 E
Jiminghe	100	30.36 N	115.32 E
Jim Ned Creek ≃	196	31.50 N	99.07 W
Jimo	98	36.23 N	120.27 E
Jimsar	86	44.00 N	89.04 E
Jim Thorpe	210	40.52 N	75.43 W
Jimuganayaji	85	38.36 N	75.39 E
Jin (Gam) ≃, Asia	110	21.55 N	105.12 E
Jin ≃, Zhg.	100	28.24 N	115.49 E
Jin ≃, Zhg.	100	24.54 N	118.35 E
Jin ≃, Zhg.	100	26.51 N	117.46 E
Jināḥ	140	25.20 N	30.31 E
Jinan (Tsinan), Zhg.	98	36.40 N	116.57 E
Jin'an, Zhg.	100	28.38 N	119.18 E
Jinbang	100	25.01 N	118.01 E
Jinbo ≃	107	28.54 N	103.40 E
Jincang	89	43.20 N	130.30 E
Jince	60	49.47 N	13.59 E
Jinchanggouliang	98	41.56 N	120.19 E
Jincheng, Zhg.	102	35.30 N	112.50 E
Jincheng, Zhg.	104	41.12 N	121.25 E
Jinchengshai	102	26.43 N	111.00 E
Jincheng Shan ∧	107	30.47 N	106.32 E
Jinchuan	102	31.25 N	102.08 E
Jinchuanqiao	102	27.18 N	101.48 E
Jincun	106	31.08 N	119.49 E
Jīnd	123	29.19 N	76.19 E
Jindabyne	171b	36.25 S	148.38 E
Jindabyne, Lake ⊜[1]	171b	36.22 S	148.37 E
Jindaichang	107	29.43 N	104.49 E
Jindālī, Bi'r ⊤[4]	142	29.55 N	31.40 E
Jindřichovice	54	50.15 N	12.37 E
Jindřichův Hradec	30	49.09 N	15.00 E
Jinfeng	100	26.01 N	119.36 E
Jinfosi	102	39.29 N	99.00 E
Jing ≃, Zhg.	86	44.52 N	82.50 E
Jing ≃, Zhg.	102	34.28 N	109.00 E
Jing'an	100	28.52 N	115.20 E
Jin'gangpo	107	29.38 N	106.25 E
Jingangtou	100	27.54 N	113.40 E
Jingangtuo	107	29.10 N	106.07 E
Jing'anji	98	34.30 N	116.55 E
Jingbian	102	37.25 N	108.21 E
Jingbohu ⊜	89	43.54 N	128.54 E
Jingcheng	100	24.36 N	117.30 E
Jingde	100	30.19 N	118.31 E
Jingdezhen (Kingtechen)	100	29.16 N	117.11 E
Jingdong	102	24.28 N	100.52 E
Jingellic	171b	35.56 S	147.42 E
Jingeryu	105	39.43 N	115.36 E
Jinggang	100	28.28 N	112.46 E
Jinggangshan (Ciping)	100	26.36 N	114.05 E
Jinggongqiao	100	29.45 N	117.11 E
Jinggu	102	23.32 N	100.41 E
Jingguanzhen	107	29.55 N	106.33 E
Jinghai, Zhg.	100	23.03 N	116.31 E
Jinghai, Zhg.	105	38.56 N	116.55 E
Jinghaiwei	98	36.52 N	122.13 E
Jinghe	86	44.39 N	82.50 E
Jinghong	102	22.01 N	100.49 E
Jinghuiling	105	40.22 N	117.27 E
Jingjiang, Zhg.	102	26.19 N	100.33 E
Jingjiang, Zhg.	106	32.01 N	120.15 E
Jingjiayu	104	41.40 N	123.51 E
Jingle	102	38.24 N	111.54 E
Jinglou	100	32.39 N	112.56 E
Jingmen	102	31.00 N	112.09 E
Jingning, Zhg.	100	27.59 N	119.38 E
Jingning, Zhg.	102	35.25 N	105.56 E
Jingou	104	41.38 N	120.35 E
Jingoutun	98	41.03 N	117.27 E
Jingshan	100	31.02 N	113.05 E
Jingtai	102	37.17 N	104.09 E
Jingu	100	25.13 N	118.07 E
Jingxi	102	23.08 N	106.29 E
Jingxian, Zhg.	98	37.42 N	116.16 E
Jingxian, Zhg.	100	30.42 N	118.24 E
Jingxian, Zhg.	102	26.40 N	109.25 E
Jingxin	100	24.14 N	115.56 E
Jingxing, Zhg.	89	47.04 N	123.01 E
Jingxing, Zhg.	98	38.02 N	114.08 E
Jingyan	107	29.40 N	104.04 E
Jingyu	98	42.22 N	126.50 E
Jingyuan, Zhg.	102	36.38 N	104.37 E
Jingyuan, Zhg.	102	35.30 N	106.48 E
Jingzhi	98	36.19 N	119.23 E
Jingzichang	107	29.00 N	104.41 E
Jinhae → Chinhae	98	35.09 N	128.40 E
Jinhu	100	33.00 N	119.02 E
Jinhua	100	29.07 N	119.39 E
Jinhua ≃	100	29.06 N	119.39 E
Jinhui	106	30.59 N	121.29 E
Jining, Zhg.	98	35.25 N	116.36 E
Jining, Zhg.	102	40.57 N	113.02 E
Jinja	154	0.26 N	33.12 E
Jinjiadian	98	41.39 N	118.18 E
Jinjiang, Zhg.	100	24.50 N	118.35 E
Jinjiang, Zhg.	110	26.19 N	100.33 E
Jinjiawopeng	104	41.38 N	122.16 E
Jinjiawopu	104	42.32 N	122.10 E
Jinjiazhen	89	42.49 N	123.40 E
Jinjing, Zhg.	100	24.37 N	118.36 E
Jinjing, Zhg.	100	28.31 N	113.25 E
Jinjini	150	7.26 N	2.39 W
Jinju → Chinju	98	35.11 N	128.05 E
Jinkeng	100	27.15 N	117.14 E
Jinkichi-mori ∧	96	33.41 N	134.07 E
Jinkou, Zhg.	98	36.35 N	120.46 E
Jinkou, Zhg.	100	30.22 N	114.10 E
Jinkou, Zhg.	100	29.18 N	115.15 E
Jinkuang	102	28.20 N	101.54 E
Jinlijing	107	29.48 N	104.45 E
Jinlingsi	104	41.42 N	120.49 E
Jinlingyu	105	40.06 N	117.32 E
Jinlingzhen	98	36.49 N	118.11 E
Jinlonggou	89	51.45 N	125.51 E
Jinmachi-chūtonchi, Rikujō-jieitai- ■	92	38.25 N	140.27 E
Jinmu Jiao ›	110	18.09 N	109.34 E
Jinnah Barrage ◆[6]	123	32.57 N	71.30 E
Jinning	102	24.41 N	102.35 E
Jinniu, Zhg.	100	31.24 N	117.12 E
Jinniu, Zhg.	100	29.59 N	114.38 E
Jinotega	236	13.06 N	86.00 W
Jinotega □[5]	236	14.00 N	85.25 W
Jinotepe	236	11.51 N	86.12 W
Jinping, Zhg.	102	26.38 N	109.03 E
Jinping, Zhg.	102	22.50 N	103.10 E
Jinpingchang	107	28.54 N	104.43 E
Jinpo	105	39.18 N	115.15 E
Jinqian ≃	102	32.52 N	110.01 E
Jinqiao	100	31.46 N	116.50 E
Jinrui	100	27.57 N	114.12 E
Jinseki	96	34.48 N	133.11 E
Jinsen → Inch'ŏn	98	37.28 N	126.38 E
Jinsha, Zhg.	100	26.12 N	118.39 E
Jinsha, Zhg.	102	27.18 N	106.10 E
Jinsha, Zhg.	106	32.06 N	121.05 E
Jinsha (Yangtze) ≃	102	28.50 N	104.36 E
Jinshan, Zhg.	89	51.51 N	126.30 E
Jinshan, Zhg.	106	30.54 N	121.09 E
Jinshanwei	106	30.44 N	121.19 E
Jinshanxiang	107	30.35 N	104.52 E
Jinshanzui	106	30.44 N	121.22 E
Jinshi	102	29.39 N	111.52 E
Jinshijing	107	29.23 N	104.08 E
Jinshuzhen	106	31.23 N	120.24 E
Jinsiniangqiao	106	30.43 N	121.15 E
Jinta	102	40.03 N	98.53 E
Jintan	106	31.45 N	119.34 E
Jintang, Zhg.	102	30.54 N	104.19 E
Jintang, Zhg.	102	30.19 N	102.19 E
Jintian	100	27.10 N	114.27 E
Jintotolo Channel ʯ	116	11.48 N	123.05 E
Jintotolo Island I	116	11.51 N	123.08 E
Jinxi, Zhg.	100	27.54 N	116.43 E
Jinxi, Zhg.	104	40.45 N	120.50 E
Jinxian, Zhg.	98	38.02 N	115.02 E
Jinxian, Zhg.	98	39.04 N	121.40 E
Jinxian, Zhg.	100	28.22 N	116.14 E
Jinxian (Dalinghe), Zhg.	104	41.11 N	121.22 E
Jinxiang, Zhg.	98	35.05 N	116.18 E
Jinxiang, Zhg.	100	27.26 N	120.35 E
Jin-ya ⊥	94	36.06 N	137.15 E
Jinyun	100	28.40 N	120.03 E
Jinz, Qā' al- ≚	132	30.45 N	36.04 E
Jinze	106	31.02 N	120.56 E
Jinzhai	100	31.44 N	115.54 E
Jinzhaizhen	100	31.32 N	115.46 E
Jinzhen	100	33.39 N	118.17 E
Jinzhong ≃	105	39.08 N	117.42 E
Jinzhou (Chinchou)	104	41.07 N	121.08 E
Jinzisi	107	29.09 N	106.22 E
Jinzū ≃	94	36.46 N	137.13 E
Jiō	270	34.58 N	135.28 E
Ji-Paraná	248	10.52 S	61.57 W
Jipijapa	246	1.20 S	80.35 W
Jipioca, Ilha I	250	1.53 N	50.12 W
Jiquí ≃	240p	21.22 N	78.32 W
Jiquilisco	236	13.19 N	88.35 W
Jiquilisco, Bahía de ⊂	236	13.10 N	88.28 W
Jiquilpan de Juárez	234	19.59 N	102.43 W
Jiquipilas	234	16.40 N	93.39 W
Jiquipilco	234	19.32 N	99.36 W
Jiquiriçá ≃	255	13.12 S	38.57 W
Jirāfī, Wādī al- (Naḥal Paran) V	132	30.24 N	35.10 E
Jirbān	140	11.03 N	30.36 E
Jiřetín	54	50.50 N	14.35 E
Jiri ≃	120	24.42 N	93.06 E
Jiřikov	54	50.59 N	13.35 E
Jirjā	140	26.20 N	31.53 E
Jirkov	54	50.30 N	13.27 E
Jīroft	128	28.40 N	57.46 E
Jīsh (Gush Ḥalav)	132	33.02 N	35.27 E
Jishou	102	28.17 N	109.29 E
Jishui, Zhg.	100	27.14 N	115.06 E
Jishui, Zhg.	100	33.46 N	115.24 E
Jisr ash-Shughūr	130	35.48 N	36.19 E
Jitan	100	24.56 N	115.43 E
Jitarning	162	32.48 S	117.59 E
Jitaúna	255	14.01 S	39.57 W
Jitianzhen	107	30.19 N	104.01 E
Jitotol	234	17.02 N	92.52 W
Jitra	114	6.16 N	100.25 E
Jituo	120	34.15 N	82.05 E
Jiu ≃	38	43.47 N	23.48 E
Jiubao	100	25.57 N	115.48 E
Jiubingtai	104	41.39 N	124.07 E
Jiucheng, Zhg.	98	38.12 N	117.18 E
Jiucheng, Zhg.	105	39.23 N	116.44 E
Jiuchuchang	107	29.55 N	104.38 E
Jiudaoliang	102	31.35 N	110.12 E
Jiudhara	126	22.24 N	89.44 E
Jiudian	106	32.10 N	120.57 E
Jiudongle	102	38.49 N	101.05 E
Jiudu	106	30.31 N	119.53 E
Jiufanxian	98	35.51 N	115.41 E
Jiufeng, Zhg.	100	24.20 N	117.02 E
Jiufeng, Zhg.	100	25.33 N	119.08 E
Jiugang	105	39.03 N	116.12 E
Jiugongan	102	29.52 N	112.00 E
Jiugongkou	105	39.50 N	114.43 E
Jiugong Shan ∧	100	29.26 N	114.42 E
Jiuguan, Zhg.	98	37.26 N	121.53 E
Jiuguan, Zhg.	106	30.51 N	120.16 E
Jiuguantao	98	36.40 N	115.25 E
Jiuhe	100	23.32 N	115.04 E
Jiuhongshui	102	37.14 N	103.57 E
Jiuhu	98	37.03 N	117.36 E
Jiuhuai'an	98	40.24 N	114.31 E
Jiuhuajie	100	30.25 N	117.51 E
Jiuhuaxian	100	23.30 N	113.16 E
Jiuhuinan	98	42.37 N	126.14 E
Jiujiang, Zhg.	100	29.44 N	115.59 E
Jiujiang, Zhg.	100	29.36 N	115.52 E
Jiujiang, Zhg.	100	22.51 N	113.02 E
Jiujiawopeng	104	40.59 N	121.22 E
Jiujiji	98	35.09 N	114.48 E
Jiujing	107	29.05 N	103.54 E
Jiukou	100	30.52 N	112.38 E
Jiuli	107	29.32 N	103.32 E
Jiulian Shan ⋏	100	24.40 N	114.46 E
Jiuliguan	100	31.50 N	114.14 E
Jiuling Shan ⋏	100	28.46 N	114.45 E
Jiulong, Zhg.	100	24.08 N	112.55 E
Jiulong, Zhg.	102	29.00 N	101.50 E
Jiulong ≃, Zhg.	100	25.59 N	117.18 E
Jiulong ≃, Zhg.	100	24.28 N	117.48 E
Jiulongchang	107	29.32 N	106.05 E
Jiulonggang	100	32.38 N	117.03 E
Jiulong → Kowloon	271d	22.18 N	114.10 E
Jiulongpo	107	29.29 N	106.32 E
Jiulongzhen	106	31.54 N	121.34 E
Jiumen	98	40.42 N	120.27 E
Jiumianyang	100	30.16 N	113.13 E
Jiumiao	104	42.24 N	121.36 E
Jiumu	100	28.11 N	118.27 E
Jiuninghe	105	39.28 N	117.46 E
Jiuningyang	100	25.38 N	117.21 E
Jiupu, Zhg.	100	32.50 N	118.45 E
Jiupu, Zhg.	105	40.21 N	115.18 E
Jiuquan (Suzhou)	102	39.45 N	98.34 E
Jiurongcheng	98	37.21 N	122.32 E
Jiushangshui	100	33.32 N	114.32 E
Jiushan Liedao II	100	29.26 N	122.12 E
Jiushenqiu	100	33.11 N	115.08 E
Jiusiyang	100	33.41 N	118.39 E
Jiusongyu	105	40.27 N	116.58 E
Jiutai	89	44.08 N	125.50 E
Jiuwuqing	105	39.31 N	116.52 E
Jiuxian, Zhg.	98	37.53 N	117.06 E
Jiuxian, Zhg.	100	31.11 N	118.04 E
Jiuxian, Zhg.	100	25.14 N	116.31 E
Jiuxian, Zhg.	100	33.15 N	115.35 E
Jiuxian, Zhg.	100	33.32 N	113.17 E
Jiuxian, Zhg.	100	25.54 N	113.22 E
Jiuxian, Zhg.	107	30.27 N	103.51 E
Jiuxian, Zhg.	107	29.51 N	106.13 E
Jiuxian ≃	100	25.07 N	116.24 E
Jiuxiangcheng	100	33.13 N	114.49 E
Jiuyingkou	105	39.42 N	114.44 E
Jiuyingzi	104	42.03 N	121.38 E
Jiuyuanqu	102	35.09 N	111.51 E
Jiuyuhang	106	30.17 N	119.56 E
Jiuyunjie	86	44.12 N	88.05 E
Jiuzhan	89	43.57 N	126.29 E
Jiuzhen	100	24.05 N	117.42 E
Jiuzhou	105	39.30 N	116.33 E
Jiuzhuangwo	105	40.11 N	115.36 E
Jiwangmiao	269b	31.14 N	121.17 E
Jiwangtun	104	41.02 N	122.58 E
Jīwani	128	25.03 N	61.45 E
Jiwen	89	50.32 N	123.15 E
Jixi, Zhg.	89	45.17 N	130.59 E
Jixi, Zhg.	100	30.06 N	118.35 E
Jixian, Zhg.	98	35.26 N	114.05 E
Jixian, Zhg.	98	37.36 N	115.31 E
Jixian, Zhg.	105	40.03 N	117.24 E
Jixiangsi	107	30.39 N	105.32 E
Jixiashi	100	28.22 N	118.44 E
Jixingji	100	32.55 N	116.46 E
Jiyang, Zhg.	98	36.59 N	117.11 E
Jiyang, Zhg.	100	27.10 N	118.07 E
Jiyang, Zhg.	105	39.38 N	115.59 E
Jiyi	102	35.50 N	110.23 E
Jiyuan	102	35.08 N	112.35 E
Jiyun ≃	105	39.07 N	117.43 E
Jiz', Wādī al- V	144	16.19 N	52.00 E
Jīzah, Ahrāmāt al- (Pyramids of Giza) ⊥	142	29.59 N	31.08 E
Jīzah, Tur'at al- ≍	273c	29.50 N	31.16 E
Jīzān	144	16.54 N	42.29 E
Jizayy	142	30.28 N	30.51 E
Jize	98	36.54 N	114.52 E
Jizera ≃	54	50.10 N	14.43 E
Jizl, Wādī al- V	128	25.38 N	38.21 E
Jizō-dake ∧	94	36.36 N	139.28 E
Jizō-zaki ›	96	35.34 N	133.20 E
Joaçaba	252	27.10 S	51.30 W
Joachimsthal	54	52.58 N	13.44 E
Joachimsthal → Jáchymov	54	50.20 N	12.55 E
Joaíma	255	16.39 S	41.02 W
Joal Fadiout	150	14.10 N	16.51 W
Joana Coeli	250	1.58 S	49.23 W
Joana Peres	250	3.18 S	49.42 W
Joanes	250	0.51 S	48.31 W
Joanicó	258	34.36 S	56.15 W
Joanna	192	34.24 N	81.48 W
Joanópolis	256	22.56 S	46.17 W
João Câmara	250	5.32 S	35.48 W
João Mendes ≃	287a	22.57 S	43.03 W
João Neiva	255	19.45 S	40.24 W
João Pessoa	250	7.07 S	34.52 W
João Pinheiro	255	17.45 S	46.10 W
Joaquim Egídio	256	22.53 S	46.59 W
Joaquim Távora	255	23.30 S	49.58 W
Joaquin	194	31.58 N	94.03 W
Joaquin Miller Park ♠	282	37.49 N	122.11 W
Joaquín Suárez	258	34.44 S	56.02 W
Joaquín V. González	252	25.05 S	64.11 W
Job	62	45.37 N	3.45 E
Jobabo	240p	20.54 N	77.17 W
Jobat	120	22.25 N	74.34 E
Jobo Point ›	116	8.42 N	126.15 E

Symbols in the index entries represent the broad categories identified in the key at the right. Symbols with superior numbers (⋏[1]) identify subcategories (see complete key on page *I · 1)*.

Symbole im Register stellen die rechts im Schlüssel erklärten Kategorien dar. Symbole mit hochgestellten Ziffern (⋏[1]) bezeichnen Unterabteilungen einer Kategorie (vgl. vollständiger Schlüssel auf Seite *I · 1)*.

Los símbolos incluídos en el texto del índice representan las grandes categorias identificadas con la clave a la derecha. Los símbolos con numeros en su parte superior (⋏[1]) identifican las subcategorías (véase la clave completa en la página *I · 1)*.

Les symboles de l'index représentent les catégories indiquées dans la légende à droite. Les symboles suivis d'un indice (⋏[1]) représentent des sous-catégories (voir légende complète à la page *I · 1)*.

Os símbolos incluídos no texto do índice representam as grandes categorias identificadas com a chave à direita. Os símbolos com números em sua parte superior (⋏[1]) identificam as subcategorias (veja-se a chave completa à página *I · 1)*.

English	Deutsch	Español	Français	Português
∧ Mountain	Berg	Montaña	Montagne	Montanha
⋏ Mountains	Gebirge	Montañas	Montagnes	Montanhas
)(Pass	Paß	Paso	Col	Passo
V Valley, Canyon	Tal, Cañon	Valle, Cañón	Vallée, Canyon	Vale, Canhão
≚ Plain	Ebene	Llano	Plaine	Planície
› Cape	Kap	Cabo	Cap	Cabo
I Island	Insel	Isla	Île	Ilha
II Islands	Inseln	Islas	Îles	Ilhas
⊥ Other Topographic Features	Andere Topographische Objekte	Otros Elementos Topográficos	Autres données topographiques	Outros acidentes topográficos

ESPAÑOL — FRANÇAIS — PORTUGUÊS

Nombre / Nom / Nome	Página / Page	Lat.°'	Long.°' W = Oeste / W = Ouest
Jobos	240m	17.58 N	66.10 W
Jobos, Bahía de	240m	17.56 N	66.13 W
Job Peak	204	39.35 N	118.14 W
Jobstown	285	40.02 N	74.41 W
Jochberg	64	47.23 N	12.24 E
Jock	212	45.16 N	75.43 W
Jocketa	54	50.33 N	12.10 E
Jockgrim	56	49.06 N	8.17 E
Jocko	202	47.20 N	114.17 W
Jocolí	252	32.35 S	68.41 W
Jo Co Marsh	276	40.37 N	73.47 W
Jocón	236	15.17 N	86.58 W
Jocoro	236	13.37 N	88.01 W
Jocotán	236	14.49 N	89.23 W
Jocotepec	234	20.18 N	103.26 W
Jocotitlán	234	19.42 N	99.48 W
Jódar	34	37.50 N	3.21 W
Jodhpur	120	26.17 N	73.02 E
Jodiya	120	22.42 N	70.18 E
Jodoigne	56	50.43 N	4.52 E
Jodrell Bank Radio Telescope	262	53.14 N	2.18 W
Joe	220	25.17 N	81.05 W
Joe Batt's Arm	186	49.44 N	54.10 W
Joel	158	28.42 S	28.21 E
Joensuu	26	62.36 N	29.46 E
Joetsu	94	37.06 N	138.15 E
Jœuf	56	49.14 N	6.01 E
Jofane	156	21.17 S	34.16 E
Joffre, Mount	182	50.32 N	115.13 W
Jōganzi	94	36.46 N	137.18 E
Jōga-shima I	94	35.08 N	139.37 E
Jōgawara	268	35.42 N	139.22 E
Jōge	96	34.42 N	133.07 E
Jogeshvari	272c	19.08 N	72.51 E
Jogeshvari Cave	272c	19.08 N	72.51 E
Jõgeva	76	58.45 N	26.24 E
Jog Falls	122	14.13 N	74.45 E
Joggins	186	45.42 N	64.27 W
Joghatāy	128	36.36 N	57.01 E
Jogindarnagar	123	31.59 N	76.46 E
Jogjakarta → Yogyakarta	115a	7.48 S	110.22 E
Jogui	255	23.45 S	54.40 W
Jōhana	94	36.31 N	136.54 E
Johannesburg, S. Afr.	158	26.12 S	28.05 E
Johannesburg, S. Afr.	273d	26.12 S	28.05 E
Johannesburg, Ca., U.S.	228	35.22 N	117.38 W
Johannesburg	273d	26.13 S	28.02 E
Johannesburg (Jan Smuts) Airport	273d	26.08 S	28.14 E
Johanngeorgenstadt	54	50.26 N	12.43 E
Johanniskreuz	56	49.20 N	7.49 E
Johannisthal	264a	52.26 N	13.30 E
Jōhen	92	32.57 N	132.35 E
Johi	120	26.41 N	67.37 E
Johilla	124	23.37 N	81.14 E
John	180	66.55 N	151.35 W
John Boyd Thacher State Park	210	42.38 N	74.01 W
John Carroll University	279a	41.29 N	81.32 W
John Day	202	44.24 N	118.57 W
John Day	202	45.44 N	120.39 W
John Day, Middle Fork	202	44.55 N	119.18 W
John Day, North Fork	202	44.45 N	119.38 W
John Day, South Fork	202	44.28 N	119.31 W
John Day Dam	224	45.43 N	120.41 W
John Day Fossil Beds National Monument	202	44.34 N	119.39 W
John Fitzgerald Kennedy Stadium	285	39.54 N	75.10 W
John F. Kennedy International Airport	210	40.38 N	73.47 W
John F. Kennedy National Historical Site	283	42.21 N	71.08 W
John F. Kennedy Space Center	220	28.40 N	80.40 W
John Forrest National Park	168a	31.53 S	116.06 E
John Hancock Center	278	41.55 N	87.37 W
John H. Kerr Reservoir	192	36.35 N	78.35 W
John J. Duffy Preserve	278	41.39 N	87.55 W
John Martin Reservoir	198	38.05 N	103.02 W
John McLaren Park	282	37.43 N	122.25 W
John Muir National Historical Site	282	37.59 N	122.08 W
Johnny Run	216	41.17 N	88.21 W
John o'Groats	46	58.38 N	3.05 W
John Pennekamp Coral Reef State Park	220	25.11 N	80.15 W
John Redmond Reservoir	198	38.18 N	95.55 W
Johns	224	46.54 N	124.01 W
Johns Creek	192	37.30 N	80.06 W
Johnshaven	46	56.47 N	2.20 W
Johns Hopkins University	284b	39.20 N	76.37 W
Johns Island I	192	32.40 N	80.05 W
Johnson, Ar., U.S.	194	36.07 N	94.09 W
Johnson, Ks., U.S.	198	37.34 N	101.45 W
Johnson, Ne., U.S.	198	40.24 N	95.59 W
Johnson, N.Y., U.S.	210	41.22 N	74.30 W
Johnson, Vt., U.S.	188	44.38 N	72.40 W
Johnson, In., U.S.	218	39.29 N	86.03 W
Johnson, Tx., U.S.	222	32.20 N	97.20 W
Johnson, Mount	226	36.37 N	121.19 W
Johnson Bay	208	38.03 N	75.20 W
Johnsonburg, N.J., U.S.	210	40.58 N	74.53 W
Johnsonburg, N.Y., U.S.	210	42.44 N	78.18 W
Johnsonburg, Pa., U.S.	214	41.29 N	78.40 W
Johnson City, N.Y., U.S.	210	42.06 N	75.57 W
Johnson City, Tn., U.S.	192	36.18 N	82.21 W
Johnson City, Tx., U.S.	196	30.16 N	98.24 W
Johnson Creek, N.Y., U.S.	210	43.15 N	78.31 W
Johnson Creek, Wi., U.S.	216	43.04 N	88.46 W
Johnson Creek, Id., U.S.	202	44.58 N	115.30 W
Johnson Creek, Ky., U.S.	218	38.27 N	84.04 W
Johnson Creek, N.Y., U.S.	210	43.22 N	78.16 W
Johnson Creek, Tx., U.S.	222	32.02 N	94.59 W
Johnson Creek, Wa., U.S.	224	46.35 N	121.42 W
Johnsondale	204	35.58 N	118.32 W
Johnson Drain	281	42.26 N	83.28 W
Johnson Draw, Tx., U.S.	196	31.58 N	101.41 W
Johnson Draw, Tx., U.S.	196	30.08 N	101.07 W
Johnson Hall State Historic Site	210	43.01 N	74.23 W
Johnson Park	276	40.30 N	74.27 W
Johnson Point	241h	13.07 N	61.12 W
Johnsons Crossing	180	60.29 N	133.16 W
Johnsons Point	240c	17.02 N	61.53 W
Johnsons Pond	283	42.44 N	71.03 W
Johnsons Station	222	32.42 N	97.08 W
Johnsonville, N.Z.	172	41.14 S	174.47 E
Johnsonville, N.Y., U.S.	210	42.55 N	73.31 W
Johnsonville, S.C., U.S.	192	33.49 N	79.26 W
Johnston, Wales, U.K.	42	51.46 N	5.00 W
Johnston, Ia., U.S.	190	41.40 N	93.41 W
Johnston, R.I., U.S.	207	41.46 N	71.21 W
Johnston, S.C., U.S.	192	33.49 N	81.48 W
Johnston, Lake	162	32.25 S	120.30 E
Johnston Atoll I	14	16.45 N	169.32 W
Johnston City	194	37.49 N	88.55 W
Johnstone	46	55.50 N	4.31 W
Johnstone Peak	280	34.10 N	117.48 W
Johnstone Strait	182	50.25 N	126.00 W
Johnston Falls	154	10.35 S	28.40 E
Johnstown, Co., U.S.	200	40.20 N	104.54 W
Johnstown, N.Y., U.S.	210	43.00 N	74.22 W
Johnstown, Oh., U.S.	214	40.09 N	82.41 W
Johnstown, Pa., U.S.	214	40.19 N	78.55 W
Johnstown Center	216	42.42 N	88.50 W
Johnstown Flood National Memorial	214	40.21 N	78.47 W
John Tyler Arboretum	285	39.56 N	75.26 W
Jōhoku	94	36.28 N	140.22 E
Johol	114	2.36 N	102.16 E
Johor	114	2.00 N	103.30 E
Johor	114	1.27 N	104.02 E
Johor, Selat	271c	1.28 N	103.48 E
Johor Baharu	114	1.28 N	103.45 E
Jöhstadt	54	50.30 N	13.05 E
Joice Island I	282	38.08 N	122.02 W
Joigny	50	47.59 N	3.24 E
Joiner	194	35.30 N	90.08 W
Joinerville	222	32.11 N	94.55 W
Joinvile	252	26.18 S	48.50 W
Joinville	58	48.27 N	5.08 E
Joinville, Lac	206	46.18 N	75.12 W
Joinville Island I	9	63.15 S	55.45 W
Joinville-le-Pont	261	48.49 N	2.28 E
Jōjima	96	33.15 N	130.26 E
Jojogan	115a	6.58 S	111.46 E
Jojutla	234	18.37 N	99.11 W
Joka	272b	22.27 N	88.18 E
Jokau	140	8.24 N	33.49 E
Jokioinen	26	60.49 N	23.28 E
Jokkmokk	24	66.37 N	19.50 E
Jökulsá á Brú	24a	65.41 N	14.13 W
Jökulsárgljúfur National Park	24a	66.00 N	16.20 W
Jolārpettai	122	12.34 N	78.35 E
Jolfā	128	38.57 N	45.38 E
Joliet, Il., U.S.	216	41.31 N	88.04 W
Joliet, Mt., U.S.	202	45.29 N	108.58 W
Joliet Correctional Center	278	41.33 N	88.04 W
Joliett	208	40.37 N	76.27 W
Joliette	206	46.01 N	73.27 W
Joliette	206	46.25 N	74.00 W
Jolietville	218	40.03 N	86.15 W
Jöllenbeck	52	52.11 N	8.45 E
Jollyville	222	30.27 N	97.47 W
Jolo	116	6.03 N	121.00 E
Jolo Group II	116	6.00 N	121.09 E
Jolo Island I	116	5.58 N	121.06 E
Jølstravatnet	26	61.32 N	6.13 E
Jomalig Island I	116	14.42 N	122.22 E
Jomba	102	31.27 N	98.15 E
Jombang	115a	7.33 S	112.14 E
Jombo	152	10.36 S	17.32 E
Jona	58	47.14 N	8.52 E
Jonacatepec	234	18.41 N	98.48 W
Jonah	222	30.38 N	97.32 W
Jönåker	40	58.44 N	16.40 E
Jonathan Dickinson State Park	220	27.01 N	80.08 W
Jonava	76	55.05 N	24.17 E
Jones, Pil.	116	16.33 N	121.42 E
Jones, Mi., U.S.	216	41.54 N	85.48 W
Jones, Ok., U.S.	196	35.33 N	97.17 W
Jones	283	42.00 N	70.42 W
Jones and Laughlin Steel Corporation, Pa., U.S.	279b	40.26 N	79.58 W
Jones and Laughlin Steel Corporation, Pa., U.S.	279b	40.37 N	80.14 W
Jones Beach State Park	210	40.35 N	73.31 W
Jonesboro, Ar., U.S.	194	35.50 N	90.42 W
Jonesboro, Ga., U.S.	192	33.31 N	84.21 W
Jonesboro, Il., U.S.	194	37.27 N	89.16 W
Jonesboro, In., U.S.	216	40.28 N	85.37 W
Jonesboro, La., U.S.	194	32.14 N	92.42 W
Jonesboro, Tn., U.S.	192	36.17 N	82.28 W
Jonesburg	219	38.51 N	91.18 W
Jones Creek	222	28.58 N	95.27 W
Jones Creek, On., Can.	212	44.30 N	75.49 W
Jones Creek, Tx., U.S.	222	29.08 N	96.03 W
Jones Falls	284b	39.18 N	76.37 W
Jones Falls, North Branch	284b	39.25 N	76.42 W
Jones Inlet	210	40.35 N	73.34 W
Jones Mill	194	34.27 N	92.50 W
Jones Mountains	9	73.32 S	94.00 W
Jonesport	188	44.31 N	67.35 W
Jones Sound	176	76.00 N	85.00 W
Jonestown	194	34.19 N	90.27 W
Jonesville, In., U.S.	218	39.04 N	85.53 W
Jonesville, La., U.S.	194	31.37 N	91.49 W
Jonesville, Mi., U.S.	216	41.59 N	84.40 W
Jonesville, N.Y., U.S.	210	42.55 N	73.49 W
Jonesville, N.C., U.S.	192	36.14 N	80.50 W
Jonesville, S.C., U.S.	192	34.50 N	81.40 W
Jonesville, Va., U.S.	192	36.41 N	83.06 W
Jong	150	7.32 N	12.23 W
Jonglei Canal	136	9.21 N	31.32 E
Jongunjärvi	26	65.17 N	27.15 E
Jónicas, Islas → Iónioi Nísoi II	38	38.30 N	20.30 E
Jónico, Mar → Ionian Sea	22	39.00 N	19.00 E
Joniškėlis	76	56.02 N	24.10 E
Joniškis	76	56.14 N	23.37 E
Jonkersberg	158	33.55 S	22.15 E
Jönköping	26	57.47 N	14.11 E
Jönköpings Län	26	57.30 N	14.30 E
Jonquière	186	48.24 N	71.15 W
Jonquières	62	44.07 N	4.54 E
Jonsdorf	54	50.51 N	14.43 E
Jonstorp	41	56.14 N	12.40 E
Jonuta	232	18.05 N	92.08 W
Jonvilliers	261	48.34 N	1.42 E
Jonzac	32	45.27 N	0.26 W
Joondalup, Lake	168a	31.45 S	115.47 E
Joplin, Mo., U.S.	194	37.05 N	94.30 W
Joplin, Mt., U.S.	202	48.33 N	110.46 W
Joppa, Il., U.S.	194	37.12 N	88.50 W
Joppa, Md., U.S.	208	39.26 N	76.21 W
Jóquei Clube	287b	23.35 S	46.41 W
Joquicingo	234	19.03 N	99.33 W
Jora	124	26.20 N	77.49 E
Jordan, Pil.	116	10.40 N	122.35 E
Jordan, Mn., U.S.	190	44.40 N	93.37 W
Jordan, Mt., U.S.	202	47.19 N	106.54 W
Jordan, N.Y., U.S.	210	43.03 N	76.28 W
Jordan (Al-Urdun), Asia	118	31.00 N	36.00 E
Jordan (Al-Urdun), Asia	128	31.00 N	36.00 E
Jordan (Nahr al-Urdunn) (HaYarden), Asia	132	31.46 N	35.33 E
Jordan, B.C., Can.	224	48.26 N	124.08 W
Jordan, Ut., U.S.	200	40.49 N	112.08 W
Jordan Creek	202	42.52 N	117.38 W
Jordânia	255	15.54 S	40.11 W
Jordania → Jordan	128	31.00 N	36.00 E
Jordanie → Jordan	128	31.00 N	36.00 E
Jordanien → Jordan	128	31.00 N	36.00 E
Jordan Lake	216	42.46 N	85.09 W
Jordanów	30	49.40 N	19.50 E
Jordans	260	51.37 N	0.36 W
Jordan Valley	202	42.58 N	117.03 W
Jordanville	210	42.55 N	74.57 W
Jordão	252	25.46 S	52.07 W
Jordbro	40	59.09 N	18.07 E
Jördenstorf	54	53.52 N	12.37 E
Jordet	26	61.25 N	12.09 E
Jorge Chávez, Aeropuerto Internacional	286d	12.02 S	77.07 W
Jorge Grego, Ilha I	256	23.13 S	44.09 W
Jorge Montt, Isla I	254	51.20 S	74.45 W
Jorge V, Costade → George V Coast	9	68.30 S	147.30 E
Jorge VI, Estrecho de → George VI Sound	9	71.00 S	68.00 W
Jorhāt	120	26.46 N	94.13 E
Jork	52	53.32 N	9.41 E
Jörlfeld	41	54.38 N	9.15 E
Jorm	120	36.52 N	70.51 E
Jörn	26	65.04 N	20.02 E
Jornado del Muerto	200	33.20 N	106.50 W
Joroinen	26	62.11 N	27.50 E
Jorong	112	3.58 S	114.56 E
Jørpeland	26	59.01 N	6.03 E
J'orzovka	80	48.56 N	44.38 E
Jos	150	9.55 N	8.53 E
Jose Abad Santos	116	5.38 N	125.27 E
José Batlle y Ordóñez	252	33.28 S	55.07 W
José Bonifácio	255	21.03 S	49.41 W
José Cardel	234	19.22 N	96.22 W
José C. Paz	258	34.30 S	58.45 W
José de Freitas	250	4.45 S	42.35 W
José de San Martín	254	44.02 S	70.29 W
José Enrique Rodó (Drabble)	258	33.41 S	57.34 W
José Francisco Vergara	252	22.28 S	69.38 W
Joselândia	248	16.32 S	56.12 W
José Martí, Aeropuerto Internacional	286b	23.00 N	82.24 W
Jose Panganiban	116	14.17 N	122.41 E
José Pedro Varela	252	33.27 S	54.32 W
Joseph	202	45.21 N	117.13 W
Joseph, Lac	176	52.45 N	65.15 W
Joseph, Lake	212	45.10 N	79.44 W
Joseph Bonaparte Gulf	164	14.15 S	128.30 E
Joseph City	200	34.57 N	110.20 W
Joseph Creek	202	46.03 N	117.01 W
Joseph Davis State Park	284a	43.13 N	79.03 W
Josephine, Pa., U.S.	214	40.29 N	79.11 W
Josephine, Tx., U.S.	222	33.04 N	96.19 W
Josephine, Lake	220	27.24 N	81.26 W
Josephine Peak	280	34.17 N	118.09 W
Josephstaal	164	4.44 S	145.01 E
José Santos Arévalo	258	35.10 S	59.14 W
Joshīmath	120	30.34 N	79.34 E
Jōshin-Etsu-kōgen-kokuritsu-kōen	94	36.46 N	138.40 E
Joshua	222	32.28 N	97.23 W
Joshuas Creek	275b	43.29 N	79.37 W
Joshua Tree	204	34.08 N	116.18 W
Joshua Tree National Monument	204	33.55 N	116.00 W
Joshua Trees State Park	228	34.41 N	117.47 W
Joškar-Ola	80	56.38 N	47.52 E
Jos Plateau	150	9.30 N	9.00 E
Jossa	56	50.14 N	9.35 E
Josselin	32	47.57 N	2.33 W
Jossigny	50	48.50 N	2.45 E
Jostedalsbreen	26	61.40 N	7.00 E
Jost Van Dyke I	240m	18.28 N	64.45 W
Jōtō	270	34.42 N	135.34 E
Jotunheimen	26	61.38 N	8.18 E
Jotunheimen Nasjonalpark	26	61.35 N	8.30 E
Jouarre	50	48.56 N	3.08 E
Jouars-Pontchartrain	261	48.47 N	1.54 E
Joubertina	158	33.50 S	23.51 E
Joué-lès-Tours	50	47.21 N	0.40 E
Jougne	58	46.46 N	6.24 E
Jouques	62	43.38 N	5.38 E
Jourdanton	196	28.55 N	98.32 W
Joure	52	52.57 N	5.47 E
Joutsa	26	61.44 N	26.07 E
Joutseno	26	61.06 N	28.30 E
Joutsijärvi	24	66.40 N	28.00 E
Joux, Lac de	58	46.38 N	6.18 E
Joux, Vallée de	58	46.35 N	6.15 E
Jouy	50	48.31 N	1.33 E
Jouy-en-Josas	261	48.46 N	2.10 E
Jouy-le-Moutier	261	49.01 N	2.03 E
Jouy-le-Potier	50	47.45 N	1.49 E
Jovellanos	240p	22.48 N	81.12 W
Jovellar	116	13.04 N	123.36 E
Jovet, Mont	62	45.30 N	6.39 E
Joveyn	128	36.48 N	56.28 E
Joviânia	255	17.49 S	49.30 W
Jowai	120	25.27 N	92.12 E
Jowhar	144	2.46 N	45.31 E
Jowlaenga, Mount	162	17.21 S	122.56 E
Jowzjān	120	36.30 N	66.00 E
Joy	190	41.12 N	90.55 W
Joy, Mount	180	63.46 N	132.55 W
Joyce	194	31.56 N	92.35 W
Joyeuse	62	44.29 N	4.14 E
Jōyō	96	34.51 N	135.47 E
Joyous Pavilion Park	271a	39.52 N	116.22 E
Joyuda	240m	18.07 N	67.11 W
Józefów	30	52.09 N	21.12 E
J. Percy Priest Lake	194	36.05 N	86.30 W
Ju, Zhg.	100	30.38 N	114.51 E
Ju, Zhg.	105	39.45 N	117.35 E
Juaba	250	2.23 S	49.33 W
Juagdan	116	10.00 N	124.35 E
Juami	246	1.45 S	67.30 W
Juanacatlán	234	20.31 N	103.10 W
Juana Díaz	240m	18.03 N	66.31 W
Juan Aldama	232	24.19 N	103.21 W
Juan Anchorena	288	34.29 S	58.30 W
Juan Atucha	258	35.32 S	59.21 W
Juan B. Arruabarrena	252	30.20 S	58.19 W
Juan Bautista Alberdi	252	27.35 S	65.37 W
Juan Blanco, Arroyo	258	35.05 S	57.26 W
Juancheng	98	35.35 N	115.29 E
Juan de Fuca, Strait of	224	48.18 N	124.00 W
Juan de Garay	254	38.52 S	64.34 W
Juan de Mena	252	24.55 S	56.44 W
Juan de Nova, Île I	138	17.03 S	42.45 E
Juan Díaz Covarrubias	234	18.07 N	95.09 W
Juan E. Barra	252	37.48 S	60.29 W
Juan Eugenio	232	25.10 N	103.20 W
Juan Fernández, Archipiélago II	244	33.00 S	80.00 W
Juan González Grande, Arroyo	258	34.00 S	58.14 W
Juan González Romero	286a	19.30 N	99.04 W
Juangriego	246	11.05 N	63.57 W
Juan Gualberto Gómez	240p	22.52 N	81.33 W
Juan Guerra	248	6.35 S	76.21 W
Juanita	224	47.42 N	122.13 W
Juan Jorba	252	33.37 S	65.16 W
Juan José Castelli	252	25.57 S	60.37 W
Juán José Perez	248	15.14 S	68.58 W
Juanjuí	248	7.11 S	76.45 W
Juankoski	26	63.04 N	28.21 E
Juan-les-Pins	62	43.34 N	7.06 E
Juan L. Lacaze	258	34.26 S	57.27 W
Juan N. Fernández	252	38.00 S	59.16 W
Juan Perez Sound	182	52.30 N	131.18 W
Juan Ramírez, Isla I	234	21.50 N	97.40 W
Juan Rodríguez Clara	234	18.00 N	95.25 W
Juan Tronconi	258	35.30 S	59.15 W
Juan Viñas	236	9.54 N	83.45 W
Juárez, Méx.	232	27.37 N	100.44 W
Juárez, Méx.	232	30.19 N	108.05 W
Juárez, Méx.	234	17.39 N	93.10 W
Juárez, Cerro	234	20.37 N	99.17 W
Juárez, Sierra	234	17.30 N	96.30 W
Juárez, Sierra de	232	32.00 N	115.50 W
Juárez → Ciudad Juárez	232	31.44 N	106.29 W
Juarzon	150	5.20 N	8.52 W
Juatinga, Ponta de	256	23.17 S	44.30 W
Juazeirinho	250	7.04 S	36.35 W
Juàzeiro	250	9.25 S	40.30 W
Juazeiro do Norte	250	7.12 S	39.20 W
Jūbā	154	4.51 N	31.37 E
Juba	248	14.59 S	57.44 W
Jubachstausee	263	51.10 N	7.37 E
Jūbāl, Maḍīq	140	27.40 N	33.55 E
Jubal, Strait of → Jūbāl, Maḍīq	140	27.40 N	33.55 E
Jubayl (Byblos)	130	34.07 N	35.39 E
Jubaysho	144	5.48 N	37.22 E
Jubayt	140	18.57 N	36.50 E
Jubba (Genale)	144	0.15 S	42.38 E
Jubbada Dhexe	144	1.00 N	43.00 E
Jubbada Hoose	144	0.00	42.00 E
Jubbah	128	28.02 N	40.56 E
Jubb al-Jarrāḥ	130	34.49 N	37.19 E
Jubbātā al-Khashab	132	33.13 N	35.49 E
Jubb Jannīn	132	33.37 N	35.47 E
Jubbulpore → Jabalpur	124	23.10 N	79.57 E
Jubilee Downs	162	18.22 S	125.17 E
Jubilee Lake, Austl.	162	29.12 S	126.38 E
Jubilee Lake, Nf., Can.	186	48.04 N	55.11 W
Jubones	246	3.13 S	79.57 W
Jūbu-san	270	34.50 N	135.55 E
Juby, Cap	148	27.58 N	12.55 W
Júcar (Xúquer)	34	39.09 N	0.14 W
Juçara	255	15.53 S	50.51 W
Júcaro	240p	21.37 N	78.51 W
Jucás	250	6.32 S	39.32 W
Jüchen	56	51.06 N	6.30 E
Juchhöh	54	50.24 N	11.52 E
Juchipila	234	21.25 N	103.07 W
Juchipila	234	21.03 N	103.25 W
Juchitán de Zaragoza	234	16.26 N	95.01 W
Juchitepec	234	19.06 N	98.53 W
Juchitlán	234	20.05 N	104.07 W
Juchnov	76	54.45 N	35.14 E
Juchoviči	76	56.02 N	28.39 E
Jucuapa	236	13.31 N	88.24 W
Jucurucu	255	17.21 S	39.13 W
Jucurutu	250	6.02 S	37.01 W
Judaea	132	31.35 N	35.00 E
Judas, Punta	236	9.31 N	84.32 W
Judaydat al-Khāṣ	132	33.24 N	36.33 E
Judaydat ʻArṭūz	132	33.26 N	36.10 E
Juddah → Jiddah	144	21.30 N	39.12 E
Jude Island I	186	47.15 N	54.49 W
Judenau	61	48.17 N	16.00 E
Judenburg	61	47.10 N	14.40 E
Judges Hill	283	42.12 N	70.49 W
Judian	102	27.20 N	99.36 E
Judinki, Ross.	82	54.37 N	37.17 E
Judinki, Ross.	82	55.27 N	35.48 E
Judino, Ross.	76	58.43 N	39.17 E
Judino, Ross.	80	55.51 N	48.55 E
Judino, Ross.	82	54.09 N	38.19 E
Judino, Ross.	265b	55.40 N	37.12 E
Judío, Rambla del	34	38.15 N	1.27 W
Judique	186	45.52 N	61.30 W
Judith	202	47.44 N	109.38 W
Judith, Point	207	41.22 N	71.29 W
Judith Gap	202	46.40 N	109.45 W
Judith Mountains	202	47.12 N	109.15 W
Judith Peak	202	47.13 N	109.13 W
Judoma	74	59.08 N	135.06 E
Judson, S.C., U.S.	192	34.50 N	82.27 W
Judson, Tx., U.S.	222	32.35 N	94.45 W
Judsonia	194	35.16 N	91.38 W
Jue	100	31.42 N	113.20 E
Juehedian	105	39.26 N	117.06 E
Juelsminde	41	55.43 N	10.01 E
Juexi	100	29.27 N	121.57 E
Juexizhen	107	28.55 N	104.16 E
Jufari	246	1.13 S	62.00 W
Jufayr, Bi'r al-	142	30.49 N	32.40 E
Jufrah, Wādī al-	142	30.24 N	31.35 E
Jug	86	57.43 N	56.10 E
Jug	24	60.45 N	46.20 E
Jughna	140	12.24 N	25.06 E
Jugo-Kamskij	86	57.42 N	55.35 E
Jugon	32	48.25 N	2.20 W
Jugo-Osetinskaja Avtonomnaja Oblast'	84	42.20 N	44.00 E
Jugoslavija → Yugoslavia	22	44.00 N	19.00 E
Jugoslawien → Yugoslavia	22	44.00 N	19.00 E
Jugo-Zapad	265b	55.40 N	37.32 E
Juḥā	144	16.41 N	42.54 E
Jühnsdorf	264a	52.18 N	13.23 E
Jühnsdorfer Heide	264a	52.19 N	13.24 E
Juhu	272c	19.07 N	72.49 E
Juhua Dao I	98	40.29 N	120.47 E
Juhu Airport	272c	19.06 N	72.50 E
Jui	272c	19.01 N	73.05 E
Juidongshan	100	23.46 N	117.31 E
Juigalpa	236	12.05 N	85.24 W
Juillac	32	45.19 N	1.19 E
Juilly	261	49.01 N	2.42 E
Juína	248	12.36 S	58.57 W
Juine	50	48.32 N	2.23 E
Juist	52	53.40 N	6.59 E
Juist I	52	53.40 N	7.00 E
Juisui	100	23.30 N	121.21 E
Juiz de Fora	256	21.45 S	43.20 W
Jūjō Base	268	35.45 N	139.43 E
Jujurieux	58	46.02 N	5.25 E
Jujuy	252	23.00 S	66.00 W
Jujuy → San Salvador de Jujuy	252	24.11 S	65.18 W
Jukagirskoje ploskogorje	74	66.00 N	155.00 E
Jukamenskoje	80	57.53 N	52.15 E
Jukonda	86	59.38 N	67.26 E
Juksa	86	56.55 N	85.10 E
Juksejevo	24	59.52 N	54.19 E
Jukskei	273d	26.06 S	28.06 E
Jukta	74	63.23 N	105.41 E
Jula	24	63.49 N	44.44 E
Julāna	124	29.08 N	76.25 E
Julayfah, Bi'r al-	142	30.43 N	29.35 E
Julbach	60	48.40 N	13.52 E
Juldybajevo	86	52.20 N	57.52 E
Julebu	98	40.09 N	113.36 E
Julesburg	198	40.59 N	102.15 W
Juli	248	16.13 S	69.27 W
Juliaca	248	15.30 S	70.08 W
Julia Creek	166	20.39 S	141.45 E
Julia Creek	166	20.00 S	141.11 E
Julian	214	40.52 N	77.56 W
Juliana, Lake	220	28.07 N	81.48 W
Julianakanaal	56	51.05 N	5.50 E
Julian Alps	36	46.00 N	14.00 E
Juliana Top	250	3.41 N	56.32 W
Julianehåb (Qaqortoq)	176	60.43 N	46.01 W
Julia Pfeiffer Burns State Park	226	36.10 N	120.40 W
Jülich	56	50.55 N	6.21 E
Juliénas	58	46.14 N	4.43 E
Juliette, Lake	192	33.05 N	83.50 W
Julijske Alpe → Julian Alps	36	46.00 N	14.00 E
Julimes	232	28.25 N	105.27 W
Júlio de Castilhos	252	29.14 S	53.41 W
Julio Prestes, Estação	287b	23.32 S	46.38 W
Julita	40	59.09 N	16.02 E
Juliuhe	104	42.03 N	122.55 E
Juliustown	285	40.00 N	74.40 W
Julu	98	37.13 N	115.01 E
Juma	24	65.07 N	33.16 E
Juma	98	39.34 N	115.42 E
Jumaguzino	86	52.54 N	56.23 E
Jumapolo	115a	7.42 S	111.00 E
Jumaševo	80	54.59 N	54.25 E
Jumay, Volcán	236	14.41 N	89.59 W
Jumbilla	248	5.54 S	77.45 W
Jumbo	154	17.28 S	30.55 E
Jumbo, Raas	144	1.39 S	41.36 E
Jumboo	144	0.15 S	42.38 E
Jumbo Peak	204	36.12 N	114.11 W
Jumeauville	261	48.55 N	1.47 E
Jumentos Cays II	238	22.42 N	75.55 W
Jumet	50	50.26 N	4.25 E
Jumièges	50	49.26 N	0.49 E
Jumilla	34	38.29 N	1.17 W
Jumlā	124	29.17 N	82.10 E
Jummayzat Banī ʻAmr	142	30.48 N	31.32 E
Jump	190	45.17 N	91.05 W
Jump, North Fork	190	45.25 N	90.40 W
Jump, South Fork	190	45.25 N	90.40 W
Jumt uul	102	44.29 N	97.10 E
Jūn	132	33.35 N	35.27 E
Jun	100	25.57 N	118.03 E
Jūnāgadh	120	21.31 N	70.28 E
Junan (Shizilu)	98	35.11 N	118.51 E
Junayfah	142	30.12 N	32.25 E
Junaynah, Ra's al-	140	29.01 N	33.58 E
Juncal, Isla I	258	33.58 S	58.24 W
Juncal do Norte	266c	38.52 N	8.59 W
Juncal do Sul	266c	38.51 N	8.58 W
Juncheng	98	38.57 N	114.41 E
Juncos	240m	18.14 N	65.55 W
Junction, Tx., U.S.	196	30.29 N	99.46 W
Junction, Ut., U.S.	200	38.14 N	112.13 W
Junction City, Ar., U.S.	194	33.00 N	92.43 W
Junction City, Il., U.S.	219	38.34 N	89.07 W
Junction City, Ks., U.S.	198	39.01 N	96.49 W
Junction City, Ky., U.S.	194	37.35 N	84.47 W
Junction City, Or., U.S.	202	44.13 N	123.12 W
Junction City, Wa., U.S.	224	46.58 N	123.46 W
Jundah	166	24.50 S	143.04 E
Jundiaí	256	23.11 S	46.52 W
Jundiaí, Bra.	256	23.32 S	46.15 W
Jundiaí, Bra.	256	23.11 S	47.16 W
Jundiaí do Sul	255	23.27 S	50.17 W
Jundiaí-mirim	256	23.10 S	46.56 W
Jundiapeba	256	23.33 S	46.15 W
Jundu Shan	105	40.30 N	116.05 E
Juneau, Ak., U.S.	180	58.20 N	134.27 W
Juneau, Wi., U.S.	190	43.24 N	88.42 W
Junee	166	34.52 S	147.35 E
June in Winter, Lake	220	27.18 N	81.24 W
June Lake	226	37.46 N	119.04 W
June Park	220	28.04 N	80.41 W
Jungapeo de Juárez	234	19.27 N	100.29 W
Jungar Qi	102	39.49 N	111.10 E
Jungbluth Ditch	279a	41.27 N	82.07 W
Jungfernheide	264a	52.34 N	13.17 E
Jungfern-Inseln → Virgin Islands	240m	18.20 N	64.50 W
Jungfern-See	264a	52.25 N	13.05 E
Jungfrau	58	46.32 N	7.58 E
Jungfraujoch	58	46.33 N	7.58 E
Junggar Pendi (Dzungarian Basin)	86	45.00 N	88.00 E
Jungle Habitat	276	41.08 N	74.21 W
Junglinster	56	49.43 N	6.15 E
Jungshāhi	120	24.51 N	67.46 E
Juniata	198	40.35 N	98.30 W
Juniata	208	40.34 N	77.24 W
Juniata	285	40.01 N	75.07 W
Juniata	188	40.24 N	77.01 W
Juniata, Frankstown Branch	214	40.34 N	78.03 W
Juniata, Raystown Branch	214	40.25 N	77.58 W
Juniata Gap	214	40.33 N	78.26 W
Juniata Terrace	208	40.35 N	77.34 W
Junín, Arg.	252	34.35 S	60.57 W
Junín, Ec.	246	0.56 S	80.13 W
Junín, Perú	248	11.10 S	76.00 W
Junín	248	11.30 S	75.00 W
Junín, Lago de	248	11.02 S	76.06 W
Junín de los Andes	254	39.56 S	71.05 W
Junior	188	38.59 N	79.57 W
Juniper	186	46.33 N	67.13 W
Junipero Serra Peak	226	36.08 N	121.25 W
Juniville	50	49.24 N	4.23 E
Jūniyah	130	33.59 N	35.38 E
Junk Bay	271d	22.17 N	114.15 E
Jun Kharchanai	123	36.52 N	75.01 E
Junk Island I	271d	22.17 N	114.16 E
Junkou	100	26.42 N	116.49 E
Junlian	102	28.08 N	104.35 E
Junliangcheng	105	39.04 N	117.27 E
Junling	100	28.17 N	116.28 E
Junnar	122	19.12 N	73.53 E
Juno Beach	220	26.52 N	80.04 W
Junokommunarskoje	83	48.13 N	38.18 E
Junqalī	140	7.30 N	32.20 E
Junqueiro	250	9.56 S	36.29 W
Junqueirópolis	255	21.32 S	51.26 W
Junsele	26	63.41 N	16.54 E
Juntas	236	10.16 N	85.00 W
Jun Ul Shan	102	37.30 N	97.00 E
Junxian	102	32.31 N	111.30 E
Jūō	94	36.40 N	140.41 E
Juodkrantė	76	55.33 N	21.08 E
Juodupė	76	56.05 N	25.37 E
Juojärvi	26	62.43 N	28.33 E
Juparanã, Lagoa	255	19.35 S	40.18 W
Jupilingo	236	14.48 N	89.14 W
Jupille	56	50.39 N	5.38 E
Jupiter	220	26.56 N	80.05 W
Jupiter	186	49.29 N	63.37 W
Jupiter Inlet	220	26.57 N	80.04 W
Jupiter Island I	220	27.04 N	80.07 W
Juqueri	256	23.24 S	46.52 W
Juqueri, Reservatório do	256	23.20 S	46.38 W
Juqueriquerê, Serra do	256	23.43 S	45.37 W
Juquiá	252	24.19 S	47.38 W
Juquiá	256	23.56 S	47.09 W
Juquiá, Ponta do	252	24.25 S	47.00 W
Juquiá-guaçu	256	24.00 S	47.16 W
Juquitiba	256	23.57 S	47.03 W
Jur, Česko.	30	48.15 N	17.13 E
Jur, Ross.	74	59.52 N	137.39 E
Jur	140	8.39 N	29.18 E
Jura	58	47.20 N	7.15 E
Jura	58	46.50 N	5.50 E
Jura	58	46.45 N	6.30 E
Jura I	46	56.00 N	5.50 W
Jūra	76	55.03 N	22.09 E
Jura, Sound of	46	55.57 N	5.48 W
Juramento	255	16.50 S	43.35 W
Juratiški	76	54.02 N	25.54 E
Jurayrah, Jabal al-	128	24.06 N	39.16 E
Jurays wa ʻIzbatuhā	142	30.19 N	30.55 E
Jurbarkas	76	55.05 N	22.48 E
Jurcevo	76	60.02 N	32.36 E
Juréia	256	21.17 S	46.22 W
Jurenino	76	59.24 N	42.47 E
Jurevići	78	51.57 N	29.32 E
Jurf ad-Darāwīsh	132	30.42 N	35.52 E
Jurga	86	55.42 N	84.51 E
Jurgamyš	86	55.21 N	64.28 E
Jurgenson Woods	278	41.34 N	87.36 W
Jurien	162	30.19 S	115.02 E
Juriesfontein	158	31.40 S	22.08 E
Juring	164	6.26 S	134.20 E
Jurino	80	56.18 N	46.18 E
Jurja	24	59.03 N	49.14 E
Jurjevec	80	57.18 N	43.06 E
Jurjevka, Ukr.	78	48.44 N	36.02 E
Jurjevka, Ukr.	83	48.30 N	39.00 E
Jurjev-Pol'skij	80	56.30 N	39.41 E
Jurjevskoje	82	55.05 N	36.13 E
Jurjev → Tartu	76	58.23 N	26.43 E
Jurla	86	59.17 N	54.19 E
Jurlovo, Ross.	82	55.54 N	37.16 E
Jurlovo, Ross.	82	55.19 N	35.52 E
Jūrmala	76	56.58 N	23.42 E
Jurong, Sing.	271c	1.19 N	103.43 E
Jurong, Zhg.	106	31.57 N	119.10 E
Jurong	271c	1.18 N	103.44 E
Jurong, Selat	271c	1.18 N	103.42 E
Jurovo, Ross.	80	57.30 N	43.50 E
Jurovo, Ross.	82	55.30 N	38.22 E
Jurovo, Ukr.	78	51.22 N	27.50 E
Jurovskoje	86	59.29 N	69.02 E
Jursla	40	58.40 N	16.11 E
Jurty	88	56.03 N	97.37 E
Juruá	246	3.27 S	66.03 W
Juruá	242	2.37 S	65.44 W
Juruaia	256	21.15 S	46.35 W
Juruá-mirim	248	8.08 S	72.48 W
Juruena	248	7.20 S	58.03 W
Jurujuba, Enseada de	287a	22.56 S	43.07 W
Jurumirim, Reprêsa	255	23.20 S	49.15 W
Jurumkuvejem	180	66.14 N	173.35 E
Jurupari	248	7.45 S	70.10 W
Jurupari, Arquipélago II	250	0.07 N	50.30 W
Jurupari, Ilha de I	250	0.20 N	50.07 W
Juruti	250	2.09 S	56.04 W
Jur'uzan'	86	54.52 N	58.26 E
Jur'uzan'	86	55.42 N	57.00 E
Jurva	26	62.41 N	21.59 E
Jušala	86	57.04 N	64.17 E
Juscelândia	255	15.20 S	51.19 W
Jusepín	246	9.45 N	63.31 W
Jushiguan	102	24.47 N	97.38 E
Jūshiyama	94	35.06 N	136.46 E
Juskatla	182	53.37 N	132.18 W
Jus'ki	80	56.39 N	53.05 E
Juškovo	76	59.46 N	45.11 E
Juškozero	24	64.44 N	32.06 E
Jūsō	270	34.43 N	135.28 E
Jussey	58	47.49 N	5.54 E
Justa	80	47.07 N	46.18 E
Justice	278	41.44 N	87.50 W
Justin	222	33.05 N	97.18 W
Justineberg	40	58.43 N	15.04 E
Justiniano Posse	252	32.53 S	62.40 W
Justo Daract	252	33.52 S	65.11 W
Justus	214	40.42 N	81.35 W
Jušut	80	56.12 N	48.23 E
Jus'va	24	58.56 N	54.57 E
Jutaí	248	5.11 S	68.54 W
Jutaí	242	2.43 S	66.57 W
Jutaza	80	54.35 N	53.16 E
Jütchendorf	264a	52.16 N	13.10 E
Jüterbog	54	51.59 N	13.04 E
Juththah, Jabal al-	132	30.12 N	35.36 E
Juti	255	22.52 S	54.37 W
Jutiapa	236	14.17 N	89.54 W
Jutiapa	236	14.10 N	89.50 W
Juticalpa	236	14.42 N	86.15 W
Jutiquile	236	14.45 N	86.08 W
Jutland → Jylland	26	56.00 N	9.15 E
Jutogh	123	31.06 N	77.07 E
Jutrosin	30	51.40 N	17.10 E
Juupajoki	26	61.47 N	24.27 E
Juuru	76	59.04 N	24.59 E
Juva	26	61.54 N	27.51 E
Juventud, Isla de la (Isla de Pinos) I	240p	21.40 N	82.50 W
Juvisy-sur-Orge	50	48.41 N	2.23 E
Juvuln	26	63.43 N	13.09 E
Juwana	115a	6.42 S	111.09 E
Juwangi	115a	7.10 S	110.45 E
Juxi	100	27.30 N	119.08 E
Juxian	98	35.37 N	118.54 E
Juxing	106	31.56 N	121.33 E
Juyanhai → Gaxun Nur	102	42.22 N	100.34 E
Juye	98	35.23 N	116.06 E
Jūyom	128	28.34 N	53.56 E
Juyongguan	105	40.18 N	116.04 E
Juža	80	56.35 N	42.01 E
Juzennecourt	58	48.11 N	4.59 E
Juzi	98	40.18 N	123.35 E
Juziers	261	49.00 N	1.51 E
Južna Morava	38	43.41 N	21.24 E
Južno-Aleksandrovka	88	55.51 N	96.10 E
Južno-Aličurskij chrebet	120	37.30 N	73.20 E
Južno-Golodnostepskij kanal	85	40.15 N	69.08 E
Južno-Jenisejskij	86	58.48 N	94.39 E
Južno-Mujskij chrebet	88	55.40 N	114.00 E
Južno-Sachalinsk	89	46.58 N	142.42 E
Južno-Suchokumsk	84	44.37 N	45.34 E
Južno-Ural'sk	86	54.26 N	61.15 E
Južnyj, Kaz.	86	49.21 N	73.01 E
Južnyj, Ross.	80	56.08 N	44.09 E
Južnyj, Ross.	80	47.20 N	41.51 E
Južnyj, Ross.	86	53.14 N	83.42 E
Južnyj, Ross.	86	53.33 N	60.02 E
Južnyj, mys	74	57.45 N	156.45 E
Južnyj-Alamyšik	85	40.46 N	72.38 E
Južnyj Bug	78	46.59 N	31.58 E
Južnyj Prijut	84	43.12 N	41.55 E
Južnyj Ural	86	54.00 N	58.30 E
Juzovka → Doneck	83	48.00 N	37.48 E
Jwālahari	272a	28.40 N	77.06 E

English	Deutsch	Español	Français	Português
River	Fluß	Río	Rivière	Rio
Canal	Kanal	Canal	Canal	Canal
Waterfall, Rapids	Wasserfall, Stromschnellen	Cascada, Rápidos	Chute d'eau, Rapides	Cascata, Rápidos
Strait	Meeresstraße	Estrecho	Détroit	Estreito
Bay, Gulf	Bucht, Golf	Bahía, Golfo	Baie, Golfe	Baía, Golfo
Lake, Lakes	See, Seen	Lago, Lagos	Lac, Lacs	Lago, Lagos
Swamp	Sumpf	Pantano	Marais	Pântano
Ice Features, Glacier	Eis- und Gletscherformen	Accidentes Glaciales	Formes glaciaires	Acidentes glaciares
Other Hydrographic Features	Andere Hydrographische Objekte	Otros Elementos Hidrográficos	Autres données hydrographiques	Outros acidentes hidrográficos
Submarine Features	Untermeerische Objekte	Accidentes Submarinos	Formes de relief sous-marin	Acidentes submarinos
Political Unit	Politische Einheit	Unidad Politica	Entité politique	Unidade política
Cultural Institution	Kulturelle Institution	Institución Cultural	Institution culturelle	Instituição cultural
Historical Site	Historische Stätte	Sitio Histórico	Site historique	Sitio histórico
Recreational Site	Erholungs- und Ferienort	Sitio de Recreo	Centre de loisirs	Area de Lazer
Airport	Flughafen	Aeropuerto	Aéroport	Aeroporto
Military Installation	Militäranlage	Instalación Militar	Installation militaire	Instalação militar
Miscellaneous	Verschiedenes	Misceláneo	Divers	Diversos

Name	Page	Lat.°′	Long.°′
Jwayyā	**132**	33.14 N	35.19 E
Jyderup	**41**	55.40 N	11.26 E
Jylland (Jutland) ◆[1]	**26**	56.00 N	9.15 E
Jyllinge	**41**	55.45 N	12.07 E
Jyväskylä	**26**	62.14 N	25.44 E
K			
K2 (Qogir Feng) ∧	**123**	35.53 N	76.30 E
Ka ≃	**150**	11.40 N	4.10 E
Kaaawa	**229c**	21.33 N	157.51 W
Kaabong	**154**	3.31 N	34.08 E
Kaachka	**128**	37.21 N	59.36 E
Kaala ∧	**229c**	21.31 N	158.09 W
Kaalaea	**229c**	21.28 N	157.51 W
Kaala-Gomén	**175f**	20.40 S	164.25 E
Kaalspruit	**158**	29.15 S	26.10 E
Kaapahu Bay ⊂	**229a**	20.39 N	156.05 W
Kaapmuiden	**156**	25.33 S	31.20 E
Kaappunt ≻	**158**	34.21 S	18.30 E
Kaapstad → Cape Town	**158**	33.55 S	18.22 E
Kaarli	**76**	59.24 N	26.27 E
Kaarssen	**54**	53.12 N	11.02 E
Kaarst	**56**	51.14 N	6.37 E
Kaaterskill Creek ≃	**210**	42.13 N	73.53 W
Kaatoan, Mount ∧	**116**	8.07 N	124.55 E
Kaatsheuvel	**52**	51.40 N	5.02 E
Kaavi	**26**	62.59 N	28.30 E
Kaba	**150**	10.09 N	11.40 W
Kaba ≃	**86**	47.53 N	86.12 E
Kaba, Goulbin V	**150**	13.42 N	6.19 E
Kabacan	**116**	7.08 N	124.49 E
Kabacan ≃	**116**	7.08 N	124.50 E
Kabadak	**126**	22.13 N	89.19 E
Kabadak ≃[1]	**126**	22.13 N	89.18 E
Kabadüz	**130**	40.53 N	37.56 E
Kabaena, Pulau I	**112**	5.15 S	121.55 E
Kabaena, Selat ʊ	**112**	5.00 S	122.00 E
Kabah ⊥	**232**	20.07 N	89.29 W
Kabala	**150**	9.35 N	11.33 W
Kabale	**154**	1.15 S	29.59 E
Kabalebo ≃	**250**	5.02 N	57.21 W
Kabalega Falls ⌞	**154**	2.17 N	31.41 E
Kabalega Falls National Park ♦	**154**	2.15 N	31.50 E
Kabali, Indon.	**112**	1.42 S	121.54 E
Kabalı, Tür.	**130**	41.52 N	35.05 E
Kabalo	**154**	6.03 S	26.55 E
Kabambare	**154**	4.42 S	27.43 E
Kaban'	**86**	54.39 N	66.28 E
Kabangu Kuta	**154**	14.00 S	24.03 E
Kabanjahe	**114**	3.06 N	98.30 E
Kabanje	**83**	49.13 N	38.12 E
Kabankalan	**116**	9.59 N	122.49 E
Kabanovka	**80**	53.39 N	51.18 E
Kabanovo	**86**	55.20 N	70.52 E
Kabansk	**88**	52.03 N	106.39 E
Kabardinka	**78**	44.39 N	37.57 E
Kabardino-Balkarskaja Avtonomnaja Sovetskaja Socialističeskaja Respublika □[3]	**84**	43.30 N	43.30 E
Kabasalan	**116**	7.48 N	122.45 E
Kabayan	**116**	16.37 N	120.51 E
Kabba	**150**	7.50 N	6.03 E
Kabbani ≃	**122**	12.13 N	76.54 E
Kåbdalis	**24**	66.10 N	20.00 E
Kabd aṣ-Ṣārim ◆[1]	**130**	34.34 N	39.33 E
Kabd Warqah ◆[1]	**130**	34.20 N	39.37 E
Kabel ◆[8]	**263**	51.24 N	7.29 E
Kabenung Lake ⊜	**190**	48.16 N	85.00 W
Kabetogama Lake ⊜	**190**	48.28 N	92.59 W
Kabeya	**154**	5.40 S	27.58 E
Kab-hegy ∧	**30**	47.03 N	17.39 E
Kabia ≃	**146**	9.54 N	15.10 E
Kabid, Wādī V	**132**	30.08 N	36.31 E
Kabinakagami Lake ⊜	**190**	48.54 N	84.25 W
Kabin Buri	**110**	13.59 N	101.43 E
Kabinda	**152**	6.08 S	24.29 E
Kabinu	**112**	4.00 N	116.05 E
Kabir	**112**	8.17 S	124.13 E
Kabira	**175d**	24.27 N	124.08 E
Kabīr Kili	**123**	33.11 N	71.19 E
Kabīr Kūh ⋌	**128**	33.25 N	46.45 E
Kabīrwāla	**123**	30.24 N	71.52 E
Kabkābīyah	**140**	13.39 N	24.05 E
Kablow	**264a**	52.18 N	13.44 E
Kablower Ziegelei	**264a**	52.19 N	13.43 E
Kablukovo, Ross.	**82**	56.50 N	36.12 E
Kablukovo, Ross.	**82**	56.02 N	38.10 E
Kablumgu, Cape ≻	**164**	6.20 S	150.00 E
Kabna	**140**	19.10 N	32.41 E
Kabo	**152**	7.39 N	18.37 E
Kabobo	**154**	5.07 S	29.03 E
Kaboe ≃	**158**	28.55 S	19.17 E
Kābol	**120**	34.31 N	69.12 E
Kābol □[4]	**120**	34.30 N	69.15 E
Kābol ≃	**120**	33.55 N	72.14 E
Kabompo	**154**	13.36 S	24.12 E
Kabompo ≃	**138**	14.10 S	23.11 E
Kabondo-Dianda	**154**	8.53 S	25.40 E
Kabongo, Zaïre	**154**	7.19 S	25.35 E
Kabongo, Zaïre	**154**	8.43 S	28.11 E
Kabongo-Lunda, Chutes ⌞	**152**	7.34 S	17.17 E
Kaboro	**152**	6.59 N	17.33 E
Kabot	**150**	10.48 N	14.57 W
Kabotshome	**154**	3.46 S	26.54 E
Kabou, Centraf.	**152**	5.20 N	21.43 E
Kabou, Togo	**150**	9.27 N	0.49 E
Kaboudia, Rass ≻	**148**	35.14 N	11.10 E
Kaboul → Kābol	**120**	34.31 N	69.12 E
Kabr	**140**	10.54 N	26.50 E
Kabri	**132**	33.01 N	35.09 E
Kabūdarāhang	**128**	35.12 N	48.44 E
Kabūd Gonbad	**128**	37.00 N	59.45 E
Kābul → Kābol	**120**	34.30 N	69.11 E
Kabunda	**154**	12.25 S	29.22 E
Kabunga	**154**	1.42 S	28.08 E
Kabura ≃	**94**	36.17 N	139.04 E
Kaburuang, Pulau I	**108**	3.48 N	126.48 E
Kabūshīyah	**140**	16.53 N	33.42 E
Kabwanga	**152**	7.01 S	22.37 E
Kabwe (Broken Hill)	**154**	14.27 S	28.27 E
Kabwe-Katanda	**152**	7.59 S	24.29 E
Kabyčovka	**83**	49.28 N	39.45 E
Kabylie ◆[1]	**34**	36.30 N	4.30 E
Kača	**78**	44.47 N	33.32 E
Kačalinskaja	**80**	49.07 N	44.03 E
Kačanik	**38**	42.13 N	21.14 E
Kačanovo	**76**	57.28 N	27.46 E
Kacbachskij	**86**	52.58 N	59.40 E
Kačerginė	**76**	54.56 N	23.44 E
Kacha ≃[1]	**126**	22.23 N	89.54 E
Kachagalau ∧	**154**	2.19 N	35.03 E
Kach'ang-ni	**98**	38.24 N	126.11 E
Kachati	**84**	42.30 N	41.46 E
Kachchh, Gulf of ⊂	**120**	22.36 N	69.30 E
Kachemak Bay ⊂	**180**	59.35 N	151.30 W
Kachess Lake ⊜[1]	**224**	47.20 N	121.14 W
Kachhwa	**124**	25.13 N	82.43 E
Kachi	**84**	41.26 N	46.56 E
Kachia	**150**	9.53 N	7.58 E
Kachib	**84**	42.25 N	46.36 E
Kachin □[3]	**102**	26.00 N	97.30 E
Kach'i-ri	**98**	34.27 N	126.08 E
Kachisi	**144**	9.39 N	37.50 E
Kachovka	**78**	46.47 N	33.30 E
Kachovskoje vodochranilišče ⊜[1]	**78**	47.25 N	34.10 E
Kachowka-Stausee → Kachovskoje vodochranilišče ⊜[1]	**78**	47.25 N	34.10 E
K'achta	**88**	50.26 N	106.25 E
Kachua, Bngl.	**126**	22.39 N	89.53 E
Kachua, Bngl.	**126**	23.21 N	90.54 E
Kachul	**78**	45.54 N	28.11 E
Kačiry	**86**	53.05 N	76.07 E
Kačkanar	**86**	58.42 N	59.38 E
Kačkanar, gora ∧	**86**	58.47 N	59.23 E
Kaçkar Dağı ∧	**130**	40.50 N	41.10 E
Kačkarovka	**78**	47.06 N	33.44 E
Kačug	**88**	53.58 N	105.52 E
Kada ≃	**88**	55.03 N	102.04 E
Kadada ≃	**80**	53.09 N	46.01 E
Kadaingti	**110**	17.37 N	97.32 E
Kadaiyanallūr	**122**	9.05 N	77.21 E
Kadamatt Island I	**122**	11.14 N	72.47 E
Kadaň	**54**	50.20 N	13.15 E
Kadanai (Kadaney) ≃	**120**	31.02 N	66.09 E
Kadaney (Kadanai) ≃	**120**	31.02 N	66.09 E
Kadan Kyun I	**110**	12.30 N	98.22 E
Kadapongan, Pulau I	**112**	4.43 S	115.44 E
Kadassa ≃	**115b**	9.24 S	120.02 E
Kaddam ⊜[1]	**122**	19.07 N	78.46 E
Kade	**150**	6.05 N	0.50 W
Kadéï ≃	**152**	3.31 N	16.05 E
Kadena	**174m**	26.22 N	127.45 E
Kadena Airfield ⊠	**174m**	26.22 N	127.45 E
Kadeshiki	**80**	58.08 N	49.11 E
Kadetrenden (Kadet Rinne) ʊ	**41**	54.30 N	12.15 E
Kadgo, Lake ⊜	**162**	26.42 S	127.18 E
Kadi	**120**	23.18 N	72.20 E
Kadiana	**150**	10.45 N	6.30 W
Kadıköy	**130**	40.46 N	26.46 E
Kadina	**168b**	33.58 S	137.43 E
Kading ≃	**110**	18.19 N	104.00 E
Kadınhanı	**130**	38.15 N	32.14 E
Kadiolo	**150**	10.33 N	5.46 W
Kadipaten	**115a**	6.46 S	108.10 E
Kādīpur	**124**	26.10 N	82.23 E
Kadiri	**122**	14.07 N	78.10 E
Kadirli	**130**	37.23 N	36.05 E
Kadışehri	**130**	40.00 N	35.49 E
Kadiyevka → Stachanov	**83**	48.34 N	38.40 E
Kadja, Ouadi (Wādī Kaja) V	**146**	12.02 N	22.28 E
Kadkan	**128**	35.35 N	58.50 E
Kadnikov	**76**	59.30 N	40.20 E
Kadnikovskij	**76**	60.19 N	40.15 E
Kado	**150**	7.39 N	9.44 E
Ka-do I	**98**	39.33 N	124.40 E
Kadodo	**140**	11.04 N	29.31 E
Kadogawa	**92**	32.28 N	131.39 E
Kadoka	**198**	43.50 N	101.30 W
Kadom	**80**	54.34 N	42.30 E
Kadoma, Nihon	**270**	34.44 N	135.35 E
Kadoma, Zimb.	**154**	18.21 S	29.55 E
Kadoškino	**80**	54.01 N	44.25 E
Kadov	**60**	49.24 N	13.47 E
Kaduj	**76**	59.12 N	37.09 E
Kadumbul ≃	**115b**	9.42 S	120.32 E
Kaduna	**150**	10.33 N	7.27 E
Kaduna □[3]	**150**	10.30 N	7.45 E
Kaduna ≃	**150**	8.45 N	5.45 E
Kāduqlī	**140**	11.01 N	29.43 E
Kadūr	**122**	13.34 N	76.01 E
Kadyj	**80**	57.47 N	43.11 E
Kadykčan	**74**	63.02 N	146.50 E
Kadyšovo	**80**	54.20 N	46.45 E
Kadžerom	**24**	64.41 N	55.54 E
Kadži-Saj	**85**	42.08 N	77.10 E
Kaech'ŏn	**98**	39.42 N	125.53 E
Kaédi	**150**	16.09 N	13.30 W
Kaedo-ri	**98**	34.35 N	127.39 E
Kaegudeck Lake ⊜	**186**	48.07 N	55.11 W
Kaélé	**146**	10.07 N	14.27 E
Kaena Point ≻	**229c**	21.35 N	158.17 W
Kaeo	**172**	35.06 S	173.47 E
Kaesŏng	**98**	37.59 N	126.33 E
Kāf	**128**	31.24 N	37.24 E
Kafakumba	**152**	9.41 S	23.44 E
Kafan, Haya.	**84**	39.13 N	46.24 E
Kafan, Haya.	**84**	39.11 N	46.08 E
Kafanchan	**150**	9.36 N	8.17 E
Kaffraria □[9]	**158**	31.30 S	28.30 E
Kaffrine	**150**	14.06 N	15.33 W
Kafia Kingi	**140**	9.16 N	24.25 E
Kafin	**150**	9.30 N	7.04 E
Kafinda	**154**	12.39 S	30.20 E
Kafin Madaki	**150**	10.41 N	9.46 E
Kafirévs, Ákra ≻	**38**	38.09 N	24.36 E
Kafirnigan ≃	**120**	36.58 N	68.02 E
Kafo ≃	**154**	1.08 N	31.05 E
Kafr ad-Dawwār	**142**	31.08 N	30.07 E
Kafr ad-Difrāwī	**142**	31.03 N	30.40 E
Kafr al-ʿĀ'id	**142**	30.27 N	31.35 E
Kafr al-Baṭṭīkh	**142**	31.24 N	31.44 E
Kafr al-Jarā'idah	**142**	31.13 N	31.16 E
Kafr ash-Shaykh	**142**	31.07 N	30.56 E
Kafr ash-Shaykh □[4]	**142**	31.15 N	30.50 E
Kafrat Ṭā'il Mūsā	**142**	30.53 N	29.44 E
Kafr at-Tamīmī	**142**	30.37 N	31.21 E
Kafr az-Zayyāt	**142**	30.49 N	30.49 E
Kafr Diyamā	**142**	30.48 N	30.52 E
Kafr el-Zaiyat → Kafr az-Zayyāt	**142**	30.49 N	30.49 E
Kafr Ḥakīm	**273c**	30.05 N	31.07 E
Kafr Ḥūnah	**132**	33.29 N	35.35 E
Kafr Kanna	**132**	32.45 N	35.20 E
Kafr Kilā al-Bāb	**142**	30.41 N	31.09 E
Kafr Nabrakh	**132**	33.42 N	35.38 E
Kafr Naffākh	**132**	33.04 N	35.44 E
Kafr Nāsij	**132**	33.09 N	36.03 E
Kafr Rabīʿ	**142**	30.42 N	30.50 E
Kafr Saʿd	**142**	31.19 N	31.39 E
Kafr Salīm	**142**	31.09 N	30.06 E
Kafr Ṣaqr	**142**	30.48 N	31.37 E
Kafr Shanawān	**142**	30.30 N	31.01 E
Kafr Shibīn	**142**	30.18 N	31.18 E
Kafr Shīmā	**132**	33.49 N	35.32 E
Kafr Shukr	**142**	30.33 N	31.16 E
Kafr Sūsah	**132**	33.29 N	36.16 E
Kafr Takhārīm	**130**	36.07 N	36.31 E
Kafr Ṭarkhān al-Gharbī	**142**	29.29 N	31.13 E
Kafr Yasif	**132**	32.57 N	35.10 E
Kafue	**154**	15.47 S	28.11 E
Kafue ≃	**154**	15.56 S	28.55 E
Kafue Flats ≚	**154**	15.40 S	27.25 E
Kafue Gorge V	**154**	15.54 S	28.34 E
Kafue National Park ♦	**154**	15.00 S	25.45 E
Kafulwe Mission	**154**	9.00 S	29.02 E
Kafumba	**152**	5.23 S	18.55 E
Kafwira	**154**	12.10 S	27.33 E
Kaga	**94**	36.18 N	136.18 E
Kaga Bandoro	**152**	6.59 N	19.11 E
Kagalaska Island I	**180**	51.47 N	176.23 W
Kagal'nickaja	**83**	46.53 N	40.09 E
Kagal'nik	**83**	47.05 N	39.19 E
Kagal'nik ≃	**83**	47.04 N	39.18 E
Kagami	**96**	33.37 N	133.26 E
Kagamigahara	**94**	35.24 N	136.54 E
Kagamil Island I	**180**	53.00 N	169.43 W
Kagamino	**96**	35.05 N	133.56 E
Kāgān, Pāk.	**123**	34.47 N	73.32 E
Kagan, Uzb.	**128**	39.43 N	64.33 E
Kagan Valley V	**123**	34.25 N	73.17 E
Kagarko	**150**	9.29 N	7.41 E
Kagarlyk	**78**	49.51 N	30.50 E
Kagawa	**96**	34.15 N	134.02 E
Kagawa □[5]	**96**	34.15 N	134.00 E
Kagawong, Lake ⊜	**190**	45.49 N	82.18 W
Kagaznagar	**122**	19.18 N	79.50 E
Kåge	**26**	64.50 N	20.59 E
Kagelike	**120**	37.20 N	87.02 E
Kagera (Akagera) ≃	**154**	0.57 S	31.47 E
Kågeröd	**41**	56.01 N	13.06 E
Kâgheṭ ◆[1]	**148**	24.00 N	7.30 W
Kâğıthane ◆[8]	**267b**	41.04 N	28.58 E
Kagitumba	**154**	1.04 S	30.27 E
Kağızman	**84**	40.09 N	43.08 E
Käglan ⋌[2]	**40**	59.23 N	15.31 E
Kagmar	**140**	14.24 N	30.25 E
Kagopal	**146**	8.17 N	16.27 E
Kagoshima	**92**	31.36 N	130.33 E
Kagoshima □[5]	**93b**	29.00 N	129.30 E
Kagoshima-wan ⊂	**92**	31.25 N	130.38 E
Kagran ◆[8]	**264b**	48.15 N	16.27 E
Kagulu	**154**	1.15 N	33.18 E
Kagyo-ri	**98**	34.25 N	126.48 E
Kahalīya, Jabal ∧	**142**	29.55 N	32.09 E
Kahaluu	**229c**	21.27 N	157.50 W
Kahama	**154**	3.50 S	32.36 E
Kahana Bay ⊂	**229c**	21.34 N	157.52 W
Kahayan ≃	**112**	3.20 S	114.04 E
Kahe	**154**	3.30 S	37.26 E
Kahemba	**152**	7.17 S	19.00 E
Kahia	**154**	6.21 S	28.24 E
Kahiu Point ≻	**229a**	21.13 N	156.58 W
Kaḥk	**142**	29.25 N	30.38 E
Kahl ≃	**56**	50.04 N	9.00 E
Kahla	**54**	50.48 N	11.35 E
Kahl am Main	**56**	50.04 N	9.00 E
Kahlenberg ∧	**264b**	48.16 N	16.21 E
Kahler Asten ∧	**56**	51.11 N	8.29 E
Kahlersberg ∧	**64**	47.32 N	13.02 E
Kāhna	**123**	31.22 N	74.22 E
Kahnūj	**128**	27.58 N	57.45 E
Kahoka	**194**	40.25 N	91.43 W
Kahoku, Nihon	**96**	33.39 N	133.47 E
Kahoku, Nihon	**96**	33.06 N	130.41 E
Kahoku-gata ⊜	**94**	36.40 N	136.41 E
Kahoolawe I	**229a**	20.33 N	156.37 W
Kahouanne, Îlet à I	**241o**	16.22 N	61.47 W
Kahoué, Mont ∧	**150**	7.06 N	7.15 W
Kahramanmaraş	**130**	37.36 N	36.55 E
Kahraman Maraş □[4]	**130**	38.00 N	37.05 E
Kahror Pakka	**123**	29.37 N	71.55 E
Kahshe Lake ⊜	**212**	44.52 N	79.16 W
Kâhta	**130**	37.46 N	38.36 E
Kahuku	**229c**	21.40 N	157.57 W
Kahuku Point ≻	**229c**	21.43 N	157.59 W
Kahului	**229a**	20.54 N	156.28 W
Kahului Airport ⊠	**229a**	20.54 N	156.26 W
Kahului Bay ⊂	**229a**	20.54 N	156.28 W
Kahurangi Point ≻	**172**	40.47 S	172.13 E
Kahūta	**123**	33.35 N	73.23 E
Kahuzi-Biega, Parc National de ♦	**154**	1.50 N	28.40 E
Kahyŏn-bong ∧	**271b**	37.38 N	126.39 E
Kahyŏn-ni	**271b**	37.32 N	126.44 E
Kai	**164**	2.15 S	136.32 E
Kai, Kepulauan II	**164**	5.35 S	132.45 E
Kai, Tanjung ≻	**112**	2.52 S	118.45 E
Kaia, Wādī V	**140**	11.31 N	24.15 E
Kaiai, Jabal ∧	**140**	19.54 N	36.48 E
Kaiama	**150**	9.37 N	3.58 E
Kaiapit	**164**	6.15 S	146.15 E
Kaiapoi	**172**	43.23 S	172.40 E
Kaibab Indian Reservation ◆[4]	**200**	36.55 N	112.40 W
Kaibab Plateau ⋌[1]	**200**	36.30 N	112.15 W
Kaibara	**96**	35.08 N	135.05 E
Kai Beab	**164**	7.29 S	139.40 E
Kaibing	**61**	47.12 N	15.50 E
Kaibito Plateau ⋌[1]	**200**	36.40 N	111.20 W
Kaichengqiao	**100**	31.18 N	117.44 E
Kaida	**94**	35.56 N	137.36 E
Kaidori	**268**	35.37 N	139.27 E
Kaidu ≃	**90**	41.55 N	86.38 E
Kaiedin	**140**	9.45 N	32.11 E
Kaieteur Fall ⌞	**246**	5.10 N	59.28 W
Kaieteur National Park ♦	**246**	5.10 N	59.45 W
Kaifeng	**98**	34.51 N	114.21 E
Kaifu	**96**	33.35 N	134.21 E
Kaifu ≃	**96**	33.35 N	134.22 E
Kaihe	**98**	35.42 N	116.20 E
Kaihu	**172**	35.46 S	173.42 E
Kaihua	**100**	29.09 N	118.23 E
Kai Iwi	**172**	39.51 S	174.56 E
Kaijian	**102**	23.42 N	111.48 E
Kaijiang	**102**	31.05 N	107.55 E
Kaijo → Kaesŏng	**98**	37.59 N	126.33 E
Kai Kecil I	**164**	5.45 S	132.40 E
Kaikohe	**172**	35.25 S	173.48 E
Kaikoura	**172**	42.25 S	173.41 E
Kaikoura Peninsula ≻[1]	**172**	42.26 S	173.42 E
Kaikukang	**89**	53.07 N	124.46 E
Kailahun	**150**	8.17 N	10.34 W
Kailāshahar	**120**	24.20 N	92.01 E
Kailas → Kangrinboqê Feng ∧	**120**	31.04 N	81.18 E
Kaili	**102**	26.35 N	107.55 E
Kailu	**89**	43.36 N	121.14 E
Kailua	**229c**	21.24 N	157.44 W
Kailua Bay ⊂	**229c**	21.25 N	157.44 W
Kailua Kona	**229d**	19.22 N	155.59 W
Kaim ≃	**164**	6.40 S	141.45 E
Kaimai Range ⋌	**172**	37.45 S	175.55 E
Kaïmaktsalán ∧	**38**	40.58 N	21.48 E
Kaimana	**164**	3.39 S	133.45 E
Kaimanawa Mountains ⋌	**172**	39.15 S	175.54 E
Kaiman-Inseln → Cayman Islands □[2]	**238**	19.30 N	80.40 W
Kaimenshan	**104**	41.03 N	123.08 E
Kaimganj	**124**	27.34 N	79.21 E
Kaimon-dake ∧	**92**	31.11 N	130.32 E
Kain	**50**	50.38 N	3.22 E
Käina	**76**	58.50 N	22.45 E
Kainab ≃	**158**	28.31 S	19.35 E
Kainach ≃	**61**	46.54 N	15.31 E
Kainan, Nihon	**96**	33.36 N	134.22 E
Kainan, Nihon	**96**	34.09 N	135.12 E
Kainantu	**164**	6.15 S	145.55 E
Kainda	**85**	42.50 N	73.41 E
Kai-Ndunda	**152**	5.42 S	12.42 E
Kaingan ≃	**115a**	7.44 S	107.54 E
Kainji Lake ⊜[1]	**150**	10.30 N	4.35 E
Kaioba	**112**	5.20 S	122.37 E
Kaipara Harbour ⊂	**172**	36.25 S	174.13 E
Kaiparowits Plateau ⋌[1]	**200**	37.20 N	111.15 W
Kaiping, Zhg.	**102**	22.23 N	112.35 E
Kaiping, Zhg.	**105**	39.41 N	118.16 E
Kaipuri, Pulau I	**164**	1.51 S	137.01 E
Kairābani	**126**	24.08 N	87.02 E
Kairaku-en ♦	**94**	36.22 N	140.27 E
Kairāna	**124**	29.24 N	77.12 E
Kairatu	**164**	3.21 S	128.22 E
Kairiru Island I	**164**	3.20 S	143.35 E
Kairo → Al-Qāhirah	**142**	30.03 N	31.15 E
Kairouan	**148**	35.41 N	10.07 E
Kairouan □[8]	**148**	35.30 N	9.55 E
Kairuku	**164**	8.50 S	146.35 E
Kairy	**78**	46.57 N	33.43 E
Kaisarganj	**124**	27.15 N	81.33 E
Kaisarianí	**267c**	37.58 N	23.47 E
Kaisariani Monastery ⊍[1]	**267c**	37.58 N	23.47 E
Kaisergebirge ⋌	**64**	47.36 N	12.20 E
Kaisermühlen ◆[8]	**264b**	48.14 N	16.26 E
Kaiser Pass)(	**226**	37.17 N	119.06 W
Kaisersesch	**56**	50.14 N	7.08 E
Kaiserslautern	**56**	49.26 N	7.46 E
Kaiserstuhl ⋌[2]	**58**	48.06 N	7.40 E
Kaiserswerth ◆[8]	**263**	51.18 N	6.44 E
Kaiser-Wilhelm-Museum ⊍	**263**	51.20 N	6.34 E
Kaishantun	**98**	42.43 N	129.43 E
Kaisheim	**56**	48.46 N	10.48 E
Kaišiadorys	**76**	54.52 N	24.27 E
Kait, Tanjung ≻	**112**	3.14 S	106.05 E
Kaita	**96**	34.20 N	132.32 E
Kaitaia	**172**	35.07 S	173.16 E
Kaitaichi-chūtonchi, Rikujō-jieitai- ■	**96**	34.21 N	132.32 E
Kai Tak Airport ⊠	**271d**	22.20 N	114.12 E
Kaitangata	**172**	46.18 S	169.51 E
Kaitersberg ⋌	**60**	49.11 N	12.57 E
Kaithal	**124**	29.48 N	76.23 E
Kaituma ≃	**246**	8.11 N	59.41 W
Kaiwaka	**172**	36.10 S	174.27 E
Kaiwatu	**164**	8.07 S	127.49 E
Kaiwi Channel ʊ	**229b**	21.15 N	157.30 W
Kaixian	**102**	31.13 N	108.25 E
Kaiyang	**102**	26.58 N	106.40 E
Kaiyuan, Zhg.	**102**	23.44 N	103.11 E
Kaiyuan, Zhg.	**104**	42.32 N	124.01 E
Kaiyuancheng	**98**	42.37 N	124.04 E
Kaiyuh Mountains ⋌	**180**	64.00 N	158.00 W
Kaizhou	**104**	41.22 N	121.19 E
Kaizu	**94**	35.13 N	136.38 E
Kaizuka	**96**	34.27 N	135.21 E
Kaja, Wādī (Ouadi Kadja) V	**146**	12.02 N	22.28 E
Kajaani	**26**	64.14 N	27.41 E
Kajabbi	**166**	20.02 S	140.02 E
Kajakī, Band-e ⊜[1]	**128**	32.22 N	65.16 E
Kajang, Indon.	**112**	5.20 S	120.21 E
Kajang, Malay.	**114**	2.59 N	101.47 E
Kajang, Gunong ∧	**114**	2.46 N	104.09 E
Kajasan	**86**	55.12 N	62.16 E
Kajasula	**84**	44.19 N	44.59 E
Kajen	**115a**	7.02 S	109.34 E
Kajgy	**86**	50.55 N	64.43 E
Kajiado	**154**	1.51 S	36.47 E
Kajikazawa	**94**	35.33 N	138.27 E
Kajiki	**92**	31.44 N	130.40 E
Kājlāgarh	**126**	22.02 N	87.47 E
Kajmanačicha	**86**	53.32 N	75.11 E
Kajmonovo	**88**	56.50 N	104.54 E
Kajmysovy	**86**	59.48 N	76.31 E
Kajnar	**86**	49.12 N	77.25 E
Kajo Kaji	**154**	3.53 N	31.40 E
Kajrakkum	**85**	40.16 N	69.49 E
Kajrakkumskoje vodochranilišče ⊜[1]	**85**	40.20 N	70.10 E
Kajrakty	**86**	48.31 N	73.14 E
Kajsackoje	**80**	49.44 N	46.51 E
Kājū ≃	**128**	25.34 N	61.13 E
Kājulia	**126**	23.01 N	89.57 E
Kajuru	**150**	10.21 N	7.40 E
Kaka, Centraf.	**140**	6.01 N	26.30 E
Kākā, Sūd.	**140**	10.36 N	32.11 E
Kaka, Lae o ≻	**229a**	20.31 N	156.33 W
Kakabeka Falls ⌞	**190**	48.24 N	89.37 W
Kakabia, Pulau I	**112**	6.54 S	122.13 E
Kakadu National Park ♦	**164**	13.00 S	132.45 E
Kakagi Lake ⊜	**184**	49.13 N	93.52 W
Kakamas	**158**	28.45 S	20.33 E
Kakamega	**154**	0.17 N	34.45 E
Kakamigahara	**94**	35.24 N	136.54 E
Kakana	**110**	9.07 N	92.49 E
Kakanui Mountains ⋌	**172**	45.09 S	170.26 E
Kaka Point	**172**	46.23 S	169.47 E
Kakaramea	**172**	39.43 S	174.27 E
Kakasa	**164**	9.20 S	148.45 E
Kakata	**150**	6.35 N	10.19 W
Kakatahi	**172**	39.41 S	175.20 E
Kākdwīp	**126**	21.53 N	88.11 E
Kake, Nihon	**96**	34.36 N	132.19 E
Kake, Ak., U.S.	**180**	56.58 N	133.56 W
Kakegawa	**94**	34.46 N	138.01 E
Kakehashi ≃	**94**	36.25 N	136.25 E
Kakelwe	**154**	4.49 S	29.00 E
Kakenge	**152**	4.51 S	21.55 E
Kakeya	**96**	35.11 N	132.49 E
Kakhonak	**180**	59.26 N	154.51 W
Kakhra	**126**	21.38 N	87.27 E
Kākī	**128**	28.19 N	51.34 E
Kākināda	**122**	16.56 N	82.13 E
Kakino	**80**	55.12 N	44.53 E
Kakinoki	**96**	34.26 N	131.52 E
Kakisa Lake ⊜	**176**	60.55 N	117.40 W
Kakizaki	**92**	37.15 N	138.25 E
Kako ≃, Guy.	**246**	5.46 N	60.35 W
Kako ≃, Nihon	**96**	34.44 N	134.49 E
Kakoaka	**156**	18.40 S	24.22 E
Kakogawa	**96**	34.46 N	134.51 E
Kakrāla	**272a**	28.33 N	77.25 E
Kāksa	**126**	23.28 N	87.28 E
Kaktovik	**180**	70.08 N	143.37 W
Kakuda	**92**	37.58 N	140.47 E
Kakui-shima I	**96**	34.43 N	134.19 E
Kakuma	**154**	3.43 N	34.52 E
Kakunodate	**92**	39.35 N	140.34 E
Kakus ≃	**112**	2.46 N	113.01 E
Kakwa ≃	**182**	54.36 N	118.28 W
Kala	**146**	12.05 N	14.27 E
Kala ≃	**122**	8.18 N	79.50 E
Kalaa Kebira	**148**	35.52 N	10.32 E
Kalaallit Nunaat → Greenland □[2]	**16**	70.00 N	40.00 W
Kalaa Sghira	**36**	35.49 N	10.33 E
Kālābāgh	**123**	32.58 N	71.34 E
Kalabahi	**112**	8.13 S	124.31 E
Kalabáka	**38**	39.42 N	21.43 E
Kalabakan	**112**	4.25 N	117.29 E
Kalabo	**152**	14.57 S	22.40 E
Kalabula	**86**	43.24 N	83.06 E
Kalač	**78**	50.25 N	41.01 E
Kalačinsk	**86**	55.03 N	74.34 E
Kalač-Kurtlak	**80**	49.00 N	42.26 E
Kalač-na-Donu	**80**	48.43 N	43.31 E
Kalačskaja vozvyšennost' ⋌[1]	**80**	50.30 N	41.30 E
Kaladan ≃	**110**	20.09 N	92.57 E
Kaladar	**212**	44.39 N	77.07 W
Kalae	**229a**	21.10 N	157.00 W
Ka Lae ≻	**229d**	18.55 N	155.41 W
Kalaena ≃	**112**	2.40 S	120.53 E
Kalagan	**89**	50.30 N	119.55 E
Kalagwe	**110**	22.31 N	96.31 E
Kalahari Desert ◆[2]	**156**	24.00 S	21.30 E
Kalahari Gemsbok National Park ♦	**156**	25.30 S	20.30 E
Kalaheo	**229b**	21.55 N	159.31 W
Kālaia	**126**	22.23 N	90.36 E
Kalai-Chumb	**85**	38.28 N	70.46 E
Kalai-Mor	**128**	35.39 N	62.33 E
Kalais	**80**	52.38 N	42.38 E
Kalaiyā	**124**	27.02 N	85.00 E
Kalajka	**88**	58.28 N	111.46 E
Kalajoki	**26**	64.15 N	23.57 E
Kalajoki ≃	**26**	64.17 N	23.55 E
Kalakamate	**156**	20.39 S	27.21 E
Kalakan	**88**	55.08 N	116.45 E
Kalakan ≃	**88**	55.07 N	116.46 E
Kalakepen	**114**	2.45 N	97.50 E
Kalām	**123**	35.32 N	72.35 E
Kalama, Wa., U.S.	**224**	46.00 N	122.50 W
Kalama, Zaïre	**154**	2.55 S	28.33 E
Kalama ≃	**224**	46.02 N	122.52 W
Kalama, Pulau I	**112**	3.15 N	125.28 E
Kalámai	**38**	37.04 N	22.07 E
Kalamákion	**267c**	37.55 N	23.43 E
Kalamalka Lake ⊜	**182**	50.09 N	119.22 W
Kalamariá	**38**	40.35 N	22.58 E
Kalamazoo	**216**	42.17 N	85.35 W
Kalamazoo □[6]	**216**	42.14 N	85.32 W
Kalamazoo ≃	**216**	42.40 N	86.10 W
Kalamazoo, North Branch ≃	**216**	42.14 N	84.44 W
Kalamazoo, South Branch ≃	**216**	42.14 N	84.44 W
Kalamazoo Lake ⊂	**216**	42.39 N	86.13 W
Kalamb	**122**	19.03 N	73.57 E
Kalamba	**152**	0.26 S	18.17 E
Kalambau, Pulau I	**112**	4.55 S	115.39 E
Kalambo Falls ⌞	**154**	8.36 S	31.14 E
Kalamboli	**272c**	19.01 N	73.06 E
Kalamitskij zaliv ⊂	**78**	45.05 N	33.23 E
Kalamo	**216**	42.32 N	85.01 W
Kalampáka	**38**	39.42 N	21.39 E
Kalampising	**112**	3.44 N	116.42 E
Kalamunda	**168a**	31.57 S	116.03 E
Kalamunda National Park ♦	**168a**	31.59 S	116.04 E
Kalana	**150**	10.47 N	8.12 W
Kalančak	**78**	46.16 N	33.17 E
Kalandula	**152**	9.06 S	15.57 E
Kalange-Bushimaie ≃	**152**	7.55 S	23.11 E
Kalanguj	**88**	51.01 N	116.31 E
Kalankalan	**150**	10.07 N	8.54 W
Kalannie	**162**	30.21 S	117.04 E
Kalanshiyū ar-Ramlī al-Kabīr, Sarīr ⊥[8]	**146**	28.00 N	23.00 E
Kālānwāli	**123**	29.51 N	74.57 E
Kalao, Pulau I	**112**	7.18 S	120.58 E
Kalaong	**116**	6.04 N	124.28 E
Kalaotoa, Pulau I	**112**	7.22 S	121.47 E
Kalapana	**229d**	19.21 N	154.58 W
Kalāpāra	**126**	21.59 N	90.14 E
Kalar ≃	**88**	55.23 N	116.18 E
Kalar, Kūh-e ∧	**128**	31.50 N	50.53 E
Kalaraš	**78**	47.16 N	28.19 E
Kälarne	**26**	62.59 N	16.05 E
Kālāroa	**126**	22.52 N	89.02 E
Kalasarv	**84**	39.11 N	48.03 E
Kalasi	**86**	48.43 N	86.59 E
Kalasin, Indon.	**112**	0.12 N	114.16 E
Kalasin, Thai	**110**	16.29 N	103.30 E
Kalašnikovo	**76**	57.17 N	35.13 E
Kalāt	**120**	29.02 N	66.35 E
Kalatungan Mountain ∧	**116**	7.58 N	124.47 E
Kalaupapa	**229a**	21.11 N	156.59 W
Kalaupapa National Historical Park ♦	**229a**	21.12 N	156.58 W
Kalaupapa Peninsula ≻[1]	**229a**	21.13 N	156.58 W
Kalauri	**84**	41.49 N	45.42 E
Kalaus ≃	**80**	45.43 N	44.07 E
Kalaus-Kr'akovka	**83**	48.46 N	38.52 E
Kalavárdha	**38**	36.20 N	27.57 E
Kalávrita	**38**	38.01 N	22.06 E
Kalaw	**110**	20.38 N	96.34 E
Kalawao □[6]	**229a**	21.12 N	156.58 W
Kal'azin	**76**	57.15 N	37.52 E
Kalb, Nahr al- ≃	**132**	33.57 N	35.35 E
Kalb, Ra's al- ≻	**144**	14.02 N	48.41 E
Kalbā'	**128**	25.03 N	56.21 E
Kalbar	**171a**	27.56 S	152.37 E
Kalbarri	**162**	27.42 S	114.09 E
Kalbarri National Park ♦	**162**	27.45 S	114.25 E
Kalbe	**54**	52.40 N	11.25 E
Kalbinskij chrebet ⋌	**86**	49.10 N	83.00 E
Kalchās	**120**	29.21 N	69.42 E
Kal'čik ≃	**83**	47.07 N	37.36 E
Kaldırım ≃	**267b**	41.10 N	29.12 E
Kaldygajty ≃	**80**	49.20 N	52.38 E
Kale, Tür.	**130**	36.14 N	29.59 E
Kale, Tür.	**130**	40.23 N	39.39 E
Kale, Tür.	**130**	37.26 N	28.51 E
Kalecik, Tür.	**130**	40.06 N	33.25 E
Kalecik, Tür.	**130**	37.17 N	39.02 E
Kaleden	**182**	49.23 N	119.35 W
Kaledupa, Pulau I	**112**	5.32 S	123.47 E
Kalegauk Island I	**110**	15.32 N	97.40 E
Kalehe	**154**	2.06 S	28.55 E
Kaleindaung ≃	**110**	18.50 N	94.00 E
Kalema, Tan.	**154**	1.12 S	31.50 E
Kalema, Zaïre	**152**	4.08 S	24.15 E
Kalemie (Albertville)	**154**	5.56 S	29.12 E
Kalemyo	**120**	23.12 N	94.10 E
Kalene Hill	**152**	11.11 S	24.10 E
Kaleščatovka	**83**	49.35 N	39.55 E
Kaletwa	**110**	21.45 N	92.48 E
Kalety	**30**	50.34 N	18.54 E
Kalevala	**24**	65.13 N	31.08 E
Kalewa	**110**	23.12 N	94.17 E
Kale Water ≃	**46**	55.32 N	2.28 W
Kaleybar	**128**	38.47 N	47.02 E
Kálfafell	**24a**	63.58 N	17.40 W
Kalga	**88**	50.57 N	118.48 E
Kalgačicha	**24**	63.20 N	36.44 E
Kalgan	**162**	34.53 S	118.01 E
Kalgan → Zhangjiakou	**105**	40.50 N	114.53 E
Kalgin Island I	**180**	60.28 N	151.55 W
Kalgoorlie	**162**	30.45 S	121.28 E
Kalhe	**272c**	18.52 N	73.06 E
Kali	**150**	12.10 N	11.29 W
Kāli ≃[1]	**126**	23.40 N	89.12 E
Kālia	**126**	23.03 N	89.38 E
Kāliāganj	**124**	25.38 N	88.19 E
Kāliāghaj ≃	**126**	22.10 N	87.50 E
Kāliākair	**126**	24.05 N	90.14 E
Kaliakra, nos ≻	**38**	43.21 N	28.27 E
Kalianda	**115a**	5.45 S	105.38 E
Kalianget	**115a**	7.03 S	113.56 E
Kalibek, ozero ⊜	**86**	53.52 N	70.40 E
Kālībhīt Hills ⋌[2]	**124**	22.10 N	77.30 E
Kalibo	**116**	11.43 N	122.22 E
Kalida	**216**	40.59 N	84.12 W
Kalifornien, Golf von → California, Golfo de ⊂	**232**	28.00 N	112.00 W
Kālī Gaṇḍakī ≃	**124**	27.42 N	84.25 E
Kāliganga ≃	**126**	23.43 N	90.15 E
Kālīganj, Bngl.	**126**	23.25 N	89.08 E
Kālīganj, Bngl.	**126**	23.55 N	90.34 E
Kālīganj, Bngl.	**126**	22.28 N	89.02 E
Kāliganj, India	**126**	23.44 N	88.14 E
Kalihiwai ≃	**229b**	22.13 N	159.26 W
Kalijati	**115a**	6.32 S	107.40 E
Kālikāpur, Bngl.	**126**	22.43 N	89.26 E
Kālikāpur, Bngl.	**126**	23.46 N	89.55 E
Kālikāpur, India	**126**	22.37 N	86.17 E
Kālikāpur, India	**272b**	22.29 N	88.32 E
Kalikino, Ross.	**76**	52.57 N	39.50 E
Kalikino, Ross.	**80**	52.55 N	54.05 E
Kalima, Zaïre	**154**	2.34 S	26.37 E
Kalima, Zhg.	**104**	41.32 N	122.40 E
Kalimantan Barat □[4]	**112**	0.30 N	110.00 E
Kalimantan → Borneo I	**112**	0.30 N	114.00 E
Kalimantan Selatan □[4]	**112**	2.30 S	115.30 E
Kalimantan Tengah □[4]	**112**	2.00 S	113.30 E
Kalimantan Timur □[4]	**112**	1.30 N	116.30 E
Kálimnos	**38**	36.57 N	26.59 E
Kálimnos I	**38**	37.00 N	27.00 E
Kālimpang	**124**	27.04 N	88.29 E
Kalina, Pointe de ≻	**273b**	4.18 S	15.16 E
Kālīnadi ≃	**122**	14.50 N	74.08 E
Kālinagar	**126**	22.26 N	88.51 E
Kalinga-Apayao □[4]	**116**	17.50 N	121.10 E
Kalinga Bil ⊜	**272b**	22.33 N	88.33 E
Kalinin	**80**	47.11 N	42.10 E
Kalininabad	**85**	39.45 N	69.08 E
Kaliningrad (Königsberg), Ross.	**76**	54.43 N	20.30 E
Kaliningrad, Ross.	**82**	55.55 N	37.49 E
Kalinino, Haya.	**84**	41.07 N	44.17 E
Kalinino, Ross.	**78**	45.07 N	39.00 E
Kalinino, Ross.	**80**	46.21 N	48.53 E
Kalinino, Ross.	**86**	57.20 N	56.20 E
Kalinino, Ross.	**89**	49.24 N	129.20 E
Kalinino, Ukr.	**83**	47.27 N	37.28 E
Kalininsk, Kyrg.	**85**	42.29 N	72.06 E
Kalininsk, Ross.	**80**	51.30 N	44.28 E
Kalininskaja, Ross.	**78**	45.29 N	38.40 E
Kalininskaja, Ross.	**80**	47.52 N	42.15 E
Kalininskij	**83**	48.01 N	39.36 E
Kalininskoje, Kyrg.	**85**	42.50 N	73.49 E
Kalininskoje, Ukr.	**78**	47.07 N	32.59 E
Kalinin → Tver'	**82**	56.52 N	35.55 E
Kalinkoviči	**78**	52.08 N	29.21 E
Kalinku	**154**	11.12 S	33.12 E
Kalinovik	**38**	43.31 N	18.26 E
Kalinovka, Kaz.	**86**	49.58 N	55.22 E
Kalinovka, Ross.	**78**	51.54 N	34.28 E
Kalinovka, Ukr.	**78**	50.14 N	30.14 E
Kalinovka, Ukr.	**78**	49.27 N	28.32 E
Kalinovo, Ross.	**82**	54.54 N	37.17 E
Kalinovo, Ukr.	**83**	48.34 N	38.31 E
Kālipur	**272b**	22.41 N	88.17 E
Kaliro	**154**	0.54 N	33.30 E
Kalis	**144**	8.23 N	49.05 E
Kalisat	**115a**	8.08 S	113.48 E
Kalisch → Kalisz	**30**	51.46 N	18.06 E
Kāli Sindh ≃	**124**	25.32 N	76.17 E
Kalispell	**202**	48.11 N	114.18 W
Kalistraticha	**86**	52.59 N	83.35 E
Kalisz	**30**	51.46 N	18.06 E
Kalisz □[4]	**30**	51.40 N	17.45 E
Kalisz Pomorski	**30**	53.19 N	15.54 E
Kalitva ≃	**78**	48.10 N	40.46 E
Kaliua	**154**	5.04 S	31.48 E
Kaliveli Tank ⊜[1]	**122**	12.05 N	79.50 E
Kaliwiro	**115a**	7.27 S	109.51 E
Kaliwungu	**115a**	6.57 S	110.14 E
Kalix	**26**	65.51 N	23.08 E
Kalixälven ≃	**24**	65.50 N	23.11 E
Kālka	**123**	30.50 N	76.56 E
Kālkāji ◆[8]	**272a**	28.33 N	77.16 E
Kalkaman	**86**	51.58 N	76.02 E
Kalkan	**130**	36.15 N	29.24 E
Kalkar	**52**	50.36 N	6.46 E
Kalkaska	**190**	44.44 N	85.10 W
Kalkfeld	**156**	20.53 S	16.11 E
Kalkfontein	**156**	22.08 S	20.53 E
Kalkfonteindam ⊜[1]	**158**	29.30 S	25.15 E
Kalkhorst	**54**	53.58 N	11.02 E
Kalkım	**130**	39.48 N	27.13 E
Kālkini	**126**	23.06 N	90.16 E
Kalkmond	**158**	28.40 S	20.26 E
Kalkrand	**156**	24.03 S	17.33 E
Kalksburg ◆[8]	**264b**	48.08 N	16.15 E
Kalk-See ⊜	**264a**	52.26 N	13.46 E
Kalkstasie	**158**	30.00 S	18.55 E
Kalkum ◆[8]	**263**	51.18 N	6.46 E
Kalkutta → Calcutta	**126**	22.32 N	88.22 E
Kalkwerf	**158**	28.39 S	21.43 E
Kall	**56**	50.32 N	6.32 E
Kallakkurichchi	**122**	11.44 N	78.58 E
Kallakoopah Creek ≃	**166**	27.29 S	138.15 E
Kållandsö I	**26**	58.40 N	13.09 E
Kallang ≃	**271c**	1.19 N	103.52 E
Kallar Kahār	**123**	32.47 N	72.42 E
Kallaste	**76**	58.39 N	27.09 E
Kallavesi ⊜	**26**	62.50 N	27.45 E
Kalletal	**52**	52.06 N	8.56 E
Källfallet	**40**	59.50 N	15.31 E
Kallhäll	**40**	59.27 N	17.48 E
Kalliecahoolie Lake ⊜	**184**	54.14 N	95.29 W
Kallinge	**26**	56.14 N	15.17 E
Kallista	**274b**	37.53 S	145.22 E
Kallithéa	**267c**	37.57 N	23.42 E
Kallmünz	**60**	49.09 N	11.58 E
Kallnach	**58**	47.01 N	7.14 E
Kallsjön ⊜	**26**	63.37 N	13.00 E
Kalmakkora	**86**	44.03 N	78.44 E
Kalmakkyrgan ≃	**86**	46.58 N	64.30 E
Kalmar	**26**	56.40 N	16.22 E
Kalmar Län □[6]	**26**	57.20 N	16.00 E
Kalmarsund ʊ	**26**	56.40 N	16.25 E
Kalmit ∧	**56**	49.19 N	8.05 E
Kal'mius ≃	**83**	47.05 N	37.34 E
Kalmthout	**50**	51.23 N	4.28 E
Kalmyckaja Avtonomnaja Sovetskaja Socialističeskaja Respublika □[3]	**80**	46.30 N	45.30 E
Kalmyckije Mysy	**86**	51.53 N	82.16 E
Kalmykov	**80**	49.01 N	42.49 E
Kalmykovka, Ukr.	**83**	49.17 N	38.39 E
Kalmykovka, Ukr.	**83**	49.17 N	39.52 E
Kalmykovo	**80**	49.03 N	51.47 E
Kālna	**126**	23.13 N	88.22 E
Kalnciems	**76**	56.50 N	23.37 E
Kal'niboloto	**78**	48.44 N	31.00 E
Kalnibolotskaja	**78**	46.01 N	40.28 E
Kalničko Gorje ⋌	**36**	46.10 N	16.30 E
Kalo	**164**	10.00 S	147.45 E
Kálócfa	**61**	46.45 N	16.34 E
Kalocsa	**30**	46.32 N	18.59 E
Kalofer	**38**	42.37 N	24.59 E
Kalohi Channel ʊ	**229a**	21.00 N	156.56 W
Kaloko	**154**	6.47 S	25.48 E
Kalol, India	**120**	22.36 N	73.27 E
Kālol, India	**120**	23.15 N	72.29 E
Kalole	**154**	3.42 S	27.22 E
Kalolio	**112**	0.11 S	121.38 E
Kaloli Point ≻	**229d**	19.38 N	154.57 W
Kalomo	**154**	17.02 S	26.30 E
Kalomo ≃	**154**	17.57 S	26.24 E
Kalona	**190**	41.28 N	91.42 W
Kalonda	**152**	4.48 S	17.33 E
Kalone Peak ∧	**182**	52.38 N	126.37 W
Kalonga	**154**	9.10 S	27.25 E
Kalorama	**274b**	37.49 S	145.22 E
Kaloran	**115a**	7.15 S	110.15 E
Kalø Vig ⊂	**41**	56.15 N	10.25 E
Kalpáki	**38**	39.55 N	20.20 E
Kalpeni Island I	**122**	10.05 N	73.38 E
Kālpi	**124**	26.07 N	79.44 E
Kāl Qalʿeh	**128**	32.38 N	62.32 E
Kalri	**123**	31.39 N	72.33 E
Kalsdorf bei Graz	**61**	46.57 N	15.28 E
Kalskag	**180**	61.30 N	160.23 W
Kalsūbai ∧	**122**	19.36 N	73.43 E
Kaltag	**180**	64.20 N	158.44 W
Kaltan	**86**	53.30 N	87.17 E
Kaltbrunn	**58**	47.12 N	9.02 E
Kalte Herberge ∧	**56**	50.03 N	7.59 E
Kalteneber	**56**	51.19 N	10.08 E
Kaltenhouse	**56**	48.48 N	7.50 E
Kaltenkirchen	**52**	53.50 N	9.58 E
Kaltenleutgeben	**264b**	48.07 N	16.12 E
Kaltennordheim	**56**	50.38 N	10.10 E
Kaltensundheim	**56**	50.36 N	10.10 E
Kalter Gang ≃	**264b**	48.02 N	16.25 E
Kalthof	**263**	51.26 N	7.40 E
Kal'tino	**265a**	59.58 N	30.40 E
Kaltungo	**146**	9.50 N	11.19 E
Kaluga	**82**	54.31 N	36.16 E
Kaluga □[8]	**82**	54.45 N	36.30 E
Kalugino, Kaz.	**80**	48.22 N	51.33 E
Kalugino, Ross.	**82**	54.59 N	37.11 E
Kalukalukuang, Pulau I	**112**	5.14 S	117.38 E
Kālu Khuhar	**120**	25.08 N	67.46 E
Kalulushi	**154**	12.50 S	28.03 E
Kalumba, Mount ∧	**166**	31.49 S	146.22 E
Kalumburu	**164**	14.18 S	126.39 E
Kalumburu Aboriginal Reserve ◆[4]	**164**	14.15 S	126.50 E
Kalundborg	**41**	55.41 N	11.06 E
Kalundborg Fjord ⊂	**41**	55.41 N	11.00 E
Kālundri	**272c**	18.59 N	73.08 E
Kalundu, Zaïre	**154**	3.26 S	29.08 E
Kalundu, Zam.	**154**	10.16 S	29.24 E
Kalungwishi ≃	**154**	9.01 S	28.57 E
Kalūr Kot	**123**	32.09 N	71.16 E
Kaluš	**78**	49.03 N	24.23 E
Kałuszyn	**30**	52.13 N	21.49 E
Kalutara	**122**	6.35 N	79.58 E
Kalvåg	**26**	61.46 N	4.53 E
Kalvarija	**76**	54.21 N	23.14 E
K'alvaz	**84**	38.39 N	48.18 E
Kalvehave	**41**	55.00 N	12.10 E
Kälviä	**26**	63.52 N	23.26 E
Kalwa	**272c**	19.12 N	72.59 E
Kalwang	**61**	47.26 N	14.46 E
Kalwaria Zebrzydowska	**30**	49.52 N	19.41 E
Kalyān	**122**	19.15 N	73.09 E
Kalyāndurg	**122**	14.33 N	77.06 E

Symbols in the index entries represent the broad categories identified in the key at the right. Symbols with superior numbers (⋌[1]) identify subcategories (see complete key on page *I* · *1*).

Symbole im Register stellen die rechts im Schlüssel erklärten Kategorien dar. Symbole mit hochgestellten Ziffern (⋌[1]) bezeichnen Unterabteilungen einer Kategorie (vgl. vollständiger Schlüssel auf Seite *I* · *1*).

Los símbolos incluídos en el texto del índice representan las grandes categorias identificadas con la clave a la derecha. Los símbolos con numeros en su parte superior (⋌[1]) identifican las subcategorías (véase la clave completa en la página *I* · *1*).

Les symboles de l'index représentent les catégories indiquées dans la légende à droite. Les symboles suivis d'un indice (⋌[1]) représentent des sous-catégories (voir légende complète à la page *I* · *1*).

Os símbolos incluídos no texto do índice representam as grandes categorias identificadas com a chave à direita. Os símbolos com números em sua parte superior (⋌[1]) identificam as subcategorias (veja-se a chave completa à página *I* · *1*).

	English	Deutsch	Español	Français	Português
∧	Mountain	Berg	Montaña	Montagne	Montanha
⋌	Mountains	Gebirge	Montañas	Montagnes	Montanhas
)(	Pass	Paß	Paso	Col	Passo
V	Valley, Canyon	Tal, Cañon	Valle, Cañón	Vallée, Canyon	Vale, Canhão
≚	Plain	Ebene	Llano	Plaine	Planície
≻	Cape	Kap	Cabo	Cap	Cabo
I	Island	Insel	Isla	Île	Ilha
II	Islands	Inseln	Islas	Îles	Ilhas
⊥	Other Topographic Features	Andere Topographische Objekte	Otros Elementos Topográficos	Autres données topographiques	Outros acidentes topográficos

ESPAÑOL

Nombre	Página	Lat.°′	Long.°′ W = Oeste
Kam ≃	146	8.15 N	11.00 E
Kama, Mya.	110	19.02 N	95.06 E
Kama, Ross.	80	56.19 N	54.06 E
Kama, Ross.	86	60.08 N	62.10 E
Kama, Zaïre	154	3.32 S	27.07 E
Kama ≃, Ross.	72	55.45 N	52.00 E
Kama ≃, Ross.	86	55.35 N	76.54 E
Kamachumu	154	1.35 S	31.37 E
Kamado-zaki ≻	96	33.04 N	132.02 E
Kamae	92	32.48 N	131.56 E
Kamagaya	94	35.45 N	140.01 E
Kamaiki Point ≻	229a	20.46 N	156.50 W
Kamaishi	92	39.16 N	141.53 E
Kama-iwa I	174f	24.47 N	141.17 E
Kamajai	76	55.49 N	25.30 E
Kamajri	84	40.48 N	43.50 E
Kamakou ∧	229a	21.07 N	156.52 W
Kamakura	94	35.19 N	139.33 E
Kamakwie	150	9.30 N	12.14 W
Kamal	115a	7.10 S	112.42 E
Kamālia	123	30.44 N	72.39 E
Kamamaung	110	17.21 N	97.40 E
Kāman, India	124	27.39 N	77.16 E
Kaman, Tür.	130	39.22 N	33.44 E
Kaman ≃	110	14.48 N	106.51 E
Kamana	154	5.59 S	24.56 E
Kamanashi ≃	94	35.33 N	138.28 E
Kamango	154	0.39 N	29.53 E
Kamaniskeg Lake ⊜	212	45.25 N	77.42 W
Kamanjab	156	19.35 S	14.51 E
Kamapanda	152	12.00 S	24.10 E
Kamara Forest ♠	264c	47.26 N	19.00 E
Kamarān I	144	15.21 N	42.35 E
Kamaran, Hadjer ∧	146	12.41 N	21.46 E
Kamarang ≃	246	5.53 N	60.35 W
Kāmāreddi	122	18.19 N	78.21 E
Kāmārhāti	272b	22.40 N	88.22 E
Kamarik	130	39.37 N	39.18 E
Kāmārkhāli Ghāt	126	23.32 N	89.33 E
Kāmārkunda	272b	22.49 N	88.13 E
Kamas	200	40.38 N	111.16 W
Kamata ◆8	268	35.33 N	139.43 E
Kamatsi Lake ⊜	184	56.10 N	102.15 W
Kamay	196	33.51 N	98.48 W
Kamba	150	11.53 N	3.36 E
Kamba Kota	152	7.10 N	17.54 E
Kambalda	162	31.12 S	121.40 E
Kambam	122	9.44 N	77.18 E
Kambang	112	1.42 S	100.42 E
Kambanga	152	13.23 S	23.03 E
Kambar	120	27.36 N	68.00 E
Kambara	94	35.07 N	138.36 E
Kambara Island I	175g	18.57 S	178.57 W
Kambara-tunnel ◆5	94	35.02 N	138.31 E
Kambarka	80	56.17 N	54.12 E
Kambia	150	9.07 N	12.55 W
Kambja	76	58.14 N	26.42 E
Kambolé	150	8.45 N	1.36 E
Kambole Mission	154	8.46 S	30.46 E
Kambove	154	10.52 S	26.38 E
Kambu	115b	8.23 S	118.20 E
Kambuye	152	7.18 S	22.50 E
Kamčatka ≃	74	56.15 N	162.30 E
Kamčatka, poluostrov (Kamchatka) ≻1	74	56.00 N	160.00 E
Kamčatskij poluostrov ≻1	74	56.15 N	163.00 E
Kamčatskij zaliv c	74	55.35 N	162.21 E
Kamchatka → Kamčatka, poluostrov ≻1	74	56.00 N	160.00 E
Kâmchay Méa	110	11.35 N	105.40 E
Kamčija ≃	38	43.02 N	27.53 E
Kāmdebpur, India	272b	22.47 N	88.30 E
Kāmdebpur, India	272b	22.54 N	88.20 E
Kāmdeysh	123	35.24 N	71.20 E
Kameari ◆8	268	35.46 N	139.51 E
Kameda	92	37.52 N	139.07 E
Kameel	158	26.38 S	24.58 E
Kamegamori ∧	96	33.47 N	133.12 E
Kameido ◆8	268	35.42 N	139.50 E
Kamelik ≃	80	52.06 N	49.30 E
Kamen', Bela.	76	55.01 N	28.53 E
Kamen, Dtsch.	52	51.35 N	7.40 E
Kamen', gora ∧	74	69.06 N	94.48 E
Kamenda	154	6.28 S	24.33 E
Kamenec	76	52.24 N	23.49 E
Kamenec-Podol'skij	78	48.41 N	26.36 E
Kameng ≃	120	26.38 N	92.54 E
Kamenický Šenov	54	50.45 N	14.29 E
Kamenjak, Rt ≻	36	44.46 N	13.55 E
Kamenka, Kaz.	80	51.07 N	50.19 E
Kamenka, Kaz.	85	42.55 N	72.50 E
Kamenka, Kaz.	86	52.22 N	69.04 E
Kamenka, Mol.	78	48.03 N	28.42 E
Kamenka, Ross.	24	65.54 N	44.05 E
Kamenka, Ross.	78	50.43 N	39.25 E
Kamenka, Ross.	80	56.11 N	45.35 E
Kamenka, Ross.	80	57.23 N	41.49 E
Kamenka, Ross.	80	53.13 N	44.03 E
Kamenka, Ross.	80	52.04 N	41.49 E
Kamenka, Ross.	82	54.43 N	38.19 E
Kamenka, Ross.	82	56.11 N	37.18 E
Kamenka, Ross.	82	55.13 N	36.59 E
Kamenka, Ross.	86	58.33 N	95.51 E
Kamenka, Ross.	89	44.28 N	136.01 E
Kamenka, Ross.	265a	59.59 N	30.53 E
Kamenka, Ukr.	78	49.02 N	32.06 E
Kamenka, Ukr.	83	49.38 N	39.22 E
Kamenka, Ukr.	83	49.07 N	37.18 E
Kamenka, Ukr.	83	47.25 N	37.42 E
Kamenka ◆8	265a	60.03 N	30.11 E
Kamenka ≃, Ross.	83	47.30 N	38.54 E
Kamenka ≃, Ross.	88	58.33 N	95.51 E
Kamenka ≃, Ross.	265a	60.01 N	30.12 E
Kamenka ≃, Ukr.	78	49.47 N	30.01 E
Kamenka ≃, Ukr.	78	47.39 N	34.02 E
Kamenka ≃, Ukr.	83	49.35 N	39.05 E
Kamenka-Bugskaja	78	50.07 N	24.20 E
Kamenka-Dneprovskaja	78	47.29 N	34.25 E
Kamen'-Kaširskij	78	51.38 N	24.58 E
Kamen'-na-Obi	86	53.47 N	81.20 E
Kamennogorsk	24	60.58 N	29.07 E
Kamennoje, Ukr.	78	51.31 N	27.38 E
Kamennoje, Ukr.	78	47.53 N	35.25 E
Kamennomostskij	84	44.18 N	40.12 E
Kamennye Mogily, zapovednik ♠	78	47.18 N	37.04 E
Kamennyj Brod, Ross.	83	47.26 N	39.51 E
Kamennyj Brod, Ukr.	78	50.25 N	27.49 E
Kamennyj Jar	80	48.27 N	45.34 E
Kamenolomni	83	47.40 N	40.13 E
Kamen'-Rybolov	89	44.46 N	132.02 E
Kamensk	88	51.58 N	106.36 E
Kamenskij	80	50.53 N	45.29 E
Kamenskoje, Ross.	74	62.30 N	166.12 E
Kamenskoje, Ross.	82	55.16 N	36.50 E
Kamenskoje, Ukr.	78	45.49 N	29.16 E
Kamensk-Šachtinskij	83	48.21 N	40.19 E
Kamensk-Ural'skij	86	56.28 N	61.54 E
Kamenz	54	51.16 N	14.06 E
Kameoka	96	35.00 N	135.35 E
Kamerik	52	52.06 N	4.54 E
Kamerunberg → Cameroon Mountain ∧	152	4.12 N	9.11 E
Kamerun → Cameroon □1	134	6.00 N	12.00 E
Kames	46	55.54 N	5.15 W
Kameškovo	80	56.21 N	41.00 E
Kāmet ∧	120	30.54 N	79.37 E
Kameur, Bahr ≃	146	9.26 N	20.50 E
Kameyama	94	34.51 N	136.27 E
Kami, Nihon	94	34.41 N	137.42 E
Kami, Nihon	96	35.05 N	134.53 E
Kamiah	202	46.13 N	116.01 W
Kamiak Butte ∧	202	46.52 N	117.10 W
Kamiakotani	270	34.56 N	135.23 E

FRANÇAIS

Nom	Page	Lat.°′	Long.°′ W = Ouest
Kamiasō	268	35.35 N	139.30 E
Kamień Krajeńskie	30	53.33 N	17.32 E
Kamienna ≃	30	51.06 N	21.47 E
Kamienna Góra	30	50.47 N	16.01 E
Kamień Pomorski	30	53.58 N	14.46 E
Kamieńsk	30	51.12 N	19.30 E
Kamieskroon	156	30.09 S	17.56 E
Kamifukuoka	94	35.52 N	139.32 E
Kamigōri	96	34.52 N	134.22 E
Kamigyō ◆8	270	35.02 N	135.45 E
Kamiichi	94	36.42 N	137.22 E
Kamiishihara	268	35.39 N	139.32 E
Kamiiso	92a	41.49 N	140.39 E
Kamiita	96	34.07 N	134.24 E
Kami-jima I	94	34.33 N	136.59 E
Kamikamagari-jima I	96	34.11 N	132.44 E
Kamikatsu	96	33.53 N	134.24 E
Kamikawa, Nihon	92a	43.51 N	142.46 E
Kamikawa, Nihon	94	36.13 N	139.07 E
Kamikitazawa ◆8	268	35.40 N	139.38 E
Kamikume	270	34.55 N	135.03 E
Kâmil	130	41.07 N	34.47 E
Kamilukuak Lake ⊜	176	62.22 N	101.40 W
Kamimaki	270	34.34 N	135.43 E
Kamimizo	268	35.33 N	139.22 E
Kamina	154	8.44 S	25.00 E
Kaminaka, Nihon	94	35.28 N	135.51 E
Kaminaka, Nihon	96	33.48 N	134.22 E
Kaminak Lake ⊜	176	62.10 N	95.00 W
Kaminaljuyú ⊥	236	14.38 N	90.33 W
Kaminoho	94	35.37 N	137.03 E
Kaminokawa	94	36.26 N	139.55 E
Kaminokuni	92a	41.48 N	140.06 E
Kaminoseki	96	33.49 N	132.07 E
Kaminoyama	92	38.09 N	140.17 E
Kaminskij	80	57.10 N	41.28 E
Kaminuriak Lake ⊜	176	63.00 N	95.40 W
Kamioka	94	36.16 N	137.18 E
Kamiotawa	270	34.54 N	135.31 E
Kamioyamada	268	35.35 N	139.24 E
Kámiros ⊥	38	36.19 N	27.57 E
Kamisato	94	36.15 N	139.09 E
Kamishak Bay c	180	59.15 N	153.45 W
Kamishii	94	36.04 N	136.24 E
Kamishinden	270	34.49 N	135.30 E
Kamisunagawa	92a	43.30 N	142.00 E
Kamitaira	94	36.24 N	136.54 E
Kamitakara	94	36.17 N	137.22 E
Kamitakino	270	34.57 N	134.59 E
Kamitomi	268	35.49 N	139.31 E
Kamitonda	96	33.43 N	135.27 E
Kamitsuruma	268	35.31 N	139.25 E
Kamitsushima	92	34.50 N	129.28 E
Kamituga	154	3.04 S	28.11 E
Kamiura	96	33.03 N	131.55 E
Kamiyahagi	94	35.18 N	137.29 E
Kamiyama	96	33.58 N	134.23 E
Kamiyamada	94	36.28 N	138.09 E
Kamiyama-jima I	174m	26.15 N	127.35 E
Kamiyugi	268	35.37 N	139.23 E
Kamīzgān	84	38.58 N	47.44 E
Kamkhat Muḩaywir ∧2	132	31.08 N	36.30 E
Kamku	120	27.30 N	96.30 E
Kamla (Kamlā) ≃	124	25.37 N	86.40 E
Kamlach ≃	58	48.30 N	10.22 E
Kamloops	182	50.40 N	120.20 W
Kamloops Indian Reserve ◆4	182	50.42 N	120.20 W
Kamloops Lake ⊜	182	50.43 N	120.33 W
Kammon-kaikyō ∪	96	33.56 N	130.56 E
Kammon-kyō ◆5	96	33.56 N	130.55 E
Kammuri-yama ∧	96	34.28 N	132.05 E
Kamnik	36	46.13 N	14.37 E
Kamniokan	88	56.17 N	111.57 E
Kamo, Haya.	84	40.22 N	45.08 E
Kamo, N.Z.	172	35.41 S	174.19 E
Kamo, Nihon	92	37.39 N	139.03 E
Kamo, Nihon	94	34.50 N	138.46 E
Kamo, Nihon	96	34.45 N	135.52 E
Kamo, Nihon	96	35.10 N	134.04 E
Kamo, Nihon	96	35.20 N	132.55 E
Kamo, Nihon	270	34.55 N	135.13 E
Kamo ≃, Nihon	94	35.06 N	140.06 E
Kamo ≃, Nihon	96	33.56 N	133.09 E
Kamo ≃, Nihon	270	34.56 N	135.44 E
Kamoa Mountains ⋏	246	1.37 N	59.00 W
Kamoda-misaki ≻	96	33.50 N	134.45 E
Kamogata	96	34.32 N	133.35 E
Kamogawa, Nihon	94	35.06 N	140.06 E
Kamogawa, Nihon	96	34.51 N	133.49 E
Kamohio Bay c	229a	20.31 N	156.36 W
Kamojima	96	34.04 N	134.21 E
Kāmoke	123	31.58 N	74.13 E
Kamoshida ◆8	268	35.34 N	139.30 E
Kamoto	96	33.00 N	130.45 E
Kamp	56	50.14 N	7.37 E
Kamp ≃	61	48.23 N	15.48 E
Kāmpa	272b	22.56 N	88.28 E
Kampala	154	0.19 N	32.25 E
Kampar	114	4.18 N	101.09 E
Kampar ≃	112	0.32 N	103.08 E
Kamparkalns ∧2	76	57.18 N	22.47 E
Kampar Kanan ≃	112	0.16 N	101.41 E
Kampen	52	52.33 N	5.54 E
Kampene	154	3.36 S	26.40 E
Kampfe, Lake ⊜	276	41.02 N	74.21 W
Kamphaeng, Khao ∧	110	14.37 N	99.18 E
Kamphaeng Phet	110	16.28 N	99.30 E
Kampil	124	27.37 N	79.17 E
Kampinoski Park Narodowy ♠	30	52.20 N	20.35 E
Kampire Dior ∧	123	36.38 N	74.23 E
Kamp-Lintfort	52	51.30 N	6.31 E
Kamp'o	98	35.48 N	129.29 E
Kampolombo, Lake ⊜	154	11.37 S	29.42 E
Kampong Ayer Puteh	114	4.16 N	103.12 E
Kampong Baharu	114	3.43 N	103.17 E
Kampong Benta	114	3.32 N	103.22 E
Kampong Buloh	114	5.32 N	102.45 E
Kâmpóng Cham	110	12.00 N	105.27 E
Kampong Chenor	114	3.29 N	102.36 E
Kâmpóng Chhnăng	110	12.15 N	104.40 E
Kampong Dong	114	3.54 N	101.54 E
Kampong Guchil	114	5.33 N	102.14 E
Kampong Jabor	114	3.57 N	103.20 E
Kampong Jerangau	114	4.51 N	103.12 E
Kampong Kandang	114	2.11 N	102.18 E
Kâmpóng Kântuŏt	110	11.26 N	104.49 E
Kampong Kenyam	114	4.31 N	102.28 E
Kampong Kuala Kemaman	114	4.14 N	103.27 E
Kampong Lamir	114	3.36 N	103.21 E
Kampong Lawa	114	5.40 N	101.42 E
Kampong Mengkarak	114	3.19 N	102.27 E
Kampong Merang	114	5.32 N	102.57 E
Kampong Nuri	114	5.02 N	102.23 E
Kampong Penarek	114	5.37 N	102.48 E
Kampong Raja	114	5.48 N	102.35 E
Kampong Renggong	114	4.33 N	102.35 E
Kâmpóng Saôm	110	10.38 N	103.30 E
Kâmpóng Saôm, Chhâk c	110	10.50 N	103.32 E
Kampong Sebuyau	112	1.31 N	110.56 E
Kampong Sekendi	114	3.43 N	100.56 E
Kampong Surau	114	5.49 N	100.54 E
Kampong Tanjong Batu	114	3.12 N	103.27 E
Kampong Tebing Runtoh	271c	1.26 N	103.40 E
Kâmpóng Thum	110	12.42 N	104.54 E
Kâmpóng Trâlach	110	11.54 N	104.47 E
Kampong Ulu	110	10.03 N	98.33 E
Kampong Ulu Chalok	114	5.26 N	102.50 E
Kâmpôt	110	10.37 N	104.11 E
Kampsville	194	39.18 N	90.37 W
Kampti	150	10.08 N	3.27 W
Kâmpŭchéa → Cambodia □1	110	13.00 N	105.00 E
Kampung ≃	164	5.44 S	138.24 E

PORTUGUÊS

Nome	Página	Lat.°′	Long.°′ W = Oeste
Kampungbaru	112	1.12 S	102.57 E
Kampville	219	38.51 N	90.33 W
Kāmrānga	126	23.14 N	90.47 E
Kamrau, Teluk c	164	3.32 S	133.37 E
Kamsack	184	51.34 N	101.54 W
Kamsdorf	54	50.38 N	11.28 E
Kamskij	24	60.04 N	53.13 E
Kamskoje Ustje	80	55.13 N	49.16 E
Kamskoje vodochranilišče ⊜1	86	58.52 N	56.15 E
Kamslybas, ozero ⊜	86	46.12 N	61.48 E
Kamsu-ri	98	38.03 N	125.54 E
Kamsuuma	144	0.15 N	42.47 E
Kāmthi	120	21.14 N	79.12 E
Kam Tin	271d	22.27 N	114.03 E
Kamuchawie Lake ⊜	184	56.18 N	101.59 W
Kamudilo	154	7.42 S	27.18 E
Kamuela (Waimea)	229d	20.01 N	155.48 W
Kamui-misaki ≻	92a	43.20 N	140.21 E
Kámuk, Cerro ∧	236	9.17 N	83.04 W
Kamuli	154	0.57 N	33.07 E
Kamundan ≃	164	2.17 S	132.39 E
Kamutambaie ≃	152	7.17 S	23.41 E
Kamwandu	152	6.04 S	22.42 E
Kamyšet	88	55.12 N	98.42 E
Kamyšev, Ross.	80	46.39 N	42.38 E
Kamyšev, Ross.	80	46.53 N	42.31 E
Kamyševacha, Ukr.	78	47.43 N	35.32 E
Kamyševacha, Ukr.	83	48.42 N	38.23 E
Kamyševatskaja	78	46.25 N	37.57 E
Kamyševskaja	80	47.37 N	41.49 E
Kamyšin	80	50.06 N	45.24 E
Kamyškurgon	85	40.34 N	70.24 E
Kamyšla	80	54.07 N	52.10 E
Kamyšlov	86	56.52 N	62.43 E
Kamyslybas	86	46.11 N	61.57 E
Kamyšnaja ≃	83	48.55 N	39.55 E
Kamyšnoje	86	51.58 N	61.47 E
Kamyšovyj	80	46.26 N	45.12 E
Kamyš-Samarskich Ozer, razlivy ☷	80	48.50 N	50.50 E
Kamyz'ak	80	46.07 N	48.05 E
Kamyz'ak ≃	80	46.00 N	48.06 E
Kan, Īrān	128	35.45 N	51.16 E
Kan, Sūd.	140	9.01 N	31.47 E
Kan ≃	86	56.31 N	93.47 E
Kana ≃	154	18.30 S	27.22 E
Kanaaupscow ≃	176	53.39 N	77.09 W
Kanab	200	37.02 N	112.31 W
Kanab Creek ≃	200	36.24 N	112.38 W
Kanab Plateau ⋏1	200	36.40 N	112.45 W
Kanada	96	33.41 N	130.47 E
Kanada → Canada □1	176	60.00 N	95.00 W
Kanadej	80	53.10 N	47.30 E
Kanae	94	35.30 N	137.49 E
Kanafis	140	9.48 N	25.40 E
Kanaga Island I	180	51.45 N	177.10 W
Kanaga Volcano ∧1	180	51.50 N	177.09 W
Kanagawa □5	94	35.30 N	139.30 E
Kanagawa ◆8	268	35.28 N	139.38 E
Kanagi	96	34.53 N	132.11 E
Kanai	268	35.35 N	139.28 E
Kānāipur	126	23.33 N	89.47 E
Kanairiktok ≃	176	55.05 N	60.20 W
Kanā'is, Ra's al- ≻	140	31.15 N	27.51 E
Kanajevka, Ross.	80	53.07 N	45.35 E
Kanajevka, Ross.	80	52.12 N	49.40 E
Kanaka Creek ≃	226	39.25 N	120.57 W
Kanakapura	122	12.33 N	77.25 E
Kanakeswar	126	23.09 N	90.25 E
Kanákia I	267c	37.55 N	23.24 E
Kanākir	132	33.15 N	36.05 E
Kanal	64	46.05 N	13.38 E
Kanal-Inseln → Channel Islands II	28	49.20 N	2.20 W
Kanam	164	3.25 S	152.10 E
Kanamachi ◆8	268	35.46 N	139.53 E
Kanamori	268	35.32 N	139.28 E
Kanan	270	34.29 N	135.38 E
Kananaskis ≃	182	51.05 N	115.03 W
Kananga (Luluabourg)	152	5.54 S	22.25 E
Kananggar	115b	10.03 S	120.22 E
Kanangra-Boyd National Park ♠	170	34.00 S	150.06 E
Kananikol'skoje	86	52.47 N	57.29 E
Kanaoka	270	34.33 N	135.32 E
Kanapou Bay c	229a	20.33 N	156.33 W
Kanarase-yama ∧	96	33.26 N	131.15 E
Kanarraville	200	37.32 N	113.10 W
Kanaš	80	55.31 N	47.30 E
Kanasagō	94	36.33 N	140.28 E
Kanata	212	45.19 N	75.54 W
Kanaudi	124	23.36 N	81.23 E
Kanava, Ross.	24	61.07 N	54.58 E
Kanava, Ross.	80	47.13 N	45.24 E
Kanavka	80	50.19 N	48.33 E
Kanawha	190	42.56 N	93.47 W
Kanawha ≃	188	38.50 N	82.08 W
Kanaya, Nihon	94	34.49 N	138.08 E
Kanaya, Nihon	96	34.04 N	135.15 E
Kanaya, Nihon	268	35.10 N	139.50 E
Kanayama	94	35.39 N	137.09 E
Kanazawa	94	36.34 N	136.39 E
Kanazawa ◆8	268	35.20 N	139.38 E
Kanazu	94	36.13 N	136.14 E
Kanbalu	110	23.12 N	95.31 E
Kanbauk	110	14.36 N	98.02 E
Kančalan ≃	180	65.08 N	176.25 E
Kanchanaburi	110	14.01 N	99.32 E
Kanchanadit	110	9.10 N	99.28 E
Kānchenjunga (Kañchanjanggā) ∧	124	27.42 N	88.08 E
Kānchipuram	122	12.50 N	79.43 E
Kanchow → Ganzhou	100	25.54 N	114.55 E
Kānchrāpāra	126	22.57 N	88.28 E
Kańczuga	30	49.59 N	22.24 E
Kanda	96	33.47 N	130.59 E
Kanda ◆8	268	35.42 N	139.46 E
Kandabulak	80	53.58 N	50.44 E
Kandāghāt	123	30.59 N	77.07 E
Kandahar	184	51.46 N	104.21 W
Kandāhu	120	27.33 N	69.24 E
Kanda-Kanda	152	6.56 S	23.36 E
Kandala	152	6.02 S	19.24 E
Kandalakša	24	67.09 N	32.21 E
Kandalakšskaja guba c	24	66.55 N	32.45 E
Kandalakšskij zapovednik ♠	24	68.50 N	37.30 E
Kandang	114	3.03 N	97.20 E
Kandangan	112	2.47 S	115.16 E
Kandanghaur	115a	6.21 S	108.06 E
Kandat	86	57.08 N	89.02 E
Kandava	76	57.05 N	22.49 E
Kandavu Island I	175g	19.03 S	178.13 E
Kandavu Passage ∪	175g	18.45 S	178.00 E
Kandé	150	9.57 N	1.03 E
Kandel	56	49.05 N	8.11 E
Kandel ∧	58	48.04 N	8.01 E
Kander ≃	58	46.43 N	7.38 E
Kandern	58	47.43 N	7.40 E
Kandersteg	58	46.30 N	7.40 E
Kandhkot	120	28.14 N	69.11 E
Kāndhla	124	29.19 N	77.16 E
Kandi, Bénin	150	11.08 N	2.56 E
Kandi, India	126	23.57 N	88.02 E
Kandi, Tanjung ≻	112	1.19 N	121.28 E
Kandia ≃	123	35.28 N	73.18 E
Kandiāro	120	27.04 N	68.13 E
Kandik ≃	180	65.24 N	142.34 W
Kandilli ◆8	267b	41.04 N	29.03 E
Kandıra	130	41.04 N	30.09 E
Kandivli ◆8	272c	19.12 N	72.51 E
Kandla	120	23.02 N	70.14 E
Kando ≃	96	35.22 N	132.40 E
Kandor, Ouadi ∨	146	17.13 N	20.52 E
Kandos	170	32.52 S	149.58 E
Kāndra	126	23.44 N	87.58 E
Kandrāch	120	25.29 N	65.29 E
Kandreho	157b	17.29 S	46.06 E
Kandrian	164	6.15 S	149.35 E
Kandry	80	54.34 N	54.07 E
Kandufuri I	122	7.05 N	72.48 E
Kandute I	122	6.20 N	72.57 E
Kandy	122	7.18 N	80.38 E
Kane, Il., U.S.	219	39.11 N	90.21 W
Kane, Pa., U.S.	214	41.39 N	78.48 W
Kane □6	216	41.53 N	88.18 W
Kaneda	268	35.28 N	139.22 E
Kaneilio Point ≻	229c	21.27 N	158.12 W
Kanektok ≃	180	59.45 N	161.55 W
Kanem □5	146	15.00 N	16.00 E
Kanemi	116	6.55 N	123.58 E
Kaneohe	229c	21.25 N	157.48 W
Kaneohe Bay c	229c	21.28 N	157.49 W
Kaneohe Bay Marine Corps Air Station ■	229c	21.27 N	157.46 W
Kaneville	216	41.50 N	88.31 W
Kanevskaja	78	46.05 N	38.57 E
Kaneyama	94	35.28 N	137.06 E
Kanfanar	64	45.07 N	13.51 E
Kang	156	23.41 S	22.50 E
Kangaba	150	11.56 N	8.25 W
Kangal	130	39.15 N	37.24 E
Kangalassy	74	62.23 N	129.59 E
Kangān	128	27.50 N	52.03 E
Kānganheri ◆8	272a	28.33 N	76.59 E
Kanganpur	123	30.46 N	74.08 E
Kangar	114	6.26 N	100.12 E
Kangaré	150	11.35 N	8.10 W
Kangarilla	168b	35.09 S	138.40 E
Kangaroo ≃	170	34.46 S	150.18 E
Kangaroo Creek Reservoir ⊜1	168b	34.52 S	138.46 E
Kangaroo Flat	168b	34.33 S	138.40 E
Kangaroo Ground	274b	37.41 S	145.13 E
Kangaroo Island I	166	35.50 S	137.06 E
Kangaroo Valley	170	34.44 S	150.32 E
Kangasala	26	61.28 N	24.05 E
Kangasniemi	26	61.59 N	26.38 E
Kangāvar	128	34.30 N	47.58 E
Kangaz	78	46.07 N	28.33 E
Kangbao	98	41.53 N	114.40 E
Kangding	102	30.03 N	102.02 E
Kangdong	98	39.09 N	126.05 E
Kangdu	100	27.00 N	116.36 E
Kangean, Kepulauan II	112	6.55 S	115.30 E
Kangean, Pulau I	112	6.54 S	115.20 E
Kangen ≃	140	6.47 N	33.09 E
Kanggezhuang	105	40.26 N	116.44 E
Kanggup'o	98	41.07 N	127.31 E
Kanggye	98	40.58 N	126.34 E
Kanggyŏng	98	36.10 N	127.00 E
Kanghwa	98	37.45 N	126.30 E
Kanghwa-do I	98	37.40 N	126.27 E
Kanghwa-man c	98	37.20 N	126.35 E
Kangil	88	52.15 N	116.20 E
Kangiqsualujjuaq	176	58.41 N	65.57 W
Kangiqsujuaq	176	61.36 N	71.58 W
Kangirsuk	176	60.01 N	70.01 W
Kangjin	98	34.39 N	126.45 E
Kangjinjing	89	46.12 N	126.48 E
Kangkar Lenggor	114	2.16 N	103.44 E
Kangkar Teberau	114	1.32 N	103.45 E
Kangley	216	41.09 N	88.53 W
Kangly	85	40.07 N	67.54 E
Kangmaer	124	30.45 N	85.34 E
Kangmar	120	28.34 N	89.51 E
Kangnam ◆8	271b	37.30 N	127.01 E
Kangnam-sanmaek ⋏	98	40.30 N	125.30 E
Kangnichumike	120	33.10 N	80.59 E
Kangnŭng	98	37.45 N	128.54 E
Kango	152	0.09 N	10.08 E
Kangoku-iwa I	174f	24.48 N	141.17 E
Kangombe	152	14.03 S	23.40 E
Kangongo	152	17.57 S	21.02 E
Kangowa	152	9.55 S	22.48 E
Kangping	98	42.44 N	123.21 E
Kāngpokpi	120	25.08 N	93.58 E
Kangpu	102	27.43 N	99.00 E
Kāngra	123	32.06 N	76.16 E
Kangrinboqê Feng ∧	120	31.29 N	80.45 E
Kangshan	100	22.48 N	120.17 E
Kangsŏ	98	38.58 N	125.26 E
Kangsŏ-ri	98	38.06 N	126.58 E
Kangto ∧	120	27.52 N	92.30 E
Kangtuyingzi	104	41.47 N	121.31 E
Känguruh-Insel → Kangaroo Island I	166	35.50 S	137.06 E
Kangwŏn Do □4, C.M.I.K.	98	38.45 N	127.35 E
Kangwŏn Do □4, Taehan	98	37.45 N	128.15 E
Kangxianzhuang	105	39.06 N	116.27 E
Kangyidaung	110	16.56 N	94.54 E
Kangzhuang	105	40.23 N	115.53 E
Kanhar ≃	124	24.28 N	83.08 E
Kanheri Caves ⊥5	272c	19.13 N	72.52 E
Kanholmsfjärden ∪	40	59.20 N	18.47 E
Kanhsien → Ganzhou	100	25.54 N	114.55 E
Kani, C. Iv.	150	8.29 N	6.36 W
Kani, Mya.	110	22.26 N	94.50 E
Kani, Nihon	94	35.22 N	137.04 E
Kaniama	152	7.31 S	24.11 E
Kaniamba	154	7.27 S	26.57 E
Kanibadam	85	40.17 N	70.25 E
Kanie	94	35.08 N	136.48 E
Kaniepa	154	9.00 S	27.21 E
Kaniere	172	42.45 S	171.00 E
Kaniere, Lake ⊜	172	42.50 S	171.09 E
Kaniet Islands II	164	0.53 S	145.30 E
Kanifay	174q	9.32 N	138.06 E
Kanigiri	122	15.24 N	79.31 E
Kanihāula ◆8	272a	28.44 N	77.01 E
Kanin	54	52.17 N	12.50 E
Kanin, poluostrov ≻1	24	68.00 N	45.00 E
Kanina	124	28.20 N	76.19 E
Kaningo	154	0.49 S	38.32 E
Kanin-Kamen' ∧	24	68.18 N	45.00 E
Kanin Nos	24	68.39 N	43.14 E
Kanin Nos, mys ≻	24	68.39 N	43.16 E
Kaniva	166	36.23 S	141.15 E
Kanjiža	38	46.04 N	20.04 E
Kānjur ◆8	272c	19.08 N	72.56 E
Kanjut Sār ∧	123	36.14 N	75.22 E
Kankaanpää	26	61.48 N	22.25 E
Kankakee	216	41.07 N	87.51 W
Kankakee □6	216	41.07 N	87.52 W
Kankakee ≃	216	41.23 N	88.16 W
Kankakee River State Park ♠	216	41.12 N	87.59 W
Kankan	150	10.23 N	9.18 W
Kankar ◆8	272a	28.46 N	77.06 E
Kankéla	150	10.50 N	6.40 W
Kānker	122	20.17 N	81.29 E
Kankō → Hamhŭng	98	39.54 N	127.32 E
Kankossa	150	15.56 N	11.31 W
Kankunskij	74	57.37 N	126.08 E
Kanlıavşar	130	37.13 N	38.16 E
Kanlıca ◆8	267b	41.06 N	29.04 E
Kanmaw Kyun I	110	11.40 N	98.28 E
Kanmen	100	28.06 N	121.16 E
Kanmuri-jima I	96	35.41 N	135.25 E
Kanmuri-yama ∧	92	34.28 N	132.05 E
Kanna ≃	94	36.17 N	139.09 E
Kannabe	96	34.32 N	133.23 E
Kannabi-san ∧2	270	34.48 N	135.44 E
Kannack	110	14.07 N	108.37 E
Kannad	122	20.16 N	75.08 E
Kanna-kō c	174m	26.28 N	127.58 E
Kannami	94	35.05 N	138.57 E
Kannapolis	192	35.29 N	80.37 W
Kannauj	124	27.04 N	79.55 E
Kanniyākumari	122	8.05 N	77.34 E
Kannod	124	22.40 N	76.44 E
Kannonkoski	26	62.58 N	25.15 E
Kannon-zaki ≻	268	35.15 N	139.45 E
Kannose ≃	96	34.54 N	132.49 E
Kannus	26	63.54 N	23.54 E
Kano, Nig.	150	12.00 N	8.30 E
Kano, Nihon	96	34.14 N	131.49 E
Kano □3	150	11.45 N	9.00 E
Kano ≃, Nig.	150	11.50 N	8.31 E
Kano ≃, Nihon	94	35.05 N	138.52 E
Kanona	210	42.22 N	77.22 W
Kanoneiland	158	28.39 S	21.05 E
Kanonerskij, ostrov I	265a	59.54 N	30.13 E
Kanonji	96	34.07 N	133.39 E
Kanopolis	198	38.42 N	98.09 W
Kanopolis Lake ⊜1	198	38.38 N	98.00 W
Kanorado	198	39.19 N	102.02 W
Kanosh	200	38.48 N	112.26 W
Kanouse Brook ≃	276	41.02 N	74.26 W
Kanouse Mountain ∧	276	41.04 N	74.25 W
Kan'ov	78	49.44 N	31.28 E
Kan'ovka	24	67.08 N	39.40 E
Kanovlei	156	19.10 S	19.23 E
Kan'ovskoje vodochranilišče ⊜1	78	50.00 N	31.20 E
Kanowit	112	2.06 N	112.09 E
Kanoya	92	31.23 N	130.51 E
Kanō-zan ∧2	268	35.15 N	139.57 E
Kanpetlet	110	21.12 N	94.02 E
Kanpoli	272c	19.04 N	73.09 E
Kānpur	124	26.28 N	80.21 E
Kanra	94	36.13 N	138.55 E
Kansa ≃	94	34.55 N	137.34 E
Kansaj	85	40.30 N	69.41 E
Kansanshi	154	12.05 S	26.26 E
Kānsāripāra	272b	22.56 N	88.14 E
Kansas, Il., U.S.	194	39.33 N	87.56 W
Kansas, Oh., U.S.	214	41.14 N	83.17 W
Kansas □3, U.S.	178	38.45 N	98.15 W
Kansas □3, U.S.	198	38.45 N	98.15 W
Kansas ≃	198	39.07 N	94.36 W
Kansas City, Ks., U.S.	198	39.06 N	94.37 W
Kansas City, Mo., U.S.	194	39.05 N	94.34 W
Kansau	110	23.50 N	93.35 E
Kansei Gakuin University ʋ2	270	34.46 N	135.21 E
Kansei University ʋ2	270	34.46 N	135.31 E
Kansenia	154	10.19 S	26.02 E
Kanshan	106	30.12 N	120.25 E
Kanshi	100	24.56 N	116.54 E
Kansk	86	56.13 N	95.41 E
Kansŏng	98	38.22 N	128.29 E
Kansu	85	39.45 N	75.02 E
Kansu → Gansu □4	102	37.00 N	103.00 E
Kansyat	164	2.15 S	138.51 E
Kant	85	42.55 N	74.55 E
Kantabrisches Gebirge → Cantábrica, Cordillera ⋏	34	43.00 N	5.00 W
Kantalvi	272c	18.54 N	73.03 E
Kantang	110	7.25 N	99.31 E
Kāntāphor	124	22.35 N	76.34 E
Kantchari	150	12.29 N	1.31 E
Kantché	150	13.33 N	8.28 E
Kantemirovka, Kaz.	85	42.51 N	70.20 E
Kantemirovka, Ross.	83	49.41 N	39.51 E
Kānth	124	29.04 N	78.38 E
Kantharalak	110	14.39 N	104.39 E
Kānthi Coastal Plain ≍	126	21.45 N	87.45 E
Kantishna ≃	180	64.45 N	149.58 W
Kantner	214	40.06 N	78.56 W
Kantō-heiya ≍	94	36.00 N	139.30 E
Kanton (Canton) I	174h	2.50 S	171.40 W
Kanton → Guangzhou	100	23.06 N	113.16 E
Kantorp	40	59.01 N	16.28 E
Kantō-sanchi ⋏, Nihon	92	35.50 N	138.50 E
Kantō-sanchi ⋏, Nihon	94	35.59 N	138.43 E
Kantuanji	100	32.59 N	116.19 E
Kantubek	86	45.07 N	59.16 E
Kantu-long	110	19.57 N	97.36 E
Kantunilkin	232	21.06 N	87.29 W
Kanturk	48	52.10 N	8.55 W
Kanuku Mountains ⋏	246	3.12 N	59.30 W
Kanuma	94	36.33 N	139.44 E
Kanus	156	27.54 S	18.40 E
Kanuti ≃	180	66.26 N	153.02 W
Kan'utino	76	55.33 N	33.14 E
Kanye	156	24.59 S	25.19 E
Kanygtokynmangkyn, laguna c	180	69.20 N	178.45 E
Kanyu	156	20.05 S	24.39 E
Kanyutkwin	110	18.21 N	96.30 E
Kanzaki ≃	270	34.42 N	135.25 E
Kanzanavolok	24	62.23 N	36.58 E
Kanzenze	154	10.31 S	25.12 E
Kanzi	98	39.34 N	122.39 E
Kaohiung → Kaohsiung	100	22.38 N	120.17 E
Kaohsiung	100	22.38 N	120.17 E
Kaohsiunghsien	100	22.38 N	120.21 E
Kaoje	150	11.14 N	4.07 E
Kaoka Bay c	175e	9.42 S	160.40 E
Kaokoland □5	156	18.15 S	13.00 E
Kaoko Otavi	156	18.14 S	13.40 E
Kaoko Veld ⋏1	156	20.00 S	14.00 E
Kaolack	150	14.09 N	16.04 W
Kaolack □4	150	14.00 N	15.30 W
Kaolin	285	39.48 N	75.43 W
Kaolun → Kowloon	271d	22.18 N	114.10 E
Kaoma	154	14.47 S	24.48 E
Kaongweshi ≃	152	7.53 S	22.20 E
Kaoping → Changzhi	102	36.11 N	113.08 E
Kaoshanji	105	40.11 N	117.17 E
Kaoshanpu	100	30.54 N	114.32 E
Kaouadja ≃	140	6.45 N	24.15 E
Kaouar ◆1	146	19.00 N	12.40 E
Kao Valley ∨	158	28.54 S	18.06 E
Kapaa	229b	22.04 N	159.19 W
Kapadvanj	120	23.01 N	73.04 E
Kapahiang	112	3.39 S	102.34 E
Kapal	86	45.08 N	79.03 E
Kapalong	116	7.35 N	125.42 E
Kapan	112	9.44 S	124.17 E
Kapanga, Zaïre	152	8.21 S	22.35 E
Kapanga, Zaïre	152	5.04 S	16.58 E
Kapangan	116	16.35 N	120.35 E
Kapaonik ⋏	38	43.20 N	20.50 E
Kāpāsia	126	24.07 N	90.32 E
Kapatagan	116	7.52 N	123.44 E
Kapatu	154	9.43 S	30.42 E
Kapčagaj	85	43.53 N	77.12 E
Kapčagajskoje vodochranilišče ⊜1	86	43.50 N	78.00 E
Kapchorwa	154	1.24 N	34.27 E
Kapedo	154	1.10 N	36.06 E
Kapelle	52	51.28 N	3.58 E
Kapellen, Bel.	50	51.19 N	4.26 E
Kapellen, Dtsch.	56	51.25 N	6.35 E
Kapellen, Dtsch.	263	51.08 N	6.38 E
Kapellen, Öst.	61	47.38 N	15.37 E
Kapelle-op-den-Bos	50	51.01 N	4.22 E
Kapellerfeld	264b	48.19 N	16.30 E
Kapelln	61	48.15 N	15.45 E
Kapellskär	40	59.43 N	19.04 E
Kapema	154	10.42 S	28.24 E
Kapenguria	154	1.04 N	35.07 E
Kapfenberg	61	47.26 N	15.18 E
Kapia	152	4.17 S	19.46 E
Kapıdağ Yarımadası ≻1	130	40.28 N	27.50 E
Kapikik Lake ⊜	184	51.32 N	91.57 W
Kapikog Lake ⊜	212	45.09 N	79.53 W
Kapilmuni	126	22.42 N	89.20 E
Kapingamarangi I1	14	1.04 N	154.46 E
Kapiri Mposhi	154	13.58 S	28.41 E
Kāpīsā □4	120	34.45 N	69.30 E
Kapiskau ≃	176	52.47 N	81.55 W
Kapit	112	2.01 N	112.56 E
Kapitanovka	78	48.54 N	31.42 E
Kapiti Island I	172	40.52 S	174.54 E
Kapiura ≃	164	5.45 S	150.35 E
Kapka, Massif du ⋏	146	15.07 N	21.45 E
Kapkataš	85	40.23 N	74.20 E
Kapkatas, chrebet ⋏	85	41.50 N	76.10 E
Kapkinka	80	48.08 N	43.51 E
Kaplan	194	29.59 N	92.17 W
Kaplice	61	48.45 N	14.30 E
Kapoe	110	9.35 N	98.40 E
Kapoeta	154	4.47 N	33.35 E
Kapona	154	7.11 S	29.09 E
Kaponga	172	39.26 S	174.09 E
Kaporskoje	265a	59.45 N	29.58 E
Kapos ≃	30	46.44 N	18.30 E
Kaposvár	30	46.22 N	17.47 E
Kaposvar Creek ≃	184	50.31 N	101.55 W
Kapotn'a ◆8	265b	55.38 N	37.48 E
Kapowsin	224	46.59 N	122.13 W
Kapowsin, Lake ⊜	224	46.58 N	122.13 W
Kapp	26	60.42 N	10.52 E
Kappar	128	25.19 N	62.42 E
Kappel	56	50.00 N	7.21 E
Kappeln	41	54.40 N	9.56 E
Kappelshamn	26	57.51 N	18.47 E
Kapps	156	22.22 S	17.52 E
Kapralicha	86	56.11 N	67.15 E
Kaprijke	50	51.13 N	3.36 E
Kaprun	64	47.16 N	12.46 E
Kapsabet	154	0.12 N	35.06 E
Kapsan	98	41.04 N	128.19 E
Kapstadt → Cape Town	158	33.55 S	18.22 E
Kaptai	120	22.21 N	92.17 E
Kaptipada	126	21.31 N	86.32 E
Kaptol	38	45.26 N	17.44 E
Kapuas ≃, Indon.	112	0.25 S	109.40 E
Kapuas ≃, Indon.	112	3.01 S	114.20 E
Kapuas Hulu, Pegunungan ⋏	112	1.15 N	113.30 E
Kapulo	154	8.18 S	29.15 E
Kapunda	168b	34.21 S	138.54 E
Kapūrthala	123	31.23 N	75.23 E
Kapur Utara, Pegunungan ⋏	115a	6.52 S	111.30 E
Kapuskasing	176	49.25 N	82.26 W
Kapuskasing ≃	176	49.49 N	82.00 W
Kapuskasing Lake ⊜	190	48.30 N	82.55 W
Kapustin Jar	80	48.36 N	45.45 E
Kapustino	78	48.57 N	31.14 E
Kapuvár	30	47.36 N	17.02 E
Kap Verde → Cape Verde □1	150a	16.00 N	24.00 W
Kapyrevščina	76	55.15 N	32.53 E
Kapytdžuch, gora ∧	84	39.13 N	46.00 E
Kara	74	69.14 N	65.00 E
Kara ≃	150	10.01 N	0.25 E
Karaali	130	39.40 N	32.57 E
Karaaul	86	48.57 N	79.15 E
Karababa Dağı ∧	130	39.31 N	36.10 E
Karabachskij chrebet ⋏	84	39.42 N	46.36 E
Karabagl'ar	84	39.26 N	45.12 E
Kara-Balta	85	42.50 N	73.52 E
Karabanovo	82	56.19 N	38.42 E
Karabaš, Ross.	80	54.42 N	52.36 E
Karabaš, Ross.	86	55.29 N	60.14 E
Karabau	80	48.26 N	52.54 E
Karabekaul	128	38.30 N	64.08 E
Karabiğa	130	40.24 N	27.18 E
Karabil', vozvyšennost' ⋏1	128	36.25 N	64.00 E
Kara-Bogaz-Gol, zaliv c	72	41.00 N	53.15 E
Karabudachkent	84	42.41 N	47.34 E
Karabük	130	41.12 N	32.37 E
Karabula	88	58.08 N	97.23 E
Karabula ≃	88	58.22 N	97.02 E
Karabulak, Kaz.	85	42.32 N	69.46 E
Karabulak, Kaz.	86	44.54 N	78.30 E
Karabulak, Kaz.	86	47.34 N	84.41 E
Karabulak, Kyrg.	85	39.51 N	69.38 E
Karabulduk	130	40.50 N	38.34 E
Karaburun	130	38.37 N	26.31 E
Karabutak	86	49.59 N	60.10 E
Karacabey	130	40.13 N	28.21 E
Karacadağ, Tür.	130	37.43 N	39.37 E
Karacadağ, Tür.	130	41.57 N	27.40 E
Karaca Dağ ∧	130	37.40 N	39.50 E
Karačaj ≃	84	41.28 N	49.00 E
Karačajevo-Čerkesskaja Avtonomnaja Sovetskaja Socialističeskaja Respublika □3	84	44.00 N	42.00 E
Karačajevsk	84	43.45 N	41.54 E
Karacaköy	130	41.24 N	28.22 E
Karačala	84	39.48 N	48.57 E
Karacaoğlan	130	41.31 N	27.07 E
Karacasu	130	37.43 N	28.37 E
Karacaviran	130	39.44 N	38.08 E
Karaçay	130	36.10 N	36.02 E
Karaçayır	130	39.55 N	37.01 E
Karačev	76	53.07 N	35.00 E
Karāchi	120	24.52 N	67.03 E
Karachtaj	85	40.55 N	69.46 E
Karači	80	57.59 N	50.28 E
Karād	122	17.17 N	74.12 E
Kara Dağ ∧	130	40.22 N	39.05 E
Karadarja ≃	85	40.54 N	71.45 E
Karadeniz → Black Sea ⫧2	22	43.00 N	35.00 E
Karadere	130	40.40 N	30.50 E
Karadirek	130	38.34 N	30.11 E
Karaftit	88	54.12 N	111.54 E
Karagaj, Kaz.	80	48.39 N	47.38 E
Karagaj, Ross.	80	58.16 N	54.56 E
Karagajly	86	49.20 N	75.48 E
Karaganda	86	49.50 N	73.10 E
Karagel	128	39.23 N	53.11 E
Karagičevskij	80	50.11 N	42.55 E
Karaginskij, ostrov I	74	58.50 N	164.00 E
Karaginskij zaliv c	74	58.50 N	164.00 E
Karagola Road	124	25.29 N	87.23 E
Karagöl Dağı ∧	130	40.32 N	38.10 E
Kara Gölü ⊜	130	36.42 N	29.50 E
Karagoš, gora ∧	86	51.44 N	89.24 E
Karagužicha	86	50.47 N	83.00 E
Karahallı	130	38.20 N	29.32 E
Karaia	124	25.54 N	78.01 E
Karaičev	80	48.37 N	42.13 E
Karaidel'	86	55.50 N	56.53 E
Karaidel'skij	86	55.49 N	57.05 E
Kāraikāl	122	10.55 N	79.50 E
Kāraikkudi	122	10.04 N	78.47 E
Karaisalı	130	37.16 N	35.03 E
Karaitivu I	122	8.23 N	79.47 E
Karaj	128	35.48 N	50.59 E
Karaj ≃	267d	35.35 N	51.11 E
Karajantak	85	40.03 N	67.54 E
Karak	114	3.24 N	102.02 E
Karakabak	86	50.33 N	75.09 E
Karakain	85	41.26 N	74.19 E
Kara-Kala	128	38.26 N	56.18 E
Karakalpakskaja Avtonomnaja Sovetskaja Socialističeskaja Respublika □3	86	43.00 N	59.00 E

≃	River	Fluß	Río	Rivière	Rio
≚	Canal	Kanal	Canal	Canal	Canal
∟	Waterfall, Rapids	Wasserfall, Stromschnellen	Cascada, Rápidos	Chute d'eau, Rapides	Cascata, Rápidos
∪	Strait	Meeresstraße	Estrecho	Détroit	Estreito
c	Bay, Gulf	Bucht, Golf	Bahía, Golfo	Baie, Golfe	Baía, Golfo
⊜	Lake, Lakes	See, Seen	Lago, Lagos	Lac, Lacs	Lago, Lagos
☷	Swamp	Sumpf	Pantano	Marais	Pântano
⊓	Ice Features, Glacier	Eis- und Gletscherformen	Accidentes Glaciales	Formes glaciaires	Acidentes glaciares
⫧	Other Hydrographic Features	Andere Hydrographische Objekte	Otros Elementos Hidrográficos	Autres données hydrographiques	Outros acidentes hidrográficos

⊹	Submarine Features	Untermeerische Objekte	Accidentes Submarinos	Formes de relief sous-marin	Acidentes submarinos
□	Political Unit	Politische Einheit	Unidad Politica	Entité politique	Unidade política
ʋ	Cultural Institution	Kulturelle Institution	Institución Cultural	Institution culturelle	Institução cultural
⊥	Historical Site	Historische Stätte	Sitio Histórico	Site historique	Sitio histórico
♠	Recreational Site	Erholungs- und Ferienort	Sitio de Recreo	Centre de loisirs	Area de Lazer
⊠	Airport	Flughafen	Aeropuerto	Aéroport	Aeroporto
■	Military Installation	Militäranlage	Instalación Militar	Installation militaire	Instalação militar
◆	Miscellaneous	Verschiedenes	Misceláneo	Divers	Diversos

Name	Page	Lat.°′	Long.°′
Karakaralong, Pulau II	112	4.30 N	125.30 E
Karakastek	85	43.08 N	76.06 E
Karakavak	85	39.41 N	72.43 E
Karakax ≏	120	37.00 N	79.45 E
Karakaya Barajı ⊜ [1]	130	38.25 N	38.45 E
Karakeçı	130	37.26 N	39.26 E
Karakeçili	130	39.36 N	33.23 E
Karakelong, Pulau I	108	4.15 N	126.48 E
Karakemer	85	42.55 N	75.20 E
Karakendža	85	39.14 N	71.31 E
Karakitang, Pulau I	112	3.11 N	125.32 E
Karakoin, ozero ⊜	86	46.10 N	68.45 E
Karakojsu ≏	84	42.33 N	46.58 E
Karakojun ≏	85	41.10 N	75.45 E
Karakol (Prževal'sk)	85	42.29 N	78.24 E
Karakolka	85	41.32 N	77.23 E
Karakoram Pass)(	120	35.30 N	77.50 E
Karakoram Range ⩘	120	35.30 N	77.00 E
Karakoro ≏	150	14.43 N	12.03 W
Karaksar	88	51.16 N	115.58 E
Karakudžur ≏	85	41.59 N	75.42 E
Karakul', Ross.	86	57.26 N	70.51 E
Karakul', Taj.	85	39.02 N	73.33 E
Karakul', Uzb.	128	39.32 N	63.50 E
Karakul', ozero ⊜	85	39.05 N	73.25 E
Karakulak	130	39.59 N	40.01 E
Kara-Kul'dža	85	40.37 N	73.35 E
Karakul'dža ≏	85	40.39 N	73.26 E
Karakulino	80	56.01 N	53.43 E
Karakul'skoje	86	54.04 N	62.26 E
Karakum	86	46.49 N	79.33 E
Karakumskij kanal ≡	128	37.35 N	61.50 E
Karakumy ⬥ [2]	72	39.00 N	60.00 E
Karakuni	270	34.28 N	135.28 E
Karakurt	130	40.10 N	42.36 E
Karala ⬥ [8]	272a	28.44 N	77.02 E
Karalat	80	45.55 N	48.18 E
Karalon	88	57.02 N	115.52 E
Karalundi	162	26.07 S	118.41 E
Karam	88	55.09 N	107.37 E
Karama ≏	112	2.18 S	119.06 E
Karamağara	130	39.42 N	35.31 E
Karamai → Karamay	86	45.30 N	84.55 E
Karaman	130	37.11 N	33.14 E
Karamanlı	130	37.22 N	29.49 E
Karamay	86	45.30 N	84.55 E
Karambu	112	3.51 S	116.04 E
Karamea	172	41.15 S	172.07 E
Karamea ≏	172	41.16 S	172.06 E
Karamea Bight ⊂ [3]	172	41.30 S	171.40 E
Karamıkbataklığı ≡	130	38.25 N	30.50 E
Karamnisa Nāla ⊜ [1]	124	25.42 N	83.25 E
Karamoja □ [5]	154	2.50 N	34.15 E
Karamola, gora ∧	86	47.58 N	66.35 E
Karamürsel	130	40.42 N	29.36 E
Karamurt	85	42.19 N	69.58 E
Karamyš ≏	80	51.20 N	45.00 E
Karamyševo, Ross.	76	57.45 N	28.45 E
Karamyševo, Ross.	82	54.46 N	36.07 E
Karamyševo, Ross.	88	57.34 N	100.55 E
Karamzino	76	56.00 N	34.33 E
Karang, Gunung ∧	115a	6.16 S	106.03 E
Karang, Tanjung ≻	112	0.38 S	119.44 E
Karangagung	112	2.22 S	104.27 E
Karangampel	115a	6.28 S	108.27 E
Karangana	150	12.13 N	5.02 W
Karangasem	115b	8.27 S	115.37 E
Karangbinangun	115a	7.01 S	112.30 E
Karangbolang, Ujung ≻	115a	7.46 S	109.02 E
Karangbolong	115a	7.45 S	109.28 E
Karanggede	115a	7.22 S	110.37 E
Karangkates, Waduk ⊜ [1]	115a	8.11 S	112.34 E
Karangkobar	115a	7.16 S	109.44 E
Karangnunggal	115a	7.38 S	108.06 E
Karangpandan	115a	7.37 S	111.04 E
Karangsembung	115a	6.51 S	108.39 E
Kāranja	122	20.29 N	77.29 E
Karanjia	120	21.47 N	85.58 E
Karanpura	123	29.50 N	73.27 E
Karaoba, Kaz.	86	53.17 N	65.06 E
Karaoba, Kaz.	86	47.03 N	56.20 E
Karaoğlan	130	39.14 N	39.13 E
Karaoj	86	45.54 N	74.45 E
Karaozek, Kaz.	85	43.43 N	77.23 E
Karaozek, Kaz.	86	45.03 N	65.18 E
Karaozek, Uzb.	86	43.16 N	58.40 E
Karapınar, Tür.	130	37.43 N	33.33 E
Karapınar, Tür.	130	41.30 N	32.12 E
Karapyši	78	49.38 N	30.47 E
Karaš	80	56.54 N	39.24 E
Karas, Pulau I	164	3.27 S	132.40 E
Karasaj	85	41.34 N	77.49 E
Kara-Sal ≏	80	47.22 N	43.38 E
Karaşar	130	40.20 N	32.00 E
Karasay	120	36.47 N	83.48 E
Karasburg	156	28.00 S	18.43 E
Karasburg □ [5]	156	28.00 S	18.45 E
Kara Sea → Karskoje more ⊤ [2]	72	76.00 N	80.00 E
Karašengel'	86	47.29 N	75.35 E
Karašjåkka ≏	24	69.26 N	25.49 E
Karasjok	24	69.27 N	25.30 E
Karaskan	85	41.03 N	71.49 E
Karasor, ozero ⊜, Kaz.	86	51.57 N	75.45 E
Karasor, ozero ⊜, Kaz.	86	49.54 N	75.32 E
Karasu, Azer.	84	40.11 N	48.41 E
Karasu, Kaz.	86	52.40 N	65.28 E
Karasu, Kaz.	86	51.20 N	62.21 E
Karasu, Kyrg.	85	43.03 N	73.57 E
Kara-Su, Kyrg.	85	40.44 N	72.53 E
Karasu, Nihon	94	34.39 N	136.32 E
Karasu, Tür.	130	41.06 N	30.41 E
Karasu ≏, Nihon	94	36.15 N	139.17 E
Karasu ≏, Tür.	130	39.07 N	38.44 E
Karasuk	86	53.44 N	78.02 E
Karasuk ≏	86	53.35 N	77.30 E
Karasuyama	94	36.39 N	140.09 E
Karata	84	42.35 N	46.21 E
Karatal, Kaz.	86	45.07 N	77.54 E
Karatal, Kaz.	86	47.36 N	85.12 E
Karatal ≏	86	46.26 N	77.10 E
Karataş, Tür.	130	36.36 N	35.21 E
Karataş, Tür.	130	38.34 N	28.17 E
Karataş Burun ≻	130	36.35 N	35.22 E
Karatau	85	43.10 N	70.28 E
Karatau, chrebet ⩘, Kaz.	72	43.50 N	68.30 E
Karatau, chrebet ⩘, Taj.	85	38.10 N	69.00 E
Karateginskij chrebet ⩘	85	38.50 N	69.40 E
Karatepe Milli Parkı ♦	130	37.17 N	36.13 E
Karatia	126	24.14 N	89.58 E
Karatobe	80	49.41 N	53.31 E
Karatogaj	86	48.42 N	59.40 E
Karaton	86	46.25 N	53.30 E
Karatoya ≏	124	24.13 N	89.36 E
Karatschi → Karāchi	120	24.52 N	67.03 E
Karatsu	92	33.26 N	129.58 E
Karaturuk	85	43.33 N	77.59 E
Karatuzskoje	86	53.36 N	92.53 E
Karau	164	3.45 S	144.20 E
Karaul	74	70.06 N	83.08 E
Karauli	124	26.30 N	77.01 E
Karault'ob'o	85	40.33 N	75.57 E
Karaunk'ur ≏	85	40.54 N	72.20 E
Karaurğan	130	40.15 N	42.17 E
Karauzak	86	42.59 N	60.02 E
Karauzek	80	47.15 N	48.25 E
Karavan	85	41.30 N	71.45 E
Karavannoje, Ross.	80	45.59 N	47.08 E
Karavannoje, Ross.	80	57.47 N	47.41 E
Karavás	38	36.21 N	22.57 E
Karave	272c	19.01 N	73.01 E
Karawa	152	3.20 N	20.18 E
Karawang	115a	6.19 S	107.17 E
Karawang, Tanjung ≻	115a	5.56 S	107.00 E
Karawanken ⩘	36	46.30 N	14.25 E
Karayaka	130	40.45 N	36.37 E
Karayazı	130	39.41 N	42.08 E
Karaye	150	11.48 N	8.02 E
Karayün	130	39.41 N	37.19 E
Karažal	86	48.02 N	70.49 E
Karbalā'	128	32.36 N	44.02 E
Karbalā' □ [4]	128	32.00 N	42.15 E
Karbenning	40	60.02 N	16.04 E
Kårberg	40	58.58 N	14.57 E
Karbeyaz	130	36.02 N	36.12 E
Kårböle	26	61.59 N	15.19 E
Karby	40	59.34 N	18.13 E
Karcag	30	47.19 N	20.56 E
Karczew	30	52.06 N	21.15 E
Kardail ≏	80	50.43 N	42.54 E
Kardašova Řečice	61	49.11 N	14.53 E
Karden	56	50.11 N	7.17 E
Kardhámaina	38	36.47 N	27.09 E
Kardhámila	38	38.32 N	26.05 E
Kardhítsa	38	39.21 N	21.55 E
Kärdla	76	59.00 N	22.45 E
Kardymovo	76	54.54 N	32.26 E
Kârdžali	38	41.39 N	25.22 E
Kardžin	84	43.16 N	44.16 E
Karea	272b	22.42 N	88.33 E
Kareeberge ⩘	158	30.53 S	21.57 E
Kareedouw	158	33.57 S	24.18 E
Kareli	84	42.01 N	43.54 E
Karelia □ [9]	24	63.00 N	32.00 E
Karelskaja Avtonomnaja Sovetskaja Socialističeskaja Respublika □ [3]	24	64.00 N	32.30 E
Karel'skij Gorodok	76	58.04 N	36.30 E
Karema, Pap. N. Gui.	164	9.12 S	147.14 E
Karema, Tan.	154	6.49 S	30.26 E
Karen	110	12.51 N	92.53 E
Karenga ≏	88	54.28 N	116.32 E
Karepino	24	61.02 N	57.02 E
Karera	272a	28.41 N	77.23 E
Karesuando	24	68.25 N	22.30 E
Kärevere	76	58.26 N	26.29 E
Kāreyz-e Elyās	128	35.25 N	61.20 E
Kargali	80	55.12 N	50.54 E
Kargalinskaja	84	43.44 N	46.30 E
Karganaj	180	65.21 N	175.25 E
Kargapazarı Dağları ⩘	130	40.07 N	41.35 E
Kargapolje	86	55.57 N	64.27 E
Kargasok	86	59.07 N	80.53 E
Kargat	86	55.10 N	80.17 E
Kargat ≏	86	54.37 N	78.12 E
Kargı	130	41.08 N	34.30 E
Kargil	123	34.34 N	76.06 E
Karginskaja	80	49.21 N	41.38 E
Karginskij ≏	265a	59.50 N	30.01 E
Kargopol'	24	61.30 N	38.58 E
Karguéri	146	13.27 N	10.25 E
Karhal	124	27.01 N	78.57 E
Karhijärvi ⊜	26	61.35 N	22.30 E
Karhula	26	60.31 N	26.57 E
Kari	146	11.14 N	10.34 E
Karia-Ba-Mohammed	148	34.19 N	5.10 W
Kariaí	38	40.16 N	24.15 E
Karianga	157b	22.22 S	47.26 E
Kariba	154	16.30 S	28.45 E
Kariba, Lake ⊜ [1]	154	17.00 S	28.00 E
Karibib	156	21.58 S	15.51 E
Karibib □ [5]	156	22.20 S	16.00 E
Karibisches Meer → Caribbean Sea ⊤ [2]	230	15.00 N	73.00 W
Karibumba	154	0.22 N	29.22 E
Kariega ≏	158	33.03 S	23.28 E
Karigasniemi	24	69.24 N	25.50 E
Karikari, Cape ≻	172	34.47 S	173.24 E
Karimata	175d	24.54 N	125.17 E
Karimata, Kepulauan II	112	1.25 S	109.05 E
Karimata, Pulau I	112	1.36 S	108.55 E
Karimata, Selat (Karimata Strait) ⴾ	112	2.05 S	108.40 E
Karīmganj	120	24.52 N	92.21 E
Karīmnagar	122	18.26 N	79.09 E
Karīmpur	126	23.58 N	88.37 E
Karimun, Pulau I	114	1.03 N	103.22 E
Karimunjawa, Kepulauan II	115a	5.50 S	110.25 E
Karimunjawa, Pulau I	115a	5.51 S	110.27 E
Karin, Som.	144	10.59 N	49.13 E
Karin, Som.	144	10.51 N	45.47 E
Karino	82	54.42 N	38.56 E
Karin Seamount ⬥ [3]	14	17.55 N	168.58 W
Karinskoje	82	55.42 N	36.41 E
Karintorf	80	58.33 N	50.11 E
Karis (Karjaa)	26	60.05 N	23.40 E
Karise	41	55.18 N	12.13 E
Karisimbi, Volcan ∧ [1]	154	1.30 S	29.27 E
Káristos	38	38.00 N	24.24 E
Kariya	94	34.59 N	136.59 E
Kariye Museum ⊍ [1]	267b	41.01 N	28.55 E
Kārīz	128	34.49 N	60.47 E
Karjaa → Karis	26	60.05 N	23.40 E
Karjala ⬥ [1]	26	64.00 N	32.00 E
Karjepolje	24	65.34 N	43.40 E
Kārkal	122	13.12 N	74.59 E
Karkalaj	80	57.00 N	52.24 E
Karkaralinsk	86	49.23 N	75.21 E
Karkar Dūmān ⬥ [8]	272a	28.39 N	77.18 E
Karkar Island I	164	4.40 S	146.00 E
Karkas, Kūh-e ∧	128	33.29 N	51.50 E
Karkheh ≏	128	31.46 N	47.55 E
Karkīndar	128	25.47 N	59.15 E
Karkinitskij zaliv ⊂	78	45.55 N	33.00 E
Karkkila	26	60.32 N	24.11 E
Karkku	26	61.25 N	23.01 E
Karkom, Har ∧	132	30.17 N	34.44 E
Karkonoski Park Narodowy ♦	30	50.45 N	15.35 E
Kärla	76	58.20 N	22.15 E
Karlholmsbruk	40	60.31 N	17.35 E
Karlik Shan ∧	102	43.08 N	94.20 E
Karlino	30	54.03 N	15.51 E
Karlıova	130	39.18 N	41.01 E
Karlobag	36	44.32 N	15.05 E
Karlo-Libknechtovsk	83	48.42 N	38.04 E
Karlo-Marksovo	83	48.16 N	38.09 E
Karloske ≏	184	55.41 N	93.56 W
Karlovac	36	45.29 N	15.34 E
Karlovka	78	49.27 N	35.08 E
Karlovo	38	42.38 N	24.48 E
Karlovy Vary (Carlsbad)	54	50.11 N	12.52 E
Karlsbad → Karlovy Vary	54	50.11 N	12.52 E
Karlsborg, Sve.	26	58.32 N	14.31 E
Karlsborg, Sve.	26	65.48 N	23.17 E
Karlsburg → Alba Iulia	38	46.04 N	23.35 E
Karlsby	40	58.38 N	15.08 E
Karlsfeld	60	48.13 N	11.28 E
Karlshafen	52	51.38 N	9.27 E
Karlshamn	26	56.10 N	14.51 E
Karlshorst ⬥ [8]	264a	52.29 N	13.32 E
Karlshorst, Trabrennbahn ♦	264a	52.29 N	13.31 E
Karlshuld	60	48.41 N	11.18 E
Karlskoga	40	59.20 N	14.31 E
Karlskrona	26	56.10 N	15.35 E
Karlslunde Strand	41	55.34 N	12.14 E
Karlsöarna II	26	57.17 N	17.58 E
Karlsruhe	56	49.03 N	8.24 E
Karlsruhe □ [5], Dtsch.	56	49.20 N	8.45 E
Karlsruhe □ [5], Dtsch.	58	48.30 N	8.30 E
Karlstad, Sve.	40	59.22 N	13.30 E
Karlstad, Mn., U.S.	198	48.34 N	96.31 W
Karlstadt	56	49.57 N	9.45 E
Karlstift	61	48.35 N	14.45 E
Karluk, Ross.	88	53.27 N	105.58 E
Karluk, Ak., U.S.	180	57.34 N	154.28 W
Karl'uk, Uzb.	85	38.12 N	67.42 E
Karma	150	13.40 N	1.49 E
Karma, Ouadi ∨	146	15.38 N	20.01 E
Karmah	140	19.38 N	30.25 E
Karmāla	122	18.25 N	75.12 E
Karmanovka	80	49.24 N	50.22 E
Karmanovo	76	55.52 N	34.52 E
Karmansbo	40	59.42 N	15.44 E
Karmatānr	126	24.05 N	86.42 E
Karmel, Har (Mount Carmel) ∧	132	32.44 N	35.02 E
Karmi'el	132	32.55 N	35.18 E
Karmiyya	132	31.36 N	34.33 E
Karmøy I	26	59.15 N	5.15 E
Karnack	194	32.40 N	94.10 W
Karnak	194	37.17 N	88.58 W
Karnak → Al-Karnak	140	25.43 N	32.39 E
Karnāl	124	29.41 N	76.59 E
Karnāla Fort ⫠	272c	18.53 N	73.07 E
Karṇālī □ [8]	124	29.30 N	82.30 E
Karṇālī ≏	124	28.15 N	81.05 E
Karnap ⬥ [8]	263	51.31 N	7.01 E
Karnaphuli Reservoir ⊜ [1]	120	22.42 N	92.12 E
Karnātaka □ [3]	122	14.00 N	76.00 E
Karnauchovka	78	48.28 N	34.44 E
Karnes □ [6]	222	29.00 N	97.47 W
Karnes City	196	28.53 N	97.54 W
Karni	150	10.40 N	2.37 W
Karniki	82	54.12 N	38.05 E
Karnische Alpen (Alpi Carniche) ⩘	64	46.40 N	13.00 E
Karnobat	38	42.39 N	26.59 E
Karns City	214	41.00 N	79.44 W
Kärnten □ [3]	30	46.50 N	13.50 E
Karnzow	54	52.59 N	12.26 E
Karoi	154	16.50 S	29.40 E
Karokh	128	34.28 N	62.35 E
Karoli	124	22.55 N	79.04 E
Karolinenhof ⬥ [8]	264a	52.23 N	13.38 E
Karomatan	116	7.46 N	123.44 E
Karompa Lompo, Pulau I	112	7.15 S	121.45 E
Karon	126	24.07 N	86.44 E
Karonga	154	9.56 S	33.56 E
Karonie	162	30.58 S	122.32 E
Karoonda	166	35.06 S	139.54 E
Karor	123	31.13 N	70.57 E
Karora	140	17.42 N	38.22 E
Karos	158	28.24 S	21.35 E
Karosa	112	1.48 S	119.20 E
Karoso, Tanjung ≻	115b	9.33 S	118.50 E
Karotho Post	154	5.11 N	35.50 E
Karou	150	15.07 N	0.39 E
Karow, Dtsch.	54	52.20 N	12.15 E
Karow, Dtsch.	54	53.32 N	12.15 E
Karow ⬥ [8]	264a	52.37 N	13.29 E
Karpathen → Carpathian Mountains ⩘	22	48.00 N	24.00 E
Kárpathos, Ellás	38	35.30 N	27.14 E
Kárpathos, Ellás	130	35.31 N	27.12 E
Kárpathos I	38	35.40 N	27.10 E
Karpenísion	38	38.55 N	21.40 E
Karpinsk	86	59.45 N	60.01 E
Karpogory	24	64.00 N	44.24 E
Karpovka, Ukr.	83	49.10 N	37.43 E
Karpovka, Ukr.	83	47.57 N	39.36 E
Karpovo, Ross.	76	60.02 N	36.43 E
Karpovo, Ross.	82	55.35 N	38.34 E
Karpunicha	80	57.42 N	45.20 E
Karpuninskij	86	58.43 N	61.50 E
Karpuzlu	130	37.33 N	27.50 E
Karratha	162	20.44 S	116.51 E
Karrats Fjord ⊂ [2]	176	71.20 N	54.00 W
Karrebæksminde	41	55.11 N	11.40 E
Karres	58	47.13 N	10.47 E
Kärrgruvan	40	60.05 N	15.56 E
Karridale	162	34.13 S	115.05 E
Kars	84	40.36 N	43.05 E
Kars □ [4]	84	40.35 N	43.00 E
Kars ≏	84	40.37 N	43.41 E
Karša	80	49.48 N	51.27 E
Karsakpaj	86	47.49 N	66.41 E
Karsakuwigamak Lake ⊜	184	56.22 N	99.30 W
Kärsämäki	26	63.58 N	25.46 E
Karsantı	130	37.33 N	35.24 E
Kārsava	76	56.47 N	27.40 E
Karsdorf	54	51.17 N	11.39 E
Karši	128	38.53 N	65.48 E
Karsin	30	53.54 N	17.56 E
Karšinskaja step' ≚	128	39.10 N	65.00 E
Karskije Vorota, proliv ⴾ	72	70.30 N	58.00 E
Karskoje more (Kara Sea) ⊤ [2]	72	76.00 N	80.00 E
Karsovaj	80	58.14 N	53.11 E
Kårsta, Sve.	40	59.39 N	18.14 E
Kärsta, Sve.	40	59.40 N	16.49 E
Karstädt	54	53.09 N	11.44 E
Karst → Kras ⩘ [1]	64	45.48 N	14.00 E
Karstula	26	62.52 N	24.47 E
Karsun	80	54.11 N	46.59 E
Kartajol'	24	64.32 N	53.14 E
Kartala ∧	157a	11.45 S	43.22 E
Kartaly	86	53.03 N	60.40 E
Kartārpur	123	31.27 N	75.30 E
Karthaus	214	41.07 N	78.07 W
Kartlijskij chrebet ⩘	84	42.10 N	44.55 E
Kartosuro	115a	7.33 S	110.44 E
Karttula	26	62.53 N	26.58 E
Kartuzy	30	54.20 N	18.12 E
Kartzow	54	52.29 N	12.58 E
Käru	76	58.50 N	25.11 E
Karuah ≏	170	32.39 S	151.58 E
Karufa	164	3.50 S	133.27 E
Karuizawa	94	36.21 N	138.38 E
Karukuwisa	156	18.56 S	19.40 E
Karumai	92	40.19 N	141.28 E
Karumba	166	17.29 S	140.50 E
Kārūn ≏	128	30.26 N	48.10 E
Karungi	26	66.03 N	23.57 E
Karungu	154	0.51 S	34.09 E
Karuni	115b	9.26 S	119.19 E
Karunjie	164	16.18 S	127.12 E
Karunki	26	66.02 N	24.01 E
Karup	41	56.18 N	9.10 E
Karup Å ≏	41	56.18 N	9.10 E
Karūr	122	10.57 N	78.05 E
Karuscia, Punta ≻	70	36.49 N	11.59 E
Karvala	265a	59.41 N	30.09 E
Karviná	30	49.50 N	18.30 E
Kārwār	122	14.48 N	74.08 E
Karwendel ⩘	64	47.27 N	11.20 E
Karwi	124	25.12 N	80.54 E
Karym	86	60.07 N	66.41 E
Karymskoje, Ross.	88	51.37 N	114.21 E
Karymskoje, Ross.	88	54.07 N	101.49 E
Karza	86	58.35 N	80.50 E
Karzachi	84	41.15 N	43.16 E
Kas, Sūd.	140	12.30 N	24.17 E
Kaş, Tür.	130	36.12 N	29.38 E
Kas ≏	86	59.40 N	90.00 E
Kasaan	182	55.32 N	132.24 W
Kasabi	152	14.48 S	23.42 E
Kasach ≏	84	40.03 N	43.52 E
Kasadi ≏	272c	19.01 N	73.03 E
Kasa-do I	98	34.28 N	126.03 E
Kasado-shima I	96	33.57 N	131.51 E
Kasagi	94	34.45 N	135.56 E
Kasagi-sanchi ⩘	270	34.37 N	135.56 E
Kasagi-yama ∧	94	35.31 N	137.21 E
Kasahara	94	35.17 N	137.09 E
Kasahata	268	35.54 N	139.25 E
Kasai	96	34.56 N	134.50 E
Kasai ⬥ [8]	268	35.39 N	139.53 E
Kasai (Cassai) ≏, Afr.	152	3.02 S	16.57 E
Kāsai ≏, India	124	22.09 N	87.50 E
Kasai-Occidental □ [4]	152	5.30 S	21.40 E
Kasai-Oriental □ [4]	152	4.00 S	23.30 E
Kasaji	152	10.22 S	23.27 E
Kasakake	94	36.23 N	139.17 E
Kasama, Nihon	94	36.23 N	140.16 E
Kasama, Zam.	154	10.13 S	31.12 E
Kasamatsu	94	35.22 N	136.46 E
Kasan	128	39.02 N	65.35 E
Kasan-dong	98	41.18 N	126.55 E
Kasane	156	17.50 S	25.05 E
Kasanga	154	8.28 S	31.09 E
Kasangale	152	6.20 S	22.42 E
Kasangeshi ≏	152	8.24 S	21.56 E
Kasangulu	152	4.36 S	15.10 E
Kasanka National Park ♦	154	12.35 S	30.12 E
Kasan → Kazan'	80	55.49 N	49.08 E
Kasano-misaki ≻	94	36.21 N	136.18 E
Kasansaj	85	41.15 N	71.32 E
Kasansaj ≏	85	40.57 N	71.30 E
Kasaoka	96	34.30 N	133.30 E
Kāsaragod	122	12.30 N	75.00 E
Kasari ≏	76	58.45 N	23.49 E
Kašary	78	49.03 N	41.00 E
Kasatori-yama ∧, Nihon	94	34.44 N	136.18 E
Kasatori-yama ∧, Nihon	96	33.33 N	132.55 E
Kasauli	123	30.55 N	76.57 E
Kasba	124	25.51 N	87.33 E
Kasbagoas	126	24.11 N	88.30 E
Kasba Kamarda	126	21.46 N	87.21 E
Kasba Lake ⊜	176	60.18 N	102.07 W
Kasba Mirgoda	126	21.42 N	87.28 E
Kasba Nārāyangarh	126	22.10 N	87.23 E
Kasba Patāspur	126	22.02 N	87.32 E
Kasba-Tadla	148	32.34 N	6.18 W
Kaschau → Košice	30	48.43 N	21.15 E
Kåseberga	26	55.23 N	14.04 E
Kaseda	92	31.25 N	130.19 E
Kasempa	154	13.27 S	25.50 E
Kasenga	154	10.22 S	28.38 E
Kasenyi	154	1.24 N	30.26 E
Kasese, Ug.	154	0.10 N	30.05 E
Kasese, Zaïre	154	1.38 S	27.07 E
Kaset Sombun	110	16.17 N	101.57 E
Kasfareet Military Base ■	142	30.15 N	32.24 E
Kāsganj	124	27.49 N	78.39 E
Kashabowie Lake ⊜	190	48.42 N	90.25 W
Kashaf ≏	128	35.58 N	61.07 E
Kashagawigamog Lake ⊜	212	44.59 N	78.37 W
Kāshān	128	33.59 N	51.29 E
Kashasha	154	1.44 S	31.37 E
Kashegelok	180	60.50 N	157.50 W
Kashgar → Kashi	85	39.29 N	75.59 E
Kashi	85	39.29 N	75.59 E
Kashiba	96	34.33 N	135.42 E
Kashihara	96	34.30 N	135.46 E
Kashiji Plain ≚	152	13.20 S	22.30 E
Kashileshi ≏	152	9.46 S	23.05 E
Kashima, Nihon	92	33.07 N	130.06 E
Kashima, Nihon	94	35.58 N	140.38 E
Kashima, Nihon	94	36.58 N	136.55 E
Kashima, Nihon	96	35.30 N	133.01 E
Kashima-jingū ⊍ [1]	94	35.59 N	140.40 E
Kashima-nada ⊤ [2]	94	36.15 N	140.45 E
Kashima-Yariga-take ∧	94	36.37 N	137.45 E
Kashimo	94	35.43 N	137.23 E
Kāshināthpur	126	23.58 N	89.37 E
Kashing → Jiaxing	106	30.46 N	120.45 E
Kashio ⬥ [8]	268	35.25 N	139.33 E
Kāshīpur, India	124	29.13 N	78.57 E
Kāshipur, India	126	23.26 N	86.40 E
Kashitu	154	13.42 S	28.40 E
Kashiwa	94	35.52 N	139.59 E
Kashiwara	96	34.35 N	135.37 E
Kashiwazaki, Nihon	92	37.22 N	138.33 E
Kashiwazaki, Nihon	268	35.56 N	139.42 E
Kāshmar	128	35.12 N	58.27 E
Kashmir, Vale of ∨	123	34.00 N	75.00 E
Kashmir → Jammu and Kashmīr □ [2]	120	34.00 N	76.00 E
Kashmor	120	28.26 N	69.35 E
Kashmūnd Ghar ⩘	123	34.42 N	70.31 E
Kashunuk ≏	180	61.18 N	165.36 W
Kashwakamak Lake ⊜	212	44.50 N	77.04 W
Kasia	124	26.45 N	83.55 E
Kāsiāni	126	23.14 N	89.45 E
Kasiāri	126	22.08 N	87.14 E
Kasidiji ≏	152	7.57 S	23.12 E
Kasigau ∧	154	3.50 S	38.40 E
Kasigluk	180	60.52 N	162.32 W
Kasilof	180	60.24 N	151.18 W
Kasilovo	78	50.38 N	35.37 E
Kasimbar	112	0.09 S	120.00 E
Kasimov	80	54.56 N	41.24 E
Kāsimpur, Bngl.	126	23.59 N	90.19 E
Kāsimpur, India	272b	22.46 N	88.31 E
Kašin	76	57.21 N	37.37 E
Kāsināthpur	272b	22.35 N	88.31 E
Kasinge	154	6.20 S	26.59 E
Kasinka	156	18.13 S	24.22 E
Kāsipur	272b	22.25 N	88.10 E
Kaširа	82	54.51 N	38.10 E
Kaširka ≏	82	54.52 N	38.13 E
Kasiruta, Pulau I	108	0.25 S	127.12 E
Kasiui, Pulau I	164	4.30 S	131.40 E
Kasiwa → Kashiwa	94	35.52 N	139.59 E
Kaskabulak	86	49.34 N	79.52 E
Kaškadarjinskaja Oblast' □ [8]	85	39.00 N	67.00 E
Kaskaden-Kette → Cascade Range ⩘	202	45.00 N	121.30 W
Kaskana	85	40.45 N	69.36 E
Kaskaskia ≏	194	37.59 N	89.56 W
Kaskaskia, East Fork ≏	219	38.43 N	89.09 W
Kaskaskia, North Fork ≏	219	38.46 N	89.09 W
Kaskattama ≏	176	57.03 N	90.07 W
Kaskelen	85	43.12 N	76.37 E
Kaskelen ≏	85	43.53 N	77.08 E
Kaskinen → Kaskö	26	62.23 N	21.13 E
Kaskö (Kaskinen)	26	62.23 N	21.13 E
Kašlagač ≏	83	47.45 N	37.16 E
Kaslātu ∧	124	23.58 N	84.54 E
Kasli	86	55.53 N	60.46 E
Kaslo	182	49.55 N	116.55 W
Kasn'a	76	55.24 N	34.20 E
Kasn'a ≏	76	55.51 N	34.25 E
Kaso ≏	115a	7.25 S	106.40 E
Kasongo	154	4.27 S	26.40 E
Kasongo-Lunda	152	6.28 S	16.49 E
Kásos I	38	35.22 N	26.56 E
Kasota	190	44.18 N	93.57 W
Kašperovka	78	49.26 N	29.41 E
Kaspi	84	41.57 N	44.25 E
Kaspijsk	84	42.52 N	47.38 E
Kaspijskij	22	45.22 N	47.24 E
Kaspijskoje more → Caspian Sea ⊤ [2]	72	42.00 N	50.30 E
Kaspische Senke → Prikaspijskaja nizmennost' ≚	80	48.00 N	52.00 E

ENGLISH

Name	Page	Lat.°′	Long.°′
Kaspisches Meer → Caspian Sea ⊤ [2]	72	42.00 N	50.30 E
Kaspl'a	76	55.00 N	31.38 E
Kaspl'a ≏	76	55.24 N	30.43 E
Kasr, Ra's ≻	140	18.02 N	38.35 E
Kasrik	130	38.13 N	41.54 E
Kassab	130	35.56 N	35.59 E
Kassai → Cassai (Kasai) ≏	152	3.02 S	16.57 E
Kassa → Košice	30	48.43 N	21.15 E
Kassalā	140	15.28 N	36.24 E
Kassalā □ [4]	140	15.00 N	35.00 E
Kassándra ≻ [1]	38	40.06 N	23.22 E
Kassándras, Kólpos ⊂	38	40.06 N	23.30 E
Kassel	56	51.19 N	9.29 E
Kassel □ [5]	56	51.10 N	9.20 E
Kasserine	148	35.11 N	8.48 E
Kasserine □ [8]	148	35.00 N	8.45 E
Kasshabog Lake ⊜	212	44.38 N	77.58 W
Kassikaityu ≏	246	1.49 N	58.32 W
Kassinger	140	18.45 N	31.54 E
Kassîr, Sabkhat al- ⊜	130	35.03 N	41.07 E
Kasslerfeld ⬥ [8]	263	51.26 N	6.45 E
Kasson	190	44.01 N	92.45 W
Kassou	150	11.35 N	2.03 W
Kassoum	150	13.05 N	3.18 W
Kastamonu	130	41.22 N	33.47 E
Kastamonu □ [4]	130	41.40 N	33.45 E
Kastanéai	38	41.38 N	26.28 E
Kastelholm	26	60.14 N	20.04 E
Kastellaun	56	50.04 N	7.26 E
Kastellórizon I	130	36.08 N	29.34 E
Kasterlee	56	51.15 N	4.57 E
Kastiyu, Puntan ≻	174n	14.57 N	145.40 E
Kastl, Dtsch.	60	49.22 N	11.42 E
Kastl, Dtsch.	60	49.50 N	11.54 E
Kastorf	52	53.44 N	10.34 E
Kastoría	38	40.31 N	21.15 E
Kastorías, Límni ⊜	38	40.30 N	21.17 E
Kastornoje	78	51.50 N	38.06 E
Kastrávion, Tekhnití Límni ⊜ [1]	38	38.50 N	21.20 E
Kastrup Lufthavn ⊠	41	55.38 N	12.39 E
Kasuga, Nihon	94	35.28 N	136.29 E
Kasuga, Nihon	96	33.32 N	130.27 E
Kasuga, Nihon	96	35.10 N	135.06 E
Kasugai, Nihon	94	35.14 N	136.58 E
Kasugai, Nihon	94	35.39 N	138.39 E
Kasuga-kōkūkichi, Kaijō-jieitai- ■	96	33.31 N	130.28 E
Kasuga Shrine ⊍ [1]	270	34.41 N	135.51 E
Kasuka	158	33.40 S	26.41 E
Kasukabe	94	35.58 N	139.45 E
Kasukawa	94	36.24 N	139.13 E
Kasulu	154	4.34 S	30.06 E
Kasumi	96	35.38 N	134.38 E
Kasumiga-ura ⊜	94	36.00 N	140.25 E
Kasum-Ismailov	84	40.36 N	46.47 E
Kasumkent	84	41.41 N	48.07 E
Kasungan	112	1.58 S	113.24 E
Kasungu	154	13.01 S	33.30 E
Kasungu National Park ♦	154	12.55 S	33.15 E
Kasupe	154	15.10 S	35.15 E
Kasūr	123	31.07 N	74.27 E
Kaszuby ⬥ [1]	30	54.10 N	18.15 E
Kata	88	58.46 N	102.40 E
Kataba	154	16.05 S	25.10 E
Kataeregi	150	9.22 N	6.17 E
Katagum	146	12.17 N	10.21 E
Katahdin, Mount ∧	188	45.55 N	68.55 W
Katai	272c	19.10 N	73.05 E
Katajevo	88	50.57 N	108.41 E
Katajsk	86	56.18 N	62.35 E
Katako-Kombe	152	3.24 S	24.25 E
Katakura	270	34.29 N	135.31 E
Katakwi	154	1.55 N	33.57 E
Katale	154	4.59 S	31.03 E
Katalla	180	60.12 N	144.31 W
Katanda	154	0.50 S	29.22 E
Katanga □ [9]	138	10.00 S	26.00 E
Katanga ≏	74	60.08 N	102.13 E
Katangi	124	23.27 N	79.47 E
Katanglad Mountains ⩘	116	8.06 N	124.54 E
Katangli	89	51.42 N	143.14 E
Katanimara	126	22.17 N	87.11 E
Katanning	162	33.42 S	117.33 E
Katano	270	34.47 N	135.40 E
Katano-hana ≻	174f	24.49 N	141.20 E
Katanti	154	2.18 S	27.08 E
Kataoka	270	35.03 N	135.58 E
Katapakishi	152	8.15 S	22.49 E
Katara, Depresión de → Qaṭṭārah, Munkhafaḍ al- ⫠ [7]	140	30.00 N	27.30 E
Katârniān Ghāt	124	28.20 N	81.09 E
Katar → Qatar □ [1]	128	25.00 N	51.10 E
Katase	268	35.19 N	139.29 E
Katashina	94	36.46 N	139.14 E
Katašin	76	52.36 N	32.10 E
Katav-Ivanovsk	86	54.45 N	58.12 E
Katayama	268	35.46 N	139.34 E
Katchall Island I	110	7.57 N	93.22 E
Katchewanooka Lake ⊜	212	44.27 N	78.16 W
Katchin-wan ⊂	174m	26.18 N	127.53 E
Katchirga	150	14.03 N	0.06 E
Katchiungo	152	12.35 S	16.13 E
Katech	84	41.39 N	46.34 E
Kateel ≏	180	65.28 N	157.35 W
Katélé	150	10.38 N	5.37 W
Katena-wan ⊂	174m	26.50 N	128.05 E
Katepwa Beach	184	50.42 N	103.38 W
Katerbow	54	52.59 N	12.39 E
Kateríni	38	40.16 N	22.30 E
Katerinopol'	78	48.56 N	30.59 E
Katerloch ⫠ [5]	61	47.16 N	15.32 E
Katernberg ⬥ [8], Dtsch.	263	51.16 N	7.06 E
Katernberg ⬥ [8], Dtsch.	263	51.29 N	7.04 E
Katesbridge	48	54.18 N	6.08 W
Kates Needle ∧	180	57.03 N	132.03 W
Katešovo	82	54.08 N	37.00 E
Katete, Malaŵi	154	12.17 S	33.39 E
Katete, Zam.	154	14.05 S	32.07 E
Katghora	124	22.30 N	82.33 E
Katha	110	24.11 N	96.21 E
Kathangor, Jabal ∧	140	5.45 N	33.59 E
Katherine	164	14.28 S	132.16 E
Katherine ≏	164	14.39 S	131.42 E
Katherine Creek ≏	166	23.48 S	143.42 E
Katherine Gorge National Park ♦	164	14.10 S	132.30 E
Kāthgodām	124	29.16 N	79.32 E
Kathiār	120	25.32 N	87.35 E
Kāthiāwār Peninsula ≻ [1]	120	22.00 N	71.00 E
Kathīb, Ra's ≻	144	14.55 N	42.53 E
Kathla	123	31.59 N	76.47 E
Kathleen	220	28.07 N	82.01 W
Kathleen Valley	162	27.23 S	120.38 E
Kathlow	54	51.43 N	14.29 E
Kāṭhmāṇḍau	124	27.43 N	85.19 E
Kathmandu → Kāṭhmāṇḍau	124	27.43 N	85.19 E
Kathor	120	21.18 N	72.56 E
Kathrabbā	132	31.08 N	35.37 E
Kathua	123	32.22 N	75.31 E
Kāthuli	126	23.52 N	88.40 E
Kati	150	12.44 N	8.04 W
Kātiādi	126	24.15 N	90.48 E
Katibas ≏	112	2.01 N	112.33 E
Katihār	124	25.32 N	87.35 E
Katikati	172	37.33 S	175.55 E
Katima Mulilo	152	17.27 S	24.14 E

DEUTSCH

Name	Seite	Breite°′	Länge°′ E = Ost
Katimik Lake ⊜	184	52.54 N	99.22 W
Katiola	150	8.08 N	5.06 W
Katipunan	116	8.31 N	123.17 E
Katiti Aboriginal Land Reserve ⬥ [4]	162	25.10 S	131.15 E
Kātlang	123	34.22 N	72.05 E
Katlehong	273d	26.19 S	28.09 E
Katlenburg-Duhm	52	51.41 N	10.06 E
Katmai, Mount ∧	180	58.17 N	154.56 W
Katmai National Park ♦	180	58.30 N	155.00 W
Kātmāndu → Kāṭhmāṇḍau	124	27.43 N	85.19 E
Katni	80	57.59 N	47.46 E
Katni → Murwāra	124	23.51 N	80.24 E
Káto Akhaïa	38	38.09 N	21.32 E
Kātol	120	21.16 N	78.35 E
Katompi	154	6.11 S	26.20 E
Katonah	210	41.16 N	73.41 W
Katonga ≏	154	0.34 N	31.50 E
Katon-Karagaj	86	49.11 N	85.37 E
Katoomba	170	33.42 S	150.18 E
Katopa	154	2.45 S	25.06 E
Katori-jingū ⊍ [1]	94	35.52 N	140.30 E
Katoúna	38	38.47 N	21.07 E
Katovice	60	49.16 N	13.49 E
Katowice	30	50.16 N	19.00 E
Katowice □ [4]	30	50.15 N	19.00 E
Katra	123	32.59 N	74.57 E
Kātrās	126	23.48 N	86.17 E
Katričev	80	49.23 N	45.33 E
Kātrīnā, Jabal ∧	140	28.31 N	33.57 E
Katrine, Loch ⊜	46	56.15 N	4.31 W
Katrineholm	40	59.00 N	16.12 E
Katsch, Golf von → Kutch, Gulf of ⊂	120	22.36 N	69.30 E
Katschbach ≏	61	47.08 N	14.17 E
Katschberg)(	64	47.03 N	13.37 E
Katsepe	157b	15.45 S	46.15 E
Katshungu	154	2.27 S	27.23 E
Katsina	150	13.00 N	7.32 E
Katsina □ [3]	150	12.20 N	7.45 E
Katsina Ala	150	7.10 N	9.17 E
Katsina Ala ≏	152	7.48 N	8.52 E
Katsunuma	94	35.39 N	138.44 E
Katsura ⬥ [8]	270	34.59 N	135.42 E
Katsura ≏, Nihon	94	35.36 N	139.15 E
Katsura ≏, Nihon	94	34.53 N	135.42 E
Katsura ≏, Nihon	96	34.02 N	134.35 E
Katsura ≏, Nihon	270	34.53 N	135.42 E
Katsuragi	96	34.15 N	135.30 E
Katsuragi-san ∧	96	34.20 N	135.27 E
Katsushika ⬥ [8]	268	35.43 N	139.51 E
Katsuta, Nihon	94	36.24 N	140.30 E
Katsuta, Nihon	96	35.04 N	134.11 E
Katsuura, Nihon	94	35.08 N	140.18 E
Katsuura, Nihon	96	33.56 N	134.30 E
Katsuyama, Nihon	94	36.03 N	136.30 E
Katsuyama, Nihon	96	35.05 N	133.41 E
Kattakurgan	72	39.55 N	66.15 E
Kattara-Senke → Qaṭṭārah, Munkhafaḍ al- ⫠ [7]	140	30.00 N	27.30 E
Kattarp	41	56.09 N	12.46 E
Katta-Taldyk	85	40.19 N	73.12 E
Kattaviá	38	35.57 N	27.46 E
Kattegat ⴾ	26	57.00 N	11.00 E
Katternberg ⬥ [8]	263	51.09 N	7.02 E
Katthammarsvik	26	57.26 N	18.50 E
Kattowitz → Katowice	30	50.16 N	19.00 E
Kattrup	41	55.57 N	9.56 E
Kāttuputtūr	122	10.59 N	78.14 E
Katul, Jabal ∧	140	14.16 N	29.23 E
Katuma	154	6.10 S	30.34 E
Katumba	154	7.45 S	25.18 E
Katun' ≏	86	52.25 N	85.05 E
Katunino	80	58.01 N	45.39 E
Katunki	80	56.50 N	43.14 E
Kātūria	124	24.44 N	86.43 E
Katu Shan ∧	86	45.40 N	82.55 E
Katusice	54	50.26 N	14.50 E
Kātwa	126	23.39 N	88.08 E
Katwijk aan de Rijn	52	52.11 N	4.26 E
Katwijk aan Zee	52	52.13 N	4.24 E
Katy	222	29.47 N	95.49 W
Katyn	76	54.47 N	31.44 E
Kąty Wrocławskie	30	51.02 N	16.46 E
Katzenbuckel ∧	56	49.28 N	9.02 E
Katzenelnbogen	56	50.17 N	7.59 E
Katzenfurt	56	50.37 N	8.21 E
Katzhütte	54	50.33 N	11.03 E
Kaua ≏	156	19.24 S	22.03 E
Kauai □ [6]	229b	21.59 N	159.22 W
Kauai I	229b	22.00 N	159.30 W
Kauai Channel ⴾ	229b	21.45 N	158.50 W
Kaub	56	50.05 N	7.46 E
Kau Desert ⬥ [2]	229d	19.21 N	155.19 W
Kaufbeuren	58	47.53 N	10.37 E
Kaufering	58	48.05 N	10.52 E
Kaufman	222	32.35 N	96.18 W
Kaufman □ [6]	222	32.38 N	96.18 W
Kaufungen, Dtsch.	52	51.17 N	9.38 E
Kaufungen, Dtsch.	56	51.17 N	9.38 E
Kaugama	150	12.28 N	9.44 E
Kauhajoki	26	62.26 N	22.11 E
Kauhanevan-Pohjankankaan kansallispuisto ♦	26	63.08 N	22.25 E
Kauhava	26	63.06 N	23.05 E
Kauiki Head ≻	229a	20.45 N	155.59 W
Kaukapakapa	172	36.37 S	174.30 E
Kaukasus → Bol'šoj Kavkaz ⩘	84	42.30 N	45.00 E
Kaukauna	190	44.16 N	88.16 W
Kaukau Veld ⩘ [1]	156	19.30 S	20.30 E
Kaukhāli	126	22.38 N	90.04 E
Kaukura I [1]	14	15.45 S	146.42 W
Kaula I	229d	21.45 N	160.30 W
Kaulakahi Channel ⴾ	229b	22.00 N	159.53 W
Kaulille	56	51.11 N	5.31 E
Kauliranta	24	66.27 N	23.41 E
Kaŭl-li	98	37.58 N	124.37 E
Kaulsdorf	54	50.37 N	11.26 E
Kaulsdorf ⬥ [8]	264a	52.31 N	13.33 E
Kaulsdorf-Süd ⬥ [8]	264a	52.29 N	13.34 E
Kaumakani	229b	21.55 N	159.37 W
Kaumalapau	229a	20.47 N	156.59 W
Kaunakakai	229a	21.05 N	157.01 W
Kaunas	76	54.54 N	23.54 E
Kauneonga Lake	210	41.41 N	74.50 W
Kauner Tal ∨	58	47.01 N	10.44 E
Kaunghein	110	25.40 N	95.26 E
Kauniainen → Grankulla	26	60.13 N	24.45 E
Kaununui ≻	229b	21.56 N	160.10 W
Kaup	164	3.50 S	144.00 E
Kaupanger	26	61.11 N	7.14 E
Kaura Namoda	150	12.35 N	6.35 E
Kauriyāla Ghāt	124	28.23 N	81.02 E
Kauru	150	10.33 N	8.12 E
Kausa	272c	19.10 N	73.02 E
Kau Sai Chau I	271d	22.22 N	114.18 E
Kausala	26	60.54 N	26.22 E
Kaušany	78	46.38 N	29.25 E
Kaustinen	26	63.32 N	23.42 E
Kauswagan	116	8.11 N	124.05 E
Kautokeino	24	69.00 N	23.02 E
Kauttua	26	61.06 N	22.10 E
Kau-ye Kyun I	110	11.01 N	98.32 E
Kavača	74	60.16 N	169.51 E
Kavacık	130	39.40 N	28.30 E
Kavadarci	38	41.26 N	22.00 E
Kavajë	38	41.11 N	19.33 E
Kavak, Tür.	130	38.24 N	39.26 E
Kavak, Tür.	130	41.05 N	36.03 E
Kavak, Tür.	130	39.18 N	37.30 E
Kavakbaşı	130	38.29 N	41.49 E
Kavaklıdere	130	37.26 N	28.22 E

Symbols in the index entries represent the broad categories identified in the key at the right. Symbols with superior numbers (⩘[1]) identify subcategories (see complete key on page *I · 1).*

Symbole im Register stellen die rechts im Schlüssel erklärten Kategorien dar. Symbole mit hochgestellten Ziffern (⩘[1]) bezeichnen Unterabteilungen einer Kategorie (vgl. vollständiger Schlüssel auf Seite *I · 1).*

Los símbolos incluídos en el texto del índice representan las grandes categorias identificadas con la clave a la derecha. Los símbolos con numeros en su parte superior (⩘[1]) identifican las subcategorías (véase la clave completa en la página *I · 1).*

Les symboles de l'index représentent les catégories indiquées dans la légende à droite. Les symboles suivis d'un indice (⩘[1]) représentent des sous-catégories (voir légende complète à la page *I · 1).*

Os símbolos incluídos no texto do índice representam as grandes categorias identificadas com a chave à direita. Os símbolos com números em sua parte superior (⩘[1]) identificam as subcategorias (veja-se a chave completa à página *I · 1).*

∧ Mountain	Berg	Montaña	Montagne	Montanha
⩘ Mountains	Gebirge	Montañas	Montagnes	Montanhas
)(Pass	Paß	Paso	Col	Passo
∨ Valley, Canyon	Tal, Cañon	Valle, Cañón	Vallée, Canyon	Vale, Canhão
≚ Plain	Ebene	Llano	Plaine	Planície
≻ Cape	Kap	Cabo	Cap	Cabo
I Island	Insel	Isla	Île	Ilha
II Islands	Inseln	Islas	Îles	Ilhas
⫠ Other Topographic Features	Andere Topographische Objekte	Otros Elementos Topográficos	Autres données topographiques	Outros acidentes topográficos

ESPAÑOL

Nombre	Página	Lat.°′	Long.°′ W = Oeste
Kavála	38	40.56 N	24.25 E
Kavalerovo	89	44.15 N	135.04 E
Kāvali	122	14.55 N	79.59 E
Kavango □[5]	156	18.30 S	20.15 E
Kavaratti	122	10.34 N	72.39 E
Kavaratti Island I	122	10.33 N	72.38 E
Kavarna	38	43.25 N	28.20 E
Kavendou, Mont ʌ	150	10.41 N	12.12 W
Kāveri ≃	122	11.09 N	79.52 E
Kāveri Falls ∟	122	12.18 N	77.17 E
Kaverino, Ross.	80	54.10 N	41.47 E
Kaverino, Ross.	82	56.11 N	36.15 E
Kavieng	164	2.35 S	150.50 E
Kavimba	156	18.02 S	24.38 E
Kavīr, Dasht-e ◆[2]	128	34.40 N	54.30 E
Kavkazskij zapovednik ♠	84	43.55 N	40.30 E
Kävlinge	41	55.48 N	13.06 E
Kävlingeån ≃	41	55.47 N	13.06 E
Kavungo	152	11.31 S	23.03 E
Kavuu ≃	154	7.40 S	31.46 E
Kavykuči-Gazimurskije	88	51.22 N	118.10 E
Kaw, Guy. fr.	250	4.29 N	52.02 W
Kaw, Ok., U.S.	196	36.46 N	96.50 W
Kawa	110	17.05 N	96.28 E
Kawaba	94	36.41 N	139.07 E
Kawabe, Nihon	94	35.29 N	137.04 E
Kawabe, Nihon	96	33.55 N	135.11 E
Kawachi, Nihon	94	36.24 N	136.38 E
Kawachi, Nihon	94	36.37 N	139.56 E
Kawachi, Nihon	94	35.53 N	140.15 E
Kawachi-nagano	96	34.27 N	135.34 E
Kawagama Lake ⊜	212	45.18 N	78.45 W
Kawage	94	34.47 N	136.33 E
Kawagoe	94	35.55 N	139.29 E
Kawaguchi	94	35.48 N	139.43 E
Kawaguchiko	94	35.30 N	138.46 E
Kawaguchi-ko ⊜	94	35.31 N	138.45 E
Kawahara	96	35.24 N	134.12 E
Kawai, Nihon	94	36.18 N	137.07 E
Kawai, Nihon	270	34.35 N	135.45 E
Kawaihae Bay c	229d	20.02 N	155.50 W
Kawaihoa ›	229b	21.47 N	160.12 W
Kawaikini ʌ	229b	22.05 N	159.29 W
Kawailoa	229c	21.36 N	158.05 W
Kawailoa Beach	229c	21.37 N	158.04 W
Kawajiri	96	34.14 N	132.42 E
Kawakami, Nihon	94	35.58 N	138.35 E
Kawakami, Nihon	96	34.44 N	133.29 E
Kawakami, Nihon	96	35.17 N	133.39 E
Kawakawa	172	35.23 S	174.04 E
Kawakubo	270	34.54 N	135.38 E
Kawali	115a	7.11 S	108.22 E
Kawama Mission	154	10.04 S	28.37 E
Kawamata	92	37.39 N	140.36 E
Kawambwa	154	9.47 S	29.05 E
Kawamoto, Nihon	94	36.09 N	139.17 E
Kawamoto, Nihon	96	34.59 N	132.30 E
Kawane	94	34.57 N	138.05 E
Kawanishi, Nihon	94	37.09 N	138.45 E
Kawanishi, Nihon	96	34.49 N	135.24 E
Kawanishi, Nihon	270	34.35 N	135.47 E
Kawanoe	96	34.01 N	133.34 E
Kawara, Nihon	96	33.40 N	130.51 E
Kawara, Nihon	270	34.59 N	135.18 E
Kawara Débé	150	12.20 N	3.26 E
Kawarai	268	35.25 N	140.05 E
Kawardha	124	22.01 N	81.15 E
Kawartha Park	212	44.32 N	78.12 W
Kawasaki, Nihon	94	35.32 N	139.43 E
Kawasaki, Nihon	96	33.35 N	130.49 E
Kawasaki-kō c	268	35.30 N	139.47 E
Kawasaki Stadium ♠	268	35.32 N	139.43 E
Kawashima, Nihon	94	35.21 N	136.50 E
Kawashima, Nihon	94	35.59 N	139.30 E
Kawashima, Nihon	96	34.04 N	134.19 E
Kawashima ◆[8]	268	35.28 N	139.35 E
Kawashiri-misaki ›	96	34.26 N	130.58 E
Kawatana	92	33.04 N	129.52 E
Kawauchi	96	33.48 N	132.55 E
Kawau Island I	172	36.25 S	174.51 E
Kawawa ◆[8]	268	35.31 N	139.33 E
Kawayan	116	11.41 N	124.21 E
Kawazu	94	34.44 N	138.59 E
Kawbein	110	16.33 N	97.52 E
Kawdut	110	15.31 N	97.47 E
Kawe	164	7.50 S	138.14 E
Kawe, Pulau I	164	0.03 S	130.07 E
Kaweenakumik Lake ⊜	184	52.52 N	99.30 W
Kaweka ʌ	172	39.17 S	176.23 E
Kaweka Range ϰ	172	39.15 S	176.20 E
Kawerau	172	38.03 S	176.43 E
Kawhia	172	38.04 S	174.49 E
Kawhia Harbour c	172	38.05 S	174.50 E
Kawich Peak ʌ	204	37.58 N	116.27 W
Kawich Range ϰ	204	37.40 N	116.30 W
Kawin	164	2.45 S	150.45 E
Kawinda	115b	8.07 S	118.04 E
Kawit	269f	14.27 N	120.54 E
Kawkabān	144	15.40 N	43.52 E
Kawkareik	110	16.33 N	98.14 E
Kaw Lake ⊜[1]	196	36.55 N	96.57 W
Kawludo	110	18.29 N	97.19 E
Kawm	140	13.31 N	22.50 E
Kawm al-Farā'in (Buto) ⊥	142	31.11 N	30.45 E
Kawm ar-Rāhib	142	28.20 N	30.37 E
Kawm Birah	273c	30.05 N	31.08 E
Kawm Dafanah (Daphnæ) ⊥	142	30.52 N	32.11 E
Kawm Ḥamādah	142	30.46 N	30.42 E
Kawm Ishfīn	273c	30.11 N	31.15 E
Kawm Ishū	142	31.07 N	30.00 E
Kawm Ju'ayf (Naucratis) ⊥	142	30.54 N	30.36 E
Kawm Umbū	140	24.28 N	32.57 E
Kawnglanghpu	102	27.04 N	98.21 E
Kawnipi Lake ⊜	190	48.24 N	91.14 W
Kawthaung	110	9.59 N	98.33 E
Kax ≃	86	43.40 N	81.45 E
Kaxgar ≃	85	39.40 N	78.00 E
Kaya, Burkina	150	13.05 N	1.05 W
Kaya, Nihon	96	35.30 N	135.06 E
Kayaapu	112	5.26 S	102.24 E
Kayadibi, Tür.	130	39.29 N	36.43 E
Kayadibi, Tür.	130	39.55 N	34.15 E
Kayah □[3]	110	19.15 N	97.30 E
Kayak Island I	180	59.52 N	144.30 W
Kāyalpattinam	122	8.34 N	78.07 E
Kāyamba	272b	22.41 N	88.32 E
Kayambi	154	9.27 S	31.58 E
Kayan	110	16.54 N	96.34 E
Kayan ≃	112	2.55 N	117.35 E
Kayangel Islands II	108	8.04 N	134.43 E
Kayang-san ʌ[2]	271b	37.33 N	126.43 E
Kāyankulam	122	9.11 N	76.30 E
Kayapa	116	16.22 N	120.53 E
Kayapınar	130	37.34 N	41.10 E
Kayaş	130	39.56 N	32.58 E
Kaya-san ʌ	98	35.49 N	128.07 E
Kaya-san Kukrip Kongwŏn ♠	98	35.47 N	128.06 E
Kaycee	200	43.42 N	106.38 W
Kayeli	164	3.23 S	127.06 E
Kayembe-Mukulu	152	9.03 S	23.57 E
Kayen	115a	6.54 S	110.59 E
Kayenta	200	36.43 N	110.15 W
Kayes, Congo	152	4.25 S	11.41 E
Kayes, Mali	150	14.27 N	11.26 W
Kayes □[4]	150	14.00 N	11.00 W
Kay Gardens	285	39.45 N	75.25 W
Kayima	150	8.53 N	11.10 W
Kayin □[3]	110	17.30 N	97.45 E
Kayış Dağı ʌ	267b	40.59 N	29.10 E
Kaymakçı	130	38.10 N	28.08 E
Kaymaz, Tür.	130	39.31 N	31.11 E
Kaymaz, Tür.	130	40.55 N	30.18 E
Kayna	54	50.59 N	12.14 E

FRANÇAIS

Nom	Page	Lat.°′	Long.°′ W = Ouest
Kaynar	130	38.55 N	36.28 E
Kayō, Nihon	96	34.51 N	133.42 E
Kayō, Nihon	174m	26.33 N	128.07 E
Kayoa, Pulau I	164	0.05 S	127.25 E
Kayombo	154	9.36 S	25.37 E
Kaypak	130	37.08 N	36.27 E
Kay Point ›	180	69.18 N	138.22 W
Kayser Gebergte ϰ	250	3.03 N	56.35 W
Kayseri	130	38.43 N	35.30 E
Kayseri □[4]	130	38.30 N	35.55 E
Kaysersberg	58	48.08 N	7.15 E
Kaysville	200	41.02 N	111.56 W
Kayuadi, Pulau I	112	6.49 S	120.47 E
Kayuagung	112	3.24 S	104.50 E
Kayumas	115a	7.50 S	114.08 E
Kayuta Lake ⊜	210	43.25 N	75.12 W
Kayuyu	154	3.39 S	26.21 E
Kazach	84	41.06 N	45.22 E
Kazachskij melkosopočnik ϰ[2]	86	49.00 N	72.00 E
Kazachstan → Kazakhstan □[1]	72	48.00 N	68.00 E
Kazačij	83	46.58 N	40.03 E
Kazačinskoje, Ross.	86	57.49 N	93.17 E
Kazačinskoje, Ross.	88	56.16 N	107.36 E
Kazačja Lopan'	78	50.21 N	36.11 E
Kazačje	74	70.44 N	136.13 E
Kazačji Lageri	78	46.42 N	32.59 E
Kazačka	80	51.28 N	43.56 E
Kazackij	86	49.20 N	58.31 E
Kazackoje	78	51.18 N	33.29 E
Kazakdarja	86	43.27 N	59.46 E
Kazakevičevo	89	48.17 N	134.46 E
Kazakhstan □[1], Asia	72	48.00 N	68.00 E
Kazakhstan □[1], Asia	86	47.00 N	76.00 E
Kazaki	76	52.38 N	38.16 E
Kazaklija	78	46.00 N	28.37 E
Kazakstan → Kazakhstan □[1]	72	48.00 N	68.00 E
Kazal'cevo	86	59.18 N	80.30 E
Kazalinsk	86	45.46 N	62.07 E
Kazan'	80	55.49 N	49.08 E
Kazan ≃	176	64.02 N	95.30 W
Kazanbulak	84	40.38 N	46.41 E
Kazancı	130	36.30 N	32.53 E
Kazandžik	128	39.16 N	55.32 E
Kazanka, Kaz.	86	53.20 N	67.27 E
Kazanka, Ukr.	78	47.50 N	32.49 E
Kazanka ≃	80	55.48 N	49.01 E
Kazanlăk	38	42.38 N	25.21 E
Kazan Lake ⊜	184	55.33 N	108.21 W
Kazanlı	130	36.50 N	34.45 E
Kazanovka	76	53.46 N	38.34 E
Kazan-rettō (Volcano Islands) II	14	25.00 N	141.00 E
Kazanskaja	78	49.48 N	41.09 E
Kazanskoje, Ross.	82	54.59 N	37.39 E
Kazanskoje, Ross.	86	55.38 N	69.14 E
Kazan' Station ◆[5]	265b	55.46 N	37.40 E
Kazantip, mys ›	78	45.28 N	35.51 E
Kazarman	85	41.24 N	74.03 E
Kazatin	78	49.43 N	28.50 E
Kazatkul'	86	55.02 N	76.03 E
Kazbegi	84	42.39 N	44.39 E
Kazbek, gora ʌ	84	42.42 N	44.31 E
Kaz Dağı ʌ	130	39.42 N	26.50 E
Kazembe	154	12.11 S	32.37 E
Kāzerūn	128	29.37 N	51.38 E
Kazgorodok, Kaz.	86	52.53 N	70.42 E
Kazgorodok, Kaz.	86	49.56 N	71.36 E
Kažim	24	60.20 N	51.30 E
Kazi-Magomed	84	40.03 N	48.56 E
Kazimierza Wielka	30	50.16 N	20.30 E
Kazimierz Dolny	30	51.20 N	21.58 E
Kazincbarcika	30	48.16 N	20.37 E
Kazinka, Ross.	76	52.32 N	39.42 E
Kazinka, Ross.	78	50.14 N	37.50 E
Kāzipāra	272b	22.43 N	88.31 E
Kāzīr Char	126	22.46 N	90.33 E
Kaziza	152	10.42 S	23.52 E
Kazlų Rūda	76	54.46 N	23.30 E
Kaz'minskoje	84	44.35 N	41.41 E
Kaznačejevo	82	54.31 N	37.16 E
Kazo	94	36.07 N	139.36 E
Kaz'onnyj Torec ≃	83	48.54 N	37.46 E
Kaztalovka	80	49.46 N	48.42 E
Kazuma Pan National Park ♠	154	18.15 S	25.33 E
Kazumba	152	6.25 S	22.02 E
Kazungula	154	17.45 S	25.20 E
Kazuno	92	40.11 N	140.47 E
Kazvin → Qazvīn	128	36.16 N	50.00 E
Kazy	128	39.13 N	57.30 E
Kazym	74	63.40 N	67.14 E
Kazym ≃	74	63.54 N	65.50 E
Kazyr ≃	86	53.47 N	92.53 E
Kbal Dâmrei	110	14.07 N	105.21 E
Kbelnice	60	49.18 N	13.59 E
Kbely ◆[8]	54	50.07 N	14.32 E
Kcynia	30	53.00 N	17.30 E
Kdyně	60	49.23 N	13.02 E
Kéa	38	37.38 N	24.21 E
Kéa I	38	37.34 N	24.22 E
Keaau	229d	19.37 N	155.02 W
Keady	48	54.15 N	6.42 W
Keahole Point ›	229d	19.44 N	156.03 W
Keal, Loch na c	46	56.28 N	6.04 W
Kealaikahiki, Lae o ›	229a	20.32 N	156.42 W
Kealaikahiki Channel ʯ	229a	20.37 N	156.50 W
Kealakekua Bay c	229d	19.28 N	155.56 W
Kealia	229b	22.06 N	159.18 W
Keams Canyon	200	35.48 N	110.11 W
Keanae	229a	20.51 N	156.09 W
Keanapapa Point ›	229a	20.54 N	157.04 W
Kean College of New Jersey ʊ[2]	276	40.41 N	74.14 W
Keansburg	208	40.25 N	74.12 W
Kearney, Mo., U.S.	194	39.22 N	94.21 W
Kearney, Ne., U.S.	198	40.41 N	99.04 W
Kearney, Pa., U.S.	214	40.08 N	78.12 W
Kearns	200	40.39 N	111.59 W
Kearny, Az., U.S.	200	33.03 N	110.54 W
Kearny, N.J., U.S.	210	40.46 N	74.08 W
Kearsley	262	53.32 N	2.23 W
Kearsley Creek ≃	216	43.04 N	83.40 W
Keasbey	276	40.31 N	74.19 W
Keb' ≃	76	57.44 N	28.28 E
Kebajoran ◆[8]	269e	6.13 S	106.46 E
Keban	130	38.48 N	38.45 E
Keban Barajı ⊜[1]	130	38.50 N	39.20 E
Kebanyartimur	115a	7.09 S	112.52 E
Kébara	152	2.27 S	14.25 E
Kebbi	150	12.08 N	4.44 E
Kebeiti	120	36.47 N	79.29 E
Kébémer	150	15.22 N	16.27 W
Kébi, Mayo ≃	146	9.18 N	13.33 E
Kebili	148	33.42 N	8.58 E
Kebîr, Oued el ≃	34	36.50 N	6.07 E
Kebnekaise ʌ	24	67.53 N	18.33 E
Kebock Head ›	46	58.01 N	6.20 W
Kebri Dehar	144	6.47 N	44.17 E
Kebumen	115a	7.40 S	109.39 E
Keb'uty	80	45.50 N	44.14 E
Keče	85	43.14 N	71.22 E
Kecel	30	46.32 N	19.16 E
Kech ≃	128	26.00 N	62.44 E
Kechika ≃	176	59.36 N	127.05 W
Keçiborlu	130	37.57 N	30.18 E
Kecksburg	214	40.11 N	79.28 W
Kecskemét	30	46.54 N	19.42 E
Kedabek	84	40.34 N	45.49 E
Kedah □[3]	114	6.00 N	100.40 E
Kėdainiai	76	55.17 N	24.00 E
Kédange-sur-Canner	56	49.19 N	6.20 E
Kedārnāth	124	30.44 N	79.04 E
Kedārpur	126	23.18 N	90.27 E
Kedges Straits ʯ	208	38.03 N	76.02 W
Kedgwick	186	47.39 N	67.21 W

PORTUGUÊS

Nome	Página	Lat.°′	Long.°′ W = Oeste
Kedgwick ≃	186	47.40 N	67.29 W
Kédhron	38	39.13 N	22.03 E
Kedian	100	31.23 N	112.51 E
Kediri	115a	7.49 S	112.01 E
Kedjebi	150	8.12 N	0.25 E
Kedon	74	64.08 N	159.14 E
Kedong	89	48.02 N	126.15 E
Kédougou	150	12.33 N	12.11 W
Kedrasju	24	64.36 N	60.24 E
Kedrovka	86	55.32 N	86.03 E
Kedu	102	26.33 N	104.21 E
Kedungdung	115a	7.06 S	113.15 E
Kedungjati	115a	7.10 S	110.37 E
Kedungwuni	115a	6.58 S	109.39 E
Kedvavom	24	64.15 N	53.27 E
Kędzierzyn Kozle	30	50.20 N	18.12 E
Keecheus Lake ⊜	224	47.22 N	121.22 W
Keefer	218	38.32 N	84.38 W
Keefers	182	50.02 N	121.33 W
Keego Harbor	216	42.36 N	83.20 W
Keelby	44	53.34 N	0.15 W
Keele	42	53.00 N	2.17 W
Keele ≃	180	64.24 N	124.50 W
Keele Peak ʌ	180	63.26 N	130.19 W
Keeley Lake ⊜	184	54.54 N	108.08 W
Keeling Islands → Cocos Islands □[2]	12	12.10 S	96.55 E
Keels	186	48.36 N	53.24 W
Keelung → Chilung	100	25.08 N	121.44 E
Keen, Mount ʌ	46	56.58 N	2.54 W
Keene, On., Can.	212	44.15 N	78.10 W
Keene, Ca., U.S.	228	35.13 N	118.33 W
Keene, Ky., U.S.	192	37.56 N	84.38 W
Keene, N.H., U.S.	188	42.56 N	72.16 W
Keene, Oh., U.S.	214	40.21 N	81.52 W
Keene, Tx., U.S.	222	32.23 N	97.19 W
Keenesburg	200	40.06 N	104.31 W
Keeney Knob ʌ	192	37.47 N	80.42 W
Keeneyville	278	41.59 N	88.07 W
Keep River National Park ♠	164	15.48 S	129.03 E
Keerbergen	56	51.00 N	4.37 E
Keer-Weer, Cape ›	164	13.58 S	141.30 E
Keeseg ʌ	64	46.58 N	12.14 E
Keeseville	188	44.30 N	73.28 W
Keesler Air Force Base ■	194	30.26 N	88.55 W
Keetmanshoop	156	26.36 S	18.08 E
Keetmanshoop □[5]	156	26.30 S	19.00 E
Keewatin, On., Can.	184	49.46 N	94.34 W
Keewatin, Mn., U.S.	190	47.23 N	93.04 W
Kefa □[4]	144	6.50 N	36.00 E
Kefallinía I	38	38.15 N	20.35 E
Kéfalos	38	36.45 N	27.00 E
Kefamenanu	112	9.27 S	124.29 E
Kefar 'Azza	132	31.29 N	34.32 E
Kefar Blum	132	33.10 N	35.36 E
Kefar 'Eẓyon	132	31.39 N	35.08 E
Kefar Naḥum (Capernaum) ⊥	132	32.53 N	35.34 E
Kefar Sava	132	32.10 N	34.54 E
Kefar Shammay	132	32.57 N	35.27 E
Kefar Szold	132	33.11 N	35.39 E
Kefar Vitkin	132	32.23 N	34.53 E
Kefar Warburg	132	31.43 N	34.44 E
Kefar Yona	132	32.19 N	34.55 E
Kefermarkt	61	48.26 N	14.32 E
Keffi	150	8.51 N	7.52 E
Keffin Hausa	150	12.15 N	9.58 E
Keflavík	24a	64.02 N	22.36 W
Keftya	144	13.54 N	37.07 E
Kega	24	65.10 N	36.54 E
Ke Ga, Mui ›, Viet	110	12.53 N	109.28 E
Ke Ga, Mui ›, Viet	110	10.42 N	107.58 E
Kegalla	122	7.15 N	80.21 E
Kégashka	186	50.12 N	61.17 W
Kégashka, Lac ⊜	186	50.20 N	61.25 W
Kegejli	86	42.45 N	59.35 E
Kegičovka	78	49.17 N	35.46 E
Kegnæs ›[1]	41	54.52 N	9.59 E
Kegon-no-taki ∟	94	36.44 N	139.31 E
Kegonsa, Lake ⊜	216	42.58 N	89.15 W
Kegonzhake	120	33.00 N	87.53 E
Keg River	176	57.48 N	117.52 W
Kegums	76	56.46 N	24.45 E
Kegworth	42	52.50 N	1.16 W
Kehdingen, Land ◆[1]	52	53.45 N	9.15 E
Kehiwin Indian Reserve ◆[4]	182	54.07 N	110.48 W
Kehl	56	48.35 N	7.50 E
Kehlen	58	47.41 N	9.33 E
Kehoe	218	38.28 N	83.03 W
Kehra	76	59.20 N	25.20 E
Kehrigk	54	52.09 N	13.55 E
Ke-hsi Mānsām	110	21.56 N	97.50 E
Keig	46	57.15 N	2.39 W
Keighley	44	53.52 N	1.54 W
Keihoku	96	35.09 N	135.38 E
Keijō → Sŏul	98	37.33 N	126.58 E
Keila	76	59.18 N	24.25 E
Keilor	169	37.43 S	144.50 E
Keimoes	158	28.41 S	21.00 E
Kei Mouth	158	32.41 S	28.22 E
Keio University ʊ[2]	268	35.38 N	139.45 E
Kei Road	158	32.42 S	27.32 E
Keiser	194	35.40 N	90.05 W
Keiskammahoek	158	32.41 S	27.09 E
Keiskammapunt ›	158	32.40 S	27.10 E
Keïta	150	14.46 N	5.46 E
Kéita, Bahr ≃	146	9.14 N	18.21 E
Keitele	26	63.11 N	26.22 E
Keitele ⊜	26	62.55 N	26.00 E
Keith, Austl.	166	36.06 S	140.21 E
Keith, Scot., U.K.	46	57.32 N	2.57 W
Keith Arm c	176	65.20 N	122.15 W
Keithley Creek	182	52.45 N	121.24 W
Keithsburg	190	41.05 N	90.56 W
Keiyasi	175g	17.54 S	177.45 E
Keizer	224	44.59 N	123.01 W
Kejaman	112	2.39 N	113.45 E
Kejimkujik National Park ♠	186	44.21 N	65.18 W
Kejngypil'gyn, laguna c	180	63.30 N	178.50 E
Kejni, gora ʌ	180	64.30 N	174.54 W
Kejvy ϰ	24	67.35 N	38.00 E
Kekaha	229b	21.58 N	159.42 W
Kekek ≃	190	48.24 N	75.48 W
Kekerengu	172	42.00 S	174.01 E
Kékes ʌ	30	47.55 N	20.02 E
Kekeyaer	85	38.02 N	75.05 E
Kek Lok Si ʊ[1]	114	5.23 N	100.14 E
Kekpāra	126	22.27 N	86.35 E
Kekri	120	25.58 N	75.09 E
Kekurnoi, Cape ›	180	57.44 N	155.15 W
Kelafo	144	5.40 N	44.20 E
Kelai ≃	112	2.10 N	117.29 E
Kelan	102	38.43 N	111.32 E
Kelanang	114	2.48 N	101.26 E
Kelang	114	3.02 N	101.27 E
Kelang, Pulau I, Indon.	164	3.12 S	127.44 E
Kelang, Pulau I, Malay.	114	3.00 N	101.18 E
Kelani ≃	122	6.58 N	79.52 E
Kelantan	114	0.51 N	101.40 E
Kelantan □[3]	114	5.20 N	102.00 E
Kelantan ≃	114	6.11 N	102.15 E
Kelapa	112	1.52 S	105.42 E
Kelasuri	84	43.08 N	41.13 E
Kelat	218	38.32 N	84.19 W
Kelayres	210	40.54 N	76.00 W
Kelb, Ouadi V	146	15.19 N	18.51 E
Kel'badžar	84	40.07 N	46.02 E
Kelberg	56	50.17 N	6.55 E
Kelbia, Sebkhet ⊜	36	35.51 N	10.16 E
Kelbra	54	51.26 N	11.02 E

Keld Ula ʌ	86	43.20 N	85.25 E
Kel'd'ušovo	80	55.01 N	44.59 E
Keleft	128	37.21 N	66.15 E
Kelegou	98	41.57 N	118.11 E
Kélékélé	273b	4.20 S	15.08 E
Kelem	144	4.48 N	35.58 E
Kelenföld ◆[8]	264c	47.28 N	19.03 E
Kelenken, gora ʌ	180	66.07 N	170.52 W
Keles, Tür.	130	39.55 N	29.14 E
Keles, Uzb.	85	41.24 N	69.12 E
Keles ≃	85	41.02 N	68.37 E
Keleti-főcsatorna ≊	30	48.01 N	21.20 E
Keleti Pályaudvar ◆[5]	264c	47.30 N	19.06 E
Kelheim	60	48.55 N	11.52 E
Kelibia	148	36.51 N	11.06 E
Kelkheim	56	50.08 N	8.26 E
Kelkit	130	40.08 N	39.27 E
Kelkit ≃	130	40.46 N	36.32 E
Kell	219	38.30 N	88.54 W
Kellé	152	0.06 S	14.33 E
Kellen	52	51.48 N	6.10 E
Kellenhusen	54	54.11 N	11.03 E
Keller, Tx., U.S.	222	32.56 N	97.15 W
Keller, Va., U.S.	208	37.37 N	75.45 W
Keller, Wa., U.S.	182	48.04 N	118.41 W
Kellerberg	64	46.40 N	13.42 E
Kellerberrin	162	31.38 S	117.43 E
Kellerjoch ʌ	64	47.19 N	11.46 E
Keller Lake ⊜, N.T., Can.	176	64.00 N	121.30 W
Keller Lake ⊜, Sk., Can.	184	56.04 N	106.46 W
Kellerovka	86	53.50 N	69.17 E
Keller Peak ʌ	228	34.12 N	117.03 W
Kellett, Cape ›	176	71.59 N	125.34 W
Kellettville	214	41.33 N	79.16 W
Kelleys Island	214	41.36 N	82.42 W
Kelleys Island I	214	41.36 N	82.42 W
Kelliher	184	51.15 N	103.44 W
Kellinghusen	52	53.57 N	9.43 E
Kellmünz	58	48.07 N	10.08 E
Kelloe	44	54.43 N	1.28 W
Kellogg, Id., U.S.	202	47.32 N	116.07 W
Kellogg, Ia., U.S.	190	41.43 N	92.54 W
Kellogg, Mn., U.S.	190	44.18 N	91.59 W
Kellogg Marsh	224	48.05 N	122.07 W
Kelloggsville	214	41.52 N	80.36 W
Kellojärvi ⊜	26	64.16 N	29.03 E
Kelloselkä	24	66.56 N	28.50 E
Kells, N. Ire., U.K.	44	54.48 N	6.13 E
Kells, N. Ire., U.K.	48	54.48 N	6.13 E
Kells → Ceanannus Mór	48	53.44 N	6.53 W
Kelly Air Force Base ■	196	29.24 N	98.35 W
Kelly Lake ⊜	180	65.30 N	126.10 W
Kelly Run ≃, Pa., U.S.	279b	40.15 N	79.55 W
Kelly Run ≃, Pa., U.S.	279b	40.13 N	79.45 W
Kellyville, Austl.	274a	33.43 S	150.57 E
Kellyville, Ok., U.S.	196	35.56 N	96.12 W
Kelmė	76	55.38 N	22.56 E
Kel'mency	78	48.27 N	26.50 E
Kelmet	144	16.04 N	38.55 E
Kelmscott	168a	32.07 S	116.01 E
Kelo	146	9.19 N	15.48 E
Kelolokan	112	1.08 N	117.54 E
Kelottijärvi	24	68.31 N	22.04 E
Kelowna	182	49.53 N	119.29 W
Kelsall	44	53.13 N	2.43 W
Kelsey Bay	182	50.24 N	125.57 W
Kelsey Head ›	42	50.24 N	5.08 W
Kelsey Lake ⊜	184	53.37 N	101.02 W
Kelseyville	204	38.58 N	122.50 W
Kelso, Scot., U.K.	46	55.36 N	2.25 W
Kelso, Wa., U.S.	224	46.08 N	122.54 W
Kelsterbach	56	50.04 N	8.32 E
Kel'temašat	85	42.30 N	70.17 E
Kelty	46	56.08 N	3.23 W
Keluang	114	2.02 N	103.19 E
Keluang, Tanjung ›	112	3.02 S	110.39 E
Kelud, Gunung ʌ	115a	7.56 S	112.18 E
Keluo ≃	89	49.22 N	125.15 E
Keluotun	89	49.16 N	125.44 E
Kelvedon	42	51.51 N	0.42 E
Kelvedon Hatch	260	51.40 N	0.16 E
Kelvington	184	52.10 N	103.30 W
Kelvin Seamount ✣[3]	16	38.50 N	64.00 W
Kelyexeed	144	8.46 N	49.12 E
Kelzenberg	263	51.07 N	6.30 E
Kem'	24	64.57 N	34.36 E
Kem' ≃, Ross.	24	64.57 N	34.41 E
Kem' ≃, Ross.	86	58.31 N	92.04 E
Kema	112	1.23 N	125.04 E
Kema ≃, Ross.	76	60.16 N	37.20 E
Kema ≃, Ross.	76	59.21 N	44.29 E
Ké Macina	150	13.58 N	5.22 W
Kémah, Congo	273b	4.11 S	15.13 E
Kemah, Tür.	130	39.36 N	39.02 E
Kemah, Tx., U.S.	222	29.32 N	95.01 W
Kemaliye	130	39.16 N	38.29 E
Kemalpaşa, Tür.	130	41.30 N	41.30 E
Kemalpaşa, Tür.	130	38.25 N	27.26 E
Kemano	182	53.34 N	127.56 W
Kemasik	114	4.25 N	103.27 E
Kemayan	114	3.08 N	102.22 E
Kemayoran Airport ⊠	269e	6.09 S	106.51 E
Kembani	112	1.34 S	122.54 E
Kembé	152	4.36 N	21.54 E
Kemberg	54	51.46 N	12.38 E
Kemblesville	208	39.45 N	75.50 W
Kembolcha	144	11.02 N	39.43 E
Kembs	58	47.41 N	7.30 E
Kembul	164	5.55 S	150.40 E
Kemčug ≃	86	57.14 N	90.31 E
Kemena ≃	112	3.10 N	113.03 E
Kemeneshát ϰ[2]	61	46.58 N	16.40 E
Kemer, Tür.	130	36.38 N	29.21 E
Kemer, Tür.	130	36.36 N	30.34 E
Kemer, Tür.	130	37.21 N	30.04 E
Kemer ≃	267b	41.04 N	29.07 E
Kemer Barajı ⊜[1]	130	37.34 N	28.31 E
Kemerburgaz ◆[8]	267b	41.09 N	28.54 E
Kemerhisar	130	37.49 N	34.36 E
Kemerovo	86	55.20 N	86.05 E
Kemi	24	65.49 N	24.32 E
Kemie	26	62.14 N	30.20 E
Kemijärvi	24	66.40 N	27.25 E
Kemijärvi ⊜	24	66.36 N	27.24 E
Kemijoki ≃	26	65.47 N	24.30 E
Kemiö → Kimito	26	60.10 N	22.45 E
Keml'a	80	54.42 N	45.15 E
Kemmel	50	50.47 N	2.49 E
Kemmelberg ʌ[2]	50	50.47 N	2.50 E
Kemmerer	200	41.47 N	110.32 W
Kemminghausen ◆[8]	263	51.34 N	7.29 E
Kemmuna (Comino) I	36	36.00 N	14.20 E
Kemnader See ⊜	263	51.25 N	7.15 E
Kemnath	60	49.52 N	11.54 E
Kemnay	46	57.14 N	2.27 W
Kemnitz	54	54.04 N	13.31 E
Kémo-Gribingui □[5]	152	6.00 N	19.00 E
Kemp	222	32.26 N	96.13 W
Kemp, Lake ⊜[1]	196	33.45 N	99.13 W
Kemparana	150	12.50 N	4.56 W
Kemp Coast ⊤[2]	9	67.10 S	58.00 E
Kempele	26	64.55 N	25.30 E
Kempen	56	51.22 N	6.25 E
Kempen □[9]	56	51.10 N	5.20 E
Kempener Land ◆[1]	263	51.19 N	6.29 E
Kempenfelt Bay c	212	44.23 N	79.36 W
Kempenich	56	50.25 N	7.07 E
Kemper → Quimper	32	48.00 N	4.06 W
Kempisch Kanaal ≊	56	51.10 N	4.49 E
Kemp Mill	284c	39.02 N	77.01 W
Kempner	196	31.05 N	98.00 W
Kemp Peninsula ›[1]	9	73.08 S	60.15 W

Kemps Bay	238	24.02 N	77.33 W
Kemps Creek ≃	274a	33.51 S	150.46 E
Kempsey, Austl.	166	31.05 S	152.50 E
Kempsey, Eng., U.K.	42	52.08 N	2.12 W
Kempston	42	52.07 N	0.30 W
Kempt, Lac ⊜	176	47.25 N	74.22 W
Kempten (Allgäu)	58	47.43 N	10.19 E
Kempton, Il., U.S.	216	40.56 N	88.14 W
Kempton, In., U.S.	216	40.17 N	86.13 W
Kempton Park	158	26.06 S	28.14 E
Kempton Park □[5]	273d	26.06 S	28.14 E
Kempton Park Race Course ♠	260	51.25 N	0.23 W
Kemptville	212	45.01 N	75.38 W
Kemptville Creek ≃	212	45.03 N	75.39 W
Kemsing	260	51.18 N	0.14 E
Kemubu	114	5.18 N	102.01 E
Kemujan, Pulau I	115a	5.48 S	110.28 E
Kemul, Kong ʌ	112	1.52 N	116.11 E
Ken ≃	124	25.46 N	80.31 E
Ken, Loch ⊜	44	55.02 N	4.02 W
Ken, Water of ≃	44	55.04 N	4.08 W
Kena ≃	24	62.05 N	39.06 E
Kenai	180	60.33 N	151.15 W
Kenai Fjords National Park ♠	180	59.45 N	150.00 W
Kenai Mountains ϰ	180	60.00 N	150.00 W
Kenai Peninsula ›[1]	180	60.10 N	150.00 W
Kenamuke Swamp ≡	140	6.15 N	33.48 E
Kenansville, Fl., U.S.	220	27.52 N	80.59 W
Kenansville, N.C., U.S.	192	34.57 N	77.57 W
Kenaral	85	42.32 N	72.08 E
Kenašči	80	50.32 N	53.20 E
Kenashiga-sen ʌ	96	35.14 N	133.31 E
Kenaston	184	51.30 N	106.18 W
Kenberma	283	42.17 N	70.52 W
Kenbridge	192	36.57 N	78.07 W
Kenda	126	23.12 N	86.32 E
Kendai	124	22.45 N	82.37 E
Kendal, Sk., Can.	184	50.15 N	103.37 W
Kendal, Indon.	115a	6.55 S	110.12 E
Kendal, S. Afr.	158	26.04 S	28.58 E
Kendal, Eng., U.K.	44	54.20 N	2.45 W
Kendall, Austl.	166	31.38 S	152.43 E
Kendall, Fl., U.S.	220	25.40 N	80.19 W
Kendall, Mi., U.S.	216	42.22 N	85.49 W
Kendall, N.Y., U.S.	210	43.20 N	78.02 W
Kendall, Wi., U.S.	190	43.47 N	90.22 W
Kendall □[6]	216	41.38 N	88.27 W
Kendall, Cape ›	176	63.36 N	87.09 W
Kendall, Mount ʌ	172	41.22 S	172.24 E
Kendall Park	208	40.31 N	74.24 W
Kendallville	216	41.26 N	85.15 W
Kendari	112	3.57 S	122.35 E
Kendari, Teluk c	112	3.57 S	122.38 E
Kendawangan	112	2.32 S	110.12 E
Kende	150	11.30 N	4.12 E
Kendenup	162	34.29 S	117.39 E
Kendghāta	126	24.05 N	87.10 E
Kendikolu I	122	5.57 N	73.24 E
Kendiktas ϰ	85	43.35 N	74.45 E
Kendleton	222	29.27 N	96.00 W
Kendrāparha	120	20.30 N	86.25 E
Kendrew	158	32.31 S	24.30 E
Kendrick, Fl., U.S.	192	29.22 N	82.12 W
Kendrick, Id., U.S.	202	46.36 N	116.38 W
Kendrick Creek ≃	226	38.00 N	119.50 W
Kendua	272b	22.34 N	88.10 E
Kendu Bay	154	0.22 S	34.39 E
Kendujhargarh	120	21.38 N	85.35 E
Kendyrlik	86	47.30 N	85.12 E
Kenedy	196	28.49 N	97.50 W
Kenefick	222	30.07 N	94.51 W
Kenema	150	7.52 N	11.12 W
Kenes, Kaz.	85	43.41 N	67.49 E
Kenes, Kaz.	85	43.59 N	73.35 E
Kenesaw	198	40.37 N	98.39 W
Kenga	86	57.27 N	80.57 E
Kenga ≃	86	58.05 N	80.37 E
Kenge	152	4.52 S	16.59 E
Kengeja	154	5.25 S	39.44 E
Kēng Hkam, Mya.	110	21.01 N	98.29 E
Keng Hkam, Mya.	110	21.27 N	97.03 E
Kengkou, Zhg.	100	29.48 N	117.22 E
Kengkou, Zhg.	100	28.27 N	120.26 E
Kengtian	100	25.54 N	119.26 E
Kēng Tung	110	21.17 N	99.36 E
Kengun-chūtonchi, Rikujō-jieitai- ■	92	32.46 N	130.45 E
Kenhardt	158	29.19 S	21.12 E
Kenhorst	208	40.18 N	75.57 W
Kenia	152	2.43 S	17.04 E
Kenia → Kenya □[1]	154	1.00 N	38.00 E
Kenia → Kirinyaga ʌ	154	0.10 S	37.20 E
Kéniéba	150	12.50 N	11.14 W
Kenilworth, Eng., U.K.	42	52.21 N	1.34 W
Kenilworth, Il., U.S.	278	42.05 N	87.43 W
Kenilworth, N.J., U.S.	276	40.40 N	74.17 W
Kenilworth, Pa., U.S.	208	40.14 N	75.38 W
Kenilworth, Ut,. U.S.	200	39.41 N	110.48 W
Kenilworth Castle ⊥	42	52.21 N	1.34 W
Keningau	112	5.20 N	116.10 E
Kenitra	148	34.16 N	6.40 W
Kenitra □[4]	148	34.30 N	6.00 W
Kenley ◆[8]	260	51.19 N	0.06 W
Kenli (Xishuanghe)	98	37.40 N	118.35 E
Kenly	192	35.35 N	78.07 W
Kenmare, Ire.	48	51.53 N	9.35 W
Kenmare, N.D., U.S.	198	48.40 N	102.04 W
Kenmare River ≃	48	51.45 N	10.00 W
Kenmawr	279b	40.28 N	80.06 W
Kenmore, Scot., U.K.	46	56.34 N	3.59 W
Kenmore, N.Y., U.S.	210	42.57 N	78.52 W
Kenmore, Wa., U.S.	224	47.45 N	122.14 W
Kennard, In., U.S.	218	39.54 N	85.31 W
Kennard, Pa., U.S.	214	41.28 N	80.20 W
Kennard, Tx., U.S.	222	31.22 N	95.11 W
Kennebec	198	43.54 N	99.51 W
Kennebec ≃	188	44.00 N	69.50 W
Kennebecasis Bay c	186	45.25 N	66.00 W
Kennebec Lake ⊜	212	44.43 N	77.00 W
Kennebunk	188	43.23 N	70.32 W
Kennedale	222	32.38 N	97.13 W
Kennedy, Al., U.S.	194	33.35 N	87.59 W
Kennedy, N.Y., U.S.	214	42.09 N	79.06 W
Kennedy, Zimb.	154	18.52 S	27.10 E
Kennedy, Cape → Canaveral, Cape ›	220	28.27 N	80.32 W
Kennedy, Mount ʌ, B.C., Can.	182	50.49 N	125.33 W
Kennedy, Mount ʌ, Yk., Can.	180	60.30 N	139.00 W
Kennedy Entrance ʯ	180	59.00 N	152.00 W
Kennedy Lake ⊜	182	49.05 N	125.40 W
Kennedy Peak ʌ	110	23.19 N	93.45 E
Kennedy Range ϰ	162	24.30 S	115.00 E
Kennedyville	208	39.18 N	75.59 W
Kennemerduinen, Nationale Park de ♠	52	52.25 N	4.35 E
Kenner	194	29.59 N	90.14 W
Kennerdell	214	41.16 N	79.51 W
Kennet ≃, Eng., U.K.	42	52.26 N	0.28 E
Kennet ≃, Eng., U.K.	42	51.28 N	0.57 W
Kennetcook	186	45.11 N	63.44 W
Kenneth City	220	27.49 N	82.44 W
Kennett	194	36.14 N	90.03 W
Kennett Square	208	39.50 N	75.42 W
Kennewick	202	46.12 N	119.08 W
Kenney	219	40.06 N	89.05 W
Kenney Dam ◆[6]	182	53.37 N	124.58 W
Kennington, Eng., U.K.	42	51.43 N	1.15 W
Kennington, Eng., U.K.	42	51.10 N	0.54 E

Kennisis Lake ⊜	212	45.13 N	78.39 W
Kenn Reef ✣[2]	160	21.12 S	155.46 E
Kenny	222	30.03 N	96.20 W
Kennydale	224	47.31 N	122.12 W
Kennywood Park ♠	279b	40.23 N	79.52 W
Kénogami	186	48.26 N	71.14 W
Kenogami ≃	176	51.06 N	84.28 W
Kénogami, Lac ⊜	186	48.20 N	71.23 W
Kenogamissi Lake ⊜	190	48.15 N	81.31 W
Keno Hill	180	63.55 N	135.18 W
Kenora	184	49.47 N	94.29 W
Kenosha	216	42.35 N	87.49 W
Kenosha □[6]	216	42.35 N	88.03 W
Kenova	188	38.23 N	82.34 W
Kenoza Lake	210	41.44 N	74.57 W
Kenoza Lake ⊜	283	42.47 N	71.03 W
Kenozero, ozero ⊜	24	62.03 N	38.14 E
Ken Rock	216	42.15 N	89.03 W
Kensal	198	47.18 N	98.43 W
Kense	86	46.49 N	68.20 E
Kensett	194	35.13 N	91.40 W
Kensico Lake ⊜	276	41.07 N	73.45 W
Kensico Reservoir ⊜[1]	210	41.05 N	73.46 W
Kensington, Austl.	274a	33.55 S	151.14 E
Kensington, P.E., Can.	186	46.26 N	63.38 W
Kensington, Ca., U.S.	226	37.54 N	122.16 W
Kensington, Ct., U.S.	207	41.38 N	72.46 W
Kensington, Ks., U.S.	198	39.46 N	99.01 W
Kensington, Md., U.S.	284c	39.01 N	77.04 W
Kensington, Oh., U.S.	214	40.44 N	80.57 W
Kensington ◆[8], S. Afr.	273d	26.12 S	28.06 E
Kensington ◆[8], N.Y., U.S.	276	40.39 N	73.58 W
Kensington ◆[8], Pa., U.S.	285	39.58 N	75.08 W
Kensington and Chelsea ◆[8]	260	51.29 N	0.11 W
Kensington Estates	284c	39.02 N	77.05 W
Kensington Metropolitan Park ♠	281	42.32 N	83.39 W
Kensington Park	220	27.22 N	82.31 W
Kent, S.L.	150	8.10 N	13.10 W
Kent, Ct., U.S.	207	41.43 N	73.28 W
Kent, N.Y., U.S.	210	43.20 N	78.08 W
Kent, Oh., U.S.	214	41.09 N	81.21 W
Kent, Or., U.S.	224	45.11 N	120.41 W
Kent, Wa., U.S.	224	47.22 N	122.14 W
Kent □[6], On., Can.	214	42.25 N	82.10 W
Kent □[6], Eng., U.K.	42	51.15 N	0.40 E
Kent □[6], De., U.S.	208	39.10 N	75.32 W
Kent □[6], Md., U.S.	208	39.13 N	76.04 W
Kent □[6], Mi., U.S.	216	42.56 N	85.33 W
Kent □[6], R.I., U.S.	207	41.40 N	71.38 W
Kent ≃	44	54.15 N	2.48 W
Kent, Vale of V	42	51.10 N	0.30 E
Kent Acres	208	39.07 N	75.31 W
Kentallen	46	56.39 N	5.15 W
Kentani	158	32.31 S	28.19 E
Kentau	85	43.36 N	68.36 E
Kent Bridge	214	42.31 N	82.04 W
Kent County Airport ⊠	216	42.54 N	85.39 W
Kentfield	282	37.57 N	122.33 W
Kent Group II	166	39.27 S	147.20 E
Kenthurst	274a	33.40 S	151.00 E
Kent Island I	208	38.55 N	76.20 W
Kent Lake ⊜	216	42.32 N	83.40 W
Kentland, In., U.S.	216	40.46 N	87.26 W
Kentland, Md., U.S.	284c	38.55 N	76.53 W
Kenton, Eng., U.K.	42	50.38 N	3.28 W
Kenton, De., U.S.	208	39.13 N	75.39 W
Kenton, Mi., U.S.	190	46.29 N	88.53 W
Kenton, Oh., U.S.	216	40.38 N	83.36 W
Kenton, Tn., U.S.	194	36.12 N	89.00 W
Kenton □[6]	218	38.56 N	84.33 W
Kent Park	283	42.06 N	70.41 W
Kent Park ♠	273d	26.08 S	28.04 E
Kent Peninsula ›[1]	176	68.30 N	107.00 W
Kent Point ›	208	38.50 N	76.22 W
Kentucky □[3]	178	37.30 N	85.15 W
Kentucky ≃	218	38.41 N	85.11 W
Kentucky, Middle Fork ≃	192	37.35 N	83.40 W
Kentucky, North Fork ≃	192	37.34 N	83.42 W
Kentucky, South Fork ≃	192	37.34 N	83.42 W
Kentucky Horse Park ♠	218	38.08 N	84.31 W
Kentucky Lake ⊜[1]	194	36.25 N	88.05 W
Kent Village	284c	38.55 N	76.53 W
Kentville	186	45.05 N	64.30 W
Kentwood, La., U.S.	194	30.56 N	90.30 W
Kentwood, Mi., U.S.	216	42.52 N	85.38 W
Kent Woodlands	282	37.57 N	122.34 W
Kenvil	276	40.52 N	74.37 W
Kenwick	168a	32.02 S	115.58 E
Kenwood, Ca., U.S.	226	38.25 N	122.33 W
Kenwood, Md., U.S.	284b	39.21 N	76.31 W
Kenwood, Oh., U.S.	218	39.12 N	84.22 W
Kenwood ◆[8]	278	41.49 N	87.36 W
Kenwood ⊥	260	51.34 N	0.10 W
Kenya □[1]	154	1.00 N	38.00 E
Kenya, Mount → Kirinyaga ʌ	154	0.10 S	37.20 E
Kenyon, Eng., U.K.	262	53.27 N	2.34 W
Kenyon, Mn., U.S.	190	44.16 N	92.59 W
Kenyon, R.I., U.S.	207	41.26 N	71.37 W
Ken-zaki ›	268	35.08 N	139.41 E
Kenzingen	58	48.11 N	7.46 E
Kenzou	152	4.10 N	15.02 E
Keokea	229a	20.42 N	156.21 W
Keokuk	190	40.23 N	91.23 W
Keoladeo National Park ♠	124	27.10 N	77.20 E
Keonchi	124	22.38 N	81.47 E
Keo Neua, Col de)(	110	18.23 N	105.09 E
Keon Park	274b	37.42 S	145.01 E
Keosauqua	190	40.43 N	91.57 W
Keota, Ia., U.S.	190	41.21 N	91.57 W
Keota, Ok., U.S.	196	35.15 N	94.55 W
Keowee, Lake ⊜[1]	192	34.45 N	82.55 W
Kepa (Mittagskogel) ʌ	61	46.31 N	13.57 E
Kepala Batas	114	5.31 N	100.26 E
Kepanjen	115a	8.07 S	112.34 E
Kepi	164	6.32 S	139.19 E
Kępice	30	54.15 N	16.52 E
Kepina	24	65.24 N	41.50 E
Keping Shan ϰ	85	40.00 N	77.10 E
Kępno	30	51.17 N	17.59 E
Kepo	112	2.56 S	106.33 E
Keppel Bay c	166	23.21 S	150.55 E
Keppel Harbour c	271c	1.16 N	103.50 E
Kepsut	130	39.41 N	28.09 E
Keptown	219	39.05 N	88.40 W
Kequan	98	36.04 N	114.00 E
Kerala □[3]	122	10.00 N	76.30 E
Keram ≃	164	4.07 S	144.07 E
Keramian, Pulau I	112	5.04 S	114.36 E
Kerandin	112	0.12 S	104.46 E
Kerang	166	35.44 S	143.55 E
Keranyo	144	5.04 N	38.18 E
Keratéa	38	37.48 N	23.59 E
Keratsínion	267c	37.58 N	23.37 E
Keraudren, Cape ›	162	19.57 S	119.45 E
Kerava	26	60.24 N	25.07 E
Keravat	164	4.19 S	152.01 E
Kerbat ≃	114	5.01 N	102.51 E
Kerbela → Karbalā'	128	32.36 N	44.02 E
Kerbi ≃	89	52.28 N	136.25 E
Kerby	202	42.11 N	123.39 W
Kerč'	78	45.22 N	36.27 E
Kerčel'	86	59.18 N	64.46 E
Kerčemja	24	61.28 N	53.50 E

Symbol	English	Deutsch	Español	Français	Português
≃	River	Fluß	Río	Rivière	Rio
≊	Canal	Kanal	Canal	Canal	Canal
∟	Waterfall, Rapids	Wasserfall, Stromschnellen	Cascada, Rápidos	Chute d'eau, Rapides	Cascata, Rápidos
ʯ	Strait	Meeresstraße	Estrecho	Détroit	Estreito
c	Bay, Gulf	Bucht, Golf	Bahía, Golfo	Baie, Golfe	Baía, Golfo
⊜	Lake, Lakes	See, Seen	Lago, Lagos	Lac, Lacs	Lago, Lagos
≡	Swamp	Sumpf	Pantano	Marais	Pântano
⊼	Ice Features, Glacier	Eis- und Gletscherformen	Accidentes Glaciales	Formes glaciaires	Acidentes glaciares
⊤	Other Hydrographic Features	Andere Hydrographische Objekte	Otros Elementos Hidrográficos	Autres données hydrographiques	Outros acidentes hidrográficos
✣	Submarine Features	Untermeerische Objekte	Accidentes Submarinos	Formes de relief sous-marin	Acidentes submarinos
□	Political Unit	Politische Einheit	Unidad Politica	Entité politique	Unidade política
ʊ	Cultural Institution	Kulturelle Institution	Institución Cultural	Institution culturelle	Institução cultural
⊥	Historical Site	Historische Stätte	Sitio Histórico	Site historique	Sitio histórico
♠	Recreational Site	Erholungs- und Ferienort	Sitio de Recreo	Centre de loisirs	Area de Lazer
⊠	Airport	Flughafen	Aeropuerto	Aéroport	Aeroporto
■	Military Installation	Militäranlage	Instalación Militar	Installation militaire	Instalação militar
◆	Miscellaneous	Verschiedenes	Misceláneo	Divers	Diversos

Name	Page	Lat.	Long.
Kerčenskij poluostrov ≻[1]	**78**	45.15 N	36.00 E
Kerčenskij proliv ⊔	**78**	45.22 N	36.38 E
Kerčevskij	**24**	59.55 N	56.17 E
Kerch → Kerč'	**78**	45.22 N	36.27 E
Kerckhoff Lake ⊜[1]	**226**	37.09 N	119.31 W
Kéré	**154**	5.16 N	26.11 E
Kéré ≃	**140**	5.19 N	25.40 E
Kerec, mys ≻	**24**	65.20 N	39.40 E
Kerej, ozero ⊜	**86**	50.08 N	68.45 E
Kerema	**164**	8.00 S	145.45 E
Keremeos	**182**	49.12 N	119.50 W
Kerem Maharal	**132**	32.39 N	34.59 E
Kerempe Burnu ≻	**130**	42.01 N	33.21 E
Keren	**144**	15.46 N	38.28 E
Kerend	**128**	34.16 N	46.15 E
Kerens	**222**	32.07 N	96.13 W
Kerepes	**264c**	47.34 N	19.18 E
Keret'	**24**	66.16 N	33.34 E
Keret', ozero ⊜	**24**	65.55 N	32.56 E
Kerewan	**150**	13.29 N	16.10 W
Kerga	**24**	62.39 N	46.00 E
Kergez	**84**	40.18 N	49.38 E
Kerguélen, Îles II	**6**	49.15 S	69.10 E
Kerguelen Plateau ✦[3]	**6**	55.00 S	75.00 E
Kerhonkson	**210**	41.46 N	74.17 W
Kerian ≃	**114**	5.10 N	100.26 E
Kericho	**154**	0.22 S	35.17 E
Keri Kera	**140**	12.21 N	32.46 E
Kerikeri	**172**	35.13 S	173.58 E
Kerimäki	**26**	61.55 N	29.17 E
Kerinci, Gunung ∧	**112**	1.42 S	101.16 E
Kerio ≃	**154**	2.59 N	36.07 E
Keríon	**38**	37.40 N	20.48 E
Keritang	**112**	0.51 S	102.39 E
Keriya ≃	**120**	38.30 N	82.10 E
Kerka ≃	**61**	46.28 N	16.36 E
Kerkafalva	**61**	46.46 N	16.30 E
Kerkdriel	**52**	51.46 N	5.20 E
Kerkebet	**144**	16.18 N	37.24 E
Kerken	**56**	51.27 N	6.22 E
Kerkenna, Îles II	**148**	34.44 N	11.12 E
Kerkhove	**50**	50.48 N	3.30 E
Kerkhoven	**198**	45.11 N	95.19 W
Kerki, Ross.	**24**	63.43 N	54.05 E
Kerki, Turk.	**128**	37.50 N	65.12 E
Kérkira (Corfu)	**38**	39.36 N	19.56 E
Kérkira I	**38**	39.40 N	19.42 E
Kerkrade [-Holz]	**56**	50.52 N	6.04 E
Kerling	**114**	3.35 N	101.36 E
Kermadec Islands II	**14**	29.16 S	177.55 W
Kermadec Ridge ✦[3]	**14**	30.30 S	178.30 W
Kermadec Trench ✦[1]	**14**	30.00 S	177.00 W
Kermajärvi ⊜	**26**	62.28 N	28.40 E
Kermān, Īrān	**128**	30.17 N	57.05 E
Kerman, Ca., U.S.	**226**	36.43 N	120.04 W
Kermān □[4]	**128**	29.00 N	57.30 E
Kermit	**196**	31.51 N	103.05 W
Kermit Roosevelt Seamount ✦[3]	**16**	39.35 N	146.00 W
Kermode, Mount ∧	**182**	52.57 N	131.51 W
Kern □[6]	**228**	35.20 N	118.55 W
Kern ≃	**204**	35.13 N	119.17 W
Kern, South Fork ≃	**204**	35.40 N	118.27 W
Kern City	**228**	35.18 N	119.05 W
Kernersville	**192**	36.07 N	80.04 W
Kernforschungszentrum ʊ[3]	**56**	49.07 N	8.26 E
Kernhof	**61**	47.49 N	15.32 E
Kern Island Canal ≡	**228**	35.22 N	119.01 W
Kern Lake Bed ⊜	**228**	35.10 N	119.05 W
Kern River Channel ≃[1]	**226**	35.49 N	119.40 W
Kernville	**204**	35.45 N	118.25 W
Keroh	**114**	5.43 N	101.00 E
Keros	**24**	60.44 N	52.50 E
Kérou	**150**	10.50 N	2.06 E
Kérouané	**150**	9.16 N	9.01 W
Kerowagi	**164**	5.50 S	144.50 E
Kerpen	**56**	50.52 N	6.41 E
Kerpinen'	**78**	46.47 N	28.22 E
Kerr	**214**	41.03 N	78.25 W
Kerrera I	**46**	56.23 N	5.34 W
Kerridge	**262**	53.17 N	2.06 W
Kerridge Hill ∧[2]	**262**	53.17 N	2.06 W
Kerrobert	**184**	51.55 N	109.08 W
Kerrtown	**214**	41.38 N	80.10 W
Kerruish Park ♦	**279a**	41.26 N	81.34 W
Kerrville	**196**	30.02 N	99.08 W
Kerry	**42**	52.30 N	3.16 W
Kerry □[6]	**48**	52.10 N	9.30 W
Kerry Head ≻	**48**	52.25 N	9.57 W
Kersa	**144**	9.28 N	41.53 E
Kersbrook	**168b**	34.47 S	138.51 E
Kersey	**214**	41.21 N	78.35 W
Kershaw	**192**	34.33 N	80.35 W
Kersinyane	**150**	15.24 N	10.10 W
Kersley	**182**	52.49 N	122.25 W
Kerspestausee ⊜[1]	**263**	51.08 N	7.30 E
Kerstenhausen	**56**	51.04 N	9.13 E
Kert, Oued ≃	**34**	35.15 N	3.15 W
Kertamulia	**112**	0.23 S	109.09 E
Kerteh	**114**	4.31 N	103.27 E
Kerteminde	**41**	55.27 N	10.40 E
Kertosono	**115a**	7.35 S	112.06 E
Kerulen (Cherlen) (Herlen) ≃	**90**	48.48 N	117.00 E
Kerva	**80**	55.37 N	39.35 E
Kerzaz	**148**	29.30 N	1.37 W
Kerzendorf	**264a**	52.16 N	13.17 E
Kerženec	**80**	56.28 N	44.26 E
Kerženec ≃	**80**	56.05 N	45.03 E
Kerzers	**58**	46.58 N	7.12 E
Kesabpur	**126**	22.55 N	89.13 E
Ke Sach	**110**	9.46 N	105.59 E
Kesagami Lake ⊜	**176**	50.23 N	80.15 W
Kesälahti	**26**	61.54 N	29.50 E
Keşan	**130**	40.51 N	26.37 E
Keşap	**130**	40.55 N	38.31 E
Kesbern	**263**	51.20 N	7.42 E
Kesch, Piz ∧	**58**	46.38 N	9.52 E
Kesem ≃	**144**	9.14 N	40.06 E
Kesennuma	**92**	38.54 N	141.35 E
Kesh	**48**	54.32 N	7.43 W
Keshan	**89**	48.02 N	125.51 E
Keshena	**190**	44.53 N	88.38 W
Keshendeh	**120**	36.05 N	66.51 E
Keshequa Creek ≃	**210**	42.43 N	77.50 W
Keshod	**120**	21.18 N	70.15 E
Keşiş Dağları ⋏	**130**	39.50 N	39.45 E
Keskastel	**56**	48.58 N	7.02 E
Keskin	**130**	39.41 N	33.37 E
Keski-Suomen lääni □[4]	**26**	62.30 N	25.30 E
Keskozero	**24**	61.24 N	33.12 E
Keskuvejem, gora ∧	**180**	66.12 N	177.40 W
Kes'ma	**76**	58.27 N	37.04 E
Kesova Gora	**76**	57.35 N	37.17 E
Kespur	**126**	22.35 N	87.29 E
Kesra	**36**	35.49 N	9.22 E
Kessebüren	**263**	51.31 N	7.43 E
Kessel	**56**	51.08 N	4.37 E
Kesselsdorf	**54**	51.02 N	13.35 E
Kessingland	**42**	52.25 N	1.42 E
Kesswil	**58**	47.36 N	9.20 E
Kestel Gölü ⊜	**130**	37.24 N	30.28 E
Kestell	**158**	28.19 S	28.38 E
Kesten'ga	**24**	65.55 N	31.47 E
Kestilä	**26**	64.21 N	26.17 E
Keston ◆[8]	**260**	51.22 N	0.02 E
Keswick, On., Can.	**212**	44.15 N	79.28 W
Keswick, Eng., U.K.	**44**	54.37 N	3.08 W
Keszthely	**30**	46.46 N	17.15 E
Ket' ≃	**86**	58.55 N	81.32 E
Keta	**150**	5.55 N	1.00 E
Keta ≃	**94**	34.56 N	137.50 E
Keta, ozero ⊜	**74**	68.44 N	90.00 E
Ketaka	**96**	35.30 N	134.03 E
Keta Lagoon ⊂	**150**	5.54 N	0.56 E
Ketam, Pulau I	**271c**	1.24 N	103.57 E
Ketama	**34**	34.50 N	4.37 W
Ketang	**100**	22.58 N	115.28 E
Ketapang, Indon.	**112**	1.52 S	109.59 E
Ketapang, Indon.	**115a**	6.54 S	113.17 E
Ketapang, Indon.	**115a**	5.44 S	105.48 E
Ketaun	**112**	3.23 S	101.49 E
Ketčenery	**80**	47.18 N	44.31 E
Ketchikan	**182**	55.21 N	131.35 W
Ketchum	**202**	43.40 N	114.21 W
Kete Krachi	**150**	7.46 N	0.03 W
Ketelmeer ⊜	**52**	52.35 N	5.45 E
Keti Bandar	**120**	24.08 N	67.27 E
Ketingwan ∧	**154**	0.40 N	35.50 E
Ketoj, ostrov I	**74**	47.20 N	152.28 E
Kétou	**150**	7.22 N	2.36 E
Ketovo	**86**	55.21 N	65.18 E
Kętrzyn (Rastenburg)	**30**	54.06 N	21.23 E
Ketsch	**56**	49.22 N	8.31 E
Ketta	**152**	1.28 N	15.56 E
Kettering, Eng., U.K.	**42**	52.24 N	0.44 W
Kettering, Md., U.S.	**284c**	38.53 N	76.49 W
Kettering, Oh., U.S.	**218**	39.41 N	84.10 W
Kettinge	**41**	54.42 N	11.45 E
Kettle ≃, Mb., Can.	**184**	56.23 N	94.34 W
Kettle ≃, N.A.	**182**	48.42 N	118.07 W
Kettle ≃, Mn., U.S.	**190**	45.52 N	92.45 W
Kettle Creek ≃, On., Can.	**212**	42.40 N	81.13 W
Kettle Creek ≃, Pa., U.S.	**210**	41.18 N	77.51 W
Kettle Creek State Park ♦	**214**	41.23 N	77.56 W
Kettle Falls	**202**	48.36 N	118.03 W
Kettleman City	**226**	36.00 N	119.57 W
Kettleman Hills ⋏[2]	**226**	36.00 N	120.00 W
Kettle Rapids Dam ◆[6]	**184**	56.23 N	94.38 W
Kettlersville	**216**	40.22 N	84.16 W
Kettleshulme	**262**	53.19 N	2.01 W
Kettlewell	**44**	54.09 N	2.02 W
Kettwig	**56**	51.22 N	6.56 E
Kęty	**30**	49.53 N	19.13 E
Ketzin	**54**	52.28 N	12.50 E
Keudemane	**114**	5.15 N	96.55 E
Keudepasi	**114**	4.18 N	95.56 E
Keudeteunom	**114**	4.27 N	95.48 E
Keudeunga	**114**	5.01 N	95.22 E
Keuka Lake ⊜	**210**	42.27 N	77.10 W
Keuka Lake, West Branch ⊂	**210**	42.33 N	77.09 W
Keuka Park	**210**	42.37 N	77.06 W
Keukenhof ♦	**52**	52.16 N	4.33 E
Keul'	**88**	58.25 N	102.49 E
Keula	**54**	51.20 N	10.31 E
Keum ≃	**86**	59.32 N	70.35 E
Keurboomsrivier	**158**	34.00 S	23.24 E
Keurusselkä ⊜	**26**	62.10 N	24.40 E
Keuruu	**26**	62.16 N	24.42 E
Kevdo-Mel'sitovo	**80**	53.09 N	43.54 E
Kevelaer	**52**	51.35 N	6.15 E
Kevin	**202**	48.44 N	111.57 W
Kevsala	**80**	45.48 N	42.41 E
Kew, Austl.	**169**	37.49 S	145.02 E
Kew, T./C. Is.	**238**	21.54 N	72.02 W
Kewanee	**190**	41.14 N	89.55 W
Kewanna	**216**	41.01 N	86.25 W
Kewaunee	**190**	44.27 N	87.30 W
Keweenaw Bay ⊂	**190**	46.56 N	88.23 W
Keweenaw Peninsula ≻[1]	**190**	47.12 N	88.25 W
Keweenaw Point ≻	**190**	47.30 N	87.50 W
Kew Gardens ♦, On., Can.	**275b**	43.40 N	79.18 W
Kew Gardens ♦, Eng., U.K.	**260**	51.28 N	0.18 W
Keyala	**154**	4.27 N	32.52 E
Keyangkeer Shan ∧	**120**	31.20 N	87.13 E
Keya Paha ≃	**198**	42.54 N	99.00 W
Key Biscayne	**220**	25.42 N	80.10 W
Keyes, Ca., U.S.	**226**	37.33 N	120.54 W
Keyes, Ok., U.S.	**196**	36.48 N	102.15 W
Keyesport	**219**	38.44 N	89.17 W
Keyhole Reservoir ⊜[1]	**198**	44.21 N	104.51 W
Keyhole State Park ♦	**198**	44.19 N	104.48 W
Keyihe	**89**	50.40 N	122.27 E
Keyingham	**44**	53.42 N	0.07 W
Key Largo	**220**	25.04 N	80.28 W
Key Largo I	**220**	25.16 N	80.19 W
Keymer	**42**	50.55 N	0.08 W
Keynes Hill ∧[2]	**168b**	34.37 S	139.06 E
Keyneton	**168b**	34.34 S	139.08 E
Keynsham	**42**	51.26 N	2.30 W
Keynshamburg	**154**	19.15 S	29.39 E
Keyport, N.J., U.S.	**276**	40.25 N	74.12 W
Keyport, Wa., U.S.	**224**	47.42 N	122.38 W
Keyport Harbor ⊂	**276**	40.26 N	74.12 W
Keysborough	**274b**	38.00 S	145.10 E
Keysbrook	**168a**	32.26 S	115.59 E
Keyser	**188**	39.26 N	78.58 W
Keystone, In., U.S.	**216**	40.36 N	85.16 W
Keystone, Ia., U.S.	**190**	41.59 N	92.11 W
Keystone, S.D., U.S.	**198**	43.53 N	103.25 W
Keystone, W.V., U.S.	**192**	37.24 N	81.27 W
Keystone Lake ⊜[1], Ok., U.S.	**196**	36.15 N	96.25 W
Keystone Lake ⊜[1], Pa., U.S.	**214**	40.45 N	79.15 W
Keystone Peak ∧	**200**	31.53 N	111.13 W
Keystone Race Track ♦	**285**	40.07 N	74.57 W
Keystone State Park ♦	**214**	40.23 N	79.24 W
Keysville, Fl., U.S.	**220**	27.52 N	82.06 W
Keysville, Va., U.S.	**192**	37.02 N	78.29 W
Keytesville	**194**	39.26 N	92.56 W
Key West	**220**	24.33 N	81.46 W
Key West Island I	**220**	24.33 N	81.47 W
Key West Naval Air Station ■	**220**	24.34 N	81.41 W
Keyworth	**42**	52.52 N	1.05 W
Kez	**80**	57.53 N	53.43 E
Kezar Stadium ♦	**282**	37.46 N	122.27 W
Kezi	**154**	20.58 S	28.32 E
Kezilesu Zizhizhou □[8]	**85**	40.00 N	75.30 E
Kežma	**88**	58.59 N	101.09 E
Kežmarok	**30**	49.08 N	20.25 E
Kgalagadi □[5]	**156**	25.00 S	22.00 E
Kgatleng □[5]	**156**	24.28 S	26.05 E
Kgokgole ≃	**158**	26.44 S	22.28 E
Kgun Lake ⊜	**180**	61.32 N	163.45 W
Khaanziir, Ras ≻	**144**	10.55 N	45.47 E
Khabab	**132**	33.00 N	36.16 E
Khabīr, Kūh-e ∧	**128**	28.48 N	56.26 E
Khābūr, Nahr al- (Habur) ≃	**130**	35.08 N	40.26 E
Khādar	**272a**	28.33 N	77.22 E
Khadari, Wādī al- V	**140**	10.29 N	26.15 E
Khadaungnge Taung ∧	**110**	18.57 N	94.37 E
Khadki (Kirkee)	**122**	18.34 N	73.52 E
Khadra	**34**	36.15 N	0.35 E
Khafūrī, Wādī V	**142**	29.37 N	32.04 E
Khagaria	**124**	25.30 N	86.29 E
Khagdon ≃[1]	**126**	22.09 N	90.05 E
Khāgrāmuri	**272b**	22.26 N	88.14 E
Khaïdhárion	**267c**	37.33 N	22.53 E
Khair	**124**	27.57 N	77.50 E
Khairābād	**124**	27.32 N	80.45 E
Khairāgarh	**120**	21.25 N	80.58 E
Khairbani	**126**	24.14 N	87.05 E
Khairna	**272c**	19.06 N	73.01 E
Khairpur, Pāk.	**120**	27.32 N	68.46 E
Khairpur, Pāk.	**123**	29.35 N	72.14 E
Khairwāra	**120**	23.59 N	73.35 E
Khajrāho	**120**	24.50 N	79.58 E
Khajuri	**126**	21.52 N	87.58 E
Khajuri ◆[8]	**272a**	28.43 N	77.16 E
Kha Khaeng ≃	**110**	14.55 N	99.07 E
Khakhea	**156**	24.51 S	23.20 E
Khalándrion	**267c**	38.01 N	23.48 E
Khalatse	**123**	34.20 N	76.49 E
Khālidī, Khirbat al- ⊥	**132**	29.39 N	35.14 E
Khalkhāl	**128**	37.37 N	48.32 E
Khalkhalah	**132**	33.04 N	36.32 E
Khálki I	**130**	36.17 N	27.35 E
Khalkidhikí □[9]	**38**	40.25 N	23.27 E
Khalkís	**38**	38.28 N	23.36 E
Khālsar	**120**	34.31 N	77.41 E
Khambhāliya	**120**	22.12 N	69.39 E
Khambhāt	**120**	22.18 N	72.37 E
Khambhāt, Gulf of ⊂	**122**	21.00 N	72.30 E
Khāmgaon	**122**	20.41 N	76.34 E
Khamir	**144**	16.05 N	43.55 E
Khāmis, Ash-Shallāl al- (Fifth Cataract) L	**140**	18.23 N	33.47 E
Khamīs Mushayṭ	**144**	18.18 N	42.44 E
Khamkeut	**110**	18.15 N	104.43 E
Khamma	**70**	36.47 N	12.02 E
Khammam	**122**	17.15 N	80.09 E
Khamsah	**142**	30.25 N	32.23 E
Khan ≃, Lao	**110**	19.54 N	102.09 E
Khan ≃, Namibia	**156**	22.37 S	14.56 E
Khāna	**126**	23.20 N	87.44 E
Khānābād	**120**	36.41 N	69.07 E
Khān Abū Shāmāt	**132**	33.40 N	36.54 E
Khānākul	**126**	22.43 N	87.51 E
Khān al-Baghdādī	**128**	33.51 N	42.33 E
Khānaqīn	**128**	34.21 N	45.22 E
Khān Arnabah	**132**	33.11 N	35.53 E
Khancoban	**171b**	36.12 S	148.05 E
Khandaghosh	**126**	23.13 N	87.41 E
Khandela	**120**	27.36 N	75.30 E
Khandwa	**124**	21.50 N	76.20 E
Khān-e Chahār Bāgh, Afg.	**120**	35.58 N	69.38 E
Khān-e Chahār Bāgh, Afg.	**128**	37.00 N	65.14 E
Khāneh Khvodī	**128**	36.02 N	55.59 E
Khānewāl	**123**	30.18 N	71.56 E
Khāngāh Dogrān	**123**	31.50 N	73.37 E
Khāngarh, Pāk.	**120**	28.22 N	71.43 E
Khāngarh, Pāk.	**123**	29.55 N	71.10 E
Khangkhai	**110**	19.28 N	103.15 E
Khaniá	**38**	35.31 N	24.02 E
Khaníon, Kólpos ⊂	**38**	35.34 N	23.48 E
Khānkurda	**126**	22.00 N	87.25 E
Khanna	**123**	30.42 N	76.13 E
Khannā, Qā' ≚	**132**	32.04 N	36.26 E
Khānozai	**120**	30.37 N	67.19 E
Khānpur, India	**272b**	22.40 N	88.16 E
Khānpur, Pāk.	**123**	28.39 N	70.39 E
Khānpur ◆[8], India	**272a**	28.34 N	77.01 E
Khānpur ◆[8], India	**272a**	28.31 N	77.14 E
Khān Shaykhūn	**130**	35.26 N	36.38 E
Khanty-Mansiysk → Chanty-Mansijsk	**74**	61.00 N	69.06 E
Khān Yūnus	**132**	31.21 N	34.19 E
Khao Laem Reservoir ⊜[1]	**110**	14.50 N	98.30 E
Khao Saming	**110**	12.21 N	102.27 E
Khao Sok National Park ♦	**110**	8.55 N	98.35 E
Khao Yoi	**110**	13.14 N	99.50 E
Khapalu	**123**	35.10 N	76.20 E
Khaptad National Park ♦	**124**	29.28 N	81.10 E
Kharab, Ghoubet al ⊂	**144**	11.30 N	42.35 E
Kharabā	**132**	32.34 N	36.27 E
Kharagdiha	**124**	24.25 N	86.10 E
Kharagpur, India	**124**	25.07 N	86.33 E
Kharagpur, India	**126**	22.20 N	87.20 E
Kharak	**123**	33.07 N	71.06 E
Khārān	**120**	28.35 N	65.25 E
Kharānoq	**128**	32.20 N	54.39 E
Kharar, India	**123**	30.45 N	76.39 E
Kharar, India	**126**	22.42 N	87.41 E
Khāravli ∧[2]	**272c**	18.54 N	72.55 E
Kharāyij, Sabkhat al- ⊜	**130**	35.40 N	37.20 E
Kharaz, Jabal ∧	**144**	12.44 N	44.09 E
Kharbatā	**132**	31.57 N	35.04 E
Kharbine → Harbin	**89**	45.45 N	126.41 E
Khardaha	**126**	22.44 N	88.22 E
Khārghar	**272c**	19.03 N	73.04 E
Kharg Island → Khārk, Jazīreh-ye I	**128**	29.15 N	50.20 E
Khargon	**120**	21.49 N	75.36 E
Khāriān Cantonment	**123**	32.49 N	73.52 E
Khariār Road	**122**	20.54 N	82.31 E
Khārijah, Al-Wāḥāt al- ⫪[4]	**140**	25.20 N	30.35 E
Kharīm, Jabal ∧	**132**	30.17 N	33.58 E
Kharīṭ, Wādī al- V	**140**	24.26 N	33.03 E
Khārk, Jazīreh-ye (Kharg Island) I	**128**	29.15 N	50.20 E
Kharkov → Char'kov	**78**	50.00 N	36.15 E
Kharmān, Kūh-e ∧	**128**	29.13 N	53.35 E
Kharri	**272b**	22.55 N	88.14 E
Kharsāwān	**124**	22.48 N	85.50 E
Kharsia	**124**	21.58 N	83.07 E
Khartoum → Al-Kharṭūm	**140**	15.36 N	32.32 E
Khartoum North → Al-Kharṭūm Baḥrī	**140**	15.38 N	32.33 E
Khartum → Al-Kharṭūm	**140**	15.36 N	32.32 E
Kharumwa	**154**	3.12 S	32.39 E
Khāsbāti	**272b**	22.55 N	88.25 E
Khasebake	**156**	20.41 S	24.29 E
Khāsh, Afg.	**128**	31.31 N	62.52 E
Khāsh, Īrān	**128**	28.14 N	61.14 E
Khāsh ≃	**128**	31.11 N	62.05 E
Khāsh, Dasht-e ◆[2]	**128**	31.50 N	62.30 E
Khashab, Jabal al- ∧[2]	**142**	29.56 N	31.01 E
Khashm al-Qirbah	**140**	14.58 N	35.55 E
Khashm al-Qirbah, Khazzān ⊜[1]	**140**	14.40 N	35.55 E
Khashshab, Tur'at al- ≡	**273c**	29.53 N	31.17 E
Khashum	**140**	12.27 N	28.02 E
Khāş Konar	**120**	34.39 N	70.54 E
Khaskovo → Haskovo	**38**	41.56 N	25.33 E
Khatauli	**124**	29.17 N	77.43 E
Khātegaon	**124**	22.36 N	76.55 E
Khātra	**126**	22.59 N	86.51 E
Khatt, Oued al V	**148**	26.45 N	13.03 W
Khaur	**123**	33.16 N	72.28 E
Khāvda	**120**	23.51 N	69.43 E
Khawrah	**144**	14.26 N	46.09 E
Khawsa	**110**	15.03 N	97.50 E
Khayāla ◆[8]	**272a**	28.40 N	77.06 E
Khaybar, Ḥarrat ⊥[9]	**128**	25.30 N	39.45 E
Khayerpur	**272b**	22.35 N	88.33 E
Khayl, Kathīb al- ⊥[8]	**142**	30.33 N	32.28 E
Khayra Bil ⊜	**272b**	22.52 N	88.29 E
Khayrasole	**126**	23.48 N	87.16 E
Khayung ≃	**110**	15.07 N	104.42 E
Kheardaha	**272b**	22.29 N	88.28 E
Khe Bo	**110**	19.08 N	104.41 E
Khed	**122**	17.43 N	73.23 E
Khefapur	**272a**	28.30 N	77.05 E
Khejurdaha	**272b**	22.59 N	88.10 E
Khemis	**148**	36.16 N	2.13 E
Khemis el Khechna	**34**	36.39 N	3.20 E
Khemisset	**148**	33.50 N	6.03 W
Khemisset □[4]	**148**	33.50 N	6.05 W
Khem Karan	**123**	31.09 N	74.34 E
Khemmarat	**110**	16.03 N	105.13 E
Khenchla	**148**	35.28 N	7.11 E
Khenifra	**148**	33.00 N	5.40 W
Khenifra □[4]	**148**	32.35 N	5.10 W
Khenjān	**120**	35.36 N	70.59 E
Khenyen	**272b**	22.59 N	88.19 E
Khera ◆[8]	**272a**	28.46 N	77.08 E
Kheri	**124**	27.54 N	80.48 E
Kheri Branch ≡	**124**	28.11 N	80.25 E
Kherli	**124**	27.12 N	77.02 E
Kherrata	**148**	36.31 N	5.26 E
Khersān ≃	**128**	31.33 N	50.22 E
Kherson → Cherson	**78**	46.38 N	32.35 E
Khetia	**120**	21.40 N	74.35 E
Khevāj	**120**	38.13 N	71.02 E
Khewāri	**120**	26.36 N	68.52 E
Khewra	**123**	32.39 N	73.01 E
Kheyr Khāneh	**128**	34.57 N	63.37 E
Khichīwāra Plateau ⋏[1]	**124**	24.25 N	77.30 E
Khichripur ◆[8]	**272a**	28.37 N	77.19 E
Khilchipur	**124**	24.02 N	76.34 E
Khilkāpur	**272b**	22.46 N	88.29 E
Khimki → Chimki	**82**	55.54 N	37.26 E
Khíos	**38**	38.22 N	26.08 E
Khíos I	**38**	38.22 N	26.00 E
Khipro	**120**	25.50 N	69.22 E
Khirbat al-Ghazālah	**132**	32.44 N	36.12 E
Khirbat 'Awwād	**132**	32.19 N	36.43 E
Khirbat Qanāfār	**132**	33.38 N	35.43 E
Khirbat Umm as-Surab	**132**	32.26 N	36.19 E
Khirbitā	**142**	30.45 N	30.40 E
Khiri Mat	**110**	16.50 N	99.48 E
Khirpai	**126**	22.42 N	87.37 E
Khirr, Wādī al- V	**128**	31.51 N	44.29 E
Khisfīn	**132**	32.51 N	35.49 E
Khiuri Khala ∧	**124**	29.58 N	81.18 E
Khiva → Chiva	**72**	41.24 N	60.22 E
Khlong Khlung	**110**	16.12 N	99.43 E
Khlong Thom	**110**	7.56 N	99.09 E
Khlong Yai	**110**	11.46 N	102.54 E
Khlung	**110**	12.27 N	102.14 E
Khmel'nitskiy → Chmel'nickij	**78**	49.25 N	27.00 E
Khoai, Hon I	**110**	8.26 N	104.50 E
Khogali	**140**	6.08 N	27.47 E
Khojāng ∧	**124**	28.41 N	85.09 E
Khok Kloi	**110**	8.17 N	98.19 E
Khok Pho	**110**	6.43 N	101.06 E
Khoksa	**126**	23.48 N	89.17 E
Khok Samrong	**110**	15.04 N	100.44 E
Kholargós	**267c**	38.00 N	23.48 E
Kholm	**120**	36.42 N	67.41 E
Kholombidzo Falls L	**154**	15.54 S	34.44 E
Khomām	**128**	37.22 N	49.40 E
Khomas Hochland ⋏[1]	**156**	22.30 S	16.30 E
Khomeyn	**128**	33.38 N	50.04 E
Khomeynīshahr	**128**	32.41 N	51.31 E
Khomodimo	**156**	22.46 S	23.52 E
Khondmāl Hills ⋏[2]	**122**	20.20 N	84.00 E
Khong → Mekong ≃	**12**	10.33 N	105.24 E
Khoni	**272c**	19.10 N	73.07 E
Khon Kaen	**110**	16.26 N	102.50 E
Khóra	**38**	37.04 N	21.43 E
Khorāsān □[4]	**128**	35.00 N	58.00 E
Khóra Sfakíon	**38**	35.12 N	24.09 E
Khordha	**120**	20.11 N	85.37 E
Khorel	**272b**	22.42 N	88.19 E
Khorramābād	**128**	33.30 N	48.20 E
Khorram Daraq	**128**	36.26 N	48.36 E
Khorramshahr	**128**	30.25 N	48.11 E
Khoru	**272b**	22.51 N	88.31 E
Khossanto	**150**	13.08 N	11.58 W
Khouribga	**148**	32.54 N	6.57 W
Khouribga □[4]	**148**	32.50 N	6.30 W
Khowai	**120**	24.06 N	91.38 E
Khowāng	**120**	27.16 N	94.53 E
Khowst	**120**	33.22 N	69.57 E
Khrisokhoús, Kólpos ⊂	**130**	35.06 N	32.25 E
Khrisoúpolis	**38**	40.58 N	24.42 E
Khudiān	**123**	30.59 N	74.17 E
Khuff	**128**	24.57 N	44.42 E
Khugaung	**110**	26.07 N	98.18 E
Khūgīānī Šānī	**120**	31.31 N	66.12 E
Khuis	**156**	26.37 S	21.45 E
Khuīyāla	**120**	27.14 N	70.30 E
Khu Khan	**110**	14.42 N	104.12 E
Khulna	**124**	22.48 N	89.33 E
Khulna □[5]	**126**	22.45 N	89.30 E
Khŭm Bathéay	**110**	11.59 N	104.57 E
Khumbur Khūlē Ghar ∧	**120**	32.49 N	68.47 E
Khungdugang ∧	**124**	27.31 N	89.02 E
Khūnjerāb Pass)(	**123**	36.52 N	75.27 E
Khun Tan, Doi ∧	**110**	18.30 N	99.20 E
Khunti	**124**	23.05 N	85.17 E
Khūr	**128**	32.57 N	58.26 E
Khurai	**124**	24.03 N	78.19 E
Khuralji Khās ◆[8]	**272a**	28.39 N	77.17 E
Khuria Tank ⊜[1]	**124**	22.25 N	81.36 E
Khurigāchi	**272b**	22.49 N	88.20 E
Khurīyā Murīyā, Jazā'ir II	**118**	17.30 N	56.00 E
Khurja	**124**	28.15 N	77.51 E
Khurli	**120**	28.59 N	65.52 E
Khurramshahr → Khorramshahr	**128**	30.25 N	48.11 E
Khūsf	**128**	32.46 N	58.53 E
Khushāb	**123**	32.18 N	72.21 E
Khushālgarh	**123**	33.30 N	71.54 E
Khushk Khurd ◆[8]	**272a**	28.46 N	77.10 E
Khutubi ≃	**86**	44.45 N	86.25 E
Khuwayy	**140**	13.05 N	29.14 E
Khuzdār	**120**	27.48 N	66.37 E
Khūzestān □[4]	**128**	31.00 N	49.00 E
Khvāf	**128**	34.33 N	60.08 E
Khvājeh Moḥammad, Kūh-e ⋏	**120**	36.22 N	70.17 E
Khvājeh Ra'ūf	**120**	33.19 N	64.43 E
Khvor	**128**	33.47 N	55.03 E
Khvormūj	**128**	28.39 N	51.23 E
Khvoy	**128**	38.33 N	44.58 E
Khwae Noi ≃	**110**	14.01 N	99.32 E
Khyber Pass)(	**123**	34.05 N	71.10 E
Kia	**175e**	7.33 S	158.26 E
Kialwe	**154**	9.22 S	27.08 E
Kiama, Austl.	**170**	34.41 S	150.51 E
Kiama, Zaïre	**152**	7.15 S	17.44 E
Kiamba	**116**	5.59 N	124.37 E
Kiambi	**154**	7.20 S	28.01 E
Kiamboni, Kap → Jumbo, Raas ≻	**144**	1.39 S	41.36 E
Kiambu	**154**	1.10 S	36.50 E
Kiamesha Lake	**210**	41.41 N	74.40 W
Kiamichi ≃	**194**	33.57 N	95.14 W
Kiamika ≃	**206**	46.38 N	75.15 W
Kiamika, Barrage ◆[6]	**206**	46.37 N	75.08 W
Kiamika, Réservoir ⊜[1]	**206**	46.40 N	75.05 W
Kiamusze → Jiamusi	**89**	46.50 N	130.21 E
Kiana	**180**	66.59 N	160.25 W
Kiandra	**171b**	35.53 S	148.30 E
Kiangara	**157b**	17.58 S	47.02 E
Kiangarow, Mount ∧	**166**	26.49 S	151.33 E
Kiangsi → Jiangxi □[4]	**100**	28.00 N	116.00 E
Kiangsu → Jiangsu □[4]	**90**	33.00 N	120.00 E
Kian → Ji'an	**100**	27.07 N	114.58 E
Kiantajärvi ⊜	**26**	65.03 N	29.07 E
Kiaohsien → Jiaoxian	**98**	36.18 N	119.58 E
Kibæk	**41**	56.02 N	8.51 E
Kibaha	**154**	6.46 S	38.55 E
Kibali ≃	**154**	3.37 N	28.34 E
Kibali-Sturi Game Reserve ◆[4]	**154**	2.45 N	29.33 E
Kibamba	**154**	4.53 S	26.33 E
Kibanga Port	**154**	0.11 N	32.52 E
Kibangou	**152**	3.27 S	12.21 E

ENGLISH

Name	Page	Lat.°′	Long.°′
Kibanseke	**273b**	4.26 S	15.23 E
Kibar	**120**	32.20 N	78.01 E
Kibara	**154**	2.09 S	33.27 E
Kibāsī	**128**	30.34 N	47.50 E
Kibau Iyayi	**154**	8.52 S	34.32 E
Kibawe	**116**	7.34 N	125.00 E
Kibaya	**154**	5.18 S	36.34 E
Kibenga	**152**	7.55 S	17.35 E
Kibeni	**164**	7.25 S	143.48 E
Kiberashi	**154**	5.23 S	37.26 E
Kiberege	**154**	7.57 S	36.52 E
Kibi	**150**	6.10 N	0.33 W
Kibi-kōgen ⋏[1]	**96**	34.45 N	133.15 E
Kibila	**154**	8.14 S	26.23 E
Kibiti	**154**	7.44 S	38.57 E
Kibler Park	**273d**	26.18 S	28.00 E
Kiboga	**154**	1.02 N	30.58 E
Kiboko	**154**	2.15 S	37.42 E
Kibombo	**154**	3.54 S	25.55 E
Kibondo	**154**	3.35 S	30.42 E
Kibouendé, Congo	**273b**	4.19 S	15.11 E
Kibouendé, Congo	**273b**	4.17 S	15.09 E
Kibouendé I	**273b**	4.11 S	15.09 E
Kibouendé II	**273b**	4.12 S	15.09 E
Kibre Mengist	**144**	5.52 N	39.00 E
Kıbrısçık	**130**	40.25 N	31.51 E
Kıbrıs → Cyprus □[1]	**130**	35.00 N	33.00 E
Kibumbu	**154**	3.32 S	29.45 E
Kibungo	**154**	2.10 S	30.32 E
Kibuye, Bdi.	**154**	3.40 S	29.59 E
Kibuye, Rw.	**154**	2.03 S	29.21 E
Kibwesa	**154**	6.28 S	29.57 E
Kibwezi	**154**	2.25 S	37.58 E
Kibworth Harcourt	**42**	52.32 N	0.59 W
Kičevo	**38**	41.31 N	20.57 E
Kichčik	**74**	53.24 N	156.03 E
Kichijōji	**268**	35.42 N	139.35 E
Kickany	**78**	46.47 N	29.36 E
Kickapoo ≃	**190**	43.05 N	90.53 W
Kickapoo Creek ≃, Il., U.S.	**194**	40.08 N	89.27 W
Kickapoo Creek ≃, Il., U.S.	**219**	40.08 N	89.27 W
Kickapoo Creek ≃, Tx., U.S.	**196**	31.31 N	99.58 W
Kickapoo Creek ≃, Tx., U.S.	**222**	30.47 N	95.08 W
Kickapoo Creek ≃, Tx., U.S.	**222**	32.16 N	95.28 W
Kicking Horse Pass)(	**182**	51.27 N	116.18 W
Kičkino	**80**	47.05 N	44.02 E
Kičma	**80**	57.12 N	48.55 E
Kicman'	**78**	48.27 N	25.44 E
Kičmengskij Gorodok	**24**	59.59 N	45.48 E
Kičuj ≃	**80**	55.13 N	51.16 E
Kidal	**150**	18.26 N	1.24 E
Kidapawan	**116**	7.01 N	125.03 E
Kidatu	**154**	7.42 S	36.57 E
Kidbrooke ◆[8]	**260**	51.28 N	0.02 E
Kidderminster	**42**	52.23 N	2.14 W
Kidderpore ◆[8]	**272b**	22.31 N	88.19 E
Kidderpore Docks ◆[5]	**272b**	22.33 N	88.19 E
Kidd's Beach	**158**	33.09 S	27.42 E
Kidepo National Park ♦	**154**	3.50 N	33.40 E
Kidete, Tan.	**154**	6.25 S	37.16 E
Kidete, Tan.	**154**	6.39 S	36.42 E
Kidira	**150**	14.28 N	12.13 W
Kidlington	**42**	51.50 N	1.17 W
Kidnappers, Cape ≻	**172**	39.39 S	177.07 E
Kido	**164**	9.15 S	146.55 E
Kidričevo	**61**	46.24 N	15.47 E
Kidron	**214**	40.44 N	81.45 W
Kidsgrove	**44**	53.06 N	2.15 W
Kidston	**166**	18.53 S	144.10 E
Kidugallo	**154**	6.47 S	38.12 E
Kidul, Pegunungan ⋏	**115a**	8.13 S	111.30 E
Kidwelly	**42**	51.45 N	4.18 W
Kiefersfelden	**64**	47.37 N	12.11 E
Kiekebusch	**264a**	52.21 N	13.33 E
Kiel, Dtsch.	**41**	54.20 N	10.08 E
Kiel, Wi., U.S.	**190**	43.54 N	88.02 W
Kiel Canal → Nord-Ostsee-Kanal ≡	**30**	53.53 N	9.08 E
Kielce	**30**	50.52 N	20.37 E
Kielce □[4]	**30**	50.30 N	20.30 E
Kielder	**44**	55.14 N	2.35 W
Kielder Reservoir ⊜[1]	**44**	55.11 N	2.30 W
Kieler Bucht (Kiel Bay) ⊂	**41**	54.35 N	10.35 E
Kieler Förde ⊂	**41**	54.24 N	10.12 E
Kiembara	**150**	13.15 N	2.44 W
Kienberg	**264a**	52.40 N	12.54 E
Kienge	**154**	10.34 S	27.33 E
Kienitz	**54**	52.40 N	14.26 E
Kiens → Chienes	**64**	46.48 N	11.50 E
Kiental	**58**	46.35 N	7.43 E
Kierling	**264b**	48.19 N	16.17 E
Kierspe	**56**	51.08 N	7.35 E
Kierspe-Bahnhof	**263**	51.08 N	7.37 E
Kiester	**190**	43.32 N	93.42 W
Kieta	**175e**	6.13 S	155.38 E
Kietrz	**30**	50.05 N	18.01 E
Kietz	**54**	52.34 N	14.36 E
Kiev → Kijev	**78**	50.26 N	30.31 E
Kiev Station ◆[5]	**265b**	55.45 N	37.34 E
Kiew → Kijev	**78**	50.26 N	30.31 E
Kifaya	**150**	12.10 N	13.04 W
Kiffa	**150**	16.37 N	11.24 W
Kifisiá	**38**	38.04 N	23.48 E
Kifisós ≃, Ellás	**38**	38.26 N	23.15 E
Kifisós ≃, Ellás	**267c**	38.06 N	23.45 E
Kifrī	**128**	34.42 N	44.58 E
Kifrī, Jabal ∧	**142**	27.48 N	32.50 E
Kigač ≃	**80**	46.28 N	49.12 E
Kigali	**154**	1.57 S	30.04 E
Kiği	**130**	39.19 N	40.21 E
Kigille	**140**	8.40 N	34.02 E
Kigoma	**154**	4.52 S	29.38 E
Kigoma □[4]	**154**	4.30 S	30.30 E
Kigun, Cape ≻	**180**	52.00 N	175.21 W
Kigwa	**154**	5.10 S	33.08 E
Kihei	**229a**	20.47 N	156.27 W
Kihikihi	**172**	38.02 S	175.21 E
Kihniö	**26**	62.12 N	23.11 E
Kihnu I	**76**	58.08 N	24.00 E
Kiholo Bay ⊂	**229d**	19.52 N	155.56 W
Kihundo	**154**	9.25 S	38.59 E
Kihurio	**154**	4.28 S	38.04 E
Kii-hantō ≻[1]	**92**	34.00 N	135.45 E
Kiik	**86**	47.31 N	72.55 E
Kiikkaškan	**86**	49.28 N	77.04 E
Kiiminginjoki ≃	**26**	65.12 N	25.18 E
Kii-nagashima	**92**	34.12 N	136.20 E
Kiirun → Chilung	**100**	25.08 N	121.44 E
Kii-sanchi ⋏	**92**	34.00 N	135.50 E
Kii-suidō ⊔	**96**	33.55 N	134.55 E
Kija ≃	**86**	56.52 N	86.39 E
Kijabe	**154**	0.56 S	36.34 E
Kijakty, ozero ⊜	**86**	50.00 N	69.15 E
Kijal	**114**	4.21 N	103.29 E
Kijaly	**86**	54.17 N	69.41 E
Kijasovo	**80**	56.21 N	53.07 E
Kijev (Kiev)	**78**	50.26 N	30.31 E
Kijevka, Kaz.	**86**	50.16 N	71.34 E
Kijevka, Ross.	**80**	46.05 N	42.57 E
Kijevka, Ross.	**80**	50.46 N	48.28 E
Kijevskoje	**78**	45.03 N	37.52 E
Kijevskoje vodochranilišče ⊜[1]	**78**	51.00 N	30.25 E
Kijima-chosuichi ⊜	**96**	35.04 N	132.44 E
Kijimadaira	**94**	36.51 N	138.24 E
Kijima-dam ◆[6]	**96**	35.05 N	132.44 E
Kijma	**86**	51.35 N	67.34 E

DEUTSCH

Name	Seite	Breite°′	Länge°′ E = Ost
Kijoka	**174m**	26.42 N	128.09 E
Kikagati	**154**	1.02 S	30.40 E
Kikai-shima I	**93b**	28.19 N	129.59 E
Kikale	**154**	7.50 S	39.12 E
Kikati ≃	**152**	14.48 S	12.28 E
Kikenka ≃	**265a**	59.52 N	30.04 E
Kikerino	**76**	59.28 N	29.35 E
Kikerk Lake ⊜	**176**	67.20 N	113.20 W
Kikimi	**273b**	4.26 S	15.25 E
Kikimorka	**80**	58.10 N	49.27 E
Kikinda	**38**	45.50 N	20.28 E
Kikládhes (Cyclades) II	**38**	37.30 N	25.00 E
Kiklah	**146**	32.05 N	12.41 E
Kiknur	**80**	57.19 N	47.14 E
Kikombo, Zaïre	**152**	5.59 S	18.09 E
Kikombo, Zaïre	**152**	5.40 S	18.48 E
Kikongo	**152**	4.16 S	17.11 E
Kikori	**164**	7.25 S	144.15 E
Kikori ≃	**164**	7.10 S	144.05 E
Kikorze	**54**	53.39 N	15.01 E
Kiku ≃	**94**	34.39 N	138.04 E
Kikuchi	**96**	32.59 N	130.49 E
Kikuchi ≃	**96**	32.56 N	130.35 E
Kikugawa, Nihon	**94**	34.45 N	138.05 E
Kikugawa, Nihon	**96**	34.07 N	131.02 E
Kikuka	**96**	33.02 N	130.46 E
Kikuma	**96**	34.03 N	132.53 E
Kikuna	**268**	35.10 N	139.40 E
Kikusui	**96**	32.58 N	130.36 E
Kikvidze, Ross.	**80**	50.53 N	42.46 E
Kikvidze, Ross.	**80**	50.44 N	43.03 E
Kikvorsberg ⋏	**158**	31.17 S	25.20 E
Kikwit	**152**	5.02 S	18.49 E
Kil	**26**	59.30 N	13.19 E
Kilaån ≃	**40**	58.44 N	17.01 E
Kilafors	**26**	61.14 N	16.34 E
Kila Kila	**164**	9.30 S	147.10 E
Kīlakkarai	**122**	9.14 N	78.47 E
Kilambé, Cerro ∧	**236**	13.34 N	85.42 W
Kilauea	**229b**	22.12 N	159.24 W
Kilauea Crater ⊥[6]	**229d**	19.25 N	155.17 W
Kilauea Point ≻	**229b**	22.14 N	159.24 W
Kilb	**61**	48.06 N	15.24 E
Kilbaha	**48**	52.33 N	9.52 W
Kilbarchan	**46**	55.50 N	4.33 W
Kılbasan	**130**	37.20 N	33.12 E
Kilbeggan	**48**	53.22 N	7.29 W
Kilbirnie	**46**	55.46 N	4.41 W
Kilbourne, Il., U.S.	**219**	40.09 N	90.01 W
Kilbourne, Oh., U.S.	**214**	40.20 N	82.58 W
Kilbrannan Sound ⊔	**46**	55.40 N	5.25 W
Kilbride	**46**	57.05 N	7.27 W
Kilbuck Mountains ⋏	**180**	60.50 N	159.45 W
Kilbuck Run ≃	**279b**	40.31 N	80.08 W
Kilcar	**48**	54.38 N	8.35 W
Kilchberg	**58**	47.19 N	8.33 E
Kilchis ≃	**224**	45.30 N	123.52 W
Kilchoan	**46**	56.42 N	6.06 W
Kilchreest	**48**	53.10 N	8.38 W
Kilchrenan	**46**	56.21 N	5.11 W
Kilchu	**98**	40.58 N	129.20 E
Kilcock	**48**	53.24 N	6.40 W
Kilcolgan	**48**	53.13 N	8.52 W
Kilconnell	**48**	53.20 N	8.25 W
Kilcoole	**48**	53.06 N	6.04 W
Kilcormac	**48**	53.10 N	7.43 W
Kilcoy	**171a**	26.57 S	152.33 E
Kilcreggan	**46**	55.59 N	4.50 W
Kilcullen	**48**	53.08 N	6.45 W
Kildare (Saint-Ambroise-de-Kildare), P.Q., Can.	**206**	46.05 N	73.32 W
Kildare, Ire.	**48**	53.10 N	6.55 W
Kildare □[6]	**48**	53.15 N	6.45 W
Kildare, Cape ≻	**186**	46.52 N	63.58 W
Kildeer	**278**	42.10 N	88.03 W
Kil'din, ostrov I	**24**	69.22 N	34.12 E
Kil'dinstroj	**24**	68.48 N	33.06 E
Kildonan, B.C., Can.	**182**	49.00 N	125.00 W
Kildonan, Scot., U.K.	**46**	58.10 N	3.51 W
Kildonan, Zimb.	**154**	17.21 S	30.37 E
Kildonan, Strath of V	**46**	58.09 N	3.51 W
Kildorrery	**48**	52.14 N	8.26 W
Kildrummy Castle ⊥	**46**	57.14 N	2.52 W
Kildurk	**164**	16.26 S	129.37 E
Kilemary	**80**	56.47 N	46.52 E
Kilembe, Ug.	**154**	0.12 N	30.00 E
Kilembe, Zaïre	**152**	5.42 S	19.55 E
Kilfenora	**48**	52.59 N	9.13 W
Kilfinnane	**48**	52.21 N	8.28 W
Kilgard	**224**	49.03 N	122.12 W
Kilgarvan	**48**	51.45 N	9.26 W
Kilgore, Oh., U.S.	**214**	40.28 N	81.00 W
Kilgore, Tx., U.S.	**222**	32.23 N	94.52 W
Kilham	**44**	54.04 N	0.23 W
Kili I	**14**	5.39 N	169.04 E
Kilian Island I	**176**	73.35 N	107.53 W
Kilibo	**150**	8.34 N	2.36 E
Kılıç	**130**	40.38 N	29.23 E
Kilifi	**154**	3.38 S	39.51 E
Kilija	**78**	45.27 N	29.16 E
Kilikollūr	**122**	8.54 N	76.39 E
Kilima	**154**	0.59 S	29.12 E
Kilimanjaro □[4]	**154**	3.45 S	37.45 E
Kilimanjaro ∧	**154**	3.04 S	37.22 E
Kilimanjaro Game Reserve ◆[4]	**154**	3.05 S	37.20 E
Kilimatinde	**154**	5.51 S	34.57 E
Kilimavony	**157b**	23.48 S	43.41 E
Kilimli	**130**	41.28 N	31.50 E
Kilindoni	**154**	7.55 S	39.39 E
Kilingi-Nõmme	**76**	58.09 N	24.58 E
Kilis	**130**	36.44 N	37.05 E
Kilkare Woods	**282**	37.38 N	121.55 W
Kilkee	**48**	52.41 N	9.38 W
Kilkeel	**48**	54.04 N	6.00 W
Kilkelly	**48**	53.53 N	8.51 W
Kilkenny (Cill Chainnigh)	**48**	52.39 N	7.15 W
Kilkenny □[6]	**48**	52.40 N	7.20 W
Kilkerrin	**48**	53.33 N	8.34 W
Kilkhampton	**42**	50.53 N	4.29 W
Kilkieran	**48**	53.19 N	9.43 W
Kilkieran Bay ⊂	**48**	53.15 N	9.45 W
Kilkís	**38**	41.00 N	22.53 E
Killadoon	**48**	53.42 N	9.56 W
Killadysert	**48**	52.41 N	9.06 W
Killala	**48**	54.13 N	9.13 W
Killala Bay ⊂	**48**	54.15 N	9.10 W
Killaloe	**48**	52.48 N	8.27 W
Killaloe Station	**190**	45.33 N	77.25 W
Killam	**182**	52.47 N	111.51 W
Killara	**274a**	33.46 S	151.09 E
Killarney, Austl.	**166**	28.20 S	152.18 E
Killarney, Mb., Can.	**184**	49.12 N	99.42 W
Killarney, On., Can.	**190**	45.58 N	81.31 W
Killarney, Ire.	**48**	52.03 N	9.30 W
Killarney, Lake ⊜	**240b**	25.03 N	77.27 W
Killarney, Lakes of ⊜	**48**	52.01 N	9.30 W
Killarney Heights	**274a**	33.46 S	151.13 E
Killarney Provincial Park ♦	**190**	46.05 N	81.30 W
Killashandra	**48**	54.00 N	7.32 W
Killavally	**48**	53.45 N	9.23 W
Killawog	**210**	42.24 N	76.01 W
Killbear Provincial Park ♦	**212**	45.21 N	80.12 W
Kill Buck, N.Y., U.S.	**210**	42.10 N	78.41 W
Killbuck, Oh., U.S.	**214**	40.29 N	81.59 W
Killbuck Creek ≃, Il., U.S.	**216**	42.10 N	89.06 W
Killbuck Creek ≃, In., U.S.	**218**	40.07 N	85.41 W
Killbuck Creek ≃, Oh., U.S.	**214**	40.20 N	81.57 W
Killdeer	**198**	47.22 N	102.45 W
Killean	**46**	55.39 N	5.40 W
Killearn	**46**	56.03 N	4.22 W
Killeen	**222**	31.07 N	97.43 W
Killen	**194**	34.51 N	87.32 W

Symbols in the index entries represent the broad categories identified in the key at the right. Symbols with superior numbers (⋏[1]) identify subcategories (see complete key on page *I · 1*).

Symbole im Register stellen die rechts im Schlüssel erklärten Kategorien dar. Symbole mit hochgestellten Ziffern (⋏[1]) bezeichnen Unterabteilungen einer Kategorie (vgl. vollständiger Schlüssel auf Seite *I · 1*).

Los símbolos incluídos en el texto del índice representan las grandes categorias identificadas con la clave a la derecha. Los símbolos con numeros en su parte superior (⋏[1]) identifican las subcategorías (véase la clave completa en la página *I · 1*).

Les symboles de l'index représentent les catégories indiquées dans la légende à droite. Les symboles suivis d'un indice (⋏[1]) représentent des sous-catégories (voir légende complète à la page *I · 1*).

Os símbolos incluídos no texto do índice representam as grandes categorias identificadas com a chave à direita. Os símbolos com números em sua parte superior (⋏[1]) identificam as subcategorias (veja-se a chave completa à página *I · 1*).

∧ Mountain	Berg	Montaña	Montagne	Montanha
⋏ Mountains	Gebirge	Montañas	Montagnes	Montanhas
)(Pass	Paß	Paso	Col	Passo
V Valley, Canyon	Tal, Cañon	Valle, Cañón	Vallée, Canyon	Vale, Canhão
≚ Plain	Ebene	Llano	Plaine	Planície
≻ Cape	Kap	Cabo	Cap	Cabo
I Island	Insel	Isla	Île	Ilha
II Islands	Inseln	Islas	Îles	Ilhas
⊥ Other Topographic Features	Andere Topographische Objekte	Otros Elementos Topográficos	Autres données topographiques	Outros acidentes topográficos

ESPAÑOL

Nombre	Página	Lat.°′	Long.°′ W = Oeste
Killenaule	48	52.34 N	7.40 W
Killeter	48	54.40 N	7.41 W
Killıdağ ∧	130	40.21 N	42.10 E
Killik ≃	180	69.00 N	153.58 W
Killilan	46	57.19 N	5.25 W
Killimor	48	53.10 N	8.17 W
Killin	46	56.28 N	4.19 W
Killington Peak ∧	188	43.36 N	72.49 W
Killingworth	207	41.21 N	72.33 W
Killíni	38	37.55 N	21.09 E
Killíni ∧	38	37.57 N	22.23 E
Killiniq Island I	176	60.24 N	64.40 W
Killinkoski	26	62.24 N	23.52 E
Killorglin	48	52.06 N	9.47 W
Killough	48	54.16 N	5.39 W
Killpecker Creek ≃	202	41.35 N	109.14 W
Killucan	48	53.31 N	7.07 W
Kill Van Kull ᵿ	276	40.39 N	74.05 W
Killybegs	48	54.38 N	8.27 W
Killyleagh	48	54.24 N	5.39 W
Kilmacolm	46	55.54 N	4.38 W
Kilmacthomas	48	52.12 N	7.25 W
Kilmaine	48	53.34 N	9.09 W
Kilmallock	48	52.23 N	8.34 W
Kilmaluag	46	57.41 N	6.17 W
Kilmarnock, Scot., U.K.	46	55.36 N	4.30 W
Kilmarnock, Va., U.S.	208	37.42 N	76.22 W
Kilmartin	46	56.07 N	5.29 W
Kilmar Tor ∧[2]	42	50.33 N	4.28 W
Kilmaurs	46	55.39 N	4.32 W
Kilmelford	46	56.16 N	5.29 W
Kil'mez', Ross.	80	56.57 N	51.04 E
Kil'mez', Ross.	80	57.04 N	51.21 E
Kil'mez' ≃	80	56.58 N	50.28 E
Kilmichael	194	33.26 N	89.34 W
Kilmichael Point ›	48	52.44 N	6.10 W
Kilmore	169	37.18 S	144.57 E
Kilmore Creek ≃	216	40.20 N	86.38 W
Kilmory	46	57.03 N	6.22 W
Kilnaleck	48	53.52 N	7.19 W
Kilninver	46	56.20 N	5.31 W
Kilo	115b	8.21 S	118.24 E
Kilokri ◆[8]	272a	28.35 N	77.16 E
Kiloli	154	6.50 S	33.23 E
Kilombero ≃	154	8.31 S	37.22 E
Kilomines	154	1.48 N	30.14 E
Kilondo	154	9.46 S	34.21 E
Kilosa	154	6.50 S	36.59 E
Kilpisjärvi	24	69.03 N	20.48 E
Kilrea	48	54.58 N	6.35 W
Kilrenny	46	56.14 N	2.41 W
Kilrush	48	52.39 N	9.30 W
Kilsbergen ⋏[2]	40	59.20 N	14.47 E
Kilsmo	40	59.04 N	15.31 E
Kilsyth, Austl.	274b	37.48 S	145.19 E
Kilsyth, Scot., U.K.	46	55.59 N	4.04 W
Kiltealy	48	52.34 N	6.45 W
Kiltimagh	48	53.51 N	9.01 W
Kiltoom	48	53.28 N	8.01 W
Kilttān Island I	122	11.29 N	73.00 E
Kiltu-ri	98	34.35 N	127.20 E
Kilwa	154	9.18 S	28.25 E
Kilwa Island I	154	9.20 S	28.33 E
Kilwa Kivinje	154	8.45 S	39.24 E
Kilwa Masoko	154	8.56 S	39.31 E
Kilwinning	44	55.40 N	4.42 W
Kim	198	37.14 N	103.21 W
Kim ≃	152	5.28 N	11.07 E
Kima	154	1.26 S	26.43 E
Kimaam	164	7.58 S	138.53 E
Kimamba	154	6.47 S	37.08 E
Kimande	154	7.22 S	35.30 E
Kīmān Fāris (Crocodilopolis) (Arsinoe) ⊥	142	29.19 N	30.50 E
Kimba	166	33.09 S	136.25 E
Kimball, Mn., U.S.	190	45.19 N	94.18 W
Kimball, Ne., U.S.	198	41.14 N	103.39 W
Kimball, S.D., U.S.	198	43.44 N	98.57 W
Kimball, Mount ∧	180	63.14 N	144.39 W
Kimbanda	152	4.07 S	17.59 E
Kimbe	164	5.31 S	150.10 E
Kimbe Bay ⊂	164	5.30 S	150.30 E
Kimberley, B.C., Can.	182	49.41 N	115.59 W
Kimberley, S. Afr.	158	28.43 S	24.46 E
Kimberley, Eng., U.K.	44	52.59 N	1.16 W
Kimberley Downs	162	17.24 S	124.22 E
Kimberley Plateau ⋏[1]	160	17.00 S	127.00 E
Kimberling City	194	36.38 N	93.28 W
Kimberly, Id., U.S.	202	42.32 N	114.21 W
Kimberly, Wi., U.S.	190	44.16 N	88.20 W
Kimberton	208	40.08 N	75.34 W
Kimbolton, N.Z.	172	40.03 S	175.47 E
Kimbolton, Eng., U.K.	42	52.18 N	0.24 W
Kimbolton, Oh., U.S.	214	40.09 N	81.34 W
Kimbongo	152	6.08 S	18.01 E
Kimbwala	273b	4.22 S	15.12 E
Kimch'aek (Sŏngjin)	98	40.41 N	129.12 E
Kimch'ŏn	98	36.07 N	128.05 E
Kimerka ≃	82	56.52 N	37.22 E
Kimhae	98	35.14 N	128.52 E
Kimhwa	98	38.26 N	127.36 E
Kími	38	38.37 N	24.06 E
Kimil'tej	88	54.08 N	101.59 E
Kimito (Kemiö)	26	60.10 N	22.45 E
Kimito I	26	60.07 N	22.40 E
Kimi-tōge ∧[2]	270	34.43 N	135.06 E
Kimi-tōge)(	96	34.23 N	135.37 E
Kimitsu	94	35.20 N	139.54 E
Kimiwan Lake ◎	182	55.45 N	116.54 W
Kimje	98	35.48 N	126.52 E
Kim Kim ≃	271c	1.26 N	103.58 E
Kimmell	216	41.23 N	85.32 W
Kim-me-ni-oli Wash V	200	36.07 N	108.11 W
Kímolos I	38	36.48 N	24.34 E
Kimongo	152	4.29 S	12.58 E
Kimovsk	76	53.58 N	38.32 E
Kimpangu	152	5.51 S	15.01 E
Kim Plan	279b	40.20 N	79.44 W
Kimp'o	271b	37.37 N	126.43 E
Kimp'o Airport ⊠	271b	37.33 N	126.48 E
Kimpombo	273b	4.17 S	15.10 E
Kimpō-zan ∧	94	35.53 N	138.38 E
Kimry	82	56.52 N	37.21 E
Kimsquit	182	52.49 N	126.58 W
Kimstad	40	58.32 N	15.58 E
Kimu ≃	268	35.56 N	139.57 E
Kimuenza	273b	4.27 S	15.17 E
Kimvula	152	5.44 S	15.58 E
Kimwanga	154	7.08 S	28.42 E
Kin	174m	26.26 N	127.55 E
Kinabalian, Mount ∧	116	8.14 N	125.25 E
Kinabalu, Gunong ∧	112	6.05 N	116.33 E
Kinabalu National Park ♠	112	6.05 N	116.33 E
Kinabatangan ≃	112	5.42 N	118.23 E
Kınalı ◆[8]	267b	40.55 N	29.03 E
Kınalı Ada I	267b	40.55 N	29.03 E
Kinangaly ∧	157b	19.12 S	45.40 E
Kinango	154	4.08 S	39.19 E
Kinapusan Island I	116	5.13 N	120.40 E
Kinara	164	2.16 S	132.44 E
Kinasa	94	36.42 N	138.01 E
Kinaūni	272a	28.39 N	77.23 E
Kinbasket Lake ◎[1]	182	51.58 N	118.03 W
Kinbrace	46	58.15 N	3.56 W
Kinbuck	46	56.13 N	3.57 W
Kincaid, Sk., Can.	184	49.39 N	107.00 W
Kincaid, Il., U.S.	219	39.35 N	89.24 W
Kincardine, On., Can.	190	44.11 N	81.38 W
Kincardine, Scot., U.K.	46	56.04 N	3.44 W
Kinchafoonee Creek ≃	192	31.38 N	84.10 W
Kinchang	110	26.32 N	98.02 E
Kinchara	272b	22.53 N	88.32 E
Kinchega National Park ♠	166	32.30 S	142.20 E

FRANÇAIS

Nom	Page	Lat.°′	Long.°′ W = Ouest
Kincheloe Air Force Base ■	190	46.15 N	84.28 W
Kincolith	182	55.00 N	129.57 W
Kincraig	46	57.08 N	3.55 W
Kinda, Zaïre	152	4.47 S	21.48 E
Kinda, Zaïre	154	9.18 S	25.04 E
Kindadal	112	1.35 S	123.11 E
Kindanba	152	3.44 S	14.31 E
Kindarun Mountain ∧	170	32.49 S	150.41 E
Kindberg	61	47.31 N	15.27 E
Kinde	190	43.56 N	82.59 W
Kindeje	152	7.07 S	13.44 E
Kindel'a	80	51.36 N	52.58 E
Kindel'a ≃	80	51.30 N	52.45 E
Kindelbrück	54	51.16 N	11.05 E
Kindele	152	8.39 S	24.11 E
Kinder	194	30.29 N	92.51 W
Kinderhook, Il., U.S.	219	39.42 N	91.09 W
Kinderhook, Mi., U.S.	216	41.48 N	85.00 W
Kinderhook, N.Y., U.S.	210	42.23 N	73.41 W
Kinderhook Creek ≃	210	42.19 N	73.45 W
Kinder Reservoir ◎[1]	262	53.23 N	1.55 W
Kinder Scout ∧	44	53.23 N	1.52 W
Kindersley	184	51.27 N	109.10 W
Kindia	150	10.04 N	12.51 W
Kindikan	88	56.02 N	115.15 E
Kinding	60	49.00 N	11.23 E
Kindley Field ⊠	240a	32.22 N	64.40 W
Kindred	198	46.38 N	97.01 W
Kindu	154	2.57 S	25.56 E
Kindykty, ozero ◎	86	51.15 N	62.14 E
Kinel'	80	53.14 N	50.39 E
Kinel'-Čerkasy	80	53.29 N	51.29 E
Kinel'skije jary ⋏[1]	80	53.42 N	52.00 E
Kineo, Mount ∧	188	45.42 N	69.44 W
Kinesi	154	1.28 S	33.52 E
Kinešma	80	57.26 N	42.09 E
Kineton	42	52.10 N	1.30 W
Kinfauns	46	56.22 N	3.21 W
King	192	36.16 N	80.21 W
King □[6]	224	47.26 N	121.48 W
King ≃, Austl.	164	14.41 S	131.59 E
King ≃, Austl.	169	36.41 S	146.25 E
King, Lake ◎	162	25.38 S	120.06 E
King, Mont ∧	212	45.29 N	75.52 W
King, Mount ∧	166	25.10 S	147.31 E
Kingabwa ◆[8]	273b	4.19 S	15.20 E
King and Queen □[6]	208	37.42 N	76.50 W
King and Queen Court House	208	37.40 N	76.52 W
Kingaroy	166	26.33 S	151.50 E
Kingarth	46	55.46 N	5.03 W
King City, On., Can.	212	43.56 N	79.32 W
King City, Ca., U.S.	226	36.12 N	121.07 W
King City, Mo., U.S.	194	40.03 N	94.31 W
King Cove	180	55.04 N	162.19 W
Kingdom City	219	38.58 N	91.56 W
King Edward ≃	164	14.14 S	126.35 E
Kingersheim	58	47.48 N	7.20 E
King Ferry	210	42.39 N	76.37 W
Kingfield	188	44.57 N	70.09 W
Kingfisher	196	35.51 N	97.55 W
King George	208	38.16 N	77.11 W
King George □[6]	208	38.15 N	77.10 W
King George, Mount ∧	182	50.35 N	115.24 W
King George Bay ⊂	254	51.33 S	60.37 W
King George Island I	9	62.00 S	58.15 W
King George Islands II	176	57.20 N	78.25 W
King George's Dock ◆[5]	272b	22.32 N	88.18 E
King George Sound ᵿ	162	35.03 S	117.57 E
King George's Reservoir ◎[1]	260	51.39 N	0.01 W
King Hill	202	43.00 N	115.12 W
Kinghorn	46	56.04 N	3.10 W
Kingie ≃	46	57.04 N	5.08 W
Kingisepp	76	59.22 N	28.36 E
King Island I, Austl.	166	39.50 S	144.00 E
King Island I, B.C., Can.	182	52.12 N	127.42 W
King Island I, Ak., U.S.	180	64.58 N	168.05 W
Kinglake National Park ♠	169	37.35 S	145.25 E
King Lear Peak ∧	204	41.12 N	118.34 W
King Leopold Ranges ⋏	160	17.30 S	125.45 E
Kingman, Az., U.S.	200	35.11 N	114.03 W
Kingman, Ks., U.S.	198	37.38 N	98.06 W
Kingman Reef ✢[2]	14	6.24 N	162.22 W
King Mountain ∧, B.C., Can.	180	58.17 N	128.54 W
King Mountain ∧, Ok., U.S.	196	34.52 N	99.17 W
King Mountain ∧, Or., U.S.	202	42.42 N	123.14 W
King Mountain ∧, Or., U.S.	202	43.49 N	118.52 W
King of Prussia	208	40.05 N	75.23 W
King of Prussia Plaza ◆[9]	285	40.05 N	75.25 W
Kingoma	152	5.11 S	13.34 E
Kingoma-Ngoma	152	5.50 S	16.49 E
Kingombe, Zaïre	154	3.56 S	26.35 E
Kingombe, Zaïre	154	7.24 S	26.11 E
Kingoonya	162	30.54 S	135.18 E
Kingoué	152	3.43 S	14.09 E
King Peak ∧	204	40.10 N	124.08 W
Kingri	120	30.27 N	69.49 E
Kings, Il., U.S.	216	42.00 N	89.06 W
Kings, Ms., U.S.	194	32.23 N	90.51 W
Kings □[6], Ca., U.S.	226	36.20 N	119.39 W
Kings □[6], N.Y., U.S.	210	40.42 N	74.00 W
Kings ≃, Ar., U.S.	194	36.29 N	93.35 W
Kings ≃, Ca., U.S.	226	36.03 N	119.49 W
Kings ≃, Nv., U.S.	204	41.31 N	118.08 W
Kings, Middle Fork ≃	204	36.50 N	118.52 W
Kings, North Fork ≃, Ca., U.S.	204	36.52 N	119.08 W
Kings, North Fork ≃, Ca., U.S.	226	36.18 N	119.52 W
Kings, South Fork ≃	226	36.18 N	119.52 W
King Salmon	180	58.41 N	156.39 W
King Salmon ≃	180	58.15 N	157.30 W
Kingsbarns	46	56.18 N	2.39 W
Kings Beach	226	39.14 N	120.01 W
Kingsbridge	42	50.17 N	3.46 W
Kingsburg	226	36.30 N	119.33 W
Kingsbury, Eng., U.K.	42	52.35 N	1.40 W
Kingsbury, In., U.S.	216	41.31 N	86.42 W
Kingsbury ◆[8]	260	51.35 N	0.17 W
Kings Canyon National Park ♠	204	36.48 N	118.30 W
Kingsclere	42	51.20 N	1.14 W
Kingscote	168b	35.40 S	137.38 E
Kingscourt	48	53.53 N	6.48 W
Kings Creek	218	40.10 N	83.44 W
Kings Creek ≃, Austl.	171a	27.57 S	151.42 E
Kings Creek ≃, Tx., U.S.	222	32.25 N	96.15 W
King's Cross Station ◆[5]	260	51.32 N	0.07 W
Kings Dominion ♠	208	37.51 N	77.27 W
Kingsdown, Eng., U.K.	42	51.11 N	1.25 E
Kingsdown, Eng., U.K.	260	51.21 N	0.17 E
Kings Falls ʟ	212	43.55 N	75.38 W
Kingsford, Austl.	274a	33.56 S	151.14 E
Kingsford, Mi., U.S.	190	45.47 N	88.04 W
Kingsford Heights	216	41.29 N	86.42 W
Kingsford Smith Airport ⊠	170	33.57 S	151.11 E
Kingsgate	182	49.00 N	116.11 W
Kingsgrove	274a	33.57 S	151.06 E

PORTUGUÊS

Nome	Página	Lat.°′	Long.°′ W = Oeste
Kingshill	241n	17.44 N	64.48 W
Kingshouse	46	56.21 N	4.19 W
Kings Island ♠	218	39.21 N	84.16 W
Kingskerswell	42	50.30 N	3.33 W
Kingsland, Eng., U.K.	42	52.15 N	2.47 W
Kingsland, Ar., U.S.	194	33.51 N	92.17 W
Kingsland, Ga., U.S.	192	30.47 N	81.41 W
Kingsland, Tx., U.S.	196	30.40 N	98.26 W
Kingsland, Va., U.S.	208	37.24 N	77.26 W
Kings Langley	42	51.43 N	0.28 W
Kingsley, S. Afr.	158	27.55 S	30.33 E
Kingsley, Eng., U.K.	42	53.01 N	1.59 W
Kingsley, Eng., U.K.	262	53.16 N	2.40 W
Kingsley, Ia., U.S.	198	42.35 N	95.58 W
Kingsley, Mi., U.S.	190	44.35 N	85.32 W
Kingsley, Pa., U.S.	210	41.46 N	75.45 W
Kingsley Dam ◆[6]	198	41.11 N	101.39 W
King's Lynn	42	52.45 N	0.24 E
Kings Manor	285	40.05 N	75.21 W
Kingsmere Lake ◎	184	54.06 N	106.27 W
Kings Mills	218	39.21 N	84.14 W
Kings Mountain	192	35.14 N	81.20 W
Kings Mountain National Military Park ♠	192	35.07 N	81.33 W
King Solomon's Mines → Mikhrot Shelomo Hamelekh ⊥	132	29.45 N	34.56 E
King Sound ᵿ	162	17.00 S	123.30 E
Kings Park, N.Y., U.S.	210	40.53 N	73.16 W
Kings Park, Va., U.S.	284c	38.48 N	77.14 W
Kings Park ♠	168a	31.57 S	115.49 E
Kings Peak ∧	200	40.46 N	110.22 W
Kings Plaza ◆[9]	276	40.37 N	73.55 W
King's Point, Nf., Can.	186	49.35 N	56.11 W
Kings Point, N.Y., U.S.	210	40.49 N	73.44 W
Kingsport	192	36.32 N	82.33 W
King's Sutton	42	52.01 N	1.16 W
Kingsteignton	42	50.33 N	3.35 W
King Sterndale	262	53.15 N	1.52 W
Kingsthorpe	171a	27.29 S	151.49 E
Kingston, Austl.	171a	27.40 S	153.07 E
Kingston, N.S., Can.	186	44.59 N	64.57 W
Kingston, On., Can.	212	44.14 N	76.30 W
Kingston, Jam.	241q	18.00 N	76.48 W
Kingston, N.Z.	172	45.20 S	168.42 E
Kingston, Norf. I.	174c	29.03 S	167.58 E
Kingston, Eng., U.K.	28	51.25 N	0.19 W
Kingston, Ga., U.S.	192	34.14 N	84.56 W
Kingston, Il., U.S.	216	42.06 N	88.46 W
Kingston, Ma., U.S.	207	41.59 N	70.43 W
Kingston, Mo., U.S.	194	39.38 N	94.02 W
Kingston, N.J., U.S.	276	40.22 N	74.36 W
Kingston, N.Y., U.S.	210	41.55 N	73.59 W
Kingston, Oh., U.S.	218	39.28 N	82.54 W
Kingston, Ok., U.S.	196	33.59 N	96.43 W
Kingston, Pa., U.S.	210	41.15 N	75.53 W
Kingston, R.I., U.S.	207	41.29 N	71.31 W
Kingston, Tn., U.S.	192	35.52 N	84.30 W
Kingston, Wa., U.S.	224	47.48 N	122.30 W
Kingston ◆[8]	42	51.25 N	0.19 W
Kingston Bay ⊂	283	42.00 N	70.42 W
Kingston Mills	212	44.17 N	76.27 W
Kingston Southeast	166	36.50 S	139.51 E
Kingston upon Hull	44	53.45 N	0.20 W
Kingston upon Thames ◆[8]	260	51.25 N	0.19 W
Kingstown	241h	13.09 N	61.14 W
Kingstown → Dún Laoghaire	48	53.17 N	6.08 W
Kingstree	192	33.40 N	79.49 W
Kingsville, Austl.	274b	37.49 S	144.52 E
Kingsville, On., Can.	214	42.02 N	82.45 W
Kingsville, Md., U.S.	284b	39.26 N	76.25 W
Kingsville, Oh., U.S.	214	41.53 N	80.41 W
Kingsville, Tx., U.S.	196	27.30 N	97.51 W
Kingsville Naval Air Station ■	196	27.31 N	97.47 W
Kingswear	42	50.21 N	3.34 W
Kingswinford	42	52.29 N	2.10 W
Kingswood, Austl.	274a	33.46 S	150.43 E
Kingswood, S. Afr.	158	27.29 S	25.46 E
Kingswood, Eng., U.K.	42	51.27 N	2.22 W
Kingswood, Eng., U.K.	260	51.17 N	0.13 W
Kingswood Park	285	40.07 N	74.51 W
King's Worthy	42	51.06 N	1.18 W
Kingtechen → Jingdezhen	100	29.16 N	117.11 E
Kington	42	52.12 N	3.01 W
Kingunda	152	6.34 S	16.58 E
Kingungi	152	5.24 S	17.56 E
Kingussie	46	57.05 N	4.03 W
King William	208	37.41 N	77.00 W
King William □[6]	208	37.42 N	77.05 W
King William Island I	176	69.00 N	97.30 W
King William's Town	158	32.51 S	27.22 E
Kingwood, Tx., U.S.	222	29.54 N	95.18 W
Kingwood, W.V., U.S.	188	39.28 N	79.41 W
Kinh Duc	110	11.49 N	107.58 E
Kinhwa → Jinhua	100	29.07 N	119.39 E
Kınık	130	39.05 N	27.23 E
Kinira ≃	158	31.12 S	29.17 E
Kinistino	184	52.57 N	105.00 W
Kinjar Khās	123	29.55 N	70.58 E
Kinkala	152	4.22 S	14.46 E
Kinker Creek ≃	282	38.02 N	121.52 W
Kinkony, Lac ◎	157b	16.08 S	45.50 E
Kinkora	285	40.07 N	74.45 W
Kinleith	172	38.16 S	175.54 E
Kinloch	46	57.01 N	6.17 W
Kinlochbervie	46	58.28 N	5.03 W
Kinlocheil	46	56.51 N	5.20 W
Kinlochewe	46	57.36 N	5.20 W
Kinloch Hourn	46	57.06 N	5.22 W
Kinlochleven	46	56.42 N	4.58 W
Kinloch Rannoch	46	56.42 N	4.11 W
Kinloss	46	57.37 N	3.34 W
Kinmount	212	44.47 N	78.39 W
Kinmundy	219	38.46 N	88.50 W
Kinn	26	61.36 N	4.45 E
Kinna	26	57.30 N	12.41 E
Kinnaird	182	49.17 N	117.39 W
Kinnaird Head ›	46	57.42 N	2.00 W
Kinnegad	48	53.26 N	7.05 W
Kinnekulle ∧[2]	26	58.35 N	13.23 E
Kinnelon	210	40.59 N	74.23 W
Kinnel Water ≃	44	55.08 N	3.25 W
Kinneret	132	32.43 N	35.33 E
Kinneret, Yam (Sea of Galilee) ◎	132	32.48 N	35.35 E
Kinneret-Negev Conduit ≊[1]	132	32.52 N	35.32 E
Kinnerley	42	52.47 N	2.59 W
Kinniconick Creek ≃	218	38.37 N	83.09 W
Kinnula	26	63.22 N	24.58 E
Kino ≃	96	34.13 N	135.09 E
Kinoe	96	34.14 N	132.55 E
Kinogitan	116	9.00 N	124.48 E
Kinojévis ≃	190	48.23 N	78.21 W
Kinomoto	94	35.30 N	136.13 E
Kinonge ≃	206	45.39 N	74.55 W
Kinoni	154	0.39 S	30.27 E
Kinosaki	96	35.37 N	134.49 E
Kinpoku-san ∧	92	38.05 N	138.22 E
Kinrola	166	23.46 S	148.45 E
Kinross, S. Afr.	158	26.22 S	29.03 E
Kinross, Scot., U.K.	46	56.13 N	3.27 W
Kin-saki ›	174m	26.26 N	127.57 E
Kinsale, Ire.	48	51.42 N	8.32 W
Kinsale, Va., U.S.	208	38.01 N	76.34 W
Kinsale, Old Head of ›	48	51.36 N	8.32 W
Kinsale Harbour ⊂	48	51.41 N	8.30 W
Kinsarvik	26	60.23 N	6.43 E
Kinschasa → Kinshasa	152	4.18 S	15.18 E
Kinshasa (Léopoldville), Zaïre	152	4.18 S	15.18 E
Kinshasa (Léopoldville), Zaïre	273b	4.18 S	15.18 E
Kinshasa □[4]	152	4.18 S	15.18 E
Kinshasa (Ndolo) Airport ⊠, Zaïre	273b	4.20 S	15.19 E
Kinshasa (Ndjili) Airport ⊠, Zaïre	273b	4.23 S	15.27 E
Kinshasa-Est ◆[8]	273b	4.18 S	15.18 E
Kinshasa-Ouest ◆[8]	273b	4.20 S	15.15 E
Kinsley	198	37.55 N	99.24 W
Kinsman, Il., U.S.	216	41.11 N	88.34 W
Kinsman, Oh., U.S.	214	41.27 N	80.36 W
Kinston, Al., U.S.	194	31.12 N	86.10 W
Kinston, N.C., U.S.	192	35.15 N	77.34 W
Kintamani	115b	8.14 S	115.19 E
Kintamo, Rapides de ʟ	273b	4.19 S	15.15 E
Kintampo	150	8.03 N	1.43 W
Kintap	112	3.51 S	115.13 E
Kintari, Mont ∧[2]	273b	4.08 S	15.23 E
Kintélé	273b	4.09 S	15.21 E
Kintinian	150	11.36 N	9.23 W
Kintinku	154	5.53 S	35.14 E
Kintobongo-Bunge	154	8.54 S	26.23 E
Kintore	46	57.13 N	2.21 W
Kintore, Mount ∧	162	26.34 S	130.30 E
Kintore Range ⋏	162	23.25 S	129.20 E
Kintsana	273b	4.19 S	15.10 E
Kintus	86	60.09 N	71.25 E
Kintyre ›[1]	46	55.32 N	5.35 W
Kintyre, Mull of ›	46	55.17 N	5.55 W
Kinu ≃	94	35.56 N	139.57 E
Kinuseo Falls ʟ	182	54.47 N	121.12 W
Kinuso	182	55.20 N	115.25 W
Kinvarra	48	53.08 N	8.55 W
Kinver	42	52.27 N	2.14 W
Kin-wan ⊂	174m	26.25 N	127.54 E
Kinwood	222	29.56 N	95.23 W
Kinyangiri	154	4.27 S	34.37 E
Kinyeti ∧	154	3.57 N	32.54 E
Kinzia	152	3.36 S	18.26 E
Kinzig ≃, Dtsch.	56	50.08 N	8.54 E
Kinzig ≃, Dtsch.	58	48.37 N	7.49 E
Kinzua	202	44.59 N	120.03 W
Kinzua Creek ≃	214	41.47 N	78.50 W
Kinzua Dam ◆[6]	214	41.50 N	79.01 W
Kioga-See → Kyoga, Lake ◎	154	1.30 N	33.00 E
Kioshkokwi Lake ◎	190	46.05 N	78.52 W
Kioto → Kyōto	94	35.00 N	135.45 E
Kiowa, Co., U.S.	198	39.20 N	104.27 W
Kiowa, Ks., U.S.	198	37.01 N	98.29 W
Kiowa, Ok., U.S.	196	34.43 N	95.53 W
Kiowa Creek ≃, U.S.	196	36.46 N	99.55 W
Kiowa Creek ≃, Co., U.S.	198	40.20 N	104.05 W
Kipahigan Lake ◎	184	55.20 N	101.55 W
Kipandi	152	5.19 S	16.46 E
Kipanga	154	6.14 S	35.21 E
Kiparissía	38	37.14 N	21.40 E
Kiparissiakós Kólpos ⊂	38	37.37 N	21.24 E
Kipatimu	154	8.29 S	38.56 E
Kipawa ≃	190	47.03 N	79.23 W
Kipawa, Lac ◎	190	46.55 N	79.00 W
Kipawa, Réserve ♠	190	47.15 N	78.15 W
Kipembawe	154	7.39 S	33.24 E
Kipengere Range ⋏	154	9.10 S	34.15 E
Kiperčeny	78	47.32 N	28.50 E
Kipijevo	24	65.40 N	54.30 E
Kipili	154	7.26 S	30.36 E
Kipini	154	2.32 S	40.31 E
Kipling	184	50.10 N	102.38 W
Kipnuk	180	59.56 N	164.03 W
Kippax	44	53.46 N	1.22 W
Kippen	46	56.08 N	4.11 W
Kippenheim	58	48.17 N	7.49 E
Kippure ∧	48	53.10 N	6.18 W
Kípros → Cyprus □[1]	130	35.00 N	33.00 E
Kipsdorf	54	50.47 N	13.32 E
Kipton	214	41.16 N	82.18 W
Kipushi	154	11.46 S	27.14 E
Kipushia, Zaïre	154	6.10 S	25.12 E
Kipushia, Zaïre	154	12.58 S	29.30 E
Kira, Nihon	94	34.49 N	137.05 E
Kir'a, Ross.	80	55.04 N	46.53 E
Kirakira	175e	10.27 S	161.55 E
Kirandul	122	18.40 N	81.16 E
Kirane	150	15.25 N	10.14 W
Kiranlık	130	39.07 N	41.41 E
Kiranomena	157b	18.17 S	46.03 E
Kīratpur	124	29.31 N	78.12 E
Kiraz	130	38.13 N	28.13 E
Kirazlı	130	40.02 N	26.41 E
Kırbaçbayırı ∧	267b	40.56 N	29.10 E
Kırbaşı	130	40.01 N	31.50 E
Kirbla	76	58.44 N	23.57 E
Kirby Muxloe	42	52.38 N	1.13 W
Kirbys Creek ≃	208	36.28 N	77.06 W
Kirbyville	194	30.39 N	93.53 W
Kırçal	130	41.39 N	35.16 E
Kırcasalih	130	41.23 N	26.48 E
Kirchardt	56	49.12 N	8.59 E
Kirchbach in Steiermark	61	46.54 N	15.44 E
Kirchberg, Dtsch.	54	50.37 N	12.32 E
Kirchberg, Dtsch.	56	49.12 N	9.58 E
Kirchberg, Dtsch.	56	49.56 N	7.24 E
Kirchberg, Dtsch.	60	48.54 N	13.11 E
Kirchberg, Schw.	58	47.05 N	7.35 E
Kirchberg, Schw.	58	47.25 N	9.03 E
Kirch-Berg ∧[2]	264a	52.27 N	13.02 E
Kirchberg am Wagram	61	48.26 N	15.53 E
Kirchberg an der Pielach	61	48.02 N	15.26 E
Kirchberg in Tirol	64	47.27 N	12.19 E
Kirchbichl	64	47.31 N	12.05 E
Kirchderne ◆[8]	263	51.33 N	7.30 E
Kirchdorf, Dtsch.	52	52.36 N	8.49 E
Kirchdorf, Dtsch.	54	54.00 N	11.26 E
Kirchdorf an der Krems	61	47.56 N	14.07 E
Kirchdorf im Wald	60	48.55 N	13.16 E
Kirchen	56	50.48 N	7.53 E
Kirchende	263	51.25 N	7.26 E
Kirchenlaibach	60	49.53 N	11.46 E
Kirchenlamitz	54	50.09 N	11.56 E
Kirchenthumbach	60	49.45 N	11.43 E
Kirchhain	56	50.49 N	8.55 E
Kirchham	60	48.21 N	13.16 E
Kirchheiligen	54	51.11 N	10.42 E
Kirchheimbolanden	56	49.40 N	8.00 E
Kirchheim in Schwaben	58	48.10 N	10.30 E
Kirchheim unter Teck	56	48.39 N	9.27 E
Kirchhellen	52	51.36 N	6.55 E
Kirchhellen Heide ◆[3]	263	51.36 N	6.53 E
Kirchhofen	264a	52.22 N	13.53 E
Kirchhörde ◆[8]	263	51.27 N	7.27 E
Kirchhundem	56	51.05 N	8.05 E
Kirchlengern	52	52.12 N	8.35 E
Kirchlinde ◆[8]	263	51.32 N	7.22 E
Kirchlinteln	52	52.56 N	9.19 E
Kirchmöser	54	52.22 N	12.25 E
Kirchroth	60	48.57 N	12.33 E
Kirchschlag in der Buckligen Welt	61	47.31 N	16.18 E
Kirchveischede	56	51.05 N	7.59 E
Kirchwalsede	52	53.01 N	9.23 E
Kirchwerder ◆[8]	52	53.25 N	10.11 E
Kirchzarten	58	47.58 N	7.56 E
Kircubbin	48	54.29 N	5.32 W
Kirda	85	41.06 N	69.00 E
Kirdāsah	142	30.02 N	31.07 E
Kireç	130	39.33 N	28.22 E
Kirej ≃	88	54.12 N	100.40 E
Kirejevo	80	50.01 N	44.29 E
Kirejevsk	76	53.56 N	37.56 E
Kirejkovo	76	53.38 N	35.49 E
Kirenga ≃	88	57.47 N	108.07 E
Kirensk	88	57.46 N	108.08 E
Kirghizia → Kyrgyzstan □[1]	72	41.30 N	75.00 E
Kirgili	85	40.24 N	71.43 E
Kirgizija → Kyrgyzstan □[1]	72	41.30 N	75.00 E
Kirgiziya → Kyrgyzstan □[1]	72	41.30 N	75.00 E
Kirgiz-Mijaki	86	53.38 N	54.47 E
Kirgizskij chrebet ⋏	85	42.30 N	74.00 E
Kiri	152	1.27 S	19.00 E
Kiribati □[1]	14	5.00 S	170.00 W
Kiribati II	14	0.30 S	174.00 E
Kiries West	158	26.34 S	19.00 E
Kiriga-mine ∧	94	36.06 N	138.12 E
Kırıkhan, Tür.	130	39.32 N	41.20 E
Kırıkhan, Tür.	130	36.32 N	36.19 E
Kirikiri Prisons ♁	273a	6.27 N	3.19 E
Kırıkkale	130	39.50 N	33.31 E
Kirikovka	78	50.22 N	35.07 E
Kirillov	76	59.52 N	38.23 E
Kirillovka	265b	55.57 N	37.20 E
Kirillovo, Ross.	80	57.07 N	45.27 E
Kirillovo, Ross.	80	53.47 N	42.40 E
Kirillovskoje	76	60.28 N	29.17 E
Kirin → Jilin	89	43.51 N	126.33 E
Kirin → Jilin □[4]	90	44.00 N	126.00 E
Kirinyaga (Mount Kenya) ∧	154	0.10 S	37.20 E
Kirishima-Yaku-kokuritsu-kōen ♠	92	31.55 N	130.51 E
Kirishima-yama ∧	92	31.56 N	130.52 E
Kiriši	76	59.27 N	32.02 E
Kiritimati (Christmas Island) I[1]	174o	1.52 N	157.20 W
Kiriwina Island I	164	8.35 S	151.05 E
Kiriwina Islands II	164	8.35 S	151.05 E
Kirizume-tōge ∧[2]	270	34.56 N	135.16 E
Kirjanovskaja Kontora	88	58.18 N	104.13 E
Kirka	130	39.17 N	30.33 E
Kirkabister	46a	60.07 N	1.08 W
Kırkağaç	130	39.06 N	27.40 E
Kirkbride	44	54.54 N	3.12 W
Kirkburton	44	53.37 N	1.42 W
Kirkby ◆[8]	44	53.29 N	2.54 W
Kirkby in Ashfield	44	53.06 N	1.15 W
Kirkby Lonsdale	44	54.13 N	2.36 W
Kirkby Malzeard	44	54.11 N	1.38 W
Kirkbymoorside	44	54.16 N	0.55 W
Kirkby Stephen	44	54.28 N	2.20 W
Kirkcaldy	46	56.07 N	3.10 W
Kirkcolm	44	54.58 N	5.05 W
Kirkconnel	44	55.23 N	4.00 W
Kirkcudbright	44	54.50 N	4.03 W
Kirkcudbright Bay ⊂	44	54.48 N	4.04 W
Kirkdale ◆[8]	262	53.26 N	2.59 W
Kirkeby	41	56.09 N	9.27 E
Kirkee → Khadki	122	18.34 N	73.52 E
Kirkenær	26	60.28 N	12.03 E
Kirkenes	24	69.40 N	30.03 E
Kirke Stillinge	41	55.26 N	11.15 E
Kirkham	44	53.47 N	2.53 W
Kirkhill	46	57.28 N	4.26 W
Kirkintilloch	46	55.57 N	4.10 W
Kirkjubæjarklaustur	24a	63.47 N	18.04 W
Kirkkonummi → Kyrkslätt	26	60.07 N	24.26 E
Kirkland, P.Q., Can.	275a	45.27 N	73.52 W
Kirkland, Il., U.S.	216	42.05 N	88.51 W
Kirkland, Tx., U.S.	196	34.23 N	100.04 W
Kirkland, Wa., U.S.	224	47.40 N	122.12 W
Kirkland Creek ≃	200	34.32 N	113.00 W
Kirkland Lake	190	48.09 N	80.02 W
Kırklar Dağı ∧	130	40.32 N	40.35 E
Kırklareli	130	41.44 N	27.12 E
Kırklareli □[4]	130	41.40 N	27.30 E
Kirklees □[8]	262	53.36 N	1.52 W
Kirkleyditch	262	53.18 N	2.12 W
Kirklin	194	40.11 N	86.21 W
Kirkliston	46	55.58 N	3.25 W
Kirk Michael, I. of Man	44	54.17 N	4.35 W
Kirkmichael, Scot., U.K.	46	56.43 N	3.29 W
Kirkmuirhill	46	55.40 N	3.55 W
Kirkness Lake ◎	184	51.32 N	93.56 W
Kirkpatrick, Mount ∧	9	84.20 S	166.19 E
Kirkpatrick Lake ◎	182	51.52 N	111.18 W
Kirk Sandall	44	53.33 N	1.04 W
Kirksville, Il., U.S.	219	39.34 N	88.40 W
Kirksville, Mo., U.S.	194	40.11 N	92.34 W
Kirkton of Culsalmond	46	57.23 N	2.34 W
Kirkton of Glenisla	46	56.44 N	3.17 W
Kirktown of Auchterless	46	57.27 N	2.28 W
Kirkūk	128	35.28 N	44.28 E
Kirkville	210	43.05 N	75.57 W
Kirkwall	46	58.59 N	2.58 W
Kirkwood, S. Afr.	158	33.24 S	25.26 E
Kirkwood, De., U.S.	208	39.34 N	75.41 W
Kirkwood, Il., U.S.	190	40.51 N	90.44 W
Kirkwood, Mo., U.S.	219	38.35 N	90.24 W
Kirkwood, N.J., U.S.	285	39.50 N	75.01 W
Kirkwood, N.Y., U.S.	210	42.02 N	75.48 W
Kirmir ≃	130	40.07 N	31.43 E
Kirn	56	49.47 N	7.28 E
Kirnāhar	126	23.45 N	87.52 E
Kirotshe	154	1.37 S	29.02 E
Kirov, Ross.	76	54.05 N	34.20 E
Kirov, Ross.	80	58.38 N	49.42 E
Kirova, zaliv ⊂	84	39.09 N	49.03 E
Kirovabad → Gjandža	84	40.40 N	46.22 E
Kirovakan	84	40.48 N	44.30 E
Kirovgrad	86	57.26 N	60.04 E
Kirovka	86	47.07 N	82.00 E
Kirovo, Bela.	78	51.29 N	29.24 E
Kirovo, Ross.	86	55.33 N	63.46 E
Kirovo, Ukr.	78	47.41 N	35.46 E
Kirovo, Ukr.	83	48.23 N	37.55 E
Kirovo, Ukr.	83	48.50 N	38.03 E
Kirovo, Uzb.	85	40.26 N	70.34 E
Kirovo-Čepeck	80	58.33 N	50.01 E
Kirovograd	78	48.30 N	32.18 E
Kirovograd □[8]	38	48.10 N	30.20 E
Kirovsk, Azer.	84	38.48 N	48.43 E
Kirovsk, Bela.	76	53.16 N	29.29 E
Kirovsk, Ross.	24	67.37 N	33.35 E
Kirovsk, Ross.	265a	59.52 N	31.00 E
Kirovsk, Turk.	128	37.42 N	60.23 E
Kirovsk, Ukr.	83	48.38 N	38.39 E
Kirovsk, Ukr.	83	49.01 N	37.56 E
Kirovskij, Azer.	84	40.26 N	49.51 E
Kirovskij, Kaz.	86	44.52 N	78.12 E
Kirovskij, Ross.	74	54.18 N	155.47 E
Kirovskij, Ross.	80	45.51 N	48.07 E
Kirovskij, Ross.	89	54.26 N	126.55 E
Kirovskij, Ross.	89	45.07 N	133.30 E
Kirovskije ostrova II	265a	59.58 N	30.15 E
Kirovskoje, Kyrg.	85	42.39 N	71.35 E
Kirovskoje, Ukr.	78	48.33 N	34.53 E
Kirovskoje, Ukr.	78	45.14 N	35.13 E
Kirovskoje, Ukr.	83	48.09 N	38.21 E
Kirov Stadium ♠	265a	59.58 N	30.14 E
Kirov Theatre ♁	265a	59.55 N	30.18 E
Kirpičnyj Zavod	265a	60.01 N	30.48 E
Kirpil'skaja	78	45.23 N	39.43 E
Kirriemuir	46	56.41 N	3.01 W
Kirs	86	59.21 N	52.14 E
Kirsanov	80	52.38 N	42.43 E
Kirsanovka	80	52.30 N	52.53 E
Kirschau	54	51.04 N	14.27 E
Kırşehir	130	39.09 N	34.10 E
Kırşehir □[4]	130	39.20 N	34.10 E
Kīrthar National Park ♠	120	25.50 N	67.40 E
Kīrthar Range ⋏	120	27.00 N	67.10 E
Kirtland, N.M., U.S.	200	36.44 N	108.21 W
Kirtland, Oh., U.S.	214	41.37 N	81.21 W
Kirtland Air Force Base ■	200	35.02 N	106.37 W
Kirtland Hills	214	41.37 N	81.24 W
Kirtle Water ≃	44	54.58 N	3.05 W
Kirton	42	52.56 N	0.04 W
Kirton in Lindsey	44	53.28 N	0.36 W
Kirton of Largo	46	56.13 N	2.55 W
Kirtorf	56	50.46 N	9.06 E
Kiruna	24	67.51 N	20.16 E
Kirundu	154	0.44 S	25.32 E
Kirurumo	154	5.53 S	34.11 E
Kirvin	222	31.46 N	96.20 W
Kirwan Heights	279b	40.22 N	80.06 W
Kirwee	172	43.30 S	172.13 E
Kirwin	198	39.40 N	99.07 W
Kirwin Reservoir ◎[1]	198	39.39 N	99.10 W
Kiryandongo	154	1.53 N	32.03 E
Kiryū	94	36.24 N	139.20 E
Kirza	86	54.14 N	81.40 E
Kirżač	82	56.09 N	38.52 E
Kirżač ≃	82	55.52 N	39.04 E
Kisa, Nihon	96	34.43 N	132.59 E
Kisa, Sve.	26	57.59 N	15.37 E
Kisai	94	36.06 N	139.35 E
Kisaichi	270	34.46 N	135.42 E
Kisakata	92	39.13 N	139.54 E
Kisaki	154	7.28 S	37.36 E
Kišaly	76	54.23 N	43.12 E
Kisambo	152	6.25 S	18.14 E
Kisanga	154	2.29 N	26.35 E
Kisangani (Stanleyville)	154	0.30 S	25.12 E
Kisantu	152	5.07 S	15.05 E
Kisar, Pulau I	112	8.05 S	127.10 E
Kisaralik ≃	180	60.51 N	161.16 W
Kisaran	114	2.59 N	99.37 E
Kisarawe	154	6.54 S	39.04 E
Kisarazu	94	35.23 N	139.55 E
Kisarazu-Kichi, Kōkū-jieitai ■	94	35.24 N	139.55 E
Kisawa	96	33.49 N	134.18 E
K.I. Sawyer Air Force Base ■	190	46.21 N	87.25 W
Kisbér	30	47.30 N	18.02 E
Kisbey	184	49.38 N	102.41 W
Kise ≃	94	35.06 N	138.53 E
Kiselevsk → Kisel'ovsk	86	54.00 N	86.39 E
Kisel'ovka	80	47.18 N	44.07 E
Kisel'ovsk	86	54.00 N	86.39 E
Kisengwa	154	6.00 S	25.50 E
Kisen-yama ∧[2]	270	34.54 N	135.51 E
Kiser Lake ◎	218	40.11 N	83.58 W
Kīsh, Jazīreh-ye I	128	26.32 N	53.56 E
Kishanda	154	1.42 S	31.34 E
Kishanganga ≃	123	34.22 N	73.30 E
Kishanganj	124	26.07 N	87.56 E
Kishangarh	120	27.52 N	70.34 E
Kishangarh ◆[8]	272a	28.31 N	77.08 E
Kishangarh Bās	120	26.34 N	74.52 E
Kishb, Ḥarrat al- ⊥[9]	144	23.00 N	41.25 E
Kishi, Nig.	150	9.05 N	3.52 E
Kishi, Zaïre	154	10.04 S	26.26 E
Kishida ≃	96	35.38 N	134.27 E
Kishigawa	96	34.13 N	135.20 E
Kishikas ≃	184	52.45 N	91.43 W
Kishimoto	96	35.23 N	133.25 E
Kishinev → Kišin'ov	78	47.00 N	28.50 E
Kishiwada	96	34.28 N	135.22 E
Kishorganj	124	24.26 N	90.46 E
Kishorn, Loch ⊂	46	57.21 N	5.41 W
Kishtwār	123	33.19 N	75.46 E
Kishwaukee ≃	216	42.11 N	89.08 W
Kishwaukee, South Branch ≃	216	42.12 N	88.59 W
Kisia	152	4.35 S	18.22 E
Kisigo ≃	154	7.03 S	35.50 E
Kisii	154	0.41 S	34.46 E
Kisiju	154	7.24 S	39.20 E
Kiši-Karoj, ozero ◎	86	54.03 N	71.20 E
Kisika-zaki ›	93b	30.50 N	131.04 E
Kısıklı ◆[8]	267b	41.01 N	29.03 E
Kišin	78	51.08 N	27.41 E
Kišin'ov (Kishinev)	78	47.00 N	28.50 E
Kısır Dağı ∧	84	40.58 N	43.04 E
Kısırkaya ◆[8]	267b	41.14 N	28.58 E
Kısırmandıra ◆[8]	267b	41.14 N	28.49 E
Kisiwada → Kishiwada	96	34.28 N	135.22 E
Kisiwani	154	4.08 S	37.57 E
Kisizi	154	1.00 S	29.56 E
Kiska Island I	181a	52.00 N	177.30 E
Kiskatinaw ≃	182	56.06 N	120.08 W
Kiska Volcano ∧[1]	181a	52.07 N	177.36 E
Kis-Kevély ∧[2]	264c	47.38 N	18.59 E
Kiski Lake ◎	184	54.46 N	98.55 W
Kiskimere	279b	40.37 N	79.35 W
Kiskiminetas ≃	214	40.41 N	79.40 W
Kiskittogisu Lake ◎	184	54.13 N	98.20 W
Kiskitto Lake ◎	184	54.16 N	98.34 W
Kiskörei-víztároló ◎[1]	30	47.35 N	20.40 E
Kiskőrös	30	46.38 N	19.17 E
Kiskunfélegyháza	30	46.43 N	19.52 E
Kiskunhalas	30	46.26 N	19.30 E
Kiskunmajsa	30	46.30 N	19.45 E
Kiskunsági Nemzeti Park ♠	30	46.40 N	19.25 E
Kisl'akovka	78	46.44 N	31.59 E
Kisl'akovskaja	78	46.27 N	39.40 E
Kislovka	83	49.38 N	37.53 E
Kislovo	80	49.54 N	45.25 E
Kislovodsk	84	43.55 N	42.44 E
Kismaayo	144	0.22 S	42.32 E
Kismet	276	40.38 N	73.12 W
Kisnema	76	60.20 N	37.39 E
Kiso, Nihon	94	35.56 N	137.47 E
Kiso, Nihon	268	35.34 N	139.26 E
Kiso ≃	94	35.02 N	136.45 E
Kisofukushima	94	35.51 N	137.42 E
Kisogawa	94	35.20 N	136.47 E
Kisoripur	126	22.05 N	88.34 E
Kisoro	154	1.17 S	29.41 E
Kiso-sammyaku ⋏	94	35.43 N	137.50 E
Kisozaki	94	35.04 N	136.44 E
Kispest ◆[8]	264c	47.27 N	19.08 E
Kispiox	182	55.21 N	127.41 W
Kispiox ≃	182	55.16 N	127.41 W
Kispiox Mountain ∧	182	55.25 N	127.57 W
Kissamos	38	35.30 N	23.38 E
Kissena Park ♠	276	40.45 N	73.49 W
Kisseynew Lake ◎	184	54.58 N	101.35 W
Kissidougou	150	9.11 N	10.06 W
Kissimmee	220	28.17 N	81.24 W
Kissimmee ≃	220	27.10 N	80.53 W
Kissimmee, Lake ◎	220	27.55 N	81.16 W
Kissing	60	48.18 N	10.59 E
Kississing	184	55.07 N	101.07 W
Kississing Lake ◎	184	55.10 N	101.20 W
Kisslegg	58	47.47 N	9.53 E
Kissū, Jabal ∧	140	21.35 N	25.09 E
Kista	80	46.05 N	43.06 E
Kistanje	36	43.59 N	15.58 E
Kistarcsa	264c	47.33 N	19.16 E
Kistendej	80	52.08 N	43.39 E
Kistigan Lake ◎	184	54.38 N	92.37 W
Kistler	214	40.22 N	77.51 W
Kisújszállás	30	47.13 N	20.46 E

≃	River	Fluß	Río	Rivière	Rio
≊	Canal	Kanal	Canal	Canal	Canal
ʟ	Waterfall, Rapids	Wasserfall, Stromschnellen	Cascada, Rápidos	Chute d'eau, Rapides	Cascata, Rápidos
ᵿ	Strait	Meeresstraße	Estrecho	Détroit	Estreito
⊂	Bay, Gulf	Bucht, Golf	Bahía, Golfo	Baie, Golfe	Baía, Golfo
◎	Lake, Lakes	See, Seen	Lago, Lagos	Lac, Lacs	Lago, Lagos
⩸	Swamp	Sumpf	Pantano	Marais	Pântano
⊓	Ice Features, Glacier	Eis- und Gletscherformen	Accidentes Glaciales	Formes glaciaires	Acidentes glaciares
⫪	Other Hydrographic Features	Andere Hydrographische Objekte	Otros Elementos Hidrográficos	Autres données hydrographiques	Outros acidentes hidrográficos

✢	Submarine Features	Untermeerische Objekte	Accidentes Submarinos	Formes de relief sous-marin	Acidentes submarinos
□	Political Unit	Politische Einheit	Unidad Politica	Entité politique	Unidade política
♁	Cultural Institution	Kulturelle Institution	Institución Cultural	Institution culturelle	Instituição cultural
⊥	Historical Site	Historische Stätte	Sitio Histórico	Site historique	Sitio histórico
♠	Recreational Site	Erholungs- und Ferienort	Sitio de Recreo	Centre de loisirs	Area de Lazer
⊠	Airport	Flughafen	Aeropuerto	Aéroport	Aeroporto
■	Military Installation	Militäranlage	Instalación Militar	Installation militaire	Instalação militar
◆	Miscellaneous	Verschiedenes	Misceláneo	Divers	Diversos

ENGLISH: Name, Page, Lat.°′, Long.°′ — DEUTSCH: Name, Seite, Breite°′, Länge°′ E = Ost

Name	Page	Lat.°′	Long.°′
Kisuki	96	35.17 N	132.54 E
Kisumu	154	0.06 S	34.45 E
Kisvárda	30	48.13 N	22.05 E
Kiswere	154	9.26 S	39.33 E
Kita	150	13.03 N	9.29 W
Kita ◆[8], Nihon	268	35.45 N	139.44 E
Kita ◆[8], Nihon	270	34.45 N	135.08 E
Kita ◆[8], Nihon	270	34.42 N	135.30 E
Kita ◆[8], Nihon	270	35.03 N	135.45 E
Kitaaiki	94	36.04 N	138.34 E
Kita-Daitō-jima I	90	25.57 N	131.18 E
Kitafuji-enshūjō ■	94	35.25 N	138.48 E
Kitagata	94	35.26 N	136.41 E
Kitagawa	96	33.27 N	134.03 E
Kitagi-shima I	96	34.23 N	133.32 E
Kitaibaraki	94	36.48 N	140.45 E
Kitain Temple ᵾ[1]	268	35.54 N	139.30 E
Kita-Iō-jima I	14	25.26 N	141.17 E
Kitairiso	268	35.50 N	139.26 E
Kitajima	96	34.05 N	134.35 E
Kitakami	92	39.18 N	141.07 E
Kitakami ≃	92	38.25 N	141.19 E
Kitakami-kōchi ⋏	92	39.30 N	141.30 E
Kitakata	92	37.39 N	139.52 E
Kitakyuschu → Kitakyūshū	96	33.53 N	130.50 E
Kitakyūshū	96	33.53 N	130.50 E
Kitakyushu-kokutei-kōen ♠	96	33.45 N	130.50 E
Kitale	154	1.01 N	35.00 E
Kitamachi ◆[8]	268	35.46 N	139.39 E
Kitamba ◆[8]	273b	4.19 S	15.14 E
Kitami	92a	43.48 N	143.54 E
Kitami-sanchi ⋏	92a	44.22 N	142.43 E
Kitamoto	94	36.02 N	139.32 E
Kita-Nagato-kaigan-kokutei-kōen ♠	96	34.24 N	131.16 E
Kitanakagusuku	174m	26.21 N	127.51 E
Kitanda, Zaïre	154	6.36 S	26.27 E
Kitanda, Zaïre	154	9.59 S	27.28 E
Kitangari	154	10.39 S	39.20 E
Kitangiri, Lake ⊜	154	4.05 S	34.19 E
Kitangua	152	6.17 S	20.22 E
Kitano, Nihon	96	33.20 N	130.35 E
Kitano, Nihon	268	35.47 N	139.26 E
Kitanoshinden	268	35.48 N	139.26 E
Kitatachibana	94	36.29 N	139.03 E
Kitatajima	268	35.56 N	139.30 E
Kitatawara	270	34.44 N	135.42 E
Kitaura	94	36.04 N	140.32 E
Kita-ura ⊜	94	36.00 N	140.34 E
Kitava Island I	164	8.40 S	151.20 E
Kitaya	154	10.39 S	40.10 E
Kit Carson, Ca., U.S.	226	38.41 N	120.07 W
Kit Carson, Co., U.S.	198	38.45 N	102.47 W
Kitchener, Austl.	162	31.02 S	124.11 E
Kitchener, On., Can.	212	43.27 N	80.29 W
Kitee	26	62.06 N	30.09 E
Kitega → Gitega	154	3.26 S	29.56 E
Kiteiyab	140	17.12 N	33.43 E
Kitenda	152	6.53 S	17.21 E
Kitenevo	82	56.21 N	36.13 E
Kitengo	152	7.26 S	24.08 E
Kitéssa	154	5.20 N	25.20 E
Kitgum	154	3.18 N	32.53 E
Kíthira	38	36.09 N	23.00 E
Kíthira I	38	36.20 N	22.58 E
Kíthnos	38	37.26 N	24.26 E
Kíthnos I	38	37.25 N	24.28 E
Kitimat	182	54.03 N	128.33 W
Kitimat ≃	182	54.06 N	128.38 W
Kitimat Ranges ⋏	182	53.30 N	128.50 W
Kitinen ≃	24	67.08 N	27.29 E
Kitíou, Akrotírion ➤	130	34.48 N	33.36 E
Kitlope ≃	182	53.10 N	127.45 W
Kitlope Lake ⊜	182	53.07 N	127.47 W
Kitō, Nihon	94	34.42 N	138.03 E
Kitō, Nihon	96	33.46 N	134.12 E
Kitoj ≃	88	52.39 N	103.56 E
Kitridge Point ➤	241g	13.09 N	59.25 W
Kitsap □[6]	224	47.41 N	122.44 W
Kitscoty	184	53.20 N	110.20 W
Kit's Coty House ᵾ	260	51.19 N	0.30 E
Kitshua-Nseke	152	4.26 S	19.36 E
Kitsuki	92	33.25 N	131.37 E
Kitsuregawa	94	36.43 N	140.01 E
Kittanning	214	40.48 N	79.31 W
Kittatinny Mountain ʌ	210	41.10 N	74.55 W
Kittatinny Tunnel ◆[5]	214	40.09 N	77.41 W
Kittendorf	54	53.37 N	12.54 E
Kittery	188	43.05 N	70.44 W
Kitt Green	262	53.33 N	2.41 W
Kittilä	24	67.40 N	24.54 E
Kittitas	202	46.59 N	120.24 W
Kittitas □[6]	224	47.13 N	121.01 W
Kitt Peak National Observatory ᵾ[3]	200	31.58 N	111.36 W
Kittsee	61	48.05 N	17.04 E
Kitu	154	7.38 S	27.42 E
Kitui	154	1.22 S	38.01 E
Kitumbeine ʌ[1]	154	2.44 S	36.16 E
Kitunda	154	6.48 S	33.13 E
Kitutu	154	3.17 S	28.05 E
Kitwanga	182	55.06 N	128.03 W
Kitwangar Indian Reserve ◆[4]	182	55.06 N	128.04 W
Kitwe	154	12.49 S	28.13 E
Kitwitwi	156	17.25 S	18.25 E
Kityang → Jieyang	100	23.35 N	116.21 E
Kitzbühel	64	47.27 N	12.23 E
Kitzbüheler Alpen ⋏	64	47.20 N	12.20 E
Kitzingen	56	49.44 N	10.09 E
Kitzscher	54	51.09 N	12.33 E
Kiukiang → Jiujiang	100	29.44 N	115.59 E
Kiukiu, Pointe ➤	174x	9.47 S	139.09 W
Kiul	124	25.09 N	86.06 E
Kiunga, Kenya	154	1.45 S	41.29 E
Kiunga, Pap. N. Gui.	164	6.10 S	141.15 E
Kiuruvesi	26	63.39 N	26.37 E
Kiuschu → Kyūshū I	92	33.00 N	131.00 E
Kivak	180	64.16 N	172.57 W
Kivalina	180	67.44 N	164.33 W
Kivercy	78	50.50 N	25.27 E
Kiveriči	76	57.22 N	36.36 E
Kivijärvi	26	63.04 N	25.03 E
Kivijärvi ⊜	26	63.10 N	25.09 E
Kivik	26	55.41 N	14.15 E
Kiviõli	76	59.21 N	26.57 E
Kivu □[4]	154	2.30 S	27.00 E
Kivu, Lac ⊜	154	2.00 S	29.10 E
Kiwaba N'zogi	152	8.57 S	16.32 E
Kiwai Island I	164	8.30 S	143.25 E
Kiwalik	180	66.02 N	161.50 W
Kiwanis Lake	214	41.28 N	81.09 W
Kiyama	96	33.25 N	130.32 E
Kīyāmakī Dāgh ʌ	84	38.47 N	45.51 E
Kiyan	174m	26.05 N	127.40 E
Kiyan-zaki ➤	174m	26.05 N	127.39 E
Kıyıköy	130	41.38 N	28.05 E
Kiyiu Lake ⊜	184	51.38 N	108.55 W
Kiyl ≃	86	49.25 N	54.50 E
Kiyokawa	94	35.29 N	139.17 E
Kiyomi	94	36.07 N	137.11 E
Kiyosawa	94	35.03 N	138.15 E
Kiyose	94	35.47 N	139.32 E
Kiyosu	94	35.13 N	136.50 E
Kiyosumi-yama ʌ	94	35.09 N	140.09 E
Kiyotani	270	34.52 N	134.59 E
Kiyotsu ≃	94	37.03 N	138.41 E
Kizel	86	59.03 N	57.40 E
Kizevatovo	80	53.13 N	45.18 E
Kızıl ≃	130	41.44 N	35.58 E
Kızıl Adalar II	130	40.52 N	29.05 E
Kızılcabölük	130	37.37 N	29.01 E
Kızılcadağ	130	37.01 N	29.58 E
Kızılcahamam	130	40.28 N	32.39 E
Kızılçakçak	84	40.46 N	43.37 E
Kızıldağ Milli Parkı ♠	130	37.58 N	31.28 E
Kızıldikme	130	39.05 N	37.01 E
Kızılhisar	130	37.33 N	29.18 E
Kızılırmak	130	40.21 N	33.59 E
Kızılören	130	37.52 N	32.07 E
Kizil'skoje	86	52.44 N	58.54 E
Kızılsu	130	37.28 N	42.13 E
Kiziltašskij liman c	78	45.07 N	37.05 E
Kızıltepe	130	37.12 N	40.36 E
Kızıltoprak ◆[8]	267b	40.58 N	29.03 E
Kizil'unt	84	43.12 N	46.53 E
Kızılyaka	130	37.09 N	32.54 E
Kižimiz, gora ʌ	24	63.12 N	58.48 E
Kizimkazi	154	6.27 S	39.28 E
Kižinga	88	51.51 N	109.55 E
Kizir ≃	86	53.51 N	93.06 E
Kızkalesi ⊥	130	36.28 N	34.04 E
Kızkulesi ◆[5]	267b	41.01 N	29.00 E
Kizl'ar	84	43.50 N	46.40 E
Kizl'arskij zaliv c	84	44.33 N	46.55 E
Kizner	80	56.17 N	51.31 E
Kiz'oma	24	61.08 N	44.50 E
Kizu	96	34.44 N	135.49 E
Kizu ≃	94	34.53 N	135.42 E
Kizuki	268	35.34 N	139.40 E
Kizuri	270	34.39 N	135.34 E
Kizyl-Ajak	128	37.40 N	65.23 E
Kizyl-Arvat	128	38.58 N	56.15 E
Kizyl-Atrek	128	37.36 N	54.46 E
Kizyl-Su	128	39.48 N	53.01 E
Kjellerup	41	56.17 N	9.26 E
Kjøbenhavn → København	41	55.40 N	12.35 E
Kjustendil	38	42.17 N	22.41 E
Klaarstroom	158	33.20 S	22.32 E
Klaaswaal	52	51.46 N	4.26 E
Klabat, Gunung ʌ	112	1.28 N	125.02 E
Kladanj	38	44.13 N	18.41 E
Kladbišči	80	55.32 N	45.33 E
Kläden	54	52.38 N	11.39 E
Kladkovo	82	55.24 N	38.51 E
Kladno	54	50.08 N	14.05 E
Kladovo	38	44.37 N	22.37 E
Kladow ◆[8]	264a	52.27 N	13.09 E
Kladruby	60	49.43 N	12.59 E
Klaeng	110	12.47 N	101.39 E
Klagan	112	5.58 N	117.27 E
Klagenfurt	61	46.37 N	14.18 E
Klågerup	41	55.36 N	13.15 E
Klagshamn	41	55.32 N	12.55 E
Klagstorp	41	55.24 N	13.22 E
Klahoose Indian Reserve ◆[4]	182	50.31 N	124.19 W
Klaipėda (Memel)	76	55.43 N	21.07 E
Klakah	115a	7.59 S	113.15 E
Klamath	204	41.31 N	124.02 W
Klamath ≃	204	41.33 N	124.04 W
Klamath Falls	202	42.13 N	121.46 W
Klamath Marsh ≋	202	42.54 N	121.44 W
Klamath Mountains ⋏	204	41.40 N	123.20 W
K. Lamido	146	9.21 N	11.12 E
Klämmingen ⊜	40	59.07 N	17.15 E
Klammpass)(	64	47.17 N	13.05 E
Klamono	164	1.08 S	131.30 E
Klangenan	115a	6.42 S	108.26 E
Klang → Kelang	114	3.02 N	101.27 E
Klangpi	110	22.59 N	93.20 E
Klarälven (Trysilelva) ≃	26	59.23 N	13.32 E
Kl'as'ma	265b	55.59 N	37.50 E
Klášterec	54	50.24 N	13.10 E
Kl'asticy	76	55.53 N	28.36 E
Klaten	115a	7.42 S	110.35 E
Klatovy	60	49.24 N	13.18 E
Klausdorf, Dtsch.	54	54.20 N	13.01 E
Klausdorf, Dtsch.	54	54.18 N	10.15 E
Klausenburg → Cluj-Napoca	38	46.47 N	23.36 E
Klausenpass)(	58	46.52 N	8.51 E
Kl'avlino	80	54.17 N	52.01 E
Klawer	158	31.44 S	18.36 E
Klawock	182	55.33 N	133.06 W
Klazienaveen	52	52.44 N	7.00 E
Kl'az'ma	82	55.58 N	37.27 E
Kl'az'ma ≃	80	56.10 N	42.58 E
Kl'az'minskoje vodochranilišče ⊜[1]	265b	55.59 N	37.35 E
Kleberg	222	32.40 N	96.37 W
Kleck	76	53.04 N	26.38 E
Kłecko	30	52.38 N	17.26 E
Kleczew	30	52.23 N	18.10 E
Kledering ◆[8]	264b	48.08 N	16.26 E
Kleef	263	51.11 N	6.56 E
Kleena Kleene	182	51.57 N	124.50 W
Kleinasien → Asia Minor □[9]	22	39.00 N	32.00 E
Kleinbeeren	264a	52.22 N	13.20 E
Kleinbegin	158	28.50 S	21.36 E
Klein-Blesbokspruit ≃	273d	26.16 S	28.29 E
Kleinbodungen	54	51.28 N	10.32 E
Klein Bonaire I	241s	12.10 N	68.18 W
Klein Bünzow	54	53.53 N	13.48 E
Kleinburg	275b	43.50 N	79.38 W
Klein Curaçao I	241s	12.00 N	68.40 W
Kleine Elster ≃	54	51.32 N	13.23 E
Kleine Emme ≃	58	47.04 N	8.17 E
Kleine Emscher ≃	263	51.31 N	6.43 E
Kleine Erlauf ≃	61	48.07 N	15.08 E
Kleineichen	263	51.08 N	7.21 E
Kleine Laber ≃	60	48.55 N	12.31 E
Kleinenberg	52	51.35 N	8.58 E
Kleinenbroich	263	51.12 N	6.35 E
Kleinengstingen	58	48.23 N	9.18 E
Kleiner Jasmunder Bodden c	54	54.28 N	13.32 E
Kleiner Ravens-Berg ʌ[2]	264a	52.22 N	13.04 E
Kleiner Wannsee ⊜	264a	52.25 N	13.10 E
Kleiner Zern-See ⊜	264a	52.26 N	12.55 E
Kleine Spree ≃	54	51.31 N	14.24 E
Kleines Walsertal V	64	47.23 N	10.12 E
Kleinfeltersville	208	40.18 N	76.15 W
Kleinglödnitz	61	46.51 N	14.08 E
Kleinhammer	263	51.14 N	7.46 E
Klein-Jukskei ≃	273d	26.08 S	27.56 E
Klein-Karas	156	27.32 S	18.06 E
Klein Karroo → Little Karroo ⋏[1]	158	33.45 S	21.30 E
Klein Kienitz	264a	52.18 N	13.29 E
Kleinlützel	58	47.26 N	7.25 E
Kleinmachnow	54	52.24 N	13.15 E
Klein Marzehns	54	52.01 N	12.37 E
Kleinmond	158	34.21 S	19.03 E
Klein-Olifants ≃	158	25.41 S	29.19 E
Kleinschönebeck	264a	52.29 N	13.43 E
Klein-Soutpan	158	30.26 S	22.26 E
Klein-Vis ≃	158	33.05 S	26.00 E
Klein Wanzleben	54	52.04 N	11.21 E
Klein Ziethen	264a	52.23 N	13.27 E
Klein Ziethener-Berge ʌ[2]	264a	52.22 N	13.26 E
Klekovača ʌ	36	44.26 N	16.31 E
Klementjevka	86	50.16 N	80.56 E
Klementjevo	82	55.38 N	36.01 E
Klemme	190	43.00 N	93.36 W
Klemtu	182	52.36 N	128.31 W
Klenovka	80	57.45 N	54.19 E
Klenovo	82	55.19 N	37.21 E
Klerksdorp	158	26.58 S	26.39 E
Klerkskraal	158	26.15 S	27.10 E
Klesov	78	51.19 N	26.54 E
Klésso	150	10.57 N	3.59 W
Klet' ʌ	61	48.52 N	14.17 E
Kletn'a	76	53.23 N	33.12 E
Kletskij	80	49.19 N	43.04 E
Kletsko-Počtovskij	80	49.36 N	43.03 E
Klettgau ◆[1]	58	47.40 N	8.25 E
Klettwitz	54	51.32 N	13.53 E
Klevan'	78	50.44 N	26.02 E
Kleve	52	51.48 N	6.09 E
Klevenka	80	52.07 N	49.33 E
Kley ◆[8]	263	51.30 N	7.22 E
Klibreck, Ben ʌ	46	58.14 N	4.22 W
Kličev	76	53.29 N	29.21 E
Klička	88	50.26 N	118.00 E
Klickitat	224	45.49 N	121.09 W
Klickitat □[6]	224	45.50 N	121.07 W
Klickitat ≃	224	45.42 N	121.17 W
Kliedbruch ◆[1]	263	51.22 N	6.33 E
Klietz	54	52.40 N	12.04 E
Klimino	88	58.39 N	98.42 E
Klimoviči	76	53.37 N	31.58 E
Klimovo, Ross.	76	52.23 N	32.11 E
Klimovo, Ross.	82	55.22 N	38.52 E
Klimovsk	82	55.22 N	37.32 E
Klimovskoje	82	54.42 N	37.48 E
Klimov Zavod	76	54.50 N	34.55 E
Klimpfjäll	24	65.04 N	14.52 E
Klin, Ross.	82	56.20 N	36.44 E
Klin, Ross.	82	55.19 N	36.20 E
Klinaklini ≃	182	51.05 N	125.36 W
Klin-Bel'din	82	54.45 N	39.13 E
Klincovka	80	51.41 N	49.11 E
Klincy	76	52.47 N	32.14 E
Kline Ditch ≡	279a	41.28 N	82.04 W
Kling	116	5.58 N	124.42 E
Klingbach ≃	56	50.17 N	9.22 E
Klingenberg	54	50.55 N	13.31 E
Klingenberg am Main	56	49.47 N	9.11 E
Klingenmünster	56	49.08 N	8.01 E
Klingenthal	54	50.21 N	12.28 E
Klinger Lake ⊜	216	41.47 N	85.33 W
Klingerstown	208	40.40 N	76.41 W
Klinghardtberge ʌ	156	27.18 S	15.48 E
Klingnau	58	47.35 N	8.15 E
Klink	54	53.29 N	12.37 E
Klinkino	83	47.17 N	38.15 E
Klínovec ʌ	54	50.24 N	12.58 E
Klinsko-Dmitrovskaja gr'ada ʌ	82	56.15 N	37.30 E
Klintehamn	26	57.24 N	18.12 E
Klintsy → Klincy	76	52.47 N	32.14 E
Klip ≃, S. Afr.	158	27.03 S	29.03 E
Klip ≃, S. Afr.	273d	26.19 S	27.53 E
Klipbakken	158	28.50 S	21.21 E
Klipdale	158	34.19 S	19.57 E
Klipdam	158	27.35 S	19.56 E
Kliplev	41	54.56 N	9.25 E
Klippan	41	56.08 N	13.06 E
Klipplaat	158	33.02 S	24.21 E
Klippoortjie	273d	26.13 S	28.10 E
Klipriviersberg ⋏	273d	26.17 S	28.02 E
Kliptown	273d	26.17 S	27.53 E
Klipwerf	158	31.09 S	19.52 E
Kliškovcy	78	48.26 N	26.15 E
Klisura	38	42.42 N	24.27 E
Klitmøller	26	57.02 N	8.31 E
Klitten	54	51.20 N	14.36 E
Klixbüll	41	54.48 N	8.53 E
Ključ	36	44.32 N	16.47 E
Klobbicke	264a	52.46 N	13.48 E
Klobouky	61	49.00 N	16.52 E
Kłobuck	30	50.55 N	18.57 E
Klobuticy	76	58.35 N	29.35 E
Kłodawa	30	52.16 N	18.55 E
Kłodzko	30	50.27 N	16.39 E
Kløfta	26	60.04 N	11.09 E
Kłomnice	30	50.56 N	19.21 E
Klondike	216	40.28 N	86.57 W
Klondike □[9]	180	63.30 N	139.00 W
Klondike ≃	180	64.05 N	139.26 W
Klöntaler See ⊜	58	47.02 N	8.58 E
Klooga	76	59.19 N	24.16 E
Kloosterveen	52	52.59 N	6.33 E
Kloosterzande	52	51.22 N	4.02 E
Kloster	54	54.35 N	13.06 E
Klosterfelde	54	52.48 N	13.28 E
Klosterhardt ◆[8]	263	51.31 N	6.53 E
Klösterle	58	47.08 N	10.05 E
Klostermansfeld	54	51.35 N	11.29 E
Klosterneuburg	264b	48.18 N	16.20 E
Kloster Oesede	52	52.12 N	8.07 E
Klosters	58	46.54 N	9.53 E
Klostertal V	58	47.08 N	9.59 E
Kloster Zinna	54	52.01 N	13.07 E
Kloten, Schw.	58	47.27 N	8.35 E
Kloten, Sve.	40	59.54 N	15.17 E
Klotz, Lac ⊜	176	60.32 N	73.40 W
Klötze	54	52.38 N	11.10 E
Kloulklubed	175b	7.02 N	134.15 E
Klouto	150	6.57 N	0.34 E
Kluane ≃	180	61.53 N	139.43 W
Kluane Lake ⊜	180	61.15 N	138.40 W
Kluane National Park ♠	180	60.45 N	139.30 W
Kluang	112	2.41 S	103.54 E
Kl'učevaja	24	65.16 N	41.32 E
Kl'učevskaja Sopka, vulkan ʌ[1]	74	56.04 N	160.38 E
Kl'učevskij	88	53.33 N	119.26 E
Kluchorskij, pereval)(	84	43.15 N	41.54 E
Kl'uči, Ross.	74	56.18 N	160.51 E
Kl'uči, Ross.	80	51.59 N	46.31 E
Kl'uči, Ross.	80	51.26 N	45.11 E
Kl'uči, Ross.	86	52.16 N	79.10 E
Kl'učovka, Kyrg.	85	42.34 N	71.48 E
Kl'učovka, Ross.	86	51.22 N	55.48 E
Kluczbork	30	50.59 N	18.13 E
Kluess	54	53.46 N	12.14 E
Kluet ≃	114	3.04 N	97.20 E
Kl'ukvenka	86	58.34 N	85.55 E
Klukwan	180	59.24 N	135.54 W
Klundert	52	51.40 N	4.32 E
Klungkung	115b	8.32 S	115.24 E
Klüppelberg	56	51.06 N	7.28 E
Klüterthöhle ⊥[5]	52	51.18 N	7.21 E
Klutina Lake ⊜	180	61.37 N	146.55 W
Klütz	54	53.58 N	11.10 E
Knaben gruver	26	58.39 N	7.04 E
Knaddah	130	35.45 N	36.12 E
Kn'aginino	80	55.49 N	45.03 E
Knaik ≃	46	56.14 N	3.52 W
Knapdaar	158	30.43 S	26.09 E
Knapdale ◆[1]	46	55.55 N	5.30 W
Knaphill	260	51.19 N	0.37 W
Knapp	190	44.57 N	92.04 W
Knapp Creek	210	42.00 N	78.30 W
Knappenberg	61	46.56 N	14.35 E
Knäred	26	56.32 N	13.19 E
Knaresborough	44	54.00 N	1.27 W
Knargram	126	24.01 N	87.59 E
Knauertown	285	40.10 N	75.44 W
Knauthain ◆[8]	54	51.16 N	12.18 E
Kn'ažaja Bajgora	76	52.23 N	40.02 E
Kn'azevka	86	57.35 N	74.10 E
Kn'ažji Gory	76	56.05 N	35.14 E
Kn'ažovo	76	59.40 N	43.54 E
Knebel	41	56.13 N	10.30 E
Knebworth	42	51.52 N	0.12 W
Kneehills Creek ≃	182	51.30 N	112.50 W
Knee Lake ⊜, Mb., Can.	184	55.03 N	94.40 W
Knee Lake ⊜, Sk., Can.	184	55.51 N	107.00 W
Knesebeck	54	52.41 N	10.42 E
Knesselare	50	51.08 N	3.25 E
Knetzgau	56	50.00 N	10.33 E
Knevicy	76	57.56 N	32.14 E
Kneža	38	43.30 N	24.05 E
Knić	38	43.55 N	20.43 E
Knickerbocker	196	31.16 N	100.38 W
Kniebis	58	48.28 N	8.17 E
Knife ≃	198	47.20 N	101.23 W
Knife Lake ⊜	184	53.47 N	91.20 W
Knife River Indian Villages National Historical Site ⊥	198	47.21 N	101.23 W
Knight Inlet c	182	50.41 N	125.40 W
Knight Island I	180	60.20 N	147.45 W
Knighton	42	52.21 N	3.03 W
Knightsen	226	37.58 N	121.40 W
Knights Landing	226	38.47 N	121.43 W
Knightstown	218	39.47 N	85.31 W
Knightville Dam ◆[6]	207	42.17 N	72.52 W
Knik Arm c	180	61.25 N	149.45 W
Knin	36	44.02 N	16.12 E
Knippa	196	29.18 N	99.38 W
Knislinge	26	56.11 N	14.05 E
Knittelfeld	61	47.14 N	14.50 E
Knittlingen	56	49.01 N	8.45 E
Knivsbjerg ʌ[2]	41	55.08 N	9.27 E
Knivsta	40	59.43 N	17.48 E
Knjaževac	38	43.34 N	22.16 E
Knob, Cape ➤	162	34.32 S	119.16 E
Knobby Head ➤	162	29.40 S	114.58 E
Knob Noster	194	38.45 N	93.33 W
Knob Peak ʌ	116	12.28 N	121.21 E
Knoc	48	52.38 N	9.20 W
Knock	46	57.33 N	2.45 W
Knockholt	260	51.18 N	0.06 E
Knockholt Pound	260	51.19 N	0.08 E
Knocklayd ʌ	48	55.09 N	6.15 W
Knocklong	48	52.26 N	8.24 W
Knockmealdown Mountains ⋏	48	52.10 N	8.00 W
Knokke	50	51.21 N	3.17 E
Knole ⊥	260	51.16 N	0.12 E
Knolls Green	262	53.19 N	2.18 W
Knollwood, Ct., U.S.	207	41.16 N	72.23 W
Knollwood, Il., U.S.	278	42.17 N	87.53 W
Knollwood, Md., U.S.	284c	39.02 N	76.58 W
Knollwood Park	216	42.14 N	84.22 W
Knon ⊜	40	60.12 N	13.40 E
Knossós ⊥	38	35.20 N	25.10 E
Knottingley	44	53.43 N	1.14 W
Knott's Berry Farm ♠	280	33.50 N	118.00 W
Knotts Island	208	36.31 N	75.56 W
Knotty Ash ◆[8]	262	53.25 N	2.54 W
Knotty Green	260	51.37 N	0.39 W
Knowland State Arboretum and Park ♠	282	37.45 N	122.09 W
Knowle	42	52.23 N	1.43 W
Knowlesville	210	43.14 N	78.19 W
Knowlton Lake ⊜	212	44.28 N	76.41 W
Knowltonwood	285	39.53 N	75.24 W
Knowsley ◆[8], Eng., U.K.	262	53.27 N	2.51 W
Knowsley ◆[8], Eng., U.K.	262	53.27 N	2.50 W
Knowsley Hall ᵾ	262	53.26 N	2.50 W
Knowsley Park ♠	262	53.27 N	2.49 W
Knox, In., U.S.	216	41.17 N	86.37 W
Knox, N.Y., U.S.	210	42.40 N	74.07 W
Knox, Pa., U.S.	214	41.14 N	79.32 W
Knox □[6], Mo., U.S.	219	40.08 N	92.09 W
Knox □[6], Oh., U.S.	214	40.23 N	82.29 W
Knox, Cape ➤	182	54.11 N	133.04 W
Knoxboro	210	42.58 N	75.36 W
Knox City, Mo., U.S.	219	40.08 N	92.00 W
Knox City, Tx., U.S.	196	33.25 N	99.49 W
Knox Coast ⊥[2]	9	66.30 S	105.00 E
Knox Dale	214	41.05 N	79.02 W
Knoxfield	274b	37.53 S	145.15 E
Knox Lake ⊜[1]	214	40.31 N	82.30 W
Knoxville, Ga., U.S.	192	32.43 N	83.59 W
Knoxville, Il., U.S.	190	40.54 N	90.17 W
Knoxville, Ia., U.S.	190	41.19 N	93.06 W
Knoxville, Pa., U.S.	210	41.57 N	77.26 W
Knoxville, Tn., U.S.	192	35.57 N	83.55 W
Knuckles ʌ	122	7.24 N	80.48 E
Knudshoved Odde ➤[1]	41	55.03 N	11.45 E
Knüll ʌ	56	50.53 N	9.24 E
Knutby	40	59.55 N	18.15 E
Knuthenborg	41	54.50 N	11.30 E
Knutsford	44	53.19 N	2.22 W
Knysna	158	34.02 S	23.02 E
Knyszyn	30	53.19 N	22.55 E
Koala Sanctuary ◆[4]	274a	33.40 S	151.10 E
Koani	154	6.08 S	39.17 E
Kob'	88	55.25 N	101.24 E
Koba	112	2.29 S	106.24 E
Kob'aj	74	63.34 N	126.30 E
Kőbánya ◆[8]	264c	47.29 N	19.10 E
Kobarid	36	46.15 N	13.35 E
Kobar Sink ⊥[7]	144	13.35 N	40.50 E
Kobayashi	92	31.59 N	130.59 E
Kōbe, Nihon	96	34.41 N	135.10 E
Kōbe, Nihon	270	34.41 N	135.10 E
Kōbe-kō c	270	34.40 N	135.12 E
Kobel'aki	78	49.09 N	34.12 E
København (Copenhagen)	41	55.40 N	12.35 E
København □[6]	41	55.45 N	12.25 E
Kōbe University ᵾ[2]	270	34.43 N	135.14 E
Kobi	84	42.33 N	44.32 E
Koblenz, Dtsch.	56	50.21 N	7.35 E
Koblenz, Schw.	58	47.37 N	8.14 E
Koblenz □[5]	56	50.10 N	7.30 E
Kobo, Ityo.	144	12.11 N	39.33 E
Kobo, Zaïre	152	4.54 S	17.09 E
Ko-boke ♠	96	33.50 N	133.46 E
Koboko	154	3.25 N	30.58 E
Koboldo	89	52.58 N	132.42 E
Kobona	76	60.01 N	31.36 E
Kobou ≃	152	6.13 N	23.19 E
Kobowen Swamp ≋	144	5.38 N	33.54 E
Koboža	76	58.49 N	35.01 E
Koboža ≃	76	58.52 N	36.17 E
Kobra	24	60.03 N	50.44 E
Kobrin	76	52.13 N	24.21 E
Kobrinskoje	76	59.25 N	30.07 E
Kobroor, Pulau I	164	6.12 S	134.32 E
Kobuchizawa	94	35.52 N	138.19 E
Kobuga-hara ♠	94	36.40 N	139.35 E
Kobuk	180	66.54 N	156.52 W
Kobuk ≃	180	66.45 N	161.00 W
Kobuk Valley National Park ♠	180	67.20 N	159.00 W
Kobuleti	84	41.50 N	41.47 E
Kobushiga-take ʌ	94	35.54 N	138.44 E
Kobylanka	54	53.19 N	14.50 E
Kobylin	30	51.43 N	17.13 E
Kobyl'nik	76	54.56 N	26.41 E
Kobyžča	78	50.49 N	31.30 E
Kocaali	130	41.03 N	30.52 E
Kocaaliler	130	37.19 N	30.44 E
Kocaavşar ≃	130	40.08 N	27.57 E
Kocaeli □[4]	130	40.55 N	29.55 E
Kocaeli → İzmit	130	40.46 N	29.55 E
Koçali	130	37.55 N	38.15 E
Kočani	38	41.55 N	22.25 E
Koçarlı	130	37.45 N	27.42 E
Kocasinan ◆[8]	267b	41.01 N	28.50 E
Koçbaşı Tepe ʌ	84	39.25 N	43.21 E
Kočečum ≃	74	64.17 N	101.10 E
Kočelajevo	80	54.01 N	44.02 E
Kočemary	80	54.50 N	40.58 E
Kočen'ajevka	80	53.52 N	46.59 E
Kočen'ga, Ross.	76	60.09 N	43.33 E
Kočenga, Ross.	88	55.55 N	104.06 E
Kočenga ≃	88	55.55 N	104.06 E
Kočerdyk	86	54.35 N	62.58 E
Kočerga	88	55.15 N	103.46 E
Kočerov	78	50.21 N	29.21 E
Kočetovka, Ross.	80	55.16 N	46.07 E
Kočetovka, Ross.	80	52.58 N	40.29 E
Kočevar	76	60.26 N	42.11 E
Kočevje	36	45.38 N	14.52 E
Kočevo	86	59.36 N	54.18 E
Koch'am-ni	98	41.06 N	129.23 E
Kŏch'ang, Taehan	98	35.26 N	126.42 E
Kŏch'ang, Taehan	98	35.41 N	127.55 E
Kochanoviči	76	55.52 N	28.08 E
Kochanovo	76	54.28 N	30.01 E
Koch Bihār	124	26.19 N	89.26 E
Kochel	64	47.39 N	11.22 E
Kochelsee ⊜	64	47.38 N	11.20 E
Kochena	158	27.00 S	18.50 E
Kocher ≃	56	49.14 N	9.12 E
Kōchi, Nihon	96	34.28 N	132.53 E
Kōchi, Nihon	96	33.33 N	133.33 E
Kōchi □[5]	96	33.40 N	133.30 E
Kōchi-dani ♠	94	34.34 N	136.10 E
Kochinda	174m	26.08 N	127.43 E
Koch Island I	176	69.38 N	78.15 W
Kochiu → Gejiu	90	23.22 N	103.06 E
Kochma	80	56.56 N	41.06 E
Koch Peak ʌ	202	45.02 N	111.28 W
Kochugaon	124	26.34 N	90.04 E
Kock	30	51.39 N	22.27 E
Kočki, Ross.	86	52.24 N	80.40 E
Kočki, Ross.	86	54.20 N	80.29 E
Kočkor-Ata	85	41.04 N	72.29 E
Kočkorka	85	42.14 N	75.45 E
Kocksoord	273d	26.13 S	27.39 E
Kočkurovo	80	54.02 N	45.26 E
Kočmes	24	66.12 N	60.44 E
Kočon'ovo	86	55.02 N	82.12 E
Kočov	60	49.49 N	12.44 E
Kočubej	84	44.24 N	46.33 E
Kočubejevskoje	84	44.41 N	41.41 E
Kōda, Nihon	94	34.52 N	137.10 E
Kōda, Nihon	96	34.42 N	132.45 E
Kodačdikost	24	63.11 N	55.49 E
Kodaikānal	122	10.14 N	77.29 E
Kodaira	94	35.44 N	139.29 E
Kodama	94	36.11 N	139.08 E
Kodar, chrebet ⋏	88	57.15 N	118.10 E
Kodāri	124	27.56 N	85.56 E
Kodarma	124	24.28 N	85.36 E
Kodera ◆[8]	270	34.41 N	135.04 E
Kodersdorf	54	51.15 N	14.53 E
Kodi	152	3.34 S	22.12 E
Kodiak	180	57.48 N	152.23 W
Kodiak Island I	180	57.30 N	153.30 W
Kodiang	114	6.24 N	100.18 E
Kodinār	120	20.47 N	70.42 E
Kodino	24	63.43 N	39.41 E
Kodo ≃	152	7.05 N	19.10 E
Kodo, Jabal ʌ	140	12.26 N	23.38 E
Kodok	140	9.53 N	32.07 E
Kodori ≃	84	42.47 N	41.10 E
Kodorskij chrebet ⋏	84	43.00 N	42.00 E
Kodra	78	50.36 N	29.34 E
Kodry ⋏[2]	78	47.10 N	28.25 E
Kodyma	78	48.07 N	29.07 E
Kodyma ≃	78	48.01 N	30.48 E
Kodžori	84	41.40 N	44.41 E
Koegas	158	29.16 S	22.20 E
Koehn Lake ⊜	228	35.20 N	117.53 W
Koekelare	50	51.05 N	2.58 E
Koekenaap	158	31.30 S	18.18 E
Koeltztown	219	38.19 N	92.03 W
Koenigsmacker	56	49.24 N	6.17 E
Koersel	56	51.04 N	5.16 E
Koes	156	25.59 S	19.08 E
Kofa Mountains ⋏	200	33.20 N	114.00 W
Kofçaz	130	41.58 N	27.12 E
Kofeld	58	47.44 N	9.41 E
Köfering	60	48.56 N	12.12 E
Koffiefontein	158	29.30 S	25.00 E
Kofiau, Pulau I	164	1.11 S	129.50 E
Köflach	61	47.04 N	15.05 E
Koforidua	150	6.03 N	0.17 W
Kōfu, Nihon	94	35.39 N	138.35 E
Kōfu, Nihon	96	35.17 N	133.30 E
Koga, Nihon	94	36.11 N	139.43 E
Koga, Nihon	96	33.40 N	130.30 E
Koga, Tan.	154	6.14 S	32.25 E
Kogaluc ≃	176	59.40 N	77.35 W
Kogaluc, Baie c	176	59.20 N	77.50 W
Kogaluk ≃	176	56.12 N	61.44 W
Kogan	166	27.03 S	150.46 E
Kogane	268	35.50 N	139.56 E
Koganei	94	35.42 N	139.32 E
Kogarah	274a	33.58 S	151.08 E
Kogarah Bay c	274a	33.59 S	151.07 E
Køge, Dan.	41	55.27 N	12.11 E
Kōge, Nihon	96	35.24 N	134.15 E
Køge Bugt c, Dan.	41	55.30 N	12.20 E
Køge Bugt c, Kal. Nun.	176	65.00 N	40.30 W
Kogil'nik ≃	78	45.51 N	29.38 E
Kogin Baba	146	7.55 N	11.30 E
Koglhof	61	47.19 N	15.40 E
Kogon ≃	150	11.09 N	14.42 W
Kogoni	150	14.44 N	6.02 W
Kŏgŭm-do I	98	34.27 N	127.11 E
Kohak	128	25.44 N	62.33 E
Kohala Mountains ⋏	229d	20.05 N	155.45 W
Kohama-shima I	175d	24.19 N	123.59 E
Kohāt	123	33.35 N	71.26 E
Kohāt ≃	123	33.24 N	71.48 E
Kohatk Wash V	200	32.38 N	111.55 W
Kohila	76	59.10 N	24.45 E
Kohīma	120	25.40 N	94.07 E
Kohistān □[9]	123	35.03 N	72.52 W
Kohlberg ʌ[2]	263	51.18 N	7.46 E
Kohler	190	43.44 N	87.46 W
Kohlstädt	52	51.50 N	8.52 E
Kohoku	94	35.26 N	136.15 E
Kōhoku ◆[8]	268	35.31 N	139.38 E
Kohren-Sahlis	54	51.01 N	12.36 E
Kohsān	128	34.39 N	61.12 E
Kohtla-Järve	76	59.24 N	27.15 E
Kohu → Kōfu	94	35.39 N	138.35 E
Kohukohu	172	35.21 S	173.32 E
Kohŭng	98	34.37 N	127.16 E
Kohunlich ⊥	232	18.27 N	89.01 W
Kohuratahi	172	39.06 S	174.46 E
Koide	94	37.13 N	138.57 E
Koidern	180	61.58 N	140.25 W
Koidu	150	8.38 N	10.59 W
Koigi	76	58.50 N	25.45 E
Koihoa	110	8.12 N	93.29 E
Koil-Aligarh → Alīgarh	124	27.53 N	78.05 E
Koimbani	157a	11.37 S	43.23 E
Koindu	150	8.26 N	10.19 W
Koin-ni	98	40.28 N	126.22 E
Koitere ⊜	26	62.58 N	30.45 E
Koito ≃	94	35.21 N	139.52 E
Kojandy	86	49.51 N	75.40 E
Kojda	24	66.23 N	42.31 E
Kŏje-do I	98	34.52 N	128.37 E
Kojetin	30	49.21 N	17.18 E
Kojgorodok	24	60.26 N	50.58 E
Ko-jima I	92a	41.22 N	139.48 E
Kojima-ko ⊜[1]	96	34.37 N	134.00 E
Kojŏ	98	38.57 N	127.51 E
Kojonup	162	33.50 S	117.09 E
Kojsary	85	42.33 N	78.10 E
Kojsug	83	47.07 N	39.41 E
Kojtas, Kaz.	86	51.32 N	76.15 E
Kojtaš, Uzb.	85	40.11 N	67.19 E
Kok (Hkok) ≃	110	20.14 N	100.09 E
Kōka	94	34.54 N	136.13 E
Koka, Lake ⊜[1]	144	8.23 N	39.05 E
Kokai ≃	94	35.52 N	140.08 E
K'okajgyr	85	40.43 N	75.37 E
Kokalaat	86	49.47 N	64.15 E
Kokand	85	40.33 N	70.57 E
Kokanee Glacier Provincial Park ♠	182	49.47 N	117.10 W
Kokankišlak	85	40.56 N	72.30 E
Kökar I	26	59.56 N	20.55 E
Kokas	164	2.42 S	132.26 E
Kokašice	60	49.53 N	12.57 E
Kokava nad Rimavicou	30	48.34 N	19.50 E
Kokawa	96	34.16 N	135.24 E
K'okbel'	85	40.17 N	72.55 E
Kokčetav	86	53.17 N	69.25 E
Kokčetavskaja vozvyšennost' ⋏[1]	86	52.50 N	69.00 E
Kokee State Park ♠	229b	22.08 N	159.40 W
Kokemäenjoki ≃	26	61.33 N	21.42 E
Kokemäki	26	61.15 N	22.21 E
Kokenau	164	4.43 S	136.26 E
Ko Kha	110	18.11 N	99.24 E
Kokhav HaYarden (Belvoir) ⊥	132	32.36 N	35.31 E
Kókhi, Ákra ➤	267c	37.53 N	23.27 E
Koki	150	15.30 N	15.59 W
Kokinu	268	35.59 N	139.59 E
Kokiu → Gejiu	102	23.22 N	103.06 E
Kok-Jangak	85	41.02 N	73.12 E
Kokka	140	20.00 N	30.35 E
Kokkilai Lagoon c	122	9.00 N	80.56 E
Kokkola (Karleby)	26	63.50 N	23.07 E
Kokku	98	40.22 N	128.44 E
Koknese	76	56.39 N	25.29 E
Koko	150	11.26 N	4.32 E
Kokoda	164	8.52 S	147.45 E
Koko Head ➤	229c	21.16 N	157.42 W
Kokola	154	0.47 N	29.36 E
Kokole Point ➤	229b	21.59 N	159.46 W
Kokolik ≃	180	69.46 N	163.00 W
Kokolopozo	150	5.08 N	6.05 W
K'ok'omeren ≃	85	41.43 N	73.54 E
Kokomo, Hi., U.S.	229a	20.52 N	156.18 W
Kokomo, In., U.S.	216	40.29 N	86.08 W
Kokomo, Ms., U.S.	194	31.11 N	90.00 W
Kokong	156	24.27 S	23.03 E
Kokonoe	96	33.10 N	131.10 E
Koko Nor → Qinghai Hu ⊜	102	36.50 N	100.20 E
Kokopo	164	4.20 S	152.15 E
Kokorevka	76	52.35 N	34.16 E
Kokosing ≃	214	40.22 N	82.12 W
Kokos-Inseln → Cocos (Keeling) Islands □[2]	14	12.10 S	96.55 E
Kokoškino	265b	55.38 N	37.11 E
Kokpāra Narsinghgarh	126	22.31 N	86.33 E
Kokpaš	86	51.12 N	87.45 E
Kokpekty	86	48.45 N	82.24 E
Kokrājhār	124	26.24 N	90.16 E
Kokrines	180	64.56 N	154.42 W
Kokrines Hills ⋏[2]	180	65.15 N	154.00 W
Koksa ≃	86	50.16 N	85.36 E
Kokšaalatau, chrebet ⋏	72	41.00 N	78.00 E
Koksan	98	38.46 N	126.40 E
Koksaraj	85	42.40 N	68.08 E
Kokšekol', ozero ⊜	86	46.05 N	62.00 E
Koksijde	50	51.07 N	2.38 E
Koksilah	224	48.40 N	123.38 W
Koksilah ≃	224	48.45 N	123.39 W
Koksoak ≃	176	58.32 N	68.10 W
Koksŏng	98	35.17 N	127.17 E
Koksovyj	78	48.12 N	40.39 E
Kokstad	158	30.32 S	29.29 E
Koksu, Kaz.	85	41.27 N	68.01 E
Koksu, Kaz.	86	44.59 N	77.56 E
Koktal	86	44.09 N	79.48 E
Koktas, Kaz.	86	47.33 N	70.55 E
Koktas, Kaz.	86	45.59 N	73.32 E
Kok-Taš, Kyrg.	85	41.12 N	72.25 E
Kokterek	80	49.25 N	49.15 E
Koktubek	86	48.07 N	56.51 E
Kokubu, Nihon	92	31.44 N	130.46 E
Kokubu, Nihon	96	34.56 N	132.07 E
Kokubunji, Nihon	94	36.22 N	139.51 E
Kokubunji, Nihon	96	34.18 N	133.58 E
Kokubunji, Nihon	268	35.42 N	139.29 E
Kokubunji Temple ᵾ[1]	268	35.44 N	139.55 E
Kokufu	96	35.28 N	134.16 E
Kokuj	88	52.13 N	117.33 E
Kokujbel' ≃	85	38.21 N	72.46 E
Kokžar	86	49.01 N	60.10 E
Kol ≃	128	26.59 N	55.47 E
Kola, Indon.	164	5.26 S	134.29 E
Kola, Ross.	24	68.53 N	33.01 E
Kola ≃	24	68.53 N	33.02 E
Kolachel	122	8.10 N	77.15 E
Kolāchi ≃	120	27.08 N	67.02 E
Kol'adovka	83	49.05 N	39.12 E
Kolageran	84	40.58 N	44.37 E
Kolahun	150	8.24 N	10.02 W
Kolaka	112	4.03 S	121.36 E
Kolambo	152	7.34 S	21.58 E
Kolambugan	116	8.07 N	123.55 E
Kolangār	120	34.02 N	69.01 E
Kola Peninsula → Kol'skij poluostrov ➤[1]	24	67.30 N	37.00 E
Kolār	122	13.08 N	78.08 E
Kolāras	124	25.14 N	77.36 E
Kolār Gold Fields	122	12.55 N	78.17 E
Kolari	24	67.20 N	23.48 E
Kolarovgrad → Šumen	38	43.16 N	26.55 E
Kolárovo	30	47.52 N	18.02 E
Kolašin	38	42.49 N	19.31 E
Kolāyat	120	27.50 N	72.57 E
Kolbači	89	54.22 N	123.02 E
Kolbäck	40	59.34 N	16.15 E
Kolbäcksån ≃	40	59.32 N	16.16 E
Kol'baj, gora ʌ[2]	86	43.43 N	53.57 E
Kolbano	112	10.02 S	124.31 E
Kolbasna	78	47.47 N	29.13 E
Kolbča	76	53.39 N	29.14 E
Kolberg → Kołobrzeg	30	54.12 N	15.33 E
Kolbermoor	64	47.51 N	12.04 E
Kolbio	144	1.10 S	41.15 E
Kolbnitz	64	46.52 N	13.19 E
Kolbotn	26	59.49 N	10.48 E
Kolbuszowa	30	50.15 N	21.47 E
Kolby Kås	41	55.48 N	10.33 E
Kolchida ≚	84	42.15 N	42.00 E
Kolchozabad	120	37.27 N	68.31 E
Kol'covo	82	54.27 N	36.40 E
Kol'čuga	82	55.43 N	37.12 E
Kol'čugino	80	56.18 N	39.23 E
Kołczewo	54	53.58 N	14.38 E
Kolda	150	12.53 N	14.57 W
Kolda □[4]	150	12.50 N	14.50 W
Kolding	41	55.31 N	9.29 E
Kolding Fjord c	41	55.30 N	9.35 E
Kole, Zaïre	152	3.27 S	22.29 E
Kole, Zaïre	154	2.07 N	25.26 E
Kolea	34	36.38 N	2.46 E
Kolebīra	124	22.43 N	84.42 E
Kole Kalyan ◆[8]	272c	19.06 N	72.51 E
Kolenfeld	52	52.24 N	9.27 E
Koleno	80	51.52 N	44.07 E
Kolenté	150	10.06 N	12.37 W
Kolenté (Great Scarcies) ≃	150	8.55 N	13.08 W
Kolga	76	59.32 N	25.42 E
Kolgujev, ostrov I	24	69.05 N	49.15 E
Kolhāpur, India	122	16.06 N	78.16 E
Kolhāpur, India	122	16.42 N	74.13 E
Kolho	26	62.08 N	24.31 E
Koli	76	59.30 N	34.30 E
Koli ʌ[2]	26	63.06 N	29.48 E
Koli, Jabal ʌ	140	14.05 N	25.31 E
Kolia	150	9.46 N	6.28 W
Koliba (Corubal) ≃	150	11.57 N	15.06 W
Koliganek	180	59.48 N	157.25 W
Kolima ⊜	26	63.16 N	25.50 E
Kolimbine ≃	150	14.26 N	11.23 W
Kolín	30	50.01 N	15.13 E
Kolka	76	57.45 N	22.35 E
Kølkær	41	56.04 N	9.06 E
Kolkasrags ➤	76	57.47 N	22.36 E
Kolki, Ukr.	78	51.37 N	26.37 E
Kolki, Ukr.	78	51.07 N	25.41 E
Kolkwitz	54	51.45 N	14.15 E
Kollbach ≃	60	48.36 N	12.58 E
Kölleda	54	51.11 N	11.15 E
Kollegāl	122	12.09 N	77.07 E
Kolleru Lake ⊜	122	16.39 N	81.13 E
Kollum	52	53.16 N	6.09 E
Kollund	41	54.51 N	9.27 E

Symbols in the index entries represent the broad categories identified in the key at the right. Symbols with superior numbers (⋏[1]) identify subcategories (see complete key on page *I · 1).*

Symbole im Register stellen die rechts im Schlüssel erklärten Kategorien dar. Symbole mit hochgestellten Ziffern (⋏[1]) bezeichnen Unterabteilungen einer Kategorie (vgl. vollständiger Schlüssel auf Seite *I · 1).*

Los símbolos incluídos en el texto del índice representan las grandes categorias identificadas con la clave a la derecha. Los símbolos con numeros en su parte superior (⋏[1]) identifican las subcategorías (véase la clave completa en la página *I · 1).*

Les symboles de l'index représentent les catégories indiquées dans la légende à droite. Les symboles suivis d'un indice (⋏[1]) représentent des sous-catégories (voir légende complète à la page *I · 1).*

Os símbolos incluídos no texto do índice representam as grandes categorias identificadas com a chave à direita. Os símbolos com números em sua parte superior (⋏[1]) identificam as subcategorias (veja-se a chave completa à página *I · 1).*

ʌ Mountain	Berg	Montaña	Montagne	Montanha
⋏ Mountains	Gebirge	Montañas	Montagnes	Montanhas
)(Pass	Paß	Paso	Col	Passo
V Valley, Canyon	Tal, Cañon	Valle, Cañón	Vallée, Canyon	Vale, Canhão
≚ Plain	Ebene	Llano	Plaine	Planície
➤ Cape	Kap	Cabo	Cap	Cabo
I Island	Insel	Isla	Île	Ilha
II Islands	Inseln	Islas	Îles	Ilhas
⊥ Other Topographic Features	Andere Topographische Objekte	Otros Elementos Topográficos	Autres données topographiques	Outros acidentes topográficos

ESPAÑOL

Nombre	Página	Lat.°′	Long.°′ W = Oeste
Kolmanskop	156	26.40 S	15.12 E
Kolmården	40	58.40 N	16.23 E
Kolmården ⩘[2]	40	58.41 N	16.35 E
Kolmårdens Djurpark ♠	40	58.40 N	16.29 E
Kolmogorovo	86	59.15 N	91.20 E
Köln (Cologne)	56	50.56 N	6.59 E
Köln □[5]	56	50.55 N	6.40 E
Köln-Bonn, Flughafen ⊠	56	50.50 N	7.10 E
Kolno	30	53.25 N	21.56 E
Kolo, Niger	150	13.14 N	2.20 E
Koło, Pol.	30	52.12 N	18.38 E
Kolo, Tan.	154	4.44 S	35.50 E
Koloa	229b	21.54 N	159.28 W
Kolobovo	80	56.42 N	41.21 E
Kołobrzeg	30	54.12 N	15.33 E
Koloč' ≃	82	55.34 N	35.52 E
Kolochau	54	51.44 N	13.16 E
Kolodn'a	76	54.48 N	32.09 E
Kologriv	76	58.51 N	44.17 E
Kologrivovka	80	51.44 N	45.20 E
Kolojar	80	52.34 N	46.58 E
Kolok (Golok) ≃	114	6.15 N	102.05 E
Kolokani	150	13.35 N	8.02 W
Koloko	150	11.05 N	5.19 W
Kolokol'covka, Ross.	80	52.36 N	49.48 E
Kolokol'covka, Ross.	80	51.12 N	44.36 E
Kololo	144	7.29 N	41.58 E
Kolom'agi ◆[8]	265a	60.00 N	30.17 E
Kolom'agi Airport ⊠	265a	60.01 N	30.17 E
Kolomak	78	49.50 N	35.18 E
Kolombangara Island I	175e	8.00 S	157.05 E
Kolomea → Kolomyja	78	48.32 N	25.04 E
Kolomenka ≃	82	55.06 N	38.46 E
Kolomenskaja Sloboda	82	54.22 N	38.15 E
Kolomenskoje ◆[8]	265b	55.40 N	37.41 E
Kolomna	82	55.05 N	38.49 E
Kolomyja	78	48.32 N	25.04 E
Kolondiéba	150	11.05 N	6.54 W
Kolonga	174w	21.08 S	175.04 W
Kolonia	174r	6.58 N	158.13 E
Kolonie Stolp	264a	52.28 N	13.46 E
Kolono	112	4.18 S	122.41 E
Kolonodale	112	2.00 S	121.19 E
Kolora	272b	22.55 N	88.22 E
Kolosib	120	24.14 N	92.42 E
Kol'osnoje	78	46.02 N	29.56 E
Kolosovka	86	56.28 N	73.36 E
Kolovai	174w	21.06 S	175.20 W
Kolovertnoje	80	50.36 N	51.06 E
Kolowana Watobo, Teluk c	112	5.00 S	123.06 E
Kolozsvár → Cluj-Napoca	38	46.47 N	23.36 E
Kolp' ≃	76	59.20 N	36.49 E
Kolpaševo	86	58.20 N	82.50 E
Kolpino	76	59.45 N	30.36 E
Kölpinsee ⊜	54	53.30 N	12.34 E
Kolpny	76	52.15 N	37.02 E
Kölsa	54	51.28 N	12.13 E
Kol'skij poluostrov (Kola Peninsula) ›[1]	24	67.30 N	37.00 E
Kolsnaren ⊜	40	59.02 N	16.01 E
Kolsva	40	59.36 N	15.50 E
Kol'togan	85	43.51 N	67.25 E
Koltovskaja	80	52.47 N	44.16 E
Koltubanovskij	80	52.57 N	52.02 E
Koltuši	265a	59.56 N	30.40 E
Kol'ubakino	82	55.40 N	36.32 E
Kolubara ≃	38	44.40 N	20.15 E
Kol'učinskaja guba c	180	66.40 N	174.30 W
Koluel Kayke	254	46.43 S	68.14 W
Kolumbien → Colombia □[1]	246	4.00 N	72.00 W
Kol'upanovo	82	54.26 N	36.14 E
Koluškino	78	48.39 N	40.56 E
Koluszki	30	51.44 N	19.49 E
Koluton	86	51.43 N	69.25 E
Koluton ≃	86	51.42 N	69.10 E
Kolva ≃	24	65.55 N	57.15 E
Kolvereid	24	64.51 N	11.32 E
Kølvrå	41	56.18 N	9.08 E
Kolwezi	154	10.43 S	25.28 E
Kolyberovo	82	55.16 N	38.44 E
Kolyčevo	82	55.30 N	37.52 E
Kolyma ≃	74	69.30 N	161.00 E
Kolymskaja	74	68.44 N	158.44 E
Kolymskaja nizmennost' ≚	74	68.30 N	154.00 E
Kolyšlej	80	52.42 N	44.32 E
Kolyšovo	82	54.54 N	36.57 E
Kolyvan', Ross.	86	51.18 N	82.34 E
Kolyvan', Ross.	86	55.18 N	82.45 E
Kom ʌ	38	43.10 N	23.03 E
Kom ≃	152	2.18 N	11.40 E
Koma, Ityo.	144	8.27 N	36.52 E
Koma, Mya.	110	15.39 N	98.12 E
Koma, Ross.	86	55.02 N	91.19 E
Koma ≃	94	35.59 N	139.26 E
Komadougou Yobé (Komadugu Yobe) ≃	146	13.43 N	13.20 E
Komadugu Gana ≃	146	13.05 N	12.24 E
Komadugu Yobe (Komadougou Yobé) ≃	146	13.43 N	13.20 E
Komae	94	35.38 N	139.35 E
Komagane	94	35.43 N	137.55 E
Komaga-take ʌ, Nihon	92a	42.04 N	140.41 E
Komaga-take ʌ, Nihon	94	35.45 N	138.14 E
Komaga-take ʌ, Nihon	94	35.47 N	137.48 E
Komagome ◆[8]	268	35.44 N	139.45 E
Komaki	94	35.17 N	136.55 E
Komandorskije ostrova II	74	55.00 N	167.00 E
Komandorski Village	226	37.43 N	121.54 W
Komariči	76	52.27 N	34.47 E
Komarin	78	51.26 N	30.31 E
Komarniki	78	49.00 N	23.04 E
Komárno, Česko.	30	47.45 N	18.09 E
Komarno, Ukr.	78	49.38 N	23.42 E
Komárom	30	47.44 N	18.08 E
Komárom-Esztergom □[6]	30	47.40 N	18.15 E
Komarovka	78	51.14 N	32.07 E
Komarovo	76	58.39 N	33.26 E
Komarovy	86	60.26 N	75.50 E
Komati (Incomáti) ≃	156	25.46 S	32.43 E
Komatipoort	156	25.25 S	31.55 E
Komatsu, Nihon	94	36.24 N	136.27 E
Komatsu, Nihon	96	33.53 N	133.07 E
Komatsu-kūkō ⊠	94	36.24 N	136.26 E
Komatsushima	96	34.00 N	134.35 E
Kombissiri	150	12.04 N	1.20 W
Kombone	152	4.37 N	9.19 E
Komdhārā	272b	22.53 N	88.14 E
Kome Island I	154	0.06 S	32.45 E
Komen	64	45.49 N	13.44 E
Komenda	150	5.03 N	1.29 W
Komenoi	268	35.55 N	140.01 E
Komering ≃	112	2.59 S	104.50 E
Komeshia	154	8.01 S	27.07 E
Komfane	164	5.39 S	134.44 E
Komga	158	32.35 S	27.55 E
Komi Avtonomnaja Sovetskaja Socialističeskaja Respublika □[3]	24	64.00 N	54.00 E
Kominato → Amatsu-kominato	94	35.07 N	140.10 E
Kominternovskoje	78	46.49 N	30.56 E
Komin Yanga	150	11.42 N	0.08 E

FRANÇAIS

Nom	Page	Lat.°′	Long.°′ W = Ouest
Komi-Perm'ackij Avtonomnyj Okrug □[8]	24	60.00 N	54.30 E
Komissarovka, Ross.	83	48.07 N	40.09 E
Komissarovka, Ukr.	83	48.23 N	38.32 E
Komissarovo	89	44.59 N	131.46 E
Komissarovskij	80	47.29 N	42.59 E
Komkans	158	31.16 S	18.09 E
Komló	30	46.12 N	18.16 E
Kommadagga	158	33.09 S	25.55 E
Kommandodrif	158	27.30 S	26.14 E
Kommandokraal	158	33.06 S	22.51 E
Kommetjie	158	34.08 S	18.21 E
Kommunal'naja	88	52.03 N	115.06 E
Kommunar, Ross.	80	58.10 N	43.33 E
Kommunar, Ross.	86	54.20 N	89.18 E
Kommunarka	265b	55.34 N	37.29 E
Kommunarsk	83	48.30 N	38.47 E
Kommunary	26	60.54 N	29.47 E
Kommunizma, pik ʌ	85	38.57 N	72.01 E
Komo ≃	152	0.09 N	9.50 E
Komodo	115b	8.35 S	119.30 E
Komodo, Pulau I	115b	8.36 S	119.30 E
Komoé ≃	150	5.12 N	3.44 W
Komoé, Parc National de la ♠	150	9.00 N	3.30 W
Komoka	214	42.57 N	81.26 W
Komono, Congo	152	3.15 S	13.14 E
Komono, Nihon	94	35.00 N	136.31 E
Komoran, Pulau I	164	8.18 S	138.45 E
Komoren → Comoros □[1]	157a	12.10 S	44.10 E
Komorin, Kap → Comorin, Cape ›	122	8.04 N	77.34 E
Komorn → Komárno	30	47.45 N	18.09 E
Komoro	94	36.19 N	138.26 E
Komotau → Chomutov	54	50.28 N	13.26 E
Komotiní	38	41.08 N	25.25 E
Kompanejevka	78	48.15 N	32.12 E
Kompasberg ʌ	158	31.45 S	24.32 E
Kompiam	164	5.20 S	143.55 E
Kompot	112	0.24 N	124.10 E
Kom → Qom	128	34.39 N	50.54 E
Komrat	78	46.18 N	28.38 E
Komsomolabad	85	38.52 N	69.57 E
Komsomolec	86	53.45 N	62.02 E
Komsomolec, ostrov I	74	80.30 N	95.00 E
Komsomolec, zaliv c	72	45.30 N	52.45 E
Komsomol'sk, Ross.	80	57.02 N	40.21 E
Komsomol'sk, Ross.	86	57.27 N	86.02 E
Komsomol'sk, Ross.	86	55.38 N	88.11 E
Komsomol'sk, Turk.	128	39.02 N	63.36 E
Komsomol'skij, Kaz.	86	47.20 N	53.42 E
Komsomol'skij, Kaz.	86	51.40 N	66.39 E
Komsomol'skij, Ross.	80	54.27 N	45.49 E
Komsomol'skij, Ross.	89	50.22 N	142.10 E
Komsomol'skij, Ukr.	83	47.40 N	37.26 E
Komsomol'sk-na-Amure	89	50.35 N	137.02 E
Komsomol'sk-na-Ust'urte	86	44.03 N	58.20 E
Komsomol'skoje, Ross.	80	55.16 N	47.33 E
Komsomol'skoje, Ross.	80	50.46 N	47.03 E
Komsomol'skoje, Ross.	88	52.29 N	111.06 E
Komsomol'skoje, Ukr.	78	49.43 N	28.40 E
Komsomol'skoje, Ukr.	78	49.35 N	36.30 E
Komsomol'skoje, Ukr.	83	47.40 N	38.05 E
Komsomol'skoj Pravdy, ostrova II	74	77.20 N	107.40 E
Kŏmun-do I	98	34.02 N	127.19 E
Kömürcüpinar ◆[8]	267b	41.15 N	28.51 E
Komusan	98	42.08 N	129.41 E
Komyšn'a	78	50.12 N	33.41 E
Kona, India	272b	22.37 N	88.18 E
Kona, Mali	150	14.57 N	3.53 W
Kona Coast ∸[2]	229d	19.25 N	155.55 W
Konagkend	84	41.04 N	48.37 E
Konakovo	82	56.42 N	36.46 E
Konakpınar, Tür.	130	39.26 N	27.53 E
Konakpınar, Tür.	130	38.53 N	37.22 E
Konan, C. Iv.	150	8.21 N	8.00 W
Kōnan, Nihon	94	35.20 N	136.53 E
Kōnan, Nihon	94	34.56 N	136.11 E
Kōnan ◆[8]	268	35.22 N	139.35 E
Konan → Hŭngnam	98	39.50 N	127.38 E
Konar (Kunar) ≃	123	34.25 N	70.32 E
Konārak	120	19.54 N	86.07 E
Konār Dam ◆[6]	124	23.58 N	85.45 E
Konarhā □[4]	120	35.15 N	71.00 E
Konawa	196	34.57 N	96.45 W
Končanskoje-Suvorovskoje	76	58.39 N	34.04 E
Konceba	78	48.07 N	29.56 E
Konch	124	25.59 N	79.09 E
Konda	74	61.20 N	63.58 E
Konda ≃, Ross.	86	60.40 N	69.46 E
Konda ≃, Ross.	88	53.30 N	113.32 E
Kondagaon	122	19.36 N	81.40 E
Konde	154	4.57 S	39.45 E
Kondega	76	60.14 N	33.30 E
Kondiaronk, Lac ⊜	190	46.56 N	76.45 W
Kondinin	162	32.30 S	118.16 E
Kondinskoje	86	59.40 N	67.22 E
Kondli ◆[8]	272a	28.37 N	77.19 E
Kondoa	154	4.54 S	35.47 E
Kondol'	80	52.49 N	45.03 E
Kondolole	154	1.20 N	25.58 E
Kondopoga	24	62.12 N	34.17 E
Kondorfa	61	46.54 N	16.24 E
Kondratjevo, Ross.	76	60.38 N	28.08 E
Kondratjevo, Ross.	88	57.21 N	98.11 E
Kondrovka	80	54.36 N	43.17 E
Kondrovo	82	54.48 N	35.56 E
Konduga	146	11.39 N	13.24 E
Kondukūr	122	15.13 N	79.55 E
Kondurča ≃	80	53.31 N	50.24 E
Kondūz	120	37.45 N	68.51 E
Kondūz □[4]	120	36.45 N	68.30 E
Koné	175f	21.04 S	164.52 E
Koné, Passe de ⊔	175f	21.08 S	164.41 E
Konecbor	24	64.52 N	57.44 E
Konergino	180	65.54 N	178.50 W
Konfara	150	11.55 N	8.50 W
Kong, C. Iv.	150	9.09 N	4.37 W
Køng, Dan.	41	55.07 N	11.50 E
Kông ≃	110	13.32 N	105.58 E
Kông, Kaôh I	110	11.20 N	103.00 E
Kongakut ≃	180	69.48 N	141.50 W
Kongbo	152	4.44 N	21.23 E
Kongcheng	100	31.02 N	117.05 E
Kongeå ≃	41	55.23 N	8.40 E
Kongens Lyngby	41	55.46 N	12.31 E
Kongfang	100	27.58 N	116.53 E
Kongiganak	180	59.58 N	162.45 W
Konginkangas	26	62.46 N	25.48 E
Kongjiamatou	105	39.07 N	116.10 E
Kongjiatun	104	40.42 N	124.04 E
Kongjiawopeng	89	43.58 N	122.41 E
Kongjiazhuang	105	40.47 N	114.48 E
Kongju	98	36.27 N	127.07 E
Konglong	100	29.56 N	115.54 E
Konglongshan	105	40.33 N	117.17 E
Konglu	102	27.16 N	97.56 E
Kongmoon → Jiangmen	100	22.35 N	113.05 E
Kongo, Republik → Zaire □[1]	138	4.00 S	25.00 E
Kongo → Congo ≃	138	6.04 S	12.24 E

PORTUGUÊS

Nome	Página	Lat.°′	Long.°′ W = Oeste
Kongō-Ikoma-kokutei-kōen ♠	96	34.28 N	135.40 E
Kongolo, Zaïre	154	5.26 S	24.49 E
Kongolo, Zaïre	154	5.23 S	27.00 E
Kongor	140	7.10 N	31.21 E
Kongō-sanchi ⩘	270	34.27 N	135.41 E
Kongoussi	150	13.19 N	1.32 W
Kongō-zan ʌ	96	34.25 N	135.41 E
Kongsberg	26	59.39 N	9.39 E
Kongsvinger	26	60.12 N	12.00 E
Kongsvoll	26	62.18 N	9.37 E
Kongtan	107	29.10 N	104.42 E
Kongur Shan ʌ, Zhg.	85	38.37 N	75.20 E
Kongur Shan ʌ, Zhg.	120	38.37 N	75.20 E
Kongwa	154	6.12 S	36.25 E
Kongyangcun	106	31.23 N	118.54 E
Kongzhen	106	31.29 N	119.00 E
Koni	154	10.42 S	27.15 E
Koni ≃	150	13.05 N	5.37 W
Koniakari	150	14.34 N	10.54 W
Konice	30	49.35 N	16.53 E
Koniecpol	30	50.48 N	19.41 E
Königgrätz → Hradec Králové	30	50.12 N	15.50 E
Königheim	56	49.37 N	9.35 E
Königin Alexandra-Kette → Queen Alexandra Range ⩘	9	84.00 S	168.00 E
Königin Fabiola-Gebirge → Queen Fabiola Mountains ⩘	9	71.30 S	35.40 E
Königin Mary-Küste → Queen Mary Coast ∸[2]	9	67.00 S	96.00 E
Königin Maud-Land → Queen Maud Land ◆[1]	9	72.30 S	12.00 E
König-Otto-Höhe ∸[5]	60	49.15 N	11.42 E
Königsbach	56	48.58 N	8.36 E
Königsberg	56	50.05 N	10.34 E
Königsberg → Kaliningrad	76	54.43 N	20.30 E
Königsborn	263	51.33 N	7.41 E
Königsbrück	54	51.16 N	13.54 E
Königsbrunn, Dtsch.	58	48.16 N	10.53 E
Königsbrunn, Öst.	264b	48.21 N	16.25 E
Königsdorf	64	47.49 N	11.28 E
Königsee	54	50.39 N	11.05 E
Königsfelden ʊ[1]	58	47.29 N	8.14 E
Königsfeld im Schwarzwald	58	48.08 N	8.25 E
Königshain	54	51.11 N	14.52 E
Königshardt ◆[8]	263	51.33 N	6.51 E
Königsheim	58	48.06 N	8.51 E
Königslutter	54	52.15 N	10.49 E
Königsmoor ◆[3]	52	53.15 N	9.40 E
Königssee	64	47.33 N	12.58 E
Königssee ⊜	64	47.36 N	12.59 E
Königsstuhl ∸[4]	54	54.34 N	13.40 E
Königstein, Dtsch.	54	50.55 N	14.04 E
Königstein, Dtsch.	56	50.11 N	8.29 E
Königstein, Dtsch.	60	49.37 N	11.38 E
Königstetten	264b	48.18 N	16.09 E
Königswalde	54	50.33 N	13.02 E
Königswartha	54	51.18 N	14.20 E
Königswiesen	61	48.24 N	14.50 E
Königswinter	56	50.40 N	7.11 E
Königs Wusterhausen	54	52.18 N	13.37 E
Konin	30	52.13 N	18.16 E
Konin □[4]	30	52.20 N	18.20 E
Konispol	38	39.39 N	20.10 E
Kónitsa	38	40.02 N	20.45 E
Köniz	58	46.56 N	7.25 E
Konjic	38	43.39 N	17.57 E
Konka ≃	78	47.40 N	35.22 E
Könkämäälven ≃	24	68.29 N	22.17 E
Konkapot ≃	210	42.03 N	73.20 W
Konkiep ≃	156	28.03 S	17.21 E
Konkō	96	34.32 N	133.37 E
Kon'-Kolodez'	76	52.08 N	39.11 E
Konkouré ≃	150	9.58 N	13.42 W
Kon'kovo	83	47.20 N	38.10 E
Konkudera	88	57.33 N	112.30 E
Konkug University ʊ[2]	271b	37.32 N	127.05 E
Konnagar	126	22.42 N	88.22 E
Könnern	54	51.40 N	11.46 E
Konnevesi ⊜	26	62.40 N	26.35 E
Konnur	122	16.12 N	74.45 E
Kōno	94	35.49 N	136.04 E
Konobejevo	82	55.24 N	38.40 E
Konohana ◆[8]	270	34.41 N	135.26 E
Kōnoike	270	34.42 N	135.37 E
Konolfingen	58	46.53 N	7.38 E
Konongo	150	6.37 N	1.11 W
Konoša	24	60.58 N	40.15 E
Kōno-shima I	96	34.28 N	133.31 E
Kōnosu	94	36.03 N	139.31 E
Konotop	78	51.14 N	33.12 E
Konovalovka	80	53.06 N	51.34 E
Kon'ovo, Ross.	24	62.08 N	39.16 E
Kon'ovo, Ross.	86	56.18 N	70.43 E
Konqi ≃	90	40.40 N	90.10 E
Konradshöhe ◆[8]	264a	52.35 N	13.14 E
Konradsreuth	54	50.16 N	11.50 E
Konsankoro	150	9.02 N	9.00 W
Konsen-daichi ⩘[1]	92a	43.25 N	144.52 E
Końskie	30	51.12 N	20.26 E
Konstabel	158	33.16 S	20.17 E
Konstantinopel → İstanbul	130	41.01 N	28.58 E
Konstantinovka, Ross.	80	56.41 N	50.53 E
Konstantinovka, Ross.	265a	59.47 N	30.08 E
Konstantinovka, Ukr.	78	49.57 N	35.07 E
Konstantinovka, Ukr.	78	47.51 N	31.09 E
Konstantinovka, Ukr.	83	48.32 N	37.43 E
Konstantinovka, Ukr.	83	47.52 N	37.24 E
Konstantinovo	82	56.33 N	38.02 E
Konstantinovsk	80	47.35 N	41.06 E
Konstantinovskij	76	57.50 N	39.36 E
Konstantinovskije Porogi	76	60.34 N	37.04 E
Konstantynów Łódzki	30	51.45 N	19.20 E
Konstanz	58	47.40 N	9.10 E
Kontagora	150	10.24 N	5.28 E
Kontcha	152	7.58 N	12.14 E
Kontejevo	80	58.26 N	41.21 E
Kontha	110	19.30 N	96.03 E
Kontich	50	51.08 N	4.27 E
Kontiolahti	26	62.46 N	29.51 E
Kontiomäki	26	64.21 N	28.09 E
Kon Tum	110	14.21 N	108.00 E
Kontum, Plateau du ⩘[1]	110	13.55 N	108.05 E
Kōnu	96	34.42 N	133.05 E
Kon'uchovo	86	55.08 N	70.38 E
Konus, gora ʌ	180	67.34 N	178.10 E
Konya	130	37.52 N	32.31 E
Konya □[4]	130	38.00 N	33.00 E
Konyr	80	50.25 N	53.25 E
Konyrat	80	49.36 N	47.01 E
Konyrolen	86	44.16 N	79.19 E
Konyševka	78	51.51 N	35.18 E
Konystanu	80	48.51 N	53.20 E
Konz	56	49.42 N	6.34 E
Konza	154	1.45 S	37.07 E
Konžakovskij Kamen', gora ʌ	86	59.38 N	59.08 E
Konzell	60	49.04 N	12.43 E
Koocanusa, Lake ⊜[1]	202	49.00 N	115.10 W
Koog [aan de Zaan]	52	52.27 N	4.49 E
Kookynie	162	29.20 S	121.29 E
Koolamarra	166	20.12 S	140.14 E
Koolatah	164	15.53 S	142.27 E
Koolau Range ⩘	229c	21.35 N	158.00 W
Kooloonong	166	34.53 S	143.09 E
Koolskamp	50	51.00 N	3.12 E
Koolyanobbing	162	30.50 S	119.35 E
Koolywurtie	168b	34.38 S	137.37 E
Koombana Bay c	168a	33.18 S	115.36 E
Koonap ≃	158	33.03 S	26.39 E
Koondrook	166	35.39 S	144.08 E
Koonga	76	58.35 N	24.12 E
Koonibba	162	31.58 S	133.27 E
Koontz Lake	216	41.25 N	86.29 W
Koontz Lake ⊜	216	41.25 N	86.28 W
Koopan-Noord	158	26.53 S	20.41 E
Koopan-Suid	158	27.15 S	20.22 E
Koopmansfontein	158	28.14 S	24.01 E
Koorawatha	166	34.02 S	148.33 E
Koorda	162	30.50 S	117.29 E
Koosa	76	58.33 N	27.07 E
Koosfontein	158	27.22 S	25.27 E
Koosharem	200	38.30 N	111.52 W
Kooskia	202	46.08 N	115.58 W
Koossa	150	9.32 N	8.32 W
Kootenai (Kootenay) ≃	182	49.15 N	117.39 W
Kootenay (Kootenai) ≃	182	49.15 N	117.39 W
Kootenay Indian Reserve ◆[4]	182	49.37 N	115.45 W
Kootenay Lake ⊜	182	49.35 N	116.50 W
Kootenay National Park ♠	182	51.00 N	116.00 W
Kootjieskolk	158	31.15 S	20.21 E
Kootwijk	52	52.12 N	5.45 E
Koo-wee-rup	169	38.12 S	145.30 E
Kopa	85	43.32 N	75.50 E
Kopa ≃	85	43.40 N	76.15 E
Kopāganj	124	26.01 N	83.34 E
Kopāi ≃	126	23.48 N	87.47 E
Kopajgorod	78	48.51 N	27.48 E
Kopanbulak	86	48.56 N	80.52 E
Kopang	115b	8.39 S	116.21 E
Kopanovka	80	47.27 N	46.48 E
Kopanskaja	78	46.17 N	38.29 E
Kopapan	80	50.20 N	50.26 E
Kopargaon	122	19.53 N	74.29 E
Koparkhairna	272c	19.06 N	72.59 E
Koparpāda	272c	19.02 N	73.04 E
Kópasker	24a	66.20 N	16.24 W
Kopatkeviči	76	52.19 N	28.49 E
Kópavogur	24a	64.06 N	21.50 W
Kopceviči	78	52.14 N	28.19 E
Kopé, Mont ʌ[2]	150	4.59 N	7.27 W
Kopejsk	86	55.07 N	61.37 E
Kopenhagen → København	41	55.40 N	12.35 E
Köpenick ◆[8]	54	52.27 N	13.34 E
Köpenick, Schloss ʊ	264a	52.27 N	13.34 E
Koper	36	45.33 N	13.44 E
Köpernitz	54	53.04 N	12.56 E
Kopervik	26	59.17 N	5.18 E
Kopetdag, chrebet ⩘	128	37.50 N	58.00 E
Kopeysk → Kopejsk	86	55.07 N	61.37 E
Kop Geçidi)(	130	40.03 N	40.33 E
Kopice	54	53.44 N	14.32 E
Köping	40	59.31 N	16.00 E
Kopisty	54	50.34 N	13.35 E
Kopjevo	86	55.03 N	89.50 E
Koplik	38	42.13 N	19.26 E
Köpmanholmen	26	63.10 N	18.34 E
Kopnino	82	56.53 N	38.29 E
Kopondei, Tanjung ›	115b	8.04 S	122.52 E
Koporje	76	59.44 N	29.01 E
Koporskaja guba c	76	59.52 N	28.55 E
Koppal	122	15.21 N	76.09 E
Koppang	26	61.34 N	11.04 E
Koppány ≃	30	46.35 N	18.26 E
Kopparberg	40	59.52 N	14.59 E
Kopparbergs Län □[6]	26	61.00 N	14.30 E
Koppel	214	40.50 N	80.19 W
Kopperå	26	63.24 N	11.51 E
Kopperby	41	54.38 N	9.56 E
Kopperl	222	32.04 N	97.30 W
Koppi	89	48.32 N	140.07 E
Koppi ≃	89	48.33 N	140.08 E
Koppies	158	27.20 S	27.30 E
Koppom	26	59.43 N	12.09 E
Kopri	272c	19.11 N	72.58 E
Koprivnica	36	46.10 N	16.50 E
Köprü ≃	130	36.50 N	31.10 E
Köprülü Kanyon Milli Parkı ♠	130	37.20 N	31.18 E
Köprüören	130	39.30 N	29.47 E
Kopt'ovo	80	56.43 N	40.31 E
Kopyčincy	78	49.06 N	25.55 E
Kopyl'	76	53.09 N	27.05 E
Kopylovka	86	58.40 N	82.22 E
Kopylovo, Ross.	24	60.35 N	45.02 E
Kopylovo, Ross.	82	56.26 N	36.25 E
Kopys'	76	54.19 N	30.18 E
Kor ≃	128	29.36 N	53.18 E
Kōra	94	35.12 N	136.15 E
Koraa Shiir	144	3.18 N	46.16 E
Korab ⩘	38	41.47 N	20.34 E
Kor Aban	144	3.58 N	42.44 E
Korablino	80	53.55 N	40.01 E
Korahe	144	6.35 N	44.23 E
Kor'akovka	86	52.24 N	77.08 E
Kor'akskaja Sopka, vulkan ʌ[1]	74	53.20 N	158.43 E
Kor'akskoje nagorje ⩘	74	62.30 N	172.00 E
Kōrakuen ♠	96	34.38 N	133.53 E
Korakuen Stadium ♠	268	35.43 N	139.45 E
Korallenmeer → Coral Sea ⫧[2]	14	20.00 S	158.00 E
Koralpe ⩘	61	46.50 N	14.58 E
Korannaberg ⩘	158	27.25 S	22.32 E
Korapun	164	5.25 S	152.00 E
Korāput	122	18.49 N	82.43 E
Korarou, Lac ⊜	150	15.15 N	3.16 W
Koratla	122	18.49 N	78.43 E
Korat → Nakhon Ratchasima	110	14.58 N	102.07 E
Kor'ažma	24	61.18 N	47.06 E
Korba, India	124	22.21 N	82.41 E
Korba, Tun.	36	36.35 N	10.52 E
Korbach	56	51.16 N	8.52 E
Korbeta	144	13.03 N	39.43 E
Korbol	146	10.01 N	17.43 E
Korbous	36	36.49 N	10.35 E
Korbu, Gunong ʌ	114	4.43 N	101.17 E
Korçë	38	40.37 N	20.46 E
Korcovo	76	58.52 N	42.13 E
Korčula	36	42.58 N	17.08 E
Korčula, Otok I	36	42.57 N	16.50 E
Korčulanski Kanal ⊔	36	43.03 N	16.40 E
Kordestān □[4]	128	35.30 N	47.00 E
Kord Kūy	128	36.48 N	54.07 E
Kordovo	86	54.06 N	93.17 E
Korea, North □[1], Asia	90	40.00 N	127.00 E
Korea, North □[1], Asia	98	40.00 N	127.00 E
Korea, South □[1], Asia	90	36.30 N	128.00 E
Korea, South □[1], Asia	98	36.30 N	128.00 E
Korea Bay c	98	39.00 N	124.00 E
Korea Strait ⊔	90	34.00 N	129.00 E
Korea University ʊ[2]	271b	37.36 N	127.02 E
Korec	78	50.37 N	27.09 E
Korekozevo	82	54.20 N	36.11 E
Korelakša	24	65.33 N	32.22 E
Koreliči	76	53.34 N	26.08 E
Korem	144	12.30 N	39.30 E
Koré Mayroua	150	13.18 N	3.55 E
Koren (Die Wurzen))(	64	46.31 N	13.45 E
Korenkovo	78	45.07 N	36.24 E
Koren'ovo, Ross.	78	51.25 N	34.55 E
Koren'ovo, Ross.	265b	55.40 N	38.00 E
Korenovsk	78	45.29 N	39.28 E
Korf	74	60.19 N	165.50 E
Korfovskij	89	48.13 N	135.03 E
Korga	158	30.12 S	20.28 E
Korgan	130	40.44 N	37.13 E
Korgašino	82	54.45 N	37.41 E
Kõrgessaare	76	58.59 N	22.28 E
Korgonskij chrebet ⩘	86	50.45 N	84.30 E
Korgus	140	19.13 N	33.29 E
Korhogo	150	9.27 N	5.38 W
Kōri	270	34.47 N	135.39 E
Koridhallós	267c	37.59 N	23.39 E
Korido	164	0.50 S	135.35 E
Koriella	169	37.10 S	145.39 E
Korienzé	150	15.24 N	3.47 W
Korim	164	0.54 S	136.02 E
Korima, Oued el V	148	33.51 N	0.23 W
Koringberg	158	33.01 S	18.40 E
Koringplaas	158	32.48 S	20.58 E
Korinth	41	55.08 N	10.21 E
Korinthiakós Kólpos c	38	38.19 N	22.04 E
Kórinthos (Corinth)	38	37.56 N	22.56 E
Korínthou, Dhiórix ≊	38	37.57 N	22.56 E
Kőris-hegy ʌ	30	47.18 N	17.45 E
Koritsa → Korçë	38	40.37 N	20.46 E
Köritz	54	52.51 N	12.27 E
Kōriyama	92	37.24 N	140.23 E
Kōriyama → Yamato-kōriyama	96	34.38 N	135.47 E
Korizo, Passe de)(	146	22.28 N	15.27 E
Korkino, Ross.	86	54.54 N	61.23 E
Korkino, Ross.	88	54.23 N	105.14 E
Korkinskoje, ozero ⊜	265a	59.55 N	30.44 E
Korkuteli	130	37.04 N	30.13 E
Korla	90	41.44 N	86.09 E
Korl'aki	80	57.06 N	46.57 E
Korliki	74	61.31 N	82.22 E
Korma, Bela.	76	52.21 N	31.31 E
Korma, Bela.	76	53.08 N	30.48 E
Körmend	61	47.01 N	16.37 E
Kormilovka	86	55.00 N	74.06 E
Kormovoje	80	46.17 N	43.30 E
Kornat, Otok I	36	43.50 N	15.16 E
Körnebach ≃	263	51.35 N	7.38 E
Kornejevka, Kaz.	86	54.01 N	68.27 E
Kornejevka, Kaz.	86	50.12 N	74.19 E
Kornejevka, Ross.	80	51.45 N	48.46 E
Kornelimünster	56	50.43 N	6.11 E
Körner, Dtsch.	54	51.13 N	10.35 E
Korner, Mt., U.S.	182	48.59 N	112.15 W
Kornešty	78	47.22 N	27.59 E
Korneuburg	264b	48.21 N	16.20 E
Kórnik	30	52.17 N	17.04 E
Kornilovo	86	53.32 N	81.05 E
Kornin	78	50.06 N	29.32 E
Kornouchovo	80	55.33 N	49.53 E
Korn'ovo	265a	60.03 N	30.45 E
Kornsjø	26	58.57 N	11.39 E
Kornwestheim	56	48.52 N	9.11 E
Koro, C. Iv.	150	8.34 N	7.28 W
Koro, Mali	150	14.04 N	3.05 W
Koro I	175g	17.19 S	179.23 E
Koroba	164	5.40 S	142.45 E
Koroča	78	50.48 N	37.11 E
Korodougou Markala	150	12.26 N	6.17 W
Köroğlu Tepesi ʌ	130	40.31 N	31.53 E
Korogwe	154	5.09 S	38.29 E
Koroit	166	38.17 S	142.22 E
Korolenko, gora ʌ	88	58.15 N	115.01 E
Korolevskij Belok, gora ʌ	86	51.00 N	83.43 E
Korol'ovo	78	48.09 N	23.08 E
Korol'ovščina	76	55.49 N	31.45 E
Korom, Bahr ≃	146	10.35 N	19.45 E
Koromba ʌ	175g	17.53 S	177.34 E
Koromiri I	174k	21.15 S	159.43 W
Koromo → Toyota	94	35.05 N	137.09 E
Koronadal	116	6.30 N	124.51 E
Koróni	38	36.48 N	21.56 E
Korónia, Límni ⊜	38	40.41 N	23.05 E
Koronowo	30	53.19 N	17.57 E
Korop	78	51.34 N	32.56 E
Koropélé	152	4.44 N	17.11 E
Koropíon	38	37.54 N	23.53 E
Koror	175b	7.20 N	134.29 E
Koror I	175b	7.20 N	134.30 E
Kororoit Creek ≃	274b	37.52 S	144.52 E
Körös ≃	30	46.43 N	20.12 E
Koro Sea ⫧[2]	175g	18.00 S	179.50 E
Korosten'	78	50.57 N	28.39 E
Korostyšev	78	50.19 N	29.03 E
Korotkova	88	56.43 N	107.55 E
Korotojak	78	50.59 N	39.10 E
Koro Toro	146	16.05 N	18.30 E
Korotovo	76	58.57 N	37.28 E
Korotyš	76	52.22 N	37.27 E
Korovincy	78	50.48 N	33.45 E
Korovin Island I	180	55.25 N	160.15 W
Korovino, Ross.	78	51.25 N	36.45 E
Korovino, Ross.	80	53.49 N	53.03 E
Korovin Volcano ʌ[1]	180	52.22 N	174.10 W
Korovou	175g	17.57 S	178.21 E
Koroyanitu ʌ	175g	17.40 S	177.35 E
Korožečna ≃	76	57.32 N	38.18 E
Korpilahti	26	62.01 N	25.33 E
Korpo (Korppoo)	26	60.10 N	21.34 E
Korså	40	60.38 N	16.08 E
Korsakov	89	46.38 N	142.46 E
Korsakovo	76	53.16 N	37.21 E
Korschenbroich	56	51.11 N	6.31 E
Korselbränna	26	64.27 N	15.35 E
Korševo	78	51.11 N	40.07 E
Korsika → Corse I	36	42.00 N	9.00 E
Korsnäs, Suomi	26	62.47 N	21.12 E
Korsnäs, Sve.	40	60.35 N	15.43 E
Korsør	41	55.20 N	11.09 E
Korsør Nor c	41	55.20 N	11.11 E
Korsun'	83	48.12 N	38.05 E
Koršunovo	88	58.37 N	110.10 E
Korsun'-Ševčenkovskij	78	49.26 N	31.16 E
Korsze	30	54.10 N	21.09 E
Kortgene	52	51.34 N	3.48 E
Kortilisy	78	51.51 N	24.25 E
Kortkeros	24	61.49 N	51.28 E
Kortrijk (Courtrai)	50	50.50 N	3.16 E
Kortuz, gora ʌ	86	54.33 N	91.56 E
Koruçam Burnu ›	130	35.24 N	32.56 E
Korucu	130	39.28 N	27.22 E
Kor'ukovka	78	51.46 N	32.14 E
Korumburra	169	38.26 S	145.49 E
Korwai	124	24.08 N	78.03 E
Kōryō	96	34.33 N	135.45 E
Koryŏng	98	35.44 N	128.15 E
Koryst'	78	50.35 N	27.01 E
Koryta	60	49.24 N	13.13 E
Korženevskoj, pik ʌ	85	39.04 N	72.00 E
Korževc'	78	48.13 N	27.02 E
Korževka	80	54.12 N	46.22 E
Kos	38	36.53 N	27.18 E
Kos I	38	36.50 N	27.10 E
Kosa, Ityo.	144	7.51 N	36.51 E
Kosa, Ross.	24	59.56 N	54.55 E
Kosa, Ross.	88	54.47 N	108.52 E
Kosa ≃, Ross.	24	60.11 N	55.10 E
Kosa ≃, Ross.	80	58.26 N	51.15 E
Kosa ⊥	150	15.50 N	7.00 W
Koš-Agač	86	50.00 N	88.40 E
Kosai	94	34.43 N	137.33 E
Kosaja, šivera ʟ	88	58.24 N	97.48 E
Kosaja Gora	82	54.07 N	37.33 E
Kosaka	92	40.19 N	140.44 E
Kosan	98	38.52 N	127.24 E
Košankol'	80	49.56 N	48.11 E
Koščagyl	86	46.51 N	53.48 E
Kösching	60	48.49 N	11.30 E
Kościan	30	52.06 N	16.38 E
Kościerzyna	30	54.08 N	18.00 E
Kosciusko	194	33.03 N	89.35 W
Kosciusko □[6]	216	41.14 N	85.51 W
Kosciusko, Mount ʌ	171b	36.27 S	148.16 E
Kosciusko National Park ♠	166	36.10 S	148.15 E
Kös Dağı ʌ	130	40.59 N	34.25 E
Kosdaulet, peski ◆[2]	80	47.45 N	49.30 E
Kose, Eesti	76	59.11 N	25.10 E
Kose, Nihon	270	34.25 N	135.46 E
Köse, Tür.	130	40.13 N	39.39 E
Kösedağı ʌ	130	39.54 N	42.39 E
Kösefakılı	130	39.36 N	34.09 E
Košelevka	82	55.09 N	38.05 E
Košelicha	80	55.02 N	43.33 E
Košerovo	82	55.38 N	38.22 E
Koserow	54	54.03 N	13.59 E
Kosha	140	20.49 N	30.32 E
Koshien Stadium ♠	270	34.42 N	135.22 E
Koshigaya	94	35.54 N	139.48 E
Koshigoe	268	35.18 N	139.30 E
Koshikijima-rettō II	92	31.45 N	129.49 E
Koshino	94	36.02 N	136.01 E
Koshk-e Kohneh	128	34.52 N	62.31 E
Koshkonong	194	36.35 N	91.38 W
Koshkonong, Lake ⊜	216	42.52 N	88.58 W
Koshkonong Creek ≃	216	42.53 N	88.59 W
Koshlong Lake ⊜	212	44.58 N	78.29 W
Kōshoku	94	36.32 N	138.06 E
Koshu → Kwangju	98	35.09 N	126.54 E
Kosī □[8]	124	27.15 N	87.15 E
Kosi ≃	124	25.26 N	87.22 E
Košice	30	48.43 N	21.15 E
Kosigi	122	15.51 N	77.16 E
Kosi Kalan	124	27.48 N	77.26 E
Kosikovo	76	59.52 N	43.23 E
Kosimeer ⊜	158	26.55 S	32.52 E
Kosino, Ross.	80	58.23 N	51.17 E
Kosino, Ross.	82	55.43 N	37.52 E
Kosju	24	65.38 N	59.03 E
Kosju ≃	24	66.18 N	59.53 E
Kosjuvom	24	66.17 N	59.50 E
Köşk	130	37.51 N	28.03 E
Koskaecodde Lake ⊜	186	48.00 N	55.20 W
Koškar	80	47.27 N	53.29 E
Koški, Ross.	80	54.12 N	50.28 E
Koski, Suomi	26	60.39 N	23.09 E
Koškino	80	56.20 N	50.49 E
Koskol'	86	49.31 N	67.05 E
Koskuduk	86	44.06 N	77.22 E
Koskullskulle	24	67.12 N	20.50 E
Koslan	24	63.28 N	48.52 E
Köslin → Koszalin	30	54.12 N	16.09 E
Kosmonosy	54	50.26 N	15.00 E
Kosmynino	80	57.35 N	40.46 E
Kosoba, gora ʌ	86	48.15 N	79.40 E
Kosogor	80	57.07 N	47.34 E
Kosoj, porog ʟ, Ross.	86	57.30 N	95.30 E
Kosoj, porog ʟ, Ross.	88	57.44 N	96.20 E
Kosolapovo	80	56.57 N	49.37 E
Kosŏng, C.M.I.K.	98	38.40 N	128.19 E
Kosŏng, Taehan	98	34.58 N	128.18 E
Kosov	78	48.19 N	25.05 E
Kosovo-Metohija □[4]	38	42.35 N	21.00 E
Kosový potok ≃	60	49.46 N	12.48 E
Kosrae I	14	5.19 N	162.59 E
Kösreli	130	37.11 N	35.59 E
Kossdorf	54	51.29 N	13.14 E
Kosse	222	31.18 N	96.38 W
Kössen	64	47.40 N	12.24 E
Kossindi	152	3.51 N	16.19 E
Kösslarn	60	48.22 N	13.07 E
Kossol Passage ⊔	175b	7.52 N	134.36 E
Kossol Reef ✧[2]	175b	7.57 N	134.41 E
Kossou, Lac de ⊜[1]	150	7.25 N	5.45 W
Kossovo	76	52.45 N	25.09 E
Kossuth	214	41.17 N	79.35 W
Kosta	26	56.51 N	15.23 E
Košt'ahy	54	50.39 N	13.45 E
Kostajnica	36	45.14 N	16.33 E
Koš-Tegirmen	85	42.47 N	73.53 E
Kostelec nad Labem	54	50.11 N	14.35 E
Kostenec	38	42.16 N	23.49 E
Koster	158	25.57 S	26.42 E
Kosterevo	80	55.56 N	39.37 E
Kosteröarna I	26	58.54 N	11.02 E
Kostešty	78	46.52 N	28.44 E
Kostešty-Stynka, vodochranilišče (Lacul Stînca-Costeşti) ⊜[1]	38	47.55 N	27.10 E
Koštice	54	50.24 N	13.55 E
Kostino, Ross.	80	52.11 N	51.20 E
Kostino, Ross.	80	52.24 N	51.39 E
Kostino, Ross.	82	56.18 N	37.43 E
Kostino, Ross.	265b	55.55 N	37.51 E
Kostino-Otdelec	78	51.33 N	41.26 E
Kost'kovo	76	60.02 N	33.14 E
Košt'ob'o	85	41.06 N	74.15 E
Kostomukša	24	64.41 N	30.49 E
Kostonjärvi ⊜	26	65.47 N	28.27 E
Kostopol'	78	50.53 N	26.26 E
Kostriževka	78	48.38 N	25.41 E
Kostroma	76	57.46 N	40.55 E
Kostroma ≃	24	57.47 N	40.55 E
Kostrovo	82	55.53 N	36.42 E
Kostrzyn	30	52.37 N	14.39 E
Kost'ukoviči	76	53.20 N	32.03 E
Kost'ukovka	76	52.32 N	30.56 E
Kosugaya ◆[8]	268	35.22 N	139.33 E
Kosuge	94	35.45 N	138.57 E
Kosugi	94	36.43 N	137.06 E
Kosum Phisai	110	16.13 N	103.01 E
Koszalin (Köslin)	30	54.12 N	16.09 E
Koszalin □[4]	30	54.00 N	16.00 E
Kőszeg	61	47.23 N	16.33 E
Koszyce	30	50.11 N	20.35 E
Kota, India	120	25.11 N	75.50 E
Kota, India	124	22.18 N	82.02 E
Kota, Malay.	114	5.35 N	100.23 E
Kota, Malay.	114	2.31 N	102.10 E
Kotaagung	112	5.30 S	104.38 E
Kotabaharu, Indon.	112	0.48 S	111.33 E
Kota Baharu, Malay.	114	6.08 N	102.15 E
Kotabangun	112	0.16 S	116.35 E
Kotabaru, Indon.	112	3.14 S	116.13 E
Kotabaru, Indon.	112	1.08 S	101.43 E
Kotabaru → Jayapura	164	2.32 S	140.42 E
Kota Belud	112	6.25 N	116.31 E
Kotabumi	112	4.50 S	104.54 E
Kotabunan	112	0.49 N	124.38 E
Kotadabok	112	0.30 S	104.33 E
Kot Addu	123	30.28 N	70.58 E
Kotagiri	122	11.26 N	76.53 E
Kot'ajevka	80	46.33 N	48.46 E
Kotake	96	33.41 N	130.43 E
Kota Kinabalu (Jesselton)	112	5.59 N	116.04 E
Kota Kota → Nkhotakota	154	12.57 S	34.17 E
Kotālpur	126	23.02 N	87.36 E
Kotamobagu	112	0.46 N	124.19 E
Kotanemel', gora ʌ	86	47.43 N	77.18 E
Kotapinang	114	1.53 N	100.05 E
Kotari ⩘	36	44.05 N	15.30 E
Kotaringin	114	0.53 N	102.03 E
Kota Sarang Semut	114	5.59 N	100.24 E
Kotatengah	114	1.05 N	100.33 E
Kota Tinggi	114	1.44 N	103.54 E
Kotawaringin	112	2.29 S	111.25 E
Kotchāndpur	124	23.24 N	89.01 E
Kotcho Lake ⊜	176	59.05 N	121.10 W
Kot Chutta	123	29.53 N	70.39 E
Kotdwāra	124	29.45 N	78.32 E
Kotel	38	42.53 N	26.27 E

≃	River	Fluß	Río	Rivière	Rio
≊	Canal	Kanal	Canal	Canal	Canal
ʟ	Waterfall, Rapids	Wasserfall, Stromschnellen	Cascada, Rápidos	Chute d'eau, Rapides	Cascata, Rápidos
⊔	Strait	Meeresstraße	Estrecho	Détroit	Estreito
c	Bay, Gulf	Bucht, Golf	Bahía, Golfo	Baie, Golfe	Baía, Golfo
⊜	Lake, Lakes	See, Seen	Lago, Lagos	Lac, Lacs	Lago, Lagos
☷	Swamp	Sumpf	Pantano	Marais	Pântano
⍓	Ice Features, Glacier	Eis- und Gletscherformen	Accidentes Glaciales	Formes glaciaires	Acidentes glaciares
⫧	Other Hydrographic Features	Andere Hydrographische Objekte	Otros Elementos Hidrográficos	Autres données hydrographiques	Outros acidentes hidrográficos

✧	Submarine Features	Untermeerische Objekte	Accidentes Submarinos	Formes de relief sous-marin	Acidentes submarinos
□	Political Unit	Politische Einheit	Unidad Politica	Entité politique	Unidade política
ʊ	Cultural Institution	Kulturelle Institution	Institución Cultural	Institution culturelle	Instituição cultural
⊥	Historical Site	Historische Stätte	Sitio Histórico	Site historique	Sitio histórico
♠	Recreational Site	Erholungs- und Ferienort	Sitio de Recreo	Centre de loisirs	Area de Lazer
⊠	Airport	Flughafen	Aeropuerto	Aéroport	Aeroporto
■	Military Installation	Militäranlage	Instalación Militar	Installation militaire	Instalação militar
◆	Miscellaneous	Verschiedenes	Misceláneo	Divers	Diversos

ENGLISH: Name | Page | Lat.°′ | Long.°′ — DEUTSCH: Name | Seite | Breite°′ | Länge°′ E = Ost

Name	Page	Lat.°′	Long.°′
Kotel'nič	80	58.18 N	48.20 E
Kotel'niki	82	55.39 N	37.52 E
Kotel'nikovo	80	47.38 N	43.09 E
Kotel'nyj, ostrov I	74	75.45 N	138.44 E
Kotel'va	78	50.05 N	34.45 E
Kot Fateh	123	30.07 N	75.05 E
Köthen	54	51.45 N	11.58 E
Kotido	154	3.00 N	34.06 E
Koti → Kōchi	96	33.33 N	133.33 E
Kotikovo	89	49.08 N	144.13 E
Kotka	26	60.28 N	26.55 E
Kot Kapūra	123	30.35 N	74.54 E
Kotkino	24	67.02 N	51.03 E
Kotla	123	32.15 N	76.02 E
Kotl'akovo	82	56.17 N	35.49 E
Kotlas	24	61.16 N	46.35 E
Kotli	123	33.31 N	73.55 E
Kotlik	180	63.02 N	163.33 W
Kotlin, ostrov I	76	60.00 N	29.46 E
Kotly	76	59.36 N	28.45 E
Kot Mūmin	123	32.11 N	73.02 E
Kotō	94	35.08 N	136.14 E
Kōtō ⊕[8]	268	35.41 N	139.48 E
Koto ≏, Nihon	96	33.58 N	131.13 E
Kotō ≏, Nihon	96	34.21 N	134.02 E
Kotobiki-san ∧	96	35.03 N	132.47 E
Kotohira	96	34.11 N	133.49 E
Kotohira-gu ʊ[1]	96	34.11 N	133.49 E
Kotohira-yama ∧	96	34.11 N	133.48 E
Kotonami	96	34.10 N	133.56 E
Koton-Karifi	150	8.08 N	6.48 E
Kotonkoro	150	11.02 N	5.58 E
Kotor	38	42.25 N	18.46 E
Kotoriba	36	46.21 N	16.49 E
Kotorovo	80	54.54 N	41.35 E
Kotor Varoš	36	44.37 N	17.23 E
Kotouba	150	8.41 N	3.12 W
Kotovka	78	49.08 N	34.57 E
Kotovo	80	50.18 N	44.50 E
Kotovsk, Ross.	80	52.36 N	41.32 E
Kotovsk, Ukr.	78	47.45 N	29.33 E
Kot Pūtli	124	27.43 N	76.12 E
Kotra, India	120	24.22 N	73.10 E
Kotra, India	272b	22.46 N	88.34 E
Kot Rādha Kishan	123	31.10 N	74.06 E
Kotri	120	25.22 N	68.18 E
Kotri Allāhrakhio	120	24.24 N	67.50 E
Kotrung → Uttarpara-Kotrung	272b	22.40 N	88.21 E
Kötschach	64	46.40 N	13.00 E
Kot Sultān	123	30.46 N	70.56 E
Kōtsu-zan ∧	96	34.01 N	134.12 E
Kottagūdem	122	17.33 N	80.38 E
Kottas Mountains ⋏	9	74.20 S	12.00 W
Kottayam	122	9.35 N	76.31 E
Kotte → Sri Jayawardenepura	122	6.54 N	79.54 E
Kottingbrunn	61	47.57 N	16.14 E
Kotto ≏	136	4.14 N	22.02 E
Kotton	144	9.35 N	50.28 E
Kottūru	122	14.49 N	76.13 E
Kotuj ≏	74	71.55 N	102.05 E
Kot'užen'	78	47.51 N	28.36 E
Kotwālīpāra	126	22.59 N	89.59 E
Kotzebue	180	66.53 N	162.39 W
Kotzebue Sound ⋓	180	66.20 N	163.00 W
Kötzting	60	49.11 N	12.52 E
Koualé	150	11.24 N	7.01 W
Kou'an	106	32.19 N	119.52 E
Kouandé	150	10.20 N	1.42 E
Kouango	152	4.58 N	19.59 E
Kouassi-Datékro	150	7.49 N	3.31 W
Koubansaki	273b	4.22 S	15.09 E
Koubia	150	11.35 N	11.54 W
Kouchibouguac National Park ♠	186	46.50 N	65.00 W
Koudougou	150	12.15 N	2.22 W
Kouéré	150	10.27 N	3.59 W
Kouffo ≏	150	6.35 N	1.59 E
Kouga	146	9.56 N	21.03 E
Kouga ≏	158	33.37 S	22.14 E
Kougaberge ⋏	158	33.40 S	23.50 E
Kougarok Mountain ∧	180	65.41 N	165.13 W
K'ouhu	100	23.35 N	120.11 E
Kouilou □[5]	152	4.30 S	12.00 E
Kouilou ≏	152	4.28 S	11.41 E
Koukdjuak ≏	176	66.45 N	73.09 W
Kouki	152	7.10 N	17.18 E
Koúklia	130	34.42 N	32.34 E
Koukourou ≏	152	7.32 N	19.42 E
Koukourou-Bamingui, Réserve de Faune du ⊕[4]	152	7.20 N	20.00 E
Koula ≏	229b	21.54 N	159.36 W
Koulamoutou	152	1.08 S	12.29 E
Koulikoro	150	12.53 N	7.33 W
Koulikoro □[4]	150	13.00 N	8.00 W
Koulouguidi	150	13.27 N	11.03 W
Koulountou ≏	150	13.15 N	13.37 W
Koumac	175f	20.33 S	164.17 E
Koumac, Grand Récif de ⊤[2]	175f	20.32 S	164.04 E
Koumala	166	21.37 S	149.15 E
Koumaméyong	152	0.11 N	11.51 E
Koumankou	150	12.06 N	6.08 W
Koumbakara	150	12.42 N	14.29 W
Koumbal	146	9.26 N	22.39 E
Koumbala ≏	146	9.14 N	20.42 E
Koumbia, Burkina	150	11.14 N	3.42 W
Koumbia, Guinée	150	11.48 N	13.30 W
Koumbisaleh ⊥	150	15.46 N	7.59 W
Koumbouma	150	10.24 N	12.56 W
Koumi	94	36.05 N	138.29 E
Koumpentoum	150	13.59 N	14.34 W
Koumra	146	8.55 N	17.33 E
Koundara	150	12.29 N	13.18 W
Koundé	152	6.07 N	14.38 E
Koundian ⊥	150	13.10 N	10.41 W
Koundougou	150	11.44 N	4.31 W
Koun-Fao	150	7.29 N	3.15 W
Koungheul	150	13.59 N	14.48 W
Koungoulou	152	3.32 S	13.20 E
Kouniohou	150	7.40 N	0.48 E
Kounradskij	86	46.59 N	75.00 E
Kountze	194	30.22 N	94.18 W
Koupé, Mont ∧	152	4.47 N	9.43 E
Koupéla	150	12.11 N	0.21 W
Kouragué	150	12.18 N	10.02 W
Kourak	86	54.50 N	84.40 E
Kouriles, Détroit des → Pervyj Kuril'skij proliv ⋓	74	50.50 N	156.36 E
Kouri-shima I	174m	26.42 N	128.01 E
Kourou	250	5.09 N	52.39 W
Kouroukoto	150	12.35 N	10.05 W
Kourouma	150	11.37 N	4.48 W
Kourouninkoto	150	13.52 N	9.35 W
Kouroussa	150	10.39 N	9.53 W
Koury	150	12.11 N	4.48 W
Koussanar	150	13.52 N	14.05 W
Koussané, Mali	150	14.53 N	11.14 W
Koussane, Sén.	150	14.08 N	12.26 W
Kousser, Massif de ∧	148	32.02 N	5.59 W
Koussi, Emi ∧	146	19.50 N	18.30 E
Koussili	150	13.30 N	11.38 W
Koutia Ba	150	14.11 N	14.28 W
Koutiala	150	12.23 N	5.28 W
Kouto	150	9.53 N	6.25 W
Koutou	98	38.35 N	114.24 E
Koutoumo, Île I	175f	22.40 S	167.33 E
Kouts	216	41.19 N	87.01 W
Kouvola	26	60.52 N	26.42 E
Kouya ≏	150	10.09 N	9.45 W
Kouyou ≏	152	0.45 S	16.38 E
Kova	88	58.18 N	100.21 E
Kova ≏	88	58.18 N	100.18 E
Kovada Milli Parkı ♠	130	37.32 N	30.53 E
Kovaksa	80	55.31 N	43.30 E
Koval'ovka	78	47.16 N	31.43 E
Kovarskas	76	55.26 N	24.55 E
Kovarzino	76	60.09 N	38.33 E
Kovdor	24	67.34 N	30.22 E
Kovdozero, ozero ⊜	24	66.47 N	32.00 E
Kovel'	78	51.14 N	24.41 E
Kovernino	80	57.07 N	43.49 E
Kovilpatti	122	9.10 N	77.52 E
Kovin	38	44.45 N	20.59 E
Kovno → Kaunas	76	54.54 N	23.54 E
Kovpyta	78	51.23 N	30.50 E
Kovrina Vtoraja	80	47.01 N	41.44 E
Kovrov	80	56.22 N	41.18 E
Kovševata	78	49.29 N	30.38 E
Kovsug ≏	83	48.48 N	39.17 E
Kovūr	122	14.29 N	79.59 E
Kovvur	122	17.01 N	81.44 E
Kovylkin	80	48.16 N	41.28 E
Kovylkino	80	54.02 N	43.56 E
Kovža	24	61.09 N	38.58 E
Kovžinskij Zavod	76	60.24 N	37.04 E
Kowal	30	52.32 N	19.09 E
Kowalewo Pomorskie	30	53.10 N	18.53 E
Kowangge	115b	8.16 S	118.32 E
Kowanyama	164	15.28 S	141.44 E
Kowanyama Aboriginal Reserve ⊕[4]	164	15.15 S	141.45 E
Kowār	126	24.13 N	86.11 E
Koweït → Kuwait □[1]	128	29.30 N	47.45 E
Kowel → Kovel'	78	51.14 N	24.41 E
Kowghān ≏	128	34.15 N	62.57 E
Kowhitirangi	172	42.52 S	171.01 E
Kowie → Port Alfred	158	33.36 S	26.55 E
Kowkcheh ≏	120	37.10 N	69.23 E
Kowloon (Jiulong)	100	22.18 N	114.10 E
Kowloon City	271d	22.19 N	114.11 E
Kowloon Peak ∧	271d	22.21 N	114.13 E
Kowmung ≏	170	33.52 S	150.16 E
Kowŏn	98	39.26 N	127.14 E
Kowt-e 'Ashrow	120	34.27 N	68.48 E
Koxtag	120	37.23 N	78.05 E
Kōya	96	34.12 N	135.35 E
Koyadaira	96	33.56 N	134.13 E
Kōyaguchi	96	34.18 N	135.33 E
Koyama ⊕[8]	268	35.37 N	139.43 E
Koyama-ike ⊜	96	35.30 N	134.09 E
Kōyama-misaki >	96	34.40 N	131.36 E
Koyambattur → Coimbatore	122	11.00 N	76.58 E
Koyang-ni	98	37.42 N	126.56 E
Kōya-Ryūjin-kokutei-kōen ♠	96	34.10 N	135.35 E
Köyceğiz	130	36.57 N	28.41 E
Köyceğiz Gölü ⊜	130	36.55 N	28.40 E
Koyna Reservoir ⊜[1]	122	17.25 N	73.45 E
Koyra ≏[1]	126	22.27 N	89.16 E
Koyuk	180	64.56 N	161.08 W
Koyuk ≏	180	64.55 N	161.12 W
Koyukuk	180	64.53 N	157.43 W
Koyukuk ≏	180	64.56 N	157.30 W
Koyukuk, Middle Fork ≏	180	67.03 N	151.04 W
Koyukuk, North Fork ≏	180	67.03 N	151.04 W
Koyukuk, South Fork ≏	180	66.35 N	151.57 W
Koyulhisar	130	40.18 N	37.51 E
Koža	80	57.47 N	48.57 E
Kozakai	94	34.48 N	137.22 E
Kōzaki	94	35.54 N	140.24 E
Kō-zaki >	92	34.05 N	129.13 E
Kozaklı	130	39.14 N	34.49 E
Kōzan, Nihon	96	34.35 N	133.03 E
Kozan, Tür.	130	37.27 N	35.49 E
Kozáni	38	40.18 N	21.47 E
Kožanka	78	49.58 N	29.46 E
Koz'any, Bela.	76	55.18 N	26.52 E
Kožany, Ross.	76	52.48 N	31.44 E
Kozara ⋏	36	45.00 N	16.50 E
Kozarac	36	44.58 N	16.51 E
Kozdinga	24	63.43 N	47.32 E
Kozelec	78	50.55 N	31.08 E
Kozel'ščina	78	49.13 N	33.51 E
Kozel'sk	82	54.02 N	35.48 E
Koževnikovo	86	56.16 N	84.00 E
Kozhikode → Calicut	122	11.15 N	75.46 E
Koziegłowy	30	50.36 N	19.09 E
Kozienice	30	51.35 N	21.33 E
Kožim	24	65.48 N	59.28 E
Kozin	78	50.14 N	30.39 E
Kozino	265b	55.54 N	37.11 E
Kozjak (Possruck) ⋏	61	46.37 N	15.28 E
Kozlov	78	49.33 N	25.20 E
Kozlov Bereg	76	58.57 N	27.44 E
Kozlovka, Ross.	78	51.39 N	41.16 E
Kozlovka, Ross.	78	50.52 N	40.27 E
Kozlovka, Ross.	80	55.52 N	48.14 E
Kozlovka, Ross.	80	52.33 N	45.41 E
Kozlovo, Ross.	76	57.34 N	35.29 E
Kozlovo, Ross.	82	56.31 N	36.16 E
Kozlovščina	76	53.19 N	25.18 E
Kozlu, Tür.	130	41.26 N	31.46 E
Kozlu, Tür.	130	40.37 N	36.30 E
Kozluk	130	38.11 N	41.29 E
Koźmin	30	51.50 N	17.28 E
Koz'mino	24	61.56 N	48.19 E
Koz'modemjansk	80	56.20 N	46.36 E
Koz'mogorodskoje	24	65.32 N	44.55 E
Kozova	78	49.26 N	25.09 E
Kožpos'olok	24	63.10 N	38.06 E
Kožuchovo	265b	55.43 N	37.54 E
Kożuchów	30	51.45 N	15.35 E
Kozuka	268	35.09 N	139.57 E
Kōzuki	96	34.59 N	134.20 E
Kozukue ⊕[8]	268	35.30 N	139.36 E
Kozul'ka	86	56.10 N	91.24 E
Kožurla	86	55.21 N	79.02 E
Kōzu-shima I	92	34.13 N	139.10 E
Kozuya	270	34.52 N	135.45 E
Kpandae	150	8.28 N	0.01 W
Kpandu	150	7.00 N	0.18 E
Kpong	150	6.09 N	0.04 E
Kpo Range ⋏	150	7.15 N	10.15 W
Kra, Isthmus of ⊥[3]	110	10.20 N	99.00 E
Kraai ≏	158	30.40 S	26.45 E
Kraaifontein	158	33.50 S	18.43 E
Kraal	158	26.34 S	28.26 E
Kraankuil	158	29.52 S	24.10 E
Krabbendijke	52	51.26 N	4.07 E
Krabi	110	8.04 N	98.55 E
Krâchéh	110	12.29 N	106.01 E
Krackow	54	53.20 N	14.16 E
Kraftsdorf	54	50.52 N	11.55 E
Kragan	115a	6.42 S	111.37 E
Kragenæs	41	54.55 N	11.22 E
Kragerø	26	58.52 N	9.25 E
Kraghave	41	54.48 N	11.53 E
Kragujevac	38	44.01 N	20.55 E
Krahenhöhe ⊕[8]	263	51.10 N	7.06 E
Kraiburg	60	48.10 N	12.26 E
Kraichgau □[9]	56	49.10 N	8.50 E
Krainburg → Kranj	36	46.15 N	14.21 E
Krainka	82	54.07 N	36.21 E
Krai-Russkije	80	57.23 N	46.50 E
Krajčikovo	86	56.16 N	73.20 E
Krajenka	30	53.19 N	17.00 E
Krajeva	89	44.54 N	131.08 E
Krajneje	80	47.29 N	46.01 E
Krajnik Dolny	54	53.05 N	14.25 E
Krajnovka	84	43.57 N	47.24 E
Krakatau ∧[1]	115a	6.07 S	105.24 E
Krakatoa → Krakatau ∧[1]	115a	6.07 S	105.24 E
Krakau → Kraków	30	50.03 N	19.58 E
Krâkôr	110	12.32 N	104.12 E
Krakovec	78	49.57 N	23.07 E
Krakovo	80	53.36 N	50.51 E
Krakow, Dtsch.	54	53.39 N	12.16 E
Kraków, Pol.	30	50.03 N	19.58 E
Kraków □[4]	30	49.50 N	20.00 E
Krakower See ⊜	54	53.37 N	12.17 E
Kraksaan	115a	7.46 S	113.25 E
Kraksdorf	54	54.18 N	11.04 E
Kralendijk	241s	12.10 N	68.17 W
Kralice	61	49.11 N	16.12 E
Kraljevica	36	45.16 N	14.34 E
Kraljevo	38	43.43 N	20.41 E
Kralovice	60	49.59 N	13.29 E
Královské Vinohrady ⊕[8]	54	50.01 N	14.29 E
Kralupy nad Vltavou	54	50.11 N	14.18 E
Kralupy u Chomutova	54	50.25 N	13.20 E
Králův Dvůr	60	49.56 N	14.02 E
Kramatorsk	83	48.43 N	37.32 E
Kramer	216	40.20 N	87.17 W
Kramfors	26	62.56 N	17.47 E
Krammer ⋓	52	51.38 N	4.15 E
Krampen	61	47.40 N	15.32 E
Krampnitz	264a	52.28 N	13.04 E
Krampnitzsee ⊜	264a	52.27 N	13.03 E
Kramsach	64	47.27 N	11.52 E
Kranebitten, Flughafen ⊠	64	47.16 N	11.20 E
Kranenburg	52	51.47 N	6.03 E
Krångede	26	63.09 N	16.05 E
Kranichfeld	54	50.51 N	11.12 E
Kranídhion	38	37.22 N	23.10 E
Kranj	36	46.15 N	14.21 E
Kranji, Sing.	271c	1.26 N	103.46 E
Kranji, Sing.	271c	1.26 N	103.45 E
Kranji ≏	271c	1.26 N	103.45 E
Kranji Reservoir ⊜[1]	271c	1.26 N	103.45 E
Kranji War Memorial ⊥	271c	1.26 N	103.45 E
Kranjska Gora	64	46.29 N	13.47 E
Kransaja Pol'ana	84	43.41 N	40.13 E
Kranskop	158	29.00 S	30.47 E
Kranskop ∧	158	27.43 S	29.41 E
Kranzberg	156	21.55 S	15.43 E
Krapina	36	46.10 N	15.52 E
Krapivinskij	86	55.00 N	86.49 E
Krapivna	76	53.38 N	35.31 E
Krapkowice	30	50.29 N	17.56 E
Krapperup	41	56.16 N	12.31 E
Krapuh	114	3.39 N	98.10 E
Kras ⋏[1]	64	45.48 N	14.00 E
Krasavino	24	60.58 N	46.26 E
Krasavka	80	51.11 N	43.24 E
Krasieo ≏	110	14.49 N	100.05 E
Krasilov	78	49.39 N	26.59 E
Krasino	72	70.45 N	54.27 E
Krasivaja Meča ≏	76	52.55 N	39.03 E
Krasivka	80	52.16 N	42.31 E
Krasivoje	86	51.54 N	66.46 E
Kraskino	89	42.44 N	130.48 E
Kraskovo	265b	55.39 N	37.59 E
Krāslava	76	55.54 N	27.10 E
Kraslice	54	50.18 N	12.31 E
Krasnaja ≏	83	49.01 N	38.15 E
Krasnaja Gora, Ross.	76	53.01 N	31.37 E
Krasnaja Gora, Ross.	76	60.16 N	35.42 E
Krasnaja Gorbatka	80	55.52 N	41.46 E
Krasnaja Gorka	80	56.12 N	43.04 E
Krasnaja Jaranga	180	65.40 N	172.50 W
Krasnaja Jaruga	78	50.48 N	35.39 E
Krasnaja Pachra	82	55.27 N	37.17 E
Krasnaja Pol'ana, Ross.	80	56.15 N	51.09 E
Krasnaja Pol'ana, Ross.	80	52.13 N	53.38 E
Krasnaja Pol'ana, Ross.	80	46.06 N	41.30 E
Krasnaja Pol'ana, Ukr.	78	47.33 N	37.05 E
Krasnaja Popovka	83	49.08 N	38.09 E
Krasnaja Sloboda, Azer.	84	41.24 N	48.31 E
Krasnaja Sloboda, Bela.	76	52.51 N	27.10 E
Krasnaja Talovka	83	48.51 N	39.51 E
Krasnaja Vol'a	76	52.23 N	27.04 E
Krasnaja Zar'a	76	52.47 N	37.41 E
Krásná Lípa	54	50.54 N	14.31 E
Krasn'anka	80	51.04 N	47.56 E
Krasneno	180	64.38 N	174.48 E
Kraśnik	30	50.56 N	22.13 E
Krasnoarmejsk, Kaz.	86	53.50 N	69.42 E
Krasnoarmejsk, Ross.	80	51.02 N	45.42 E
Krasnoarmejsk, Ross.	82	56.08 N	38.08 E
Krasnoarmejsk, Ukr.	83	48.17 N	37.11 E
Krasnoarmejskaja	78	45.23 N	38.12 E
Krasnoarmejskij, Ross.	74	69.35 N	172.00 E
Krasnoarmejskij, Ross.	80	47.01 N	42.12 E
Krasnoarmejskoje, Ross.	80	55.46 N	47.11 E
Krasnoarmejskoje, Ross.	80	52.44 N	50.02 E
Krasnoarmejskoje, Ukr.	83	47.14 N	37.56 E
Krasnoborsk, Ross.	24	61.34 N	45.53 E
Krasnoborsk, Ross.	80	53.46 N	48.04 E
Krasnobród	30	50.33 N	23.13 E
Krasnobrodskij	86	54.10 N	86.28 E
Krasnodar	78	45.02 N	39.00 E
Krasnodar □[8]	80	44.10 N	40.30 E
Krasnodarskij	83	48.15 N	39.51 E
Krasnodarskoje vodochranilišče ⊜[1]	78	45.06 N	39.31 E
Krasnodon	83	48.17 N	39.48 E
Krasnofarfornyj	76	59.08 N	31.51 E
Krasnoflotskoje	80	50.04 N	41.14 E
Krasnogorka	85	43.15 N	75.10 E
Krasnogorodskoje	76	56.50 N	28.17 E
Krasnogorovka	83	48.00 N	37.31 E
Krasnogorsk, Ross.	82	55.50 N	37.20 E
Krasnogorsk, Ross.	89	48.24 N	142.06 E
Krasnogorskij, Ross.	80	56.09 N	48.20 E
Krasnogorskij, Ross.	86	54.36 N	61.15 E
Krasnogorskij, Uzb.	85	41.09 N	69.39 E
Krasnogorskoje, Ross.	80	57.42 N	52.30 E
Krasnogorskoje, Ross.	86	52.18 N	86.12 E
Krasnogovardejskij	86	57.22 N	62.20 E
Krasnograd	78	49.22 N	35.27 E
Krasnogvardejsk	85	39.46 N	67.16 E
Krasnogvardejskij	82	54.04 N	37.46 E
Krasnogvardejskoje, Kaz.	86	51.24 N	69.18 E
Krasnogvardejskoje, Ross.	78	50.39 N	38.24 E
Krasnogvardejskoje, Ross.	80	45.51 N	41.31 E
Krasnogvardejskoje, Ukr.	78	45.29 N	34.17 E
Krasnoil'sk	78	48.01 N	25.34 E
Krasnojar	80	48.54 N	51.46 E
Krasnojarka, Ross.	86	55.20 N	73.04 E
Krasnojarka, Ross.	86	59.26 N	60.30 E
Krasnoj Armii, proliv ⋓	74	80.00 N	94.35 E
Krasnojarovo	89	51.27 N	128.28 E
Krasnojarsk	86	56.01 N	92.50 E
Krasnojarsk □[8]	88	56.00 N	94.00 E
Krasnojarskij	86	51.58 N	59.55 E
Krasnojarskoje vodochranilišče ⊜[1]	86	55.00 N	92.00 E
Krasnoje, Bela.	76	54.14 N	27.05 E
Krasnoje, Mol.	78	46.38 N	29.50 E
Krasnoje, Ross.	24	59.12 N	47.49 E
Krasnoje, Ross.	76	53.06 N	33.55 E
Krasnoje, Ross.	76	52.51 N	38.47 E
Krasnoje, Ross.	78	50.21 N	38.50 E
Krasnoje, Ross.	78	46.44 N	39.34 E
Krasnoje, Ross.	78	50.56 N	38.41 E
Krasnoje, Ross.	82	54.26 N	38.38 E
Krasnoje, Ross.	86	54.37 N	85.23 E
Krasnoje, Ukr.	83	48.23 N	39.31 E
Krasnoje, Ukr.	83	48.25 N	37.19 E
Krasnoje, ozero ⊜	74	64.30 N	174.24 E
Krasnoje Echo	80	55.48 N	40.42 E
Krasnoje Gorodišče	82	54.04 N	38.44 E
Krasnoje-na-Volge	80	57.31 N	41.14 E
Krasnoje Selo, Ross.	80	48.02 N	45.13 E
Krasnoje Selo, Ross.	80	48.46 N	42.20 E
Krasnoje Selo, Ross.	265a	59.44 N	30.05 E
Krasnoje Znam'a, Ross.	76	57.26 N	35.13 E
Krasnoje Znam'a, Turk.	128	36.58 N	62.30 E
Krasnokamsk	86	58.04 N	55.48 E
Krasnokutsk, Kaz.	86	53.01 N	75.59 E
Krasnokutsk, Ukr.	78	50.06 N	35.09 E
Krasnolesje	76	54.24 N	22.23 E
Krasnolesnyj	78	51.53 N	39.35 E
Krasnoluki	76	54.37 N	28.50 E
Krasnomajskij	76	57.37 N	34.22 E
Krasnookt'abr'skij, Kyrg.	85	42.50 N	74.18 E
Krasnookt'abr'skij, Ross.	80	56.40 N	47.45 E
Krasnookt'abr'skij, Ross.	80	48.53 N	44.45 E
Krasnooskol'skoje vodochranilišče ⊜[1]	83	49.17 N	37.37 E
Krasnoostrovskij	76	60.18 N	28.40 E
Krasnopavlovka	78	49.08 N	36.19 E
Krasnoperekopsk	78	45.57 N	33.47 E
Krasnopolje, Bela.	76	53.20 N	31.24 E
Krasnopolje, Ukr.	78	50.46 N	35.16 E
Krasnorečenskij	89	44.41 N	135.14 E
Krasnoščelje	24	67.21 N	37.02 E
Krasnoščokovo	86	51.40 N	82.45 E
Krasnosel'kup	74	65.41 N	82.28 E
Krasnosel'sk	84	40.36 N	45.21 E
Krasnosel'skoje	78	45.25 N	32.42 E
Krasnosielc	30	53.03 N	21.10 E
Krasnoslobodsk, Ross.	80	54.26 N	43.48 E
Krasnoslobodsk, Ross.	80	48.42 N	44.34 E
Krasnotorka	83	48.41 N	37.31 E
Krasnoturansk	86	54.16 N	91.29 E
Krasnoturjinsk	86	59.46 N	60.12 E
Krasnoufimsk	86	56.37 N	57.46 E
Krasnoural'sk	86	58.21 N	60.03 E
Krasnousol'skij	86	53.54 N	56.27 E
Krasnovidovo	80	55.21 N	49.04 E
Krasnovišersk	24	60.23 N	56.59 E
Krasnovka, Ross.	83	48.47 N	40.07 E
Krasnovka, Ukr.	83	47.24 N	37.26 E
Krasnovodsk → Nebit-Dag	128	40.00 N	53.00 E
Krasnovodskij poluostrov >[1]	128	40.30 N	53.15 E
Krasnovodskij zaliv ⊂	128	39.55 N	53.15 E
Krasnoyarsk → Krasnojarsk	86	56.01 N	92.50 E
Krasnozatonskij	24	61.41 N	50.58 E
Krasnozavodsk	82	56.27 N	38.13 E
Krasnoznamensk	76	54.57 N	22.30 E
Krasnoznamenskij	86	51.03 N	69.30 E
Krasnoz'orskoje	86	53.59 N	79.14 E
Krásný Dvůr	54	50.10 N	13.24 E
Krasnyj, Ross.	76	54.34 N	31.26 E
Krasnyj, Ross.	92a	46.15 N	141.15 E
Krasnyj Aul	86	51.03 N	81.02 E
Krasnyj Bazar	84	39.41 N	46.58 E
Krasnyj Bogatyr'	80	56.02 N	41.08 E
Krasnyj Bor, Ross.	80	55.17 N	43.59 E
Krasnyj Bor, Ross.	80	55.53 N	53.06 E
Krasnyj Bor, Ross.	265a	59.41 N	30.41 E
Krasnyj Cholm, Ross.	76	58.03 N	37.07 E
Krasnyj Cholm, Ross.	80	54.11 N	40.42 E
Krasnyj Cholm, Ross.	86	51.35 N	54.09 E
Krasnyj Čhuduk	80	46.18 N	46.56 E
Krasnyj Čikoj	88	50.22 N	108.15 E
Krasnyje Baki	80	57.08 N	45.10 E
Krasnyje Barrikady	80	46.14 N	47.53 E
Krasnyje Četai	80	55.42 N	46.09 E
Krasnyje Gory	76	58.57 N	29.29 E
Krasnyje Okny	78	47.32 N	29.27 E
Krasnyje Partizany	78	50.57 N	31.47 E
Krasnyje Tkači	80	57.30 N	39.45 E
Krasnyj Gorodok	76	57.11 N	33.44 E
Krasnyj Gul'aj	80	54.01 N	48.22 E
Krasnyj Jar, Kaz.	86	53.20 N	69.14 E
Krasnyj Jar, Ross.	80	46.33 N	48.21 E
Krasnyj Jar, Ross.	80	53.30 N	50.22 E
Krasnyj Jar, Ross.	80	51.38 N	46.25 E
Krasnyj Jar, Ross.	80	50.37 N	45.47 E
Krasnyj Jar, Ross.	80	50.42 N	44.46 E
Krasnyj Jar, Ross.	86	55.54 N	86.57 E
Krasnyj Jar, Ross.	86	55.14 N	72.56 E
Krasnyj Jar, Ross.	86	57.07 N	84.33 E
Krasnyj Kl'ič	86	55.26 N	56.12 E
Krasnyj Kut, Ross.	80	50.57 N	46.58 E
Krasnyj Kut, Ukr.	83	48.12 N	38.48 E
Krasnyj Liman, Ross.	78	51.32 N	39.50 E
Krasnyj Liman, Ukr.	83	48.59 N	37.49 E
Krasnyj Log	78	51.23 N	39.46 E
Krasnyj Luč, Ross.	76	57.04 N	30.05 E
Krasnyj Luč, Ukr.	83	48.08 N	38.56 E
Krasnyj Majak	80	56.03 N	41.23 E
Krasnyj Manyč, Ross.	80	46.33 N	42.10 E
Krasnyj Manyč, Ross.	80	45.31 N	44.42 E
Krasnyj Manyč, Ross.	80	46.59 N	41.07 E
Krasnyj Meliorator	80	50.02 N	46.06 E
Krasnyj Okt'abr', Kaz.	86	46.50 N	75.59 E
Krasnyj Okt'abr', Ross.	80	51.33 N	45.42 E
Krasnyj Okt'abr', Ross.	80	56.06 N	41.23 E
Krasnyj Okt'abr', Ross.	82	56.07 N	38.53 E
Krasnyj Okt'abr', Ross.	82	55.37 N	36.30 E
Krasnyj Okt'abr', Ross.	86	55.37 N	64.48 E
Krasnyj Okt'abr', Ukr.	83	48.15 N	38.12 E
Krasnyj Okt'abr', Ukr.	83	48.56 N	39.23 E
Krasnyj Oskol	83	49.11 N	37.26 E
Krasnyj Partizan	80	46.20 N	43.10 E
Krasnyj Perekop	78	46.41 N	33.46 E
Krasnyj Profintern	80	57.45 N	40.27 E
Krasnyj Rog	76	52.57 N	33.45 E
Krasnyj Steklovar	80	56.13 N	48.47 E
Krasnyj Stroitel' ⊕[8]	265b	55.35 N	37.37 E
Krasnyj Sulin	83	47.54 N	40.03 E
Krasnyj Tekstil'ščik	80	51.23 N	45.50 E
Krasnyj Tkač	82	55.28 N	39.05 E
Krasnystaw	30	50.59 N	23.10 E
Krasnyy Luch → Krasnyj Luč	83	48.08 N	38.56 E
Krasucha	76	57.23 N	33.12 E
Kras'ukovskaja	83	47.31 N	40.06 E
Kraszna (Crasna) ≏	38	48.09 N	22.20 E
Kratovo	38	42.05 N	22.11 E
Krauchenwies	58	48.01 N	9.14 E
Kraul Mountains ⋏	9	73.10 S	14.10 W
Krauschwitz	54	51.31 N	14.41 E
Kräuterin ⋏	61	47.41 N	15.05 E
Krautheim	56	49.23 N	9.38 E
Kravaře, Česko.	30	49.56 N	18.01 E
Kravaře, Česko.	54	50.38 N	14.23 E
Kray ⊕[8]	263	51.28 N	7.05 E
Kražiai	76	55.36 N	22.40 E
Krbava ⊕[1]	36	44.40 N	15.35 E
Kreamer Island I	220	26.46 N	80.44 W
Kreba	54	51.20 N	14.40 E
Krebs	196	34.55 N	95.42 W
Krečetovo	24	60.56 N	38.30 E
Krečevicy	76	58.37 N	31.21 E
Krefeld	56	51.20 N	6.34 E
Kregme	41	55.57 N	12.04 E
Kreiensen	52	51.51 N	9.58 E
Kreischa	54	50.56 N	13.45 E
Kremastón, Tekhnití Límni ⊜[1]	38	38.55 N	21.30 E
Kremenčug	78	49.04 N	33.25 E
Kremenčugskoje vodochranilišče ⊜[1]	78	49.20 N	32.30 E
Kremenec	78	50.07 N	25.45 E
Kremennaja	83	49.03 N	38.14 E
Kremen'ovka	83	47.20 N	37.29 E
Kremenskoj	80	47.49 N	41.08 E
Kremenskoje	82	55.06 N	35.57 E
Kremlin ʊ	265b	55.45 N	37.37 E
Kremmen	54	52.45 N	13.01 E
Kremmling	200	40.03 N	106.23 W
Kremnica	30	48.43 N	18.54 E
Krempe	52	53.50 N	9.29 E
Krems ≏, Öst.	61	48.14 N	14.19 E
Krems ≏, Öst.	61	48.25 N	15.36 E
Krems an der Donau	61	48.25 N	15.36 E
Kremsbrücke	64	46.57 N	13.37 E
Kremsmünster	61	48.03 N	14.08 E
Krenitzin Islands II	180	54.08 N	166.00 W
Krensitz	54	51.29 N	12.27 E
Krepenskij	83	48.06 N	39.03 E
Krepkaja ≏	83	47.35 N	39.23 E
Krepoljin	38	44.16 N	21.37 E
Kreščhonka	86	55.52 N	80.06 E
Kresgeville	210	40.54 N	75.30 W
Kress	196	34.22 N	101.45 W
Kressbronn	58	47.35 N	9.36 E
Kressey Lake ⊜	285	39.44 N	75.07 W
Kresta, zaliv ⊂	180	66.00 N	179.15 W
Krestcy, Ross.	76	58.23 N	39.00 E
Krestcy, Ross.	76	58.15 N	32.31 E
Krestjanskij	85	40.32 N	69.02 E
Krestjanskoje	80	45.34 N	42.56 E
Krest-Major	74	67.37 N	144.45 E
Krestovaja Guba	72	74.07 N	55.33 E
Krestovo-Gorodišče	80	54.10 N	48.36 E
Krestovyj, pereval)(	84	42.32 N	44.28 E
Kresty	82	55.16 N	37.06 E
Kreta → Kríti I	38	35.29 N	24.42 E
Kretek	115a	7.59 S	110.19 E
Kretinga	76	55.53 N	21.13 E
Kreuth	64	47.38 N	11.44 E
Kreuzau	56	50.45 N	6.29 E
Kreuzberg	263	51.09 N	7.27 E
Kreuzberg ⊕[8]	264a	52.30 N	13.23 E
Kreuzberg ∧	56	50.22 N	9.58 E
Kreuzeck-Gruppe ⋏	64	46.51 N	13.06 E
Kreuzen	64	46.40 N	13.35 E
Kreuzlingen	58	47.39 N	9.11 E
Kreuznach → Bad Kreuznach	56	49.52 N	7.51 E
Kreuztal	56	50.58 N	7.59 E
Krevo	76	54.19 N	26.17 E
Kreyenhagen	54	52.55 N	10.52 E
Krian	115a	7.24 S	112.35 E
Kría Vrísi	38	40.41 N	22.18 E
Kribi	152	2.57 N	9.55 E
Kričov	76	53.42 N	31.43 E
Kriebstein, Burg ⊥	54	51.02 N	13.00 E
Krieglach	61	47.33 N	15.34 E
Kriel	158	26.16 S	29.14 E
Kriens	58	47.02 N	8.17 E
Krigujgun, mys >	180	65.30 N	171.05 W
Kriljon, mys >	89	45.53 N	142.05 E
Křimice	60	49.46 N	13.15 E
Krim-Krim	146	8.58 N	15.48 E
Krim → Krymskij poluostrov >[1]	78	45.00 N	34.00 E
Krimmler Wasserfälle ∟	64	47.12 N	12.10 E
Krimnicksee ⊜	264a	52.18 N	13.39 E
Krimpen aan de IJssel	52	51.54 N	4.35 E
Krimskij	80	47.39 N	40.44 E
Kriničcno-Lugskoje	83	47.45 N	39.12 E
Krinički	78	48.22 N	34.27 E
Kriničnaja	83	48.08 N	38.02 E
Kriničnoje	78	45.32 N	28.40 E
Krishna ≏	122	15.57 N	80.59 E
Krishna, Mouths of the ≏[1]	122	15.43 N	80.55 E
Krishnachaadrapur	126	21.50 N	86.49 E
Krishnagiri	122	12.32 N	78.14 E
Krishnamāti	272b	22.40 N	88.32 E
Krishnanagar, India	126	23.24 N	88.30 E
Krishnanagar, India	126	23.13 N	87.33 E
Krishnapur, Bngl.	126	23.30 N	89.56 E
Krishnapur, India	272b	22.36 N	88.26 E
Krishnarāja Sāgara ⊜[1]	122	12.30 N	76.26 E
Krishnarājpet	122	12.40 N	76.30 E
Krishnarāmpur	126	22.43 N	88.14 E
Kristdala	26	57.24 N	16.11 E
Kristiania → Oslo	26	59.55 N	10.45 E
Kristianopel	26	56.15 N	16.02 E
Kristiansand	26	58.10 N	8.00 E
Kristianstad	26	56.02 N	14.08 E
Kristianstads Län □[6]	26	56.15 N	14.00 E
Kristiansund	26	63.07 N	7.45 E
Kristiinankaupunki → Kristinestad	26	62.17 N	21.23 E
Kristineberg	26	65.04 N	18.35 E
Kristinehamn	40	59.20 N	14.07 E
Kristinestad (Kristiinankau-Punki)	26	62.17 N	21.23 E
Kríti (Crete) I	38	35.29 N	24.42 E
Kritikón Pélagos (Sea of Crete) ⊤[2]	38	35.46 N	23.54 E
Kritzendorf	264b	48.20 N	16.18 E
Kriul'any	78	47.13 N	29.09 E
Kriuša	82	54.28 N	36.24 E
Kriv'ačka	80	58.40 N	45.27 E
Krivaja ≏	38	44.27 N	18.09 E
Krivaja, kosa >[2]	83	47.02 N	38.06 E
Krivaja Ruda	78	49.31 N	32.59 E
Kriv'anskaja	83	47.24 N	40.10 E
Kriva Palanka	38	42.12 N	22.20 E
Krivcy	82	55.28 N	38.12 E
Kriviči	76	54.43 N	27.17 E
Krivinka	86	51.08 N	78.10 E
Krivodol	38	43.23 N	23.29 E
Krivoj Buzan	80	46.31 N	48.33 E
Krivoje Ozero	78	47.56 N	30.21 E
Krivoj Rog	78	47.55 N	33.21 E
Krivoj Torec ≏	83	48.39 N	37.32 E
Křivoklát	60	50.02 N	13.54 E
Krivonosovo	78	49.55 N	39.16 E
Krivorožje, Ross.	78	48.51 N	40.45 E
Krivorožje, Ukr.	78	48.31 N	38.40 E
Krivorožje, Ukr.	83	48.31 N	38.40 E
Krivošeino	86	57.20 N	83.57 E
Krivošin	76	52.52 N	26.08 E
Krivoy Rog → Krivoj Rog	78	47.55 N	33.21 E
Kriwoi-Rog → Krivoj Rog	78	47.55 N	33.21 E
Križevci	36	46.02 N	16.33 E
Krizskoje	83	49.28 N	39.38 E
Krk, Otok I	36	45.05 N	14.35 E
Krkonošský národní park ♠	30	50.45 N	15.35 E
Krn ∧	64	46.16 N	13.40 E
Krnov	30	50.05 N	17.41 E
Krobia	30	51.47 N	16.58 E
Krøderen ⊜	26	60.15 N	9.38 E
Krogager	41	55.42 N	8.51 E
Krögis	54	51.07 N	13.22 E
Krokek	40	58.40 N	16.24 E
Kroken	24	65.22 N	14.20 E
Krokodil ≏, S. Afr.	156	24.12 S	26.52 E
Krokodil ≏, S. Afr.	156	25.26 S	31.58 E
Krokom	26	63.19 N	14.30 E
Krokowa	30	54.48 N	18.11 E
Krolevec	78	51.33 N	33.23 E
Kröller-Müller, Rijksmuseum ʊ	52	52.05 N	5.50 E
Krölpa	54	50.41 N	11.32 E
Krom ≏	158	30.53 S	19.01 E
Krombi Pits	156	19.30 S	25.02 E
Kroměříž	30	49.18 N	17.24 E
Krommenie	52	52.29 N	4.45 E
Krompachy	30	48.56 N	20.52 E
Kromy	76	52.43 N	35.46 E
Kronach	54	50.14 N	11.20 E
Kronberg	56	50.10 N	8.30 E
Kronborg ⊥	41	56.02 N	12.38 E
Krone	263	51.27 N	7.20 E
Krong Ana ⊜[1]	110	12.30 N	108.00 E
Krŏng Kaôh Kŏng	110	11.37 N	102.59 E
Krŏng Kêb	110	10.29 N	104.19 E
Kronobergs Län □[6]	26	56.40 N	14.40 E
Kronoby (Kruunupyy)	26	63.43 N	23.02 E
Kronockaja Sopka, vulkan ∧[1]	74	54.44 N	160.31 E
Kronockij zaliv ⊂	74	54.12 N	160.36 E
Kronoki	74	54.36 N	161.10 E
Kronshagen	41	54.20 N	10.05 E
Kronštadt	76	59.59 N	29.45 E
Kronstadt → Brașov	38	45.39 N	25.37 E
Kronwa	110	15.25 N	98.26 E
Kroondal	158	25.45 S	27.19 E
Kroonstad	158	27.46 S	27.12 E
Kröpelin	54	54.04 N	11.48 E
Kropotkin, Ross.	72	45.26 N	40.34 E
Kropotkin, Ross.	88	58.30 N	115.17 E
Kropotkina, gora ∧	88	53.43 N	117.32 E
Kropp	41	54.24 N	9.31 E
Kroppefjäll ∧[2]	26	58.40 N	12.13 E
Kroppenstedt	54	51.56 N	11.18 E
Kropstädt	54	51.58 N	12.44 E
Kropufino	76	60.23 N	39.10 E
Krościenko	30	49.27 N	20.26 E
Kröslin	54	54.07 N	13.45 E
Krošn'a	78	50.18 N	28.39 E
Krośniewice	30	52.16 N	19.10 E
Krosno	30	49.42 N	21.46 E
Krosno □[4]	30	49.30 N	22.00 E
Krosno Odrzańskie	30	52.04 N	15.05 E
Krossen	54	50.58 N	11.59 E
Krostitz	54	51.28 N	12.27 E
Krotoszyn	30	51.42 N	17.26 E
Krotovka	80	53.18 N	51.12 E
Krotovo	86	56.57 N	69.20 E
Krotz Springs	194	30.32 N	91.45 W
Kröv	56	49.59 N	7.05 E
Kroya	115a	7.38 S	109.14 E
Krško	36	45.58 N	15.29 E
Krsy	60	49.54 N	13.03 E
Kr'učkov	80	48.01 N	45.40 E
Kr'učkovo	76	57.03 N	35.34 E
Kruckow	54	53.54 N	13.14 E
Krudenburg	263	51.39 N	6.45 E
Kruenggeukueh	114	5.15 N	97.02 E
Kruengluak	114	2.50 N	97.45 E
Kruft	56	50.23 N	7.20 E
Kruger National Park ♠	156	24.00 S	31.40 E
Krugersdorp	158	26.05 S	27.35 E
Krugersdorp □[5]	273d	26.05 S	27.35 E
Krugersdorp Race Course ♠	273d	26.08 S	27.45 E
Krugersdorp West	273d	26.06 S	27.45 E
Krugloje, Bela.	76	54.15 N	29.48 E
Krugloje, Ross.	83	47.01 N	39.15 E
Kruglooz'ornoje	86	55.13 N	79.01 E
Kruglooz'ornyj	80	51.06 N	51.17 E
Kruglyži	80	58.31 N	47.42 E
Krugzell	58	47.47 N	10.16 E
Krui	112	5.11 S	103.56 E
Kruidfontein	158	32.51 S	21.57 E
Kruiningen	52	51.27 N	4.02 E
Kruis, Kaap >	156	21.49 S	13.57 E
Kruisfontein	158	34.00 S	24.43 E
Kruishoutem	50	50.54 N	3.31 E
Kruisland	52	51.34 N	4.24 E
Kruisrivier	158	33.26 S	21.55 E
Kruisvallei	158	33.53 S	23.10 E
Krujë	38	41.30 N	19.48 E
Krukira, Laguna de ⊂	236	13.56 N	83.30 W
Kr'ukov	80	47.24 N	42.28 E
Kr'ukovo, Ross.	74	66.30 N	159.31 E
Kr'ukovo, Ross.	82	55.59 N	37.10 E
Kr'ukovo, Ross.	82	55.28 N	36.32 E
Kr'ukovo, Ross.	83	47.40 N	39.13 E
Krukut, Kali ≏	269e	6.12 S	106.48 E
Krulevščina	76	55.02 N	27.45 E
Krumasye	164	1.40 S	133.09 E
Krumbach, Dtsch.	58	47.58 N	9.02 E
Krumbach, Dtsch.	58	48.14 N	10.22 E
Krumme Lanke ⊜	264a	52.27 N	13.14 E
Krummendammer Heide ⊕[3]	264a	52.28 N	13.39 E
Krummenerl	263	51.05 N	7.45 E
Krummensee	264a	52.36 N	13.42 E
Krumme Steyrling ≏	61	47.54 N	14.14 E
Krummhörn	52	53.26 N	7.06 E
Krummhörn ⊕[1]	52	53.25 N	7.10 E
Krumovgrad	38	41.28 N	25.39 E
Krumroy	214	39.58 N	81.24 W
Krün	64	47.30 N	11.16 E
Krung Thep (Bangkok), Thai	110	13.45 N	100.31 E
Krung Thep (Bangkok), Thai	269a	13.45 N	100.31 E
Krung Thep Mahanakhon □[4]	269a	13.47 N	100.43 E
Krung Thon Bridge ⊕[5]	269a	13.47 N	100.30 E
Krupá	54	50.08 N	13.41 E
Krupec	78	51.38 N	34.21 E
Krüpel-See ⊜	264a	52.18 N	13.42 E
Krupka	54	50.43 N	13.46 E
Krupki	76	54.19 N	29.08 E
Kruså	41	54.50 N	9.25 E
Kruščica jezero ⊜[1]	36	44.39 N	15.19 E
Krusenstern, Cape >	180	67.07 N	163.43 W
Kruševac	38	43.35 N	21.20 E
Kruševo	38	41.22 N	21.14 E
Krušinovka	76	53.14 N	29.50 E
Krušné hory (Erzgebirge) ⋏	54	50.30 N	13.15 E
Kruszwica	30	52.41 N	18.19 E
Krutaja, Ross.	24	63.02 N	54.38 E
Krutaja, Ross.	86	57.24 N	76.27 E
Krutaja Gorka	86	55.25 N	73.15 E
Krutcy	76	57.10 N	29.23 E
Krutec, Ross.	76	60.17 N	39.25 E
Krutec, Ross.	82	56.10 N	38.33 E
Kruticha, Ross.	86	53.58 N	81.14 E
Kruticha, Ross.	86	56.49 N	77.10 E
Krutinka	86	56.01 N	71.31 E
Krutoje	76	52.26 N	37.28 E
Krutoj Log	86	57.53 N	58.14 E
Krutoj Majdan	80	55.35 N	44.04 E
Krutyje Verchi	82	54.19 N	36.26 E
Kruunupyy → Kronoby	26	63.43 N	23.02 E
Kruzenšterna, proliv ⋓	74	48.30 N	153.50 E
Kruzof Island I	180	57.10 N	135.40 W
Krydor	184	52.47 N	107.03 W
Krylatskoje ⊕[8]	265b	55.45 N	37.26 E
Krylbo	40	60.08 N	16.13 E
Krylovskaja	78	46.07 N	39.19 E

Symbols in the index entries represent the broad categories identified in the key at the right. Symbols with superior numbers (⋏[1]) identify subcategories (see complete key on page *I · 1*).

Symbole im Register stellen die rechts im Schlüssel erklärten Kategorien dar. Symbole mit hochgestellten Ziffern (⋏[1]) bezeichnen Unterabteilungen einer Kategorie (vgl. vollständiger Schlüssel auf Seite *I · 1*).

Los símbolos incluidos en el texto del índice representan las grandes categorías identificadas con la clave a la derecha. Los símbolos con números en su parte superior (⋏[1]) identifican las subcategorías (véase la clave completa en la página *I · 1*).

Les symboles de l'index représentent les catégories indiquées dans la légende à droite. Les symboles suivis d'un indice (⋏[1]) représentent des sous-catégories (voir légende complète à la page *I · 1*).

Os símbolos incluídos no texto do índice representam as grandes categorias identificadas com a chave à direita. Os símbolos com números em sua parte superior (⋏[1]) identificam as subcategorias (veja-se a chave completa na página *I · 1*).

∧ Mountain	Berg	Montaña	Montagne	Montanha
⋏ Mountains	Gebirge	Montañas	Montagnes	Montanhas
)(Pass	Paß	Paso	Col	Passo
∨ Valley, Canyon	Tal, Cañon	Valle, Cañón	Vallée, Canyon	Vale, Canhão
⌣ Plain	Ebene	Llano	Plaine	Planície
> Cape	Kap	Cabo	Cap	Cabo
I Island	Insel	Isla	Île	Ilha
II Islands	Inseln	Islas	Îles	Ilhas
⊥ Other Topographic Features	Andere Topographische Objekte	Otros Elementos Topográficos	Autres données topographiques	Outros acidentes topográficos

ESPAÑOL Nombre	Página	Lat.°′	Long.°′ W = Oeste
FRANÇAIS Nom	Page	Lat.°′	Long.°′ W = Ouest
PORTUGUÊS Nome	Página	Lat.°′	Long.°′ W = Oeste

Krym 83 47.19 N 39.31 E
Krymsk 78 44.56 N 37.59 E
Krymskaja Avtonomnaja Sovetskaja Socialističeskaja Respublika □³ 78 45.00 N 34.00 E
Krymskij 78 47.40 N 40.46 E
Krymskije gory ∧ 78 44.45 N 34.25 E
Krymskij poluostrov (Crimea) >¹ 78 45.00 N 34.00 E
Krymskij Zapovednik ✦⁴ 78 44.42 N 34.12 E
Krymskoje 83 48.45 N 38.48 E
Krynica 30 49.25 N 20.56 E
Krynka ≃ 83 47.36 N 38.47 E
Kryžina, chrebet ∧ 88 54.00 N 95.00 E
Kryžopol' 78 48.23 N 28.52 E
Krzepice 30 50.58 N 18.44 E
Krzeszowice 30 50.09 N 19.39 E
Krzeszyce 54 52.36 N 15.01 E
Krzna ≃ 30 52.08 N 23.31 E
Krzywiń 30 51.58 N 16.49 E
Krzyż 30 52.54 N 16.01 E
Ksar Chellala 148 35.13 N 2.18 E
Ksar el Barka 150 18.24 N 12.13 W
Ksar-el-Kebir 148 35.01 N 5.54 W
Ksar-el-Seghir 34 35.50 N 5.32 W
Ksar Hellal 36 35.39 N 10.54 E
Ksaverovka 78 50.03 N 30.12 E
Ksel, Djebel ∧ 148 33.44 N 1.10 E
Kšen' ≃ 76 52.23 N 37.44 E
Ksenjevka 88 53.34 N 118.44 E
Ksenofontova 24 60.58 N 56.12 E
Kšenskij 78 51.52 N 37.43 E
Książ Wielkopolski 30 52.05 N 17.14 E
Ksob, Oued ≃ 36 35.49 N 7.53 E
Ksour, Monts des ∧ 148 32.45 N 0.30 W
Ksour Essaf 148 35.25 N 11.00 E
Kstovo 80 56.11 N 44.11 E
Kū', Wādī al- ∨ 140 13.37 N 25.15 E
Kuah 114 6.19 N 99.51 E
Kuai ≃ 100 33.09 N 117.32 E
Kuala, Indon. 112 2.55 N 105.48 E
Kuala, Indon. 114 3.32 N 98.24 E
Kualabee 114 4.24 N 96.03 E
Kuala Berang 114 5.04 N 103.01 E
Kualabesi 112 0.28 S 102.40 E
Kuala Kangsar 114 4.46 N 100.56 E
Kualakapuas 112 3.01 S 114.21 E
Kuala Kedah 114 6.06 N 100.18 E
Kuala Kelawang 114 2.56 N 102.05 E
Kuala Kerai 114 5.32 N 102.12 E
Kuala Kerau 114 3.43 N 102.22 E
Kualakeriau 112 0.50 N 113.20 E
Kuala Ketil 114 5.36 N 100.39 E
Kuala Kubu Baharu 114 3.34 N 101.39 E
Kuala Kurau 114 5.01 N 100.26 E
Kualakurun 112 1.07 S 113.53 E
Kualalangsa 114 4.32 N 98.01 E
Kuala Lipis 114 4.11 N 102.03 E
Kuala Lumpur 114 3.10 N 101.42 E
Kuala Lumpur □³ 114 3.10 N 101.42 E
Kualamanjual 112 1.25 S 112.00 E
Kuala Nerang 114 6.15 N 100.36 E
Kualapesaguan 112 2.01 S 110.08 E
Kuala Pilah 114 2.44 N 102.15 E
Kualapuu 229a 21.09 N 157.02 W
Kuala Selangor 114 3.21 N 101.15 E
Kualasimpang 114 4.17 N 98.03 E
Kuala Terengganu 114 5.20 N 103.08 E
Kualu ≃ 114 2.45 N 100.00 E
Kuamut 112 5.13 N 117.30 E
Kuamut ≃ 112 5.13 N 117.32 E
Kuanbang 98 40.29 N 120.04 E
Kuancheng, Zhg. 98 40.37 N 118.31 E
Kuancheng, Zhg. 105 40.38 N 118.27 E
Kuandang 112 0.52 N 122.55 E
Kuandian 98 40.43 N 124.44 E
Kuando — Cuando ≃ 152 18.27 S 23.32 E
Kuanhsi 100 24.48 N 121.10 E
Kuanmiao 100 22.58 N 120.19 E
Kuanshan 100 23.03 N 121.09 E
Kuan Shan ∧ 100 23.14 N 120.54 E
Kuantan 114 3.48 N 103.20 E
Kuantan ≃ 114 3.50 N 103.17 E
Kuanyin 100 25.02 N 121.04 E
Kuanyün — Guanyun 98 34.20 N 119.17 E
Kuanza — Cuanza ≃ 152 9.19 S 13.08 E
Kuba 84 41.22 N 48.31 E
Kuba — Cuba □¹ 240p 21.30 N 80.00 W
Kuban' ≃ 72 45.20 N 37.30 E
Kubatly 84 39.22 N 46.34 E
Kubbī 140 11.08 N 25.14 E
Kubbum 140 11.47 N 23.47 E
Kubena ≃ 76 59.36 N 39.39 E
Kubenskoje 76 59.26 N 39.40 E
Kubenskoje, ozero ⊜ 76 59.40 N 39.25 E
Kubiki 94 37.11 N 138.20 E
Kubinka 82 55.35 N 36.43 E
Kubitzer Bodden ⊂ 54 54.24 N 13.12 E
Küblis 58 46.55 N 9.47 E
Kubn'a ≃ 80 55.31 N 48.27 E
Kubokawa 96 33.12 N 133.08 E
Kubor, Mount ∧ 164 6.05 S 144.45 E
Kubr' ≃ 82 56.52 N 38.17 E
Kubrat 38 43.48 N 26.30 E
Kubu 115b 8.16 S 115.35 E
Kubuchaj 88 50.30 N 114.48 E
Kubu Gajah 114 5.10 N 100.41 E
Kubumesaai 112 1.31 N 115.06 E
Kubutambahan 115b 8.05 S 115.10 E
Kučema 24 65.37 N 42.28 E
Kučen'ajevo 80 54.44 N 46.24 E
Kučevo 38 44.27 N 21.44 E
Kuchaiburi 126 22.16 N 86.10 E
Kuchaman 120 27.09 N 74.52 E
Kuch'ang-ni 98 40.09 N 124.46 E
Kuchelebai 154 1.29 N 35.01 E
Kuchen Spitze ∧ 58 47.03 N 10.14 E
Kuchinarai 110 16.32 N 104.04 E
Kuching 112 1.33 N 110.20 E
Kuchinoerabu-jima I 93b 30.28 N 130.11 E
Kuchino-shima I 93b 29.57 N 129.57 E
Kuchiwa 96 34.53 N 132.55 E
Kuchl 64 47.37 N 13.09 E
Küchnay Darweyshān 128 30.59 N 64.11 E
Kuchterin Lug 89 52.25 N 128.05 E
Kuchtinka 82 54.29 N 38.10 E
Kučino 265b 55.45 N 37.58 E
Kučkak 85 40.15 N 70.20 E
Kučki 80 53.01 N 44.29 E
Kučovë 38 40.48 N 19.54 E
Küçük Ağrı Dağı ∧ 84 39.40 N 44.25 E
Küçükbahçe 130 38.33 N 26.24 E
Küçükbakkal ✦⁸ 267b 40.58 N 29.06 E
Küçükçekmece ✦⁸ 267b 40.59 N 28.46 E
Küçükçekmece Gölü ⊜ 267b 41.00 N 28.46 E
Küçükköy ✦⁸ 267b 41.04 N 28.54 E
Küçükkuyu 130 39.32 N 26.36 E
Kučukskoje, ozero ⊜ 86 52.42 N 79.46 E
Kucur, Tanjung > 115a 8.39 S 114.34 E
Kučurgan ≃ 78 46.43 N 29.53 E
Kūd 123 33.05 N 75.17 E
Kuda ≃ 88 52.25 N 104.08 E
Kudaka-jima I 174m 26.09 N 127.54 E
Kudamatsu 96 34.00 N 131.52 E
Kudanggou 104 41.06 N 124.00 E
Kudap 114 1.17 N 102.26 E
Kudara, Ross. 88 52.13 N 106.39 E
Kudara, Taj. 85 38.25 N 72.41 E
Kudara ≃ 85 38.19 N 72.28 E
Kudara-Somon 88 50.10 N 107.25 E
Kudat 112 6.53 N 116.50 E
Kudbrooke ✦⁸ 260 51.28 N 0.03 E
Kudejevskij 86 54.52 N 56.46 E
Kudene 164 6.14 S 134.39 E
Kudever' 76 56.47 N 29.23 E
Kudinovo 82 55.45 N 38.12 E
Kudirkos Naumiestis 76 54.46 N 22.53 E
Kudongho 98 35.31 N 126.29 E
Kudoyama 96 34.17 N 135.34 E
Kudremukh ∧ 122 13.08 N 75.16 E
Kudrovo 265a 59.54 N 30.31 E
Kudus 115a 6.48 S 110.50 E
Kudyat al-Islām 142 27.32 N 30.45 E
Kudymkar 86 59.01 N 54.37 E
Kuee Ruins ⊥ 229d 19.21 N 155.23 W
Kueishan Tao I 100 24.51 N 121.57 E
Kueisui — Hohhot 102 40.51 N 111.40 E
Kueiyang — Guiyang 102 26.35 N 106.43 E
Kuekvun' ≃ 180 69.14 N 179.25 E
Kuenlun — Kunlun Shan ∧ 120 36.30 N 88.00 E
Kuerbin 89 49.25 N 128.59 E
K'uerhlo — Korla 90 41.44 N 86.09 E
Kufayr az-Zayt 132 33.26 N 35.44 E
Kufayr Yābūs 132 33.42 N 36.01 E
Kufrinjah 132 32.18 N 35.42 E
Kufstein 64 47.35 N 12.10 E
Kufūr Bilshāy 142 30.51 N 30.48 E
Kufūr Najm 142 30.44 N 31.35 E
Kuga, Nihon 96 34.05 N 132.05 E
Kuga, Nihon 96 33.56 N 132.16 E
Kuga, Zhg. 90 41.43 N 82.54 E
Kugaluk ≃ 180 69.10 N 131.00 W
Kugaly 86 44.29 N 78.40 E
Kugarčino 80 55.33 N 50.29 E
Kugart ≃ 85 40.52 N 72.53 E
Kugas 85 38.21 N 70.48 E
Kugej 83 46.53 N 39.19 E
Kugesi 80 56.02 N 47.18 E
Kugmallit Bay ⊂ 180 69.33 N 133.25 W
Kugojeja ≃ 78 46.34 N 39.38 E
Kuguno 94 36.03 N 137.16 E
Kuhaylī 140 19.25 N 32.50 E
Kühbach 60 48.29 N 11.11 E
Kühdasht 128 33.32 N 47.36 E
Kūh Lab, Ra's-e > 128 25.17 N 60.28 E
Kuhlīyah, Wādī ∨ 142 30.05 N 31.58 E
Kühlungsborn 54 54.09 N 11.43 E
Kuhmo 26 64.08 N 29.31 E
Kuhmoinen 26 61.34 N 25.11 E
Kühnhausen 54 51.02 N 10.58 E
Kühnsdorf 61 46.37 N 14.37 E
Kūhpāyeh 128 32.43 N 52.26 E
Kūhren 54 51.20 N 12.50 E
Kuhstedt 52 53.23 N 8.58 E
Kui 164 7.30 S 147.15 E
Kuibyschew — Samara 80 53.12 N 50.09 E
Kuidesu 98 41.46 N 119.29 E
Kuidou 100 25.10 N 118.11 E
Kuikkol', ozero ⊜ 86 50.57 N 64.30 E
Kuikui, Lae o > 229a 20.36 N 156.35 W
Kuilāpāl 126 22.50 N 86.38 E
Kuinre 52 52.47 N 5.50 E
Kuiseb ≃ 156 22.59 S 14.31 E
Kuishi-yama ∧, Nihon 96 33.51 N 133.35 E
Kuishi-yama ∧, Nihon 96 33.40 N 133.01 E
Kuitan 100 23.05 N 115.58 E
Kuito 152 12.22 S 16.56 E
Kuiu Island I 180 56.45 N 134.10 W
Kuivaniemi 26 65.35 N 25.11 E
Kuivastu 76 58.35 N 23.22 E
Kuja, Ross. 24 67.46 N 53.10 E
Kuja, Ross. 24 65.09 N 40.06 E
Kujal'nickij liman ⊜ 78 46.40 N 30.42 E
Kujang 98 39.52 N 126.01 E
Kujani Game Reserve ✦⁴ 150 7.10 N 0.50 W
Kujawy ✦¹ 30 52.45 N 18.30 E
Kujbyšev 86 55.27 N 78.19 E
Kujbyševka 78 47.37 N 31.42 E
Kujbyševo, Ross. 83 47.49 N 38.55 E
Kujbyševo, Ukr. 78 44.38 N 33.52 E
Kujbyševo, Ukr. 78 47.22 N 36.39 E
Kujbyševo, Uzb. 85 40.22 N 71.17 E
Kujbyšev — Samara 80 53.12 N 50.09 E
Kujbyševskij, Kaz. 86 53.15 N 66.51 E
Kujbyševskij, Uzb. 72 37.52 N 68.44 E
Kujbyševskij Zaton 80 55.09 N 49.12 E
Kujbyševskoje vodochranilišče ⊜¹ 80 54.30 N 48.30 E
Kujeda 86 56.26 N 55.35 E
Kujgan 86 45.25 N 74.10 E
Kujgenkol' 80 49.17 N 47.59 E
Kuji 92 40.11 N 141.46 E
Kuji ≃ 94 36.29 N 140.37 E
Kujirai 268 35.56 N 139.27 E
Kujl'uk 85 41.15 N 69.20 E
Kujman' 76 52.52 N 39.16 E
Kujong-ni 98 37.53 N 125.54 E
Kujtun 88 54.21 N 101.29 E
Kujū 96 33.01 N 131.18 E
Kujūkuri 94 35.32 N 140.25 E
Kujūkuri-hama ⊥² 94 35.35 N 140.30 E
Kujū-san ∧ 96 33.05 N 131.15 E
Kuk ≃ 180 70.36 N 160.00 W
Kukaklek Lake ⊜ 180 59.09 N 155.20 W
Kukalaya ≃ 236 13.39 N 83.37 W
Kukan 89 49.12 N 133.28 E
Kukarino 82 55.31 N 35.36 E
Kukawa 146 12.56 N 13.35 E
Kukerin 162 33.11 S 118.05 E
Kukës 38 42.05 N 20.24 E
Kuke Shan ∧ 85 40.00 N 75.00 E
Kuki 94 36.04 N 139.40 E
Kukipi 164 8.10 S 146.05 E
Kukkola 26 65.59 N 24.04 E
Kukmor 80 56.13 N 50.54 E
Kukoboj 76 58.42 N 39.54 E
Kukoy ≃ 76 59.52 N 32.35 E
Kukong — Shaoguan 100 24.50 N 113.37 E
Kukpowruk ≃ 180 69.35 N 163.00 W
Kukpuk ≃ 180 68.23 N 166.24 W
Kukshi 120 22.12 N 74.45 E
Kukuj 76 59.21 N 32.33 E
Kuku-Nor — Qinghai Hu ⊜ 102 36.50 N 100.20 E
Kukup 114 1.19 N 103.27 E
Kuku Point > 174a 19.19 N 166.37 E
Kukuri Mukuri Char I 126 21.56 N 90.39 E
Kukuštan 86 57.38 N 56.30 E
Kula, Blg. 38 43.53 N 22.31 E
Kula, Jugo. 38 45.36 N 19.32 E
Kula, Tür. 130 38.33 N 28.39 E
Kula, Hi., U.S. 229a 20.52 N 156.40 W
Kula ≃ 120 37.55 N 69.46 E
Kulāchi 123 31.56 N 70.27 E
Kulagi 76 52.56 N 34.50 E
Kula Gulf Ʉ 175e 8.05 S 157.18 E
Kulai 114 1.40 N 103.36 E
Kulaj 86 57.42 N 75.15 E
Kula Kangri ∧ 124 28.03 N 90.27 E
Kulākh 144 21.18 N 40.21 E
Kulakovo, Ross. 82 55.06 N 37.56 E
Kulakovo, Ross. 86 58.06 N 93.57 E
Kulakši 84 47.12 N 55.24 E
Kulal, Mount ∧ 154 2.43 N 36.56 E
Kulanak 85 41.22 N 75.31 E
Kulandy 86 46.08 N 59.31 E
Kulaneutpes ≃ 86 50.21 N 69.08 E
Kular 74 70.41 N 134.22 E
Kulassein Island I 116 6.25 N 120.41 E
Kulaura 120 24.32 N 92.03 E
Kulautuva 76 54.58 N 23.38 E
Kulaykilī 140 11.21 N 25.36 E
Kul'či 89 53.33 N 139.36 E
Kuldīga 76 56.58 N 21.59 E
Kuldja — Yining 86 43.54 N 81.21 E
Kul'dur 89 49.13 N 131.38 E
Kule 156 23.05 S 20.05 E
Kulebaki 80 55.24 N 42.32 E
Kulejevo 86 59.40 N 80.59 E
Kulen Vakuf 36 44.34 N 16.06 E
Kulešovka 83 47.05 N 39.33 E
Kulevčinskij 86 53.12 N 61.26 E
Kulgām 123 33.39 N 75.01 E
Kulgera 162 25.50 S 133.18 E
Kulgunino 86 53.35 N 56.56 E
Kuligi 80 58.11 N 53.46 E
Kulikov 78 49.58 N 24.04 E
Kulikovka, Ross. 80 52.14 N 47.36 E
Kulikovka, Ukr. 78 51.23 N 31.37 E
Kulikovo 76 52.14 N 39.35 E
Kulikovskij 80 50.51 N 42.34 E
Kulim 114 5.22 N 100.34 E
Kulin 162 32.40 S 118.10 E
Kuliushucun 105 40.07 N 116.34 E
Kulju 26 61.23 N 23.46 E
Kulkyne Creek ≃ 166 30.16 S 144.12 E
Kullaberg ∧² 41 56.18 N 12.30 E
Kullamaa 76 58.53 N 24.05 E
Küllenhahn ✦⁸ 263 51.14 N 7.08 E
Küllstedt 56 51.16 N 10.17 E
Kullu 123 31.58 N 77.06 E
Kulm 198 46.18 N 98.57 W
Kulmbach 54 50.06 N 11.27 E
Kulnura 170 33.14 S 151.13 E
Kuloj, Ross. 24 64.58 N 43.28 E
Kuloj, Ross. 24 61.02 N 42.29 E
Kuloj ≃, Ross. 24 66.03 N 43.22 E
Kuloj ≃, Ross. 76 60.25 N 42.30 E
Kuloli 85 39.22 N 68.03 E
Kulongshan 98 41.43 N 116.54 E
Kulongshanpuzi 104 41.16 N 123.59 E
Kulotino 76 58.27 N 33.21 E
Kulp 130 38.30 N 41.02 E
Kulpahar 124 25.19 N 79.38 E
Kulpara 168b 34.04 S 138.02 E
Kulpawn ≃ 150 10.21 N 1.05 W
Kulpi 126 22.06 N 88.15 E
Kul'pino 82 56.18 N 36.16 E
Kulpmont 208 40.47 N 76.28 W
Kulpsville 285 40.15 N 75.20 W
Kul'sary 86 46.59 N 54.01 E
Kulsbjerge ∧² 41 55.01 N 12.01 E
Külsheim 56 49.40 N 9.31 E
Kültepe ⊥ 130 38.44 N 35.34 E
Kulti 126 23.44 N 86.51 E
Kultikri 126 22.10 N 87.09 E
Kulttu 88 51.44 N 103.42 E
Kuluk 130 39.06 N 33.05 E
Kuluha, Jabal ∧ 140 15.31 N 23.25 E
Kulumadau 164 9.03 S 152.43 E
Kulunda 86 52.35 N 78.57 E
Kulunda ≃ 86 52.59 N 79.48 E
Kulundinskaja step' 86 53.00 N 79.00 E
Kulundinskoje, ozero ⊜ 86 53.00 N 79.36 E
Kuluqi 89 50.23 N 124.13 E
Kulwin 166 35.02 S 142.33 E
Kum ≃ 98 38.38 N 27.32 E
Kuma 96 33.39 N 132.54 E
Kuma ≃, Nihon 92 32.30 N 130.34 E
Kuma ≃, Ross. 72 44.56 N 47.00 E
Kuma ≃, Ross. 86 59.32 N 66.45 E
Kumagaya 94 36.08 N 139.23 E
Kumai, Indon. 112 3.23 S 112.33 E
Kumai, Indon. 112 2.44 S 111.43 E
Kumai, Teluk ⊂ 112 3.00 S 111.43 E
Kumaishi 92a 42.08 N 139.59 E
Kumajri 84 40.48 N 43.50 E
Kumakanda 88 52.44 N 116.55 E
Kumalarang 116 7.44 N 123.08 E
Kumamba, Kepulauan II 164 1.36 S 138.45 E
Kumamoto 92 32.48 N 130.43 E
Kumamoto □⁵ 96 32.58 N 130.55 E
Kumano, Nihon 92 33.54 N 136.05 E
Kumano, Nihon 96 34.20 N 132.34 E
Kumano ≃ 92 33.44 N 136.01 E
Kumano-nada ▾² 92 33.47 N 136.20 E
Kumanovo 38 42.08 N 21.43 E
Kumār ≃¹, Bngl. 126 23.11 N 90.10 E
Kumār ≃¹, Bngl. 126 23.31 N 89.28 E
Kumara, N.Z. 172 42.38 S 171.11 E
Kumara, Ross. 89 51.37 N 126.47 E
Kumārapālaiyam 122 11.28 N 77.43 E
Kumārdhubi 126 23.48 N 86.43 E
Kumārganj 126 22.59 N 87.44 E
Kumārghāt 120 24.04 N 92.04 E
Kumārgrām 124 26.37 N 89.50 E
Kumāri ≃ 126 22.57 N 86.48 E
Kumārkhāli 124 23.51 N 89.15 E
Kumarl 162 32.47 S 121.33 E
Kumasi 150 6.41 N 1.35 W
Kumatori 270 34.24 N 135.22 E
Kumawa, Pegunungan ∧ 164 3.50 S 132.50 E
Kumba 152 4.38 N 9.25 E
Kumbakonam 122 10.58 N 79.23 E
Kumba Pits 168b 18.45 S 24.45 E
Kumbar 120 12.03 N 30.16 E
Kumbarilla 166 27.19 S 150.53 E
Kumbe 164 8.21 S 140.13 E
Kumbel' 85 42.30 N 73.11 E
Kümch'ŏn 98 38.10 N 126.29 E
Kum-Dag 128 39.16 N 54.36 E
Kumdah ▾⁴ 144 20.23 N 45.05 E
Kumdan ∧ 123 35.09 N 77.35 E
Kumdanlı 130 38.19 N 30.59 E
Kume 96 35.03 N 133.54 E
Kume-jima I 93b 26.20 N 126.47 E
Kumenan 96 34.56 N 133.58 E
Kumeny 80 58.07 N 49.56 E
Kŭm-gang ≃ 98 36.00 N 126.40 E
Kümgang-san ∧ 98 38.40 N 128.06 E
Kümhwa 98 38.17 N 127.28 E
Kumi 154 1.29 N 33.56 E
Kumihama 96 35.36 N 134.55 E
Kuminovskij 86 53.07 N 56.44 E
Kumiskij 86 58.40 N 66.04 E
Kumiyama 270 34.53 N 135.43 E
Kumizawa ✦⁸ 268 35.23 N 139.31 E
Kumköy ✦⁸ 267b 41.15 N 29.02 E
Kuml 40 59.08 N 15.08 E
Kumli 83 43.58 N 46.04 E
Kumlinge I 40 60.15 N 20.45 E
Kumluca 130 36.22 N 30.18 E
Kumluca, Tür. 130 41.27 N 32.28 E
Kummelnäs 40 59.21 N 18.17 E
Kummerow 54 54.17 N 12.53 E
Kummerower See ⊜ 54 53.49 N 12.52 E
Kummersbruck 60 49.25 N 11.53 E
Kumo 146 10.03 N 11.13 E
Kumo-do I 98 34.31 N 127.45 E
Kumon Range ∧ 102 26.30 N 97.15 E
Kumora 88 55.53 N 111.13 E
Kumosō-yama ∧ 96 33.54 N 134.18 E
Kumotori-yama ∧ 94 35.51 N 138.57 E
Kumphawapi 110 17.07 N 103.01 E
Kumrābād 126 20.16 N 82.01 E
Kumrah 130 40.53 N 37.16 E
Kümsan 98 36.07 N 127.30 E
Kümsan-ni 98 37.55 N 125.54 E
Kumsenga 154 3.47 S 30.25 E
Kumta 122 14.25 N 74.24 E
Kumu 154 2.08 N 25.10 E
Kumuchanji 154 1.24 N 100.43 E
Kumuch 84 42.11 N 47.07 E
Kumukahi, Cape > 229d 19.31 N 154.49 W
Kumukuli 120 37.30 N 89.00 E
Kumusi ≃ 164 8.35 S 148.00 E
Kümüx 86 42.14 N 88.11 E
Kumžār 128 26.20 N 56.25 E
Kuna 202 43.29 N 116.25 W
Kunar (Konar) ≃ 123 34.25 N 70.32 E
Kunašak 86 55.43 N 61.36 E
Kunashiri-tō — Kunašir, ostrov I 92a 44.10 N 146.00 E
Kunašir, ostrov (Kunashiri-tō) I 92a 44.10 N 146.00 E
Kun'batar 84 44.17 N 45.34 E
Kuncheng Hu ⊜ 106 31.35 N 120.45 E
Kunchha 124 28.08 N 84.20 E
Kunc'ovo ✦⁸ 265b 55.44 N 37.26 E
Kunda, Eesti 76 59.29 N 26.32 E
Kunda, Zaïre 154 3.57 S 26.35 E
Kunda Hills ∧² 122 11.10 N 76.30 E
Kundahit 126 23.58 N 87.10 E
Kundam 124 23.13 N 80.21 E
Kundāpura 122 13.38 N 74.42 E
Kundar ≃ 120 31.56 N 69.19 E
Kundat 86 55.14 N 87.51 E
Kundelungu, Parc National de ♦ 154 10.30 S 27.45 E
Kunderu ≃ 122 14.38 N 78.42 E
Kundi 154 1.08 S 40.41 E
Kundiān 123 32.27 N 71.28 E
Kundiawa 164 6.00 S 145.00 E
Kundima 164 4.14 S 143.52 E
Kundl 64 47.28 N 11.59 E
Kundla 120 21.20 N 71.18 E
Kundr'učje ≃ 83 47.52 N 40.15 E
Kundur, Pulau I 112 0.45 N 103.26 E
Kunene (Cunene) ≃ 152 17.20 S 11.50 E
Kunersdorf, Forst ✦³ 264a 52.17 N 12.59 E
Kunes 24 70.21 N 26.31 E
Künes ≃ 86 43.55 N 80.55 E
Kunga ≃¹ 126 21.45 N 89.30 E
Kungälv 26 57.52 N 11.58 E
Kungana 146 7.50 N 10.42 E
Kungchuling — Huaide 89 43.32 N 124.50 E
Kungej-Alatau, chrebet ∧ 85 42.50 N 77.00 E
Kunggyü Yumco ⊜ 124 30.35 N 82.09 E
Kunghit Island I 182 52.06 N 131.04 W
Kunghsi 100 24.37 N 121.16 E
Kung-pei-tien 269d 25.06 N 121.38 E
Kungrad 86 43.06 N 58.54 E
Kungsängen 40 59.29 N 17.45 E
Kungsängen flygplats ⊠ 40 58.36 N 16.15 E
Kungsbacka 26 57.29 N 12.04 E
Kungsgården 40 60.36 N 16.37 E
Kungshamn 26 58.22 N 11.15 E
Kungsör 40 59.25 N 16.05 E
Kungu 152 2.47 N 19.12 E
Kungur 86 57.25 N 56.57 E
Kunhār ≃ 123 34.17 N 73.29 E
Kunhegyes 30 47.22 N 20.38 E
Kunhing 110 21.18 N 98.26 E
Kuni 94 36.35 N 138.38 E
Kunia 229c 21.29 N 158.07 W
Kunigami 174m 26.45 N 128.10 E
Kuningan 115a 6.59 S 108.29 E
Kunisaki 96 33.33 N 131.45 E
Kunisaki-hantō >¹ 96 33.30 N 131.40 E
Kunitachi 268 35.41 N 139.26 E
Kuni Vyselki 82 54.18 N 38.41 E
Kunja 76 56.18 N 30.59 E
Kunja ≃, Ross. 76 57.09 N 31.10 E
Kunja ≃, Ross. 82 56.31 N 38.12 E
Kunjāh 123 32.32 N 73.59 E
Kunje 83 49.23 N 37.15 E
Kunkle 216 41.38 N 84.30 W
Kunkletown 210 40.51 N 75.27 W
Kunkuri 124 22.45 N 83.57 E
Kunlong 110 23.25 N 98.39 E
Kunlun Shan ∧ 120 36.30 N 88.00 E
Kunming 102 25.05 N 102.40 E
Kunming Hu ⊜ 271a 39.59 N 116.15 E
Kunmunya Aboriginal Reserve ✦⁴ 164 15.45 S 124.45 E
Kunnamkulam 122 10.39 N 76.05 E
Kunost' 76 60.01 N 37.38 E
Kunovice 30 49.03 N 17.29 E
Kunow 54 53.00 N 12.07 E
Kunowice 54 52.20 N 14.50 E
Kunrau 54 52.35 N 11.01 E
Kunsan 98 35.58 N 126.41 E
Kunshan 106 31.23 N 120.57 E
Kunszentmárton 30 46.51 N 20.18 E
Kuntair 150 13.40 N 14.48 W
Kuntiki 86 58.29 N 76.24 E
Kunting 100 29.48 N 121.56 E
Kuntshankoie 152 3.20 S 23.34 E
Kuntuolun 102 45.13 N 115.21 E
Kununurra 164 15.47 S 128.44 E
Kunwi 98 36.15 N 128.34 E
Kunya 150 12.14 N 8.34 E
Kunyo 144 6.17 N 42.33 E
Künzak 30 49.07 N 15.11 E
Künzell 56 50.33 N 9.42 E
Künzelsau 56 49.16 N 9.41 E
Künzing 60 48.40 N 13.05 E
Kuolajarvi 100 — Kuoluo ...

Kutkai 110 23.27 N 97.56 E
Kutkašen 84 40.59 N 47.50 E
Kutluškino 80 55.14 N 50.24 E
Kutná Hora 30 49.57 N 15.16 E
Kutno 30 52.15 N 19.23 E
Kutoarjo 115a 7.43 S 109.54 E
Kutomara 88 51.06 N 118.49 E
Kutse Game Reserve ◆[4] 156 23.30 S 24.05 E
Kutsuki 94 35.21 N 135.55 E
Küttigen 58 47.25 N 8.03 E
Kuttura 24 68.24 N 26.28 E
Kuttusoja 24 67.46 N 28.50 E
Kuttuzi 265a 59.45 N 30.04 E
Kutu 152 2.44 S 18.09 E
Kutubdia Island I 120 21.50 N 91.52 E
Kutubu, Lake ⊜ 164 6.23 S 143.18 E
Kutukovo 80 54.26 N 40.31 E
Kutulik 88 53.21 N 102.48 E
Kutulo, Lagh ≃ 154 2.08 N 40.56 E
Kutuluk ≃ 80 53.19 N 51.09 E
Kutum 140 14.12 N 24.40 E
Kutu-Moke 152 3.12 S 17.21 E
Kúty, Česko. 30 48.40 N 17.03 E
Kuty, Ukr. 78 48.16 N 25.10 E
Kutztown 210 40.31 N 75.46 W
Kuujjuaq 176 58.06 N 68.25 W
Kuuli-Majak 128 40.14 N 52.42 E
Kuurne 50 50.51 N 3.17 E
Kuusamo 26 65.58 N 29.11 E
Kuusankoski 26 60.54 N 26.38 E
Kuva 85 40.32 N 72.05 E
Kuvak-Nikol'skoje 80 53.37 N 43.30 E
Kuvandyk 86 51.28 N 57.21 E
Kuvango 152 14.28 S 16.20 E
Kuvasaj 85 40.18 N 71.58 E
Kuvet ≃ 180 69.14 N 175.00 E
Kuvšinovo 76 57.02 N 34.10 E
Kuwabara 270 34.53 N 135.15 E
Kuwait (Al-Kuwayt) □[1], Asia 118 29.30 N 47.45 E
Kuwait (Al-Kuwayt) □[1], Asia 128 29.30 N 47.45 E
Kuwait → Al-Kuwayt 128 29.20 N 47.59 E
Kuwait Bay → Kuwayt, Jūn al- c 128 29.30 N 48.00 E
Kuwana 94 35.04 N 136.42 E
Kuwayt, Jūn al- (Kuwait Bay) c 128 29.30 N 48.00 E
Kuyāli 126 22.31 N 86.11 E
Kuybyshev → Samara 80 53.12 N 50.09 E
Kuye ≃ 102 38.30 N 110.44 E
Kūysanjaq 128 36.05 N 44.38 E
Kuyucak, Tür. 130 37.51 N 38.21 E
Kuyucak, Tür. 130 37.55 N 28.28 E
Kuyuwini ≃ 246 2.16 N 58.16 W
Kuyuyukak, Cape › 180 56.54 N 156.50 W
Kuzaranda 24 62.22 N 35.37 E
Kuze 94 35.33 N 136.30 E
Kuze ◆[8] 270 34.57 N 135.43 E
Kuzedejevo 86 53.20 N 87.10 E
Kuzemin 78 50.09 N 34.39 E
Kuzemovka 83 49.31 N 37.59 E
Kužener 80 56.48 N 48.56 E
Kuženkino 76 57.44 N 33.59 E
Kuzitrin ≃ 180 65.10 N 165.28 W
Kuzkejevo 80 55.46 N 52.48 E
Kuz'miniči 76 54.16 N 33.42 E
Kuz'minka ≃ 265a 59.48 N 30.31 E
Kuz'minki ◆[8] 265b 55.42 N 37.48 E
Kuz'mino, Ross. 82 55.09 N 37.53 E
Kuz'mino, Ross. 82 56.36 N 37.55 E
Kuzmiščevo 82 54.46 N 37.12 E
Kuz'movka 74 62.19 N 92.02 E
Kuznečicha 80 54.43 N 49.38 E
Kuznečikovo 82 56.13 N 36.35 E
Kuzneck 80 53.07 N 46.36 E
Kuzneckij Alatau ⋏ 86 54.45 N 88.00 E
Kuzneck → Novokuzneck 86 53.45 N 87.06 E
Kuznečnoje 26 61.09 N 29.52 E
Kuznecova 89 46.16 N 138.03 E
Kuznecovka 76 56.18 N 28.33 E
Kuznecovo, Ross. 82 55.30 N 38.21 E
Kuznecovo, Ross. 82 55.27 N 36.57 E
Kuznecovo, Ross. 86 59.15 N 63.28 E
Kuznecovo-Michajlovka 83 47.27 N 38.13 E
Kuznecovskij 80 47.25 N 40.57 E
Kuznecy 82 55.51 N 38.40 E
Kuznetsk → Kuzneck 80 53.07 N 46.36 E
Kuznetsovsk 78 51.22 N 25.53 E
Kuzomen', Ross. 24 64.17 N 42.53 E
Kuzomen', Ross. 24 66.17 N 36.54 E
Kuzovatovo 80 53.33 N 47.41 E
Kuzucubelen 130 36.51 N 34.27 E
Kuzuha 270 34.52 N 135.41 E
Kuzuryū ≃ 94 36.13 N 136.08 E
Kuzuu 94 36.24 N 139.37 E
Kuzyaka 130 41.14 N 33.44 E
Kvænangen c[2] 24 70.05 N 21.13 E
Kværndrup 41 55.10 N 10.32 E
Kvaisi 84 42.31 N 43.40 E
Kvaløy I 24 69.40 N 18.30 E
Kvaløya I 24 70.37 N 23.52 E
Kvam 26 61.40 N 9.42 E
Kvanløse 41 55.39 N 11.41 E
Kvanndal 26 60.29 N 6.36 E
Kvareli 84 41.56 N 45.54 E
Kvarner c 36 44.45 N 14.15 E
Kvarnerić ʮ 36 44.45 N 14.35 E
Kvarnsveden 40 60.31 N 15.24 E
Kvarntorp 40 59.08 N 15.15 E
Kvarsa 80 56.58 N 53.57 E
Kvarsebo 40 58.39 N 16.39 E
Kvašenki 82 56.48 N 37.33 E
Kvenna ≃ 26 60.01 N 7.56 E
Kverkfjöll ∧ 24a 64.43 N 16.38 W
Kvichak Bay c 180 58.48 N 157.30 W
Kvicksund 40 59.27 N 16.19 E
Kvidinge 41 56.08 N 13.04 E
Kvien ⊜ 40 60.24 N 13.48 E
Kvikkjokk 24 66.55 N 17.50 E
Kvilda 60 49.01 N 13.35 E
Kvina ≃ 26 58.17 N 6.56 E
Kvismare kanal ≋ 40 59.12 N 15.11 E
Kvissleby 26 62.17 N 17.21 E
Kvistbro 40 59.09 N 14.49 E
Kvistgård 41 55.59 N 12.30 E
Kvitok 88 56.03 N 98.30 E
Kwa ≃ 152 3.10 S 16.11 E
Kwachaga 154 5.38 S 38.08 E
Kwada 164 6.09 S 141.53 E
Kwahae-ri ◆[8] 271b 37.33 N 126.50 E
Kwahu Plateau ⋏[1] 150 6.30 N 0.30 W
Kwai → Khwae Noi ≃ 110 14.00 N 99.33 E
Kwajalein I[1] 14 9.05 N 167.20 E
Kwajok 140 8.19 N 28.00 E
Kwakoegron 250 5.15 N 55.20 W
Kwale, Kenya 154 4.11 S 39.27 E
Kwale, Nig. 150 5.46 N 6.26 E
Kwambilo ≃ 273b 4.26 S 15.20 E
Kwa-Mbonambi 158 28.36 S 32.05 E
Kwamisa ∧ 150 7.08 N 1.53 W
Kwamouth 152 3.10 S 16.12 E
Kwa Mtoro 154 5.14 S 35.26 E
Kwanak-san ∧ 271b 37.27 N 126.58 E
Kwando (Cuando) ≃ 152 18.27 S 23.32 E
Kwangchow → Guangzhou 100 23.06 N 113.16 E
Kwangju 98 35.09 N 126.54 E
Kwangju □[4] 98 35.09 N 126.55 E
Kwango (Cuango) ≃ 152 3.14 S 17.23 E
Kwangsi Chuang Autonomous Region → Guangxi Zhuangzu Zizhiqu □[4] 102 24.00 N 109.00 E
Kwangtung → Guangdong □[4] 90 23.00 N 113.00 E
Kwangwazi 154 7.47 S 38.15 E
Kwangyang 98 34.59 N 127.34 E
Kwania, Lake ⊜ 154 1.45 N 32.45 E
Kwanmo-bong ∧ 98 41.42 N 129.13 E
Kwansan-ni 271b 37.43 N 126.51 E
Kwanto Plain → Kantō-heiya ≚ 94 36.00 N 139.30 E
Kwara □[3] 150 8.45 N 5.00 E
Kware 150 13.12 N 5.14 E
Kwa-Thema 273d 26.18 S 28.23 E
Kwatisore 164 3.15 S 134.57 E
Kweichow → Guizhou □[4] 102 27.00 N 107.00 E
Kweihwa → Hohhot 102 40.51 N 111.40 E
Kweijang → Guiyang 102 26.35 N 106.43 E
Kweilin → Guilin 102 25.17 N 110.17 E
Kweisui → Hohhot 102 40.51 N 111.40 E
Kweiyang → Guiyang 102 26.35 N 106.43 E
Kwekwe 154 18.55 S 29.49 E
Kweneng □[5] 156 24.00 S 24.00 E
Kwenge (Caengo) ≃ 152 4.50 S 18.42 E
Kwesimintim 150 4.54 N 1.47 W
Kwethluk 180 60.49 N 161.27 W
Kwethluk ≃ 180 60.46 N 161.26 W
Kwidzyn 30 53.45 N 18.56 E
Kwigillingok 180 59.51 N 163.08 W
Kwiguk 180 62.45 N 164.28 W
Kwiha 144 13.31 N 39.32 E
Kwikila 164 9.48 S 147.41 E
Kwilu (Cuilo) ≃ 152 3.22 S 17.22 E
Kwinana 168a 32.15 S 115.48 E
Kwitaro ≃ 246 3.19 N 58.47 W
Kwobrup 162 33.37 S 117.46 E
Kwoka, Gunung ∧ 164 0.31 S 132.27 E
Kwolla 150 9.00 N 9.15 E
Kwun Tong 271d 22.19 N 114.12 E
Kyabé 146 9.27 N 18.57 E
Kyabra 166 26.18 S 143.10 E
Kyabra Creek ≃ 166 25.36 S 142.55 E
Kyabram 166 36.19 S 145.03 E
Kyaikkami 110 16.04 N 97.34 E
Kyaiklat 110 16.26 N 95.44 E
Kyaikto 110 17.18 N 97.01 E
Kya-in 110 16.02 N 98.08 E
Kyaka 154 1.16 S 31.25 E
Kyalite 166 34.57 S 143.29 E
Kyancutta 166 33.08 S 135.34 E
Ky Anh 110 18.05 N 106.18 E
Kyat-aw 110 12.29 N 98.19 E
Kyaukhnyat 110 18.15 N 97.31 E
Kyaukkyi 110 18.19 N 96.46 E
Kyaukme 110 22.32 N 97.02 E
Kyaukpa 110 13.05 N 98.59 E
Kyaukpyu, Mya. 110 19.05 N 93.52 E
Kyaukpyu, Mya. 110 19.26 N 93.33 E
Kyaukse 110 21.36 N 96.08 E
Kyauktaw 110 20.51 N 92.59 E
Kyaunggon 110 17.06 N 95.11 E
Kybartai 76 54.39 N 22.45 E
Kybean 171b 36.22 S 149.25 E
Kybeyan Range ⋏ 171b 36.10 S 149.30 E
Kyburz 226 38.47 N 120.18 W
Kydra 171b 36.27 S 149.23 E
Kyeamba 171b 35.26 S 147.37 E
Kyeamba Creek ≃ 171b 35.06 S 147.29 E
Kyebang-san ∧ 98 37.43 N 128.29 E
Kyegegwa 154 0.29 N 31.03 E
Kyeikdon 110 16.00 N 98.24 E
Kyeintali 110 18.00 N 94.29 E
Kyenjojo 154 0.37 N 30.38 E
Kyeryong-san Kukrip Kongwŏn ♠ 98 36.21 N 127.13 E
Kyes Peak ∧ 224 47.57 N 121.19 W
Kyffhäuser-Denkmal ⊥ 54 51.23 N 11.06 E
Kyffhäuser Gebirge ⋏ 54 51.23 N 11.05 E
Kyidaunggan 110 19.53 N 96.12 E
Kyindwe 110 20.58 N 93.51 E
Kyje ◆[8] 54 50.04 N 14.32 E
Kyjov 30 49.01 N 17.08 E
Kykladen → Kikládhes II 38 37.30 N 25.00 E
Kykotsmovi Village 200 35.52 N 110.37 W
Kykva 80 57.22 N 53.50 E
Kylās ∧ 124 25.18 N 90.45 E
Kyle, Sk., Can. 184 50.50 N 108.02 W
Kyle, S.D., U.S. 198 43.25 N 102.10 W
Kyle, Tx., U.S. 196 29.59 N 97.52 W
Kyle □[9] 44 55.29 N 4.24 W
Kyle, Lake ⊜[1] 154 20.14 S 31.00 E
Kyleakin 46 57.16 N 5.44 W
Kyle of Lochalsh 46 57.17 N 5.43 W
Kylerhea 46 57.14 N 5.41 W
Kylertown 214 41.00 N 78.10 W
Kylestrome 46 58.16 N 5.02 W
Kyll ≃ 56 49.48 N 6.42 E
Kyllburg 56 50.02 N 6.35 E
Kym ≃ 42 52.14 N 0.17 W
Kymen lääni □[4] 26 61.00 N 28.00 E
Kymijoki ≃ 26 60.30 N 26.52 E
Kyn 86 57.52 N 58.38 E
Kyndby 41 55.48 N 11.56 E
Kyneton 169 37.15 S 144.27 E
Kynnefjäll ∧[2] 26 58.42 N 11.41 E
Kynšperk nad Ohří 54 50.04 N 12.32 E
Kynuna 166 21.35 S 141.55 E
Kyodong-do I 98 37.45 N 126.16 E
Kyoga, Lake ⊜ 154 1.30 N 33.00 E
Kyōga-misaki › 96 35.46 N 135.13 E
Kyogle 166 28.37 S 153.00 E
Kyoha-ri 271b 37.46 N 126.46 E
Kyohyŏn-ni 271b 37.43 N 126.58 E
Kyom ≃ 140 8.58 N 28.13 E
Kyŏmip'o → Songnim 98 38.44 N 125.38 E
Kyonan 94 35.07 N 139.50 E
Kyondo 110 16.35 N 98.03 E
Kyŏnggi Do □[4] 98 37.30 N 127.15 E
Kyŏnggi-man c 98 37.25 N 126.00 E
Kyŏngju 98 35.51 N 129.14 E
Kyŏngju Kukrip Kongwŏn ♠ 98 35.47 N 129.15 E
Kyŏngsan 98 35.48 N 128.43 E
Kyŏngsang Namdo □[4] 98 35.15 N 128.30 E
Kyŏngsang Pukdo □[4] 98 36.15 N 128.45 E
Kyŏngsŏng 98 41.35 N 129.36 E
Kyŏngsŏng → Sŏul 98 37.33 N 126.58 E
Kyŏngwŏn 98 42.48 N 130.09 E
Kyônkadun 110 16.04 N 95.38 E
Kyonmange 110 16.30 N 95.50 E
Kyonpyaw 110 17.18 N 95.12 E
Kyotera 154 0.33 S 31.19 E
Kyōto, Nihon 94 35.00 N 135.45 E
Kyōto, Nihon 270 35.00 N 135.45 E
Kyōto □[5] 94 35.05 N 135.45 E
Kyōto-bonchi ⋏ 270 35.03 N 135.45 E
Kyōto Race Track ♠ 270 34.54 N 135.44 E
Kyōto University ʊ[2] 270 35.02 N 135.46 E
Kyōwa 94 36.19 N 140.03 E
Kyōyomi-dake ∧ 96 33.31 N 131.02 E
Kypšak, ozero ⊜ 86 50.09 N 68.28 E
Kyra 88 49.36 N 111.58 E
Kyra ≃ 88 49.24 N 112.19 E
Kyrčany 80 57.37 N 50.10 E
Kyren 88 51.41 N 102.08 E
Kyrenia → Girne 130 35.20 N 33.19 E
Kyrgyzstan □[1], Asia 72 41.30 N 75.00 E
Kyrgyzstan □[1], Asia 85 41.30 N 75.00 E
Kyritz 54 52.56 N 12.23 E
Kyrkheden 40 60.10 N 13.29 E
Kyrkkazyk 85 42.30 N 72.20 E
Kyrksæterøra 26 63.17 N 9.06 E
Kyrkslätt (Kirkkonummi) 26 60.07 N 24.26 E
Kyrö 26 60.42 N 22.45 E
Kyrönjoki ≃ 26 63.14 N 21.45 E
Kyrösjärvi ⊜ 26 61.45 N 23.10 E
Kyröskoski 26 61.40 N 23.11 E
Kyrta 24 64.04 N 57.42 E
Kyrykkuduk 80 49.51 N 51.54 E
Ky Son 110 19.24 N 104.08 E
Kyštovka 86 56.33 N 76.38 E
Kyštym 86 55.42 N 60.34 E
Kysykkamys 80 49.14 N 50.19 E
Kyte ≃ 190 42.00 N 89.19 W
Kytlym 86 59.30 N 59.12 E
Kytmanovo 86 53.28 N 85.28 E
Kyūhōji 270 34.38 N 135.35 E
Kyunchaung 110 15.33 N 98.15 E
Kyundon 110 20.31 N 95.44 E
Kyungyi I 110 15.04 N 97.44 E
Kyunhla 110 23.21 N 95.18 E
Kyuquot 182 50.02 N 127.23 W
Kyuquot Sound ʮ 182 50.05 N 127.15 W
Kyūroku-jima I 92 40.32 N 139.29 E
Kyū-shizudani-gakkō ⊥ 96 34.45 N 134.13 E
Kyūshū I 92 33.00 N 131.00 E
Kyushu-Palau Ridge ✧[3] 14 20.00 N 136.00 E
Kyūshū-sanchi ⋏ 92 32.35 N 131.17 E
Kywebwe 110 18.42 N 96.25 E
Kywong 166 34.59 S 146.44 E
Kyyjärvi 26 63.02 N 24.34 E
Kyyvesi ⊜ 26 61.58 N 27.07 E
Kyzas 86 52.20 N 89.20 E
Kyzyl 88 51.42 N 94.27 E
Kyzylagadžskij zapovednik ◆[4] 84 39.10 N 49.00 E
Kyzylagaš 86 45.54 N 81.37 E
Kyzylaryk 85 43.57 N 70.42 E
Kyzylbejit 85 41.30 N 72.24 E
Kyzyl-Chaja 86 50.03 N 89.54 E
Kyzyl-Chem (Šišchid) ≃ 88 51.21 N 96.58 E
Kyzyl-Džar 85 41.17 N 72.02 E
Kyzylemgek 85 41.57 N 74.56 E
Kyzylespe 86 47.27 N 73.53 E
Kyzylkak, ozero ⊜ 86 53.25 N 73.48 E
Kyzyl-Kija 85 40.16 N 72.08 E
Kyzyl-Kommuna 86 48.44 N 67.32 E
Kyzylkum ◆[2] 72 42.00 N 64.00 E
Kyzylkup 128 40.38 N 53.58 E
Kyzyl-Mažalyk 86 51.10 N 90.32 E
Kyzylmazar 85 39.39 N 68.25 E
Kyzyloba 80 49.37 N 50.38 E
Kyzylsu ≃ 85 39.17 N 71.23 E
Kyzyltas, gory ⋏ 86 48.30 N 74.50 E
Kyzyltau 86 47.53 N 72.05 E
Kyzylt'ob'o 85 42.13 N 75.16 E
Kyzyltu, Kaz. 86 47.46 N 59.08 E
Kyzyltu, Kaz. 86 47.43 N 75.42 E
Kyzyltu, Kyrg. 85 42.11 N 76.40 E
Kyzyluj 86 48.07 N 65.28 E
Kyzylžar 86 48.17 N 69.39 E
Kzyl-Kuga 80 48.28 N 53.01 E
Kzyl-Orda 86 44.48 N 65.28 E
Kzyl-Orda □[8] 85 43.30 N 67.00 E
Kzyltu 86 53.38 N 72.20 E

L

La'a 102 29.44 N 101.26 E
Laa an der Thaya 61 48.43 N 16.23 E
Laaben 61 48.06 N 15.52 E
Laaber 60 49.04 N 11.53 E
Laaberberg 60 48.46 N 12.01 E
Laab im Walde 264b 48.09 N 16.11 E
Laacher See ⊜ 56 50.25 N 7.16 E
Laaerberg ∧[2] 264b 48.09 N 16.24 E
Laage 54 53.56 N 12.20 E
La Aguja, Cabo de › 246 11.18 N 74.12 W
Laakajärvi ⊜ 26 63.50 N 27.55 E
Laaken ◆[8] 263 51.15 N 7.15 E
Laakirchen 64 47.58 N 13.49 E
La Albuera 34 38.43 N 6.49 W
La Alcarria ◆[1] 34 40.45 N 2.45 W
La Aldea 234 20.54 N 101.29 W
La Aldehuela 266a 40.18 N 3.36 W
La Algaba 34 37.28 N 6.01 W
La Almarcha 34 39.41 N 2.22 W
La Almunia de Doña Godina 34 41.29 N 1.22 W
Laanecoorie Reservoir ⊜[1] 169 36.52 S 143.53 E
La Antigua, Salina ≚ 252 30.00 S 66.06 W
La Antorcha, Cerro ∧ 234 21.43 N 102.45 W
Laar ◆[8] 263 51.28 N 6.43 E
La Araucanía □[4] 252 38.45 S 72.30 W
La Arena, Pan. 236 7.58 N 80.28 W
La Arena, Perú 248 5.20 S 80.44 W
Laas Caanood 144 8.28 N 47.21 E
La Ascención 232 24.20 N 99.55 W
Laas Dawaco 144 10.28 N 49.05 E
Laas Dhaareed 144 10.10 N 45.59 E
Laase 54 53.04 N 11.18 E
Laas → Lasa 64 46.37 N 10.42 E
Laas Qoray 144 11.10 N 48.13 E
La Asunción 246 11.02 N 63.53 W
La Atravesada, Loma ∧[2] 232 29.57 N 112.12 W
Laatzen 52 52.19 N 9.47 E
Laau Point › 229a 21.06 N 157.19 W
La Aurora 286e 33.36 S 70.38 W
La Azufrosa 196 28.14 N 100.50 W
Laba ≃ 78 45.11 N 39.42 E
La Babia 232 28.34 N 102.04 W
Labadie 219 38.31 N 90.51 W
Labadieville 194 29.50 N 90.57 W
La Baie 186 48.19 N 70.53 W
La Balme-de-Sillingy 58 45.58 N 6.02 E
La Balme-les-Grottes 62 45.51 N 5.20 E
Laban 208 37.24 N 76.17 W
La Banda 252 27.44 S 64.15 W
La Bandera, Cerro ∧ 232 24.35 N 105.07 W
La Bañeza 34 42.18 N 5.54 W
La Barca 234 20.17 N 102.34 W
La Barceloneta ◆[8] 266d 41.22 N 2.11 E
La Barge 200 42.15 N 110.11 W
La Barge Creek ≃ 200 42.14 N 110.10 W
La Barra 236 12.54 N 83.32 W
La Barre-en-Ouche 50 48.57 N 0.40 E
La Barrita 236 14.05 N 91.03 W
La Barr Meadows 226 39.11 N 121.02 W
Labason 116 8.04 N 122.31 E
La Bassée 50 50.32 N 2.48 E
Labastide-Murat 32 44.39 N 1.34 E
La Bastide-Puylaurent 62 44.36 N 3.54 E
La Bâte 261 48.35 N 2.01 E
La Baule-Escoublac 32 47.17 N 2.24 W
La Bazoche-Gouet 50 48.08 N 0.59 E
L'Abbé 261 48.34 N 1.50 E
Labdah (Leptis Magna) ⊥ 146 32.38 N 14.18 E
Labé 150 11.19 N 12.17 W
Labe (Elbe) ≃ 30 53.50 N 9.00 E
Labégude 62 44.39 N 4.22 E
La Bégude-Blanche 62 43.55 N 6.08 E
La Bégude-de-Mazenc 62 44.32 N 4.56 E
Labelle, P.Q., Can. 206 46.16 N 74.44 W
La Belle, Fl., U.S. 220 26.45 N 81.26 W
La Belle, Mo., U.S. 219 40.07 N 91.54 W
Labelle □[6] 206 46.20 N 75.00 W
Labelle, Lac ⊜, P.Q., Can. 206 46.13 N 74.52 W
La Belle, Lac ⊜, Wi., U.S. 216 43.08 N 88.31 W
Labengke, Pulau I 112 3.27 S 122.25 E
La Bérarde 62 44.56 N 6.18 E
Laberge, Lake ⊜ 180 61.11 N 135.12 W
La Berra ∧ 58 46.41 N 7.11 E
Laberweinting 60 48.48 N 12.19 E
La Besace 56 49.34 N 4.58 E
Labette Creek ≃ 198 37.03 N 95.05 W
Labi 112 4.25 N 114.22 E
La Biche ≃ 182 55.01 N 112.44 W
Labico 66 41.47 N 12.53 E
Labin 36 45.05 N 14.07 E
Labinsk 84 44.38 N 40.44 E
Labis 114 2.23 N 103.02 E
La Bisbal 34 41.57 N 3.03 E
Łabiszyn 30 52.57 N 17.55 E
Lablābah, Wādī al- V 273c 30.02 N 31.19 E
La Blanca 286e 33.31 S 70.41 W
La Blanca Grande, Laguna ⊜ 252 38.26 S 63.55 W
Labná ⊥ 232 20.11 N 89.34 W
Labo 116 14.09 N 122.51 E
Labo ≃ 116 14.11 N 122.56 E
Labo, Mount ∧ 116 14.01 N 122.48 E
Laboe 54 54.24 N 10.15 E
La Boissière 261 48.46 N 1.59 E
La Boissière-Ecole 261 48.41 N 1.39 E
La Bollène-Vésubie 62 43.59 N 7.20 E
La Bonneville-sur-Iton 50 49.00 N 1.02 E
Laboratory 214 40.09 N 80.13 W
Laborde, Arg. 252 33.09 S 62.51 W
La Borde, Fr. 261 48.32 N 2.50 E
Laborec ≃ 30 48.36 N 22.00 E
Laborie 241f 13.45 N 61.00 W
Labouchere, Mount ∧ 162 25.12 S 118.18 E
Labouheyre 32 44.13 N 0.55 W
Laboulaye 252 34.07 S 63.24 W
La Bouverie 50 50.24 N 3.52 E
La Boyera, Ven. 286c 10.25 N 66.50 W
La Boyera, Ven. 286c 10.23 N 66.57 W
Lābpur 126 23.50 N 87.49 E
Labrador ◆[1] 176 54.00 N 62.00 W
Labrador Basin ✧[1] 16 53.00 N 48.00 W
Labrador City 176 52.57 N 66.55 W
Labrador Sea ⊤[2] 176 57.00 N 53.00 W
Lábrea, Bra. 248 7.16 S 64.47 W
La Brea, Trin. 241r 10.15 N 61.37 W
Labrède 32 44.41 N 0.31 W
La Bresse 58 48.00 N 6.53 E
La Brévine 58 46.59 N 6.36 E
Labrieville, Réserve ♠ 186 49.20 N 69.40 W
La Brigue 62 44.04 N 7.37 E
La Brillanne 62 43.55 N 5.53 E
Labrit 32 44.07 N 0.33 W
La Broquerie 184 49.28 N 96.27 W
Labroye 50 50.17 N 1.59 E
Labry 56 49.10 N 5.52 E
Labuan, Pulau I 112 5.21 N 115.13 E
Labuha 164 0.37 S 127.29 E
Labuhan 115a 6.22 S 105.50 E
Labuhanbajo 115b 8.29 S 119.54 E
Labuhanbatu 114 2.12 N 100.12 E
Labuhanbilik 114 2.31 N 100.10 E
Labuhandeli 114 3.45 N 98.41 E
Labuhanhaji, Indon. 114 3.33 N 97.00 E
Labuhanhaji, Indon. 115b 8.42 S 116.34 E
Labuhanmarege 112 7.06 S 120.40 E
Labuhanmaringgai 115a 5.21 S 105.48 E
Labuhanruku 114 3.13 N 99.35 E
Labuk ≃ 112 5.54 N 117.30 E
Labuk, Telukan c 116 6.07 N 117.46 E
Labu Kananga 115b 8.08 S 117.47 E
Labutta 110 16.09 N 94.46 E
Labytnangi 72 66.39 N 66.21 E
Lač, Ross. 24 63.18 N 54.28 E
Laç, Shq. 38 41.38 N 19.43 E
Lac □[5] 146 13.30 N 14.15 E
Lača, ozero ⊜ 24 61.20 N 38.48 E
La Cadena 196 25.53 N 104.12 W
L'Acadie 275a 45.19 N 73.21 W
L'Acadie ≃ 206 45.29 N 73.16 W
La Cadière-d'Azur 62 43.12 N 5.46 E
Lacadivas, Islas → Lakshadweep II 122 10.00 N 73.00 E
Laca Jahuira ≃ 248 19.21 S 67.54 W
La Cal ≃ 248 17.27 S 58.15 W
Lac-à-la-Tortue 206 46.37 N 72.38 W
La Calera, Chile 252 32.47 S 71.12 W
La Calera, Perú 286d 12.12 S 76.54 W
Lac-Allard 186 50.33 N 63.25 W
Lacamas Creek ≃ 224 46.20 N 122.55 W
Lacamas Lake ⊜ 224 45.37 N 122.26 W
La Campana, Esp. 34 37.34 N 5.26 W
La Campana, Méx. 234 22.45 N 105.35 W
La Cañada 234 20.37 N 100.19 W
La Cañada, Cerro ∧ 234 21.24 N 99.13 W
La Canada Flintridge 228 34.12 N 118.12 W
La Canada Verde Creek ≃ 280 33.52 N 118.02 W
Lacanau 32 44.59 N 1.05 W
Lacanau, Lac de c 32 44.58 N 1.07 W
La Candelaria, Arg. 252 26.06 S 65.06 W
La Candelaria, Méx. 200 31.07 N 106.29 W
La Cañiza 34 42.13 N 8.16 W
La Canourgue 32 44.26 N 3.13 E
Lacantún ≃ 232 16.36 N 90.39 W
La Capelle-en-Thiérache 50 49.58 N 3.55 E
La Capelle-lès-Boulogne 50 50.44 N 1.42 E
Lacapelle-Marival 32 44.44 N 1.54 E
La Carlota, Arg. 252 33.26 S 63.18 W
La Carlota, Pil. 116 10.25 N 122.55 E
Lacarne 214 41.31 N 83.03 W
La Carolina 34 38.15 N 3.37 W
La Casita 234 23.43 N 104.46 W
La Castellana 116 10.20 N 123.03 E
Lacaune 32 43.43 N 2.42 E
Lac-Bellemare 206 46.34 N 72.55 W
Lac-Brome 206 45.13 N 72.31 W
Laccadive, Minicoy, and Amīndīvi → Lakshadweep □[3] 122 10.00 N 73.00 E
Laccadive Islands → Lakshadweep II 122 10.00 N 73.00 E
Laccadive Sea ⊤[2] 12 7.00 N 76.00 E
Lacchiarella 62 45.19 N 9.08 E
Lacco Ameno 68 40.45 N 13.54 E
Lac Courte Oreilles Indian Reservation ◆[4] 190 45.55 N 91.19 W
Lac du Flambeau 190 45.59 N 89.51 W
Lac du Flambeau Indian Reservation ◆[4] 190 45.59 N 89.53 W
Laceby 44 53.32 N 0.10 W
Lacedonia 68 41.03 N 15.25 E
La Ceiba, Hond. 236 15.47 N 86.50 W
La Ceiba, Ven. 246 9.28 N 71.04 W
La Celle-les-Bordes 261 48.38 N 1.57 E
La Celle-Saint-Cloud 261 48.51 N 2.08 E
La Celle-Saint-Cyr 50 47.58 N 3.18 E
La Center, Ky., U.S. 194 37.04 N 88.58 W
La Center, Wa., U.S. 224 45.52 N 122.40 W
Lacepede Bay c 166 36.47 S 139.45 E
Lacerdónia 156 18.01 S 35.30 E
Laces (Latsch) 64 46.37 N 10.52 E
Lac-Etchemin 186 46.24 N 70.30 W
Lacey 224 47.02 N 122.49 W
Lacey Creek ≃ 278 41.50 N 88.03 W
Laceyville 210 41.39 N 76.10 W
Lac-Frontière 186 46.42 N 70.00 W
La Chaise-Dieu 62 45.19 N 3.42 E
La Chambre 62 45.22 N 6.18 E
La Chapelle-d'Angillon 50 47.22 N 2.26 E
La Chapelle-en-Vercors 62 44.58 N 5.25 E
La Chapelle-Gauthier 261 48.33 N 2.54 E
La Chapelle-la-Reine 50 48.19 N 2.35 E
La Chapelle-Saint-Luc 50 48.20 N 4.03 E
La Chapelle-Vendômoise 50 47.40 N 1.15 E
La Charité-sur-Loire 50 47.11 N 3.01 E
La Chartre-sur-le-Loir 50 47.44 N 0.35 E
La Châtaigneraie 32 46.39 N 0.44 W
La Châtre 32 46.35 N 1.59 E
Lachaussée, Étang de ⊜ 56 49.02 N 5.48 E
La Chaux-de-Fonds 58 47.06 N 6.50 E
Lachay, Punta › 248 11.18 S 77.39 W
Lach Dennis 262 53.15 N 2.26 W
Lachdenpochja 24 61.31 N 30.08 E
Lachen 58 47.12 N 8.51 E
Lachenaie 275a 45.42 N 73.34 W
Lachendorf 52 52.37 N 10.14 E
Lachhmangarh Sīkar 120 27.49 N 75.02 E
L'achi 80 55.20 N 41.56 E
Lachine 206 45.26 N 73.40 W
Lachine, Canal de ≋ 275a 45.26 N 73.40 W
Lachine, Rapides de ∟ 275a 45.25 N 73.36 W
La Chira, Punta › 286d 12.13 S 77.03 W
La Chivera 286c 10.37 N 66.54 W
Lachkaltsap Indian Reserve ◆[4] 182 55.03 N 129.34 W
Lachlan ≃ 166 34.21 S 143.57 E
La Chorrera, Col. 246 0.44 S 73.01 W
La Chorrera, Pan. 236 8.53 N 79.47 W
L'achoviči, Bela. 76 53.02 N 26.16 E
L'achoviči, Bela. 76 52.23 N 27.55 E
L'achovskije ostrova II 74 73.30 N 141.00 E
La Choza 258 34.47 S 59.07 W
La Choza, Arroyo ≃ 258 34.40 S 58.58 W
Lachta ◆[8] 265a 60.00 N 30.09 E
Lachtinskij Razliv, ozero ⊜ 265a 60.00 N 30.11 E
Lachute 206 45.38 N 74.20 W
Lachva 78 52.13 N 27.04 E
La Ciénaga 252 27.30 S 66.57 W
La Ciénega 234 16.54 N 96.46 W
Lâçin 130 40.47 N 34.54 E
La Cinta Creek ≃ 196 35.24 N 104.06 W
La Ciotat 62 43.10 N 5.36 E
La Cisterna 286e 33.33 S 70.41 W
La Citadelle ⊥ 238 19.35 N 72.14 W
La Ciudad 234 23.44 N 105.42 W
Lack 48 54.33 N 7.35 W
Lackawanna 210 42.49 N 78.49 W
Lackawanna □[6] 210 41.24 N 75.40 W
Lackawanna ≃ 210 41.21 N 75.47 W
Lackawanna, Lake ⊜ 276 40.57 N 74.42 W
Lackawanna State Park ♠ 210 41.33 N 75.44 W
Lackawaxen 210 41.29 N 74.59 W
Lackawaxen ≃ 210 41.29 N 74.59 W
Lackey 208 37.14 N 76.33 W
Lackland Air Force Base ■ 196 29.27 N 98.37 W
Läckö 26 58.41 N 13.13 E
Lackoje 76 58.05 N 38.08 E
Lac La Belle 216 43.09 N 88.32 W
Lac la Biche 182 54.46 N 111.58 W
Lac la Hache 182 51.49 N 121.28 W
Lac la Ronge Provincial Park ♠ 184 55.15 N 104.55 W
La Clayette 32 46.18 N 4.19 E
Laclede, Id., U.S. 182 48.10 N 116.45 W
La Clede, Il., U.S. 219 38.53 N 88.43 W
Laclede, Mo., U.S. 194 39.47 N 93.09 W
La Clotilde 252 27.08 S 60.40 W
La Clusaz 58 45.54 N 6.25 E
La Cluse 58 46.10 N 5.34 E
La Cluse-et-Mijoux 58 46.53 N 6.23 E
Lacmalac 171b 35.19 S 148.19 E
Lac-Masson 206 46.02 N 74.04 W
Lac-Mégantic 188 45.36 N 70.53 W
Lacob ti-duyong, Mount ∧ 116 17.35 N 121.09 E
La Cocha 252 27.47 S 65.34 W
Lacolle 206 45.05 N 73.22 W
Lacolle ≃ 206 45.04 N 73.20 W
La Colle-sur-Loup 62 43.41 N 7.06 E
La Colmena 286a 19.36 N 99.18 W
La Colorada 232 28.41 N 110.25 W
La Columna → Bolívar, Pico ∧ 246 8.30 N 71.02 W
La Coma 232 24.28 N 98.19 W
Lacombe, Ab., Can. 182 52.28 N 113.44 W
Lacombe, La., U.S. 194 30.18 N 89.56 W
Lacon 190 41.01 N 89.24 W
Lacona, Ia., U.S. 190 41.11 N 93.22 W
Lacona, N.Y., U.S. 212 43.38 N 76.04 W
La Concepción, Pan. 236 8.31 N 82.37 W
La Concepción, Ven. 246 10.38 N 71.50 W
La Condamine-Châtelard 62 44.27 N 6.45 E
Laconi 71 39.51 N 9.03 E
Laconia 188 43.31 N 71.28 W
La Conner 224 48.23 N 122.29 W
La Consulta 252 33.44 S 69.07 W
Lacoochee 220 28.27 N 82.10 W
La Coruña 34 43.22 N 8.23 W
La Coruña □[4] 34 43.00 N 8.35 W
Lacoste, Fr. 62 43.50 N 5.18 E
La Coste, Tx., U.S. 196 29.19 N 98.49 W
La Côte-Saint-André 62 45.23 N 5.15 E
La Courneuve 261 48.56 N 2.23 E
La Couronne 62 43.20 N 5.03 E
La Courtine 32 45.42 N 2.16 E
Lac qui Parle ≃ 198 45.01 N 95.53 W
Lac qui Parle, West Branch ≃ 198 44.55 N 96.02 W
La Crau 62 43.09 N 6.04 E
Lacre Punt › 241s 12.02 N 68.15 W
La Crescent 190 43.49 N 91.18 W
La Crescenta 228 34.13 N 118.14 W
La Croft 214 40.39 N 80.35 W
Lacroix-Saint-Ouen 50 49.21 N 2.47 E
La Crosse, In., U.S. 216 41.19 N 86.53 W
La Crosse, Ks., U.S. 198 38.31 N 99.18 W
La Crosse, Va., U.S. 192 36.41 N 78.05 W
Lacrosse, Wa., U.S. 202 46.49 N 117.53 W
La Crosse, Wi., U.S. 190 43.48 N 91.14 W
La Crosse ≃ 190 43.49 N 91.16 W
La Cruz, Arg. 252 29.10 S 56.38 W
La Cruz, Col. 246 1.35 N 76.58 W
La Cruz, C.R. 236 11.04 N 85.39 W
La Cruz, Méx. 196 28.33 N 100.48 W
La Cruz, Ur. 258 33.56 S 56.15 W
La Cruz, Cerro ∧ 234 17.55 N 101.31 W
La Cruz de Río Grande 236 13.06 N 84.10 W
Lac-Saguay 206 46.30 N 75.09 W
Lac Seul 184 50.20 N 92.16 W
Lac Seul Indian Reserve ◆[4] 184 50.15 N 92.10 W
La Cuchilla 234 18.54 N 103.19 W
La Cuesta, C.R. 236 8.30 N 82.50 W
La Cuesta, Méx. 234 20.10 N 104.51 W
La Cuesta, P.R. 240m 18.25 N 66.49 W
La Cumbre, Arg. 252 30.58 S 64.30 W
La Cumbre, Ven. 286c 10.32 N 66.57 W
La Cumbre, Volcán ∧[1] 246a 0.20 S 91.30 W
La Cure 58 46.28 N 6.05 E
Lacy Fork ≃ 222 32.24 N 96.08 W
La Cygne 198 38.21 N 94.45 W
Lacy-Lakeview 222 31.37 N 97.06 W
Lada, Teluk c 115a 6.29 S 105.44 E
Ladainha 255 17.39 S 41.44 W
Ladākh □[9] 120 35.10 N 76.10 E
Ladākh Range ⋏ 120 34.00 N 78.00 E
Ladan 78 50.31 N 32.35 E
La Dang, Ko I 114 6.33 N 99.18 E
Ladang Jagor 114 4.42 N 101.35 E
Ladara 114 1.28 N 97.28 E
Ladário 248 19.01 S 57.35 W
Ladbergen 52 52.08 N 7.44 E
Ladby 41 55.26 N 10.38 E
Ladd 190 41.22 N 89.13 W
Ladder Creek ≃ 198 38.48 N 100.52 W
Laddingford 260 51.12 N 0.25 E
Laddonia 219 39.14 N 91.38 W
Ladeburg 264a 52.42 N 13.35 E
La Défense ʊ 261 48.53 N 2.15 E
La Dehesa 286e 33.22 S 70.33 W
La Dent d'Oche ∧ 58 46.21 N 6.44 E
Ladera Heights 280 33.59 N 118.22 W
La Désirade I 241o 16.19 N 61.03 W
Ládhi 38 41.27 N 26.17 E
Ladhurka 126 23.22 N 86.32 E
La Digue I 138 4.21 S 55.50 E
Lâdik 130 40.55 N 35.55 E
Ladinger Spitze ∧ 61 46.51 N 14.39 E
L'adiny 24 61.33 N 38.20 E
Ladismith 158 33.30 S 21.16 E
Ladispoli 66 41.56 N 12.05 E
Lādīz 128 28.56 N 61.19 E
Ladner 224 49.05 N 123.05 W
Lādnūn 120 27.39 N 74.23 E
Ladoga 194 39.54 N 86.48 W
Ladoga, Lake → Ladožskoje ozero ⊜ 24 61.00 N 31.30 E
La Dolorita 286c 10.29 N 66.47 W
Ladon 50 48.00 N 2.32 E
Ladonia 196 33.25 N 95.56 W
La Dorada 246 5.27 N 74.40 W
La Dormida 252 33.21 S 67.55 W
Lado Sarāi ◆[8] 272a 28.32 N 77.12 E
L'adova ≃ 78 48.28 N 27.37 E
Ladovskaja Balka 80 45.38 N 41.25 E
Ladožskaja 78 45.19 N 39.54 E
Ladožskoje Ozero 76 60.08 N 31.04 E
Ladožskoje ozero (Lake Ladoga) ⊜ 24 61.00 N 31.30 E
Lādpur ◆[8] 272a 28.44 N 76.59 E
Ladrillero, Golfo c 254 49.20 S 75.37 W
Ladson 192 32.59 N 80.06 W
Ladue 219 38.38 N 90.23 W
Ladue ≃ 180 63.09 N 140.25 W
Laduozong 102 31.27 N 97.19 E
Laduškin 76 54.36 N 20.11 E
Ladva 24 61.21 N 34.34 E
Ladva-Vetka 24 61.21 N 34.27 E
Lādwa 124 29.59 N 77.03 E
L'ady, Bela. 76 54.36 N 31.10 E
Lady, Fr. 261 48.35 N 2.54 E
L'ady, Ross. 76 58.38 N 28.47 E
Lady Ann Strait ʮ 176 75.40 N 79.50 W
Ladybank 46 56.16 N 3.08 W
Lady Barron 166 40.12 S 148.14 E
Ladybower Reservoir ⊜[1] 44 53.20 N 1.45 W
Ladybrand 158 29.19 S 27.25 E
Lady Elliot Island I 166 24.07 S 152.42 E
Lady Evelyn Lake ⊜ 190 47.20 N 80.10 W
Lady Frere 158 31.44 S 27.16 E
Lady Grey 158 30.45 S 27.13 E
Lady Lake 220 28.55 N 81.55 W
Ladysmith, Austl. 171b 35.12 S 147.31 E
Ladysmith, B.C., Can. 182 48.58 N 123.49 W
Ladysmith, S. Afr. 158 28.34 S 29.45 E
Ladysmith, Wi., U.S. 190 45.27 N 91.06 W
Ladyženka 86 51.00 N 68.42 E
Ladyžin 78 48.41 N 29.15 E
Ladžanurges 84 42.37 N 42.50 E
Lae 164 6.45 S 147.00 E
Lae I[1] 14 8.56 N 166.14 E
Laem, Khao ∧ 110 14.27 N 101.30 E
Laem Ngop 110 12.10 N 102.26 E
La Encantada 232 25.17 N 101.04 W
La Encarnacion 234 23.23 N 98.01 W
Laer 52 52.03 N 7.21 E
Laer ◆[8] 263 51.28 N 7.16 E
Lærdalsøyri 26 61.06 N 7.29 E
La Escondida 196 26.17 N 99.46 W
La Esmeralda, Méx. 232 27.17 N 103.39 W
La Esmeralda, Para. 252 22.13 S 62.38 W
La Esmeralda, Ven. 246 3.10 N 65.33 W
Læsø I 26 57.16 N 11.01 E
La Esperanza, Cuba 240p 22.46 N 83.44 W
La Esperanza, Hond. 236 14.20 N 88.10 W
La Esperanza, Méx. 196 26.46 N 104.00 W
La Esperanza, Méx. 200 32.06 N 114.47 W
La Esperanza, Perú 248 8.05 S 79.04 W
La Esperanza, P.R. 240m 18.22 N 66.07 W
La Estación ◆[8] 266a 40.27 N 3.48 W
La Estrada 34 42.41 N 8.29 W
La Estrella, Bol. 248 16.30 S 63.45 W
La Estrella, Ven. 286c 10.25 N 66.48 W
La Estrella, Cerro ∧ 286a 19.20 N 99.05 W
Lafa 89 43.50 N 127.19 E
La Falda 252 31.05 S 64.30 W
La Farge 190 43.34 N 90.38 W
LaFargeville 212 44.11 N 75.57 W
Lafayette, Fr. 62 45.35 N 5.04 E
Lafayette, Al., U.S. 194 32.53 N 85.24 W
Lafayette, Ca., U.S. 226 37.53 N 122.07 W
Lafayette, Co., U.S. 198 39.59 N 105.05 W
Lafayette, Ga., U.S. 192 34.42 N 85.16 W
Lafayette, In., U.S. 216 40.25 N 86.52 W
Lafayette, La., U.S. 194 30.13 N 92.01 W
Lafayette, Mn., U.S. 190 44.26 N 94.23 W
Lafayette, N.J., U.S. 210 41.05 N 74.41 W
La Fayette, N.Y., U.S. 210 42.54 N 76.06 W
Lafayette, Oh., U.S. 216 40.46 N 83.57 W
Lafayette, Or., U.S. 224 45.14 N 123.06 W
La Fayette, R.I., U.S. 207 41.34 N 71.28 W
Lafayette, Tn., U.S. 194 36.31 N 86.01 W
La Fayette, Tx., U.S. 222 32.54 N 94.51 W
Lafayette, Mount ∧ 188 44.10 N 71.38 W
Lafayette Hill 285 40.05 N 75.15 W
Lafayette Reservoir ⊜[1] 282 37.53 N 122.08 W
Lafayette Water Tunnel ◆[5] 282 37.54 N 122.12 W
La Fé 240p 21.45 N 82.45 W
La Fère 50 49.40 N 3.22 E
La Feria 196 26.09 N 97.49 W
Laferrere 288 34.45 S 58.35 W
La Ferrière-sur-Risle 50 48.59 N 0.48 E
La Ferté-Alais 50 48.29 N 2.21 E
La Ferté-Bernard 50 48.11 N 0.40 E
La Ferté-Frênel 50 48.50 N 0.30 E
La Ferté-Gaucher 50 48.47 N 3.18 E
La Ferté-Imbault 50 47.23 N 1.58 E
La Ferté-Macé 32 48.36 N 0.22 W
La Ferté-Milon 50 49.10 N 3.07 E
La Ferté-Saint-Aubin 50 47.43 N 1.56 E
La Ferté-sous-Jouarre 50 48.57 N 3.08 E
Laferté-sur-Amance 58 47.50 N 5.42 E
La Ferté-Vidame 50 48.37 N 0.55 E
La Ferté-Villeneuil 50 47.59 N 1.21 E
Lafferty 214 40.06 N 81.01 W
Laffrey 62 45.02 N 5.46 E
Lafia 150 8.30 N 8.30 E
Lafiagi 150 8.52 N 5.25 E
Laflamme ≃ 190 48.56 N 77.18 W
Laflèche, P.Q., Can. 275a 45.30 N 73.28 W
Lafleche, Sk., Can. 184 49.43 N 106.35 W
La Flèche, Fr. 32 47.42 N 0.05 W
La Floresta 266d 41.27 N 2.04 E
La Florida, Chile 286e 33.33 S 70.34 W
La Florida, Esp. 266d 41.31 N 2.12 E
La Florida, Guat. 232 16.33 N 90.27 W
Lafnitz ≃ 61 46.57 N 16.16 E
La Foa 175f 21.43 S 165.50 E
La Foce 62 44.08 N 9.47 E

Symbols in the index entries represent the broad categories identified in the key at the right. Symbols with superior numbers (⋏[1]) identify subcategories (see complete key on page *I · 1).*

Symbole im Register stellen die rechts im Schlüssel erklärten Kategorien dar. Symbole mit hochgestellten Ziffern (⋏[1]) bezeichnen Unterabteilungen einer Kategorie (vgl. vollständiger Schlüssel auf Seite *I · 1).*

Los símbolos incluídos en el texto del índice representan las grandes categorias identificadas con la clave a la derecha. Los símbolos con numeros en su parte superior (⋏[1]) identifican las subcategorías (véase la clave completa en la página *I · 1).*

Les symboles de l'index représentent les catégories indiquées dans la légende à droite. Les symboles suivis d'un indice (⋏[1]) représentent des sous-catégories (voir légende complète à la page *I · 1).*

Os símbolos incluídos no texto do índice representam as grandes categorias identificadas com a chave à direita. Os símbolos com números em sua parte superior (⋏[1]) identificam as subcategorias (veja-se a chave completa à página *I · 1).*

∧	Mountain	Berg	Montaña	Montagne	Montanha
⋏	Mountains	Gebirge	Montañas	Montagnes	Montanhas
)(	Pass	Paß	Paso	Col	Passo
V	Valley, Canyon	Tal, Cañon	Valle, Cañón	Vallée, Canyon	Vale, Canhão
≚	Plain	Ebene	Llano	Plaine	Planície
›	Cape	Kap	Cabo	Cap	Cabo
I	Island	Insel	Isla	Île	Ilha
II	Islands	Inseln	Islas	Îles	Ilhas
≛	Other Topographic Features	Andere Topographische Objekte	Otros Elementos Topográficos	Autres données topographiques	Outros acidentes topográficos

ESPAÑOL — Nombre · Página · Lat.°′ · Long.°′ W = Oeste
FRANÇAIS — Nom · Page · Lat.°′ · Long.°′ W = Ouest
PORTUGUÊS — Nome · Página · Lat.°′ · Long.°′ W = Oeste

Nombre / Nom / Nome	Página / Page	Lat.°′	Long.°′
La Follette	192	36.22 N	84.07 W
Lafon	154	5.02 N	32.27 E
Lafontaine, P.Q., Can.	206	45.48 N	74.01 W
La Fontaine, In., U.S.	216	40.40 N	85.43 W
Lafontaine, Parc ♠	275a	45.32 N	73.34 W
Lafourche, Bayou ≃	194	29.05 N	90.14 W
La Foux, Fr.	62	43.16 N	6.35 E
La Foux, Fr.	62	44.17 N	6.34 E
La Fragua	252	26.05 S	64.20 W
La Francia	252	31.24 S	62.38 W
La Fregeneda	34	40.59 N	6.52 W
La Frette-sur-Seine	261	48.58 N	2.11 E
La Fría	246	8.13 N	72.15 W
Lafrimbolle	58	48.36 N	7.01 E
La Fuente de San Esteban	34	40.48 N	6.15 W
Laga, Monti della ⩕	66	42.37 N	13.24 E
La Gacilly	28	47.46 N	2.09 W
Lagaip ≃	164	5.05 S	142.40 E
La Galite I	36	37.32 N	8.56 E
La Gallareta	252	29.34 S	60.23 W
La Gallega	34	41.54 N	3.16 W
Lagan	26	56.55 N	13.59 E
Lagan ≃, Sve.	26	56.33 N	12.56 E
Lagan ≃, N. Ire., U.K.	44	54.37 N	5.53 W
Lagan ≃, N. Ire., U.K.	48	54.37 N	5.53 W
Lagangzong	120	28.05 N	91.04 E
Lagantu	102	42.20 N	108.22 E
La Garde	62	43.07 N	6.01 E
La Garde-Freinet	62	43.19 N	6.28 E
La Garenne-Colombes	261	48.55 N	2.15 E
Lagarina, Val ∨	64	45.50 N	11.10 E
Lagarto, Bra.	250	10.54 S	37.41 W
Lagarto, C.R.	236	10.07 N	84.56 W
Lagarto Creek ≃	196	28.08 N	97.56 W
Lagawe	116	16.49 N	121.06 E
Lagay	116	14.06 N	122.12 E
Lagayan	116	17.43 N	120.42 E
Lage, Dtsch.	52	51.59 N	8.48 E
Lage, Esp.	34	43.13 N	9.00 W
Lage, Zhg.	120	29.26 N	85.51 E
Lagedu	102	26.24 N	101.11 E
Lågen ≃, Nor.	26	59.03 N	10.05 E
Lågen ≃, Nor.	26	61.08 N	10.25 E
Lägerdorf	52	53.53 N	9.34 E
Lages	252	27.48 S	50.19 W
Lageuen	114	4.44 N	95.31 E
Lage Zwaluwe	52	51.43 N	4.41 E
Laggan	46	57.02 N	4.16 W
Laggan, Loch ◎[1]	46	56.57 N	4.28 W
Laggan Bay c	46	55.41 N	6.19 W
Lagginhorn ∧	58	46.11 N	8.01 E
Laghmān □[4]	120	35.00 N	70.15 E
Laghouat	148	33.50 N	2.59 E
Laghouat □[5]	148	32.00 N	3.30 E
Laghy	48	54.37 N	8.05 W
Lagič	84	40.51 N	48.24 E
La Giettaz	62	45.52 N	6.30 E
La Giganta, Cerro ∧	234	21.08 N	101.19 W
La Giustiniana ◆[8]	267a	41.59 N	12.24 E
La Gleize	56	50.25 N	5.51 E
La Gloria	246	8.37 N	73.48 W
Lagnieu	58	45.54 N	5.21 E
Lagny	50	48.52 N	2.43 E
Lagny-le-Sac	261	49.05 N	2.45 E
Lago	68	39.10 N	16.09 E
Lago, Mount ∧	224	48.51 N	120.32 W
Lagoa Branca	256	21.54 S	47.02 W
Lagoa da Prata	255	20.01 S	45.33 W
Lagoa Formosa	255	18.47 S	46.24 W
Lago Argentino → Calafate	254	50.20 S	72.18 W
Lagoa Santa	255	19.38 S	43.53 W
Lagoa Vermelha	252	28.13 S	51.32 W
Lago Blanco	254	45.55 S	71.15 W
Lago da Pedra	250	4.20 S	45.10 W
Lagodechi	84	41.49 N	46.18 E
Lagodechskij zapovednik ♠	84	41.53 N	46.22 E
Lagoinha	256	23.06 S	45.11 W
Lagolândia	255	15.37 S	49.02 W
Lagolovo	265a	59.42 N	30.00 E
Lagonegro	68	40.07 N	15.46 E
Lagonglong	116	8.48 N	124.47 E
Lagonoy	116	13.44 N	123.31 E
Lagonoy Gulf c	116	13.35 N	123.45 E
Lagopesole, Castel di ⊥	68	40.48 N	15.45 E
Lago Posadas	254	47.32 S	71.45 W
Lagorai, Catena del ⩕	64	46.18 N	11.35 E
Lago Ranco	254	40.20 S	72.38 W
La Gorgue	50	50.38 N	2.42 E
Lagos, Ang.	152	16.04 S	17.03 E
Lagos, Nig.	150	6.27 N	3.24 E
Lagos, Nig.	273a	6.27 N	3.24 E
Lagos, Port.	34	37.06 N	8.40 W
Lagos □[3]	150	6.30 N	3.30 E
Lagos (Ikeja) Airport ⊠	273a	6.35 N	3.20 E
Lagos, University of ʋ[2]	273a	6.32 N	3.24 E
Lagosanto	66	44.46 N	12.08 E
Lagos de Moreno	234	21.21 N	101.55 W
Lagos Harbour c	273a	6.26 N	3.24 E
Lagos Island I	273a	6.27 N	3.26 E
Lagos Lagoon c	273a	6.30 N	3.26 E
Lagos Terminus ◆[5]	273a	6.28 N	3.23 E
La Gouèra	148	20.48 N	17.08 W
La Goulette	148	36.49 N	10.18 E
Lago Viedma	254	49.48 S	72.07 W
La Granadella	34	41.21 N	0.40 E
La Grand'Combe	62	44.13 N	4.02 E
La Grande	202	45.19 N	118.05 W
La Grande Deux, Réservoir ◎[1]	176	53.40 N	76.55 W
La Grande Moucherolle ∧	62	45.00 N	5.34 E
La Grande Quatre, Réservoir ◎[1]	176	54.00 N	73.15 W
La Grange, Austl.	162	18.41 S	121.45 E
LaGrange, Ca., U.S.	226	37.40 N	120.28 W
La Grange, Ga., U.S.	192	33.02 N	85.01 W
La Grange, Il., U.S.	216	41.48 N	87.52 W
Lagrange, In., U.S.	216	41.39 N	85.25 W
La Grange, Ky., U.S.	218	38.24 N	85.22 W
La Grange, Mo., U.S.	219	40.02 N	91.29 W
La Grange, N.C., U.S.	192	35.18 N	77.47 W
Lagrange, Oh., U.S.	214	41.14 N	82.07 W
La Grange, Tx., U.S.	222	29.54 N	96.52 W
Lagrange, Wy., U.S.	198	41.38 N	104.10 W
Lagrange □[6]	216	41.39 N	85.25 W
Lagrange Bay c	162	18.38 S	121.42 E
La Grange Highlands	278	41.50 N	87.51 W
La Grange Lock and Dam ◆[5]	219	39.57 N	90.32 W
La Grange Park	278	41.50 N	87.51 W
Lagrangeville	210	41.39 N	73.46 W
La Granja	286e	33.32 S	70.39 W
La Gran Piedra ∧	240p	20.01 N	75.38 W
La Gran Sabana ⠿	246	5.30 N	61.30 W
La Grave	62	45.03 N	6.18 E
La Grita	246	8.08 N	71.59 W
Lagro	216	40.50 N	85.43 W
La Groise	50	50.05 N	3.41 E
La Grue Bayou ≃	194	34.05 N	91.10 W
Lagu	102	26.26 N	101.30 E
La Guadeloupe (Saint-Évariste)	188	45.57 N	70.56 W
La Guajira □[5]	246	11.30 N	72.30 W
La Guajira, Península de ≻[1]	246	12.00 N	71.40 W
La Guardia, Arg.	252	29.33 S	65.27 W
La Guardia, Bol.	248	17.54 S	63.20 W
Laguardia, Esp.	34	42.33 N	2.35 W
La Guardia, Esp.	34	41.54 N	8.53 W
La Guardia Airport ⊠	210	40.46 N	73.53 W
La Gudiña	34	42.04 N	7.08 W
La Guêpière	261	48.35 N	1.50 E
La Guerche-de-Bretagne	32	47.56 N	1.14 W
La Guerche-sur-l'Aubois	32	46.57 N	2.57 E
Laguiole	32	44.41 N	2.51 E
Laguna, Bra.	252	28.29 S	48.47 W
Laguna, N.M., U.S.	200	35.02 N	107.22 W
Laguna □[4]	116	14.10 N	121.20 E
Laguna ≃	226	38.16 N	121.23 W
Laguna, Ilha da I	250	1.40 S	51.00 W
Laguna Beach	228	33.32 N	117.46 W
Laguna Blanca	240p	20.27 N	76.07 W
Laguna Blanca, Parque Nacional ♠	254	39.00 S	70.18 W
Laguna Creek ≃	200	36.54 N	109.45 W
Laguna Dam ◆[6]	200	32.50 N	114.31 W
Laguna de Pozuelos, Monumento Natural ♠, Arg.	248	22.20 S	66.00 W
Laguna de Pozuelos, Monumento Natural ♠, Arg.	252	22.20 S	66.00 W
Laguna Hills	228	33.36 N	117.42 W
Laguna Indian Reservation ◆[4]	200	35.00 N	107.20 W
Laguna Lake ◎	226	35.16 S	120.42 W
Laguna Larga	252	31.46 S	63.48 W
Laguna Limpia	252	26.29 S	59.41 W
Laguna Niguel	228	33.31 N	117.43 W
Laguna Paiva	252	31.19 S	60.39 W
Laguna Park	222	31.52 N	97.23 W
Lagunas	248	5.14 S	75.38 W
Laguna San Rafael, Parque Nacional ♠	254	47.00 S	73.30 W
Lagunas de Chacagua, Parque Nacional ♠	234	16.00 N	97.00 W
Lagunas de Montebello, Parque Nacional ♠	236	16.05 N	91.45 W
Lagunas de Zempoala, Parque Nacional ♠	234	19.08 N	99.20 W
Lagundo	64	46.41 N	11.08 E
Lagunillas, Bol.	248	19.38 S	63.43 W
Lagunillas, Méx.	234	21.34 N	99.35 W
Lagunillas, Ven.	246	8.31 N	71.24 W
Lagunillas, Laguna ◎	248	15.44 S	70.43 W
Lagunillas → Ciudad Ojeda	246	10.12 N	71.19 W
Laguntara c	236	15.35 N	84.05 W
L'agušje	86	54.24 N	77.59 E
Laguyu	104	41.43 N	123.49 E
Laha	89	48.10 N	124.39 E
La Habana (Havana), Cuba	240p	23.08 N	82.22 W
La Habana (Havana), Cuba	286b	23.08 N	82.22 W
La Habana □[4]	240p	22.45 N	82.10 W
La Habana, Universidad de ʋ[2]	286b	23.08 N	82.22 W
La Habra	228	33.55 N	117.56 W
La Habra Heights	280	33.57 N	117.57 W
Lahad Datu	112	5.02 N	118.19 E
Lahad Datu, Telukan c	112	4.50 N	118.30 E
Lahaina	229a	20.52 N	156.40 W
Laham	112	0.22 N	115.24 E
Lahār	124	26.12 N	78.57 E
La Harpe, Il., U.S.	190	40.35 N	90.58 W
La Harpe, Ks., U.S.	198	37.55 N	95.17 W
Lāharpur	124	27.43 N	80.54 E
Lahaska	208	40.21 N	75.02 W
Lahat, Indon.	112	3.48 S	103.32 E
Lahat, Malay.	114	4.33 N	101.02 E
La Hauteville	261	48.42 N	1.37 E
La Havane → La Habana	240p	23.08 N	82.22 W
LaHave ≃	186	44.14 N	64.20 W
La Haye-du-Puits	32	49.18 N	1.33 W
La Haye → 's-Gravenhage	52	52.06 N	4.18 E
La Häy-les-Rosas	261	48.47 N	2.21 E
Lähden	52	52.45 N	7.34 E
Lāhe	110	26.20 N	95.26 E
Laheria Sarai	124	26.07 N	85.54 E
Lahewa	114	1.24 N	97.11 E
Lahfān, Bi'r ⍑[4]	132	31.01 N	33.52 E
Lahi, Ava ʯ	174w	21.02 S	175.11 W
La Higuera	252	29.30 S	71.17 W
Lahij	144	13.02 N	44.54 E
Lāhījān	128	37.12 N	50.01 E
Lāhithah	132	32.59 N	36.35 E
Lahn ≃	56	50.18 N	7.37 E
Lahnstein	56	50.19 N	7.36 E
Laholm	26	56.31 N	13.02 E
Laholmsbukten c	26	56.35 N	12.50 E
La Honda	226	37.19 N	122.16 W
La Honda Creek ≃	282	37.18 N	122.16 W
Lahontan Reservoir ◎[1]	226	39.23 N	119.09 W
Lahontan State Recreation Area ♠	226	39.28 N	119.03 W
Lāhor	123	34.03 N	72.22 E
Lahore	123	31.35 N	74.18 E
Lahor → Lahore	123	31.35 N	74.18 E
La Horqueta	246	3.06 N	72.50 W
La Horqueta, Arroyo ≃	288	34.41 S	58.51 W
La Houssaye-en-Brie	261	48.45 N	2.53 E
Lahr	58	48.20 N	7.52 E
Lahri	120	29.11 N	68.13 E
Lāhrūd	128	38.30 N	47.49 E
Lahṭah, Wādī ∨	142	29.44 N	32.45 E
Lahti	26	60.58 N	25.40 E
La Huaca	248	4.54 S	80.57 W
La Huacana	234	18.58 N	101.49 W
La Huerta, Méx.	234	19.28 N	104.39 W
La Huerta, N.M., U.S.	196	32.27 N	104.13 W
La Hunière	261	48.36 N	1.52 E
Lahuy Island I	116	13.56 N	123.50 E
Laï	146	9.24 N	16.18 E
Laiagam	164	5.30 S	143.20 E
Lai'an	100	32.27 N	118.25 E
Laibach → Ljubljana	36	46.03 N	14.31 E
Laibin	102	23.42 N	109.22 E
Lai Chau	110	22.02 N	103.10 E
Laichingen	58	48.29 N	9.41 E
Laichow Bay → Laizhou Wan c	98	37.36 N	119.30 E
Laide	46	57.52 N	5.32 W
Laidley	171a	27.38 S	152.24 E
Laidley Creek ≃	171a	27.31 S	152.24 E
Laidon, Loch ◎	46	56.39 N	4.40 W
Laie	229c	21.39 N	157.55 W
Laifang	100	25.56 N	116.54 E
Laifeng, Zhg.	102	29.31 N	109.15 E
Laifeng, Zhg.	107	30.14 N	105.17 E
Laifengzhen	107	29.26 N	106.13 E
L'Aigle	50	48.45 N	0.38 E
L'Aigle Creek ≃	194	33.12 N	92.08 W
Laignes	50	47.50 N	4.22 E
Laigou	100	33.56 N	117.06 E
Laigueglia	62	43.58 N	8.09 E
Laihia	26	62.58 N	22.01 E
Lai-hka	110	21.16 N	97.40 E
Lailly-en-Val	50	47.46 N	1.41 E
Laïmbélé, Mont ∧	175f	16.20 S	167.31 E
Lainate	266b	45.34 N	9.02 E
Lainbach	61	47.38 N	14.46 E
La Independencia, Bahía de c	248	14.15 S	76.10 W
Laingsburg, S. Afr.	158	33.11 S	20.51 E
Laingsburg, Mi., U.S.	216	42.53 N	84.21 W
Lainioälven ≃	24	67.22 N	23.39 E
La Inmaculada	232	29.55 N	111.48 W
Laino Borgo	68	39.57 N	15.59 E
Lainsitz (Lužnice) ≃	61	49.13 N	14.42 E
Lainville	261	49.04 N	1.49 E
Lainz ◆[8]	264b	48.11 N	16.17 E
Lainzer Tiergarten ♠	264b	48.10 N	16.14 E
Lair, Scot., U.K.	46	57.29 N	5.20 W
Lair, Ky., U.S.	218	38.20 N	84.18 W
Laird Hill	222	32.21 N	94.54 W
Lairdsville	210	41.14 N	76.37 W
Lairg	46	58.01 N	4.25 W
Laïri	146	10.49 N	17.06 E
Laïri, Batha de ≃	146	12.28 N	16.45 E
Laïriri, Pic ∧	175f	15.27 S	166.48 E
Lais, Indon.	112	0.47 N	120.27 E
Lais, Indon.	112	3.32 S	102.03 E
Lais, Pil.	116	6.20 N	125.39 E
Laisamis	154	1.36 N	37.48 E
Laiševo	80	55.24 N	49.32 E
Laishan	98	37.24 N	121.23 E
Laishui	105	39.23 N	115.42 E
Laissac	32	44.23 N	2.49 E
Laissey	58	47.18 N	6.14 E
Laisu	107	29.16 N	105.47 E
Laisvall	24	66.05 N	17.10 E
Laitan	107	29.06 N	106.10 E
Laitila	26	60.53 N	21.41 E
Laives (Leifers)	64	46.26 N	11.20 E
Laiwu	98	36.12 N	117.38 E
Laiwui	164	1.22 S	127.40 E
Laixi (Shuiji)	98	36.51 N	120.29 E
Laiya	116	13.40 N	121.24 E
Laiyang	98	36.58 N	120.44 E
Laiyuan, Zhg.	98	39.18 N	114.44 E
Laiyuan, Zhg.	100	25.36 N	117.01 E
Laizhou Wan (Laichow Bay) c	98	37.36 N	119.30 E
Laja ≃, Chile	252	37.16 S	72.43 W
Laja ≃, Méx.	234	20.30 N	100.46 W
Laja ≃, Ross.	24	66.20 N	56.16 E
Laja, Laguna de la ◎	252	37.21 S	71.19 W
Laja, Salto del ∟	252	37.22 S	71.25 W
Lajajalpan ≃	234	20.17 N	97.32 W
La Jalca	248	6.29 S	77.43 W
La Jara	200	37.16 N	105.57 W
La Jara ◆[1]	34	39.42 N	4.54 W
La Jara Canyon ∨	200	36.50 N	107.30 W
La Jara Creek ≃	200	37.22 N	105.46 W
La Jarrie	32	46.08 N	1.00 W
Lajas, Cuba	240p	22.25 N	80.18 W
Lajas, P.R.	240m	18.03 N	67.04 W
La Javie	62	44.10 N	6.21 E
Laje	255	13.10 S	39.25 W
Laje, Ilha da I	287a	22.57 S	43.09 W
Laje, Ponta da ≻	266c	38.40 N	9.19 W
Laje, Ribeira de ≃	266c	38.41 N	9.19 W
Lajeado	252	29.27 S	51.58 W
Lajeado Velho ◆[8]	287b	23.32 S	46.23 W
Lajedo	250	8.40 S	36.19 W
Lajes	250	5.41 S	36.14 W
Lajes, Ribeirão das ≃	256	22.38 S	43.42 W
Lajinha	255	20.09 S	41.37 W
Laji Shan ⩕	102	36.13 N	102.15 E
Lajkovo	265b	55.42 N	37.13 E
La Jolla, Ca., U.S.	204	32.51 N	117.16 W
La Jolla, Ca., U.S.	228	32.51 N	117.16 W
La Jolla, Point ≻	228	32.51 N	117.17 W
Lajord	184	50.14 N	104.09 W
La Jose	214	40.50 N	78.41 W
Lajosmizse	30	47.02 N	19.34 E
La Joya, Méx.	196	26.26 N	101.08 W
La Joya, Perú	248	16.44 S	71.51 W
La Joya, Cerro ∧	234	20.06 N	101.38 W
La Joya, Laguna c	234	15.55 N	93.40 W
La Joya de Atotonilco	234	23.35 N	104.20 W
Lajta (Leitha) ≃	61	47.54 N	17.17 E
Lajtamak	86	58.25 N	67.25 E
Lajturi	84	41.55 N	41.55 E
La Junta	198	37.59 N	103.32 W
Lakaband	120	31.00 N	69.30 E
Lakahia, Teluk c	164	4.00 S	134.38 E
Lakamané	150	14.31 N	9.55 W
Lakar Kūh ∧	128	31.02 N	57.06 E
Lakatoro	175f	16.07 S	167.25 E
Lake	194	32.20 N	89.19 W
Lake □[6], Ca., U.S.	226	39.01 N	122.33 W
Lake □[6], Fl., U.S.	220	28.42 N	81.39 W
Lake □[6], Il., U.S.	216	42.22 N	87.50 W
Lake □[6], In., U.S.	216	41.25 N	87.22 W
Lake □[6], Oh., U.S.	214	41.43 N	81.15 W
Lake Accotink Park ♠	284c	38.48 N	77.14 W
Lake Albert	171b	35.10 S	147.23 E
Lake Alfred	220	28.05 N	81.43 W
Lake Alpine	226	38.28 N	120.00 W
Lake Andes	198	43.09 N	98.32 W
Lake Angelus	281	42.42 N	83.19 W
Lake Ariel	210	41.27 N	75.23 W
Lake Arrowhead	228	34.14 N	117.11 W
Lake Arthur, La., U.S.	194	30.04 N	92.40 W
Lake Arthur, N.M., U.S.	196	32.59 N	104.21 W
Lake Barcroft	284c	38.51 N	77.09 W
Lake Bathurst	170	35.01 S	149.36 E
Lake Benton	198	44.15 N	96.17 W
Lake Beseck	207	41.31 N	72.44 W
Lake Bluff	216	42.16 N	87.50 W
Lake Brownwood	196	31.49 N	99.02 W
Lake Buena Vista	220	28.23 N	81.31 W
Lake Butler	192	30.01 N	82.20 W
Lake Cable	214	40.52 N	81.27 W
Lake Camm	162	32.59 S	119.35 E
Lake Cargelligo	166	33.18 S	146.23 E
Lake Carmel	210	41.27 N	73.40 W
Lake Charles	194	30.13 N	93.13 W
Lake Chelan National Recreation Area ♠	224	48.20 N	120.40 W
Lake City, Ar., U.S.	194	35.48 N	90.26 W
Lake City, Co., U.S.	200	38.01 N	107.18 W
Lake City, Fl., U.S.	192	30.11 N	82.38 W
Lake City, Il., U.S.	219	39.45 N	88.43 W
Lake City, Ia., U.S.	198	42.16 N	94.44 W
Lake City, Mi., U.S.	190	44.20 N	85.12 W
Lake City, Mn., U.S.	190	44.26 N	92.16 W
Lake City, Pa., U.S.	214	42.00 N	80.20 W
Lake City, S.C., U.S.	192	33.52 N	79.45 W
Lake City, Tn., U.S.	192	36.13 N	84.09 W
Lake Clarke Shores	220	26.39 N	80.04 W
Lake Clark National Park ♠	180	60.30 N	153.15 W
Lake Coleridge	172	43.22 S	171.32 E
Lake Como, N.Y., U.S.	210	42.41 N	76.18 W
Lake Como, Pa., U.S.	210	41.51 N	75.20 W
Lake Corpus Christi State Park ♠	196	28.05 N	97.52 W
Lake Cowichan	224	48.50 N	124.03 W
Lake Creek ≃	222	30.16 N	95.29 W
Lake Crescent	224	48.06 N	123.50 W
Lake Crystal	190	44.06 N	94.13 W
Lake Dalecarlia	216	41.20 N	87.24 W
Lake Dallas	222	33.07 N	97.02 W
Lake Delta	210	43.17 N	75.28 W
Lake Delton	190	43.36 N	89.47 W
Lakedemonovka	83	47.12 N	38.33 E
Lake Dennison State Park ♠	207	42.38 N	72.05 W
Lake District ◆[1]	44	54.30 N	3.10 W
Lake District National Park ♠	44	54.30 N	3.05 W
Lake Eliza	216	41.26 N	87.10 W
Lake Elsinore	228	33.38 N	117.20 W
Lake Elsinore State Recreation Area ♠	228	33.41 N	117.22 W
Lake Entrance ʯ	170	33.05 S	151.39 E
Lake Errock	224	49.13 N	122.02 W
Lake Eyre National Park ♠	166	28.30 S	137.30 E
Lake Fairfax County Park ♠	284c	38.58 N	77.19 W
Lake Fenton	216	42.52 N	83.43 W
Lakefield, On., Can.	212	44.26 N	78.16 W
Lakefield, S. Afr.	273d	26.11 S	28.18 E
Lakefield, Mn., U.S.	198	43.40 N	95.10 W
Lakefield National Park ♠	164	15.00 S	144.05 E
Lake Forest, Fl., U.S.	192	25.58 N	80.11 W
Lake Forest, Il., U.S.	216	42.12 N	87.53 W
Lake Forest, N.J., U.S.	276	40.58 N	74.36 W
Lake Forest Park	224	47.45 N	122.17 W
Lake Fork	219	39.58 N	89.21 W
Lake Fork ≃, Il., U.S.	219	40.05 N	89.25 W
Lake Fork ≃, Ut,. U.S.	200	40.13 N	110.07 W
Lake Fork, North Fork ≃	219	39.56 N	89.14 W
Lake Fork Creek ≃	222	32.36 N	95.21 W
Lake Fork Reservoir ◎[1]	222	32.50 N	95.35 W
Lake Geneva	216	42.36 N	88.26 W
Lake George	188	43.25 N	73.42 W
Lake Grace	162	33.06 S	118.28 E
Lake Grinnell	276	41.06 N	74.38 W
Lake Grove	276	40.51 N	73.06 W
Lake Hamilton	220	28.07 N	81.42 W
Lake Harbor	220	26.42 N	80.48 W
Lake Harbour	176	62.51 N	69.53 W
Lake Harmony	210	41.04 N	75.36 W
Lake Havasu City	200	34.29 N	114.19 W
Lake Havasu State Park ♠	200	34.29 N	114.21 W
Lake Helen	220	28.58 N	81.14 W
Lake Hiawatha	210	40.52 N	74.22 W
Lake Hill	210	42.04 N	74.11 W
Lake Hills, In., U.S.	216	41.28 N	87.27 W
Lake Hills, Wa., U.S.	224	47.36 N	122.08 W
Lake Hopatcong	210	40.55 N	74.39 W
Lake Hughes	228	34.40 N	118.26 W
Lake Huntington	210	41.41 N	75.00 W
Lakehurst	208	40.00 N	74.18 W
Lakehurst Naval Air Station ■	208	40.01 N	74.18 W
Lake Illawarra	170	34.33 S	150.52 E
Lake Intervale	276	40.53 N	74.25 W
Lake in the Hills	216	42.10 N	88.19 W
Lake Isabella	204	35.39 N	118.28 W
Lake Jackson	222	29.02 N	95.26 W
Lake Jem	220	28.45 N	81.40 W
Lakekamu ≃	164	8.10 S	146.15 E
Lake Katrine	210	41.59 N	73.59 W
Lake King	162	33.05 S	119.40 E
Lake Lackawanna	210	40.57 N	74.42 W
Lakeland, Fl., U.S.	220	28.03 N	81.57 W
Lakeland, Ga., U.S.	192	31.02 N	83.04 W
Lakeland, Mi., U.S.	216	42.28 N	83.51 W
Lakeland, N.Y., U.S.	210	43.06 N	76.15 W
Lakeland Park	216	42.21 N	88.17 W
Lakeland Village	228	33.39 N	117.22 W
Lake Lenape	210	41.01 N	74.44 W
Lake Linden	190	47.11 N	88.26 W
Lake Lookover	276	41.09 N	74.24 W
Lake Loramie State Park ♠	216	40.23 N	84.20 W
Lake Louise, Ab., Can.	182	51.26 N	116.11 W
Lake Louise, Wa., U.S.	224	47.05 N	122.36 W
Lake Lucerne	214	41.24 N	81.21 W
Lake Luzerne	210	43.18 N	73.50 W
Lake Mackay Reserve ◆[4]	162	22.00 S	129.45 E
Lake Magdalene	220	28.05 N	82.28 W
Lake Malawi National Park ♠	154	14.00 S	34.55 E
Lake Manyara National Park ♠	154	3.30 S	36.25 E
Lake Mary	220	28.45 N	81.19 W
Lakemba	274a	33.55 S	151.05 E
Lakemba Island I	175g	18.13 S	178.47 W
Lakemba Passage ʯ	175g	17.53 S	178.32 W
Lake Mead National Recreation Area ♠	200	36.00 N	114.30 W
Lake Meredith National Recreation Area ♠	196	35.40 N	101.40 W
Lake Mills, Ia., U.S.	190	43.25 N	93.31 W
Lake Mills, Wi., U.S.	216	43.04 N	88.54 W
Lake Milton	214	41.06 N	80.58 W
Lake Minchumina	180	63.53 N	152.19 W
Lake Monroe	220	28.50 N	81.19 W
Lakemont, N.Y., U.S.	210	42.31 N	76.56 W
Lakemont, Pa., U.S.	214	40.28 N	78.23 W
Lakemoor	216	42.20 N	88.12 W
Lakemore	214	41.01 N	81.25 W
Lake Mountain ∧	169	37.31 S	145.54 E
Lake Murray	164	7.00 S	141.29 E
Lake Murray State Park ♠	196	34.01 N	97.00 W
Lake Nakuru National Park ♠	154	0.20 S	36.05 E
Lake Nash	166	21.00 S	137.55 E
Lake Nepessing	216	43.02 N	83.22 W
Lakenheath	42	52.25 N	0.31 E
Lake Norden	198	44.34 N	97.12 W
Lake Normandy Estates	284c	39.03 N	77.11 W
Lake Odessa	216	42.47 N	85.08 W
Lake of the Ozarks State Park ♠	194	38.08 N	92.40 W
Lake of the Woods	216	41.26 N	86.14 W
Lake on the Mountain Provincial Park ♠	212	44.02 N	77.05 W
Lake Orion	216	42.47 N	83.14 W
Lake Orion Heights	216	42.46 N	83.18 W
Lake Oroville State Recreational Area ♠	226	39.32 N	121.27 W
Lake Oswego	224	45.25 N	122.39 W
Lake Ozark	194	38.11 N	92.38 W
Lakepa	174v	18.59 S	169.48 W
Lake Panasoffkee	220	28.46 N	82.07 W
Lake Paringa	172	43.43 S	169.29 E
Lake Park, Fl., U.S.	220	26.48 N	80.04 W
Lake Park, Ia., U.S.	198	43.27 N	95.19 W
Lake Park, Mn., U.S.	198	46.53 N	96.05 W
Lake Pine	208	39.52 N	74.51 W
Lake Placid, Fl., U.S.	220	27.17 N	81.21 W
Lake Placid, N.Y., U.S.	188	44.16 N	73.58 W
Lake Pleasant	188	43.28 N	74.25 W
Lakeport, Ca., U.S.	204	39.02 N	122.54 W
Lakeport, Mi., U.S.	190	43.07 N	82.30 W
Lakeport, N.Y., U.S.	210	43.09 N	75.52 W
Lake Preston	198	44.21 N	97.22 W
Lake Providence	194	32.48 N	91.10 W
Lake Pukaki	172	44.11 S	170.09 E
Lakeridge, Nv., U.S.	226	39.02 N	119.56 W
Lake Ridge, N.J., U.S.	276	40.24 N	74.15 W
Lake Riviera	208	40.03 N	74.10 W
Lake Ronkonkoma	276	40.50 N	73.07 W
Lake Saint Louis	219	38.48 N	90.45 W
Lake Sammamish State Park ♠	224	47.33 N	122.03 W
Lake San Marcos	228	33.09 N	117.12 W
Lake Sawyer	224	47.20 N	122.03 W
Lakes Bay c	208	39.22 N	74.30 W
Lakes District	224	47.10 N	122.31 W
Lakes Entrance	166	37.53 S	147.59 E
Lake Shawnee	276	40.59 N	74.36 W
Lakeshore, Ca., U.S.	226	37.15 N	119.12 W
Lake Shore, Md., U.S.	208	39.06 N	76.29 W
Lake Shore, Mi., U.S.	216	42.38 N	86.14 W
Lakeshore, Ms., U.S.	194	30.14 N	89.26 W
Lake Shore, Wa., U.S.	224	45.42 N	122.42 W
Lakeside, N.S., Can.	186	44.38 N	63.41 W
Lakeside, S. Afr.	273d	26.06 S	28.09 E
Lakeside, Az., U.S.	200	34.09 N	109.58 W
Lakeside, Ca., U.S.	228	32.51 N	116.55 W
Lakeside, Ct., U.S.	207	41.25 N	73.13 W
Lakeside, Ct., U.S.	207	41.40 N	73.14 W
Lakeside, Mi., U.S.	216	41.51 N	86.40 W
Lakeside, Mt., U.S.	202	48.01 N	114.13 W
Lakeside, Oh., U.S.	214	41.32 N	82.44 W
Lakeside, Or., U.S.	202	43.34 N	124.10 W
Lakeside, Va., U.S.	208	37.36 N	77.28 W
Lakeside ◆[9]	281	42.37 N	83.00 W
Lakeside Village	222	32.02 N	97.30 W
Lake Station	216	41.34 N	87.14 W
Lake Stevens	224	48.01 N	122.04 W
Lake Stockholm	276	41.04 N	74.31 W
Lake Success	276	40.46 N	73.43 W
Lake Superior Provincial Park ♠	190	47.32 N	84.50 W
Lake Swannanoa	276	41.01 N	74.31 W
Lake Taghkanic State Park ♠	210	42.06 N	73.43 W
Lake Tahoe Airport ⊠	226	38.54 N	120.00 W
Lake Tahoe-Nevada State Park ♠	226	39.13 N	119.55 W
Lake Tamarack	210	41.06 N	74.32 W
Lake Tekapo	172	44.01 S	170.30 E
Lake Telemark	276	40.57 N	74.30 W
Lake Temescal Regional Park ♠	282	37.51 N	122.14 W
Laketon	216	40.58 N	85.50 W
Laketown	200	41.49 N	111.19 W
Lake Varley	162	32.46 S	119.27 E
Lake View, Ar., U.S.	194	34.24 N	90.50 W
Lakeview, Ca., U.S.	228	33.50 N	117.07 W
Lakeview, Ga., U.S.	192	34.58 N	85.15 W
Lake View, Ia., U.S.	198	42.18 N	95.03 W
Lakeview, Mi., U.S.	190	43.26 N	85.16 W
Lake View, N.Y., U.S.	210	42.42 N	78.56 W
Lakeview, Oh., U.S.	216	40.29 N	83.56 W
Lakeview, Or., U.S.	202	42.11 N	120.20 W
Lake View, S.C., U.S.	192	34.20 N	79.09 W
Lakeview, Tx., U.S.	194	29.55 N	93.54 W
Lakeview, Tx., U.S.	196	34.40 N	100.42 W
Lakeview, Wa., U.S.	224	47.10 N	122.30 W
Lakeview ◆[8]	278	41.57 N	87.39 W
Lakeview Mountain ∧, B.C., Can.	182	49.03 N	120.09 W
Lakeview Mountain ∧, Wa., U.S.	224	46.22 N	121.24 W
Lakeview Park ♠	285	40.12 N	75.32 W
Lake Village, Ar., U.S.	194	33.19 N	91.16 W
Lake Village, In., U.S.	216	41.08 N	87.27 W
Lakeville, Ct., U.S.	207	41.57 N	73.26 W
Lakeville, In., U.S.	216	41.31 N	86.16 W
Lakeville, Mi., U.S.	214	42.49 N	83.09 W
Lakeville, Mn., U.S.	190	44.38 N	93.14 W
Lakeville, N.Y., U.S.	210	42.50 N	77.42 W
Lakeville, Oh., U.S.	214	40.40 N	82.07 W
Lakeville Lake ◎	214	42.50 N	83.09 W
Lake Wales	220	27.54 N	81.35 W
Lake Whitney State Park ♠	222	31.55 N	97.22 W
Lake Wilson	198	43.59 N	95.57 W
Lake Winola	210	41.30 N	75.50 W
Lakewood, Ca., U.S.	228	33.51 N	118.07 W
Lakewood, Co., U.S.	200	39.42 N	105.04 W
Lakewood, Il., U.S.	216	39.19 N	88.54 W
Lakewood, Mi., U.S.	216	42.18 N	85.31 W
Lakewood, N.J., U.S.	208	40.05 N	74.13 W
Lakewood, N.Y., U.S.	214	42.06 N	79.20 W
Lakewood, Oh., U.S.	214	41.28 N	81.47 W
Lakewood, Pa., U.S.	210	41.51 N	75.22 W
Lakewood, Wa., U.S.	224	48.09 N	122.12 W
Lakewood, Wi., U.S.	190	45.18 N	88.31 W
Lakewood Center ◆[9]	280	33.51 N	118.09 W
Lakewood Park	198	48.04 N	98.56 W
Lakewood Park ♠	279a	41.29 N	81.47 W
Lakewood Shores	216	41.17 N	88.10 W
Lake Worth, Fl., U.S.	220	26.36 N	80.03 W
Lake Worth, Tx., U.S.	222	32.49 N	97.27 W
Lake Zurich	216	42.11 N	88.05 W
Lakhdaria	34	36.34 N	3.35 E
Lākheri	124	25.40 N	76.10 E
Lakhīmpur	124	27.57 N	80.46 E
Lakhipur, India	120	24.48 N	93.01 E
Lakhipur, India	124	26.02 N	90.18 E
Lakhish	132	31.34 N	34.51 E
Lakhish ∨	132	31.49 N	34.38 E
Lakhnādon	124	22.36 N	79.36 E
Lakhya ≃	126	23.35 N	90.31 E
L'aki	84	40.34 N	47.26 E
Laki ≃	115a	7.30 S	107.25 E
Lakin	198	37.56 N	101.15 W
Lakinsk	80	56.01 N	39.57 E
Lakkadiven → Lakshadweep II	122	10.00 N	73.00 E
Lakki	123	32.36 N	70.55 E
Laknau → Lucknow	124	26.51 N	80.55 E
Lakonikós Kólpos c	38	36.25 N	22.37 E
Lakor, Pulau I	164	8.14 S	128.10 E
Lakota, C. Iv.	150	5.51 N	5.41 W
Lakota, Ia., U.S.	190	43.22 N	94.05 W
Lakota, N.D., U.S.	198	48.02 N	98.20 W
Laksefjorden c[2]	24	70.58 N	27.00 E
Lakselv	24	70.04 N	24.56 E
Lakshadweep □[8]	122	10.00 N	73.00 E
Lakshadweep II	122	10.00 N	73.00 E
Lākshām	124	23.14 N	91.08 E
Lakshamannāth	126	21.51 N	87.13 E
Lakshmanpur	272b	22.38 N	88.16 E
Lakshmeshwar	122	15.08 N	75.28 E
Lakshmi, Char I	126	21.57 N	90.33 E
Lakshmikantapur	126	22.07 N	88.20 E
Lakshmi Narayan Temple ʋ[1]	272a	28.38 N	77.12 E
Lakshmīpur	126	22.57 N	90.50 E
Lakshmisāgar	126	22.55 N	87.01 E
Lala	116	7.59 N	123.46 E
Lalafuta ≃	154	13.57 S	24.41 E
La Laguna → San Cristóbal de la Laguna	148	28.29 N	16.19 W
La Lagunita	234	23.41 N	105.44 W
La Laja	252	37.16 S	72.42 W
La Lajilla	232	26.47 N	99.37 W
Lāla Mūsa	123	32.42 N	73.58 E
Lalana ≃	234	17.49 N	95.09 W
Lalapansi	154	19.16 S	30.15 E
Lâlapaşa	130	41.50 N	26.44 E
Lalatuncun	104	41.44 N	122.00 E
La Lava	248	19.55 S	65.38 W
Lalbenque	32	44.20 N	1.33 E
L'Albufera ◎	34	39.20 N	0.22 W
Laleham, Austl.	166	23.58 S	148.46 E
Laleham, Eng., U.K.	260	51.25 N	0.30 W
Lāleh Zār, Kūh-e ∧	128	29.24 N	56.45 E
La Leona	196	25.52 N	101.05 W
La Leonesa	252	27.03 S	58.43 W
Lalera	152	0.22 N	11.28 E
Lalevade-d'Ardèche	62	44.39 N	4.19 E
Lālganj	124	25.52 N	85.11 E
Lālgarh	126	22.35 N	87.03 E
Lāliān	123	31.49 N	72.48 E
Lalibela	144	12.02 N	39.02 E
La Libertad, El Sal.	236	13.29 N	89.19 W
La Libertad, Guat.	232	16.47 N	90.07 W
La Libertad, Hond.	236	14.43 N	87.36 W
La Libertad, Nic.	236	12.13 N	85.10 W
La Libertad □[5]	248	8.00 S	78.30 W
La Ligua	252	32.27 S	71.14 W
La Lima, Hond.	236	15.24 N	87.56 W
La Lima, It.	66	44.04 N	10.46 E
La Limpia, Laguna ◎	258	35.37 S	57.49 W
Lalín	34	42.39 N	8.07 W
Lalin ≃	89	45.29 N	125.26 E
Lalinde	32	44.51 N	0.44 E
Lalindi	115b	10.12 S	120.10 E
Lalindu ≃	112	3.28 S	122.05 E
La Línea	34	36.10 N	5.19 W
L'alino	82	54.29 N	39.06 E
Lalitpur	124	24.41 N	78.25 E
La Llagosta	266d	41.31 N	2.12 E
Lalla Khedidja, Tamgout de ∧	34	36.27 N	4.15 E
Lal Lal Reservoir ◎[1]	169	37.40 S	144.04 E
Lālmanir Hāt	124	25.54 N	89.27 E
Lālmohan	126	22.13 N	90.42 E
Laloa	112	4.50 S	121.54 E
La Loche	184	56.29 N	109.27 W
La Loche ≃	184	56.09 N	109.08 W
La Loche, Lac ◎	184	56.25 N	109.30 W
Laloki	164	9.25 S	147.15 E
La Londe	62	43.08 N	6.14 E
La Lora ⩕[1]	34	42.45 N	4.00 W
Lalor Park	274a	33.45 S	150.56 E
La Loupe	50	48.28 N	1.01 E
Lalouvesc	62	45.07 N	4.32 E
La Louvière	50	50.28 N	4.11 E
L'Alpe-d'Huez	62	45.06 N	6.04 E
Lālpur, Bngl.	126	24.11 N	88.58 E
Lālpur, India	120	22.12 N	69.58 E
Lal'sk	24	60.44 N	47.34 E
Lālsot	124	26.34 N	76.20 E
Lālua	126	21.57 N	90.18 E
La Luz, Méx.	196	25.52 N	97.37 W
La Luz, Méx.	232	24.12 N	97.52 W
La Luz, Nic.	236	13.44 N	84.47 W
La Luz, N.M., U.S.	200	32.58 N	105.56 W
Lam	60	49.12 N	13.03 E
Lama ≃, Ross.	82	56.29 N	36.10 E
Lama ≃, Zhg.	104	42.11 N	123.29 E
Lama, ozero ◎	74	69.30 N	90.30 E
L'Amable Lake ◎	212	45.01 N	77.49 W
La Macarena, Parque Nacional ♠	246	2.40 N	73.45 W
La Macarena, Serranía de ⩕	246	2.45 N	73.55 W
La Maddalena	71	41.13 N	9.24 E
Lama dei Peligni	66	42.02 N	14.11 E
La Madeleine	50	50.39 N	3.04 E
Lamadong	98	40.39 N	119.39 E
La Madrague	62	43.14 N	5.22 E
La Madrid, Arg.	252	27.38 S	65.15 W
Lamadrid, Méx.	196	27.05 N	101.50 W
Lamag	112	5.29 N	117.49 E
La Magdalena, Río de ≃	286a	19.21 N	99.11 W
Lamagoumen	105	40.52 N	116.39 E
Lamahuang	104	42.27 N	121.33 E
La Mailleraye-sur-Seine	50	49.29 N	0.46 E
Lamainong	114	3.49 N	96.46 E
La Majada	286c	10.27 N	67.01 W
Lama-Kara	150	9.33 N	1.12 E
La Malbaie	186	47.39 N	70.10 W
La Malinche, Parque Nacional ♠	234	19.15 N	98.05 W
Lamaline	186	46.52 N	55.49 W
La Malmaison ⊥	261	48.52 N	2.10 E
Lamaload Reservoir ◎[1]	262	53.16 N	2.02 W
Lama Mocogno	64	44.18 N	10.45 E
La Mancha ◆[1]	34	38.50 N	3.00 W
La Mancha, Canal de → English Channel ʯ	28	50.20 N	1.00 W
Lamandau ≃	112	2.42 S	111.34 E
Lamap	175f	16.26 S	167.43 E
Lamar, Co., U.S.	198	38.05 N	102.37 W
Lamar, Mo., U.S.	194	37.29 N	94.16 W
Lamar, Pa., U.S.	210	41.01 N	77.32 W
Lamar, S.C., U.S.	192	34.10 N	80.03 W
Lamar ≃	202	44.56 N	110.24 W
La Marañosa	266a	40.17 N	3.35 W
Lamarche	58	48.04 N	5.47 E
Lamarche-sur-Saône	58	47.16 N	5.23 E
Lamari ≃	164	6.54 S	145.25 E
La Mariposa, Embalse ◎[1]	286c	10.24 N	66.56 W
La Mariscala	252	34.03 S	54.47 W
La Marmora, Punta ∧	71	39.59 N	9.20 E
La Marolle-en-Sologne	50	47.35 N	1.47 E
La Maroma	196	28.34 N	100.45 W
Lamarque, Arg.	252	39.24 S	65.42 W
La Marque, Tx., U.S.	222	29.22 N	94.58 W
La Marsa	36	36.53 N	10.20 E
La Martre	62	43.46 N	6.36 E
Lamas	248	6.25 S	76.35 W
La Masica	236	15.37 N	87.07 W
Lamastre	62	44.59 N	4.35 E
La Matanza □[5]	288	34.46 S	58.37 W
La Matanza → San Justo	258	34.40 S	58.33 W
Lama Temple ʋ[1]	271a	39.56 N	116.25 E
La Mauricie, Parc National de (La Mauricie National Park) ♠	206	46.50 N	73.00 W
La Maya, Cuba	240p	20.10 N	75.39 W
Lamaya, Zhg.	102	29.50 N	99.53 E
Lamayingzi	104	42.09 N	121.50 E
Lambach	60	48.05 N	13.53 E
Lamballe	32	48.28 N	2.31 W
Lambaréné	152	0.42 S	10.13 E
Lambari	256	21.58 S	45.21 W
Lambari ≃, Bra.	255	19.30 S	45.00 W
Lambari ≃, Bra.	256	21.47 S	45.13 W
Lambasa	175g	16.26 S	179.24 E
Lambayeque	248	6.42 S	79.55 W
Lambayeque □[5]	248	6.20 S	80.00 W
Lambayeque ≃	248	6.43 S	79.54 W
Lambay Island I	48	53.29 N	6.01 W
Lambe	273a	6.42 N	3.21 E
Lambersart	50	50.39 N	3.02 E
Lambert, Ms., U.S.	194	34.12 N	90.17 W
Lambert, Mt., U.S.	198	47.41 N	104.37 W
Lambert, Cape ≻, Austl.	162	20.35 S	117.10 E
Lambert, Cape ≻, Pap. N. Gui.	164	4.12 S	151.32 E
Lambert Glacier ⍓	9	71.00 S	70.00 E
Lamberton	198	44.13 N	95.15 W
Lambert-Saint Louis International Airport ⊠	219	38.45 N	90.22 W
Lambertsbaai → Lambert's Bay	158	32.05 S	18.17 E
Lambert's Bay	158	32.05 S	18.17 E
Lambertville, Mi., U.S.	216	41.45 N	83.37 W
Lambertville, N.J., U.S.	208	40.21 N	74.56 W
Lambesc	62	43.39 N	5.16 E
Lambeth	214	42.54 N	81.18 W
Lambeth ◆[8]	42	51.30 N	0.07 W
L'ambir'	80	54.17 N	45.07 E
Lambo Katenga	154	5.02 S	28.48 E
Lambomakondro	157b	22.41 S	44.44 E
Lambourn	42	51.31 N	1.31 W
Lambourne ≃	42	51.24 N	1.18 W
Lambourne End	260	51.38 N	0.08 E
Lambrama	248	13.52 S	72.46 W
Lambrate ◆[8]	266b	45.29 N	9.15 E
Lambrecht	56	50.08 N	8.56 E
Lambrechten	60	48.19 N	13.31 E
Lambrechts Drift	158	28.31 S	21.43 E
Lambro ≃	62	45.08 N	9.32 E
Lambro, Parco ♠	266b	45.30 N	9.15 E
Lambs Creek	210	41.51 N	77.06 W
Lambs Terrace	285	39.46 N	75.02 W

Symbol	English	Deutsch	Español	Français	Português
≃	River	Fluß	Río	Rivière	Rio
≍	Canal	Kanal	Canal	Canal	Canal
∟	Waterfall, Rapids	Wasserfall, Stromschnellen	Cascada, Rápidos	Chute d'eau, Rapides	Cascata, Rápidos
ʯ	Strait	Meeresstraße	Estrecho	Détroit	Estreito
c	Bay, Gulf	Bucht, Golf	Bahía, Golfo	Baie, Golfe	Baía, Golfo
◎	Lake, Lakes	See, Seen	Lago, Lagos	Lac, Lacs	Lago, Lagos
⠿	Swamp	Sumpf	Pantano	Marais	Pântano
⍓	Ice Features, Glacier	Eis- und Gletscherformen	Accidentes Glaciales	Formes glaciaires	Acidentes glaciares
⍑	Other Hydrographic Features	Andere Hydrographische Objekte	Otros Elementos Hidrográficos	Autres données hydrographiques	Outros acidentes hidrográficos
✦	Submarine Features	Untermeerische Objekte	Accidentes Submarinos	Formes de relief sous-marin	Acidentes submarinos
□	Political Unit	Politische Einheit	Unidad Politica	Entité politique	Unidade política
ʋ	Cultural Institution	Kulturelle Institution	Institución Cultural	Institution culturelle	Instituição cultural
⊥	Historical Site	Historische Stätte	Sitio Histórico	Site historique	Sitio histórico
♠	Recreational Site	Erholungs- und Ferienort	Sitio de Recreo	Centre de loisirs	Area de Lazer
⊠	Airport	Flughafen	Aeropuerto	Aéroport	Aeroporto
■	Military Installation	Militäranlage	Instalación Militar	Installation militaire	Instalação militar
◆	Miscellaneous	Verschiedenes	Misceláneo	Divers	Diversos

ENGLISH | DEUTSCH

Name / Name	Page / Seite	Lat.°′ / Breite°′	Long.°′ / Länge°′ E = Ost
Lambton	273d	26.15 S	28.10 E
Lambton □6	214	42.45 N	82.15 W
Lambton, Cape ›	176	71.05 N	123.10 W
Lambu	164	3.09 S	151.41 E
Lambunao	116	11.03 N	122.29 E
L'amca	24	64.27 N	37.04 E
Lamdessar	164	7.12 S	131.58 E
Lame, Nig.	150	10.23 N	9.13 E
Lamé, Tchad	146	9.15 N	14.32 E
La Meca → Makkah	144	21.27 N	39.49 E
La Mecque → Makkah	144	21.27 N	39.49 E
Lame Deer	202	45.37 N	106.39 W
La Media Luna, Arrecifes de ⬥2	236	15.13 N	82.36 W
La Méditerranée → Mediterranean Sea ▾2	10	35.00 N	20.00 E
Lamego	34	41.06 N	7.49 W
La Meije ∧	62	45.00 N	6.18 E
Lameirão, Morro do ∧2	287a	22.54 S	43.31 W
La Membrolle-sur-Choisille	50	47.26 N	0.38 E
La Mendieta	252	24.19 S	64.58 W
L'amen'ga	76	59.51 N	44.31 E
Lamentin	241o	16.16 N	61.38 W
Lamèque	186	47.47 N	64.38 W
Lamèque, Île I	186	47.48 N	64.36 W
La Merced, Arg.	252	28.10 S	65.41 W
La Merced, Arg.	252	24.58 S	65.29 W
La Merced, Perú	248	11.03 S	75.19 W
Lameroo	166	35.20 S	140.31 E
La Mesa, Pan.	236	8.09 N	81.11 W
La Mesa, Ca., U.S.	228	32.46 N	117.01 W
La Mesa, N.M., U.S.	200	32.07 N	106.42 W
Lamesa, Tx., U.S.	196	32.44 N	101.57 W
La Mesa Dam ⬥6	269f	14.43 N	121.04 E
La Meta ∧	66	41.41 N	13.56 E
Lamía	38	38.54 N	22.26 E
L'amin ≃	74	61.18 N	71.48 E
Lamine ≃	194	38.59 N	92.51 W
La Minerve	206	46.15 N	74.56 W
Laming ≃	61	47.25 N	15.16 E
Lamington ≃	210	40.38 N	74.41 W
Lamington, Mount ∧1	164	8.56 S	148.10 E
Lamington National Park ♦	166	28.15 S	153.12 E
La Mira	234	18.02 N	102.19 W
La Mirada	228	33.55 N	118.00 W
La Mirada Creek ≃	280	33.53 N	118.01 W
La Misión	204	32.05 N	116.50 W
Lamitan	116	6.39 N	122.08 E
Lamlam, Mount ∧2	174p	13.20 N	144.40 E
Lamlash	46	55.32 N	5.08 W
Lamma Island I	271d	22.12 N	114.07 E
Lammefjord ⊂	41	55.48 N	11.43 E
Lammerlaw Top ∧	172	45.40 S	169.38 E
Lammermuir ⬥1	46	55.50 N	2.25 W
Lammermuir Hills ⋏2	46	55.50 N	2.44 W
Lammeulo	114	5.15 N	95.56 E
Lammhult	26	57.10 N	14.35 E
Lammi	26	61.05 N	25.01 E
Lamming Mills	182	53.22 N	120.18 W
Lamogai	164	5.50 S	149.20 E
La Moille, Il., U.S.	190	41.31 N	89.16 W
Lamoille, Nv., U.S.	204	40.43 N	115.28 W
Lamoille ≃	188	44.35 N	73.10 W
La Moine ≃	194	39.59 N	90.31 W
La Moine, East Fork ≃	194	40.24 N	90.56 W
Lamoka Lake ⊜	210	42.24 N	77.05 W
La Molina	286d	12.05 S	76.57 W
Lamon Bay ⊂	116	14.25 N	122.00 E
Lamone ≃	66	44.31 N	12.15 E
Lamongan	115a	7.07 S	112.25 E
Lamongan, Gunung ∧	115a	7.58 S	113.20 E
Lamoni	190	40.37 N	93.56 W
Lamont, Ab., Can.	182	53.46 N	112.48 W
Lamont, Ca., U.S.	228	35.15 N	118.54 W
Lamont, Ia., U.S.	190	42.35 N	91.38 W
Lamont, Mi., U.S.	216	43.01 N	86.09 W
Lamont, Ok., U.S.	196	36.41 N	97.33 W
La Monte	194	38.46 N	93.25 W
La Mosquitia □9	236	15.00 N	83.45 W
La Mothe, Lac ⊜1	186	48.46 N	71.09 W
La Mothe-Achard	32	46.37 N	1.40 W
Lamotrek I1	14	7.30 N	146.20 E
La Mott	285	40.04 N	75.08 W
La Motte, Lac ⊜	190	48.24 N	78.03 W
Lamotte-Beuvron	50	47.36 N	2.01 E
La Motte-Chalançon	62	44.29 N	5.23 E
La Motte-du-Caire	62	44.21 N	6.02 E
Lamoura	58	46.24 N	5.58 E
La Moure	198	46.21 N	98.17 W
La Moustique ≃	241o	16.11 N	61.35 W
Lampa	248	15.21 S	70.22 W
Lampang	110	18.18 N	99.31 E
Lampasas	196	31.03 N	98.10 W
Lampasas ≃	196	30.59 N	97.24 W
Lampazos de Naranjo	232	27.01 N	100.31 W
Lampedusa	70a	35.30 N	12.56 E
Lampedusa, Isola di I	70a	35.31 N	12.35 E
Lampertheim	56	49.35 N	8.28 E
Lampeter, Wales, U.K.	42	52.07 N	4.05 W
Lampeter, Pa., U.S.	208	39.58 N	76.14 W
Lamphun	110	18.35 N	99.01 E
Lampinsaari	26	64.25 N	25.09 E
Lampione, Isolotto di I	70a	35.34 N	12.19 E
Lampman	184	49.23 N	102.45 W
Lamprechtshausen	64	47.59 N	12.57 E
Lampung □4	112	5.00 S	105.00 E
Lampung, Teluk ⊂	115a	5.40 S	105.20 E
Lamskoje	76	52.57 N	38.02 E
Lamspringe	52	51.58 N	10.00 E
Lamstedt	52	53.38 N	9.05 E
Lāmta	124	22.08 N	80.07 E
Lam Tong Hoi Hap ʮ	271d	22.15 N	114.15 E
Lamu, Kenya	154	2.16 S	40.54 E
Lāmu, Mya.	110	19.14 N	94.10 E
Lamud	248	6.09 S	77.55 W
La Muerte, Cerro ∧	236	9.33 N	83.44 W
Lam Uk Wei	271d	22.26 N	114.22 E
La Mure	62	44.54 N	5.47 E
Lamure-sur-Azergues	58	46.04 N	4.30 E
La Mutua	234	22.23 N	99.18 W
Lan' ≃, Bela.	76	52.09 N	27.18 E
Lan ≃, Zhg.	104	41.14 N	123.32 E
Lan, Loi ∧	110	19.40 N	97.55 E
Lana	64	46.37 N	11.09 E
Lanai I	229a	20.50 N	156.55 W
Lanai City	229a	20.49 N	156.55 W
Lanaihale ∧	229a	20.49 N	156.52 W
Lanaken	56	50.53 N	5.39 E
Lanalhue, Lago ⊜	252	37.55 S	73.18 W
La Nana, Bayou ≃	222	31.27 N	94.43 W
Lanao del Norte □4	116	8.10 N	124.00 E
Lanao del Sur □4	116	7.50 N	124.25 E
La Napoule	62	43.31 N	6.56 E
Lanarce	62	44.44 N	4.00 E
Lanark, On., Can.	212	45.01 N	76.22 W
Lanark, Scot., U.K.	46	55.41 N	3.46 W
Lanark, Il., U.S.	190	42.06 N	89.50 W
Lanark, Pa., U.S.	208	40.33 N	75.26 W
Lanark □6	212	45.05 N	76.20 W
La Nartelle	62	43.19 N	6.39 E
Lanas	112	5.20 N	116.30 E
La Nava de Ricomalillo	34	39.39 N	4.59 W
Lanbi Kyun I	110	10.50 N	98.15 E
Lanboyan Point ›	116	8.18 N	122.56 E
Lancang	102	23.00 N	100.02 E
Lancang → Mekong ≃	12	10.33 N	105.24 E
Lancashire	285	39.49 N	75.29 W
Lancashire □6	44	53.45 N	2.40 W
Lancashire Plain ≚	44	53.40 N	2.45 W
Lancaster, On., Can.	206	45.08 N	74.30 W
Lancaster, Eng., U.K.	44	54.03 N	2.48 W
Lancaster, Ca., U.S.	228	34.41 N	118.08 W
Lancaster, Ky., U.S.	192	37.37 N	84.34 W
Lancaster, Ma., U.S.	207	42.27 N	71.40 W
Lancaster, Mn., U.S.	198	48.51 N	96.48 W
Lancaster, Mo., U.S.	194	40.31 N	92.31 W
Lancaster, N.H., U.S.	188	44.29 N	71.34 W
Lancaster, N.Y., U.S.	210	42.54 N	78.40 W
Lancaster, Oh., U.S.	188	39.43 N	82.36 W
Lancaster, Pa., U.S.	208	40.02 N	76.18 W
Lancaster, S.C., U.S.	192	34.43 N	80.46 W
Lancaster, Tx., U.S.	222	32.38 N	96.47 W
Lancaster, Va., U.S.	208	37.46 N	76.28 W
Lancaster, Wi., U.S.	190	42.50 N	90.42 W
Lancaster □6, Pa., U.S.	208	40.02 N	76.19 W
Lancaster □6, Va., U.S.	208	37.45 N	76.30 W
Lancaster Canal ≅	262	53.46 N	2.43 W
Lancaster Sound ʮ	176	74.13 N	84.00 W
Lancaster Village	285	39.45 N	75.35 W
Lančchuti	84	42.06 N	42.01 E
Lance Creek	200	43.01 N	104.38 W
Lance Creek ≃	198	43.22 N	104.16 W
Lancefield	169	37.17 S	144.44 E
Lancelin	162	31.02 S	115.20 E
Lancelot, Mount ∧	162	26.13 S	123.12 E
Lancey	62	45.14 N	5.53 E
Lanchang	114	3.30 N	102.11 E
Lanchester	44	54.49 N	1.44 W
Lanchow → Lanzhou	102	36.03 N	103.41 E
Lanciano	66	42.14 N	14.23 E
Lancin, Fr.	62	45.43 N	5.24 E
Lančin, Ukr.	78	48.34 N	24.45 E
Lancing	42	50.50 N	0.19 W
Lanco	254	39.24 S	72.46 W
Lancones	246	4.35 S	80.30 W
Lancun	98	36.24 N	120.10 E
Łańcut	30	50.05 N	22.13 E
Lancy	58	46.11 N	6.07 E
Lândana	152	5.13 S	12.08 E
Landang Gua	116	6.58 N	122.15 E
Landau	56	49.12 N	8.07 E
Landau an der Isar	60	48.40 N	12.43 E
Landay	128	30.31 N	63.47 E
Land Between the Lakes ♦	194	36.55 N	88.05 W
Landeck	58	47.08 N	10.34 E
Landen	56	50.45 N	5.05 E
Landenberg	208	39.47 N	75.46 W
Landenhausen	56	50.36 N	9.28 E
Lander	200	42.49 N	108.43 W
Lander ≃	162	20.25 S	132.00 E
Landerneau	32	48.27 N	4.15 W
Landes □5	32	44.20 N	1.00 W
Landes ⬥1	32	44.15 N	1.00 W
Landesbergen	52	52.33 N	9.07 E
Landeskrone ∧2	54	51.08 N	14.56 E
Landess	216	40.37 N	85.34 W
Landete	34	39.54 N	1.22 W
Landham Brook ≃	283	42.22 N	71.25 W
Landhausen	263	51.24 N	7.45 E
Landi	98	36.35 N	119.59 E
Landi Kotal	123	34.06 N	71.09 E
Landina	86	59.12 N	67.02 E
Landing	210	40.54 N	74.40 W
Landing Lake ⊜	184	55.17 N	97.26 W
Landis, Sk., Can.	184	52.12 N	108.28 W
Landis, N.C., U.S.	192	35.32 N	80.36 W
Landisburg	208	40.20 N	77.18 W
Landisville	208	40.06 N	76.25 W
Landivisiau	32	48.31 N	4.04 W
Landkey	42	51.04 N	4.00 W
Landkirchen	54	54.27 N	11.08 E
Lando	192	34.46 N	81.00 W
Land O'Lakes, Fl., U.S.	220	28.11 N	82.34 W
Land O'Lakes, Wi., U.S.	190	46.10 N	89.13 W
Landor	162	25.09 S	116.54 E
Landos	62	44.51 N	3.50 E
Landösjön ⊜	26	63.35 N	14.04 E
Landover Estates	284c	38.56 N	76.54 W
Landover Hills	284c	38.57 N	76.53 W
Landover Mall ⬥9	284c	38.55 N	76.51 W
Landquart	58	46.58 N	9.33 E
Landquart ≃	58	46.58 N	9.32 E
Landrecies	50	50.08 N	3.42 E
Landres	56	49.19 N	5.48 E
Landreth Draw V	196	31.14 N	102.29 W
Landriano	62	45.19 N	9.15 E
Landri Sales	250	7.16 S	43.55 W
Landro (Höhlenstein)	64	46.39 N	12.14 E
Landrum	192	35.10 N	82.11 W
Landry	62	45.34 N	6.45 E
Landsberg	54	51.31 N	12.10 E
Landsberg am Lech	58	48.05 N	10.55 E
Landsberg an der Warthe → Gorzów Wielkopolski	30	52.44 N	15.15 E
Landsborough	166	26.49 S	152.58 E
Landsborough Creek ≃	166	22.30 S	144.33 E
Landsbro	26	57.22 N	14.54 E
Land's End ›, Eng., U.K.	42	50.03 N	5.44 W
Lands End ›, Ca., U.S.	228	33.28 N	118.36 W
Lands End ›, R.I., U.S.	207	41.27 N	71.19 W
Landshut	60	48.33 N	12.09 E
Landskrona	41	55.52 N	12.50 E
Landsman Creek ≃	198	39.35 N	102.19 W
Landsmeer	52	52.26 N	4.52 E
Landštejn	61	49.00 N	15.13 E
Landstuhl	56	49.25 N	7.34 E
Landweg	263	51.29 N	7.37 E
Landwehrbach ≃	263	51.26 N	6.26 E
Land Wursten ⬥1	52	53.40 N	8.35 E
Lane	219	40.07 N	88.51 W
Lane ≃	50	47.17 N	0.05 E
Lane City	222	29.13 N	96.02 W
Lane Cove	274a	33.49 S	151.10 E
Lane Cove ≃	274a	33.48 S	151.09 E
Lane Cove River Park ♦	274a	33.47 S	151.09 E
La Negra	252	23.45 S	70.19 W
Lane Mountain ∧	228	35.05 N	116.56 W
Lanersbach	64	47.09 N	11.44 E
Lanesboro, Ma., U.S.	207	42.31 N	73.14 W
Lanesboro, Mn., U.S.	190	43.43 N	91.58 W
Lanesboro, Pa., U.S.	210	41.57 N	75.35 W
Lanester	32	47.46 N	3.21 W
Lanesville, In., U.S.	218	38.14 N	85.59 W
Lanesville, N.Y., U.S.	210	42.08 N	74.16 W
Lanesville, Va., U.S.	208	37.37 N	76.59 W
Lanett	194	32.52 N	85.11 W
La Neuveville	58	47.04 N	7.06 E
Laneville	222	31.58 N	94.49 W
Lanexa	208	37.24 N	76.55 W
Lanezi Lake ⊜	182	53.03 N	120.56 W
Lang	184	49.56 N	104.23 W
La'nga Co ⊜	124	30.42 N	81.16 E
Langadhás	38	40.45 N	23.04 E
Langádhia	38	37.41 N	22.02 E
Langa-Langa	152	3.54 S	15.56 E
Langan Creek ≃	216	40.57 N	87.49 W
Langano, Lake ⊜	144	7.35 N	38.48 E
Langao	102	32.13 N	109.02 E
Langar, Afg.	120	37.02 N	73.47 E
L'angar, Kyrg.	85	40.25 N	73.07 E
L'angar, Taj.	123	37.02 N	72.42 E
Langara	112	4.02 S	123.00 E
Langara Island I	182	54.14 N	133.00 W
Langarūd	128	37.11 N	50.10 E
L'angasovo	80	58.32 N	49.30 E
Langat ≃	114	2.54 N	101.22 E
Langau	61	48.49 N	15.42 E
Langavat, Loch ⊜	46	58.04 N	6.48 W
Långban	40	59.51 N	14.15 E
Langbank	184	50.05 N	102.20 W
Lang Bay	182	49.47 N	124.21 W
Langberg ⋏	158	28.20 S	22.35 E
Langburkersdorf	54	51.02 N	14.14 E
Langda	102	31.12 N	96.59 E
Langdai	102	26.06 N	105.20 E
Langdon	198	48.45 N	98.22 W
Langdondale	214	40.08 N	78.15 W
Langdon Hills	260	51.34 N	0.25 E
Langeac	32	45.06 N	3.30 E
Langeais	50	47.20 N	0.24 E
Langebaan	158	33.06 S	18.02 E
Langeberg ⋏	158	33.55 S	20.30 E
Lange Berge ⋏2	56	50.20 N	10.55 E
Langebrück	54	51.07 N	13.50 E
Langeland I	41	55.00 N	10.50 E
Langelandsbælt ʮ	41	54.50 N	10.55 E
Längelmävesi ⊜	26	61.32 N	24.22 E
Langeloth	214	40.21 N	80.24 W
Langelsheim	52	51.56 N	10.19 E
Langemark	50	50.55 N	2.55 E
Langen, Dtsch.	52	53.36 N	8.35 E
Langen, Dtsch.	56	49.59 N	8.41 E
Langenargen	58	47.35 N	9.32 E
Langenau, Dtsch.	54	50.50 N	13.18 E
Langenau, Dtsch.	58	48.30 N	10.07 E
Langenberg, Dtsch.	52	51.46 N	8.19 E
Langenberg, Dtsch.	56	51.21 N	7.09 E
Langenbernsdorf	54	50.45 N	12.19 E
Langenbielau → Bielawa	30	50.41 N	16.38 E
Langenbochum	263	51.37 N	7.07 E
Langenbruck	58	47.21 N	7.46 E
Langenburg, Sk., Can.	184	50.50 N	101.43 W
Langenburg, Dtsch.	56	49.15 N	9.50 E
Langendorf	54	51.11 N	11.58 E
Langendreer ⬥8	263	51.28 N	7.19 E
Langeneichstädt	54	51.20 N	11.41 E
Langenfeld, Dtsch.	56	51.07 N	6.56 E
Längenfeld, Öst.	64	47.04 N	10.58 E
Langenhagen	52	52.27 N	9.44 E
Langenhessen	54	50.45 N	12.22 E
Langenhorn	41	54.41 N	8.53 E
Langenhorst	263	51.22 N	7.02 E
Langenlois	61	48.28 N	15.40 E
Langennaundorf	54	51.36 N	13.20 E
Langenneufnach	58	48.16 N	10.36 E
Langenselbold	56	50.10 N	9.02 E
Langensteinach	56	49.30 N	10.10 E
Langenthal	58	47.13 N	7.47 E
Langenwang	61	47.34 N	15.37 E
Langenweddingen	54	52.02 N	11.31 E
Langenwetzendorf	54	50.41 N	12.05 E
Langenzenn	56	49.30 N	10.48 E
Langenzersdorf	61	48.18 N	16.22 E
Langeoog	52	53.45 N	7.29 E
Langeoog I	52	53.46 N	7.32 E
Langerfeld ⬥8	263	51.16 N	7.15 E
Langer See ⊜	264a	52.25 N	13.38 E
Langerwehe	56	50.49 N	6.22 E
Langeskov	41	55.22 N	10.36 E
Langesund	26	59.00 N	9.45 E
Langevåg	26	62.27 N	6.12 E
Langewiesen	54	50.40 N	10.58 E
Langfang → Anci	105	39.31 N	116.41 E
Langfjorden ⊂2	26	62.43 N	7.30 E
Langford, B.C., Can.	224	48.27 N	123.30 W
Langford, Eng., U.K.	260	51.45 N	0.40 E
Langford, N.Y., U.S.	210	42.35 N	78.51 W
Langford, S.D., U.S.	198	45.36 N	97.49 W
Langförden	52	52.47 N	8.14 E
Langgam	112	0.15 N	101.43 E
Langgapayung	114	1.43 N	99.59 E
Langgöns	56	50.30 N	8.40 E
Långhalsen ⊜	40	58.56 N	16.41 E
Langham	184	52.22 N	106.57 W
Langhe □9	62	44.30 N	8.00 E
Langhirano	64	44.37 N	10.16 E
Langho	262	53.48 N	2.27 W
Langholm	44	55.09 N	3.00 W
Langhorne	208	40.10 N	74.55 W
Langhorne Acres	284c	38.51 N	77.16 W
Langhorne Creek	168b	35.18 S	139.02 E
Langhorne Gardens	285	40.11 N	74.53 W
Langhorne Manor	285	40.10 N	74.55 W
Langhorne Terrace	285	40.10 N	74.57 W
Langji Shan I	100	28.32 N	121.36 E
Langjökull ⊓	24a	64.42 N	20.12 W
Langju	100	27.52 N	116.36 E
Lang Ka, Doi ∧	110	19.00 N	99.24 E
Langkawi, Pulau I	114	6.22 N	99.50 E
Langkesi, Kepulauan II	112	5.18 S	124.20 E
Langklip	158	28.12 S	20.20 E
Langkrans	158	27.47 S	31.03 E
Langlade I	186	46.50 N	56.20 W
Lang Lang ≃	169	38.17 S	145.31 E
Langley, B.C., Can.	224	49.06 N	122.39 W
Langley, Eng., U.K.	260	51.30 N	0.33 W
Langley, Eng., U.K.	260	51.14 N	0.35 E
Langley, Eng., U.K.	262	53.15 N	2.05 W
Langley, Ok., U.S.	196	36.27 N	95.02 W
Langley, S.C., U.S.	192	33.31 N	81.50 W
Langley, Va., U.S.	284c	38.57 N	77.10 W
Langley, Wa., U.S.	224	48.02 N	122.24 W
Langley Air Force Base ■	208	37.05 N	76.21 W
Langley Hill ∧2	282	37.20 N	122.14 W
Langley Park	284c	38.59 N	76.58 W
Langleyville	219	39.34 N	89.21 W
Langlo ≃	166	26.26 S	146.05 E
Langlois	202	42.55 N	124.26 W
Langmazong	120	30.52 N	89.58 E
Lang Mo	110	17.14 N	106.27 E
Långnäs	26	60.06 N	20.17 E
Langnau	58	46.57 N	7.47 E
Langogne	62	44.43 N	3.51 E
Langon	32	44.33 N	0.15 W
Langøya I	24	68.44 N	14.50 E
Langping	102	30.38 N	110.21 E
Langport	42	51.02 N	2.50 W
Langqiao	100	30.30 N	118.24 E
Langquaid	60	48.49 N	12.03 E
Langreo → Sama [de Langreo]	34	43.18 N	5.41 W
Langres	58	47.52 N	5.20 E
Langres, Plateau de ⋏1	58	47.41 N	5.03 E
Langruth	184	50.24 N	98.38 W
Langruzong	120	31.50 N	91.25 E
Langsa	114	4.28 N	97.58 E
Langsa, Teluk ⊂	114	4.35 N	98.00 E
Langschede	263	51.29 N	7.43 E
Långsele	26	63.11 N	17.04 E
Langshan, Zhg.	102	41.12 N	107.22 E
Langshan, Zhg.	105	40.22 N	115.41 E
Långshyttan	40	60.27 N	16.01 E
Långsjön ⊜	40	59.00 N	17.27 E
Langsnek ⊥	158	27.28 S	29.55 E
Lang Son	110	21.50 N	106.44 E
Langstaff	275b	43.50 N	79.25 W
Langst-Kierst	263	51.18 N	6.43 E
Lang Suan	110	9.57 N	99.04 E
Långsvan ⊜	40	59.43 N	15.49 E
Langtang National Park ♦	124	28.10 N	85.30 E
Langtian	100	25.11 N	113.28 E
Langting	120	25.30 N	93.07 E
Langton	212	42.45 N	80.35 W
Langtoutun	89	46.51 N	121.54 E
Langtuozi	104	41.01 N	121.43 E
Langu	100	27.56 N	118.11 E
Langue	236	13.37 N	87.39 W
Languedoc □9	32	44.00 N	4.00 E
Langui Layo, Laguna de ⊜	248	14.29 S	71.13 W
L'Anguille ≃	194	34.44 N	90.40 W
Langula	54	51.09 N	10.25 E
Langundu, Tanjung ›	115b	8.49 S	118.58 E
Langwarden	52	53.36 N	8.19 E
Langwedel	52	52.59 N	9.12 E
Langweer	52	52.57 N	5.43 E
Langweid	58	48.29 N	10.51 E
Langweiler	56	49.40 N	7.31 E
Langwies	58	46.49 N	9.43 E
Langwo	104	41.13 N	121.44 E
Langwozhuang	105	39.05 N	115.37 E
Langxi	106	31.08 N	119.10 E
Langxi ≃	106	31.10 N	118.59 E
Langzhong	102	31.35 N	105.59 E
Langzishan	104	41.02 N	123.23 E
Lanham	284c	38.58 N	76.51 W
Lanhil Island I	116	6.46 N	122.22 E
Lanibga, Mount ∧	116	10.27 N	123.56 E
Lanigan	184	51.52 N	105.02 W
Lanigan Creek ≃	184	51.23 N	105.13 W
Lanín, Parque Nacional ♦	254	39.36 S	71.24 W
Lanín, Volcán ∧1	254	39.38 S	71.30 W
Lanjiang	107	30.24 N	105.11 E
Lankao (Lanfeng)	98	34.50 N	114.49 E
Lanker See ⊜	54	54.12 N	10.17 E
Lankeys Creek	171b	35.49 S	147.39 E
Länkipohja	26	61.44 N	24.48 E
Lanklaar	56	51.01 N	5.44 E
Lank-Latum	263	51.18 N	6.41 E
Lankou	100	23.59 N	115.05 E
Lankoviri	146	9.00 N	11.25 E
Lankwitz ⬥8	264a	52.26 N	13.21 E
Lanling	89	45.15 N	126.12 E
Lannabruk	40	59.14 N	14.56 E
Lannach	61	46.56 N	15.19 E
Lännaholm	40	59.53 N	17.57 E
Lannaja	78	49.21 N	35.16 E
Lannemezan	32	43.08 N	0.23 E
Lannilis	32	48.34 N	4.31 W
Lannion	32	48.44 N	3.28 W
Lannon	216	43.08 N	88.09 W
L'Annonciation	206	46.25 N	74.52 W
Lanoka Harbor	208	39.52 N	74.10 W
Lanoraie	206	45.58 N	73.13 W
La Noria	258	35.10 S	58.48 W
Lanovcy	78	49.52 N	26.05 E
Lanping	102	26.29 N	99.23 E
Lanqibao	104	40.56 N	122.25 E
Lanqikoucun	104	40.52 N	122.26 E
Lanqipuzi	104	42.12 N	123.15 E
Lanquín	236	15.34 N	89.58 W
Lans, Montagnes de ⋏	62	44.52 N	5.29 E
Lansdale	208	40.14 N	75.17 W
Lansdowne, Austl.	162	17.53 S	126.39 E
Lansdowne, Austl.	274a	33.54 S	150.59 E
Lansdowne, On., Can.	212	44.24 N	76.01 W
Lansdowne, India	124	29.50 N	78.41 E
Lansdowne, Md., U.S.	284b	39.14 N	76.39 W
Lansdowne, Pa., U.S.	285	39.56 N	75.16 W
L'Anse, Mi., U.S.	190	46.45 N	88.27 W
Lanse, Pa., U.S.	214	40.59 N	78.08 W
L'Anse-aux-Meadows National Historic Park ♦	186	51.36 N	55.32 W
L'anse Creuse Bay ⊂	214	42.34 N	82.49 W
L'Anse Indian Reservation ⬥4	190	46.48 N	88.22 W
Lans-en-Vercors	62	45.07 N	5.35 E
Lansford, N.D., U.S.	198	48.37 N	101.22 W
Lansford, Pa., U.S.	210	40.49 N	75.52 W
Lanshan	102	25.18 N	111.52 E
Lanshantou	98	35.07 N	119.21 E
Lansing, Il., U.S.	216	41.33 N	87.32 W
Lansing, Ia., U.S.	190	43.21 N	91.12 W
Lansing, Ks., U.S.	198	39.14 N	94.54 W
Lansing, Mi., U.S.	216	42.43 N	84.33 W
Lansing, N.Y., U.S.	210	42.32 N	76.30 W
Lansing, Oh., U.S.	214	40.04 N	80.47 W
Lansing ⬥8	275b	43.45 N	79.25 W
Lansing, Lake ⊜	216	42.46 N	84.25 W
Lansing Municipal Airport ⊠	278	41.32 N	87.32 W
Lanškroun	30	49.55 N	16.37 E
Lanslebourg	62	45.17 N	6.52 E
Lanslevillard	62	45.17 N	6.55 E
Lanstrop ⬥8	263	51.34 N	7.34 E
Lantana	220	26.35 N	80.03 W
Lantang	100	23.25 N	114.56 E
Lantau Island I	100	22.17 N	113.59 E
Lanta Yai, Ko I	110	7.35 N	99.05 E
Lanterne ≃	58	47.44 N	6.03 E
Lantewa	146	12.16 N	11.44 E
Lantian	102	34.03 N	109.12 E
Lantianba	107	28.52 N	105.26 E
Lantianchang	271a	39.58 N	116.17 E
Lantsch	58	46.41 N	9.34 E
Lantsch → Laces	64	46.37 N	10.52 E
Lantschou → Lanzhou	102	36.03 N	103.41 E
Lantzville	224	49.15 N	124.05 W
La Nurra ⬥1	71	40.45 N	8.15 E
Lanús	258	34.43 S	58.24 W
Lanús □5	288	34.42 S	58.28 W
Lanusei	71	39.53 N	9.32 E
Lanuvio	66	41.40 N	12.42 E
Lanuza	116	9.14 N	126.04 E
Lanuza Bay ⊂	116	9.17 N	126.04 E
Lanxi, Zhg.	89	46.15 N	126.14 E
Lanxi, Zhg.	100	29.12 N	119.28 E
Lanxian	102	38.22 N	111.46 E
Lány	54	50.06 N	13.58 E
Lan Yü I	100	22.03 N	121.32 E
Lanzada	64	46.15 N	9.51 E
Lanzarote I	148	29.00 N	13.40 W
Lanzendorf	264b	48.06 N	16.26 E
Lanzhou (Lanchow)	102	36.03 N	103.41 E
Lanzo Torinese	62	45.16 N	7.28 E
Lao ≃, It.	68	39.47 N	15.48 E
Lao ≃, Thai	110	19.55 N	99.54 E
Lao ≃, Zhg.	100	29.11 N	116.00 E
Laoag	116	18.12 N	120.36 E
Laoag ≃	116	18.12 N	120.31 E
Laoang	116	12.34 N	125.00 E
Laoang Island I	116	12.35 N	125.01 E
Lao Bao	110	16.37 N	106.36 E
Laobian, Zhg.	104	40.42 N	122.21 E
Laobian, Zhg.	104	41.58 N	123.10 E
Lao Cai	110	22.30 N	103.57 E
Laochang, Zhg.	102	24.34 N	104.11 E
Laochang, Zhg.	107	29.30 N	106.36 E
Laocheng	104	42.37 N	124.04 E
Laodafang	104	41.40 N	122.40 E
Laodao ≃	100	28.16 N	112.58 E
Laodaodian	89	51.16 N	126.40 E
Laofengkou	86	46.11 N	83.38 E
Laofu	98	42.13 N	118.17 E
Laogang	106	31.01 N	121.49 E
Laoge	100	32.49 N	119.52 E
Laoguan	100	27.38 N	113.36 E
Laoguanpu	104	40.53 N	120.51 E
Laoha ≃	90	43.24 N	120.39 E
Laohaotuo	104	41.25 N	122.46 E
Laoheba	107	28.51 N	103.49 E
Laoheishan	89	43.45 N	130.52 E
Laoheshangtai	104	40.43 N	120.49 E
Laohokow → Guanghua	102	32.25 N	111.36 E
Laohuk'ou	100	24.53 N	121.03 E
Laohumiao	271a	39.58 N	116.20 E
Laohutuozi	104	42.25 N	122.34 E
Laois □6	48	53.00 N	7.24 W
Laojunguan	105	40.22 N	114.47 E
Laojunmiao → Yumen	102	39.56 N	97.51 E
Laoka	89	52.47 N	125.52 E
Laolao, Bahia ⊂	174n	15.08 N	145.46 E
Lao → Laos □1	110	18.00 N	105.00 E
Lao Ling ∧	89	43.27 N	130.11 E
Laolong ≃	106	32.11 N	120.00 E
Laolongtan	107	30.01 N	104.48 E
Laomocun	106	30.51 N	119.11 E
Laon	50	49.34 N	3.40 E
Laona, N.Y., U.S.	214	42.25 N	79.19 W
Laona, Wi., U.S.	190	45.33 N	88.40 W
La Orchila, Isla I	246	11.48 N	66.09 W
La Orotava	148	28.23 N	16.31 W
La Oroya	248	11.32 S	75.54 W
Laos (Lao) □1, Asia	108	18.00 N	105.00 E
Laos (Lao) □1, Asia	110	18.00 N	105.00 E
Laoshan (Licun)	98	36.10 N	120.25 E
Laoshan Wan ⊂	98	36.24 N	120.45 E
Laosolu	114	3.11 N	98.02 E
Laotto	216	41.17 N	85.12 W
Laou, Oued ≃	34	35.29 N	5.04 W
Laowushi	106	31.43 N	121.00 E
Laoxinkou	100	30.12 N	112.50 E
Laoyemiao	98	41.03 N	119.53 E
Laoyezhuang	106	32.16 N	120.04 E
Laoyingpan	100	26.34 N	115.10 E
Laozha	106	31.35 N	121.07 E
Laozhen	100	31.34 N	118.19 E
Laozhong	98	33.56 N	114.51 E
Laozhuangzi	105	39.44 N	118.05 E
Laozishan	100	33.11 N	118.36 E
Lapa	252	25.45 S	49.42 W
Lapa ⬥8, Bra.	287a	22.55 S	43.11 W
Lapa ⬥8, Bra.	287b	23.32 S	46.42 W
Lapac Island I	116	5.32 N	120.47 E
Lapai	150	9.06 N	6.45 E
Lapaich, Sgurr na ∧	46	57.21 N	5.04 W
Lapalisse	32	46.15 N	3.38 E
La Palma, Col.	246	5.22 N	74.24 W
La Palma, Cuba	240p	22.45 N	83.33 W
La Palma, El Sal.	236	14.19 N	89.11 W
La Palma, Méx.	234	17.05 N	99.29 W
La Palma, Méx.	234	20.09 N	102.46 W
La Palma, Pan.	246	8.25 N	78.09 W
La Palma, Pan.	246	7.42 N	80.12 W
La Palma, Ca., U.S.	280	33.50 N	118.02 W
La Palma I	148	28.40 N	17.52 W
La Palma ≃	240p	23.03 N	80.54 W
La Palma de Cervelló	266d	41.25 N	1.58 E
La Palma del Condado	34	37.23 N	6.33 W
La Palmita	196	25.57 N	99.18 W
La Paloma	252	34.40 S	54.10 W
La Palud	62	43.47 N	6.20 E
La Pampa □4	252	37.00 S	66.00 W
La Panza Range ⋏	226	35.18 N	120.18 W
Lapão	250	11.24 S	41.50 W
La Paragua	246	6.50 N	63.20 W
Laparan Island I	116	5.54 N	119.59 E
La Parota	234	18.20 N	101.08 W
La Pasión, Laguna ⊂	234	15.59 N	97.40 W
La Pasión, Río de ≃	232	16.28 N	90.33 W
La Patrie	206	45.24 N	71.15 W
La Paz, Arg.	252	30.45 S	59.39 W
La Paz, Arg.	252	33.28 S	67.33 W
La Paz, Bol.	248	16.30 S	68.09 W
La Paz, Col.	246	10.23 N	73.10 W
La Paz, Hond.	236	14.16 N	87.40 W
La Paz, Méx.	232	24.10 N	110.18 W
La Paz, Méx.	234	23.41 N	100.43 W
La Paz, Pil.	116	8.19 N	125.43 E
Lapaz, In., U.S.	216	41.28 N	86.18 W
La Paz, Ur.	258	34.21 S	57.18 W
La Paz, Ur.	258	34.46 S	56.15 W
La Paz □5, Bol.	248	15.30 S	68.00 W
La Paz □5, Hond.	236	14.15 N	87.50 W
La Paz, Bahía ⊂	232	24.09 N	110.25 W
La Paz, Río de ≃	248	16.27 S	67.19 W
La Paz Centro	236	12.20 N	86.41 W
Lape	115b	8.39 S	117.37 E
La Pedrera	246	1.18 S	69.43 W
Lapeer	216	43.03 N	83.19 W
Lapeer □6	216	43.00 N	83.20 W
Lapel	218	40.04 N	85.50 W
La Penne-sur-Huveaune	62	43.17 N	5.31 E
La Perla, Méx.	196	28.18 N	104.33 W
La Perla, Méx.	232	28.18 N	104.38 W
La Perla, Perú	286d	12.05 S	77.08 W
La Perouse	170	33.59 S	151.14 E
La Perouse, Bahía ⊂	174z	27.04 S	109.18 W
La Perouse Bay ⊂	229a	20.35 N	156.25 W
La Perouse Strait ʮ	89	45.45 N	142.00 E
La Pesca	234	23.46 N	97.47 W
La Pesse	58	46.18 N	5.51 E
La Petite-Pierre	56	48.52 N	7.19 E
Lapford	42	50.55 N	3.47 W
Lapham Hill ∧2	216	43.02 N	88.24 W
L'apičev	80	48.30 N	43.32 E
La Piedad de Cabadas	234	20.21 N	102.00 W
La Pimienta	234	21.28 N	99.01 W
La Pine	202	43.40 N	121.30 W
Lapinin Island I	116	10.06 N	124.34 E
Lapinjärvi (Lappträsk)	26	60.38 N	26.13 E
Lapin lääni □4	26	66.00 N	27.00 E
Lapinlahti	26	63.22 N	27.24 E
Lapino	82	54.57 N	37.49 E
La Pintada	236	8.36 N	80.27 W
La Pintana	286e	33.37 S	70.38 W
La Pizzuta ∧	70	38.00 N	13.16 E
La Place, Il., U.S.	219	39.48 N	88.43 W
La Place, La., U.S.	194	30.03 N	90.28 W
Lap Lae	110	17.39 N	100.02 E
La Plaine	240d	15.20 N	61.15 W
Lapland □9	24	68.00 N	25.00 E
Laplandija	24	68.16 N	33.19 E
Laplandskij Zapovednik ⬥4	24	67.50 N	32.10 E
La Plata, Arg.	258	34.55 S	57.57 W
La Plata, Col.	246	2.23 N	75.53 W
La Plata, Md., U.S.	208	38.31 N	76.58 W
La Plata, Mo., U.S.	194	40.01 N	92.29 W
La Plata □5	288	34.55 S	58.04 W
La Plata ≃	200	36.54 N	108.15 W
La Plata, Lago ⊜	254	44.53 S	71.50 W
La Plata, Lago ⊜1	240m	18.20 N	66.14 W
La Plata, Universidad Nacional de ʊ2	288	35.55 S	57.57 W
La Plata Peak ∧	200	39.02 N	106.28 W
La Playa ⬥8	286b	23.06 N	82.27 W
La Playa Corrida de San Juan, Punta ›	234	18.36 N	103.42 W
La Plonge Indian Reserve ⬥4	184	55.15 N	107.36 W
La Plume	210	41.34 N	75.45 W
La Pobla de Segur	34	42.14 N	0.59 E
La Pocatière	186	47.22 N	70.02 W
La Poile	186	47.41 N	58.24 W
La Poile Bay ⊂	186	47.38 N	58.20 W
Lapominka	24	64.48 N	40.28 E
La Pomme	62	43.25 N	5.35 E
Laponie → Lapland □9	24	68.00 N	25.00 E
Laporte, Co., U.S.	200	40.38 N	105.08 W
La Porte, In., U.S.	216	41.36 N	86.43 W
La Porte, Oh., U.S.	279a	41.19 N	82.05 W
Laporte, Pa., U.S.	210	41.25 N	76.30 W
La Porte, Tx., U.S.	222	29.39 N	95.01 W
La Porte □6	216	41.36 N	86.43 W
La Porte City	190	42.18 N	92.11 W
Laposo, Bulu ∧	112	4.29 S	119.47 E
La Potherie, Lac ⊜	176	58.50 N	72.24 W
Lapoutroie	58	48.09 N	7.10 E
La Poveda	266a	40.19 N	3.29 W
La Poza Grande	232	25.50 N	112.05 W
Lappago (Lappach)	64	46.55 N	11.48 E
Lappajärvi	26	63.12 N	23.38 E
Lappajärvi ⊜	26	63.08 N	23.40 E
Lappeenranta	26	61.04 N	28.11 E
Lappfjärd (Lapväärtti)	26	62.15 N	21.32 E
Lappi	26	61.06 N	21.50 E
Lappland → Lapland □9	24	68.00 N	25.00 E
Lappträsk → Lapinjärvi	26	60.38 N	26.13 E
La Prairie	206	45.25 N	73.30 W
Laprairie □6	206	45.20 N	73.35 W
La Prele Creek ≃	198	42.50 N	105.30 W
La Presa ≃	232	24.25 N	111.34 W
Laprida, Arg.	252	37.33 S	60.49 W
Laprida, Arg.	252	28.23 S	64.33 W
La Pryor	196	28.57 N	99.51 W
Lapšanga	80	57.27 N	45.03 E
Lâpseki	130	40.20 N	26.41 E
Lapta	130	35.20 N	33.10 E
Laptev Sea → Laptevych, more ▾2	74	76.00 N	126.00 E
Laptevych, more (Laptev Sea) ▾2	74	76.00 N	126.00 E
Lapua	26	62.57 N	23.00 E
Lapuanjoki ≃	26	63.34 N	22.30 E
La Puebla de Cazalla	34	37.14 N	5.19 W
La Puebla de Montalbán	34	39.52 N	4.21 W
La Puente	228	34.01 N	117.56 W
La Puerta	252	28.10 S	65.48 W
Lapu-Lapu (Opon)	116	10.19 N	123.57 E
La Punt	58	46.35 N	9.55 E
La Punta	286d	12.05 S	77.11 W
La Purísima, Chile	286e	33.34 S	70.39 W
La Purísima, Méx.	232	26.10 N	112.04 W
Lăpuș	38	47.30 N	24.01 E
La Push	224	47.54 N	124.38 W
Lapuyan	116	7.36 N	123.12 E
Lapväärtti → Lappfjärd	26	62.15 N	21.32 E
Lapwai	202	46.24 N	116.48 W
Łapy	30	53.00 N	22.53 E
La Queue-en-Brie	261	48.47 N	2.35 E
La Queue-lès-Yvelines	261	48.48 N	1.46 E
La Quiaca	252	22.06 S	65.37 W
L'Aquila	66	42.22 N	13.22 E
L'Aquila □4	66	42.05 N	13.40 E
Lār	128	27.41 N	54.17 E
Lara	169	38.01 S	144.24 E
Lara □3	246	10.10 N	69.50 W
Larabanga	150	9.13 N	1.51 W
Laracha	34	43.15 N	8.35 W
Larache	148	35.12 N	6.10 W
Laragne-Montéglin	62	44.19 N	5.49 E
Lārak, Jazīreh-ye I	128	26.52 N	56.22 E
Laramate	248	14.15 S	74.52 W
La Rambla	34	37.36 N	4.44 W
Laramie	200	41.18 N	105.35 W
Laramie ≃	200	42.12 N	104.32 W
Laramie Mountains ⋏	200	42.00 N	105.40 W
Laramie Peak ∧	200	42.17 N	105.27 W
Laranjaí ≃	255	23.12 S	53.45 W
Laranjal	255	21.22 S	42.28 W
Laranjeiras	250	10.48 S	37.10 W
Laranjeiras ⬥8	287a	22.56 S	43.11 W
Laranjeiras do Sul	252	25.25 S	52.25 W
Larantuka	115b	8.21 S	122.59 E
Laraos	248	12.17 S	75.50 W
Larap	116	14.18 N	122.39 E
Larat	164	7.09 S	131.45 E
Larat, Pulau I	164	7.10 S	131.50 E
Laravale	171a	28.05 S	152.56 E
La Raya, Abra)(	248	14.35 S	70.59 W
L'Arbaa Naït Irathen	34	36.38 N	4.12 E
Larb Creek ≃	202	48.25 N	107.16 W
L'Arbresle	62	45.50 N	4.37 E
Lärbro	26	57.47 N	18.47 E
Larbut, Jazīrat I	140	18.47 N	37.33 E
Larche, Col de (Colle della Maddalena))(	62	44.25 N	6.53 E
Larchmont	210	40.55 N	73.45 W
Larchmont Harbor ⊂	276	40.55 N	73.45 W
Larchwood	198	43.27 N	96.26 W
Lardaro	64	45.58 N	10.39 E
Larde	154	16.28 S	39.43 E
Lardeau	182	50.09 N	116.57 W
Larderello	66	43.14 N	10.53 E
Larder Lake ⊜	190	48.05 N	79.36 W
Lardier, Cap ›	62	43.09 N	6.37 E
L'Ardoise	186	45.37 N	60.45 W
Lardy	261	48.31 N	2.16 E
Lare	154	0.20 N	37.56 E
Laredo, Esp.	34	43.24 N	3.25 W
Laredo, Tx., U.S.	196	27.30 N	99.30 W
Laredo Sound ʮ	182	52.32 N	128.53 W
La Reforma, Méx.	232	25.06 N	108.05 W
La Reforma, Méx.	234	16.34 N	97.51 W
La Reina	286e	33.27 S	70.33 W
Laren	52	52.15 N	5.14 E
Larena	116	9.15 N	123.35 E
La Réole	32	44.35 N	0.02 W
Lares, Perú	248	13.04 S	72.05 W
Lares, P.R.	240m	18.18 N	66.53 W
Larga	78	48.23 N	26.50 E
Larga, Laguna ⊜	196	27.30 N	97.25 W
Large, Île du I	275a	45.19 N	73.52 W
Largentière	62	44.32 N	4.18 E
L'Argentière-la-Bessée	62	44.47 N	6.33 E
Lar Gerd	120	35.29 N	66.40 E
Largo	220	27.54 N	82.47 W
Largo, Cañon V	200	36.40 N	107.43 W
Largo, Cayo I	240p	21.38 N	81.28 W
Largo Creek ≃	200	34.29 N	108.51 W
Largoward	46	56.15 N	2.51 W
Largs	46	55.48 N	4.52 W
Largue ≃	62	43.51 N	5.52 E
Lari, It.	66	43.34 N	10.35 E
Lari, Perú	248	15.37 S	71.46 W
Lariang	112	1.26 S	119.17 E
Lariang ≃	112	1.25 S	119.17 E
La Ricamarie	62	45.24 N	4.22 E
Larimer	214	40.21 N	79.44 W
Larimore	198	47.54 N	97.37 W
Larino, It.	66	41.48 N	14.54 E
Larino, Ukr.	83	47.53 N	37.56 E
La Rioja	252	29.26 S	66.51 W
La Rioja □4, Arg.	252	30.00 S	67.30 W
La Rioja □4, Esp.	34	42.15 N	2.30 W
Lárisa	38	39.38 N	22.25 E
Larisa Station ⬥5	267c	37.58 N	23.42 E
Larjak	74	61.16 N	80.15 E
Larjan	76	59.30 N	33.47 E
Larjegan ≃	86	60.30 N	77.44 E
Lārkāna	120	27.33 N	68.13 E
Larkhall	46	55.45 N	3.59 W
Lark Harbour	186	49.06 N	58.23 W
Larkhill	42	51.12 N	1.50 W
Larkspur	226	37.56 N	122.30 W
Larksville	210	41.14 N	75.55 W
Larnaca → Lárnax	130	34.55 N	33.38 E
Lárnakos, Kólpos ⊂	130	34.55 N	33.45 E
Lárnax (Larnaca)	130	34.55 N	33.38 E
Larne	48	54.51 N	5.49 W
Larned	198	38.10 N	99.05 W
Larne Lake ⊜	44	54.47 N	5.45 W
Laro	146	8.17 N	12.18 E
La Robla	34	42.48 N	5.37 W
La Roca de la Sierra	34	39.07 N	6.41 W
La Roche	58	46.42 N	7.08 E
La Roche-Bernard	32	47.31 N	2.18 W
La Roche-de-Rame	62	44.45 N	6.35 E
La Roche-Derrien	28	48.45 N	3.16 W
La Roche-des-Arnauds	62	44.34 N	5.57 E
La Roche-en-Ardenne	56	50.11 N	5.35 E
La Roche-en-Brenil	50	47.22 N	4.10 E
La Rochefoucauld	32	45.45 N	0.23 E
La Roche-Guyon	50	49.05 N	1.38 E
La Rochelle	32	46.10 N	1.10 W
Laroche-Saint-Cydroine	50	47.58 N	3.31 E

Symbols in the index entries represent the broad categories identified in the key at the right. Symbols with superior numbers (⋏1) identify subcategories (see complete key on page *I · 1).*

Symbole im Register stellen die rechts im Schlüssel erklärten Kategorien dar. Symbole mit hochgestellten Ziffern (⋏1) bezeichnen Unterabteilungen einer Kategorie (vgl. vollständiger Schlüssel auf Seite *I · 1).*

Los símbolos incluídos en el texto del índice representan las grandes categorias identificadas con la clave a la derecha. Los símbolos con numeros en su parte superior (⋏1) identifican las subcategorías (véase la clave completa en la página *I · 1).*

Les symboles de l'index représentent les catégories indiquées dans la légende à droite. Les symboles suivis d'un indice (⋏1) représentent des sous-catégories (voir légende complète à la page *I · 1).*

Os símbolos incluídos no texto do índice representam as grandes categorias identificadas com a chave à direita. Os símbolos com números em sua parte superior (⋏1) identificam as subcategorias (veja-se a chave completa à página *I · 1).*

∧ Mountain	Berg	Montaña	Montagne	Montanha
⋏ Mountains	Gebirge	Montañas	Montagnes	Montanhas
)(Pass	Paß	Paso	Col	Passo
V Valley, Canyon	Tal, Cañon	Valle, Cañón	Vallée, Canyon	Vale, Canhão
≚ Plain	Ebene	Llano	Plaine	Planície
› Cape	Kap	Cabo	Cap	Cabo
I Island	Insel	Isla	Île	Ilha
II Islands	Inseln	Islas	Îles	Ilhas
⊥ Other Topographic Features	Andere Topographische Objekte	Otros Elementos Topográficos	Autres données topographiques	Outros acidentes topográficos

ESPAÑOL — Nombre | Página | Lat.°′ | Long.°′ W = Oeste
FRANÇAIS — Nom | Page | Lat.°′ | Long.°′ W = Ouest
PORTUGUÊS — Nome | Página | Lat.°′ | Long.°′ W = Oeste

La Roche-sur-Foron 58 46.04 N 6.19 E
La Roche-sur-Yon 32 46.40 N 1.26 W
La Rochette, Fr. 62 45.28 N 6.07 E
La Rochette, Fr. 261 48.30 N 2.40 E
Larochette, Lux. 56 49.47 N 6.15 E
La Roda 34 39.13 N 2.09 W
La Romaine 186 50.13 N 60.40 W
La Romana 238 18.25 N 68.58 W
Larona 112 2.45 S 121.20 E
La Ronge 184 55.06 N 105.17 W
Laroquebrou 32 44.58 N 2.11 E
La Roquebrussanne 62 43.20 N 5.59 E
Larose 194 29.34 N 90.22 W
La Rosita 236 13.53 N 84.24 W
La Route 261 48.48 N 2.47 E
Larrabee State Park ♠ 224 48.41 N 122.29 W
Larreynaga 236 12.40 N 86.34 W
Larrey Point ➤ 162 19.58 S 119.07 E
Larrimah 164 15.35 S 133.12 E
Larringes 58 46.22 N 6.35 E
Larrison Creek ≃ 222 31.27 N 95.03 W
Larroque 252 33.02 S 59.01 W
Larrys Creek ≃ 210 41.13 N 77.13 W
Larrys River 186 45.13 N 61.23 W
Larsen Air Park ⊠ 281 42.11 N 83.33 W
Larsen Bay 180 57.33 N 154.00 W
Larsen Ice Shelf ⍓ 9 68.30 S 62.30 W
Larteh Aheneasi 150 5.56 N 0.04 E
La Rubia 252 30.06 S 61.48 W
La Rue, Oh., U.S. 214 40.35 N 83.23 W
Larue, Tx., U.S. 222 32.07 N 95.41 W
La Rumorosa 204 32.34 N 116.06 W
Laruns 32 42.59 N 0.25 W
Larus Lake ⊜ 184 51.17 N 94.40 W
Larvik 26 59.04 N 10.00 E
Larwill 216 41.10 N 85.37 W
Larzac, Causse du ⛰[1] 32 44.00 N 3.15 E
Lasa (Laas) 64 46.37 N 10.42 E
La Sabana 252 27.52 S 59.57 W
Las Adjuntas 286c 10.26 N 67.01 W
La Sagne 58 47.03 N 6.48 E
La Sal 200 38.18 N 109.14 W
La Salada, Laguna ⊜ 234 22.28 N 98.20 W
La Salette-Fallavaux 62 44.51 N 5.59 E
La Salle, On., Can. 214 42.14 N 83.06 W
La Salle, P.Q., Can. 206 45.26 N 73.38 W
Lasalle, Fr. 62 44.03 N 3.51 E
La Salle, It. 62 45.45 N 7.04 E
La Salle, Co., U.S. 200 40.20 N 104.42 W
La Salle, Il., U.S. 216 41.20 N 89.06 W
La Salle □[6] 216 41.21 N 88.51 W
La Salle ≃ 184 49.45 N 97.08 W
Lasalle, Parc ♠ 275a 45.26 N 73.40 W
La Salle College ♜[2] 285 40.02 N 75.09 W
La Salle Gardens 216 42.39 N 83.21 W
Las Almejas, Bahía ⊂ 232 24.29 N 111.44 W
La Sal Mountains ⛰ 200 38.30 N 109.10 W
Lasan 112 1.14 N 115.13 E
Lasanga Island I 164 7.25 S 147.16 E
Las Animas 198 38.04 N 103.13 W
La Santa, Cerro ʌ 240m 18.07 N 66.03 W
Las Arenas 240m 18.02 N 67.09 W
La Sarraz 58 46.40 N 6.31 E
La Sarre 190 48.48 N 79.12 W
La Sarre ≃ 190 48.43 N 79.16 W
Las Arrias 252 30.21 S 63.35 W
La Sauceda 196 28.26 N 100.38 W
La Saulce 62 44.25 N 6.01 E
Las Auras 196 26.25 N 99.20 W
Las Aves, Isla I 238 15.42 N 63.38 W
Las Aves, Islas II 246 12.00 N 67.30 W
Las Ballenas, Canal de ⊔ 232 29.10 N 113.29 W
Lasberg 61 48.28 N 14.32 E
Las Blancas 196 25.42 N 97.35 W
Las Bonitas 246 7.52 N 65.40 W
Las Breñas 252 27.05 S 61.05 W
Låsby 41 56.09 N 9.49 E
Las Cabezas de San Juan 34 36.59 N 5.56 W
Las Cabras 252 34.18 S 71.19 W
Las Cañas ≃ 234 22.29 N 105.36 W
Lascano 252 33.40 S 54.12 W
Lascar, Volcán ʌ[1] 252 23.23 S 67.45 W
Lascari 70 38.00 N 13.56 E
Las Casas → San Cristóbal de las Casas 234 16.45 N 92.38 W
Las Catitas 252 33.18 S 68.02 W
Las Catonas, Arroyo ≃ 288 34.37 S 58.43 W
Lascaux, Grotte de ⊥[5] 32 45.01 N 1.08 E
Las Cejas 252 26.53 S 64.44 W
L'Ascension 206 46.33 N 74.50 W
L'aščevka 78 49.33 N 32.41 E
Las Chacras 258 35.05 S 59.10 W
Las Choapas 234 17.55 N 94.05 W
La Scie 186 49.57 N 55.36 W
Las Coloradas 254 39.33 S 70.35 W
Las Condes 286e 33.22 S 70.31 W
Lascone, Monte ʌ[2] 267a 41.59 N 12.23 E
Las Cruces 200 32.18 N 106.46 W
Las Cuevas 232 29.38 N 101.19 W
Las Delicias 232 15.58 N 91.50 W
La Selle, Morne ʌ 238 18.22 N 71.59 W
La Selva Beach 226 36.55 N 121.51 W
Lasem 115a 6.42 S 111.26 E
La Serena 252 29.54 S 71.16 W
La Serena ◆[1] 34 38.45 N 5.30 W
La Seyne 32 43.06 N 5.53 E
La Seyne-sur-Mer 62 43.06 N 5.53 E
Las Flores, Arg. 252 36.03 S 59.07 W
Las Flores, Arg. 252 30.19 S 69.12 W
Las Flores, Méx. 234 18.22 N 93.10 W
Las Flores, P.R. 240m 18.03 N 66.22 W
Las Flores, Ven. 286c 10.34 N 66.56 W
Las Flores, Arroyo ≃ 252 35.36 S 59.01 W
Las Flores, Cerro ʌ 234 16.43 N 95.30 W
Las Flores Canyon V 280 34.03 N 118.38 W
Las Flores Chica, Laguna ⊜ 258 35.30 S 59.01 W
Las Flores Grande, Laguna ⊜ 258 35.34 S 59.02 W
Las Garcitas 252 26.35 S 59.48 W
Las Guacamayas 234 18.02 N 102.12 W
Las Guayabas 232 24.00 N 97.45 W
Lasham 42 51.11 N 1.03 W
Las Harquetas, Arroyo ≃ 288 34.29 S 58.38 W
Lashburn 184 53.08 N 109.36 W
Lāsh-e Joveyn 128 31.43 N 61.37 E
Las Heras, Arg. 252 32.51 S 68.49 W
Las Heras, Arg. 254 46.33 S 68.57 W
Lashio 110 22.56 N 97.45 E
Lashkar Gāh 128 31.35 N 64.21 E
Lashkar → Gwalior 124 26.13 N 78.10 E
Las Hormigas 232 25.30 N 98.44 W
Lasht 123 36.48 N 73.01 E
Lasia, Pulau I 114 2.10 N 96.39 E
La Sierra, Montaña ⛰ 236 14.04 N 87.54 W
Las Iglesias 196 27.35 N 101.21 W
Las Iglesias, Cerro ʌ 232 26.16 N 106.38 W
La Sila ⛰ 68 39.15 N 16.30 E
La Siligata 66 43.56 N 12.45 E
La Silla de Caracas ʌ 286c 10.33 N 66.51 W
Łasin 30 53.32 N 19.05 E
Lašino 80 58.16 N 49.59 E
Lāsjerd 128 35.24 N 53.04 E
Łask 30 51.36 N 19.07 E
Łaskarzew 30 51.48 N 21.35 E
L'askel'a 24 61.45 N 30.59 E
Laško 36 46.09 N 15.14 E
L'askoviči 78 52.07 N 28.09 E
Las Lajas, Arg. 252 38.31 S 70.22 W
Las Lajas, Pan. 236 8.15 N 81.52 W
Las Lajitas 252 24.41 S 64.15 W

Las Lomas 246 4.40 S 80.15 W
Las Lomitas 252 24.42 S 60.36 W
Lašma 80 54.56 N 41.09 E
Las Malvinas 252 34.50 S 68.15 W
Lašmanka 80 54.44 N 51.28 E
Las Mareas 240m 17.56 N 66.09 W
Las Margaritas 232 16.19 N 91.59 W
Las Margaritas, Laguna ⊜ 258 35.28 S 57.56 W
Las Marianas 258 35.04 S 59.31 W
Las Marías 240m 18.15 N 67.00 W
Las Marismas ≣ 34 37.00 N 6.15 W
Las Mayas 286c 10.26 N 66.56 W
Las Mercedes 246 9.07 N 66.24 W
Las Mesas de San Isidro 234 21.55 N 100.15 W
Las Minas 286c 10.27 N 66.52 W
Las Minas, Cerro ʌ 236 14.33 N 88.39 W
Las Minillas, Cerro ʌ 286e 33.31 S 70.29 W
Las Moras Creek ≃ 196 29.00 N 100.39 W
Las Mulas, Laguna ⊜ 258 35.32 S 57.54 W
Las Navas 116 12.21 N 125.02 E
Las Nieves 232 26.24 N 105.22 W
Las Nopaleras, Cerro ʌ 232 25.08 N 103.14 W
La Solana 34 38.56 N 3.14 W
La Soledad, Cerro ʌ 232 26.32 N 107.17 W
Lasolo 112 3.29 S 122.04 E
Lasolo ≃ 112 3.28 S 122.06 E
Las Ortegas, Arroyo ≃ 288 34.45 S 58.32 W
Las Ovejas 252 37.01 S 70.45 W
Las Palmas, Arg. 252 27.04 S 58.42 W
Las Palmas, Arg. 258 34.05 S 59.10 W
Las Palmas, Pan. 236 8.08 N 81.27 W
Las Palmas, P.R. 240m 17.59 N 66.02 W
Las Palmas □[4] 148 28.25 N 14.15 W
Las Palmas de Gran Canaria 148 28.06 N 15.24 W
Las Palomas 200 31.44 N 107.37 W
Las Perdices, Canal ≅ 286e 33.31 S 70.33 W
La Spezia 62 44.07 N 9.50 E
La Spezia □[4] 62 44.15 N 9.42 E
Las Piedras, P.R. 240m 18.11 N 65.52 W
Las Piedras, Ur. 258 34.44 S 56.13 W
Las Piedras, Río de ≃ 248 12.30 S 69.14 W
Las Piñas, Pil. 269f 14.29 N 120.59 E
Las Piñas, P.R. 240m 18.15 N 65.55 W
Las Plumas 254 43.43 S 67.15 W
Lasqueti Island I 182 49.29 N 124.17 W
Las Raices Creek ≃ 196 28.09 N 99.02 W
Las Ratas, Cerro ʌ 234 18.37 N 103.37 W
Las Rejas 286e 33.28 S 70.44 W
Las Rosas, Arg. 252 32.28 S 61.34 W
Las Rosas, Chile 286e 33.35 S 70.37 W
Las Rosas, Méx. 232 16.24 N 92.23 W
Las Rozas de Madrid 266a 40.29 N 3.52 W
Las Sales, Canal ≅ 286a 19.26 N 99.03 W
Lassan 54 53.57 N 13.50 E
Lassance 255 17.54 S 44.34 W
Lassater 222 32.49 N 94.30 W
Lassay 32 48.26 N 0.30 W
Lassee 61 48.13 N 16.49 E
Lassellsville 210 43.03 N 74.36 W
Lassen Peak ʌ[1] 204 40.29 N 121.31 W
Lassen Volcanic National Park ♠ 204 40.30 N 121.19 W
Lassigny 50 49.35 N 2.51 E
Lassnitz ≃ 61 46.46 N 15.32 E
Lassnitzhöhe 61 47.05 N 15.35 E
Lasso ʌ[2] 174n 15.02 N 145.38 E
L'Assomption 206 45.50 N 73.25 W
L'Assomption □[6] 206 45.48 N 73.35 W
L'Assomption ≃ 206 45.43 N 73.29 W
Lasswade 46 55.53 N 3.08 W
Lassy 261 49.06 N 2.27 E
Las Tablas 246 7.46 N 80.17 W
Lastarrio, Parque Nacional ♠ 254 44.50 S 72.05 W
Las Tinajas 252 27.27 S 62.55 W
Last Mountain ʌ 184 51.07 N 104.54 W
Last Mountain Lake ⊜ 184 51.05 N 105.10 W
Las Toscas 252 28.21 S 59.17 W
Lastoursville 152 0.49 S 12.42 E
Lastovo, Otok I 36 42.45 N 16.53 E
Lastovski Kanal ⊔ 36 42.50 N 16.59 E
Lastra a Signa 66 43.46 N 11.06 E
Las Trampas Creek ≃ 282 37.53 N 122.03 W
Las Trampas Peak ʌ 282 37.50 N 122.03 W
Las Trampas Regional Park ♠ 282 37.50 N 122.03 W
Las Trampas Ridge ʌ 282 37.49 N 122.02 W
Lästringe 40 58.54 N 17.18 E
Las Truchas 234 17.55 N 102.12 W
Lastrup 52 52.48 N 7.52 E
Las Tunas 240p 20.58 N 76.57 W
Las Tunas □[4] 240p 21.00 N 77.00 W
Las Tunas, Arroyo ≃ 288 34.27 S 58.41 W
Las Tunas, Punta ➤ 240m 18.30 N 66.38 W
Las Tunas Beach ♠ 280 34.02 N 118.36 W
Las Tunas Grandes, Laguna ⊜ 252 35.58 S 62.25 W
La Suze 32 47.54 N 0.02 E
Las Varas, Méx. 232 29.29 N 108.01 W
Las Varas, Méx. 234 21.10 N 105.10 W
Las Varillas 252 31.52 S 62.43 W
Las Vegas, P.R. 240m 18.11 N 67.02 W
Las Vegas, Nv., U.S. 204 36.10 N 115.08 W
Las Vegas, N.M., U.S. 200 35.36 N 105.13 W
Las Vegas, Ven. 246 9.35 N 68.37 W
Las Vigas de Ramirez 234 19.38 N 97.05 W
La Tabatière 186 50.50 N 58.58 W
Latacunga 246 0.56 S 78.37 W
Latady Island I 9 70.45 S 74.35 W
La Tagua 246 0.03 S 74.40 W
Latakia □[9] 130 35.20 N 36.00 E
Latakia → Al-Lādhiqīyah 130 35.31 N 35.47 E
Latambar 123 33.07 N 70.52 E
Lata Mountain ʌ 174y 14.14 S 169.29 W
La Tapona 234 22.48 N 100.38 W
Låtefossen ∟ 26 59.57 N 6.37 E
Latehar 124 23.45 N 84.30 E
Lately Common 262 53.29 N 2.30 W
Latera 66 42.38 N 11.50 E
Laterina 66 43.31 N 11.43 E
Laterns 58 47.16 N 9.43 E
Laterrière 186 48.18 N 71.06 W
Laterza 68 40.37 N 16.48 E
La Teste-de-Buch 32 44.38 N 1.09 W
La Tetilla, Cerro ʌ 234 20.21 N 104.59 W
Latexo 222 31.24 N 95.29 W
Latgale □[9] 76 56.20 N 27.10 E
Latham, Austl. 162 29.45 S 116.26 E
Latham, Il., U.S. 219 39.58 N 89.10 W
Latham, N.Y., U.S. 210 42.44 N 73.45 W
Latham, Oh., U.S. 218 39.06 N 83.15 W
Lathan ≃ 50 47.27 N 0.08 E
Lathen 52 52.52 N 7.19 E
Latheron 46 58.17 N 3.23 W
Lāthi 120 21.43 N 71.23 E
Lathrop, Ca., U.S. 226 37.49 N 121.16 W
Lathrop, Mo., U.S. 194 39.32 N 94.19 W
Lathrup Village 281 42.29 N 83.14 W
La Thuile 62 45.43 N 6.57 E
La Tiama 286c 10.26 N 66.46 W
Latian, Mount ʌ 116 6.13 N 125.30 E
Latiano 68 40.33 N 17.43 E
Latimer, Eng., U.K. 260 51.41 N 0.33 W
Latimer, Ia., U.S. 190 42.45 N 93.22 W
Latina 66 41.28 N 12.52 E
Latina □[4] 66 41.27 N 13.06 E
Latiri 140 9.10 N 25.43 E
Latisana 64 45.47 N 13.00 E

Latjuga 24 64.16 N 48.46 E
Latnaja 78 51.43 N 38.55 E
La Toma 252 33.03 S 65.37 W
Laton 226 36.26 N 119.41 W
Latonovo 83 47.29 N 38.38 E
Latorica ≃ 30 48.28 N 21.50 E
Latornell ≃ 182 54.58 N 118.00 W
La Torrecilla ʌ 240m 18.12 N 66.20 W
La Tortuga, Isla I 246 10.56 N 65.20 W
Latouche Island I 180 60.00 N 147.55 W
Latouche Treville, Cape ➤ 162 18.27 S 121.49 E
La Tour 62 43.57 N 7.11 E
La Tour-d'Aigues 62 43.44 N 5.33 E
La Tour-d'Auvergne 32 45.32 N 2.41 E
La Tour-de-Peilz 58 46.27 N 6.49 E
La Tour-du-Pin 62 45.34 N 5.27 E
La Tourette Park ♠ 276 40.35 N 74.08 W
Latowicz 30 52.02 N 21.48 E
Lat Phrao, Khlong ≅ 269a 13.48 N 100.35 E
La Tremblade 32 45.46 N 1.08 W
La Trimouille 32 46.28 N 1.02 E
La Trinidad, Arg. 252 27.24 S 65.31 W
La Trinidad, Nic. 236 12.58 N 86.14 W
La Trinidad, Pil. 116 16.28 N 120.35 E
La Trinidad, Ven. 286c 10.27 N 66.52 W
La Trinidad de Orichuna 246 7.07 N 69.45 W
La Trinitaria 232 16.07 N 92.03 W
La Trinité 240e 14.44 N 60.58 W
Latrobe, Austl. 166 41.14 S 146.24 E
Latrobe, Pa., U.S. 214 40.19 N 79.22 W
La Trobe ≃ 169 38.10 S 146.32 E
Latrobe University ♜[2] 274b 37.43 S 145.03 E
La Tronche 62 45.12 N 5.44 E
Latronico 68 40.05 N 16.01 E
Latta 192 34.20 N 79.25 W
Lattarico 68 39.28 N 16.08 E
Lattasburg 214 40.53 N 82.06 W
Latterbach 58 46.40 N 7.35 E
Lattingtown 276 40.54 N 73.36 W
Latty 216 41.05 N 84.35 W
La Tuilerie 261 48.34 N 2.08 E
La Tuilière 62 44.11 N 5.32 E
Latuna 112 8.23 S 124.06 E
La Tuque 176 47.26 N 72.47 W
Lātūr 122 18.24 N 76.35 E
La Turbie 62 43.45 N 7.24 E
Latvia (Latvija) □[1], Europe 22 57.00 N 25.00 E
Latvia (Latvija) □[1], Europe 76 57.00 N 25.00 E
Lau, Nig. 146 9.13 N 11.17 E
Lau, Pap. N. Gui. 164 5.50 S 151.20 E
Laubach 56 50.33 N 8.59 E
Lau Basin ✣[1] 14 20.00 S 177.00 W
Laubusch 54 51.28 N 14.10 E
Laubuseschbach 56 50.24 N 8.20 E
Lauca ≃ 248 19.10 S 68.10 W
Lauca, Parque Nacional ♠ 248 18.20 S 69.15 W
Laucha 54 51.13 N 11.41 E
Lauchhammer 54 51.30 N 13.47 E
Lauchheim 56 48.52 N 10.14 E
Lauda-Königshofen 56 49.34 N 9.41 E
Lauder 46 55.43 N 2.45 W
Lauderdale 194 32.31 N 88.30 W
Lauderdale V 46 55.43 N 2.42 W
Lauderdale-by-the-Sea 220 26.12 N 80.07 W
Lauderdale Lakes 220 26.09 N 80.12 W
Lauderhill 220 26.08 N 80.12 W
Laudun 62 44.06 N 4.40 E
Lauenbrück 52 53.12 N 9.33 E
Lauenburg 52 53.22 N 10.33 E
Lauenburg → Lębork 30 54.33 N 17.44 E
Lauenförde 52 51.39 N 9.23 E
Lauenstein, Dtsch. 52 52.04 N 9.33 E
Lauenstein, Dtsch. 54 50.47 N 13.49 E
Lauenstein, Dtsch. 54 50.31 N 11.20 E
Lauer ≃ 56 50.18 N 10.10 E
Lauerzer See ⊜ 58 47.02 N 8.36 E
Lauf an der Pegnitz 60 49.30 N 11.17 E
Läufelfingen 58 47.24 N 7.51 E
Laufen, Dtsch. 64 47.57 N 12.56 E
Laufen, Schw. 58 47.25 N 7.30 E
Laufenburg (Baden), Dtsch. 58 47.35 N 8.04 E
Laufenburg (Baden), Schw. 58 47.33 N 8.04 E
Laufersfort, Schloss ⊥ 263 51.25 N 6.37 E
Lauffen am Neckar 56 49.05 N 9.10 E
Laugharne 42 51.47 N 4.28 W
Laughery Creek ≃ 218 39.02 N 84.53 W
Laughlen, Mount ʌ 162 23.23 S 134.23 E
Laughlin Air Force Base ■ 196 29.22 N 100.47 W
Laughlin Peak ʌ 196 36.38 N 104.12 W
Laughlintown 214 40.13 N 79.12 W
Lau Group II 175g 18.20 S 178.30 W
Lauingen 56 48.34 N 10.25 E
Lauis → Lugano 58 46.01 N 8.58 E
Laukaa 26 62.25 N 25.57 E
Laukuva 76 55.37 N 22.14 E
Laul'u 89 45.46 N 135.16 E
Laun 110 10.07 N 98.46 E
Launceston, Austl. 166 41.26 S 147.08 E
Launceston, Eng., U.K. 42 50.38 N 4.21 W
Laundi, Tanjung ➤ 115b 9.28 S 120.12 E
Laune ≃ 48 52.07 N 9.48 W
Launglon 110 13.58 N 98.07 E
Laungowāl 123 30.13 N 75.41 E
La Unión, Chile 254 40.17 S 73.05 W
La Unión, Col. 246 1.36 N 77.09 W
La Unión, El Sal. 236 13.20 N 87.51 W
La Unión, Esp. 34 37.37 N 0.52 W
La Unión, Méx. 234 17.58 N 101.49 W
La Unión, Perú 248 9.46 S 76.48 W
La Unión, Perú 248 5.24 S 80.45 W
La Union, Pil. 116 6.42 N 126.05 E
La Union, N.M., U.S. 200 31.57 N 106.39 W
La Unión, Ven. 246 8.13 N 67.46 W
La Unión, Ven. 286c 10.25 N 66.48 W
La Union □[4] 116 16.35 N 120.25 E
Launois-sur-Vence 56 49.39 N 4.32 E
Launsdorf 61 46.46 N 14.27 E
Laupen 58 46.54 N 7.14 E
Laupendahl ◆[8] 263 51.21 N 6.56 E
Laupheim 58 48.14 N 9.52 E
Laur 116 15.35 N 121.11 E
Laura, Austl. 164 15.34 S 144.28 E
Laura, Oh., U.S. 218 39.59 N 84.24 W
La Urbana 246 7.08 N 66.56 W
Laureana di Borrello 68 38.30 N 16.05 E
Laurel, De., U.S. 208 38.33 N 75.34 W
Laurel, Fl., U.S. 220 27.07 N 82.27 W
Laurel, In., U.S. 218 39.30 N 85.11 W
Laurel, Md., U.S. 208 39.05 N 76.50 W
Laurel, Ms., U.S. 194 31.41 N 89.07 W
Laurel, Mt., U.S. 202 45.40 N 108.46 W
Laurel, Ne., U.S. 198 42.25 N 97.05 W
Laurel, Va., U.S. 208 37.38 N 77.30 W
Laurel, Wa., U.S. 224 45.57 N 121.23 W
Laurel ≃ 192 36.57 N 84.18 W
Laurel, Mount ʌ[2] 285 39.56 N 74.53 W
Laurel Bay 192 32.33 N 80.44 W
Laureldale, N.J., U.S. 208 39.29 N 74.41 W
Laureldale, Pa., U.S. 208 40.23 N 75.55 W
Laureles 252 31.22 S 55.51 W
Laureles, Isla de los I 258 33.45 S 59.23 W
Laurel Gardens 279b 40.31 N 80.01 W
Laurel Hill, Austl. 171b 35.37 S 148.05 E
Laurel Hill, N.C., U.S. 192 34.48 N 79.32 W
Laurel Hill ʌ 214 40.15 N 79.05 W
Laurel Hollow 276 40.52 N 73.28 W
Laurel Reservoir ⊜[1] 276 41.10 N 73.33 W

Laurel Ridge State Park ♠ 188 39.58 N 79.23 W
Laurel River Lake ⊜[1] 192 36.55 N 84.15 W
Laurel Run 210 41.13 N 75.51 W
Laurel Run ≃ 208 40.20 N 77.20 W
Laurel Springs 285 39.49 N 75.00 W
Laurelton 210 40.52 N 77.11 W
Laurelville, Oh., U.S. 188 39.28 N 82.44 W
Laurelville, Pa., U.S. 214 40.09 N 79.29 W
Laurenburg 56 50.20 N 7.54 E
Laurence Harbor 276 40.27 N 74.14 W
Laurencekirk 46 56.50 N 2.29 W
Laurens, Ia., U.S. 198 42.50 N 94.51 W
Laurens, N.Y., U.S. 210 42.32 N 75.06 W
Laurens, S.C., U.S. 192 34.29 N 82.00 W
Laurentides 206 45.51 N 73.46 W
Laurentides, Les ⛰[1] 176 48.00 N 71.00 W
Laurentides, Parc Provincial des ♠ 186 47.40 N 71.30 W
Laurenzana 68 40.28 N 15.58 E
Lauria 68 40.02 N 15.50 E
Lau Ridge ✣[3] 14 21.00 S 178.30 W
Laurie Island I 9 60.45 S 44.35 W
Laurie Lake ⊜ 184 56.34 N 101.54 W
Laurier, Mb., Can. 184 50.54 N 99.33 W
Laurier, P.Q., Can. 206 46.32 N 71.38 W
Laurière 32 46.05 N 1.28 E
Laurierville 206 46.18 N 71.39 W
Laurinburg 192 34.46 N 79.27 W
Laurino 68 40.20 N 15.20 E
Laurito 68 40.10 N 15.24 E
Lauritsala 26 61.04 N 28.16 E
Lauritzen Bay ⊂ 9 69.05 S 156.50 E
Laurium 190 47.14 N 88.26 W
Lauriya Nandangarh 124 26.59 N 84.24 E
Lauro, Monte ʌ 70 37.07 N 14.49 E
Laurys Station 208 40.43 N 75.32 W
Lausanne 58 46.31 N 6.38 E
Lauscha 54 50.28 N 11.10 E
Laut 86 59.18 N 66.02 E
Laut, Pulau I, Indon. 112 3.40 S 116.10 E
Laut, Pulau I, Indon. 112 4.43 N 107.59 E
Laut, Selat ⊔ 112 3.25 S 116.03 E
Lauta 54 51.27 N 14.04 E
Lautaro 252 38.31 S 72.27 W
Lautaro, Volcán ʌ[1] 254 49.00 S 73.32 W
Lautem 112 8.22 S 126.54 E
Lautenbach 58 47.57 N 7.09 E
Lautenthal 52 51.52 N 10.17 E
Lauter ≃, Dtsch. 56 49.39 N 7.35 E
Lauter ≃, Europe 56 48.58 N 8.11 E
Lauterach 58 47.29 N 9.44 E
Lauterbach, Dtsch. 56 50.38 N 9.24 E
Lauterbach, Dtsch. 58 48.14 N 8.20 E
Lauterbourg 56 48.59 N 8.11 E
Lauterbrunnen 58 46.36 N 7.55 E
Lauterecken 56 49.39 N 7.35 E
Lauterhofen 60 49.22 N 11.37 E
Lauter [Sachsen] 54 50.33 N 12.44 E
Laut Kecil, Kepulauan II 112 4.50 S 115.45 E
Lautoka 175g 17.37 S 177.27 E
Lauttakylä → Huittinen 26 61.11 N 22.42 E
Laut Tawar, Danau ⊜ 114 4.38 N 96.54 E
Lauwe 50 50.48 N 3.11 E
Lauwerszee ⊂ 52 53.20 N 6.12 E
Lauzerte 32 44.15 N 1.08 E
Lauzon 206 46.50 N 71.10 W
Lauzun 32 44.38 N 0.28 E
Lava (Łyna) ≃ 76 54.37 N 21.14 E
Lava, Nosy I 157b 14.33 S 47.36 E
Lava Beds National Monument ♠ 204 41.42 N 121.30 W
Lavaca □[6] 222 29.22 N 96.55 W
Lavaca ≃ 196 28.50 N 96.36 W
Lavaca Bay ⊂ 196 28.35 N 96.35 W
La Vacherie 62 44.53 N 5.11 E
Lavagh More ʌ 48 54.45 N 8.05 W
Lavagna 62 44.18 N 9.20 E
Lavagna ≃ 62 44.21 N 9.20 E
Lava Hot Springs 202 42.37 N 112.00 W
Lavaisse 252 33.49 S 65.25 W
Laval, P.Q., Can. 206 45.35 N 73.45 W
Laval, Fr. 32 48.04 N 0.46 W
Laval-des-Rapides ◆[8] 275a 45.33 N 73.42 W
La Valette-du-Var 62 43.08 N 5.59 E
La Valette → Valletta 36 35.54 N 14.31 E
La Vall d'Uixo 34 39.49 N 0.14 W
Lavalle, Arg. 252 29.01 S 59.11 W
Lavalle, Arg. 252 28.12 S 65.08 W
Lavalleja → Minas 252 34.23 S 55.14 W
Lavallette 208 39.58 N 74.04 W
La Valley 200 37.06 N 105.20 W
Laval-Ouest ◆[8] 275a 45.33 N 73.52 W
Lavaltrie 206 45.53 N 73.17 W
Lavamünd 61 46.39 N 14.56 E
Lāvān, Jazīreh-ye I 128 26.48 N 53.15 E
Lavan, Naḥal V 132 30.57 N 34.21 E
Lavanono 157b 25.24 S 44.55 E
Lavant ≃ 61 46.38 N 14.57 E
Lavapié, Punta ➤ 252 37.09 S 73.35 W
Lávara 38 41.16 N 26.22 E
Lavaraty 157b 23.16 S 46.59 E
Lavardac 32 44.11 N 0.18 E
Lavarone 64 45.56 N 11.15 E
Lavassaare 76 58.31 N 24.22 E
Lava-Tudo ≃ 252 28.26 S 50.25 W
Laveaga Peak ʌ 226 36.53 N 121.11 W
La Vecilla de Curueño 34 42.51 N 5.24 W
La Vega 238 19.13 N 70.31 W
La Vega ◆[8] 286c 10.28 N 66.57 W
Lavela 24 63.38 N 45.31 E
La Vela, Cabo de ➤ 246 12.15 N 72.11 W
La Vela de Coro 246 11.27 N 69.34 W
Lavelanet 32 42.56 N 1.51 E
Lavelle 208 40.46 N 76.22 W
Lavello 68 41.03 N 15.48 E
Laven 41 56.07 N 9.43 E
La Venada 196 25.50 N 97.30 W
Lavendon 42 52.11 N 0.40 W
Lavenham 42 52.06 N 0.47 E
Laveno 58 45.55 N 8.37 E
Lavenone 64 45.44 N 10.26 E
La Venta ≃ 234 16.59 N 93.46 W
La Venta ⊥ 234 18.08 N 94.03 W
Laventie 50 50.38 N 2.46 E
La Ventura 232 24.38 N 100.54 W
Laver ≃ 44 54.08 N 1.30 W
Lavéra 62 43.23 N 5.02 E
La Vera ◆[1] 34 40.20 N 5.30 W
La Verde, Arg. 252 27.08 S 59.23 W
La Verde, Arg. 258 34.44 S 59.16 W
Laverdière, Lac ⊜ 206 46.50 N 74.28 W
L'Averdy, Cape ➤ 175e 5.33 S 155.04 E
La Vérendrye, Réserve ♠ 190 47.30 N 77.30 W
La Vergne 194 36.00 N 86.34 W
La Verna ♜[1] 66 43.42 N 11.54 E
La Verne, Ca., U.S. 280 34.06 N 117.46 W
Laverne, Ok., U.S. 196 36.42 N 99.53 W
La Vernia 196 29.21 N 98.07 W
Laverock 285 40.05 N 75.11 W
La Verpillière 62 45.38 N 5.09 E
La Verrière 261 48.45 N 1.57 E
Lavers Hill 169 38.40 S 143.24 E
Laverton, Austl. 162 28.38 S 122.25 E
Laverton, Austl. 169 37.52 S 144.45 E
Laverton Royal Australian Air Force Base ■ 169 37.52 S 144.43 E
La Veta 200 37.30 N 105.00 W
Lavezares 116 12.32 N 124.20 E
Lavezzi, Îles II 71 41.20 N 9.15 E
Lavezzola 66 44.34 N 11.52 E
Lavia 26 61.36 N 22.36 E

Laviano 68 40.47 N 15.18 E
Lavic Lake ⊜ 204 34.40 N 116.21 W
La Victoria, Perú 286d 12.04 S 77.02 W
La Victoria, Ven. 246 10.14 N 67.20 W
Lavieille, Lake ⊜ 190 45.51 N 78.14 W
Lavik 26 61.06 N 5.30 E
La Vila Joiosa 34 38.30 N 0.14 W
La Villa 64 46.36 N 11.54 E
La Villa ≃ 236 7.59 N 80.23 W
La Ville-du-Bois 261 48.40 N 2.16 E
La Villeneuve-Saint-Martin 261 49.04 N 1.58 E
Lavillette 186 47.16 N 65.18 W
Lavin 58 46.46 N 10.06 E
La Viña, Arg. 252 25.27 S 65.35 W
Lavina, Mt., U.S. 202 46.17 N 108.56 W
Lavinio Lido di Enea 66 41.30 N 12.05 E
Laviolette, Lac ⊜ 206 46.51 N 73.58 W
La Virginia 246 4.54 N 75.53 W
Lavis 64 46.08 N 11.07 E
La Vista 198 41.11 N 96.01 W
Lavon 222 33.02 N 96.26 W
Lavonia 192 34.26 N 83.06 W
Lavon Lake ⊜[1] 222 33.05 N 96.28 W
Lavougba 152 5.46 N 23.21 E
La Voulte-sur-Rhône 62 44.48 N 4.47 E
Lavoûte-sur-Loire 62 45.07 N 3.54 E
Lavoutte, Anse ⊂ 241f 14.06 N 60.56 W
Lavradia 266c 38.40 N 9.03 W
Lavras 256 21.14 S 45.00 W
Lavras ≃ 287a 23.00 S 43.33 W
Lavras da Mangabeira 250 6.45 S 38.57 W
Lavras do Sul 252 30.49 S 53.55 W
Lavrentija 180 65.35 N 171.00 W
Lavrentija, zaliv ⊂ 180 65.40 N 171.15 W
Lavrinhas 256 22.35 S 44.54 W
Lávrion 38 37.44 N 24.04 E
Lavumisa 158 27.19 S 31.54 E
Lavushi Manda National Park ♠ 154 12.20 S 30.50 E
Lawa 116 6.12 N 125.41 E
Lawai 229b 21.55 N 159.30 W
Lawang 115a 7.49 S 112.42 E
La Wantzenau 58 48.40 N 7.50 E
La Ward 222 28.51 N 96.28 W
Lawas 112 4.51 N 115.24 E
Lawatu 112 2.53 S 120.18 E
Lawdar 144 13.53 N 45.52 E
Lawele 112 5.13 S 122.57 E
Lawers, Ben ʌ 46 56.34 N 4.13 W
Laweueng 114 5.31 N 95.52 E
Lawford Lake ⊜ 184 54.30 N 96.43 W
Lawgi 166 24.34 S 150.39 E
Lawin 114 5.18 N 101.04 E
Lawin, Pulau I 164 1.31 S 128.44 E
Lawit, Gunong ʌ 114 5.25 N 102.35 E
Lawksawk 110 21.15 N 96.52 E
Lawler 190 43.04 N 92.09 W
Lawlor, Mount ʌ 280 34.16 N 118.06 W
Lawn, Nf., Can. 186 46.57 N 55.32 W
Lawn, Pa., U.S. 208 40.13 N 76.32 W
Lawn, Tx., U.S. 196 32.08 N 99.49 W
Lawn Bay ⊂ 186 46.53 N 55.35 W
Lawndale, Ca., U.S. 228 33.53 N 118.21 W
Lawndale, Il., U.S. 219 40.13 N 89.17 W
Lawndale, N.C., U.S. 192 35.24 N 81.33 W
Lawndale ◆[8], Il., U.S. 278 41.51 N 87.43 W
Lawndale ◆[8], Pa., U.S. 285 40.03 N 75.05 W
Lawnes Creek ≃ 208 37.08 N 76.40 W
Lawn Hill 166 18.35 S 138.35 E
Lawn Hill Creek ≃ 166 18.03 S 139.09 E
Lawn Hill National Park ♠ 166 18.45 S 138.27 E
Lawnside 285 39.51 N 75.01 W
Lawowa 112 4.26 S 122.56 E
Lawqah 128 29.49 N 42.45 E
Lawra 150 10.39 N 2.52 W
Lawrence, N.Z. 172 45.55 S 169.41 E
Lawrence, In., U.S. 218 39.50 N 86.01 W
Lawrence, Ks., U.S. 198 38.58 N 95.14 W
Lawrence, Ma., U.S. 207 42.42 N 71.09 W
Lawrence, Mi., U.S. 216 42.13 N 86.03 W
Lawrence, Ne., U.S. 198 40.17 N 98.15 W
Lawrence, N.Y., U.S. 276 40.36 N 73.43 W
Lawrence, Pa., U.S. 279b 40.18 N 80.09 W
Lawrence, Tx., U.S. 222 32.45 N 96.21 W
Lawrence □[6], In., U.S. 218 38.52 N 86.29 W
Lawrence □[6], Pa., U.S. 214 41.00 N 80.20 W
Lawrence, Lake ⊜ 224 46.51 N 122.34 W
Lawrence Brook ≃ 276 40.29 N 74.24 W
Lawrenceburg, In., U.S. 218 39.05 N 84.51 W
Lawrenceburg, Ky., U.S. 218 38.02 N 84.54 W
Lawrenceburg, Tn., U.S. 194 35.14 N 87.20 W
Lawrence Fork ≃ 198 41.36 N 103.14 W
Lawrence Institute of Technology ♜[2] 281 42.28 N 83.15 W
Lawrence Marsh ≣ 276 40.36 N 73.42 W
Lawrence Municipal Airport ⊠ 283 42.43 N 71.07 W
Lawrence Park 214 42.09 N 80.01 W
Lawrencepur 123 33.50 N 72.30 E
Lawrenceville, Il., U.S. 194 38.43 N 87.40 W
Lawrenceville, N.J., U.S. 208 40.17 N 74.43 W
Lawrenceville, Pa., U.S. 210 42.00 N 77.08 W
Lawrenceville, Va., U.S. 192 36.45 N 77.50 W
Lawrenceville ◆[8] 279b 40.28 N 79.57 W
Lawson, Austl. 170 33.43 S 150.26 E
Lawson, Mo., U.S. 194 39.26 N 94.12 W
Lawson Heights 214 40.18 N 79.23 W
Lawsonia 208 37.58 N 75.50 W
Lawsons Creek ≃ 170 32.35 S 149.43 E
Lawtey 192 30.02 N 82.04 W
Lawton, Ky., U.S. 218 38.16 N 83.13 W
Lawton, Mi., U.S. 216 42.10 N 85.50 W
Lawton, N.D., U.S. 198 48.18 N 98.22 W
Lawton, Ok., U.S. 196 34.36 N 98.23 W
Lawton ◆[8] 286b 23.06 N 82.21 W
Lawu, Gunung ʌ 115a 7.38 S 111.11 E
Lawyer Creek ≃ 202 46.14 N 116.01 W
Lawyersville 210 42.42 N 74.30 W
Lawz, Jabal al- ʌ 128 28.40 N 35.18 E
Laxå 40 58.59 N 14.37 E
Laxay 46 58.09 N 6.35 W
Laxenburg 264b 48.04 N 16.21 E
Laxenburger Park ♠ 264b 48.04 N 16.22 E
Laxey 44 54.14 N 4.23 W
Laxford, Loch ⊂ 46 58.23 N 5.06 W
Lax Kw'alaams 182 54.33 N 130.25 W
Laxou 58 48.41 N 6.09 E
Layang Layang 114 1.49 N 103.29 E
Laye ≃ 62 43.54 N 5.48 E
La Yesca 234 21.19 N 104.02 W
Layhill 208 39.05 N 77.03 W
Laylā 144 22.17 N 46.45 E
Lay Lake ⊜[1] 194 33.10 N 86.35 W
Layou 241h 13.12 N 61.17 W
Layou ≃ 240d 15.23 N 61.26 W
La'youn □[4] 148 27.55 N 12.15 W
Lay-Saint-Christophe 56 48.45 N 6.12 E
Laysan Island I 14 25.50 N 171.50 W
Layton, N.J., U.S. 210 41.13 N 74.50 W
Layton, Ut,. U.S. 200 41.03 N 111.58 W
Laytons Lake ⊜ 285 39.42 N 75.26 W
Laytonville 204 39.41 N 123.28 W
Laytown 48 53.40 N 6.14 W
Laž 80 57.11 N 49.14 E
La Zarca 232 25.50 N 104.44 W
Lazarev 89 52.13 N 141.32 E

Lazarevo 80 56.49 N 50.15 E
Lazarevskoje 84 43.55 N 39.20 E
Lazarivo 157b 23.54 S 44.59 E
Lazaro Cárdenas, Méx. 196 25.23 N 103.10 W
Lázaro Cárdenas, Méx. 232 30.33 N 115.56 W
Lázaro Cárdenas, Méx. 234 17.57 N 102.12 W
Lázaro Cárdenas, Presa ⊜[1] 232 25.35 N 105.02 W
Lazdijai 76 54.14 N 23.31 E
Lazha 102 26.26 N 101.50 E
Lazhulong 120 35.08 N 81.33 E
Lazi 116 9.08 N 123.38 E
Lazio □[4] 66 42.00 N 12.30 E
Lazise 64 45.30 N 10.44 E
Lazo 89 43.25 N 133.55 E
Lazorki 78 50.06 N 32.39 E
La Zorra, Quebrada ≃ 286c 10.36 N 67.03 W
Lazovskij zapovednik ♠ 89 43.00 N 133.55 E
Lazzaro 68 37.58 N 15.40 E
Lazzate 266b 45.40 N 9.05 E
Lea ≃ 42 51.30 N 0.01 E
Léach 110 12.21 N 103.46 E
Leach ≃ 42 51.41 N 1.39 W
Leach Pond ⊜ 283 42.04 N 71.09 W
Leachville 194 35.56 N 90.15 W
Leacock 208 40.05 N 76.12 W
Lead 198 44.21 N 103.45 W
Leadbetter Point ➤ 224 46.38 N 124.03 W
Leadburn 46 55.47 N 3.14 W
Leadenham 44 53.05 N 0.34 W
Leaden Roding 260 51.48 N 0.19 E
Leader 184 50.53 N 109.31 W
Leader Water ≃ 46 55.36 N 2.41 W
Leadgate 44 54.52 N 1.48 W
Lead Hill ʌ[2] 194 37.06 N 92.38 W
Leadhills 44 55.25 N 3.47 W
Leadon ≃ 42 51.53 N 2.16 W
Leadore 202 44.40 N 113.21 W
Leadville 200 39.15 N 106.17 W
Leaf ≃, Mn., U.S. 198 46.29 N 94.53 W
Leaf ≃, Ms., U.S. 194 31.00 N 88.45 W
Leaf Lake ⊜ 184 53.02 N 102.07 W
Leaghur, Lake ⊜ 166 33.35 S 143.04 E
League ʌ 48 54.39 N 8.44 W
League City 222 29.30 N 95.05 W
Leakesville 194 31.09 N 88.33 W
Leakey 196 29.43 N 99.45 W
Leakin Park ♠ 284b 39.18 N 76.42 W
Leak Run ≃ 279b 40.27 N 79.47 W
Leaksville 192 36.29 N 79.53 W
Lealman 220 27.49 N 82.40 W
Lealui 152 15.10 S 23.02 E
Leam ≃ 42 52.17 N 1.14 W
Leamington 214 42.03 N 82.36 W
Leamington Spa → Royal Leamington Spa 42 52.18 N 1.31 W
Le'an 100 27.24 N 115.48 E
Leán ≃ 236 15.47 N 87.20 W
Leander Point ➤ 162 29.16 S 114.56 E
Leandro 250 5.59 S 44.55 W
Leandro N. Alem 252 27.36 S 55.19 W
Leane, Lough ⊜ 48 52.05 N 9.35 W
Leannan ≃ 48 55.02 N 7.38 W
Leano, Monte ʌ 66 41.20 N 13.13 E
Learmonth 162 22.15 S 114.05 E
Leary 192 31.29 N 84.30 W
Leaside □[8] 275b 43.42 N 79.22 W
Leask 184 53.00 N 106.45 W
Leatherhead 42 51.18 N 0.20 W
Leatherman Peak ʌ 202 44.05 N 113.44 W
Leatherwood Creek ≃ 218 38.49 N 86.30 W
Lea Town 262 53.46 N 2.48 W
Leavenworth, Ks., U.S. 198 39.18 N 94.55 W
Leavenworth, Wa., U.S. 224 47.35 N 120.39 W
Leavesden Aerodrome ⊠ 260 51.42 N 0.27 W
Leavittsburg 214 41.14 N 80.52 W
Leawood 194 37.03 N 94.31 W
Łeba 30 54.47 N 17.33 E
Łeba ≃ 30 54.47 N 17.33 E
Lebach 56 49.24 N 6.54 E
Lebak 116 6.32 N 124.03 E
Lebam 224 46.33 N 123.32 W
Lébamba 152 2.12 S 11.30 E
Lebango 152 0.22 N 14.49 E
Lebanon, Ct., U.S. 207 41.38 N 72.13 W
Lebanon, Il., U.S. 219 38.36 N 89.48 W
Lebanon, In., U.S. 218 40.02 N 86.28 W
Lebanon, Ks., U.S. 198 39.48 N 98.33 W
Lebanon, Ky., U.S. 194 37.34 N 85.15 W
Lebanon, Mo., U.S. 194 37.40 N 92.39 W
Lebanon, N.H., U.S. 188 43.38 N 72.15 W
Lebanon, N.J., U.S. 210 40.38 N 74.50 W
Lebanon, N.Y., U.S. 210 42.47 N 75.39 W
Lebanon, Oh., U.S. 218 39.26 N 84.12 W
Lebanon, Or., U.S. 202 44.32 N 122.54 W
Lebanon, Pa., U.S. 208 40.20 N 76.24 W
Lebanon, S.D., U.S. 198 45.04 N 99.46 W
Lebanon, Tn., U.S. 194 36.12 N 86.17 W
Lebanon, Va., U.S. 192 36.54 N 82.04 W
Lebanon □[6] 208 40.20 N 76.25 W
Lebanon (Lubnān) □[1], Asia 118 34.00 N 36.00 E
Lebanon (Lubnān) □[1], Asia 128 34.00 N 36.00 E
Lebanon Junction 194 37.50 N 85.43 W
Lebanon Mountains → Lubnān, Jabal ⛰ 132 34.00 N 36.00 E
Lebanon Springs 210 42.29 N 73.23 W
Le Ban-Saint-Martin 56 49.07 N 6.09 E
Le Bar-sur-le-Loup 62 43.42 N 6.59 E
Leb'ažje, Kaz. 86 51.28 N 77.46 E
Leb'ažje, Ross. 80 57.25 N 49.32 E
Leb'ažje, Ross. 86 55.16 N 66.29 E
Lebbeke 50 51.00 N 4.08 E
Le Béage 62 44.51 N 4.07 E
Le Beausset 62 43.12 N 5.48 E
Lebec 228 34.50 N 118.51 W
Lebed'an' 76 53.01 N 39.09 E
Lebedevka, Kaz. 86 50.09 N 54.07 E
Lebedevka, Ross. 80 51.06 N 47.09 E
Lebedevka, Ross. 86 56.48 N 66.57 E
Lebedi 78 51.17 N 37.38 E
Lebedin, Ukr. 78 48.59 N 31.31 E
Lebedin, Ukr. 78 50.36 N 34.30 E
Lebedino 80 55.14 N 49.50 E
Leben, Oued el V 148 34.37 N 10.01 E
Lebesby 24 70.34 N 26.59 E
Le Bessat 62 45.22 N 4.31 E
Le Bihan Falls ∟ 158 29.51 S 28.03 E
Le Biot 58 46.16 N 6.38 E
Lebir ≃ 114 5.33 N 102.12 E
Le Blanc 32 46.38 N 1.04 E
Le Blanc-Mesnil 261 48.56 N 2.28 E
Le Bleymard 62 44.29 N 3.44 E
Leblon ◆[8] 287a 22.59 S 43.13 W
Lebo, Ks., U.S. 198 38.25 N 95.51 W
Lebo, Zaïre 152 4.29 N 23.57 E
Le Bois-de-Cise 50 50.05 N 1.26 E
Le Bois-Dieu 261 48.39 N 1.43 E
Le Bois-d'Oingt 58 45.55 N 4.35 E
Lebombo Mountains ⛰[2] 156 25.15 S 32.00 E
Lebongtandai 112 3.01 S 101.54 E
Le Boréon 62 44.07 N 7.17 E
Lębork 30 54.33 N 17.44 E
Le Boulay 261 48.47 N 1.40 E
Le Bourg-d'Oisans 62 45.03 N 6.02 E
Le Bourget 261 48.56 N 2.26 E
Le Bourget-du-Lac 62 45.39 N 5.52 E
Le Brassus 58 46.35 N 6.13 E

Symbol	English	Deutsch	Español	Français	Português
≃	River	Fluß	Río	Rivière	Rio
≅	Canal	Kanal	Canal	Canal	Canal
∟	Waterfall, Rapids	Wasserfall, Stromschnellen	Cascada, Rápidos	Chute d'eau, Rapides	Cascata, Rápidos
⊔	Strait	Meeresstraße	Estrecho	Détroit	Estreito
⊂	Bay, Gulf	Bucht, Golf	Bahía, Golfo	Baie, Golfe	Baía, Golfo
⊜	Lake, Lakes	See, Seen	Lago, Lagos	Lac, Lacs	Lago, Lagos
≣	Swamp	Sumpf	Pantano	Marais	Pântano
⍓	Ice Features, Glacier	Eis- und Gletscherformen	Accidentes Glaciales	Formes glaciaires	Acidentes glaciares
⊤	Other Hydrographic Features	Andere Hydrographische Objekte	Otros Elementos Hidrográficos	Autres données hydrographiques	Outros acidentes hidrográficos

Symbol	English	Deutsch	Español	Français	Português
✣	Submarine Features	Untermeerische Objekte	Accidentes Submarinos	Formes de relief sous-marin	Acidentes submarinos
□	Political Unit	Politische Einheit	Unidad Política	Entité politique	Unidade política
♜	Cultural Institution	Kulturelle Institution	Institución Cultural	Institution culturelle	Institução cultural
⊥	Historical Site	Historische Stätte	Sitio Histórico	Site historique	Sitio histórico
♠	Recreational Site	Erholungs- und Ferienort	Sitio de Recreo	Centre de loisirs	Area de Lazer
⊠	Airport	Flughafen	Aeropuerto	Aéroport	Aeroporto
■	Military Installation	Militäranlage	Instalación Militar	Installation militaire	Instalação militar
◆	Miscellaneous	Verschiedenes	Misceláneo	Divers	Diversos

ENGLISH / DEUTSCH

Name	Page / Seite	Lat.°′ / Breite°′	Long.°′ / Länge°′ E = Ost
Lebrija	34	36.55 N	6.04 W
Lebrija ≃	246	8.08 N	73.47 W
Le Broc	62	43.49 N	7.10 E
Le Brugeron	62	45.43 N	3.43 E
Łebsko, Jezioro c	30	54.44 N	17.24 E
Lebu	252	37.37 S	73.39 W
Le Bugue	32	44.55 N	0.56 E
Le Buisson de Massoury ⩩	261	48.30 N	2.43 E
Lebus	54	52.25 N	14.32 E
Le Caire → Al-Qāhirah	142	30.03 N	31.15 E
Le Camp-du-Castellet	62	43.15 N	5.45 E
Le Cannet	62	43.34 N	7.01 E
Lecanto	220	28.51 N	82.29 W
Le Cap → Cape Town	158	33.55 S	18.22 E
Le Cap → Cap-Haïtien	238	19.45 N	72.12 W
Le Carbet	240e	14.43 N	61.11 W
Le Cateau	50	50.06 N	3.33 E
Le Catelet	50	50.00 N	3.15 E
Lecce	68	40.23 N	18.11 E
Lecce □[4]	68	40.13 N	18.10 E
Lecce, Tavoliere di ≚	68	40.30 N	17.35 E
Lecce nei Marsi	66	41.56 N	13.41 E
Lečchumskij chrebet ⋏	84	42.45 N	43.05 E
Lecco	62	45.51 N	9.23 E
Lecco, Lago di ⊜	58	45.55 N	9.19 E
Le Center	190	44.23 N	93.43 W
Lech	58	47.12 N	10.09 E
Lech ≃	30	48.44 N	10.56 E
Le Châble, Fr.	58	46.06 N	6.06 E
Le Châble, Schw.	58	46.05 N	7.12 E
L'Échalp	62	44.45 N	7.00 E
Le Chambon-Feugerolles	62	45.24 N	4.19 E
Le Chambon-sur-Lignon	62	45.03 N	4.18 E
Le Champ-Renault	261	49.06 N	2.31 E
Lechang	100	25.09 N	113.21 E
Le Chasseral ∧	58	47.08 N	7.03 E
Le-Château-d'Oléron	32	45.53 N	1.11 W
Le Châtelard, Fr.	62	45.41 N	6.08 E
Le Châtelard, Schw.	58	46.04 N	6.58 E
Le Châtelet	32	46.39 N	2.17 E
Le Châtelet-en-Brie	50	48.30 N	2.48 E
Lechbruck	58	47.42 N	10.47 E
Leche, Laguna de la c	240p	22.13 N	78.38 W
Le Chêne-Rogneux	261	48.46 N	1.46 E
Le Chesnay	261	48.50 N	2.07 E
Le Chesne	56	49.31 N	4.46 E
Le Cheylard	62	44.54 N	4.25 E
Lechfeld ≚	58	48.10 N	10.50 E
Lechiguanas, Islas de las II	252	33.26 S	59.42 W
Lechlade	42	51.43 N	1.41 W
Lechleiten	58	47.16 N	10.12 E
Lechta	24	60.49 N	48.28 E
Lechtaler Alpen ⋏	64	47.15 N	10.30 E
Lechuga, Arroyo ≃	286b	23.01 N	82.16 W
Lechuguilla, Cerro ∧	234	22.19 N	104.15 W
Lecinone, Monte ∧	267a	41.59 N	12.48 E
Leck	41	54.46 N	8.58 E
Le Claire	190	41.36 N	90.21 W
Lecompte	194	31.05 N	92.24 W
Leconfield	44	53.52 N	0.27 W
Léconi	152	1.35 S	14.14 E
Lecontes Mills	214	41.05 N	78.17 W
Le Cornate ∧	66	43.10 N	10.57 E
Le Coudray-Montceaux	261	48.34 N	2.31 E
Le Coudray-Saint-Germer	50	49.25 N	1.50 E
Le Creusot	58	46.48 N	4.26 E
Le Croci di Acerno)(	68	40.47 N	15.02 E
Le Croisic	32	47.18 N	2.31 W
Le Crotoy	50	50.13 N	1.37 E
Łęczna	30	51.19 N	22.52 E
Łęczyca	30	52.04 N	19.13 E
Leda ≃	52	53.12 N	7.26 E
Ledaig	46	56.30 N	5.23 W
Led'anaja, gora ∧	74	61.53 N	171.09 E
Ledang, Gunong ∧	114	2.22 N	102.37 E
Ledava ≃	61	46.29 N	16.35 E
Ledbetter	222	30.09 N	96.48 W
Ledbury	42	52.02 N	2.25 W
Lede	50	50.58 N	3.58 E
Ledenice	61	48.57 N	14.37 E
Lederach	285	40.16 N	75.24 W
Le Deschaux	58	46.57 N	5.30 E
Ledesma	34	41.05 N	6.00 W
Ledgewood	276	40.52 N	74.39 W
Ledi, Ben ∧	46	56.15 N	4.19 W
Le Diamant	240e	14.29 N	61.02 W
Lediba	152	3.03 S	16.32 E
Lédignan	62	43.59 N	4.06 E
Ledkovo	24	67.14 N	50.30 E
Lednice	61	48.48 N	16.48 E
Ledo, India	120	27.18 N	95.44 E
Ledo, Indon.	112	1.02 N	109.36 E
Lêdo, Cabo ≻	152	9.41 S	13.12 E
Ledong	110	18.45 N	109.12 E
Le Donjon	32	46.21 N	3.48 E
Le Dorat	32	46.13 N	1.05 E
Le Doré, Lac ⊜	186	51.17 N	61.23 W
Ledra ≃	64	46.13 N	13.02 E
Ledsham	262	53.16 N	2.58 W
Ledu	102	36.32 N	102.25 E
Leduc	182	53.16 N	113.33 W
Ledung	114	2.45 N	99.59 E
Ledyard Bay c	180	69.30 N	164.30 W
Lędyczek	30	53.33 N	16.58 E
Lee, Il., U.S.	216	41.48 N	88.56 W
Lee, Ma., U.S.	207	42.18 N	73.14 W
Lee □[6], Fl., U.S.	220	26.34 N	81.55 W
Lee □[6], Il., U.S.	216	41.50 N	89.29 W
Lee □[6], Tx., U.S.	222	30.20 N	96.55 W
Lee ≃	48	51.54 N	8.22 W
Lee Boulevard Heights	284c	38.52 N	77.09 W
Lee Center	210	43.18 N	75.31 W
Leechburg	214	40.37 N	79.36 W
Leechburg Airport ⊠	279b	40.37 N	79.34 W
Leech Lake ⊜, Sk., Can.	184	51.04 N	102.30 W
Leech Lake ⊜, Mn., U.S.	190	47.09 N	94.23 W
Leech Lake Indian Reservation ◆[4]	190	47.30 N	94.27 W
Leechtown	224	48.30 N	123.42 W
Leedey	196	35.52 N	99.20 W
Leedom Estates	285	39.41 N	75.35 W
Leeds, Eng., U.K.	44	53.50 N	1.35 W
Leeds, Al., U.S.	194	33.32 N	86.32 W
Leeds, N.Y., U.S.	210	42.15 N	73.54 W
Leeds, N.D., U.S.	198	48.17 N	99.26 W
Leeds and Bradford (Yeadon) Airport ⊠	44	53.52 N	1.38 W
Leeds and Grenville □[6]	212	44.45 N	75.50 W
Leeds and Liverpool Canal ≋	262	53.25 N	2.59 W
Leeds Point	208	39.29 N	74.25 W
Leedstown	42	50.10 N	5.22 W
Leegebruch	54	52.43 N	13.11 E
Leek, Ned.	52	53.09 N	6.24 E
Leek, Eng., U.K.	44	53.06 N	2.01 W
Leelanau, Lake ⊜	190	44.55 N	85.43 W
Leelanau Peninsula ≻[1]	190	45.10 N	85.35 W
Leeming	44	54.17 N	1.32 W
Leenaun	48	53.36 N	9.45 W
Leende	52	51.21 N	5.33 E
Lee-on-the-Solent	42	50.47 N	1.12 W
Lee Park	210	41.14 N	75.55 W
Leeper	214	41.22 N	79.18 W
Leer	52	53.14 N	7.26 E
Leerdam	52	51.54 N	5.05 E
Leerhafe	52	53.32 N	7.47 E
Leersum	52	52.01 N	5.26 E
Lees	262	53.32 N	2.04 W
Leesburg, Fl., U.S.	220	28.48 N	81.52 W
Leesburg, Ga., U.S.	192	31.43 N	84.10 W
Leesburg, In., U.S.	216	41.19 N	85.51 W
Leesburg, N.J., U.S.	208	39.15 N	74.59 W
Leesburg, Oh., U.S.	218	39.20 N	83.33 W
Leesburg, Tx., U.S.	222	32.59 N	95.05 W
Leesburg, Va., U.S.	208	39.06 N	77.33 W
Lees Creek ≃	218	39.21 N	83.29 W
Leese	52	52.30 N	9.06 E
Leesport	208	40.27 N	75.58 W
Lees Summit	194	38.55 N	94.23 W
Leeste	52	52.59 N	8.49 E
Leeston	172	43.46 S	172.18 E
Leesville, Il., U.S.	216	41.01 N	87.33 W
Leesville, In., U.S.	218	38.51 N	86.18 W
Leesville, La., U.S.	194	31.08 N	93.15 W
Leesville, Oh., U.S.	214	40.27 N	81.13 W
Leesville, S.C., U.S.	192	33.54 N	81.30 W
Leesville, Tx., U.S.	222	29.24 N	97.45 W
Leesville Lake ⊜[1], Oh., U.S.	214	40.30 N	81.10 W
Leesville Lake ⊜[1], Va., U.S.	192	37.05 N	79.25 W
Leeton	166	34.33 S	146.24 E
Leetonia	214	40.52 N	80.45 W
Leetsdale	214	40.33 N	80.12 W
Leeudoringstad	158	27.15 S	26.10 E
Leeu-Gamka	158	32.47 S	21.59 E
Leeupan ≚	273d	26.14 S	28.19 E
Leeuwarden	52	53.12 N	5.46 E
Leeuwin, Cape ≻	162	34.22 S	115.08 E
Lee Vining	226	37.57 N	119.07 W
Le Faouët	28	48.02 N	3.29 W
Le Fayet	58	45.55 N	6.42 E
Lefèvre, Pointe ≻	175f	20.54 S	167.01 E
Leffe	62	45.48 N	9.53 E
Lefferts, Lake ⊜	276	40.25 N	74.14 W
Léfini ≃	152	2.57 S	16.10 E
Léfini, Réserve de Chasse de la ◆[4]	152	2.58 S	15.25 E
Lefke	130	35.07 N	32.51 E
Le Focette	64	43.55 N	10.13 E
Leforest	50	50.26 N	3.04 E
Lefors	196	35.26 N	100.48 W
Le François	240e	14.37 N	60.54 W
Le Freney-d'Oisans	62	45.02 N	6.07 E
Lefroy	212	44.16 N	79.34 W
Lefroy, Lake ⊜	162	31.15 S	121.40 E
Leftrook Lake ⊜	184	56.05 N	98.36 W
Lega Hida	144	7.56 N	41.04 E
Legal	182	53.57 N	113.35 W
Leganés	34	40.19 N	3.45 W
Le Gardeur	206	45.45 N	73.28 W
Legaspi	116	13.08 N	123.44 E
Legau	58	47.51 N	10.07 E
Legden	52	52.02 N	7.07 E
Legendre ≃	206	45.44 N	71.08 W
Legendre Island I	162	20.23 S	116.54 E
Leggett, Ca., U.S.	204	39.51 N	123.42 W
Leggett, Tx., U.S.	222	30.49 N	94.52 W
Leghorn → Livorno	66	43.33 N	10.19 E
Legion Mine	154	21.23 S	28.33 E
Legion of Honor, Palace of the ✿	282	37.47 N	122.30 W
Legionowo	30	52.25 N	20.56 E
Legnago	64	45.11 N	11.18 E
Legnano	62	45.36 N	8.54 E
Legnica (Liegnitz)	30	51.13 N	16.09 E
Legnica □[4]	30	51.25 N	16.10 E
Le Gosier	241o	16.12 N	61.30 W
Le Grand	226	37.13 N	120.14 W
LeGrand, Cape ≻	162	34.01 S	122.06 E
Le Grand-Lucé	50	47.52 N	0.28 E
Le Grand-Quevilly	50	49.25 N	1.02 E
Le Grand-Serre	62	45.16 N	5.06 E
Le Grand Wintersberg ∧[2]	56	48.59 N	7.37 E
Le Grau-du-Roi	62	43.32 N	4.08 E
Le Gua	62	45.01 N	5.37 E
Le Guelta	34	36.22 N	0.50 E
Leguga	154	3.23 N	25.02 E
Legume	166	28.25 S	152.19 E
Legundi, Pulau I	115a	5.50 S	105.16 E
Leh	123	34.10 N	77.35 E
Le Havre	50	49.30 N	0.08 E
Lehčevo	38	43.32 N	23.32 E
Le Hérie-la-Viéville	50	49.49 N	3.38 E
Lehesten	54	50.29 N	11.28 E
Lehi	200	40.23 N	111.50 W
Lehigh, Ia., U.S.	190	42.21 N	94.03 W
Lehigh, Ok., U.S.	196	34.28 N	96.12 W
Lehigh □[6]	208	40.36 N	75.29 W
Lehigh ≃	210	40.41 N	75.12 W
Lehigh Acres	220	26.37 N	81.37 W
Lehighton	210	40.50 N	75.42 W
Lehinch	48	52.56 N	9.21 W
Lehnin	54	52.19 N	12.44 E
Lehnitz	54	52.44 N	13.15 E
Lehnitz See ⊜	264a	52.45 N	13.16 E
Leho	140	7.07 N	33.52 E
Le Hohwald	58	48.24 N	7.20 E
Le Houlme	50	49.31 N	1.02 E
Lehr	198	45.59 N	99.32 W
Lehra Gāga	123	29.55 N	75.49 E
Lehrbach	56	50.47 N	9.04 E
Lehrberg	56	49.21 N	10.30 E
Lehre	54	52.19 N	10.40 E
Lehrte	52	52.22 N	9.59 E
Lehstedt	52	52.14 N	10.12 E
Lehtimäki	26	62.47 N	23.55 E
Lehtrār Bāla	123	33.42 N	73.26 E
Lehtse	76	59.15 N	25.50 E
Lehua I	229b	22.01 N	160.06 W
Lehututu	156	23.58 S	21.51 E
Lei ≃	100	26.54 N	112.39 E
Leiah	123	30.58 N	70.56 E
Leião	266c	38.44 N	9.18 W
Leibnitz	61	46.47 N	15.32 E
Leibo	102	28.19 N	103.21 E
Leicester, Eng., U.K.	42	52.38 N	1.05 W
Leicester, Ma., U.S.	207	42.14 N	71.54 W
Leicester, N.Y., U.S.	210	42.46 N	77.53 W
Leicestershire □[6]	42	52.40 N	1.10 W
Leichhardt	274a	33.53 S	151.07 E
Leichhardt ≃	166	17.35 S	139.48 E
Leichhardt Falls ⌊	166	18.14 S	139.53 E
Leichhardt Range ⋏	166	20.40 S	147.25 E
Leichlingen	56	51.06 N	7.01 E
Leiden	52	52.09 N	4.30 E
Leiderdorp	52	52.09 N	4.32 E
Leidschendam	52	52.05 N	4.24 E
Leie (Lys) ≃	50	51.03 N	3.43 E
Leiferde	52	52.26 N	10.26 E
Leigh, N.Z.	172	36.17 S	174.49 E
Leigh, Eng., U.K.	44	53.30 N	2.33 W
Leigh, Eng., U.K.	260	51.12 N	0.13 E
Leigh ≃	169	38.06 S	144.03 E
Leigh Canal ≋	262	53.28 N	2.21 W
Leigh Creek	166	30.28 S	138.25 E
Leighlinbridge	48	52.44 N	6.59 W
Leigh-on-Sea	42	51.33 N	0.38 E
Leighton	194	34.42 N	87.31 W
Leighton Buzzard	42	51.55 N	0.40 W
Leikanger	26	61.10 N	6.52 E
Leiktho	110	19.13 N	96.35 E
Leimbach	54	51.36 N	11.28 E
Leimstruth	56	50.59 N	8.19 E
Lein ≃	56	48.54 N	10.01 E
Leinan	184	50.30 N	107.46 W
Leinburg	60	49.27 N	11.19 E
Leine ≃	52	52.43 N	9.36 E
Leinefelde	54	51.23 N	10.20 E
Leinfelden-Echterdingen	56	48.41 N	9.08 E
Leinster	162	27.51 S	120.36 E
Leinster □[9]	48	53.05 N	7.00 W
Leinster, Mount ∧	48	52.37 N	6.44 W
Leintwardine	42	52.23 N	2.51 W
Leipalingis	76	54.05 N	23.51 E
Leipheim	58	48.27 N	10.13 E
Leipoldtville	158	32.14 S	18.30 E
Leipsic, De., U.S.	208	39.14 N	75.31 W
Leipsic, In., U.S.	218	38.40 N	86.22 W
Leipsic, Oh., U.S.	216	41.05 N	83.59 W
Leipsic ≃	208	39.15 N	75.24 W
Leipzig	54	51.19 N	12.20 E
Leiria	34	39.45 N	8.48 W
Leirvik	26	59.45 N	5.30 E
Leisach	64	46.48 N	12.45 E
Leishendian	107	28.58 N	106.40 E
Leisi	76	58.34 N	22.39 E
Leisler, Mount ∧	162	23.28 S	129.17 E
Leisnig	54	51.09 N	12.56 E
Leiston	42	52.12 N	1.34 E
Leisure City	220	25.29 N	80.25 W
Leitariegos, Puerto de)(	34	43.00 N	6.25 W
Leitchfield	194	37.28 N	86.17 W
Leiters Ford	216	41.07 N	86.23 W
Leith	46	55.59 N	3.10 W
Leith, Water of ≃	46	55.59 N	3.11 W
Leitha (Lajta) ≃, Europe	61	47.54 N	17.17 E
Leitha ≃, Öst.	264b	48.00 N	16.35 E
Leithagebirge ⋏	61	47.52 N	16.35 E
Leithe ◆[8]	263	51.29 N	7.06 E
Leith Hill ∧[2]	42	51.11 N	0.23 W
Leitre	164	2.50 S	141.40 E
Leitrim	48	54.00 N	8.04 W
Leitrim □[6]	48	54.20 N	8.20 W
Leitzkau	54	52.03 N	11.57 E
Leixi	100	27.10 N	112.52 E
Leixlip	48	53.22 N	6.29 W
Leiyang	100	26.24 N	112.51 E
Lei Yue Mun ⊻	271d	22.16 N	114.14 E
Leizhou Bandao ≻[1]	102	21.15 N	110.09 E
Leizhuang	98	39.47 N	118.34 E
Lejasciems	76	57.17 N	26.35 E
Lek ≃	52	51.55 N	4.34 E
Lékana	152	2.19 S	14.36 E
Le Kef → El Kef	148	36.11 N	8.43 E
Lékéti ≃	152	1.36 S	14.57 E
Lekhainá	38	37.56 N	21.17 E
Lekir	114	4.07 N	100.44 E
Lekitobi	112	1.58 S	124.33 E
Lekkeroog	158	30.43 S	20.00 E
Lekkerwater	156	23.38 S	17.14 E
Lekma ≃	80	58.18 N	52.04 E
Łeknice	54	51.35 N	14.45 E
Lékoni ≃	152	1.11 S	13.16 E
Lekotero	152	0.46 S	23.51 E
Lékoumou □[5]	152	3.00 S	13.30 E
Le Kreïder	148	34.06 N	0.02 E
Le Kremlin-Bicêtre	261	48.49 N	2.21 E
Leksand	26	60.44 N	14.59 E
Leksberg	40	59.41 N	13.49 E
Leksozero, ozero ⊜	24	63.46 N	30.58 E
Leksvik	26	63.40 N	10.37 E
Lela	152	5.03 S	12.29 E
Le Lac-d'Issarlès	62	44.49 N	4.04 E
Le Lamentin	240e	14.37 N	61.01 W
Leland, Il., U.S.	216	41.37 N	88.48 W
Leland, Mi., U.S.	190	45.01 N	85.45 W
Leland, Ms., U.S.	194	33.24 N	90.53 W
Leland Grove	219	39.47 N	89.41 W
Leland Lake ⊜	224	47.53 N	122.53 W
Lelång ⊜	26	59.08 N	12.10 E
Lelant	42	50.11 N	5.26 W
Le Laus	62	44.31 N	6.09 E
Le Lauzet-Ubaye	62	44.26 N	6.26 E
Le Lavandou	62	43.08 N	6.22 E
Lel'čicy	78	51.47 N	28.19 E
Leleiwi Point ≻	229d	19.44 N	155.00 W
Leleque	254	42.23 S	71.03 W
Leles	115a	7.07 S	107.53 E
Lelewau	112	3.02 S	121.05 E
Lélex	58	46.18 N	5.57 E
Le Liège	50	47.13 N	1.06 E
Le Limbé	238	19.42 N	72.24 W
Leling	98	37.45 N	117.12 E
Lelingluang	164	7.09 S	131.43 E
Lelintah	164	2.03 S	130.16 E
Le Lion-d'Angers	32	47.38 N	0.43 W
Leli Shan ∧	120	33.26 N	81.42 E
Le Locle	58	47.03 N	6.45 E
Lelogama	112	9.44 S	123.57 E
Le Lorrain	240e	14.50 N	61.04 W
Le Luc	62	43.23 N	6.19 E
Le Lude	50	47.39 N	0.09 E
Lelydrop	250	5.42 N	55.16 W
Lelystad	52	52.31 N	5.27 E
Lema	150	12.57 N	4.14 E
Le Madonie ⋏	70	37.52 N	13.58 E
Lemahabang	115a	6.17 S	107.27 E
Le Maire, Estrecho de ⊻	254	54.50 S	65.00 W
Léman, Lac → Geneva, Lake ⊜	58	46.25 N	6.30 E
Lemankoa	175e	5.02 S	154.35 E
Le Mans	50	48.00 N	0.12 E
Le Marin	240e	14.28 N	60.53 W
Le Markstein	58	47.56 N	7.02 E
Le Mars	198	42.47 N	96.09 W
Lema Shilindi	144	4.55 N	42.02 E
Lemay	219	38.32 N	90.17 W
Lemay, Lac ⊜	186	50.35 N	68.25 W
Lembach	56	49.00 N	7.48 E
Lembach im Mühlkreis	60	48.29 N	13.53 E
Lemba-Gaba	273b	4.27 S	15.18 E
Lembak	112	0.52 N	117.32 E
Lembang	115a	6.49 S	107.36 E
Lembeck	52	51.45 N	7.00 E
Lembeek	50	50.43 N	4.13 E
Lembeh, Pulau I	112	1.26 N	125.13 E
Lembeni	154	3.47 S	37.37 E
Lemberg, Sk., Can.	184	50.44 N	103.13 W
Lemberg, Fr.	56	49.00 N	7.23 E
Lemberg ∧	58	48.09 N	8.45 E
Lemberg → L'vov	78	49.50 N	24.00 E
Lembruch	52	52.31 N	8.22 E
Lembu, Gunung ∧	114	4.12 N	97.24 E
Lemdiyya	148	36.12 N	2.50 E
Lemdiyya □[5]	148	35.50 N	3.00 E
Leme	255	22.12 S	47.24 W
Leme, Morro do ∧[2]	287a	22.58 S	43.10 W
Le Mée-sur-Seine	261	48.32 N	2.38 E
Lemei Rock ∧	224	46.01 N	121.46 W
Lemele	52	52.27 N	6.25 E
Le Mêle-sur-Sarthe	50	48.31 N	0.21 E
Lemene ≃	64	45.37 N	12.53 E
Lemeris, Cape ≻	164	3.15 S	152.03 E
Le Merlerault	50	48.42 N	0.18 E
Lemery	116	13.53 N	120.55 E
Lemeškino	80	51.01 N	44.27 E
Le Mesle	261	48.43 N	1.41 E
Le Mesnil-Amelot	261	49.01 N	2.36 E
Le Mesnil-Aubry	261	49.03 N	2.24 E
Le Mesnil-le-Roi	261	48.56 N	2.08 E
Le Mesnil-Saint-Denis	261	48.45 N	1.58 E
Le Mesnil-sur-Oger	50	48.57 N	4.01 E
Lemesós (Limassol)	130	34.40 N	33.02 E
Lemešovka	78	52.04 N	31.38 E
Lemeta	180	64.52 N	147.44 W
Lemförde	52	52.28 N	8.22 E
Lemfu	152	5.18 S	15.13 E
Lemgo	52	52.02 N	8.54 E
Lemhi ≃	202	45.12 N	113.53 W
Lemhi Pass)(	202	44.58 N	113.27 W
Lemhi Range ⋏	202	44.30 N	113.25 W
Lemie	62	45.14 N	7.17 E
Lemierzyce	54	52.35 N	14.56 E
Lemieux Islands II	176	64.30 N	64.40 W
Lemin	102	21.11 N	109.42 E
Leming	196	29.04 N	98.29 W
Lemitar	200	34.09 N	106.54 W
Lemke	52	52.39 N	9.09 E
Lemland I	26	60.03 N	20.09 E
Lemmatsi	76	58.20 N	26.37 E
Lemmenjoen Kansallispuisto ♦	24	68.40 N	26.00 E
Lemmer	52	52.50 N	5.42 E
Lemmon	198	45.56 N	102.09 W
Lemmon, Mount ∧	200	32.26 N	110.47 W
Lemnos → Límnos I	38	39.54 N	25.21 E
Lemoenshoek	158	33.51 S	20.51 E
Lemoine, Lac ⊜	190	48.00 N	78.00 W
Lemon, Lake ⊜	218	39.16 N	86.25 W
Le Monastier	62	44.56 N	4.00 E
Lemoncove	204	36.23 N	119.01 W
Lemon Creek ≃	276	40.31 N	74.12 W
Le Monêtier-les-Bains	62	44.59 N	6.31 E
Lemon Grove	228	32.44 N	117.01 W
Lemon Heights	280	33.46 N	117.48 W
Lemont, Il., U.S.	216	41.40 N	88.00 W
Lemont, Pa., U.S.	214	40.49 N	77.49 W
Le Montet	32	46.25 N	3.03 E
Le Mont-Saint-Michel ✿[1]	32	48.38 N	1.32 W
Lemoore	226	36.18 N	119.46 W
Lemoore Naval Air Station ■	226	36.15 N	119.57 W
Lemoro	112	1.25 S	121.05 E
Le Moule	241o	16.20 N	61.21 W
Le Moutier	261	48.50 N	1.42 E
LeMoyne, P.Q., Can.	275a	45.31 N	73.29 W
Lemoyne, Oh., U.S.	214	41.30 N	83.28 W
Lemoyne, Pa., U.S.	208	40.15 N	76.54 W
Lempa ≃	236	13.14 N	88.49 W
Lempäälä	26	61.19 N	23.45 E
Lempe	112	1.40 S	120.14 E
Lempira □[5]	236	14.20 N	88.40 W
Lemro ≃	110	20.25 N	93.20 E
Lemsid	148	26.32 N	13.49 W
Lemukutan, Pulau I	112	0.45 N	108.43 E
Le Murge ⋏[1]	68	40.52 N	16.42 E
Lemutan	112	3.03 N	115.49 E
Le Muy	62	43.28 N	6.33 E
Lemva ≃	24	66.30 N	61.48 E
Lemvig	26	56.32 N	8.18 E
Lemyethna	110	17.36 N	95.09 E
Len ≃	260	51.16 N	0.31 E
Lena, Il., U.S.	190	42.22 N	89.49 W
Lena, Wi., U.S.	190	44.57 N	88.02 W
Lena ≃	74	72.25 N	126.40 E
Lenangguar	115b	8.44 S	117.24 E
Lenape	285	39.55 N	75.38 W
Lenart	61	46.35 N	15.50 E
Lenasia	273d	26.17 S	27.50 E
Lenawee □[6]	216	41.53 N	84.04 W
Lencloître	32	46.49 N	0.20 E
Lençóis	255	12.34 S	41.23 W
Lençois Maranhenses, Parque Nacional dos ♦	250	2.25 S	43.15 W
Lend	64	47.18 N	13.04 E
Lenda ≃	154	1.20 N	28.01 E
Lendava	61	46.34 N	16.27 E
Lendelede	50	50.53 N	3.14 E
Lendery	24	63.26 N	31.03 E
Lendinara	64	45.05 N	11.36 E
Lendorf	64	46.50 N	13.26 E
Lendringsen	56	51.24 N	7.49 E
Le Neubourg	50	49.09 N	0.55 E
Lenga	114	2.17 N	102.49 E
Lengduqiao	106	30.27 N	119.15 E
Lengede	52	52.12 N	10.18 E
Lengefeld	54	50.43 N	13.11 E
Lengelscheid	263	51.08 N	7.40 E
Lengenfeld, Dtsch.	54	50.34 N	12.22 E
Lengenfeld, Dtsch.	56	51.13 N	10.13 E
Lenger	85	42.12 N	69.54 E
Lengerich, Dtsch.	52	52.11 N	7.50 E
Lengerich, Dtsch.	52	52.33 N	7.32 E
Lenggor ≃	114	2.25 N	103.37 E
Lenggries	64	47.41 N	11.34 E
Lenghu	90	38.30 N	93.15 E
Lengjiagou	104	41.40 N	121.37 E
Lengkong	115a	7.32 S	112.04 E
Lenglingen ⊜	26	64.14 N	13.45 E
Lengnau	58	47.11 N	7.22 E
Lengoué	152	1.13 N	15.43 E
Lengoué ≃	152	0.49 N	15.47 E
Lengshuichang	107	29.27 N	106.26 E
Lengshuikeng	100	27.55 N	117.08 E
Lengshuitan	102	26.27 N	111.35 E
Lengua de Vaca, Punta ≻	252	30.14 S	71.38 W
Lengulu	154	3.15 N	26.30 E
Lengwe National Park ♦	154	16.15 S	34.45 E
Lengzipu	104	41.42 N	122.47 E
Lenham	42	51.14 N	0.43 E
Lenhartsville	208	40.34 N	75.53 W
Lenhovda	26	57.00 N	15.17 E
Lenina, gora ∧[2]	265b	55.42 N	37.31 E
Lenina, ozero ⊜	78	48.33 N	35.12 E
Lenina, pik ∧	85	39.20 N	72.55 E
Leninabad → Chudžand	85	40.17 N	69.37 E
Leninakan → Kamajri	84	40.48 N	43.50 E
Lenin Central Stadium ♦	265b	55.43 N	37.33 E
Lenin-Džol	85	41.03 N	72.38 E
Leningori	84	42.07 N	44.29 E
Leningrad □[8]	265a	59.55 N	30.15 E
Leningrado → Sankt-Peterburg	76	59.55 N	30.15 E
Leningrad → Sankt-Peterburg	76	59.55 N	30.15 E
Leningradskaja	78	46.19 N	39.24 E
Leningradskaja ✿[3]	9	69.30 S	159.23 E
Leningradskaja Oblast' □[8]	76	60.00 N	32.00 E
Leningradskij	85	38.06 N	70.01 E
Leningradskoje	86	53.33 N	71.35 E
Lenino	78	45.18 N	35.47 E
Lenino ◆[8]	265b	55.37 N	37.41 E
Leninogorsk, Kaz.	86	50.27 N	83.32 E
Leninogorsk, Ross.	80	54.36 N	52.30 E
Leninpol'	85	42.29 N	71.55 E
Leninsk, Kaz.	86	45.40 N	63.20 E
Leninsk, Ross.	80	46.08 N	43.46 E
Leninsk, Ross.	80	48.42 N	45.11 E
Leninsk, Ross.	86	54.55 N	59.54 E
Leninsk, Uzb.	85	40.38 N	72.15 E
Leninskaja Sloboda	80	56.05 N	44.28 E
Leninskij, Kaz.	86	52.13 N	76.47 E
Leninskij, Mol.	78	47.53 N	28.23 E
Leninskij, Ross.	80	46.31 N	44.28 E
Leninskij, Ross.	80	56.34 N	45.56 E
Leninskij, Ross.	82	54.18 N	37.28 E
Leninskij, Ukr.	83	48.05 N	39.31 E
Leninsk-Kuzneckij	86	54.38 N	86.10 E
Leninskoje, Kaz.	80	49.03 N	49.56 E
Leninskoje, Kaz.	85	41.45 N	69.23 E
Leninskoje, Kaz.	86	50.44 N	57.53 E
Leninskoje, Kaz.	86	54.04 N	65.22 E
Leninskoje, Kyrg.	85	40.42 N	73.11 E
Leninskoje, Ross.	80	58.19 N	47.06 E
Leninskoje, Ross.	89	47.56 N	132.38 E
Leninskoje, Ukr.	78	45.16 N	35.54 E
Leninskoje, Ukr.	78	51.27 N	33.18 E
Lenin-Stausee → Kujbyševskoje vodochranilišče ⊜[1]	80	54.30 N	48.30 E
Leninžol	80	49.20 N	47.05 E
Lenk	58	46.28 N	7.27 E
Lenkerville	208	40.32 N	76.58 W
Len'ki	86	52.57 N	80.26 E
Lenkoran'	84	38.45 N	48.50 E
Lenmalu	164	1.44 S	130.13 E
Lennard, Mount ∧[2]	168a	33.21 S	115.53 E
Lenne ≃	56	51.25 N	7.30 E
Lennegebirge ⋏	52	51.15 N	8.00 E
Lennep	56	51.11 N	7.15 E
Lennep ◆[8]	52	51.12 N	7.15 E
Lennestadt	56	51.08 N	8.01 E
Lenni	285	39.54 N	75.27 W
Lennon	216	42.59 N	83.56 W
Lennonville	162	27.58 S	117.50 E
Lennox, Ca., U.S.	228	33.56 N	118.21 W
Lennox, S.D., U.S.	198	43.21 N	96.53 W
Lennox □[9]	46	56.02 N	4.15 W
Lennox, Isla I	254	55.18 S	66.50 W
Lennox and Addington □[6]	212	44.30 N	77.00 W
Lennoxtown	46	55.59 N	4.12 W
Lennoxville	206	45.22 N	71.51 W
Leno	64	45.22 N	10.13 E
Lenoir	192	35.54 N	81.32 W
Lenoir City	192	35.47 N	84.15 W
Le Noirmont	58	47.13 N	6.58 E
Lenola	66	41.24 N	13.28 E
Lenora	60	48.56 N	13.48 E
Lenore Lake ⊜	184	52.30 N	105.00 W
Le Nouvion-en-Thiérache	50	50.01 N	3.47 E
Lenox, Ga., U.S.	192	31.16 N	83.27 W
Lenox, Ia., U.S.	198	40.52 N	94.33 W
Lenox, Ma., U.S.	207	42.22 N	73.17 W
Lenox, Tn., U.S.	194	36.05 N	89.29 W
Lenox Dale	207	42.20 N	73.14 W
Lens	50	50.26 N	2.50 E
Lensahn	54	54.13 N	10.52 E
Lensk	74	61.00 N	114.50 E
Lenskoje	86	58.09 N	63.11 E
Lenswood	168b	34.55 S	138.49 E
Lentate sul Seveso	266b	45.41 N	9.07 E
Lentechi	84	42.48 N	42.44 E
Lenti	61	46.37 N	16.33 E
Lenting	60	48.48 N	11.28 E
Lentini	70	37.17 N	15.00 E
Lentner	219	39.43 N	92.09 W
Lentua ⊜	26	64.14 N	29.36 E
Lentvaris	76	54.39 N	25.03 E
Lenwood	228	34.53 N	117.07 W
Lenya	110	11.28 N	99.00 E
Lenya ≃	110	11.40 N	98.43 E
Lenz	273d	26.19 S	27.49 E
Lenzburg	58	47.23 N	8.11 E
Lenzen	54	53.05 N	11.28 E
Lenzerheide (Lai)	58	46.44 N	9.33 E
Lenzinghausen	52	52.07 N	8.28 E
Lenzkirch	58	47.52 N	8.12 E
Léo, Burkina	150	11.06 N	2.06 W
Leo, In., U.S.	216	41.13 N	85.00 W
Leoben	61	47.23 N	15.06 E
Leo Carrillo State Beach ♦	228	34.03 N	118.56 W
Léogâne	238	18.31 N	72.38 W
Leogang	64	47.26 N	12.45 E
Leola, Ar., U.S.	194	34.10 N	92.35 W
Leola, Pa., U.S.	208	40.05 N	76.11 W
Leola, S.D., U.S.	198	45.43 N	98.56 W
Leominster, Eng., U.K.	42	52.14 N	2.45 W
Leominster, Ma., U.S.	207	42.31 N	71.45 W
León, Esp.	34	42.36 N	5.34 W
Léon, Fr.	32	43.53 N	1.18 W
León, Nic.	236	12.26 N	86.53 W
Leon, Pil.	116	10.47 N	122.23 E
Leon, Ia., U.S.	190	40.44 N	93.44 W
Leon, Ks., U.S.	198	37.41 N	96.46 W
Leon, N.Y., U.S.	210	42.18 N	79.01 W
León □[4]	34	42.35 N	6.00 W
León □[5]	236	12.35 N	86.35 W
Leon □[6]	222	31.18 N	95.55 W
León □[9]	34	42.00 N	6.00 W
Leon ≃	196	30.59 N	97.24 W
Leon, Arroyo ≃	282	37.28 N	122.25 W
León, Montes de ⋏	34	42.30 N	6.18 W
Leona	222	31.09 N	95.58 W
Leona ≃	196	28.45 N	99.11 W
Leona, Punta ≻	236	9.41 N	84.41 W
Leonard, Mi., U.S.	214	42.51 N	83.08 W
Leonard, Mo., U.S.	219	39.53 N	92.10 W
Leonard, N.D., U.S.	198	46.39 N	97.14 W
Leonard, Tx., U.S.	196	33.22 N	96.14 W
Leonardo	276	40.25 N	74.03 W
Leonardo da Vinci, Aeroporto Intercontinentale ⊠	66	41.48 N	12.13 E
Leonardsburg	214	40.21 N	82.59 W
Leonardsville	210	42.48 N	75.15 W
Leonardtown	208	38.17 N	76.38 W
Leonardville, Namibia	156	23.29 S	18.49 E
Leonardville, Ks., U.S.	198	39.21 N	96.51 W
Leona Vicario	200	32.10 N	115.10 W
Leonberg	56	48.48 N	9.01 E
Leonbronn	56	49.03 N	8.53 E
Leondale	273d	26.18 S	28.12 E
Leondárion	267c	37.59 N	23.51 E
León [de los Aldamas]	234	21.07 N	101.40 W
Leonding	61	48.16 N	14.15 E
Leone	174u	14.20 S	170.47 W
Leone, Golfo del → Lion, Golfe du c	32	43.00 N	4.00 E
Leone, Monte ∧	58	46.15 N	8.06 E
Leones	252	32.39 S	62.18 W
Leonessa	66	42.34 N	12.58 E
Leonforte	70	37.38 N	14.23 E
Leongatha	169	38.29 S	145.57 E
León Guzmán	196	25.31 N	103.34 W
Leonia	276	40.51 N	73.59 W
Leonicha	76	59.37 N	38.51 E
Leonidas	216	42.01 N	85.21 W
Leonídhion	38	37.10 N	22.52 E
Leonidovo	89	49.17 N	142.50 E
Leon Junction	222	31.20 N	97.36 W
Leonora	162	28.53 S	121.20 E
Leonovo	82	55.26 N	38.42 E
Leontjevka	85	43.03 N	69.50 E
Leontjevo	76	58.58 N	36.37 E
Leonville	194	30.28 N	91.58 W
Leopard	285	40.01 N	75.27 W
Leopold	169	38.11 S	144.28 E
Leopold and Astrid Coast ±[2]	9	67.10 S	84.10 E
Leopoldau ◆[8]	264b	48.16 N	16.27 E
Leopold Downs	162	17.52 S	125.25 E
Léopold II, Lac → Mai-Ndombe, Lac ⊜	152	2.00 S	18.20 E
Leopoldina	256	21.32 S	42.38 W
Leopoldkanaal ≋	50	51.14 N	3.46 E
Leopoldo de Bulhões	255	16.37 S	48.46 W
Leopoldo y Astrid, Costa → Leopold and Astrid Coast ±[2]	9	67.10 S	84.10 E
Leopoldsburg	56	51.07 N	5.15 E
Leopoldsdorf	264b	48.06 N	16.24 E
Leopoldshagen	54	53.46 N	13.53 E
Leopoldstadt ◆[8]	264b	48.13 N	16.23 E
Léopoldville → Kinshasa	152	4.18 S	15.18 E
Leoti	198	38.28 N	101.21 W
Leoville	184	53.37 N	107.35 W
Leovo	78	46.29 N	28.15 E
Le Pailly	58	47.48 N	5.25 E
Le Palais	32	47.21 N	3.09 W
Lepanto, C.R.	236	9.57 N	85.02 W
Lepanto, Ar., U.S.	194	35.36 N	90.19 W
Lepanto → Návpaktos	38	38.23 N	21.50 E
Lepar, Pulau I	112	2.57 S	106.50 E
Le Parcq	50	50.23 N	2.06 E
Le Pâté	261	48.32 N	2.18 E
Lepe	34	37.15 N	7.12 W
Le Péage-de-Roussillon	62	45.22 N	4.48 E
Le Pecq	261	48.54 N	2.07 E
Lepel'	76	54.53 N	28.42 E
Le Pellerin	32	47.12 N	1.45 W
Lepembusu, Keli ∧	115b	8.40 S	121.49 E
Le Perray-en-Yuelines	261	48.42 N	1.51 E
Le Perreux-sur-Marne	261	48.51 N	2.30 E
Lepeški	82	56.05 N	38.07 E
Le Petit-Clamart ✿	261	48.47 N	2.14 E
Le Petit-Couronne	50	49.23 N	1.01 E
Le Petit-Quevilly	50	49.26 N	1.02 E
Lephepe	156	23.20 S	25.50 E
Lépi	152	12.52 S	15.26 E
Le Piastre	66	44.00 N	10.50 E
Lepihué	254	41.37 S	73.36 W
Le Pin	261	48.55 N	2.38 E
Le Pin-au-Haras	50	48.44 N	0.09 E
L'Épine, Fr.	56	48.58 N	4.28 E
L'Épine, Fr.	261	48.32 N	2.21 E
Leping	100	28.57 N	117.05 E
Lepini, Monti ⋏	66	41.35 N	13.00 E
Lépin-le-Lac	62	45.32 N	5.47 E
L'Épiphanie	206	45.51 N	73.30 W
Lepl'avo	78	49.48 N	31.32 E
Le Plessis-aux-Bois	261	49.00 N	2.46 E
Le Plessis-Belleville	50	49.06 N	2.46 E
Le Plessis-Bouchard	261	49.00 N	2.14 E
Le Plessis-Pâté	261	48.37 N	2.20 E
Le Plessis-Trévise	261	48.49 N	2.34 E
Lépo, Lagoa de ⊜	152	17.08 S	19.00 E
Le Poët	62	44.17 N	5.53 E
Le Pont	58	46.40 N	6.20 E
Le Pont-de-Beauvoisin	62	45.32 N	5.40 E
Le Pont-de-Montvert	62	44.22 N	3.45 E
Le Pontel	261	48.49 N	1.53 E
Lepontine, Alpi ⋏	58	46.25 N	8.40 E
Leporano	68	40.23 N	17.20 E
Le Port	157c	20.55 S	55.18 E
Le Portel	50	50.42 N	1.34 E
Le Port-Marly	261	48.53 N	2.06 E
Le Pouzin	62	44.45 N	4.45 E
Leppävirta	26	62.29 N	27.47 E
Lepperton	172	39.04 S	174.13 E
Leppin	54	52.53 N	11.34 E
Leppington	274a	33.58 S	150.49 E
Le Pradet	62	43.06 N	6.01 E
Lepreau, Point ≻	186	45.04 N	66.27 W
Le Prêcheur	240e	14.48 N	61.14 W
Le Pré-Saint-Gervais	261	48.53 N	2.25 E
Le Prese	58	46.18 N	10.04 E
Lepsinsk	86	45.32 N	80.37 E
Lepsy, Kaz.	86	46.18 N	78.20 E
Lepsy, Kaz.	86	46.15 N	78.55 E
Le Puy	62	45.02 N	3.53 E
Le Quesnoy	50	50.15 N	3.38 E
Léraba ≃	150	9.42 N	4.35 W
Le Raincy	261	48.54 N	2.31 E
Le Rayol-Canadel-sur-Mer	62	43.10 N	6.28 E
Le Raysville	210	41.51 N	76.11 W
Lerberget	41	56.11 N	12.33 E
Lercara Friddi	70	37.45 N	13.36 E
Lerche ◆[8]	263	51.37 N	7.43 E
Lerderderg ≃	169	37.42 S	144.30 E
Lerdo → Ciudad Lerdo	196	25.32 N	103.32 W
Léré, Fr.	50	47.28 N	2.52 E
Léré, Mali	150	15.43 N	4.55 W
Lere, Nig.	150	9.43 N	9.21 E
Léré, Tchad	146	9.39 N	14.13 E
Lereh	164	3.08 S	139.54 E
Lerek ∧	114	3.47 N	102.47 E
Le Reposoir	58	46.00 N	6.33 E
Leri ≃	42	52.32 N	4.02 W
Leribe	158	28.58 S	28.00 E
Lerici	64	44.04 N	9.55 E
Lérida	246	0.10 N	70.42 W
Lérida → Lleida	34	41.37 N	0.37 E
Lerik	84	38.46 N	48.25 E
Lérins, Îles de II	62	43.31 N	7.03 E
Lerma	34	42.02 N	3.45 W
Lerma ≃	234	20.13 N	102.46 W
Lermontovka	89	47.10 N	134.20 E
Lermoos	58	47.24 N	10.53 E
Lerno, Monte ∧	71	40.37 N	9.10 E
Le Robert	240e	14.41 N	60.57 W
Léros I, Ellás	38	37.08 N	26.52 E
Léros I, Ellás	267c	37.59 N	23.34 E
Lérouville	56	48.47 N	5.33 E
Leroux Wash V	200	34.54 N	110.12 W
Le Roy, Il., U.S.	216	40.21 N	88.45 W
Leroy, In., U.S.	216	41.22 N	87.16 W
Le Roy, Ks., U.S.	198	38.05 N	95.38 W
Le Roy, Mn., U.S.	190	43.30 N	92.30 W
Le Roy, N.Y., U.S.	210	42.58 N	77.59 W
Le Roy, Pa., U.S.	210	41.41 N	76.43 W
Leroy, Tx., U.S.	222	31.44 N	97.01 W
Lerum	26	57.46 N	12.16 E
Le Russey	58	47.10 N	6.44 E
Lerwick	46a	60.09 N	1.09 W
Léry	206	45.21 N	73.48 W
Lesa	62	45.50 N	8.34 E
Les Abrets	62	45.32 N	5.35 E
Les Abymes	241o	16.16 N	61.31 W
Lesage, Lac ⊜	206	46.19 N	75.03 W
Le Saint-Esprit	240e	14.34 N	60.57 W
Les Aix-d'Angillon	50	47.12 N	2.34 E
Les Allues	62	45.26 N	6.33 E
Les Alluets-le-Roi	261	48.55 N	1.55 E
Les Andelys	50	49.15 N	1.25 E
Les Anses-d'Arlets	240e	14.29 N	61.05 W
Le Sappy-en-Chartreuse	62	45.16 N	5.47 E
Les Arcs	62	43.27 N	6.29 E
Lesatima, Oldoinyo ∧	154	0.19 S	36.37 E
Le Sauze	62	44.22 N	6.41 E
Les Baux-en-Provence	62	43.45 N	4.48 E
Les Bézards	50	47.48 N	2.44 E
Les Bordes	261	48.39 N	1.58 E
Les Borges Blanques	34	41.31 N	0.52 E
Lesbos → Lésvos I	38	39.10 N	26.20 E
Les Bouchoux	58	46.18 N	5.49 E
Les Bréviaires	261	48.42 N	1.49 E
Lesbury	44	55.24 N	1.36 W
L'Escarène	62	43.50 N	7.21 E
Les Cayes	238	18.12 N	73.45 W
Les Chaises	261	48.39 N	1.42 E
Les Chapieux	62	45.42 N	6.44 E
Leschenault, Cape ≻	162	31.18 S	115.27 E
Leschenault Estuary c[1]	168a	33.15 S	115.42 E
Lesches	261	48.54 N	2.47 E
Leščinovka	78	49.16 N	34.14 E
Les Clayes-sous-Bois	261	48.49 N	1.59 E
Les Contamines-Montjoie	62	45.50 N	6.44 E
Les Diablerets	58	46.21 N	7.10 E
Les Diablerets ∧	58	46.19 N	7.12 E
Lesdiboderi	146	8.28 N	12.35 E
Les Echarmeaux	58	46.10 N	4.27 E
Les Échelles	62	45.26 N	5.45 E
Les Écureuils	206	46.39 N	71.43 W
Le Semnoz ∧	62	45.48 N	6.07 E
Leseru	154	0.35 N	35.10 E
Les Essarts	32	46.46 N	1.14 W
Les Essarts-le-Roi	261	48.43 N	1.54 E
Les Estables	62	44.54 N	4.10 E
Les Étangs	56	49.09 N	6.23 E
Les Fonts	266d	41.32 N	2.02 E
Les Fourgs	58	46.50 N	6.25 E
Les Galleries d'Anjou ◆[9]	275a	45.35 N	73.34 W
Les Gâtines	261	48.48 N	1.58 E
Les Gets	58	46.09 N	6.40 E
Les Granges-le-Roi	261	48.30 N	2.01 E
Les Grésillons	261	48.56 N	2.01 E
Les Halles	62	45.43 N	4.26 E
Leshan	107	29.34 N	103.45 E

Symbols in the index entries represent the broad categories identified in the key at the right. Symbols with superior numbers (⋏[1]) identify subcategories (see complete key on page *I · 1).*

Symbole im Register stellen die rechts im Schlüssel erklärten Kategorien dar. Symbole mit hochgestellten Ziffern (⋏[1]) bezeichnen Unterabteilungen einer Kategorie (vgl. vollständiger Schlüssel auf Seite *I · 1).*

Los símbolos incluídos en el texto del índice representan las grandes categorias identificadas con la clave a la derecha. Los símbolos con numeros en su parte superior (⋏[1]) identifican las subcategorías (véase la clave completa en la página *I · 1).*

Les symboles de l'index représentent les catégories indiquées dans la légende à droite. Les symboles suivis d'un indice (⋏[1]) représentent des sous-catégories (voir légende complète à la page *I · 1).*

Os símbolos incluídos no texto do índice representam as grandes categorias identificadas com a chave à direita. Os símbolos com números em sua parte superior (⋏[1]) identificam as subcategorias (veja-se a chave completa à página *I · 1).*

English	Deutsch	Español	Français	Português
∧ Mountain	Berg	Montaña	Montagne	Montanha
⋏ Mountains	Gebirge	Montañas	Montagnes	Montanhas
)(Pass	Paß	Paso	Col	Passo
V Valley, Canyon	Tal, Cañon	Valle, Cañón	Vallée, Canyon	Vale, Canhão
≚ Plain	Ebene	Llano	Plaine	Planície
≻ Cape	Kap	Cabo	Cap	Cabo
I Island	Insel	Isla	Île	Ilha
II Islands	Inseln	Islas	Îles	Ilhas
± Other Topographic Features	Andere Topographische Objekte	Otros Elementos Topográficos	Autres données topographiques	Outros acidentes topográficos

ESPAÑOL Nombre	Página	Lat.°′	Long.°′ W = Oeste	FRANÇAIS Nom	Page	Lat.°′	Long.°′ W = Ouest	PORTUGUÊS Nome	Página	Lat.°′	Long.°′ W = Oeste

Les Haudères 58 46.05 N 7.31 E
Les Hautes-Rivières 56 49.53 N 4.50 E
Les Herbiers 32 46.52 N 1.01 W
Les Houches 62 45.53 N 6.48 E
Lesignano de'Bagni 64 44.39 N 10.18 E
Lésigny 261 48.45 N 2.37 E
Lesima, Monte ʌ 62 44.41 N 9.15 E
Lesina 68 41.52 N 15.21 E
Lesina, Lago di c 68 41.53 N 15.26 E
Les Islettes 56 49.06 N 5.00 E
Lesjaskog 26 62.15 N 8.22 E
Lesjöfors 40 59.59 N 14.11 E
Lesken 84 43.16 N 43.48 E
Les'ki 78 49.19 N 32.13 E
Lesko 30 49.29 N 22.21 E
Leskovac 38 42.59 N 21.57 E
Leskov Island I 18 56.40 S 28.10 W
Les Laumes 58 47.32 N 4.27 E
Les Lecques 62 43.11 N 5.40 E
Leslie, S. Afr. 158 26.27 S 28.55 E
Leslie, Scot., U.K. 46 56.12 N 3.13 W
Leslie, Ar., U.S. 194 35.49 N 92.33 W
Leslie, Ga., U.S. 192 31.57 N 84.05 W
Leslie, Mi., U.S. 216 42.27 N 84.25 W
Leslie, W.V., U.S. 188 38.02 N 80.43 W
Les Lilas 261 48.53 N 2.25 E
Les Loges 261 48.34 N 2.03 E
Les Loges-en-Josas 261 48.46 N 2.09 E
Lesmahagow 46 55.39 N 3.55 W
Les Marécottes 58 46.07 N 7.00 E
Les Mées 62 44.02 N 5.59 E
Les Mesnuls 50 48.45 N 1.50 E
Lesmo 266b 45.39 N 9.18 E
Les Molières 261 48.40 N 2.04 E
Les Monges ʌ 62 44.16 N 6.12 E
Lesmont 50 48.26 N 4.25 E
Les Mosses 58 46.24 N 7.07 E
Lesmurdie Falls National Park ♦ 168a 32.01 S 116.04 E
Les Mureaux 261 49.00 N 1.55 E
Leśna 30 51.02 N 15.16 E
Lesna ≃ 76 52.10 N 23.33 E
Lesnaja 76 52.59 N 25.46 E
Lesneven 32 48.34 N 4.19 W
Les Neyrolles 58 46.08 N 5.38 E
Lešnica 38 44.39 N 19.19 E
Lesnoj, Ross. 24 59.48 N 52.08 E
Lesnoj, Ross. 80 54.11 N 40.27 E
Lesnoj, Ross. 86 56.57 N 67.15 E
Lesnoj ◆[8] 265a 60.00 N 30.19 E
Lesnoje 76 58.17 N 35.32 E
Lesnoje Konobejevo 80 54.02 N 41.55 E
Lesnoje Mat'unino 80 53.27 N 47.26 E
Lesnoj Gorodok 265b 55.39 N 37.13 E
Lesnoj park ♦ 265a 59.59 N 30.21 E
Lesnyj ʌ 60 50.02 N 12.37 E
Lesnyje Pol'any, Ross. 24 58.58 N 52.26 E
Lesnyje Pol'any, Ross. 265b 55.57 N 37.53 E
Lesogorsk, Ross. 80 55.06 N 43.56 E
Lesogorsk, Ross. 88 56.03 N 99.33 E
Lesogorsk, Ross. 89 49.27 N 142.08 E
Lesogorskij 24 61.02 N 28.53 E
Lesong, Gunong ʌ 114 2.44 N 103.17 E
Lesopil'noje 89 46.44 N 134.20 E
Lesosibirsk 86 58.16 N 92.29 E
Lesotho □[1], Afr. 138 29.30 S 28.30 E
Lesotho □[1], Afr. 158 29.30 S 28.30 E
Lesovščina 78 50.47 N 28.35 E
Lesozavodsk 89 45.28 N 133.27 E
Lesozavodskij 24 66.44 N 32.49 E
Lesparre-Médoc 32 45.18 N 0.56 W
Les Pavillons-sous-Bois 261 48.55 N 2.30 E
Les Pieux 32 49.31 N 1.48 W
Les Planches-en-Montagne 58 46.40 N 6.01 E
Les Ponts-de-Martel 58 46.54 N 6.41 E
Les Posets ʌ 34 42.39 N 0.25 E
Les Praz-de-Chamonix 58 45.56 N 6.52 E
Lesquin 50 50.35 N 3.07 E
Les Riceys 50 47.59 N 4.22 E
Les Roches-l'Evêque 50 47.47 N 0.53 E
Les Rousses 58 46.29 N 6.04 E
Les Ruelles 261 48.40 N 1.37 E
Les Sables-d'Olonne 32 46.30 N 1.47 W
Lessach 64 47.11 N 13.49 E
Les Saintes II 241o 15.52 N 61.37 W
Les Salles-sur-Verdon 62 43.46 N 6.12 E
Lessay 32 49.13 N 1.32 W
Les Scaffarels 62 43.57 N 6.41 E
Lesse ≃ 56 50.14 N 4.54 E
Lessebo 26 56.45 N 15.16 E
Lessen
— Lessines 50 50.43 N 3.50 E
Lesser Antilles II 238 15.00 N 61.00 W
Lesser Khingan Range
— Xiao Hinggan Ling ʌ 89 48.45 N 127.00 E
Lesser Slave ≃ 182 55.10 N 114.03 W
Lesser Slave Lake @ 182 55.25 N 115.30 W
Lesser Sunda Islands
— Tenggara, Nusa II 108 9.00 S 120.00 E
Lessines (Lessen) 50 50.43 N 3.50 E
Lessini, Monti ʌ 64 45.41 N 11.13 E
L'Estaque 62 43.22 N 5.20 E
Leste ≃ 250 6.20 S 57.46 W
Lester, Pa., U.S. 285 39.52 N 75.17 W
Lester, Wa., U.S. 224 47.12 N 121.29 W
Lester B. Pearson International Airport ⊠ 212 43.41 N 79.38 W
Les Tessiers 62 44.24 N 4.16 E
Les Thilliers-en-Vexin 50 49.14 N 1.36 E
Lestijärvi 26 63.32 N 24.39 E
Lestijoki ≃ 26 64.04 N 23.38 E
Lestkov 60 49.54 N 12.52 E
Lestock 184 51.18 N 104.00 W
L'Estréchure 62 44.06 N 3.47 E
Les Trois-Îlets 240e 14.32 N 61.02 W
Les Trois Lacs @ 206 45.48 N 71.54 W
Le Sueur 190 44.30 N 93.52 W
Le Sueur ≃ 190 44.07 N 94.03 W
Lesueur, Mount ʌ[2] 162 30.10 S 115.11 E
Lešukonskoje 24 64.54 N 45.40 E
Les Ulis 261 48.41 N 2.11 E
Lesung, Tanjung › 115a 6.28 S 105.40 E
Lesuvo 80 55.40 N 43.07 E
Les Vans 62 44.24 N 4.08 E
Les Verrières 58 46.54 N 6.30 E
Lésvos I 38 39.10 N 26.20 E
Leszno 30 51.51 N 16.35 E
Leszno □[4] 30 51.45 N 16.45 E
Letälven ≃ 40 59.05 N 14.20 E
L'Étang-La-Ville 261 48.52 N 2.05 E
Letcher 198 43.53 N 98.08 W
Letchmore Heath 260 51.40 N 0.20 W
Letchworth 42 51.58 N 0.14 W
Letchworth State Park ♦ 210 42.42 N 77.56 W
Letea, Ostrovul I 38 45.20 N 29.20 E
Le Teil 62 44.33 N 4.41 E
Le Temple 261 49.00 N 1.58 E
Letenye 30 46.26 N 16.43 E
Le Tertre-Saint-Denis 261 48.56 N 1.36 E
Lethbridge, Austl. 274a 33.44 S 150.48 E
Lethbridge, Ab., Can. 182 49.42 N 112.50 W
Lethbridge, Nf., Can. 186 48.21 N 53.52 W
Le Theil-sur-Huisne 50 48.16 N 0.42 E
Lethem 246 3.23 N 59.48 W
Le Thillay 261 49.00 N 2.28 E
Le Thillot 58 47.53 N 6.46 E
Le Tholy 58 48.05 N 6.45 E
Le Thor 62 43.56 N 5.00 E
Le Thoronet 62 43.27 N 6.18 E
Leti, Kepulauan II 164 8.13 S 127.50 E
Leti, Pulau I 112 8.12 S 127.41 E
Letičev 78 49.23 N 27.37 E
Leticia 246 4.09 S 69.57 W
Letiing 98 39.27 N 118.53 E
Letino 68 41.26 N 14.17 E
Letjiesbos 158 32.34 S 22.16 E
Letka 24 59.36 N 49.22 E
Letlhakane 156 21.27 S 25.30 E
Letlhakeng 156 24.08 S 25.02 E
Letmathe 56 51.22 N 7.37 E
Letn'aja Zolotica 24 64.57 N 36.50 E
Letnerečenskij 24 64.17 N 34.23 E
Le Touquet-Paris-Plage 50 50.31 N 1.35 E
Le Touvet 62 45.21 N 5.57 E
Letovo 265b 55.34 N 37.24 E
Letpadan 110 17.47 N 95.45 E
Le Trait 50 49.28 N 0.49 E
Le Trayas 62 43.28 N 6.55 E
Le Tremblay-sur-Mauldre 261 48.47 N 1.53 E
Le Tréport 50 50.04 N 1.22 E
Letschin 54 52.39 N 14.21 E
Letsôk-aw Kyun I 110 11.37 N 98.15 E
Letter 52 52.24 N 9.38 E
Letterfrack 48 53.33 N 10.00 W
Letterkenny 48 54.57 N 7.44 W
Lettermullan 48 53.13 N 9.42 W
Letterston 42 51.56 N 5.00 W
Lettonie
— Latvia □[1] 72 57.00 N 25.00 E
Letts 218 39.14 N 85.35 W
Letung 112 2.58 N 105.42 E
Letzlingen 54 52.26 N 11.29 E
Leu 38 44.11 N 24.00 E
Léua 152 11.34 S 20.32 E
Leubnitz 54 50.43 N 12.21 E
Leubsdorf 54 50.48 N 13.08 E
Leuca 68 39.48 N 18.21 E
Leucadia 228 33.04 N 117.18 W
Leucate, Étang de c 32 42.51 N 3.00 E
Leuchars 46 56.23 N 2.53 W
Leuchtenberg 60 49.36 N 12.15 E
Leudeville 261 48.34 N 2.20 E
Leuenberger Forst ◆[3] 264a 52.40 N 13.53 E
Leuglay 58 47.49 N 4.48 E
Leuk 58 46.19 N 7.38 E
Leukerbad 58 46.23 N 7.38 E
Leulumoega 175a 13.49 S 171.55 W
Leumeah 274a 34.03 S 150.50 E
Leuna 54 51.19 N 12.01 E
Leupoldsgrün 54 50.17 N 11.47 E
Leura 170 33.43 S 150.20 E
Leura, Mount ʌ[2] 169 38.15 S 143.09 E
Leuser, Gunung ʌ 114 3.45 N 97.11 E
Leušinskij Tuman, ozero @ 86 59.42 N 65.35 E
Leutenberg 54 50.34 N 11.28 E
Leutersdorf 54 50.57 N 14.40 E
Leutershausen 56 49.18 N 10.24 E
Leutesdorf 56 50.27 N 7.23 E
Leutkirch 58 47.49 N 10.01 E
Leuven (Louvain) 56 50.53 N 4.42 E
Leuville-sur-Orge 261 48.37 N 2.16 E
Leuwiliang 115a 6.34 S 106.37 E
Leuze, Bel. 50 50.36 N 3.36 E
Leuze, Bel. 56 50.34 N 4.54 E
Levack 190 46.38 N 81.23 W
Levádhia 38 38.25 N 22.54 E
Levaja Mama ≃ 88 57.10 N 111.54 E
Le Val-d'Ajol 58 47.55 N 6.29 E
Le Val-d'Albian 261 48.45 N 2.11 E
Levallois-Perret 261 48.54 N 2.18 E
Le Val-Saint-Germain 261 48.34 N 2.04 E
Levan 200 39.33 N 111.51 W
Levanger 26 63.45 N 11.18 E
Levanna, Monte ʌ 62 45.24 N 7.12 E
Levant, Île du I 62 43.03 N 6.28 E
Levante, Riviera di ≛[2] 62 44.15 N 9.30 E
Levanto 62 44.10 N 9.38 E
Levanzo 70 37.59 N 12.20 E
Levanzo, Isola di I 70 38.00 N 12.20 E
Levaši 84 42.27 N 47.20 E
Le Vauclin 240e 14.33 N 60.51 W
Levdym 86 60.29 N 66.19 E
Leveaux Mountain ʌ[2] 190 47.37 N 90.47 W
Levél 61 47.54 N 17.12 E
Level, Isla I 254 44.29 S 74.23 W
Level Green 279b 40.24 N 79.43 W
Levelland 196 33.35 N 102.22 W
Levelock 180 59.07 N 156.52 W
Level Park 216 42.22 N 85.18 W
Leven, Eng., U.K. 44 53.53 N 0.19 W
Leven, Scot., U.K. 46 56.12 N 3.00 W
Leven ≃, Eng., U.K. 44 54.14 N 3.01 W
Leven ≃, Eng., U.K. 44 54.31 N 1.21 W
Leven, Loch @, Scot., U.K. 46 56.12 N 3.22 W
Leven, Loch @, Scot., U.K. 46 56.41 N 5.07 W
Leven Point › 158 27.55 S 32.35 E
Levens 62 43.52 N 7.13 E
Levenshulme ◆[8] 262 53.27 N 2.12 W
Levent 130 38.27 N 37.52 E
Leventina, Valle V 58 46.25 N 8.52 E
Leveque, Cape › 162 16.24 S 122.56 E
Leverano 68 40.17 N 18.00 E
Leverburgh 46 57.45 N 7.00 W
Leveretts Chapel 222 32.19 N 94.55 W
Levering 190 45.38 N 84.47 W
Leverkusen 56 51.03 N 6.59 E
Levern 52 52.22 N 8.26 E
Lever Park ♦ 262 53.37 N 2.34 W
Le Vésinet 261 48.54 N 2.08 E
Le Vésuve
— Vesuvio ʌ[1] 68 40.49 N 14.26 E
Leviathan Peak ʌ 226 38.41 N 119.37 W
Levice 30 48.13 N 18.37 E
Levicha 86 57.36 N 59.55 E
Levick, Mount ʌ 9 74.08 S 163.12 E
Levico 64 46.01 N 11.18 E
Levie 36 41.42 N 9.07 E
Levier 58 46.57 N 6.08 E
Le Vigan 32 43.59 N 3.35 E
Levin 172 40.37 S 175.17 E
Levino 76 60.29 N 37.30 E
Lévis 206 46.48 N 71.11 W
Lévis □[6] 206 46.40 N 71.15 W
Levisa Fork ≃ 188 38.06 N 82.36 W
Lévis-Saint Nom 261 48.43 N 1.58 E
Levitha I 38 37.00 N 26.28 E
Levittown, P.R. 240m 18.27 N 66.14 W
Levittown, N.Y., U.S. 210 40.43 N 73.30 W
Levittown, Pa., U.S. 208 40.09 N 74.49 W
Levittown Discount World ◆[9] 285 40.09 N 74.49 W
Levittown
— Willingboro 208 40.03 N 74.53 W
Lévka Óri ʌ 38 35.18 N 24.01 E
Levkás 38 38.50 N 20.41 E
Levkás I 38 38.39 N 20.27 E
Levkimmi 38 39.25 N 20.04 E
Levoča 30 49.02 N 20.36 E
Levokumskoje 84 44.48 N 44.39 E
Levroux 32 46.59 N 1.37 E
Levski 38 43.22 N 25.08 E
Lev Tolstoj 76 53.13 N 39.27 E
Levuka 175g 17.41 S 178.50 E
Levuo ≃ 76 56.04 N 24.23 E
Levyj Tuzlov ≃ 83 47.35 N 39.23 E
Lewapaku 115b 9.43 S 119.55 E
Lewbeach 210 42.00 N 74.47 W
Lewe 110 19.38 N 96.07 E
Lewedorp 52 51.30 N 3.45 E
Lewellen 198 41.19 N 102.08 W
Lewer ≃ 156 25.30 S 17.45 E
Lewes, Eng., U.K. 42 50.52 N 0.01 E
Lewes, De., U.S. 208 38.46 N 75.08 W
Lewin Brzeski 30 50.46 N 17.37 E
Lewis, Ia., U.S. 198 41.18 N 95.04 W
Lewis, Ks., U.S. 198 37.56 N 99.15 W
Lewis □[6], Ky., U.S. 218 38.32 N 83.21 W
Lewis □[6], Mo., U.S. 219 40.08 N 91.45 W
Lewis □[6], N.Y., U.S. 212 43.47 N 75.29 W
Lewis □[6], Wa., U.S. 224 46.35 N 122.22 W
Lewis ≃ 224 45.51 N 122.48 W
Lewis, Butt of › 46 58.31 N 6.16 W
Lewis, East Fork ≃ 224 45.52 N 122.43 W
Lewis, Isle of I 46 58.10 N 6.40 W
Lewis, Mount ʌ 204 40.24 N 116.51 W
Lewis and Clark ≃ 224 46.10 N 123.52 W
Lewis and Clark Cavern State Park ♦ 202 45.49 N 111.13 W
Lewis and Clark Lake @[1] 198 42.50 N 97.45 W
Lewis and Clark Range ʌʌ 202 47.30 N 113.00 W
Lewisberry 208 40.08 N 76.52 W
Lewisburg, Ky., U.S. 194 36.59 N 86.56 W
Lewisburg, Oh., U.S. 218 39.50 N 84.32 W
Lewisburg, Pa., U.S. 210 40.57 N 76.53 W
Lewisburg, Tn., U.S. 194 35.26 N 86.47 W
Lewisburg, W.V., U.S. 188 37.48 N 80.26 W
Lewis Center 214 40.12 N 83.01 W
Lewis Creek ≃, Ca., U.S. 226 35.17 N 120.58 W
Lewis Creek ≃, In., U.S. 218 39.22 N 85.51 W
Lewis Creek Reservoir @[1] 222 30.26 N 95.32 W
Lewisdale 284c 38.58 N 76.58 W
Lewisetta 208 38.01 N 76.28 W
Lewis Gut c 276 41.09 N 73.09 W
Lewisham 273d 26.07 S 27.49 E
Lewisham ◆[8] 42 51.27 N 0.01 E
Lewisham Location 273d 26.10 S 27.47 E
Lewis-Lockport Airport ⊠ 278 41.36 N 88.05 W
Lewis Pass)(172 42.23 S 172.24 E
Lewisport 194 37.56 N 86.54 W
Lewisporte 186 49.15 N 55.03 W
Lewis Range ʌʌ, Austl. 162 20.20 S 128.40 E
Lewis Range ʌʌ, Mt., U.S. 202 48.35 N 113.40 W
Lewis Run 214 41.52 N 78.39 W
Lewis Run ≃ 279b 40.17 N 79.55 W
Lewis Smith Lake @[1] 194 34.05 N 87.07 W
Lewiston, Ca., U.S. 204 40.43 N 122.48 W
Lewiston, Id., U.S. 202 46.25 N 117.01 W
Lewiston, Me., U.S. 188 44.06 N 70.12 W
Lewiston, Mi., U.S. 190 44.53 N 84.18 W
Lewiston, Mn., U.S. 190 43.59 N 91.52 W
Lewiston, N.Y., U.S. 210 43.10 N 79.02 W
Lewiston, Ut., U.S. 200 41.58 N 111.51 W
Lewiston Orchards 202 46.23 N 116.59 W
Lewistown, Il., U.S. 190 40.23 N 90.09 W
Lewistown, Md., U.S. 208 39.32 N 77.24 W
Lewistown, Mo., U.S. 219 40.05 N 91.48 W
Lewistown, Mt., U.S. 202 47.03 N 109.25 W
Lewistown, Oh., U.S. 216 40.25 N 83.53 W
Lewistown, Pa., U.S. 208 40.35 N 77.34 W
Lewisville, N.B., Can. 186 46.06 N 64.46 W
Lewisville, Ar., U.S. 194 33.21 N 93.34 W
Lewisville, In., U.S. 218 39.48 N 85.21 W
Lewisville, Pa., U.S. 208 39.43 N 75.53 W
Lewisville, Tx., U.S. 222 33.02 N 96.59 W
Lewisville Dam ◆[6] 222 33.05 N 96.55 W
Lewisville Lake @[1] 196 33.08 N 97.00 W
Lewoleba 112 8.23 S 123.24 E
Lewotobi-lakilaki, Ili ʌ 115b 8.32 S 122.46 E
Lewvan 184 50.00 N 104.06 W
Lexa 194 34.35 N 90.44 W
Lexington, Ga., U.S. 192 33.52 N 83.06 W
Lexington, Il., U.S. 216 40.38 N 88.47 W
Lexington, In., U.S. 218 38.39 N 85.37 W
Lexington, Ky., U.S. 218 38.02 N 84.30 W
Lexington, Ma., U.S. 207 42.26 N 71.13 W
Lexington, Mi., U.S. 190 43.16 N 82.31 W
Lexington, Ms., U.S. 194 33.06 N 90.03 W
Lexington, Mo., U.S. 194 39.11 N 93.52 W
Lexington, Ne., U.S. 198 40.46 N 99.44 W
Lexington, N.Y., U.S. 210 42.15 N 74.22 W
Lexington, N.C., U.S. 192 35.49 N 80.15 W
Lexington, Oh., U.S. 214 40.40 N 82.34 W
Lexington, Ok., U.S. 196 35.00 N 97.20 W
Lexington, Or., U.S. 202 45.26 N 119.41 W
Lexington, S.C., U.S. 192 33.58 N 81.14 W
Lexington, Tn., U.S. 194 35.39 N 88.23 W
Lexington, Tx., U.S. 222 30.25 N 97.01 W
Lexington, Va., U.S. 192 37.47 N 79.26 W
Lexington Park 208 38.16 N 76.27 W
Lexington Reservoir @[1] 226 37.12 N 121.59 W
Lexton 169 37.17 S 143.31 E
Leybourne 260 51.18 N 0.25 E
Leyburn 44 54.19 N 1.49 W
Leyden
— Leiden 52 52.09 N 4.30 E
Leye 102 24.48 N 106.34 E
Leyland 44 53.42 N 2.42 W
Leyond ≃ 184 51.40 N 96.32 W
Léyou ≃ 152 1.07 S 13.08 E
Leyre ≃ 32 44.39 N 1.01 W
Leysdown-on-Sea 42 51.24 N 0.55 E
Leysin 58 46.21 N 7.01 E
Leyte 116 11.22 N 124.29 E
Leyte □[4] 116 10.50 N 124.55 E
Leyte I 116 10.50 N 124.50 E
Leyte Gulf c 116 10.50 N 125.25 E
Leyu 106 31.55 N 120.43 E
Lèz ≃ 62 43.13 N 4.43 E
Lèze ≃ 62 43.31 N 1.26 E
Leža 76 58.56 N 40.45 E
Leža ≃ 76 59.15 N 40.10 E
Ležajsk 30 50.16 N 22.24 E
Lezama 246 9.43 N 66.24 W
Lézarde ≃ 240e 14.36 N 61.01 W
Lézat 58 46.30 N 5.56 E
Lézat 62 43.10 N 5.28 E
Lezhë 38 41.47 N 19.39 E
Lezhi 107 30.17 N 105.02 E
Ležn'ovo 80 56.46 N 40.53 E
Lezzeno 58 45.56 N 9.11 E
L'gov 78 51.43 N 35.17 E
Lhasa 120 29.40 N 91.09 E
Lhasa ≃ 120 29.21 N 90.45 E
L'Hautil 261 49.00 N 2.01 E
Lhazê 120 29.10 N 87.42 E
L'Hillil 34 35.41 N 0.19 E
Lhokkruet 114 4.52 N 95.24 E
Lhoknga 114 5.29 N 95.15 E
Lhokseumawe 114 5.10 N 97.08 E
Lhoksukon 114 5.03 N 97.19 E
L'Hôpital-sous-Rochefort 62 45.46 N 3.56 E
Lhorong 102 30.45 N 96.09 E
L'Hospitalet de Llobregat 34 41.22 N 2.08 E
Lhotse ʌ 124 27.57 N 86.56 E
Lhozhag 120 28.24 N 90.49 E
Lhuis 62 45.45 N 5.32 E
Lhuntsi Dzong 120 27.39 N 91.09 E
Lhünzê 120 28.25 N 92.31 E
Li 110 17.48 N 98.57 E
Li ≃, Thai 110 18.26 N 98.42 E
Li ≃, Zhg. 100 33.11 N 115.07 E
Li ≃, Zhg. 102 29.24 N 112.01 E
Lian ≃, Zhg. 100 24.02 N 113.18 E
Lian ≃, Zhg. 100 25.46 N 115.38 E
Lian ≃, Zhg. 102 24.02 N 113.18 E
Lian ≃, Zhg. 102 27.48 N 112.52 E
Liancheng 100 25.44 N 116.46 E
Liancourt 50 49.20 N 2.28 E
Liane ≃ 50 50.43 N 1.36 E
Liang 164 3.30 S 128.19 E
Lianga 116 8.38 N 126.06 E
Lianga Bay c 116 8.37 N 126.12 E
Liang'anchang 107 30.30 N 104.56 E
Liangbao 102 34.37 N 110.45 E
Liangbingbao 89 45.48 N 128.19 E
Liangbingtai 89 43.12 N 128.47 E
Liangbuaya 112 0.05 N 116.46 E
Liangchahe 107 29.03 N 106.18 E
Liangcheng 98 35.35 N 119.35 E
Liangcun 100 26.36 N 115.34 E
Liangdang 102 33.56 N 106.12 E
Liangdawa 105 40.39 N 117.37 E
Liangfengwu 107 30.11 N 105.22 E
Lianggezhuang 105 39.21 N 115.22 E
Lianghe, Zhg. 89 45.09 N 128.45 E
Lianghe, Zhg. 102 24.51 N 98.25 E
Liangheguan 102 32.52 N 109.19 E
Lianghekou, Zhg. 102 33.42 N 104.25 E
Lianghekou, Zhg. 102 29.14 N 108.40 E
Lianghekou, Zhg. 102 31.27 N 102.13 E
Lianghekou, Zhg. 107 28.55 N 106.03 E
Liangiu 98 35.12 N 117.47 E
Liangjia 107 29.29 N 105.33 E
Liangjiadian 98 39.10 N 121.54 E
Liangjiafang 98 41.04 N 117.18 E
Liangjianfang 105 40.45 N 117.20 E
Liangjiang 102 23.23 N 108.22 E
Liangjiangkou 98 42.38 N 128.05 E
Liangjiawazi 104 40.40 N 120.42 E
Liangjiazi 104 42.13 N 122.31 E
Liangkou 100 23.43 N 113.43 E
Lianglukou 107 29.18 N 106.15 E
Liangmen 98 35.34 N 114.54 E
Liangmentou 100 28.58 N 121.12 E
Liangmushi 106 30.46 N 119.35 E
Liangpa 102 24.10 N 106.13 E
Liangpeng 106 30.47 N 119.38 E
Liangping 102 30.41 N 107.49 E
Liang Shan ʌ 102 23.45 N 99.45 E
Liangshui ≃ 271a 39.49 N 116.40 E
Liangtian 100 25.37 N 113.00 E
Liangtinghe 100 30.20 N 116.12 E
Liangtoumen 100 29.31 N 120.45 E
Liangtun 98 40.14 N 122.34 E
Liangwangzhuang 105 39.01 N 116.58 E
Liangxiangzhen 105 39.44 N 116.08 E
Liangying 100 23.14 N 116.21 E
Liangyuan 100 32.00 N 117.34 E
Liangzhu 106 30.23 N 120.03 E
Liangzi Hu @ 100 30.16 N 114.34 E
Lianhe 98 42.36 N 125.37 E
Lian Hu @ 106 32.02 N 119.32 E
Lianhua 100 27.07 N 113.57 E
Lianhuachi 105 40.28 N 116.33 E
Lianhuapao 89 45.32 N 129.50 E
Lianhua Shan ʌʌ 100 23.40 N 116.00 E
Lianjiang, Zhg. 100 26.12 N 119.31 E
Lianjiang, Zhg. 102 21.38 N 110.15 E
Lianjiechang 107 29.41 N 104.30 E
Liannan (Sanjiang) 102 24.38 N 112.10 E
Lianozovo ◆[8] 265b 55.54 N 37.35 E
Lianping 100 24.22 N 114.31 E
Lianpu 100 26.02 N 118.38 E
Lianshanguan 104 40.58 N 123.46 E
Lianshi 106 30.42 N 120.26 E
Lianshui 100 33.47 N 119.16 E
Liansiji 98 33.58 N 114.24 E
Liantang 106 31.37 N 120.38 E
Lianxian 102 24.48 N 112.25 E
Lianyin 89 53.28 N 123.51 E
Lianyuan (Lantian) 102 27.42 N 111.19 E
Lianyungang, Zhg. 98 34.44 N 119.30 E
Lianyungang (Xinpu), Zhg. 98 34.39 N 119.16 E
Lianyun Shan ʌ 100 28.32 N 113.50 E
Lianzhou
— Hepu 102 21.39 N 109.11 E
Liao ≃ 90 40.50 N 121.48 E
Liaobinta 104 42.08 N 123.04 E
Liaocheng 98 36.30 N 115.59 E
Liaodong Bandao (Liaotung Peninsula) ›[1] 98 40.00 N 122.20 E
Liaodong Wan (Gulf of Liaotung) c 98 40.30 N 121.30 E
Liaohe Kou c[1] 104 40.42 N 122.05 E
Liaojiangshi 100 26.05 N 113.17 E
Liaoning □[4] 90 41.00 N 123.00 E
Liaotung, Gulf of
— Liaodong Wan c 98 40.30 N 121.30 E
Liaotung Peninsula
— Liaodong Bandao ›[1] 98 40.00 N 122.20 E
Liaoyang 104 41.17 N 123.11 E
Liaoyangwopu 89 43.00 N 123.28 E
Liaoyuan 89 42.54 N 125.07 E
Liaozhong 104 41.31 N 122.44 E
Liapádhes 38 39.40 N 19.44 E
Liāquatpur 123 28.56 N 70.57 E
Liard ≃ 176 61.52 N 121.18 W
Liāri 120 25.41 N 66.29 E
Liart 50 49.46 N 4.20 E
Liat, Pulau I 112 2.53 S 107.05 E
Liathach ʌ 46 57.35 N 5.29 W
Lib I 14 8.19 N 167.25 E
Libagon 116 10.18 N 125.03 E
Libanga 152 0.19 N 18.41 E
Liban
— Lebanon □[1] 128 34.00 N 36.00 E
Líbano 246 4.55 N 75.04 W
Libano
— Lebanon □[1] 128 34.00 N 36.00 E
Libanon
— Lebanon □[1] 128 34.00 N 36.00 E
Libau
— Liepāja 76 56.31 N 21.01 E
Libby 202 48.23 N 115.33 W
Libby Dam ◆[6] 202 48.24 N 115.20 W
Libčeves 54 50.26 N 13.50 E
Libčice nad Vltavou 54 50.10 N 14.20 E
Liběchov 54 50.20 N 14.28 E
Libenge 152 3.39 N 18.38 E
Liberal, Ks., U.S. 198 37.02 N 100.55 W
Liberal, Mo., U.S. 194 37.33 N 94.31 W
Liberdade 256 22.01 S 44.19 W
Liberdade ◆[8] 287b 23.35 S 46.37 W
Liberdade ≃, Bra. 248 7.10 S 71.51 W
Liberdade ≃, Bra. 250 9.40 S 52.17 W
Liberec 30 50.46 N 15.03 E
Liberia 236 10.38 N 85.27 W
Liberia □[1], Afr. 134 6.30 N 9.30 W
Liberia □[1], Afr. 150 6.30 N 9.30 W
Liberta 240c 17.02 N 61.47 W
Libertad, Arg. 258 34.42 S 58.41 W
Libertad, Ur. 258 34.38 S 56.39 W
Libertad, Ven. 246 8.20 N 69.37 W
Libertad, Ven. 246 9.23 N 68.44 W
Libertador □[5] 286c 10.27 N 66.57 W
Libertador General Bernardo O'Higgins □[4] 252 34.30 S 71.00 W
Libertador General San Martín 252 23.48 S 64.48 W
Liberty, Il., U.S. 219 39.53 N 91.06 W
Liberty, In., U.S. 218 39.38 N 84.55 W
Liberty, Ky., U.S. 194 37.19 N 84.56 W
Liberty, Ms., U.S. 194 31.09 N 90.48 W
Liberty, Mo., U.S. 194 39.14 N 94.25 W
Liberty, Ne., U.S. 198 40.05 N 96.28 W
Liberty, N.Y., U.S. 210 41.48 N 74.44 W
Liberty, N.C., U.S. 192 35.51 N 79.34 W
Liberty, Pa., U.S. 210 41.34 N 77.06 W
Liberty, Pa., U.S. 279b 40.20 N 79.51 W
Liberty, S.C., U.S. 192 34.47 N 82.41 W
Liberty, Tx., U.S. 222 30.03 N 94.47 W
Liberty □[6] 222 30.12 N 94.50 W
Liberty Acres 280 34.04 N 118.12 W
Liberty Bell Race Track ♦ 285 40.05 N 74.58 W
Liberty Center, In., U.S. 216 40.41 N 85.16 W
Liberty Center, Oh., U.S. 216 41.26 N 84.00 W
Liberty City 222 32.27 N 94.57 W
Liberty Corner 276 40.39 N 74.34 W
Liberty Ditch ≍ 226 36.31 N 120.02 W
Liberty Farms 226 38.19 N 121.42 W
Liberty Hill 196 30.40 N 97.55 W
Liberty Island I 276 40.41 N 74.03 W
Liberty Lake @[1] 208 39.25 N 76.53 W
Liberty Manor 284b 39.21 N 76.47 W
Liberty Mills 216 41.02 N 85.44 W
Liberty Park 216 41.26 N 87.22 W
Libertytown 208 39.29 N 77.14 W
Liberty Tree Mall ◆[9] 283 42.33 N 70.57 W
Liberty Tunnel ◆[5] 279b 40.26 N 80.01 W
Libertyville 216 42.16 N 87.57 W
Líbeznice 54 50.10 N 14.30 E
Libia
— Libya □[1] 146 27.00 N 17.00 E
Libibi 152 14.42 S 17.44 E
Libishan 106 30.45 N 119.20 E
Lībīyah, Aṣ-Ṣaḥrā' al- (Libyan Desert) ◆[2] 136 24.00 N 25.00 E
Lībiyā
— Libya □[1] 146 27.00 N 17.00 E
Liblín 60 49.55 N 13.32 E
Libni, Jabal ʌ[2] 132 30.44 N 33.50 E
Libo 102 25.28 N 107.53 E
Libobo, Tanjung › 164 0.54 S 128.28 E
Liboc ≃ 54 50.10 N 13.31 E
Libochovice 54 50.22 N 14.03 E
Libode 158 31.33 S 29.02 E
Liboi 154 0.24 N 40.57 E
Liboko 152 2.43 N 21.28 E
Libomyšl 60 49.52 N 14.00 E
Libona 116 8.20 N 124.44 E
Liboumba ≃ 152 0.38 N 12.54 E
Libourne 32 44.55 N 0.14 W
Libramont 56 49.55 N 5.23 E
Library 214 40.18 N 80.02 W
Librazhd 38 41.11 N 20.19 E
Libres 234 19.28 N 97.41 W
Libreville 152 0.23 N 9.27 E
Librizzi 70 38.06 N 14.57 E
Libro Point › 116 11.26 N 119.29 E
Libu 102 23.41 N 111.30 E
Libucan Island I 116 11.54 N 124.39 E
Libuganon ≃ 116 7.27 N 125.47 E
Libunga 154 1.49 N 26.35 E
Liburung 112 3.55 S 120.09 E
Libušín 54 50.09 N 14.04 E
Libya (Lībiyā) □[1], Afr. 136 27.00 N 17.00 E
Libya (Lībiyā) □[1], Afr. 146 27.00 N 17.00 E
Libyan Desert
— Lībīyah, Aṣ-Ṣaḥrā' al- ◆[2] 136 24.00 N 25.00 E
Libyan Plateau
— Aḍ-Ḍiffah ʌʌ[1] 140 30.30 N 25.30 E
Libye
— Libya □[1] 146 27.00 N 17.00 E
Libyen
— Libya □[1] 146 27.00 N 17.00 E
Libysche Wüste
— Lībīyah, Aṣ-Ṣaḥrā' al- ◆[2] 136 24.00 N 25.00 E
Licancábur, Volcán ʌ[1] 248 22.50 S 67.50 W
Licantén 252 34.59 S 72.00 W
Licata 70 37.06 N 13.56 E
Licciana Nardi 64 44.16 N 10.02 E
Lice 130 38.28 N 40.39 E
Lich 56 50.33 N 8.50 E
Lichačova, mys › 89 42.44 N 132.51 E
Lichaja ≃ 83 48.08 N 40.15 E
Lichang 107 28.53 N 104.26 E
Licheng 102 36.30 N 113.21 E
Lichères-Près-Aigremont 50 47.43 N 3.51 E
Lichfield 42 52.42 N 1.48 W
Lichinga 154 13.18 S 35.14 E
Lichitiseni 38 46.23 N 27.17 E
Lichoborka ≃ 265b 55.50 N 37.38 E
Lichoslavl' 76 57.07 N 35.28 E
Lichovka 78 48.41 N 33.55 E
Lichovskoj 83 48.07 N 40.12 E
Lichtaart 56 51.14 N 4.54 E
Lichte 54 50.31 N 11.10 E
Lichtenau 56 48.43 N 8.01 E
Lichtenberg, Dtsch. 54 50.23 N 11.40 E
Lichtenberg, Fr. 56 48.55 N 7.29 E
Lichtenberg ◆[8] 264a 52.31 N 13.29 E
Lichtenburg 158 26.08 S 26.08 E
Lichtendorf 263 51.28 N 7.37 E
Lichtenfels 56 50.09 N 11.04 E
Lichtenplatz ◆[8] 263 51.15 N 7.12 E
Lichtenrade ◆[8] 264a 52.23 N 13.25 E
Lichtensee 54 51.23 N 13.22 E
Lichtensteig 58 47.19 N 9.05 E
Lichtenstein 54 50.45 N 12.37 E
Lichtenstein, Schloss ʊ 58 48.24 N 9.15 E
Lichtentanne 54 50.42 N 12.25 E
Lichtenvoorde 52 51.59 N 6.34 E
Lichterfelde ◆[8] 264a 52.26 N 13.19 E
Lichtervelde 50 51.02 N 3.09 E
Lichuan, Zhg. 100 27.18 N 116.53 E
Lichuan, Zhg. 102 30.18 N 108.51 E
Lick Creek ≃, Il., U.S. 219 39.42 N 89.41 W
Lick Creek ≃, In., U.S. 218 38.33 N 86.31 W
Lick Creek ≃, Mo., U.S. 219 39.31 N 91.39 W
Lick Creek ≃, Oh., U.S. 216 41.21 N 84.25 W
Lick Creek ≃, Tn., U.S. 192 36.11 N 83.10 W
Lickershamn 26 57.50 N 18.31 E
Licking 194 37.29 N 91.51 W
Licking □[6] 214 40.10 N 82.30 W
Licking ≃, Ky., U.S. 188 39.06 N 84.30 W
Licking ≃, Oh., U.S. 214 40.03 N 82.20 W
Licking, North Fork ≃, Ky., U.S. 218 38.35 N 84.13 W
Licking, North Fork ≃, Oh., U.S. 214 40.03 N 82.23 W
Licking, South Fork ≃ 218 38.41 N 84.20 W
Lickingville 214 41.23 N 79.22 W
Lick Observatory ʊ[3] 226 37.22 N 121.37 W
Ličko Polje ≚ 36 44.35 N 15.25 E
Lick Run ≃, Pa., U.S. 210 41.12 N 77.32 W
Lick Run ≃, Pa., U.S. 279b 40.17 N 79.57 W
Licodia Eubea 70 37.09 N 14.42 E
Licosa, Punta › 68 40.15 N 14.54 E
Licun 98 38.32 N 117.08 E
Licungo ≃ 154 17.40 S 37.15 E
Lid' 76 59.39 N 35.05 E
Lida 76 53.53 N 25.18 E
Lidan ≃ 26 58.31 N 13.09 E
Lidao 98 37.15 N 122.32 E
Lidarentuncun 104 41.32 N 123.12 E
Lidcombe 274a 33.52 S 151.03 E
Liddel Water ≃ 44 55.04 N 2.57 W
Liddesdale V 44 55.12 N 2.46 W
Liddon Gulf c 176 75.03 N 113.00 W
Liden 26 62.42 N 16.48 E
Lidesi 100 33.33 N 115.53 E
Lidgerwood 198 46.04 N 97.09 W
Lidgetton 158 29.25 S 30.05 E
Lidian 107 28.57 N 103.44 E
Lídice, Bra. 256 22.51 S 44.12 W
Lídice, Pan. 236 8.45 N 79.54 W
Lidice ⊥ 54 50.03 N 14.08 E
Lidingö 40 59.22 N 18.08 E
Lidköping 26 58.30 N 13.10 E
Lido 64 45.25 N 12.22 E
Lido, Litorale di ≛[2] 64 45.23 N 12.21 E
Lido, Porto di c 64 45.26 N 12.25 E
Lido Beach 276 40.35 N 73.38 W
Lido di Camaiore 64 43.54 N 10.13 E
Lido di Castel Fusano ◆[8] 66 41.43 N 12.20 E
Lido di Iesolo 64 45.30 N 12.39 E
Lido di Metaponto 68 40.22 N 16.50 E
Lido di Ostia ◆[8] 66 41.44 N 12.14 E
Lido di Pomposa 66 44.45 N 12.14 E
Lido di Siponto 68 41.37 N 15.55 E
Lido Key I 220 27.19 N 82.35 W
Lidsjön @ 40 58.55 N 16.51 E
Lidu 107 30.35 N 106.04 E
Lidzbark 30 53.17 N 19.49 E
Lidzbark Warmiński 30 54.09 N 20.35 E
Liebenau, Dtsch. 52 52.36 N 9.05 E
Liebenau, Öst. 61 48.32 N 14.49 E
Liebenbergsvlei ≃ 158 27.20 S 28.31 E
Liebenburg 52 52.01 N 10.26 E
Liebenwalde 54 52.52 N 13.23 E
Lieberhausen 56 51.03 N 7.40 E
Lieberose 54 51.59 N 14.17 E
Liebertwolkwitz 54 51.17 N 12.28 E
Liebig, Mount ʌ 162 23.18 S 131.22 E
Liebstadt 54 50.52 N 13.51 E
Liechtenstein □[1], Europe 22 47.09 N 9.35 E
Liechtenstein □[1], Europe 58 47.09 N 9.35 E
Liechtensteinklamm V 64 47.18 N 13.12 E
Liedberg 263 51.10 N 6.32 E
Liedekerke 50 50.52 N 4.05 E
Liège (Luik) 56 50.38 N 5.34 E
Liège □[4] 56 50.30 N 5.30 E
Liège, Aéroport ⊠ 56 50.39 N 5.30 E
Liegnitz
— Legnica 30 51.13 N 16.09 E
Lieja
— Liège 56 50.38 N 5.34 E
Lieksa 26 63.19 N 30.01 E
Lielais Liepu kalns ʌ[2] 76 56.25 N 27.50 E
Lielupe ≃ 76 57.01 N 23.56 E
Lielvārde 76 56.43 N 24.51 E
Liemienzhen 107 30.29 N 106.05 E
Lienart 154 3.04 N 25.31 E
Lienchou
— Hepu 102 21.39 N 109.11 E
Lienen 52 52.09 N 7.58 E
Lienz 64 46.50 N 12.47 E
Liepāja 76 56.31 N 21.01 E
Liepājas ezers @ 76 56.27 N 21.03 E
Liepe 54 53.58 N 13.56 E
Liepna 76 57.25 N 27.25 E
Liepnitzsee @ 264a 52.45 N 13.30 E
Lièpvre 58 48.16 N 7.17 E
Lier (Lierre) 50 51.08 N 4.34 E
Lierenfeld ◆[8] 263 51.13 N 6.51 E
Lierna 58 45.57 N 9.18 E
Liernais 50 47.12 N 4.17 E
Lierneux 56 50.18 N 5.48 E
Liershizhai 104 41.49 N 123.43 E
Liesborn 52 51.43 N 8.15 E
Lieser ≃, Dtsch. 56 49.55 N 7.01 E
Lieser ≃, Öst. 64 46.47 N 13.39 E
Lieshout 52 51.32 N 5.35 E
Liesing ◆[8] 264b 48.08 N 16.17 E
Liesing ≃ 264b 48.08 N 16.28 E
Liesingbach ≃ 61 47.20 N 15.02 E
Liesjärven Kansallispuisto ♦ 26 60.40 N 23.54 E
Lieskau 54 51.37 N 13.48 E
Liesse 50 49.37 N 3.48 E
Liessies 50 50.07 N 4.05 E
Liestal 58 47.29 N 7.44 E
Liești 38 45.38 N 27.32 E
Lietuva
— Lithuania □[1] 72 56.00 N 24.00 E
Lietzow 54 54.29 N 13.30 E
Lieurey 50 49.14 N 0.29 E
Lieusaint 261 48.38 N 2.33 E
Lieutel ≃ 261 48.49 N 1.52 E
Lieutenant Robert J. Palenscar Memorial Airport ⊠ 285 39.51 N 75.03 W
Liévin 50 50.25 N 2.46 E
Lièvre, Rivière du ≃ 176 45.31 N 75.26 W
Lièvres, Île aux I 186 47.51 N 69.44 W
Liezen 61 47.35 N 14.15 E
Lifanga 152 0.19 N 21.57 E
Liffey ≃ 48 53.21 N 6.16 W
Liffol-le-Grand 58 48.19 N 5.35 E
Lifford 48 54.50 N 7.29 W
Liffré 32 48.13 N 1.30 W
Lifjell ʌ 26 59.30 N 8.52 E
Lifoku 152 0.04 S 21.18 E
Lifou I 175f 20.53 S 167.13 E
Lifoula 273b 4.06 S 15.25 E
Lifton 42 50.39 N 4.17 W
Liftwood 285 39.47 N 75.31 W
Lifune ≃ 152 8.21 S 13.22 E
Ligačovo 265b 55.56 N 37.15 E
Ligang 100 30.04 N 121.52 E
Ligao, Pil. 116 13.14 N 123.32 E
Ligao, Pil. 116 6.17 N 124.09 E
Ligasa 152 0.42 N 23.45 E
Līgatne 76 57.14 N 25.02 E
Ligezhuang, Zhg. 105 39.49 N 115.56 E
Ligezhuang, Zhg. 105 39.42 N 118.12 E
Light ≃ 168b 34.35 S 138.22 E
Lightfoot 208 37.20 N 76.45 W
Lighthouse Beach ≛[2] 273a 6.24 N 3.22 E
Lighthouse Point 220 26.16 N 80.05 W
Lighthouse Point ›, On., Can. 214 41.50 N 82.38 W
Lighthouse Point ›, Fl., U.S. 192 29.54 N 84.21 W
Lighthouse Point ›, Mi., U.S. 190 45.13 N 85.32 W
Lighthouse Reef ✧[2] 232 17.20 N 87.32 W
Lightning Creek ≃, Sk., Can. 184 49.12 N 101.43 W
Lightning Creek ≃, N.A. 224 48.50 N 121.03 W
Lightning Creek ≃, Wy., U.S. 198 43.11 N 104.44 W
Lightning Ridge 166 29.26 S 147.59 E
Lightstreet 210 41.02 N 76.25 W
Lightsville 216 40.18 N 84.42 W
Ligist 61 46.59 N 15.12 E
Lignano Pineta 64 45.40 N 13.07 E
Lignano Sabbiadoro 64 45.42 N 13.09 E
Lignières 32 46.45 N 2.11 E
Lignite 198 48.52 N 102.33 W
Lignon ≃ 62 45.44 N 4.08 E
Lignumvitae Key I 220 24.55 N 80.42 W
Ligny-en-Barrois 58 48.41 N 5.20 E
Ligny-en-Cambrésis 50 50.06 N 3.22 E
Ligny-le-Châtel 50 47.54 N 3.45 E
Ligny-le-Ribault 50 47.41 N 1.47 E
Ligonha ≃ 154 16.54 S 39.09 E
Ligonier, In., U.S. 216 41.27 N 85.35 W
Ligonier, Pa., U.S. 214 40.14 N 79.14 W
Ligovka 78 49.08 N 36.03 E
Ligovo 76 60.13 N 31.48 E
Ligovo ◆[8] 265a 59.50 N 30.12 E
Ligovskij kanal ≍ 265a 59.47 N 30.10 E
Liguantu 105 40.24 N 115.45 E
Ligueil 32 47.03 N 0.49 E
Ligui 232 25.43 N 111.16 W
Ligure, Mar
— Ligurian Sea ⩪[2] 36 43.30 N 9.00 E
Liguria □[4] 62 44.30 N 8.50 E
Liguria, Mar de
— Ligurian Sea ⩪[2] 36 43.30 N 9.00 E
Ligurian Sea ⩪[2] 36 43.30 N 9.00 E
Ligurisches Meer
— Ligurian Sea ⩪[2] 36 43.30 N 9.00 E

Symbol	English	Deutsch	Español	Français	Português
≃	River	Fluß	Río	Rivière	Rio
≍	Canal	Kanal	Canal	Canal	Canal
⊾	Waterfall, Rapids	Wasserfall, Stromschnellen	Cascada, Rápidos	Chute d'eau, Rapides	Cascata, Rápidos
⋓	Strait	Meeresstraße	Estrecho	Détroit	Estreito
c	Bay, Gulf	Bucht, Golf	Bahía, Golfo	Baie, Golfe	Baía, Golfo
@	Lake, Lakes	See, Seen	Lago, Lagos	Lac, Lacs	Lago, Lagos
≚	Swamp	Sumpf	Pantano	Marais	Pântano
⁂	Ice Features, Glacier	Eis- und Gletscherformen	Accidentes Glaciales	Formes glaciaires	Acidentes glaciares
⩪	Other Hydrographic Features	Andere Hydrographische Objekte	Otros Elementos Hidrográficos	Autres données hydrographiques	Outros acidentes hidrográficos
✧	Submarine Features	Untermeerische Objekte	Accidentes Submarinos	Formes de relief sous-marin	Acidentes submarinos
□	Political Unit	Politische Einheit	Unidad Politica	Entité politique	Unidade política
ʊ	Cultural Institution	Kulturelle Institution	Institución Cultural	Institution culturelle	Institução cultural
⊥	Historical Site	Historische Stätte	Sitio Histórico	Site historique	Sitio histórico
♦	Recreational Site	Erholungs- und Ferienort	Sitio de Recreo	Centre de loisirs	Area de Lazer
⊠	Airport	Flughafen	Aeropuerto	Aéroport	Aeroporto
■	Military Installation	Militäranlage	Instalación Militar	Installation militaire	Instalação militar
◆	Miscellaneous	Verschiedenes	Misceláneo	Divers	Diversos

ENGLISH / DEUTSCH

Name / Name	Page / Seite	Lat.°′ / Breite°′	Long.°′ / Länge°′ E = Ost
Lihir Group II	164	3.05 S	152.40 E
Lihir Island I	164	3.05 S	152.35 E
Lihou Reef and Cays ◆[2]	166	17.25 S	151.40 E
Lihu	100	23.23 N	116.03 E
Lihue	229b	21.58 N	159.22 W
Lihue Airport ⊠	229b	21.59 N	159.21 W
Lihuel Calel, Parque Nacional ♠, Arg.	252	37.58 S	65.32 W
Lihuel Calel, Parque Nacional ♠, Arg.	254	37.58 S	65.32 W
Lihula	76	58.41 N	23.50 E
Liji, Zhg.	100	31.59 N	115.51 E
Liji, Zhg.	100	33.48 N	117.48 E
Lijia, Zhg.	98	37.49 N	118.01 E
Lijia, Zhg.	104	41.43 N	122.20 E
Lijiaba	107	29.37 N	105.33 E
Lijiadian	104	42.07 N	121.14 E
Lijiajie	107	29.49 N	105.30 E
Lijiakou	105	39.12 N	116.29 E
Lijiang	102	26.57 N	100.15 E
Lijiapuzi	104	40.59 N	123.38 E
Lijiaqiao, Zhg.	105	40.03 N	116.40 E
Lijiaqiao, Zhg.	105	39.47 N	117.47 E
Lijiaqiao, Zhg.	106	31.38 N	120.00 E
Lijiatun	104	41.19 N	121.23 E
Lijiatuo	107	29.28 N	106.33 E
Lijiawobao	104	41.00 N	122.26 E
Lijiaxiang	106	30.57 N	119.59 E
Lijiazao	105	39.17 N	118.19 E
Lijin, Zhg.	98	37.29 N	118.16 E
Lijin, Zhg.	104	41.40 N	121.20 E
Lik ≃	110	18.31 N	102.31 E
Likako	152	0.15 N	21.00 E
Likang	100	22.47 N	120.29 E
Likasi (Jadotville)	154	10.59 S	26.44 E
Likati	152	3.21 N	23.53 E
Likati ≃	152	2.53 N	24.03 E
Likely	182	52.37 N	121.34 W
Likėnai	76	56.12 N	24.37 E
Likete	152	0.43 S	21.25 E
Likhu ≃	124	27.15 N	86.12 E
Liki	112	1.36 S	101.11 E
Likimi	152	2.50 N	20.45 E
Likino	82	55.38 N	37.08 E
Likino-Dulevo	82	55.43 N	38.58 E
Liknes	26	58.19 N	6.59 E
Likoma Island I	154	12.05 S	34.45 E
Likou, Zhg.	100	29.53 N	117.28 E
Likou, Zhg.	100	33.51 N	113.20 E
Likou, Zhg.	106	31.24 N	120.37 E
Likouala □[5]	152	2.00 N	17.30 E
Likouala ≃	152	1.13 S	16.48 E
Likouala aux Herbes ≃	152	0.50 S	17.11 E
Likova ≃	265b	55.34 N	37.21 E
Likstammen ⊜	40	58.58 N	17.12 E
Liku	174v	19.02 S	169.47 W
Likupang	112	1.41 N	125.04 E
Likus ≃	236	14.14 N	83.35 W
Likuyu	154	10.20 S	36.14 E
Lilanchengzhen	105	39.12 N	116.43 E
Lilanga	152	0.34 S	23.55 E
Lilasi	124	29.22 N	84.30 E
Lilbert	222	31.44 N	94.54 W
Lilbourn	194	36.35 N	89.36 W
L'Île-Bouchard	32	47.07 N	0.25 E
Lilenga	152	0.54 N	22.06 E
L'Île-Rousse	32	42.38 N	8.56 E
Lili	106	31.00 N	120.42 E
Lilian Point ›	174d	0.53 S	169.35 E
Lilienfeld	61	48.03 N	15.36 E
Lilienthal	52	53.08 N	8.55 E
Liling	100	27.40 N	113.30 E
Lilio	116	14.08 N	121.26 E
Liljendal	40	60.08 N	14.04 E
Lilla Bharwana	123	32.34 N	72.45 E
Lilla Edet	26	58.08 N	12.08 E
Lillån	40	59.19 N	15.13 E
Lillby	26	63.28 N	23.00 E
Lille	50	50.38 N	3.04 E
Lillebælt U	41	55.20 N	9.45 E
Lillebonne	50	49.31 N	0.33 E
Lillehammer	26	61.08 N	10.30 E
Lille-Lesquin, Aéroport ⊠	50	50.35 N	3.07 E
Lillerød	41	55.52 N	12.22 E
Lillers	50	50.34 N	2.29 E
Lillesand	26	58.15 N	8.24 E
Lilleshall	42	52.44 N	2.21 W
Lillestrøm	26	59.57 N	11.05 E
Lille Værløse	41	55.47 N	12.23 E
Lillhärdal	26	61.51 N	14.04 E
Lillian	222	32.30 N	97.11 W
Lillington	192	35.23 N	78.48 W
Lillinonah Lake ⊜[1]	207	41.28 N	73.21 W
Lilli Pilli	274a	34.04 S	151.07 E
Lillo	34	39.43 N	3.18 W
Lillooet	182	50.42 N	121.56 W
Lillooet ≃	182	49.45 N	122.08 W
Lillooet Lake ⊜	182	50.13 N	122.29 W
Lilly	214	40.25 N	78.37 W
Lilly Creek ≃	222	32.47 N	94.56 W
Liloan	116	10.09 N	125.07 E
Lilongwe	154	13.59 S	33.44 E
Lilo Viejo	252	26.56 S	62.58 W
Liloy	116	8.08 N	122.40 E
Liluāh	272b	22.35 N	88.23 E
Lily	192	37.01 N	84.04 W
Lily Cache Creek ≃	278	41.41 N	88.07 W
Lilydale, Austl.	166	41.15 S	147.13 E
Lilydale, Austl.	169	37.45 S	145.21 E
Lily Dale, N.Y., U.S.	214	42.21 N	79.19 W
Lilyfield	274a	33.52 S	151.10 E
Lilyvale	273d	26.06 S	28.25 E
Lim ≃, Afr.	152	7.54 N	15.46 E
Lim ≃, Europe	38	43.45 N	19.13 E
Lima, Arg.	258	34.03 S	59.12 W
Lima, Para.	252	23.54 S	56.20 W
Lima, Perú	248	12.03 S	77.03 W
Lima, Perú	286d	12.03 S	77.03 W
Lima, Sve.	26	60.56 N	13.26 E
Lima, Il., U.S.	219	40.11 N	91.23 W
Lima, Mt., U.S.	202	44.38 N	112.35 W
Lima, N.Y., U.S.	210	42.54 N	77.36 W
Lima, Oh., U.S.	216	40.44 N	84.06 W
Lima, Pa., U.S.	285	39.55 N	75.26 W
Lima □[5]	248	12.00 S	76.35 W
Lima (Limia) ≃, Europe	34	41.41 N	8.50 W
Lima ≃, It.	64	44.00 N	10.35 E
Lima, Punta ›	240m	18.11 N	65.41 W
Lima Center	216	42.47 N	88.49 W
Limache	252	33.01 S	71.16 W
Lima Duarte	256	21.51 S	43.48 W
Liman, Ross.	80	45.47 N	47.14 E
Liman, Ukr.	78	49.36 N	36.27 E
Liman, Ukr.	78	45.41 N	29.45 E
Liman, Ukr.	83	49.21 N	38.57 E
Liman, Yis.	132	33.03 N	35.06 E
Liman ≃	115a	6.29 S	105.48 E
Limanowa	30	49.43 N	20.26 E
Limanskoje	78	46.38 N	30.00 E
Limão ◆[8]	287b	23.30 S	46.40 W
Limapuluh	114	3.10 N	99.26 E
Lima Reservoir ⊜[1]	202	44.38 N	112.17 W
Limarí ≃	252	30.44 S	71.43 W
Limas	112	0.14 N	104.31 E
Limasawa Island I	116	9.56 N	125.05 E
Limassa	152	4.14 N	22.02 E
Limassol → Lemesós	130	34.40 N	33.02 E
Limavady	48	55.03 N	6.57 W
Limaville	214	40.59 N	81.09 W
Limay, Fr.	50	49.00 N	1.44 E
Limay, Pil.	116	14.34 N	120.36 E
Limay ≃	254	38.59 S	68.00 W
Limay Mahuida	252	37.12 S	66.42 W
Limbach-Oberfrohna	54	50.51 N	12.45 E
Limbadi	68	38.33 N	15.58 E
Limbang	112	4.45 N	115.00 E
Limbang ≃	112	4.50 N	115.01 E
Limbani	248	14.08 S	69.42 W
Limbara, Monte ʌ	71	40.51 N	9.10 E
Limbaži	76	57.31 N	24.42 E
Līmbdi	120	22.34 N	71.48 E
Limbe	154	15.49 S	35.03 E
Limbiate	62	45.36 N	9.07 E
Limboto	112	0.37 N	122.57 E
Limbourg	56	50.37 N	5.56 E
Limbrick	262	53.38 N	2.36 W
Limbueta	152	12.30 S	18.42 E
Limbunya	164	17.14 S	129.50 E
Limburg □[4], Bel.	56	51.00 N	5.30 E
Limburg □[4], Ned.	52	51.14 N	5.50 E
Limburg an der Lahn	56	50.23 N	8.04 E
Limburgerhof	56	49.25 N	8.24 E
Lim Chu Kang	271c	1.26 N	103.43 E
Limecrest	218	39.54 N	83.48 W
Limefield	262	53.37 N	2.18 W
Limeira	255	22.34 S	47.24 W
Limekiln Canyon V	280	34.18 N	118.33 W
Lime Lake	210	42.26 N	78.29 W
Limen	100	27.07 N	119.19 E
Limena	64	45.29 N	11.50 E
Limentra ≃	64	44.14 N	11.03 E
Limerick, Sk., Can.	184	49.40 N	106.15 W
Limerick, Ire.	48	52.40 N	8.38 W
Limerick, Pa., U.S.	285	40.14 N	75.32 W
Limerick (Luimneach) □[6]	48	52.30 N	8.45 W
Limerick Lake ⊜	212	44.54 N	77.37 W
Limerock	207	41.55 N	71.28 W
Lime Springs	190	43.27 N	92.17 W
Limestone, Austl.	162	21.11 S	119.50 E
Limestone, Fl., U.S.	220	27.21 N	81.53 W
Limestone, Me., U.S.	186	46.54 N	67.49 W
Limestone, N.Y., U.S.	210	42.01 N	78.37 W
Limestone, Pa., U.S.	214	41.08 N	79.20 W
Limestone □[6]	222	31.35 N	96.35 W
Limestone ≃	184	56.31 N	94.07 W
Limestone, Lake ⊜[1]	222	31.25 N	96.20 W
Limestone Bay c	184	53.50 N	98.50 W
Limestone Canyon V	280	33.45 N	117.41 W
Limestone Creek ≃	210	43.06 N	75.58 W
Limestone Lake ⊜, Mb., Can.	184	56.35 N	96.00 W
Limestone Lake ⊜, Sk., Can.	184	54.36 N	103.18 W
Limestone Point ›[1]	184	53.50 N	98.50 W
Limestone Point Lake ⊜	184	55.07 N	100.32 W
Lime Street Station ◆[5]	262	53.25 N	2.59 W
Lime Village	180	61.21 N	155.28 W
Limfjorden U	26	56.55 N	9.10 E
Limhamn ◆[8]	41	55.35 N	12.54 E
Limia (Lima) ≃	34	41.41 N	8.50 W
Limina	70	37.56 N	15.17 E
Liminka	26	64.49 N	25.24 E
Liminzhen	98	34.31 N	115.56 E
Limit Brook ≃	283	42.42 N	71.25 W
Limmared	26	57.32 N	13.21 E
Limmaren ⊜	40	59.44 N	18.43 E
Limmen	52	52.34 N	4.41 E
Limmen Bight c[3]	164	14.45 S	135.40 E
Limmen Bight ≃	164	15.07 S	135.44 E
Límnos I	38	39.54 N	25.21 E
Limoeiro	250	7.52 S	35.27 W
Limoeiro do Norte	250	5.08 S	38.05 W
Limoges, On., Can.	212	45.20 N	75.15 W
Limoges, Fr.	32	45.50 N	1.16 E
Limoges-Fourches	261	48.38 N	2.40 E
Limogne	32	44.24 N	1.46 E
Limón, Hond.	236	15.52 N	85.33 W
Limon, Co., U.S.	198	39.15 N	103.41 W
Limón □[4]	236	10.00 N	83.15 W
Limonar	240p	22.57 N	81.24 W
Limone Piemonte	62	44.12 N	7.34 E
Limone sul Garda	64	45.49 N	10.47 E
Limours	50	48.39 N	2.05 E
Limousin, Plateaux du ⋏[1]	32	45.30 N	1.15 E
Limoux	32	43.04 N	2.14 E
Limpopo ≃	156	25.15 S	33.30 E
Limpsfield	42	51.16 N	0.01 E
Limski kanal c	64	45.07 N	13.38 E
Limu	102	25.02 N	110.51 E
Limuru	154	1.06 S	36.39 E
Linachamari	24	69.40 N	31.20 E
Līnah	128	28.42 N	43.48 E
Lin'an	106	30.14 N	119.43 E
Linanäs	40	59.28 N	18.31 E
Linao Bay c	116	6.45 N	124.00 E
Linapacan Island I	116	11.27 N	119.49 E
Linapacan Strait U	116	11.37 N	119.56 E
Linares, Chile	252	35.51 S	71.36 W
Linares, Col.	246	1.23 N	77.31 W
Linares, Esp.	34	38.05 N	3.38 W
Linares, Méx.	232	24.52 N	99.34 W
Linariá	38	37.24 N	24.57 E
Linaro, Capo ›	66	42.02 N	11.50 E
Linas	261	48.38 N	2.16 E
Linas, Monte ʌ	71	39.27 N	8.37 E
Linas-Montlhéry, Domaine Militaire de ■	261	48.37 N	2.13 E
Linate, Aeroporto di ⊠	62	45.27 N	9.16 E
Lincai	100	33.50 N	114.56 E
Lincang	102	23.45 N	102.20 E
Lince	286d	12.06 S	77.03 W
Linch	200	43.36 N	106.11 W
Lincheng, Zhg.	98	37.27 N	114.29 E
Lincheng, Zhg.	106	30.55 N	119.47 E
Linch'ing → Linqing	98	36.53 N	115.41 E
Lincoln, Arg.	252	34.52 S	61.32 W
Lincoln, On., Can.	212	43.10 N	79.29 W
Lincoln, N.Z.	172	43.39 S	172.29 E
Lincoln, Eng., U.K.	44	53.14 N	0.33 W
Lincoln, Ar., U.S.	194	35.56 N	94.25 W
Lincoln, Ca., U.S.	226	38.53 N	121.17 W
Lincoln, De., U.S.	208	38.52 N	75.25 W
Lincoln, Il., U.S.	219	40.08 N	89.21 W
Lincoln, In., U.S.	216	40.37 N	86.12 W
Lincoln, Ks., U.S.	198	39.02 N	98.08 W
Lincoln, Me., U.S.	188	45.21 N	68.30 W
Lincoln, Ma., U.S.	207	42.25 N	71.18 W
Lincoln, Mi., U.S.	190	44.41 N	83.24 W
Lincoln, Mo., U.S.	194	38.23 N	93.20 W
Lincoln, Mt., U.S.	202	46.57 N	112.40 W
Lincoln, Ne., U.S.	198	40.48 N	96.40 W
Lincoln, N.H., U.S.	188	44.02 N	71.40 W
Lincoln, Pa., U.S.	208	40.12 N	76.12 W
Lincoln, Pa., U.S.	279b	40.18 N	79.51 W
Lincoln, R.I., U.S.	207	41.54 N	71.25 W
Lincoln, Tx., U.S.	222	30.17 N	96.52 W
Lincoln □[6], Mo., U.S.	219	39.05 N	90.57 W
Lincoln □[6], Or., U.S.	224	44.59 N	123.52 W
Lincoln, Mount ʌ	200	39.21 N	106.07 W
Lincoln Acres	228	32.40 N	117.04 W
Lincoln Boyhood National Memorial ⊥	194	38.10 N	86.58 W
Lincoln Cathedral ʋ[1]	44	53.14 N	0.33 W
Lincoln Center ʋ	276	40.46 N	73.59 W
Lincoln City	224	44.57 N	124.00 W
Lincoln Creek ≃, Ne., U.S.	198	40.54 N	97.06 W
Lincoln Creek ≃, Wa., U.S.	224	46.45 N	123.02 W
Lincolndale	210	41.19 N	73.43 W
Lincoln Estates	278	41.31 N	87.49 W
Lincoln Heights, Oh., U.S.	214	40.47 N	82.30 W
Lincoln Heights, Oh., U.S.	218	39.15 N	84.28 W
Lincoln Heights, Pa., U.S.	279b	40.19 N	79.37 W
Lincoln Home National Historical Site ⊥	219	39.47 N	89.38 W
Lincolnia Heights	284c	38.50 N	77.09 W
Lincoln Memorial ⊥	284c	38.53 N	77.03 W
Lincoln Park, Co., U.S.	200	38.25 N	105.13 W
Lincoln Park, Ga., U.S.	192	32.52 N	84.19 W
Lincoln Park, Mi., U.S.	216	42.15 N	83.10 W
Lincoln Park, N.J., U.S.	276	40.55 N	74.18 W
Lincoln Park, N.Y., U.S.	210	41.57 N	74.00 W
Lincoln Park ♠, Ca., U.S.	282	37.46 N	122.30 W
Lincoln Park ♠, Il., U.S.	278	41.56 N	87.38 W
Lincoln Park Airport ⊠	276	40.57 N	74.19 W
Lincoln Place ◆[8]	279b	40.22 N	79.55 W
Lincoln Sea ⊤[2]	16	83.00 N	56.00 W
Lincolnshire	216	42.11 N	87.54 W
Lincolnshire □[6]	42	52.55 N	0.22 W
Lincoln's New Salem State Park ♠	219	39.58 N	89.52 W
Lincoln Tomb State Memorial ⊥	219	39.50 N	89.39 W
Lincolnton, Ga., U.S.	192	33.47 N	82.28 W
Lincolnton, N.C., U.S.	192	35.28 N	81.15 W
Lincoln Tunnel ◆[5]	276	40.46 N	74.01 W
Lincoln University	208	39.48 N	75.55 W
Lincoln Village, Ca., U.S.	226	38.00 N	121.19 W
Lincoln Village, Oh., U.S.	218	39.57 N	83.08 W
Lincolnville	214	41.47 N	79.51 W
Lincolnwood	278	42.00 N	87.43 W
Lincolnwood Hills	278	41.31 N	87.54 W
Linconia	285	40.08 N	74.59 W
Lincroft	208	40.19 N	74.07 W
Lind	202	46.58 N	118.36 W
Linda, Ross.	80	56.37 N	44.07 E
Linda, Ca., U.S.	226	39.07 N	121.32 W
Linda-a-Velha	266c	38.43 N	9.14 W
Lindale, Ga., U.S.	192	34.11 N	85.10 W
Lindale, Tx., U.S.	222	32.30 N	95.24 W
Lindau, Dtsch.	41	54.36 N	9.47 E
Lindau, Dtsch.	52	51.39 N	10.07 E
Lindau, Dtsch.	54	52.02 N	12.06 E
Lindau, Dtsch.	58	47.33 N	9.41 E
Lindbergh	219	39.02 N	92.08 W
Lindbergh Field ⊠	228	32.44 N	117.11 W
Lind Coulee V	202	47.00 N	119.10 W
Linde ≃	74	64.57 N	124.36 E
Lindelse	41	54.52 N	10.44 E
Linden, Guy.	246	6.00 N	58.18 W
Linden, Al., U.S.	194	32.18 N	87.47 W
Linden, Ca., U.S.	226	38.01 N	121.05 W
Linden, In., U.S.	194	40.11 N	86.54 W
Linden, Mi., U.S.	216	42.48 N	83.46 W
Linden, N.J., U.S.	210	40.37 N	74.14 W
Linden, Pa., U.S.	210	41.14 N	77.08 W
Linden, Pa., U.S.	279b	40.14 N	80.08 W
Linden, Tn., U.S.	194	35.37 N	87.50 W
Linden, Tx., U.S.	194	33.00 N	94.21 W
Linden ◆[8]	273d	26.08 S	28.00 E
Linden Airport ⊠	276	40.37 N	74.15 W
Lindenberg, Dtsch.	54	53.02 N	12.07 E
Lindenberg, Dtsch.	54	52.36 N	13.31 E
Lindenberg, Dtsch.	54	52.12 N	14.07 E
Lindenberg im Allgäu	58	47.36 N	9.53 E
Linden-Dahlhausen ◆[8]	263	51.26 N	7.09 E
Lindenfels	56	49.41 N	8.47 E
Lindenhorst ◆[8]	263	51.33 N	7.27 E
Lindenhurst, Il., U.S.	216	42.24 N	88.01 W
Lindenhurst, N.Y., U.S.	210	40.41 N	73.22 W
Lindenhurst, Pa., U.S.	285	40.14 N	74.54 W
Linden Park	216	40.13 N	85.23 W
Lindenthal	54	51.24 N	12.20 E
Lindenwold	208	39.49 N	74.59 W
Lindenwood, Il., U.S.	216	42.03 N	89.02 W
Lindenwood, In., U.S.	218	39.41 N	86.09 W
Linderhausen	263	51.18 N	7.17 E
Linderhof, Schloss ⊥	64	47.34 N	10.57 E
Lindern	52	52.50 N	7.46 E
Linderöd	41	55.56 N	13.49 E
Linderödsåsen ⋏[2]	26	55.53 N	13.56 E
Lindesay, Mount ʌ[2]	162	34.49 S	117.18 E
Lindesberg	40	59.35 N	15.15 E
Lindesnäs	40	60.20 N	14.32 E
Lindesnes ›	26	58.00 N	7.02 E
Lindfield, Austl.	274a	33.47 S	151.10 E
Lindfield, Eng., U.K.	42	51.01 N	0.05 W
Lindfors	40	59.36 N	13.49 E
Lindholmen	40	59.35 N	18.06 E
Lindhorst	52	52.21 N	9.17 E
Líndhos	38	36.06 N	28.04 E
Líndhos ⊥	38	36.06 N	28.05 E
Lindi	154	10.00 S	39.43 E
Lindi □[4]	154	9.15 S	38.45 E
Lindi ≃	154	0.33 N	25.05 E
Lindian	89	47.11 N	124.52 E
Lindis Pass)(	172	44.36 S	169.40 E
Lindkirchen	60	48.40 N	11.47 E
Lindlar	56	51.01 N	7.23 E
Lindley, S. Afr.	158	28.00 S	27.57 E
Lindley, N.Y., U.S.	210	42.02 N	77.08 W
Lind National Park ♠	166	37.35 S	149.05 E
Lindö	40	58.37 N	16.15 E
Lindóia	256	22.31 S	46.39 W
Lindome	26	57.34 N	12.05 E
Lindon	198	39.44 N	103.24 W
Lindong, Zhg.	100	26.03 N	118.49 E
Lindong, Zhg.	105	39.51 N	117.41 E
Lindow	54	52.58 N	13.00 E
Lind Point ›	240m	18.20 N	64.48 W
Lindre, Étang de ⊜[1]	56	48.47 N	6.45 E
Lindsay, On., Can.	212	44.21 N	78.44 W
Lindsay, Ca., U.S.	204	36.12 N	119.05 W
Lindsay, Ne., U.S.	198	41.42 N	97.41 W
Lindsay, Ok., U.S.	196	34.50 N	97.36 W
Lindsborg	198	38.34 N	97.40 W
Lindsey	214	41.25 N	83.13 W
Lindved	41	55.47 N	9.35 E
Lindy Lake	276	41.05 N	74.22 W
Lineboro	208	39.43 N	76.50 W
Line Creek ≃	194	33.34 N	88.42 W
Line Islands II	14	0.05 N	157.00 W
Line Lexington	208	40.17 N	75.16 W
Line Mountain ʌ	210	40.45 N	76.37 W
Linesville	214	41.39 N	80.25 W
Lineville, Al., U.S.	194	33.18 N	85.45 W
Lineville, Ia., U.S.	190	40.34 N	93.31 W
Línevo	86	54.05 N	83.24 E
Linfen	102	36.05 N	111.32 E
Linfield	208	40.13 N	75.34 W
Linford	260	51.29 N	0.25 E
Ling ≃	46	57.19 N	5.27 W
Ling'an	106	30.36 N	120.30 E
Linganamakki Reservoir ⊜[1]	122	14.04 N	74.54 E
Lingao	102	19.54 N	109.40 E
Lingayen	116	16.01 N	120.14 E
Lingayen Gulf c	116	16.15 N	120.14 E
Lingbi	100	33.33 N	117.33 E
Lingbo	26	61.03 N	16.41 E
Lingchuan, Zhg.	102	25.26 N	110.15 E
Lingchuan, Zhg.	102	35.46 N	113.26 E
Lingda	106	31.12 N	119.18 E
Lingdale	44	54.32 N	0.57 W
Lingdianzhen	106	31.51 N	121.25 E
Lingdou	100	26.22 N	118.56 E
Lingen	52	52.31 N	7.19 E
Lingesestausee ⊜[1]	263	51.06 N	7.32 E
Lingfengwei	100	24.44 N	115.35 E
Lingfield	42	51.11 N	0.01 W
Lingga, Kepulauan II	112	0.05 S	104.35 E
Lingga, Pulau I	112	0.12 S	104.35 E
Lingham Lake ⊜	212	44.46 N	77.25 W
Linghe	98	36.23 N	119.03 E
Linghu	106	30.44 N	120.10 E
Lingig	116	8.02 N	126.24 E
Lingjiachang	107	29.28 N	104.54 E
Lingjiaqiao	106	30.09 N	120.04 E
Lingkar Dzong	124	28.45 N	90.36 E
Lingkou, Zhg.	100	29.16 N	120.38 E
Lingkou, Zhg.	106	31.57 N	119.38 E
Lingle	200	42.08 N	104.20 W
Linglestown	208	40.21 N	76.48 W
Lingling	102	26.13 N	111.37 E
Linglongta	98	40.54 N	119.59 E
Lingma	102	23.22 N	107.53 E
Lingolsheim	58	48.34 N	7.41 E
Lingomo	152	0.38 N	21.59 E
Lingqiu	98	39.24 N	114.13 E
Lingshan, Zhg.	98	36.33 N	120.27 E
Lingshan, Zhg.	102	22.28 N	109.17 E
Lingshanwei	98	35.58 N	120.13 E
Lingshi	102	36.54 N	111.43 E
Lingshou	98	38.18 N	114.24 E
Lingshui	110	18.31 N	110.01 E
Lingtangqiao	100	32.43 N	119.14 E
Linguaglossa	70	37.50 N	15.08 E
Linguère	150	15.24 N	15.07 W
Lingwala	273b	4.22 S	15.17 E
Lingwood	42	52.37 N	1.29 E
Lingwu	102	38.06 N	106.21 E
Lingxian, Zhg.	98	37.21 N	116.34 E
Lingxian, Zhg.	100	26.30 N	113.46 E
Lingxiazhu	100	29.03 N	119.46 E
Lingyuan	98	41.15 N	119.16 E
Lingzhuangzi	105	39.04 N	117.09 E
Lingzinan	105	39.29 N	115.15 E
Linh, Ngoc ʌ	110	15.04 N	107.59 E
Linhai	100	28.51 N	121.07 E
Linhares	255	19.25 S	40.04 W
Linh Cam	110	18.31 N	105.34 E
Linhe	102	40.51 N	107.30 E
Linhezhuang	105	40.04 N	117.39 E
Linhigh	284b	39.21 N	76.31 W
Linhó	266c	38.46 N	9.23 W
Linhsia → Linxia	102	35.35 N	103.13 E
Linhuaiguan	100	32.55 N	117.40 E
Linhuanji	100	33.42 N	116.33 E
Lini → Linyi	98	35.04 N	118.22 E
Linjiang, Zhg.	98	41.44 N	126.55 E
Linjiang, Zhg.	100	27.50 N	118.26 E
Linjiang, Zhg.	100	28.04 N	115.21 E
Linjiang, Zhg.	102	33.01 N	105.01 E
Linjiangchang	107	29.14 N	105.58 E
Linjianghu	100	28.41 N	117.54 E
Linjiangsi	107	30.15 N	104.37 E
Linjiatai	104	40.43 N	123.57 E
Linkenheim	56	49.07 N	8.24 E
Linköping	26	58.25 N	15.37 E
Linkou	89	45.15 N	130.16 E
Linksfield ◆[8]	273d	26.10 S	28.06 E
Linksmakalnis	76	54.45 N	23.55 E
Linksness	46	58.56 N	3.19 W
Linkuva	76	56.05 N	23.59 E
Linkwood	208	38.32 N	75.57 W
Linli	102	29.18 N	111.30 E
Linlithgow	46	55.59 N	3.37 W
Linmeyer	273d	26.16 S	28.04 E
Linn, Ks., U.S.	198	39.40 N	97.05 W
Linn, Mo., U.S.	219	38.29 N	91.51 W
Linn ◆[8]	263	51.20 N	6.38 E
Linnancang	105	39.50 N	117.37 E
Linnansaaren Kansallispuisto ♠	26	62.07 N	28.31 E
Linndale	279a	41.27 N	81.46 W
Linne	52	51.10 N	5.57 E
Linnell	226	36.21 N	119.11 W
Linnés Hammarby ⊥	40	59.49 N	17.46 E
Linney Head ›	42	51.38 N	5.04 W
Linn Grove	216	40.38 N	85.01 W
Linnhe, Loch c	46	56.39 N	5.21 W
Linnich	56	50.59 N	6.16 E
Linntown	210	40.58 N	76.54 W
Linnville Bayou ≃	222	28.57 N	95.42 W
Linosa	70a	35.51 N	12.52 E
Linosa, Isola di I	70a	35.51 N	12.52 E
Linovica	78	50.28 N	32.22 E
Lin'ovo	80	50.53 N	44.51 E
Linow	54	53.06 N	12.49 E
Linping → Yuhang	106	30.25 N	120.18 E
Linpu	100	30.03 N	120.15 E
Linqi, Zhg.	98	35.48 N	113.53 E
Linqi, Zhg.	100	29.51 N	119.06 E
Linqing	98	36.53 N	115.41 E
Linqu	98	36.32 N	118.31 E
Linquan	100	33.06 N	115.13 E
Linru	100	34.11 N	112.49 E
Linruzhen	100	34.17 N	112.35 E
Lins	255	21.40 S	49.45 W
Linshan	100	30.09 N	120.59 E
Linshanhe	100	30.44 N	114.52 E
Linshengpu	104	41.34 N	123.20 E
Linshui	102	30.21 N	106.59 E
Linslade	42	51.55 N	0.41 W
Linstead	241q	18.08 N	77.02 W
Linta ≃	157b	25.02 S	44.05 E
Lintan	102	34.37 N	103.40 E
Lintao	102	35.27 N	103.46 E
Linté	152	5.24 N	11.42 E
Linth ≃	58	47.07 N	9.07 E
Linthal, Fr.	58	47.56 N	7.08 E
Linthal, Schw.	58	46.55 N	9.00 E
Linthicum Heights	284b	39.12 N	76.39 W
Linthkanal ≅	58	47.13 N	8.57 E
Linthwaite	262	53.37 N	1.51 W
Lintingkou	105	39.39 N	117.30 E
Linton, Austl.	169	37.41 S	143.34 E
Linton, N.Z.	172	40.26 S	175.33 E
Linton, Eng., U.K.	42	52.06 N	0.17 E
Linton, Eng., U.K.	260	51.13 N	0.31 E
Linton, In., U.S.	194	39.02 N	87.09 W
Linton, N.D., U.S.	198	46.16 N	100.13 W
Lintong	102	34.21 N	109.11 E
Linton Park ♠	260	51.13 N	0.31 E
Linum	264a	52.46 N	12.53 E
Linville, Austl.	171a	26.51 S	152.16 E
Linville, N.C., U.S.	192	36.03 N	81.52 W
Linwood, Austl.	168b	34.21 S	138.46 E
Linwood, In., U.S.	218	40.12 N	85.41 W
Linwood, Ma., U.S.	207	42.05 N	71.38 W
Linwood, N.J., U.S.	208	39.20 N	74.34 W
Linwood, Pa., U.S.	285	39.49 N	75.24 W
Linworth	214	40.06 N	83.04 W
Linwu, Zhg.	98	36.14 N	119.17 E
Linwu, Zhg.	102	25.16 N	112.20 E
Linxi, Zhg.	90	43.30 N	118.00 E
Linxi, Zhg.	98	36.52 N	115.32 E
Linxia	102	35.35 N	103.13 E
Linxian, Zhg.	98	36.04 N	113.50 E
Linxian, Zhg.	102	37.58 N	110.59 E
Linxiang	100	29.28 N	113.30 E
Linyanti	156	18.04 S	24.01 E
Linyanti ≃	156	17.58 S	24.16 E
Linyi, Zhg.	98	35.04 N	118.22 E
Linyi, Zhg.	98	37.13 N	116.51 E
Linyi, Zhg.	102	35.15 N	110.59 E
Linying	100	33.50 N	113.57 E
Linyüan	100	22.30 N	120.23 E
Linyü → Shanhaiguan	98	40.01 N	119.44 E
Linz, Dtsch.	56	50.34 N	7.17 E
Linz, Öst.	61	48.18 N	14.18 E
Linze, Zhg.	100	33.03 N	119.38 E
Linze, Zhg.	102	39.19 N	100.17 E
Linzgau ◆[1]	58	47.45 N	9.16 E
Linzhai	100	24.18 N	115.03 E
Linzhang	98	36.21 N	114.36 E
Linzhi	120	29.25 N	94.22 E
Linzikou	100	28.42 N	112.46 E
Linzolo	152	4.25 S	15.07 E
Lioko, Zaïre	152	0.02 N	22.04 E
Lioko, Zaïre	152	1.25 N	23.07 E
Lio Matoh	112	3.10 N	115.14 E
Liomer	50	49.51 N	1.49 E
Lion, Golfe du c	32	43.00 N	4.00 E
Lionel Town	241q	17.48 N	77.14 W
Lioni	68	40.52 N	15.11 E
Lion Rock ʌ[2]	271d	22.22 N	114.11 E
Lion Rock Tunnel ◆[5]	271d	22.21 N	114.09 E
Lions Den	154	17.16 S	30.02 E
Lion's Head	212	44.59 N	81.15 W
Lionville	208	40.03 N	75.39 W
Lioppa	112	7.40 S	126.00 E
Liouesso	152	1.02 N	15.43 E
Liozno	76	55.02 N	30.48 E
Lipa	116	13.57 N	121.10 E
Lipan	196	32.31 N	98.03 W
Lipany	30	49.10 N	20.58 E
Lipari	70	38.28 N	14.57 E
Lipari, Isola I	70	38.29 N	14.56 E
Lipatkain	112	0.01 S	101.13 E
Lipayan	104	42.13 N	123.23 E
Lipcy	78	50.13 N	36.25 E
Lipeck	76	52.37 N	39.35 E
Lipeck □[8]	80	52.15 N	40.30 E
Lipeckoje Vtoroje	78	47.46 N	29.41 E
Liperi	26	62.32 N	29.22 E
Lipetsk → Lipeck	76	52.37 N	39.35 E
Lipez, Cerro ʌ	248	21.53 S	66.52 W
Liphook	42	51.05 N	0.49 W
Lipiany	30	53.00 N	14.59 E
Lipicy	76	53.22 N	37.17 E
Lipin Bor	76	60.16 N	37.57 E
Liping	102	26.17 N	109.00 E
Lipis ≃	114	4.10 N	102.04 E
Lipiyu	104	41.09 N	123.36 E
Lipka ≃	265b	55.45 N	37.11 E
Lipkany	78	48.16 N	26.48 E
Lipki	76	53.58 N	37.42 E
Lipník nad Bečvou	30	49.31 N	17.35 E
Lipniški	76	54.00 N	25.37 E
Lipno	30	52.51 N	19.10 E
Lipno, údolní nádrž ⊜[1]	60	48.43 N	14.04 E
Lipno nad Vltavou	61	48.38 N	14.14 E
Lipoa Point ›	229a	21.02 N	156.38 W
Lipova	38	46.05 N	21.40 E
Lipovaja Dolina	78	50.35 N	33.48 E
Lipovcy	89	44.11 N	131.44 E
Lipovec	78	49.14 N	29.03 E
Lipovka, Ross.	78	50.52 N	40.02 E
Lipovka, Ross.	80	52.26 N	46.11 E
Lipovka, Ross.	80	49.46 N	44.56 E
Lippborg	52	51.40 N	8.02 E
Lippe ≃	52	51.39 N	6.38 E
Lipperode	52	51.41 N	8.22 E
Lippetal	52	51.40 N	8.06 E
Lippoldsberg	52	51.37 N	9.33 E
Lippstadt	52	51.40 N	8.19 E
Lipscomb	196	36.14 N	100.16 W
Lipsko	30	51.09 N	21.39 E
Lipsoí I, Ellás	38	37.20 N	26.45 E
Lipsoí I, Ellás	130	37.20 N	26.45 E
Lipton	184	50.54 N	103.50 W
Liptovská Teplička	30	48.59 N	20.06 E
Liptovský Mikuláš	30	49.06 N	19.37 E
Liptrap, Cape ›	166	38.54 S	145.55 E
Lipu	102	24.25 N	110.29 E
Lipu La)(	124	30.21 N	81.05 E
Liqiao	107	29.03 N	104.48 E
Lira, Ug.	154	2.15 N	32.54 E
Lira, Ven.	286c	10.26 N	66.46 W
Liranga	152	0.40 S	17.36 E
Lirangdian	105	39.14 N	116.14 E
Lircay	248	12.56 S	74.43 W
Liren	100	33.55 N	118.47 E
Lirentuncun	104	41.24 N	122.59 E
Liri ≃	66	41.25 N	13.52 E
Liro	175f	16.27 S	168.13 E
Liro ≃	58	46.18 N	9.23 E
Lisakovsk	86	52.36 N	62.37 E
Lisala	152	2.09 N	21.31 E
Lisavy	82	56.33 N	38.32 E
Lisboa (Lisbon), Port.	34	38.43 N	9.08 W
Lisboa (Lisbon), Port.	266c	38.43 N	9.08 W
Lisboa □[5]	266c	38.48 N	9.16 W
Lisbon, Il., U.S.	216	41.29 N	88.29 W
Lisbon, Md., U.S.	208	39.20 N	77.04 W
Lisbon, N.H., U.S.	188	44.12 N	71.54 W
Lisbon, N.D., U.S.	198	46.26 N	97.40 W
Lisbon, Oh., U.S.	214	40.46 N	80.46 W
Lisbon Falls	188	43.59 N	70.03 W
Lisbon → Lisboa	34	38.43 N	9.08 W
Lisbonne → Lisboa	34	38.43 N	9.08 W
Lisburn	48	54.31 N	6.03 W
Lisburne, Cape ›	180	68.52 N	166.14 W
Lisburne Peninsula ›[1]	180	68.30 N	165.15 W
Liscannor Bay c	48	52.55 N	9.25 W
Liscarney	48	53.43 N	9.35 W
Liscia ≃	71	41.11 N	9.19 E
Liscia, Lago di ⊜	71	41.00 N	9.16 E
Lisdoonvarna	48	53.01 N	9.15 W
Lisec	78	48.52 N	24.36 E
Liseleje	41	56.01 N	11.59 E
Lishan, Zhg.	100	31.50 N	113.16 E
Lishan, Zhg.	104	41.10 N	123.00 E
Lishangzhuang	105	39.35 N	118.11 E
Lishanke	98	40.41 N	119.53 E
Lishe	100	29.48 N	121.28 E
Lishe ≃	102	24.18 N	101.32 E
Lishi, Zhg.	102	37.32 N	111.09 E
Lishi, Zhg.	106	31.14 N	120.37 E
Lishi, Zhg.	107	29.10 N	105.42 E
Lishizhen, Zhg.	107	29.04 N	106.15 E
Lishizhen, Zhg.	107	29.20 N	105.24 E
Lishu	89	43.21 N	124.37 E
Lishui, Zhg.	100	28.27 N	119.54 E
Lishui, Zhg.	106	31.39 N	119.01 E
Lishuzhen	89	45.05 N	130.41 E
Lisianski Island I	14	26.02 N	174.00 W
Lisica ≃	86	58.34 N	85.11 E
Lisičansk	83	48.55 N	38.26 E
Lisichansk → Lisičansk	83	48.55 N	38.26 E
Lisicy	82	56.47 N	36.21 E
Lisieux, Sk., Can.	184	49.17 N	105.59 W
Lisieux, Fr.	50	49.09 N	0.14 E
Lisij Nos	265a	60.01 N	30.00 E
Líšina	60	49.37 N	13.10 E
Lisitu	154	9.39 S	34.39 E
Lisizhuang	105	38.55 N	115.07 E
Lisja	80	57.15 N	54.22 E
Liska ≃	80	48.32 N	43.08 E
Liskeard	42	50.28 N	4.28 W
Liski, Ross.	78	50.56 N	39.29 E
Liski, Ross.	78	50.59 N	39.30 E
Lískova	60	49.25 N	12.43 E
L'Isle, Schw.	58	46.37 N	6.25 E
Lisle, Il., U.S.	216	41.48 N	88.04 W
Lisle, N.Y., U.S.	210	42.21 N	76.00 W
L'Isle-Adam	50	49.07 N	2.14 E
L'Isle Jourdain	32	46.14 N	0.41 E
L'Isle-sur-la-Sorgue	62	43.55 N	5.03 E
L'Isle-sur-le-Doubs	58	47.27 N	6.35 E
L'Isle-sur-Serein	50	47.35 N	4.00 E
Lisman	194	32.10 N	88.16 W
Lismore, Austl.	166	28.48 S	153.17 E
Lismore, Austl.	169	37.58 S	143.20 E
Lismore, N.S., Can.	186	45.42 N	62.16 W
Lismore, Ire.	48	52.08 N	7.55 W
Lismore Castle ⊥	48	52.08 N	7.52 W
Lismore Island I	46	56.29 N	5.33 W
Lisnaskea	48	54.15 N	7.27 W
Lišn'ovka	78	51.28 N	25.25 E
Lisö ›[1]	40	58.55 N	17.45 E
Lišov	61	49.01 N	14.37 E
Liss	42	51.03 N	0.55 W
Lissabon → Lisboa	34	38.43 N	9.08 W
Lissberg	56	50.22 N	9.05 E
Lisse	52	52.15 N	4.33 E
Lisses	261	48.36 N	2.26 E
Lissewege	50	51.18 N	3.11 E
Lissie	222	29.33 N	96.13 W
Lissingen	56	50.14 N	6.38 E
Lissone	62	45.37 N	9.14 E
Lissy	261	48.38 N	2.42 E
Lista	80	47.44 N	45.54 E
Lista ›[1]	26	58.07 N	6.40 E
Lister ≃	263	51.05 N	7.45 E
Lištica	36	43.23 N	17.36 E
Listowel, On., Can.	212	43.44 N	80.57 W
Listowel, Ire.	48	52.27 N	9.29 W
Listv'anka	88	51.52 N	104.51 E
Listv'anskij	86	54.27 N	83.29 E
Lisui	105	40.05 N	116.44 E
Lit	26	63.19 N	14.49 E
Lita	100	27.22 N	116.34 E
Litang, Malay.	112	5.20 N	118.31 E
Litang, Zhg.	102	23.11 N	109.05 E
Litang, Zhg.	102	30.00 N	100.16 E
Litang ≃	102	28.04 N	101.30 E
Litani ≃	250	3.40 N	54.00 W
Līṭānī, Nahr al- ≃	132	33.20 N	35.14 E
Litava ≃	61	49.02 N	16.36 E
Litcham	42	52.44 N	0.47 E
Litchfield, Ct., U.S.	207	41.44 N	73.11 W
Litchfield, Il., U.S.	219	39.10 N	89.39 W
Litchfield, Mi., U.S.	216	42.02 N	84.45 W
Litchfield, Mn., U.S.	190	45.07 N	94.31 W
Litchfield, Ne., U.S.	198	41.09 N	99.09 W
Litchfield, Oh., U.S.	214	41.10 N	82.02 W
Litchfield □[6]	207	41.45 N	73.11 W
Litchfield Park	200	33.29 N	112.21 W
Litchville	198	46.39 N	98.11 W
Literberry	219	39.51 N	90.12 W
Līth, Wādī al- V	144	20.40 N	40.35 E
Litherland	44	53.28 N	2.59 W
Lithgow	170	33.29 S	150.09 E
Lithia	220	27.51 N	82.10 W
Líthinon, Ákra ›	38	34.55 N	24.44 E
Lithonia	192	33.42 N	84.06 W
Lithuania (Lietuva) □[1], Europe	22	56.00 N	24.00 E
Lithuania (Lietuva) □[1], Europe	76	56.00 N	24.00 E
Litian	100	26.58 N	114.10 E
Litija	36	46.03 N	14.50 E
Litin	78	49.20 N	28.05 E
Litipāra	124	24.42 N	87.37 E
Lititz	208	40.09 N	76.18 W
Litke	89	53.57 N	140.15 E
Litókhoron	38	40.06 N	22.30 E
Litoko	154	1.13 S	24.47 E
Litoměřice	54	50.35 N	14.09 E
Litomyšl	30	49.52 N	16.19 E
Litoo	154	9.54 S	38.24 E
Litouqiao	106	31.15 N	118.54 E
Litovel	30	49.42 N	17.05 E
Litovko	89	49.15 N	135.11 E
Litschau	61	48.57 N	15.03 E
Littau	58	47.03 N	8.16 E
Little ≃, Austl.	169	38.01 S	144.35 E
Little ≃, On., Can.	281	42.20 N	82.56 W
Little ≃, U.S.	194	35.32 N	90.25 W
Little ≃, U.S.	194	33.37 N	93.52 W
Little ≃, Al., U.S.	194	31.18 N	87.46 W
Little ≃, Al., U.S.	194	34.16 N	85.40 W
Little ≃, Ct., U.S.	207	41.36 N	72.03 W
Little ≃, Ga., U.S.	192	30.51 N	83.21 W
Little ≃, Ga., U.S.	192	33.14 N	83.24 W
Little ≃, Ga., U.S.	192	33.39 N	82.32 W
Little ≃, In., U.S.	216	40.53 N	85.32 W
Little ≃, Ky., U.S.	194	36.51 N	87.58 W
Little ≃, La., U.S.	194	31.38 N	91.49 W
Little ≃, Ma., U.S.	283	42.37 N	70.42 W
Little ≃, Ma., U.S.	283	42.46 N	70.51 W
Little ≃, N.Y., U.S.	210	43.18 N	75.43 W
Little ≃, N.C., U.S.	192	35.15 N	78.42 W
Little ≃, N.C., U.S.	192	35.21 N	78.02 W
Little ≃, Ok., U.S.	196	35.00 N	96.25 W
Little ≃, S.C., U.S.	192	34.10 N	81.11 W
Little ≃, S.C., U.S.	192	33.56 N	82.25 W
Little ≃, S.C., U.S.	192	34.11 N	81.45 W
Little ≃, Tn., U.S.	192	35.51 N	83.57 W
Little ≃, Tx., U.S.	222	30.51 N	96.41 W
Little ≃, Va., U.S.	192	37.05 N	80.32 W
Little ≃, Va., U.S.	208	37.49 N	77.26 W
Little, Mountain Fork ≃	194	33.57 N	94.34 W
Little Abaco I	238	26.53 N	77.43 W
Little Amwell	260	51.47 N	0.02 W
Little Andaman I	110	10.45 N	92.30 E
Little Arkansas ≃	198	37.43 N	97.22 W
Little Auglaize ≃	216	41.07 N	84.25 W
Little Averill Lake ⊜	206	44.57 N	71.44 W
Little Baddow	260	51.44 N	0.35 E
Little Barrier Island I	172	36.12 S	175.05 E
Little Bay	186	47.41 N	58.24 W
Little Bay c	276	40.48 N	73.47 W
Little Bay Islands	186	49.39 N	55.47 W
Little Bear ≃	200	41.42 N	111.57 W
Little Bear Creek ≃	196	37.43 N	101.43 W
Little Bear Creek Reservoir ⊜[1]	194	34.25 N	87.57 W
Little Beaver Creek ≃, U.S.	198	46.17 N	103.56 W
Little Beaver Creek ≃, U.S.	198	39.49 N	101.03 W
Little Beaver Creek ≃, U.S.	214	40.38 N	80.31 W
Little Beaver Creek ≃, Wa., U.S.	224	48.54 N	121.06 W
Little Beaver Creek, Middle Fork ≃	214	40.43 N	80.37 W
Little Beaver Creek, North Fork ≃	214	40.43 N	80.33 W
Little Beaver Creek, West Fork ≃	214	40.43 N	80.37 W
Little Belt → Lillebælt U	41	55.20 N	9.45 E
Little Belt Mountains ⋏	202	46.45 N	110.35 W
Little Berkhamsted	260	51.45 N	0.08 W
Little Bighorn ≃	202	45.44 N	107.34 W
Little Billabong	171b	35.35 S	147.32 E
Little Bitter Lake → Murrah aṣ-Ṣughrā, Al-Buḥayrah al- ⊜	142	30.13 N	32.33 E
Little Bitterroot ≃	202	47.30 N	114.19 W
Little Black ≃, U.S.	194	36.25 N	90.45 W
Little Black ≃, Ak., U.S.	180	66.26 N	143.49 W
Little Black Bear Indian Reserve ◆[4]	184	51.00 N	103.23 W
Little Blackfoot ≃	202	46.31 N	112.48 W
Little Blue ≃, U.S.	198	39.41 N	96.40 W
Little Blue ≃, In., U.S.	218	39.32 N	85.46 W
Littleborough	44	53.39 N	2.05 W
Little Bow ≃	182	49.53 N	112.29 W
Little Brazos ≃	222	30.38 N	96.31 W
Little Brokenstraw Creek ≃	214	41.50 N	79.23 W
Little Brosna ≃	48	53.10 N	8.05 W
Little Buffalo ≃	176	61.00 N	113.46 W
Little Bullhead	184	51.40 N	96.51 W
Little Burstead	260	51.36 N	0.24 E
Little Calumet ≃	278	41.39 N	87.34 W
Little Catalina	186	48.33 N	53.02 W
Little Cayman I	238	19.41 N	80.03 W
Little Cedar ≃	190	42.57 N	92.31 W
Little Chalfont	260	51.40 N	0.34 W
Little Chartiers Creek ≃	279b	40.17 N	80.08 W
Little Choptank River c	208	38.32 N	76.13 W
Little Churchill ≃	184	57.15 N	95.21 W
Little Chute	190	44.16 N	88.19 W

Symbols in the index entries represent the broad categories identified in the key at the right. Symbols with superior numbers (⋏[1]) identify subcategories (see complete key on page *I · 1*).

Symbole im Register stellen die rechts im Schlüssel identifizierten Kategorien dar. Symbole mit hochgestellten Ziffern (⋏[1]) bezeichnen Unterabteilungen einer Kategorie (vgl. vollständiger Schlüssel auf Seite *I · 1*).

Los símbolos incluídos en el texto del índice representan las grandes categorias identificadas con la clave a la derecha. Los símbolos con numeros en su parte superior (⋏[1]) identifican las subcategorías (véase la clave completa en la página *I · 1*).

Les symboles de l'index représentent les catégories indiquées dans la légende à droite. Les symboles suivis d'un indice (⋏[1]) représentent des sous-catégories (voir légende complète à la page *I · 1*).

Os símbolos incluídos no texto do índice representam as grandes categorias identificadas com a chave à direita. Os símbolos com números em sua parte superior (⋏[1]) identificam as subcategorias (veja-se a chave completa à página *I · 1*).

ʌ Mountain	Berg	Montaña	Montagne	Montanha
⋏ Mountains	Gebirge	Montañas	Montagnes	Montanhas
)(Pass	Paß	Paso	Col	Passo
V Valley, Canyon	Tal, Cañon	Valle, Cañón	Vallée, Canyon	Vale, Canhão
≅ Plain	Ebene	Llano	Plaine	Planície
› Cape	Kap	Cabo	Cap	Cabo
I Island	Insel	Isla	Île	Ilha
II Islands	Inseln	Islas	Îles	Ilhas
⊥ Other Topographic Features	Andere Topographische Objekte	Otros Elementos Topográficos	Autres données topographiques	Outros acidentes topográficos

ESPAÑOL — Nombre | Página | Lat.°′ | Long.°′ W = Oeste
FRANÇAIS — Nom | Page | Lat.°′ | Long.°′ W = Ouest
PORTUGUÊS — Nome | Página | Lat.°′ | Long.°′ W = Oeste

Little Coco Island I	110	14.00 N	93.13 E
Little Colorado ≃	200	36.11 N	111.48 W
Little Compton	207	41.30 N	71.10 W
Little Cooley	214	41.44 N	79.53 W
Little Cottonwood ≃	198	44.15 N	94.20 W
Little Creek	208	39.10 N	75.26 W
Little Creek ≃	285	39.56 N	74.48 W
Little Creek Naval Amphibious Base ■	208	36.55 N	76.10 W
Little Creek Reservoir ⊜[1]	208	37.20 N	76.50 W
Little Cumbrae Island I	46	55.43 N	4.57 W
Little Current	190	45.58 N	81.56 W
Little Current ≃	176	50.57 N	84.36 W
Little Cypress Bayou ≃	194	32.41 N	94.15 W
Little Cypress Creek ≃	222	32.39 N	94.42 W
Little Darby Creek ≃	218	39.53 N	83.13 W
Little Dart ≃	42	50.54 N	3.51 W
Little Deep Creek ≃	198	48.35 N	100.52 W
Little Deer Creek ≃, In., U.S.	216	40.36 N	86.28 W
Little Deer Creek ≃, Pa., U.S.	279b	40.33 N	79.50 W
Little Deschutes ≃	202	43.51 N	121.27 W
Little Desert ◆[2]	166	36.35 S	141.20 E
Little Desert National Park ♦	166	36.25 S	141.25 E
Little Diomede Island I	180	65.45 N	168.57 W
Little Don ≃	275b	43.42 N	79.20 W
Little Dry Creek ≃, Ca., U.S.	226	39.22 N	121.52 W
Little Dry Creek ≃, Mt., U.S.	202	47.21 N	106.22 W
Little Ease Run ≃	285	39.39 N	75.04 W
Little Eau Pleine ≃	190	44.40 N	89.41 W
Little Egg Harbor c	208	39.35 N	74.18 W
Little Elkhart ≃	216	41.43 N	85.49 W
Little End	260	51.41 N	0.14 E
Little Etobicoke Creek ≃	275b	43.37 N	79.34 W
Little Exuma I	238	23.27 N	75.37 W
Little Fabius ≃	219	39.59 N	91.59 W
Little Falls, Mn., U.S.	190	45.58 N	94.21 W
Little Falls, N.J., U.S.	276	40.52 N	74.12 W
Little Falls, N.Y., U.S.	210	43.02 N	74.51 W
Little Falls ≃	208	39.36 N	76.38 W
Little Falls Dam ◆[6]	284c	38.57 N	77.08 W
Little Farms	218	39.57 N	83.10 W
Little Ferry	276	40.51 N	74.02 W
Littlefield	196	33.55 N	102.19 W
Little Flatrock ≃	218	39.26 N	85.33 W
Littlefork	190	48.23 N	93.33 W
Little Fork ≃	190	48.31 N	93.35 W
Little Fort	182	51.25 N	120.12 W
Little Genesee	210	42.02 N	78.13 W
Little Gold ≃	162	18.01 S	126.29 E
Little Gunpowder Falls ≃	208	39.23 N	76.22 W
Littlehampton	42	50.48 N	0.33 W
Little Harbour Deep	186	50.15 N	56.33 W
Little Haw Creek ≃	192	29.23 N	81.24 W
Little Hawk Lake ⊜	212	45.10 N	78.42 W
Little Hoosic ≃	210	42.49 N	73.20 W
Little Hope	214	42.06 N	79.49 W
Little Hulton	262	53.32 N	2.25 W
Little Humboldt ≃	204	41.00 N	117.43 W
Little Humboldt, North Fork ≃	204	41.24 N	117.10 W
Little Humboldt, South Fork ≃	204	41.24 N	117.10 W
Little Hurricane Creek ≃	192	31.23 N	82.19 W
Little Inagua I	238	21.30 N	73.00 W
Little Indian Creek ≃, Il., U.S.	216	41.31 N	88.46 W
Little Indian Creek ≃, In., U.S.	218	38.12 N	86.08 W
Little Island Pond ⊜	283	42.43 N	71.17 W
Littlejohns Creek ≃	226	37.52 N	121.14 W
Little Juniata ≃	214	40.34 N	78.03 W
Little Juniata Creek ≃	208	40.23 N	77.02 W
Little Kanawha ≃	188	39.16 N	81.34 W
Little Kanawha, West Fork ≃	188	38.57 N	81.16 W
Little Karroo (Klein Karroo) ⋀[1]	158	33.45 S	21.30 E
Little Kentucky ≃	218	38.41 N	85.12 W
Little Klickitat ≃	224	45.51 N	121.04 W
Little Koniuji Island I	180	55.01 N	159.26 W
Little Lake ⊜, On., Can.	212	44.26 N	79.40 W
Little Lake ⊜, La., U.S.	194	29.30 N	90.10 W
Little Laramie ≃	200	41.28 N	105.44 W
Little Laver	260	51.46 N	0.14 E
Little Leigh	262	53.17 N	2.35 W
Little Lever	262	53.34 N	2.22 W
Little Limestone Lake ⊜	184	53.46 N	99.18 W
Little London	241q	18.15 N	78.13 W
Little Lost ≃	202	43.46 N	112.58 W
Little Lun ≃	116	6.02 N	125.17 E
Little Mahoning Creek ≃	214	40.49 N	79.00 W
Little Maitland ≃	212	43.52 N	81.18 W
Little Manatee ≃	220	27.42 N	82.28 W
Little Manatee, South Fork ≃	220	27.39 N	82.18 W
Little Manistee ≃	190	44.15 N	86.19 W
Little Manitou Lake ⊜	184	51.45 N	105.30 W
Little Marco Pass c	220	26.01 N	81.46 W
Little Marsh	210	41.53 N	77.24 W
Little Meadows	210	41.59 N	76.08 W
Little Mecatina ≃	176	50.28 N	59.35 W
Little Medicine Bow ≃	200	41.58 N	106.18 W
Little Mexico	196	30.57 N	102.52 W
Little Miami ≃	218	39.05 N	84.26 W
Little Miami, East Fork ≃	218	39.09 N	84.18 W
Little Miami, North Fork ≃	218	39.48 N	83.47 W
Little Miami, Todd Fork ≃	218	39.21 N	84.08 W
Little Miami, Todd Fork, East Fork ≃	218	39.24 N	84.00 W
Littlemill	46	57.32 N	3.49 W
Little Mississippi ≃	212	45.17 N	77.35 W
Little Missouri ≃, U.S.	198	47.30 N	102.25 W
Little Missouri ≃, Ar., U.S.	194	33.49 N	92.54 W
Little Mountain ∧	208	40.47 N	76.40 W
Little Muddy ≃, Il., U.S.	194	37.50 N	89.11 W
Little Muddy ≃, N.D., U.S.	198	48.12 N	103.36 W
Little Mulberry Creek ≃	194	32.26 N	86.51 W
Little Naches ≃	224	46.58 N	121.08 W
Little Nahant	283	42.25 N	70.56 W
Little Namaqualand □[9]	156	29.00 S	17.00 E
Little Neck	283	42.42 N	70.48 W
Little Neck ◆[8]	276	40.46 N	73.44 W
Little Neck Bay c	276	40.47 N	73.46 W
Little Nemaha ≃	198	40.19 N	95.40 W
Little Neshaminy Creek ≃	285	40.15 N	75.02 W
Little Niangua ≃	194	38.04 N	92.54 W
Little Nicobar I	110	7.20 N	93.40 E
Little Ohoopee ≃	192	32.27 N	82.24 W
Little Osage ≃	194	38.02 N	94.14 W
Little Otter Creek ≃	212	42.44 N	80.51 W
Little Ouse ≃	42	52.30 N	0.22 E
Little Panoche Creek ≃	226	36.50 N	120.42 W
Little Patuxent ≃	284b	39.11 N	76.52 W
Little Paxton	42	52.15 N	0.15 W
Little Peconic Bay c	207	40.59 N	72.24 W
Little Pee Dee ≃	192	33.42 N	79.11 W
Little Pic ≃	190	48.48 N	86.37 W
Little Pine and Lucky Man Indian Reserve ◆[4]	184	52.56 N	109.05 W
Little Pine Creek ≃, Pa., U.S.	210	41.18 N	77.22 W
Little Pine Creek ≃, Pa., U.S.	279b	40.31 N	79.57 W
Little Pine Island I	220	26.36 N	82.05 W
Little Pine Key I	220	24.44 N	81.19 W
Little Pine State Park ♦	210	41.22 N	77.20 W
Little Pipe Creek ≃	208	39.36 N	77.16 W
Little Platte ≃	194	39.24 N	94.41 W
Little Plum Creek ≃	279b	40.30 N	79.51 W
Little Popo Aggie ≃	202	42.54 N	108.35 W
Little Porcupine Creek ≃, Mt., U.S.	202	48.02 N	106.04 W
Little Porcupine Creek ≃, Mt., U.S.	202	46.18 N	106.34 W
Littleport	42	52.28 N	0.19 E
Little Portage Creek ≃	216	42.00 N	85.27 W
Little Powder ≃	198	45.28 N	105.20 W
Little Pucketa Creek ≃	279b	40.33 N	79.45 W
Little Quill Lake ⊜	184	51.55 N	104.05 W
Little Rann of Kachchh ≚	120	23.25 N	71.15 E
Little Red ≃	194	35.11 N	91.27 W
Little Red, Middle Fork ≃	194	35.37 N	92.11 W
Little Red Deer ≃	182	52.04 N	114.09 W
Little Red River Indian Reserve ◆[4]	184	53.30 N	105.58 W
Little Redstone Lake ⊜	212	45.13 N	78.34 W
Little River, Austl.	169	37.58 S	144.30 E
Little River, N.Z.	172	43.46 S	172.47 E
Little River, Ks., U.S.	198	38.23 N	98.00 W
Little River, Tx., U.S.	222	30.59 N	97.22 W
Little Rock, Ar., U.S.	194	34.44 N	92.17 W
Littlerock, Ca., U.S.	228	34.31 N	117.59 W
Little Rock, Il., U.S.	216	41.43 N	88.34 W
Little Rock, Ia., U.S.	198	43.26 N	95.52 W
Littlerock, Wa., U.S.	224	46.54 N	123.01 W
Little Rock ≃	198	43.16 N	96.15 W
Little Rock Air Force Base ■	194	34.55 N	92.10 W
Little Rock Creek ≃	228	34.28 N	118.01 W
Little Rock Wash V	228	34.42 N	118.02 W
Little Rocky Mountains ⋀	202	47.50 N	108.10 W
Little Rouge Creek ≃	212	43.48 N	79.08 W
Little Ruaha ≃	154	7.17 S	35.28 E
Little Sable Point >	190	43.38 N	86.32 W
Little Sac ≃	194	37.39 N	93.46 W
Little Sachigo Lake ⊜	184	54.09 N	92.11 W
Little Saint Bernard Pass → Petit-Saint-Bernard, Col du)(	62	45.41 N	6.53 E
Little Salkehatchie ≃	192	32.37 N	80.53 W
Little Salmon ≃, Id., U.S.	202	45.25 N	116.19 W
Little Salmon ≃, N.Y., U.S.	212	43.32 N	76.16 W
Little Salmon, North Branch ≃	212	43.24 N	76.09 W
Little Salmon, South Branch ≃	212	43.24 N	76.09 W
Little Salmon Lake ⊜	180	62.12 N	134.45 W
Little Salt Lake ⊜	200	37.55 N	112.53 W
Little Sandy ≃	188	38.35 N	82.51 W
Little Sandy, East Fork ≃	188	38.30 N	82.50 W
Little Sandy Creek ≃	200	42.06 N	109.27 W
Little Sandy Desert ◆[2]	162	24.20 S	120.50 E
Little Saskatchewan ≃	184	49.52 N	100.07 W
Little Scarcies ≃	150	8.51 N	13.09 W
Little Scioto ≃, Oh., U.S.	214	40.31 N	83.12 W
Little Scioto ≃, Oh., U.S.	218	38.46 N	82.53 W
Little Sewickley Creek ≃, Pa., U.S.	279b	40.15 N	79.45 W
Little Sewickley Creek ≃, Pa., U.S.	279b	40.33 N	80.12 W
Little Silver	276	40.20 N	74.02 W
Little Sioux ≃	198	41.49 N	96.04 W
Little Sioux, West Fork ≃	198	42.04 N	96.00 W
Little Sitkin Island I	181a	51.55 N	178.30 E
Little Smoky ≃	182	55.42 N	117.38 W
Little Snake ≃	200	40.27 N	108.26 W
Little Sodus Bay c	210	43.20 N	76.43 W
Little Southwest Miramichi ≃	186	46.57 N	65.50 W
Little Stanney	262	53.15 N	2.53 W
Little Stony Creek ≃	226	39.20 N	122.31 W
Little Stour ≃	42	51.19 N	1.15 E
Littlestown	208	39.44 N	77.05 W
Little Stukeley	42	52.21 N	0.13 W
Little Sugarloaf ∧[2]	274b	37.41 S	145.19 E
Little Sur ≃	226	36.20 N	121.54 W
Little Sutton	262	53.17 N	2.57 W
Little Swatara Creek ≃	208	40.24 N	76.29 W
Little Tallapoosa ≃	192	33.18 N	85.34 W
Little Tanaga Island I	180	51.48 N	176.10 W
Little Tennessee ≃	192	35.47 N	84.15 W
Little Thurrock	260	51.28 N	0.21 E
Little Timber Creek ≃	285	39.53 N	75.08 W
Little Tinicum Island I	285	39.51 N	75.17 W
Little Tobago I, Br. Vir. Is.	240m	18.26 N	64.51 W
Little Tobago I, Trin.	241r	11.18 N	60.30 W
Little Toby Creek ≃	214	41.22 N	78.49 W
Littleton, Eng., U.K.	260	51.24 N	0.28 W
Littleton, Co., U.S.	200	39.36 N	105.00 W
Littleton, Ma., U.S.	207	42.32 N	71.30 W
Littleton, N.H., U.S.	188	44.18 N	71.46 W
Littleton, N.C., U.S.	192	36.26 N	77.54 W
Littleton, W.V., U.S.	188	39.41 N	80.31 W
Little Traverse Bay c	190	45.24 N	85.03 W
Little Truckee ≃	226	39.25 N	120.05 W
Little Turtle ≃	184	48.46 N	92.36 W
Little Turtle State Recreation Area ♦	216	40.50 N	85.26 W
Little Valley	210	42.15 N	78.48 W
Little Vermilion ≃	216	41.20 N	89.05 W
Little Vermilion Lake ⊜	184	51.16 N	93.50 W
Little Vienna Estates	284c	38.54 N	77.18 W
Little Wabash ≃	194	37.54 N	88.05 W
Little Walsingham	42	52.54 N	0.51 E
Little Waltham	260	51.47 N	0.29 E
Little Warley	260	51.35 N	0.19 E
Little Washita ≃	196	34.58 N	97.51 W
Little Wellington, Isla I	254	48.30 S	74.45 W
Little White ≃	198	43.44 N	100.40 W
Little White Mountain ∧	182	49.42 N	119.20 W
Little White Salmon ≃	224	45.43 N	121.38 W
Little Wichita ≃	196	33.54 N	97.59 W
Little Wichita, East Fork ≃	196	33.52 N	98.07 W
Little Wind ≃	202	42.57 N	108.29 W
Little Wind, North Fork ≃	202	43.01 N	108.53 W
Little Wind, South Fork ≃	202	43.01 N	108.53 W
Little Wolf ≃	190	44.23 N	88.48 W
Little Wood ≃	202	42.57 N	114.21 W
Little York, In., U.S.	218	38.42 N	85.54 W
Little York, N.Y., U.S.	210	42.42 N	76.10 W
Little Zab (Zāb-e Kūchek) (Az-Zāb aṣ-Ṣaghīr) ≃	128	35.12 N	43.25 E
Littoral □[4]	152	4.13 N	10.25 E
Litunga	152	13.17 S	16.43 E
Litvínov	54	50.37 N	13.36 E
Litvinovka	83	49.18 N	39.27 E
Litvinovo	76	59.34 N	38.01 E
Litvinskoje	86	50.42 N	72.42 E
Litzmannstadt → Łódź	30	51.46 N	19.30 E
Liu ≃, Zhg.	98	41.48 N	122.43 E
Liu ≃, Zhg.	98	42.45 N	126.04 E
Liu ≃, Zhg.	98	40.38 N	118.09 E
Liu ≃, Zhg.	102	23.52 N	109.45 E
Liu ≃, Zhg.	105	40.38 N	118.09 E
Liu ≃, Zhg.	106	31.31 N	121.18 E
Liuanzhuang	105	39.14 N	117.11 E
Liuba	102	33.32 N	107.07 E
Liubotong	100	31.26 N	116.00 E
Liucao	106	31.07 N	121.41 E
Liuchen	102	23.09 N	110.29 E
Liucheng, Zhg.	100	24.03 N	115.08 E
Liucheng, Zhg.	100	28.36 N	119.34 E
Liucheng, Zhg.	102	24.32 N	109.21 E
Liuchengba	102	27.27 N	102.53 E
Liuch'iu Hsü I	100	22.21 N	120.22 E
Liuchow → Liuzhou	102	24.19 N	109.24 E
Liucun	106	30.44 N	119.23 E
Liucura	252	38.39 S	71.05 W
Liudaogou	98	41.34 N	127.12 E
Liudaohe	105	40.39 N	116.12 E
Liudongqiao	106	31.03 N	119.32 E
Liudu	100	26.44 N	119.33 E
Liuduo	100	34.01 N	120.17 E
Liuduzhuang	105	39.27 N	117.50 E
Liuerbao	104	41.13 N	122.55 E
Liufang	100	27.56 N	116.22 E
Liufangling	100	30.27 N	114.27 E
Liufentzu	269d	24.57 N	121.35 E
Liugezhuang, Zhg.	98	38.33 N	116.30 E
Liugezhuang, Zhg.	105	40.03 N	118.16 E
Liugou	105	40.57 N	118.18 E
Liugu ≃	98	40.22 N	120.26 E
Liuguan	100	29.56 N	113.08 E
Liuguantun	104	41.20 N	121.21 E
Liuhang	106	31.21 N	121.22 E
Liuhe, Zhg.	98	42.15 N	125.43 E
Liuhe, Zhg.	100	33.20 N	112.48 E
Liuhe, Zhg.	100	30.20 N	115.36 E
Liuhe, Zhg.	100	30.46 N	113.12 E
Liuhe, Zhg.	100	32.22 N	118.49 E
Liuhe, Zhg.	105	39.31 N	118.17 E
Liuhe, Zhg.	106	31.30 N	121.15 E
Liuhegou	104	41.56 N	122.44 E
Liuheita	104	42.09 N	123.56 E
Liuhejie	102	24.26 N	101.35 E
Liuhekou	105	40.39 N	118.09 E
Liuheng Dao I	100	29.43 N	122.08 E
Liuhuang	100	23.58 N	116.28 E
Liuhudang	104	42.31 N	122.22 E
Liujia	102	24.54 N	107.49 E
Liujiachang	107	29.46 N	103.49 E
Liujiachuan	105	40.07 N	114.47 E
Liujiadai	106	31.57 N	120.23 E
Liujiadian	89	50.07 N	124.17 E
Liujiadu	106	32.15 N	120.33 E
Liujiafen	105	39.58 N	115.47 E
Liujiagangzi	104	41.28 N	122.33 E
Liujiagou	98	37.47 N	120.53 E
Liujiahe, Zhg.	100	32.06 N	113.21 E
Liujiahe, Zhg.	104	40.40 N	123.58 E
Liujiang	98	40.04 N	119.34 E
Liujiashan	105	40.14 N	114.49 E
Liujiatun, Zhg.	104	41.52 N	122.44 E
Liujiatun, Zhg.	104	41.51 N	122.05 E
Liujiatun, Zhg.	104	42.08 N	122.44 E
Liujiawopeng	104	42.16 N	123.01 E
Liujiazhai	269b	31.21 N	121.27 E
Liujiazhen	106	32.04 N	121.30 E
Liujiazi, Zhg.	98	41.00 N	120.13 E
Liujiazi, Zhg.	104	42.36 N	122.15 E
Liujiazi, Zhg.	104	41.48 N	123.47 E
Liujingcun	105	39.27 N	115.26 E
Liujisu	105	40.01 N	117.13 E
Liukeshu	86	44.59 N	90.12 E
Liuku	102	25.48 N	98.52 E
Liuli	154	11.05 S	34.38 E
Liulicun	271a	39.56 N	116.28 E
Liulidian	106	31.31 N	119.17 E
Liuligou	104	41.24 N	121.29 E
Liulihezhen	105	39.36 N	116.01 E
Liulin	100	31.34 N	113.14 E
Liuliwei	100	24.20 N	114.03 E
Liulongtai	104	41.32 N	120.56 E
Liumachang	107	29.51 N	104.54 E
Liumaogou	89	48.12 N	127.13 E
Liupangtun	104	41.36 N	123.28 E
Liupan Shan ⋀	102	35.40 N	106.40 E
Liuqianhutun	104	42.01 N	123.41 E
Liuqiao	106	32.11 N	120.51 E
Liuquan, Zhg.	98	34.27 N	117.20 E
Liuquan, Zhg.	105	39.22 N	116.18 E
Liurenba	100	29.57 N	114.49 E
Liushi, Zhg.	98	38.33 N	115.44 E
Liushi, Zhg.	100	28.03 N	120.51 E
Liushilipu	100	32.45 N	115.58 E
Liushi Shan ∧	120	36.15 N	82.05 E
Liushouying	98	39.48 N	119.19 E
Liushudian	98	35.54 N	119.30 E
Liushudixia	104	42.26 N	121.14 E
Liushui	89	44.17 N	124.15 E
Liushuigou	100	31.34 N	112.27 E
Liushuquan	105	39.21 N	118.06 E
Liusiqiao	100	29.47 N	116.21 E
Liusong	105	39.40 N	117.08 E
Liuta	98	35.52 N	115.18 E
Liutai	98	41.20 N	113.43 E
Liutaizi	104	41.46 N	122.39 E
Liutang	102	24.58 N	110.21 E
Liutiaozhaicun	104	41.29 N	123.12 E
Liutuan	98	36.56 N	119.22 E
Liutuhutun	104	40.44 N	120.32 E
Liuwanglou	98	34.48 N	116.28 E
Liuwa Plain ≚	152	14.30 S	22.40 E
Liuwa Plain National Park ♦	152	14.30 S	22.40 E
Liuwei	106	32.16 N	119.28 E
Liuwudian	100	24.36 N	118.13 E
Liuxi ≃	100	23.22 N	112.54 E
Liuxia	106	30.15 N	120.03 E
Liuyang	100	28.09 N	113.38 E
Liuyang ≃	100	28.13 N	112.58 E
Liuyuan	98	36.10 N	114.34 E
Liuyuankou	98	34.54 N	114.20 E
Liuzhai	102	25.15 N	107.20 E
Liuzhou	102	24.19 N	109.24 E
Liuzhuang	100	33.10 N	120.19 E
Livada	38	47.52 N	23.07 E
Livadija	89	42.50 N	132.39 E
Livanátai	38	38.42 N	23.03 E
Līvāni	76	56.22 N	26.11 E
Livanjsko Polje ≚	36	43.55 N	16.45 E
Livanovka	86	52.06 N	61.59 E
Livarot	50	49.01 N	0.09 E
Lively, On., Can.	190	46.26 N	81.09 W
Lively, Va., U.S.	208	37.47 N	76.31 W
Lively Island I	254	52.02 S	58.30 W
Livengood	180	65.32 N	148.33 W
Livenka, Ross.	78	50.26 N	38.18 E
Livenka, Ross.	78	50.44 N	40.14 E
Livenza ≃	64	45.35 N	12.51 E
Live Oak, Ca., U.S.	226	39.16 N	121.39 W
Live Oak, Fl., U.S.	192	30.17 N	82.59 W
Live Oak Creek ≃	196	30.39 N	101.42 W
Liverdun	56	48.45 N	6.03 E
Liverdy-en-Brie	261	48.42 N	2.47 E
Livergnano	66	44.19 N	11.21 E
Liveringa	162	18.03 S	124.10 E
Livermore, Ca., U.S.	226	37.40 N	121.46 W
Livermore, Ia., U.S.	190	42.52 N	94.11 W
Livermore, Ky., U.S.	194	37.29 N	87.07 W
Livermore, Mount ∧	196	30.38 N	104.10 W
Livermore Falls	188	44.28 N	70.11 W
Liverpool, Austl.	170	33.54 S	150.56 E
Liverpool, N.S., Can.	186	44.02 N	64.43 W
Liverpool, Eng., U.K.	44	53.25 N	2.55 W
Liverpool, Eng., U.K.	262	53.25 N	2.55 W
Liverpool, In., U.S.	216	41.34 N	87.18 W
Liverpool, N.Y., U.S.	210	43.06 N	76.13 W
Liverpool, Pa., U.S.	208	40.34 N	76.59 W
Liverpool, Tx., U.S.	222	29.18 N	95.17 W
Liverpool □[8]	262	53.25 N	2.55 W
Liverpool ≃	164	12.02 S	134.13 E
Liverpool (Speke) Airport ⊠	44	53.21 N	2.52 W
Liverpool, Cape >	176	73.38 N	78.06 W
Liverpool, University of ᵾ[2]	262	53.24 N	2.58 W
Liverpool Bay c, N.T., Can.	180	69.45 N	130.00 W
Liverpool Bay c, N.S., Can.	186	44.02 N	64.41 W
Liverpool Bay c, Eng., U.K.	44	53.30 N	3.16 W
Liverpool Football Ground ♦	262	53.26 N	2.57 W
Liverpool Heights	210	43.07 N	76.13 W
Liverpool Range ⋀	166	31.40 S	150.30 E
Liverpool Street Station ◆[5]	260	51.31 N	0.05 W
Livet-et-Gavet	62	45.06 N	5.56 E
Livigno	64	46.32 N	10.04 E
Livilliers	261	49.06 N	2.06 E
Lívingston, Guat.	236	15.50 N	88.45 W
Livingston, Scot., U.K.	46	55.53 N	3.32 W
Livingston, Al., U.S.	194	32.35 N	88.11 W
Livingston, Ca., U.S.	226	37.23 N	120.43 W
Livingston, Il., U.S.	194	38.58 N	89.45 W
Livingston, Ky., U.S.	192	37.17 N	84.12 W
Livingston, La., U.S.	194	30.30 N	90.44 W
Livingston, Mt., U.S.	202	45.39 N	110.33 W
Livingston, N.J., U.S.	210	40.47 N	74.18 W
Livingston, N.Y., U.S.	210	42.09 N	73.47 W
Livingston, Tn., U.S.	194	36.23 N	85.19 W
Livingston, Tx., U.S.	222	30.42 N	94.55 W
Livingston, Wi., U.S.	190	42.54 N	90.25 W
Livingston □[6], Il., U.S.	216	40.53 N	88.38 W
Livingston □[6], Mi., U.S.	216	42.38 N	83.50 W
Livingston □[6], N.Y., U.S.	210	42.48 N	77.49 W
Livingstone	154	17.50 S	25.53 E
Livingstone, Chutes de (Livingstone Falls) └	152	4.50 S	14.30 E
Livingstone, Lake ⊜[1]	222	30.50 N	95.30 W
Livingstone Falls → Livingstone, Chutes de └	152	4.50 S	14.30 E
Livingstone Lake ⊜	212	45.22 N	78.43 W
Livingstonia	154	10.36 S	34.07 E
Livingston Island I	9	62.35 S	60.30 W
Livingston Mall ◆[9]	276	40.47 N	74.21 W
Livingston Manor	210	41.54 N	74.49 W
Livno	36	43.50 N	17.01 E
Livny	76	52.25 N	37.37 E
Livojoki ≃	26	65.24 N	26.48 E
Livonia, In., U.S.	218	38.34 N	86.17 W
Livonia, La., U.S.	194	30.33 N	91.33 W
Livonia, Mi., U.S.	216	42.22 N	83.21 W
Livonia, N.Y., U.S.	210	42.49 N	77.40 W
Livonia Center	210	42.49 N	77.38 W
Livonia Mall ◆[9]	281	42.26 N	83.20 W
Livorno (Leghorn)	66	43.33 N	10.19 E
Livorno □[4]	66	43.14 N	10.35 E
Livorno Ferraris	62	45.17 N	8.05 E
Livourne → Livorno	66	43.33 N	10.19 E
Livramento do Brumado	255	13.39 S	41.50 W
Livramento → Santana do Livramento	252	30.53 S	55.31 W
Livron-sur-Drôme	62	44.46 N	4.51 E
Livry-Gargan	261	48.56 N	2.33 E
Livry-sur-Seine	261	48.31 N	2.41 E
Liwa	112	5.04 S	104.06 E
Liwale	154	9.46 S	37.56 E
Liwale Chini	154	9.41 S	38.01 E
Liwan	154	4.54 N	35.40 E
Liwonde	154	14.52 S	35.28 E
Liwonde National Park ♦	154	14.50 S	35.20 E
Liwung ≃	115a	6.08 S	106.49 E
Lixi, Zhg.	100	29.15 N	114.46 E
Lixi, Zhg.	100	27.39 N	116.19 E
Lixian, Zhg.	98	38.29 N	115.34 E
Lixian, Zhg.	102	34.11 N	105.02 E
Lixian, Zhg.	102	29.30 N	111.37 E
Lixian, Zhg.	105	39.33 N	116.26 E
Lixian → Black ≃	110	21.15 N	105.20 E
Lixin, Zhg.	100	26.52 N	116.42 E
Lixin, Zhg.	100	33.06 N	116.08 E
Lixing	100	33.28 N	115.28 E
Lixingzhuang	105	39.25 N	117.56 E
Lixoúrion	38	38.12 N	20.26 E
Lixus ⊥	34	35.16 N	6.13 W
Liyang, Zhg.	98	37.28 N	113.37 E
Liyang, Zhg.	106	31.26 N	119.29 E
Liyuanbao	100	25.16 N	112.55 E
Liyujiang	100	25.57 N	113.15 E
Lizard	42	49.58 N	5.12 W
Lizarda	250	9.36 S	46.41 W
Lizard Head Peak ∧	200	42.47 N	109.11 W
Lizard Island I	164	14.40 S	145.28 E
Lizard Point >	42	49.56 N	5.13 W
Lizard Point Indian Reserve ◆[4]	184	50.40 N	100.57 W
Lize	107	30.08 N	106.11 E
Lizhai	106	31.34 N	121.45 E
Lizhou	102	28.08 N	102.10 E
Lizhu	100	29.56 N	120.30 E
Lizhuang, Zhg.	100	34.24 N	116.30 E
Lizhuang, Zhg.	107	28.47 N	104.46 E
Lizhuangqiao	106	31.48 N	119.37 E
Lizino	83	49.33 N	38.51 E
Lizinovka	78	50.08 N	39.28 E
Liziwei	107	30.19 N	106.39 E
Lizy-sur-Ourcq	50	49.01 N	3.02 E
Lizzana	64	45.51 N	11.03 E
Lizzanello	68	40.18 N	18.13 E
Lizzano	68	40.23 N	17.27 E
Lizzano in Belvedere	64	44.10 N	10.53 E
Ljalovo	82	56.03 N	37.14 E
Ljan	26	59.51 N	10.48 E
Ljubelj (Loiblpass))(	61	46.26 N	14.16 E
Ljubija	36	44.56 N	16.37 E
Ljubimec	38	41.50 N	26.05 E
Ljubinje	38	42.57 N	18.05 E
Ljubljana	36	46.03 N	14.31 E
Ljubovija	38	44.11 N	19.22 E
Ljubuški	36	43.12 N	17.33 E
Ljugarn	26	57.19 N	18.42 E
Ljunga	40	58.31 N	16.21 E
Ljungan ≃	26	62.19 N	17.23 E
Ljungaverk	26	62.29 N	16.03 E
Ljungby	26	56.50 N	13.56 E
Ljungbyhed	41	56.04 N	13.12 E
Ljungbyholm	26	56.38 N	16.10 E
Ljungdalen	26	62.51 N	12.47 E
Ljungsbro	26	58.31 N	15.30 E
Ljungskile	26	58.14 N	11.55 E
Ljusdal	26	61.50 N	16.05 E
Ljusfallshammar	40	58.47 N	15.29 E
Ljusnan ≃	26	61.12 N	17.08 E
Ljusnaren ⊜	40	59.51 N	14.56 E
Ljusne	26	61.13 N	17.08 E
Ljusterö I	40	59.31 N	18.37 E
Ljutomer	61	46.31 N	16.12 E
Llagas Creek ≃	226	36.58 N	121.31 W
Llaima, Volcán ∧[1]	252	38.43 S	71.43 W
Llamara, Salar de ≚	248	21.13 S	69.40 W
Llanaber	42	52.45 N	4.05 W
Llanaelhaearn	42	52.59 N	4.24 W
Llanarth	42	52.12 N	4.18 W
Llanarthney	42	51.52 N	4.09 W
Llanbedrog	42	52.52 N	4.29 W
Llanberis, Pass of V	44	53.06 N	4.04 W
Llanbister	42	52.21 N	3.27 W
Llanboidy	42	51.54 N	4.36 W
Llanbryde	46	57.37 N	3.13 W
Llanbrynmair	42	52.37 N	3.57 W
Llançà	34	42.22 N	3.09 E
Llancanelo, Laguna ⊜	252	35.35 S	69.09 W
Llandaff	42	51.30 N	3.14 W
Llandaff Cathedral ᵾ[1]	42	51.29 N	3.15 W
Llanddewi Brefi	42	52.10 N	3.57 W
Llandeilo	42	51.52 N	3.59 W
Llandilo	274a	33.43 S	150.45 E
Llandinam	42	52.29 N	3.26 W
Llandissilio	42	51.53 N	4.44 W
Llandovery	42	51.59 N	3.48 W
Llandrindod Wells	42	52.15 N	3.23 W
Llandudno	44	53.19 N	3.49 W
Llandybie	42	51.50 N	4.00 W
Llandysul	42	52.02 N	4.19 W
Llanelli	42	51.42 N	4.10 W
Llanelltyd	42	52.45 N	3.54 W
Llanelly	169	36.44 S	143.51 E
Llanenddwyn	42	52.49 N	4.06 W
Llanerchymedd	44	53.20 N	4.22 W
Llanes	34	43.25 N	4.45 W
Llanfaethlu	44	53.21 N	4.32 W
Llanfair-Caereinion	42	52.39 N	3.20 W
Llanfairfechan	44	53.15 N	3.58 W
Llanfairpwllgwyngyll	44	53.13 N	4.12 W
Llanfrynach	42	51.56 N	3.21 W
Llanfyllin	42	52.46 N	3.17 W
Llanfynydd	42	51.56 N	4.06 W
Llanfyrnach	42	51.57 N	4.35 W
Llangadog	42	51.56 N	3.53 W
Llangefni	44	53.16 N	4.18 W
Llangennech	42	51.41 N	4.04 W
Llangollen	42	52.58 N	3.10 W
Llangollen Estates	208	39.39 N	75.37 W
Llangranog	42	52.09 N	4.29 W
Llangurig	42	52.25 N	3.36 W
Llangwyryfon	42	52.19 N	4.03 W
Llangynog	42	52.50 N	3.25 W
Llanharan	42	51.33 N	3.25 W
Llanidloes	42	52.27 N	3.32 W
Llanilar	42	52.21 N	4.01 W
Llanllyfni	44	53.03 N	4.17 W
Llano	196	30.45 N	98.40 W
Llano ≃	196	30.35 N	98.25 W
Llano Colorado	204	31.38 N	115.55 W
Llanon	42	52.17 N	4.10 W
Llanos ≚	246	5.00 N	70.00 W
Llanpumsaint	42	51.56 N	4.18 W
Llanquihue	254	41.15 S	73.01 W
Llanquihue, Lago ⊜	254	41.08 S	72.48 W
Llanrhaeadr-ym-Mochnant	42	52.51 N	3.17 W
Llanrhidian	42	51.37 N	4.11 W
Llanrhystud	42	52.18 N	4.09 W
Llanrwst	44	53.08 N	3.48 W
Llansantffraid-ym-Mechain	42	52.47 N	3.08 W
Llansawel	42	52.01 N	4.00 W
Llantrisant	42	51.33 N	3.23 W
Llantwit Major	42	51.25 N	3.30 W
Llanuwchllyn	42	52.52 N	3.41 W
Llanwenog	42	52.06 N	4.12 W
Llanwrda	42	51.58 N	3.53 W
Llanwrtyd Wells	42	52.07 N	3.38 W
Llanybydder	42	52.04 N	4.09 W
Llata	248	9.25 S	76.47 W
Llavallol ◆[8]	288	34.48 S	58.28 W
Llay	44	53.06 N	2.59 W
Lleida	34	41.37 N	0.37 E
Lleida □[4]	34	42.00 N	1.10 E
Llentrisca, Cap >	34	38.51 N	1.14 E
Llera de Canales	234	23.19 N	99.01 W
Llerena	34	38.14 N	6.01 W
Lleulleu, Lago ⊜	252	38.09 S	73.20 W
Lleyn Peninsula >[1]	42	52.54 N	4.30 W
Llica	248	19.52 S	68.16 W
Llico	252	34.46 S	72.05 W
Lliria	34	39.38 N	0.36 W
Llivia	32	42.28 N	1.59 E
Llobregat ≃	34	41.19 N	2.09 E
Llobregat, Delta del ≚[2]	266d	41.17 N	2.08 E
Llorente	116	11.25 N	125.33 E
Llorente ≃	116	11.25 N	125.33 E
Llorona, Punta >	236	8.39 N	83.45 W
Lloyd	218	38.37 N	82.51 W
Lloyd Harbor	210	40.54 N	73.27 W
Lloyd Harbor c	276	40.55 N	73.27 W
Lloydminster	184	53.17 N	110.00 W
Lloyd Neck >[1]	276	40.56 N	73.28 W
Lloyd Point >	210	40.57 N	73.29 W
Lloyds ≃	186	48.33 N	57.13 W
Llucena	34	40.08 N	0.17 W
Llucmajor	34	39.29 N	2.54 E
Llullaillaco, Volcán ∧[1]	252	24.43 S	68.33 W
Llusco	248	14.21 S	72.07 W
Lluta ≃	248	18.24 S	70.19 W
Llyn Brianne Reservoir ⊜[1]	42	52.08 N	3.45 W
Llyswen	42	52.02 N	3.17 W
Llys-y-frân Reservoir ⊜[1]	42	51.53 N	4.51 W
Lnáře	60	49.28 N	13.47 E
Lo (Panlong) ≃	110	21.18 N	105.25 E
Loa	200	38.24 N	111.38 W
Loa ≃, Chile	244	21.26 S	70.04 W
Loa ≃, Congo	273b	4.20 S	15.11 E
Loami	194	39.40 N	89.51 W
Loanda, Bra.	255	22.54 S	53.10 W
Loanda, Gabon	152	0.55 S	9.00 E
Loanda → Luanda	152	8.48 S	13.14 E
Loande ≃	152	8.41 S	17.56 E
Loange (Luangue) ≃	152	4.17 S	20.02 E
Loango Buele	152	5.10 S	12.59 E
Loanhead	46	55.53 N	3.09 W
Loanja ≃	154	17.22 S	24.48 E
Loano	62	44.08 N	8.15 E
Loantaka Brook ≃	276	40.43 N	74.28 W
Lo Aranguiz	286e	33.23 S	70.40 W
Loay	116	9.36 N	124.01 E
Lob' ≃	82	56.29 N	35.51 E
Lobamba	158	26.27 S	31.12 E
Loban	24	65.44 N	45.25 E
Loban' ≃	80	56.58 N	51.12 E
Lobanovo	76	53.04 N	38.14 E
Lobanovskije Vyselki	82	54.18 N	38.58 E
Lo Barnechea	286e	33.21 S	70.31 W
Lobaski	80	54.38 N	45.09 E
Lobatos	234	22.49 N	103.24 W
Lobatse	156	25.11 S	25.40 E
Löbau	54	51.05 N	14.40 E
Lobau ≚	264b	48.10 N	16.32 E
Lobaye □[5]	152	4.00 N	18.30 E
Lobaye ≃	152	3.41 N	18.35 E
Lobbes	50	50.21 N	4.15 E
Lobbs Run ≃	279b	40.15 N	79.55 W
Lobdell Lake ⊜	216	42.48 N	83.48 W
Löbejün	54	51.38 N	11.53 E
Lobelville	194	35.46 N	87.47 W
Lo Benitez	286e	33.34 S	70.42 W
Lobenstein	54	50.26 N	11.38 E
Lobería	252	38.09 S	58.47 W
Lo Bernales	286e	33.34 S	70.34 W
Löberöd	41	55.47 N	13.30 E
Lobethal	168b	34.54 S	138.52 E
Łobez	30	53.39 N	15.36 E
Lobito	152	12.20 S	13.34 E
Lobitos	246	4.26 S	81.17 W
Lobitos Creek ≃	282	37.22 N	122.24 W
Lobkoviči	76	53.50 N	31.45 E
Lobn'a	82	56.01 N	37.30 E
Löbnitz, Dtsch.	54	51.35 N	12.28 E
Löbnitz, Dtsch.	54	54.17 N	12.43 E
Lobo, Indon.	164	3.45 S	134.05 E
Lobo, Pil.	116	13.39 N	121.13 E
Lobo ≃	150	6.02 N	6.47 W
Loboko	152	0.45 S	16.38 E
Lobos	258	35.11 S	59.06 W
Lobos, Cay I	238	22.24 N	77.32 W
Lobos, Isla I	232	27.20 N	110.36 W
Lobos, Isla de I, Esp.	148	28.45 N	13.49 W
Lobos, Isla de I, Méx.	234	21.27 N	97.13 W
Lobos, Laguna de ⊜	258	35.17 S	59.07 W
Lobos, Point >	226	37.47 N	122.31 W
Lobos, Punta >	248	21.01 S	70.11 W
Lobos de Afuera, Islas II	248	6.57 S	80.42 W
Lobos de Tierra, Isla I	248	6.27 S	80.52 W
Lo Boza	286e	33.23 S	70.46 W
Lobskoje	24	62.45 N	35.16 E
Lobstädt	54	51.08 N	12.29 E
Löbtau ◆[8]	54	51.03 N	13.42 E
Loburg	54	52.07 N	12.05 E
Lobva	86	59.12 N	60.30 E
Łobżenica	30	53.16 N	17.15 E
Locana	62	45.25 N	7.27 E
Locana, Val di V	62	45.25 N	7.27 E
Locarno	58	46.10 N	8.48 E
Lo Castillo, Aeropuerto ⊠	286e	33.23 S	70.36 W
Locate Triulzi	62	45.21 N	9.13 E
Loccum	52	52.27 N	9.08 E
Loceri	71	39.51 N	9.35 E
Loch	169	38.22 S	145.43 E
Lochaber ◆[1]	46	56.57 N	5.06 W
Lochailort	46	56.53 N	5.40 W
Lochaline	46	56.32 N	5.47 W
Locharbriggs	44	55.06 N	3.35 W
Lochar Water ≃	44	54.59 N	3.27 W
Lochboisdale	46	57.09 N	7.19 W
Lochcarron	46	57.24 N	5.30 W
Lochdon	46	56.26 N	5.41 W
Lochearn	284b	39.21 N	76.43 W
Lochearnhead	46	56.23 N	4.17 W
Lochem	52	52.09 N	6.25 E
Loches	50	47.08 N	1.00 E
Lochgair	46	56.03 N	5.20 W
Loch Garman → Wexford	48	52.20 N	6.27 W
Lochgelly	46	56.08 N	3.19 W
Lochgilphead	46	56.03 N	5.26 W
Lochgoilhead	46	56.10 N	4.54 W
Lochiel	168b	33.56 S	138.10 E
Lochindorb ⊜	46	57.24 N	3.43 W
Lochino	265b	55.42 N	37.19 E
Lochinvar National Park ♦	154	15.55 S	27.15 E
Lochinver	46	58.09 N	5.15 W
Lochmaben	44	55.08 N	3.27 W
Lochmaddy	46	57.36 N	7.11 W
Lochnagar ∧	46	56.57 N	3.16 W
Lochovice	60	49.51 N	13.59 E
Lochranza	46	55.42 N	5.18 W
Loch Raven Dam ◆[6]	284b	39.26 N	76.33 W
Loch Raven Reservoir ⊜[1]	208	39.27 N	76.34 W
Lochristi	50	51.06 N	3.50 E
Lochsa ≃	202	46.08 N	115.36 W
Loch Sheldrake	210	41.46 N	74.39 W
Loch Sport	166	38.03 S	147.36 E
Lochvica	78	50.22 N	33.16 E
Lochwinnoch	46	55.48 N	4.39 W
Lochy, Loch ⊜	46	56.57 N	4.53 W
Lock	166	33.34 S	135.46 E
Lock and Dam No. 20 ◆[6], U.S.	219	40.09 N	91.30 W
Lock and Dam No. 21 ◆[6], U.S.	219	39.54 N	91.26 W
Lock and Dam No. 24 ◆[6], U.S.	219	39.22 N	90.55 W
Lock and Dam No. 25 ◆[6], U.S.	219	39.01 N	90.41 W
Lock and Dam No. 22 ◆[6], U.S.	219	39.39 N	91.16 W
Locke, Ca., U.S.	226	38.15 N	121.31 W
Locke, In., U.S.	216	41.28 N	86.00 W
Locke, N.Y., U.S.	210	42.39 N	76.25 W
Lockeford	226	38.10 N	121.09 W
Lockenhaus	61	47.24 N	16.25 E
Lockeport	186	43.42 N	65.07 W
Lockerbie	44	55.07 N	3.22 W
Lockesburg	194	33.58 N	94.10 W
Lockhart, Austl.	166	35.14 S	146.43 E
Lockhart, Fl., U.S.	220	28.37 N	81.26 W
Lockhart, Tx., U.S.	222	29.53 N	97.40 W
Lockhart River Aboriginal Reserve ◆[4]	164	13.00 S	143.15 E
Lock Haven	210	41.08 N	77.26 W
Lockheed Aircraft Corporation ᵾ[3], Ca., U.S.	280	34.12 N	118.22 W
Lockheed Aircraft Corporation ᵾ[3], Ca., U.S.	282	37.25 N	122.02 W
Lockington	216	40.12 N	84.13 W
Lock Mountain ∧	214	40.25 N	78.18 W
Lockney	196	34.07 N	101.26 W
Löcknitz	54	53.27 N	14.12 E
Löcknitz ≃, Dtsch.	54	53.07 N	11.16 E
Löcknitz ≃, Dtsch.	264a	52.25 N	13.49 E
Lockport, Mb., Can.	184	50.05 N	96.56 W
Lockport, Il., U.S.	216	41.35 N	88.03 W
Lockport, La., U.S.	194	29.39 N	90.32 W
Lockport, N.Y., U.S.	210	43.10 N	78.41 W
Lockport Lock ◆[5]	278	41.35 N	88.04 W
Locks Heath	42	50.52 N	1.15 W
Locksley Park	210	42.45 N	78.52 W
Lockvattnet ⊜	40	59.03 N	17.05 E
Lockview	279b	40.10 N	79.55 W
Lockwood, Ca., U.S.	226	35.56 N	121.05 W
Lockwood, Mo., U.S.	194	37.23 N	93.57 W
Lockwood Corners	214	41.00 N	81.34 W
Lockyer Creek ≃	171a	27.25 S	152.36 E
Locminé	28	47.53 N	2.50 W
Loc Ninh	110	11.51 N	106.36 E
Loco, Bayou ≃	222	31.28 N	94.44 W
Locon	50	50.34 N	2.40 E
Locorotondo	68	40.45 N	17.20 E
Locri	68	38.14 N	16.16 E
Locri Epizefiri ⊥	68	38.12 N	16.13 E
Locroja	248	12.41 S	74.26 W
Locsin	116	13.09 N	123.43 E
Locumba	248	17.36 S	70.46 W
Locumba ≃	248	17.54 S	70.57 W
Locust	208	40.18 N	73.59 W
Locust Creek ≃	194	39.40 N	93.17 W
Locust Fork ≃	194	33.33 N	87.11 W
Locust Grove, N.Y., U.S.	276	40.48 N	73.30 W
Locust Grove, Ok., U.S.	196	36.12 N	95.10 W
Locust Lake State Park ♦	208	40.46 N	76.08 W
Locust Point >	276	40.49 N	73.48 W
Locust Valley	210	40.53 N	73.36 W

Symbol	English	Deutsch	Español	Français	Português
≃	River	Fluß	Río	Rivière	Rio
≍	Canal	Kanal	Canal	Canal	Canal
└	Waterfall, Rapids	Wasserfall, Stromschnellen	Cascada, Rápidos	Chute d'eau, Rapides	Cascata, Rápidos
)(	Strait	Meeresstraße	Estrecho	Détroit	Estreito
c	Bay, Gulf	Bucht, Golf	Bahía, Golfo	Baie, Golfe	Baía, Golfo
⊜	Lake, Lakes	See, Seen	Lago, Lagos	Lac, Lacs	Lago, Lagos
≚	Swamp	Sumpf	Pantano	Marais	Pântano
⌂	Ice Features, Glacier	Eis- und Gletscherformen	Accidentes Glaciales	Formes glaciaires	Acidentes glaciares
⊤	Other Hydrographic Features	Andere Hydrographische Objekte	Otros Elementos Hidrográficos	Autres données hydrographiques	Outros acidentes hidrográficos
✢	Submarine Features	Untermeerische Objekte	Accidentes Submarinos	Formes de relief sous-marin	Acidentes submarinos
□	Political Unit	Politische Einheit	Unidad Politica	Entité politique	Unidade política
ᵾ	Cultural Institution	Kulturelle Institution	Institución Cultural	Institution culturelle	Institução cultural
⊥	Historical Site	Historische Stätte	Sitio Histórico	Site historique	Sitio histórico
♦	Recreational Site	Erholungs- und Ferienort	Sitio de Recreo	Centre de loisirs	Area de Lazer
⊠	Airport	Flughafen	Aeropuerto	Aéroport	Aeroporto
■	Military Installation	Militäranlage	Instalación Militar	Installation militaire	Instalação militar
◆	Miscellaneous	Verschiedenes	Misceláneo	Divers	Diversos

Lod (Lydda) 132 31.58 N 34.54 E
Lod, Nemel-Te'Ufa (Ben Gurion Airport) ⊠ 132 31.59 N 34.53 E
Loda 216 40.31 N 88.04 W
Lodal Creek ≃ 285 40.14 N 75.27 W
Löddeköpinge 41 55.46 N 13.01 E
Loddenhøj ∧² 41 56.13 N 9.48 E
Loddon 42 52.32 N 1.29 E
Loddon ≃, Austl. 166 35.32 S 143.52 E
Loddon ≃, Eng., U.K. 42 51.30 N 0.53 W
Lodè 71 40.35 N 9.32 E
Lodejnoje Pole 76 60.44 N 33.30 E
Lodenau 54 51.24 N 14.57 E
Löderburg 54 51.52 N 11.32 E
Lodève 32 43.43 N 3.19 E
Lodge Creek ≃ 202 48.35 N 109.10 W
Lodge Grass 202 45.18 N 107.21 W
Lodgepole, Ab., Can. 182 53.06 N 115.19 W
Lodgepole, Ne., U.S. 198 41.08 N 102.38 W
Lodgepole Creek ≃ 198 40.57 N 102.22 W
Lodhāsuli 126 22.19 N 87.03 E
Lodhrān 123 29.32 N 71.38 E
Lodi, It. 62 45.19 N 9.30 E
Lodi, Ca., U.S. 226 38.07 N 121.16 W
Lodi, N.J., U.S. 210 40.52 N 74.05 W
Lodi, N.Y., U.S. 210 42.36 N 76.49 W
Lodi, Oh., U.S. 214 41.02 N 82.00 W
Lodi, Wi., U.S. 190 43.18 N 89.31 W
Lodi Park ♦ 272a 28.36 N 77.13 E
Lodi Vecchio 62 45.18 N 9.24 E
Lodja 152 3.29 S 23.26 E
Lodosa 34 42.25 N 2.05 W
Lodoyo 115a 8.10 S 112.13 E
Lodrone 64 45.50 N 10.32 E
Lods 58 47.03 N 6.15 E
Lodsch → Łódź 30 51.46 N 19.30 E
Lodwar 154 3.07 N 35.36 E
Łódź 30 51.46 N 19.30 E
Łódź □⁴ 30 51.50 N 19.25 E
Loe Āgra 123 34.35 N 71.43 E
Loei 110 17.29 N 101.35 E
Loei ≃ 110 17.51 N 101.37 E
Loen 26 61.52 N 6.52 E
Loenen 52 52.07 N 6.01 E
Loengo 154 4.45 S 26.27 E
Loeriesfontein 158 30.56 S 19.26 E
Lo Espejo 286e 33.32 S 70.43 W
Lo Espejo, Canal ≊ 286e 33.32 S 70.43 W
Lofa ≃ 150 6.36 N 11.08 W
Lofer 64 47.35 N 12.41 E
Löffingen 58 47.53 N 8.20 E
Lofoten II 24 68.30 N 15.00 E
Lofoten Basin ✣¹ 10 70.00 N 4.00 E
Lofthouse 44 53.44 N 1.29 W
Lofthus 26 60.20 N 6.40 E
Loftus, Austl. 274a 34.03 S 151.03 E
Loftus, Eng., U.K. 44 54.33 N 0.53 W
Lofty, Mount ∧, Austl. 168b 34.59 S 138.42 E
Lofty, Mount ∧, Austl. 274b 37.43 S 145.17 E
Log 80 49.29 N 43.52 E
Loga, Dtsch. 52 53.14 N 7.29 E
Loga, Niger 150 13.37 N 3.14 E
Logačovka 80 52.23 N 52.21 E
Logan, Ia., U.S. 198 41.38 N 95.47 W
Logan, Ks., U.S. 198 39.39 N 99.34 W
Logan, N.M., U.S. 196 35.22 N 103.25 W
Logan, Oh., U.S. 188 39.32 N 82.24 W
Logan, Ut,. U.S. 200 41.44 N 111.50 W
Logan, W.V., U.S. 188 37.50 N 81.59 W
Logan □⁶, Il., U.S. 219 40.09 N 89.22 W
Logan □⁶, Oh., U.S. 216 40.22 N 83.46 W
Logan ➝⁸ 285 40.02 N 75.09 W
Logan ≃, Austl. 171a 27.43 S 153.18 E
Logan ≃, Ab., Can. 182 55.09 N 111.42 W
Logan ≃, Ut,. U.S. 200 41.44 N 111.57 W
Logan, Mount ∧, Yk., Can. 180 60.34 N 140.24 W
Logan, Mount ∧, Wa., U.S. 224 48.32 N 120.57 W
Logan Creek ≃, Ca., U.S. 226 39.22 N 122.06 W
Logan Creek ≃, Mo., U.S. 194 37.11 N 90.49 W
Logan Creek ≃, Ne., U.S. 198 41.37 N 96.29 W
Logandale 204 36.35 N 114.29 W
Logan International Airport ⊠ 283 42.22 N 71.00 W
Logan Lake ◎ 212 44.52 N 78.59 W
Logan Martin Lake ◎¹ 194 33.40 N 86.15 W
Logan Mountains ⋀ 180 61.45 N 128.38 W
Logan Pass)(202 48.42 N 113.43 W
Logansport, In., U.S. 216 40.45 N 86.21 W
Logansport, La., U.S. 194 31.58 N 93.59 W
Logan Square ➝⁸ 278 41.56 N 87.42 W
Loganton 210 41.02 N 77.18 W
Loganville, Ga., U.S. 192 33.50 N 83.54 W
Loganville, Pa., U.S. 208 39.52 N 76.42 W
Logärden ◎ 40 60.37 N 16.00 E
Lögdeälven ≃ 26 63.33 N 19.25 E
Logduz 76 60.00 N 44.41 E
Loge ≃, Ang. 152 10.12 S 17.00 E
Loge ≃, Ang. 152 7.49 S 13.06 E
Logia 164 2.55 S 151.27 E
Loginovo 82 55.42 N 38.44 E
Logirim 154 4.43 N 33.14 E
Logišin 76 52.20 N 25.59 E
Lognes 261 48.50 N 2.38 E
Lognes-Émerainville, Aérodrome de ⊠ 261 48.49 N 2.37 E
Logo 154 5.20 N 30.18 E
Logojsk 76 54.12 N 27.49 E
Logone ≃ 146 12.06 N 15.02 E
Logone Birni 146 11.47 N 15.06 E
Logone Gana 146 11.33 N 15.09 E
Logone-Occidental □⁵ 146 8.50 N 16.00 E
Logone Occidental ≃ 146 9.07 N 16.26 E
Logone-Oriental □⁵ 146 8.15 N 16.20 E
Logone Oriental ≃ 146 9.07 N 16.26 E
Logoualé 150 7.07 N 7.33 W
Logovskij 80 48.26 N 43.23 E
Log pod Mangartom 64 46.24 N 13.36 E
Logroño 34 42.28 N 2.27 W
Logrosán 34 39.20 N 5.29 W
Løgstør 26 56.58 N 9.15 E
Logtāk Lake ◎ 120 24.33 N 93.50 E
Løgten 41 56.17 N 10.19 E
Logudoro ➝¹ 71 40.35 N 8.40 E
Logue Brook Dam ➝⁶ 168a 33.00 S 115.57 E
Løgumgårde 41 55.05 N 8.57 E
Løgumkloster 41 55.03 N 8.57 E
Logumukum 154 0.27 N 36.05 E
Logy Creek ≃ 224 46.11 N 120.35 W
Loh I 175f 13.21 S 166.38 E
Lohāgara 126 23.11 N 89.39 E
Lohals 41 55.08 N 10.55 E
Lohārdaga 124 23.26 N 84.41 E
Lohāru 120 28.27 N 75.49 E
Lohatlha 158 28.02 S 23.04 E
Lohausen ➝⁸ 263 51.16 N 6.44 E
Lohauserholz ➝⁸ 263 51.39 N 7.48 E
Lohberg 263 51.35 N 6.46 E
Löhdorf ➝⁸ 263 51.09 N 7.01 E
Lo Hermida 286e 33.29 S 70.33 W
Lohfelden 56 51.16 N 9.32 E
Lohheide ➝⁸ 263 51.30 N 6.40 E
Lohiān 123 31.10 N 75.11 E
Lohiniva 24 67.10 N 24.58 E
Lohit ≃ 120 27.48 N 95.28 E
Lohja 26 60.15 N 24.05 E
Lohjan harju ∧ 26 60.15 N 24.30 E
Lohjanjärvi ◎ 26 60.15 N 23.55 E
Löhlbach 56 51.04 N 8.58 E
Lohmar 56 50.50 N 7.13 E
Lohme, Dtsch. 54 54.35 N 13.37 E
Löhme, Dtsch. 264a 52.37 N 13.40 E
Lohmen, Dtsch. 54 50.59 N 13.59 E
Lohmen, Dtsch. 54 53.41 N 12.05 E
Lohmühle 263 51.31 N 6.40 E
Lohne, Dtsch. 52 52.42 N 8.12 E
Löhne, Dtsch. 52 52.11 N 8.41 E
Löhnen 263 51.36 N 6.39 E
Lohnsburg 60 48.09 N 13.24 E
Loho → Luohe 100 33.35 N 114.01 E
Lohr am Main 56 50.00 N 9.34 E
Lohrville 198 42.16 N 94.32 W
Lohsa 54 51.23 N 14.24 E
Loi ≃ 110 21.19 N 100.44 E
Loi, Phou ∧ 110 20.16 N 103.12 E
Loiano 66 44.16 N 11.19 E
Loiblpass (Ljubelj))(61 46.26 N 14.16 E
Loiborsoit 154 3.52 S 36.26 E
Loi-kaw 110 19.41 N 97.13 E
Loile ≃ 152 0.52 S 20.12 E
Loimaa 26 60.51 N 23.03 E
Loimijoki ≃ 26 61.13 N 22.38 E
Loi Mwe 110 21.11 N 99.46 E
Loing ≃ 50 48.23 N 2.48 E
Loing, Canal du ≊ 50 48.22 N 2.50 E
Loir ≃ 32 47.33 N 0.32 W
Loira → Loire ≃ 32 47.16 N 2.11 W
Loire 62 45.33 N 4.48 E
Loire □⁵ 32 45.30 N 4.00 E
Loire ≃ 32 47.16 N 2.11 W
Loire, Canal latéral à la ≊ 50 47.37 N 2.44 E
Loire-Atlantique □⁵ 32 47.20 N 1.35 W
Loiret □⁵ 50 47.55 N 2.20 E
Loiret ≃ 50 47.52 N 1.48 E
Loir-et-Cher □⁵ 50 47.30 N 1.30 E
Loïs, Lac ◎ 190 48.34 N 78.44 W
Loisach ≃ 64 47.56 N 11.27 E
Loisdale 284c 38.46 N 77.11 W
Loisia 58 46.29 N 5.27 E
Loison ≃ 56 49.30 N 5.17 E
Loitz 54 53.58 N 13.07 E
Loíza, Lago ◎¹ 240m 18.17 N 66.00 W
Loíza Aldea 240m 18.26 N 65.53 W
Loja, Ec. 246 4.00 S 79.13 W
Loja, Esp. 34 37.10 N 4.09 W
Loja □⁴ 246 4.10 S 79.30 W
Lojang → Luoyang 102 34.41 N 112.28 E
Lojev 78 51.56 N 30.46 E
Lojga 24 61.05 N 44.37 E
Lojno 24 59.44 N 52.39 E
Løjt Kirkeby 41 55.05 N 9.28 E
Loka, Sūd. 154 4.16 N 31.01 E
Loka, Zaïre 152 0.20 N 17.57 E
Loka brunn 40 59.36 N 14.28 E
Lokači 78 50.44 N 24.39 E
Lokako 152 2.14 S 21.45 E
Lokalema 152 1.59 N 22.17 E
Lokan ≃ 116 5.25 N 117.44 E
Lokandu 154 2.31 S 25.47 E
Lokan tekojärvi ◎¹ 24 67.55 N 27.40 E
Lokbatan 84 40.20 N 49.43 E
Løken 26 59.48 N 11.29 E
Lokeren 50 51.06 N 4.00 E
Loket 54 50.09 N 12.43 E
Lokichar 154 2.23 N 35.39 E
Lokichokio 154 4.12 N 34.21 E
Lokitaung 154 4.16 N 35.45 E
Lokka 24 67.49 N 27.44 E
Løkken 26 57.22 N 9.43 E
Løkken verk 26 63.08 N 9.42 E
Lokn'a 76 56.50 N 30.09 E
Loknaš ≃ 82 56.11 N 36.04 E
Loko 150 8.02 N 7.49 E
Lokofa-Bokolongo 152 0.12 N 19.22 E
Lokoja 150 7.47 N 6.45 E
Lokolama 152 2.34 S 19.53 E
Lokolenge 152 1.11 N 22.40 E
Lokolo ≃ 152 0.43 S 19.40 E
Lokomo 152 2.41 N 15.19 E
Lokoro ≃ 152 1.43 S 18.23 E
Lokossa 150 6.38 N 1.43 E
Lokosso 150 10.19 N 3.40 W
Lokot', Ross. 76 52.34 N 34.34 E
Lokot', Ross. 86 51.11 N 81.11 E
Lokoua ≃ 273b 4.06 S 15.16 E
Loksa 76 59.35 N 25.45 E
Loks Land I 176 62.26 N 64.38 W
Loktyši 76 52.50 N 26.43 E
Lokve 64 46.01 N 13.49 E
Loky 157b 12.47 S 49.39 E
Lol 140 6.26 N 29.37 E
Lol ≃ 140 9.13 N 28.59 E
Lóla, Ang. 152 14.22 S 13.42 E
Lola, Guinée 150 7.48 N 8.32 W
Lola, Mount ∧ 226 39.26 N 120.22 W
Lolengi 152 0.07 N 20.59 E
Loleta 204 40.38 N 124.13 W
Lolingo 152 0.55 N 22.38 E
Loliondo 154 2.03 S 35.37 E
Lolita 222 28.50 N 96.32 W
Lolland I 41 54.46 N 11.30 E
Lollar 56 50.39 N 8.42 E
Lolo, Mt., U.S. 202 46.45 N 114.04 W
Lolo, Zaïre 152 2.13 N 23.00 E
Lolo ≃ 152 1.07 S 12.28 E
Lolobau Island I 164 4.55 S 151.10 E
Lolo Creek ≃, Id., U.S. 202 46.26 N 116.10 W
Lolo Creek ≃, Mt., U.S. 202 46.45 N 114.03 W
Lolodorf 152 3.14 N 10.44 E
Lolo Pass)(202 46.38 N 114.35 W
Lolotique 236 13.33 N 88.21 W
Lolowai 175f 15.18 S 168.00 E
Loltong 175f 15.33 S 168.08 E
Lolvavana, Passage ʮ 175f 15.26 S 168.12 E
Lolwa 154 1.22 N 29.31 E
Lolworth Range ⋀ 166 20.20 S 145.15 E
Lom, Blg. 38 43.49 N 23.14 E
Lom, Česko. 54 50.37 N 13.40 E
Lom, Nor. 26 61.50 N 8.33 E
Lom, Ross. 80 57.54 N 39.12 E
Lom ∧ 60 49.54 N 13.12 E
Lom ≃, Afr. 152 5.20 N 13.24 E
Lom ≃, Blg. 38 43.50 N 23.15 E
Loma 144 6.55 N 37.34 E
Loma, Point › 228 32.41 N 117.14 W
Loma Blanca, Chile 286e 33.30 S 70.47 W
Loma Blanca, Méx. 200 31.35 N 106.17 W
Loma Bonita 234 18.07 N 95.53 W
Loma Echegareña 234 22.53 N 105.51 W
Lomakino 85 40.05 N 68.10 E
Lomako ≃ 152 0.50 N 20.50 E
Loma Linda 228 34.02 N 117.15 W
Lomaloma 175g 17.17 S 178.59 W
Lomami ≃ 138 0.46 N 24.16 E
Loma Mountains ⋀ 150 9.10 N 11.07 W
Loma Ridge ∧ 280 33.45 N 117.43 W
Lomas, Bahía c 254 52.35 S 69.05 W
Lomas Alegres 234 17.38 N 92.36 W
Lomas Chapultepec ➝⁸ 286a 19.26 N 99.13 W
Lomas del Real 234 22.30 N 97.54 W
Lomas de Monreal 200 31.17 N 110.56 W
Lomas de Zamora 258 34.46 S 58.24 W
Lomas de Zamora □⁵ 288 34.45 S 58.24 W
Loma Verde 258 35.16 S 58.24 W
Lomax, Il., U.S. 190 40.41 N 91.04 W
Lomax, Tx., U.S. 222 29.41 N 95.04 W
Łomazy 30 51.55 N 23.10 E
Lomazzo 62 45.42 N 9.02 E
Lomba ≃ 152 15.36 S 21.32 E
Lombagin 112 0.55 N 124.04 E
Lombard 216 41.52 N 88.00 W
Lombardia □⁴ 36 45.40 N 9.30 E
Lombardy East 273d 26.07 S 28.08 E
Lombe 152 9.27 S 16.13 E
Lomblen, Pulau I 112 8.25 S 123.30 E
Lombo do Tejo, Mouchão do I 266c 38.52 N 9.00 W
Lombok 115b 8.30 S 116.40 E
Lombok I 115b 8.45 S 116.30 E
Lombok, Selat ʮ 115b 8.30 S 115.50 E
Lombong 114 1.48 N 103.51 E
Lomé 150 6.08 N 1.13 E
Lomela 152 2.18 S 23.17 E
Lomela ≃ 152 0.14 S 20.42 E
Lomellina □⁹ 62 45.15 N 8.45 E
Lomello 62 45.07 N 8.47 E
Lometa 196 31.13 N 98.23 W
Lomi 24 67.05 N 16.09 E
Lomié 152 3.10 N 13.37 E
Lomira 190 43.35 N 88.26 W
Lo Miranda 252 34.11 S 70.54 W
Lomita 228 33.47 N 118.18 W
Lom Kao 110 16.53 N 101.14 E
Lomma 41 55.41 N 13.05 E
Lommabukten c 41 55.40 N 12.58 E
Lommatzsch 54 51.12 N 13.18 E
Lomme 50 50.39 N 2.59 E
Lomme ≃ 56 50.08 N 5.10 E
Lommel 56 51.14 N 5.18 E
Lomnice ≃ 60 49.26 N 14.04 E
Lomnice nad Popelkou 30 50.32 N 15.22 E
Lomond 182 50.21 N 112.39 W
Lomond, Loch ◎, N.S., Can. 186 45.46 N 60.35 W
Lomond, Loch ◎, On., Can. 190 48.15 N 89.20 W
Lomond, Loch ◎, Scot., U.K. 46 56.08 N 4.38 W
Lomond, Loch ◎, Il., U.S. 278 42.17 N 88.01 W
Lomonosov 265a 59.55 N 29.46 E
Lomonosov Moscow State University ʊ² 265b 55.43 N 37.32 E
Lomonosovskij 86 52.50 N 66.28 E
Lomovatka 83 48.27 N 38.34 E
Lomovoje 24 64.01 N 40.40 E
Lompobatang, Gunung ∧ 112 5.20 S 119.55 E
Lompoc 204 34.38 N 120.27 W
Lom Sak 110 16.47 N 101.15 E
Lomy 88 52.17 N 117.59 E
Łomża 30 53.11 N 22.05 E
łomźa □⁴ 30 53.00 N 22.15 E
Lonaconing 188 39.33 N 78.58 W
Lonate Pozzolo 62 45.36 N 8.45 E
Lonato 64 45.27 N 10.29 E
Lonāvale 122 18.45 N 73.25 E
Lončakovo 89 47.05 N 134.10 E
Loncoche 254 39.22 S 72.38 W
Loncon ≃ 64 45.42 N 12.47 E
Loncopué 252 38.04 S 70.37 W
Londela-Kaye 152 4.51 S 13.24 E
Londerzeel 50 51.00 N 4.18 E
Londinières 50 49.50 N 1.24 E
Londo 154 2.03 N 25.43 E
Londoko 89 49.02 N 131.59 E
London, On., Can. 212 42.59 N 81.14 W
London, Kiribati 174o 1.58 N 157.28 W
London, Eng., U.K. 42 51.30 N 0.10 W
London, Eng., U.K. 260 51.30 N 0.10 W
London, Ar., U.S. 194 35.19 N 93.15 W
London, Ca., U.S. 226 36.30 N 119.25 W
London, Ky., U.S. 192 37.07 N 84.05 W
London, Oh., U.S. 218 39.53 N 83.26 W
London, Tx., U.S. 196 30.41 N 99.35 W
London, Wi., U.S. 216 43.03 N 89.01 W
London (Gatwick) Airport ⊠, Eng., U.K. 42 51.09 N 0.21 W
London (Heathrow) Airport ⊠, Eng., U.K. 42 51.27 N 0.28 W
London Bridge Station ➝⁵ 260 51.30 N 0.05 W
London Colney 260 51.43 N 0.18 W
Londonderry, N.S., Can. 186 45.29 N 63.36 W
Londonderry (Derry), N. Ire., U.K. 48 54.59 N 7.20 W
Londonderry, N.H., U.S. 207 42.51 N 71.22 W
Londonderry, Oh., U.S. 214 39.16 N 82.47 W
Londonderry, Cape › 164 13.45 S 126.55 E
Londonderry, Isla I 254 55.03 S 70.35 W
Londontowne 208 38.59 N 76.32 W
London Zoo ♦ 260 51.32 N 0.09 W
Londres 252 27.43 S 67.07 W
Londres → London 42 51.30 N 0.10 W
Londrina 255 23.18 S 51.09 W
Lonedell 219 38.18 N 90.50 W
Lone Grove 196 34.10 N 97.15 W
Lonely Lake ◎ 184 51.09 N 99.05 W
Lonelyville 276 40.39 N 73.11 W
Lone Mountain ∧ 204 38.02 N 117.29 W
Lone Oak, Ky., U.S. 194 37.02 N 88.39 W
Lone Oak, Tx., U.S. 222 33.01 N 95.57 W
Lone Pine 204 36.36 N 118.03 W
Lone Pine Koala Sanctuary ♦ 171a 27.32 S 152.57 E
Lone Rock 190 43.11 N 90.11 W
Lone Star 222 32.56 N 94.43 W
Lone Tree 190 41.29 N 91.25 W
Lone Tree Creek ≃, U.S. 200 40.25 N 104.35 W
Lone Tree Creek ≃, Ca., U.S. 226 37.53 N 121.14 W
Lone Wolf 196 34.59 N 99.14 W
Long 110 18.05 N 99.50 E
Long ≃, Fr. 50 47.41 N 0.28 E
Long ≃, Zhg. 100 23.26 N 114.38 E
Long ≃, Zhg. 102 24.32 N 109.15 E
Long ≃, Zhg. 105 39.23 N 116.49 E
Longa 152 14.42 S 18.32 E
Longa ≃, Ang. 152 16.25 N 19.04 E
Longa ≃, Ang. 152 10.15 S 13.30 E
Longá ≃, Bra. 250 3.09 S 41.56 W
Longa, proliv ʮ 74 70.20 N 178.00 E
Longairo 154 4.30 N 32.17 E
Long Akah 112 3.19 N 114.47 E
Long'an 102 25.03 N 109.00 E
Longana 175f 15.20 S 167.55 E
Long'anqiao 89 47.31 N 124.27 E
Longare 64 45.29 N 11.36 E
Longarone 64 46.16 N 12.18 E
Long Arroyo V 196 33.04 N 104.17 W
Longasy 24 61.58 N 35.09 E
Longaví 252 35.58 S 71.41 W
Longbangun 112 0.36 N 115.11 E
Long Bar Harbor 208 39.27 N 76.15 W
Long Barn 226 38.05 N 120.08 W
Long Bay c, Austl. 274a 33.58 S 151.16 E
Long Bay c, U.S. 192 33.35 N 78.45 W
Long Beach, Ca., U.S. 228 33.46 N 118.11 W
Long Beach, In., U.S. 216 41.44 N 86.51 W
Long Beach, Ms., U.S. 194 30.21 N 89.09 W
Long Beach, N.Y., U.S. 210 40.35 N 73.39 W
Long Beach, Wa., U.S. 224 46.21 N 124.03 W
Long Beach ⊥² 208 39.39 N 74.11 W
Long Beach Breakwater ➝⁵ 280 33.43 N 118.09 W
Long Beach Middle Harbor c 280 33.45 N 118.13 W
Long Beach Municipal Airport ⊠ 280 33.49 N 118.09 W
Long Beach Naval Station ■ 280 33.45 N 118.14 W
Longbeleh 112 0.16 N 116.11 E
Long Belepai 112 2.45 N 114.04 E
Longbenton 44 55.02 N 1.35 W
Longboat Key 220 27.24 N 82.39 W
Longboat Key I 220 27.23 N 82.39 W
Long Branch, N.J., U.S. 208 40.18 N 73.59 W
Longbranch, Wa., U.S. 224 47.12 N 122.45 W
Long Branch □⁸ 275b 43.35 N 79.32 W
Long Branch ≃ 219 39.23 N 91.49 W
Long Branch Lake ◎¹ 194 39.49 N 92.31 W
Longbu 100 25.32 N 115.24 E
Long Buckby 42 52.19 N 1.04 W
Long Cane Creek ≃ 192 33.57 N 82.24 W
Long Canyon V 226 38.59 N 120.41 W
Long Cay I 238 22.37 N 74.20 W
Longchamp, Hippodrome de ♦ 261 48.51 N 2.14 E
Longchamps, Arg. 258 34.52 S 58.23 W
Longchamps, Bel. 56 50.03 N 5.42 E
Longchang, Zhg. 104 40.53 N 123.08 E
Longchang, Zhg. 107 29.21 N 105.17 E
Longchaumois 58 46.27 N 5.56 E
Longchêne 261 48.38 N 2.00 E
Longchuan, Zhg. 100 24.07 N 115.17 E
Longchuan, Zhg. 102 24.14 N 97.45 E
Longchuan (Shweli) ≃ 102 23.56 N 96.17 E
Long Creek, Il., U.S. 219 39.48 N 88.50 W
Long Creek, Or., U.S. 202 44.42 N 119.06 W
Long Creek ≃ 184 49.07 N 103.00 W
Long Crendon 42 51.47 N 1.01 W
Longcun 100 23.34 N 115.33 E
Longde 102 35.28 N 106.22 E
Longdendale V 262 53.29 N 1.56 W
Long Ditton 260 51.23 N 0.20 W
Longdongtuo 107 29.59 N 106.21 E
Longdor, gora ∧ 88 58.24 N 116.47 E
Longdou 100 27.25 N 117.24 E
Longdu 106 31.51 N 118.56 E
Long Eaton 42 52.54 N 1.15 W
Longeau 58 47.46 N 5.18 E
Long Eddy 210 41.51 N 75.08 W
Longfellow National Historical Site ⊥ 283 42.23 N 71.08 W
Longfengchang 107 30.26 N 105.38 E
Longfengkan 104 41.51 N 124.01 E
Longfengyutun 104 40.39 N 122.57 E
Longfield 260 51.24 N 0.18 E
Longford, Austl. 166 38.10 S 147.05 E
Longford, Ire. 48 53.44 N 7.47 W
Longford, Md., U.S. 284b 39.25 N 76.39 W
Longford □⁶ 48 53.40 N 7.40 W
Longford Park ♦ 262 53.27 N 2.17 W
Longframlington 44 55.18 N 1.47 W
Longgang, Zhg. 100 29.38 N 114.57 E
Longgang, Zhg. 100 33.22 N 120.04 E
Longgang, Zhg. 102 24.41 N 101.09 E
Longgangzi 104 42.09 N 123.26 E
Long Green 208 39.28 N 76.31 W
Long Grove 216 42.11 N 88.00 W
Longguan 105 40.47 N 115.34 E
Longgudu 100 27.45 N 116.14 E
Longguntur 112 0.13 N 112.12 E
Long Harbour 186 47.26 N 53.48 W
Long Harbour c, Nf., Can. 186 47.44 N 55.01 W
Long Harbour c, H.K. 271d 22.27 N 114.20 E
Longhorn Cavern State Park ♦ 196 30.20 N 98.30 W
Longhorsley 44 55.15 N 1.46 W
Longhoughton 44 55.26 N 1.36 W
Long Hu ◎ 100 29.58 N 116.10 E
Longhua, Zhg. 98 41.17 N 117.37 E
Longhua, Zhg. 100 22.42 N 113.59 E
Longhua, Zhg. 100 23.37 N 114.14 E
Longhua, Zhg. 106 31.09 N 121.26 E
Longhua Airport ⊠ 269b 31.10 N 121.26 E
Longhua Pagoda ʊ¹ 269b 31.11 N 121.26 E
Longhui, Zhg. 100 25.32 N 114.47 E
Longhui (Taohuaping), Zhg. 102 27.00 N 110.59 E
Longhui, Zhg. 107 29.32 N 104.48 E
Longhutang 106 31.52 N 119.59 E
Longi 70 38.01 N 14.45 E
Longido 154 2.44 S 36.41 E
Longiram 112 0.02 S 115.38 E
Long Island I, Antig. 240c 17.08 N 61.45 W
Long Island I, Austl. 166 22.09 S 149.54 E
Long Island I, Ba. 238 23.15 N 75.07 W
Long Island I, Nf., Can. 186 47.35 N 54.05 W
Long Island I, N.T., Can. 176 54.50 N 79.20 W
Long Island I, N.S., Can. 186 44.20 N 66.15 W
Long Island I, Ak., U.S. 182 54.54 N 132.45 W
Long Island I, Ma., U.S. 283 42.19 N 70.58 W
Long Island I, N.Y., U.S. 188 40.50 N 73.00 W
Long Island I, Wa., U.S. 224 46.27 N 123.58 W
Long Island City ➝⁸ 276 40.45 N 73.56 W
Long Island MacArthur Airport ⊠ 210 40.48 N 73.06 W
Long Island Sound ʮ 188 41.05 N 72.58 W
Long Island University ʊ², N.Y., U.S. 276 40.41 N 73.59 W
Long Island University (C.W. Post Center) ʊ², N.Y., U.S. 276 40.49 N 73.36 W
Longitudinal, Valle V 252 36.00 S 72.00 W
Long Jetty 170 33.22 S 151.29 E
Longji 107 29.23 N 106.04 E
Longjiadian 104 42.10 N 120.47 E
Longjiang, Zhg. 89 47.19 N 123.12 E
Longjiang, Zhg. 100 22.53 N 113.04 E
Longjiang, Zhg. 100 22.59 N 116.13 E
Longjiang, Zhg. 107 29.48 N 105.03 E
Longjie 107 29.53 N 104.32 E
Longjin 100 28.37 N 116.37 E
Longjing 100 23.53 N 112.52 E
Longjohn Slough ≃ 278 41.43 N 87.53 W
Longjumeau 50 48.42 N 2.18 E
Longka 120 33.12 N 79.47 E
Longkamp 56 49.53 N 7.07 E
Longkangji 100 33.09 N 116.54 E
Long Ke 271d 22.23 N 114.22 E
Long Key I, Fl., U.S. 220 24.49 N 80.49 W
Long Key I, Fl., U.S. 220 27.44 N 82.45 W
Long King Creek ≃ 222 30.34 N 94.58 W
Longkou, Zhg. 98 37.38 N 120.18 E
Longkou, Zhg. 100 32.56 N 114.57 E
Longkou, Zhg. 100 29.57 N 113.47 E
Longkou, Zhg. 100 26.11 N 115.15 E
Longkouqiao 85 39.40 N 77.09 E
Long Lake, Il., U.S. 216 42.22 N 88.08 W
Long Lake, N.Y., U.S. 188 43.58 N 74.25 W
Long Lake, Tx., U.S. 222 31.39 N 95.47 W
Long Lake ◎, On., Can. 212 44.41 N 76.45 W
Long Lake ◎, Mi., U.S. 190 45.12 N 83.30 W
Long Lake ◎, Mi., U.S. 281 42.37 N 83.44 W
Long Lake ◎, Mi., U.S. 281 42.36 N 83.28 W
Long Lake ◎, N.Y., U.S. 188 44.04 N 74.20 W
Long Lake ◎, N.D., U.S. 198 46.43 N 100.07 W
Long Lake ◎, Wa., U.S. 224 47.03 N 122.47 W
Long Lake ◎¹ 202 47.50 N 117.40 W
Long Lake Creek ≃ 198 46.40 N 100.13 W
Long Lake Shores 281 42.35 N 83.19 W
Long Lama 112 3.46 N 114.24 E
Longlaville 56 49.32 N 5.47 E
Longleaf 194 31.00 N 92.34 W
Long Leaf Park 192 34.12 N 77.56 W
Longleat ʊ 42 51.12 N 2.17 W
Longlegged Lake ◎ 184 50.46 N 94.08 W
Longli 102 26.26 N 106.58 E
Longlin 102 24.49 N 105.31 E
Longling 102 24.39 N 98.40 E
Longmeadow 207 42.03 N 72.35 W
Long Melford 42 52.05 N 0.43 E
Longmen, Zhg. 89 48.55 N 126.54 E
Longmen, Zhg. 100 29.53 N 119.57 E
Longmen, Zhg. 100 24.56 N 118.04 E
Longmen, Zhg. 100 25.06 N 116.58 E
Longmen, Zhg. 100 23.44 N 114.15 E
Longmen, Zhg. 107 29.12 N 106.13 E
Longmen, Zhg. 107 29.27 N 104.59 E
Longmenchang 107 30.53 N 106.10 E
Longmensuo 98 40.56 N 115.54 E
Longmenzhang 107 28.59 N 106.13 E
Longming 102 22.59 N 107.11 E
Longmire 224 46.45 N 121.49 W
Long Moc 110 18.51 N 105.01 E
Longmont 200 40.10 N 105.06 W
Longmorn 46 57.36 N 3.17 W
Long Mountain ∧ 194 36.41 N 92.26 W
Long Mountain ∧² 42 52.39 N 3.09 W
Longmu 100 24.16 N 115.28 E
Longnan 100 24.54 N 114.48 E
Longnawan 112 1.54 N 114.53 E
Long Neck ›¹ 276 41.03 N 73.29 W
Long Neck Point › 276 41.02 N 73.29 W
Longniddry 46 55.58 N 2.53 W
Longnüsi 107 30.23 N 106.11 E
Longny-au-Perche 50 48.32 N 0.45 E
Longobucco 68 39.27 N 16.37 E
Longperrier 261 49.03 N 2.40 E
Long Pine 198 42.32 N 99.42 W
Longping 100 29.53 N 115.41 E
Long Plains 168b 34.21 S 138.22 E
Long Point, Austl. 274a 34.01 S 150.54 E
Long Point, Il., U.S. 216 41.00 N 88.54 W
Long Point ›, Ba. 240b 25.01 N 77.20 W
Long Point ›, Nf., Can. 186 48.48 N 58.46 W
Long Point ›, N.S., Can. 186 46.51 N 60.18 W
Long Point ›, On., Can. 212 44.06 N 76.29 W
Long Point ›, On., Can. 212 44.32 N 80.18 W
Long Point ›, Pil. 116 9.39 N 118.20 E
Long Point ›, Ca., U.S. 280 33.44 N 118.23 W
Long Point ›, Vir. Is., U.S. 240m 18.18 N 64.53 W
Long Point ›¹, Mb., Can. 184 53.02 N 98.40 W
Long Point ›¹, On., Can. 214 42.34 N 80.15 W
Long Point Bay c 212 42.40 N 80.14 W
Long Point Creek ≃ 216 41.02 N 88.48 W
Long Point Provincial Park ♦ 214 42.35 N 80.35 W
Long Pond ◎, U.S. 283 42.41 N 71.21 W
Long Pond ◎, Ma., U.S. 207 41.43 N 70.04 W
Long Pond ◎, Ma., U.S. 207 41.48 N 70.57 W
Longpont, Fr. 50 49.16 N 3.13 E
Longpont, Fr. 261 48.38 N 2.17 E
Longport 208 39.18 N 74.31 W
Long Prairie 198 45.58 N 94.51 W
Long Prairie ≃ 198 46.20 N 94.36 W
Longpré-les-Corps-Sants 50 50.01 N 1.59 E
Long Preston 44 54.02 N 2.15 W
Longqiantai 104 41.23 N 120.52 E
Longqu, Zhg. 98 34.16 N 114.49 E
Longqu, Zhg. 98 34.54 N 116.47 E
Longquan 100 28.04 N 119.07 E
Longquan ≃ 100 28.17 N 119.44 E
Longquanguan 98 38.55 N 113.51 E
Longquan Shan ⋀ 107 30.25 N 104.15 E
Longquanyi 107 30.34 N 104.16 E
Longquanzhen 107 30.21 N 104.39 E
Long Range Mountains ⋀ 186 49.20 N 57.30 W
Longreach 166 23.26 S 144.15 E
Long Reach c 186 45.26 N 66.09 W
Long Reach ʮ 212 44.07 N 77.04 W
Long Reef ✣² 164 11.11 S 151.40 E
Long Reef Point › 274a 33.45 S 151.19 E
Longridge 44 53.51 N 2.36 W
Long Run ≃, Il., U.S. 278 41.37 N 88.03 W
Long Run ≃, Pa., U.S. 279b 40.20 N 79.48 W
Long-Sault 206 45.02 N 74.53 W
Long Sault Dam ➝⁶ 206 45.00 N 74.45 W
Long Sault Islands II 206 45.00 N 74.55 W
Longsegah 112 2.15 N 116.42 E
Longshan, Zhg. 100 33.36 N 116.18 E
Longshan, Zhg. 102 29.28 N 109.20 E
Longshansuo 100 30.05 N 121.33 E
Longsheng, Zhg. 102 25.48 N 110.00 E
Longsheng, Zhg. 107 30.36 N 105.21 E
Longshizhen, Zhg. 107 30.12 N 106.26 E
Longshizhen, Zhg. 107 29.23 N 105.10 E
Longshu 107 29.33 N 105.45 E
Longs Peak ∧ 200 40.15 N 105.37 W
Long Stratton 42 52.29 N 1.14 E
Long Sutton 42 52.47 N 0.08 E
Longtaichang 107 30.04 N 105.34 E
Longtan, Zhg. 100 23.40 N 113.24 E
Longtan, Zhg. 102 28.20 N 108.52 E
Longtan, Zhg. 106 32.11 N 119.04 E
Longtan, Zhg. 106 31.20 N 118.45 E
Longtansi 107 30.42 N 104.10 E
Longtanzhen 107 29.19 N 104.35 E
Long Teru 112 3.52 N 114.15 E
Long Thanh 110 10.47 N 106.57 E
Longtian 100 25.38 N 119.28 E
Longtian'an 106 31.10 N 120.49 E
Long Tom ≃ 202 44.23 N 123.15 W
Longton, Eng., U.K. 44 53.43 N 2.48 W
Longton, Eng., U.K. 262 53.43 N 2.48 W
Longton, Ks., U.S. 198 37.22 N 96.04 W
Longtou 98 38.51 N 121.18 E
Longtoupu 100 27.54 N 113.12 E
Longtouwei 100 25.14 N 115.24 E
Longtown 44 55.01 N 2.58 W
Long Truong 269c 10.49 N 106.49 E
Longué 32 47.23 N 0.06 W
Longueau 50 49.52 N 2.21 E
Longuenesse 50 50.44 N 2.14 E
Longuesse 261 49.04 N 1.56 E
Longueuil 206 45.32 N 73.30 W
Longueville, Austl. 274a 33.50 S 151.10 E
Longueville, Fr. 50 48.31 N 3.15 E
Longueville-sur-Scie 50 49.48 N 1.06 E
Longuyon 56 49.26 N 5.36 E
Long Valley 210 40.47 N 74.46 W
Long Valley Creek ≃, Ca., U.S. 226 39.03 N 122.34 W
Long Valley Creek ≃, Nv., U.S. 226 39.31 N 119.39 W
Longvic 58 47.17 N 5.04 E
Longview, Ab., Can. 182 50.32 N 114.14 W
Longview, N.C., U.S. 192 35.43 N 81.23 W
Longview, Tx., U.S. 222 32.30 N 94.44 W
Longview, Wa., U.S. 224 46.08 N 122.56 W
Longview Heights 222 32.30 N 94.41 W
Longvilliers 261 48.35 N 2.00 E
Longvilly 56 50.01 N 5.50 E
Longwai 112 0.42 N 116.39 E
Longwan 105 38.57 N 116.10 E
Longwangmiao, Zhg. 98 36.12 N 115.13 E
Longwangmiao, Zhg. 102 40.36 N 95.52 E
Longwangmiao, Zhg. 104 41.38 N 121.04 E
Longwangmiao, Zhg. 104 42.35 N 123.42 E
Longwarry 169 38.07 S 145.46 E
Longwen 100 24.36 N 116.21 E
Longwo 100 23.28 N 115.17 E
Longwokou 106 32.18 N 119.52 E
Longwood 220 28.42 N 81.20 W
Longwood Gardens ♦ 285 39.52 N 75.40 W
Longwood Lake 276 40.59 N 74.52 W
Longwood Park 192 34.55 N 79.42 W
Longworth 182 53.55 N 121.28 W
Longwy 56 49.31 N 5.46 E
Longxi, Zhg. 102 34.56 N 104.47 E
Longxi, Zhg. 107 29.59 N 106.09 E
Longxian, Zhg. 102 34.51 N 106.59 E
Longxian, Zhg. 107 29.09 N 105.50 E
Longxi → Zhangzhou 100 24.33 N 117.39 E
Long Xuyen 110 10.23 N 105.25 E
Longyan 100 25.08 N 117.02 E
Longyao 98 37.23 N 114.41 E
Longyou 100 29.02 N 119.10 E
Longyou ≃ 106 32.08 N 120.38 E
Longyuanba 100 24.56 N 114.27 E
Longzhaogou 98 40.49 N 124.36 E
Longzhen 89 48.41 N 126.42 E
Longzhou 102 22.22 N 106.52 E
Loni 272a 28.45 N 77.17 E
Lonigo 64 45.23 N 11.23 E
Löningen 52 52.44 N 7.46 E
Lonja ≃ 36 45.27 N 16.41 E
Lonkala 152 4.37 S 23.14 E
Lönnewitz 54 51.34 N 13.11 E
Lonny 56 49.49 N 4.35 E
Lonoke 194 34.47 N 91.53 W
Lonquimay, Volcán ∧¹ 252 38.22 S 71.34 W
Lönsboda 26 56.24 N 14.19 E
Lønsdal 24 66.44 N 15.28 E
Lonsdale 190 44.28 N 93.25 W
Lonsdale, Point › 169 38.17 S 144.37 E
Lons-le-Saunier 58 46.40 N 5.33 E
Lonton 110 25.06 N 96.17 E
Lontra ≃ 250 6.37 S 48.39 W
Lontra, Ribeirão da ≃ 255 21.28 S 53.37 W
Lonua ≃ 152 1.16 N 22.38 E
Lonzhen 107 30.00 N 103.59 E
Loo 84 43.43 N 39.36 E
Looc 116 12.16 N 121.59 E
Looe 42 50.21 N 4.28 W
Loogootee 194 38.40 N 86.54 W
Looking Glass ≃ 216 42.52 N 84.54 W
Lookout 210 41.47 N 75.11 W
Lookout, Cape ›, N.C., U.S. 192 34.35 N 76.32 W
Lookout, Cape ›, Or., U.S. 224 45.20 N 124.00 W
Lookout, Point ›, Austl. 171a 27.26 S 153.33 E
Lookout, Point ›, Md., U.S. 208 38.02 N 76.19 W
Lookout Mountain ∧, U.S. 194 34.25 N 85.40 W
Lookout Mountain ∧, Or., U.S. 202 44.20 N 120.22 W
Lookout Mountain ∧, Or., U.S. 224 45.21 N 121.31 W
Lookout Mountain ∧, Wa., U.S. 224 48.40 N 122.22 W
Lookout Pass)(202 47.27 N 115.42 W
Lookout Point Lake ◎¹ 202 43.52 N 122.40 W
Lookout Ridge ⋀ 180 69.07 N 158.36 W
Loolmalassin ∧¹ 154 3.03 S 35.49 E
Loomis, Ca., U.S. 226 38.49 N 121.12 W
Loomis, Ne., U.S. 198 40.28 N 99.30 W
Loomis, Wa., U.S. 182 48.49 N 119.37 W
Loon 116 9.48 N 123.47 E
Loon ≃ 184 55.50 N 101.59 W
Loon Creek ≃ 202 44.49 N 114.49 W
Loongana 162 30.57 S 127.02 E
Loon Lake ◎, Can. 184 55.51 N 102.00 W
Loon Lake ◎, Mi., U.S. 281 42.41 N 83.22 W
Loon Lake ◎¹ 226 39.00 N 120.18 W
Loon op Zand 52 51.38 N 5.04 E
Loop 196 32.55 N 102.25 W
Loop ➝⁸ 278 41.53 N 87.38 W
Loop Head › 48 52.34 N 9.56 W
Loos 50 50.37 N 3.01 E
Loosdorf 61 48.12 N 15.24 E
Loosduinen ➝⁸ 52 52.04 N 4.13 E
Loose, Dtsch. 41 54.31 N 9.53 E
Loose, Eng., U.K. 260 51.14 N 0.31 E
Loose Creek 219 38.30 N 91.57 W
Lop 120 37.02 N 80.15 E
Lop ≃ 110 13.18 N 107.37 E
Lopandino 76 52.28 N 34.49 E
Lopanka 80 46.24 N 40.59 E
Lopar'ovo 80 58.20 N 42.41 E
Lopasn'a ≃ 82 54.51 N 37.52 E
Lopatiči 76 53.34 N 30.53 E
Lopatin, Ross. 84 43.53 N 47.41 E
Lopatin, Ukr. 78 50.13 N 24.50 E
Lopatina, gora ∧ 89 50.52 N 143.10 E
Lopatino, Ross. 80 52.37 N 45.47 E
Lopatino, Ross. 82 54.45 N 37.00 E
Lopatino, Ross. 89 48.24 N 142.15 E
Lopatinskij 82 55.21 N 38.34 E
Lopatka, mys › 74 50.52 N 156.40 E
Lopatovo 76 56.08 N 29.12 E
Lop Buri 110 14.48 N 100.37 E
Lopé-Okanda, Réserve de Chasse de ➝⁴ 152 0.30 S 11.40 E
Lopévi I 175f 16.30 S 168.21 E
López, Méx. 232 27.00 N 105.02 W
Lopez, Pa., U.S. 210 41.27 N 76.20 W
Lopez, Wa., U.S. 224 48.31 N 122.54 W
López, Arroyo de ≃ 258 35.26 S 57.35 W
Lopez, Cap › 152 0.37 S 8.43 E
Lopez Bay c 116 13.56 N 122.12 E
Lopez Island I 224 48.30 N 122.54 W
Lopez Lake ◎¹ 226 35.12 N 120.28 W
Lopik 52 51.58 N 4.56 E
Lop Nor → Lop Nur ◎ 90 40.20 N 90.15 E
Lop Nur (Lop Nor) ◎ 90 40.20 N 90.15 E
Lopori ≃ 152 1.14 N 19.49 E
Lopotovo 82 56.04 N 36.49 E
Loppersum 52 53.19 N 6.45 E
Loppi 26 60.43 N 24.27 E
Lo Prado 286e 33.26 S 70.45 W
Lopšen'ga 24 64.58 N 37.41 E
L'Opton Ruisseau ≃ 261 48.52 N 1.29 E
Lopt'uga 24 63.16 N 47.56 E
Lopuchovka, Ross. 80 51.59 N 44.42 E
Lopuchovka, Ross. 80 50.37 N 44.29 E
Łopuszno 30 50.57 N 20.15 E
Lora 123 33.53 N 73.17 E
Lora ≃ 246 9.25 N 72.25 W
Lora, Hāmūn-i- ◎ 128 29.20 N 64.50 E
Lora Creek ≃ 162 28.10 S 135.22 E
Lora del Río 34 37.39 N 5.32 W
Lorain 214 41.27 N 82.10 W
Lorain □⁶ 214 41.22 N 82.06 W
Lorain County Regional Airport ⊠ 279a 41.20 N 82.11 W
Loraine, Ca., U.S. 228 35.19 N 118.25 W
Loraine, Il., U.S. 219 40.09 N 91.13 W
Loraine, Tx., U.S. 196 32.24 N 100.42 W
Loralai 120 30.22 N 68.36 E
Loramie, Lake ◎¹ 216 40.23 N 84.18 W
Loramie Creek ≃ 216 40.11 N 84.14 W
Lorca 34 37.40 N 1.42 W
Lorch, Dtsch. 56 48.49 N 9.40 E
Lorch, Dtsch. 56 50.02 N 7.48 E
Lorchhausen 56 50.03 N 7.47 E
Lord Howe Island I 160 31.33 S 159.05 E
Lord Howe Rise ✣³ 14 32.00 S 162.00 E

Symbols in the index entries represent the broad categories identified in the key at the right. Symbols with superior numbers (⋀¹) identify subcategories (see complete key on page *I · 1).*

Symbole im Register stellen die rechts im Schlüssel erklärten Kategorien dar. Symbole mit hochgestellten Ziffern (⋀¹) bezeichnen Unterabteilungen einer Kategorie (vgl. vollständiger Schlüssel auf Seite *I · 1).*

Los símbolos incluídos en el texto del índice representan las grandes categorias identificadas con la clave a la derecha. Los símbolos con numeros en su parte superior (⋀¹) identifican las subcategorías (véase la clave completa en la página *I · 1).*

Les symboles de l'index représentent les catégories indiquées dans la légende à droite. Les symboles suivis d'un indice (⋀¹) représentent des sous-catégories (voir légende complète à la page *I · 1).*

Os símbolos incluídos no texto do índice representam as grandes categorias identificadas com a chave à direita. Os símbolos com números em sua parte superior (⋀¹) identificam as subcategorias (veja-se a chave completa à página *I · 1).*

∧ Mountain	Berg	Montaña	Montagne	Montanha
⋀ Mountains	Gebirge	Montañas	Montagnes	Montanhas
)(Pass	Paß	Paso	Col	Passo
V Valley, Canyon	Tal, Cañon	Valle, Cañón	Vallée, Canyon	Vale, Canhão
≚ Plain	Ebene	Llano	Plaine	Planície
› Cape	Kap	Cabo	Cap	Cabo
I Island	Insel	Isla	Île	Ilha
II Islands	Inseln	Islas	Îles	Ilhas
⊥ Other Topographic Features	Andere Topographische Objekte	Otros Elementos Topográficos	Autres données topographiques	Outros acidentes topográficos

ESPAÑOL

Nombre	Página	Lat.°′	Long.°′ W = Oeste
Lord Howe Seamounts ✤ [3]	14	28.00 S	159.00 E
Lord Mayor Bay ⊂	176	69.44 N	92.00 W
Lordsburg	200	32.21 N	108.42 W
Lord's Cricket Ground ♠	260	51.32 N	0.10 W
Lordstown	214	41.09 N	80.53 W
Lords Valley	210	41.23 N	75.04 W
Loreauville	194	30.03 N	91.44 W
Loreley ♠	56	50.08 N	7.44 E
Lorena, Bra.	256	22.44 S	45.08 W
Lorena, Tx., U.S.	222	31.23 N	97.13 W
Lorengau	164	2.00 S	147.15 E
Lorentz ≃	164	5.23 S	138.04 E
Lorentzen	56	48.57 N	7.10 E
Lorenzago di Cadore	64	46.29 N	12.28 E
Lorenzo	196	33.40 N	101.32 W
Lorenzo Geyres (Queguay)	252	32.05 S	57.55 W
Loreo	64	45.04 N	12.11 E
Lorestān □ [4]	128	33.30 N	48.30 E
Loreto, Arg.	252	27.46 S	57.17 W
Loreto, Bol.	248	15.13 S	64.40 W
Loreto, Bra.	250	7.05 S	45.09 W
Loreto, It.	66	43.26 N	13.36 E
Loreto, Méx.	232	26.01 N	111.21 W
Loreto, Méx.	234	22.16 N	101.58 W
Loreto, Para.	252	23.16 S	57.11 W
Loreto, Pil.	116	8.12 N	125.45 E
Loreto, Pil.	116	10.21 N	125.34 E
Loreto □ [5]	246	3.00 S	75.00 W
Loreto Aprutino	66	42.26 N	13.59 E
Loreto Mocagua	246	3.48 S	70.15 W
Lorette, Mb., Can.	184	49.44 N	96.52 W
Lorette, Fr.	62	45.31 N	4.35 E
Loretteville	206	46.51 N	71.21 W
Loretto, Ky., U.S.	194	37.38 N	85.24 W
Loretto, Pa., U.S.	214	40.30 N	78.37 W
Loretto, Tn., U.S.	194	35.04 N	87.26 W
Loretto → Loreto	66	43.26 N	13.36 E
Lorgues	62	43.29 N	6.22 E
Lorian Swamp ≡	154	0.40 N	39.35 E
Lorica	246	9.14 N	75.49 W
Lorida	220	27.26 N	81.15 W
Lorient	32	47.45 N	3.22 W
L'Orignal	206	45.37 N	74.42 W
Lorimer Park ♠	285	40.06 N	75.05 W
Lorimor	194	41.07 N	94.03 W
Loring, Aeródromo de ⊠	266a	40.22 N	3.47 W
Loring Air Force Base ■	186	46.57 N	67.54 W
Lorino	180	65.30 N	171.43 W
Loriol-sur-Drôme	62	44.45 N	4.49 E
Loris	192	34.03 N	78.53 W
Lorman	194	31.49 N	91.03 W
L'Orme	261	48.39 N	1.41 E
Lormes	50	47.17 N	3.49 E
Lorn, Firth of ⊂ [1]	46	56.20 N	5.45 W
Lorna Glen	162	26.14 S	121.33 E
Lorne, Austl.	169	38.33 S	143.59 E
Lorne, N.B., Can.	186	47.53 N	66.08 W
Loro Ciuffenna	66	43.35 N	11.38 E
Loronyo	154	4.39 N	32.38 E
Lorquin	58	48.40 N	7.00 E
Lörrach	58	47.37 N	7.40 E
Lorraine □ [9]	32	49.00 N	6.00 E
Lorrez-le-Bocage	50	48.14 N	2.54 E
Lorris	50	47.53 N	2.31 E
Lorsch	56	49.39 N	8.34 E
Lorsica	62	44.26 N	9.16 E
Lorup	52	52.55 N	7.38 E
Lorze ≃	58	47.15 N	8.25 E
Los	26	61.44 N	15.10 E
Los, Îles de II	150	9.30 N	13.48 W
Losa, Nuraghe ⊥	71	40.07 N	8.46 E
Losada ≃	246	2.12 N	73.55 W
Los Aguacates	286c	10.35 N	66.48 W
Los Alamitos	280	33.48 N	118.04 W
Los Alamitos Armed Forces Reserve Center ■	280	33.47 N	118.03 W
Los Alamitos Race Course ♠	280	33.48 N	118.03 W
Los Alamos, Ca., U.S.	204	34.44 N	120.16 W
Los Alamos, N.M., U.S.	200	35.53 N	106.19 W
Los Aldamas	232	26.03 N	99.11 W
Los Alerces, Parque Nacional ♠	254	42.50 S	71.52 W
Los Altos, Méx.	196	26.14 N	98.28 W
Los Altos, Ca., U.S.	226	37.23 N	122.06 W
Los Altos Hills	226	37.22 N	122.08 W
Los Amates, Guat.	236	15.16 N	89.06 W
Los Amates, Méx.	234	18.08 N	102.15 W
Los Americanos, Barra I	232	24.50 N	97.35 W
Los Andes	252	32.50 S	70.37 W
Los Ángeles, Chile	252	37.28 S	72.21 W
Los Angeles, Ca., U.S.	228	34.03 N	118.14 W
Los Angeles, Ca., U.S.	280	34.03 N	118.14 W
Los Angeles □ [6]	228	34.20 N	118.10 W
Los Angeles ≃	228	33.46 N	118.12 W
Los Angeles Aqueduct ≊ [1]	204	35.22 N	118.05 W
Los Angeles Coliseum and Sports Arena ♠	280	34.01 N	118.17 W
Los Angeles Convention Center ⊍	280	34.03 N	118.17 W
Los Angeles County Fairgrounds ♠	280	34.05 N	117.46 W
Los Angeles County Museum of Art ⊍	280	34.05 N	118.22 W
Los Angeles Harbor ⊂	280	33.42 N	118.16 W
Los Angeles International Airport ⊠	228	33.56 N	118.24 W
Los Antiguos	254	46.33 S	71.37 W
Losantville	218	40.01 N	85.10 W
Losap I [1]	14	6.54 N	152.44 E
Los Arabos	240p	22.44 N	80.43 W
Losarang	115a	6.24 S	108.10 E
Los Aros	234	22.46 N	102.57 W
Los Banos	226	37.03 N	120.50 W
Los Banos Creek ≃	226	37.20 N	120.57 W
Los Banos Creek, North Fork ≃	226	36.57 N	121.07 W
Los Banos Creek, South Fork ≃	226	36.57 N	121.07 W
Los Banos Reservoir ⊜ [1]	226	36.59 N	120.57 W
Los Berros	252	31.57 S	68.39 W
Los Blancos	252	23.36 S	62.36 W
Los Bolones, Cerro ∧, Méx.	232	16.50 N	92.38 W
Los Bolones, Cerro ∧, Méx.	234	16.39 N	92.34 W
Los Cardales	258	34.20 S	58.59 W
Los Cerrillos, Arg.	252	31.57 S	65.28 W
Los Cerrillos, Ur.	258	34.37 S	56.22 W
Los Cerrillos, Aeropuerto ⊠	286e	33.30 S	70.43 W
Los Cerritos Center ➜ [9]	280	33.52 N	118.05 W
Los Chacos	248	14.33 S	62.11 W
Löschenrod	56	50.30 N	9.41 E
Los Chiles	236	11.02 N	84.43 W
Los Conquistadores	252	30.36 S	58.28 W
Los Coronados, Islas II	204	32.25 N	117.15 W
Los Coyotes Indian Reservation ➜ [4]	204	33.20 N	116.35 W
Los Cuatro Álamos	286e	33.32 S	70.44 W

FRANÇAIS

Nom	Page	Lat.°′	Long.°′ W = Ouest
Los Dos Caminos	286c	10.31 N	66.50 W
Los Ebanos	196	26.14 N	98.34 W
Loseley House ⊥	260	51.13 N	0.36 W
Los Esclavos ≃	236	13.50 N	90.20 W
Losevo	78	50.40 N	40.02 E
Los Flamencos, Laguna ⊜	258	35.36 S	58.42 W
Los Frailes, Picacho ∧	234	23.53 N	106.03 W
Los Frentones	252	26.25 S	61.25 W
Los Fresnos	196	26.04 N	97.29 W
Los Garzas	196	26.23 N	99.46 W
Los Gatos	226	37.13 N	121.58 W
Los Gatos Creek ≃, Ca., U.S.	226	36.13 N	120.08 W
Los Gatos Creek ≃, Ca., U.S.	226	37.20 N	121.54 W
Los Glaciares, Parque Nacional ♠	254	49.52 S	73.05 W
Los Guerras	196	26.25 N	99.05 W
Loshan → Leshan	107	29.34 N	103.45 E
Losheim	56	49.30 N	6.44 E
Los Hermanos, Islas II	246	11.45 N	64.25 W
Los Herreras	196	25.55 N	99.24 W
Los Huacales, Cerro ∧	234	22.19 N	101.34 W
Losi	273a	6.40 N	3.31 E
Łosice	30	52.14 N	22.43 E
Los Idolos, Parque Arquelógico de ⊥	246	1.55 N	76.10 W
Lošinj, Otok I	36	44.36 N	14.24 E
Losinoborskaja	86	58.27 N	89.28 E
Losino-Petrovskij	82	55.52 N	38.12 E
Losinovka	78	50.51 N	31.54 E
Los Jazmines, Presa ⊜ [1]	286a	19.25 N	99.16 W
Los Juríes	252	28.28 S	62.06 W
Loškar'ovka	78	47.57 N	34.12 E
Loskopdam ⊜ [1]	156	25.23 S	29.20 E
Loskop Dam Game Reserve ➜ [4]	156	25.23 S	29.20 E
Los Lagos	254	39.51 S	72.50 W
Los Lagos □ [4]	254	41.45 S	73.00 W
Los Llanos	240m	18.03 N	66.24 W
Los Llanos [de Aridane]	148	28.39 N	17.54 W
Los López	196	26.15 N	99.05 W
Los Lunas	200	34.48 N	106.43 W
Los Manglares de Tumbes, Santuario Nacional ♠	246	2.25 S	80.20 W
Los Maribios, Cordillera ⋀	236	12.35 N	86.50 W
Los Médanos, Istmo de ⩡ [3]	241s	11.35 N	69.45 W
Los Menucos	254	40.50 S	68.08 W
Los Micos, Laguna de ⊂	236	15.45 N	87.36 W
Los'mino	76	55.04 N	34.24 E
Los Mochis	232	25.45 N	108.57 W
Los Molinos	204	40.01 N	122.05 W
Los Muermos	254	41.24 S	73.29 W
Los Naranjos	286c	10.27 N	66.48 W
Los Navalmorales	34	39.43 N	4.38 W
Lošnica	76	54.17 N	28.46 E
Los Nietos	280	33.58 N	118.04 W
Løsning	41	55.48 N	9.42 E
Los Nogales	196	26.16 N	99.43 W
Losolava	175f	14.11 S	167.34 E
Los Olmos Creek ≃, Tx., U.S.	196	27.20 N	97.40 W
Los Olmos Creek ≃, Tx., U.S.	196	26.21 N	98.48 W
Los Osos	226	35.19 N	120.50 W
Los Oyameles	234	19.43 N	97.32 W
Los Padillas	200	34.58 N	106.41 W
Los Palacios, Arg.	252	29.22 S	68.11 W
Los Palacios, Cuba	240p	22.35 N	83.15 W
Los Palacios y Villafranca	34	37.10 N	5.56 W
Los Perros, Arroyo ≃	288	34.37 S	58.46 W
Los Pinos ➜ [8]	286b	23.04 N	82.23 W
Los Pinos ≃	200	36.56 N	107.36 W
Los Placeres del Oro	234	18.13 N	100.54 W
Los Polvorines	288	34.30 S	58.41 W
Los Quillayes	286e	33.34 S	70.37 W
Los Quirquinchos	252	33.22 S	61.43 W
Los Rábanos	240m	18.11 N	66.50 W
Los Ramones	196	25.42 N	99.37 W
Los Remedios ≃	286a	19.31 N	99.05 W
Los Reyes de Salgado	234	19.35 N	102.29 W
Los Reyes la Paz	286a	19.21 N	98.58 W
Los Ríos □ [4]	246	1.30 S	79.25 W
Los Rodríguez	232	27.11 N	101.21 W
Los Roques, Islas II	246	11.50 N	66.45 W
Lossa	54	51.13 N	11.25 E
Lossa ≃	54	51.18 N	11.10 E
Los Santos □ [4]	236	7.55 N	80.25 W
Los Santos de Maimona	34	38.27 N	6.23 W
Los Sauces	252	37.58 S	72.50 W
Lossburg	58	48.25 N	8.27 E
Lössel	263	51.21 N	7.39 E
Losser	52	52.15 N	7.00 E
Los Serranos	228	33.59 N	117.42 W
Lossie ≃	46	57.43 N	3.16 W
Lossiemouth	46	57.43 N	3.18 W
Lössnitz	54	50.37 N	12.43 E
Lost ≃, U.S.	202	41.56 N	121.30 W
Lost ≃, In., U.S.	194	38.33 N	86.49 W
Lost ≃, Mn., U.S.	198	47.51 N	96.02 W
Lost ≃, W.V., U.S.	188	39.05 N	78.36 W
Lostant	216	41.09 N	89.04 W
Los Taques	246	11.50 N	70.16 W
Lost Bridge State Recreation Area ♠	216	40.45 N	85.37 W
Lost Creek ≃, Al., U.S.	194	33.38 N	87.14 W
Lost Creek ≃, Ar., U.S.	194	34.10 N	92.31 W
Lost Creek ≃, Oh., U.S.	218	39.58 N	84.09 W
Lost Creek ≃, Ut,. U.S.	200	41.04 N	111.32 W
Lost Creek ≃, Wy., U.S.	200	42.01 N	108.11 W
Lost Draw ∨	196	32.58 N	102.02 W
Los Telares	252	28.59 S	63.26 W
Los Teques	246	10.21 N	67.02 W
Los Testigos, Islas II	246	11.22 N	63.06 W
Lost Hills	226	35.36 N	119.41 W
Lostine ≃	202	45.33 N	117.29 W
Lost Lake ⊜, Or., U.S.	224	45.29 N	121.49 W
Lost Lake ⊜, Wa., U.S.	224	47.20 N	121.24 W
Lost Nation	190	41.57 N	90.49 W
Lostock ≃	262	53.40 N	2.48 W
Lostock Gralam	262	53.16 N	2.28 W
Los Trancos Creek ≃	282	37.25 N	122.12 W
Los Trancos Woods	282	37.21 N	122.12 W
Lost River Range ⋀	202	44.10 N	113.35 W
Lost Trail Pass)(	202	45.41 N	113.57 W
Lostwithiel	42	50.25 N	4.40 W
Losuia	164	8.32 S	151.04 E
Los Vidrios	232	31.59 N	113.28 W
Los Vilos	252	31.55 S	71.31 W
Los Yébenes	34	39.34 N	3.53 W
Lot □ [5]	32	44.35 N	1.40 E
Lot ≃	32	44.18 N	0.20 E
Lota	252	37.05 S	73.10 W
Lotagipi Swamp (Lotikipi Plain) ≚	144	4.36 N	34.55 E
Lotak	112	0.11 S	115.54 E
Lotbinière □ [6]	206	46.30 N	71.40 W
Lotela, Lake ⊜	220	27.34 N	81.29 W
Løten	26	60.49 N	11.19 E

PORTUGUÊS

Nome	Página	Lat.°′	Long.°′ W = Oeste
Lot-et-Garonne □ [5]	32	44.20 N	0.20 E
Lotfābād	128	37.32 N	59.20 E
Lothair, S. Afr.	158	26.26 S	30.27 E
Lothair, Ky., U.S.	192	37.14 N	83.10 W
Lothian □ [4]	46	55.55 N	3.05 W
Lothringen → Lorraine □ [9]	32	49.00 N	6.00 E
Lotikipi Plain (Lotagipi Swamp) ≚	144	4.36 N	34.55 E
Loto	152	2.49 S	22.29 E
Loto ≃	152	1.55 S	22.09 E
Lotofaga	175a	13.59 S	171.50 W
Lotoi ≃	152	1.35 S	18.30 E
Lotorp	40	58.44 N	15.50 E
Lotošino	76	56.14 N	35.38 E
Lotrului, Munții ⋀	38	45.30 N	23.52 E
Lotsane ≃	156	22.41 S	28.11 E
Lötschberg Tunnel ➜ [5]	58	46.25 N	7.45 E
Lötschental ∨	58	46.25 N	7.50 E
Lotseninsel I	41	54.40 N	10.01 E
Lott	222	31.12 N	97.02 W
Lotta ≃	24	68.36 N	31.06 E
Lottaville	278	41.31 N	87.22 W
Lotte	52	52.17 N	7.55 E
Lottivue	214	42.40 N	82.46 W
Löttringhausen ➜ [8]	263	51.27 N	7.27 E
Lottsburg	208	37.57 N	76.31 W
Lotts Creek ≃	192	32.09 N	81.47 W
Lottsford Branch ≃	284c	38.55 N	76.49 W
Lottstetten	58	47.38 N	8.34 E
Lotuke, Jabal ∧	154	4.07 N	33.48 E
Lotung	100	24.41 N	121.46 E
Lotzorai	71	39.58 N	9.39 E
Louang Namtha	110	20.57 N	101.25 E
Louangphrabang	110	19.52 N	102.08 E
L'Ouarsenis, Massif de ⋀	34	35.40 N	1.50 E
Loubaresse	62	44.36 N	4.03 E
Loube, Montagne de la ∧	62	43.22 N	5.59 E
Loubetsi	152	3.12 S	12.10 E
Louchi	24	66.04 N	33.00 E
Loučim	60	49.22 N	13.07 E
Loučná ∧	54	50.39 N	13.37 E
Loude	98	35.54 N	117.18 E
Loudéac	32	48.10 N	2.45 W
Louden Cove ⊂	276	41.05 N	73.43 W
Loudes	62	45.05 N	3.45 E
Loudima Poste	152	4.07 S	13.04 E
Loudon	192	35.43 N	84.20 W
Loudonville, N.Y., U.S.	210	42.42 N	73.45 W
Loudonville, Oh., U.S.	214	40.38 N	82.14 W
Loudoun □ [6]	208	39.05 N	77.30 W
Loudun	32	47.01 N	0.05 E
Loué	32	48.00 N	0.09 W
Loue ≃	58	47.01 N	5.27 E
Louga	150	15.37 N	16.13 W
Louga □ [4]	150	15.25 N	15.30 W
Louge	252	36.57 S	61.40 W
Louge ≃	32	43.27 N	1.20 E
Lougguéré ≃	150	15.35 N	14.47 W
Loughborough	42	52.47 N	1.11 W
Loughborough Lake ⊜	212	44.23 N	76.30 W
Loughermore ∧ [2]	48	54.59 N	7.05 W
Loughman	220	28.14 N	81.34 W
Loughor	42	51.40 N	4.04 W
Loughor ≃	42	51.40 N	4.04 W
Loughrea	48	53.12 N	8.34 W
Loughros More Bay ⊂	48	54.47 N	8.35 W
Loughton	260	51.39 N	0.03 E
Louhans	58	46.38 N	5.13 E
Louin	194	32.04 N	89.15 W
Louisa, Ky., U.S.	192	38.06 N	82.36 W
Louisa, Va., U.S.	192	38.01 N	78.00 W
Louisa, Lake ⊜, On., Can.	212	45.28 N	78.30 W
Louisa, Lake ⊜, Fl., U.S.	220	28.29 N	81.44 W
Louisbourg	186	45.55 N	59.58 W
Louis Bull Indian Reserve ➜ [4]	182	52.53 N	113.31 W
Louisburg, Ks., U.S.	198	38.37 N	94.40 W
Louisburg, N.C., U.S.	192	36.05 N	78.18 W
Louisburgh	48	53.46 N	9.51 W
Louisdale	186	45.36 N	61.04 W
Louise, Ms., U.S.	194	32.58 N	90.35 W
Louise, Tx., U.S.	222	29.06 N	96.25 W
Louise, Lac ⊜, P.Q., Can.	206	45.46 N	74.25 W
Louise, Lac ⊜, P.Q., Can.	206	45.43 N	71.25 W
Louise, Lake ⊜	180	62.20 N	146.30 W
Louise Island I	182	52.58 N	131.50 W
Louiseville	206	46.15 N	72.57 W
Louis Gentil → Youssoufia	148	32.16 N	8.33 W
Louisiade Archipelago II	160	11.00 S	153.00 E
Louisiana	219	39.26 N	91.03 W
Louisiana □ [3], U.S.	178	31.15 N	92.15 W
Louisiana □ [3], U.S.	194	31.15 N	92.15 W
Louisiana ⊍	41	55.58 N	12.33 E
Lou Island I	164	2.25 S	147.20 E
Louis Trichardt	156	23.01 S	29.43 E
Louisvale	158	28.33 S	21.12 E
Louisville, On., Can.	214	42.28 N	82.07 W
Louisville, Al., U.S.	194	31.47 N	85.33 W
Louisville, Ga., U.S.	192	33.00 N	82.24 W
Louisville, Il., U.S.	194	38.46 N	88.30 W
Louisville, Ky., U.S.	218	38.15 N	85.45 W
Louisville, Ms., U.S.	194	33.07 N	89.03 W
Louisville, Ne., U.S.	198	40.59 N	96.09 W
Louisville, Oh., U.S.	214	40.50 N	81.15 W
Louisville Ridge ✤ [3]	14	31.00 S	172.30 W
Louisville Seamount ✤ [3]	14	31.15 S	172.15 W
Louis-XIV, Pointe ›	176	54.37 N	79.45 W
Loujiaying	98	42.04 N	116.04 E
Loukanga	273b	4.20 S	15.09 E
Loukkos, Oued ≃	34	35.12 N	6.09 W
Loukoua ≃	273b	4.09 S	15.08 E
Loulé	34	37.08 N	8.02 W
Loum	152	4.43 N	9.44 E
Loumou	273b	4.08 S	15.09 E
Lount Lake ⊜	184	50.10 N	94.20 W
Louny	54	50.19 N	13.46 E
Loup ≃, Fr.	62	43.38 N	7.09 E
Loup ≃, Ne., U.S.	198	41.24 N	97.19 W
Loup, Gorge du ∨	56	49.47 N	6.23 E
Loup, Rivière du ≃	206	46.13 N	72.55 W
Loup City	198	41.16 N	98.57 W
Loups Marins, Lacs des ⊜	176	56.30 N	73.45 W
Lourches	50	50.19 N	3.21 E
Lourdes, Nf., Can.	186	48.39 N	59.00 W
Lourdes, Fr.	32	43.06 N	0.03 W
Lourel de Baixo	266c	38.49 N	9.22 W
Lourenço	250	2.30 N	51.40 W
Lourenço Marques → Maputo	156	25.58 S	32.35 E
Lourenço Velho	256	22.22 S	45.19 W
Lourenço Velho ≃, Bra.	256	23.26 S	45.35 W
Lourenço Velho ≃, Bra.	256	22.22 S	45.31 W
Loures	34	38.50 N	9.10 W
Loures ≃	266c	38.50 N	9.08 W
Lourinhã	34	39.14 N	9.19 W
Lourmarin	62	43.46 N	5.22 E
Lourosa	34	40.19 N	7.56 W
Loury	50	48.00 N	2.05 E
Lousã, Port.	34	40.07 N	8.15 W
Lousa, Port.	266c	38.53 N	9.12 W
Louse Creek ≃	198	46.22 N	100.57 W
Lou Shan ∧	89	45.15 N	128.58 E
Louta	150	13.30 N	3.10 W

Loutang	106	31.26 N	121.12 E
Loutézou, Île de I	273b	4.22 S	15.10 E
Louth, Austl.	166	30.32 S	145.07 E
Louth, Ire.	44	53.57 N	6.33 W
Louth, Ire.	48	53.37 N	6.53 W
Louth, Eng., U.K.	44	53.22 N	0.01 W
Louth □ [6]	48	53.55 N	6.30 W
Louth Bay ⊂	166	34.34 S	136.02 E
Louti, Mayo ≃	146	9.38 N	13.56 E
Loutit Bay ⊂	169	38.33 S	144.00 E
Loutrá Aidhipsoú	38	38.51 N	23.02 E
Loutre ≃	219	38.42 N	91.25 W
Loutre, Bayou de ≃	194	32.41 N	92.08 W
Loutrópirgos	267c	38.02 N	23.28 E
Louvain → Leuven	56	50.53 N	4.42 E
Louveciennes	261	48.52 N	2.07 E
Louveigné	56	50.32 N	5.42 E
Louveira	256	23.04 S	46.58 W
Louviers, Fr.	50	49.13 N	1.10 E
Louviers, Co., U.S.	200	39.28 N	105.00 W
Louvre ⊍	261	48.52 N	2.20 E
Louvres	50	49.02 N	2.30 E
Louvroil	50	50.16 N	3.58 E
Louwsburg	158	27.37 S	31.07 E
Lou Yaeger, Lake ⊜ [1]	219	39.10 N	89.37 W
Lövånger	26	64.22 N	21.18 E
Lovászi	61	46.33 N	16.34 E
Lovat' ≃	76	58.14 N	31.28 E
Lovcy	82	55.00 N	39.15 E
Love	184	53.29 N	104.09 W
Loveč	38	43.08 N	24.43 E
Love Clough	262	53.44 N	2.17 W
Lovedale	279b	40.17 N	79.52 W
Lovejoy	219	38.39 N	90.10 W
Lovelady	222	31.08 N	95.27 W
Loveland, Co., U.S.	200	40.23 N	105.04 W
Loveland, Oh., U.S.	218	39.16 N	84.16 W
Lovell	202	44.50 N	108.23 W
Lovell Island I	283	42.20 N	70.56 W
Lovelock	204	40.10 N	118.28 W
Lovely	192	37.49 N	82.24 W
Love Point ›	208	39.02 N	76.18 W
Lovere	64	45.49 N	10.04 E
Lovering, Lac ⊜	206	45.10 N	72.09 W
Lovero	64	46.14 N	10.14 E
Loves Green	260	51.43 N	0.24 E
Loves Park	216	42.19 N	89.03 W
Loviisa → Lovisa	26	60.27 N	26.14 E
Lovilia	190	41.08 N	92.54 W
Loving, N.M., U.S.	196	32.17 N	104.05 W
Loving, Tx., U.S.	196	33.16 N	98.31 W
Lovingston	192	37.45 N	78.52 W
Lovington, Il., U.S.	219	39.42 N	88.37 W
Lovington, N.M., U.S.	196	32.56 N	103.20 W
Lovisa (Loviisa)	26	60.27 N	26.14 E
Lövő	61	47.30 N	16.47 E
Lovö I	40	59.20 N	17.50 E
Lovoi ≃	154	8.14 S	26.39 E
Lovosice	54	50.31 N	14.03 E
Lovozero, Ross.	24	68.00 N	35.00 E
Lovozero, Ross.	24	65.00 N	29.50 E
Lovozero, ozero ⊜	24	67.54 N	35.12 E
Lovrenc	61	46.32 N	15.23 E
Lövstabruk	40	60.24 N	17.53 E
Lövstabukten ⊂	40	60.35 N	17.45 E
Lövstad slott ⊥	40	58.33 N	16.02 E
Lóvua, Ang.	152	11.36 S	23.53 E
Lóvua, Ang.	152	7.20 S	20.16 E
Lovua (Lóvua) ≃	152	6.07 S	20.35 E
Low	188	45.48 N	75.57 W
Low, Cape ›	176	63.07 N	85.18 W
Lowa	154	1.24 S	25.51 E
Lowa ≃	154	1.24 S	25.51 E
Lowāda	126	22.27 N	87.37 E
Lowat → Lovat' ≃	76	58.14 N	31.28 E
Lowber	279b	40.15 N	79.46 W
Lowden	190	41.51 N	90.55 W
Lowder Brook ≃	283	43.14 N	71.11 W
Lowell, Ar., U.S.	194	36.15 N	94.07 W
Lowell, In., U.S.	216	41.17 N	87.25 W
Lowell, Ma., U.S.	207	42.38 N	71.19 W
Lowell, Mi., U.S.	216	42.56 N	85.20 W
Lowell, Or., U.S.	202	43.55 N	122.46 W
Lowell, Lake ⊜ [1]	202	43.33 N	116.40 W
Lowell, University of ⊍ [2]	283	42.39 N	71.20 W
Lowell-Dracut State Forest ♠	283	42.40 N	71.22 W
Lowelli	140	5.59 N	33.45 E
Lowellville	214	41.02 N	80.32 W
Löwen ≃	158	26.51 S	18.17 E
Löwenberg	54	52.54 N	13.08 E
Löwenbruch	264a	52.18 N	13.19 E
Löwen → Leuven	56	50.53 N	4.42 E
Löwenstein	56	49.06 N	9.22 E
Lowe Pond ⊜	283	42.41 N	70.59 W
Lower Aetna Lake ⊜	285	39.51 N	74.48 W
Lower Arrow Lake ⊜	182	49.40 N	118.08 W
Lower Bay ⊂	208	40.33 N	74.02 W
Lower Bear River Reservoir ⊜ [1]	226	38.33 N	120.14 W
Lower Bershire Valley	276	40.54 N	74.37 W
Lower Beverley Lake ⊜	212	44.36 N	76.09 W
Lower Broughton ➜ [8]	262	53.29 N	2.15 W
Lower Brule Indian Reservation ➜ [4]	198	44.05 N	99.44 W
Lower Buckhorn Lake ⊜	212	44.33 N	78.17 W
Lower Burrell	214	40.33 N	79.45 W
Lower California → Baja California › [1]	232	28.00 N	113.30 W
Lower Chittering	168a	31.34 S	116.06 E
Lower Crystal Springs Reservoir ⊜ [1]	226	37.32 N	122.22 W
Lower Darwen	262	53.43 N	2.28 W
Lower Egypt → Mişr Baḥrī □ [9]	140	31.00 N	31.00 E
Lower Eltham Park ♠	274b	37.45 S	145.09 E
Lower Elwha Indian Reservation ➜ [4]	224	48.09 N	123.33 W
Lower Fort Garry National Historic Park ♠	184	50.07 N	96.55 W
Lower Ganga Canal ≊	124	26.27 N	80.17 E
Lower Gap ⊂	212	44.10 N	76.35 W
Lower Halstow	260	51.22 N	0.40 E
Lower Hay Lake ⊜	212	45.25 N	78.13 W
Lower Higham	260	51.26 N	0.28 E
Lower Huron Metropolitan Park ♠	281	42.12 N	83.25 W
Lower Hutt	172	41.13 S	174.55 E
Lower Kalskag	180	61.31 N	160.22 W
Lower Keechi Creek ≃	222	31.08 N	95.46 W
Lower Klamath Lake ⊜	204	41.55 N	121.42 W
Lower Lake	226	38.55 N	122.36 W
Lower Lake ⊜	204	41.15 N	120.02 W
Lower Loteni	158	29.32 S	29.36 E
Lower Manitou Lake ⊜	184	49.15 N	93.00 W
Lower Matecumbe Key I	220	24.51 N	80.43 W
Lower Montville	276	40.54 N	74.22 W
Lower Mystic Lake ⊜	283	42.26 N	71.09 W
Lower Nazeing	260	51.44 N	0.01 E
Lower Otay Lake ⊜ [1]	228	32.37 N	116.55 W
Lower Paia	229a	20.55 N	156.23 W
Lower Paudash Lake ⊜	212	44.58 N	78.01 W

Lower Peirce Reservoir ⊜ [1]	271c	1.22 N	103.49 E
Lower Peover	262	53.16 N	2.23 W
Lower Place	262	53.36 N	2.09 W
Lower Plenty	274b	37.44 S	145.06 E
Lower Portland	170	33.27 S	150.53 E
Lower Post	176	59.55 N	128.30 W
Lower Red Lake ⊜	198	48.00 N	94.50 W
Lower River Rouge ≃	281	42.18 N	83.14 W
Lower Rouge Parkway ♠	281	42.18 N	83.20 W
Lower Saxony → Niedersachsen □ [3]	30	52.40 N	9.00 E
Lower Stoke	260	51.27 N	0.38 E
Lower Trajan's Wall ⊥	38	45.40 N	28.30 E
Lower Ugashik Lake ⊜	180	57.30 N	156.56 W
Lower Van Norman Lake ⊜ [1]	280	34.17 N	118.29 W
Lower West Pubnico	186	43.38 N	65.48 W
Lower Whitley	262	53.18 N	2.35 W
Lower Wood's Harbour	186	43.31 N	65.44 W
Lowery, Lake ⊜	220	28.07 N	81.41 W
Lower Zambezi International Game Park ➜ [4]	154	15.30 S	29.35 E
Lowestoft	42	52.29 N	1.45 E
Lowgar □ [4]	120	33.50 N	69.00 E
Lowick	44	55.38 N	2.00 W
Łowicz	30	52.07 N	19.56 E
Lowman	210	42.02 N	76.44 W
Lowmoor	192	37.47 N	79.53 W
Lowood	171a	27.28 S	152.35 E
Lowrah (Pishīn Lora) ≃	120	29.09 N	64.55 E
Lowries Run ≃	279b	40.30 N	80.05 W
Low Rocky Point ›	166	43.00 S	145.30 E
Lowry Air Force Base ■	198	39.43 N	104.53 W
Lowry City	194	38.08 N	93.43 W
Lowther ≃	44	54.39 N	2.44 W
Lowther Hills ⋀ [2]	44	55.19 N	3.38 W
Lowton	262	53.28 N	2.35 W
Lowton Common	262	53.29 N	2.33 W
Lowville, N.Y., U.S.	212	43.47 N	75.29 W
Lowville, Pa., U.S.	214	42.01 N	79.49 W
Loxahatchee	220	26.49 N	80.13 W
Loxley	194	30.37 N	87.45 W
Loxstedt	52	53.28 N	8.38 E
Loxten	52	52.03 N	8.08 E
Loxton, Austl.	166	34.27 S	140.35 E
Loxton, S. Afr.	158	31.30 S	22.22 E
Loyal	190	44.44 N	90.29 W
Loyal, Loch ⊜	46	58.23 N	4.22 W
Loyalhanna	214	40.19 N	79.21 W
Loyalhanna Creek ≃	214	40.28 N	79.27 W
Loyalhanna Lake ⊜ [1]	214	40.25 N	79.28 W
Loyalsock Creek ≃	210	41.14 N	76.56 W
Loyalton	204	39.40 N	120.14 W
Loyalty Islands → Loyauté, Îles II	175f	21.00 S	167.00 E
Loyang	271c	1.22 N	103.58 E
Loyang → Luoyang	102	34.41 N	112.28 E
Loyauté, Îles (Loyalty Islands) II	175f	21.00 S	167.00 E
Loyne, Loch ⊜	46	57.06 N	5.00 W
Loyola College ⊍ [2]	284b	39.21 N	76.37 W
Loyola University ⊍ [2], Ca., U.S.	280	33.58 N	118.25 W
Loyola University ⊍ [2], Il., U.S.	278	42.00 N	87.39 W
Loyoro	154	3.21 N	34.16 E
Loysburg	214	40.10 N	78.23 W
Loysville	208	40.22 N	77.21 W
Lozano	258	34.51 S	59.03 W
Lozère □ [5]	32	44.30 N	3.30 E
Lozère, Mont ∧	62	44.25 N	3.46 E
Loznica	38	44.32 N	19.13 E
Ložnikovo, Ross.	86	56.54 N	73.56 E
Ložnikovo, Ross.	88	51.22 N	117.03 E
Lozno-Aleksandrovka	78	49.50 N	38.44 E
Loznoje	80	49.17 N	44.26 E
L'Ozone ➜ [8]	273b	4.21 S	15.14 E
Lozovaja, Kaz.	86	53.17 N	77.45 E
Lozovaja, Ukr.	78	48.54 N	36.20 E
Lozovaja, Ukr.	83	49.28 N	37.54 E
Lozovoje, Ukr.	78	49.18 N	27.18 E
Lozovoje, Ukr.	83	49.13 N	37.36 E
Lozovskij	83	48.33 N	38.54 E
Lozoyuela	34	40.55 N	3.37 W
Loz'va ≃	86	59.36 N	62.20 E
Lozzo di Cadore	64	46.29 N	12.27 E
Lu	62	45.00 N	8.29 E
Lu ≃	100	27.04 N	115.00 E
Lua ≃	152	2.46 N	18.26 E
Luabo	156	18.30 S	36.10 E
Luabu ≃	152	2.46 S	18.19 E
Luachimo ≃	152	6.33 S	20.59 E
Luaha-sibuha	110	0.31 S	98.28 E
Luala ≃	154	17.57 S	36.30 E
Lualaba ≃	154	0.26 N	25.20 E
Luali	152	5.06 S	12.29 E
Lualoje ≃	152	12.18 S	21.38 E
Luama ≃	154	4.46 S	26.53 E
Luambe National Park ♠	154	12.25 S	32.15 E
Luambimba ≃	152	15.00 S	22.48 E
Luampa	154	15.03 S	24.28 E
Luampa ≃	154	14.33 S	24.10 E
Lu'an	100	31.44 N	116.31 E
Luan ≃	98	39.20 N	119.10 E
Luana ≃	152	7.56 S	21.06 E
Luan Balu	114	2.38 N	96.13 E
Luancheng, Zhg.	98	37.53 N	114.39 E
Luancheng, Zhg.	102	22.45 N	108.51 E
Luanchuan	102	33.51 N	111.36 E
Luancundo ≃	152	16.25 S	21.27 E
Luanda	152	8.48 S	13.14 E
Luanda □ [5]	152	9.00 S	13.15 E
Luando ≃	152	10.19 S	16.40 E
Luando, Réserva do ➜ [4]	152	11.10 S	17.30 E
Luang, Khao ∧	110	8.31 N	99.47 E
Luang, Thale ⊂	110	7.30 N	100.15 E
Luang Chiang Dao, Doi ∧	110	19.23 N	98.54 E
Luanginga (Luanguinga) ≃	152	15.11 S	22.56 E
Luang Prabang → Louangphrabang	110	19.52 N	102.08 E
Luang Prabang Range ⋀	110	18.30 N	101.15 E
Luangue	152	7.19 S	19.38 E
Luangue (Loange) ≃	152	4.17 S	20.02 E
Luanguinga (Luanginga) ≃	152	15.11 S	22.56 E
Luangwa (Aruângua) ≃	154	15.36 S	30.25 E
Luanhaizi	120	34.27 N	93.12 E
Luanhe	105	40.57 N	117.44 E
Luannan (Bencheng)	98	39.32 N	118.39 E
Luanping (Anjiangying)	98	40.57 N	117.20 E
Luanshishan	104	42.10 N	123.41 E
Luanshya	154	13.08 S	28.24 E
Luán Toro	252	36.12 S	65.06 W
Luanxian	98	39.45 N	118.44 E
Luanza	154	8.42 S	28.42 E
Luapula □ [4]	154	10.55 S	29.00 E
Luapula ≃	154	9.26 S	28.33 E
Luar, Danau ⊜	112	0.55 N	112.15 E
Luarca	34	43.32 N	6.32 W
Luashi	152	10.56 S	23.37 E
Luashi ≃	152	10.41 S	22.55 E

Luassinga ≃	152	15.47 S	18.50 E
Luati	152	14.35 S	21.13 E
Luatira	152	12.52 S	17.14 E
Luau	152	10.42 S	22.12 E
Lua-Vindu ≃	152	3.38 N	19.16 E
Luba	152	3.27 N	8.33 E
Lubaantun ⊥	232	16.17 N	88.58 W
Lubaczów	30	50.10 N	23.07 E
Lubalo	152	9.12 S	19.16 E
Lubalo ≃	152	7.22 S	19.20 E
Lubamiti	152	2.29 S	17.47 E
L'uban', Bela.	76	52.37 N	29.08 E
L'uban', Bela.	76	52.48 N	27.59 E
Lubań, Pol.	30	51.08 N	15.18 E
L'uban', Ross.	76	59.21 N	31.13 E
Lubāna	76	56.54 N	26.43 E
Lubānas ezers ⊜	76	56.46 N	26.53 E
Lubang	116	13.52 N	120.07 E
Lubang Island I	116	13.46 N	120.11 E
Lubang Islands II	116	13.46 N	120.15 E
Lubango	152	14.55 S	13.30 E
Lubanowo	54	53.09 N	14.36 E
Lubansenshi ≃	154	11.21 S	30.35 E
Lub'any	80	56.02 N	51.24 E
Lubao	100	23.22 N	112.55 E
L'ubar	78	49.55 N	27.44 E
Lübars, Dtsch.	54	52.39 N	12.02 E
Lübars, Dtsch.	54	52.10 N	12.09 E
Lübars ➜ [8]	264a	52.37 N	13.22 E
Lubartów	30	51.28 N	22.38 E
L'ubašovka	78	47.51 N	30.15 E
Lubawa	30	53.30 N	19.45 E
Lubaynī, Baḥr al- ≊	273c	29.56 N	31.11 E
Lübbecke	52	52.18 N	8.36 E
Lübben	54	51.56 N	13.53 E
Lübbenau	54	51.52 N	13.57 E
Lubber Brook ≃	283	42.33 N	71.09 W
Lubbers Run ≃	276	40.56 N	74.43 W
Lübbesee ⊜	54	53.05 N	13.34 E
Lubbock	196	33.34 N	101.51 W
Lübbow	54	52.54 N	11.10 E
Lubbub Creek ≃	194	33.04 N	88.10 W
L'ubča	76	53.45 N	26.03 E
L'ubeč, Ukr.	78	51.42 N	30.39 E
Lubec, Me., U.S.	188	44.51 N	66.59 W
Lübeck	52	53.52 N	10.40 E
Lübecker Bucht ⊂	54	54.00 N	10.55 E
Lubefu	152	4.43 S	24.25 E
Lubefu ≃	152	4.10 S	23.00 E
Lubelska, Wyżyna ⋀ [2]	30	51.00 N	23.00 E
Lubembe (Luembe) ≃	152	6.37 S	21.05 E
Lubenec	54	50.06 N	13.20 E
Lüben → Lubin	30	51.24 N	16.13 E
L'ubercy	82	55.41 N	37.53 E
Lubéron, Montagne du ⋀	62	43.48 N	5.22 E
Lubersac	32	45.27 N	1.24 E
L'ubešov	78	51.46 N	25.31 E
Lübesse	54	53.29 N	11.28 E
Lubi ≃	152	4.58 S	23.26 E
Lubiana → Ljubljana	36	46.03 N	14.31 E
Lubic Island I	116	10.58 N	120.44 E
L'ubickoje	80	51.46 N	49.19 E
Lubień Kujawski	30	52.25 N	19.10 E
Lubilash ≃	152	6.02 S	23.45 E
Lubile	154	2.55 S	26.45 E
L'ubim	80	58.22 N	40.41 E
L'ubimovka, Kaz.	86	52.15 N	66.45 E
L'ubimovka, Ross.	78	51.31 N	35.37 E
L'ubimovka, Ukr.	78	46.47 N	33.34 E
L'ubimyj	83	47.53 N	39.28 E
Lubin, Pol.	30	51.24 N	16.13 E
Lubin, Pol.	54	53.50 N	14.25 E
L'ubino	86	57.30 N	88.47 E
L'ubinskij	86	55.09 N	72.42 E
Lubishi ≃	152	6.54 S	24.09 E
Lubja ≃	265a	59.58 N	30.30 E
Lublin	30	51.15 N	22.35 E
Lublin □ [4]	30	51.30 N	22.30 E
Lubliniec	30	50.40 N	18.41 E
L'ublino ➜ [8]	265b	55.41 N	37.44 E
Lubmin	54	54.08 N	13.37 E
Lubnān, Jabal (Lebanon Mountains) ⋀	132	34.00 N	36.00 E
Lubnān → Lebanon □ [1]	128	34.00 N	36.00 E
L'ubnica	76	57.58 N	32.42 E
Lubny	78	50.01 N	33.00 E
L'ubochna	76	53.31 N	34.23 E
Lubok China	114	2.27 N	102.04 E
Lubomierz	30	51.01 N	15.30 E
L'uboml'	78	51.14 N	24.01 E
Luboń	30	52.23 N	16.54 E
Lubondai	152	6.34 S	22.39 E
Lubondoi	154	8.02 S	26.31 E
L'ubostan'	78	51.19 N	35.44 E
L'ubotin	78	49.57 N	35.57 E
Lubraniec	30	52.33 N	18.50 E
Lubsko	30	51.46 N	14.59 E
Lubsza ≃	54	51.56 N	14.43 E
Lübtheen	54	53.18 N	11.04 E
Lubu, Indon.	112	0.46 S	122.30 E
Lubu, Zhg.	102	23.09 N	112.13 E
Lubuagan	116	17.21 N	121.10 E
L'ubučany	82	55.15 N	37.33 E
Lubudi, Zaïre	152	6.51 S	21.18 E
Lubudi, Zaïre	154	9.57 S	25.58 E
Lubudi ≃, Zaïre	152	4.03 S	21.23 E
Lubudi ≃, Zaïre	154	9.13 S	25.38 E
Lubue	152	4.09 S	19.52 E
Lubue ≃	152	4.10 S	19.53 E
Lubukambacang	112	0.37 S	101.25 E
Lubukbatang	112	4.03 S	104.12 E
Lubukbertubung	112	0.02 N	102.08 E
Lubuklinggau	112	3.18 S	102.52 E
Lubukpakam	114	3.33 N	98.52 E
Lubukraya, Dolok ∧	114	1.29 N	99.13 E
Lubuksikaping	112	0.08 N	100.10 E
Lubumbaschi → Lubumbashi	154	11.40 S	27.28 E
Lubumbashi (Élisabethville)	154	11.40 S	27.28 E
Lubunda	154	5.10 S	26.40 E
Lubutu	154	0.44 S	26.35 E
Luby	54	50.12 N	12.25 E
L'ubytino	76	58.49 N	33.23 E
Lübz	54	53.27 N	12.01 E
Lučak	85	38.23 N	67.25 E
Lucala	152	9.16 S	15.15 E
Lucala ≃, Ang.	152	6.38 S	12.34 E
Lucala ≃, Ang.	152	9.37 S	14.14 E
Lucan, On., Can.	190	43.11 N	81.24 W
Lucan, Ire.	48	53.22 N	6.27 W
Lucanas	248	14.36 S	74.15 W
Lucania □ [9]	68	40.30 N	16.00 E
Lucania, Mount ∧	180	61.01 N	140.28 W
Lucano	152	11.16 S	21.38 E
Lucaogou	102	42.26 N	96.55 E
Lucapa	152	8.36 S	20.54 E
Lucas, Ia., U.S.	190	41.01 N	93.27 W
Lucas, Ks., U.S.	198	39.03 N	98.32 W
Lucas, Oh., U.S.	214	40.45 N	82.30 W
Lucas, Tx., U.S.	222	33.05 N	96.35 W
Lucas □ [6]	214	41.39 N	83.32 W
Lucas González	252	32.24 S	59.33 W
Lucas Heights	274a	34.02 S	150.58 E
Lucas Valley	282	38.03 N	122.35 W
Lucasville	218	38.52 N	82.59 W
Lucban	116	14.06 N	121.33 E
Lucca	66	43.50 N	10.29 E
Lucca □ [4]	64	44.02 N	10.27 E
Lucca Sicula	70	37.35 N	13.18 E
Lucé	50	48.26 N	1.28 E
Luce, Water of ≃	44	54.52 N	4.48 W
Lucea	241q	18.27 N	78.10 W
Luce Bay ⊂	44	54.47 N	4.50 W

≃	River	Fluß	Río	Rivière	Rio
≊	Canal	Kanal	Canal	Canal	Canal
⌞	Waterfall, Rapids	Wasserfall, Stromschnellen	Cascada, Rápidos	Chute d'eau, Rapides	Cascata, Rápidos
⊔	Strait	Meeresstraße	Estrecho	Détroit	Estreito
⊂	Bay, Gulf	Bucht, Golf	Bahía, Golfo	Baie, Golfe	Baía, Golfo
⊜	Lake, Lakes	See, Seen	Lago, Lagos	Lac, Lacs	Lago, Lagos
≡	Swamp	Sumpf	Pantano	Marais	Pântano
⊓	Ice Features, Glacier	Eis- und Gletscherformen	Accidentes Glaciales	Formes glaciaires	Acidentes glaciares
⊤	Other Hydrographic Features	Andere Hydrographische Objekte	Otros Elementos Hidrográficos	Autres données hydrographiques	Outros acidentes hidrográficos

✤	Submarine Features	Untermeerische Objekte	Accidentes Submarinos	Formes de relief sous-marin	Acidentes submarinos
□	Political Unit	Politische Einheit	Unidad Politica	Entité politique	Unidade política
⊍	Cultural Institution	Kulturelle Institution	Institución Cultural	Institution culturelle	Institução cultural
⊥	Historical Site	Historische Stätte	Sitio Histórico	Site historique	Sitio histórico
♠	Recreational Site	Erholungs- und Ferienort	Sitio de Recreo	Centre de loisirs	Area de Lazer
⊠	Airport	Flughafen	Aeropuerto	Aéroport	Aeroporto
■	Military Installation	Militäranlage	Instalación Militar	Installation militaire	Instalação militar
➜	Miscellaneous	Verschiedenes	Misceláneo	Divers	Diversos

Name	Page	Lat.	Long.
Luce Bayou ≃	222	30.03 N	95.07 W
Lucedale	194	30.55 N	88.35 W
Lucena, Esp.	34	37.24 N	4.29 W
Lucena, Pil.	116	13.56 N	121.37 E
Lucenay-L'Évêque	32	47.05 N	4.15 E
Luc-en-Diois	62	44.37 N	5.27 E
Lučenec	30	48.20 N	19.40 E
Lucens	58	46.42 N	6.50 E
Luceque	152	14.41 S	15.04 E
Lucera	68	41.30 N	15.20 E
Lucéram	62	43.53 N	7.22 E
Lucerne, Ca., U.S.	204	39.05 N	122.47 W
Lucerne, In., U.S.	216	40.52 N	86.24 W
Lucerne, Lake → Vierwaldstätter See ⊜	58	47.00 N	8.28 E
Lucerne Lake ⊜	228	34.31 N	116.57 W
Lucerne → Luzern	58	47.03 N	8.18 E
Lucernemines	214	40.33 N	79.09 W
Lucerne Valley	228	34.26 N	116.58 W
Lucero	200	30.49 N	106.30 W
Lucero, Lake ⊜	200	32.42 N	106.25 W
Lučesa ≃	76	55.10 N	30.11 E
Luch	80	57.01 N	42.15 E
Luch ≃	80	56.14 N	42.25 E
Luchang	102	26.23 N	102.18 E
Luchena ≃	34	37.44 N	1.50 W
Lucheng, Zhg.	102	24.21 N	106.00 E
Lücheng, Zhg.	106	31.55 N	119.44 E
Lucheng, Zhg.	106	31.47 N	120.02 E
Luché-Pringé	50	47.42 N	0.05 E
Lucheringo ≃	154	11.43 S	36.17 E
Luchibe ≃	152	12.07 S	21.13 E
Luchico (Lushiko) ≃	152	6.13 S	19.40 E
Luchou	269d	25.05 N	121.28 E
Luchovicy	82	54.59 N	39.03 E
Lüchow	54	52.58 N	11.10 E
Luchow → Luzhou	107	28.54 N	105.27 E
Lüchtringen	52	51.47 N	9.25 E
Luchuan	102	22.19 N	110.11 E
Luci	100	29.52 N	119.47 E
Luciara	250	10.27 S	50.32 W
Lucie ≃	250	3.35 N	57.38 W
Lucikou	100	28.56 N	116.04 E
Lučin	76	53.01 N	30.01 E
Lucinda, Austl.	166	18.32 S	146.20 E
Lucinda, Pa., U.S.	214	41.19 N	79.22 W
Lucindale	166	36.59 S	140.22 E
Lucio Vázquez	234	22.47 N	99.46 W
Lucipara, Kepulauan II	164	5.30 S	127.33 E
Lucira	152	13.51 S	12.31 E
Lucito	66	41.44 N	14.41 E
Luci Yu I	100	25.07 N	119.22 E
Luck, Ukr.	78	50.44 N	25.20 E
Luck, Wi., U.S.	190	45.34 N	92.28 W
Luck, Mount ∧[2]	162	28.47 S	123.33 E
Lucka	54	51.06 N	12.20 E
Luckau	54	51.51 N	13.43 E
Luckeesarai	124	25.11 N	86.05 E
Luckenwalde	54	52.05 N	13.10 E
Luckey	214	41.27 N	83.29 W
Luckhoff	158	29.44 S	24.43 E
Luckiamute ≃	202	44.45 N	123.09 W
Luck Lake ⊜	184	51.05 N	107.07 W
Lucknow, On., Can.	190	43.57 N	81.31 W
Lucknow, India	124	26.51 N	80.55 E
Lucknow, Pa., U.S.	208	40.20 N	76.54 W
Lucknow Branch ≍	124	27.57 N	80.03 E
Lucky Lake	184	51.00 N	107.10 W
Lucky Peak Lake ⊜[1]	202	43.33 N	116.00 W
Luco dei Marsi	66	41.58 N	13.28 E
Lucomagno, Passo del)(	58	46.33 N	8.49 E
Luçon, Fr.	32	46.27 N	1.10 W
Lucon, Pa., U.S.	285	40.14 N	75.25 W
Luconha ≃	152	12.54 S	21.15 E
Lucun, Zhg.	98	36.12 N	118.01 E
Lucun, Zhg.	106	30.49 N	119.26 E
Lucunga ≃	152	6.57 S	12.48 E
Lucungu ≃	152	6.41 S	14.26 E
Lucusse	152	12.32 S	20.48 E
Lucy Creek	166	22.25 S	136.20 E
Lüda → Dalian	98	38.53 N	121.35 E
Luda Kamčija ≃	38	43.03 N	27.29 E
Ludao	89	43.51 N	129.19 E
Ludbreg	36	46.15 N	16.37 E
Luddan	123	29.54 N	72.34 E
Luddenden	262	53.44 N	1.56 W
Luddenham	274a	33.53 S	150.41 E
Luddesdown	260	51.22 N	0.24 E
Lüdenscheid	56	51.13 N	7.38 E
Lüder ≃	56	50.31 N	9.27 E
Lüderitz, Dtsch.	54	52.30 N	11.44 E
Lüderitz, Namibia	156	26.38 S	15.10 E
Lüderitz □[5]	156	26.30 S	15.45 E
Lüdersdorf	54	53.47 N	10.46 E
Ludgershall	42	51.16 N	1.37 W
Ludgo	40	58.55 N	17.08 E
Ludhiāna	123	30.54 N	75.51 E
Ludian	102	27.11 N	103.33 E
Luding	102	29.55 N	102.15 E
Lüdinghausen	52	51.46 N	7.26 E
Ludington	190	43.57 N	86.27 W
Ludingtonville	210	41.29 N	73.39 W
L'udinovo	76	53.52 N	34.27 E
L'udkovo	76	54.36 N	34.43 E
Ludlam Bay ⊂	208	39.10 N	74.42 W
Ludlow, Eng., U.K.	42	52.22 N	2.43 W
Ludlow, Il., U.S.	216	40.23 N	88.08 W
Ludlow, Ky., U.S.	218	39.05 N	84.32 W
Ludlow, Ma., U.S.	207	42.09 N	72.28 W
Ludlow, Pa., U.S.	214	41.43 N	78.56 W
Ludlow, Vt., U.S.	188	43.23 N	72.42 W
Ludlow Falls	218	40.00 N	84.20 W
Ludlowville	210	42.33 N	76.32 W
Ludogorie ◆[1]	38	43.46 N	26.56 E
Ludonghe	102	25.53 N	103.33 E
Ludoni	76	58.12 N	29.21 E
Ludowici	192	31.42 N	81.44 W
Ludus	38	46.29 N	24.05 E
Ludvika	40	60.09 N	15.11 E
Ludwigkanal ≍	60	49.05 N	11.27 E
Ludwigsburg	56	48.53 N	9.11 E
Ludwigsfelde	54	52.17 N	13.16 E
Ludwigsfelder-Heide ◆[3]	264a	52.18 N	13.14 E
Ludwigshafen	56	49.29 N	8.26 E
Ludwigshafen am Bodensee	58	47.49 N	9.03 E
Ludwigslust	54	53.19 N	11.30 E
Ludwigsort → Laduškin	76	54.36 N	20.11 E
Ludwigsstadt	54	50.30 N	11.23 E
Ludwigstein, Burg ⊥	56	51.20 N	9.55 E
Ludza	76	56.33 N	27.43 E
Lue	170	32.39 S	149.51 E
Luebo	152	5.21 S	21.25 E
Lueders	196	32.48 N	99.37 W
Lueg, Pass)(	64	47.34 N	13.12 E
Lueki	154	3.22 S	25.51 E
Luele ≃	152	7.55 S	20.09 E
Luemba	154	3.42 S	28.40 E
Luembe (Lubembe) ≃, Afr.	152	6.37 S	21.05 E
Luembé ≃, Zaïre	154	6.43 S	24.11 E
Luena, Ang.	152	11.47 S	19.52 E
Luena, Zaïre	154	9.27 S	25.47 E
Luena ≃, Ang.	152	12.31 S	22.34 E
Luena ≃, Zam.	152	14.45 S	23.25 E
Luena Flats ≋	152	14.50 S	23.20 E
Luengué ≃	152	16.54 S	21.52 E
Luenha (Ruenya) ≃	154	16.24 S	33.48 E
Lueo ≃	152	9.06 S	23.51 E
Luepa	246	5.43 N	61.31 W
Lueta	152	7.19 S	22.06 E
Lueta ≃	152	7.04 S	21.40 E
Lueyang	102	33.20 N	106.10 E
Lüfangsicun	104	41.25 N	123.22 E
Lufeng, Zhg.	100	22.57 N	115.38 E
Lufeng, Zhg.	102	25.07 N	102.07 E
Lufico	152	6.24 S	13.23 E
Lufira ≃	154	8.16 S	26.27 E
Lufkin	222	31.20 N	94.43 W
Luftekopf ∧[2]	56	50.05 N	7.37 E
Lufubu ≃	154	8.36 S	30.47 E
Lufuidje ≃	152	12.52 S	22.47 E
Lufupa	154	10.37 S	24.56 E
Lufupa ≃	154	14.37 S	26.12 E
Luga	76	58.44 N	29.52 E
Luga ≃	76	59.40 N	28.18 E
Lugagnano Val d'Arda	62	44.49 N	9.50 E
Lugan' ≃	83	48.37 N	39.27 E
Lugančik ≃	83	48.35 N	39.32 E
Lugang, Zhg.	100	31.17 N	118.22 E
Lugang, Zhg.	100	27.23 N	115.36 E
Luganga	154	7.31 S	35.32 E
Lugano	58	46.01 N	8.58 E
Lugano, Lago di ⊜	58	46.00 N	9.00 E
Lugansk (Vorošilovgrad)	83	48.34 N	39.20 E
Lugansk □[8]	83	49.00 N	39.00 E
Luganskoje	83	48.26 N	38.15 E
Luganville	175f	15.32 S	167.10 E
Lugards Falls ∟	154	3.03 S	38.42 E
Lugareño	240p	21.33 N	77.28 W
Lugarno	274a	33.59 S	151.03 E
Lugau	54	50.44 N	12.44 E
Lügde	52	51.57 N	9.15 E
Lugela	154	16.25 S	36.43 E
Lugenda	154	12.30 S	37.43 E
Lugenda ≃	154	11.25 S	38.33 E
Lugg ≃	42	52.02 N	2.38 W
Luggarus → Locarno	58	46.10 N	8.48 E
Luginino	76	57.43 N	35.17 E
Luginy	78	51.04 N	28.24 E
Lugnano in Teverina	66	42.34 N	12.20 E
Lugnaquillia Mountain ∧	48	52.58 N	6.27 W
Lugnås	40	58.39 N	13.42 E
Lugny	58	46.28 N	4.49 E
Lugo, Esp.	34	43.00 N	7.34 W
Lugo, It.	66	44.25 N	11.54 E
Lugo □[4]	34	43.00 N	7.25 W
Lugoj	38	45.41 N	21.54 E
Lugongshi	106	31.38 N	121.12 E
Lugos → Lugoj	38	45.41 N	21.54 E
Lugouqiao	105	39.51 N	116.13 E
Lugovaja Subbota	86	59.52 N	69.45 E
Lugovoj, Kaz.	85	42.56 N	72.45 E
Lugovoj, Ross.	86	59.44 N	65.55 E
Lugovoje	85	42.55 N	72.43 E
Lugovskij	88	58.02 N	112.54 E
Lugovskoje	80	50.38 N	46.28 E
Lugu	102	28.21 N	102.09 E
Lugulu ≃	154	2.17 S	26.32 E
Lugunga ∧	154	6.47 S	36.19 E
Luguru	154	2.55 S	33.58 E
Lugus Island I	116	5.41 N	120.50 E
Luhanka	26	61.47 N	25.42 E
Luhe	60	49.35 N	12.09 E
Luhe ≃	52	53.18 N	10.11 E
Lühedian	100	32.33 N	114.28 E
Lühmannsdorf	54	54.00 N	13.38 E
Luhombero ≃	154	8.24 S	37.12 E
Luhsien → Luzhou	107	28.54 N	105.27 E
Luhuo	102	31.26 N	100.48 E
Lui ≃, Ang.	152	8.41 S	17.56 E
Lui ≃, Zam.	152	16.21 S	23.18 E
Lui, Beinn ∧	46	56.24 N	4.49 W
Luia	152	8.26 S	21.45 E
Luia (Ruya) ≃, Afr.	154	16.34 S	33.12 E
Luia ≃, Ang.	152	8.24 S	21.42 E
Lúia ≃, Moç.	154	15.34 S	32.58 E
Luiana	152	17.23 S	23.03 E
Luiana ≃	152	17.27 S	23.14 E
Luichart, Loch ⊜	46	57.37 N	4.46 W
Luido	156	21.31 S	34.41 E
Luie ≃	152	4.33 S	17.41 E
Luik → Liège	56	50.38 N	5.34 E
Luilaka ≃	152	0.52 S	20.12 E
Luilu ≃	152	6.22 S	23.50 E
Luimbale	152	12.15 S	15.19 E
Luimneach → Limerick	48	52.40 N	8.38 W
Luing I	46	56.13 N	5.40 W
Luino	58	46.00 N	8.44 E
Luio ≃	152	13.15 S	21.39 E
Luipaardsvlei	273d	26.16 S	27.42 E
Luiro ≃	24	67.08 N	27.29 E
Luisant	50	48.25 N	1.29 E
Luís Correia	250	2.53 S	41.40 W
Luisen-Berg ∧[2]	264a	52.27 N	13.07 E
Luisenthal	54	50.47 N	10.43 E
Luís Gomes	250	6.25 S	38.23 W
Luis Guillón	288	34.48 S	58.27 W
Luishia	154	11.10 S	27.02 E
Luis Moya, Méx.	234	22.25 N	102.15 W
Luis Moya, Méx.	234	23.05 N	103.56 W
Luis Muñoz Marin, Aeropuerto Internacional ⊠	240m	18.27 N	66.00 W
Luis Peña, Cayo de I	240m	18.18 N	65.20 W
Luis Pereira, Arroyo ≃	258	34.33 S	57.02 W
Luita	152	8.04 S	19.25 E
Luitpold Coast ⊥[2]	9	78.30 S	32.00 W
Luiza	152	7.12 S	22.25 E
Luiza ≃	152	7.35 S	22.40 E
Luizavo ≃	152	11.42 S	23.12 E
Luizi	154	6.03 S	27.28 E
Luiziânia	255	21.41 S	50.17 W
Luján, Arg.	252	33.03 S	68.52 W
Luján, Arg.	252	32.22 S	65.57 W
Luján, Arg.	258	34.34 S	59.07 W
Luján ≃	288	34.26 S	58.32 W
Lujia, Zhg.	106	31.15 N	121.37 E
Lujia, Zhg.	106	31.19 N	121.03 E
Lujia, Zhg.	269b	31.22 N	121.18 E
Lujiabang	106	31.20 N	121.01 E
Lujiachang	107	30.14 N	105.34 E
Lujiagangzi	104	42.05 N	122.59 E
Lujiang	100	31.14 N	117.17 E
Lujiao	100	29.10 N	112.52 E
Lujiaoxi	107	28.55 N	105.48 E
Lujiaqiao, Zhg.	106	31.47 N	120.27 E
Lujiaqiao, Zhg.	107	28.50 N	106.21 E
Lujiatun, Zhg.	98	40.14 N	122.11 E
Lujiatun, Zhg.	104	41.10 N	121.56 E
Lujiatun, Zhg.	104	41.58 N	122.38 E
Lujiatun, Zhg.	104	42.18 N	124.15 E
Lujiazhou	100	28.16 N	114.35 E
L'uk	80	56.55 N	52.48 E
Lukachukai Wash V	200	36.39 N	109.36 W
Lukačok	89	53.03 N	132.16 E
Lukala	152	5.31 S	14.32 E
Lukang	100	24.03 N	120.25 E
Lukanga, Zaïre	152	1.00 S	18.08 E
Lukanga, Zaïre	152	1.41 S	18.09 E
Lukanga Swamp ≋	154	14.25 S	27.45 E
Luk'anovo	82	54.52 N	37.25 E
Lukašin	84	40.12 N	44.01 E
Lukaškin Jar	86	60.20 N	78.24 E
Luke, Mount ∧	162	27.13 S	116.48 E
Luke Air Force Base ■	200	33.32 N	112.22 W
Lukenie ≃	152	2.44 S	18.09 E
Lukens, Mount ∧	280	34.16 N	118.14 W
Lukeville	200	31.52 N	112.48 W
Luki	76	53.29 N	26.15 E
Lukino, Ross.	82	55.26 N	37.04 E
Lukino, Ross.	82	55.50 N	36.49 E
Lukka	140	14.33 N	23.42 E
Luknovo	80	56.12 N	42.03 E
Lukojanov	80	55.02 N	44.30 E
Lukolela, Zaïre	152	5.23 S	24.32 E
Lukolela, Zaïre	152	1.03 S	17.12 E
Lukong	107	29.31 N	105.39 E
Lukoshi ≃	152	10.05 S	22.59 E
Lukosi	154	18.30 S	26.30 E
Lukoškino	82	55.19 N	37.16 E
Lukou, Zhg.	100	27.14 N	114.04 E
Lukou, Zhg.	106	31.48 N	118.52 E
Lukoupu	100	29.30 N	113.26 E
Lukouyu	100	28.24 N	113.18 E
Lukov	78	51.13 N	24.19 E
Lukovit	38	43.12 N	24.10 E
Lukovskaja	80	50.35 N	41.52 E
Łuków	30	51.56 N	22.23 E
Lükqün	86	42.44 N	89.42 E
Lukuga ≃	154	5.40 S	26.55 E
Lukula	152	5.23 S	12.57 E
Lukula ≃, Afr.	152	5.08 S	12.28 E
Lukula ≃, Zaïre	152	4.13 S	17.58 E
Lukuledi ≃	154	10.05 S	39.42 E
Lukulu	152	14.25 S	23.12 E
Lukulu ≃	154	10.56 S	31.05 E
Lukumburu	154	9.45 S	35.09 E
Lukunga ≃	273b	4.25 S	15.14 E
Lukuni	152	5.52 S	17.11 E
Lukusashi ≃	154	14.38 S	30.00 E
Lukusuzi National Park ♠	154	12.50 S	32.35 E
Lula, It.	71	40.28 N	9.29 E
Lula, Ms., U.S.	194	34.27 N	90.28 W
Lula, Zaïre	152	5.22 S	16.02 E
Luleå	26	65.34 N	22.10 E
Luleälven ≃	24	65.35 N	22.03 E
Lüleburgaz	130	41.24 N	27.21 E
Lules	252	26.56 S	65.21 W
Luliang	102	25.05 N	103.36 E
Lüliang Shan ⩘	102	37.25 N	111.20 E
Luliāni	123	31.15 N	74.25 E
Luliao	269d	25.07 N	121.39 E
Luling	222	29.40 N	97.38 W
Lullingstone Castle ⊥	260	51.21 N	0.12 E
Lulo ≃	152	9.25 S	18.14 E
Lulong	98	39.54 N	118.50 E
Lulonga	152	0.37 N	18.23 E
Lulonga ≃	152	0.43 N	18.23 E
Lulu ≃	152	1.18 N	23.42 E
Lulua ≃	152	5.02 S	21.07 E
Luluabourg → Kananga	152	5.54 S	22.25 E
Lulu Island I, B.C., Can.	224	49.09 N	123.05 W
Lulu Island I, Ak., U.S.	182	55.28 N	133.30 W
Luluo	98	37.06 N	113.58 E
Lulworth, Mount ∧	162	26.53 S	117.42 E
Lumai	152	13.31 S	21.21 E
Lumajang	115a	8.08 S	113.13 E
Lumajangdong Co ⊜	120	34.00 N	81.45 E
Lumaku, Gunong ∧	112	4.52 N	115.38 E
Lumaling	120	29.53 N	92.37 E
Lumb	262	53.42 N	1.58 W
Lumbala ≃	152	12.38 S	22.34 E
Lumbala Kaquengue	152	12.39 S	22.34 E
Lumbala N'guimbo	152	14.08 S	21.25 E
Lumbangaraga	114	1.53 N	99.04 E
Lumbanlobu	114	2.31 N	99.08 E
Lumbe ≃	152	16.42 S	23.42 E
Lumber ≃	192	34.12 N	79.10 W
Lumber City	192	31.55 N	82.40 W
Lumberport	188	39.22 N	80.20 W
Lumberton, Ms., U.S.	194	31.00 N	89.27 W
Lumberton, N.J., U.S.	285	39.57 N	74.48 W
Lumberton, N.C., U.S.	192	34.37 N	79.00 W
Lumberton, Tx., U.S.	194	30.16 N	94.10 W
Lumbinī □[8]	124	27.45 N	83.30 E
Lumbis	112	4.18 N	116.15 E
Lumbo	154	15.00 S	40.44 E
Lumbovka	24	67.44 N	40.30 E
Lumbrales	34	40.56 N	6.43 W
Lumbrein	58	46.41 N	9.08 E
Lumbres	50	50.42 N	2.08 E
Lumbwa	154	0.12 S	35.28 E
Lumby	182	50.15 N	118.58 W
Lumding	120	25.45 N	93.10 E
Lumege ≃	152	11.55 S	20.58 E
Lumerau ≃	116	5.21 N	118.53 E
Lumi	164	3.29 S	142.02 E
Lumiei ≃	64	46.24 N	12.51 E
Luminárias	256	21.30 S	44.54 W
Luminosa	256	22.35 S	45.38 W
Lumintao ≃	116	12.43 N	120.55 E
Lummen	56	50.59 N	5.12 E
Lummi Bay ⊂	224	48.46 N	122.41 W
Lummi Indian Reservation ◆[4]	224	48.48 N	122.38 W
Lummi Island	224	48.42 N	122.40 W
Lummi Island I	224	48.42 N	122.40 W
Lumphanan	46	57.07 N	2.41 W
Lumphät	110	13.30 N	106.59 E
Lumphini Park ♠	269a	13.44 N	100.33 E
Lumpkin	192	32.03 N	84.47 W
Lumpun ≃	80	57.01 N	51.22 E
Lumsån ≃	40	59.59 N	15.26 E
Lumsås	41	55.57 N	11.31 E
Lumsden, Nf., Can.	186	49.19 N	53.37 W
Lumsden, Sk., Can.	184	50.34 N	104.53 W
Lumsden, N.Z.	172	45.44 S	168.27 E
Lumsden, Scot., U.K.	46	57.15 N	2.52 W
Lumsheden	40	60.43 N	16.15 E
Lums Pond State Park ♠	208	39.34 N	75.43 W
Lumu, Indon.	112	2.11 S	119.09 E
Lumu, Zhg.	106	31.22 N	120.37 E
Lumuna	154	3.46 S	26.24 E
Lumuna ≃	152	16.59 S	21.25 E
Lumut, Indon.	114	1.33 N	98.56 E
Lumut, Malay.	114	4.14 N	100.38 E
Lumut, Tanjung ≻	112	3.50 S	105.57 E
Lumwana	154	11.50 S	25.10 E
Lün, Mong.	88	47.24 N	102.52 E
Lün, Mong.	88	47.52 N	105.15 E
Luna, Pil.	116	16.51 N	120.23 E
Luna, Pil.	116	18.18 N	121.21 E
Luna ≃	246	4.32 S	60.41 W
Lunada Bay ⊂	280	33.46 N	118.25 W
Lunain ≃	50	48.20 N	2.47 E
Lunamatrona	71	39.39 N	8.54 E
Lunan	102	24.49 N	103.16 E
Lunan Bay ⊂	46	56.39 N	2.28 W
Lunano	66	43.44 N	12.26 E
Luna Pier	216	41.48 N	83.26 W
Lūnāvāda	120	23.08 N	73.37 E
Luncarty	46	56.27 N	3.28 W
Lund, B.C., Can.	182	49.58 N	124.44 W
Lund, Sve.	41	55.42 N	13.11 E
Lund, Nv., U.S.	204	38.51 N	115.00 W
Lunda ≃, Ang.	152	6.07 S	13.52 E
L'unda ≃, Ross.	80	56.32 N	46.03 E
Lundåkrabukten ⊂	41	55.48 N	12.53 E
Lundale	188	37.48 N	81.44 W
Lunda Norte □[5]	152	8.45 S	19.45 E
Lundar	184	50.42 N	98.02 W
Lunda Sul □[5]	152	10.00 S	20.30 E
Lundazi	154	12.19 S	33.13 E
Lundby	41	55.07 N	11.53 E
Lunde	41	55.29 N	10.21 E
Lundeborg	41	55.08 N	10.47 E
Lunden	41	54.20 N	9.01 E
Lunderskov	41	55.29 N	9.18 E
Lundevatn ⊜	26	58.22 N	6.36 E
Lundi ≃	154	21.43 S	32.34 E
Lundsberg	40	59.30 N	14.10 E
Lundsfjärden ⊜	40	59.38 N	14.41 E
Lundy I	42	51.10 N	4.40 W
Lundys Lane	214	41.53 N	80.21 W
Lune ≃	44	54.02 N	2.50 W
Lüneburg	52	53.15 N	10.23 E
Lüneburg □[6]	52	53.15 N	10.00 E
Lüneburger Heide ◆[1]	52	53.10 N	10.20 E
Lunel	62	43.41 N	4.08 E
Lünen	52	51.36 N	7.32 E
Lunenburg, N.S., Can.	186	44.23 N	64.19 W
Lunenburg, Ma., U.S.	207	42.35 N	71.43 W
Lunenburg, Va., U.S.	192	36.57 N	78.15 W
Luneray	50	49.50 N	0.55 E
Lünern	263	51.33 N	7.46 E
Lunéville	56	48.36 N	6.30 E
Lunga I	46	56.13 N	5.42 W
Lunga ≃, Ang.	152	5.59 S	16.20 E
Lunga ≃, Zam.	154	14.34 S	26.25 E
Lungälven ≃	40	59.34 N	14.10 E
Lunga Reservoir ⊜[1]	208	38.32 N	77.28 W
Lungau ◆[1]	64	47.07 N	13.39 E
Lungavilla	62	45.02 N	9.04 E
Lungch'i → Zhangzhou	100	24.33 N	117.39 E
Lunge	152	12.12 S	16.05 E
Lunge'nake	120	31.45 N	85.55 E
Lungern	58	46.47 N	8.10 E
Lunggar	120	31.10 N	84.00 E
Lunghezza ◆[8]	267a	41.55 N	12.35 E
Lungi	150	8.38 N	13.13 W
Lunglei	120	22.53 N	92.44 E
Lungro	68	39.44 N	16.07 E
Lungsang	124	29.51 N	88.41 E
Lungt'an	100	24.52 N	121.12 E
Lungué-Bungo (Lungwebungu) ≃	152	14.19 S	23.14 E
Lunguya	154	3.23 S	32.24 E
Lungwebungu (Lungué-Bungo) ≃	152	14.19 S	23.14 E
Lūni	120	26.00 N	73.00 E
Lūni ≃	120	24.41 N	71.15 E
Luni ⊥	64	44.04 N	10.01 E
Lunia-Bubi	154	7.30 S	24.49 E
Lunigiana ◆[1]	64	44.15 N	9.50 E
Lunin	76	52.18 N	26.38 E
Luninec	76	52.15 N	26.48 E
Lunino, Ross.	80	53.35 N	45.14 E
Lunino, Ross.	82	54.09 N	38.29 E
Lunjiao	100	22.53 N	113.13 E
Lūnkaransar	120	28.29 N	73.44 E
Lunnaja, gora ∧	180	68.14 N	174.20 E
Lunndörrsfjällen ∧	26	63.00 N	13.00 E
Lunno	76	53.27 N	24.16 E
Lunongzha	106	31.59 N	120.55 E
Lunsar	150	8.41 N	12.32 W
Lunsemfwa ≃	154	14.54 S	30.12 E
Lunt	262	53.31 N	2.59 W
Lunteren	52	52.05 N	5.37 E
Lunyuk	115b	8.57 S	117.14 E
Lunz am See	61	47.51 N	15.03 E
Lunzenau	54	50.58 N	12.45 E
Lunzhen	98	36.47 N	116.34 E
Luo ≃, Zhg.	102	34.48 N	113.04 E
Luo ≃, Zhg.	102	34.42 N	110.15 E
Luoba, Zhg.	100	24.51 N	114.13 E
Luoba, Zhg.	107	29.08 N	106.11 E
Luobei (Fengxiang)	89	47.34 N	130.50 E
Luobo	102	28.22 N	101.38 E
Luobu	102	24.30 N	109.40 E
Luobumiao	102	40.19 N	107.30 E
Luochanghe	100	31.01 N	117.18 E
Luocheng, Zhg.	102	24.51 N	108.59 E
Luocheng, Zhg.	107	29.23 N	104.01 E
Luochuan	102	35.55 N	109.26 E
Luoci	102	25.19 N	102.18 E
Luodian	106	31.25 N	121.20 E
Luoding	102	22.47 N	111.31 E
Luoduzhen	107	30.22 N	106.35 E
Luofa	105	39.25 N	116.50 E
Luofang, Zhg.	100	28.40 N	115.04 E
Luofang, Zhg.	100	27.52 N	115.06 E
Luofu, Zaïre	154	0.10 S	29.14 E
Luofu, Zhg.	100	24.32 N	115.35 E
Luogang, Zhg.	100	23.11 N	113.30 E
Luogang, Zhg.	100	24.25 N	115.38 E
Luogosanto	71	41.03 N	9.13 E
Luoguhe	89	53.18 N	121.30 E
Luohan Shan ∧	100	25.51 N	119.13 E
Luohe	100	33.35 N	114.01 E
Luoheya	98	35.46 N	118.54 E
Luohua	100	26.35 N	118.43 E
Luoji	100	32.06 N	117.16 E
Luojiachang	107	30.49 N	106.32 E
Luojiang	102	31.21 N	104.28 E
Luojiatang	106	30.18 N	120.13 E
Luojiatun, Zhg.	98	40.11 N	118.34 E
Luojiatun, Zhg.	104	42.06 N	122.44 E
Luojiatun, Zhg.	104	40.55 N	122.04 E
Luojiawei	100	26.55 N	115.02 E
Luoke	100	24.07 N	114.28 E
Luokeng	100	24.32 N	113.23 E
Luokou, Zhg.	100	28.54 N	117.24 E
Luokou, Zhg.	100	25.46 N	115.39 E
Luolong	107	28.49 N	104.46 E
L'Uomo di Cagna ∧	71	41.33 N	9.04 E
Luonan	102	34.05 N	110.04 E
Luoning	102	34.25 N	111.42 E
Luoping	102	24.59 N	104.21 E
Luoqi	102	29.48 N	106.56 E
Luoqiao	100	26.28 N	119.01 E
Luoquanzhen	107	29.50 N	104.31 E
Luoshan, Zhg.	100	29.41 N	113.18 E
Luoshan, Zhg.	100	32.13 N	114.32 E
Luoshan, Zhg.	105	39.55 N	117.33 E
Luoshe, Zhg.	106	31.39 N	120.11 E
Luoshe, Zhg.	106	30.41 N	120.04 E
Luoshuihe	98	39.27 N	114.19 E
Luossa ≃	152	8.24 S	17.03 E
Luotian	100	30.48 N	115.22 E
Luotuodian	100	32.13 N	113.49 E
Luotuoqiao	100	29.56 N	121.32 E
Luotuo Shan ∧	104	42.14 N	121.42 E
Luowenba	102	31.48 N	107.48 E
Luowenyu	105	40.16 N	117.57 E
Luoxi	100	29.05 N	114.58 E
Luoxiao Shan ⩘	100	26.00 N	114.00 E
Luoyang (Loyang), Zhg.	102	34.41 N	112.28 E
Luoyang, Zhg.	106	31.39 N	120.05 E
Luoyuan	100	26.31 N	119.32 E
Luoyuan Wan ⊂	100	26.25 N	119.43 E
Luoyukou	102	38.23 N	110.43 E
Luozhexi	107	29.02 N	103.54 E
Luozi	152	4.57 S	14.08 E
Lupala	156	17.50 S	19.06 E
Lupani	154	18.54 S	27.44 E
Lupao	116	15.53 N	120.54 E
Lupar ≃	112	1.30 N	111.00 E
Łupawa	30	54.26 N	17.24 E
Lupberg	60	49.09 N	11.45 E
Lupembe	154	9.15 S	35.15 E
Lupeni	38	45.22 N	23.13 E
Lupire	152	14.36 S	19.29 E
Lupiro	154	8.23 S	36.40 E
Lupon	116	6.54 N	126.00 E
Luppa	54	51.20 N	12.57 E
Luputa	152	7.10 S	23.42 E
Luqiao, Zhg.	100	32.34 N	117.14 E
Luqiao, Zhg.	100	28.35 N	121.22 E
Luqu	102	34.41 N	102.22 E
Luque	34	37.33 N	4.16 W
Luquillo	240m	18.22 N	65.43 W
Luquillo, Sierra de ⩘	240m	18.17 N	65.47 W
Lūrah ≃	120	31.33 N	66.33 E
Luray	188	38.39 N	78.27 W
Lure	58	47.41 N	6.30 E
Lure, Montagne de ⩘	62	44.07 N	5.47 E
Lureco ≃	154	12.28 S	37.40 E
Luremo	152	8.31 S	17.50 E
Lurgan	48	54.28 N	6.20 W
Luribay	248	17.06 S	67.39 W
Lurigancho	286d	12.02 S	77.01 W
Lurín	248	12.17 S	76.52 W
Lúrio	154	13.35 S	40.30 E
Lúrio ≃	154	13.35 S	40.32 E

ENGLISH

Name	Page	Lat.°'	Long.°'
Lurisia	62	44.18 N	7.42 E
Lurnea	274a	33.56 S	150.54 E
Lurö I	26	58.48 N	13.14 E
Lürrip ◆[8]	263	51.12 N	6.28 E
Lusahunga	154	2.52 S	31.15 E
Lusaka, Zaïre	154	7.10 S	29.27 E
Lusaka, Zam.	154	15.25 S	28.17 E
Lusaka □[4]	154	15.25 S	29.00 E
Lusakert	84	40.23 N	44.36 E
Lusambo	152	4.58 S	23.27 E
Lusancay Islands and Reefs II	164	8.25 S	150.20 E
Lusanga	152	4.50 S	18.44 E
Lusangaye	154	4.54 S	26.00 E
Lusangi	154	4.37 S	27.08 E
Luscar	182	53.04 N	117.24 W
Luseke	152	2.51 S	23.08 E
Luseland	184	52.05 N	109.24 W
Lusen ∧	60	48.56 N	13.31 E
Lusenga Plain National Park ♠	154	9.30 S	29.10 E
Lusengo	152	1.46 N	19.29 E
Luserna San Giovanni	62	44.48 N	7.15 E
Lush, Mount ∧	164	17.02 S	127.30 E
Lushan, Zhg.	100	33.45 N	112.53 E
Lushan, Zhg.	102	30.15 N	102.58 E
Lu Shan ∧	100	29.31 N	115.58 E
Lu Shan ⩘	98	36.05 N	118.05 E
Lushanguanliju	100	29.33 N	115.58 E
Lushi	102	34.05 N	111.01 E
Lushiko (Luchico) ≃	152	6.13 S	19.40 E
Lüshikou	100	29.16 N	120.17 E
Lushnje	38	40.56 N	19.42 E
Lushoto	154	4.47 S	38.17 E
Lushui	102	26.00 N	98.51 E
Lüshun (Port Arthur)	98	38.48 N	121.16 E
Lüsi	106	32.03 N	121.36 E
Lusi ≃	115a	7.05 S	110.55 E
Lusiana	64	45.47 N	11.34 E
Lusignan	32	46.26 N	0.07 E
Lusignan, Lac ⊜	206	46.40 N	74.09 W
Lusigny-sur-Barse	50	48.15 N	4.16 E
Lusikisiki	158	31.25 S	29.30 E
L'usino	76	52.38 N	26.31 E
Lusk, Ire.	48	53.32 N	6.10 W
Lusk, Wy., U.S.	200	42.45 N	104.27 W
Lus-la-Croix-Haute	62	44.40 N	5.42 E
Lusongwa	152	12.58 S	24.16 E
Luspebryggan	24	67.01 N	19.51 E
Lussac-les-Châteaux	32	46.24 N	0.44 E
Lussan	62	44.09 N	4.22 E
Luṣṣān, Wādī V	132	30.30 N	34.18 E
Lustenau	58	47.26 N	9.39 E
Luster	26	61.26 N	7.24 E
Lustin	56	50.23 N	4.53 E
Lustrafjorden ⊂[2]	26	61.20 N	7.22 E
Lüstringen	52	52.16 N	8.08 E
Lusutfu (Maputo) (Great Usutu) ≃	158	26.11 S	32.42 E
Luswishi ≃	154	13.55 S	27.24 E
Lūt, Dasht-e ◆[2]	128	32.00 N	58.00 E
L'uta ≃	76	58.37 N	28.40 E
Lü-ta → Dalian	98	38.53 N	121.35 E
Lutago (Luttach)	64	46.57 N	11.55 E
Lutai	100	33.32 N	115.03 E
Lütan, Zhg.	98	34.07 N	114.27 E
Lütan, Zhg.	100	28.57 N	119.46 E
Lutang	100	25.39 N	112.46 E
Lutao	116	10.00 N	124.04 E
Lü Tao I	100	22.40 N	121.29 E
Lutcher	194	30.02 N	90.41 W
Lute	284c	39.04 N	77.03 W
Lutembo	152	13.26 S	21.16 E
Lutembo ≃	152	12.03 S	22.15 E
L'uten'ka	78	50.13 N	34.02 E
Lutesville	194	37.18 N	89.58 W
Lutéte ≃	152	9.21 S	15.14 E
Lutexu ≃	273b	4.24 S	15.12 E
Lütgendortmund ◆[8]	263	51.30 N	7.21 E
Luthe	52	52.26 N	9.28 E
Luther, Mi., U.S.	190	44.02 N	85.40 W
Luther, Ok., U.S.	196	35.39 N	97.11 W
Luther Lake ⊜	212	43.55 N	80.26 W
Luthersburg	214	41.03 N	78.43 W
Lutherville-Timonium	284b	39.25 N	76.37 W
Luthrie	46	56.21 N	3.05 W
Luti	175e	7.14 S	156.59 E
Lutian, Zhg.	100	26.33 N	114.38 E
Lütian, Zhg.	100	23.48 N	113.56 E
Lütjenburg	54	54.17 N	10.35 E
Lütjensee	52	53.39 N	10.22 E
Luton, Eng., U.K.	42	51.53 N	0.25 W
Luton, Eng., U.K.	260	51.22 N	0.32 E
Lutong	112	4.28 N	114.00 E
Lutosn'a ≃	82	56.26 N	36.52 E
Lutou	100	32.16 N	112.53 E
Lutry	58	46.30 N	6.41 E
Lutshi	154	4.09 S	26.30 E
Lutshima ≃	152	5.22 S	18.59 E
Lutsk → Luck	78	50.44 N	25.20 E
Luttach → Lutago	64	46.57 N	11.55 E
Lutter am Barenberge	52	51.59 N	10.16 E
Lutterbach	58	47.46 N	7.17 E
Lutterworth	42	52.28 N	1.10 W
Lüttich → Liège	56	50.38 N	5.34 E
Luttrell	192	36.11 N	83.44 W
Lüttringhausen ◆[8]	263	51.13 N	7.14 E
Lutuai ≃	152	12.33 S	20.16 E
Lutugino	83	48.24 N	39.13 E
Lutz	220	28.09 N	82.27 W
Lützel	56	50.58 N	8.10 E
Lutzelbourg	56	48.44 N	7.15 E
Lützelflüh	58	47.00 N	7.41 E
Lützen	54	51.15 N	12.08 E
Lutzerath	56	50.07 N	7.00 E
Lutz Hill	284b	39.20 N	76.32 W
Lützow	54	53.40 N	11.11 E
Lützow-Holm Bay ⊂	9	69.10 S	37.30 E
Lutzputs	158	28.03 S	20.40 E
Lützschena	54	51.23 N	12.16 E
Lutzville	158	31.33 S	18.22 E
Luud, Waadi V	144	10.17 N	50.14 E
Luuq	144	3.48 N	42.33 E
Luus	102	45.30 N	105.45 E
Luverne, Al., U.S.	194	31.42 N	86.15 W
Lu Verne, Ia., U.S.	190	42.54 N	94.04 W
Luverne, Mn., U.S.	198	43.39 N	96.12 W
Luvo	152	5.51 S	14.05 E
Luvo ≃	152	10.18 S	17.08 E
Luvua	154	8.48 S	25.19 E
Lúvua ≃, Ang.	152	11.57 S	22.30 E
Luvua ≃, Zaïre	154	6.46 S	26.58 E
Luvuvhu ≃	156	22.40 S	30.55 E
Luwegu ≃	154	8.31 S	37.23 E
Luwingu	154	10.15 S	29.55 E
Luwuk	112	0.56 S	122.47 E
Luwuk → Banggai	112	1.34 S	123.30 E
Luxana Bay ⊂	182	52.03 N	131.00 W
Luxapallila Creek ≃	194	33.28 N	88.26 W
Luxembourg	56	49.36 N	6.09 E
Luxembourg □[4]	56	50.00 N	5.30 E
Luxembourg □[1], Europe	22	49.45 N	6.05 E
Luxembourg □[1], Europe	56	49.45 N	6.05 E
Luxembourg, Aéroport de ⊠	56	49.37 N	6.10 E
Luxembourg, Jardin du ♠	261	48.51 N	2.19 E
Luxemburg	190	44.32 N	87.42 W
Luxemburg → Luxembourg □[1]	56	49.45 N	6.05 E
Luxemburgo → Luxembourg □[1]	56	49.45 N	6.05 E

DEUTSCH

Name	Seite	Breite°'	Länge°' E = Ost
Luxeuil-les-Bains	58	47.49 N	6.23 E
Luxi, Zhg.	102	24.32 N	103.41 E
Luxi (Mangshi), Zhg.	102	24.20 N	98.25 E
Lüxia	100	26.41 N	120.06 E
Luxian	107	28.55 N	105.29 E
Luxiang, Zhg.	106	31.32 N	120.45 E
Lüxiang, Zhg.	106	30.50 N	121.10 E
Luxi Dao I	100	27.59 N	121.11 E
Luxikou	100	29.54 N	113.42 E
Luxmanor	284c	39.02 N	77.07 W
Luxor	214	40.20 N	79.28 W
Luxora	194	35.45 N	89.55 W
Luxor → Al-Uqṣur	140	25.41 N	32.39 E
Luxu	106	31.01 N	120.50 E
Lu Xun Museum ⊽	269b	31.16 N	121.28 E
Lüxuqiao	106	31.50 N	119.31 E
Luy ≃	32	43.39 N	1.08 W
Luyan	106	30.25 N	120.53 E
Lüyang	104	41.23 N	121.40 E
Luyanó ≃	286b	23.07 N	82.21 W
Luyeh	100	22.55 N	121.08 E
Luyi	100	33.53 N	115.28 E
Luynes	50	47.23 N	0.33 E
Luyu	106	31.34 N	121.41 E
Luyuan, Zhg.	106	31.51 N	120.38 E
Luyuan, Zhg.	271a	39.54 N	116.27 E
Luz, Bra.	255	19.48 S	45.40 W
Luz, Bra.	287a	22.48 S	43.05 W
Luz ◆[8]	266c	38.46 N	9.10 W
Luz, Estação da ◆[5]	287b	23.32 S	46.38 W
Luz, Isla I	254	45.30 S	73.59 W
Luz, Ponta da ≻	287a	22.47 S	43.05 W
Luza, Ross.	24	62.42 N	37.06 E
Luza, Ross.	24	60.39 N	47.10 E
Luža, Ross.	76	59.58 N	31.56 E
Luža ≃	82	55.03 N	36.35 E
Luzarches	50	49.07 N	2.25 E
Luzern	58	47.03 N	8.18 E
Luzern □[3]	58	47.05 N	8.05 E
Luzerne	210	41.17 N	75.54 W
Luzerne □[6]	210	41.14 N	75.53 W
Luzhai, Zhg.	102	24.31 N	109.50 E
Luzhai, Zhg.	269b	31.20 N	121.22 E
Luzhi	106	31.16 N	120.52 E
Luzhou	107	28.54 N	105.27 E
Luziânia	255	16.15 S	47.56 W
Lužické hory ⩘	54	50.48 N	14.40 E
Luzilândia	250	3.28 S	42.22 W
Lužki, Bela.	76	55.21 N	27.52 E
Lužki, Ross.	82	54.51 N	37.36 E
Lužná	54	50.06 N	13.45 E
Lužnice ≃, Europe	30	49.14 N	14.23 E
Lužnice (Lainsitz) ≃, Europe	61	49.13 N	14.42 E
Lužniki ◆[8]	265b	55.43 N	37.33 E
Luzon I	116	16.00 N	121.00 E
Luzon Strait ∪	108	20.30 N	121.00 E
Lužskaja guba ⊂	76	59.45 N	28.20 E
Luzy	32	46.48 N	3.58 E
Luzzara	64	44.58 N	10.41 E
Luzzi	68	39.27 N	16.17 E
L'va ≃	78	52.00 N	27.36 E
L'va Tolstogo	82	54.37 N	36.03 E
L'vov	78	49.50 N	24.00 E
L'vovskij	82	55.19 N	37.31 E
Lwówek	30	52.28 N	16.10 E
Lwówek Śląski	30	51.07 N	15.35 E
Lwów → L'vov	78	49.50 N	24.00 E
Lyall, Mount ∧	172	45.17 S	167.34 E
Lyallpur → Faisalabad	123	31.25 N	73.05 E
Lyantonde	154	0.24 S	31.09 E
Lybster	46	58.18 N	3.18 W
Lycaonia □[9]	130	37.50 N	33.15 E
Lychen	54	53.12 N	13.19 E
Lycia □[9]	130	36.20 N	30.00 E
Lyckeby	26	56.12 N	15.39 E
Lyck → Ełk	30	53.50 N	22.22 E
Lyčkovo, Ross.	76	57.55 N	32.24 E
Lyčkovo, Ukr.	78	49.06 N	35.12 E
Lycksele	26	64.36 N	18.40 E
Lycoming □[6]	210	41.14 N	77.00 W
Lycoming Creek ≃	210	41.13 N	77.02 W
Lydd	42	50.57 N	0.55 E
Lydda → Lod	132	31.58 N	34.54 E
Lydden ≃	42	50.56 N	2.22 W
Lydenburg	156	25.10 S	30.29 E
Lydenburgh County Park ♠	276	40.50 N	73.14 W
Lydford	42	50.39 N	4.06 W
Lydgate	262	53.44 N	2.07 W
Lydham	42	52.31 N	2.58 W
Lydia □[9]	130	38.40 N	27.30 E
Lydia Mills	192	34.28 N	81.55 W
Lydiate	262	53.32 N	2.57 W
Lydick	216	41.42 N	86.22 W
Lydney	42	51.44 N	2.32 W
Lye Green	260	51.43 N	0.35 W
Lyell, Mount ∧, Can.	182	51.57 N	117.06 W
Lyell, Mount ∧, Ca., U.S.	226	37.44 N	119.16 W
Lyell Brown, Mount ∧	162	23.21 S	130.24 E
Lyell Island I	182	52.40 N	131.30 W
Lyerly	192	34.24 N	85.24 W
Lyford	196	26.24 N	97.47 W
Lygnern ⊜	26	57.29 N	12.20 E
Lykens	208	40.34 N	76.42 W
Lykošino	76	58.07 N	33.43 E
Lyle, Mn., U.S.	190	43.30 N	92.56 W
Lyle, Wa., U.S.	224	45.41 N	121.17 W
Lyles	194	35.55 N	87.20 W
Lyman, Ne., U.S.	198	41.55 N	104.02 W
Lyman, S.C., U.S.	192	34.56 N	82.07 W
Lyman, Wa., U.S.	224	48.31 N	122.03 W
Lyman, Wy., U.S.	200	41.19 N	110.17 W
Lymbel'karamo	86	60.15 N	83.32 E
Lyme	207	41.18 N	72.19 W
Lyme Bay ⊂	42	50.38 N	3.00 W
Lyme Hall ⊥	262	53.20 N	2.03 W
Lyme Park ♠	262	53.21 N	2.04 W
Lyme Regis	42	50.44 N	2.57 W
Lyminge	42	51.08 N	1.05 E
Lymington	42	50.46 N	1.33 W
Lymkoj	86	59.31 N	70.22 E
Lymm	262	53.23 N	2.29 W
Lympne	42	51.05 N	1.02 E
Lympstone	42	50.39 N	3.25 W
Lyn	212	44.35 N	75.47 W
Łyna (Lava) ≃	76	54.37 N	21.14 E
Lynæs	41	55.57 N	11.52 E
Lynbrook	276	40.39 N	73.41 W
Lynch, Ky., U.S.	192	36.57 N	82.55 W
Lynch, Ne., U.S.	198	42.49 N	98.27 W
Lynch, Lac ⊜	190	46.25 N	77.05 W
Lynchburg, Oh., U.S.	218	39.14 N	83.47 W
Lynchburg, S.C., U.S.	192	34.03 N	80.04 W
Lynchburg, Tn., U.S.	194	35.16 N	86.22 W
Lynchburg, Va., U.S.	192	37.24 N	79.08 W
Lynches ≃	192	33.50 N	79.22 W
Lynchville	214	41.26 N	78.34 W
Lynd ≃	164	16.28 S	143.18 E
Lynde Creek ≃	212	43.51 N	78.57 W
Lynden, On., Can.	212	43.14 N	80.09 W
Lynden, Wa., U.S.	224	48.56 N	122.27 W
Lyndhurst, Austl.	166	19.12 S	144.23 E
Lyndhurst, Austl.	166	30.17 S	138.21 E
Lyndhurst, Austl.	274b	38.03 S	145.15 E
Lyndhurst, Eng., U.K.	42	50.52 N	1.34 W
Lyndhurst, N.J., U.S.	276	40.48 N	74.07 W
Lyndhurst, Oh., U.S.	214	41.31 N	81.29 W
Lyndoch	168b	34.37 S	138.53 E
Lyndon, Austl.	162	23.37 S	115.15 E
Lyndon, Ks., U.S.	198	38.38 N	95.41 W
Lyndon, Ky., U.S.	218	38.15 N	85.36 W
Lyndon ≃	162	23.29 S	114.06 E

Symbols in the index entries represent the broad categories identified in the key at the right. Symbols with superior numbers (⩘[1]) identify subcategories (see complete key on page *I · 1).*

Symbole im Register stellen die rechts im Schlüssel erklärten Kategorien dar. Symbole mit hochgestellten Ziffern (⩘[1]) bezeichnen Unterabteilungen einer Kategorie (vgl. vollständiger Schlüssel auf Seite *I · 1).*

Los símbolos incluídos en el texto del índice representan las grandes categorias identificadas con la clave a la derecha. Los símbolos con numeros en su parte superior (⩘[1]) identifican las subcategorías (véase la clave completa en la página *I · 1).*

Les symboles de l'index représentent les catégories indiquées dans la légende à droite. Les symboles suivis d'un indice (⩘[1]) représentent des souscatégories (voir légende complète à la page *I · 1).*

Os símbolos incluídos no texto do índice representam as grandes categorias identificadas com a chave à direita. Os símbolos com números em sua parte superior (⩘[1]) identificam as subcategorias (vejase a chave completa à página *I · 1).*

	English	Deutsch	Español	Français	Português
∧	Mountain	Berg	Montaña	Montagne	Montanha
⩘	Mountains	Gebirge	Montañas	Montagnes	Montanhas
)(	Pass	Paß	Paso	Col	Passo
V	Valley, Canyon	Tal, Cañon	Valle, Cañón	Vallée, Canyon	Vale, Canhão
≚	Plain	Ebene	Llano	Plaine	Planície
≻	Cape	Kap	Cabo	Cap	Cabo
I	Island	Insel	Isla	Île	Ilha
II	Islands	Inseln	Islas	Îles	Ilhas
⊥	Other Topographic Features	Andere Topographische Objekte	Otros Elementos Topográficos	Autres données topographiques	Outros acidentes topográficos

ESPAÑOL

Nombre	Página	Lat.°′	Long.°′ W = Oeste
Lyndon B. Johnson, Lake ⊜[1]	196	30.35 N	98.25 W
Lyndon B. Johnson Historical Park ⊥	196	30.15 N	98.38 W
Lyndon B. Johnson Space Center ♁[3]	222	29.34 N	95.05 W
Lyndonville, N.Y., U.S.	210	43.19 N	78.23 W
Lyndonville, Vt., U.S.	188	44.32 N	72.00 W
Lyndora	214	40.51 N	79.55 W
Lyne	260	51.23 N	0.33 W
Lyne ≏	44	54.58 N	3.01 W
Lyneham	42	51.31 N	1.58 W
Lynemouth	44	55.12 N	1.31 W
Lyne Water ≏	46	55.39 N	3.16 W
Lynga	80	57.17 N	53.04 E
Lyngdal	26	58.08 N	7.05 E
Lynge	41	55.51 N	12.17 E
Lyngen	24	69.34 N	20.10 E
Lyngen c[2]	24	69.58 N	20.30 E
Lyngør	26	58.38 N	9.10 E
Lynher ≏	42	50.28 N	4.12 W
Lynmouth	42	51.15 N	3.50 W
Lynn, Al., U.S.	194	34.02 N	87.32 W
Lynn, In., U.S.	218	40.02 N	84.56 W
Lynn, Ma., U.S.	207	42.28 N	70.57 W
Lynn ≏	212	42.47 N	80.12 W
Lynn Canal c	180	58.50 N	135.15 W
Lynndyl	200	39.31 N	112.22 W
Lynne Acres	284b	39.21 N	76.45 W
Lynnfield	207	42.32 N	71.02 W
Lynn Garden	192	36.34 N	82.34 W
Lynn Harbor c	283	42.27 N	70.57 W
Lynn Haven	194	30.14 N	85.38 W
Lynn Lake	184	56.51 N	101.03 W
Lynnville	190	41.34 N	92.47 W
Lynnwood, Pa., U.S.	210	41.14 N	75.56 W
Lynnwood, Pa., U.S.	214	40.07 N	79.51 W
Lynnwood, Wa., U.S.	224	47.49 N	122.18 W
Lynn Woods ♠	283	42.29 N	70.59 W
Lynton	42	51.15 N	3.50 W
Lyntupy	76	55.03 N	26.19 E
Lynwood, Ca., U.S.	228	33.55 N	118.12 W
Lynwood, Il., U.S.	278	41.32 N	87.32 W
Lynx Lake ⊜	176	62.25 N	106.15 W
Lyø I	41	55.02 N	10.10 E
Lyon	62	45.45 N	4.51 E
Lyon □[6]	226	39.00 N	119.15 W
Lyon ≏	46	56.37 N	4.01 W
Lyon, Gare ◆[5]	261	48.51 N	2.23 E
Lyon, Glen V	46	56.35 N	4.20 W
Lyon, Loch ⊜	46	56.32 N	4.36 W
Lyon Inlet c	176	66.32 N	83.53 W
Lyon Mountain	188	44.43 N	73.54 W
Lyon Mountain ∧	188	44.41 N	73.53 W
Lyonnais □[9]	62	45.45 N	4.30 E
Lyonnais, Monts du ⨯	62	45.40 N	4.30 E
Lyons, Co., U.S.	200	40.13 N	105.16 W
Lyons, Ga., U.S.	192	32.12 N	82.19 W
Lyons, Il., U.S.	216	41.48 N	87.49 W
Lyons, In., U.S.	194	38.59 N	87.04 W
Lyons, Ks., U.S.	198	38.20 N	98.12 W
Lyons, Mi., U.S.	216	42.58 N	84.56 W
Lyons, Ne., U.S.	198	41.56 N	96.28 W
Lyons, N.Y., U.S.	210	43.03 N	76.59 W
Lyons, Oh., U.S.	216	41.41 N	84.04 W
Lyons, Tx., U.S.	222	30.23 N	96.34 W
Lyons, Wi., U.S.	216	42.39 N	88.21 W
Lyons ≏	162	25.02 S	115.09 E
Lyon-Satolas, Aéroport de ⊠	62	45.43 N	5.04 E
Lyons Creek ≏	284a	43.03 N	79.04 W
Lyons Falls	212	43.37 N	75.22 W
Lyons-la-Forêt	50	49.24 N	1.28 E
Lyons Plains	207	41.13 N	73.21 W
Lyons Run ≏	279b	40.25 N	79.43 W
Lyon Station	208	40.28 N	75.45 W
Lyonsville	276	40.57 N	74.25 W
Lyracrumpane	48	52.20 N	9.30 W
Lyrestad	40	58.48 N	14.04 E
Lys (Leie) ≏, Europe	50	51.03 N	3.43 E
Lys ≏, It.	62	45.36 N	7.47 E
Lysá ∧	60	49.29 N	12.42 E
Lysaja Gora	78	48.11 N	31.06 E
Lysaker	26	59.54 N	10.36 E
Lys'anka	78	49.16 N	30.50 E
Lysá pod Makytou	30	49.12 N	18.13 E
Lysefjorden c[2]	26	59.00 N	6.14 E
Lysekil	26	58.16 N	11.26 E
Łysica ∧	30	50.54 N	20.55 E
Lysjön ⊜	40	60.07 N	14.18 E
Lyskovo	80	56.04 N	45.02 E
Lysogorka	83	47.42 N	39.12 E
Lyss	58	47.04 N	7.18 E
Lysterfield	274b	37.56 S	145.18 E
Lysterfield ∧[2]	274b	37.56 S	145.16 E
Lysterfield Reservoir ⊜[1]	274b	37.58 S	145.18 E
Lyster Station	206	46.22 N	71.37 W
Lys'va	86	58.07 N	57.47 E
Lys'va ≏	80	58.15 N	54.47 E
Lysyje Gory	80	51.32 N	44.46 E
Lytham Saint Anne's	44	53.45 N	2.57 W
Lytkarino	82	55.35 N	37.54 E
Lytle	196	29.13 N	98.47 W
Lytle Creek ≏	228	34.09 N	117.23 W
Lyttelton, N.Z.	172	43.35 S	172.42 E
Lyttelton, S. Afr.	158	25.50 S	28.11 E
Lytton	182	50.14 N	121.34 W
Lytton Springs	222	30.00 N	97.37 W
Lyubertsy → L'ubercy	82	55.41 N	37.53 E

M

Nombre	Página	Lat.°′	Long.°′ W = Oeste
Ma ≏	110	19.47 N	105.56 E
Ma, Oued el V, Alg.	148	27.45 N	7.45 W
Ma, Oued el V, Maur.	148	24.03 N	9.10 W
Maadid, Djebel ∧	34	35.52 N	4.46 E
Maalaea Bay c	229a	20.47 N	156.29 W
Ma'alot-Tarshiḥa	132	33.01 N	35.17 E
Maam Cross	48	53.27 N	9.31 W
Ma'ān	132	30.12 N	35.44 E
Ma'ān □[8]	132	30.20 N	36.30 E
Maaninka	26	63.09 N	27.18 E
Ma'anshan, Zhg.	100	31.42 N	118.30 E
Maanshan, Zhg.	107	29.52 N	104.59 E
Ma-ao	116	10.29 N	122.59 E
Maap I	174q	9.35 N	138.11 E
Maar	140	6.54 N	31.33 E
Maardu	76	59.28 N	25.02 E
Maarianhamina → Mariehamn	26	60.06 N	19.57 E
Ma'ārik, Qārat al- ∧[2]	142	29.59 N	30.52 E
Ma'arrat an-Nu'mān	130	35.38 N	36.40 E
Ma'arrat Miṣrīn	130	36.01 N	36.40 E
Ma'arrat Ṣaydnāyā	132	33.41 N	36.23 E
Maarssen	52	52.08 N	5.08 E
Maas	48	54.50 N	8.22 W
Maas (Meuse) ≏	30	51.49 N	5.01 E
Maasbracht	52	51.08 N	5.53 E
Maasdam	52	51.47 N	4.32 E
Maaseik	56	51.06 N	5.48 E
Maasholm	41	54.41 N	9.59 E
Maasin	116	10.08 N	124.50 E
Maasmechelen (Mechelen)	56	50.58 N	5.42 E
Maasniel	52	51.13 N	6.01 E
Maassluis	52	51.55 N	4.15 E
Maastricht	56	50.52 N	5.43 E
Maave	156	21.03 S	34.47 E
Ma-ayon ≏	116	11.25 N	122.46 E
Maba	100	32.59 N	118.48 E
Maba, Ouadi V	146	15.10 N	21.00 E
Mababe Depression ⏚[7]	156	18.50 S	24.15 E
Mabaduan	164	9.16 S	142.44 E

FRANÇAIS

Nom	Page	Lat.°′	Long.°′ W = Ouest
Mabaho, Mount ∧	116	9.15 N	125.42 E
Mabaia	152	7.13 S	14.03 E
Mabalacat	116	15.14 N	120.34 E
Mabalane	156	23.37 S	32.31 E
Mabana	224	48.05 N	122.24 W
Mabanga	152	1.30 N	19.06 E
Mabank	222	32.21 N	96.06 W
Mabaoquan	105	40.09 N	115.53 E
Ma'barot	132	32.22 N	34.54 E
Mabaruma	246	8.12 N	59.47 W
Mabashi	268	35.49 N	139.55 E
Mabau	112	2.14 S	111.54 E
Mabay	240p	20.16 N	76.40 W
Mabber, Ras ≻	144	9.28 N	50.50 E
Mabel Creek	162	29.01 S	134.17 E
Mabeleapodi	156	20.58 S	22.36 E
Mabel Lake ⊜	182	50.35 N	118.44 W
Maben	194	33.33 N	89.05 W
Mabenga-Cité	152	3.39 S	18.40 E
Mabenge	152	4.14 N	24.09 E
Maberry, Loch ⊜	44	55.02 N	4.41 W
Mabeti ≏	92	40.31 N	141.31 E
Mabeul	36	36.27 N	10.46 E
Mabi, Nihon	96	34.38 N	133.41 E
Mabi, Zhg.	100	26.21 N	119.36 E
Mabi, Zhg.	102	35.59 N	112.15 E
Mabian	107	28.48 N	103.41 E
Mabian ≏	107	29.08 N	103.58 E
Mablethorpe	44	53.21 N	0.15 E
Mableton	192	33.49 N	84.34 W
Mabole ≏	150	9.01 N	12.44 W
Maboma	154	2.32 N	28.13 E
Mabonto	150	8.52 N	11.49 W
Mabote	156	22.03 S	34.09 E
Mabou	186	46.05 N	61.22 W
Mabrak, Jabal ∧	132	30.13 N	35.29 E
Mabrous ⍑[4]	146	21.13 N	13.38 E
Mabrūk, Lībiyā	146	29.50 N	17.10 E
Mabrūk, Sūd.	140	8.07 N	29.25 E
Mabton	202	46.12 N	119.59 W
Mabuasehube Game Reserve ◆[4]	156	25.10 S	22.10 E
Mabuguai	100	29.49 N	112.42 E
Mabuki	154	2.59 S	33.11 E
Mabuni	174m	26.05 N	127.43 E
Mabwe	154	8.39 S	26.31 E
Mača, Ross.	74	59.54 N	117.35 E
Maca, Ven.	286c	10.28 N	66.48 W
Maca, Cerro ∧	254	45.06 S	73.12 W
Macachín	252	37.09 S	63.39 W
Macaco, Morro do ∧[2]	287a	22.56 S	43.07 W
Macacos, Ilha dos I	250	1.20 S	50.35 W
Macacu ≏	256	22.42 S	43.02 W
Macaé	255	22.23 S	41.47 W
Macaíba	250	5.51 S	35.21 W
Macajalar Bay c	116	8.37 N	124.38 E
Macajuba	255	12.09 S	40.22 W
Macalaya	116	12.53 N	123.46 E
Macalelon	116	13.45 N	122.08 E
Macalister	182	52.27 N	122.24 W
Macalister ≏	166	38.02 S	146.59 E
Macalister, Mount ∧	170	34.27 S	149.45 E
Macallum Lake ⊜	184	55.02 N	108.25 W
Macaloge	154	12.25 S	35.25 E
MacAlpine Lake ⊜	176	66.40 N	103.15 W
Macamic, Lac ⊜	190	48.48 N	78.59 W
Macan, Kepulauan II	112	7.00 S	121.00 E
Macão	34	39.33 N	8.00 W
Macao → Macau □[2]	100	22.10 N	113.33 E
Macapá	250	0.02 N	51.03 W
Macará	246	4.23 S	79.57 W
Macarani	255	15.33 S	40.24 W
Macarao	286c	10.26 N	67.02 W
Macarao ≏	286c	10.26 N	67.01 W
Macareo, Caño ≏[1]	246	9.47 N	61.37 W
Macari ≏	250	1.52 N	50.31 W
MacArthur, Pil.	116	10.50 N	125.00 E
MacArthur, Il., U.S.	278	41.39 N	87.44 W
Macas	246	2.19 S	78.07 W
Macatawa ≏	216	42.48 N	86.05 W
Macatawa, Lake c	216	42.47 N	86.10 W
Macaterick, Loch ⊜	44	55.12 N	4.26 W
Macau, Bra.	250	5.07 S	36.38 W
Macau (Aomen), Macau	100	22.14 N	113.35 E
Macau □[2], Asia	90	22.10 N	113.33 E
Macau □[2], Asia	100	22.10 N	113.33 E
Macau, Ilha I	156	20.55 S	35.05 E
Macauã ≏	248	9.13 S	68.44 W
Macaúbas	255	13.02 S	42.42 W
Macaya, Pic ∧	238	18.25 N	74.00 W
Macaza ≏	206	46.21 N	74.47 W
Maccarese ◆[8]	267a	41.53 N	12.13 E
Maccarese, Bonifica di ◆[1]	267a	41.51 N	12.13 E
Macchiagodena	66	41.33 N	14.24 E
MacClenny	192	30.16 N	82.07 W
Macclesfield, Austl.	168b	35.10 S	138.50 E
Macclesfield, Eng., U.K.	44	53.16 N	2.07 W
Macclesfield □[8]	262	53.17 N	2.15 W
Macclesfield Canal ≊	262	53.24 N	2.03 W
Macclesfield Forest ◆[3]	262	53.15 N	2.03 W
Macdhui, Ben ∧	158	30.39 S	27.58 E
MacDill Air Force Base ■	220	27.51 N	82.29 W
Macdonald ≏	170	33.23 S	150.59 E
Macdonald, Lake ⊜	162	23.30 S	129.00 E
MacDonald Downs	162	22.27 S	135.13 E
Macdonald Lake ⊜	212	45.14 N	78.34 W
MacDonald Pass)(	202	46.34 N	112.18 W
Macdonald Range ⨯	182	49.12 N	114.46 W
MacDonnell Ranges ⨯	162	23.45 S	133.20 E
Macdonnel Peninsula ≻[1]	168b	35.47 S	138.00 E
MacDowell Lake ⊜	184	52.15 N	92.45 W
Macduff	46	57.40 N	2.29 W
Macdui, Ben ∧	46	57.05 N	3.38 W
Mačecha	80	50.48 N	43.17 E
Mačechi	78	49.31 N	34.26 E
Maceday Lake ⊜	281	42.42 N	83.26 W
Macedo de Cavaleiros	34	41.32 N	6.58 W
Macedon, Austl.	169	37.25 S	144.34 E
Macedon, N.Y., U.S.	210	43.04 N	77.17 W
Macedonia, Ct., U.S.	207	41.47 N	73.30 W
Macedonia, Oh., U.S.	214	41.18 N	81.30 W
Macedonia □[9]	38	41.00 N	23.00 E
Macedonia (Makedonija) □[1]	38	41.50 N	22.00 E
Macedonia Brook State Park ♠	207	41.47 N	73.29 W
Maceió	250	9.40 S	35.43 W
Maceira	266c	38.52 N	9.19 W
Macenta	150	8.33 N	9.28 W
Maceo	246	6.33 N	74.47 W
Macerata	66	43.18 N	13.27 E
Macerata □[4]	66	43.12 N	13.10 E
Macerata Feltria	66	43.48 N	12.26 E
MacFarlane ≏	176	59.12 N	107.58 W
Macfarlane, Lake ⊜	166	31.55 S	136.42 E
Macfarlane, Mount ∧	172	43.56 S	169.23 E
Macgillycuddy's Reeks ⨯	48	51.55 N	9.45 W
MacGregor	184	49.57 N	98.49 W
Machacamarca	248	18.10 S	67.02 W
Machache ∧	158	29.21 S	27.55 E
Machachi	246	0.30 S	78.34 W
Machačkala	84	42.58 N	47.30 E
Machada, Mata Nacional da ♠	266c	38.36 N	9.02 W
Machadinho ≏	248	9.00 S	61.52 W
Machado	256	21.41 S	45.56 W
Machado ≏, Bra.	248	8.03 S	62.52 W
Machado ≏, Bra.	256	21.38 S	45.52 W
Machadodorp	156	25.40 S	30.14 E

PORTUGUÊS

Nome	Página	Lat.°′	Long.°′ W = Oeste
Machagai	252	26.56 S	60.03 W
Machaila	156	22.15 S	32.55 E
Machakos	154	1.31 S	37.16 E
Machala	246	3.16 S	79.58 W
Machalí	252	34.11 S	70.40 W
Machalilla, Parque Nacional ♠	246	1.30 S	80.45 W
Machalino	80	53.05 N	46.14 E
Māchalpur	124	24.08 N	76.18 E
Machaneng	156	23.10 S	27.26 E
Machang, Malay.	114	5.46 N	102.13 E
Machang, Zhg.	98	34.06 N	119.02 E
Machang, Zhg.	98	42.05 N	119.42 E
Machanga	156	20.58 S	34.59 E
Machangcun	105	38.54 N	115.26 E
Machangfu	102	25.14 N	103.45 E
Machang Jianhe ≏	105	39.00 N	117.40 E
Machaquilá ≏	236	16.13 N	90.01 W
Machattie, Lake ⊜	166	24.50 S	139.48 E
Machault	50	49.21 N	4.30 E
Machava	156	25.54 S	32.29 E
Machaze	156	20.51 S	33.26 E
Machecoul	32	47.00 N	1.50 W
Macheke	154	18.05 S	31.51 E
Machelen	50	50.55 N	4.26 E
Macheng	100	31.13 N	115.00 E
Macherio	266b	45.38 N	9.16 E
Māčherla	122	16.29 N	79.26 E
Machern	54	51.21 N	12.37 E
Machery	261	48.36 N	2.05 E
Machesna Mountain ∧	226	35.17 N	120.14 W
Machesney Park	216	42.20 N	89.03 W
Māchhīwāra	123	30.55 N	76.12 E
Machhlīshahr	124	25.41 N	82.25 E
Machias, Me., U.S.	188	44.42 N	67.27 W
Machias, N.Y., U.S.	210	42.25 N	78.30 W
Machias ≏	188	44.43 N	67.22 W
Machias Bay c	188	44.40 N	67.20 W
Machichaco, Cabo ≻	34	43.27 N	2.45 W
Machichi ≏	184	57.03 N	92.06 W
Machico	148	32.42 N	16.46 W
Machida	94	35.32 N	139.27 E
Machile ≏	154	17.26 S	25.02 E
Machilīpatnam (Bandar)	122	16.10 N	81.08 E
Machindžauri	84	41.40 N	41.43 E
Machiques	246	10.04 N	72.34 W
Machiya ≏	94	35.01 N	136.42 E
Machkund ⊜[1]	122	18.26 N	82.35 E
Machmud-Mekteb	84	44.26 N	45.13 E
Machn'ovo	86	58.27 N	61.42 E
Macho, Arroyo del V	196	33.36 N	104.28 W
Machočen, porog ⌞	88	57.23 N	121.29 E
Machona, Laguna c	234	18.20 N	93.40 W
Machrihanish	46	55.26 N	5.45 W
Machtaly	85	41.22 N	68.02 E
Machupicchu	248	13.07 S	72.34 W
Machupicchu ⊥	248	13.07 S	72.34 W
Machupo ≏	248	12.34 S	64.25 W
Machynlleth	42	52.35 N	3.51 W
Maciá, Arg.	252	32.10 S	59.23 W
Macia, Moç.	156	25.03 S	33.10 E
Maciel, Arroyo ≏, Ur.	258	33.36 S	56.31 W
Maciel, Arroyo ≏, Ur.	258	33.42 S	57.59 W
Măcin	38	45.15 N	28.08 E
Macina → Massina ◆[1]	150	14.30 N	5.00 W
Macintyre ≏, Austl.	166	29.25 S	148.45 E
Macintyre ≏, Austl.	166	28.38 S	150.47 E
Maçka	130	40.48 N	39.38 E
Mačkassy	80	52.46 N	45.34 E
Mackay, Austl.	166	21.09 S	149.11 E
Mackay, Id., U.S.	202	43.54 N	113.36 W
MacKay ≏	184	57.03 N	111.55 W
Mackay, Lake ⊜	162	22.30 S	129.00 E
MacKay Lake ⊜	176	63.55 N	110.25 W
Mackenrode	54	51.33 N	10.33 E
Mackenzie	246	6.00 N	58.17 W
Mackenzie ≏, Austl.	166	23.38 S	149.46 E
Mackenzie ≏, N.T., Can.	176	69.15 N	134.08 W
MacKenzie Bay c, Ant.	9	68.20 S	71.15 E
Mackenzie Bay c, Can.	180	69.00 N	136.30 W
Mackenzie Delta ≚[2]	180	68.50 N	135.25 W
Mackenzie Mountains ⨯	180	64.00 N	130.00 W
Mackeyville	210	41.03 N	77.28 W
Mackinac, Straits of ⋓	190	45.49 N	84.42 W
Mackinac Bridge ◆[5]	190	45.50 N	84.45 W
Mackinac Island	190	45.50 N	84.37 W
Mackinac Island I	190	45.51 N	84.38 W
Mackinac Island State Park ♠	190	45.52 N	84.40 W
Mackinaw	190	40.32 N	89.21 W
Mackinaw ≏	194	40.33 N	89.44 W
Mackinaw City	190	45.47 N	84.43 W
Mackinnon Road	154	3.44 S	39.03 E
Macklin	184	52.20 N	109.56 W
Mačkovci	61	46.47 N	16.09 E
M'ačkovo, Ross.	82	55.13 N	38.40 E
M'ačkovo, Ross.	82	56.21 N	39.03 E
Macksville, Austl.	166	30.43 S	152.55 E
Macksville, Ks., U.S.	198	38.57 N	98.58 W
Maclean	166	29.28 S	153.13 E
Macleantown	158	32.47 S	27.45 E
Maclear	158	31.02 S	28.23 E
Macleay ≏	166	30.52 S	153.01 E
Macleod	274b	37.43 S	145.04 E
Macleod, Lake ⊜	162	24.00 S	113.35 E
Maclovia Herrera	232	29.05 N	105.08 W
Macmillan ≏	180	62.52 N	135.55 W
Macocolo	152	6.47 S	16.08 E
Macolin	58	47.09 N	7.14 E
Macolla, Punta ≻	241s	12.06 N	70.13 W
Macolo	152	7.05 S	16.48 E
Macomb	190	40.27 N	90.40 W
Macomb □[6]	214	42.40 N	82.54 W
Macomb Mall ◆[9]	281	42.32 N	82.55 W
Macomer	71	40.16 N	8.47 E
Macomia	154	12.15 S	40.08 E
Macon, Bel.	50	50.03 N	4.13 E
Mâcon, Fr.	58	46.18 N	4.50 E
Macon, Ga., U.S.	192	32.50 N	83.37 W
Macon, Il., U.S.	219	39.42 N	88.59 W
Macon, Ms., U.S.	194	33.06 N	88.33 W
Macon, Mo., U.S.	194	39.44 N	92.28 W
Macon □[6], Il., U.S.	219	39.51 N	89.32 W
Macon □[6], Mo., U.S.	219	39.50 N	92.20 W
Macon, Bayou ≏	194	31.55 N	91.33 W
Macon Creek ≏	216	41.58 N	83.38 W
Macondo	152	12.35 S	23.44 E
Macondo ≏	152	13.23 S	23.03 E
Mâconnais, Monts du ⨯	58	46.18 N	4.45 E
Macorís, Cabo ≻	238	19.47 N	70.28 W
Macosquin	48	55.06 N	6.43 W
Macossa	156	17.52 S	33.56 E
Macouba, Pointe de ≻	240e	14.53 N	61.09 W
Macoun Lake ⊜	184	56.32 N	103.50 W
Macoupin □[6]	219	39.17 N	89.53 W
Macoupin Creek ≏	219	39.11 N	90.36 W
Macovane	156	21.28 S	35.04 E
Macpherson, Mount ∧[2]	162	21.49 S	121.35 E
Macquarie ≏, Austl.	166	41.44 S	147.08 E
Macquarie ≏, Austl.	166	30.07 S	147.24 E
Macquarie, Lake ⊜	170	33.05 S	151.35 E
Macquarie Fields	274a	33.59 S	150.53 E
Macquarie Harbour c	166	42.19 S	145.23 E
Macquarie Island I	9	54.30 S	158.56 E
Macquarie Marshes ☷	166	30.50 S	147.32 E
Macquarie Pass National Park ♠	170	34.34 S	150.39 E
Macquarie Ridge ✣[3]	9	57.00 S	159.00 E

Nome	Página	Lat.°′	Long.°′
Macquarie University ♁[2]	274a	33.46 S	151.06 E
MacRitchie Reservoir ⊜[1]	271c	1.21 N	103.50 E
Mac. Robertson Land ◆[1]	9	68.10 S	65.00 E
Macrohon	116	10.05 N	124.56 E
Macroom	48	51.54 N	8.57 W
Mactan Island I	116	10.18 N	123.58 E
MacTier	212	45.08 N	79.47 W
Macuco de Minas	256	21.46 S	44.47 W
Macucuau ≏	246	0.37 S	61.24 W
Macuelizo	236	15.18 N	88.31 W
Macugnaga	58	45.58 N	7.58 E
Macujer	246	0.23 N	72.55 W
Macul	286e	33.30 S	70.34 W
Maculabo Island I	116	14.24 N	122.49 E
Macumba ≏	162	27.52 S	137.12 E
Macungie	208	40.30 N	75.33 W
Macunqiao	100	33.50 N	116.13 E
Macuro	246	10.39 N	61.56 W
Macusani	248	14.05 S	70.26 W
Macuspana	234	17.46 N	92.36 W
Macusse	152	17.51 S	20.21 E
Macuto	286c	10.37 N	66.53 W
Macuze	156	17.42 S	37.11 E
Macy	216	40.57 N	86.07 W
Mad ≏, On., Can.	212	44.25 N	79.54 W
Mad ≏, Ca., U.S.	204	40.57 N	124.07 W
Mad ≏, N.Y., U.S.	212	43.20 N	75.44 W
Mad ≏, Oh., U.S.	188	39.46 N	84.11 W
Mad ≏, Vt., U.S.	188	44.18 N	72.41 W
Mada ≏	150	7.59 N	7.55 E
Ma'dabā	132	31.43 N	35.48 E
Madagascar (Madagasikara) □[1], Afr.	138	19.00 S	46.00 E
Madagascar (Madagasikara) □[1], Afr.	157b	19.00 S	46.00 E
Madagascar Basin ✣[1]	12	27.00 S	53.00 E
Madagascar Plateau ✣[3]	10	30.00 S	45.00 E
Madagasikara → Madagascar □[1]	157b	19.00 S	46.00 E
Madagaskar → Madagascar □[1]	157b	19.00 S	46.00 E
Madagiz	84	40.19 N	46.44 E
Madagoi, Bohol V	144	0.44 N	42.56 E
Madā'in Ṣāliḥ	128	26.48 N	37.53 E
Madajevo	80	54.48 N	44.31 E
Madama	146	21.58 N	13.39 E
Madame, Isle I	186	45.33 N	61.02 W
Madan	38	41.30 N	24.57 E
Madanapalle	122	13.33 N	78.30 E
Madang, Pap. N. Gui.	164	5.15 S	145.50 E
Madang, Zhg.	100	29.58 N	116.40 E
Madang □[5]	164	5.00 S	145.30 E
Madanpur	272b	22.40 N	88.32 E
Madanpur Dabās ◆[8]	272a	28.43 N	77.02 E
Madaoua	150	14.05 N	5.58 E
Mādār Gāng ≏[1]	126	22.12 N	89.04 E
Mādāri Hāt	124	26.42 N	89.17 E
Mādārīpur	124	23.10 N	90.12 E
Madarounfa	150	13.18 N	7.09 E
Mādārpur	272b	22.54 N	88.27 E
Madau Island I	164	8.58 S	152.28 E
Madawaska, On., Can.	212	45.30 N	77.59 W
Madawaska, Me., U.S.	186	47.21 N	68.19 W
Madawaska ≏	212	45.27 N	76.21 W
Madawaska Highlands ⨯[1]	212	45.15 N	77.35 W
Madawaska Lake ⊜	212	45.20 N	78.23 W
Madaxmaroodi	144	2.39 N	44.36 E
Madaya, Mya.	110	22.13 N	96.07 E
Maḍāyā, Sūrīy.	132	33.41 N	36.06 E
Madbar	140	6.19 N	30.40 E
Mad Creek ≏	210	42.55 N	77.59 W
Maddalena, Colle della (Col de Larche))(	62	44.25 N	6.53 E
Maddalena, Isola I	71	41.14 N	9.25 E
Maddaloni	68	41.02 N	14.23 E
Maddela	116	16.21 N	121.41 E
Madden, Mount ∧	162	33.12 S	119.51 E
Maddington	168a	32.03 S	115.59 E
Maddock	198	47.57 N	99.31 W
Maddy, Loch c	46	57.36 N	7.08 W
Made	52	51.41 N	4.46 E
Madeir	140	7.50 N	29.12 E
Madeira	218	39.11 N	84.21 W
Madeira I	148	32.44 N	17.00 W
Madeira ≏	242	3.22 S	58.45 W
Madeira, Arquipélago da II	148	32.40 N	16.45 W
Madeira Beach	220	27.48 N	82.48 W
Madeirinha ≏	248	8.31 S	60.46 W
Madeirinha, Paraná ≏[1]	246	3.25 S	58.51 W
M'adel'	76	54.53 N	26.57 E
Mädelegabel ∧	58	47.18 N	10.18 E
Madeleine, Îles de la II	186	47.30 N	61.45 W
Madeleine, Pointe ≻	275a	45.27 N	73.57 W
Madeleine-Centre	186	49.15 N	65.21 W
Madeley, Eng., U.K.	42	52.59 N	2.20 W
Madeley, Eng., U.K.	42	52.39 N	2.28 W
Madelia	190	44.03 N	94.25 W
Madeline Island I	190	46.50 N	90.40 W
Maden, Tür.	130	38.23 N	39.40 E
Maden, Tür.	130	40.11 N	40.25 E
Madenijet	86	47.53 N	78.37 E
Madera, Méx.	232	29.12 N	108.07 W
Madera, Ca., U.S.	226	36.57 N	120.03 W
Madera, Pa., U.S.	214	40.49 N	78.26 W
Madera □[6]	226	37.15 N	119.45 W
Madera Canal ≊	226	37.05 N	119.59 W
Madera Lake ⊜[1]	226	37.02 N	119.59 W
Madera Peak ∧	226	37.32 N	119.23 W
Maderas, Islas → Madeira, Arquipélago da II	148	32.40 N	16.45 W
Maderas, Volcán ∧[1]	236	11.27 N	85.31 W
Maderno	64	45.38 N	10.35 E
Madgaon (Margao)	122	15.18 N	73.57 E
Madh ◆[8]	272c	19.08 N	72.47 E
Madhepura	124	25.55 N	86.47 E
Madhkūr, Bi'r ⍑[4]	142	30.42 N	32.32 E
Mādhopur	123	32.22 N	75.36 E
Madhubani	124	26.22 N	86.05 E
Madhudaha	272b	22.31 N	88.25 E
Madhugiri	122	13.40 N	77.12 E
Madhumati ≏[1]	126	22.53 N	89.52 E
Madhupar	126	22.54 N	86.28 E
Madhupur	126	24.16 N	86.39 E
Madhya Bhārat Pathār ◆[1]	124	25.00 N	77.00 E
Madhyamgrām	272b	22.42 N	88.27 E
Madhya Pradesh □[3]	118	23.00 N	79.00 E
Madia	154	7.08 S	26.00 E
Madian	106	32.15 N	119.58 E
Madibi	152	4.18 S	18.24 E
Madibira	154	8.12 S	34.49 E
Madibogo	158	26.25 S	25.10 E
Madida	98	42.57 N	130.48 E
Madidi ≏	248	12.32 S	66.52 W
Madill	196	34.05 N	96.46 W
Madimba, Ang.	152	6.31 S	14.21 E
Madimba, Zaïre	152	4.58 S	15.08 E
Madina	150	13.24 N	8.51 W
Madina do Boé	150	11.45 N	14.13 W
Madinani	150	9.37 N	6.57 W
Madinat al-Abyār	146	32.11 N	20.36 E
Madīnat ash-Sha'b (Al-Ittihad)	144	12.50 N	44.56 E
Madīnat ath Thawrah	130	35.52 N	38.34 E
Madine, Lac de ⊜	56	48.54 N	5.42 E

Nome	Página	Lat.°′	Long.°′
Madingo	152	4.07 S	11.22 E
Madingou	152	4.09 S	13.34 E
Madingzi	104	42.08 N	120.52 E
Madi Opei	154	3.37 N	33.05 E
Madirobe	157b	16.04 S	46.15 E
Madirovalo	157b	16.26 S	46.30 E
Madison, Al., U.S.	194	34.41 N	86.44 W
Madison, Ca., U.S.	226	38.41 N	121.58 W
Madison, Ct., U.S.	207	41.16 N	72.35 W
Madison, Fl., U.S.	192	30.28 N	83.24 W
Madison, Ga., U.S.	192	33.35 N	83.28 W
Madison, Il., U.S.	219	38.40 N	90.09 W
Madison, In., U.S.	218	38.44 N	85.22 W
Madison, Ks., U.S.	198	38.08 N	96.08 W
Madison, Me., U.S.	188	44.47 N	69.52 W
Madison, Md., U.S.	208	38.30 N	76.13 W
Madison, Mn., U.S.	198	45.00 N	96.11 W
Madison, Mo., U.S.	219	39.28 N	92.12 W
Madison, Ne., U.S.	198	41.49 N	97.27 W
Madison, N.J., U.S.	210	40.45 N	74.25 W
Madison, N.Y., U.S.	210	42.53 N	75.30 W
Madison, N.C., U.S.	192	36.23 N	79.57 W
Madison, Oh., U.S.	214	41.46 N	81.03 W
Madison, Pa., U.S.	279b	40.15 N	79.41 W
Madison, S.D., U.S.	198	44.00 N	97.06 W
Madison, Va., U.S.	188	38.22 N	78.15 W
Madison, W.V., U.S.	188	38.04 N	81.49 W
Madison, Wi., U.S.	216	43.04 N	89.24 W
Madison □[6], Il., U.S.	219	38.49 N	89.58 W
Madison □[6], In., U.S.	218	40.10 N	85.41 W
Madison □[6], N.Y., U.S.	210	43.05 N	75.42 W
Madison □[6], Oh., U.S.	218	39.53 N	83.27 W
Madison □[6], Tx., U.S.	222	30.58 N	95.55 W
Madison ≏	202	45.56 N	111.30 W
Madison, West Fork ≏	202	44.55 N	111.35 W
Madisonburg, Oh., U.S.	214	40.51 N	81.55 W
Madisonburg, Pa., U.S.	210	40.55 N	77.31 W
Madison Heights, Mi., U.S.	216	42.29 N	83.06 W
Madison Heights, Va., U.S.	192	37.25 N	79.07 W
Madison Mills	218	39.40 N	83.20 W
Madison-on-the-Lake	214	41.42 N	81.24 W
Madison Park	276	40.26 N	74.19 W
Madison Range ⨯	202	45.15 N	111.20 W
Madison Square Garden ♠	276	40.45 N	74.00 W
Madisonville, Ky., U.S.	194	37.19 N	87.29 W
Madisonville, La., U.S.	194	30.24 N	90.09 W
Madisonville, Tn., U.S.	192	35.31 N	84.21 W
Madisonville, Tx., U.S.	222	30.56 N	95.54 W
Madiun	115a	7.37 S	111.31 E
Madiun ≏	115a	7.23 S	111.27 E
Madiyi	102	28.14 N	110.30 E
Madjingo	152	1.23 N	14.06 E
Madjoari	150	11.26 N	1.15 E
Madley, Mount ∧	162	24.31 S	123.58 E
Madoc	212	44.30 N	77.28 W
Mado Gashi	154	0.44 N	39.10 E
Madoi	102	34.53 N	98.24 E
Madol	140	9.02 N	27.46 E
Madon ≏	58	48.36 N	6.06 E
Madona	76	56.51 N	26.13 E
Madonna (Unserfrau)	64	46.43 N	10.52 E
Madonna della Guardia ♁[1]	62	44.29 N	8.51 E
Madonna della Quercia ♁[1]	66	42.25 N	12.06 E
Madonna dell'Olmo	62	44.25 N	7.32 E
Madonna del Sasso ♁[1]	58	46.11 N	8.33 E
Madonna di Campiglio	64	46.14 N	10.49 E
Madonna di Tirano	64	46.13 N	10.09 E
Madora	76	53.09 N	30.11 E
Madougou	150	14.24 N	3.05 W
Madrakah	144	21.59 N	39.59 E
Madrakah, Ra's al- ≻	118	19.00 N	57.50 E
Madras, India	122	13.05 N	80.17 E
Madras, Or., U.S.	202	44.38 N	121.07 W
Madras → Tamil Nādu □[3]	122	11.00 N	78.15 E
Madre, Laguna c, Méx.	232	25.00 N	97.40 W
Madre, Laguna c, Tx., U.S.	196	27.00 N	97.35 W
Madre, Sierra ⨯	116	16.20 N	122.00 E
Madre de Chiapas, Sierra ⨯	232	15.30 N	92.35 W
Madre de Deus de Minas	256	21.29 S	44.20 W
Madre de Dios □[5]	248	12.00 S	70.15 W
Madre de Dios ≏	248	10.23 S	65.24 W
Madre de Dios, Isla I	254	50.15 S	75.05 W
Madre del Sur, Sierra ⨯	234	17.00 N	100.00 W
Madre Occidental, Sierra ⨯	232	25.00 N	105.00 W
Madre Oriental, Sierra ⨯	232	22.00 N	99.30 W
Madre Vieja ≏	236	14.01 N	91.26 W
Madrid, Col.	246	4.44 N	74.16 W
Madrid, Esp.	34	40.24 N	3.41 W
Madrid, Esp.	266a	40.24 N	3.41 W
Madrid, Pil.	116	9.15 N	126.00 E
Madrid, Al., U.S.	194	31.02 N	85.23 W
Madrid, Ia., U.S.	190	41.52 N	93.49 W
Madrid, Ne., U.S.	198	40.51 N	101.32 W
Madrid □[4], Esp.	34	40.30 N	3.40 W
Madrid □[4], Esp.	34	40.30 N	3.40 W
Madridejos, Esp.	34	39.28 N	3.32 W
Madridejos, Pil.	116	11.18 N	123.44 E
Madrigalejo	34	39.09 N	5.37 W
Madrillon	284c	38.55 N	77.14 W
Madriz □[5]	236	13.30 N	86.30 W
Madroñera	34	39.26 N	5.46 W
Madruga	240p	22.55 N	81.51 W
Madrūsah	146	24.48 N	14.32 E
Madsen	184	50.58 N	93.55 W
Madsūs, Bi'r ⍑[4]	142	29.15 N	32.19 E
Maducang Island I	116	10.42 N	120.15 E
Maduda	152	4.55 S	13.06 E
Maduo	152	1.24 S	20.44 E
Madura	162	31.55 S	127.00 E
Madura I	115a	7.00 S	113.20 E
Madura, Selat ⋓	115a	7.25 S	113.25 E
Madurai	122	9.56 N	78.07 E
Madura → Madurai	122	9.56 N	78.07 E
Madurāntakam	122	12.31 N	79.54 E
Madureira, Serra de ⨯	287a	22.49 S	43.31 W
Maduru ≏	122	7.52 N	81.31 E
Madwar al-Bighāl ∧[2]	142	29.09 N	29.54 E
Madžalis	84	42.08 N	47.50 E
Mãe, Ilha da I	287a	22.59 S	43.04 W
Maeander Reef ✣[2]	116	8.05 N	119.18 E
Maebaru	92	33.33 N	130.12 E
Maebashi	94	36.23 N	139.04 E
Maeda	270	34.55 N	135.08 E
Mãe dos Homens	256	22.52 S	46.37 W
Maegye-ri	98	34.45 N	126.18 E
Mae Hong Son	110	19.16 N	97.56 E
Mae Klong ≏	110	13.21 N	100.00 E
Maenclochog	42	51.54 N	4.48 W
Maengsan	98	39.40 N	126.30 E
Maeno ◆[8]	268	35.46 N	139.42 E
Maenza	66	41.31 N	13.11 E
Mae Ramat	110	16.58 N	98.31 E
Mae Rim	110	18.54 N	98.57 E

Nome	Página	Lat.°′	Long.°′
Maerkansu	85	39.19 N	73.53 E
Ma'erna	102	31.13 N	102.02 E
Maershan ∧	102	26.18 N	100.20 E
Mae Sariang	110	18.10 N	97.56 E
Maeser	200	40.28 N	109.35 W
Mae Sot	110	16.43 N	98.34 E
Maesteg	42	51.37 N	3.40 W
Maestra, Sierra ⨯	240p	20.00 N	76.45 W
Maestre de Campo Island I	116	12.56 N	121.42 E
Maestu	34	42.44 N	2.27 W
Mae Tha	110	18.28 N	99.08 E
Maevarano ≏	157b	14.35 S	47.58 E
Maevatanana	157b	16.56 S	46.49 E
Maéwo I	175f	15.10 S	168.10 E
Ma'fan	146	25.55 N	14.29 E
Mafang	105	40.02 N	117.01 E
Mafangchang	107	29.24 N	106.06 E
Mafangcun	105	40.09 N	116.24 E
Ma Faro ✣[2]	122	5.50 N	73.26 E
Mafeking	184	52.41 N	101.06 W
Mafembage	152	14.32 S	21.42 E
Mafengtun	104	40.49 N	122.54 E
Mafeteng	158	29.51 S	27.15 E
Maffliers	261	49.05 N	2.19 E
Maffra	166	37.58 S	146.59 E
Mafia Channel ⋓	154	8.10 S	39.40 E
Mafia Island I	154	7.50 S	39.50 E
Mafikeng	156	25.53 S	25.39 E
Mafou ≏	150	10.32 N	10.08 W
Mafra, Bra.	252	26.07 S	49.49 W
Mafra, Port.	34	38.56 N	9.20 W
Magadan	74	59.34 N	150.48 E
Magadi	154	1.54 S	36.17 E
Magadi, Lake ⊜	154	1.52 S	36.17 E
Magaguadavic Lake ⊜	186	45.43 N	67.12 W
Magai-butsu ♁[1]	96	33.05 N	131.45 E
Magalhães Bastos ◆[8]	287a	22.53 S	43.23 W
Magalhães de Almeida	250	3.24 S	42.12 W
Magaliesberg ⨯	158	25.50 S	27.30 E
Magallanes	116	12.50 N	123.50 E
Magallanes, Estrecho de (Strait of Magellan) ⋓	254	54.00 S	71.00 W
Magallanes → Punta Arenas	254	53.09 S	70.55 W
Magallanes y de la Antártica Chilena □[4]	254	53.00 S	72.00 W
Maganga	154	0.51 N	26.22 E
Magangué	246	9.14 N	74.45 W
Magansk	88	55.52 N	93.15 E
Maganuy ≏	116	6.55 N	124.30 E
Magara, India	126	22.34 N	87.34 E
Mağara, Tür.	130	36.43 N	33.52 E
Magaramkent	84	41.37 N	48.21 E
Magaria	150	13.00 N	8.54 E
Magat ≏	116	17.02 N	121.49 E
Magazine Mountain ∧	194	35.10 N	93.38 W
Magazzolo ≏	70	37.25 N	13.15 E
Magboro	273a	6.43 N	3.24 E
Magburaka	150	8.43 N	11.57 W
Magdagači	89	53.27 N	125.48 E
Magdalena, Arg.	258	35.04 S	57.32 W
Magdalena, Bol.	248	13.20 S	64.08 W
Magdalena, Méx.	234	20.55 N	103.57 W
Magdalena, Perú	248	6.21 S	77.49 W
Magdalena, Perú	286d	12.06 S	77.05 W
Magdalena, N.M., U.S.	200	34.07 N	107.14 W
Magdalena □[5]	246	10.00 N	74.00 W
Magdalena ≏, Col.	246	11.06 N	74.51 W
Magdalena ≏, Méx.	232	30.48 N	112.32 W
Magdalena, Bahía c	232	24.35 N	112.00 W
Magdalena, Isla I, Chile	254	44.40 S	73.10 W
Magdalena, Isla I, Méx.	232	24.55 N	112.15 W
Magdalena, Punta ≻	246	3.56 N	77.21 W
Magdalena Contreras ◆[8]	286a	19.18 N	99.17 W
Magdalena de Kino	232	30.38 N	110.57 W
Magdalena Peñasco	234	17.14 N	97.34 W
Magdalena Teitipac	234	16.54 N	96.34 W
Magdalena Tequisistlán	234	16.22 N	95.15 W
Magdalen Laver	260	51.45 N	0.11 E
Magdalinovka	78	48.55 N	34.54 E
Magdeborn	54	51.14 N	12.26 E
Magdeburg	54	52.07 N	11.38 E
Magdeburger Börde ≚	54	52.00 N	11.30 E
Magdeburgo → Magdeburg	54	52.07 N	11.38 E
Magdiwang	116	12.30 N	122.31 E
Magdonskij, porog ⌞	88	57.45 N	100.55 E
Māge	110	26.33 N	98.33 E
Magé □[7]	287a	22.41 S	43.07 W
Magee	194	31.52 N	89.44 W
Magee, Island ≻[1]	48	54.49 N	5.42 W
Magelang	115a	7.28 S	110.13 E
Magellan, Strait of → Magallanes, Estrecho de ⋓	254	54.00 S	71.00 W
Magellan-Strasse → Magallanes, Estrecho de ⋓	254	54.00 S	71.00 W
Magén	132	31.18 N	34.26 E
Magenta	62	45.28 N	8.53 E
Magenta, Lake ⊜	162	33.26 S	119.10 E
Magerov	78	50.08 N	23.43 E
Magerøy I	24	71.03 N	25.45 E
Magetan	115a	7.39 S	111.20 E
Magezhuang	105	40.08 N	117.59 E
Maggia	58	46.15 N	8.42 E
Maggia ≏	58	46.09 N	8.48 E
Maggia, Valle V	58	46.17 N	8.40 E
Maggie Creek ≏	204	40.43 N	116.05 W
Maggiorasca, Monte ∧	62	44.33 N	9.29 E
Maggiore ≏, It.	267a	41.54 N	12.16 E
Maggiore ≏, It.	267a	43.43 N	13.06 E
Maggiore, Lago ⊜	36	46.00 N	8.40 E
Maggiore, Monte ∧	68	41.14 N	14.12 E
Maghāghah	142	28.39 N	30.50 E
Maghama	150	15.31 N	12.51 W
Maghar	132	32.53 N	35.24 E
Maghdūshah	132	33.31 N	35.23 E
Maghera	48	54.51 N	6.40 W
Magherafelt	48	54.45 N	6.36 W
Maghniyya	148	34.50 N	1.50 W
Magholpur ◆[8]	272a	28.42 N	77.06 E
Maghull	44	53.32 N	2.57 W
Magician Lake ⊜	216	42.04 N	86.10 W
Magic Mountain ♠	228	34.26 N	118.36 W
Magic Reservoir ⊜[1]	202	43.17 N	114.23 W
Magill, Lac ⊜	206	45.35 N	71.17 W
Magill Heights	279b	40.37 N	79.52 W
Magill Lake ⊜	184	54.45 N	94.58 W
Mágina ∧	34	37.43 N	3.28 W
Maginu	268	35.35 N	139.36 E
Magione	66	43.08 N	12.12 E
Magisano	68	39.01 N	16.27 E
Magiscatzín	234	22.48 N	98.42 W
Magiss Lake ⊜	184	52.59 N	91.40 W
Maglaj	38	44.33 N	18.06 E
Magliana ◆[8]	267a	41.50 N	12.25 E
Magliana, Fosso ≏	267a	41.49 N	12.25 E
Magliano dei Marsi	66	42.05 N	13.22 E
Magliano in Toscana	66	42.36 N	11.17 E
Magliano Sabina	66	42.22 N	12.29 E
Maglie	68	40.07 N	18.19 E
Maglód	264c	47.27 N	19.21 E
M'aglovo	265a	59.53 N	30.41 E
Magnago	266b	45.35 N	8.48 E
Magnanville	261	48.58 N	1.41 E
Magnet	184	51.19 N	99.30 W

Symbol	English	Deutsch	Español	Français	Português
≏	River	Fluß	Río	Rivière	Rio
≊	Canal	Kanal	Canal	Canal	Canal
⌞	Waterfall, Rapids	Wasserfall, Stromschnellen	Cascada, Rápidos	Chute d'eau, Rapides	Cascata, Rápidos
⋓	Strait	Meeresstraße	Estrecho	Détroit	Estreito
c	Bay, Gulf	Bucht, Golf	Bahía, Golfo	Baie, Golfe	Baía, Golfo
⊜	Lake, Lakes	See, Seen	Lago, Lagos	Lac, Lacs	Lago, Lagos
☷	Swamp	Sumpf	Pantano	Marais	Pântano
⊓	Ice Features, Glacier	Eis- und Gletscherformen	Accidentes Glaciales	Formes glaciaires	Acidentes glaciares
⍑	Other Hydrographic Features	Andere Hydrographische Objekte	Otros Elementos Hidrográficos	Autres données hydrographiques	Outros acidentes hidrográficos
✣	Submarine Features	Untermeerische Objekte	Accidentes Submarinos	Formes de relief sous-marin	Acidentes submarinos
□	Political Unit	Politische Einheit	Unidad Politica	Entité politique	Unidade política
♁	Cultural Institution	Kulturelle Institution	Institución Cultural	Institution culturelle	Instituição cultural
⊥	Historical Site	Historische Stätte	Sitio Histórico	Site historique	Sitio histórico
♠	Recreational Site	Erholungs- und Ferienort	Sitio de Recreo	Centre de loisirs	Area de Lazer
⊠	Airport	Flughafen	Aeropuerto	Aéroport	Aeroporto
■	Military Installation	Militäranlage	Instalación Militar	Installation militaire	Instalação militar
◆	Miscellaneous	Verschiedenes	Misceláneo	Divers	Diversos

Magnetawan ≃ **190** 45.46 N 80.37 W
Magnetic Island I **166** 19.08 S 146.50 E
Magnetic Springs **214** 40.21 N 83.16 W
Magnetischer Nordpol → North Magnetic Pole ◆ **16** 77.19 N 101.49 W
Magnetischer Südpol → South Magnetic Pole ◆ **9** 65.18 S 139.30 E
Magnières **58** 48.27 N 6.34 E
Magnitka **86** 55.21 N 59.43 E
Magnitogorsk **86** 53.27 N 59.04 E
Magnitostroj **80** 51.43 N 53.05 E
Magnolia, Ar., U.S. **194** 33.16 N 93.14 W
Magnolia, De., U.S. **208** 39.04 N 75.28 W
Magnolia, Ma., U.S. **283** 42.35 N 70.43 W
Magnolia, Mn., U.S. **198** 43.38 N 96.04 W
Magnolia, Ms., U.S. **194** 31.08 N 90.27 W
Magnolia, N.J., U.S. **285** 39.51 N 75.02 W
Magnolia, Oh., U.S. **214** 40.39 N 81.17 W
Magnolia, Tx., U.S. **222** 30.13 N 95.45 W
Magnor **26** 59.57 N 12.12 E
Magny-en-Vexin **50** 49.09 N 1.47 E
Magny-le-Hongre **261** 48.52 N 2.49 E
Magny-les-Hameaux **261** 48.44 N 2.04 E
Mago **89** 53.15 N 140.13 E
Magog **206** 45.16 N 72.09 W
Magog ≃ **206** 45.24 N 71.54 W
Magog, Lake ⊜ **206** 45.18 N 72.03 W
Magoito **266c** 38.52 N 9.26 W
Magome ◆[8] **268** 35.35 N 139.43 E
Mago National Park ♦ **144** 5.30 N 36.15 E
Magonoy **116** 6.54 N 124.33 E
Magoro **154** 1.44 N 34.06 E
Magothy Bay c **208** 37.10 N 75.55 W
Magothy River c **208** 39.04 N 76.28 W
Magoúla **267c** 38.04 N 23.32 E
Magoye **154** 16.00 S 27.37 E
Magozal, Méx. **232** 21.34 N 97.59 W
Magozal, Méx. **234** 21.34 N 97.59 W
M'agozero **76** 60.21 N 34.50 E
Magpie **186** 50.19 N 64.30 W
Magpie ≃, On., Can. **190** 47.56 N 84.50 W
Magpie ≃, P.Q., Can. **186** 50.19 N 64.27 W
Magpie, Lac ⊜ **186** 51.00 N 64.41 W
Magpie Ouest ≃ **186** 51.02 N 64.42 W
Magra **126** 22.59 N 88.22 E
Magra ≃ **64** 44.03 N 9.58 E
Magra Hāt **126** 22.14 N 88.23 E
Magrath **182** 49.25 N 112.52 W
Magrè (Margreid) **64** 46.17 N 11.12 E
Magro ≃ **34** 39.11 N 0.25 W
Magruder Mountain ∧ **204** 37.25 N 117.33 W
Magsaysay (Linugos) **116** 9.01 N 125.11 E
Magsingal **116** 17.41 N 120.25 E
Magu ≃ **250** 2.56 S 41.55 W
Maguan **102** 22.59 N 104.19 E
Maguanying **271a** 39.52 N 116.17 E
Maguari, Cabo ≻ **250** 0.18 S 48.22 W
Magude **156** 25.02 S 32.40 E
Magudu **158** 27.31 S 31.40 E
Magueyes **196** 25.44 N 97.47 W
Maguindanao □[4] **116** 6.55 N 124.20 E
Magumeri **146** 12.08 N 12.50 E
Māgura **124** 23.29 N 89.25 E
Maguru **150** 12.28 N 6.35 E
Maguse Lake ⊜ **176** 61.40 N 95.10 W
Maguzhan **120** 31.15 N 88.00 E
Magway, Mya. **110** 20.09 N 94.55 E
Magway, Mya. **110** 20.30 N 94.30 E
Magwe **154** 4.08 N 32.17 E
Magwood Park ♦ **275b** 43.39 N 79.30 W
Magyarország → Hungary □[1] **30** 47.00 N 20.00 E
Mahābād **128** 36.45 N 45.43 E
Mahābaleshwar **122** 17.55 N 73.40 E
Mahabe **157b** 17.05 S 45.20 E
Mahābhārat Lek ⋏ **124** 27.40 N 84.30 E
Mahabo, Madag. **157b** 23.40 S 46.08 E
Mahabo, Madag. **157b** 20.23 S 44.40 E
Mahād **122** 18.05 N 73.25 E
Mahadday Weyn **144** 2.58 N 45.32 E
Mahādebpur **126** 23.51 N 89.53 E
Mahādeo Hills ⋏[2] **122** 22.22 N 78.34 E
Mahādeo Range ⋏ **122** 17.50 N 74.15 E
Mahaffey **214** 40.52 N 78.43 W
Mahagi **154** 2.18 N 30.59 E
Mahagi Port **154** 2.09 N 31.14 E
Mahai **102** 38.17 N 94.13 E
Mahaica-Berbice □[4] **246** 6.20 N 57.50 W
Mahaicony Village **246** 6.36 N 57.48 W
Mahajamba ≃ **157b** 15.33 S 47.08 E
Mahajamba, Helodranon' i c **157b** 15.24 S 47.05 E
Mahājan **123** 28.47 N 73.50 E
Mahajanga **157b** 15.43 S 46.19 E
Mahajanga □[4] **157b** 17.00 S 46.00 E
Mahajilo ≃ **157b** 19.42 S 45.22 E
Mahajjah **132** 32.57 N 36.14 E
Mahākālī □[8] **124** 29.30 N 80.30 E
Mahākālī (Sārda) ≃ **124** 27.21 N 81.23 E
Mahakam ≃ **112** 0.35 S 117.17 E
Mahālandi **126** 24.04 N 88.07 E
Mahalatswe **156** 23.05 S 26.51 E
Mahalla el-Kubra → Al-Maḥallah al-Kubrā **142** 30.58 N 31.10 E
Maḥallāt **128** 33.55 N 50.27 E
Maḥallat Kayl **142** 31.01 N 30.17 E
Maḥallat Marḥūm **142** 30.48 N 30.57 E
Maḥallat Minūf **142** 30.53 N 30.58 E
Maḥallat Zayyād **142** 31.02 N 31.14 E
Maham **124** 28.59 N 76.18 E
Mahamba **158** 27.07 S 31.10 E
Mahānadi ≃ **118** 20.19 N 86.45 E
Mahānadpati **126** 23.00 N 88.16 E
Mahānanda ≃ **124** 24.29 N 88.18 E
Mahanay Island I **116** 10.12 N 124.14 E
Mahanoro **157b** 19.54 S 48.48 E
Mahanoy City **208** 40.48 N 76.08 W
Mahanoy Creek ≃ **208** 40.42 N 76.51 W
Mahantango Creek ≃ **208** 40.47 N 76.56 W
Mahantango Mountain ∧ **208** 40.40 N 76.45 W
Mahao **89** 43.10 N 127.59 E
Mahape **272c** 19.07 N 73.01 E
Mahārājganj, India **124** 27.09 N 83.34 E
Mahārājganj, India **124** 26.07 N 84.29 E
Mahārājpur, India **124** 25.01 N 79.44 E
Mahārājpur, India **272a** 28.39 N 77.20 E
Mahārāshtra □[3] **122** 19.00 N 76.00 E
Mahārīq, Wādī V **142** 27.48 N 31.47 E
Mahārlū, Daryācheh-ye ⊜ **128** 29.25 N 52.50 E
Mahāsamund **120** 21.06 N 82.06 E
Maha Sarakham **110** 16.11 N 103.18 E
Maha Sawat, Khlong ≍ **269a** 13.47 N 100.28 E
Mahasoa **157b** 22.12 S 46.06 E
Mahasolo **157b** 19.07 S 46.22 E
Mahates **246** 10.14 N 75.12 W
Mahatsinjo **157b** 21.26 S 45.51 E
Maḥaṭṭat al-Ḥafīf **132** 32.12 N 37.08 E
Mahaut **240d** 15.21 N 61.25 W
Mahavavy ≃, Madag. **157b** 15.57 S 45.54 E
Mahavavy ≃, Madag. **157b** 13.00 S 48.55 E
Mahaweli ≃ **122** 8.27 N 81.13 E
Mahaxai **110** 17.25 N 105.12 E
Maḥbas, Wādī al- V **140** 15.50 N 29.45 E
Mahbūbābād **122** 17.37 N 80.01 E
Mahbūbnagar **122** 16.44 N 77.59 E
Mahd adh-Dhahab **128** 23.30 N 40.52 E
Mahdāt, Bi'r al- ⊤[4] **142** 30.44 N 32.32 E
Mahdia, Guy. **246** 5.16 N 59.09 W
Mahdia, Tun. **148** 35.30 N 11.04 E
Mahdia □[8] **148** 35.18 N 10.45 E
Mahe **122** 11.42 N 75.32 E
Mahébourg **157c** 20.24 S 57.42 E
Mahé Island I **138** 4.40 S 55.28 E
Mahendraganj **124** 25.20 N 89.45 E
Mahendragarh **124** 28.17 N 76.09 E
Mahendra Giri ∧ **122** 18.58 N 84.21 E
Mahendranagar **124** 28.52 N 80.17 E
Mahenge, Tan. **154** 7.38 S 36.16 E
Mahenge, Tan. **154** 8.41 S 36.43 E
Maheno **172** 45.10 S 170.50 E
Mahesāna **120** 23.36 N 72.24 E
Mahesgādi **272b** 22.39 N 88.33 E
Maheshmunda **126** 24.13 N 86.24 E
Maheshtala **272b** 22.30 N 88.15 E
Maheshwar **120** 22.11 N 75.35 E
Mahespur **124** 23.21 N 88.55 E
Mahgawān **124** 26.29 N 78.37 E
Mahi ≃ **120** 22.16 N 72.58 E
Mahia Peninsula ≻[1] **172** 39.10 S 177.53 E
Mahiāri **272b** 22.35 N 88.14 E
Māhikpur **272b** 22.32 N 88.14 E
Mahilāra **126** 22.56 N 90.16 E
Māhīm ◆[8] **272c** 19.03 N 72.49 E
Māhīm ≃ **272c** 19.03 N 72.51 E
Māhīm Bay c **272c** 19.02 N 72.50 E
Mahina, Mali **150** 13.46 N 10.51 W
Mahina, Poly. fr. **174s** 17.31 S 149.30 W
Mahinerangi, Lake ⊜ **172** 45.51 S 169.57 E
Mahinog **116** 9.09 N 124.47 E
Mahīshādal **126** 22.11 N 87.59 E
Mahishdānga **272b** 22.54 N 88.11 E
Mahlabatini **158** 28.14 S 31.30 E
Mahlangasi **158** 27.37 S 31.42 E
Mahlberg **58** 48.17 N 7.48 E
Mahlow **54** 52.22 N 13.24 E
Mahlsdorf **54** 52.47 N 11.13 E
Mahlsdorf-Süd ◆[8] **264a** 52.29 N 13.36 E
Mahmūdābād, India **124** 27.18 N 81.07 E
Maḥmūdābād, Īrān **128** 36.38 N 52.15 E
Maḥmūd-e Rāqī **120** 35.01 N 69.20 E
Maḥmūdīyah, Tur'at al- ≍ **142** 31.11 N 29.53 E
Mahmudiye **130** 39.30 N 31.00 E
Mahmūdpur, India **272a** 28.46 N 77.22 E
Mahmudpur, India **272b** 22.41 N 88.09 E
Mahmutbey ◆[8] **267b** 41.03 N 28.49 E
Mahmutşevketpaşa **130** 41.05 N 29.19 E
Mahmutşevketpaşa ◆[8] **267b** 41.09 N 29.11 E
Mahnomen **198** 47.18 N 95.58 W
Mahoba **124** 25.17 N 79.52 E
Mahogany Mountain ∧ **202** 43.14 N 117.16 W
Mahomet **216** 40.11 N 88.24 W
Mahone Bay **186** 44.27 N 64.23 W
Mahone Bay c **186** 44.30 N 64.15 W
Mahoning □[6] **214** 41.06 N 80.39 W
Mahoning ≃ **214** 40.58 N 80.23 W
Mahoning, West Branch ≃ **214** 41.12 N 80.57 W
Mahoning Creek ≃ **214** 40.55 N 79.27 W
Mahoning Creek Lake ⊜[1] **214** 40.50 N 79.10 W
Mahony Lake ⊜ **180** 65.30 N 125.20 W
Mahood Falls **182** 51.50 N 120.39 W
Mahood Lake ⊜ **182** 51.55 N 120.24 W
Mahopac **210** 41.22 N 73.44 W
Mahopac Falls **210** 41.22 N 73.46 W
Mahora **34** 39.13 N 1.44 W
Mahoras Brook ≃ **276** 40.25 N 74.08 W
Mahrāt, Jabal ⋏[1] **144** 17.05 N 51.30 E
Mahrauli ◆[8] **272a** 28.31 N 77.11 E
Mahrauni **124** 24.35 N 78.43 E
Mähren → Morava □[9] **30** 49.20 N 17.00 E
Mahres **148** 34.32 N 10.30 E
Mähring **60** 49.55 N 12.32 E
Mahuiling **100** 29.24 N 115.48 E
Māhul ◆[8] **272c** 19.01 N 72.53 E
Mahulia **126** 22.39 N 86.24 E
Mahur Island I **164** 2.50 S 152.40 E
Mahuta **154** 10.52 S 39.27 E
Mahuva **120** 21.05 N 71.48 E
Mahwa **124** 27.03 N 76.56 E
Mahwah **276** 41.06 N 74.09 W
Mahwah ≃ **276** 41.06 N 74.10 W
Mai, Île de I **275a** 45.36 N 73.50 W
Maia, Am. Sam. **174y** 14.13 S 169.28 W
Maia, Port. **34** 41.14 N 8.37 W
Mai Aini **144** 14.47 N 39.06 E
Maiala National Park ♦ **171a** 27.19 S 152.46 E
Maianga **152** 14.12 S 21.45 E
Maiano **64** 46.11 N 13.04 E
Maiauatá **250** 1.51 S 49.02 W
Maicao **246** 11.23 N 72.13 W
Maîche **58** 47.15 N 6.48 E
Maichen **102** 20.29 N 109.59 E
Maici ≃ **248** 6.30 S 61.43 W
Maicuru ≃ **250** 2.14 S 54.17 W
Maida **68** 38.51 N 16.22 E
Maidan ♦ **272b** 22.33 N 88.21 E
Maiden **192** 35.34 N 81.12 W
Maidenhead **42** 51.32 N 0.44 W
Maiden Newton **42** 50.46 N 2.35 W
Maidstone, Austl. **274b** 37.47 S 144.52 E
Maidstone, On., Can. **214** 42.13 N 82.53 W
Maidstone, Sk., Can. **184** 53.06 N 109.18 W
Maidstone, Eng., U.K. **42** 51.17 N 0.32 E
Maidstone □[8] **260** 51.17 N 0.35 E
Maiduguri **146** 11.51 N 13.10 E
Maie **154** 2.46 N 30.34 E
Maiella, Montagna della ⋏ **66** 42.05 N 14.07 E
Maienfeld **58** 47.00 N 9.32 E
Maierato **68** 38.42 N 16.11 E
Maifeld □[9] **56** 50.20 N 7.20 E
Maigatari **150** 12.46 N 9.27 E
Maignelay **50** 49.33 N 2.31 E
Maigo **116** 8.10 N 123.57 E
Mai Gudo ∧ **144** 7.29 N 37.12 E
Maihar **124** 24.16 N 80.45 E
Maihara **94** 35.19 N 136.17 E
Maijoma **196** 28.55 N 104.21 W
Maikala Plateau ⋏[1] **124** 22.30 N 81.00 E
Maikala Range ⋏ **122** 22.30 N 81.30 E
Maikammer **56** 49.18 N 9.07 E
Maiko ≃ **154** 0.14 N 25.33 E
Maiko, Parc National de la ♦ **154** 3.30 N 27.45 E
Maikoor, Pulau I **164** 6.15 S 134.15 E
Mailand → Milano **62** 45.28 N 9.12 E
Mailāni **124** 28.17 N 80.21 E
Mailasqui **256** 23.33 S 47.04 W
Maili **229c** 21.25 N 158.10 W
Maillane **62** 43.50 N 4.47 E
Mailley-et-Chazelot **58** 47.32 N 6.03 E
Maillezais **32** 46.22 N 0.44 W
Mailly-le-Camp **50** 48.40 N 4.13 E
Mailly-le-Château **50** 47.36 N 3.38 E
Mailly-Maillet **50** 50.04 N 2.36 E
Mailsi **123** 29.48 N 72.11 E
Maimbung **116** 5.56 N 121.02 E
Mai Mefales **144** 14.59 N 38.16 E
Mā'īn **132** 31.41 N 35.44 E
Main ≃, Dtsch. **30** 50.00 N 8.18 E
Main ≃, N. Ire., U.K. **48** 54.43 N 6.18 W
Maināguri **124** 26.34 N 88.49 E
Mainau **58** 47.42 N 9.11 E
Mainburg **60** 48.38 N 11.47 E
Main Camp **174o** 2.01 N 157.25 W
Main Canal ≍, Ca., U.S. **226** 37.25 N 121.05 W
Main Canal ≍, Ca., U.S. **226** 37.23 N 120.26 W
Main Canal ≍, Wa., U.S. **224** 47.07 N 120.44 W
Main Channel ⋓ **190** 45.22 N 81.50 W
Maincourt-sur-Yvette **261** 48.43 N 1.58 E
Main Creek ≃ **276** 40.34 N 74.11 W
Maincy **261** 48.33 N 2.42 E
Mai-Ndombe, Lac ⊜ **152** 2.00 S 18.20 E
Main-Donau-Kanal ≍ **60** 49.02 N 11.36 E
Main Duck Island I **212** 43.56 N 76.37 W
Maine **210** 42.11 N 76.03 W
Maine □[9] **32** 48.15 N 0.05 W
Maine □[3], U.S. **178** 45.15 N 69.15 W
Maine □[3], U.S. **188** 45.15 N 69.15 W
Maine ≃ **48** 52.09 N 9.45 W
Maine, Gulf of c **178** 43.00 N 68.00 W
Mainebene □[9] **56** 50.00 N 8.45 E
Maine-et-Loire □[5] **32** 47.25 N 0.30 W
Mainesburg **210** 41.47 N 77.07 W
Maïné-Soroa **146** 13.12 N 12.02 E
Maineville **218** 39.18 N 84.13 W
Mainguerin **261** 48.32 N 1.51 E
Mainhardt **56** 49.04 N 9.33 E
Mainit **116** 9.32 N 125.32 E
Mainit, Lake ⊜ **116** 9.26 N 125.32 E
Mainland **285** 40.15 N 75.22 W
Mainland I, Scot., U.K. **46** 59.00 N 3.15 W
Mainland I, Scot., U.K. **46a** 60.16 N 1.16 W
Mainleus **54** 50.06 N 11.22 E
Mainoru **164** 14.02 S 134.05 E
Mainpuri **124** 27.14 N 79.01 E
Main Range National Park ♦ **171a** 28.01 S 152.22 E
Maintal **56** 50.09 N 8.54 E
Maintenon **50** 48.35 N 1.35 E
Maintirano **157b** 18.03 S 44.01 E
Main Topsail ∧ **186** 49.08 N 56.33 W
Mainvilliers **50** 48.27 N 1.28 E
Mainz **56** 50.01 N 8.16 E
Maio I **150a** 15.15 N 23.10 W
Maiolati Spontini **66** 43.28 N 13.06 E
Maiori **68** 40.39 N 14.38 E
Maiori, Nuraghe ⊥ **71** 40.56 N 9.06 E
Maipa **164** 8.21 S 146.33 E
Maipo ≃ **252** 33.37 S 71.39 W
Maipo, Volcán ∧[1] **252** 34.10 S 69.50 W
Maipú, Arg. **252** 36.52 S 57.52 W
Maipú, Arg. **252** 32.58 S 68.47 W
Maipú, Chile **252** 33.31 S 70.46 W
Maiqihamiao **89** 43.22 N 120.46 E
Maiquetía **246** 10.36 N 66.57 W
Maira ≃ **62** 44.49 N 7.38 E
Maira, Valle V **62** 44.30 N 7.08 E
Mairābāri **120** 26.28 N 92.26 E
Mairi **250** 11.43 S 40.08 W
Mairinque **256** 23.33 S 47.10 W
Mairiporã **256** 23.19 S 46.35 W
Mairiporã □[7] **287b** 23.24 S 46.37 W
Mairipotaba **255** 17.18 S 49.28 W
Maisach **60** 48.13 N 11.16 E
Maisaka **94** 34.41 N 137.37 E
Maishi **100** 29.11 N 113.58 E
Maišiagala **76** 54.52 N 25.04 E
Maiskhāl Island I **120** 21.36 N 91.56 E
Maison de Pierre, Lac de la ⊜ **206** 46.53 N 74.42 W
Maisonneuve, Parc ♦ **275a** 45.33 N 73.34 W
Maisons-Alfort **261** 48.48 N 2.26 E
Maisons-Laffitte **50** 48.57 N 2.09 E
Maisons-Laffitte, Château de ⊥ **261** 48.57 N 2.09 E
Maisse **50** 48.24 N 2.23 E
Maissin **56** 49.58 N 5.11 E
Maitani **270** 34.49 N 135.22 E
Maitengwe **156** 20.06 S 27.13 E
Maitengwe ≃ **156** 19.59 S 26.26 E
Maithon Reservoir ⊜[1] **126** 23.50 N 86.43 E
Maitland, Austl. **168b** 34.22 S 137.40 E
Maitland, Austl. **170** 32.44 S 151.33 E
Maitland, N.S., Can. **186** 45.19 N 63.30 W
Maitland, On., Can. **212** 44.38 N 75.37 W
Maitland, Fl., U.S. **220** 28.37 N 81.21 W
Maitland ≃ **190** 43.45 N 81.43 W
Maitland, Lake ⊜ **162** 27.11 S 121.03 E
Maixie **100** 27.38 N 115.29 E
Maíz ≃ **236** 11.17 N 83.52 W
Maíz, Islas del II **236** 12.15 N 83.00 W
Maizefield **158** 26.28 S 29.31 E
Maizhokunggar **120** 29.50 N 91.45 E
Maizières-lès-Metz **56** 49.13 N 6.09 E
Maizières-lès-Vic **58** 48.43 N 6.46 E
Maizuru **96** 35.28 N 135.24 E
Maja ≃, Ross. **74** 60.24 N 134.30 E
Maja ≃, Ross. **89** 54.31 N 134.41 E
Majābirah, Minqār al- ≗[4] **142** 30.16 N 29.49 E
Majačka ≃ **83** 48.44 N 37.33 E
Majačnyj **86** 52.41 N 55.44 E
Majadahonda **266a** 40.29 N 3.52 W
Majagua **240p** 21.55 N 79.00 W
Majagual **246** 8.33 N 74.38 W
Majaki, Ukr. **78** 46.25 N 30.16 E
Majaki, Ukr. **83** 48.57 N 37.37 E
Majalaya **115a** 7.03 S 107.45 E
Majalengka **115a** 6.50 S 108.13 E
Majana, Ensenada de c **240p** 22.41 N 82.45 W
Majanji **154** 0.15 N 33.59 E
Majari ≃ **246** 3.29 N 60.58 W
Majayjay **116** 14.09 N 121.28 E
Majchura **85** 39.02 N 68.35 E
Majdantal **85** 43.41 N 68.02 E
Majd el Kurūm **132** 32.55 N 35.15 E
Majé **256** 22.39 S 43.02 W
Majeigha **140** 11.33 N 24.40 E
Majenang **115a** 7.18 S 108.45 E
Majene **112** 3.33 S 118.57 E
Majenica **216** 40.46 N 85.27 W
Majevica ⋏ **38** 44.30 N 18.55 E
Maji **144** 6.11 N 35.38 E
Majia **100** 32.32 N 118.50 E
Majia ≃ **98** 38.09 N 117.53 E
Majiacun **106** 30.08 N 119.58 E
Majiahe **102** 35.20 N 104.46 E
Majian, Zhg. **100** 29.19 N 119.36 E
Majian, Zhg. **100** 29.43 N 120.00 E
Majiang, Zhg. **102** 23.48 N 111.09 E
Majiang, Zhg. **110** 26.28 N 107.28 E
Majiangzong **120** 30.27 N 90.03 E
Majiaoba **102** 32.14 N 104.35 E
Majiaping **102** 36.31 N 103.20 E
Majiasi **105** 39.03 N 117.05 E
Majiawopu **104** 41.46 N 121.06 E
Majiayan **100** 27.26 N 112.56 E
Majiazhai **104** 42.22 N 124.04 E
Majiazhou **100** 26.46 N 114.47 E
Majidun Creek ≃ **273a** 6.38 N 3.28 E
Majie, Zhg. **102** 23.50 N 105.07 E
Majie, Zhg. **102** 25.03 N 103.45 E
Majin **100** 29.18 N 118.24 E
Majin ≃ **100** 29.00 N 118.21 E
Majinzhuangzi **104** 41.55 N 123.53 E
Maji Shan I **106** 31.26 N 120.06 E
Majītha **123** 31.46 N 74.57 E
Majja **74** 61.44 N 130.18 E
Majkain **86** 51.27 N 75.52 E
Majkop **84** 44.35 N 40.07 E
Majkor **86** 59.01 N 55.54 E
Majlibaš **86** 45.49 N 62.39 E
Majli-Saj **85** 41.17 N 72.29 E
Majlispur **126** 24.13 N 90.53 E
Majmak **85** 42.40 N 71.15 E
Majna, Ross. **80** 54.07 N 47.37 E
Majna, Ross. **86** 53.00 N 91.28 E
Majnan **272b** 22.59 N 88.09 E
Majnic, ozero ⊜ **180** 63.15 N 176.40 E
Majno-Gytkino **180** 63.36 N 176.30 E
Majŏn-ni, C.M.I.K. **98** 39.06 N 127.07 E
Majŏn-ni, Taehan **271b** 37.36 N 126.41 E
Major, Puig ∧ **34** 39.48 N 2.48 E
Majorca → Mallorca I **34** 39.30 N 3.00 E
Major Creek ≃ **169** 36.51 S 145.05 E
Major Isidoro **250** 9.32 S 37.00 W
Majorque, Île → Mallorca I **34** 39.30 N 3.00 E
Majrūr **140** 14.01 N 30.27 E
Majrūr, Wādī V **140** 15.44 N 26.26 E
Majsk **86** 57.49 N 77.16 E
Majskij, Ross. **83** 47.43 N 40.03 E
Majskij, Ross. **84** 43.38 N 44.04 E
Majskij, Ross. **89** 52.18 N 129.38 E
Majskij, Ross. **89** 49.00 N 140.10 E
Majskoje, Kaz. **86** 50.55 N 78.15 E
Majskoje, Ross. **82** 56.08 N 37.55 E
Majtan **86** 45.46 N 74.20 E
Majtobe **85** 43.01 N 70.35 E
Māju **126** 22.37 N 88.05 E
Majuba Hill ⊥ **158** 27.28 S 29.51 E
Majuqiao **105** 39.46 N 116.32 E
Majuro I[1] **14** 7.09 N 171.12 E
Majuzigou **104** 41.49 N 121.38 E
Maka **150** 13.40 N 14.17 W
Makabana **152** 2.48 S 12.29 E
Makabe **94** 36.16 N 140.06 E
Makadasa ≃ **116** 7.22 N 124.36 E
Makaha, Hi., U.S. **229c** 21.28 N 158.13 W
Makaha, Zimb. **154** 17.17 S 32.37 E
Makaha Point ≻ **229b** 22.08 N 159.44 W
Makah Indian Reservation ◆[4] **224** 48.20 N 124.41 W
Makahuena Point ≻ **229b** 21.52 N 159.27 W
Makak **152** 3.33 N 11.02 E
Makala **273b** 4.25 S 15.17 E
Makalamabedi **156** 20.19 S 23.51 E
Makale **112** 3.06 S 119.51 E
Makallé **252** 27.13 S 59.17 W
Makālu ∧ **124** 27.54 N 87.06 E
Makamba **154** 4.08 S 29.49 E
Makanapur **272a** 28.38 N 77.21 E
Makanči **86** 46.48 N 82.00 E
Makanya **154** 4.20 S 37.51 E
Makanza **152** 1.36 N 19.07 E
Makaoo Indian Reserve ◆[4] **184** 53.40 N 110.02 W
Makapu Point ≻ **174v** 18.59 S 169.56 W
Makapuu Head ≻ **229c** 21.19 N 157.39 W
Makarakomburu, Mount ∧ **175e** 9.43 S 160.02 E
Makarakskij **86** 55.36 N 88.03 E
Makarapan Mountain ∧ **246** 4.00 N 58.51 W
Makarewa **172** 46.20 S 168.21 E
Makari **146** 12.35 N 14.28 E
Makar-Ib **24** 63.39 N 49.24 E
Makaricha **24** 66.15 N 58.20 E
Makarje **80** 58.35 N 48.11 E
Makarjev **80** 57.52 N 43.48 E
Makarjevo **80** 56.06 N 45.06 E
Makarov, Ross. **89** 48.38 N 142.48 E
Makarov, Ukr. **78** 50.28 N 29.49 E
Makarovo, Ross. **80** 52.18 N 43.20 E
Makarovo, Ross. **82** 54.22 N 36.40 E
Makarovo, Ross. **88** 57.29 N 107.52 E
Makarska **36** 43.18 N 17.02 E
Makasar, Selat (Makassar Strait) ⋓ **112** 2.00 S 117.30 E
Makasar → Ujungpandang **112** 5.07 S 119.24 E
Makaševka **80** 51.30 N 42.36 E
Makassar Strait → Makasar, Selat ⋓ **112** 2.00 S 117.30 E
Makasuko **154** 6.00 S 34.56 E
Makat **80** 47.39 N 53.19 E
Makatea I **14** 15.50 S 148.15 W
Makati **269f** 14.34 N 121.02 E
Makaw, Mya. **110** 26.27 N 96.42 E
Makaw, Zaïre **152** 3.29 S 18.19 E
Makawao **229a** 20.51 N 156.18 W
Makaweli **229b** 21.55 N 159.38 W
Makay, Massif du ⋏ **157b** 21.15 S 45.15 E
Makaya **152** 3.22 S 18.02 E
Makedonija → Macedonia □[1] **38** 41.50 N 22.00 E
Makefu **174v** 18.59 S 169.55 W
Makejevka, Ukr. **78** 50.40 N 31.50 E
Makejevka, Ukr. **83** 48.02 N 37.58 E
Makejevka, Ukr. **83** 49.14 N 37.59 E
Makemie Park **208** 37.55 N 75.34 W
Makemo I[1] **14** 16.35 S 143.40 W
Makena **229a** 20.39 N 156.27 W
Makeni **150** 8.53 N 12.03 W
Makere **154** 4.17 S 30.25 E
Maketu **172** 37.46 S 176.27 E
Makeyevka → Makejevka **83** 48.02 N 37.58 E
Makgadikgadi ≚ **156** 20.45 S 25.30 E
Makgadikgadi Pans Game Reserve ◆[4] **156** 20.30 S 24.45 E
Makhachkala → Machačkala **84** 42.58 N 47.30 E
Makhad **123** 33.08 N 71.44 E
Makhaleng ≃ **158** 30.20 S 27.23 E
Mākhālpur **272b** 22.56 N 88.10 E
Makham **110** 12.40 N 102.12 E
Makhdūmnagar **124** 26.28 N 82.46 E
Makhfar al-Quwayrah **132** 29.48 N 35.19 E
Makhfar Ramn **132** 29.42 N 35.25 E
Makhrūq, Wādī al- V **132** 31.30 N 37.10 E
Makhyah, Wādī V **144** 17.40 N 49.01 E
Maki, Indon. **164** 3.11 S 134.14 E
Maki, Nihon **92** 37.45 N 138.53 E
Maki, Nihon **94** 37.05 N 138.23 E
Maki, Nihon **270** 34.52 N 135.04 E
Makika, Lua ≗[6] **229a** 20.34 N 156.34 W
Makikihi **172** 44.38 S 171.09 E
Makilala **116** 6.55 N 125.05 E
Makindu **154** 2.17 S 37.49 E
Makino, Nihon **94** 35.28 N 136.05 E
M'akino, Ross. **265b** 55.48 N 37.22 E
Makinsk **86** 52.37 N 70.26 E
Makio-dam ◆[6] **94** 35.50 N 137.36 E
Makioka **94** 35.45 N 138.43 E
Makira □[4] **175e** 11.00 S 162.30 E
Makira Harbour c **175e** 10.25 S 161.29 E
M'akiševo **76** 56.34 N 28.53 E
M'akit **74** 61.24 N 152.09 E
Makkah (Mecca) **144** 21.27 N 39.49 E
Makkavejevo **88** 51.44 N 113.58 E
Makkum **52** 53.04 N 5.24 E
Makó, Magy. **30** 46.13 N 20.29 E
Mako, Sén. **150** 12.52 N 12.21 W
Makoaneng ∧ **158** 29.47 S 28.57 E
Makobe Lake ⊜ **190** 47.27 N 80.25 W
Makoka **154** 2.34 S 25.29 E
Makok-ni **271b** 37.43 N 126.38 E
Makokou **152** 0.34 N 12.52 E
Makoli **154** 17.27 S 26.05 E
Makongai Island I **175g** 17.27 S 178.58 E
Makongo **154** 3.25 N 26.22 E
Makongolosi **154** 8.24 S 33.09 E
Makopse **84** 43.59 N 39.13 E
Makorako ∧ **172** 39.09 S 176.02 E
Makoro **154** 3.08 N 29.44 E
Makoshika State Park ♦ **198** 47.03 N 104.41 W
Makošino **78** 51.27 N 32.18 E
Makotuku **172** 40.07 S 176.14 E
Makoua **152** 0.01 N 15.39 E
Makov **30** 49.23 N 18.30 E
Makovskoje **86** 58.12 N 90.52 E
Maków Mazowiecki **30** 52.52 N 21.06 E
Maków Podhalański **30** 49.44 N 19.41 E
Makrai **124** 22.04 N 77.06 E
Makrampur **126** 22.44 N 90.14 E
Makrāna **120** 27.03 N 74.43 E
Makran Coast ≗[2] **128** 25.15 N 61.00 E
M'aksa **76** 58.54 N 38.12 E
Maksaticha **76** 57.48 N 35.53 E
Maksimicha **88** 53.15 N 108.43 E
Maksimkin Jar **86** 58.42 N 86.48 E
Maksimoviči **78** 51.13 N 29.37 E
Maksimovka, Ross. **80** 52.59 N 51.10 E
Maksimovka, Ross. **89** 46.04 N 137.51 E
Maksimovka, Ukr. **83** 47.38 N 37.34 E
Maksimovo **82** 56.20 N 35.58 E
Maksudangarh **124** 24.03 N 77.15 E
Maktar **148** 35.51 N 9.12 E
Maktau **154** 3.24 S 38.08 E
Mākū, Īrān **128** 39.17 N 44.31 E
Maku, Zhg. **105** 39.33 N 114.46 E
Makuhari **268** 35.39 N 140.03 E
Makuliro **154** 9.35 S 37.26 E
Makumbako **154** 8.51 S 34.50 E
Makumbi **152** 5.51 S 20.41 E
Makung (P'enghu) **100** 23.34 N 119.34 E
Makunudu I **122** 6.25 N 72.41 E
Makunudu Atoll I[1] **122** 6.20 N 72.36 E
Makuragi-san ∧ **96** 35.32 N 133.08 E
Makurazaki **92** 31.16 N 130.19 E
Makurdi **150** 7.45 N 8.32 E
Makushin Volcano ∧[1] **180** 53.53 N 166.50 W
Makušino **86** 55.13 N 67.13 E
Makuyuni **154** 3.33 S 36.06 E
Makwa Lake ⊜ **184** 54.04 N 109.15 W
Makwassie **158** 27.26 S 26.00 E
Makwende-Bayo **154** 7.08 S 28.06 E
Makwiro **154** 17.58 S 30.28 E
Māl, India **124** 26.52 N 88.44 E
Mal, Maur. **150** 16.58 N 13.23 W
Mala, Perú **248** 12.39 S 76.38 W
Malå, Sve. **26** 65.11 N 18.44 E
Mala ≃ **248** 12.40 S 76.41 W
Mala, Punta ≻ **246** 7.28 N 80.00 W
Malabang **116** 7.38 N 124.03 E
Malabar, Austl. **274a** 33.58 S 151.15 E
Malabar, Fl., U.S. **220** 28.00 N 80.33 W
Malabar Coast ≗[2] **122** 11.00 N 75.00 E
Malabar Farm State Park ♦ **214** 40.38 N 82.25 W
Malabar Hill ∧[2] **272c** 18.57 N 72.48 E
Malabar Point ≻ **272c** 18.57 N 72.47 E
Malabo **152** 3.45 N 8.47 E
Mal Abrigo **258** 34.09 S 56.57 W
Malabrigo Point ≻ **116** 13.36 N 121.15 E
Malabuyoc **116** 9.39 N 123.19 E
Malaca, Estrecho de → Malacca, Strait of ⋓ **110** 2.30 N 101.20 E
Malacacheta **255** 17.50 S 42.05 W
Malacañang Palace ⚜ **269f** 14.36 N 120.59 E
Malacatepec, Volcán ∧[1] **286a** 19.10 N 99.16 W
Malacca, Strait of ⋓ **110** 2.30 N 101.20 E
Malachovka **82** 55.39 N 38.00 E
Malachovo, Ross. **82** 54.45 N 37.27 E
Malachovo, Ross. **82** 54.22 N 37.31 E
Malachovskij **80** 49.08 N 41.43 E
Malacky **30** 48.27 N 17.00 E
Mālād ◆[8] **272c** 19.11 N 72.51 E
Malad ≃ **200** 41.35 N 112.07 W
Malad City **202** 42.11 N 112.15 W
Malad Creek ≃ **272c** 19.08 N 72.48 E
Malafede ≃ **267a** 41.47 N 12.24 E
Málaga, Col. **246** 6.42 N 72.44 W
Málaga, Esp. **34** 36.43 N 4.25 W
Malaga, Ca., U.S. **226** 36.42 N 119.46 W
Malaga, N.J., U.S. **208** 39.34 N 75.02 W
Malaga, N.M., U.S. **196** 32.13 N 104.04 W
Málaga □[4] **34** 36.50 N 4.40 W
Malagarasi **154** 5.06 S 30.50 E
Malagarasi ≃ **154** 5.12 S 29.47 E
Malagash **186** 45.46 N 63.23 W
Malagasy Republic → Madagascar □[1] **157b** 19.00 S 46.00 E
Malago ≃ **116** 10.55 N 123.02 E
Malagón **34** 39.10 N 3.51 W
Malagón ≃ **34** 37.35 N 7.29 W
Malagrotta ◆[8] **66** 41.53 N 12.20 E
Mal'agurt **80** 57.39 N 52.32 E
Malahat **224** 48.32 N 123.34 W
Malahide **48** 53.27 N 6.09 W
Malaimbandy **157b** 20.20 S 45.36 E
Malaisie → Malaysia □[1] **112** 2.30 N 112.30 E
Malaita □[4] **175e** 9.00 S 161.00 E
Malaita I **175e** 9.00 S 161.00 E
Malaja Beloz'orka **78** 47.14 N 34.56 E
Malaja Bessergenovka **83** 47.09 N 38.36 E
Malaja Borščovka **82** 56.33 N 36.53 E
Malaja Bykovka **80** 51.54 N 47.45 E
Malaja Čuja ≃ **88** 58.56 N 112.13 E
Malaja Devica **78** 50.41 N 32.10 E
Malaja Doroginka **82** 54.06 N 38.56 E
Malaja Dubna **82** 55.52 N 38.58 E
Malaja Istra ≃ **82** 55.54 N 36.50 E
Malaja Ižmora **80** 53.32 N 42.48 E
Malaja Janisol' **83** 47.22 N 37.20 E
Malaja Jekaterinovka **80** 51.26 N 44.17 E
Malaja Kinel' ≃ **80** 53.29 N 51.30 E
Malaja Kokšaga ≃ **80** 56.09 N 47.53 E
Malaja Konkudera ≃ **88** 57.26 N 112.37 E
Malaja Kuril'skaja Gr'ada (Habomai-Shotō) II **92a** 43.30 N 146.10 E
Malaja Laba ≃ **84** 44.16 N 40.53 E
Malaja Neva ≃[1] **265a** 59.57 N 30.15 E
Malaja Ochta ◆[8] **265a** 59.56 N 30.24 E
Malaja Orlovka **80** 47.18 N 41.24 E
Malaja Pera **24** 64.11 N 54.47 E
Malaja Serdoba **80** 52.28 N 44.56 E
Malaja Sestra ≃ **82** 56.17 N 35.57 E
Malaja Tokmačevka **78** 47.32 N 35.54 E
Malaja Višera **76** 58.51 N 32.14 E
Malaja Viska **78** 48.39 N 31.38 E
Malaka, Sempitan ⋓ **114** 5.44 N 95.30 E
Malakāl **140** 9.31 N 31.39 E
Malaka → Melaka **114** 2.12 N 102.15 E
Malākand **123** 34.34 N 71.56 E
Mala Kapela ⋏ **36** 44.50 N 15.30 E
Malakka, Strasse von → Malacca, Strait of ⋓ **110** 2.30 N 101.20 E
Malakoff, Fr. **261** 48.49 N 2.19 E
Malakoff, Tx., U.S. **222** 32.10 N 96.00 W
Malakpur ◆[8] **272a** 28.42 N 77.12 E
Malakula □[8] **175f** 16.20 S 167.20 E
Malakula I **175f** 16.15 S 167.30 E
Malakwāl **123** 32.34 N 73.13 E
Malala **164** 5.15 S 147.10 E
Malalag **116** 6.36 N 125.24 E
Malalbergo **64** 44.43 N 11.32 E
Malamala **112** 3.21 S 120.55 E
Mala Mala Game Reserve ◆[4] **156** 24.52 S 31.30 E
Malamaui Island I **116** 6.44 N 121.58 E
Malambo **246** 10.52 N 74.47 W
Malambo, Arroyo ≃ **258** 33.43 S 58.46 W
Malambunga **116** 9.02 N 117.38 E
Malamocco **64** 45.22 N 12.20 E
Malampaya Sound ⋓ **116** 10.51 N 119.20 E
Malān **110** 25.37 N 96.21 E
Malān, Rās ≻ **128** 25.18 N 65.11 E
Malanao Island I **116** 9.27 N 118.37 E
Malanas ≃ **116** 17.41 N 120.43 E
Mālancha **272b** 22.55 N 88.26 E
Mālancha ≃[1] **126** 21.40 N 89.20 E
Mālandighi **126** 23.33 N 87.24 E
Malandji **152** 5.56 S 22.18 E
Malang **115a** 7.59 S 112.37 E
Malang, Gunung ∧ **115a** 7.02 S 107.01 E
Malangali **154** 8.34 S 34.51 E
Malangas **116** 7.37 N 123.01 E
Malanggwā **124** 26.52 N 85.34 E
Malangka, Tanjung ≻ **112** 1.20 N 120.48 E
Malan Guan)(**105** 40.16 N 117.39 E
Malanipa Island I **116** 6.53 N 122.16 E
Malanje **152** 9.32 S 16.20 E
Malanje □[5] **152** 9.30 S 16.30 E
Malanut Bay c **116** 9.16 N 117.59 E
Malanville **150** 11.52 N 3.23 E
Malanyu **105** 40.11 N 117.42 E
Malanzán **252** 30.48 S 66.37 W
Mała Panew ≃ **30** 50.44 N 17.52 E
Malapantao, Mount ∧ **116** 9.54 N 122.37 E
Malapardis Brook ≃ **276** 40.49 N 74.25 W
Mälaren ⊜ **40** 59.30 N 17.12 E
Malargüe **252** 35.28 S 69.35 W
Mälar-See → Mälaren ⊜ **40** 59.30 N 17.12 E
Malartic **190** 48.08 N 78.08 W
Malartic, Lac ⊜ **190** 48.15 N 78.07 W
Malasia → Malaysia □[1] **112** 2.30 N 112.30 E
Malasiqui **116** 15.55 N 120.25 E
Malaspina **254** 44.56 S 66.54 W
Malaspina Glacier ⊓ **180** 59.50 N 140.30 W
Malaspina Strait ⋓ **182** 49.44 N 124.20 W
Malassis **261** 48.38 N 2.03 E
Malāṭīyah **142** 28.42 N 30.51 E
Malatya **130** 38.21 N 38.19 E
Malatya □[4] **130** 38.30 N 38.10 E
Malau **175f** 15.10 S 166.48 E
Malaucène **62** 44.10 N 5.08 E
Malaunay **50** 49.32 N 1.02 E
Malaut **123** 30.13 N 74.29 E
Malavalli **122** 12.23 N 77.05 E
Malawali, Pulau I **116** 7.03 N 117.18 E
Malawi □[1], Afr. **138** 13.30 S 34.00 E
Malawi □[1], Afr. **154** 13.30 S 34.00 E
Malawi, Lake → Nyasa, Lake ⊜ **154** 12.00 S 34.30 E
Malawiya **140** 15.16 N 36.12 E
Malayagiri ∧ **120** 21.23 N 85.16 E
Malayal **116** 7.12 N 121.57 E
Malaya → Semenanjung Malaysia □[9] **114** 4.00 N 102.00 E
Malaybalay **116** 8.09 N 125.05 E
Malāyer **128** 34.17 N 48.50 E
Malay Peninsula ≻[1] **110** 6.00 N 101.00 E
Malay Reef ✢[2] **166** 17.59 S 149.18 E
Malaysia □[1], Asia **108** 2.30 N 112.30 E
Malaysia □[1], Asia **112** 2.30 N 112.30 E
Malazgirt **130** 39.09 N 42.31 E
Malbaie ≃ **186** 47.39 N 70.09 W
Malbaie, La c **186** 48.35 N 64.14 W
Malbon **166** 21.04 S 140.18 E
Malbooma **162** 30.41 S 134.11 E
Malborghetto Valbruna **64** 46.30 N 13.26 E
Malbork **30** 54.02 N 19.01 E
Malbrán **252** 29.21 S 62.27 W
Malbuisson **58** 46.48 N 6.18 E
Malbun **58** 47.35 N 9.33 E
Malcesine **64** 45.46 N 10.48 E
Mal'cevo **265b** 55.56 N 37.57 E
Mal'čevskaja **78** 49.04 N 40.21 E
Mal'čevsko-Polnenskaja **83** 48.58 N 40.12 E
Malchanskij chrebet ⋏ **88** 50.45 N 109.30 E
Malchin **54** 53.44 N 12.46 E
Malchiner See ⊜ **54** 53.43 N 12.38 E
Malching **60** 48.19 N 13.12 E
Malchow **54** 53.28 N 12.25 E
Malchow ◆[8] **264a** 52.35 N 13.29 E
Malčin **88** 49.44 N 93.18 E
Malcolm **162** 28.56 S 121.30 E
Malcolm, Point ≻ **162** 33.48 S 123.45 E
Malcolm Island I **182** 50.40 N 127.00 W
Malcom **190** 41.42 N 92.33 W
Malcompeth → Mahābaleshwar **122** 17.55 N 73.40 E
Malcontenta **64** 45.25 N 12.13 E
Malczyce **30** 51.14 N 16.29 E
Māldah **124** 25.02 N 88.09 E
Maldegem **50** 51.13 N 3.27 E
Malden, Ma., U.S. **207** 42.25 N 71.04 W
Malden, Mo., U.S. **194** 36.33 N 89.57 W
Malden I **14** 4.03 S 154.59 W
Malden ≃ **283** 42.24 N 71.05 W
Malden Bridge **210** 42.28 N 73.35 W
Malden on Hudson **210** 42.06 N 73.56 W
Maldivas → Maldives □[1] **12** 3.15 N 73.00 E
Maldive Islands → Maldives □[1] **12** 3.15 N 73.00 E
Mal di Ventre, Isola di I **71** 39.59 N 8.18 E
Maldives □[1] **12** 3.15 N 73.00 E
Maldon, Austl. **169** 37.00 S 144.04 E
Maldon, Eng., U.K. **42** 51.45 N 0.40 E
Maldon □[8] **260** 51.43 N 0.40 E
Maldonado **252** 34.54 S 54.57 W
Maldonado, Punta ≻ **234** 16.20 N 98.35 W
Male, It. **64** 46.21 N 10.55 E
Male, Mald. **12** 4.10 N 73.30 E
Male, Mya. **110** 23.02 N 95.58 E
Maléa, Ákra ≻ **38** 36.26 N 23.12 E
Malea, Dolok ∧ **114** 0.56 N 99.38 E
Malebo, Pool ⊜ **152** 4.17 S 15.20 E
Malediven → Maldives □[1] **12** 3.15 N 73.00 E
Mālegaon **122** 20.33 N 74.32 E
Malegno, It. **64** 45.56 N 10.14 E
Malegno, It. **64** 46.40 N 11.08 E
Malehra **124** 24.34 N 79.19 E
Maleit, Lake ⊜ **140** 7.55 N 28.35 E
Malejevka **78** 47.29 N 32.43 E
Malek, Kaz. **85** 40.47 N 68.37 E
Malek, Sūd. **140** 6.04 N 31.36 E
Malé Karpaty ⋏ **30** 48.30 N 17.20 E
Malek Dīn **120** 32.25 N 68.04 E
Malek Kandī **128** 37.09 N 46.06 E
Malek Sīāh, Kūh-e ∧ **128** 29.51 N 60.52 E
Malela, Zaïre **154** 2.28 S 26.09 E
Malela, Zaïre **154** 4.22 S 26.08 E
Malema **154** 14.57 S 37.20 E
Malen'ga **24** 63.50 N 36.25 E
Malengoya **154** 3.32 N 25.25 E
Malente **54** 54.10 N 10.33 E
Maleo **62** 45.10 N 9.46 E
Māler Kotla **124** 30.31 N 75.53 E
Malesco **58** 46.08 N 8.30 E
Malesherbes **50** 48.18 N 2.25 E
Malestroit **32** 47.49 N 2.23 W
Maleta **88** 50.50 N 108.25 E
Maletto **70** 37.49 N 14.52 E
Malfa **70** 38.35 N 14.50 E
Malgas **158** 34.18 S 20.35 E
Malgersdorf **60** 48.32 N 12.45 E
Malgobek **84** 43.32 N 44.34 E
Malgomaj ⊜ **26** 64.47 N 16.12 E
Malha Wells **140** 15.08 N 26.12 E
Malheur ≃ **202** 44.03 N 116.59 W
Malheur, North Fork ≃ **202** 43.45 N 118.04 W
Malheur, South Fork ≃ **202** 43.33 N 118.10 W
Malheureux, Cap ≻ **157c** 19.59 S 57.36 E
Malheur Lake ⊜ **202** 43.20 N 118.45 W
Mali, Guinée **150** 12.05 N 12.18 W
Mali, Zaïre **154** 2.48 S 26.08 E
Mali □[1], Afr. **134** 17.00 N 4.00 W
Mali □[1], Afr. **150** 17.00 N 4.00 W
Mali ≃ **102** 25.43 N 97.29 E
Maliangping **102** 31.29 N 111.20 E
Malianjingzi **102** 41.32 N 95.23 E
Malibamatšo ≃ **158** 29.20 S 29.28 E
Malibu **228** 34.02 N 118.42 W
Malibu Lake ⊜[1] **228** 34.07 N 118.45 W
Malien ≃ **269d** 25.11 N 121.41 E
Malienkang **269d** 25.10 N 121.39 E
Maligay Bay c **116** 7.30 N 123.14 E
Malighati **126** 22.33 N 87.40 E
Maligne ≃ **182** 52.56 N 118.02 W
Maligne Lake ⊜ **182** 52.40 N 117.31 W
Malīhābād **124** 26.55 N 80.43 E
Māliḥah, Wādī V **142** 29.21 N 32.35 E
Malik **112** 0.34 S 123.14 E
Malik, Wādī al- V **140** 18.02 N 30.58 E
Mali Kyun I **110** 13.06 N 98.16 E
Malili **112** 2.38 S 121.06 E
Målilla **26** 57.23 N 15.48 E
Malimba, Monts ⋏ **154** 7.32 S 29.30 E
Malim Nawar **114** 4.21 N 101.07 E
Malimono **116** 9.34 N 125.25 E
Malin, Ire. **48** 55.18 N 7.15 W

Symbols in the index entries represent the broad categories identified in the key at the right. Symbols with superior numbers (⋏[1]) identify subcategories (see complete key on page *I · 1).*

Symbole im Register stellen die rechts im Schlüssel erklärten Kategorien dar. Symbole mit hochgestellten Ziffern (⋏[1]) bezeichnen Unterabteilungen einer Kategorie (vgl. vollständiger Schlüssel auf Seite *I · 1).*

Los símbolos incluídos en el texto del índice representan las grandes categorias identificadas con la clave a la derecha. Los símbolos con numeros en su parte superior (⋏[1]) identifican las subcategorías (véase la clave completa en la página *I · 1).*

Les symboles de l'index représentent les catégories indiquées dans la légende à droite. Les symboles suivis d'un indice (⋏[1]) représentent des sous-catégories (voir légende complète à la page *I · 1).*

Os símbolos incluídos no texto do índice representam as grandes categorias identificadas com a chave à direita. Os símbolos com números em sua parte superior (⋏[1]) identificam as subcategorias (veja-se a chave completa à página *I · 1).*

	English	Deutsch	Español	Français	Português
∧	Mountain	Berg	Montaña	Montagne	Montanha
⋏	Mountains	Gebirge	Montañas	Montagnes	Montanhas
)(	Pass	Paß	Paso	Col	Passo
V	Valley, Canyon	Tal, Cañon	Valle, Cañón	Vallée, Canyon	Vale, Canhão
≚	Plain	Ebene	Llano	Plaine	Planície
≻	Cape	Kap	Cabo	Cap	Cabo
I	Island	Insel	Isla	Île	Ilha
II	Islands	Inseln	Islas	Îles	Ilhas
≗	Other Topographic Features	Andere Topographische Objekte	Otros Elementos Topográficos	Autres données topographiques	Outros acidentes topográficos

ESPAÑOL — Nombre | Página | Lat.°′ | Long.°′ W = Oeste
FRANÇAIS — Nom | Page | Lat.°′ | Long.°′ W = Ouest
PORTUGUÊS — Nome | Página | Lat.°′ | Long.°′ W = Oeste

Malin, Ukr. 78 50.46 N 29.15 E
Malin, Or., U.S. 202 42.00 N 121.24 W
Malinalco ⊥ 234 18.57 N 99.30 W
Malinaltepec 234 17.03 N 98.40 W
Malinau 112 3.35 N 116.38 E
Malin Beg 48 54.40 N 8.48 W
Malindang, Mount ∧ 116 8.13 N 123.38 E
Malindi 154 3.13 S 40.07 E
Malindi Marine National Park ♠ 154 3.15 S 40.10 E
Malines
→ Mechelen 50 51.02 N 4.28 E
Malinga 152 2.25 S 12.14 E
Malingping 115a 6.46 S 106.01 E
Malingsbosjön ⊜ 40 59.55 N 15.27 E
Malin Head › 48 55.23 N 7.24 W
Malinki 82 54.05 N 38.59 E
Malinniki 82 56.17 N 38.24 E
Malino, Indon. 112 5.15 S 119.51 E
Malino, Ross. 82 55.06 N 38.11 E
Malino, Ross. 265b 55.58 N 37.13 E
Malino, Bukit ∧ 112 0.45 N 120.47 E
Malinoa I 174w 21.02 S 175.08 W
Malinovka, Ross. 80 51.47 N 43.26 E
Malinovka, Ross. 86 53.24 N 87.17 E
Malinovka, Ukr. 78 49.47 N 36.43 E
Malinta 216 41.19 N 84.02 W
Malinyi 154 8.56 S 36.08 E
Malipara 272b 22.57 N 88.14 E
Mali Rajinac ∧ 36 44.48 N 15.02 E
Malita 116 6.25 N 125.36 E
Malitbog 116 10.10 N 125.00 E
Maliuchang 107 29.05 N 104.07 E
Maliuping 107 29.55 N 106.23 E
Ma Liu Shui 271d 22.25 N 114.12 E
Malivo 82 55.07 N 39.02 E
Maliwun 110 10.14 N 98.37 E
Malizhen 102 23.10 N 104.35 E
Maljamar 196 32.51 N 103.46 W
Malka, Ross. 74 53.20 N 157.30 E
Malka, Ross. 84 43.47 N 43.21 E
Malka ≃ 84 43.44 N 44.15 E
Malkāpur 120 20.53 N 76.12 E
Malkara 130 40.53 N 26.54 E
Malkerns 158 26.32 S 31.11 E
Malko Târnovo 38 41.59 N 27.32 E
Mallāḥ 132 32.30 N 36.51 E
Mallaig, Ab., Can. 182 54.13 N 111.22 W
Mallaig, Scot., U.K. 46 57.00 N 5.50 W
Mallala 168b 34.26 S 138.30 E
Mallaoua 150 13.02 N 9.36 E
Mallapunyah 164 16.59 S 135.49 E
Mallaranny 48 53.54 N 9.49 W
Mallard Reservoir ⊜[1] 282 38.01 N 122.03 W
Mallawī 142 27.44 N 30.50 E
Mallee Cliffs National Park ♠ 166 34.15 S 142.40 E
Mallemort 62 43.44 N 5.11 E
Mallersdorf 60 48.47 N 12.16 E
Mallery Lake ⊜ 176 63.55 N 98.25 W
Malles Venosta (Mals) 64 46.41 N 10.32 E
Mallet 252 25.55 S 50.50 W
Mallig 116 17.08 N 121.41 E
Malligasta 252 29.11 S 67.26 W
Mallina 162 20.53 S 118.02 E
Malling 41 56.02 N 10.10 E
Mallnitz 64 46.59 N 13.10 E
Mallorca I 34 39.30 N 3.00 E
Mallorytown 212 44.29 N 75.53 W
Mallow 48 52.08 N 8.39 W
Mallwood 216 42.51 N 89.02 W
Malm 26 64.04 N 11.13 E
Malmbäck 26 57.35 N 14.28 E
Malmberget 24 67.10 N 20.40 E
Malmédy 56 50.25 N 6.02 E
Malmesbury, S. Afr. 158 33.28 S 18.44 E
Malmesbury, Eng., U.K. 42 51.36 N 2.06 W
Malmesbury, Vale of V 42 51.22 N 2.10 W
Malmköping 40 59.08 N 16.44 E
Malmlången ⊜ 40 59.27 N 14.42 E
Malmö 41 55.36 N 13.00 E
Malmöhus Län □[6] 26 55.45 N 13.30 E
Malmsbury 169 37.12 S 144.23 E
Malmsbury Reservoir ⊜[1] 169 37.13 S 144.22 E
Malmslätt 26 58.25 N 15.30 E
Malmstrom Air Force Base ■ 202 47.30 N 111.10 W
Malmyž 80 56.31 N 50.41 E
Malna 116 8.08 N 124.27 E
Malnate 62 45.48 N 8.53 E
Malnoue 261 48.50 N 2.36 E
Malo 64 45.39 N 11.24 E
Malo I 175f 15.40 S 167.11 E
Malo, Arroyo ≃ 258 33.43 S 58.52 W
Maloarchangel'sk 76 52.24 N 36.30 E
Maloarchangel'skoje 88 50.24 N 108.50 E
Maloba 154 6.18 S 27.39 E
Malodel'skaja 80 50.11 N 43.53 E
Maloduša 78 52.09 N 30.14 E
Maloelap I[1] 14 8.45 N 171.03 E
Malo-Iljinovka -◆-[8] 83 48.38 N 37.59 E
Maloja 58 46.24 N 9.41 E
Malojapass)(58 46.24 N 9.41 E
Malojaroslavec 82 55.01 N 36.28 E
Malojaz 86 55.13 N 58.09 E
Maloje Goloustnoje 88 52.18 N 105.18 E
Malojekaterinovka 78 47.39 N 35.16 E
Maloje Kozino 80 56.26 N 43.41 E
Maloje Polesje -◆-[1] 78 50.10 N 25.00 E
Maloje-Ščerbedino 80 51.59 N 42.50 E
Maloje Skuratovo 76 53.33 N 37.00 E
Malokirsanovka 83 47.28 N 38.31 E
Malokrasnojarka 86 56.28 N 76.01 E
Malo-les-Bains 50 51.03 N 2.24 E
Malolo 154 7.18 S 36.35 E
Malolos, Guam 174p 13.18 N 144.46 E
Malolos, Pil. 116 14.51 N 120.49 E
Malom 164 3.10 S 151.50 E
Maloma 158 27.00 S 31.40 E
Malombe, Lake ⊜ 154 14.38 S 35.12 E
Malomichajlovka 78 48.06 N 36.23 E
Malonabatovskij 80 48.57 N 43.40 E
Malone, Fl., U.S. 192 30.57 N 85.09 W
Malone, N.Y., U.S. 188 44.50 N 74.17 W
Malone, Tx., U.S. 222 31.55 N 96.54 W
Malone, Wa., U.S. 224 46.58 N 123.20 W
Malonga 152 10.24 S 23.10 E
Malonno 64 46.07 N 10.18 E
Malonty 61 48.41 N 14.35 E
Małopolska -◆-[1] 30 50.10 N 21.30 E
Malor'azancevo 83 48.53 N 38.23 E
Malorita 78 51.47 N 24.05 E
Malorossijskij 86 53.12 N 62.30 E
Malošujka 24 63.45 N 37.22 E
Malott 182 48.16 N 119.42 W
Måløv 41 55.45 N 12.20 E
Małowice 30 51.34 N 15.27 E
Måløy 26 61.56 N 5.07 E
Malozemel'skaja Tundra -◆-[1] 24 67.50 N 51.00 E
Malpaisillo 236 12.35 N 86.41 W
Malpartida de Plasencia 34 39.59 N 6.02 W
Malpas, Austl. 166 34.43 S 140.37 E
Malpas, Eng., U.K. 44 53.01 N 2.46 W
Malpaso 234 22.37 N 102.46 W
Malpe 122 13.21 N 74.43 E
Malpelo, Isla de I 242 3.59 N 81.35 W
Malpensa, Aeroporto della ⊠ 62 45.38 N 8.44 E
Malpeque Bay ⊂ 186 46.30 N 63.47 W
Malprabha ≃ 122 16.12 N 76.03 E
Mālpura 120 26.17 N 75.23 E
Mälsåker slott ⊥ 40 59.23 N 17.18 E
Malsch 56 48.53 N 8.19 E
Malše (Maltsch) ≃ 61 48.58 N 14.28 E
Målselva ≃ 24 69.14 N 18.30 E
Mals
→ Malles Venosta 64 46.41 N 10.32 E
Malta, Bra. 250 6.54 S 37.31 W
Malta, Lat. 76 56.21 N 27.10 E
Malta, Öst. 64 46.57 N 13.30 E
Malta, Il., U.S. 216 41.56 N 88.52 W
Malta, Mt., U.S. 202 48.21 N 107.52 W
Malta, Oh., U.S. 188 39.38 N 81.51 W
Malta □[1], Europe 22 35.50 N 14.35 E
Malta □[1], Europe 36 35.50 N 14.35 E
Malta I 36 35.53 N 14.27 E
Malta ≃ 76 56.44 N 26.53 E
Malta Channel ʊ 36 36.20 N 15.00 E
Maltahöhe 156 24.50 S 17.00 E
Maltahöhe □[5] 156 25.00 S 16.30 E
Malta-Tal V 64 47.03 N 13.24 E
Maltby 44 53.26 N 1.11 W
Malte Brun ∧ 172 43.34 S 170.18 E
Malte
→ Malta □[1] 36 35.50 N 14.35 E
Maltepe -◆-[8] 267b 40.55 N 29.08 E
Malton 44 54.08 N 0.48 W
Malton -◆-[8] 275b 43.42 N 79.38 W
Maltrata 234 18.48 N 97.16 W
Maltsch (Malše) ≃ 61 48.58 N 14.28 E
Malugou 89 43.39 N 128.27 E
Maluku □[4] 164 5.00 S 130.00 E
Maluku (Moluccas) II 108 2.00 S 128.00 E
Maluku, Laut (Molucca Sea) ⊤[2] 108 0.00 125.00 E
Maluku-Maes 152 4.06 S 15.31 E
Ma'lūlā 130 33.50 N 36.33 E
Ma'lūlā, Jabal ∧ 132 33.54 N 36.36 E
Malu Mare 38 44.15 N 23.51 E
Malumfashi 150 11.47 N 7.37 E
Malunda 112 3.00 S 118.50 E
Malung 26 60.40 N 13.44 E
Maluso 116 6.33 N 121.53 E
Malūṭ 140 10.26 N 32.12 E
Maluti 126 24.09 N 87.41 E
Maluwe 150 8.40 N 2.17 W
Maluzhen 106 31.20 N 121.16 E
Malvaglia 58 46.25 N 8.59 E
Malvaglio 266b 45.31 N 8.47 E
Malvagna 70 37.55 N 15.04 E
Mālvan 122 16.04 N 73.28 E
Malveira 266c 38.45 N 9.27 W
Malvern, Austl. 274b 37.52 S 145.02 E
Malvern, Ar., U.S. 194 34.21 N 92.48 W
Malvern, Ia., U.S. 198 41.00 N 95.35 W
Malvern, Oh., U.S. 214 40.41 N 81.10 W
Malvern, Pa., U.S. 285 40.02 N 75.31 W
Malvern -◆-[8] 273d 26.12 S 28.06 E
Malverne 276 40.40 N 73.40 W
Malvern Hills ⋏[2] 42 52.05 N 2.21 W
Malvérnia 156 22.06 S 31.42 E
Malvern Link 42 52.08 N 2.18 W
Malvinas 252 29.37 S 58.59 W
Malvinas, Islas
→ Falkland Islands □[2] 254 51.45 S 59.00 W
Malvito 68 39.36 N 16.03 E
Malwal 140 9.19 N 31.35 E
Mālwa Plateau ⋏[1] 124 23.50 N 77.30 E
Malybaj 85 43.30 N 78.25 E
Malý Dunaj ≃ 30 47.45 N 18.09 E
Malyi Nesvetaj ≃ 83 47.32 N 39.49 E
Malyj, ostrov I 76 60.02 N 28.02 E
Malyj An'uj ≃ 74 68.30 N 160.49 E
Malyj Čeremšan ≃ 80 54.18 N 50.01 E
Malyj Chamar-Daban, chrebet ⋏ 88 51.00 N 105.00 E
Malyj Civil' ≃ 80 55.54 N 47.28 E
Malyje Alabuchi 80 51.33 N 42.10 E
Malyje Čany, ozero ⊜ 86 54.33 N 78.02 E
Malyje Gorod'atiči 76 52.33 N 28.20 E
Malyje Jagury 80 45.26 N 43.01 E
Malyje Kamkaly 86 44.44 N 71.31 E
Malyje Karmakuly 72 72.23 N 52.44 E
Malyje Porogi 265a 59.47 N 30.42 E
Malyj Irgiz ≃ 80 52.12 N 47.58 E
Malyj Jenisej (Ka-Chem) ≃ 88 51.43 N 94.26 E
Malyj Jugan ≃ 86 60.40 N 73.54 E
Malyj Kavkaz ⋏ 84 41.00 N 44.35 E
Malyj Kundyš ≃ 80 56.22 N 47.53 E
Malyj Šantar, ostrov I 89 54.30 N 137.36 E
Malyj Sarybulak 86 52.10 N 72.35 E
Malyj Tajmyr, ostrov I 74 78.08 N 107.12 E
Malyj T'uters, ostrov I 76 59.49 N 26.56 E
Malyj Uran ≃ 80 52.30 N 53.01 E
Malyj Uzen' ≃ 80 48.50 N 49.39 E
Malyj Zelenčuk ≃ 84 44.24 N 41.56 E
Malyn' 82 54.36 N 38.40 E
Malyševo 76 57.50 N 35.36 E
Malzéville 58 48.43 N 6.12 E
Mama 88 58.18 N 112.54 E
Mama ≃ 88 58.18 N 112.55 E
Ma Ma Creek ≃ 171a 27.35 S 152.13 E
Mamadyš 80 55.44 N 51.25 E
Mamagota 175e 6.46 S 155.24 E
Mamahuolang 104 42.24 N 124.12 E
Mamajiecun 104 41.26 N 122.51 E
Mamakan 88 57.48 N 114.01 E
Mamaku 172 38.06 S 176.05 E
Mamakwash Lake ⊜ 184 51.38 N 92.56 W
Mamala Bay ⊂ 229a 21.18 N 157.57 W
Mamalu Bay ⊂ 229a 20.37 N 156.09 W
Mamanguape 250 6.50 S 35.07 W
Mama'o, Hakau -✦-[2] 174w 21.00 S 175.12 W
Mamara 248 14.14 S 72.35 W
Mamaroneck 210 40.56 N 73.43 W
Mamaroneck ≃ 276 40.57 N 73.44 W
Mamaroneck Harbor ⊂ 276 40.56 N 73.43 W
Mamasa 112 2.56 S 119.22 E
Mamasa ≃ 112 3.30 S 119.42 E
Mamba 94 36.07 N 138.55 E
Mambaí 255 14.28 S 46.07 W
Mambajao 116 9.15 N 124.43 E
Mambajao, Mount ∧ 116 9.10 N 124.44 E
Mambali 154 4.33 S 32.41 E
Mambalot 116 8.51 N 117.55 E
Mambare ≃ 164 8.20 S 147.55 E
Mambasa 154 1.21 N 29.03 E
Mamberamo ≃ 164 1.26 S 137.53 E
Mambéré ≃ 152 3.31 N 16.03 E
Mambili ≃ 152 0.07 N 16.08 E
Mambrui 154 3.07 S 40.09 E
Mambucaba 256 23.01 S 44.31 W
Mambucaba ≃ 256 23.02 S 44.32 W
Mamburao 116 13.14 N 120.35 E
Mambusao ≃ 116 11.24 N 122.41 E
Mamdūh, Rujm ∧ 132 32.14 N 36.15 E
Mamedkala 84 42.10 N 48.06 E
Mamehaktebo 112 0.08 N 115.32 E
Mamelodi 158 25.45 S 28.18 E
Ma-Me-O Beach 182 52.58 N 113.59 W
Mamera 286c 10.27 N 66.59 W
Mamera, Quebrada ≃ 286c 10.27 N 66.59 W
Mamers 50 48.21 N 0.23 E
Mamfe 152 5.46 N 9.17 E
Mamiá ≃ 250 1.55 S 55.07 W
Mamiá, Lago ⊜ 246 4.15 S 63.03 W
Mamiao 98 35.04 N 116.10 E
Mamie 192 36.07 N 75.50 W
Mamiña 248 20.05 S 69.14 W
Maminigui 150 7.24 N 5.50 W
Mamirolle 58 47.12 N 6.10 E
Mamisonskij, pereval)(84 42.43 N 43.48 E
Maml'utka 86 54.57 N 68.35 E
Mammendorf 60 48.12 N 11.09 E
Mammola 68 38.22 N 16.15 E
Mammoth, Az., U.S. 200 32.43 N 110.38 W
Mammoth, W.V., U.S. 188 38.15 N 81.22 W
Mammoth Cave National Park ♠ 194 37.08 N 86.13 W
Mammoth Lakes 204 37.38 N 118.58 W
Mammoth Pool Reservoir ⊜[1] 226 37.20 N 119.20 W
Mammoth Spring 194 36.29 N 91.32 W
Mamoiada 71 40.13 N 9.17 E
Mamonovo, Ross. 76 54.28 N 19.57 E
Mamonovo, Ross. 265b 55.36 N 37.49 E
Mamonovo, Ross. 265b 55.41 N 37.19 E
Mamont 279b 40.29 N 79.36 W
Mamontovo, Ross. 86 52.43 N 81.37 E
Mamontovo, Ross. 86 51.45 N 81.25 E
Mamoré ≃ 248 10.23 S 65.23 W
Mamori, Lago ⊜ 246 3.38 S 60.07 W
Mamoriá ≃ 248 7.30 S 66.21 W
Mamou, Guinée 150 10.23 N 12.05 W
Mamou, La., U.S. 194 30.38 N 92.25 W
Mamoutzou 157a 12.47 S 45.14 E
Mampikony 157b 16.06 S 47.38 E
Mampong 150 7.04 N 1.24 W
Mamraš 84 41.44 N 48.19 E
Mamre 158 33.30 S 18.29 E
Mamry, Jezioro ⊜ 30 54.08 N 21.42 E
Mamuchi 98 35.41 N 118.17 E
Mamué 152 13.35 S 13.13 E
Mamuil, Paso de)(254 39.35 S 71.28 W
Mamuju 112 2.41 S 118.54 E
Mamulique 196 26.08 N 100.20 W
Ma'mūn 140 12.15 N 22.41 E
Mamuno 156 22.16 S 20.01 E
Mamuripi (Manuripe) ≃ 248 11.06 S 67.36 W
Mamuru ≃ 250 2.42 S 56.44 W
Mamykovo 80 54.38 N 50.37 E
Mamyl' 24 61.57 N 56.41 E
Man, C. Iv. 150 7.24 N 7.33 W
Man, India 120 33.51 N 78.32 E
Man, W.V., U.S. 192 37.44 N 81.52 W
Man (Île de)
→ Isle of Man □[2] 44 54.15 N 4.30 W
Man, Isle of
→ Isle of Man □[2] 44 54.15 N 4.30 W
Mana, Guy. fr. 250 5.40 N 53.47 W
Mana, Hi., U.S. 229b 22.02 N 159.46 W
Mana ≃, Guy. fr. 250 5.44 N 53.54 W
Mana ≃, Ross. 86 55.57 N 92.28 E
Manabí □[4] 246 0.40 S 80.05 W
Manacacías ≃ 246 4.23 N 72.04 W
Manacapuru 246 3.18 S 60.37 W
Manacapuru ≃ 246 3.18 S 60.38 W
Manacle Point › 42 50.03 N 5.03 W
Manacor 34 39.34 N 3.12 E
Manado 112 1.29 N 124.51 E
Managua 236 12.09 N 86.17 W
Managua □[5] 236 12.00 N 86.25 W
Managua, Aeropuerto ⊠ 286b 23.00 N 82.17 W
Managua, Lago de ⊜ 236 12.20 N 86.20 W
Manahawkin 208 39.41 N 74.15 W
Manahawkin Bay ⊂ 208 39.40 N 74.12 W
Manaia 172 39.33 S 174.08 E
Manā'if, Bi'r al- ⊤[4] 142 30.31 N 32.12 E
Manajenki 76 53.42 N 36.27 E
Manakalampona ∧ 157b 15.23 S 48.50 E
Manakara 157b 22.08 S 48.01 E
Manakau 172 40.43 S 175.13 E
Manakau ∧ 172 42.14 S 173.37 E
Manākhah 144 15.07 N 43.44 E
Manalapan Brook ≃ 276 40.24 N 74.23 W
Manāli 123 32.15 N 77.10 E
Manama
→ Al-Manāmah 128 26.13 N 50.35 E
Manambaho ≃ 157b 17.41 S 44.04 E
Manambato, Madag. 157b 13.14 S 49.54 E
Manambato, Madag. 157b 13.43 S 49.07 E
Manambolo ≃ 157b 19.18 S 44.24 E
Manambolosy 157b 16.02 S 49.40 E
Manam Island I 164 4.05 S 145.05 E
Mánamo, Caño ≃[1] 246 9.55 N 62.16 W
Manamoc Island I 116 11.19 N 120.41 E
Manana Island I 229c 21.20 N 157.40 W
Mananantanana ≃ 157b 21.25 S 45.33 E
Mananao 116 13.30 N 120.34 E
Mananara 157b 16.10 S 49.46 E
Mananara ≃ 157b 23.21 S 47.42 E
Manandaza 157b 19.19 S 45.23 E
Mananjary 157b 21.13 S 48.20 E
Manankoro 150 10.28 N 7.27 W
Manantenina 157b 24.17 S 47.19 E
Manantiales Behr 254 45.41 S 67.31 W
Manaoag 116 16.03 N 120.29 E
Manáos
→ Manaus 246 3.08 S 60.01 W
Manapatrana 157b 21.40 S 47.35 E
Manapiare ≃ 246 5.04 N 66.30 W
Manapire ≃ 246 7.42 N 66.07 W
Manapla 116 10.58 N 123.07 E
Mana Point › 229b 22.03 N 159.47 W
Mana Pools National Park ♠ 154 16.00 S 28.35 E
Manapouri 172 45.34 S 167.36 E
Manapouri, Lake ⊜ 172 45.30 S 167.30 E
Manappārai 122 10.36 N 78.25 E
Manaquiri, Lago ⊜ 246 3.29 S 60.31 W
Manār ≃ 122 18.39 N 77.44 E
Manaravolo 157b 23.59 S 45.39 E
Manas, Som. 144 2.57 N 43.28 E
Manas, Zhg. 86 44.18 N 86.13 E
Manās ≃, Asia 120 26.13 N 90.38 E
Manas ≃, Zhg. 86 45.38 N 85.12 E
Manas, gora ∧ 85 42.18 N 71.01 E
Manasarowar Lake
→ Mapam Yumco ⊜ 120 30.42 N 81.27 E
Manas Hu ⊜ 86 45.45 N 85.55 E
Manāslu ∧ 124 28.33 N 84.33 E
Manasota Key I 220 26.58 N 82.23 W
Manasquan 208 40.07 N 74.02 W
Manasquan ≃ 208 40.06 N 74.02 W
Manassa 200 37.10 N 105.56 W
Manassas 208 38.45 N 77.28 W
Manassas National Battlefield Park ♠ 208 38.50 N 77.32 W
Manassas Park 208 38.46 N 77.27 W
Manastash Creek ≃ 224 46.59 N 120.35 W
Manastash Creek, North Fork ≃ 224 46.57 N 120.44 W
Manastash Creek, South Fork ≃ 224 46.57 N 120.44 W
Manastash Ridge ∧ 224 46.55 N 120.30 W
Manatang 112 8.26 S 124.28 E
Manatawny 208 40.17 N 75.41 W
Manatawny Creek ≃ 208 40.14 N 75.39 W
Manatee □[6] 220 27.26 N 82.25 W
Manatee ≃ 220 27.32 N 82.38 W
Manatee, Lake ⊜[1] 220 27.29 N 82.20 W
Manatí, Col. 246 10.27 N 74.58 W
Manatí, Cuba 240p 21.19 N 76.56 W
Manatí, P.R. 240m 18.26 N 66.29 W
Manatí ≃ 240p 21.40 N 79.50 W
Manatí, Bahía de ⊂ 240p 21.24 N 76.48 W
Manatuto 112 8.30 S 126.01 E
Manaul 116 12.27 N 121.25 E
Manaung 110 18.51 N 93.44 E
Manaus 246 3.08 S 60.01 W
Manavgat 130 36.47 N 31.26 E
Manawa 190 44.27 N 88.55 W
Mānāwāla 123 31.35 N 73.41 E
Manawan Lake ⊜ 184 55.24 N 103.14 W
Manāwar 120 22.14 N 75.05 E
Manawatu ≃ 172 40.28 S 175.13 E
Manawoka, Pulau I 164 4.05 S 131.20 E
Manay 116 7.13 N 126.32 E
Manayunk -◆-[8] 285 40.01 N 75.13 W
Manazuru 94 35.09 N 139.08 E
Manazuru-misaki › 94 35.08 N 139.10 E
Manban 102 23.04 N 103.11 E
Mānbāzār 126 23.04 N 86.39 E
Manbian 102 24.19 N 100.32 E
Manbij 130 36.31 N 37.57 E
Manby 44 53.22 N 0.06 E
Mancelona 190 44.54 N 85.03 W
Mancha Blanca 254 40.47 S 65.27 W
Mancha Real 34 37.47 N 3.37 W
Manchaug 207 42.05 N 71.44 W
Manche □[5] 32 49.00 N 1.10 W
Mancheng 105 38.56 N 115.20 E
Mancherāl 122 18.52 N 79.26 E
Manchester, Eng., U.K. 44 53.28 N 2.15 W
Manchester, Eng., U.K. 262 53.28 N 2.15 W
Manchester, Ct., U.S. 207 41.46 N 72.31 W
Manchester, Ga., U.S. 192 32.51 N 84.37 W
Manchester, Il., U.S. 219 39.33 N 90.20 W
Manchester, Ia., U.S. 190 42.29 N 91.27 W
Manchester, Ky., U.S. 192 37.09 N 83.45 W
Manchester, Md., U.S. 208 39.39 N 76.53 W
Manchester, Ma., U.S. 207 42.34 N 70.46 W
Manchester, Mi., U.S. 216 42.09 N 84.02 W
Manchester, N.H., U.S. 188 42.59 N 71.27 W
Manchester, N.Y., U.S. 210 42.58 N 77.13 W
Manchester, Oh., U.S. 218 38.41 N 83.36 W
Manchester, Pa., U.S. 208 40.03 N 76.43 W
Manchester, Tn., U.S. 194 35.28 N 86.05 W
Manchester, Vt., U.S. 210 43.09 N 73.04 W
Manchester, Wa., U.S. 224 47.33 N 122.33 W
Manchester □[8] 262 53.27 N 2.13 W
Manchester Airport ⊠ 44 53.21 N 2.15 W
Manchester Bridge 210 41.41 N 73.52 W
Manchester City Football Ground ♠ 262 53.27 N 2.14 W
Manchester Docks -◆-[5] 262 53.28 N 2.17 W
Manchester Race Course ♠ 262 53.30 N 2.16 W
Manchester Ship Canal ≊ 262 53.19 N 2.57 W
Manchester United Football Ground ♠ 262 53.28 N 2.18 W
Manching 60 48.43 N 11.30 E
Manchioneal 241q 18.02 N 76.17 W
Manchón 236 14.23 N 92.02 W
Manchouli
→ Manzhouli 88 49.35 N 117.22 E
Manchuria □[9] 90 47.00 N 125.00 E
Manciano 66 42.35 N 11.31 E
Mancieulles 56 49.17 N 5.53 E
Máncora 246 4.06 S 81.05 W
Mancos 200 37.20 N 108.17 W
Mancos ≃ 200 36.59 N 108.59 W
Mand 128 26.07 N 62.03 E
Mānd ≃, India 120 21.42 N 83.15 E
Mand ≃, Īrān 128 28.11 N 51.17 E
Manda, India 126 22.06 N 86.14 E
Manda, Tan. 154 7.58 S 32.26 E
Manda, Tan. 154 8.30 S 32.44 E
Manda, Tan. 154 10.28 S 34.35 E
Manda, Tchad 146 9.12 N 18.10 E
Manda, Jabal ∧ 140 8.39 N 24.27 E
Mandabe, Madag. 157b 21.03 S 44.55 E
Mandabe, Madag. 157b 20.55 S 45.49 E
Mandach 102 44.28 N 108.11 E
Mandaguari 255 23.32 S 51.42 W
Mandai Orchard Gardens ♠ 271c 1.24 N 103.47 E
Manda Island I 154 2.15 S 40.57 E
Mandal 26 58.02 N 7.27 E
Mandal, Jibāl ∧[2] 140 12.09 N 29.31 E
Mandala, Puncak ∧ 164 4.44 S 140.20 E
Mandalay 110 22.00 N 96.05 E
Mandalay □[5] 110 21.00 N 96.00 E
Mandale 216 41.01 N 84.20 W
Mandale Station -◆-[5] 272c 19.03 N 72.56 E
Mandalgov' 102 45.45 N 106.12 E
Mandalī 128 33.45 N 45.32 E
Mandalkia 272b 22.43 N 88.08 E
Mandal-Ovoo 102 44.35 N 104.05 E
Mandalselva ≃ 26 58.02 N 7.28 E
Mandaluyong 269f 14.35 N 121.02 E
Mandan 198 46.49 N 100.53 W
Mandanici 70 38.00 N 15.19 E
Mandāoli -◆-[8] 272a 28.38 N 77.18 E
Mandaon 116 12.14 N 123.17 E
Mandapur 126 23.00 N 88.29 E
Mandar, Teluk ⊂ 112 3.40 S 119.15 E
Mandara Mountains (Monts Mandara) ⋏ 146 10.45 N 13.40 E
Mandas 71 39.38 N 9.07 E
Mandatoriccio 68 39.28 N 16.50 E
Mandau ≃ 114 0.48 N 101.47 E
Mandaue 116 10.20 N 123.56 E
Mandāwar 124 29.30 N 78.08 E
Mandeb, Bab el ʊ 144 12.40 N 43.20 E
Mandehu 104 42.07 N 121.33 E
Mandel 128 33.17 N 61.52 E
Mandélia 146 11.43 N 15.15 E
Mandelieu 62 43.33 N 6.56 E
Mandello del Lario 58 45.54 N 9.19 E
Mandera 154 3.56 N 41.52 E
Manderfeld 56 50.20 N 6.20 E
Manderscheid 56 50.05 N 6.49 E
Manderson 202 44.16 N 107.57 W
Mandeure 58 47.27 N 6.48 E
Mandeville, P.Q., Can. 206 46.22 N 73.22 W
Mandeville, Jam. 241q 18.02 N 77.30 W
Mandeville, N.Z. 172 46.00 S 168.49 E
Mandeville, La., U.S. 194 30.21 N 90.03 W
Mandi 123 31.43 N 76.55 E
Mandiana 150 10.38 N 8.41 W
Mandiangin 112 2.01 S 102.58 E
Mandi Angin, Gunong ∧ 114 4.42 N 102.52 E
Mandi Bahāuddīn 123 32.35 N 73.30 E
Mandi Būrewāla 123 30.09 N 72.41 E
Mandi Dabwāli 123 29.58 N 74.42 E
Mandié 154 16.30 S 33.30 E
Mandimba 154 14.21 S 35.39 E
Mandini 158 29.09 S 31.25 E
Mandioli, Pulau I 108 0.44 S 127.14 E
Mandioré, Lagoa ⊜ 248 18.08 S 57.33 W
Mandira ⊜[1] 124 22.20 N 84.35 E
Mandiri ≃ 115a 7.02 S 106.32 E
Mandi Sādiqganj 123 30.10 N 73.44 E
Mandjafa 146 11.11 N 15.25 E
Mandjé, Lac ⊜ 152 2.50 S 10.22 E
Mandji 152 1.36 S 10.26 E
Mandla 124 22.36 N 80.23 E
Mandora 162 19.44 S 120.51 E
Mandoto 157b 19.34 S 46.17 E
Mandoul ≃ 146 8.56 N 17.58 E
Mandouri 150 10.51 N 0.49 E
Mándra, Ellás 267c 38.04 N 23.30 E
Māndrā, India 272b 22.55 N 88.07 E
Mandra, Pāk. 123 33.22 N 73.14 E
Mandrare ≃ 157b 25.10 S 46.27 E
Mandres-les-Roses 261 48.42 N 2.33 E
Mandriola -◆-[8] 267a 41.45 N 12.30 E
Mandriole 64 44.33 N 12.14 E
Mandrioli, Passo dei)(64 43.48 N 11.55 E
Mandritsara 157b 15.50 S 48.49 E
Mandronarivo 157b 21.07 S 45.38 E
Mandsaur 120 24.04 N 75.04 E
Māndu 122 22.22 N 75.23 E
Mandu, Ribeirão do ≃ 256 22.14 S 45.55 W
Manduba, Ponta › 256 24.05 S 46.18 W
Manduhu 104 41.36 N 122.38 E
Mandun 102 22.17 N 100.05 E
Mandurah 168a 32.32 S 115.43 E
Manduria 68 40.24 N 17.38 E
Māndvi, India 120 21.15 N 73.18 E
Māndvi, India 120 22.50 N 69.22 E
Mandvi -◆-[8] 272c 18.57 N 72.50 E
Mandya 122 12.33 N 76.54 E
Mané 150 12.59 N 1.21 W
Måne ≃ 26 59.00 N 9.40 E
Manea 42 52.30 N 0.11 E
Manebach 54 50.41 N 10.51 E
Manek Urai 114 5.23 N 102.14 E
Manendragarh 124 23.13 N 82.13 E
Manera 157b 22.55 S 44.20 E
Manerbio 64 45.21 N 10.08 E
Manětin 60 49.59 N 13.14 E
Manevīči 78 51.17 N 25.33 E
Manfalūṭ 142 27.19 N 30.58 E
Manfredonia 68 41.38 N 15.55 E
Manfredonia, Golfo di ⊂ 68 41.35 N 16.05 E
Manga, Bra. 255 14.46 S 43.56 W
Manga, Burkina 150 11.40 N 1.04 W
Manga, Ur. 258 34.49 S 56.06 W
Manga -◆-[1] 146 15.00 N 14.00 E
Mangabeiras, Chapada das ⋏[2] 250 10.00 S 46.30 W
Mangagoy 116 8.11 N 126.21 E
Mangahao ≃ 172 40.23 S 175.50 E
Mangai 164 2.45 S 151.05 E
Mangaia I 14 21.55 S 157.55 W
Mangakino 172 38.22 S 175.47 E
Mangala 152 1.02 N 23.50 E
Mangalagiri 122 16.26 N 80.33 E
Mangaldai 120 26.26 N 92.02 E
Mangaldan 116 16.04 N 120.24 E
Mangalia 38 43.50 N 28.35 E
Mangalkot 126 23.33 N 87.54 E
Mangalmé 146 12.21 N 19.37 E
Mangalore 122 12.52 N 74.53 E
Mangalpaita 126 23.19 N 89.11 E
Mangalvedha 122 17.31 N 75.28 E
Mangamahu 172 39.49 S 175.22 E
Manganês ≃ 250 10.21 S 48.27 W
Manganji 268 35.40 N 139.26 E
Mangaoka 157b 12.19 S 49.07 E
Mangapehi 172 38.31 S 175.18 E
Mangaratiba 256 22.57 S 44.02 W
Mangart, Monte (Mangrt) ∧ 64 46.25 N 13.40 E
Mangatarem 116 15.47 N 120.17 E
Mangawān 124 24.41 N 81.33 E
Mangaweka 172 39.48 S 175.47 E
Mangaweka ∧ 172 39.49 S 176.05 E
Mangcao Point › 116 11.02 N 123.54 E
Mangchang 102 25.08 N 107.31 E
Mangde ≃ 124 27.35 N 90.28 E
Mange, S.L. 150 8.55 N 12.51 W
Mange, Zaïre 152 0.54 N 20.30 E
Mange, Zhg. 120 32.25 N 83.35 E
Mangeigne 146 10.31 N 21.19 E
Mangerton Mountain ∧ 48 51.57 N 9.29 W
Mangfall ≃ 64 47.51 N 12.08 E
Manggar 112 2.53 S 108.16 E
Manggeng 114 3.36 N 96.55 E
Manggonggri 164 3.30 S 133.19 E
Mangguar, Tanjung › 164 2.53 S 134.51 E
Mangham 194 32.18 N 91.46 W
Mangichu ≃ 126 23.24 N 90.48 E
Mangindrano 157b 14.17 S 48.58 E
Mangin Range ⋏ 110 24.20 N 95.42 E
Mangkalihat, Tanjung › 112 1.02 N 118.59 E
Mangkutana 112 2.24 S 120.48 E
Manglares, Cabo › 246 1.36 N 79.02 W
Mangla Reservoir ⊜[1] 123 33.10 N 73.40 E
Manglaur 124 29.48 N 77.52 E
Manglisi 84 41.43 N 44.24 E
Mangnai 120 37.40 N 91.50 E
Mangniu ≃, Zhg. 104 41.45 N 120.53 E
Mangniu ≃, Zhg. 105 39.04 N 116.26 E
Mangnuiyingzi 104 41.37 N 120.43 E
Mango 220 28.00 N 82.19 W
Mangochi 154 14.28 S 35.16 E
Mango Island I 175g 17.27 S 179.09 W
Mangoky ≃, Madag. 157b 21.29 S 43.41 E
Mangoky ≃, Madag. 157b 23.27 S 45.13 E
Mangole, Pulau I 112 1.53 S 125.50 E
Mangombe 154 1.25 S 26.54 E
Mangone 68 39.12 N 16.20 E
Mangonia Park 220 26.46 N 80.05 W
Mangonui 172 34.59 S 173.32 E
Mangoplah 171b 35.23 S 147.15 E
Mangoro ≃ 157b 20.00 S 48.45 E
Mangotsfield 42 51.28 N 2.28 W
Mangoupa 140 5.53 N 24.40 E
Mangrol 120 21.07 N 70.07 E
Mangrove Cay I 238 24.10 N 77.45 W
Mangrove Creek ≃ 170 33.28 S 151.10 E
Mangrove Creek Dam -◆-[6] 170 33.13 S 151.07 E
Mangrove Mountain 170 33.19 S 151.14 E
Mangrove Point › 220 26.56 N 82.08 W
Mangrt (Monte Mangart) ∧ 64 46.25 N 13.40 E
Mangrullo, Cuchilla ⋏[2] 258 34.34 S 56.42 W
Mangrūl Pīr 122 20.19 N 77.21 E
Mångsälven ≃ 40 59.59 N 14.36 E
Mangsang 112 2.10 S 104.00 E
Mangu ≃ 273b 4.24 S 15.24 E
Mangualde 34 40.36 N 7.46 W
Mangueira, Lagoa ⊂ 252 33.06 S 52.48 W
Mangueirinha 252 25.57 S 52.09 W
Manguéni, Plateau du ⋏[1] 146 22.35 N 12.40 E
Mangui 89 52.03 N 122.13 E
Manguito 240p 22.35 N 80.55 W
Mangulile 236 15.03 N 86.49 W
Mangum 196 34.52 N 99.30 W
Mangungu 152 5.13 S 19.35 E
Mangut, Ross. 86 55.47 N 70.46 E
Mangut, Ross. 88 49.46 N 112.38 E
Mangya 90 37.40 N 90.50 E
Man'gyŏng 98 35.52 N 126.48 E
Mangyšlak □[8] 86 44.00 N 54.30 E
Manhan ≃ 207 42.17 N 72.38 W
Manhartsberg ∧ 61 48.32 N 15.44 E
Manhasset 276 40.47 N 73.42 W
Manhasset Bay ⊂ 276 40.50 N 73.43 W
Manhasset Hills 276 40.46 N 73.41 W
Manhasset Neck ›[1] 276 40.50 N 73.42 W
Manhattan, Il., U.S. 216 41.25 N 87.59 W
Manhattan, Ks., U.S. 198 39.11 N 96.34 W
Manhattan, Mt., U.S. 202 45.51 N 111.19 W
Manhattan □[8] 276 40.46 N 73.55 W
Manhattan Beach 228 33.53 N 118.24 W
Manhattan Beach State Park ♠ 280 33.54 N 118.25 W
Manhattan Bridge -◆-[5] 276 40.42 N 73.59 W
Manhattan College ⊽[2] 276 40.53 N 73.54 W
Manheim 208 40.09 N 76.23 W
Manhiça 156 25.24 S 32.48 E
Mān Hpāng 110 22.41 N 98.36 E
Manhuaçu 255 20.15 S 42.02 W
Manhuaçu ≃ 255 19.30 S 41.06 W
Manhumirim 255 20.22 S 41.57 W
Maní, P.R. 240m 18.15 N 67.10 W
Mani, Zaïre 154 6.27 S 25.20 E
Māni', Jabal al- ∧ 132 33.19 N 36.17 E
Mania ≃ 157b 19.42 S 45.22 E
Maniago 64 46.10 N 12.43 E
Maniamba 154 12.43 S 35.00 E
Manianga 273b 4.10 S 15.19 E
Manica □[5] 156 19.00 S 33.15 E
Manicahan 116 7.01 N 122.12 E
Manicaland □[4] 154 19.30 S 32.15 E
Manicani Island I 116 10.59 N 125.38 E
Manicaragua 240p 22.09 N 79.58 W
Manic Deux, Réservoir ⊜[1] 186 49.25 N 68.25 W
Manicoré 248 5.49 S 61.17 W
Manicoré ≃ 248 5.51 S 61.19 W
Manicouagan ≃ 186 49.11 N 68.13 W
Manicouagan, Réservoir ⊜[1] 186 51.30 N 68.19 W
Manic Trois, Réservoir ⊜[1] 186 50.00 N 68.40 W
Manifold ≃ 44 53.03 N 1.47 W
Maniganggo 102 32.01 N 99.11 E
Manignan 150 10.00 N 7.50 W
Manigotagan 184 51.06 N 96.18 W
Manigotagan ≃ 184 51.07 N 96.20 W
Manihāri 124 25.21 N 87.38 E
Manihiki I[1] 14 10.24 S 161.01 W
Manika, Plateau de la ⋏[1] 154 10.00 S 26.00 E
Manikanāli 126 23.19 N 87.03 E
Mānikganj 124 23.52 N 90.00 E
Mānikpur 124 25.04 N 81.07 E
Manila, Pil. 116 14.35 N 121.00 E
Manila, Pil. 269f 14.35 N 121.00 E
Manila, Ar., U.S. 194 35.52 N 90.10 W
Manila, Ut,. U.S. 200 40.59 N 109.43 W
Manila Bay ⊂ 116 14.30 N 120.45 E
Manila Cathedral ⊽[1] 269f 14.35 N 120.59 E
Manila International Airport ⊠ 269f 14.31 N 121.01 E
Manilla, Austl. 166 30.45 S 150.43 E
Manilla, In., U.S. 218 39.34 N 85.37 W
Manilla, Ia., U.S. 198 41.53 N 95.13 W
Manille
→ Manila 116 14.35 N 121.00 E
Manily 74 62.29 N 165.36 E
Mani Majra 123 30.43 N 76.50 E
Manimbaya, Tanjung › 112 0.01 N 119.36 E
Manimpé 150 14.09 N 5.31 W
Maningory ≃ 157b 17.13 S 49.28 E
Maningrida 164 12.03 S 134.13 E
Maninjau, Danau ⊜ 112 0.20 S 100.11 E
Manino 76 53.58 N 34.20 E
Manipa, Pulau I 164 3.17 S 127.35 E
Manipa, Selat ʊ 164 3.20 S 127.23 E
Manipur □[3] 120 25.00 N 94.00 E
Manipur ≃ 110 22.52 N 94.05 E
Manique de Baixo 266c 38.44 N 9.22 W
Maniquin Island I 116 11.36 N 121.45 E
Manirāmpur 126 23.01 N 89.14 E
Manisa 130 38.36 N 27.26 E
Manisa □[4] 130 38.50 N 28.10 E
Manissauá-Miçu ≃ 250 10.58 S 53.20 W
Manistee 190 44.14 N 86.19 W
Manistee ≃ 190 44.15 N 86.21 W
Manistique 190 45.57 N 86.14 W
Manistique ≃ 190 45.57 N 86.15 W
Manistique, West Branch ≃ 190 46.02 N 86.09 W
Manistique Lake ⊜ 190 46.15 N 85.45 W
Manito 194 40.25 N 89.46 W
Manitoba □[4], Can. 176 54.00 N 97.00 W
Manitoba □[4], Can. 184 54.00 N 97.00 W
Manitoba, Lake ⊜ 184 51.00 N 98.45 W
Manitou 184 49.15 N 98.31 W
Manitou ≃, On., Can. 184 48.58 N 93.20 W
Manitou ≃, P.Q., Can. 186 50.18 N 65.15 W
Manitou, Lac ⊜, P.Q., Can. 186 50.29 N 63.54 W
Manitou, Lac ⊜, P.Q., Can. 186 50.54 N 65.18 W
Manitou, Lac ⊜, P.Q., Can. 206 46.03 N 74.23 W
Manitou, Lake ⊜, On., Can. 190 45.48 N 82.00 W
Manitou, Lake ⊜, In., U.S. 216 41.03 N 86.11 W
Manitou Beach, Sk., Can. 184 51.43 N 105.26 W
Manitou Beach, Mi., U.S. 216 41.58 N 84.19 W
Manitou Lake ⊜, On., Can. 190 46.01 N 79.00 W
Manitou Lake ⊜, Sk., Can. 184 52.45 N 109.45 W
Manitoulin Island I 190 45.50 N 82.20 W
Manitou Springs 200 38.51 N 104.55 W
Manitouwabing Lake ⊜ 212 45.29 N 79.54 W
Manitowaning 190 45.45 N 81.49 W
Manitowik Lake ⊜ 190 48.10 N 84.24 W
Manitowish Waters 190 46.09 N 89.53 W
Manitowoc 190 44.05 N 87.39 W
Manitowoc ≃ 190 44.05 N 87.39 W
Maniwaki 188 46.23 N 75.58 W
Ma'nīyā 142 30.50 N 30.39 E
Manizales 246 5.05 N 75.32 W
Manja, Madag. 157b 21.26 S 44.20 E
Manjā, Urd. 132 31.45 N 35.51 E
Manjacaze 156 24.44 S 33.53 E
Manjakandriana 157b 18.55 S 47.47 E
Manjeri 122 11.07 N 76.07 E
Manjiang 98 41.57 N 127.36 E
Manjimup 162 34.14 S 116.09 E
Manjing 107 29.55 N 104.07 E
Mānjra ≃ 122 18.49 N 77.52 E
Manjuyod 116 9.41 N 123.09 E
Mank 61 48.06 N 15.20 E
Mankanaj 86 48.58 N 60.58 E
Månkarbo 40 60.14 N 17.28 E
Mān Kāt 110 22.05 N 98.01 E
Mankato, Ks., U.S. 198 39.47 N 98.12 W
Mankato, Mn., U.S. 190 44.09 N 93.59 W
Mankayane 158 26.42 S 31.00 E
Mankent 85 42.25 N 69.50 E
Mankera 123 31.23 N 71.26 E
Mankim 152 5.01 N 12.00 E
Mankinholes 262 53.42 N 2.03 W
Mankono 150 8.04 N 6.12 W
Mankota 184 49.25 N 107.04 W
Man'kovka, Ukr. 78 48.58 N 30.20 E
Man'kovka, Ukr. 83 49.34 N 38.27 E
Man'kovo 83 49.24 N 40.17 E
Man'kovo-Ber'ozovskaja 80 48.47 N 41.33 E
Mankoya 154 14.47 S 24.48 E
Mānkundu 272b 22.50 N 88.22 E
Mānkur, India 126 22.30 N 87.54 E
Mānkur, India 126 23.20 N 87.33 E
Manlaj 102 44.07 N 106.50 E
Manley 262 53.14 N 2.45 W
Manley Hot Springs 180 65.00 N 150.37 W
Manleys Corner 283 42.03 N 71.04 W
Manlius 210 43.00 N 75.58 W
Manlleu 34 42.00 N 2.17 E
Manly, Austl. 170 33.48 S 151.17 E
Manly, Austl. 171a 27.28 S 153.15 E
Manly, Ia., U.S. 190 43.17 N 93.12 W
Manly Warringah War Memorial Park ♠ 274a 33.46 S 151.15 E
Manmād 122 20.15 N 74.27 E
Mann ≃ 164 12.20 S 134.07 E
Mann, Mount ∧ 162 25.59 S 129.42 E
Manna, Indon. 112 4.27 S 102.55 E
Mān Na, Mya. 110 23.27 N 97.14 E
Mannahill 166 32.26 S 139.59 E
Mannar 122 8.59 N 79.54 E
Mannar, Gulf of ⊂ 122 8.30 N 79.00 E
Mannārgudi 122 10.40 N 79.26 E
Mannar Island I 122 9.03 N 79.50 E
Mann Creek ≃ 281 42.32 N 83.44 W
Männedorf 58 47.15 N 8.42 E
Mannersdorf am Leithagebirge 61 47.58 N 16.36 E
Mannersdorf an der Rabnitz 61 47.25 N 16.31 E

Symbol	English	Deutsch	Español	Français	Português
≃	River	Fluß	Río	Rivière	Rio
≊	Canal	Kanal	Canal	Canal	Canal
⌊	Waterfall, Rapids	Wasserfall, Stromschnellen	Cascada, Rápidos	Chute d'eau, Rapides	Cascata, Rápidos
ʊ	Strait	Meeresstraße	Estrecho	Détroit	Estreito
⊂	Bay, Gulf	Bucht, Golf	Bahía, Golfo	Baie, Golfe	Baía, Golfo
⊜	Lake, Lakes	See, Seen	Lago, Lagos	Lac, Lacs	Lago, Lagos
≡	Swamp	Sumpf	Pantano	Marais	Pântano
⊓	Ice Features, Glacier	Eis- und Gletscherformen	Accidentes Glaciales	Formes glaciaires	Acidentes glaciares
⊤	Other Hydrographic Features	Andere Hydrographische Objekte	Otros Elementos Hidrográficos	Autres données hydrographiques	Outros acidentes hidrográficos
-✦-	Submarine Features	Untermeerische Objekte	Accidentes Submarinos	Formes de relief sous-marin	Acidentes submarinos
□	Political Unit	Politische Einheit	Unidad Politica	Entité politique	Unidade política
⊽	Cultural Institution	Kulturelle Institution	Institución Cultural	Institution culturelle	Institução cultural
⊥	Historical Site	Historische Stätte	Sitio Histórico	Site historique	Sitio histórico
♠	Recreational Site	Erholungs- und Ferienort	Sitio de Recreo	Centre de loisirs	Area de Lazer
⊠	Airport	Flughafen	Aeropuerto	Aéroport	Aeroporto
■	Military Installation	Militäranlage	Instalación Militar	Installation militaire	Instalação militar
-◆-	Miscellaneous	Verschiedenes	Misceláneo	Divers	Diversos

ENGLISH: Name / Page / Lat.°′ / Long.°′ — DEUTSCH: Name / Seite / Breite°′ / Länge°′ E = Ost

Name	Page	Lat.°′	Long.°′
Mannford	196	36.09 N	96.23 W
Mannheim	56	49.29 N	8.29 E
Manni	120	34.48 N	87.15 E
Manning, Ia., U.S.	198	41.54 N	95.03 W
Manning, N.D., U.S.	198	47.13 N	102.46 W
Manning, S.C., U.S.	192	33.41 N	80.12 W
Manning, Cape ›	174o	2.02 N	157.26 W
Manning Provincial Park ♠	224	49.07 N	120.54 W
Manning Strait ʮ	175e	7.24 S	158.00 E
Mannington	188	39.31 N	80.20 W
Manningtree	42	51.57 N	1.04 E
Mannō	96	34.11 N	133.51 E
Mann Ranges ⋏	162	26.00 S	129.30 E
Mannsville	212	43.42 N	76.03 W
Mannswörth ◆[8]	264b	48.09 N	16.31 E
Mannu	71	39.18 N	8.58 E
Mannu ≃	71	40.50 N	8.23 E
Mannu, Capo ›	71	40.47 N	8.09 E
Mannu, Monte ∧	71	40.23 N	8.25 E
Mannum	166	34.55 S	139.18 E
Mannus	171b	35.48 S	147.57 E
Mannus Creek ≃	171b	35.58 S	148.03 E
Mannville	182	53.20 N	111.10 W
Mano	150	8.02 N	12.06 W
Mano ≃	150	6.56 N	11.31 W
Manoa	248	9.40 S	65.27 W
Manoel Ribas	252	24.31 S	51.39 W
Manohardi	126	24.08 N	90.43 E
Manoharpur, India	124	22.23 N	85.12 E
Manoharpur, India	126	21.59 N	87.18 E
Manokin ≃	208	38.05 N	75.55 W
Manokotak	180	58.40 N	159.09 W
Manokwari	164	0.52 S	134.05 E
Manolo Fortich (Maluko)	116	8.25 N	124.58 E
Manoma ≃	89	49.18 N	136.37 E
Manombo	157b	22.57 S	43.28 E
Manomet	207	41.55 N	70.34 W
Manomet Hill ∧[2]	207	41.55 N	70.36 W
Manong	114	4.36 N	100.53 E
Manonga ≃	154	4.08 S	34.12 E
Manono	154	7.18 S	27.25 E
Manono I	175a	13.50 S	172.05 W
Manoora	168b	34.00 S	138.49 E
Manoppello	66	42.15 N	14.03 E
Manor, Sk., Can.	184	49.36 N	102.05 W
Manor, Pa., U.S.	214	40.20 N	79.40 W
Manor, Tx., U.S.	222	30.20 N	97.33 W
Manorbier	42	51.39 N	4.48 W
Manorhamilton	48	54.18 N	8.10 W
Manorhaven	276	40.50 N	73.42 W
Manor Hill	214	40.38 N	77.55 W
Manori ◆[8]	272c	19.12 N	72.47 E
Manori Creek c	272c	19.12 N	72.48 E
Manorina National Park ♠	171a	27.23 S	152.47 E
Manori Point ›	272c	19.11 N	72.47 E
Manoron	110	11.38 N	99.04 E
Manorville	214	40.47 N	79.31 W
Manosque	62	43.50 N	5.47 E
Manotick	212	45.13 N	75.41 W
Manouane ≃	186	49.30 N	71.11 W
Manouane, Lac ⊜	186	50.41 N	70.45 W
Manouanis ≃	186	50.28 N	70.08 W
Manouanis, Lac ⊜	186	50.51 N	70.20 W
Manown	279b	40.13 N	79.54 W
Manpaka	273b	4.18 S	15.12 E
Manpitou	100	22.17 N	112.52 E
Manp'o	98	41.10 N	126.17 E
Mānpur, India	122	20.22 N	80.43 E
Mānpur, India	124	23.46 N	81.08 E
Manqabād	142	27.12 N	31.07 E
Manqaṭīn	142	28.20 N	30.40 E
Manquehue, Cerro ∧	286e	33.21 S	70.36 W
Manra I[1]	14	4.27 S	171.15 W
Manresa	34	41.44 N	1.50 E
Manresa Island I	276	41.04 N	73.25 W
Mānsa, India	120	23.26 N	72.40 E
Mānsa, India	123	29.59 N	75.23 E
Mansa (Fort Rosebery), Zam.	154	11.12 S	28.53 E
Mansabá	150	12.18 N	15.15 W
Mansafīs	142	28.00 N	30.49 E
Mansalay	116	12.31 N	121.26 E
Mansara	150	13.20 N	4.39 W
Manse ≃	50	47.08 N	0.25 E
Manseau	206	46.22 N	72.00 W
Mānsehra	123	34.20 N	73.12 E
Mansein	110	25.12 N	95.58 E
Mansel Island I	176	62.00 N	79.50 W
Mansfeld	54	51.35 N	11.27 E
Mansfield, Austl.	169	37.03 S	146.05 E
Mansfield, Eng., U.K.	44	53.09 N	1.11 W
Mansfield, Ar., U.S.	194	35.04 N	94.13 W
Mansfield, Ga., U.S.	192	33.31 N	83.44 W
Mansfield, Il., U.S.	216	40.12 N	88.30 W
Mansfield, La., U.S.	194	32.02 N	93.42 W
Mansfield, Ma., U.S.	207	42.02 N	71.13 W
Mansfield, Mo., U.S.	194	37.06 N	92.34 W
Mansfield, N.J., U.S.	285	40.05 N	74.43 W
Mansfield, Oh., U.S.	214	40.45 N	82.30 W
Mansfield, Pa., U.S.	210	41.48 N	77.04 W
Mansfield, Tx., U.S.	222	32.33 N	97.08 W
Mansfield, Mount ∧	188	44.33 N	72.49 W
Mansfield Center	207	41.45 N	72.11 W
Mansfield Hollow Lake ⊜[1]	207	41.45 N	72.11 W
Mansfield Hollow State Park ♠	207	41.46 N	72.10 W
Mansfield Municipal Airport ⊠	283	42.00 N	71.12 W
Mansfield Woodhouse	44	53.11 N	1.12 W
Man Shan I	106	31.14 N	120.17 E
Mansieville Location	273d	26.05 S	27.45 E
Mānsinhapur	272b	22.39 N	88.09 E
Mansión	236	10.06 N	85.22 W
Manskoje belogorje ⋏	88	54.35 N	94.00 E
Mansle	32	45.53 N	0.11 E
Manso ≃	248	14.42 S	56.16 W
Mansôa	150	12.10 N	14.36 W
Manson, Ia., U.S.	198	42.32 N	94.32 W
Manson, Wa., U.S.	182	47.53 N	120.09 W
Manson ≃	182	55.42 N	123.47 W
Manson Creek	182	55.41 N	124.29 W
Mansonville	206	45.03 N	72.23 W
Mansourah	34	36.04 N	4.28 E
Mansucum	246	9.02 N	77.49 W
Mansura	194	31.03 N	92.02 W
Mansura → Al-Manṣūrah	142	31.03 N	31.23 E
Manṣūrīyah, Tur'at al- ≡	142	31.03 N	31.24 E
Mansurovo	82	55.52 N	36.36 E
Manta, Ec.	246	0.57 S	80.44 W
Manta, It.	62	44.37 N	7.29 E
Manta, Bahía de c	246	0.54 S	80.42 W
Mantabuan Island I	116	5.02 N	120.13 E
Mantagao ≃	184	51.50 N	97.48 W
Mantalingajan, Mount ∧	116	8.48 N	117.40 E
Mantalingajan Range ⋏	116	8.46 N	117.40 E
Mantanani Besar, Pulau I	112	6.45 N	116.17 E
Mantangule Island I	116	8.10 N	117.10 E
Mantantale	152	2.10 S	20.06 E
Mantare	154	2.43 S	33.13 E
Mantaro ≃	248	12.15 S	73.58 W
Manteca	226	37.47 N	121.12 W
Mantecal	246	7.33 N	69.09 W
Mantel	60	49.39 N	12.03 E
Mantena	255	18.47 S	40.59 W
Manteno	216	41.15 N	87.49 W
Manteo	192	35.54 N	75.40 W
Mantes-Chérence, Aérodrome de ⊠	261	49.05 N	1.41 E
Mantes-la-Jolie	50	48.59 N	1.43 E
Mantes-la-Ville	261	48.58 N	1.42 E
Manteswar	126	23.26 N	88.06 E
Manteuil-le-Haudouin	50	49.08 N	2.48 E
Manthelan	50	47.08 N	0.47 E
Manti	200	39.16 N	111.38 W
Manticao	116	8.24 N	124.17 E
Mantilla ◆[8]	286b	23.04 N	82.20 W
Mantin	114	2.49 N	101.54 E
Mantiqueira, Serra da ⋏	256	22.00 S	44.45 W
Mantok	112	1.09 S	123.14 E
Manton	190	44.24 N	85.23 W
Mantorville	190	44.04 N	92.45 W
Mantos Blancos	252	23.25 S	70.05 W
Mantou	104	42.27 N	122.26 E
Mantova	64	45.09 N	10.48 E
Mantova □[4]	64	45.10 N	10.47 E
Māntri	126	21.39 N	86.49 E
Mänttä	26	62.02 N	24.38 E
Mantua, Cuba	240p	22.17 N	84.17 W
Mantua, N.J., U.S.	208	39.47 N	75.10 W
Mantua, Oh., U.S.	214	41.17 N	81.13 W
Mantua, Va., U.S.	284c	38.51 N	77.15 W
Mantua ≃	240p	22.12 N	84.25 W
Mantua Creek ≃	285	39.51 N	75.14 W
Mantua Creek, Chestnut Branch ≃	285	39.47 N	75.10 W
Mantua Creek, Porch Branch ≃	285	39.46 N	75.07 W
Mantua Hills	284c	38.51 N	77.16 W
Mantua → Mantova	64	45.09 N	10.48 E
Mantua Terrace	285	39.48 N	75.10 W
Manturovo, Ross.	78	51.28 N	37.07 E
Manturovo, Ross.	80	58.20 N	44.46 E
Mäntyharju	26	61.25 N	26.53 E
Mäntyluoto	26	61.35 N	21.29 E
Manu	248	12.15 S	70.50 W
Manú ≃	248	12.16 S	70.51 W
Manu, Parque Nacional del ♠	248	12.15 S	71.40 W
Manuae I[1], Cook Is.	14	19.21 S	158.56 W
Manuae I[1], Poly. fr.	14	16.30 S	154.40 W
Manua Islands II	174y	14.13 S	169.35 W
Manuel	234	22.44 N	98.19 W
Manuel Alves ≃	250	11.19 S	48.28 W
Manuel Alves Grande ≃	250	7.27 S	47.35 W
Manuel Antonio, Parque Nacional ♠	236	9.25 N	84.10 W
Manuel Avila Camacho, Presa ⊜[1]	234	18.55 N	98.10 W
Manuel Benavides	232	29.05 N	103.55 W
Manuel Derqui	252	27.50 S	58.48 W
Manuel Duarte	256	22.06 S	43.34 W
Manuel Ribeiro	256	22.54 S	42.47 W
Manuel Rodríguez, Isla I	254	52.35 S	73.50 W
Manuel Urbano	248	8.53 S	69.18 W
Manués-Açu ≃	250	3.22 S	57.44 W
Manuguru	122	17.59 N	80.43 E
Manuhangi I[1]	14	19.12 S	141.16 W
Manuherikia ≃	172	45.16 S	169.24 E
Manui, Pulau I	112	3.35 S	123.08 E
Manuilovskaja	76	60.29 N	40.40 E
Manu Island I	164	1.17 S	143.35 E
Manūjān	128	27.24 N	57.32 E
Manuk ≃	115a	6.14 S	108.13 E
Manuk, Pulau I	164	5.33 S	130.18 E
Manukan	116	8.31 N	123.06 E
Manukau	172	37.02 S	174.54 E
Manukau Harbour c	172	37.01 S	174.44 E
Manulla ≃	48	53.57 N	9.12 W
Manulu Lagoon c	174o	1.56 N	157.20 W
Manumuskin ≃	208	39.18 N	75.00 W
Manundi, Tanjung ›	164	0.38 S	135.22 E
Manunui	172	38.53 S	175.20 E
Manuoha ∧	172	38.39 S	177.07 E
Manuripe (Mamuripi) ≃	248	11.06 S	67.36 W
Manuripi ≃	248	11.42 S	67.16 W
Manursing Island I	276	40.58 N	73.40 W
Manursing Island Park ♠	276	40.58 N	73.40 W
Manus □[5]	164	2.00 S	147.00 E
Mānushmuria	126	22.22 N	86.47 E
Manus Island I	164	2.05 S	147.00 E
Manutahi	172	39.40 S	174.24 E
Manutuke	172	38.41 S	177.55 E
Manvel, N.D., U.S.	198	48.04 N	97.10 W
Manvel, Tx., U.S.	222	29.28 N	95.22 W
Manville, N.J., U.S.	210	40.32 N	74.35 W
Manville, R.I., U.S.	207	41.58 N	71.28 W
Mānwat	122	19.18 N	76.30 E
Many	194	31.34 N	93.29 W
Manyal Shīḥah	273c	29.57 N	31.14 E
Manyana	156	23.23 S	21.44 E
Manyani	154	3.05 S	38.30 E
Manyara, Lake ⊜	154	3.35 S	35.50 E
Manyas	130	40.02 N	27.58 E
Manyberries	184	49.24 N	110.42 W
Manyč ≃	72	47.15 N	40.00 E
Manyč-Gudilo, ozero ⊜	80	46.24 N	42.38 E
Manyeleti Game Reserve ◆[4]	156	25.42 S	31.30 E
Many Island Lake ⊜	184	50.08 N	110.03 W
Manyoni	154	5.45 S	34.50 E
Many Peaks	166	24.33 S	151.23 E
Manytsch → Manyč ≃	72	47.15 N	40.00 E
Manz'a	86	58.29 N	96.15 E
Mānzai	120	30.07 N	68.52 E
Manzanares	34	39.00 N	3.22 W
Manzanares ≃	34	40.19 N	3.32 W
Manzanares, Canal del ≡	266a	40.23 N	3.41 W
Manzanillo, Cuba	240p	20.21 N	77.07 W
Manzanillo, Méx.	234	19.03 N	104.20 W
Manzanillo, Bahía c	234	19.04 N	104.22 W
Manzanillo, Bahía de c	234	19.12 N	104.43 W
Manzanillo, Punta ›, Pan.	236	9.38 N	79.32 W
Manzanillo, Punta ›, Ven.	241s	11.32 N	69.17 W
Manzanillo Bay c	238	19.45 N	71.46 W
Manzanita, Or., U.S.	224	45.43 N	123.56 W
Manzanita, Wa., U.S.	224	47.42 N	122.33 W
Manzano, It.	64	45.59 N	13.23 E
Manzano, N.M., U.S.	200	34.38 N	106.20 W
Manzanola	198	38.06 N	103.51 W
Manzano Peak ∧	200	34.35 N	106.26 W
Manželija	78	49.19 N	33.38 E
Manzhouli	88	49.35 N	117.22 E
Manziana	66	42.08 N	12.08 E
Manzil	128	29.15 N	63.05 E
Manzilah, Birkat al- ⊜	142	31.08 N	31.56 E
Manzilah, Buḥayrat al- ⊜	142	31.15 N	32.00 E
Manzini	158	26.30 S	31.25 E
Manzone	258	34.29 S	58.52 W
Manzurka	88	53.30 N	106.04 E
Maó, Esp.	34	39.53 N	4.15 E
Mao, Rep. Dom.	238	19.34 N	71.05 W
Mao, Tchad	136	14.07 N	15.19 E
Maoba	102	30.02 N	108.59 E
Maocifan	100	31.40 N	112.53 E
Maocun	98	34.25 N	117.16 E
Maodianzi, Zhg.	107	30.42 N	104.25 E
Maodianzi, Zhg.	107	29.45 N	104.55 E
Mao'ertuo	107	29.19 N	106.24 E
Maojiagou	104	40.58 N	120.51 E
Maojiaji	100	31.32 N	114.16 E
Maojiakou	100	29.53 N	112.58 E
Maojiaping	105	40.34 N	114.43 E
Maojiapuzi	104	41.10 N	123.32 E
Maojiatun	104	41.05 N	121.58 E
Maojiazao	98	39.53 N	113.26 E
Maoke, Pegunungan ⋏	164	4.00 S	138.00 E
Maolin, Zhg.	89	43.58 N	123.24 E
Maolin, Zhg.	100	30.32 N	118.14 E
Maomao Shan ∧	102	37.12 N	103.10 E
Maoming	102	21.39 N	110.54 E
Maomu	102	40.18 N	99.28 E
Ma On Shan ∧	271d	22.25 N	114.15 E
Ma On Shan Tsuen	271d	22.24 N	114.14 E
Maoping	102	30.23 N	110.33 E
Maopora, Pulau I	112	7.35 S	127.35 E
Maoshan	105	40.17 N	117.26 E
Mao Shan ⋏	106	31.43 N	119.17 E
Maoshi	100	26.57 N	113.05 E
Maospati	115a	7.36 S	111.26 E
Maouri, Dallol V	150	12.05 N	3.32 E
Maowen	102	31.30 N	103.39 E
Maoxing	89	45.32 N	124.33 E
Mao Yü I	100	23.19 N	119.19 E
Maozhou	105	38.51 N	116.06 E
Mapaga	112	0.06 S	119.48 E
Mapam Yumco ⊜	120	30.42 N	81.27 E
Mapan	112	2.21 S	111.10 E
Mapanda	152	9.32 S	24.16 E
Mapane	112	1.24 S	120.40 E
Mapanza	154	16.15 S	26.55 E
Mapaoni ≃	250	1.55 N	54.13 W
Mapari ≃, Bra.	246	1.49 S	66.48 W
Mapari ≃, Bra.	250	0.45 N	53.07 W
Mapastepec	234	15.26 N	92.54 W
Mapaville	219	38.14 N	90.29 W
Mapi	164	7.07 S	139.23 E
Mapi ≃	164	7.00 S	139.16 E
Mapia, Kepulauan II	108	0.50 N	134.20 E
Mapida	112	0.33 S	119.46 E
Mapimí	232	25.49 N	103.51 W
Mapimí, Bolsón de ◆[2]	232	26.30 N	104.00 W
Mapimí, Bufa de ∧	196	25.47 N	103.48 W
Maping, Zhg.	100	24.16 N	117.54 E
Maping, Zhg.	100	31.36 N	113.32 E
Mapinga	154	6.36 S	39.04 E
Mapinhane	156	22.19 S	35.03 E
Mapire	246	7.45 N	64.42 W
Mapiri	248	15.15 S	68.10 W
Mapiri ≃	248	9.52 S	66.21 W
Mapixari, Ilha I	246	2.10 S	65.08 W
Maple ◆[8]	275b	43.51 N	79.31 W
Maple ≃, U.S.	198	45.47 N	98.33 W
Maple ≃, Ia., U.S.	198	42.00 N	95.59 W
Maple ≃, Mi., U.S.	190	42.59 N	84.57 W
Maple ≃, Mn., U.S.	190	44.05 N	94.00 W
Maple ≃, N.D., U.S.	198	46.56 N	96.55 W
Maple Airfield ⊠	275b	43.51 N	79.32 W
Maple Bay	224	48.49 N	123.36 W
Maple Bluff	216	43.07 N	89.22 W
Maple Creek	184	49.55 N	109.27 W
Maple Creek ≃	198	41.33 N	96.27 W
Maplecrest	210	42.17 N	74.11 W
Maple Cross	260	51.37 N	0.30 W
Mapledale	214	41.23 N	79.51 W
Maple Falls	224	48.55 N	122.04 W
Maple Glen	285	40.11 N	75.11 W
Maple Grove, On., Can.	212	43.55 N	78.44 W
Maple Grove, P.Q., Can.	206	45.19 N	73.50 W
Maple Heights	214	41.24 N	81.33 W
Maple Lake	190	45.13 N	94.00 W
Maple Lake ⊜	212	45.06 N	78.40 W
Maple Lane	216	41.45 N	86.14 W
Maple Leaf Gardens ♠	275b	43.40 N	79.23 W
Maple Meadow Brook ≃	283	42.33 N	71.09 W
Maple Mount	194	37.42 N	87.26 W
Maple Park	216	41.55 N	88.36 W
Maples	216	41.01 N	84.58 W
Maple Shade	285	39.57 N	74.59 W
Maple Springs	214	42.12 N	79.25 W
Maplesville	194	32.47 N	86.52 W
Mapleton, S. Afr.	158	26.20 S	28.14 E
Mapleton, Ia., U.S.	198	42.09 N	95.47 W
Mapleton, Mn., U.S.	190	43.55 N	93.57 W
Mapleton, Or., U.S.	202	44.01 N	123.51 W
Mapleton, Ut,. U.S.	200	40.07 N	111.34 W
Mapleton Depot	214	40.24 N	77.57 W
Maple Valley	224	47.25 N	122.03 W
Mapleville	207	41.56 N	71.38 W
Maplewood, Mo., U.S.	219	38.36 N	90.19 W
Maplewood, N.J., U.S.	276	40.43 N	74.14 W
Maplewood, Oh., U.S.	216	40.23 N	84.02 W
Maplewood, Wa., U.S.	224	47.30 N	122.07 W
Maplewood Terrace	279b	40.17 N	79.32 W
Mapocho ≃	286e	33.25 S	70.47 W
Mapocho, Estación ◆[5]	286e	33.26 S	70.40 W
Mapoi	154	5.28 N	27.40 E
Mapoon Aboriginal Reserve ◆[4]	164	11.40 S	142.25 E
Mappsville	208	37.51 N	75.34 W
Maprik	164	3.40 S	143.05 E
Mapuera ≃	250	1.05 S	57.02 W
Mapujiang	105	40.24 N	114.56 E
Mapulanguene	156	24.29 S	32.06 E
Mapumulo	158	29.11 S	31.02 E
Maputa	158	26.59 S	32.46 E
Maputo	156	25.58 S	32.35 E
Maputo □[5]	156	26.00 S	32.25 E
Maputo (Great Usutu) (Lusutfu) ≃	158	26.11 S	32.42 E
Maputo, Baia de c	158	25.48 S	32.51 E
Maqên Gangri ∧	102	34.55 N	99.18 E
Maqiangou	105	39.30 N	115.02 E
Maqiao, Zhg.	100	29.48 N	114.22 E
Maqiao, Zhg.	106	30.28 N	120.42 E
Maqna	128	28.24 N	34.45 E
Maqṭeïr ⊤[4]	148	22.10 N	10.50 W
Maquan ≃	124	29.35 N	84.10 E
Maqueda	34	40.04 N	4.22 W
Maqueda Bay c	116	11.44 N	124.58 E
Maqueda Channel ʮ	116	13.42 N	124.01 E
Maquela do Zombo	152	6.03 S	15.07 E
Maquereau, Pointe au ›	186	48.12 N	64.47 W
Maquilaú ≃	246	1.23 N	63.24 W
Maquiling, Mount ∧	116	14.08 N	121.12 E
Maquinchao	254	41.15 S	68.44 W
Maquinchao ≃	254	41.13 S	69.25 W
Maquoketa	190	42.04 N	90.39 W
Maquoketa ≃	190	42.11 N	90.19 W
Maquoketa, North Fork ≃	190	42.05 N	90.40 W
Mar, Laguna c	286b	23.05 N	82.30 W
Mar, Serra do ⊥[4]	252	26.00 S	48.00 W
Mara, India	120	28.11 N	94.06 E
Mara, Perú	248	14.06 S	72.07 W
Mara, Zhg.	120	28.11 N	94.08 E
Mara □[4]	154	1.45 S	34.30 E
Mara ≃, Afr.	154	1.31 S	33.56 E
Mara ≃, Ross.	88	58.06 N	104.06 E
Maraã, Bra.	246	1.50 S	65.22 W
Maraa, Poly. fr.	174s	17.46 S	149.34 W
Marabá	250	5.21 S	49.07 W
Marabahan	112	3.00 S	114.45 E
Marabut	116	11.07 N	125.13 E
Maracá, Ilha de I, Bra.	246	3.25 N	61.40 W
Maracá, Ilha de I, Bra.	250	2.05 N	50.25 W
Maracaçumé ≃	250	1.23 S	45.42 W
Maracaí	255	22.36 S	50.39 W
Maracaibo	246	10.40 N	71.37 W
Maracaibo, Lago de ⊜	246	9.50 N	71.30 W
Maracaju	255	21.38 S	55.09 W
Maracaju, Serra de ⋏[2]	255	20.45 S	55.00 W
Maracalagonis	71	39.17 N	9.13 E
Maracanã	250	0.46 S	47.27 W
Maracanã ◆[8]	287a	22.54 S	43.14 W
Maracanã ≃	248	8.22 S	59.41 W
Maracanã, Estádio do ♠	287a	22.55 S	43.14 W
Maracanaú	250	3.52 S	38.38 W
Maracás	255	13.26 S	40.27 W
Maracay	246	10.15 N	67.36 W
Maracossic Creek ≃	208	37.53 N	77.11 W
Marādah	146	29.14 N	19.13 E
Maradi	150	13.29 N	7.06 E
Maradi □[5]	150	14.00 N	7.00 E
Maradi, Goulbin ≃	150	13.38 N	6.20 E
Marāghah, Sabkhat al- ⊜	130	35.39 N	37.39 E
Marāgheh	128	37.23 N	46.13 E
Maragiu, Capo ›	71	40.20 N	8.23 E
Maragogi	250	9.01 S	35.13 W
Maragogipe	255	12.46 S	38.55 W
Marahoué, Parc National de la ♠	150	7.00 N	6.00 W
Mārahra	124	27.44 N	78.35 E
Marahuaca, Cerro ∧	246	3.34 N	65.27 W
Maraial	250	8.47 S	35.50 W
Maraiche Lake ⊜	184	54.28 N	102.01 W
Marainviller	58	48.35 N	6.36 E
Maraisburg → Roodepoort-Maraisburg	273d	26.11 S	27.56 E
Marais des Cygnes ≃	194	38.02 N	94.14 W
Marais Temps Clair ⊜	219	38.54 N	90.24 W
Marajó, Baía de c	250	1.00 S	48.30 W
Marajó, Ilha de I	250	1.00 S	49.30 W
Marakabei	158	29.32 S	28.09 E
Ma'rakah	132	33.16 N	35.18 E
Mārākand	84	38.52 N	45.14 E
Marakwini	164	3.42 S	141.31 E
Maralal	154	1.06 N	36.42 E
Maralaleng	156	25.47 S	22.45 E
Maralal Game Sanctuary ◆[4]	154	1.09 N	36.38 E
Maraldy	86	52.26 N	77.45 E
Marali	152	6.01 N	18.24 E
Maralik	84	40.35 N	43.52 E
Maralinga	162	30.10 S	131.35 E
Maralinga Lands ◆[4]	162	29.15 S	130.50 E
Maram	120	25.25 N	94.06 E
Maramag	116	7.46 N	125.00 E
Maramasike I	175e	9.32 S	161.27 E
Marambaia ≃	256	21.44 S	46.25 W
Marambaia, Ilha da I	256	23.04 S	43.58 W
Marambaia, Pico da ∧	256	23.04 S	43.59 W
Marambaia, Restinga de ⊥[2]	256	23.04 S	43.45 W
Marambio ʋ[3]	9	64.14 S	56.43 W
Marampa	150	8.41 N	12.28 W
Maramsilli Reservoir ⊜[1]	122	20.32 N	81.41 E
Maramureș □[6]	38	47.40 N	24.00 E
Maran	114	3.35 N	102.46 E
Mārān, Koh-i- ∧	120	29.26 N	66.48 E
Marana, Mali	150	14.38 N	11.55 W
Marana, Az., U.S.	200	32.26 N	111.13 W
Maranalgo	162	29.23 S	117.48 E
Maranboy	164	14.30 S	132.45 E
Maranchón	34	41.03 N	2.12 W
Marand	128	38.26 N	45.46 E
Maranello	64	44.32 N	10.52 E
Marang, Malay.	114	5.12 N	103.13 E
Marang, Mya.	110	10.27 N	98.47 E
Marangá ≃	287a	22.51 S	43.23 W
Marangani	248	14.22 S	71.10 W
Marangas	116	8.40 N	117.38 E
Marange-Zondrange	56	49.07 N	6.32 E
Maranguape	250	3.53 S	38.40 W
Maranhão □[3]	250	5.00 S	45.00 W
Maranhão ≃	255	13.51 S	48.20 W
Marano	266b	45.38 N	8.38 E
Marano, Laguna di c	64	45.44 N	13.10 E
Maranoa ≃	166	27.50 S	148.37 E
Marano di Napoli	68	40.54 N	14.11 E
Marano Lagunare	64	45.46 N	13.10 E
Marañón ≃	242	4.30 S	73.27 W
Marano sul Panaro	64	44.27 N	10.58 E
Marano Vicentino	64	45.41 N	11.25 E
Marans	32	46.19 N	1.00 W
Maraoli ◆[8]	272c	19.03 N	72.54 E
Marapanim	250	0.42 S	47.42 W
Marapendi, Lagoa de c	287a	23.01 S	43.24 W
Marapi ≃	250	0.37 N	55.58 W
Marapicu, Morro do ∧	287a	22.50 S	43.36 W
Mararoa ≃	172	45.34 S	167.36 E
Mararui	154	1.56 S	41.18 E
Maras	248	13.20 S	72.09 W
Marasany	80	57.27 N	54.25 E
Marasende, Pulau I	112	5.08 S	118.09 E
Mărășești	38	45.52 N	27.14 E
Maraş → Kahramanmaraş	130	37.36 N	36.55 E
Maratasã ≃	250	4.14 S	42.15 W
Maratea	68	39.59 N	15.45 E
Marathon, Austl.	166	20.49 S	143.34 E
Marathon, On., Can.	190	48.43 N	86.23 W
Marathón, Ellás	38	38.10 N	23.58 E
Marathon, Fl., U.S.	220	24.42 N	81.05 W
Marathon, N.Y., U.S.	210	42.26 N	76.01 W
Marathon, Tx., U.S.	196	30.12 N	103.15 W
Marathon, Wi., U.S.	190	44.55 N	89.50 W
Maratua, Pulau I	112	2.15 N	118.36 E
Marau, Bra.	252	28.27 S	52.12 W
Maraú, Bra.	255	14.06 S	39.00 W
Marauiá ≃	246	0.23 S	65.13 W
Marausa	70	37.56 N	12.30 E
Maravari	175e	7.51 S	156.42 E
Maravatío de Ocampo	234	19.54 N	100.27 W
Maravilha	252	26.47 S	53.09 W
Maravillas	232	27.22 N	104.29 W
Maravillas Creek ≃	196	29.34 N	102.47 W
Mara Vista	207	41.33 N	70.34 W
Marav Lake ⊜	120	29.04 N	69.18 E
Maravovo	175e	9.17 S	159.38 E
Marāwah	146	32.29 N	21.25 E
Marawi, Pil.	116	8.01 N	124.18 E
Marawī, Sūd.	140	18.29 N	31.49 E
Marawwaḥ I	128	24.18 N	53.18 E
Maraye-en-Othe	50	48.10 N	3.51 E
Marayes	252	31.29 S	67.20 W
Marayong	274a	33.45 S	150.54 E
Maraza	84	40.33 N	48.56 E
Marazion	42	50.08 N	5.28 W
Marbach, Dtsch.	54	51.02 N	13.13 E
Marbach, Dtsch.	56	50.37 N	9.43 E
Marbach, Schw.	58	46.52 N	7.55 E
Marbach am Neckar	56	48.56 N	9.14 E
Marbache	56	48.48 N	6.05 E
Marbais	50	50.33 N	4.31 E
Marbeck	52	51.49 N	6.52 E
Marbella	34	36.31 N	4.53 W
Marble, Mn., U.S.	190	47.19 N	93.17 W
Marble, N.C., U.S.	192	35.10 N	83.55 W
Marble, Pa., U.S.	214	41.20 N	79.26 W
Marble Arch ⊥	146	30.29 N	18.35 E
Marble Bar	162	21.11 S	119.44 E
Marble Canyon V	200	36.30 N	111.50 W
Marble Falls	196	30.34 N	98.16 W
Marble Hall	156	24.57 S	29.13 E
Marblehead, Il., U.S.	219	39.50 N	91.22 W
Marblehead, Ma., U.S.	207	42.30 N	70.51 W
Marblehead, Oh., U.S.	214	41.32 N	82.44 W
Marblehead Neck ›[1]	283	42.29 N	70.51 W
Marble Hill	194	37.18 N	89.58 W
Marble Lake ⊜	216	41.54 N	84.54 W
Marblemount	224	48.31 N	121.26 W
Marble Rock	190	42.57 N	92.52 W
Marbleton	206	45.37 N	71.35 W
Marburg, Austl.	171a	27.34 S	152.35 E
Marburg, Dtsch.	56	50.49 N	8.46 E
Marburg, S. Afr.	158	30.44 S	30.26 E
Marburg, Lake ⊜[1]	208	39.48 N	76.53 W
Marburg an der Drau → Maribor	36	46.33 N	15.39 E
Marbury	208	38.34 N	77.09 W
Marc ≃	50	50.43 N	3.50 E
Marca, Ponta da ›	152	16.31 S	11.42 E
Marcal ≃	30	47.41 N	17.32 E
Marcala	236	14.07 N	88.00 W
Marcali	30	46.35 N	17.25 E
Marcallo con Casone	266b	45.29 N	8.52 E
Marcaria	64	45.07 N	10.32 E
Marceau, Lac ⊜	186	51.25 N	66.41 W
Marcedusa	68	39.02 N	16.50 E
Marcelin	184	52.55 N	106.47 W
Marceline	194	39.42 N	92.56 W
Marcelino Ramos	252	27.28 S	51.54 W
Marcella	276	40.59 N	74.28 W
Marcellina	66	42.01 N	12.48 E
Marcellus, Mi., U.S.	216	42.01 N	85.48 W
Marcellus, N.Y., U.S.	210	42.59 N	76.20 W
Marcellus Falls	210	43.00 N	76.20 W
Marcevo	83	47.15 N	38.53 E
March	42	52.33 N	0.06 E
March (Morava) ≃	30	48.10 N	16.59 E
Marcha	74	60.37 N	123.18 E
Marcha ≃	74	63.28 N	118.50 E
March Air Force Base ■	228	33.54 N	117.15 W
Marchais	261	48.31 N	2.03 E
Marchal	152	5.16 S	14.58 E
Marchamat	85	40.30 N	72.19 E
Marchand	214	40.51 N	79.02 W
Marchaux	58	47.19 N	6.08 E
Marche □[4]	66	43.30 N	13.15 E
Marche □[9]	32	46.05 N	2.10 E
Marche-en-Famenne	56	50.12 N	5.20 E
Marchegg	61	48.17 N	16.55 E
Marche-les-Dames	56	50.29 N	4.58 E
Marchémoret	261	49.03 N	2.46 E
Marchena	34	37.20 N	5.24 W
Marchena, Isla I	246a	0.21 N	90.29 W
Marchenoir	50	47.49 N	1.24 E
Marchesato	68	39.07 N	16.58 E
Marchfeld ◆[1]	264b	48.17 N	16.31 E
Marchienne-au-Pont	50	50.24 N	4.23 E
Marchinbar Island I	164	11.15 S	136.45 E
Marching	60	48.49 N	11.43 E
Mar Chiquita, Laguna c	252	37.37 S	57.24 W
Mar Chiquita, Laguna ⊜	252	30.42 S	62.36 W
Marchtrenk	61	48.11 N	14.07 E
Marciana	66	42.47 N	10.10 E
Marciana Marina	66	42.48 N	10.12 E
Marcianise	68	41.02 N	14.17 E
Marciano della Chiana	66	43.18 N	11.47 E
Marčichina Buda	78	51.58 N	34.03 E
Marcigny	32	46.17 N	4.02 E
Marcillac-Vallon	32	44.29 N	2.28 E
Marcilloles	62	45.20 N	5.11 E
Marcilly	261	49.02 N	2.53 E
Marcilly-la-Campagne	50	48.50 N	1.13 E
Marcilly-le-Hayer	50	48.21 N	3.38 E
Marcilly-sur-Eure	50	48.49 N	1.21 E
Marck	50	50.57 N	1.57 E
Marckolsheim	58	48.10 N	7.33 E
Marco, Bra.	250	3.08 S	40.09 W
Marco, It.	64	45.51 N	11.01 E
Marco, Fl., U.S.	220	25.58 N	81.43 W
Marcoing	50	50.07 N	3.11 E
Marco Island I	220	25.55 N	81.45 W
Marcola	202	44.10 N	122.51 W
Marcolino, Igarapé ≃	250	11.03 S	58.35 W
Marcona	248	15.03 S	75.01 W
Marco Polo, Aeroporto ⊠	64	45.30 N	12.21 E
Marco Polo Bridge ◆[5]	271a	39.52 N	116.12 E
Marcos Juárez	252	32.42 S	62.06 W
Marcos Paz	258	34.46 S	58.50 W
Marcos Paz □[5]	288	34.49 S	58.49 W
Marcotte, Lac ⊜	206	46.47 N	73.12 W
Marcoussis	261	48.39 N	2.14 E
Marcq	261	48.52 N	1.49 E
Marcq-en-Barœul	50	50.40 N	3.05 E
Marčugi	82	55.21 N	38.33 E
Marcus	198	42.49 N	95.48 W
Marcus Baker, Mount ∧	180	61.26 N	147.45 W
Marcus Hook	208	39.49 N	75.25 W
Marcus Hook Creek ≃	285	39.49 N	75.25 W
Marcus Island → Minami-Tori-shima I	14	24.18 N	153.58 E
Marcy, Mount ∧	188	44.07 N	73.56 W
Marda	162	30.13 S	119.17 E
Mardakert	84	40.12 N	46.48 E
Mardalsfossen ⌞	26	62.30 N	8.07 E
Mardān	123	34.12 N	72.02 E
Mardarovka	78	47.32 N	29.44 E
Mar de Cães, Vala de ≡	266c	38.51 N	8.59 W
Mar de Espanha	256	21.52 S	43.00 W
Mardela Springs	208	38.27 N	75.45 W
Mar del Plata	252	38.00 S	57.33 W
Marden	42	51.10 N	0.29 E
Mardie	162	21.11 S	115.57 E
Mardin	130	37.18 N	40.44 E
Mardin □[4]	128	37.25 N	41.00 E
Mar Dyke ≃	260	51.29 N	0.14 E
Maré I	175f	21.30 S	168.00 E
Mare a Brăilei, Insula I	38	45.00 N	28.00 E
Marea de Portillo	240p	19.55 N	77.11 W
Marecchia ≃	66	44.04 N	12.34 E
Marechal Cândido Rondon	252	24.34 S	54.04 W
Marechal Deodoro	250	9.43 S	35.54 W
Marechal Taumaturgo	248	8.57 S	72.48 W
Maree, Loch ⊜	46	57.42 N	5.30 W
Mareeba	166	17.00 S	145.26 E
Mareetsane	158	26.09 S	25.25 E
Mareil-en-France	261	49.04 N	2.26 E
Mareil-le-Guyon	261	48.47 N	1.51 E
Mareil-Marly	261	48.53 N	2.05 E
Mare Island I	226	38.06 N	122.16 W
Mare Island Naval Shipyard ■	226	38.06 N	122.17 W
Mare Island Strait ʮ	282	38.06 N	122.17 W
Mareje, Gunung ∧	115b	8.46 S	116.08 E
Marek	112	4.48 S	120.21 E
Maremma ◆[1]	66	42.30 N	11.30 E
Marene	62	44.39 N	7.44 E
Marengo, Il., U.S.	216	42.14 N	88.36 W
Marengo, In., U.S.	218	38.22 N	86.20 W
Marengo, Ia., U.S.	190	41.47 N	92.04 W
Marengo, Mi., U.S.	216	42.17 N	84.51 W
Marengo, Oh., U.S.	214	40.24 N	82.49 W
Marengo ◆[1]	62	44.55 N	8.40 E
Marengo ⊥	62	44.49 N	8.40 E
Marengo Cave ⊥[5]	218	38.23 N	86.21 W
Marenisco	190	46.22 N	89.41 W
Marennes	32	45.50 N	1.06 W
Marerano	157b	21.23 S	44.52 E
Maresias	256	23.48 S	45.33 W
Marettimo	70	37.58 N	12.04 E
Marettimo, Isola I	70	37.58 N	12.03 E
Mareuil-en-Brie	50	48.57 N	3.45 E
Mareuil-lès-Meaux	261	48.56 N	2.52 E
Mareuil-sur-Aÿ	50	49.03 N	4.02 E
Mareuil-sur-Belle	32	45.28 N	0.28 E
Marevo	76	57.19 N	32.05 E
Marey-sur-Tille	58	47.35 N	5.03 E
Marfa	196	30.18 N	104.01 W
Marfinka	83	47.36 N	38.32 E
Marfino	80	46.25 N	48.44 E
Mar Forest ◆[3]	46	57.00 N	3.35 W
Margai Caka ⊜	120	35.00 N	87.00 E
Margam, Īrān	84	39.09 N	44.57 E
Margam, Wales, U.K.	42	51.34 N	3.44 W
Marganec	78	47.38 N	34.40 E
Margao → Madgaon	122	15.18 N	73.57 E
Margaree	186	46.24 N	61.05 W
Margaree Harbour	186	46.26 N	61.07 W
Margaret ≃	162	18.10 S	125.37 E
Margaret, Mount ∧	224	46.18 N	122.08 W
Margaret Bay	182	51.20 N	127.29 W
Margaret Creek ≃	166	29.26 S	137.07 E
Margarethenhöhe ◆[8]	263	51.26 N	6.58 E
Margaret River, Austl.	162	33.57 S	115.04 E
Margaret River, Austl.	162	18.38 S	126.52 E
Margaret Roding	260	51.47 N	0.19 E
Margaretting	260	51.41 N	0.25 E
Margarettsville	208	36.32 N	77.21 W
Margaretville	210	42.08 N	74.38 W
Margarita, Bahía → Marguerite Bay c	9	68.30 S	68.30 W
Margarita, Isla I	246	9.05 N	74.30 W
Margarita, Isla de I	246	11.00 N	64.00 W
Margarita Belén	252	27.16 S	58.58 W
Margarita Peak ∧	228	33.26 N	117.23 W
Margaritovka	83	46.55 N	38.52 E
Margate, S. Afr.	158	30.55 S	30.15 E
Margate, Eng., U.K.	42	51.24 N	1.24 E
Margate, Fl., U.S.	220	26.14 N	80.12 W
Margate City	208	39.19 N	74.30 W
Margecany	30	48.54 N	21.01 E
Margelan → Margilan	85	40.28 N	71.44 E
Margeride, Monts de la ⋏	32	44.50 N	3.30 E
Margès	62	45.09 N	5.03 E
Mārgherita	120	27.17 N	95.41 E
Margherita di Savoia	68	41.23 N	16.09 E
Margherita → Jamaame	144	0.04 N	42.45 E
Margherita Peak ∧	154	0.22 N	29.51 E
Marghī	120	34.58 N	66.31 E
Marghita	38	47.21 N	22.21 E
Margi ≃	70	37.16 N	14.58 E
Margilan	85	40.28 N	71.44 E
Margit Híd ◆[5]	264c	47.31 N	19.02 E
Margit-sziget I	264c	47.32 N	19.03 E
Margny-lès-Compiègne	50	49.26 N	2.49 E
Margone	62	45.13 N	7.11 E
Margonin	30	52.59 N	17.05 E
Margos	248	10.04 S	76.26 W
Margosatubig	116	7.34 N	123.10 E
Margot Lake ⊜	184	52.28 N	93.10 W
Māŕgow, Dasht-e ◆[2]	128	30.45 N	63.10 E
Margreid → Magrè	64	46.17 N	11.12 E
Marguerite, Pic → Margherita Peak ∧	154	0.22 N	29.51 E
Marguerite Bay c	9	68.30 S	68.30 W
Marguerittes	62	43.51 N	4.27 E
Margut	56	49.35 N	5.16 E
Margyang	124	29.57 N	90.09 E
Mari	164	9.10 S	141.40 E
Maria	116	9.12 N	123.39 E
Maria, Îles II	14	21.48 S	154.41 W
Mariabrunn ◆[8]	264b	48.12 N	16.14 E
María Cleofas, Isla I	234	21.16 N	106.14 W
Maria da Fé	256	22.18 S	45.23 W
María Elena	252	22.21 S	69.40 W
Maria Enzersdorf	61	48.06 N	16.17 E
Maria Gail	64	46.36 N	13.52 E
Mariager	26	56.39 N	10.00 E
Mariāhu	124	25.37 N	82.37 E
María Ignacia (Vela)	252	37.24 S	59.30 W
Maria Island I, Austl.	164	14.52 S	135.40 E
Maria Island I, Austl.	166	42.39 S	148.04 E
Maria Island National Park ♠	166	42.39 S	148.06 E
Mariakani	154	3.52 S	39.28 E
Maria Laach ʋ[1]	56	50.24 N	7.14 E
María la Baja	246	9.59 N	75.17 W
Maria Lanzendorf	264b	48.06 N	16.25 E
Maria Luggau	64	46.42 N	12.45 E
María Madre, Isla I	234	21.35 N	106.33 W
María Magdalena, Isla I	234	21.25 N	106.24 W
Marian, Lake ⊜	220	27.52 N	81.06 W
Mariana	255	20.23 S	43.25 W
Mariana Basin ✢[1]	14	17.30 N	145.00 E
Mariana Islands II	108	16.00 N	145.30 E
Mariana Ridge ✢[3]	14	17.00 N	146.00 E
Mariana Trench ✢[1]	14	15.00 N	147.30 E
Mariāni	120	26.40 N	94.20 E
Marian Lake ⊜	176	63.00 N	116.10 W
Marianna, Ar., U.S.	194	34.46 N	90.45 W
Marianna, Fl., U.S.	192	30.46 N	85.13 W
Mariannelund	26	57.37 N	15.34 E
Mariannhill	158	29.52 S	30.50 E
Mariano Acosta	258	34.43 S	58.48 W
Mariano Comense	62	45.42 N	9.11 E
Mariano del Friuli	64	45.55 N	13.27 E
Mariano I. Loza	252	29.22 S	58.12 W
Mariano J. Haedo	288	34.38 S	58.36 W
Mariano Moreno	252	38.44 S	70.01 W
Mariano Moreno → Moreno	258	34.39 S	58.48 W
Marianopoli	70	37.36 N	13.55 E
Mariánské Lázně	60	49.59 N	12.43 E
Mariar	164	2.48 S	132.50 E
Mariarano	157b	15.29 S	46.42 E
Marias ≃	202	47.56 N	110.30 W
Marias, Dry Fork ≃	202	48.22 N	111.45 W
Marías, Islas II	234	21.25 N	106.28 W
Maria Saal	61	46.41 N	14.21 E
Marias Pass)(	202	48.19 N	113.21 W
Maria Stein	216	40.24 N	84.28 W
María Teresa	252	34.01 S	61.54 W
Maria-Theresiopel → Subotica	38	46.06 N	19.39 E
Mariato, Punta ›	246	7.13 N	80.53 W
Maria van Diemen, Cape ›	172	34.28 S	172.39 E
Mariaville	210	42.49 N	74.08 W
Mariazell	61	47.47 N	15.19 E
Ma'rib	144	15.30 N	45.20 E
Maribo	41	54.46 N	11.31 E
Maribojoc Bay c	116	9.42 N	123.50 E
Maribor	61	46.33 N	15.39 E
Maribyrnong	274b	37.46 S	144.54 E
Marica, Blg.	38	42.02 N	25.50 E
Maricá, Bra.	256	22.55 S	42.49 W
Marica, Ross.	78	51.45 N	35.16 E
Maricá □[7]	287a	22.57 S	42.59 W
Marica (Évros) (Meriç) ≃	38	40.52 N	26.12 E
Maricá, Lagoa de c	256	22.56 S	42.50 W
Maricaban Island I	116	13.39 N	120.53 E
Maricao	240m	18.11 N	66.59 W
Maricás, Ilhas II	256	23.01 S	42.55 W
Maricha Bil ⊜	272b	22.55 N	88.31 E
Marico ≃	156	24.12 S	26.52 E
Maricopa, Az., U.S.	200	33.03 N	112.02 W
Maricopa, Ca., U.S.	204	35.03 N	119.24 W
Maricopa Indian Reservation ◆[4]	200	33.02 N	112.05 W
Maricunga, Salar de ≚	252	26.55 S	69.05 W
Maridagao ≃	116	7.13 N	124.41 E
Marīdī	154	4.55 N	29.28 E
Maridi ≃	140	6.05 N	29.24 E
Marié ≃	246	0.27 S	66.26 W
Marie Byrd Land ◆[1]	9	80.00 S	120.00 W
Marie Curtis Park ♠	275b	43.35 N	79.33 W
Mariedamm	40	58.51 N	15.09 E

Symbols in the index entries represent the broad categories identified in the key at the right. Symbols with superior numbers (⋏[1]) identify subcategories (see complete key on page *I · 1)*.

Symbole im Register stellen die rechts im Schlüssel erklärten Kategorien dar. Symbole mit hochgestellten Ziffern (⋏[1]) bezeichnen Unterabteilungen einer Kategorie (vgl. vollständiger Schlüssel auf Seite *I · 1)*.

Los símbolos incluídos en el texto del índice representan las grandes categorias identificadas con la clave a la derecha. Los símbolos con numeros en su parte superior (⋏[1]) identifican las subcategorías (véase la clave completa en la página *I · 1)*.

Les symboles de l'index représentent les catégories indiquées dans la légende à droite. Les symboles suivis d'un indice (⋏[1]) représentent des sous-catégories (voir légende complète à la page *I · 1)*.

Os símbolos incluídos no texto do índice representam as grandes categorias identificadas com a chave à direita. Os símbolos com números em sua parte superior (⋏[1]) identificam as subcategorias (veja-se a chave completa à página *I · 1)*.

Symbol	English	Deutsch	Español	Français	Português
∧	Mountain	Berg	Montaña	Montagne	Montanha
⋏	Mountains	Gebirge	Montañas	Montagnes	Montanhas
)(	Pass	Paß	Paso	Col	Passo
V	Valley, Canyon	Tal, Cañon	Valle, Cañón	Vallée, Canyon	Vale, Canhão
≚	Plain	Ebene	Llano	Plaine	Planície
›	Cape	Kap	Cabo	Cap	Cabo
I	Island	Insel	Isla	Île	Ilha
II	Islands	Inseln	Islas	Îles	Ilhas
⊥	Other Topographic Features	Andere Topographische Objekte	Otros Elementos Topográficos	Autres données topographiques	Outros acidentes topográficos

ESPAÑOL — Nombre | Página | Lat.°′ | Long.°′ W = Oeste

Mariefred 40 59.16 N 17.13 E
Marie-Galante I 241o 15.56 N 61.16 W
Mariehamn 26 60.06 N 19.57 E
Marieholm 41 55.52 N 13.09 E
Mariel 240p 22.59 N 82.45 W
Marie Lake ⊜ 184 54.37 N 110.18 W
Marie-Lefranc, Lac ⊜ 206 46.08 N 75.00 W
Mariembourg 50 50.06 N 4.31 E
Marienbad → Mariánské Lázně 60 49.59 N 12.43 E
Marienbaum 52 51.41 N 6.22 E
Marienberg, Dtsch. 54 50.39 N 13.10 E
Marienberg, Dtsch. 56 50.39 N 7.57 E
Marienberg, Pap. N. Gui. 164 3.55 S 144.15 E
Marien-Berg ∧[2] 264a 52.22 N 13.32 E
Marienborn 54 52.12 N 11.08 E
Marienburg → Malbork 30 54.02 N 19.01 E
Mariendorf ◆[8] 264a 52.26 N 13.23 E
Marienfelde ◆[8] 264a 52.25 N 13.22 E
Marienhafe 52 53.31 N 7.16 E
Marienheide 56 51.05 N 7.32 E
Mariental, Dtsch. 54 52.16 N 10.59 E
Mariental, Namibia 156 24.36 S 17.59 E
Mariental □[5] 156 25.00 S 19.00 E
Marienville 214 41.28 N 79.07 W
Maries □[6] 219 38.15 N 91.56 W
Maries ≃ 194 38.30 N 92.01 W
Mariestad 40 58.43 N 13.51 E
Marieta ≃ 246 5.02 N 66.38 W
Marietta, Ga., U.S. 192 33.57 N 84.33 W
Marietta, In., U.S. 218 39.26 N 85.53 W
Marietta, Mn., U.S. 198 45.00 N 96.25 W
Marietta, Oh., U.S. 188 39.24 N 81.27 W
Marietta, Ok., U.S. 196 33.56 N 97.06 W
Marietta, Pa., U.S. 208 40.03 N 76.33 W
Marietta, Tx., U.S. 222 33.10 N 94.33 W
Marietta, Wa., U.S. 224 48.47 N 122.34 W
Marieville 206 45.26 N 73.10 W
Mariga ≃ 150 9.40 N 5.55 E
Marigliano 66 40.56 N 14.27 E
Marignane 62 43.25 N 5.13 E
Marignier 58 46.06 N 6.31 E
Marigny-le-Châtel 50 48.24 N 3.44 E
Marigny-L'Église 50 47.22 N 3.56 E
Marigot, Dom. 240d 15.32 N 61.18 W
Marigot, Guad. 238 18.04 N 63.06 W
Marihatag 116 8.48 N 126.18 E
Mariinsk 86 56.13 N 87.45 E
Mariinskoje 89 51.43 N 140.13 E
Marijampole 76 54.33 N 23.21 E
Marijec 80 56.32 N 49.50 E
Marijskaja Avtonomnaja Sovetskaja Socialističeskaja Respublika □[3] 80 56.30 N 48.00 E
Marikana 158 25.42 S 27.30 E
Marikina 269f 14.38 N 121.06 E
Marikina ≃ 269f 14.33 N 121.04 E
Marília 255 22.13 S 49.56 W
Marilla 210 42.50 N 78.33 W
Mari-Malmyž 80 56.30 N 50.52 E
Marimari ≃ 246 3.58 S 58.49 W
Marimba 152 8.28 S 17.08 E
Marín 34 42.23 N 8.42 W
Marin □[6] 226 38.03 N 122.33 W
Marina 226 36.41 N 121.48 W
Marina ◆[8] 282 37.47 N 122.27 W
Marina del Rey 280 33.50 N 118.25 W
Marina del Rey ⊂ 280 33.58 N 118.27 W
Marina di Andora 62 43.57 N 8.08 E
Marina di Campo 66 42.44 N 10.14 E
Marina di Caronia 70 38.02 N 14.28 E
Marina di Carrara 64 44.02 N 10.02 E
Marina di Cecina 66 43.18 N 10.29 E
Marina di Gioiosa Ionica 68 38.18 N 16.20 E
Marina di Grosseto 66 42.43 N 10.59 E
Marina di Massa 64 44.00 N 10.06 E
Marina di Minturno 66 41.16 N 13.45 E
Marina di Orosei 71 40.22 N 9.43 E
Marina di Palma ◆[8] 70 37.10 N 13.43 E
Marina di Pietrasanta 64 43.56 N 10.12 E
Marina di Pisa 66 43.40 N 10.16 E
Marina di Ragusa 70 36.47 N 14.33 E
Marina di Ravenna 66 44.29 N 12.17 E
Marina Fall ⌞ 246 5.22 N 59.29 W
Marin City 282 37.52 N 122.21 W
Marinduque □[4] 116 13.25 N 121.55 E
Marinduque Island I 116 13.24 N 121.58 E
Marine 219 38.47 N 89.46 W
Marine City 214 42.43 N 82.29 W
Marine-Ehrenmal ⊥ 54 54.23 N 10.15 E
Marineland of the Pacific ʊ[3] 228 33.44 N 118.24 W
Marinella 70 37.35 N 12.50 E
Marine Museum ʊ 280 33.43 N 118.17 W
Marineo 70 37.57 N 13.25 E
Marine Park ♠ 283 42.20 N 71.01 W
Marine Parkway Bridge ◆[5] 276 40.34 N 73.53 W
Mariners Museum ʊ 208 37.03 N 76.30 W
Marines 50 49.09 N 1.59 E
Marinette 190 45.06 N 87.37 W
Marine World/Africa USA ♠ 282 37.32 N 122.16 W
Maringá 255 23.25 S 51.55 W
Maringa ≃ 152 1.14 N 19.48 E
Maringouin 194 30.29 N 91.31 W
Marínguè 154 17.55 S 34.24 E
Marinha Grande 34 39.45 N 8.56 W
Marinho ≃ 287a 23.00 S 43.27 W
Marin Mall ◆[9] 282 37.56 N 122.31 W
Marino, It. 66 41.46 N 12.39 E
Marino, Vanuatu 175f 15.00 S 168.09 E
Marinovka, Ross. 80 48.41 N 43.49 E
Marinovka, Ukr. 78 47.46 N 30.53 E
Marinovka, Ukr. 83 47.54 N 38.51 E
Marin Peninsula ≻[1] 282 37.51 N 122.31 W
Marinskij Posad 80 56.07 N 47.43 E
Marintu 112 0.34 N 110.00 E
Marinwood 226 38.02 N 122.32 W
Mario, Monte ∧[2] 267a 41.55 N 12.27 E
Marion, Austl. 168b 35.01 S 138.34 E
Marion, Al., U.S. 194 32.37 N 87.19 W
Marion, Ar., U.S. 194 35.12 N 90.11 W
Marion, Ct., U.S. 207 41.33 N 72.55 W
Marion, Il., U.S. 194 37.43 N 88.55 W
Marion, In., U.S. 216 40.33 N 85.39 W
Marion, Ia., U.S. 190 42.02 N 91.35 W
Marion, Ks., U.S. 198 38.20 N 97.01 W
Marion, Ky., U.S. 194 37.19 N 88.04 W
Marion, La., U.S. 194 32.54 N 92.14 W
Marion, Ma., U.S. 207 41.42 N 70.45 W
Marion, Mi., U.S. 190 44.06 N 85.08 W
Marion, Ms., U.S. 194 32.25 N 88.38 W
Marion, N.Y., U.S. 210 43.08 N 77.11 W
Marion, N.C., U.S. 192 35.41 N 82.00 W
Marion, N.D., U.S. 198 46.36 N 98.19 W
Marion, Oh., U.S. 214 40.35 N 83.07 W
Marion, S.C., U.S. 192 34.10 N 79.24 W
Marion, S.D., U.S. 198 43.25 N 97.15 W
Marion, Va., U.S. 192 36.50 N 81.30 W
Marion, Wi., U.S. 190 44.40 N 88.53 W
Marion □[6], Fl., U.S. 220 29.00 N 82.03 W
Marion □[6], Il., U.S. 219 38.38 N 88.57 W
Marion □[6], In., U.S. 218 39.46 N 86.09 W
Marion □[6], Mo., U.S. 219 39.50 N 91.37 W
Marion □[6], Oh., U.S. 214 40.35 N 83.08 W
Marion □[6], Or., U.S. 224 45.06 N 122.47 W
Marion □[6], Tx., U.S. 222 32.48 N 94.33 W
Marion, Lake ⊜ 220 28.05 N 81.32 W
Marion, Lake ⊜[1] 192 33.30 N 80.25 W
Marion Bay ⊂ 166 42.48 S 147.55 E
Marion Center 214 40.46 N 79.03 W
Marion Downs 166 23.22 S 139.39 E
Marion Heights 210 40.48 N 76.28 W

FRANÇAIS — Nom | Page | Lat.°′ | Long.°′ W = Ouest

Marion Hill 214 40.44 N 80.18 W
Marion Hills 278 41.45 N 87.57 W
Marion Junction 194 32.26 N 87.14 W
Marion Lake ⊜[1] 198 38.24 N 97.08 W
Marion Reef ✥[2] 166 19.10 S 152.17 E
Marion Station 208 38.02 N 75.46 W
Marionville 194 37.00 N 93.38 W
Marièpolis 252 26.20 S 52.33 W
Maripa 246 7.26 N 65.09 W
Maripá de Minas 256 21.48 S 42.58 W
Maripasoula 250 3.38 N 54.02 W
Maripipi Island I 116 11.47 N 124.19 E
Mariposa 226 37.29 N 119.57 W
Mariposa □[6] 226 37.29 N 119.58 W
Mariposa Creek ≃ 226 37.14 N 120.26 W
Mariposa Slough ≃ 226 37.12 N 120.46 W
Mariquita 246 5.12 N 74.54 W
Marisa 112 0.28 N 121.56 E
Marisa ≃ 112 0.28 N 121.56 E
Mariscal Estigarribia 252 22.02 S 60.38 W
Marisco, Ponta do ≻ 287a 23.01 S 43.17 W
Mariškino 82 55.21 N 38.37 E
Marissa 219 38.15 N 89.45 W
Maritime Alps (Alpes Maritimes) (Alpi Marittime) ⩘ 62 44.15 N 7.10 E
Maritimes, Alpes → Maritime Alps ⩘ 62 44.15 N 7.10 E
Marittime, Alpi → Maritime Alps ⩘ 62 44.15 N 7.10 E
Mari-Turek 80 56.47 N 49.36 E
Maritzburg → Pietermaritzburg 158 29.37 S 30.16 E
Mariupol' (Ždanov) 83 47.06 N 37.33 E
Mariusa, Caño ≃[1] 246 9.43 N 61.26 W
Mariusa, Isla I 241r 9.39 N 61.19 W
Marīvān 128 35.31 N 46.10 E
Mariveles 116 14.26 N 120.29 E
Märjamaa 76 58.54 N 24.26 E
Marjanovka, Ross. 86 54.58 N 72.38 E
Marjanovka, Ukr. 78 50.28 N 24.48 E
Marjanskaja 78 45.06 N 38.38 E
Marjevka 86 53.46 N 67.24 E
Marjina Gorka 76 53.31 N 28.09 E
Marjinka 83 47.56 N 37.31 E
Marjino, Ross. 82 54.28 N 37.12 E
Marjino, Ross. 89 48.31 N 130.38 E
Marjino, Ross. 265a 59.50 N 29.56 E
Marjino, Ross. 265a 59.54 N 31.00 E
Marjino, Ross. 265b 55.52 N 37.18 E
Marjinskaja 84 43.53 N 43.29 E
Marjinsko 76 58.49 N 28.32 E
Mār Jirjis, Jūn ⊂ 132 33.54 N 35.33 E
Marj 'Uyūn 132 33.22 N 35.35 E
Marka, Som. 144 1.43 N 44.53 E
Mārkā, Urd. 132 31.59 N 35.59 E
Markā I 144 18.13 N 41.19 E
Mark Acres 279b 40.21 N 79.42 W
Markakol', ozero ⊜ 86 48.45 N 85.48 E
Markala 150 13.41 N 6.05 W
Markam 102 29.40 N 98.30 E
Markansu 85 39.18 N 73.20 E
Mārkāpur 122 15.44 N 79.17 E
Markaryd 26 56.26 N 13.36 E
Markazī □[4] 128 34.30 N 50.30 E
Markdale 212 44.19 N 80.39 W
Markdorf 58 47.43 N 9.23 E
Marked Tree 194 35.31 N 90.25 W
Markelo 52 52.14 N 6.30 E
Markelovo 86 56.42 N 83.33 E
Marken I 52 52.28 N 5.03 E
Markendorf 54 51.59 N 13.10 E
Markermeer ⊜ 52 52.33 N 5.15 E
Markesan 190 43.42 N 88.59 W
Märket I 40 60.18 N 19.08 E
Market Bosworth 42 52.37 N 1.24 W
Market Deeping 42 52.41 N 0.19 W
Market Drayton 42 52.54 N 2.29 W
Market Harborough 42 52.29 N 0.55 W
Markethill 48 54.18 N 6.31 W
Market Lavington 42 51.18 N 1.59 W
Market Rasen 44 53.24 N 0.21 W
Market Weighton 44 53.52 N 0.40 W
Markfield 42 52.40 N 1.17 W
Markgröningen 56 48.54 N 9.05 E
Markham, On., Can. 212 43.52 N 79.16 W
Markham, Il., U.S. 278 41.35 N 87.41 W
Markham, Tx., U.S. 222 28.57 N 96.04 W
Markham ≃ 164 6.35 S 146.25 E
Markham, Mount ∧ 9 82.51 S 161.21 E
Markham Bay ⊂ 176 63.30 N 71.48 W
Markinch 46 56.12 N 3.08 W
Märkisch Buchholz 54 52.07 N 13.46 E
Markit 85 38.55 N 77.38 E
Markkleeberg 54 51.17 N 12.23 E
Markland Dam ◆[6] 218 38.47 N 84.58 W
Markle, In., U.S. 216 40.50 N 85.20 W
Markle, Pa., U.S. 279b 40.34 N 79.39 W
Markleeville 226 38.41 N 119.46 W
Markleville 218 39.58 N 85.36 W
Markley Canyon V 282 38.00 N 121.50 W
Marknesse 52 52.43 N 5.52 E
Markneukirchen 54 50.18 N 12.19 E
Markoldendorf 52 51.48 N 9.46 E
Markópoulon 267c 37.54 N 23.54 E
Markounda 152 7.37 N 16.59 E
Markovka 83 49.31 N 39.34 E
Markovo, Ross. 74 64.40 N 170.25 E
Markovo, Ross. 80 57.01 N 40.30 E
Markovo, Ross. 82 55.52 N 39.17 E
Markovo, Ross. 88 57.20 N 107.04 E
Markoy 150 14.39 N 0.02 E
Markranstädt 54 51.18 N 12.13 E
Marks, Ross. 80 51.42 N 46.46 E
Marks, Ms., U.S. 194 34.15 N 90.16 W
Marks Tey 42 51.52 N 0.47 E
Markssuhl 56 50.55 N 10.11 E
Marksville 194 31.07 N 92.03 W
Markt Bibart 56 49.39 N 10.26 E
Marktbreit 56 49.40 N 10.08 E
Markt Erlbach 56 49.29 N 10.38 E
Marktheidenfeld 56 49.50 N 9.36 E
Markt Indersdorf 60 48.22 N 11.23 E
Marktl 60 48.15 N 12.51 E
Marktleugast 54 50.10 N 11.38 E
Marktleuthen 54 50.08 N 12.00 E
Marktoberdorf 58 47.47 N 10.37 E
Marktredwitz 30 50.00 N 12.06 E
Markt Rettenbach 58 47.57 N 10.23 E
Marktschellenberg 64 47.42 N 13.02 E
Markt Schwaben 60 48.11 N 11.51 E
Mark Twain Cave ⊥[5] 219 39.42 N 91.21 W
Mark Twain Lake ⊜[1] 219 39.30 N 91.45 W
Mark Twain State Park ♠ 219 39.29 N 91.48 W
Markulešty 78 47.52 N 28.14 E
Markundi 140 11.33 N 23.49 E
Markvue Manor 279b 40.20 N 79.46 W
Mark West Creek ≃ 226 38.30 N 122.42 W
Marl 52 51.38 N 7.05 E
Marlasi 164 5.30 S 134.38 E
Marlboro, Ab., Can. 182 53.33 N 116.45 W
Marlboro, N.J., U.S. 208 40.18 N 74.14 W
Marlboro, N.Y., U.S. 210 41.36 N 73.58 W
Marlboro, Oh., U.S. 214 40.53 N 81.12 W
Marlboro, Pa., U.S. 285 39.54 N 75.42 W
Marlborough, Austl. 166 22.49 S 149.53 E
Marlborough, Guy. 246 7.29 N 58.38 W
Marlborough, Eng., U.K. 42 51.26 N 1.43 W
Marlborough, Ct., U.S. 207 41.37 N 72.27 W
Marlborough, Ma., U.S. 207 42.20 N 71.33 W
Marlborough Downs ⩘[1] 42 51.30 N 1.45 W
Marldon 42 50.28 N 3.36 W
Marle 50 49.44 N 3.46 E
Marlenheim 58 48.37 N 7.30 E
Marles-en-Brie 261 48.44 N 2.53 E

PORTUGUÊS — Nome | Página | Lat.°′ | Long.°′ W = Oeste

Marles-les-Mines 50 50.30 N 2.31 E
Marlette 190 43.19 N 83.04 W
Marlette Lake ⊜ 226 39.10 N 119.54 W
Marley, Il., U.S. 278 41.33 N 87.55 W
Marley, Md., U.S. 208 39.09 N 76.35 W
Marley Creek ≃ 278 41.31 N 87.57 W
Marley Neck ≻[1] 284b 39.12 N 76.33 W
Marlieux 58 46.04 N 5.04 E
Marlin 222 31.18 N 96.53 W
Marlinton 188 38.13 N 80.05 W
Marl-Loemühle, Flughafen ⊠ 263 51.39 N 7.10 E
Marlow, Dtsch. 54 54.09 N 12.34 E
Marlow, Eng., U.K. 42 51.35 N 0.48 W
Marlow, Ok., U.S. 196 34.38 N 97.57 W
Marlpit Hill 260 51.13 N 0.04 E
Marlton 208 39.53 N 74.55 W
Marlton Heights 285 39.40 N 75.21 W
Marly 50 50.20 N 3.32 E
Marly, Forêt de ♠ 261 48.50 N 2.00 E
Marly-la-Ville 261 49.05 N 2.30 E
Marly-le-Roi 50 48.52 N 2.05 E
Marma, Sve. 26 61.16 N 16.52 E
Marma, Sve. 40 60.30 N 17.25 E
Marmaduke 194 36.11 N 90.22 W
Marmagne 58 46.50 N 4.21 E
Marmande 32 44.30 N 0.10 E
Marmara, Sea of → Marmara Denizi ⏚[2] 130 40.40 N 28.15 E
Marmara Adası I 130 40.38 N 27.37 E
Marmara Denizi (Sea of Marmara) ⏚[2] 130 40.40 N 28.15 E
Marmara Ereğlisi 130 40.58 N 27.57 E
Marmara Gölü ⊜ 130 38.37 N 28.02 E
Marmaris 130 36.51 N 28.16 E
Marmarītā 130 34.47 N 36.15 E
Marmarth 198 46.17 N 103.55 W
Marmaton ≃ 194 38.00 N 94.19 W
Marmelopolis 256 22.27 S 45.10 W
Marmelos 248 6.08 S 61.50 W
Marmelos, Rio dos ≃ 248 6.06 S 61.46 W
Marmet 188 38.14 N 81.34 W
Marmion Lake ⊜[1] 190 48.54 N 91.30 W
Marmirolo 64 45.13 N 10.45 E
Marmolada ∧ 64 46.26 N 11.51 E
Marmora, On., Can. 212 44.29 N 77.41 W
Marmora, N.J., U.S. 208 39.16 N 74.38 W
Marmore 66 42.33 N 12.43 E
Marmore ≃ 62 45.44 N 7.37 E
Marmore, Cascàta delle ⌞ 66 42.33 N 12.43 E
Marmot Bay ⊂ 180 58.00 N 152.20 W
Marmot Island I 180 58.13 N 151.51 W
Marmoutier 58 48.41 N 7.23 E
Mar Muerto, Laguna ⊂ 234 16.10 N 94.10 W
Marnate 266b 45.38 N 8.54 E
Marnay 58 47.17 N 5.46 E
Marnaz 58 46.04 N 6.32 E
Marne, Dtsch. 52 53.57 N 9.00 E
Marne, Mi., U.S. 216 43.02 N 85.49 W
Marne □[5] 32 48.55 N 4.10 E
Marne ≃, Austl. 168b 34.40 S 139.18 E
Marne ≃, Fr. 32 48.49 N 2.24 E
Marne à la Saône, Canal de la ≚ 58 48.44 N 4.36 E
Marne au Rhin, Canal de la ≚ 56 48.35 N 7.47 E
Marneuli 84 41.28 N 44.50 E
Marnhull 42 50.58 N 2.18 W
Marnitz 54 53.19 N 11.56 E
Maroa, Il., U.S. 219 40.02 N 88.57 W
Maroa, Ven. 246 2.43 N 67.33 W
Maroala 157b 15.23 S 47.59 E
Maroantsetra 157b 15.26 S 49.44 E
Marobi Raghza 120 32.36 N 69.52 E
Maroc → Morocco □[1] 148 32.00 N 5.00 W
Maroelaboom 156 19.15 S 18.53 E
Marofandilia 157b 20.07 S 44.34 E
Maroglio ≃ 70 37.03 N 14.15 E
Marokko → Morocco □[1] 148 32.00 N 5.00 W
Marol ◆[8] 272c 19.07 N 72.53 E
Marolambo 157b 20.02 S 48.07 E
Maroldsweisach 56 50.12 N 10.39 E
Marolles-en-Brie 261 48.44 N 2.33 E
Marolles-en-Hurepoix 261 48.34 N 2.18 E
Marolles-les-Braults 50 48.15 N 0.19 E
Maromandia 157b 14.13 S 48.08 E
Maromme 50 49.28 N 1.02 E
Maromokotro ∧ 157b 14.01 S 48.59 E
Marondera 154 18.10 S 31.36 E
Marone 64 45.44 N 10.05 E
Marong 102 31.07 N 99.20 E
Maronghi Creek ≃ 171a 26.58 S 152.22 E
Maroni (Marowijne) ≃ 250 5.45 N 53.58 W
Maroon 171a 28.10 S 152.44 E
Maroon, Mount ∧ 171a 28.13 S 152.44 E
Maroondah Aqueduct ≚[1] 274b 37.42 S 145.01 E
Maros 112 5.00 S 119.34 E
Maros (Mureș) ≃ 38 46.15 N 20.13 E
Maroseranana 157b 18.32 S 48.51 E
Marostica 64 45.45 N 11.39 E
Marosvásárhely → Tîrgu Mureș 38 46.33 N 24.33 E
Marotandrano 157b 16.10 S 48.50 E
Marotiri, Îles II 14 27.55 S 143.26 W
Marotta 66 43.46 N 13.08 E
Maroua 146 10.36 N 14.20 E
Maroubra 274a 33.57 S 151.16 E
Marouini ≃ 250 3.18 N 54.04 W
Marovato, Madag. 157b 13.59 S 48.36 E
Marovato, Madag. 157b 15.48 S 48.05 E
Marovato, Madag. 157b 16.28 S 48.25 E
Marovoay 157b 16.06 S 46.39 E
Marovoay Nord 157b 16.57 S 44.34 E
Marowijne □[5] 250 5.40 N 54.20 W
Marowijne (Maroni) ≃ 250 5.45 N 53.58 W
Marpent 50 50.18 N 4.05 E
Marple 44 53.24 N 2.03 W
Marquam 224 45.04 N 122.41 W
Marquand 194 37.25 N 90.10 W
Marquard 158 28.54 S 27.28 E
Marquardt 54 52.27 N 12.57 E
Marquartstein 64 47.45 N 12.28 E
Marquesas Islands → Marquises, Îles II 6 9.00 S 139.30 W
Marquesas Keys II 220 24.34 N 82.08 W
Marquette, Ks., U.S. 198 38.33 N 97.50 W
Marquette, Mi., U.S. 190 46.32 N 87.23 W
Marquette Park ♠ 278 41.46 N 87.42 W
Márquez, Perú 286d 11.57 S 77.08 W
Marquez, Tx., U.S. 222 31.14 N 96.15 W
Marquion 50 50.13 N 3.05 E
Marquis 241k 12.06 N 61.37 W
Marquis, Cape ≻ 241f 14.03 N 60.54 W
Marquise 50 50.49 N 1.42 E
Marquises, Îles (Marquesas Islands) II 6 9.00 S 139.30 W
Marrabel 168b 34.08 S 138.53 E
Marra Creek ≃ 166 30.05 S 147.05 E
Marradi 66 44.04 N 11.37 E
Marradong 168a 32.52 S 116.27 E
Marrah, Jabal ∧ 140 13.04 N 24.21 E
Marra Hills ⩘[2] 140 6.05 N 27.33 E
Marrakech 148 31.38 N 8.00 W
Marrakech □[4] 148 31.30 N 8.05 W
Marramarra National Park ♠ 170 33.32 S 151.04 E
Marrawah 166 40.56 S 144.41 E
Marree 166 29.39 S 138.04 E
Marrero 194 29.53 N 90.06 W
Marrickville 274a 33.55 S 151.09 E
Marromeu 156 18.20 S 35.56 E
Marrowstone Island I 224 48.04 N 122.41 W

Marrubiu 71 39.45 N 8.38 E
Marruecos → Morocco □[1] 148 32.00 N 5.00 W
Marrupa 154 13.08 S 37.30 E
Mars 214 40.41 N 80.00 W
Marsā al-Burayqah 146 30.25 N 19.34 E
Marsabit 154 2.20 N 37.59 E
Marsabit National Park ♠ 154 2.20 N 38.00 E
Marsac-en-Livradois 62 45.29 N 3.44 E
Marṣafā wa Kafr Aḥmad Hashīsh 142 30.25 N 31.15 E
Marsal 56 48.48 N 6.36 E
Marsala 70 37.48 N 12.26 E
Marsā Maṭrūḥ 140 31.21 N 27.14 E
Marsā Maṭrūḥ □[4] 142 29.00 N 30.00 E
Marsange ≃ 261 48.43 N 2.45 E
Marsangue ≃ 261 48.40 N 2.47 E
Marsannay-la-Côte 58 47.16 N 4.59 E
Marsanne 62 44.39 N 4.52 E
Marsassoum 150 12.50 N 16.00 W
Mars'aty 86 60.05 N 60.29 E
Marscheid ◆[8] 263 51.14 N 7.14 E
Marsciano 66 42.54 N 12.20 E
Marsden, Austl. 166 33.45 S 147.32 E
Marsden, Eng., U.K. 262 53.36 N 1.56 W
Marsden, Point ≻ 168b 35.35 S 137.38 E
Marsden Park 274a 33.42 S 150.50 E
Marsdiep ɥ 52 52.59 N 4.45 E
Marseille 62 43.18 N 5.24 E
Marseille-en-Beauvaisis 50 49.35 N 1.57 E
Marseille-Marignane, Aéroport de ⊠ 62 43.27 N 5.13 E
Marseilles, Il., U.S. 216 41.19 N 88.42 W
Marseilles, Oh., U.S. 214 40.42 N 83.23 W
Marsella → Marseille 62 43.18 N 5.24 E
Marsfield 274a 33.47 S 151.07 E
Marsfjället ∧ 24 65.05 N 15.28 E
Marshall, Liber. 150 6.10 N 10.23 W
Marshall, Ar., U.S. 194 35.54 N 92.37 W
Marshall, Il., U.S. 194 39.23 N 87.41 W
Marshall, Mi., U.S. 216 42.16 N 84.57 W
Marshall, Mn., U.S. 198 44.26 N 95.47 W
Marshall, Mo., U.S. 194 39.07 N 93.11 W
Marshall, N.C., U.S. 192 35.47 N 82.41 W
Marshall, Tx., U.S. 194 32.32 N 94.22 W
Marshall, Va., U.S. 188 38.51 N 77.51 W
Marshall, Wi., U.S. 216 43.10 N 89.04 W
Marshall □[6], Il., U.S. 216 41.02 N 89.24 W
Marshall □[6], In., U.S. 216 41.21 N 86.19 W
Marshall ≃ 162 22.59 S 136.59 E
Marshall Bennett Islands II 164 8.50 S 151.50 E
Marshallberg 192 34.43 N 76.30 W
Marshall Canyon Regional Park ♠ 280 34.09 N 117.43 W
Marshall Gold Discovery State Historical Park ♠ 226 38.48 N 120.53 W
Marshall Hall 208 38.41 N 77.06 W
Marshall Islands □[1] 14 11.00 N 168.00 E
Marshall Islands II 14 9.00 N 168.00 E
Marshalls Creek 210 41.03 N 75.08 W
Marshallton, De., U.S. 208 39.43 N 75.39 W
Marshallton, Pa., U.S. 210 40.47 N 76.33 W
Marshallton, Pa., U.S. 285 39.57 N 75.41 W
Marshalltown 190 42.02 N 92.54 W
Marshallville, Ga., U.S. 192 32.27 N 83.56 W
Marshallville, Oh., U.S. 214 40.54 N 81.44 W
Marshbank Metropolitan Park ♠ 281 42.36 N 83.23 W
Marsh Creek ≃, Ca., U.S. 282 37.53 N 121.49 W
Marsh Creek ≃, Mi., U.S. 281 42.06 N 83.13 W
Marsh Creek ≃, Pa., U.S. 214 41.03 N 77.36 W
Marsh Creek ≃, Pa., U.S. 285 40.03 N 75.43 W
Marsh Creek ≃, Wi., U.S. 216 42.13 N 89.04 W
Marsh Creek Lake ⊜[1] 208 40.04 N 75.44 W
Marshes Creek ≃ 276 40.36 N 74.13 W
Marshfield, Eng., U.K. 42 51.28 N 2.19 W
Marshfield, Ma., U.S. 207 42.05 N 70.42 W
Marshfield, Mo., U.S. 194 37.20 N 92.54 W
Marshfield, Wi., U.S. 190 44.40 N 90.10 W
Marshfield Airport ⊠ 283 42.06 N 70.40 W
Marshfield Center 283 42.07 N 70.43 W
Marshfield Hills 207 42.08 N 70.44 W
Marsh Harbour 238 26.33 N 77.03 W
Marsh Hill 210 41.29 N 76.58 W
Mars Hill, In., U.S. 218 39.43 N 86.09 W
Mars Hill, Me., U.S. 186 46.30 N 67.52 W
Mars Hill, N.C., U.S. 192 35.49 N 82.32 W
Marsh Island I 194 29.35 N 91.53 W
Marsh Lake ⊜ 180 60.25 N 134.18 W
Marsh Peak ∧ 200 40.43 N 109.50 W
Marshside 262 53.40 N 2.58 W
Marshville 192 34.59 N 80.22 W
Marshyhope Creek ≃ 208 38.32 N 75.45 W
Marsica ◆[1] 66 41.50 N 13.45 E
Marsico Nuovo 68 40.25 N 15.44 E
Marsico Vetere 68 40.23 N 15.49 E
Marsillargues 62 43.40 N 4.11 E
Marsimang, Tanjung ≻ 164 3.27 S 130.49 E
Marsing 202 43.32 N 116.48 W
Marske-by-the-Sea 44 54.36 N 1.01 W
Mars-la-Tour 56 49.06 N 5.54 E
Marson 56 48.55 N 4.32 E
Marssum 52 53.12 N 5.42 E
Märsta 40 59.37 N 17.51 E
Marstal 41 54.51 N 10.31 E
Marsteller 214 40.39 N 78.48 W
Märstetten 58 47.36 N 9.04 E
Marston 262 53.16 N 2.30 W
Marston Moor ≡ 44 53.57 N 1.17 W
Marston Moor Battlesite ⊥ 44 53.57 N 1.17 W
Marstons Mills 207 41.39 N 70.25 W
Marstrand 26 57.53 N 11.35 E
Marsyāngdī ≃ 124 28.05 N 84.28 E
Mart 222 31.32 N 96.50 W
Marta 66 42.32 N 11.55 E
Marta ≃ 66 42.14 N 11.42 E
Martaban 110 16.32 N 97.37 E
Martaban, Gulf of ⊂ 110 16.30 N 97.00 E
Martano 68 40.12 N 18.18 E
Martap 152 6.54 N 13.03 E
Martapura, Indon. 112 3.25 S 114.51 E
Martapura, Indon. 112 4.19 S 104.22 E
Marte 146 12.22 N 13.51 E
Marteg ≃ 42 52.20 N 3.33 W
Martel, Fr. 32 44.56 N 1.37 E
Martel, Oh., U.S. 214 40.40 N 82.55 W
Martelange 56 49.50 N 5.44 E
Martell 226 38.22 N 120.48 W
Martello 64 46.34 N 10.47 E
Martello, Val V 64 46.31 N 10.45 E
Martemjanovskij 86 55.54 N 80.22 E
Marten ◆[8] 263 51.31 N 7.23 E
Marten Lake ⊜ 190 46.42 N 79.41 W
Marten Mountain ∧ 182 55.28 N 114.43 W
Marte R. Gomez, Presa ⊜[1] 196 26.10 N 99.00 W
Martfeld 52 52.52 N 9.04 E
Marthaguy Creek ≃ 166 30.16 S 147.35 E
Martha Lake 224 47.51 N 122.20 W
Marthall 262 53.17 N 2.18 W
Martham 42 52.42 N 1.38 E
Marthasville 219 38.37 N 91.03 W

Martha's Vineyard I 207 41.25 N 70.40 W
Martí, Cuba 240p 21.09 N 77.27 W
Martí, Cuba 240p 22.57 N 80.55 W
Martí, Pico ∧ 240p 20.01 N 76.35 W
Martignacco 64 46.05 N 13.08 E
Martignat 58 46.13 N 5.36 E
Martigny 58 46.06 N 7.04 E
Martigny-les-Bains 58 48.06 N 5.49 E
Martigues 62 43.24 N 5.03 E
Martil 34 35.37 N 5.17 W
Martim Francisco 256 22.31 S 46.57 W
Martin, Česko. 30 49.05 N 18.55 E
Martin, Ky., U.S. 192 37.34 N 82.45 W
Martin, Mi., U.S. 216 42.32 N 85.38 W
Martin, N.D., U.S. 198 47.49 N 100.06 W
Martin, Oh., U.S. 214 41.33 N 83.20 W
Martin, S.D., U.S. 198 43.10 N 101.43 W
Martin, Tn., U.S. 194 36.20 N 88.51 W
Martin □[6] 220 27.07 N 80.31 W
Martín ≃ 34 41.18 N 0.19 W
Martín, Arroyo ≃ 288 34.51 S 58.04 W
Martin, Isle I 46 57.55 N 5.14 W
Martina 58 46.53 N 10.30 E
Martina Franca 68 40.42 N 17.21 E
Martinborough 172 41.13 S 175.28 E
Martín Chico, Punta ≻ 258 34.10 S 58.13 W
Martindale 196 29.50 N 97.51 W
Martindale Creek ≃, Austl. 170 32.32 S 150.42 E
Martindale Creek ≃, In., U.S. 218 39.48 N 85.09 W
Martindale Pond ⊜ 284a 43.11 N 79.16 W
Martin-Église 50 49.54 N 1.09 E
Martinengo 62 45.34 N 9.46 E
Mărtinești 38 45.30 N 27.18 E
Martinez, Ca., U.S. 226 38.01 N 122.07 W
Martinez, Ga., U.S. 192 33.31 N 82.04 W
Martínez ◆[8] 258 34.29 S 58.30 W
Martínez de la Torre 234 20.04 N 97.03 W
Martín García, Isla I 258 34.13 S 58.15 W
Martinho Campos 255 19.20 S 45.13 W
Martinica → Martinique □[2] 240e 14.40 N 61.00 W
Martini Creek ≃ 282 37.33 N 122.31 W
Martinique □[2], N.A. 230 14.40 N 61.00 W
Martinique □[2], N.A. 240e 14.40 N 61.00 W
Martinique Passage ɥ 238 15.10 N 61.15 W
Martin Lake ⊜[1], Al., U.S. 194 32.50 N 85.55 W
Martin Lake ⊜[1], Tx., U.S. 222 32.15 N 94.35 W
Martin Marietta Corporation ʊ[3] 284b 39.20 N 76.26 W
Martinniemi 26 65.13 N 25.18 E
Martinópole 250 3.15 S 40.41 W
Martin Peninsula ≻[1] 9 74.25 S 114.10 W
Martín Pérez ≃ 286b 23.07 N 82.20 W
Martin Point ≻ 180 70.08 N 143.16 W
Martin Run ≃ 279a 41.27 N 82.12 W
Martins 250 6.05 S 37.55 W
Martinsberg 61 48.22 N 15.09 E
Martins Brook ≃ 283 42.34 N 71.06 W
Martinsburg, Mo., U.S. 219 39.06 N 91.38 W
Martinsburg, N.Y., U.S. 212 43.44 N 75.28 W
Martinsburg, Oh., U.S. 214 40.16 N 82.21 W
Martinsburg, Pa., U.S. 214 40.18 N 78.19 W
Martinsburg, W.V., U.S. 188 39.27 N 77.57 W
Martins Creek 208 40.47 N 75.11 W
Martins Creek ≃ 210 41.37 N 75.46 W
Martinscroft 262 53.24 N 2.31 W
Martins Ferry 214 40.05 N 80.43 W
Martins Mills 222 32.25 N 95.47 W
Martins Pond ⊜ 283 42.36 N 71.08 W
Martinstein 56 49.48 N 7.32 E
Martinsthal 56 50.03 N 8.07 E
Martinsville, Austl. 170 33.03 S 151.25 E
Martinsville, Il., U.S. 194 39.20 N 87.52 W
Martinsville, In., U.S. 218 39.25 N 86.25 W
Martinsville, N.J., U.S. 276 40.36 N 74.34 W
Martinsville, Oh., U.S. 218 39.19 N 83.48 W
Martinsville, Va., U.S. 192 36.41 N 79.52 W
Martinton 216 40.55 N 87.44 W
Martintown 206 45.09 N 74.42 W
Martin Van Buren National Historic Site ⊥ 210 42.22 N 73.43 W
Martin Vaz, Ilhas II 244 20.30 S 28.51 W
Martis 71 40.47 N 8.49 E
Martisovo 76 56.34 N 31.55 E
Martock 42 50.59 N 2.46 W
Martofte 41 55.33 N 10.40 E
Marton, N.Z. 172 40.05 S 175.23 E
Marton, Eng., U.K. 262 53.12 N 2.13 W
Martorell 266d 41.28 N 1.56 E
Martorelles de Baix 266d 41.32 N 2.14 E
Martos 34 37.43 N 3.58 W
Martovaja 78 49.57 N 36.57 E
Martre, Lac la ⊜ 176 63.15 N 117.55 W
Martti 24 67.28 N 28.28 E
Martūbah 146 32.35 N 22.46 E
Martuk 86 50.46 N 56.31 E
Martuni, Azer. 84 39.48 N 47.06 E
Martuni, Haya. 84 40.08 N 45.19 E
Martvili 84 42.25 N 42.22 E
Martville 210 43.17 N 76.38 W
Martynoviči 78 51.17 N 29.37 E
Martynovka 78 49.38 N 31.18 E
Martynovo 80 50.43 N 50.23 E
Martynovskij 80 50.29 N 42.18 E
Maru 150 12.22 N 6.22 E
Marua 164 9.30 S 149.20 E
Marudi 112 4.11 N 114.19 E
Marudu, Telukan ⊂ 112 6.45 N 116.55 E
Marugame 96 34.17 N 133.47 E
Maruggio 68 40.19 N 17.34 E
Maruia 172 42.11 S 172.13 E
Maruia ≃ 172 41.47 S 172.12 E
Maruim 250 10.45 S 37.05 W
Maruko 94 36.19 N 138.16 E
Marula 154 20.26 S 28.06 E
Marulan 170 34.43 S 150.00 E
Marulan South 170 34.46 S 150.02 E
Marum 52 53.08 N 6.16 E
Marum, Mont ∧ 175f 16.15 S 168.07 E
Marunga 152 17.27 S 20.02 E
Marungu 154 3.44 S 30.48 E
Marungu ⩘ 154 7.42 S 30.00 E
Maruoka 94 36.09 N 136.16 E
Mårup 41 55.57 N 10.35 E
Marusino 265b 55.42 N 37.59 E
Maruškino 82 55.36 N 37.12 E
Ma'rūt 120 31.34 N 67.03 E
Marutea I[1] 14 17.00 S 143.10 W
Maruyama 94 35.01 N 139.58 E
Maruyama ≃ 96 35.39 N 134.50 E
Marv Dasht 128 29.50 N 52.40 E
Marve ◆[8] 272c 19.12 N 72.49 E
Marvejols 32 44.33 N 3.18 E
Marvell 194 34.33 N 90.54 W
Marvel Loch 162 31.28 S 119.28 E
Marviken 40 58.34 N 16.51 E
Marvila ◆[8] 266c 38.44 N 9.06 W
Marville 56 49.27 N 5.27 E
Marvin Creek ≃ 214 41.48 N 78.26 W
Marvine, Mount ∧ 200 38.40 N 111.39 W
Mar Vista ◆[8] 280 34.00 N 118.27 W
Mārwār 120 25.44 N 73.36 E
Marwayne 184 53.32 N 110.20 W
Marwitz 264a 52.41 N 13.09 E
Marwitzer Heide ◆[3] 264a 52.40 N 13.06 E
Marwood 214 40.48 N 79.47 W
Marxhagen 54 53.37 N 12.36 E
Marxloh ◆[8] 263 51.31 N 6.46 E
Mary 128 37.36 N 61.50 E

Mary □[8] 128 37.30 N 62.30 E
Mary ≃, Austl. 164 12.53 S 131.38 E
Mary ≃, Austl. 166 25.26 S 152.55 E
Mary Anne Group II 162 21.13 S 115.32 E
Maryborough, Austl. 166 25.32 S 152.42 E
Maryborough, Austl. 169 37.03 S 143.45 E
Maryborough → Port Laoise 48 53.02 N 7.17 W
Mary D 208 40.45 N 76.04 W
Marydale 158 29.23 S 22.05 E
Marydel 208 39.06 N 75.44 W
Maryfield 184 49.48 N 101.32 W
Maryhill 224 45.41 N 120.49 W
Mary Jane, Lake ⊜ 220 28.22 N 81.11 W
Mary Kathleen 166 20.49 S 139.58 E
Maryknoll 210 41.11 N 73.50 W
Mary Lake ⊜ 212 45.15 N 79.15 W
Maryland 210 42.32 N 74.53 W
Maryland □[3], U.S. 178 39.00 N 76.45 W
Maryland □[3], U.S. 188 39.00 N 76.45 W
Maryland, University of (Baltimore County Campus) ʊ[2], Md., U.S. 284b 39.15 N 76.43 W
Maryland, University of ʊ[2], Md., U.S. 284c 38.59 N 76.57 W
Maryland City 208 39.05 N 76.49 W
Maryland Gardens Park ♠ 275b 43.47 N 79.32 W
Maryland Heights 219 38.42 N 90.25 W
Maryland Historical Society ʊ 284b 39.18 N 76.37 W
Maryland Line 208 39.42 N 76.39 W
Maryland Park 284c 38.53 N 76.54 W
Marylebone 262 53.34 N 2.38 W
Maryneal 196 32.14 N 100.27 W
Marypark 46 57.26 N 3.21 W
Maryport 44 54.43 N 3.30 W
Marys ≃, Il., U.S. 194 37.53 N 89.47 W
Marys ≃, Nv., U.S. 204 41.04 N 115.16 W
Marys Creek ≃ 202 42.18 N 115.48 W
Mary's Igloo 180 65.09 N 165.04 W
Marys Peak ∧ 202 44.30 N 123.33 W
Marystown 186 47.10 N 55.09 W
Marysvale 200 38.26 N 112.13 W
Marysville, Austl. 169 37.31 S 145.45 E
Marysville, B.C., Can. 182 49.38 N 115.57 W
Marysville, N.B., Can. 186 45.59 N 66.35 W
Marysville, Ca., U.S. 226 39.08 N 121.35 W
Marysville, Ks., U.S. 198 39.50 N 96.38 W
Marysville, Mi., U.S. 214 42.54 N 82.29 W
Marysville, Oh., U.S. 214 40.14 N 83.22 W
Marysville, Pa., U.S. 208 40.20 N 76.55 W
Marysville, Wa., U.S. 224 48.03 N 122.10 W
Maryūṭ, Buḥayrat ⊜ 142 31.08 N 29.56 E
Maryvale 171a 28.05 S 152.15 E
Maryvale ◆[8] 275b 43.46 N 79.18 W
Maryville, Mo., U.S. 194 40.20 N 94.52 W
Maryville, Tn., U.S. 192 35.45 N 83.58 W
Marywell 46 57.02 N 2.42 W
Marywood 216 41.48 N 88.18 W
Marzabotto 64 44.20 N 11.12 E
Marzagão 255 17.59 S 48.39 W
Marzahn ◆[8] 264a 52.33 N 13.33 E
Marzahna 54 52.00 N 12.46 E
Marzahne 54 52.31 N 12.31 E
Marzal, Aven de ⊥[5] 62 44.22 N 4.31 E
Marzo, Punta ≻ 246 6.50 N 77.42 W
Marzolara 64 44.38 N 10.10 E
Marzūq 146 25.55 N 13.55 E
Marzūq, Ḥamādat ◆[2] 146 26.10 N 12.45 E
Marzūq, Ṣaḥrā' ◆[2] 146 24.30 N 13.00 E
Masa 152 3.45 S 15.29 E
Masachapa 236 11.47 N 86.31 W
Mas'adah (Cæsarea Philippi) 132 33.14 N 35.45 E
Masada → Meẓada, Ḥorvot ⊥ 132 31.19 N 35.21 E
Más Afuera, Isla → Alejandro Selkirk, Isla I 244 33.45 S 80.46 W
Masagua 236 14.12 N 90.51 W
Masaguisi 116 12.41 N 121.32 E
Masai 114 1.29 N 103.53 E
Masai Mara Game Reserve ◆[4] 154 1.15 S 35.15 E
Masai Steppe ⩘[1] 154 4.45 S 37.00 E
Masak 85 43.37 N 78.18 E
Masaka 154 0.20 S 31.44 E
Masaki, Nihon 96 33.47 N 132.42 E
Masaki, Nihon 268 35.13 N 140.02 E
Masalembu Besar, Pulau I 112 5.34 S 114.26 E
Masally 84 39.03 N 48.40 E
Masalok, Puntan ≻ 174n 15.01 N 145.41 E
Masamba 112 2.32 S 120.20 E
Masan 98 35.11 N 128.32 E
Masangwe ∧ 154 5.28 S 30.05 E
Masānjor 126 24.07 N 87.19 E
Masapelid Island I 116 9.42 N 125.39 E
Masapun 112 7.47 S 126.38 E
Masāraḥ 142 27.29 N 30.50 E
Masaran 115a 7.28 S 110.55 E
Ma'ṣarat Samālūṭ 142 28.19 N 30.43 E
Masaryktown 220 28.26 N 82.27 W
Masasi 154 10.43 S 38.48 E
Masatepe 236 11.55 N 86.09 W
Más a Tierra, Isla → Róbinson Crusoe, Isla I 244 33.38 S 78.52 W
Masaya 236 11.58 N 86.06 W
Masaya □[5] 236 12.00 N 86.10 W
Masba 146 11.30 N 13.00 E
Masbate 116 12.22 N 123.36 E
Masbate □[4] 116 12.20 N 123.30 E
Masbate Island I 116 12.15 N 123.30 E
Masbate Pass ɥ 116 12.30 N 123.35 E
Mascali 70 37.45 N 15.12 E
Mascarene Basin ✥[1] 12 15.00 S 56.00 E
Mascarene Islands II 157c 21.00 S 57.00 E
Mascarene Plateau ✥[3] 12 10.00 S 60.00 E
Mascasín 252 31.22 S 66.59 W
Maschen 52 53.24 N 10.02 E
Maschito 68 40.54 N 15.50 E
Mascot, Austl. 274a 33.56 S 151.12 E
Mascot, Tn., U.S. 192 36.03 N 83.44 W
Mascota 234 20.32 N 104.49 W
Mascota ≃ 234 20.38 N 104.59 W
Mascotte 220 28.35 N 81.53 W
Mascouche 206 45.45 N 73.36 W
Mascouche ≃ 206 45.41 N 73.40 W
Mascoutah 219 38.29 N 89.47 W
Mascuppic Lake ⊜ 283 42.41 N 71.23 W
Mase 102 27.16 N 104.08 E
Masefield 184 49.09 N 107.48 W
Masela, Pulau I 164 8.09 S 129.50 E
Masenberg ∧ 61 47.21 N 15.53 E
Maser 64 45.48 N 11.59 E
Maserada sul Piave 64 45.45 N 12.17 E
Maseru 158 29.28 S 27.30 E
Masevaux 58 47.47 N 7.00 E
Maševka 78 49.26 N 34.52 E
Maševo 78 52.06 N 32.48 E
Masha 100 27.26 N 117.50 E
Mashaba 154 20.02 S 30.29 E
Mashaba Mountains ⩘ 154 18.45 S 30.32 E
Mash'abbe' Sade 132 31.00 N 34.47 E
Mashābih I 128 25.37 N 36.29 E
Mashalah 142 30.44 N 31.08 E
Masham 44 54.13 N 1.40 W
Mashan, Zhg. 89 45.13 N 130.35 E
Mashan, Zhg. 100 27.33 N 113.46 E
Mashan, Zhg. 102 23.50 N 108.16 E
Mashar 140 9.14 N 26.52 E
Mashbury 260 51.47 N 0.24 E
Mashel ≃ 224 46.51 N 122.20 W

≃ River	Fluß	Río	Rivière	Rio
≚ Canal	Kanal	Canal	Canal	Canal
⌞ Waterfall, Rapids	Wasserfall, Stromschnellen	Cascada, Rápidos	Chute d'eau, Rapides	Cascata, Rápidos
ɥ Strait	Meeresstraße	Estrecho	Détroit	Estreito
⊂ Bay, Gulf	Bucht, Golf	Bahía, Golfo	Baie, Golfe	Baía, Golfo
⊜ Lake, Lakes	See, Seen	Lago, Lagos	Lac, Lacs	Lago, Lagos
≡ Swamp	Sumpf	Pantano	Marais	Pântano
⍓ Ice Features, Glacier	Eis- und Gletscherformen	Accidentes Glaciales	Formes glaciaires	Acidentes glaciares
⏚ Other Hydrographic Features	Andere Hydrographische Objekte	Otros Elementos Hidrográficos	Autres données hydrographiques	Outros acidentes hidrográficos

✥ Submarine Features	Untermeerische Objekte	Accidentes Submarinos	Formes de relief sous-marin	Acidentes submarinos
□ Political Unit	Politische Einheit	Unidad Politica	Entité politique	Unidade política
ʊ Cultural Institution	Kulturelle Institution	Institución Cultural	Institution culturelle	Instituição cultural
⊥ Historical Site	Historische Stätte	Sitio Histórico	Site historique	Sitio histórico
♠ Recreational Site	Erholungs- und Ferienort	Sitio de Recreo	Centre de loisirs	Area de Lazer
⊠ Airport	Flughafen	Aeropuerto	Aéroport	Aeroporto
▪ Military Installation	Militäranlage	Instalación Militar	Installation militaire	Instalação militar
◆ Miscellaneous	Verschiedenes	Misceláneo	Divers	Diversos

ENGLISH / DEUTSCH

Name	Page	Lat.°′	Long.°′
Mashenqiao	**105**	40.04 N	117.36 E
Masherbrum ∧	**123**	35.43 N	76.18 E
Mashgharah	**132**	33.32 N	35.39 E
Mashhad, Īrān	**128**	36.18 N	59.36 E
Mash-had, Yis.	**132**	32.44 N	35.19 E
Mashi, Nig.	**150**	13.00 N	7.54 E
Mashi, Zhg.	**100**	29.05 N	114.22 E
Mashi, Zhg.	**100**	25.01 N	114.09 E
Mashike	**92a**	43.51 N	141.31 E
Mashiko	**94**	36.28 N	140.06 E
Mashita ≏	**94**	35.40 N	137.10 E
Mashīz	**128**	29.56 N	56.37 E
Mashkai ≏	**128**	26.02 N	65.19 E
Māshkel, Hāmūn-i- ⊜	**128**	28.15 N	63.00 E
Māshkel, Rūd-i- (Māshkīd) ≏	**128**	28.02 N	63.25 E
Mashki Chāh	**128**	29.01 N	62.27 E
Māshkīd (Rūd-i-Māshkel) ≏	**128**	28.02 N	63.25 E
Mashonaland North □[4]	**154**	16.30 S	30.00 E
Mashonaland South □[4]	**154**	18.15 S	30.45 E
Mashpee	**207**	41.38 N	70.28 W
Mashra'ur-Raqq	**140**	8.25 N	29.16 E
Mashtūl as-Sūq	**142**	30.22 N	31.22 E
Mashū-ko ⊜	**92a**	43.35 N	144.32 E
Masibi	**152**	11.08 S	22.42 E
Masihi	**114**	2.47 N	99.40 E
Masīlah, Wādī al- V	**144**	15.10 N	51.08 E
Masi-Manimba	**152**	4.46 S	17.55 E
Masin	**164**	6.15 S	139.19 E
Masina	**272b**	22.55 N	88.32 E
Masindi	**154**	1.41 N	31.43 E
Masini Port	**154**	1.42 N	32.05 E
Masinloc	**116**	15.32 N	119.57 E
Masīr	**142**	31.03 N	31.00 E
Maṣīrah I	**118**	20.25 N	58.50 E
Maṣīrah, Khalīj c	**118**	20.10 N	58.15 E
Masis	**84**	40.00 N	44.29 E
Masisea	**248**	8.36 S	74.19 W
Masisi	**154**	1.24 S	28.49 E
Masjed-e Soleymān	**128**	31.58 N	49.18 E
Masjid Tanah	**114**	2.21 N	102.07 E
Mask, Lough ⊜	**48**	53.35 N	9.20 W
Maska	**150**	11.20 N	7.20 E
Maskan, Ras ›	**144**	11.10 N	43.33 E
Maskanah	**130**	36.01 N	38.05 E
Maskin	**128**	23.35 N	56.39 E
Maškino	**82**	54.53 N	36.08 E
Maskinongé □[6]	**206**	46.35 N	73.30 W
Maskinongé ≏, P.Q., Can.	**206**	46.10 N	73.01 W
Maskinongé ≏, P.Q., Can.	**206**	45.49 N	74.40 W
Maskinongé, Lac ⊜	**206**	46.19 N	73.23 W
Maškoviči	**82**	54.11 N	36.17 E
Masku	**26**	60.34 N	22.06 E
Maskūtān	**128**	26.51 N	59.49 E
Maskwa ≏	**184**	50.33 N	96.08 W
Masl'anino	**86**	54.20 N	84.13 E
Masl'anskaja	**86**	55.56 N	70.08 E
Maslova	**265a**	59.47 N	30.48 E
Maslovka	**78**	51.33 N	39.14 E
Maslovo	**86**	60.07 N	60.30 E
Masnières	**50**	50.07 N	3.13 E
Maso	**150**	7.14 N	2.53 W
Masoala	**157b**	15.59 S	50.10 E
Masoala, Cap ›	**157b**	15.59 S	50.13 E
Masoala, Presqu'île de ›[1]	**157b**	15.40 S	50.12 E
Masoarivo	**157b**	19.03 S	44.19 E
Masomeloka	**157b**	20.17 S	48.37 E
Mason, Mi., U.S.	**216**	42.34 N	84.26 W
Mason, Oh., U.S.	**218**	39.21 N	84.18 W
Mason, Tn., U.S.	**194**	35.24 N	89.31 W
Mason, Tx., U.S.	**196**	30.44 N	99.13 W
Mason, W.V., U.S.	**188**	39.01 N	82.01 W
Mason □[6], Il., U.S.	**219**	40.18 N	90.04 W
Mason □[6], Ky., U.S.	**218**	38.35 N	83.48 W
Mason □[6], Wa., U.S.	**224**	47.20 N	123.09 W
Mason, Lake ⊜	**162**	27.39 S	119.34 E
Mason Bay c	**172**	46.56 S	167.44 E
Mason City, Il., U.S.	**219**	40.12 N	89.41 W
Mason City, Ia., U.S.	**190**	43.09 N	93.12 W
Mason City, Ne., U.S.	**198**	41.13 N	99.18 W
Masone	**62**	44.30 N	8.42 E
Masonicus Brook ≏	**276**	41.06 N	74.09 W
Mason Lake ⊜	**224**	47.20 N	122.57 W
Masons Creek ≏	**285**	39.59 N	74.51 W
Mason Valley V	**226**	39.07 N	119.10 W
Masonville, N.J., U.S.	**285**	39.59 N	74.52 W
Masonville, N.Y., U.S.	**210**	42.15 N	75.23 W
Maspeth ◆[8]	**276**	40.43 N	73.55 W
Masqat (Muscat)	**128**	23.37 N	58.35 E
Maṣra'	**142**	27.14 N	31.02 E
Massa	**64**	44.01 N	10.09 E
Massa-Carrara □[4]	**64**	44.15 N	10.03 E
Massachusetts □[3], U.S.	**178**	42.15 N	71.50 W
Massachusetts □[3], U.S.	**207**	42.15 N	71.50 W
Massachusetts (Boston), University of ʊ[2]	**283**	42.19 N	71.03 W
Massachusetts Bay c	**207**	42.20 N	70.50 W
Massachusetts Correctional Institution ʊ	**283**	42.07 N	71.18 W
Massachusetts Institute of Technology ʊ[2]	**283**	42.21 N	71.06 W
Massaciuccoli, Lago di ⊜	**66**	43.50 N	10.20 E
Massacre Lake ⊜	**204**	41.39 N	119.35 W
Massa Fermana	**66**	43.09 N	13.28 E
Massa Fiscaglia	**66**	44.48 N	12.01 E
Massafra	**68**	40.35 N	17.07 E
Massaguet	**146**	12.28 N	15.26 E
Massakory	**146**	13.00 N	15.44 E
Massalassef	**146**	11.43 N	17.08 E
Massa Lombarda	**66**	44.27 N	11.49 E
Massa Lubrense	**68**	40.36 N	14.20 E
Massa Marittima	**66**	43.03 N	10.53 E
Massa Martana	**66**	42.46 N	12.31 E
Massandra	**78**	44.32 N	34.12 E
Massangano	**152**	9.37 S	14.15 E
Massangena	**156**	21.32 S	32.57 E
Massapê	**250**	3.31 S	40.19 W
Massapequa	**210**	40.40 N	73.28 W
Massapequa Park	**276**	40.40 N	73.27 W
Massapequa Reserve County Park ♣	**276**	40.42 N	73.27 W
Massapoag Brook ≏	**283**	42.09 N	71.09 W
Massapoag Lake ⊜	**283**	42.06 N	71.11 W
Massara	**156**	18.20 S	34.09 E
Massarosa	**66**	43.52 N	10.20 E
Massasoit State Park ♣	**207**	41.53 N	71.01 W
Massaua → Mitsiwa	**144**	15.38 N	39.28 E
Massawa → Mitsiwa	**144**	15.38 N	39.28 E
Massawippi ≏	**206**	45.22 N	71.51 W
Massawippi, Lake ⊜	**206**	45.14 N	72.00 W
Massay	**50**	47.09 N	2.00 E
Massé, Ruisseau ≏	**275a**	45.28 N	73.17 W
Massello	**62**	44.57 N	7.04 E
Massen	**52**	51.32 N	7.38 E
Massena, Ia., U.S.	**198**	41.15 N	94.46 W
Massena, N.Y., U.S.	**206**	44.55 N	74.53 W
Massenya	**146**	11.24 N	16.10 E
Masset	**182**	54.02 N	132.09 W
Masset Inlet c	**182**	53.42 N	132.20 W
Masseube	**32**	43.26 N	0.35 E
Massey	**190**	46.12 N	82.05 W
Massiac	**32**	45.15 N	3.12 E
Massiaru	**76**	58.00 N	24.35 E
Massico, Monte ∧	**68**	41.10 N	13.55 E
Massieville	**218**	39.16 N	82.58 W
Massif Central → Central, Massif ⋏	**32**	45.00 N	3.10 E
Massillon	**214**	40.48 N	81.32 W
Massima Camp	**152**	1.27 S	11.42 E
Massina	**273b**	4.22 S	15.22 E
Massina ◆[1]	**150**	14.30 N	5.00 W
Massinga	**156**	23.20 S	35.25 E
Massingir	**156**	23.51 S	32.04 E
Massive, Mount ∧	**200**	39.12 N	106.28 W
Masson, Lac ⊜	**206**	46.03 N	74.02 W
Masson Island I	**9**	66.08 S	96.34 E
Massy	**261**	48.44 N	2.17 E
Mastābah	**144**	20.49 N	39.20 E
Maštaga	**84**	40.32 N	50.00 E
Masterson	**196**	35.38 N	101.58 W
Masterton	**172**	40.57 S	175.40 E
Mas-Thibert	**62**	43.34 N	4.44 E
Mastic Point	**192**	25.03 N	77.57 W
Mastigouche ≏	**206**	46.20 N	73.24 W
Mastigouche Nord ≏	**206**	46.24 N	73.25 W
Mastūj	**123**	36.17 N	72.31 E
Mastūj ≏	**123**	35.54 N	71.49 E
Mastung	**120**	29.48 N	66.51 E
Mastūrah	**128**	23.06 N	38.50 E
Masu	**146**	12.10 N	13.19 E
Masua	**126**	24.16 N	90.46 E
Masuda	**96**	34.40 N	131.51 E
Masuho	**94**	35.34 N	138.28 E
Masuika	**152**	7.37 S	22.32 E
Masuku	**154**	17.12 S	27.07 E
Māsūleh	**128**	37.10 N	48.59 E
Masulipatam → Machilīpatnam	**122**	16.10 N	81.08 E
Masura	**126**	23.16 N	90.24 E
Masurai, Gunung ∧	**112**	2.30 S	101.51 E
Masury	**214**	41.12 N	80.32 W
Masvingo	**154**	20.05 S	30.50 E
Maṣyāf	**130**	35.03 N	36.21 E
Maszewo, Pol.	**30**	53.29 N	15.02 E
Maszewo, Pol.	**54**	52.06 N	14.55 E
Mat ≏	**38**	41.39 N	19.34 E
Mata, Indon.	**115b**	8.12 S	122.56 E
Mata, Zaïre	**152**	7.53 S	21.58 E
Mata Amarilla	**254**	49.36 S	71.13 W
Mataba, Mount ∧	**269f**	14.42 N	121.10 E
Matabeleland North □[4]	**154**	19.00 S	27.15 E
Matabeleland South □[4]	**154**	21.00 S	29.15 E
Mātābhānga	**124**	26.20 N	89.13 E
Matabuena	**34**	41.10 N	3.40 W
Matachel ≏	**34**	38.50 N	6.17 W
Matachewan	**190**	47.56 N	80.39 W
Matacuni ≏	**246**	3.02 N	65.16 W
Matad	**88**	46.58 N	115.18 E
Mata de Plátano, Quebrada ≏	**286c**	10.35 N	66.46 W
Matadero Creek ≏	**282**	37.26 N	122.08 W
Mata de São João	**255**	12.31 S	38.17 W
Matadi	**152**	5.49 S	13.27 E
Matador	**196**	34.00 N	100.49 W
Matagalpa	**236**	12.55 N	85.55 W
Matagalpa □[5]	**236**	13.00 N	85.30 W
Matagami	**176**	49.45 N	77.38 W
Matag-ob	**116**	11.07 N	124.29 E
Matagorda	**196**	28.41 N	95.58 W
Matagorda □[6]	**222**	28.57 N	96.00 W
Matagorda Bay c	**196**	28.35 N	96.20 W
Matagorda Island I	**196**	28.15 N	96.30 W
Matagorda Peninsula ›[1]	**196**	28.32 N	96.07 W
Mata Grande	**250**	9.07 S	37.44 W
Matahiae, Pointe ›	**174s**	17.49 S	149.17 W
Mataiea	**174s**	17.45 S	149.23 W
Mataiva I[1]	**14**	14.53 S	148.40 W
Mataj	**86**	45.53 N	78.43 E
Matajing	**107**	29.32 N	104.00 E
Matak, Pulau I	**112**	3.18 N	106.16 E
Matakana, Austl.	**166**	33.00 S	145.54 E
Matakana, N.Z.	**172**	36.21 S	174.43 E
Matakana Island I	**172**	37.35 S	176.05 E
Matakitaki ≏	**172**	41.48 S	172.19 E
Matala	**152**	14.46 S	15.04 E
Matale	**122**	7.28 N	80.37 E
Matam	**150**	15.40 N	13.15 W
Matama	**96**	33.36 N	131.28 E
Matama, Cerro ∧	**236**	9.47 N	83.15 W
Matamata	**172**	37.49 S	175.47 E
Matameye	**150**	13.26 N	8.28 E
Matamoras	**210**	41.22 N	74.42 W
Matamoros, Méx.	**232**	25.53 N	97.30 W
Matamoros, Méx.	**232**	25.32 N	103.15 W
Matan	**112**	1.52 S	110.00 E
Matana	**154**	3.46 S	29.41 E
Matana, Danau ⊜	**112**	2.28 S	121.20 E
Matanalem, Cape ›	**164**	2.28 S	149.57 E
Matandu ≏	**154**	8.45 S	39.19 E
Matane	**186**	48.51 N	67.32 W
Matang, Malay.	**114**	4.49 N	100.41 E
Matang, Zhg.	**100**	29.17 N	113.05 E
Matang, Zhg.	**100**	32.20 N	121.04 E
Matangi	**172**	37.49 S	175.25 E
Matani	**84**	42.06 N	45.13 E
Matanni	**123**	33.48 N	71.34 E
Matanuska ≏	**180**	61.30 N	149.15 W
Matanza, Aeródromo ⊠	**288**	34.44 S	58.30 W
Matanza, Río de la ≏	**258**	34.42 S	58.28 W
Matanzas, Cuba	**240p**	23.03 N	81.35 W
Matanzas, Méx.	**234**	21.37 N	101.38 W
Matanzas □[4]	**240p**	22.40 N	81.20 W
Matanzas, Bahía de c	**240p**	23.04 N	81.30 W
Matanza → San Justo	**258**	34.40 S	58.33 W
Matapa	**156**	23.11 S	24.39 E
Matapalo, Cabo ›	**236**	8.23 N	83.19 W
Matape ≏	**232**	28.25 N	110.26 W
Matapédia	**186**	47.58 N	66.57 W
Matapédia, Lac ⊜	**186**	48.33 N	67.33 W
Matapi ≏	**250**	0.03 S	51.12 W
Mata Point ›	**174v**	19.07 S	169.51 W
Matapu	**172**	39.29 S	174.14 E
Mataquito ≏	**252**	34.59 S	72.12 W
Matará, Perú	**248**	7.16 S	78.16 W
Matara, S. Lan.	**122**	5.56 N	80.33 E
Mataram	**115b**	8.35 S	116.07 E
Matarani	**248**	17.00 S	72.06 W
Mataranka	**164**	14.56 S	133.07 E
Matārimah, Ra's ›	**142**	29.27 N	32.42 E
Matarinao Bay c	**116**	11.14 N	125.34 E
Mataró	**34**	41.32 N	2.27 E
Matarraña ≏	**34**	41.14 N	0.22 E
Matas ∧	**266d**	41.30 N	2.16 E
Matasiri, Pulau I	**112**	4.48 S	115.48 E
Mätäsvaara	**26**	63.26 N	29.36 E
Matata	**172**	37.53 S	176.45 E
Matatepai, Pointe ›	**174x**	9.43 S	139.02 W
Matatiele	**158**	30.24 S	28.43 E
Mātātīla Dam ◆[6]	**124**	25.06 N	78.22 E
Matatindoc Point ›	**116**	9.43 N	122.23 E
Matatula, Cape ›	**174u**	14.15 S	170.34 W
Mataura	**172**	46.11 S	168.52 E
Matauré ≏, Bra.	**248**	5.30 S	60.45 W
Mataura ≏, N.Z.	**172**	46.34 S	168.43 E
Matāutu	**175a**	13.57 S	171.56 W
Mataval, Baie de c	**174s**	17.30 S	149.30 W
Matavera	**174k**	21.13 S	159.44 W
Mataveri	**174z**	27.10 S	109.27 E
Mataveri Airstrip ⊠	**174z**	27.10 S	109.25 W
Matawai	**172**	38.21 S	177.32 E
Matawan	**208**	40.24 N	74.13 W
Matawin ≏	**206**	46.54 N	72.56 W
Matāy	**142**	28.25 N	30.46 E
Matbūl	**142**	31.05 N	31.02 E
Matča	**85**	39.27 N	69.39 E
Matchaponix Brook ≏	**276**	40.23 N	74.23 W
Matchi-Manitou, Lac ⊜	**190**	48.00 N	77.04 W
Matching	**260**	51.47 N	0.13 E
Matching Green	**260**	51.47 N	0.14 E
Matching Tye	**260**	51.47 N	0.12 E
Mateare	**236**	12.14 N	86.26 W
Mateba, Île de I	**152**	5.54 S	12.50 E
Matehuala	**234**	23.39 N	100.39 W
Mateke Hills ⋏[2]	**154**	21.48 S	31.00 E
Mateko	**152**	4.03 S	18.55 E
Matelica	**66**	43.15 N	13.00 E
Matemo, Ilha I	**154**	12.13 S	40.36 E
Matera	**68**	40.40 N	16.37 E
Matera □[4]	**68**	40.30 N	16.25 E
Materborn	**52**	51.46 N	6.06 E
Matese, Lago del ⊜	**68**	41.25 N	14.25 E
Matese, Monti del ⋏	**66**	41.27 N	14.22 E
Mátészalka	**30**	47.57 N	22.19 E
Matete ≏	**273b**	4.24 S	15.20 E
Matetsi	**154**	18.16 S	25.56 E
Mateur	**148**	37.03 N	9.40 E
Matewan	**192**	37.37 N	82.09 W
Matfield	**207**	42.02 N	70.59 W
Matfors	**26**	62.21 N	17.02 E
Matha	**32**	45.52 N	0.19 W
Mathbaria	**126**	22.18 N	89.57 E
Mathematicians Seamounts ✣[3]	**16**	15.00 N	111.00 W
Mather, Mb., Can.	**184**	49.06 N	99.07 W
Mather, Ca., U.S.	**226**	37.53 N	119.52 W
Mather, Pa., U.S.	**188**	39.56 N	80.04 W
Mather Air Force Base ■	**226**	38.34 N	121.18 W
Mather Gorge V	**284c**	38.59 N	77.15 W
Matheson	**190**	48.32 N	80.28 W
Matheson Island	**184**	51.44 N	96.56 W
Matheu	**258**	34.22 S	58.50 W
Mathews	**208**	37.26 N	76.19 W
Mathews □[6]	**208**	37.25 N	76.20 W
Mathews, Lake ⊜	**228**	33.51 N	117.26 W
Mathi	**62**	45.15 N	7.32 E
Mathis	**196**	28.05 N	97.49 W
Māthle	**272b**	22.35 N	88.14 E
Mathry	**42**	51.57 N	5.05 W
Mathura, India	**122**	10.57 N	78.27 E
Mathura, India	**124**	27.30 N	77.41 E
Mathura Bil ⊜	**272b**	22.56 N	88.29 E
Mathurai → Madurai	**122**	9.56 N	78.07 E
Mathurāpur, Bngl.	**126**	24.02 N	88.47 E
Mathurāpur, Bngl.	**126**	23.17 N	89.15 E
Mati	**116**	6.57 N	126.13 E
Matiacoali	**150**	12.22 N	1.02 E
Matiakhola	**126**	23.16 N	86.56 E
Mātiāli	**124**	26.56 N	88.49 E
Matiāri	**120**	25.36 N	68.27 E
Matias Barbosa	**256**	21.53 S	43.20 W
Matías Romero	**234**	16.53 N	95.02 W
Mātibhānga	**126**	22.49 N	89.56 E
Matícora ≏	**246**	11.03 N	71.09 W
Matiere	**172**	38.45 S	175.06 E
Matignon	**32**	48.36 N	2.18 W
Matiguás	**236**	12.50 N	85.28 W
Matinecock	**276**	40.53 N	73.38 W
Matinenda Lake ⊜	**190**	46.22 N	82.57 W
Matinha	**250**	3.06 S	45.02 W
Matinicock Point ›	**276**	40.54 N	73.38 W
Matinicus Island I	**188**	43.54 N	68.55 W
Matino	**68**	40.02 N	18.08 E
Matipó	**255**	20.17 S	42.21 W
Matir Ṭāris	**142**	29.22 N	30.54 E
Matiyure ≏	**246**	7.36 N	67.39 W
Matjiesfontein	**158**	33.14 S	20.35 E
Matkasel'kja	**26**	61.58 N	30.33 E
Mātla ≏[1]	**126**	22.04 N	88.38 E
Matlab Bāzār	**126**	23.20 N	90.43 E
Matlacha	**220**	26.37 N	82.05 W
Matlacha Pass)(	**220**	26.37 N	82.04 W
Matlamanyane	**156**	19.33 S	25.57 E
Matlapa	**234**	21.15 N	98.50 W
M'atlevo	**76**	54.54 N	35.39 E
Mātli	**120**	25.02 N	68.39 E
Matlock, Eng., U.K.	**44**	53.08 N	1.32 W
Matlock, Wa., U.S.	**224**	47.14 N	123.25 W
Matlock, Mount ∧	**169**	37.35 S	146.11 E
Matmata	**148**	33.33 N	9.58 E
Matnog	**116**	12.35 N	124.05 E
Mato	**154**	8.01 S	24.55 E
Mato ≏	**246**	7.09 N	65.07 W
Mato, Cerro ∧	**246**	7.15 N	65.14 W
Matoaca	**208**	37.13 N	77.28 W
Matobe	**112**	2.42 S	100.11 E
Matočkin Šar	**72**	73.16 N	56.27 E
Matočkin Šar, proliv)(	**72**	73.20 N	55.21 E
Mato Grosso □[3]	**242**	12.00 S	57.00 W
Mato Grosso, Planalto do ⋏[1]	**242**	15.30 S	56.00 W
Mato Grosso do Sul □[3]	**242**	20.00 S	55.00 W
Matola-Rio	**156**	25.58 S	32.26 E
Matombo	**154**	7.03 S	37.46 E
Mato Mole, Serra do ⋏[2]	**256**	23.00 S	46.12 W
Matong	**164**	5.35 S	151.45 E
Matonipi ≏	**186**	51.21 N	69.45 W
Matope	**154**	15.20 S	34.59 E
Matopo Hills ⋏[2]	**154**	20.36 S	28.28 E
Matopos	**154**	20.24 S	28.28 E
Matos ≏	**248**	14.07 S	65.25 W
Matosinhos	**34**	41.11 N	8.42 W
Matoso, Ponta do ›	**287a**	22.50 S	43.11 W
Matou, T'aiwan	**100**	23.11 N	120.14 E
Matou, Zhg.	**98**	36.29 N	114.26 E
Matou, Zhg.	**100**	29.49 N	115.35 E
Matou, Zhg.	**100**	25.14 N	118.22 E
Matou, Zhg.	**100**	30.48 N	118.29 E
Matou, Zhg.	**105**	39.46 N	116.49 E
Matou, Zhg.	**105**	39.18 N	116.45 E
Matou, Zhg.	**105**	39.33 N	116.07 E
Matouji	**98**	35.02 N	115.07 E
Matour	**58**	46.18 N	4.29 E
Matoury	**250**	4.51 N	52.20 W
Matouxi	**107**	30.15 N	106.31 E
Matouying	**98**	39.18 N	118.47 E
Matouzhen, Zhg.	**98**	34.39 N	118.18 E
Matouzhen, Zhg.	**100**	33.32 N	118.56 E
Mato Verde	**255**	15.23 S	42.52 W
Matozinhos	**255**	19.35 S	44.07 W
Mátra ⋏	**30**	47.55 N	20.00 E
Maṭraḥ	**128**	23.38 N	58.34 E
Matraville	**274a**	33.54 S	151.18 E
Matrei am Brenner	**64**	47.08 N	11.27 E
Matrei in Osttirol	**64**	47.00 N	12.32 E
Matru	**150**	7.36 N	12.11 W
Matsap	**158**	28.38 S	22.47 E
Matsapha	**158**	26.29 S	31.23 E
Matsari	**152**	5.21 N	12.14 E
Matsena	**150**	13.05 N	10.05 E
Matsiatra ≏	**157b**	21.25 S	45.33 E
Matsieng	**158**	29.36 S	27.32 E
Matsknutsgårdarna	**40**	60.28 N	15.22 E
Matsqui	**224**	49.12 N	122.25 W
Matsubara	**96**	34.34 N	135.33 E
Matsubushi	**268**	35.55 N	139.49 E
Matsuda	**94**	35.21 N	139.09 E
Matsudai	**94**	37.08 N	138.37 E
Matsudo	**94**	35.47 N	139.54 E
Matsudo Race Track ♣	**268**	35.48 N	139.55 E
Matsue	**96**	35.28 N	133.04 E
Matsugasaki	**268**	35.53 N	139.58 E
Matsuida	**94**	36.19 N	138.48 E
Matsukawa, Nihon	**94**	36.25 N	137.51 E
Matsukawa, Nihon	**94**	35.36 N	137.55 E
Matsumae	**92**	41.26 N	140.07 E
Matsu → Matsu Tao I	**100**	26.09 N	119.56 E
Matsumoto	**94**	36.14 N	137.58 E
Matsuno	**96**	33.13 N	132.42 E
Matsunoyama	**94**	37.05 N	138.37 E
Matsuo	**94**	35.38 N	140.28 E
Matsuōji	**268**	35.08 N	140.01 E
Matsuoka	**94**	36.05 N	136.18 E
Matsuo-san ∧	**270**	34.38 N	135.44 E
Matsusaka	**94**	34.34 N	136.32 E
Matsushima	**92**	38.22 N	141.04 E
Matsu Tao I	**100**	26.09 N	119.56 E
Matsutō	**94**	36.31 N	136.34 E
Matsuura	**92**	33.22 N	129.42 E
Matsuyama	**96**	33.50 N	132.45 E
Matsuzaki	**94**	34.45 N	138.47 E
Matta ≏	**208**	38.07 N	77.26 W
Mattagami ≏	**176**	50.43 N	81.29 W
Mattagami Heights	**190**	48.29 N	81.22 W
Mattagami Lake ⊜	**190**	47.54 N	81.35 W
Mattamuskeet, Lake ⊜	**192**	35.30 N	76.11 W
Mattapan ◆[8]	**283**	42.16 N	71.06 W
Mattapoisett	**207**	41.39 N	70.49 W
Mattaponi	**208**	37.32 N	76.46 W
Mattaponi ≏	**208**	37.31 N	76.47 W
Mattarana	**62**	44.15 N	9.37 E
Mattarello	**64**	46.00 N	11.07 E
Mattawa, On., Can.	**190**	46.19 N	78.42 W
Mattawa, Wa., U.S.	**202**	46.44 N	119.54 W
Mattawa ≏	**190**	46.19 N	78.43 W
Mattawamkeag	**188**	45.30 N	68.21 W
Mattawamkeag ≏	**188**	45.30 N	68.24 W
Mattawan	**216**	42.12 N	85.47 W
Mattawana	**214**	40.30 N	77.44 W
Mattawoman Creek ≏	**208**	38.34 N	77.12 W
Matterhorn (Cervino) ∧, Europe	**58**	45.59 N	7.43 E
Matterhorn ∧, Nv., U.S.	**204**	41.49 N	115.23 W
Mattersburg	**61**	47.44 N	16.25 E
Mattertal V	**58**	46.10 N	7.49 E
Matteson	**216**	41.30 N	87.42 W
Matteson Lake ⊜	**216**	41.56 N	85.12 W
Matthew Flinders Memorial ⊥	**169**	38.19 S	145.04 E
Matthews	**216**	40.23 N	85.29 W
Matthews Mountain ∧[2]	**194**	37.29 N	90.21 W
Matthews Ridge	**246**	7.30 N	60.10 W
Matthew Town	**238**	20.57 N	73.40 W
Matthias Church ʊ[1]	**264c**	47.30 N	19.02 E
Matthiessen State Park ♣	**216**	41.17 N	89.01 W
Mattī, Sabkhat ⊜	**128**	23.30 N	52.00 E
Mattie, Lake ⊜	**220**	28.08 N	81.46 W
Mattig ≏	**60**	48.10 N	13.07 E
Mattighofen	**60**	48.06 N	13.09 E
Mattinata	**68**	41.42 N	16.03 E
Mattishall	**42**	52.39 N	1.02 E
Mattituck	**207**	40.59 N	72.32 W
Mattole ≏	**204**	40.18 N	124.21 W
Mattoon, Il., U.S.	**194**	39.28 N	88.22 W
Mattoon, Wi., U.S.	**190**	45.00 N	89.02 W
Mattox Creek ≏	**208**	38.12 N	76.58 W
Mattox Draw V	**198**	38.03 N	101.11 W
Mattsee	**64**	47.58 N	13.06 E
Mattsee ⊜	**60**	47.59 N	13.07 E
Mattydale	**210**	43.05 N	76.08 W
Matu	**112**	2.41 N	111.32 E
Matua	**112**	2.59 S	110.45 E
Matuba	**156**	24.27 S	32.55 E
Matucana	**248**	11.51 S	76.24 W
Matudo → Matsudo	**94**	35.47 N	139.54 E
Matue → Matsue	**96**	35.28 N	133.04 E
Matuku Island I	**175g**	19.10 S	179.46 E
Matumoto → Matsumoto	**94**	36.14 N	137.58 E
Matungo ≏	**152**	16.25 S	21.27 E
Matunuck	**207**	41.23 N	71.32 W
Matuog	**116**	9.55 N	123.09 E
Matura Bay c	**241r**	10.38 N	61.01 W
Maturín	**246**	9.45 N	63.11 W
Maturino	**76**	59.06 N	37.55 E
Matusadona National Park ♣	**154**	16.25 S	28.35 E
Matusov	**78**	49.03 N	31.34 E
Matutina	**255**	19.13 S	45.58 W
Matuto	**154**	14.46 S	35.59 E
Matutum, Mount ∧	**116**	6.22 N	125.05 E
Matuzaka → Matsusaka	**94**	34.34 N	136.32 E
Matvejevka	**80**	53.32 N	53.29 E
Matvejev Kurgan	**83**	47.35 N	38.52 E
Matvejevo, Ross.	**76**	58.38 N	43.30 E
Matvejevo, Ross.	**86**	57.47 N	57.51 E
Mátyásföld ◆[8]	**264c**	47.31 N	19.13 E
Matyra ≏	**76**	52.38 N	39.38 E
Matyševo	**80**	50.49 N	44.12 E
Mau	**124**	25.17 N	81.23 E
Maú (Ireng) ≏	**246**	3.33 N	59.51 W
Mauá, Bra.	**256**	23.40 S	46.27 W
Maúa, Moç.	**154**	13.51 S	37.10 E
Mauá □[7]	**287b**	23.40 S	46.27 W
Mau Aimma	**124**	25.42 N	81.55 E
Mauban	**116**	14.12 N	121.44 E
Maubara	**112**	8.37 S	125.12 E
Maubeuge	**50**	50.17 N	3.58 E
Mauchamps	**261**	48.32 N	2.12 E
Mauchline	**46**	55.31 N	4.24 W
Maud, Scot., U.K.	**46**	57.31 N	2.06 W
Maud, Mo., U.S.	**219**	39.37 N	92.15 W
Maud, Oh., U.S.	**218**	39.21 N	84.23 W
Maud, Ok., U.S.	**196**	35.08 N	96.46 W
Maud, Tx., U.S.	**194**	33.20 N	94.21 W
Maud, Point ›	**162**	23.06 S	113.45 E
Maudaha	**124**	25.41 N	80.07 E
Maude	**166**	34.28 S	144.18 E
Maudétour-en-Vexin	**261**	49.06 N	1.47 E
Mau-é-ele	**156**	24.21 S	34.07 E
Mauensee	**58**	47.10 N	8.04 E
Mauer ◆[8]	**264b**	48.09 N	16.16 E
Mauerbach	**264b**	48.15 N	16.10 E
Mauerbach ≏	**264b**	48.12 N	16.14 E
Mauerkirchen	**60**	48.11 N	13.08 E
Maués	**250**	3.24 S	57.42 W
Maués ≏	**246**	3.22 S	57.44 W
Maug ≏	**116**	8.20 N	125.53 E
Mauganj	**124**	24.41 N	81.53 E
Mauga Silisili ∧	**175a**	13.35 S	172.27 W
Maughold	**44**	54.18 N	4.17 W
Maug Islands II	**108**	20.01 N	145.13 E
Mauguio	**62**	43.37 N	4.01 E
Mauguio, Étang de c	**62**	43.35 N	4.02 E
Maui □[6]	**229a**	20.53 N	156.30 W
Maui I	**229a**	20.45 N	156.15 W
Mauk	**115a**	6.04 S	106.30 E
Mauke I	**14**	20.09 S	157.23 W
Maulbach	**56**	50.43 N	9.04 E
Maulbronn	**56**	49.00 N	8.49 E
Maulde	**50**	50.30 N	3.26 E
Mauldin	**192**	34.46 N	82.18 W
Mauldre ≏	**261**	48.58 N	1.49 E
Maule	**50**	48.55 N	1.51 E
Maule □[4]	**252**	35.30 S	71.30 W
Maule ≏	**252**	35.19 S	72.25 W
Maule, Laguna del ⊜	**252**	36.04 S	70.30 W
Mauléon	**32**	46.56 N	0.45 W
Mauléon-Licharre	**32**	43.14 N	0.53 W
Maulette	**261**	48.48 N	1.37 E
Maullín	**254**	41.38 S	73.37 W
Maulvi Bāzār	**120**	24.29 N	91.47 E
Maumaupaki ∧	**172**	36.58 S	175.35 E
Maumee	**214**	41.33 N	83.39 W
Maumee ≏	**216**	41.42 N	83.28 W
Maumee Bay c	**214**	41.43 N	83.26 W
Maumelle, Lake ⊜[1]	**194**	34.55 N	92.40 W
Maumere	**115b**	8.37 S	122.14 E
Maun	**156**	20.00 S	23.25 E
Maunabo	**240m**	18.01 N	65.54 W
Mauna Kea ∧[1]	**229d**	19.50 N	155.28 W
Maunaloa	**229a**	21.08 N	157.13 W
Mauna Loa ∧[1]	**229d**	19.29 N	155.36 W
Maunalua Bay c	**229c**	21.17 N	157.44 W
Maunath Bhanjan	**124**	25.57 N	83.33 E
Maunatlala	**156**	22.32 S	27.28 E
Maunesha ≏	**216**	43.13 N	88.57 W
Maungahaumi ∧	**172**	38.18 S	177.40 E
Maunga Roa ∧	**174k**	21.13 S	159.48 W
Maungatapere	**172**	35.45 S	174.12 E
Maungaturoto	**172**	36.06 S	174.22 E
Maungdaw	**110**	20.50 N	92.21 E
Maungmagan	**110**	14.09 N	98.06 E
Maungu	**154**	3.33 S	38.45 E
Maunoir, Lac ⊜	**180**	67.30 N	125.00 W
Maupihaa I[1]	**14**	16.50 S	153.55 W
Maupin	**224**	45.10 N	121.04 W
Maur	**123**	30.05 N	75.15 E
Mau Rānīpur	**124**	25.15 N	79.08 E
Maurecourt	**261**	49.00 N	2.04 E
Maure-de-Bretagne	**32**	47.54 N	1.59 W
Mauregard	**261**	49.02 N	2.35 E
Maurepas	**261**	48.45 N	1.55 E
Maurepas, Lake ⊜	**194**	30.15 N	90.30 W
Maures ⋏	**62**	43.16 N	6.23 E
Mauretanien → Mauritania □[1]	**134**	20.00 N	12.00 W
Mauri ≏	**248**	17.18 S	68.41 W
Mauria, Passo della)(	**64**	46.27 N	12.31 E
Mauriac	**32**	45.13 N	2.20 E
Maurice (Île) → Mauritius □[1]	**157c**	20.17 S	57.33 E
Maurice ≏	**208**	39.13 N	75.02 W
Maurice, Lake ⊜	**162**	29.28 S	130.58 E
Maurice K. Goddard State Park ♣	**214**	41.23 N	81.10 W
Mauricetown	**208**	39.17 N	74.58 W
Mauriceville	**172**	40.47 S	175.42 E
Mauricio → Mauritius □[1]	**157c**	20.17 S	57.33 E
Maurienne V	**62**	45.13 N	6.30 E
Maurino, Canal ≋	**286e**	33.34 S	70.32 W
Mauritania (Mauritanie) □[1]	**134**	20.00 N	12.00 W
Mauritanie → Mauritania □[1]	**134**	20.00 N	12.00 W
Mauriti	**250**	7.23 S	38.46 W
Mauritius □[1], Afr.	**138**	20.17 S	57.33 E
Mauritius □[1], Afr.	**157c**	20.17 S	57.33 E
Mauritius I	**157c**	20.17 S	57.33 E
Mauron	**32**	48.05 N	2.18 W
Maurs	**32**	44.43 N	2.11 E
Maurui	**154**	5.07 S	38.23 E
Maury ≏	**192**	37.37 N	79.27 W
Maury Channel)(	**176**	75.44 N	94.40 W
Maury Island ›[1]	**224**	47.20 N	122.24 W
Maussane	**62**	43.43 N	4.48 E
Mauston	**190**	43.47 N	90.04 W
Mautala	**126**	22.25 N	89.05 E
Mautau, Pointe ›	**174x**	9.42 S	138.58 W
Mautern an der Donau	**61**	48.24 N	15.35 E
Mauterndorf	**64**	47.08 N	13.40 E
Mautern in Steiermark	**61**	47.24 N	14.50 E
Mauth	**60**	48.53 N	13.35 E
Mauthausen	**61**	48.14 N	14.32 E
Mauthen	**64**	46.40 N	13.00 E
Mauvais Coulee V	**198**	48.21 N	99.06 W
Mauvaise Terre Creek ≏	**219**	39.43 N	90.38 W
Mauvaise Terre Lake ⊜[1]	**219**	39.42 N	90.12 W
Mauvezin	**32**	43.44 N	0.55 E
Mava	**164**	6.50 S	141.25 E
Mavaca ≏	**246**	2.31 N	65.11 W
Mavanza	**156**	22.43 S	35.08 E
Māvelikara	**122**	9.16 N	76.33 E
Maverick	**200**	33.43 N	109.32 W
Mavinga	**152**	15.50 S	20.21 E
Mavita	**156**	19.33 S	33.10 E
Mavonde	**156**	18.32 S	33.02 E
Mavuradona Mountains ⋏	**154**	16.30 S	31.20 E
Mawa	**154**	2.43 N	26.42 E
Mawai	**114**	1.52 N	103.57 E
Ma Wan I	**271d**	22.21 N	114.03 E
Mawāna	**124**	29.06 N	77.55 E
Mawangkanli Shan ∧	**120**	34.19 N	80.03 E
Mawangtang	**106**	30.42 N	120.42 E
Mawasangka	**112**	5.17 S	122.18 E
Mawchi	**110**	18.49 N	97.09 E
Maw-daung Pass)(	**110**	11.47 N	99.39 E
Mawdesley	**262**	53.38 N	2.46 W
Mawdesley Lake ⊜	**184**	54.01 N	100.39 W
Mawgan	**42**	50.06 N	5.06 W
Mawi	**272a**	28.39 N	77.25 E
Mawiwi	**154**	3.06 N	27.40 E
Māwiyah	**144**	13.35 N	44.21 E
Mawjib, Wādī al- V	**132**	31.28 N	35.34 E
Mawkhi	**110**	16.17 N	98.53 E
Mawlaik	**110**	23.38 N	94.24 E
Mawlamyaing → Mawlamyine	**110**	16.30 N	97.38 E
Mawlamyine (Moulmein)	**110**	16.30 N	97.38 E
Mawr, Wādī V	**144**	15.41 N	42.42 E
Mawshij	**144**	13.43 N	43.17 E
Mawson ʊ[3]	**9**	67.40 S	63.43 E
Mawson Escarpment ⫠[4]	**9**	73.05 S	68.10 E
Mawson Peninsula ›[1]	**9**	68.35 S	154.11 E
Maw Taung ∧	**110**	11.39 N	99.35 E
Mawuba	**102**	29.50 N	108.11 E
Max	**198**	47.49 N	101.17 W
Maxaranguape	**250**	5.31 S	35.16 W
Maxatawny	**208**	40.33 N	75.41 W
Maxcanú	**232**	20.35 N	89.59 W
Maxéville	**58**	48.43 N	6.10 E
Maxglan, Flughafen ⊠	**64**	47.48 N	13.02 E
Maxhütte Haidhof	**60**	49.12 N	12.05 E
Maxiang	**100**	24.41 N	118.15 E
Maximo	**214**	40.53 N	81.11 W
Maximo Paz	**258**	34.56 S	58.37 W
Maxinkuckee, Lake ⊜	**216**	41.12 N	86.24 W
Maxixe	**156**	23.51 S	35.21 E
Maxon Creek ≏	**196**	29.53 N	102.24 W
Maxton	**192**	34.44 N	79.20 W
Maxville	**206**	45.17 N	74.51 W
Maxwell, Ca., U.S.	**226**	39.16 N	122.11 W
Maxwell, In., U.S.	**218**	39.51 N	85.46 W
Maxwell, Ia., U.S.	**190**	41.53 N	93.23 W
Maxwell, Ne., U.S.	**198**	41.04 N	100.31 W
Maxwell, N.M., U.S.	**196**	36.32 N	104.32 W
Maxwell, Tx., U.S.	**222**	29.53 N	97.48 W
Maxwell Air Force Base ■	**194**	32.23 N	86.21 W
Maxwell Bay c	**176**	74.35 N	89.00 W
May	**196**	31.59 N	98.55 W
May ≏, Austl.	**162**	17.07 S	123.50 E
May ≏, Ab., Can.	**182**	55.43 N	111.22 W
May ≏, Pap. N. Gui.	**164**	4.35 S	141.35 E
May, Cape ›[1]	**208**	38.58 N	74.55 W
May, Isle of I	**46**	56.11 N	2.34 W
May, Mount ∧	**182**	54.02 N	119.58 W
Maya, Pulau I	**112**	1.10 S	109.35 E
May Aché	**146**	12.00 N	15.44 E
Mayaguana I	**238**	22.23 N	72.57 W
Mayaguana Passage)(	**238**	22.32 N	73.15 W
Mayagüez	**240m**	18.12 N	67.09 W
Mayagüez, Aeropuerto ⊠	**240m**	18.15 N	67.09 W
Mayagüez, Bahía de c	**240m**	18.12 N	67.10 W
Mayahi	**150**	13.58 N	7.40 E
Mayajigua	**240p**	22.14 N	79.04 W
Mayaka	**152**	5.17 N	16.52 E
Mayala	**273b**	4.21 S	15.09 E
Mayales, Punta ›	**236**	11.52 N	85.26 W
Mayama	**152**	3.51 S	14.54 E
Mayamba	**152**	4.46 S	16.52 E
Mayāmey	**128**	36.24 N	55.42 E
Maya Mountains ⋏	**232**	16.40 N	88.50 W
Mayang	**102**	27.41 N	109.35 E
Mayang-do I	**98**	40.00 N	128.12 E
Mayantoc	**116**	15.37 N	120.23 E
Mayao	**106**	30.50 N	120.23 E
Mayapan ⊥	**232**	20.38 N	89.27 W
Māyāpur	**272b**	22.27 N	88.08 E
Mayarí	**240p**	20.40 N	75.41 W
Mayarí Arriba	**240p**	20.25 N	75.32 W
Mayaro Bay c	**241r**	10.15 N	60.58 W
Maya-san ∧	**96**	34.44 N	135.12 E
Maybee	**216**	42.00 N	83.30 W
Maybeury	**192**	37.22 N	81.22 W
Maybole	**44**	55.21 N	4.41 W
Maybrook	**210**	41.29 N	74.13 W
Maychew	**144**	13.02 N	39.34 E
Maydelle	**222**	31.48 N	95.18 W
Maydena	**166**	42.55 S	146.30 E
Maydh	**144**	11.00 N	47.07 E
Maydī	**144**	16.20 N	42.46 E
Maydolong	**116**	11.30 N	125.30 E
Maydūm	**142**	29.22 N	31.10 E
Mayen	**56**	50.19 N	7.13 E
Mayence → Mainz	**56**	50.01 N	8.16 E
Mayenne	**32**	48.18 N	0.37 W
Mayenne □[5]	**32**	48.05 N	0.40 W
Mayenne ≏	**32**	47.30 N	0.33 W
Mayer	**200**	34.23 N	112.14 W
Mayerling	**61**	48.03 N	16.06 E
Mayersville	**194**	32.54 N	91.03 W
Mayerthorpe	**182**	53.57 N	115.08 W
Mayet	**50**	47.46 N	0.17 E
Mayfair ◆[8], S. Afr.	**273d**	26.12 S	28.01 E
Mayfair ◆[8], Pa., U.S.	**285**	40.02 N	75.03 W
Mayfield, N.Z.	**172**	43.49 S	171.25 E
Mayfield, Eng., U.K.	**42**	51.01 N	0.15 E
Mayfield, Eng., U.K.	**44**	53.01 N	1.45 W
Mayfield, Scot., U.K.	**46**	55.52 N	3.02 W
Mayfield, In., U.S.	**218**	40.11 N	85.21 W
Mayfield, Ky., U.S.	**194**	36.44 N	88.38 W
Mayfield, N.Y., U.S.	**210**	43.06 N	74.15 W
Mayfield, Oh., U.S.	**279a**	41.33 N	81.26 W
Mayfield, Pa., U.S.	**210**	41.32 N	75.32 W
Mayfield, Ut,. U.S.	**200**	39.06 N	111.42 W
Mayfield Creek ≏	**194**	36.57 N	89.05 W
Mayfield Dam ◆[6]	**224**	46.30 N	122.35 W
Mayfield Heights	**214**	41.31 N	81.27 W
Mayfield Lake ⊜[1]	**224**	46.31 N	122.32 W
Mayflower	**194**	34.57 N	92.25 W
Mayford	**260**	51.18 N	0.34 W
May Inlet c	**176**	76.15 N	100.45 W
Māyir, Sūrīy.	**130**	36.28 N	37.11 E
Māyir, Sūrīy.	**130**	36.23 N	37.02 E
May Jirgui	**150**	13.44 N	8.08 E
Maykop → Majkop	**84**	44.35 N	40.07 E
Mayland	**42**	51.39 N	0.47 E
Maymont	**184**	52.33 N	107.40 W
Maymūn, Wādī V	**146**	30.10 N	10.27 E
Maymyo	**110**	22.02 N	96.28 E
Mayna	**126**	22.14 N	87.47 E
Maynāmati	**124**	23.29 N	91.07 E
Maynard, Ia., U.S.	**190**	42.46 N	91.52 W
Maynard, Ma., U.S.	**207**	42.26 N	71.27 W
Maynard, Oh., U.S.	**214**	40.07 N	80.53 W
Maynardville	**192**	36.15 N	83.47 W
Mayne	**224**	48.51 N	123.18 W
Mayne ≏	**166**	23.34 S	141.18 E
Mayne Island I	**224**	48.51 N	123.17 W
Maynooth	**48**	53.23 N	6.35 W
Mayo, Yk., Can.	**180**	63.35 N	135.54 W
Mayo, Fl., U.S.	**192**	30.03 N	83.10 W
Mayo, Md., U.S.	**208**	38.53 N	76.30 W
Mayo □[6]	**48**	53.54 N	9.15 W
Mayo ≏, Arg.	**254**	45.46 S	69.43 W
Mayo ≏, Col.	**246**	1.40 N	77.21 W
Mayo ≏, Méx.	**232**	26.45 N	109.47 W
Mayo ≏, Perú	**248**	6.37 S	76.16 W
Mayoba	**154**	17.13 S	26.16 E
Mayo Bay c	**116**	6.56 N	126.22 E
Mayodan	**192**	36.24 N	79.58 W
Mayo Faran	**146**	8.57 N	12.04 E
Mayo-Kébbi □[5]	**146**	10.00 N	15.30 E
Mayoko, Congo	**152**	2.18 S	12.49 E
Mayoko, Zaïre	**152**	1.05 S	23.49 E
Mayola ≏	**44**	54.45 N	6.31 W
Mayo Lake ⊜	**180**	63.46 N	135.10 W
Mayo Ndaga	**146**	6.54 N	11.25 E
Mayon Volcano ∧[1]	**116**	13.15 N	123.41 E
Mayor Buratovich	**252**	39.15 S	62.37 W
Mayo Reservoir ⊜[1]	**192**	36.00 N	78.53 W
Mayor Island I	**172**	37.18 S	176.16 E
Mayor Pablo Lagerenza	**248**	19.58 S	60.45 W
Mayotte □[2], Afr.	**138**	12.50 S	45.10 E
Mayotte □[2], Afr.	**157a**	12.50 S	45.10 E
Mayoyao	**116**	16.59 N	121.14 E
Mayoyoque	**246**	0.41 N	75.18 W
Maypearl	**222**	32.19 N	97.01 W
May Pen	**241q**	17.58 N	77.14 W
Mayport Naval Station ■	**192**	30.22 N	81.24 W
Mayraira Point ›	**116**	18.39 N	120.51 E
Mayrán, Desierto de ◆[2]	**196**	25.45 N	102.45 W
Mayres	**62**	44.40 N	4.07 E
Mayrhofen	**64**	47.10 N	11.52 E
Mays	**218**	39.45 N	85.26 W
Maysah, Tall al- ∧	**132**	31.08 N	35.40 E
Maysān □[4]	**128**	32.00 N	47.00 E
Maysfield	**222**	30.54 N	96.51 W
Mays Landing	**208**	39.27 N	74.43 W
Mays Lick	**218**	38.31 N	83.50 W
Maysville, Ky., U.S.	**218**	38.38 N	83.44 W
Maysville, Mo., U.S.	**194**	39.53 N	94.21 W
Maysville, N.C., U.S.	**192**	34.54 N	77.13 W
Maysville, Ok., U.S.	**196**	34.49 N	97.24 W
Maythalūn	**132**	32.21 N	35.16 E
Maytiguid Island I	**116**	11.03 N	119.36 E
Maytown	**208**	40.04 N	76.35 W
Mayu	**100**	27.48 N	120.26 E
Mayumba	**152**	3.25 S	10.39 E
Mayung	**114**	0.49 N	103.03 E
Māyūram	**122**	11.06 N	79.40 E
Mayville, Mi., U.S.	**190**	43.20 N	83.21 W
Mayville, N.Y., U.S.	**214**	42.15 N	79.30 W
Mayville, N.D., U.S.	**198**	47.29 N	97.19 W
Mayville, Wi., U.S.	**190**	43.29 N	88.32 W
Maywood, Ca., U.S.	**280**	33.59 N	118.11 W
Maywood, Il., U.S.	**216**	41.52 N	87.50 W
Maywood, Mo., U.S.	**219**	39.57 N	91.36 W
Maywood, Ne., U.S.	**198**	40.39 N	100.37 W
Maywood, N.J., U.S.	**276**	40.54 N	74.03 W
Maywood, N.Y., U.S.	**210**	42.42 N	73.52 W
Maywood Race Track ♣	**278**	41.44 N	87.50 W
Mayyit, Al-Baḥr al- → Dead Sea ⊜	**132**	31.30 N	35.30 E
Maza, Arg.	**252**	36.50 S	63.19 W
Maza, Ross.	**80**	57.14 N	44.13 E
Mazabuka	**154**	15.51 S	27.46 E
Mazagan → El-Jadida	**148**	33.16 N	8.30 W
Mazagão	**250**	0.07 S	51.17 W
Mazagaon ◆[8]	**272c**	18.57 N	72.50 E
Mazagão Velho	**250**	0.13 S	51.25 W
Ma'zah, Jabal ∧	**130**	35.51 N	40.38 E
Mazamet	**32**	43.30 N	2.24 E
Mazamitla	**234**	19.55 N	103.02 W
Mazán ≏	**246**	3.28 S	73.11 W
Māzandarān □[4]	**128**	36.30 N	53.30 E
Mazanovo	**89**	51.40 N	128.52 E
Mazār, Jabal ∧	**132**	33.34 N	36.03 E
Mazar, Oued V	**148**	31.50 N	1.36 E
Mazara, Val di ◆[1]	**70**	37.50 N	13.00 E
Mazara del Vallo	**70**	37.39 N	12.35 E
Mazār-e Sharīf	**120**	36.42 N	67.06 E
Mazargues	**62**	43.15 N	5.24 E
Mazaro ≏	**70**	37.39 N	12.35 E
Mazarredo	**254**	47.05 S	66.42 W
Mazarrón	**34**	37.36 N	1.19 W
Mazarrón, Golfo de c	**34**	37.30 N	1.18 W

Symbols in the index entries represent the broad categories identified in the key at the right. Symbols with superior numbers (⋏[1]) identify subcategories (see complete key on page *I · 1).*

Symbole im Register stellen die rechts im Schlüssel erklärten Kategorien dar. Symbole mit hochgestellten Ziffern (⋏[1]) bezeichnen Unterabteilungen einer Kategorie (vgl. vollständiger Schlüssel auf Seite *I · 1).*

Los símbolos incluídos en el texto del índice representan las grandes categorias identificadas con la clave a la derecha. Los símbolos con numeros en su parte superior (⋏[1]) identifican las subcategorías (véase la clave completa en la página *I · 1).*

Les symboles de l'index représentent les catégories indiquées dans la légende à droite. Les symboles suivis d'un indice (⋏[1]) représentent des sous-catégories (voir légende complète à la page *I · 1).*

Os símbolos incluídos no texto do índice representam as grandes categorias identificadas com a chave à direita. Os símbolos com números em sua parte superior (⋏[1]) identificam as subcategorias (veja-se a chave completa à página *I · 1).*

English	Deutsch	Español	Français	Português
∧ Mountain	Berg	Montaña	Montagne	Montanha
⋏ Mountains	Gebirge	Montañas	Montagnes	Montanhas
)(Pass	Paß	Paso	Col	Passo
V Valley, Canyon	Tal, Cañon	Valle, Cañón	Vallée, Canyon	Vale, Canhão
≚ Plain	Ebene	Llano	Plaine	Planície
› Cape	Kap	Cabo	Cap	Cabo
I Island	Insel	Isla	Île	Ilha
II Islands	Inseln	Islas	Îles	Ilhas
⫠ Other Topographic Features	Andere Topographische Objekte	Otros Elementos Topográficos	Autres données topographiques	Outros acidentes topográficos

ESPAÑOL

Nombre	Página	Lat.°′	Long.°′ W = Oeste
Mazarsu	85	41.56 N	72.40 E
Mazaruni ≃	246	6.25 N	58.38 W
Mazatenango	236	14.32 N	91.30 W
Mazatlán	234	23.13 N	106.25 W
Mazatlán Villa de Flores	234	18.02 N	96.54 W
Mazatzal Mountains ⋏	200	34.00 N	111.55 W
Mazatzal Peak ∧	200	34.03 N	111.28 W
Maze	94	35.52 N	137.10 E
Maze ≃	94	35.40 N	137.10 E
Mažeikiai	76	56.19 N	22.20 E
Mazenod	184	49.53 N	106.14 W
Mazeppa, Mn., U.S.	190	44.16 N	92.32 W
Mazeppa, Pa., U.S.	210	40.59 N	76.59 W
Mazha	100	23.27 N	114.00 E
Māzhān, Īrān	128	32.35 N	59.01 E
Mazhan, Zhg.	98	36.04 N	118.45 E
Mazhangfang, Zhg.	104	40.44 N	120.53 E
Mazhangfang, Zhg.	104	42.23 N	122.26 E
Mazhuang, Zhg.	98	37.47 N	115.17 E
Mazhuang, Zhg.	100	32.54 N	114.03 E
Mazhuang, Zhg.	105	39.11 N	116.15 E
Mazhūr, Khubb al- ⊥[8]	128	27.45 N	43.55 E
Mazıdağı	130	37.30 N	40.30 E
Mazigou	105	40.28 N	114.48 E
Mazilovo ◆[8]	265b	55.44 N	37.26 E
Mazīnān	128	36.18 N	56.46 E
Mazinaw Lake ⊜	212	44.55 N	77.12 W
Mazirbe	76	57.41 N	22.21 E
Mazoco	154	11.40 S	35.48 E
Mazoe ≃	154	16.32 S	33.25 E
Mazomanie	190	43.10 N	89.47 W
Mazomba ≃	256	22.53 S	43.45 W
Mazon	216	41.14 N	88.25 W
Mazon ≃	216	41.21 N	88.25 W
Mazon, East Fork ≃	216	41.11 N	88.18 W
Mazon, West Fork ≃	216	41.15 N	88.21 W
Mazong Shan ∧	102	41.28 N	97.10 E
Mazong Shan ⋏	102	41.30 N	97.30 E
Mazou ≃	50	47.15 N	2.59 E
Mazra'at-Bayt Jinn	132	33.19 N	35.55 E
Mazsalaca	76	57.52 N	25.03 E
Mazul'skij	86	56.16 N	90.28 E
Mazunga	154	21.45 S	29.52 E
Mazury ◆[1]	30	53.45 N	21.00 E
Mazzarino	70	37.18 N	14.13 E
Mazzarrà Sant'andrea	70	38.05 N	15.08 E
Mazzin	64	46.27 N	11.42 E
Mba	175g	17.33 S	177.41 E
Mbabala Island I	154	11.18 S	29.44 E
Mbabane	158	26.18 S	31.06 E
Mbabo, Tchabal ∧	152	7.16 N	12.09 E
Mbacké	150	14.48 N	15.55 W
Mbaéré ≃	152	3.47 N	17.31 E
Mbage	140	5.30 N	25.13 E
M'bahiakro	150	7.27 N	4.20 W
Mbaïki	152	3.53 N	18.00 E
Mbakaou, Barrage de ◆[5]	152	6.15 N	12.46 E
Mbala, Centraf.	152	7.48 N	20.51 E
Mbala (Abercorn), Zam.	154	8.50 S	31.22 E
Mbalam	152	2.13 N	13.49 E
Mbale	154	1.05 N	34.10 E
Mbali	152	2.50 S	16.12 E
Mbali ≃	152	4.26 N	18.20 E
Mbalizi	154	8.56 S	33.22 E
Mbalmayo	152	3.31 N	11.30 E
Mbalouro ≃	273b	4.09 S	15.21 E
Mbalourou	273b	4.09 S	15.21 E
Mbam ≃	152	4.24 N	11.17 E
Mbamba Bay	154	11.17 S	34.46 E
Mbamou, Île I	152	4.13 S	15.25 E
Mbamou, Pointe ≻	273b	4.16 S	15.19 E
Mbandaka (Coquilhatville)	152	0.04 N	18.16 E
Mbanga	152	4.30 N	9.34 E
Mbanika Island I	175e	9.05 S	159.12 E
M'banza Congo	152	6.16 S	14.15 E
Mbanza-Ngungu	152	5.15 S	14.52 E
Mbarangandu ≃	154	8.57 S	37.24 E
Mbarara	154	0.37 S	30.39 E
Mbari ≃	152	4.34 N	22.43 E
Mbarizunga Game Reserve ◆[4]	154	4.45 N	28.06 E
Mbashe ≃	158	32.15 S	28.53 E
Mbassay	146	7.39 N	15.40 E
Mbate	154	8.52 S	39.10 E
M'batto	150	6.28 N	4.22 W
Mbava Island I	175e	7.49 S	156.33 E
Mbé, Cam.	152	7.43 N	13.30 E
Mbé, Congo	152	3.18 S	15.54 E
Mbé ≃	152	0.27 N	9.41 E
Mbemba	154	10.03 S	38.36 E
Mbengga I	175g	18.23 S	178.08 E
M'bengué	150	10.00 N	5.54 W
Mbéré	146	10.49 N	15.44 E
Mbéré ≃	152	7.45 N	15.36 E
Mberengwa	154	20.30 S	29.53 E
Mbereshi Mission	154	9.45 S	28.46 E
Mberubu	150	6.10 N	7.38 E
Mbeya	154	8.54 S	33.27 E
Mbeya □[4]	154	8.00 S	33.30 E
Mbi ≃	152	4.26 N	18.16 E
Mbia	140	6.15 N	29.19 E
M'bigou	152	1.53 S	11.56 E
Mbinda	152	2.00 S	12.55 E
Mbindawina	152	15.57 S	23.18 E
Mbinga	154	10.56 S	35.01 E
Mbini	152	1.35 N	9.37 E
Mbini ≃	152	1.35 N	9.37 E
Mbirira	154	4.21 S	30.10 E
Mbirizi	154	0.23 S	31.27 E
Mbogo	154	7.26 S	33.26 E
Mboie	152	6.56 S	21.54 E
Mbola	175e	9.37 S	160.39 E
Mboli	152	4.08 N	23.09 E
Mbomou □[5]	152	5.00 N	23.30 E
Mbomou (Bomu) ≃	136	4.08 N	22.26 E
Mbonge	152	4.33 N	9.05 E
Mboro, Sén.	150	15.09 N	16.54 W
Mboro, Sūd.	140	6.18 N	28.45 E
Mborokua I	175e	9.00 S	158.40 E
Mborong	115b	8.49 S	120.37 E
Mboté	152	3.56 S	12.43 E
Mbotou ≃	152	6.49 N	24.14 E
Mbouda	152	5.38 N	10.15 E
Mboula	152	4.27 N	16.29 E
Mbour	150	14.24 N	16.58 W
Mbout	150	16.02 N	12.35 W
Mbrès	152	6.40 N	19.48 E
M'Bridge ≃	152	7.14 S	12.52 E
Mbua	175g	16.48 S	178.37 E
Mbua Bay ⊂	175g	16.49 S	178.35 E
Mbuji-Mayi (Bakwanga)	152	6.09 S	23.38 E
Mbulu	154	3.51 S	35.32 E
Mbulula	154	5.26 S	27.26 E
Mbuluzane ≃	158	26.08 S	31.52 E
Mbuluzi ≃	158	26.08 S	31.52 E
Mbuma	154	3.32 N	24.50 E
Mburucuyá	252	28.03 S	58.14 W
Mbutha	175g	16.39 S	179.50 E
Mbwemkuru ≃	154	9.29 S	39.39 E
McAdam	186	45.36 N	67.20 W
McAdam National Park ♦	164	7.15 S	145.40 E
McAdams Peak ∧[2]	219	38.58 N	90.32 W
McAdoo	210	40.54 N	75.59 W
McAdoo Heights	210	40.54 N	76.01 W
McAfee	210	41.10 N	74.32 W
McAlester	196	34.56 N	95.46 W
McAlisterville	208	40.38 N	77.16 W
McAllen	196	26.12 N	98.13 W
McAlpine	208	39.16 N	76.50 W
McAlpine Dam ◆[6]	218	38.16 N	85.47 W
McAlveys Fort	214	40.39 N	77.50 W

FRANÇAIS

Nom	Page	Lat.°′	Long.°′ W = Ouest
McArthur	188	39.14 N	82.28 W
McArthur ≃	164	15.54 S	136.40 E
McArthur River	164	16.27 S	136.07 E
McAuley	184	50.16 N	101.23 W
McBain	190	44.11 N	85.12 W
McBee	192	34.28 N	80.15 W
McBeth	222	29.11 N	95.30 W
McBeth Fjord ⊂[2]	176	69.38 N	68.30 W
McBride	182	53.18 N	120.10 W
McCall	202	44.54 N	116.05 W
McCall Creek	194	31.30 N	90.41 W
McCallum	186	47.38 N	56.15 W
McCallum Creek ≃	169	37.03 S	143.49 E
McCamey	196	31.08 N	102.13 W
McCammon	202	42.39 N	112.11 W
McCandless, Pa., U.S.	214	40.35 N	80.01 W
McCandless, Pa., U.S.	279b	40.34 N	80.02 W
McCarteney Creek ≃	202	47.13 N	120.05 W
McCarthy	180	61.26 N	142.55 W
McCauley Island I	182	53.40 N	130.15 W
McCaysville	192	34.59 N	84.22 W
McChord Air Force Base ■	224	47.08 N	122.29 W
McClarens Run ≃	279b	40.27 N	80.12 W
McClarty Lake ⊜	184	54.28 N	100.20 W
McCleary	224	47.03 N	123.15 W
McClees Creek ≃	276	40.22 N	74.03 W
McClellan Air Force Base ■	226	38.39 N	121.23 W
McClellan Creek ≃	196	35.22 N	100.34 W
McClellanville	192	33.05 N	79.27 W
McClintock, Mount ∧	9	80.13 S	157.26 E
McCloud	204	41.15 N	122.08 W
McCloud ≃	204	40.46 N	122.18 W
McClure, Il., U.S.	194	37.19 N	89.26 W
McClure, Oh., U.S.	216	41.22 N	83.56 W
McClure, Pa., U.S.	210	40.42 N	77.18 W
McClure, Lake ⊜[1]	226	37.37 N	120.16 W
McClusky	198	47.29 N	100.26 W
McColl	192	34.40 N	79.32 W
McComas	192	37.23 N	81.17 W
McComb, Ms., U.S.	194	31.14 N	90.27 W
McComb, Oh., U.S.	216	41.06 N	83.47 W
McConaughy, Lake ⊜[1]	198	41.15 N	101.50 W
McConnell Air Force Base ■	198	37.38 N	97.15 W
McConnell Range ⋏	180	64.00 N	123.50 W
McConnellsburg	188	39.55 N	77.59 W
McConnells Mill	279b	40.15 N	80.15 W
McConnells Mill State Park ♦	214	40.57 N	80.11 W
McConnellstown	214	40.27 N	78.05 W
McConnellsville	210	43.16 N	75.42 W
McConnelsville	188	39.38 N	81.51 W
McCook, Il., U.S.	278	41.48 N	87.50 W
McCook, Ne., U.S.	198	40.12 N	100.37 W
McCordsville	218	39.53 N	85.55 W
McCormick	192	33.54 N	82.17 W
McCormick Place ⊌	278	41.51 N	87.37 W
McCoy	224	45.03 N	123.13 W
McCoy Creek ≃	202	43.02 N	118.50 W
McCoy Lake ⊜	184	52.35 N	92.19 W
McCraney Creek ≃	219	39.39 N	91.12 W
McCreary	184	50.46 N	99.30 W
McCrory	194	35.15 N	91.12 W
McCulloch, Mount ∧	162	25.10 S	129.52 E
McCullom Lake	216	42.22 N	88.18 W
McCullough	279b	40.22 N	79.38 W
McCullough Mountain ∧	204	35.36 N	115.11 W
McCune	198	37.21 N	95.00 W
McCurtain	196	35.08 N	94.58 W
McCusker ≃	184	55.32 N	108.40 W
McCutchenville	214	40.59 N	83.15 W
McDade	222	30.17 N	97.15 W
McDavid	194	30.51 N	87.19 W
McDermitt	204	41.59 N	117.43 W
McDermott	218	38.50 N	83.03 W
McDonald, Ks., U.S.	198	39.47 N	101.22 W
McDonald, Pa., U.S.	214	40.22 N	80.14 W
McDonald, Lac ⊜	206	45.52 N	74.35 W
McDonald, Lake ⊜	202	48.35 N	113.55 W
McDonald Park ♦	282	37.18 N	122.17 W
McDonogh	284c	39.24 N	76.46 W
McDonough, Ga., U.S.	192	33.26 N	84.08 W
McDonough, N.Y., U.S.	210	42.30 N	75.46 W
McDouall Peak	162	29.51 S	134.55 E
McDougal, Mount ∧	200	42.54 N	110.36 W
McDowell Peak ∧	200	33.40 N	111.50 W
McElhattan	210	41.09 N	77.22 W
McElmo Creek ≃	200	37.13 N	109.12 W
Mc Ennen Airport ⊠	281	42.12 N	83.37 W
Mcensk	76	53.17 N	36.35 E
McEwen	194	36.06 N	87.37 W
McEwensville	210	41.05 N	76.49 W
McFadden	200	41.39 N	106.07 W
McFarland, Ca., U.S.	226	35.40 N	119.13 W
McFarland, Wi., U.S.	216	43.00 N	89.17 W
McGavock Lake ⊜	184	56.32 N	101.25 W
McGehee	194	33.37 N	91.23 W
McGill	204	39.24 N	114.46 W
McGill, Université ⊌[2]	275a	45.30 N	73.35 W
McGillivray, Lac ⊜	190	46.04 N	77.06 W
McGinnis Slough Wildlife Refuge ◆[4]	278	41.39 N	87.52 W
McGovern	214	40.14 N	80.13 W
McGrann	214	40.47 N	79.31 W
McGrath	180	62.58 N	155.38 W
McGraw	210	42.35 N	76.05 W
McGregor, On., Can.	214	42.09 N	82.58 W
McGregor, S. Afr.	158	33.57 S	19.50 E
McGregor, Ia., U.S.	190	43.01 N	91.10 W
McGregor, Tx., U.S.	222	31.26 N	97.24 W
McGregor ≃	182	54.11 N	122.00 W
McGregor Creek ≃	214	42.24 N	82.11 W
McGregor Lake ⊜	182	50.31 N	112.53 W
McGregor Range ⋏	166	26.40 S	142.45 E
McGuffey	216	40.41 N	83.47 W
McGuire, Mount ∧	202	45.10 N	114.36 W
McGuire Air Force Base ■	208	40.02 N	74.35 W
McGuire Reservoir ⊜	224	45.19 N	123.26 W
M'Chedallah	34	36.21 N	4.16 E
McHenry, Il., U.S.	216	42.20 N	88.16 W
McHenry, Ms., U.S.	194	30.42 N	89.08 W
McHenry □[6]	216	42.19 N	88.27 W
Mcherrah ◆[1]	148	27.00 N	4.40 W
Mchinga	154	9.44 S	39.42 E
Mchinji	154	13.41 S	32.55 E
Mchungo	154	7.42 S	39.17 E
McInnes Lake ⊜	184	52.12 N	93.45 W
McIntosh, Al., U.S.	194	31.15 N	88.01 W
McIntosh, Il., U.S.	216	42.03 N	88.23 W
McIntosh, Mn., U.S.	198	47.38 N	95.53 W
McIntosh, S.D., U.S.	198	45.55 N	101.20 W
McIntosh Lake ⊜	184	55.45 N	105.08 W
McIntyre	214	40.34 N	79.17 W
McIntyre Bay ⊂	182	54.05 N	131.55 W
McKay, Mount ∧	162	22.26 S	120.01 E
McKay Creek ≃	202	45.40 N	118.50 W
McKean	214	41.59 N	80.09 W
McKean □[6]	214	41.49 N	78.27 W
McKeand ≃	176	65.26 N	68.10 W
McKee	192	37.25 N	83.59 W
McKee City	208	39.27 N	74.38 W
McKee Creek ≃	219	39.46 N	90.36 W
McKeesport	214	40.20 N	79.51 W
McKees Rocks	214	40.27 N	80.03 W
McKenna	224	46.56 N	122.33 W
McKenzie, Al., U.S.	194	31.32 N	86.42 W
McKenzie, Tn., U.S.	194	36.07 N	88.31 W
McKenzie ≃	202	44.07 N	123.06 W
McKenzie Bridge	202	44.10 N	122.09 W
McKenzie Creek ≃	212	43.02 N	79.53 W
McKenzie Island	184	51.05 N	93.48 W

PORTUGUÊS

Nome	Página	Lat.°′	Long.°′ W = Oeste
McKenzie Lake ⊜, On., Can.	212	45.22 N	78.02 W
McKenzie Lake ⊜, Sk., Can.	184	54.12 N	102.30 W
McKerrow, Lake ⊜	172	44.26 S	168.03 E
McKillip Ditch ≊	216	40.50 N	86.51 W
McKinlay	166	21.16 S	141.17 E
McKinlay ≃	166	20.50 S	141.28 E
McKinley, Mount ∧	180	63.04 N	151.00 W
McKinley Airport ⊠	281	42.33 N	82.58 W
McKinley Park ♦	279b	40.25 N	80.00 W
McKinleyville, Ca., U.S.	204	40.56 N	124.05 W
McKinleyville, W.V., U.S.	214	40.15 N	80.36 W
McKinney	222	33.11 N	96.36 W
McKittrick, Ca., U.S.	226	35.18 N	119.37 W
McKittrick, Mo., U.S.	219	38.44 N	91.27 W
McKittrick Summit ∧	226	35.18 N	119.46 W
McKnight Lake ⊜	184	56.03 N	101.08 W
McKnightstown	208	39.52 N	77.20 W
McKnight Village	279b	40.31 N	80.00 W
McKownville	210	42.41 N	73.50 W
McLain	194	31.06 N	88.49 W
McLaren Vale	168b	35.14 S	138.32 E
McLarty Hills ⋏[2]	162	19.29 S	123.33 E
McLaughlin	198	45.48 N	100.48 W
McLaughlin ≃	184	53.46 N	97.38 W
McLaughlin Run ≃	279b	40.22 N	80.07 W
McLaurin	194	31.10 N	89.13 W
McLean, Sk., Can.	184	50.30 N	104.04 W
McLean, Il., U.S.	194	40.18 N	89.10 W
McLean, N.Y., U.S.	210	42.33 N	76.17 W
McLean, Tx., U.S.	196	35.13 N	100.35 W
McLean, Va., U.S.	208	38.56 N	77.10 W
McLean □[6]	216	40.29 N	88.45 W
McLean Hamlet	284c	38.56 N	77.13 W
McLean Lake ⊜	184	56.27 N	109.15 W
McLean Mountain ∧	186	47.07 N	68.50 W
McLeansboro	194	38.05 N	88.32 W
McLennan	182	55.42 N	116.54 W
McLennan □[6]	222	31.35 N	97.13 W
McLeod ≃	182	54.08 N	115.42 W
McLeod Bay ⊂	176	62.53 N	110.00 W
McLeodganj	123	30.15 N	73.42 E
McLeod Lake	182	54.59 N	123.02 W
M'Clintock Channel ⊔	176	72.00 N	102.00 W
McLoughlin, Mount ∧	202	42.27 N	122.19 W
McLoughlin Bay ⊂	176	67.50 N	99.00 W
McLoughlin House National Historic Site ⊥	224	45.20 N	122.33 W
McLouth	198	39.11 N	95.12 W
McLure	182	51.03 N	120.14 W
M'Clure Strait ⊔	176	74.30 N	116.00 W
McMahan	222	29.51 N	97.31 W
McMahon	184	50.05 N	107.32 W
McMasterville	206	45.33 N	73.15 W
McMichael Art Collection ⊌	275b	43.50 N	79.37 W
McMillan, Lake ⊜[1]	196	32.40 N	104.20 W
McMinnville, Or., U.S.	224	45.12 N	123.11 W
McMinnville, Tn., U.S.	194	35.41 N	85.46 W
McMurdo ⊌[3]	9	77.50 S	166.25 E
McMurdo Sound ⊔	9	77.30 S	165.00 E
McMurray	214	40.17 N	80.05 W
McNair	222	29.48 N	95.02 W
McNary	200	34.04 N	109.51 W
McNeil, Ar., U.S.	194	33.20 N	93.12 W
McNeil, Tx., U.S.	222	30.27 N	97.43 W
McNeil, Mount ∧	182	54.35 N	130.14 W
McNeil Island I	224	47.13 N	122.41 W
McNeill	194	30.40 N	89.38 W
McNulty	224	45.50 N	122.50 W
McPhail ≃	184	52.44 N	96.31 W
McPhee Bay ⊂	212	44.35 N	79.19 W
McPhee Reservoir ⊜[1]	200	37.32 N	108.35 W
McPherson	198	38.22 N	97.39 W
McPherson Range ⋏	166	28.20 S	153.00 E
McQueeney	196	29.35 N	98.02 W
McRae, Ar., U.S.	194	35.06 N	91.49 W
McRae, Ga., U.S.	192	32.04 N	82.54 W
McRae, Mount ∧	162	22.17 S	117.35 E
McRae Point Provincial Park ♦	212	44.34 N	79.19 W
McRoberts	192	37.12 N	82.40 W
McSherrystown	208	39.48 N	77.00 W
McVeigh	192	37.32 N	82.15 W
McVeytown	214	40.30 N	77.44 W
McVickers Brook ≃	276	40.45 N	74.38 W
McVille	198	47.45 N	98.10 W
McWilliams	194	31.49 N	87.05 W
Mdandu	154	9.09 S	34.42 E
Mdantsana	158	32.56 S	27.42 E
M'Daourouch	36	36.05 N	7.49 E
Meacham	184	52.08 N	105.45 W
Mead	198	41.14 N	96.30 W
Mead, Lake ⊜[1]	200	36.05 N	114.25 W
Meade, Ks., U.S.	198	37.17 N	100.20 W
Meade, Mi., U.S.	214	42.43 N	82.52 W
Meade ≃	180	70.50 N	156.25 W
Meaden Peak ∧	200	40.46 N	107.03 W
Meade Peak ∧	202	42.30 N	111.15 W
Meadie, Loch ⊜	46	58.20 N	4.33 W
Meadow, Tx., U.S.	196	33.20 N	102.12 W
Meadow, Ut,. U.S.	200	38.53 N	112.24 W
Meadowbank Park ♦	274a	33.49 S	151.06 E
Meadowbrook, Il., U.S.	219	38.54 N	90.01 W
Meadowbrook, In., U.S.	216	41.03 N	85.03 W
Meadow Brook ≃, Ma., U.S.	283	42.03 N	70.58 W
Meadow Brook ≃, Pa., U.S.	285	40.07 N	75.04 W
Meadow Creek ≃	202	46.03 N	115.18 W
Meadowdale	278	41.32 N	87.21 W
Meadow Flat	170	33.26 S	149.56 E
Meadow Island I	276	40.36 N	73.33 W
Meadow Lake	184	54.08 N	108.26 W
Meadow Lake ⊜, Sk., Can.	184	54.07 N	108.20 W
Meadow Lake ⊜, N.Y., U.S.	276	40.44 N	73.50 W
Meadow Lake Provincial Park ♦	184	54.28 N	109.10 W
Meadow Lands	214	40.13 N	80.13 W
Meadowlands Sports Complex ♦	276	40.49 N	74.05 W
Meadowlark Airport ⊠	280	33.43 N	118.02 W
Meadowood, De., U.S.	285	39.43 N	75.47 W
Meadowood, Md., U.S.	284c	39.04 N	77.00 W
Meadows	168b	35.11 S	138.46 E
Meadows, Island of I	276	40.34 N	74.12 W
Meadows Field ⊠	226	35.26 N	119.03 W
Meadowvale ◆[8]	275b	43.37 N	79.43 W
Meadow Valley Wash V	204	36.39 N	114.35 W
Meadowview	192	36.46 N	81.52 W
Meadow Vista	226	39.06 N	121.01 W
Meads Creek ≃	210	42.10 N	77.07 W
Meadville, Ms., U.S.	194	31.28 N	90.53 W
Meadville, Mo., U.S.	194	39.47 N	93.18 W
Meadville, Pa., U.S.	214	41.38 N	80.09 W
Meaford	212	44.36 N	80.35 W
Meaghers Grant	186	44.55 N	63.15 W
Me-akan-dake ∧	92a	43.23 N	144.01 E
Mealasta Isle I	46	58.05 N	7.08 W
Mealhada	34	40.22 N	8.27 W
Méan	56	50.22 N	5.20 E
Meana	128	36.55 N	60.30 E
Meana Sardo	71	39.57 N	9.04 E
Meandarra	166	27.20 S	149.53 E
Meander Creek Reservoir ⊜[1]	214	41.09 N	80.47 W
Meander River	176	59.02 N	117.42 W
Mearim ≃	250	3.04 S	44.35 W

Measham	42	52.43 N	1.29 W
Meath □[6]	48	53.35 N	6.40 W
Meath □[9]	48	53.40 N	7.00 W
Meaux	50	48.57 N	2.52 E
Meaux-Esbly, Aérodrome de ⊠	261	48.55 N	2.50 E
Mebane	192	36.05 N	79.16 W
Mebisere	273a	6.42 N	3.31 E
Mebtoûh, Oued el ≃	34	35.16 N	0.32 W
Meča ≃	82	54.50 N	39.10 E
Meca, La → Makkah	144	21.27 N	39.49 E
Mecanhelas	154	15.12 S	35.54 E
Mecatán	234	21.32 N	105.08 W
Mecatlán	234	20.13 N	97.41 W
Mecaya ≃	246	0.29 N	75.11 W
Mecca → Makkah	144	21.27 N	39.49 E
Mečebilovo	78	49.04 N	36.41 E
Mečetinskaja	78	46.46 N	40.27 E
Mečetka	78	50.54 N	40.05 E
Mechanic Falls	188	44.06 N	70.23 W
Mechanicsburg, Il., U.S.	219	39.48 N	89.24 W
Mechanicsburg, In., U.S.	218	40.09 N	86.28 W
Mechanicsburg, Oh., U.S.	218	40.04 N	83.33 W
Mechanicsburg, Pa., U.S.	208	40.12 N	77.00 W
Mechanicstown, N.Y., U.S.	210	41.27 N	74.24 W
Mechanicstown, Oh., U.S.	214	40.37 N	80.57 W
Mechanicsville, Ia., U.S.	190	41.54 N	91.15 W
Mechanicsville, Md., U.S.	208	38.26 N	76.44 W
Mechanicsville, Va., U.S.	192	37.36 N	77.22 W
Mechanicville	210	42.54 N	73.41 W
Mechara	144	8.32 N	40.22 E
Mechelen (Malines)	50	51.02 N	4.28 E
Mechel'ta	84	42.48 N	46.30 E
Mechernich	56	50.35 N	6.38 E
Mechī □[8]	124	27.15 N	87.45 E
Mechī ≃	124	26.14 N	87.58 E
Mechita	252	35.04 S	60.24 W
Mechlin → Mechelen	50	51.02 N	4.28 E
Mechonskoje	86	56.09 N	64.34 E
Mechra Safsaf	34	34.52 N	2.36 W
Mechren'ga	24	61.46 N	40.57 E
Mechrenga ≃	24	63.15 N	41.20 E
Mechriyya	148	33.35 N	0.18 W
Mechroha	36	36.21 N	7.51 E
Mecidiye, Tür.	130	40.38 N	26.32 E
Mecidiye, Tür.	130	38.53 N	27.42 E
Mečigmen	180	65.28 N	172.05 W
Mečigmeskij zaliv ⊂	180	65.25 N	172.00 W
Meçitözü	130	40.31 N	35.19 E
Meckelfeld	52	53.25 N	10.01 E
Meckenbeuren	58	47.42 N	9.34 E
Meckenheim	56	50.37 N	7.07 E
Meckering	162	31.38 S	117.01 E
Meckesheim	56	49.19 N	8.49 E
Meckinghoven	263	51.37 N	7.19 E
Mecklenburg, Dtsch.	54	53.47 N	11.28 E
Mecklenburg, N.Y., U.S.	210	42.27 N	76.43 W
Mecklenburg □[9]	54	53.30 N	13.00 E
Mecklenburger Bucht ⊂	54	54.20 N	11.40 E
Mecklenburgische Seenplatte ◆[1]	54	53.30 N	12.00 E
Mecklenburg-Vorpommern □[3]	30	53.45 N	12.30 E
Meclov	60	49.31 N	12.52 E
Meco	210	43.03 N	74.23 W
Mecoacán	234	18.23 N	93.07 W
Mecoacán, Laguna ⊂	234	18.22 N	93.09 W
Meconta	154	14.49 S	39.50 E
Mecox Bay ⊂	207	40.54 N	72.20 W
Mecque, La → Makkah	144	21.27 N	39.49 E
Mecsek ⋏	30	46.15 N	18.05 E
Mecubúri	154	14.39 S	38.54 E
Mecubúri ≃	154	14.10 S	40.31 E
Mecúfi	154	13.17 S	40.30 E
Mecula	154	12.04 S	37.40 E
Meda, It.	62	45.40 N	9.09 E
Meda, Port.	34	40.58 N	7.16 W
Medak	122	18.02 N	78.16 E
Medākul	126	23.03 N	90.11 E
Médan, Fr.	261	48.57 N	2.00 E
Medan, Indon.	114	3.35 N	98.40 E
Medang	114	2.06 N	101.38 E
Medang, Pulau I	115b	8.09 S	117.23 E
Medang, Tanjung ≻	114	2.08 N	101.39 E
Médanos	252	38.50 S	62.41 W
Medanosa, Punta ≻	254	48.06 S	65.55 W
Medaryville	216	41.04 N	86.53 W
Mede	62	45.06 N	8.44 E
Medebach	56	51.12 N	8.42 E
Medeiros Neto	255	17.20 S	40.14 W
Medel, Val V	58	46.37 N	8.50 E
Medellín, Col.	246	6.15 N	75.35 W
Medellin, Pil.	116	11.08 N	123.58 E
Medelpad □[9]	26	62.40 N	16.15 E
Medemblik	52	52.46 N	5.06 E
Měděnec	54	50.25 N	13.05 E
Medenica	78	49.26 N	23.45 E
Médenine	148	33.21 N	10.30 E
Médenine □[8]	148	32.00 N	10.00 E
Mederdra	150	16.55 N	15.39 W
Medesano	64	44.45 N	10.08 E
Medevi	40	58.40 N	14.57 E
Medfield	207	42.11 N	71.18 W
Medford, Ma., U.S.	207	42.25 N	71.06 W
Medford, N.J., U.S.	208	39.54 N	74.49 W
Medford, N.Y., U.S.	210	40.49 N	73.00 W
Medford, Ok., U.S.	196	36.48 N	97.44 W
Medford, Or., U.S.	202	42.19 N	122.52 W
Medford, Wi., U.S.	190	45.08 N	90.20 W
Medford Farms	285	39.52 N	74.45 W
Medford Lakes	285	39.51 N	74.48 W
Medfra	180	63.06 N	154.44 W
Medgidia	38	44.15 N	28.16 E
Medgyes → Mediaș	38	46.10 N	24.21 E
Medi	154	5.04 N	30.44 E
Media	208	39.55 N	75.23 W
Mediapolis	190	41.00 N	91.09 W
Mediaș	38	46.10 N	24.21 E
Medical Lake	202	47.34 N	117.40 W
Medicina	66	44.28 N	11.38 E
Medicine Bow	200	41.53 N	106.12 W
Medicine Bow ≃	200	42.00 N	106.40 W
Medicine Bow Mountains ⋏	200	41.10 N	106.10 W
Medicine Bow Peak ∧	200	41.21 N	106.19 W
Medicine Creek ≃, Mo., U.S.	194	39.43 N	93.24 W
Medicine Creek ≃, Ne., U.S.	198	40.17 N	100.10 W
Medicine Creek ≃, S.D., U.S.	198	44.06 N	99.42 W
Medicine Hat	184	50.03 N	110.40 W
Medicine Knoll Creek ≃	198	44.19 N	100.05 W
Medicine Lake	198	48.30 N	104.30 W
Medicine Lake ⊜	198	48.28 N	104.24 W
Medicine Lodge	198	37.16 N	98.34 W
Medicine Lodge ≃	196	36.49 N	98.20 W
Medicine Rocks State Park ♦	198	46.01 N	104.35 W
Medina, Bra.	255	16.15 S	41.29 W
Medina, Pil.	116	8.55 N	125.01 E
Medina, N.Y., U.S.	210	43.13 N	78.23 W
Medina, N.D., U.S.	198	46.53 N	99.17 W
Medina, Oh., U.S.	214	41.08 N	81.51 W
Medina, Tx., U.S.	196	29.48 N	99.15 W
Medina, Wa., U.S.	224	47.37 N	122.13 W
Medina □[6]	214	41.08 N	81.52 W
Medina ≃	196	29.12 N	98.20 W
Medina → Al-Madīnah	128	24.28 N	39.36 E
Medinaceli	34	41.10 N	2.26 W
Medina del Campo	34	41.18 N	4.55 W
Medina de Rioseco	34	41.53 N	5.02 W
Médina Gonasse	150	13.08 N	13.45 W
Medinah	278	41.59 N	88.01 W
Medina Lake ⊜[1]	196	29.35 N	98.58 W
Médina Sabak	150	13.36 N	15.35 W
Medina-Sidonia	34	36.27 N	5.55 W
Medinat al-Faiyum → Al-Fayyūm	142	29.19 N	30.50 E
Medininkai	76	54.32 N	25.40 E
Medinīpur	126	22.26 N	87.20 E
Medino	164	9.40 S	149.40 E
Medio, Arroyo del ≃	258	33.49 S	57.43 W
Medio, Punta ≻	252	27.07 S	70.57 W
Medio Creek ≃	196	28.19 N	97.19 W
Mediterranean Sea ⊤[2]	10	35.00 N	20.00 E
Mediterraneo, Mare → Mediterranean Sea ⊤[2]	10	35.00 N	20.00 E
Medjana	34	36.08 N	4.41 E
Medje	154	2.25 N	27.18 E
Medjerda, Monts de la ⋏	36	36.35 N	8.15 E
Medkovec	38	43.37 N	23.10 E
Mednogorsk	86	51.24 N	57.37 E
Mednoje	76	56.56 N	35.29 E
Mednyj, ostrov I	74	54.45 N	167.35 E
Médoc ◆[1]	32	45.20 N	1.00 W
Mêdog	120	29.20 N	95.15 E
Medolla	64	44.51 N	11.04 E
Medora, Il., U.S.	219	39.11 N	90.09 W
Medora, In., U.S.	218	38.49 N	86.10 W
Medora, N.D., U.S.	198	46.54 N	103.31 W
Médouneu	152	0.57 N	10.47 E
Medow	54	53.50 N	13.32 E
Medstead, Sk., Can.	184	53.19 N	108.02 W
Medstead, Eng., U.K.	42	51.08 N	1.04 W
Medua	126	22.38 N	90.44 E
Meductic	186	46.00 N	67.29 W
Medulla	220	27.58 N	81.58 W
Međumurje ◆[1]	61	46.25 N	16.30 E
Meduna ≃	64	45.49 N	12.34 E
Medveđa	38	42.50 N	21.35 E
Medvedevo, Ross.	76	60.02 N	43.01 E
Medvedevo, Ross.	80	56.37 N	47.47 E
Medvedevo, Ross.	86	60.37 N	77.21 E
Medvedevskoje	76	58.58 N	35.58 E
Medvedica ≃, Ross.	76	57.05 N	37.32 E
Medvedica ≃, Ross.	80	49.35 N	42.41 E
Medvedickij	80	50.47 N	44.43 E
Medvědí hora ∧	60	48.59 N	13.25 E
Medvedkovo ◆[8]	265b	55.53 N	37.38 E
Medvedok	80	57.23 N	50.05 E
Medvedovskaja	78	45.27 N	39.01 E
Medvenka, Ross.	78	51.26 N	36.07 E
Medvenka, Ross.	82	54.15 N	37.42 E
Medvežij, ostrov I	89	54.41 N	136.18 E
Medvežinka	83	48.10 N	39.31 E
Medvežje, ozero ⊜	86	55.07 N	68.00 E
Medvežjegorsk	24	62.55 N	34.23 E
Medvežji ostrova II	74	70.52 N	161.26 E
Medvežji ozera ⊜	265b	55.52 N	38.00 E
Medvežji Oz'ora	265b	55.52 N	37.59 E
Medvežskaja	24	64.57 N	57.34 E
Medviagalis ∧[2]	76	55.38 N	22.45 E
Medvin	78	49.23 N	30.47 E
Medv'onka ≃	265b	55.44 N	37.12 E
Medway, Ma., U.S.	207	42.08 N	71.23 W
Medway, Oh., U.S.	218	39.53 N	83.59 W
Medway □[8]	260	51.24 N	0.31 E
Medway ≃, N.S., Can.	186	44.08 N	64.36 W
Medway ≃, Eng., U.K.	42	51.27 N	0.44 E
Medyn'	82	54.58 N	35.52 E
Medynka ≃	82	54.44 N	36.02 E
Medynskij Zavorot, mys ≻	24	68.58 N	59.17 E
Medžibož	78	49.26 N	27.25 E
Medzilaborce	30	49.16 N	21.55 E
Meeberrie	162	26.58 S	115.58 E
Meekatharra	162	26.36 S	118.29 E
Meeker, Co., U.S.	200	40.02 N	107.54 W
Meeker, Oh., U.S.	214	40.39 N	83.18 W
Meeks Bay	226	39.02 N	120.08 W
Meelpaeg Lake ⊜[1]	186	48.16 N	56.35 W
Meenaar	168a	31.38 S	116.53 E
Meentheena	162	21.17 S	120.28 E
Meer	52	51.27 N	4.44 E
Meeralpen → Maritime Alps ⋏	62	44.15 N	7.10 E
Meerane	54	50.51 N	12.28 E
Meerbeck	263	51.28 N	6.39 E
Meerbeke	50	50.50 N	4.02 E
Meerbusch	56	51.15 N	6.41 E
Meerhout	56	51.08 N	5.05 E
Meerhusener Moor ◆[3]	52	53.35 N	7.30 E
Meerkerk	52	51.45 N	5.00 E
Meerle	52	51.28 N	4.48 E
Meersburg	58	47.41 N	9.16 E
Meerssen	56	50.53 N	5.45 E
Meerut	124	28.59 N	77.42 E
Meese ≃	42	52.40 N	2.39 W
Meeteetse	202	44.09 N	108.52 W
Mega, Indon.	164	0.41 S	131.53 E
Mega, Ityo.	144	4.07 N	38.16 E
Mega, Pulau I	112	4.00 S	101.02 E
Megalo	144	6.55 N	41.48 E
Megálon Khoríon	38	36.27 N	27.21 E
Megalópolis	38	37.24 N	22.08 E
Meganom, mys ≻	78	44.48 N	35.05 E
Mégantic □[6]	206	46.10 N	71.30 W
Mégantic, Lac ⊜	188	45.32 N	70.53 W
Mégantic, Mont ∧	206	45.28 N	71.09 W
Mégara	38	38.01 N	23.21 E
Megargel	196	33.27 N	98.56 W
Mégaron, Kólpos ⊂	267c	37.56 N	23.20 E
Megaruma ≃	154	13.28 S	40.32 E
Megasini ∧	126	21.38 N	86.21 E
Meget	88	52.24 N	104.03 E
Megève	62	45.52 N	6.37 E
Mégevette	58	46.12 N	6.30 E
Megezez ∧	144	9.17 N	39.32 E
Megget Reservoir ⊜[1]	46	55.29 N	3.17 W
Meghālaya □[3]	120	25.30 N	91.15 E
Meghna ≃	120	22.50 N	90.50 E
Megi-jima I	96	34.24 N	134.03 E
Mégiscane ≃	190	48.29 N	77.08 W
Mégiscane, Lac ⊜	190	48.35 N	75.55 W
Meglino, ozero ⊜	76	58.25 N	35.07 E
Megra, Ross.	24	66.09 N	41.37 E
Megra, Ross.	76	60.10 N	37.13 E
Megri	84	38.56 N	46.16 E
Meguro ◆[8]	268	35.38 N	139.42 E
Meguro ≃	268	35.37 N	139.45 E
Mehadia	38	44.55 N	22.22 E
Méhaigne ≃	56	50.32 N	5.13 E
Mehaïguene, Oued V	148	32.15 N	2.59 E
Mehakit	112	2.51 S	115.57 E
Mehar	120	27.11 N	67.49 E
Meharry, Mount ∧	162	22.59 S	118.35 E
Mehdia	148	35.26 N	1.40 E
Mehede	40	60.27 N	17.24 E
Mehedinți □[6]	38	44.30 N	22.50 E
Meheisa	140	19.37 N	32.57 E
Mehekar	122	20.09 N	76.34 E
Mehendiganj	126	22.49 N	90.32 E
Meherpur	124	23.46 N	88.38 E
Meherrin ≃	192	36.26 N	76.57 W
Mehetia I	14	17.52 S	148.03 W
Mehidpur	120	23.49 N	75.40 E
Mehikoorma	76	58.14 N	27.28 E
Mehlteuer	54	50.32 N	12.02 E
Mehlville	219	38.30 N	90.19 W
Mehnagar	124	25.53 N	83.07 E
Mehndāwal	124	26.59 N	83.07 E
Mehoopany	210	41.34 N	76.04 W
Mehoopany Creek ≃	210	41.34 N	76.03 W
Mehpālpur ◆[8]	272a	28.33 N	77.08 E
Mehr	52	51.43 N	6.29 E
Mehrābād	128	36.53 N	47.55 E
Mehrābād ◆[8]	267d	35.40 N	51.20 E
Mehram Nagar ◆[8]	272a	28.34 N	77.07 E
Mehrān	128	33.07 N	46.10 E
Mehrān ≃	128	26.52 N	55.24 E
Mehring	56	49.48 N	6.49 E
Mehrīz	128	31.35 N	54.28 E
Mehrow	264a	52.34 N	13.37 E
Mehrum	263	51.35 N	6.37 E
Mè-hsa-tè	110	19.33 N	97.38 E
Mehtarlām	120	34.39 N	70.10 E
Mehun-sur-Yèvre	50	47.09 N	2.13 E
Mei ≃, Zhg.	100	24.24 N	116.34 E
Mei ≃, Zhg.	100	26.00 N	115.23 E
Mei ≃, Zhg.	105	39.21 N	117.50 E
Meia Meia	154	5.49 S	35.48 E
Meia Ponte, Rio da ≃	255	18.32 S	49.36 W
Meichang	105	39.22 N	117.10 E
Meichuan	100	30.10 N	115.36 E
Meicun, Zhg.	100	25.30 N	116.56 E
Meicun, Zhg.	106	30.22 N	119.01 E
Meicun, Zhg.	106	30.40 N	119.04 E
Meicun, Zhg.	106	31.33 N	120.24 E
Meide	263	51.11 N	6.55 E
Meiderich ◆[8]	263	51.28 N	6.46 E
Meidling ◆[8]	264b	48.11 N	16.20 E
Meierij ◆[1]	52	51.35 N	5.40 E
Meierkaisong	120	30.54 N	84.31 E
Meiersberg	263	51.17 N	6.57 E
Meig ≃	46	57.34 N	4.41 W
Meiganga	152	6.31 N	14.11 E
Meigle	46	56.35 N	3.09 W
Meigs	192	31.04 N	84.05 W
Meigs Field ⊠	278	41.51 N	87.36 W
Meihsien → Meixian	100	24.21 N	116.08 E
Meihua	100	26.02 N	119.40 E
Meihuajie	100	25.14 N	113.05 E
Meijel	52	51.21 N	5.53 E
Meijino-Mori-Minō-kokutei-kōen ♦	94	34.51 N	135.29 E
Meiji Shrine ⊌[1]	268	35.41 N	139.42 E
Meikeng	100	23.59 N	114.05 E
Meikle Millyea ∧	44	55.07 N	4.19 W
Meikle Says Law ∧	46	55.55 N	2.40 W
Meiktila	110	20.52 N	95.52 E
Meila	54	51.09 N	13.13 E
Meilen	58	47.16 N	8.38 E
Meili	106	31.42 N	120.53 E
Meilie	100	26.18 N	117.38 E
Meilin, Zhg.	100	23.18 N	115.58 E
Meilin, Zhg.	106	30.35 N	119.04 E
Meillerie	58	46.24 N	6.43 E
Meilong	100	22.56 N	115.17 E
Meilunyingzi	104	42.18 N	122.10 E
Meina	62	45.47 N	8.32 E
Meine	52	52.23 N	10.32 E
Meiners Oaks	228	34.26 N	119.17 W
Meinerzhagen	56	51.06 N	7.38 E
Meiningen	54	50.34 N	10.25 E
Meinung	100	22.54 N	120.32 E
Meio, Ilha do I	287a	23.02 S	43.17 W
Meiringen	58	46.43 N	8.12 E
Meisburg	56	50.06 N	6.41 E
Meisenheim	56	49.42 N	7.40 E
Meishan, Zhg.	106	31.06 N	119.43 E
Meishan, Zhg.	107	30.02 N	103.49 E
Meissen	54	51.10 N	13.28 E
Meissendorf	52	52.43 N	9.50 E
Meiss Lake ⊜	204	41.52 N	122.04 W
Meissner ∧	56	51.12 N	9.50 E
Meitan	102	27.46 N	107.35 E
Meitian	100	25.21 N	112.47 E
Meitingen	56	48.32 N	10.50 E
Meiwa	94	34.33 N	136.39 E
Meixi	106	30.48 N	119.45 E
Meixian, Zhg.	100	24.21 N	116.08 E
Meixian, Zhg.	100	28.52 N	113.38 E
Meiyao	89	49.37 N	124.30 E
Meiyino	140	6.12 N	34.40 E
Meizhai	102	25.30 N	108.50 E
Meizhou	100	23.50 N	117.20 E
Meizhou Dao I	100	25.06 N	119.07 E
Meizhou Wan ⊂	100	25.06 N	119.00 E
Meizhu	106	31.16 N	119.13 E
Meječkyn, ostrov I	180	65.26 N	178.00 W
Mejerda, Oued (Oued Medjerda) ≃	36	37.07 N	10.13 E
Mejez el Bab	148	36.39 N	9.37 E
Mejia	126	23.34 N	87.06 E
Mejicanos	236	13.43 N	89.12 W
Mejillones	252	23.06 S	70.27 W
Mejillones, Península ≻[1]	252	23.17 S	70.34 W
Mejillones del Sur, Bahía de ⊂	252	23.03 S	70.27 W
Mejnypil'gyno	74	62.32 N	177.02 E
Mejorada del Campo	266a	40.24 N	3.29 W
Meka	162	27.26 S	116.48 E
Mekada, Garaet el ⩩	36	36.48 N	8.00 E
Mékambo	152	1.01 N	13.56 E
Mekele	144	13.33 N	39.30 E
Mekerra, Oued ≃	34	35.00 N	0.45 W
Mekhé	150	15.07 N	16.38 W
Mekhliganj	124	26.21 N	88.55 E
Mekhtar	120	30.28 N	69.22 E
Mékinac ≃	206	46.51 N	72.46 W
Mekka → Makkah	144	21.27 N	39.49 E
Meknès	148	33.53 N	5.37 W
Meknès □[4]	148	33.50 N	5.30 W
Mekong ≃	12	10.33 N	105.24 E
Mekongga, Gunung ∧	112	3.38 S	121.15 E
Mekongga, Pegunungan ⋏	112	3.35 S	121.15 E
Mékôngk → Mekong ≃	12	10.33 N	105.24 E
Mekoryuk	180	60.23 N	166.12 W
Mékrou ≃	150	12.24 N	2.49 E
Mel	64	46.04 N	12.05 E
Melado ≃	252	35.43 S	71.05 W
Melah, Oued el V, Alg.	148	28.21 N	6.00 E
Melah, Oued el V, Tun.	148	34.03 N	8.06 E
Melah, Sebkhet el ⊜	148	29.05 N	1.10 W
Melaka	114	2.12 N	102.15 E
Melaka □[3]	114	2.15 N	102.15 E
Melalap	112	5.14 N	116.00 E
Melandro ≃	68	40.37 N	15.27 E
Melanesia II	14	13.00 S	164.00 E
Melanesian Basin ✦[1]	14	0.05 N	160.35 E
Melappālaiyam	122	8.42 N	77.43 E
Melara	64	45.03 N	11.11 E
Melaune	54	51.11 N	14.44 E
Melawi ≃	112	0.05 N	111.29 E
Melayu ≃	271c	1.27 N	103.42 E
Melbern	216	41.28 N	84.39 W
Melbost	46	58.15 N	6.22 W
Melbourn	42	52.05 N	0.01 E
Melbourne, Austl.	169	37.49 S	144.58 E
Melbourne, Austl.	274b	37.49 S	144.58 E
Melbourne, On., Can.	214	42.49 N	81.33 W
Melbourne, Eng., U.K.	42	52.49 N	1.25 W
Melbourne, Ar., U.S.	194	36.03 N	91.54 W
Melbourne, Fl., U.S.	220	28.04 N	80.36 W

≃	River	Fluß	Río	Rivière	Rio
≊	Canal	Kanal	Canal	Canal	Canal
∟	Waterfall, Rapids	Wasserfall, Stromschnellen	Cascada, Rápidos	Chute d'eau, Rapides	Cascata, Rápidos
⊔	Strait	Meeresstraße	Estrecho	Détroit	Estreito
⊂	Bay, Gulf	Bucht, Golf	Bahía, Golfo	Baie, Golfe	Baía, Golfo
⊜	Lake, Lakes	See, Seen	Lago, Lagos	Lac, Lacs	Lago, Lagos
⩩	Swamp	Sumpf	Pantano	Marais	Pântano
⊓	Ice Features, Glacier	Eis- und Gletscherformen	Accidentes Glaciales	Formes glaciaires	Acidentes glaciares
⊤	Other Hydrographic Features	Andere Hydrographische Objekte	Otros Elementos Hidrográficos	Autres données hydrographiques	Outros acidentes hidrográficos
✦	Submarine Features	Untermeerische Objekte	Accidentes Submarinos	Formes de relief sous-marin	Acidentes submarinos
□	Political Unit	Politische Einheit	Unidad Politica	Entité politique	Unidade política
⊌	Cultural Institution	Kulturelle Institution	Institución Cultural	Institution culturelle	Instituição cultural
⊥	Historical Site	Historische Stätte	Sitio Histórico	Site historique	Sitio histórico
♦	Recreational Site	Erholungs- und Ferienort	Sitio de Recreo	Centre de loisirs	Area de Lazer
⊠	Airport	Flughafen	Aeropuerto	Aéroport	Aeroporto
■	Military Installation	Militäranlage	Instalación Militar	Installation militaire	Instalação militar
◆	Miscellaneous	Verschiedenes	Misceláneo	Divers	Diversos

Name	Page	Lat.°′	Long.°′
Melbourne, Ia., U.S.	190	41.56 N	93.06 W
Melbourne, University of ʊ²	274b	37.48 S	144.58 E
Melbourne Beach	220	28.04 N	80.33 W
Melbourne Island I	176	68.30 N	104.45 W
Melbourne Regional Airport ⊠	220	28.06 N	80.38 W
Mel'cany	80	54.28 N	44.43 E
Melcher	190	41.13 N	93.14 W
Melchor, Isla I	254	45.08 S	73.57 W
Melchor Múzquiz	232	27.53 N	101.31 W
Melchor Ocampo	196	26.03 N	99.33 W
Melchor Romero ⬥⁸	258	34.56 S	58.03 W
Melchtal	58	46.50 N	8.17 E
Melcroft	214	40.03 N	79.24 W
Melderskin ∧	26	60.01 N	6.05 E
Meldola	66	44.07 N	12.05 E
Meldorf	30	54.05 N	9.05 E
Meldrum Bay	190	45.56 N	83.07 W
Meldrum Creek	182	52.07 N	122.20 W
Mélé, Centraf.	146	9.46 N	21.33 E
Mele, India	272b	22.49 N	88.09 E
Mele, It.	62	44.27 N	8.45 E
Mélé, Baie c	175f	17.43 S	168.15 E
Mele, Capo ≻	62	43.57 N	8.10 E
Melechovo	80	56.17 N	41.17 E
Meleck	86	57.25 N	90.12 E
Meleden	144	10.25 N	49.51 E
Melegnano	62	45.21 N	9.19 E
Meleješt'	78	46.59 N	29.33 E
Melekeok	175b	7.29 N	134.38 E
Melekess → Dimitrovgrad	80	54.14 N	49.39 E
Melela ≃	154	17.04 S	38.36 E
Melena del Sur	240p	22.47 N	82.09 W
Melendiz Dağı ∧	130	38.07 N	34.25 E
Melendugno	68	40.16 N	18.20 E
Melenki	80	55.20 N	41.38 E
Meleškoviči	78	51.56 N	28.59 E
Meleuz	86	52.58 N	55.55 E
Mélèzes, Rivière aux ≃	176	57.40 N	69.29 W
Melfa	208	37.39 N	75.45 W
Melfa ≃	66	41.30 N	13.35 E
Melfi, It.	68	41.00 N	15.39 E
Melfi, Tchad	146	11.04 N	17.56 E
Melfort, Sk., Can.	184	52.52 N	104.36 W
Melfort, Zimb.	154	17.59 S	31.19 E
Melfort, Loch c	46	56.15 N	5.31 W
Melgaço, Bra.	250	1.47 S	50.44 W
Melgaço, Port.	34	42.07 N	8.16 W
Melgar	246	4.12 N	74.39 W
Melghir, Chott ⊜	148	34.20 N	6.20 E
Mel'guny	80	52.09 N	40.52 E
Melhus	26	63.17 N	10.16 E
Meli ≃	150	8.16 N	10.42 W
Meliane, Oued ≃	36	36.46 N	10.18 E
Meliau	112	0.08 S	110.18 E
Meliau, Gunong ∧	116	5.50 N	117.14 E
Melibocus ∧	56	49.42 N	8.40 E
Melichovo, Ross.	78	50.42 N	36.48 E
Melichovo, Ross.	82	55.07 N	37.39 E
Melicuccà	68	38.18 N	15.53 E
Melide, Esp.	34	42.55 N	8.00 W
Melide, Schw.	58	45.57 N	8.57 E
Meligalás	38	37.13 N	21.59 E
Melilla	34	35.19 N	2.58 W
Melilli	70	37.11 N	15.07 E
Melimoyu, Cerro ∧	254	44.05 S	72.52 W
Melincué	252	33.39 S	61.27 W
Melipilla	252	33.42 S	71.13 W
Mélisey	58	47.45 N	6.35 E
Melissa	68	39.18 N	17.01 E
Melissano	68	39.58 N	18.07 E
Melíssia	267c	38.03 N	23.50 E
Melita	184	49.16 N	101.00 W
Melito di Porto Salvo	68	37.55 N	15.47 E
Melitopol'	78	46.50 N	35.22 E
Melívoia	38	39.45 N	22.48 E
Melk	61	48.14 N	15.20 E
Melk ≃	61	48.14 N	15.19 E
Melk ʊ¹	61	48.14 N	15.20 E
Melka Teka	144	6.05 N	43.08 E
Melkbosstrand	158	33.43 S	18.27 E
Melksham	42	51.23 N	2.09 W
Mella ≃	64	45.13 N	10.13 E
Mellansel	26	63.26 N	18.19 E
Mellau	58	47.21 N	9.53 E
Melle, Dtsch.	52	52.12 N	8.20 E
Melle, Fr.	32	46.13 N	0.09 W
Melleck	64	47.40 N	12.45 E
Mellègue, Oued ≃	36	36.32 N	8.51 E
Mellen	190	46.19 N	90.39 W
Mellendorf	52	52.33 N	9.43 E
Mellenville	210	42.15 N	73.40 W
Mellerud	26	58.42 N	12.28 E
Mellette	198	45.09 N	98.29 W
Mellier ≃	56	49.43 N	5.32 E
Melling	262	53.30 N	2.56 W
Mellingen	54	50.56 N	11.23 E
Mellish Reef I¹	160	17.25 S	155.50 E
Mellish Rise ✦³	14	17.00 S	156.00 E
Mellit	140	14.08 N	25.33 E
Mellone, Monte ∧	267a	41.50 N	12.43 E
Mellong Range ⋏	170	33.06 S	150.43 E
Mellon Udrigle	46	57.55 N	5.39 W
Mellor	262	53.46 N	2.32 W
Mellor Brook	262	53.47 N	2.33 W
Mellösa	40	59.06 N	16.33 E
Mellrichstadt	56	50.26 N	10.18 E
Mellum I	52	53.40 N	8.10 E
Melmerby	44	54.44 N	2.35 W
Melmore	214	41.02 N	83.07 W
Melmoth	158	28.38 S	31.24 E
Mel'nica-Podol'skaja	78	48.37 N	26.10 E
Mělník	54	50.20 N	14.29 E
Mel'nikovo, Ross.	26	61.05 N	29.22 E
Mel'nikovo, Ross.	86	56.34 N	84.05 E
Mel'nikovo, Taj.	85	40.19 N	70.19 E
Melo	252	32.22 S	54.11 W
Melo ≃	248	21.27 S	57.52 W
Melo, Ilha de I	150	11.02 N	15.13 W
Melocheville	206	45.19 N	73.56 W
Meloco	154	13.25 S	39.08 E
Melolo	115b	9.53 S	120.40 E
Melolo ≃	115b	9.52 S	120.41 E
Melong	152	5.07 N	9.57 E
Melos → Mílos I	38	36.41 N	24.15 E
Melovaja ≃	83	49.23 N	40.16 E
Melovatka	83	49.21 N	38.11 E
Melovoje	83	49.22 N	40.06 E
Melovoj Syrt ∧	80	52.15 N	52.35 E
Melozitna ≃	180	64.46 N	155.29 W
Melrose, Austl.	162	27.56 S	121.19 E
Melrose, Austl.	166	32.42 S	146.58 E
Melrose, Scot., U.K.	46	55.36 N	2.44 W
Melrose, Ma., U.S.	207	42.27 N	71.04 W
Melrose, Mn., U.S.	198	45.40 N	94.48 W
Melrose, N.M., U.S.	196	34.25 N	103.37 W
Melrose, N.Y., U.S.	210	42.50 N	73.37 W
Melrose, Oh., U.S.	216	41.05 N	84.25 W
Melrose, Wi., U.S.	190	44.07 N	90.59 W
Melrose ⬥⁸	276	40.49 N	73.55 W
Melrose Abbey ʊ¹	46	55.37 N	2.45 W
Melrose Park, Fl., U.S.	220	26.06 N	80.12 W
Melrose Park, Il., U.S.	216	41.54 N	87.51 W
Melrose Park, N.Y., U.S.	212	42.54 N	76.32 W
Melrose Park, Pa., U.S.	285	40.04 N	75.08 W
Mels	58	47.03 N	9.25 E
Melstone	202	46.35 N	107.52 W
Melsungen	56	51.08 N	9.32 E
Meltaus	24	66.54 N	25.22 E
Meltham, Eng., U.K.	44	53.35 N	1.51 W
Meltham, Eng., U.K.	262	53.36 N	1.51 W
Melton, Austl.	168b	34.05 S	137.59 E
Melton, Austl.	169	37.41 S	144.35 E
Melton Constable	42	52.53 N	1.01 E
Melton Hill Lake ⊜¹	192	36.00 N	84.15 W
Melton Mowbray	42	52.46 N	0.53 W
Melton Reservoir ⊜¹	169	37.43 S	144.32 E
Melúa	246	3.55 N	72.50 W
Meluan	112	1.52 N	111.56 E
Meluco	154	12.36 S	39.38 E
Melúli ≃	154	16.28 S	39.44 E
Melun, Fr.	50	48.32 N	2.40 E
Melun, Mya.	110	20.14 N	93.24 E
Melunga	152	17.16 S	16.24 E
Melūr	122	10.03 N	78.20 E
Melvaig	46	57.48 N	5.49 W
Melvern	198	38.30 N	95.38 W
Melvern Lake ⊜¹	198	38.30 N	95.50 W
Melvich	46	58.33 N	3.55 W
Melville, Austl.	168a	32.03 S	115.49 E
Melville, Sk., Can.	184	50.55 N	102.48 W
Melville, La., U.S.	194	30.41 N	91.44 W
Melville, N.Y., U.S.	276	40.47 N	73.24 W
Melville ⬥⁸	273d	26.11 S	28.00 E
Melville, Cape ≻, Austl.	164	14.11 S	144.30 E
Melville, Cape ≻, Pil.	116	7.49 N	117.01 E
Melville, Détroit de → Viscount Melville Sound ᵿ	176	74.10 N	108.00 W
Melville, Lake ⊜	176	53.45 N	59.30 W
Melville Bugt c	16	75.30 N	63.00 W
Melville Hall Airport ⊠	240d	15.33 N	61.18 W
Melville Hills ⋏²	180	69.15 N	124.00 W
Melville Island I, Austl.	164	11.40 S	131.00 E
Melville Island I, N.T., Can.	16	75.15 N	110.00 W
Melville Island Aboriginal Reserve ⬥⁴	164	11.40 S	131.00 E
Melville Peninsula ≻¹	176	68.00 N	84.00 W
Melville Sound ᵿ, N.T., Can.	176	68.05 N	107.30 W
Melville Sound ᵿ, On., Can.	212	44.57 N	81.05 W
Melvin, Il., U.S.	216	40.34 N	88.15 W
Melvin, Ky., U.S.	192	37.21 N	82.41 W
Melvin, Tx., U.S.	196	31.13 N	99.35 W
Melvin, Lough ⊜	48	54.26 N	8.10 W
Melvindale	214	42.16 N	83.10 W
Melvin Lake ⊜	184	57.08 N	100.15 W
Melyana	148	36.15 N	2.15 E
Mélykút	30	46.13 N	19.24 E
Melzo	62	45.30 N	9.25 E
Memala	112	1.44 S	112.36 E
Mêmar Co ⊜	120	34.15 N	82.20 E
Memāri	126	23.12 N	88.07 E
Memba	154	14.11 S	40.30 E
Membalong	112	3.09 S	107.38 E
Memboro	115b	9.22 S	119.32 E
Membre	56	49.52 N	4.54 E
Même ≃	50	48.11 N	0.39 E
Memel	158	27.43 S	29.30 E
Mēmele ≃	76	56.24 N	24.10 E
Memel → Klaipėda	76	55.43 N	21.07 E
Memel → Nemunas ≃	76	55.18 N	21.23 E
Memewin, Lac ⊜	190	46.29 N	78.42 W
Memmert I	52	53.39 N	6.53 E
Memmingen	58	47.59 N	10.11 E
Memo ≃	246	9.16 N	66.40 W
Memori, Tanjung ≻	164	0.52 S	134.08 E
Memorial Bridge ⬥⁵	269a	13.44 N	100.30 E
Memorial Stadium ♦	284b	39.20 N	76.36 W
Mémót	110	11.49 N	106.11 E
Mempawah	112	0.22 N	108.58 E
Memphis, Fl., U.S.	220	27.32 N	82.33 W
Memphis, In., U.S.	218	38.29 N	85.45 W
Memphis, Mi., U.S.	214	42.54 N	82.46 W
Memphis, Mo., U.S.	194	40.27 N	92.10 W
Memphis, Tn., U.S.	194	35.08 N	90.02 W
Memphis, Tx., U.S.	196	34.43 N	100.32 W
Memphis → Mīt Ruhaynah ⊥	142	29.51 N	31.15 E
Memphis Naval Air Station ■	194	35.21 N	89.52 W
Memphremagog, Lake ⊜	206	45.05 N	72.15 W
Memsie	46	57.39 N	2.02 W
Mena, Ityo.	144	6.25 N	39.51 E
Mena, Ukr.	78	51.31 N	32.13 E
Mena, Ar., U.S.	194	34.35 N	94.14 W
Menado → Manado	112	1.29 N	124.51 E
Menaggio	58	46.01 N	9.14 E
Menahga	198	46.45 N	95.06 W
Menai	274a	34.01 S	151.01 E
Menai Bridge	44	53.14 N	4.10 W
Menai Strait ᵿ	44	53.12 N	4.12 W
Ménaka	150	15.55 N	2.24 E
Menaldum	52	53.12 N	5.39 E
Menan	202	43.43 N	111.59 W
Menands	210	42.41 N	73.43 W
Menangina	162	29.50 S	121.54 E
Menantico Creek ≃	208	39.20 N	75.00 W
Menarandra ≃	157b	25.17 S	44.30 E
Menard	196	30.55 N	99.47 W
Menard □⁶	219	40.01 N	89.51 W
Menard Creek ≃	222	30.29 N	94.50 W
Menars	50	47.38 N	1.24 E
Menasha	190	44.12 N	88.26 W
Menate	112	0.14 S	113.02 E
Menawashei	140	12.40 N	24.59 E
Menchang	105	38.54 N	117.01 E
Menčikury	78	47.04 N	34.48 E
Mencué	254	40.25 S	69.38 W
Mend	89	43.40 N	123.08 E
Mendanau, Pulau I	112	2.51 S	107.26 E
Mendarik, Pulau I	112	1.18 N	107.02 E
Mendatai	102	38.51 N	94.39 E
Mendatica	62	44.05 N	7.49 E
Mendawai	112	2.59 S	113.16 E
Mendawai ≃	112	3.17 S	113.21 E
Mendaya	115a	8.23 S	114.42 E
Mende	32	44.30 N	3.30 E
Mendebo ⋏	144	6.50 N	39.40 E
Mendel' ≃	86	58.13 N	90.08 E
Mendelejevsk	80	55.54 N	52.20 E
Menden	56	51.26 N	7.47 E
Menden ⬥⁸	263	51.24 N	6.54 E
Mendenhall, Ms., U.S.	194	31.57 N	89.52 W
Mendenhall, Pa., U.S.	285	39.51 N	75.38 W
Mendenhall, Cape ≻	180	59.51 N	166.15 W
Mendes	256	22.32 S	43.44 W
Méndez	232	25.07 N	98.34 W
Mendez-Nuñez	116	14.08 N	120.54 E
Mendham	210	40.46 N	74.36 W
Mendi, Ityo.	144	9.50 N	35.06 E
Mendi, Pap. N. Gui.	164	6.10 S	143.40 E
Mendig	56	50.21 N	7.15 E
Mendip Hills ⋏²	42	51.15 N	2.40 W
Mendlesham	42	52.16 N	1.05 E
Mendocino	204	39.18 N	123.47 W
Mendocino, Cape ≻	204	40.25 N	124.25 W
Mendocino Fracture Zone ✦	16	40.00 N	145.00 W
Mendola ≃	70	37.44 N	13.32 E
Mendon, Il., U.S.	219	40.05 N	91.17 W
Mendon, Ma., U.S.	207	42.06 N	71.33 W
Mendon, Mi., U.S.	216	42.00 N	85.27 W
Mendon, N.Y., U.S.	210	43.00 N	77.34 W
Mendon, Oh., U.S.	216	40.40 N	84.31 W
Mendon, Pa., U.S.	279b	40.11 N	79.41 W
Mendota, Ca., U.S.	226	36.45 N	120.22 W
Mendota, Il., U.S.	216	41.32 N	89.07 W
Mendota, Lake ⊜	216	43.05 N	89.25 W
Mendoza, Arg.	252	32.53 S	68.49 W
Mendoza, Perú	248	6.20 S	77.24 W
Mendoza, Ur.	258	34.17 S	56.13 W
Mendoza □⁴	252	34.30 S	68.30 W
Mendoza ≃	252	32.21 S	68.18 W
Mendoza, Arroyo de ≃	258	34.21 S	56.18 W
Mendrisio	58	45.52 N	8.59 E
Mend'ukino	82	54.47 N	38.51 E
Mendung	112	0.31 N	103.13 E
Ménéac	32	48.09 N	2.28 W
Mene de Mauroa	246	10.43 N	71.01 W
Mene Grande	246	9.49 N	70.56 W
Menemen	130	38.36 N	27.04 E
Menen	50	50.48 N	3.07 E
Meneng Point ≻	174b	0.32 S	166.57 E
Menes	115a	6.23 S	105.55 E
Menfi	70	37.36 N	12.58 E
Mengalum, Pulau I	112	6.16 N	115.12 E
Mengban	102	23.08 N	100.19 E
Mengbang	102	21.28 N	101.19 E
Mengcheng	100	33.17 N	116.33 E
Mengchi ≃	107	29.47 N	104.56 E
Mengcun	98	38.06 N	117.05 E
Mengdapu	104	41.35 N	123.12 E
Mengede ⬥⁸	263	51.34 N	7.23 E
Mengeh Jek	120	37.02 N	66.07 E
Mengen, Dtsch.	58	48.03 N	9.20 E
Mengen, Tür.	130	40.56 N	32.04 E
Mengeringhausen	56	51.22 N	8.59 E
Mengersgereuth-Hämmern	54	50.24 N	11.07 E
Menges Mills	208	39.52 N	76.54 W
Menggala	112	4.28 S	105.17 E
Menggu	102	26.34 N	102.57 E
Menggubao	104	42.27 N	122.23 E
Menggudai	102	38.10 N	108.15 E
Menghai	102	22.00 N	100.26 E
Menghe	106	32.03 N	119.47 E
Menghun	102	21.44 N	100.23 E
Mengjiacun	106	31.33 N	118.46 E
Mengjiagang	89	46.22 N	130.40 E
Mengjiatai	104	42.06 N	123.21 E
Mengjiawan	102	38.35 N	109.25 E
Mengjiawopeng	104	41.22 N	121.51 E
Mengjiayuanjia	105	40.52 N	118.08 E
Mengjiazhai	269b	31.18 N	121.19 E
Mengka	102	25.10 N	98.01 E
Mengkibol	114	1.58 N	103.20 E
Mengkuang	114	3.11 N	102.24 E
Menglian	102	22.20 N	99.38 E
Menglinghausen ⬥⁸	263	51.28 N	7.25 E
Mengluchang	107	29.19 N	103.35 E
Mengmucun	106	31.59 N	119.01 E
Mengong	152	2.56 N	11.25 E
Mengqigou	104	42.00 N	121.08 E
Mengshan	102	24.07 N	110.33 E
Meng Shan ⋏, Zhg.	98	35.44 N	117.45 E
Meng Shan ⋏, Zhg.	104	41.50 N	121.10 E
Mengtong	107	30.44 N	105.53 E
Mengulek, gora ∧	86	50.58 N	89.30 E
Mengwang	102	22.26 N	100.34 E
Mengyin	98	35.45 N	117.57 E
Mengzhe	102	22.02 N	100.16 E
Mengzhi	102	24.10 N	99.46 E
Mengzi	102	23.22 N	103.20 E
Menihek Lakes ⊜	176	54.00 N	66.35 W
Ménil-la-Tour	56	48.46 N	5.52 E
Menindee	166	32.24 S	142.26 E
Menindee Lake ⊜	166	32.21 S	142.20 E
Meningie	166	35.42 S	139.20 E
Menjiaqiangzi	104	42.29 N	121.19 E
Menkoutang	106	31.01 N	119.27 E
Menlo	224	46.37 N	123.38 W
Menlo Park	226	37.27 N	122.10 W
Menlo Park Mall ⬥⁹	276	40.32 N	74.20 W
Menlo Park Terrace	276	40.32 N	74.20 W
Mennecy	261	48.34 N	2.26 E
Mennetou-sur-Cher	50	47.16 N	1.53 E
Mennighüffen	52	52.13 N	8.43 E
Menno	198	43.14 N	97.34 W
Meno, Indon.	164	3.52 S	135.31 E
Meno, Ok., U.S.	196	36.23 N	98.10 W
Menominee	190	45.06 N	87.36 W
Menominee ≃	190	45.05 N	87.36 W
Menominee Indian Reservation ⬥⁴	190	45.00 N	88.45 W
Menomonee ≃	216	43.02 N	87.54 W
Menomonee Falls	216	43.10 N	88.07 W
Menomonie	190	44.52 N	91.55 W
Menongue	152	14.36 S	17.48 E
Menor, Mar c	34	37.43 N	0.48 W
Menorca I	34	40.00 N	4.00 E
Mens	62	44.49 N	5.45 E
Menslage	52	52.41 N	7.49 E
Menston	44	53.53 N	1.44 W
Menstrup	41	55.13 N	11.36 E
Mentana	66	42.02 N	12.38 E
Mentasta Lake	180	62.55 N	143.45 W
Mentasta Mountains ⋏	180	62.40 N	143.07 W
Mentawai, Kepulauan II	108	2.00 S	99.30 E
Mentawai, Selat ᵿ	108	1.45 S	100.00 E
Mentekab	114	3.29 N	102.21 E
Menteke, peski ⬥²	80	47.20 N	50.40 E
Menteng ⬥⁸	269e	6.12 S	106.50 E
Menteroda	54	51.18 N	10.33 E
Menthon-Saint-Bernard	62	45.51 N	6.12 E
Menton	62	43.47 N	7.30 E
Mentone, Austl.	274b	37.59 S	145.05 E
Mentone, Ca., U.S.	228	34.05 N	117.08 W
Mentone, In., U.S.	216	41.10 N	86.02 W
Mentone, Tx., U.S.	196	31.42 N	103.36 W
Mentone → Menton	62	43.47 N	7.30 E
Mentor, Ky., U.S.	218	38.53 N	84.14 W
Mentor, Oh., U.S.	214	41.39 N	81.20 W
Mentor-on-the-Lake	214	41.42 N	81.21 W
Mentougou	105	39.56 N	116.03 E
Mentzdam ⊜¹	158	33.10 S	25.09 E
Menucourt	261	49.02 N	1.59 E
Menuma	94	36.13 N	139.23 E
Men'uša	76	58.23 N	30.42 E
Menyamya	164	7.10 S	146.00 E
Menyapa, Gunung ∧	112	1.05 N	116.05 E
Menyuan	102	37.27 N	101.48 E
Menza ≃	88	50.14 N	108.38 E
Menzel Bourguiba	148	37.10 N	9.48 E
Menzel Bou Zelfa	36	36.41 N	10.36 E
Menzel Djemil	36	37.14 N	9.55 E
Menzelen	52	51.37 N	6.32 E
Menzelerheide	263	51.37 N	6.31 E
Menzelinsk	80	55.43 N	53.08 E
Menzel Temime	148	36.47 N	10.59 E
Menzenschwand	58	47.49 N	8.04 E
Menzies	162	29.41 S	121.02 E
Menzies, Mount ∧	9	73.30 S	61.50 E
Menziken	58	47.14 N	8.12 E
Meobbaai c	156	24.25 S	14.34 E
Meola Āgri	272a	28.42 N	77.23 E
Meolo	64	45.37 N	12.27 E
Meon ≃	42	50.48 N	1.15 W
Meopham	260	51.22 N	0.22 E
Meopham Station	260	51.23 N	0.21 E
Meoqui	232	28.17 N	105.29 W
Meota	184	53.02 N	108.27 W
Méouge ≃	62	44.16 N	5.50 E
Méounes-lès-Montrieux	62	43.17 N	5.58 E
Mepal	42	52.24 N	0.07 E
Mepisckaro, gora ∧	84	41.50 N	42.40 E
Meppel	52	52.42 N	6.11 E
Meppen	52	52.41 N	7.17 E
Meqerghane, Sebkha ≚	148	26.19 N	1.20 E
Meqruur	174q	9.31 N	138.09 E
Mequinenza, Embalse de ⊜¹	34	41.20 N	0.05 E
Mequon	216	43.13 N	87.59 W
Mer	50	47.42 N	1.30 E
Mera ≃	58	46.11 N	9.25 E
Merah	112	0.50 N	116.48 E
Merai	164	4.50 S	152.20 E
Meråker	26	63.26 N	11.45 E
Merakurak	115a	6.53 S	111.59 E
Meramangye, Lake ⊜	162	28.25 S	132.13 E
Merambéllou, Kólpos c	38	35.14 N	25.47 E
Meramec ≃	194	38.23 N	90.21 W
Meramec Caverns ≗⁵	219	38.15 N	91.06 W
Meramec State Park ♦	219	38.14 N	91.05 W
Meran	273a	6.38 N	3.16 E
Meranggau	112	0.12 S	110.17 E
Merangin ≃	112	2.09 S	102.47 E
Meran → Merano	64	46.40 N	11.09 E
Merano (Meran)	64	46.40 N	11.09 E
Merapi, Gunung ∧	115a	8.03 S	114.15 E
Merapoh	114	4.41 N	101.59 E
Merasheen	186	47.25 N	54.21 W
Merasheen Island I	186	47.30 N	54.15 W
Merate	62	45.42 N	9.25 E
Meratus, Pegunungan ⋏	112	2.45 S	115.40 E
Merauke	164	8.28 S	140.20 E
Merauke ≃	164	8.30 S	140.24 E
Merbabu, Gunung ∧	115a	7.27 S	110.26 E
Merbau, Indon.	114	2.16 N	99.50 E
Merbau, Indon.	114	1.07 N	102.33 E
Merbein	166	34.11 S	142.04 E
Mercaderes	246	1.47 N	77.10 W
Merca → Marka	144	1.43 N	44.53 E
Mercantour, Parc National du ♦	62	44.10 N	7.00 E
Mercāra	122	12.25 N	75.44 E
Mercatale	66	43.15 N	12.08 E
Mercato San Severino	68	40.47 N	14.46 E
Mercato Saraceno	66	43.57 N	12.12 E
Merced	226	37.18 N	120.28 W
Merced □⁶	226	37.15 N	120.40 W
Merced ≃	226	37.21 N	120.58 W
Merced, Lake ⊜	282	37.43 N	122.29 W
Merced, North Fork ≃	226	37.37 N	120.03 W
Merced, South Fork ≃	226	37.39 N	119.53 W
Merced Airport ⊠	226	37.17 N	120.31 W
Mercedario, Cerro ∧	252	31.59 S	70.07 W
Mercedes, Arg.	252	29.12 S	58.05 W
Mercedes, Arg.	252	33.40 S	65.28 W
Mercedes, Arg.	258	34.39 S	59.27 W
Mercedes, Pil.	116	14.07 N	123.01 E
Mercedes, Tx., U.S.	196	26.08 N	97.54 W
Mercedes, Ur.	252	33.16 S	58.01 W
Mercer, N.Z.	172	37.16 S	175.03 E
Mercer, Mo., U.S.	194	40.30 N	93.31 W
Mercer, Oh., U.S.	216	40.40 N	84.35 W
Mercer, Pa., U.S.	214	41.13 N	80.14 W
Mercer, Wi., U.S.	190	46.09 N	90.03 W
Mercer □⁶, N.J., U.S.	208	40.13 N	74.45 W
Mercer □⁶, Oh., U.S.	216	40.33 N	84.34 W
Mercer □⁶, Pa., U.S.	214	41.14 N	80.15 W
Mercer Island	224	47.35 N	122.15 W
Mercersburg	188	39.49 N	77.54 W
Mercerville	208	40.14 N	74.41 W
Mercês, Bra.	256	21.12 S	43.21 W
Mercês, Port.	266c	38.47 N	9.19 W
Merchants Bay c	176	67.10 N	62.50 W
Merchants Millpond ⊜	208	36.26 N	76.41 W
Merchantville	285	39.56 N	75.04 W
Merchong ≃	114	3.03 N	103.27 E
Merchtem	50	50.58 N	4.14 E
Mercier (Saint-Philomène)	275a	45.19 N	73.45 W
Mercier, Pont ⬥⁵	275a	45.25 N	73.39 W
Mercoal	182	53.10 N	117.05 W
Mercogliano	68	40.55 N	14.44 E
Mercury	204	36.40 N	115.59 W
Mercury Islands II	172	36.35 S	175.55 E
Mercy, Cape ≻	176	64.53 N	63.32 W
Mercy Bay c	176	74.05 N	119.00 W
Mercy-le-Bas	56	49.23 N	5.45 E
Merdeka Bridge ⬥⁵	271c	1.18 N	103.53 E
Méré, Fr.	261	48.47 N	1.49 E
Mere, Eng., U.K.	42	51.06 N	2.16 W
Mere, Eng., U.K.	262	53.20 N	2.25 W
Mere Brow	262	53.40 N	2.53 W
Mereckij	85	43.48 N	74.42 E
Mereclough	262	53.46 N	2.11 W
Meredale	273d	26.17 S	27.59 E
Meredith, Austl.	169	37.51 S	144.04 E
Meredith, N.H., U.S.	188	43.39 N	71.30 W
Meredith, Cape ≻	254	52.15 S	60.39 W
Meredith, Lake ⊜¹	196	35.36 N	101.42 W
Meredosia	219	39.50 N	90.34 W
Meredosia Lake ⊜	219	39.52 N	90.33 W
Mereeg	144	3.46 N	47.18 E
Merefa	78	49.49 N	36.03 E
Méré Lava I	175f	14.25 S	168.03 E
Merelbeke	50	51.00 N	3.45 E
Merenkurkku (Norra Kvarken) ᵿ	26	63.36 N	20.43 E
Mereny	78	46.58 N	29.04 E
Merevari ≃	246	4.28 N	63.57 W
Méréville	50	48.19 N	2.05 E
Merewa	144	7.40 N	37.00 E
Merewether	170	32.57 S	151.46 E
Mereworth	260	51.15 N	0.23 E
Mergenevo	80	49.56 N	51.17 E
Mergozzo	58	45.58 N	8.26 E
Mergui (Myeik)	110	12.26 N	98.36 E
Mergui Archipelago II	110	12.00 N	98.00 E
Merḥavya	132	32.36 N	35.19 E
Meria	272b	22.59 N	88.20 E
Meribah	166	34.42 S	140.51 E
Méribel	62	45.25 N	6.34 E
Meriç	130	41.11 N	26.25 E
Meriç (Marica) (Évros) ≃	38	40.52 N	26.12 E
Méricourt	50	50.24 N	2.52 E
Mérida, Esp.	34	38.55 N	6.20 W
Mérida, Méx.	200	32.39 N	114.58 W
Mérida, Méx.	232	20.58 N	89.37 W
Merida, Pil.	116	10.55 N	124.32 E
Mérida, Ven.	246	8.36 N	71.08 W
Mérida □³	246	8.30 N	71.10 W
Mérida, Cordillera de ⋏	246	8.40 N	71.00 W
Meridale	210	42.22 N	74.57 W
Meriden, Eng., U.K.	42	52.26 N	1.37 W
Meriden, Ct., U.S.	207	41.32 N	72.48 W
Meriden, N.J., U.S.	276	40.57 N	74.28 W
Meridian, Ca., U.S.	226	39.09 N	121.55 W
Meridian, Ga., U.S.	192	31.27 N	81.22 W
Meridian, Id., U.S.	202	43.36 N	116.23 W
Meridian, Ms., U.S.	194	32.21 N	88.42 W
Meridian, N.Y., U.S.	210	43.09 N	76.32 W
Meridian, Pa., U.S.	214	40.51 N	79.58 W
Meridian, Tx., U.S.	222	31.55 N	97.39 W
Meridian Hills	218	39.53 N	86.09 W
Meridian Naval Air Station ■	194	32.33 N	88.34 W
Meridianville	194	34.51 N	86.34 W
Mériel	261	49.05 N	2.12 E
Mérignac	32	44.50 N	0.42 W
Merigold	194	33.50 N	90.43 W
Merikarvia	26	61.51 N	21.30 E
Merille, Laga ≃	154	1.25 N	38.26 E
Merimbula	166	36.53 S	149.54 E
Merín, Laguna (Lagoa Mirim) c	252	32.45 S	52.50 W
Merinda	166	20.01 S	148.10 E
Mering	60	48.16 N	10.59 E
Meringa	146	10.44 N	12.09 E
Merin Gubai	144	1.26 N	44.20 E
Meringur	166	34.24 S	141.16 E
Merino	198	40.28 N	103.21 W
Merinos	252	32.24 S	56.54 W
Merion Station	285	39.59 N	75.15 W
Merir I	108	4.19 N	132.19 E
Merishausen	58	47.45 N	8.37 E
Merit	222	33.13 N	96.17 W
Merivale Gardens	212	45.19 N	75.44 W
Meriwether Farms	285	39.58 N	75.34 W
Merizo	174p	13.16 N	144.40 E
Merke	85	42.52 N	73.11 E
Merkel	196	32.28 N	100.00 W
Merkem	50	50.57 N	2.51 E
Merkendorf	56	49.12 N	10.42 E
Merkinė	76	54.10 N	24.10 E
Merklin	60	49.34 N	13.07 E
Merklingen	58	48.30 N	9.44 E
Merkourovoúni ∧	267c	37.54 N	23.48 E
Merksem	50	51.15 N	4.27 E
Merksplas	56	51.22 N	4.52 E
Merkulovići	76	52.58 N	30.36 E
Merkys ≃	76	54.10 N	24.11 E
Merlara	64	45.10 N	11.26 E
Merlejevo	82	55.05 N	37.13 E
Merlimau, Pulau I	271c	1.17 N	103.42 E
Merlimont-Plage	50	50.28 N	1.35 E
Merlin, On., Can.	214	42.14 N	82.14 W
Merlin, Or., U.S.	202	42.31 N	123.25 W
Merlin Seamount ✦³	14	9.05 S	150.44 W
Merlo, Arg.	252	32.21 S	65.02 W
Merlo, Arg.	258	34.40 S	58.45 W
Merlo □⁵	288	34.40 S	58.45 W
Merlo, Aeródromo ⊠	288	34.41 S	58.45 W
Merlynston	274b	37.43 S	144.58 E
Mermaid Beach	171a	28.03 S	153.27 E
Mern	41	55.03 N	12.04 E
Merna	198	41.29 N	99.45 W
Mernye	30	46.30 N	17.50 E
Meroe ⊥	140	16.56 N	33.43 E
Meron	132	32.59 N	35.26 E
Meron, Hare ∧	132	32.58 N	35.25 E
Meros, Ponta dos ≻	256	23.13 S	44.21 W
Merotai Besar	112	4.26 N	117.46 E
Merouana	34	35.38 N	5.55 E
Merouane, Chott ⊜	148	34.00 N	6.02 E
Mer'oža	76	59.02 N	36.23 E
Merredin	162	31.29 S	118.16 E
Merrick	276	40.39 N	73.33 W
Merrick ∧	44	55.08 N	4.29 W
Merrick Bay c	276	40.38 N	73.33 W
Merrickville	212	44.55 N	75.50 W
Merri Creek ≃	169	37.48 S	145.01 E
Merriewold Lake	210	41.22 N	74.12 W
Merrifield	284c	38.52 N	77.13 W
Merrill, Ia., U.S.	198	42.43 N	96.14 W
Merrill, Mi., U.S.	190	43.24 N	84.19 W
Merrill, Or., U.S.	202	42.01 N	121.35 W
Merrill, Wi., U.S.	190	45.10 N	89.41 W
Merrillan	190	44.27 N	90.50 W
Merrill C. Meigs Field ⊠	278	41.52 N	87.37 W
Merrill Lake ⊜	212	44.55 N	77.24 W
Merrillville	216	41.28 N	87.19 W
Merrimac	207	42.49 N	71.00 W
Merrimack ≃	188	42.49 N	70.49 W
Merrimack College ʊ²	283	42.40 N	71.08 W
Merrimac Terrace	283	42.49 N	71.00 W
Merriman, S. Afr.	158	31.13 S	23.38 E
Merriman, Ne., U.S.	198	42.55 N	101.42 W
Merrionette Park	278	41.41 N	87.42 W
Merriott	42	50.54 N	2.48 W
Merritt, B.C., Can.	182	50.07 N	120.47 W
Merritt, Wa., U.S.	224	47.47 N	120.51 W
Merritt, Lake ⊜¹	282	37.48 N	122.16 W
Merritt Island	220	28.21 N	80.42 W
Merritt Island I	220	28.33 N	80.40 W
Merritt Reservoir ⊜¹	198	42.35 N	100.55 W
Merriwa	166	32.08 S	150.21 E
Mer Rouge	194	32.46 N	91.47 W
Merrow	207	41.49 N	72.18 W
Merrygoen	166	31.50 S	149.14 E
Merrylands	274a	33.50 S	150.59 E
Merrymount Park ♦	283	42.16 N	71.01 W
Merryville	194	30.45 N	93.32 W
Mersa Fatma	144	14.55 N	40.20 E
Mersa Matruh → Marsā Maṭrūḥ	140	31.21 N	27.14 E
Mersch	56	49.46 N	6.06 E
Merscheid ⬥⁸	263	51.10 N	7.01 E
Merse V	46	55.39 N	2.15 W
Merse ≃	66	43.05 N	11.22 E
Mersea Island I	42	51.47 N	0.55 E
Merseburg	54	51.21 N	11.59 E
Mersey ≃, Austl.	166	41.10 S	146.22 E
Mersey ≃, N.S., Can.	186	44.02 N	64.43 W
Mersey ≃, Eng., U.K.	44	53.25 N	3.00 W
Merseyside □⁶	44	53.25 N	2.50 W
Mersey Tunnel ⬥⁵	262	53.24 N	3.00 W
Mersing	114	2.26 N	103.50 E
Mersin → İçel	130	36.48 N	34.38 E
Mers-les-Bains	50	50.04 N	1.23 E
Mērsrags	76	57.21 N	23.07 E
Mersthaw	260	51.16 N	0.09 W
Merta	120	26.39 N	74.02 E
Merta Road	120	26.43 N	73.55 E
Merthyr Tydfil	42	51.46 N	3.23 W
Merti	154	1.04 N	38.40 E
Mertingen	56	48.39 N	10.47 E
Mértola	34	37.38 N	7.40 W
Merton, Austl.	169	36.59 S	145.42 E
Merton, Wi., U.S.	216	43.08 N	88.18 W
Merton ⬥⁸	42	51.25 N	0.12 W
Mertz Glacier Tongue ⊓	9	67.40 S	144.45 E
Mertzon	196	31.16 N	100.49 W
Mertztown	208	40.30 N	75.40 W
Méru, Fr.	50	49.14 N	2.08 E
Meru, Kenya	154	0.03 N	37.39 E
Meru, Mount ∧	154	3.14 S	36.45 E
Meru National Park ♦	154	0.10 N	38.15 E
Meruoca	250	3.28 S	40.28 W
Mervans	58	46.48 N	5.11 E
Merville	50	50.38 N	2.38 E
Mervin	184	53.20 N	108.53 W
Merv → Mary	128	37.36 N	61.50 E
Merwede	158	31.38 S	23.48 E
Merweville	158	32.40 S	21.31 E
Merwin, Lake ⊜¹	224	45.59 N	122.26 W
Merxleben	54	51.07 N	10.40 E
Mery	82	55.49 N	36.36 E
Méry-la-Bataille	50	49.33 N	2.38 E
Méry-sur-Oise	261	49.04 N	2.11 E
Méry-sur-Seine	50	48.30 N	3.53 E
Merzdorf	54	51.23 N	14.32 E
Merzhausen	58	47.58 N	7.49 E
Merzifon	130	40.53 N	35.29 E
Merzig	56	49.27 N	6.36 E
Mesa, Micron.	175c	7.21 N	151.51 E
Mesa, Moç.	154	13.00 S	39.33 E
Mesa, S. Afr.	158	26.29 S	26.59 E
Mesa, Az., U.S.	200	33.25 N	111.49 W
Mesa ≃	34	41.15 N	1.48 W
Mesa, Cerro ∧	254	48.46 S	71.29 W
Mesabi Range ⋏²	190	47.30 N	92.50 W
Mesachie Lake	224	48.49 N	124.07 W
Mesa del Nayar	234	22.16 N	104.35 W
Mesa de Santa Rita	234	23.04 N	105.31 W
Mesagne	68	40.33 N	17.49 E
Mes'agutovo	86	55.35 N	58.20 E
Mesaména	152	3.44 N	12.50 E
Mesa Mountain ∧	200	37.55 N	106.38 W
Mesarás, Kólpos c	38	34.58 N	24.36 E
Mesa Verde National Park ♦	200	37.13 N	108.30 W
Mescalero	200	33.09 N	105.46 W
Mescalero Apache Indian Reservation ⬥⁴	200	33.12 N	105.40 W
Meščerino, Ross.	76	53.37 N	37.23 E
Meščerino, Ross.	82	55.11 N	38.21 E
Meščerskij	265b	55.40 N	37.25 E
Meščerskoje	82	55.17 N	37.38 E
Meschede	56	51.20 N	8.17 E
Meschetskij chrebet ⋏	84	41.48 N	42.30 E
Mescit Tepe ∧	130	40.22 N	41.11 E
Meščovsk	76	54.19 N	35.17 E
Meščura	24	63.20 N	50.52 E
Mese	58	46.17 N	9.21 E
Mèsè Atet	110	18.38 N	97.39 E
Mesen-Bucht → Mezenskaja guba c	24	66.40 N	43.45 E
Mesero	266b	45.30 N	8.51 E
Mesewa → Mitsiwa	144	15.38 N	39.28 E
Mesfinto	144	13.20 N	37.19 E
Mesgarābād	267d	35.37 N	51.31 E
Mesgouez, Lac ⊜	176	51.24 N	75.05 W
Meshed → Mashhad	128	36.18 N	59.36 E
Meshgīn Shahr	128	38.24 N	47.40 E
Meshomasic Mountain ∧	207	41.38 N	72.32 W
Meshoppen	210	41.34 N	76.03 W
Meshoppen Creek ≃	210	41.37 N	76.03 W
Mesick	190	44.24 N	85.42 W
Mesier, Canal ᵿ	254	48.20 S	74.33 W
Mesilinka ≃	182	56.09 N	124.28 W
Mesilla	200	32.16 N	106.48 W
Mesillas, Méx.	234	23.14 N	106.03 W
Mesillas, Méx.	234	23.33 N	103.35 W
Mesima ≃	68	38.30 N	16.15 E
Meskiana	148	35.39 N	7.41 E
Meskiana, Oued ≃	36	35.49 N	7.53 E
Meskine	146	11.25 N	15.21 E
Meškuičiai	76	56.05 N	23.28 E
Meskum	114	1.34 N	102.01 E
Meslay-du-Maine	32	47.57 N	0.33 W
Meslay-le-Grenet	50	48.22 N	1.23 E
Mesnil-Val-Plage	50	50.03 N	1.20 E
Mesocco	58	46.23 N	9.14 E
Mesola	66	44.55 N	12.14 E
Mesolcina, Valle V	58	46.20 N	9.10 E
Mesolóngion	38	38.21 N	21.17 E
Mesomikenda Lake ⊜	190	47.40 N	81.53 W
Mesopotamia	214	41.27 N	80.57 W
Mesopotamia □⁹	128	34.00 N	44.00 E
Mesoraca	68	39.05 N	16.48 E
Mesóyia □⁹	267c	37.56 N	23.53 E
Mespelbrunn ⊥	56	49.54 N	9.19 E
Mesquita, Bra.	255	19.13 S	42.35 W
Mesquita, Bra.	256	22.48 S	43.26 W
Mesquite, Nv., U.S.	204	36.48 N	114.03 W
Mesquite, Tx., U.S.	222	32.46 N	96.35 W
Messach Mellet ⋏²	146	24.30 N	11.35 E
Messalo ≃	154	11.40 S	40.26 E
Messaoud, Oued V	148	27.28 N	0.21 W
Messdorf	54	52.43 N	11.33 E
Messina, It.	70	38.11 N	15.33 E
Messina, S. Afr.	156	22.23 S	30.00 E
Messina □⁴	70	38.03 N	14.52 E
Messina, Stretto di ᵿ	70	38.15 N	15.35 E
Messinge ≃	154	11.34 S	35.25 E
Messingham	44	53.32 N	0.39 W
Messíni	38	37.04 N	22.00 E
Messíni ⊥	38	37.11 N	21.57 E
Messiniakós Kólpos c	38	36.58 N	22.00 E
Messix Peak ∧	202	41.29 N	112.31 W
Messkirch	58	47.59 N	9.07 E
Messojacha ≃	74	67.52 N	77.27 E
Messondo	152	3.43 N	10.28 E
Messstetten	58	48.11 N	8.58 E
Messy	261	48.58 N	2.42 E
Mestá	38	38.15 N	25.55 E
Mesta (Néstos) ≃	38	40.41 N	24.44 E
Mestasa	148	35.07 N	4.25 W
Městečko	60	50.03 N	13.52 E
Mestghanem	148	35.51 N	0.07 E
Mestghanem □⁵	148	36.00 N	0.30 E
Mestia	84	43.03 N	42.43 E
Mestlin	54	53.35 N	11.56 E
Město Touškov	60	49.46 N	13.15 E
Mestre	64	45.29 N	12.15 E
Mestrino	64	45.26 N	11.45 E
Mesudiye	130	40.28 N	37.46 E
Mesuji ≃	112	4.08 S	105.52 E
Mesum	52	52.13 N	7.29 E
Meszah Peak ∧	180	58.28 N	131.26 W
Meta, It.	68	40.39 N	14.24 E
Meta, Mo., U.S.	219	38.18 N	92.09 W
Meta □⁵	246	3.30 N	73.00 W
Meta ≃	246	6.12 N	67.28 W
Métabief	58	46.47 N	6.21 E
Metagācha	272b	22.38 N	88.31 E
Metahara	144	8.54 N	39.55 E
Meta Incognita Peninsula ≻¹	176	62.45 N	68.30 W
Metairie	194	29.59 N	90.09 W
Metaline Falls	202	48.51 N	117.22 W
Metallifere, Colline ⋏	66	43.15 N	11.00 E
Metallostroj	265a	59.47 N	30.33 E
Metamora, Il., U.S.	190	40.47 N	89.21 W
Metamora, In., U.S.	218	39.26 N	85.08 W
Metamora, Mi., U.S.	216	42.56 N	83.17 W
Metamora, Oh., U.S.	216	41.42 N	83.54 W
Metán	252	25.29 S	64.57 W
Metangula	154	12.43 S	34.49 E
Metapán	236	14.20 N	89.27 W
Metapontum ⊥	68	40.23 N	16.50 E
Metarica	154	14.20 S	36.48 E
Metates	234	23.46 N	106.02 W
Metaurilia	66	43.49 N	13.03 E
Metauro ≃	66	43.50 N	13.03 E
Metcalfe	212	45.14 N	75.28 W
Metchosin	224	48.22 N	123.33 W
Metechi	84	41.55 N	44.21 E
Metedeconk, South Branch ≃	208	40.04 N	74.09 W
Meteghan	186	44.11 N	66.10 W
Metelen	52	52.08 N	7.12 E
Metema	144	12.57 N	36.12 E
Metéora ʊ¹	38	39.46 N	21.36 E
Meteor Crater ≗⁶	200	35.02 N	111.02 W
Meteor Seamount ✦³	8	48.00 S	8.30 E
Metepec, Méx.	234	19.15 N	99.36 W
Metepec, Méx.	234	18.56 N	98.28 W
Metharaw	110	16.12 N	98.08 E
Metheringham	44	53.08 N	0.24 W
Methil	46	56.10 N	3.01 W
Methler	263	51.35 N	7.37 E
Methlick	46	57.25 N	2.14 W
Methóni	38	36.50 N	21.43 E
Methow	182	48.07 N	120.00 W
Methow ≃	202	48.03 N	119.53 W
Methuen	207	42.43 N	71.11 W
Methven	172	43.38 S	171.39 E
Methwold	42	52.31 N	0.33 E
Methyen	46	56.25 N	3.34 W
Metica ≃	246	4.09 N	72.55 W
Metiskow	184	52.24 N	110.38 W
Metković	36	43.03 N	17.39 E
Metlakatla, B.C., Can.	182	54.20 N	130.27 W
Metlakatla, Ak., U.S.	182	55.08 N	131.35 W
Metlaoui	148	34.20 N	8.24 E
Metlatonoc	234	17.11 N	98.20 W
Metlika	36	45.39 N	15.19 E
Metlili, Oued V	148	31.54 N	4.53 E
Metlili ech Chaâmba	148	32.18 N	3.40 E
Metnitz	61	46.59 N	14.13 E
Meto, Bayou ≃	194	34.05 N	91.26 W
Metolius ≃	202	44.36 N	121.17 W
Metompkin Bay c	208	37.43 N	75.35 W
Metompkin Inlet c	208	37.41 N	75.35 W
Metro	115a	5.05 S	105.20 E
Metropolis	194	37.09 N	88.43 W
Metropolitan	190	46.00 N	87.53 W
Metropolitan Beach ♦	281	42.35 N	82.48 W
Metropolitan Museum of Art ʊ	276	40.47 N	73.58 W
Metropolitan Oakland International Airport ⊠	226	37.43 N	122.13 W

Symbols in the index entries represent the broad categories identified in the key at the right. Symbols with superior numbers (⋏¹) identify subcategories (see complete key on page *I · 1).*

Symbole im Register stellen die rechts im Schlüssel erklärten Kategorien dar. Symbole mit hochgestellten Ziffern (⋏¹) bezeichnen Unterabteilungen einer Kategorie (vgl. vollständiger Schlüssel auf Seite *I · 1).*

Los símbolos incluídos en el texto del índice representan las grandes categorias identificadas con la clave a la derecha. Los símbolos con numeros en su parte superior (⋏¹) identifican las subcategorías (véase la clave completa en la página *I · 1).*

Les symboles de l'index représentent les catégories indiquées dans la légende à droite. Les symboles suivis d'un indice (⋏¹) représentent des sous-catégories (voir légende complète à la page *I · 1).*

Os símbolos incluídos no texto do índice representam as grandes categorias identificadas com a chave à direita. Os símbolos com números em sua parte superior (⋏¹) identificam as subcategorias (veja-se a chave completa à página *I · 1).*

	ENGLISH	DEUTSCH			
∧	Mountain	Berg	Montaña	Montagne	Montanha
⋏	Mountains	Gebirge	Montañas	Montagnes	Montanhas
)(	Pass	Paß	Paso	Col	Passo
V	Valley, Canyon	Tal, Cañon	Valle, Cañón	Vallée, Canyon	Vale, Canhão
≚	Plain	Ebene	Llano	Plaine	Planície
≻	Cape	Kap	Cabo	Cap	Cabo
I	Island	Insel	Isla	Île	Ilha
II	Islands	Inseln	Islas	Îles	Ilhas
≗	Other Topographic Features	Andere Topographische Objekte	Otros Elementos Topográficos	Autres données topographiques	Outros acidentes topográficos

ESPAÑOL — Nombre / Página / Lat.°′ / Long.°′ W = Oeste
FRANÇAIS — Nom / Page / Lat.°′ / Long.°′ W = Ouest
PORTUGUÊS — Nome / Página / Lat.°′ / Long.°′ W = Oeste

Nombre / Nom / Nome	Página / Page	Lat.°′	Long.°′
Metschow	54	53.49 N	12.58 E
Metsematluku	156	24.01 S	24.40 E
Metsera	154	2.35 S	26.07 E
Métsovon	38	39.46 N	21.11 E
Mettawa	278	42.14 N	87.56 W
Metten	60	48.52 N	12.55 E
Mettendorf	56	49.57 N	6.19 E
Metter	192	32.23 N	82.03 W
Mettet	56	50.19 N	4.40 E
Mettetal Airport ⊠	281	42.21 N	83.27 W
Mettingen	52	52.18 N	7.46 E
Mettlach	56	49.30 N	6.36 E
Mettmach	60	48.10 N	13.21 E
Mettmann	56	51.15 N	6.58 E
Mettray	50	47.27 N	0.39 E
Mettuppālaiyam	122	11.18 N	76.57 E
Mettūr	122	11.48 N	77.48 E
Metu	144	8.20 N	35.36 E
Metuchen	210	40.32 N	74.21 W
Metuge	154	12.58 S	40.20 E
Metulla	132	33.16 N	35.35 E
Metundo, Ilha I	154	11.10 S	40.41 E
Metz	56	49.08 N	6.10 E
Metzervisse	56	49.19 N	6.17 E
Metzger	224	45.26 N	122.45 W
Metzingen	56	48.32 N	9.17 E
Metzkausen	263	51.16 N	6.57 E
Metztitlán	234	20.36 N	98.45 W
Metztitlán, Laguna ⊜	234	20.40 N	98.50 W
Meu ≃	32	48.02 N	1.47 W
Meudon	261	48.48 N	2.14 E
Meudon, Bois de ♠	261	48.47 N	2.12 E
Meul ≃	158	27.56 S	28.50 E
Meulaboh	114	4.09 N	96.08 E
Meulan	50	49.01 N	1.54 E
Meulebeke	50	50.57 N	3.17 E
Meung-sur-Loire	50	47.50 N	1.42 E
Meureubo ≃	114	4.09 N	96.09 E
Meureudu	114	5.16 N	96.16 E
Meursault	58	46.59 N	4.46 E
Meurthe ≃	32	48.47 N	6.09 E
Meurthe-et-Moselle □[5]	32	48.35 N	6.10 E
Meuse	58	47.59 N	5.33 E
Meuse □[5]	56	49.00 N	5.30 E
Meuse (Maas) ≃	30	51.49 N	5.01 E
Meuselwitz	54	51.02 N	12.17 E
Meuvette ≃	50	48.45 N	1.08 E
Meux Creek ≃	212	44.07 N	81.02 W
Mevagissey	42	50.16 N	4.48 W
Mevang	152	0.07 N	11.05 E
Mewāt Plain ≚	124	27.40 N	77.15 E
Mexborough	44	53.30 N	1.17 W
Mexia	222	31.40 N	96.28 W
Mexia Lake ⊜[1]	222	31.39 N	96.36 W
Mexiana, Ilha I	250	0.02 S	49.35 W
Mexicali	232	32.40 N	115.29 W
Mexican Hat	200	37.09 N	109.52 W
Mexico, In., U.S.	216	40.49 N	86.06 W
Mexico, Me., U.S.	188	44.33 N	70.32 W
Mexico, Mo., U.S.	219	39.10 N	91.52 W
Mexico, N.Y., U.S.	212	43.27 N	76.13 W
Mexico, Pa., U.S.	208	40.32 N	77.21 W
México □[3]	234	19.20 N	99.45 W
Mexico (México) □[1], N.A.	230	23.00 N	102.00 W
Mexico (México) □[1], N.A.	232	23.00 N	102.00 W
México, Golfo de → Mexico, Gulf of c	230	25.00 N	90.00 W
Mexico, Gulf of c	230	25.00 N	90.00 W
Mexico Basin ✣[1]	16	25.00 N	92.00 W
Mexico Bay c	212	43.31 N	76.17 W
Mexico Beach	192	29.58 N	85.24 W
Mexico City → Ciudad de México	234	19.24 N	99.09 W
Mexiko, Golf von → Mexico, Gulf of c	230	25.00 N	90.00 W
Mexiko → Ciudad de México	234	19.24 N	99.09 W
Mexiko → Mexico □[1]	232	23.00 N	102.00 W
Meximieux	58	45.54 N	5.12 E
Mexique, Golfe du → Mexico, Gulf of c	230	25.00 N	90.00 W
Mexique → Mexico □[1]	230	23.00 N	102.00 W
Mexticacán	234	21.13 N	102.43 W
Mey, Castle of ⊥	46	58.38 N	3.14 W
Meyanodas	164	7.38 S	131.38 E
Meycauayan	116	14.44 N	120.58 E
Meydan	130	38.21 N	41.47 E
Meydancık	130	41.25 N	42.14 E
Meydān-e Gel ≚	128	29.04 N	54.50 E
Meydān Khvolah	120	33.36 N	69.51 E
Meyenburg	54	53.18 N	12.14 E
Meyers Chuck	182	55.44 N	132.15 W
Meyersdale	188	39.48 N	79.01 W
Meyers Lake	214	40.52 N	81.24 W
Meyersville	222	28.55 N	97.21 W
Meyerton	158	26.33 S	28.01 E
Meyísti I	130	36.08 N	29.34 E
Meymac	32	45.32 N	2.09 E
Meymaneh	120	35.55 N	64.47 E
Meymeh	128	33.27 N	51.10 E
Meymeh ≃	128	32.05 N	47.16 E
Meynypilgino	180	62.32 N	177.02 E
Meyo Centre	152	2.33 N	11.02 E
Meyrargues	62	43.38 N	5.32 E
Meyrin	58	46.14 N	6.05 E
Meyronne	184	49.39 N	106.50 W
Meyrueis	32	44.10 N	3.26 E
Meyungs	175b	7.20 N	134.27 E
Meža ≃	61	46.35 N	15.02 E
Mezada, Horvot (Masada) ⊥	132	31.19 N	35.21 E
Mezapa	236	15.33 N	87.23 W
Mezcala	234	17.56 N	99.37 W
Mezcala ≃	234	18.00 N	99.47 W
Mezcalapa	234	17.37 N	93.22 W
Mezcalapa ≃	234	18.00 N	92.54 W
Mezdra	38	43.09 N	23.42 E
Meždurečensk	86	53.42 N	88.03 E
Meždurečenskij	86	59.36 N	65.53 E
Mèze	32	43.25 N	3.36 E
Mézel	62	43.59 N	6.12 E
Mezen'	24	65.50 N	44.13 E
Mezen' ≃	24	66.11 N	43.59 E
Mézenc, Mont ∧	62	44.55 N	4.11 E
Mezenskaja guba c	24	66.40 N	43.45 E
Meževaja	78	48.16 N	36.44 E
Mežgorje	78	48.32 N	23.30 E
Meziadin Lake ⊜	182	56.04 N	129.18 W
Mežica	61	46.31 N	14.52 E
Mézières-en-Brenne	32	46.49 N	1.13 E
Mézières-sur-Seine	261	48.58 N	1.48 E
Mézilhac	62	44.48 N	4.21 E
Mézin	32	44.03 N	0.16 E
Mezinovskij	76	55.30 N	40.21 E
Mežirič	78	50.43 N	34.29 E
Mezőberény	30	46.50 N	21.02 E
Mezőcsát	30	47.49 N	20.55 E
Mezőkovácsháza	30	46.25 N	20.55 E
Mezőkövesd	30	47.50 N	20.34 E
Mezőtúr	30	47.00 N	20.38 E
Mežoz'ornyj	86	54.09 N	59.23 E
Mezquital	234	23.29 N	104.23 W
Mezquital ≃	232	22.35 N	104.54 W
Mezquital del Oro	234	21.10 N	103.23 W
Mezquitic	234	22.23 N	103.41 W
Mezraa	130	41.12 N	35.08 E
Mézy	261	49.00 N	1.53 E
Mezzana	64	46.19 N	10.48 E
Mezzano	64	46.09 N	11.48 E
Mezzenile	62	45.17 N	7.23 E
Mezzocorona	64	46.13 N	11.07 E
Mezzoiuso	70	37.52 N	13.28 E
Mezzola, Lago di ⊜	58	46.12 N	9.26 E
Mezzoldo	58	46.01 N	9.40 E
Mezzolombardo	64	46.13 N	11.05 E
Mezzomerico	266b	45.37 N	8.36 E
Mfangano Island I	154	0.28 S	34.01 E
Mfolozi ≃	158	28.25 S	32.26 E
Mfou	152	3.43 N	11.38 E
Mfuwe	154	13.04 S	31.46 E
Mgači	89	51.05 N	142.17 E
Mgeni ≃	158	29.48 S	31.02 E
Mgeta	154	8.19 S	36.08 E
Mglin	76	53.04 N	32.51 E
M'goun, Irhil ∧	148	31.31 N	6.25 W
M'hai, B'nom ∧	110	11.21 N	107.50 E
Mhasvād	122	17.38 N	74.47 E
Mhlatuze ≃	158	28.47 S	32.06 E
Mhlume	158	26.02 S	31.50 E
Mholach, Beinn ∧[2]	46	56.45 N	4.18 W
Mhòr, Beinn ∧	46	57.17 N	7.19 W
Mhòr, Loch ⊜	46	57.14 N	4.26 W
Mhow	120	22.33 N	75.46 E
Mi ≃, Zhg.	98	37.12 N	119.10 E
Mi ≃, Zhg.	100	27.09 N	112.51 E
Mia, Oued V	148	30.47 N	4.54 E
Miacatlán	234	18.46 N	99.22 W
Mia-dong ◆[8]	271b	37.37 N	127.01 E
Miagao	116	10.39 N	122.14 E
Miahuatlán de Porfirio Díaz	234	16.20 N	96.36 W
Miajadas	34	39.09 N	5.54 W
Miaméré	146	8.52 N	19.50 E
Miami, Mb., Can.	184	49.21 N	98.11 W
Miami, Az., U.S.	200	33.23 N	110.52 W
Miami, Fl., U.S.	220	25.46 N	80.11 W
Miami, In., U.S.	216	40.36 N	86.06 W
Miami, Ok., U.S.	196	36.52 N	94.52 W
Miami, Tx., U.S.	196	35.42 N	100.38 W
Miami □[6], In., U.S.	216	40.45 N	86.04 W
Miami □[6], Oh., U.S.	218	40.02 N	84.13 W
Miami ≃	224	45.33 N	123.53 W
Miami Beach, On., Can.	212	44.13 N	79.29 W
Miami Beach, Fl., U.S.	220	25.47 N	80.07 W
Miami Canal ≅	220	25.47 N	80.15 W
Miami Creek ≃	226	37.21 N	119.44 W
Miami International Airport ⊠	220	25.48 N	80.17 W
Miami Lakes	220	25.53 N	80.18 W
Miamisburg	218	39.38 N	84.17 W
Miamisburg Mound State Memorial ⊥	218	39.38 N	84.17 W
Miami Shores	220	25.51 N	80.11 W
Miami Springs	220	25.49 N	80.17 W
Miami State Recreation Area ♠	216	40.40 N	85.55 W
Miamiville	218	39.13 N	84.18 W
Miān Channūn	123	30.27 N	72.22 E
Mianchi	102	34.48 N	111.49 E
Miāndoāb	128	36.58 N	46.06 E
Miandrivazo	157b	19.31 S	45.28 E
Mianduhe	89	49.05 N	121.06 E
Miane	64	45.57 N	12.06 E
Miāneh	128	37.26 N	47.42 E
Miang, Phu ∧	110	17.42 N	101.01 E
Miangas, Pulau I	108	5.35 N	126.35 E
Mianhu	100	23.28 N	116.09 E
Mianhuadi	104	41.15 N	120.49 E
Miāni	123	32.32 N	73.04 E
Miāni Hōr c	120	25.34 N	66.19 E
Mianning	102	28.39 N	102.09 E
Mianus ≃	207	41.03 N	73.35 W
Mianus, East Branch ≃	276	41.06 N	73.35 W
Mianus Reservoir ⊜[1]	276	41.08 N	73.37 W
Miānwāli	123	32.35 N	71.33 E
Mianxian	102	33.09 N	106.48 E
Mianyang, Zhg.	100	30.23 N	113.25 E
Mianyang, Zhg.	102	31.30 N	104.49 E
Mianzhu	102	31.20 N	104.09 E
Miao Dao I	98	37.56 N	120.45 E
Miaodao Qundao II	98	38.10 N	120.40 E
Miao'ergou	86	45.32 N	83.52 E
Miaofengshan	105	40.04 N	116.13 E
Miaogou	104	41.12 N	120.40 E
Miaojiagou	104	42.16 N	123.22 E
Miaojiatun	104	40.54 N	120.55 E
Miaokou	98	35.48 N	114.09 E
Miaoli	100	24.34 N	120.49 E
Miao Ling ⨯	102	26.15 N	107.26 E
Miaopu	106	31.00 N	118.44 E
Miaoqian	100	30.33 N	117.44 E
Miaotou	106	30.58 N	120.33 E
Miaowan	100	33.07 N	114.41 E
Miaoyang	98	40.49 N	124.24 E
Miaozhen	106	31.43 N	121.21 E
Miaozigou	107	30.17 N	104.35 E
Miarayon	116	8.04 N	124.50 E
Miarinarivo, Madag.	157b	16.38 S	48.15 E
Miarinarivo, Madag.	157b	18.57 S	46.55 E
Miarinavaratra	157b	20.13 S	47.31 E
Miasa	94	36.34 N	137.53 E
Miass	86	54.59 N	60.06 E
Miass ≃	86	56.06 N	64.30 E
Miasteczko Krajeńskie	30	53.06 N	17.01 E
Miastko	30	54.01 N	17.00 E
Miboro-dam ◆[6]	94	36.08 N	136.55 E
Mibu	94	36.25 N	139.48 E
Mibu ≃	94	35.49 N	137.57 E
Mica	156	24.10 S	30.48 E
Mica Mountain ∧	200	32.13 N	110.33 W
Micang Shan ⨯	102	32.45 N	107.20 E
Micanopy	192	29.30 N	82.16 W
Micaúne	156	18.18 S	36.35 E
Mičavičevnik	24	64.14 N	57.58 E
Miccosukee, Lake ⊜[1]	192	30.34 N	83.58 W
Miccosukee Indian Reservation ◆[4]	220	26.10 N	80.50 W
Michael, Mount ∧	164	6.25 S	145.20 E
Michael J. Kirwan Reservoir ⊜[1]	214	41.10 N	81.10 W
Michajlo-Koc'ubinskoje	78	51.27 N	31.04 E
Michajlov	82	54.14 N	39.02 E
Michajlovka, Kaz.	85	42.50 N	75.42 E
Michajlovka, Kaz.	85	43.06 N	71.36 E
Michajlovka, Kaz.	86	53.51 N	76.32 E
Michajlovka, Kyrg.	85	42.37 N	78.20 E
Michajlovka, Ross.	78	49.53 N	39.38 E
Michajlovka, Ross.	80	47.38 N	46.54 E
Michajlovka, Ross.	80	50.05 N	43.15 E
Michajlovka, Ross.	86	51.49 N	79.45 E
Michajlovka, Ross.	86	56.26 N	78.53 E
Michajlovka, Ross.	88	50.26 N	104.10 E
Michajlovka, Ross.	88	55.30 N	114.09 E
Michajlovka, Ross.	88	51.07 N	119.20 E
Michajlovka, Ross.	88	52.57 N	103.18 E
Michajlovka, Ross.	89	49.13 N	129.56 E
Michajlovka, Ross.	89	43.56 N	132.00 E
Michajlovka, Ross.	265a	60.04 N	30.14 E
Michajlovka, Ross.	265a	59.43 N	30.01 E
Michajlovka, Ukr.	78	49.19 N	36.28 E
Michajlovka, Ukr.	78	47.16 N	35.14 E
Michajlovka, Ukr.	83	48.30 N	38.54 E
Michajlovka, Ukr.	83	48.09 N	37.22 E
Michajlovka, Ukr.	83	48.44 N	37.16 E
Michajlovo	80	56.56 N	45.04 E
Michajlovo-Aleksandrovskij	83	49.13 N	40.15 E
Michajlovskaja	80	50.58 N	41.52 E
Michajlovskaja Celina, zapovednik ♠	78	50.45 N	34.10 E
Michajlovskij, Kaz.	86	50.17 N	55.23 E
Michajlovskij, Ross.	76	60.05 N	43.29 E
Michajlovskij, Ross.	86	51.41 N	79.47 E
Michajlovskoje, Ross.	76	58.23 N	37.40 E
Michajlovskoje, Ross.	80	56.11 N	45.47 E
Michajlovskoje, Ross.	82	55.50 N	36.20 E
Michajlovskoje, Ross.	265b	55.35 N	37.35 E
Michalevo	82	55.27 N	38.26 E
Michali	82	55.17 N	39.05 E
Michalkovo	82	54.11 N	37.33 E
Michalovce	30	48.45 N	21.55 E
Michalovy Hory	60	49.55 N	12.47 E
Michanoviči	76	53.45 N	27.40 E
Michaud, Point ›	186	45.34 N	60.40 W
Micheal Peak ∧	182	53.35 N	126.26 W
Michejevo	88	57.10 N	104.53 E
Michel	182	49.43 N	114.49 W
Michelago	171b	35.43 S	149.10 E
Michelau	56	50.10 N	11.06 E
Micheldever	42	51.09 N	1.15 W
Micheldorf in Oberösterreich	61	47.52 N	14.08 E
Michelsneukirchen	60	49.08 N	12.33 E
Michelson, Mount ∧	180	69.19 N	144.17 W
Michel'sonovskij	265b	55.42 N	37.54 E
Michelstadt	56	49.41 N	9.00 E
Michendorf	54	52.18 N	13.01 E
Miches	238	18.59 N	69.03 W
Micheta	84	41.52 N	44.44 E
Michiana	216	41.46 N	86.48 W
Michiana Regional Airport ⊠	216	41.42 N	86.19 W
Michigamme ≃	190	46.04 N	88.13 W
Michigan	198	48.01 N	98.07 W
Michigan □[3], U.S.	178	44.00 N	85.00 W
Michigan □[3], U.S.	190	44.00 N	85.00 W
Michigan ≃	200	40.52 N	106.20 W
Michigan, Lake ⊜	190	44.00 N	87.00 W
Michigan, University of ʋ[2]	281	42.17 N	83.44 W
Michigan Center	216	42.13 N	84.19 W
Michigan City	216	41.42 N	86.53 W
Michigan International Speedway ♠	216	42.03 N	84.15 W
Michigan Stadium ♠	281	42.16 N	83.45 W
Michigan State Fair Grounds ♠	281	42.27 N	83.07 W
Michigantown	216	40.19 N	86.23 W
Michika	146	10.38 N	13.24 E
Michillinda	280	34.07 N	118.05 W
Michinmahuida, Volcán ∧[1]	254	42.49 S	72.28 W
Michipicoten Bay c	190	47.55 N	84.56 W
Michipicoten Island I	190	47.45 N	85.45 W
Michnevo	82	55.07 N	37.58 E
Michninskaja	24	60.26 N	46.14 E
Michoacán	204	32.28 N	115.20 W
Michoacán □[3]	234	19.10 N	101.50 W
Michoacanejo	234	21.33 N	102.36 W
Michów	30	51.32 N	22.19 E
Michurinsk → Mičurinsk	80	52.54 N	40.30 E
Mickle Fell ∧	44	54.37 N	2.18 W
Mickleham	260	51.16 N	0.19 W
Mickleover	42	52.24 N	1.34 W
Mickleton	285	39.47 N	75.14 W
Mickle Trafford	262	53.13 N	2.50 W
Mickleyville	218	39.45 N	86.16 W
Mico ≃	236	12.11 N	84.16 W
Mico, Montañas del ⨯	236	15.30 N	88.55 W
Miconge	152	4.26 S	12.51 E
Micoud	241f	13.50 N	60.54 W
Micronesia II	14	11.00 N	159.00 E
Micronesia, Federated States of □[1]	14	5.00 N	152.00 E
Mičurin	38	42.10 N	27.51 E
Mičurinsk	80	52.54 N	40.30 E
Midai, Pulau I	112	3.00 N	107.47 E
Midale	184	49.22 N	103.27 W
Midar	148	34.58 N	3.30 W
Mid-Atlantic Ridge ✣[3]	8	0.00	20.00 W
Midbar Yehuda → Wilderness of Judæa ◆[2]	132	31.30 N	35.18 E
Middalya	162	23.55 S	114.45 E
Middelburg, Ned.	52	51.30 N	3.37 E
Middelburg, S. Afr.	158	31.30 S	25.00 E
Middelburg, S. Afr.	158	25.47 S	29.28 E
Middelfart	41	55.30 N	9.45 E
Middelharnis	52	51.45 N	4.11 E
Middelkerke	50	51.11 N	2.49 E
Middelkerke, Vliegveld ⊠	50	51.12 N	2.52 E
Middelpos	158	31.55 S	20.13 E
Middelstum	52	53.20 N	6.38 E
Middelwater	156	23.17 S	30.16 E
Middelwit	156	24.58 S	27.00 E
Middenbeemster	52	52.33 N	4.55 E
Middenin	158	27.43 S	28.02 E
Middenmeer	52	52.47 N	5.00 E
Middle ≃, B.C., Can.	182	54.50 N	125.08 W
Middle ≃, Ca., U.S.	226	38.03 N	121.31 W
Middle ≃, Ia., U.S.	194	41.29 N	93.24 W
Middle ≃, Mn., U.S.	198	48.22 N	97.04 W
Middle ≃, Mo., U.S.	219	38.39 N	91.53 W
Middle Alkali Lake ⊜	204	41.28 N	120.04 W
Middle America Trench ✣[1]	16	15.00 N	95.00 W
Middle Andaman I	110	12.30 N	92.50 E
Middle Barton	42	51.56 N	1.22 W
Middle Bass	214	41.41 N	82.50 W
Middle Bass Island I	214	41.41 N	82.49 W
Middle-Bay	186	51.28 N	57.30 W
Middle Bay c	276	40.37 N	73.36 W
Middleboro	207	41.53 N	70.54 W
Middle Bosque ≃	222	31.31 N	97.16 W
Middlebourne	188	39.29 N	80.54 W
Middlebranch	214	40.54 N	81.20 W
Middle Breakwater ◆[5]	280	33.43 N	118.13 W
Middlebro	184	49.01 N	95.21 W
Middle Brook	186	48.45 N	54.13 W
Middle Brook ≃, N.J., U.S.	276	40.39 N	74.41 W
Middle Brook ≃, N.J., U.S.	276	40.33 N	74.33 W
Middle Brook, East Branch ≃	276	40.35 N	74.33 W
Middle Brook, West Branch ≃	276	40.35 N	74.33 W
Middleburg, Md., U.S.	208	39.35 N	77.12 W
Middleburg, N.Y., U.S.	210	42.36 N	74.20 W
Middleburg, Oh., U.S.	216	40.17 N	83.34 W
Middleburg, Pa., U.S.	208	40.47 N	77.02 W
Middleburg Heights	214	41.22 N	81.48 W
Middlebury, Ct., U.S.	207	41.31 N	73.07 W
Middlebury, In., U.S.	216	41.40 N	85.42 W
Middlebury, Vt., U.S.	188	44.00 N	73.10 W
Middlebush	276	40.29 N	74.32 W
Middle Caicos I	238	21.47 N	71.43 W
Middle Cape ›	220	25.09 N	81.09 W
Middle Castor ≃	212	45.16 N	75.24 W
Middle Channel ≃[1], N.T., Can.	180	69.21 N	135.33 W
Middle Channel ≃[1], Mi., U.S.	281	42.33 N	82.42 W
Middle Concho ≃	196	31.27 N	100.25 W
Middle Creek ≃, U.S.	208	39.41 N	76.18 W
Middle Creek ≃, Pa., U.S.	210	40.46 N	76.52 W
Middle Creek ≃, Pa., U.S.	210	41.28 N	75.11 W
Middle Fabius ≃	194	39.58 N	91.35 W
Middle Falls	210	43.07 N	73.32 W
Middlefield, Ct., U.S.	207	41.31 N	72.42 W
Middlefield, N.Y., U.S.	210	42.41 N	74.50 W
Middlefield, Oh., U.S.	214	41.27 N	81.04 W
Middle Fork Reservoir ⊜[1]	218	39.51 N	84.51 W
Middle Ground I	272c	18.55 N	72.51 E
Middle Ground ✣[2]	174g	28.15 N	177.25 W
Middle Grove, Mo., U.S.	219	39.24 N	92.16 W
Middle Grove, N.Y., U.S.	210	43.05 N	73.55 W
Middle Haddam	207	41.33 N	72.33 W
Middleham	44	54.17 N	1.49 W
Middle Harbour c	274a	33.48 S	151.14 E
Middle Head ›	274a	33.50 S	151.16 E
Middle Hope	210	41.34 N	74.01 W
Middle Island	210	40.53 N	72.56 W
Middle Island I	162	34.07 S	123.12 E
Middle Level Main Drain ≅	42	52.43 N	0.22 E
Middle Loup ≃	198	41.17 N	98.23 W
Middle Maitland ≃	212	43.53 N	81.19 W
Middlemarch	172	45.31 S	170.07 E
Middlemount	166	22.49 S	148.40 E
Middle Musquodoboit	186	45.03 N	63.09 W
Middle Nodaway ≃	194	40.54 N	95.00 W
Middle Pease ≃	196	34.15 N	100.07 W
Middle Point	216	40.51 N	84.27 W
Middleport, N.Y., U.S.	210	43.12 N	78.28 W
Middleport, Oh., U.S.	188	39.00 N	82.02 W
Middleport, Pa., U.S.	208	40.44 N	76.05 W
Middle Raccoon ≃	198	41.34 N	94.12 W
Middle Reservoir ⊜[1]	283	42.27 N	71.07 W
Middle River	208	39.20 N	76.26 W
Middle River c	208	39.19 N	76.25 W
Middle River Neck ›[1]	284b	39.22 N	76.23 W
Middle River Rouge ≃	281	42.20 N	83.15 W
Middle Rouge Parkway ♠	281	42.21 N	83.21 W
Middle Run ≃	285	39.41 N	75.43 W
Middlesboro	192	36.36 N	83.43 W
Middlesbrough	44	54.35 N	1.14 W
Middlesex, Belize	232	17.02 N	88.31 W
Middlesex, N.J., U.S.	276	40.34 N	74.29 W
Middlesex, N.Y., U.S.	210	42.42 N	77.16 W
Middlesex, N.C., U.S.	192	35.47 N	78.12 W
Middlesex □[6], On., Can.	212	43.00 N	81.08 W
Middlesex □[6], Ct., U.S.	207	41.33 N	72.39 W
Middlesex □[6], Ma., U.S.	207	42.30 N	71.25 W
Middlesex □[6], N.J., U.S.	208	40.29 N	74.27 W
Middlesex □[6], Va., U.S.	208	37.40 N	76.35 W
Middlesex Fells Reservation ♠	283	42.27 N	71.07 W
Middlesex Reservoir ⊜[1]	276	40.37 N	74.19 W
Middle Stewiacke	186	45.13 N	63.08 W
Middle Swan	168a	31.52 S	116.00 E
Middle Thames ≃	212	42.59 N	80.58 W
Middleton, Austl.	166	22.22 S	141.32 E
Middleton, N.S., Can.	186	44.57 N	65.04 W
Middleton, Eng., U.K.	42	52.43 N	0.28 E
Middleton, Eng., U.K.	44	53.33 N	2.13 W
Middleton, Ma., U.S.	207	42.35 N	71.01 W
Middleton, Mi., U.S.	190	43.11 N	84.42 W
Middleton, Tn., U.S.	194	35.03 N	88.53 W
Middleton, Wi., U.S.	216	43.05 N	89.30 W
Middleton-in-Teesdale	44	54.38 N	2.04 W
Middleton Island I	180	59.25 N	146.25 W
Middleton-on-the-Wolds	44	53.56 N	0.33 W
Middleton Pond ⊜	283	42.36 N	71.02 W
Middleton Reef I[1]	160	29.28 S	159.06 E
Middleton Saint George	44	54.30 N	1.28 W
Middletown, N. Ire., U.K.	48	54.18 N	6.50 W
Middletown, Ca., U.S.	226	38.45 N	122.36 W
Middletown, Ct., U.S.	207	41.33 N	72.39 W
Middletown, De., U.S.	208	39.26 N	75.43 W
Middletown, Il., U.S.	219	40.11 N	89.35 W
Middletown, In., U.S.	218	40.03 N	85.32 W
Middletown, Ky., U.S.	218	38.14 N	85.32 W
Middletown, Md., U.S.	208	39.26 N	77.32 W
Middletown, Mo., U.S.	219	39.07 N	91.24 W
Middletown, N.J., U.S.	208	40.23 N	74.07 W
Middletown, N.Y., U.S.	210	41.26 N	74.25 W
Middletown, Oh., U.S.	218	39.30 N	84.23 W
Middletown, Pa., U.S.	208	40.11 N	76.43 W
Middletown, R.I., U.S.	207	41.32 N	71.17 W
Middletown, Va., U.S.	188	39.01 N	78.16 W
Middletown Park	218	40.09 N	85.26 W
Middle Tuolumne ≃	226	37.50 N	120.01 W
Middleville, Mi., U.S.	216	42.42 N	85.27 W
Middleville, N.Y., U.S.	210	43.08 N	74.58 W
Middleville, N.Y., U.S.	276	43.08 N	74.58 W
Middlewich	44	53.11 N	2.27 W
Middle Yegua Creek ≃	222	30.19 N	96.47 W
Middle Yuba ≃	226	39.22 N	121.12 W
Midelt	148	32.41 N	4.43 W
Midfield	222	28.56 N	96.13 W
Midge Hall	262	53.42 N	2.45 W
Midgic	186	45.59 N	64.18 W
Mid Glamorgan □[6]	42	51.40 N	3.30 W
Midgley	262	53.44 N	1.58 W
Midhurst, On., Can.	212	44.27 N	79.44 W
Midhurst, Eng., U.K.	42	50.59 N	0.45 W
Midi, Aiguille du ∧	62	45.52 N	6.53 E
Midi, Canal du ≅	32	43.26 N	1.58 E
Midi de Bigorre, Pic du ∧	32	42.56 N	0.08 E
Mid Illovo	158	29.59 S	30.25 E
Mid-Indian Basin ✣[1]	12	10.00 S	80.00 E
Mid-Indian Ridge ✣[3]	6	30.00 S	75.00 E
Midland, Austl.	168a	31.53 S	116.00 E
Midland, On., Can.	212	44.45 N	79.53 W
Midland, Ca., U.S.	204	33.52 N	114.48 W
Midland, Mi., U.S.	190	43.36 N	84.14 W
Midland, N.C., U.S.	192	35.13 N	80.30 W
Midland, Oh., U.S.	218	39.18 N	83.54 W
Midland, Pa., U.S.	214	40.37 N	80.26 W
Midland, Pa., U.S.	214	40.37 N	80.26 W
Midland, S.D., U.S.	198	44.04 N	101.09 W
Midland, Tx., U.S.	196	31.59 N	102.04 W
Midland, Wa., U.S.	224	47.10 N	122.24 W
Midland Bay c	212	44.47 N	79.52 W
Midland Beach ◆[8]	276	40.34 N	74.05 W
Midland City	219	40.09 N	89.08 W
Midland Park, Mi., U.S.	216	42.23 N	85.22 W
Midland Park, N.J., U.S.	276	40.59 N	74.08 W
Midland Park Lake ⊜	212	44.44 N	79.53 W
Midlands □[4]	154	19.00 S	29.45 E
Midleton	48	51.55 N	8.10 W
Midlothian, Il., U.S.	216	41.37 N	87.43 W
Midlothian, Tx., U.S.	222	32.28 N	96.59 W
Midlothian Creek ≃	278	41.39 N	87.40 W
Midlum	52	53.43 N	8.37 E
Midnapore	182	50.55 N	114.05 W
Midnapore Canal ≅	126	22.25 N	87.53 E
Midnapore Plain ≚	126	22.00 N	87.45 E
Mid-Ohio Sports Car Course ♠	214	40.40 N	82.38 W
Midongy Nord	157b	20.45 S	46.13 E
Midongy Sud	157b	23.35 S	47.01 E
Midori	96	34.43 N	132.37 E
Midori ◆[8]	268	35.32 N	139.34 E
Midori ≃	92	32.42 N	130.37 E
Midou ≃	32	43.54 N	0.30 W
Mid-Pacific Mountains ✣[3]	14	20.00 N	170.00 E
Midpines	226	37.32 N	119.55 W
Midreshet Ben Gurion	132	30.21 N	34.46 E
Midsayap	116	7.12 N	124.32 E
Midshipman Point ›	282	38.07 N	122.27 W
Midsland	52	53.22 N	5.16 E
Midsomer Norton	42	51.18 N	2.28 W
Midu	102	25.22 N	100.31 E
Midvale, De., U.S.	285	39.39 N	75.37 W
Midvale, Id., U.S.	202	44.28 N	116.44 W
Midvale, Oh., U.S.	214	40.26 N	81.22 W
Midville	192	32.49 N	82.14 W
Midway, B.C., Can.	182	49.01 N	118.47 W
Midway, B.C., Can.	202	49.01 N	118.46 W
Midway, Al., U.S.	194	32.04 N	85.31 W
Midway, In., U.S.	216	41.37 N	85.55 W
Midway, Ky., U.S.	218	38.09 N	84.41 W
Midway, Pa., U.S.	279b	40.22 N	80.17 W
Midway, Tx., U.S.	222	31.02 N	95.45 W
Midway, Ut,. U.S.	200	40.30 N	111.28 W
Midway City	280	33.45 N	118.00 W
Midway Islands □[2], Oc.	6	28.13 N	177.22 W
Midway Islands □[2], Oc.	174g	28.13 N	177.22 W
Midway Mall ◆[9]	279a	41.24 N	82.07 W
Midway Naval Station ■	174g	28.13 N	177.26 W
Midway Park	192	34.43 N	77.21 W
Midwest	200	43.24 N	106.16 W
Midwest City	196	35.26 N	97.23 W
Midwolda	52	53.12 N	7.00 E
Midyan ◆[1]	128	27.40 N	35.35 E
Midyat	130	37.25 N	41.23 E
Midyobe	152	1.21 N	10.18 E
Midžor (Midžur) ∧	38	43.23 N	22.42 E
Mie	96	32.58 N	131.35 E
Mie □[5]	92	34.30 N	136.30 E
Miechów	30	50.23 N	20.01 E
Miedwie, Jezioro ⊜	54	53.17 N	14.52 E
Międzybórz	30	51.24 N	17.40 E
Międzychód	30	52.36 N	15.55 E
Międzylesie	30	50.10 N	16.40 E
Międzyrzec Podlaski	30	52.00 N	22.47 E
Międzyrzecz	30	52.28 N	15.35 E
Międzyzdroje	30	53.55 N	14.28 E
Miehuapu	105	39.11 N	117.44 E
Miejska Górka	30	51.40 N	16.58 E
Miélan	32	43.26 N	0.19 E
Mielec	30	50.18 N	21.25 E
Mielno	30	54.16 N	16.01 E
Mien ⊜	26	56.25 N	14.51 E
Mienga	152	17.17 S	19.48 E
Mienhua Yü I	100	25.29 N	122.06 E
Mient'ienhuo Shan ∧	269d	25.11 N	121.30 E
Mier	232	26.26 N	99.09 W
Miercurea-Ciuc	38	46.22 N	25.48 E
Mieres	34	43.15 N	5.46 W
Mierlo	52	51.27 N	5.37 E
Mieroszów	30	50.41 N	16.10 E
Miersdorf	264a	52.20 N	13.37 E
Miersig	38	46.53 N	21.51 E
Mier y Noriega	234	23.25 N	100.07 W
Miesaituo	120	35.52 N	93.40 E
Miesbach	64	47.47 N	11.50 E
Miesenbach	61	47.22 N	15.46 E
Mieso	144	9.15 N	40.48 E
Mieste	54	52.28 N	11.11 E
Miesterhorst	54	52.27 N	11.09 E
Mieszkowice	30	52.46 N	14.30 E
Mifflin, Oh., U.S.	214	40.47 N	82.22 W
Mifflin, Pa., U.S.	208	40.34 N	77.24 W
Mifflin □[6]	210	40.40 N	77.33 W
Mifflinburg	210	40.55 N	77.02 W
Mifflintown	208	40.34 N	77.23 W
Mifflinville	210	41.01 N	76.18 W
Miftāḥ, Wādī V	142	30.15 N	31.46 E
Migdal	132	32.50 N	35.30 E
Migdal Ha'Emeq	132	32.41 N	35.15 E
Migdol	158	26.54 S	25.27 E
Migennes	50	47.58 N	3.31 E
Migliarino	66	44.46 N	11.56 E
Migliaro	64	44.48 N	11.58 E
Miglionico	68	40.34 N	16.30 E
Mignano Monte Lungo	68	41.23 N	13.58 E
Mignone ≃	66	42.11 N	11.44 E
Mignovillard	58	46.48 N	6.08 E
Migori ≃	154	0.59 S	34.15 E
Miguel Alemán, Presa ⊜[1]	234	18.13 N	96.32 W
Miguel Alves	250	4.10 S	42.54 W
Miguel Auza	232	24.18 N	103.25 W
Miguel Calmon	250	11.26 S	40.36 W
Miguel Couto	287a	22.43 S	43.27 W
Miguel de la Borda	236	9.09 N	80.19 W
Migueles, Arroyo de los ≃	266a	40.20 N	3.32 W
Miguelete	258	34.01 S	57.39 W
Miguelete, Arroyo ≃	258	34.14 S	57.54 W
Miguel Hidalgo, Presa ⊜[1]	232	26.30 N	108.35 W
Miguelópolis	255	20.12 S	48.03 W
Miguel Pereira	256	22.27 S	43.22 W
Miguel Riglos	252	36.51 S	63.42 W
Migulinskaja	80	49.42 N	41.16 E
Migvie	46	57.08 N	2.56 W
Migyaunglaung	110	14.40 N	98.09 E
Mihăeşti	38	45.07 N	25.00 E
Mihai Viteazu	38	44.39 N	28.41 E
Mihajlovgrad	38	43.25 N	23.13 E
Mihalgazi	130	40.02 N	30.34 E
Mihalıççık	130	39.52 N	31.30 E
Mihama, Nihon	94	34.46 N	136.54 E
Mihama, Nihon	94	35.36 N	135.56 E
Mihama, Nihon	96	33.54 N	135.08 E
Mihara, Nihon	96	34.24 N	133.05 E
Mihara, Nihon	96	34.17 N	134.46 E
Mihara, Nihon	96	34.32 N	135.34 E
Mihara-yama ∧	94	34.43 N	139.23 E
Mihla	54	51.04 N	10.20 E
Miho	94	36.00 N	140.18 E
Mihonoseki	96	35.34 N	133.19 E
Miho-wan c	96	35.30 N	133.23 E
Mihuangzhuang	105	39.07 N	116.12 E
Mijaly	86	48.57 N	53.42 E
Mijares ≃	34	39.55 N	0.01 W
Mijdaḥah	144	14.00 N	48.26 E
Mijdrecht	52	52.13 N	4.52 E
Mijiang	98	43.01 N	130.08 E
Mijoux	58	46.22 N	6.00 E
Mikabo-yama ∧	94	36.09 N	138.55 E
Mikame	96	33.25 N	132.27 E
Mikamo, Nihon	96	35.09 N	133.37 E
Mikamo, Nihon	96	34.05 N	133.57 E
Mikasa	92a	43.14 N	141.53 E
Mikaševiči	78	52.13 N	27.28 E
Mikata	94	35.33 N	135.55 E
Mikata-ko ⊜	94	35.34 N	135.53 E
Mikatou	273b	4.16 S	15.08 E
Mikawa, Nihon	94	36.29 N	136.29 E
Mikawa, Nihon	96	33.37 N	132.58 E
Mikawa-wan c	94	34.43 N	137.10 E
Mikawa-wan-kokutei-kōen ♠	94	34.42 N	137.10 E
Mikazuki	96	34.58 N	134.27 E
Mikese	154	6.46 S	37.54 E
Mikhaylov, Cape ›	9	66.51 S	118.33 E
Mikhrot Shelomo Hamelekh (Timna') (King Solomon's Mines) ⊥	132	29.45 N	34.56 E
Miki, Nihon	96	34.48 N	134.59 E
Miki, Nihon	96	34.17 N	134.05 E
Mikínai ⊥	38	37.44 N	22.45 E
Mikindani	154	10.17 S	40.07 E
Mikinduri	154	0.07 N	37.50 E
Mikkabi	94	34.48 N	137.33 E
Mikkaichi	270	34.26 N	135.35 E
Mikkeli	26	61.41 N	27.15 E
Mikkelin lääni □[4]	26	62.00 N	27.30 E
Mikkwa ≃	176	58.25 N	114.45 W
Mikołajki	30	53.49 N	21.36 E
Mikolów	30	50.11 N	18.55 E
Mikomeseng	152	2.08 N	10.37 E
Mikomoto-jima I	94	34.34 N	138.56 E
Míkonos	38	37.26 N	25.20 E
Míkonos I	38	37.29 N	25.25 E
Mikope	152	5.03 S	20.48 E
Mikre	38	43.02 N	24.31 E
Mikrí Préspa, Límni ⊜	38	40.46 N	21.04 E
Miksimil	126	22.52 N	89.23 E
Mikšino	76	57.15 N	35.43 E
Mikstat	30	51.32 N	17.59 E
Mikulášovice	54	50.58 N	14.20 E
Mikulincy	78	49.24 N	25.38 E
Mikulino	76	55.02 N	31.07 E
Mikulkin, mys ›	24	67.48 N	46.40 E
Mikulov	61	48.49 N	16.39 E
Mikumi	154	7.24 S	36.59 E
Mikumi National Park ♠	154	7.12 S	37.05 E
Mikun'	24	62.21 N	50.06 E
Mikuni	94	36.13 N	136.09 E
Mikuni-sammyaku ⨯	94	36.50 N	138.40 E
Mikuni-tōge)(	94	36.46 N	138.50 E
Mikuni-yama ∧	94	35.59 N	138.43 E
Mikura-jima I	92	33.52 N	139.36 E
Mila	34	36.27 N	6.16 E
Milaca	190	45.45 N	93.39 W
Miladummadulu Atoll I[1]	122	6.15 N	73.15 E
Milagre	256	21.18 S	47.00 W
Milagres	250	7.17 S	38.57 W
Milagro	246	2.07 S	79.36 W
Milagros	116	12.13 N	123.30 E
Milam □[6]	222	30.47 N	96.57 W
Milan, Ga., U.S.	192	32.01 N	83.03 W
Milan, In., U.S.	218	39.07 N	85.07 W
Milan, Mi., U.S.	216	42.05 N	83.40 W
Milan, Mn., U.S.	198	45.06 N	95.54 W
Milan, Mo., U.S.	194	40.12 N	93.07 W
Milan, N.M., U.S.	200	35.10 N	107.53 W
Milan, Oh., U.S.	214	41.17 N	82.36 W
Milan, Pa., U.S.	210	41.54 N	76.32 W
Milan, Tn., U.S.	194	35.55 N	88.45 W
Milando	152	8.45 S	17.36 E
Milan Federal Correctional Institution ʋ	281	42.06 N	83.40 W
Milang	168b	35.25 S	138.58 E
Milan → Milano	62	45.28 N	9.12 E
Milano (Milan), It.	62	45.28 N	9.12 E
Milano (Milan), It.	266b	45.28 N	9.12 E
Milano, Tx., U.S.	222	30.43 N	96.52 W
Milano □[4]	62	45.30 N	9.30 E
Milanoa	157b	13.35 S	49.47 E
Milano Marittima	66	44.16 N	12.21 E
Milanville	210	41.40 N	75.04 W
Milâs	130	37.19 N	27.47 E
Milaševiči	78	51.39 N	27.56 E
Mil'atino, Ross.	76	54.29 N	34.18 E
Mil'atino, Ross.	82	55.41 N	35.48 E
Milazzo	70	38.13 N	15.14 E
Milazzo, Capo di ›	70	38.16 N	15.14 E
Milazzo, Golfo di c	70	38.15 N	15.20 E
Milbank	198	45.13 N	96.38 W
Milbanke Sound ɥ	182	52.18 N	128.33 W
Milborne Port	42	50.58 N	2.27 W
Milbuk	116	6.10 N	124.16 E
Milburn	196	34.14 N	96.32 W
Milburn Creek ≃	276	40.38 N	73.36 W
Milden	184	51.30 N	107.31 W
Mildenau	54	50.35 N	13.04 E
Mildenhall	42	52.21 N	0.30 E
Milders	64	47.06 N	11.16 E
Mildmay	212	44.03 N	81.07 W
Mildred, Il., U.S.	219	39.46 N	89.38 W
Mildred, Pa., U.S.	210	41.28 N	76.22 W
Mildura	166	34.12 S	142.09 E
Mile	102	24.26 N	103.26 E
Miléai	38	39.20 N	23.09 E
Milena	70	37.28 N	13.44 E
Milendella	168b	34.49 S	139.12 E
Milepa	154	11.43 S	36.20 E
Miles, Austl.	166	26.40 S	150.11 E
Miles, Tx., U.S.	196	31.35 N	100.10 W
Miles ≃	283	42.40 N	70.51 W
Milesburg	214	40.56 N	77.47 W
Miles City	202	46.24 N	105.50 W
Miles Creek c	208	38.46 N	76.12 W
Miles Creek ≃	226	37.12 N	120.21 W
Mile Seven Hundred Thirty Three	180	60.03 N	131.07 W
Milešovka ∧	54	50.33 N	13.56 E
Milestone	184	50.00 N	104.30 W
Milesville	279b	40.12 N	79.52 W
Milet (Miletus) ⊥	130	37.28 N	27.15 E
Mileto	68	38.36 N	16.04 E
Miletto, Monte ∧	68	41.27 N	14.22 E
Miletus → Milet ⊥	130	37.28 N	27.15 E
Mileura	162	26.23 S	117.20 E
Milevsko	30	49.27 N	14.22 E
Milford, Eng., U.K.	42	51.11 N	1.38 W
Milford, Ct., U.S.	207	41.13 N	73.04 W
Milford, De., U.S.	208	38.54 N	75.25 W
Milford, Il., U.S.	216	40.37 N	87.41 W
Milford, In., U.S.	216	41.24 N	85.50 W
Milford, Ia., U.S.	198	43.19 N	95.08 W
Milford, Ky., U.S.	218	38.34 N	84.09 W
Milford, Me., U.S.	188	44.56 N	68.38 W
Milford, Md., U.S.	284b	39.21 N	76.44 W
Milford, Ma., U.S.	207	42.08 N	71.31 W
Milford, Mi., U.S.	216	42.35 N	83.35 W
Milford, N.H., U.S.	207	42.50 N	71.38 W
Milford, N.J., U.S.	210	40.34 N	75.05 W
Milford, N.Y., U.S.	210	42.35 N	74.56 W
Milford, Oh., U.S.	218	39.10 N	84.17 W
Milford, Pa., U.S.	210	41.19 N	74.48 W
Milford, Tx., U.S.	222	32.07 N	96.57 W
Milford, Ut,. U.S.	200	38.23 N	113.00 W
Milford, Va., U.S.	208	38.01 N	77.22 W
Milford Brook ≃	276	40.19 N	74.17 W
Milford Center	218	40.10 N	83.26 W
Milford Cross Roads	285	39.43 N	75.44 W
Milford Haven	42	51.40 N	5.02 W
Milford Haven c	42	51.42 N	5.03 W
Milford Lake ⊜[1]	198	39.15 N	97.00 W
Milford on Sea	42	50.44 N	1.36 W
Milford Ridge	284b	39.21 N	76.45 W
Milford Sound	172	44.40 S	167.54 E
Milford Sound ɥ	172	44.35 S	167.47 E
Milford Station	186	45.03 N	63.26 W
Milgis ≃	154	1.48 N	38.06 E
Milgoo ∧	162	28.51 S	118.07 E
Mil'guvejem ≃	180	68.22 N	171.30 E
Milḥ, Baḥr al- ⊜	128	32.40 N	43.35 E
Milḥat Ashqar ⊜	128	35.18 N	41.55 E
Milḥat Ashqar ≡	130	35.18 N	41.55 E
Milhaud	62	43.47 N	4.18 E
Mili I[1]	14	6.08 N	171.55 E
Milian ≃	112	5.13 N	117.25 E
Milibangalala, Ponta ›	158	26.26 S	32.56 E
Milicia ≃	70	38.04 N	13.33 E
Milicz	30	51.32 N	17.17 E
Milieu, Rivière du ≃	206	46.47 N	73.56 W
Milīj	142	30.36 N	31.03 E
Milim	164	5.10 S	152.00 E
Milín	60	49.39 N	14.02 E
Miling	162	30.30 S	116.21 E
Milis	71	40.03 N	8.38 E
Militello in Val di Catania	70	37.16 N	14.48 E
Militello Rosmarino	70	38.03 N	14.41 E
Milk ≃	202	48.05 N	106.15 W

Symbol	English	Deutsch	Español	Français	Português
≃	River	Fluß	Río	Rivière	Rio
≅	Canal	Kanal	Canal	Canal	Canal
∟	Waterfall, Rapids	Wasserfall, Stromschnellen	Cascada, Rápidos	Chute d'eau, Rapides	Cascata, Rápidos
ɥ	Strait	Meeresstraße	Estrecho	Détroit	Estreito
c	Bay, Gulf	Bucht, Golf	Bahía, Golfo	Baie, Golfe	Baía, Golfo
⊜	Lake, Lakes	See, Seen	Lago, Lagos	Lac, Lacs	Lago, Lagos
≡	Swamp	Sumpf	Pantano	Marais	Pântano
⊓	Ice Features, Glacier	Eis- und Gletscherformen	Accidentes Glaciales	Formes glaciaires	Acidentes glaciares
⫪	Other Hydrographic Features	Andere Hydrographische Objekte	Otros Elementos Hidrográficos	Autres données hydrographiques	Outros acidentes hidrográficos
✣	Submarine Features	Untermeerische Objekte	Accidentes Submarinos	Formes de relief sous-marin	Acidentes submarinos
□	Political Unit	Politische Einheit	Unidad Politica	Entité politique	Unidade política
ʋ	Cultural Institution	Kulturelle Institution	Institución Cultural	Institution culturelle	Instituição cultural
⊥	Historical Site	Historische Stätte	Sitio Histórico	Site historique	Sitio histórico
♠	Recreational Site	Erholungs- und Ferienort	Sitio de Recreo	Centre de loisirs	Area de Lazer
⊠	Airport	Flughafen	Aeropuerto	Aéroport	Aeroporto
■	Military Installation	Militäranlage	Instalación Militar	Installation militaire	Instalação militar
◆	Miscellaneous	Verschiedenes	Misceláneo	Divers	Diversos

Name	Page	Lat. °′	Long. °′
Milk Creek ≃, Co., U.S.	200	40.24 N	107.45 W
Milk Creek ≃, Or., U.S.	224	45.15 N	122.41 W
Milk Hill ∧ 2	42	51.23 N	1.51 W
Mil'kovo	74	54.43 N	158.37 E
Milk River	182	49.09 N	112.05 W
Milk River Ridge Reservoir ⊜ 1	182	49.22 N	112.35 W
Mill	52	51.41 N	5.47 E
Mill ≃, Ct., U.S.	276	41.08 N	73.16 W
Mill ≃, Ma., U.S.	207	42.18 N	72.37 W
Mill ≃, Ma., U.S.	283	42.38 N	70.41 W
Mill ≃, Ma., U.S.	283	42.12 N	70.57 W
Mill ≃, Ma., U.S.	283	42.08 N	71.21 W
Mill ≃, Ma., U.S.	283	42.44 N	70.52 W
Mill ≃, N.Y., U.S.	276	40.38 N	73.39 W
Millard	198	41.13 N	96.07 W
Millau	32	44.06 N	3.05 E
Mill Bay	224	48.39 N	123.34 W
Millboro	192	37.59 N	79.36 W
Millbourne	285	39.58 N	75.15 W
Millbrae	226	37.35 N	122.23 W
Millbrook, On., Can.	212	44.09 N	78.27 W
Millbrook, Eng., U.K.	42	50.20 N	4.13 W
Millbrook, Ma., U.S.	283	42.03 N	70.41 W
Millbrook, N.J., U.S.	276	40.52 N	74.33 W
Millbrook, N.Y., U.S.	210	41.47 N	73.41 W
Mill Brook ≃, Ma., U.S.	283	42.31 N	71.18 W
Mill Brook ≃, N.J., U.S.	276	40.53 N	74.32 W
Mill Brook ≃, N.J., U.S.	276	40.25 N	74.06 W
Mill Brook ≃, N.J., U.S.	276	40.29 N	74.23 W
Millburn	276	40.44 N	74.18 W
Millbury, Ma., U.S.	207	42.11 N	71.45 W
Millbury, Oh., U.S.	214	41.33 N	83.25 W
Mill City	202	44.45 N	122.29 W
Mill Creek, Pa., U.S.	214	40.26 N	77.56 W
Millcreek, Ut,. U.S.	200	40.27 N	111.54 W
Mill Creek, W.V., U.S.	188	38.43 N	79.58 W
Mill Creek ≃, Austl.	274a	33.59 S	151.01 E
Mill Creek ≃, Ca., U.S.	226	36.49 N	119.21 W
Mill Creek ≃, Ca., U.S.	228	34.05 N	117.06 W
Mill Creek ≃, De., U.S.	285	39.42 N	75.39 W
Mill Creek ≃, Il., U.S.	219	39.50 N	91.24 W
Mill Creek ≃, In., U.S.	194	39.30 N	86.57 W
Mill Creek ≃, In., U.S.	216	41.01 N	86.36 W
Mill Creek ≃, Ia., U.S.	198	42.47 N	95.31 W
Mill Creek ≃, Ks., U.S.	198	39.55 N	96.56 W
Mill Creek ≃, Ky., U.S.	218	38.28 N	84.20 W
Mill Creek ≃, N.J., U.S.	276	40.48 N	74.03 W
Mill Creek ≃, N.J., U.S.	285	40.02 N	74.55 W
Mill Creek ≃, N.Y., U.S.	212	43.57 N	76.08 W
Mill Creek ≃, Oh., U.S.	214	41.06 N	80.40 W
Mill Creek ≃, Oh., U.S.	214	40.14 N	83.09 W
Mill Creek ≃, Oh., U.S.	218	39.06 N	84.32 W
Mill Creek ≃, Oh., U.S.	279a	41.25 N	81.38 W
Mill Creek ≃, Or., U.S.	224	45.36 N	121.11 W
Mill Creek ≃, Pa., U.S.	208	40.00 N	76.18 W
Mill Creek ≃, Pa., U.S.	210	41.53 N	77.08 W
Mill Creek ≃, Pa., U.S.	214	41.09 N	79.03 W
Mill Creek ≃, Pa., U.S.	285	40.03 N	75.16 W
Mill Creek ≃, Pa., U.S.	285	40.08 N	74.52 W
Mill Creek ≃, Tx., U.S.	222	32.46 N	95.46 W
Mill Creek ≃, Tx., U.S.	222	29.50 N	96.07 W
Mill Creek ≃, Tx., U.S.	222	30.08 N	95.37 W
Mill Creek ≃, Va., U.S.	208	38.09 N	77.10 W
Mill Creek, North Fork ≃	224	45.33 N	121.18 W
Mill Creek, South Fork ≃	224	45.36 N	121.12 W
Millcreek Township	214	42.05 N	80.10 W
Milldale	207	41.33 N	72.53 W
Milledgeville, Ga., U.S.	192	33.04 N	83.13 W
Milledgeville, Il., U.S.	190	41.57 N	89.46 W
Milledgeville, Oh., U.S.	218	39.36 N	83.35 W
Mille Îles, Rivière des ≃	206	45.42 N	73.32 W
Mille Lacs, Lac des ⊜	190	48.50 N	90.30 W
Mille Lacs Kathio State Park ♦	190	46.08 N	93.43 W
Mille Lacs Lake ⊜	190	46.15 N	93.40 W
Millemont	261	48.49 N	1.45 E
Millen	192	32.48 N	81.56 W
Millendon	168a	31.48 S	116.02 E
Miller, Mo., U.S.	194	37.13 N	93.50 W
Miller, S.D., U.S.	198	44.31 N	98.59 W
Miller □ 6	219	38.15 N	92.15 W
Miller, Mount ∧	180	60.25 N	142.23 W
Miller City	216	41.06 N	84.08 W
Miller Creek ≃	282	38.02 N	122.30 W
Miller House	180	65.32 N	145.11 W
Miller Mountain ∧	204	38.03 N	118.12 W
Millerovo, Ross.	78	48.55 N	40.25 E
Millerovo, Ross.	83	47.49 N	39.15 E
Miller Peak ∧	200	31.23 N	110.17 W
Miller Place	210	40.58 N	73.00 W
Millers ≃	207	42.35 N	72.30 W
Millersburg, In., U.S.	216	41.31 N	85.41 W
Millersburg, In., U.S.	218	41.31 N	85.41 W
Millersburg, Ky., U.S.	218	38.18 N	84.08 W
Millersburg, Mi., U.S.	190	45.20 N	84.03 W
Millersburg, Oh., U.S.	214	40.33 N	81.55 W
Millersburg, Pa., U.S.	208	40.32 N	76.57 W
Millers Creek ≃	196	33.27 N	99.14 W
Miller Seamount ✣ 3	16	53.30 N	144.20 W
Millers Falls	207	42.34 N	72.29 W
Millers Ferry	194	32.05 N	87.22 W
Millers Flat	172	45.40 S	169.25 E
Millers Island	284b	39.14 N	76.24 W
Millers Pond ⊜	276	40.51 N	73.12 W
Millersport	188	39.54 N	82.32 W
Millers Run ≃	279b	40.22 N	80.07 W
Millerstown	210	40.32 N	77.09 W
Millersville, Il., U.S.	219	39.25 N	89.07 W
Millersville, Oh., U.S.	214	41.18 N	83.16 W
Millersville, Pa., U.S.	208	39.59 N	76.21 W
Millerton, N.Y., U.S.	210	41.57 N	73.30 W
Millerton, Pa., U.S.	210	41.59 N	76.56 W
Millerton Lake ⊜ 1	226	37.01 N	119.41 W
Millerton Lake State Recreation Area ♦	226	37.02 N	119.37 W
Millertown	186	48.49 N	56.33 W
Millertown Junction	186	49.01 N	56.21 W
Millesimo	62	44.22 N	8.12 E
Millet	182	53.06 N	113.28 W
Millett, Mi., U.S.	216	42.42 N	84.38 W
Millett, Tx., U.S.	196	28.35 N	99.12 W
Milleur Point >	44	55.01 N	5.06 W
Millevaches, Plateau de ⋏ 1	32	45.30 N	2.10 E
Millford	48	55.07 N	7.43 W
Mill Green	260	51.41 N	0.22 E
Mill Grove	216	40.25 N	85.17 W
Mill Hall	210	41.06 N	77.29 W
Millheim	210	40.53 N	77.28 W
Mill Hill ◆ 8	260	51.37 N	0.13 W
Mill Hill ∧ 2	262	53.25 N	1.54 W
Millhousen	218	39.13 N	85.26 W
Millican	222	30.28 N	96.12 W
Millicent	166	37.36 S	140.22 E
Milligan, Fl., U.S.	194	30.45 N	86.38 W
Milligan, Ne., U.S.	198	40.30 N	97.23 W
Milligan Gulch ∨	200	33.37 N	107.02 W
Milligantown	279b	40.33 N	79.41 W
Milliken	275b	43.49 N	79.18 W
Millingen aan de Rijn	52	51.52 N	6.02 E
Millington, Il., U.S.	216	41.34 N	88.36 W
Millington, Md., U.S.	208	39.15 N	75.50 W
Millington, Mi., U.S.	190	43.16 N	83.31 W
Millington, N.J., U.S.	210	40.40 N	74.31 W
Millington, Tn., U.S.	194	35.20 N	89.53 W
Millinocket	188	45.39 N	68.42 W
Millionnyj	89	54.30 N	126.19 E
Millis	207	42.10 N	71.21 W
Mill Island I, Ant.	9	65.30 S	100.40 E
Mill Island I, N.T., Can.	176	64.00 N	78.00 W
Millisle	48	54.36 N	5.32 W
Mill Lake ⊜	212	45.22 N	80.00 W
Millmerran	166	27.52 S	151.16 E
Millmont	210	40.53 N	77.08 W
Mill Neck	276	40.52 N	73.34 W
Mill Neck > 1	276	40.53 N	73.33 W
Mill Neck Creek C	276	40.54 N	73.33 W
Millom	44	54.13 N	3.18 W
Mill Pond ⊜	276	40.53 N	73.22 W
Millport, Scot., U.K.	46	55.46 N	4.55 W
Millport, Al., U.S.	194	33.33 N	88.04 W
Millport, N.Y., U.S.	210	42.16 N	76.50 W
Millport, Pa., U.S.	214	41.55 N	78.07 W
Millrift	210	41.25 N	74.45 W
Mill River	207	42.06 N	73.16 W
Mill Run Acres	284c	38.58 N	77.17 W
Millry	194	31.38 N	88.18 W
Mills, Pa., U.S.	214	41.57 N	77.41 W
Mills, Wy., U.S.	202	42.50 N	106.21 W
Mills, Lake ⊜ 1	224	47.59 N	123.36 W
Millsboro	208	38.35 N	75.17 W
Mills Creek ≃, Austl.	166	22.23 S	143.05 E
Mills Creek ≃, Ca., U.S.	282	37.27 N	122.25 W
Mills Lake ⊜	176	61.30 N	118.10 W
Mills Mansion State Historic Site ⊥	210	41.52 N	73.57 W
Millstadt	219	38.27 N	90.05 W
Millstatt	64	46.48 N	13.35 E
Millstätter See ⊜	64	46.47 N	13.35 E
Millstone	276	40.29 N	74.35 W
Millstone ≃	276	40.33 N	74.34 W
Millstream, Austl.	162	21.35 S	117.04 E
Millstream, B.C., Can.	224	48.30 N	123.31 W
Millstream Chichester National Park ♦	162	21.25 S	117.20 E
Millstreet	48	52.03 N	9.04 W
Milltown, Scot., U.K.	46	57.14 N	2.52 W
Milltown, In., U.S.	218	38.20 N	86.16 W
Milltown, Mt., U.S.	202	46.52 N	113.52 W
Milltown, N.J., U.S.	208	40.27 N	74.26 W
Milltown, Wi., U.S.	190	45.31 N	92.30 W
Milltown Malbay	48	52.50 N	9.23 W
Millvale	279b	40.28 N	79.58 W
Mill Valley	226	37.54 N	122.32 W
Mill Village	214	41.53 N	79.58 W
Millville, Ma., U.S.	207	42.01 N	71.34 W
Millville, N.J., U.S.	208	39.24 N	75.02 W
Millville, Oh., U.S.	218	39.24 N	84.40 W
Millville, Pa., U.S.	210	41.07 N	76.31 W
Millville Lake	283	42.48 N	71.13 W
Millville Lake ⊜	283	42.48 N	71.13 W
Millwood, Md., U.S.	284c	38.53 N	76.53 W
Millwood, N.Y., U.S.	210	41.11 N	73.48 W
Millwood, Va., U.S.	188	39.04 N	78.02 W
Millwood Lake ⊜ 1	194	33.45 N	94.00 W
Milly-la-Forêt	50	48.24 N	2.28 E
Milly-Lamartine	58	46.21 N	4.42 E
Milmay	208	39.26 N	74.51 W
Milmersdorf	54	53.06 N	13.38 E
Milmine	219	39.54 N	88.39 W
Milmont Park	285	39.53 N	75.20 W
Milne Bay □ 5	164	10.00 S	152.30 E
Milne Bay C	164	10.22 S	150.30 E
Milner	224	49.20 N	122.42 W
Milnesville	210	40.59 N	75.59 W
Milngavie	46	55.57 N	4.20 W
Milnor	198	46.15 N	97.27 W
Milnrow	44	53.37 N	2.06 W
Milnthorpe	44	54.14 N	2.46 W
Milo, Ab., Can.	182	50.34 N	112.53 W
Milo, Ia., U.S.	190	41.17 N	93.26 W
Milo, Me., U.S.	188	45.15 N	68.59 W
Milo ≃	150	11.04 N	9.14 W
Milon-la-Chapelle	261	48.44 N	2.03 E
Mílos	38	36.45 N	24.27 E
Mílos I	38	36.41 N	24.15 E
Miloslaviči	76	53.41 N	32.15 E
Miloslavskoje	76	53.34 N	39.24 E
Miłosław	30	52.13 N	17.29 E
Milow, Dtsch.	54	53.11 N	11.32 E
Milow, Dtsch.	54	52.31 N	12.18 E
Milpa Alta ◆ 8	286a	19.11 N	99.01 W
Milparinka	166	29.44 S	141.53 E
Milpitas	226	37.25 N	121.54 W
Milpitas Wash ∨	204	33.18 N	114.44 W
Milroy, In., U.S.	218	39.29 N	85.28 W
Milroy, Pa., U.S.	208	40.42 N	77.35 W
Milseburg ∧	56	50.32 N	9.53 E
Mil'skaja ravnina ≚	84	40.00 N	48.00 E
Milspe	263	51.18 N	7.21 E
Miltach	60	49.09 N	12.46 E
Miltenberg	56	49.42 N	9.15 E
Miltitz	54	51.19 N	12.16 E
Milton, Austl.	170	35.19 S	150.26 E
Milton, On., Can.	212	43.31 N	79.53 W
Milton, N.Z.	172	46.07 S	169.58 E
Milton, Eng., U.K.	42	52.14 N	0.09 W
Milton, De., U.S.	208	38.46 N	75.18 W
Milton, Fl., U.S.	194	30.37 N	87.02 W
Milton, Il., U.S.	219	39.34 N	90.39 W
Milton, In., U.S.	218	39.47 N	85.09 W
Milton, In., U.S.	218	38.58 N	85.01 W
Milton, Ia., U.S.	190	40.40 N	92.09 W
Milton, Ky., U.S.	218	38.43 N	85.22 W
Milton, Ma., U.S.	207	42.15 N	71.05 W
Milton, N.J., U.S.	276	41.02 N	74.32 W
Milton, N.Y., U.S.	210	41.39 N	73.57 W
Milton, N.D., U.S.	198	48.37 N	98.02 W
Milton, Pa., U.S.	210	41.00 N	76.50 W
Milton, Vt., U.S.	188	44.38 N	73.06 W
Milton, Wa., U.S.	224	47.14 N	122.18 W
Milton, W.V., U.S.	188	38.26 N	82.07 W
Milton, Wi., U.S.	216	42.46 N	88.56 W
Milton, Lake ⊜	214	41.06 N	80.58 W
Milton Abbot	42	50.35 N	4.15 W
Milton-Freewater	202	45.55 N	118.23 W
Milton Harbor C	276	40.57 N	73.42 W
Milton Keynes	42	52.02 N	0.42 W
Milton Point >	276	40.57 N	73.42 W
Miltonvale	198	39.20 N	97.26 W
Miltou	146	10.14 N	17.26 E
Miltzow	54	54.12 N	13.13 E
Milumba	154	7.06 S	31.04 E
Miluo	100	28.50 N	113.04 E
Miluo ≃	100	28.50 N	113.06 E
Mil'utinskaja	80	48.38 N	41.40 E
Mil'utkej, gora ∧	180	65.42 N	178.03 W
Milverton, On., Can.	212	43.34 N	80.55 W
Milverton, Eng., U.K.	42	51.02 N	3.16 W
Milwaukee	216	43.02 N	87.54 W
Milwaukee □ 6	216	43.02 N	87.58 W
Milwaukee ≃	190	43.02 N	87.54 W
Milwaukee Bay C	216	43.02 N	87.53 W
Milwaukie	224	45.26 N	122.38 W
Mim	150	6.54 N	2.34 W
Mima	96	33.17 N	132.36 E
Mimasaka	96	35.00 N	134.10 E
Mimbres ≃	200	32.13 N	107.28 W
Mimbres Mountains ⋏	200	32.45 N	107.45 W
Mimi ≃	92	32.20 N	131.37 E
Mimico ◆ 8	275b	43.37 N	79.30 W
Mimico Creek ≃	275b	43.37 N	79.29 W
Mimizan	32	44.12 N	1.14 W
Mimmaya	92	41.12 N	140.26 E
Mimoň	54	50.40 N	14.44 E
Mimongo	152	1.11 S	11.36 E
Mimoso, Bra.	248	16.17 S	55.48 W
Mimoso, Bra.	255	15.10 S	48.05 W
Mimoso do Sul	255	21.04 S	41.22 W
Mims	220	28.39 N	80.50 W
Mimuro-yama ∧	96	35.14 N	134.28 E
Min ≃, Zhg.	100	26.05 N	119.32 E
Min ≃, Zhg.	102	28.46 N	104.38 E
Mina, Méx.	196	26.01 N	100.32 W
Mina, Nv., U.S.	204	38.23 N	118.06 W
Mina ≃	112	10.09 S	124.12 E
Mîna, Oued ≃	34	35.47 N	0.30 E
Mīnā' al-Aḥmadī	128	29.04 N	48.08 E
Mīnāb	128	27.09 N	57.05 E
Mīnāb ≃	128	27.01 N	56.53 E
Minabe	96	33.46 N	135.19 E
Minabegawa	96	33.47 N	135.20 E
Mina El Limón	236	12.45 N	86.44 W
Minago ≃	184	54.34 N	98.08 W
Minahasa > 1	112	1.00 N	124.35 E
Minàj ≃ 1	126	22.31 N	89.22 E
Minakami	94	36.46 N	138.58 E
Minakuchi	94	34.58 N	136.10 E
Minam ≃	202	45.37 N	117.43 W
Minamata	92	32.13 N	130.24 E
Minami	94	35.39 N	136.57 E
Minami ◆ 8, Nihon	268	35.24 N	139.36 E
Minami ◆ 8, Nihon	270	34.40 N	135.31 E
Minami ◆ 8, Nihon	270	34.58 N	135.45 E
Minami ≃	94	35.30 N	135.49 E
Minamiaiki	94	36.02 N	138.33 E
Minami-Alps-kokuritsu-kōen ♦	94	35.40 N	138.13 E
Minamiashigara	94	35.19 N	139.07 E
Minami-Bōsō-kokutei-kōen ♦	94	35.10 N	140.05 E
Minamichita	94	34.44 N	136.52 E
Minami-Daitō-jima I	90	25.50 N	131.15 E
Minami-Iō-jima I	14	24.14 N	141.28 E
Minamiizu	94	34.39 N	138.50 E
Minamimaki	94	36.00 N	138.30 E
Minaminasu	94	36.39 N	140.06 E
Minamisenju ◆ 8	268	35.44 N	139.48 E
Minamishinano	94	35.19 N	137.56 E
Minami-Tori-shima (Marcus Island) I	14	24.18 N	153.58 E
Minano	94	36.04 N	139.06 E
Mina Pirquitas	252	22.41 S	66.31 W
Minard, S. Afr.	158	31.17 S	27.35 E
Minard, Scot., U.K.	46	56.07 N	5.15 W
Minas, Cuba	240p	21.29 N	77.37 W
Minas, Indon.	114	0.50 N	101.29 E
Minas, Ur.	252	34.23 S	55.14 W
Minas, Sierra de las ⋏	236	15.10 N	89.40 W
Minas Basin C	186	45.20 N	64.00 W
Minas Channel U	186	45.15 N	64.45 W
Minas de Barroterán	232	27.40 N	101.20 W
Minas de Corrales	252	31.35 S	55.28 W
Minas de Matahambre	240p	22.35 N	83.57 W
Minas de Oro	236	14.46 N	87.20 W
Minas de Ríotinto	34	37.42 N	6.35 W
Minas Gerais □ 3	255	18.00 S	44.00 W
Minas Novas	255	17.15 S	42.36 W
Mînăstirea	38	44.13 N	26.54 E
Minatare	198	41.48 N	103.30 W
Minatitlán	234	17.59 N	94.31 W
Minato	268	35.13 N	139.52 E
Minato ◆ 8, Nihon	268	35.39 N	139.45 E
Minato ◆ 8, Nihon	270	34.39 N	135.26 E
Minato ≃	268	35.13 N	139.52 E
Minbāl	142	28.24 N	30.41 E
Minbu	110	20.11 N	94.52 E
Minbulak	85	41.30 N	75.53 E
Minbya	110	20.22 N	93.15 E
Minbyin	110	19.17 N	93.32 E
Minchinābād	123	30.10 N	73.34 E
Minchinhampton	42	51.42 N	2.10 W
Minchumina, Lake ⊜	180	63.52 N	152.15 W
Mincio ≃	64	45.04 N	10.59 E
Minco	196	35.18 N	97.56 W
Minčol ∧	30	49.15 N	20.59 E
Mind'ak	86	54.02 N	58.48 E
Mindanao I	116	8.00 N	125.00 E
Mindanao ≃	116	7.07 N	124.24 E
Mindego Creek ≃	282	37.18 N	122.15 W
Mindego Hill ∧ 2	282	37.18 N	122.13 W
Mindel ≃	58	48.31 N	10.23 E
Mindelheim	58	48.03 N	10.29 E
Mindelo	150a	16.53 N	25.00 W
Mindemoya	190	45.44 N	82.10 W
Minden, On., Can.	212	44.55 N	78.43 W
Minden, Dtsch.	52	52.17 N	8.55 E
Minden, La., U.S.	194	32.36 N	93.17 W
Minden, Ne., U.S.	198	40.29 N	98.56 W
Minden, Nv., U.S.	226	38.57 N	119.45 W
Minden, W.V., U.S.	188	37.58 N	81.07 W
Minden City	190	43.40 N	82.46 W
Mindenmines	194	37.28 N	94.35 W
Minderoo	162	22.00 S	115.02 E
Mindif	146	10.24 N	14.26 E
Mindiptana	164	5.45 S	140.42 E
Mindon	110	19.21 N	94.44 E
Mindoro I	116	12.50 N	121.05 E
Mindoro Occidental □ 4	116	13.00 N	121.00 E
Mindoro Oriental □ 4	116	13.00 N	121.20 E
Mindoro Strait U	116	12.20 N	120.40 E
Mindouli	152	4.17 S	14.21 E
Mindourou, Cam.	152	4.06 N	14.34 E
Mindourou, Cam.	152	3.25 N	13.32 E
Minduri	256	21.41 S	44.37 W
Mindživan	84	39.03 N	46.42 E
Mine, Ityo.	144	8.20 N	40.09 E
Mine, Nihon	96	33.17 N	130.26 E
Mine, Nihon	96	34.10 N	131.13 E
Minear Lake ⊜	278	42.17 N	87.57 W
Minebank Run ≃	284b	39.25 N	76.32 W
Mine Brook ≃, Ma., U.S.	283	42.09 N	71.15 W
Mine Brook ≃, Ma., U.S.	283	42.08 N	71.26 W
Mine Brook ≃, N.J., U.S.	276	40.41 N	74.38 W
Mine Centre	190	48.45 N	92.37 W
Minehead	42	51.13 N	3.29 W
Mine Hill	210	40.52 N	74.35 W
Mineiros	255	17.34 S	52.34 W
Mineo	70	37.16 N	14.42 E
Mineola, N.Y., U.S.	210	40.44 N	73.38 W
Mineola, Tx., U.S.	222	32.39 N	95.29 W
Miner ≃	180	66.30 N	138.25 W
Mineral	224	46.43 N	122.10 W
Mineral City	214	40.36 N	81.21 W
Mineral Creek ≃	224	46.45 N	122.08 W
Mineral de Cucharas	234	22.52 N	105.19 W
Mineral del Monte	234	20.08 N	98.40 W
Mineral de Pozos	234	21.14 N	100.29 W
Mineral'nyje Vody	84	44.12 N	43.08 E
Mineral Point, Pa., U.S.	214	40.23 N	78.50 W
Mineral Point, Wi., U.S.	190	42.51 N	90.10 W
Mineral Ridge	214	41.08 N	80.46 W
Mineral Springs, Ar., U.S.	194	33.52 N	93.54 W
Mineral Springs, Pa., U.S.	214	41.00 N	78.22 W
Mineral Wells	196	32.48 N	98.06 W
Minerbe	64	45.14 N	11.20 E
Minerbio	64	44.37 N	11.29 E
Minersville, Pa., U.S.	208	40.41 N	76.16 W
Minersville, Ut,. U.S.	200	38.12 N	112.55 W
Mine Run ≃	285	40.15 N	75.28 W
Minerva, Ky., U.S.	218	38.42 N	83.55 W
Minerva, Oh., U.S.	214	40.43 N	81.06 W
Minerva, Tx., U.S.	222	30.46 N	96.59 W
Minerva, Embalse ⊜ 1	240p	22.25 N	79.48 W
Minerva Park	214	40.04 N	83.00 W
Minervino Murge	68	41.05 N	16.05 E
Minesing Swamp ≡	212	44.23 N	79.51 W
Minetto	210	43.23 N	76.28 W
Mineville	188	44.05 N	73.31 W
Mineyama	96	35.37 N	135.04 E
Minfeng	120	37.05 N	82.40 E
Minga	154	11.08 S	27.57 E
Mingala	152	5.06 N	21.49 E
Mingan	186	50.18 N	64.02 W
Mingan ≃	186	50.18 N	63.59 W
Mingan, Îles de II	186	50.12 N	63.35 W
Mingan Archipelago National Park ♦	186	50.12 N	63.35 W
Mingan Mountains ⋏	116	15.29 N	121.24 E
Mingāora	123	34.47 N	72.22 E
Mingardo ≃	68	40.02 N	15.18 E
Mingary	166	32.08 S	140.44 E
Mingcheng	89	43.11 N	125.59 E
Mingečaur	84	40.45 N	47.03 E
Mingečaurskoje vodochranilišče ⊜ 1	84	40.50 N	46.50 E
Mingela	166	19.53 S	146.38 E
Mingenew	162	29.11 S	115.26 E
Mingera Creek ≃	166	20.38 S	138.10 E
Minggang	100	32.29 N	114.03 E
Minggao	100	34.20 N	112.15 E
Minghuang	106	31.41 N	119.56 E
Mingin	110	22.52 N	94.39 E
Mingjuesi	106	31.34 N	118.53 E
Minglanilla	34	39.32 N	1.36 W
Ming Ming	164	5.30 S	146.10 E
Mingo, Congo	152	1.55 S	14.59 E
Mingo, Oh., U.S.	216	40.13 N	83.38 W
Mingo Creek ≃, Pa., U.S.	279b	40.13 N	79.57 W
Mingo Creek ≃, Pa., U.S.	285	40.10 N	75.32 W
Mingo Junction	214	40.19 N	80.36 W
Mingorría	34	40.45 N	4.40 W
Mingoville	214	40.56 N	77.39 W
Mingoyo	154	10.06 S	39.38 E
Mingrel'skaja	78	45.01 N	38.20 E
Mingshantou	100	29.18 N	112.33 E
Mingshui, Zhg.	89	47.10 N	125.55 E
Mingshui, Zhg.	102	42.06 N	96.04 E
Mingulay I	46	56.49 N	7.38 W
Mingwan	106	31.04 N	120.17 E
Mingxi	100	26.24 N	117.13 E
Mingyuegou	89	43.07 N	128.54 E
Mingyuelu	85	39.34 N	75.26 E
Minhang	106	31.01 N	121.24 E
Minhla, Mya.	110	19.58 N	95.03 E
Minhla, Mya.	110	17.59 N	95.43 E
Minho □ 9	34	41.40 N	8.30 W
Minho (Miño) ≃	34	41.52 N	8.51 W
Minhou	100	26.12 N	119.06 E
Minianko	150	9.58 N	8.22 W
Minićevo	38	43.41 N	22.18 E
Minicoy Island I	122	8.17 N	73.02 E
Minier	194	40.26 N	89.18 W
Minigwal, Lake ⊜	162	29.35 S	123.12 E
Minija ≃	76	55.21 N	21.17 E
Minilya	162	23.51 S	113.58 E
Minilya ≃	162	23.56 S	113.51 E
Minimarg	123	34.47 N	75.05 E
Minīn	132	33.39 N	36.18 E
Miniota	184	50.08 N	101.00 W
Minisinakwa Lake ⊜	190	47.40 N	81.43 W
Ministikwan Lake ⊜	184	54.01 N	109.39 W
Ministro Ramos Mexía	254	40.30 S	67.17 W
Ministro Rivadavia	288	34.51 S	58.22 W
Minitonas	184	52.07 N	101.00 W
Minj	164	5.54 S	144.39 E
Minjar	86	55.04 N	57.33 E
Minjary, Mount ∧	171b	35.14 S	148.08 E
Minjiadianzi	104	41.35 N	121.41 E
Minjiaji	100	31.08 N	115.01 E
Minkamman	140	6.03 N	31.32 E
Min'kovo	76	59.42 N	43.28 E
Min-Kuš	85	41.41 N	74.28 E
Minlaton	168b	34.46 S	137.36 E
Minle, Zhg.	100	22.59 N	112.58 E
Minle, Zhg.	102	38.27 N	100.56 E
Minna	150	9.37 N	6.33 E
Minna Bluff > 1	9	78.32 S	166.30 E
Minna-shima I, Nihon	174m	26.39 N	127.49 E
Minna-shima I, Nihon	175d	24.45 N	124.42 E
Minneapolis, Ks., U.S.	198	39.07 N	97.42 W
Minneapolis, Mn., U.S.	190	44.58 N	93.15 W
Minnechaduza Creek ≃	198	42.54 N	100.29 W
Minnedosa	184	50.14 N	99.51 W
Minnehaha	224	45.39 N	122.37 W
Minnehaha, Lake ⊜	220	28.31 N	81.46 W
Minneola, Fl., U.S.	220	28.35 N	81.45 W
Minneola, Ks., U.S.	198	37.26 N	100.00 W
Minneola, Lake ⊜	220	28.34 N	81.46 W
Minneosa Creek ≃	196	35.31 N	102.48 W
Minneota	198	44.34 N	95.59 W
Minnertsga	52	53.15 N	5.35 E
Minnesota □ 3	178	46.00 N	94.15 W
Minnesota ≃	178	44.54 N	93.10 W
Minnesota Lake	190	43.50 N	93.49 W
Minnewanka, Lake ⊜	182	51.15 N	115.20 W
Minnewaukan	198	48.04 N	99.15 W
Minnie Creek	162	24.02 S	115.42 E
Minnigaff	44	54.58 N	4.30 W
Minnipa	162	32.51 S	135.09 E
Minnitaki Lake ⊜	184	49.58 N	92.00 W
Minnoch, Water of ≃	44	55.02 N	4.33 W
Mino, Nihon	94	35.32 N	136.55 E
Minō, Nihon	96	34.50 N	135.28 E
Miño (Minho) ≃, Europe	34	41.52 N	8.51 W
Minō ≃, Nihon	270	34.47 N	134.57 E
Minoa	210	43.04 N	76.00 W
Minobu	94	35.22 N	138.26 E
Minobu-san ∧	94	35.24 N	138.25 E
Minobu-sanchi ⋏	94	35.14 N	138.20 E
Minocqua	190	45.52 N	89.42 W
Minokamo	94	35.26 N	137.01 E
Mino-Mikawa-kōgen ⋏ 1	94	35.11 N	137.23 E
Minong	190	46.05 N	91.49 W
Minonk	216	40.54 N	89.02 W
Minooka	216	41.27 N	88.16 W
Minorca → Menorca I	34	40.00 N	4.00 E
Minori	94	36.14 N	140.21 E
Minorsville	218	38.20 N	84.42 W
Minoshō	270	34.39 N	135.49 E
Minot, Ma., U.S.	283	42.14 N	70.45 W
Minot, N.D., U.S.	198	48.13 N	101.17 W
Minot Air Force Base ■	198	48.26 N	101.21 W
Minowa	94	35.55 N	137.59 E
Minqiao	100	32.53 N	119.13 E
Minqin	102	38.42 N	103.11 E
Minqing	100	26.12 N	118.51 E
Minquadale	285	39.42 N	75.34 W
Minquan	98	34.41 N	115.11 E
Minquiers, Plateau des II	32	48.57 N	2.09 W

ENGLISH

Name	Page	Lat. °′	Long. °′
Minsen	52	53.42 N	7.58 E
Min Shan ⋏	102	33.35 N	103.00 E
Minshāt adh-Dhahab	142	28.00 N	30.42 E
Minshat al-Amir Muhammad 'Ali	142	29.10 N	30.38 E
Minshāt al-Bakkārī	273c	30.01 N	31.08 E
Minshāt al-Ikhwah	142	30.56 N	31.21 E
Minshāt al-Mughālaqah	142	27.44 N	30.47 E
Minshāt Būlīn	142	31.11 N	30.10 E
Minshāt Sulṭān	142	30.32 N	30.55 E
Minsk	76	53.54 N	27.34 E
Minsk □ 8	24	54.30 N	28.00 E
Minskaja vozvyšennost' ⋏ 1	76	54.00 N	27.10 E
Mińsk Mazowiecki	30	52.11 N	21.34 E
Minster, Eng., U.K.	42	51.20 N	1.19 E
Minster, Eng., U.K.	42	51.26 N	0.49 E
Minster, Oh., U.S.	216	40.24 N	84.23 W
Minsterley	42	52.39 N	2.55 W
Minta	152	4.35 N	12.48 E
Mintaka Pass)(	123	37.00 N	74.50 E
Mintard	263	51.22 N	6.54 E
Mintaro	168b	33.55 S	138.43 E
Mint Canyon	228	34.26 N	118.25 W
Mintlaw	46	57.31 N	2.00 W
Minto, Austl.	274a	34.01 S	150.51 E
Minto, Mb., Can.	184	49.25 N	100.01 W
Minto, N.B., Can.	186	46.05 N	66.05 W
Minto, Yk., Can.	180	62.34 N	136.51 W
Minto, Ak., U.S.	180	65.09 N	149.21 W
Minto, N.D., U.S.	198	48.17 N	97.22 W
Minto, Lac ⊜	176	57.13 N	75.00 W
Minto, Mount ∧	9	71.55 S	169.33 E
Minto Inlet C	176	71.20 N	117.00 W
Mintom II	152	2.42 N	13.17 E
Minton	184	49.10 N	104.35 W
Mintoum	152	0.27 N	12.16 E
Minturn	200	39.35 N	106.25 W
Minturnae ⊥	68	41.14 N	13.45 E
Minturno	66	41.15 N	13.45 E
Minūf	142	30.28 N	30.56 E
Minulovo	265a	60.03 N	30.45 E
Minumadai-yōsui ≅	268	35.50 N	139.42 E
Minur'uk	85	40.56 N	73.22 E
Minusinsk	86	53.43 N	91.42 E
Minutang	120	28.13 N	96.32 E
Minute Man National Historical Park ♦	207	42.27 N	71.17 W
Minvoul	152	2.09 N	12.08 E
Minwakh	144	16.50 N	48.05 E
Minxian	102	34.26 N	104.02 E
Minya → Al-Minyā	142	28.06 N	30.45 E
Minyā al-Qamḥ	142	30.31 N	31.21 E
Minya Konka → Gongga Shan ∧	102	29.35 N	101.51 E
Minyat an-Naṣr	142	31.07 N	31.39 E
Minyat as-Sīrij ◆ 8	273c	30.05 N	31.15 E
Minyat Sandūb	142	31.00 N	31.23 E
Minžir	78	46.40 N	28.19 E
Minzow	54	53.23 N	12.30 E
Mio	190	44.39 N	84.07 W
Mioglia	62	44.29 N	8.25 E
Mionica	38	44.15 N	20.05 E
Miory	76	55.37 N	27.38 E
Mipi	120	28.57 N	95.48 E
Miquan	86	44.06 N	87.35 E
Miquelon I	186	47.03 N	56.20 W
Miquihuana	234	23.34 N	99.47 W
Miquon	285	40.04 N	75.16 W
Mir, Bela.	76	53.27 N	26.28 E
Mir, Cuba	240p	20.46 N	76.36 W
Mīr, Miṣr	142	27.27 N	30.44 E
Mir, Niger	146	14.05 N	11.59 E
Mira	34	40.26 N	8.44 W
Mira ≃, N.S., Can.	186	46.03 N	60.00 W
Mira ≃, Col.	246	1.36 N	79.01 W
Mira ≃, Port.	34	37.43 N	8.47 W
Mīrābād	128	30.25 N	61.50 E
Mira Bay C	186	46.02 N	59.56 W
Mirabeau	62	43.42 N	5.39 E
Mirabel	206	45.39 N	74.05 W
Mirabel, Aéroport International de ⊠	206	45.41 N	74.02 W
Mirabella Eclano	68	41.02 N	14.59 E
Mirabella Imbaccari	70	37.19 N	14.27 E
Mirabello, Ippodromo ♦	266b	45.36 N	9.17 E
Mirabello Monferrato	62	45.02 N	8.31 E
Miracema do Tocantins	250	9.33 S	48.24 W
Mirada Hills → La Mirada	228	33.54 N	118.01 W
Mirador	250	6.22 S	44.22 W
Mirador, Cerro ∧	286d	11.57 S	77.02 W
Mirador, Paso de)(	254	40.42 S	71.56 W
Miradouro	255	20.53 S	42.21 W
Miraflores, Arg.	252	28.36 S	65.55 W
Miraflores, Col.	246	5.12 N	73.12 W
Miraflores, Col.	246	1.25 N	72.13 W
Miraflores, Perú	286d	12.07 S	77.02 W
Miraflores, Esclusas de ◆ 5	236	9.00 N	79.36 W
Miraflores, Palacio ◎	286c	10.31 N	66.55 W
Mīrah, Wādī al- ∨	128	32.26 N	41.42 E
Miraí	256	21.12 S	42.37 W
Miraj	122	16.50 N	74.38 E
Miraki	85	39.02 N	67.10 E
Miraleste	228	33.46 N	118.19 W
Mira Loma	228	34.01 N	117.31 W
Miramar, Arg.	252	38.16 S	57.51 W
Miramar, Arg.	252	30.54 S	62.40 W
Miramar, C.R.	236	10.06 N	84.44 W
Miramar, Fr.	62	43.30 N	6.57 E
Miramar, Moç.	156	23.50 S	35.34 E
Miramar, Fl., U.S.	220	25.59 N	80.13 W
Miramar ◆ 8	286b	23.07 N	82.25 W
Miramar, Laguna ⊜	236	16.23 N	91.16 W
Miramare	66	44.02 N	12.38 E
Miramare, Aeroporto di ⊠	66	44.02 N	12.35 E
Miramare, Castello di ⊥	64	45.42 N	13.43 E
Miramar Naval Air Station ■	228	32.52 N	117.07 W
Miramas	62	43.35 N	5.00 E
Mirambeau	32	45.23 N	0.34 W
Miramichi Bay C	186	47.08 N	65.08 W
Mira Monte	228	36.42 N	119.03 W
Mīram Shāh	120	33.01 N	70.04 E
Mīrān	123	31.24 N	70.43 E
Miranda, Austl.	274a	34.02 S	151.06 E
Miranda, Bra.	248	20.14 S	56.22 W
Miranda, Col.	246	3.15 N	76.14 W
Miranda, Ca., U.S.	204	40.14 N	123.49 W
Miranda □ 3	246	10.15 N	66.25 W
Miranda ≃	248	19.25 S	57.20 W
Miranda, Aerodromo ⊠	286c	10.29 N	66.50 W
Miranda de Ebro	34	42.41 N	2.57 W
Miranda do Douro	34	41.30 N	6.16 W
Mirande	32	43.31 N	0.25 E
Mirandela	34	41.29 N	7.11 W
Mirando City	196	27.26 N	99.00 W
Mirandola	64	44.53 N	11.04 E
Mirano	64	45.30 N	12.07 E
Mirantão	256	22.15 S	44.30 W
Mirante do Paranapanema	255	22.17 S	51.54 W
Mirapuxi ≃	255	13.06 S	51.10 W
Mirasaka	96	34.46 N	132.58 E
Mira Taglio	64	45.26 N	12.08 E
Miravalles, Volcán ∧ 1	236	10.45 N	85.10 W
Miravete, Puerto de)(	34	39.43 N	5.43 W
Mīr Bacheh Kowt	120	34.45 N	69.08 E
Mir-Bašir	84	40.20 N	46.55 E
Mirbāṭ	118	17.00 N	54.45 E
Mirboo North	169	38.24 S	146.10 E
Mirebeau-sur-Bèze	58	47.24 N	5.19 E

DEUTSCH

Name	Seite	Breite °′	Länge °′ E = Ost
Mirecourt	58	48.18 N	6.08 E
Miren	64	45.54 N	13.37 E
Mirfield	44	53.40 N	1.41 W
Mirgorod	78	49.58 N	33.36 E
Mirgorodka	80	50.58 N	53.33 E
Miri	112	4.23 N	113.59 E
Miriam Vale	166	24.20 S	151.34 E
Mirim, Lagoa (Laguna Merín) C	252	32.45 S	52.50 W
Mirimichi, Lake ⊜	283	42.02 N	71.18 W
Mirina	38	39.52 N	25.04 E
Miriñay ≃	252	30.10 S	57.39 W
Mirinzal	250	2.01 S	44.43 W
Miritiparaná ≃	246	1.11 S	70.02 W
Miriyama	164	3.57 S	141.45 E
Mīrjāveh	128	29.01 N	61.28 E
Mirke ◆ 8	263	51.16 N	7.09 E
Mirna ≃	64	45.19 N	13.36 E
Mirnock ∧	64	46.46 N	13.43 E
Mirnoje Ozero	86	57.44 N	78.45 E
Mirnyj, Ross.	74	62.33 N	113.53 E
Mirnyj, Ross.	80	53.30 N	50.18 E
Mirnyj, Ukr.	78	50.57 N	28.34 E
Mirnyy ◎ 3	9	66.33 S	93.00 E
Mirond Lake ⊜	184	55.06 N	102.47 W
Mironeasa	38	46.58 N	27.25 E
Mironovka	78	49.39 N	30.59 E
Mironovo	88	58.19 N	109.38 E
Mironovskij	83	48.29 N	38.17 E
Miropol'	78	50.07 N	27.41 E
Miropolje	78	51.02 N	35.16 E
Miroslav	61	48.57 N	16.18 E
Mirosławiec	30	53.21 N	16.05 E
Mirošov	60	49.41 N	13.40 E
Mirovice	60	49.31 N	14.02 E
Mirovoje	78	47.45 N	34.45 E
Mirovskoje	78	48.05 N	33.23 E
Mirow	54	53.16 N	12.49 E
Mīrpur, Bngl.	126	23.47 N	90.21 E
Mīrpur, Bngl.	126	23.56 N	88.59 E
Mīrpur, Pāk.	123	33.11 N	73.47 E
Mīrpur Batoro	120	24.44 N	68.16 E
Mīrpur Bībīwāri	120	28.32 N	67.44 E
Mīrpur Khās	120	25.32 N	69.00 E
Mīrpur Sakro	120	24.33 N	67.37 E
Mirria	150	13.43 N	9.07 E
Mirror	182	52.28 N	113.07 W
Mirror Lake ⊜, Ma., U.S.	283	42.05 N	71.20 W
Mirror Lake ⊜, N.J., U.S.	276	40.29 N	74.22 W
Mirtağ	130	38.23 N	41.56 E
Mirto	70	38.05 N	14.45 E
Mirtóön Pélagos ⊤ 2	38	36.51 N	23.18 E
Miryang	98	35.31 N	128.44 E
Miry Run ≃	285	40.15 N	74.49 W
Mirza-Aki	85	40.45 N	73.25 E
Mirzaani	84	41.23 N	46.09 E
Mirzāganj	126	22.21 N	90.14 E
Mīrzākalu	126	22.29 N	90.48 E
Mirzāpur, Bngl.	126	24.06 N	90.06 E
Mirzāpur, India	124	25.09 N	82.35 E
Mirzāpur, India	272b	22.50 N	88.24 E
Mis	64	46.12 N	11.57 E
Misa ≃	66	43.43 N	13.14 E
Misāḥah, Bi'r ⊤ 4	140	22.12 N	27.57 E
Misailovo	265b	55.34 N	37.49 E
Misaka	94	35.38 N	138.40 E
Misaka-tōge)(	96	33.42 N	132.52 E
Misaki, Nihon	94	35.18 N	140.22 E
Misaki, Nihon	96	33.23 N	132.07 E
Misaki, Nihon	96	34.19 N	135.09 E
Misaki → Miura	94	35.08 N	139.37 E
Misakubo	94	35.09 N	137.52 E
Misallah, Ra's >	142	29.50 N	32.36 E
Misamis Occidental □ 4	116	8.20 N	123.42 E
Misamis Oriental □ 4	116	8.45 N	125.00 E
Misano Adriatico	66	43.57 N	12.39 E
Misantla	234	19.56 N	96.50 W
Misasa	96	35.24 N	133.54 E
Misasagi → Fujiidera	96	34.34 N	135.36 E
Misato, Nihon	94	36.23 N	138.57 E
Misato, Nihon	94	34.43 N	136.24 E
Misato, Nihon	94	36.15 N	137.54 E
Misato, Nihon	96	34.09 N	135.22 E
Misato, Nihon	268	35.50 N	139.53 E
Misawa	92	40.41 N	141.24 E
Misbourne ≃	260	51.34 N	0.29 W
Misburg	52	52.23 N	9.51 E
Miscou Centre	186	47.57 N	64.34 W
Miscou Island I	186	47.57 N	64.33 W
Miscou Point >	186	48.03 N	64.32 W
Mišelevka	88	52.51 N	103.09 E
Misema ≃	190	47.54 N	79.53 W
Mi-sen ∧	96	34.16 N	132.19 E
Misenheimer	192	35.29 N	80.17 W
Miseno	68	40.47 N	14.05 E
Misericórdia, Serra da ∧	287a	22.51 S	43.17 W
Misery, Mount ∧	169	37.24 S	143.36 E
Misgār	123	36.47 N	74.47 E
Mish'āb, Ra's al- >	128	28.12 N	48.39 E
Mishagua ≃	248	11.13 S	72.59 W
Mishan	89	45.33 N	131.52 E
Mishawaka	216	41.39 N	86.09 W
Mishawum Lake ⊜	283	42.30 N	71.08 W
Mishbiḥ, Jabal ∧	140	22.38 N	34.44 E
Misheguk Mountain ∧	180	68.15 N	161.03 W
Mishe-Mokwa, Lake ⊜	285	39.52 N	74.48 W
Mishibishu Lake ⊜	190	48.05 N	85.25 W
Mishicot	190	44.14 N	87.38 W
Mishima	94	35.07 N	138.55 E
Mi-shima I	96	34.46 N	131.09 E
Mishima → Settsu	96	34.46 N	135.33 E
Mishmar HaNegev	132	31.21 N	34.43 E
Mishmi Hills ⋏ 2	120	29.00 N	96.00 E
Mishō	96	32.57 N	132.34 E
Mishqal, Jabal al- ∧	132	31.53 N	36.08 E
Mišicha	88	51.38 N	105.35 E
Misikan	120	35.45 N	89.25 E
Misilmeri	70	38.02 N	13.27 E
Misima Island I	164	10.40 S	152.45 E
Misinto	266b	45.40 N	9.05 E
Misiones □ 4	252	27.00 S	55.00 W
Misiones □ 5	252	27.00 S	57.00 W
Misión San Francisco de Laishí	252	26.14 S	58.38 W
Misión San Vicente	232	31.20 N	116.15 W
Misirevo	82	56.16 N	36.45 E
Miskī	140	14.51 N	24.13 E
Miski, Enneri ∨	146	20.00 N	17.55 E
Miškino, Ross.	86	55.20 N	63.55 E
Miškino, Ross.	265a	59.42 N	30.45 E
Miskito Channel U	236	14.20 N	83.08 W
Miskitos, Cayos II	236	14.23 N	82.46 W
Miskitos Reef ✣ 2	236	14.28 N	82.42 W
Miskolc	30	48.06 N	20.47 E
Misli	130	38.10 N	34.52 E
Mislinja	61	46.28 N	15.14 E
Mislinja ≃	61	46.35 N	15.02 E
Mislippi	146	10.00 N	15.37 E
Mislivna ∧	61	48.40 N	14.44 E
Mismār	140	18.13 N	35.38 E
Mismār, Jabal ∧	140	18.06 N	35.42 E
Mismi, Nevado ∧	248	15.30 S	71.42 W
Mišn'ovo	76	53.58 N	36.21 E
Misoke	154	1.06 S	28.38 E
Misool, Pulau I	164	1.52 S	130.10 E
Mispillion ≃	208	38.57 N	75.20 W
Misquamaebin Lake ⊜	184	53.30 N	91.05 W
Misquamicut	207	41.20 N	71.49 W
Miṣr al-Jadīdah (Heliopolis) ◆ 8	273c	30.06 N	31.20 E
Miṣr al-Qadīmah (Old Cairo) ◆ 8	273c	30.00 N	31.14 E

Symbols in the index entries represent the broad categories identified in the key at the right. Symbols with superior numbers (⋏ 1) identify subcategories (see complete key on page *I · 1)*.

Symbole im Register stellen die rechts im Schlüssel erklärten Kategorien dar. Symbole mit hochgestellten Ziffern (⋏ 1) bezeichnen Unterabteilungen einer Kategorie (vgl. vollständiger Schlüssel auf Seite *I · 1)*.

Los símbolos incluídos en el texto del índice representan las grandes categorias identificadas con la clave a la derecha. Los símbolos con numeros en su parte superior (⋏ 1) identifican las subcategorías (véase la clave completa en la página *I · 1)*.

Les symboles de l'index représentent les catégories indiquées dans la légende à droite. Les symboles suivis d'un indice (⋏ 1) représentent des sous-catégories (voir légende complète à la page *I · 1)*.

Os símbolos incluídos no texto do índice representam as grandes categorias identificadas com a chave à direita. Os símbolos com números em sua parte superior (⋏ 1) identificam as subcategorias (veja-se a chave completa à página *I · 1)*.

∧	Mountain	Berg	Montaña	Montagne	Montanha
⋏	Mountains	Gebirge	Montañas	Montagnes	Montanhas
)(	Pass	Paß	Paso	Col	Passo
∨	Valley, Canyon	Tal, Cañon	Valle, Cañón	Vallée, Canyon	Vale, Canhão
≚	Plain	Ebene	Llano	Plaine	Planície
>	Cape	Kap	Cabo	Cap	Cabo
I	Island	Insel	Isla	Île	Ilha
II	Islands	Inseln	Islas	Îles	Ilhas
⊥	Other Topographic Features	Andere Topographische Objekte	Otros Elementos Topográficos	Autres données topographiques	Outros acidentes topográficos

ESPAÑOL

Nombre	Página	Lat.°′	Long.°′ W = Oeste
Misrātah	146	32.23 N	15.06 E
Mişr Baḥrī □[9]	140	31.00 N	31.00 E
Mişr → Egypt □[1]	140	27.00 N	30.00 E
Misrikh	124	27.27 N	80.31 E
Missanello	68	40.17 N	16.10 E
Missão Santa Cruz	152	16.14 S	21.57 E
Missão Velha	250	7.15 S	39.08 W
Misserghin	34	35.37 N	0.45 W
Missinaibi ≏	176	50.44 N	81.29 W
Missinaibi Lake ⊜	190	48.23 N	83.40 W
Missinaibi Lake Provincial Park ♦	190	48.25 N	83.35 W
Mission, S.D., U.S.	198	43.18 N	100.39 W
Mission, Tx., U.S.	196	26.12 N	98.19 W
Mission ✦[8]	282	37.45 N	122.25 W
Mission Bay c	228	32.47 N	117.15 W
Mission Beach	166	17.52 S	146.06 E
Mission City	224	49.08 N	122.18 W
Mission Creek ≏	282	37.32 N	121.55 W
Mission Hills ✦[8]	280	34.16 N	118.27 W
Mission Mountain ʌ[2]	194	36.02 N	94.35 W
Mission Peak ʌ	282	37.31 N	121.53 W
Mission Range ⋏	202	47.30 N	113.55 W
Mission Texas State Historic Park ♦	222	31.33 N	95.15 W
Mission Valley	222	28.54 N	97.12 W
Mission Viejo	228	33.36 N	117.40 W
Missisquoi □[6]	206	45.10 N	72.55 W
Missisquoi ≏	206	45.00 N	73.08 W
Missisquoi Bay c	206	45.05 N	73.10 W
Missisquoi-Nord ≏	206	45.02 N	72.26 W
Mississagagon Lake ⊜	212	44.52 N	77.05 W
Mississagi ≏	190	46.10 N	83.01 W
Mississagi Provincial Park ♦	190	46.35 N	82.45 W
Mississagua ≏	212	44.34 N	78.20 W
Mississagua Lake ⊜	212	44.42 N	78.19 W
Mississauga	212	43.35 N	79.39 W
Mississinewa ≏	216	40.46 N	86.02 W
Mississinewa Lake ⊜[1]	216	40.42 N	85.52 W
Mississippi □[3], U.S.	178	32.50 N	89.30 W
Mississippi □[3], U.S.	194	32.50 N	89.30 W
Mississippi ≏, On., Can.	212	45.26 N	76.16 W
Mississippi ≏, U.S.	178	29.00 N	89.15 W
Mississippi Bay c	162	34.00 S	122.17 E
Mississippi Delta ≚[2]	194	29.10 N	89.15 W
Mississippi Lake ⊜	212	45.05 N	76.12 W
Mississippi Sound ʯ	194	30.15 N	88.40 W
Mississippi State	194	33.26 N	88.47 W
Missolonghi → Mesolóngion	38	38.21 N	21.17 E
Missoula	202	46.52 N	113.59 W
Missouri □[3], U.S.	178	38.30 N	93.30 W
Missouri □[3], U.S.	194	38.30 N	93.30 W
Missouri ≏	178	38.50 N	90.08 W
Missouri, Coteau du ⋏[2]	198	46.00 N	99.30 W
Missouri Buttes ʌ	198	44.37 N	104.47 W
Missouri City	222	29.37 N	95.32 W
Missouri Creek ≏	219	40.07 N	90.43 W
Missouri Valley	198	41.33 N	95.53 W
Mistake, Mount ʌ	171a	27.52 S	152.20 E
Mistake Creek	164	17.06 S	129.04 E
Mistake Creek ≏	166	21.38 S	146.50 E
Mistake Mountains ⋏	171a	27.52 S	152.22 E
Mistaken Point ≻	186	46.38 N	53.10 W
Mistanipisipou ≏	186	51.32 N	61.50 W
Mistassibi ≏	176	48.53 N	72.13 W
Mistassibi Nord-Est ≏	186	49.50 N	71.56 W
Mistassini	176	50.25 N	73.52 W
Mistassini, Lac ⊜	176	51.00 N	73.37 W
Mistatim	184	52.52 N	103.22 W
Mistawasis Indian Reserve ✦[4]	184	53.06 N	106.48 W
Mistelbach, Dtsch.	60	49.55 N	11.31 E
Mistelbach, Öst.	61	48.34 N	16.35 E
Mistelgau	60	49.55 N	11.28 E
Misteln ⊜	40	59.07 N	16.57 E
Misterbianco	70	37.31 N	15.00 E
Misterei	140	13.07 N	22.09 E
Misteriosa Bank ✧[2]	238	18.50 N	83.50 W
Misterton, Eng., U.K.	42	50.52 N	2.47 W
Misterton, Eng., U.K.	44	53.27 N	0.51 W
Misti, Volcán ʌ[1]	248	16.18 S	71.24 W
Mistikokan ≏	184	57.01 N	91.27 W
Mistley	42	51.56 N	1.05 E
Mistrás ⊥	38	37.04 N	22.21 E
Mistretta	70	37.56 N	14.22 E
Misugi	94	34.33 N	136.16 E
Misumi, Nihon	92	32.37 N	130.27 E
Misumi, Nihon	96	34.46 N	131.58 E
Misumi, Nihon	96	34.22 N	131.15 E
Misumi ≏	96	34.47 N	131.56 E
Misurina	64	46.35 N	12.15 E
Mišurin Rog	78	48.50 N	33.58 E
Mišutino, Ross.	76	59.31 N	36.01 E
Mišutino, Ross.	82	56.23 N	38.06 E
Mita, Punta ≻	234	20.47 N	105.33 W
Mīt Abū Ghālib	142	31.17 N	31.40 E
Mita Hills Dam ✦[6]	154	14.15 S	29.06 E
Mit'ajevo, Ross.	82	55.16 N	36.32 E
Mit'ajevo, Ross.	86	60.17 N	61.06 E
Mitaka	94	35.40 N	139.33 E
Mitake, Nihon	94	35.25 N	137.08 E
Mitake, Nihon	94	35.51 N	137.37 E
Mit'akinka ≏	83	48.35 N	39.50 E
Mit'akino	82	54.24 N	38.50 E
Mit'akinskaja	83	48.36 N	39.47 E
Mīt al-ʿĀmil	142	30.54 N	31.21 E
Mitatib	140	16.03 N	36.11 E
Mitau → Jelgava	76	56.39 N	23.42 E
Mīt Badr Ḥalāwah	142	30.51 N	31.14 E
Mīt Bashshār	142	30.31 N	31.24 E
Mitcham, Austl.	168b	34.59 S	138.36 E
Mitcham, Austl.	274b	37.49 S	145.12 E
Mitcham ✦[8]	260	51.24 N	0.10 W
Mitcheldean	42	51.53 N	2.30 W
Mitchell, Austl.	166	26.29 S	147.58 E
Mitchell, On., Can.	212	43.28 N	81.12 W
Mitchell, Il., U.S.	219	38.46 N	90.06 W
Mitchell, In., U.S.	218	38.43 N	86.28 W
Mitchell, Ne., U.S.	198	41.56 N	103.48 W
Mitchell, Or., U.S.	202	44.34 N	120.09 W
Mitchell, S.D., U.S.	198	43.42 N	98.01 W
Mitchell ≏, Austl.	164	15.12 S	141.35 E
Mitchell ≏, Austl.	164	14.28 S	125.43 E
Mitchell ≏, Austl.	166	37.53 S	147.41 E
Mitchell, Lake ⊜[1]	194	32.50 N	86.30 W
Mitchell, Mount ʌ	192	35.46 N	82.16 W
Mitchell and Alice Rivers National Park ♦	164	15.30 S	142.05 E
Mitchell Bay c	214	42.28 N	82.26 W
Mitchell Corners	212	43.57 N	78.48 W
Mitchell Field ⊠	278	41.55 N	88.15 W
Mitchell Lake ⊜, B.C., Can.	182	52.53 N	120.36 W
Mitchell Lake ⊜, On., Can.	212	44.34 N	78.58 W
Mitchell Point ≻	214	42.26 N	82.26 W
Mitchellville	190	41.40 N	93.21 W
Mitchelstown	48	52.16 N	8.16 W
Mīt Fāris	142	31.02 N	31.36 E
Mīt Ghamr	142	30.43 N	31.16 E
Mīt Ḥalfah	273c	30.10 N	31.14 E
Mīt Ḥamal	142	30.26 N	31.32 E
Mithapur	120	22.25 N	69.00 E
Mitha Tiwāna	123	32.15 N	72.07 E
Mithi	120	24.44 N	69.48 E
Mithimna	38	39.22 N	26.10 E
Mitiaro I	14	19.49 S	157.43 W
Mitidja, Plaine de la ≚	34	36.45 N	3.00 E
Mitilíni	38	39.06 N	26.32 E

FRANÇAIS

Nom	Page	Lat.°′	Long.°′ W = Ouest
Mitino	265b	55.51 N	37.21 E
Mitis, Lac ⊜	186	48.17 N	67.45 W
Mitishto ≏	184	54.50 N	98.58 W
Mitiškovo	76	54.40 N	33.31 E
Mitiwanga	214	41.22 N	82.27 W
Mitkof Island I	180	56.45 N	132.50 W
Mitla ⊥	234	16.55 N	96.17 W
Mitla, Laguna c	234	17.03 N	100.25 W
Mitla, Mamarr (Mitla Pass))(	142	30.00 N	32.53 E
Mitla Pass → Mitla, Mamarr)(	142	30.00 N	32.53 E
Mito, Nihon	94	34.49 N	137.19 E
Mito, Nihon	94	36.22 N	140.28 E
Mito, Nihon	96	34.40 N	131.59 E
Mitō, Nihon	96	34.13 N	131.21 E
Mito, Nihon	268	35.10 N	139.37 E
Mitomi	94	35.47 N	138.44 E
Mitoya	96	35.17 N	132.52 E
Mitra, Monte ʌ	152	1.23 N	9.57 E
Mitra do Bispo ʌ	256	22.10 S	44.34 W
Mitre ʌ	172	40.48 S	175.27 E
Mitre, Península ≻[1]	254	54.48 S	65.40 W
Mitre Peak ʌ	172	44.38 S	167.50 E
Mitrofania Island I	180	55.51 N	158.49 W
Mitrofanovka	78	49.58 N	39.42 E
Mitrofanovo	24	63.13 N	56.00 E
Mīt Ruhaynah	273c	29.51 N	31.15 E
Mīt Ruhaynah (Memphis) ⊥	142	29.51 N	31.15 E
Mitry-le-Neuf	261	48.57 N	2.36 E
Mitry-Mory	261	48.59 N	2.37 E
Mitsamiouli	157a	11.23 S	43.18 E
Mitsinjo	157b	16.01 S	45.52 E
Mitsio, Nosy I	157b	12.54 S	48.36 E
Mitsiwa (Massawa)	144	15.38 N	39.28 E
Mitsiwa Channel ʯ	144	15.30 N	40.00 E
Mitsu, Nihon	96	34.47 N	134.33 E
Mitsu, Nihon	96	34.48 N	133.56 E
Mitsubori	268	35.56 N	139.56 E
Mitsue	94	34.29 N	136.10 E
Mitsugi	96	34.30 N	133.09 E
Mitsuike Park ♦	268	35.31 N	139.39 E
Mitsukaidō	94	36.01 N	139.59 E
Mitsuke	92	37.32 N	138.56 E
Mitsumarenge-dake ʌ	94	36.23 N	137.35 E
Mitsushima	92	34.16 N	129.19 E
Mitsuzaku	268	35.25 N	140.00 E
Mitsuzawa Park Race Track ♦	268	35.27 N	139.36 E
Mitta, Oued el V	148	34.20 N	6.44 E
Mittagong	170	34.27 S	150.27 E
Mittagskogel (Kepa) ʌ	61	46.31 N	13.57 E
Mittainville	261	48.40 N	1.39 E
Mitta Mitta ≏	171b	36.12 S	147.11 E
Mitte ✦[8]	264a	52.31 N	13.24 E
Mittelberg, Dtsch.	58	47.38 N	10.25 E
Mittelberg, Öst.	58	47.20 N	10.10 E
Mittelfischach	56	49.02 N	9.52 E
Mittelfranken □[5]	56	49.20 N	10.40 E
Mittellandkanal ≍	30	52.16 N	11.41 E
Mittelmeer → Mediterranean Sea ⊤[2]	10	35.00 N	20.00 E
Mittelsaida	54	50.46 N	13.18 E
Mittelstetten	60	48.15 N	11.06 E
Mittenwald	64	47.27 N	11.15 E
Mittenwalde, Dtsch.	54	53.11 N	13.39 E
Mittenwalde, Dtsch.	54	52.16 N	13.32 E
Mitterndorf	64	47.33 N	13.55 E
Mittersill	64	47.16 N	12.29 E
Mitterskirchen	60	48.21 N	12.44 E
Mitterteich	60	49.57 N	12.15 E
Mittewald an der Drau	64	46.46 N	12.36 E
Mittweida	54	50.59 N	12.59 E
Mitú	246	1.08 N	70.03 W
Mitumba, Monts ⋏	154	6.00 S	29.00 E
Mituo	107	28.53 N	105.37 E
Mitwaba	154	8.38 S	27.20 E
Mitwitz	56	50.15 N	11.12 E
Mityana	154	0.24 N	32.03 E
Mīt Yazīd	142	30.30 N	31.20 E
Mitzic	152	0.47 N	11.34 E
Miura	94	35.08 N	139.37 E
Miura-chosuichi ⊜[1]	94	35.49 N	137.23 E
Miura-dam ✦[6]	94	35.49 N	137.24 E
Miura-hantō ≻[1]	94	35.15 N	139.39 E
Mius	80	51.26 N	47.56 E
Mius ≏	83	47.18 N	38.49 E
Miusinsk	83	48.05 N	38.53 E
Miusskij liman c[1]	83	47.15 N	38.40 E
Miwa, Nihon	94	35.11 N	136.47 E
Miwa, Nihon	94	36.39 N	140.18 E
Miwa, Nihon	96	35.12 N	135.14 E
Miwa, Nihon	96	34.39 N	132.51 E
Miwa, Nihon	96	34.13 N	132.06 E
Miwa, Nihon	270	34.31 N	135.51 E
Mi-Wuk Village	226	38.05 N	120.13 W
Mixcoac ✦[8]	286a	19.23 N	99.12 W
Mixcoac, Presa de ⊜[1]	286a	19.22 N	99.14 W
Mixco Viejo ⊥	236	14.52 N	90.40 W
Mixian	100	34.31 N	113.22 E
Mixin	107	30.23 N	105.46 E
Mixquiahuala	234	20.14 N	99.13 W
Mixtán	234	17.55 N	95.51 W
Mixteco ≏	234	18.11 N	98.30 W
Mixtlán	234	20.26 N	104.25 W
Miya	94	36.05 N	137.15 E
Miya ≏, Nihon	94	34.32 N	136.44 E
Miya ≏, Nihon	94	36.28 N	137.15 E
Miyagawa, Nihon	94	36.19 N	137.09 E
Miyagawa, Nihon	94	34.22 N	136.21 E
Miyagi □[5]	92	38.22 N	140.52 E
Miyagi-jima I	174m	26.21 N	127.57 E
Miyāh, Wādī al- V	140	25.00 N	33.23 E
Miyahara	268	35.56 N	139.37 E
Miyajima	96	34.18 N	132.19 E
Miyake	270	34.35 N	135.47 E
Miyake-jima I	92	34.05 N	139.32 E
Miyako	92	39.38 N	141.57 E
Miyakojima ✦[8]	270	34.43 N	135.33 E
Miyako-jima I	175d	24.47 N	125.20 E
Miyakonojō	92	31.44 N	131.04 E
Miyako-rettō II	175d	24.24 N	125.00 E
Miyama, Nihon	92	34.06 N	136.14 E
Miyama, Nihon	94	36.00 N	136.22 E
Miyama, Nihon	94	35.33 N	136.45 E
Miyama, Nihon	96	35.16 N	135.33 E
Miyama, Nihon	96	33.59 N	135.22 E
Miyāni	120	21.51 N	69.23 E
Miyanojō	92	31.54 N	130.27 E
Miyanoura-dake ʌ	93b	30.20 N	130.31 E
Miyara	175d	24.20 N	124.14 E
Miyata	96	33.44 N	130.40 E
Miyazaki, Nihon	92	31.54 N	131.26 E
Miyazaki, Nihon	94	35.56 N	136.05 E
Miyazakino-hana ≻	96	34.04 N	135.05 E
Miyazu	96	35.32 N	135.11 E
Miyi	102	27.00 N	102.08 E
Miyoshi, Nihon	96	33.57 N	133.03 E
Miyoshi, Nihon	96	34.48 N	132.51 E
Miyoshi, Nihon	96	34.02 N	133.52 E
Miyoshi, Nihon	268	35.50 N	139.31 E
Miyota	94	36.18 N	138.30 E
Miyun	105	40.22 N	116.50 E
Miyun Shuiku ⊜[1]	105	40.30 N	116.58 E
Mizan Teferi	144	6.53 N	35.28 E
Mizdah	146	31.26 N	12.59 E
Mize	194	31.52 N	89.33 W
Mizen Head ≻, Ire.	48	52.51 N	6.01 W
Mizen Head ≻, Ire.	48	51.27 N	9.49 W
Miževiči	76	52.59 N	25.05 E
Mizhi	102	37.49 N	110.02 E
Mizil	38	45.00 N	26.26 E
Mizoč	78	50.24 N	26.09 E
Mizoguchi	96	35.21 N	133.26 E
Mizonokuchi	268	35.36 N	139.37 E

PORTUGUÊS

Nome	Página	Lat.°′	Long.°′ W = Oeste
Mizonuma	268	35.48 N	139.36 E
Mizoram □[3]	120	23.30 N	93.00 E
Mizpah	208	39.29 N	74.50 W
Mizpah Creek ≏	198	46.16 N	105.17 W
Mizpé Ramon	132	30.36 N	34.48 E
Mizque	248	17.56 S	65.19 W
Mizque ≏	248	18.39 S	64.20 W
Mizue ✦[8]	268	35.41 N	139.54 E
Mizuho, Nihon	94	35.46 N	139.21 E
Mizuho, Nihon	96	35.10 N	135.22 E
Mizuho, Nihon	96	34.51 N	132.31 E
Mizukaidō → Mitsukaidō	94	36.01 N	139.59 E
Mizuko	268	35.50 N	139.34 E
Mizumaki	96	33.51 N	130.42 E
Mizunami	94	35.22 N	137.15 E
Mizunoko-jima I	96	33.02 N	132.11 E
Mizusawa	92	39.08 N	141.08 E
Mizushima-nada c	96	34.25 N	133.40 E
Mizutori	270	34.47 N	135.45 E
Mizuwake-tōge)(	96	33.15 N	131.17 E
Mjälgen	40	60.33 N	15.07 E
Mjällom	26	62.59 N	18.26 E
Mjangad	86	48.15 N	91.57 E
Mjanyana	158	31.50 S	28.10 E
Mjölby	26	58.19 N	15.08 E
Mjøndalen	26	59.45 N	10.01 E
Mjörn ⊜	26	57.54 N	12.25 E
Mjøsa ⊜	26	60.40 N	11.00 E
Mkalama	154	4.07 S	34.38 E
Mkata	154	5.47 S	38.17 E
Mkhondvo ≏	158	26.39 S	31.25 E
Mkokotoni	154	5.52 S	39.15 E
Mkomazi ≏	158	30.12 S	30.50 E
Mkomazi Game Reserve ✦[4]	154	4.10 S	38.10 E
Mkulwe	154	8.35 S	32.19 E
Mkumvura ≏	154	15.55 S	31.07 E
Mkunumbi	154	2.18 S	40.42 E
Mkushi	154	13.40 S	29.20 E
Mkushi ≏	154	14.40 S	29.07 E
Mkushi River	154	13.32 S	29.45 E
Mkuze	158	27.37 S	32.02 E
Mkuze ≏	158	27.53 S	32.29 E
Mkuzi Game Reserve ✦[4]	158	27.40 S	32.15 E
Mkwaja	154	5.47 S	38.51 E
Mkwaya	154	10.06 S	39.40 E
Mladá Boleslav	54	50.23 N	14.59 E
Mladenovac	38	44.26 N	20.42 E
Mladotice	60	49.58 N	13.18 E
Mlala Hills ⋏[2]	154	6.47 S	31.45 E
M'Lang	116	6.55 N	124.53 E
M'Lang ≏	116	6.52 N	124.45 E
Mlanje Peak → Sapitwa ʌ	154	15.57 S	35.36 E
Mlava ≏	38	44.45 N	21.13 E
Mława	30	53.06 N	20.23 E
Mlawula	158	26.11 S	32.01 E
Mliba	158	26.14 S	31.36 E
Mlinov	78	50.31 N	25.37 E
Mljet, Otok I	36	42.45 N	17.30 E
Mljet Nacionalni Park ♦	36	42.47 N	17.25 E
Mljetski Kanal ʯ	36	42.48 N	17.35 E
Mmabatho	138	25.51 S	25.38 E
Mmadinare	156	21.57 S	27.52 E
Mnazi	154	8.54 S	39.06 E
Mnevniki ✦[8]	265b	55.45 N	37.28 E
Mnichov	60	50.03 N	12.49 E
Mníšek pod Brdy	30	49.52 N	14.16 E
Mo	24	66.15 N	14.08 E
Mo ≏	150	8.45 N	0.11 E
Moa	240p	20.40 N	74.56 W
Moa ≏, Afr.	150	6.59 N	11.36 W
Moa ≏, Bra.	248	7.39 S	72.41 W
Moa, Pulau I	164	8.10 S	127.56 E
Moab	200	38.34 N	109.32 W
Moabi	152	2.15 S	11.00 E
Moaco ≏	248	7.41 S	68.18 W
Moa Island I	164	10.12 S	142.16 E
Moala Island I	175g	18.36 S	179.53 E
Moalboal	116	9.56 N	123.23 E
Moama	166	36.07 S	144.47 E
Moamba	156	25.35 S	32.13 E
Moana	168b	35.13 S	138.29 E
Moanda	152	1.34 S	13.11 E
Moanza	152	5.25 S	17.30 E
Moar Lake ⊜	184	52.00 N	95.09 W
Moate	48	53.24 N	7.58 W
Moatize	154	16.08 S	33.45 E
Moawhango	172	39.35 S	175.52 E
Moba, Nig.	273a	6.27 N	3.28 E
Moba, Zaïre	154	7.03 S	29.47 E
Mobara	94	35.25 N	140.18 E
Mobārakpur	126	22.58 N	89.10 E
Mobaye	152	4.19 N	21.11 E
Mobayi-Mbongo	152	4.18 N	21.11 E
Mobberley	262	53.19 N	2.20 W
Mobeetie	196	35.31 N	100.26 W
Mobeka	152	1.53 N	19.46 E
Mobenzélé	152	0.54 N	17.51 E
Moberly	194	39.25 N	92.26 W
Moberly ≏	182	56.12 N	120.55 W
Moberly Lake	182	55.48 N	121.45 W
Moberly Lake ⊜	182	55.49 N	121.45 W
Mobile, Al., U.S.	194	30.41 N	88.02 W
Mobile, Az., U.S.	200	33.03 N	112.16 W
Mobile ≏	194	30.29 N	88.01 W
Mobile Bay c	194	30.25 N	88.00 W
Mobjack	208	37.23 N	76.21 W
Mobjack Bay c	208	37.19 N	76.21 W
Mobridge	198	45.32 N	100.25 W
Moca, P.R.	240m	18.24 N	67.07 W
Moca, Rep. Dom.	238	19.24 N	70.31 W
Moča ≏	82	55.25 N	37.28 E
Mocajuba	250	2.35 S	49.30 W
Mocal ≏	236	14.00 N	88.33 W
Močalejevka	80	53.38 N	51.46 E
Močališče	80	56.21 N	48.23 E
Moçambique	154	15.03 S	40.45 E
Moçambique → Mozambique □[1]	138	18.15 S	35.00 E
Mocanaqua	210	41.08 N	76.08 W
Mocanguê Grande, Ilha I	287a	22.52 S	43.08 W
Mocassins, Lac des ⊜	206	46.35 N	74.25 W
Mo Cay	110	10.08 N	106.20 E
Moccasin, Ca., U.S.	226	37.49 N	120.18 W
Moccasin, Il., U.S.	219	39.09 N	88.45 W
Moc Chau	110	20.51 N	104.37 E
Moccoidumis	144	1.36 N	44.26 E
Mocha, Isla I	252	38.22 S	73.56 W
Mocha → Al-Makhā'	144	13.19 N	43.15 E
Moche ≏	248	8.10 S	79.03 W
Moche ⊥	248	8.06 S	79.05 W
Mocheng	106	31.35 N	120.43 E
Mochh	123	32.45 N	71.31 E
Mochigase	96	35.20 N	134.12 E
Mochitlan	234	17.30 N	99.18 W
Mochizuki	94	36.16 N	138.22 E
Mocho, Arroyo ≏	226	37.41 N	121.55 W
Mochov	54	50.08 N	14.50 E
Mochtín	60	49.22 N	13.21 E
Mochudi	156	24.28 S	26.05 E
Močily	82	54.20 N	38.41 E
Mocímboa da Praia	154	11.20 S	40.21 E
Mocímboa do Rovuma	154	11.20 S	39.18 E
Möckeln ⊜, Sve.	26	56.40 N	14.10 E
Möckeln ⊜, Sve.	40	59.18 N	14.30 E
Möckern	54	52.08 N	11.57 E
Mockfjärd	40	60.30 N	14.58 E
Mockhorn Island I	208	37.13 N	75.53 W
Möckmühl	56	49.19 N	9.22 E
Mockrehna	54	51.30 N	12.49 E
Mocksville	192	35.53 N	80.33 W
Moclips	224	47.14 N	124.12 W

Môco, Serra do ʌ	152	12.28 S	15.10 E
Mocoa	246	1.09 N	76.37 W
Mococa	256	21.28 S	47.01 W
Mocoduene	156	23.40 S	35.10 E
Mocoretá	252	30.38 S	57.58 W
Mocorito	232	25.29 N	107.55 W
Moctezuma, Méx.	232	29.48 N	109.42 W
Moctezuma, Méx.	234	22.45 N	101.05 W
Moctezuma ≏, Méx.	232	29.09 N	109.40 W
Moctezuma ≏, Méx.	234	21.59 N	98.34 W
Mocuba	154	16.50 S	36.59 E
Močurica ≏	38	42.31 N	26.32 E
Modane	62	45.12 N	6.40 E
Modāsa	120	23.28 N	73.18 E
Modau ≏	56	49.49 N	8.28 E
Modbury	42	50.21 N	3.53 W
Modder ≏	158	29.02 S	24.37 E
Modderbee	273d	26.10 S	28.24 E
Modder East	273d	26.11 S	28.26 E
Modderfontein	273d	26.06 S	28.09 E
Modderfontein ≏	273d	26.13 S	28.10 E
Modderrivier	158	29.02 S	24.38 E
Model City	284a	43.11 N	78.59 W
Modena, It.	64	44.40 N	10.55 E
Modena, N.Y., U.S.	210	41.40 N	74.07 W
Modena □[4]	64	44.30 N	10.54 E
Moder ≏	56	48.49 N	8.06 E
Möderbrugg	61	47.17 N	14.29 E
Modern Art, Museum of ʊ	276	40.46 N	73.58 W
Modeste, Mount ʌ	224	48.37 N	124.06 W
Modesto, Ca., U.S.	226	37.38 N	120.59 W
Modesto, Il., U.S.	219	39.29 N	89.59 W
Modesto City-County Airport ⊠	226	37.39 N	120.57 W
Modesto Main Canal ≍	226	37.39 N	120.27 W
Modesto Reservoir ⊜[1]	226	37.26 N	121.58 W
Modica	70	36.52 N	14.46 E
Modigliana	66	44.09 N	11.47 E
Modinagar	124	28.51 N	77.37 E
Modione ≏	70	37.34 N	12.49 E
Modjamboli	152	2.28 N	22.06 E
Modjeska	280	33.43 N	117.37 W
Mödling	264b	48.05 N	16.17 E
Mödling ≏	264b	48.04 N	16.22 E
Modoc	218	40.02 N	85.07 W
Modon ≏	50	47.16 N	1.27 E
Modowi	164	4.05 S	134.39 E
Modra, Česko.	30	48.21 N	17.17 E
Modra, Tchad	146	20.43 N	17.42 E
Modra špilja ⫠[5]	36	43.00 N	16.02 E
Mödrath	56	50.53 N	6.43 E
Modriča	38	44.57 N	18.18 E
Modřice	61	49.07 N	16.37 E
Mo Duc	110	14.57 N	108.53 E
Modugno	68	41.05 N	16.47 E
Moe	169	38.10 S	146.15 E
Moe ≏, Austl.	169	38.08 S	146.17 E
Moe ≏, P.Q., Can.	206	45.19 N	71.49 W
Moecherville	216	41.44 N	88.17 W
Moeda	255	20.20 S	44.03 W
Moehau ʌ	172	36.35 S	175.24 E
Moel Fferna ʌ	42	52.57 N	3.18 W
Moelv	26	60.56 N	10.42 E
Moema	255	19.50 S	45.24 W
Moen	50	50.46 N	3.24 E
Moen I	175c	7.26 N	151.52 E
Moena	64	46.22 N	11.39 E
Moengo	250	5.37 N	54.24 W
Moen-jo-Daro ⊥	120	27.18 N	68.15 E
Moenkopi	200	36.06 N	111.13 W
Moenkopi Wash V	200	35.54 N	111.26 W
Moeraki Point ≻	172	45.22 S	170.52 E
Moerbeke, Bel.	50	50.45 N	3.55 E
Moerbeke, Bel.	50	51.10 N	3.56 E
Moerdijk	52	51.43 N	4.38 E
Moerewa	172	35.23 S	174.02 E
Moergestel	52	51.33 N	5.11 E
Moero, Lago → Mweru, Lake ⊜	154	9.00 S	28.45 E
Moers	56	51.27 N	6.37 E
Moersbach ≏	263	51.33 N	6.36 E
Moesa ≏	58	46.13 N	9.03 E
Moffat	44	55.20 N	3.27 W
Moffat Peak ʌ	172	45.02 S	168.07 E
Moffatt	222	31.12 N	97.28 W
Moffatt, Lac ⊜	206	45.34 N	71.19 W
Moffat Water ≏	44	55.18 N	3.25 W
Moffet Point ≻	180	55.26 N	162.32 W
Moffett Field Naval Air Station ■	226	37.24 N	122.03 W
Moffit	198	46.40 N	100.17 W
Mofoluku	273a	6.33 N	3.20 E
Moga	123	30.48 N	75.10 E
Mogadiscio → Muqdisho	144	2.04 N	45.22 E
Mogadishu → Muqdisho	144	2.04 N	45.22 E
Mogadore	214	41.02 N	81.23 W
Mogadore Reservoir ⊜[1]	214	41.04 N	81.21 W
Mogador → Essaouira	148	31.30 N	9.47 W
Mogadouro	34	41.20 N	6.39 W
Mogalakwena ≏	156	23.00 S	28.40 E
Mogalo	152	3.10 N	19.04 E
Mogami ≏	92	38.55 N	139.48 E
Mogan Shan ʌ	106	30.36 N	119.52 E
Mogapinyana	156	22.19 S	27.27 E
Mogaung	110	25.18 N	96.56 E
Mogdy	89	50.35 N	133.51 E
Mogees	285	40.06 N	75.19 W
Møgeltønder	41	54.56 N	8.49 E
Mogenstrup	41	55.11 N	11.53 E
Mogent ≏	266d	41.33 N	2.15 E
Moggio Udinese	64	46.25 N	13.12 E
Mogi, Serra do ⋏	287b	23.47 S	46.20 W
Mogielnica	30	51.42 N	20.43 E
Mogila-Bel'mak, gora ʌ[2]	78	47.20 N	36.35 E
Mogila-Mečetnaja, gora ʌ[2]	83	48.16 N	38.53 E
Mogilev → Mogil'ov	76	53.54 N	30.21 E
Mogilno	30	52.40 N	17.58 E
Mogil'ov, Bela.	76	53.54 N	30.21 E
Mogil'ov, Ukr.	78	48.52 N	34.29 E
Mogil'ov-Podol'skij	78	48.27 N	27.48 E
Mogincual	154	15.35 S	40.25 E
Moglal, Wādī V	140	19.18 N	34.29 E
Moglia	64	44.56 N	10.55 E
Mogliano Veneto	64	45.33 N	12.14 E
Mogoča	88	53.44 N	119.44 E
Mogoča ≏	76	58.00 N	36.26 E
Mogočin	86	57.43 N	83.34 E
Mogod	88	48.24 N	103.00 E
Mogogh	140	8.26 N	31.19 E
Mogojto	88	54.25 N	110.27 E
Mogojtuj	88	51.17 N	114.55 E
Mogok	110	22.55 N	96.30 E
Mogollon Mountains ⋏	200	33.25 N	108.40 W
Mogollon Rim ⫠[4]	200	34.25 N	110.50 W
Mogor	120	32.52 N	67.47 E
Mogorella	71	39.52 N	8.51 E
Mogoro	71	39.41 N	8.47 E
Mogotes	246	6.30 N	72.58 W
Mogotón ʌ	236	13.45 N	86.23 W
Mograt Island I	140	19.30 N	33.15 E
Mogroum	146	11.06 N	15.25 E
Moguer	34	37.16 N	6.50 W
Mogyoród	264c	47.36 N	19.15 E
Mogyoródi-patak ≏	264c	47.36 N	19.05 E
Mogzon	88	51.45 N	111.58 E
Mohács	30	45.59 N	18.42 E
Mohaka	172	39.07 S	177.11 E
Mohaka ≏	172	39.07 S	177.12 E
Mohall	198	48.45 N	101.30 W

Moḥammadābād	128	30.53 N	61.28 E
Mohammedia (Fedala)	148	33.44 N	7.24 W
Mohana	124	25.54 N	77.45 E
Mohangi	154	0.03 N	29.05 E
Mohania	124	25.11 N	83.37 E
Mohanpur, Bngl.	126	23.24 N	90.36 E
Mohanpur, India	126	21.51 N	87.26 E
Mohanpur, India	272a	28.44 N	77.10 E
Mohave, Lake ⊜[1]	204	35.25 N	114.38 W
Mohawk, Mi., U.S.	190	47.18 N	88.21 W
Mohawk, N.Y., U.S.	210	43.00 N	75.00 W
Mohawk ≏	210	42.47 N	73.42 W
Mohawk, East Branch ≏	212	43.22 N	75.28 W
Mohawk, Lake ⊜	276	41.02 N	74.41 W
Mohawk Dam ✦[6]	214	40.20 N	82.05 W
Mohawk Mountain ʌ	207	41.49 N	73.17 W
Mohawk Point ≻	212	42.51 N	79.29 W
Mohe	89	53.29 N	122.19 E
Moheda	26	57.00 N	14.34 E
Mohegan	207	41.28 N	72.06 W
Mohegan Lake	210	41.19 N	73.51 W
Mohelnice	30	49.46 N	16.55 E
Moher, Cliffs of ⫠[4]	48	52.57 N	9.26 W
Mohican ≏	214	40.22 N	82.09 W
Mohican, Black Fork ≏	214	40.35 N	82.17 W
Mohican, Cape ≻	180	60.12 N	167.28 W
Mohican, Clear Fork ≏	214	40.35 N	82.12 W
Mohican, Jerome Fork ≏	214	40.45 N	82.23 W
Mohican, Lake Fork ≏	214	40.27 N	82.12 W
Mohican, Muddy Fork ≏	214	40.45 N	82.08 W
Mohican State Park ♦	214	40.37 N	82.16 W
Mohicanville Dam ✦[6]	214	40.44 N	82.09 W
Mohili ✦[8]	272c	19.06 N	72.53 E
Mohill	48	53.54 N	7.52 W
Mohlakeng	273d	26.13 S	27.42 E
Möhlau	54	51.44 N	12.21 E
Möhlin	58	47.34 N	7.51 E
Möhne ≏	52	51.27 N	7.57 E
Möhnestausee ⊜[1]	52	51.29 N	8.08 E
Mohns Ridge ✧[3]	16	72.30 N	5.00 E
Mohnton	208	40.17 N	75.59 W
Mohnyin	110	24.47 N	96.22 E
Moho ≏	236	16.04 N	88.52 W
Mohokare (Caledon) ≏	158	30.31 S	26.05 E
Moholm	40	58.37 N	14.02 E
Mohon	56	49.45 N	4.44 E
Mohorn	54	51.00 N	13.28 E
Mohoro	154	8.08 S	39.10 E
Möhringen	58	47.57 N	8.46 E
Mohrsville	208	40.28 N	75.59 W
Moi	26	58.28 N	6.32 E
Moiano, It.	68	40.39 N	14.28 E
Moiano, It.	68	41.05 N	14.32 E
Moindou	175f	21.42 S	165.41 E
Moinești	38	46.28 N	26.29 E
Moingbi	140	5.46 N	28.49 E
Moinkum	85	43.48 N	73.41 E
Mointy	86	47.13 N	73.21 E
Moio Alcantara	70	37.54 N	15.03 E
Moiporá	255	16.34 S	50.42 W
Moira	48	54.30 N	6.17 W
Moira ≏	212	44.09 N	77.23 W
Moiraba	250	2.27 S	49.25 W
Moira Lake ⊜	212	44.29 N	77.27 W
Moirans	62	45.20 N	5.34 E
Moirans-en-Montagne	58	46.26 N	5.44 E
Mõisaküla	76	58.06 N	25.11 E
Moisdon	32	47.37 N	1.22 W
Moisejeviči	76	53.13 N	28.17 E
Moisejevka, Ross.	86	58.05 N	76.16 E
Moisejevka, Ukr.	83	49.14 N	39.51 E
Moisejevo Alabuška	76	51.54 N	42.06 E
Moisenay	261	48.34 N	2.44 E
Moisés Ville	252	30.43 S	61.29 W
Moisie	186	50.11 N	66.05 W
Moisie ≏	176	50.11 N	66.05 W
Moisie, Baie de c	186	50.16 N	65.56 W
Moisling ✦[8]	52	53.50 N	10.38 E
Moison Creek ≏	281	42.18 N	82.40 W
Moissac	32	44.06 N	1.05 E
Moïssala	146	8.21 N	17.46 E
Moisselles	261	49.03 N	2.20 E
Moisson	261	49.05 N	1.40 E
Moisson, Forêt de ♦	261	49.03 N	1.39 E
Moissy-Cramayel	261	48.38 N	2.36 E
Moita	34	38.39 N	8.59 W
Moitaco	246	8.01 N	64.21 W
Moivre ≏	56	48.52 N	4.28 E
Mojácar	34	37.08 N	1.51 W
Mojana, Brazo ≏[1]	246	9.02 N	74.46 W
Mojave	228	35.03 N	118.10 W
Mojave ≏	204	35.06 N	116.04 W
Mojave Desert ✦[2]	204	35.00 N	117.00 W
Mojave River Forks Reservoir ⊜[1]	228	34.20 N	117.15 W
Moji	85	38.59 N	74.24 E
Mojiang	102	23.28 N	101.39 E
Mojicuaçu ≏	255	20.53 S	48.10 W
Moji das Cruzes	256	23.31 S	46.11 W
Mojiguaçu	256	22.22 S	46.57 W
Mojimirim	256	22.26 S	46.57 W
Mojjero ≏	74	68.44 N	103.42 E
Mojnalyk	88	51.18 N	95.33 E
Mojo	144	8.36 N	39.07 E
Mojoagung	115a	7.34 S	112.21 E
Mojokerto	115a	7.28 S	112.26 E
Mojosari	115a	7.31 S	112.33 E
Mojstrana	64	46.27 N	13.56 E
Moju	250	1.53 S	48.46 W
Moju ≏	250	1.40 S	48.25 W
Mōka	94	36.26 N	140.01 E
Mokai	172	38.32 S	175.54 E
Mokāma	124	25.24 N	85.55 E
Mokambo	154	12.25 S	28.21 E
Mokane	219	38.40 N	91.52 W
Mokapu Peninsula ≻[1]	229c	21.27 N	157.45 W
Mokaria	152	2.00 N	23.20 E
Mokarta, Castello di ⊥	70	37.48 N	12.45 E
Mokau	172	38.41 S	174.37 E
Mokau ≏	172	38.42 S	174.37 E
Moke	102	30.14 N	100.01 E
Mokelumne ≏	226	38.13 N	121.28 W
Mokelumne, Middle Fork ≏	226	38.22 N	120.37 W
Mokelumne, North Fork ≏	226	38.22 N	120.37 W
Mokelumne, South Fork ≏	226	38.23 N	120.35 W
Mokelumne Aqueduct ≍[1]	226	37.54 N	122.07 W
Mokelumne Hill	226	38.18 N	120.42 W
Mokena	216	41.31 N	87.53 W
Mokhotlong	158	29.22 S	29.02 E
Mokil I[1]	14	6.40 N	159.47 E
Mokimbo	154	6.20 S	28.42 E
Mokino	80	57.27 N	49.11 E
Moklakan	88	54.56 N	118.56 E
Möklinta	40	60.05 N	16.32 E
Moknine	148	35.38 N	10.54 E
Mokochu, Khao ʌ	110	15.56 N	99.06 E
Mokohinau Islands II	172	35.55 S	175.07 E
Mokokchūng	120	26.20 N	94.32 E
Mokolo, Cam.	146	10.45 N	13.48 E
Mokolo, Zaïre	152	1.57 N	18.05 E
Mokolo ≏	156	23.14 S	27.43 E
Mokombe	152	0.14 S	23.48 E
Mokoreta ≏	172	46.21 S	168.51 E
Mokou	273b	4.13 S	15.13 E
Mokpalin	110	17.26 N	96.53 E
Mokp'o	98	34.48 N	126.22 E
Mokraja Jel'muta	80	46.51 N	41.41 E

Mokraja Ol'chovka	80	50.28 N	44.59 E
Mokraja Sura ≏	78	48.19 N	35.09 E
Mokraja Volnovacha ≏	83	47.30 N	37.15 E
Mokrany	78	51.50 N	24.14 E
Mokrisset	34	34.59 N	5.20 W
Mokro-Jelančik	83	47.42 N	38.31 E
Mokrous	80	51.14 N	47.37 E
Mokrousovo	86	55.48 N	66.45 E
Mokrušinskoje	86	57.31 N	93.11 E
Mokryje Jaly ≏	78	48.05 N	36.44 E
Mokryj Gašun	80	46.53 N	42.45 E
Mokryj Jelančik ≏	83	47.08 N	38.20 E
Mokryj Kor	82	54.34 N	37.58 E
Mokša ≏	80	54.44 N	41.53 E
Mokšan	80	53.26 N	44.37 E
Moku	154	2.57 N	29.22 E
Mokuleia	229c	21.35 N	158.09 W
Mokumbusu	152	1.44 N	21.04 E
Mokvin	78	50.57 N	26.48 E
Mokwa	150	9.20 N	5.02 E
Mol	56	51.11 N	5.06 E
Mola di Bari	68	41.04 N	17.05 E
Molale	144	10.08 N	39.42 E
Molalla	224	45.08 N	122.34 W
Molalla ≏	224	45.18 N	122.43 W
Molalla, North Fork ≏	224	45.05 N	122.29 W
Molanda	152	2.28 N	20.48 E
Molango	234	20.53 N	98.46 W
Molanosa	184	54.30 N	105.33 W
Moláoi	38	36.48 N	22.52 E
Molara, Isola I	71	40.52 N	9.43 E
Molaretto	62	45.10 N	7.00 E
Molat, Otok I	36	44.15 N	14.49 E
Molbergen	52	52.51 N	7.55 E
Molčanovka	83	46.52 N	38.37 E
Molčanovo	86	57.35 N	83.48 E
Mold	44	53.10 N	3.08 W
Moldary	86	50.47 N	78.29 E
Moldau → Vltava ≏	30	50.21 N	14.30 E
Moldavia □[9]	38	47.00 N	27.15 E
Moldavia → Moldova □[1]	78	47.00 N	29.00 E
Moldavija → Moldova □[1]	72	47.00 N	29.00 E
Molde	26	62.44 N	7.11 E
Moldotau, chrebet ⋏	85	41.35 N	74.40 E
Moldova □[1], Europe	22	47.00 N	29.00 E
Moldova □[1], Europe	78	47.00 N	29.00 E
Moldova ≏	38	46.54 N	26.58 E
Moldova Nouă	38	44.44 N	21.40 E
Moldoveanu, Vîrful ʌ	38	45.36 N	24.44 E
Môle ≏, Fr.	62	43.15 N	6.32 E
Mole ≏, Eng., U.K.	42	50.57 N	3.54 W
Mole ≏, Eng., U.K.	42	51.24 N	0.21 W
Môle, Cap du ≻	238	19.50 N	73.25 W
Mole Creek	166	41.33 S	146.24 E
Moledet	132	32.35 N	35.26 E
Molega Lake ⊜	186	44.22 N	64.53 W
Mole Game Reserve ✦[4]	150	9.30 N	2.00 W
Molegbe	152	4.14 N	20.53 E
Molenbeek-St.-Jean	50	50.51 N	4.19 E
Molepolole	156	24.25 S	25.30 E
Moléson ʌ	58	46.33 N	7.01 E
Molėtai	76	55.14 N	25.25 E
Mole Valley □[8]	260	51.16 N	0.18 W
Molfetta	68	41.12 N	16.36 E
Molibagu	112	0.23 N	123.59 E
Molières-sur-Cèze	62	44.15 N	4.09 E
Molimiao	89	43.34 N	121.54 E
Molina	252	35.07 S	71.17 W
Molina de Aragón	34	40.51 N	1.53 W
Molina de Segura	34	38.03 N	1.12 W
Molina di Ledro	64	45.56 N	10.46 E
Molinara	68	41.18 N	14.54 E
Moline, Il., U.S.	190	41.30 N	90.30 W
Moline, Ks., U.S.	198	37.21 N	96.18 W
Moline, Mi., U.S.	216	42.44 N	85.39 W
Molinella	64	44.37 N	11.40 E
Molinges	58	46.21 N	5.46 E
Molingguan	106	31.50 N	118.50 E
Molini di Tures (Mühlen)	64	46.54 N	11.56 E
Molinière Point ≻	241k	12.05 N	61.45 W
Molino	194	30.43 N	87.18 W
Molino de Rosas ✦[8]	286a	19.22 N	99.13 W
Molinos	252	25.25 S	66.19 W
Molins de Rei	34	41.25 N	2.01 E
Moliro	154	8.13 S	30.34 E
Molise □[4]	66	41.35 N	14.30 E
Moliterno	68	40.14 N	50.52 E
Mölkau	54	51.20 N	12.26 E
Molkom	40	59.36 N	13.43 E
Möll ≏	64	46.50 N	13.26 E
Mollahasan	130	39.22 N	42.37 E
Mollāhāt	126	22.56 N	89.48 E
Mollakendi	130	38.36 N	39.20 E
Mollaro	64	46.16 N	11.05 E
Möllbrücke	64	46.50 N	13.22 E
Mölle	41	56.17 N	12.29 E
Möllen	263	51.35 N	6.42 E
Möllenbeck, Dtsch.	54	53.17 N	11.44 E
Möllenbeck, Dtsch.	54	53.23 N	13.20 E
Mollendo	248	17.02 S	72.01 W
Möllensee ⊜	264a	52.26 N	13.51 E
Mollepata	248	13.31 S	72.32 W
Moller, Port c	180	55.51 N	160.25 W
Möllersdorf	264b	48.02 N	16.18 E
Mollet del Vallès	266d	41.33 N	2.13 E
Mollia	62	45.49 N	8.02 E
Molliens-Vidame	50	49.53 N	2.01 E
Mollington	262	53.13 N	2.55 W
Mollis	58	47.05 N	9.04 E
Mölln, Dtsch.	54	53.37 N	10.41 E
Molln, Öst.	61	47.53 N	14.15 E
Mollösund	26	58.04 N	11.28 E
Mollusk	208	37.43 N	76.32 W
Molly Ann Brook ≏	276	40.55 N	74.11 W
Mölnbo	40	59.03 N	17.25 E
Mölndal	26	57.39 N	12.01 E
Mölnlycke	26	57.39 N	12.09 E
Mölntorp	40	59.33 N	16.15 E
Molocaboc Island I	116	10.58 N	123.34 E
Moločansk	78	47.12 N	35.36 E
Molochio	68	38.18 N	16.02 E
Moločnaja ≏	78	46.42 N	35.20 E
Moločnoje	76	59.17 N	39.41 E
Moločnoje, ozero ⊜	78	46.30 N	35.20 E
Molócuè ≏	154	17.03 S	38.52 E
Molodečno	76	54.19 N	26.49 E
Molodežnaja ʊ[3]	9	67.35 S	46.35 E
Molodi	82	55.17 N	37.31 E
Molodo	150	14.14 N	6.02 W
Molodogvardejsk	83	48.20 N	39.40 E
Molodoj Tud	76	56.26 N	33.36 E
Molod'ožnyj	89	50.23 N	136.48 E
Mologa ≏	76	58.50 N	37.11 E
Molokai I	229a	21.07 N	157.00 W
Molokai Fracture Zone ✧	14	23.00 N	148.00 W
Molokai Fracture Zone ✧	16	23.00 N	130.00 W
Molokča ≏	82	56.15 N	38.45 E
Molokini I	229a	20.38 N	156.30 W
Molokovo, Ross.	76	58.10 N	36.45 E
Molokovo, Ross.	82	55.34 N	37.52 E
Moloma ≏	24	58.20 N	48.28 E
Molong	166	33.06 S	148.52 E
Molonglo ≏	171b	35.15 S	148.58 E
Molopo ≏	156	28.30 S	20.13 E
Molotkoviči	78	52.07 N	25.56 E
Molotov → Perm'	86	58.00 N	56.15 E
Molotovsk → Severodvinsk	24	64.34 N	39.50 E
Molou	146	13.42 N	21.44 E
Moloundou	152	2.03 N	15.10 E
Molowaie	152	5.47 S	23.20 E

≏ River	Fluß	Río	Rivière	Rio
≍ Canal	Kanal	Canal	Canal	Canal
ʟ Waterfall, Rapids	Wasserfall, Stromschnellen	Cascada, Rápidos	Chute d'eau, Rapides	Cascata, Rápidos
ʯ Strait	Meeresstraße	Estrecho	Détroit	Estreito
c Bay, Gulf	Bucht, Golf	Bahía, Golfo	Baie, Golfe	Baía, Golfo
⊜ Lake, Lakes	See, Seen	Lago, Lagos	Lac, Lacs	Lago, Lagos
≚ Swamp	Sumpf	Pantano	Marais	Pântano
⌑ Ice Features, Glacier	Eis- und Gletscherformen	Accidentes Glaciales	Formes glaciaires	Acidentes glaciares
⊤ Other Hydrographic Features	Andere Hydrographische Objekte	Otros Elementos Hidrográficos	Autres données hydrographiques	Outros acidentes hidrográficos

✧ Submarine Features	Untermeerische Objekte	Accidentes Submarinos	Formes de relief sous-marin	Acidentes submarinos
□ Political Unit	Politische Einheit	Unidad Politica	Entité politique	Unidade política
ʊ Cultural Institution	Kulturelle Institution	Institución Cultural	Institution culturelle	Instituição cultural
⊥ Historical Site	Historische Stätte	Sitio Histórico	Site historique	Sitio histórico
♦ Recreational Site	Erholungs- und Ferienort	Sitio de Recreo	Centre de loisirs	Area de Lazer
⊠ Airport	Flughafen	Aeropuerto	Aéroport	Aeroporto
■ Military Installation	Militäranlage	Instalación Militar	Installation militaire	Instalação militar
✦ Miscellaneous	Verschiedenes	Misceláneo	Divers	Diversos

Moloy 58 47.32 N 4.55 E
Molsheim 58 48.32 N 7.29 E
Molson Lake ⊜ 184 54.12 N 96.45 W
Molteno 158 31.22 S 26.22 E
Moltrasio 58 45.52 N 9.05 E
Molu, Pulau I 164 6.45 S 131.33 E
Moluca, Mar de la → Maluku, Laut ≂[2] 108 0.00 125.00 E
Molucas, Islas → Maluku II 108 2.00 S 128.00 E
Molucca Sea → Maluku, Laut ≂[2] 108 0.00 125.00 E
Moluccas → Maluku II 108 2.00 S 128.00 E
Molukken → Maluku II 108 2.00 S 128.00 E
Molumbo 154 15.27 S 30.15 E
Molundo 116 7.56 N 124.23 E
Moluques → Maluku II 108 2.00 S 128.00 E
Molveno, Lago di ⊜ 64 46.08 N 10.57 E
Molvoticy 76 57.25 N 32.20 E
Molžaninovo 82 55.56 N 37.22 E
Moma, Moç. 154 16.44 S 39.14 E
Moma, Zaïre 152 1.36 S 23.57 E
Moma ≏ 74 66.26 N 143.06 E
Momanga 156 18.12 S 21.42 E
Momats ≏ 164 5.20 S 137.47 E
Momax 234 21.56 N 103.19 W
Momba ≏ 154 8.28 S 32.40 E
Mombaça 250 5.45 S 39.38 W
Mombaça, Corrego ≏ 287b 23.46 S 46.47 W
Mombachito, Cerro ∧ 236 12.24 N 85.34 W
Mombacho, Volcán ∧[1] 236 11.50 N 85.58 W
Mombango 152 1.45 N 24.26 E
Mombaruzzo 62 44.46 N 8.27 E
Mombasa 154 4.03 S 39.40 E
Mombetsu 92a 44.21 N 143.22 E
Mombo 154 4.53 S 38.17 E
Mombongo 152 1.39 N 23.09 E
Momboyo ≏ 152 0.16 S 19.00 E
Mombuey 34 42.02 N 6.20 W
Mombum 164 8.23 S 138.51 E
Momčilgrad 38 41.32 N 25.25 E
Momence 216 41.10 N 87.39 W
Momfafa, Tanjung › 164 0.18 S 131.20 E
Momi 175g 17.55 S 177.17 E
Momignies 50 50.02 N 4.10 E
Mommark 41 54.55 N 10.03 E
Mommenheim 56 48.45 N 7.39 E
Momo 152 1.52 N 11.48 E
Momotombo, Volcán ∧[1] 236 12.26 N 86.33 W
Momozaka 270 34.51 N 135.02 E
Mompog Island I 116 13.31 N 122.11 E
Mompog Pass ʮ 116 13.34 N 122.13 E
Mompono 152 0.04 N 21.48 E
Mompós 246 9.14 N 74.26 W
Momskij chrebet ⋏ 74 66.00 N 146.00 E
Mon 110 18.31 N 96.38 E
Mon □[8] 110 17.30 N 97.00 E
Møn I 41 55.00 N 12.20 E
Mon ≏ 110 20.20 N 94.54 E
Mona 200 39.48 N 111.51 W
Mona, Canal de la ʮ 238 18.30 N 67.45 W
Mona, Isla de I 238 18.05 N 67.54 W
Mona, Punta › 236 9.38 N 82.37 W
Monaca 214 40.41 N 80.16 W
Monach, Sound of ʮ 46 57.34 N 7.35 W
Monach Islands II 46 57.31 N 7.40 W
Monachovo 83 48.09 N 38.07 E
Monaci, Fiume dei ≏ 70 37.24 N 14.48 E
Monaco 62 43.42 N 7.23 E
Monaco □[1], Europe 22 43.45 N 7.25 E
Monaco □[1], Europe 62 43.45 N 7.25 E
Monadhliath Mountains ⋏ 46 57.10 N 4.00 W
Monadnock Mountain ∧ 207 42.52 N 72.07 W
Monagas □[3] 246 9.20 N 63.00 W
Monaghan 48 54.15 N 6.58 W
Monaghan □[6] 48 54.10 N 7.00 W
Monagrillo 236 7.59 N 80.26 W
Monahans 196 31.35 N 102.53 W
Monahans Draw V 196 31.55 N 101.46 W
Monahans Sandhills State Park ♠ 196 31.38 N 102.50 W
Monakino 89 43.24 N 133.29 E
Mona Lake ⊜ 216 43.11 N 86.17 W
Monamolin 48 52.33 N 6.20 W
Monango 198 46.10 N 98.35 W
Monapo 154 14.57 S 40.17 E
Monapo ≏ 154 15.07 S 40.33 E
Mona Quimbundo 152 9.55 S 19.58 E
Monar, Loch ⊜ 46 57.25 N 5.06 W
Monarch 192 34.43 N 81.35 W
Monarch Mountain ∧ 182 51.54 N 125.53 W
Monarch Pass)(200 38.30 N 106.19 W
Monaro Range ⋏ 171b 36.22 S 149.03 E
Monarto South 168b 35.08 S 139.08 E
Monaš 80 46.58 N 50.36 E
Monashee Mountains ⋏ 182 50.30 N 118.30 W
Monashee Provincial Park ♠ 182 50.28 N 118.11 W
Monash University ♥[2] 274b 37.55 S 145.08 E
Monasterace 68 38.27 N 16.33 E
Monasterevin 48 53.07 N 7.02 W
Monasterolo di Savigliano 62 44.40 N 7.37 E
Monastir, It. 71 39.23 N 9.02 E
Monastir, Tun. 148 35.47 N 10.50 E
Monastir □[8] 148 35.15 N 10.45 E
Monastir → Bitola 38 41.01 N 21.20 E
Monastyrišče 78 49.00 N 29.49 E
Monastyriska 78 49.06 N 25.11 E
Monastyrščina 76 54.21 N 31.50 E
Monatélé 152 4.16 N 11.12 E
Mona Vale 170 33.41 S 151.18 E
Monbulk 274b 37.52 S 145.25 E
Monbulk Creek ≏ 274b 37.54 S 145.15 E
Moncada 116 15.44 N 120.34 E
Moncalieri 62 45.00 N 7.41 E
Moncalvo 62 45.03 N 8.16 E
Monção, Bra. 250 3.30 S 45.15 W
Monção, Port. 34 42.05 N 8.29 W
Monceau-sur-Sambre 50 50.25 N 4.22 E
Mončegorsk 24 67.54 N 32.58 E
Mönchdorf 61 48.21 N 14.48 E
Mönchengladbach 56 51.12 N 6.28 E
Mönchengladbach, Flughafen ⊠ 263 51.14 N 6.29 E
Mönchhof 61 47.52 N 16.56 E
Monchique 34 37.19 N 8.33 W
Mönchweiler 58 48.06 N 8.25 E
Moncks Corner 192 33.11 N 80.00 W
Monclova 232 26.54 N 101.25 W
Moncontour 32 48.21 N 2.39 W
Moncoutant 32 46.43 N 0.35 W
Moncton 186 46.06 N 64.47 W
Mondaí 252 27.05 S 53.25 W
Mondaino 66 43.51 N 12.41 E
Mondavio 66 43.40 N 12.58 E
Monday ≏ 252 25.33 S 54.41 W
Mondego ≏ 34 40.09 N 8.52 W
Mondego, Cabo › 34 40.11 N 8.55 W
Mondello 70 38.13 N 13.20 E
Mondeodo 112 3.33 S 122.12 E
Mondeor 273d 26.17 S 28.00 E
Mondimbi 152 1.43 N 22.58 E
Mondo, Tan. 154 4.59 S 35.54 E
Mondo, Tchad 146 13.47 N 15.32 E
Mondolè, Monte ∧ 62 44.13 N 7.46 E
Mondolfo 66 43.45 N 13.06 E
Mondombe 152 0.53 S 22.45 E
Mondoñedo 34 43.26 N 7.22 W
Mondorf-les-Bains 56 49.31 N 6.16 E
Mondoro 150 14.40 N 1.57 W
Mondoubleau 50 47.59 N 0.54 E
Mondovi 190 44.34 N 91.40 W
Mondragon, Fr. 62 44.14 N 4.43 E
Mondragon, Pil. 116 12.31 N 124.45 E
Mondragone 68 41.07 N 13.53 E
Mondrain Island I 162 34.08 S 122.15 E
Mondsee 64 47.52 N 13.21 E
Mondsee ⊜ 64 47.49 N 13.23 E
Monds Island I 285 39.50 N 75.19 W
Mondy 88 51.40 N 100.59 E
Monee 216 41.25 N 87.45 W
Moneglia 62 44.14 N 9.30 E
Monemvasía 38 36.41 N 23.03 E
Monero 200 36.54 N 106.52 W
Moneron, ostrov I 89 46.17 N 141.15 E
Monesiglio 62 44.28 N 8.07 E
Monessen 214 40.08 N 79.53 W
Monesterio 34 38.05 N 6.16 W
Monestier-de-Clermont 62 44.54 N 5.38 E
Monetnyj 86 57.03 N 60.53 E
Monett 194 36.55 N 93.55 W
Monette 194 35.53 N 90.20 W
Money Creek ≏ 216 40.40 N 88.58 W
Moneygall 48 52.53 N 7.57 W
Moneymore 48 54.42 N 6.40 W
Monfalcone 64 45.49 N 13.32 E
Monferrato □[9] 62 44.55 N 8.05 E
Monflanquin 32 44.32 N 0.46 E
Monforte 34 39.03 N 7.26 W
Monforte de Lemos 34 42.31 N 7.30 W
Monforte San Giorgio 70 38.09 N 15.23 E
Monfort Heights 218 39.12 N 84.37 W
Monga 152 4.12 N 22.49 E
Mongaguá 256 24.06 S 46.37 W
Mongai-Musenge 152 4.04 S 19.34 E
Mongala ≏ 152 1.53 N 19.46 E
Mongalla 154 5.12 N 31.46 E
Mongalla Game Reserve ◆[4] 154 5.12 N 31.33 E
Mongandjo 152 1.21 N 24.20 E
Mongarlowe ≏ 170 35.15 S 149.52 E
Mongat 266d 41.28 N 2.17 E
Mongaup ≏ 210 41.25 N 74.45 W
Mongaup Valley 210 41.40 N 74.47 W
Mongbwalu 154 1.57 N 30.02 E
Mongbyŏn-ni 271b 37.40 N 126.44 E
Mong Cai 110 21.32 N 107.58 E
Monge ∧ 266c 38.46 N 9.26 W
Monger, Îles II 186 51.05 N 58.45 W
Mongeri 150 8.19 N 11.44 W
Mongers Lake ⊜ 162 29.15 S 117.05 E
Monggon Qulu 89 48.35 N 119.49 E
Monggŭmp'o 98 38.09 N 124.47 E
Möng Hai 110 20.46 N 99.49 E
Möng Hawm 110 23.51 N 98.20 E
Monghidoro 66 44.13 N 11.19 E
Möng Hpāyak 110 20.53 N 99.54 E
Möng Hsat 110 20.32 N 99.15 E
Monghyr → Munger 124 25.23 N 86.28 E
Mongi ≏ 164 6.35 S 147.35 E
Mongiana 68 38.31 N 16.19 E
Mongibello → Etna, Monte ∧[1] 70 37.46 N 15.00 E
Mongiuffi 70 37.55 N 15.17 E
Möng Küng 110 21.36 N 97.32 E
Möng Ma 110 21.37 N 99.54 E
Möng Mit 110 23.07 N 96.41 E
Möng Nai 110 20.31 N 97.52 E
Möng Nawng 110 21.39 N 98.08 E
Mongo, Tchad 146 12.11 N 18.42 E
Mongo, In., U.S. 216 41.41 N 85.17 W
Mongo ≏ 150 9.34 N 12.11 W
Mongoj 88 53.57 N 113.50 E
Mongol Altajn nuruu ⋏ 90 46.30 N 93.00 E
Mongol Ard Uls → Mongolia □[1] 90 46.00 N 105.00 E
Mongolei → Mongolia □[1] 90 46.00 N 105.00 E
Mongol els ◆[2] 88 47.45 N 94.30 E
Mongolia (Mongol Ard Uls) □[1] 90 46.00 N 105.00 E
Mongolie → Mongolia □[1] 90 46.00 N 105.00 E
Mongomo 152 1.38 N 11.19 E
Möngön Mor't 88 48.11 N 108.29 E
Mongororo 146 12.01 N 22.28 E
Mongoumba 152 3.38 N 18.36 E
Möng Pai 110 19.44 N 97.05 E
Möng Pan 110 20.19 N 98.22 E
Möng Pawn 110 20.49 N 97.28 E
Möng Ping 110 22.22 N 99.02 E
Mongpong ≏ 116 12.44 N 120.48 E
Mongrando 62 45.31 N 8.00 E
Möng Si 110 23.40 N 98.23 E
Mong Tung Hang 271d 22.20 N 114.02 E
Mongu 152 15.15 S 23.09 E
Môngua 152 16.43 S 15.23 E
Monguelfo (Welsberg) 64 46.45 N 12.06 E
Monguno 146 12.40 N 13.38 E
Möng Yai 110 22.25 N 98.02 E
Möng Yawng 110 21.11 N 100.22 E
Monheim, Dtsch. 56 48.50 N 10.51 E
Monheim, Dtsch. 56 51.05 N 6.52 E
Moniaive 44 55.12 N 3.55 W
Mönichkirchen 61 47.31 N 16.02 E
Monico 190 45.34 N 89.09 W
Monida Pass)(202 44.33 N 112.18 W
Mon Idée 50 49.53 N 4.23 E
Monie 152 4.00 S 17.22 E
Monie Bay ⊂ 208 38.13 N 75.51 W
Monie Creek ≏ 208 38.14 N 75.50 W
Monifieth 46 56.29 N 2.49 W
Monimail 46 56.18 N 3.08 W
Moninger 214 40.14 N 80.13 W
Monino 82 55.50 N 38.11 E
Moniquirá 246 5.52 N 73.36 W
Mõniste 76 57.35 N 26.33 E
Monistrol-d'Allier 62 44.57 N 3.38 E
Monistrol-sur-Loire 62 45.17 N 4.10 E
Monitor Range ⋏ 204 38.45 N 116.30 W
Monitor Valley V 204 39.00 N 116.40 W
Monívea 48 53.23 N 8.43 W
Monjolo 256 22.49 S 42.57 W
Monk, Pointe › 275a 45.29 N 73.57 W
Monkayo 116 7.50 N 126.03 E
Mönkebude 54 53.46 N 13.57 E
Monken Hadley ◆[8] 260 51.40 N 0.11 W
Monkey Bay 154 14.05 S 34.55 E
Monkey River 236 16.22 N 88.29 W
Mońki 30 53.24 N 22.49 E
Monkira 166 24.49 S 140.34 E
Monkoto 152 1.38 S 20.39 E
Monks Heath 262 53.16 N 2.14 W
Monkton 212 43.35 N 81.05 W
Monmouth, Wales, U.K. 42 51.50 N 2.43 W
Monmouth, Il., U.S. 190 40.54 N 90.38 W
Monmouth, In., U.S. 216 40.52 N 84.57 W
Monmouth, Or., U.S. 202 44.50 N 123.13 W
Monmouth □[6] 208 40.16 N 74.17 W
Monmouth Beach 276 40.19 N 73.58 W
Monmouth Hills 276 40.24 N 74.00 W
Monmouth Junction 208 40.22 N 74.32 W
Monmouth Mountain ∧ 182 51.00 N 123.47 W
Monnickendam 52 52.27 N 5.02 E
Monnow ≏ 42 51.48 N 2.42 W
Mono □[5] 150 6.45 N 1.50 E
Mono □[6] 226 38.18 N 119.22 W
Mono ≏ 150 6.17 N 1.51 E
Mono, Caño ≏ 246 4.25 N 67.47 W
Mono, Punta › 236 11.36 N 83.39 W
Monobe 96 33.42 N 133.53 E
Monobe ≏ 96 33.32 N 133.41 E
Monocacy ≏ 208 39.13 N 77.27 W
Monocacy Station 208 40.16 N 75.46 W
Monogarovo 82 54.42 N 38.45 E
Mono Island I 175e 7.21 S 155.34 E
Mono Lake ⊜ 204 38.00 N 119.00 W
Monolith 228 35.07 N 118.22 W
Monomoy Island I 207 41.35 N 69.59 W
Monomoy Point › 207 41.33 N 70.02 W
Monon 216 40.52 N 86.52 W
Monona, Ia., U.S. 190 43.03 N 91.23 W
Monona, Wi., U.S. 216 43.03 N 89.20 W
Monona, Lake ⊜ 216 43.03 N 89.22 W
Monongahela 214 40.12 N 79.55 W
Monongahela ≏ 188 40.27 N 80.00 W
Monongahela Brook ≏ 285 39.47 N 75.09 W
Monopoli 68 40.57 N 17.19 E
Monor 30 47.21 N 19.27 E
Mono Road Station 275b 43.51 N 79.51 W
Monòver 34 38.26 N 0.50 W
Monowai, Lake ⊜ 172 45.52 S 167.27 E
Monponsett 207 42.01 N 70.50 W
Monponsett Pond ⊜ 283 42.01 N 70.51 W
Monreal 34 42.42 N 1.30 W
Monreal del Campo 34 40.47 N 1.21 W
Monreale 70 38.05 N 13.17 E
Monreale, Castello di ⊥ 71 39.38 N 8.49 E
Monroe, Ct., U.S. 207 41.19 N 73.12 W
Monroe, Fl., U.S. 220 25.52 N 81.06 W
Monroe, Ga., U.S. 192 33.47 N 83.42 W
Monroe, In., U.S. 216 40.44 N 84.56 W
Monroe, Ia., U.S. 190 41.31 N 93.06 W
Monroe, La., U.S. 194 32.30 N 92.07 W
Monroe, Mi., U.S. 214 41.54 N 83.23 W
Monroe, Ne., U.S. 198 41.28 N 97.35 W
Monroe, N.J., U.S. 276 41.06 N 74.38 W
Monroe, N.Y., U.S. 210 41.19 N 74.11 W
Monroe, N.C., U.S. 192 34.59 N 80.32 W
Monroe, Oh., U.S. 218 39.26 N 84.21 W
Monroe, Or., U.S. 202 44.18 N 123.17 W
Monroe, Ut,. U.S. 200 38.37 N 112.07 W
Monroe, Va., U.S. 192 37.30 N 79.07 W
Monroe, Wa., U.S. 224 47.51 N 121.58 W
Monroe, Wi., U.S. 190 42.36 N 89.38 W
Monroe □[6], Fl., U.S. 220 25.10 N 81.10 W
Monroe □[6], Il., U.S. 219 38.20 N 90.09 W
Monroe □[6], In., U.S. 218 39.10 N 86.26 W
Monroe □[6], Mi., U.S. 216 41.55 N 83.26 W
Monroe □[6], Mo., U.S. 219 39.30 N 92.00 W
Monroe □[6], N.Y., U.S. 210 43.10 N 77.36 W
Monroe □[6], Pa., U.S. 210 40.59 N 75.12 W
Monroe, Lake ⊜ 220 28.52 N 81.16 W
Monroe Bridge 207 42.43 N 72.56 W
Monroe Center, Ct., U.S. 207 41.20 N 73.12 W
Monroe Center, Il., U.S. 216 42.06 N 89.00 W
Monroe City, In., U.S. 194 38.36 N 87.21 W
Monroe City, Mo., U.S. 219 39.39 N 91.44 W
Monroe City, Tx., U.S. 222 29.47 N 94.35 W
Monroe Lake ⊜[1] 218 39.05 N 86.25 W
Monroe Manor 216 41.36 N 86.40 W
Monroeton 210 41.43 N 76.30 W
Monroeville, Al., U.S. 194 31.31 N 87.19 W
Monroeville, In., U.S. 216 40.58 N 84.52 W
Monroeville, N.J., U.S. 208 39.37 N 75.09 W
Monroeville, Oh., U.S. 214 41.14 N 82.41 W
Monroeville, Pa., U.S. 214 40.26 N 79.47 W
Monroeville Mall ◆[9] 279b 40.26 N 79.48 W
Monrovia, Liber. 150 6.18 N 10.47 W
Monrovia, Ca., U.S. 228 34.08 N 117.59 W
Monrovia, In., U.S. 218 39.34 N 86.28 W
Monrovia Mountain Park ♠ 280 34.10 N 118.10 W
Monrovia Peak ∧ 280 34.13 N 117.58 W
Mons (Bergen), Bel. 50 50.27 N 3.56 E
Mons, Fr. 62 43.41 N 6.43 E
Monschau 56 50.33 N 6.14 E
Monse 112 4.07 S 123.15 E
Monsefú 248 6.52 S 79.52 W
Monselice 64 45.14 N 11.45 E
Monsenhor Hipólito 250 6.59 S 41.07 W
Monsenhor Paulo 256 21.46 S 45.33 W
Monsenhor Tabosa 250 4.47 S 40.04 W
Monserrato 71 39.15 N 9.08 E
Monsey 210 41.06 N 74.04 W
Monsheim, Dtsch. 56 49.38 N 8.12 E
Mönsheim, Dtsch. 56 48.52 N 8.52 E
Møns Klint ≗[4] 41 54.58 N 12.33 E
Monsols 58 46.13 N 4.31 E
Monson, Me., U.S. 188 45.17 N 69.30 W
Monson, Ma., U.S. 207 42.06 N 72.19 W
Monster 52 52.02 N 4.10 E
Mönsterås 26 57.02 N 16.26 E
Monsummano Terme 66 43.52 N 10.49 E
Montà 62 44.48 N 7.57 E
Montabaur 56 50.26 N 7.50 E
Montabaur □[5] 56 50.30 N 7.40 E
Montafon V 58 47.02 N 9.57 E
Montagano 66 41.39 N 14.40 E
Montagnana 64 45.14 N 11.28 E
Montagnareale 70 38.07 N 14.57 E
Montagne d'Ambre, Parque National de la ♠ 157b 12.40 S 49.05 E
Montagnola ⋏ 66 43.17 N 11.11 E
Montagrier 32 45.16 N 0.29 E
Montagu 158 33.45 S 20.08 E
Montague, P.E., Can. 186 46.10 N 62.39 W
Montague, Ca., U.S. 204 41.43 N 122.31 W
Montague, Ma., U.S. 207 42.32 N 72.32 W
Montague, Mi., U.S. 190 43.25 N 86.21 W
Montague, Tx., U.S. 196 33.40 N 97.43 W
Montague, Isla I 232 31.45 N 114.48 W
Montague City 207 42.35 N 72.35 W
Montague Island I 180 60.00 N 147.30 W
Montague Peak ∧ 180 60.15 N 147.01 W
Montagu Island I 18 58.25 S 26.20 W
Montaigle, Château de ⊥ 56 50.18 N 4.49 E
Montaigu 32 46.59 N 1.19 W
Montaigut-en-Combraille 32 46.11 N 2.48 E
Montainville 261 48.53 N 1.52 E
Montaione 66 43.33 N 10.55 E
Montaj-Taš 85 42.06 N 68.58 E
Montalba 222 31.53 N 95.38 W
Montalbán 34 40.50 N 0.48 W
Montalbancito 286c 10.28 N 66.59 W
Montalbano Elicona 70 38.02 N 15.01 E
Montalbano Ionico 68 40.17 N 16.34 E
Montalcino 66 43.03 N 11.29 E
Montaldo di Cosola 62 44.40 N 9.11 E
Montale 66 43.56 N 11.01 E
Montalegre 34 41.49 N 7.48 W
Montalet-le-Bois 261 49.03 N 1.50 E
Montalieu-Vercieu 62 45.49 N 5.24 E
Montallegro 70 37.23 N 13.21 E
Mont Alto 208 39.50 N 77.33 W
Montalto ∧ 68 38.10 N 15.55 E
Montalto delle Marche 66 42.59 N 13.36 E
Montalto di Castro 66 42.21 N 11.37 E
Montalto Ligure 62 43.56 N 7.51 E
Montalto Uffugo 68 39.25 N 16.10 E
Montalvin Manor 226 37.59 N 122.21 W
Montalvo 228 34.15 N 119.12 W
Montana, Schw. 58 46.18 N 7.29 E
Montana, Ak., U.S. 180 62.05 N 150.04 W
Montana □[3], U.S. 178 47.00 N 110.00 W
Montana □[3], U.S. 202 47.00 N 110.00 W
Montana de Oro State Park ♠ 226 35.15 N 120.50 W
Montana Indian Reserve ◆[4] 182 52.43 N 113.25 W
Montanaro 62 45.14 N 7.51 E
Montánchez 34 39.13 N 6.09 W
Montandon 210 40.58 N 76.51 W
Montanha 255 18.08 S 40.21 W
Montano Antilia 68 40.10 N 15.22 E
Montara 226 37.33 N 122.31 W
Montara Beach ♠ 282 37.33 N 122.31 W
Montara Mountain ⋏ 282 37.32 N 122.27 W
Montargil 34 39.05 N 8.10 W
Montargis 50 48.00 N 2.45 E
Montataire 50 49.16 N 2.26 E
Montauban 32 44.01 N 1.21 E
Montauban, Lac ⊜ 206 46.52 N 72.10 W
Montauban-les-Mines 206 46.50 N 72.20 W
Montauk 207 41.02 N 71.57 W
Montauk, Lake ⊜ 207 41.04 N 71.55 W
Montauk Point › 207 41.04 N 71.52 W
Montauroux 62 43.37 N 6.46 E
Monta Vista 226 37.19 N 122.03 W
Montazzoli 66 41.57 N 14.26 E
Montbard 50 47.37 N 4.20 E
Montbarrey 58 47.01 N 5.39 E
Montbazon 50 47.17 N 0.43 E
Montbéliard 58 47.31 N 6.48 E
Mont Belvieu 222 29.50 N 94.53 W
Montbenoît 58 46.59 N 6.28 E
Montblanc 34 41.22 N 1.10 E
Mont Blanc, Tunnel du ◆[5] 58 45.50 N 6.53 E
Mont-Bonvillers 56 49.20 N 5.51 E
Montbovon 58 46.29 N 7.03 E
Montbozon 58 47.28 N 6.16 E
Montbrison 62 45.36 N 4.03 E
Montbron 32 45.40 N 0.30 E
Montbronn 56 48.59 N 7.19 E
Montcada i Reixas 266d 41.29 N 2.11 E
Montcalm □[6] 206 46.20 N 74.20 W
Montceau-les-Mines 58 46.40 N 4.22 E
Montcenis 58 46.47 N 4.23 E
Mont Cenis, Col du)(62 45.15 N 6.54 E
Mont Cenis, Lac du ⊜ 62 45.14 N 6.55 E
Montcevelles, Lac ⊜ 186 51.07 N 60.38 W
Montchanin, Fr. 58 46.45 N 4.27 E
Montchanin, De., U.S. 285 39.47 N 75.35 W
Montchauvet 261 48.54 N 1.38 E
Montclair, Ca., U.S. 228 34.06 N 117.41 W
Montclair, N.J., U.S. 210 40.49 N 74.12 W
Montclair State College ♥[2] 276 40.51 N 74.12 W
Mont Clare 285 40.08 N 75.30 W
Montcornet 50 49.41 N 4.01 E
Montdale 210 41.32 N 75.37 W
Mont-de-Marsan 32 43.53 N 0.30 W
Montdidier 50 49.39 N 2.34 E
Mont-Dore 175f 22.16 S 166.34 E
Monte, Castel del ⊥ 68 41.05 N 16.16 E
Monte, Laguna del ⊜, Arg. 252 37.00 S 62.28 W
Monte, Laguna del ⊜, Arg. 258 35.28 S 58.49 W
Montea ∧ 68 39.40 N 15.57 E
Monte Adone, Galleria di ◆[5] 64 44.21 N 11.25 E
Monteagle 194 35.15 N 85.50 W
Monteagudo 248 19.49 S 63.59 W
Monte Albán ⊥ 234 17.02 N 96.45 W
Monte Alegre, Bra. 250 2.01 S 54.04 W
Monte Alegre, Bra. 250 6.04 S 35.20 W
Monte Alegre de Goiás 255 13.14 S 47.10 W
Monte Alegre de Minas 255 18.52 S 48.52 W
Monte Alegre de Sergipe 250 10.02 S 37.33 W
Monte Alegre do Piauí 250 9.46 S 45.18 W
Monte Alegre do Sul 256 22.40 S 46.41 W
Monte Azul 255 15.09 S 42.53 W
Monte Azul Paulista 255 20.55 S 48.38 W
Montebello, P.Q., Can. 206 45.39 N 74.56 W
Montebello, It. 62 45.00 N 9.06 E
Montebello, P.R. 240m 18.22 N 66.31 W
Montebello, Ca., U.S. 228 34.00 N 118.06 W
Montebello Iónico 68 37.59 N 15.45 E
Monte Bello Islands II 162 20.25 S 115.32 E
Montebello Vicentino 64 45.27 N 11.23 E
Montebelluna 64 45.47 N 12.03 E
Monte Belo 256 21.20 S 46.23 W
Montebruno 62 44.31 N 9.15 E
Monte Buey 252 32.55 S 62.27 W
Montecalvo Irpino 68 41.11 N 15.02 E
Monte Campatri 267a 41.48 N 12.44 E
Montecarlo 252 26.34 S 54.47 W
Monte Carlo ◆[8] 62 43.44 N 7.25 E
Monte Carmelo 255 18.43 S 47.29 W
Montecarotto 66 43.31 N 13.04 E
Monte Caseros 252 30.15 S 57.39 W
Montecassiano 66 43.21 N 13.26 E
Montecassino, Abbazia di ♥[1] 66 41.29 N 13.48 E
Montecastrilli 66 42.39 N 12.29 E
Montecatini-Terme 66 43.53 N 10.46 E
Monte Cavallo 66 42.59 N 13.00 E
Montecchio 66 43.51 N 12.46 E
Montecchio Emilia 64 44.42 N 10.27 E
Montecchio Maggiore 64 45.30 N 11.24 E
Montecelio 66 42.01 N 12.44 E
Montechiaro d'Asti 62 45.01 N 8.07 E
Montechiarugolo 64 44.42 N 10.25 E
Monte Chingolo ◆[8] 288 34.45 S 58.20 W
Monteciccardo 66 43.49 N 12.48 E
Montecilfone 66 41.54 N 14.50 E
Montecillos, Cordillera de ⋏ 236 14.25 N 87.51 W
Montecito 204 34.26 N 119.37 W
Monte Comán 252 34.36 S 67.54 W
Montecorice 68 40.14 N 14.59 E
Montecorvino Pugliano 68 40.41 N 14.57 E
Montecorvino Rovella 68 40.42 N 14.59 E
Montecosaro 66 43.19 N 13.37 E
Monte Creek 182 50.39 N 119.57 W
Montecreto 64 44.14 N 10.41 E
Montecristi, Ec. 246 1.03 S 80.40 W
Monte Cristi, Rep. Dom. 238 19.52 N 71.39 W
Monte Cristo 248 14.43 S 61.14 W
Montecristo, Isola di I 36 42.20 N 10.19 E
Montecuccolo ♥[1] 64 44.19 N 10.50 E
Montedinove 66 42.58 N 13.35 E
Monte di Procida 68 40.48 N 14.03 E
Monte do Carmo 250 10.45 S 48.07 W
Montedoro 70 37.27 N 13.49 E
Monte Escobedo 234 22.18 N 103.35 W
Monte Estoril 266c 38.42 N 9.24 W
Montefalcione 68 40.58 N 14.53 E
Montefalco 66 42.54 N 12.39 E
Montefalcone di Val Fortore 68 41.20 N 15.00 E
Montefano 66 43.25 N 13.26 E
Montefeltro ◆[1] 66 43.50 N 12.15 E
Montefiascone 66 42.32 N 12.02 E
Montefiorino 64 44.22 N 10.37 E
Monteforte d'Alpone 64 45.25 N 11.17 E
Monteforte Irpino 68 40.54 N 14.42 E
Montefrío 34 37.19 N 4.01 W
Montegallo 66 42.50 N 13.19 E
Montegiordano 68 40.02 N 16.32 E
Montegiorgio 66 43.08 N 13.32 E
Monte Giovi, Passo di (Jaufen Pass))(64 46.50 N 11.19 E
Montego Bay 241q 18.28 N 77.55 W
Montegranaro 66 43.14 N 13.38 E
Monte Grande 252 30.06 S 70.31 W
Monte Grimano 66 43.52 N 12.29 E
Montegrotto Terme 64 45.19 N 11.46 E
Montegut 194 29.28 N 90.33 W
Monteiasi 68 40.30 N 17.23 E
Monteiro 250 7.53 S 37.07 W
Monteiro Lobato 256 22.58 S 45.50 W
Monteith, Mount ∧ 182 55.45 N 122.30 W
Montejicar 34 37.34 N 3.30 W
Montejinni 164 16.40 S 131.45 E
Montelavar 266c 38.51 N 9.20 W
Monteleone di Puglia 68 41.10 N 15.15 E
Monteleone di Spoleto 66 42.39 N 12.58 E
Monteleone Rocco Doria 71 40.29 N 8.34 E
Monteleone Sabino 66 42.14 N 12.51 E
Montelepre 70 38.05 N 13.10 E
Montelíbano 246 8.05 N 75.29 W
Montélimar 62 44.34 N 4.45 E
Montelindo ≏ 252 23.56 S 57.12 W
Montella 68 40.51 N 15.01 E
Montellano 34 37.00 N 5.34 W
Montello, Nv., U.S. 204 41.15 N 114.11 W
Montello, Wi., U.S. 190 43.47 N 89.19 W
Monteluco ♥[1] 66 42.43 N 12.45 E
Montelungo 64 44.24 N 9.54 E
Montelupo Fiorentino 66 43.44 N 11.01 E
Montemaggiore Belsito 70 37.51 N 13.46 E
Montemagno 62 44.59 N 8.20 E
Monte Maíz 252 33.12 S 62.36 W
Montemarano 68 40.55 N 15.00 E
Montemarciano 66 43.38 N 13.19 E
Montemayor, Meseta de ⋏[1] 254 44.20 S 66.10 W
Montemesola 68 40.34 N 17.20 E
Montemiletto 68 41.01 N 14.54 E
Montemilone 68 41.02 N 15.38 E
Montemor 266c 38.49 N 9.12 W
Montemor ∧ 266c 38.49 N 9.12 W
Montemorelos 232 25.12 N 99.49 W
Montemor-o-Novo 34 38.39 N 8.13 W
Montemor-o-Vehlo 34 40.10 N 8.41 W
Montemuro ∧ 34 40.58 N 7.56 W
Montemurro 68 40.18 N 15.59 E
Montendre 32 45.17 N 0.24 W
Montenegro 252 29.42 S 51.28 W
Montenegro → Crna Gora □[3] 38 42.30 N 19.18 E
Montenero 66 43.30 N 10.21 E
Montenero ∧ 68 39.13 N 16.35 E
Montenero di Bisaccia 66 41.57 N 14.47 E
Monteodorisio 66 42.05 N 14.39 E
Monte Oliveto Maggiore, Abbazia del ♥[1] 66 43.12 N 11.32 E
Monte Pascoal, Parque Nacional de ♠ 255 16.54 S 39.24 W
Monte Patria 252 30.42 S 70.58 W
Montepescali 66 42.53 N 11.05 E
Monte Porzio Catone 267a 41.49 N 12.43 E
Monteprandone 66 42.55 N 13.50 E
Montepuez 154 13.07 S 39.00 E
Montepuez ≏ 154 12.32 S 40.27 E
Montepulciano 66 43.05 N 11.47 E
Monte Quemado 252 25.48 S 62.52 W
Monterado 112 0.45 N 109.08 E
Monterchi 66 43.29 N 12.07 E
Montereale 66 42.31 N 13.15 E
Montereale Valcellina 64 46.10 N 12.39 E
Montereau 50 47.51 N 2.34 E
Montereau-Faut-Yonne 50 48.23 N 2.57 E
Montereau-sur-le-Jard 261 48.35 N 2.40 E
Monterey, Ca., U.S. 226 36.36 N 121.53 W
Monterey, In., U.S. 216 41.09 N 86.28 W
Monterey, Ky., U.S. 218 38.25 N 84.52 W
Monterey, Ma., U.S. 207 42.10 N 73.12 W
Monterey, N.Y., U.S. 210 42.18 N 77.03 W
Monterey, Tn., U.S. 194 36.08 N 85.16 W
Monterey, Va., U.S. 188 38.24 N 79.34 W
Monterey □[6] 226 36.40 N 121.38 W
Monterey Bay ⊂ 226 36.45 N 121.55 W
Monterey Park 228 34.03 N 118.07 W
Monterey Peninsula Airport ⊠ 226 36.35 N 121.51 W
Montería 246 8.46 N 75.53 W
Monteriggioni 66 43.23 N 11.13 E
Montero 248 17.20 S 63.15 W
Monte Romano 66 42.16 N 11.54 E
Monteroni d'Arbia 66 43.14 N 11.25 E
Monteroni di Lecce 68 40.19 N 18.06 E
Monteros 252 27.10 S 65.30 W
Monterosso al Mare 62 44.09 N 9.39 E
Monterosso Almo 70 37.05 N 14.46 E
Monterosso Calabro 68 38.43 N 16.17 E
Monterotondo 66 42.03 N 12.37 E
Monterotondo Marittimo 66 43.09 N 10.51 E
Monterrey, Méx. 232 25.40 N 100.19 W
Monterrey, Méx. 234 16.05 N 93.23 W
Monterrico, Hipódromo de ♠ 286d 12.06 S 76.59 W
Monterubbiano 66 43.05 N 13.43 E
Montes Altos 250 5.50 S 47.04 W
Monte San Biagio 66 41.21 N 13.21 E
Monte San Giovanni Campano 66 41.38 N 13.31 E
Montesano, It. 36 40.16 N 15.43 E
Montesano, Wa., U.S. 224 46.58 N 123.36 W
Montesano sulla Marcellana 68 40.16 N 15.42 E
Monte San Savino 66 43.20 N 11.43 E
Monte Santa Maria Tiberina 66 43.26 N 12.09 E
Monte Sant'Angelo 68 41.42 N 15.57 E
Monte Santo 250 10.26 S 39.20 W
Monte Santo de Minas 256 21.12 S 46.59 W
Monte Santu, Capo di › 71 40.05 N 9.44 E
Montesarchio 68 41.04 N 14.38 E
Montescaglioso 68 40.33 N 16.40 E
Montes Claros 255 16.43 S 43.52 W
Montescudaio 66 43.18 N 10.40 E
Montese 64 44.16 N 10.56 E
Monte Sereno 226 37.15 N 122.01 W
Monte Sião 256 22.26 S 46.34 W
Montesilvano Marina 66 42.31 N 14.09 E
Montespaccato ◆[8] 267a 41.54 N 12.23 E
Montespertoli 66 43.38 N 11.04 E
Montespluga 58 46.30 N 9.21 E
Montets, Col des)(58 46.00 N 6.55 E
Monteux 62 44.02 N 5.00 E
Montevago 70 37.42 N 12.58 E
Montevallo 194 33.06 N 86.51 W
Montevarchi 66 43.31 N 11.34 E
Monteverde 68 41.00 N 15.32 E
Monte Verde ≏ 256 21.55 S 43.33 W
Monteverde Nuovo ◆[8] 267a 41.51 N 12.27 E
Montevergine, Santuario di ♥[1] 68 40.55 N 14.45 E
Montevideo, Mn., U.S. 198 44.56 N 95.43 W
Montevideo, Ur. 258 34.53 S 56.11 W
Montevideo □[5] 258 34.50 S 56.12 W
Montevideo, Cerro de ∧[2] 258 33.54 S 56.15 W
Monte Vista 200 37.34 N 106.08 W
Montévrain 261 48.53 N 2.45 E
Montezemolo 62 44.22 N 8.08 E
Montezuma, Ca., U.S. 282 38.05 N 121.53 W
Montezuma, Ga., U.S. 192 32.18 N 84.01 W
Montezuma, In., U.S. 194 39.47 N 87.22 W
Montezuma, Ia., U.S. 190 41.35 N 92.31 W
Montezuma, Ks., U.S. 198 37.35 N 100.26 W
Montezuma, N.Y., U.S. 210 43.00 N 76.42 W
Montezuma, Oh., U.S. 216 40.29 N 84.33 W
Montezuma Castle National Monument ♠ 200 34.38 N 110.49 W
Montezuma Creek ≏ 200 37.17 N 109.20 W
Montezuma Hills ⋏[2] 282 38.07 N 121.51 W
Montezuma Slough ≏ 226 38.04 N 121.52 W
Montfaucon, Fr. 56 49.17 N 5.08 E
Montfaucon, Fr. 62 45.10 N 4.18 E
Montfaucon, Schw. 58 47.17 N 7.03 E
Montfermeil 261 48.54 N 2.34 E
Montfleur 58 46.19 N 5.26 E
Montfort, Fr. 32 48.08 N 1.58 W
Montfort, Wi., U.S. 190 42.58 N 90.25 W
Montfort-l'Amaury 50 48.47 N 1.49 E
Montfort-le-Rotrou 50 48.03 N 0.25 E
Montfort-sur-Risle 50 49.18 N 0.40 E
Montfrin 62 43.53 N 4.36 E
Montgé 261 49.02 N 2.45 E
Montgenèvre 62 44.56 N 6.43 E
Montgenèvre, Col de)(62 44.56 N 6.44 E
Montgeron 261 48.42 N 2.27 E
Montgeroult 261 49.05 N 2.00 E
Montgesoye 58 47.05 N 6.12 E
Montgomery, Wales, U.K. 42 52.33 N 3.03 W
Montgomery, Al., U.S. 194 32.23 N 86.18 W
Montgomery, Il., U.S. 216 41.43 N 88.20 W
Montgomery, La., U.S. 194 31.40 N 92.53 W
Montgomery, Mi., U.S. 216 41.46 N 84.48 W
Montgomery, Mn., U.S. 190 44.26 N 93.34 W
Montgomery, N.Y., U.S. 210 41.31 N 74.14 W
Montgomery, Oh., U.S. 218 39.13 N 84.21 W
Montgomery, Pa., U.S. 210 41.10 N 76.52 W
Montgomery, Tx., U.S. 222 30.23 N 95.42 W
Montgomery, W.V., U.S. 188 38.11 N 81.19 W
Montgomery □[6], Il., U.S. 219 39.09 N 89.29 W
Montgomery □[6], Md., U.S. 208 39.05 N 77.09 W
Montgomery □[6], Mo., U.S. 219 38.57 N 91.27 W
Montgomery □[6], N.Y., U.S. 210 42.57 N 74.22 W
Montgomery □[6], Oh., U.S. 218 39.45 N 84.15 W
Montgomery □[6], Pa., U.S. 208 40.07 N 75.21 W
Montgomery □[6], Tx., U.S. 222 30.18 N 95.30 W
Montgomery City 219 38.58 N 91.30 W
Montgomery Dam ◆[6] 214 40.39 N 80.24 W
Montgomery Knolls 284b 39.14 N 76.48 W
Montgomery Mall ◆[9] 284c 39.01 N 77.09 W
Montgomery → Sāhīwāl 123 30.40 N 73.06 E
Montgomery Square 284c 39.04 N 77.09 W
Montgomeryville 285 40.15 N 75.15 W
Montgomeryville Airport ⊠ 285 40.15 N 75.14 W
Montguyon 32 45.13 N 0.11 W
Monthermé 56 49.53 N 4.44 E
Monthey 58 46.15 N 6.57 E
Monthois 56 49.19 N 4.43 E
Monthureux-sur-Saône 58 48.02 N 5.58 E
Monthyon 261 49.00 N 2.50 E
Monti 71 40.49 N 9.19 E
Monticelli d'Ongina 64 45.05 N 9.56 E
Monticello, Ar., U.S. 194 33.37 N 91.47 W
Monticello, Fl., U.S. 192 30.32 N 83.52 W
Monticello, Ga., U.S. 192 33.18 N 83.41 W
Monticello, Il., U.S. 194 40.01 N 88.34 W
Monticello, In., U.S. 216 40.44 N 86.45 W
Monticello, Ia., U.S. 190 42.14 N 91.11 W
Monticello, Ky., U.S. 194 36.49 N 84.50 W
Monticello, Mn., U.S. 190 45.18 N 93.47 W
Monticello, Ms., U.S. 194 31.33 N 90.06 W
Monticello, Mo., U.S. 219 40.07 N 91.42 W
Monticello, N.Y., U.S. 210 41.39 N 74.41 W
Monticello, Ut,. U.S. 200 37.52 N 109.20 W
Monticello, Wi., U.S. 190 42.44 N 89.35 W
Monticello ⊥ 188 38.00 N 78.30 W
Monticello Conte Otto 64 45.35 N 11.35 E
Monticello Dam ◆[6] 226 38.30 N 122.07 W
Monticello Woods 284c 38.47 N 77.10 W
Montichiari 64 45.25 N 10.23 E
Monticiano 66 43.08 N 11.11 E
Montiel, Campo de ≚ 34 38.46 N 2.44 W
Montier-en-Der 58 48.29 N 4.46 E
Montieri 66 43.08 N 11.01 E
Montieri, Poggio di ∧ 66 43.08 N 11.00 E
Montiers-sur-Saulx 58 48.32 N 5.16 E
Montignac 32 45.04 N 1.10 E
Montigny 58 48.31 N 6.48 E
Montigny-Devant-Sassey 56 49.26 N 5.09 E
Montigny-le-Bretonneux 261 48.46 N 2.02 E
Montigny-le-Roi 58 48.00 N 5.30 E
Montigny-lès-Cormeilles 261 48.59 N 2.12 E
Montigny-lès-Metz 56 49.06 N 6.09 E
Montigny-sur-Aube 58 47.57 N 4.46 E
Montijo, Esp. 34 38.55 N 6.37 W
Montijo, Pan. 236 7.59 N 81.03 W
Montijo, Port. 34 38.42 N 8.58 W
Montijo, Aeroporto ⊠ 266c 38.42 N 9.02 W
Montijo, Golfo de ⊂ 246 7.40 N 81.07 W
Montilla 34 37.35 N 4.38 W
Montividiu 255 17.24 S 51.14 W
Montivilliers 50 49.33 N 0.12 E
Montjay-la-Tour 261 48.55 N 2.40 E
Montjoie, Lac ⊜, P.Q., Can. 206 46.17 N 75.08 W
Montjoie, Lac ⊜, P.Q., Can. 206 45.25 N 72.06 W
Mont-Joli 186 48.35 N 68.11 W
Montjovet 62 45.43 N 7.40 E
Montjuich, Estadio de ♠ 266d 41.22 N 2.09 E
Montjuich, Faro de ◆[5] 266d 41.21 N 2.11 E
Montjuich, Parque de ♠ 266d 41.21 N 2.09 E
Mont-Laurier 176 46.33 N 75.30 W
Montlebon 58 47.02 N 6.37 E
Montlhéry 50 48.38 N 2.16 E
Montlhéry, Tour de ♥ 261 48.38 N 2.16 E
Montlhéry, Tour de ♠ 261 48.38 N 2.16 E
Montlignon 261 49.01 N 2.17 E
Montlouet 261 48.31 N 1.43 E
Mont-Louis 32 42.31 N 2.07 E
Montlouis-sur-Loire 50 47.23 N 0.50 E
Montluçon 32 46.21 N 2.36 E
Montluel 62 45.51 N 5.03 E
Montmagny, P.Q., Can. 186 46.59 N 70.33 W
Montmagny, Fr. 261 48.58 N 2.21 E
Montmajour, Abbaye de ♥[1] 62 43.43 N 4.40 E
Montmartre ◆[8] 261 48.53 N 2.21 E
Montmédy 56 49.31 N 5.22 E
Montmélian 62 45.30 N 6.04 E
Montmeló 266d 41.33 N 2.15 E
Montmerle-sur-Saône 58 46.05 N 4.46 E
Montmin 62 45.48 N 6.16 E

Symbols in the index entries represent the broad categories identified in the key at the right. Symbols with superior numbers (⋏[1]) identify subcategories (see complete key on page *I · 1).*

Symbole im Register stellen die rechts im Schlüssel erklärten Kategorien dar. Symbole mit hochgestellten Ziffern (⋏[1]) bezeichnen Unterabteilungen einer Kategorie (vgl. vollständiger Schlüssel auf Seite *I · 1).*

Los símbolos incluídos en el texto del índice representan las grandes categorias identificadas con la clave a la derecha. Los símbolos con numeros en su parte superior (⋏[1]) identifican las subcategorías (véase la clave completa en la página *I · 1).*

Les symboles de l'index représentent les catégories indiquées dans la légende à droite. Les symboles suivis d'un indice (⋏[1]) représentent des sous-catégories (voir légende complète à la page *I · 1).*

Os símbolos incluídos no texto do índice representam as grandes categorias identificadas com a chave à direita. Os símbolos com números em sua parte superior (⋏[1]) identificam as subcategorias (veja-se a chave completa à página *I · 1).*

∧	Mountain	Berg	Montaña	Montagne	Montanha
⋏	Mountains	Gebirge	Montañas	Montagnes	Montanhas
)(	Pass	Paß	Paso	Col	Passo
V	Valley, Canyon	Tal, Cañon	Valle, Cañón	Vallée, Canyon	Vale, Canhão
≚	Plain	Ebene	Llano	Plaine	Planície
›	Cape	Kap	Cabo	Cap	Cabo
I	Island	Insel	Isla	Île	Ilha
II	Islands	Inseln	Islas	Îles	Ilhas
⊥	Other Topographic Features	Andere Topographische Objekte	Otros Elementos Topográficos	Autres données topographiques	Outros acidentes topográficos

ESPAÑOL / FRANÇAIS / PORTUGUÊS

Nombre / Nom / Nome	Página / Page	Lat.°′	Long.°′ W = Oeste / W = Ouest
Montmirail, Fr.	50	48.52 N	3.32 E
Montmirail, Fr.	50	48.06 N	0.48 E
Montmirey-le-Château	58	47.13 N	5.32 E
Montmoreau-Saint-Cybard	32	45.24 N	0.08 E
Montmorenci	216	40.28 N	87.02 W
Montmorency, Austl.	274b	37.43 S	145.07 E
Montmorency, Fr.	261	49.00 N	2.20 E
Montmorency ≃	186	46.53 N	71.07 W
Montmorency, Forêt de ♠	261	49.02 N	2.16 E
Montmorency → Beauport	186	46.52 N	71.11 W
Montmorillon	32	46.26 N	0.52 E
Montmort	50	48.55 N	3.49 E
Monto	166	24.52 S	151.07 E
Montodine	62	45.17 N	9.42 E
Montoggio	62	44.31 N	9.03 E
Montoire-sur-le-Loir	50	47.45 N	0.52 E
Montone	66	43.22 N	12.20 E
Montone ≃, It.	64	44.24 N	12.14 E
Montone ≃, It.	66	43.22 N	12.20 E
Montopoli in Val d'Arno	66	43.40 N	10.45 E
Mont Orford, Parc du ♠	206	45.22 N	72.05 W
Montorio al Vomano	66	42.35 N	13.38 E
Montorio nei Frentani	66	41.46 N	14.55 E
Montoro	34	38.01 N	4.23 W
Mont'Orso, Galleria di ➜[5]	66	41.20 N	13.15 E
Montour □[6]	210	40.58 N	76.37 W
Montour Falls	210	42.20 N	76.50 W
Montour Run ≃, Pa., U.S.	279b	40.36 N	79.57 W
Montour Run ≃, Pa., U.S.	279b	40.31 N	80.08 W
Montoursville	210	41.15 N	76.55 W
Mont Park	274b	37.43 S	145.04 E
Montparnasse, Gare ➜[5]	261	48.51 N	2.19 E
Mont Peko, Parc National du ♠	150	7.00 N	7.15 W
Montpelier, Jam.	241q	18.22 N	77.56 W
Montpelier, Id., U.S.	202	42.19 N	111.17 W
Montpelier, In., U.S.	216	40.33 N	85.16 W
Montpelier, Md., U.S.	284c	39.04 N	76.51 W
Montpelier, Ms., U.S.	194	33.43 N	88.56 W
Montpelier, Oh., U.S.	216	41.35 N	84.36 W
Montpelier, Vt., U.S.	188	44.15 N	72.34 W
Montpellier	62	43.36 N	3.53 E
Montpellier-Fréjorgues, Aéroport de ⊠	62	43.33 N	4.00 E
Montpezat-sous-Bauzon	62	44.43 N	4.12 E
Mont-Pichet	261	48.53 N	2.54 E
Montpon-Ménesterol	32	45.00 N	0.10 E
Montpont-en-Bresse	58	46.33 N	5.09 E
Montréal, P.Q., Can.	206	45.31 N	73.34 W
Montréal, P.Q., Can.	275a	45.31 N	73.34 W
Montréal, Fr.	50	47.32 N	4.02 E
Montreal, Wi., U.S.	190	46.25 N	90.14 W
Montreal ≃, On., Can.	190	47.14 N	84.39 W
Montreal ≃, On., Can.	190	47.08 N	79.27 W
Montreal ≃, Sk., Can.	184	55.06 N	105.19 W
Montreal ≃, U.S.	190	46.44 N	90.25 W
Montréal, Base des Forces Canadiennes ■	275a	45.31 N	73.25 W
Montréal, Île de I	206	45.30 N	73.40 W
Montréal, Université de ♉[2]	275a	45.30 N	73.37 W
Montréal-Est	206	45.38 N	73.31 W
Montreal International Airport ⊠	206	45.28 N	73.45 W
Montreal Lake	184	54.03 N	105.46 W
Montreal Lake ⊜	184	54.20 N	105.40 W
Montreal Lake Indian Reserve ➜[4]	184	54.00 N	105.45 W
Montréal-Nord	206	45.36 N	73.38 W
Montréal-Quest	275a	45.27 N	73.39 W
Montreal Water Works Aqueduct ≅[1]	275a	45.26 N	73.36 W
Montrésor	50	47.09 N	1.12 E
Montresta	71	40.22 N	8.30 E
Montret	58	46.41 N	5.07 E
Montreuil	261	48.52 N	2.26 E
Montreuil-Bellay	32	47.08 N	0.09 W
Montreuil-sous-Bois	50	48.52 N	2.26 E
Montreuil-sur-Mer	50	50.28 N	1.46 E
Montreux	58	46.26 N	6.55 E
Montrevel-en-Bresse	58	46.20 N	5.08 E
Montrichard	50	47.21 N	1.11 E
Montriond	58	46.12 N	6.41 E
Mont-Rolland	206	45.57 N	74.07 W
Montrond-les-Bains	62	45.38 N	4.14 E
Montrose, Austl.	274b	37.49 S	145.21 E
Montrose, Scot., U.K.	46	56.43 N	2.29 W
Montrose, Ca., U.S.	228	34.12 N	118.13 W
Montrose, Co., U.S.	200	38.28 N	107.52 W
Montrose, Ia., U.S.	190	40.31 N	91.24 W
Montrose, Mi., U.S.	190	43.10 N	83.53 W
Montrose, N.Y., U.S.	210	41.15 N	73.56 W
Montrose, Oh., U.S.	214	41.08 N	81.37 W
Montrose, Pa., U.S.	210	41.50 N	75.52 W
Montrose, S.D., U.S.	198	43.41 N	97.11 W
Montrose Harbor c	278	41.58 N	87.38 W
Montrose Hill	279b	40.30 N	79.51 W
Montross	208	38.05 N	76.49 W
Montrouge	261	48.49 N	2.19 E
Mont-Royal	206	45.31 N	73.39 W
Mont Royal, Parc ♠	275a	45.31 N	73.35 W
Mont Royal Tunnel ➜[5]	275a	45.31 N	73.38 W
Montry	261	48.53 N	2.50 E
Monts	50	47.17 N	0.37 E
Monts, Pointe des ›	186	49.20 N	67.23 W
Mont-Saint-Aignan	50	49.28 N	1.05 E
Mont-Sainte-Anne, Parc du ♠	186	47.08 N	70.55 W
Mont-Saint-Hilaire	206	45.34 N	73.11 W
Mont-Saint-Martin	56	49.32 N	5.47 E
Mont-Saint-Michel → Le Mont-Saint-Michel ♉[1]	32	48.38 N	1.32 W
Mont-Saint-Vincent	58	46.38 N	4.29 E
Montsauche	50	47.13 N	4.01 E
Montsec	56	48.53 N	5.43 E
Montserrat □[2], N.A.	230	16.45 N	62.12 W
Montserrat □[2], N.A.	238	16.45 N	62.12 W
Montserrat, Monasterio de ♉[1]	34	41.36 N	1.49 E
Montsoult	261	49.04 N	2.19 E
Montsûrs	28	48.08 N	0.33 W
Mont-sur-Vaudrey	58	46.58 N	5.36 E
Mont-Tremblant, Parc provincial du ♠	206	46.42 N	74.20 W
Montuenga	34	41.03 N	4.37 W
Montvale, N.J., U.S.	276	41.02 N	74.01 W
Montvale, Va., U.S.	192	37.23 N	79.43 W
Montverde	220	28.36 N	81.41 W
Montville, Ct., U.S.	207	41.27 N	72.08 W
Montville, N.J., U.S.	276	40.54 N	74.23 W
Montville, Oh., U.S.	214	41.36 N	81.03 W
Montville Airpark ⊠	276	40.56 N	74.20 W
Monument, S. Afr.	273d	26.06 S	27.43 E
Monument, Or., U.S.	202	44.49 N	119.25 W
Monument, Pa., U.S.	214	41.07 N	77.42 W
Monument Beach	207	41.43 N	70.36 W
Monument Draw V, U.S.	196	32.27 N	102.20 W
Monument Draw V, Tx., U.S.	196	30.51 N	102.33 W
Monument Hill State Historic Site ⊥	222	29.53 N	96.54 W
Monumento	256	22.44 S	43.51 W
Monument Peak ʌ, Co., U.S.	200	39.43 N	107.55 W
Monument Peak ʌ, Id., U.S.	202	42.07 N	114.14 W
Monument Valley V	200	37.05 N	110.20 W
Monundilla, Mount ʌ	170	32.45 S	150.29 E
Monveda	152	2.57 N	21.27 E
Monymusk	46	57.13 N	2.31 W
Monyo	110	17.59 N	95.30 E
Monywa	110	22.05 N	95.08 E
Monza	62	45.35 N	9.16 E
Monze	154	16.16 S	27.28 E
Monzen	92	37.17 N	136.46 E
Monzie	46	56.24 N	3.48 W
Monzón, Esp.	34	41.55 N	0.12 E
Monzón, Perú	248	9.10 S	76.23 W
Moóca ➜[8]	287b	23.33 S	46.35 W
Moóca, Ribeirão da ≃	287b	23.36 S	46.35 W
Moodie Island I	176	64.37 N	65.30 W
Moodus	207	41.30 N	72.27 W
Moodus Reservoir ⊜[1]	207	41.30 N	72.24 W
Moody	222	31.18 N	97.21 W
Moody Air Force Base ■	192	30.59 N	83.11 W
Moody Wood Dale Airport ⊠	278	41.59 N	87.58 W
Mooers	206	44.58 N	73.35 W
Mooi ≃, S. Afr.	158	28.45 S	30.34 E
Mooi ≃, S. Afr.	158	26.53 S	26.56 E
Mooirivier	158	29.13 S	29.50 E
Mook	52	51.45 N	5.54 E
Mookane	156	24.59 S	24.33 E
Mooketsi	156	23.35 S	30.05 E
Moolawatana	166	29.55 S	139.43 E
Moolman	158	27.10 S	30.53 E
Mooloogool	162	26.06 S	119.05 E
Moon	214	40.31 N	80.14 W
Moon ≃	212	45.08 N	79.59 W
Moon, Mountains of the → Ruwenzori Range ⩘	154	0.23 N	29.54 E
Moonachie	276	40.50 N	74.02 W
Moonachie Creek ≃	276	40.48 N	74.03 W
Moonah Creek ≃	166	22.03 S	138.33 E
Moon Crest	279b	40.32 N	80.11 W
Moondarra Reservoir ⊜[1]	169	38.04 S	146.22 E
Moonee Valley Racecourse ♠	274b	37.46 S	144.56 E
Moonie	166	27.43 S	150.22 E
Moonie ≃	166	29.19 S	148.43 E
Moon Island I, On., Can.	212	45.09 N	80.01 W
Moon Island I, Ma., U.S.	283	42.18 N	71.00 W
Moon Run	214	40.27 N	80.06 W
Moonta	168b	34.04 S	137.35 E
Moor, Kepulauan II	164	2.57 S	135.45 E
Moora	162	30.39 S	116.00 E
Moorabbin	169	37.56 S	145.02 E
Moorabbin Airport ⊠	274b	37.59 S	145.09 E
Mooraberree	166	25.14 S	140.59 E
Moorabool ≃	169	38.09 S	144.19 E
Moorarie	162	25.56 S	117.35 E
Moorburg	52	53.17 N	7.53 E
Moorcroft	198	44.15 N	104.56 W
Moordorf	52	53.28 N	7.23 E
Moordrecht	52	51.59 N	4.40 E
Moore, Austl.	171a	26.53 S	152.18 E
Moore, Eng., U.K.	262	53.21 N	2.38 W
Moore, Id., U.S.	202	43.44 N	113.21 W
Moore, Mt., U.S.	202	46.58 N	109.41 W
Moore, Ok., U.S.	196	35.20 N	97.29 W
Moore, Tx., U.S.	196	29.03 N	99.01 W
Moore ≃	162	31.22 S	115.29 E
Moore, Lake ⊜	162	29.50 S	117.35 E
Moorea I	174s	17.32 S	149.50 W
Moorebank	274a	33.56 S	150.56 E
Moore Creek ≃	212	45.29 N	77.58 W
Moorefield, Ky., U.S.	218	38.16 N	83.55 W
Moorefield, Oh., U.S.	214	40.12 N	81.10 W
Moorefield, W.V., U.S.	188	39.03 N	78.58 W
Moore Haven	220	26.49 N	81.05 W
Moore Haven Lock ➜[5]	220	26.51 N	81.05 W
Moore Lake ⊜, On., Can.	212	45.26 N	78.01 W
Moore Lake ⊜, On., Can.	212	44.48 N	78.48 W
Moore Lake ⊜, Mi., U.S.	281	42.37 N	83.36 W
Mooreland, In., U.S.	218	39.59 N	85.15 W
Mooreland, Ok., U.S.	196	36.26 N	99.12 W
Moore Point ›	275b	43.48 N	79.03 W
Moore Reservoir ⊜[1]	188	44.25 N	71.50 W
Mooresburg	210	40.59 N	76.43 W
Moores Creek National Battlefield ♠	192	34.24 N	78.08 W
Moores Hill	218	39.06 N	85.05 W
Moore Station	222	32.11 N	95.35 W
Moorestown	208	39.58 N	74.56 W
Moorestown Mall ➜[9]	285	39.56 N	74.58 W
Mooresville, In., U.S.	218	39.36 N	86.22 W
Mooresville, N.C., U.S.	192	35.35 N	80.48 W
Mooreville	281	42.06 N	83.44 W
Moorfoot Hills ⩘[2]	46	55.45 N	3.02 W
Moorhead, Mn., U.S.	198	46.52 N	96.46 W
Moorhead, Ms., U.S.	194	33.27 N	90.30 W
Mooring	222	30.41 N	96.33 W
Mooringsport	194	32.41 N	93.57 W
Moormerland	52	53.20 N	7.27 E
Moornanyah Lake ⊜	166	33.02 S	143.58 E
Moorooka	171a	27.32 S	153.02 E
Mooroolbark	274b	37.47 S	145.19 E
Moorpark	228	34.17 N	118.53 W
Moorreesburg	158	33.08 S	18.40 E
Moorrege	52	53.40 N	9.39 E
Moorriem	52	53.15 N	8.19 E
Moorsel	50	50.57 N	4.06 E
Moorside	262	53.34 N	2.04 W
Moorslede	50	50.53 N	3.04 E
Moosach ➜[8]	60	48.11 N	11.31 E
Moosbrunn	264b	48.01 N	16.28 E
Moosburg, Dtsch.	30	48.29 N	11.57 E
Moosburg, Öst.	61	46.39 N	14.10 E
Moosburg an der Isar	60	48.29 N	11.57 E
Moose ≃, Me., U.S.	188	45.40 N	69.42 W
Moose ≃, N.Y., U.S.	212	43.37 N	75.22 W
Moose Creek	206	45.15 N	74.58 W
Moose Creek ≃	206	45.23 N	75.04 W
Moosehead Lake ⊜	188	45.40 N	69.40 W
Mooseheart	216	41.49 N	88.20 W
Moose Heights	182	53.05 N	122.30 W
Moose Hill ʌ[2]	283	42.07 N	71.13 W
Moose Island I	184	51.42 N	97.10 W
Moose Jaw	184	50.23 N	105.32 W
Moose Jaw ≃	184	50.34 N	105.17 W
Moose Lake, Mb., Can.	184	53.43 N	100.20 W
Moose Lake, Mn., U.S.	190	46.27 N	92.45 W
Moose Lake ⊜, Ab., Can.	182	54.15 N	110.55 W
Moose Lake ⊜, Mb., Can.	184	53.55 N	99.45 W
Moose Lake ⊜, On., Can.	212	45.09 N	78.28 W
Mooselookmeguntic Lake ⊜	188	44.53 N	70.48 W
Moose Mountain ʌ	184	49.45 N	102.37 W
Moose Mountain Creek ≃	184	49.12 N	102.10 W
Moose Mountain Provincial Park ♠	184	49.48 N	102.25 W
Moose Pass	180	60.29 N	149.22 W
Moos → Moso	64	46.41 N	12.23 E
Moos → Moso in Passiria	64	46.50 N	11.10 E
Moosomin	184	50.07 N	101.40 W
Moosomin Indian Reserve ➜[4]	184	53.06 N	108.14 W
Moosonee	176	51.17 N	80.39 W
Moosup	207	41.42 N	71.52 W
Mooti	144	0.35 N	41.56 E
Moots Creek ≃	216	40.32 N	86.47 W
Mootwingee National Park ♠	166	31.07 S	142.23 E
Mopane	156	22.37 S	29.52 E
Mopeia Velha	156	17.59 S	35.44 E
Mopipi	156	21.07 S	24.55 E
Mopo	100	33.07 N	113.02 E
Moppo → Mokp'o	98	34.48 N	126.22 E
Mopti	150	14.30 N	4.12 W
Mopti □[4]	150	14.40 N	4.15 W
Moqokorei	144	4.04 N	46.08 E
Moquegua	248	17.12 S	70.56 W
Moquegua □[5]	248	16.50 S	70.55 W
Mór	30	47.23 N	18.12 E
Mor ≃	126	24.01 N	88.03 E
Mòr, Glen V	46	57.10 N	4.40 W
Mor, Sgurr ʌ	46	57.42 N	5.03 W
Mora, Cam.	146	11.03 N	14.09 E
Mora, Esp.	34	39.41 N	3.46 W
Mora, India	272c	18.54 N	72.56 E
Mora, Port.	34	38.56 N	8.10 W
Mora, Sve.	26	61.00 N	14.33 E
Mora, Mn., U.S.	190	45.52 N	93.17 W
Mora, N.M., U.S.	200	35.58 N	105.19 W
Mora ≃	196	35.44 N	104.23 W
Mora, Arroyo de la ≃	196	34.05 N	104.18 W
Moraby	40	60.23 N	15.35 E
Morača, Manastir ♉[1]	38	42.44 N	19.20 E
Morada	226	38.01 N	121.15 W
Morādābād	124	28.50 N	78.47 E
Morada Nova	250	5.07 S	38.23 W
Morada Nova de Minas	255	18.37 S	45.22 W
Moradel, Montaña de ʌ	236	15.06 N	86.16 W
Mora de Rubielos	34	40.15 N	0.45 W
Moraduccio	66	44.10 N	11.29 E
Morafenobe	157b	17.49 S	44.55 E
Morąg	30	53.56 N	19.56 E
Moraga	226	37.50 N	122.08 W
Mórahalom	30	46.13 N	19.54 E
Moraine	218	39.42 N	84.13 W
Moraine Hills State Park ♠	216	42.18 N	88.15 W
Moraine State Park ♠	214	40.56 N	80.07 W
Morainvilliers	261	48.56 N	1.56 E
Morākhi ≃	126	24.01 N	88.10 E
Morākhi Reservoir ⊜[1]	126	24.10 N	87.15 E
Mor'akovskij Zaton	86	56.45 N	84.41 E
Moral de Calatrava	34	38.50 N	3.35 W
Moraleda, Canal ⊔	254	44.30 S	73.30 W
Morales, Guat.	236	15.29 N	88.49 W
Morales, Perú	248	6.28 S	76.28 W
Morales, Arroyo ≃	258	34.48 S	58.36 W
Morales, Laguna c	234	23.35 N	97.47 W
Moramanga	157b	18.56 S	48.12 E
Moran, Ks., U.S.	198	37.54 N	95.10 W
Moran, Mi., U.S.	190	45.59 N	84.49 W
Moran, Tx., U.S.	196	32.33 N	99.10 W
Moran ≃	164	15.16 S	125.33 E
Moranbah	166	22.00 S	148.02 E
Morangis	261	48.42 N	2.20 E
Morangup Hill ʌ[2]	168a	31.41 S	116.19 E
Morann	214	40.48 N	78.21 W
Morano Calabro	68	39.50 N	16.08 E
Morano sul Po	62	45.10 N	8.22 E
Moran State Park ♠	224	48.41 N	122.52 W
Morant Bay	241q	17.53 N	76.25 W
Morant Cays II	238	17.24 N	75.59 W
Morant Point ›	241q	17.55 N	76.10 W
Morar, Loch ⊜	46	56.57 N	5.43 W
Mörarp	41	56.04 N	12.52 E
Morasverdes	34	40.36 N	6.16 W
Morat, Lac de (Murtensee) ⊜	58	46.55 N	7.05 E
Moratalla	34	38.12 N	1.53 W
Morattico	208	37.47 N	76.37 W
Moratuwa	122	6.46 N	79.53 E
Morava □[9]	30	49.30 N	17.00 E
Morava (March) ≃	30	48.10 N	16.59 E
Morāveh Tappeh	128	37.55 N	55.57 E
Moravia, C.R.	236	9.51 N	83.26 W
Moravia, Ia., U.S.	190	40.53 N	92.48 W
Moravia, N.Y., U.S.	210	42.42 N	76.25 W
Moravia → Morava □[9]	30	49.20 N	17.00 E
Moravian Indian Reserve ➜[4]	214	42.34 N	81.53 W
Moravská Dyje ≃	61	48.51 N	15.30 E
Moravská Ostrava → Ostrava	30	49.50 N	18.17 E
Moravská Třebová	30	49.45 N	16.40 E
Moravské Budějovice	61	49.03 N	15.49 E
Moravský Krumlov	61	49.03 N	16.19 E
Morawa	162	29.13 S	116.00 E
Morawhanna	246	8.16 N	59.45 W
Moraya	248	21.45 S	65.32 W
Morayfield	171a	27.07 S	152.57 E
Moray Firth c[1]	46	57.50 N	3.30 W
Morazán, Guat.	236	14.56 N	90.09 W
Morazán, Hond.	236	15.17 N	87.34 W
Morbach	56	49.48 N	7.07 E
Morbegno	36	46.08 N	9.34 E
Morbi	120	22.49 N	70.50 E
Morbihan □[5]	32	47.55 N	2.50 W
Mörbisch am See	61	47.45 N	16.40 E
Morbras ≃	261	48.47 N	2.29 E
Mörbylånga	26	56.31 N	16.23 E
Morcenx	32	44.02 N	0.55 W
Morciano di Romagna	66	43.55 N	12.38 E
Morcone	68	41.20 N	14.40 E
Morcote	58	45.56 N	8.55 E
Morcy	80	51.18 N	47.51 E
Morden	184	49.11 N	98.05 W
Morden ➜[8]	260	51.24 N	0.12 W
Mordialloc	169	38.00 S	145.05 E
Mordino	24	61.21 N	51.52 E
Mordoğan	130	38.30 N	26.37 E
Mordovo, Ross.	80	51.07 N	45.48 E
Mordovo, Ross.	80	52.05 N	40.46 E
Mordovo-Adel'akovo	80	53.47 N	51.36 E
Mordovskaja Avtonomnaja Sovetskaja Socialističeskaja Respublika □[1]	80	54.30 N	44.00 E
Mordovskij Buguruslan	80	53.48 N	52.31 E
Mordovskij Zapovednik ➜[4]	80	54.48 N	43.20 E
Mordves	82	54.34 N	38.13 E
Mordy	30	52.13 N	22.31 E
More, Ben ʌ, Scot., U.K.	46	56.21 N	4.35 W
More, Ben ʌ, Scot., U.K.	46	56.25 N	6.01 W
More, Loch ⊜	46	58.17 N	4.52 W
More Assynt, Ben ʌ	46	58.08 N	4.53 W
Moreau ≃, Mo., U.S.	219	38.33 N	92.06 W
Moreau ≃, S.D., U.S.	198	45.18 N	100.43 W
Moreau, North Fork ≃	198	45.09 N	102.50 W
Moreau, South Fork ≃	198	45.09 N	102.50 W
Moreau Peak ʌ	198	45.21 N	103.43 W
Moreauville	194	31.02 N	91.58 W
Morec	80	51.03 N	44.03 E
Morecambe	44	54.04 N	2.53 W
Morecambe Bay c	44	54.07 N	3.00 W
Moree, Austl.	166	29.28 S	149.51 E
Morée, Fr.	50	47.54 N	1.14 E
Morehead, Pap. N. Gui.	164	8.40 S	141.35 E
Morehead, Ky., U.S.	218	38.11 N	83.25 W
Morehead ≃	164	9.00 S	141.25 E
Morehead City	192	34.43 N	76.43 W
Morehouse	194	36.50 N	89.41 W
Moreira César	256	22.55 S	45.22 W
Moreland, Austl.	274b	37.45 S	144.58 E
Moreland, Ga., U.S.	192	33.17 N	84.46 W
Moreland, Ky., U.S.	194	37.30 N	84.48 W
Moreland Hills	279a	41.27 N	81.29 W
Morelia	234	19.42 N	101.07 W
Morell	186	46.25 N	62.42 W
Morella, Austl.	166	22.59 S	143.52 E
Morella, Esp.	34	40.37 N	0.06 W
Morello ≃	70	37.29 N	14.08 E
Morelos, Méx.	196	28.25 N	100.53 W
Morelos, Méx.	232	26.42 N	107.40 W
Morelos, Méx.	234	22.53 N	102.37 W
Morelos □[3]	234	18.45 N	99.00 W
Moremi Wildlife Reserve ➜[4]	156	19.10 S	23.15 E
Morena	124	26.30 N	78.09 E
Morena, Sierra ʌ	282	37.25 N	122.18 W
Morena, Sierra ⩘	34	38.00 N	5.00 W
Morenci, Az., U.S.	200	33.04 N	109.21 W
Morenci, Mi., U.S.	216	41.43 N	84.13 W
Moreni	38	45.00 N	25.39 E
Moreno, Arg.	258	34.39 S	58.48 W
Moreno, Ca., U.S.	228	33.55 N	117.09 W
Moreno □[5]	288	34.36 S	58.48 W
Moreno, Bahía c	252	23.35 S	70.30 W
Møre og Romsdal □[6]	26	62.40 N	7.50 E
Mores	71	40.33 N	8.50 E
Moresby Island I, B.C., Can.	182	52.50 N	131.55 W
Moresby Island I, B.C., Can.	224	48.40 N	123.20 W
Mores Island I	238	26.18 N	77.33 W
Moresnet	56	50.43 N	5.59 E
Morestel	62	45.40 N	5.28 E
Moreton, Austl.	164	12.28 S	142.38 E
Moreton, Eng., U.K.	44	53.24 N	3.07 W
Moreton, Eng., U.K.	260	51.44 N	0.14 E
Moreton, Cape ›	171a	27.02 S	153.28 E
Moreton Bay c	171a	27.20 S	153.15 E
Moretonhampstead	42	50.40 N	3.45 W
Moreton-in-Marsh	42	51.59 N	1.42 W
Moreton Island I	171a	27.10 S	153.25 E
Moreton Island National Park ♠	171a	27.09 S	153.25 E
Moret-sur-Loing	50	48.22 N	2.49 E
Moretta	62	44.46 N	7.32 E
Moreuil	50	49.46 N	2.29 E
Morey Park	210	42.33 N	73.43 W
Morey Peak ʌ	204	38.37 N	116.17 W
Morez	58	46.31 N	6.02 E
Morfa Nefyn	42	52.56 N	4.33 W
Mörfelden-Walldorf	56	49.58 N	8.34 E
Morga	80	54.26 N	46.29 E
Morgan, Austl.	166	34.02 S	139.40 E
Morgan, Ga., U.S.	192	31.32 N	84.35 W
Morgan, Ky., U.S.	218	38.36 N	84.23 W
Morgan, Mn., U.S.	198	44.25 N	94.55 W
Morgan, Pa., U.S.	279b	40.22 N	80.08 W
Morgan, Tx., U.S.	222	32.01 N	97.37 W
Morgan, Ut,. U.S.	200	41.02 N	111.40 W
Morgan □[6], Il., U.S.	219	39.44 N	90.14 W
Morgan □[6], In., U.S.	218	39.30 N	86.25 W
Morgan, Mount ʌ	171b	35.44 S	148.47 E
Morgan City, Al., U.S.	194	34.28 N	86.34 W
Morgan City, La., U.S.	194	29.41 N	91.12 W
Morgan Creek ≃	196	32.19 N	100.55 W
Morganfield	194	37.41 N	87.55 W
Morgan Hill	226	37.07 N	121.39 W
Morganito	246	5.04 N	67.44 W
Morgan Park ➜[8]	278	41.42 N	87.40 W
Morgan's Bay	158	32.43 S	28.20 E
Morgan's Point	222	29.41 N	94.59 W
Morgans Point ›	212	42.52 N	79.21 W
Morgan State College ♉[2]	284b	39.21 N	76.35 W
Morgantina ⊥	70	37.25 N	14.29 E
Morganton	192	35.44 N	81.41 W
Morgantown, In., U.S.	218	39.22 N	86.15 W
Morgantown, Ky., U.S.	194	37.13 N	86.41 W
Morgantown, Md., U.S.	208	38.21 N	76.58 W
Morgantown, Ms., U.S.	194	31.18 N	89.54 W
Morgantown, Ms., U.S.	194	31.34 N	91.20 W
Morgantown, Oh., U.S.	218	39.08 N	83.13 W
Morgantown, Pa., U.S.	208	40.09 N	75.54 W
Morgantown, W.V., U.S.	188	39.37 N	79.57 W
Morganville	208	40.23 N	74.15 W
Morgan Whyalla Pipeline ≅[1]	168b	33.48 S	138.56 E
Morganza	194	30.44 N	91.35 W
Morgårdshammar	40	60.09 N	15.23 E
Morgauši	80	55.58 N	46.47 E
Morgenzon	158	26.45 S	29.36 E
Morges	58	46.31 N	6.30 E
Morgex	62	45.45 N	7.02 E
Morghāb (Murgab) ≃	128	38.18 N	61.12 E
Morghar	126	23.40 N	89.37 E
Morghūm, Kūh-e ʌ	128	33.06 N	57.30 E
Morgongåva	40	59.56 N	16.57 E
Morgongiori	71	39.45 N	8.46 E
Morguilla, Punta ›	252	37.46 S	73.40 W
Morhange	56	48.55 N	6.38 E
Mori, It.	64	45.51 N	10.59 E
Mori, Nihon	92a	42.06 N	140.35 E
Mori, Nihon	94	34.50 N	137.56 E
Mori, Nihon	270	34.32 N	135.00 E
Mori ≃	164	10.00 S	148.30 E
Moriah	241r	11.15 N	60.43 W
Moriah, Mount ʌ	204	39.17 N	114.12 W
Morialta Conservation Park ♠	168b	34.55 S	138.40 E
Moriarty	200	34.59 N	106.02 W
Moriarty, Mount ʌ	224	49.08 N	124.26 W
Morib	114	2.45 N	101.26 E
Moribaya	150	9.53 N	9.33 W
Morice ≃	182	54.24 N	126.45 W
Morice Lake ⊜	182	54.00 N	127.37 W
Morichal Largo ≃	246	9.27 N	62.25 W
Moricsala ♠	76	57.17 N	22.11 E
Morie, Loch ⊜	46	57.44 N	4.28 W
Morienval	50	49.18 N	2.56 E
Morigerati	68	40.08 N	15.33 E
Moriguchi	96	34.44 N	135.34 E
Morija	158	29.34 S	27.31 E
Moriki	150	12.52 N	6.30 E
Morin Dawa	89	48.28 N	124.27 E
Moringen	52	51.42 N	9.52 E
Morino, It.	66	41.53 N	13.25 E
Morino, Ross.	76	57.54 N	30.22 E
Morinville	182	53.48 N	113.39 W
Morioka	92	39.42 N	141.09 E
Morīri, Tso ⊜	120	32.54 N	78.20 E
Morisset	170	33.06 S	151.29 E
Moriston ≃	46	57.12 N	4.36 W
Moritzburg ⊥	54	51.09 N	13.40 E
Morivione ➜[8]	266b	45.26 N	9.12 E
Moriya	94	35.56 N	140.00 E
Moriyama	94	35.04 N	135.59 E
Moriyama-chūtonchi, Rikujō-jieitai- ■	94	35.12 N	136.57 E
Moriyoshi-zan ʌ	92	39.58 N	140.33 E
Morki	80	56.25 N	49.01 E
Morkill ≃	182	53.42 N	120.30 W
Morkiny Gory	76	57.33 N	36.18 E
Mörkö I	40	58.59 N	17.40 E
Morkoka ≃	74	65.10 N	115.52 E
Mørkøv	41	55.40 N	11.32 E
Morlaix	32	48.35 N	3.50 W
Morlanwelz	50	50.27 N	4.14 E
Morles	56	50.38 N	9.51 E
Morley, Eng., U.K.	44	53.46 N	1.36 W
Morley, Mi., U.S.	190	43.29 N	85.26 W
Morley, N.Y., U.S.	212	44.40 N	75.12 W
Morley Green	262	53.20 N	2.16 W
Mörlunda	26	57.19 N	15.51 E
Mormal'	76	52.45 N	29.53 E
Mormanno	68	39.53 N	16.00 E
Mormant	50	48.36 N	2.53 E
Mormoiron	62	44.04 N	5.11 E
Mormon Bar	226	37.28 N	119.57 W
Mormon Lake ⊜	200	34.57 N	111.27 W
Mormon Peak ʌ	204	36.57 N	114.30 W
Mormon Reservoir ⊜[1]	202	43.16 N	114.49 W
Mormon Slough ≃	226	37.57 N	121.18 W
Mormon Station Historical State Monument ♠	226	39.00 N	119.50 W
Mormugao	122	15.24 N	73.48 E
Morna	272a	28.35 N	77.22 E
Mornant	62	45.37 N	4.40 E
Mornas	62	44.12 N	4.44 E
Morne-à-l'Eau	241o	16.21 N	61.31 W
Morne Trois Pitons National Park ♠	240d	15.19 N	61.19 W
Morney	166	25.22 S	141.28 E
Morningdale	207	42.18 N	71.45 W
Morningside	284c	38.50 N	76.53 W
Morningside Park ♠	275b	43.47 N	79.12 W
Morningstar ≃	48	52.27 N	8.41 W
Morning Sun	190	41.05 N	91.15 W
Mornington	169	38.13 S	145.03 E
Mornington, Isla I	254	49.45 S	75.23 W
Mornington Island I	164	16.33 S	139.24 E
Mornington Island Aboriginal Land Trust ➜[4]	164	16.20 S	139.20 E
Mornington Peninsula ›[1]	169	38.20 S	145.05 E
Morno	150	8.41 N	1.31 W
Mornou, Hadjer ʌ	146	17.12 N	23.08 E
Moro, Indon.	114	0.46 N	103.43 E
Moro, Or., U.S.	224	45.29 N	120.43 W
Moro ≃	150	7.25 N	11.03 W
Morobe	164	7.45 S	147.35 E
Morobe □[5]	164	7.00 S	146.30 E
Moroč'	76	52.34 N	27.36 E
Moroč' ≃	76	52.35 N	27.35 E
Morocco	216	40.56 N	87.27 W
Morocco (Al-Magreb) □[1], Afr.	134	32.00 N	5.00 W
Morocco (Al-Magreb) □[1], Afr.	148	32.00 N	5.00 W
Morococala	248	18.10 S	66.44 W
Morococha	248	11.37 S	76.09 W
Moro Creek ≃	194	33.18 N	92.22 W
Morogoro	154	6.49 S	37.40 E
Morogoro □[4]	154	8.00 S	37.15 E
Moro Gulf c	116	6.51 N	123.00 E
Moroka	273d	26.16 S	27.52 E
Morokweng	158	26.12 S	23.45 E
Moroleón	234	20.08 N	101.12 W
Morombe	157b	21.45 S	43.22 E
Morón, Arg.	258	34.39 S	58.37 W
Morón, Cuba	240p	22.06 N	78.38 W
Mörön, Mong.	88	48.15 N	100.23 E
Mörön, Mong.	88	47.24 N	110.16 E
Mörön, Mong.	88	49.38 N	100.10 E
Morón, Ven.	246	10.29 N	68.11 W
Morón □[5]	288	34.37 S	58.37 W
Mörön ≃	88	47.14 N	110.37 E
Morón, Aeródromo ⊠	288	34.41 S	58.38 W
Morón, Arroyo ≃	288	34.33 S	58.37 W
Morona ≃	246	4.45 S	77.04 W
Morona-Santiago □[4]	246	2.30 S	78.00 W
Morondava	157b	20.17 S	44.17 E
Morón de Almazán	34	41.25 N	2.25 W
Morón de la Frontera	34	37.08 N	5.27 W
Morones, Sierra ⩘	234	21.45 N	103.10 W
Morong	116	14.41 N	120.16 E
Morongo Indian Reservation ➜[4]	204	33.59 N	116.50 W
Moroni, Comores	157a	11.41 S	43.16 E
Moroni, Ut,. U.S.	200	39.31 N	111.35 W
Moron Us ≃, Zhg.	90	34.42 N	94.50 E
Moron Us ≃, Zhg.	120	34.42 N	94.50 E
Moros ≃	34	41.03 N	4.15 W
Morošečnoje	74	56.24 N	156.12 E
Morotai I	108	2.20 N	128.25 E
Moroto	154	2.32 N	34.39 E
Moroto ʌ	154	2.32 N	34.46 E
Morouba	152	6.11 N	20.13 E
Morovis	240m	18.20 N	66.24 W
Morovsk	78	51.06 N	30.50 E
Morowali	112	1.52 S	121.30 E
Moroyama	94	35.56 N	139.19 E
Morozkovo	86	59.29 N	61.01 E
Morozovka, Ross.	78	50.09 N	39.38 E
Morozovka, Ukr.	83	49.28 N	39.54 E
Morozovsk	80	48.22 N	41.50 E
Morozovskaja	24	61.10 N	50.18 E
Morpeth, On., Can.	214	42.23 N	81.51 W
Morpeth, Eng., U.K.	44	55.10 N	1.41 W
Morphett Vale	168b	35.07 S	138.31 E
Morra, Monte ʌ	267a	42.02 N	12.50 E
Morral	214	40.41 N	83.12 W
Morral, Arroyo del ≃	266d	41.29 N	2.03 E
Morrelganj	126	22.28 N	89.51 E
Morrice	216	42.50 N	84.11 W
Morrill	198	41.57 N	103.55 W
Morrilton	194	35.09 N	92.44 W
Morrin	182	51.40 N	112.47 W
Morrinhos, Bra.	250	3.14 S	40.07 W
Morrinhos, Bra.	255	17.44 S	49.07 W
Morrinsville	172	37.39 S	175.32 E
Morris, Mb., Can.	184	49.21 N	97.22 W
Morris, Ct., U.S.	207	41.41 N	73.11 W
Morris, Il., U.S.	216	41.21 N	88.25 W
Morris, In., U.S.	218	39.16 N	85.10 W
Morris, Mn., U.S.	198	45.35 N	95.54 W
Morris, N.Y., U.S.	210	42.32 N	75.14 W
Morris, Ok., U.S.	196	35.36 N	95.51 W
Morris, Pa., U.S.	210	41.36 N	77.18 W
Morris □[6], N.J., U.S.	210	40.48 N	74.29 W
Morris □[6], Tx., U.S.	222	33.05 N	94.45 W
Morris ≃	184	49.21 N	97.22 W
Morris, Mount ʌ	162	26.09 S	131.04 E
Morrisburg	212	44.54 N	75.11 W
Morrisdale	214	40.56 N	78.13 W
Morris Dam ➜[6]	280	34.11 N	117.53 W
Morris Jesup, Kap ›	16	83.38 N	33.52 W
Morris Lake ⊜	276	41.03 N	74.37 W
Morrison, Arg.	252	32.36 S	62.50 W
Morrison, Il., U.S.	190	41.48 N	89.57 W
Morrison, Mo., U.S.	219	38.40 N	91.38 W
Morrison, Point ›	168b	35.44 S	137.47 E
Morrison Creek ≃	275b	43.28 N	79.39 W
Morrison Lake ⊜, On., Can.	212	44.52 N	79.28 W
Morrison Lake ⊜, Mi., U.S.	216	42.53 N	85.13 W
Morrisonville	219	39.25 N	89.27 W
Morris Park ♠	285	39.59 N	75.15 W
Morris Plains	210	40.49 N	74.28 W
Morris Reservoir ⊜[1]	228	34.12 N	117.52 W
Morris Run	210	41.40 N	77.01 W
Morristown, Az., U.S.	200	33.51 N	112.37 W
Morristown, Il., U.S.	216	42.10 N	89.03 W
Morristown, In., U.S.	218	39.40 N	85.41 W
Morristown, Mn., U.S.	190	44.14 N	93.26 W
Morristown, N.J., U.S.	210	40.47 N	74.28 W
Morristown, N.Y., U.S.	212	44.35 N	75.38 W
Morristown, Oh., U.S.	214	40.04 N	81.05 W
Morristown, S.D., U.S.	198	45.56 N	101.43 W
Morristown, Tn., U.S.	192	36.12 N	83.17 W
Morristown Airport ⊠	276	40.48 N	74.25 W
Morristown National Historical Park ♠	210	40.46 N	74.32 W
Morrisville, N.Y., U.S.	210	42.53 N	75.38 W
Morrisville, Pa., U.S.	208	40.12 N	74.47 W
Morrisville, Vt., U.S.	188	44.33 N	72.35 W
Morrito	236	11.37 N	85.05 W
Morro	246	2.39 S	80.19 W
Morro, Castillo del (Morro Castle) ⊥	286b	23.09 N	82.21 W
Morro, Punta ›	232	19.39 N	90.42 W
Morro Agudo	287a	22.45 S	43.29 W
Morro Bay	226	35.21 N	120.50 W
Morro Bay c	226	35.20 N	120.51 W
Morro Bay State Park ♠	226	35.20 N	120.52 W
Morro Creek ≃	226	35.23 N	120.52 W
Morro do Chapéu	250	11.33 S	41.09 W
Morro d'Oro	66	42.39 N	13.54 E
Morro Mazatán	234	16.07 N	95.27 W
Morrone del Sannio	66	41.43 N	14.47 E
Morropón	248	5.15 S	80.00 W
Morros	250	2.52 S	44.03 W
Morrosquillo, Golfo de c	246	9.35 N	75.40 W
Morrow, La., U.S.	194	30.49 N	92.04 W
Morrow, Oh., U.S.	218	39.21 N	84.07 W
Morrow □[6]	214	40.33 N	82.50 W
Morrow Island I	282	38.07 N	122.05 W
Morrow Mountain State Park ♠	192	35.23 N	80.05 W
Morrow Point Reservoir ⊜[1]	200	38.25 N	107.30 W
Mörrum	26	56.11 N	14.45 E
Morrumbala	154	17.22 S	35.36 E
Morrumbene	156	23.39 S	35.20 E
Mörrumsån ≃	26	56.09 N	14.44 E
Mors I	26	56.50 N	8.45 E
Morsains	50	48.48 N	3.32 E
Morsang-sur-Orge	261	48.40 N	2.21 E
Moršansk	80	53.26 N	41.49 E
Morsbach	56	50.52 N	7.43 E
Mörsch	56	48.58 N	8.17 E
Morschwiller-le-Bas	58	47.45 N	7.16 E
Morščichino	265b	55.56 N	37.20 E
Morse, Sk., Can.	184	50.25 N	107.03 W
Morse, La., U.S.	194	30.07 N	92.29 W
Morse, Tx., U.S.	196	36.04 N	101.29 W
Morse Mill	219	38.17 N	90.40 W
Mörsenbroich ➜[8]	263	51.15 N	6.48 E
Morse Reservoir ⊜[1]	218	40.06 N	86.02 W
Morses Pond ⊜	283	42.18 N	71.19 W
Morsi	120	21.21 N	78.00 E
Morskaja Masel'ga	24	63.06 N	34.54 E
Morskoj Bir'učok, ostrov I	84	44.42 N	47.02 E
Morson	184	49.03 N	94.18 W
Morsott	36	35.40 N	8.01 E
Morstein	285	40.01 N	75.35 W
Mort	272a	28.43 N	77.25 E
Morta	272a	28.44 N	77.27 E
Mortagne	32	48.31 N	0.33 E
Mortagne ≃	58	48.33 N	6.27 E
Mortagne-au-Perche	50	48.31 N	0.33 E
Mortagne-sur-Sèvre	32	47.00 N	0.57 W
Mortain	32	48.39 N	0.56 W
Mortana	162	33.02 S	134.07 E
Mortara	62	45.15 N	8.44 E
Morteau	58	47.04 N	6.37 E
Mortefontaine	50	49.07 N	2.36 E
Mortegliano	64	45.57 N	13.10 E
Morte Point ›	42	51.11 N	4.13 W
Morteratsch, Piz ʌ	58	46.22 N	9.51 E
Morteros	252	30.42 S	62.00 W
Mortes, Rio das ≃, Bra.	255	11.45 S	50.44 W
Mortes, Rio das ≃, Bra.	256	21.18 S	43.58 W
Mortesoro	140	10.12 N	34.09 E
Mort-Homme, Forêt du ➜[3]	56	49.15 N	5.15 E
Mortimer	42	51.22 N	1.04 W
Mortlach	184	50.28 N	106.03 W
Mortlake, Austl.	166	38.05 S	142.48 E
Mortlake, Austl.	274a	33.51 S	151.07 E
Mortlake ➜[8]	260	51.28 N	0.16 W
Mortlock ≃	168a	31.42 S	116.55 E
Mortlock North ≃	168a	31.38 S	116.42 E
Mortola Inferiore	62	43.47 N	7.33 E
Morton, Il., U.S.	190	40.36 N	89.27 W
Morton, Mn., U.S.	198	44.33 N	94.59 W
Morton, Ms., U.S.	194	32.21 N	89.39 W
Morton, N.Y., U.S.	210	43.20 N	78.00 W
Morton, Pa., U.S.	285	39.55 N	75.20 W
Morton, Tx., U.S.	196	33.43 N	102.45 W
Morton, Wa., U.S.	224	46.33 N	122.16 W
Morton, Mount ʌ[2]	274b	37.56 S	145.20 E
Morton Arboretum ➜[4]	278	41.49 N	88.04 W
Morton Craig Range ⩘	162	28.12 S	124.41 E
Morton Grove	216	42.02 N	87.46 W
Morton National Park ♠	170	35.00 S	150.10 E
Mortons Gap	194	37.14 N	87.28 W
Mortorio, Isola I	71	41.05 N	9.36 E
Mortornès del Vallès	266d	41.33 N	2.16 E
Mortrée	50	48.38 N	0.05 E
Mörtschach	64	46.55 N	12.55 E
Mortsel	50	51.10 N	4.28 E
M'ortvyj Donec ≃	83	47.15 N	39.14 E
Morty	80	55.49 N	51.44 E
Morua	175f	16.54 S	168.32 E
Morumbi ➜[8]	287b	23.36 S	46.42 E
Morumbi, Estádio do ♠	287b	23.37 S	46.43 W
Morungaba	256	22.52 S	46.48 W
Morungole ʌ	154	3.49 N	34.02 E
Moruya	166	35.55 S	150.05 E
Morvan ⩘	32	47.05 N	4.00 E
Morvant	241r	10.39 N	61.28 W
Morven, Austl.	166	26.25 S	147.07 E
Morven, N.Z.	172	44.50 S	171.07 E
Morven, Ga., U.S.	192	30.56 N	83.29 W
Morven, N.C., U.S.	192	34.51 N	80.00 W
Morven ʌ, Scot., U.K.	46	58.14 N	3.42 W
Morven ʌ, Scot., U.K.	46	57.07 N	3.02 W
Morwell	169	38.14 S	146.24 E
Morwell ≃	169	38.10 S	146.23 E
Morwenstow	42	50.54 N	4.33 W
Moryń	30	52.49 N	14.13 E
Morženga	76	59.37 N	40.12 E
Morzhovoi	180	54.55 N	163.18 W
Morzine	58	46.11 N	6.43 E
Moržovec, ostrov I	24	66.44 N	42.35 E
Moša ≃, Ross.	24	62.25 N	39.46 E
M'oša ≃, Ross.	80	55.25 N	49.22 E
Mosal'sk	76	54.29 N	34.59 E
Mosambik → Mozambique □[1]	138	18.15 S	35.00 E
Mošanicy	82	54.56 N	38.23 E
Mosås	40	59.12 N	15.08 E
Mosbach	56	49.21 N	9.08 E
Mosborough	44	53.19 N	1.22 W

Symbol	English	Deutsch	Español	Français	Português
≃	River	Fluß	Río	Rivière	Rio
≅	Canal	Kanal	Canal	Canal	Canal
∟	Waterfall, Rapids	Wasserfall, Stromschnellen	Cascada, Rápidos	Chute d'eau, Rapides	Cascata, Rápidos
⊔	Strait	Meeresstraße	Estrecho	Détroit	Estreito
c	Bay, Gulf	Bucht, Golf	Bahía, Golfo	Baie, Golfe	Baía, Golfo
⊜	Lake, Lakes	See, Seen	Lago, Lagos	Lac, Lacs	Lago, Lagos
⩧	Swamp	Sumpf	Pantano	Marais	Pântano
⊟	Ice Features, Glacier	Eis- und Gletscherformen	Accidentes Glaciales	Formes glaciaires	Acidentes glaciares
⍑	Other Hydrographic Features	Andere Hydrographische Objekte	Otros Elementos Hidrográficos	Autres données hydrographiques	Outros acidentes hidrográficos
➜	Submarine Features	Untermeerische Objekte	Accidentes Submarinos	Formes de relief sous-marin	Acidentes submarinos
□	Political Unit	Politische Einheit	Unidad Politica	Entité politique	Unidade política
♉	Cultural Institution	Kulturelle Institution	Institución Cultural	Institution culturelle	Instituição cultural
⊥	Historical Site	Historische Stätte	Sitio Histórico	Site historique	Sitio histórico
♠	Recreational Site	Erholungs- und Ferienort	Sitio de Recreo	Centre de loisirs	Area de Lazer
⊠	Airport	Flughafen	Aeropuerto	Aéroport	Aeroporto
■	Military Installation	Militäranlage	Instalación Militar	Installation militaire	Instalação militar
✦	Miscellaneous	Verschiedenes	Misceláneo	Divers	Diversos

ENGLISH / DEUTSCH

Name	Page (Seite)	Lat.°′ (Breite°′)	Long.°′ (Länge°′ E = Ost)
Mosby	**26**	58.14 N	7.54 E
Mosby Woods	**284c**	38.52 N	77.18 W
Moscavide	**266c**	38.47 N	9.06 W
Mosciano Sant'Angelo	**66**	42.45 N	13.53 E
Moščnyj, ostrov I	**76**	60.01 N	27.50 E
Moscos Islands II	**110**	14.00 N	97.45 E
Moscou → Moskva	**82**	55.45 N	37.35 E
Moscow, Id., U.S.	**202**	46.43 N	116.59 W
Moscow, In., U.S.	**218**	39.29 N	85.34 W
Moscow, Oh., U.S.	**218**	38.51 N	84.13 W
Moscow, Pa., U.S.	**210**	41.20 N	75.31 W
Moscow, Tx., U.S.	**222**	30.55 N	94.50 W
Moscow Air Terminal ⊠	**265b**	55.48 N	37.32 E
Moscow Circus ♠	**265b**	55.43 N	37.33 E
Moscow Mills	**219**	38.56 N	90.55 W
Moscow → Moskva	**82**	55.45 N	37.35 E
Moscow Station ➛[5]	**265a**	59.56 N	30.22 E
Moscow Victory Park ♠	**265a**	59.52 N	30.20 E
Moscow Zoo ♠	**265b**	55.46 N	37.34 E
Moscufo	**66**	42.25 N	14.03 E
Moscú → Moskva	**82**	55.45 N	37.35 E
Mosel	**54**	50.47 N	12.28 E
Mosel (Moselle) ≃	**32**	50.22 N	7.36 E
Moselebe ≃	**156**	25.03 S	23.13 E
Moselle, Ms., U.S.	**194**	31.30 N	89.16 W
Moselle, Mo., U.S.	**219**	38.23 N	90.54 W
Moselle □[5]	**56**	49.00 N	6.30 E
Moselle (Mosel) ≃	**32**	50.22 N	7.36 E
Moselotte ≃	**58**	48.01 N	6.38 E
Mošenskoje	**76**	58.31 N	34.35 E
Mosermandl ∧	**64**	47.12 N	13.24 E
Mosers River	**186**	44.59 N	62.15 W
Moses Lake	**202**	47.07 N	119.16 W
Moses Lake ⊜[1]	**202**	47.10 N	119.20 W
Moses Point	**180**	64.42 N	162.03 W
Moses Power Plant ➛[6]	**284a**	43.09 N	79.02 W
Mosetse	**156**	20.37 S	26.32 E
Mosgiel	**172**	45.53 S	170.21 E
Moshannon	**214**	41.02 N	78.00 W
Moshannon Creek ≃	**214**	41.04 N	78.06 W
Moshanpu	**100**	29.34 N	112.41 E
Moshaweng ≃	**158**	26.35 S	22.50 E
Mosheim, Tn., U.S.	**192**	36.11 N	82.57 W
Mosheim, Tx., U.S.	**222**	31.38 N	97.36 W
Moshi	**154**	3.21 S	37.20 E
Moshi ≃	**150**	9.18 N	4.38 E
Moshiyu	**104**	41.15 N	124.05 E
Mosier	**224**	45.41 N	121.23 W
Mosier Hill ∧[2]	**214**	40.06 N	80.24 W
Mosina	**30**	52.16 N	16.51 E
Mosinee	**190**	44.47 N	89.42 W
Mosjøen	**24**	65.50 N	13.10 E
Moskal'onki	**86**	54.59 N	71.54 E
Moskal'vo	**89**	53.35 N	142.30 E
Moskau → Moskva	**82**	55.45 N	37.35 E
Moskenesøya I	**24**	67.59 N	13.00 E
Moskhāton	**267c**	37.57 N	23.41 E
Moškino	**80**	57.45 N	45.20 E
Moskito-Golf → Mosquitos, Golfo de los ⊂	**236**	9.00 N	81.15 W
Moškovo	**86**	55.18 N	83.37 E
Moskovskaja Slav'anka	**265a**	59.45 N	30.30 E
Moskovskaja vozvyšennost' ⋏[1]	**76**	56.15 N	37.30 E
Moskva (Moscow), Ross.	**82**	55.45 N	37.35 E
Moskva (Moscow), Ross.	**265b**	55.45 N	37.35 E
Moskva □[8]	**82**	55.45 N	37.30 E
Moskva ≃	**76**	55.05 N	38.50 E
Moskva, Gorod □[7]	**265b**	55.45 N	37.35 E
Moskva, pik ∧	**85**	38.57 N	71.49 E
Moskvy, kanal imeni ≍	**82**	56.43 N	37.08 E
Mosman	**170**	33.49 S	151.14 E
Mosman Park	**168a**	32.01 S	115.46 E
Mošny	**78**	49.32 N	31.44 E
Moso (Moos)	**64**	46.41 N	12.23 E
Moso in Passiria (Moos)	**64**	46.50 N	11.10 E
Mošok	**80**	55.48 N	41.17 E
Mosolovo	**80**	54.17 N	40.32 E
Mosomane	**156**	24.04 S	26.15 E
Mosoni-Duna ≃	**61**	47.54 N	17.17 E
Mosonmagyaróvár	**30**	47.51 N	17.17 E
Mosonszolnok	**61**	47.51 N	17.11 E
Mosopa	**156**	24.50 S	25.31 E
Mospino	**83**	47.53 N	38.03 E
Mosqueiro	**250**	1.10 S	48.28 W
Mosquera	**246**	2.30 N	78.29 W
Mosquero	**196**	35.46 N	103.57 W
Mosquic, Lac ⊜	**206**	46.39 N	74.28 W
Mosquito, Punta ≻	**246**	9.07 N	77.53 W
Mosquito, Riacho ≃	**252**	22.02 S	57.57 W
Mosquito Brook ≃	**283**	42.40 N	71.02 W
Mosquito Creek ≃, Ia., U.S.	**198**	41.11 N	95.50 W
Mosquito Creek ≃, Oh., U.S.	**214**	41.10 N	80.45 W
Mosquito Creek ≃, Pa., U.S.	**214**	41.07 N	78.07 W
Mosquito Creek Lake ⊜[1]	**214**	41.22 N	80.45 W
Mosquito Creek State Park ♠	**214**	41.22 N	80.45 W
Mosquito Indian Reserve ➛[4]	**184**	52.30 N	108.15 W
Mosquito Lagoon ⊂	**220**	28.45 N	80.45 W
Mosquitos, Costa de □[9]	**236**	13.00 N	83.45 W
Mosquitos, Golfo de los ⊂	**236**	9.00 N	81.15 W
Moss	**26**	59.26 N	10.42 E
Mossaka	**152**	1.13 S	16.48 E
Mossâmedes	**255**	16.07 S	50.11 W
Mossbank, Sk., Can.	**184**	49.55 N	105.59 W
Moss Bank, Eng., U.K.	**262**	53.29 N	2.44 W
Mossbank, Scot., U.K.	**46a**	60.27 N	1.12 W
Moss Bank Park ♠	**262**	53.36 N	2.28 W
Moss Beach	**282**	37.32 N	122.31 W
Mossburn	**172**	45.40 S	168.15 E
Mosselbaai (Mossel Bay)	**158**	34.11 S	22.08 E
Mosselbaai ⊂	**158**	34.06 S	22.20 E
Mossendjo	**152**	2.57 S	12.44 E
Mosses, Col des)(	**58**	46.24 N	7.06 E
Mossgiel	**166**	33.15 S	144.34 E
Moss Hill	**222**	30.15 N	94.45 W
Mossig ≃	**58**	48.33 N	7.30 E
Mössingen	**58**	48.24 N	9.03 E
Moss Landing	**226**	36.48 N	121.47 W
Mossleigh	**182**	50.43 N	113.20 W
Mossley	**262**	53.32 N	2.02 W
Mossley Hill ➛[8]	**262**	53.23 N	2.55 W
Mossman	**164**	16.28 S	145.22 E
Mossmans Brook ≃	**276**	41.03 N	74.27 W
Moss Moor ➛[3]	**262**	53.37 N	2.00 W
Moss Mountain ∧	**194**	34.50 N	92.40 W
Mossø ⊜	**41**	56.02 N	9.48 E
Mosson ≃	**62**	43.33 N	3.54 E
Mossoró	**250**	5.11 S	37.20 W
Mosso Santa Maria	**62**	45.38 N	8.08 E
Moss Point	**194**	30.24 N	88.32 W
Moss Point ≻	**279a**	41.37 N	81.32 W
Moss Side	**262**	53.46 N	2.57 W
Mossuril	**154**	14.58 S	40.42 E
Moss Vale	**170**	34.33 S	150.22 E
Mossy ≃, Mb., Can.	**184**	51.39 N	99.55 W
Mossy ≃, Sk., Can.	**184**	54.05 N	103.00 W
Mossyrock	**224**	46.31 N	122.29 W
Mossyrock Dam ➛[6]	**224**	46.32 N	122.25 W
Most	**54**	50.32 N	13.39 E
Mosta	**80**	56.32 N	42.10 E
Mostar	**36**	43.20 N	17.49 E
Mostardas, Bra.	**252**	31.06 S	50.57 W
Mostardas, Bra.	**256**	23.44 S	46.38 W
Møsting, Kap ≻	**176**	64.00 N	41.00 W
Mostiska	**78**	49.48 N	23.09 E
Mostiștea ≃	**38**	44.15 N	27.10 E
Mostizzolo	**64**	46.24 N	11.01 E
Mostki	**83**	49.19 N	38.30 E
Most na Soči	**64**	46.09 N	13.44 E
Mostok	**76**	53.59 N	30.28 E
Móstoles	**266a**	40.19 N	3.51 W
Mostoos Hills ⋏[2]	**184**	55.00 N	109.15 W
Mostovaja	**76**	56.13 N	33.08 E
Mostovka	**86**	58.10 N	65.31 E
Mostovoje	**78**	47.24 N	30.59 E
Mostovskoj	**84**	44.25 N	40.48 E
Mostovskoje	**86**	55.46 N	66.22 E
Mostrim (Edgeworthstown)	**48**	53.42 N	7.36 W
Mostva ≃	**78**	52.00 N	27.33 E
Mosty	**76**	53.25 N	24.32 E
Mostyn, Malay.	**112**	4.40 N	118.11 E
Mostyn, Wales, U.K.	**44**	53.19 N	3.16 W
Mosul → Al-Mawṣil	**128**	36.20 N	43.08 E
Møsvatnet ⊜	**26**	59.52 N	8.05 E
Mota	**144**	11.02 N	37.52 E
Mota I	**175f**	13.49 S	167.42 E
Motaba ≃	**152**	2.03 N	18.03 E
Mota del Cuervo	**34**	39.30 N	2.52 W
Mota del Marqués	**34**	41.38 N	5.10 W
Motagua ≃	**236**	15.44 N	88.14 W
Motala	**26**	58.33 N	15.03 E
Motala ström ≃	**40**	58.38 N	16.10 E
Mota Lava I	**175f**	13.40 S	167.40 E
Motane I	**174x**	9.59 S	138.49 W
Motatán	**246**	9.24 N	70.36 W
Motaze	**156**	24.48 S	32.52 E
Motegi	**94**	36.32 N	140.11 E
Mote Park ♠	**260**	51.17 N	0.34 E
Moteve, Cap ≻	**174x**	9.58 S	139.02 W
Moth	**124**	25.43 N	78.57 E
Mother Brook ≍	**283**	42.15 N	71.10 W
Motherwell	**46**	55.48 N	4.00 W
Motihāri	**124**	26.39 N	84.55 E
Motilla del Palancar	**34**	39.34 N	1.53 W
Motiong	**116**	11.47 N	125.00 E
Motiti Island I	**172**	37.38 S	176.26 E
Motjärnshyttan	**40**	59.56 N	13.58 E
Motloutse	**156**	21.28 S	27.24 E
Motloutse ≃	**156**	22.15 S	29.00 E
Moto-ara ≃	**94**	35.53 N	139.50 E
Motobu	**174m**	26.39 N	127.54 E
Motol'	**76**	52.19 N	25.36 E
Motola, Monte ∧	**68**	40.22 N	15.26 E
Motopu	**174x**	9.55 S	139.03 W
Motor Island I	**284a**	42.58 N	78.56 W
Motorki	**80**	56.53 N	51.29 E
Motorovo	**86**	56.31 N	71.10 E
Motosu	**94**	35.29 N	136.40 E
Motosu-ko ⊜	**94**	35.28 N	138.35 E
Motou	**106**	32.18 N	120.34 E
Motovilovo	**80**	55.36 N	43.51 E
Motovun	**64**	45.20 N	13.50 E
Motoyama	**96**	33.45 N	133.35 E
Moto-yama ∧[2]	**174f**	24.48 N	141.20 E
Motozintla de Mendoza	**232**	15.22 N	92.14 W
Motril	**34**	36.45 N	3.31 W
Motrone	**64**	43.54 N	10.12 E
Motru	**38**	44.50 N	23.00 E
Mott	**198**	46.22 N	102.19 W
Motta	**64**	45.36 N	11.29 E
Motta Camastra	**70**	37.54 N	15.10 E
Motta d'Affermo	**70**	37.59 N	14.18 E
Motta di Livenza	**64**	45.47 N	12.36 E
Mottafollone	**68**	39.39 N	16.04 E
Motta Montecorvino	**68**	41.30 N	15.07 E
Motta San Giovanni	**70**	38.00 N	15.41 E
Motta Sant'Anastasia	**70**	37.31 N	14.58 E
Motta Visconti	**62**	45.17 N	8.59 E
Möttingen	**56**	48.48 N	10.35 E
Mottingham ➛[8]	**260**	51.26 N	0.03 E
Mottisfont	**42**	51.02 N	1.32 W
Mottola	**68**	40.38 N	17.03 E
Mottram in Longdendale	**262**	53.27 N	2.01 W
Motts Creek ≃	**276**	40.38 N	73.45 W
Mottville, Mi., U.S.	**216**	41.48 N	85.45 W
Mottville, N.Y., U.S.	**210**	42.59 N	76.27 W
Motu ≃	**172**	37.51 S	177.35 E
Motueka	**172**	41.07 S	173.00 E
Motueka ≃	**172**	41.05 S	173.01 E
Motul [de Felipe Carrillo Puerto]	**232**	21.06 N	89.17 W
Motu One I[1]	**14**	15.48 S	154.33 W
Motupe	**248**	6.09 S	79.44 W
Motupena Point ≻	**175e**	6.32 S	155.09 E
Motutapu I	**174k**	21.14 S	159.43 W
Motygino	**86**	58.11 N	94.40 E
Motyklejka	**74**	59.26 N	148.38 E
Motyžin	**78**	50.23 N	29.55 E
Motyzlej	**80**	54.54 N	42.54 E
Mou	**175f**	21.05 S	165.26 E
Mouanko	**152**	3.39 N	9.49 E
Mouans-Sartoux	**62**	43.37 N	6.58 E
Mouaskar	**148**	35.45 N	0.01 E
Mouaskar □[5]	**148**	35.10 N	0.00
Mouchard	**58**	46.58 N	5.48 E
Mouchoir Bank ✦[2]	**238**	20.57 N	70.42 W
Mouchoir Passage ʮ	**238**	21.10 N	71.00 W
Moúdhros	**38**	39.52 N	25.16 E
Mouding	**102**	25.24 N	101.35 E
Moudjéria	**150**	17.53 N	12.20 W
Moudon	**58**	46.40 N	6.48 E
Moudongouma ≃	**152**	1.36 N	17.24 E
Mouila	**152**	1.52 S	11.01 E
Mouit	**150**	16.35 N	13.05 W
Mouka	**152**	7.16 N	21.52 E
Moukden → Shenyang	**104**	41.48 N	123.27 E
Moulamein	**166**	35.05 S	144.02 E
Moulay-bou-Selham	**34**	34.53 N	6.15 W
Moulay-Idriss	**148**	34.02 N	5.27 W
Mouldsworth	**262**	53.14 N	2.44 W
Moule à Chique, Cap ≻	**241f**	13.43 N	60.57 W
Moulhoulé	**144**	12.36 N	43.12 E
Moulin, Île du I	**275a**	45.41 N	73.32 W
Moulin-des-Ponts	**58**	46.20 N	5.19 E
Moulineaux	**50**	49.21 N	0.58 E
Moulinet	**62**	43.57 N	7.25 E
Moulins	**32**	46.34 N	3.20 E
Moulins-la-Marche	**50**	48.39 N	0.29 E
Moulmeingyun	**110**	16.23 N	95.16 E
Moulmein → Mawlamyine	**110**	16.30 N	97.38 E
Moulouya, Oued ≃	**148**	35.05 N	2.25 W
Moulton, Eng., U.K.	**262**	53.13 N	2.31 W
Moulton, Al., U.S.	**194**	34.28 N	87.17 W
Moulton, Ia., U.S.	**190**	40.41 N	92.40 W
Moulton, Tx., U.S.	**222**	29.34 N	97.09 W
Moultrie	**192**	31.10 N	83.47 W
Moultrie □[6]	**219**	39.36 N	88.37 W
Moultrie, Lake ⊜[1]	**192**	33.20 N	80.05 W
Mouly	**175f**	20.42 S	166.25 E
Mound	**222**	31.21 N	97.38 W
Mound Bayou	**194**	33.52 N	90.43 W
Mound City, Il., U.S.	**194**	37.05 N	89.09 W
Mound City, Ks., U.S.	**198**	38.08 N	94.48 W
Mound City, Mo., U.S.	**194**	40.07 N	95.13 W
Mound City, S.D., U.S.	**198**	45.43 N	100.04 W
Mound City Group National Monument ♠	**218**	39.23 N	83.00 W
Mound Lake ⊜	**219**	40.05 N	90.17 W
Moundou	**146**	8.34 N	16.05 E
Moundridge	**198**	38.12 N	97.31 W
Mounds, Il., U.S.	**194**	37.06 N	89.11 W
Mounds, Ok., U.S.	**196**	35.52 N	96.03 W
Mounds State Park ♠	**218**	40.07 N	85.37 W
Mounds State Recreation Area ♠	**218**	39.30 N	84.59 W
Moundsville	**188**	39.55 N	80.44 W
Moundville	**194**	32.59 N	87.37 W
Moungali ➛[8]	**273b**	4.15 S	15.17 E
Moung Roessei	**110**	12.46 N	103.27 E
Mounianzé ≃	**152**	0.32 N	12.52 E
Mounier, Mont ∧	**62**	44.09 N	6.58 E
Mounlapamôk	**110**	14.20 N	105.52 E
Mount Aetna	**208**	40.25 N	76.18 W
Mountain	**190**	45.11 N	88.28 W
Mountain □[4]	**116**	17.20 N	121.10 E
Mountain ≃	**180**	65.41 N	128.50 W
Mountainair	**200**	34.31 N	106.14 W
Mountainaire	**200**	35.05 N	111.39 W
Mountain Ash	**42**	51.42 N	3.24 W
Mountain Brook	**194**	33.30 N	86.45 W
Mountain Chute Dam ➛[6]	**212**	45.11 N	76.54 W
Mountain City, Ga., U.S.	**192**	34.55 N	83.23 W
Mountain City, Nv., U.S.	**204**	41.50 N	115.57 W
Mountain City, Tn., U.S.	**192**	36.28 N	81.48 W
Mountain Creek	**194**	32.43 N	86.29 W
Mountain Creek ≃, Pa., U.S.	**208**	40.09 N	77.11 W
Mountain Creek ≃, Tx., U.S.	**222**	32.42 N	96.58 W
Mountain Creek Lake ⊜[1]	**222**	32.43 N	96.58 W
Mountain Dale	**210**	41.41 N	74.31 W
Mountain Grove	**194**	37.07 N	92.15 W
Mountain Home, Ar., U.S.	**194**	36.20 N	92.23 W
Mountain Home, Id., U.S.	**202**	43.07 N	115.41 W
Mountainhome, Pa., U.S.	**210**	41.11 N	75.17 W
Mountain Home Air Force Base ■	**202**	43.03 N	115.52 W
Mountain Iron	**190**	47.31 N	92.37 W
Mountain Lake, Fl., U.S.	**220**	27.57 N	81.36 W
Mountain Lake, Mn., U.S.	**198**	43.56 N	94.55 W
Mountain Lake ⊜, On., Can.	**212**	44.42 N	81.03 W
Mountain Lake ⊜, On., Can.	**212**	44.59 N	78.43 W
Mountain Lake ⊜, N.J., U.S.	**276**	40.53 N	74.27 W
Mountain Lakes	**210**	40.53 N	74.26 W
Mountain Lodge	**210**	41.23 N	74.09 W
Mountain Nile (Baḥr al-Jabal) ≃	**136**	9.30 N	30.30 E
Mountain Park	**182**	52.55 N	117.14 W
Mountain Pine	**194**	34.34 N	93.10 W
Mountain Point	**182**	55.18 N	131.32 W
Mountain Ranch	**226**	38.14 N	120.33 W
Mountainside	**208**	40.40 N	74.21 W
Mountain Spring Lakes	**276**	41.02 N	74.23 W
Mountain Valley Lake ⊜	**279b**	40.18 N	79.35 W
Mountain View, Ar., U.S.	**194**	35.52 N	92.07 W
Mountain View, Ca., U.S.	**226**	37.23 N	122.04 W
Mountain View, Mo., U.S.	**194**	36.59 N	91.42 W
Mountain View, Ok., U.S.	**196**	35.05 N	98.44 W
Mountain View, Wy., U.S.	**200**	41.16 N	110.20 W
Mountain View, Wy., U.S.	**200**	42.51 N	106.23 W
Mountain View Acres	**228**	34.31 N	117.24 W
Mountain Village	**180**	62.05 N	163.44 W
Mountain Zebra National Park ♠	**158**	32.16 S	25.29 E
Mount Airy, Md., U.S.	**208**	39.22 N	77.09 W
Mount Airy, N.C., U.S.	**192**	36.29 N	80.36 W
Mount Airy ➛[8]	**285**	40.04 N	75.12 W
Mount Albert	**212**	44.08 N	79.19 W
Mount Alford	**171a**	28.04 S	152.36 E
Mount Alida	**158**	29.09 S	30.18 E
Mount Alverno	**285**	39.53 N	75.25 W
Mount Angel	**224**	45.04 N	122.47 W
Mount Ann Park ♠	**283**	42.37 N	70.44 W
Mount Arlington	**210**	40.55 N	74.38 W
Mount Assiniboine Provincial Park ♠	**182**	50.54 N	115.40 W
Mount Auburn	**219**	39.46 N	89.16 W
Mount Augustus	**162**	24.19 S	116.54 E
Mount Ayliff	**158**	30.54 S	29.20 E
Mount Ayr, In., U.S.	**216**	40.57 N	87.18 W
Mount Ayr, Ia., U.S.	**198**	40.42 N	94.14 W
Mount Baldy	**280**	34.14 N	117.40 W
Mount Barker, Austl.	**162**	34.38 S	117.40 E
Mount Barker, Austl.	**168b**	35.04 S	138.52 E
Mount Bellew Bridge	**48**	53.28 N	8.29 W
Mount Berry	**194**	34.17 N	85.11 W
Mount Bethel	**210**	40.54 N	75.07 W
Mount Blanchard	**216**	40.53 N	83.33 W
Mount Bold Reservoir ⊜[1]	**168b**	35.07 S	138.42 E
Mount Brydges	**214**	42.54 N	81.29 W
Mount Buffalo National Park ♠	**166**	36.45 S	146.45 E
Mount Buller	**169**	37.10 S	146.27 E
Mount Calm	**222**	31.45 N	96.53 W
Mount Carleton Provincial Park ♠	**186**	47.23 N	66.50 W
Mount Carmel, Nf., Can.	**186**	47.09 N	53.29 W
Mount Carmel, Il., U.S.	**194**	38.24 N	87.45 W
Mount Carmel, Ky., U.S.	**218**	38.29 N	83.38 W
Mount Carmel, Oh., U.S.	**218**	39.06 N	84.18 W
Mount Carmel, Pa., U.S.	**208**	40.47 N	76.24 W
Mount Carmel Heights	**218**	39.07 N	84.18 W
Mount Carroll	**190**	42.05 N	89.58 W
Mount Cavenagh	**162**	25.58 S	133.15 E
Mount Charles	**275b**	43.41 N	79.40 W
Mount Clare	**188**	39.13 N	80.21 W
Mount Clemens	**214**	42.35 N	82.52 W
Mount Colah	**274a**	33.41 S	151.07 E
Mount Compass	**168b**	35.22 S	138.37 E
Mount Cook	**172**	43.44 S	170.06 E
Mount Cook National Park ♠	**172**	43.35 S	170.15 E
Mount Coot-tha Park ♠	**171a**	27.28 S	152.56 E
Mount Cory	**216**	40.56 N	83.50 W
Mount Crawford	**168b**	34.40 S	138.57 E
Mount Crosby	**171a**	27.32 S	152.48 E
Mount Currie Indian Reserve ➛[4]	**182**	50.19 N	122.42 W
Mount Dandenong	**274b**	37.50 S	145.22 E
Mount Dennis ➛[8]	**275b**	43.42 N	79.30 W
Mount Desert Island I	**188**	44.20 N	68.20 W
Mount Diablo Creek ≃	**282**	38.02 N	122.02 W
Mount Diablo State Park ♠	**226**	37.51 N	121.55 W
Mount Dora	**220**	28.48 N	81.38 W
Mount Doreen	**162**	22.03 S	131.18 E
Mount Druitt	**274a**	33.46 S	150.49 E
Mount Eaton	**214**	40.42 N	81.42 W
Mount Eba	**166**	30.12 S	135.40 E
Mount Eden	**226**	37.38 N	122.06 W
Mount Edgecumbe	**180**	57.03 N	135.21 W
Mount Edwards	**171a**	28.01 S	152.31 E
Mount Elgon National Park ♠	**154**	1.07 N	34.44 E
Mount Elizabeth	**164**	16.15 S	126.12 E
Mount Emu Creek ≃	**169**	38.18 S	142.55 E
Mount Enterprise	**222**	31.55 N	94.41 W
Mount Ephraim	**285**	39.52 N	75.05 W
Mount Evelyn	**274b**	37.47 S	145.23 E
Mount Fern	**276**	40.52 N	74.34 W
Mount Field National Park ♠	**166**	42.40 S	146.35 E
Mount Fletcher	**158**	30.40 S	28.30 E
Mount Forest	**212**	43.59 N	80.44 W
Mount Freedom	**210**	40.49 N	74.34 W
Mount Frere	**158**	31.00 S	28.58 E
Mount Gambier	**166**	37.50 S	140.46 E
Mount Garnet	**166**	17.41 S	145.07 E
Mount Gay	**188**	37.51 N	82.00 W
Mount Gilead, N.C., U.S.	**192**	35.12 N	80.00 W
Mount Gilead, Oh., U.S.	**214**	40.32 N	82.49 W
Mount Gravatt	**171a**	27.33 S	153.06 E
Mount Greenwood ➛[8]	**278**	41.42 N	87.43 W
Mount Gunson	**162**	31.27 S	137.11 E
Mount Hagen	**164**	5.50 S	144.15 E
Mount Hawke	**42**	50.17 N	5.12 W
Mount Hawthorn	**168a**	31.55 S	115.50 E
Mount Healthy	**218**	39.14 N	84.32 W
Mount Hebron	**284b**	39.18 N	76.50 W
Mount Helena	**168a**	31.53 S	116.13 E
Mount Hermon, Ca., U.S.	**226**	37.03 N	122.04 W
Mount Hermon, Ma., U.S.	**207**	42.40 N	72.29 W
Mount Holly, N.J., U.S.	**208**	39.59 N	74.47 W
Mount Holly, N.C., U.S.	**192**	35.17 N	81.00 W
Mount Holly Springs	**208**	40.07 N	77.11 W
Mount Hope, Austl.	**166**	34.07 S	135.23 E
Mount Hope, On., Can.	**212**	43.09 N	79.55 W
Mount Hope, Ks., U.S.	**198**	37.52 N	97.39 W
Mount Hope, N.J., U.S.	**276**	40.56 N	74.33 W
Mount Hope, Oh., U.S.	**214**	40.38 N	81.47 W
Mount Hope, W.V., U.S.	**188**	37.53 N	81.09 W
Mount Hope Lake ⊜	**276**	40.56 N	74.32 W
Mount Horeb	**190**	43.00 N	89.44 W
Mount Houston	**222**	29.54 N	95.18 W
Mount Howitt	**166**	26.31 S	142.16 E
Mount Hunter Rivulet ≃	**274a**	34.02 S	150.40 E
Mount Ida	**194**	34.33 N	93.38 W
Mount Isa	**166**	20.44 S	139.30 E
Mount Jackson, Pa., U.S.	**214**	40.58 N	80.26 W
Mount Jackson, Va., U.S.	**188**	38.44 N	78.38 W
Mount Jewett	**214**	41.43 N	78.38 W
Mount Juliet	**194**	36.12 N	86.31 W
Mount Kaputar National Park ♠	**166**	30.16 S	150.10 E
Mount Kenya National Park ♠	**154**	0.09 S	37.19 E
Mount Kisco	**210**	41.12 N	73.43 W
Mount Kokeby	**168a**	32.13 S	116.58 E
Mountlake Terrace	**224**	47.47 N	122.18 W
Mount Laurel	**285**	39.56 N	74.54 W
Mount Lebanon	**214**	40.21 N	80.02 W
Mount Liberty	**214**	40.21 N	82.38 W
Mount Lofty Ranges ⋏	**168b**	34.45 S	139.00 E
Mount Magnet	**162**	28.04 S	117.49 E
Mount Manara	**166**	32.29 S	143.56 E
Mount Margaret, Austl.	**162**	28.47 S	122.11 E
Mount Margaret, Austl.	**166**	26.54 S	143.21 E
Mount Marion	**210**	42.02 N	73.59 W
Mount Martha	**169**	38.17 S	145.01 E
Mount Maunganui	**172**	37.37 S	176.11 E
Mount McKinley National Park → Denali National Park ♠	**180**	63.15 N	150.30 W
Mount Mee	**171a**	27.04 S	152.46 E
Mountmellick	**48**	53.07 N	7.20 W
Mount Misery Point ≻	**276**	40.58 N	73.05 W
Mount Mistake National Park ♠	**171a**	27.53 S	152.20 E
Mount Molloy	**164**	16.41 S	145.20 E
Mount Monger	**162**	30.59 S	121.53 E
Mount Moorosi	**158**	30.16 S	27.53 E
Mount Morgan	**166**	23.39 S	150.23 E
Mount Morris, Il., U.S.	**190**	42.03 N	89.25 W
Mount Morris, Mi., U.S.	**190**	43.07 N	83.41 W
Mount Morris, N.Y., U.S.	**210**	42.43 N	77.52 W
Mount Morris Dam ➛[6]	**210**	42.44 N	77.53 W
Mount Mulligan	**166**	16.51 S	144.52 E
Mount Nebo	**279b**	40.33 N	80.06 W
Mountnessing	**260**	51.39 N	0.21 E
Mount Olive, Il., U.S.	**219**	39.04 N	89.43 W
Mount Olive, Ms., U.S.	**194**	31.45 N	89.39 W
Mount Olive, N.C., U.S.	**192**	35.11 N	78.04 W
Mount Oliver	**279b**	40.28 N	79.59 W
Mount Olivet	**218**	38.31 N	84.02 W
Mount Orab	**218**	39.01 N	83.55 W
Mount Penn	**208**	40.20 N	75.54 W
Mount Perry	**166**	25.11 S	151.39 E
Mount Pleasant, Austl.	**168b**	34.47 S	139.02 E
Mount Pleasant, On., Can.	**212**	43.05 N	80.19 W
Mount Pleasant, In., U.S.	**218**	38.07 N	86.31 W
Mount Pleasant, Ia., U.S.	**190**	40.57 N	91.33 W
Mount Pleasant, Mi., U.S.	**190**	43.35 N	84.46 W
Mount Pleasant, N.C., U.S.	**192**	35.23 N	80.26 W
Mount Pleasant, Oh., U.S.	**214**	40.11 N	80.48 W
Mount Pleasant, Pa., U.S.	**214**	40.08 N	79.32 W
Mount Pleasant, S.C., U.S.	**192**	32.47 N	79.51 W
Mount Pleasant, Tn., U.S.	**194**	35.32 N	87.12 W
Mount Pleasant, Tx., U.S.	**222**	33.09 N	94.58 W
Mount Pleasant, Ut,. U.S.	**200**	39.32 N	111.27 W
Mount Pleasant Mills	**208**	40.43 N	77.01 W
Mount Pleasant Park ♠	**284b**	39.22 N	76.35 W
Mount Pocono	**210**	41.07 N	75.21 W
Mount Pritchard	**274a**	33.54 S	150.54 E
Mount Prospect, S. Afr.	**158**	27.29 S	29.53 E
Mount Prospect, Il., U.S.	**216**	42.03 N	87.56 W
Mount Pulaski	**219**	40.00 N	89.16 W
Mount Rainier	**284c**	38.56 N	76.57 W
Mount Rainier National Park ♠	**224**	46.52 N	121.43 W
Mountrath	**48**	53.00 N	7.27 W
Mount Repose	**218**	39.10 N	84.14 W
Mount Revelstoke National Park ♠	**182**	51.06 N	118.00 W
Mount Riddock	**162**	23.03 S	134.40 E
Mount Robson Provincial Park ♠	**182**	52.58 N	118.50 W
Mount Rogers National Recreation Area ♠	**192**	36.42 N	81.30 W
Mount Roskill	**172**	36.55 S	174.45 E
Mount Royal	**285**	39.49 N	75.13 W
Mount Rushmore National Memorial ⊥	**198**	43.50 N	103.24 W
Mount Saint Helens National Volcanic Monument ♠	**224**	46.12 N	122.11 W
Mount Sandiman	**162**	24.24 S	115.23 E
Mount Sarah	**162**	26.57 S	135.22 E
Mount Savage	**188**	39.41 N	78.52 W
Mount's Bay ⊂	**42**	50.03 N	5.25 W
Mount Selinda	**154**	20.25 S	32.43 E
Mount Selman	**222**	32.04 N	95.17 W
Mount Seymour Provincial Park ♠	**182**	49.23 N	122.57 W
Mount Shasta	**204**	41.18 N	122.18 W
Mount Sinai	**276**	40.57 N	73.02 W
Mount Sinai Harbor ⊂	**276**	40.57 N	73.02 W
Mount Sinai Ridge ∧	**218**	39.04 N	84.58 W
Mount Somers	**172**	43.43 S	171.24 E
Mountsorrel	**42**	52.44 N	1.07 W
Mount Spokane State Park ♠	**202**	47.58 N	117.13 W
Mount Sterling, Il., U.S.	**219**	39.59 N	90.45 W
Mount Sterling, Ky., U.S.	**192**	38.03 N	83.56 W
Mount Sterling, Mo., U.S.	**219**	38.28 N	91.38 W
Mount Sterling, Oh., U.S.	**218**	39.43 N	83.15 W
Mount Stewart, P.E., Can.	**186**	46.22 N	62.52 W
Mount Stewart, S. Afr.	**158**	33.10 S	24.26 E
Mount Stromlo Observatory ⱱ[3]	**171b**	35.20 S	149.00 E
Mount Summit	**218**	40.00 N	85.23 W
Mount Surprise	**166**	18.09 S	144.19 E
Mount Sylvia	**171a**	27.44 S	152.14 E
Mount Tamalpais State Park ♠	**226**	37.54 N	122.34 W
Mount Torrens	**168b**	34.52 S	138.57 E
Mount Tremper	**210**	42.03 N	74.17 W
Mount Uniacke	**186**	44.54 N	63.50 W
Mount Union	**214**	40.23 N	77.52 W
Mount Upton	**210**	42.25 N	75.23 W
Mount Vernon, Austl.	**162**	24.13 S	118.14 E
Mount Vernon, Al., U.S.	**194**	31.05 N	88.00 W
Mount Vernon, Ga., U.S.	**192**	32.10 N	82.35 W
Mount Vernon, Il., U.S.	**219**	38.19 N	88.54 W
Mount Vernon, In., U.S.	**194**	37.55 N	87.53 W
Mount Vernon, Ia., U.S.	**190**	41.55 N	91.25 W
Mount Vernon, Ky., U.S.	**192**	37.21 N	84.20 W
Mount Vernon, Md., U.S.	**208**	38.14 N	75.49 W
Mount Vernon, Mo., U.S.	**194**	37.06 N	93.49 W
Mount Vernon, N.Y., U.S.	**210**	42.45 N	78.53 W
Mount Vernon, N.Y., U.S.	**210**	40.54 N	73.50 W
Mount Vernon, Oh., U.S.	**214**	40.23 N	82.29 W
Mount Vernon, Or., U.S.	**202**	44.25 N	119.06 W
Mount Vernon, Pa., U.S.	**279b**	40.17 N	79.48 W
Mount Vernon, S.D., U.S.	**198**	43.42 N	98.15 W
Mount Vernon, Tx., U.S.	**222**	33.11 N	95.13 W
Mount Vernon, Wa., U.S.	**224**	48.25 N	122.19 W
Mount Vernon ⊥	**208**	38.47 N	77.06 W
Mount Victoria	**170**	33.35 S	150.15 E
Mount Victory	**216**	40.32 N	83.31 W
Mount View	**207**	41.38 N	71.24 W
Mountville	**208**	40.02 N	76.26 W
Mount Vision	**210**	42.35 N	75.04 W
Mount Washington	**284b**	39.23 N	76.41 W
Mount Washington ➛[8]	**284b**	39.22 N	76.40 W
Mount Waverley	**274b**	37.53 S	145.08 E
Mount Wedge, Austl.	**162**	22.45 S	132.09 E
Mount Wedge, Austl.	**162**	33.29 S	135.10 E
Mount Wellington	**172**	36.54 S	174.51 E
Mount Wilhelm National Park ♠	**164**	5.45 S	145.05 E
Mount William National Park ♠	**166**	40.56 S	148.15 E
Mount Willoughby	**162**	27.58 S	134.08 E
Mount Wilson Observatory ⱱ[3]	**228**	34.14 N	118.03 W
Mount Wolf	**208**	40.03 N	76.42 W
Mount Zion	**219**	39.46 N	88.53 W
Mounyaz	**146**	10.41 N	21.18 E
Moura, Austl.	**166**	24.35 S	149.58 E
Moura, Bra.	**246**	1.27 S	61.38 W
Moura, Port.	**34**	38.08 N	7.27 W
Moura, Tchad	**146**	13.47 N	21.13 E
Moura Brasil	**256**	22.07 S	43.09 W
Mouraya	**146**	11.27 N	20.59 E
Mourdi, Dépression du ⊥[7]	**146**	18.10 N	23.00 E
Mourdiah	**150**	14.28 N	7.28 W
Mouriès	**62**	43.41 N	4.52 E
Mourindi	**152**	2.32 S	10.48 E
Mourmelon-le-Grand	**50**	49.08 N	4.22 E
Mourne ≃	**48**	54.49 N	7.28 W
Mourne Beg ≃	**48**	54.41 N	7.39 W
Mourne Mountains ⋏	**48**	54.10 N	6.04 W
Mousa I	**46a**	60.00 N	1.11 W
Mouscron	**50**	50.44 N	3.13 E
Mousgougou	**146**	10.47 N	16.09 E
Moussa Ali ∧	**144**	12.28 N	42.24 E
Mousseaux-sur-Seine	**261**	49.03 N	1.39 E
Moussey	**58**	48.40 N	6.47 E
Moussoro	**146**	13.39 N	16.29 E
Moussy-le-Neuf	**261**	49.04 N	2.36 E
Moussy-le-Vieux	**261**	49.03 N	2.38 E
Moustiers-Sainte-Marie	**62**	43.51 N	6.13 E
Moustique, Morne ∧	**241o**	16.06 N	61.44 W
Mouthe	**58**	46.43 N	6.12 E
Mouthier-Haute-Pierre	**58**	47.02 N	6.16 E
Moutier	**58**	47.17 N	7.23 E
Moûtiers	**62**	45.29 N	6.32 E
Moutiers-au-Perche	**50**	48.29 N	0.51 E
Moutnice	**61**	49.02 N	16.46 E
Moutohora	**172**	38.17 S	177.32 E
Moutomoukadi	**152**	4.41 S	13.15 E
Moutong	**112**	0.28 N	121.13 E
Mouy	**50**	49.19 N	2.19 E
Mouydir ⋏	**148**	24.45 N	4.05 E
Mouyondzi	**152**	3.58 S	13.57 E
Mouzákion	**38**	39.26 N	21.40 E
Mouzarak	**146**	13.11 N	15.58 E
Mouzon	**56**	49.36 N	5.05 E
Mouzon ≃	**58**	48.21 N	5.41 E
Moville, Ire.	**48**	55.11 N	7.03 W
Moville, Ia., U.S.	**198**	42.29 N	96.04 W
Mowang	**100**	30.31 N	113.34 E
Moweaqua	**219**	39.37 N	89.01 W
Mowein	**140**	7.36 N	28.11 E
Mowry Slough ≃	**282**	37.29 N	122.03 W
Mowrystown	**218**	39.02 N	83.44 W
Mowu	**100**	26.50 N	117.42 E
Moxhe	**56**	50.38 N	5.05 E
Moxi	**107**	30.18 N	105.41 E
Moxico □[5]	**152**	13.00 S	20.30 E
Moxotó ≃	**250**	9.19 S	38.14 W
Moy	**48**	54.27 N	6.42 W
Moy ≃	**48**	54.12 N	9.08 W
Moy, Cnoc ∧[2]	**46**	55.22 N	5.46 W
Moya, Comores	**157a**	12.18 S	44.27 E
Moya, Perú	**248**	12.24 S	75.10 W
Moyagee	**162**	27.45 S	117.54 E
Moyahua	**234**	21.16 N	103.10 W
Moyale, Ityo.	**144**	3.30 N	39.07 E
Moyale, Kenya	**154**	3.32 N	39.03 E
Moyamba	**150**	8.10 N	12.26 W
Moycullen	**48**	53.21 N	9.09 W
Moydans	**62**	44.24 N	5.30 E
Moÿ-de-l'Aisne	**50**	49.45 N	3.22 E
Moye Dao I	**98**	36.55 N	122.32 E
Moyen Atlas ⋏	**148**	33.30 N	5.00 W
Moyen-Chari □[5]	**146**	9.00 N	18.00 E
Moyenmoutier	**58**	48.23 N	6.55 E
Moyenne-Sido	**146**	8.13 N	18.43 E
Moyenneville	**50**	50.04 N	1.45 E
Moyen-Ogooué □[4]	**152**	0.30 S	10.30 E
Moyenvic	**56**	48.47 N	6.33 E
Moyeuvre-Grande	**56**	49.15 N	6.02 E
Moyie	**182**	49.17 N	115.50 W
Moyie ≃	**202**	48.42 N	116.11 W
Moyie Springs	**202**	48.43 N	116.11 W
Moylan	**285**	39.54 N	75.23 W
Moyle ≃	**48**	52.24 N	7.39 W
Moyo	**154**	3.39 N	31.43 E
Moyo ≃	**115b**	8.26 S	117.28 E
Moyo, Pulau I	**115b**	8.15 S	117.34 E
Moyobamba	**248**	6.03 S	76.58 W
Moyock	**208**	36.31 N	76.10 W
Moyogalpa	**236**	11.32 N	85.42 W
Moyowosi ≃	**154**	4.50 S	31.24 E
Moyu	**120**	37.17 N	79.44 E
Moyuta, Volcán ∧[1]	**236**	14.02 N	90.06 W
M'oža ≃, Europe	**76**	55.27 N	30.43 E
M'oža ≃, Ross.	**80**	58.23 N	44.54 E
Možajevka	**83**	48.44 N	39.45 E
Možajsk	**82**	55.30 N	36.01 E
Možajskij	**265a**	59.43 N	30.07 E
Možajskoje vodochranilišče ⊜[1]	**82**	55.35 N	35.50 E
Mozambique (Moçambique) □[1]	**138**	18.15 S	35.00 E
Mozambique Channel ʮ	**138**	19.00 S	41.00 E
Mozambique → Moçambique	**154**	15.03 S	40.42 E
Mozambique Plateau ✦[3]	**10**	32.00 S	35.00 E
Mozarlândia	**255**	14.47 S	50.35 W
Možarovka	**86**	51.09 N	59.05 E
Možarov Majdan	**80**	55.37 N	45.53 E
Možary	**80**	53.53 N	41.02 E
Mozdok	**84**	43.44 N	44.38 E
Možga	**80**	56.23 N	52.17 E
Mozhabong Lake ⊜	**190**	46.57 N	82.05 W
Mozia ⊥	**70**	37.52 N	12.28 E
Mozichang	**107**	29.20 N	103.53 E
Mozolevo	**76**	59.19 N	33.51 E
Mozu	**270**	34.34 N	135.29 E
Mozuli	**76**	56.36 N	28.11 E
Mozyr'	**78**	52.03 N	29.14 E
Mozzanica	**62**	45.29 N	9.41 E
Mozzano	**66**	42.50 N	13.31 E
Mozzate	**266b**	45.41 N	8.57 E
Mpaka	**158**	26.26 S	31.47 E
Mpala	**154**	6.45 S	29.31 E
Mpama ≃	**152**	0.57 S	15.39 E
Mpanda	**154**	6.22 S	31.02 E
Mpé	**152**	2.54 S	14.43 E
Mpese	**152**	5.14 S	15.33 E
Mpessoba	**150**	12.40 N	5.43 W
Mphoengs	**154**	21.10 S	27.51 E
Mpigi	**154**	0.13 N	32.42 E
Mpika	**154**	11.54 S	31.26 E
Mpila ➛[8]	**273b**	4.14 S	15.18 E
Mpoka	**152**	1.26 S	17.02 E
Mpoko ≃	**152**	4.19 N	18.33 E
Mporokoso	**154**	9.23 S	30.05 E
Mpouya	**152**	2.37 S	16.13 E
Mpraeso	**150**	6.35 N	0.44 W
Mpui	**154**	8.21 S	31.50 E
Mpulungu	**154**	8.46 S	31.07 E
Mpwapwa	**154**	6.21 S	36.29 E
Mqanduli	**158**	31.48 S	28.46 E
Mrągowo	**30**	53.52 N	21.19 E
Mrakovo	**86**	52.43 N	56.38 E
M'Ramani	**157a**	12.21 S	44.32 E
Mranggen	**115a**	7.01 S	110.31 E
Mras-Su ≃	**86**	53.45 N	87.49 E
Mrhila, Jebel ∧	**36**	35.25 N	9.14 E
Mrijo	**154**	5.10 S	36.15 E
Mrkonjić Grad	**36**	44.25 N	17.05 E
Mrkopalj	**36**	45.19 N	14.51 E
Mrocza	**30**	53.14 N	17.36 E
Msagali	**154**	6.21 S	36.18 E
M'Saken	**148**	35.44 N	10.35 E
Msata	**154**	6.20 S	38.23 E
Mšec	**54**	50.10 N	13.54 E
Mšeno	**54**	50.27 N	14.38 E
M'Sila	**148**	35.46 N	4.31 E
M'Sila □[5]	**148**	35.00 N	4.20 E
M'Sila, Oued ≃	**34**	35.46 N	4.34 E
Mšinskaja	**76**	59.01 N	29.57 E
Msoro	**154**	13.36 S	31.55 E
Msta	**76**	57.55 N	34.29 E
Msta ≃	**76**	58.25 N	31.20 E
Mstera	**80**	56.23 N	41.56 E
Mstislavl'	**76**	54.02 N	31.42 E
Mstiž	**76**	54.34 N	28.10 E
Mszana Dolna	**30**	49.42 N	20.05 E
Mszczonów	**30**	51.58 N	20.31 E
Mtakataka	**154**	14.12 S	34.32 E
Mtakuja	**154**	7.22 S	30.37 E
Mtama	**154**	10.18 S	39.22 E
Mtamvuna ≃	**158**	31.06 S	30.12 E
Mtarazi National Park ♠	**154**	18.36 S	32.50 E
Mtata ≃	**158**	31.58 S	29.10 E
Mtelo ∧	**154**	1.39 N	35.23 E
Mtilikwe ≃	**154**	21.09 S	31.30 E
Mtito Andei	**154**	2.41 S	38.10 E
Mtowabaga	**154**	2.30 S	35.53 E
Mtsensk → Mcensk	**76**	53.17 N	36.35 E
Mtubatuba	**158**	28.30 S	32.08 E
Mtunzini	**158**	28.57 S	31.46 E
Mtwara	**154**	10.16 S	40.11 E
Mtwara □[4]	**154**	11.00 S	39.00 E
Mtyangimbori	**154**	10.16 S	35.31 E
Mu ≃, Mya.	**110**	21.56 N	95.38 E
Mu ≃, Nihon	**92a**	42.33 N	141.56 E
Mu, Cerro ∧	**246**	9.29 N	73.07 W
Mu'a	**174w**	21.11 S	175.07 W
Muacandala	**152**	10.02 S	19.40 E
Mualama	**154**	16.53 S	38.17 E
Mualang	**112**	0.42 N	111.18 E
Mu'allaqah, Lubnān	**132**	33.50 N	35.54 E
Mu 'Allaqah, Sūd.	**140**	13.28 N	23.57 E
Muan	**98**	34.58 N	126.26 E
Muaná	**250**	1.32 S	49.13 W
Muanda	**152**	5.56 S	12.21 E
Muangai	**152**	12.32 S	19.51 E
Muang Bèng	**110**	20.22 N	101.44 E
Muang Hay	**110**	21.03 N	101.49 E
Muang Hinboun	**110**	17.35 N	104.36 E
Muang Hôngsa	**110**	19.43 N	101.20 E

Symbols in the index entries represent the broad categories identified in the key at the right. Symbols with superior numbers (⋏[1]) identify subcategories (see complete key on page *I* · 1).

Symbole im Register stellen die rechts im Schlüssel erklärten Kategorien dar. Symbole mit hochgestellten Ziffern (⋏[1]) bezeichnen Unterabteilungen einer Kategorie (vgl. vollständiger Schlüssel auf Seite *I* · 1).

Los símbolos incluídos en el texto del índice representan las grandes categorias identificadas con la clave a la derecha. Los símbolos con numeros en su parte superior (⋏[1]) identifican las subcategorías (véase la clave completa en la página *I* · 1).

Les symboles de l'index représentent les catégories indiquées dans la légende à droite. Les symboles suivis d'un indice (⋏[1]) représentent des sous-catégories (voir légende complète à la page *I* · 1).

Os símbolos incluídos no texto do índice representam as grandes categorias identificadas com a chave à direita. Os símbolos com números em sua parte superior (⋏[1]) identificam as subcategorias (veja-se a chave completa à página *I* · 1).

	English	Deutsch	Español	Français	Português
∧	Mountain	Berg	Montaña	Montagne	Montanha
⋏	Mountains	Gebirge	Montañas	Montagnes	Montanhas
)(	Pass	Paß	Paso	Col	Passo
V	Valley, Canyon	Tal, Cañon	Valle, Cañón	Vallée, Canyon	Vale, Canhão
≚	Plain	Ebene	Llano	Plaine	Planície
≻	Cape	Kap	Cabo	Cap	Cabo
I	Island	Insel	Isla	Île	Ilha
II	Islands	Inseln	Islas	Îles	Ilhas
⊥	Other Topographic Features	Andere Topographische Objekte	Otros Elementos Topográficos	Autres données topographiques	Outros acidentes topográficos

ESPAÑOL — Nombre | Página | Lat.°′ | Long.°′ W = Oeste
FRANÇAIS — Nom | Page | Lat.°′ | Long.°′ W = Ouest
PORTUGUÊS — Nome | Página | Lat.°′ | Long.°′ W = Oeste

Muang Houn 110 20.09 N 101.27 E
Muang Hounxianghoung 110 21.37 N 102.18 E
Muang Huang 110 18.45 N 103.42 E
Muang Khammouan 110 17.24 N 104.48 E
Muang Khao 110 19.47 N 103.29 E
Muang Khi 110 18.27 N 101.46 E
Muang Không 110 14.07 N 105.51 E
Muang Khôngxédôn 110 15.34 N 105.49 E
Muang La 110 20.52 N 102.07 E
Muang Liap 110 18.29 N 101.40 E
Muang Long 110 20.57 N 100.48 E
Muang Meung 110 20.43 N 100.28 E
Muang Ngoy, Lao 102 20.43 N 102.41 E
Muang Ngoy, Lao 110 20.43 N 102.41 E
Muang Nong 110 16.22 N 106.30 E
Muang Ou Nua 110 22.18 N 101.48 E
Muang Ou Tai 110 22.07 N 101.48 E
Muang Pakbèng 110 19.54 N 101.08 E
Muang Pak-Lay 110 18.12 N 101.25 E
Muang Paktha 110 20.06 N 100.36 E
Muang Pakxan 110 18.22 N 103.39 E
Muang Peun 110 20.13 N 103.52 E
Muang Phalan 110 16.39 N 105.34 E
Muang Phiang 110 19.06 N 101.32 E
Muang Phônthong 110 15.05 N 105.39 E
Muang Phoun 110 19.07 N 102.43 E
Muang Sam Sip 110 15.31 N 104.44 E
Muang Sing 110 21.11 N 101.09 E
Muang Soum 110 18.45 N 102.36 E
Muang Souvannakhili 110 15.23 N 105.49 E
Muang Souy 110 19.33 N 102.52 E
Muang Sung 110 20.19 N 102.27 E
Muang Thadua 110 19.26 N 101.50 E
Muang Thatèng 110 15.26 N 106.23 E
Muang Thathôm 110 19.00 N 103.36 E
Muang Va 110 21.53 N 102.19 E
Muang Vangviang 110 18.56 N 102.27 E
Muang Vapi 110 15.40 N 105.55 E
Muang Xaignabouri 110 19.15 N 101.45 E
Muang Xamtong 110 19.51 N 103.51 E
Muang Xay 110 20.42 N 101.59 E
Muang Xépôn 110 16.41 N 106.14 E
Muang Xon 110 20.27 N 103.19 E
Muang Yo 110 21.31 N 101.51 E
Muang You 110 19.49 N 102.50 E
Muanza 156 18.59 S 34.48 E
Muar (Bandar Maharani) 114 2.02 N 102.34 E
Muar ≃ 114 2.03 N 102.35 E
Muara 112 5.02 N 115.02 E
Muaraaman 112 3.07 S 102.12 E
Muaraancalung 112 0.27 N 116.41 E
Muarabeliti 112 3.15 S 103.02 E
Muarabenangin 112 0.58 S 115.19 E
Muarabinuangeun 115a 6.50 S 105.53 E
Muarabulian 112 1.43 S 103.15 E
Muarabungo 112 1.28 S 102.07 E
Muaradua 112 4.32 S 104.05 E
Muaraenim 112 3.39 S 103.48 E
Muaragusung 112 1.35 N 117.17 E
Muarajuloi 112 0.12 S 114.03 E
Muarakaman 112 0.09 S 116.43 E
Muarakelingi 112 3.05 S 103.14 E
Muarakumpe 112 1.24 S 104.00 E
Muaralabuh 112 1.29 S 101.03 E
Muaralakitan 112 2.51 S 103.19 E
Muaralasan 112 1.48 N 117.12 E
Muaralembu 112 0.24 S 101.21 E
Muaramawai 112 0.37 N 116.49 E
Muarapangean 112 2.38 N 116.41 E
Muarapantai 112 0.45 S 101.43 E
Muarapayang 112 1.32 S 115.48 E
Muararupit 112 2.44 S 102.54 E
Muarasabak 112 1.08 S 103.51 E
Muarasiberut 108 1.36 S 99.11 E
Muarasipongi 112 0.37 N 99.51 E
Muaratais 114 1.17 N 99.21 E
Muaratebo 112 1.30 S 102.26 E
Muarateladang 112 2.50 S 103.58 E
Muaratembesi 112 1.42 S 103.07 E
Muaratewe 112 0.57 S 114.53 E
Muaratuhup 112 0.37 S 114.50 E
Muaratunan 112 1.24 S 116.39 E
Muarawahau 112 1.02 N 116.52 E
Muāri, Rās > 120 24.49 N 66.40 E
Muasdale 46 55.36 N 5.41 W
Muá Ximica 152 9.50 S 18.41 E
Mubārakpur 124 26.05 N 83.18 E
Mubārakpur Dabās ◆[8] 272a 28.43 N 77.03 E
Mubayyad ⫪[4] 142 30.55 N 32.48 E
Mubende 154 0.35 N 31.23 E
Mubi 146 10.18 N 13.20 E
Mubur, Pulau I 112 3.20 N 106.12 E
Mucaitá ≃ 250 6.59 S 42.40 W
Mucajaí ≃ 246 2.25 N 60.52 W
Mucambo 250 3.54 S 40.44 W
Mucári 152 9.30 S 16.54 E
Muccan 162 20.38 S 120.04 E
Muccia 66 43.05 N 13.02 E
Much 56 50.54 N 7.25 E
Mucha 269d 24.59 N 121.34 E
Muchangpu 100 31.55 N 116.35 E
Muchanovo 82 56.31 N 38.20 E
Muchavec ≃ 76 52.05 N 23.39 E
Much Dewchurch 42 51.59 N 2.46 W
Muchea 168a 31.35 S 115.59 E
Mücheln 54 51.18 N 11.48 E
Muchen 89 48.10 N 136.13 E
Muchengzhen 107 29.47 N 103.29 E
Much Hoole 262 53.42 N 2.48 W
Muchinga Escarpment ⊓[4] 154 14.45 S 29.30 E
Muchinga Mountains ⛰ 154 12.20 S 31.00 E
Muchino, Ross. 80 58.11 N 51.02 E
Muchino, Ross. 89 52.16 N 127.14 E
Muchor-Konduj 88 52.25 N 113.16 E
Muchrani 84 41.56 N 44.35 E
Muchtadir 84 41.41 N 48.46 E
Muchtolovo 80 55.27 N 43.13 E
Muchuan 107 28.55 N 103.58 E
Much Wenlock 42 52.36 N 2.34 W
Mucifal 266c 38.48 N 9.26 W
Mučikan 88 53.02 N 120.27 E
Muck I 46 56.50 N 6.15 W
Mücka 54 51.18 N 14.40 E
Muckadilla 166 26.35 S 148.23 E
Muckalee Creek ≃ 192 31.38 N 84.09 W
Muckamore 48 54.41 N 6.10 W
Mučkapskij 80 51.52 N 42.28 E
Mučkas 24 64.02 N 48.27 E
Mücke 56 50.38 N 9.03 E
Muckendorf an der Donau 264b 48.20 N 16.09 E
Mucking 260 51.30 N 0.26 E
Muckle Roe I 46a 60.22 N 1.27 W
Muckleshoot Indian Reservation ◆[4] 224 47.16 N 122.09 W
Muckno Lough ⊜ 48 54.07 N 6.42 W
Mucojo 154 12.04 S 40.28 E
Mucoma 152 15.18 S 13.39 E
Muconda 152 10.34 S 21.17 E
Mucope, Ang. 152 16.24 S 14.53 E
Mucope, Ang. 152 8.42 S 21.43 E
Mucrone, Monte ∧ 62 45.36 N 7.56 E
Mucubela 154 16.55 S 37.52 E
Mucuchíes 246 8.45 N 70.55 W
M'uc'ucl'u 84 40.28 N 47.55 E
Mucugê 255 13.00 S 41.23 W
Mucuim ≃ 248 6.33 S 64.18 W
Muculo 152 16.47 S 14.51 E
Muçum 252 29.10 S 51.53 W
Mucumbura 154 16.09 S 31.31 E
Mucun 100 26.44 N 114.00 E
Mucupia 156 18.01 S 36.48 E
Mucupina, Monte ∧ 236 15.08 N 86.38 W
Mucur 130 39.04 N 34.23 E
Mucuri 255 18.05 S 39.34 W

Mucuri ≃ 255 18.05 S 39.34 W
Mucusso 152 18.01 S 21.25 E
Mud ≃, Ky., U.S. 194 37.13 N 86.54 W
Mud ≃, W.V., U.S. 188 38.25 N 82.17 W
Muda ≃ 114 5.33 N 100.22 E
Mudan ≃ 89 46.22 N 129.33 E
Mudanjiang 89 44.35 N 129.36 E
Mudanya 130 40.22 N 28.52 E
Mudau 56 49.32 N 9.11 E
Mudaysīsāt, Jabal ∧ 132 31.39 N 36.14 E
Mud Creek ≃, N.A. 206 45.01 N 72.24 W
Mud Creek ≃, U.S. 198 43.17 N 96.15 W
Mud Creek ≃, Il., U.S. 219 38.21 N 89.48 W
Mud Creek ≃, In., U.S. 216 41.06 N 86.21 W
Mud Creek ≃, In., U.S. 216 40.26 N 85.55 W
Mud Creek ≃, Ne., U.S. 198 41.01 N 98.54 W
Mud Creek ≃, N.Y., U.S. 210 42.17 N 77.13 W
Mud Creek ≃, N.Y., U.S. 210 42.59 N 77.23 W
Mud Creek ≃, N.Y., U.S. 210 43.05 N 78.43 W
Mud Creek ≃, Ok., U.S. 196 33.55 N 97.28 W
Mud Creek ≃, S.D., U.S. 198 45.11 N 98.24 W
Mud Creek ≃, Tx., U.S. 222 31.48 N 94.58 W
Muddus Nationalpark ♠ 24 67.00 N 20.16 E
Muddy ≃, Nv., U.S. 204 36.27 N 114.22 W
Muddy ≃, Wa., U.S. 224 46.04 N 122.01 W
Muddy Boggy Creek ≃ 196 34.03 N 95.47 W
Muddy Branch ≃ 284c 39.03 N 77.18 W
Muddy Brook ≃ 276 41.07 N 73.20 W
Muddy Creek ≃, U.S. 276 41.03 N 74.02 W
Muddy Creek ≃, Mo., U.S. 194 38.51 N 93.03 W
Muddy Creek ≃, Mt., U.S. 202 47.56 N 111.46 W
Muddy Creek ≃, Oh., U.S. 214 41.27 N 83.03 W
Muddy Creek ≃, Pa., U.S. 208 39.47 N 76.18 W
Muddy Creek ≃, Ut., U.S. 200 38.24 N 110.42 W
Muddy Creek ≃, Wy., U.S. 198 42.35 N 104.57 W
Muddy Creek ≃, Wy., U.S. 200 41.59 N 106.08 W
Muddy Creek ≃, Wy., U.S. 200 41.32 N 110.13 W
Muddy Creek ≃, Wy., U.S. 200 41.01 N 107.42 W
Muddy Creek ≃, Wy., U.S. 202 43.17 N 108.14 W
Muddy Fork ≃ 224 46.22 N 121.34 W
Muddy Gut c 284b 39.17 N 76.26 W
Muddy Peak ∧ 204 36.18 N 114.42 W
Müden, Dtsch. 52 52.52 N 10.07 E
Müden, Dtsch. 54 52.31 N 10.22 E
Mudgee 166 32.36 S 149.35 E
Mudgeeraba 171a 28.04 S 153.22 E
Mudhol 122 16.21 N 75.17 E
Mud Island I 171a 27.20 S 153.15 E
Mud Islands II 169 38.17 S 144.45 E
Mudjatik ≃ 184 56.02 N 107.36 W
Mudjuga 24 63.46 N 39.15 E
Mud Lake ⊜, Id., U.S. 202 43.53 N 112.24 W
Mud Lake ⊜, Nv., U.S. 204 37.52 N 117.04 W
Mud Lake ⊜, N.Y., U.S. 212 44.30 N 75.28 W
Mud Lake Reservoir ⊜[1] 198 45.50 N 98.10 W
Mudon 110 16.15 N 97.44 E
Mudongzhen 102 29.35 N 106.51 E
Mudu 106 31.15 N 120.30 E
Mudug □[4] 144 6.15 N 48.00 E
Mudurnu 130 40.28 N 31.13 E
Mudurnu ≃ 130 40.49 N 30.33 E
M'ud'ur'um ≃ 85 40.53 N 76.36 E
Mueda 154 11.39 S 39.33 E
Muelle de los Bueyes 236 12.04 N 84.32 W
Mueller, Mount ∧[2] 162 19.54 S 127.51 E
Muenster 196 33.39 N 97.23 W
Mu'er 107 29.48 N 106.37 E
Muerte, Valle de la → Death Valley V 204 36.30 N 117.00 W
Muerto ≃ 252 23.02 S 62.29 W
Muerto, Mar → Dead Sea ⊜ 132 31.30 N 35.30 E
Mufulira 154 12.33 S 28.14 E
Mufuma 152 9.04 S 17.06 E
Mufu Shan ∧ 100 29.02 N 113.54 E
Mufu Shan ⛰ 100 29.00 N 114.00 E
Mugang 100 29.44 N 115.14 E
Muganskaja ravnina ≡ 84 39.40 N 48.15 E
Mugazine 158 26.07 S 32.30 E
Mugegawa 94 35.31 N 136.51 E
Mugello V 66 43.55 N 11.30 E
Mügeln 54 51.14 N 13.02 E
Muger ≃ 144 9.54 N 37.57 E
Müggelberge ⛰[2] 264a 52.25 N 13.39 E
Müggelheim ◆[8] 264a 52.25 N 13.40 E
Muggia 64 45.36 N 13.46 E
Muggio 266b 45.36 N 9.14 E
Mughal Sarāi 124 25.18 N 83.07 E
Mugi, Nihon 94 35.34 N 137.01 E
Mugi, Nihon 96 33.40 N 134.25 E
Mu Gia, Deo)(110 17.40 N 105.47 E
Muginga 152 8.20 S 17.37 E
Muğla 130 37.12 N 28.22 E
Muğla □[4] 130 37.10 N 28.30 E
Mugodžarskaja 86 48.36 N 58.27 E
Mugodžary, gory ⛰[2] 86 49.00 N 58.40 E
Mugombazi 154 5.50 S 30.14 E
Mugo-ri 98 38.58 N 126.31 E
Mugrejevskij 80 56.36 N 42.21 E
Mugron 32 43.45 N 0.45 W
Mugu Karṇālī ≃ 124 29.38 N 81.52 E
Mugur-Aksy 86 50.21 N 90.30 E
Mūḥ, Sabkhat al- ⊜ 130 34.30 N 38.20 E
Muhala 154 5.40 S 28.43 E
Muhamdi 124 27.57 N 80.13 E
Muḥammad, Ra's > 140 27.44 N 34.15 E
Muhammadābād 124 26.02 N 83.23 E
Muhammadpur 126 23.24 N 89.36 E
Muḥammad Qawl 140 20.54 N 37.05 E
Muḥayshir, Birkat ⊜ 142 30.43 N 31.56 E
Muheza 154 5.10 S 38.47 E
Muḥīṭ, Maṣrif al- ≊ 273c 30.07 N 31.06 E
Mühlacker 56 48.57 N 8.50 E
Mühlau 54 50.54 N 12.45 E
Mühlbach am Hochkönig 64 47.22 N 13.08 E
Muhlbach-sur-Munster 58 48.02 N 7.05 E
Mühlberg 54 51.26 N 13.13 E
Mühldorf 61 48.22 N 15.21 E
Mühldorf am Inn 60 48.15 N 12.32 E
Mühlenbeck 54 52.40 N 13.22 E
Mühlenbecker See ⊜ 264a 52.41 N 13.24 E
Muhlenberg 210 41.14 N 76.09 W
Mühlen-Berg ∧[2] 264a 52.23 N 13.15 E
Mühlen Eichsen 54 53.45 N 11.15 E
Mühlenfliess ≃ 264a 52.26 N 13.41 E
Mühlen → Molini di Tures 64 46.54 N 11.56 E
Mühlenrahmede 263 51.16 N 7.40 E
Mühlhausen, Dtsch. 54 51.12 N 10.27 E
Mühlhausen, Dtsch. 263 51.33 N 7.44 E
Mühlhausen im Täle 56 48.34 N 9.39 E
Mühlheim 56 50.07 N 8.50 E

Mühlheim an der Donau 58 48.01 N 8.53 E
Mühlig-Hofmann Mountains ⛰ 9 72.00 S 5.20 E
Mühlleiten 264b 48.10 N 16.34 E
Mühltroff 54 50.32 N 11.55 E
Mühlviertel ◆[1] 30 48.25 N 14.10 E
Muhola 26 63.20 N 25.05 E
Muhoro 154 1.01 S 34.07 E
Muhos 26 64.48 N 25.59 E
Muḥradah 130 35.15 N 36.35 E
Mühringen 58 48.25 N 8.46 E
Muhu I 76 58.38 N 23.15 E
Muhula 154 13.53 S 39.30 E
Muhulu 154 1.03 S 27.17 E
Muhutwe 154 1.33 S 31.42 E
Muhu väin ⊍ 76 58.45 N 23.20 E
Muhuwesi ≃ 154 11.16 S 37.58 E
Muick, Loch ⊜ 46 56.55 N 3.10 W
Muiden 52 52.19 N 5.04 E
Muiderslot ⊥ 52 52.20 N 5.10 E
Muides-sur-Loire 50 47.40 N 1.31 E
Muié 152 14.25 S 20.36 E
Mui Hopohoponga Point > 174w 21.09 S 175.02 W
Muikaichi 96 34.21 N 131.56 E
Muikamachi 94 37.04 N 138.53 E
Muine Bheag 48 52.41 N 6.58 W
Muir, Mi., U.S. 216 42.59 N 84.56 W
Muir, Pa., U.S. 208 40.36 N 76.31 W
Muir, Mount ∧ 180 61.06 N 148.24 W
Muir Beach 282 37.52 N 122.35 W
Muirdrum 46 56.31 N 2.42 W
Muirkirk, Scot., U.K. 46 55.31 N 4.04 W
Muirkirk, Md., U.S. 284c 39.03 N 76.53 W
Muir of Ord 46 57.31 N 4.27 W
Muiron Islands II 162 21.35 S 114.20 E
Muir Seamount ✢[3] 16 33.41 N 62.30 W
Muirtown 46 56.16 N 3.45 W
Muir Woods 282 37.53 N 122.34 W
Muir Woods National Monument ♠ 226 37.54 N 122.33 W
Muiskraal 158 33.56 S 21.13 E
Muisne 246 0.36 N 80.02 W
Muite 154 14.02 S 39.00 E
Mui Wo 271d 22.16 N 113.59 E
Muizen 50 51.01 N 4.31 E
Muja, Ityo. 144 12.02 N 39.29 E
Muja, Ross. 88 56.24 N 115.39 E
Muja ≃ 88 56.24 N 115.39 E
Mujāhidpur ◆[8] 272a 28.34 N 77.13 E
Mujang-ni 98 35.26 N 126.32 E
Mujezerskij 24 63.57 N 31.55 E
Mujiapucun 104 41.06 N 122.48 E
Mujiayu 105 40.24 N 116.55 E
Mujimbeji Mission 154 12.11 S 24.57 E
Mujnak 86 43.48 N 59.02 E
Muju 98 36.02 N 127.40 E
Mujunkum, peski ◆[2] 86 44.20 N 71.00 E
Mukačevo 78 48.27 N 22.45 E
Mukah 112 2.54 N 112.06 E
Mukaishima 96 34.20 N 133.10 E
Mukalla → Al-Mukallā 144 14.32 N 49.08 E
Mukandpur ◆[8] 272a 28.44 N 77.11 E
Mukandwara 120 24.49 N 75.59 E
Mukawa 94 35.47 N 138.23 E
Mukāwir 132 31.34 N 35.38 E
Mukāwir ⊥ 132 31.34 N 35.38 E
Mukawwar I 140 20.48 N 37.13 E
Mukdahan 110 16.32 N 104.43 E
Mukden → Shenyang 104 41.48 N 123.27 E
Muke Arba 144 8.57 N 42.09 E
Mukebo 154 6.49 S 28.03 E
Mukeriān 123 31.57 N 75.37 E
Mukharram al-Fawqānī 130 34.49 N 37.04 E
Mukhmās 132 31.52 N 35.17 E
Mukho 98 37.33 N 129.06 E
Mukilteo 224 47.56 N 122.18 W
Mukinbudin 162 30.54 S 118.13 E
Mukinge Hill 154 13.29 S 25.52 E
Mukō 96 34.56 N 135.42 E
Muko ≃ 96 34.41 N 135.23 E
Mukomuko 112 2.35 S 101.07 E
Mukomwenze 154 6.52 S 27.16 E
Mukoshima-rettō II 14 27.37 N 142.10 E
Mukry 128 37.36 N 65.44 E
Muksi-ri 98 39.52 N 125.54 E
Muksu ≃ 85 39.15 N 71.23 E
Muksūdpur 126 23.18 N 89.51 E
Muktāgācha 126 24.46 N 90.14 E
Muktsar 123 30.29 N 74.31 E
Mukuku 154 12.09 S 29.49 E
Mukuleshi ≃ 154 10.21 S 24.30 E
Mukur 86 48.03 N 54.30 E
Mukusaki 115b 8.33 S 121.37 E
Mukutan 154 0.38 N 36.16 E
Mukutawa ≃ 184 53.10 N 97.28 W
Mukwela 154 17.02 S 26.39 E
Mukwonago 216 42.51 N 88.19 W
Mūl 122 20.04 N 79.40 E
Mula, Esp. 34 38.03 N 1.30 W
Mula, Zhg. 102 29.40 N 100.39 E
Mula ≃, India 122 18.34 N 74.20 E
Mula ≃, India 122 19.32 N 74.50 E
Mūla ≃, Pāk. 120 27.57 N 67.36 E
Mulādi 126 22.54 N 90.25 E
Muladu I 122 7.01 N 72.59 E
Mulaly 86 45.27 N 78.19 E
Mulan 89 45.57 N 128.03 E
Muland ◆[8] 272c 19.10 N 72.57 E
Mulanda 152 14.41 S 21.48 E
Mulanje, Malaŵi 154 16.03 S 35.31 E
Mulanje, Moç. 154 16.03 S 35.45 E
Mulargia, Lago ⊜ 71 39.37 N 9.14 E
Mulas, Punta > 240m 18.09 N 65.27 W
Mulas, Punta de > 240p 21.01 N 75.35 W
Mulatos 232 28.39 N 108.51 W
Mulayit Taung ∧ 110 16.11 N 98.32 E
Mulazzo 64 44.19 N 9.53 E
Mulbāgal 122 13.10 N 78.24 E
Mulben 46 57.31 N 3.06 W
Mulberry, Ar., U.S. 194 35.30 N 94.03 W
Mulberry, Fl., U.S. 220 27.53 N 81.58 W
Mulberry, In., U.S. 216 40.20 N 86.39 W
Mulberry, Oh., U.S. 218 39.11 N 84.14 W
Mulberry ≃ 194 35.28 N 94.03 W
Mulberry Creek ≃, Al., U.S. 194 32.27 N 86.52 W
Mulberry Creek ≃, Tx., U.S. 196 34.37 N 100.55 W
Mulberry Fork ≃ 194 33.33 N 87.11 W
Mulberry Grove 219 38.55 N 89.16 W
Mulberry Mountain ∧ 194 35.42 N 92.56 W
Mulchatna ≃ 180 59.39 N 157.08 W
Mulchén 252 37.43 S 72.14 W
Mulda, Dtsch. 54 50.48 N 13.25 E
Mul'da, Ross. 24 67.28 N 63.34 E
Mulde ≃ 54 51.52 N 12.15 E
Muldenstein 54 51.40 N 12.19 E
Muldersdrif se Loop ≃ 273d 26.06 S 27.51 E
Muldersvlei 158 30.41 S 22.13 E
Muldoon 222 29.49 N 97.04 W
Muldraugh 194 37.56 N 85.59 W
Muldrow 194 35.24 N 94.35 W
Mule, Lac la ⊜ 186 51.33 N 65.35 W
Muleba 154 1.49 S 31.40 E
Mule Creek ≃ 198 37.05 N 99.00 W
Mulegé 232 26.53 N 112.01 W
Mulegns 58 46.33 N 9.37 E
Mulei 86 43.49 N 90.11 E
Mules (Mauls) 64 46.51 N 11.31 E
Mules, Pulau I 115b 8.54 S 120.17 E
Muleshoe 196 34.13 N 102.43 W
Mulevala 154 16.30 S 37.30 E
Mulga Downs 162 22.08 S 118.26 E
Mulgathing 162 30.15 S 134.00 E

Mulgathing Rocks ∧ 162 30.14 S 133.58 E
Mulghar 126 22.46 N 89.45 E
Mulgoa 170 33.50 S 150.40 E
Mulgoa Creek ≃ 274a 33.46 S 150.39 E
Mulgowie 171a 27.43 S 152.22 E
Mulgrave, Austl. 274b 37.56 S 145.12 E
Mulgrave, N.S., Can. 186 45.37 N 61.23 W
Mulgrave Hills ⛰[2] 180 67.42 N 163.24 W
Mulgul 162 24.49 S 118.26 E
Mulhacén ∧ 34 37.03 N 3.19 W
Mulhall 196 36.03 N 97.24 W
Mülhausen → Mulhouse 58 47.45 N 7.20 E
Mülheim 56 49.54 N 7.01 E
Mülheim an der Ruhr 56 51.24 N 6.54 E
Mülheimer Ruhrtalbrüke ◆[5] 263 51.23 N 6.54 E
Mülheim-Karlich 56 50.21 N 7.28 E
Mulhouse (Mülhausen) 58 47.45 N 7.20 E
Muli 102 27.50 N 101.15 E
Muling, Zhg. 89 44.56 N 130.31 E
Muling, Zhg. 89 44.31 N 130.13 E
Muling ≃ 89 45.53 N 133.30 E
Mulini, Capo > 70 37.34 N 15.10 E
Mulino 224 45.13 N 122.34 W
Mulinu'u, Cape > 175a 13.26 S 172.43 W
Mulita ≃ 116 7.18 N 124.52 E
Mulkear ≃ 48 52.40 N 8.33 W
Mūlki 122 13.06 N 74.48 E
Mull, Island of I 46 56.27 N 6.00 W
Mull, Sound of ⊍ 46 56.32 N 5.50 W
Mullagh 48 53.49 N 6.57 W
Mullaghareirk Mountains ⛰ 48 52.20 N 9.10 W
Mullaghcleevaun ∧ 48 53.06 N 6.24 W
Mullaghmore ∧ 48 54.52 N 6.51 W
Mullaloo Point > 168a 31.48 S 115.44 E
Mullan 202 47.28 N 115.48 W
Mullen 198 42.02 N 101.02 W
Müllenbach 56 50.19 N 6.55 E
Mullengudgery 166 31.41 S 147.26 E
Mullens 192 37.34 N 81.22 W
Muller, Pegunungan ⛰ 112 0.40 N 113.50 E
Muller Creek ≃ 162 22.29 S 134.30 E
Muller Range ⛰ 164 5.35 S 142.15 E
Mullerup 41 55.30 N 11.13 E
Mullet Key I 220 27.37 N 82.44 W
Mullet Peninsula >[1] 48 54.12 N 10.00 W
Mullett Lake ⊜ 190 45.30 N 84.30 W
Mullewa 162 28.33 S 115.31 E
Mull Head >, Scot., U.K. 46 59.23 N 2.54 W
Mull Head >, Scot., U.K. 46 58.58 N 2.43 W
Müllheim 58 47.48 N 7.38 E
Mullhyttan 40 59.09 N 14.41 E
Mullica ≃ 208 39.33 N 74.25 W
Mullica, Alquatka Branch ≃ 285 39.47 N 74.48 W
Mullica, Sleeper Branch ≃ 285 39.39 N 74.40 W
Mullica Hill 208 39.44 N 75.13 W
Mulligan ≃ 166 25.00 S 138.30 E
Mulliken 216 42.45 N 84.53 W
Mullin 196 31.33 N 98.40 W
Mullinahone 48 52.30 N 7.30 W
Mullinavat 48 52.21 N 7.10 W
Mullingar 48 53.32 N 7.20 W
Mullins 192 34.12 N 79.15 W
Mullinville 198 37.35 N 99.28 W
Mullion 42 50.01 N 5.15 W
Mulloon Creek ≃ 171b 35.12 S 149.38 E
Mullovka 80 54.13 N 49.25 E
Müllrose 54 52.14 N 14.25 E
Mullsjö 26 57.55 N 13.53 E
Mullumbimby 166 28.33 S 153.30 E
Mullum Mullum Creek ≃ 274b 37.44 S 145.10 E
Mulobezi 154 16.48 S 25.09 E
Mulonda Funda 154 11.06 S 25.28 E
Mulondo 152 15.39 S 15.14 E
Mulongo 154 7.50 S 27.00 E
Mulshi Lake ⊜ 122 18.30 N 73.30 E
Multai 120 21.46 N 78.15 E
Multān 123 30.11 N 71.29 E
Multen ⊜ 40 59.10 N 14.37 E
Multia 26 62.25 N 24.47 E
Multnomah □[6] 224 45.30 N 122.22 W
Multnomah Channel ≃[1] 224 45.51 N 122.52 W
Multnomah Falls ⌞ 224 45.35 N 122.07 W
Mulu, Gunong ∧ 112 4.04 N 114.56 E
Mulumbe, Monts ⛰ 154 8.16 S 28.16 E
Mulungushi 154 14.40 S 28.50 E
Mulungushi Dam ◆[6] 154 14.40 S 28.50 E
Mulvane 198 37.28 N 97.14 W
Mulwad 140 18.39 N 30.35 E
Mulyah Mountain ∧ 166 30.37 S 144.31 E
Muma 152 3.24 N 23.15 E
Mumbles Head > 42 51.35 N 3.59 W
Mumbondo 152 10.09 S 14.15 E
Mumbra 272c 19.11 N 73.01 E
Mumbwa 154 14.59 S 27.04 E
Mumcular 130 37.05 N 27.40 E
Mume 154 9.40 S 27.26 E
Mumen 102 32.09 N 106.28 E
Mumeng 164 7.00 S 146.35 E
Mumford, N.Y., U.S. 210 42.59 N 77.52 W
Mumford, Tx., U.S. 222 30.44 N 96.34 W
Mumias 154 0.20 N 34.29 E
Mümling ≃ 56 49.50 N 9.09 E
Mumoni ∧ 154 0.31 S 38.01 E
Mumra 80 45.47 N 47.41 E
Mumu 140 12.06 N 23.42 E
Mumungwe 156 21.59 S 26.24 E
Mun ≃ 110 15.19 N 105.30 E
Mun, Jabal ∧ 140 14.08 N 22.42 E
Munā, Ar. Su. 144 21.25 N 39.52 E
Muna, Méx. 232 20.29 N 89.43 W
Muna ≃ 74 67.52 N 123.06 E
Muna, Pulau I 112 5.00 S 122.30 E
Muna, Selat ⊍ 112 5.15 S 122.10 E
Munā al-Amīr 142 29.54 N 31.15 E
Munābāo 120 25.45 N 70.17 E
Munajly 86 46.47 N 54.31 E
Munakata 96 33.50 N 130.35 E
Munam-ni 98 38.41 N 126.54 E
Munam-san ∧ 98 40.26 N 127.22 E
Munbong-ni 271b 37.43 N 126.49 E
Muncar 115a 8.26 S 114.20 E
Münchberg 54 50.11 N 11.47 E
Müncheberg 54 52.30 N 14.08 E
Münchehofe 264a 52.30 N 13.40 E
München 60 48.08 N 11.34 E
Münchenbernsdorf 54 50.49 N 11.56 E
Münchenbuchsee 58 47.01 N 7.27 E
Münchendorf 264b 48.02 N 16.23 E
München-Gladbach → Mönchengladbach 56 51.12 N 6.28 E
München-Riem, Flughafen ⊠ 60 48.08 N 11.41 E
Münchenstein 58 47.31 N 7.37 E
Münchhausen 56 50.57 N 8.43 E
Munchique, Cerro ∧ 246 2.32 N 76.57 W
Munchique, Parque Nacional ♠ 246 2.30 N 77.10 W
Munch'ŏn 98 39.16 N 127.15 E
Muncie 216 40.11 N 85.23 W
Muncusun 130 38.54 N 35.38 E
Muncy 210 41.12 N 76.47 W
Muncy Creek ≃ 210 41.13 N 76.48 W
Muncy Valley 210 41.21 N 76.35 W
Mundare 182 53.36 N 112.20 W
Mundaring 168a 31.54 S 116.10 E
Munday 196 33.26 N 99.37 W
Mundelein 216 42.15 N 88.00 W
Mündelheim ◆[8] 263 51.21 N 6.41 E

Münden 56 51.25 N 9.39 E
Munderfing 60 48.05 N 13.11 E
Munderkingen 58 48.14 N 9.38 E
Munderoo ∧ 171b 35.48 S 147.47 E
Mundesley 42 52.53 N 1.26 E
Mundijong 168a 32.18 S 115.59 E
Mundiwindi 162 23.52 S 120.09 E
Mūndka ◆[8] 272a 28.41 N 77.02 E
Mundo ≃ 34 38.19 N 1.40 W
Mundolsheim 58 48.39 N 7.42 E
Mundon Hill 260 51.41 N 0.42 E
Mundo Novo 255 11.52 S 40.28 W
Mundra 120 22.51 N 69.44 E
Mundrabilla 162 31.52 S 127.51 E
Mundubbera 166 25.36 S 151.18 E
Mundybaš 86 53.14 N 87.19 E
Mundytau, gora ∧ 85 38.00 N 68.27 E
Munene 154 20.38 S 30.03 E
Munenga 152 10.02 S 14.41 E
Munera 34 39.02 N 2.28 W
Munford 194 35.26 N 89.48 W
Munfordville 194 37.16 N 85.53 W
Mungallala 166 26.27 S 147.33 E
Mungallala Creek ≃ 166 28.05 S 147.15 E
Mungana 166 17.07 S 144.24 E
Mungaoli 124 24.25 N 78.06 E
Mungári 154 17.12 S 33.31 E
Mungar Junction 166 25.36 S 152.36 E
Mungau 152 13.56 S 21.55 E
Mungbere 154 2.38 N 28.30 E
Mungeli 124 22.04 N 81.41 E
Munger 124 25.23 N 86.28 E
Mungeranie 162 28.00 S 138.36 E
Mungindi 166 28.58 S 148.59 E
Munglinup 162 33.43 S 120.51 E
Mungo 152 11.49 S 16.16 E
Mungo National Park ♠ 166 33.44 S 143.02 E
Mungra Badshāhpur 124 25.40 N 82.11 E
Mungun-Tajga, gora ∧ 86 50.16 N 90.05 E
Mun'gyŏng 98 36.44 N 128.07 E
Munhall 214 40.23 N 79.54 W
Munhamade 154 16.37 S 36.58 E
Munhango 152 12.12 S 18.42 E
Munhango ≃ 152 11.20 S 19.50 E
Munhoz 256 22.37 S 46.22 W
Munhye-ri 98 38.10 N 127.19 E
Munich → München 60 48.08 N 11.34 E
Muniesa 34 41.02 N 0.48 W
Munim ≃ 250 2.45 S 44.04 W
Munirka ◆[8] 272a 28.34 N 77.10 E
Munising 190 46.24 N 86.38 W
Munith 216 42.23 N 84.15 W
Muñiz 258 34.33 S 58.42 W
Muniz Freire 255 20.28 S 41.25 W
Munkács → Mukačevo 78 48.27 N 22.45 E
Munka-Ljungby 41 56.15 N 12.58 E
Munkebjerg ∧[2] 41 55.41 N 9.37 E
Munkebo 41 55.27 N 10.34 E
Munkedal 26 58.29 N 11.41 E
Munkerud 40 59.50 N 13.31 E
Munkfors 40 59.50 N 13.32 E
Munksund 26 65.17 N 21.29 E
Munktorp 40 59.32 N 16.08 E
Munku-Sardyk, gora ∧ 88 51.45 N 100.32 E
Munlochy 46 57.32 N 4.15 W
Münnerstadt 56 50.15 N 10.11 E
Munnsville 210 42.58 N 75.35 W
Muñoz 116 15.43 N 120.54 E
Munozero 24 67.05 N 34.12 E
Muñoz Gamero, Península >[1] 254 52.30 S 73.10 W
Munpal-li 271b 37.45 N 126.43 E
Munro ◆[8] 288 34.32 S 58.31 W
Munroe Falls 214 41.08 N 81.26 W
Munro Lake ⊜ 184 54.38 N 95.16 W
Munsan 98 37.51 N 126.48 E
Munsarpur 126 24.18 N 88.26 E
Munsey Park 276 40.48 N 73.41 W
Munshiganj 124 23.33 N 90.32 E
Münsing 64 47.54 N 11.22 E
Münsingen, Dtsch. 58 48.25 N 9.29 E
Münsingen, Schw. 58 46.53 N 7.34 E
Munsö I 40 59.23 N 17.35 E
Munson, Ab., Can. 182 51.34 N 112.45 W
Munson, Pa., U.S. 214 40.57 N 78.10 W
Munson Knob ∧[2] 214 40.40 N 81.54 W
Munsons Corners 210 42.35 N 76.13 W
Münster, Dtsch. 52 51.57 N 7.37 E
Munster, Dtsch. 52 52.59 N 10.05 E
Münster, Dtsch. 56 49.55 N 8.52 E
Munster, Fr. 56 48.55 N 6.54 E
Munster, Fr. 58 48.03 N 7.08 E
Münster, Schw. 58 46.29 N 8.16 E
Munster, In., U.S. 216 41.33 N 87.30 W
Münster □[6] 52 51.50 N 7.25 E
Munster □[9] 48 52.25 N 8.20 W
Munster ≃ 48 52.33 N 7.12 W
Münsterkirche ⚜[1] 263 51.27 N 7.01 E
Münsterland ◆[1] 52 52.00 N 7.30 E
Münsterlingen 58 47.38 N 9.14 E
Münstermaifeld 56 50.15 N 7.22 E
Muntadgin 162 31.45 S 118.34 E
Muntahak ∧ 114 1.52 N 103.47 E
Munte 112 0.30 N 119.55 E
Muntele Mare, Vîrful ∧ 38 46.29 N 23.14 E
Muntendam 52 53.07 N 6.53 E
Muntok 112 2.04 S 105.11 E
Mununzi 154 0.36 N 29.15 E
Munuscong Lake ⊜ 190 46.10 N 84.08 W
Münzenberg 56 50.27 N 8.46 E
Münzkirchen 60 48.29 N 13.34 E
Munzur Dağları ⛰ 130 39.30 N 39.10 E
Munzur Vadisi Milli Parkı ♠ 130 39.25 N 39.30 E
Muojärvi ⊜ 26 65.56 N 29.36 E
Muolea Point > 229a 20.41 N 156.01 W
Muong Het 110 20.49 N 104.01 E
Muong Hinh 110 19.49 N 105.03 E
Muong Khoua 110 21.05 N 102.31 E
Muong Saiapoun 110 18.24 N 101.31 E
Muong Te 110 22.28 N 102.37 E
Muonio 24 67.57 N 23.42 E
Muoro 36 40.20 N 9.20 E
Muotathal 58 46.59 N 8.46 E
Mupa 152 16.10 S 15.44 E
Mupa, Parque Nacional da ◆[4] 152 16.00 S 15.35 E
Muping 98 37.24 N 121.35 E
Mupini 156 17.50 S 19.40 E
Mup'ungjang 98 35.58 N 127.49 E
Muqaddam, Wādī V 140 18.04 N 31.30 E
Muqaṭṭa' 140 14.40 N 35.51 E
Muqaybirah, Bi'r al- ⫪[4] 142 30.53 N 32.50 E
Muqayshiṭ I 128 24.10 N 53.45 E
Muqdisho (Mogadishu) 144 2.04 N 45.22 E
Muqi 98 41.46 N 124.39 E
Muqsam, Jabal ∧ 140 13.38 N 27.42 E
Muquequete 152 14.50 S 14.16 E
Muqui 255 20.57 S 41.20 W
Mur (Mura) ≃ 30 46.18 N 16.53 E
Mura (Mur) ≃, Europe 30 46.18 N 16.53 E
Mura ≃, Ross. 88 58.27 N 98.34 E
Muradiye, Tür. 84 38.59 N 43.46 E
Muradiye, Tür. 130 38.39 N 27.21 E
Murādnagar 124 28.47 N 77.30 E
Murafa ≃ 78 48.13 N 28.14 E
Murāgācha 126 23.32 N 88.24 E
Muraglione, Passo del)(66 43.56 N 11.39 E
Murai Reservoir ⊜[1] 271c 1.24 N 103.41 E
Murajá 250 0.47 S 47.57 W

Murakami 92 38.14 N 139.29 E
Murallón, Cerro ∧ 254 49.48 S 73.25 W
Murambi 154 1.46 S 30.23 E
Muramvya 154 3.16 S 29.37 E
Muráň 30 48.46 N 20.02 E
Murana 164 3.33 S 133.49 E
Murang'a 154 0.43 S 37.09 E
Murano, Isola di I 64 45.28 N 12.21 E
Muranskij porog ⌞ 88 58.02 N 112.16 E
Muraoka 96 35.28 N 134.35 E
Muraši 24 59.24 N 48.55 E
Muraški 265b 55.59 N 37.45 E
Murat 32 45.07 N 2.52 E
Murat ≃ 84 38.39 N 39.50 E
Murat Dağı ∧ 130 38.55 N 29.43 E
Muratkovo 86 58.26 N 62.23 E
Muratlı 130 41.10 N 27.30 E
Muratovo 83 48.48 N 38.45 E
Muratpur 272b 22.59 N 88.27 E
Murau 61 47.07 N 14.10 E
Muravera 71 39.25 N 9.34 E
Muravjovka 89 49.50 N 127.44 E
Muravjovo 76 56.14 N 34.14 E
Murayama 92 38.28 N 140.22 E
Murayama-chosuichi ⊜[1] 268 35.45 N 139.25 E
Muraysah, Ra's al- > 146 31.55 N 25.02 E
Murča 34 41.24 N 7.27 W
Murcanyo 144 11.41 N 50.27 E
Mūrcheh Khvort 128 33.06 N 51.30 E
Murchin 54 53.54 N 13.44 E
Murchison, Austl. 166 36.37 S 145.14 E
Murchison, N.Z. 172 41.48 S 172.20 E
Murchison, Tx., U.S. 222 32.17 N 95.45 W
Murchison ≃ 162 27.42 S 114.09 E
Murchison, Mount ∧, Austl. 162 26.46 S 116.25 E
Murchison, Mount ∧, N.Z. 172 43.01 S 171.22 E
Murchison Falls → Kabalega Falls ⌞ 154 2.17 N 31.41 E
Murchison Range ⛰ 162 20.11 S 134.26 E
Murcia, Esp. 34 37.59 N 1.07 W
Murcia, Pil. 116 10.36 N 123.02 E
Murcia □[4], Esp. 34 38.00 N 1.30 W
Murcia □[4], Esp. 34 38.00 N 1.30 W
Murcia □[4], Esp. 148 37.55 N 1.30 W
Murciélago, Islas II 236 10.51 N 85.57 W
Murcielagos Bay c 116 8.39 N 123.33 E
Mur-de-Barrez 32 44.51 N 2.39 E
Murdeduke, Lake ⊜ 169 38.11 S 143.53 E
Murder Creek ≃, Al., U.S. 194 31.04 N 87.06 W
Murder Creek ≃, N.Y., U.S. 210 43.05 N 78.31 W
Murderkill ≃ 208 39.03 N 75.24 W
Murdo 198 43.53 N 100.42 W
Murdock 220 27.00 N 82.08 W
Mure 94 36.45 N 138.14 E
Mureaux, Aérodrome des ⊠ 261 49.00 N 1.57 E
Mureck 61 46.42 N 15.46 E
Mürefte 130 40.40 N 27.14 E
Mureş □[6] 38 46.35 N 24.40 E
Mureş (Maros) ≃ 38 46.15 N 20.13 E
Muret 32 43.28 N 1.21 E
Murewa 154 17.39 S 31.47 E
Murfreesboro, Ar., U.S. 194 34.03 N 93.41 W
Murfreesboro, N.C., U.S. 192 36.26 N 77.05 W
Murfreesboro, Tn., U.S. 194 35.50 N 86.23 W
Murg 58 47.33 N 8.01 E
Murg ≃ 56 48.55 N 8.10 E
Murgab 85 38.10 N 73.59 E
Murgab (Morghāb) ≃, Asia 128 38.18 N 61.12 E
Murgab ≃, Taj. 120 38.20 N 72.30 E
Murgenella 164 11.33 S 132.55 E
Murgeni 38 46.12 N 28.01 E
Murgenthal 58 47.16 N 7.50 E
Murgha Faqīrzai 120 31.03 N 67.48 E
Murgha Kibzai 120 30.44 N 69.25 E
Murgon 166 26.15 S 151.57 E
Muri, Cook Is. 174k 21.14 S 159.43 W
Muri, Nig. 146 9.11 N 10.53 E
Muri, Schw. 58 46.56 N 7.29 E
Muri, Schw. 58 47.16 N 8.21 E
Muria, Gunung ∧ 115a 6.36 S 110.53 E
Muriaé 255 21.08 S 42.22 W
Muriaé ≃ 255 21.43 S 41.22 W
Murias de Paredes 34 42.51 N 6.11 W
Muribeca 250 10.26 S 36.59 W
Muribeca dos Guararapes 250 8.10 S 35.01 W
Murici 250 9.19 S 35.56 W
Muricizal ≃ 250 6.40 S 48.40 W
Murīdke 123 31.48 N 74.16 E
Muriége 152 9.58 S 21.11 E
Muriel Lake ⊜ 182 54.10 N 110.40 W
Murih, Pulau I 112 1.54 N 108.38 E
Murila 152 10.44 S 20.20 E
Murilo I[1] 14 8.40 N 152.11 E
Mūrinda 123 30.47 N 76.29 E
Murinja 88 54.47 N 107.21 E
Murino, Ross. 88 51.30 N 104.23 E
Murino, Ross. 265a 60.03 N 30.27 E
Murinskij ≃ 265a 60.01 N 30.28 E
Muriqui 256 22.56 S 43.57 W
Muriqui ≃ 287a 22.52 S 43.02 W
Murisengo 62 45.05 N 8.08 E
Mūrītāniyā → Mauritania □[1] 134 20.00 N 12.00 W
Müritz ⊜ 54 53.25 N 12.43 E
Muriwai 172 38.46 S 177.55 E
Murkong Selek 120 27.49 N 95.16 E
Murlīganj 124 25.54 N 86.59 E
Murlo 66 43.09 N 11.23 E
Murmansk 24 68.58 N 33.05 E
Murmansk Rise ✢[3] 12 75.00 N 37.00 E
Murmerwoude 52 53.16 N 6.00 E
Murmino 80 54.36 N 40.03 E
Murnau 64 47.40 N 11.12 E
Murnei 140 12.57 N 22.52 E
Murō 94 34.34 N 136.02 E
Murō-Akame-Aoyama-kokutei-kōen ♠ 94 34.30 N 136.10 E
Muro Lucano 68 40.45 N 15.29 E
Murom 80 55.34 N 42.02 E
Muromcevo 86 56.23 N 75.14 E
Muroran 92a 42.18 N 140.59 E
Muros 34 42.47 N 9.02 W
Muros y Noya, Ría de c[1] 34 42.45 N 9.00 W
Muroto 96 33.18 N 134.09 E
Muroto-Anan-kaigan-kokutei-kōen ♠ 96 33.41 N 134.32 E
Muroto-zaki > 96 33.15 N 134.11 E
Murovanyje Kurilovcy 78 48.43 N 27.31 E
Murowana Goślina 30 52.35 N 17.01 E
Murphy, Id., U.S. 202 43.13 N 116.33 W
Murphy, Mo., U.S. 219 38.29 N 90.29 W
Murphy, N.C., U.S. 192 35.05 N 84.02 W
Murphy Lake ⊜ 182 52.03 N 121.14 W
Murphys 226 38.08 N 120.27 W
Murphysboro 194 37.45 N 89.20 W
Murphy Slough ≃ 226 36.28 N 120.00 W
Murr ≃ 56 48.57 N 9.16 E
Murr, Wādī V 142 28.27 N 32.18 E
Murrah, Qārat al- ∧[2] 142 30.00 N 32.41 E
Murrah al-Kubrā, Al-Buḥayrah al- (Great Bitter Lake) ⊜ 142 30.20 N 32.23 E
Murrah aṣ-Ṣughrā, Al-Buḥayrah al- (Little Bitter Lake) ⊜ 142 30.13 N 32.33 E

Symbol	English	Deutsch	Español	Français	Português
≃	River	Fluß	Río	Rivière	Rio
≊	Canal	Kanal	Canal	Canal	Canal
⌞	Waterfall, Rapids	Wasserfall, Stromschnellen	Cascada, Rápidos	Chute d'eau, Rapides	Cascata, Rápidos
⊍	Strait	Meeresstraße	Estrecho	Détroit	Estreito
c	Bay, Gulf	Bucht, Golf	Bahía, Golfo	Baie, Golfe	Baía, Golfo
⊜	Lake, Lakes	See, Seen	Lago, Lagos	Lac, Lacs	Lago, Lagos
≡	Swamp	Sumpf	Pantano	Marais	Pântano
⊓	Ice Features, Glacier	Eis- und Gletscherformen	Accidentes Glaciales	Formes glaciaires	Acidentes glaciares
⫪	Other Hydrographic Features	Andere Hydrographische Objekte	Otros Elementos Hidrográficos	Autres données hydrographiques	Outros acidentes hidrográficos
✢	Submarine Features	Untermeerische Objekte	Accidentes Submarinos	Formes de relief sous-marin	Acidentes submarinos
□	Political Unit	Politische Einheit	Unidad Política	Entité politique	Unidade política
⚜	Cultural Institution	Kulturelle Institution	Institución Cultural	Institution culturelle	Instituição cultural
⊥	Historical Site	Historische Stätte	Sitio Histórico	Site historique	Sitio histórico
♠	Recreational Site	Erholungs- und Ferienort	Sitio de Recreo	Centre de loisirs	Area de Lazer
⊠	Airport	Flughafen	Aeropuerto	Aéroport	Aeroporto
■	Military Installation	Militäranlage	Instalación Militar	Installation militaire	Instalação militar
◆	Miscellaneous	Verschiedenes	Misceláneo	Divers	Diversos

Murra Murra 166 28.16 S 146.48 E
Murrāt, Ābār ⊽4 140 21.03 N 32.55 E
Murray, Ia., U.S. 190 41.02 N 93.56 W
Murray, Ky., U.S. 194 36.36 N 88.18 W
Murray, Ut,. U.S. 200 40.40 N 111.53 W
Murray ≃, Austl. 166 35.22 S 139.22 E
Murray ≃, Austl. 168a 32.35 S 115.46 E
Murray ≃, B.C., Can. 182 55.40 N 121.10 W
Murray, Lake ⊜ 164 7.00 S 141.30 E
Murray, Lake ⊜1 192 34.04 N 81.23 W
Murray, Mount ʌ, Yk., Can. 180 60.54 N 128.49 W
Murray, Mount ʌ, Pap. N. Gui. 164 6.46 S 144.01 E
Murray Bay → La Malbaie 186 47.39 N 70.10 W
Murray Bridge 168b 35.07 S 139.17 E
Murray Canal ≅ 212 44.04 N 77.35 W
Murray City 188 39.30 N 82.09 W
Murray Downs 162 21.04 S 134.40 E
Murray Fracture Zone ✦ 16 34.00 N 135.00 W
Murray Harbour 186 46.00 N 62.31 W
Murray Head > 186 46.00 N 62.28 W
Murray Maxwell Bay c 176 70.00 N 80.00 W
Murray Mouth ≃1 168b 35.34 S 138.54 E
Murray River 186 46.01 N 62.37 W
Murraysburg 158 31.58 S 23.47 E
Murrayville, B.C., Can. 224 49.10 N 122.36 W
Murrayville, Il., U.S. 194 39.35 N 90.15 W
Murrébuè 154 13.02 S 40.30 E
Murree 123 33.54 N 73.24 E
Mürren 58 46.34 N 7.54 E
Murrhardt 56 48.59 N 9.34 E
Murrí ≃ 246 6.33 N 76.52 W
Murrieta 228 33.33 N 117.12 W
Murro di Porca, Capo > 70 37.00 N 15.20 E
Murrumbidgee ≃ 166 34.43 S 143.12 E
Murrumburrah 166 34.33 S 148.21 E
Murrupula 154 15.27 S 38.47 E
Murrurundi 166 31.46 S 150.50 E
Murry Hill 279b 40.17 N 80.09 W
Murrysville 279b 40.25 N 79.41 W
Mursal 130 39.11 N 37.59 E
Mursala, Pulau I 114 1.38 N 98.32 E
Murshidābād 126 24.11 N 88.16 E
Mürşitpınar 130 36.54 N 38.19 E
Murska Sobota 61 46.40 N 16.10 E
Murskij, porog ⊾ 88 58.27 N 98.30 E
Mursko Središće 61 46.31 N 16.27 E
Murtajāpur 122 20.44 N 77.23 E
Murtal 266c 38.42 N 9.22 W
Murtee 166 31.35 S 143.30 E
Murten 58 46.56 N 7.07 E
Murtensee → Morat, Lac de ⊜ 58 46.55 N 7.05 E
Murter, Otok I 36 43.48 N 15.37 E
Murtle Lake ⊜ 182 52.08 N 119.38 W
Murtoa 166 36.37 S 142.28 E
Murton 44 54.49 N 1.24 W
Murtosa 34 40.44 N 8.38 W
Muru 140 6.36 N 29.15 E
Muru ≃ 248 8.09 S 70.45 W
Muru, Capu di > 36 41.44 N 8.40 E
Murud 122 18.19 N 72.58 E
Murud, Gunong ʌ 112 3.52 N 115.30 E
Murukta 74 67.46 N 102.01 E
Murung ≃ 112 0.12 S 114.03 E
Murupara 172 38.28 S 176.42 E
Mururoa I1 6 21.52 S 138.55 W
Murutinga 246 3.26 S 59.12 W
Murvaul, Lake ⊜1 222 32.03 N 94.28 W
Murvaul Creek ≃ 194 32.05 N 94.12 W
Murwāra 124 23.51 N 80.24 E
Murwillumbah 166 28.19 S 153.24 E
Mürz ≃ 61 47.24 N 15.17 E
Mürzsteg 61 47.40 N 15.29 E
Mürzzuschlag 61 47.36 N 15.41 E
Muş 130 38.44 N 41.30 E
Muş □4 128 39.00 N 42.00 E
Musa 152 2.40 N 19.18 E
Mūša ≃, Europe 76 56.24 N 24.10 E
Musa ≃, Pap. N. Gui. 164 9.25 S 148.50 E
Mūsā, Jabal (Mount Sinai) ʌ 140 28.32 N 33.59 E
Mūsā, ʿUyūn (Springs of Moses) ⊽4 142 29.52 N 32.39 E
Musabeyli 130 39.51 N 34.37 E
Musadi 152 2.34 S 22.47 E
Musaid 146 31.35 N 25.03 E
Mūsa Khel 123 32.38 N 71.44 E
Mūsa Khel Bāzār 120 30.52 N 69.49 E
Musala ʌ 38 42.11 N 23.34 E
Musan 98 42.14 N 129.13 E
Musandam Peninsula >1 128 26.18 N 56.24 E
Musao 154 7.43 S 26.17 E
Mūsā Qalʿeh 120 32.22 N 64.46 E
Mūsā Qalʿeh ≃ 128 32.05 N 64.51 E
Musar 272b 22.54 N 88.14 E
Musasa 154 3.21 S 31.33 E
Musashi 96 33.30 N 131.43 E
Musashi → Iruma 94 35.50 N 139.24 E
Musashimurayama 268 35.45 N 139.23 E
Musashino 94 35.42 N 139.34 E
Musashino-daichi ⋏1 268 35.45 N 139.35 E
Musau 58 47.32 N 10.40 E
Musayʿīd 128 24.59 N 51.32 E
Musaymīr 144 13.27 N 44.37 E
Mūsāzai 120 30.23 N 66.32 E
Muscat and Oman → Oman □1 118 22.00 N 58.00 E
Muscatatuck ≃ 218 38.46 N 86.10 W
Muscatatuck, Grassy Fork ≃ 218 38.45 N 85.07 W
Muscatatuck, Vernon Fork ≃ 218 38.46 N 85.54 W
Muscatine 190 41.25 N 91.03 W
Muscat → Masqaṭ 128 23.37 N 58.35 E
Müsch 56 50.23 N 6.49 E
Mus-Chaja, gora ʌ 74 62.35 N 140.50 E
Muschu Island I 164 3.25 S 143.35 E
Muschwitz 54 51.11 N 12.07 E
Muscle Shoals 194 34.44 N 87.40 W
Musclow, Mount ʌ 182 53.17 N 127.09 W
Musclow Lake ⊜ 184 51.25 N 94.56 W
Muscoda 190 43.11 N 90.26 W
Musconetcong ≃ 210 40.36 N 75.11 W
Musconetcong, Lake ⊜ 276 40.54 N 74.42 W
Muscongus Bay c 188 43.55 N 69.20 W
Muscote Bay c 212 44.06 N 77.18 W
Muscowpetung Indian Reserve ◆4 184 50.45 N 104.15 W
Muscoy 228 34.09 N 117.20 W
Muse 214 40.17 N 80.12 W
Musengezi ≃ 154 15.43 S 31.14 E
Museum, Bergbau ✦ 263 51.29 N 7.13 E
Musgrave, Austl. 164 14.47 S 143.30 E
Musgrave, B.C., Can. 224 48.45 N 123.32 W
Musgrave, Mount ʌ 172 43.48 S 170.43 E
Musgrave Ranges ⋏ 162 26.10 S 131.50 E
Musgravetown 186 48.24 N 53.53 W
Mūshā 142 27.08 N 31.18 E
Mushābani 126 22.31 N 86.27 E
Mushāsh, Jabal al- ʌ2 142 28.54 N 31.11 E
Mushenge 152 4.32 S 21.21 E
Mushie 152 3.01 S 16.54 E
Mushima 154 14.13 S 25.05 E
Mushin 150 6.32 N 3.22 E
Mūsi ≃, India 122 16.41 N 79.40 E
Musi ≃, Indon. 112 2.20 S 104.56 E
Musicians Seamounts ✦3 6 31.00 N 162.00 W
Muskauer Heide ◆3 54 51.25 N 14.40 E
Muskeg ≃ 182 54.01 N 119.03 W
Muskeget Channel ⊻ 207 41.25 N 70.20 W
Muskeget Island I 207 41.20 N 70.18 W
Muskeg Lake Indian Reserve ◆4 184 52.58 N 106.57 W
Muskego 216 42.54 N 88.08 W
Muskego Lake ⊜ 216 42.53 N 88.07 W
Muskegon 216 43.14 N 86.14 W
Muskegon □6 216 43.12 N 86.08 W
Muskegon ≃ 190 43.14 N 86.20 W
Muskegon County Airport ⊠ 216 43.10 N 86.14 W
Muskegon Heights 216 43.12 N 86.14 W
Muskegon Lake ⊜ 216 43.14 N 86.17 W
Muskegon State Park ♦ 216 43.14 N 86.20 W
Muškętova, gora ʌ 88 53.35 N 113.32 E
Muskingum □6 214 40.06 N 81.51 W
Muskingum ≃ 188 39.27 N 81.30 W
Muskingum Brook ≃ 285 39.48 N 74.44 W
Muskira 124 25.40 N 79.48 E
Muskö I 40 59.00 N 18.06 E
Muskoday Indian Reserve ◆4 184 53.06 N 105.30 W
Muskogee 196 35.44 N 95.22 W
Muskoka □6 212 45.05 N 79.03 W
Muskoka, Lake ⊜ 212 45.00 N 79.25 W
Muskoka, North Branch ≃ 212 45.02 N 79.19 W
Muskoka, South Branch ≃ 212 45.02 N 79.19 W
Muskosh Channel ⊻ 212 44.55 N 79.53 W
Muskowekwan Indian Reserve ◆4 184 51.19 N 104.06 W
Muskrat Creek ≃ 202 43.09 N 108.11 W
Muskrat Dam Lake ⊜ 184 53.25 N 91.40 W
Muskrat Lake ⊜ 190 45.40 N 76.55 W
Muskwa ≃ 176 58.45 N 122.35 W
Muskwa Lake ⊜ 182 56.09 N 114.38 W
Muslimbāgh 120 30.49 N 67.45 E
Musl'umovo 80 55.18 N 53.12 E
Muşmuş 132 32.32 N 35.09 E
Musocco ◆8 266b 45.30 N 9.08 E
Musofu Mission 154 13.31 S 29.02 E
Musoma 154 1.30 S 33.48 E
Musone ≃, It. 64 45.50 N 11.55 E
Musone ≃, It. 66 43.28 N 13.38 E
Musoshi 154 11.54 S 27.46 E
Musquanousse, Lac ⊜ 186 50.22 N 61.05 W
Musquapsink Brook ≃ 276 40.59 N 74.01 W
Musquaro, Lac ⊜ 186 50.38 N 61.05 W
Musquash ≃ 212 44.57 N 79.52 W
Musquash Brook ≃ 283 42.42 N 71.26 W
Musquashcut Pond ⊜ 283 42.13 N 70.46 W
Musquodoboit Harbour 186 44.47 N 63.09 W
Mussau Island I 164 1.30 S 149.40 E
Musselburgh 46 55.57 N 3.04 W
Musselkanaal 52 52.56 N 7.00 E
Musselshell ≃ 202 47.21 N 107.58 W
Mussende 152 10.32 S 16.05 E
Mussidan 32 45.02 N 0.22 E
Mussolo 152 9.59 S 17.19 E
Mussomeli 70 37.35 N 13.45 E
Mussoorie 124 30.27 N 78.05 E
Mussuco 152 17.08 S 19.05 E
Mussum 52 51.48 N 6.34 E
Mussuma 152 14.14 S 21.59 E
Mussy-sur-Seine 58 47.58 N 4.30 E
Mustafakemalpaşa 130 40.02 N 28.24 E
Mustafa Kemal Paşa ≃ 130 40.07 N 28.33 E
Mustafino 80 55.01 N 53.38 E
Mustahil 144 5.12 N 44.17 E
Müstair 58 46.37 N 10.27 E
Mustajevo 80 51.48 N 53.25 E
Mustajõe 76 57.59 N 26.58 E
Mustāng 124 29.11 N 83.58 E
Mustang Draw V 196 32.12 N 101.36 W
Mustang Island I 196 28.00 N 96.55 W
Mustāy 142 30.37 N 31.09 E
Musters, Lago ⊜ 254 45.27 S 69.13 W
Mustinka ≃ 198 45.45 N 96.38 W
Mustjala 76 58.28 N 22.14 E
Mustla 76 58.14 N 25.52 E
Musṭurud 273c 30.08 N 31.17 E
Mustvee 76 58.51 N 26.56 E
Musu-dan > 98 40.50 N 129.43 E
Musun 84 39.42 N 43.49 E
Muswellbrook 166 32.16 S 150.53 E
Muszyna 30 49.21 N 20.54 E
Mūt, Mişr 140 25.29 N 28.59 E
Mut, Tür. 130 36.39 N 33.27 E
Muta 61 46.37 N 15.10 E
Mutá, Ponta do > 255 13.52 S 38.56 W
Muʾtah 132 31.06 N 35.42 E
Mutalau 174v 18.56 S 169.50 W
Mutambara 154 19.36 S 32.33 E
Mutanchiang → Mudanjiang 89 44.35 N 129.36 E
Mutanda, Moç. 156 21.02 S 33.31 E
Mutanda, Zaïre 152 5.17 S 16.34 E
Mutanda Mission 154 12.24 S 26.16 E
Mutankiang → Mudanjiang 89 44.35 N 129.36 E
Mutarammil, Jabal al- ʌ 132 31.04 N 36.06 E
Mutare 154 18.58 S 32.40 E
Mutbīn 132 33.09 N 36.15 E
Mutějovice 54 50.09 N 13.41 E
Mutha 154 1.48 S 38.26 E
Muthill 46 56.19 N 3.50 W
Mutiko 154 1.39 S 28.12 E
Muting 164 7.23 S 140.20 E
Mutis, Gunung ʌ 112 9.34 S 124.14 E
Mutlu (Rezovska) ≃ 130 41.59 N 28.01 E
Mutoko 154 17.24 S 32.13 E
Mutombo-Mukulu 152 7.58 S 24.00 E
Mutoraj 74 61.20 N 100.30 E
Mutoto 152 5.42 S 22.42 E
Mutouchengzi 98 41.20 N 119.59 E
Mutouhao 107 28.49 N 105.04 E
Mutsamudu 157a 12.09 S 44.25 E
Mutshatsha 152 10.39 S 24.27 E
Mutsu 92 41.17 N 141.10 E
Mutsuai 268 35.08 N 139.38 E
Mutsumi 96 34.26 N 131.34 E
Mutsuura ◆8 268 35.19 N 139.37 E
Mutsu-wan c 92 41.05 N 140.55 E
Muttaburra 166 22.36 S 144.33 E
Mutte Kopf ʌ 58 47.16 N 10.39 E
Muttenz 58 47.32 N 7.39 E
Mutters 64 47.14 N 11.23 E
Mutterstadt 56 49.26 N 8.21 E
Muttonbird Islands II 172 47.15 S 167.24 E
Muttontown 276 40.49 N 73.33 W
Muttra → Mathura 124 27.30 N 77.41 E
Mutual, Oh., U.S. 218 40.05 N 83.38 W
Mutual, Pa., U.S. 279b 40.14 N 79.30 W
Muṭūbis 142 31.18 N 30.31 E
Mutuca, Ribeirão da ≃ 256 21.36 S 45.39 W
Mutuco, Lago ⊜ 250 1.21 N 50.24 W
Mutuípe 255 13.15 S 39.31 W
Mutum 255 19.49 S 41.26 W
Mutum ≃ 246 4.25 S 68.03 W
Mutum Biyu 146 8.38 N 10.46 E
Mutumbo 152 13.14 S 17.17 E
Mutunópolis 255 13.40 S 49.15 W
Muturi 164 2.06 S 133.43 E
Muturi ≃ 164 2.13 S 133.40 E
Mututi, Ilha do I 250 0.45 S 51.00 W
Mutzig 58 48.32 N 7.28 E
Mutzschen 54 51.16 N 12.53 E
Mu Us Shamo ◆2 102 38.45 N 109.10 E
Mūvattupula 122 9.58 N 76.35 E
Muvukoni 154 0.24 S 38.14 E
Muwopu 104 41.03 N 121.12 E
Muxaluando 152 8.07 S 14.17 E
Muxihe 100 31.03 N 115.21 E
Muxima 152 9.31 S 13.56 E
Muyaga 154 3.14 S 30.33 E
Muyang 100 27.06 N 119.34 E
Muyang ≃ 100 27.00 N 119.41 E
Muyinga 154 2.51 S 30.20 E
Muymano ≃ 248 11.27 S 69.03 W
Muy Muy 236 12.46 N 85.38 W
Muyua Island I 164 9.05 S 152.50 E
Muyuka 152 4.17 N 9.25 E
Muyumba 154 7.15 S 26.59 E
Mužač' 82 54.22 N 36.21 E
Muzaffarābād 123 34.22 N 73.28 E
Muzaffargarh 123 30.04 N 71.12 E
Muzaffarnagar 124 29.28 N 77.41 E
Muzaffarpur 124 26.07 N 85.24 E
Muzambinho 256 21.22 S 46.32 W
Muzambinho ≃ 256 21.15 S 46.26 W
Muzambo ≃ 256 21.17 S 46.16 W
Muzat ≃ 90 41.15 N 83.27 E
Muzayrīb 132 32.42 N 36.01 E
Muzbek, gora ʌ 85 40.23 N 69.39 E
Muzbel' ◆1 86 50.15 N 70.50 E
Muzeze 152 15.03 S 17.43 E
Muzhen 100 30.43 N 117.56 E
Muži 74 65.22 N 64.40 E
Mužiči 84 43.03 N 44.59 E
Mužiksu 86 47.42 N 84.58 E
Muzillac 32 47.33 N 2.29 W
Muzkol, chrebet ⋏ 85 38.25 N 73.30 E
Muzoka 154 16.41 S 27.19 E
Muzon, Cape > 182 54.41 N 132.44 W
Muztag ʌ, Zhg. 120 36.25 N 87.25 E
Muztag ʌ, Zhg. 120 36.03 N 80.07 E
Muztagata ʌ 85 38.17 N 75.11 E
Muz Tau ʌ 86 43.50 N 85.40 E
Muzūrah 142 28.53 N 30.48 E
Muzzana del Turgnano 64 45.49 N 13.08 E
Mvam 152 0.13 S 9.39 E
Mvangan 152 2.38 N 11.44 E
Mvela 154 14.46 S 35.16 E
Mvengué 152 3.17 N 11.01 E
Mvolo 140 6.03 N 29.56 E
Mvomero 154 6.20 S 37.25 E
Mvoti ≃ 158 29.24 S 31.22 E
Mvoung ≃ 152 0.04 N 12.18 E
Mvouti 152 4.15 S 12.29 E
Mvuha 154 7.12 S 37.51 E
Mvuma 154 19.19 S 30.35 E
Mwadi-Kalumba 152 7.53 S 18.46 E
Mwadui 154 3.33 S 33.36 E
Mwali (Mohéli) I 157a 12.15 S 43.45 E
Mwami 154 16.40 S 29.46 E
Mwanangumune 152 15.31 S 23.30 E
Mwango 152 6.51 S 24.13 E
Mwanza, Malaŵi 154 15.37 S 34.31 E
Mwanza, Tan. 154 2.31 S 32.54 E
Mwanza, Zaïre 154 7.54 S 26.45 E
Mwanza, Zam. 152 17.02 S 24.27 E
Mwanza □4 154 2.45 S 32.45 E
Mwanza Gulf c 154 2.35 S 32.51 E
Mwaya, Tan. 154 9.33 S 33.57 E
Mwaya, Tan. 154 8.55 S 36.50 E
Mweelrea ʌ 48 53.38 N 9.50 W
Mwehu 154 5.44 S 26.40 E
Mweka 152 4.51 S 21.34 E
Mwemena 154 10.19 S 27.28 E
Mwenda 154 12.01 S 28.44 E
Mwendjila 152 7.12 S 18.51 E
Mwene-Ditu 152 7.03 S 23.27 E
Mwenezi 154 21.22 S 30.45 E
Mwenga 154 3.02 S 28.26 E
Mwepo 154 11.56 S 26.11 E
Mwerasandu 154 0.59 S 30.23 E
Mwereni 154 4.20 S 39.08 E
Mweru, Lake ⊜ 154 9.00 S 28.45 E
Mweru Mantipa National Park ♦ 154 8.45 S 29.30 E
Mweru Wantipa, Lake ⊜ 154 8.45 S 29.40 E
Mwetshi 152 4.42 S 22.39 E
Mwilambwe 154 8.07 S 25.00 E
Mwilitau Islands II 164 2.50 S 146.20 E
Mwimbi 154 8.39 S 31.40 E
Mwingi 154 0.56 S 38.04 E
Mwinilunga 152 11.44 S 24.26 E
Mwitikira 154 6.31 S 35.39 E
Mwombezhi ≃ 154 12.52 S 25.00 E
Myaing 110 21.37 N 94.51 E
Myājlār 120 26.15 N 70.23 E
Myakka ≃ 220 26.56 N 82.11 W
Myakka, Lake ⊜ 220 27.16 N 82.17 W
Myakka City 220 27.20 N 82.09 W
Myakka River State Park ♦ 220 27.15 N 82.17 W
Myall Lakes National Park ♦ 166 32.28 S 152.22 E
Myall Range ⋏ 170 32.58 S 151.22 E
Myanaung 110 18.17 N 95.19 E
Myanmar → Burma □1 110 22.00 N 98.00 E
Myaungmya 110 16.36 N 94.56 E
Myawadi 110 16.41 N 98.31 E
Mybster 46 58.27 N 3.25 W
Myckelgensjö 26 63.34 N 17.37 E
Myebon 110 20.03 N 93.22 E
Myeik → Mergui 110 12.26 N 98.36 E
Myers, Ky., U.S. 218 38.21 N 83.57 W
Myers, N.Y., U.S. 210 42.32 N 76.32 W
Myerstown 208 40.22 N 76.19 W
Myingyan 110 21.28 N 95.23 E
Myinmoletkat Taung ʌ 110 13.28 N 98.48 E
Myitkyinā 110 25.23 N 97.24 E
Myitnge ≃ 110 21.52 N 95.59 E
Myitta 110 14.10 N 98.31 E
Myittha 110 21.25 N 96.08 E
Myittha ≃ 110 23.12 N 94.17 E
Myjava 30 48.45 N 17.34 E
Myjeldino 24 61.46 N 54.48 E
Myjlybulak 86 48.57 N 75.13 E
Myla 24 65.25 N 50.48 E
Mylau 54 50.37 N 12.16 E
Myl'džino 86 59.03 N 78.29 E
Myllendonk, Schloss ⊥ 263 51.13 N 6.29 E
Myllykoski 26 60.47 N 26.48 E
Myllymäki 26 62.32 N 24.17 E
Mylor 168b 35.03 S 138.45 E
Mymensingh 124 24.45 N 90.24 E
Mynämäki 26 60.40 N 22.00 E
Mynaral 86 45.25 N 73.41 E
Mynbulak, gora ʌ 85 41.43 N 69.49 E
Mynfontein 158 30.55 S 23.57 E
Mynydd Bach ʌ2 42 52.15 N 4.05 W
Mynydd Eppynt ʌ 42 52.05 N 3.30 W
Mynydd Hiraethog ʌ 44 53.05 N 3.33 W
Mynydd Pencarreg ʌ2 42 52.04 N 4.04 W
Mynydd Preseli ʌ 42 51.58 N 4.42 W
Myōgata 94 35.51 N 137.02 E
Myōgi 94 36.17 N 138.49 E
Myōgi-Arafune-Saku-kōgen-kokutei-kōen ♦ 94 36.12 N 138.10 E
Myōgi-san ʌ 94 36.17 N 138.44 E
Myo-gyi 110 21.27 N 96.22 E
Myohaung 110 20.36 N 93.10 E
Myohyang-san ʌ 98 40.02 N 126.17 E
Myohyang-sanmaek ⋏ 98 40.30 N 127.00 E
Myojin-dake ʌ 270 34.57 N 135.36 E
Myōjin-san ʌ 96 33.34 N 133.04 E
Myōken-san ʌ 96 35.24 N 134.39 E
Myōken-zan ʌ 270 34.56 N 135.28 E
Myōken-zan ʌ2 270 34.30 N 134.57 E
Myōkō 94 36.56 N 138.13 E
Myōkō-kōgen 94 36.52 N 138.12 E
Myōkō-san ʌ 94 36.52 N 138.07 E
Myŏnmong-ni ◆8 271b 37.35 N 127.05 E
Myponga 168b 35.24 S 138.28 E
Myponga Reservoir ⊜1 168b 35.24 S 138.26 E
Myra ⊥ 130 36.15 N 29.54 E
Mýrdalsjökull ⊓ 24a 63.40 N 19.05 W
Myrnam 182 53.40 N 111.14 W
Myroodah 162 18.08 S 124.16 E
Myrskylä (Mörskom) 26 60.40 N 25.51 E
Myrtle Beach 192 33.41 N 78.53 W
Myrtle Beach Air Force Base ■ 192 33.41 N 78.56 W
Myrtle Beach State Park ♦ 192 33.37 N 78.58 W
Myrtle Creek 202 43.01 N 123.17 W
Myrtle Grove 194 30.25 N 87.18 W
Myrtle Point 202 43.03 N 124.08 W
Myrtle Springs 222 32.37 N 95.56 W
Myrtletowne 204 40.47 N 124.04 W
Myrtleville 170 34.29 S 149.49 E
Myšega 82 54.31 N 37.02 E
Mysen 26 59.33 N 11.20 E
Mysia □9 130 39.15 N 28.00 E
Mysingen ⊻ 40 59.00 N 18.15 E
Myski 86 53.42 N 87.48 E
Myškino 76 57.47 N 38.27 E
Myśla ≃ 54 52.40 N 14.29 E
Myślenice 30 49.51 N 19.56 E
Myślibórz 30 52.55 N 14.52 E
Mysłowice 30 50.15 N 19.07 E
Mysore 122 12.18 N 76.39 E
Mys Šmidta 180 68.56 N 179.26 W
Mystic, Ct., U.S. 207 41.21 N 71.58 W
Mystic, Ia., U.S. 190 40.46 N 92.56 W
Mystic ≃ 283 42.23 N 71.03 W
Mystic Seaport ✦ 207 41.22 N 71.58 W
Mys Vchodnoj 74 73.53 N 86.43 E
Mysy 24 60.34 N 53.57 E
Mys Želanija 72 76.56 N 68.35 E
Myszków 30 50.36 N 19.20 E
Myszyniec 30 53.24 N 21.21 E
Myt 80 56.48 N 42.21 E
My Tho 110 10.21 N 106.21 E
Mytholm 262 53.44 N 2.01 W
Mytholmroyd 262 53.44 N 1.59 W
Mytilene → Mitilíni 38 39.06 N 26.32 E
Mytišči 82 55.55 N 37.46 E
Mytishchi → Mytišči 82 55.55 N 37.46 E
Mytišino 76 54.48 N 34.01 E
Mýto 60 49.47 N 13.44 E
Myton 200 40.11 N 110.03 W
Mývatn ⊜ 24a 65.37 N 16.58 W
Myzovo 78 51.22 N 24.31 E
M'zab, Oued V 148 32.19 N 5.24 E
Mže ≃ 60 49.46 N 13.24 E
Mzenga 154 6.56 S 38.43 E
Mziha 154 5.54 S 37.47 E
Mzimba 154 11.52 S 33.34 E
Mzimkulu ≃ 158 30.44 S 30.28 E
Mzimvubu ≃ 158 31.38 S 29.32 E
Mzintlava ≃ 158 31.12 S 29.18 E
Mzuzu 154 11.27 S 33.55 E
Mzymta ≃ 84 43.27 N 39.56 E

N

Na I 174r 6.52 N 158.22 E
Na (Tengtiao) ≃ 110 22.05 N 103.09 E
Naab ≃ 60 49.01 N 12.02 E
Naach, Jbel ʌ 34 34.53 N 3.22 W
Naachtpunkt Brook ≃ 276 40.54 N 74.15 W
Naaldwijk 52 52.00 N 4.12 E
Naalehu 229d 19.03 N 155.35 W
Naʿām 140 9.42 N 28.27 E
Naʿâma, Sebkhet en ≡ 148 33.20 N 0.16 W
Naaman Creek ≃ 285 39.48 N 75.27 W
Naaman Creek, South Branch ≃ 285 39.49 N 75.27 W
Naamans Garden 285 39.49 N 75.31 W
Naantali 26 60.27 N 22.02 E
Naarden 52 52.17 N 5.09 E
Naarn ≃ 61 48.11 N 14.49 E
Naas 48 53.13 N 6.39 W
Naas ≃ 171b 35.36 S 149.04 E
Naast, Bel. 50 50.33 N 4.05 E
Naast, Scot., U.K. 46 57.47 N 5.39 W
Naʿaẓuz, Har ʌ 132 30.01 N 35.00 E
Nabā, Jabal an- (Mount Nebo) ʌ 132 31.46 N 35.45 E
Nababiep 156 29.36 S 17.46 E
Nabābpur 272b 22.42 N 88.12 E
Nabaganga ≃1 126 22.59 N 89.34 E
Nabagram 126 24.12 N 88.06 E
Nabalat Al-Ḥajanah 140 13.13 N 29.02 E
Nabari 94 34.37 N 136.05 E
Nabari ≃ 94 34.45 N 136.01 E
Nabarūh 142 31.06 N 31.18 E
Nabas 116 11.50 N 122.05 E
Nabasta 126 23.15 N 88.01 E
Nabawa 162 28.31 S 114.47 E
Nabb 218 38.36 N 85.38 W
Nabberu, Lake ⊜ 162 25.36 S 120.30 E
Nabburg 60 49.28 N 12.11 E
Nabeina 174t 1.26 N 173.05 E
Naberera 154 4.12 S 36.56 E
Naberežnoje 265b 55.57 N 37.58 E
Naberežnyje Čelny 80 55.42 N 52.19 E
Nabesna 180 62.22 N 143.00 W
Nabesna ≃ 180 63.03 N 141.52 W
Nabeul 148 36.27 N 10.44 E
Nabeul □8 148 36.35 N 10.45 E
Nābha 123 30.22 N 76.09 E
Nab Hill ʌ2 262 53.47 N 1.57 W
Nabigou 152 1.12 S 9.31 E
Nabī Hārūn, Jabal an- ʌ 132 30.19 N 35.24 E
Nabileque ≃ 248 20.55 S 57.49 W
Nabire 164 3.22 S 135.29 E
Nabī Shuʿayb, Jabal an- ʌ 144 15.17 N 43.59 E
Nabisipi ≃ 186 50.14 N 62.13 W
Nabiswera 154 1.28 N 32.16 E
Nabī Yūnus, Ra's an- > 132 33.39 N 35.24 E
Nabnasset 207 42.36 N 71.25 W
Nabnasset Pond ⊜ 283 42.37 N 71.26 W
Nabogame 232 26.14 N 106.57 W
Naboomspruit 156 24.32 S 28.36 E
Nabordo 150 10.10 N 9.20 E
Nabou 150 11.27 N 2.43 W
Nabq 140 28.04 N 34.25 E
Nabua 116 13.24 N 123.22 E
Nabula 120 31.55 N 80.10 E
Nābulus 132 32.13 N 35.16 E
Nabunturan 116 7.35 N 125.58 E
Nacajuca 234 18.08 N 93.01 W
Nacala 154 14.34 S 40.41 E
Nacala-Velha 154 14.32 S 40.37 E
Načalovo 80 46.20 N 48.11 E
Nacaome 236 13.31 N 87.30 W
Nacastillo 234 19.35 N 104.55 W
Nacchie 144 7.23 N 40.10 E
Nacereddine 34 36.08 N 3.26 E
Nachabinka ≃ 265b 55.51 N 37.12 E
Nachabino 82 55.51 N 37.11 E
Naches 224 46.43 N 120.41 W
Naches ≃ 202 46.38 N 120.31 W
Nachičevan' 84 39.13 N 45.24 E
Nachičevanskaja Avtonomnaja Sovetskaja Socialističeskaja Respublika □3 84 39.20 N 45.30 E

ENGLISH
Name Page Lat.°′ Long.°′

Nachi-katsuura 92 33.30 N 135.55 E
Nāchinda 126 21.53 N 87.46 E
Nachingwea 154 10.23 S 38.46 E
Nāchna 120 27.30 N 71.43 E
Náchod 30 50.25 N 16.10 E
Nachodka 89 42.48 N 132.52 E
Nächstebreck ◆8 263 51.18 N 7.14 E
Nachterstedt 54 51.49 N 11.20 E
Nachuge 110 10.45 N 92.22 E
Nachvak Fiord c2 176 59.03 N 63.45 W
Naci, Pil. 116 14.19 N 120.46 E
Naci, Pil. 116 6.19 N 124.46 E
Nacimiento 252 37.30 S 72.40 W
Nacimiento ≃ 226 35.49 N 120.45 W
Nacimiento, Lake ⊜1 226 35.45 N 121.00 W
Načinskij Golec, gora ʌ 89 52.24 N 118.53 E
Nacka 40 59.18 N 18.10 E
Naco, Méx. 232 31.20 N 109.56 W
Naco, Az., U.S. 200 31.20 N 109.56 W
Nacogdoches 222 31.36 N 94.39 W
Nacogdoches □6 222 31.40 N 94.45 W
Nacogdoches, Lake ⊜1 222 31.37 N 94.50 W
Nácori Chico 232 29.39 N 109.01 W
Nacozari de García 232 30.24 N 109.39 W
Ñacunday 252 26.01 S 54.46 W
Nada 222 29.24 N 96.23 W
Nada ◆8 270 34.44 N 135.14 E
Nadābhānga 272b 22.24 N 88.14 E
Nadachi 94 37.09 N 138.06 E
Nadaleen Mountain ʌ 180 64.15 N 133.04 W
Nadasaki 96 34.32 N 133.52 E
Nádasd 61 46.58 N 16.37 E
Nadbai 124 27.14 N 77.12 E
Nadder ≃ 42 51.03 N 1.48 W
Nadela 34 42.58 N 7.30 W
Nadelkap → Agulhas, Cape > 158 34.52 S 20.00 E
Naden Harbour c 182 54.00 N 132.35 W
Nadeždinskoje 89 48.18 N 133.11 E
Nadi 140 18.40 N 33.42 E
Nadiād 120 22.42 N 72.52 E
Nādir, Mişr 142 30.33 N 30.51 E
Nadir, Vir. Is., U.S. 240m 18.19 N 64.53 W
Nădlac 38 46.10 N 20.45 E
Nador 148 35.12 N 2.55 W
Nador □4 148 35.09 N 3.04 W
Nadporožje 76 60.28 N 34.17 E
Nadrin 56 50.10 N 5.41 E
Nadterečnaja 84 43.37 N 45.22 E
Nadvoicy 24 63.52 N 34.15 E
Nadvornaja 78 48.38 N 24.34 E
Nadym 72 65.35 N 72.42 E
Nadym ≃ 74 66.12 N 72.00 E
Nadyrovo 80 54.53 N 52.28 E
Naeba-san ʌ 94 36.51 N 138.41 E
Nae-dong 98 37.16 N 126.27 E
Naejang-san Kukrip Kongwŏn ♦ 98 35.28 N 126.52 E
Naenwa 120 25.46 N 75.51 E
Nærbø 26 58.40 N 5.39 E
Næsby 41 55.25 N 10.22 E
Næstved 41 55.14 N 11.46 E
Nafada 146 11.08 N 11.20 E
Nafadji 150 12.37 N 11.37 W
Nafarros 266c 38.49 N 9.25 W
Nafāzah, ʿAlam ʌ2 142 30.30 N 29.42 E
Näfels 58 47.06 N 9.04 E
Nafī 128 24.57 N 43.42 E
Nafīshah 142 30.34 N 32.15 E
Naftalan 84 40.31 N 46.50 E
Naftan, Puntan I > 174n 15.05 N 145.45 E
Nāfūrah 146 29.20 N 21.20 E
Nafūsah, Jabal ⋏2 146 31.50 N 12.00 E
Nāg 120 27.24 N 65.08 E
Naga, Nihon 96 34.16 N 135.26 E
Naga, Pil. 116 13.37 N 123.11 E
Naga, Pil. 116 10.13 N 123.45 E
Nâga, Kreb en ±4 148 24.00 N 6.00 W
Naga, Oued en V 148 27.53 N 7.10 W
Nagaga 154 10.54 S 39.07 E
Nagahama, Nihon 94 35.23 N 136.16 E
Nagahama, Nihon 96 33.36 N 132.29 E
Nagahama, Nihon 174m 26.25 N 127.44 E
Naga Hills ⋏ 110 26.00 N 95.00 E
Nagai, Nihon 92 38.06 N 140.02 E
Nagai, Nihon 268 35.12 N 139.37 E
Nagai Island I 180 55.11 N 159.55 W
Nagai Park ♦ 270 34.36 N 135.31 E
Nagaizumi 94 35.08 N 138.54 E
Nāgāland □3 120 26.00 N 95.00 E
Nagambie 169 36.47 S 145.10 E
Nagannu-shima I 174m 26.16 N 127.33 E
Nagano 94 36.39 N 138.11 E
Nagano □5 94 36.00 N 138.00 E
Nagano-dam ◆6 94 35.50 N 136.33 E
Naganohara 94 36.33 N 138.38 E
Nagao, Nihon 96 34.16 N 134.10 E
Nagao, Nihon 270 34.50 N 135.43 E
Nagao-hana > 96 35.32 N 134.01 E
Nagaoka 92 37.27 N 138.51 E
Nagaokakyō 94 34.55 N 135.42 E
Nagaon 120 26.20 N 92.40 E
Nāgappattinam 122 10.46 N 79.50 E
Nagar, India 123 32.07 N 77.10 E
Nagar, India 124 27.26 N 77.06 E
Nagara 270 34.26 N 135.44 E
Nagara ≃ 94 35.01 N 136.43 E
Nagareyama 94 35.51 N 139.54 E
Nāgārjuna Sāgar ⊜1 122 16.35 N 79.21 E
Nagarote 236 12.16 N 86.34 W
Nagar Pārkar 120 24.22 N 70.45 E
Nāgarpur 124 24.03 N 89.53 E
Nagar Untāri 124 24.17 N 83.30 E
Nagarzê 124 28.59 N 90.25 E
Nagas 116 13.06 N 123.18 E
Nagasaka 94 35.49 N 138.22 E
Nagasaki 92 32.48 N 129.55 E
Nagasawa 268 35.12 N 139.41 E
Nagashima 94 35.05 N 136.42 E
Naga-shima I, Nihon 96 33.49 N 132.05 E
Naga-shima I, Nihon 96 34.41 N 134.15 E
Nagashino ⊥ 94 34.56 N 137.32 E
Nagasin Lake ⊜ 190 47.44 N 83.37 W
Nagasu 96 32.56 N 130.27 E
Nagasu → Usa 96 33.31 N 131.22 E
Nagata ◆8 270 34.40 N 135.09 E
Nagataki 270 34.23 N 135.20 E
Nagatino ◆8 265b 55.41 N 37.41 E
Nagato, Nihon 94 36.15 N 138.16 E
Nagato, Nihon 96 34.21 N 131.10 E
Nagatsuda ◆8 268 35.32 N 139.30 E
Nāgaur 120 27.12 N 73.44 E
Nāgāvali ≃ 122 18.13 N 83.56 E
Nagavskaja 80 47.47 N 42.50 E
Nagawa 94 36.05 N 137.41 E
Nagawicka Lake ⊜ 216 43.05 N 88.23 W
Nagcarlan 116 14.08 N 121.25 E
Nagda 120 23.27 N 75.25 E
Nagele 52 52.37 N 5.44 E
Nāgercoil 122 8.10 N 77.26 E
Nagi 96 35.07 N 134.11 E
Nagiba 116 13.41 N 120.53 E
Nagibino 86 55.46 N 72.43 E
Nagichot 154 4.16 N 33.34 E
Nagīna 124 29.27 N 78.27 E
Nāgirāt 126 23.38 N 89.18 E
Nagi-san ʌ 96 35.10 N 134.11 E
Nagiso 94 35.36 N 137.37 E
Nagla 272a 28.31 N 77.22 E
Naglarby 40 60.25 N 15.34 E
Nagles Mountains ⋏ 48 52.05 N 8.30 W
Nagłowice 30 50.41 N 20.06 E
Nago 174m 26.35 N 127.59 E
Nāgod 124 24.34 N 80.36 E
Nagog Pond ⊜ 283 42.31 N 71.26 W
Nagoja → Nagoya 94 35.10 N 136.55 E
Nagold 56 48.33 N 8.43 E

DEUTSCH
Name Seite Breite°′ Länge°′ E = Ost

Nagold ≃ 56 48.52 N 8.42 E
Nagol'naja ≃ 83 47.57 N 38.58 E
Nagol'no-Tarasovka 83 48.00 N 39.29 E
Nagorje 76 56.55 N 38.16 E
Nagornoje 78 45.26 N 28.27 E
Nagorno-Karabachskaja Avtonomnaja Oblast' □8 84 40.00 N 46.40 E
Nagornyj, Ross. 74 55.58 N 124.57 E
Nagornyj, Ross. 265a 59.43 N 30.16 E
Nagorsk 24 59.18 N 50.48 E
Nagorskoje 82 56.54 N 38.06 E
Nago-wan c 174m 26.34 N 127.57 E
Nagoya 94 35.10 N 136.55 E
Nagoya-kūkō ⊠ 94 35.15 N 136.55 E
Nāgpur 120 21.09 N 79.06 E
Nagqu 120 31.34 N 92.00 E
Nagrai 123 34.23 N 72.41 E
Nāgrākāta 124 26.54 N 88.55 E
Nagrota 123 32.03 N 76.05 E
Nagu I 26 60.10 N 21.48 E
Nagua 238 19.23 N 69.50 W
Naguabo 240m 18.13 N 65.44 W
Naguilian 116 17.01 N 121.50 E
Nagumbuaya Point > 116 13.34 N 124.21 E
Naguri 94 35.53 N 139.11 E
Naguri I 122 6.39 N 72.55 E
Nagyatád 30 46.14 N 17.22 E
Nagybajom 30 46.23 N 17.31 E
Nagybánya → Baia Mare 38 47.40 N 23.35 E
Nagycenk 61 47.36 N 16.42 E
Nagyecsed 30 47.52 N 22.24 E
Nagykálló 78 47.53 N 21.51 E
Nagykanizsa 30 46.27 N 17.00 E
Nagykáta 30 47.25 N 19.45 E
Nagy-Kevély ʌ2 264c 47.37 N 18.59 E
Nagykőrös 30 47.02 N 19.43 E
Nagy-Milic ʌ 30 48.35 N 21.28 E
Nagytarcsa 264c 47.32 N 19.17 E
Nagytétény ◆8 264c 47.24 N 18.58 E
Nagyvarad → Oradea 38 47.03 N 21.57 E
Naha 174m 26.13 N 127.40 E
Naha Airfield ⊠ 174m 26.13 N 127.40 E
Nahabuan 112 0.49 N 114.05 E
Nahakki 123 34.25 N 71.20 E
Nahalal 132 32.41 N 35.12 E
Naḥal ʿOz 132 31.28 N 34.30 E
Naḥam 132 31.46 N 35.00 E
Nāhan 124 30.33 N 77.18 E
Nahang (Nihing) ≃ 128 26.00 N 62.44 E
Nahanni National Park ♦ 180 61.40 N 126.00 W
Nahant 207 42.25 N 70.55 W
Nahant Bay c 207 42.27 N 70.55 W
Nahant Beach ±2 283 42.27 N 70.56 W
Nahari 96 33.25 N 134.01 E
Nahari ≃ 96 33.25 N 134.01 E
Nahariyya 132 33.00 N 35.05 E
Naharpur ◆8 272a 28.42 N 77.07 E
Nahāta 126 23.20 N 89.31 E
Nahāvand 128 34.12 N 48.22 E
Nahcotta 224 46.30 N 124.02 W
Nahe 89 48.28 N 124.52 E
Nahe ≃ 56 49.58 N 7.57 E
Naḥf 132 32.56 N 35.19 E
Nahma 190 45.50 N 86.39 W
Nahmer ◆8 263 51.20 N 7.35 E
Nahmer ≃ 263 51.21 N 7.35 E
Nahoe 174x 9.45 S 138.55 W
Nahoï, Cap > 175f 14.39 S 166.37 E
Nahon ≃ 50 47.14 N 1.39 E
Nahrīn 120 36.01 N 69.06 E
Nahr Ouassel, Oued ≃ 148 35.42 N 2.33 E
Nahualate ≃ 236 14.03 N 91.32 W
Nahuatzén 234 19.42 N 101.50 W
Nahuel Huapi 254 41.03 S 71.09 W
Nahuel Huapi, Lago ⊜ 254 40.58 S 71.30 W
Nahuel Huapi, Parque Nacional ♦ 254 41.00 S 71.48 W
Nahuel Niyeu 254 40.30 S 66.33 W
Nahunta 192 31.12 N 81.58 W
Nāhyā 142 30.03 N 31.07 E
Naia ≃ 66 42.46 N 12.22 E
Naica 232 27.53 N 105.31 W
Naicam 184 52.25 N 104.30 W
Nai Ga 102 27.48 N 97.30 E
Naiguatá, Pico ʌ 286c 10.33 N 66.46 W
Naihāti, Bngl. 126 22.49 N 89.37 E
Naihāti, India 126 22.54 N 88.25 E
Naij Gol ≃, Zhg. 102 36.20 N 94.49 E
Naij Gol ≃, Zhg. 120 36.20 N 94.49 E
Naikliu 112 9.30 S 123.50 E
Naikoon Provincial Park ♦ 182 53.50 N 131.50 W
Naila 54 50.19 N 11.42 E
Nailin 98 41.53 N 119.15 E
Nails Creek ≃ 222 30.16 N 96.44 W
Nailsea 42 51.26 N 2.43 W
Nailsworth 42 51.42 N 2.14 W
Nāʾim, Jabal an- ʌ 132 31.04 N 35.55 E
Naiman Qi 89 42.55 N 120.43 E
Nain, Nf., Can. 176 56.32 N 61.41 W
Nāʾīn, Īrān 128 32.52 N 53.05 E
Nain ⊜ 40 60.14 N 13.50 E
Naini Tāl 124 29.23 N 79.27 E
Nainpur 124 22.26 N 80.07 E
Nairai I 175g 17.49 S 179.24 E
Nairn, Scot., U.K. 46 57.35 N 3.53 W
Nairn, La., U.S. 194 29.27 N 89.38 W
Nairn ≃ 46 57.35 N 3.52 W
Nairne 168b 35.02 S 138.54 E
Nairobi 154 1.17 S 36.49 E
Nairobi Airport ⊠ 276 41.08 N 74.21 W
Nairobi National Park ♦ 154 1.24 S 36.50 E
Naissaar I 76 59.33 N 24.32 E
Naita ʌ 144 5.30 N 35.18 E
Naitamba Island I 175g 17.31 S 179.17 W
Naivasha 154 0.43 S 36.26 E
Naivasha, Lake ⊜ 154 0.46 S 36.21 E
Naivos 114 2.30 N 96.10 E
Naizifang 105 39.36 N 116.47 E
N'aizishen 89 43.41 N 127.29 E
Najac 32 44.13 N 1.59 E
Najafābād 128 32.37 N 51.21 E
Najafgarh ◆8 272a 28.37 N 76.59 E
Najafgarh Drain ≅ 272a 28.43 N 77.14 E
Najasa ≃ 240p 20.42 N 77.55 W
Najd □8 144 21.00 N 46.00 E
Najd □9 118 25.00 N 44.30 E
Nájera 34 42.25 N 2.44 W
Najhā 132 33.23 N 36.22 E
Najʿ Ḥammādī 140 26.03 N 32.15 E
Najībābād 124 29.38 N 78.20 E
Najin 98 42.15 N 130.18 E
Najinkouzi 89 50.23 N 126.57 E
Najio 270 34.50 N 135.18 E
Najstenjarvi 24 62.16 N 32.38 E
Naju 98 35.03 N 126.43 E
Najza, gora ʌ 86 49.24 N 70.42 E
Naka, Nihon 94 36.27 N 140.30 E
Naka, Nihon 96 35.02 N 134.55 E
Naka, Nihon 268 35.49 N 140.03 E
Naka, Nihon 270 34.50 N 135.48 E
Naka, Nihon 270 34.42 N 135.45 E
Naka, Nihon 270 34.50 N 135.56 E
Naka ◆8 268 35.27 N 139.39 E
Naka ≃, Nihon 94 36.20 N 140.36 E
Naka ≃, Nihon 96 33.56 N 134.42 E
Naka ≃, Nihon 268 35.39 N 139.51 E
Nakadōri-shima I 92 32.57 N 129.04 E
Nakagami 268 35.49 N 139.21 E
Nakagawa 94 35.38 N 137.56 E
Nakagawa ◆8 268 35.33 N 139.35 E
Nakagō 94 36.58 N 138.14 E
Nakagusuku 174m 26.15 N 127.49 E

Symbols in the index entries represent the broad categories identified in the key at the right. Symbols with superior numbers (⋏1) identify subcategories (see complete key on page *I · 1)*.

Symbole im Register stellen die rechts im Schlüssel erklärten Kategorien dar. Symbole mit hochgestellten Ziffern (⋏1) bezeichnen Unterabteilungen einer Kategorie (vgl. vollständiger Schlüssel auf Seite *I · 1)*.

Los símbolos incluídos en el texto del índice representan las grandes categorias identificadas con la clave a la derecha. Los símbolos con numeros en su parte superior (⋏1) identifican las subcategorías (véase la clave completa en la página *I · 1)*.

Les symboles de l'index représentent les catégories indiquées dans la légende à droite. Les symboles suivis d'un indice (⋏1) représentent des sous-catégories (voir légende complète à la page *I · 1)*.

Os símbolos incluídos no texto do índice representam as grandes categorias identificadas com a chave à direita. Os símbolos com números em sua parte superior (⋏1) identificam as subcategorias (veja-se a chave completa à página *I · 1)*.

ʌ Mountain	Berg	Montaña	Montagne	Montanha
⋏ Mountains	Gebirge	Montañas	Montagnes	Montanhas
)(Pass	Paß	Paso	Col	Passo
V Valley, Canyon	Tal, Cañon	Valle, Cañón	Vallée, Canyon	Vale, Canhão
≚ Plain	Ebene	Llano	Plaine	Planície
> Cape	Kap	Cabo	Cap	Cabo
I Island	Insel	Isla	Île	Ilha
II Islands	Inseln	Islas	Îles	Ilhas
± Other Topographic Features	Andere Topographische Objekte	Otros Elementos Topográficos	Autres données topographiques	Outros acidentes topográficos

Nakagusuku-wan c 174m 26.14 N 127.53 E
Nakagyō ✦ 8 270 35.01 N 135.45 E
Nakaheji 96 33.47 N 135.31 E
Nakai 94 35.20 N 139.14 E
Nakaizu 94 34.57 N 139.00 E
Nakajima, Nihon 94 37.07 N 136.51 E
Nakajima, Nihon 96 33.58 N 132.07 E
Nakajima, Nihon 268 35.26 N 139.56 E
Nakajima, Nihon 268 35.18 N 139.58 E
Naka-jima I 96 33.58 N 132.37 E
Nakajō, Nihon 92 38.03 N 139.24 E
Nakajō, Nihon 94 36.36 N 138.02 E
Nakakawane 94 35.03 N 138.05 E
Nāka Khārari 120 25.15 N 66.44 E
Nakalele Point ➤ 229a 21.02 N 156.35 W
Nākālia 126 24.02 N 89.40 E
Nakama, Nihon 96 33.50 N 130.43 E
Nakama, Nihon 174m 26.16 N 127.44 E
Nakaminato 94 36.21 N 140.36 E
Nakamura 96 32.59 N 132.56 E
Nakanai Mountains ⋏ 164 5.35 S 151.10 E
Nakano, Nihon 94 36.45 N 138.22 E
Nakano, Nihon 268 35.20 N 139.54 E
Nakano, Nihon 270 34.58 N 135.58 E
Nakano ✦ 8 268 35.42 N 139.42 E
Nakanobu ✦ 8 268 35.36 N 139.43 E
Nakanojō 94 36.35 N 138.51 E
Nakano-shima I 93b 29.49 N 129.52 E
Nakanoshima-suidō ≌ 93b 29.44 N 129.49 E
Nakanouqan-jima I 175d 24.11 N 123.33 E
Nakaosu 174m 26.37 N 128.02 E
Nakaōzō ✦ 8 270 34.51 N 135.11 E
Nakape 140 5.47 N 28.37 E
Nakashibetsu 92a 43.33 N 144.59 E
Nākāsipāra 126 23.35 N 88.21 E
Nakasongola 154 1.19 N 32.28 E
Nakatō 268 35.45 N 139.24 E
Nakatomi, Nihon 94 35.28 N 138.26 E
Nakatomi, Nihon 268 35.49 N 139.30 E
Nakatosa 96 33.20 N 133.14 E
Nakatsu, Nihon 96 33.34 N 131.13 E
Nakatsu, Nihon 96 33.57 N 135.18 E
Nakatsu, Nihon 268 35.30 N 139.20 E
Nakatsu ≃ 94 37.00 N 138.39 E
Nakatsue 96 33.08 N 130.56 E
Nakatsugawa 94 35.29 N 137.30 E
Nakatsumine-yama ∧ 96 33.58 N 134.31 E
Nakauchigami 270 34.56 N 135.10 E
Naka-umi c 96 35.28 N 133.12 E
Nakayama, Nihon 96 33.38 N 132.42 E
Nakayama, Nihon 96 35.31 N 133.35 E
Nakayama ✦ 8 268 35.31 N 139.33 E
Nakayama ≃ 96 33.55 N 133.08 E
Nakazato, Nihon 94 36.05 N 138.50 E
Nakazato, Nihon 94 37.03 N 138.42 E
Nakazuma 268 35.58 N 139.35 E
Nakéty 175f 21.33 S 166.03 E
Nakfa 144 16.43 N 38.32 E
Nakhola 120 26.07 N 92.11 E
Nakhon Nayok 110 14.12 N 101.13 E
Nakhon Pathom 110 13.49 N 100.03 E
Nakhon Phanom 110 17.24 N 104.47 E
Nakhon Ratchasima 110 14.58 N 102.07 E
Nakhon Sawan 110 15.41 N 100.07 E
Nakhon Si Thammarat 110 8.26 N 99.58 E
Nakhon Thai 110 17.07 N 100.50 E
Nakhtarana 120 23.20 N 69.15 E
Nakina 176 50.10 N 86.42 W
Nakkaş ≃ 267b 41.00 N 28.45 E
Nakło nad Notecią 30 53.08 N 17.35 E
Naknek 180 58.44 N 157.02 W
Naknek Lake ⊜ 180 58.40 N 156.15 W
Nako 150 10.38 N 3.04 W
Nakodar 123 31.07 N 75.29 E
Nakonde 154 9.20 S 32.42 E
Nakoso-no-seki-ato ⊥ 94 36.53 N 140.46 E
Nakou 100 27.09 N 117.38 E
Nakskov 41 54.50 N 11.09 E
Nakskov Fjord c 41 54.50 N 11.02 E
Näkten ⊜ 26 62.52 N 14.38 E
Naktong-gang ≃ 98 35.07 N 128.57 E
Nakur 124 29.55 N 77.18 E
Nakuru 154 0.17 S 36.04 E
Nakuru, Lake ⊜ 154 0.22 S 36.05 E
Nakusp 182 50.15 N 117.48 W
Nāl ≃ 120 26.02 N 65.19 E
Nālāgarh 123 31.03 N 76.43 E
Nalajch 88 47.45 N 107.16 E
Nalanda 124 25.07 N 85.25 E
Nalao 102 24.22 N 105.23 E
Nalázi 156 24.03 S 33.20 E
Nalbāri 120 26.25 N 91.26 E
Nalcayec, Isla I 254 46.06 S 73.49 W
Nalchik — Nal'čik 84 43.29 N 43.37 E
Nālchiti 124 22.38 N 90.17 E
Nal'čik 84 43.29 N 43.37 E
Naldānga 126 23.26 N 89.11 E
Nāldera 123 31.11 N 77.11 E
Näldsjön ⊜ 26 63.23 N 14.17 E
Nałęczów 30 51.18 N 22.11 E
Nalgonda 122 17.03 N 79.16 E
Nalgora 126 22.52 N 90.39 E
Nalhāti 124 24.18 N 87.49 E
Naliagrām 126 23.36 N 89.37 E
Naliang 102 21.43 N 107.51 E
Nālikul 272b 22.49 N 88.11 E
Nallıhan 130 40.11 N 31.21 E
Nalinnes 50 50.19 N 4.26 E
Nalisan 104 42.06 N 122.12 E
Nallamalla Hills ⋏ 122 15.30 N 78.45 E
Nalles (Nals) 64 46.32 N 11.12 E
Nallıhan 130 40.11 N 31.21 E
Na Logu 64 46.23 N 13.45 E
Nalolo 152 15.35 S 23.07 E
Nalón ≃ 34 43.32 N 6.04 W
Nalong 102 23.35 N 106.05 E
Nalusa 152 14.55 S 22.13 E
Nālūt 146 31.52 N 10.59 E
Nalžovské Hory 60 49.20 N 13.33 E
Nam ≃ 110 21.33 N 98.38 E
Namaacha 156 25.58 S 32.01 E
Namachire 152 11.26 S 22.43 E
Namacunde 152 17.18 S 15.50 E
Namacurra 154 17.29 S 37.01 E
Namadgi National Park ✦ 171b 35.45 S 148.57 E
Namak, Daryācheh-ye ⊜ 128 34.30 N 51.50 E
Namak, Kavīr-e ✦ 2 128 34.45 N 57.45 E
Namakan Lake ⊜ 190 48.27 N 92.35 W
Nāmakkal 122 11.14 N 78.10 E
Namaksār, Kowl-e ⊜ 128 34.00 N 64.30 E
Namakula 174v 18.57 S 169.54 W
Namaland □ 5 156 25.50 S 18.00 E
Namamugi ✦ 8 268 35.29 N 139.41 E
Namanga 154 2.33 S 36.46 E
Namangan 85 41.00 N 71.40 E
Namanyere 154 7.31 S 31.03 E
Namapa 154 13.43 S 39.50 E
Namarodu, Cape ➤ 164 3.38 S 152.30 E
Namarrói 154 15.58 S 36.51 E
Namasagali 154 1.01 N 32.57 E
Namatanai 164 3.40 S 152.25 E
Nambe Indian Reservation ✦ 4 200 35.52 N 105.57 W
Namber 164 1.04 S 134.49 E
Nambi 162 28.54 S 121.26 E
Nambour 166 26.38 S 152.58 E
Nambouwalu 175g 16.59 S 178.42 E
Nambuangongo 152 8.01 S 14.12 E
Nambucca Heads 166 30.39 S 153.00 E
Nam Can 110 8.46 N 104.59 E
Namcha Barwa — Namjagbarwa Feng ∧ 102 29.38 N 95.04 E
Namch'ang 98 35.26 N 129.16 E
Nam Co ⊜ 120 30.42 N 90.30 E
Namdae-ch'ŏn ≃ 98 40.26 N 128.57 E
Namdanak 85 41.11 N 69.42 E
Nam Dinh 110 20.25 N 106.10 E
Namdö I 40 59.12 N 18.41 E
Nämdöfjärden ≌ 40 59.12 N 18.34 E
Nam Du, Quan Dao II 110 9.42 N 104.22 E
Namegawa 94 36.04 N 139.22 E
Nameh 112 2.34 N 116.21 E
Nameigos Lake ⊜ 190 48.46 N 84.43 W
Namekagon ≃ 190 46.05 N 92.06 W
Namen — Namur 56 50.28 N 4.52 E
Namerikawa 94 36.46 N 137.20 E
Náměšť 61 49.12 N 16.10 E
Námestovo 30 49.25 N 19.30 E
Nametil 154 15.43 S 39.21 E
Namew Lake ⊜ 184 54.13 N 101.56 W
Nam-gang ≃ 98 39.03 N 125.52 E
Namhae 98 34.50 N 127.54 E
Namhae-do I 98 34.48 N 127.57 E
Namhan-gang ≃ 98 37.31 N 127.18 E
Namhkam 110 23.50 N 97.41 E
Namho-ri 98 38.07 N 125.10 E
Namhsan 110 22.58 N 97.10 E
Namiai 94 35.22 N 137.41 E
Namib Desert ✦ 2 156 23.00 S 15.00 E
Namibe 152 15.10 S 12.09 E
Namibe □ 5 152 15.20 S 12.30 E
Namibia □ 1, Afr. 138 22.00 S 17.00 E
Namibia □ 1, Afr. 156 22.00 S 17.00 E
Namibie — Namibia □ 1 156 22.00 S 17.00 E
Namib-Naukluft Park ✦ 156 23.30 S 15.30 E
Namie 92 37.29 N 141.00 E
Namies 158 29.18 S 19.13 E
Namīn 128 38.25 N 48.30 E
Naminga 88 56.33 N 118.41 E
Namjagbarwa Feng ∧ 102 29.38 N 95.04 E
Nāmja La ✕ 124 29.27 N 82.34 E
Namji-ri 98 35.23 N 128.29 E
Nāmkhāna 126 21.46 N 88.14 E
Nam Kwo Chau I 271d 22.15 N 114.21 E
Namlan 110 22.15 N 97.24 E
Nämlang ≃ 124 29.28 N 82.50 E
Namlea 164 3.18 S 127.06 E
Namling 120 29.41 N 89.04 E
Namlos 58 47.21 N 10.40 E
Nam Ngum Reservoir ⊜ 1 110 18.30 N 102.40 E
Namoi, Khao ∧ 110 10.36 N 98.38 E
Namo 112 1.24 S 119.57 E
Namoi ≃ 166 30.00 S 148.07 E
Namoluk I 1 14 5.55 N 153.08 E
Namonuito I 1 14 8.46 N 150.02 E
Namorik I 1 14 5.36 N 168.07 E
Namoruputh 154 4.34 N 35.57 E
Namounou 150 11.52 N 1.42 E
Namous, Oued en V 148 31.00 N 0.15 W
Namoya 154 4.01 S 27.34 E
Nampa, Ab., Can. 182 56.02 N 117.08 W
Nampa, Id., U.S. 202 43.32 N 116.33 W
Nampala 150 15.17 N 5.33 W
Nam Pat 110 17.43 N 100.41 E
Nampawng 110 23.35 N 96.27 E
Nam Phan □ 9 110 11.00 N 107.00 E
Nam Phong 110 16.42 N 102.52 E
Nampicuan 116 15.44 N 120.38 E
Namp'o 98 38.45 N 125.23 E
Nampont-Saint-Martin 50 50.21 N 1.45 E
Namp'ot'ae-san ∧ 98 41.44 N 128.24 E
Nampuecha 154 13.59 S 40.18 E
Nampula 154 15.07 S 39.15 E
Nampula □ 5 154 15.00 S 39.00 E
Namsang 110 20.53 N 97.43 E
Namsan Park ✦ 271b 37.34 N 126.59 E
Namsanyŏng-ni 98 38.59 N 127.26 E
Namsen ≃ 24 64.27 N 11.28 E
Namsi 98 39.54 N 124.36 E
Namsos 24 64.29 N 11.30 E
Nam Tok 110 14.14 N 99.04 E
Namtu 110 23.05 N 97.24 E
Namu 182 51.49 N 127.52 W
Namu I 1 14 8.00 N 168.10 E
Namuka-I-Lau I 175g 18.51 S 178.39 W
Namúli, Serra ⋏ 154 15.15 S 37.08 E
Namur, Bel. 56 50.28 N 4.52 E
Namur, P.Q., Can. 206 45.54 N 74.56 W
Namur □ 4 56 50.20 N 4.50 E
Namuruputh 154 4.34 N 35.57 E
Namutoni 156 18.49 S 16.55 E
Namwala 154 15.45 S 26.26 E
Namwera 154 14.22 S 35.30 E
Namwŏn 98 35.25 N 127.21 E
Namyang, C.M.I.K. 98 42.57 N 129.53 E
Namyang, Taehan 98 37.14 N 126.44 E
Namyit Island I 108 10.11 N 114.22 E
Namysłów 30 51.05 N 17.42 E
Nan 110 18.47 N 100.47 E
Nan ≃, Thai 110 15.42 N 100.09 E
Nan ≃, Zhg. 100 28.15 N 120.43 E
Nana ≃ 152 5.00 N 15.50 E
Nana Barya ≃ 146 7.59 N 17.43 E
Nana Barya, Réserve de Faune de la ✦ 4 146 7.30 N 17.30 E
Nanacamilpa 234 19.29 N 98.33 W
Nanaimo 224 49.10 N 123.56 W
Nanaimo ≃ 224 49.08 N 123.54 W
Nanaimo Lakes ⊜ 224 49.07 N 124.11 W
Nānākheri ✦ 8 272a 28.31 N 77.06 E
Nana Kru 150 4.50 N 8.44 W
Nanakuli 229c 21.23 N 158.09 W
Nanam 98 41.43 N 129.41 E
Nana-Mambéré □ 5 152 5.30 N 15.30 E
Nan'an 100 24.58 N 118.23 E
Nan'anba 107 28.46 N 104.38 E
Nanango 166 26.40 S 152.00 E
Nanantun 110 24.45 N 95.41 E
Nanao, Nihon 94 37.03 N 136.58 E
Nanao, T'aiwan 100 24.28 N 121.48 E
Nan'ao, Zhg. 100 23.27 N 117.02 E
Nan'ao Dao I 100 23.26 N 117.03 E
Nanao-wan c 94 37.06 N 137.00 E
Nanas Channel ≌ 271c 1.25 N 103.58 E
Nanatsu-jima II 92 37.36 N 136.53 E
Nanatsuka 94 36.44 N 136.41 E
Nanay ≃ 246 3.42 S 73.16 W
Nanba 102 32.20 N 104.58 E
Nanbaita 105 38.58 N 115.39 E
Nanbaixia 98 35.46 N 117.21 E
Nanbaozhen 106 31.32 N 121.37 E
Nanbu, Nihon 94 35.17 N 138.27 E
Nanbu, Zhg. 102 31.23 N 106.02 E
Nancaicun 105 39.28 N 117.01 E
Nancefield 273d 26.17 S 27.53 E
Nancha 89 47.08 N 129.19 E
Nanchang, Zhg. 100 28.41 N 115.53 E
Nanchang (Liantang), Zhg. 100 28.34 N 115.56 E
Nancheng, Zhg. 100 25.39 N 116.26 E
Nancheng, Zhg. 100 27.35 N 116.40 E
Nancheng — Hanzhong 102 33.08 N 107.02 E
Nanching — Nanjing 106 32.03 N 118.47 E
Nanchital 234 18.04 N 94.24 W
Nanchong 107 30.48 N 106.04 E
Nanchuan 102 29.08 N 107.07 E
Nanchuang 100 24.36 N 120.59 E
Nanch'ung — Nanchong 107 30.48 N 106.04 E
Nancowry Island I 110 7.59 N 93.32 E
Nancroix 62 45.32 N 6.46 E
Nancun, Zhg. 98 36.32 N 120.06 E
Nancun, Zhg. 98 39.46 N 114.07 E
Nancy 58 48.41 N 6.12 E
Nanda Devi ∧ 124 30.23 N 79.59 E
Nandāha 272b 22.50 N 88.17 E
Nandaime 236 11.46 N 86.03 W
Nanda Kot ∧ 124 30.17 N 80.05 E
Nandan 96 34.15 N 134.43 E
Nandarivatu 175g 17.34 S 177.58 E
Nandashan 100 29.01 N 112.43 E
Nānded 122 19.09 N 77.20 E
Nāndgaon, India 122 20.19 N 74.39 E
Nāndgaon, India 272c 18.58 N 73.08 E
Nandi 175g 17.48 S 177.25 E
Nandi Bay c 175g 17.44 S 177.25 E
Nandi Drug ∧ 122 13.25 N 77.42 E
Nandigrām 126 22.01 N 87.58 E
Nandikotkūr 122 15.52 N 78.16 E
Nanding ≃, Asia 102 23.25 N 98.41 E
Nanding ≃, Asia 110 23.25 N 98.41 E
Nandlstadt 60 48.32 N 11.48 E
Nandom 150 10.51 N 2.45 W
N'andoma 24 61.40 N 40.12 E
Nandu 106 31.27 N 119.19 E
Nandu ≃ 110 20.04 N 110.22 E
Nanduluohe 105 40.11 N 117.13 E
Nāndūra 122 20.50 N 76.27 E
Nandurbār 122 21.22 N 74.15 E
Nanduri 175g 16.27 S 179.09 E
Nandy 261 48.35 N 2.34 E
Nandyāl 122 15.29 N 78.29 E
Nanfangquan 106 31.26 N 120.16 E
Nanfen 104 41.06 N 123.44 E
Nanfeng, Zhg. 100 27.15 N 116.32 E
Nanfeng, Zhg. 100 29.16 N 116.30 E
Nangabadau 112 1.02 N 111.54 E
Nangade 154 11.05 S 39.36 E
Nanga Eboko 152 4.41 N 12.22 E
Nangahale 115b 8.34 S 122.32 E
Nangakelawit 112 0.23 N 112.29 E
Nāngal 123 31.24 N 76.14 E
Nangalangki 112 1.15 S 111.40 E
Nangalao Island I 116 11.27 N 120.11 E
Nangal Dewat ✦ 8 272a 28.33 N 77.06 E
Nangamau 112 0.06 S 111.55 E
Nangamesi, Teluk c 115b 9.37 S 120.20 E
Nangamuntatai 112 0.22 S 112.25 E
Nangang 100 31.22 N 116.59 E
Nan Gang c 100 23.30 N 117.00 E
Nan'gangwa 105 39.46 N 116.09 E
Nangaobat 112 0.57 N 113.13 E
Nangaocun 105 39.25 N 115.58 E
Nanga Parbat ∧ 123 35.15 N 74.36 E
Nangapinoh 112 0.20 S 111.44 E
Nangaraun 112 0.38 N 113.11 E
Nangarhār □ 4 120 34.15 N 70.30 E
Nangatayap 112 1.32 S 110.34 E
Nangezhuang 105 39.31 N 116.23 E
Nanggala Hill ∧ 175e 8.16 S 157.43 E
Nangguan 115a 7.46 S 110.12 E
Nangi 272b 22.31 N 88.13 E
Nangin 110 10.31 N 98.31 E
Nangis 50 48.33 N 3.00 E
Nangka ≃ 269f 14.41 N 121.06 E
Nanglai ≃ 126 24.20 N 90.04 E
Nangloi ✦ 8, India 272a 28.41 N 77.04 E
Nangloi ✦ 8, India 272a 28.40 N 77.02 E
Nangloi Jat ✦ 8 272a 28.41 N 77.04 E
Nangnim 98 40.58 N 127.08 E
Nangnim-sanmaek ⋏ 98 40.30 N 127.00 E
Nangō, Nihon 92 31.32 N 131.23 E
Nangō, Nihon 94 37.13 N 139.33 E
Nangola 150 12.40 N 6.36 W
Nangoma 152 15.30 S 23.08 E
Nangong 98 37.24 N 115.22 E
Nangou 89 43.17 N 128.37 E
Nangō-yama-tunnel ✦ 6 94 35.12 N 139.10 E
Nangqên 102 32.22 N 96.21 E
Nang Rong 110 14.38 N 102.48 E
Nanguan 100 37.00 N 112.31 E
Nangweshi 152 16.26 S 23.17 E
Nanhai — Foshan 100 23.03 N 113.09 E
Nanhai — South China Sea ≂ 2 108 10.00 N 113.00 E
Nanhe 98 37.01 N 114.41 E
Nanhedian 100 33.23 N 112.25 E
Nanhekan 100 30.24 N 103.27 E
Nanhezhao 105 39.05 N 115.56 E
Nanhsi 100 23.11 N 120.29 E
Nanhu 102 39.57 N 94.13 E
Nanhua 102 25.14 N 101.23 E
Nanhualou 104 42.30 N 123.53 E
Nanhuang 98 36.58 N 121.47 E
Nanhui 106 31.03 N 121.45 E
Nan Hulsan Hu ⊜ 102 36.39 N 96.20 E
Nanhuta Shan ∧ 100 24.29 N 121.23 E
Nanhutou 89 43.44 N 128.55 E
Nanika Lake ⊜ 182 53.45 N 127.40 W
Naniwa ✦ 8 270 34.39 N 135.30 E
Nanjangūd 122 12.06 N 76.42 E
Nanjemoy 208 38.27 N 77.13 W
Nanjemoy Creek c 208 38.25 N 77.07 W
Nanji 100 27.28 N 121.04 E
Nanjing, Zhg. 100 32.44 N 120.52 E
Nanjing, Zhg. 102 32.33 N 107.30 E
Nanjiangqiao 100 28.58 N 113.44 E
Nanjie 107 29.11 N 105.00 E
Nanjing, Zhg. 100 24.41 N 114.25 E
Nanjing, Zhg. 100 24.32 N 117.22 E
Nanjing (Nanking), Zhg. 106 32.03 N 118.47 E
Nanjing, Zhg. 107 28.49 N 105.12 E
Nanjinyi 107 30.02 N 104.42 E
Nanjinji 154 9.35 N 39.04 E
Nanjō 96 35.50 N 136.12 E
Nanjuma ≃ 105 39.24 N 115.43 E
Nankan 100 30.33 N 120.32 E
Nankāna Sāhib 123 31.27 N 73.42 E
Nankang 100 25.42 N 114.44 E
Nankang ✦ 8 269d 25.03 N 121.36 E
Nankoku 96 33.39 N 133.44 E
Nanking — Nanjing 106 32.03 N 118.47 E
Nanko-kōen ✦ 94 37.05 N 140.14 E
Nankoku 96 33.39 N 133.44 E
Nankou 105 40.14 N 116.08 E
Nankuozhen 100 27.51 N 115.04 E
Nanku 106 31.06 N 120.37 E
Nanle 98 36.04 N 115.10 E
Nanlei ≃ 110 22.10 N 98.11 E
Nanling 106 30.56 N 118.20 E
Nanling, Zhg. 100 23.21 N 115.25 E
Nanling, Zhg. 100 25.20 N 113.00 E
Nan Ling ⋏ 90 25.00 N 112.00 E
Nanlinqiao 100 29.35 N 114.19 E
Nanliu ≃ 102 21.38 N 109.02 E
Nanliu ≃ 107 24.17 N 101.03 E
Nanliucun 105 40.10 N 116.04 E
Nanlou 102 28.02 N 107.36 E
Nanlou Shan ∧ 100 27.27 N 117.32 E
Nanma 89 43.27 N 126.42 E
Nanmatang 102 24.17 N 103.14 E
Nanmeng 105 39.11 N 116.22 E
Nanmoku 94 36.10 N 138.44 E
Nannerch 262 53.13 N 3.15 W
Nannine 162 26.53 S 118.20 E
Nanning 102 22.48 N 108.20 E
Nanniwan 102 36.29 N 109.42 E
Nannō 94 35.31 N 136.38 E
Nannup 162 33.59 S 115.45 E
Nannzhi 102 31.55 N 106.47 E
Nanny ≃ 48 53.40 N 6.14 W
Na Noi 110 18.19 N 100.43 E
Nanole ✦ 8 272c 19.01 N 72.55 E
Nanoose Bay 224 49.16 N 124.12 W
Nanoose Harbour c 224 49.20 N 124.10 W
Nanortalik 272c 18.56 N 73.05 E
Nanowin ≃ 184 53.13 N 97.13 W
Nanpan ≃, Zhg. 102 25.07 N 106.00 E
Nanpan ≃, Zhg. 107 24.34 N 103.04 E
Nānpāra 124 27.52 N 81.30 E
Nanpengchang 107 29.21 N 106.38 E
Nanpi 98 38.02 N 116.42 E
Nanpiao 104 41.12 N 120.39 E
Nanping, Zhg. 89 43.24 N 129.05 E
Nanping, Zhg. 100 26.45 N 118.10 E
Nanping, Zhg. 100 26.38 N 118.10 E
Nanping, Zhg. 100 21.50 N 107.28 E
Nanping, Zhg. 102 33.07 N 104.20 E
Nanpingji 100 33.30 N 116.51 E
Nanpu 105 39.16 N 118.12 E
Nanpu ≃ 100 27.02 N 118.18 E
Nanqingtuo 105 39.37 N 117.53 E
Nanqu 104 40.44 N 122.08 E
Nanquan 98 36.24 N 120.17 E
Nanri Dao I 100 25.13 N 119.30 E
Nansa ≃ 34 43.22 N 4.29 W
Nansei 92 34.22 N 136.41 E
Nansei-shotō (Ryukyu Islands) II 90 26.30 N 128.00 E
Nansemond □ 6 208 36.43 N 76.40 W
Nansen, Lago ⊜ 254 47.57 S 72.21 W
Nan Sha I 106 31.36 N 121.22 E
Nanshahe 98 35.03 N 117.12 E
Nanshan, Zhg. 100 26.38 N 118.20 E
Nanshan, Zhg. 105 39.21 N 115.34 E
Nanshanba 100 25.34 N 116.32 E
Nanshanchengzi 98 42.09 N 125.19 E
Nanshan Island I 108 10.45 N 115.49 E
Nanshankou 102 43.09 N 93.41 E
Nanshanlingcun 105 39.09 N 117.26 E
Nanshan — Qilian Shan ⋏ 102 39.06 N 98.40 E
Nanshuang Dao I 100 26.35 N 120.08 E
Nanshui 100 22.02 N 113.16 E
Nansifa 105 39.27 N 116.27 E
Nansio 154 2.08 S 33.03 E
Nans-les-Pins 62 43.22 N 5.47 E
Nansunzhai 269b 31.21 N 121.27 E
Nant 32 44.01 N 3.18 E
Nant ≃ 50 47.30 N 1.14 E
Nantai 104 40.55 N 122.47 E
Nantais, Lac ⊜ 176 60.59 N 74.00 W
Nantai-san ∧ 94 36.43 N 140.26 E
Nantai-zan ∧ 94 36.46 N 139.29 E
Nantang 100 26.08 N 115.12 E
Nantangdun 106 31.15 N 120.56 E
Nantangmei 105 38.51 N 114.56 E
Nantasket Beach 283 42.16 N 70.52 W
Nantawarra 168b 34.00 S 138.14 E
Nant Bran ≃ 42 51.57 N 3.28 W
Nanterre 50 48.53 N 2.12 E
Nantes 32 47.13 N 1.33 W
Nanteuil-le-Haudouin 50 49.08 N 2.48 E
Nanteuil-lès-Meaux 261 48.56 N 2.54 E
Nantian, Zhg. 100 27.57 N 119.56 E
Nantian, Zhg. 100 29.08 N 121.56 E
Nantianmen 104 40.56 N 123.04 E
Nanticoke, On., Can. 212 42.54 N 80.11 E
Nanticoke, Md., U.S. 208 38.16 N 75.54 W
Nanticoke, Pa., U.S. 210 41.12 N 76.00 W
Nanticoke ≃ 208 38.16 N 75.56 W
Nanticoke Creek ≃, On., Can. 212 42.48 N 80.04 W
Nanticoke Creek ≃, N.Y., U.S. 210 42.05 N 76.05 W
Nantmeal Village 285 40.08 N 75.42 W
Nanto 92 34.20 N 136.31 E
Nanton 182 50.21 N 113.46 W
Nantong 106 32.02 N 120.53 E
Nant'ou, T'aiwan 100 23.55 N 120.41 E
Nantou, Zhg. 100 22.33 N 113.55 E
Nantouillet 261 49.00 N 2.42 E
Nantschang — Nanchang 100 28.41 N 115.53 E
Nantua 58 46.09 N 5.37 E
Nantuantingzhuang 105 40.17 N 118.17 E
Nantucket 207 41.17 N 70.06 W
Nantucket □ 6 207 41.17 N 70.06 W
Nantucket Island I 207 41.16 N 70.03 W
Nantucket Sound ≌ 207 41.30 N 70.15 W
Nantuego 154 11.21 S 38.24 E
Nantulo 154 12.17 S 39.03 E
Nantung — Nantong 106 32.02 N 120.53 E
Nantwich 44 53.04 N 2.32 W
Nanty Glo 214 40.28 N 78.50 W
Nant-y-Moch Reservoir ⊜ 1 42 52.27 N 3.50 W
Nanu 164 8.50 S 142.40 E
Nanuet 210 41.05 N 74.00 W
Nanuet Mall ✦ 9 276 41.06 N 74.01 W
Nanuku Passage ≌ 175g 16.45 S 179.15 W
Nanumanga I 14 6.18 S 176.20 E
Nanumea I 1 14 5.39 S 176.08 E
Nanuque 255 17.50 S 40.21 W
Nanūr 126 23.42 N 87.52 E
Nanusa, Kepulauan II 116 4.42 N 127.06 E
Nanushuk ≃ 180 69.18 N 151.00 W
Nanwan 100 32.09 N 114.02 E
Nan Wan c 100 21.55 N 120.47 E
Nanwengkouzi 89 51.10 N 125.25 E
Nanwenquan 107 29.26 N 106.35 E
Nanxi, Zhg. 100 31.31 N 115.36 E
Nanxi, Zhg. 107 28.51 N 104.58 E
Nanxi ≃, Zhg. 100 29.20 N 112.19 E
Nanxian 100 29.20 N 112.19 E
Nanxiang 106 31.17 N 121.18 E
Nanxiao 105 39.31 N 117.07 E
Nanxin, Zhg. 98 35.33 N 117.12 E
Nanxin, Zhg. 105 39.11 N 115.52 E
Nanxing Hu ⊜ 106 31.08 N 120.48 E
Nanxinzhuang 98 36.39 N 115.15 E
Nanxiong 100 25.10 N 114.20 E
Nanxu 102 22.23 N 110.53 E
Nanxun 106 30.53 N 120.26 E
Nanya 106 26.52 N 118.19 E
Nanyandang Shan ∧ 100 27.24 N 120.25 E
Nanyang, Zhg. 100 27.24 N 119.39 E
Nanyang, Zhg. 100 33.00 N 112.32 E
Nanyang, Zhg. 100 32.59 N 112.29 E
Nanyang, Zhg. 100 33.25 N 120.13 E
Nanyangcun 100 31.53 N 121.43 E
Nanyangangzi 89 48.43 N 125.27 E
Nanyang Hu ⊜ 98 35.12 N 116.41 E
Nanyang Shan ∧ 106 31.20 N 120.28 E
Nanyang Technological Institute ✦ 2 271c 1.21 N 103.41 E
Nanyi Hu ⊜ 106 31.07 N 118.57 E
Nan-yō 92 38.04 N 140.07 E
Nanyu 100 25.59 N 119.14 E
Nanyuan 105 39.48 N 116.23 E
Nanyuan Airport ✈ 271a 39.47 N 116.23 E
Nanyue 100 27.13 N 112.43 E
Nanyuki 154 0.01 N 37.04 E
Nanzamu 98 41.56 N 124.23 E
Nanzha 106 31.51 N 120.15 E
Nanzhao 106 31.34 N 120.22 E
Nanzhao 100 33.30 N 112.24 E
Nanzhang, Zhg. 102 31.50 N 111.41 E
Nanzhang, Zhg. 100 29.33 N 116.12 E
Nanzhao 100 33.30 N 112.27 E
Nanzhaoji 100 32.26 N 117.41 E
Nanzhe 100 26.59 N 119.57 E
Nanzhenjie 106 31.48 N 119.17 E
Nanzhi 154 16.05 S 26.07 E
Nanzhuang, Zhg. 105 40.22 N 116.21 E
Nanzhuang, Zhg. 105 40.43 N 114.58 E
Nanzhuang, Zhg. 105 39.07 N 116.34 E
Nao 152 4.35 N 15.09 E
Naoābād 272b 22.29 N 88.23 E
Naoāpāra 126 22.45 N 89.39 E
Naococane, Lac ⊜ 176 52.52 N 70.40 W
Naoetsu 94 37.11 N 138.15 E
Naogaon 124 24.47 N 88.56 E
Naoiri 174l 1.38 N 173.56 E
Naokot 120 24.51 N 69.24 E
Naoli ≃ 89 47.20 N 134.10 E
Naolinco 234 19.39 N 96.51 W
Nāo-me-Toque 252 28.28 S 52.49 W
Naong, Bukit ∧ 112 2.40 N 112.36 E
Nāopāra 126 24.09 N 88.54 E
Naopukura 272b 22.55 N 88.16 E
Naosap Lake ⊜ 184 54.51 N 101.24 W
Naoshima 96 34.27 N 133.59 E
Naours 50 50.02 N 2.17 E
Náousa 38 40.37 N 22.05 E
Naozhou Dao I 102 20.57 N 110.34 E
Napa 226 38.17 N 122.17 W
Napa □ 6 226 38.18 N 122.17 W
Napa ≃ 226 38.07 N 122.18 W
Napacao Point ➤ 116 9.43 N 124.31 E
Napajedla 30 49.10 N 17.31 E
Napakiak 180 60.42 N 161.57 W
Napaku 112 2.32 N 115.58 E
Na Pali Coast State Park ✦ 229b 22.09 N 159.41 W
Napalkovo 74 70.03 N 73.47 E
Napamute 180 61.33 N 158.42 W
Napanee 212 44.15 N 76.57 W
Napanee ≃ 212 44.12 N 77.02 W
Napanoch 210 41.44 N 74.22 W
Napareuli 84 42.03 N 45.31 E
Napas 86 59.53 N 81.58 E
Napaskiak 180 60.42 N 161.45 W
Napa Valley V 226 38.18 N 122.18 W
Napavine 224 46.34 N 122.54 W
Napayauan Island I 116 12.22 N 123.14 E
Napé 110 18.18 N 105.06 E
Napenay 252 26.44 S 60.37 W
Naperville 216 41.47 N 88.08 W
Napetipi ≃ 186 51.21 N 58.08 W
Napf ∧ 58 47.00 N 7.56 E
Napido 164 0.41 S 135.23 E
Napiéolédougou 150 9.18 N 5.35 W
Napier, N.Z. 172 39.29 S 176.55 E
Napier, S. Afr. 158 34.29 S 19.53 E
Napier, Mount ∧ 2 162 17.32 S 129.10 E
Napier Mountains ⋏ 9 66.30 S 53.40 E
Napierville 206 45.11 N 73.25 W
Napierville □ 6 206 45.10 N 73.35 W
Napinka 184 49.17 N 100.50 W
Naplate 216 41.20 N 88.54 W
Naples, Fl., U.S. 220 26.08 N 81.47 W
Naples, Id., U.S. 202 48.34 N 116.23 W
Naples, Il., U.S. 219 39.45 N 90.36 W
Naples, N.Y., U.S. 210 42.36 N 77.24 W
Naples, Tx., U.S. 222 33.12 N 94.40 W
Naples — Napoli 68 40.51 N 14.17 E
Naples Park 220 26.16 N 81.48 W
Napo 102 23.16 N 105.54 E
Napo □ 4 246 0.30 S 77.00 W
Napo ≃ 246 3.20 S 72.40 W
Napola 70 37.59 N 12.38 E
Napoleon, In., U.S. 218 39.12 N 85.19 W
Napoleon, Ky., U.S. 218 38.46 N 84.47 W
Napoleon, Mi., U.S. 216 42.10 N 84.15 W
Napoleon, N.D., U.S. 198 46.30 N 99.46 W
Napoleon, Oh., U.S. 216 41.23 N 84.07 W
Napoleonville 194 29.56 N 91.01 W
Nápoles — Napoli 68 40.51 N 14.17 E
Napoli (Naples) 68 40.51 N 14.17 E
Napoli □ 4 68 40.53 N 14.25 E
Napoli, Golfo di c 68 40.43 N 14.10 E
Napopo 154 4.12 N 28.02 E
Napparmerry 166 27.36 S 141.07 E
Nappanee 216 41.26 N 86.00 W
Nappan Island I 212 44.23 N 77.49 W
Napton on the Hill 42 52.15 N 1.24 W
Napu 115b 9.24 S 119.56 E
Napudalutai Shan ∧ 89 51.06 N 122.13 E
Naqādah 140 25.54 N 32.43 E
Naqadeh 128 36.57 N 45.23 E
Naqb, Ra's an- ∧ 132 29.50 N 35.40 E
Nar ≃ 42 52.45 N 0.24 E
Nara, Mali 150 15.10 N 7.17 W
Nara, Nihon 96 34.41 N 135.50 E
Nara □ 5 96 34.30 N 135.50 E
Nara ≃, Pāk. 120 24.07 N 69.07 E
Nara ≃, Ross. 82 54.53 N 37.26 E
Nara-bonchi ≃ 1 270 34.38 N 135.50 E
Naracoorte 166 36.58 S 140.44 E
Naradhan 166 33.37 S 146.19 E
Narai ≃ 94 36.20 N 137.55 E
Narail 126 23.10 N 89.30 E
Naraina ✦ 8 272a 28.37 N 77.08 E
Naraini 124 25.11 N 80.29 E
Narainpur 126 24.03 N 86.36 E
Narakawa 94 35.59 N 137.50 E
Naramata 182 49.36 N 119.35 W
Naran 88 48.34 N 98.17 E
Naran Bulag 86 49.22 N 93.52 E
Nārang 123 31.54 N 74.31 E
Narangba 171a 27.12 S 152.58 E
Naranja 220 25.31 N 80.25 W
Naranjal, Ec. 246 2.42 S 79.37 W
Naranjal, Ven. 286c 10.28 N 67.02 W
Naranjito, Hond. 236 14.57 N 88.41 W
Naranjito, P.R. 240m 18.18 N 66.15 W
Naranjo 236 10.06 N 84.22 W
Naranjo ≃ 236 14.30 N 92.11 W
Naranjo Islands II 116 12.23 N 124.03 E
Naranjos 234 21.21 N 97.41 W
Narao 92 32.50 N 129.04 E
Nara Park ✦ 270 34.41 N 135.52 E
Narasannapeta 122 18.25 N 84.03 E
Narasapur 122 16.27 N 81.40 E
Narasaraopet 122 16.15 N 80.04 E
Narashino 94 35.41 N 140.02 E
Narasun 88 50.06 N 112.58 E
Narat 86 43.28 N 83.44 E
Narathiwat 110 6.26 N 101.50 E
Nara Visa 196 35.36 N 103.05 W
Nara Women's University ✦ 2 270 34.42 N 135.49 E
Nārāyanganj 124 23.37 N 90.30 E
Nārāyanī ≃ 8 124 27.15 N 84.03 E
Nārāyani ≃ 124 25.39 N 85.13 E
Nārāyanpāra 272b 22.54 N 88.19 E
Nārāyanpet 122 16.44 N 77.30 E
Nārāyanpur 272b 22.29 N 88.34 E
Narazeni 84 42.27 N 41.57 E
Narberth, Wales, U.K. 42 51.48 N 4.45 W
Narberth, Pa., U.S. 285 40.00 N 75.15 W
Narbonne 32 43.11 N 3.00 E
Narcao 71 39.10 N 8.40 E
Narcea ≃ 34 43.28 N 6.06 W
Narcondam Island I 110 13.20 N 94.16 E
Narcoossi Creek ≃ 220 28.19 N 81.06 W
Nardò 68 40.11 N 18.02 E
Nare ≃ 246 6.12 N 74.35 W
Narellan 170 34.02 S 150.44 E
Narembeen 162 32.04 S 118.24 E
Narenbulake 89 49.52 N 120.23 E
Narendranagar 124 30.10 N 78.18 E
Nares Strait ≌ 16 80.30 N 68.00 W
Naretha 162 31.00 S 124.50 E
Narew ≃ 30 52.26 N 20.42 E
Nargund 122 15.43 N 75.23 E
Narhan 272c 19.08 N 73.07 E
Nāri ≃ 120 28.35 N 67.50 E
Narib 156 24.11 S 17.46 E
Nariel 171b 36.26 S 147.50 E
Narijn ≃ 88 50.20 N 93.24 E
Narijnteel 102 45.57 N 101.29 E
Nārikelbāria 126 23.17 N 89.21 E
Nariman 85 40.34 N 72.48 E
Narimanabad 84 38.53 N 48.52 E
Narimba, Her Majesty's Air Station (Royal Australian Navy Airfield) ■ 274a 33.43 S 150.53 E
Narin ≃ 120 36.54 N 52.51 E
Narince 130 37.52 N 38.46 E
Narin Gol ≃ 102 37.24 N 91.21 E
Narinjāra 126 22.38 N 89.33 E
Narita 94 35.47 N 140.19 E
Nariva 96 34.47 N 133.33 E
Nariwa ≃ 96 34.46 N 133.32 E
Nar'jan-Mar 24 67.39 N 53.00 E
Nārkanda 123 31.16 N 77.27 E
Narkatiāganj 124 27.06 N 84.28 E
Närke ≃ 9 40 59.06 N 15.03 E
Närkes Marieberg 40 59.12 N 15.10 E
Narli 130 37.27 N 37.09 E
Narma 80 54.46 N 42.01 E
Narmada ≃ 120 21.38 N 72.36 E
Narmada Valley V 124 22.30 N 77.00 E
Narmak ✦ 8 267d 35.43 N 51.29 E
Narman 130 40.21 N 41.52 E
Narmušad' 80 54.40 N 41.07 E
Nar-Nar-Goon 169 38.05 S 145.34 E
Nārnaul 124 28.03 N 76.07 E
Narni 66 42.31 N 12.31 E
Naro 70 37.18 N 13.47 E
Naro ≃ 70 37.14 N 13.37 E
Naroč' ≃ 76 54.26 N 26.39 E
Naroč', ozero ⊜ 76 54.52 N 26.45 E
Narodiči 78 51.13 N 29.03 E
Narodnaja, gora ∧ 24 65.04 N 60.09 E
Naro-Fominsk 82 55.23 N 36.43 E
Naro Island I 116 11.53 N 123.40 E
Narok 154 1.05 S 35.52 E
Narol 30 50.22 N 23.21 E
Narón 34 43.32 N 8.10 W
Narooma 166 36.14 S 150.03 E
Naro-Osakovo 82 55.33 N 36.33 E
Narovčat 80 53.52 N 43.41 E
Narovl'a 78 51.48 N 29.29 E
Narōwāl 123 32.06 N 74.53 E
Närpes (Närpiö) 26 62.28 N 21.20 E
Närpiö — Närpes 26 62.28 N 21.20 E
Narrabeen 274a 33.43 S 151.18 E
Narrabeen Lagoon c 274a 33.43 S 151.17 E
Narrabri 166 30.19 S 149.47 E
Narragansett 207 41.25 N 71.27 W
Narragansett Bay c 207 41.40 N 71.20 W
Narran ≃ 166 29.45 S 147.20 E
Narran Narra ∧ 171b 35.50 S 147.27 E
Narrandera 166 34.45 S 146.33 E
Narraway ≃ 182 54.48 N 119.56 W
Narraweena 274a 33.45 S 151.16 E
Narre Warren 274b 38.02 S 145.19 E
Narre Warren North 274b 37.59 S 145.19 E
Narrogin 162 32.56 S 117.10 E
Narromine 166 32.14 S 148.15 E
Narrows, Md., U.S. 208 38.58 N 76.15 W
Narrows, Va., U.S. 192 37.19 N 80.48 W
Narrowsburg 210 41.36 N 75.03 W
Närsen ⊜ 40 60.17 N 14.23 E
Narsimhapur 124 22.57 N 79.12 E
Narsinghdi 124 23.55 N 90.43 E
Narsinghgarh 124 23.42 N 77.06 E
Narsīpatnam 122 17.40 N 82.37 E
Narskije Prudy, ozero ⊜ 1 82 55.32 N 36.36 E
Narssaq 176 60.54 N 46.00 W
Nartkala 84 43.33 N 43.50 E
Nartuby ≃ 62 43.28 N 6.34 E
Naru 92 32.49 N 128.56 E
Narubis, Namibia 158 27.10 S 19.05 E
Narubis, Namibia 158 26.55 S 18.35 E
Naruko 92 38.44 N 140.43 E
Narukosovo 80 54.37 N 44.33 E
Naruo 270 34.43 N 135.23 E
Narusawa 94 35.29 N 138.41 E
Narutō, Nihon 94 35.36 N 140.25 E
Naruto, Nihon 96 34.11 N 134.37 E
Naruto-kaikyō ≌ 96 34.14 N 134.39 E
Narva, Eesti 76 59.23 N 28.12 E
Narva, Ross. 86 55.25 N 93.39 E
Narva ≃ 76 59.27 N 28.02 E
Narvacan 116 17.25 N 120.28 E
Narva-Jõesuu 76 59.27 N 28.03 E
Narva laht (Narvskij zaliv) c 76 59.30 N 27.40 E
Narvan 85 40.15 N 67.12 E
Narvik 24 68.26 N 17.25 E
Narvskij zaliv (Narva laht) c 76 59.30 N 27.40 E
Narvskoje vodochranilišče ⊜ 1 76 59.18 N 28.14 E
Narwāna 124 29.37 N 76.07 E
Narwietooma 162 23.15 S 132.35 E
Narym 86 58.58 N 81.30 E
Naryn, Kyrg. 85 41.26 N 75.59 E
Naryn, Ross. 88 50.13 N 96.27 E
Naryn ≃ 85 40.54 N 71.45 E
Narynkol 72 42.43 N 80.12 E
Naryntau, gory ⋏ 85 41.25 N 76.50 E
Naryškino 76 52.58 N 35.44 E
Naryū-zaki ➤ 96 35.36 N 135.28 E
Narzole 62 44.35 N 7.52 E
Nås, Sve. 40 60.27 N 14.29 E
Näs, Sve. 40 58.41 N 15.50 E
Nasadkino 82 56.29 N 37.21 E
Nåsåker 26 63.26 N 16.54 E
Na San, Thai 110 8.48 N 99.22 E
Na San, Viet 110 21.12 N 104.02 E
Nasarawa 150 8.30 N 7.40 E
Nåsåud 38 47.17 N 24.24 E
Nasawa 175f 15.13 S 168.09 E
NASA Wallops Station ✦ 3 208 37.52 N 75.28 W
Nasbinals 32 44.40 N 3.03 E
Naschel 252 32.55 S 65.23 W
Naseby, N.Z. 172 45.02 S 170.09 E
Naseby, Eng., U.K. 42 52.25 N 0.59 W
Naselle 224 46.21 N 123.48 W
Naselle ≃ 224 46.25 N 123.55 W
Nase — Naze 93b 28.23 N 129.30 E
Nash 194 33.27 N 94.08 W
Nashawena Island I 207 41.26 N 70.53 W
Nashik 122 19.59 N 73.48 E
Nashoba Brook ≃ 283 42.28 N 71.24 W
Nashport 214 40.04 N 82.09 W
Nashū', Wādī an- V 146 26.25 N 14.15 E
Nashua, Ia., U.S. 190 42.57 N 92.32 W
Nashua, Mt., U.S. 202 48.07 N 106.21 W
Nashua, N.H., U.S. 207 42.45 N 71.28 W
Nashua ≃ 207 42.46 N 71.27 W
Nashuixi 102 30.09 N 108.40 E
Näshultasjön ⊜ 40 59.14 N 16.21 E
Nashville, Ar., U.S. 275b 43.50 N 79.40 W
Nashville, Ga., U.S. 194 33.56 N 93.50 W
Nashville, Il., U.S. 192 31.12 N 83.15 W
Nashville, In., U.S. 219 38.20 N 89.22 W
Nashville, Mi., U.S. 218 39.12 N 86.15 W
Nashville, N.C., U.S. 216 42.36 N 85.05 W
Nashville, Oh., U.S. 192 35.58 N 77.57 W
Nashville, Tn., U.S. 214 40.36 N 82.07 W
Nashwaak ≃ 194 36.09 N 86.47 W
Nashwaaksis 186 45.57 N 66.37 W
Nashwah 186 45.59 N 66.39 W
Nashwauk 142 30.30 N 31.29 E
Nasia 190 47.22 N 93.10 W
Nasīb 150 10.09 N 0.48 W
Našice 132 32.33 N 36.11 E
Nasielsk 38 45.29 N 18.06 E
Näsijärvi ⊜ 30 52.36 N 20.48 E
Nāsir 26 61.37 N 23.42 E
Nāşir, Buhayrat (Lake Nasser) ⊜ 1 140 8.36 N 33.04 E
Nasīrābād, India 140 22.40 N 32.00 E
Nasīrābād, Pāk. 120 26.18 N 74.44 E
Naskaftym 120 28.23 N 68.24 E
Naskaupi ≃ 80 52.57 N 45.38 E
Näsnaren ⊜ 176 53.45 N 60.50 W
Naso 40 58.51 N 16.18 E
Nasondoye 70 38.07 N 14.47 E
Naso Point ➤ 154 10.22 S 25.06 E
Nasorolevu ∧ 116 10.25 N 121.57 E
Nasosnyj 175g 16.38 S 178.42 E
Nasr 84 40.37 N 49.34 E
Nasrābād 142 30.36 N 30.52 E
Nasrānī, Jabal an- ∧ 128 34.08 N 51.26 E
Nasriddinbek 132 32.33 N 36.11 E
Nasriganj 85 40.41 N 71.55 E
Nass ≃ 124 25.03 N 84.20 E
Nassau, Ba. 182 55.00 N 129.50 W
Nassau, Dtsch. 240b 25.05 N 77.21 W
Nassau, Dtsch. 54 50.18 N 7.48 E
Nassau, N.Y., U.S. 56 50.19 N 7.47 E
210 42.30 N 73.36 W

≃ River — Fluß — Río — Rivière — Rio
≃ Canal — Kanal — Canal — Canal — Canal
⌐ Waterfall, Rapids — Wasserfall, Stromschnellen — Cascada, Rápidos — Chute d'eau, Rapides — Cascata, Rápidos
≌ Strait — Meeresstraße — Estrecho — Détroit — Estreito
c Bay, Gulf — Bucht, Golf — Bahía, Golfo — Baie, Golfe — Baía, Golfo
⊜ Lake, Lakes — See, Seen — Lago, Lagos — Lac, Lacs — Lago, Lagos
≡ Swamp — Sumpf — Pantano — Marais — Pântano
⌘ Ice Features, Glacier — Eis- und Gletscherformen — Accidentes Glaciales — Formes glaciaires — Acidentes glaciares
≂ Other Hydrographic Features — Andere Hydrographische Objekte — Otros Elementos Hidrográficos — Autres données hydrographiques — Outros acidentes hidrográficos

✦ Submarine Features — Untermeerische Objekte — Accidentes Submarinos — Formes de relief sous-marin — Acidentes submarinos
□ Political Unit — Politische Einheit — Unidad Política — Entité politique — Unidade política
✦ Cultural Institution — Kulturelle Institution — Institución Cultural — Institution culturelle — Instituição cultural
⊥ Historical Site — Historische Stätte — Sitio Histórico — Site historique — Sitio histórico
✦ Recreational Site — Erholungs- und Freizeitort — Sitio de Recreo — Centre de loisirs — Area de Lazer
✈ Airport — Flughafen — Aeropuerto — Aéroport — Aeroporto
■ Military Installation — Militäranlage — Instalación Militar — Installation militaire — Instalação militar
✦ Miscellaneous — Verschiedenes — Misceláneo — Divers — Diversos

ENGLISH / DEUTSCH

Name / Name	Page / Seite	Lat.°′ / Breite°′	Long.°′ / Länge°′ E = Ost
Nassau □⁶	210	40.45 N	73.38 W
Nassau, Bahía c	254	55.25 S	67.40 W
Nassau Bay	222	29.32 N	95.05 W
Nassau Coliseum ♦	276	40.43 N	73.36 W
Nassau International Airport ⊠	240b	25.02 N	77.28 W
Nassau Island I	14	11.33 S	165.25 W
Nassau Shores	276	40.39 N	73.26 W
Nassawadox	208	37.28 N	75.51 W
Nassawango Creek ≃	208	38.10 N	75.25 W
Nassenfels	60	48.48 N	11.16 E
Nassenheide	54	52.49 N	13.12 E
Nasser, Lake → Nāṣir, Buḥayrat ⊜¹	140	22.40 N	32.00 E
Nassereith	58	47.19 N	10.50 E
Nassian	150	8.27 N	3.29 W
Nässjö	26	57.39 N	14.41 E
Nastapoca ≃	176	56.55 N	76.33 W
Nastapoka Islands II	176	57.00 N	76.50 W
Nastasjino	82	54.28 N	38.16 E
Nastaška	78	49.39 N	30.19 E
Nastätten	56	50.12 N	7.51 E
Nastauli	272a	28.43 N	77.22 E
Nastf, Bi'r ⊤⁴	142	30.18 N	30.28 E
Nasu	94	37.01 N	140.07 E
Nasu-dake ∧, Nihon	92	37.07 N	139.58 E
Nasu-dake ∧, Nihon	94	37.09 N	139.58 E
Nasugbu	116	14.05 N	120.38 E
Nasukoin Mountain ∧	202	48.48 N	114.35 W
Nasva	76	56.35 N	30.10 E
Nat ≃	190	48.48 N	82.07 W
Nata, Bots.	156	20.12 S	26.12 E
Natá, Pan.	236	8.20 N	80.31 W
Nata ≃	156	20.14 S	26.10 E
Natagaima	246	3.37 N	75.06 W
Nātāgarh	272b	22.42 N	88.25 E
Natal, Bra.	250	5.47 S	35.13 W
Natal, B.C., Can.	182	49.44 N	114.50 W
Natal, Indon.	110	0.33 N	99.07 E
Natal □⁴	158	28.40 S	30.40 E
Natal Basin ✦¹	10	30.00 S	40.00 E
Natalia	196	29.11 N	98.51 W
Nataljevka	83	47.10 N	38.29 E
Nataljin Jar	80	51.46 N	50.35 E
Nataljino	80	52.56 N	49.02 E
Natalkuz Lake ⊜	182	53.26 N	125.20 W
Natalspruit ≃	273d	26.19 S	28.10 E
Natanes Plateau ⋏¹	200	33.35 N	110.15 W
Natash, Wādī V	140	24.25 N	33.26 E
Natashō	96	35.24 N	135.38 E
Natashquan	186	50.12 N	61.49 W
Natashquan ≃	176	50.06 N	61.49 W
Natashquan, Pointe de ≻	186	50.06 N	61.44 W
Natashquan Est ≃	186	51.20 N	61.40 W
Natchez	194	31.33 N	91.24 W
Natchez Trace Parkway ♠	194	32.00 N	91.00 W
Natchitoches	194	31.45 N	93.05 W
Natco Lake ⊜	276	40.26 N	74.09 W
Natércia	256	22.07 S	45.30 W
Naters	58	46.20 N	7.59 E
Natewa Bay c	175g	16.35 S	179.40 E
Na Thawi	110	6.45 N	100.42 E
Nāthdwāra	120	24.56 N	73.49 E
Nathia Gali	123	34.04 N	73.24 E
Nathkaw	102	26.53 N	96.13 E
Nathula I	175g	16.53 S	177.25 E
Natick	207	42.17 N	71.21 W
Natick Laboratories ■	283	42.17 N	71.22 W
Natimuk	166	36.45 S	141.57 E
Nation ≃	182	55.28 N	123.35 W
National Agricultural Research Center ʊ³	284c	39.02 N	76.52 W
National Airport ⊠	281	42.19 N	83.25 W
National Arboretum ♠	284c	38.54 N	76.58 W
National Assembly ʊ	269a	13.46 N	100.31 E
National Baseball Hall of Fame and Museum ʊ	210	42.42 N	74.57 W
National City	228	32.40 N	117.05 W
National Gallery ʊ	260	51.31 N	0.08 W
National Institute of Health ʊ	284c	39.00 N	77.06 W
National Maritime Museum ʊ	260	51.29 N	0.00
National Park	285	39.51 N	75.10 W
National Taiwan Normal University ʊ²	269d	25.02 N	121.31 E
National Taiwan University ʊ²	269d	25.01 N	121.32 E
National Zoological Park ♠	284c	38.56 N	77.03 W
Natipi, Lac ⊜	186	51.27 N	71.23 W
Natisone ≃	64	45.57 N	13.22 E
Natitingou	150	10.19 N	1.22 E
Native Bay c	176	63.52 N	82.30 W
Natividade	250	11.43 S	47.47 W
Natividade da Serra	256	23.24 S	45.26 W
Natívitas ◆⁸	286a	19.14 N	99.05 W
Nativity, Church of the ʊ¹	132	31.43 N	35.12 E
Natkyizin	110	14.55 N	97.57 E
Natl	132	31.39 N	35.52 E
Natoma	198	39.11 N	99.01 W
Natong	102	23.01 N	107.50 E
Nator	124	24.25 N	88.59 E
Natori	92	38.08 N	140.55 E
Natorp	263	51.30 N	7.38 E
Natron, Lake ⊜	154	2.25 S	36.00 E
Natrona Heights	214	40.37 N	79.43 W
Naṭrūn, Wādī an- ⊥⁷	142	30.25 N	30.13 E
Natsui ≃	94	37.03 N	140.59 E
Nattai ≃	170	34.05 S	150.25 E
Nattai River	170	34.04 S	150.27 E
Nattam	122	10.14 N	78.14 E
Nåttarö I	40	58.52 N	18.07 E
Nattaset ∧	24	68.12 N	27.20 E
Nattaung ∧	110	18.48 N	97.02 E
Natters	64	47.14 N	11.22 E
Nattwerder	264a	52.26 N	12.56 E
Natuchajevskaja	78	44.54 N	37.34 E
Nātudaha	126	23.39 N	88.41 E
Natukanaoka Pan ≍	156	18.40 S	15.45 E
Natuna Besar I	112	4.00 N	108.15 E
Natuna Besar, Kepulauan II	112	4.40 N	108.00 E
Natuna Selatan, Kepulauan II	112	2.45 N	109.00 E
Natural Bridge	212	44.04 N	75.29 W
Natural Bridge ♠	192	37.38 N	79.33 W
Natural Bridges National Monument ♠	200	37.30 N	110.08 W
Natural Bridge State Resort Park ♠	192	37.47 N	83.42 W
Naturaliste, Cape ≻	162	33.32 S	115.01 E
Naturaliste Channel ⊔	162	25.25 S	113.00 E
Naturita	200	38.13 N	108.34 W
Naturita Creek ≃	200	38.13 N	108.32 W
Naturno (Naturns)	64	46.39 N	11.00 E
Natzungen	52	51.36 N	9.14 E
Nau	85	40.09 N	69.22 E
Nau, Cap de la ≻	34	38.44 N	0.14 E
Naucalpan de Juárez	286a	19.28 N	99.14 W
Naucelle	32	44.12 N	2.20 E
Naučnyj	78	44.44 N	34.01 E
Naude	272c	19.03 N	73.06 E
Nauders	58	46.53 N	10.30 E
Nauen	54	52.36 N	12.52 E
Nauener Luch ≡	264a	52.37 N	12.55 E
Nauener Stadtforst ♠	264a	52.38 N	12.58 E
Naugachhia	124	25.24 N	87.06 E
Naugatuck	207	41.30 N	73.05 W
Naugatuck ≃	207	41.19 N	73.05 W
Naughton	190	46.24 N	81.12 W
Naugol'noje	82	56.22 N	38.11 E
Naui	140	18.28 N	30.43 E
Naujamiestis	76	55.41 N	24.04 E
Naujan	116	13.20 N	121.18 E
Naujan, Lake ⊜	116	13.10 N	121.21 E
Naujoji Akmenė	76	56.19 N	22.55 E
Naukan	180	66.01 N	169.43 W
Naulavaara ∧²	26	63.53 N	28.13 E
Naulila	152	17.12 S	14.42 E
Naumburg, Dtsch.	54	51.09 N	11.48 E
Naumburg, Dtsch.	56	51.15 N	9.10 E
Naumovščina	76	58.23 N	28.20 E
Naunak	86	59.00 N	80.13 E
Naundorf	54	50.56 N	13.25 E
Naunglon	110	16.48 N	97.45 E
Naungpale	110	19.33 N	97.08 E
Naunhof	54	51.16 N	12.35 E
Naupada ◆⁸	272c	19.04 N	72.50 E
Nā'ūr	132	31.53 N	35.50 E
Nauraushaun Brook ≃	276	41.03 N	73.59 W
Nauroth	56	50.42 N	7.52 E
Nauroz Kalāt	128	28.47 N	65.38 E
Naurskaja	84	43.38 N	45.19 E
Nauru □¹, Oc.	14	0.32 S	166.55 E
Nauru □¹, Oc.	174b	0.32 S	166.55 E
Naurzumskij zapovednik ♠	86	51.30 N	64.20 E
Naushahro Fīroz	120	26.50 N	68.07 E
Naushon Island I	207	41.29 N	70.45 W
Nauški	88	50.28 N	106.07 E
Nausori	175g	18.02 S	178.32 E
Naussac, Barrage de ◆⁶	62	44.46 N	3.49 E
Naustdal	26	61.31 N	5.43 E
Nauta	246	4.32 S	73.33 W
Nautanwa	124	27.26 N	83.25 E
Nautilus Park	207	41.22 N	72.05 W
Nautla	234	20.13 N	96.47 W
Nauvoo	190	40.33 N	91.23 W
Nava	232	28.25 N	100.46 W
Nava, Arroyo de la ≃	266a	40.31 N	3.46 W
Nava, Colle di)(	62	44.05 N	7.53 E
Nava del Rey	34	41.20 N	5.05 W
Navadwip	126	23.25 N	88.22 E
Navahermosa	34	39.38 N	4.28 W
Navajo	200	35.55 N	109.01 W
Navajo ≃	200	37.01 N	107.10 W
Navajo Creek ≃	200	36.59 N	111.24 W
Navajo Hopi Joint Use Area ◆⁴	200	36.15 N	110.30 W
Navajo Indian Reservation ◆⁴	200	36.25 N	110.00 W
Navajo Mountain ∧	200	37.02 N	110.52 W
Navajo National Monument ♠	200	36.40 N	110.33 W
Navajo Reservoir ⊜¹	200	36.55 N	107.30 W
Naval	116	11.34 N	124.23 E
Navalmoral de la Mata	34	39.54 N	5.32 W
Naval Ordnance Test Station ■	228	35.32 N	117.05 W
Navalvillar de Pela	34	39.06 N	5.28 W
Navan	48	53.39 N	6.41 W
Navāpur	122	21.09 N	73.48 E
Navarin, mys ≻	180	62.16 N	179.10 E
Navarino, Isla I	254	55.05 S	67.40 W
Navarino → Pílos	38	36.55 N	21.43 E
Navarra □⁴, Esp.	34	42.40 N	1.30 W
Navarra □⁴, Esp.	34	42.45 N	1.30 W
Navarre, Austl.	169	36.54 S	143.07 E
Navarre, Oh., U.S.	214	40.43 N	81.31 W
Navarro	258	35.01 S	59.16 W
Navarro □⁶	222	32.05 N	96.30 W
Navarro ≃	204	39.11 N	123.45 W
Navarro, Cañada ≃	258	35.00 S	59.18 W
Navarro, Laguna ⊜	258	35.01 S	59.18 W
Navarro Mills Lake ⊜¹	222	31.56 N	96.45 W
Navašino	80	55.32 N	42.12 E
Navasota	222	30.23 N	96.05 W
Navasota ≃	222	30.20 N	96.09 W
Navassa	192	34.15 N	78.00 W
Navassa Island I	238	18.24 N	75.01 W
Nave	64	45.35 N	10.17 E
Nävekvarn	40	58.38 N	16.49 E
Navenne	58	47.36 N	6.10 E
Naver ≃	46	58.32 N	4.15 W
Naver, Loch ⊜	46	58.17 N	4.23 W
Navesink	276	40.23 N	74.02 W
Navesink River c	276	40.23 N	73.58 W
Navesnoje	76	52.17 N	37.57 E
Nâves-Parmelan	58	45.56 N	6.11 E
Navesti ≃	76	58.30 N	24.54 E
Navestock	260	51.39 N	0.13 E
Navestock Side	260	51.39 N	0.16 E
Navia, Arg.	252	34.47 S	66.35 W
Navia, Esp.	34	43.32 N	6.43 W
Navia ≃	34	43.33 N	6.44 W
Navidad	252	33.57 S	71.50 W
Navidad ≃	196	28.41 N	96.35 W
Navidad, Bahía de c	234	19.17 N	104.50 W
Navidad Bank ✦³	238	20.00 N	68.50 W
Navio, Riacho do ≃	250	8.39 S	38.36 W
Naviraí	255	23.08 S	54.13 W
Navis	64	47.07 N	11.32 E
Naviti I	175g	17.07 S	177.15 E
Navl'a	76	52.51 N	34.30 E
Navl'a ≃	76	52.42 N	34.01 E
Năvodari	38	44.19 N	28.36 E
Navoi	72	40.15 N	65.15 E
Navojoa	232	27.06 N	109.26 W
Navolato	232	24.47 N	107.42 W
Navoloki	80	57.28 N	41.59 E
Navotas	269f	14.39 N	120.57 E
Návpaktos	38	38.23 N	21.50 E
Návplion	38	37.34 N	22.48 E
Navrongo	150	10.54 N	1.06 W
Navsāri	120	20.51 N	72.55 E
Navua	175g	18.14 S	178.10 E
Navy Island I	284a	43.04 N	79.01 W
Navy Pier ◆⁵	278	41.53 N	87.36 W
Navy Yard City	224	47.32 N	122.41 W
Nawa, Nihon	96	35.30 N	133.30 E
Nawá, Sūrīy.	132	32.53 N	36.03 E
Nawābganj, Bngl.	124	24.36 N	88.17 E
Nawābganj, Bngl.	126	23.40 N	90.10 E
Nawābganj, India	124	28.33 N	79.38 E
Nawābganj, India	124	26.52 N	82.08 E
Nawābganj, India	124	26.56 N	81.13 E
Nawābshāh	120	26.15 N	68.25 E
Nawāda	124	24.53 N	85.32 E
Nāwah	120	32.19 N	67.53 E
Nawa Kot	120	28.20 N	71.22 E
Nawalapitiya	122	7.03 N	80.32 E
Nawalgarh	120	27.51 N	75.16 E
Nawa → Naha	174m	26.13 N	127.40 E
Nawān Kot	123	31.06 N	71.32 E
Nawanshahr	123	31.07 N	76.08 E
Nawāpāra, Bngl.	126	23.02 N	89.23 E
Nawāpāra, India	122	20.58 N	81.51 E
Nawapārā, India	126	23.29 N	88.15 E
Nawasā al-Ghayṭ	142	30.58 N	31.19 E
Nawāshahr	123	34.10 N	73.16 E
Nawāṣīf, Ḥarrat ⊥⁹	144	21.20 N	42.10 E
Nawāy	142	27.47 N	30.46 E
Nawiliwili Bay c	229b	21.57 N	159.21 W
Nawinda Kuta	152	16.25 S	24.28 E
Nawŏn-ni	98	36.25 N	126.40 E
Naxera	208	37.20 N	76.27 W
Naxi	107	28.47 N	105.22 E
Náxos	38	37.06 N	25.23 E
Náxos I	38	37.02 N	25.35 E
Naxos ⊥	70	37.49 N	15.17 E
Nayābās	272a	28.35 N	77.19 E
Nayāgaon	126	23.32 N	90.46 E
Nayāgarh	120	20.08 N	85.06 E
Nayāgrām	126	22.02 N	87.11 E
Nayak	120	34.44 N	66.57 E
Nayāpāra	126	21.35 N	87.01 E
Nayarit	204	32.20 N	115.19 W
Nayarit □³	234	22.00 N	105.00 W
Nayau Island I	175g	17.58 S	179.03 W
Nāy Band, Īrān	128	32.20 N	57.34 E
Nāy Band, Īrān	128	27.23 N	52.38 E
Nāy Band, Kūh-e ∧	128	32.26 N	57.22 E
Nayland	42	51.59 N	0.52 E
Naylor	194	36.34 N	90.36 W
Nayong	102	26.50 N	105.13 E
Nayoro	92a	44.21 N	142.28 E
Nazālī Ṭāḥā'	142	28.11 N	30.42 E
Nazaré, Bra.	250	6.23 S	47.40 W
Nazaré, Bra.	255	13.02 S	39.00 W
Nazaré, Port.	34	39.36 N	9.04 W
Nazaré da Mata	250	7.44 S	35.14 W
Nazaré do Piauí	250	6.59 S	42.40 W
Nazareno	256	21.13 S	44.37 W
Nazaré Paulista	256	23.11 S	46.24 W
Nazareth, Bel.	50	50.58 N	3.36 E
Nazareth, Pa., U.S.	208	40.44 N	75.18 W
Nazareth, Vanuatu	175f	15.29 S	168.10 E
Nazareth Bank ✦⁴	12	14.30 S	60.45 E
Nazareth → Naẓerat	132	32.42 N	35.18 E
Nazário	255	16.36 S	49.54 W
Nazarjevo, Ross.	82	55.22 N	36.24 E
Nazarjevo, Ross.	265b	55.59 N	37.16 E
Nazarovo	86	56.01 N	90.26 E
Nazarovskij	78	49.33 N	40.56 E
Nazas	232	25.14 N	104.08 W
Nazas ≃	232	25.35 N	105.00 W
Nazca	248	14.50 S	74.57 W
Nazca Ridge ✦³	18	22.00 S	82.00 W
Naze	93b	28.23 N	129.30 E
Nazeing	260	51.44 N	0.03 E
N'azepetrovsk	86	56.03 N	59.36 E
Naẓerat (Nazareth)	132	32.42 N	35.18 E
Naẓerat 'Illit	132	32.42 N	35.19 E
Nazija	76	59.50 N	31.35 E
Nazik Gölü ⊜	130	38.50 N	42.16 E
Nazilli	130	37.55 N	28.21 E
Nazimicha	265b	55.59 N	38.08 E
Nazımiye	130	39.11 N	39.50 E
Nazimovo	86	59.30 N	90.58 E
Nazina	86	60.07 N	78.52 E
Nāzira	120	26.55 N	94.44 E
Nāzir Hāt	120	22.38 N	91.47 E
Nāzirpur	126	22.43 N	89.58 E
Nazko ≃	182	53.07 N	123.34 W
Nazlat al-'Amūdayn	142	28.14 N	30.42 E
Nazlat al-Badramān	142	27.40 N	30.44 E
Nazlat as-Sammān	273c	29.59 N	31.08 E
Nazlat Khalīfah	273c	30.01 N	31.10 E
Nazlat Quftan Bāshā	142	28.57 N	30.49 E
Nazlat Thābit	142	28.25 N	30.47 E
Nazran'	84	43.13 N	44.46 E
Nazret	144	8.33 N	39.16 E
Nazyvajevsk	86	55.34 N	71.21 E
N. B. C. Studios ʊ³	280	34.09 N	118.20 W
Nchanga	154	12.30 S	27.53 E
Nchelenge	154	9.20 S	28.50 E
Ncue	152	2.01 N	10.28 E
Ndabala	154	13.28 S	29.50 E
Ndala	154	4.46 S	33.16 E
N'dalatando	152	9.18 S	14.54 E
Ndali	150	9.51 N	2.43 E
Ndanda	152	5.12 N	22.21 E
Ndande	150	15.16 N	16.30 W
Ndarassa	152	6.49 N	22.15 E
Ndélé	146	8.24 N	20.39 E
Ndélélé	152	4.02 N	14.56 E
Ndemba	152	0.11 N	14.19 E
Ndendé	152	2.23 S	11.23 E
Ndikiniméki	152	4.46 N	10.50 E
Ndindi	152	3.46 S	11.09 E
N'Djamena	146	12.07 N	15.03 E
Ndji ≃	152	6.47 N	22.14 E
Ndjili ◆⁸	273b	4.20 S	15.22 E
Ndjili ≃	273b	4.19 S	15.24 E
Ndjili, Grande Île de la I	273b	4.19 S	15.24 E
Ndjim ≃	152	4.38 N	11.24 E
Ndjo	152	1.15 S	14.30 E
Ndjolé	152	0.11 S	10.45 E
Ndogo, Lagune c	152	2.35 S	10.00 E
Ndola	154	12.58 S	28.38 E
Ndolo ◆⁸	273b	4.19 S	15.19 E
Ndona	115b	8.46 S	121.45 E
Ndongo	152	2.19 S	13.38 E
Ndouba	152	0.11 S	14.09 E
Ndougou	152	1.39 S	9.40 E
Ndu	152	4.41 N	22.49 E
Nduguti	154	4.18 S	34.42 E
Nduindui	175f	15.24 S	167.46 E
Ndumbwe	154	10.14 S	39.58 E
Ndumu Game Reserve ◆⁴	158	26.53 S	32.15 E
Nduye	154	1.50 N	29.01 E
Ne	268	35.47 N	140.03 E
Nea ≃	26	63.13 N	11.02 E
Neabul Creek ≃	166	27.45 S	147.32 E
Néa Erithraía	267c	38.05 N	23.49 E
Néa Filadhélfia	267c	38.02 N	23.44 E
Neagari	94	36.27 N	136.27 E
Neagh, Lough ⊜	48	54.38 N	6.24 W
Neah Bay	224	48.22 N	124.37 W
Néa Ionía	267c	38.02 N	23.45 E
Neajlov ≃	38	44.11 N	26.12 E
Néa Khalkidhón	267c	38.02 N	23.43 E
Neale, Lake ⊜	162	24.22 S	130.00 E
Neales ≃	162	28.08 S	136.47 E
Neales Flat	168b	34.15 S	139.10 E
Néa Liósia	267c	38.02 N	23.42 E
Neamț □⁶	38	47.00 N	26.30 E
Neandertal, Naturschutzgebiet ♠	263	51.15 N	7.00 E
Néa Páfos (Paphos)	130	34.45 N	32.25 E
Neapel → Napoli	68	40.51 N	14.17 E
Néa Pendéli	267c	38.04 N	23.52 E
Néa Péramos	267c	38.00 N	23.26 E
Neápolis, Ellás	38	36.30 N	23.04 E
Neápolis, Ellás	38	35.15 N	25.37 E
Neapolis, Oh., U.S.	216	41.29 N	83.52 W
Néa Psará	38	38.23 N	23.48 E
Near Islands II	181a	52.40 N	173.30 E
Near North Side ◆⁸	278	41.54 N	87.38 W
Néa Smírni	267c	37.57 N	23.43 E
Neasons Hill	214	41.37 N	80.08 W
Neatahwanta, Lake ⊜	210	43.18 N	76.27 W
Neath	42	51.40 N	3.48 W
Neath ≃	42	51.37 N	3.50 W
Neauphle-le-Château	50	48.49 N	1.54 E
Neauphle-le-Vieux	261	48.49 N	1.52 E
Neavitt	208	38.43 N	76.16 W
Neba	94	35.15 N	137.35 E
Nebaj	236	15.24 N	91.08 W
Nebbou	150	11.18 N	1.53 W
Nebelhorn ∧	58	47.25 N	10.20 E
Nebesnaja, gora ∧	86	43.19 N	80.44 E
Nebeur	36	36.17 N	8.47 E
Nebine Creek ≃	166	29.07 S	146.56 E
Nebit-Dag (Krasnovodsk)	128	40.00 N	53.00 E
Nebit-Dag, Turk.	128	39.30 N	54.22 E
Neblina, Pico da ∧	246	0.48 N	66.02 W
Nebo	194	39.27 N	90.47 W
Nebo, Mount ∧	200	39.49 N	111.46 W
Nebo, Mount → Nabā, Jabal an- ∧	132	31.46 N	35.45 E
Nebolči	76	59.08 N	33.18 E
Nebra	54	51.17 N	11.34 E
Nebraska	218	39.04 N	85.28 W
Nebraska □³, U.S.	178	41.30 N	100.00 W
Nebraska □³, U.S.	198	41.30 N	100.00 W
Nebraska City	198	40.40 N	95.51 W
Nebrodi ⋏	70	37.54 N	14.35 E
Nebyloje	80	56.22 N	39.59 E
Nečajannoje	78	46.57 N	31.33 E
Nečajevka	80	53.17 N	44.27 E
Nečajevo	82	54.42 N	37.23 E
Necaxa ≃	234	20.16 N	97.27 W
Necedah	190	44.01 N	90.04 W
Nechajevskij	80	50.25 N	41.44 E
Nechako ≃	182	53.56 N	122.42 W
Nechako Plateau ⋏¹	182	54.00 N	124.30 W
Nechako Range ⋏	182	53.20 N	124.30 W
Nechako Reservoir ⊜¹	182	53.25 N	125.10 W
Neche	198	48.59 N	97.33 W
Neches	222	31.52 N	95.30 W
Neches ≃	194	29.55 N	93.52 W
Nechí	246	8.07 N	74.46 W
Nechí ≃	246	8.08 N	74.46 W
Nechisar National Park ♠	144	6.00 N	37.50 E
Nechmeya	36	36.36 N	7.31 E
Nechranická Přehradová Nádrž ⊜¹	54	50.20 N	13.20 E
Nechvoroščа	78	49.09 N	34.44 E
Neckar ≃	30	49.31 N	8.26 E
Neckarbischofsheim	56	49.17 N	8.57 E
Neckarelz	56	49.20 N	9.06 E
Neckargemünd	56	49.23 N	8.47 E
Neckarsteinach	56	49.25 N	8.53 E
Neckarsulm	56	49.12 N	9.13 E
Neckartailfingen	56	48.36 N	9.16 E
Neckartenzlingen	56	48.35 N	9.14 E
Neck Creek ≃	276	40.36 N	74.12 W
Necker	284b	39.23 N	76.29 W
Necker Island I, Br. Vir. Is.	240m	18.33 N	64.21 W
Necker Island I, Hi., U.S.	14	23.35 N	164.42 W
Necker Ridge ✦³	14	22.00 N	167.15 W
Necochea	252	38.33 S	58.45 W
Necrópolis ◆	266a	40.25 N	3.38 W
Nedalssjön ⊜	26	62.56 N	12.11 E
Nedančiči	78	51.30 N	30.37 E
Ned Brown Preserve ♠	278	42.02 N	88.01 W
Nedel'noje	82	54.50 N	36.39 E
Nederland	194	29.58 N	93.59 W
Nederland → Netherlands □¹	30	52.15 N	5.30 E
Nederlandse Antillen → Netherlands Antilles □²	241s	12.15 N	69.00 W
Neder-Rijn ≃¹	52	51.58 N	5.20 E
Nederweert	52	51.17 N	5.45 E
Nederzwalm-Hermelgem	50	50.53 N	3.41 E
Nedlands	168a	31.59 S	115.49 E
Nedlitz	54	52.04 N	12.14 E
Nedlitz ◆⁸	264a	52.26 N	13.03 E
Nêdong	120	29.14 N	91.46 E
Nedre Soppero	24	68.01 N	21.44 E
Nedre Vättern ⊜	40	59.49 N	15.40 E
Nedrigajlov	78	50.50 N	33.53 E
Nédroma	148	35.01 N	1.45 W
Nedrow	210	42.58 N	76.08 W
Nedstrand	26	59.21 N	5.51 E
Neebish Island I	190	46.16 N	84.09 W
Neede	52	52.08 N	6.36 E
Needham, In., U.S.	218	39.32 N	85.58 W
Needham, Ma., U.S.	207	42.17 N	71.14 W
Needham Market	42	52.09 N	1.03 E
Needhams Point ≻	241g	13.05 N	59.36 W
Needle Mountain ∧	202	44.05 N	109.37 W
Needles	204	34.50 N	114.36 W
Needling Hill ∧²	168a	31.53 S	116.56 E
Needville	222	29.23 N	95.50 W
Neelyton	214	40.10 N	77.50 W
Ñeembucú □⁵	252	27.00 S	58.00 W
Neenah	190	44.11 N	88.27 W
Neepawa	184	50.13 N	99.29 W
Neerabup National Park ♠	168a	31.41 S	115.43 E
Neerim South	169	38.01 S	145.58 E
Neermoor	52	53.18 N	7.26 E
Neeroeteren	56	51.05 N	5.42 E
Neerpelt	56	51.13 N	5.25 E
Neersen	263	51.15 N	6.29 E
Nee Soon	271c	1.24 N	103.49 E
Neetze	52	53.15 N	10.39 E
Neetze ≃	54	53.20 N	10.28 E
Nefedjevo, Ross.	82	54.39 N	37.56 E
Nefedjevo, Ross.	265b	55.54 N	37.10 E
Neffs	208	40.42 N	75.37 W
Neffsville	208	40.06 N	76.18 W
Nef'odovo	86	58.48 N	72.34 E
Nefta	148	33.52 N	7.33 E
Nefteabad	85	40.12 N	70.34 E
Neftečala	84	39.23 N	49.16 E
Neftegorsk	84	44.22 N	39.42 E
Neftekumsk	84	44.45 N	44.48 E
Nefyn	42	52.57 N	4.31 W
Nefza	36	36.58 N	9.05 E
Negage	152	7.45 S	15.16 E
Négala	150	12.52 N	8.27 W
Negapatam → Nāgappattinam	122	10.46 N	79.50 E
Negara, Indon.	112	2.37 S	115.06 E
Negara, Indon.	115a	8.22 S	114.37 E
Negara ≃	112	3.00 S	114.45 E
Negast	54	54.15 N	13.01 E
Negaunee	190	46.29 N	87.36 W
Negba	132	31.40 N	34.41 E
Negele	144	5.20 N	39.36 E
Negenborn	52	51.53 N	9.34 E
Negeribatin	112	4.35 S	104.32 E
Negeri Sembilan □³	114	2.45 N	102.10 E
Negev Desert → HaNegev ◆¹	132	30.30 N	34.55 E
Negishi	268	35.51 N	139.23 E
Negley	214	40.47 N	80.32 W
Negola	152	14.10 S	14.30 E
Negomano	154	11.27 S	38.31 E
Negombo	122	7.13 N	79.50 E
Negonego I¹	14	18.47 S	141.48 W
Negoreloje	76	53.36 N	27.04 E
Negotin	38	44.14 N	22.32 E
Negra, Laguna ⊜	252	34.03 S	53.40 W
Negra, Ponta ≻	256	22.58 S	42.42 W
Negra, Punta ≻, Belize	232	16.17 N	88.34 W
Negra, Punta ≻, Perú	248	6.06 S	81.09 W
Negrais	266c	38.53 N	9.17 W
Negras, Lomas ∧²	286d	11.55 S	77.06 W
Negreira	34	42.54 N	8.44 W
Nègres, Pointe des ≻	240e	14.36 N	61.06 W
Negrești	38	46.50 N	27.27 E
Negrești-Oaș	38	47.52 N	23.25 E
Negrine	148	34.30 N	7.30 E
Negritos	246	4.38 S	81.19 W
Negro ≃, Arg.	254	41.02 S	62.47 W
Negro ≃, Bol.	248	14.11 S	63.07 W
Negro ≃, Bol.	248	9.49 S	65.42 W
Negro ≃, Bra.	248	5.15 S	70.53 W
Negro ≃, Bra.	248	19.13 S	57.17 W
Negro ≃, Bra.	250	9.15 S	47.34 W
Negro ≃, Bra.	252	26.01 S	50.30 W
Negro ≃, Col.	246	5.44 N	74.39 W
Negro ≃, N.A.	236	13.02 N	87.17 W
Negro ≃, Para.	252	24.23 S	57.11 W
Negro ≃, S.A.	246	3.08 S	59.55 W
Negro ≃, S.A.	252	33.24 S	58.22 W
Negro, Baia del c	144	7.55 N	49.55 E
Negro, Cerro ∧, Arg.	254	46.55 S	70.12 W
Negro, Cerro ∧, Arg.	254	44.09 S	69.30 W
Negro, Cerro ∧, Méx.	234	17.19 N	97.25 W
Negro, Mar → Black Sea ⊤²	22	43.00 N	35.00 E
Negros I	116	10.00 N	123.00 E
Negros Occidental □⁴	116	10.20 N	123.00 E
Negros Oriental □⁴	116	9.40 N	123.00 E
Negru-Vodă	38	43.50 N	28.12 E
Neguac	186	47.15 N	65.05 W
Nehalem	224	45.43 N	123.53 W
Nehalem ≃	224	45.40 N	123.56 W
Nehawka	198	40.49 N	95.59 W
Nehbandān	128	31.32 N	60.02 E
Neheim-Hüsten	56	51.27 N	7.57 E
Nehonsey Brook ≃	285	39.49 N	75.18 W
Néhoué, Baie de c	175f	20.21 S	164.09 E
Nehru Planetarium ʊ	272c	18.59 N	72.49 E
Neiba	238	18.28 N	71.25 W
Neichiang → Neijiang	107	29.35 N	105.03 E
Neidpath	184	50.13 N	107.15 W
Neige, Crêt de la ∧	58	46.16 N	5.56 E
Neiges, Piton des ∧	157c	21.05 S	55.29 E
Neihart	202	46.56 N	110.44 W
Neihe ≃	100	22.54 N	115.38 E
Neihu	269d	25.05 N	121.34 E
Neihuang	98	35.59 N	114.55 E
Neijiang	107	29.35 N	105.03 E
Neikiang → Neijiang	107	29.35 N	105.03 E
Neilburg	184	52.50 N	109.38 W
Neillsville	190	44.33 N	90.35 W
Neilston	46	55.47 N	4.27 W
Neimen	263	51.29 N	7.48 E
Nei Monggol Zizhiqu (Inner Mongolia) □⁴	90	43.00 N	115.00 E
Nein	132	32.38 N	35.21 E
Neindorf	54	52.20 N	10.50 E
Neinstedt	54	51.45 N	11.05 E
Neiqiu	98	37.17 N	114.31 E
Neira	246	5.10 N	75.32 W
Neirone	62	44.27 N	9.11 E
Neishuishan	269d	25.09 N	121.43 E
Neisse (Nysa Łużycka) (Nisa) ≃	30	52.04 N	14.46 E
Neiva	246	2.56 N	75.18 W
Neiwufuquan	105	40.11 N	117.39 E
Neixiang	102	33.12 N	111.57 E
Neixpa ≃	234	18.05 N	102.46 W
Neizeng Shan ∧	100	24.02 N	117.32 E
Neja, Ross.	80	58.24 N	46.31 E
Neja, Ross.	80	58.18 N	43.54 E
Neja ≃	80	57.48 N	43.42 E
Nejapa de Madero	234	16.37 N	95.59 W
Nejdek	54	50.17 N	12.42 E
Nejd → Najd □⁹	118	25.00 N	44.30 E
Nejo	144	9.30 N	35.30 E
Nejva ≃	86	57.54 N	62.18 E
Nejvo-Šajtanskij	86	57.44 N	61.15 E
Nekalagba	154	2.50 N	28.01 E
Nekemte	144	9.02 N	36.31 E
Nekhab ⊥	140	25.10 N	32.48 E
Nekoosa	190	44.18 N	89.54 W
Nekor, Oued ≃	34	35.14 N	3.45 W
Neko-zaki ≻	96	35.40 N	134.46 E
Nekrasino	82	56.18 N	36.33 E
Nekrasovka	265b	55.41 N	37.56 E
Nekrasovo, Ross.	80	51.10 N	45.18 E
Nekrasovo, Ross.	82	54.30 N	38.57 E
Nekrasovskoje	80	57.41 N	40.22 E
Nekselø I	41	55.47 N	11.18 E
Neksø	26	55.04 N	15.09 E
Nela Park ♠	279a	41.33 N	81.33 W
Nel'aty	88	56.29 N	115.41 E
Nelichu ∧	140	6.08 N	34.25 E
Nelidovo	76	56.13 N	32.46 E
Neligh	198	42.07 N	98.01 W
Nel'kan	74	57.40 N	136.13 E
Nellie	214	40.20 N	82.04 W
Nellikuppam	122	11.46 N	79.41 E
Nellingen	56	48.33 N	9.47 E
Nellis Air Force Base ■	204	36.14 N	115.02 W
Nelliston	210	42.56 N	74.37 W
Nellis Weapons Range ■	204	37.15 N	116.20 W
Nellore	122	14.26 N	79.58 E
Nel'ma	89	47.39 N	139.09 E
Nelson, B.C., Can.	182	49.29 N	117.17 W
Nelson, N.Z.	172	41.17 S	173.17 E
Nelson, Eng., U.K.	44	53.51 N	2.13 W
Nelson, Ne., U.S.	198	40.12 N	98.04 W
Nelson, Pa., U.S.	210	41.59 N	77.14 W
Nelson ≃	184	57.04 N	92.30 W
Nelson, Cape ≻, Austl.	166	38.26 S	141.33 E
Nelson, Cape ≻, Pap. N. Gui.	164	9.00 S	149.15 E
Nelson, Estrecho ⊔	254	51.37 S	75.00 W
Nelson Creek ≃	222	30.56 N	95.31 W
Nelson House	184	55.47 N	98.51 W
Nelson Island I	180	60.35 N	164.45 W
Nelson-Kennedy Ledges State Park ♠	214	41.18 N	81.04 W
Nelson Lake ⊜	184	55.44 N	100.00 W
Nelson Lakes National Park ♠	172	41.50 S	172.40 E
Nelson Reservoir ⊜¹	202	48.30 N	107.34 W
Nelson's Dockyard ⊥	240c	17.00 N	61.46 W
Nelsonville, N.Y., U.S.	210	41.25 N	73.57 W
Nelsonville, Oh., U.S.	188	39.27 N	82.14 W
Nelspoort	158	32.07 S	23.00 E
Nelspoortjie	158	29.58 S	22.25 E
Nelspruit	156	25.30 S	30.58 E
Néma, Maur.	150	16.37 N	7.15 W
Nema, Ross.	80	57.31 N	50.31 E
Néma, Dahr ⊥⁴	150	16.40 N	7.13 W
Nemadji ≃	190	46.41 N	92.02 W
Nemah	224	46.31 N	123.51 W
Nemaha	198	40.20 N	95.40 W
Neman	76	55.02 N	22.02 E
Neman (Nemunas) ≃	76	55.18 N	21.23 E
Nematābād ◆⁸	267d	35.38 N	51.21 E
Nembe	150	4.35 N	6.26 E
Nembrala	112	10.53 S	122.50 E
Nembro	62	45.45 N	9.45 E
Nemčinovka	265b	55.43 N	37.23 E
Nemda ≃, Ross.	80	57.35 N	48.56 E
Nemda ≃, Ross.	80	57.21 N	43.08 E
Nemegosenda ≃	190	48.31 N	82.53 W
Nemegt uul ⋏	102	43.40 N	101.10 E
Nemeiben Lake ⊜	184	55.20 N	105.20 W
Nemenčinė	76	54.51 N	25.29 E
Nementcha, Monts de ⋏	148	34.52 N	7.05 E
Nemeriči	76	53.51 N	33.59 E
Nemi	66	41.43 N	12.43 E
Nemi, Lago di ⊜	267a	41.43 N	12.42 E
Nemira Mare, Vîrful ∧	38	46.15 N	26.19 E
Nemirov, Ukr.	78	50.07 N	23.25 E
Nemirov, Ukr.	78	48.58 N	28.50 E
Nemirovo	82	55.54 N	36.12 E
Nemo	222	32.16 N	97.39 W
Nemoli	68	40.04 N	15.48 E
Nemor ≃	89	48.23 N	124.32 E
Nemours	50	48.16 N	2.42 E
Nemoviči	78	51.16 N	26.38 E
Nemrut Gölü ⊜	130	38.37 N	42.12 E
Nemuna, Bjeshkët e ⋏	38	42.27 N	19.47 E
Nemunas (Neman) ≃	76	55.18 N	21.23 E
Nemuro	92a	43.20 N	145.35 E
Nemuro-hantō ≻¹	92a	43.21 N	145.42 E
Nemuro Strait ⊔	92a	44.00 N	145.20 E
Nemzeti Museum ʊ	264c	47.29 N	19.05 E
Nen ≃	89	45.25 N	124.40 E
Nena Creek ≃	224	45.07 N	121.07 W
Nenagh	48	52.52 N	8.12 W
Nenagh ≃	48	52.56 N	8.17 W
Nenana	180	64.34 N	149.07 W
Nenana ≃	180	64.30 N	149.00 W
Nenaševo	82	54.34 N	37.28 E
Nenasi	114	3.08 N	103.27 E
Nendaz	58	46.11 N	7.18 E
Nendeln	58	47.12 N	9.32 E
Nendo I	14	10.45 S	165.54 E
Nene ≃	42	52.48 N	0.13 E
Neneckij Avtonomnyj Okrug □⁸	24	67.30 N	54.00 E
Nenggiri ≃	114	4.53 N	101.48 E
Nengjia	104	41.38 N	120.46 E
Nengo ≃	152	14.27 S	22.09 E
Nenneper ≃	263	51.32 N	6.26 E
Neno	154	15.24 S	34.39 E
Nentón ≃	236	15.48 N	91.52 W
Nenzing	58	47.11 N	9.42 E
Neo	94	35.38 N	136.37 E
Neo ≃	94	35.24 N	136.34 E
Neodesha	198	37.25 N	95.40 W
Neoga	194	39.19 N	88.27 W
Neola, Ia., U.S.	198	41.26 N	95.36 W
Neola, Ut,. U.S.	200	40.26 N	110.01 W
Neoneli	71	40.04 N	8.57 E
Néon Fáliron	267c	37.57 N	23.40 E
Néon Karlovásion	38	37.48 N	26.44 E
Néon Psikhikón	267c	38.00 N	23.47 E
Neopit	190	44.58 N	88.49 W
Neópolis	250	10.18 S	36.35 W
Neoshera	123	33.09 N	74.14 E
Neosho	194	36.52 N	94.22 W
Neosho ≃	194	35.48 N	95.18 W
Neotsu	224	45.00 N	123.58 W
Nepa ≃	88	59.16 N	108.16 E
Nepal (Nepāl) □¹, Asia	118	28.00 N	84.00 E
Nepal (Nepāl) □¹, Asia	124	28.00 N	84.00 E
Nepālgañj	124	28.03 N	81.37 E
Nepa Nagar	120	21.28 N	76.23 E
Nepaug Reservoir ⊜¹	207	41.48 N	72.57 W
Nepean	212	45.18 N	75.47 W
Nepean ≃	170	33.27 S	150.53 E
Nepean, Point ≻	169	38.18 S	144.39 E
Nepean Bay c	168b	35.42 S	137.44 E
Nepean Island I	174c	29.04 S	167.58 E
Nepean Reservoir ⊜¹	170	34.22 S	150.35 E
Nepecino	82	55.12 N	38.37 E
Nepeña	248	9.10 S	78.23 W
Nepewassi Lake ⊜	190	46.20 N	80.40 W
Nephi	200	39.42 N	111.50 W
Nephin ∧	48	54.01 N	9.22 W
Nephin Beg Range ⋏	48	54.00 N	9.35 W
Nepi	66	42.14 N	12.21 E
Nepisiguit ≃	186	47.37 N	65.38 W
Nepisiguit Bay c	186	47.46 N	65.32 W
Népliget ♠	264c	47.29 N	19.07 E
Nepoko ≃	154	1.40 N	27.01 E
Nepomuceno	256	21.14 S	45.15 W
Nepomuk	60	49.29 N	13.36 E
Neponset ≃	283	42.17 N	71.02 W
Neponset Reservoir ⊜¹	283	42.05 N	71.15 W
Neponset River Reservation ♠	283	42.13 N	71.08 W
Neppermin	54	53.56 N	14.02 E
Nepr'adva ≃	76	53.40 N	38.39 E
Nép-sziget I	264c	47.34 N	19.05 E
Neptune, N.J., U.S.	208	40.12 N	74.02 W
Neptune, Oh., U.S.	216	40.36 N	84.30 W
Neptune Beach	192	30.18 N	81.23 W
Neptune City	208	40.12 N	74.02 W
Neqarot, Naḥal V	132	30.40 N	35.15 E
Nera ≃, Europe	38	44.49 N	21.22 E
Nera ≃, It.	66	42.26 N	12.24 E
Nérac	32	44.08 N	0.20 E
Nerákion	267c	38.01 N	23.27 E
Nerang	171a	28.00 S	153.20 E
Nerang ≃	171a	28.03 S	153.17 E
Neratovice	54	50.14 N	14.31 E
Nerča ≃	88	51.56 N	116.40 E
Nerchau	54	51.16 N	12.47 E
Nerčinsk	88	51.58 N	116.35 E
Nerčinskij Zavod	88	51.19 N	119.36 E
Nère ≃	50	47.34 N	2.18 E
Nerechta	80	57.28 N	40.34 E
Nerenstetten	56	48.31 N	10.06 E
Neresheim	56	48.45 N	10.15 E
Nereta	76	56.13 N	25.18 E
Nereto	66	42.49 N	13.49 E
Neretva ≃	36	43.01 N	17.27 E
Nerevoznoje	80	56.53 N	53.54 E
Nerima ◆⁸	268	35.44 N	139.39 E
Neringa	76	55.18 N	21.01 E
Neris ≃	76	54.54 N	23.53 E
Nerito	66	42.32 N	13.28 E
Nerja	34	36.44 N	3.52 W
Nerka, Lake ⊜	180	59.30 N	158.45 W
Nerl', Ross.	76	57.03 N	37.59 E
Nerl', Ross.	80	56.40 N	40.24 E
Nerl' ≃, Ross.	76	57.07 N	37.39 E
Nerl' ≃, Ross.	80	56.11 N	40.34 E
Nero, ozero ⊜	80	57.07 N	39.27 E
Neroj	88	54.28 N	97.49 E
Néronde	62	45.50 N	4.14 E
Nérondes	32	47.00 N	2.49 E
Nerópolis	255	16.25 S	49.14 W
Nerriga	170	35.07 S	150.05 E
Nerrima	162	18.24 S	124.29 E
Nerrimunga Creek ≃	170	34.57 S	150.04 E
Nersingen	58	48.25 N	10.07 E
Nerskaja ≃	82	55.23 N	38.35 E
Nerul	272c	19.02 N	73.01 E
Nerus ≃	114	5.20 N	103.05 E
Nerussa ≃	76	52.33 N	33.47 E
Nerva	34	37.42 N	6.32 W
Nervi	62	44.23 N	9.02 E
Nervia ≃	62	43.47 N	7.38 E
Nerviano	266b	45.33 N	8.58 E
Nerville-la-Forêt	261	49.05 N	2.17 E
Nes, Ned.	52	53.04 N	5.51 E
Nes, Ned.	52	53.26 N	5.45 E
Nes, Nor.	26	60.34 N	9.59 E
Nes', Ross.	24	66.37 N	44.36 E
Nes, Har ∧	132	30.22 N	34.37 E
Nesbyen	26	60.34 N	9.09 E
Neščerdo, ozero ⊜	76	55.54 N	29.04 E
Neščeretovo	83	49.24 N	38.48 E
Nesco	208	39.38 N	74.41 W
Nescochague Creek ≃	285	39.39 N	74.41 W
Nescochague Creek, Great Swamp Branch ≃	285	39.41 N	74.43 W
Nesconset	276	40.51 N	73.09 W
Nescopeck	210	41.03 N	76.13 W
Nescopeck Creek ≃	210	41.03 N	76.14 W
Nescopeck Mountain ∧	210	41.03 N	76.05 W
Nesebâr	38	42.39 N	27.44 E
Neshaminy Creek ≃	208	40.04 N	74.55 W
Neshaminy Hills	285	40.10 N	74.57 W
Neshaminy Mall ◆⁹	285	40.08 N	74.57 W
Neshaminy State Park ♠	285	40.05 N	74.55 W
Neshaminy Woods	285	40.10 N	74.57 W
Neshannock Creek ≃	214	40.59 N	80.21 W
Nesher	132	32.46 N	35.03 E
Nesjøen ⊜¹	26	63.02 N	12.01 E
Neškan	180	67.03 N	173.01 W
Neskaupstaður	24a	65.10 N	13.43 W
Neskowin	224	45.06 N	123.58 W
Neskynpil'gyn, laguna c	180	66.57 N	172.45 W
Nesle	50	49.46 N	2.55 E
Nesna	24	66.12 N	13.02 E
Nespelem	182	48.10 N	118.58 W
Nesque ≃	62	43.59 N	4.59 E
Nesquehoning	210	40.51 N	75.48 W
Ness	262	53.17 N	3.03 W
Ness, Loch ⊜	46	57.15 N	4.30 W
Ness City	198	38.27 N	99.54 W
Nesse ≃	54	50.59 N	10.32 E
Nesselrode, Mount ∧	180	58.58 N	134.18 W
Nesselwang	58	47.37 N	10.30 E
Nesselwängle	58	47.29 N	10.37 E
Nesslau	58	47.13 N	9.13 E
Nessmersiel	52	53.40 N	7.21 E
Nesso	58	45.55 N	9.08 E

Symbols in the index entries represent the broad categories identified in the key at the right. Symbols with superior numbers (⋏¹) identify subcategories (see complete key on page *I · 1).*

Symbole im Register stellen die rechts im Schlüssel erklärten Kategorien dar. Symbole mit hochgestellten Ziffern (⋏¹) bezeichnen Unterabteilungen einer Kategorie (vgl. vollständiger Schlüssel auf Seite *I · 1).*

Los símbolos incluídos en el texto del índice representan las grandes categorias identificadas con la clave a la derecha. Los símbolos con numeros en su parte superior (⋏¹) identifican las subcategorías (véase la clave completa en la página *I · 1).*

Les symboles de l'index représentent les catégories indiquées dans la légende à droite. Les symboles suivis d'un indice (⋏¹) représentent des sous-catégories (voir légende complète à la page *I · 1).*

Os símbolos incluídos no texto do índice representam as grandes categorias identificadas com a chave à direita. Os símbolos com números em sua parte superior (⋏¹) identificam as subcategorias (veja-se a chave completa à página *I · 1).*

∧ Mountain	Berg	Montaña	Montagne	Montanha
⋏ Mountains	Gebirge	Montañas	Montagnes	Montanhas
)(Pass	Paß	Paso	Col	Passo
V Valley, Canyon	Tal, Cañon	Valle, Cañón	Vallée, Canyon	Vale, Canhão
≍ Plain	Ebene	Llano	Plaine	Planície
≻ Cape	Kap	Cabo	Cap	Cabo
I Island	Insel	Isla	Île	Ilha
II Islands	Inseln	Islas	Îles	Ilhas
⊥ Other Topographic Features	Andere Topographische Objekte	Otros Elementos Topográficos	Autres données topographiques	Outros acidentes topográficos

ESPAÑOL

Nombre	Página	Lat.°′	Long.°′ W = Oeste
Neštěmice	54	50.40 N	14.07 E
Nesterkovo	76	59.10 N	30.33 E
Nesterov, Ross.	76	54.38 N	22.34 E
Nesterov, Ukr.	78	50.04 N	23.58 E
Nesterovka	80	52.26 N	53.42 E
Nesterovo, Ross.	80	54.31 N	41.49 E
Nesterovo, Ross.	82	56.45 N	36.30 E
Nesterovo, Ross.	88	52.22 N	107.53 E
Nestiary	80	56.34 N	45.21 E
Nestoita	78	47.47 N	29.21 E
Neston	44	53.18 N	3.04 W
Nestore ≃	66	43.21 N	12.15 E
Néstos (Mesta) ≃	38	40.41 N	24.44 E
Nesttun	26	60.19 N	5.20 E
Nestucca ≃	224	45.12 N	123.57 W
Nesvetaj	83	47.27 N	39.40 E
Nesviž	76	53.13 N	26.40 E
Nes Ziyyona	132	31.55 N	34.48 E
Netanya	132	32.20 N	34.51 E
Netarhāt	124	23.29 N	84.16 E
Netarts	224	45.26 N	123.56 W
Netarts Bay ⊂	224	45.24 N	123.56 W
Netcong	210	40.53 N	74.42 W
Nethan ≃	46	55.42 N	3.52 W
Nether Alderley	262	53.17 N	2.14 W
Netherdale	166	21.08 S	148.32 E
Netherlands (Nederland) □[1], Europe	22	52.15 N	5.30 E
Netherlands (Nederland) □[1], Europe	30	52.15 N	5.30 E
Netherlands Antilles (Nederlandse Antillen) □[2], N.A.	230	12.15 N	68.45 W
Netherlands Antilles (Nederlandse Antillen) □[2], N.A.	241s	12.15 N	68.45 W
Netherton	262	53.30 N	2.58 W
Nethy Bridge	46	57.16 N	3.38 W
Netia	154	14.48 S	39.59 E
Netley Marsh	42	50.53 N	1.21 W
Neto ≃	68	39.13 N	17.08 E
Netolice	61	49.03 N	14.12 E
Netphen	56	50.55 N	8.06 E
Netra	56	51.06 N	10.05 E
Netrakona	124	24.53 N	90.43 E
Netstal	58	47.03 N	9.03 E
Nettancourt	56	48.52 N	4.57 E
Nette	52	52.02 N	10.05 E
Nette ◆[8]	263	51.33 N	7.25 E
Nettelstedt	52	52.18 N	8.41 E
Nettetal	56	51.18 N	6.16 E
Nettilling Fiord ⊂[2]	176	66.02 N	68.12 W
Nettilling Lake ⊜	176	66.30 N	70.40 W
Nett Lake ⊜	190	48.10 N	93.10 W
Nett Lake Indian Reservation ◆[4]	190	48.06 N	93.10 W
Nettlebed	42	51.35 N	1.00 W
Nettle Creek ≃	218	40.03 N	83.48 W
Nettleden	260	51.47 N	0.32 W
Nettleham	44	53.16 N	0.29 W
Nettlestead	260	51.15 N	0.25 E
Nettlestead Green	260	51.14 N	0.25 E
Nettleton	194	34.05 N	88.37 W
Nettuno	66	41.27 N	12.39 E
Nettuno, Grotta di ⊥[5]	71	40.34 N	8.09 E
Netzschkau	54	50.36 N	12.14 E
Neualbenreuth	60	49.59 N	12.27 E
Neu-Anspach	56	50.17 N	8.29 E
Neuastenberg	56	51.10 N	8.29 E
Neubeckum	52	51.48 N	8.01 E
Neubrandenburg	54	53.33 N	13.15 E
Neubraunschweig → New Brunswick □[4]	186	46.30 N	66.15 W
Neubritannien → New Britain I	164	6.00 S	150.00 E
Neu Büddenstedt	54	52.10 N	10.31 E
Neubukow	54	54.02 N	11.40 E
Neuburg am Inn	60	48.30 N	13.27 E
Neuburg an der Donau	60	48.44 N	11.11 E
Neuchâtel	58	46.59 N	6.56 E
Neuchâtel □[3]	58	47.00 N	6.55 E
Neuchâtel, Lac de ⊜	58	46.52 N	6.50 E
Neu-Delhi → New Delhi	124	28.36 N	77.12 E
Neudenau	56	49.17 N	9.16 E
Neudietendorf	54	50.55 N	10.55 E
Neudorf, Sk., Can.	184	50.44 N	102.59 W
Neudorf, Dtsch.	54	50.29 N	12.58 E
Neudorf ◆[8]	263	51.25 N	6.47 E
Neudörfl	61	47.48 N	16.17 E
Neue Hebriden → Vanuatu □[1]	175f	16.00 S	167.00 E
Neuemühle	264a	52.18 N	13.39 E
Neuenburg, Dtsch.	52	53.23 N	7.57 E
Neuenbürg, Dtsch.	56	48.50 N	8.35 E
Neuenburg, Dtsch.	58	47.49 N	7.35 E
Neuenburg → Neuchâtel	58	46.59 N	6.56 E
Neuendettelsau	56	49.17 N	10.47 E
Neuendorf	54	54.31 N	13.05 E
Neuendorfer See ⊜	54	52.07 N	13.55 E
Neuenegg	58	46.54 N	7.18 E
Neuenhagen bei Berlin	54	52.32 N	13.41 E
Neuenhaus	52	52.30 N	6.59 E
Neuenhof ◆[8]	263	51.10 N	7.13 E
Neuenhoven	263	51.08 N	6.31 E
Neue Niers ≃	263	51.16 N	6.26 E
Neuenkamp ◆[8]	263	51.26 N	6.44 E
Neuenkirchen, Dtsch.	52	52.30 N	8.04 E
Neuenkirchen, Dtsch.	52	53.14 N	8.31 E
Neuenkirchen, Dtsch.	52	53.02 N	9.42 E
Neuenkirchen, Dtsch.	52	52.14 N	7.22 E
Neuenkirchen, Dtsch.	52	53.46 N	8.53 E
Neuenkirchen, Dtsch.	52	51.50 N	8.26 E
Neuenkirchen, Dtsch.	54	54.32 N	13.20 E
Neuenrade	56	51.17 N	7.47 E
Neuensalz	54	50.30 N	12.13 E
Neuenstadt am Kocher	56	49.14 N	9.20 E
Neuenwalde	52	53.40 N	8.40 E
Neuerburg	56	50.00 N	6.17 E
Neu-Erlaa ◆[8]	264b	48.08 N	16.19 E
Neues Palais ⊥	264a	52.24 N	13.01 E
Neu Fahrland	264a	52.26 N	13.03 E
Neufahrn bei Freising	60	48.19 N	11.40 E
Neufahrn in Niederbayern	60	48.44 N	12.11 E
Neuf-Brisach	58	48.01 N	7.32 E
Neufchâteau, Bel.	56	49.50 N	5.26 E
Neufchâteau, Fr.	58	48.21 N	5.42 E
Neufchâtel-en-Bray	50	49.44 N	1.27 E
Neufchâtel-sur-Aisne	50	49.26 N	4.02 E
Neufelden	61	48.29 N	14.00 E
Neuffen	56	48.33 N	9.22 E
Neuffossé, Canal de ≊	50	50.45 N	2.15 E
Neufmanil	56	49.49 N	4.48 E
Neuf-Marché	50	49.25 N	1.43 E
Neufmontiers-lès-Meaux	261	48.58 N	2.50 E
Neufundland → Newfoundland □[4]	176	52.00 N	56.00 W
Neufvilles	50	50.34 N	4.00 E
Neugersdorf	54	50.59 N	14.36 E
Neuglobsow	54	53.09 N	13.02 E
Neugraben-Fischbek ◆[8]	52	53.28 N	9.52 E
Neuguinea → New Guinea I	164	5.00 S	140.00 E
Neuharlingersiel	52	53.42 N	7.42 E
Neu-Hartmannsdorf	264a	52.22 N	13.51 E
Neuhaus, Dtsch.	54	50.30 N	11.08 E
Neuhaus, Dtsch.	54	53.17 N	10.55 E
Neuhaus, Dtsch.	58	47.48 N	8.34 E

FRANÇAIS

Nom	Page	Lat.°′	Long.°′ W = Ouest
Neuhaus, Öst.	61	47.47 N	15.11 E
Neuhaus an der Oste	52	53.48 N	9.02 E
Neuhausen, Dtsch.	54	50.41 N	13.28 E
Neuhausen, Dtsch.	58	47.58 N	8.55 E
Neuhausen, Schw.	58	47.41 N	8.37 E
Neuhaus im Solling	52	51.45 N	9.31 E
Neuhaus-Schierschnitz	54	50.19 N	11.14 E
Neuheum	114	5.34 N	95.32 E
Neuhof	56	50.27 N	9.40 E
Neuhof an der Zenn	56	49.27 N	10.38 E
Neuhofen	56	49.25 N	8.26 E
Neuhofen an der Krems	61	48.08 N	14.14 E
Neuillé-Pont-Pierre	50	47.33 N	0.33 E
Neuilly-en-Thelle	50	49.13 N	2.17 E
Neuilly-L'Évêque	58	47.55 N	5.26 E
Neuilly-Saint-Front	50	49.10 N	3.16 E
Neuilly-sur-Marne	261	48.51 N	2.32 E
Neuilly-sur-Seine	50	48.53 N	2.16 E
Neuirland → New Ireland I	164	3.20 S	152.00 E
Neu-Isenburg	56	50.03 N	8.41 E
Neukagran ◆[8]	264b	48.14 N	16.27 E
Neu-Kaledonien → New Caledonia □[2]	175f	21.30 S	165.30 E
Neukalen	54	53.49 N	12.47 E
Neu Kaliss	54	53.10 N	11.17 E
Neukieritzsch	54	51.10 N	12.25 E
Neukirch, Dtsch.	54	51.17 N	13.58 E
Neukirch, Dtsch.	54	51.05 N	14.20 E
Neukirch, Dtsch.	58	47.39 N	9.41 E
Neukirchen, Dtsch.	41	54.52 N	8.44 E
Neukirchen, Dtsch.	54	54.19 N	11.01 E
Neukirchen, Dtsch.	54	51.05 N	12.32 E
Neukirchen, Dtsch.	54	50.47 N	12.22 E
Neukirchen, Dtsch.	54	50.46 N	12.52 E
Neukirchen, Dtsch.	56	50.46 N	9.41 E
Neukirchen, Dtsch.	56	49.29 N	6.50 E
Neukirchen, Dtsch.	60	49.05 N	11.45 E
Neukirchen, Dtsch.	263	51.07 N	6.41 E
Neukirchen, Öst.	64	47.15 N	12.17 E
Neukirchen am Walde	60	48.24 N	13.46 E
Neukirchen bei Sulzbach-Rosenberg	60	49.32 N	11.38 E
Neukirchen-Vluyn	56	51.27 N	6.33 E
Neukloster	54	53.52 N	11.41 E
Neukölln ◆[8]	264a	52.29 N	13.27 E
Neu Kosenow	54	53.47 N	13.46 E
Neulangerwisch	264a	52.19 N	13.04 E
Neulengbach	61	48.12 N	15.55 E
Neulienken	54	53.27 N	14.22 E
Neu Lübbenau	54	52.04 N	13.53 E
Neulussheim	56	49.17 N	8.31 E
Neumagen	56	49.51 N	6.53 E
Neuman Creek ≃	284a	42.42 N	78.48 W
Neumark	54	50.39 N	12.21 E
Neumark ◆[1]	54	52.40 N	14.50 E
Neumarkt am Wallersee	64	47.57 N	13.14 E
Neumarkt im Hausruckkreis	60	48.16 N	13.45 E
Neumarkt in der Oberpfalz	60	49.16 N	11.28 E
Neumarkt in Steiermark	61	47.04 N	14.25 E
Neumarkt-Sankt Veit	60	48.22 N	12.30 E
Neumarkt → Tîrgu Mureș	38	46.33 N	24.33 E
Neumarkt → Tîrgu-Secuiesc	38	46.00 N	26.08 E
Neumünster	30	54.04 N	9.59 E
Neun ≃	110	19.42 N	104.03 E
Neunburg vorm Wald	60	49.21 N	12.24 E
Neundorf	54	51.49 N	11.34 E
Neung-sur-Beuvron	50	47.32 N	1.48 E
Neunkirchen, Dtsch.	56	50.32 N	8.06 E
Neunkirchen, Dtsch.	56	49.20 N	7.10 E
Neunkirchen, Dtsch.	56	50.48 N	8.00 E
Neunkirchen, Öst.	61	47.43 N	16.05 E
Neunkirchen am Brand	60	49.37 N	11.08 E
Neunkirchen am Potzberg	56	49.30 N	7.29 E
Neunkirchen-Seelscheid	56	50.51 N	7.20 E
Neuötting	60	48.14 N	12.42 E
Neupetershain	54	51.36 N	14.09 E
Neuquén	252	38.57 S	68.04 W
Neuquén □[4]	254	39.00 S	70.00 W
Neuquén ≃	252	38.59 S	68.00 W
Neurara	252	24.10 S	68.29 W
Neuravensburg	58	47.38 N	9.46 E
Neureisenberg	264b	48.01 N	16.30 E
Neurode → Nowa Ruda	30	50.35 N	16.31 E
Neuruppin	54	52.55 N	12.48 E
Neusalza-Spremberg	54	51.02 N	14.32 E
Neusalz → Nowa Sól	30	51.48 N	15.44 E
Neu Sankt Johann	58	47.14 N	9.12 E
Neusatz → Novi Sad	38	45.15 N	19.50 E
Neuschottland → Nova Scotia □[4]	186	45.00 N	63.00 W
Neuschwanstein, Schloss ʋ	64	47.35 N	10.44 E
Neuse ≃	192	35.06 N	76.30 W
Neuseddin	264a	52.18 N	12.59 E
Neuseeland → New Zealand □[1]	172	41.00 S	174.00 E
Neusibirische Inseln → Novosibirskije ostrova II	74	75.00 N	142.00 E
Neusiedl am See	61	47.57 N	16.51 E
Neusiedler See (Fertő) ⊜	61	47.50 N	16.45 E
Neusohl → Banská Bystrica	30	48.44 N	19.07 E
Neusorg	60	49.56 N	11.58 E
Neuss	56	51.12 N	6.41 E
Neusserweyhe	263	51.13 N	6.39 E
Neustadt, On., Can.	212	44.05 N	81.00 W
Neustadt, Dtsch.	54	52.52 N	12.25 E
Neustadt, Dtsch.	54	51.01 N	14.13 E
Neustadt, Dtsch.	54	50.44 N	11.44 E
Neustadt, Dtsch.	56	50.51 N	9.07 E
Neustadt, Dtsch.	56	50.37 N	7.26 E
Neustadt ◆[8]	52	53.04 N	8.47 E
Neustadt am Rübenberge	52	52.30 N	9.28 E
Neustadt an der Aisch	56	49.34 N	10.37 E
Neustadt an der Donau	60	48.48 N	11.46 E
Neustadt an der Waldnaab	60	49.44 N	12.11 E
Neustadt an der Weinstrasse	56	49.21 N	8.08 E
Neustadt bei Coburg	56	50.19 N	11.07 E
Neustädter Bucht ⊂	54	54.02 N	10.50 E
Neustadt-Glewe	54	53.25 N	11.36 E
Neustadt in Holstein	54	54.06 N	10.48 E
Neustettin → Szczecinek	30	53.43 N	16.42 E
Neustift am Walde ◆[8]	264b	48.15 N	16.18 E
Neustift im Stubaital	64	47.07 N	11.19 E
Neustrelitz	54	53.21 N	13.04 E
Neu Töplitz	264a	52.27 N	12.54 E
Neutral Hills ⋏[2]	184	52.10 N	110.50 W
Neutraubling	60	48.59 N	12.12 E
Neutrebbin	54	52.40 N	14.13 E
Neu-Ulm	58	48.23 N	10.01 E
Neuve-Chapelle	50	50.35 N	2.47 E
Neuves-Maisons	58	48.37 N	6.06 E
Neuvic	32	45.23 N	2.16 E

PORTUGUÊS

Nome	Página	Lat.°′	Long.°′ W = Oeste
Neuville-aux-Bois	50	48.04 N	2.03 E
Neuville-de-Poitou	32	46.41 N	0.15 E
Neuville-en-Condroz	56	50.32 N	5.27 E
Neuville-lès-Dieppe	50	49.55 N	1.06 E
Neuville-sur-Oise	261	49.01 N	2.04 E
Neuville-sur-Saône	62	45.52 N	4.51 E
Neuvy-le-Roi	50	47.36 N	0.36 E
Neuvy-sur-Barangeon	50	47.19 N	2.15 E
Neuvy-sur-Loire	50	47.31 N	2.53 E
Neuwaldegg ◆[8]	264b	48.14 N	16.17 E
Neuwerk ◆[8]	263	51.13 N	6.28 E
Neuwerk I	52	53.55 N	8.30 E
Neuwied	56	50.25 N	7.27 E
Neuwiller-lès-Saverne	56	48.49 N	7.24 E
Neu Wulmstorf	52	53.28 N	9.48 E
Neuzelle	54	52.05 N	14.38 E
Neu Zittau	54	52.23 N	13.44 E
Neva ≃	265a	59.57 N	30.20 E
Névache	62	45.01 N	6.37 E
Nevada, Ia., U.S.	190	42.01 N	93.27 W
Nevada, Mo., U.S.	194	37.50 N	94.21 W
Nevada, Oh., U.S.	214	40.49 N	83.07 W
Nevada, Tx., U.S.	222	33.02 N	96.22 W
Nevada □[6]	226	39.16 N	121.01 W
Nevada □[3], U.S.	178	39.00 N	117.00 W
Nevada □[3], U.S.	204	39.00 N	117.00 W
Nevada, Sierra ⋏, Esp.	34	37.05 N	3.10 W
Nevada, Sierra ⋏, Ca., U.S.	204	38.00 N	119.15 W
Nevada City	226	39.15 N	121.00 W
Nevada Creek ≃	202	46.54 N	113.02 W
Nevado, Cerro ∧, Arg.	252	35.35 S	68.30 W
Nevado, Cerro ∧, Col.	246	3.59 N	74.04 W
Nevado de Colima, Parque Nacional del ♠	234	19.30 N	103.35 W
Nevado de Toluca, Parque Nacional ♠	234	19.10 N	99.44 W
Neval'cevo	86	58.38 N	81.53 E
Nevali	272c	19.01 N	73.07 E
Nevanka	88	56.30 N	98.54 E
Neve, Serra da ⋏	152	13.52 S	13.26 E
Nevel'	76	56.02 N	29.55 E
Nevel'sk	89	46.40 N	141.53 E
Nevel'skogo, proliv Ʉ	89	52.05 N	141.35 E
Nevendon	260	51.36 N	0.30 E
Never	89	53.58 N	124.05 E
Neverkino	80	52.47 N	46.44 E
Neverovo	80	55.07 N	44.24 E
Nevers	32	47.00 N	3.09 E
Neversink ≃	210	41.21 N	74.42 W
Neversink Reservoir ⊜[1]	210	41.48 N	74.42 W
Nevertire	166	31.52 S	147.39 E
Neves	256	22.51 S	43.06 W
Nevesinje	38	43.15 N	18.07 E
Nevėžis ≃	76	54.56 N	23.46 E
Nevežkino	80	53.07 N	43.19 E
Neviano	68	40.06 N	18.06 E
Neviano degli Arduini	64	44.35 N	10.19 E
Neviges	56	51.19 N	7.05 E
Neville Island	279b	40.31 N	80.08 W
Neville Island I	279b	40.31 N	80.08 W
Nevinnomyssk	84	44.38 N	41.56 E
Nevis I	238	17.10 N	62.34 W
Nevis ≃	46	56.50 N	5.00 W
Nevis, Ben ∧	46	56.48 N	5.01 W
Nevis, Loch ⊂	46	57.01 N	5.43 W
Nevjansk	86	57.32 N	60.13 E
Nevlunghamn	26	58.58 N	9.52 E
Nevon	88	58.07 N	102.49 E
Nevşehir	130	38.38 N	34.43 E
Nevşehir □[4]	130	38.50 N	34.40 E
Nevskoje	76	58.08 N	30.26 E
New ≃, Belize	232	18.22 N	88.24 W
New ≃, Guy.	246	3.23 N	57.36 W
New ≃, N.A.	204	33.08 N	115.44 W
New ≃, Eng., U.K.	260	51.40 N	0.01 W
New ≃, U.S.	192	38.10 N	81.12 W
New ≃, Az., U.S.	200	33.31 N	112.18 W
New ≃, Fl., U.S.	192	29.50 N	84.40 W
New ≃, Fl., U.S.	192	29.55 N	82.25 W
New ≃, N.C., U.S.	192	34.32 N	77.20 W
New ≃, S.C., U.S.	192	32.09 N	80.50 W
New ≃, Tn., U.S.	192	36.25 N	84.38 W
New, North Fork ≃	192	36.33 N	81.21 W
Newabāgam	272b	22.48 N	88.24 E
New Abbey	44	54.59 N	3.38 W
New Addington ◆[8]	260	51.21 N	0.01 W
Newala	154	10.56 S	39.18 E
New Albany, In., U.S.	218	38.17 N	85.49 W
New Albany, Ms., U.S.	194	34.29 N	89.00 W
New Albany, Oh., U.S.	214	40.05 N	82.49 W
New Albany, Pa., U.S.	210	41.36 N	76.27 W
New Albin	190	43.29 N	91.17 W
New Alexandria, Oh., U.S.	214	40.17 N	80.40 W
New Alexandria, Pa., U.S.	214	40.24 N	79.25 W
New Alexandria, Va., U.S.	284c	38.47 N	77.03 W
New Alfa	140	15.10 N	35.40 E
New Almaden	226	37.11 N	121.49 W
New Alresford	42	51.06 N	1.10 W
New Amsterdam	246	6.15 N	57.31 W
New Angledool	166	29.07 S	147.57 E
Newark, Ar., U.S.	194	35.42 N	91.26 W
Newark, Ca., U.S.	226	37.31 N	122.02 W
Newark, De., U.S.	208	39.41 N	75.45 W
Newark, Il., U.S.	216	41.32 N	88.35 W
Newark, Md., U.S.	208	38.15 N	75.17 W
Newark, Mo., U.S.	219	39.59 N	91.59 W
Newark, N.J., U.S.	210	40.44 N	74.10 W
Newark, N.Y., U.S.	210	43.02 N	77.05 W
Newark, Oh., U.S.	214	40.04 N	82.24 W
Newark, Tx., U.S.	222	33.00 N	97.29 W
Newark Bay ⊂, U.S.	276	40.39 N	74.09 W
Newark Bay ⊂, N.J., U.S.	276	40.40 N	74.08 W
Newark Bay Bridge ◆[5]	276	40.42 N	74.07 W
Newark International Airport ⊠	210	40.42 N	74.10 W
Newark Lake ⊜	204	39.41 N	115.44 W
Newark-on-Trent	42	53.05 N	0.49 W
Newark Slough ≃	282	37.31 N	122.05 W
Newark Valley	210	42.13 N	76.11 W
New Athens, Il., U.S.	219	38.19 N	89.52 W
New Athens, Oh., U.S.	214	40.11 N	80.59 W
New Augusta	194	31.12 N	89.02 W
Newaukum, North Fork ≃	224	46.36 N	122.51 W
Newaukum, South Fork ≃	224	46.36 N	122.51 W
Newaygo	190	43.25 N	85.48 W
New Baden, Il., U.S.	219	38.32 N	89.42 W
New Baden, Tx., U.S.	222	31.03 N	96.26 W
New Baltimore, Mi., U.S.	214	42.40 N	82.44 W
New Baltimore, N.Y., U.S.	210	42.26 N	73.47 W
New Bavaria	216	41.12 N	84.10 W
New Bedford, Ma., U.S.	207	41.38 N	70.56 W
New Bedford, Pa., U.S.	214	41.06 N	80.30 W
New Bedford ≃	42	52.35 N	0.20 E
Newberg	224	45.18 N	122.58 W
New Berlin, Il., U.S.	219	39.43 N	89.54 W
New Berlin, N.Y., U.S.	210	42.37 N	75.19 W
New Berlin, Pa., U.S.	210	40.53 N	76.59 W
New Berlin, Wi., U.S.	216	42.58 N	88.06 W
New Berlinville	208	40.20 N	75.38 W
Newbern, Al., U.S.	194	32.35 N	87.31 W
Newbern, Il., U.S.	219	39.01 N	90.20 W
New Bern, N.C., U.S.	192	35.06 N	77.02 W
Newbern, Tn., U.S.	194	36.06 N	89.15 W
Newberry, Fl., U.S.	192	29.38 N	82.36 W
Newberry, Mi., U.S.	190	46.21 N	85.30 W
Newberry, S.C., U.S.	192	34.16 N	81.37 W
Newbery, Aeroparque ⊠, Arg.	258	34.35 S	58.24 W
Newbery, Aeroparque ⊠, Arg.	288	34.35 S	58.24 W
New Bethlehem	214	41.00 N	79.19 W
Newbiggin-by-the-Sea	44	55.11 N	1.30 W
New Bight	238	24.19 N	75.24 W
New Bloomfield, Mo., U.S.	219	38.43 N	92.05 W
New Bloomfield, Pa., U.S.	208	40.25 N	77.11 W
New Bloomington	214	40.35 N	83.19 W
Newbold Island I	285	40.08 N	74.45 W
Newboro	212	44.39 N	76.19 W
Newboro Lake ⊜	212	44.38 N	76.20 W
Newborough, Austl.	169	38.11 S	146.17 E
Newborough, Wales, U.K.	44	53.09 N	4.22 W
New Boston, Il., U.S.	190	41.10 N	90.59 W
New Boston, Mi., U.S.	216	42.09 N	83.24 W
New Boston, Oh., U.S.	218	38.45 N	82.56 W
New Boston, Tx., U.S.	194	33.27 N	94.24 W
New Braintree	207	42.19 N	72.07 W
New Braunfels	196	29.42 N	98.07 W
New Bremen	216	40.26 N	84.22 W
Newbridge → Droichead Nua	48	53.11 N	6.48 W
Newbridge on Wye	42	52.13 N	3.27 W
New Brighton, N.Z.	172	43.31 S	172.44 E
New Brighton, Eng., U.K.	262	53.26 N	3.03 W
New Brighton, Pa., U.S.	214	40.43 N	80.18 W
New Brighton ◆[8]	276	40.38 N	74.06 W
New Britain, Ct., U.S.	207	41.39 N	72.46 W
New Britain, Pa., U.S.	208	40.18 N	75.11 W
New Britain I	164	6.00 S	150.00 E
New Britain Trench ✣[1]	14	6.00 S	153.00 E
New Brockton	194	31.23 N	85.55 W
Newbrook	182	54.19 N	112.57 W
New Brooklyn County Park ♠	285	39.43 N	74.57 W
New Brunswick, In., U.S.	218	39.57 N	86.31 W
New Brunswick, N.J., U.S.	208	40.29 N	74.27 W
New Brunswick □[4], Can.	176	46.30 N	66.15 W
New Brunswick □[4], Can.	186	46.30 N	66.15 W
New Buffalo, Mi., U.S.	216	41.47 N	86.44 W
New Buffalo, Pa., U.S.	208	40.27 N	76.58 W
New Buildings	48	54.57 N	7.21 W
New Bullards Bar Lake ⊜[1]	226	39.25 N	121.08 W
Newburg, Mo., U.S.	194	37.54 N	91.54 W
Newburg, Pa., U.S.	208	40.08 N	77.32 W
Newburg, Pa., U.S.	214	40.31 N	78.25 W
Newburgh, On., Can.	212	44.19 N	76.52 W
Newburgh, Eng., U.K.	262	53.35 N	2.47 W
Newburgh, Scot., U.K.	46	57.18 N	2.00 W
Newburgh, Scot., U.K.	46	56.20 N	3.15 W
Newburgh, In., U.S.	194	37.56 N	87.24 W
Newburgh, N.Y., U.S.	210	41.30 N	74.00 W
Newburgh Heights	279a	41.27 N	81.39 W
Newburn	44	54.59 N	1.43 W
Newbury, On., Can.	214	42.41 N	81.48 W
Newbury, Eng., U.K.	42	51.25 N	1.20 W
Newbury, Ma., U.S.	207	42.49 N	70.53 W
Newbury Old Town	207	42.46 N	70.51 W
Newbury Park	228	34.11 N	118.53 W
Newburyport	207	42.48 N	70.52 W
Newby	44	54.20 N	0.28 W
Newby Bridge	44	54.16 N	2.58 W
New Caledonia (Nouvelle-Calédonie) □[2], Oc.	14	21.30 S	165.30 E
New Caledonia (Nouvelle-Calédonie) □[2], Oc.	175f	21.30 S	165.30 E
New Caledonia Basin ✣[1]	14	30.00 S	165.00 E
New Canaan	207	41.08 N	73.29 W
New Canada ◆[8]	273d	26.13 S	27.57 E
New Caney	222	30.09 N	95.13 W
New Canton	219	39.38 N	91.06 W
New-Carlisle, P.Q., Can.	186	48.01 N	65.20 W
New Carlisle, In., U.S.	216	41.42 N	86.30 W
New Carlisle, Oh., U.S.	218	39.56 N	84.01 W
New Carrollton	284c	38.58 N	76.52 W
New Cassel	276	40.45 N	73.34 W
Newcastle, Austl.	170	32.56 S	151.46 E
Newcastle, N.B., Can.	186	47.00 N	65.34 W
Newcastle, On., Can.	212	43.55 N	78.35 W
Newcastle, Ire.	48	52.16 N	7.48 W
Newcastle, S. Afr.	158	27.49 S	29.55 E
Newcastle, Eng., U.K.	42	52.26 N	3.06 W
Newcastle, N. Ire., U.K.	48	54.12 N	5.54 W
Newcastle, Ca., U.S.	226	38.53 N	121.08 W
New Castle, Co., U.S.	200	39.34 N	107.32 W
New Castle, De., U.S.	208	39.39 N	75.34 W
New Castle, In., U.S.	218	39.55 N	85.22 W
New Castle, Ky., U.S.	218	38.26 N	85.10 W
Newcastle, Ne., U.S.	198	42.33 N	96.42 W
Newcastle, Oh., U.S.	214	40.20 N	82.10 W
Newcastle, Ok., U.S.	196	35.15 N	97.36 W
New Castle, Pa., U.S.	214	41.00 N	80.20 W
Newcastle, Tx., U.S.	196	33.11 N	98.44 W
New Castle, Va., U.S.	192	37.30 N	80.06 W
Newcastle, Wy., U.S.	198	43.51 N	104.12 W
New Castle □[6]	208	39.44 N	75.33 W
Newcastle Airport ⊠	44	55.03 N	1.43 W
Newcastle Bay ⊂	164	10.50 S	142.37 E
Newcastle Bight ⊂[3]	170	32.51 S	151.54 E
Newcastle Creek ≃	164	17.20 S	133.23 E
Newcastle Emlyn	42	52.02 N	4.28 W
Newcastle Mine	182	51.28 N	112.46 W
Newcastleton	44	55.11 N	2.49 W
Newcastle-under-Lyme	44	53.00 N	2.14 W
Newcastle upon Tyne	44	54.59 N	1.35 W
Newcastle Waters	162	17.24 S	133.24 E
Newcastle West	48	52.27 N	9.03 W
New Centerville	285	40.04 N	75.26 W
Newcestown	48	51.47 N	8.51 W
New Chicago	216	41.34 N	87.16 W
Newchurch, Wales, U.K.	42	52.09 N	3.08 W
New Church, Va., U.S.	208	37.59 N	75.32 W
New City	210	41.08 N	73.59 W
Newclare ◆[8]	273d	26.11 S	27.58 E
New Columbia	210	41.02 N	76.52 W
New Columbus	210	41.10 N	76.18 W
Newcomerstown	214	40.16 N	81.36 W
New Concord	188	39.59 N	81.44 W
New Corydon	216	40.34 N	84.51 W
New Croton Aqueduct ≊[1]	276	41.11 N	73.49 W
New Croton Reservoir ⊜[1]	210	41.14 N	73.46 W
New Cumberland, Pa., U.S.	208	40.13 N	76.53 W
New Cumberland, W.V., U.S.	214	40.29 N	80.36 W
New Cumberland Dam ◆[6]	214	40.32 N	80.37 W
New Cumnock	44	55.24 N	4.12 W
New Dayton	182	49.25 N	112.23 W
New Deer	46	57.30 N	2.12 W
Newdegate	162	33.06 S	119.01 E
New Delhi, India	124	28.36 N	77.12 E
New Delhi, India	272a	28.36 N	77.12 E
New Delhi Railroad Station ◆[5]	272a	28.39 N	77.13 E
New Denver	182	49.59 N	117.22 W
New Derry	214	40.21 N	79.19 W
New Dundee	212	43.21 N	80.31 W
New Eagle	214	40.12 N	79.56 W
New Edinburg	194	33.45 N	92.14 W
New Effington	198	45.51 N	96.55 W
New Egypt	208	40.04 N	74.31 W
Newell, Ia., U.S.	198	42.36 N	95.00 W
Newell, S.D., U.S.	198	44.42 N	103.25 W
Newell, W.V., U.S.	214	40.37 N	80.36 W
Newell, Lake ⊜, Austl.	162	24.50 S	126.10 E
Newell, Lake ⊜, Ab., Can.	182	50.25 N	111.56 W
New Ellenton	192	33.25 N	81.41 W
Newellton	194	32.04 N	91.14 W
New Eltham ◆[8]	260	51.26 N	0.04 E
New England	198	46.32 N	102.52 W
New England National Park ♠	166	30.30 S	152.15 E
New England Range ⋏	166	30.00 S	151.50 E
Newenham, Cape ≻	180	58.37 N	162.12 W
Newent	42	51.56 N	2.24 W
New Enterprise	214	40.10 N	78.25 W
New Ermelo	158	26.32 S	30.02 E
New Falconwood	284a	42.59 N	78.58 W
Newfane, N.Y., U.S.	210	43.17 N	78.42 W
Newfane, Vt., U.S.	188	42.59 N	72.39 W
New Ferry	262	53.22 N	2.59 W
Newfield, N.J., U.S.	208	39.32 N	75.01 W
Newfield, N.Y., U.S.	210	42.22 N	76.35 W
Newfield Pond ⊜	283	42.38 N	71.22 W
New Florence, Mo., U.S.	219	38.54 N	91.26 W
New Florence, Pa., U.S.	214	40.22 N	79.04 W
New Forest ◆[3]	42	50.53 N	1.35 W
New Fork ≃	200	42.33 N	109.58 W
Newfound Gap)(	192	35.37 N	83.25 W
Newfoundland, N.J., U.S.	276	40.44 N	74.29 W
Newfoundland, Pa., U.S.	210	41.19 N	75.19 W
Newfoundland □[4]	176	52.00 N	56.00 W
Newfoundland I	186	48.30 N	56.00 W
Newfoundland Basin ✣[1]	8	45.00 N	40.00 W
Newfoundland Ridge ✣[3]	8	40.30 N	48.00 W
New Franklin	194	39.01 N	92.44 W
New Freedom	208	39.44 N	76.42 W
New Galilee	214	40.50 N	80.24 W
New Galloway	44	55.05 N	4.10 W
New Garden	285	39.49 N	75.45 W
Newgate	182	49.00 N	115.10 W
Newgate Street	260	51.44 N	0.07 W
New Georgia I	175e	8.15 S	157.30 E
New Georgia Group II	175e	8.30 S	157.20 E
New Georgia Sound Ʉ	175e	8.00 S	158.10 E
New Germantown	208	40.18 N	77.34 W
New Germany	186	44.33 N	64.43 W
New Glarus	190	42.48 N	89.38 W
New Glasgow	186	45.35 N	62.39 W
New Gretna	208	39.35 N	74.27 W
New Guinea I	164	5.00 S	140.00 E
Newgulf	222	29.16 N	95.54 W
Newhalem	224	48.40 N	121.14 W
Newhalen	180	59.43 N	154.54 W
Newhall, Eng., U.K.	42	52.48 N	1.34 W
Newhall, Ca., U.S.	228	34.23 N	118.31 W
Newham ◆[8]	42	51.32 N	0.03 E
New Hamburg, On., Can.	212	43.23 N	80.42 W
New Hamburg, N.Y., U.S.	210	41.35 N	73.57 W
New Hampshire	216	40.33 N	83.57 W
New Hampshire □[3], U.S.	178	43.35 N	71.40 W
New Hampshire □[3], U.S.	188	43.35 N	71.40 W
New Hampton, Ia., U.S.	190	43.03 N	92.19 W
New Hampton, N.Y., U.S.	210	41.25 N	74.24 W
New Hanover, S. Afr.	158	29.28 S	30.28 E
New Hanover, Il., U.S.	219	38.23 N	90.13 W
New Hanover I	164	2.30 S	150.15 E
New Harmony	194	38.07 N	87.56 W
New Hartford, Ct., U.S.	207	41.52 N	72.58 W
New Hartford, Ia., U.S.	190	42.34 N	92.37 W
New Hartford, Mo., U.S.	219	39.12 N	91.16 W
New Hartford, N.Y., U.S.	210	43.04 N	75.18 W
Newhaven, Eng., U.K.	42	50.47 N	0.03 E
New Haven, Ct., U.S.	207	41.18 N	72.56 W
New Haven, Il., U.S.	194	37.54 N	88.07 W
New Haven, In., U.S.	216	41.04 N	85.00 W
New Haven, Ky., U.S.	194	37.39 N	85.35 W
New Haven, Mi., U.S.	214	42.43 N	82.48 W
New Haven, Mo., U.S.	219	38.36 N	91.13 W
New Haven, N.Y., U.S.	212	43.29 N	76.19 W
New Haven, Oh., U.S.	214	41.02 N	82.41 W
New Haven, W.V., U.S.	188	38.59 N	81.58 W
New Haven □[6]	207	41.18 N	72.56 W
New Hazelton	182	55.15 N	127.35 W
New Hebrides II	175f	16.00 S	167.00 E
New Hebrides Trench ✣[1]	14	22.30 S	170.00 E
New Hebrides → Vanuatu □[1]	175f	16.00 S	167.00 E
Newhebron	194	31.44 N	89.58 W
New Hempstead	276	41.08 N	74.03 W
New Hey	262	53.36 N	2.06 W
New Hogan Lake ⊜[1]	226	38.09 N	120.48 W
New Holland, Eng., U.K.	44	53.42 N	0.22 W
New Holland, Il., U.S.	219	40.11 N	89.36 W
New Holland, Oh., U.S.	218	39.33 N	83.15 W
New Holland, Pa., U.S.	208	40.06 N	76.05 W
New Holstein	190	43.57 N	88.05 W
New Hope, Al., U.S.	194	34.32 N	86.23 W
New Hope, Pa., U.S.	208	40.21 N	74.57 W
New Hudson	281	42.30 N	83.36 W
New Hyde Park	276	40.44 N	73.41 W
New Hythe	260	51.19 N	0.27 E
New Iberia	194	30.00 N	91.49 W
Newick	42	50.58 N	0.01 E
Newington, On., Can.	206	45.07 N	75.01 W
Newington, Eng., U.K.	42	51.05 N	1.08 E
Newington, Eng., U.K.	260	51.21 N	0.40 E
Newington, Ct., U.S.	207	41.42 N	72.43 W
Newinn	48	52.26 N	7.53 W
New Ipswich	207	42.44 N	71.51 W
New Ireland □[5]	164	3.00 S	151.30 E
New Ireland I	164	3.20 S	152.00 E
New Island I	126	21.31 N	88.12 E
New Jersey □[3], U.S.	178	40.15 N	74.30 W
New Jersey □[3], U.S.	188	40.15 N	74.30 W
New Jersey Institute of Technology ʋ[2]	276	40.45 N	74.11 W
New Johnsonville	194	36.01 N	87.58 W
New Kensington	214	40.34 N	79.45 W
New Kent	208	37.31 N	76.58 W
New Kent □[6]	208	37.30 N	77.00 W
New Kingstown	208	40.13 N	77.07 W
Newkirk	196	36.52 N	97.03 W
Newkirk Estates	285	39.42 N	75.36 W
New Knoxville	216	40.29 N	84.18 W
New Kowloon (Xinjiulong)	271d	22.20 N	114.10 E
New Lagos ◆[8]	273a	6.30 N	3.22 E
New Lake ⊜	192	35.38 N	76.20 W
Newland	192	36.05 N	81.55 W
Newland Head ≻	168b	35.39 S	138.31 E
Newland Range ⋏	162	27.53 S	123.58 E
Newlands	166	21.11 S	147.54 E
Newlands ◆[8]	273d	26.11 S	27.58 E
New Lane	262	53.37 N	2.52 W
New Lebanon, N.Y., U.S.	210	42.27 N	73.23 W
New Lebanon, Oh., U.S.	218	39.45 N	84.23 W
New Lebanon, Pa., U.S.	214	41.25 N	80.04 W
New Lebanon Center	210	42.28 N	73.25 W
New Leipzig	198	46.22 N	101.56 W
New Lenox	216	41.30 N	87.57 W
New Lexington	188	39.42 N	82.12 W
New Liberty	218	38.36 N	84.54 W
New Lisbon	190	43.52 N	90.09 W
New Liskeard	190	47.30 N	79.40 W
Newllano	194	31.06 N	93.16 W
New London, Ct., U.S.	207	41.21 N	72.07 W
New London, Ia., U.S.	190	40.55 N	91.23 W
New London, Mn., U.S.	198	45.18 N	94.56 W
New London, Mo., U.S.	219	39.35 N	91.24 W
New London, N.H., U.S.	188	43.24 N	71.59 W
New London, Oh., U.S.	214	41.05 N	82.24 W
New London, Pa., U.S.	208	39.47 N	75.52 W
New London, Tx., U.S.	222	32.15 N	94.56 W
New London, Wi., U.S.	190	44.23 N	88.44 W
New London □[6]	207	41.21 N	72.07 W
New London Submarine Base ■	207	41.24 N	72.05 W
New Longton	262	53.44 N	2.45 W
Newlonsburg	279b	40.25 N	79.40 W
New Lyme	214	41.36 N	80.47 W
Newlyn, Austl.	169	37.25 S	143.59 E
Newlyn, Eng., U.K.	42	50.06 N	5.33 W
Newlyn East	42	50.22 N	5.03 W
Newmachar	46	57.16 N	2.11 W
New Machavie	158	26.48 S	26.57 E
New Madison	218	39.58 N	84.42 W
New Madrid	194	36.35 N	89.31 W
Newmains	44	55.47 N	3.53 W
Newman, Austl.	162	23.20 S	119.46 E
Newman, Ca., U.S.	226	37.18 N	121.01 W
Newman, Il., U.S.	194	39.47 N	87.59 W
Newman, Mount ∧	162	23.16 S	119.33 E
New Manchester	214	40.31 N	80.34 W
Newman Grove	198	41.45 N	97.46 W
Newmanstown	208	40.20 N	76.12 W
Newmansville	219	40.00 N	90.01 W
New Marion	218	39.00 N	85.22 W
Newmarket, Austl.	171a	27.25 S	153.01 E
Newmarket, On., Can.	212	44.03 N	79.28 W
Newmarket, Ire.	48	52.13 N	9.00 W
Newmarket, S. Afr.	273d	26.17 S	28.08 E
Newmarket, Eng., U.K.	42	52.15 N	0.25 E
New Market, Al., U.S.	194	34.54 N	86.25 W
New Market, Ia., U.S.	198	40.43 N	94.53 W
New Market, Md., U.S.	208	39.22 N	77.16 W
Newmarket, N.H., U.S.	188	43.04 N	70.56 W
New Market, N.J., U.S.	276	40.34 N	74.27 W
New Market, Va., U.S.	188	38.39 N	78.40 W
Newmarket on Fergus	48	52.45 N	8.53 W
Newmarket Race Course ♠	273d	26.17 S	28.08 E
New Marske	44	54.34 N	1.02 W
New Martinsville	188	39.38 N	80.51 W
New Meadows	202	44.58 N	116.16 W
New Melle	219	38.42 N	90.52 W
New Melones Lake ⊜[1]	226	38.00 N	120.32 W
New Memphis	219	38.29 N	89.41 W
New Mexico □[3]	178	34.30 N	106.00 W
New Miami	218	39.26 N	84.32 W
New Middletown	214	40.58 N	80.34 W
New Milford, Ct., U.S.	207	41.34 N	73.24 W
New Milford, Il., U.S.	216	42.11 N	89.04 W
New Milford, N.J., U.S.	276	40.56 N	74.01 W
New Milford, Pa., U.S.	210	41.52 N	75.43 W
New Millpond ⊜	276	40.50 N	73.13 W
New Millport	214	40.54 N	78.32 W
New Mills	44	53.23 N	2.00 W
Newmilns	46	55.37 N	4.20 W
New Milton	42	50.44 N	1.40 W
New Minden	219	38.26 N	89.22 W
New Munster	216	42.34 N	88.13 W
Newnan	192	33.22 N	84.47 W
Newnans Lake ⊜	192	29.39 N	82.13 W
Newnham	42	51.49 N	2.27 W
New Norcia	162	30.58 S	116.13 E
New Norfolk	166	42.47 S	147.03 E
New Norway	182	52.53 N	112.58 W
New Orleans	194	29.57 N	90.04 W
New Orleans Naval Air Station ■	194	29.51 N	90.01 W
New Oxford	208	39.51 N	77.03 W
New Palestine	218	39.43 N	85.53 W
New Paltz	210	41.44 N	74.05 W
New Paris, In., U.S.	216	41.30 N	85.49 W
New Paris, Oh., U.S.	218	39.51 N	84.47 W
New Paris, Pa., U.S.	214	40.06 N	78.39 W
New Philadelphia, Oh., U.S.	214	40.30 N	81.27 W
New Philadelphia, Pa., U.S.	208	40.43 N	76.06 W
New Pine Creek	202	41.59 N	120.17 W

English	Deutsch	Español	Français	Português
≃ River	Fluß	Río	Rivière	Rio
≊ Canal	Kanal	Canal	Canal	Canal
⌞ Waterfall, Rapids	Wasserfall, Stromschnellen	Cascada, Rápidos	Chute d'eau, Rapides	Cascata, Rápidos
Ʉ Strait	Meeresstraße	Estrecho	Détroit	Estreito
⊂ Bay, Gulf	Bucht, Golf	Bahía, Golfo	Baie, Golfe	Baía, Golfo
⊜ Lake, Lakes	See, Seen	Lago, Lagos	Lac, Lacs	Lago, Lagos
⋮⋮ Swamp	Sumpf	Pantano	Marais	Pântano
⊓ Ice Features, Glacier	Eis- und Gletscherformen	Accidentes Glaciales	Formes glaciaires	Acidentes glaciares
⊤ Other Hydrographic Features	Andere Hydrographische Objekte	Otros Elementos Hidrográficos	Autres données hydrographiques	Outros acidentes hidrográficos
✣ Submarine Features	Untermeerische Objekte	Accidentes Submarinos	Formes de relief sous-marin	Acidentes submarinos
□ Political Unit	Politische Einheit	Unidad Politica	Entité politique	Unidade política
ʋ Cultural Institution	Kulturelle Institution	Institución Cultural	Institution culturelle	Institução cultural
⊥ Historical Site	Historische Stätte	Sitio Histórico	Site historique	Sitio histórico
♠ Recreational Site	Erholungs- und Ferienort	Sitio de Recreo	Centre de loisirs	Area de Lazer
⊠ Airport	Flughafen	Aeropuerto	Aéroport	Aeroporto
■ Military Installation	Militäranlage	Instalación Militar	Installation militaire	Instalação militar
◆ Miscellaneous	Verschiedenes	Misceláneo	Divers	Diversos

ENGLISH

Name	Page	Lat.°′	Long.°′
New Pitsligo	46	57.35 N	2.11 W
New Pittsburg	214	40.50 N	82.06 W
New Plymouth, N.Z.	172	39.04 S	174.05 E
New Plymouth, Id., U.S.	202	43.58 N	116.49 W
New Point	218	39.18 N	85.19 W
New Point Comfort ≻	208	37.18 N	76.17 W
Newport, Austl.	274a	33.40 S	151.19 E
Newport, Austl.	274b	37.51 S	144.53 E
Newport, P.Q., Can.	186	48.16 N	64.45 W
Newport, Ire.	48	52.42 N	8.24 W
Newport, Ire.	48	53.53 N	9.34 W
Newport, Eng., U.K.	42	50.42 N	1.18 W
Newport, Eng., U.K.	42	52.47 N	2.22 W
Newport, Eng., U.K.	42	51.59 N	0.15 E
Newport, Wales, U.K.	42	52.01 N	4.51 W
Newport, Wales, U.K.	42	51.35 N	3.00 W
Newport, Ar., U.S.	194	35.36 N	91.16 W
Newport, De., U.S.	208	39.42 N	75.36 W
Newport, In., U.S.	194	39.53 N	87.24 W
Newport, Ky., U.S.	218	39.05 N	84.29 W
Newport, Me., U.S.	188	44.50 N	69.16 W
Newport, Md., U.S.	208	38.25 N	76.54 W
Newport, Mi., U.S.	216	42.00 N	83.18 W
Newport, N.H., U.S.	188	43.21 N	72.10 W
Newport, N.J., U.S.	208	39.17 N	75.10 W
Newport, N.Y., U.S.	210	43.11 N	75.00 W
Newport, N.C., U.S.	192	34.47 N	76.51 W
Newport, Oh., U.S.	216	39.23 N	81.13 W
Newport, Or., U.S.	202	44.38 N	124.03 W
Newport, Pa., U.S.	208	40.28 N	77.07 W
Newport, R.I., U.S.	207	41.29 N	71.18 W
Newport, Tn., U.S.	192	35.58 N	83.11 W
Newport, Vt., U.S.	206	44.56 N	72.12 W
Newport, Wa., U.S.	202	48.11 N	117.02 W
Newport □[6]	207	41.35 N	71.15 W
Newport Bay c	208	38.14 N	75.13 W
Newport Beach	228	33.37 N	117.55 W
Newport Center	206	44.57 N	72.18 W
Newport Hills	224	47.32 N	122.10 W
Newport News	208	36.58 N	76.25 W
Newport-on-Tay	46	56.26 N	2.55 W
Newport Pagnell	42	52.05 N	0.44 W
New Port Richey	220	28.14 N	82.43 W
Newportville	285	40.09 N	74.53 W
Newportville Terrace	285	40.07 N	74.54 W
New Prague	190	44.32 N	93.34 W
New Preston	207	41.40 N	73.21 W
New Providence, N.J., U.S.	210	40.41 N	74.24 W
New Providence, Pa., U.S.	208	39.56 N	76.12 W
New Providence, Tn., U.S.	194	36.32 N	87.23 W
New Providence I	240b	25.02 N	77.24 W
Newquay, Eng., U.K.	42	50.25 N	5.05 W
New Quay, Wales, U.K.	42	52.13 N	4.22 W
New Redruth	273d	26.16 S	28.07 E
New Richland	190	43.53 N	93.29 W
New-Richmond, P.Q., Can.	186	48.10 N	65.52 W
New Richmond, Oh., U.S.	218	38.56 N	84.16 W
New Richmond, Wi., U.S.	190	45.07 N	92.32 W
New Riegel	214	41.03 N	83.19 W
New Rim Ditch ≡	228	35.08 N	118.58 W
New Ringgold	208	40.41 N	76.00 W
New Road	186	44.45 N	63.28 W
New Roads	194	30.42 N	91.26 W
New Rochelle	210	40.54 N	73.46 W
New Rockford	198	47.40 N	99.08 W
New Romney	42	50.59 N	0.57 E
New Ross, N.S., Can.	186	44.44 N	64.27 W
New Ross, Ire.	48	52.24 N	6.56 W
New Rossington	44	53.29 N	1.04 W
Newry, N. Ire., U.K.	48	54.11 N	6.20 W
Newry, Pa., U.S.	214	40.24 N	78.26 W
Newry, S.C., U.S.	192	34.43 N	82.54 W
New Salem, In., U.S.	218	39.32 N	85.22 W
New Salem, N.D., U.S.	198	46.50 N	101.24 W
New Salisbury	218	38.19 N	86.06 W
New Sarum → Salisbury	42	51.05 N	1.48 W
New Schwabenland ◆[1]	9	72.30 S	1.00 E
New Scone	46	56.25 N	3.24 W
Newsham Park ♠	262	53.25 N	2.56 W
New Sharon	190	41.28 N	92.39 W
New Sheffield	214	40.36 N	80.17 W
New Shrewsbury	276	40.19 N	74.04 W
New Siberian Islands → Novosibirskoje ostrova II	74	75.00 N	142.00 E
New Smyrna Beach	220	29.01 N	80.55 W
Newsome	222	32.59 N	95.08 W
Newsoms	208	36.37 N	77.07 W
New South Wales □[3]	166	33.00 S	146.00 E
New South Wales, University of ʊ[2]	274a	33.55 S	151.14 E
New South Wales Lawn Tennis Association Courts ♠	274a	33.53 S	151.14 E
New Springfield	214	40.55 N	80.36 W
New Square	276	41.08 N	74.02 W
New Stanton	214	40.13 N	79.37 W
Newstead	169	37.07 S	144.04 E
New Stuyahok	180	59.29 N	157.20 W
New Suffolk	207	41.00 N	72.28 W
New Summerfield	222	31.59 N	95.06 W
New Tazewell	192	36.27 N	83.33 W
New Terrell City Lake ⊜[1]	222	32.44 N	96.14 W
New Territories □[8]	271d	22.24 N	114.10 E
New Thunderchild Indian Reserve ◆[4]	184	53.30 N	108.50 W
Newtok	180	60.56 N	164.38 W
Newton, Eng., U.K.	44	53.57 N	2.27 W
Newton, Eng., U.K.	262	53.16 N	2.43 W
Newton, Ga., U.S.	192	31.18 N	84.20 W
Newton, Il., U.S.	194	38.59 N	88.09 W
Newton, Ia., U.S.	190	41.41 N	93.02 W
Newton, Ks., U.S.	198	38.02 N	97.20 W
Newton, Ma., U.S.	207	42.20 N	71.12 W
Newton, Ms., U.S.	194	32.19 N	89.09 W
Newton, N.J., U.S.	210	41.03 N	74.45 W
Newton, N.C., U.S.	192	35.40 N	81.13 W
Newton, Tx., U.S.	194	30.50 N	93.45 W
Newton □[6]	216	40.46 N	87.27 W
Newton Abbot	42	50.32 N	3.36 W
Newton Arlosh	44	54.53 N	3.15 W
Newton Aycliffe	44	54.36 N	1.32 W
Newton Brook ◆[8]	275b	43.48 N	79.24 W
Newton Center	283	42.20 N	71.12 W
Newton Falls, N.Y., U.S.	188	44.12 N	74.59 W
Newton Falls, Oh., U.S.	214	41.11 N	80.58 W
Newton Ferrers	42	50.18 N	4.02 W
Newton Flotman	42	52.32 N	1.16 E
Newton Hamilton	214	40.24 N	77.51 W
Newton Highlands	283	42.19 N	71.13 W
Newton-le-Willows	44	53.28 N	2.37 W
Newton Longville	42	51.58 N	0.46 W
Newton Lower Falls	283	42.19 N	71.23 W
Newtonmore	46	57.04 N	4.08 W
Newton Stewart	44	54.57 N	4.29 W
Newtonsville	218	39.11 N	84.05 W
Newton Upper Falls	283	42.19 N	71.13 W
Newtonville, On., Can.	212	43.56 N	78.30 W
Newtonville, Ma., U.S.	283	42.21 N	71.13 W
Newtonville, N.J., U.S.	208	39.33 N	74.51 W
New Toronto ◆[8]	275b	43.36 N	79.30 W
Newtown, Austl.	169	38.09 S	144.20 E
Newtown, Nf., Can.	186	49.12 N	53.31 W
Newtown, Eng., U.K.	262	53.21 N	2.00 W
Newtown, Wales, U.K.	42	52.32 N	3.19 W
Newtown, Ct., U.S.	207	41.24 N	73.18 W
Newtown, In., U.S.	216	40.12 N	87.08 W
Newtown, Ky., U.S.	218	38.13 N	84.57 W
New Town, N.D., U.S.	198	47.58 N	102.29 W
Newtown, Pa., U.S.	208	40.14 N	74.56 W
Newtown ◆[8]	274a	33.54 S	151.11 E
Newtownabbey	48	54.42 N	5.54 W
Newtownards	48	54.36 N	5.41 W
Newtownbutler	48	54.12 N	7.23 W
Newtown Creek ≃, N.Y., U.S.	276	40.44 N	73.58 W
Newtown Creek ≃, Pa., U.S.	285	40.13 N	74.56 W
Newtown Crommelin	48	54.59 N	6.13 W
Newtown Forbes	48	53.46 N	7.50 W
Newtownhamilton	48	54.12 N	6.35 W
Newtown Mount Kennedy	48	53.05 N	6.07 W
Newtown Saint Boswells	46	55.34 N	2.40 W
Newtown Square	208	39.59 N	75.24 W
Newtownstewart	48	54.43 N	7.24 W
New Tredegar	42	51.43 N	3.14 W
New Tripoli	208	40.41 N	75.45 W
New Troy	216	41.53 N	86.33 W
New Truxton	219	38.58 N	91.15 W
New Ulm, Mn., U.S.	190	44.18 N	94.27 W
New Ulm, Tx., U.S.	222	29.53 N	96.29 W
New Utrecht ◆[8]	276	40.36 N	73.59 W
New Vernon	276	40.45 N	74.30 W
New Vienna	218	39.19 N	83.41 W
Newville, In., U.S.	216	41.21 N	84.51 W
Newville, Pa., U.S.	208	40.10 N	77.23 W
New Vineyard	188	44.48 N	70.07 W
New Waltham	44	53.32 N	0.04 W
New Washington, Pil.	116	11.39 N	122.26 E
New Washington, In., U.S.	218	38.33 N	85.32 W
New Washington, Oh., U.S.	214	40.57 N	82.51 W
New Waterford, N.S., Can.	186	46.15 N	60.05 W
New Waterford, Oh., U.S.	214	40.50 N	80.36 W
New Waverly, In., U.S.	216	40.46 N	86.12 W
New Waverly, Tx., U.S.	222	30.32 N	95.29 W
New Westminster	224	49.12 N	122.55 W
New Whiteland	218	39.33 N	86.05 W
New Wilmington	214	41.07 N	80.19 W
New Windsor, Md., U.S.	208	39.32 N	77.06 W
New Windsor, N.Y., U.S.	210	41.30 N	74.01 W
New Windsor → Windsor	42	51.29 N	0.38 W
New Woodbine Racetrack ♠	275b	43.43 N	79.36 W
New Woodstock	210	42.50 N	75.51 W
New World Island I	186	49.35 N	54.40 W
New Year Creek ≃	222	30.08 N	96.12 W
New York, N.Y., U.S.	210	40.43 N	74.01 W
New York, N.Y., U.S.	276	40.43 N	74.01 W
New York □[6]	276	40.47 N	73.58 W
New York □[3], U.S.	178	43.00 N	75.00 W
New York □[3], U.S.	188	43.00 N	75.00 W
New York, City College of ʊ[2]	276	40.49 N	73.57 W
New York, Polytechnic Institute of ʊ[2]	276	40.42 N	73.59 W
New York, State University of (Stony Brook) ʊ[2], N.Y., U.S.	276	40.55 N	73.08 W
New York, State University of (Buffalo) ʊ[2], N.Y., U.S.	284a	42.57 N	78.49 W
New York, State University of, College at Buffalo ʊ[2]	284a	42.56 N	78.53 W
New York at Buffalo, State University of ʊ[2]	284a	42.56 N	78.49 W
New York Mills, Mn., U.S.	198	46.31 N	95.22 W
New York Mills, N.Y., U.S.	210	43.06 N	75.18 W
New York State Barge Canal ≡	210	43.05 N	78.43 W
New York Stock Exchange ʊ	276	40.42 N	74.01 W
New Zealand □[1]	172	41.00 S	174.00 E
Nexapa ≃	234	18.07 N	98.46 W
Nexon	32	45.41 N	1.11 E
Ney	216	41.23 N	84.32 W
Neyagawa	96	34.46 N	135.38 E
Neye	263	51.07 N	7.22 E
Neyestausee ⊜[1]	263	51.08 N	7.24 E
Ney Lake ⊜	184	54.38 N	92.25 W
Neyland	42	51.43 N	4.57 W
Neylandville	222	33.12 N	96.00 W
Neyrīz	128	29.12 N	54.19 E
Neyshābūr	128	36.12 N	58.50 E
Neyyāttinkara	122	8.24 N	77.05 E
Nezahualcóyotl	234	19.27 N	99.03 W
Nezahualcóyotl, Presa ⊜[1]	234	17.10 N	93.40 W
Nezamajevskaja	78	46.09 N	40.16 E
Nezameno-toko ♠	94	35.46 N	137.42 E
Nežárka ≃	61	49.11 N	14.41 E
Nezavertajlovka	78	46.37 N	29.56 E
Nežin	78	51.03 N	31.54 E
Nezlobnaja	84	44.08 N	43.23 E
Neznanka ≃	265b	55.34 N	37.21 E
Neznanovo	80	54.02 N	40.06 E
Nezperce	202	46.14 N	116.14 W
Nez Perce Indian Reservation ◆[4]	202	46.20 N	116.30 W
Nez Perce National Historical Park ♠	202	45.50 N	116.15 W
Nezpique, Bayou ≃	194	30.12 N	92.35 W
Nezvěstice	60	49.39 N	13.32 E
Ngabang	112	0.23 N	109.57 E
Ngabé	152	3.12 S	16.11 E
Ngabordamlu, Tanjung ≻	164	6.56 S	134.11 E
Ngadda ≃	146	12.40 N	13.50 E
Ngadirojo	115a	8.13 S	111.19 E
Ngadza	152	5.10 N	20.12 E
Ngahere	172	42.24 S	171.27 E
Ngala	146	12.20 N	14.10 E
Ngale	152	2.56 N	21.20 E
Ngali	152	2.27 S	19.20 E
Ngaliema, Baie de c	273b	4.19 S	15.16 E
Ngalipaeng	112	3.24 N	125.37 E
Ngaloa Harbour c	175g	19.06 S	178.11 E
Ngamaba	273b	4.14 S	15.16 E
Ngamba ◆[8]	273b	4.15 S	15.18 E
Ngambé	152	4.14 N	10.37 E
Ngamdu	146	11.48 N	12.18 E
Ngami, Lake ⊜	156	20.37 S	22.40 E
Ngamiland □[5]	156	19.09 S	22.47 E
Ngamo	154	19.08 S	27.32 E
Ngamouéri	273b	4.14 S	15.14 E
Ngamring	124	29.14 N	87.10 E
Nganda ∧	154	10.25 S	33.50 E
Ngangala	154	4.42 N	31.55 E
Ngangla Ringco ⊜	120	31.40 N	83.00 E
Nganglong Kangri ∧	120	32.45 N	81.12 E
Nganglong Kangri ⋏	120	32.00 N	83.00 E
Ngangzê Co ⊜	120	31.05 N	86.55 E
Nganjuk	115a	7.36 S	111.55 E
Ngao	110	18.46 N	99.59 E
Ngaoui, Mont ∧	152	6.40 N	14.57 E
Ngaoundéré	152	7.19 N	13.35 E
Ngapali	110	18.26 N	94.19 E
Ngapara	172	44.57 S	170.45 E
Ngape	110	20.04 N	94.38 E
Ngaputaw	110	16.32 N	94.42 E
Ngara	154	2.28 S	30.39 E
Ngaramasch	175b	6.54 N	134.08 E
Ngarimbi	154	8.28 S	38.36 E
Ngaruawahia	172	37.40 S	175.09 E
Ngaruroro ≃	172	39.34 S	176.56 E
Ngasamo	154	2.33 S	33.53 E
Ngat ≃	110	19.09 N	99.01 E
Ngatangiia	174k	21.14 S	159.43 W
Ngatangiia Harbour c	174k	21.14 S	159.45 W
Ngatea	172	37.17 S	175.30 E
Ngathainggyaung	110	17.24 N	95.05 E
Ngatik I[1]	14	5.51 N	157.16 E
Ngau I	175g	18.02 S	179.18 E
Ngauruhoe, Mount ∧	172	39.09 S	175.38 E
Ngau Tau Kok → Kwun Tong	271d	22.19 N	114.12 E
Ngawen	115a	7.00 S	111.18 E
Ngawi	115a	7.24 S	111.26 E
Ngay Nua	110	21.50 N	101.54 E
Ngebel	115a	7.46 S	111.37 E
Ngele	152	0.29 S	20.25 E
Ngemelis Islands II	175b	7.07 N	134.15 E
Ngerengere	154	6.45 S	38.07 E
Ngerkeel	175b	7.25 N	134.30 E
Ngermechau	175b	7.35 N	134.39 E
Ngeruktabel I	175b	7.15 N	134.24 E
Ngetbong	175b	7.37 N	134.35 E
Ngetera	146	12.31 N	12.38 E
Nggamea Island I	175g	16.46 S	179.46 W
Nggatokae Island I	175e	8.46 S	158.11 E
Nggela Pile I	175e	9.05 S	160.15 E
Nggela Sule I	175e	9.05 S	160.15 E
Nggelelevu I	175g	16.05 S	179.09 W
Nggwavuma ≃	158	26.58 S	32.17 E
Nghia Dan	110	19.18 N	105.26 E
Nghia Hanh	110	15.03 N	108.47 E
Nghia Lo	110	21.36 N	104.31 E
Ngiap ≃	110	18.24 N	103.36 E
Ngidinga	152	5.37 S	15.17 E
Ngimbang	115a	7.17 S	112.12 E
Ng'iro ∧	154	2.08 N	36.51 E
Ngiro, Ewaso ≃, Kenya	154	2.04 S	36.07 E
Ng'iro, Ewaso ≃, Kenya	154	0.28 N	39.55 E
Ngo	152	2.29 S	15.45 E
Ngoangoa ≃	140	5.48 N	25.09 E
Ngoboli	154	4.57 N	32.37 E
Ngoko ≃, Afr.	152	1.40 N	16.03 E
Ngoko ≃, Congo	152	0.25 S	15.29 E
Ngol-Kedju Hill ∧[2]	152	6.20 N	9.45 E
Ngolo	146	9.56 N	22.16 E
Ngom ≃	102	31.11 N	97.15 E
Ngomahuru	154	20.26 S	30.43 E
Ngomba	154	8.23 S	32.53 E
Ngomba ∧	154	5.43 S	35.52 E
Ngombe, Zaïre	152	6.35 S	20.42 E
Ngombe, Zaïre	273b	4.24 S	15.11 E
Ngome	158	27.46 S	31.28 E
Ngomedzap	152	3.15 N	11.12 E
Ngomeni, Ras ≻	154	2.59 S	40.14 E
Ngong	154	1.22 S	36.39 E
Ngongotaha	172	38.05 S	176.12 E
Ngono ≃	154	1.08 S	31.35 E
Ngonye Falls ∟	152	16.40 S	23.35 E
Ngop	140	6.16 N	30.12 E
Ngora	154	1.27 N	33.46 E
Ngorengore	154	1.02 S	35.30 E
Ngoring Hu ⊜	102	34.50 N	97.35 E
Ngoro	115a	7.41 S	112.16 E
Ngorongoro Crater ⊼[6]	154	3.10 S	35.35 E
Ngote	154	2.14 N	30.48 E
Ngoto	152	4.00 N	17.21 E
Ngotwane ≃	156	23.35 S	26.58 E
Ngoulémakong	152	3.07 N	11.25 E
Ngouma	150	15.38 N	3.22 W
Ngounié □[4]	152	1.30 S	11.00 E
Ngounié ≃	152	0.37 S	10.18 E
Ngouri	146	13.38 N	15.22 E
Ngouroundou	152	6.27 N	22.37 E
Ngourti	146	15.19 N	13.12 E
Ngoywa	154	5.56 S	32.48 E
Ngozi	154	2.54 S	29.50 E
Ngqeleni	158	31.40 S	29.02 E
Ngudiabaka ≃	273b	4.25 S	15.11 E
Nguélémendouka	152	4.23 N	12.55 E
Ngugha ≃	156	19.21 S	23.15 E
Nguigmi	146	14.15 N	13.07 E
Nguila	152	4.43 N	11.41 E
Nguiu	164	11.45 S	130.38 E
Ngulu I[1]	108	8.27 N	137.29 E
Ngum ≃	110	18.09 N	103.06 E
Nguna, Île I	175f	17.26 S	168.21 E
Ngunga	154	3.41 S	33.34 E
Ngunju, Tanjung ≻	115b	10.19 S	120.28 E
Ngunut	115a	8.06 S	112.01 E
Ngurore	146	9.18 N	12.14 E
Nguru	146	12.52 N	10.27 E
Ngwempisi ≃	158	26.42 S	31.26 E
Ngweni	158	27.56 S	32.15 E
Ngwenya ∧	158	26.11 S	31.02 E
Ngwerere	154	15.18 S	28.20 E
Ngweze ≃	154	17.40 S	25.07 E
Nha Be	269c	10.42 N	106.44 E
Nhabe ≃, Bots.	156	20.22 S	22.58 E
Nha Be ≃, Viet	269c	10.39 N	106.44 E
Nhacoongo	156	24.18 S	35.14 E
Nhamacolomo	156	18.05 S	34.26 E
Nhamundá	250	2.14 S	56.43 W
Nhamundá ≃	246	2.12 S	56.41 W
Nha Nam	110	21.27 N	106.06 E
Nhandeara	255	20.40 S	50.02 W
Nhareia	152	11.25 S	17.03 E
Nha Trang	110	12.15 N	109.11 E
Nhia ≃	152	10.15 S	14.12 E
Nhill	166	36.20 S	141.39 E
Nhlangano	158	27.06 S	31.12 E
Nhlazatshe	158	28.10 S	31.14 E
Nhoma ≃	156	18.52 S	20.53 E
Nhon Trach	269c	10.43 N	106.51 E
Nhulunbuy	164	12.11 S	136.47 E
Nhundo	152	14.25 S	21.23 E
Nhunguaçu	256	22.21 S	42.53 W
Niabembe	154	2.14 S	27.44 E
Niafounké	150	15.56 N	4.00 W
Niagara	190	45.46 N	87.59 W
Niagara □[6], On., Can.	212	43.05 N	79.20 W
Niagara □[6], N.Y., U.S.	210	43.10 N	78.42 W
Niagara ≃	212	43.15 N	79.04 W
Niagara County Historical Center ʊ	284a	43.10 N	78.43 W
Niagara Falls, On., Can.	212	43.06 N	79.04 W
Niagara Falls, On., Can.	284a	43.06 N	79.04 W
Niagara Falls, N.Y., U.S.	210	43.05 N	79.03 W
Niagara Falls, N.Y., U.S.	284a	43.05 N	79.03 W
Niagara Falls ∟	212	43.05 N	79.04 W
Niagara Falls Airport ⊠	284a	43.02 N	79.08 W
Niagara Falls International Airport ⊠	284a	43.06 N	78.56 W
Niagara-on-the-Lake	212	43.15 N	79.04 W
Niagara University ʊ[2]	284a	43.08 N	79.02 W
Niagassola	150	12.19 N	9.07 W
Niah	112	3.52 N	113.44 E
Niakaramandougou	150	8.40 N	5.17 W
Niamey	150	13.31 N	2.07 E
Niamey □[5]	150	14.00 N	2.00 E
Niamtougou	150	9.46 N	1.06 E
Nianbadu	100	28.17 N	118.28 E
Niandan ≃	150	10.30 N	10.26 W
Niandan Koro	150	11.05 N	9.15 W
Nianforando	150	9.32 N	10.31 W
Niangara	154	3.42 N	27.52 E
Niangay, Lac ⊜	150	15.50 N	3.00 W
Niangmake	102	30.14 N	99.40 E
Niangnianggong	104	41.00 N	121.13 E
Niangniangmiao	98	42.34 N	118.05 E
Niangniangwa	105	40.33 N	117.30 E
Niangoloko	150	10.17 N	4.55 W
Niangua ≃	194	37.58 N	92.48 W
Niangzizhuang	105	40.02 N	118.05 E
Nia-Nia	154	1.24 N	27.36 E
Nianpan	104	41.48 N	124.02 E
Niantic, Ct., U.S.	207	41.19 N	72.11 W
Niantic, Il., U.S.	219	39.51 N	89.10 W
Nianyugou	104	42.00 N	123.59 E
Nianyushan	100	29.11 N	117.04 E
Nianzhuang	98	34.19 N	117.47 E
Nianzigang	100	31.03 N	114.18 E
Nianzishan	89	47.32 N	122.52 E
Niapu	154	2.25 N	26.28 E
Niari □[5]	152	3.15 S	12.30 E
Niari ≃	152	3.56 S	12.12 E
Niaro	140	10.38 N	31.31 E
Nias, Pulau I	114	1.05 N	97.35 E
Niassa □[5]	154	13.30 S	36.00 E
Niatupo	246	9.33 N	78.54 W
Nibbiano	62	44.54 N	9.19 E
Nibe	26	56.59 N	9.38 E
Nibong Tebal	114	5.10 N	100.29 E
Nibra	272b	22.36 N	88.16 E
Nīca	76	56.19 N	21.04 E
Nica ≃	86	57.29 N	64.33 E
Nicaea → İznik	130	40.26 N	29.43 E
Nicaragua □[1], N.A.	230	13.00 N	85.00 W
Nicaragua □[1], N.A.	236	13.00 N	85.00 W
Nicaragua, Lago de ⊜	236	11.30 N	85.30 W
Nicaro	240p	20.42 N	75.33 W
Nicastro	68	38.59 N	16.20 E
Ničatka, ozero ⊜	88	57.45 N	117.30 E
Nice	62	43.42 N	7.15 E
Nice-Côte d'Azur, Aéroport de ⊠	62	43.40 N	7.14 E
Niceville	194	30.31 N	86.28 W
Nichelino	62	44.59 N	7.38 E
Nicheng	106	30.55 N	121.49 E
Nichihara	96	34.33 N	131.50 E
Nichinan, Nihon	92	31.36 N	131.23 E
Nichinan, Nihon	96	35.09 N	133.16 E
Nicholas □[6]	218	38.20 N	84.02 W
Nicholas Channel Ʉ	238	23.25 N	80.05 W
Nicholasville	192	37.52 N	84.34 W
Nicholls	192	31.31 N	82.38 W
Nicholl's Town	238	25.08 N	78.00 W
Nichols, Ca., U.S.	282	38.02 N	121.59 W
Nichols, Fl., U.S.	220	27.54 N	82.02 W
Nichols, N.Y., U.S.	210	42.01 N	76.22 W
Nichols Brook ≃	283	42.37 N	70.59 W
Nicholson, Austl.	162	18.02 S	128.54 E
Nicholson, Ky., U.S.	218	38.54 N	84.33 W
Nicholson, Ms., U.S.	194	30.28 N	89.41 W
Nicholson, Pa., U.S.	210	41.37 N	75.46 W
Nicholson ≃, Austl.	162	17.34 S	128.38 E
Nicholson ≃, Austl.	166	17.31 S	139.36 E
Nicholson Island I	212	43.56 N	77.31 W
Nicholson Range ⋏	162	27.15 S	116.45 E
Nicholson River Aboriginal Reserve ◆[4]	162	18.00 S	137.30 E
Nichols Run ≃	284b	39.03 N	77.18 W
Nickerie □[5]	250	5.40 N	56.50 W
Nickerie ≃	250	5.59 N	57.00 W
Nickerson	198	38.08 N	98.05 W
Nickol Bay c	162	20.39 S	116.52 E
Nicktown	214	40.37 N	78.48 W
Nicobar Islands II	110	8.00 N	93.30 E
Nicola	182	50.10 N	120.40 W
Nicola ≃	182	50.25 N	121.18 W
Nicolae Bălcescu	38	47.34 N	26.52 E
Nicolai Mountain ∧	224	46.05 N	123.28 W
Nicola Lake ⊜	182	50.10 N	120.25 W
Nicola Mameet Indian Reserve ◆[4]	182	50.11 N	120.49 W
Nicolaus	226	38.54 N	121.35 W
Nicolet	206	46.13 N	72.37 W
Nicolet □[6]	206	46.15 N	72.20 W
Nicolet ≃	206	46.14 N	72.39 W
Nicolet, Lac ⊜	206	45.50 N	71.33 W
Nicolet, Lake ⊜	190	46.20 N	84.15 W
Nicolet Centre ≃	206	45.46 N	71.50 W
Nicolet Sud-Ouest ≃	206	46.13 N	72.36 W
Nicoll Bay c	276	40.43 N	73.07 W
Nicollet	190	44.16 N	94.11 W
Nicoll Point ≻	276	40.42 N	73.09 W
Nicolosi	70	37.37 N	15.01 E
Nicosia, It.	70	37.45 N	14.24 E
Nicosia (Levkosía), Kípros	130	35.10 N	33.22 E
Nicosia (Lefkoşa), Kıbrıs	130	35.10 N	33.22 E
Nicotera	68	38.34 N	15.57 E
Nicoya	236	10.09 N	85.27 W
Nicoya, Golfo de c	236	9.47 N	84.48 W
Nicoya, Península de ≻[1]	236	10.00 N	85.25 W
Nictheroy → Niterói	256	22.53 S	43.07 W
Nida ≃	30	50.18 N	20.52 E
Nidadavole	122	16.55 N	81.40 E
Nidau	58	47.07 N	7.14 E
Nidd ≃	44	54.01 N	1.12 W
Nidda	56	50.24 N	9.00 E
Nidda ≃	56	50.06 N	8.34 E
Nidder ≃	56	50.12 N	8.47 E
Nidderau	56	50.14 N	8.52 E
Nide	102	31.51 N	96.19 E
Nideggen	56	50.47 N	6.29 E
Nidelva ≃	26	58.24 N	8.48 E
Nidwalden □[3]	58	46.55 N	8.28 E
Nidž	84	40.56 N	47.41 E
Nidzica	30	53.22 N	20.26 E
Niebüll	41	54.48 N	8.50 E
Nied ≃	56	49.23 N	6.40 E
Nied Allemande ≃	56	49.10 N	6.26 E
Nieddu, Monte ∧	71	40.45 N	9.34 E
Niederanven	56	49.39 N	6.16 E
Niederau	54	51.10 N	13.32 E
Niederaula	56	50.48 N	9.36 E
Niederbayern □[5]	60	48.45 N	12.45 E
Niederbipp	58	47.16 N	7.39 E
Niederbobritzsch	54	50.54 N	13.26 E
Niederbonsfeld	263	51.23 N	7.08 E
Niederbronn-Les-Bains	56	48.57 N	7.38 E
Niederdonk	263	51.14 N	6.41 E
Niederelfringhausen	263	51.21 N	7.10 E
Niedere Tauern ⋏	30	47.18 N	14.00 E
Niederfinow	54	52.50 N	13.55 E
Niederfrohna	54	50.53 N	12.43 E
Niederhaverbeck	52	53.09 N	9.54 E
Niederheimbach	56	50.02 N	7.48 E
Niederhone	56	51.13 N	10.06 E
Niederkassel	56	50.49 N	7.02 E
Nieder-Kassel ◆[8]	263	51.14 N	6.45 E
Niederkrüchten	56	51.12 N	6.13 E
Niederlande → Netherlands □[1]	30	52.15 N	5.30 E
Niederländische Antillen → Netherlands Antilles □[2]	241s	12.15 N	69.00 W
Niederlausitz □[9]	54	51.40 N	14.15 E
Niederlehme	54	52.19 N	13.39 E
Niedermarsberg	56	51.28 N	8.50 E
Niedermarschacht	52	53.25 N	10.21 E
Nieder-Mörlen	56	50.23 N	8.43 E
Niederndodeleben	54	52.08 N	11.30 E
Nieder-Neuendorf	264a	52.37 N	13.12 E
Niedernhall	56	49.17 N	9.36 E
Niedernwöhren	52	52.21 N	9.08 E
Niederoderwitz	54	50.57 N	14.44 E
Nieder-Ohmen	56	50.38 N	9.02 E
Nieder-Olm	56	49.55 N	8.11 E
Niederorschel	54	51.22 N	10.25 E
Niederösterreich □[3]	61	48.20 N	15.50 E
Niedersachsen □[3]	30	52.40 N	9.00 E
Niedersachswerfen	54	51.33 N	10.46 E
Niederschöneweide ◆[8]	264a	52.27 N	13.31 E
Niederschönhausen ◆[8]	54	52.35 N	13.23 E
Niedersonthofen	58	47.38 N	10.13 E
Niederstetten	56	49.24 N	9.55 E
Niederstotzingen	56	48.32 N	10.14 E
Niedersulz	61	48.29 N	16.40 E
Niederurnen	58	47.07 N	9.03 E
Niederwald	58	46.26 N	8.12 E
Niederwalgern	56	50.44 N	8.41 E
Niederweningen	58	47.30 N	8.23 E
Niederwiesa	54	50.51 N	13.01 E
Niederwürschnitz	54	50.43 N	12.45 E
Nied Française ≃	56	49.10 N	6.26 E
Niedu	100	25.28 N	114.08 E
Niefang	152	1.50 N	10.14 E
Nieheim	52	51.48 N	9.06 E
Niekerkshoop	158	29.19 S	22.51 E
Niel	50	51.07 N	4.20 E
Niellé	150	10.12 N	5.38 W
Niellim	146	9.42 N	17.49 E
Niem	152	6.12 N	15.14 E
Niemba	154	5.57 S	28.26 E
Niemegk	54	52.04 N	12.41 E
Niemeyer ◆[8]	287a	23.00 S	43.15 W
Niemodlin	30	50.39 N	17.37 E
Niéna	150	11.26 N	6.21 W
Nienberge	52	52.00 N	7.34 E
Nienborg-Wigbold	52	52.08 N	7.06 E
Nienburg, Dtsch.	52	52.38 N	9.13 E
Nienburg, Dtsch.	54	51.50 N	11.46 E
Niendorf	54	53.59 N	10.50 E
Nienhagen, Dtsch.	52	52.33 N	10.05 E
Nienhagen, Dtsch.	54	51.57 N	11.09 E
Niénokoué, Mont ∧[2]	150	5.26 N	7.10 W
Niepkuhlen ≃	263	51.29 N	6.31 E
Niepołomice	30	50.03 N	20.13 E
Nieppe	50	50.42 N	2.50 E
Nier ≃	48	52.17 N	7.48 W
Niéré	146	14.30 N	21.09 E
Niéré, Hadjer ∧	146	14.21 N	21.40 E
Niéri Ko ≃	150	13.21 N	13.23 W
Niers ≃	52	51.43 N	5.57 E
Nierst	263	51.19 N	6.43 E
Nierstein	56	49.52 N	8.20 E
Niesen ∧	58	46.39 N	7.39 E
Niesky	54	51.17 N	14.49 E
Nieszawa	30	52.50 N	18.55 E
Nieto, Cañada de ≃	258	34.00 S	58.15 W
Nieu Bethesda	158	31.51 S	24.34 E
Nieuw-Amsterdam, Ned.	52	52.44 N	6.51 E
Nieuw Amsterdam, Sur.	250	5.53 N	55.05 W
Nieuw-Buinen	52	52.57 N	6.55 E
Nieuwefontein	158	28.01 S	19.06 E
Nieuwegein	52	52.03 N	5.05 E
Nieuwe-Niedorp	52	52.45 N	4.54 E
Nieuwe-Pekela	52	53.04 N	6.58 E
Nieuweschans	52	53.11 N	7.12 E
Nieuwkoop	52	52.08 N	4.47 E
Nieuw Nickerie	250	5.57 N	56.59 W
Nieuwolda	52	53.14 N	6.59 E
Nieuwoudtville	158	31.23 S	19.07 E
Nieuwpoort, Bel.	50	51.08 N	2.45 E
Nieuwpoort, Ned. Ant.	241s	12.03 N	68.49 W
Nieuwpoort-Bad	50	51.09 N	2.42 E
Nieuw-Schoonebeek	52	52.38 N	6.59 E
Nieuw-Vennep	52	52.16 N	4.38 E
Nieuw-Weerdinge	52	52.52 N	6.59 E
Nieva ≃	246	4.35 S	77.53 W
Nievenheim	56	51.07 N	6.46 E
Nievería	286d	11.59 S	76.55 W
Nièvre □[5]	32	47.05 N	3.30 E
Nièvre ≃	50	47.10 N	3.13 E
Niga	150	13.38 N	5.27 W
Nigan	126	23.30 N	87.59 E
Niğde	130	37.59 N	34.42 E
Niğde □[4]	130	38.15 N	34.15 E
Nigei Island I	182	50.55 N	127.50 W
Nigel	158	26.30 S	28.28 E
Niger □[3]	150	10.00 N	6.00 E
Niger □[1]	134	16.00 N	8.00 E
Niger ≃	150	5.33 N	6.33 E
Niger Delta ≚[2]	150	4.50 N	6.00 E
Nigeria □[1]	134	10.00 N	8.00 E
Nigerian Museum ʊ	273a	6.20 N	3.24 E
Nigg	46	57.43 N	4.00 W
Nighāsan	124	28.14 N	80.52 E
Nightcaps	172	45.58 S	168.02 E
Nighthawk	182	48.58 N	119.38 W
Night Hawk Lake ⊜	190	48.28 N	81.00 W
Nightingale Island I	10	37.24 S	12.28 W
Nightmute	180	60.29 N	164.43 W
Nigríta	38	40.55 N	23.30 E
Nihe	104	41.27 N	121.13 E
Nihing (Nahang) ≃	128	26.00 N	62.44 E
Nihoa I	14	23.06 N	161.58 W
Nihommatsu	92	37.35 N	140.26 E
Nihonbashi ◆[8]	268	35.41 N	139.47 E
Nihon → Japan □[1]	92	36.00 N	138.00 E
Nihon-kai → Japan, Sea of ⊤[2]	90	40.00 N	135.00 E
Nihon University ʊ[2]	268	35.42 N	139.45 E
Nihtaur	124	29.20 N	78.23 E
Nihuil, Embalse del ⊜[1]	252	35.05 S	68.45 W
Niida ≃	96	33.11 N	132.58 E
Niigata	92	37.55 N	139.03 E
Niigata □[5]	94	37.08 N	138.30 E
Niihama	96	33.58 N	133.16 E
Niihari	94	36.07 N	140.09 E
Niiharu	94	36.41 N	138.55 E
Niihau I	229b	21.55 N	160.10 W
Nii-jima I	92	34.22 N	139.16 E
Niimi	96	34.59 N	133.28 E
Niinisalo	26	61.50 N	22.29 E
Niitsu	92	37.48 N	139.07 E
Niiza	94	35.48 N	139.34 E
Níjar	34	36.58 N	2.12 W
Nijiaqiao	269b	31.14 N	121.21 E
Nijil	132	30.31 N	35.33 E
Nijkerk	52	52.13 N	5.30 E
Nijlen	56	51.10 N	4.39 E
Nijmegen	52	51.50 N	5.50 E
Nijo Castle ⊥	270	35.01 N	135.45 E
Nijvel → Nivelles	50	50.36 N	4.20 E
Nijverdal	52	52.22 N	6.27 E
Níkaia	267c	37.58 N	23.39 E
Nikel'	24	69.24 N	30.12 E
Nikel'tau	86	50.23 N	58.13 E
Nikiforovo	265b	55.50 N	38.05 E
Nikiniki	112	9.49 S	124.28 E
Nikip Lake ⊜	184	52.53 N	91.53 W
Nikitovka, Ross.	78	50.23 N	38.25 E
Nikitovka, Ukr.	83	48.21 N	38.02 E
Nikitsch	61	47.32 N	16.40 E
Nikitskoje, Ross.	82	55.18 N	38.28 E
Nikitskoje, Ross.	82	55.13 N	35.46 E
Nikki	150	9.56 N	3.12 E
Nikkō	94	36.45 N	139.37 E
Nikkō-kokuritsu-kōen ♠	94	36.49 N	139.33 E
Niklā al-ʻInab	142	30.55 N	30.46 E
Niklasdorf	61	47.24 N	15.10 E

DEUTSCH

Name	Seite	Breite°′	Länge°′ E = Ost
Nikobaren → Nicobar Islands II	110	8.00 N	93.30 E
Nikolai	180	62.58 N	154.09 W
Nikolajev, Ukr.	78	49.32 N	23.58 E
Nikolajev, Ukr.	78	46.58 N	32.00 E
Nikolajevka, Kaz.	86	49.10 N	81.59 E
Nikolajevka, Ross.	80	46.21 N	47.44 E
Nikolajevka, Ross.	80	52.28 N	49.14 E
Nikolajevka, Ross.	80	52.11 N	48.04 E
Nikolajevka, Ross.	80	53.08 N	47.12 E
Nikolajevka, Ross.	83	47.18 N	38.50 E
Nikolajevka, Ross.	86	56.29 N	95.06 E
Nikolajevka, Ross.	86	54.57 N	75.44 E
Nikolajevka, Ross.	88	55.46 N	98.10 E
Nikolajevka, Ross.	89	48.34 N	134.47 E
Nikolajevka, Ukr.	78	47.38 N	33.12 E
Nikolajevka, Ukr.	78	47.06 N	34.14 E
Nikolajevka, Ukr.	78	44.58 N	33.37 E
Nikolajevka, Ukr.	78	46.23 N	29.24 E
Nikolajevka, Ukr.	78	47.33 N	30.25 E
Nikolajevka, Ukr.	78	51.04 N	34.02 E
Nikolajevka, Ukr.	83	48.46 N	38.20 E
Nikolajevka, Ukr.	83	47.39 N	37.41 E
Nikolajevka, Ukr.	83	48.51 N	37.46 E
Nikolajevo	76	58.16 N	29.29 E
Nikolajevo-Kozlovskij	83	47.13 N	38.21 E
Nikolajevsk	80	50.01 N	45.28 E
Nikolajevskaja	80	47.37 N	41.29 E
Nikolajevsk-Na-Amure	89	53.08 N	140.44 E
Nikolajevskoje, Ross.	78	45.08 N	39.36 E
Nikolajevskoje, Ross.	88	51.04 N	111.48 E
Nikolajevskoje, Ross.	88	52.21 N	117.00 E
Nikolassee ◆[8]	264a	52.26 N	13.12 E
Nikolayev → Nikolajev	78	46.58 N	32.00 E
Nikolo-Berezovec	76	58.38 N	42.17 E
Nikolo-Berjozovka	80	56.06 N	54.17 E
Nikolo-Chovanskoje	265b	55.36 N	37.27 E
Nikologory	80	56.09 N	41.59 E
Nikolo-Kropotki	82	56.44 N	37.55 E
Nikolo-L'vovsk	89	43.54 N	131.23 E
Nikolo-Makarovo	80	57.38 N	43.34 E
Nikolsdorf	64	46.47 N	12.55 E
Nikol'sk, Ross.	24	59.30 N	45.27 E
Nikol'sk, Ross.	80	53.45 N	46.05 E
Nikolski	180	52.56 N	168.52 W
Nikol'skij, Ross.	24	60.55 N	34.00 E
Nikol'skij, Ross.	86	56.18 N	68.58 E
Nikol'skij Toržok	76	59.53 N	38.46 E
Nikol'skoje, Ross.	74	55.12 N	166.00 E
Nikol'skoje, Ross.	76	52.39 N	36.04 E
Nikol'skoje, Ross.	76	55.26 N	35.04 E
Nikol'skoje, Ross.	76	59.23 N	44.36 E
Nikol'skoje, Ross.	76	59.30 N	42.32 E
Nikol'skoje, Ross.	78	50.35 N	41.10 E
Nikol'skoje, Ross.	80	52.37 N	43.49 E
Nikol'skoje, Ross.	80	47.46 N	46.24 E
Nikol'skoje, Ross.	82	55.15 N	36.04 E
Nikol'skoje, Ross.	82	56.09 N	36.43 E
Nikol'skoje, Ross.	82	55.53 N	36.26 E
Nikol'skoje, Ross.	82	54.51 N	35.53 E
Nikol'skoje, Ross.	82	54.27 N	36.24 E
Nikol'skoje, Ross.	82	54.30 N	36.50 E
Nikol'skoje, Ross.	82	54.03 N	37.10 E
Nikol'skoje, Ross.	82	54.18 N	35.53 E
Nikol'skoje, Ross.	82	55.37 N	36.41 E
Nikol'skoje, Ross.	86	57.12 N	84.21 E
Nikol'skoje, Ross.	86	52.02 N	55.43 E
Nikol'skoje, Ross.	265a	59.41 N	30.47 E
Nikol'skoje, Ross.	265b	55.46 N	37.54 E
Nikol'skoje, Ukr.	83	47.46 N	37.18 E
Nikol'skoje-na-Čeremšane	80	54.03 N	49.14 E
Nikol'skoje-na-Dnepre	78	48.12 N	35.12 E
Nikol'skoje-Ur'upino	265b	55.48 N	37.13 E
Nikonga ≃	154	4.40 S	31.28 E
Nikonorovka	83	49.07 N	39.59 E
Nikonova Gora	76	60.22 N	36.07 E
Nikonovskoje	82	55.17 N	38.10 E
Nikopol, Blg.	38	43.42 N	24.54 E
Nikopol', Ukr.	78	47.35 N	34.25 E
Niksar	130	40.36 N	36.58 E
Nīkshahr	128	26.13 N	60.12 E
Nikšić	38	42.46 N	18.56 E
Nikulino, Ross.	76	55.16 N	33.46 E
Nikulino, Ross.	80	58.05 N	44.14 E
Nikulino, Ross.	82	56.48 N	35.50 E
Nikulino ◆[8]	265b	55.40 N	37.28 E
Nikulkino	82	56.07 N	38.38 E
Nikul'skoje	82	55.10 N	38.41 E
Nikumaroro I[1]	14	4.40 S	174.32 W
Nikunau I	14	1.23 S	176.26 E
Nīl, Nahr an- → Nile ≃	140	30.10 N	31.06 E
Nila, Pulau I	164	6.44 S	129.31 E
Nilakka ⊜	26	63.07 N	26.33 E
Niland	204	33.14 N	115.31 W
Nil Blanc → White Nile ≃	140	15.38 N	32.31 E
Nile □[5]	154	3.00 N	31.30 E
Nile (Nahr an-Nīl) ≃	140	30.10 N	31.06 E
Niles, Il., U.S.	216	42.01 N	87.48 W
Niles, Mi., U.S.	216	41.49 N	86.15 W
Niles, Oh., U.S.	214	41.10 N	80.45 W
Niles Pond ⊜	283	42.35 N	70.40 W
Nilgani	272b	22.46 N	88.26 E
Nilgaut, Lac ⊜	190	46.36 N	77.15 W
Nīlgiri	126	21.28 N	86.46 E
Nilka	86	43.47 N	82.20 E
Nilkitkwa ≃	182	55.27 N	126.43 W
Nillahcootie, Lake ⊜[1]	169	36.54 S	146.00 E
Nil → Nile ≃	140	30.10 N	31.06 E
Nilo Azul → Blue Nile ≃	140	15.38 N	32.31 E
Nilo Blanco → White Nile ≃	140	15.38 N	32.31 E
Nilo → Nile ≃	140	30.10 N	31.06 E
Nilópolis	256	22.49 S	43.25 W
Nilópolis □[7]	287a	22.49 S	43.26 W
Nilphāmāri	124	25.56 N	88.51 E
Nilsiä	26	63.12 N	28.05 E
Niltepec	234	16.34 N	94.37 W
Nilüfer ≃	130	40.18 N	28.27 E
Nīlwāl ◆[8]	272a	28.40 N	76.59 E
Nilwood	219	39.24 N	89.49 W
Nima	96	35.09 N	132.24 E
Nīmach	120	24.28 N	74.52 E
Niman ≃	89	51.24 N	132.45 E
Nimančik	89	52.09 N	133.47 E
Nimba, Mount ∧	150	7.37 N	8.25 W
Nimbāhera	120	24.37 N	74.41 E
Nimba Range ⋏	150	7.30 N	8.30 W
Nimboran, Pegunungan ⋏	164	2.45 S	140.20 E
Nimelen ≃	89	52.27 N	136.32 E
Nîmes	62	43.50 N	4.21 E
Nimis	64	46.12 N	13.16 E
Nimishillen Creek ≃	214	40.38 N	81.22 W
Nimisila	214	40.56 N	81.34 W
Nimisila Reservoir ⊜[1]	214	40.57 N	81.31 W
Nīm Ka Thāna	120	27.44 N	75.48 E
Nimmitabel	166	36.31 S	149.16 E
Nimmonsburg	210	42.09 N	75.55 W
Nimpkish Lake ⊜	182	50.25 N	126.59 W
Nimrod Lake ⊜[1]	194	34.55 N	93.20 W
Nīmrūz □[4]	128	30.30 N	62.00 E
Nims ≃	56	49.51 N	6.28 E
Nimta	272b	22.40 N	88.25 E
Nimule	154	3.36 N	32.03 E
Nimule National Park ♠	154	3.50 N	31.35 E
Nimy	50	50.28 N	3.57 E
Niña Bonita, Presa ⊜[1]	286b	23.02 N	82.29 W
Nīnah, Wādī V	146	30.02 N	15.22 E
Nīnawā □[4]	128	36.10 N	42.35 E
Nīnawá (Nineveh) ⊥	128	36.25 N	43.10 E

Symbols in the index entries represent the broad categories identified in the key at the right. Symbols with superior numbers (⋏[1]) identify subcategories (see complete key on page *I · 1*).

Symbole im Register stellen die rechts im Schlüssel erklärten Kategorien dar. Symbole mit hochgestellten Ziffern (⋏[1]) bezeichnen Unterabteilungen einer Kategorie (vgl. vollständiger Schlüssel auf Seite *I · 1*).

Los símbolos incluídos en el texto del índice representan las grandes categorias identificadas con la clave a la derecha. Los símbolos con numeros en su parte superior (⋏[1]) identifican las subcategorías (véase la clave completa en la página *I · 1*).

Les symboles de l'index représentent les catégories indiquées dans la légende à droite. Les symboles suivis d'un indice (⋏[1]) représentent des sous-catégories (voir légende complète à la page *I · 1*).

Os símbolos incluídos no texto do índice representam as grandes categorias identificadas com a chave à direita. Os símbolos com números em sua parte superior (⋏[1]) identificam as subcategorias (veja-se a chave completa à página *I · 1*).

Symbol	English	Deutsch	Español	Français	Português
∧	Mountain	Berg	Montaña	Montagne	Montanha
⋏	Mountains	Gebirge	Montañas	Montagnes	Montanhas
)(	Pass	Paß	Paso	Col	Passo
V	Valley, Canyon	Tal, Cañon	Valle, Cañón	Vallée, Canyon	Vale, Canhão
≚	Plain	Ebene	Llano	Plaine	Planície
≻	Cape	Kap	Cabo	Cap	Cabo
I	Island	Insel	Isla	Île	Ilha
II	Islands	Inseln	Islas	Îles	Ilhas
⊼	Other Topographic Features	Andere Topographische Objekte	Otros Elementos Topográficos	Autres données topographiques	Outros acidentes topográficos

ESPAÑOL Nombre Página Lat.°′ Long.°′ W = Oeste
FRANÇAIS Nom Page Lat.°′ Long.°′ W = Ouest
PORTUGUÊS Nome Página Lat.°′ Long.°′ W = Oeste

Nin Bay c 116 12.13 N 123.15 E
Ninda 152 14.47 S 21.24 E
Nindigully 166 28.21 S 148.49 E
Nindiri 236 12.00 N 86.08 W
Nine Ashes 260 51.42 N 0.18 E
Nine Degree Channel ꟾ 122 9.00 N 73.00 E
Ninemile Creek ≐, N.Y., U.S. 210 43.11 N 75.20 W
Ninemile Creek ≐, N.Y., U.S. 210 43.06 N 76.14 W
Ninemile Creek ≐, N.Y., U.S. 210 43.24 N 76.38 W
Nine Mile Creek ≐, Ut., U.S. 200 39.50 N 109.53 W
Ninemile Island I 279b 40.29 N 79.52 W
Nine Mile Lake ⊜ 212 44.57 N 79.34 W
Nine Mile Point ≻ 212 44.09 N 76.34 W
Ninepin Group II 271d 22.16 N 114.21 E
Nineteen Hundred Five Memorial Cemetery ✦ 265a 59.51 N 30.27 E
Ninette 184 49.24 N 99.38 W
Ninetyeast Ridge ✢³ 6 4.00 S 90.00 E
Ninety Mile Beach ⊥², Austl. 166 38.13 S 147.23 E
Ninety Mile Beach ⊥², N.Z. 172 34.48 S 173.00 E
Ninety Six 192 34.10 N 82.01 W
Nineveh, In., U.S. 218 39.22 N 86.05 W
Nineveh, N.Y., U.S. 210 42.12 N 75.36 W
Nineveh — Nīnawá ⊥ 128 36.25 N 43.10 E
Ninfa ⊥ 66 41.36 N 12.58 E
Ninfas, Punta ≻ 254 42.56 S 64.20 W
Ninfield 42 50.53 N 0.25 E
Ninga 184 49.13 N 99.51 W
Ningaloo 162 22.42 S 113.40 E
Ning'an 89 44.22 N 129.25 E
Ningari 150 14.40 N 3.16 W
Ningbo 100 29.52 N 121.31 E
Ningcheng (Tianyi) 98 41.33 N 119.20 E
Ningde 100 26.43 N 119.33 E
Ningdu 100 26.31 N 115.58 E
Ningerum 164 5.41 S 141.08 E
Ninggang 100 26.50 N 114.02 E
Ningguo 106 30.38 N 118.58 E
Ninghai 100 29.17 N 121.25 E
Ninghe (Lutai) 105 39.20 N 117.48 E
Ninghepu 105 40.43 N 116.07 E
Ninghua 100 26.15 N 116.38 E
Ningi 150 11.04 N 9.32 E
Ningjin, Zhg. 98 37.37 N 114.55 E
Ningjin, Zhg. 98 37.39 N 116.48 E
Ningjing Shan ⩘ 102 29.45 N 98.45 E
Ningling 98 34.27 N 115.21 E
Ningming 102 22.07 N 107.05 E
Ningnan 102 27.11 N 102.36 E
Ningpo — Ningbo 100 29.52 N 121.31 E
Ningqiang 102 32.44 N 106.19 E
Ningshan 102 33.04 N 108.39 E
Ningsia Hui Autonomous Region — Ningxia Huizu Zizhiqu □⁴ 102 37.00 N 106.00 E
Ningsia — Yinchuan 102 38.30 N 106.18 E
Ningwu 102 39.01 N 112.21 E
Ningxi 100 28.35 N 121.00 E
Ningxia Huizu Zizhiqu (Ningsia Hui) □⁴ 102 37.00 N 106.00 E
Ningxian 102 35.31 N 108.01 E
Ningxiang 100 28.15 N 112.33 E
Ningyang 98 35.47 N 116.47 E
Ningyō-tōge ✕ 96 35.19 N 133.56 E
Ningyuan 102 25.37 N 111.46 E
Ningyuanbao 102 38.38 N 102.36 E
Ningyuanpu 105 40.44 N 114.54 E
Ninh Binh 110 20.15 N 105.59 E
Ninh Hoa 110 12.29 N 109.08 E
Ninhue 252 36.24 S 72.24 W
Ninigo Group II 164 1.15 S 144.15 E
Ninilchik 180 60.03 N 151.41 W
Ninnescah ≐ 198 37.20 N 97.10 W
Ninnescah, North Fork ≐ 198 37.34 N 97.42 W
Ninnescah, South Fork ≐ 198 37.34 N 97.42 W
Ninnis Glacier Tongue ⊓ 9 68.12 S 147.12 E
Ninohe 92 40.16 N 141.18 E
Ninomiya, Nihon 94 35.18 N 139.16 E
Ninomiya, Nihon 94 36.22 N 139.58 E
Ninove 50 50.50 N 4.01 E
Niny 84 44.29 N 43.57 E
Nio 96 34.12 N 133.39 E
Nioaque 248 21.08 S 55.48 W
Niobe ≐ 248 20.46 S 56.04 W
Niobe 214 42.01 N 79.27 W
Niobrara 198 42.45 N 98.01 W
Niobrara ≐ 198 42.45 N 98.00 W
Nioka 154 2.10 N 30.39 E
Niokl 152 2.43 S 17.41 E
Niokolo Koba 150 13.04 N 12.43 W
Niokolo Koba, Parc National du ♦ 150 13.00 N 13.00 W
Niono 150 14.15 N 6.00 W
Nionsamoridougou 150 8.43 N 8.50 W
Niono du Rip 150 13.45 N 15.48 W
Nioro du Sahel 150 15.15 N 9.35 W
Niort 32 46.19 N 0.27 W
Niota 192 35.30 N 84.32 W
Nioût ✢⁴ 150 16.03 N 6.52 W
Nipan 166 24.47 S 150.01 E
Nipāni 122 16.24 N 74.23 E
Nipawin 184 53.22 N 104.00 W
Nipawin Provincial Park ♦ 184 54.00 N 104.40 W
Nipe, Bahía de c 240p 20.47 N 75.42 W
Nipekamew ≐ 184 54.59 N 104.52 W
Nipekamew Lake ⊜ 184 54.24 N 104.58 W
Nipepe 154 14.01 S 37.55 E
Nipigon 190 49.01 N 88.16 W
Nipigon, Lake ⊜ 176 49.50 N 88.30 W
Nipigon Bay c 190 48.53 N 87.50 W
Nipin ≐ 184 55.45 N 109.02 W
Nipisi Lake ⊜ 182 55.47 N 114.57 W
Nipissing c⁸ 212 45.30 N 78.50 W
Nipissing, Lake ⊜ 190 46.17 N 80.00 W
Nipissis, Lac ⊜ 186 51.02 N 66.10 W
Nipissis, Lac ⊜ 186 50.52 N 65.50 W
Nipomo 204 35.02 N 120.28 W
Nippenicket, Lake ⊜ 283 41.58 N 71.03 W
Nippers Harbour 186 49.48 N 55.52 W
Nippersink Creek ≐ 216 42.23 N 88.22 W
Niqiu 100 33.27 N 115.38 E
Niquelândia 255 14.27 S 48.27 W
Niquero 240p 20.03 N 77.35 W
Niquivil 252 30.25 S 68.42 W
Nīr 128 38.02 N 47.59 E
Nīr, Jabal an- ⩘² 128 24.10 N 43.20 E
Nira ≐ 122 17.59 N 75.07 E
Nir'am 132 31.31 N 34.35 E
Nirasaki 94 35.42 N 138.27 E
Nirayama 94 35.03 N 138.57 E
Nirgua 246 10.09 N 68.34 W
Nirim 132 31.20 N 34.24 E
Nirmal 122 19.06 N 78.21 E
Nirmāli 124 26.19 N 86.35 E
Nirsa 126 23.47 N 86.43 E
Niš 38 43.19 N 21.54 E
Nisa 34 39.31 N 7.39 W
Nisa (Neisse) (Nysa Łużycka) ≐ 30 52.04 N 14.46 E
Nisāb, Ar. Su. 128 29.11 N 44.43 E
Nisāb, Yaman 144 14.31 N 46.30 E
Nišava ≐ 38 43.22 N 21.46 E
Nisbet 210 41.13 N 77.07 W
Niscemi 70 37.09 N 14.23 E
Nischintāpur 272b 22.26 N 88.22 E
Nīsf Thānī Bashbīsh 142 31.07 N 31.11 E
Nishan 120 33.35 N 85.30 E
Nishi ✦⁸, Nihon 268 35.27 N 139.38 E
Nishi ✦⁸, Nihon 270 34.41 N 135.30 E
Nishiarai ✦⁸ 268 35.47 N 139.47 E
Nishiazai 94 35.31 N 136.10 E
Nishibetsuin 270 34.58 N 135.31 E
Nishi-Chūgoku-sanchi-kokutei-kōen ♦ 96 34.40 N 132.10 E
Nishigō 94 37.09 N 140.10 E
Nishiiyayama 96 33.53 N 133.49 E
Nishiizu 94 34.46 N 138.47 E
Nishi-jima I 96 34.39 N 134.29 E
Nishikata 94 36.28 N 139.45 E
Nishikatsura 94 35.31 N 138.51 E
Nishiki 96 34.16 N 131.57 E
Nishiki ≐ 96 34.09 N 132.15 E
Nishikiori 270 34.29 N 135.34 E
Nishikyō ✦⁸ 270 34.59 N 135.40 E
Nishimori ✦⁸ 270 34.45 N 135.01 E
Nishinari ✦⁸ 270 34.38 N 135.28 E
Nishinasuno 94 36.53 N 139.59 E
Nishinomiya 96 34.43 N 135.20 E
Nishinoomote 93b 30.44 N 131.00 E
Nishio 94 34.52 N 137.03 E
Nishitoda ✦⁸ 270 34.43 N 135.00 E
Nishitosa 96 33.09 N 132.47 E
Nishiwaki 96 34.59 N 134.58 E
Nishiyodogawa ✦⁸ 270 34.42 N 135.27 E
Nish — Niš 38 43.19 N 21.54 E
Nisinomiya — Nishinomiya 96 34.43 N 135.20 E
Nisiros I 38 36.35 N 27.10 E
Niska Lake ⊜ 184 55.35 N 108.38 W
Niskayuna 210 42.46 N 73.50 W
Nisling ≐ 180 62.27 N 139.30 W
Nismes 50 50.05 N 4.33 E
Nispen 52 51.29 N 4.28 E
Nisporeny 78 47.06 N 28.11 E
Nisqually ≐ 224 47.06 N 122.42 W
Nisqually Indian Reservation ✦⁴ 224 47.02 N 122.42 W
Nisqually Reach c 224 47.07 N 122.45 W
Nissan ≐ 26 56.40 N 12.51 E
Nissequogue 276 40.54 N 73.12 W
Nissequogue ≐ 276 40.54 N 73.13 W
Nissequogue, Northeast Branch ≐ 276 40.50 N 73.13 W
Nissequogue River State Park ♦ 276 40.51 N 73.13 W
Nisser ⊜ 26 59.10 N 8.30 E
Nisshin 94 35.08 N 137.02 E
Nissoria 70 37.39 N 14.27 E
Nissum Bredning c 26 56.38 N 8.22 E
Nissum Fjord c² 26 56.21 N 8.14 E
Nisswa 190 46.31 N 94.17 W
Nisteirode 52 51.43 N 5.33 E
Nister ≐ 56 50.47 N 7.43 E
Nisutlin ≐ 180 60.10 N 132.30 W
Nita, Indon. 115b 8.40 S 122.11 E
Nita, Nihon 96 35.12 N 133.01 E
Nitalas 272c 19.06 N 73.08 E
Nitaure 76 57.10 N 25.10 E
Niterói 256 22.53 S 43.07 W
Niterói □⁷ 287a 22.56 S 43.04 W
Nith ≐, On., Can. 212 43.12 N 80.22 W
Nith ≐, Scot., U.K. 44 55.00 N 3.35 W
Nithāri 272a 28.35 N 77.21 E
Nithāri ✦⁸ 272a 28.42 N 77.03 E
Nithi River 182 54.01 N 125.01 W
Nithsdale ∨ 44 55.14 N 3.46 W
Nitibe 112 9.19 S 124.12 E
Nitinat ≐ 224 48.55 N 124.29 W
Nitinat ≐ 224 48.49 N 124.37 W
Nitinat Lake ⊜ 182 48.45 N 124.45 W
Niton 42 50.35 N 1.16 W
Nitra 30 48.20 N 18.05 E
Nitra ≐ 30 47.46 N 18.10 E
Nitro 188 38.24 N 81.50 W
Nitry 50 47.40 N 3.53 E
Nítse Óros (Nidže) ʌ 38 40.58 N 21.49 E
Nitta 94 36.17 N 139.18 E
Nittälven ≐ 40 59.51 N 14.50 E
Nittany Mountain ʌ 210 41.00 N 77.25 W
Nittedal 26 60.04 N 10.53 E
Nittendorf 60 49.12 N 12.16 E
Nittenau 60 49.02 N 11.58 E
Niu Aunfo Point ≻ 174w 21.04 S 175.20 W
Niubaotun 105 39.46 N 116.41 E
Niubu 100 31.02 N 117.39 E
Niuchutuncun 104 41.28 N 122.58 E
Niudouguang 100 24.51 N 115.44 E
Niue □², Oc. 14 19.02 S 169.52 W
Niue □², Oc. 174v 19.02 S 169.52 W
Niu'erhe 89 51.30 N 121.49 E
Niufentai 89 47.05 N 120.02 E
Niufozhen 107 29.23 N 105.02 E
Niuhang 100 28.44 N 115.51 E
Niuhuaxi 107 29.29 N 103.43 E
Niujie 102 27.47 N 104.16 E
Niujingjie 110 25.46 N 100.33 E
Niuke 120 30.41 N 82.01 E
Niulakita I 14 10.45 S 179.30 E
Niulan ≐ 102 27.28 N 103.10 E
Niulanshan 105 40.13 N 116.39 E
Niumaowu 98 40.58 N 124.59 E
Niupeng 106 31.32 N 121.50 E
Niupichang 107 30.35 N 103.40 E
Niushitun 98 35.18 N 114.24 E
Niut, Gunung ʌ 112 1.00 N 109.55 E
Niutan 107 29.05 N 105.21 E
Niutao I 14 6.06 S 177.17 E
Niuti 100 32.58 N 113.35 E
Niutian 100 27.17 N 115.44 E
Niutoushan 89 45.09 N 126.45 E
Niutou Shan I 100 29.07 N 121.56 E
Niutuo 105 39.15 N 116.35 E
Niutoushan 106 31.04 N 119.37 E
Niuxichang 107 28.47 N 104.31 E
Niuxintai 104 41.21 N 123.53 E
Niuxintun 104 41.56 N 121.21 E
Niuyuanzi 105 40.20 N 117.42 E
Niuzhuang, Zhg. 98 37.21 N 118.29 E
Niuzhuang, Zhg. 104 40.58 N 122.32 E
Nivå 41 55.56 N 12.31 E
Nivala 26 63.55 N 24.58 E
Nive ≐, Austl. 166 26.02 S 146.25 E
Nive ≐, Fr. 32 43.30 N 1.29 W
Nivelles (Nijvel) 50 50.36 N 4.20 E
Nivernais □⁹ 32 47.00 N 3.30 E
Nivernais, Canal du ≋ 50 47.40 N 3.40 E
Niverville, Mb., Can. 184 49.37 N 97.01 W
Niverville, N.Y., U.S. 210 42.26 N 73.40 W
Nivillers 50 49.28 N 2.10 E
Nivnoje 76 53.11 N 32.35 E
Nivskij 24 67.16 N 32.23 E
Niwāno 128 26.22 N 62.43 E
Nixa 194 37.02 N 93.17 W
Nixi 102 27.58 N 99.27 E
Nixis 107 30.08 N 106.19 E
Nixizhen 107 29.02 N 104.12 E
Nixon, Nv., U.S. 204 39.49 N 119.21 W
Nixon, Pa., U.S. 214 40.45 N 79.56 W
Nixon, Tx., U.S. 222 29.16 N 97.45 W
Niyodo ≐ 96 33.32 N 133.08 E
Niyodo 96 33.29 N 133.05 E
Niyor 114 2.05 N 103.17 E
Niyu Shan I 100 27.51 N 121.03 E
Niža 24 66.20 N 43.16 E
Nizāmābād 122 18.40 N 78.07 E
Nizamghāt 120 28.16 N 95.42 E
Nizām Sāgar ⊜¹ 122 18.10 N 77.55 E
Nižankoviči 78 49.40 N 22.47 E
Nizgān ≐ 128 33.13 N 63.40 E
Nižniy Tagil — Nižnij Tagil 86 57.55 N 59.57 E
Nižin 76 52.38 N 28.10 E
Nizino 265a 59.50 N 29.53 E
Nizip 130 37.01 N 37.46 E
Nízke Tatry ⩘ 30 48.54 N 19.40 E
Nízke Tatry, národní park ♦ 30 47.48 N 19.35 E
Nižn'aja 80 56.34 N 49.07 E
Nižn'aja Čvorovaja 86 59.11 N 77.31 E
Nižnaja Dobrinka 80 50.18 N 45.42 E
Nižn'aja Duvanka 83 49.35 N 38.10 E
Nižn'aja-Gerasimovka 83 48.46 N 39.44 E
Nižn'aja Grajvoronka 78 51.47 N 37.45 E
Nižn'aja Irga 86 56.51 N 57.26 E
Nižn'aja Ivanovka ✦⁸ 83 48.09 N 38.46 E
Nižn'aja Karelina 88 57.55 N 107.44 E
Nižn'aja Keul'skaja, šivera ∟ 88 58.25 N 102.46 E
Nižn'aja Krynka 83 48.07 N 38.11 E
Nižnaja Matrenka 80 52.16 N 40.06 E
Nižn'aja-Ol'chovaja 83 48.44 N 39.35 E
Nižn'aja Omka 86 55.26 N 74.55 E
Nižn'aja Omra 24 62.46 N 55.46 E
Nižn'aja Ošma 80 55.44 N 51.18 E
Nižn'aja Peša 24 66.43 N 47.36 E
Nižn'aja Pojma 88 56.11 N 97.13 E
Nižn'aja Pokrovka 80 51.40 N 50.07 E
Nižn'aja Šachtama 88 51.24 N 117.40 E
Nižn'aja Salda 86 58.05 N 60.43 E
Nižn'aja Syzran' 80 53.04 N 48.34 E
Nižn'aja Tavda 86 57.40 N 66.12 E
Nižn'aja Tunguska ≐ 74 65.48 N 88.04 E
Nižn'aja Tura 86 58.37 N 59.49 E
Nižn'aja Vol'dža 86 58.19 N 79.20 E
Nižn'aja Zaimka 88 56.09 N 98.14 E
Nižneangarsk 88 55.47 N 109.33 E
Nižnebakanskij 78 44.52 N 37.52 E
Nižne-Baranikovka 83 49.05 N 39.51 E
Nižnečujskij 85 43.12 N 74.21 E
Nižnedevick 78 51.33 N 38.20 E
Nižne-Gnilovskoj ✦⁸ 83 47.11 N 39.36 E
Nižnegnutov 80 48.02 N 42.22 E
Nižnegorskij 78 45.27 N 34.44 E
Nižneilimsk 88 57.11 N 103.16 E
Nižneje 83 48.46 N 38.37 E
Nižneje Al'kejevo 80 54.46 N 50.03 E
Nižn'eje Gir'unino 88 51.12 N 116.58 E
Nižneje Kučukovo 80 56.13 N 52.57 E
Nižneje Kujto, ozero ⊜ 24 64.58 N 31.38 E
Nižneje M'ačkovo 82 55.33 N 37.59 E
Nižneje Platino 83 48.48 N 39.30 E
Nižnejepravalje ≐ 83 48.17 N 39.57 E
Nižneje Romanovo 86 59.47 N 69.35 E
Nižneje Sančelejevo 80 53.40 N 49.27 E
Nižnekamsk 80 55.32 N 51.58 E
Nižnekamskoje vodochranilišče ⊜¹ 24 55.50 N 53.00 E
Nižnekundr'učen-Skaja 80 47.45 N 40.57 E
Nižnelemskij 24 64.01 N 56.16 E
Nižne-Mit'akin Pervyj 83 48.41 N 40.02 E
Nižne-Nagol'naja 83 49.00 N 39.59 E
Nižneoz'ornoje 80 51.37 N 53.56 E
Nižne-Podpol'nyj 83 47.12 N 40.01 E
Nižne-Pokrovka 83 49.13 N 38.38 E
Nižnetambovskoje 89 50.54 N 138.13 E
Nižne-T'oploje 83 48.48 N 39.23 E
Nižnetroickij 80 54.20 N 53.41 E
Nižneudinsk 88 54.54 N 99.03 E
Nižnevartovsk 74 60.56 N 76.31 E
Nižnij Baskunčak 80 48.13 N 46.50 E
Nižnij Časučej 88 50.31 N 115.08 E
Nižnij Čir 80 48.22 N 43.03 E
Nižnij Čulym 86 54.37 N 78.56 E
Nižnije Černi 80 47.41 N 43.26 E
Nižnije Čeršely 80 54.40 N 52.08 E
Nižnije Ostrovcy 82 55.35 N 38.01 E
Nižnije Sergi 86 56.40 N 59.18 E
Nižnije Serogozy 78 46.50 N 34.23 E
Nižnije Timers'any 80 54.34 N 47.45 E
Nižnije V'azovyje 80 55.49 N 48.32 E
Nižnij Ingaš 88 56.12 N 96.31 E
Nižnij Kisl'aj 78 50.50 N 40.11 E
Nižnij Kuranach 88 58.49 N 125.32 E
Nižnij Lomov 80 53.32 N 43.41 E
Nižnij Mamon 78 50.11 N 40.30 E
Nižnij Novgorod (Gorky) 80 56.20 N 44.00 E
Nižnij Odes 24 63.40 N 54.52 E
Nižnij Ol'šan 78 50.45 N 38.55 E
Nižnij P'andž 120 37.08 N 68.32 E
Nižnij Paramonov 80 47.57 N 41.55 E
Nižnij Rogačik 78 47.21 N 34.02 E
Nižnij Šerebr'akov 80 47.58 N 41.02 E
Nižnij Škaft 80 53.36 N 45.40 E
Nižnij Stan 88 52.18 N 115.44 E
Nižnij Tagil 86 57.55 N 59.57 E
Nižnij Takanyš 80 55.57 N 51.04 E
Nižnij Ufalej 86 55.55 N 59.59 E
Nižnij V'aloz'orskij 24 66.44 N 35.10 E
Nižnyj Nagol'čik 83 48.01 N 39.04 E
Nizwā 128 22.56 N 57.32 E
Nizy 78 50.47 N 34.46 E
Nizy-le-Comte 50 49.34 N 4.03 E
Nizza Monferrato 62 44.46 N 8.21 E
Nizzana 132 30.53 N 34.27 E
Nizzana, Nahal ∨ 132 30.57 N 34.23 E
Nizzanim 132 31.43 N 34.38 E
Njassa-See — Nyasa, Lake ⊜ 154 12.00 S 34.30 E
Njazidja (Grande Comore) I 157a 11.35 S 43.20 E
Njinjo 154 8.48 S 38.54 E
Njoko ≐ 152 17.10 S 24.05 E
Njombe 154 9.20 S 34.46 E
Njombe ≐ 154 6.56 S 35.06 E
Njupeskär ∟ 26 61.38 N 12.41 E
Njurunda 26 62.16 N 17.22 E
Nkambe 152 6.38 N 10.40 E
Nkandla 158 28.37 S 31.05 E
Nkawkaw 150 6.33 N 0.47 W
Nkayi 154 19.00 S 28.54 E
Nkhata Bay 154 11.33 S 34.18 E
Nkhotakota 154 12.57 S 34.17 E
Nkolabona 152 1.14 N 11.43 E
Nkomi, Lagune c 152 1.35 S 9.17 E
Nkongsamba 152 4.57 N 9.56 E
Nkonko 154 6.20 S 34.58 E
Nkoso 152 2.42 S 22.39 E
Nkoto 152 1.56 S 19.41 E
Nkunga 152 4.41 S 18.34 E
Nkurenkuru 152 17.38 S 18.35 E
Nkwalini 158 28.45 S 31.33 E
Nmai ≐ 102 25.42 N 97.30 E
Nnewi 150 6.00 N 6.59 E
Nō 96 37.05 N 137.59 E
Noābād 272b 22.34 N 88.31 E
Noailles 50 49.20 N 2.12 E
Noākhāli 124 22.49 N 91.06 E
Noak Hill ✦⁸ 260 51.37 N 0.14 E
Noale 64 45.32 N 12.04 E
Noamundi 124 22.09 N 85.32 E
Noane 207 41.19 N 71.59 W
Noarlunga 168b 35.11 S 138.30 E
Noasca 62 45.27 N 7.19 E
Noatak 180 67.34 N 162.59 W
Noatak ≐ 180 67.00 N 162.30 W
Nobby 171a 27.51 S 151.54 E
Nobel 212 45.25 N 80.06 W
Nobeoka 92 32.35 N 131.40 E
Nobidome 268 35.48 N 139.35 E
Nobidome-yōsui ≋¹ 268 35.44 N 139.27 E
Nōbi-heiya ≡ 94 35.15 N 136.45 E
Nobili 110 11.33 N 1.12 W
Nobitz 54 50.58 N 12.29 E
Noble, Il., U.S. 194 38.41 N 88.13 W
Noble, Ok., U.S. 196 35.08 N 97.23 W
Noble □⁶ 216 41.24 N 85.25 W
Noble Park 274b 37.58 S 145.10 E
Noblestown 279b 40.24 N 80.12 W
Noblesville 218 40.02 N 86.00 W
Nobleton, On., Can. 212 43.54 N 79.40 W
Nobleton, Fl., U.S. 220 28.38 N 82.15 W
Noboribetsu 92a 42.27 N 141.11 E
Noborito 268 35.37 N 139.34 E
Nobres 248 14.44 S 56.20 W
Nobsa 246 5.46 N 72.57 W
Nocatee 220 27.09 N 81.52 W
Noccundra 166 27.50 S 142.36 E
Nocé 50 48.22 N 0.42 E
Noce ≐ 64 46.09 N 11.04 E
Nocera Inferiore 68 40.44 N 14.38 E
Nocera Superiore 68 40.44 N 14.40 E
Nocera Tirinese 68 39.02 N 16.09 E
Nocera Umbra 66 43.05 N 12.47 E
Noceto 64 44.48 N 10.11 E
Nochistlán 234 21.22 N 102.51 W
Nochten 54 51.26 N 14.36 E
Noci 68 40.48 N 17.08 E
Nociglia 68 40.02 N 18.20 E
Nockamixon Lake ⊜¹ 208 40.28 N 75.14 W
Nockamixon State Park ♦ 208 40.27 N 75.16 W
Nockatunga 166 27.43 S 142.43 E
Nocona 196 33.47 N 97.43 W
Nocupétaro 234 18.48 N 101.04 W
Noda 94 35.56 N 139.52 E
Nodagawa 96 35.31 N 135.06 E
Nodaway ≐ 194 39.54 N 94.58 W
Nodera 270 34.45 N 134.56 E
Nods 58 47.06 N 6.20 E
Noé, Ouadi ∨ 146 15.39 N 21.19 E
Noel 194 36.32 N 94.29 W
Noenieput 158 27.29 S 20.06 E
Noepoli 68 40.05 N 16.20 E
Noer 41 54.27 N 10.00 E
Noetinger 252 32.22 S 62.19 W
Nœux-les-Mines 50 50.29 N 2.40 E
Nofels 58 47.15 N 9.34 E
Nogah 132 31.37 N 34.42 E
Nogajskaja step' ≡ 84 44.17 N 46.05 E
Nogales, Chile 252 32.44 S 71.15 W
Nogales, Méx. 232 31.20 N 110.56 W
Nogales, Méx. 234 18.49 N 97.10 W
Nogales, Az., U.S. 200 31.20 N 110.56 W
Nogami 94 36.07 N 139.07 E
Nogangjin 98 39.30 N 125.23 E
Nogara, It. 64 45.11 N 11.04 E
Nogara, Ityo. 144 13.53 N 36.32 E
Nogaro 32 43.46 N 0.02 W
Nōgata 96 33.44 N 130.44 E
Nogent-en-Bassigny 58 48.02 N 5.21 E
Nogent-le-Roi 50 48.39 N 1.32 E
Nogent-le-Rotrou 50 48.19 N 0.50 E
Nogent-sur-Marne 261 48.50 N 2.29 E
Nogent-sur-Oise 50 49.16 N 2.28 E
Nogent-sur-Seine 50 48.29 N 3.30 E
Nogent-sur-Vernisson 50 47.51 N 2.45 E
Nogi 94 36.14 N 139.44 E
Nogies Creek ≐ 212 44.35 N 78.31 W
Noginsk 82 55.51 N 38.27 E
Nogisaki 268 35.57 N 139.58 E
Nogliki 89 51.48 N 143.10 E
Nogmung 102 27.30 N 97.49 E
Nogoa ≐ 166 23.33 S 148.32 E
Nōgohaku-san ʌ 94 35.46 N 136.31 E
Nogoon Nuur 86 49.33 N 90.17 E
Nogoyá 252 32.24 S 59.48 W
Nógrád □⁶ 30 48.00 N 19.35 E
Noguera Pallaresa ≐ 34 42.15 N 0.54 E
Noguera Ribagorzana ≐ 34 41.40 N 0.43 E
Nohain ≐ 50 47.24 N 2.55 E
Nohar 123 29.11 N 74.46 E
Noheji 92 40.52 N 141.08 E
Nohili Point ≻ 229b 22.04 N 159.47 W
Nohjhīl 124 27.51 N 77.39 E
Nohta 124 23.40 N 79.34 E
Nohwa-do I 98 34.12 N 126.35 E
Noicattaro 68 41.02 N 16.59 E
Noichi 96 33.33 N 133.42 E
Noir, Causse ⩘¹ 32 44.10 N 3.15 E
Noir, Isla I 254 54.29 S 73.02 W
Noire ≐, P.Q., Can. 190 45.54 N 76.57 W
Noire ≐, P.Q., Can. 206 45.33 N 72.58 W
Noire ≐, P.Q., Can. 206 46.39 N 72.08 W
Noire, Mer du — Black Sea ✢² 22 43.00 N 35.00 E
Noire, Montagne ʌ 206 46.14 N 74.18 W
Noire, Montagne ⩘ 32 43.28 N 2.18 E
Noirétable 62 45.49 N 3.46 E
Noirmoutier 32 47.00 N 2.15 W
Noirmoutier, Île de I 32 47.00 N 2.15 W
Noiseau 261 48.47 N 2.33 E
Noisiel 261 48.51 N 2.37 E
Noisy ≐ 212 44.19 N 80.08 W
Noisy-le-Grand 261 48.51 N 2.33 E
Noisy-le-Roi 261 48.51 N 2.04 E
Noisy-le-Sec 261 48.53 N 2.28 E
Nojember'an 84 41.12 N 45.01 E
Nojima-zaki ≻ 94 34.56 N 139.53 E
Nojiri-ko ⊜ 94 36.49 N 138.13 E
Nojon 102 43.10 N 102.07 E
Nojon uul ⩘ 102 43.10 N 101.30 E
Nokami 96 34.15 N 135.20 E
Nokaneng 156 19.40 S 22.16 E
Nokha 124 27.36 N 73.29 E
Nokha Mandi 120 27.35 N 73.29 E
Nokia 26 61.28 N 23.30 E
Nokilalaki, Bulu ʌ 112 1.13 S 120.08 E
Nok Kundi 128 28.46 N 62.46 E
Nokogiri-yama ʌ² 268 35.09 N 139.51 E
Nokomis, Sk., Can. 184 51.30 N 105.00 W
Nokomis, Fl., U.S. 220 27.07 N 82.26 W
Nokomis, Il., U.S. 219 39.18 N 89.17 W
Nokomis Lake ⊜ 190 45.50 N 89.50 W
Nokou 146 14.35 N 14.47 E
Nokpan-ni ✦⁸ 271b 37.36 N 126.56 E
Nokrek ʌ 120 25.27 N 90.20 E
Nokuku 175f 14.53 S 166.35 E
Nola, Centraf. 152 3.32 N 16.04 E
Nola, It. 68 40.55 N 14.33 E
Nolan 222 32.27 N 100.15 W
Nolan Creek ≐ 222 31.02 N 97.26 W
Nolanville 222 31.05 N 97.36 W
Nolay 58 46.57 N 4.38 E
Noli 62 45.15 N 7.35 E
Noli, Capo di ≻ 62 44.12 N 8.25 E
Nolichucky ≐ 192 36.07 N 83.14 W
Nolin ≐ 194 37.13 N 86.15 W
Nolin Lake ⊜¹ 194 37.20 N 86.10 W
Nolinsk 80 57.33 N 49.57 E
Nomad 164 6.18 S 142.14 E
Nomahegan Brook ≐ 276 40.41 N 74.18 W
Nomans Land I 207 41.15 N 70.49 W
Nombre de Dios, Méx. 234 23.51 N 104.14 W
Nombre de Dios, Pan. 236 9.35 N 79.28 W
Nombre de Dios, Cordillera ⩘ 236 15.35 N 86.55 W
Nome 180 64.30 N 165.24 W
Nomeny 56 48.54 N 6.14 E
Nomexy 58 48.18 N 6.23 E
Nomgon, Mong. 102 45.26 N 105.08 E
Nomgon, Mong. 102 42.50 N 105.08 E
Nomgon uul ⩘ 102 42.50 N 104.20 E
Nomingue, Petit lac ⊜ 206 46.21 N 75.00 W
Nomingue, Lac ⊜ 206 46.24 N 75.02 W
Nominingue 206 46.24 N 75.02 W
Nominingue, Lac ⊜ 206 46.26 N 74.59 W
Nomoi Islands II 14 5.27 N 153.40 E
Nomoneas II 175c 7.24 N 151.53 E
Nomozaki 92 32.35 N 129.45 E
Nomtsas 156 24.22 S 16.47 E
Nomuka 96 33.22 N 132.38 E
Nona, Lake ⊜ 220 28.24 N 81.15 W
Nonacho Lake ⊜ 176 61.42 N 109.40 W
Nonancourt 50 48.46 N 1.12 E
Nonant-le-Pin 50 48.42 N 0.13 E
Nonantola 64 44.41 N 11.02 E
Nonburg 24 65.34 N 50.32 E
Nonceveux 56 50.28 N 5.44 E
Nondalton 180 60.00 N 154.49 W
Nondwa 154 6.26 S 35.20 E
Nondweni 158 28.11 S 30.49 E
None 62 44.56 N 7.32 E
Nonette ≐ 50 49.12 N 2.24 E
None-yama ʌ 96 33.29 N 134.10 E
Nong'an 89 44.25 N 125.10 E
Nong Bua Lamphu 110 17.11 N 102.25 E
Nong Han 110 17.21 N 103.07 E
Nong Hèt 110 19.29 N 103.59 E
Nong Khai 110 17.52 N 102.44 E
Nongoma 158 27.58 S 31.35 E
Nongpoh 120 25.54 N 91.53 E
Nongstoin 120 25.31 N 91.16 E
Nonnenhorn 58 47.34 N 9.36 E
Nonnevitz 54 54.39 N 13.17 E
Nonning 166 32.30 S 136.30 E
Nonnweiler 56 49.36 N 6.58 E
Nono 144 8.32 N 37.26 E
Nonoai 252 27.21 S 52.47 W
Nonoava 232 27.28 N 106.44 W
Nonoc Island I 116 9.51 N 125.37 E
Nono de Julho, Túnel ✦⁵ 287b 23.34 S 46.39 W
Nonogasta 252 29.18 S 67.30 W
Nonoichi 94 36.32 N 136.37 E
Nonouti I¹ 14 0.40 S 174.21 E
Nonsan 98 36.12 N 127.05 E
Nonsuch Bay c 240c 17.03 N 61.42 W
Non Sung 110 15.11 N 102.16 E
Nonthaburi 110 13.50 N 100.29 E
Nonthaburi □⁴ 269a 13.52 N 100.27 E
Nontron 32 45.32 N 0.40 E
Nonvianuk Lake ⊜ 180 59.00 N 155.15 W
Noojee 169 37.55 S 146.00 E
Nookawarra 162 26.19 S 116.52 E
Nooksack 224 48.55 N 122.19 W
Nooksack ≐ 224 48.46 N 122.35 W
Nooksack, Middle Fork ≐ 224 48.50 N 122.08 W
Nooksack, North Fork ≐ 224 48.50 N 122.11 W
Nooksack, South Fork ≐ 224 48.50 N 122.11 W
Noonamah 164 12.38 S 131.04 E
Noonan 198 48.53 N 103.00 W
Noon Hill ʌ² 283 42.09 N 71.19 W
Noonkanbah 162 18.30 S 124.50 E
Noorat 169 38.12 S 142.56 E
Noord-Beveland I 52 51.35 N 3.45 E
Noord-Brabant □⁴ 52 51.30 N 5.00 E
Noord-Holland □⁴ 52 52.40 N 4.50 E
Noordhorn 52 53.16 N 6.24 E
Noordoewer 156 28.45 S 17.37 E
Noordoost Polder ✢¹ 52 52.42 N 5.45 E
Noordpunt ≻ 241s 12.21 N 69.09 W
Noord-Scharwoude 52 52.43 N 4.47 E
Noordwijk aan Zee 52 52.14 N 4.26 E
Noordwijk-Binnen 52 52.13 N 4.27 E
Noordwijkerhout 52 52.15 N 4.30 E
Noordwolde 52 52.54 N 6.09 E
Noormarkku 26 61.35 N 21.52 E
Noorvik 180 66.50 N 161.12 W
Noosaville 166 26.24 S 153.04 E
Nootka Island I 182 49.32 N 126.42 W
Nootka Sound ꟾ 182 49.33 N 126.38 W
Nopaltepec 234 18.17 N 95.59 W
No Point, Point ≻ 276 41.09 N 73.08 W
Nóqui 152 5.51 S 13.25 E
Nora, Sve. 40 59.31 N 15.02 E
Nora, In., U.S. 218 39.55 N 86.08 W
Nora ≐ 89 52.26 N 129.58 E
Nora ⊥ 71 39.00 N 9.01 E
Nor Ačin 84 40.19 N 44.35 E
Norah Head ≻ 170 33.17 S 151.35 E
Nora Islands II 144 16.02 N 40.03 E
Norala 116 6.28 N 124.38 E
Noralee 182 53.59 N 126.26 W
Noranda 190 48.15 N 79.02 W
Noraskög ⩘ 40 59.39 N 14.50 E
Nora Springs 190 43.08 N 93.00 W
Norberg 40 60.04 N 15.56 E
Norberto de la Riestra 252 35.16 S 59.46 W
Norborne 194 39.18 N 93.40 W
Norcan Lake ⊜ 212 45.10 N 76.53 W
Norcatur 198 39.50 N 100.11 W
Norchia ⊥ 66 42.20 N 11.54 E
Norcia 66 42.48 N 13.05 E
Norco 228 33.56 N 117.33 W
Norcott, Mount ʌ 162 32.07 S 121.59 E
Norcross 192 33.56 N 84.12 W
Nord □⁴ 146 9.00 N 13.30 E
Nord □⁵ 50 50.20 N 3.40 E
Nord, Canal du ≋ 50 50.16 N 3.05 E
Nord, Cap — Nordkapp ≻ 24 71.11 N 25.48 E
Nord, Gare ✦⁵ 261 48.53 N 2.21 E
Nord, Grand lac du ⊜ 186 50.54 N 67.06 W
Nord, Petit lac du ⊜ 186 50.51 N 67.10 W
Nord, Rivière du ≐ 206 45.31 N 74.20 W
Nordamerika — North America ✢¹ 16 45.00 N 100.00 W
Nordanholen 40 60.30 N 14.57 E
Nordausques 50 50.49 N 2.05 E
Nordaustlandet I 12 79.48 N 22.24 E
Nordbögge 263 51.37 N 7.44 E
Nordborg 41 55.03 N 9.45 E
Nordby 41 55.58 N 10.34 E
Nord Dakota — North Dakota □³ 198 47.30 N 100.15 W
Norddeich 52 53.37 N 7.09 E
Nordegg 182 52.28 N 116.04 W
Nordegg ≐ 182 52.53 N 115.18 W
Norden, Dtsch. 52 53.36 N 7.12 E
Norden, Eng., U.K. 262 53.38 N 2.13 W
Norden, Ca., U.S. 226 39.20 N 120.22 W
Nordendorf 58 48.36 N 10.50 E
Nordenham 52 53.29 N 8.28 E
Nordenšel'da, archipelag II 74 76.45 N 96.00 E
Nordenskiold ≐ 180 62.05 N 136.18 W
Norderney 52 53.42 N 7.08 E
Norderney I 52 53.42 N 7.15 E
Norderstedt 41 54.21 N 9.14 E
Norderstedt 52 53.43 N 10.00 E
Nordfjord c² 26 61.54 N 5.12 E
Nordfjordeid 26 61.54 N 6.00 E
Nordfold 24 67.46 N 15.12 E
Nordfriesische Inseln — North Frisian Islands II 24 54.50 N 8.12 E
Nordfriesland ✦¹ 41 54.40 N 9.10 E
Nordgermersleben 54 52.13 N 11.20 E
Nordhalben 54 50.22 N 11.30 E
Nordhausen 54 51.30 N 10.47 E
Nordheim 222 28.55 N 97.36 W
Nordheim von der Rhön 56 50.28 N 10.11 E
Nordhelle ʌ² 263 51.09 N 7.46 E
Nordhorn 52 52.27 N 7.05 E
Nordic Park 278 41.57 N 88.02 W
Nordingrå 26 62.56 N 18.16 E
Nordirland — Northern Ireland □⁸ 44 54.40 N 6.45 W
Nordiyya 132 32.19 N 34.54 E
Nordkanal ≋ 263 51.10 N 6.42 E
Nordkapp ≻ 24 71.11 N 25.48 E
Nordkinnhalvøya ≻¹ 24 70.55 N 27.45 E
Nordkirchen 52 51.44 N 7.31 E
Nordkjosbotn 24 69.13 N 19.30 E
Nord-Korea — Korea, North □¹ 98 40.00 N 127.00 E
Nordland 224 48.03 N 122.41 W
Nordland □⁶ 24 67.00 N 14.40 E
Nördliche Dwina — Severnaja Dvina ≐ 24 64.32 N 40.30 E
Nördliches Eismeer — Arctic Ocean ✢¹ 16 85.00 N 170.00 E
Nördlingen 56 48.51 N 10.30 E
Nordmaling 26 63.34 N 19.30 E
Nordmark 40 59.50 N 14.06 E
Nordmarka ✦¹ 26 60.00 N 10.25 E
Nordostrundingen ≻ 16 81.36 N 12.09 W
Nord-Ostsee-Kanal ≋ 30 53.53 N 9.08 E
Nord-Ouest □⁴ 152 6.30 N 10.30 E
Nordpfälzer Bergland ⩘ 56 49.40 N 7.40 E
Nordradde ≐ 52 52.43 N 7.17 E
Nordreisa 24 69.46 N 21.03 E
Nordre Strømfjord c² 176 67.50 N 52.00 W
Nordrhein-Westfalen □³ 30 51.30 N 7.30 E
Nordsee — North Sea ✢² 22 55.20 N 3.00 E
Nordstemmen 52 52.09 N 9.46 E
Nordstrand I 41 54.30 N 8.53 E
Nordstrandischmoor I 41 54.33 N 8.48 E
Nord-Trøndelag □⁶ 24 64.25 N 12.00 E
Nordvik 74 74.02 N 111.32 E
Nordwalde 52 52.05 N 7.28 E
Nordwest-Kap — North West Cape ≻ 162 21.45 S 114.10 E
Nore 26 60.10 N 9.01 E
Nore ≐ 48 52.25 N 6.58 W
Noremberg — Nürnberg 60 49.27 N 11.04 E
Norf 263 51.09 N 6.43 E
Norf ≐ 263 51.11 N 6.44 E
Norfolk, Ct., U.S. 207 41.59 N 73.12 W
Norfolk, Ma., U.S. 283 42.07 N 71.19 W
Norfolk, Ne., U.S. 198 42.02 N 97.25 W
Norfolk, Va., U.S. 208 36.50 N 76.17 W
Norfolk □⁶, On., Can. 214 42.48 N 80.25 W
Norfolk □⁶, Eng., U.K. 42 52.35 N 1.00 E
Norfolk □⁶, Ma., U.S. 207 42.10 N 71.15 W
Norfolk Broads ✦¹ 42 52.40 N 1.30 E
Norfolk-Insel — Norfolk Island □² 174c 29.02 S 167.57 E
Norfolk International Airport ⊠ 208 36.54 N 76.12 W
Norfolk Island □², Oc. 14 29.02 S 167.57 E
Norfolk Island □², Oc. 174c 29.02 S 167.57 E
Norfolk Island Aerodrome ⊠ 174c 29.03 S 167.56 E
Norfolk Naval Shipyard ■ 208 36.49 N 76.18 W
Norfolk Naval Station ■ 208 36.57 N 76.18 W
Norfolk Ridge ✢³ 14 29.00 S 168.00 E
Norfork Lake ⊜¹ 194 36.25 N 92.10 W
Norg 52 53.04 N 6.27 E
Norge 208 37.22 N 76.46 W
Norge — Norway □¹ 24 62.00 N 10.00 E
Norham 44 55.43 N 2.10 W
Norheimsund 26 60.22 N 6.08 E
Noria de Ángeles 234 22.27 N 101.56 W
Norikura-dake ʌ 94 36.06 N 137.33 E
Noril'sk 74 69.20 N 88.06 E
Noring, Gunong ʌ 114 5.24 N 101.44 E
Norland, On., Can. 212 44.43 N 78.49 W
Norland, Fl., U.S. 220 25.57 N 80.12 W
Norlane 169 38.06 S 144.21 E
Norley 262 53.15 N 2.39 W
Norlina 192 36.26 N 78.11 W
Norma, It. 66 41.35 N 12.58 E
Norma, N.J., U.S. 208 39.29 N 75.05 W
Normal, Al., U.S. 194 34.47 N 86.34 W
Normal, Il., U.S. 216 40.30 N 88.59 W
Norman, Ar., U.S. 194 34.27 N 93.40 W
Norman, In., U.S. 218 38.57 N 86.16 W
Norman, Ok., U.S. 196 35.13 N 97.26 W
Norman ≐ 166 17.28 S 140.49 E
Norman, Lake ⊜¹ 192 35.35 N 80.55 W
Normanby, Austl. 171a 27.28 S 153.01 E
Normanby, N.Z. 172 39.32 S 174.17 E
Normanby ≐ 164 14.25 S 144.08 E
Normanby Island I 164 10.05 S 151.05 E
Norman Creek ≐ 284b 39.18 N 76.25 W
Normandie □⁹ 32 49.00 N 0.05 W
Normandie, Collines de ⩘² 32 48.40 N 0.30 W
Normandien 158 27.57 S 29.47 E
Normandy Heights 284b 39.17 N 76.48 W
Normandy — Normandie □⁹ 32 49.00 N 0.05 W
Normandy Park 224 47.27 N 122.21 W
Normangee 222 31.02 N 96.07 W
Normanhurst 274a 33.43 S 151.06 E
Normanhurst, Mount ʌ 162 25.04 S 122.32 E
Norman Island I 240m 18.20 N 64.37 W
Normannische Inseln — Channel Islands II 28 49.20 N 2.20 W
Norman Park 192 31.16 N 83.41 W
Normans Kill ≐ 210 42.36 N 73.44 W
Normanton, Austl. 166 17.40 S 141.05 E
Normanton, Eng., U.K. 44 53.41 N 1.27 W
Normanville 168b 35.27 S 138.19 E
Norman Wells 180 65.17 N 126.51 W
Nor Marsh ⊞ 260 51.24 N 0.38 E
Normalup 162 35.00 S 116.49 E
Norogachi 232 27.15 N 107.07 W
Noroton ≐ 276 41.03 N 73.31 W
Noroton Point ≻ 276 41.03 N 73.26 W
Norovlin 88 48.40 N 112.00 E
Noroy-le-Bourg 58 47.37 N 6.18 E
Norphlet 194 33.18 N 92.39 W
Norquay 184 51.53 N 102.05 W
Ñorquinco 254 41.51 S 70.54 W
Norra Barken ⊜ 40 60.07 N 15.31 E
Norra Björkfjärden c 40 59.27 N 17.28 E
Norrahammar 26 57.42 N 14.06 E
Norra Hörken ⊜ 40 60.04 N 14.53 E
Norra Kvarken (Merenkurkku) ꟾ 26 63.36 N 20.43 E
Norra Kvills Nationalpark ♦ 26 57.44 N 15.37 E
Norrälgen ⊜ 40 59.50 N 14.34 E
Norra Rörum 41 56.01 N 13.30 E
Norra Storfjället ʌ 24 65.52 N 15.18 E
Norra Yngern ⊜ 40 59.09 N 17.22 E
Norrboda 40 60.28 N 18.25 E
Norrbotten □⁹ 26 66.45 N 23.00 E
Norrbottens Län □⁶ 24 66.00 N 20.00 E
Nørre Åby 41 55.27 N 9.54 E
Nørre Alslev 41 54.54 N 11.54 E
Nørre Broby 41 55.15 N 10.14 E
Nørre Nærå 41 55.34 N 10.17 E
Norrent-Fontes 50 50.35 N 2.24 E
Nørre Snede 41 55.58 N 9.25 E
Nørresundby 26 57.04 N 9.55 E
Nørre Vejrup 41 55.31 N 8.47 E
Norrfjärden 26 65.25 N 21.29 E
Norridge 216 41.57 N 87.49 W
Norridgewock 188 44.42 N 69.47 W
Norris 192 36.11 N 84.04 W
Norris, Lake ⊜ 220 28.57 N 81.32 W
Norris Arm 186 49.05 N 55.15 W
Norris Bridge ✦⁵ 208 37.37 N 76.26 W
Norris City 194 37.58 N 88.19 W
Norris Dam State Park ♦ 192 36.14 N 84.07 W

≐ River · Fluß · Río · Rivière · Rio
≋ Canal · Kanal · Canal · Canal · Canal
∟ Waterfall, Rapids · Wasserfall, Stromschnellen · Cascada, Rápidos · Chute d'eau, Rapides · Cascata, Rápidos
ꟾ Strait · Meeresstraße · Estrecho · Détroit · Estreito
c Bay, Gulf · Bucht, Golf · Bahía, Golfo · Baie, Golfe · Baía, Golfo
⊜ Lake, Lakes · See, Seen · Lago, Lagos · Lac, Lacs · Lago, Lagos
⊞ Swamp · Sumpf · Pantano · Marais · Pântano
⊓ Ice Features, Glacier · Eis- und Gletscherformen · Accidentes Glaciales · Formes glaciaires · Acidentes glaciares
✢ Other Hydrographic Features · Andere Hydrographische Objekte · Otros Elementos Hidrográficos · Autres données hydrographiques · Outros acidentes hidrográficos

✢ Submarine Features · Untermeerische Objekte · Accidentes Submarinos · Formes de relief sous-marin · Acidentes submarinos
□ Political Unit · Politische Einheit · Unidad Política · Entité politique · Unidade política
ʊ Cultural Institution · Kulturelle Institution · Institución Cultural · Institution culturelle · Instituição cultural
⊥ Historical Site · Historische Stätte · Sitio Histórico · Site historique · Sitio histórico
♦ Recreational Site · Erholungs- und Ferienort · Sitio de Recreo · Centre de loisirs · Area de Lazer
⊠ Airport · Flughafen · Aeropuerto · Aéroport · Aeroporto
■ Military Installation · Militäranlage · Instalación Militar · Installation militaire · Instalação militar
✦ Miscellaneous · Verschiedenes · Misceláneo · Divers · Diversos

Name	Page	Lat.°′	Long.°′
Norrish Creek ≃	224	49.10 N	122.08 W
Norris Lake ⊜[1]	192	36.20 N	83.55 W
Norris Point	186	49.31 N	57.53 W
Norristown	208	40.07 N	75.20 W
Norrköping	40	58.36 N	16.11 E
Norroway Brook ≃	283	42.11 N	71.03 W
Norrskedika	40	60.17 N	18.17 E
Norrsundet	26	60.56 N	17.08 E
Norrtälje	40	59.46 N	18.42 E
Norrtäljeviken C	40	59.47 N	18.53 E
Norseman	162	32.12 S	121.46 E
Norsewood	172	40.04 S	176.13 E
Norsjå ⊜	26	59.18 N	9.20 E
Norsjö	26	64.55 N	19.29 E
Norsk	89	52.20 N	129.55 E
Norsminde	41	56.01 N	10.16 E
Norsup	175f	16.05 S	167.23 E
Norte, Cabo ➤, Bra.	250	1.40 N	49.55 W
Norte, Cabo ➤, Chile	174z	27.03 S	109.24 W
Norte, Cabo → Nordkapp ➤	24	71.11 N	25.48 E
Norte, Canal ʊ	288	34.37 S	58.15 W
Norte, Canal do ʊ	250	0.30 N	50.30 W
Norte, Cayo I	240m	18.20 N	65.15 W
Norte, Estación del ◆[5], Esp.	266a	40.25 N	3.43 W
Norte, Estación del ◆[5], Esp.	266d	41.24 N	2.02 E
Norte, Mar del → North Sea ⊤[2]	22	55.20 N	3.00 E
Norte, Punta ➤	254	42.04 S	63.45 W
Norte, Serra do ⋏[1]	248	11.20 S	59.00 W
Norte de Santander □[3]	238	9.15 N	73.00 W
Norte de Santander □[5]	246	8.00 N	73.00 W
Nortelândia	248	14.25 S	56.48 W
Nörten-Hardenberg	52	51.38 N	9.56 E
North, S.C., U.S.	192	33.36 N	81.06 W
North, Va., U.S.	208	37.26 N	76.24 W
North ≃, Nf., Can.	176	57.30 N	62.05 W
North ≃, On., Can.	212	44.44 N	79.39 W
North ≃, Al., U.S.	194	33.15 N	87.30 W
North ≃, Ia., U.S.	194	41.31 N	93.27 W
North ≃, Ma., U.S.	283	42.10 N	70.43 W
North ≃, Mo., U.S.	219	39.52 N	91.27 W
North ≃, Wa., U.S.	224	46.45 N	123.53 W
North, Cape ➤	186	47.02 N	60.25 W
North Abington	207	42.07 N	70.57 W
North Adams, Ma., U.S.	207	42.42 N	73.06 W
North Adams, Mi., U.S.	216	41.58 N	84.32 W
North Albany	202	44.39 N	123.06 W
Northallerton	44	54.20 N	1.26 W
Northam, Austl.	168a	31.39 S	116.40 E
Northam, S. Afr.	156	25.03 S	27.11 E
Northam, Eng., U.K.	42	51.02 N	4.12 W
North America ≛[1]	4	45.00 N	100.00 W
North America ≛[1]	16	45.00 N	100.00 W
North American Basin ✦[1]	8	30.00 N	60.00 W
North Amherst	207	42.24 N	72.31 W
North Amityville	276	40.41 N	73.25 W
Northampton, Austl.	162	28.21 S	114.37 E
Northampton, Eng., U.K.	42	52.14 N	0.54 W
Northampton, Md., U.S.	284c	38.52 N	76.49 W
Northampton, Ma., U.S.	207	42.19 N	72.38 W
Northampton, N.Y., U.S.	207	40.54 N	72.40 W
Northampton, Pa., U.S.	208	40.41 N	75.29 W
Northampton □[6], N.C., U.S.	208	36.28 N	77.21 W
Northampton □[6], Pa., U.S.	210	40.45 N	75.18 W
Northampton □[6], Va., U.S.	208	37.20 N	75.50 W
Northamptonshire □[6]	42	52.20 N	0.50 W
North Andaman I	110	13.15 N	92.55 E
North Andover	207	42.41 N	71.08 W
North Andrews Gardens	220	26.12 N	80.07 W
North Anna ≃	192	37.48 N	77.25 W
North Anson	188	44.51 N	69.54 W
North Apollo	214	40.35 N	79.33 W
North Arlington	276	40.47 N	74.08 W
North Arm ≃[1]	224	49.12 N	123.10 W
North Asheboro	192	35.44 N	79.49 W
North Atlanta	192	33.51 N	84.20 W
North Attleboro	207	41.59 N	71.20 W
North Attleboro National Fish Hatchery ♠	283	42.00 N	71.17 W
North Auburn	274a	33.50 S	151.02 E
North Augusta	192	33.30 N	81.57 W
North Aulatsivik Island I	176	59.50 N	64.00 W
North Aurora	216	41.48 N	88.19 W
North Australian Basin ✦[1]	14	14.30 S	116.30 E
Northaw	260	51.42 N	0.09 W
North Babylon	276	40.42 N	73.19 W
North Balabac Strait ʊ	116	8.10 N	117.04 E
North Baltimore	216	41.10 N	83.40 W
North Balwyn	274b	37.48 S	145.05 E
North Bannister	168a	32.35 S	116.26 E
North Bārākpur	126	22.46 N	88.22 E
North Bass Island I	214	41.43 N	82.49 W
North Battleford	184	52.47 N	108.17 W
North Bay, On., Can.	190	46.19 N	79.28 W
North Bay, N.Y., U.S.	210	43.14 N	75.45 W
North Bay, Wi., U.S.	216	42.46 N	87.47 W
North Bay C, On., Can.	212	44.53 N	79.48 W
North Bay C, Wa., U.S.	224	46.59 N	124.04 W
North Bay Village	220	25.51 N	80.08 W
North Beach	168a	31.52 S	115.45 E
North Beach ◆[8]	282	37.48 N	122.25 W
North Beach Peninsula ➤[1]	224	46.30 N	124.02 W
North Belle Vernon	214	40.08 N	79.52 W
North Bellmore	276	40.41 N	73.32 W
North Bend, B.C., Can.	182	49.53 N	121.27 W
North Bend, Ne., U.S.	198	41.27 N	96.46 W
North Bend, Oh., U.S.	218	39.09 N	84.44 W
North Bend, Or., U.S.	202	43.24 N	124.13 W
North Bend, Pa., U.S.	214	41.21 N	77.42 W
North Bend, Wa., U.S.	224	47.29 N	121.47 W
North Benfleet	260	51.35 N	0.32 E
North Bengal Plains ≚, Asia	124	26.20 N	88.30 E
North Bengal Plains ≚, Asia	124	26.15 N	88.35 E
North Bennington	210	42.55 N	73.14 W
North Bergen	276	40.47 N	74.02 W
North Berwick, Scot., U.K.	46	56.04 N	2.44 W
North Berwick, Me., U.S.	188	43.18 N	70.44 W
North Bethlehem	210	42.40 N	73.50 W
North Bihar Plains ≚	124	26.20 N	86.00 E
North Billerica	207	42.35 N	71.17 W
North Bloomfield	214	41.27 N	80.52 W
North Boggy Creek ≃	196	34.23 N	96.04 W
North Bonneville	224	45.38 N	121.58 W
Northborough	207	42.19 N	71.38 W
North Bosque ≃	196	31.40 N	97.24 W
North Boston	210	42.41 N	78.47 W
North Bourke	166	30.03 S	145.57 E
North Box Hill	274b	37.48 S	145.07 E
North Braddock	279b	40.23 N	79.50 W
North Branch, Mi., U.S.	190	43.13 N	83.11 W
North Branch, Mn., U.S.	190	45.30 N	92.58 W
North Branch, N.J., U.S.	210	40.36 N	74.41 W
North Branch Canal ≍	224	47.12 N	120.40 W
North Branford	207	41.19 N	72.46 W
North Breakers ✦[2]	174g	28.14 N	177.25 W
Northbridge, Austl.	274a	33.49 S	151.13 E
Northbridge, Ma., U.S.	207	42.09 N	71.39 W
North Bristol	214	41.24 N	80.52 W
Northbrook, On., Can.	212	44.44 N	77.10 W
Northbrook, Il., U.S.	216	42.07 N	87.49 W
Northbrook, Pa., U.S.	285	39.55 N	75.41 W
North Brookfield, Ma., U.S.	207	42.16 N	72.05 W
North Brookfield, N.Y., U.S.	210	42.51 N	75.24 W
North Brunswick	208	40.28 N	74.28 W
North Buganda □[5]	154	1.00 N	32.15 E
North Caicos I	238	21.56 N	71.59 W
North Caldwell	276	40.51 N	74.16 W
North Canadian ≃	196	35.17 N	95.31 W
North Canton, Ct., U.S.	207	41.53 N	72.53 W
North Canton, Ga., U.S.	192	34.14 N	84.29 W
North Canton, Oh., U.S.	214	40.52 N	81.24 W
North Cape	216	42.47 N	88.05 W
North Cape ➤, P.E., Can.	186	47.05 N	64.00 W
North Cape ➤, N.Z.	172	34.25 S	173.02 E
North Cape ➤, Pap. N. Gui.	164	2.32 S	150.49 E
North Cape ➤, Mi., U.S.	216	41.44 N	83.25 W
North Cape May	208	38.58 N	74.57 W
North Cape → Nordkapp ➤	24	71.11 N	25.48 E
North Captiva Island I	220	26.35 N	82.13 W
North Caribou Lake ⊜	176	52.50 N	90.40 W
North Carolina □[3], U.S.	178	35.30 N	80.00 W
North Carolina □[3], U.S.	192	35.30 N	80.00 W
North Carver	207	41.55 N	70.48 W
North Cascades National Park ♠	224	48.30 N	121.00 W
North Castor ≃	212	45.16 N	75.24 W
North Catasauqua	208	40.40 N	75.29 W
North Chagrin Reservation ♠	279a	41.34 N	81.26 W
North Channel ʊ, On., Can.	190	46.02 N	82.50 W
North Channel ʊ, On., Can.	212	44.10 N	76.45 W
North Channel ʊ, U.K.	44	55.10 N	5.40 W
North Channel ʊ, N.Y., U.S.	276	40.36 N	73.53 W
North Channel ≃[1]	281	42.38 N	82.40 W
North Charleroi	214	40.09 N	79.54 W
North Charleston	192	32.51 N	79.58 W
North Chatham	210	42.29 N	73.38 W
North Chelmsford	207	42.38 N	71.23 W
North Chicago	216	42.19 N	87.50 W
North Chili	210	43.06 N	77.45 W
Northchurch	260	51.46 N	0.36 W
North City	224	47.45 N	122.18 W
North Cleveland	222	30.21 N	95.06 W
Northcliff ◆[8]	273d	26.09 S	27.58 E
Northcliffe	162	34.36 S	116.07 E
North Clymer	214	42.04 N	79.34 W
North Cohasset	283	42.15 N	70.50 W
North Cohocton	210	42.34 N	77.28 W
North College Hill	218	39.13 N	84.33 W
North Collins	210	42.35 N	78.56 W
North Commerce Lake ⊜	281	42.35 N	83.30 W
North Concho ≃	196	31.27 N	100.25 W
North Conway	188	44.03 N	71.07 W
North Cotabato □[4]	116	7.15 N	124.50 E
Northcote	274b	37.46 S	145.00 E
North Cray ◆[8]	260	51.26 N	0.08 E
North Creek	188	43.41 N	73.59 W
North Creek ≃	278	41.33 N	87.37 W
Northcrest	222	31.38 N	97.06 W
North Crossett	194	33.09 N	91.56 W
North Crosswicks	285	40.10 N	74.39 W
North Croton Creek ≃	196	33.24 N	100.00 W
North Dakota □[3], U.S.	178	47.30 N	100.15 W
North Dakota □[3], U.S.	198	47.30 N	100.15 W
North Dandalup	168a	32.31 S	115.58 E
North Dandalup ≃	168a	32.36 S	115.53 E
North Dartmouth	207	41.38 N	70.58 W
North Dighton	207	41.51 N	71.07 W
North Dorset Downs ⋏[1]	42	50.47 N	2.30 W
North Downs ⋏[1]	42	51.20 N	0.10 E
North Dum Dum	126	22.38 N	88.23 E
North Eagle Butte	198	45.02 N	101.15 W
North East, Md., U.S.	208	39.36 N	75.56 W
North East, Pa., U.S.	214	42.12 N	79.50 W
North-East □[5]	156	21.00 S	27.30 E
Northeast Cape	180	63.18 N	168.42 W
Northeast Cape ➤	180	63.17 N	168.45 W
Northeast Cape Fear ≃	192	34.11 N	77.57 W
Northeast Creek ≃	284b	39.18 N	76.29 W
North Eastern □[4]	154	1.00 N	40.15 E
Northeastern University ʋ[2]	283	42.20 N	71.05 W
North Eastham	207	41.51 N	69.59 W
Northeast Henrietta	210	43.04 N	77.36 W
Northeast Islands II	175c	7.36 N	151.57 E
North Easton	207	42.04 N	71.06 W
Northeast Pass ʊ	175c	7.30 N	151.59 E
North East Point ➤, Ba.	238	21.20 N	73.01 W
North East Point ➤, Ba.	238	22.43 N	73.50 W
North East Point ➤, Kiribati	174o	1.57 N	157.16 W
Northeast Point ➤, St. Vin.	241h	13.03 N	61.13 W
Northeast Providence Channel ʊ	238	25.40 N	77.09 W
North Edwards	228	35.01 N	117.44 W
North Egremont	207	42.11 N	73.26 W
Northeim	52	51.42 N	10.00 E
North Elkhorn Creek ≃	218	38.13 N	84.48 W
North Elm Creek ≃	222	30.53 N	97.00 W
North English	190	41.30 N	92.04 W
Northern □[4], Ghana	150	9.30 N	1.00 W
Northern □[4], Malaŵi	154	11.00 S	34.00 E
Northern □[4], S.L.	150	9.15 N	11.45 W
Northern □[4], Zam.	154	11.00 S	31.00 E
Northern □[5], Pap. N. Gui.	164	9.00 S	148.30 E
Northern □[5], Ug.	154	2.50 N	32.45 E
Northern Aire Estates	278	42.08 N	88.02 W
Northern Arm	186	49.10 N	55.23 W
Northern Cheyenne Indian Reservation ◆[4]	202	45.31 N	106.45 W
Northern Circārs ⋏[2]	122	18.00 N	83.15 E
Northern Cook Islands II	14	10.00 S	161.00 W
Northern Division □[5]	175g	16.30 S	179.30 E
Northern Dvina → Severnaja Dvina ≃	24	64.32 N	40.30 E
Northern Indian Lake ⊜	176	57.20 N	97.20 W
Northern Ireland □[8]	48	54.40 N	6.45 W
Northern Light Lake ⊜	190	48.15 N	90.38 W
Northern Mariana Islands □[2]	14	16.00 N	149.00 E
Northern Samar □[4]	116	12.30 N	124.30 E
Northern Territory □[8]	160	20.00 S	134.00 E
North Esk ≃, Scot., U.K.	46	56.44 N	2.28 W
North Esk ≃, Scot., U.K.	46	55.54 N	3.04 W
North Essendon	274b	37.45 S	144.54 E
North Evans	210	42.42 N	78.56 W
Northey Island I	260	51.44 N	0.43 E
North Fabius ≃	194	39.54 N	91.30 W
North Fairfield	214	41.06 N	82.36 W
North Fair Oaks	282	37.28 N	122.12 W
North Falmouth	207	41.38 N	70.37 W
North Ferriby	44	53.43 N	0.30 W
Northfield, B.C., Can.	224	49.11 N	123.59 W
Northfield, Ct., U.S.	207	41.41 N	73.06 W
Northfield, Il., U.S.	278	42.05 N	87.46 W
Northfield, Ma., U.S.	207	42.41 N	72.27 W
Northfield, Mn., U.S.	190	44.27 N	93.09 W
Northfield, N.J., U.S.	208	39.22 N	74.33 W
Northfield, Oh., U.S.	214	41.20 N	81.32 W
Northfield, Vt., U.S.	188	44.09 N	72.39 W
Northfield Airport ⊠	279a	41.17 N	81.31 W
Northfield Center	279a	41.19 N	81.32 W
Northfield Park Race Track ♠	279a	41.21 N	81.31 W
Northfield Village	279a	41.21 N	81.31 W
Northfield Woods	278	42.05 N	87.52 W
North Fiji Basin ✦[1]	14	16.00 S	174.00 E
North Fillmore	228	34.24 N	118.56 W
North Fitzroy	274b	37.47 S	144.59 E
Northfleet	42	51.27 N	0.21 E
North Flinders Range ⋏	166	31.00 S	139.00 E
North Fond du Lac	190	43.48 N	88.29 W
Northford	207	41.23 N	72.47 W
North Foreland ➤	42	51.23 N	1.27 E
North Fork	226	37.13 N	119.30 W
North Fork ≃	194	36.13 N	92.17 W
North Fork Lake ⊜[1]	226	38.56 N	121.00 W
North Fork Reservoir ⊜[1]	224	45.13 N	122.15 W
North Fork Village	218	39.21 N	83.02 W
North Fort Myers	220	26.40 N	81.52 W
North Freedom	190	43.27 N	89.52 W
North Frisian Islands II	24	54.50 N	8.12 E
Northgate	216	43.01 N	85.36 W
Northgate ◆[9]	282	38.00 N	122.33 W
North Georgetown	214	40.51 N	80.59 W
North Glanford	212	43.11 N	79.54 W
North Glen Ellyn	278	41.54 N	88.04 W
Northglenn	200	39.53 N	104.59 W
North Gower	212	45.08 N	75.43 W
North Grafton	207	42.14 N	71.42 W
North Granby	207	41.59 N	72.49 W
North Grand Island Bridge ◆[5]	284a	43.04 N	78.59 W
North Great River	276	40.44 N	73.10 W
North Greece	212	43.15 N	77.44 W
North Grosvenordale	207	41.59 N	71.53 W
North Grove	216	40.37 N	85.58 W
North Gulfport	194	30.24 N	89.06 W
North Hadley	207	42.23 N	72.36 W
North Haledon	276	40.57 N	74.11 W
North Hampton	218	39.59 N	83.56 W
North Hanover	283	42.08 N	70.52 W
North Harbor C	269f	14.36 N	120.57 E
North Harbour C	274a	33.49 S	151.17 E
North Haven	207	41.23 N	72.51 W
North Head ➤, Austl.	274a	33.49 S	151.18 E
North Head ➤, N.Z.	172	36.25 S	174.03 E
North Henderson	192	36.21 N	78.22 W
North Henik Lake ⊜	176	61.45 N	97.40 W
North Hero	188	44.49 N	73.17 W
North Highlands	226	38.41 N	121.22 W
North Hill	42	50.34 N	4.25 W
North Hills, De., U.S.	285	39.46 N	75.30 W
North Hills, Il., U.S.	278	42.18 N	88.01 W
North Hills, N.Y., U.S.	276	40.47 N	73.41 W
North Hinksey	42	51.45 N	1.16 W
North Hogan Creek ≃	218	39.03 N	84.54 W
North Hollywood ◆[8]	280	34.10 N	118.23 W
North Holmwood	260	51.13 N	0.20 W
North Honcut Creek ≃	226	39.19 N	121.36 W
North Hoosick	210	42.56 N	73.21 W
North Hornell	210	42.21 N	77.40 W
North Horr	154	3.19 N	37.04 E
North Houston	222	29.54 N	95.31 W
Northiam	42	50.59 N	0.36 E
North Industry	214	40.44 N	81.22 W
North Irwin	279b	40.20 N	79.43 W
North Island I, India	122	10.08 N	72.20 E
North Island I, Kenya	154	4.04 N	36.03 E
North Island I, N.Z.	172	39.00 S	176.00 E
North Island Naval Air Station ■	228	32.42 N	117.12 W
North Islet I	116	8.56 N	120.02 E
North Jackson	214	41.06 N	80.52 W
North Java	210	42.41 N	78.20 W
North Judson	216	41.12 N	86.46 W
North Kenai	180	60.44 N	151.19 W
North Kingstown	207	41.38 N	71.25 W
North Kingsville	214	41.54 N	80.42 W
North Knife Lake ⊜	176	58.05 N	97.05 W
North Knob ∧	210	41.43 N	75.33 W
North Korea → Korea, North □[1]	98	40.00 N	127.00 E
North La Junta	198	37.59 N	103.31 W
Northlake, Il., U.S.	278	41.50 N	87.58 W
North Lake, Wi., U.S.	216	43.09 N	88.22 W
North Lake ⊜, N.Y., U.S.	276	41.09 N	73.41 W
North Lake ⊜, Tx., U.S.	222	32.57 N	96.58 W
North Lakhimpur	120	27.14 N	94.07 E
Northland ◆[9]	281	42.27 N	83.13 W
North Landing ≃	208	36.31 N	76.01 W
North Laramie ≃	198	42.08 N	104.56 W
North Las Vegas	204	36.11 N	115.07 W
North La Veta Pass)(	200	37.37 N	105.11 W
North Lawrence	214	40.51 N	81.38 W
Northleach	42	51.51 N	1.50 W
North Lewisburg	216	40.13 N	83.33 W
North Liberty	216	41.32 N	86.25 W
North Lima	214	40.56 N	80.39 W
North Lindenhurst	276	40.42 N	73.22 W
North Line Island I	276	40.38 N	73.29 W
Northline Terrace	222	29.55 N	95.25 W
North Little Rock	194	34.46 N	92.16 W
North Llano ≃	196	30.30 N	99.46 W
North Logan	202	41.46 N	111.48 W
North Loma Linda	228	34.02 N	117.05 W
North Loon Mountain ∧	202	45.07 N	115.52 W
North Loup	198	41.29 N	98.46 W
North Loup ≃	198	41.17 N	98.23 W
North Luangwa National Park ♠	154	11.50 S	32.15 E
North Luconia Shoals ✦[2]	108	5.40 N	112.35 E
North Macmillan ≃	180	63.03 N	133.18 W
North Madison	214	41.48 N	81.03 W
North Magnetic Pole ◆	16	77.19 N	101.49 W
North Malosmadulu Atoll I[1]	122	5.35 N	72.55 E
North Mamm Peak ∧	200	39.23 N	107.52 W
North Manchester	216	41.00 N	85.46 W
North Manitou Island I	190	45.06 N	86.01 W
North Mankato	190	44.10 N	94.02 W
North Manly	274a	33.46 S	151.16 E
North Maroota	170	33.29 S	150.56 E
North Marshfield	283	42.08 N	70.46 W
North Marysville	224	48.07 N	122.09 W
North Massapequa	276	40.42 N	73.27 W
Northmead, Austl.	274a	33.47 S	151.00 E
Northmead, S. Afr.	273d	26.10 S	28.20 E
North Merrick	276	40.41 N	73.33 W
North Miami	220	25.53 N	80.11 W
North Miami Beach	220	25.55 N	80.09 W
North Middleboro	207	41.56 N	70.58 W
North Milk ≃	202	49.08 N	112.23 W
North Mokelumne ≃	226	38.08 N	121.35 W
North Moose Lake ⊜	184	54.08 N	100.13 W
North Moreau Creek ≃	194	38.30 N	92.18 W
North Muskegon	216	43.15 N	86.16 W
North Myrtle Beach	192	33.49 N	78.40 W
North Nahanni ≃	180	62.05 N	124.30 W
North Naples	220	26.13 N	81.47 W
North Narrabeen	274a	33.42 S	151.18 E
North Nemah ≃	224	46.30 N	123.53 W
North New Hyde Park	276	40.44 N	73.41 W
North New River Canal ≍	220	26.05 N	80.12 W
North Newton	198	38.04 N	97.21 W
North Niles	216	41.52 N	86.15 W
North Norwich	210	42.37 N	75.31 W
North Oaks	222	30.22 N	97.41 W
North Ockendon ◆[8]	260	51.32 N	0.18 E
North Ogden	200	41.18 N	111.57 W
North Olmsted	214	41.24 N	81.55 W
Northolt Aerodrome ⊠	260	51.33 N	0.23 W
Northome	190	47.52 N	94.16 W
Northop	262	53.12 N	3.08 W
North Ore Creek ≃	281	42.43 N	83.47 W
North Orwell	210	41.55 N	76.19 W
Northowram	262	53.44 N	1.50 W
North Oxford	207	42.09 N	71.52 W
North Palisade ∧	204	37.06 N	118.31 W
North Palm Beach	220	26.49 N	80.04 W
North Para ≃	168b	34.36 S	138.45 E
North Park ◆[8]	278	41.59 N	87.43 W
North Park ♠	279b	40.36 N	80.00 W
North Park Lake ⊜	279b	40.36 N	80.00 W
North Parramatta	274a	33.48 S	151.00 E
North Pass ʊ	175c	7.41 N	151.48 E
North Patchogue	276	40.47 N	73.00 W
North Peak ∧, Ak., U.S.	180	62.34 N	162.23 W
North Peak ∧, Ca., U.S.	282	37.33 N	122.28 W
North Pease ≃	196	34.15 N	100.07 W
North Pelham, N.H., U.S.	283	42.46 N	71.21 W
North Pelham, N.Y., U.S.	276	40.55 N	73.48 W
North Pembroke	207	42.05 N	70.47 W
North Pender Island I	224	48.49 N	123.17 W
North Perry	214	41.47 N	81.07 W
North Petherton	42	51.06 N	3.01 W
North Philadelphia ◆[8]	285	39.58 N	75.09 W
North Philadelphia Airport ⊠	285	40.05 N	75.01 W
North Pine ≃	171a	27.17 S	153.01 E
North Pine Grove	214	41.24 N	79.13 W
North Piney Creek ≃	200	42.31 N	110.05 W
North Pitcher	210	42.37 N	75.49 W
North Plainfield	210	40.37 N	74.25 W
North Plains	224	45.35 N	122.59 W
North Plains ≚	200	34.40 N	108.15 W
North Platte	198	41.07 N	100.45 W
North Platte ≃	178	41.07 N	100.42 W
North Pleasureville	218	38.22 N	85.07 W
North Plympton	283	41.59 N	70.48 W
North Point, H.K.	271d	22.17 N	114.12 E
Northpoint, Pa., U.S.	214	40.54 N	79.08 W
North Point ➤, Barb.	241g	13.20 N	59.36 W
North Point ➤, Md., U.S.	284b	39.12 N	76.27 W
North Point ➤, Mi., U.S.	190	45.02 N	83.16 W
North Pole	180	64.45 N	147.21 W
North Pole ◆	16	90.00 N	0.00
Northport, Al., U.S.	194	33.13 N	87.34 W
North Port, Fl., U.S.	220	27.03 N	82.15 W
Northport, Mi., U.S.	190	45.07 N	85.37 W
Northport, N.Y., U.S.	210	40.53 N	73.20 W
Northport, Wa., U.S.	202	48.54 N	117.46 W
North Portal	184	49.00 N	102.33 W
Northport Bay C	276	40.55 N	73.23 W
Northport Harbor C	276	40.53 N	73.22 W
North Powder	202	45.01 N	117.55 W
North Pownal	207	42.47 N	73.15 W
North Prairie	216	42.56 N	88.24 W
North Providence	207	41.50 N	71.25 W
North Puyallup	224	47.12 N	122.17 W
North Queensferry	46	56.01 N	3.25 W
North Quincy	219	39.58 N	91.24 W
North Raccoon ≃	198	41.50 N	94.08 W
North Raisin ≃	206	45.09 N	74.43 W
North Ram ≃	182	52.16 N	115.38 W
North Randall	279a	41.27 N	81.32 W
North Reading	207	42.34 N	71.04 W
North Reservoir ⊜[1]	283	42.28 N	71.07 W
North Richland Hills	222	32.50 N	97.13 W
North Richmond	282	37.57 N	122.22 W
Northridge, Oh., U.S.	218	39.59 N	83.46 W
Northridge, Oh., U.S.	218	39.48 N	84.11 W
Northridge ◆[8]	280	34.14 N	118.33 W
Northridge Fashion Center ◆[9]	280	34.13 N	118.33 W
North Ridge Village	218	39.57 N	86.09 W
North Ridgeville	214	41.23 N	82.01 W
North Rim	200	36.12 N	112.03 W
North River C	208	37.25 N	76.25 W
North Riverside	278	41.50 N	87.49 W
North Riverside Park Mall ◆[9]	278	41.51 N	87.49 W
North Robinson	214	40.48 N	82.51 W
North Rocks	274a	33.46 S	151.02 E
North Ronaldsay I	46	59.22 N	2.26 W
North Ronaldsay Firth ʊ	46	59.20 N	2.25 W
North Rose	210	43.11 N	76.53 W
North Royalton	214	41.18 N	81.43 W
North Rustico	186	46.27 N	63.19 W
North Ryde	274a	33.48 S	151.07 E
North Salem	214	40.09 N	81.33 W
North Salt Lake	200	40.50 N	111.54 W
North San Juan	226	39.22 N	121.06 W
North Santiam ≃	202	44.41 N	123.00 W
North Saskatchewan ≃	176	53.15 N	105.05 W
North Saugeen ≃	212	44.19 N	81.17 W
North Scituate, Ma., U.S.	207	42.13 N	70.47 W
North Scituate, R.I., U.S.	207	41.49 N	71.35 W
North Sea ⊤[2]	22	56.00 N	3.00 E
North Seaton Colliery	44	55.11 N	1.32 W
North Sentinel Island I	110	11.33 N	92.15 E
North Shafter	226	35.31 N	119.18 W
North Shields	44	55.01 N	1.27 W
Norths Highland ⋏[1]	9	66.40 S	126.00 E
North Shoal Lake ⊜	184	50.29 N	97.40 W
North Shore	216	42.16 N	88.23 W
Northshore ◆[9]	283	42.32 N	70.57 W
North Shore Channel ≍	278	42.05 N	87.41 W
North Shores	216	41.50 N	83.25 W
North Shoshone Peak ∧	204	39.09 N	117.29 W
North Siberian Lowland → Severo-Sibirskaja nizmennost' ≚	74	73.00 N	100.00 E
Northside	174h	2.47 S	171.43 W
North Singa	126	23.16 N	89.30 E
North Sioux City	198	42.31 N	96.28 W
North Skunk ≃	190	41.15 N	92.02 W
North Somercotes	44	53.28 N	0.08 E
North Sound ʊ, Antig.	240c	17.07 N	61.45 W
North Sound ʊ, Ire.	48	53.11 N	9.43 W
North Sound ʊ, Scot., U.K.	46	59.18 N	2.46 W
North Spicer Island I	176	68.30 N	78.55 W
North Spirit Lake ⊜	184	52.30 N	92.53 W
North Spot I	236	16.15 N	88.11 W
North Springfield, Pa., U.S.	214	41.59 N	80.26 W
North Springfield, Va., U.S.	284c	38.48 N	77.12 W
North Stamford Reservoir ⊜[1]	276	41.08 N	73.32 W
North Star, De., U.S.	285	39.46 N	75.43 W
North Star, Oh., U.S.	216	40.19 N	84.34 W
North Sterling Reservoir ⊜[1]	198	40.47 N	103.17 W
North Stradbroke Island I	171a	27.35 S	153.28 E
North Sudbury	283	42.24 N	71.24 W
North Sulphur ≃	196	33.23 N	95.18 W
North Sunday Creek ≃	202	46.27 N	105.54 W
North Sunderland	44	55.34 N	1.39 W
North Swansea	207	41.46 N	71.15 W
North Sydenham ≃	214	42.35 N	82.23 W
North Sydney, Austl.	274a	33.50 S	151.13 E
North Sydney, N.S., Can.	186	46.13 N	60.15 W
North Syracuse	210	43.08 N	76.07 W
North Tamborine	171a	27.56 S	153.11 E
North Taranaki Bight C[3]	172	38.42 S	174.15 E
North Tarrytown	276	41.05 N	73.51 W
North Tawton	42	50.48 N	3.53 W
North Tea Lake ⊜	190	45.56 N	79.03 W
North Terre Haute	194	39.31 N	87.21 W
North Tewksbury	283	42.38 N	71.14 W
North Thames ≃	212	42.59 N	81.16 W
North Thompson ≃	182	50.41 N	120.21 W
North Thoresby	44	53.28 N	0.03 W
North Tidworth	42	51.16 N	1.40 W
North Toe ≃	192	36.00 N	82.16 W
North Tolsta	46	58.20 N	6.13 W
North Tonawanda	210	43.02 N	78.51 W
North Towanda	210	41.47 N	76.28 W
North Troy	206	44.59 N	72.24 W
North Truro	207	42.02 N	70.05 W
North Tule Draw V	196	34.30 N	101.36 W
North Tunica	194	34.42 N	90.23 W
North Turlock	226	37.31 N	120.51 W
North Turramurra	274a	33.43 S	151.09 E
North Twin Lake ⊜	186	49.16 N	55.56 W
North Tyne ≃	44	54.59 N	2.08 W
North Ubian Island I	116	6.09 N	120.27 E
North Uist I	46	57.36 N	7.18 W
Northumberland	210	40.53 N	76.47 W
Northumberland □[6], On., Can.	212	44.10 N	78.00 W
Northumberland □[6], Eng., U.K.	44	55.15 N	2.05 W
Northumberland □[6], Pa., U.S.	210	40.49 N	76.39 W
Northumberland □[6], Va., U.S.	208	37.50 N	76.25 W
Northumberland Isles II	166	21.40 S	150.00 E
Northumberland National Park ♠	44	55.15 N	2.20 W
Northumberland Strait ʊ	186	46.00 N	63.30 W
North Umpqua ≃	202	43.16 N	123.27 W
North Uxbridge	207	42.05 N	71.38 W
Northvale	276	41.00 N	73.56 W
North Valley Hills ⋏[2]	285	40.02 N	75.40 W
North Valley Stream	276	40.41 N	73.42 W
North Vancouver	224	49.19 N	123.04 W
North Vandergrift	279b	40.36 N	79.34 W
North Vernon	218	39.00 N	85.37 W
North Versailles	279b	40.22 N	79.48 W
North Vietnam → Vietnam □[1]	108	16.00 N	108.00 E
Northville, Mi., U.S.	216	42.25 N	83.29 W
Northville, N.Y., U.S.	210	43.13 N	74.10 W
Northville Downs ♠	281	42.26 N	83.29 W
Northvue	214	40.54 N	79.56 W
North Wabasca Lake ⊜	182	56.00 N	113.55 W
North Wales	208	40.12 N	75.16 W
Northwall	46	59.16 N	2.17 W
North Walsham	42	52.50 N	1.24 E
North Wantagh	276	40.41 N	73.30 W
North Warren	214	41.52 N	79.09 W
North Washington, Pa., U.S.	214	41.03 N	79.49 W
North Washington, Pa., U.S.	279b	40.32 N	79.36 W
North Watuppa Pond ⊜	207	41.42 N	71.06 W
Northway	180	62.58 N	141.56 W
North Weald Bassett	42	51.43 N	0.10 E
North Webster	216	41.19 N	85.41 W
North Weissport	210	40.50 N	75.41 W
Northwest ≃	208	36.31 N	76.05 W
North West Cape ➤, Austl.	162	21.45 S	114.10 E
Northwest Cape ➤, Ak., U.S.	180	63.46 N	171.45 W
Northwest Cape ➤, Fl., U.S.	220	25.13 N	81.11 W
North Westchester	207	41.34 N	72.24 W
North Western	210	43.20 N	75.22 W
North-Western □[4]	154	13.00 S	25.00 E
Northwestern University ʋ[2], Il., U.S.	278	42.04 N	87.40 W
Northwestern University (Chicago Campus) ʋ[2], Il., U.S.	278	41.54 N	87.37 W
Northwest Frontier □[4]	120	34.30 N	72.00 E
Northwest Gander ≃	186	48.50 N	55.00 W
Northwest Harbor C	284b	39.16 N	76.35 W
Northwest Head ➤	116	10.08 N	118.45 E
Northwest Miramichi ≃	186	46.58 N	65.35 W
Northwest Pacific Basin ✦[1]	6	40.00 N	155.00 E
North West Point ➤	174o	2.02 N	157.29 W
Northwest Providence Channel ʊ	238	26.10 N	78.20 W
North West River	176	53.32 N	60.08 W
Northwest Territories □[4]	176	70.00 N	100.00 W
North Weymouth	283	42.15 N	70.57 W
Northwich	44	53.16 N	2.32 W
North Wichita ≃	196	33.43 N	99.29 W
North Wilbraham	207	42.09 N	72.25 W
North Wildwood	208	39.00 N	74.47 W
North Wilkesboro	192	36.09 N	81.08 W
North Willow Creek ≃	202	46.51 N	107.54 W
North Wilmington	283	42.34 N	71.09 W
North Windham, Ct., U.S.	207	41.44 N	72.09 W
North Windham, Me., U.S.	188	43.50 N	70.26 W
Northwold	42	52.33 N	0.35 E
Northwood, Eng., U.K.	42	50.44 N	1.19 W
Northwood, Ia., U.S.	190	43.26 N	93.13 W
Northwood, Mi., U.S.	216	42.19 N	85.38 W
Northwood, N.D., U.S.	198	47.44 N	97.33 W
Northwood, Oh., U.S.	214	41.36 N	83.28 W
Northwood ◆[8]	260	51.37 N	0.25 W
North Woodslee	281	42.13 N	82.43 W
Northwood Village	284c	39.02 N	77.01 W
North Yamhill ≃	224	45.13 N	123.08 W
North Yelta	168b	34.03 S	137.37 E
North York	212	43.46 N	79.25 W
North York Moors ⋏[2]	44	54.24 N	0.53 W
North York Moors National Park ♠	44	54.23 N	0.50 W
North Yorkshire □[6]	44	54.15 N	1.30 W
North Yuba ≃	226	39.22 N	121.08 W
North Zulch	222	30.55 N	96.07 W
Norton, N.B., Can.	186	45.38 N	65.42 W
Norton, Eng., U.K.	44	54.09 N	0.47 W
Norton, Eng., U.K.	262	53.20 N	2.40 W
Norton, Ks., U.S.	198	39.50 N	99.53 W
Norton, Ma., U.S.	207	41.58 N	71.11 W
Norton, Oh., U.S.	214	41.01 N	81.39 W
Norton, Vt., U.S.	206	45.00 N	71.47 W
Norton, Va., U.S.	192	36.56 N	82.37 W
Norton, Zimb.	154	17.53 S	30.42 E
Norton Air Force Base ■	228	34.06 N	117.14 W
Norton Basin C	276	40.36 N	73.47 W
Norton Bay C	180	64.45 N	161.15 W
Norton Creek ≃	281	42.34 N	83.34 W
Norton Fitzwarren	42	51.02 N	3.09 W
Norton Grove	207	42.00 N	71.12 W
Norton Heath	260	51.43 N	0.19 E
Norton Hill	210	42.25 N	74.04 W
Norton Pond ⊜	206	44.56 N	71.51 W
Norton Reservoir ⊜[1]	283	41.59 N	71.12 W
Norton Shores	216	43.10 N	86.15 W
Norton Sound ʊ	180	63.50 N	164.00 W
Nortonville, On., Can.	275b	43.43 N	79.44 W
Nortonville, Ks., U.S.	198	39.25 N	95.20 W
Nortorf, Dtsch.	30	54.10 N	9.50 E
Nortorf, Dtsch.	52	53.55 N	9.16 E
Nort-sur-Erdre	32	47.26 N	1.30 W
Noruega, Mar de → Norwegian Sea ⊤[2]	10	70.00 N	2.00 E
Noruega → Norway □[1]	24	62.00 N	10.00 E
Norumbega Reservoir ⊜[1]	283	42.20 N	71.18 W
Nørup	41	55.43 N	9.19 E
Norval	212	43.39 N	79.51 W
Norvalspont	158	30.38 S	25.27 E
Norvège → Norway □[1]	24	62.00 N	10.00 E
Norvegia, Cape ➤	9	71.25 S	12.18 W
Norvell	216	42.10 N	84.11 W
Norvelt	214	40.12 N	79.32 W
Norvin Green State Forest ♠	276	41.03 N	74.20 W
Norwalk, Ca., U.S.	228	33.54 N	118.04 W
Norwalk, Ct., U.S.	207	41.07 N	73.24 W
Norwalk, Ia., U.S.	190	41.28 N	93.40 W
Norwalk, Oh., U.S.	214	41.14 N	82.36 W
Norwalk ≃	207	41.06 N	73.25 W
Norwalk Harbor C	276	41.06 N	73.24 W
Norwalk Islands II	276	41.03 N	73.23 W
Norway, In., U.S.	216	40.47 N	86.46 W
Norway, Ia., U.S.	190	41.54 N	91.55 W
Norway, Me., U.S.	188	44.12 N	70.32 W
Norway, Mi., U.S.	190	45.47 N	87.54 W
Norway (Norge) □[1], Europe	22	62.00 N	10.00 E
Norway (Norge) □[1], Europe	24	62.00 N	10.00 E
Norway Bay C	176	71.08 N	104.35 W
Norway House	184	53.59 N	97.50 W
Norway Lake ⊜	212	45.20 N	76.43 W
Norwegen → Norway □[1]	24	62.00 N	10.00 E
Norwegian Basin ✦[1]	10	68.00 N	2.00 W
Norwegian Sea ⊤[2]	10	70.00 N	2.00 E
Norwegian Trench ✦[1]	10	59.00 N	4.30 E
Norwell	283	42.09 N	70.47 W
Norwich, On., Can.	212	42.59 N	80.36 W
Norwich, Eng., U.K.	42	52.38 N	1.18 E
Norwich, Ct., U.S.	207	41.32 N	72.05 W
Norwich, Ks., U.S.	198	37.27 N	97.50 W
Norwich, N.Y., U.S.	210	42.31 N	75.31 W
Norwich Airport ⊠	42	52.31 N	1.15 E
Norwin Heights	279b	40.20 N	79.44 W
Norwood, On., Can.	212	44.23 N	77.59 W
Norwood, Co., U.S.	200	38.07 N	108.17 W
Norwood, Ma., U.S.	207	42.11 N	71.12 W
Norwood, Mn., U.S.	190	44.46 N	93.55 W
Norwood, N.J., U.S.	276	40.59 N	73.57 W
Norwood, N.Y., U.S.	188	44.45 N	74.59 W
Norwood, N.C., U.S.	192	35.13 N	80.07 W
Norwood, Oh., U.S.	218	39.10 N	84.27 W
Norwood, Pa., U.S.	285	39.53 N	75.17 W
Norwood ◆[8]	273d	26.10 S	28.04 E
Norwood Memorial Airport ⊠	283	42.11 N	71.10 W
Norwood Park ◆[8]	278	41.59 N	87.48 W
Norwood Pond ⊜	283	42.35 N	70.52 W
Norwoodville	190	41.39 N	93.33 W
Noryang	98	34.56 N	127.52 E
Nosaka	94	35.39 N	140.34 E
Nosappu-misaki ➤	92a	43.23 N	145.49 E
Nosate	266b	45.33 N	8.43 E
Nosbonsing, Lake ⊜	190	46.12 N	79.13 W
Nose	96	34.58 N	135.24 E
Nose ◆[8]	270	34.49 N	135.09 E
Nose Creek ≃	182	54.52 N	119.38 W
Noshiro	92	40.12 N	140.02 E
Noska ≃	86	58.53 N	68.40 E
Nosop (Nossob) ≃	156	26.55 S	20.37 E
Nosova	86	59.30 N	63.13 E
Nosovaja, Ross.	24	68.15 N	54.35 E
Nosovaja, Ross.	80	57.15 N	45.35 E
Nosovka	78	50.55 N	31.35 E
Nosovo, Ross.	76	57.07 N	27.50 E
Nosovo, Ross.	83	47.16 N	38.40 E
Nosovščina	24	62.56 N	37.03 E
Noṣratābād	128	29.54 N	59.59 E
Noss, Isle of I	46a	60.09 N	1.01 W
Nossa Senhora da Aparecida	256	22.02 S	42.48 W
Nossa Senhora das Dores	250	10.29 S	37.13 W
Nossa Senhora do Amparo	256	22.22 S	44.05 W
Nossa Senhora do Livramento	248	15.48 S	56.22 W
Nossa Senhora do Ó ◆[8]	287b	23.30 S	46.41 W
Nossebro	26	58.11 N	12.43 E
Nossen	54	51.03 N	13.17 E
Nossentiner Heide ◆[3]	54	53.35 N	12.25 E
Noss Head ➤	46	58.28 N	3.04 W
Nossob	156	22.18 S	17.10 E
Nossob (Nosop) ≃	156	26.55 S	20.37 E
Nossombougou	150	13.06 N	7.56 W
Nošul'	24	60.09 N	49.28 E
Nosy Varika	157b	20.35 S	48.32 E
Notasulga	194	32.33 N	85.40 W
Notch Cliff	284b	39.27 N	76.31 W
Notch Hill	182	50.52 N	119.26 W
Notch Peak ∧	200	39.08 N	113.24 W
Noteć ≃	30	52.44 N	15.26 E
Notigi Lake ⊜	184	55.57 N	99.18 W
Notikewin ≃	176	57.15 N	117.05 W
Noto, It.	70	36.53 N	15.04 E
Noto, Nihon	92	37.18 N	137.09 E
Noto, Golfo di C	70	36.50 N	15.12 E
Noto, Val di ◆[1]	70	37.05 N	14.35 E

Symbols in the index entries represent the broad categories identified in the key at the right. Symbols with superior numbers (⋏[1]) identify subcategories (see complete key on page *I · 1).*

Symbole im Register stellen die rechts im Schlüssel erklärten Kategorien dar. Symbole mit hochgestellten Ziffern (⋏[1]) bezeichnen Unterabteilungen einer Kategorie (vgl. vollständiger Schlüssel auf Seite *I · 1).*

Los símbolos incluídos en el texto del índice representan las grandes categorias identificadas con la clave a la derecha. Los símbolos con numeros en su parte superior (⋏[1]) identifican las subcategorías (véase la clave completa en la página *I · 1).*

Les symboles de l'index représentent les catégories indiquées dans la légende à droite. Les symboles suivis d'un indice (⋏[1]) représentent des sous-catégories (voir légende complète à la page *I · 1).*

Os símbolos incluídos no texto do índice representam as grandes categorias identificadas com a chave à direita. Os símbolos com números em sua parte superior (⋏[1]) identificam as subcategorias (veja-se a chave completa à página *I · 1).*

∧	Mountain	Berg	Montaña	Montagne	Montanha
⋏	Mountains	Gebirge	Montañas	Montagnes	Montanhas
)(	Pass	Paß	Paso	Col	Passo
V	Valley, Canyon	Tal, Cañon	Valle, Cañón	Vallée, Canyon	Vale, Canhão
≚	Plain	Ebene	Llano	Plaine	Planície
➤	Cape	Kap	Cabo	Cap	Cabo
I	Island	Insel	Isla	Île	Ilha
II	Islands	Inseln	Islas	Îles	Ilhas
≛	Other Topographic Features	Andere Topographische Objekte	Otros Elementos Topográficos	Autres données topographiques	Outros acidentes topográficos

ESPAÑOL

Nombre	Página	Lat. °′	Long. °′ W = Oeste
Noto Antica ⊥	70	36.56 N	15.02 E
Notodden	26	59.34 N	9.17 E
Notogawa	94	35.10 N	136.10 E
Noto-hantō ›[1]	92	37.20 N	137.00 E
Noto-hantō-kokutei-kōen ♠	94	37.10 N	136.50 E
Noto-jima	94	37.08 N	137.00 E
Noto-jima I	94	37.07 N	137.00 E
Nōtori-dake ∧	94	35.37 N	138.15 E
Notoro-ko ⊜	92a	44.05 N	144.10 E
Notozero, ozero ⊜	24	66.28 N	32.05 E
Notre-Dame	186	46.19 N	64.43 W
Notre-Dame ✝[1]	261	48.51 N	2.21 E
Notre-Dame, Bois ♠	261	48.45 N	2.35 E
Notre-Dame, Monts ⋏	186	48.10 N	68.00 W
Notre-Dame, Ruisseau ≃	275a	45.41 N	73.26 W
Notre Dame Bay ⊂	186	49.45 N	55.15 W
Notre-Dame-de-Bellecombe	62	45.48 N	6.31 E
Notre-Dame-de-Lorette ✝[1]	50	50.25 N	2.42 E
Notre-Dame-de-Lourdes	184	49.32 N	98.33 W
Notre-Dame-de-Pierreville	206	46.06 N	72.53 W
Notre-Dame-des-Victoires ◆[8]	275a	45.35 N	73.34 W
Notre-Dame-du-Haut ✝[1]	58	47.43 N	6.37 E
Notre-Dame-du-Laus	188	46.05 N	75.37 W
Notre-Dame-du-Nord	190	47.36 N	79.30 W
Notrees	196	31.55 N	102.45 W
Notreure ≃	50	47.41 N	2.36 E
Notsu	96	33.02 N	131.42 E
Notsuharu	96	33.09 N	131.32 E
Nottawa	216	41.55 N	85.27 W
Nottawa Creek ≃	216	42.01 N	85.24 W
Nottawasaga ≃	212	44.32 N	80.01 W
Nottawasaga Bay ⊂	212	44.35 N	80.15 W
Nottaway ≃	176	51.22 N	79.55 W
Nottingham, Eng., U.K.	42	52.58 N	1.10 W
Nottingham, Pa., U.S.	208	39.45 N	76.01 W
Nottingham, Pa., U.S.	285	40.07 N	74.58 W
Nottingham Island I	176	63.20 N	77.55 W
Nottingham Park	278	41.46 N	87.48 W
Nottingham Road	158	29.22 S	30.00 E
Nottinghamshire □[6]	44	53.00 N	1.00 W
Notting Hill	274b	37.54 S	145.08 E
Nottleben	54	50.58 N	10.50 E
Nottoway	192	37.08 N	78.05 W
Nottoway ≃	192	36.33 N	76.55 W
Nottuln	52	51.55 N	7.22 E
Notukeu Creek ≃	184	49.55 N	106.30 W
Nouâdhibou	148	20.54 N	17.04 W
Nouâdhibou, Râs ›	148	20.46 N	17.03 W
Nouakchott	150	18.06 N	15.57 W
Nouâmghâr	150	19.22 N	16.31 W
Nouan-le-Fuzelier	50	47.32 N	2.02 E
Nouans-les-Fontaines	50	47.08 N	1.18 E
Nouméa	175f	22.16 S	166.27 E
Noun ≃	152	4.55 N	11.06 E
Nouna	150	12.44 N	3.52 W
Nounsley	260	51.46 N	0.36 E
Noupoort	158	31.10 S	24.57 E
Nous	158	28.44 S	19.52 E
Nouveau Brunswick → New Brunswick □[4]	186	46.30 N	66.15 W
Nouveau Mexique → New Mexico □[3]	178	34.30 N	106.00 W
Nouveau-Québec, Cratère du ⌓[6]	176	61.17 N	73.40 W
Nouvelle	186	48.08 N	66.19 W
Nouvelle ≃	186	48.07 N	66.18 W
Nouvelle-Calédonie (New Caledonia) I	175f	21.30 S	165.30 E
Nouvelle-Calédonie → New Caledonia □[2]	175f	21.30 S	165.30 E
Nouvelle Écosse → Nova Scotia □[4]	186	45.00 N	63.00 W
Nouvelle-France, Cap de ›	176	62.27 N	73.42 W
Nouvelle Galles du Sud → New South Wales □[3]	166	33.00 S	146.00 E
Nouvelle-Orléans → New Orleans	194	29.58 N	90.07 W
Nouvelles-Hébrides → Vanuatu □[1]	175f	16.00 S	167.00 E
Nouvelle Zélande → New Zealand □[1]	172	41.00 S	174.00 E
Nouvelle Zemble → Novaja Zeml'a II	72	74.00 N	57.00 E
Nouvion-en-Ponthieu	50	50.12 N	1.47 E
Nouvion-sur-Meuse	56	49.42 N	4.48 E
Nouzonville	56	49.49 N	4.45 E
Nova, Magy.	61	46.41 N	16.41 E
Nova, Oh., U.S.	214	41.02 N	82.18 W
Nova América	255	15.01 S	49.56 W
Nova Andradina	255	22.10 S	53.15 W
Novabad, Taj.	85	39.01 N	70.09 E
Novabad, Taj.	85	38.37 N	68.45 E
Nová Baňa	30	48.26 N	18.39 E
Nová Bystřice	61	49.01 N	15.06 E
Nova Cachoeirinha ◆[8]	287b	23.28 S	46.40 W
Nova Caipemba	152	7.26 S	14.38 E
Novacella ✝[1]	64	46.44 N	11.39 E
Nova Era	255	19.45 S	43.03 W
Nova Esperança	255	23.08 S	52.13 W
Novafeltria	66	43.53 N	12.17 E
Nova Friburgo	256	22.16 S	42.32 W
Nova Goa → Panaji	122	15.29 N	73.50 E
Nova Gorica	64	45.57 N	13.39 E
Nova Gradiška	36	45.16 N	17.23 E
Nova Granada	255	20.29 S	49.19 W
Nova Iguaçu	256	22.45 S	43.27 W
Nova Iguaçu □[7]	287a	22.45 S	43.29 W
Novaja, Ross.	82	55.13 N	38.54 E
Novaja, Ross.	265b	55.48 N	38.03 E
Novaja ◆[8]	265a	60.02 N	30.28 E
Novaja Astrachan'	83	49.07 N	38.36 E
Novaja Belaja	78	49.46 N	39.11 E
Novaja Belokoroviči	78	51.07 N	28.02 E
Novaja Binaradka	80	53.48 N	49.56 E
Novaja Borovaja	78	50.42 N	28.39 E
Novaja Čigla	78	51.13 N	40.28 E
Novaja Derevn'a, Ross.	82	54.01 N	38.53 E
Novaja Derevn'a, Ross.	88	57.15 N	103.08 E
Novaja Ivanovka	78	45.55 N	29.05 E
Novaja Janisol'	83	47.17 N	37.16 E
Novaja Kachovka	78	46.45 N	33.23 E
Novaja Kalitva	78	50.06 N	40.01 E
Novaja Kazanka	80	48.57 N	49.36 E
Novaja Kazmaska	80	56.49 N	53.31 E
Novaja Kriuša	78	50.16 N	41.16 E
Novaja Ladoga	76	60.05 N	32.16 E
Novaja L'al'a	86	59.03 N	60.36 E
Novaja Majačka	78	46.36 N	33.14 E
Novaja Maluksa	76	59.39 N	31.21 E
Novaja Malykla	80	54.13 N	49.57 E
Novaja Mojgora	82	54.27 N	38.32 E
Novaja Odessa	78	47.19 N	31.47 E
Novaja Porubežka	80	51.45 N	49.40 E
Novaja Praga	78	48.33 N	32.54 E
Novaja Ropša	265a	59.45 N	29.53 E
Novaja Sibir', ostrov I	74	75.00 N	149.00 E
Novaja Sloboda	78	51.23 N	34.08 E
Novaja Slobodka	82	54.56 N	36.47 E
Novaja Šul'ba	86	50.33 N	81.20 E
Novaja Uda	88	54.07 N	103.33 E
Novaja Ušica	78	48.49 N	27.16 E
Novaja Usman'	78	51.37 N	39.24 E

FRANÇAIS

Nom	Page	Lat. °′	Long. °′ W = Ouest
Novaja Vodolaga	78	49.43 N	35.52 E
Novaja Zburjevka	78	46.28 N	32.24 E
Novaja Zeml'a II	72	74.00 N	57.00 E
Nováky	30	48.43 N	18.34 E
Nova Lamego	150	12.19 N	14.11 W
Novale (Rauth)	64	46.24 N	11.30 E
Novalesa	62	45.11 N	7.01 E
Novaliches Reservoir ⊜[1]	269f	14.43 N	121.05 E
Nova Lima	255	19.59 S	43.51 W
Nova Lisboa → Huambo	152	12.44 S	15.47 E
Nova Lusitânia	156	19.54 S	34.35 E
Nova Mambone	156	20.59 S	35.01 E
Nova Milanese	266b	45.35 N	9.12 E
Nova Nabúri	154	16.46 S	38.57 E
Nova Odessa	256	23.09 S	46.51 W
Nova Olinda	250	7.06 S	39.40 W
Nova Olinda do Norte	246	3.45 S	59.03 W
Nová Paka	30	50.29 N	15.31 E
Nova Ponente (Deutschnofen)	64	46.25 N	11.25 E
Nova Ponte	255	19.08 S	47.41 W
Nova Prata	252	28.47 S	51.36 W
Novar	212	45.27 N	79.15 W
Novara	62	45.28 N	8.38 E
Novara □[4]	62	45.40 N	8.30 E
Novara di Sicilia	70	38.01 N	15.08 E
Nová Role	54	50.15 N	12.47 E
Nova Roma	255	13.51 S	46.57 W
Nova Russas	250	4.42 S	40.34 W
Nova Scotia □[4], Can.	176	45.00 N	63.00 W
Nova Scotia □[4], Can.	186	45.00 N	63.00 W
Nova Siri	68	40.09 N	16.32 E
Nova Sofala	156	20.09 S	34.42 E
Nova Soure	250	11.14 S	38.29 W
Novate Mezzola	58	46.15 N	9.27 E
Novate Milanese	266b	45.32 N	9.08 E
Nova Timboteua	250	1.12 S	47.24 W
Novato	226	38.06 N	122.34 W
Novato Creek ≃	282	38.06 N	122.29 W
Nova Vandúzi	156	18.57 S	33.16 E
Nova Varoš	38	43.28 N	19.48 E
Nova Venécia	255	18.43 S	40.24 W
Nova Viçosa	255	17.53 S	39.22 W
Nova Vida	248	10.11 S	62.47 W
Nova Vida, Cachoeira ∟	248	9.25 S	63.36 W
Nova Zagora	38	42.29 N	26.01 E
Nove	64	45.43 N	11.40 E
Nové Hrady	61	48.47 N	14.37 E
Novelda	34	38.23 N	0.46 W
Novellara	64	44.51 N	10.44 E
Novelty	219	40.00 N	92.12 W
Nové Město	30	50.21 N	16.09 E
Nové Město nad Váhom	30	48.46 N	17.49 E
Nové Město na Moravě	30	49.34 N	16.04 E
Nové Mlýny, údolní nádrž ⊜[1]	61	48.54 N	16.34 E
Noventa di Piave	64	45.39 N	12.31 E
Noventa Padovana	64	45.24 N	11.58 E
Noventa Vicentina	64	45.17 N	11.32 E
Noves	62	43.52 N	4.54 E
Nové Sedlo	54	50.10 N	12.42 E
Nové Strašecí	54	50.07 N	13.53 E
Nové Údolí	60	48.48 N	13.48 E
Nové Zámky	30	47.59 N	18.11 E
Novgorod	76	58.31 N	31.17 E
Novgorodka	78	48.21 N	32.39 E
Novgorod-Severskij	78	51.59 N	33.16 E
Novgorodskoje	83	48.20 N	37.50 E
Novi	216	42.28 N	83.28 W
Novi Bečej	38	45.36 N	20.08 E
Novi Beograd	38	44.49 N	20.27 E
Novice	196	31.59 N	99.37 W
Novičicha	86	52.13 N	81.24 E
Novi di Modena	64	44.54 N	10.54 E
Novigrad, Cro.	36	45.19 N	13.34 E
Novigrad, Cro.	36	44.11 N	15.33 E
Novikovo, Ross.	86	58.15 N	80.39 E
Novikovo, Ross.	89	46.23 N	143.20 E
Novi Ligure	62	44.46 N	8.47 E
Noville	56	50.40 N	5.23 E
Novi Lyon Drain ≅	281	42.30 N	83.38 W
Novinger	194	40.13 N	92.42 W
Novinka	76	59.49 N	33.20 E
Novion-Porcien	50	49.36 N	4.25 E
Novi Pazar, Blg.	38	43.21 N	27.12 E
Novi Pazar, Jugo.	38	43.08 N	20.31 E
Novi Sad	38	45.15 N	19.50 E
Novi Vinodolski	36	45.08 N	14.48 E
Novka	76	55.27 N	30.24 E
Novki	80	56.22 N	41.06 E
Novl'anka	80	55.48 N	41.44 E
Novlenskoje	76	59.37 N	39.20 E
Novo ≃, Bra.	248	4.55 S	70.33 W
Novo ≃, Bra.	250	6.22 S	55.42 W
Novo ≃, Bra.	250	4.30 S	53.50 W
Novo ≃, Bra.	256	21.23 S	42.44 W
Novo, Lago ⊜	250	1.30 N	50.40 W
Novoachtyrka	83	48.55 N	38.49 E
Nôvo Acôrdo	255	13.10 S	46.48 W
Novoajdar	83	48.57 N	39.00 E
Novoaleksandrovka, Kaz.	86	51.47 N	68.49 E
Novoaleksandrovka, Ross.	80	51.56 N	52.26 E
Novoaleksandrovka, Ukr.	83	48.17 N	39.37 E
Novoaleksandrovka, Ukr.	83	49.08 N	39.17 E
Novoaleksandrovo	265b	55.59 N	37.33 E
Novoaleksandrovsk	80	45.29 N	41.16 E
Novoaleksejevka, Kaz.	86	52.47 N	74.54 E
Novoaleksejevka, Kaz.	86	52.56 N	64.41 E
Novoaleksejevka, Kaz.	86	50.08 N	55.39 E
Novoaleksejevka, Ukr.	78	46.06 N	32.30 E
Novoaleksejevka, Ukr.	78	46.13 N	34.39 E
Novoaltajsk	86	53.24 N	83.58 E
Novoamvrosijevskoje	83	47.49 N	38.29 E
Novoanninskij	80	50.32 N	42.41 E
Novoarchangel'sk	78	48.39 N	30.48 E
Novoarchangel'skoje	265b	55.55 N	37.33 E
Novo Aripuanã	246	5.08 S	60.22 W
Novoasbest	86	57.44 N	60.45 E
Novoazovsk	83	47.08 N	38.05 E
Novobachmutovka	83	48.15 N	37.48 E
Novobatajsk	83	46.54 N	39.47 E
Novobelaja	78	49.49 N	39.18 E
Novobessergenovka	83	47.11 N	38.51 E
Novobogatinskoje	80	47.22 N	51.11 E
Novobogdanovka	78	47.06 N	35.29 E
Novobogordskoje	80	53.11 N	53.56 E
Novoborovaja	83	49.15 N	38.33 E
Novo Brasil	255	16.11 S	50.38 W
Novobratcevskij	82	55.51 N	37.23 E
Novoburejskij	89	49.49 N	129.54 E
Novočeboksarsk	80	56.08 N	47.30 E
Novo Čeremšansk	80	54.21 N	50.10 E
Novočerkassk	83	47.25 N	40.06 E
Novočernorečenskij	86	56.16 N	91.06 E
Novocharitonovo	82	55.35 N	38.30 E
Novocherkassk → Novočerkassk	83	47.25 N	40.06 E
Novochop'orsk	80	51.07 N	41.37 E
Novochop'orskij	80	51.06 N	41.33 E
Novochovrino ◆[8]	265b	55.52 N	37.30 E
Novociml'anskaja	80	47.59 N	42.17 E
Novo Cruzeiro	255	17.29 S	41.53 W
Novodanilovka	78	46.38 N	35.00 E
Novoderev'ankov-Skaja	78	46.19 N	38.45 E
Novoderkul	83	49.08 N	39.38 E

PORTUGUÊS

Nome	Página	Lat. °′	Long. °′ W = Oeste
Novodevičje	80	53.37 N	48.52 E
Novodolinka	86	51.12 N	72.33 E
Novodolinskij	86	49.44 N	72.45 E
Novodoroninskoje	88	51.08 N	112.08 E
Novodružesk	83	48.58 N	38.21 E
Novodubovoje	76	52.19 N	39.13 E
Novodugino	76	55.38 N	34.18 E
Novodvinsk	24	64.26 N	40.47 E
Novodžerelijevskaja	78	45.46 N	38.41 E
Novoekonomičeskoje	83	48.18 N	37.15 E
Novofetinino	82	56.14 N	39.17 E
Novogaritovo	80	52.47 N	40.07 E
Novogirejevo ◆[8]	265b	55.45 N	37.49 E
Novogorbovo	82	55.43 N	36.29 E
Novogornyj	86	55.37 N	60.47 E
Novograd-Volynskij	78	50.36 N	27.36 E
Novogrigorjevka	78	46.24 N	34.59 E
Novogrigorjevskaja	80	49.26 N	43.37 E
Novogrodovka	83	48.13 N	37.20 E
Novogroznenskij	84	43.15 N	46.15 E
Novogrudok	76	53.36 N	25.50 E
Novogupalovka	78	48.02 N	35.26 E
Novo Hamburgo	252	29.41 S	51.08 W
Novo Horizonte	255	21.28 S	49.13 W
Novoignatjevka	83	47.38 N	37.41 E
Novoiljinsk	88	51.42 N	108.41 E
Novoiljinskij	86	57.54 N	55.30 E
Novoivanovka, Kaz.	85	43.08 N	71.26 E
Novoivanovka, Ukr.	78	49.44 N	33.28 E
Novoivanovka, Ukr.	83	47.41 N	38.23 E
Novoivanovskoje	265b	55.43 N	37.22 E
Novoizborsk	76	57.50 N	27.59 E
Novojampol'	89	52.55 N	127.38 E
Novojamskoje	76	52.14 N	34.28 E
Novoje, Ross.	82	55.38 N	38.55 E
Novoje, Ross.	86	58.53 N	68.40 E
Novoje Alechnovo	82	56.02 N	36.49 E
Novojegorjevskoje	86	51.46 N	80.53 E
Novojekaterinovka	83	47.43 N	38.07 E
Novoje Koval'ovo	265a	59.59 N	30.34 E
Novoje Leušino	80	56.48 N	40.32 E
Novojel'n'a	76	53.28 N	25.35 E
Novojenisejsk	86	58.16 N	92.24 E
Novoje Pavšino	82	54.15 N	37.07 E
Novoje Zarečje	76	57.43 N	34.22 E
Novokačalinsk	89	45.06 N	132.01 E
Novokadinsk	88	54.46 N	101.24 E
Novokamala	88	55.58 N	94.58 E
Novokarasuk	86	56.16 N	71.46 E
Novokaširovo	80	54.58 N	52.32 E
Novokaširsk	82	54.51 N	38.15 E
Novokazalinsk	86	45.50 N	62.10 E
Novokijevskij	80	50.27 N	43.08 E
Novokorsunskaja	78	45.38 N	39.09 E
Novokrasn'anka	83	49.08 N	38.18 E
Novokrasnoje	78	48.01 N	31.21 E
Novokručininskij	88	51.46 N	113.48 E
Novokubanka	86	51.40 N	70.44 E
Novokujbyševsk	80	53.07 N	49.58 E
Novokurovka	89	48.51 N	134.20 E
Novokuzneck	86	53.45 N	87.06 E
Novokuznetsk → Novokuzneck	86	53.45 N	87.06 E
Novolakskoje	84	43.07 N	46.29 E
Novolazarevskaja ✝[3]	9	70.45 S	11.50 E
Novoleuškovskaja	78	45.59 N	39.58 E
Novoli	68	40.23 N	18.03 E
Novolimarevka	83	49.17 N	39.36 E
Novolukoml'	76	54.40 N	29.08 E
Novol'vovsk	76	53.55 N	38.47 E
Novomalorossijskaja	78	45.38 N	39.53 E
Novomansurkino	80	53.52 N	51.52 E
Novomargaritovka	83	46.54 N	38.50 E
Novomariinka	88	55.27 N	96.01 E
Novomarkovka	86	51.44 N	72.17 E
Novomel'nikov	84	43.56 N	45.09 E
Novomelovatka	78	50.27 N	40.46 E
Novomelovoje	78	51.23 N	38.13 E
Novo Mesto	36	45.48 N	15.10 E
Novomichajlovka, Ross.	86	55.13 N	81.57 E
Novomichajlovka, Ukr.	78	47.19 N	36.04 E
Novomichajlovka, Ukr.	83	47.51 N	37.29 E
Novomichajlovskij	78	44.15 N	38.51 E
Novomichajlovskoje	82	55.25 N	37.10 E
Novominskaja	78	46.19 N	38.57 E
Novomirgorod	78	48.47 N	31.39 E
Novomoskovsk, Ross.	82	54.05 N	38.13 E
Novomoskovsk, Ukr.	78	48.37 N	35.12 E
Novomyšastovskaja	78	45.12 N	38.35 E
Novonagajevo	80	55.56 N	54.15 E
Novonikolajevka, Kaz.	85	42.26 N	70.28 E
Novonikolajevka, Ross.	83	46.59 N	39.36 E
Novonikolajevka, Ukr.	78	47.59 N	35.55 E
Novonikolajevka, Ukr.	78	46.13 N	32.45 E
Novonikolajevskij	80	50.58 N	42.22 E
Novonikolayevsk → Novosibirsk	86	55.02 N	82.55 E
Novonikol'skoje, Ross.	76	59.25 N	33.13 E
Novonikol'skoje, Ross.	80	49.09 N	45.00 E
Novonikol'skoje, Ross.	86	59.46 N	79.12 E
Novonikol'skoje, Ross.	265b	55.50 N	37.15 E
Novonikol'skoje, Ukr.	83	49.21 N	39.51 E
Novoomel'kovo	83	49.08 N	39.05 E
Novo Oriente	250	5.32 S	40.42 W
Novoorsk	86	51.23 N	58.58 E
Novopavlovka	88	51.13 N	109.14 E
Novopavlovskaja	84	43.58 N	43.38 E
Novopavlovskoje	88	50.56 N	111.35 E
Novopetrovo	86	57.11 N	69.10 E
Novopetrovskoje	82	55.59 N	36.28 E
Novopiscovo	76	57.19 N	41.54 E
Novopodrezkovo	82	55.57 N	37.21 E
Novopokrovka, Kaz.	86	50.41 N	80.28 E
Novopokrovka, Kaz.	86	53.43 N	67.45 E
Novopokrovka, Kyrg.	85	42.52 N	74.45 E
Novopokrovka, Ross.	89	45.52 N	134.28 E
Novopokrovka, Ukr.	78	48.03 N	34.37 E
Novopokrovskoje	80	51.35 N	43.36 E
Novopolevodino	80	51.46 N	47.29 E
Novopolock	76	55.31 N	28.38 E
Novopskov	83	49.33 N	39.05 E
Novorajčichinsk	89	49.47 N	129.38 E
Novor'ažsk	80	53.44 N	40.07 E
Novorepnoje	80	51.06 N	48.24 E
Novorossijka	85	42.44 N	76.07 E
Novorossijsk	78	44.45 N	37.45 E
Novorossijskoje	86	50.13 N	58.00 E
Novorossiysk → Novorossijsk	78	44.45 N	37.45 E
Novorossoš'	83	49.32 N	39.15 E
Novorudnyj	86	51.30 N	58.10 E
Novorybinka	86	51.51 N	71.14 E
Novorybnoje	74	72.50 N	105.50 E
Novoržev	76	57.02 N	29.20 E
Novošachtinsk	83	47.47 N	39.56 E
Novosaratovka	265a	59.50 N	30.32 E
Novoščerbinovskaja	78	46.28 N	38.38 E
Novosel'e	86	54.10 N	76.53 E
Novoselenginsk	88	51.06 N	106.37 E
Novoselica	78	48.14 N	26.17 E
Novoselickoje	84	44.45 N	43.26 E
Novoseliščе	78	49.48 N	25.03 E
Novoselje	265a	59.48 N	30.05 E
Novoselki, Ross.	82	55.08 N	37.33 E
Novoselki, Ross.	82	54.49 N	38.55 E
Novosel'nyj	86	50.00 N	54.38 E
Novoselovka Pervaja	83	48.12 N	37.31 E
Novoselovo	82	56.04 N	39.04 E
Novosel'skoje	78	45.20 N	28.33 E
Novosemejkino	80	53.23 N	50.22 E
Novosergijevka, Ross.	80	52.06 N	53.39 E
Novosergijevka, Ross.	265a	59.54 N	30.34 E
Novoseslavino	80	53.21 N	40.26 E
Novošešminsk	80	55.04 N	51.15 E
Novoshakhtinsk → Novošachtinsk	83	47.47 N	39.56 E
Novosibirsk	86	55.02 N	82.55 E
Novosibirskije ostrova II	74	75.00 N	142.00 E
Novosibirskoje vodochranilišče ⊜[1]	86	54.35 N	82.35 E
Novosil'	76	52.58 N	37.03 E
Novosil'skoje	78	51.56 N	38.31 E
Novosokol'niki	76	56.21 N	30.10 E
Novos'olki, Bela.	76	52.24 N	28.33 E
Novos'olki, Bela.	78	52.02 N	24.21 E
Novos'olki, Ross.	76	56.01 N	33.37 E
Novos'olki, Ross.	80	54.50 N	39.46 E
Novos'olki, Ross.	80	55.48 N	42.41 E
Novos'olki, Ross.	265a	59.42 N	30.17 E
Novos'olovka	83	49.04 N	37.42 E
Novos'olovo, Ross.	86	55.04 N	91.07 E
Novos'olovo, Ross.	88	56.04 N	107.42 E
Novos'olovskoje	78	45.26 N	33.34 E
Novospasovka	83	47.42 N	39.04 E
Novospasskoje	80	53.08 N	47.45 E
Novostrel'covka	83	49.20 N	39.55 E
Novostrojevo	76	54.27 N	21.50 E
Novosvetlovka	83	48.30 N	39.30 E
Novosysojevka	89	44.14 N	133.22 E
Novotavolžanka	78	50.22 N	36.50 E
Novotitarovskaja	78	45.14 N	39.00 E
Novotroick, Ross.	86	56.11 N	78.41 E
Novotroick, Ross.	86	51.12 N	58.20 E
Novotroickoje, Kaz.	85	43.42 N	73.46 E
Novotroickoje, Ross.	80	58.28 N	47.06 E
Novotroickoje, Ukr.	78	46.22 N	34.20 E
Novotroickoje, Ukr.	83	47.43 N	37.35 E
Novo-Troitsk → Novotroick	86	51.12 N	58.20 E
Novotulka, Ross.	80	52.38 N	48.45 E
Novotulka, Ross.	80	50.50 N	47.34 E
Novotul'skij	82	54.10 N	37.43 E
Novoukolovo	78	51.02 N	38.25 E
Novoukrainka	78	48.19 N	31.32 E
Novouljanovsk	80	54.08 N	48.24 E
Novoural'sk	86	51.15 N	57.16 E
Novouzensk	80	50.28 N	48.08 E
Novovaršavka	86	54.11 N	74.42 E
Novovasiljevka, Ukr.	78	46.51 N	36.46 E
Novovasiljevka, Ukr.	78	46.48 N	35.44 E
Novov'atsk	80	58.29 N	49.44 E
Novov'azniki	80	56.12 N	42.10 E
Novovolynsk	78	50.50 N	24.05 E
Novovoroncovka	78	47.29 N	33.54 E
Novovoronežskij	78	51.16 N	39.11 E
Novovoskresenovka	85	42.50 N	73.32 E
Novovoskresenskoje	78	47.21 N	33.37 E
Novozacharkino	80	52.11 N	48.29 E
Novozagorje	82	55.39 N	38.38 E
Novozavidovskij	82	56.33 N	36.26 E
Novožilovskaja	24	64.50 N	51.20 E
Novozizevka	80	50.48 N	49.08 E
Novozybkov	76	52.32 N	31.56 E
Novska	36	45.21 N	16.59 E
Nový Bohumín	30	49.56 N	18.20 E
Nový Bor	54	50.45 N	14.33 E
Novyj	86	55.39 N	86.39 E
Novyj Afon	84	43.06 N	40.48 E
Novyj Bor	24	66.43 N	52.16 E
Novyj Bug	78	47.41 N	32.30 E
Novyj Bujan	80	53.41 N	50.04 E
Novyj Bykov	78	50.36 N	31.39 E
Novyj Donbass ◆[8]	83	48.05 N	38.46 E
Novyj Dvor	76	52.50 N	24.21 E
Novyje Ajbesi	80	54.49 N	47.02 E
Novyje Aneny	78	46.52 N	29.14 E
Novyje Basy	78	50.53 N	34.51 E
Novyje Burasy	80	52.08 N	46.06 E
Novyje Denisoviči	76	54.12 N	29.13 E
Novyje Gorki	80	56.42 N	41.06 E
Novyje Maty	80	55.15 N	54.04 E
Novyje Salty	80	54.06 N	53.26 E
Novyje Senžary	78	49.21 N	34.19 E
Novyje Z'atcy	80	57.27 N	52.36 E
Nový Jičín	30	49.36 N	18.00 E
Novyj Jaryčev	78	49.55 N	24.18 E
Novyj Jegorlyk	80	46.24 N	41.54 E
Novyj Karačaj	84	43.49 N	41.56 E
Novyj Karamass	80	56.11 N	48.58 E
Novyj Kiner	80	56.24 N	49.44 E
Novyj Multan	80	57.09 N	52.19 E
Novyj Nekouz	76	57.54 N	38.04 E
Novyj Oskol	78	50.46 N	37.53 E
Novyj Pogost	76	55.30 N	27.29 E
Novyj Port	74	67.40 N	72.52 E
Novyj Put'	85	43.29 N	73.52 E
Novyj Ropsk	76	52.18 N	32.19 E
Novyj Stan	82	56.18 N	37.00 E
Novyj Svet	83	47.48 N	38.00 E
Novyj Tap	86	57.04 N	67.49 E
Novyj Terek ≃	84	43.37 N	47.25 E
Novyj Tevriz	86	59.04 N	78.08 E
Novyj Uzen	72	43.18 N	52.48 E
Novyj Vas'ugan	86	58.34 N	76.29 E
Novy Torjal	80	57.00 N	48.44 E
Nowa Dęba	30	50.26 N	21.46 E
Nowaja Semlja → Novaja Zeml'a II	72	74.00 N	57.00 E
Nowa Ruda	30	50.35 N	16.31 E
Nowa Sól (Neusalz)	30	51.48 N	15.44 E
Nowata	196	36.42 N	95.38 W
Nowater Creek ≃	202	43.57 N	108.00 W
Nowbarān	128	35.08 N	48.42 E
Nowe	30	53.40 N	18.43 E
Nowe Miasto Lubawskie	30	53.27 N	19.35 E
Nowe Miasto nad Pilicą	30	51.38 N	20.35 E
Nowendoc	166	31.32 S	151.43 E
Nowe Warpno	30	53.44 N	14.16 E
Nowfel low Shātow	128	34.23 N	50.32 E
Nowgong	124	25.04 N	79.27 E
Nowingi	166	34.36 S	142.14 E
Nowitna ≃	180	65.55 N	154.17 W
Nowogard	30	53.40 N	15.08 E
Nowogród	30	53.15 N	21.53 E
Nowogrodziec	30	51.12 N	15.25 E
Nowokusnezk → Novokuzneck	86	53.45 N	87.06 E
Nowood ≃	202	44.17 N	107.58 W
Nowosibirsk → Novosibirsk	86	55.02 N	82.55 E
Nowra	170	34.53 S	150.36 E
Nowrangapur	122	19.14 N	82.33 E
Nowshāk ∧	123	36.26 N	71.50 E
Nowshera	123	34.01 N	71.59 E
Nowy Dwór Gdański	30	54.13 N	19.06 E
Nowy Dwór Mazowiecki	30	52.26 N	20.43 E
Nowy Sącz	30	49.38 N	20.42 E
Nowy Sącz □[4]	30	49.30 N	20.15 E
Nowy Staw	30	54.09 N	19.00 E
Nowy Targ	30	49.29 N	20.02 E
Nowy Tomyśl	30	52.20 N	16.07 E
Now Zād	120	32.24 N	64.28 E
Noxapater	194	32.59 N	89.03 W
Noxe ≃	50	48.33 N	3.35 E
Noxen	210	41.25 N	76.03 W
Noxon	202	48.00 N	115.47 W
Noxon Reservoir ⊜[1]	202	47.54 N	115.40 W
Noxubee ≃	194	32.50 N	88.10 W
Noy ≃	110	17.05 N	105.02 E
Noya	34	42.47 N	8.53 W
Noya ≃	152	0.58 N	9.48 E
Noyant	50	47.31 N	0.08 E
Noye ≃	50	49.51 N	2.20 E
Noyelles-sur Mer	50	50.11 N	1.43 E
Noyers	50	47.42 N	4.00 E
Noyers, Ruisseau des ≃	275a	45.21 N	73.22 W
Noyes Island I	182	55.30 N	133.40 W
Noyon	50	49.35 N	3.00 E
Nožaj-Jurt	84	43.05 N	46.24 E
Nozawa-onsen	94	36.55 N	138.27 E
Nozay, Fr.	32	47.34 N	1.38 W
Nozay, Fr.	261	48.40 N	2.14 E
Nozeroy	58	46.47 N	6.02 E
Nozori-dam ◆[6]	94	36.43 N	138.39 E
Nozori-ko ⊜	94	36.42 N	138.39 E
Nozuta	268	35.35 N	139.27 E
Nqamakwe	158	32.12 S	27.56 E
Nqutu	158	28.13 S	30.32 E
N'Riquinha	152	15.45 S	21.42 E
N'Rougas	158	29.07 S	21.09 E
Nsa, Oued en ∨	148	32.28 N	5.24 E
Nsaba	150	5.39 N	0.45 W
Nsah	152	2.22 S	15.19 E
Nsang	152	2.02 N	10.56 E
Nsanje	154	16.55 S	35.12 E
Nsawam	150	5.50 N	0.20 W
Nsefu Game Reserve ◆[4]	154	13.07 S	32.10 E
Nsele ≃	152	4.14 S	15.33 E
Nseleni	158	28.33 S	31.39 E
Nsok	152	1.08 N	11.16 E
Nsoko	158	27.02 S	31.57 E
Nsontin	152	3.09 S	18.00 E
Nsouélé	273b	4.12 S	15.11 E
Nsukka	150	6.52 N	7.24 E
Nsuta	150	5.17 N	1.58 W
Ntakat	150	16.49 N	11.43 W
Ntambanana	158	28.36 S	31.45 E
Ntandembele	152	2.11 S	17.08 E
Ntcheu	154	14.49 S	34.38 E
Ntem ≃	152	2.15 N	9.45 E
Ntoum	152	0.23 N	9.47 E
Ntsama	152	0.32 S	14.38 E
N'Tsaoueni	157a	11.27 S	43.18 E
Ntui	152	4.27 N	11.38 E
Ntumba	154	8.20 S	32.05 E
Ntusi	154	0.03 N	31.13 E
Ntwetwe Pan ≚	156	20.30 S	25.20 E
Nuala	154	13.27 S	28.16 E
Nuanchitang	104	41.02 N	120.41 E
Nuanetsi ≃	156	22.40 S	31.50 E
Nuangola	210	41.09 N	75.58 W
Nuanli	102	23.26 N	100.51 E
Nuannuan	269d	25.06 N	121.44 E
Nuanshui	100	28.53 N	117.51 E
Nuanzhouying	100	25.22 N	117.22 E
Nuasjärvi ⊜	26	64.10 N	28.05 E
Nuatabu	174t	1.33 N	172.59 E
Nuatja	150	6.57 N	1.10 E
Nu'aymah	132	32.38 N	36.10 E
Nūbah	142	30.29 N	31.33 E
Nūbah, Jibāl an- ⋏	140	11.00 N	30.45 E
Nūbārīyah, Tur'at an- ≅	142	30.43 N	30.46 E
Nubian Desert ◆[2]	140	20.30 N	33.00 E
Ñuble ≃	252	36.39 S	72.27 W
Nubra ≃	123	34.39 N	77.36 E
Nucet	38	46.28 N	22.35 E
Nucetto	62	44.20 N	8.04 E
Nucha → Šeki	84	41.12 N	47.12 E
Nuchatlitz Inlet ⊂	182	49.45 N	126.55 W
N'uchča	24	63.27 N	46.28 E
Nuch'ŏn-ni	98	38.14 N	126.16 E
Nucla	200	38.16 N	108.32 W
Núcleo Colonial São Bento	287a	22.44 S	43.18 W
N'učpas	24	60.51 N	51.18 E
Nucuray ≃	246	5.02 S	75.34 W
Nuda, Monte la ∧	64	44.17 N	10.15 E
Nudaybah	142	30.59 N	30.22 E
Nudol' ≃	82	56.07 N	36.42 E
Nudol'-Šarino	82	56.06 N	36.31 E
Nudow	264a	52.20 N	13.10 E
Nueces ≃	196	27.50 N	97.30 W
Nueces Plains ≚	196	28.30 N	99.15 W
Nueltin Lake ⊜	176	60.20 N	99.50 W
Nuenen	52	51.29 N	5.33 E
Nü'er ≃	98	40.57 N	121.19 E
Nü'erhe	104	41.04 N	121.00 E
Nuestra Señora de Talavera	252	25.26 S	63.48 W
Nueva, Isla I	254	55.13 S	66.30 W
Nueva Antioquia	246	6.05 N	69.26 W
Nueva Asunción □[5]	248	21.00 S	61.00 W
Nueva Atzacoalco ◆[8]	286a	19.29 N	99.05 W
Nueva Brunswick → New Brunswick □[4]	186	46.30 N	66.15 W
Nueva Caledonia → New Caledonia □[2]	175f	21.30 S	165.30 E
Nueva Chicago ◆[8]	288	34.40 S	58.30 W
Nueva Ciudad Guerrero	232	26.35 N	99.15 W
Nueva Concepción	236	14.08 N	89.18 W
Nueva Cuadrilla	234	18.04 N	101.33 W
Nueva Ecija □[4]	116	15.35 N	121.00 E
Nueva Escocia → Nova Scotia □[4]	186	45.00 N	63.00 W
Nueva Esparta □[3]	246	11.00 N	64.00 W
Nueva Francia	252	28.11 S	64.12 W
Nueva Galia	252	35.07 S	65.15 W
Nueva Germania	252	23.54 S	56.45 W
Nueva Gerona	240p	21.53 N	82.48 W
Nueva Guinea, Isla → New Guinea I	164	5.00 S	140.00 E
Nueva Hébridas → Vanuatu □[1]	175f	16.00 S	167.00 E
Nueva Helvecia	258	34.19 S	57.13 W
Nueva Imperial	252	38.44 S	72.57 W
Nueva Italia de Ruiz	234	19.01 N	102.06 W
Nueva Loja	246	0.06 N	76.52 W
Nueva Lubecka	254	44.32 S	70.24 W
Nueva Ocotepeque	236	14.24 N	89.13 W
Nueva Palmira	258	33.53 S	58.25 W
Nueva Paz	240p	22.46 N	81.45 W
Nueva Pompeya ◆[8]	288	34.39 S	58.25 W
Nueva Rosita	232	27.57 N	101.13 W
Nueva San Salvador	236	13.41 N	89.17 W
Nueva Segovia □[5]	236	13.40 N	86.10 W
Nueva Siberia, Islas → Novosibirskije ostrova II	74	75.00 N	142.00 E
Nueva Venecia	236	14.03 N	91.33 W
Nueva Vizcaya □[4]	116	16.25 N	121.10 E
Nueva Zelandia → New Zealand □[1]	172	41.00 S	174.00 E
Nueva Zembla, Isla de → Novaja Zeml'a II	72	74.00 N	57.00 E
Nueve, Canal Numero ≅	252	36.11 S	57.18 W
Nueve de Julio	252	35.27 S	60.52 W
Nuevitas	240p	21.33 N	77.16 W
Nuevitas, Bahía de ⊂	240p	21.30 N	77.12 W
Nuevo	228	33.48 N	117.09 W
Nuevo, Bajo ✢[4]	238	15.55 N	78.30 W
Nuevo, Cayo I	232	21.51 N	92.05 W
Nuevo, Golfo ⊂	254	42.42 S	64.36 W
Nuevo Berlín	252	32.59 S	58.03 W
Nuevo Camarón	196	27.05 N	99.55 W
Nuevo Casas Grandes	232	30.25 N	107.55 W
Nuevo Chagres	236	9.14 N	80.05 W
Nuevo Delicias	232	26.15 N	102.50 W
Nuevo Laredo	232	27.30 N	99.31 W
Nuevo Léon	204	32.20 N	115.12 W
Nuevo León □[3]	232	25.40 N	100.00 W
Nuevo Morelos	234	17.31 N	95.02 W
Nuevo Necaxa	234	20.13 N	98.00 W
Nuevo Poblado el Oro	196	26.50 N	101.19 W
Nuevo Primero de Mayo	196	26.01 N	98.02 W
Nuevo Progreso	232	18.38 N	92.18 W
Nuevo Rocafuerte	246	0.56 S	75.24 W
Nuevo Saucillo	196	27.20 N	104.54 W
Nufcor	273d	26.17 S	27.44 E
Nugaal □[4]	144	8.30 N	49.00 E
Nugaaleed, Dooxo ∨	144	8.35 N	48.35 E
Nugget Point ›	172	46.27 S	169.49 E
Nûgssuaq ›[1]	176	70.25 N	52.30 W
Nugu ⊜[1]	122	11.58 N	76.28 E
Nuguria Islands II	14	3.20 S	154.45 E
Nūh	124	28.07 N	77.01 E
Nūh, Rās ›	128	25.05 N	62.24 E
Nuhaka	172	39.03 S	177.45 E
Nuhaydāt as-Sūd, Jabal an- ∧	142	28.01 N	32.21 E
Nuhūd, Jabal an- ∧	140	14.50 N	29.53 E
Nui I[1]	14	7.15 S	177.10 E
Nuia	76	58.04 N	25.33 E
Nuits-Saint-Georges	58	47.08 N	4.57 E
Nuits-sur-Armançon	50	47.44 N	4.12 E
N'uja	74	60.32 N	116.14 E
N'uja ≃	74	60.32 N	116.20 E
Nujiang	102	29.58 N	97.25 E
N'uk, ozero ⊜	24	64.27 N	31.45 E
Nuka Island I	180	59.21 N	150.42 W
Nukan	175c	7.23 N	151.53 E
Nukata	94	34.55 N	137.17 E
Nukatl', chrebet ⋏	84	42.15 N	46.35 E
Nukey Bluff ⌓[4]	166	32.33 S	135.40 E
Nukhayb	128	32.02 N	42.15 E
Nukhaylah ⊤[4]	140	19.03 N	26.19 E
Nukhaylah, Wādī an- ∨	132	31.27 N	35.49 E
Nukiki	175e	6.46 S	156.28 E
N'uksenica	24	60.25 N	44.13 E
Nuku'alofa	174w	21.08 S	175.12 W
Nukufetau I[1]	14	8.00 S	178.22 E
Nukuhu	164	5.35 S	149.25 E
Nukulaelae I[1]	14	9.23 S	179.52 E
Nukumanu Islands II	14	4.30 S	159.30 E
Nukunonu I	14	9.12 S	171.54 W
Nukunuku	174w	21.08 S	175.18 W
Nukuoro I[1]	14	3.51 N	154.58 E
Nukus	72	42.50 N	59.29 E
Nul	175f	16.49 S	168.24 E
Nulato	180	64.43 N	158.06 W
Nullagine	162	21.53 S	120.06 E
Nullagine ≃	162	20.43 S	120.33 E
Nullarbor	162	31.26 S	130.55 E
Nullarbor National Park ♠	162	31.30 S	130.30 E
Nullarbor Plain ≚	162	31.00 S	129.00 E
Nulltown	218	39.35 N	85.10 W
Nul'vand	85	38.16 N	70.32 E
Nulvi	71	40.47 N	8.45 E
Num, Mios I	164	1.30 S	135.13 E
Numabin Bay ⊂	184	56.30 N	103.08 W
Numakuma	96	34.23 N	133.20 E
Numan	146	9.28 N	12.02 E
Numana	66	43.31 N	13.37 E
Numancia	116	9.52 N	125.58 E
Numancia ⊥	34	41.48 N	2.25 W
Numansdorp	52	51.44 N	4.26 E
Numara I	122	6.26 N	73.03 E
Numata, Nihon	92a	43.48 N	141.57 E
Numata, Nihon	94	36.38 N	139.03 E
Numata, Nihon	96	34.27 N	132.24 E
Numatinna ≃	140	7.14 N	27.37 E
Numazu	94	35.06 N	138.52 E
Numbargulme, Mount ∧	164	14.56 S	145.03 E
Number 5 Mine	214	41.08 N	80.11 W
Numedal ∨	26	60.06 N	9.06 E
Numeralla	171b	36.11 S	149.20 E
Numeralla ≃	171b	36.06 S	149.11 E
Numfoor, Pulau I	164	1.03 S	134.54 E
Numidia	210	40.53 N	76.24 W
Numila	229b	21.54 N	159.33 W
Nu Mine	214	40.48 N	79.18 W
Numto	74	63.40 N	71.20 E
Numurkah	166	36.06 S	145.26 E
Nun ≃[1]	150	4.20 N	6.00 E
Nun'amo	180	65.37 N	170.40 W
Nunapitchuk	180	60.54 N	162.29 W
Nunawading	169	37.49 S	145.10 E
Nünchritz	54	51.18 N	13.23 E
Nunda	210	42.34 N	77.56 W
Nundah	171a	27.24 S	153.04 E
Nundu	154	3.49 S	29.05 E
Nuneaton	42	52.32 N	1.28 W
Núñes, Isla I	254	53.31 S	73.48 W
Núñez ◆[8]	288	34.33 S	58.27 W
Nunez ≃	150	10.36 N	14.40 W
Nungarin	162	31.11 S	118.06 E
Nungesser Lake ⊜	184	51.28 N	93.35 W
Nungwe	154	2.46 S	32.01 E
Nunica	216	43.04 N	86.04 W
Nunivak Island I	180	60.00 N	166.30 W
Nunjiang	89	49.10 N	125.11 E
Nunjikompita	162	32.16 S	134.19 E
Nunkini	232	20.20 N	90.11 W
Nunkun ∧	123	33.59 N	76.01 E
Nunligran	180	64.48 N	175.24 W
Nunnelly	194	35.51 N	87.28 W
Ñuñoa	286e	33.28 S	70.36 W
Nunshan	89	48.59 N	125.14 E
Nunspeet	52	52.23 N	5.46 E
Nuomin ≃	89	48.06 N	124.26 E
Nuomin Dashan ∧	89	50.15 N	122.46 E
Nuon ≃	150	6.30 N	8.36 W
Nuoro	71	40.19 N	9.20 E
Nuoro □[4]	71	40.10 N	9.20 E
Nuqruș, Jabal ∧	140	24.49 N	34.36 E
Nuquí	246	5.42 N	77.17 W
Nura	86	48.53 N	62.20 E
Nura ≃	86	50.30 N	69.59 E
Nurallao	71	39.47 N	9.05 E
Nuraminis	71	39.26 N	9.01 E
Nuratau, chrebet ⋏	85	40.20 N	67.15 E
Nuraxi, Nuraghe su ⊥	71	39.42 N	9.00 E
N'urba	74	63.17 N	118.20 E
Nürburg	56	50.21 N	6.57 E
Nürburgring ♠	56	50.21 N	6.58 E
Nur Dağları ⋏	130	36.45 N	36.20 E
Nure ≃	62	45.03 N	9.49 E
Nurek	85	38.23 N	69.19 E
Nurekskoje vodochranilišče ⊜[1]	85	38.30 N	69.30 E
Nuremberg	210	40.56 N	76.10 W
Nuremberg → Nürnberg	60	49.27 N	11.04 E
Nürenbei	107	30.11 N	106.04 E
Nūrestān □[9]	123	35.30 N	70.45 E
Nurettin	130	39.14 N	42.25 E
Nurhak	130	37.58 N	37.25 E
Nuria, Monte ∧	66	42.21 N	13.05 E
Nuriootpa	168b	34.29 S	139.00 E
Nurlat	80	54.26 N	50.46 E
Nurlaty	80	55.37 N	48.18 E
Nūrmahal	123	31.06 N	75.36 E
Nurmes	26	63.33 N	29.07 E
Nurmijärvi	26	60.28 N	24.48 E
Nūrnagar	126	22.20 N	89.03 E
Nürnberg	60	49.27 N	11.04 E
Nürnberg, Flughafen ⊠	60	49.30 N	11.06 E
Nūrpur, India	123	31.10 N	76.29 E
Nūrpur, India	123	32.18 N	75.54 E
Nurpur, India	126	22.13 N	88.05 E
Nūrpur, Pāk.	123	31.53 N	71.54 E
Nurrari Lakes ⊜	162	29.01 S	130.05 E
Nurri	71	39.43 N	9.14 E
Nurri, Mount ∧[2]	166	31.42 S	146.02 E
Nursery	222	28.56 N	97.06 W
Nürtingen	56	48.38 N	9.20 E
Nus	62	45.45 N	7.28 E

Symbol	English	Deutsch	Español	Français	Português
≃	River	Fluß	Río	Rivière	Rio
≅	Canal	Kanal	Canal	Canal	Canal
∟	Waterfall, Rapids	Wasserfall, Stromschnellen	Cascada, Rápidos	Chute d'eau, Rapides	Cascata, Rápidos
⊔	Strait	Meeresstraße	Estrecho	Détroit	Estreito
⊂	Bay, Gulf	Bucht, Golf	Bahía, Golfo	Baie, Golfe	Baía, Golfo
⊜	Lake, Lakes	See, Seen	Lago, Lagos	Lac, Lacs	Lago, Lagos
≚	Swamp	Sumpf	Pantano	Marais	Pântano
⊓	Ice Features, Glacier	Eis- und Gletscherformen	Accidentes Glaciales	Formes glaciaires	Acidentes glaciares
⊤	Other Hydrographic Features	Andere Hydrographische Objekte	Otros Elementos Hidrográficos	Autres données hydrographiques	Outros acidentes hidrográficos
✢	Submarine Features	Untermeerische Objekte	Accidentes Submarinos	Formes de relief sous-marin	Acidentes submarinos
□	Political Unit	Politische Einheit	Unidad Politica	Entité politique	Unidade política
✝	Cultural Institution	Kulturelle Institution	Institución Cultural	Institution culturelle	Institução cultural
⊥	Historical Site	Historische Stätte	Sitio Histórico	Site historique	Sitio histórico
♠	Recreational Site	Erholungs- und Ferienort	Sitio de Recreo	Centre de loisirs	Area de Lazer
⊠	Airport	Flughafen	Aeropuerto	Aéroport	Aeroporto
▪	Military Installation	Militäranlage	Instalación Militar	Installation militaire	Instalação militar
◆	Miscellaneous	Verschiedenes	Misceláneo	Divers	Diversos

Nūsah 144 14.00 N 46.43 E
Nusa Tenggara Barat □[4] 115b 8.50 S 117.30 E
Nusa Tenggara Timur □[4] 112 9.30 S 122.00 E
Nusaybin 130 37.03 N 41.13 E
Nuṣayrīyah, Jabal an- ⋏ 130 35.30 N 36.12 E
Nusco 68 40.53 N 15.05 E
Nushagak ≃ 180 59.00 N 158.30 W
Nushagak Bay c 180 58.40 N 158.40 W
Nushagak Peninsula ≻[1] 180 58.30 N 159.00 W
Nu Shan ⋏ 102 27.00 N 99.00 E
Nüshan Hu ⊜ 100 32.57 N 118.03 E
Nu-shima I 96 34.10 N 134.50 E
Nushki 120 29.33 N 66.01 E
Nusplingen 58 48.08 N 8.53 E
Nušpoly 82 56.39 N 37.44 E
Nussdorf ◆[8] 264b 48.15 N 16.22 E
Nussdorf am Attersee 64 47.53 N 13.31 E
Nuta ≃ 96 34.23 N 133.04 E
Nutauge, laguna c 180 67.55 N 176.45 W
Nutepel'men, Ross. 180 67.26 N 174.56 W
Nutepelmen, Ross. 180 65.31 N 178.30 W
Nutfield 260 51.14 N 0.07 W
Nuth 56 50.55 N 5.54 E
Nuthe ≃, Dtsch. 54 51.58 N 11.53 E
Nuthe ≃, Dtsch. 54 52.23 N 13.04 E
Nut Lake Indian Reserve ◆[4] 184 52.20 N 103.30 W
Nutley 210 40.49 N 74.09 W
Nutrioso 200 33.57 N 109.12 W
Nut Swamp Brook ≃ 276 40.21 N 74.06 W
Nuttby Mountain ∧[2] 186 45.33 N 63.13 W
Nutter Fort 188 39.15 N 80.19 W
Nutting Lake 207 42.32 N 71.16 W
Nutting Lake ⊜ 283 42.32 N 71.16 W
Nutwood 219 39.05 N 90.39 W
Nutwood Downs 164 15.49 S 134.10 E
Nutzotin Mountains ⋏ 180 62.10 N 141.40 W
Nu'ūmīyah, Wādī an- V 142 29.31 N 31.17 E
Nuupere, Pointe ≻ 174s 17.36 S 149.47 W
Nu'uuli 174u 14.18 S 170.42 W
N'uvčim 24 61.22 N 50.42 E
Nuwākot 124 28.08 N 83.53 E
Nuwaybi' al-Muzayyinah 140 28.58 N 34.39 E
Nuwerus 158 31.08 S 18.24 E
Nuweveldberge ⋏ 158 32.13 S 22.10 E
Nuxis 71 39.09 N 8.44 E
Nuyakuk Lake ⊜ 180 60.00 N 158.40 W
Nuyts, Point ≻ 162 35.04 S 116.37 E
Nuyts Archipelago II 162 32.35 S 133.17 E
Nūzvīd 122 16.47 N 80.51 E
N'Vinda 152 13.04 S 18.57 E
Nwa 152 6.30 N 11.00 E
Nxainxai 156 19.50 S 21.13 E
Nxai Pan National Park ♠ 156 19.45 S 24.50 E
Nxaunxau 156 18.19 S 21.04 E
Nyaake 150 4.52 N 7.37 W
Nyabéssan 152 2.24 N 10.24 E
Nyabing 162 33.32 S 118.09 E
Nyac 180 61.01 N 159.57 W
Nyack 210 41.05 N 73.55 W
Nyack Beach State Park ♠ 276 41.07 N 73.55 W
Nyadiri ≃ 154 16.44 S 32.33 E
Nyahanga 154 2.23 S 33.33 E
Nyahua 154 5.24 S 33.19 E
Nyahururu Falls 154 0.02 N 36.22 E
Nyah West 166 35.11 S 143.22 E
Nyainqêntanglha Feng ∧ 124 30.22 N 90.35 E
Nyainqêntanglha Shan ⋏ 120 30.00 N 90.00 E
Nyainrong 120 32.09 N 92.11 E
Nyakabindi 154 2.38 S 33.59 E
Nyakakiri 154 2.15 S 31.28 E
Nyakanazi 154 3.00 S 31.15 E
Nyakrom 150 5.37 N 0.48 W
Nyakulenga 152 13.03 S 23.29 E
Nyala 140 12.03 N 24.53 E
Nyalam 120 28.11 N 85.58 E
Nyalas 114 2.26 N 102.28 E
Nyamandhlovu 154 19.50 S 28.16 E
Nyamina 150 13.19 N 6.59 W
Nyamlell 140 9.07 N 26.58 E
Nyamougo 154 1.29 S 34.33 E
Nyamtumbo 154 10.29 S 36.02 E
Nyamwage 154 8.08 S 39.00 E
Nyandekwa 154 3.55 S 32.30 E
Nyanding, Khawr V 140 8.40 N 32.41 E
Nyang ≃ 124 29.25 N 94.22 E
Nyanga □[4] 152 3.00 S 11.00 E
Nyanga ≃ 152 2.58 S 10.15 E
Nyanga, Lake ⊜ 162 29.57 S 126.10 E
Nyangana 156 18.00 S 20.41 E
Nyangui ∧ 154 17.53 S 32.44 E
Nyanji Mission 154 14.23 S 31.48 E
Nyanza □[4] 154 0.30 S 34.30 E
Nyanza-Lac 154 4.21 S 29.36 E
Nyasa, Lake (Lake Malawi) ⊜ 154 12.00 S 34.30 E
Nyaunglebin 110 17.57 N 96.44 E
Nyavikungu 154 11.26 S 25.54 E
Nyazura 154 18.43 S 32.10 E
Nyazvidzi ≃ 154 20.00 S 32.17 E
Nybergsund 26 61.15 N 12.19 E
Nyborg 41 55.19 N 10.48 E
Nybro 26 56.45 N 15.54 E
Nyda 74 66.36 N 72.54 E
Nyêmo 124 29.25 N 90.08 E
Nyengo Swamp ≡ 152 14.51 S 22.07 E
Nyeri 154 0.25 S 36.57 E
Nyerol 140 8.41 N 32.02 E
Nyfer ≃ 42 52.02 N 4.50 W
Nygčigen, mys ≻ 180 65.05 N 172.06 W
Nyhammar 40 60.17 N 14.58 E
Nyhyttan 40 59.40 N 14.48 E
Nyiel 140 6.06 N 31.13 E
Nyika National Park ♠ 154 10.48 S 33.48 E
Nyika Plateau ⋏[1] 154 10.40 S 33.50 E
Nyimba 154 14.35 S 30.52 E
Nyingchi 120 29.32 N 94.25 E
Nyíradony 30 47.41 N 21.55 E
Nyírbátor 30 47.50 N 22.08 E
Nyíregyháza 30 47.59 N 21.43 E
Nykøbing, Dan. 26 56.48 N 8.52 E
Nykøbing, Dan. 41 55.55 N 11.41 E
Nykøbing, Dan. 41 54.46 N 11.53 E
Nyköping 40 58.45 N 17.00 E
Nykroppa 40 59.38 N 14.18 E
Nykvarn 40 59.11 N 17.26 E
Nyland 26 63.00 N 17.46 E
Nyland Acres 228 34.14 N 119.09 W
Nylga, Ross. 80 56.46 N 52.22 E
Nylga, Ross. 89 51.38 N 127.35 E
Nylstroom 156 24.42 S 28.20 E
Nymagee 166 32.04 S 146.20 E
Nymboida ≃ 166 29.39 S 152.30 E
Nymburk 30 50.11 N 15.03 E
Nymphenburg ◆[8] 60 48.09 N 11.30 E
Nynäshamn 40 58.54 N 17.57 E
Nyngan 166 31.34 S 147.11 E
Nyoma 120 33.11 N 78.38 E
Nyon 58 46.23 N 6.14 E
Nyong ≃ 152 3.17 N 9.54 E
Nyons 62 44.22 N 5.08 E
Nyord I 41 55.03 N 12.13 E
Nyou 150 12.46 N 1.56 W
Nýřany 60 49.43 N 13.12 E
Nyrov 24 60.42 N 56.40 E
Nýrsko 60 49.18 N 13.09 E
Nyš 89 51.31 N 142.46 E
Nysa, Pol. 30 50.29 N 17.20 E
Nyša, Ross. 80 56.23 N 51.51 E
Nysa Kłodzka ≃ 30 50.49 N 17.50 E
Nysa Łużycka (Neisse) (Nisa) ≃ 30 52.04 N 14.46 E
Nyslott → Savonlinna 26 61.52 N 28.53 E
Nysø 41 55.08 N 12.02 E
Nyssa 202 43.52 N 116.59 W
Nysted 41 54.40 N 11.45 E
Nytva 86 57.56 N 55.20 E
Nyūdō-zaki ≻ 92 40.00 N 139.42 E
Nyugati Pályaudvar ◆[5] 264c 47.31 N 19.04 E
Nyūkawa 94 36.10 N 137.19 E
Nyumba ya Mungu Dam ◆[6] 154 3.51 S 37.28 E
Nyungwe 154 10.16 S 34.07 E
Nyunzu 154 5.57 S 28.01 E
Nyuri 120 27.42 N 92.13 E
Nyūzen 94 36.56 N 137.30 E
Nyvång 41 56.08 N 12.54 E
Nyvrovo 89 54.19 N 142.36 E
Nzaba 273b 4.06 S 15.16 E
Nzébéla 150 8.05 N 9.06 W
Nzega 154 4.13 S 33.11 E
Nzéla 152 1.25 S 12.39 E
Nzérékoré 150 7.45 N 8.49 W
N'zeto 152 7.14 S 12.52 E
Nzheleledam ⊜[1] 156 22.44 S 30.06 E
Nzi ≃ 150 5.57 N 4.50 W
Nzima 154 3.03 S 32.48 E
Nziro 152 3.17 N 24.06 E
Nzo ≃ 150 6.16 N 7.03 W
Nzoia ≃ 154 0.03 N 33.57 E
Nzubuka 154 4.45 S 32.50 E
Nzwani (Anjouan) I 157a 12.15 S 44.25 E

O

Oa, Mull of ≻ 46 55.35 N 6.20 W
Oacoma 198 43.47 N 99.23 W
Oadby 42 52.36 N 1.04 W
Oad Street 260 51.20 N 0.41 E
Oahe, Lake ⊜[1] 198 45.30 N 100.25 W
Oahe Dam ◆[6] 198 44.21 N 100.23 W
Oahu I 229c 21.30 N 158.00 W
Oak ≃ 184 49.51 N 100.28 W
O-Akan-dake ∧ 92a 43.27 N 144.10 E
Oakbank, Austl. 162 33.03 S 140.35 E
Oakbank, Austl. 168b 34.59 S 138.51 E
Oak Bay 224 48.27 N 123.18 W
Oak Beach 276 40.38 N 73.17 W
Oak Bluffs 207 41.27 N 70.33 W
Oakboro 192 35.13 N 80.19 W
Oak Brook 278 41.49 N 87.55 W
Oakbrook Center ◆[9] 278 41.52 N 87.57 W
Oakbrook Terrace 278 41.52 N 87.58 W
Oakburn 184 50.35 N 100.32 W
Oak City, N.C., U.S. 192 35.57 N 77.18 W
Oak City, Ut,. U.S. 200 39.22 N 112.20 W
Oak Creek, Co., U.S. 200 40.16 N 106.57 W
Oak Creek, Wi., U.S. 216 42.53 N 87.55 W
Oak Creek ≃, U.S. 198 45.39 N 100.31 W
Oak Creek ≃, Az., U.S. 200 34.41 N 111.56 W
Oak Creek ≃, Co., U.S. 200 40.25 N 106.50 W
Oak Creek ≃, Ks., U.S. 198 39.29 N 98.28 W
Oak Creek ≃, N.D., U.S. 198 48.38 N 100.24 W
Oak Creek ≃, Tx., U.S. 196 31.48 N 100.13 W
Oakdale, Ca., U.S. 226 37.46 N 120.50 W
Oakdale, Ct., U.S. 207 41.27 N 72.09 W
Oakdale, Il., U.S. 219 38.16 N 89.30 W
Oakdale, La., U.S. 194 30.48 N 92.39 W
Oakdale, Ma., U.S. 207 42.23 N 71.47 W
Oakdale, Ne., U.S. 198 42.04 N 97.58 W
Oakdale, N.J., U.S. 285 39.59 N 74.49 W
Oakdale, N.Y., U.S. 210 40.44 N 73.08 W
Oakdale, Pa., U.S. 214 40.23 N 80.11 W
Oakdale, Tn., U.S. 192 35.59 N 84.33 W
Oakdale Woods 278 41.56 N 87.58 W
Oakengates 42 52.42 N 2.28 W
Oakes 198 46.08 N 98.05 W
Oakesdale 202 47.07 N 117.14 W
Oakey 171a 27.26 S 151.43 E
Oakeys Brook ≃ 276 40.25 N 74.30 W
Oakfield, Me., U.S. 188 46.05 N 68.09 W
Oakfield, N.Y., U.S. 210 43.03 N 78.16 W
Oakfield, Wi., U.S. 190 43.41 N 88.32 W
Oakford, Il., U.S. 219 40.06 N 89.58 W
Oakford, In., U.S. 216 40.25 N 86.06 W
Oakford, Pa., U.S. 208 40.09 N 74.58 W
Oak Forest 216 41.36 N 87.44 W
Oakgrove, Eng., U.K. 262 53.13 N 2.07 W
Oak Grove, La., U.S. 194 32.51 N 91.23 W
Oak Grove, Or., U.S. 224 45.25 N 122.38 W
Oak Hall 208 37.56 N 75.33 W
Oakham 42 52.40 N 0.43 W
Oak Harbor, Oh., U.S. 214 41.30 N 83.09 W
Oak Harbor, Wa., U.S. 224 48.17 N 122.38 W
Oak Hill, De., U.S. 285 39.44 N 75.36 W
Oak Hill, Fl., U.S. 220 28.51 N 80.51 W
Oak Hill, Mi., U.S. 190 44.13 N 86.18 W
Oak Hill, N.Y., U.S. 210 42.25 N 74.09 W
Oak Hill, Oh., U.S. 188 38.54 N 82.34 W
Oak Hill, W.V., U.S. 188 37.58 N 81.08 W
Oakhurst, Ca., U.S. 226 37.19 N 119.40 W
Oakhurst, N.J., U.S. 208 40.16 N 74.01 W
Oakhurst, Tx., U.S. 222 30.44 N 95.19 W
Oak Island I, N.S., Can. 186 44.31 N 64.18 W
Oak Island I, N.Y., U.S. 276 40.39 N 73.18 W
Oak Knolls 204 34.51 N 120.27 W
Oak Lake 184 49.47 N 100.38 W
Oak Lake ⊜, Mb., Can. 184 49.40 N 100.45 W
Oak Lake ⊜, On., Can. 184 50.26 N 93.50 W
Oak Lake ⊜, On., Can. 212 44.36 N 77.55 W
Oakland, On., Can. 214 42.09 N 82.36 W
Oakland, Ca., U.S. 226 37.48 N 122.16 W
Oakland, Ca., U.S. 282 37.48 N 122.16 W
Oakland, Fl., U.S. 220 28.33 N 81.38 W
Oakland, Il., U.S. 194 39.39 N 88.01 W
Oakland, Ia., U.S. 198 41.18 N 95.23 W
Oakland, Me., U.S. 188 44.32 N 69.43 W
Oakland, Md., U.S. 188 39.24 N 79.24 W
Oakland, Md., U.S. 284c 38.51 N 76.55 W
Oakland, Ms., U.S. 194 34.03 N 89.54 W
Oakland, Ne., U.S. 198 41.50 N 96.28 W
Oakland, N.J., U.S. 210 41.00 N 74.15 W
Oakland, Or., U.S. 202 43.25 N 123.17 W
Oakland, Pa., U.S. 210 41.57 N 75.36 W
Oakland, Pa., U.S. 214 40.59 N 80.22 W
Oakland, Tx., U.S. 222 29.36 N 96.50 W
Oakland □[6] 216 42.40 N 83.23 W
Oakland ◆[8] 279b 40.26 N 79.58 W
Oakland-Alameda County Coliseum ♠ 282 37.45 N 122.12 W
Oakland Army Base ■ 282 37.49 N 122.19 W
Oakland Beach 214 41.37 N 80.18 W
Oakland City 194 38.20 N 87.20 W
Oakland Gardens ◆[8] 276 40.45 N 73.45 W
Oakland Mall ◆[9] 281 42.32 N 83.07 W
Oakland Park 220 26.10 N 80.07 W
Oakland-Pontiac Airport ⊠ 281 42.40 N 83.24 W
Oaklands 168b 35.00 S 137.41 E
Oaklands ◆[8] 273d 26.09 S 28.04 E
Oakland Southwest Airport ⊠ 281 42.30 N 83.37 W
Oakland University ⊽[2] 281 42.41 N 83.13 W
Oak Lane Manor 285 39.47 N 75.32 W
Oak Lawn, Il., U.S. 216 41.43 N 87.45 W
Oaklawn, Ks., U.S. 198 37.36 N 97.17 W
Oaklawn, Md., U.S. 284c 38.47 N 76.57 W
Oakleigh 169 37.54 S 145.06 E
Oakleigh South 274b 37.56 S 145.05 E
Oakley, Eng., U.K. 42 51.15 N 1.11 W
Oakley, Scot., U.K. 46 56.04 N 3.33 W
Oakley, Ca., U.S. 226 37.58 N 121.43 W
Oakley, Id., U.S. 202 42.14 N 113.52 W
Oakley, Il., U.S. 219 39.53 N 88.48 W
Oakley, Ks., U.S. 198 39.08 N 100.51 W
Oakley Park 216 42.34 N 83.30 W
Oaklyn 285 39.54 N 75.05 W
Oakman 194 33.42 N 87.23 W
Oakmont 214 40.31 N 79.50 W
Oak Mountain State Park ♠ 194 33.22 N 86.41 W
Oakmulgee Creek ≃ 194 32.28 N 87.09 W
Oak Neck ≻[1] 276 40.54 N 73.34 W
Oak Neck Point ≻ 276 40.55 N 73.34 W
Oakohay Creek ≃ 194 31.44 N 89.25 W
Oak Orchard Creek ≃ 210 43.22 N 78.12 W
Oak Orchard Swamp ≡ 210 43.07 N 78.18 W
Oakover ≃ 162 20.43 S 120.33 E
Oak Park, Austl. 274b 37.43 S 144.55 E
Oak Park, Ca., U.S. 228 34.11 N 118.45 W
Oak Park, Il., U.S. 216 41.53 N 87.47 W
Oak Park, Mi., U.S. 216 42.27 N 83.10 W
Oak Park, Pa., U.S. 285 40.15 N 75.18 W
Oak Point 184 50.30 N 98.00 W
Oakridge, Ca., U.S. 226 38.03 N 121.20 W
Oak Ridge, N.J., U.S. 210 41.03 N 74.29 W
Oakridge, Or., U.S. 202 43.44 N 122.27 W
Oak Ridge, Pa., U.S. 214 41.00 N 79.18 W
Oak Ridge, Tn., U.S. 192 36.00 N 84.16 W
Oak Ridge Lake 276 41.00 N 74.32 W
Oak Ridge National Laboratory ⊽[3] 192 36.00 N 84.15 W
Oak Ridge Reservoir ⊜[1] 276 41.03 N 74.30 W
Oaks 285 40.08 N 81.28 W
Oaks Corners 210 42.56 N 77.01 W
Oak Shades 276 40.26 N 74.13 W
Oakton 284c 38.52 N 77.18 W
Oaktown 194 38.52 N 87.26 W
Oakura 172 39.07 S 173.57 E
Oak Valley, N.J., U.S. 208 39.48 N 75.09 W
Oak Valley, Va., U.S. 284c 38.54 N 77.18 W
Oak View, Ca., U.S. 228 34.24 N 119.18 W
Oak View, Md., U.S. 284c 39.01 N 76.59 W
Oakview, N.J., U.S. 285 39.51 N 75.09 W
Oakview Beach 212 44.29 N 80.03 W
Oakville, Mb., Can. 184 49.56 N 97.58 W
Oakville, On., Can. 212 43.27 N 79.41 W
Oakville, Ct., U.S. 207 41.35 N 73.05 W
Oakville, In., U.S. 218 40.05 N 85.23 W
Oakville, Mo., U.S. 219 38.28 N 90.18 W
Oakville, Wa., U.S. 224 46.50 N 123.13 W
Oakwood, On., Can. 212 44.20 N 78.53 W
Oakwood, N.J., U.S. 285 39.52 N 74.50 W
Oakwood, Oh., U.S. 214 41.23 N 81.29 W
Oakwood, Oh., U.S. 216 41.05 N 84.22 W
Oakwood, Oh., U.S. 218 39.44 N 84.10 W
Oakwood, Tx., U.S. 222 31.35 N 95.50 W
Oakwood Beach 208 39.33 N 75.31 W
Oakwood Park ♠ 279a 41.26 N 82.06 W
Oamaru 172 45.06 S 170.58 E
Ōamishirasato 94 35.31 N 140.19 E
Ōana 268 35.45 N 140.04 E
Oancea 38 45.55 N 28.06 E
Ōarai 94 36.18 N 140.34 E
Oaro 172 42.31 S 173.30 E
Ōasa 96 34.46 N 132.28 E
Oat Creek ≃ 226 38.50 N 121.56 W
Oates Coast ±[2] 9 70.00 S 160.00 E
Oatka Creek ≃ 210 43.01 N 77.44 W
Oatlands 166 42.18 S 147.21 E
Oatley 274a 33.59 S 151.05 E
Oatley Park ♠ 274a 33.59 S 151.04 E
Oatman 200 35.01 N 114.22 W
Oaxaca □[3] 234 17.00 N 96.30 W
Oaxaca [de Juárez] 234 17.03 N 96.43 W
Ob' ≃ 72 66.45 N 69.30 E
Oba ≃ 190 48.55 N 84.17 W
Obaba 152 2.00 S 16.10 E
Obabika Lake ⊜ 190 47.05 N 80.17 W
Obala 152 4.10 N 11.32 E
Oba Lake ⊜ 190 48.38 N 84.18 W
Obama, Nihon 92 32.43 N 130.13 E
Obama, Nihon 94 35.30 N 135.45 E
Obama-wan c 94 35.30 N 135.42 E
Oban, Austl. 166 21.14 S 139.03 E
Oban, Nig. 150 5.17 N 8.35 E
Oban, Scot., U.K. 46 56.25 N 5.29 W
Obanazawa 92 38.36 N 140.24 E
Obando 269f 14.43 N 120.56 E
Oban Hills ⋏[2] 150 5.35 N 8.35 E
Obara 94 35.15 N 137.18 E
Obata 94 34.30 N 136.40 E
Ob' Bay c 9 70.35 S 163.22 E
Obbo 144 3.36 N 38.54 E
Obbola 26 63.42 N 20.19 E
Občuga 76 54.30 N 29.22 E
Obdach 61 47.04 N 14.41 E
Obed 182 53.33 N 117.12 W
Obed ≃ 192 36.04 N 84.39 W
Obeliai 76 55.56 N 25.48 E
Obelisk ∧ 172 45.20 S 169.12 E
Oberá 252 27.29 S 55.08 W
Oberägeri 58 47.08 N 8.37 E
Oberalppass)(58 46.39 N 8.40 E
Oberalpstock ∧ 58 46.44 N 8.46 E
Oberammergau 64 47.35 N 11.04 E
Oberau 64 47.33 N 11.08 E
Oberaudorf 64 47.39 N 12.10 E
Oberbauer 263 51.17 N 7.26 E
Oberbayern □[5] 60 48.15 N 11.45 E
Oberbieber 56 50.28 N 7.29 E
Oberbonsfeld 263 51.22 N 7.08 E
Oberbrügge 263 51.11 N 7.34 E
Obercunnersdorf 54 51.02 N 14.40 E
Oberdiessbach 58 46.51 N 7.38 E
Oberdolling 60 48.50 N 11.35 E
Oberdorla 54 51.10 N 10.25 E
Oberdrauburg 64 46.45 N 12.58 E
Oberelfringhausen 263 51.20 N 7.11 E
Ober Engadin V 58 46.37 N 9.58 E
Oberengstringen 58 47.25 N 8.28 E
Oberer See → Superior, Lake ⊜ 190 48.00 N 88.00 W
Oberfranken □[5] 60 49.50 N 11.20 E
Obergeis 56 50.54 N 9.35 E
Ober-Grafendorf 61 48.09 N 15.33 E
Obergum 52 53.20 N 6.31 E
Obergünzburg 58 47.51 N 10.25 E
Obergurgl 64 46.52 N 11.01 E
Obergurig 54 51.07 N 14.24 E
Oberhaan 263 51.13 N 7.02 E
Oberhaching 60 48.02 N 11.37 E
Oberharmersbach 58 48.22 N 8.07 E
Oberhaslach 58 48.33 N 7.20 E
Oberhausen 56 51.28 N 6.50 E
Oberhof 54 50.41 N 10.44 E
Oberhofen 58 46.44 N 7.40 E
Oberinntal V 64 47.13 N 10.45 E
Oberjettingen 56 48.34 N 8.46 E
Oberjoch 58 47.31 N 10.23 E
Ober-Kassel ◆[8] 263 51.14 N 6.46 E
Oberkirch 58 48.31 N 8.05 E
Ober-Kirchbach 264b 48.17 N 16.12 E
Oberkirchen 56 51.09 N 8.22 E
Oberkochen 56 48.47 N 10.06 E
Oberkotzau 54 50.16 N 11.56 E
Oberlaa ◆[8] 264b 48.08 N 16.24 E
Oberlaapark ◆[8] 264b 48.08 N 16.25 E
Oberlausitz □[9] 54 51.15 N 14.40 E
Oberlin, Ks., U.S. 198 39.49 N 100.31 W
Oberlin, La., U.S. 194 30.37 N 92.45 W
Oberlin, Oh., U.S. 214 41.17 N 82.13 W
Oberlin, Pa., U.S. 208 40.14 N 76.49 W
Oberloisdorf 61 47.27 N 16.30 E
Oberlungwitz 54 50.47 N 12.44 E
Obermarchtal 58 48.14 N 9.34 E
Obermeiser 56 51.26 N 9.19 E
Obermieming 64 47.18 N 10.59 E
Obermodern 56 48.51 N 7.32 E
Obermoschel 56 49.44 N 7.46 E
Obermünstertal 58 47.52 N 7.49 E
Obernai 58 48.28 N 7.29 E
Obernbeck 52 52.12 N 8.41 E
Obernberg am Inn 60 48.19 N 13.20 E
Obernburg am Main 56 49.50 N 9.08 E
Oberndorf 52 53.45 N 9.08 E
Oberndorf am Neckar 58 48.18 N 8.34 E
Oberndorf bei Salzburg 64 47.57 N 12.56 E
Oberndorf in Tirol 64 47.30 N 12.23 E
Oberne 171b 35.24 S 147.50 E
Oberne Hill ∧[2] 171b 35.26 S 147.53 E
Obernhausen 56 50.29 N 9.56 E
Obernkirchen 52 52.16 N 9.07 E
Obernzell 60 48.34 N 13.39 E
Oberoderwitz 54 50.58 N 14.42 E
Oberon 170 33.43 S 149.52 E
Oberösterreich □[3] 30 48.15 N 14.00 E
Oberpfalz □[5] 60 49.30 N 12.10 E
Oberpleis 56 50.43 N 7.16 E
Oberpullendorf 61 47.31 N 16.31 E
Ober-Ramstadt 56 49.49 N 8.44 E
Oberried 58 46.44 N 7.58 E
Oberriet 58 47.19 N 9.33 E
Oberrimsingen 58 47.59 N 7.40 E
Oberröblingen 54 51.26 N 11.18 E
Ober Sankt Veit ◆[8] 264b 48.11 N 16.16 E
Oberscheidental 56 49.30 N 9.09 E
Oberscheinfeld 56 49.42 N 10.26 E
Oberscheld 56 50.44 N 8.20 E
Oberschleissheim 60 48.15 N 11.34 E
Oberschöneweide ◆[8] 264a 52.28 N 13.31 E
Oberseebach 56 48.58 N 7.59 E
Obersickte 54 52.13 N 10.38 E
Oberspier 54 51.19 N 10.51 E
Oberstadtfeld 56 50.10 N 6.46 E
Oberstaufen 58 47.33 N 10.01 E
Oberstdorf 58 47.24 N 10.16 E
Obersteinbach 56 49.02 N 7.41 E
Oberstreu 56 50.24 N 10.17 E
Obersuhl 56 50.56 N 10.02 E
Obersulm 56 49.08 N 9.27 E
Obertheres 56 50.01 N 10.26 E
Obertilliach 64 46.42 N 12.37 E
Obertin 78 48.42 N 25.11 E
Obertraubling 60 48.58 N 12.10 E
Obertraun 64 47.33 N 13.41 E
Obertrum 64 47.56 N 13.05 E
Obertrumer See ⊜ 60 47.58 N 13.06 E
Obertürken 60 48.19 N 12.50 E
Oberueckersee ⊜ 54 53.12 N 13.52 E
Oberursel 56 50.11 N 8.35 E
Oberuzwil 58 47.26 N 9.08 E
Obervellach 64 46.56 N 13.12 E
Oberviechtach 60 49.28 N 12.25 E
Obervolta → Burkina Faso □[1] 150 13.00 N 1.30 W
Oberwald 58 46.32 N 8.21 E
Oberwart 61 47.17 N 16.13 E
Oberweissbach 54 50.35 N 11.08 E
Oberwengern 263 51.23 N 7.22 E
Oberwesel 56 50.06 N 7.43 E
Oberwiesenthal 54 50.25 N 12.59 E
Oberwolfach 58 48.19 N 8.12 E
Oberwölz Stadt 61 47.13 N 14.17 E
Oberzeiring 61 47.15 N 14.29 E
Obetz 218 39.52 N 82.57 W
Obey, East Fork ≃ 192 36.27 N 85.07 W
Obey, West Fork ≃ 192 36.27 N 85.09 W
Obgruiten 263 51.13 N 7.01 E
Obhausen 54 51.23 N 11.39 E
Obi 150 8.22 N 8.46 E
Obi, Kepulauan II 164 1.30 S 127.45 E
Obi, Pulau I 164 1.30 S 127.45 E
Obi, Selat ᴗ 164 0.52 S 127.33 E
Obiaruku 150 5.51 N 6.09 E
Obichingou ≃ 85 38.53 N 70.01 E
Obichody 78 51.02 N 28.59 E
Óbidos 250 1.55 S 55.31 W
Obi-Garm 85 38.43 N 69.42 E
Obihiro 92a 42.55 N 143.12 E
Obikanda 85 39.10 N 67.10 E
Obilatu, Pulau I 108 1.25 S 127.20 E
Obil'noje 80 47.31 N 44.25 E
Obing 60 48.00 N 12.24 E
Obion 194 36.15 N 89.11 W
Obion ≃ 194 35.55 N 89.39 W
Obion, Middle Fork ≃ 194 36.13 N 88.56 W
Obion, Rutherford Fork ≃ 194 36.17 N 89.01 W
Obion, South Fork ≃ 194 36.17 N 89.03 W
Obion Creek ≃ 194 36.35 N 89.11 W
Obiou, Grande Tête de l' ∧ 62 44.46 N 5.50 E
Obira 92a 44.00 N 141.35 E
Obitočnaja kosa ≻[2] 78 46.33 N 36.13 E
Obitočnyj zaliv c 78 46.35 N 36.00 E
Obitsu ≃ 94 35.24 N 139.54 E
Objačevo 24 60.20 N 49.34 E
Oblačnaja, gora ∧ 89 43.45 N 134.10 E
Öblarn 61 47.27 N 13.59 E
Oblastnaja 80 56.59 N 52.37 E
Oblivskaja 80 48.32 N 42.30 E
Oblong 194 39.00 N 87.54 W
Oblučje 89 49.03 N 131.04 E
Obninsk 82 55.05 N 36.37 E
Obnora ≃ 76 58.14 N 40.58 E
Obnova 38 43.26 N 24.59 E
Obo 154 5.24 N 26.30 E
Obobogorap 158 27.18 S 20.04 E
Obock 144 11.59 N 43.16 E
Obojan' 78 51.13 N 36.16 E
Ō-boke ♠ 96 33.55 N 133.46 E
Obokote 154 0.52 S 26.19 E
Obol' 76 55.22 N 29.17 E
Obol' ≃ 76 55.24 N 29.02 E
Oboldino 265b 55.53 N 37.56 E
Obolon' 78 49.36 N 32.52 E
Oborniki 30 52.39 N 16.51 E
Obot 144 4.30 N 37.20 E
Obouya 152 0.56 S 15.43 E
Oboz'orskij 24 63.28 N 40.18 E
Obra ≃ 30 52.36 N 15.28 E
Obrazcovo-Travino 80 45.58 N 48.02 E
Obree, Mount ∧ 164 9.30 S 148.05 E
Obrenovac 38 44.39 N 20.12 E
O'Brien 202 42.04 N 123.42 W
O'Brien Coulee V 202 48.38 N 110.22 W
Obrighoven-Lackhausen 52 51.40 N 6.38 E
Obrovac 36 44.12 N 15.41 E
Obrovo 76 52.30 N 25.34 E
Obručeva, gora ∧ 88 53.36 N 113.52 E
Obručevka 85 42.30 N 69.05 E
Obruk 130 38.10 N 33.12 E
Obryta 54 53.13 N 14.59 E
Obryvistoje 89 48.46 N 144.40 E
Obša ≃ 76 55.55 N 32.32 E
Obšarovka 80 53.07 N 48.52 E
Obščij Syrt ∧ 80 52.00 N 51.30 E
Observation Peak ∧ 204 40.46 N 120.10 W
Observatoire, Caye de l' I 160 21.25 S 158.50 E
Observatorio Cerro Tololo ⊽[3] 252 30.05 S 71.00 W
Observatory Inlet c 182 55.10 N 129.54 W
Obskaja guba c 72 69.00 N 73.00 E
Obsteig 64 47.18 N 10.56 E
Obtovo 38 43.29 N 25.42 E
Ob' Trench ⊤[1] 14 33.00 S 98.00 E

ENGLISH
Name Page Lat.°′ Long.°′

Ōbu 94 35.00 N 136.58 E
Obu ◆[8] 270 34.44 N 135.09 E
Obuasi 150 6.14 N 1.39 W
Obubra 150 6.05 N 8.21 E
Obuchov 78 50.08 N 30.37 E
Obuchova 76 56.06 N 32.22 E
Obuchoviči 78 51.00 N 29.46 E
Obuchovka 86 46.13 N 81.05 E
Obuchovo, Ross. 82 55.50 N 38.16 E
Obuchovo, Ross. 82 56.09 N 36.55 E
Óbuda ◆[8] 264c 47.33 N 19.02 E
Óbudai-sziget I 264c 47.33 N 19.04 E
Obudu 150 6.40 N 9.09 E
Obuse 94 36.42 N 138.19 E
Obushkong Lake ⊜ 190 47.42 N 80.48 W
Obuškovo 82 55.47 N 37.02 E
Obu-tōge)(270 34.44 N 135.10 E
Obva ≃ 86 58.32 N 55.18 E
Obvinsk 86 58.29 N 54.51 E
Obwalden □[3] 58 46.50 N 8.14 E
Obžericha 80 57.11 N 42.58 E
Očakov 78 46.37 N 31.33 E
Očakovo ◆[8] 265b 55.41 N 37.27 E
Ocala 192 29.11 N 82.08 W
Ocallí 248 6.09 S 78.18 W
Očamčira 84 42.44 N 41.28 E
Ocamo ≃ 246 2.48 N 65.14 W
Ocampo, Méx. 232 28.11 N 108.23 W
Ocampo, Méx. 232 27.20 N 102.21 W
Ocampo, Méx. 234 21.39 N 101.30 W
Ocampo, Méx. 234 22.50 N 99.20 W
Ocaña, Col. 246 8.15 N 73.20 W
Ocaña, Esp. 34 39.56 N 3.31 W
Ocate Creek ≃ 196 36.17 N 104.30 W
Occaquan ≃ 208 38.40 N 77.14 W
Occaquan Reservoir ⊜[1] 208 38.43 N 77.22 W
Očchamuri 84 41.52 N 41.50 E
Occhieppo Inferiore 62 45.33 N 8.01 E
Occhiobello 64 44.55 N 11.35 E
Occidental, Cordillera ⋏, Col. 246 5.00 N 76.00 W
Occidental, Cordillera ⋏, Perú 248 10.00 S 77.00 W
Occidental College ⊽[2] 280 34.08 N 118.13 W
Occidental de Zapata, Ciénaga ≡ 240p 22.25 N 81.20 W
Occimiano 62 45.03 N 8.30 E
Occoquan 208 38.41 N 77.15 W
Occoquan Bay c 208 38.37 N 77.13 W
Ocean □[6] 208 39.58 N 74.12 W
Oceana 192 37.41 N 81.37 W
Oceana Naval Air Station ■ 208 36.50 N 76.02 W
Ocean Bay Park 276 40.39 N 73.08 W
Ocean Beach 276 40.38 N 73.18 W
Ocean Bluff 207 42.05 N 70.39 W
Ocean Breeze Park 220 27.15 N 80.14 W
Ocean Cape ≻ 180 59.30 N 139.45 W
Ocean City, Md., U.S. 208 38.20 N 75.05 W
Ocean City, N.J., U.S. 208 39.16 N 74.34 W
Ocean City, Wa., U.S. 224 47.04 N 124.09 W
Ocean Falls 182 52.21 N 127.40 W
Ocean Gate 208 39.55 N 74.08 W
Ocean Grove, Austl. 169 38.16 S 144.32 E
Ocean Grove, Ma., U.S. 207 41.43 N 71.12 W
Ocean Heights 207 41.24 N 70.33 W
Ocean Island → Banaba I 174d 0.52 S 169.35 E
Ocean Lake ⊜[1] 202 43.11 N 108.36 W
Oceano 204 35.06 N 120.37 W
Ocean Park, B.C., Can. 224 49.02 N 122.53 W
Ocean Park, Wa., U.S. 224 46.29 N 124.02 W
Ocean Park ♠ 271d 22.15 N 114.09 E
Ocean Port 276 40.19 N 74.00 W
Ocean Shores 224 47.01 N 124.09 W
Oceanside, Ca., U.S. 228 33.11 N 117.22 W
Oceanside, N.Y., U.S. 210 40.38 N 73.38 W
Ocean Springs 194 30.24 N 88.49 W
Ocean View, De., U.S. 208 38.32 N 75.05 W
Ocean View, N.J., U.S. 208 39.10 N 74.44 W
Oceanville 208 39.28 N 74.27 W
Oceola 214 40.51 N 83.06 W
Očer 80 57.53 N 54.42 E
Očeretino 83 48.14 N 37.36 E
O. C. Fisher Lake ⊜[1] 196 31.30 N 100.30 W
Ocha 89 53.34 N 142.56 E
Ochagavía, Canal ≚ 286e 33.30 S 70.49 W
Ochanomizu Women's University ⊽[2] 268 35.43 N 139.44 E
Ochansk 86 57.43 N 55.23 E
Ochapowace Indian Reserve ◆[4] 184 50.30 N 102.24 W
Ocheyedan 198 43.24 N 95.32 W
Ocheyedan ≃ 198 43.08 N 95.09 W
Ochi, Nihon 96 33.32 N 133.15 E
Ōchi, Nihon 96 34.16 N 134.18 E
Ōchi, Nihon 96 35.04 N 132.36 E
Ochiai 96 35.01 N 133.45 E
Ochiai ◆[8] 268 35.43 N 139.42 E
O'Chiese Indian Reserve ◆[4] 182 52.50 N 115.28 W
Ochil Hills ⋏[2] 46 56.14 N 3.40 W
Ochiltree 44 55.28 N 4.23 W
Ōchise ≃ 94 35.03 N 137.46 E
Ochlocknee 192 30.58 N 84.03 W
Ochlockonee ≃ 192 29.58 N 84.21 W
Ochoco Creek ≃ 202 44.19 N 120.53 W
Ochoco Mountains ⋏ 202 44.30 N 120.35 W
Ochopee 220 25.54 N 81.18 W
Ocho Rios 241q 18.25 N 77.07 W
Ochota ≃ 74 59.20 N 143.04 E
Ochotsk 74 59.23 N 143.18 E
Ochotskisches Meer → Okhotsk, Sea of ⊤[2] 74 53.00 N 150.00 E
Ochotskoje more → Okhotsk, Sea of ⊤[2] 74 53.00 N 150.00 E
Ochre River 184 51.03 N 99.47 W
Ochsenfurt 56 49.40 N 10.03 E
Ochsenhausen 58 48.04 N 9.56 E
Ochsenwerder ◆[8] 52 53.28 N 10.05 E
Ochta ≃ 265a 59.57 N 30.24 E
Ochtrup 52 52.13 N 7.11 E
Ochvat 76 56.46 N 32.27 E
Oci ≃ 152 15.14 S 15.16 E
Ocilla 192 31.35 N 83.15 W
Ock ≃ 42 51.39 N 1.17 W
Ockelbo 26 60.53 N 16.43 E
Öckerö 26 57.43 N 11.39 E
Ockham 260 51.18 N 0.27 W
Ockholm 41 54.40 N 8.49 E
Ockies 158 31.31 S 21.41 E
Ocklawaha, Lake ⊜[1] 192 29.30 N 81.50 W
Ocmulgee ≃ 192 31.58 N 82.32 W
Ocmulgee National Monument ♠ 192 32.43 N 83.38 W
Ocna Mureș 38 46.23 N 23.51 E
Ocoa, Bahía de c 238 18.22 N 70.39 W
Ocoee 220 28.34 N 81.32 W
Ocoee (Toccoa) ≃ 192 35.12 N 84.40 W
Ocoña 248 16.26 S 73.07 W
Ocoña ≃ 248 16.28 S 73.07 W
Oconee 219 39.17 N 89.07 W
Oconee ≃ 192 31.58 N 82.32 W
Oconee, Lake ⊜[1] 192 33.30 N 83.15 W
Ocongate 248 13.38 S 71.24 W
O'Connell 170 33.32 S 149.44 E
Oconomowoc 216 43.06 N 88.29 W
Oconomowoc Lake 216 43.07 N 88.28 W

DEUTSCH
Name Seite Breite°′ Länge°′ E = Ost

Oconomowoc Lake ⊜ 216 43.06 N 88.27 W
Oconto 190 44.53 N 87.51 W
Oconto ≃ 190 44.53 N 87.50 W
Oconto, North Branch ≃ 190 45.00 N 88.23 W
Oconto Falls 190 44.52 N 88.08 W
Ocós 236 14.31 N 92.11 W
Ocosingo 232 16.54 N 92.07 W
Ocotal 236 13.38 N 86.29 W
Ocotepec 234 17.13 N 93.09 W
Ocotepeque □[5] 236 14.30 N 89.00 W
Ocotlán 234 20.21 N 102.46 W
Ocotlán de Morelos 234 16.48 N 96.40 W
Ocoyoacac 234 19.16 N 99.26 W
Ocozocoautla [de Espinosa] 234 16.46 N 93.22 W
Ocracoke 192 35.06 N 75.58 W
Ocracoke Island I 192 35.09 N 75.53 W
Ocre, Monte ∧ 66 42.15 N 13.26 E
Ocros 248 10.24 S 77.24 W
Octoraro Creek ≃ 208 39.39 N 76.09 W
Octoraro Creek, East Branch ≃ 208 39.49 N 76.02 W
Octoraro Creek, West Branch ≃ 208 39.49 N 76.05 W
Octoraro Lake ⊜[1] 208 39.48 N 76.02 W
Ocú 236 7.57 N 80.47 W
Ocuilán de Arteaga 234 18.58 N 99.25 W
Ocumare del Tuy 246 10.07 N 66.46 W
Ocuri 248 18.50 S 65.50 W
Ocussi 112 9.12 S 124.21 E
Oda, Ghana 150 5.55 N 0.59 W
Oda, Nihon 96 33.34 N 132.48 E
Ōda, Nihon 96 35.11 N 132.30 E
Oda ≃ 96 34.37 N 133.44 E
Oda, Jabal ∧ 140 20.21 N 36.39 E
Ŏdaejin 98 41.34 N 129.40 E
Odae-san Kukrip Kongwŏn ♠ 98 37.46 N 128.37 E
Ōdai 94 34.24 N 136.25 E
Ōdaigahara-zan ∧ 92 34.11 N 136.05 E
Odaka 92 37.34 N 141.00 E
Ödåkra 41 56.06 N 12.44 E
Odanakumadona 156 20.53 S 24.45 E
Ōdate 92 40.16 N 140.34 E
Odawara 94 35.15 N 139.10 E
Odayeri ◆[8] 267b 41.14 N 28.51 E
Odda 26 60.04 N 6.33 E
Odden 41 55.58 N 11.22 E
Odder 41 55.58 N 10.10 E
Oddville 218 38.27 N 84.15 W
Odebolt 198 42.18 N 95.15 W
Ödeby 40 59.24 N 15.25 E
Odei ≃ 184 56.06 N 96.55 W
Odeleite, Ribeira de ≃ 34 37.21 N 7.27 W
Odell, Il., U.S. 216 41.00 N 88.31 W
Odell, Ne., U.S. 198 40.03 N 96.48 W
Odell, Or., U.S. 224 45.37 N 121.32 W
Odell, Tx., U.S. 196 34.21 N 99.25 W
Odell Lake ⊜ 202 43.34 N 122.00 W
Odelzhausen 60 48.19 N 11.12 E
Odem 196 27.57 N 97.34 W
Odemira 34 37.36 N 8.38 W
Ödemiș 130 38.13 N 27.59 E
Ödenburg → Sopron 61 47.41 N 16.36 E
Odendaalsrus 158 27.48 S 26.45 E
Odenkirchen ◆[8] 263 51.08 N 6.27 E
Odensbacken 40 59.10 N 15.32 E
Odense 41 55.24 N 10.23 E
Odense Å ≃ 41 55.26 N 10.26 E
Odense Fjord c 41 55.30 N 10.34 E
Odenthal 56 51.02 N 7.07 E
Odenton 208 39.05 N 76.42 W
Odenwald ⋏ 56 49.40 N 9.00 E
Oder ≃, Dtsch. 52 51.40 N 10.06 E
Oder (Odra) ≃, Europe 30 53.32 N 14.38 E
Oderberg 54 52.52 N 14.02 E
Oderbruch ◆[1] 54 52.40 N 14.15 E
Oderen 58 47.55 N 6.59 E
Oderhaff (Zalew Szczeciński) c 54 53.46 N 14.14 E
Oder-Havel-Kanal ≚ 54 52.52 N 14.02 E
Oder-Spree-Kanal ≚ 54 52.23 N 13.41 E
Odertalsperre ◆[6] 54 51.38 N 10.30 E
Oderzo 64 45.47 N 12.29 E
Odesa → Odessa 78 46.28 N 30.44 E
Ödeshög 26 58.14 N 14.39 E
Odessa, On., Can. 212 44.17 N 76.43 W
Odessa, Ukr. 78 46.28 N 30.44 E
Odessa, De., U.S. 208 39.27 N 75.39 W
Odessa, Fl., U.S. 220 28.11 N 82.35 W
Odessa, Mo., U.S. 194 38.59 N 93.57 W
Odessa, N.Y., U.S. 210 42.20 N 76.47 W
Odessa, Tx., U.S. 196 31.50 N 102.22 W
Odessa, Wa., U.S. 202 47.20 N 118.41 W
Odessa □[8] 38 47.30 N 30.00 E
Odessa Lake ⊜ 212 44.19 N 76.41 W
Odesskoje 86 54.13 N 72.58 E
Odiakwe 156 20.01 S 25.17 E
Odib, Wādī V 140 22.38 N 36.06 E
Odiel ≃ 34 37.10 N 6.54 W
Odienné 150 9.30 N 7.34 W
Odiham 42 51.15 N 0.57 W
Odin 219 38.37 N 89.03 W
Odin, Mount ∧ 182 50.33 N 118.08 W
Odincovo, Ross. 82 54.40 N 38.00 E
Odincovo, Ross. 82 55.41 N 37.17 E
Odiongan 116 12.24 N 121.59 E
Odiongan Bay c 116 12.25 N 121.58 E
Odivelas 266c 38.47 N 9.11 W
Odobești 38 45.45 N 27.04 E
Odojev 76 53.56 N 36.41 E
Odolanów 30 51.35 N 17.39 E
Ōdomari-chosuichi ⊜ 96 34.43 N 132.18 E
Odon 194 38.50 N 86.59 W
Ŏdŏngk 110 11.48 N 104.45 E
O'Donnell 196 32.57 N 101.49 W
O'Donnell ≃ 162 18.22 S 126.36 E
Odoorn 52 52.51 N 6.51 E
Odorheiu Secuiesc 38 46.18 N 25.18 E
Odra (Oder) ≃ 30 53.32 N 14.38 E
Odra Port 54 53.52 N 14.14 E
Odrinhas 266c 38.53 N 9.22 W
Odrzywół 30 51.32 N 20.33 E
Ødsted 41 55.39 N 9.25 E
Odum 192 31.39 N 82.01 W
Odžaci 38 45.30 N 19.16 E
Odzala, Parc National d' ♠ 152 1.00 S 15.00 E
Odzi 154 18.58 S 32.23 E
Odzi ≃ 154 19.45 S 32.24 E
Odziba 152 3.35 S 15.31 E
Ōe 96 35.23 N 135.09 E
Oebisfelde 54 52.25 N 10.59 E
Oedelem 50 51.10 N 3.20 E
Oederan 54 50.52 N 13.09 E
Oeding 52 51.56 N 6.49 E
Oedt 56 51.19 N 6.22 E
Oegstgeest 52 52.10 N 4.29 E
Oeiras, Bra. 250 7.01 S 42.08 W
Oeiras, Port. 266c 38.41 N 9.21 W
Oeiras do Pará 250 1.58 S 49.51 W
Oelde 52 51.49 N 8.08 E
Oelemari ≃ 250 3.13 N 54.09 W
Oella 284b 39.16 N 76.47 W
Oelsig 54 51.41 N 13.22 E
Oelsnitz, Dtsch. 54 50.24 N 12.10 E
Oelsnitz, Dtsch. 54 50.43 N 12.41 E
Oels → Oleśnica 30 51.13 N 17.23 E
Oelwein 190 42.40 N 91.54 W
Oenpelli 164 12.20 S 133.04 E
Oensingen 58 47.17 N 7.44 E
Oepping 60 48.36 N 13.56 E
Oeraro-do I 98 34.27 N 127.30 E
Oer-Erkenschwick 52 51.39 N 7.15 E
Oerlinghausen 52 51.57 N 8.39 E

Symbols in the index entries represent the broad categories identified in the key at the right. Symbols with superior numbers (⋏[1]) identify subcategories (see complete key on page I · 1).

Symbole im Register stellen die rechts im Schlüssel erklärten Kategorien dar. Symbole mit hochgestellten Ziffern (⋏[1]) bezeichnen Unterabteilungen einer Kategorie (vgl. vollständiger Schlüssel auf Seite I · 1).

Los símbolos incluidos en el texto del índice representan las grandes categorías identificadas con la clave a la derecha. Los símbolos con números en su parte superior (⋏[1]) identifican las subcategorías (véase la clave completa en la página I · 1).

Les symboles de l'index représentent les catégories indiquées dans la légende à droite. Les symboles suivis d'un indice (⋏[1]) représentent des sous-catégories (voir légende complète à la page I · 1).

Os símbolos incluídos no texto do índice representam as grandes categorias identificadas com a chave à direita. Os símbolos com números em sua parte superior (⋏[1]) identificam as subcategorias (veja-se a chave completa à página I · 1).

∧ Mountain	Berg	Montaña	Montagne	Montanha
⋏ Mountains	Gebirge	Montañas	Montagnes	Montanhas
)(Pass	Paß	Paso	Col	Passo
V Valley, Canyon	Tal, Cañon	Valle, Cañón	Vallée, Canyon	Vale, Canhão
≡ Plain	Ebene	Llano	Plaine	Planície
≻ Cape	Kap	Cabo	Cap	Cabo
I Island	Insel	Isla	Île	Ilha
II Islands	Inseln	Islas	Îles	Ilhas
± Other Topographic Features	Andere Topographische Objekte	Otros Elementos Topográficos	Autres données topographiques	Outros acidentes topográficos

ESPAÑOL — Nombre, Página, Lat.°′, Long.°′ W = Oeste
FRANÇAIS — Nom, Page, Lat.°′, Long.°′ W = Ouest
PORTUGUÊS — Nome, Página, Lat.°′, Long.°′ W = Oeste

Nombre	Página	Lat.°′	Long.°′ W = Oeste
Oermten	263	51.29 N	6.27 E
Oesede	52	52.12 N	8.04 E
Oespel ◆[8]	263	51.30 N	7.23 E
Oeste, Canal del ≍	266a	40.32 N	3.42 W
Oeste, Parque del ♠	266a	40.26 N	3.44 W
Oesterdam ◆[5]	52	51.29 N	4.15 E
Oestrich	263	51.22 N	7.38 E
Oestrich ◆[8]	263	51.34 N	7.22 E
Oestrum ◆[8]	263	51.25 N	6.40 E
Ōetaka-yama ∧	96	35.04 N	132.26 E
Oettingen in Bayern	56	48.57 N	10.36 E
Oetz	58	47.12 N	10.54 E
Oeuf ≃	50	48.11 N	2.21 E
Oeventrop	56	51.23 N	8.08 E
Oeversee	41	54.42 N	9.26 E
Ōe-yama ∧	96	35.27 N	135.07 E
Oeyŏn-do I	98	36.14 N	126.05 E
Of	130	40.57 N	40.18 E
O'Fallon, Il., U.S.	219	38.35 N	89.54 W
O'Fallon, Mo., U.S.	219	38.48 N	90.41 W
O'Fallon Creek ≃	198	46.50 N	105.09 W
Ofanto ≃	68	41.22 N	16.13 E
Ofaqim	132	31.17 N	34.37 E
Ofenpass → Fuorn, Pass dal)(	58	46.37 N	10.15 E
Offa	150	8.09 N	4.44 E
Offaly □[6]	48	53.20 N	7.30 W
Offanengo	62	45.22 N	9.44 E
Offemont	58	47.40 N	6.53 E
Offenbach	56	50.08 N	8.47 E
Offenburg	58	48.28 N	7.57 E
Offendorf	58	48.43 N	7.55 E
Offerdal	26	63.28 N	14.00 E
Offham	260	51.17 N	0.23 E
Officer	274b	38.04 S	145.25 E
Officer Creek ≃	162	27.45 S	132.24 E
Offida	66	42.56 N	13.41 E
Offingen	58	48.29 N	10.21 E
Offranville	50	49.52 N	1.03 E
Offutt Air Force Base ■	198	41.08 N	95.56 W
Oficina Alemania	252	25.10 S	69.55 W
Oficina Alianza	248	20.46 S	69.42 W
Oficina Chile	252	25.09 S	69.54 W
Oficina Pedro de Valdivia	252	22.36 S	69.40 W
Oficina Victoria	248	20.44 S	69.42 W
Ofin	273a	6.33 N	3.30 E
Öflingen	58	47.35 N	7.55 E
Ofotfjorden ⊂[2]	24	68.23 N	16.10 E
Oftringen	58	47.19 N	7.56 E
Ofu	174y	14.10 S	169.42 W
Ofu I	174y	14.11 S	169.42 W
Ōfukuroshinden	268	35.53 N	139.27 E
Ōfuna	268	35.21 N	139.32 E
Ōfunato	92	39.04 N	141.43 E
Oga	92	39.53 N	139.51 E
Ogaden ◆[1]	144	8.00 N	44.00 E
Oga-hantō >[1]	92	39.55 N	139.50 E
Ōgaki, Nihon	94	35.21 N	136.37 E
Ōgaki, Nihon	96	34.06 N	132.30 E
Ogallala	198	41.07 N	101.43 W
Ogan ≃	112	3.01 S	104.44 E
Ogano	94	36.01 N	139.00 E
Ogasa	94	34.41 N	138.06 E
Ogasawara-guntō (Bonin Islands) II	14	27.00 N	142.10 E
Ōgata, Nihon	94	37.13 N	138.20 E
Ōgata, Nihon	96	33.01 N	133.01 E
Ogata, Nihon	96	32.58 N	131.29 E
Ōga-tō ∧	94	36.13 N	138.06 E
Ogatsu	92	38.31 N	141.28 E
Ogawa, Nihon	92	32.35 N	130.43 E
Ogawa, Nihon	94	36.10 N	140.21 E
Ogawa, Nihon	94	36.37 N	137.58 E
Ogawa, Nihon	94	36.03 N	139.16 E
Ogawa, Nihon	94	36.45 N	140.08 E
Ogawa, Nihon	268	35.44 N	139.28 E
Ogawara-ko ⊜	92	40.47 N	141.20 E
Ogbomosho	150	8.08 N	4.15 E
Ogden, Ia., U.S.	190	42.02 N	94.01 W
Ogden, Ks., U.S.	198	39.06 N	96.42 W
Ogden, Pa., U.S.	208	39.49 N	75.27 W
Ogden, Ut,. U.S.	200	41.13 N	111.58 W
Ogden, Mount ∧	180	58.26 N	133.23 W
Ogden Dunes	216	41.38 N	87.12 W
Ogden Island I	212	44.52 N	75.12 W
Ogden Reservoir ⊜[1]	262	53.42 N	2.22 W
Ogdensburg, N.J., U.S.	210	41.04 N	74.35 W
Ogdensburg, N.Y., U.S.	212	44.41 N	75.29 W
Ogeechee ≃	192	31.51 N	81.06 W
Ōge-jima I	96	34.12 N	134.38 E
Ogema	184	49.35 N	104.55 W
Oggersheim	56	49.29 N	8.22 E
Oghi Fort	123	34.31 N	73.01 E
Ogibalovo	76	60.34 N	39.40 E
Ogidaki Mountain ∧[2]	190	46.58 N	83.58 W
Ogies	158	26.02 S	29.04 E
Ogi-jima I	96	34.26 N	134.04 E
Ogijo	273a	6.42 N	3.31 E
Ogilvie, Austl.	162	28.09 S	114.38 E
Ogilvie, Mn., U.S.	190	45.49 N	93.25 W
Ogilvie ≃	180	65.52 N	137.16 W
Ogilvie Mountains ⋏	180	65.00 N	139.30 W
Ogilville	218	39.08 N	86.01 W
Ōgimi	174m	26.42 N	128.07 E
Ōgino-sen ∧	96	35.26 N	134.26 E
Ogle □[6]	216	42.01 N	89.20 W
Oglesby, Il., U.S.	216	41.17 N	89.03 W
Oglesby, Tx., U.S.	222	31.25 N	97.31 W
Oglethorpe	192	32.17 N	84.03 W
Ogliastra ◆[1]	71	39.56 N	9.37 E
Ogliastro Cilento	68	40.21 N	15.03 E
Oglio ≃	64	45.02 N	10.39 E
Ogmore	166	22.37 S	149.40 E
Ogmore ≃	42	51.28 N	3.38 W
Ogmore Vale	42	51.38 N	3.31 W
Ogni	86	51.54 N	83.31 E
Ognica	54	53.07 N	14.27 E
Ognon ≃	58	47.20 N	5.29 E
Ogn'ov Jar	86	58.23 N	76.29 E
Ogn'ovka	86	49.36 N	83.25 E
Ōgo	94	36.25 N	139.10 E
Ōgo ◆[8]	270	34.49 N	135.06 E
Ōgo ≃	270	34.47 N	135.04 E
Ogoamas, Bulu ∧	112	0.40 N	120.12 E
Ogōchi-dam ◆[6]	94	35.47 N	139.04 E
Ogodža	89	52.44 N	132.31 E
Ogoja	150	6.40 N	8.48 E
Ogoki ≃	176	51.38 N	85.57 W
'Ogol, Khaṭṭ el V	150	20.01 N	15.29 W
Ogooué ≃	152	0.49 S	9.00 E
Ogooué-Ivindo □[4]	152	1.00 N	13.00 E
Ogooué-Lolo □[4]	152	1.00 S	12.30 E
Ogooué-Maritime □[4]	152	2.00 S	9.30 E
Ogōri, Nihon	96	33.22 N	130.32 E
Ogōri, Nihon	96	34.06 N	131.24 E
Ogorodnoje	78	45.53 N	28.50 E
Ogose	94	35.58 N	139.18 E
Ogosta ≃	38	43.45 N	23.51 E
Ogou ≃	150	7.50 N	1.19 E
Ogoyo	273a	6.26 N	3.29 E
Ogr	140	12.02 N	27.06 E
Ogre	76	56.51 N	24.36 E
Ogre ≃	76	56.48 N	24.36 E
Ogrodzieniec	30	50.27 N	19.31 E
Ogrosen	54	51.42 N	14.02 E
Ōguchi	94	35.20 N	136.55 E
Ōgu-dong	98	38.57 N	126.56 E
Ogudu	273a	6.34 N	3.24 E
Ogulin	36	45.16 N	15.14 E
Ogun □[3]	150	6.45 N	3.25 E
Ogun ≃	150	6.36 N	3.27 E
Ogun Forest Reserve ♠	273a	6.37 N	3.26 E
Oguni, Nihon	92	38.04 N	139.45 E
Oguni, Nihon	96	33.07 N	131.04 E
Ogunlogun	273a	6.41 N	3.28 E
Ogunquit	188	43.14 N	70.35 W
Ogura-san ∧	94	36.02 N	138.37 E
Ogurčinskij, ostrov I	128	38.55 N	53.02 E
Oguta	150	5.44 N	6.44 E
Oğuz, Tür.	130	37.49 N	41.22 E
Oğuz, Tür.	130	39.32 N	38.51 E
Oğuzeli	130	36.59 N	37.30 E
Ogwashi-Uku	150	6.10 N	6.31 E
Ohakune	172	39.25 S	175.24 E
Ohanapecosh ≃	224	46.38 N	121.37 W
Ohanet	148	28.45 N	8.55 E
Ohār	124	27.21 N	84.37 E
Ōhara, Nihon	94	35.15 N	140.23 E
Ōhara, Nihon	96	35.07 N	134.20 E
Ōharano ◆[8]	270	34.58 N	135.40 E
Ōhara-tunnel ◆[5]	94	35.12 N	137.50 E
Ōhata	92	41.24 N	141.10 E
Ōhatake	268	35.57 N	139.46 E
Ohau, Lake ⊜	172	44.15 S	169.51 E
Ohaupo	172	37.55 S	175.19 E
Ohey	56	50.26 N	5.08 E
O'Higgins, Cabo >	174z	27.05 S	109.15 W
O'Higgins, Cerro ∧	254	48.48 S	73.11 W
O'Higgins, Lago (Lago San Martín) ⊜	254	49.00 S	72.40 W
Ohingaiti	172	39.52 S	175.43 E
Ohio	190	41.34 N	89.28 W
Ohio □[6], In., U.S.	218	38.57 N	84.51 W
Ohio □[6], W.V., U.S.	214	40.09 N	80.35 W
Ohio □[3], U.S.	178	40.15 N	82.45 W
Ohio □[3], U.S.	188	40.15 N	82.45 W
Ohio ≃	178	36.59 N	89.08 W
Ohio Brush Creek ≃	218	38.41 N	83.27 W
Ohio Brush Creek, Baker Fork ≃	218	39.02 N	83.26 W
Ohio Brush Creek, Little West Fork ≃	218	38.58 N	83.34 W
Ohio Brush Creek, West Fork ≃	218	38.56 N	83.28 W
Ohio Canal ≍	279a	41.26 N	81.40 W
Ohio Caverns ♠[5]	216	40.14 N	83.43 W
Ohio City	216	40.46 N	84.36 W
Ohio Peak ∧	200	38.49 N	107.07 W
Ohiopyle State Park ♠	188	39.50 N	79.31 W
Ohioville, N.Y., U.S.	210	41.45 N	74.03 W
Ohioville, Pa., U.S.	214	40.40 N	80.29 W
Ōhira	94	36.20 N	139.42 E
Ōhira-yama ∧	96	34.20 N	133.57 E
Ōhito	94	35.01 N	138.56 E
Ohlau → Oława	30	50.57 N	17.17 E
Ohligs ◆[8]	263	51.09 N	7.00 E
Ohlman	219	39.21 N	89.13 W
Ohlsdorf	64	47.57 N	13.47 E
Ohm ≃	56	50.51 N	8.48 E
Ōho	94	36.08 N	140.06 E
Ohoitom	164	5.56 S	132.41 E
'Ohonua	174w	21.20 S	174.57 W
Ohoopee ≃	192	31.54 N	82.07 W
Ōhori	268	35.20 N	139.52 E
Ohorn	54	51.10 N	14.02 E
Ohra Stausee ⊜[1]	54	50.46 N	10.42 E
Ohrdruf	54	50.50 N	10.44 E
Ohre ≃, Dtsch.	54	52.18 N	11.47 E
Ohře (Eger) ≃, Europe	54	50.32 N	14.08 E
Ohrid	38	41.07 N	20.47 E
Ohrid, Lake ⊜	38	41.02 N	20.43 E
Ohrigstad	156	24.49 S	30.33 E
Öhringen	56	49.12 N	9.29 E
Ohrnberg	56	49.15 N	9.27 E
Ohuira, Bahía ⊂	232	25.38 N	108.58 W
Ohura	172	38.50 S	174.59 E
Ōi, Nihon	96	35.28 N	135.37 E
Ōi, Nihon	268	35.51 N	139.30 E
Oi ◆[8]	268	35.35 N	139.45 E
Ōi ≃, Nihon	94	34.46 N	138.18 E
Ōi ≃, Nihon	96	35.01 N	135.39 E
Oiapoque	250	3.50 N	51.50 W
Oiapoque (Oyapock) ≃	250	4.08 N	51.40 W
Oies, Île aux I	186	47.07 N	70.30 W
Ōigawa	94	34.48 N	138.17 E
Oignies	50	50.28 N	2.59 E
Oil Center	196	32.29 N	103.15 W
Oil City, La., U.S.	194	32.44 N	93.58 W
Oil City, Pa., U.S.	214	41.26 N	79.42 W
Oil Creek ≃	214	41.26 N	79.42 W
Oil Creek State Park ♠	214	41.33 N	79.40 W
Oildale	226	35.25 N	119.01 W
Oilmont	182	48.44 N	111.50 W
Oil Springs	214	42.47 N	82.07 W
Oilton, Ok., U.S.	196	36.05 N	96.35 W
Oilton, Tx., U.S.	196	27.33 N	98.59 W
Oil Trough	194	35.37 N	91.27 W
Oinville-sur-Montcient	261	49.02 N	1.51 E
Oir, Beinn an ∧	46	55.54 N	6.00 W
Oirschot	52	51.30 N	5.18 E
Oise □[5]	50	49.30 N	2.30 E
Oise ≃	50	49.00 N	2.04 E
Oise à l'Aisne, Canal de l' ≍	50	49.36 N	3.11 E
Oisemont	50	49.57 N	1.46 E
Ōiso, Nihon	94	35.18 N	139.19 E
Ōiso, Nihon	270	34.33 N	135.01 E
Oissel	50	49.20 N	1.06 E
Oissery	261	49.04 N	2.49 E
Oisterwijk	52	51.35 N	5.12 E
Oistins	241g	13.04 N	59.32 W
Ōita	96	33.14 N	131.36 E
Ōita □[5]	96	33.15 N	131.30 E
Ōita ≃	96	33.15 N	131.37 E
Oiticica	250	5.03 S	41.05 W
Oituz, Pasul)(	38	46.03 N	26.23 E
Ōiwa	270	34.53 N	135.33 E
Oiyung	124	29.39 N	89.46 E
Ōizumi, Nihon	94	36.15 N	139.25 E
Ōizumi, Nihon	94	35.52 N	138.23 E
Oizuruga-dake ∧	94	36.18 N	136.47 E
Öja I	40	58.45 N	17.52 E
Oja ≃	86	53.26 N	91.55 E
Ojai	228	34.26 N	119.14 W
Öjaren ⊜	40	60.43 N	16.50 E
Ojat' ≃	76	60.31 N	33.00 E
Ojcowski Park Narodowy ♠	30	50.15 N	19.50 E
Öje	26	60.49 N	13.51 E
Ojgon nuur ⊜	88	49.10 N	96.36 E
Ojgor	86	49.10 N	89.17 E
Ōji	96	34.35 N	135.42 E
Ōjima	94	36.15 N	139.20 E
Ojinaga	232	29.34 N	104.25 W
Ojiya	92	37.18 N	138.48 E
Ojm'akon	74	63.28 N	142.49 E
Ojocaliente	234	22.34 N	102.15 W
Ojo de la Casa	200	31.23 N	106.32 W
Ojo del Carrizo	232	29.58 N	105.16 W
Ojo de Liebre, Laguna ⊂	232	27.45 N	114.15 W
Ojok	88	52.35 N	104.27 E
Ojos del Salado, Nevado ∧	252	27.06 S	68.32 W
Ojos Negros	232	31.52 N	116.16 W
Ojota	273a	6.35 N	3.23 E
Ojtal, Kaz.	85	42.55 N	73.17 E
Ojtal, Kyrg.	85	40.24 N	74.06 E
Oju	150	6.53 N	8.26 E
Ojuelos de Jalisco	234	21.52 N	101.35 W
Ojus	220	25.57 N	80.09 W
Oka	150	7.29 N	5.49 E
Oka ≃, Ross.	80	56.20 N	43.59 E
Oka ≃, Ross.	88	55.15 N	102.10 E
Okaba	164	8.06 S	139.42 E
Okabe, Nihon	94	36.12 N	139.15 E
Okabe, Nihon	94	34.55 N	138.17 E
Okagaki	96	33.50 N	130.38 E
Okahandja	156	21.59 S	16.58 E
Okahandja □[5]	156	21.30 S	17.00 E
Okahukura	172	38.47 S	175.13 E
Okahumpka	220	28.45 N	81.54 W
Okaihau	172	35.19 S	173.47 E
Okalataka	152	0.20 S	14.59 E
Okaloacoochee Slough ≃	220	26.16 N	81.17 W
Okamoto	270	34.59 N	135.58 E
Okamoto ◆[8]	270	34.44 N	135.16 E
Okanagan (Okanogan) ≃	182	48.06 N	119.43 W
Okanagan Centre	182	50.03 N	119.27 W
Okanagan Falls	182	49.21 N	119.34 W
Okanagan Indian Reserve ◆[4]	182	50.21 N	119.17 W
Okanagan Lake ⊜	182	50.00 N	119.28 W
Okanagan Landing	182	50.14 N	119.22 W
Okanagan Mountain Provincial Park ♠	182	49.45 N	119.40 W
Okanagan Range (Okanogan Range) ⋏	182	49.00 N	120.00 W
Okanogan	202	48.21 N	119.34 W
Okanogan □[6]	224	48.39 N	120.41 W
Okanogan (Okanagan) ≃	182	48.06 N	119.43 W
Okanogan Range (Okanagan Range) ⋏	182	49.00 N	120.00 W
Okapilco Creek ≃	192	30.45 N	83.30 W
Okaputa	156	20.09 S	16.56 E
Okāra	123	30.49 N	73.27 E
Okarche	196	35.44 N	97.58 W
Okarito	172	43.14 S	170.11 E
Okasaki	270	34.46 N	135.52 E
Okatibbee Reservoir ⊜[1]	194	32.30 N	88.47 W
Okato	172	39.12 S	173.53 E
Okauchee	216	43.06 N	88.26 W
Okauchee Lake ⊜	216	43.07 N	88.26 W
Okaukuejo	156	19.10 S	15.54 E
Okavango (Cubango) ≃	138	18.50 S	22.25 E
Okavango Delta ⩸[2]	156	18.45 S	22.45 E
Ōkawa, Nihon	92	33.12 N	130.23 E
Ōkawa, Nihon	94	35.05 N	138.15 E
Ōkawa, Nihon	96	33.47 N	133.26 E
Ōkawachi	96	35.04 N	134.45 E
Ōkawado	268	35.56 N	139.50 E
Okawville	219	38.26 N	89.33 W
Okaya	94	36.03 N	138.03 E
Okayama	96	34.39 N	133.55 E
Okayama □[5]	96	35.00 N	134.00 E
Okazaki	94	34.57 N	137.10 E
Okch'ŏn	98	36.20 N	127.34 E
Oke-Aro	273a	6.41 N	3.19 E
Okeechobee	220	27.14 N	80.49 W
Okeechobee □[6]	220	27.25 N	80.52 W
Okeechobee, Lake ⊜	220	26.55 N	80.45 W
O'Keefe Centre ʊ	275b	43.37 N	79.22 W
Okeene	196	36.06 N	98.19 W
Okefenokee Swamp ⩸	192	30.42 N	82.20 W
Okegawa	94	36.00 N	139.35 E
Okehampton	42	50.44 N	4.00 W
Okeigbo	150	7.09 N	4.43 E
Okemah	196	35.25 N	96.18 W
Okement ≃	42	50.50 N	4.01 W
Okemos	216	42.43 N	84.25 W
Okene	150	7.33 N	6.15 E
Oke-Ode	150	8.33 N	5.02 E
Oke Ogbe	273a	6.24 N	3.23 E
Oker	52	51.54 N	10.29 E
Oker ≃	54	52.30 N	10.22 E
Okere ≃	154	2.07 N	33.55 E
Okhaldunggā	124	27.19 N	86.30 E
Okhla ◆[8]	272a	28.34 N	77.18 E
Okhotsk, Sea of (Ochotskoje more) ⊤[2]	74	53.00 N	150.00 E
Okhotsk Basin ✣[1]	12	53.00 N	148.00 E
Okiep	156	29.39 S	17.53 E
Okinawa	174m	26.20 N	127.50 E
Okinawa □[5]	93b	26.31 N	127.59 E
Okinawa-jima I	174m	26.30 N	128.00 E
Okinawa-shotō II	93b	26.40 N	128.00 E
Okino-Daitō-jima I	90	24.28 N	131.11 E
Okino-Erabu-shima I	93b	27.22 N	128.35 E
Okino-Kl'uči	88	50.36 N	107.06 E
Okino-shima I, Nihon	94	35.12 N	136.04 E
Okino-shima I, Nihon	96	34.07 N	135.06 E
Okino-Tori-shima (Parece Vela) I	90	20.25 N	136.00 E
Oki-shotō II	92	36.15 N	133.15 E
Okitipupa	150	6.29 N	4.46 E
Okitsu-zaki >	96	33.09 N	133.14 E
Okkang-ni	98	40.18 N	124.42 E
Okkerbil' ≃	265a	59.56 N	30.26 E
Okladnevo	76	58.36 N	33.39 E
Oklahoma, Pa., U.S.	214	41.07 N	78.44 W
Oklahoma, Pa., U.S.	279b	40.35 N	79.35 W
Oklahoma □[3], U.S.	178	35.30 N	98.00 W
Oklahoma □[3], U.S.	196	35.30 N	98.00 W
Oklahoma City	196	35.28 N	97.30 W
Oklawaha	220	29.02 N	81.55 W
Oklawaha ≃, Fl., U.S.	192	29.28 N	81.41 W
Oklawaha ≃, Fl., U.S.	220	29.03 N	81.52 W
Oklee	198	47.50 N	95.51 W
Okmulgee	196	35.37 N	95.57 W
Oknica	78	48.24 N	27.29 E
Okno	78	48.34 N	25.58 E
Oko, Wādī V	140	21.15 N	35.56 E
Okobojo Creek ≃	198	44.38 N	100.28 W
Okok ≃	154	2.06 N	33.53 E
Okoka	152	2.57 S	23.27 E
Okola	152	4.01 N	11.23 E
Okollo	154	2.40 N	31.08 E
Okolo	152	3.46 S	23.55 E
Okolona, Ar., U.S.	194	33.59 N	93.20 W
Okolona, Ky., U.S.	194	38.08 N	85.41 W
Okolona, Ms., U.S.	194	34.00 N	88.45 W
Okombahe	156	21.23 S	15.22 E
Okondja	152	0.41 S	13.47 E
Okonek	30	53.33 N	16.50 E
Okonešnikovo	86	54.50 N	75.05 E
Okotoks	182	50.44 N	113.59 W
Okoyo	152	1.28 S	15.04 E
Okpara ≃	150	7.40 N	2.35 E
Okrika	150	4.47 N	7.04 E
Oksbøl	26	55.38 N	8.17 E
Okskij Zapovednik ◆[4]	80	54.45 N	40.45 E
Oksko-Donskaja ravnina ⩸	80	53.00 N	40.30 E
Oksovskij	24	62.37 N	39.55 E
Oksskolten ∧	24	65.59 N	14.15 E
Oksu ≃, Asia	85	40.12 N	69.16 E
Oksu ≃, Taj.	120	38.09 N	73.57 E
Okt'abr', Kaz.	85	43.41 N	77.12 E
Okt'abr', Kaz.	86	45.45 N	61.34 E
Okt'abr', Ross.	76	57.50 N	37.26 E
Okt'abr'sk, Kaz.	86	49.28 N	57.25 E
Okt'abr'sk, Ross.	80	53.11 N	48.40 E
Okt'abr'skij, Bela.	76	52.38 N	28.53 E
Okt'abr'skij, Kaz.	86	52.35 N	62.40 E
Okt'abr'skij, Kaz.	86	49.38 N	83.35 E
Okt'abr'skij, Ross.	24	61.04 N	43.08 E
Okt'abr'skij, Ross.	24	59.29 N	48.50 E
Okt'abr'skij, Ross.	76	53.47 N	39.29 E
Okt'abr'skij, Ross.	78	44.56 N	39.00 E
Okt'abr'skij, Ross.	78	50.26 N	36.22 E
Okt'abr'skij, Ross.	80	54.28 N	53.28 E
Okt'abr'skij, Ross.	80	56.17 N	44.12 E
Okt'abr'skij, Ross.	80	57.08 N	40.20 E
Okt'abr'skij, Ross.	80	58.19 N	44.19 E
Okt'abr'skij, Ross.	80	56.35 N	53.58 E
Okt'abr'skij, Ross.	80	47.58 N	43.38 E
Okt'abr'skij, Ross.	82	55.37 N	37.58 E
Okt'abr'skij, Ross.	82	54.14 N	38.54 E
Okt'abr'skij, Ross.	83	47.28 N	40.04 E
Okt'abr'skij, Ross.	86	56.31 N	57.12 E
Okt'abr'skij, Ross.	88	50.04 N	118.04 E
Okt'abr'skij, Ross.	88	56.05 N	99.26 E
Okt'abr'skij, Ross.	89	53.01 N	128.37 E
Okt'abr'skij, Ross.	89	49.02 N	140.11 E
Okt'abr'skij, Taj.	85	38.33 N	68.22 E
Okt'abr'skoje, Kaz.	86	52.07 N	65.40 E
Okt'abr'skoje, Ross.	74	62.28 N	66.03 E
Okt'abr'skoje, Ross.	76	52.18 N	39.44 E
Okt'abr'skoje, Ross.	80	45.37 N	42.49 E
Okt'abr'skoje, Ross.	80	52.54 N	46.30 E
Okt'abr'skoje, Ross.	86	52.20 N	55.30 E
Okt'abr'skoje, Ross.	86	54.26 N	62.44 E
Okt'abr'skoje, Ukr.	78	48.38 N	33.04 E
Okt'abr'skoje, Ukr.	78	45.18 N	34.09 E
Okt'abr'skoje, Ukr.	83	48.28 N	37.22 E
Okt'abr'skoj Revol'ucii, ostrov I	74	79.30 N	97.00 E
Ok Tedi	164	5.44 S	141.09 E
Oktember'an	84	40.09 N	44.02 E
Oktong-ni	98	38.27 N	127.07 E
Oktwin	110	18.49 N	96.26 E
Oktyabr'skiy → Okt'abr'skij	80	54.28 N	53.28 E
Oku, Nihon	96	34.40 N	134.05 E
Oku, Nihon	174m	26.50 N	128.17 E
Ōkubo, Nihon	268	35.21 N	139.56 E
Ōkubo, Nihon	270	34.41 N	134.57 E
Ōkubo ◆[8]	268	35.24 N	139.35 E
Okučani	36	45.16 N	17.12 E
Ōkuchi, Nihon	92	32.04 N	130.37 E
Okuchi, Nihon	94	36.17 N	136.39 E
Okuku ≃	172	43.16 S	172.28 E
Okulovka	76	58.26 N	33.18 E
Okumi	84	42.43 N	41.45 E
Okundi	150	6.22 N	8.44 E
Okun'ov Nos	24	66.15 N	52.28 E
Ōkura-yama ∧	96	35.08 N	133.22 E
Okusawa ◆[8]	268	35.36 N	139.40 E
Okushiri	92a	42.10 N	139.31 E
Okushiri-tō I	92a	42.10 N	139.27 E
Ōkusu-yama ∧[2]	268	35.15 N	139.38 E
Okuta	150	9.14 N	3.15 E
Okutadami Dam ◆[6]	94	37.09 N	139.15 E
Okutama	94	35.47 N	139.02 E
Okutama-ko ⊜	94	35.47 N	139.02 E
Okutsu	96	35.14 N	133.56 E
Ōkuwa	94	35.41 N	137.40 E
Okwa (Chapman's) ≃	156	22.30 S	23.00 E
Okwoga	150	7.01 N	7.50 E
Olá, Pan.	236	8.25 N	80.39 W
Ola, Ross.	74	59.35 N	151.17 E
Ola, Ar., U.S.	194	35.01 N	93.13 W
Ola ≃	76	52.41 N	29.39 E
Ólafsfjörður	24a	66.06 N	18.38 W
Olambwe Valley Game Reserve ◆[4]	154	0.37 S	34.15 E
Olancha	204	36.16 N	118.00 W
Olancha Peak ∧	204	36.16 N	118.07 W
Olanchito	236	15.30 N	86.35 W
Olancho □[5]	236	14.45 N	86.00 W
Öland I	26	56.45 N	16.38 E
Olandsån ≃	40	60.20 N	18.14 E
Olango Island I	116	10.16 N	124.03 E
Olanta	192	33.56 N	79.55 W
Olar	192	33.10 N	81.11 W
Olarevo	76	59.22 N	40.04 E
Olaria, Bra.	256	21.52 S	43.56 W
Olaria, Bra.	287a	22.41 S	43.08 W
Olaria ◆[8]	287a	22.52 S	43.15 W
Olary	166	32.17 S	140.19 E
Olascoaga	252	35.12 S	60.36 W
Olasore	273a	6.40 N	3.17 E
Olathe, Co., U.S.	200	38.36 N	107.58 W
Olathe, Ks., U.S.	198	38.52 N	94.49 W
Olavarría	252	36.54 S	60.17 W
Olavinlinna ⊥	26	61.52 N	29.00 E
Oława	30	50.57 N	17.17 E
Olbernhau	54	50.39 N	13.20 E
Olbersdorf	54	50.52 N	14.46 E
Olbersleben	54	51.09 N	11.20 E
Olbia	71	40.55 N	9.31 E
Olbia, Golfo di ⊂	71	40.55 N	9.39 E
Ølby Lyng	41	55.29 N	12.09 E
Olca, Volcán ∧[1]	248	20.57 S	68.30 W
Ol'chi	80	53.53 N	41.28 E
Olching	60	48.12 N	11.20 E
Ol'chon, ostrov I	88	53.09 N	107.24 E
Ol'chovaja ≃, Ross.	80	48.47 N	40.51 E
Ol'chovaja ≃, Ukr.	83	48.35 N	39.17 E
Ol'chovatka, Ross.	78	50.18 N	39.17 E
Ol'chovatka, Ukr.	83	48.15 N	38.25 E
Ol'chovka, Ross.	80	49.52 N	44.34 E
Ol'chovka, Ross.	86	56.22 N	63.46 E
Ol'chovoje	83	48.40 N	39.34 E
Olcott	210	43.20 N	78.42 W
Old ≃, Ca., U.S.	226	38.04 N	121.35 W
Old ≃, Tx., U.S.	222	30.25 N	96.19 W
Old Bahama Channel ʯ	238	22.30 N	78.50 W
Old Bedford ≃	42	52.35 N	0.20 E
Old Bennington	210	42.52 N	73.12 W
Old Bethpage	276	40.45 N	73.27 W
Old Bethpage Village ⊥	276	40.47 N	73.28 W
Old Brazoria	222	29.04 N	95.34 W
Old Bridge	276	40.24 N	74.21 W
Old Brookville	276	40.49 N	73.36 W
Oldbury	42	52.30 N	2.00 W
Old Cairo → Miṣr al-Qadīmah ◆[8]	273c	30.00 N	31.14 E
Oldcastle	48	53.46 N	7.10 W
Old Colwyn	44	53.18 N	3.43 W
Old Cork	166	22.56 S	141.52 E
Old Creek Estates	284c	38.50 N	77.16 W
Old Crow	180	67.35 N	139.50 W
Old Crow ≃	180	67.35 N	139.50 W
Oldeani	154	3.21 S	35.33 E
Oldebroek	52	52.26 N	5.54 E
Old Economy ⊥	279b	40.36 N	80.14 W
Olden, Nor.	26	61.50 N	6.49 E
Olden, Tx., U.S.	196	32.25 N	98.45 W
Oldenbrok	52	53.17 N	8.23 E
Oldenburg, Dtsch.	52	53.08 N	8.13 E
Oldenburg, In., U.S.	218	39.20 N	85.12 W
Oldenburg □[9]	52	53.00 N	8.00 E
Oldenburg in Holstein	54	54.17 N	10.52 E
Oldendorf	52	53.35 N	9.14 E
Oldenstadt	52	52.58 N	10.35 E
Oldenswort	41	54.22 N	8.56 E
Oldenzaal	52	52.19 N	6.56 E
Oldersum	52	53.20 N	7.20 E
Old Faithful Geyser ⊤[4]	202	44.30 N	110.45 W
Old Farm	284c	39.03 N	77.09 W
Old Field	276	40.57 N	73.08 W
Old Field Point >	276	40.58 N	73.07 W
Old Forge, N.Y., U.S.	188	43.42 N	74.58 W
Old Forge, Pa., U.S.	210	41.22 N	75.44 W
Old Forge Village	276	40.49 N	74.29 W
Old Fort	214	41.15 N	83.09 W
Old Fort Erie ⊥	284a	42.53 N	78.56 W
Old Fort Henry ⊥	212	44.14 N	76.28 W
Old Fort Mountain ∧	182	55.05 N	126.30 W
Old Fort Niagara ⊥	284a	43.16 N	79.03 W
Old Fort Parker State Historic Site ⊥	222	31.34 N	96.34 W
Old Fort Point >	240b	25.03 N	77.29 W
Old Greenwich	276	41.02 N	73.34 W
Oldham, Eng., U.K.	44	53.33 N	2.07 W
Oldham, S.D., U.S.	198	44.13 N	97.18 W
Oldham □[6]	218	38.23 N	85.27 W
Oldham □[8]	262	53.34 N	2.03 W
Oldham Pines	283	42.05 N	70.50 W
Oldham Pond ⊜	283	42.03 N	70.51 W
Oldham Village	207	42.04 N	70.49 W
Old Harbor	180	57.12 N	153.19 W
Old Harbour	241q	17.56 N	77.07 W
Old Hickory Lake ⊜[1]	194	36.18 N	86.30 W
Old Howe ≃	44	53.57 N	0.21 W
Oldisleben	54	51.18 N	11.10 E
Old Lyme	207	41.18 N	72.19 W
Old Malden ◆[8]	260	51.23 N	0.15 W
Oldman ≃	182	49.56 N	111.42 W
Old Man House ⊥	224	47.43 N	122.34 W
Old Man Mountain ∧	186	49.08 N	57.43 W
Old Manor	276	40.24 N	74.11 W
Oldmans Creek ≃	208	39.47 N	75.27 W
Oldmeldrum	46	57.20 N	2.20 W
Old Mkushi	154	14.22 S	29.22 E
Old Monroe	219	38.55 N	90.44 W
Old Mystic	207	41.23 N	71.57 W
Old Nene ≃	42	52.40 N	0.10 E
Old North Bridge ⊥	283	42.28 N	71.21 W
Old North Church ʊ[1]	283	42.22 N	71.03 W
Old Ocean	222	29.05 N	95.45 W
Ol Doinyo Sapuk National Park ♠	154	1.09 S	37.12 E
Ol'doj ≃	89	53.33 N	123.21 E
Old Orchard ◆[9]	278	42.04 N	87.45 W
Old Orchard Beach	188	43.31 N	70.22 W
Old Perlican	186	48.05 N	53.01 W
Old Place Creek ≃	276	40.38 N	74.12 W
Old Point Comfort >	208	37.00 N	76.19 W
Old Rhodes Key I	220	25.22 N	80.14 W
Old Ripley	219	38.54 N	89.34 W
Old Road Bay ⊂	284b	39.12 N	76.27 W
Old Road Bluff >	240c	16.59 N	61.50 W
Old Round Rock	222	30.31 N	97.42 W
Olds	182	51.47 N	114.06 W
Old Saybrook	207	41.17 N	72.22 W
Oldsmar	220	28.02 N	82.39 W
Old Speck Mountain ∧	188	44.34 N	70.57 W
Old Sturbridge Village ⊥	207	42.07 N	72.07 W
Old Swamp ≃	283	42.11 N	70.57 W
Old Swedes Church ʊ[1]	285	39.44 N	75.32 W
Old Tampa Bay ⊂	220	27.56 N	82.35 W
Old Tappan	276	41.00 N	73.59 W
Old Tate	156	21.22 S	27.46 E
Old Town	188	44.56 N	68.38 W
Old Trafford Cricket Ground ♠	262	53.28 N	2.17 W
Old Trap	192	36.15 N	76.02 W
Olduvai Gorge V	154	2.58 S	35.22 E
Old Westbury	276	40.47 N	73.37 W
Old Westbury Gardens ♠	276	40.46 N	73.36 W
Oldwick	210	40.40 N	74.44 W
Old Windsor	260	51.28 N	0.35 W
Old Wives Lake ⊜	184	50.06 N	106.00 W
Old Woman Creek ≃	198	43.19 N	104.21 W
Öldzijt, Mong.	88	48.07 N	102.34 E
Öldzijt, Mong.	102	45.18 N	106.12 E
Old Zoinsville	208	40.29 N	75.31 W
Olean	210	42.04 N	78.25 W
Olean Creek ≃	210	42.04 N	78.25 W
O'Leary	186	46.42 N	64.13 W
Olecko	30	54.03 N	22.30 E
Olegário Maciel	256	22.19 S	45.35 W
Oleggio	62	45.36 N	8.38 E
Olekma → Ol'okma ≃	74	60.22 N	120.42 E
Olema	24	64.30 N	46.08 E
Olen, Bel.	56	51.09 N	4.51 E
Ølen, Nor.	26	59.36 N	5.48 E
Ölen ⊜	40	59.13 N	14.31 E
Olenegorsk	24	68.09 N	33.15 E
Olenevka	78	45.23 N	32.32 E
Olenica	24	66.29 N	35.20 E
Olenij, ostrov I	74	72.25 N	77.45 E
Olenino	76	56.12 N	33.29 E
Olenja Rečka	86	52.48 N	93.14 E
Olen'kovo	82	54.34 N	38.06 E
Olen'ok	74	68.33 N	112.18 E
Olen'ok ≃	74	73.00 N	119.55 E
Olen'okskij zaliv ⊂	74	73.20 N	121.00 E
Olentangy ≃	214	39.58 N	83.06 W
Olenty	80	50.02 N	52.07 E
Olenty ≃	80	49.50 N	52.03 E
Oleopolis	214	41.27 N	79.37 W
Oléron, Île d' I	32	45.56 N	1.15 W
Olesko	78	49.58 N	24.53 E
Olešná	60	49.46 N	13.48 E
Oleśnica	30	51.13 N	17.23 E
Olesno	30	50.53 N	18.25 E
Olevano Romano	66	41.52 N	13.02 E
Olevano sul Tusciano	68	40.40 N	15.01 E
Olevsk	78	51.13 N	27.39 E
Oley	208	40.23 N	75.47 W
Olfen	52	51.42 N	7.23 E
Ol'ga, Ross.	89	43.45 N	135.18 E
Olga, Wa., U.S.	224	48.37 N	122.50 W
Olga, Mount ∧, Austl.	162	25.19 S	130.46 E
Olga, Mount ∧, Vt., U.S.	207	42.51 N	72.48 W
Olgiata	267a	42.02 N	12.22 E
Olgiate Comasco	62	45.48 N	8.58 E
Olgiate Olona	62	45.38 N	8.53 E
Ölgij, Mong.	86	48.59 N	92.01 E
Ölgij, Mong.	86	48.56 N	89.57 E
Olginate	62	45.48 N	9.24 E
Ol'ginka, Ross.	78	44.14 N	38.53 E
Ol'ginka, Ukr.	83	47.42 N	37.31 E
Ol'gino	89	52.53 N	125.47 E
Ol'gino ◆[8]	265a	60.00 N	30.09 E
Ol'ginskaja, Ross.	78	45.57 N	38.34 E
Ol'ginskaja, Ross.	83	47.11 N	39.56 E
Ølgod	26	55.49 N	8.37 E
Ol'gopol'	78	48.12 N	29.29 E
Ol'govo	82	56.16 N	37.21 E
Olhão	34	37.02 N	7.50 W
Olho d'Água das Cunhãs	250	4.43 S	44.34 W
Olho d'Água das Flores	250	9.33 S	37.17 W
Oli ≃	150	9.45 N	4.38 E
Olib, Otok I	36	44.22 N	14.48 E
Oliden	258	35.11 S	57.57 W
Oliena	71	40.16 N	9.24 E
Olifants (Rio dos Elefantes) ≃, Afr.	156	24.10 S	32.40 E
Olifants ≃, Namibia	156	25.30 S	19.30 E
Olifants ≃, S. Afr.	158	31.42 S	18.12 E
Olifants ≃, S. Afr.	158	33.41 S	21.42 E
Olifants ≃, S. Afr.	158	29.39 S	21.10 E
Olifantshoek	158	27.57 S	22.42 E
Olifantsrivierberge ⋏	158	32.40 S	19.00 E
Oliki	265a	59.46 N	29.55 E
Olimarao I[1]	108	7.41 N	145.52 E
Olimbía ⊥	38	37.38 N	21.41 E
Ólimbos	38	35.44 N	27.11 E
Ólimbos ∧, Ellás	38	40.05 N	22.21 E
Ólimbos ∧, Kípros	130	34.56 N	32.52 E
Olímpia	255	20.44 S	48.54 W
Olímpico, Estadio ♠	286a	19.20 N	99.12 W
Olímpio Noronha	256	22.04 S	45.16 W
Olimpo → Ólimbos ∧	38	40.05 N	22.21 E
Olin	190	41.59 N	91.08 W
Olinalá	234	17.50 N	98.51 W
Olinda, Austl.	170	32.50 S	150.08 E
Olinda, Austl.	274b	37.51 S	145.22 E
Olinda, Bra.	250	8.01 S	34.51 W
Olinda, Bra.	256	22.49 S	43.25 W
Olinda, Mount ∧	274b	37.52 S	145.21 E
Olinda Creek ≃	274b	37.41 S	145.21 E
Olindina	250	11.22 S	38.21 W
Olinsk	88	52.24 N	116.13 E
Olio	166	21.54 S	143.13 E
Olišovka	78	51.13 N	31.18 E
Olite	34	42.29 N	1.39 W
Oliva, Arg.	252	32.03 S	63.34 W
Oliva, Esp.	34	38.55 N	0.07 W
Oliva de la Frontera	34	38.16 N	6.55 W
Olivais ◆[8]	266c	38.46 N	9.06 E
Olival Basto	266c	38.47 N	9.10 W
Olivares, Cerro de ∧	252	30.18 S	69.55 W
Olive Branch	194	34.57 N	89.49 W
Olivebridge	210	41.55 N	74.13 W
Olive Hill	218	38.18 N	83.10 W
Olivehurst	226	39.05 N	121.33 W
Oliveira	255	20.41 S	44.49 W
Oliveira dos Brejinhos	255	12.19 S	42.54 W
Oliveira Fortes	256	21.20 S	43.27 W
Olivelifuri I	122	5.17 N	73.35 E
Olive Mount ◆[8]	262	53.24 N	2.55 W
Olivença	154	11.47 S	35.13 E
Olivenza	34	38.41 N	7.06 W
Oliver	182	49.11 N	119.33 W
Olivera	258	34.38 S	59.15 W
Oliver Creek ≃	222	33.06 N	97.17 W
Oliver Ditch ≍	216	41.00 N	87.10 W
Oliverea	210	42.04 N	74.28 W
Oliver Estates	284c	38.59 N	77.18 W
Oliveri	70	38.07 N	15.03 E
Oliver Lake ⊜	184	56.56 N	103.22 W
Oliver Springs	192	36.02 N	84.20 W
Olivet, Fr.	50	47.52 N	1.54 E
Olivet, Mi., U.S.	216	42.26 N	84.55 W
Olivet, S.D., U.S.	198	43.14 N	97.40 W
Oliveto Citra	68	40.41 N	15.14 E
Oliveto Lucano	68	40.32 N	16.11 E
Olivette	219	38.39 N	90.22 W
Olivia	198	44.46 N	94.59 W
Olivine Range ⋏	172	44.18 S	168.30 E
Olivo	116	10.52 N	123.53 E
Olivo ≃	70	37.22 N	14.15 E
Olivone	58	46.32 N	8.57 E
Olivos ◆[8]	258	34.32 S	58.29 W
Öljaren ⊜	40	59.08 N	16.02 E
Olji Moron ≃	89	44.16 N	121.42 E
Olla	194	31.54 N	92.14 W
Ollagüe	248	21.14 S	68.16 W
Ollagüe, Volcán ∧[1]	248	21.18 S	68.12 W
Ollainville	261	48.35 N	2.13 E
Ollantaitambo	248	13.16 S	72.16 W
Ollatrim ≃	48	52.52 N	8.13 W
Ollei	175b	7.43 N	134.37 E
Ollerton	262	53.17 N	2.20 W
Ollerup	41	55.04 N	10.30 E
Olliergues	62	45.40 N	3.38 E
Ollioules	62	43.08 N	5.51 E
Ollomont	62	45.50 N	7.22 E
Ollon	58	46.18 N	7.00 E
Olloua	152	0.56 S	14.34 E
Olmedillo de Roa	34	41.47 N	3.56 W
Olmedo, Esp.	34	41.23 N	4.41 W
Olmedo, It.	71	40.39 N	8.23 E
Olmo al Brembo	58	45.58 N	9.39 E
Olmos	248	5.59 S	79.46 W
Olmsted	214	41.24 N	81.44 W
Olmsted Falls	279a	41.22 N	81.54 W
Olmütz → Olomouc	30	49.36 N	17.16 E
Olney, Eng., U.K.	42	52.09 N	0.42 W
Olney, Il., U.S.	194	38.43 N	88.05 W
Olney, Md., U.S.	208	39.09 N	77.04 W
Olney, Mo., U.S.	219	39.05 N	91.15 W
Olney, Mt., U.S.	182	48.32 N	114.34 W
Olney, Tx., U.S.	196	33.22 N	98.45 W
Olney ◆[8]	285	40.02 N	75.08 W
Oloči	89	51.21 N	119.55 E
Olofström	26	56.16 N	14.30 E
Oloj ≃	74	66.29 N	159.29 E
Ol'okma ≃	74	60.22 N	120.42 E
Ol'okminsk	74	60.24 N	120.24 E
Ol'okminskij Stanovik ⋏	88	54.30 N	120.00 E
Olokui ∧	229a	21.08 N	156.51 W
Olomane ≃	186	50.14 N	60.37 W
Olombo	152	1.18 S	15.53 E
Olomega, Laguna ⊜	236	13.19 N	88.04 W
Olomouc	30	49.36 N	17.16 E
Olona ≃	62	45.06 N	9.21 E
Olonec	24	61.00 N	32.57 E
Olongapo	116	14.50 N	120.16 E
Olonki	88	52.54 N	103.45 E
Olorgasailie National Monument ♠	154	1.40 S	36.22 E
Oloron, Gave d' ≃	32	43.33 N	1.05 W
Oloron-Sainte-Marie	32	43.12 N	0.36 W
Olosega	174y	14.11 S	169.39 W
Olosega I	174y	14.11 S	169.39 W
Olot	34	42.11 N	2.29 E
Olov'annaja, Ross.	88	50.56 N	115.35 E
Olov'annaja, Ross.	180	66.10 N	178.59 W
Oloví	54	50.11 N	12.33 E
Olpe, Dtsch.	56	51.02 N	7.52 E
Olpe, Ks., U.S.	198	38.15 N	96.10 W
Olperer ∧	64	47.03 N	11.39 E
Olsabach ≃	61	46.56 N	14.25 E
Ol'šana, Ukr.	78	49.47 N	37.46 E
Ol'šana, Ukr.	78	50.48 N	34.02 E
Ol'šana, Ukr.	78	49.13 N	31.13 E
Ol'šanka, Ross.	78	51.46 N	35.25 E
Ol'šanka, Ukr.	78	48.14 N	30.52 E
Ol'šany, Bela.	78	52.05 N	27.20 E
Olšany, Česko.	60	49.24 N	13.38 E
Ol'šany, Ukr.	78	50.03 N	35.53 E
Olsberg	56	51.21 N	8.29 E
Ølsemagle	41	55.30 N	12.10 E
Olshammar	40	58.45 N	14.48 E
Olst	52	52.20 N	6.06 E
Ølstykke	41	55.47 N	12.11 E
Olsufjevo	76	53.36 N	33.40 E
Olsztyn (Allenstein)	30	53.48 N	20.29 E
Olsztyn □[4]	30	53.50 N	20.40 E
Olsztynek	30	53.36 N	20.17 E
Olt □[6]	38	44.20 N	24.30 E
Olt ≃	38	43.43 N	24.51 E
Olta	252	30.37 S	66.16 W
Olten	58	47.21 N	7.54 E
Olteni	38	44.10 N	25.18 E
Oltenița	38	44.05 N	26.39 E
Olteț ≃	38	44.14 N	24.27 E
Olton	196	34.11 N	102.08 W
Oltre il Colle	64	45.54 N	9.46 E
Oltu	130	40.33 N	41.59 E
Oltu ≃	130	40.49 N	41.40 E
Oluan Pi >	100	21.54 N	120.51 E
Olukonda	156	18.03 S	16.00 E
Olur	130	40.50 N	42.08 E
Olustee, Fl., U.S.	192	30.12 N	82.26 W
Olustee, Ok., U.S.	196	34.32 N	99.25 W
Olustee Creek ≃	192	29.57 N	82.32 W
Oluta	234	17.55 N	94.54 W
Olutanga (Suba Nipa)	116	7.26 N	122.54 E
Olutanga Island I	116	7.22 N	122.52 E
Olutayan Island I	116	11.39 N	122.50 E
Olute	273a	6.28 N	3.16 E
Ol'utorskij, mys >	74	59.55 N	170.27 E
Ol'utorskij zaliv ⊂	74	60.15 N	168.30 E
Oluwo	273a	6.42 N	3.18 E
Olvenstedt	54	52.09 N	11.34 E
Olvera	34	36.56 N	5.16 W
Olychovatka	78	50.12 N	37.31 E
Olyka	78	50.42 N	25.51 E
Olym	78	51.42 N	38.10 E
Olympe, Mont → Ólimbos ∧	38	40.05 N	22.21 E
Olympia	224	47.02 N	122.53 W
Olympia Fields	216	41.32 N	87.42 W
Olympia Heights	220	25.43 N	80.21 W
Olympia → Olimbía ⊥	38	37.38 N	21.41 E
Olympia Park ♠	273d	26.15 S	28.26 E
Olympia-Stadion ♠	264a	52.31 N	13.14 E
Olympic Mountains ⋏	224	47.50 N	123.45 W
Olympic National Park ♠	224	47.48 N	123.30 W
Olympic Valley	226	39.13 N	120.14 W
Olympic View	224	47.43 N	122.45 W
Olympieion ⊥	267c	37.58 N	23.44 E

Symbol	English	Deutsch	Español	Français	Português
≃	River	Fluß	Río	Rivière	Rio
≍	Canal	Kanal	Canal	Canal	Canal
⌊	Waterfall, Rapids	Wasserfall, Stromschnellen	Cascada, Rápidos	Chute d'eau, Rapides	Cascata, Rápidos
ʯ	Strait	Meeresstraße	Estrecho	Détroit	Estreito
⊂	Bay, Gulf	Bucht, Golf	Bahía, Golfo	Baie, Golfe	Baía, Golfo
⊜	Lake, Lakes	See, Seen	Lago, Lagos	Lac, Lacs	Lago, Lagos
⩸	Swamp	Sumpf	Pantano	Marais	Pântano
⍓	Ice Features, Glacier	Eis- und Gletscherformen	Accidentes Glaciales	Formes glaciaires	Acidentes glaciares
⊤	Other Hydrographic Features	Andere Hydrographische Objekte	Otros Elementos Hidrográficos	Autres données hydrographiques	Outros acidentes hidrográficos
✣	Submarine Features	Untermeerische Objekte	Accidentes Submarinos	Formes de relief sous-marin	Acidentes submarinos
□	Political Unit	Politische Einheit	Unidad Politica	Entité politique	Unidade política
ʊ	Cultural Institution	Kulturelle Institution	Institución Cultural	Institution culturelle	Instituição cultural
⊥	Historical Site	Historische Stätte	Sitio Histórico	Site historique	Sitio histórico
♠	Recreational Site	Erholungs- und Ferienort	Sitio de Recreo	Centre de loisirs	Area de Lazer
⊠	Airport	Flughafen	Aeropuerto	Aéroport	Aeroporto
■	Military Installation	Militäranlage	Instalación Militar	Installation militaire	Instalação militar
◆	Miscellaneous	Verschiedenes	Misceláneo	Divers	Diversos

ENGLISH

Name	Page	Lat.°′	Long.°′

DEUTSCH

Name	Seite	Breite°′	Länge°′ E = Ost

Name	Page	Lat.	Long.
Olympique, Stade ♦	275a	45.33 N	73.33 W
Olymp → Ólimbos ∧	38	40.05 N	22.21 E
Olympus, Mount ∧	224	47.48 N	123.43 W
Olympus, Mount ∧[2]	192	38.03 N	83.39 W
Olympus, Mount → Ólimbos ∧	38	40.05 N	22.21 E
Olyphant	210	41.28 N	75.36 W
Olzai	71	40.11 N	9.09 E
Ol'zony	88	52.57 N	105.15 E
Om ≃, Pap. N. Gui.	164	5.09 S	142.22 E
Om' ≃, Ross.	86	54.59 N	73.22 E
Ōma	92	41.32 N	140.55 E
Ōmachi, Nihon	94	36.30 N	137.52 E
Ōmachi, Nihon	270	34.28 N	135.25 E
Omaezaki	94	34.35 N	138.13 E
Omae-zaki ≻	94	34.36 N	138.14 E
Ōmagari	92	39.27 N	140.29 E
Omagh, On., Can.	275b	43.30 N	79.49 W
Omagh, N. Ire., U.K.	48	54.36 N	7.18 W
Ōmagi	268	35.52 N	139.42 E
Omaguas	246	4.08 S	73.15 W
Omaha, Ne., U.S.	198	41.15 N	95.56 W
Omaha, Tx., U.S.	222	33.11 N	94.45 W
Omaha Indian Reservation ◆[4]	198	42.08 N	96.22 W
Omak	202	48.24 N	119.31 W
Omakau	172	45.05 S	169.36 E
Omak Lake ⊜	202	48.16 N	119.23 W
Omalo	84	42.23 N	45.38 E
Ōmama	94	36.26 N	139.17 E
Oman ('Umān) □[1]	118	22.00 N	58.00 E
Oman, Gulf of c	118	24.30 N	58.30 E
Omapere, Lake ⊜	172	35.21 S	173.47 E
Omar	192	37.45 N	81.59 W
Omarama	172	44.29 S	169.58 E
Omaruru	156	21.28 S	15.56 E
Omaruru □[5]	156	21.00 S	16.00 E
Omaruru ≃	156	22.07 S	14.15 E
Omas	248	12.31 S	76.17 W
Omatako ∧	156	21.07 S	16.43 E
Omatako ≃	156	17.59 S	20.30 E
Omate	248	16.41 S	70.59 W
Omatena	115b	9.53 S	119.47 E
Ōma-zaki ≻	92	41.32 N	140.55 E
Ombai, Selat Ʉ	112	8.30 S	125.00 E
Ombella-Mpoko □[5]	152	5.00 N	18.00 E
Omberg ∧[2]	26	58.20 N	14.39 E
Ombersley	42	52.17 N	2.13 W
Ombombo	156	18.43 S	13.53 E
Omboué	152	1.34 S	9.15 E
Ombrone ≃	66	42.39 N	11.00 E
Ombúes de Lavalle	258	33.55 S	57.47 W
Ombutosu ∧	156	21.22 S	16.50 E
Ombwe	154	4.22 S	25.35 E
Omčak	74	61.38 N	147.55 E
Omčaly	128	40.47 N	53.43 E
Omdraaisvlei	158	30.08 S	23.08 E
Omdurman → Umm Durmān	140	15.38 N	32.30 E
Ōme	94	35.47 N	139.15 E
Omega, Ga., U.S.	192	31.20 N	83.35 W
Omega, Oh., U.S.	218	39.09 N	82.55 W
Omegna	62	45.53 N	8.24 E
Omel'nik	78	49.12 N	33.32 E
Omemee	212	44.18 N	78.33 W
Omeo	166	37.06 S	147.36 E
Ömerköy	130	39.48 N	28.03 E
Ömerli	130	37.24 N	40.58 E
Ömerli Barajı ⊜[1]	130	41.00 N	29.20 E
Omerville	206	45.17 N	72.07 W
Ometepe, Isla de I	236	11.30 N	85.35 W
Ometepec	234	16.41 N	98.25 W
Ometepec ≃	234	16.30 N	98.45 W
Om Hajer	144	14.24 N	36.46 E
Omi, Nihon	94	36.27 N	138.03 E
Ōmi, Nihon	94	37.01 N	137.48 E
Ōmi, Nihon	94	35.20 N	136.24 E
Omigawa	94	35.51 N	140.37 E
Ōmi-hachiman	94	35.08 N	136.06 E
Ōminato → Mutsu	92	41.17 N	141.10 E
Omineca ≃	182	56.05 N	124.30 W
Omineca Mountains ⩘	182	56.00 N	125.00 W
Omin-ni ◆[8]	271b	37.27 N	127.01 E
Ōmino	270	34.32 N	135.33 E
Omišalj	36	45.13 N	14.34 E
Ōmi-shima I, Nihon	96	34.25 N	131.13 E
Omi-shima I, Nihon	96	34.15 N	133.00 E
Omitara	156	22.18 S	18.01 E
Omitlán ≃	234	17.06 N	99.34 W
Ōmiya, Nihon	94	36.33 N	140.25 E
Ōmiya, Nihon	94	35.54 N	139.38 E
Ōmiya, Nihon	96	35.35 N	135.06 E
Ōmiya-daichi ⩘[1]	268	35.56 N	139.38 E
Ōmiya Park Race Track ♦	268	35.55 N	139.38 E
Øm Kloster ⊥	41	56.03 N	9.45 E
Ommaney, Cape ≻	180	56.10 N	134.39 W
Ommanney Bay c	176	73.07 N	100.11 W
Omme ≃	41	55.53 N	8.40 E
Ommen	52	52.32 N	6.25 E
Ömnödelger	88	47.52 N	109.55 E
Ömnögov'	86	49.06 N	91.43 E
Ömnögov' □[4]	102	43.00 N	104.00 E
Omø I	41	55.09 N	11.10 E
Omo ≃	144	43.10 N	35.59 E
Omoa, Bahía de c	236	15.45 N	88.10 W
Omodeo, Lago ⊜	71	40.08 N	8.55 E
Omogo	96	33.41 N	133.02 E
Omoi ≃	94	36.09 N	139.41 E
Omoko	150	5.20 N	6.39 E
Omole	273a	6.38 N	3.22 E
Omoloj ≃	74	71.10 N	132.08 E
Omolon ≃	74	68.42 N	158.36 E
Omo National Park ♦	144	6.00 N	35.45 E
Omono ≃	92	39.46 N	140.03 E
Omont	56	49.36 N	4.44 E
Omo Ranch	226	38.35 N	120.35 W
Ōmori ◆[8]	268	35.34 N	139.44 E
Omotegō	94	37.03 N	140.18 E
Omoy	152	1.21 S	13.09 E
Omrel'kaj ≃	180	68.34 N	170.30 E
Omro	190	44.02 N	88.44 W
Omsino	80	58.36 N	50.28 E
Omsk	86	55.00 N	73.24 E
Omsukčan	74	62.32 N	155.48 E
O-mu, Mya.	110	22.58 N	99.18 E
Ōmu, Nihon	92a	44.34 N	142.58 E
Omu-Aran	150	8.09 N	5.07 E
Ōmuda → Ōmuta	96	33.02 N	130.27 E
Omul, Vîrful ∧	38	45.26 N	25.26 E
Omulew ≃	30	53.05 N	21.32 E
Ōmura	92	32.54 N	129.57 E
Ōmura-wan c	92	32.57 N	129.52 E
Ōmuro	268	35.54 N	139.58 E
Omurtag	38	43.06 N	26.25 E
Ōmuta	96	33.02 N	130.27 E
Omutinskij	86	56.31 N	67.41 E
Omutninsk	86	58.40 N	52.12 E
Ōmyōnbo	98	41.16 N	127.36 E
On	110	21.40 N	106.35 E
Ona, Nor.	26	62.52 N	6.34 E
Ona, Fl., U.S.	220	27.28 N	81.55 W
Ona ≃	86	52.34 N	89.50 E
Onabas	232	28.35 N	109.34 W
Ona → Bir'usa ≃	88	57.43 N	95.24 E
Onadikondo	152	3.52 S	24.10 E
Onaga	198	39.29 N	96.10 W
Onagawa	92	38.26 N	141.27 E
Onahama	94	36.57 N	140.54 E
Onalaska, Tx., U.S.	222	30.48 N	95.07 W
Onalaska, Wa., U.S.	224	46.34 N	122.43 W
Onamia	190	46.04 N	93.40 W
Onancock	208	37.42 N	75.44 W
Onangué, Lac ⊜	152	0.57 S	10.04 E
Onaping ≃	190	46.37 N	81.18 W
Onaping Lake ⊜	190	47.00 N	81.30 W
Onarga	216	40.42 N	88.00 W
Ōnari	268	35.55 N	139.37 E
Onatchiway, Lac ⊜	186	49.00 N	71.03 W
Onawa	198	42.01 N	96.05 W
Onaway	190	45.21 N	84.13 W
Oncativo	252	31.55 S	63.40 W
Once, Canal Numero ≊	252	36.09 S	58.36 W
Onchāi	272b	22.57 N	88.19 E
Onchan	44	54.11 N	4.27 W
Onch'ŏn-dong	98	40.51 N	129.07 E
Oncócua	152	16.34 S	13.28 E
Onda, Esp.	34	39.58 N	0.15 W
Onda, India	126	23.08 N	87.12 E
Ondangwa	156	17.55 S	16.00 E
Ondas, Rio de ≃	255	12.08 S	45.00 W
Ondava ≃	30	48.27 N	21.48 E
Onderdijk	52	52.45 N	5.07 E
Onderstedorings	158	30.13 S	20.37 E
Ondjiva	152	17.03 S	15.47 E
Ondo, Nig.	150	7.04 N	4.47 E
Ondo, Nihon	96	34.11 N	132.32 E
Ondo □[3]	150	7.00 N	5.15 E
Ondo-ōhashi ◆[5]	96	34.12 N	132.33 E
Öndörchaan	88	47.19 N	110.39 E
Öndörchangaj	88	49.20 N	94.50 E
Öndör-Önc	102	45.51 N	103.11 E
Öndöršireet	88	47.27 N	104.50 E
Öndör-Ulaan	88	48.03 N	100.30 E
Ondozero, ozero ⊜	24	63.48 N	33.20 E
O'Neals	226	37.08 N	119.42 W
One Arrow Indian Reserve ◆[4]	184	52.48 N	106.03 W
Oneco, Ct., U.S.	207	41.41 N	71.48 W
Oneco, Fl., U.S.	220	27.26 N	82.32 W
Onega	24	63.55 N	38.05 E
Onega ≃	24	63.58 N	37.55 E
Onega, Lake → Onežskoje ozero ⊜	24	61.30 N	35.45 E
Oneglia	62	43.53 N	8.02 E
One Hundred and Two ≃	194	39.44 N	94.43 W
One Hundred and Two, West Fork ≃	194	40.26 N	94.49 W
One Hundred Fifty Mile House	182	52.06 N	121.55 W
One Hundred Mile House	182	51.39 N	121.18 W
Oneida, Il., U.S.	190	41.04 N	90.13 W
Oneida, Ky., U.S.	192	37.16 N	83.38 W
Oneida, N.Y., U.S.	210	43.05 N	75.39 W
Oneida, Oh., U.S.	218	39.28 N	84.23 W
Oneida, Pa., U.S.	210	40.54 N	76.08 W
Oneida, Tn., U.S.	192	36.29 N	84.30 W
Oneida □[6]	210	43.10 N	75.20 W
Oneida ≃	210	43.12 N	76.17 W
Oneida Castle	210	43.05 N	75.40 W
Oneida County Airport ⊠	210	43.09 N	75.23 W
Oneida Creek ≃	210	43.10 N	75.44 W
Oneida Indian Reservation ◆[4]	190	44.30 N	88.10 W
Oneida Indian Reserve ◆[4]	214	42.49 N	81.24 W
Oneida Lake ⊜	210	43.13 N	76.00 W
O'Neil Forebay ⊜[1]	226	37.05 N	121.03 W
O'Neill	198	42.27 N	98.38 W
Onekama	190	44.21 N	86.12 W
Onekotan, ostrov I	74	49.25 N	154.45 E
Onema	152	4.33 S	24.31 E
Onemen, zaliv c	180	64.45 N	176.35 E
Oneonta, Al., U.S.	194	33.56 N	86.28 W
Oneonta, N.Y., U.S.	210	42.27 N	75.03 W
Oneroa I	174k	21.15 S	159.43 W
One Tree Hill	168b	34.43 S	138.46 E
One Tree Hill ∧[2]	274b	37.52 S	145.19 E
One Tree Hill Lookout ♦	169	36.48 S	144.18 E
Onevai I	174w	21.05 S	175.07 W
Onex	58	46.10 N	6.06 E
Onežskaja guba c	24	64.20 N	36.30 E
Onežskij poluostrov ≻[1]	24	64.35 N	38.00 E
Onežskoje ozero (Lake Onega) ⊜	24	61.30 N	35.45 E
Onga ≃	96	33.54 N	130.39 E
Ongaonga	172	39.55 S	176.25 E
Ongarue	172	38.43 S	175.17 E
Ong Con, Cu Lao I	269c	10.45 N	106.50 E
Ongea Levu I	175g	19.08 S	178.24 W
Ongeluks ≃	158	32.24 S	19.46 E
Ongers ≃	158	31.04 S	23.13 E
Ongerup	162	33.58 S	118.29 E
Ongijn ≃	102	44.30 N	103.40 E
Ongjin	98	37.57 N	125.21 E
Ongoka	154	1.23 S	26.02 E
Ongole	122	15.31 N	80.04 E
Ongon	102	45.21 N	113.09 E
Ongudaj	86	50.45 N	86.09 E
Oni	84	42.34 N	43.27 E
Onich	46	56.42 N	5.13 W
Onida	198	44.42 N	100.03 W
Onifai	71	40.24 N	9.39 E
Oniferi	71	40.16 N	9.10 E
Onigajō-yama ∧	96	33.07 N	132.41 E
Onilahy ≃	157b	23.34 S	43.45 E
Onin, Jazirah ≻[1]	164	2.50 S	132.05 E
Onion Creek ≃	222	30.12 N	97.35 W
Onion Peak ∧	224	45.49 N	123.53 W
Onishi	94	36.09 N	139.04 E
Onistagane, Lac ⊜	186	50.42 N	71.19 W
Onitsha	150	6.09 N	6.47 E
Onji	270	34.37 N	135.38 E
Onjuku	94	35.11 N	140.22 E
Onkaparinga ≃	168b	35.10 S	138.28 E
Onkivesi ⊜	26	63.18 N	27.18 E
Onko	152	4.07 S	19.59 E
Onley	208	37.41 N	75.42 W
Onna	174m	26.30 N	127.51 E
Onnaing	50	50.23 N	3.36 E
Onno	58	45.55 N	9.17 E
Onny ≃	42	52.23 N	2.45 W
Ōno, Nihon	94	35.59 N	136.29 E
Ōno, Nihon	94	35.28 N	136.38 E
Ōno, Nihon	96	34.18 N	132.17 E
Ono, Nihon	96	34.51 N	134.56 E
Ōno, Nihon	96	33.02 N	131.30 E
Ono, Nihon	270	34.57 N	135.14 E
Ono, Pa., U.S.	208	40.24 N	76.32 W
Ono I	175g	18.55 S	178.29 E
Ōno ≃	96	33.15 N	131.43 E
Onochoj	88	51.58 N	108.01 E
Onoda	96	33.59 N	131.11 E
Ōno-dam ◆[6]	96	35.15 N	135.27 E
Onogami	94	36.33 N	138.56 E
Ōnohara	96	34.05 N	133.40 E
Ono-I-Lau I	14	20.39 S	178.42 W
Ōnojō	96	33.32 N	130.28 E
Onolimbu	114	1.03 N	97.53 E
Ōnomi	96	33.21 N	133.09 E
Onomichi	96	34.25 N	133.12 E
Onon	88	49.08 N	112.38 E
Onon ≃	88	51.42 N	115.50 E
Onondaga, Mi., U.S.	216	42.26 N	84.33 W
Onondaga, N.Y., U.S.	210	43.00 N	76.11 W
Onondaga □[6]	210	43.03 N	76.09 W
Onondaga Creek ≃	210	43.04 N	76.11 W
Onondaga Indian Reservation ◆[4]	210	42.55 N	76.09 W
Onor	89	50.11 N	142.40 E
Onota Lake ⊜	207	42.28 N	73.17 W
Onoto	246	9.36 N	65.12 W
Onotoa I[1]	14	1.52 S	175.34 E
Onoway	182	53.42 N	114.12 W
Ons, Isla de I	34	42.23 N	8.56 W
Onsbjerg	41	55.51 N	10.35 E
Onseepkans	158	28.46 S	19.14 E
Onsen	96	35.33 N	134.29 E
Onset	207	41.44 N	70.39 W
Onslow	162	21.39 S	115.06 E
Onslow Bay c	192	34.20 N	77.20 W
Onslow Village	260	51.14 N	0.36 W
Onsted	216	42.00 N	84.11 W
Onstmettingen	58	48.17 N	9.00 E
Onstwedde	52	53.02 N	7.02 E
On-take ∧	92	31.35 N	130.39 E
Ontake-san ∧	94	35.53 N	137.29 E
Ontario, Ca., U.S.	228	34.03 N	117.39 W
Ontario, In., U.S.	216	41.43 N	85.23 W
Ontario, N.Y., U.S.	210	43.13 N	77.17 W
Ontario, Oh., U.S.	214	40.45 N	82.35 W
Ontario, Or., U.S.	202	44.01 N	116.57 W
Ontario □[6]	210	42.54 N	77.17 W
Ontario □[4]	176	51.00 N	85.00 W
Ontario, Lake ⊜	212	43.45 N	78.00 W
Ontario Agricultural Museum ʊ	212	43.30 N	79.56 W
Ontario Center	210	43.14 N	77.19 W
Ontario International Airport ⊠	228	34.04 N	117.36 W
Ontario Place ♦	275b	43.38 N	79.25 W
Ontario Science Centre ʊ	275b	43.43 N	79.21 W
Ontelaunee, Lake ⊜	208	40.27 N	75.55 W
Ontinyent (Onteniente)	34	38.49 N	0.37 W
Ontojärvi ⊜	26	64.08 N	29.09 E
Ontonagon	190	46.52 N	89.18 W
Ontonagon ≃	190	46.52 N	89.20 W
Ontonagon, East Branch ≃	190	46.42 N	89.11 W
Ontonagon, Middle Branch ≃	190	46.42 N	89.10 W
Ontonagon, West Branch ≃	190	46.42 N	89.11 W
Ontong Java I[1]	175e	5.20 S	159.30 E
Onufrijevka	78	48.54 N	33.26 E
Onufrijevo	82	55.51 N	36.31 E
Ōnuma	268	35.32 N	139.25 E
Onverwacht	250	5.36 N	55.12 W
Onward	216	40.42 N	86.12 W
Ŏnyang, Taehan	98	36.47 N	127.00 E
Ŏnyang, Taehan	98	35.34 N	129.07 E
Onzain	50	47.30 N	1.11 E
Onzo ≃	152	8.12 S	13.16 E
Oobagooma	162	16.46 S	123.59 E
Oodnadatta	162	27.33 S	135.28 E
Ood Weyne	144	9.25 N	45.04 E
Ōoka	94	36.30 N	137.59 E
Ooldea	162	30.27 S	131.50 E
Oolitic	218	38.54 N	86.31 W
Oologah	196	36.26 N	95.42 W
Oologah Lake ⊜[1]	196	36.33 N	95.36 W
Ooma	174d	0.53 S	169.36 E
Oombergen	50	50.54 N	3.50 E
Oona River	182	53.57 N	130.18 W
Ooratippra	162	22.00 S	136.00 E
Ooratippra Creek ≃	162	21.55 S	136.05 E
Oorlogskloof ≃	158	31.52 S	19.01 E
Oos	56	48.47 N	8.11 E
Oos-Londen → East London	158	33.00 S	27.55 E
Oostakker	50	51.06 N	3.46 E
Oostburg, Ned.	52	51.20 N	3.30 E
Oostburg, Wi., U.S.	190	43.37 N	87.47 W
Oost-Cappel	50	50.55 N	2.36 E
Oostduinkerke	50	51.07 N	2.41 E
Oostelijk Flevoland ◆[1]	52	52.30 N	5.45 E
Oostende (Ostende)	50	51.13 N	2.55 E
Oosterbeek	52	52.00 N	5.50 E
Oosterend	52	53.05 N	4.52 E
Oosterhout	52	51.38 N	4.51 E
Oosterschelde c	52	51.30 N	4.00 E
Oosterscheldedam ◆[6]	52	51.38 N	3.42 E
Oosterwolde	52	52.59 N	6.17 E
Oosterzele	50	50.57 N	3.48 E
Oosthuizen	52	52.35 N	5.00 E
Oostkamp	50	51.09 N	3.14 E
Oostmahorn	52	53.24 N	6.09 E
Oostmalle	56	51.18 N	4.44 E
Oostpunt ≻	241s	12.02 N	68.45 W
Oostrozebeke	50	50.55 N	3.20 E
Oost-Souburg	52	51.27 N	3.35 E
Oost-Vlaanderen □[4]	50	51.00 N	3.45 E
Oostvleteren	50	50.56 N	2.44 E
Oost-Vlieland	52	53.17 N	5.04 E
Oostvoorne	52	51.55 N	4.06 E
Ootmarsum	52	52.25 N	6.54 E
Ootsa Lake	182	53.47 N	126.03 W
Ootsa Lake ⊜	182	53.49 N	126.18 W
Ootsi	156	25.02 S	25.45 E
Ootua, Mont ∧	174x	9.47 S	138.58 W
Opaka	38	43.27 N	26.10 E
Opala	152	0.37 S	24.21 E
Opalaca, Cordillera ⩘	236	14.30 N	88.20 W
Opal Cliffs	226	36.57 N	121.57 W
Opale, Côte d' ⩦[2]	50	50.40 N	1.35 E
Opalenica	30	52.19 N	16.23 E
Opalicha	265b	55.49 N	37.15 E
Opa-Locka	220	25.54 N	80.15 W
Opari	154	3.56 N	32.03 E
Oparino	24	59.52 N	48.17 E
Opasatica, Lac ⊜	190	48.05 N	79.18 W
Opasatika Lake ⊜	190	49.04 N	83.08 W
Opasquia	184	53.16 N	93.35 W
Opasquia Lake ⊜	184	53.18 N	93.34 W
Opatija	36	45.21 N	14.19 E
Opatów	30	50.49 N	21.26 E
Opava	30	49.56 N	17.54 E
Opava ≃	30	49.50 N	18.13 E
Opečenskij Posad	76	58.16 N	34.07 E
Opeepeesway Lake ⊜	190	47.38 N	82.14 W
Opeilu	273a	6.42 N	3.18 E
Opelika	194	32.38 N	85.22 W
Opelousas	194	30.32 N	92.04 W
Open Bay c	164	4.50 S	151.20 E
Open Door	258	34.30 S	59.05 W
Opeongo ≃	190	45.30 N	77.57 W
Opeongo Lake ⊜	190	45.42 N	78.23 W
Opequon Creek ≃	188	39.35 N	77.52 W
Opfikon	58	47.26 N	8.35 E
Ophain-Bois-Seigneur-Isaac	50	50.40 N	4.21 E
Ophasselt	50	50.49 N	3.53 E
Opheim	202	48.51 N	106.24 W
Opherdicke	263	51.29 N	7.38 E
Opheusden	52	51.56 N	5.38 E
Ophir, Ak., U.S.	180	63.10 N	156.31 W
Ophir, Or., U.S.	202	42.33 N	124.22 W
Ophirton ◆[8]	273d	26.14 S	28.01 E
Ophthalmia Range ⩘	162	23.17 S	119.30 E
Opi	66	41.47 N	13.50 E
Opienge	154	0.12 N	27.30 E
Opihikao	229d	19.25 N	154.53 W
Opinaca ≃	176	52.15 N	78.02 W
Opinan	46	57.43 N	5.47 W
Opinicon Lake ⊜	212	44.33 N	76.20 W
Opiscotéo, Lac ⊜	176	53.10 N	68.10 W
Opladen	56	51.04 N	7.00 E
Opmeer	52	52.43 N	4.56 E
Opobo	150	4.34 N	7.27 E
Opobo Town	150	4.30 N	7.30 E
Opočka	76	56.43 N	28.38 E
Opoczno	30	51.23 N	20.17 E
Opol	116	8.31 N	124.34 E
Opole (Oppeln)	30	50.41 N	17.55 E
Opole □[4]	30	50.30 N	17.45 E
Opole Lubelskie	30	51.09 N	21.58 E
Opon → Lapu-Lapu	116	10.19 N	123.57 E
Opononο, Lake ⊜	156	18.08 S	15.45 E
Opopeo	234	19.24 N	101.36 W
Oporto → Porto	34	41.11 N	8.36 W
Opošn'a	78	49.58 N	34.37 E
Opotiki	172	38.00 S	177.17 E
Opp	194	31.16 N	86.15 W
Oppach	54	51.03 N	14.30 E
Oppdal	26	62.36 N	9.40 E
Oppelhain	54	51.33 N	13.35 E
Oppeln → Opole	30	50.41 N	17.55 E
Oppenau	58	48.28 N	8.10 E
Oppenberg	61	47.29 N	14.16 E
Oppenheim, Dtsch.	56	49.51 N	8.21 E
Oppenheim, N.Y., U.S.	210	43.04 N	74.42 W
Oppenheim Park ♦	284a	43.06 N	78.54 W
Oppenhuizen	52	53.00 N	5.42 E
Oppido Lucano	68	40.47 N	16.00 E
Oppido Mamertina	68	38.16 N	16.00 E
Oppio	66	44.03 N	10.50 E
Oppland □[6]	26	61.10 N	9.40 E
Opportunity, Mt., U.S.	202	46.07 N	112.49 W
Opportunity, Wa., U.S.	202	47.39 N	117.14 W
Oppum ◆[8]	263	51.19 N	6.37 E
Opsa	76	55.32 N	26.47 E
Opsaheden	40	60.28 N	13.59 E
Optic Lake	184	54.46 N	101.13 W
Optima Lake ⊜[1]	196	36.40 N	101.10 W
Opua	172	35.19 S	174.07 E
Opunake	172	39.27 S	173.51 E
Opunohu, Baie d' c	174s	17.30 S	149.51 W
Opuwo	152	18.03 S	13.45 E
Opwijk	50	50.58 N	4.11 E
Oquawka	190	40.55 N	90.56 W
Oquendo, Perú	286d	11.58 S	77.08 W
Oquendo, Pil.	116	12.08 N	124.32 E
O'Quinn	222	29.50 N	96.58 W
Or' ≃	86	51.12 N	58.30 E
Or, Côte d' ∧	58	47.10 N	4.50 E
Or, Étang d' ⊜	261	48.38 N	1.51 E
Ora (Auer), It.	64	46.21 N	11.18 E
Ora, Lībiyā	146	28.33 N	19.24 E
Ōra, Nihon	174m	26.33 N	128.02 E
Ora Banda	162	30.22 S	121.04 E
Oracle	200	32.36 N	110.46 W
Oradea	38	47.03 N	21.57 E
Oradell	276	40.57 N	74.02 W
Oradell Reservoir ⊜[1]	276	40.58 N	74.01 W
Öræfajökull ⊓	24a	64.03 N	16.38 W
Orahovica	38	45.31 N	17.53 E
Orai	124	25.59 N	79.28 E
Oraibi Wash V	200	35.26 N	110.49 W
Oraison	62	43.55 N	5.55 E
Oran	194	37.05 N	89.39 W
Oran, Sebkha d' ⊜	34	35.32 N	0.48 W
Orange, Austl.	166	33.17 S	149.06 E
Orange, Fr.	62	44.08 N	4.48 E
Orange, Ca., U.S.	228	33.47 N	117.51 W
Orange, Ct., U.S.	207	41.16 N	73.01 W
Orange, Ma., U.S.	207	42.35 N	72.18 W
Orange, N.J., U.S.	276	40.46 N	74.13 W
Orange, Oh., U.S.	279a	41.26 N	81.29 W
Orange, Tx., U.S.	194	30.05 N	93.44 W
Orange, Va., U.S.	188	38.14 N	78.06 W
Orange □[6], Ca., U.S.	228	33.43 N	117.54 W
Orange □[6], Fl., U.S.	220	28.32 N	81.16 W
Orange □[6], In., U.S.	218	38.33 N	86.28 W
Orange □[6], N.Y., U.S.	210	41.24 N	74.20 W
Orange (Oranje) ≃	156	28.41 S	16.28 E
Orange, Cabo ≻	250	4.24 N	51.33 W
Orange Bowl ♦	220	25.46 N	80.14 W
Orangeburg, Ky., U.S.	218	38.35 N	83.39 W
Orangeburg, N.Y., U.S.	210	41.03 N	73.57 W
Orangeburg, S.C., U.S.	192	33.29 N	80.51 W
Orange City, Fl., U.S.	220	28.57 N	81.17 W
Orange City, Ia., U.S.	198	43.00 N	96.03 W
Orange County Airport ⊠	228	33.40 N	117.51 W
Orange Cove	226	36.37 N	119.19 W
Orange Free State (Oranje-Vrystaat) □[4]	158	28.30 S	27.00 E
Orange Grove	196	27.57 N	97.56 W
Orange Grove ◆[8]	273d	26.10 S	28.05 E
Orange Lake, Fl., U.S.	192	29.25 N	82.13 W
Orange Lake, N.Y., U.S.	210	41.33 N	74.06 W
Orange Lake ⊜	192	29.29 N	82.10 W
Orangemouth → Oranjemund	156	28.38 S	16.24 E
Orange Park	192	30.09 N	81.42 W
Orange Park Acres	280	33.48 N	117.47 W
Orange Reservoir ⊜[1]	276	40.46 N	74.17 W
Orangevale	226	38.40 N	121.13 W
Orangeville, On., Can.	212	43.55 N	80.06 W
Orangeville, Oh., U.S.	214	41.20 N	80.31 W
Orangeville, Pa., U.S.	210	41.05 N	76.25 W
Orangeville, Ut,. U.S.	200	39.13 N	111.03 W
Orange Walk	232	18.06 N	88.33 W
Orango Grande I	150	11.10 N	16.08 W
Orani, It.	71	40.15 N	9.11 E
Orani, Pil.	116	14.49 N	120.32 E
Oranienbaum	54	51.48 N	12.24 E
Oranienburg	54	52.45 N	13.14 E
Oranje	52	52.55 N	6.28 E
Oranjefontein	156	23.25 S	27.41 E
Oranje Gebergte ⩘	250	3.00 N	55.05 W
Oranjemund	156	28.38 S	16.24 E
Oranje → Orange ≃	156	28.41 S	16.28 E
Oranjerivier	158	29.40 S	24.12 E
Oranjestad	241s	12.33 N	70.06 W
Oranjeville	158	27.00 S	28.15 E
Oranki	80	55.53 N	43.44 E
Oranmore	48	53.16 N	8.54 W
Ŏran-ni	98	34.22 N	126.29 E
Oran → Wahran	148	35.43 N	0.43 W
Oranžerei	80	45.50 N	47.36 E
Or 'Aqiva	132	32.30 N	34.55 E
Orarak	140	6.15 N	32.23 E
Orari ≃	172	44.15 S	171.25 E
Oras	116	12.09 N	125.26 E
Oras ≃	116	12.08 N	125.26 E
Oras Bay c	116	12.07 N	125.28 E
Orăştie	38	45.50 N	23.12 E
Oraşul Stalin → Braşov	38	45.39 N	25.37 E
Oratório, Ribeirão do ≃	287b	23.37 S	46.32 W
Oratov	78	49.12 N	29.32 E
Oravais (Oravainen)	26	63.18 N	22.23 E
Oraviţa	38	45.02 N	21.41 E
Orawia	172	46.03 S	167.49 E
Orb ≃	32	43.15 N	3.18 E
Orba ≃	62	44.53 N	8.37 E
Orba Co ⊜	120	34.32 N	81.03 E
Orbassano	62	45.01 N	7.32 E
Orbe	58	46.43 N	6.32 E
Orbe ≃	58	46.47 N	6.39 E
Orbec-en-Auge	50	49.01 N	0.25 E
Orbetello	66	42.27 N	11.13 E
Orbetello, Laguna di c	66	42.27 N	11.14 E
Orbey	58	48.08 N	7.10 E
Orbieu ≃	32	43.14 N	2.54 E
Orbigny	50	47.12 N	1.14 E
Órbigo ≃	34	41.58 N	5.40 W
Orbiquet ≃	50	49.09 N	0.14 E
Orbisonia	214	40.15 N	77.54 W
Orbost	166	37.42 S	148.27 E
Örbyhus	40	60.14 N	17.42 E
Orcadas ʊ[3]	9	60.45 S	44.43 W
Orcadas, Islas → Orkney Islands II	46	59.00 N	3.00 W
Orcadas del Sur, Islas → South Orkney Islands II	9	60.35 S	45.30 W
Orcades du Sud, Îles → South Orkney Islands II	9	60.35 S	45.30 W
Orcas	224	48.36 N	122.57 W
Orcas Island I	224	48.39 N	122.55 W
Orcemont	261	48.35 N	1.49 E
Orcera	34	38.19 N	2.39 W
Orchamps	58	47.09 N	5.40 E
Orchard, Ne., U.S.	198	42.20 N	98.14 W
Orchard, Tx., U.S.	222	29.36 N	95.58 W
Orchard City	200	38.49 N	107.58 W
Orchard Hills, Austl.	274a	33.47 S	150.43 E
Orchard Hills, Pa., U.S.	279b	40.35 N	79.32 W
Orchard Homes	202	46.51 N	114.02 W
Orchard Island	216	40.28 N	83.53 W
Orchard Lake ⊜	281	42.35 N	83.22 W
Orchard Lake Village	281	42.35 N	83.21 W
Orchard Mesa	200	39.02 N	108.33 W
Orchard Park	210	42.46 N	78.44 W
Orchard Park Airport ⊠	284a	42.48 N	78.45 W
Orchard Peak ∧	226	35.44 N	120.08 W
Orchards	224	45.40 N	122.33 W
Orchard Valley	200	41.05 N	104.48 W
Orchard View	285	40.04 N	74.53 W
Orchej	78	47.23 N	28.48 E
Orchha	124	25.21 N	78.39 E
Orchies	50	50.28 N	3.14 E
Orchon	88	49.09 N	105.21 E
Orchon ≃	88	50.21 N	106.05 E
Orchon Tuul	88	48.58 N	104.59 E
Orcia ≃	66	42.58 N	11.21 E
Orcières	62	44.41 N	6.20 E
Orčik ≃	78	49.10 N	35.04 E
Orco ≃	62	45.10 N	7.52 E
Ord	198	41.36 N	98.55 W
Ord ≃	160	15.30 S	128.21 E
Ord, Mount ∧	162	17.20 S	125.34 E
Orda	86	57.12 N	56.54 E
Ordenes	34	43.04 N	8.24 W
Orderville	200	37.16 N	112.38 W
Ordesa, Parque Nacional de ♦	34	42.39 N	0.02 E
Ord Mountain ∧	204	34.40 N	116.49 W
Ord Mountains ⩘	228	34.42 N	117.10 W
Ordoqui	252	35.54 S	61.10 W
Ord River	162	17.23 S	128.51 E
Ordu	130	41.00 N	37.53 E
Ordu □[4]	130	40.45 N	37.30 E
Ordubad	84	38.56 N	46.02 E
Ordway	198	38.13 N	103.45 W
Ordynskoje	86	54.22 N	81.56 E
Ordzhonikidze → Jenakijevo	83	48.14 N	38.13 E
Ordžhonikidze → Vladikavkaz, Ross.	84	43.03 N	44.40 E
Ordzhonikidze → Vladikavkaz, Ross.	84	43.03 N	44.40 E
Ordžonikidze, Azer.	84	40.53 N	47.23 E
Ordžonikidze, Kaz.	86	52.28 N	61.46 E
Ordžonikidze, Sak.	84	42.01 N	43.12 E
Ordžonikidze, Ukr.	78	47.40 N	34.04 E
Ordžonikidze, Ukr.	78	44.57 N	35.22 E
Ordžonikidzeabad	85	38.34 N	69.01 E
Ordžonikidzevskaja	84	43.18 N	45.03 E
Ordžonikidzevskij, Ross.	84	43.51 N	41.54 E
Ordžonikidzevskij, Ross.	86	54.46 N	88.59 E
Ore	150	6.44 N	4.52 E
Ore ≃	46	56.10 N	3.15 W
Öreälven ≃	26	63.32 N	19.44 E
Oreana	219	39.56 N	88.51 W
Örebro	40	59.17 N	15.13 E
Örebro Län □[6]	40	59.30 N	15.00 E
Orechov	78	47.34 N	35.47 E
Orechovka, Ross.	80	52.56 N	48.14 E
Orechovka, Ukr.	83	48.17 N	39.13 E
Orechovo	80	58.28 N	41.58 E
Orechovo-Zujevo	82	55.49 N	38.59 E
Orechovsk	76	54.41 N	30.30 E
Orechov'skij ◆[8]	83	48.01 N	38.42 E
Ore City	222	32.48 N	94.43 W
Oredež	76	58.49 N	30.20 E
Oredež ≃	76	58.49 N	30.00 E
Orefield	208	40.38 N	75.35 W
Oregon, Il., U.S.	190	42.00 N	89.19 W
Oregon, Mo., U.S.	194	39.59 N	95.08 W
Oregon, Oh., U.S.	214	41.38 N	83.29 W
Oregon, Wi., U.S.	216	42.55 N	89.23 W
Oregon □[3], U.S.	178	44.00 N	121.00 W
Oregon □[3], U.S.	202	44.00 N	121.00 W
Oregon Caves National Monument ♦	202	42.06 N	123.24 W
Oregon City	224	45.21 N	122.36 W
Oregon Creek ≃	226	39.23 N	121.05 W
Oregon Dunes National Recreation Area ♦	202	43.45 N	124.12 W
Oregon House	226	39.21 N	121.17 W
Öregrund	40	60.20 N	18.26 E
Öregrundsgrepen c	40	60.27 N	18.18 E
Orehoved	41	54.57 N	11.52 E
Orekhovo-Zuyevo → Orechovo-Zujevo	82	55.49 N	38.59 E
Orel', ozero ⊜	89	53.30 N	139.42 E
Oreland	285	40.07 N	75.10 W
Orellana	248	6.54 S	75.04 W
Orellana, Embalse de ⊜[1]	34	39.00 N	5.25 W
Orel → Or'ol	76	52.59 N	36.05 E
Orem	200	40.17 N	111.41 W
Ören	130	37.02 N	27.57 E
Orenburg	86	51.54 N	55.06 E
Orenburg □[8]	80	52.38 N	53.00 E
Örencik	130	39.16 N	29.33 E
Oreng, Indon.	114	4.33 N	96.49 E
Oreng, Indon.	114	4.03 N	97.28 E
Orense, Arg.	252	38.40 S	59.47 W
Orense, Esp.	34	42.20 N	7.51 W
Orense □[4]	34	42.15 N	7.30 W
Örenşehir	130	39.00 N	36.39 E
Orepuki	172	46.17 S	167.44 E
Oreški	82	55.43 N	36.21 E
Oressa ≃	76	52.33 N	28.45 E
Orestes	216	40.16 N	85.43 W
Orestes Pereyra	232	26.31 N	105.40 W
Orestiás	38	41.30 N	26.31 E
Orestimba Creek ≃	226	37.25 N	121.00 W
Øresund → The Sound Ʉ	41	55.50 N	12.40 E
Oreti ≃	172	46.28 S	168.17 E
Oreto ≃	70	38.06 N	13.24 E
Orewa	172	36.34 S	174.42 E
Oreye	56	50.44 N	5.22 E
Orfanoú, Kólpos c	38	40.40 N	23.50 E
Orford, Eng., U.K.	42	52.06 N	1.31 E
Orford, Eng., U.K.	262	53.25 N	2.35 W
Orford, Mont ∧	206	45.19 N	72.15 W
Orford Ness ≻	42	52.05 N	1.34 E
Orfordville	190	42.37 N	89.15 W
Organ Needle ∧	200	32.21 N	106.33 W
Organ Pipe Cactus National Monument ♦	200	32.00 N	112.55 W
Órgãos, Serra dos ⩘	256	22.22 S	42.45 W
Orgaz	34	39.39 N	3.54 W
Orge ≃	50	48.42 N	2.24 E
Orgelet	58	46.31 N	5.37 E
Orgères-en-Beauce	50	48.09 N	1.42 E
Orgerus	261	48.50 N	1.42 E
Orgeval	50	48.55 N	1.59 E
Orgeval ≃	261	49.00 N	1.54 E
Orgiano	64	45.21 N	11.28 E
Orgnac, Aven d' ⩦[5]	62	44.19 N	4.27 E
Orgnac-l'Aven	62	44.19 N	4.27 E
Orgof	144	3.03 N	41.44 E
Orgon	62	43.47 N	5.02 E
Orgosolo	71	40.12 N	9.21 E
Orgtrud	80	56.12 N	40.37 E
Orgūn	120	32.51 N	69.07 E
Orhaneli	130	39.54 N	29.00 E
Orhangazi	130	40.30 N	29.18 E
Orhanlar	130	39.54 N	27.37 E
Oria, It.	68	40.30 N	17.38 E
Oria, Zaïre	154	3.17 N	30.41 E
Orica	236	14.41 N	86.56 W
Oriçanga, Rio do ≃	256	22.18 S	47.03 W
Orichuna ≃	246	7.25 N	68.58 W
Oriči	80	58.24 N	49.05 E
Orick	204	41.17 N	124.03 W
Oricola	66	42.02 N	13.02 E
Orient, Ia., U.S.	198	41.12 N	94.24 W
Orient, N.Y., U.S.	207	41.08 N	72.18 W
Orient, Oh., U.S.	218	39.48 N	83.09 W
Orient, Wa., U.S.	182	48.53 N	118.13 W
Oriental, Méx.	234	19.22 N	97.37 W
Oriental, N.C., U.S.	192	35.01 N	76.41 W
Oriental, Cordillera ⩘, Col.	246	6.00 N	73.00 W
Oriental, Cordillera ⩘, Perú	248	11.00 S	74.00 W
Oriental, Pico ∧	286c	10.32 N	66.50 W
Oriental de Zapata, Ciénaga ≡	240p	22.15 N	80.50 W
Oriental Park	214	42.09 N	79.22 W
Oriente	252	38.44 S	60.37 W
Orientos	166	28.05 S	141.14 E
Origgio	266b	45.36 N	9.01 E
Origny-en-Thiérache	50	49.54 N	4.01 E
Origny-Sainte-Benoite	50	49.50 N	3.30 E
Orillia	212	44.37 N	79.25 W
Orimattila	26	60.48 N	25.45 E
Orinda	226	37.52 N	122.10 W
Orinduik	246	4.42 N	60.01 W
Orini	172	37.34 S	175.18 E
Orinin	78	48.46 N	26.24 E
Orinoco ≃	246	8.37 N	62.15 W
Orinoco, Delta del ≚[2]	246	9.15 N	61.30 W
Oriola (Orihuela)	34	38.05 N	0.57 W
Oriole, Md., U.S.	208	38.10 N	75.48 W
Oriole, Pa., U.S.	210	41.08 N	77.13 W
Oriolo	68	40.03 N	16.27 E
Oriomo	164	8.50 S	143.15 E
Orion, Pil.	116	14.37 N	120.34 E
Orion, Il., U.S.	190	41.21 N	90.22 W
Oripää	26	60.51 N	22.41 E
Oriskany	210	43.09 N	75.19 W
Oriskany Battlefield State Historic Site ⊥	210	43.11 N	75.23 W
Oriskany Creek ≃	210	43.10 N	75.20 W
Oriskany Falls	210	42.56 N	75.27 W
Orissa □[3]	118	20.00 N	84.00 E
Orissaare	76	58.34 N	23.05 E
Orissa Coast Canal ≊	126	21.51 N	87.41 E
Oristano	71	39.54 N	8.36 E
Oristano □[4]	71	39.55 N	8.40 E
Oristano, Golfo di c	71	39.50 N	8.29 E
Őriszentpéter	61	46.51 N	16.25 E
Orituco ≃	246	8.45 N	67.27 W
Orivesi	26	61.41 N	24.21 E
Orivesi ⊜	26	62.16 N	29.24 E
Oriximiná	250	1.45 S	55.52 W
Orizaba	234	18.51 N	97.06 W
Orizaba, Pico de (Volcán Citlatépetl) ∧[1]	234	19.01 N	97.16 W
Orizona	255	17.03 S	48.18 W
Orjahovo	38	43.45 N	23.57 E
Ørje	26	59.29 N	11.39 E
Orjen ∧	38	42.30 N	18.38 E
Orjiva	34	36.54 N	3.25 W
Ork, Ness of ≻	46	59.05 N	2.48 W
Orkanger	26	63.19 N	9.52 E
Örkelljunga	41	56.17 N	13.17 E
Orken	263	51.06 N	6.34 E
Orkla ≃	26	63.18 N	9.50 E
Orkney, Sk., Can.	184	49.08 N	107.55 W
Orkney, S. Afr.	158	27.00 S	26.39 E
Orkney □[4]	46	59.00 N	3.00 W
Orkney Islands II	46	59.00 N	3.00 W
Orl'a	76	53.30 N	24.59 E
Orla ≃	54	50.46 N	11.31 E
Orlamünde	54	50.47 N	11.31 E
Orland, Ca., U.S.	204	39.44 N	122.11 W
Orland, In., U.S.	216	41.43 N	85.10 W
Orlândia	255	20.43 S	47.53 W
Orland Lake ⊜	278	41.38 N	87.52 W
Orlando, S. Afr.	273d	26.14 S	27.55 E
Orlando, Fl., U.S.	220	28.32 N	81.22 W
Orlando, Capo d' ≻	70	38.10 N	14.45 E
Orlando Dam ⊜[1]	273d	26.16 S	27.56 E
Orlando International Airport ⊠	220	28.26 N	81.19 W
Orlando Naval Training Center ■	220	28.34 N	81.20 W
Orlando West Extension	273d	26.15 S	27.54 E
Orland Park	216	41.37 N	87.51 W
Orland Square ◆[9]	278	41.36 N	87.51 W
Orléanais □[9]	50	47.50 N	2.00 E
Orléans, On., Can.	212	45.28 N	75.31 W
Orléans, Fr.	50	47.55 N	1.54 E
Orleans, Ca., U.S.	204	41.18 N	123.32 W
Orleans, In., U.S.	218	38.39 N	86.27 W
Orleans, Ma., U.S.	207	41.47 N	69.59 W
Orleans, Ne., U.S.	198	40.07 N	99.27 W
Orleans, Vt., U.S.	188	44.48 N	72.12 W
Orleans □[6], N.Y., U.S.	210	43.15 N	78.12 W
Orleans □[6], Vt., U.S.	206	44.57 N	72.12 W
Orléans, Canal d' ≊	50	47.54 N	1.55 E
Orléans, Île d' I	186	46.55 N	70.58 W
Orléansville → Ech Cheliff	148	36.10 N	1.20 E
Orlik, Kaz.	80	48.17 N	51.32 E
Orlik, Ross.	88	52.30 N	99.55 E
Orlinaja, gora ∧	180	62.35 N	178.30 E
Orlinga	88	56.03 N	105.53 E
Orlinga ≃	88	56.03 N	105.53 E
Orlová	30	49.50 N	18.24 E
Orlov Gaj	80	50.57 N	48.12 E
Orlovista	220	28.32 N	81.28 W
Orlovka, Ross.	78	51.02 N	40.32 E
Orlovka, Ross.	86	59.03 N	85.59 E
Orlovka, Ukr.	78	51.54 N	32.47 E
Orlovka, Ukr.	78	45.40 N	33.21 E
Orlovka, Ukr.	83	48.10 N	37.39 E
Orlovka ≃	86	58.40 N	86.08 E
Orlovo, Ross.	78	51.45 N	39.35 E
Orlovo, Ross.	265b	55.38 N	37.23 E
Orlovskij	80	46.52 N	42.03 E
Orlu	150	5.47 N	7.02 E
Orly	261	48.45 N	2.24 E
Ormanlı	130	41.10 N	31.39 E
Ormāra	128	25.12 N	64.38 E
Ormāra, Rās ≻	128	25.09 N	64.35 E
Orme, Rivière à l' ≃	275a	45.27 N	73.56 W
Ormea	62	44.09 N	7.54 E
Ormesby	44	54.33 N	1.11 W
Ormesby Saint Margaret	42	52.40 N	1.42 E
Ormiston	184	49.45 N	105.22 W
Ormoc	116	11.00 N	124.37 E
Ormoc Bay c	116	10.58 N	124.35 E
Ormond	274b	37.54 S	145.03 E
Ormond Beach	192	29.17 N	81.03 W
Ormož	61	46.25 N	16.09 E
Ormsby	214	41.48 N	78.33 W
Ormsby □[6]	226	39.11 N	119.46 W
Ormsjön ⊜	26	64.23 N	16.03 E

Symbols in the index entries represent the broad categories identified in the key at the right. Symbols with superior numbers (⩘[1]) identify subcategories (see complete key on page *I* · 1).

Symbole im Register stellen die rechts im Schlüssel erklärten Kategorien dar. Symbole mit hochgestellten Ziffern (⩘[1]) bezeichnen Unterabteilungen einer Kategorie (vgl. vollständiger Schlüssel auf Seite *I* · 1).

Los símbolos incluídos en el texto del índice representan las grandes categorias identificadas con la clave a la derecha. Los símbolos con numeros en su parte superior (⩘[1]) identifican las subcategorías (véase la clave completa en la página *I* · 1).

Les symboles de l'index représentent les catégories indiquées dans la légende à droite. Les symboles suivis d'un indice (⩘[1]) représentent des sous-catégories (voir légende complète à la page *I* · 1).

Os símbolos incluídos no texto do índice representam as grandes categorias identificadas com a chave à direita. Os símbolos com números em sua parte superior (⩘[1]) identificam as subcategorias (veja-se a chave completa à página *I* · 1).

∧ Mountain	Berg	Montaña	Montagne	Montanha
⩘ Mountains	Gebirge	Montañas	Montagnes	Montanhas
⟩⟨ Pass	Paß	Paso	Col	Passo
V Valley, Canyon	Tal, Cañon	Valle, Cañón	Vallée, Canyon	Vale, Canhão
≚ Plain	Ebene	Llano	Plaine	Planície
≻ Cape	Kap	Cabo	Cap	Cabo
I Island	Insel	Isla	Île	Ilha
II Islands	Inseln	Islas	Îles	Ilhas
⩦ Other Topographic Features	Andere Topographische Objekte	Otros Elementos Topográficos	Autres données topographiques	Outros acidentes topográficos

ESPAÑOL Nombre / FRANÇAIS Nom / PORTUGUÊS Nome	Página / Page	Lat.°'	Long.°' W = Oeste / W = Ouest
Ormskirk	44	53.35 N	2.54 W
Ormstown	206	45.08 N	74.00 W
Ormtjernkampen Nasjonalpark ♦	26	61.12 N	9.48 E
Ornain ≃	58	48.46 N	4.47 E
Ornans	58	47.06 N	6.09 E
Ornäs	40	60.31 N	15.32 E
Ornavasso	58	45.58 N	8.24 E
Orne □[5]	32	48.40 N	0.05 E
Orne ≃, Fr.	32	49.19 N	0.14 W
Orne ≃, Fr.	50	48.08 N	0.11 E
Orne ≃, Fr.	56	49.17 N	6.11 E
Ornes	26	61.18 N	7.22 E
Orneta	30	54.08 N	20.08 E
Ornö I	40	59.04 N	18.24 E
Örnsköldsvik	26	63.18 N	18.43 E
Oro	98	40.02 N	127.26 E
Orø I	41	55.46 N	11.49 E
Orobie, Alpi ⛰	64	46.00 N	10.00 E
Oročanskij Golec, gora ∧	88	53.29 N	114.18 E
Oročen	74	58.28 N	125.26 E
Orocovis	240m	18.14 N	66.23 W
Orocué	246	4.48 N	71.20 W
Orocuina	236	13.26 N	87.06 W
Orodara	150	10.59 N	4.55 W
Orofino	202	46.28 N	116.15 W
Orogen Zizhiqi	89	50.34 N	123.40 E
Örög nuur ◎, Mong.	86	50.10 N	91.00 E
Orog nuur ◎, Mong.	102	45.03 N	100.42 E
Oro Grande	228	34.35 N	117.20 W
Orohena, Mont ∧	174s	17.37 S	149.28 W
Orok, Oldoinyo ∧	154	2.29 S	36.46 E
Oroku	174m	26.12 N	127.39 E
Or'ol, Ross.	76	52.59 N	36.05 E
Or'ol, Ross.	86	59.21 N	56.35 E
Or'ol □[8]	78	52.00 N	38.00 E
Or'ol' ≃	78	48.30 N	34.54 E
Oroluk I[1]	14	7.32 N	155.18 E
Oromocto	186	45.51 N	66.29 W
Oromocto Lake ◎	186	45.36 N	67.00 W
Oron, Nig.	150	4.48 N	8.14 E
Oron, Ross.	88	57.11 N	116.28 E
Oron, ozero ◎	88	57.06 N	116.30 E
Orona I[1]	14	4.29 S	172.10 W
Oron-la-Ville	58	46.34 N	6.50 E
Orono, On., Can.	212	43.59 N	78.37 W
Orono, Me., U.S.	188	44.52 N	68.40 W
Oronoque ≃	246	2.45 N	57.25 W
Oronsay I	46	56.01 N	6.16 W
Orontes → Asi ≃	130	36.02 N	35.58 E
Oropa, Santuario di ʋ[1]	62	45.38 N	7.58 E
Oropeo	234	18.50 N	101.48 W
Oroquieta	116	8.29 N	123.48 E
Orós	250	6.15 S	38.55 W
Orós, Açude ◎[1]	250	6.15 S	39.05 W
Orosei	71	40.23 N	9.42 E
Orosei, Golfo di c	71	40.15 N	9.44 E
Orosháza	30	46.34 N	20.40 E
Orosi	226	36.33 N	119.17 W
Orosí, Volcán ∧[1]	236	10.59 N	85.29 W
Oroszlány	30	47.30 N	18.19 E
Orotelli	71	40.18 N	9.07 E
Orote Peninsula ≻[1]	174p	13.26 N	144.38 E
Oroville, Ca., U.S.	226	39.30 N	121.33 W
Oroville, Wa., U.S.	202	48.56 N	119.26 W
Oroville, Lake ◎[1]	204	39.32 N	121.25 W
Orowoc Creek ≃	276	40.43 N	73.13 W
Orpheus Island I	166	18.37 S	146.30 E
Orphin	261	48.35 N	1.47 E
Orpierre	62	44.19 N	5.41 E
Orpington ◆[8]	260	51.23 N	0.06 E
Orrefors	26	56.50 N	15.45 E
Orrell, Eng., U.K.	44	53.32 N	2.42 W
Orrell, Eng., U.K.	262	53.32 N	2.43 W
Orrick	194	39.12 N	94.07 W
Orrin	198	48.05 N	100.09 W
Orrin, Glen V	46	57.30 N	4.46 W
Orrin, Loch ◎	46	57.30 N	4.45 W
Òrrius	266d	41.33 N	2.21 E
Orr Lake ◎, Mb., Can.	184	56.07 N	97.11 W
Orr Lake ◎, On., Can.	212	44.37 N	79.47 W
Orroroo	166	32.44 S	138.37 E
Orrs Island	188	43.45 N	69.58 W
Orrtanna	208	39.51 N	77.22 W
Orrville, Al., U.S.	194	32.18 N	87.14 W
Orrville, Oh., U.S.	214	40.50 N	81.45 W
Orrville, Pa., U.S.	279b	40.33 N	79.47 W
Orša, Bela.	76	54.30 N	30.24 E
Orsa, Sve.	26	61.07 N	14.37 E
Orša ≃	82	56.48 N	36.11 E
Orsago	64	45.56 N	12.25 E
Orsan	62	44.08 N	4.40 E
Oršanka	80	56.55 N	47.53 E
Orsara di Puglia	68	41.17 N	15.16 E
Orsasjön ◎	26	61.07 N	14.34 E
Orsay	50	48.48 N	2.11 E
Orsett	260	51.31 N	0.22 E
Orsières	58	46.02 N	7.09 E
Orsjön ◎	26	61.35 N	16.20 E
Orsk	86	51.12 N	58.34 E
Örskär I	40	60.31 N	18.23 E
Ørslev	41	55.02 N	11.59 E
Orsogna	66	42.13 N	14.17 E
Orsomarso	68	39.48 N	15.55 E
Orson	210	41.49 N	75.27 W
Orşova	38	44.42 N	22.24 E
Ørsta	26	62.12 N	6.09 E
Ørsted	41	55.20 N	10.04 E
Örsundaån ≃	40	59.44 N	17.21 E
Örsundsbro	40	59.44 N	17.18 E
Orta	130	40.38 N	33.06 E
Orta, Lago d' ◎	62	45.49 N	8.24 E
Ortaca	130	36.49 N	28.47 E
Ortakent	130	37.02 N	27.21 E
Ortaklar	130	37.53 N	27.30 E
Ortaköy, Tür.	130	40.17 N	35.16 E
Ortaköy, Tür.	130	38.44 N	34.03 E
Ortaköy, Tür.	130	38.00 N	34.23 E
Ortaköy, Tür.	130	40.27 N	38.02 E
Ortaköy ◆[8]	267b	41.03 N	29.01 E
Orta Nova	68	41.19 N	15.42 E
Orta San Giulio	62	45.48 N	8.25 E
Orte	66	42.27 N	12.23 E
Ortega	246	3.56 N	75.13 W
Ortegal, Cabo ≻	34	43.45 N	7.53 W
Orteguaza ≃	246	0.43 N	75.16 W
Ortelsburg → Szczytno	30	53.34 N	21.00 E
Ortenberg, Dtsch.	56	50.21 N	9.02 E
Ortenberg, Dtsch.	58	48.27 N	7.58 E
Ortenburg	60	48.33 N	13.14 E
Orth	54	54.27 N	11.03 E
Orthez	32	43.29 N	0.46 W
Orthon ≃	248	10.50 S	66.04 W
Ortigalita Creek ≃	226	36.57 N	120.52 W
Ortigalita Peak ∧	226	36.48 N	120.55 W
Ortigara, Monte ∧	64	46.00 N	11.29 E
Ortigueira	34	43.41 N	7.51 W
Ortigueira, Ría de c[1]	34	43.42 N	7.51 W
Orting	224	47.05 N	122.12 W
Ortisei (Sankt Ulrich)	64	46.34 N	11.40 E
Ortiz, Méx.	232	28.17 N	110.43 W
Ortiz, Ven.	246	9.37 N	67.17 W
Ortles (Otler) ∧	64	46.31 N	10.33 E
Örtofta	41	55.47 N	13.14 E
Ortolo ≃	71	41.30 N	8.55 E
Ortona	66	42.21 N	14.24 E
Ortona Lock ◆[5]	220	26.47 N	81.18 W
Orton Park ♦	275b	43.46 N	79.12 W
Ortonura	85	41.29 N	76.12 E
Ortonville, Mi., U.S.	216	42.51 N	83.26 W
Ortonville, Mn., U.S.	198	45.18 N	96.26 W
Ortonville State Recreation Area ♦	216	42.52 N	83.26 W
Ortoterek	85	41.56 N	71.21 E
Orto-Tokoj	85	42.21 N	76.01 E
Ortovero	62	44.03 N	8.07 E
Ortrand	54	51.22 N	13.45 E
Örträsk	26	64.08 N	18.59 E
Ortueri	71	40.02 N	8.59 E
Ortúzar, Canal ≋	286e	33.33 S	70.47 W
Örtze ≃	52	52.40 N	9.57 E
Oruanui	172	38.35 S	176.02 E
Oruba	273a	6.35 N	3.25 E
Orudjevo	82	56.26 N	37.32 E
Orūmīyeh (Reẕā'īyeh)	128	37.33 N	45.04 E
Orūmīyeh, Daryācheh-ye (Lake Urmia) ◎	128	37.40 N	45.30 E
Orune	71	40.24 N	9.22 E
Oruro	248	17.59 S	67.09 W
Oruro □[5]	248	18.40 S	67.30 W
Or'us-Mijele ≃	88	58.35 N	121.30 E
Orust I	26	58.10 N	11.38 E
Orūzgān (Qala-i-Hazār Qadam)	120	32.56 N	66.38 E
Orūzgān □[4]	120	33.15 N	66.00 E
Orval, Abbaye d' ʋ[1]	56	49.38 N	5.22 E
Orvanne ≃	50	48.22 N	2.50 E
Orvieto	66	42.43 N	12.07 E
Orvilla	208	40.16 N	75.17 W
Orvilliers	261	48.52 N	1.39 E
Orvin ≃	50	48.28 N	3.23 E
Orvinio	66	42.08 N	12.56 E
Orviston	214	41.06 N	77.45 W
Orvyn, gora ∧	180	65.14 N	175.20 W
Orwell, On., Can.	214	42.46 N	81.02 W
Orwell, N.Y., U.S.	212	43.35 N	76.00 W
Orwell, Oh., U.S.	214	41.32 N	80.52 W
Orwell ≃	42	51.57 N	1.17 E
Orwigsburg	208	40.39 N	76.06 W
Orwin	208	40.35 N	76.31 W
Orxon ≃	88	49.00 N	117.41 E
Or Yehuda	132	32.01 N	34.51 E
Oryu-dong ◆[8]	271b	37.29 N	126.51 E
Orževo	78	50.45 N	26.07 E
Orževka	80	52.43 N	42.55 E
Oržica	78	49.48 N	32.42 E
Orzinuovi	62	45.24 N	9.55 E
Orzyc ≃	30	52.47 N	21.13 E
Orzysz	30	53.49 N	21.56 E
Oš, Kyrg.	85	40.33 N	72.48 E
Os, Nor.	26	62.30 N	11.12 E
Ōsa, Nihon	96	35.05 N	133.34 E
Osa, Ross.	86	57.17 N	55.26 E
Osa, Ross.	88	53.24 N	103.53 E
Oša ≃	86	57.13 N	73.41 E
Osa, Península de ≻[1]	236	8.34 N	83.31 W
Osage, Ia., U.S.	190	43.17 N	92.48 W
Osage, Mo., U.S.	219	38.25 N	92.02 W
Osage, N.J., U.S.	285	39.51 N	75.01 W
Osage, Wy., U.S.	198	43.58 N	104.25 W
Osage □[6]	219	38.27 N	91.50 W
Osage ≃	194	38.35 N	91.57 W
Osage Beach	194	38.09 N	92.37 W
Osage City	198	38.38 N	95.49 W
Osaka, Nihon	94	35.57 N	137.16 E
Ōsaka, Nihon	96	34.40 N	135.30 E
Ōsaka, Nihon	270	34.40 N	135.30 E
Ōsaka □[5]	96	34.30 N	135.30 E
Osaka Castle ⊥	270	34.41 N	135.32 E
Ōsaka-heiya ≡	270	34.43 N	135.30 E
Ōsaka International Airport ✈	270	34.47 N	135.26 E
Ōsaka-kō c	270	34.38 N	135.26 E
Ōsaka-kokusai-kūkō ✈	96	34.47 N	135.26 E
Osakarovka	86	50.32 N	72.39 E
Ōsaka-tōge)(	270	34.56 N	135.18 E
Osaka University ʋ[2]	270	34.42 N	135.30 E
Ōsaka-wan c	96	34.30 N	135.18 E
Ōsakiga-hana ≻	96	35.11 N	132.25 E
Ōsaki-Kami-jima I	96	34.14 N	132.54 E
Osakis	198	45.52 N	95.09 W
Ōsaki-Shimo-jima I	96	34.10 N	132.50 E
Osâm ≃	38	43.42 N	24.51 E
Osan	98	37.11 N	127.04 E
Osanovo	82	54.12 N	38.41 E
Osasco	256	23.32 S	46.46 W
Osasco □[7]	287b	23.32 S	46.46 W
Ōsawano	94	36.34 N	137.12 E
Osawatomie	198	38.29 N	94.57 W
Ōsa-yama ∧	96	34.45 N	132.12 E
Osbaldeston	262	53.47 N	2.32 W
Osborne, Ks., U.S.	198	39.26 N	98.41 W
Osborne, Pa., U.S.	279b	40.32 N	80.10 W
Osburger Hochwald ◆[3]	56	49.40 N	6.50 E
Osburn	202	47.30 N	115.59 W
Osby	26	56.22 N	13.59 E
Osbyholm	41	55.51 N	13.36 E
Oscar Peak ∧	182	54.51 N	129.07 W
Oscarville	180	60.43 N	161.46 W
Oscawana Lake	210	41.23 N	73.52 W
Osceola, Ar., U.S.	194	35.42 N	89.58 W
Osceola, In., U.S.	216	41.39 N	86.04 W
Osceola, Ia., U.S.	190	41.02 N	93.45 W
Osceola, Mo., U.S.	194	38.02 N	93.42 W
Osceola, Ne., U.S.	198	41.10 N	97.32 W
Osceola, Pa., U.S.	210	41.59 N	77.21 W
Osceola, Tx., U.S.	222	32.08 N	97.14 W
Osceola, Wi., U.S.	190	45.19 N	92.42 W
Osceola □[6]	220	28.00 N	81.15 W
Osceola Mills	214	40.51 N	78.16 W
Oščepkovo	86	56.29 N	70.42 E
Oschatz	54	51.17 N	13.07 E
Oschersleben	54	52.01 N	11.13 E
Oschiri	71	40.43 N	9.06 E
Oscoda	190	44.26 N	83.20 W
Öse ≃	263	51.26 N	7.49 E
Osečenka	76	57.33 N	34.48 E
Osečina	38	44.23 N	19.36 E
Osejevskaja	82	55.53 N	38.10 E
Ošejkino	82	56.15 N	35.54 E
Osek	54	50.37 N	13.40 E
Ösel → Saaremaa I	76	58.25 N	22.30 E
Osen	24	64.17 N	10.30 E
Osetrovo	88	56.47 N	105.47 E
Ōse-zaki ≻	94	35.02 N	138.47 E
Osgood, In., U.S.	218	39.07 N	85.17 W
Osgood, Oh., U.S.	216	40.20 N	84.30 W
Osgoode	212	45.08 N	75.36 W
Oshamambe	92a	42.30 N	140.22 E
O'Shanassy ≃	166	18.59 S	138.46 E
O'Shaughnessy Dam ◆[6]	226	37.57 N	119.47 W
O'Shaughnessy Reservoir ◎[1]	214	40.12 N	83.09 W
Oshawa	212	43.54 N	78.51 W
Oshawa Creek ≃	212	43.52 N	78.49 W
Oshibe ◆[8]	270	34.45 N	135.04 E
Oshigambo	156	17.47 S	16.05 E
Oshika, Nihon	92	38.16 N	141.32 E
Ōshika, Nihon	94	35.34 N	138.02 E
Oshika-hantō ≻[1]	92	38.20 N	141.30 E
Oshikango	156	17.25 S	15.56 E
Ōshima, Nihon	92	33.03 N	129.33 E
Ōshima, Nihon	94	37.07 N	138.30 E
Ōshima, Nihon	94	34.45 N	139.22 E
Ōshima, Nihon	96	33.55 N	132.15 E
Ō-shima I, Nihon	92a	41.30 N	139.22 E
Ō-shima I, Nihon	94	34.43 N	139.23 E
Ō-shima I, Nihon	94	36.15 N	136.07 E
Ō-shima I, Nihon	96	33.54 N	130.26 E
Ō-shima I, Nihon	96	33.38 N	134.30 E
Ō-shima I, Nihon	96	34.30 N	131.25 E
Ō-shima I, Nihon	96	34.00 N	133.22 E
Ō-shima I, Nihon	96	34.09 N	133.04 E
Oshima-hantō ≻[1]	92a	42.00 N	140.30 E
Oshimizu	94	36.49 N	136.46 E
Oshino	94	35.28 N	138.51 E
Oshivre ◆[8]	272c	19.09 N	72.51 E
Oshkosh, Ne., U.S.	198	41.24 N	102.20 W
Oshkosh, Wi., U.S.	190	44.01 N	88.32 W
Oshnovīyeh	128	37.02 N	45.06 E
Oshodi	273a	6.34 N	3.21 E
Oshoek	158	26.13 S	30.59 E
Oshogbo	150	7.47 N	4.34 E
Osh → Oš	85	40.33 N	72.48 E
Oshtemo	216	42.15 N	85.41 W
Oshtorān Kūh ∧	128	33.20 N	49.16 E
Oshtorīnān	128	34.01 N	48.38 E
Oshwe	152	3.24 S	19.30 E
Osi	150	8.08 N	5.14 E
Osica de Jos	38	44.15 N	24.17 E
Osich'ŏn-ni	98	41.25 N	128.16 E
Osiek	30	50.31 N	21.28 E
Osiglia	62	44.17 N	8.12 E
Osijek	38	45.33 N	18.41 E
Osilinka ≃	182	56.05 N	124.29 W
Osilo	71	40.45 N	8.40 E
Osimo	66	43.29 N	13.29 E
Osini	71	39.50 N	9.29 E
Osinki	80	52.51 N	49.30 E
Osinniki, Ross.	80	58.03 N	47.02 E
Osinniki, Ross.	86	53.37 N	87.21 E
Osinovka, Ross.	88	50.34 N	109.27 E
Osinovka, Ross.	88	56.19 N	101.56 E
Osinovka, Ukr.	83	49.34 N	39.05 E
Osinovskij chrebet ⛰	180	67.10 N	175.00 E
Osinów Dolny	54	52.48 N	14.10 E
Osintorf	76	54.42 N	30.39 E
Osio Sotto	62	45.36 N	9.35 E
Osipaonica	38	44.33 N	21.04 E
Osipenko	78	46.54 N	36.49 E
Osipenko → Berd'ansk	78	46.45 N	36.49 E
Osipoviči	76	53.18 N	28.38 E
Osipovo Selo	76	56.51 N	30.30 E
Osire	156	20.59 S	17.19 E
Osivān	120	26.43 N	72.55 E
Oskaloosa, Ia., U.S.	190	41.17 N	92.38 W
Oskaloosa, Ks., U.S.	198	39.12 N	95.18 W
Oskar-Fredriksborg	40	59.24 N	18.26 E
Oskarshamn	26	57.16 N	16.26 E
Oskarström	26	56.48 N	12.58 E
Os'kino	78	51.14 N	39.02 E
Oskol ≃	78	49.06 N	37.25 E
Oskolkovo	24	67.58 N	53.42 E
Oskū	128	37.55 N	46.06 E
Oskuj	76	59.17 N	32.05 E
Oskuja ≃	76	59.14 N	31.54 E
Osl'anka, gora ∧	86	59.10 N	58.33 E
Oslava ≃	61	49.05 N	16.22 E
Ösling ◆[1]	56	49.55 N	6.00 E
Oslo	26	59.55 N	10.45 E
Oslob	116	9.31 N	123.26 E
Oslofjorden c[2]	26	59.20 N	10.35 E
Os'ma ≃, Ross.	76	54.55 N	33.24 E
Ošma ≃, Ross.	80	57.52 N	47.45 E
Osmānābād	122	18.10 N	76.02 E
Osmancık	130	40.59 N	34.49 E
Osmaneli	130	40.22 N	30.01 E
Osmaniye	130	37.05 N	36.14 E
Osmanpaşa	130	39.38 N	34.58 E
Ošm'anskaja vozvyšennost' ⛰[1]	76	54.20 N	26.00 E
Ošm'any	76	54.25 N	25.56 E
Osmeña	116	10.11 N	125.31 E
Osmington	42	50.38 N	2.22 W
Os'mino	76	59.01 N	29.06 E
Osminog, gora ∧	180	67.54 N	176.50 E
Ösmo	40	58.59 N	17.54 E
Osmond	198	42.21 N	97.35 W
Osmore ≃	248	17.33 S	71.12 W
Osmoy	261	48.52 N	1.43 E
Osmussaar I	76	59.18 N	23.22 E
Osnabrück	52	52.16 N	8.02 E
Ośno	30	52.28 N	14.50 E
Osny	261	49.04 N	2.04 E
Oso	224	48.16 N	121.56 W
Oso ≃	154	1.09 S	27.22 E
Oso, Gran Lago del → Great Bear Lake ◎	176	66.00 N	120.00 W
Ošoba	85	40.44 N	70.26 E
Osogna	58	46.18 N	9.00 E
Osoppo	64	46.15 N	13.05 E
Osorakan-zan ∧	96	34.36 N	132.08 E
Osore-yama ∧	92	41.18 N	141.05 E
Osorio, Quebrada ≃	286c	10.36 N	66.56 W
Osório Fonseca	250	3.40 S	58.13 W
Osorno, Chile	254	40.34 S	73.09 W
Osorno, Esp.	34	42.24 N	4.22 W
Osorno, Volcán ∧[1]	254	41.06 S	72.30 W
Osorun	273a	6.33 N	3.29 E
Os'otr ≃	82	54.58 N	38.46 E
Osoyoos	182	49.02 N	119.28 W
Osoyoos Indian Reserve ◆[4]	182	49.08 N	119.30 W
Osoyoos Lake ◎	182	49.00 N	119.26 W
Osøyra	26	60.11 N	5.28 E
Ospedaletti	62	43.48 N	7.43 E
Ospedaletto, It.	64	46.17 N	13.07 E
Ospedaletto, It.	64	46.03 N	11.33 E
Ospino	246	9.18 N	69.27 W
Ospitale di Cadore	64	46.20 N	12.19 E
Ospitaletto	64	45.33 N	10.04 E
Osprey	220	27.11 N	82.29 W
Osprey Reef ✦[2]	164	13.55 S	146.38 E
Ospwagan Lake ◎	184	55.35 N	98.03 W
Oss	52	51.46 N	5.31 E
Ossa, Mount ∧	166	41.54 S	146.01 E
Ossabaw Island I	192	31.47 N	81.06 W
Osse ≃, Fr.	32	44.07 N	0.17 E
Osse ≃, Nig.	150	6.10 N	5.20 E
Ossenberg	263	51.34 N	6.35 E
Ossendrecht	52	51.24 N	4.19 E
Osseo, Mi., U.S.	216	41.53 N	84.33 W
Osseo, Wi., U.S.	190	44.34 N	91.13 W
Ossett	44	53.41 N	1.35 W
Ossi	71	40.40 N	8.35 E
Ossiacher See ◎	64	46.40 N	13.55 E
Ossian, In., U.S.	216	40.52 N	85.09 W
Ossian, Ia., U.S.	190	43.08 N	91.45 W
Ossian, Loch ◎	46	56.46 N	4.38 W
Ossining	210	41.09 N	73.51 W
Ossipee	188	43.41 N	71.07 W
Ossjøen ◎	26	61.13 N	11.53 E
Ossling	54	51.21 N	14.09 E
Ossona	266b	45.30 N	8.54 E
Ossora	74	59.20 N	163.13 E
Ossum-Bösinghoven	263	51.18 N	6.39 E
Ošta	24	60.49 N	35.32 E
Ostaboningue, Lac ◎	190	47.09 N	78.53 W
Östanå, Sve.	40	59.33 N	18.35 E
Östanå, Sve.	40	60.38 N	16.48 E
Östanbyn	40	60.39 N	16.48 E
Ostankino ◆[8]	265b	55.49 N	37.37 E
Östansjö	40	59.03 N	14.59 E
Ostapje	78	49.33 N	33.46 E
Ostaškov	76	57.09 N	33.06 E
Ostašovo	82	55.52 N	35.52 E
Ostbevern	52	52.02 N	7.50 E
Østbirk	41	55.58 N	9.46 E
Ostbüren	263	51.31 N	7.46 E
Østby	26	61.15 N	12.32 E
Ostchinesisches Meer → East China Sea ⍑[2]	90	30.00 N	126.00 E
Oste ≃	52	53.51 N	8.59 E
Osted	41	55.34 N	11.58 E
Osteen	220	28.50 N	81.09 W
Ostellato	66	44.45 N	11.56 E
Ostende → Oostende	50	51.13 N	2.55 E
Ostenfelde	52	51.52 N	8.04 E
Oster ≃	60	48.13 N	13.29 E
Osterath	56	51.16 N	6.37 E
Osterbönen	263	51.37 N	7.48 E
Osterburg, Dtsch.	54	52.47 N	11.44 E
Osterburg, Pa., U.S.	214	40.10 N	78.31 W
Osterburken	56	49.26 N	9.26 E
Österbybruk	40	60.12 N	17.54 E
Österbymo	26	57.50 N	15.16 E
Ostercappeln	52	52.20 N	8.13 E
Österdalälven ≃	26	60.33 N	15.08 E
Østerdalen V	26	61.15 N	11.10 E
Österfärnebo	40	60.18 N	16.48 E
Osterfeld	54	51.05 N	11.56 E
Osterfeld ◆[8]	263	51.30 N	6.53 E
Östergötland □[9]	26	58.24 N	15.34 E
Östergötlands Län □[6]	26	58.25 N	15.45 E
Österhaninge	40	59.08 N	18.12 E
Osterhofen	60	48.42 N	13.01 E
Øster Højst	41	55.00 N	9.03 E
Osterholz-Scharmbeck	52	53.14 N	8.47 E
Osterley Park ♦	260	51.30 N	0.21 W
Österlövsta	40	60.26 N	17.47 E
Ostermundigen	58	46.58 N	7.29 E
Osternienburg	54	51.48 N	12.01 E
Osterode	52	51.44 N	10.11 E
Osterode → Ostróda	30	53.43 N	19.59 E
Osterøya I	26	60.33 N	5.35 E
Österreich → Austria □[1]	30	47.20 N	13.20 E
Österreichisches Freilichtmuseum ʋ	61	47.10 N	15.19 E
Osterrönfeld	41	54.17 N	9.41 E
Östersjön → Baltic Sea ⍑[2]	24	57.00 N	19.00 E
Österskär	40	59.28 N	18.18 E
Östersund	26	63.11 N	14.39 E
Östervåla	40	60.11 N	17.11 E
Osterville	207	41.37 N	70.23 W
Osterwick	52	52.01 N	7.13 E
Osterwieck	54	51.58 N	10.42 E
Ostfeld ◆[8]	263	51.40 N	7.45 E
Østfold □[6]	26	59.20 N	11.30 E
Ostfriesische Inseln II	52	53.44 N	7.25 E
Ostfriesland □[9]	52	53.20 N	7.40 E
Ost-Ghats → Eastern Ghāts ⛰	122	14.00 N	78.50 E
Östhammar	40	60.16 N	18.22 E
Ostheim vor der Rhön	56	50.27 N	10.14 E
Osthofen	56	49.42 N	8.19 E
Ostia, Bonifica di ◆[1]	267a	41.46 N	12.18 E
Ostia Antica ⊥	66	41.45 N	12.16 E
Ostiano	64	45.13 N	10.15 E
Ostiglia	64	45.04 N	11.08 E
Ostki	78	51.16 N	27.22 E
Östliche Sierra Madre → Madre Oriental, Sierra ⛰	232	22.00 N	99.30 W
Östmark	26	60.17 N	12.45 E
Ost'or, Ross.	76	54.01 N	32.48 E
Ost'or, Ukr.	78	50.57 N	30.53 E
Ost'or ≃, Europe	76	53.47 N	31.46 E
Ost'or ≃, Ukr.	78	50.56 N	30.52 E
Ostpeene ≃	54	53.43 N	12.46 E
Ostra	66	43.37 N	13.09 E
Östraby	41	55.46 N	13.41 E
Ostrach	58	47.57 N	9.23 E
Ostrach ≃	58	48.04 N	9.24 E
Östra Grevie	41	55.28 N	13.08 E
Östra Husby	40	58.35 N	16.33 E
Östra Laxsjön ◎	40	58.54 N	14.42 E
Östra Ljungby	41	56.11 N	13.04 E
Ostrander	214	40.15 N	83.12 W
Östra Ringsjön ◎	41	55.52 N	13.32 E
Ostrau	54	51.12 N	13.09 E
Ostrau → Ostrava	30	49.50 N	18.17 E
Ostrava	30	49.50 N	18.17 E
Ostra Vetere	66	43.36 N	13.03 E
Ostrhauderfehn	52	53.08 N	7.37 E
Östrich	263	51.40 N	6.55 E
Ostricourt	50	50.27 N	3.02 E
Östringen	56	49.13 N	8.43 E
Ostritz	54	51.01 N	14.56 E
Ostróda	30	53.43 N	19.59 E
Ostrog	78	50.20 N	26.31 E
Ostrogožsk	78	50.52 N	39.05 E
Ostrokonje	76	59.52 N	42.02 E
Ostrołęka	30	53.06 N	21.34 E
Ostrołęka □[4]	30	53.00 N	21.30 E
Ostroróg	30	52.39 N	16.27 E
Ostrošickij Gorodok	76	54.04 N	27.42 E
Ostrov, Bela.	76	52.53 N	25.59 E
Ostrov, Česko.	54	50.17 N	12.57 E
Ostrov, Rom.	38	44.06 N	27.22 E
Ostrov, Ross.	76	57.20 N	28.22 E
Ostrov, Ross.	76	60.34 N	37.55 E
Ostrov, Ross.	265b	55.35 N	37.51 E
Ostrov I	30	47.55 N	17.35 E
Ostrov'anskij	80	46.45 N	42.13 E
Ostrovec	76	54.37 N	25.57 E
Ostrovki	265a	59.48 N	30.50 E
Ostrovno	76	55.08 N	29.53 E
Ostrovskaja	80	50.26 N	44.27 E
Ostrovskoje	80	57.48 N	42.15 E
Ostrov-Zalit	76	58.01 N	28.04 E
Ostrowiec Świętokrzyski	30	50.57 N	21.23 E
Ostrów Lubelski	30	51.30 N	22.52 E
Ostrów Mazowiecka	30	52.49 N	21.54 E
Ostrów Wielkopolski	30	51.39 N	17.49 E
Ostryna	76	53.44 N	24.32 E
Ostrzeszów	30	51.25 N	17.57 E
Ostseebad Ahrenshoop	54	54.23 N	12.25 E
Ostseebad Boltenhagen	54	54.00 N	11.12 E
Ostseebad Dierhagen	41	54.17 N	12.22 E
Ostseebad Graal-Müritz	54	54.15 N	12.12 E
Ostseebad Nienhagen	54	54.09 N	11.58 E
Ostseebad Rerik	54	54.06 N	11.37 E
Ostseebad Wustrow	54	54.21 N	12.23 E
Ostsee → Baltic Sea ⍑[2]	24	57.00 N	19.00 E
Ost-Sümmern	263	51.26 N	7.44 E
Osttirol ◆[1]	64	46.55 N	12.30 E
Ostúa ≃	236	14.17 N	89.33 W
Ostuacán	234	17.25 N	93.18 W
Ostula	234	18.30 N	103.28 W
Ostuni	68	40.44 N	17.35 E
Ostwald	58	48.33 N	7.43 E
Osu	98	35.31 N	127.18 E
Osuga	76	56.02 N	34.18 E
Osuga ≃	76	57.16 N	34.49 E
Ōsuka	94	34.41 N	137.59 E
O'Sullivan, Lac ◎	190	47.37 N	76.05 W
Osum ≃	38	40.48 N	19.52 E
Ōsumi	270	34.50 N	135.45 E
Ōsumi-hantō ≻[1]	92	31.20 N	130.55 E
Ōsumi-kaikyō ꭒ	92	31.00 N	131.00 E
Ōsumi-shotō II	93b	30.30 N	130.00 E
Osuna	34	37.14 N	5.07 W
Osupugo ∧	154	1.40 N	35.49 E
Osvaldo Cruz	255	21.47 S	50.50 W
Osveja	76	56.01 N	28.06 E
Osvejskoje, ozero ◎	76	56.03 N	28.08 E
Ošvor	24	66.58 N	62.53 E
Oswaldtwistle	44	53.43 N	2.26 W
Oswaldtwistle Moor ◆[3]	262	53.43 N	2.23 W
Oswald West State Park ♦	224	45.45 N	123.58 W
Oswayo	214	41.55 N	78.01 W
Oswayo Creek ≃	210	42.02 N	78.21 W
Oswegatchie ≃	188	44.42 N	75.30 W
Oswegatchie, Middle Branch ≃	212	44.07 N	75.19 W
Oswegatchie, West Branch ≃	188	44.18 N	75.20 W
Oswego, Il., U.S.	216	41.40 N	88.21 W
Oswego, In., U.S.	216	41.19 N	85.47 W
Oswego, Ks., U.S.	198	37.10 N	95.06 W
Oswego, N.Y., U.S.	212	43.27 N	76.30 W
Oswego □[6]	212	43.22 N	76.15 W
Oswego ≃, N.J., U.S.	208	39.40 N	74.32 W
Oswego ≃, N.Y., U.S.	212	43.28 N	76.31 W
Oswestry	42	52.52 N	3.04 W
Oświęcim	30	50.03 N	19.12 E
Osyka	194	31.00 N	90.28 W
Ota, Nihon	94	35.58 N	136.04 E
Ōta, Nihon	94	36.18 N	139.22 E
Ōta, Nihon	96	33.31 N	131.33 E
Ōta ◆[8]	268	35.34 N	139.43 E
Ōta ≃, Nihon	94	34.40 N	137.54 E
Ōta ≃, Nihon	96	34.22 N	132.25 E
Otago Peninsula ≻[1]	172	45.52 S	170.40 E
Otahuhu	172	36.57 S	174.51 E
Ōtake	96	34.12 N	132.13 E
Otaki, N.Z.	172	40.45 S	175.09 E
Ōtaki, Nihon	94	35.17 N	140.15 E
Ōtaki, Nihon	94	35.48 N	137.33 E
Ōtaki, Nihon	94	35.57 N	138.56 E
Ōtaki ≃	94	35.49 N	137.40 E
Ōtaki-yama ∧	96	34.07 N	134.08 E
Ōta-Koizumi-hikojō ♦	94	36.16 N	139.24 E
Otane	172	39.53 S	176.38 E
Otanmäki	26	64.07 N	27.06 E
Otar	85	43.33 N	75.13 E
Otari	94	36.46 N	137.54 E
Otaru	92a	43.13 N	141.00 E
Otatara	172	46.26 S	168.18 E
Otatitlán	234	18.12 N	96.02 W
Otautau	172	46.09 S	168.00 E
Otava	26	61.39 N	27.04 E
Otava ≃	30	49.27 N	14.12 E
Otavalo	246	0.14 N	78.16 W
Otavi	156	19.39 S	17.20 E
Ōtawara	94	36.52 N	140.02 E
Otawa-yama ∧	270	34.28 N	135.53 E
Otay	228	32.35 N	117.03 W
Otchinjau	152	16.30 S	13.57 E
Oteapan	234	18.00 N	94.39 W
Otego	210	42.23 N	75.10 W
Otego Creek ≃	210	42.25 N	75.07 W
Otélé	152	3.35 N	11.15 E
Otematata	172	44.37 S	170.16 E
Oteotea	175e	9.05 S	161.11 E
Otepää	76	58.03 N	26.30 E
Oteros ≃	232	26.55 N	108.22 W
Otford, Austl.	170	34.12 S	151.01 E
Otford, Eng., U.K.	42	51.19 N	0.12 E
Otgon	88	47.11 N	97.33 E
Otgon Tenger uul ∧	88	47.36 N	97.36 E
Otham	260	51.15 N	0.35 E
Othello	202	46.49 N	119.10 W
Othery	42	51.05 N	2.53 W
Othfresen	52	52.00 N	10.23 E
Óthiris, Óros ⛰	38	39.02 N	22.37 E
Othis	261	49.04 N	2.41 E
Othonoí I	38	39.50 N	19.26 E
Oti ≃	150	8.40 N	0.13 E
Otibanda	164	7.15 S	146.30 E
Otinapa	232	24.11 N	105.02 W
Otira	172	42.50 S	171.33 E
Otis, Co., U.S.	198	40.08 N	102.57 W
Otis, In., U.S.	216	41.36 N	86.54 W
Otis, Ks., U.S.	198	38.32 N	99.03 W
Otis, Ma., U.S.	207	42.11 N	73.05 W
Otisco	218	38.32 N	85.40 W
Otisco Lake ◎	210	42.52 N	76.18 W
Otish, Monts ⛰	176	52.22 N	70.30 W
Otis Reservoir ◎[1]	207	42.09 N	73.02 W
Otisville	210	41.28 N	74.32 W
Otjassy	80	53.14 N	41.39 E
Otjikondo	156	19.50 S	15.23 E
Otjimbingue	156	22.19 S	16.10 E
Otjinene	156	21.13 S	18.42 E
Otjiwarongo	156	20.29 S	16.36 E
Otjiwarongo □[5]	156	20.45 S	16.30 E
Otjozondjou ≃	156	20.18 S	20.50 E
Otley	44	53.54 N	1.41 W
Otmanlı	130	41.52 N	34.37 E
Otm'ok, pereval)(	85	42.20 N	73.10 E
Otmuchów	30	50.28 N	17.10 E
Otnes	26	61.45 N	11.14 E
Otnice	61	49.05 N	16.49 E
Ōtō	96	33.41 N	135.35 E
Otočac	36	44.52 N	15.14 E
Otog Qi	102	39.08 N	108.00 E
Ōtomi	175d	24.19 N	123.54 E
Oton	116	10.42 N	122.29 E
Otonabee ≃	212	44.08 N	78.14 W
Otoque, Isla I	236	8.36 N	79.36 W
Ōtori-kita	270	34.33 N	135.27 E
Otorma	80	53.32 N	42.32 E
Otoro ≃	236	15.00 N	88.16 W
Otorohanga	172	38.11 S	175.12 E
Otoskwin ≃	176	52.13 N	88.06 W
Otowa	94	34.51 N	137.18 E
Otowa-yama ∧	270	34.58 N	135.51 E
Otowa-yama-tunnel ◆[5]	94	34.58 N	135.51 E
Ōtoyo	96	33.46 N	133.40 E
Otra ≃	26	58.09 N	8.00 E
Otradnaja	84	44.23 N	41.31 E
Otradnoje	265a	59.47 N	30.49 E
Otradnyj	80	53.22 N	51.21 E
Otranto	68	40.09 N	18.30 E
Otranto, Capo d' ≻	68	40.06 N	18.31 E
Otranto, Strait of ꭒ	38	40.00 N	19.00 E
Otricoli	66	42.25 N	12.29 E
Otrokovice	30	49.13 N	17.31 E
Ötscher ∧	61	47.52 N	15.12 E
Otsego	216	42.27 N	85.41 W
Otsego □[6]	210	42.42 N	74.56 W
Otsego Lake ◎	210	42.45 N	74.52 W
Otselic ≃	210	42.20 N	75.58 W
Ōtsu, Nihon	96	35.00 N	135.52 E
Ōtsu, Nihon	268	35.16 N	139.42 E
Ōtsu ≃	270	34.30 N	135.24 E
Ōtsuchi	92	39.21 N	141.54 E
Ōtsuki	94	35.36 N	138.57 E
Ōtsu-shima I	96	34.00 N	131.42 E
Otta, Nig.	150	6.42 N	3.10 E
Otta, Nor.	26	61.46 N	9.32 E
Otta ≃	26	61.46 N	9.31 E
Ottakring ◆[8]	264b	48.12 N	16.19 E
Ottana	71	40.14 N	9.02 E
Otta Pass ꭒ	175c	7.09 N	151.53 E
Ottarnic Pond ◎	283	42.46 N	71.25 W
Ottati	68	40.28 N	15.19 E
Ottavia ◆[8]	267a	41.58 N	12.24 E
Ottaviano	68	40.51 N	14.28 E
Ottawa, On., Can.	212	45.25 N	75.42 W
Ottawa, Il., U.S.	216	41.20 N	88.50 W
Ottawa, Ks., U.S.	198	38.36 N	95.16 W
Ottawa, Oh., U.S.	216	41.01 N	84.02 W
Ottawa □[6], Mi., U.S.	216	42.57 N	86.02 W
Ottawa □[6], Oh., U.S.	214	41.31 N	82.56 W
Ottawa ≃, Can.	176	45.20 N	73.58 W
Ottawa ≃, Oh., U.S.	214	41.44 N	83.28 W
Ottawa ≃, Oh., U.S.	216	41.00 N	84.15 W
Ottawa-Carleton □[6]	212	45.15 N	75.45 W
Ottawa Hills	214	41.39 N	83.38 W
Ottawa International Airport ✈	212	45.19 N	75.40 W
Ottawa Islands II	176	59.30 N	80.10 W
Ottbergen	52	51.42 N	9.18 E
Ottenby	26	56.14 N	16.25 E
Ottendorf-Okrilla	54	51.11 N	13.50 E
Ottenhöfen	58	48.34 N	8.09 E
Ottenschlag	61	48.25 N	15.13 E
Ottensheim	61	48.20 N	14.11 E
Ottenstein Stausee ◎[1]	61	48.37 N	15.17 E
Otter ≃	42	50.46 N	3.17 W
Otterbach ≃	56	49.07 N	8.21 E
Otterbäcken	40	58.57 N	14.02 E
Otterbein	216	40.29 N	87.06 W
Otterburn	44	55.14 N	2.10 W
Otterburne	184	49.30 N	97.03 W
Otterburn Park	206	45.33 N	73.13 W
Otter Creek	192	29.19 N	82.46 W
Otter Creek ≃, On., Can.	212	44.06 N	81.07 W
Otter Creek ≃, Il., U.S.	219	39.18 N	90.07 W
Otter Creek ≃, In., U.S.	218	38.58 N	85.37 W
Otter Creek ≃, Ia., U.S.	190	41.20 N	93.30 W
Otter Creek ≃, Mo., U.S.	219	39.31 N	91.51 W
Otter Creek ≃, Mt., U.S.	202	45.36 N	106.17 W
Otter Creek ≃, N.Y., U.S.	212	43.43 N	75.23 W
Otter Creek ≃, Ut., U.S.	200	38.10 N	112.02 W
Otter Creek ≃, Vt., U.S.	188	44.13 N	73.17 W
Otter Creek Reservoir ◎[1]	200	38.12 N	111.59 W
Otterhöfen	56	48.33 N	8.12 E
Otter-Lake, P.Q., Can.	188	45.51 N	76.26 W
Otter Lake, Mi., U.S.	190	43.13 N	83.28 W
Otter Lake ◎, On., Can.	212	44.47 N	76.07 W
Otter Lake ◎, On., Can.	212	45.17 N	79.56 W
Otter Lake ◎, Sk., Can.	184	55.35 N	104.39 W
Otter Lake ◎[1]	219	39.26 N	89.54 W
Otterlo	52	52.06 N	5.45 E
Otterndorf	52	53.48 N	8.53 E
Otterøya I	26	62.42 N	6.48 E
Otter River	207	42.35 N	72.03 W
Ottersberg	52	53.06 N	9.08 E
Ottershaw	260	51.22 N	0.32 W
Ottersleben ◆[8]	54	52.05 N	11.34 E
Otter Tail ≃	198	46.16 N	96.36 W
Otter Tail Lake ◎	198	46.23 N	95.40 W
Otterup	41	55.31 N	10.24 E
Otterville, On., Can.	212	42.55 N	80.36 W
Otterville, Il., U.S.	219	39.03 N	90.24 W
Otterville, Mo., U.S.	194	38.41 N	93.00 W
Ottery ≃	42	50.39 N	4.20 W
Ottery Saint Mary	42	50.45 N	3.17 W
Ottignies	56	50.40 N	4.34 E
Ottine	222	29.36 N	97.35 W
Ottleben	54	52.05 N	11.07 E
Ottmarsbocholt	52	51.49 N	7.32 E
Ottnang	60	48.06 N	13.40 E
Ottnaren ◎	40	60.29 N	16.37 E
Otto, N.Y., U.S.	210	42.21 N	78.50 W
Otto, Tx., U.S.	222	31.27 N	96.49 W
Ottobeuren	58	47.56 N	10.18 E
Ottobeuren, Klosterkirche ʋ[1]	58	47.56 N	10.18 E
Ottobiano	62	45.09 N	8.50 E
Ottobrunn	60	48.04 N	11.40 E
Ottone	62	44.37 N	9.20 E
Ottoschwanden	58	48.12 N	7.52 E
Ottosdal	158	26.58 S	26.00 E
Ottoshoop	156	25.45 S	25.59 E
Ottoville	216	40.55 N	84.20 W
Ottuk, Kyrg.	85	42.18 N	76.18 E
Ottuk, Kyrg.	85	41.38 N	75.51 E
Ottumwa	190	41.00 N	92.22 W
Ottweiler	56	49.24 N	7.09 E
Otty Lake ◎	212	44.50 N	76.13 W
Otu	150	8.14 N	3.24 E
Otukpa	150	7.09 N	7.41 E
Otumpa	252	27.19 S	62.13 W
Otun	273a	6.42 N	3.22 E
Otu → Ōtsu	96	35.00 N	135.52 E
Otuquis, Bañados de ≡	248	19.20 S	58.30 W
Oturkpo	150	7.14 N	8.08 E
Otway, Bahía ꭒ	254	53.20 S	74.00 W
Otway, Cape ≻	166	38.52 S	143.31 E
Otway, Seno c	254	53.05 S	71.30 W
Otway Range ⛰	169	38.30 S	143.50 E
Otwock	30	52.07 N	21.16 E
Otyn'a	78	48.44 N	24.51 E
Ötztal V	64	47.05 N	10.55 E
Ötztaler Ache ≃	64	47.14 N	10.50 E
Ötztaler Alpen (Alpi Venoste) ⛰	64	46.45 N	10.55 E
Ou ≃, Lao	110	20.04 N	102.13 E
Ou ≃, Zhg.	100	26.02 N	113.09 E
Ou ≃, Zhg.	100	28.01 N	120.44 E
Oua ≃	152	0.43 N	12.55 E
Ouachita ≃	194	31.38 N	91.49 W
Ouachita, Lake ◎[1]	194	34.40 N	93.25 W
Ouachita Mountains ⛰	194	34.40 N	94.25 W
Ouaco	175f	20.50 S	164.29 E
Ouadâne	148	20.56 N	11.37 W
Ouadda	152	8.04 N	22.24 E
Ouaddaï □[5]	146	13.00 N	21.00 E
Ouadey, Ouadi el V	146	13.34 N	18.03 E
Ouagadougou	150	12.22 N	1.31 W
Ouahigouya	150	13.35 N	2.25 W
Ouahran → Wahran	148	35.43 N	0.43 W
Ouaka □[5]	152	6.00 N	21.00 E
Ouaka ≃	152	4.59 N	19.56 E
Oualâta	150	17.18 N	7.02 W
Ouâlata, Dahr ⏊[4]	150	17.48 N	7.24 W
Oualé ≃	150	10.52 N	0.51 E
Oualidia	148	32.44 N	9.08 W
Ouallam	150	14.19 N	2.05 E
Ouallene	148	24.37 N	1.14 E
Oualto	150	9.01 N	10.06 W
Ouanary	250	4.13 N	51.40 W
Ouanda Djallé	146	8.54 N	22.48 E
Ouandago	146	7.10 N	18.42 E
Ouandja ≃	146	9.35 N	21.43 E
Ouandja-Vakaga, Réserve de la ◆[4]	146	9.00 N	21.30 E
Ouango	152	4.19 N	22.33 E
Ouangolodougou	150	9.58 N	5.09 W
Ouaninou	150	8.11 N	7.51 W
Ouanne ≃	50	47.57 N	2.47 E
Ouan Taredert	148	27.33 N	9.32 E
Ouaquaga	210	42.08 N	75.39 W
Ouara ≃	154	5.05 N	24.26 E
Ouarâne ◆[1]	134	21.00 N	10.30 W
Ouararda, Passe de)(	148	21.01 N	13.03 W
Ouareau ≃	206	45.56 N	73.25 W
Ouareau, Lac ◎[1]	206	46.17 N	74.09 W
Ouargaye	150	11.32 N	0.01 E
Ouarkoye	150	12.05 N	3.40 W
Ouarkziz, Jbel ⛰	148	28.50 N	9.00 W
Ouarsenis, Djebel ∧	34	35.53 N	1.38 E
Ouarville	50	48.21 N	1.46 E
Ouarzazate	148	30.57 N	6.50 W
Ouarzazate □[4]	148	30.55 N	6.45 W
Ouassoulou ≃	150	11.35 N	8.11 W
Ouatcha	150	13.22 N	9.18 E
Oubangui (Ubangi) ≃	152	0.30 S	17.42 E
Ouche ≃	58	47.06 N	5.16 E
Oucques	50	47.49 N	1.18 E
Ōuda	94	34.28 N	135.56 E
Oudaze Lake ◎	212	45.27 N	79.11 W
Oud-Beijerland	52	51.49 N	4.25 E
Ouddorp	52	51.18 N	3.56 E
Oude IJssel (Issel) ≃	52	52.00 N	6.10 E
Oudenaarde	50	50.51 N	3.36 E
Oudenbosch	52	51.35 N	4.31 E
Oudenburg	50	50.46 N	3.53 E
Oude-Pekela	52	53.04 N	6.58 E
Oude Rijn ≃	52	52.05 N	4.20 E
Oudeschild	52	53.02 N	4.50 E
Oude-Tonge	52	51.41 N	4.12 E

	English	Deutsch	Español	Français	Português
≃	River	Fluß	Río	Rivière	Rio
≋	Canal	Kanal	Canal	Canal	Canal
⌊	Waterfall, Rapids	Wasserfall, Stromschnellen	Cascada, Rápidos	Chute d'eau, Rapides	Cascata, Rápidos
ꭒ	Strait	Meeresstraße	Estrecho	Détroit	Estreito
c	Bay, Gulf	Bucht, Golf	Bahía, Golfo	Baie, Golfe	Baía, Golfo
◎	Lake, Lakes	See, Seen	Lago, Lagos	Lac, Lacs	Lago, Lagos
≡	Swamp	Sumpf	Pantano	Marais	Pântano
⍓	Ice Features, Glacier	Eis- und Gletscherformen	Accidentes Glaciales	Formes glaciaires	Acidentes glaciares
⍑	Other Hydrographic Features	Andere Hydrographische Objekte	Otros Elementos Hidrográficos	Autres données hydrographiques	Outros acidentes hidrográficos

	English	Deutsch	Español	Français	Português
✦	Submarine Features	Untermeerische Objekte	Accidentes Submarinos	Formes de relief sous-marin	Acidentes submarinos
□	Political Unit	Politische Einheit	Unidad Politica	Entité politique	Unidade política
ʋ	Cultural Institution	Kulturelle Institution	Institución Cultural	Institution culturelle	Instituição cultural
⊥	Historical Site	Historische Stätte	Sitio Histórico	Site historique	Sitio histórico
♦	Recreational Site	Erholungs- und Ferienort	Sitio de Recreo	Centre de loisirs	Area de Lazer
✈	Airport	Flughafen	Aeropuerto	Aéroport	Aeroporto
■	Military Installation	Militäranlage	Instalación Militar	Installation militaire	Instalação militar
◆	Miscellaneous	Verschiedenes	Misceláneo	Divers	Diversos

ENGLISH: Name | Page | Lat.°′ | Long.°′
DEUTSCH: Name | Seite | Breite°′ | Länge°′ E = Ost

Oudewater 52 52.02 N 4.52 E
Oud-Gastel 52 51.35 N 4.27 E
Oudjda
— Oujda 148 34.41 N 1.45 W
Oud-Loosdrecht 52 52.13 N 5.04 E
Oudtshoorn 158 33.35 S 22.14 E
Oudyoumoudi 150 14.04 N 0.28 W
Oued Athmenia 34 36.15 N 6.17 E
Oued Cheham 36 36.23 N 7.46 E
Oued edh Dheheb, Khlij c 148 23.45 N 15.47 W
Oued Fodda 34 36.11 N 1.32 E
Oued Meliz 36 36.27 N 8.34 E
Oued Rhiou 34 35.58 N 0.55 E
Oued Tlelat 34 35.34 N 0.27 W
Oued Zarga 36 36.40 N 9.25 E
Oued-Zem 148 32.55 N 6.33 W
Ouellé 150 7.18 N 4.01 W
Ouémé ◻5 150 6.20 N 2.35 E
Ouémé ≃ 150 6.29 N 2.32 E
Ouen, Île I 175f 22.26 S 166.49 E
Ouenkoro 150 13.23 N 3.50 W
Ouenza, Djebel ʌ 36 35.57 N 8.05 E
Ouenzé ✈8 273b 4.14 S 15.17 E
Ouessa 150 11.03 N 2.47 W
Ouessant, Île d' (Ushant) I 32 48.28 N 5.05 W
Ouesso 152 1.37 N 16.04 E
Ouest ◻4 152 5.23 N 10.45 E
Ouest, Pointe de l' ≻ 186 49.52 N 64.31 W
Ouest, Rivière de l' ≃ 206 45.39 N 74.21 W
Ouezzane 148 34.52 N 5.35 W
Ouffet 56 50.26 N 5.28 E
Ouganda
— Uganda ◻1 154 1.00 N 32.00 E
Ougarou 150 12.09 N 0.56 E
Oughter, Lough ⊜ 48 54.00 N 7.30 W
Oughterard 48 53.25 N 9.17 W
Oughtibridge 44 53.26 N 1.33 W
Ouham ◻5 152 7.00 N 18.00 E
Ouham ≃ 136 9.18 N 18.14 E
Ouham-Pendé ◻5 152 7.00 N 16.00 E
Ouidah 150 6.22 N 2.05 E
Ouidi 146 14.07 N 12.58 E
Ouimet Canyon V 190 48.47 N 88.40 W
Oujda 148 34.41 N 1.45 W
Oujda ◻4 148 34.05 N 2.10 W
Oulad Naïl, Monts des ʌʌ 148 34.33 N 3.28 E
Oulainen 26 64.16 N 24.48 E
Oulangan Kansallispuisto ♦ 24 66.12 N 29.30 E
Oulchy-le-Château 50 49.12 N 3.21 E
Oule ≃ 62 44.25 N 5.21 E
Ouled Agla 34 35.58 N 4.45 E
Ouleout Creek ≃ 210 42.20 N 75.18 W
Oulins 50 48.52 N 1.28 E
Oullins 62 45.43 N 4.48 E
Oulou, Bahr ≃ 146 9.48 N 21.32 E
Oulton Broad 42 52.31 N 1.42 E
Oulu 26 65.01 N 25.28 E
Oulujärvi ⊜ 26 64.20 N 27.15 E
Oulujoki ≃ 26 65.01 N 25.25 E
Oulun lääni ◻4 24 65.00 N 27.00 E
Oulx 62 45.02 N 6.50 E
Oumba 152 4.55 N 19.04 E
Oum-Chalouba 146 15.48 N 20.46 E
Oumé 150 6.23 N 5.25 W
Oum El Bouagui 148 35.53 N 7.07 E
Oum El Bouagui ◻5 148 35.50 N 7.15 E
Oum er Rbia, Oued ≃ 148 33.19 N 8.21 W
Oum-Hadjer 146 13.18 N 19.41 E
Oum Hadjer, Ouadi V 146 16.38 N 20.14 E
Oumiao 102 31.55 N 112.09 E
Oumm ed Droûs Guebli, Sebkhet ⊜ 148 24.03 N 11.45 W
Oumm ed Droûs Telli, Sebkhet ⊜ 148 24.20 N 11.30 W
Ounâne, Bir ⊽4 148 21.28 N 3.56 W
Ounara 148 31.33 N 9.26 W
Ounasjoki ≃ 24 66.30 N 25.45 E
Oundle 42 52.29 N 0.29 W
Ounianga Kébir 146 19.04 N 20.29 E
Ouolossébougou 150 12.00 N 7.55 W
Our ≃ 56 49.53 N 6.18 E
Ouragahio 150 6.19 N 5.56 W
Oura-wan c 174m 26.32 N 128.02 E
Ouray 200 38.01 N 107.40 W
Ouray, Mount ʌ 200 38.25 N 106.14 W
Ource ≃ 58 48.06 N 4.23 E
Ourcq ≃ 50 49.01 N 3.01 E
Ourcq, Canal de l' ≅ 50 48.51 N 2.22 E
Ourém 250 1.33 S 47.06 W
Ouri 146 21.34 N 19.13 E
Ouri, Tarso ʌ 146 21.25 N 18.56 E
Ouricuri 250 7.53 S 40.05 W
Ourimbah 170 33.22 S 151.23 E
Ourinhos 255 22.59 S 49.52 W
Ourique 34 37.39 N 8.13 W
Ournie 171b 35.56 S 147.51 E
Ouro, Paraná do ≃ 248 8.29 S 70.30 W
Ouro, Ponta do ≻ 158 26.51 S 32.54 E
Ouro Branco 250 6.42 S 36.57 W
Ouro Fino 256 22.17 S 46.22 W
Ouro Preto 255 20.23 S 43.30 W
Ouro Preto ≃ 248 11.02 S 65.13 W
Ouroufa, Vallée d' V 150 14.42 N 7.00 E
Ours, Grand Lac de l'
— Great Bear Lake ⊜ 176 66.00 N 120.00 W
Oursi 150 14.41 N 0.27 W
Ourthe ≃ 56 50.38 N 5.35 E
Ourthe Occidentale ≃ 56 50.08 N 5.41 E
Ourthe Orientale ≃ 56 50.08 N 5.41 E
Ourville-en-Caux 50 49.44 N 0.36 E
Ōu-sammyaku ʌʌ 92 38.45 N 140.50 E
Ouse ≃, On., Can. 212 44.17 N 78.03 W
Ouse ≃, Eng., U.K. 42 50.47 N 0.03 E
Ouse ≃, Eng., U.K. 44 53.42 N 0.41 W
Oust ≃ 32 47.39 N 2.06 W
Outaouais, Rivière des
— Ottawa ≃ 176 45.20 N 73.58 W
Outardes, Baie aux c 186 49.02 N 68.30 W
Outardes, Rivière aux ≃ 176 49.04 N 68.28 W
Outardes Est, Rivière aux ≃ 206 45.06 N 74.04 W
Outardes Quatre, Réservoir ⊜1 186 49.50 N 68.58 W
Outardes Trois, Barrage ✈6 186 49.34 N 68.48 W
Outarville 50 48.13 N 2.01 E
Outcalt 276 40.23 N 74.24 W
Outeniekwaberge ʌʌ 158 33.53 S 22.35 E
Outerbridge Crossing ✈5 276 40.31 N 74.15 W
Outer Harbour 168b 34.47 S 138.30 E
Outer Hebrides II 46 57.45 N 7.00 W
Outer Island I 190 47.03 N 90.30 W
Outer Santa Barbara Passage ע 228 33.10 N 118.30 W
Outer Sister Island I 166 39.39 S 148.00 E
Outjo 156 20.08 S 16.08 E
Outjo ◻5 156 19.53 S 15.30 E
Outlane 262 53.39 N 1.53 W
Outlet Bay c 208 37.22 N 74.56 W
Outlook, Sk., Can. 184 51.30 N 107.03 W
Outlook, Mt., U.S. 198 48.53 N 104.46 W
Outokumpu 26 62.44 N 29.01 E
Outpost Mountain ʌ 180 69.08 N 151.12 W
Outreau 50 50.42 N 1.35 E
Outremont 206 45.31 N 73.38 W
Outside Canal ≅ 226 37.13 N 121.02 W
Out Skerries II 46a 60.25 N 0.42 W
Outwell 42 52.37 N 0.14 E
Ouvéa I 175f 20.30 S 166.35 E
Ouvéa, Lagon d' c 175f 20.33 S 166.27 E
Ouvèze ≃ 62 43.59 N 4.51 E
Ouvidor 255 18.14 S 47.50 W
Ouye, Forêt de l' ♦ 261 48.32 N 2.00 E
Ouyen 166 35.04 S 142.20 E
Ouzinkie 180 57.55 N 152.30 W
Ouzouer-le-Marché 50 47.55 N 1.32 E
Ouzouer-sur-Loire 50 47.46 N 2.29 E
Ouzzal, Oued in- V 148 21.35 N 2.00 E
Ovabağ 130 37.43 N 39.59 E
Ovacık, Tür. 130 41.05 N 32.55 E
Ovacık, Tür. 130 39.22 N 39.13 E
Ovada 62 44.38 N 8.38 E
Ovakent 130 38.06 N 28.02 E
Oval 210 41.09 N 77.11 W
Ovalau I 175g 17.40 S 178.48 E
Ovalle 252 30.36 S 71.12 W
Ovamboland ◻9 156 17.45 S 16.30 E
Ovana, Cerro ʌ 246 4.38 N 66.57 W
Ovar 34 40.52 N 8.38 W
Ovaro 64 46.29 N 12.52 E
Ovčinino 82 56.02 N 39.03 E
Ovcyno 265a 59.48 N 30.37 E
Ovedskloster 41 55.41 N 13.38 E
Ovejas 246 9.32 N 75.14 W
Ovelgönne 52 53.20 N 8.25 E
Ovenden 262 53.44 N 1.53 W
Oveng 152 2.25 N 12.16 E
Overath 56 50.55 N 7.14 E
Overberge 263 51.37 N 7.41 E
Overbrook 198 38.46 N 95.33 W
Overbrook ✈8, Pa., U.S. 279b 40.24 N 79.59 W
Overbrook ✈8, Pa., U.S. 285 39.58 N 75.16 W
Overdinkel 52 52.14 N 7.01 E
Overflakkee I 52 51.45 N 4.10 E
Overflowing ≃ 184 53.10 N 101.05 W
Overhalla 24 64.30 N 11.57 E
Overijse 56 50.46 N 4.32 E
Overijssel ◻4 52 52.25 N 6.30 E
Over Jerstal 41 55.12 N 9.18 E
Överkalix 24 66.21 N 22.56 E
Overland 219 38.42 N 90.21 W
Overland Park 198 38.58 N 94.40 W
Overlea 208 39.22 N 76.31 W
Overloon 52 51.35 N 5.57 E
Övermark (Ylimarkku) 26 62.38 N 21.30 E
Overpeck Creek ≃ 276 40.51 N 74.02 W
Overpelt 56 51.13 N 5.25 E
Overseal 42 52.44 N 1.34 W
Overstrand 42 52.56 N 1.20 E
Overton, Eng., U.K. 42 51.15 N 1.15 W
Overton, Ne., U.S. 198 40.44 N 99.32 W
Overton, Nv., U.S. 204 36.32 N 114.26 W
Overton, Tx., U.S. 222 32.16 N 94.58 W
Overton Arm c 204 36.20 N 114.25 W
Övertorneå 24 66.23 N 23.40 E
Överum 26 57.59 N 16.19 E
Over Wallop 42 51.09 N 1.35 W
Ovett 194 31.29 N 89.01 W
Ovid, Mi., U.S. 216 43.00 N 84.22 W
Ovid, N.Y., U.S. 210 42.40 N 76.49 W
Ovidiopol' 78 46.17 N 30.27 E
Oviedo, Esp. 34 43.22 N 5.50 W
Oviedo, Fl., U.S. 220 28.40 N 81.13 W
Oviglio 62 44.52 N 8.29 E
Oviken 26 62.59 N 14.24 E
Oviksfjällen ʌʌ 26 63.02 N 13.51 E
Ovilla 222 32.32 N 96.53 W
Ovindoli 66 42.08 N 13.31 E
Ovinišče 76 58.22 N 37.02 E
Ovino 76 59.41 N 33.11 E
Oviši 76 57.34 N 21.45 E
Övörchangaj ◻4 102 46.00 N 102.30 E
Øvre Anarjokka Nasjonalpark ♦ 24 69.00 N 25.00 E
Øvre Årdal 26 61.19 N 7.48 E
Øvre Dividal Nasjonalpark ♦ 24 68.39 N 19.45 E
Øvre Pasvik Nasjonalpark ♦ 24 69.06 N 28.55 E
Øvre Rendal 26 61.53 N 11.05 E
Övre Vättern ⊜ 40 59.52 N 15.40 E
Ovruč 78 51.21 N 28.49 E
Ovs'anikovo 76 60.09 N 45.16 E
Ovs'anka, Ross. 86 55.57 N 92.33 E
Ovs'anka, Ross. 89 53.35 N 126.57 E
Ovs'annikovo 82 56.54 N 37.33 E
Ovstug 76 53.24 N 34.08 E
Ōwada 268 35.49 N 139.33 E
Owaka 172 46.27 S 169.40 E
Owambo ◻5 156 18.00 S 16.00 E
Owambo ≃ 156 18.45 S 17.03 E
Owando 152 0.29 S 15.55 E
Owaneco 219 39.29 N 89.12 W
Owariasahi 94 35.12 N 137.02 E
Owasco 210 42.51 N 76.28 W
Owasco Inlet ≃ 210 42.45 N 76.28 W
Owasco Lake ⊜ 210 42.52 N 76.32 W
Owasco Outlet ≃ 210 43.04 N 76.39 W
Owase 92 34.04 N 136.12 E
Owasso 196 36.16 N 95.51 W
Owatonna 190 44.05 N 93.13 W
Owbeh 128 34.22 N 63.10 E
Owe 174b 19.04 N 73.04 E
Owego 210 42.06 N 76.15 W
Owego Creek, East Branch ≃ 210 42.10 N 76.15 W
Owego Creek, West Branch ≃ 210 42.10 N 76.15 W
Owel, Lough ⊜ 48 53.34 N 7.25 W
Owen, Austl. 168b 34.16 S 138.33 E
Owen, Dtsch. 56 48.35 N 9.27 E
Owen, Wi., U.S. 190 44.57 N 90.33 W
Owen ◻6 218 38.33 N 84.49 W
Owen, Mount ʌ 172 41.33 S 172.32 E
Owenboy ≃ 48 51.48 N 8.18 W
Owendo 152 0.17 N 9.30 E
Owenea ≃ 48 54.52 N 8.26 W
Owen Falls Dam ✈6 154 0.27 N 33.11 E
Owen Fracture Zone ✦ 12 12.00 N 58.00 E
Owenkillew ≃ 48 54.44 N 7.18 W
Owenmore ≃ 48 54.07 N 9.50 W
Owen River 172 41.39 S 172.27 E
Owens ≃ 204 36.31 N 117.57 W
Owensboro 194 37.46 N 87.06 W
Owens Creek ≃, Ca., U.S. 226 37.13 N 120.42 W
Owens Creek ≃, Md., U.S. 208 39.33 N 77.20 W
Owens Lake ⊜ 204 36.25 N 117.56 W
Owen Sound 212 44.34 N 80.56 W
Owen Sound c 212 44.40 N 80.55 W
Owen Stanley Range ʌʌ 164 9.20 S 147.55 E
Owensville, In., U.S. 194 38.16 N 87.41 W
Owensville, Mo., U.S. 219 38.20 N 91.30 W
Owensville, Oh., U.S. 218 39.07 N 84.08 W
Owenton, Ky., U.S. 218 38.32 N 84.50 W
Owenton, Va., U.S. 208 37.53 N 77.06 W
Owentown 222 32.26 N 95.12 W
Owerri 150 5.29 N 7.02 E
Owhango 172 39.00 S 175.23 E
Owikeno Lake ⊜ 182 51.41 N 127.00 W
Owings 208 38.43 N 76.36 W
Owings Mills 284b 39.25 N 76.46 W
Owingsville 188 38.08 N 83.45 W
Owl ≃, Ab., Can. 182 54.54 N 111.57 W
Owl ≃, Mb., Can. 176 57.51 N 92.44 W
Owl Creek ≃, U.S. 198 44.41 N 103.29 W
Owl Creek ≃, Mt., U.S. 202 45.18 N 107.21 W
Owl Creek ≃, Wy., U.S. 202 43.41 N 108.11 W
Owl Creek, South Fork ≃ 202 43.43 N 108.32 W
Owl Creek Mountains ʌʌ 202 43.30 N 108.35 W
Owo 150 7.15 N 5.37 E
Oworonsoki 273a 6.33 N 3.24 E
Owosso 216 42.59 N 84.10 W
Owuru ≃ 273a 6.39 N 3.27 E
Owyhee 204 41.56 N 116.05 W
Owyhee ≃ 202 43.46 N 117.02 W
Owyhee, Lake ⊜1 202 43.28 N 117.20 W
Owyhee, South Fork ≃ 202 42.26 N 116.53 W
Oxapampa 248 10.34 S 75.24 W
Öxarfjördur c 24a 66.15 N 16.45 W
Oxbow, Sk., Can. 184 49.14 N 102.11 W
Oxbow, Mi., U.S. 281 42.38 N 83.28 W
Oxbow, N.Y., U.S. 212 44.17 N 75.37 W
Oxbow Lake ⊜ 281 42.38 N 83.28 W
Ox Creek ≃ 198 48.37 N 100.17 W
Oxelösund 40 58.40 N 17.06 E
Oxford, N.S., Can. 186 45.44 N 63.52 W
Oxford, N.Z. 172 43.18 S 172.11 E
Oxford, Eng., U.K. 42 51.46 N 1.15 W
Oxford, Al., U.S. 194 33.36 N 85.50 W
Oxford, Ct., U.S. 207 41.26 N 73.07 W
Oxford, Fl., U.S. 220 28.55 N 82.02 W
Oxford, In., U.S. 216 40.31 N 87.14 W
Oxford, Ia., U.S. 190 41.43 N 91.47 W
Oxford, Ks., U.S. 198 37.16 N 97.10 W
Oxford, Ky., U.S. 218 38.16 N 84.30 W
Oxford, Me., U.S. 188 44.07 N 70.29 W
Oxford, Md., U.S. 208 38.41 N 76.10 W
Oxford, Ma., U.S. 207 42.07 N 71.51 W
Oxford, Mi., U.S. 216 42.49 N 83.15 W
Oxford, Ms., U.S. 194 34.21 N 89.31 W
Oxford, Ne., U.S. 198 40.15 N 99.38 W
Oxford, N.J., U.S. 210 40.48 N 74.59 W
Oxford, N.Y., U.S. 210 42.26 N 75.35 W
Oxford, N.C., U.S. 192 36.18 N 78.35 W
Oxford, Oh., U.S. 218 39.30 N 84.44 W
Oxford, Pa., U.S. 208 39.47 N 75.58 W
Oxford, Wi., U.S. 190 43.46 N 89.34 W
Oxford ◻6 212 43.08 N 80.50 W
Oxford Falls 274a 33.44 S 151.15 E
Oxford House 184 54.56 N 95.16 W
Oxford House Indian Reserve ✈4 184 54.54 N 95.15 W
Oxford Junction 190 41.59 N 90.57 W
Oxford Lake ⊜ 184 54.51 N 95.37 W
Oxford Peak ʌ 202 42.16 N 112.06 W
Oxfordshire ◻6 42 51.50 N 1.15 W
Oxford Valley Mall ✈9 285 40.11 N 74.53 W
Oxhey 260 51.39 N 0.23 W
Oxie 41 55.33 N 13.04 E
Oxkutzcab 232 20.18 N 89.25 W
Oxley 166 34.12 S 144.06 E
Oxley Creek ≃ 171a 27.32 S 153.00 E
Oxnard 228 34.11 N 119.10 W
Oxnard Beach 228 34.09 N 119.13 W
Oxon Hill 284c 38.48 N 76.59 W
Oxon Run ≃ 284b 38.49 N 77.00 W
Ox Pasture Brook ≃ 283 42.45 N 70.54 W
Oxshott 260 51.20 N 0.21 W
Oxted 42 51.16 N 0.01 W
Oxtongue ≃ 212 45.19 N 79.01 W
Oxtongue Lake ⊜ 212 45.22 N 78.55 W
Oxus
— Amu Darya ≃ 72 43.40 N 59.01 E
Oy 58 47.38 N 10.28 E
Oya, Malay. 112 2.52 N 111.53 E
Ōya, Nihon 96 35.20 N 134.40 E
Oya ≃ 112 2.52 N 111.52 E
Oyabe 94 36.40 N 136.52 E
Oyabe ≃ 94 36.48 N 137.04 E
Ōya-ji ✦1 94 36.38 N 139.48 E
Ōyake-yama ʌ2 270 34.48 N 135.51 E
Oyalı 130 37.14 N 41.45 E
Oyama, B.C., Can. 182 50.07 N 119.22 W
Oyama, Nihon 94 36.18 N 139.48 E
Ōyama, Nihon 94 36.36 N 137.18 E
Oyama, Nihon 94 35.21 N 139.00 E
Oyama, Nihon 268 35.36 N 139.22 E
Ōyamada 94 34.46 N 136.13 E
Ōyamazaki 270 34.54 N 135.42 E
Oyameyo, Volcán ʌ1 286a 19.10 N 99.11 W
Oyan 152 0.02 N 10.17 E
Ōyano 92 32.35 N 130.26 E
Oyapock (Oiapoque) ≃ 250 4.08 N 51.40 W
Oyashirazu ♦ 94 36.59 N 137.40 E
Oybin 54 50.50 N 14.44 E
Oye-et-Pallet 58 46.51 N 6.20 E
Oyem 152 1.37 N 11.35 E
Oyen 184 51.22 N 110.28 W
Øyeren ⊜ 26 59.48 N 11.14 E
Oykel ≃ 46 57.56 N 4.25 W
Oykel Bridge 46 57.58 N 4.43 W
Oymyakon
— Ojm'akon 74 63.28 N 142.49 E
Oyo, Congo 152 0.01 N 15.54 E
Oyo, Nig. 150 7.51 N 3.56 E
Oyo ◻3 150 8.00 N 3.50 E
Oyo ≃ 115a 7.57 S 110.22 E
Ōyodo 96 34.23 N 135.48 E
Oyodo ✈8 270 34.43 N 135.30 E
Ōyodo ≃ 92 31.53 N 131.28 E
Oyón 248 10.39 S 76.47 W
Oyonnax 58 46.15 N 5.40 E
Ōyorogi-san ʌ 96 35.05 N 132.51 E
Oyotún 248 6.51 S 79.19 W
Oyster 208 37.17 N 75.55 W
Oyster Bay 210 40.51 N 73.31 W
Oyster Bay c 276 40.55 N 73.30 W
Oyster Bay Cove 276 40.52 N 73.31 W
Oyster Bay Harbor c 276 40.53 N 73.32 W
Oyster Creek 222 29.00 N 95.20 W
Oyster Creek ≃ 222 28.59 N 95.18 W
Oyster Point ʌ 282 37.50 N 121.52 W
Oyster Point ≻ 168b 34.55 S 137.48 E
Oyster Rock I2 272c 18.54 N 72.50 E
Oysterville 224 46.33 N 124.02 W
Øystese 26 60.23 N 6.13 E
Oyten 52 53.04 N 9.01 E
Ozaki 268 35.59 N 139.51 E
Ozamiz 116 8.08 N 123.50 E
Ozanne ≃ 50 48.11 N 1.22 E
Ozariči 76 52.28 N 29.16 E
Ozark, Al., U.S. 194 31.27 N 85.38 W
Ozark, Ar., U.S. 194 35.29 N 93.49 W
Ozark, Mo., U.S. 194 37.01 N 93.12 W
Ozark National Scenic Riverways ♦ 194 37.10 N 91.10 W
Ozark Plateau ʌʌ1 194 37.00 N 93.00 W
Ozark Reservoir ⊜1 194 35.35 N 94.00 W
Ozarks, Lake of the ⊜1 194 38.10 N 92.50 W
Ozaukee ◻6 216 44.14 N 88.00 W
Ozbourn Seamount ✦3 14 26.00 S 174.50 W
Ózd 30 48.14 N 20.18 E
Ozd'atiči 76 54.06 N 28.50 E
Oze ≃ 96 34.12 N 132.14 E
Ozeblin ʌ 36 44.35 N 15.53 E
Ozek 86 46.35 N 60.41 E
Ozereckoje 82 56.04 N 37.23 E
Ožerelje 82 54.48 N 38.17 E
Ožerelki 82 55.51 N 38.52 E
Ozerišče 76 54.48 N 33.13 E
Ozerki, Ross. 80 51.13 N 53.56 E
Ozerki, Ross. 80 51.32 N 45.16 E
Ozerki, Ross. 80 52.01 N 45.29 E
Ozerki, Ross. 86 53.38 N 83.44 E
Ozerki, Ross. 265a 59.54 N 30.44 E
Ozerna ≃ 82 55.44 N 36.08 E
Ozerninskoje vodochranilišče ⊜1 82 55.45 N 36.15 E
Ozernoje 78 50.11 N 28.42 E
Ozernovskij 74 51.30 N 156.31 E
Ozernyj 180 66.24 N 179.06 W
Ozero 80 56.58 N 44.43 E
Ozery 82 54.51 N 38.34 E
Ozette Lake ⊜ 224 48.06 N 124.38 W
Ozgoryš 85 41.15 N 74.45 E
Ozieri 71 40.35 N 9.00 E
Ozimek 30 50.41 N 18.13 E
Ozinki 80 51.12 N 49.45 E
Ožogino, ozero ⊜ 74 69.16 N 146.36 E
Ozoir-la-Ferrière 261 48.46 N 2.40 E
Ozona, Fl., U.S. 220 28.04 N 82.46 W
Ozona, Tx., U.S. 196 30.42 N 101.12 W
Ozone Park ✈8 276 40.40 N 73.51 W
Ozorków 30 51.58 N 19.19 E
Oz'ornaja, Kaz. 86 53.25 N 63.15 E
Oz'ornaja, Ross. 86 51.08 N 60.50 E
Oz'ornoje, Ross. 80 51.46 N 51.28 E
Oz'ornoje, Ross. 80 51.41 N 44.55 E
Oz'ornoje, Ross. 86 56.48 N 71.15 E
Oz'ornyj 80 57.10 N 40.59 E
Oz'orsk, Ross. 76 54.25 N 22.01 E
Oz'orsk, Ukr. 78 51.43 N 26.24 E
Oz'orskij 89 46.36 N 143.08 E
Oz'ory 76 53.43 N 24.11 E
Ozouer-le-Voulgis 261 48.40 N 2.47 E
Özpınar 130 37.57 N 42.16 E
Ōzu, Nihon 92 32.52 N 130.52 E
Ōzu, Nihon 96 33.30 N 132.33 E
Ozubulu 150 5.57 N 6.51 E
Ozuluama 234 21.40 N 97.51 W
Ozumba 234 19.03 N 98.48 W
Ozurgety 84 41.56 N 42.00 E

P

Pâ 150 11.33 N 3.15 W
Paagoumène 175f 20.29 S 164.11 E
Paal 56 51.02 N 5.11 E
Paama ◻8 175f 16.28 S 168.18 E
Paama I 175f 16.28 S 168.14 E
Paar ≃ 60 48.45 N 11.33 E
Paardekraal Monument ⊥ 273d 26.06 S 27.47 E
Paaren 264a 52.39 N 12.59 E
Paarl 158 33.45 S 18.56 E
Paasbach ≃ 263 51.25 N 7.11 E
Paauilo 229d 20.02 N 155.22 W
Pabarabuk 164 6.05 S 144.05 E
Pabbay I, Scot., U.K. 46 57.46 N 7.15 W
Pabbay I, Scot., U.K. 46 56.51 N 7.35 W
Pabbi 123 34.01 N 71.47 E
Pabbiring, Kepulauan II 112 4.55 S 119.25 E
Pabean 112 6.50 S 115.19 E
Pabellón, Punta ≻ 254 43.14 S 74.23 W
Pabellón de Arteaga 234 22.10 N 102.21 W
Pabellones, Ensenada c 232 24.27 N 107.36 W
Pabianice 30 51.40 N 19.22 E
Pabillonis 71 39.35 N 8.43 E
Pablo 202 47.36 N 114.07 W
Pābna 124 24.00 N 89.15 E
Pabo 154 3.00 N 32.09 E
Pabradė 76 54.59 N 25.44 E
Paca 115b 8.29 S 120.11 E
Pacaás Novos ≃ 248 10.51 S 65.20 W
Pacaás Novos, Parque Nacional ♦ 248 11.10 S 63.30 W
Pacaás Novos, Serra dos ʌʌ 248 10.45 S 64.15 W
Pacaembu 255 21.34 S 51.17 W
Pacaembú, Estádio do ♦ 287b 23.33 S 46.39 W
Pacajá ≃ 250 1.56 S 50.50 W
Pacajus 250 4.10 S 38.28 W
Pacaltsdorp 158 34.00 S 22.28 E
Pacaraima, Sierra de
— Pakaraima Mountains ʌʌ 246 5.30 N 60.40 W
Pacarán 248 12.52 S 76.03 W
Pacaraos 248 11.11 S 76.44 W
Pacasmayo 248 7.24 S 79.34 W
Pacatuba 250 3.58 S 38.37 W
Pace, Fl., U.S. 194 30.35 N 87.09 W
Pace, Ms., U.S. 194 33.47 N 90.51 W
Paceco 70 37.59 N 12.33 E
Pačelma, Ross. 80 53.15 N 43.21 E
Pačelma, Ross. 80 53.20 N 43.20 E
Pacet 115a 6.45 S 107.03 E
Pachača 74 60.34 N 169.03 E
Pachacamac ⊥ 248 12.14 S 76.52 W
Pachamba 126 24.12 N 86.16 E
Pachaug Pond ⊜ 207 41.34 N 71.54 W
Pacheco 226 37.59 N 122.04 W
Pacheco, Isla I 254 52.17 S 74.45 W
Pacheco Creek ≃ 226 36.58 N 121.28 W
Pacheco Pass)(226 37.03 N 121.13 W
Pāchh Elāsin 126 24.08 N 89.54 E
Pachino 70 36.43 N 15.05 E
Pachitea ≃ 248 8.46 S 74.32 W
Pachiza 248 7.16 S 76.46 W
Pachkoli ✈8 272c 19.08 N 72.54 E
Pachmarhi 124 22.28 N 78.26 E
Pacho 246 5.08 N 74.10 W
Pachomovo 82 54.38 N 37.33 E
Pachor 124 23.42 N 76.44 E
Pāchora 122 20.40 N 75.21 E
Pachotnyj Ugol 80 52.58 N 41.56 E
Pachra ≃ 82 55.32 N 37.59 E
Pachtaabad 85 38.28 N 68.10 E
Pachuca [de Soto] 234 20.07 N 98.44 W
Paciência ✈8 256 22.55 S 43.38 W
Pacific, B.C., Can. 182 54.46 N 128.17 W
Pacific, Mo., U.S. 219 38.28 N 90.44 W
Pacific, Wa., U.S. 224 47.15 N 122.14 W
Pacific ◻6 224 46.30 N 123.39 W
Pacifica 226 37.37 N 122.29 W
Pacific-Antarctic Ridge ✦3 6 62.00 S 157.00 W
Pacific Beach 224 47.12 N 124.12 W
Pacific City 224 45.12 N 123.57 W
Pacific Creek ≃ 200 42.08 N 109.24 W
Pacific Gardens 226 37.58 N 121.20 W
Pacific Grove 226 36.38 N 121.56 W
Pacific Islands, Trust Territory of the
— Palau ◻2 14 5.00 N 137.00 E
Pacific Missile Test Center ■ 228 34.07 N 119.07 W
Pacífico, Océano
— Pacific Ocean ⊽1 6 10.00 S 150.00 W
Pacific Ocean ⊽1 4 10.00 S 150.00 W
Pacific Ocean ⊽1 6 10.00 S 150.00 W
Pacifico Mountain ʌ 228 34.23 N 118.02 W
Pacific Palisades ✈8 280 34.03 N 118.32 W
Pacific Ranges ʌʌ 182 50.45 N 125.30 W
Pacific Rim National Park ♦ 182 48.45 N 125.40 W
Pacifique, Océan
— Pacific Ocean ⊽1 6 10.00 S 150.00 W
Pacijan Island I 116 10.39 N 124.20 E
Pacinan, Tanjung ≻ 115a 7.36 S 114.02 E
Paciran 115a 6.52 S 112.20 E
Pacitan 115a 8.12 S 111.07 E
Pack 61 46.58 N 14.59 E
Packanack Lake ⊜ 276 40.56 N 74.15 W
Packard Mountain ʌ2 207 42.28 N 72.21 W
Páckevei-Duna ≃1 264c 47.19 N 19.02 E
Pack Monadnock Mountain ʌ 207 42.52 N 71.52 W
Packsattel)(61 46.58 N 14.58 E
Packwood 224 46.36 N 121.40 W
Packwood Lake ⊜ 224 46.35 N 121.34 W
Pacllón 248 10.18 S 77.07 W
Pacock Brook ≃ 276 41.05 N 74.31 W
Paço de Arcos 266c 38.42 N 9.17 W
Paço do Lumiar 250 2.31 S 44.07 W
Pacohuaras ≃ 248 10.04 S 65.46 W
Pacoima ✈8 280 34.16 N 118.26 W
Pacolet ≃ 192 34.50 N 81.27 W
Pacolet Mills 192 34.55 N 81.44 W
Pacora 246 9.05 N 79.17 W
Pacov 30 49.28 N 15.00 E
Pacquet 186 49.59 N 55.53 W
Pacuare ≃ 236 10.14 N 83.17 W
Pacuí ≃ 255 16.46 S 45.01 W
Pacuneiro ≃ 255 13.02 S 53.25 W
Pacy-sur-Eure 50 49.01 N 1.23 E
Paczkow 30 50.27 N 17.00 E
Padada 116 6.42 N 125.22 E
Padada ≃ 116 6.42 N 125.23 E
Padaido, Kepulauan II 164 1.15 S 136.30 E
Padam 123 33.28 N 76.53 E
Padamarang, Pulau I 112 4.07 S 121.24 E
Padamo ≃ 246 2.54 N 65.17 W
Padampur 120 20.59 N 83.04 E
Padang, Indon. 112 1.39 S 108.55 E
Padang, Indon. 112 2.59 N 105.40 E
Padang, Indon. 112 6.11 S 120.26 E
Padang, Indon. 112 0.57 S 100.21 E
Padang, Pulau I 114 1.10 N 102.20 E
Padang Besar 114 6.40 N 100.19 E
Padangbetuah 112 3.39 S 102.13 E
Padang Endau 114 2.40 N 103.37 E
Padangpanjang 112 0.27 S 100.25 E
Padangsidempuan 114 1.22 N 99.16 E
Padangtiji 114 5.22 N 95.50 E
Padangtikar, Pulau I 112 0.50 S 109.30 E
Padang Tungku 114 4.14 N 101.59 E
Padany 24 63.17 N 33.22 E
Padas 115a 7.25 S 111.32 E
Padas ≃ 112 5.14 N 115.34 E
Padasjoki 26 61.21 N 25.17 E
Padauari ≃ 246 0.15 S 64.05 W
Padborg 41 54.49 N 9.22 E
Padcaya 248 21.52 S 64.48 W
Paddington ✈8 260 51.31 N 0.10 W
Paddington Station ✈5 260 51.31 N 0.11 W
Paddle ≃ 182 54.05 N 114.15 W
Paddle Prairie 176 57.57 N 117.29 W
Paddock Lake 216 42.34 N 88.06 W
Paddock Wood 42 51.11 N 0.23 E
Padea 38 44.01 N 23.52 E
Padea-besar I 112 3.30 S 123.05 E
Padeghar 272c 18.58 N 73.03 E
Paden City 188 39.36 N 80.56 W
Paderborn 52 51.43 N 8.45 E
Paderno Dugnano 266b 45.34 N 9.10 E
Paderno Ponchielli 64 45.14 N 9.55 E
Padghe 272c 19.03 N 73.07 E
Padibe 154 3.28 N 32.50 E
Padiham 44 53.49 N 2.19 W
Padilla 248 19.19 S 64.20 W
Padilla Bay c 224 48.35 N 122.32 W
Padjelanta Nationalpark ♦ 24 67.28 N 16.41 E
Padle 272c 19.09 N 73.03 E
Padloping Island I 176 67.07 N 62.35 W
Padma
— Ganges ≃ 124 23.22 N 90.32 E
Padola 64 46.36 N 12.28 E
Padoue
— Padova 64 45.25 N 11.53 E
Padova 64 45.25 N 11.53 E
Padova ◻4 64 45.21 N 11.49 E
Padovka 80 52.28 N 49.31 E
Pādra 120 22.14 N 73.05 E
Padrão, Ponta do ≻ 152 6.03 S 12.18 E
Padrauna 124 26.55 N 83.59 E
Padre Bernardo 255 15.21 S 48.30 W
Padre Brito 256 21.18 S 43.59 W
Padre Burgos 116 10.02 N 125.01 E
Padre Island I 196 27.00 N 97.15 W
Padre Island National Seashore ♦ 196 27.00 N 97.25 W
Padre Miguel ✈8 287a 22.53 S 43.26 W
Padre Paraíso 255 17.06 S 41.31 W
Padria 71 40.24 N 8.38 E
Padrón 34 42.44 N 8.40 W
Padrone, Cape ≻ 158 33.46 S 26.30 E
Padrt' 60 49.40 N 13.46 E
Padstow, Austl. 274a 33.57 S 151.02 E
Padstow, Eng., U.K. 42 50.33 N 4.56 W
Padua
— Padova 64 45.25 N 11.53 E
Paducah, Ky., U.S. 194 37.05 N 88.36 W
Paducah, Tx., U.S. 196 34.00 N 100.18 W
Padula 68 40.20 N 15.39 E
Paduli 68 41.10 N 14.53 E
Padunskaja 86 55.02 N 85.02 E
Paea 174s 17.41 S 149.35 W
Paedun 98 35.03 N 128.21 E
Paekakariki 172 40.59 S 174.57 E
Paektu-san ʌ 98 42.00 N 128.03 E
Paengaroa 172 37.49 S 176.25 E
Paengnyŏng-do I 98 37.57 N 124.40 E
Paerdegat Basin c 276 40.37 N 73.54 W
Paeroa 172 37.23 S 175.40 E
Paesana 62 44.41 N 7.16 E
Paese 64 45.40 N 12.10 E
Paestum ⊥ 68 40.25 N 15.00 E
Paete 116 14.23 N 121.29 E
Páez ≃ 246 2.28 N 75.34 W
Pafúri 156 22.27 S 31.21 E
Pag 36 44.27 N 15.04 E
Pag, Otok I 36 44.30 N 15.00 E
Paga 150 10.58 N 1.06 W
Pagadenbaru 115a 6.28 S 107.48 E
Pagadian 116 7.49 N 123.25 E
Pagadian Bay c 116 7.48 N 123.31 E
Pagai Selatan, Pulau I 112 3.00 S 100.20 E
Pagai Utara, Pulau I 112 2.42 S 100.07 E
Pagalungan 116 7.04 N 124.41 E
Pagan 110 21.10 N 94.51 E
Pagan I 108 18.07 N 145.46 E
Pagancillo 252 29.34 S 68.03 W
Paganella ʌ 64 46.08 N 11.02 E
Pagani 68 40.45 N 14.37 E
Paganica 66 42.21 N 13.28 E
Paganico 66 42.56 N 11.16 E
Pagaralam 112 4.01 S 103.16 E
Pagasitikós Kólpos c 38 39.15 N 22.51 E
Pagatan 112 3.36 S 115.56 E
Pagato ≃ 184 55.49 N 102.05 W
Pagato Lake ⊜ 184 56.08 N 102.30 W
Pagbilao 116 13.58 N 121.41 E
Pagbilao Grande Island I 116 13.55 N 121.46 E
Pagdanan Bay c 116 10.31 N 119.15 E
Page, Az., U.S. 200 36.54 N 111.28 W
Page, N.D., U.S. 198 47.09 N 97.34 W
Page Field ⊠ 220 26.35 N 81.52 W
Pagėgiai 76 55.09 N 21.54 E
Pageland 192 34.46 N 80.23 W
Page Manor 218 39.45 N 84.06 W
Pager ≃ 154 3.09 N 32.30 E
Pagerdewa 112 3.46 S 105.18 E
Paget, Mount ʌ 244 54.26 S 36.33 W
Paghmān 120 34.36 N 68.57 E
Paglia ≃ 66 42.42 N 12.11 E
Pagliara 70 37.59 N 15.22 E
Paglieta 66 42.10 N 14.30 E
Pagliete, Bonifica delle ✈1 267a 41.53 N 12.12 E
Pagny-sur-Moselle 56 48.59 N 6.01 E
Pago Bay c 174p 13.25 N 144.48 E
Pagoda Peak ʌ 200 40.10 N 107.20 W
Pagoda Point ≻ 110 15.57 N 94.15 E
Pagon, Bukit ʌ 112 4.18 N 115.19 E
Pago Pago 174u 14.16 S 170.42 W
Pago Pago Harbor c 174u 14.17 S 170.40 W
Pago Pago International Airport ⊠ 174u 14.20 S 170.43 W
Pagosa Springs 200 37.16 N 107.00 W
Pagote 272c 18.54 N 72.59 E
Pagouda 150 9.45 N 1.19 E
Pagri 124 27.44 N 89.09 E
Pagsangahan 116 13.13 N 122.33 E
Pagsanjan 116 14.15 N 121.25 E
Paguate 200 35.08 N 107.22 W
Pagudpud 116 18.34 N 120.47 E
Pagueras, Torrente de ≃ 266d 41.28 N 1.58 E
Paguyaman ≃ 112 0.31 N 122.38 E
Pagwi 164 4.03 S 143.02 E
Pah 84 39.08 N 39.40 E
Pahādi ✈8 272c 19.10 N 72.51 E
Pahala 229d 19.12 N 155.28 W
Pahalgam 123 34.02 N 75.20 E
Pahang ◻3 114 3.30 N 102.45 E
Pahang ≃ 114 3.32 N 103.28 E
Páhara, Laguna c 236 14.18 N 83.15 W
Pahāsu 124 28.11 N 78.03 E
Pahau Point ≻ 229b 21.49 N 160.15 W
Pahi 114 5.28 N 102.13 E
Pahia Point ≻ 172 46.19 S 167.41 E
Pahiatua 172 40.27 S 175.50 E
Pahlād Garhi 272a 28.40 N 77.21 E
Pahlavī
— Bandar-e Anzalī 128 37.28 N 49.27 E
Pahlevī
— Bandar-e Anzalī 128 37.28 N 49.27 E
Pahoa 229d 19.29 N 154.57 W
Pahokee 220 26.49 N 80.39 W
Pahrump 204 36.12 N 115.58 W
Pahsimeroi ≃ 202 44.41 N 114.03 W
Pahuatlán de Valle 234 20.17 N 98.09 W
Pahvant Range ʌʌ 200 38.45 N 112.15 W
Pai 110 19.19 N 98.27 E
Pai ≃ 110 19.09 N 97.33 E
Pai, Ilha do I 287a 22.59 S 43.05 W
Paia 229a 20.54 N 156.22 W
Paianía 267c 37.57 N 23.51 E
Paicines 226 36.44 N 121.17 W
Paico 248 14.02 S 73.39 W
Paide 76 58.54 N 25.33 E
Paidorzu, Monte ʌ 71 40.30 N 9.05 E
Paifangchang 107 30.31 N 106.38 E
Paige 222 30.13 N 97.07 W
Paignton 42 50.26 N 3.34 W
Paiguano 252 30.01 S 70.32 W
Paihia 172 35.17 S 174.05 E
Paiho 100 23.21 N 120.25 E
Paiján 248 7.44 S 79.19 W
Päijänne ⊜ 26 61.35 N 25.30 E
Pāikgācha 126 22.35 N 89.20 E
Paikü Co ⊜ 124 28.48 N 85.36 E
Pail 123 32.38 N 72.27 E
Paila ≃ 248 16.02 S 64.12 W
Paila, Sierra la ʌʌ 196 25.50 N 101.30 W
Pailin 110 12.51 N 102.36 E
Pailitas 246 8.58 N 73.38 W
Paillaco 254 40.04 S 72.53 W
Pailolo Channel ע 229a 21.05 N 156.42 W
Pailoutou 106 30.56 N 121.16 E
Pailoutun 104 40.44 N 122.49 E
Paimboeuf 32 47.17 N 2.02 W
Paimio 26 60.27 N 22.42 E
Paimpol 32 48.46 N 3.03 W
Painan 112 1.21 S 100.34 E
Paincourt 214 42.23 N 82.17 W
Painesdale 190 47.02 N 88.40 W
Painesville 214 41.43 N 81.14 W
Painscastle 42 52.07 N 3.12 W
Painshawfield 44 54.56 N 1.54 W
Painswick 42 51.48 N 2.11 W
Paint ≃ 190 45.58 N 88.15 W
Paint Creek ≃, Mi., U.S. 281 42.06 N 83.36 W
Paint Creek ≃, Oh., U.S. 218 39.18 N 82.56 W
Paint Creek ≃, Pa., U.S. 214 41.10 N 79.28 W
Paint Creek ≃, Tx., U.S. 196 30.18 N 99.54 W
Paint Creek, East Fork ≃ 218 39.32 N 83.25 W
Paint Creek, North Fork ≃ 218 39.18 N 83.02 W
Paint Creek Lake ⊜1 218 39.15 N 83.22 W
Painted Desert ✈2 200 36.00 N 111.20 W
Painted Post 210 42.09 N 77.05 W
Painted Rock Reservoir ⊜1 200 33.00 N 112.50 W
Painten 60 49.00 N 11.49 E
Painter 208 37.35 N 75.47 W
Painter Creek ≃ 218 40.05 N 84.21 W
Paintertown 279b 40.21 N 79.42 W
Paint Lake ⊜ 184 55.28 N 97.57 W
Paint Rock 196 31.30 N 99.55 W
Paint Rock ≃ 194 34.28 N 86.28 W
Paintsville 192 37.48 N 82.48 W
Paiolinho 256 21.52 S 45.54 W
Pai Pobre, Morro do ʌ 287b 23.40 S 46.55 W
Paisco 64 46.04 N 10.17 E
Paisha 100 23.40 N 119.35 E
Paisley, Austl. 274b 37.51 S 144.51 E
Paisley, On., Can. 212 44.18 N 81.16 W
Paisley, Scot., U.K. 46 55.50 N 4.26 W
Paisley, Fl., U.S. 220 28.59 N 81.32 W
Paisley, Or., U.S. 202 42.41 N 120.32 W
Païta, N. Cal. 175f 22.08 S 166.22 E
Paita, Perú 248 5.06 S 81.07 W
Paita, Bahía de c 248 5.04 S 81.05 W
Paitan 100 23.31 N 113.46 E
Paitan ≃ 116 6.30 N 117.30 E
Paitan, Teluk c 116 6.45 N 117.20 E
Paiton 115a 7.43 S 113.30 E
Paiva 256 21.18 S 43.25 W
Paiva ≃ 34 41.04 N 8.16 W
Paizhou 100 30.13 N 113.56 E
Paj 24 61.13 N 34.24 E
Pajala 24 67.11 N 23.22 E
Pajan 246 1.34 S 80.25 W
Pajapan 234 18.15 N 94.42 W
Pajares, Puerto de)(34 43.00 N 5.46 W
Pajaro 226 36.54 N 121.39 W
Pajaro ≃ 226 36.51 N 121.48 W
Pajaros Point ≻ 240m 18.31 N 64.18 W
Paj-Choj ʌʌ2 72 69.00 N 63.00 E
Pajdugina ≃ 86 58.50 N 81.47 E
Pajęczno 30 51.09 N 19.00 E
Pajeú ≃ 250 8.55 S 38.42 W
Pajiangkou 100 23.46 N 113.14 E
Pajjer, gora ʌ 24 66.42 N 64.25 E
Pajtug 85 40.53 N 72.15 E
Pak ≃ 110 21.05 N 102.31 E
Páka, Magy. 61 46.36 N 16.39 E
Paka, Malay. 114 4.39 N 103.26 E
Paka ≃ 114 4.40 N 103.27 E
Pākāla 122 13.28 N 79.07 E
Pakaraima Mountains ʌʌ 246 5.30 N 60.40 W
Pākaur 124 24.38 N 87.51 E
Pak Ban 110 21.14 N 102.28 E
Pakch'ŏn 98 39.45 N 125.35 E
Pak Chong 110 14.42 N 101.25 E
Pakeng 140 6.55 N 30.40 E
Pakenham, Austl. 169 38.04 S 145.29 E
Pakenham, On., Can. 212 45.20 N 76.17 W
Pākhāl ⊜1 122 17.57 N 79.59 E
Pákhi 267c 37.59 N 23.22 E
Pákhi I 267c 37.58 N 23.22 E
Pákhna 130 34.46 N 32.48 E
Pakhoi
— Beihai 102 21.29 N 109.05 E
Pakin I1 14 7.04 N 157.48 E
Pakipaki 172 39.41 S 176.48 E
Pakistan (Pākistān) ◻1, Asia 118 30.00 N 70.00 E
Pakistan (Pākistān) ◻1, Asia 120 30.00 N 70.00 E
Pakistan, East
— Bangladesh ◻1 120 24.00 N 90.00 E
Pak Kong 271d 22.23 N 114.15 E
Pak Kret 269a 13.55 N 100.30 E
Pak Kwo Chau I 271d 22.16 N 114.20 E
Paklenica Nacionalni Park ♦ 36 44.21 N 15.23 E

Symbols in the index entries represent the broad categories identified in the key at the right. Symbols with superior numbers (ʌʌ1) identify subcategories (see complete key on page *I · 1*).

Symbole im Register stellen die rechts im Schlüssel erklärten Kategorien dar. Symbole mit hochgestellten Ziffern (ʌʌ1) bezeichnen Unterabteilungen einer Kategorie (vgl. vollständiger Schlüssel auf Seite *I · 1*).

Los símbolos incluídos en el texto del índice representan las grandes categorias identificadas con la clave a la derecha. Los símbolos con numeros en su parte superior (ʌʌ1) identifican las subcategorías (véase la clave completa en la página *I · 1*).

Les symboles de l'index représentent les catégories indiquées dans la légende à droite. Les symboles suivis d'un indice (ʌʌ1) représentent des sous-catégories (voir légende complète à la page *I · 1*).

Os símbolos incluídos no texto do índice representam as grandes categorias identificadas com a chave à direita. Os símbolos com números em sua parte superior (ʌʌ1) identificam as subcategorias (veja-se a chave completa à página *I · 1*).

ʌ	Mountain	Berg	Montaña	Montagne	Montanha
ʌʌ	Mountains	Gebirge	Montañas	Montagnes	Montanhas
)(	Pass	Paß	Paso	Col	Passo
V	Valley, Canyon	Tal, Cañon	Valle, Cañón	Vallée, Canyon	Vale, Canhão
⌣	Plain	Ebene	Llano	Plaine	Planície
≻	Cape	Kap	Cabo	Cap	Cabo
I	Island	Insel	Isla	Île	Ilha
II	Islands	Inseln	Islas	Îles	Ilhas
⊥	Other Topographic Features	Andere Topographische Objekte	Otros Elementos Topográficos	Autres données topographiques	Outros acidentes topográficos

ESPAÑOL Nombre	Página	Lat.°′	Long.°′ W = Oeste
Ramsau	64	47.36 N	12.54 E
Ramsay Range ⋌	162	18.31 S	127.03 E
Ramsbeck	56	51.18 N	8.24 E
Ramsberg	40	59.46 N	15.17 E
Ramsbottom	44	53.40 N	2.19 W
Ramsden Bellhouse	260	51.37 N	0.29 E
Ramsden Heath	260	51.38 N	0.28 E
Ramsdorf	52	51.54 N	6.55 E
Ramsele	26	63.33 N	16.29 E
Ramsenthal	60	50.01 N	11.35 E
Ramseur	192	35.44 N	79.39 W
Ramsey, I. of Man	44	54.20 N	4.21 W
Ramsey, Eng., U.K.	42	51.56 N	1.14 E
Ramsey, Eng., U.K.	42	52.27 N	0.07 W
Ramsey, Il., U.S.	219	39.08 N	89.06 W
Ramsey, N.J., U.S.	210	41.03 N	74.08 W
Ramsey Bay ⊂	44	54.20 N	4.20 W
Ramsey Brook ≃	276	41.02 N	74.08 W
Ramsey Creek ≃	219	39.03 N	89.04 W
Ramsey Island I	42	51.52 N	5.10 W
Ramsey Lake ⊜	190	47.15 N	82.16 W
Ramsey Lake State Park ♠	219	39.10 N	89.08 W
Ramsgate, Austl.	274a	33.59 S	151.08 E
Ramsgate, S. Afr.	158	30.55 S	30.20 E
Ramsgate, Eng., U.K.	42	51.20 N	1.25 E
Rāmshai	124	26.44 N	88.51 E
Rāmshīr	128	30.54 N	49.24 E
Ramshorn Peak ∧	202	45.09 N	111.06 W
Rämshyttan	40	60.18 N	15.13 E
Ramsjö	26	62.11 N	15.39 E
Ramsloh	52	53.06 N	7.40 E
Ramstein	56	49.27 N	7.33 E
Rāmtek	120	21.24 N	79.20 E
Rāmu, Bngl.	120	21.25 N	92.07 E
Ramu, Kenya	154	3.56 N	41.13 E
Ramu ≃	164	4.02 S	144.41 E
Ramuševo	76	57.50 N	31.37 E
Ramvik	26	62.49 N	17.51 E
Ramville, Îlet I	240e	14.42 N	60.53 W
Ramygala	76	55.31 N	24.18 E
Ramzaj	80	53.18 N	44.44 E
Rānāghāt	126	23.11 N	88.35 E
Rana Kao, Volcán ∧[1]	174z	27.11 S	109.27 W
Ranalt	64	47.02 N	11.13 E
Rāna Pratāp Sāgar ⊜[1]	120	24.50 N	75.35 E
Rånäs	40	59.48 N	18.17 E
Ranau	112	5.58 N	116.41 E
Ranau, Danau ⊜	112	4.50 S	103.55 E
Ranbīrsinghpura	123	32.38 N	74.44 E
Ranburne	194	33.31 N	85.20 W
Ranburn Woods	278	41.33 N	87.22 W
Rancabali	115a	7.08 S	107.21 E
Rancagua	252	34.10 S	70.45 W
Rancah	115a	7.12 S	108.30 E
Rance ≃	32	48.31 N	1.59 W
Rancevo, Ross.	76	56.56 N	34.03 E
Rancevo, Ross.	76	56.40 N	33.02 E
Rancharia	255	22.15 S	50.55 W
Rancheria	180	60.05 N	130.40 W
Ranchería ≃	246	11.34 N	72.54 W
Rancheria Rock ∧	202	44.53 N	120.08 W
Ranches of Taos	200	36.22 N	105.37 W
Ranchester	202	44.54 N	107.09 W
Rānchi	124	23.21 N	85.20 E
Ranchillos	252	26.57 S	65.03 W
Rānchi Plateau ⋌[1]	124	23.20 N	84.50 E
Ranch Lake ⊜	184	52.30 N	104.46 W
Rancho Colorado, Presa de ⊜[1]	286a	19.29 N	99.17 W
Rancho Cordova	226	38.35 N	121.18 W
Rancho Del Mar	226	38.10 N	122.15 W
Rancho Nuevo, Méx.	196	26.22 N	99.54 W
Rancho Nuevo, Méx.	234	23.12 N	97.48 W
Rancho Palos Verdes	228	33.45 N	118.24 W
Rancho Rinconado	226	37.18 N	122.01 W
Rancho Santa Fe	228	33.01 N	117.12 W
Rancho Veloz	240p	22.53 N	80.23 W
Ranchuelo	240p	22.23 N	80.09 W
Ranco, Lago ⊜	254	40.14 S	72.24 W
Rancocas	208	40.00 N	74.52 W
Rancocas Creek ≃	285	40.02 N	74.59 W
Rancocas Creek, North Branch ≃	208	40.00 N	74.52 W
Rancocas Creek, South Branch ≃	208	40.00 N	74.52 W
Rancocas Creek, Southwest Branch ≃	285	39.57 N	74.48 W
Rancocas Heights	285	39.59 N	74.51 W
Rancocas State Park ♠	285	40.00 N	74.50 W
Rancocas Woods	285	39.59 N	74.51 W
Rancul	252	35.03 S	64.42 W
Rand	166	35.36 S	146.35 E
Rand (Germiston) Airport ⊠	273d	26.15 S	28.09 E
Randa	58	46.07 N	7.47 E
Randall Lake ⊜	216	41.57 N	85.02 W
Randall Park Mall ◆[9]	279a	41.26 N	81.32 W
Randalls Island I	276	40.48 N	73.55 W
Randallstown	284b	39.22 N	76.48 W
Randalstown	48	54.45 N	6.19 W
Randan	32	46.01 N	3.21 E
Rāndaveswar	126	23.43 N	87.17 E
Randazzo	70	37.53 N	14.57 E
Randbøl	41	55.42 N	9.16 E
Randburg	273d	26.06 S	27.59 E
Randers	26	56.28 N	10.03 E
Randfontein	158	26.11 S	27.42 E
Randfontein □[5]	273d	26.13 S	27.40 E
Randgate	273d	26.11 S	27.41 E
Randhurst ◆[9]	278	42.05 N	87.56 W
Randle	224	46.32 N	121.57 W
Randleman	192	35.49 N	79.48 W
Randlett	196	34.10 N	98.27 W
Randolph, Az., U.S.	200	32.55 N	111.30 W
Randolph, Me., U.S.	188	44.13 N	69.46 W
Randolph, Ma., U.S.	207	42.09 N	71.02 W
Randolph, Ne., U.S.	198	42.22 N	97.21 W
Randolph, N.Y., U.S.	210	42.09 N	78.58 W
Randolph, Oh., U.S.	214	41.01 N	81.14 W
Randolph, Ut,. U.S.	200	41.39 N	111.10 W
Randolph, Vt., U.S.	188	43.55 N	72.39 W
Randolph, Wi., U.S.	190	43.32 N	89.00 W
Randolph □[6], In., U.S.	218	40.10 N	85.00 W
Randolph □[6], Mo., U.S.	219	39.22 N	92.20 W
Randolph Air Force Base ■	196	29.32 N	98.16 W
Randolph Hills	284c	39.03 N	77.05 W
Randolph Village	284c	38.53 N	76.52 W
Random Island I	186	48.08 N	53.45 W
Random Lake	190	43.33 N	87.57 W
Randow ≃	54	53.41 N	14.04 E
Randowaya	164	1.52 S	136.31 E
Randowbruch ≡	54	53.15 N	14.10 E
Randsburg	228	35.22 N	117.39 W
Randse Afrikaanse Universiteit ʋ[2]	273d	26.11 S	27.50 E
Randsfjorden ⊜	26	60.25 N	10.24 E
Rand Stadium ♠	273d	26.14 S	28.03 E
Randublatung	115a	7.12 S	111.23 E
Randudongkal	115a	7.06 S	109.19 E
Randwick	170	33.55 S	151.15 E
Randwick Racecourse ♠	274a	33.54 S	151.14 E
Råneå	26	65.52 N	22.18 E
Ranelagh	258	34.48 S	58.12 W
Rāner	123	28.53 N	73.17 E
Ranérou	150	15.18 N	13.58 W
Rāneswar	126	24.02 N	87.25 E
Raneue	114	5.03 N	95.20 E
Ranford	168a	32.48 S	116.31 E
Ranfurly, N.Z.	172	45.08 S	170.06 E
Ranfurly, Scot., U.K.	46	55.52 N	4.33 W
Rangae	114	6.17 N	101.44 E
Rāngāmāti	120	22.38 N	92.12 E

FRANÇAIS Nom	Page	Lat.°′	Long.°′ W = Ouest
Rangantemiang	112	0.35 S	113.19 E
Rangas, Tanjung ›	112	2.38 S	118.49 E
Rangasa, Tanjung ›	112	3.33 S	118.56 E
Rangaunu Bay ⊂	172	34.50 S	173.15 E
Range Creek ≃	200	39.18 N	110.04 W
Range Indian Reserve ◆[4]	182	49.09 N	119.50 W
Rangeley	188	44.57 N	70.38 W
Rangely	200	40.05 N	108.48 W
Ranger	196	32.28 N	98.40 W
Ranger Lake ⊜	190	46.54 N	83.35 W
Rangersdorf	64	46.51 N	12.58 E
Ranghe	100	33.43 N	112.51 E
Rangia	120	26.28 N	91.38 E
Rangiora	172	43.18 S	172.36 E
Rangitaiki ≃	172	37.54 S	176.53 E
Rangitata ≃	172	44.12 S	171.30 E
Rangitikei ≃	172	40.18 S	175.14 E
Rangitukia	172	37.46 S	178.27 E
Rangkasbitung	115a	6.21 S	106.15 E
Rangkul'	85	38.29 N	74.22 E
Rangoon ≃	110	16.29 N	96.21 E
Rangoon → Yangon	110	16.47 N	96.10 E
Rangpo	124	27.11 N	88.32 E
Rangpur, Bngl.	124	25.45 N	89.15 E
Rangpur, Pāk.	123	30.31 N	71.34 E
Rangpuri ⊥	272a	28.33 N	77.08 E
Rangsang, Pulau I	114	1.00 N	102.55 E
Rangsdorf	54	52.17 N	13.25 E
Rangsdorfer See ⊜	264a	52.17 N	13.24 E
Ranguana Cay I	236	16.20 N	88.09 W
Ranguana Entrance Џ	236	16.19 N	88.09 W
Rangun → Yangon	110	16.47 N	96.10 E
Ranholas	266c	38.47 N	9.22 W
Rānibāndh	126	22.52 N	86.47 E
Rānībennur	122	14.37 N	75.37 E
Rānīganj	126	23.37 N	87.08 E
Rānikhet	124	29.39 N	79.25 E
Ranino	80	52.58 N	40.15 E
Ranis	54	50.39 N	11.34 E
Rānīwāra	120	24.45 N	72.13 E
Rāniyah	128	36.15 N	44.53 E
Rankamhaeng National Park ♠	110	17.10 N	99.58 E
Ranken ≃	166	20.31 S	137.36 E
Ranken Store	166	19.35 S	136.55 E
Rankin, Il., U.S.	216	40.27 N	87.53 W
Rankin, Mi., U.S.	216	42.55 N	83.46 W
Rankin, Pa., U.S.	279b	40.24 N	79.52 W
Rankin, Tx., U.S.	196	31.13 N	101.56 W
Rankin Inlet	176	62.45 N	92.10 W
Rankins Springs	166	33.50 S	146.16 E
Rankūs	132	33.45 N	36.23 E
Rankweil	58	47.17 N	9.39 E
Ranlo	192	35.17 N	81.07 W
Ranneje	80	51.29 N	52.37 E
Rannersdorf	264b	48.08 N	16.28 E
Rannoch, Loch ⊜	46	56.41 N	4.20 W
Rannoch Moor ◆[3]	46	56.38 N	4.40 W
Rann of Kutch → Kutch, Rann of ◆[1]	120	24.05 N	70.10 E
Ranobe ≃	157b	17.10 S	44.08 E
Ranohira	157b	22.29 S	45.24 E
Ranomafana, Madag.	157b	18.57 S	48.50 E
Ranomafana, Madag.	157b	24.36 S	46.58 E
Ranomena	157b	23.25 S	47.17 E
Ranong	110	9.58 N	98.38 E
Ranongga Island I	175e	8.05 S	156.34 E
Ranopiso	157b	25.03 S	46.40 E
Ranot	110	7.46 N	100.19 E
Ranotsara Nord	157b	22.48 S	46.36 E
Rānsai	272c	18.53 N	73.05 E
Ransäter	40	59.46 N	13.26 E
Ransiki	164	1.30 S	134.10 E
Ransom, Il., U.S.	216	41.09 N	88.39 W
Ransom, Ks., U.S.	198	38.38 N	99.56 W
Ransom, Pa., U.S.	210	41.24 N	75.50 W
Ransom Creek ≃	284a	43.04 N	78.45 W
Ransomville	210	43.14 N	78.54 W
Ranson	188	39.17 N	77.51 W
Ransta	40	59.48 N	16.38 E
Ranstadt	56	50.21 N	8.59 E
Rantabe	157b	15.42 S	49.39 E
Rantasalmi	26	62.04 N	28.18 E
Rantau, Indon.	112	2.56 S	115.09 E
Rantau, Malay.	114	2.35 N	101.58 E
Rantaukampar	114	1.24 N	100.59 E
Rantaupanjang, Indon.	112	1.51 S	102.19 E
Rantaupanjang, Indon.	112	1.16 S	101.49 E
Rantaupanjang, Indon.	114	0.58 N	99.13 E
Rantauprapat	114	2.06 N	99.50 E
Rantekombola, Bulu ∧	112	3.21 S	120.01 E
Ranten	61	47.09 N	14.05 E
Rantepao	112	2.59 S	119.54 E
Rantigny	50	49.20 N	2.26 E
Rantoul	216	40.09 N	88.20 W
Rantsila	26	64.31 N	25.39 E
Rantzau	54	54.15 N	10.30 E
Ranua	26	65.55 N	26.32 E
Rānvād	272c	18.53 N	72.55 E
Ranwanalenaus	156	19.35 S	22.47 E
Råö	26	57.24 N	11.56 E
Rao'er	100	28.48 N	117.40 E
Raohe	89	46.47 N	134.00 E
Raon-L'Étape	58	48.24 N	6.51 E
Raon-sur-Plaine	58	48.31 N	7.06 E
Raoping	100	23.43 N	117.01 E
Raoui, 'Erg er ◆[2]	148	29.17 N	2.20 W
Raoul	192	34.27 N	83.36 W
Raoul Island I	14	29.16 S	177.54 W
Raoyang	98	38.16 N	115.44 E
Raoyang ≃	104	41.50 N	122.35 E
Raoyanghe	104	41.46 N	122.26 E
Rapa I	14	27.36 S	144.20 W
Rapa, Ponta do ›	252	27.22 S	48.26 W
Rapallo	62	44.21 N	9.14 E
Rapang	112	3.50 S	119.48 E
Rāpar	120	23.34 N	70.38 E
Raparo, Monte ∧	68	40.12 N	15.59 E
Rapatovo	80	55.04 N	54.37 E
Rāpch ≃	128	25.28 N	59.21 E
Rapel ≃	252	33.55 S	71.51 W
Rapel, Embalse ⊜[1]	252	34.12 S	71.30 W
Rapelli	252	26.24 S	64.29 W
Raphoe	48	54.52 N	7.36 W
Rapid ≃, Mi., U.S.	190	45.55 N	86.58 W
Rapid ≃, Mn., U.S.	198	48.42 N	94.26 W
Rapid ≃, Wa., U.S.	224	47.48 N	121.18 W
Rapidan ≃	188	38.22 N	77.37 W
Rapid Bay	168b	35.32 S	138.12 E
Rapid City, Mb., Can.	184	50.08 N	100.02 W
Rapid City, Mi., U.S.	190	44.50 N	85.16 W
Rapid City, S.D., U.S.	198	44.04 N	103.13 W
Rapid Creek ≃	198	43.54 N	102.37 W
Rapide Taureau, Barrage du ◆[6]	206	46.52 N	73.39 W
Rapid River	190	45.55 N	86.58 W
Räpina	76	58.06 N	27.27 E
Rapkan	85	40.22 N	70.40 E
Rapla	76	59.01 N	24.47 E
Rapness	46	59.14 N	2.51 W
Rapolano Terme	66	43.17 N	11.36 E
Rapolla	68	40.58 N	15.41 E
Rapone	68	40.51 N	15.30 E
Raposo ∧[2]	266c	38.40 N	9.11 W
Rappahannock ≃	208	37.34 N	76.18 W
Rappbodestausee ⊜[1]	54	51.09 N	10.58 E
Rappenlochschlucht ⌞	58	47.23 N	9.47 E
Rappottenstein	61	48.31 N	15.05 E
Rāptī □[8]	124	28.15 N	82.30 E
Rāpti (Raptī) ≃, Asia	124	26.18 N	83.41 E

PORTUGUÊS Nome	Página	Lat.°′	Long.°′ W = Oeste
Rāptī ≃, Nepāl	124	27.33 N	84.07 E
Rapulo ≃	248	13.43 S	65.32 W
Rapu-Rapu	116	13.11 N	124.08 E
Rapu Rapu Island I	116	13.12 N	124.09 E
Raqabah, Khashm ar- ∧[2]	142	28.18 N	31.43 E
Raquette ≃	206	45.00 N	74.42 W
Raraka I[1]	14	16.10 S	144.54 W
Rara National Park ♠	124	29.35 N	82.05 E
Rārh Plains ≚	126	23.13 N	87.20 E
Rāribahāl	126	24.05 N	87.21 E
Raritan	210	40.34 N	74.38 W
Raritan ≃	208	40.29 N	74.17 W
Raritan, North Branch ≃	210	40.33 N	74.41 W
Raritan, South Branch ≃	210	40.33 N	74.41 W
Raritan Bay ⊂	208	40.28 N	74.12 W
Raroïa I	14	16.01 S	142.27 W
Raron	58	46.19 N	7.48 E
Rarotonga I	174k	21.14 S	159.46 W
Rarotonga International Airport ⊠	174k	21.12 S	159.49 W
Rarz	85	39.23 N	68.44 E
Rasa, Ilha I	287a	23.04 S	43.09 W
Rasa, Punta ›, Arg.	252	36.17 S	56.47 W
Rasa, Punta ›, Arg.	254	40.51 S	62.19 W
Rašaant	88	49.07 N	101.25 E
Rasa de Guaratiba, Ilha I	256	23.05 S	43.34 W
Rasa Island I	116	9.14 N	118.27 E
Ra's al-ʿAyn	130	36.51 N	40.04 E
Ra's al-Barr	142	31.31 N	31.50 E
Ra's al-Khalīj	142	31.15 N	31.39 E
Ra's al-Khaymah	128	25.47 N	55.57 E
Ra's al-Unūf	146	30.31 N	18.34 E
Ra's al-Ushsh ◆[8]	142	31.08 N	32.18 E
Ra's an-Naqb, Miṣr	132	29.36 N	34.51 E
Ra's an-Naqb, Urd.	132	30.00 N	35.29 E
Rasawi	164	2.04 S	134.01 E
Ra's Baʿlabakk	130	34.15 N	36.25 E
Rasbo	40	59.57 N	17.53 E
Raschau	54	50.32 N	12.50 E
Ras Dashen Terara ∧	144	13.16 N	38.24 E
Rasdorf	56	50.43 N	9.53 E
Raseborg	26	59.59 N	23.39 E
Raseiniai	76	55.24 N	23.07 E
Râs el Aïoun	36	35.30 N	8.18 E
Ras el Ma, Alg.	148	34.31 N	0.46 W
Râs el Mâ, Mali	150	16.37 N	4.28 W
Ras el Oued	34	35.57 N	5.03 E
Rasen-Antholz → Anterselva di Sopra	64	46.52 N	12.08 E
Raševka	78	50.14 N	33.54 E
Rashād	140	11.51 N	31.04 E
Rāshayyā	132	33.30 N	35.51 E
Rashīd (Rosetta)	142	31.24 N	30.25 E
Rashīd, Farʿ (Rosetta Branch) ≃	142	31.30 N	30.21 E
Rashīd, Maṣabb (Rosetta Mouth) ≃[1]	142	31.30 N	30.20 E
Rashīd Qalʿeh	120	31.31 N	67.31 E
Rashin → Najin	98	42.15 N	130.18 E
Rasht	128	37.16 N	49.36 E
Rashtrapati Bhawan ʋ	272a	28.37 N	77.12 E
Rasina ≃	38	43.37 N	21.22 E
Rāsipuram	122	11.28 N	78.10 E
Rasi Salai	110	15.20 N	104.09 E
Rāsk	128	26.13 N	61.25 E
Raška	38	43.17 N	20.37 E
Rask Mølle	41	55.52 N	9.37 E
Rās Koh ∧	128	28.50 N	65.12 E
Raškov	78	47.57 N	28.50 E
Raskunda	126	22.48 N	87.26 E
Rasm al-Arwām, Sabkhat ⊜	130	35.53 N	37.40 E
R'asna	76	54.01 N	31.12 E
R'asnopol'	78	47.04 N	31.12 E
Raso, Cabo ›	266c	38.43 N	9.29 W
Raso, Ilhéu I	150a	16.37 N	24.36 W
Rasocolmo, Capo ›	70	38.18 N	15.31 E
Rason Lake ⊜	162	28.46 S	124.20 E
Raspberry Peak ∧	194	34.23 N	94.01 W
Raspopinskaja	80	49.24 N	42.52 E
Rasra	124	25.51 N	83.51 E
Rass Jebel	36	37.13 N	10.09 E
Rasskazovka	265b	55.38 N	37.20 E
Rasskazovo	80	52.40 N	41.53 E
Rassua, ostrov I	74	47.45 N	153.01 E
Rassudovo	82	55.29 N	36.54 E
Rassvet, Ross.	84	43.58 N	46.44 E
Rassvet, Ross.	84	43.58 N	46.44 E
Rassvet, Ross.	86	57.02 N	91.34 E
Rassvet, Ross.	88	57.02 N	91.34 E
Rassypnaja	80	51.35 N	53.37 E
Rassypnoje	83	48.08 N	38.34 E
Rast	38	43.53 N	23.17 E
Rastälven ≃	40	59.37 N	14.56 E
Ra's Tannūrah	128	26.42 N	50.06 E
Rastatt	56	48.51 N	8.12 E
Rastavica ≃	78	49.44 N	30.01 E
Rastede	52	53.15 N	8.11 E
Rastegai'sa ∧	24	70.00 N	26.18 E
Rastenberg	54	51.10 N	11.25 E
Rastenburg → Kętrzyn	30	54.06 N	21.23 E
Rastorf	54	54.16 N	10.19 E
Rastorgujevo	82	55.33 N	37.41 E
Rastovcy	82	56.39 N	37.35 E
Rastunovo	82	55.16 N	37.50 E
Rasu, Monte ∧	71	40.25 N	9.00 E
Rasūl	123	32.42 N	73.34 E
Rasūlnagar	123	32.20 N	73.47 E
Rasulpur	272a	28.37 N	77.22 E
Rasulpur ◆[8]	272a	28.42 N	77.01 E
Rasun di sopra	64	46.48 N	12.03 E
Rasun di sotto	64	46.47 N	12.02 E
Rasura	58	46.06 N	9.33 E
Råsvalen ⊜	40	59.40 N	15.10 E
Răsvani	38	44.25 N	26.53 E
Rat ≃, Mb., Can.	184	55.41 N	99.04 W
Rat ≃, Mb., Can.	184	49.35 N	97.08 W
Ratahan	112	1.04 N	124.48 E
Ratak Chain II	14	9.00 N	171.00 E
Ratangarh	120	28.05 N	74.36 E
Ratanpur, India	126	23.07 N	87.04 E
Ratanpur, India	272b	22.50 N	88.14 E
Rätansbyn	26	62.29 N	14.32 E
Rat Burana	269a	13.41 N	100.30 E
Ratčino, Ross.	80	53.02 N	39.55 E
Ratčino, Ross.	82	55.16 N	38.39 E
Ratcliff	222	31.24 N	95.08 W
Rateče	64	46.30 N	13.43 E
Ratekau	54	53.57 N	10.44 E
Rāth	124	25.35 N	79.34 E
Rath ◆[8]	263	51.17 N	6.49 E
Rathangan	48	53.12 N	6.59 W
Rathbone	210	42.08 N	77.19 W
Rathbun Lake ⊜	212	44.47 N	78.12 W
Rathbun Lake ⊜[1]	190	40.54 N	93.05 W
Rathcoole	48	53.16 N	6.28 W
Rathcormack	48	52.05 N	8.17 W
Rathdowney, Austl.	171a	28.12 S	152.52 E
Rathdowney, Ire.	48	52.50 N	7.34 W
Rathdrum, Ire.	48	52.56 N	6.13 W
Rathdrum, Id., U.S.	202	47.48 N	116.53 W
Rathebur	54	53.44 N	13.46 E
Ratheim	52	51.04 N	6.10 E
Rathen	46	57.38 N	2.02 W
Rathenow	54	52.36 N	12.20 E
Rathfriland	48	54.14 N	6.10 W
Rathkeale	48	52.32 N	8.56 W
Rathlin Island I	48	55.18 N	6.13 W
Rathlin Sound Џ	48	55.15 N	6.15 W

Ráth Luirc (Charleville)	48	52.21 N	8.41 W
Rathmecke	263	51.15 N	7.38 E
Rathmelton	48	55.02 N	7.38 W
Rathmore	48	52.03 N	9.13 W
Rathmullan	48	55.06 N	7.33 W
Rathnew	48	53.00 N	6.05 W
Ratho	46	55.55 N	3.22 W
Rathowen	48	53.40 N	7.31 W
Rathstock	54	52.31 N	14.32 E
Rathwell	184	49.40 N	98.32 W
Ratibor → Racibórz	30	50.06 N	18.13 E
Raticosa, Passo della)(	66	44.10 N	11.20 E
Rätikon ⋌	58	47.03 N	9.40 E
Ratingen	56	51.18 N	6.51 E
Ratisbon → Regensburg	60	49.01 N	12.06 E
Rätische Alpen → Rhaetian Alps ⋌	58	46.30 N	10.00 E
Rat Island I	181a	51.55 N	178.20 E
Rat Islands II	181a	51.40 N	178.30 E
Rat'kovo	82	56.01 N	38.38 E
Rat Lake ⊜	184	56.10 N	99.40 W
Ratlām	120	23.19 N	75.04 E
Ratmanova, ostrov I	180	65.46 N	169.02 W
Ratnāgiri	122	16.59 N	73.18 E
Ratnapura	122	6.41 N	80.24 E
Ratno	78	51.40 N	24.31 E
Ratodero	120	27.48 N	68.18 E
Ratomka	76	53.56 N	27.21 E
Raton	196	36.54 N	104.26 W
Raton Pass)(	196	36.59 N	104.29 W
Ratqah, Wādī ar- ∨	130	34.25 N	40.55 E
Ratt ≃	224	47.27 N	124.21 W
Rattanaburi	110	15.19 N	103.51 E
Rattaphum	110	7.08 N	100.16 E
Ratten	61	47.29 N	15.43 E
Rattlesnake	202	46.56 N	113.59 W
Rattlesnake Creek ≃, Ks., U.S.	198	38.13 N	98.22 W
Rattlesnake Creek ≃, Oh., U.S.	218	39.16 N	83.23 W
Rattlesnake Creek ≃, Or., U.S.	202	42.44 N	117.47 W
Rattlesnake Creek ≃, Wa., U.S.	224	46.45 N	120.55 W
Rattlesnake Creek ≃, Wa., U.S.	224	45.48 N	121.29 W
Rattlesnake Mountain ∧	207	41.42 N	72.50 W
Rattlesnake Peak ∧	280	34.16 N	117.47 W
Rattling Brook	186	49.38 N	56.10 W
Rattling Run ≃	279b	40.33 N	79.32 W
Rattray	46	56.35 N	3.19 W
Rattray Head ›	46	57.37 N	1.49 W
Rattu	123	35.08 N	74.48 E
Rättvik	26	60.53 N	15.06 E
Ratz, Mount ∧	180	57.23 N	132.19 W
Ratzeburg	54	53.42 N	10.46 E
Ratzeburger See ⊜	54	53.45 N	10.47 E
Rätzlingen	54	52.23 N	11.08 E
Rau	112	0.34 N	100.01 E
Raub, Malay.	114	3.48 N	101.52 E
Raub, In., U.S.	216	40.44 N	87.29 W
Raubsville	208	40.38 N	75.12 W
Rauch	252	36.46 S	59.06 W
Raucheck ∧	64	47.30 N	13.14 E
Rauchenwarth	264b	48.05 N	16.32 E
Rauchtown	210	41.07 N	77.14 W
Raucourt-et-Flaba	56	49.36 N	4.57 E
Rauen	54	52.20 N	14.01 E
Rauenstein	54	50.24 N	11.03 E
Raufarhöfn	24a	66.30 N	15.57 W
Raufoss	26	60.43 N	10.37 E
Rauhe Ebrach ≃	56	49.50 N	10.56 E
Raukumara Range ⋌	172	37.47 S	178.02 E
Raul Soares	255	20.05 S	42.22 W
Rauma	26	61.08 N	21.30 E
Rauma ≃	26	62.33 N	7.43 E
Raumünzach	56	48.38 N	8.21 E
Rauna	76	57.20 N	25.43 E
Raunds	42	52.21 N	0.33 W
Raung, Gunung ∧	115a	8.08 S	114.03 E
Raunheim	56	50.01 N	8.28 E
Raupal'an	180	65.28 N	171.59 W
Raurimu	172	39.07 S	175.24 E
Rauris	64	47.13 N	13.00 E
Raurkela	124	22.13 N	84.53 E
Rauschenberg	56	50.53 N	8.55 E
Rausu	92a	44.01 N	145.12 E
Rautalampi	26	62.38 N	26.50 E
Rāutara	272b	22.51 N	88.28 E
Rautavaara	26	63.29 N	28.18 E
Ravahere I[1]	14	18.14 S	142.09 W
Ravalgaon	122	20.38 N	74.25 E
Ravanica, Manastir ʋ[1]	38	43.58 N	21.26 E
Ravānsar	128	34.43 N	46.40 E
Ravanusa	70	37.16 N	13.58 E
Rāvar	128	31.15 N	56.53 E
Ravarano	64	44.35 N	10.04 E
Ravarino	64	44.44 N	11.06 E
Rava-Russkaja	78	50.14 N	23.37 E
Ravascletto	64	46.32 N	12.57 E
Ravat	85	39.54 N	70.12 E
Ravello	68	40.39 N	14.37 E
Ravelo	248	18.48 S	65.32 W
Raven	192	37.05 N	81.51 W
Ravena	210	42.28 N	73.49 W
Ravenglass	44	54.21 N	3.24 W
Raven Lake ⊜	212	45.13 N	78.51 W
Ravenna, It.	66	44.25 N	12.12 E
Ravenna, Ky., U.S.	192	37.41 N	83.57 W
Ravenna, Mi., U.S.	216	43.11 N	85.56 W
Ravenna, Ne., U.S.	198	41.01 N	98.54 W
Ravenna, Oh., U.S.	214	41.09 N	81.14 W
Ravenna □[4]	66	44.25 N	11.59 E
Ravensbourne	171a	27.22 S	152.10 E
Ravensbourne National Park ♠	171a	27.21 S	152.15 E
Ravensburg	58	47.47 N	9.37 E
Ravenscrag	184	49.30 N	109.05 W
Ravensdale	224	47.21 N	121.58 W
Ravenshoe	166	17.37 S	145.29 E
Ravensthorpe, Austl.	162	33.35 S	120.02 E
Ravensthorpe, Eng., U.K.	44	53.42 N	1.35 W
Ravenswood, S. Afr.	273d	26.11 S	28.15 E
Ravenswood, Mi., U.S.	216	42.45 N	84.36 W
Ravenswood, W.V., U.S.	188	38.56 N	81.45 W
Ravenswood Park ♠	283	42.36 N	70.42 W
Ravenswood Point ›	282	37.30 N	122.08 W
Ravensworth	284c	38.48 N	77.13 W
Rāver	120	21.15 N	76.02 E
Ravernet ≃	48	54.30 N	6.04 W
Rāvi ≃	123	30.35 N	71.49 E
Ravières	50	47.45 N	4.17 E
Ravine	208	40.34 N	76.24 W
Ravine Lake ⊜[1]	276	40.43 N	74.38 W
Ravinia Park ♠	278	42.09 N	87.46 W
Ravna Gora	36	45.23 N	14.57 E
Ravne	61	46.33 N	14.58 E
Ravnina	128	37.57 N	62.40 E
Ravsted	41	55.01 N	9.08 E
Rāwah	128	34.28 N	41.55 E
Rawaki I[1]	14	3.43 S	170.43 W
Rāwala Kot	123	33.52 N	73.46 E
Rāwalpindi	123	33.36 N	73.04 E
Rawa Mazowiecka	30	51.46 N	20.16 E
Rāwāndūz	128	36.37 N	44.31 E
Rawang	114	3.19 N	101.35 E
Rawas ≃	112	2.42 S	103.24 E
Rāwatsar	123	29.17 N	74.23 E
Rawāwiṣ, Wādī ∨	146	30.26 N	15.24 E
Rawḍah ⊜	130	35.15 N	41.05 E
Rawḍah, Wādī ar- ∨	130	34.22 N	37.21 E

Rawd al-Faraj ◆[8]	273c	30.05 N	31.14 E
Rawḍaw, Jazīrat ar- I	273c	30.01 N	31.13 E
Rawdon	206	46.03 N	73.43 W
Rawene	172	35.24 S	173.30 E
Rawḥah	144	19.28 N	41.48 E
Rawhide Creek ≃	198	42.06 N	104.20 W
Rawhide Lake ⊜	190	46.39 N	82.37 W
Rawhide Mountain ∧	204	38.17 N	116.25 W
Rawi	112	2.07 S	113.56 E
Rawi, Ko I	114	6.33 N	99.14 E
Rawicz	30	51.37 N	16.52 E
Rawlinna	162	31.01 S	125.20 E
Rawlins	200	41.47 N	107.14 W
Rawlinson, Mount ∧	162	25.58 S	127.28 E
Rawlinson Range ⋌	162	24.51 S	128.00 E
Rawmarsh	44	53.27 N	1.21 W
Rawreth	260	51.37 N	0.35 E
Rawson, Arg.	252	34.36 S	60.04 W
Rawson, Arg.	254	43.18 S	65.06 W
Rawson, Oh., U.S.	216	40.57 N	83.47 W
Rawsonville	158	33.41 S	19.20 E
Rawtenstall	44	53.42 N	2.18 W
Rawu	102	29.30 N	96.45 E
Rax ⋌	61	47.42 N	15.43 E
Raxāul	124	26.59 N	84.51 E
Ray, Il., U.S.	219	40.12 N	90.29 W
Ray, In., U.S.	216	41.45 N	84.53 W
Ray, N.D., U.S.	198	48.20 N	103.09 W
Ray ≃	42	51.48 N	1.15 W
Ray, Cape ›	186	47.40 N	59.18 W
Raya	112	1.05 N	118.32 E
Raya, Bukit ∧	112	0.40 S	112.41 E
Raya, Gunong ∧	114	6.22 N	99.49 E
Raya, Pulau I	114	4.52 N	95.22 E
Rāyachoti	122	14.03 N	78.45 E
Rāyadurg	122	14.42 N	76.52 E
Rāyagarha	122	19.10 N	83.25 E
Rayburn	222	30.25 N	94.56 W
Rayen, Dtsch.	263	51.28 N	6.32 E
Rāyen, Īrān	128	29.34 N	57.26 E
Ray Hubbard, Lake ⊜[1]	222	32.53 N	96.35 W
Rāyikhah I	128	26.12 N	36.21 E
Rayland	214	40.11 N	80.41 W
Rayleigh	42	51.36 N	0.36 E
Raymond, Ab., Can.	182	49.27 N	112.39 W
Raymond, Ca., U.S.	226	37.13 N	119.54 W
Raymond, Il., U.S.	219	39.19 N	89.34 W
Raymond, Mn., U.S.	198	45.00 N	95.14 W
Raymond, Ms., U.S.	194	32.15 N	90.25 W
Raymond, Oh., U.S.	216	40.20 N	83.28 W
Raymond, Wa., U.S.	224	46.41 N	123.43 W
Raymond Terrace	170	32.46 S	151.44 E
Raymondville	196	26.29 N	97.47 W
Raymore	184	51.25 N	104.31 W
Ray Mountains ⋌	180	65.45 N	151.30 W
Rāyna	126	23.05 N	87.54 E
Rayne	194	30.14 N	92.16 W
Raynham	207	41.56 N	71.04 W
Raynham Dog Track ♠	283	41.59 N	71.04 W
Rayón, Méx.	232	29.43 N	110.35 W
Rayón, Méx.	234	17.12 N	93.00 W
Rayón, Méx.	234	21.51 N	99.40 W
Rayones	232	25.01 N	100.05 W
Rayong	110	12.40 N	101.17 E
Rāypur	272b	22.25 N	88.31 E
Rayrah ⫪[4]	140	15.21 N	34.41 E
Rayse Creek ≃	219	38.13 N	89.00 W
Raystown Lake ⊜[1]	214	40.20 N	78.05 W
Rayton	158	25.45 S	28.32 E
Raytown	194	39.00 N	94.27 W
Rayville	194	32.28 N	91.45 W
Raywood	222	30.02 N	94.40 W
Raz, Pointe du ›	32	48.02 N	4.44 W
Raza, Punta ›	234	21.02 N	105.20 W
Razan, Īrān	128	35.23 N	49.02 E
R'azan', Ross.	80	54.38 N	39.44 E
R'azan □[8]	82	54.15 N	39.00 E
R'azancevo	82	56.42 N	39.12 E
Ražanj	38	43.40 N	21.33 E
R'azanovo	82	55.29 N	37.31 E
Razbegaj	265a	59.47 N	29.56 E
Războeni	38	47.05 N	26.32 E
Razdan	84	40.30 N	44.46 E
Razdan ≃	84	39.58 N	44.27 E
Razdel'naja	78	46.51 N	30.05 E
Razdolinsk	86	58.25 N	94.38 E
Razdolje	88	52.27 N	103.13 E
Razdol'noje, Ross.	89	43.30 N	131.52 E
Razdol'noje, Ukr.	78	45.47 N	33.29 E
Razdol'noje, Ukr.	83	47.37 N	38.01 E
Razdol'nyj	80	46.38 N	42.57 E
Razdorskaja	78	47.33 N	40.38 E
Razdory, Ross.	265b	55.45 N	37.18 E
Razdory, Ukr.	78	48.21 N	35.42 E
R'aženoje	83	47.31 N	38.52 E
Raževo	86	56.09 N	68.25 E
Razgrad	38	43.32 N	26.31 E
Razim, Lacul ⊜	38	44.54 N	28.57 E
Razlog	38	41.53 N	23.28 E
Razmachnino	88	51.47 N	115.28 E
Razmitelevo	265a	59.54 N	30.41 E
Raznočinovka	80	46.37 N	47.57 E
Raznomojka	86	52.29 N	55.52 E
Razorback Mountain ∧	182	51.35 N	124.42 W
R'ažsk	80	53.43 N	40.04 E
Razvil'noje	80	46.14 N	41.18 E
Razzoli, Isola I	71	41.18 N	9.21 E
Ré, Île de I	32	46.12 N	1.25 W
Rea ≃	42	52.18 N	2.32 W
Read	262	53.49 N	2.21 W
Reading, Eng., U.K.	42	51.28 N	0.59 W
Reading, Il., U.S.	216	41.05 N	88.51 W
Reading, Ks., U.S.	198	38.31 N	95.57 W
Reading, Ma., U.S.	207	42.31 N	71.05 W
Reading, Mi., U.S.	216	41.50 N	84.44 W
Reading, Oh., U.S.	218	39.13 N	84.26 W
Reading, Pa., U.S.	208	40.20 N	75.55 W
Reading Center	210	42.26 N	76.56 W
Reading Station ◆[5]	285	39.57 N	75.10 W
Readington	210	40.34 N	74.44 W
Readlyn	190	42.42 N	92.13 W
Readsboro	207	42.46 N	72.56 W
Readstown	190	43.26 N	90.45 W
Reagan	222	31.13 N	96.47 W
Real	116	14.40 N	121.36 E
Real ≃	250	11.27 S	37.22 W
Real, Cordillera ⋌	248	19.00 S	66.30 W
Real, Estero ≃	236	12.55 N	87.23 W
Real del Padre	252	34.50 S	67.46 W
Real de San Carlos	258	34.26 S	57.53 W
Realengo ◆[8]	256	22.53 S	43.25 W
Real Felipe, Museo Histórico del ⊥	286d	12.04 S	77.09 W
Realicó	252	35.02 S	64.15 W
Realitos	196	27.27 N	98.32 W
Realmonte	70	37.18 N	13.28 E
Reamstown	208	40.12 N	76.07 W
Reana del Roiale	64	46.12 N	13.13 E
Reardan	202	47.40 N	117.52 W
Reata	232	26.08 N	101.05 W
Reatini, Monti ⋌	66	42.28 N	13.00 E
Réau	261	48.37 N	2.38 E
Reay	46	58.33 N	3.47 W
Reay Forest ◆[3]	46	58.19 N	4.47 W
Rebecca, Lake ⊜	162	29.53 S	122.10 E
Rebecq-Rognon	50	50.40 N	4.08 E
Rebeida, Wādī ∨	140	20.45 N	34.06 E
Rebel Hill	285	40.04 N	75.20 W
Rebersburg	210	40.57 N	77.27 W
Rebi	164	6.23 S	134.06 E
Rebiana Sand Sea → Rabyānah, Ṣaḥrā' ◆[2]	146	24.20 N	20.37 E
Rebild Bakker ♠	26	56.50 N	9.51 E
Reboly	24	63.50 N	30.47 E
Rebouças	252	25.36 S	50.42 W
Reboucas, Túnel ◆[5]	287a	22.56 S	43.14 W

Rebricha	86	53.05 N	82.20 E
Rebun-tō I	92a	45.23 N	141.02 E
Recalde	252	36.39 S	61.05 W
Recanati	66	43.24 N	13.32 E
Rečane	76	56.25 N	31.39 E
Recco	62	44.22 N	9.09 E
Recey-sur-Ource	58	47.47 N	4.52 E
Rēchah Lām	120	34.58 N	70.51 E
Rechberghausen	56	48.44 N	9.38 E
Recherche, Archipelago of the II	162	34.05 S	122.45 E
Recherche, Cape ›	175e	10.11 S	161.19 E
Réchicourt-le-Château	58	48.40 N	6.51 E
Rechlin	54	53.21 N	12.43 E
Rechna Doāb ⋌[1]	123	31.35 N	73.30 E
Rechnitz	61	47.18 N	16.27 E
Rečica, Bela.	76	52.22 N	30.25 E
Rečica, Bela.	78	51.52 N	26.48 E
Recife	250	8.03 S	34.54 W
Recife, Kaap ›	158	34.02 S	25.44 E
Recinto	252	36.48 S	71.44 W
Recke	52	52.22 N	7.43 E
Rečki	78	51.07 N	34.30 E
Recklinghausen	52	51.36 N	7.13 E
Recknitz ≃	54	54.14 N	12.28 E
Recoaro Terme	64	45.42 N	11.13 E
Recogne	56	49.55 N	5.22 E
Recoleta	286e	33.23 S	70.38 W
Recologne	58	47.16 N	5.50 E
Reconquista	252	29.09 S	59.39 W
Reconquista, Río de la ≃	288	34.25 S	58.35 W
Recovery Glacier ⍓	9	81.10 S	28.00 W
Recreio	255	21.32 S	42.28 W
Recreo	252	29.16 S	65.04 W
Rector	194	36.15 N	90.17 W
Rectorville	218	38.34 N	83.39 W
Recuay	248	9.43 S	77.28 W
Recz	30	53.16 N	15.33 E
Red (Hong) (Yuan) ≃, Asia	110	20.17 N	106.34 E
Red ≃, N.A.	178	50.24 N	96.48 W
Red ≃, U.S.	178	31.00 N	91.40 W
Red ≃, U.S.	194	36.32 N	87.22 W
Red ≃, Ky., U.S.	192	37.51 N	84.05 W
Red ≃, N.M., U.S.	200	36.39 N	105.42 W
Red ≃, Wi., U.S.	190	44.49 N	88.38 W
Red, Elm Fork ≃	196	34.53 N	99.19 W
Red, North Fork ≃	196	34.24 N	99.14 W
Red, Prairie Dog Town Fork ≃	196	34.35 N	99.58 W
Red, Salt Fork ≃	196	34.27 N	99.22 W
Red, South Fork ≃	194	36.41 N	86.56 W
Red, West Fork ≃	194	36.32 N	87.21 W
Reda	30	54.37 N	18.21 E
Redang, Pulau I	114	5.47 N	103.00 E
Redange	56	49.46 N	5.54 E
Redang Panjang	114	5.07 N	100.47 E
Red Bank, N.J., U.S.	208	40.20 N	74.03 W
Red Bank, Tn., U.S.	194	35.07 N	85.17 W
Red Bank Battle Monument ⊥	285	39.52 N	75.11 W
Redbank Creek ≃	214	40.58 N	79.33 W
Red Banks	194	34.49 N	89.33 W
Red Bay, Nf., Can.	186	51.44 N	56.25 W
Red Bay, Al., U.S.	194	34.26 N	88.08 W
Redbay, Fl., U.S.	194	30.35 N	85.56 W
Red Bay ⊂	48	55.04 N	6.02 W
Redberry Lake ⊜	184	52.40 N	107.10 W
Redbird	214	41.48 N	81.06 W
Red Bluff	204	40.10 N	122.14 W
Red Bluff Reservoir ⊜[1]	196	31.57 N	103.56 W
Red Boiling Springs	194	36.31 N	85.50 W
Redbourn	42	51.48 N	0.24 W
Redbridge ◆[8]	42	51.34 N	0.05 E
Red Bud	219	38.12 N	89.59 W
Red Canyon ∨	198	43.18 N	103.49 W
Redcar	44	54.37 N	1.04 W
Red Cedar ≃, Mi., U.S.	216	42.43 N	84.33 W
Red Cedar ≃, Wi., U.S.	190	44.42 N	91.53 W
Red Cedar Lake ⊜	190	46.45 N	79.54 W
Red Clay Creek ≃	285	39.43 N	75.39 W
Red Clay Creek, East Branch ≃	285	39.49 N	75.42 W
Red Clay Creek, West Branch ≃	285	39.49 N	75.42 W
Redcliff, Ab., Can.	184	50.05 N	110.47 W
Red Cliff, Co., U.S.	200	39.31 N	106.22 W
Redcliff, Zimb.	154	19.02 S	29.50 E
Redcliffe	171a	27.14 S	153.07 E
Redcliffe, Mount ∧	162	28.25 S	121.32 E
Red Cliff Indian Reservation ◆[4]	190	46.50 N	90.47 W
Red Cliffs	166	34.19 S	142.11 E
Red Cloud	198	40.05 N	98.31 W
Red Creek	210	43.14 N	76.43 W
Red Creek ≃	194	30.41 N	88.40 W
Red Cross Lake ⊜	184	55.05 N	92.55 W
Red Deer	182	52.16 N	113.48 W
Red Deer ≃, Can.	176	50.56 N	109.54 W
Red Deer ≃, Can.	184	52.53 N	101.01 W
Red Deer Creek ≃	196	35.56 N	100.24 W
Red Deer Lake ⊜, Ab., Can.	182	52.43 N	113.02 W
Red Deer Lake ⊜, Mb., Can.	184	52.56 N	101.20 W
Reddersburg	158	29.38 S	26.07 E
Red Devil	180	61.46 N	157.18 W
Red Dial	44	54.48 N	3.10 W
Reddick	216	41.06 N	88.15 W
Redding, Ca., U.S.	204	40.35 N	122.23 W
Redding, Ct., U.S.	207	41.18 N	73.23 W
Redding Ridge	207	41.18 N	73.21 W
Reddish	262	53.26 N	2.09 W
Redditch	42	52.19 N	1.56 W
Rede ≃	44	55.08 N	2.13 W
Redefin	54	53.21 N	11.11 E
Redelinghuys	158	32.30 S	18.33 E
Redenção	250	4.13 S	38.43 W
Redenção da Serra	256	23.16 S	45.33 W
Redesdale ∨	44	55.17 N	2.16 W
Redes Mere ⊜	262	53.15 N	2.14 W
Redeye ≃	198	46.26 N	94.49 W
Redfield, Ia., U.S.	198	41.35 N	94.11 W
Redfield, N.Y., U.S.	212	43.32 N	75.49 W
Redfield, S.D., U.S.	198	44.52 N	98.31 W
Redfish Lake ⊜	202	44.07 N	114.56 W
Redford	196	29.47 N	104.10 W
Redford ◆[8]	281	42.25 N	83.16 W
Redford Township	216	42.25 N	83.16 W
Red Fox Forest	284c	38.49 N	77.15 W
Redhead	241r	10.47 N	60.57 W
Red Hill, Austl.	162	21.59 S	116.03 E
Redhill, Eng., U.K.	42	51.14 N	0.11 W
Red Hill, Ca., U.S.	280	33.45 N	117.48 W
Red Hill, Pa., U.S.	208	40.22 N	75.29 W
Red Hill ∧	172	41.38 S	173.04 E
Redhill Aerodrome ⊠	260	51.12 N	0.07 W
Red Hill Branch ≃	284b	39.14 N	76.51 W
Red Hook	210	41.59 N	73.52 W
Redhouse Creek ≃	284b	39.18 N	76.31 W
Rédics	61	46.36 N	16.30 E
Red Indian Lake ⊜	186	48.40 N	56.50 W
Redinger Lake ⊜[1]	226	37.09 N	119.26 W
Redington Beach	220	27.49 N	82.49 W
Redington Shores	220	27.50 N	82.50 W
Red Island I	186	47.23 N	54.11 W
Redja ≃	76	58.05 N	31.33 E
Redkey	216	40.21 N	85.09 W
Redkino	82	56.38 N	36.17 E
Red Lake, On., Can.	184	51.03 N	93.49 W
Redlake, Mn., U.S.	198	47.53 N	95.01 W
Red Lake ⊜, On., Can.	184	51.01 N	94.05 W

≃ River	Fluß	Río	Rivière	Rio
≊ Canal	Kanal	Canal	Canal	Canal
⌞ Waterfall, Rapids	Wasserfall, Stromschnellen	Cascada, Rápidos	Chute d'eau, Rapides	Cascata, Rápidos
Џ Strait	Meeresstraße	Estrecho	Détroit	Estreito
⊂ Bay, Gulf	Bucht, Golf	Bahía, Golfo	Baie, Golfe	Baía, Golfo
⊜ Lake, Lakes	See, Seen	Lago, Lagos	Lac, Lacs	Lago, Lagos
≡ Swamp	Sumpf	Pantano	Marais	Pântano
⍓ Ice Features, Glacier	Eis- und Gletscherformen	Accidentes Glaciales	Formes glaciaires	Acidentes glaciares
⫪ Other Hydrographic Features	Andere Hydrographische Objekte	Otros Elementos Hidrográficos	Autres données hydrographiques	Outros acidentes hidrográficos

✢ Submarine Features	Untermeerische Objekte	Accidentes Submarinos	Formes de relief sous-marin	Acidentes submarinos
□ Political Unit	Politische Einheit	Unidad Politica	Entité politique	Unidade política
ʋ Cultural Institution	Kulturelle Institution	Institución Cultural	Institution culturelle	Instituição cultural
⊥ Historical Site	Historische Stätte	Sitio Histórico	Site historique	Sitio histórico
♠ Recreational Site	Erholungs- und Ferienort	Sitio de Recreo	Centre de loisirs	Area de Lazer
⊠ Airport	Flughafen	Aeropuerto	Aéroport	Aeroporto
■ Military Installation	Militäranlage	Instalación Militar	Installation militaire	Instalação militar
◆ Miscellaneous	Verschiedenes	Misceláneo	Divers	Diversos

Red Lake ⊜, Az., U.S. 200 35.40 N 114.04 W
Red Lake ⊜, S.D., U.S. 198 43.44 N 99.13 W
Red Lake ⊜[1] 222 31.40 N 95.58 W
Red Lake ≐ 198 47.55 N 97.01 W
Red Lake Falls 198 47.52 N 96.16 W
Red Lake Indian Reservation ◆[4] 198 48.05 N 95.05 W
Red Lake Road 184 49.58 N 93.22 W
Redland, Scot., U.K. 46 59.05 N 3.05 W
Redland, Tx., U.S. 222 31.25 N 94.43 W
Redland Bay 171a 27.37 S 153.18 E
Redlands, S. Afr. 158 29.52 S 22.57 E
Redlands, Ca., U.S. 228 34.01 N 117.12 W
Redlands, Co., U.S. 200 39.04 N 108.38 W
Red Level 194 31.24 N 86.36 W
Red Lick 194 31.47 N 90.58 W
Redlin 54 53.22 N 12.01 E
Red Lion, Pa., U.S. 208 39.54 N 76.36 W
Red Lion, Pa., U.S. 285 39.53 N 75.41 W
Red Lion Airport ⊠ 285 39.54 N 74.45 W
Red Lodge 202 45.11 N 109.14 W
Red Mill 206 46.25 N 72.28 W
Redmond, Or., U.S. 202 44.16 N 121.10 W
Redmond, Ut., U.S. 200 39.00 N 111.51 W
Redmond, Wa., U.S. 224 47.40 N 122.07 W
Red Mountain 228 35.21 N 117.36 W
Red Mountain ∧, Ca., U.S. 204 41.35 N 123.06 W
Red Mountain ∧, Ca., U.S. 228 35.21 N 117.36 W
Red Mountain ∧, Mt., U.S. 202 47.07 N 112.44 W
Red Mountain Pass)(200 37.54 N 107.43 W
Rednitz ≐ 56 49.28 N 10.59 E
Red Oak, Ia., U.S. 198 41.00 N 95.13 W
Red Oak, Ok., U.S. 196 34.57 N 95.04 W
Red Oak, Tx., U.S. 222 32.31 N 96.48 W
Red Oak Creek ≐ 222 32.28 N 96.30 W
Red Oaks Mill 210 41.40 N 73.53 W
Redon 32 47.39 N 2.05 W
Redonda I 238 16.55 N 62.19 W
Redonda, Ilha I 256 23.04 S 43.12 W
Redonda, Isla I 241r 9.52 N 61.35 W
Redonda Islands II 182 50.13 N 124.48 W
Redondela 34 42.17 N 8.36 W
Redondo, Port. 34 38.39 N 7.33 W
Redondo, Wa., U.S. 224 47.20 N 122.19 W
Redondo, Mount ∧ 116 10.21 N 125.38 E
Redondo Beach 228 33.50 N 118.23 W
Redondo Beach State Park ◆ 280 33.50 N 118.24 W
Redoubt, Mount ∧ 224 48.57 N 121.18 W
Redoubt Volcano ∧[1] 180 60.29 N 152.45 W
Red Pass 182 52.59 N 118.59 W
Red Pheasant Indian Reserve ◆[4] 184 52.30 N 108.07 W
Red Pine Lake ⊜ 212 45.12 N 78.42 W
Red Point ➤ 170 34.29 S 150.55 E
Red Rock, B.C., Can. 182 53.39 N 122.41 W
Red Rock, On., Can. 190 48.58 N 88.15 W
Red Rock, Tx., U.S. 222 29.58 N 97.27 W
Red Rock I 282 37.56 N 122.26 W
Red Rock ≐ 202 44.59 N 112.52 W
Red Rock, Lake ⊜[1] 190 41.30 N 93.02 W
Red Rock Canyon State Park ◆ 228 35.23 N 118.00 W
Red Rock Creek ≐ 196 36.36 N 97.03 W
Red Rocks Point ➤ 162 32.13 S 127.32 E
Red Root Creek ≐ 276 40.30 N 74.19 W
Red Run ≐, Md., U.S. 284b 39.24 N 76.47 W
Red Run ≐, Mi., U.S. 281 42.34 N 82.58 W
Redruth 42 50.13 N 5.14 W
Red Sea ⊤[2] 136 20.00 N 38.00 E
Red Springs 192 34.48 N 79.11 W
Redstone 182 52.08 N 123.42 W
Redstone ≐, N.T., Can. 180 64.17 N 124.33 W
Redstone ≐, On., Can. 190 48.27 N 81.03 W
Redstone Arsenal ■ 194 34.38 N 86.38 W
Redstone Creek ≐ 198 44.04 N 98.05 W
Redstone Lake ⊜ 212 45.11 N 78.32 W
Red Sucker ≐ 184 55.19 N 92.31 W
Red Sucker Lake ⊜ 184 54.09 N 93.40 W
Reduction 279b 40.11 N 79.46 W
Redut 80 47.22 N 51.53 E
Redvers 184 49.33 N 101.39 W
Redwater 182 53.57 N 113.06 W
Redwater ≐ 198 48.03 N 105.13 W
Red Wharf Bay C 44 53.18 N 4.10 W
Redwillow ≐ 182 55.04 N 119.21 W
Red Willow Creek ≐ 198 40.13 N 100.29 W
Red Wing 190 44.33 N 92.32 W
Redwood 212 44.18 N 75.48 W
Redwood ≐ 198 44.34 N 95.05 W
Redwood City 226 37.29 N 122.14 W
Redwood Creek ≐, Ca., U.S. 204 41.18 N 124.05 W
Redwood Creek ≐, Ca., U.S. 226 38.18 N 122.18 W
Redwood Creek ≐, Ca., U.S. 282 37.31 N 122.12 W
Redwood Creek ≐, Ca., U.S. 282 37.52 N 122.35 W
Redwood Estates 226 37.10 N 121.59 W
Redwood Falls 198 44.32 N 95.07 W
Redwood National Park ◆ 204 41.30 N 124.05 W
Redwood Point ➤ 282 37.32 N 122.12 W
Redwood Regional Park ◆ 282 37.38 N 122.10 W
Redwood Terrace 282 37.19 N 122.18 W
Redwood Valley 204 39.15 N 123.12 W
Ree, Lough ⊜ 48 53.35 N 8.00 W
Reed City 190 43.52 N 85.30 W
Reeder 198 46.06 N 102.56 W
Reeders 210 41.01 N 75.20 W
Reed Lake ⊜, Mb., Can. 184 54.37 N 100.30 W
Reed Lake ⊜, Sk., Can. 184 50.24 N 107.05 W
Reedley 226 36.35 N 119.26 W
Reedsburg, Oh., U.S. 214 40.49 N 82.07 W
Reedsburg, Wi., U.S. 190 43.31 N 90.00 W
Reeds Peak ∧ 200 33.09 N 107.51 W
Reedsport 202 43.42 N 124.05 W
Reedsville, Pa., U.S. 208 40.39 N 77.35 W
Reedsville, Wi., U.S. 190 44.09 N 87.57 W
Reedurban 214 40.47 N 81.26 W
Reedville 208 37.50 N 76.16 W
Reedy Creek ≐ 220 28.04 N 81.21 W
Reedy Creek Swamp ⊞ 220 28.17 N 81.31 W
Reedy Lake ⊜ 220 27.44 N 81.22 W
Reefton 172 42.07 S 171.52 E
Reelfoot Lake ⊜ 194 36.25 N 89.22 W
Reepham 42 52.46 N 1.07 E
Reersø ➤[1] 41 55.31 N 11.06 E
Rees 52 51.45 N 6.23 E
Reese 190 43.27 N 83.41 W
Reese ≐ 204 40.39 N 116.54 W
Reese Air Force Base ■ 196 33.36 N 102.02 W
Reeseville 190 43.18 N 88.50 W
Reesville 218 39.29 N 83.41 W
Reetz 54 53.11 N 11.52 E
Refaa, Djebel ∧ 34 35.34 N 5.52 E
Refahiye 130 39.54 N 38.46 E
Reform 194 33.22 N 88.00 W
Reforma de Pineda 234 16.24 N 94.28 W
Refton 208 39.57 N 76.14 W
Refuge Cove 182 50.07 N 124.50 W
Refugio 196 28.18 N 97.16 W
Refugio, Isla I 254 43.58 S 73.12 W
Refugio Creek ≐ 282 38.01 N 122.17 W
Rega ≐ 30 54.10 N 15.18 E
Regaïa 34 35.38 N 5.46 W
Regalbuto 70 37.39 N 14.38 E
Regau 64 47.59 N 13.41 E
Regen 60 48.59 N 13.07 E
Regen ≐ 60 49.01 N 12.06 E
Regência 255 19.36 S 39.49 W
Regency Estates 284c 39.03 N 77.10 W
Regeneração 250 6.15 S 42.41 W
Regensburg 60 49.01 N 12.06 E
Regensdorf 58 47.26 N 8.28 E
Regenstauf 60 49.08 N 12.08 E
Regent, Austl. 274b 37.44 S 145.00 E
Regent, N.D., U.S. 198 46.25 N 102.33 W
Regent Park 284c 39.03 N 77.10 W
Regents Park 274a 33.53 S 151.02 E
Regents Park ◆[8] 273d 26.15 S 28.04 E
Regent's Park ◆ 260 51.32 N 0.09 W
Regentville 274a 33.47 S 150.40 E
Reggane 148 26.42 N 0.10 E
Regge ≐ 52 52.31 N 6.22 E
Reggello 66 43.41 N 11.32 E
Reggio di Calabria 68 38.07 N 15.39 E
Reggio di Calabria □[4] 68 38.10 N 16.00 E
Reggiolo 64 44.55 N 10.48 E
Reggio nell'Emilia 64 44.43 N 10.36 E
Reggio nell'Emilia □[4] 64 44.37 N 10.37 E
Reghaïa 60 48.50 N 16.22 E
Reghin 38 46.47 N 24.42 E
Regina, Sk., Can. 184 50.25 N 104.39 W
Régina, Guy. fr. 250 4.19 N 52.08 W
Regina, S. Afr. 158 27.02 S 26.30 E
Regina Beach 184 50.47 N 105.00 W
Regina Elena, Canale ⊼ 266b 45.41 N 8.19 E
Región Metropolitana □[4] 252 33.30 S 70.30 W
Regis-Breitingen 54 51.05 N 12.26 E
Registro 252 24.30 S 47.50 W
Registro do Araguaia 255 15.44 S 51.50 W
Regiwar 120 25.57 N 65.44 E
Regla ◆[8] 286b 23.08 N 82.20 W
Regnéville 32 49.01 N 1.33 W
Regnitz ≐ 56 49.54 N 10.49 E
Rego Park ◆[8] 276 40.44 N 73.52 W
Regozero 24 65.28 N 31.10 E
Regresso, Cachoeira do ⌞ 250 0.58 S 54.51 W
Regstrup 41 55.40 N 11.37 E
Reguengos de Monsaraz 34 38.25 N 7.32 W
Reh 263 51.22 N 7.33 E
Rehau 54 50.15 N 12.02 E
Rehbach ≐ 56 49.27 N 8.27 E
Rehberg 54 52.43 N 12.10 E
Rehberge ∧[2] 264a 52.35 N 13.11 E
Rehberge, Volkspark ◆ 264a 52.33 N 13.20 E
Rehburg 52 52.28 N 9.13 E
Rehden 52 52.37 N 8.29 E
Rehe 56 50.38 N 8.07 E
Rehefeld-Zaunhaus 54 50.43 N 13.42 E
Rehfelde 54 52.30 N 13.54 E
Rehli 124 23.38 N 79.05 E
Rehme 52 52.12 N 8.49 E
Rehna 54 53.47 N 11.03 E
Rehoboth, Namibia 156 17.53 S 15.04 E
Rehoboth, Namibia 156 23.18 S 17.03 E
Rehoboth □[5] 156 23.30 S 17.00 E
Rehoboth Bay C 208 38.40 N 75.06 W
Rehoboth Beach 208 38.43 N 75.04 W
Rehoboth Seamount ◆[3] 16 37.30 N 59.50 W
Réhon 56 49.30 N 5.45 E
Rehovot 132 31.54 N 34.49 E
Rehti 124 22.44 N 77.26 E
Reiche Ebrach ≐ 56 49.49 N 10.58 E
Reiche Liesing ≐ 264b 48.08 N 16.16 E
Reichelsheim 56 49.43 N 8.50 E
Reichenau, Dtsch. 58 47.41 N 9.03 E
Reichenau, Schw. 58 46.49 N 9.24 E
Reichenau an der Rax 61 47.42 N 15.50 E
Reichenbach, Dtsch. 54 50.37 N 12.18 E
Reichenbach, Dtsch. 54 51.08 N 14.48 E
Reichenbach, Schw. 58 46.38 N 7.42 E
Reichenbach → Dzierżoniów 30 50.44 N 16.39 E
Reichenberg → Liberec 30 50.46 N 15.03 E
Reichenhofen 58 47.50 N 9.58 E
Reichensachsen 56 51.09 N 9.59 E
Reichen Spitze ∧ 64 47.09 N 12.07 E
Reichertshausen 60 48.28 N 11.31 E
Reichertsheim 60 48.12 N 12.17 E
Reichertshofen 60 48.40 N 11.28 E
Reichraming 61 47.53 N 14.27 E
Reichsbrücke ◆[5] 264b 48.14 N 16.25 E
Reichshoffen 56 48.56 N 7.40 E
Reid 162 30.49 S 128.26 E
Reid, Mount ∧, Austl. 162 17.58 S 130.38 E
Reid, Mount ∧, Ak., U.S. 182 55.42 N 131.15 W
Reid Lake ⊜[1] 184 50.02 N 108.05 W
Reidsville, Ga., U.S. 192 32.05 N 82.07 W
Reidsville, N.C., U.S. 192 36.21 N 79.39 W
Reiffton 208 40.19 N 75.53 W
Reigate 42 51.14 N 0.13 W
Reigate and Banstead □[8] 260 51.17 N 0.12 W
Reignac-sur-Indre 50 47.13 N 0.55 E
Reignier 58 46.08 N 6.16 E
Reigoldswil 58 47.24 N 7.41 E
Reihoku 92 32.31 N 130.02 E
Reillanne 62 43.53 N 5.40 E
Reims 50 49.15 N 4.02 E
Reims, Montagne de ∧[2] 50 49.08 N 4.00 E
Reina Alejandra → Queen Alexandra Range ∧ 9 84.00 S 168.00 E
Reina Carlota, Estrecho de la → Queen Charlotte Sound ⊔ 182 51.30 N 129.30 W
Reinach, Schw. 58 47.30 N 7.35 E
Reinach, Schw. 58 47.15 N 8.11 E
Reina Fabiola → Queen Fabiola Mountains ∧ 9 71.30 S 35.40 E
Reina Maria, Costa de la → Queen Mary Coast ⊥[2] 9 67.00 S 96.00 E
Reina Maud, Tierras de la → Queen Maud Land ◆[1] 9 72.30 S 12.00 E
Reinbeck 190 42.19 N 92.35 W
Reinbek 52 53.31 N 10.14 E
Reinberg 54 54.12 N 13.15 E
Reindeer ≐ 184 55.36 N 103.11 W
Reindeer Island I 184 52.25 N 98.00 W
Reindeer Lake ⊜ 176 57.15 N 102.40 W
Reindeer Station 180 68.42 N 134.06 W
Reine Charlotte, Détroit de la → Queen Charlotte Sound ⊔ 182 51.30 N 129.30 W
Reinerton 208 40.36 N 76.34 W
Reinfeld 52 53.49 N 10.28 E
Reinga, Cape ➤ 172 34.25 S 172.41 E
Reinhardswald ◆[3] 52 51.30 N 9.30 E
Reinhardtsdorf 54 50.53 N 14.11 E
Reinheim 56 49.49 N 8.50 E
Reinickendorf ◆[8] 264a 52.35 N 13.21 E
Reinosa 34 43.00 N 4.08 W
Reino Unido → United Kingdom □[1] 28 54.00 N 2.00 W
Reinsdorf, Dtsch. 54 50.42 N 12.33 E
Reinsdorf, Dtsch. 54 51.54 N 12.37 E
Reinshagen ◆[8] 263 51.10 N 7.09 E
Reinstorf 54 53.50 N 11.38 E
Reis 130 38.16 N 31.35 E
Reisach 64 46.39 N 13.09 E
Reisaelva ≐ 24 69.48 N 21.00 E
Reischach 60 48.17 N 12.44 E
Reisdorf 56 49.53 N 6.15 E
Reisdorf, Camp ■ 273b 4.21 S 15.15 E
Reisholz ◆[8] 263 51.11 N 6.52 E
Reisjärvi 26 63.37 N 24.54 E
Reiss 46 58.28 N 3.10 W
Reisterstown 208 39.28 N 76.49 W
Reisterstown Road Plaza ◆[9] 284b 39.02 N 76.42 W
Reitano 70 37.58 N 14.20 E
Reitdiep ⊼ 52 53.20 N 6.18 E
Reith bei Seefeld 64 47.18 N 11.12 E
Reit im Winkl 64 47.40 N 12.28 E
Reitz 158 27.53 S 28.31 E
Reitzenhain 54 50.33 N 13.13 E
Reivilo 158 27.36 S 24.08 E
Rejinagar 126 23.53 N 88.15 E
Rejmyra 40 58.50 N 15.55 E
Rejowiec Fabryczny 30 51.08 N 23.13 E
Rejštejn 60 49.09 N 13.31 E
Rekarne 40 59.26 N 16.20 E
Rekarne □[9] 40 59.17 N 16.25 E
Reken 52 51.50 N 7.02 E
Rekjoāti 272b 22.37 N 88.28 E
Reliance, N.T., Can. 176 62.42 N 109.08 W
Reliance, Wy., U.S. 200 41.40 N 109.11 W
Relief Reservoir ⊜[1] 226 38.16 N 119.44 W
Religione, Punta ➤ 70 36.42 N 14.46 E
Reliz Creek ≐ 226 36.19 N 121.18 W
Rellingen 52 53.39 N 9.49 E
Rellinghausen ◆[8] 263 51.25 N 7.04 E
Reloncaví, Seno C 254 41.40 S 72.35 W
Remada 148 32.19 N 10.24 E
Remagen 56 50.34 N 7.13 E
Rémalard 50 48.26 N 0.47 E
Remanso 250 9.37 S 42.07 W
Remarde ≐ 261 48.35 N 2.15 E
Remarkable, Mount ∧ 162 32.48 S 138.10 E
Rembang 115a 6.42 S 111.20 E
Rembau 114 2.35 N 102.06 E
Rembia 114 2.20 N 102.13 E
Remchi 34 35.04 N 1.26 W
Remecó 252 37.38 S 63.39 W
Remedios, Col. 246 7.02 N 74.41 W
Remedios, Cuba 240p 22.30 N 79.33 W
Remedios, Pan. 236 8.14 N 81.51 W
Remedios, Punta ➤ 236 13.31 N 89.49 W
Remedios, Santuario de los ◆[1] 286a 19.28 N 99.15 W
Remedios de Escalada ◆[8] 258 34.43 S 58.23 W
Remels 52 53.18 N 7.44 E
Remennicy 82 56.43 N 36.36 E
Remer 190 47.03 N 93.54 W
Remeshk 128 26.50 N 58.49 E
Remhoogte 158 29.33 S 23.01 E
Remich 56 49.33 N 6.22 E
Remich Airport ⊠ 279b 40.36 N 79.49 W
Rémigny, Lac ⊜ 190 47.51 N 79.12 W
Rémilly 56 49.01 N 6.24 E
Reminderville 214 41.20 N 81.23 W
Remington, In., U.S. 216 40.45 N 87.09 W
Remington, Va., U.S. 188 38.32 N 77.48 W
Rémire 250 4.53 N 52.17 W
Remiremont 58 48.01 N 6.35 E
Remo ⊙[8] 273a 6.42 N 3.29 E
Remolà, Estany del C 266d 41.17 N 2.04 E
Remollon 62 44.28 N 6.10 E
Remontnoje 80 46.33 N 43.39 E
Remoray 58 46.46 N 6.14 E
Remoulins 62 43.56 N 4.34 E
Removka ◆[8] 83 47.59 N 38.43 E
Rempang, Pulau I 114 0.51 N 104.10 E
Remptendorf 54 50.31 N 11.39 E
Rems ≐ 58 48.52 N 9.16 E
Remscheid 56 51.11 N 7.11 E
Remscheider-Stausee ⊜[1] 263 51.10 N 7.14 E
Remsen, Ia., U.S. 198 42.48 N 95.58 W
Remsen, N.Y., U.S. 210 43.19 N 75.11 W
Remsfeld 56 51.00 N 9.29 E
Remuna 126 21.33 N 86.54 E
Remus 190 43.36 N 85.09 W
Rémuzat 62 44.24 N 5.21 E
Rena 26 61.08 N 11.22 E
Renaix → Ronse 50 50.45 N 3.36 E
Renāla Khurd 123 30.53 N 73.36 E
Rena Point ➤ 116 16.10 N 119.45 E
Renard Islands II 164 10.50 S 153.05 E
Renata 182 49.26 N 118.06 W
Renaud Island I 182 55.45 N 9.05 E
Renca 286e 33.24 S 70.44 W
Renca, Cerro ∧ 286e 33.23 S 70.43 W
Renčeni 76 57.44 N 25.26 E
Renchen 58 48.35 N 8.01 E
Rencontre East 186 47.38 N 55.12 W
Rencun 98 36.19 N 113.53 E
Renda, Ityo. 144 14.30 N 39.53 E
Renda, Lat. 76 57.09 N 22.22 E
Rende 68 39.19 N 16.11 E
Rendena, Valle V 58 46.08 N 10.42 E
Rend Lake ⊜[1] 194 38.05 N 88.58 W
Rendova Island I 175e 8.32 S 157.20 E
Rendsburg 52 54.18 N 9.40 E
Renens 58 46.32 N 6.35 E
Renesse 52 51.44 N 3.46 E
Renews 186 46.56 N 52.56 W
Renfrew, On., Can. 212 45.28 N 76.41 W
Renfrew, Scot., U.K. 46 55.53 N 4.24 W
Renfrew, Pa., U.S. 214 40.46 N 79.58 W
Renfrew □[6] 212 45.25 N 77.05 W
Rengam 114 1.53 N 103.24 E
Ren'gang 106 32.01 N 120.50 E
Rengasdengklok 115a 6.09 S 107.17 E
Rengat 112 0.24 S 102.33 E
Rengel 115a 7.04 S 112.06 E
Rengen ⊜ 26 64.05 N 14.03 E
Rengezhuang 105 39.45 N 118.10 E
Rengit 114 1.41 N 103.09 E
Rengkang 112 1.07 N 112.10 E
Rengo 252 34.25 S 70.52 W
Rengsdorf 56 50.30 N 7.29 E
Reng Tlāng ∧ 120 21.59 N 92.36 E
Renhe, Zhg. 100 33.32 N 114.02 E
Renhe, Zhg. 100 27.41 N 115.15 E
Renhechang 107 30.30 N 105.56 E
Renheji 100 31.56 N 115.07 E
Renhua 100 25.06 N 113.44 E
Renhuai 102 27.48 N 106.18 E
Reni 78 45.27 N 28.17 E
Renick 188 37.59 N 80.21 W
Renish Point ➤ 46 57.44 N 6.59 W
Renjiawopeng 104 41.27 N 122.18 E
Renjiaxu 106 30.49 N 121.00 E
Renju 100 24.51 N 115.54 E
Renk 140 11.50 N 32.48 E
Renkiö 26 60.54 N 24.17 E
Renkum 52 51.58 N 5.45 E
Renliuchang 107 29.13 N 106.39 E
Renlong 107 30.32 N 105.47 E
Renmark 166 34.11 S 140.45 E
Renmei 100 25.50 N 117.56 E
Renmin 89 46.37 N 125.32 E
Renna, Monte ∧ 70 36.52 N 14.41 E
Rennau 54 52.17 N 10.55 E
Renne, Lac du → Reindeer Lake ⊜ 176 57.15 N 102.40 W
Rennell, Rivière le ≐ 206 45.41 N 72.39 W
Rennell I 160 11.40 S 160.10 E
Rennell, Islas II 254 52.00 S 74.00 W
Rennell Sound ⊔ 182 53.25 N 132.40 W
Renner 222 32.59 N 96.47 W
Rennerdale 279b 40.24 N 80.08 W
Rennerod 56 50.36 N 8.04 E
Renner Springs 162 18.20 S 133.48 E
Rennertshofen 60 48.45 N 11.02 E
Rennes 32 48.05 N 1.41 W
Rennick Bay C 9 70.18 S 161.45 E
Rennick Glacier ⊓ 9 70.30 S 161.35 E
Rennie 184 49.51 N 95.33 W
Rennie's Mill 271d 22.18 N 114.15 E
Renningen 58 48.46 N 8.56 E
Renntier-See → Reindeer Lake ⊜ 176 57.15 N 102.40 W
Rennweg 64 47.01 N 13.37 E
Reno, Nv., U.S. 226 39.31 N 119.48 W
Reno, Pa., U.S. 214 41.25 N 79.45 W
Reno, Tx., U.S. 222 32.56 N 97.05 W
Reno ≐ 64 44.37 N 12.16 E
Reno Beach 214 41.40 N 83.15 W
Reno Hill ∧ 200 42.35 N 106.03 W
Reno International Airport ⊠ 226 39.30 N 119.46 W
Renoster ≐ 158 31.37 S 20.37 E
Renous 186 46.49 N 65.48 W
Renous ≐ 185 46.50 N 65.50 W
Renovo 214 41.19 N 77.45 W
Renqiao 100 33.27 N 117.16 E
Renqiu 98 38.43 N 116.05 E
Rens 41 54.54 N 9.06 E
Renshan 100 22.50 N 114.48 E
Renshou, Zhg. 100 27.08 N 117.51 E
Renshou, Zhg. 107 30.00 N 104.08 E
Rensjön 24 68.05 N 19.49 E
Rensselaer, In., U.S. 216 40.56 N 87.09 W
Rensselaer, Mo., U.S. 219 39.40 N 91.33 W
Rensselaer, N.Y., U.S. 210 42.38 N 73.44 W
Rensselaer □[6] 210 42.43 N 73.40 W
Rensselaer Falls 212 44.35 N 75.19 W
Rensselaerville 210 42.30 N 74.08 W
Renteria 34 43.19 N 1.54 W
Rentfort ◆[8] 263 51.35 N 6.57 E
Renton 224 47.28 N 122.12 W
Rentuo 107 29.14 N 106.23 E
Rentweinsdorf 56 50.04 N 10.47 E
Renun ≐ 114 3.05 N 97.55 E
Renville 198 44.47 N 95.12 W
Renwez 56 49.50 N 4.36 E
Renwick, N.Z. 172 41.30 S 173.50 E
Renwick, Ia., U.S. 190 42.49 N 93.58 W
Renyichang 107 29.29 N 105.28 E
Renziehausen Park ◆ 279b 40.21 N 79.50 W
Réo, Burkina 150 12.19 N 2.28 W
Reo, Indon. 115b 8.19 S 120.30 E
Reola ◆[8] 272a 28.34 N 76.59 E
Repartimento ≐ 250 6.06 S 50.40 W
Repaupo 285 39.48 N 75.18 W
Repbäcken 40 60.31 N 15.20 E
Répce ≐ 30 47.41 N 17.03 E
Repentigny 206 45.44 N 73.28 W
Repetek 128 38.34 N 63.11 E
Repino 76 60.10 N 29.52 E
Repjovka, Ross. 78 51.05 N 38.39 E
Repjovka, Ross. 80 53.09 N 48.06 E
Repki 78 51.48 N 31.05 E
Repolka 76 59.16 N 29.34 E
Repolovo 86 60.40 N 69.50 E
Reporoa 172 38.26 S 176.21 E
Reposaari 26 61.37 N 21.27 E
Repton 194 31.24 N 87.14 W
Republic, Ks., U.S. 198 39.55 N 97.49 W
Republic, Mi., U.S. 190 46.24 N 87.58 W
Republic, Mo., U.S. 194 37.07 N 93.28 W
Republic, Oh., U.S. 214 41.07 N 83.00 W
Republic, Wa., U.S. 202 48.38 N 118.44 W
República Centroafricana → Central African Republic □[1] 136 7.00 N 21.00 E
Republic Airport ⊠ 276 40.44 N 73.25 W
Republican ≐ 198 39.03 N 96.48 W
Republican, North Fork ≐ 198 40.01 N 101.59 W
Republican, South Fork ≐ 198 40.03 N 101.31 W
Republic Observatory ◆[3] 273d 26.11 S 28.05 E
Republic Steel Corporation ◆[3] 279a 41.28 N 81.40 W
République centrafricaine → Central African Republic □[1] 136 7.00 N 21.00 E
Repueblo de Oriente 196 25.51 N 99.39 W
Repulse Bay 176 66.32 N 86.15 W
Repulse Bay C 166 20.36 S 148.43 E
Repvåg 24 70.45 N 25.41 E
Requena, Esp. 34 39.29 N 1.06 W
Requena, Perú 248 4.58 S 73.50 W
Réquista 32 44.02 N 2.32 E
Rère ≐ 50 47.22 N 1.50 E
Reriutaba 250 4.10 S 40.35 W
Reşadiye 130 40.24 N 37.21 E
Reşadiye ◆[8] 267b 41.05 N 29.15 E
Reşadiye Yarımadası ➤[1] 130 36.40 N 27.45 E
Resang, Tanjong ➤ 114 2.35 N 103.51 E
Resarö 40 59.26 N 18.20 E
Rescalda 266b 45.38 N 8.56 E
Rescaldina 266b 45.37 N 8.57 E
Reschenpass (Passo di Resia))(64 46.50 N 10.30 E
Reschenscheideck)(64 46.51 N 10.31 E
Rescue 208 36.59 N 76.33 W
Research 274b 37.42 S 145.11 E
Reseda ◆[8] 280 34.12 N 118.31 W
Resen 38 41.05 N 21.00 E
Resende 256 22.28 S 44.27 W
Reserva 252 24.38 S 50.52 W
Reserva, Parque de la ◆ 286d 12.04 S 77.02 W
Reserve, La., U.S. 194 30.03 N 90.33 W
Reserve, N.M., U.S. 200 33.42 N 108.45 W
Reserve Township 279b 40.29 N 79.59 W
Reservoir 274b 37.43 S 145.00 E
Reservoir Pond ⊜ 283 42.10 N 71.07 W
Rešetilovka 78 49.34 N 34.04 E
Rešetnikovo 82 56.27 N 36.34 E
Reshui 98 42.09 N 119.18 E
Reshuitang 102 24.10 N 103.09 E
Resia, Passo di (Reschenpass))(64 46.50 N 10.30 E
Resipol, Beinn ∧ 46 56.43 N 5.39 W
Resistencia 252 27.27 S 58.59 W
Reşita 38 45.17 N 21.53 E
Resiutta 64 46.23 N 13.13 E
Resko 30 53.47 N 15.25 E
Rešma 82 57.24 N 42.34 E
Rešn'ovka 78 49.47 N 27.25 E
Resolute 176 74.41 N 94.54 W
Resolution Island I, N.T., Can. 176 61.30 N 65.00 W
Resolution Island I, N.Z. 172 45.40 S 166.40 E
Resolven 42 51.42 N 3.42 W
Resort, Loch C 46 58.03 N 7.06 W
Rešoty 76 57.09 N 28.30 E
Resplendes 255 6.17 S 45.13 W
Resplendor 255 19.20 S 41.15 W
Ressa ≐ 76 54.45 N 35.10 E
Ressaca, Ribeirão da ≐ 287b 23.38 S 46.51 W
Resse ◆[8] 263 51.34 N 7.07 E
Resseta ≐ 76 53.49 N 35.15 E
Ressons-sur-Matz 50 49.33 N 2.45 E
Resta ≐ 76 53.30 N 30.56 E
Resthaven 216 41.16 N 88.09 W
Restigouche (Ristigouche) ≐ 186 48.04 N 66.20 W
Restin, Punta ➤ 246 4.17 S 81.15 W
Restinga 34 35.42 N 5.23 W
Restinga Seca 252 29.49 S 53.23 W
Reston, Mb., Can. 184 49.35 N 101.02 W
Reston, Scot., U.K. 46 55.51 N 2.11 W

ENGLISH: Name · Page · Lat.°′ · Long.°′ — DEUTSCH: Name · Seite · Breite°′ · Länge°′ E = Ost

Reston, Va., U.S. 208 38.58 N 77.20 W
Restoule Lake ⊜ 190 46.03 N 79.47 W
Restrepo, Col. 246 4.15 N 73.33 W
Restrepo, Col. 246 3.48 N 76.31 W
Resuttano 70 37.41 N 14.02 E
Retalhuleu 236 14.32 N 91.41 W
Retalhuleu □[5] 236 14.20 N 91.50 W
Retamosa 252 33.35 S 54.44 W
Retem, Oued er V 148 33.30 N 5.45 E
Řetenice 54 50.38 N 13.46 E
Retezat, Parcul Naţional ◆ 38 45.20 N 22.50 E
Retezatului, Munţii ∧ 38 45.25 N 23.00 E
Rethel 50 49.31 N 4.22 E
Rethem 52 52.45 N 9.23 E
Réthimnon 38 35.22 N 24.29 E
Retiche, Alpi → Rhaetian Alps ∧ 58 46.30 N 10.00 E
Retie 56 51.16 N 5.04 E
Retiers 28 47.55 N 1.23 W
Retiro, Estacion ◆[5] 288 34.36 S 58.22 W
Retiro, Parque del ◆ 266a 40.25 N 3.41 W
Retournac 62 45.12 N 4.02 E
Retreat 222 32.03 N 96.29 W
Retreat ≐ 170 34.07 S 149.38 E
Retsof 210 42.50 N 77.53 W
Rettenberg 58 47.35 N 10.17 E
Rettendon 260 51.39 N 0.33 E
Rettendon Place 260 51.38 N 0.34 E
Rettichovka 89 44.10 N 132.47 E
Rettin 54 54.06 N 10.53 E
Return Creek ≐ 226 37.56 N 119.28 W
Retz 61 48.45 N 15.57 E
Retzow 54 52.37 N 12.41 E
Reuden 54 52.04 N 12.18 E
Reungeut 114 4.34 N 96.22 E
Reunion (Réunion) □[2], Afr. 138 21.06 S 55.36 E
Reunion (Réunion) □[2], Afr. 157c 21.06 S 55.36 E
Reus 34 41.09 N 1.07 E
Reuschenberg 263 51.10 N 6.42 E
Reusel 52 51.21 N 5.22 E
Reusrath 263 51.06 N 6.57 E
Reuss ≐ 58 47.28 N 8.14 E
Reut ≐ 78 47.15 N 29.09 E
Reuterstadt Stavenhagen 54 53.42 N 12.53 E
Reutlingen 58 48.29 N 9.11 E
Reutov 82 55.46 N 37.52 E
Reutte 58 47.29 N 10.43 E
Reuver 52 51.17 N 6.05 E
Revadim 132 31.46 N 34.48 E
Rev'akino 82 54.22 N 37.40 E
Reval → Tallinn 76 59.25 N 24.45 E
Revda, Ross. 24 67.58 N 34.32 E
Revda, Ross. 86 56.48 N 59.57 E
Réveillon, Ruisseau le ≐ 261 48.42 N 2.30 E
Revel 62 45.11 N 5.52 E
Revelganj 124 25.47 N 84.40 E
Revelstoke 182 50.59 N 118.12 W
Reventazón 248 6.10 S 80.58 W
Reventazón ≐ 236 10.17 N 83.24 W
Revere, It. 64 45.03 N 11.08 E
Revere, Ma., U.S. 207 42.24 N 71.00 W
Revere, Pa., U.S. 208 40.31 N 75.10 W
Revere Beach ⊥[2] 283 42.25 N 70.59 W
Revermont ∧[2] 58 46.27 N 5.25 E
Revesby 274a 33.57 S 151.01 E
Revest-du-Bion 62 44.05 N 5.33 E
Révia 154 13.23 S 36.31 E
Reviga 38 44.42 N 27.06 E
Revigny-sur-Ornain 56 48.50 N 4.59 E
Revilla del Campo 34 42.13 N 3.32 W
Revillagigedo, Islas II 232 19.00 N 111.30 W
Revillagigedo Channel ⊔ 182 55.10 N 131.13 W
Revillagigedo Island I 182 55.35 N 131.23 W
Revillo 198 45.01 N 96.34 W
Revin 56 49.56 N 4.38 E
Revloc 214 40.29 N 78.45 W
Řevničov 54 50.08 N 13.45 E
Revò 64 46.23 N 11.03 E
Revol'ucii, pik ∧ 85 38.31 N 72.21 E
Revolución Mexicana 234 16.03 N 93.04 W
Revolution, Museum of the ◆ 265b 55.46 N 37.36 E
Revsundssjön ⊜ 26 62.49 N 15.17 E
Revúboè ≐ 154 16.13 S 33.37 E
Revuè ≐ 156 19.49 S 34.00 E
Rew 214 41.54 N 78.32 W
Rewa 124 24.32 N 81.18 E
Rewa ≐ 246 3.53 N 58.45 W
Rewāri 124 28.11 N 76.37 E
Rewataya, Taka ➤[2] 112 6.05 S 118.55 E
Rex, Mount ∧ 9 74.57 S 76.00 W
Rexburg 202 43.49 N 111.47 W
Rexdale ◆[8] 275b 43.43 N 79.35 W
Rexford, Ks., U.S. 198 39.28 N 100.44 W
Rexford, Mt., U.S. 202 48.52 N 115.13 W
Rexford, N.Y., U.S. 210 42.51 N 73.52 W
Rexhame 283 42.06 N 70.40 W
Rexton 186 46.39 N 64.52 W
Rexton 190 46.11 N 85.14 W
Rexville, In., U.S. 218 41.31 N 87.21 W
Rexville, N.Y., U.S. 210 42.05 N 77.40 W
Rey, Arroyo del ≐ 258 34.46 S 58.27 W
Rey, Embalse del ⊜[1] 266a 40.18 N 3.32 W
Rey, Estrecho del → King Sound ⊔ 162 17.00 S 123.30 E
Rey, Isla del I 246 8.22 N 78.55 W
Rey, Laguna del ⊜ 196 27.01 N 103.26 W
Rey Bouba 146 8.40 N 14.11 E
Reyes 248 14.19 S 67.23 W
Reyes, Point ➤ 204 38.00 N 123.01 W
Reyes Peak ∧ 228 34.38 N 119.17 W
Reyhanlı 130 36.18 N 36.32 E
Rey Jorge, Estrecho → King George Sound ⊔ 162 35.03 S 117.57 E
Rey Jorge, Isla → King George Island I 9 62.00 S 58.15 W
Reykjahlíð 24a 65.39 N 16.55 W
Reykjanes ➤ 24a 63.49 N 22.43 W
Reykjanes Ridge ◆[3] 10 62.00 N 27.00 W
Reykjavík 24a 64.09 N 21.51 W
Reynella 168b 35.06 S 138.32 E
Reyno 194 36.21 N 90.45 W
Reynolds, Ga., U.S. 192 32.33 N 84.05 W
Reynolds, In., U.S. 216 40.44 N 86.52 W
Reynolds, N.D., U.S. 198 47.40 N 97.06 W
Reynolds Channel ⊔ 276 40.36 N 73.40 W
Reynolds Creek ≐, Austl. 171a 27.56 S 152.36 E
Reynolds Creek ≐, On., Can. 212 43.00 N 80.58 W
Reynoldsville 214 41.05 N 78.53 W
Reynosa 232 26.07 N 98.18 W
Reyssouze ≐ 58 46.27 N 4.54 E
Rež 86 57.23 N 61.24 E
Rež ≐ 86 57.54 N 62.18 E
Reza, gora (Küh-e Rīzeh) ∧ 128 37.47 N 58.05 E
Rezé 32 47.12 N 1.34 W
Rēzekne 76 56.30 N 27.19 E
Rēzekne ≐ 76 56.46 N 26.58 E
Rezeny 78 46.46 N 28.54 E
Rezina 78 47.44 N 28.58 E
Rezino 86 55.51 N 75.18 E
Rēznas ezers ⊜ 76 56.20 N 27.27 E
Rezovo 38 41.59 N 28.02 E
Rezovska (Mutlu) ≐ 130 41.59 N 28.01 E
Rezvānshahr 128 37.33 N 49.09 E
Rezzato 64 45.31 N 10.19 E
Rezzoaglio 62 44.32 N 9.23 E
Rezzonico 58 46.04 N 9.16 E
Rhade 52 53.19 N 9.07 E
Rhadeswood Reservoir ⊜[1] 262 53.29 N 1.56 W
Rhaetian Alps (Rätische Alpen) (Alpi Retiche) ∧ 58 46.30 N 10.00 E
Rhallamane, Sebkha de ⊻ 148 23.41 N 9.50 W
Rhame 198 46.13 N 103.39 W
Rharbi, Île I 148 34.39 N 11.03 E
Rharbi, Zahrez ⊜ 148 34.50 N 2.50 E
Rhauderfehn 52 53.08 N 7.35 E
Rhaunen 56 49.52 N 7.20 E
Rhayader 42 52.18 N 3.30 W
Rhea Creek ≐ 202 45.30 N 119.46 W
Rheda-Wiedenbrück 52 51.50 N 8.18 E
Rhede, Dtsch. 52 53.03 N 7.16 E
Rhede, Dtsch. 52 51.50 N 6.11 E
Rheden 52 52.01 N 6.02 E
Rheems 208 40.08 N 76.34 W
Rheem Valley 226 37.52 N 122.07 W
Rheidol ≐ 42 52.25 N 4.05 W
Rheims → Reims 50 49.15 N 4.02 E
Rhein 184 51.22 N 102.10 W
Rheinau 56 48.41 N 7.56 E
Rheinbach 56 50.37 N 6.57 E
Rheinberg 52 51.33 N 6.35 E
Rheinböllen 56 50.00 N 7.40 E
Rheinbrohl 56 50.30 N 7.19 E
Rheinbrücke ◆[5] 263 51.12 N 6.44 E
Rheindürkheim 56 49.42 N 8.21 E
Rheine 52 52.17 N 7.26 E
Rheineck 58 47.28 N 9.35 E
Rheinen 263 51.27 N 7.38 E
Rheinfall ⌞ 58 47.41 N 8.38 E
Rheinfelden, Dtsch. 58 47.33 N 7.47 E
Rheinfelden, Schw. 58 47.33 N 7.48 E
Rheinhausen 56 51.24 N 6.44 E
Rhein-Herne-Kanal ⊼ 263 51.27 N 6.47 E
Rheinhessen □[5] 56 49.40 N 8.40 E
Rheinkamp 52 51.30 N 6.37 E
Rheinland-Pfalz □[3] 56 50.00 N 7.00 E
Rhein → Rhine ≐ 30 51.52 N 6.02 E
Rheinsberg 54 53.06 N 12.53 E
Rheinstadion ◆ 263 51.16 N 6.44 E
Rheinstein, Burg ɪ 56 50.00 N 7.50 E
Rheinwald V 58 46.32 N 9.17 E
Rheinwaldhorn ∧ 58 46.30 N 9.02 E
Rheirs, Oued V 148 30.39 N 4.26 W
Rhêmes-Notre-Dame 62 45.34 N 7.07 E
Rhenen 52 51.57 N 5.34 E
Rhens 56 50.17 N 7.37 E
Rheurdt 263 51.27 N 6.28 E
Rheydt 56 51.10 N 6.27 E
Rheydt, Schloss ɪ 263 51.11 N 6.29 E
Rhin ≐ 54 52.59 N 12.55 E
Rhinau 58 48.19 N 7.42 E
Rhine 192 31.59 N 83.12 W
Rhine (Rhein) (Rhin) ≐ 30 51.52 N 6.02 E
Rhinebeck 210 41.55 N 73.54 W
Rhinecliff 210 41.55 N 73.57 W
Rhineland 219 38.43 N 91.31 W
Rhinelander 190 45.38 N 89.24 W
Rhin Kanal ⊼ 54 52.47 N 12.24 E
Rhinluch ⊞ 54 52.50 N 12.50 E
Rhinns of Kells ∧ 44 55.07 N 4.22 W
Rhinns Point ➤ 46 55.40 N 6.30 W
Rhino Camp 154 2.58 N 31.24 E
Rhinow 54 52.45 N 12.20 E
Rhin → Rhine ≐ 30 51.52 N 6.02 E
Rhiou, Oued ≐ 34 36.00 N 0.55 E
Rhir, Cap ➤ 148 30.38 N 9.55 W
Rhis, Oued ≐ 34 35.14 N 3.57 W
Rhiw ≐ 42 52.36 N 3.11 W
Rho 62 45.32 N 9.02 E
Rhode Island □[3], U.S. 178 41.40 N 71.30 W
Rhode Island □[3], U.S. 207 41.40 N 71.30 W
Rhode Island I 207 41.33 N 71.15 W
Rhode Island Sound ⊔ 207 41.25 N 71.15 W
Rhoden 52 51.28 N 9.00 E
Rhodes, Austl. 274a 33.50 S 151.05 E
Rhodes, S. Afr. 158 30.47 S 27.59 E
Rhodes, Eng., U.K. 262 53.33 N 2.14 W
Rhodesia → Zimbabwe □[1] 154 20.00 S 30.00 E
Rhodes Inyanga National Park ◆ 154 18.12 S 32.45 E
Rhodes Matopos National Park ◆ 154 20.33 S 28.20 E
Rhodes Park ◆ 273d 26.12 S 28.06 E
Rhodes Peak ∧ 202 46.41 N 114.47 W
Rhodes → Ródhos 38 36.26 N 28.13 E
Rhodes → Ródhos I 38 36.10 N 28.00 E
Rhodes' Tomb ɪ 154 20.30 S 28.30 E
Rhododendron 224 45.20 N 121.55 W
Rhododendron State Park ◆ 207 42.47 N 72.12 W
Rhodon 261 48.43 N 2.04 E
Rhodon, Ruisseau le ≐ 261 48.42 N 2.04 E
Rhodope Mountains ∧ 38 41.30 N 24.30 E
Rhodt 56 49.16 N 8.07 E
Rhome 222 33.03 N 97.28 W
Rhondda 42 51.40 N 3.27 W
Rhône □[5] 32 45.55 N 4.40 E
Rhône ≐ 32 43.20 N 4.50 E
Rhône à Sète, Canal du ⊼ 62 43.25 N 3.42 E
Rhône au Rhin, Canal du ⊼ 58 47.06 N 5.19 E
Rhoose 42 51.24 N 3.20 W
Rhosesmor 262 53.12 N 3.10 W
Rhosllanerchrugog 44 53.00 N 3.03 W
Rhosneigr 44 53.14 N 4.31 W
Rhos-on-Sea 44 53.19 N 3.45 W
Rhossili 42 51.34 N 4.17 W
Rhourde-El-Baguel 148 31.24 N 6.57 E
Rhuddlan 44 53.18 N 3.27 W
Rhue ≐ 32 45.23 N 2.29 E
Rhum I 46 57.00 N 6.20 W
Rhum, Sound of ⊔ 46 56.56 N 6.14 W
Rhyl 44 53.19 N 3.29 W
Rhymney 42 51.46 N 3.18 W
Rhymney ≐ 42 51.28 N 3.10 W
Rhynie 46 57.19 N 2.50 W
Riaba 152 3.23 N 8.46 E
Riace 68 38.25 N 16.29 E
Riachão 250 7.22 S 46.37 W
Riachão do Dantas 250 11.04 S 37.44 W
Riachão do Jacuípe 250 11.48 S 39.21 W
Riacho de Santana 255 13.37 S 42.57 W
Riacho Grande 256 23.48 S 46.35 W
Riachos, Islas de los II 254 40.10 S 62.08 W
Riachuelo, Bra. 250 10.44 S 37.11 W
Riachuelo, Chile 254 40.49 S 73.21 W
Riachuelo, Ur. 258 34.28 S 57.43 W
Riachuelo ≐ 288 34.38 S 58.22 W
Riachuelo, Arroyo ≐ 258 34.27 S 57.44 W
Rialma 255 15.18 S 49.34 W
Rialto, Bra. 256 22.35 S 44.16 W
Rialto, Ca., U.S. 228 34.06 N 117.22 W
Riamkanan, Waduk ⊜[1] 112 3.30 S 115.05 E
Rianápolis 255 15.29 S 49.28 W
Riang 120 27.32 N 92.56 E
Riangnom 140 9.55 N 30.01 E
Riaño 34 42.58 N 5.01 W
Rians 62 43.37 N 5.45 E
Riánsares ≐ 34 39.32 N 3.18 W
Riāsi 123 33.05 N 74.50 E
Riau □[4] 112 1.00 N 102.00 E
Riau, Kepulauan II 114 1.00 N 104.30 E
Riaz 58 46.38 N 7.04 E

Symbols in the index entries represent the broad categories identified in the key at the right. Symbols with superior numbers (∧[1]) identify subcategories (see complete key on page I · 1).

Symbole im Register stellen die rechts im Schlüssel erklärten Kategorien dar. Symbole mit hochgestellten Ziffern (∧[1]) bezeichnen Unterabteilungen einer Kategorie (vgl. vollständiger Schlüssel auf Seite I · 1).

Los símbolos incluidos en el texto del índice representan las grandes categorías identificadas con la clave a la derecha. Los símbolos con números en su parte superior (∧[1]) identifican las subcategorías (véase la clave completa en la página I · 1).

Les symboles de l'index représentent les catégories indiquées dans la légende à droite. Les symboles suivis d'un indice (∧[1]) représentent des sous-catégories (voir légende complète à la page I · 1).

Os símbolos incluídos no texto do índice representam as grandes categorias identificadas com a chave à direita. Os símbolos com números em sua parte superior (∧[1]) identificam as subcategorias (veja-se a chave completa à página I · 1).

English	Deutsch	Español	Français	Português
∧ Mountain	Berg	Montaña	Montagne	Montanha
∧ Mountains	Gebirge	Montañas	Montagnes	Montanhas
)(Pass	Paß	Paso	Col	Passo
V Valley, Canyon	Tal, Cañon	Valle, Cañón	Vallée, Canyon	Vale, Canhão
⊻ Plain	Ebene	Llano	Plaine	Planície
➤ Cape	Kap	Cabo	Cap	Cabo
I Island	Insel	Isla	Île	Ilha
II Islands	Inseln	Islas	Îles	Ilhas
◆ Other Topographic Features	Andere Topographische Objekte	Otros Elementos Topográficos	Autres données topographiques	Outros acidentes topográficos

ESPAÑOL: Nombre | Página | Lat.°′ | Long.°′ W = Oeste
FRANÇAIS: Nom | Page | Lat.°′ | Long.°′ W = Ouest
PORTUGUÊS: Nome | Página | Lat.°′ | Long.°′ W = Oeste

Nombre / Nom / Nome	Página / Page	Lat.°′	Long.°′
Riaza	34	41.17 N	3.28 W
Riaza ≃	34	41.42 N	3.55 W
Ribadavia	34	42.17 N	8.08 W
Ribadeo	34	43.32 N	7.02 W
Ribadesella	34	43.28 N	5.04 W
Ribas de Jarama	266a	40.23 N	3.31 W
Ribas do Rio Pardo	255	20.27 S	53.46 W
Ribauè	154	14.57 S	38.17 E
Ribble ≃	44	53.44 N	2.50 W
Ribbleton	262	53.46 N	2.40 W
Ribble Valley □[8]	262	53.48 N	2.31 W
Ribbon Fall ∟	226	37.44 N	119.39 W
Ribchester	262	53.49 N	2.32 W
Ribe	41	55.21 N	8.46 E
Ribe □[6]	41	55.35 N	8.50 E
Ribe Å ≃	41	55.21 N	8.40 E
Ribeauvillé	58	48.12 N	7.19 E
Ribécourt	50	49.31 N	2.55 E
Ribeira	252	24.40 S	49.01 W
Ribeira do Iguape ≃	252	24.40 S	47.24 W
Ribeira do Pombal	250	10.50 S	38.32 W
Ribeira Grande, C.V.	150a	17.11 N	25.04 W
Ribeira Grande, Port.	148a	37.49 N	25.31 W
Ribeirão	250	8.31 S	35.23 W
Ribeirão das Lajes, Represa do ⊜[1]	256	22.45 S	43.55 W
Ribeirão de São Joaquim	256	22.17 S	44.11 W
Ribeirão do Pinhal	255	23.24 S	50.18 W
Ribeirão Pires	256	23.43 S	46.25 W
Ribeirão Preto	255	21.10 S	47.48 W
Ribeirao Vermelho	255	21.11 S	45.03 W
Ribeirãozinho	255	16.27 S	52.35 W
Ribeiro Gonçalves	250	7.32 S	45.14 W
Ribeiro Junqueira	256	21.28 S	42.31 W
Ribeiros	256	21.59 S	45.35 W
Ribemont	50	49.48 N	3.28 E
Ribera	70	37.30 N	13.16 E
Ribérac	32	45.15 N	0.20 E
Riberalta	248	10.59 S	66.06 W
Riberão Pires □[7]	287b	23.43 S	46.21 W
Ribiers	62	44.14 N	5.52 E
Rib Lake	190	45.19 N	90.12 W
Ribnica, Slo.	36	45.44 N	14.44 E
Ribnica, Slo.	61	46.32 N	15.16 E
Ribnitz-Damgarten	54	54.15 N	12.28 E
Ribstone Creek ≃	184	52.51 N	110.05 W
Ricadi	68	38.37 N	15.52 E
Ricarda, Estany de la ⊂	266d	41.18 N	2.07 E
Ricardo Flores Magón	232	29.58 N	106.58 W
Ricaurte	246	1.13 N	77.59 W
Riccall	44	53.50 N	1.04 W
Riccarton	172	43.32 S	172.36 E
Riccia	66	41.29 N	14.50 E
Riccione	66	43.59 N	12.39 E
Rice	222	32.15 N	96.30 W
Rice Creek ≃	216	42.16 N	84.57 W
Rice Lake	190	45.30 N	91.44 W
Rice Lake ⊜, On., Can.	190	47.42 N	82.08 W
Rice Lake ⊜, On., Can.	212	44.08 N	78.13 W
Rice Lake Indian Reserve ➜[4]	212	44.10 N	78.12 W
Riceville, Ia., U.S.	190	43.22 N	92.33 W
Riceville, Pa., U.S.	214	41.47 N	79.48 W
Riceville, Tn., U.S.	192	35.23 N	84.41 W
Rich, Cape ≻	212	44.43 N	80.38 W
Richan	184	49.59 N	92.49 W
Richard B. Russell Lake ⊜[1]	192	34.05 N	82.39 W
Richard Collinson Inlet ⊂	176	72.45 N	113.45 W
Richards	222	30.32 N	95.51 W
Richard's Bay	158	28.47 S	32.06 E
Richard's Bay ⊂	158	28.50 S	32.02 E
Richards-Gebaur Air Force Base ■	194	38.51 N	94.33 W
Richard's Harbour	186	47.37 N	56.24 W
Richards Island I	180	69.20 N	134.30 W
Richardson	222	32.56 N	96.43 W
Richardson ≃	176	58.30 N	111.30 W
Richardson, Mount ∧	162	28.49 S	119.59 E
Richardson Bay ⊂	282	37.52 N	122.29 W
Richardson Mountains ⋏, Can.	180	67.15 N	136.30 W
Richardson Mountains ⋏, N.Z.	172	44.45 S	168.31 E
Richardson Park	285	39.44 N	75.35 W
Richardsville	214	41.14 N	79.01 W
Richard-Toll	150	16.28 N	15.41 W
Richardton	198	46.53 N	102.18 W
Rîchât, Guelb er ∧[2]	148	21.07 N	11.24 W
Richboro	208	40.13 N	75.01 W
Richburg	210	42.05 N	78.09 W
Riche, Pointe ≻	186	50.42 N	57.25 W
Richebourg	261	48.49 N	1.38 E
Richelieu, P.Q., Can.	206	45.27 N	73.15 W
Richelieu, Fr.	32	47.01 N	0.19 E
Richelieu □[6]	206	45.55 N	73.00 W
Richelieu ≃	206	46.03 N	73.07 W
Richer	184	49.39 N	96.28 W
Richey	198	47.38 N	105.04 W
Richfield, Id., U.S.	202	43.02 N	114.09 W
Richfield, Mn., U.S.	190	44.53 N	93.16 W
Richfield, Oh., U.S.	214	41.14 N	81.39 W
Richfield, Pa., U.S.	208	40.41 N	77.07 W
Richfield, Ut,. U.S.	200	38.46 N	112.05 W
Richfield Springs	210	42.51 N	74.59 W
Richford, N.Y., U.S.	210	42.21 N	76.12 W
Richford, Vt., U.S.	206	44.59 N	72.40 W
Rich Fountain	219	38.24 N	91.53 W
Richgrove	226	35.48 N	119.07 W
Richhill, N. Ire., U.K.	48	54.23 N	6.33 W
Rich Hill, Mo., U.S.	194	38.05 N	94.12 W
Richibucto	186	46.41 N	64.52 W
Richisau	58	47.02 N	8.54 E
Richland, Ga., U.S.	192	32.05 N	84.40 W
Richland, Mi., U.S.	216	42.22 N	85.27 W
Richland, Mo., U.S.	194	37.51 N	92.24 W
Richland, N.J., U.S.	208	39.29 N	74.52 W
Richland, N.Y., U.S.	212	43.34 N	76.03 W
Richland, Pa., U.S.	208	40.21 N	76.16 W
Richland, Tx., U.S.	222	31.56 N	96.26 W
Richland, Tx., U.S.	222	32.57 N	95.49 W
Richland, Wa., U.S.	202	46.17 N	119.17 W
Richland □[6]	214	40.46 N	82.31 W
Richland Center	190	43.20 N	90.23 W
Richland Creek ≃, Il., U.S.	219	38.14 N	89.54 W
Richland Creek ≃, Tn., U.S.	194	35.02 N	86.55 W
Richland Creek ≃, Tx., U.S.	222	31.58 N	96.03 W
Richlands, N.C., U.S.	192	34.53 N	77.32 W
Richlands, Va., U.S.	192	37.05 N	81.47 W
Richland Springs	196	31.16 N	98.57 W
Richmond, Austl.	166	20.44 S	143.08 E
Richmond, Austl.	170	33.36 S	150.46 E
Richmond, Austl.	274b	37.49 S	145.00 E
Richmond, B.C., Can.	224	49.09 N	123.06 W
Richmond, On., Can.	212	45.11 N	75.50 W
Richmond, P.Q., Can.	206	45.40 N	72.09 W
Richmond, N.Z.	172	41.20 S	173.11 E
Richmond, S. Afr.	158	31.23 S	23.56 E
Richmond, S. Afr.	158	29.54 S	30.08 E
Richmond, Eng., U.K.	44	54.24 N	1.44 W
Richmond, Ca., U.S.	226	37.56 N	122.20 W
Richmond, Il., U.S.	216	42.28 N	88.18 W
Richmond, In., U.S.	218	39.49 N	84.53 W
Richmond, Ks., U.S.	198	38.24 N	95.15 W
Richmond, Ky., U.S.	192	37.44 N	84.17 W
Richmond, Me., U.S.	188	44.05 N	69.47 W
Richmond, Ma., U.S.	207	42.22 N	73.22 W
Richmond, Mi., U.S.	214	42.48 N	82.45 W
Richmond, Mn., U.S.	190	45.27 N	94.31 W
Richmond, Mo., U.S.	194	39.16 N	93.58 W
Richmond, Oh., U.S.	214	40.26 N	80.46 W
Richmond, Tx., U.S.	222	29.34 N	95.45 W
Richmond, Ut,. U.S.	200	41.55 N	111.48 W
Richmond, Vt., U.S.	188	44.24 N	72.59 W
Richmond, Va., U.S.	208	37.33 N	77.27 W
Richmond □[6], P.Q., Can.	206	45.40 N	72.00 W
Richmond □[6], N.Y., U.S.	210	40.38 N	74.05 W
Richmond □[6], Va., U.S.	208	37.32 N	77.28 W
Richmond ➜[8], Eng., U.K.	42	51.28 N	0.18 W
Richmond ➜[8], Ca., U.S.	282	37.46 N	122.29 W
Richmond ➜[8], Pa., U.S.	285	39.59 N	75.06 W
Richmond, Mount ∧	172	41.29 S	173.24 E
Richmond, Point ≻	282	37.55 N	122.23 W
Richmond Beach	224	47.46 N	122.23 W
Richmond Creek ≃	276	40.34 N	74.11 W
Richmond Heights, Fl., U.S.	220	25.37 N	80.22 W
Richmond Heights, Mo., U.S.	219	38.37 N	90.19 W
Richmond Heights, Oh., U.S.	214	41.33 N	81.30 W
Richmond Highlands	224	47.45 N	122.20 W
Richmond Hill, On., Can.	212	43.52 N	79.27 W
Richmond Hill, Ga., U.S.	192	31.56 N	81.18 W
Richmond Hill ➜[8]	276	40.42 N	73.49 W
Richmond International Airport ⊠	208	37.30 N	77.19 W
Richmond Mall ➜[9]	279a	41.32 N	81.30 W
Richmond National Battlefield Park ♦	208	37.25 N	77.23 W
Richmond Park ♦	260	51.26 N	0.16 W
Richmond Peak ∧	241h	13.17 N	61.13 W
Richmond Range ⋏	172	41.27 S	173.30 E
Richmond Royal Australian Air Force Base ■	170	33.37 S	150.48 E
Richmond-San Rafael Bridge ➜[5]	282	37.56 N	122.27 W
Richmondtown Restoration ⊥	276	40.34 N	74.09 W
Richmond Valley ➜[8]	276	40.31 N	74.13 W
Richmondville	210	42.38 N	74.33 W
Richrath	263	51.08 N	6.56 E
Rich Square	192	36.16 N	77.17 W
Rich Stadium ♦	284a	42.57 N	78.47 W
Richtenberg	54	54.12 N	12.53 E
Richterswil	58	47.13 N	8.42 E
Richton	194	31.20 N	88.56 W
Richton Park	216	41.29 N	87.42 W
Richvale, On., Can.	212	43.51 N	79.26 W
Richvale, Ca., U.S.	226	39.30 N	121.45 W
Richview	219	38.23 N	89.11 W
Richville, N.Y., U.S.	212	44.25 N	75.23 E
Richville, Oh., U.S.	214	40.45 N	81.27 W
Richwood, N.J., U.S.	285	39.43 N	75.10 W
Richwood, Oh., U.S.	214	40.25 N	83.17 W
Richwood, W.V., U.S.	188	38.13 N	80.32 W
Richwood Village	222	29.04 N	95.25 W
Ricinskij zapovednik ♦	84	43.25 N	40.30 E
Rickenbacker Air Force Base ■	218	39.48 N	82.56 W
Rickenpass)(	58	47.14 N	9.02 E
Ricken Tunnel ➜[5]	58	47.12 N	9.05 E
Ricketts Glen State Park ♦	210	41.20 N	76.18 W
Ricketts Point ≻	274b	38.00 S	145.02 E
Rickleån ≃	26	64.05 N	20.56 E
Rickling	54	54.01 N	10.13 E
Rickmansworth	42	51.39 N	0.29 W
Rico	200	37.41 N	108.01 W
Ricoa ≃	241s	11.30 N	69.12 W
Ricobayo, Embalse de ⊜[1]	34	41.30 N	5.55 W
Ricupe	152	14.37 S	21.25 E
Ridā'	144	14.38 N	44.54 E
Ridanna (Ridnaun)	64	46.55 N	11.15 E
Riddarhyttan	40	59.48 N	15.33 E
Ridderkerk	52	51.52 N	4.36 E
Riddes	58	46.10 N	7.13 E
Riddle	202	42.57 N	123.21 W
Riddle Mountain ∧	202	43.07 N	118.30 W
Riddlesburg	214	40.10 N	78.15 W
Riddlewood	285	39.54 N	75.26 W
Riddon, Loch ⊂	46	55.58 N	5.12 W
Rideau ≃	212	45.27 N	75.42 W
Ridge, Eng., U.K.	260	51.41 N	0.15 W
Ridge, N.Y., U.S.	207	40.54 N	72.53 W
Ridge, Tx., U.S.	222	31.09 N	96.19 W
Ridge Acres	276	40.41 N	74.32 W
Ridgecrest, Ca., U.S.	204	35.37 N	117.40 W
Ridgecrest, Wa., U.S.	224	47.45 N	122.21 W
Ridgedale	184	53.04 N	104.09 W
Ridge Farm	194	39.53 N	87.39 W
Ridgefield, Ct., U.S.	207	41.16 N	73.29 W
Ridgefield, Il., U.S.	216	42.16 N	88.22 W
Ridgefield, N.J., U.S.	210	40.50 N	74.00 W
Ridgefield, Wa., U.S.	224	45.48 N	122.44 W
Ridgefield Park	276	40.51 N	74.01 W
Ridgeland, Ms., U.S.	194	32.25 N	90.07 W
Ridgeland, S.C., U.S.	192	32.28 N	80.58 W
Ridgely, Md., U.S.	208	38.56 N	75.53 W
Ridgely, Tn., U.S.	194	36.15 N	89.29 W
Ridge Manor	220	28.31 N	82.10 W
Ridgemont	210	43.13 N	77.43 W
Ridgetown	214	42.26 N	81.54 W
Ridgeville, Mb., Can.	184	49.04 N	97.01 W
Ridgeville, In., U.S.	216	40.17 N	85.01 W
Ridgeville, S.C., U.S.	192	33.05 N	80.18 W
Ridgeville Corners	216	41.26 N	84.15 W
Ridgeway, On., Can.	284a	42.53 N	79.03 W
Ridgeway, Mi., U.S.	216	41.59 N	83.51 W
Ridgeway, Mo., U.S.	194	40.22 N	93.56 W
Ridgeway, N.J., U.S.	208	40.01 N	74.17 W
Ridgeway, Oh., U.S.	216	40.30 N	83.34 W
Ridgeway, Tx., U.S.	222	33.11 N	95.46 W
Ridgeway, Wi., U.S.	190	43.00 N	89.59 W
Ridgeway Ditch ≊	279a	41.25 N	82.05 W
Ridgewood	210	40.58 N	74.07 W
Ridgewood ➜[8]	276	40.42 N	73.53 W
Ridgewood Farm	285	39.57 N	75.34 W
Ridgewood Reservoir ⊜[1]	276	40.41 N	73.53 W
Ridgway, Co., U.S.	200	38.09 N	107.46 W
Ridgway, Il., U.S.	194	37.47 N	88.15 W
Ridgway, Pa., U.S.	214	41.25 N	78.43 W
Riding Mountain ∧	184	50.37 N	99.37 W
Riding Mountain National Park ♦	184	50.55 N	100.25 W
Ridīwajār	124	27.57 N	83.26 E
Ridley Creek ≃	285	39.51 N	75.21 W
Ridley Creek State Park ♦	285	39.57 N	75.27 W
Ridley Park	285	39.52 N	75.19 W
Ridnaun → Ridanna	64	46.55 N	11.15 E
Riebeek-Kasteel	158	33.23 S	18.53 E
Riebeek-Oos	158	33.10 S	26.10 E
Riebeek-Wes	158	33.21 S	18.52 E
Riecawr, Loch ⊜	44	55.13 N	4.27 W
Riedau	60	48.18 N	13.38 E
Riedelbach	56	50.18 N	8.23 E
Rieden	60	49.19 N	11.57 E
Riedenburg	60	48.58 N	11.41 E
Rieder	54	51.44 N	11.10 E
Riederalp	58	46.23 N	8.01 E
Riedern	56	49.40 N	9.23 E
Ried im Innkreis	60	48.13 N	13.30 E
Ried im Oberinntal	58	47.03 N	10.39 E
Riedisheim	58	47.45 N	7.22 E
Riedlingen	58	48.09 N	9.28 E
Riedstadt	56	49.50 N	8.30 E
Riegel	58	48.09 N	7.45 E
Riegelsville, N.J., U.S.	210	40.49 N	74.52 W
Riegelsville, Pa., U.S.	208	40.36 N	75.12 W
Riegelwood	192	34.20 N	78.15 W
Riegersburg	61	47.00 N	15.56 E
Riegersburg, Schloss ⊥	61	47.01 N	15.56 E
Riegersdorf	64	46.33 N	13.47 E
Riehen	58	47.35 N	7.39 E
Rieka → Rijeka	36	45.20 N	14.27 E
Rielasingen	58	47.44 N	8.50 E
Riemke ➜[8]	263	51.30 N	7.13 E
Riemst	56	50.48 N	5.36 E
Rieneck	56	50.05 N	9.38 E
Rienza (Rienz) ≃	64	46.43 N	11.39 E
Rienzi	194	34.45 N	88.31 W
Riesa	54	51.18 N	13.17 E
Riesco, Isla I	254	53.00 S	72.30 W
Rieseby	41	54.32 N	9.48 E
Riesel	222	31.28 N	96.56 W
Riesenbeck	52	52.16 N	7.37 E
Riese Pio X	64	45.44 N	11.55 E
Riesi	70	37.17 N	14.05 E
Riestedt	54	51.29 N	11.21 E
Riet ≃, S. Afr.	158	29.00 S	23.54 E
Riet ≃, S. Afr.	158	31.20 S	20.17 E
Rietavas	76	55.44 N	21.56 E
Rietberg	52	51.47 N	8.25 E
Rietbron	158	32.54 S	23.10 E
Rietfontein	156	21.58 S	20.58 E
Riethuiskraal	158	34.20 S	21.22 E
Rieti	66	42.24 N	12.51 E
Rieti □[4]	66	42.18 N	12.52 E
Rietschen	54	51.23 N	14.47 E
Rietspruit ≃, S. Afr.	273d	26.19 S	28.18 E
Rietspruit ≃, S. Afr.	273d	26.06 S	27.39 E
Rietvlei	158	30.29 S	29.51 E
Rietzer See ⊜	54	52.22 N	12.39 E
Rievaulx Abbey ⊍[1]	44	54.16 N	1.07 W
Riez	62	43.49 N	6.06 E
Riezlern	58	47.21 N	10.11 E
Rif ⋏	148	35.00 N	4.00 W
Riffe Lake ⊜[1]	224	46.30 N	122.20 W
Rifflart	273b	4.25 S	15.21 E
Rifiano (Riffian)	64	46.42 N	11.11 E
Rifle	200	39.32 N	107.46 W
Rifle ≃	190	44.00 N	83.49 W
Rifstangi ≻	24a	66.35 N	16.10 W
Rifton	210	41.50 N	74.03 W
Rift Valley □[4]	154	0.30 N	36.00 E
Rift Valley V	10	3.00 S	29.00 E
Rift Valley Lakes National Park ♦	144	7.30 N	38.30 E
Rīga, Lat.	76	56.57 N	24.06 E
Riga, Ross.	88	56.36 N	106.17 E
Riga, Mi., U.S.	216	41.49 N	83.50 W
Riga, Gulf of (Rīgas jūras līcis) (Riia laht) ⊂	76	57.30 N	23.35 E
Riga, Mount ∧	162	21.59 S	116.25 E
Rigacikun	150	10.40 N	7.28 E
Rigaih	114	4.40 N	95.34 E
Rīgān	128	28.37 N	58.58 E
Rīgas jūras līcis → Riga, Gulf of ⊂	76	57.30 N	23.35 E
Riga Station ➜[5]	265b	55.48 N	37.38 E
Rigaud	206	45.29 N	74.18 W
Rigaud ≃	206	45.29 N	74.18 W
Rigby	202	43.40 N	111.54 W
Rīgestān ➜[1]	128	31.00 N	65.00 E
Riggins	202	45.25 N	116.18 W
Riggisberg	58	46.48 N	7.29 E
Riggston	219	39.42 N	90.25 W
Righedo, Passo del)(	64	44.27 N	9.55 E
Rigi ∧	58	47.05 N	8.30 E
Rignano Flaminio	66	42.12 N	12.29 E
Rignano Garganico	68	41.40 N	15.35 E
Rignano sull'Arno	66	43.43 N	11.27 E
Rigney	58	47.23 N	6.11 E
Rigney Bluff	210	43.19 N	77.38 W
Rigny-Ussé	50	47.15 N	0.18 E
Rigo	164	9.47 S	147.34 E
Rigolet	176	54.20 N	58.35 W
Rig-Rig	146	14.16 N	14.21 E
Rigside	46	55.36 N	3.47 W
Riguldi	76	59.08 N	23.33 E
Rīh, Jazīrat ar- I	140	18.10 N	38.27 E
Rihāb	132	32.19 N	36.06 E
Rihand ≃	124	24.33 N	82.59 E
Rihand Dam ➜[6]	124	24.05 N	82.45 E
Riihimäki	26	60.45 N	24.46 E
Riiser-Larsen Peninsula ≻[1]	9	68.55 S	34.00 E
Rijau	150	11.07 N	5.14 E
Riječki Zaljev ⊂	36	45.15 N	14.25 E
Rijeka	36	45.20 N	14.27 E
Rijen	52	51.35 N	4.55 E
Rijkevorsel	56	51.21 N	4.46 E
Rijksdorp	52	52.09 N	4.25 E
Rijn → Rhine ≃	30	51.52 N	6.02 E
Rijnsburg	52	52.12 N	4.27 E
Rijssel → Lille	50	50.38 N	3.04 E
Rijssen	52	52.18 N	6.30 E
Rijswijk	52	52.04 N	4.20 E
Rike	144	10.42 N	39.55 E
Rikers Island I	276	40.47 N	73.53 W
Rikers Island Channel ʊ	276	40.47 N	73.52 W
Rikkavesi ⊜	26	62.50 N	28.44 E
Riksgränsen	24	68.24 N	18.12 E
Rikuchū-kaigan-kokuritsu-kōen ♦	92	39.25 N	141.57 E
Rikuzen-takata	92	39.01 N	141.38 E
Rila ⋏	38	42.08 N	23.33 E
Riley	198	39.17 N	96.49 W
Riley, Mount ∧	200	31.55 N	107.07 W
Riley, Point ≻	168b	33.53 S	137.36 E
Riley Creek ≃	216	41.02 N	84.00 W
Riley Lake ⊜	212	44.50 N	79.11 W
Rileys Range ⋏	170	34.21 S	150.10 E
Rilievo	70	37.55 N	12.33 E
Rillieux	62	45.49 N	4.54 E
Rillington	44	54.09 N	0.42 W
Rillito	200	32.24 N	111.09 W
Rillton	214	40.17 N	79.44 W
Rilly-la-Montagne	50	49.10 N	4.03 E
Rilski manastir ⊍[1]	38	42.08 N	23.20 E
Rima ≃	150	13.04 N	5.10 E
Rímac	286d	12.03 S	77.03 W
Rímac ≃	248	12.02 S	77.09 W
Rimachi, Laguna ⊜	246	4.25 S	76.43 W
Rimāh, Jabal ar- ∧	132	32.19 N	36.52 E
Rima San Giuseppe	62	45.52 N	8.00 E
Rimatara I	14	22.38 S	152.51 W
Rimavská Sobota	30	48.23 N	20.02 E
Rimbey	182	52.38 N	114.14 W
Rimbo	40	59.45 N	18.22 E
Rimé, Ouadi V	146	14.02 N	18.03 E
Rimersburg	214	41.02 N	79.30 W
Rimforsa	26	58.08 N	15.40 E
Rimi	150	12.58 N	7.43 E
Rimini	66	44.04 N	12.34 E
Rîmna ≃	38	45.39 N	27.19 E
Rîmnicu Sărat	38	45.23 N	27.03 E
Rîmnicu Vîlcea	38	45.06 N	24.22 E
Rimo Glacier ⊓	123	35.25 N	77.30 E
Rimogne	56	49.50 N	4.33 E
Rimouski	186	48.26 N	68.33 W
Rimouski ≃	186	48.27 N	68.32 W
Rimouski, Réserve ♦	186	48.03 N	68.15 W
Rimpar	56	49.51 N	9.57 E
Rimrock Lake ⊜[1]	224	46.38 N	121.12 W
Rimsko-Korsakovka	80	51.34 N	48.31 E
Rinbung	124	29.21 N	89.57 E
Rinca	115b	8.37 S	119.48 E
Rinca, Pulau I	115b	8.41 S	119.42 E
Rinchnach	60	48.57 N	13.12 E
Rinčin Lchumbe	88	51.07 N	99.40 E
Rincón, C.R.	236	8.42 N	83.29 W
Rincón, P.R.	240m	18.20 N	67.15 W
Rincon, Ga., U.S.	192	32.17 N	81.14 W
Rincon, N.M., U.S.	200	32.40 N	107.03 W
Rincón, Bahía de ⊂	240m	17.58 N	66.20 W
Rinconada	252	22.26 S	66.10 W
Rinconada, Hipódromo de la ♦	286c	10.26 N	66.56 W
Rincón de la Vieja, Parque Nacional ♦	236	10.48 N	85.18 W
Rincón del Bonete, Lago Artificial de ⊜[1]	252	32.45 S	56.00 W
Rincón del Ocote, Cerro ∧	236	13.36 N	87.10 W
Rincón de Romos	234	22.14 N	102.18 W
Rincon Indian Reservation ➜[4]	228	33.15 N	116.57 W
Rincon Valley	226	38.28 N	122.39 W
Rindal	26	63.03 N	9.13 E
Rindown Castle ⊥	48	53.32 N	7.59 W
Rīngas	120	27.21 N	75.34 E
Ringdove	175f	16.38 S	168.09 E
Ringe	41	55.14 N	10.29 E
Ringebu	26	61.31 N	10.10 E
Ringenwalde	54	53.03 N	13.42 E
Ringertown	279b	40.25 N	79.36 W
Ringford	44	54.54 N	4.03 W
Ringgau ➜[1]	56	51.04 N	10.04 E
Ringgit, Gunung ∧	115a	7.43 S	113.50 E
Ringgold, Ga., U.S.	192	34.54 N	85.06 W
Ringgold, La., U.S.	194	32.19 N	93.16 W
Ringgold, Pa., U.S.	214	41.00 N	79.10 W
Ringgold Isles II	175g	16.15 S	179.25 W
Ringim	150	12.08 N	9.10 E
Ringkøbing	26	56.05 N	8.15 E
Ringkøbing □[6]	41	56.10 N	8.50 E
Ringkøbing Fjord ⊂[2]	26	56.00 N	8.15 E
Ringlet	114	4.25 N	101.23 E
Ringling	196	34.10 N	97.35 W
Ringling Museums ⊍	220	27.23 N	82.34 W
Ringmer	42	50.53 N	0.04 E
Ringoes	208	40.26 N	74.52 W
Rings Island	283	42.49 N	70.52 W
Ringsted, Dan.	41	55.27 N	11.49 E
Ringsted, Ia., U.S.	198	43.17 N	94.30 W
Ringtown	210	40.51 N	76.14 W
Ringvassøy I	24	69.55 N	19.15 E
Ringville	48	52.02 N	7.34 W
Ringwood, Austl.	169	37.49 S	145.14 E
Ringwood, Eng., U.K.	42	50.51 N	1.47 W
Ringwood, N.J., U.S.	210	41.06 N	74.14 W
Ringwood Manor ⊥	276	41.08 N	74.15 W
Ringwood North	274b	37.48 S	145.14 E
Ringwood State Park ♦	210	41.08 N	74.16 W
Riñihue	254	39.49 S	72.27 W
Riñihue, Lago ⊜	254	39.50 S	72.18 W
Rinjani, Gunung ∧	115b	8.24 S	116.28 E
Rinkenæs	41	54.54 N	9.34 E
Rinkerode	52	51.50 N	7.41 E
Rinnes, Ben ∧	46	57.23 N	3.15 W
Rinnthal	56	49.13 N	7.55 E
Rín → Rhine ≃	30	51.52 N	6.02 E
Rinsumageest	52	53.18 N	5.57 E
Rinteln	52	52.11 N	9.04 E
Rinxent	50	50.48 N	1.44 E
Rio, Fl., U.S.	220	27.13 N	80.14 W
Rio, Wi., U.S.	190	43.26 N	89.14 W
Rio Azul	252	25.43 S	50.47 W
Riobamba	246	1.40 S	78.38 W
Río Blanco, Chile	252	32.55 S	70.19 W
Río Blanco (Tenango de Rio Blanco), Méx.	234	18.50 N	97.09 W
Rio Bonito	256	22.43 S	42.37 W
Rio Bonito ➜[8]	287b	23.43 S	46.41 W
Rio Branco, Bra.	248	9.58 S	67.48 W
Río Branco, Ur.	252	32.34 S	53.25 W
Río Bravo, Méx.	196	28.17 N	100.55 W
Río Bravo, Méx.	232	25.59 N	98.06 W
Rio Brilhante	255	21.48 S	54.33 W
Río Bueno	254	40.19 S	72.58 W
Río Caribe	246	10.42 N	63.07 W
Rio Casca	255	20.13 S	42.39 W
Río Cauto	240p	20.33 N	76.55 W
Río Ceballos	252	31.10 S	64.20 W
Río Chico, Arg.	254	41.43 S	70.30 W
Río Chico, Ven.	246	10.18 N	65.59 W
Rio Claro, Bra.	255	22.24 S	47.33 W
Rio Claro, Bra.	256	22.43 S	44.09 W
Rio Claro, Trin.	241r	10.18 N	61.11 W
Rio Claro, Représa do ⊜[1]	256	23.39 S	45.54 W
Río Colorado	252	39.01 S	64.05 W
Rio Comprido ➜[8]	287a	22.55 S	43.12 W
Río Cuarto	252	33.08 S	64.21 W
Rio das Flores	256	22.10 S	43.35 W
Rio das Pedras	156	23.12 S	35.23 E
Rio de Contas	255	13.36 S	41.48 W
Rio de Janeiro, Bra.	256	22.54 S	43.14 W
Rio de Janeiro, Bra.	287a	22.54 S	43.14 W
Rio de Janeiro □[3]	255	22.00 S	42.30 W
Rio de Janeiro □[7]	287a	22.55 S	43.30 W
Río de Jesús	236	7.59 N	81.10 W
Rio Dell	204	40.29 N	124.06 W
Rio de Mouro	266c	38.46 N	9.20 W
Río de Oro	246	8.17 N	73.23 W
Rio do Prado	255	16.35 S	40.34 W
Rio do Sul	252	27.13 S	49.39 W
Rio Douro	287a	22.39 S	43.32 W
Rio Espera	255	20.51 S	43.29 W
Río Gallegos	254	51.38 S	69.13 W
Río Grande, Arg.	254	53.47 S	67.42 W
Rio Grande, Bra.	252	32.02 S	52.05 W
Río Grande, Méx.	234	15.59 N	97.27 W
Río Grande, Méx.	234	23.50 N	103.02 W
Río Grande, Nic.	236	12.53 N	86.32 W
Río Grande, P.R.	240m	18.23 N	65.50 W
Rio Grande, N.J., U.S.	208	39.00 N	74.52 W
Río Grande, Ven.	286c	10.35 N	66.57 W
Rio Grande, Ponte do ➜[5]	287b	23.46 S	46.31 W
Rio Grande City	196	26.22 N	98.49 W
Rio Grande Da Serra, Bra.	256	23.44 S	46.24 W
Rio Grande da Serra, Bra.	287b	23.44 S	46.24 W
Rio Grande da Serra □[7]	287b	23.45 S	46.23 W
Rio Grande do Norte □[3]	250	5.45 S	36.00 W
Rio Grande do Sul □[3]	252	30.00 S	54.00 W
Rio Grande do Sul → Rio Grande	252	32.02 S	52.05 W
Rio Grande → Grande, Rio ≃	178	25.57 N	97.09 W
Riograndina	256	22.11 S	42.30 W
Ríohacha	246	11.33 N	72.55 W
Río Hato	236	8.23 N	80.10 W
Río Hondo, Méx.	286a	19.25 N	99.16 W
Rio Hondo, Tx., U.S.	196	26.14 N	97.34 W
Rioja	248	6.05 S	77.09 W
Rio Jaguari, Reservatório do ⊜[1]	256	22.55 S	46.25 W
Río Jueyes	240m	18.01 N	66.20 W
Riola	64	44.16 N	11.04 E
Río Lagartos	232	21.36 N	88.10 W
Riolândia	255	19.59 S	49.40 W
Rio Largo	250	9.29 S	35.51 W
Riola Sardo	71	39.59 N	8.32 E
Rio Linda	226	38.41 N	121.26 W
Riolo Terme	66	44.16 N	11.43 E
Río Luján	258	34.17 S	58.54 W
Riom	32	45.54 N	3.07 E
Riomaggiore	62	44.06 N	9.44 E
Rio Marina	66	42.49 N	10.25 E
Río Mayo	254	45.41 S	70.16 W
Rio Mulatos	248	19.42 S	66.47 W
Río Muni □[4]	152	1.30 N	10.30 E
Riondel	182	49.46 N	116.52 W
Rio Negro, Bra.	252	26.06 S	49.48 W
Rio Negro, Bra.	255	19.27 S	54.58 W
Río Negro, Chile	254	40.47 S	73.14 W
Ríonegro, Col.	246	6.09 N	75.22 W
Ríonegro, Col.	246	7.16 N	73.09 W
Río Negro □[4]	254	40.00 S	67.00 W
Rio Negro, Pantanal do ⁞	248	19.00 S	56.00 W
Rionero in Vulture	68	40.56 N	15.41 E
Rionero Sannitico	66	41.42 N	14.08 E
Rioni ≃	84	42.08 N	41.39 E
Rio Novo	256	21.29 S	43.08 W
Rio Novo do Sul	255	20.52 S	40.56 W
Riópar	34	38.30 N	2.27 W
Rio Pardo	252	29.59 S	52.22 W
Rio Pardo de Minas	255	15.37 S	42.33 W
Río Pico	254	44.13 S	71.21 W
Río Piedras, Arg.	252	25.18 S	64.54 W
Río Piedras, P.R.	240m	18.24 N	66.03 W
Río Pilcomayo, Parque Nacional ♦	252	25.10 S	58.00 W
Rio Piracicaba	255	19.55 S	43.11 W
Rio Pomba	256	21.17 S	43.11 W
Rio Prêto	256	22.06 S	43.50 W
Rio Prêto → São José do Rio Prêto	256	22.10 S	42.57 W
Rio Rancho	200	35.14 N	106.38 W
Rio Real	250	11.28 S	37.56 W
Rio Saliceto	64	44.49 N	10.49 E
Río San Juan □[5]	236	11.10 N	84.30 W
Río Segundo	252	31.40 S	63.55 W
Ríosucio, Col.	246	5.25 N	75.42 W
Ríosucio, Col.	246	7.27 N	77.07 W
Río Tercero	252	32.11 S	64.06 W
Rio Tinto	250	6.48 S	35.05 W
Riotord	62	45.14 N	4.24 E
Rio Tuba	116	8.30 N	117.25 E
Riou, Île de I	62	43.11 N	5.24 E
Rioveggio	64	44.17 N	11.14 E
Rio Verde, Bra.	255	17.43 S	50.56 W
Ríoverde, Méx.	234	21.56 N	99.59 W
Rio Verde de Mato Grosso	255	18.56 S	54.52 W
Rio Vermelho	255	18.18 S	43.00 W
Rio Vista, Ca., U.S.	226	38.09 N	121.41 W
Rio Vista, Tx., U.S.	222	32.14 N	97.23 W
Rioz	58	47.25 N	6.04 E
Riozinho ≃, Bra.	246	2.55 S	67.07 W
Riozinho ≃, Bra.	250	10.22 S	49.50 W
Riozinho ≃, Bra.	250	7.06 S	51.40 W
Riozinho ≃, Bra.	250	8.25 S	45.43 W
Říp ∧	54	50.24 N	14.18 E
Ripacandida	68	40.55 N	15.43 E
Ripalti, Punta dei ≻	66	42.42 N	10.25 E
Ripatransone	66	43.00 N	13.46 E
Ripley, Eng., U.K.	42	53.03 N	1.24 W
Ripley, Eng., U.K.	260	51.18 N	0.29 W
Ripley, Il., U.S.	219	40.01 N	90.38 W
Ripley, In., U.S.	216	41.06 N	86.39 W
Ripley, Ms., U.S.	194	34.43 N	88.57 W
Ripley, N.Y., U.S.	214	42.16 N	79.42 W
Ripley, Oh., U.S.	218	38.44 N	83.50 W
Ripley, Tn., U.S.	194	35.44 N	89.31 W
Ripley, W.V., U.S.	188	38.49 N	81.42 W
Ripley □[6]	218	39.04 N	85.15 W
Ripoll	34	42.12 N	2.12 E
Ripoll ≃	266d	41.29 N	2.12 E
Ripollet	266d	41.30 N	2.10 E
Ripon, P.Q., Can.	206	45.47 N	75.06 W
Ripon, Eng., U.K.	44	54.08 N	1.31 W
Ripon, Ca., U.S.	226	37.44 N	121.07 W
Ripon, Wi., U.S.	190	43.50 N	88.50 W
Riposto	70	37.44 N	15.12 E
Rippling Ridge	284b	39.11 N	76.37 W
Ripponden	44	53.41 N	1.57 W
Rippowam ≃	276	41.03 N	73.33 W
Riquewihr	58	48.10 N	7.18 E
Ririba, Laga ≃	154	3.34 N	37.15 E
Ririe	202	43.37 N	111.46 W
Risālpur Cantonment	123	34.04 N	72.00 E
Risaralda □[5]	246	5.00 N	76.00 W
Risasi	154	0.25 S	25.44 E
Risbäck	26	64.42 N	15.32 E
Risca	42	51.37 N	3.07 W
Rischenau	52	51.53 N	9.17 E
Riscle	32	43.40 N	0.05 W
Risco, Ilha do I	246	3.07 S	58.19 W
Rishā', Wādī ar- V	128	25.33 N	44.05 E
Rīshahr	128	28.55 N	50.50 E
Rishīkesh	124	30.07 N	78.19 E
Rishiri-Rebun-Sarobetsu-kokuritsu-kōen ♦	92a	45.10 N	141.35 E
Rishiri-suidō ʊ	92a	45.10 N	141.25 E
Rishiri-tō I	92a	45.11 N	141.15 E
Rishiri-zan ∧	92a	45.11 N	141.15 E
Rishmayyā	132	33.44 N	35.36 E
Rishon LeẒiyyon	132	31.58 N	34.48 E
Rishpon	132	32.12 N	34.49 E
Rishra	272b	22.43 N	88.21 E
Rishrāsh, Wādī V	142	29.29 N	31.16 E
Rishton	262	53.46 N	2.25 W
Rishworth	262	53.40 N	1.57 W
Rishworth Moor ➜[3]	262	53.39 N	2.01 W
Risinge	40	58.42 N	15.51 E
Rising Star	196	32.05 N	98.57 W
Rising Sun, In., U.S.	218	38.56 N	84.51 W
Rising Sun, Md., U.S.	208	39.41 N	76.03 W
Risingsun, Oh., U.S.	214	41.16 N	83.25 W
Risle ≃	50	49.26 N	0.23 E
Risnjak ∧	36	45.26 N	14.37 E
Rîșnov	38	45.36 N	25.28 E
Risø	41	55.42 N	12.06 E
Rison, Ar., U.S.	194	33.57 N	92.11 W
Rison, Md., U.S.	208	38.32 N	77.10 W
Risør	26	58.43 N	9.14 E
Ris-Orangis	50	48.39 N	2.25 E
Riss ≃	58	48.17 N	9.49 E
Rissani	148	31.23 N	4.09 W
Risskov ➜[8]	41	56.11 N	10.14 E
Risstissen	58	48.16 N	9.49 E
Risti	76	58.59 N	24.03 E
Ristigouche (Restigouche) ≃	186	48.04 N	66.20 W
Ristiina	26	61.30 N	27.16 E
Ristijärvi	26	64.44 N	28.24 E
Ristinge	41	54.50 N	10.38 E
Ristna	76	58.56 N	22.05 E
Risum-Lindholm	41	54.45 N	8.53 E
Rita Blanca Creek ≃	196	35.40 N	102.29 W
Ritchie, S. Afr.	158	29.02 S	24.38 E
Ritchie, Md., U.S.	284c	38.52 N	76.52 W
Ritchie Branch ≃	284c	38.53 N	76.52 W
Rithāla ➜[8]	272a	28.43 N	77.06 E
Ritidian Point ≻	174p	13.39 N	144.51 E
Ritscher Upland ⋏[1]	9	73.20 S	9.30 W
Ritsumeikan University ⊍[2]	270	35.01 N	135.46 E
Ritsurin-kōen ♦	96	34.21 N	134.02 E
Ritta Island I	220	26.44 N	80.48 W
Ritter, Mount ∧	226	37.42 N	119.12 W
Ritterhude	52	53.11 N	8.45 E
Rittersgrün	54	50.29 N	12.47 E
Rittman	214	40.58 N	81.46 W
Rittō	94	35.01 N	136.00 E
Ritzleben	54	52.50 N	11.21 E
Ritzville	202	47.07 N	118.22 W
Riu	120	28.19 N	95.03 E
Riva	208	38.57 N	76.35 W
Rivadavia, Arg.	252	35.28 S	62.57 W
Rivadavia, Arg.	252	33.11 S	68.28 W
Rivadavia, Arg.	252	24.11 S	62.53 W
Rivadavia, Arg.	252	31.33 S	68.37 W
Rivadavia, Chile	252	29.58 S	70.34 W
Riva del Garda	64	45.53 N	10.50 E
Riva del Sole	66	42.46 N	10.52 E
Riva di Tures (Rain)	64	46.57 N	12.04 E
Rivanazzano	62	44.56 N	9.01 E
Rivanna ≃	192	37.45 N	78.10 W
Rivare	216	40.49 N	84.50 W
Rivarolo Canavese	62	45.19 N	7.43 E
Rivarolo Mantovano	64	45.04 N	10.26 E
Rivas	236	11.26 N	85.50 W
Rivas □[5]	236	11.25 N	85.50 W
Rivasdale	273d	26.17 S	27.56 E
Rīvash	128	35.26 N	58.26 E
Rivas-Vaciamadrid	266a	40.20 N	3.31 W
Riva Trigoso	62	44.16 N	9.26 E
Rive, Île de la I	273b	4.21 S	15.26 E
Rive d'Arcano	64	46.08 N	13.02 E
Rive-de-Gier	62	45.32 N	4.37 E
Rivello	68	40.04 N	15.45 E
Rivera, Arg.	252	37.12 S	63.14 W
Rivera, Col.	246	2.47 N	75.15 W
Rivera, Ur.	252	30.54 S	55.31 W
Riverbank	226	37.44 N	120.56 W
River Cess	150	5.28 N	9.32 W
Riverdale, Ca., U.S.	226	36.25 N	119.51 W
Riverdale, Il., U.S.	278	41.38 N	87.37 W
Riverdale, Md., U.S.	284c	38.57 N	76.55 W
Riverdale, N.J., U.S.	276	40.59 N	74.18 W
Riverdale, N.D., U.S.	198	47.29 N	101.22 W
Riverdale, Or., U.S.	224	45.27 N	122.41 W
Riverdale ➜[8]	276	40.54 N	73.54 W
Riverdale Heights	284c	38.58 N	76.55 W
Riverdale Park ♦	275b	43.40 N	79.21 W
River Drive Park	212	44.08 N	79.31 W
River Edge, N.J., U.S.	276	40.55 N	74.02 W
River Edge, Oh., U.S.	279a	41.25 N	81.51 W
River Falls, Al., U.S.	194	31.21 N	86.32 W
River Falls, Wi., U.S.	190	44.51 N	92.37 W
River Forest	278	41.53 N	87.48 W
Rivergaro	62	44.55 N	9.36 E
River Grove	278	41.55 N	87.50 W
Riverhaven	216	41.05 N	85.02 W
Riverhead, Eng., U.K.	260	51.17 N	0.10 E
Riverhead, N.Y., U.S.	207	40.55 N	72.39 W
River Hébert	186	45.42 N	64.23 W
River Hill	279b	40.12 N	79.54 W
River Hills	216	43.10 N	87.55 W
Riverhurst	184	50.53 N	106.52 W
Riverina ➜[1]	166	35.30 S	145.30 E
River John	186	45.45 N	63.03 W
River Jordan	224	48.25 N	124.03 W
Riverlea	214	40.05 N	83.02 W
River Lea Navigation ≊	260	51.32 N	0.02 W
River Meadow Brook ≃	283	42.38 N	71.17 W
Rivermont	192	35.13 N	77.38 W
Rivero, Isla I	254	45.37 S	74.20 W
River Oaks	284c	38.57 N	77.11 W
River of Ponds	186	50.32 N	57.24 W
River Pines, Ca., U.S.	226	38.33 N	120.45 W
River Pines, Ma., U.S.	207	42.33 N	71.17 W
River Plaza	208	40.21 N	74.05 W
River Ridge Estates	284c	38.47 N	77.00 W
River Road	202	44.03 N	123.05 W
River Rouge	216	42.16 N	83.08 W
River Rouge Park ♦	281	42.22 N	83.15 W
Rivers	184	50.02 N	100.12 W
Rivers □[3]	150	4.30 N	6.30 E
Rivers, Lake of the ⊜	184	49.45 N	105.45 W
Riversdale, N.Z.	172	45.54 S	168.45 E
Riversdale, S. Afr.	158	34.07 S	21.15 E
Riverside, Ca., U.S.	228	33.57 N	117.23 W
Riverside, Ct., U.S.	276	41.02 N	73.35 W
Riverside, Il., U.S.	278	41.50 N	87.49 W
Riverside, Ia., U.S.	190	41.28 N	91.34 W
Riverside, Mi., U.S.	216	42.11 N	86.23 W
Riverside, Mi., U.S.	216	42.17 N	84.29 W
Riverside, N.J., U.S.	208	40.01 N	74.57 W
Riverside, N.Y., U.S.	210	42.55 N	73.40 W
Riverside, N.Y., U.S.	210	42.08 N	77.01 W
Riverside, Pa., U.S.	210	40.57 N	76.38 W
Riverside, Tx., U.S.	222	30.57 N	95.24 W
Riverside, Wa., U.S.	182	48.30 N	119.30 W
Riverside □[6]	228	33.45 N	117.10 W
Riverside ➜[8]	281	42.20 N	82.57 W
Riverside International Raceway ♦	228	33.57 N	117.17 W
Riverside Manors	284a	43.11 N	79.03 W
Riverside Park ♦, Mi., U.S.	281	42.22 N	83.26 W
Riverside Park ♦, N.Y., U.S.	284a	42.57 N	78.54 W
Rivers Inlet	182	51.41 N	127.15 W
Rivers Inlet ⊂	182	51.39 N	127.30 W
Riversleigh	166	19.02 S	138.44 E
Riverstone	170	33.40 S	150.52 E
Riverton, Austl.	168b	34.09 S	138.45 E
Riverton, Mb., Can.	184	50.59 N	96.59 W
Riverton, N.Z.	172	46.21 S	168.01 E
Riverton, Il., U.S.	219	39.51 N	89.33 W
Riverton, Ne., U.S.	198	40.05 N	98.45 W
Riverton, N.J., U.S.	208	40.00 N	75.00 W
Riverton, Ut,. U.S.	200	40.31 N	111.56 W
Riverton, Va., U.S.	188	38.56 N	78.11 W
Riverton, Wy., U.S.	200	43.01 N	108.22 W
Riverton Heights	224	47.28 N	122.18 W
River Vale	276	40.59 N	74.00 W
Riverview, S. Afr.	158	28.27 S	32.10 E
River View, Al., U.S.	194	32.47 N	85.08 W
Riverview, Fl., U.S.	220	27.51 N	82.19 W
Riverview, Ks., U.S.	198	37.47 N	97.22 W
Riverview, Mi., U.S.	216	42.10 N	83.10 W
Riverview Park ♦	279b	40.29 N	80.01 W
Riverwood, Austl.	274a	33.57 S	151.03 E
Riverwood, In., U.S.	218	40.06 N	85.58 W
Riverwoods	278	42.10 N	87.54 W
Rives, Fr.	62	45.21 N	5.30 E
Rives, Tn., U.S.	194	36.21 N	89.02 W
Rivesaltes	32	42.46 N	2.52 E
Rives Junction	216	42.23 N	84.27 W
Rive Sud, Canal de la ≊	275a	45.25 N	73.41 W
Rivesville	188	39.31 N	80.07 W
Riviera, Az., U.S.	204	35.04 N	114.35 W
Riviera, Tx., U.S.	196	27.18 N	97.49 W
Riviera V	58	46.15 N	8.58 E
Riviera Beach, Fl., U.S.	220	26.46 N	80.03 W
Riviera Beach, Md., U.S.	208	39.10 N	76.30 W
Rivière-à-Claude	186	49.13 N	65.54 W
Rivière-au-Tonnerre	186	50.16 N	64.47 W
Rivière-Bleue	186	47.26 N	69.03 W
Rivière-Bois-Clair	206	46.34 N	71.50 W
Rivière-de-la-Chaloupe	186	49.08 N	62.32 W
Rivière-des-Prairies ➜[8]	275a	45.39 N	73.33 W
Rivière-du-Loup	186	47.50 N	69.32 W
Rivière du Rempart	157c	20.06 S	57.41 E
Rivière-Matane	186	48.39 N	67.20 W
Rivière-Mékinac	206	46.47 N	72.48 W
Rivière-Pentecôte	186	49.47 N	67.10 W
Rivière-Pilote	240e	14.29 N	60.54 W
Rivière-Salée	240e	14.32 N	60.59 W
Rivière-Verte	186	47.19 N	68.09 W
Riviersonderend	158	34.09 S	19.55 E
Rivignano	64	45.52 N	13.03 E
Rivington	262	53.37 N	2.34 W
Rivington Reservoirs ⊜[1]	262	53.37 N	2.34 W
Rivisondoli	66	41.52 N	14.04 E
Rivoli	62	45.04 N	7.31 E
Rivoli Bay ⊂	166	37.32 S	140.04 E
Rivolta d'Adda	62	45.28 N	9.31 E
Rivoltella	64	45.27 N	10.33 E
Riwaka	172	41.05 S	173.00 E

≃ River	Fluß	Río	Rivière	Rio
≊ Canal	Kanal	Canal	Canal	Canal
∟ Waterfall, Rapids	Wasserfall, Stromschnellen	Cascada, Rápidos	Chute d'eau, Rapides	Cascata, Rápidos
ʊ Strait	Meeresstraße	Estrecho	Détroit	Estreito
⊂ Bay, Gulf	Bucht, Golf	Bahía, Golfo	Baie, Golfe	Baía, Golfo
⊜ Lake, Lakes	See, Seen	Lago, Lagos	Lac, Lacs	Lago, Lagos
⁞ Swamp	Sumpf	Pantano	Marais	Pântano
⊓ Ice Features, Glacier	Eis- und Gletscherformen	Accidentes Glaciales	Formes glaciaires	Acidentes glaciares
⍑ Other Hydrographic Features	Andere Hydrographische Objekte	Otros Elementos Hidrográficos	Autres données hydrographiques	Outros acidentes hidrográficos

✣ Submarine Features	Untermeerische Objekte	Accidentes Submarinos	Formes de relief sous-marin	Acidentes submarinos
□ Political Unit	Politische Einheit	Unidad Politica	Entité politique	Unidade política
⊍ Cultural Institution	Kulturelle Institution	Institución Cultural	Institution culturelle	Instituição cultural
⊥ Historical Site	Historische Stätte	Sitio Histórico	Site historique	Sitio histórico
♦ Recreational Site	Erholungs- und Ferienort	Sitio de Recreo	Centre de loisirs	Area de Lazer
⊠ Airport	Flughafen	Aeropuerto	Aéroport	Aeroporto
■ Military Installation	Militäranlage	Instalación Militar	Installation militaire	Instalação militar
➜ Miscellaneous	Verschiedenes	Misceláneo	Divers	Diversos

Rixford 214 41.55 N 78.30 W
Rixheim 58 47.46 N 7.24 E
Riyadh → Ar-Riyāḍ 128 24.38 N 46.43 E
Rīyāq 132 33.51 N 36.00 E
Rizal 116 15.43 N 121.06 E
Rizal □[4] 116 14.35 N 121.10 E
Rizal Memorial Stadium ♦ 269f 14.34 N 120.59 E
Rizal → Pasay 269f 14.33 N 121.00 E
Rize 130 41.02 N 40.31 E
Rize □[4] 130 40.55 N 40.55 E
Rīzeh, Kūh-e (gora Reza) ∧ 128 37.47 N 58.05 E
Rizhao 98 35.27 N 119.29 E
Rizziconi 68 38.25 N 15.57 E
Rizzuto, Capo › 68 38.54 N 17.06 E
Rjukan 26 59.52 N 8.34 E
Rkîz, Lac ⊜ 150 16.50 N 15.19 W
Rô 175f 21.22 S 167.50 E
Roa, Esp. 34 41.42 N 3.55 W
Roa, Nor. 26 60.17 N 10.37 E
Roa, Zaïre 154 3.49 N 24.56 E
Roachdale 194 39.50 N 86.48 W
Roade 42 52.09 N 0.53 W
Roadford Reservoir ⊜[1] 42 50.43 N 4.13 W
Roadhead 44 55.04 N 2.46 W
Roadknight, Point › 169 38.26 S 144.11 E
Roadside 158 27.31 S 28.52 E
Road Town 240m 18.27 N 64.37 W
Roag, East Loch ⊂ 46 58.14 N 6.48 W
Roag, West Loch ⊂ 46 58.13 N 6.53 W
Roaming Rock, Lake ⊜[1] 214 41.38 N 80.49 W
Roaming Shores 214 41.39 N 80.49 W
Roana 64 45.52 N 11.28 E
Roan Cliffs ⊥[4] 200 39.20 N 109.40 W
Roan Creek ≃ 200 39.20 N 108.13 W
Roan Fell ∧ 44 55.13 N 2.52 W
Roan Mountain 192 36.11 N 82.04 W
Roann 216 40.54 N 85.55 W
Roanne 32 46.02 N 4.04 E
Roanoke, Al., U.S. 194 33.09 N 85.22 W
Roanoke, Il., U.S. 190 40.47 N 89.11 W
Roanoke, In., U.S. 216 40.57 N 85.22 W
Roanoke, Tx., U.S. 222 33.01 N 97.14 W
Roanoke, Va., U.S. 192 37.16 N 79.56 W
Roanoke (Staunton) ≃ 192 35.56 N 76.43 W
Roanoke Island I 192 35.53 N 75.39 W
Roanoke Rapids 192 36.27 N 77.39 W
Roanoke Rapids Dam ◆[6] 192 36.24 N 77.40 W
Roan Plateau ⋀[1] 200 39.30 N 109.40 W
Roans Prairie 222 30.35 N 95.57 W
Roaring ≃ 224 45.13 N 122.12 W
Roaring Branch 210 41.34 N 76.57 W
Roaring Brook ≃ 212 43.44 N 75.24 W
Roaring Fork ≃ 200 39.33 N 107.20 W
Roaring River Slough ≃ 282 38.05 N 121.55 W
Roaring Run ≃ 279b 40.33 N 79.32 W
Roaring Spring 214 40.20 N 78.23 W
Roaring Springs 196 33.54 N 100.52 W
Roaringwater Bay ⊂ 48 51.25 N 9.35 W
Roatán 236 16.18 N 86.35 W
Roatán, Isla de I 236 16.23 N 86.30 W
Robâa Oued Yahia 36 36.05 N 9.35 E
Robāṭ Karīm 128 35.28 N 51.05 E
Robbeneiland I 158 33.49 S 18.22 E
Robbers Cave State Park ♦ 196 35.01 N 95.27 W
Robbins, Ca., U.S. 226 38.53 N 121.42 W
Robbins, Il., U.S. 216 41.38 N 87.42 W
Robbins, N.C., U.S. 192 35.26 N 79.35 W
Robbins, Tn., U.S. 192 36.21 N 84.35 W
Robbins Airport ⊠ 283 42.34 N 70.58 W
Robbins Ditch ≋ 216 41.21 N 86.43 W
Robbins Island I 166 40.41 S 144.57 E
Robbins Pond ⊜ 283 42.00 N 70.55 W
Robbins Rest 276 40.39 N 73.10 W
Robbinsville, N.J., U.S. 208 40.13 N 74.37 W
Robbinsville, N.C., U.S. 192 35.19 N 83.48 W
Robbio 62 45.17 N 8.35 E
Robe, Austl. 166 37.11 S 139.45 E
Robe, Ityo. 144 7.52 N 39.38 E
Robe ≃, Austl. 162 21.19 S 115.40 E
Robe ≃, Ire. 48 53.37 N 9.16 W
Robe, Mount ∧[2] 166 31.40 S 141.20 E
Robecchetto con Induno 266b 45.32 N 8.46 E
Robecco d'Oglio 64 45.15 N 10.04 E
Robecco sul Naviglio 266b 45.26 N 8.53 E
Röbel 54 53.23 N 12.35 E
Robeline 194 31.41 N 93.18 W
Röberget ∧[2] 40 59.45 N 14.54 E
Robersonville 192 35.49 N 77.15 W
Robert, Havre du ⊂ 240e 14.40 N 60.55 W
Roberta 192 32.43 N 84.00 W
Roberta Mills 192 35.22 N 80.38 W
Robert E. Lee Memorial Park ♦ 284b 39.23 N 76.39 W
Robert E. Lee's Birthplace ⊥ 208 38.10 N 76.49 W
Robert-Espagne 56 48.45 N 5.02 E
Robert F. Kennedy Memorial Stadium ♦ 284c 38.53 N 76.58 W
Robert H. Treman State Park ♦ 210 42.24 N 76.35 W
Robert Lee 196 31.54 N 100.29 W
Robert Louis Stevenson Memorial State Park ♦ 226 38.40 N 122.36 W
Robert Louis Stevenson's Tomb ⊥ 175a 13.50 S 171.44 W
Robert Morse College ʊ[2] 279b 40.31 N 80.12 W
Robert Moses State Park ♦ 210 40.37 N 73.16 W
Robert Mueller Municipal Airport ⊠ 222 30.18 N 97.42 W
Roberto Payró 258 35.10 S 57.39 W
Robert Point › 168a 32.31 S 115.42 E
Roberts, Id., U.S. 202 43.43 N 112.07 W
Roberts, Il., U.S. 216 40.37 N 88.11 W
Roberts, Mt., U.S. 202 45.21 N 109.10 W
Roberts, Mount ∧ 171a 28.13 S 152.28 E
Roberts, Point › 224 49.00 N 123.06 W
Robert's Arm 186 49.29 N 55.49 W
Robertsbridge 42 50.59 N 0.29 E
Roberts Canyon V 280 34.11 N 117.54 W
Roberts Creek Mountain ∧ 204 39.52 N 116.18 W
Robertsdale, Al., U.S. 194 30.33 N 87.42 W
Robertsdale, Pa., U.S. 214 40.11 N 78.06 W
Robertsfield 150 6.15 N 10.24 W
Robertsfors 26 64.11 N 20.51 E
Robertsganj 124 24.42 N 83.04 E
Robertsham ◆[8] 273d 26.15 S 28.00 E
Robertsholm 40 60.35 N 76.16 E
Robert S. Kerr Lake ⊜[1] 194 35.25 N 95.00 W
Roberts Mountain ∧ 180 60.03 N 166.16 W
Robertson, Austl. 170 34.35 S 150.35 E
Robertson, S. Afr. 158 33.46 S 19.50 E
Robertson □[6], Ky., U.S. 218 38.32 N 84.04 W
Robertson □[6], Tx., U.S. 222 31.00 N 96.30 W
Robertson, Lac ⊜ 186 51.00 N 59.10 W
Robertson Bay ⊂ 9 71.25 S 170.00 E
Robertson Range ⋀ 162 23.10 S 121.00 E
Robertsonville 206 46.09 N 71.13 W
Roberts Park 278 41.44 N 87.49 W
Roberts Peak ∧ 182 52.57 N 120.32 W
Robertsport 150 6.45 N 11.22 W
Robertstown, Austl. 168b 34.00 S 139.05 E
Robertstown, Ire. 48 53.15 N 6.59 W
Robertsville 214 40.46 N 81.11 W
Robertville 56 50.27 N 6.07 E
Roberval 176 48.31 N 72.13 W
Robin Hood's Bay 44 54.25 N 0.33 W
Robins Air Force Base ■ 192 32.38 N 83.35 W
Robins Island I 207 40.58 N 72.28 W
Robinson, Il., U.S. 194 39.00 N 87.44 W
Robinson, Tx., U.S. 222 31.28 N 97.06 W
Robinson ≃ 164 16.03 S 137.16 E
Robinson, Lake ⊜[1] 192 34.26 N 80.10 W
Robinson Brook ≃ 283 43.02 N 71.13 W
Robinson Creek ≃ 226 38.16 N 119.15 W
Róbinson Crusoe, Isla (Isla Más a Tierra) I 244 33.38 S 78.52 W
Robinson Gorge National Park ♦ 166 25.15 S 149.10 E
Robinson Lake ⊜ 222 29.35 N 94.36 W
Robinson Lake Aerodrome ⊠ 273d 26.08 S 27.42 E
Robinson Pond ⊜ 283 42.48 N 71.23 W
Robinson Range ⋀ 162 25.45 S 119.00 E
Robinson Run ≃ 279b 40.23 N 80.06 W
Robinson Run, North Branch ≃ 279b 40.23 N 80.11 W
Robinsons 186 48.15 N 58.48 W
Robinvale 166 34.36 S 142.46 E
Robleda 34 40.23 N 6.36 W
Robledo 34 38.46 N 2.26 W
Roblin 184 51.14 N 101.21 W
Röblingen 54 51.28 N 11.40 E
Roboré 248 18.20 S 59.45 W
Röbrinken 40 58.36 N 15.53 E
Rob Roy Island I 175e 7.25 S 157.35 E
Robson, Mount ∧ 182 53.07 N 119.09 W
Robstown 196 27.47 N 97.40 W
Roby, Eng., U.K. 262 53.25 N 2.51 W
Roby, Il., U.S. 219 39.44 N 89.24 W
Roby, Tx., U.S. 196 32.44 N 100.22 W
Roby Mill 262 53.34 N 2.44 W
Roca, Cabo da › 34 38.47 N 9.30 W
Roçado 250 6.40 S 44.19 W
Rocafuerte 246 0.55 S 80.28 W
Roça Grande 256 21.36 S 42.58 W
Rocanville 184 50.24 N 101.43 W
Roca Partida, Isla I 232 19.01 N 112.02 W
Roca Partida, Punta › 234 18.42 N 95.10 W
Rocas, Atol das I[1] 250 3.52 S 33.59 W
Roccabernarda 68 39.08 N 16.52 E
Roccacasale 66 42.07 N 13.53 E
Roccadaspide 68 40.26 N 15.12 E
Rocca di Cambio 66 42.14 N 13.29 E
Rocca di Mezzo 66 42.12 N 13.31 E
Rocca di Neto 68 39.11 N 17.00 E
Rocca di Papa 66 41.46 N 12.42 E
Roccafluvione 66 42.51 N 13.29 E
Roccagloriosa 68 40.06 N 15.26 E
Roccalbegna 66 42.47 N 11.30 E
Roccalumera 70 37.58 N 15.24 E
Rocca Massima 66 41.41 N 12.55 E
Roccamena 70 37.50 N 13.09 E
Roccamonfina 68 41.17 N 13.59 E
Roccanova 68 40.13 N 16.12 E
Roccapalumba 70 37.48 N 13.39 E
Rocca Pia 66 41.56 N 13.59 E
Rocca Pietore 64 46.26 N 11.59 E
Roccaprebalza 64 44.31 N 9.57 E
Rocca Priora 267a 41.48 N 12.45 E
Roccaraso 66 41.51 N 14.05 E
Rocca San Casciano 66 44.03 N 11.50 E
Rocca Santa Maria 66 42.41 N 13.30 E
Roccasecca 66 41.33 N 13.40 E
Roccasecca dei Volsci 66 41.29 N 13.13 E
Roccastrada 66 43.00 N 11.10 E
Roccavione 62 44.19 N 7.29 E
Roccavivara 66 41.50 N 14.36 E
Roccelito, Monte ∧ 70 37.50 N 13.47 E
Roccella Ionica 68 38.19 N 16.24 E
Roccella Valdemone 70 37.56 N 15.00 E
Rocchetta Sant'Antonio 68 41.06 N 15.27 E
Rocciamelone ∧ 62 45.12 N 7.05 E
Ročegda 24 62.42 N 43.23 E
Roch ≃ 44 53.34 N 2.18 W
Rocha, Bra. 256 21.28 S 45.49 W
Rocha, Ur. 252 34.29 S 54.20 W
Rocha Miranda ◆[8] 287a 22.52 S 43.22 W
Rocha Sobrinho 287a 22.47 S 43.25 W
Rochdale, Eng., U.K. 44 53.38 N 2.09 W
Rochdale, Ma., U.S. 207 42.11 N 71.54 W
Rochdale, N.Y., U.S. 210 41.43 N 73.50 W
Rochdale □[8] 262 53.37 N 2.08 W
Rochdale Canal ≋ 262 53.43 N 1.54 W
Roche 42 50.24 N 4.48 W
Rochebrune, Pic de ∧ 62 44.49 N 6.51 E
Rochechouart 32 45.50 N 0.50 E
Rochedinho 255 20.14 S 54.33 W
Rochedo 255 19.57 S 54.52 W
Rochedo de Minas 256 21.38 S 43.01 W
Rochefort, Bel. 56 50.10 N 5.13 E
Rochefort, Fr. 32 45.57 N 0.58 W
Rochefort-en-Yvelines 50 48.35 N 1.59 E
Rochefort-Montagne 32 45.41 N 2.48 E
Rochefort-sur-Nenon 58 47.07 N 5.34 E
Roche Harbor 224 48.36 N 123.08 W
Rochehaut 56 49.51 N 5.00 E
Roche-la-Molière 62 45.26 N 4.19 E
Roche-lez-Beaupré 58 47.17 N 6.07 E
Rochelle, Ga., U.S. 192 31.57 N 83.27 W
Rochelle, Il., U.S. 216 41.55 N 89.04 W
Rochelle, Tx., U.S. 196 31.13 N 99.13 W
Rochelle Park 276 40.54 N 74.04 W
Rochemaure 62 44.35 N 4.42 E
Roche-Percée 184 49.03 N 102.45 W
Rochepot, Château de la ⊥ 58 46.57 N 4.40 E
Rocher Fendu, Rapides du ∟ 275a 45.19 N 73.57 W
Rochester, Austl. 166 36.22 S 144.42 E
Rochester, Eng., U.K. 42 51.24 N 0.30 E
Rochester, Eng., U.K. 44 55.16 N 2.16 W
Rochester, Il., U.S. 219 39.45 N 89.32 W
Rochester, In., U.S. 216 41.03 N 86.12 W
Rochester, Ma., U.S. 207 41.43 N 70.49 W
Rochester, Mi., U.S. 214 42.40 N 83.08 W
Rochester, Mn., U.S. 190 44.01 N 92.28 W
Rochester, N.H., U.S. 188 43.18 N 70.58 W
Rochester, N.Y., U.S. 210 43.09 N 77.36 W
Rochester, Oh., U.S. 214 41.07 N 82.18 W
Rochester, Pa., U.S. 214 40.42 N 80.17 W
Rochester, Tx., U.S. 196 33.19 N 99.51 W
Rochester, Wa., U.S. 224 46.49 N 123.05 W
Rochester, Wi., U.S. 216 42.44 N 88.13 W
Rochester City Airport ⊠ 260 51.21 N 0.30 E
Rochester Hills 214 42.40 N 83.09 W
Rochester Mills 214 40.49 N 78.59 W
Rochester-Monroe County Airport ⊠ 210 43.07 N 77.40 W
Rochester-Utica State Recreation Area ♦ 214 42.39 N 83.04 W
Rochetaillée 62 45.25 N 4.27 E
Rocheuses → Rocky Mountains ⋀ 16 48.00 N 116.00 W
Rochford 42 51.36 N 0.43 E
Rochford □[8] 260 51.36 N 0.39 E
Rochfortbridge 48 53.23 N 7.17 W
Rochlitz 54 51.03 N 12.47 E
Rochon, Lac ⊜ 206 46.43 N 75.14 W
Rock 190 46.04 N 87.09 W
Rock □[6] 216 42.41 N 89.05 W
Rock ≃, U.S. 190 41.29 N 90.37 W
Rock ≃, U.S. 198 43.05 N 96.27 W
Rockall I 22 57.35 N 13.48 W
Rockall Rise ✦[3] 10 59.00 N 14.00 W
Rockanje 52 51.53 N 4.05 E
Rockaway, N.J., U.S. 210 40.54 N 74.30 W
Rockaway, Or., U.S. 224 45.36 N 123.56 W
Rockaway ≃ 210 40.51 N 74.21 W
Rockaway Inlet ⊂ 276 40.34 N 73.55 W
Rockaway Neck 276 40.51 N 74.21 W
Rockaway Park ◆[8] 276 40.35 N 73.50 W
Rockaway Point ◆[8] 276 40.33 N 73.55 W
Rockaway Point › 276 40.33 N 73.56 W
Rockaways' Playland ♦ 276 40.35 N 73.49 W
Rockbank 274b 37.43 S 144.39 E
Rock Bay 182 50.20 N 125.29 W
Rockbridge 219 39.16 N 90.12 W
Rock Bridge State Park ♦ 219 38.53 N 92.19 W
Rock Brook ≃ 276 40.25 N 74.40 W
Rock Candy Mountain ∧ 224 47.01 N 123.07 W
Rockcastle ≃ 192 36.58 N 84.21 W
Rock City Falls 210 43.04 N 73.55 W
Rockcliffe Park 212 45.27 N 75.41 W
Rockcorry 48 54.07 N 7.01 W
Rock Creek, B.C., Can. 182 49.06 N 118.58 W
Rock Creek, Oh., U.S. 214 41.39 N 80.51 W
Rock Creek ≃, N.A. 202 48.25 N 107.05 W
Rock Creek ≃, U.S. 208 39.43 N 77.13 W
Rock Creek ≃, U.S. 284c 38.54 N 77.04 W
Rock Creek ≃, Ca., U.S. 226 37.55 N 120.58 W
Rock Creek ≃, Co., U.S. 198 40.20 N 102.31 W
Rock Creek ≃, Il., U.S. 216 41.12 N 87.59 W
Rock Creek ≃, In., U.S. 216 40.42 N 86.35 W
Rock Creek ≃, In., U.S. 216 40.49 N 85.23 W
Rock Creek ≃, Mt., U.S. 202 45.31 N 108.49 W
Rock Creek ≃, Mt., U.S. 202 46.43 N 113.40 W
Rock Creek ≃, Nv., U.S. 204 40.39 N 116.54 W
Rock Creek ≃, Or., U.S. 202 42.39 N 119.08 W
Rock Creek ≃, Or., U.S. 202 45.34 N 120.25 W
Rock Creek ≃, Or., U.S. 224 45.51 N 123.12 W
Rock Creek ≃, S.D., U.S. 198 43.44 N 97.58 W
Rock Creek ≃, Ut., U.S. 200 40.17 N 110.30 W
Rock Creek ≃, Wa., U.S. 202 46.55 N 117.56 W
Rock Creek ≃, Wa., U.S. 202 45.42 N 120.29 W
Rock Creek ≃, Wy., U.S. 200 41.54 N 106.08 W
Rock Creek Butte ∧ 202 44.49 N 118.07 W
Rock Creek Hills 284c 39.01 N 77.04 W
Rock Creek Park ♦ 284c 38.58 N 77.03 W
Rock Cut State Park ♦ 216 42.20 N 89.00 W
Rockdale, Austl. 170 33.57 S 151.08 E
Rockdale, Il., U.S. 216 41.30 N 88.06 W
Rockdale, Md., U.S. 284b 39.21 N 76.45 W
Rockdale, Pa., U.S. 285 39.53 N 75.26 W
Rockdale, Tx., U.S. 222 30.39 N 97.00 W
Rockdale, W.V., U.S. 214 40.18 N 80.35 W
Rockefeller Center ʊ 276 40.45 N 74.00 W
Rockefeller Park ♦ 279a 41.32 N 81.38 W
Rockefeller Plateau ⋀[1] 9 80.00 S 135.00 W
Rockenhausen 56 49.38 N 7.49 E
Rockensüss 56 51.03 N 9.50 E
Rockfall 207 41.31 N 72.41 W
Rock Falls 190 41.46 N 89.41 W
Rock Ferry 262 53.22 N 3.00 W
Rockfield 216 40.38 N 86.34 W
Rock Flat 171b 36.21 S 149.12 E
Rock Flat Creek ≃ 171b 36.07 S 149.12 E
Rockford, Al., U.S. 194 32.53 N 86.13 W
Rockford, Il., U.S. 216 42.16 N 89.05 W
Rockford, In., U.S. 218 38.59 N 85.54 W
Rockford, Ia., U.S. 190 43.03 N 92.56 W
Rockford, Mi., U.S. 190 43.07 N 85.33 W
Rockford, Oh., U.S. 216 40.41 N 84.38 W
Rockford, Tn., U.S. 192 35.49 N 83.56 W
Rock Forest 206 45.20 N 71.59 W
Rockglen, Sk., Can. 184 49.10 N 105.57 W
Rock Glen, N.Y., U.S. 210 42.41 N 78.07 W
Rock Hall 208 39.08 N 76.14 W
Rockhammar 40 59.32 N 15.26 E
Rockhampton 166 23.23 S 150.31 E
Rockhampton Downs 162 18.57 S 135.01 E
Rock Hill, N.Y., U.S. 210 41.38 N 74.36 W
Rock Hill, S.C., U.S. 192 34.55 N 81.01 W
Rockhill Furnace 214 40.15 N 77.54 W
Rockingham, Austl. 168a 32.17 S 115.44 E
Rockingham, N.C., U.S. 192 34.56 N 79.46 W
Rockingham □[6] 207 42.50 N 71.15 W
Rockingham Bay ⊂ 166 18.10 S 146.05 E
Rockingham Forest ◆[3] 42 52.30 N 0.37 W
Rockingham State Historic Site ⊥ 276 40.24 N 74.37 W
Rock Island, P.Q., Can. 206 45.01 N 72.06 W
Rock Island, Il., U.S. 190 41.30 N 90.34 W
Rock Island, Tx., U.S. 222 29.32 N 96.35 W
Rocklake 198 48.47 N 99.15 W
Rock Lake ⊜, Mb., Can. 184 49.11 N 99.12 W
Rock Lake ⊜, On., Can. 212 45.30 N 78.23 W
Rock Lake ⊜, Il., U.S. 278 41.40 N 88.03 W
Rock Lake ⊜, N.D., U.S. 198 48.50 N 99.10 W
Rock Lake ⊜, Wi., U.S. 216 43.04 N 88.56 W
Rockland, On., Can. 188 45.33 N 75.17 W
Rockland, De., U.S. 285 39.47 N 75.34 W
Rockland, Id., U.S. 202 42.34 N 112.52 W
Rockland, Me., U.S. 188 44.06 N 69.06 W
Rockland, Ma., U.S. 207 42.07 N 70.55 W
Rockland, Mi., U.S. 190 46.44 N 89.10 W
Rockland, N.Y., U.S. 210 41.58 N 74.54 W
Rockland □[6] 210 41.09 N 73.59 W
Rockland Lake 276 41.09 N 73.55 W
Rockland Lake ⊜ 276 41.08 N 73.55 W
Rockland Lake State Park ♦ 276 41.08 N 73.55 W
Rocklands Reservoir ⊜[1] 166 37.15 S 142.00 E
Rockledge, Fl., U.S. 220 28.21 N 80.43 W
Rockledge, Pa., U.S. 285 40.03 N 75.05 W
Rockleigh 276 41.00 N 73.55 W
Rocklin 226 38.47 N 121.14 W
Rockmart 192 34.00 N 85.02 W
Rock Meadow Brook ≃ 283 42.16 N 71.13 W
Rock of Cashel ⊥ 48 52.31 N 7.53 W
Rock Point 208 38.16 N 76.50 W
Rock Point Provincial Park ♦ 212 42.51 N 79.33 W
Rock Pond ⊜ 283 42.44 N 71.00 W
Rockport, Il., U.S. 219 39.32 N 91.00 W
Rockport, Ky., U.S. 194 37.20 N 86.59 W
Rockport, Me., U.S. 188 44.11 N 69.04 W
Rockport, Ma., U.S. 207 42.39 N 70.37 W
Rock Port, Mo., U.S. 194 40.24 N 95.30 W
Rockport, Tx., U.S. 196 28.01 N 97.03 W
Rock Rapids 198 43.25 N 96.10 W
Rock River 200 41.44 N 105.58 W
Rock Run 208 39.59 N 75.50 W
Rock Run ≃ 284c 38.58 N 77.11 W
Rock Sound 238 24.54 N 76.12 W
Rocksprings, Tx., U.S. 196 30.00 N 100.12 W
Rock Springs, Wy., U.S. 200 41.35 N 109.12 W
Rockstone 246 5.59 N 58.33 W
Rock Stream 210 42.28 N 76.56 W
Rockton, Il., U.S. 216 42.27 N 89.04 W
Rockton, Pa., U.S. 214 41.05 N 78.39 W
Rock Valley 198 43.12 N 96.17 W
Rockville, N.Z. 172 40.44 S 172.38 E
Rockville, Ct., U.S. 207 41.52 N 72.27 W
Rockville, In., U.S. 194 39.45 N 87.13 W
Rockville, Md., U.S. 208 39.05 N 77.09 W
Rockville, Ma., U.S. 283 42.08 N 71.21 W
Rockville, Pa., U.S. 208 40.20 N 76.54 W
Rockville, R.I., U.S. 207 41.27 N 71.30 W
Rockville Centre 210 40.39 N 73.38 W
Rockwall 222 32.55 N 96.27 W
Rockwall □[6] 222 32.55 N 96.23 W
Rockwell, Ia., U.S. 190 42.59 N 93.11 W
Rockwell, N.C., U.S. 192 35.33 N 80.24 W
Rockwell, Lake ⊜ 214 41.12 N 81.19 W
Rockwell City 198 42.23 N 94.38 W
Rockwell International Corporation ʊ[3] 280 33.52 N 117.51 W
Rockwood, On., Can. 212 43.37 N 80.08 W
Rockwood, Me., U.S. 188 45.41 N 69.44 W
Rockwood, Mi., U.S. 216 42.04 N 83.14 W
Rockwood, Or., U.S. 224 45.31 N 122.28 W
Rockwood, Pa., U.S. 188 39.54 N 79.09 W
Rockwood, Tn., U.S. 192 35.51 N 84.41 W
Rockwood Lake ⊜ 276 41.06 N 73.38 W
Rockwood Lake Brook ≃ 276 41.03 N 73.36 W
Rocky 196 35.09 N 99.03 W
Rocky ≃, Ab., Can. 182 53.08 N 117.59 W
Rocky ≃, Mi., U.S. 216 41.57 N 85.39 W
Rocky ≃, N.C., U.S. 192 35.37 N 79.09 W
Rocky ≃, Oh., U.S. 214 41.30 N 81.49 W
Rocky, East Branch ≃ 279a 41.24 N 81.53 W
Rocky, West Branch ≃ 214 41.24 N 81.53 W
Rocky Arroyo V 196 32.32 N 104.21 W
Rocky Boy's Indian Reservation ◆[4] 202 48.18 N 109.45 W
Rocky Branch ≃ 284c 38.53 N 77.19 W
Rocky Cape National Park ♦ 166 40.56 S 145.35 E
Rocky Comfort Creek ≃ 192 32.59 N 82.25 W
Rocky Coulee V 202 47.10 N 119.16 W
Rocky Creek ≃ 192 35.53 N 80.47 W
Rockyford, Ab., Can. 182 51.13 N 113.08 W
Rocky Ford, Co., U.S. 198 38.06 N 103.43 W
Rocky Ford Creek ≃ 216 41.19 N 83.37 W
Rocky Fork Lake ⊜ 218 39.11 N 83.28 W
Rocky Fork State Park ♦ 218 39.11 N 83.30 W
Rocky Gorge Reservoir ⊜[1] 208 39.07 N 77.54 W
Rocky Grove 214 41.25 N 79.49 W
Rocky Gully 162 34.30 S 116.48 E
Rocky Harbour 186 49.36 N 57.55 W
Rocky Harbour ⊂ 271d 22.20 N 114.19 E
Rocky Hill, Ct., U.S. 207 41.40 N 72.39 W
Rocky Hill, N.J., U.S. 276 40.24 N 74.38 W
Rocky Island Lake ⊜[1] 190 46.56 N 83.04 W
Rocky Lake ⊜ 184 54.08 N 101.30 W
Rocky Mount, N.C., U.S. 192 35.57 N 77.48 W
Rocky Mount, Va., U.S. 192 36.59 N 79.53 W
Rocky Mountain ∧ 202 47.49 N 112.49 W
Rocky Mountain House 182 52.22 N 114.55 W
Rocky Mountain National Park ♦ 200 40.19 N 105.42 W
Rocky Mountains ⋀ 16 48.00 N 116.00 W
Rocky Point, N.Y., U.S. 207 40.57 N 72.56 W
Rocky Point, Wa., U.S. 224 47.35 N 122.41 W
Rocky Point ›, Ba. 192 26.00 N 77.25 W
Rocky Point ›, Ire. 48 54.42 N 8.48 W
Rocky Point ›, Namibia 156 19.03 S 12.30 E
Rocky Point ›, Norf. I. 174c 29.03 S 167.55 E
Rocky Point ›, Ak., U.S. 180 64.25 N 163.10 W
Rocky Point ›, Ma., U.S. 207 41.57 N 70.35 W
Rocky Point ›, N.Y., U.S. 276 40.55 N 73.32 W
Rocky Ridge 214 41.32 N 83.13 W
Rocky Ridge ∧ 282 37.48 N 122.03 W
Rocky River 214 41.28 N 81.50 W
Rocky River Reservation ♦ 279a 41.27 N 81.50 W
Rocky Run ≃, N.D., U.S. 198 47.38 N 99.02 W
Rocky Run ≃, Pa., U.S. 285 39.54 N 75.28 W
Rocky Run ≃, Va., U.S. 284c 38.58 N 77.15 W
Rocky Saugeen ≃ 212 44.13 N 80.53 W
Rocky Top ∧ 202 44.47 N 122.17 W
Roclenge-sur-Geer 56 50.45 N 5.36 E
Rocosas, Montañas → Rocky Mountains ⋀ 16 48.00 N 116.00 W
Rocquencourt 261 48.50 N 2.07 E
Rocroi 50 49.55 N 4.31 E
Roda 192 36.58 N 82.49 W
Roda ≃ 54 50.52 N 11.44 E
Rodach 56 50.20 N 10.46 E
Rodach ≃ 56 50.08 N 10.52 E
Rodakovo 83 48.33 N 39.02 E
Rodalben 56 49.14 N 7.38 E
Rodalquilar 34 37.40 N 2.08 W
Rodas 240p 22.20 N 80.33 W
Rodas → Ródhos I 38 36.10 N 28.00 E
Rodaun ◆[8] 264b 48.08 N 16.16 E
Rødberg 26 60.16 N 8.58 E
Rødby 41 54.42 N 11.24 E
Rødbyhavn 41 54.39 N 11.21 E
Roddickton 186 50.52 N 56.08 W
Rødding 41 55.23 N 9.06 E
Rodeiro 256 21.12 S 42.52 W
Rødekro 41 55.04 N 9.21 E
Rodel 46 57.41 N 7.05 W
Roden 52 53.07 N 6.26 E
Roden ≃ 42 52.43 N 2.36 W
Rodenberg 52 52.18 N 9.21 E
Rodenkirchen, Dtsch. 52 53.24 N 8.26 E
Rodenkirchen, Dtsch. 56 50.54 N 6.59 E
Rödentel 54 50.17 N 11.01 E
Rodeo, Arg. 252 30.12 S 69.06 W
Rodeo, Méx. 232 25.11 N 104.34 W
Rodeo, Ca., U.S. 226 38.01 N 122.15 W
Rodeo, N.M., U.S. 200 31.50 N 109.01 W
Rodeo Lagoon ⊂ 282 37.50 N 122.31 W
Röderau 54 51.19 N 13.19 E
Roderick ≃ 162 26.57 S 116.13 E
Roderick Island I 182 52.40 N 128.22 W
Rödermark 56 49.59 N 8.50 E
Rodewisch 54 50.32 N 12.24 E

ENGLISH
Name Page Lat.°′ Long.°′

Rodez 32 44.21 N 2.35 E
Rodgau 56 50.02 N 8.54 E
Rodheim-Bieber 56 50.37 N 8.35 E
Rodhópis, Orosirá → Rhodope Mountains ⋀ 38 41.30 N 24.30 E
Ródhos (Rhodes) 38 36.26 N 28.13 E
Ródhos (Rhodes) I 38 36.10 N 28.00 E
Rodi Garganico 68 41.55 N 15.53 E
Roding 60 49.12 N 12.32 E
Roding ≃ 42 51.31 N 0.06 E
Rodinka 80 57.24 N 43.34 E
Rodino, Ross. 76 58.57 N 44.59 E
Rodino, Ross. 86 52.30 N 80.15 E
Rodionovo-Nesvetajskaja 83 47.36 N 39.42 E
Rodman 180 57.28 N 135.21 W
Rodman Naval Station ■ 236 8.56 N 79.36 W
Rodn'a 76 56.22 N 34.55 E
Rodnei, Munții ⋀ 38 47.35 N 24.40 E
Rodney, On., Can. 214 42.34 N 81.41 W
Rodney, Ms., U.S. 194 31.51 N 91.11 W
Rodney, Cape ›, N.Z. 172 36.17 S 174.49 E
Rodney, Cape ›, Ak., U.S. 180 64.39 N 166.24 W
Rodney Bay ⊂ 241f 14.05 N 60.58 W
Rodney Village 208 39.07 N 75.31 W
Rodničok 80 51.26 N 42.54 E
Rodniki, Ross. 80 57.06 N 41.44 E
Rodniki, Ross. 265b 55.39 N 38.04 E
Rodnikovskij 86 50.39 N 57.12 E
Rodolfo, Lago → Rudolf, Lake ⊜ 144 3.30 N 36.05 E
Rodonit, Kep i › 38 41.35 N 19.27 E
Rodostov 78 51.58 N 24.57 E
Rødovre 41 55.41 N 12.29 E
Rodrigo de Freitas, Lagoa ⊂ 287a 22.58 S 43.13 W
Rodrigues I 12 19.42 S 63.25 E
Rodríguez, Méx. 196 27.10 N 100.01 W
Rodríguez, Ur. 258 34.23 S 56.33 W
Rodríguez, Arroyo ≃ 288 34.52 S 58.02 W
Roduco 208 36.27 N 76.48 W
Rødven 26 62.38 N 7.33 E
Rødvig 41 55.15 N 12.23 E
Roe ≃ 48 55.07 N 6.59 W
Roebling 208 40.06 N 74.47 W
Roebourne 162 20.47 S 117.09 E
Roebuck Bay ⊂ 162 18.04 S 122.17 E
Roehampton ◆[8] 260 51.27 N 0.14 W
Roe Island I 282 38.04 N 122.02 W
Roeland Park 198 39.02 N 94.37 W
Roelands 168a 33.18 S 115.50 E
Roeliff Jansen Kill ≃ 210 42.11 N 73.52 W
Roelofarendsveen 52 52.12 N 4.38 E
Roelofskamp 158 26.10 S 24.24 E
Roen, Monte ∧ 64 46.22 N 11.11 E
Roer (Rur) ≃ 56 51.12 N 5.59 E
Roermond 52 51.12 N 6.00 E
Roesbrugge-Haringe 50 50.55 N 2.37 E
Roeselare (Roulers) 50 50.57 N 3.08 E
Roesinger, Lake ⊜ 224 47.58 N 121.55 W
Roessleville 210 42.41 N 73.48 W
Roes Welcome Sound ʬ 176 64.00 N 88.00 W
Roetgen 56 50.39 N 6.12 E
Rœulx 50 50.30 N 4.06 E
Roff 196 34.37 N 96.50 W
Röfors 40 58.57 N 14.37 E
Rofrano 68 40.12 N 15.25 E
Rogačevo 82 56.26 N 37.10 E
Rogačov 76 53.05 N 30.03 E
Rogačovka 78 51.30 N 39.34 E
Rogagua, Laguna ⊜ 248 13.43 S 66.54 W
Rogaguado, Laguna ⊜ 248 12.52 S 65.43 W
Rogaland □[6] 26 59.00 N 6.15 E
Rogalik 83 48.56 N 40.03 E
Rogan' 78 49.54 N 36.29 E
Rogans Hill 274a 33.44 S 151.01 E
Rogan's Seat ∧ 44 54.25 N 2.07 W
Rogart 46 58.00 N 4.08 W
Rogäsen 54 52.19 N 12.20 E
Rogaška Slatina 36 46.14 N 15.38 E
Rogatica 38 43.48 N 19.00 E
Rogatin 78 49.25 N 24.37 E
Rogätz 54 52.19 N 11.46 E
Rogen ⊜ 26 62.19 N 12.23 E
Roger, Lac ⊜ 190 47.50 N 78.51 W
Roger Island I 283 42.43 N 70.50 W
Rogers, Ar., U.S. 194 36.19 N 94.07 W
Rogers, Ct., U.S. 207 41.50 N 71.54 W
Rogers, Oh., U.S. 214 40.48 N 80.38 W
Rogers, Tx., U.S. 222 30.55 N 97.13 W
Rogers, Mount ∧ 192 36.39 N 81.33 W
Rogers City 190 45.25 N 83.49 W
Rogers Lake ⊜ 228 34.52 N 117.51 W
Rogers Park ◆[8] 278 42.01 N 87.40 W
Rogers Pass)(182 51.17 N 117.31 W
Rogersville, N.B., Can. 186 46.44 N 65.26 W
Rogersville, Al., U.S. 194 34.49 N 87.17 W
Rogersville, Tn., U.S. 192 36.24 N 83.00 W
Roggeveldberge ⋀ 158 32.17 S 20.08 E
Roggewein, Cabo › 174z 27.07 S 109.15 W
Roggiano Gravina 68 39.37 N 16.09 E
Roghudi 68 38.03 N 15.55 E
Rogliano, Fr. 62 42.57 N 9.25 E
Rogliano, It. 68 39.11 N 16.20 E
Rognac 62 43.29 N 5.14 E
Rognedino 76 53.48 N 33.33 E
Rögnitz ≃ 54 53.19 N 10.57 E
Rognon ≃ 58 48.23 N 5.10 E
Rogny 50 47.45 N 2.53 E
Rogojampi 115a 8.19 S 114.17 E
Rogovatoje 78 51.14 N 38.22 E
Rogovo 82 55.13 N 37.05 E
Rogovskaja 78 45.44 N 38.44 E
Rogovskoje 80 58.33 N 50.43 E
Rogožkino 83 47.10 N 39.21 E
Rogoźno 30 52.46 N 17.00 E
Rogozov 78 50.14 N 31.03 E
Rogue ≃, Mi., U.S. 190 43.04 N 85.35 W
Rogue ≃, Or., U.S. 202 42.26 N 124.25 W
Rogue River 202 42.26 N 123.10 W
Rohdenhaus 263 51.18 N 7.01 E
Rohilkhand Plains ≚ 124 28.20 N 79.30 E
Rohinjan 272c 19.06 N 73.04 E
Rohitpur 126 23.42 N 90.19 E
Rohl ≃ 140 6.22 N 29.46 E
Röhlinghausen ◆[8] 263 51.36 N 7.14 E
Rohnert Park 226 38.20 N 122.42 W
Rohr 60 48.46 N 11.58 E
Rohrbach in Oberösterreich 60 48.34 N 13.59 E
Rohrbach-lès-Bitche 56 49.03 N 7.16 E
Rohrbeck 264a 52.32 N 13.02 E
Rohrberg 54 52.42 N 11.02 E
Röhrenfurth 56 51.09 N 9.32 E
Rohri 120 27.41 N 68.54 E
Röhrsdorf 54 50.51 N 12.50 E
Rohtak 123 28.54 N 76.34 E
Rohunta, Laguna ⊂ 236 15.12 N 83.30 W
Roi, Île du → King Island I 166 39.50 S 144.00 E
Roia (Roya) ≃ 62 43.48 N 7.35 E
Roi Et 110 16.03 N 103.40 E
Roi Georges, Îles du II 14 14.32 S 145.08 W
Roi Léopold, Monts du → King Leopold Ranges ⋀ 160 17.30 S 125.45 E
Roine ⊜ 26 61.24 N 24.06 E
Roinville 261 48.32 N 2.03 E
Roisel 50 49.57 N 3.06 E
Roissy 261 48.47 N 2.39 E
Roissy-en-France 261 49.00 N 2.31 E
Roitzsch 54 51.34 N 12.16 E
Roja, Lat. 76 57.30 N 22.49 E

DEUTSCH
Name Seite Breite°′ Länge°′ E = Ost

Roja, Ukr. 83 47.59 N 37.20 E
Rojas 252 34.12 S 60.44 W
Rojl'anka 78 46.17 N 29.46 E
Rojo, Cabo ›, Méx. 234 21.33 N 97.20 W
Rojo, Cabo ›, P.R. 240m 17.56 N 67.11 W
Rojo, Mar → Red Sea ⊤[2] 136 20.00 N 38.00 E
Rojo → Red ≃ 178 31.00 N 91.40 W
Rokan 112 0.34 N 100.25 E
Rokan ≃ 114 2.00 N 100.52 E
Rokan-kanan ≃ 114 1.23 N 100.56 E
Rokan-kiri ≃ 114 1.23 N 100.56 E
Röke 41 56.14 N 13.30 E
Rokeby National Park ♦ 164 13.40 S 142.55 E
Rokel ≃ 150 8.33 N 12.48 W
Rokewood 169 37.54 S 143.43 E
Rokewood Junction 169 37.51 S 143.41 E
Rokhah 120 35.16 N 69.28 E
Rokiškis 76 55.58 N 25.35 E
Rokkō-san ∧ 96 34.46 N 135.16 E
Rokkō-sanchi ⋀ 270 34.45 N 135.13 E
Roklum 54 52.04 N 10.44 E
Rokuan Kansallispuisto ♦ 26 64.32 N 26.33 E
Rokugō 94 35.29 N 138.27 E
Rokugō ◆[8] 268 35.33 N 139.43 E
Rokusei 94 36.58 N 136.52 E
Rokycany 60 49.45 N 13.36 E
Rokytná ≃ 61 49.05 N 16.22 E
Rolampont 58 47.57 N 5.16 E
Roland, Mb., Can. 184 49.25 N 97.55 W
Roland, Ar., U.S. 194 34.54 N 92.29 W
Roland, Ia., U.S. 190 42.09 N 93.30 W
Roland, Lake ⊜[1] 284b 39.23 N 76.38 W
Roland C. Nickerson State Park ♦ 207 41.46 N 70.03 W
Rolândia 255 23.18 S 51.22 W
Roland Park ◆[8] 284b 39.22 N 76.39 W
Roland Run ≃ 284b 39.23 N 76.39 W
Rolava ≃ 54 50.15 N 12.51 E
Røldal 26 59.49 N 6.48 E
Roldán 252 32.54 S 60.54 W
Roldanillo 246 4.24 N 76.09 W
Rolde 52 52.58 N 6.38 E
Roldskov ◆[3] 26 56.48 N 9.50 E
Rolette 198 48.39 N 99.50 W
Roleystone 168a 32.08 S 116.04 E
Rolfe 198 42.48 N 94.31 W
Roll, Az., U.S. 200 32.45 N 113.59 W
Roll, In., U.S. 216 40.33 N 85.23 W
Rolla, B.C., Can. 182 55.54 N 120.09 W
Rolla, Ks., U.S. 198 37.07 N 101.07 W
Rolla, Mo., U.S. 194 37.57 N 91.46 W
Rolla, N.D., U.S. 198 48.51 N 99.37 W
Rolle 58 46.28 N 6.20 E
Rolle, Passo di)(64 46.18 N 11.47 E
Rolleboise 261 49.01 N 1.36 E
Rolleston, Austl. 166 24.28 S 148.37 E
Rolleston, N.Z. 172 43.35 S 172.23 E
Rolling Acres 284b 39.17 N 76.52 W
Rollingbay 224 47.39 N 122.30 W
Rolling Fork 194 32.54 N 90.52 W
Rolling Fork ≃ 194 37.55 N 85.50 W
Rolling Hills 280 33.46 N 118.21 W
Rolling Hills Estates 280 33.47 N 118.21 W
Rolling Meadows 216 42.05 N 88.00 W
Rolling Prairie 216 41.40 N 86.37 W
Rolling River Indian Reserve ◆[4] 184 50.27 N 100.00 W
Rollingstone 166 19.03 S 146.24 E
Rollingwood 226 37.57 N 122.20 W
Rollins 182 47.54 N 114.11 W
Rollins Reservoir ⊜[1] 226 39.08 N 120.57 W
Rolvsøya I 24 71.00 N 24.00 E
Roma, Austl. 166 26.35 S 148.47 E
Roma (Rome), It. 66 41.54 N 12.29 E
Roma (Rome), It. 267a 41.54 N 12.29 E
Roma, Leso. 158 29.27 S 27.45 E
Roma, Tx., U.S. 196 26.25 N 99.01 W
Roma □[4] 66 41.58 N 12.40 E
Romagna □[9] 64 44.30 N 12.15 E
Romagnano Sesia 62 45.38 N 8.23 E
Romagne-sous-Montfaucon 56 49.20 N 5.05 E
Romain, Cape › 192 33.00 N 79.22 W
Romaine ≃ 176 50.18 N 63.47 W
Romainmôtier 58 46.42 N 6.29 E
Romainville 261 48.53 N 2.26 E
Romakloster 26 57.31 N 18.27 E
Roman, Blg. 38 43.09 N 23.55 E
Roman, Rom. 38 46.55 N 26.56 E
Roman ≃ 42 51.51 N 0.57 E
Romanche ≃ 62 45.05 N 5.43 E
Romanche Gap ✦[1] 10 0.10 S 18.15 W
Romang, Pulau I 164 7.35 S 127.26 E
Romang, Selat ʬ 164 7.30 S 127.00 E
Romania (România) □[1], Europe 22 46.00 N 25.30 E
Romania (România) □[1], Europe 38 46.00 N 25.30 E
Roman-Koš, gora ∧ 78 44.37 N 34.15 E
Romankovcy 78 48.29 N 27.13 E
Roman Nose Mountain ∧ 202 43.55 N 123.44 W
Romano, Cape › 220 25.50 N 81.41 W
Romano, Cayo I 240p 22.04 N 77.50 W
Romano Banco 266b 45.25 N 9.06 E
Romano di Lombardia 62 45.31 N 9.45 E
Romanova 88 57.04 N 103.24 E
Romanovka, Ross. 80 51.24 N 47.23 E
Romanovka, Ross. 80 51.45 N 42.45 E
Romanovka, Ross. 80 49.47 N 45.05 E
Romanovka, Ross. 86 54.38 N 76.03 E
Romanovka, Ross. 88 53.14 N 112.46 E
Romanovka, Ross. 265a 60.03 N 30.42 E
Romanovo, Ross. 82 56.39 N 39.14 E
Romanovo, Ross. 86 53.58 N 80.30 E
Romanovo, Ross. 86 52.37 N 81.14 E
Romanovo, Ross. 86 59.09 N 61.30 E
Romans d'Isonzo 64 45.53 N 13.26 E
Romanshorn 58 47.34 N 9.22 E
Romans-sur-Isère 62 45.03 N 5.03 E
Romansville 285 39.57 N 75.45 W
Romanzof Mountains ⋀ 180 69.00 N 144.00 W
Romaški 80 50.13 N 46.41 E
Romaškino 80 52.29 N 51.48 E
Romaškovo 265b 55.44 N 37.20 E
Romayor 222 30.27 N 94.50 W
Rombari 154 4.33 N 31.02 E
Romblon 116 12.35 N 122.15 E
Romblon □[4] 116 12.30 N 122.10 E
Romblon Island I 116 12.33 N 122.17 E
Romblon Passage ʬ 116 12.27 N 122.12 E
Rombo, Ilhéus do II 150a 14.58 N 24.40 W
Rome, Ga., U.S. 192 34.15 N 85.09 W
Rome, Il., U.S. 190 40.53 N 89.30 W
Rome, Ms., U.S. 194 33.57 N 90.28 W
Rome, N.Y., U.S. 210 43.12 N 75.27 W
Rome, Oh., U.S. 214 41.36 N 80.52 W
Rome, Pa., U.S. 210 41.51 N 76.21 W
Rome, Wi., U.S. 216 42.58 N 88.38 W
Rome City 216 41.29 N 85.22 W
Romeleåsen ⋀[2] 41 55.34 N 13.33 E
Romenay 58 46.30 N 5.04 E
Romeno 64 46.24 N 11.07 E
Romentino 62 45.28 N 8.42 E
Romeo 214 42.48 N 83.00 W
Romeoville 216 41.38 N 88.05 W
Römerberg 56 49.17 N 8.24 E
Romero, Isla I 258 33.48 S 59.20 W
Rome → Roma 66 41.54 N 12.29 E
Rometan 128 39.56 N 64.23 E
Rometta 70 38.10 N 15.25 E
Romfartuna 40 59.44 N 16.35 E
Romford ◆[8] 260 51.35 N 0.11 E
Römhild 54 50.24 N 10.32 E

Symbols in the index entries represent the broad categories identified in the key at the right. Symbols with superior numbers (⋀[1]) identify subcategories (see complete key on page *I · 1)*.

Symbole im Register stellen die rechts im Schlüssel erklärten Kategorien dar. Symbole mit hochgestellten Ziffern (⋀[1]) bezeichnen Unterabteilungen einer Kategorie (vgl. vollständiger Schlüssel auf Seite *I · 1)*.

Los símbolos incluídos en el texto del índice representan las grandes categorias identificadas con la clave a la derecha. Los símbolos con numeros en su parte superior (⋀[1]) identifican las subcategorías (véase la clave completa en la página *I · 1)*.

Les symboles de l'index représentent les catégories indiquées dans la légende à droite. Les symboles suivis d'un indice (⋀[1]) représentent des sous-catégories (voir légende complète à la page *I · 1)*.

Os símbolos incluídos no texto do índice representam as grandes categorias identificadas com a chave à direita. Os símbolos com números em sua parte superior (⋀[1]) identificam as subcategorias (veja-se a chave completa à página *I · 1)*.

∧ Mountain	Berg	Montaña	Montagne	Montanha
⋀ Mountains	Gebirge	Montañas	Montagnes	Montanhas
)(Pass	Paß	Paso	Col	Passo
V Valley, Canyon	Tal, Cañon	Valle, Cañón	Vallée, Canyon	Vale, Canhão
≚ Plain	Ebene	Llano	Plaine	Planície
› Cape	Kap	Cabo	Cap	Cabo
I Island	Insel	Isla	Île	Ilha
II Islands	Inseln	Islas	Îles	Ilhas
⊥ Other Topographic Features	Andere Topographische Objekte	Otros Elementos Topográficos	Autres données topographiques	Outros acidentes topográficos

ESPAÑOL Nombre / FRANÇAIS Nom / PORTUGUÊS Nome	Página / Page	Lat.°′	Long.°′ W = Oeste / W = Ouest

Romiley	262	53.25 N	2.05 W
Romilly, Mount ∧[2]	162	20.27 S	126.34 E
Romilly-sur-Seine	50	48.31 N	3.43 E
Romit	85	38.44 N	69.17 E
Romit, zapovednik ♠	85	38.52 N	69.20 E
Romita	234	20.52 N	101.31 W
Romitorio	267a	42.01 N	12.39 E
Rommani	148	34.34 N	6.37 W
Romme	40	60.26 N	15.30 E
Rommerskirchen	56	51.02 N	6.40 E
Romney, In., U.S.	216	40.14 N	86.54 W
Romney, W.V., U.S.	188	39.20 N	78.45 W
Romney Marsh ≡	42	51.03 N	0.55 E
Romny, Ross.	89	50.44 N	129.15 E
Romny, Ukr.	78	50.45 N	33.30 E
Rømø I	26	55.08 N	8.31 E
Romodan	78	49.59 N	33.19 E
Romodanovo	80	54.26 N	45.20 E
Romoland	228	33.45 N	117.10 W
Romont	58	46.42 N	6.55 E
Romorantin-Lanthenay	50	47.22 N	1.45 E
Rompin, Malay.	114	2.42 N	102.31 E
Rompin, Malay.	114	2.48 N	103.29 E
Rompin ≏	114	2.49 N	103.29 E
Romrod	56	50.43 N	9.13 E
Rom → Roma	66	41.54 N	12.29 E
Romsdalen V	26	62.15 N	8.05 E
Romsdalsfjorden ⊂[2]	26	62.39 N	7.15 E
Romsey, Austl.	169	37.21 S	144.45 E
Romsey, Eng., U.K.	42	50.59 N	1.30 W
Romsø I	41	55.31 N	10.48 E
Romulus, Mi., U.S.	216	42.13 N	83.23 W
Romulus, N.Y., U.S.	210	42.45 N	76.50 W
Røn, Nor.	26	61.03 N	9.03 E
Ron, Viet	110	17.53 N	106.27 E
Ron, Mui ›	110	18.07 N	106.27 E
Rona, Schw.	58	46.34 N	9.38 E
Rona, Zaïre	154	2.14 N	30.52 E
Rona I, Scot., U.K.	46	57.34 N	5.59 W
Rona I, Scot., U.K.	46	59.07 N	5.49 W
Ronald	224	47.14 N	121.01 W
Ronan	202	47.31 N	114.06 W
Ronas Hill ∧[2]	46a	60.31 N	1.28 W
Ronas Voe ⊂	46a	60.32 N	1.29 W
Ronay I	46	57.29 N	7.11 W
Roncade	64	45.38 N	12.22 E
Roncador, Cayos de ✦[4]	236	13.32 N	80.03 W
Roncador, Serra do ⋏[1]	242	12.00 S	52.00 W
Roncador Reef ✦[2]	175e	6.13 S	159.22 E
Roncegno	64	46.03 N	11.25 E
Roncesvalles	34	43.01 N	1.19 W
Ronceverte	192	37.44 N	80.27 W
Ronchamp	58	47.42 N	6.39 E
Ronchi dei Legionari	64	45.50 N	13.30 E
Ronchin	50	50.36 N	3.06 E
Ronchis	64	45.49 N	13.00 E
Ronciglione	66	42.17 N	12.13 E
Ronco	58	46.08 N	8.44 E
Ronco Canavese	62	45.30 N	7.32 E
Roncofreddo	66	44.02 N	12.20 E
Roncone	64	45.59 N	10.40 E
Ronco Scrivia	62	44.37 N	8.59 E
Roncq	50	50.45 N	3.07 E
Rond, Sommet ∧	206	45.05 N	72.33 W
Ronda	34	36.44 N	5.10 W
Ronda, Serranía de ⋏	34	36.44 N	5.03 W
Rondane ∧	26	61.55 N	9.45 E
Rondane Nasjonal Park ♠	26	61.50 N	9.50 E
Rønde	41	56.18 N	10.29 E
Ronde, Pointe ›	240d	15.33 N	61.29 W
Rondeau Harbour ⊂	214	42.18 N	81.53 W
Rondeau Provincial Park ♠	214	42.16 N	81.51 W
Rondebult	273d	26.18 S	28.14 E
Ronde Island I	241k	12.18 N	61.35 W
Rondissone	62	45.15 N	7.58 E
Rondon	255	23.23 S	52.48 W
Rondônia □[3]	248	11.00 S	63.00 W
Rondonópolis	255	16.28 S	54.38 W
Rondout	278	42.17 N	87.53 W
Rondout Creek ≏	210	41.55 N	73.53 W
Rondout Reservoir ⊜[1]	210	41.50 N	74.29 W
Rone ≏	50	50.46 N	3.27 E
Ronehamn	26	57.10 N	18.29 E
Rong ≏	102	24.32 N	109.15 E
Ronga	80	56.43 N	48.32 E
Rongai	154	0.10 S	35.51 E
Rong'an	102	25.10 N	109.20 E
Rongbaca	102	31.48 N	99.40 E
Rongchang	107	29.24 N	105.36 E
Rongcheng, Zhg.	98	37.08 N	122.23 E
Rongcheng, Zhg.	105	39.03 N	115.52 E
Rongding	107	28.57 N	103.40 E
Ronge, Lac la ⊜	184	55.10 N	105.00 W
Rongelap I[1]	14	11.20 N	166.50 E
Rongjiang	102	25.52 N	108.37 E
Rongkop	115a	8.10 S	110.45 E
Rongola	158	27.22 S	31.37 E
Rongotea	172	40.18 S	175.25 E
Rõngu	76	58.09 N	26.15 E
Rongui, Ilha I	154	10.50 S	40.40 E
Rongwanshi	100	28.10 N	112.57 E
Rongxian, Zhg.	102	22.50 N	110.38 E
Rongxian, Zhg.	107	29.28 N	104.25 E
Ronkiti Harbor ⊂	174r	6.48 N	158.10 E
Ronkonkoma	276	40.48 N	73.06 W
Ronkonkoma, Lake ⊜	276	40.50 N	73.07 W
Rønne	26	55.06 N	14.42 E
Rönne ≏	41	56.16 N	12.50 E
Ronneburg	54	50.51 N	12.10 E
Ronneby	26	56.12 N	15.18 E
Ronne Entrance ⊂	9	72.30 S	74.00 W
Ronne Ice Shelf ⊓	9	78.30 S	61.00 W
Ronnenberg	52	52.20 N	9.40 E
Rönneshytta	40	58.56 N	15.02 E
Rönninge	40	59.12 N	17.44 E
Ronroni	175e	9.37 S	159.58 E
Rönsahl	263	51.07 N	7.30 E
Ronsdorf ◆[8]	263	51.14 N	7.12 E
Ronse (Renaix-Gleiche)	50	50.45 N	3.36 E
Röntgenmuseum ʋ	263	51.12 N	7.16 E
Ronuro ≏	255	11.56 S	53.33 W
Roodepoort □[5]	273d	26.10 S	27.52 E
Roodepoort-Maraisburg	158	26.11 S	27.54 E
Roodeschool	52	53.25 N	6.45 E
Roodhouse	219	39.29 N	90.22 W
Roof Butte ∧	200	36.28 N	109.05 W
Rooiberge ∧	158	28.27 S	28.26 E
Rooiboklaagte ≏	156	20.50 S	21.00 E
Rooidam	158	28.07 S	21.15 E
Rooilyf	158	28.49 S	21.57 E
Rooiwal	158	27.18 S	27.32 E
Rooks Creek ≏	216	40.57 N	88.44 W
Rookwood Cemetery ◆	274a	33.53 S	151.04 E
Roon, Pulau I	164	2.23 S	134.33 E
Rooniu, Mont ∧	174s	17.49 S	149.12 W
Roordahuizum	52	53.06 N	5.46 E
Roorkee	124	29.52 N	77.53 E
Roosboom	158	28.36 S	29.44 E
Roosendaal	52	51.32 N	4.28 E
Roosevelt, Az., U.S.	200	33.40 N	111.08 W
Roosevelt, Mn., U.S.	198	48.48 N	95.05 W
Roosevelt, N.J., U.S.	208	40.13 N	74.28 W
Roosevelt, N.Y., U.S.	276	40.40 N	73.35 W
Roosevelt, Ok., U.S.	196	34.50 N	99.01 W
Roosevelt, Ut,. U.S.	200	40.17 N	109.59 W
Roosevelt ≏	248	7.35 S	60.20 W
Roosevelt Beach	210	43.19 N	78.52 W
Roosevelt Campobello International Park ♠	186	44.52 N	66.58 W
Roosevelt Field ◆[9]	276	40.45 N	73.37 W
Roosevelt Island I	9	79.30 S	162.00 W
Roosevelt Park	216	43.11 N	86.15 W
Roosevelt Park ♠	276	40.33 N	74.21 W
Roosevelt Raceway ♠	276	40.44 N	73.36 W
Roosevelt Roads Naval Station ■	240m	18.15 N	65.38 W
Roosevelt Terrace	226	38.08 N	122.16 W
Root	58	47.07 N	8.23 E
Root ≏, N.T., Can.	180	62.50 N	123.40 W
Root ≏, Mn., U.S.	190	43.46 N	91.15 W
Root ≏, Wi., U.S.	216	42.44 N	87.47 W
Root, North Branch ≏	190	43.49 N	92.10 W
Root, South Branch ≏	190	43.44 N	91.58 W
Root Lake ⊜	184	54.04 N	101.24 W
Rootstown	214	41.05 N	81.14 W
Rooty Hill	170	33.46 S	150.50 E
Ropang	115b	8.52 S	117.29 E
Ropaži	76	57.08 N	24.30 E
Ropča	24	63.02 N	52.16 E
Ropczyce	30	50.03 N	21.37 E
Roper	192	35.52 N	76.36 W
Roper ≏	164	14.43 S	135.27 E
Roper Bar	164	14.44 S	134.44 E
Roper Valley	164	14.56 S	134.00 E
Ropes Creek ≏	274a	33.43 S	150.47 E
Ropesville	196	33.26 N	102.09 W
Roppe	58	47.40 N	6.55 E
Ropša	265a	59.44 N	29.52 E
Roque	250	3.01 S	45.23 W
Roquebillière	62	44.01 N	7.18 E
Roquebrune-Cap-Martin	62	43.46 N	7.28 E
Roquebrune-sur-Argens	62	43.26 N	6.38 E
Roquefavour, Aqueduc de ≍[1]	62	43.31 N	5.19 E
Roquefort	32	44.02 N	0.19 W
Roquemaure	62	44.03 N	4.47 E
Roque Pérez	258	35.25 S	59.20 W
Roquestéron	62	43.52 N	7.00 E
Roquevaire	62	43.21 N	5.36 E
Rora Head ›	46	58.52 N	3.25 W
Roraima □[3]	246	1.00 N	61.00 W
Roraima, Mount ∧	246	5.12 N	60.44 W
Rörbäcksnäs	26	61.08 N	12.49 E
Roreto Chisone	62	44.59 N	7.06 E
Rorey Lake ⊜	180	66.55 N	128.25 W
Rorke Lake ⊜	184	54.33 N	92.30 W
Rorke's Drift ⊥	158	28.20 S	30.32 E
Rorketon	184	51.26 N	99.32 W
Røros	26	62.35 N	11.20 E
Rorschach	58	47.29 N	9.30 E
Rørvig	41	55.57 N	11.46 E
Rørvik	24	64.51 N	11.14 E
Ros' ≏	78	49.39 N	31.35 E
Rosà, It.	64	45.43 N	11.45 E
Rosa, Zam.	154	9.38 S	31.21 E
Rosa, Cap ›	36	36.58 N	8.14 E
Rosa, Lake ⊜	238	21.00 N	73.30 W
Rosa, Monte ∧	58	45.55 N	7.53 E
Rosairinho	266c	38.40 N	9.01 W
Rošal'	80	55.40 N	39.51 E
Rosales, Méx.	232	28.12 N	105.33 W
Rosales, Pil.	116	15.54 N	120.38 E
Rosalia	202	47.14 N	117.22 W
Rosalie, Lake ⊜	220	27.58 N	81.28 W
Rosalind Bank ✦[4]	238	16.30 N	80.30 W
Rosamond, Ca., U.S.	228	34.51 N	118.09 W
Rosamond, Il., U.S.	219	39.23 N	89.10 W
Rosamond Lake ⊜	228	34.50 N	118.04 W
Rosamorada	234	22.08 N	105.12 W
Rosana	255	22.33 S	53.00 W
Rosander, Mount ∧	224	48.46 N	124.42 W
Rosanky	222	29.56 N	97.18 W
Rosanna	274b	37.45 S	145.04 E
Rosans	62	44.23 N	5.28 E
Rosario, Arg.	252	32.57 S	60.40 W
Rosário, Bra.	250	2.57 S	44.14 W
Rosario, Méx.	232	27.37 N	109.16 W
Rosario, Méx.	234	23.00 N	105.52 W
Rosario, Para.	252	24.27 S	57.03 W
Rosario, Pil.	116	13.51 N	121.12 E
Rosario, Pil.	116	16.14 N	120.29 E
Rosario, Ur.	258	34.19 S	57.21 W
Rosario, Ven.	246	10.19 N	72.19 W
Rosario ≏, Arg.	252	24.50 S	65.43 W
Rosario ≏, Ur.	258	34.26 S	57.21 W
Rosario, Bahía ⊂	232	29.52 N	115.45 W
Rosario, Cayo el I	240p	21.38 N	81.53 W
Rosario, Islas del II	246	10.10 N	75.46 W
Rosario Bank ✦[2]	238	18.30 N	84.05 W
Rosario de Arriba	232	30.01 N	115.40 W
Rosario de la Frontera	252	25.48 S	64.58 W
Rosario de Lerma	252	24.59 S	65.35 W
Rosario del Tala	252	32.18 S	59.09 W
Rosário de Minas	256	21.43 S	43.38 W
Rosário do Sul	252	30.15 S	54.55 W
Rosário Oeste	248	14.50 S	56.25 W
Rosario Strait ʯ	224	48.30 N	122.45 W
Rosarito, Méx.	204	32.20 N	117.02 W
Rosarito, Méx.	232	26.27 N	111.38 W
Rosarito, Embalse de ⊜[1]	34	40.05 N	5.15 W
Rosarno	68	38.29 N	15.59 E
Rosas	196	26.09 N	103.27 W
Rosazza	62	45.41 N	7.58 E
Rošča	82	54.47 N	36.51 E
Roščino	76	60.15 N	29.37 E
Rosciolo	66	42.07 N	13.20 E
Roscoe, Il., U.S.	216	42.25 N	89.01 W
Roscoe, N.Y., U.S.	210	41.55 N	74.54 W
Roscoe, Pa., U.S.	214	40.04 N	79.51 W
Roscoe, S.D., U.S.	198	45.26 N	99.20 W
Roscoe, Tx., U.S.	196	32.26 N	100.32 W
Roscoe ≏	180	69.40 N	120.57 W
Roscoe Village ⊥	214	40.18 N	81.54 W
Roscoff	32	48.44 N	3.59 E
Roscommon, Ire.	48	53.38 N	8.11 W
Roscommon, Mi., U.S.	190	44.29 N	84.35 W
Roscommon □[6]	48	53.45 N	8.15 W
Roscrea	48	52.57 N	7.47 W
Rosdorf	52	51.30 N	9.53 E
Rose, It.	68	39.24 N	16.17 E
Rose, N.Y., U.S.	210	43.09 N	76.53 W
Rose, Monte ∧	70	37.39 N	13.25 E
Rose, Mount ∧	226	39.21 N	119.55 W
Rose, Pointe de la ›	240e	14.40 N	60.53 W
Roseau, Dom.	240d	15.18 N	61.24 W
Roseau, Mn., U.S.	198	48.50 N	95.45 W
Roseau ≏, Dom.	240d	15.18 N	61.24 W
Roseau ≏, N.A.	198	49.08 N	97.15 W
Roseau ≏, St. Luc.	241f	13.58 N	61.02 W
Rosebank ◆[8]	273d	26.09 S	28.02 E
Rosebank Station	275b	43.47 N	79.07 W
Roseberry Lakes ⊜	184	52.40 N	92.30 W
Roseberth	166	25.47 S	139.37 E
Rosebery	166	41.46 S	145.32 E
Rosebery ◆[8]	274a	33.55 S	151.12 E
Rose-Blanche	186	47.37 N	58.41 W
Roseboom	210	42.45 N	74.47 W
Roseboro	192	34.57 N	78.30 W
Rose Bowl ♠	280	34.10 N	118.09 W
Rosebud, Austl.	169	38.21 S	144.54 E
Rosebud, Mo., U.S.	219	38.23 N	91.24 W
Rosebud, Mt., U.S.	202	46.16 N	106.26 W
Rose Bud, Pa., U.S.	214	40.45 N	78.33 W
Rosebud, S.D., U.S.	198	43.13 N	100.51 W
Rosebud, Tx., U.S.	222	31.04 N	96.58 W
Rosebud ≏	182	51.25 N	112.37 W
Rosebud Creek ≏	202	46.16 N	106.28 W
Rosebud Indian Reservation ◆[4]	198	43.25 N	100.28 W
Roseburg	202	43.13 N	123.20 W
Rosebush	190	43.41 N	84.46 W
Rose City	190	44.25 N	84.07 W
Rose Creek ≏, U.S.	198	40.04 N	97.07 W
Rose Creek ≏, Ca., U.S.	226	38.07 N	120.24 W
Rosecroft Raceway ♠	284c	38.48 N	76.58 W
Rosedale, Austl.	166	24.38 S	151.55 E
Rosedale, Ab., Can.	182	51.25 N	112.38 W
Rosedale, B.C., Can.	224	49.11 N	121.48 W
Rosedale, In., U.S.	194	39.37 N	87.17 W
Rosedale, La., U.S.	194	30.27 N	91.27 W
Rosedale, Md., U.S.	284b	39.19 N	76.30 W
Rosedale, Ms., U.S.	194	33.51 N	91.01 W
Rosedale ◆[8], On., Can.	275b	43.41 N	79.22 W
Rosedale ◆[8], N.Y., U.S.	276	40.39 N	73.45 W
Rosedale Estates	284c	38.47 N	76.58 W
Rosedale Hills	218	39.42 N	86.07 W
Rosedene	158	32.01 S	22.07 E
Rosehall	246	6.16 N	57.21 W
Rosehearty	46	57.42 N	2.07 W
Rose-Hill, Maus.	157c	20.14 S	57.27 E
Rose Hill, N.C., U.S.	192	34.49 N	78.01 W
Rose Hill, Va., U.S.	192	36.40 N	83.22 W
Rose Hill, Wa., U.S.	224	47.42 N	122.10 W
Rosehill Cemetery ◆	278	41.59 N	87.41 W
Rosehill Racecourse ♠	274a	33.49 S	151.02 E
Rose Hills Memorial Park ◆	280	34.01 N	118.02 W
Roseira	256	22.54 S	45.18 W
Rose Island I, Am. Sam.	14	14.32 S	168.08 W
Rose Island I, Ba.	192	25.06 N	77.14 W
Rose Lake	182	54.24 N	126.02 W
Roseland, Ca., U.S.	226	38.30 N	122.55 W
Roseland, In., U.S.	216	41.42 N	86.15 W
Roseland, La., U.S.	194	30.45 N	90.30 W
Roseland, N.J., U.S.	276	40.49 N	74.17 W
Roseland, Oh., U.S.	214	40.47 N	82.32 W
Roseland ◆[8]	278	41.42 N	87.38 W
Roselawn	216	41.09 N	87.19 W
Roselle, Il., U.S.	216	41.59 N	88.04 W
Roselle, N.J., U.S.	276	40.39 N	74.15 W
Roselle Field ⊠	278	41.59 N	88.06 W
Rosellen	263	51.08 N	6.43 E
Roselle Park	276	40.39 N	74.15 W
Rosellerheide	263	51.07 N	6.44 E
Rose Lodge	224	45.01 N	123.52 W
Rosemary	182	50.46 N	112.05 W
Rosemary Brook ≏	283	42.19 N	71.15 W
Rosemead	280	34.04 N	118.04 W
Rosemère	206	45.38 N	73.48 W
Rosemont, Ca., U.S.	226	38.34 N	121.20 W
Rosemont, Il., U.S.	278	41.59 N	87.52 W
Rosemont, Ky., U.S.	218	38.01 N	84.32 W
Rosemont, Oh., U.S.	214	41.03 N	80.53 W
Rosemont, Pa., U.S.	285	40.01 N	75.19 W
Rosemont Horizon ♠	278	42.00 N	87.53 W
Rosenberg	222	29.33 N	95.48 W
Rosendaël	50	51.02 N	2.24 E
Rosendal, Nor.	26	59.59 N	6.01 E
Rosendal, S. Afr.	158	28.30 S	27.55 E
Rosendale	210	41.51 N	74.05 W
Roseneath	273d	26.17 S	28.11 E
Rosenfeld	58	48.17 N	8.43 E
Rosengarten	52	53.23 N	9.54 E
Rosenhayn	208	39.28 N	75.07 W
Rosenheim	64	47.51 N	12.07 E
Rosenhügel ◆[8]	263	51.10 N	7.12 E
Rosenthal, Dtsch.	54	50.51 N	14.04 E
Rosenthal, Dtsch.	56	50.58 N	8.52 E
Rosenthal ◆[8]	264a	52.36 N	13.23 E
Rose Peak ∧	200	33.26 N	109.22 W
Rosepine	194	30.55 N	93.17 W
Rose Point ›	182	54.13 N	131.35 W
Rosersberg	40	59.35 N	17.53 E
Rosersberg ⊥	40	59.34 N	17.50 E
Roses, Golf de ⊂	34	42.10 N	3.15 E
Roseto	210	40.52 N	75.12 W
Roseto Capo Spulico	68	39.59 N	16.36 E
Roseto degli Abruzzi	66	42.41 N	14.01 E
Roseto Valfortore	68	41.22 N	15.06 E
Rosetown	184	51.33 N	108.00 W
Rose Tree	285	39.56 N	75.23 W
Rose Tree Park ♠	285	39.56 N	75.24 W
Rosetta Branch → Rashīd, Far'≏	142	31.30 N	30.21 E
Rosetta Mouth → Rashīd, Maṣabb ≏[1]	142	31.30 N	30.20 E
Rosetta → Rashīd	142	31.24 N	30.25 E
Rosettenville ◆[8]	273d	26.15 S	28.03 E
Rosevale	171a	27.51 S	152.29 E
Rose Valley, Sk., Can.	184	52.18 N	103.50 W
Rose Valley, Pa., U.S.	285	39.53 N	75.23 W
Rose Valley, Pa., U.S.	285	40.10 N	75.13 W
Rose Valley, Wa., U.S.	224	46.06 N	122.50 W
Roseville, Austl.	274a	33.47 S	151.11 E
Roseville, Ca., U.S.	226	38.45 N	121.17 W
Roseville, Il., U.S.	190	40.43 N	90.39 W
Roseville, Mi., U.S.	214	42.29 N	82.56 W
Roseville, Mn., U.S.	190	45.00 N	93.09 W
Roseville, Oh., U.S.	188	39.48 N	82.04 W
Roseville, Pa., U.S.	210	41.51 N	76.57 W
Roseville Park	285	39.42 N	75.43 W
Rosewood, Austl.	171a	27.39 S	152.35 E
Rosewood, Austl.	171b	35.41 S	147.52 E
Rosewood, Oh., U.S.	216	40.13 N	83.58 W
Rosewood Heights	219	38.53 N	90.05 W
Roseworthy	168b	34.32 S	138.44 E
Roshanara Gardens ♠	272a	28.40 N	77.12 E
Rosharon	222	29.21 N	95.28 W
Rosheim	58	48.30 N	7.28 E
Rosherville Dam ⊜[1]	273d	26.14 S	28.07 E
Rosh Ha'Ayin	132	32.06 N	34.57 E
Rosholt, S.D., U.S.	198	45.52 N	96.43 W
Rosholt, Wi., U.S.	190	44.37 N	89.18 W
Rosh Pinna	132	32.58 N	35.32 E
Rosica ≏	38	43.15 N	25.42 E
Rosice	30	49.11 N	16.23 E
Rosiclare	194	37.25 N	88.20 W
Rosières-aux-Salines	58	48.36 N	6.20 E
Rosières-en-Santerre	50	49.49 N	2.43 E
Rosiers, Rivière des ≏	206	45.59 N	72.07 W
Rosignano Marittimo	66	43.24 N	10.28 E
Rosignano Solvay	66	43.23 N	10.26 E
Rosignol	246	6.17 N	57.32 W
Roșiori de Vede	38	44.07 N	25.00 E
Rositz	54	51.01 N	12.22 E
Roskilde	41	55.39 N	12.05 E
Roskilde □[6]	41	55.30 N	12.05 E
Roskilde Fjord ⊂	41	55.56 N	12.00 E
Roskow	54	52.28 N	12.42 E
Roslagen □[9]	40	59.30 N	18.40 E
Roslags-Bro	40	59.50 N	18.44 E
Rosl'akovo	24	69.03 N	33.09 E
Rosl'atino	76	59.46 N	44.15 E
Roslavl'	76	53.57 N	32.52 E
Roslev	26	56.42 N	8.59 E
Roslindale ◆[8]	283	42.18 N	71.07 W
Roslyn, N.Y., U.S.	276	40.48 N	73.39 W
Roslyn, Pa., U.S.	208	40.07 N	75.08 W
Roslyn, Pa., U.S.	285	39.57 N	75.36 W
Roslyn, Wa., U.S.	224	47.13 N	120.59 W
Roslyn Estates	276	40.47 N	73.40 W
Roslyn Harbor	276	40.49 N	73.38 W
Roslyn Heights	276	40.47 N	73.38 W
Rosmalen	52	51.43 N	5.22 E
Rosman	192	35.08 N	82.49 W
Rosmead	158	31.29 S	25.08 E
Ros Mhic Thriúin → New Ross	48	52.24 N	6.56 W
Røsnæs ›[1]	41	55.44 N	10.59 E
Rosne, Ruisseau le ≏	261	48.58 N	2.25 E
Rosneath	46	56.01 N	4.49 W
Rosny-sous-Bois	261	48.53 N	2.29 E
Rosny-sur-Seine	50	49.00 N	1.38 E
Rosolina	64	45.05 N	12.15 E
Rosolini	70	36.49 N	14.57 E
Rošore	85	38.20 N	72.19 E
Rosporden	32	47.58 N	3.50 W
Rösrath	56	50.54 N	7.11 E
Ross, Austl.	166	42.02 S	147.29 E
Ross', Bela.	76	53.17 N	24.24 E
Ross, N.Z.	172	42.54 S	170.49 E
Ross, Ca., U.S.	226	37.55 N	122.32 W
Ross, In., U.S.	278	41.32 N	87.23 W
Ross, Oh., U.S.	218	39.19 N	84.39 W
Ross □[6]	218	39.20 N	83.06 W
Ross ≏	180	61.59 N	132.26 W
Ross, Cape ›	116	10.56 N	119.13 E
Ross, Mount ∧	172	41.28 S	175.21 E
Ross, Point ›	174c	29.04 S	167.56 E
Ross, Pointe ›	275a	45.21 N	73.48 W
Rossa	58	46.22 N	9.08 E
Rossach	56	50.09 N	10.56 E
Rossano	68	39.35 N	16.39 E
Rossasna	76	54.39 N	30.53 E
Rossau	54	52.47 N	11.38 E
Rossbach	54	51.15 N	11.53 E
Ross Behy	48	52.02 N	9.58 W
Ross-Béthio	150	16.16 N	16.08 W
Rossburg	216	40.17 N	84.38 W
Rossburn	184	50.40 N	100.52 W
Ross Carbery	48	51.35 N	9.01 W
Rosscott Manor	285	39.39 N	75.44 W
Ross Dam ◆[6]	224	48.44 N	121.04 W
Rossdorf	56	49.51 N	8.45 E
Rosseau	212	45.16 N	79.39 W
Rosseau, Lake ⊜	212	45.10 N	79.35 W
Rossel, Cap ›	175f	20.23 S	166.36 E
Rossell y Rius	252	33.11 S	55.42 W
Rossen ⊜	40	60.19 N	16.26 E
Rossendale □[8]	262	53.43 N	2.14 W
Rosser	222	32.28 N	96.27 W
Rosses Bay ⊂	48	55.10 N	8.27 W
Rosses Point	48	54.18 N	8.33 W
Rossford	214	41.37 N	83.33 W
Ross Fork Creek ≏	202	47.05 N	109.43 W
Rosshaupten	58	47.39 N	10.43 E
Rosshyttan	40	60.04 N	16.21 E
Ross Ice Shelf ⊓	9	81.30 S	175.00 W
Rossiglione	62	44.34 N	8.40 E
Rossignol, Lake ⊜	186	44.10 N	65.10 W
Rossija → Russia □[1]	72	60.00 N	80.00 E
Rössing	156	22.31 S	14.52 E
Rossio, Estação do ◆[5]	266c	38.43 N	9.09 W
Ross Island I, Ant.	9	77.30 S	168.00 E
Ross Island I, Mb., Can.	184	54.14 N	97.45 W
Rossiter	214	40.53 N	78.55 W
Rossitten → Rybačij	76	55.09 N	20.51 E
Rossiya → Russia □[1]	72	60.00 N	80.00 E
Rossla	54	51.28 N	11.04 E
Ross Lake ⊜[1]	224	48.53 N	121.04 W
Ross Lake National Recreation Area ♠	224	48.45 N	121.00 W
Rossland	182	49.05 N	117.48 W
Rosslare	48	52.17 N	6.23 W
Rosslare Harbour	48	52.15 N	6.22 W
Rosslau	54	51.53 N	12.14 E
Rosslea	48	54.14 N	7.11 W
Rossleben	54	51.17 N	11.25 E
Rosslyn Farms	279b	40.26 N	80.05 W
Rossmoor	280	33.47 N	118.05 W
Rossmore	274a	33.57 S	150.46 E
Rossmoyne	208	40.13 N	76.57 W
Rosso	150	16.30 N	15.49 W
Rossön	26	63.55 N	16.21 E
Ross-on-Wye	42	51.55 N	2.35 W
Rossony	76	55.53 N	28.49 E
Rossoš', Ross.	78	51.08 N	38.29 E
Rossoš', Ross.	78	50.12 N	39.34 E
Rossouw	158	31.09 S	27.18 E
Ross R. Barnett Reservoir ⊜[1]	194	32.30 N	90.00 W
Ross River	180	61.59 N	132.27 W
Ross-Schelfeis → Ross Ice Shelf ⊓	9	81.30 S	175.00 W
Ross Sea ⊤[2]	9	76.00 S	175.00 W
Rosstal	56	49.25 N	10.52 E
Rosston	218	40.03 N	86.17 W
Rossu, Capu ›	36	42.14 N	8.33 E
Røssvatnet ⊜	24	65.45 N	14.00 E
Rossville, Ga., U.S.	192	34.58 N	85.17 W
Rossville, Il., U.S.	216	40.22 N	87.40 W
Rossville, In., U.S.	216	40.25 N	86.35 W
Rossville, Ks., U.S.	198	39.08 N	95.57 W
Rossville, Md., U.S.	284b	39.20 N	76.29 W
Rosswein	54	51.03 N	13.10 E
Røst II	24	67.28 N	11.59 E
Rostāq	120	37.07 N	69.49 E
Röstånga	41	56.00 N	13.17 E
Rosthern	184	52.40 N	106.17 W
Rostherne	262	53.21 N	2.23 W
Rostherne Mere ⊜	262	53.21 N	2.23 W
Roštkala	120	37.16 N	71.49 E
Rostock	54	54.05 N	12.07 E
Rostov	80	57.11 N	39.25 E
Rostov □[8]	83	47.30 N	39.30 E
Rostov-na-Donu	83	47.14 N	39.42 E
Rostrataville	158	26.49 S	25.39 E
Rostraver Airport ⊠	279b	40.13 N	79.50 W
Rostrevor	48	54.06 N	6.12 W
Rosvinskoje	24	66.32 N	52.26 E
Roswell, Ga., U.S.	192	34.01 N	84.21 W
Roswell, N.M., U.S.	196	33.23 N	104.31 W
Roswell, Oh., U.S.	214	40.28 N	81.21 W
Rosyth	46	56.03 N	3.26 W
Rot ≏	58	48.19 N	9.54 E
Rota	34	36.37 N	6.21 W
Rota I	108	14.10 N	145.12 E
Rot am See	56	49.15 N	10.01 E
Rotan	196	32.51 N	100.27 W
Rotanda	156	19.33 S	32.50 E
Rotary Island I	285	40.14 N	74.49 W
Rotbach ≏	263	51.34 N	6.41 E
Rotberg	264a	52.21 N	13.31 E
Rote-Erde, Stadion ♠	263	51.30 N	7.27 E
Rotenburg	52	53.06 N	9.24 E
Rotenburg an der Fulda	56	51.00 N	9.45 E
Roter Main ≏	54	50.04 N	11.24 E
Rotes Meer → Red Sea ⊤[2]	136	20.00 N	38.00 E
Roth, Dtsch.	56	50.46 N	7.42 E
Roth, Dtsch.	60	49.15 N	11.06 E
Roth ≏	58	48.27 N	10.10 E
Rötha	54	51.12 N	12.25 E
Rothaargebirge ⋏	56	51.05 N	8.15 E
Rothbury	44	55.19 N	1.55 W
Rothbury Forest ◆[3]	44	55.18 N	1.54 W
Rothemühl	54	53.36 N	13.49 E
Röthenbach, Dtsch.	58	47.37 N	9.59 E
Röthenbach, Schw.	58	46.51 N	7.45 E
Röthenbach an der Pegnitz	60	49.29 N	11.15 E
Rothenburg	54	51.20 N	14.58 E
Rothenburg ob der Tauber	56	49.23 N	10.10 E
Rothenkirchen	54	50.33 N	12.30 E
Rothenschirmbach	54	51.27 N	11.33 E
Rothenstein ∧[2]	263	51.07 N	7.41 E
Rother ≏	42	50.57 N	0.32 W
Rothera ʋ[3]	9	67.34 S	68.08 W
Rotherham, N.Z.	172	42.42 S	172.57 E
Rotherham, Eng., U.K.	44	53.26 N	1.20 W
Rothes	46	57.31 N	3.13 W
Rothesay, N.B., Can.	186	45.23 N	66.00 W
Rothesay, Scot., U.K.	46	55.51 N	5.03 W
Roth-Neusiedl ◆[8]	264b	48.08 N	16.23 E
Rothrist	58	47.19 N	7.53 E
Rothsay, Austl.	162	29.17 S	116.53 E
Rothsay, Mn., U.S.	198	46.28 N	96.16 W
Rothschild	190	44.53 N	89.37 W
Rothsville	208	40.09 N	76.15 W
Rothwell, N.B., Can.	186	46.04 N	66.04 W
Rothwell, Eng., U.K.	42	52.25 N	0.48 W
Rothwell, Eng., U.K.	44	53.46 N	1.29 W
Roti, Pulau I	112	10.45 S	123.10 E
Roti, Selat ʯ	112	10.25 S	123.25 E
Roto	166	33.03 S	145.28 E
Rotoiti, Lake ⊜, N.Z.	172	41.50 S	172.50 E
Rotoiti, Lake ⊜, N.Z.	172	38.02 S	176.25 E
Rotomanu	172	42.39 S	171.32 E
Rotonda	68	39.57 N	16.02 E
Rotondella	68	40.10 N	16.32 E
Rotondo, Monte ∧	36	42.13 N	9.03 E
Rotoroa, Lake ⊜	172	41.52 S	172.38 E
Rotorua	172	38.09 S	176.15 E
Rotorua, Lake ⊜	172	38.05 S	176.16 E
Rotowaro	172	37.36 S	175.05 E
Rott	64	47.54 N	10.59 E
Rott ≏	60	48.27 N	13.26 E
Rottach-Egern	64	47.41 N	11.46 E
Rott am Inn	64	47.59 N	12.07 E
Rotten ≏	58	46.17 N	7.33 E
Röttenbach	60	49.09 N	11.02 E
Rottenbach-Tremersdorf	56	50.21 N	10.56 E
Rottenbuch	64	47.44 N	10.58 E
Rottenburg am Neckar	58	48.28 N	8.56 E
Rottenburg an der Laaber	60	48.42 N	12.02 E
Rottenmann	61	47.31 N	14.22 E
Rotterdam, Ned.	52	51.55 N	4.28 E
Rotterdam, N.Y., U.S.	210	42.48 N	73.59 W
Rotterdam, Luchthaven ⊠	52	51.58 N	4.30 E
Rotterdam Junction	210	42.52 N	74.03 W
Rotthalmünster	60	48.21 N	13.12 E
Rotthausen ◆[8]	263	51.30 N	7.05 E
Rottingdean	42	50.48 N	0.04 W
Röttingen	56	49.30 N	9.58 E
Rottleberode	54	51.31 N	10.57 E
Rottnest Island I	168a	32.00 S	115.30 E
Rottofreno	62	45.03 N	9.34 E
Rottum	263	51.36 N	7.42 E
Rottumeroog I	52	53.30 N	6.30 E
Rottumerplaat I	52	53.32 N	6.30 E
Rottweil	58	48.10 N	8.37 E
Rotuma I	14	12.30 S	177.05 E
Rotwand ∧	64	47.39 N	11.56 E
Rötz	60	49.21 N	12.32 E
Roubaix	50	50.42 N	3.10 E
Roubideau Creek ≏	200	38.44 N	108.10 W
Roubidoux Creek ≏	194	37.51 N	92.13 W
Roubion ≏	62	44.31 N	4.42 E
Rouceux	58	48.22 N	5.41 E
Roudnice [nad Labem]	54	50.22 N	14.16 E
Rouen	50	49.26 N	1.05 E
Rougé	32	47.47 N	1.27 W
Rouge ≏, On., Can.	212	43.48 N	79.07 W
Rouge ≏, P.Q., Can.	206	45.39 N	74.42 W
Rouge ≏, P.Q., Can.	206	45.33 N	74.20 W
Rouge, Bell Branch ≏	281	42.23 N	83.16 W
Rouge, Lac ⊜	206	46.56 N	74.38 W
Rouge, Mer → Red Sea ⊤[2]	136	20.00 N	38.00 E
Rouge, River ≏	281	42.17 N	83.06 W
Rougeau, Forêt de ♠	261	48.35 N	2.30 E
Rougemont, Fr.	58	47.29 N	6.21 E
Rougemont, Schw.	58	46.29 N	7.12 E
Rougemont-le-Château	58	47.44 N	6.58 E
Rouge → Red ≏	178	31.00 N	91.40 W
Rough ≏	194	37.29 N	87.08 W
Rough And Ready	226	39.14 N	121.08 W
Rough River Lake ⊜[1]	194	37.40 N	86.25 W
Rouiba	34	36.44 N	3.17 E
Rouillac	32	45.47 N	0.04 W
Rouillon	261	48.33 N	2.00 E
Roulans	58	47.19 N	6.14 E
Rouleau	184	50.11 N	104.55 W
Roulers → Roeselare	50	50.57 N	3.08 E
Roulette	214	41.46 N	78.09 W
Roumanie → Romania □[1]	38	46.00 N	25.30 E
Round Harbour	186	49.51 N	55.40 W
Roundhead	216	40.34 N	83.50 W
Round Hill Head ›	166	24.10 S	151.53 E
Round Hill Regional Park ♠	279b	40.15 N	79.51 W
Round Knowe ∧[2]	48	55.08 N	6.55 W
Round Lake, Il., U.S.	278	42.21 N	88.05 W
Round Lake, Mn., U.S.	198	43.32 N	95.28 W
Round Lake, N.Y., U.S.	210	42.56 N	73.47 W
Round Lake ⊜, Nf., Can.	186	51.08 N	56.33 W
Round Lake ⊜, On., Can.	190	45.38 N	77.32 W
Round Lake ⊜, On., Can.	212	44.30 N	77.52 W
Round Lake ⊜, On., Can.	212	45.28 N	79.24 W
Round Lake ⊜, Sk., Can.	184	50.33 N	102.23 W
Round Lake ⊜, Il., U.S.	278	42.22 N	88.05 W
Round Lake ⊜, Mi., U.S.	216	41.58 N	84.17 W
Round Lake Beach	216	42.22 N	88.05 W
Round Lake Park	216	42.21 N	88.04 W
Round Mound ∧[2]	198	38.55 N	99.39 W
Round Mountain	204	38.42 N	117.04 W
Round Mountain ∧, Austl.	166	30.27 S	152.14 E
Round Mountain ∧, Austl.	171b	36.15 S	148.34 E
Round Pond ⊜, Nf., Can.	186	48.10 N	56.00 W
Round Pond ⊜, Ma., U.S.	283	42.36 N	70.49 W
Round Rock	222	30.30 N	97.40 W
Roundstone	48	53.23 N	9.53 W
Round Top	210	42.16 N	74.02 W
Round Top ∧[2]	208	40.30 N	76.42 W
Round Top Regional Park ♠	282	37.51 N	122.12 W
Roundup	202	46.26 N	108.32 W
Round Valley Indian Reservation ◆[4]	204	39.50 N	123.20 W
Round Valley Reservoir ⊜[1]	210	40.36 N	74.50 W
Roundwood	48	53.04 N	6.13 W
Roura	250	4.44 N	52.20 W
Rourkela → Raurkela	124	22.13 N	84.53 E
Rousay I	46	59.10 N	3.02 W
Rouse Hill	274a	33.41 S	150.56 E
Rouses Point	206	45.00 N	73.22 W
Rouseville	214	41.28 N	79.41 W
Rousies	50	50.16 N	4.00 E
Rousseau, Lake ⊜[1]	220	29.02 N	82.32 W
Rousset, Col de)(	62	44.50 N	5.24 E
Roussigny	261	48.39 N	2.06 E
Roussillon, Fr.	62	45.22 N	4.49 E
Roussillon, Fr.	62	43.54 N	5.17 E
Roussillon □[9]	32	42.30 N	2.30 E
Roussy-le-Village	56	49.27 N	6.10 E
Routhierville	186	48.11 N	67.09 W
Routot	50	49.23 N	0.44 E
Rouveen	52	52.36 N	6.11 E
Rouvignies	50	50.20 N	3.26 E
Rouville □[6]	206	45.23 N	73.04 W
Rouvray	50	47.25 N	4.06 E
Rouvray, Lac ⊜	186	49.18 N	70.49 W
Rouxville	158	30.29 S	26.46 E
Rouyn	190	48.15 N	79.01 W
Rouzerville	208	39.44 N	77.32 W
Rovaniemi	24	66.34 N	25.48 E
Rovasenda	62	45.32 N	8.19 E
Rovato	64	45.34 N	10.00 E
Rovbickskaja	76	52.40 N	24.05 E
Rove, Tunnel du ◆[5]	62	43.22 N	5.17 E
Rovegno	62	44.35 N	9.17 E
Rovellasca	62	45.40 N	9.03 E
Rovello Porro	62	45.39 N	9.02 E
Roven'ki, Ross.	78	49.56 N	38.54 E
Roven'ki, Ukr.	83	48.05 N	39.21 E
Rovenskaja Sloboda	78	52.13 N	30.19 E
Roverbella	64	45.16 N	10.46 E
Rovere	66	42.10 N	13.31 E
Roverè della Luna	64	46.15 N	11.10 E
Roveredo	58	46.14 N	9.08 E
Rovereto	64	45.53 N	11.02 E
Roverè Veronese	64	45.36 N	11.03 E
Rövershagen	54	54.10 N	12.15 E
Roversi	252	27.35 S	61.57 W
Roverud	26	60.15 N	12.03 E
Roviano	66	42.01 N	13.00 E
Rovigo	64	45.04 N	11.47 E
Rovigo □[4]	64	45.02 N	11.50 E
Rovinj	36	45.05 N	13.38 E
Rovira	246	4.14 N	75.14 W
Rovno	78	50.37 N	26.15 E
Rovnoje, Kyrg.	85	42.53 N	73.32 E
Rovnoje, Ross.	80	50.47 N	46.05 E
Rovnoje, Ukr.	78	48.15 N	31.45 E
Rovubu (Ruvubu) ≏	154	2.23 S	30.47 E
Rovuma (Ruvuma) ≏	154	10.29 S	40.28 E
Rów	54	52.58 N	14.45 E
Rowan □[6]	218	38.17 N	83.26 W
Rowan Lake ⊜	184	49.18 N	93.32 W
Rowanty Creek ≏	208	36.58 N	77.21 W
Rowena, Austl.	166	29.49 S	148.54 E
Rowena, Tx., U.S.	196	31.39 N	100.03 W
Rowe Park ♠	273a	6.30 N	3.23 E
Rowhill	273d	26.14 S	28.26 E
Rowland, N.C., U.S.	192	34.32 N	79.17 W
Rowland, Pa., U.S.	210	41.28 N	75.03 W
Rowland Flat	168b	34.35 S	138.56 E
Rowland Heights	280	33.58 N	117.54 W
Rowlands Gill	44	54.54 N	1.45 W
Rowlesburg	188	39.20 N	79.40 W
Rowlett	222	32.54 N	96.33 W
Rowlett, Isla I	254	44.48 S	74.25 W
Rowlett Creek ≏	222	32.49 N	96.31 W
Rowley	207	42.43 N	70.52 W
Rowley ≏, N.T., Can.	176	70.16 N	77.45 W
Rowley ≏, Ma., U.S.	283	42.43 N	70.49 W
Rowley Island I	176	69.08 N	78.50 W
Rowley Regis	42	52.29 N	2.03 W
Rowley Shoals ✦[2]	162	17.30 S	119.00 E
Rowntree Mill Park ♠	275b	43.45 N	79.35 W
Rowsburg	214	40.52 N	82.10 W
Rowville	274b	37.56 S	145.14 E
Roxa, Ilha I	150	11.15 N	15.40 W
Roxana	219	38.50 N	90.04 W
Roxas, Pil.	108	11.35 N	122.45 E
Roxas, Pil.	116	17.08 N	121.36 E
Roxas, Pil.	116	12.35 N	121.31 E
Roxas, Pil.	116	10.20 N	119.21 E
Roxas (Capiz), Pil.	116	11.35 N	122.45 E
Roxboro, P.Q., Can.	275a	45.31 N	73.48 W
Roxboro, N.C., U.S.	192	36.23 N	78.58 W
Roxborough	241r	11.15 N	60.35 W
Roxborough ◆[8]	285	40.02 N	75.13 W
Roxburgh, N.Z.	172	45.32 S	169.19 E
Roxburgh, Scot., U.K.	46	55.34 N	2.30 W
Roxbury, Ct., U.S.	207	41.33 N	73.18 W
Roxbury, N.Y., U.S.	210	42.17 N	74.33 W
Roxbury, Pa., U.S.	214	40.07 N	77.40 W
Roxbury, Va., U.S.	208	37.28 N	77.09 W
Roxbury ◆[8], Ma., U.S.	283	42.20 N	71.06 W
Roxbury ◆[8], N.Y., U.S.	276	40.34 N	73.54 W
Roxby Downs	162	30.43 S	136.46 E
Roxel	52	51.57 N	7.32 E
Roxen ⊜	26	58.30 N	15.41 E
Roxie	194	31.30 N	91.04 W
Roxo, Cap ›	150	12.20 N	16.43 W
Roxton	196	33.33 N	95.44 W
Roxton Pond (Sainte-Pudentienne)	206	45.29 N	72.40 W
Roxwell	260	51.45 N	0.23 E
Roy, N.M., U.S.	196	35.56 N	104.11 W
Roy, Ut,. U.S.	200	41.09 N	112.01 W
Roy, Wa., U.S.	224	47.00 N	122.32 W
Roya (Roia) ≏	62	43.48 N	7.35 E
Royal	198	43.03 N	95.17 W
Royal Albert Hall ʋ	260	51.30 N	0.11 W
Royal Australian Naval College ʋ[2]	170	35.07 S	150.42 E
Royal Bangkok Sports Club ♠	269a	13.44 N	100.33 E
Royal Botanic Gardens ♠, Austl.	274a	33.52 S	151.13 E
Royal Botanic Gardens ♠, Austl.	274b	37.50 S	144.59 E
Royal Canal ≍	48	53.21 N	6.15 W
Royal Center	216	40.51 N	86.29 W
Royal Chitwan National Park ♠	124	27.30 N	84.30 E
Royal City	202	46.54 N	119.38 W
Royale, Isle I	190	48.00 N	89.00 W
Royal Festival Hall ʋ	260	51.30 N	0.07 W
Royal Gorge V	200	38.17 N	105.45 W
Royal Island I	192	25.31 N	76.51 W
Royalla	171b	35.31 S	149.09 E
Royal Leamington Spa	42	52.18 N	1.31 W
Royal Natal National Park ♠	158	28.45 S	28.57 E
Royal National Park ♠	170	34.10 S	151.05 E
Royal Naval College ■	260	51.29 N	0.01 W
Royal Oak, B.C., Can.	224	48.30 N	123.23 W
Royal Oak, Md., U.S.	208	38.44 N	76.10 W
Royal Oak, Mi., U.S.	216	42.29 N	83.08 W
Royal Oak Township	281	42.27 N	83.10 W
Royal Ontario Museum ʋ	275b	43.40 N	79.24 W
Royal Opera House ʋ	260	51.30 N	0.08 W
Royal Palms State Beach ♠	280	33.44 N	118.19 W
Royal Park ♠	274b	37.47 S	144.57 E
Royal Roads ⊂	224	48.26 N	123.26 W
Royalton, In., U.S.	218	39.56 N	86.21 W
Royalton, Mn., U.S.	190	45.49 N	94.17 W
Royalton, Pa., U.S.	208	40.11 N	76.44 W
Royal Tunbridge Wells	42	51.08 N	0.16 E
Royal Turf Club ♠	269a	13.46 N	100.32 E
Royan	32	45.37 N	1.01 W
Royaume-Uni → United Kingdom □[1]	28	54.00 N	2.00 W
Roybon	62	45.15 N	5.15 E
Royce Brook ≏	276	40.32 N	70.35 W
Roydon, Eng., U.K.	42	51.46 N	0.03 E
Roydon, Eng., U.K.	42	52.50 N	0.32 E
Roye	50	49.42 N	2.48 E
Royersford	208	40.11 N	75.32 W

Symbol	English	Deutsch	Español	Français	Português
≏	River	Fluß	Río	Rivière	Rio
≍	Canal	Kanal	Canal	Canal	Canal
ᒪ	Waterfall, Rapids	Wasserfall, Stromschnellen	Cascada, Rápidos	Chute d'eau, Rapides	Cascata, Rápidos
ʯ	Strait	Meeresstraße	Estrecho	Détroit	Estreito
⊂	Bay, Gulf	Bucht, Golf	Bahía, Golfo	Baie, Golfe	Baía, Golfo
⊜	Lake, Lakes	See, Seen	Lago, Lagos	Lac, Lacs	Lago, Lagos
≡	Swamp	Sumpf	Pantano	Marais	Pântano
⊓	Ice Features, Glacier	Eis- und Gletscherformen	Accidentes Glaciales	Formes glaciaires	Acidentes glaciares
⊤	Other Hydrographic Features	Andere Hydrographische Objekte	Otros Elementos Hidrográficos	Autres données hydrographiques	Outros acidentes hidrográficos
✦	Submarine Features	Untermeerische Objekte	Accidentes Submarinos	Formes de relief sous-marin	Acidentes submarinos
□	Political Unit	Politische Einheit	Unidad Politica	Entité politique	Unidade política
ʋ	Cultural Institution	Kulturelle Institution	Institución Cultural	Institution culturelle	Instituição cultural
⊥	Historical Site	Historische Stätte	Sitio Histórico	Site historique	Sitio histórico
♠	Recreational Site	Erholungs- und Ferienort	Sitio de Recreo	Centre de loisirs	Area de Lazer
⊠	Airport	Flughafen	Aeropuerto	Aéroport	Aeroporto
■	Military Installation	Militäranlage	Instalación Militar	Installation militaire	Instalação militar
◆	Miscellaneous	Verschiedenes	Misceláneo	Divers	Diversos

Royerton 216 40.15 N 85.21 W
Roy Hill 162 22.38 S 119.57 E
Royse City 222 32.58 N 96.19 W
Royston, Eng., U.K. 42 52.03 N 0.01 W
Royston, Eng., U.K. 44 53.37 N 1.27 W
Royston, Ga., U.S. 192 34.17 N 83.06 W
Royton 44 53.34 N 2.08 W
Rožaj 38 42.50 N 20.10 E
Różan 30 52.53 N 21.25 E
Rozay-en-Brie 50 48.41 N 2.58 E
Roždestvenka, Kaz. 86 50.52 N 71.22 E
Roždestvenka, Ross. 86 55.21 N 77.29 E
Roždestvenka, Ross. 86 55.42 N 70.00 E
Roždestveno, Ross. 76 57.44 N 37.57 E
Roždestveno, Ross. 80 53.15 N 50.04 E
Roždestveno, Ross. 82 56.51 N 36.33 E
Roždestveno, Ross. 82 55.57 N 36.23 E
Roždestvenskaja Chava 78 51.38 N 39.40 E
Roždestvenskoje, Ross. 80 58.09 N 45.35 E
Roždestvenskoje, Ross. 80 52.47 N 42.10 E
Roždestvenskoje, Ross. 80 51.14 N 42.10 E
Roždestvo 76 57.36 N 33.48 E
Rozel 43b 49.14 N 2.03 W
Rozelle 274a 33.52 S 151.10 E
Roželov 60 49.33 N 13.48 E
Rozewie, Przylądek > 30 54.51 N 18.21 E
Rozhnof, Cape > 180 55.58 N 160.58 W
Rožišče 78 50.54 N 25.15 E
Rožki 80 56.41 N 50.31 E
Rožkov 80 51.39 N 52.19 E
Rožmberk @ 61 49.04 N 14.47 E
Rožmberk nad Vltavou 61 48.39 N 14.22 E
Rožmitál pod Třemšínem 60 49.36 N 13.52 E
Rožn'atov 78 48.56 N 24.09 E
Rožňava 30 48.40 N 20.32 E
Roznov 38 46.50 N 26.31 E
Rožnov pod Radhoštěm 30 49.28 N 18.10 E
Rożnów 30 49.46 N 20.42 E
Rozovka 78 47.23 N 37.04 E
Rozoy-sur-Serre 50 49.43 N 4.08 E
Roztocze ⋏[2] 30 50.30 N 23.20 E
Roztoky 54 50.09 N 14.22 E
Rozzano 62 45.20 N 9.06 E
Rrëshen 38 41.47 N 19.54 E
Rrogozhinë 38 41.05 N 19.40 E
Rtiščevo 80 52.16 N 43.47 E
Ru ≐ 100 32.43 N 115.01 E
Ru, Tanjong > 114 2.50 N 101.17 E
Ruabon 42 52.59 N 3.02 W
Ruacaná 152 17.25 S 14.12 E
Ruacana Falls ⌊ 152 17.22 S 14.12 E
Ruaha National Park ♦ 154 7.30 S 34.40 E
Ruahine Range ⋏ 172 40.00 S 176.06 E
Ruahmi, Ra's > 142 28.44 N 32.50 E
Ruanda 154 10.33 S 34.57 E
Ruanda → Rwanda □[1] 154 2.00 S 30.00 E
Ruango 164 5.35 S 150.10 E
Ruapehu, Mount ∧ 172 39.17 S 175.34 E
Ruapuke Island I 172 46.47 S 168.30 E
Ruatahuna 172 38.33 S 176.57 E
Ruatapu 172 42.48 S 170.53 E
Ruathair, Lochan @ 46 58.18 N 3.56 W
Ruatoria 172 37.53 S 178.20 E
Ruawai 172 36.08 S 174.02 E
Rub' al Khali → Ar-Rub' al-Khālī ◆[2] 118 20.00 N 51.00 E
Rubanovka 78 47.00 N 34.10 E
Rubbestadneset 26 59.49 N 5.17 E
Rubcovsk 86 51.33 N 81.10 E
Rubcy 83 49.12 N 37.33 E
Rubeho Mountains ⋏ 154 6.55 S 36.30 E
Rubel' 78 51.58 N 27.04 E
Rübeland 54 51.45 N 10.50 E
Rubelles 261 48.34 N 2.41 E
Rubery 42 52.24 N 2.00 W
Rubeshibe 92a 43.47 N 143.38 E
Rubežka 80 51.26 N 51.59 E
Rubežnoje 83 49.01 N 38.23 E
Rubí, Esp. 266d 41.29 N 2.02 E
Rubi, Zaïre 154 2.49 N 25.14 E
Rubí ≐, Esp. 266d 41.26 N 2.00 E
Rubi ≐, Zaïre 152 2.48 N 23.54 E
Rubiana 62 45.08 N 7.23 E
Rubiataba 255 15.08 S 49.48 W
Rubicon ≐ 226 39.00 N 120.44 W
Rubicone ≐ 66 44.08 N 12.28 E
Rubidoux 228 33.59 N 117.24 W
Rubiera 64 44.39 N 10.45 E
Rubim 255 16.23 S 40.32 W
Rubino 150 6.04 N 4.18 W
Rubio 246 7.43 N 72.22 W
Rubio Woods ♦ 278 41.38 N 87.46 W
Rubl'ovka 78 49.15 N 33.19 E
Rubl'ovo 82 55.47 N 37.21 E
Ruboani 140 8.06 N 30.45 E
Rubona 154 0.33 N 30.10 E
Rubondo Island I 154 2.20 S 31.52 E
Rubondo Island National Park ♦ 154 2.20 S 31.52 E
Rubtsovsk → Rubcovsk 86 51.33 N 81.10 E
Ruby, Ak., U.S. 180 64.44 N 155.30 W
Ruby, N.Y., U.S. 210 42.01 N 74.01 W
Ruby ≐ 202 45.34 N 112.21 W
Ruby Creek ≐ 224 48.43 N 120.59 W
Ruby Dome ∧ 204 40.37 N 115.28 W
Ruby Lake ≡ 204 40.10 N 115.30 W
Ruby Mountains ⋏ 204 40.25 N 115.35 W
Ruby Valley V 204 40.30 N 115.15 W
Rucava 76 56.09 N 21.10 E
Ruchan' 76 53.33 N 32.48 E
Ruche 261 49.02 N 2.27 E
Rucheng 100 25.34 N 113.41 E
Ruciane-Nida 30 53.39 N 21.35 E
Ručji ◆[8] 265a 60.01 N 30.24 E
Ručjuvom 24 66.42 N 61.08 E
Rucphen 52 51.32 N 4.34 E
Ruda 64 45.50 N 13.24 E
Rudall 166 33.41 S 136.16 E
Rudall ≐ 162 22.16 S 122.47 E
Rudall River National Park ♦ 162 22.25 S 122.40 E
Ruda Śląska 30 50.18 N 18.51 E
Rudauli 124 26.45 N 81.45 E
Ruḍaymat al-Liwā' 132 33.01 N 36.35 E
Rūdbār, Afg. 128 30.09 N 62.36 E
Rūdbār, Īrān 128 36.48 N 49.24 E
Rudbøl 41 54.54 N 8.45 E
Ruddervoorde 50 51.06 N 3.12 E
Ruddiman Terrace 216 43.12 N 86.17 W
Rudelsburg ⊥ 54 51.07 N 11.43 E
Ruden I 54 54.12 N 13.46 E
Rudensk 76 53.36 N 27.52 E
Rüdersdorf, Dtsch. 54 52.29 N 13.47 E
Rudersdorf, Öst. 61 47.03 N 16.07 E
Rüdersdorf, Forst ◆[3] 264a 52.26 N 13.50 E
Rüdesheim am Rhein 56 49.59 N 7.56 E
Rudeville 276 41.09 N 74.33 W
Rudewa 154 10.06 S 34.39 E
Rudge Ramos 287b 23.41 S 46.34 W
Rūdiškės 76 54.31 N 24.50 E
Rudki 78 49.39 N 23.29 E
Rudkino 78 51.27 N 39.01 E
Rudkøbing 41 54.56 N 10.43 E
Rudn'a, Ross. 76 54.57 N 31.06 E
Rudn'a, Ross. 80 50.48 N 44.33 E
Rudnaja Pristan' 89 44.22 N 135.48 E
Rudnevka ≐ 265b 55.43 N 37.56 E
Rudnevo 82 54.44 N 38.09 E
Rudnica 78 48.15 N 28.55 E
Rudničnyj, Kaz. 86 44.40 N 78.55 E
Rudničnyj, Ross. 24 59.38 N 52.27 E
Rudničnyj, Ross. 86 56.08 N 86.12 E
Rudničnyj, Ross. 86 59.42 N 60.18 E
Rudnik 30 50.28 N 22.15 E
Rüdnitz 54 52.43 N 13.37 E
Rudnyj, Kaz. 86 52.57 N 63.07 E
Rudnyj, Ross. 89 44.21 N 134.58 E
Rudo 38 43.37 N 19.22 E
Rudolf, Lake (Lake Turkana) @ 144 3.30 N 36.00 E
Rudolfov 61 48.59 N 14.34 E
Rudolph 216 41.17 N 83.40 W
Rudolstadt 54 50.43 N 11.20 E
Rudong, Zhg. 102 21.39 N 111.23 E
Rudong, Zhg. 106 32.19 N 121.12 E
Rudovka, Ross. 80 53.07 N 42.23 E
Rudovka, Ukr. 83 49.24 N 38.27 E
Rudow ◆[8] 264a 52.25 N 13.30 E
Rudrón ≐ 34 42.47 N 3.45 W
Rūdsar 128 37.08 N 50.18 E
Ruds Vedby 41 55.33 N 11.23 E
Rudyard, Mi., U.S. 190 46.13 N 84.36 W
Rudyard, Mt., U.S. 202 48.33 N 110.33 W
Rudyerd Bay c 182 55.35 N 130.44 W
Rue, Fr. 50 50.16 N 1.40 E
Rue, Schw. 58 46.37 N 6.50 E
Ruecas ≐ 34 39.00 N 5.55 W
Rueil-Malmaison 261 48.53 N 2.11 E
Ruen ∧ 38 42.10 N 22.31 E
Ruenya (Luenha) ≐ 154 16.24 S 33.48 E
Rufā'ah 140 14.46 N 33.22 E
Ruffano 68 39.59 N 18.15 E
Ruffec 32 46.01 N 0.12 E
Ruffieu 58 46.00 N 5.40 E
Ruffieux 62 45.51 N 5.50 E
Ruffin 192 33.00 N 80.48 W
Ruffle Bar I 276 40.36 N 46.51 W
Rufford 262 53.38 N 2.49 W
Rufford Old Hall ⊥ 262 53.38 N 2.49 W
Ruffs Dale 279b 40.10 N 79.37 W
Rufidschi → Rufiji ≐ 154 8.00 S 39.20 E
Rufiji ≐ 154 8.00 S 39.20 E
Rufina 66 43.49 N 11.29 E
Rufino 252 34.16 S 62.42 W
Rufisque 150 14.43 N 17.17 W
Rufunsa 154 15.05 S 29.40 E
Rufus 224 45.41 N 120.44 W
Rufus, Mount ∧ 168b 34.20 S 139.07 E
Rugāji 76 57.00 N 27.08 E
Rugao 100 32.25 N 120.36 E
Rugby, Eng., U.K. 42 52.23 N 1.15 W
Rugby, N.D., U.S. 198 48.22 N 99.59 W
Rugeley 42 52.46 N 1.55 W
Rügen I 54 54.25 N 13.24 E
Rüggeberg 263 51.16 N 7.22 E
Rugged Mountain ∧ 182 50.02 N 126.41 W
Ruggles Beach 214 41.22 N 82.29 W
Rugles 50 48.49 N 0.42 E
Rugufu ≐ 154 5.10 S 30.14 E
Ruguj 76 59.28 N 32.50 E
Ruḥama 132 31.30 N 34.42 E
Ruhea 124 26.10 N 88.25 E
Ruhengeri 154 1.30 S 29.38 E
Ruhla 54 50.53 N 10.22 E
Ruhland 54 51.27 N 13.52 E
Ruhlsdorf 264a 52.23 N 13.16 E
Ruhmannsfelden 60 48.59 N 12.59 E
Ruhner Berge ⋏[2] 54 53.17 N 11.55 E
Ruhnu saar I 76 57.48 N 23.15 E
Ruhpolding 64 47.45 N 12.38 E
Ruhr ≐ 52 51.27 N 6.44 E
Ruhrort ◆[8] 263 51.26 N 6.45 E
Ruhr-Universität ʊ[2] 263 51.27 N 7.16 E
Ruhstorf an der Rott 60 48.26 N 13.20 E
Ruhudji ≐ 154 8.52 S 36.01 E
Ruhuhu ≐ 154 10.31 S 34.34 E
Ruhunu National Park ♦ 122 6.30 N 81.30 E
Rui'an 100 27.49 N 120.38 E
Ruichang 100 29.41 N 115.40 E
Ruicheng 102 34.45 N 110.45 E
Ruidoso 200 33.19 N 105.40 W
Ruidoso, Rio ≐ 200 33.23 N 105.16 W
Ruidoso Downs 200 33.19 N 105.36 W
Ruifeng Sha I 106 31.25 N 121.36 E
Ruihong 100 28.45 N 116.23 E
Ruijin 100 25.50 N 116.00 E
Ruinen 52 52.46 N 6.22 E
Ruiselede 50 51.03 N 3.24 E
Ruislip ◆[8] 260 51.34 N 0.25 W
Ruivo, Pico ∧ 148 32.45 N 16.56 W
Ruiz 234 21.57 N 105.09 W
Ruiz, Nevado del ∧[1] 246 4.54 N 75.18 W
Ruiz de Montoya 252 26.59 S 55.03 W
Rūjiena 76 57.54 N 25.21 E
Rujm ar-Rashīd, Jabal ∧ 132 31.53 N 36.18 E
Rujm aṣ-Ṣakhrī 132 31.02 N 35.43 E
Rukan-shō ✦[2] 174m 26.06 N 127.32 E
Rukatunturi ∧[2] 26 66.09 N 29.10 E
Ruki ≐ 152 0.05 N 18.17 E
Rukni 126 23.33 N 86.33 E
Rukungiri 154 0.48 S 29.55 E
Rukwa □[4] 154 7.00 S 31.30 E
Rukwa, Lake @ 154 8.00 S 32.25 E
Rule 196 33.11 N 99.53 W
Rule Creek ≐ 198 38.02 N 103.02 W
Ruleville 194 33.43 N 90.33 W
Rulle 52 52.20 N 8.04 E
Rully 58 46.52 N 4.45 E
Rulo 198 40.03 N 95.25 W
Rülzheim 56 49.09 N 8.16 E
Rum 61 47.08 N 16.51 E
Rum ≐ 190 45.11 N 93.23 W
Ruma 38 45.00 N 19.49 E
Rumaat 164 5.49 S 132.48 E
Rumāh 128 25.34 N 47.09 E
Rumahtinggih 164 6.23 S 140.17 E
Rum'ancevo, Ross. 82 55.38 N 37.26 E
Rum'ancevo, Ross. 82 55.58 N 36.32 E
Rum'ancevo ◆[8] 83 48.21 N 38.06 E
Rumänien → Romania □[1] 38 46.00 N 25.30 E
Rumaysh 132 33.05 N 35.22 E
Rumbek 140 6.48 N 29.41 E
Rumbeke 50 50.56 N 3.10 E
Rumberpon, Pulau I 164 1.50 S 134.15 E
Rumbling Bridge 46 56.10 N 3.35 W
Rumburk 54 50.57 N 14.32 E
Rum Cay I 238 23.40 N 74.53 W
Rumelange 56 49.28 N 6.02 E
Rumelifeneri ◆[8] 267b 41.14 N 29.06 E
Rumelihisarı ◆[8] 267b 41.05 N 29.03 E
Rumelihisarı ⊥ 267b 41.05 N 29.02 E
Rumelikavağı ◆[8] 267b 41.11 N 29.04 E
Rumford 188 44.33 N 70.33 W
Rumford ≐ 283 41.58 N 71.11 W
Rumia 30 54.35 N 18.25 E
Rumigny 50 49.48 N 4.16 E
Rumilly 62 45.52 N 5.57 E
R'uminskoje 82 56.31 N 38.47 E
Rum Jungle 164 13.01 S 131.00 E
R'umki 265a 59.47 N 30.02 E
Rümlang 58 47.27 N 8.32 E
Rummah, Wādī ar- V 128 26.12 N 44.04 E
Rummānah 142 31.01 N 32.40 E
Rummānah, Bi'r ar- ⊤[4] 142 31.00 N 32.40 E
Rummel 214 40.13 N 78.48 W
Rummelsburg ◆[8] 264a 52.30 N 13.29 E
Rummenohl ◆[8] 263 51.17 N 7.32 E
Rumney 42 51.31 N 3.07 W
Rumoi 92a 43.56 N 141.39 E
Rumont 56 48.50 N 5.17 E
Rumphi 154 11.01 S 33.52 E
Rump Mountain ∧ 188 45.12 N 71.04 W
Rumson 208 40.22 N 73.59 W
Rumst 50 51.05 N 4.25 E
Rumula 164 16.35 S 145.20 E
Rumung I 174q 9.37 N 138.10 E
Rumuruti 154 0.16 N 36.32 E
Runan 100 33.01 N 114.22 E
Runanga 172 42.24 S 171.16 E
Runaway, Cape > 172 37.32 S 177.59 E
Runazi 154 2.47 S 31.28 E
Runcorn ◆[8] 44 53.20 N 2.44 W
Rundeng 114 2.39 N 97.52 E
Rundēni 76 56.16 N 27.50 E
Rundu 156 17.52 S 19.43 E
Rundvik 26 63.32 N 19.26 E
Runere 154 3.06 S 33.16 E
Rŭng, Kaôh I 110 10.44 N 103.14 E
Rungāni 120 26.38 N 65.43 E
Runge 222 28.52 N 97.42 W
Rungis 261 48.45 N 2.21 E
Rungis-Halles, Marché de ʊ 261 48.46 N 2.21 E
Rungsted 41 55.53 N 12.33 E
Rungus Point > 116 13.43 N 123.58 E
Rungwa, Tan. 154 7.21 S 31.40 E
Rungwa, Tan. 154 6.57 S 33.31 E
Rungwa ≐ 154 7.36 S 31.50 E
Rungwa Game Reserve ◆[4] 154 7.00 S 34.10 E
Rungwe 154 9.10 S 33.36 E
Runhällen 40 60.02 N 16.49 E
Runheji 100 32.30 N 116.05 E
Runkel 56 50.24 N 8.10 E
Runmarö I 40 59.17 N 18.46 E
Runn @ 40 60.33 N 15.40 E
Runnemede 285 39.51 N 75.04 W
Running Springs 228 34.12 N 117.07 W
Running Water Draw V 196 33.58 N 101.30 W
Runnymede □[8] 260 51.24 N 0.32 W
Runnymede ⊥ 260 51.26 N 0.34 W
Rünthe 263 51.39 N 7.39 E
Runwell 260 51.37 N 0.32 E
Ruo ≐, Afr. 154 16.33 S 35.09 E
Ruo ≐, Zhg. 102 41.00 N 100.10 E
Ruo'ergai 102 33.16 N 102.55 E
Ruoheng 100 28.24 N 121.31 E
Ruokolahti 26 61.17 N 28.50 E
Ruoms 62 44.27 N 4.21 E
Ruoqiang 90 38.30 N 88.05 E
Ruoti 68 40.43 N 15.41 E
Ruovesi 26 61.59 N 24.05 E
Ruoxi 100 29.18 N 115.20 E
Rupanco 254 40.46 S 72.42 W
Rupanco, Lago @ 254 40.49 S 72.28 W
Rupari 168b 35.37 S 139.09 E
Rupat, Pulau I 114 1.50 N 101.35 E
Rupat, Selat ʯ 114 1.50 N 101.25 E
Rupdia 126 23.08 N 89.18 E
Rupea 38 46.02 N 25.13 E
Rupert, Id., U.S. 202 42.37 N 113.40 W
Rupert, Vt., U.S. 210 43.15 N 73.13 W
Rupert, W.V., U.S. 188 37.57 N 80.41 W
Rupert, Rivière de ≐ 176 51.29 N 78.45 W
Rupert Creek ≐ 166 20.53 S 142.23 E
Rupganj 126 23.48 N 90.31 E
Rūpnagar 123 30.59 N 76.31 E
Rūpnārāyan ≐ 126 22.13 N 88.03 E
Ruponda 154 10.15 S 38.42 E
Ruppertenrod 56 50.37 N 9.05 E
Ruppiner See @ 54 52.48 N 12.50 E
Rupprechtseck ∧ 61 47.14 N 14.00 E
Rupt de Mad ≐ 56 49.01 N 6.02 E
Rupt-sur-Moselle 58 47.56 N 6.40 E
Rupununi ≐ 246 4.03 N 58.34 W
Ruqqād, Wādī ar- V 132 32.44 N 35.46 E
Rur (Roer) ≐ 56 51.12 N 5.59 E
Rural Hall 192 36.14 N 80.17 W
Rural Retreat 192 36.53 N 81.16 W
Rural Ridge 279b 40.35 N 79.50 W
Rural Valley 214 40.48 N 79.18 W
Rurberg 56 50.37 N 6.22 E
Ruri-kei ♦ 96 35.03 N 135.26 E
Rurrenabaque 248 14.28 S 67.34 W
Rurstausee @[1] 56 50.36 N 6.22 E
Rurutu I 14 22.26 S 151.20 W
Rusambo 154 16.35 S 32.12 E
Rušan 120 37.58 N 71.30 E
Rusanov 78 50.29 N 31.09 E
Rusanovka 78 50.32 N 33.44 E
Rusape 154 18.32 S 32.07 E
Rusavkina-Popovščina 265b 55.42 N 38.04 E
Ruṣayriṣ, Khazzān ar- @[1] 140 11.40 N 34.20 E
Ruschuk → Ruse 38 43.50 N 25.57 E
Ruscom ≐ 214 42.18 N 82.38 W
Ruscom Station 214 42.13 N 82.39 W
Ruse, Blg. 38 43.50 N 25.57 E
Ruše, Slo. 61 46.32 N 15.31 E
Rusera 124 25.45 N 86.02 E
Rush, Ire. 48 53.32 N 6.06 W
Rush, N.Y., U.S. 210 42.59 N 77.39 W
Rush, Pa., U.S. 210 41.47 N 76.03 W
Rush □[6] 218 39.37 N 85.27 W
Rush ≐, N.D., U.S. 198 47.00 N 96.54 W
Rush ≐, Wi., U.S. 190 44.34 N 92.19 W
Rushan (Xiacun) 98 36.54 N 121.29 E
Rush Center 198 38.27 N 99.18 W
Rush City 190 45.41 N 92.57 W
Rush Creek ≐, Co., U.S. 198 38.22 N 102.32 W
Rush Creek ≐, Ne., U.S. 198 41.27 N 102.32 W
Rush Creek ≐, N.Y., U.S. 284a 42.00 N 78.52 W
Rush Creek ≐, Oh., U.S. 188 39.38 N 82.33 W
Rush Creek ≐, Oh., U.S. 214 40.34 N 83.20 W
Rush Creek ≐, Ok., U.S. 196 34.42 N 97.10 W
Rushden 42 52.17 N 0.36 W
Rushford, Mn., U.S. 190 43.48 N 91.45 W
Rushford, N.Y., U.S. 210 42.23 N 78.15 W
Rush Hill 219 39.13 N 91.43 W
Rush Lake @, On., Can. 190 47.48 N 82.12 W
Rush Lake @, Wi., U.S. 190 43.56 N 88.49 W
Rushland 285 40.15 N 75.02 W
Rushmore 198 43.37 N 95.48 W
Rusholme ◆[8] 262 53.27 N 2.12 W
Rush Springs 196 34.46 N 97.57 W
Rushsylvania 216 40.27 N 83.40 W
Rushville, Il., U.S. 219 40.07 N 90.33 W
Rushville, In., U.S. 218 39.36 N 85.26 W
Rushville, Ne., U.S. 198 42.43 N 102.27 W
Rushville, N.Y., U.S. 210 42.45 N 77.13 W
Rusinga Island I 154 0.24 S 34.10 E
Rusizi (Ruzizi) ≐ 154 3.16 S 29.14 E
Rusk 222 31.47 N 95.09 W
Rusk □[6] 222 32.10 N 94.50 W
Rusken @ 26 57.17 N 14.20 E
Ruskin, B.C., Can. 224 49.12 N 122.28 W
Ruskin, Fl., U.S. 220 27.43 N 82.26 W
Ruskington 44 53.02 N 0.23 W
Rusnė 76 55.18 N 21.22 E
Rušonu ezers @ 76 56.11 N 27.02 E
Rusovce 61 48.04 N 17.10 E
Russa 272b 22.29 N 88.21 E
Russas 250 4.56 S 37.58 W
Russbach ≐ 264b 48.17 N 16.35 E
Russee 41 54.18 N 10.04 E
Russell, Mb., Can. 184 50.47 N 101.15 W
Russell, On., Can. 212 45.15 N 75.22 W
Russell, N.Z. 172 35.16 S 174.07 E
Russell, Ia., U.S. 190 40.58 N 93.11 W
Russell, Ks., U.S. 198 38.53 N 98.51 W
Russell, Ky., U.S. 188 38.31 N 82.41 W
Russell, Ma., U.S. 207 42.11 N 72.51 W
Russell, Mn., U.S. 198 44.19 N 95.57 W
Russell, Pa., U.S. 214 41.56 N 79.08 W
Russell, Cape > 176 75.15 N 117.35 W
Russell, Mount ∧ 180 62.48 N 151.52 W
Russell Cave National Monument ♦ 194 34.54 N 85.48 W
Russell Creek ≐ 194 37.14 N 85.30 W
Russell Gardens 276 40.47 N 73.43 W
Russell Island I 176 73.55 N 98.25 W
Russell Islands II 175e 9.04 S 159.12 E
Russellkonda 120 19.56 N 84.35 E
Russell Lake @ 184 56.15 N 101.30 W
Russell Range ⋏ 162 33.24 S 123.28 E
Russells Point 216 40.28 N 83.54 W
Russell Springs 194 37.03 N 85.05 W
Russellton 214 40.37 N 79.50 W
Russellville, Al., U.S. 194 34.30 N 87.43 W
Russellville, Ar., U.S. 194 35.16 N 93.08 W
Russellville, Ky., U.S. 194 36.50 N 86.53 W
Russellville, Mo., U.S. 194 38.30 N 92.26 W
Russellville, Oh., U.S. 218 38.51 N 83.47 W
Russellville, Or., U.S. 224 45.31 N 122.33 W
Rüsselsheim 56 50.00 N 8.25 E
Russi 66 44.22 N 12.02 E
Russia 216 40.14 N 84.24 W
Russia □[1], Europe 72 60.00 N 80.00 E
Russia □[1], Europe 74 60.00 N 100.00 E
Russian ≐ 204 38.27 N 123.08 W
Russian Mission 180 61.47 N 161.19 W
Russiaville 216 40.25 N 86.16 W
Russka 76 58.59 N 28.30 E
Russkaja Bujlovka 78 50.22 N 40.03 E
Russkaja Gavan' 74 76.10 N 62.35 E
Russkaja Pol'ana 86 53.47 N 73.53 E
Russkaja Ṭalovka 80 49.59 N 49.05 E
Russkaja Žuravka 80 50.21 N 40.33 E
Russkij 89 43.03 N 131.50 E
Russkij, ostrov I 74 77.00 N 96.00 E
Russkij Aktaš 80 55.02 N 52.07 E
Russkij Brod 76 52.36 N 37.22 E
Russkij Kameškir 80 52.52 N 46.06 E
Russkij Turek 80 57.03 N 50.13 E
Russkij Vožoj 80 56.57 N 53.22 E
Russkij Zavorot, mys > 24 68.58 N 54.34 E
Russkoje 83 47.45 N 38.56 E
Russkoje-Dobrino 80 54.22 N 52.28 E
Russko-Vysockoje 265a 59.42 N 29.56 E
Rust, Dtsch. 58 48.16 N 7.43 E
Rust, Öst. 61 47.48 N 16.41 E
Rustajskij 80 56.31 N 44.49 E
Rustam 123 34.21 N 72.17 E
Rustavi 84 41.33 N 45.02 E
Rustburg 192 37.16 N 79.06 W
Rustenburg 158 25.37 S 27.08 E
Rustfontein 158 30.28 S 29.17 E
Rustic Canyon V 280 34.04 N 118.31 W
Rustig 158 27.22 S 27.09 E
Rustington 42 50.48 N 0.31 W
Ruston, La., U.S. 194 32.31 N 92.38 W
Ruston, Wa., U.S. 224 47.17 N 122.30 W
Rusville 273d 26.10 S 28.18 E
Rutana 154 3.55 S 30.00 E
Rutčenkovo 83 47.57 N 37.44 E
Rute 34 37.19 N 4.22 W
Rütenbrock 52 52.50 N 7.10 E
Ruteng 115b 8.36 S 120.27 E
Rutenga 154 21.08 S 30.45 E
Rutersville 222 29.57 N 96.48 W
Rutgers University ʊ[2], N.J., U.S. 276 40.30 N 74.27 W
Rutgers University (Newark) ʊ[2], N.J., U.S. 276 40.44 N 74.10 W
Rutgers University (Camden) ʊ[2], N.J., U.S. 285 39.56 N 75.07 W
Ruth, Ms., U.S. 194 31.22 N 90.18 W
Ruth, Nv., U.S. 204 39.16 N 114.59 W
Rüthen 52 51.29 N 8.25 E
Rutherford, Ca., U.S. 226 38.28 N 122.25 W
Rutherford, N.J., U.S. 210 40.49 N 74.06 W
Rutherford, Tn., U.S. 194 36.07 N 88.59 W
Rutherfordton 192 35.22 N 81.57 W
Rutherglen, Scot., U.K. 46 55.50 N 4.12 W
Ruther Glen, Va., U.S. 208 37.56 N 77.27 W
Ruthin 44 53.07 N 3.18 W
Ruthton 198 44.10 N 96.06 W
Ruthven, On., Can. 214 42.03 N 82.40 W
Ruthven, Ia., U.S. 198 43.07 N 94.53 W
Rüti 58 47.16 N 8.51 E
Rutigliano 68 41.01 N 17.00 E
Rutino 68 40.18 N 15.04 E
Rutka ≐ 80 56.22 N 46.38 E
Rutland, B.C., Can. 182 49.53 N 119.24 W
Rutland, Fl., U.S. 220 28.51 N 82.13 W
Rutland, Il., U.S. 216 40.59 N 89.03 W
Rutland, Ma., U.S. 207 42.22 N 71.56 W
Rutland, N.D., U.S. 198 46.03 N 97.30 W
Rutland, Vt., U.S. 188 43.36 N 72.58 W
Rutland □[6] 210 43.21 N 73.15 W
Rutland Island I 110 11.25 N 92.40 E
Rutland State Park ♦ 207 42.23 N 72.01 W
Rutland Water @[1] 42 52.39 N 0.38 W
Rutledge, Ga., U.S. 192 33.37 N 83.36 W
Rutledge, Pa., U.S. 285 39.54 N 75.20 W
Rutledge, Tn., U.S. 192 36.16 N 83.30 W
Rutog 120 33.28 N 79.40 E
Rutshuru 154 1.11 S 29.27 E
Rüttenscheid ◆[8] 263 51.26 N 7.00 E
Rutter 190 46.06 N 80.40 W
Rutul 84 41.33 N 47.25 E
Ruukki 26 64.40 N 25.06 E
Ruurlo 52 52.05 N 6.26 E
Ruvo del Monte 68 40.51 N 15.32 E
Ruvo di Puglia 68 41.07 N 16.29 E
Ruvu 154 6.48 S 38.39 E
Ruvu ≐ 154 6.23 S 38.52 E
Ruvubu (Rovubu) ≐ 154 2.23 S 30.47 E
Ruvuma □[4] 154 11.00 S 36.00 E
Ruvuma (Rovuma) ≐ 154 10.29 S 40.28 E
Ruwayān, Wādī ar- ⊥[7] 142 29.07 N 30.10 E
Ruwaybah ⊤[4] 140 15.39 N 28.45 E
Ruwayfī, Jabal ar- ∧ 132 31.12 N 36.00 E
Ruwenzori National Park ♦ 154 0.15 S 30.00 E
Ruwenzori Range ⋏ 154 0.23 N 29.54 E
Ruwer 56 49.47 N 6.43 E
Ruwer ≐ 56 49.47 N 6.42 E
Ruya (Luia) ≐ 154 16.34 S 33.12 E
Ruyang 100 34.10 N 112.26 E
Ruy Barbosa 255 12.18 S 40.27 W
Ruyigi 154 3.29 S 30.15 E
Ruyton-Eleven-Towns 42 52.48 N 2.54 W
Ruza 82 55.42 N 36.12 E
Ruza ≐ 82 55.38 N 36.17 E
Ruzajevka, Kaz. 86 52.49 N 66.57 E
Ruzajevka, Ross. 80 54.04 N 44.57 E
Ružany 76 52.52 N 24.53 E
Ružičnaja 78 49.24 N 26.58 E
Ružin 78 49.43 N 29.14 E
Ruzizi (Rusizi) ≐ 154 3.16 S 29.14 E
Ružomberok 30 49.06 N 19.18 E
Ruzskoje vodochranilišče @[1] 82 55.47 N 36.00 E
Ruzyně ⊠ 54 50.06 N 14.17 E
Ruzzah, Jabal ∧[2] 142 30.01 N 30.26 E
Rwamagana 154 1.57 S 30.34 E
Rwanda □[1], Afr. 138 2.00 S 30.00 E
Rwanda □[1], Afr. 154 2.00 S 30.00 E
Rwashamaire 154 0.49 S 30.08 E
Ry 41 56.05 N 9.46 E
Ryal Fold 262 53.41 N 2.30 W
Ryan 196 34.01 N 97.57 W
Ryan ≐ 182 50.25 N 122.43 W
Ryan, Loch c 44 54.58 N 5.02 W
Ryan Peak ∧ 202 43.54 N 114.25 W
Ryans Creek ≐ 169 36.43 S 146.12 E
Ryarsh 260 51.19 N 0.24 E

ENGLISH — Name Page Lat.°′ Long.°′ / DEUTSCH — Name Seite Breite°′ Länge°′ E = Ost

Ryazan' → R'azan' 80 54.38 N 39.44 E
Rybačij 76 55.09 N 20.51 E
Rybačij, poluostrov >[1] 24 69.42 N 32.36 E
Rybačje 86 46.27 N 81.32 E
Rybackaja ◆[8] 265a 60.00 N 30.30 E
Rybackoje ◆[8] 265a 59.50 N 30.30 E
Rybakovka 78 46.37 N 31.20 E
Rybinsk 76 58.03 N 38.52 E
Rybinsker Stausee → Rybinskoje vodochranilišče @[1] 76 58.30 N 38.25 E
Rybinskije Budy 78 51.13 N 35.57 E
Rybinskoje 86 55.47 N 94.47 E
Rybinskoje vodochranilišče @[1] 76 58.30 N 38.25 E
Rybkino 80 54.15 N 43.46 E
Rybnaja Sloboda 80 55.28 N 50.09 E
Rybnica 78 47.45 N 29.01 E
Rybnik 30 50.06 N 18.32 E
Rybnoje, Ross. 76 54.44 N 39.30 E
Rybnoje, Ross. 86 58.08 N 94.30 E
Rybnovsk 89 53.12 N 141.50 E
Ryburn ≐ 262 53.43 N 1.54 W
Rybuška 80 51.17 N 45.26 E
Rychnov nad Kněžnou 30 50.10 N 16.17 E
Rychwał 30 52.05 N 18.09 E
Ryčkovo 86 58.09 N 61.43 E
Rycroft 182 55.45 N 118.43 W
Ryd 26 56.28 N 14.41 E
Rydaholm 26 56.59 N 14.16 E
Rydal, Austl. 170 33.29 S 150.02 E
Rydal, Pa., U.S. 285 40.06 N 75.06 W
Rydalmere 274a 33.49 S 151.02 E
Rydbo 40 59.28 N 18.11 E
Ryde, Austl. 170 33.49 S 151.06 E
Ryde, Eng., U.K. 42 50.44 N 1.10 W
Ryder 198 47.55 N 101.40 W
Ryder's Hill ∧[2] 42 50.31 N 3.53 W
Ryderwood 224 46.22 N 123.02 W
Rydsgård 41 55.28 N 13.35 E
Rydzyna 30 51.48 N 16.40 E
Rye, Austl. 169 38.23 S 144.49 E
Rye, Eng., U.K. 42 50.57 N 0.44 E
Rye, N.Y., U.S. 210 40.58 N 73.41 W
Rye, Tx., U.S. 222 30.27 N 94.46 W
Rye ≐ 44 54.10 N 0.45 W
Ryegate 202 46.17 N 109.15 W
Rye Hills-Rye Brook 276 41.00 N 73.41 W
Rye Lake @ 276 41.04 N 73.43 W
Ryeosu → Yŏsu 98 34.46 N 127.44 E
Rye Patch Reservoir @[1] 204 40.38 N 118.18 W
Ryer Island I 282 38.05 N 122.01 W
Ryes 32 49.19 N 0.37 W
Ryfoss 26 61.09 N 8.49 E
Ryfylke ◆[1] 26 59.30 N 5.30 E
Rygge 26 59.23 N 10.43 E
Rygnestad 26 59.16 N 7.29 E
Ryhope 44 54.52 N 1.21 W
Rykaartspos 158 26.32 S 26.39 E
Ryker Lake @ 276 41.03 N 74.33 W
Rykerts 182 49.00 N 116.35 W
Ryki 30 51.39 N 21.56 E
Rykonec 76 59.33 N 36.34 E
Ryley 182 53.17 N 112.26 W
Rylovičі 76 52.31 N 32.04 E
Ryl'sk 78 51.36 N 34.43 E
Rylstone 170 32.48 S 149.58 E
Rymanów 30 49.34 N 21.53 E
Rýmařov 30 49.56 N 17.16 E
Ryn 30 53.56 N 21.33 E
Rynfield 273d 26.09 S 28.20 E
Rynok 80 45.39 N 47.34 E
Ryn-Peski ◆[2] 80 48.24 N 49.00 E
Ryō 270 34.44 N 135.55 E
Ryōhaku-sanchi ⋏ 94 36.09 N 136.45 E
Ryojun → Lüshun 98 38.48 N 121.16 E
Ryōkami 94 36.00 N 138.58 E
Ryōke 268 35.58 N 139.33 E
Ryōnan 96 33.15 N 133.55 E
Ryōtsu 92 38.05 N 138.26 E
Rypin 30 53.05 N 19.25 E
Ryškany 78 47.58 N 27.32 E
Ryslinge 41 55.15 N 10.33 E
Rysy ∧ 30 49.12 N 20.04 E
Ryton 44 54.59 N 1.46 W
Ryton ≐ 44 53.25 N 1.00 W
Ryton-on-Dunsmore 42 52.22 N 1.26 W
Ryūga-do ⊥[5] 96 33.39 N 133.45 E
Ryūgasaki 94 35.54 N 140.11 E
Ryūjin 96 33.53 N 135.29 E
Ryukyu Islands → Nansei-shotō II 90 26.30 N 128.00 E
Ryukyu Trench ✦[1] 12 24.45 N 128.00 E
Ryūmon-dake ∧ 270 34.26 N 135.53 E
Ryūō, Nihon 94 35.04 N 136.07 E
Ryūō, Nihon 94 35.39 N 138.30 E
Ryūsen 270 34.28 N 135.37 E
Ryūyō 94 34.40 N 137.48 E
Ržaksa 80 52.09 N 42.02 E
Ržanica 76 53.26 N 33.55 E
Ržava 78 51.14 N 36.43 E
Rzepin 30 52.22 N 14.50 E
Rzeszów 30 50.03 N 22.00 E
Rzeszów □[4] 30 50.00 N 22.00 E
Ržev 76 56.16 N 34.20 E
Ržiščov 78 49.58 N 31.03 E
Ržovka ◆[8] 265a 59.58 N 30.30 E

S

Sa 110 18.34 N 100.45 E
Sa ≐ 105 40.22 N 117.58 E
Saa 152 4.22 N 11.27 E
Sa'ad 132 31.28 N 34.32 E
Sa'ādatābād 128 30.06 N 53.08 E
Sääksjärvi @ 26 61.24 N 22.24 E
Saal 54 54.19 N 12.29 E
Saalach ≐ 64 47.51 N 13.00 E
Saal an der Donau 60 48.54 N 11.56 E
Saal an der Saale 56 50.19 N 10.21 E
Saalbach 64 47.23 N 12.38 E
Saalburg 54 50.30 N 11.43 E
Saaldorf 54 50.27 N 11.41 E
Saale ≐ 54 51.57 N 11.55 E
Saaler Bodden c 54 54.20 N 12.28 E
Saales 58 48.21 N 7.07 E
Saaletalsperre ◆[6] 54 50.30 N 11.35 E
Saalfeld 54 50.39 N 11.22 E
Saalfelden 64 47.25 N 12.51 E
Šaamar 88 50.08 N 106.10 E
Saâne ≐, Fr. 50 49.54 N 0.56 E
Saane ≐, Schw. 58 46.59 N 7.16 E
Saanen 58 46.29 N 7.16 E
Saanenmöser 58 46.31 N 7.18 E
Saanich Inlet c 224 48.38 N 123.30 W
Saar (Sarre) ≐ 56 49.42 N 6.34 E
Saarbrücken 56 49.14 N 6.59 E
Saarburg 56 49.36 N 6.33 E
Sääre 76 57.56 N 22.02 E
Saarelouis → Saarlouis 56 49.21 N 6.45 E
Saaremaa I 76 58.25 N 22.30 E
Saarijärvi 26 62.43 N 25.16 E
Saaristomeren kansallispuisto ♦ 26 59.50 N 21.50 E
Saarland □[3] 56 49.20 N 7.00 E
Saarlautern → Saarlouis 56 49.21 N 6.45 E
Saarlouis 56 49.21 N 6.45 E
Saarmund 264a 52.19 N 13.07 E
Saarn ◆[8] 263 51.24 N 6.53 E
Saarnberg ◆[8] 263 51.25 N 6.53 E
Saar → Saarland □[3] 56 49.20 N 7.00 E
Saas Almagell 58 46.07 N 7.58 E
Saas Fee 58 46.07 N 7.55 E
Saas Grund 58 46.08 N 7.56 E
Saastal V 58 46.10 N 7.56 E
Saatly 84 39.56 N 48.23 E
Saavedra 252 37.45 S 62.22 W
Saba I 238 17.38 N 63.10 W
Saba ≐, Nihon 96 34.02 N 131.30 E
Saba ≐, Ross. 76 59.08 N 29.00 E
Sabā', Wādī al- V 128 28.35 N 36.35 E
Saba Bank ✦[2] 238 17.30 N 63.30 W
Šabac 38 44.45 N 19.42 E
Sabadell 34 41.33 N 2.06 E
Sabae 94 35.57 N 136.11 E
Sab'ah 142 30.15 N 32.33 E
Sabah □[3] 112 5.20 N 117.10 E
Sabajevo 80 53.59 N 45.43 E
Sabak, Cape > 181a 52.20 N 173.45 E
Sabak Bernam 114 3.46 N 100.59 E
Sabal 112 0.59 S 123.14 E
Sabalān ∧ 128 38.15 N 47.48 E
Sabalana, Kepulauan II 112 6.45 S 118.50 E
Sabalgarh 124 26.15 N 77.24 E
Sabaluka Game Reserve ◆[4] 140 16.18 N 32.40 E
Sabana 240m 18.20 N 65.44 W
Sabana, Archipiélago de II 240p 23.00 N 80.00 W
Sabana de La Mar 238 19.04 N 69.23 W
Sabana de Mendoza 246 9.26 N 70.46 W
Sabanagrande, Hond. 236 13.50 N 87.15 W
Sabana Grande, P.R. 240m 18.05 N 66.58 W
Sabanalamar, Ensenada c 240p 21.36 N 78.44 W
Sabanalarga 246 10.38 N 74.55 W
Sabana Llana 240m 18.02 N 66.15 W
Sabancuy 232 18.58 N 91.11 W
Sabaneta, Rep. Dom. 238 19.30 N 71.21 W
Sabaneta, Ven. 246 8.46 N 69.56 W
Sabaneta, Puntan > 174n 15.17 N 145.49 E
Sābang, India 126 22.11 N 87.36 E
Sabang (Dampelas), Indon. 112 0.11 N 119.51 E
Sabang, Indon. 114 5.55 N 95.19 E
Sabanillas 232 25.08 N 101.44 W
Šabanovo 82 55.38 N 38.43 E
Şabanözü 130 40.29 N 33.18 E
Sabará 255 19.54 S 43.48 W
Sabarei 154 4.20 N 36.55 E
Sābari ≐ 122 17.34 N 81.15 E
Sābarmati ≐ 120 22.18 N 72.22 E
Sabasṭīyah (Samaria) 132 32.17 N 35.12 E
Sab'atayn, Ramlat as- ⊥[8] 144 15.30 N 46.10 E
Sabathu 123 30.59 N 76.59 E
Sabatini, Monti ⋏ 66 42.10 N 12.15 E
Sabato ≐ 66 41.08 N 14.45 E
Sabaudia 66 41.18 N 13.01 E
Sabaudia, Lago di c 66 41.16 N 13.02 E
Sabaúna 256 23.29 S 46.05 W
Saba Wanak 144 10.33 N 44.08 E
Sabaya 248 19.01 S 68.23 W
Ṣabāyā, Jabal I 144 18.35 N 41.03 E
Sabažo 84 42.14 N 41.48 E
Sabbioneta 64 45.00 N 10.39 E
Ṣabe 272c 19.11 N 73.02 E
Šabel'kovka 83 48.45 N 37.29 E
Šabel'sk 83 46.51 N 38.29 E
Ṣāberī, Hāmūn-e @ 128 31.30 N 61.20 E
Sabetha 198 39.54 N 95.48 W
Sabhā, Lībiyā 146 27.03 N 14.26 E
Ṣabḥā, Urd. 132 32.20 N 36.30 E
Sābhār 126 23.51 N 90.15 E
Sabi (Save) ≐, Afr. 156 21.00 S 35.02 E
Sabi ≐, Nihon 94 36.48 N 140.04 E
Sabicy 76 58.50 N 29.18 E
Sabidana, Jabal ∧ 140 18.04 N 36.50 E
Sabie 156 25.10 S 30.48 E
Sábiè ≐ 156 25.19 S 32.18 E
Sabile 76 57.03 N 22.35 E
Sabillasville 208 39.42 N 77.27 W
Sabina 218 39.29 N 83.38 W
Sabina □[9] 36 42.15 N 12.42 E
Sabinal 196 29.19 N 99.27 W
Sabinal ≐ 196 29.06 N 99.27 W
Sabinal, Cayo I 240p 21.40 N 77.18 W
Sabiñánigo 34 42.31 N 0.22 W
Sabinas 232 27.51 N 101.07 W
Sabinas ≐, Méx. 232 27.37 N 100.42 W
Sabinas ≐, Méx. 232 26.51 N 99.34 W
Sabinas ≐, Méx. 234 22.59 N 98.58 W
Sabinas Hidalgo 232 26.30 N 100.10 W
Sabine ≐ 178 30.00 N 93.45 W
Sabine, Mount ∧ 169 38.38 S 143.44 E
Sabine, South Fork ≐ 222 32.52 N 96.10 W
Sabine Bay c 176 75.35 N 109.30 W
Sabine Lake @ 194 29.50 N 93.50 W
Sabine Pass c 194 29.44 N 93.52 W
Sabine Peninsula >[1] 176 76.20 N 109.30 W
Sabini, Monti ⋏ 66 42.13 N 12.50 E
Sabinópolis 255 18.40 S 43.06 W
Sabinov 30 49.06 N 21.06 E
Sabinsville 210 41.52 N 77.31 W
Sabir, Jabal ∧ 144 13.30 N 44.03 E
Şabirabad 84 40.01 N 48.29 E
Šabla 38 43.32 N 28.32 E
Sabl'a, gora ∧ 24 64.48 N 58.50 E
Sablayan 116 12.50 N 120.46 E
Sable, Anse au c 275a 45.21 N 73.56 W
Sable, Cape > 186 43.25 N 65.35 W
Sable, Cape >[1] 220 25.12 N 81.05 W
Sable, Île de I 160 19.15 S 159.56 E
Sable, Rivière du ≐ 176 55.30 N 68.21 W
Sable Island I 186 43.55 N 59.50 W
Sables, Lac aux @ 206 46.53 N 72.22 W
Sables, River aux ≐ 190 46.13 N 82.04 W
Sablé-sur-Sarthe 32 47.50 N 0.20 W
Sablinskoje 84 44.31 N 43.14 E
Sablūkah, Ash-Shallāl as- (Sixth Cataract) ⌊ 140 16.20 N 32.42 E
Šablykino 76 52.51 N 35.12 E
Ṣabo, Centraf. 152 7.50 N 17.49 E
Šabo, Ukr. 78 46.08 N 30.23 E
Saboeiro 250 6.32 S 39.54 W
Sabogal ≐ 236 10.55 N 84.43 W
Sāboli ◆[8] 272a 28.43 N 77.18 E
Sabonkafi 150 14.38 N 8.45 E
Sabor ≐ 34 41.10 N 7.07 W
Sabou 150 12.04 N 2.14 W
Sabourin, Lac @ 190 47.58 N 77.41 W
Sabra, Tanjung > 164 2.17 S 132.19 E
Ṣabrātah 146 32.47 N 12.29 E
Sabres 32 44.09 N 0.44 W
Sabrevois 206 45.12 N 73.14 W
Sabrina Coast ⊥[2] 9 67.00 S 119.30 E
Sabuda, Pulau I 164 2.38 S 131.36 E
Sabugal 34 40.21 N 7.05 W
Sabugo 266c 38.49 N 9.18 W
Sabuka 273b 4.27 S 15.10 E
Sabula 190 42.04 N 90.10 W
Sabunči 84 40.26 N 49.56 E
Sabuncu 130 39.33 N 30.12 E
Saburovo 265b 55.53 N 37.16 E
Saburovo ◆[8] 265b 55.38 N 37.42 E
Ṣabyā 144 17.09 N 42.37 E
Ṣabyin 110 19.06 N 94.11 E
Sabyndy 86 50.53 N 70.33 E
Sabzevār 128 36.13 N 57.42 E
Sac ≐ 194 38.01 N 93.43 W
Sacaba 248 17.23 S 66.02 W
Sacaca 248 18.05 S 66.26 W
Sacacomie, Lac @ 206 46.31 N 73.14 W
Sacagawea ≐ 202 47.27 N 107.58 W
Sacajawea Peak ∧ 202 45.15 N 117.17 W
Sacanche 248 7.05 S 76.44 W
Sacandaga ≐ 210 43.19 N 73.50 W

Symbols in the index entries represent the broad categories identified in the key at the right. Symbols with superior numbers (⋏[1]) identify subcategories (see complete key on page *I · 1*).

Symbole im Register stellen die rechts im Schlüssel erklärten Kategorien dar. Symbole mit hochgestellten Ziffern (⋏[1]) bezeichnen Unterabteilungen einer Kategorie (vgl. vollständiger Schlüssel auf Seite *I · 1*).

Los símbolos incluídos en el texto del índice representan las grandes categorias identificadas con la clave a la derecha. Los símbolos con numeros en su parte superior (⋏[1]) identifican las subcategorías (véase la clave completa en la página *I · 1*).

Les symboles de l'index représentent les catégories indiquées dans la légende à droite. Les symboles suivis d'un indice (⋏[1]) représentent des sous-catégories (voir légende complète à la page *I · 1*).

Os símbolos incluídos no texto do índice representam as grandes categorias identificadas com a chave à direita. Os símbolos com números em sua parte superior (⋏[1]) identificam as subcategorias (veja-se a chave completa à página *I · 1*).

∧ Mountain	Berg	Montaña	Montagne	Montanha
⋏ Mountains	Gebirge	Montañas	Montagnes	Montanhas
)(Pass	Paß	Paso	Col	Passo
V Valley, Canyon	Tal, Cañon	Valle, Cañón	Vallée, Canyon	Vale, Canhão
≚ Plain	Ebene	Llano	Plaine	Planície
> Cape	Kap	Cabo	Cap	Cabo
I Island	Insel	Isla	Île	Ilha
II Islands	Inseln	Islas	Îles	Ilhas
⊥ Other Topographic Features	Andere Topographische Objekte	Otros Elementos Topográficos	Autres données topographiques	Outros acidentes topográficos

ESPAÑOL Nombre | Página | Lat.°′ | Long.°′ W = Oeste
FRANÇAIS Nom | Page | Lat.°′ | Long.°′ W = Ouest
PORTUGUÊS Nome | Página | Lat.°′ | Long.°′ W = Oeste

Sacandaga, West Branch ≃ 210 43.22 N 74.17 W
Sacandica 152 5.58 S 15.56 E
Sacaola 152 12.57 S 22.25 E
Sacariúna ≃ 248 12.52 S 57.22 W
Sacaton 200 33.04 N 111.44 W
Sacavém 266c 38.47 N 9.06 W
Saĉchere 84 42.21 N 43.23 E
Sac City 198 42.25 N 94.59 W
Sacco ≃ 66 41.31 N 13.32 E
Sacedón 34 40.29 N 2.43 W
Săcele 38 45.37 N 25.42 E
Saç Geçidi ⋈ 130 39.54 N 42.22 E
Sacha ≃ 82 56.45 N 39.10 E
Sachalin □8 89 50.00 N 143.00 E
Sachalin, ostrov (Sakhalin) I 89 51.00 N 143.00 E
Sachalinskij zaliv c 89 53.45 N 141.30 E
Sachand 85 40.54 N 71.28 E
Sachayoj 252 26.41 S 61.50 W
Sachbuz 84 39.25 N 45.34 E
Sachdagskij chrebet ∧ 84 40.24 N 45.35 E
Saché 50 47.14 N 0.33 E
Sache ≃ 84 43.47 N 39.27 E
Sachicapa 152 10.21 S 19.59 E
Sachigo ≃ 176 55.06 N 88.58 W
Sachigo Lake ⊜ 184 53.49 N 92.08 W
Sachimbo 152 9.14 S 20.16 E
Sachnovščina 78 49.08 N 35.53 E
Sachovskaja 76 56.02 N 35.29 E
Sachrang 64 47.41 N 12.15 E
Sachrichan 85 40.44 N 72.03 E
Sachrinau 85 38.34 N 68.20 E
Sachrisabz 72 39.03 N 66.50 E
Sachristan 85 39.47 N 68.49 E
Sachristan, pereval ⋈ 85 39.33 N 68.33 E
Sachrovka 80 58.34 N 52.12 E
Sachse 222 32.59 N 96.36 W
Sachseln 58 46.52 N 8.15 E
Sachsen □3 30 51.00 N 13.00 E
Sachsen □9 30 52.45 N 9.30 E
Sachsen-Anhalt □3 30 52.00 N 11.30 E
Sachsenbrunn 54 50.27 N 10.56 E
Sachsenburg 64 46.50 N 13.21 E
Sachsenhagen 52 52.24 N 9.16 E
Sachsenhausen, Dtsch. 54 52.47 N 13.14 E
Sachsenhausen, Dtsch. 56 51.15 N 9.00 E
Sachs Harbour 176 72.00 N 125.00 W
Sächsische Schweiz ◆1 54 50.55 N 14.10 E
Šachterskij 180 64.42 N 177.40 E
Šachtinsk 86 49.40 N 72.37 E
Šachtnoje 83 47.57 N 38.17 E
Šacht'orsk, Ross. 89 49.11 N 142.07 E
Šacht'orsk, Ukr. 83 48.03 N 38.28 E
Šacht'orskij ◆8 83 48.09 N 39.08 E
Šachty 83 47.42 N 40.13 E
Šachunja 80 57.40 N 46.37 E
Sachy 56 49.40 N 5.08 E
Sacile 64 45.57 N 12.30 E
Šack, Bela. 76 53.25 N 27.41 E
Šack, Ross. 80 54.01 N 41.43 E
Šack, Ukr. 78 51.31 N 23.57 E
Sackets Harbor 212 43.56 N 76.07 W
Sackville 186 45.54 N 64.22 W
Saclay 261 48.44 N 2.10 E
Saclay, Étang de ⊜ 261 48.45 N 2.10 E
Saco, Me., U.S. 188 43.30 N 70.26 W
Saco, Mt., U.S. 202 48.27 N 107.20 W
Saco ≃ 188 43.27 N 70.22 W
Saco Bay c 188 43.30 N 70.15 W
Sacol Island I 116 6.58 N 122.13 E
Sacotes 266c 38.48 N 9.20 W
Sacra, Isola I 267a 41.45 N 12.15 E
Sacra Família do Tinguá 256 22.29 S 43.36 W
Sacramento, Bra. 255 19.53 S 47.27 W
Sacramento, Ca., U.S. 226 38.34 N 121.29 W
Sacramento □6 226 38.35 N 121.30 W
Sacramento ≃, Ca., U.S. 204 38.03 N 121.56 W
Sacramento ≃, N.M., U.S. 200 32.16 N 105.31 W
Sacramento, Pampa del ≋ 248 8.00 S 75.50 W
Sacramento Metropolitan Airport ≋ 226 38.42 N 121.37 W
Sacramento Mountains ∧ 200 32.45 N 105.30 W
Sacramento River Deep Water Ship Channel ≍ 226 38.15 N 121.40 W
Sacramento South 226 38.32 N 121.26 W
Sacramento Valley V 204 39.15 N 122.00 W
Sacramento Wash V 200 34.43 N 114.28 W
Sacre ≃ 248 12.56 S 58.18 W
Sacré-Cœur ᵾ1 261 48.53 N 2.21 E
Sacred Heart 198 44.47 N 95.21 W
Sacriston 44 54.49 N 1.37 W
Sacro, Monte ∧ 68 40.13 N 15.20 E
Sacro Monte ᵾ1 62 45.49 N 8.15 E
Sacrow ◆8 264a 52.26 N 13.06 E
Sacrower See ⊜ 264a 52.27 N 13.06 E
Săcueni 38 47.21 N 22.06 E
Sacul 222 31.50 N 94.56 W
Sacupana 246 8.35 N 61.39 W
Sada, Esp. 34 43.21 N 8.15 W
Sada, Nihon 96 35.15 N 132.43 E
Sádaba 34 42.17 N 1.16 W
Sadābād, India 124 27.27 N 78.03 E
Sa'dābād, Īrān 128 29.23 N 51.07 E
Sa'dābād, Īrān 128 34.51 N 50.36 E
Sadad 130 34.18 N 36.56 E
Ṣa'dah 144 16.52 N 43.37 E
Sadaik Taung ∧ 110 15.09 N 98.12 E
Sadali 71 39.49 N 9.16 E
Sada-misaki > 96 33.20 N 132.01 E
Sada-misaki-hantō >1 96 33.26 N 132.13 E
Sadamitsu 96 34.02 N 134.04 E
Sadane ≃ 115a 6.01 S 106.37 E
Sadang ≃ 112 3.43 S 119.27 E
Sadanga 116 17.09 N 121.02 E
Sadani 154 6.03 S 38.47 E
Sadao 110 6.38 N 100.26 E
Sadarpur, Bngl. 126 23.28 N 90.02 E
Sadarpur, India 272a 28.33 N 77.21 E
Sadčikovka 86 53.01 N 63.27 E
Sadda 120 33.42 N 70.20 E
Saddle ≃ 276 40.52 N 74.07 W
Saddleback ∧ 44 54.38 N 3.03 W
Saddleback, Mount ∧ 168a 32.58 S 116.28 E
Saddle Brook 276 40.54 N 74.06 W
Saddlebunch Keys II 220 24.37 N 81.37 W
Saddle Lake Indian Reserve ◆4 182 54.00 N 111.40 W
Saddle Mountain ∧, Co., U.S. 200 38.50 N 105.28 W
Saddle Mountain ∧, Or., U.S. 224 45.58 N 123.41 W
Saddle Mountains ∧ 202 46.50 N 119.55 W
Saddle Mountain State Park ♦ 224 45.58 N 123.41 W
Saddle Peak ∧ 110 13.09 N 93.01 E
Saddle River 276 40.54 N 74.05 W
Saddle Rock 276 40.48 N 73.45 W
Saddleworth, Austl. 168b 34.05 S 138.47 E
Saddleworth, Eng., U.K. 262 53.33 N 1.59 W
Saddleworth Moor ◆3 262 53.33 N 1.57 W
Sa Dec 110 10.18 N 105.46 E
Sadelkow 54 53.36 N 13.26 E
Sādhaura 124 30.23 N 77.13 E
Sādhuhāti 126 23.34 N 89.01 E
Sadieville 218 38.23 N 84.32 W
Sadiola 150 13.53 N 11.42 W
Sādiqābād 120 28.18 N 70.08 E
Sadiya 120 27.50 N 95.40 E
Sa'dīyah, Wādī V 144 20.35 N 39.38 E
Sa'dīyāt, Ra's as- > 132 33.41 N 35.25 E
Sadler Lake ⊜ 184 55.17 N 103.45 W
Sado I 92 38.00 N 138.25 E
Sado ≃ 34 38.29 N 8.55 W
Sado-kaikyō ⋈ 92 37.50 N 138.40 E
Sadon 84 42.51 N 44.00 E
Sadovoje, Ross. 80 46.56 N 44.23 E
Sadovoje, Ross. 80 47.46 N 44.30 E
Sadovoje Pervoje 78 51.33 N 40.29 E
Sadowara 92 32.02 N 131.26 E
Sādri 120 25.11 N 73.26 E
Šadrina 89 51.33 N 130.22 E
Šadrino 86 55.52 N 91.06 E
Šadrinsk 86 56.05 N 63.38 E
Sadsburyville 208 39.59 N 75.53 W
Sādulpur 123 28.38 N 75.24 E
Sādvaluspen 24 66.24 N 16.51 E
Sæby, Dan. 26 57.20 N 10.32 E
Sæby, Dan. 41 55.33 N 11.19 E
Saegertown 214 41.43 N 80.09 W
Sae Islands II 164 0.45 S 145.15 E
Saeki, Nihon 96 34.22 N 132.11 E
Saeki, Nihon 96 34.51 N 134.06 E
Saeki
→ Saiki 96 32.57 N 131.54 E
Saengil-to I 98 34.19 N 126.59 E
Saerbeck 52 52.10 N 7.38 E
Saerluojia Hu ⊜ 120 33.55 N 86.55 E
Særslev, Dan. 41 55.31 N 10.11 E
Særslev, Dan. 41 55.43 N 11.23 E
Saeul 56 49.44 N 5.59 E
Ṣafā, Tulūl aṣ- ∧1 132 33.02 N 37.12 E
Safad
→ Ẓefat 132 32.58 N 35.30 E
Ṣafājah, Jazīrat I 140 26.45 N 33.59 E
Safakulevo 86 54.59 N 62.33 E
Ṣafānīyah 142 28.49 N 30.48 E
Šafárikovo 30 48.27 N 20.20 E
Safdar Jang Airport ≋ 272a 28.37 N 77.13 E
Safdar Jang's Tomb ᵾ 272a 28.36 N 77.13 E
Safed Koh Range ∧ 123 33.58 N 70.25 E
Safe Harbor Dam ◆6 208 39.59 N 76.28 W
Safenbach ≃ 61 47.06 N 16.05 E
Safety Bay 168a 32.18 S 115.43 E
Safety Harbor 220 27.59 N 82.41 W
Säffle 26 59.08 N 12.56 E
Safford 200 32.50 N 109.42 W
Saffron Walden 42 52.01 N 0.15 E
Safi 148 32.20 N 9.17 W
Safi □4 148 32.05 N 9.00 W
Safia 164 9.35 S 148.40 E
Šafīābād 128 36.45 N 57.58 E
Safīd ≃ 120 36.44 N 65.38 E
Safīd Kūh, Selseleh-ye ∧ 128 34.30 N 63.30 E
Safidon 124 29.25 N 76.40 E
Safiental V 58 46.40 N 9.18 E
Safioune, Sebkhet ≋ 148 32.16 N 5.27 E
Safipur 126 23.01 N 90.22 E
Ṣāfītā 130 34.49 N 36.07 E
Safonovo, Ross. 24 65.42 N 47.39 E
Safonovo, Ross. 76 55.06 N 33.15 E
Safonovo, Ross. 82 55.33 N 38.17 E
Safrakköyü ◆8 267b 41.00 N 28.47 E
Safranbolu 130 41.15 N 32.45 E
Ṣaft al-'Inab 142 30.49 N 30.41 E
Ṣaft al-Khammār 142 28.02 N 30.42 E
Ṣaft al-Laban 273c 30.02 N 31.10 E
Ṣaft al-Mulūk 142 30.49 N 30.41 E
Ṣaft Rāshīn 142 28.58 N 30.55 E
Ṣaft Turāb 142 30.54 N 31.07 E
Ṣafwān 128 30.07 N 47.43 E
Saga, Kaz. 86 50.23 N 64.15 E
Saga, Kaz. 86 49.25 N 55.17 E
Saga, Nihon 92 33.15 N 130.18 E
Saga, Nihon 96 33.05 N 133.06 E
Saga, Zhg. 120 29.30 N 85.22 E
Saga □5 96 33.21 N 130.28 E
Sagaba 152 11.17 S 23.07 E
Sagae 92 38.22 N 140.17 E
Sagaing 110 21.52 N 95.59 E
Sagaing □8 110 24.00 N 95.00 E
Sagak, Cape > 180 52.48 N 169.08 W
Şagalaherang 115a 6.40 S 107.39 E
Šagalakasa 80 46.54 N 50.43 E
Sagamāthā □8 124 27.15 N 86.45 E
Sagami ≃ 94 35.19 N 139.22 E
Sagamihara 94 35.34 N 139.23 E
Sagamihara-daichi ⩘1 268 35.27 N 139.27 E
Sagamiko 94 35.37 N 139.12 E
Sagami-ko ⊜ 94 35.35 N 139.16 E
Sagami-nada c 94 35.00 N 139.30 E
Sagami-wan c 94 35.15 N 139.25 E
Sagamore, Ma., U.S. 207 41.46 N 70.31 W
Sagamore, Pa., U.S. 214 40.46 N 79.13 W
Sagamore Beach 207 41.47 N 70.31 W
Sagamore Hill National Historic Site ⊥ 276 40.53 N 73.30 W
Sagamore Hills 279a 41.02 N 81.26 W
Sagan ≃, Kaz. 86 50.37 N 73.15 E
Sagån ≃, Sve. 40 59.35 N 16.54 E
Saganaga Lake ⊜ 190 48.14 N 90.52 W
Saganashkee Slough ≋ 278 41.41 N 87.53 W
Saganash Lake ⊜ 190 49.04 N 82.35 W
Saganoseki 96 33.15 N 131.53 E
Saganthit Kyun I 110 11.56 N 98.29 E
Sagany, ozero ⊜ 78 45.43 N 29.53 E
Sagan
→ Żagań 30 51.37 N 15.19 E
Sagaon 272c 19.12 N 73.06 E
Sāgar, India 122 14.10 N 75.02 E
Sāgar, India 124 23.50 N 78.43 E
Sagara 94 34.41 N 138.12 E
Sagaranten 115a 7.13 S 106.52 E
Sagard 54 54.31 N 13.33 E
Sāgardīghi 126 24.17 N 88.06 E
Sagaredžo 84 41.44 N 45.20 E
Sāgar Island I 126 21.43 N 88.06 E
Sagarmatha
→ Everest, Mount ∧ 124 27.59 N 86.56 E
Sagarmatha National Park ♦ 124 27.50 N 86.45 E
Sāgar Plateau ⩘1 124 23.30 N 78.30 E
Sagavanirktok ≃ 180 70.20 N 148.00 W
Sagay 116 10.57 N 123.25 E
Sage, Mount ∧ 240m 18.25 N 64.39 W
Sage Creek ≃, N.A. 202 48.58 N 110.06 W
Sage Creek ≃, U.S. 202 44.50 N 108.26 W
Sage Creek ≃, Mt., U.S. 202 47.16 N 109.43 W
Sage Creek ≃, Mt., U.S. 202 48.20 N 110.03 W
Sagemace Bay c 184 51.49 N 100.03 W
Sagerton 196 33.05 N 99.58 W
Saggaubach ≃ 61 46.43 N 15.24 E
Sag Harbor 207 40.59 N 72.17 W
Ṣaghbīn 132 33.37 N 35.42 E
Ṣaghīr, Al-Baḥr aṣ- ≍ 142 31.09 N 31.56 E
Sagil 86 50.20 N 91.40 E
Saginaw, Mi., U.S. 190 43.25 N 83.56 W
Saginaw, Tx., U.S. 222 32.52 N 97.22 W
Saginaw ≃ 190 43.39 N 83.51 W
Saginaw Bay c 190 43.50 N 83.40 W
Sagiz, Kaz. 80 47.31 N 53.16 E
Sagiz, Kaz. 86 48.12 N 54.56 E
Sagiz ≃ 86 47.32 N 53.20 E
Sağkaya 130 37.11 N 35.41 E
Sagleipie 150 7.00 N 8.52 W
Saglek Bay c 176 58.35 N 63.00 W
Šaglyteniz, ozero ⊜ 86 54.08 N 69.52 E
Šagonar 86 51.32 N 92.48 E
Sagra ∧ 34 37.57 N 2.34 W
Sagrado 64 45.52 N 13.29 E
Sagres 34 37.00 N 8.56 W
Sag Sag 164 5.35 S 148.20 E
Sagsaj 86 48.54 N 89.37 E
Sagsajn ≃ 102 44.50 N 96.26 E
Sagu, Indon. 112 8.15 S 123.13 E
Şagu, Rom. 38 46.03 N 21.17 E
Saguache 200 38.05 N 106.05 W
Saguache Creek ≃ 200 37.52 N 105.51 W
Sagua de Tánamo 240p 20.35 N 75.14 W
Sagua la Chica ≃ 240p 22.45 N 79.39 W
Sagua la Grande 240p 22.49 N 80.05 W
Saguaro National Monument ♦ 200 32.12 N 110.38 W
Saguenay ≃ 176 48.08 N 69.44 W
Saguna 272b 22.59 N 88.29 E
Sagunay Lake 216 41.43 N 86.34 W
Šagunovka 78 49.17 N 32.23 E
Sagunt 34 39.41 N 0.16 W
Saguny 78 50.36 N 39.43 E
Sagutjevo 76 52.28 N 33.28 E
Sāgwāra 120 23.41 N 74.01 E
Sagy 261 49.03 N 1.57 E
Sa'gya 120 28.55 N 88.05 E
Sagyndyk, mys > 84 44.02 N 50.52 E
Sah 150 15.38 N 4.03 W
Ṣahāb 132 31.53 N 36.00 E
Sahaba 140 18.55 N 30.28 E
Sahagún, Col. 246 8.57 N 75.27 W
Sahagún, Esp. 34 42.22 N 5.02 W
Saham 132 32.42 N 35.47 E
Saham al-Jawlān 132 32.46 N 35.56 E
Sahana Ambodipont 157b 14.37 S 50.11 E
Sahand, Kūh-e ∧ 128 37.44 N 46.27 E
Sahara ◆2 10 26.00 N 13.00 E
Sahāranpur 124 29.58 N 77.33 E
Sahara Occidentale
→ Western Sahara □2 148 24.30 N 13.00 W
Sahara Occidental
→ Western Sahara □2 148 24.30 N 13.00 W
Saharsa 124 25.53 N 86.36 E
Sahasinaka 157b 21.49 S 47.49 E
Sahasrail 126 23.19 N 89.43 E
Sahaswān 124 28.05 N 78.45 E
Sahel, Canal du ≍ 150 13.44 N 6.05 W
Sahel, Oued ≃ 34 36.26 N 4.33 E
Sahel
→ Sudan ◆1 134 10.00 N 20.00 E
Sāhibābad 272a 28.40 N 77.22 E
Sāhibābad ◆8 272a 28.45 N 77.05 E
Sāhibganj 124 25.15 N 87.39 E
Sāhibi ≃ 124 28.29 N 76.44 E
Şahin 130 41.01 N 26.50 E
Sāhīwāl, Pāk. 123 31.58 N 72.20 E
Sāhīwāl, Pāk. 123 30.40 N 73.06 E
Sahlenburg 52 53.52 N 8.38 E
Şahneh 128 34.29 N 47.41 E
Ṣahrā', Bi'r ⊤4 140 22.52 N 28.37 E
Ṣahrajat al-Kubrā wa Kafr Jirjis Yūsuf 142 30.38 N 31.17 E
Sahtlam 224 48.48 N 123.54 W
Sahuaripa 232 29.03 N 109.14 W
Sahuarita 200 31.57 N 110.58 W
Sahuayo de José María Morelos 234 20.04 N 102.43 W
Sahul Shelf ◆4 14 12.30 S 125.00 E
Sa Huynh 110 14.40 N 109.04 E
Ṣahwat al-Qamḥ 132 32.36 N 36.23 E
Šahy 30 48.05 N 18.57 E
Saï 150 13.50 N 5.00 W
Sai ≃, India 124 25.39 N 82.47 E
Sai ≃, Nihon 94 36.36 N 136.35 E
Sai ≃, Nihon 94 36.37 N 138.14 E
Saibai Island I 164 9.24 S 142.40 E
Sai Buri 110 6.42 N 101.37 E
Sai Buri ≃ 110 6.43 N 101.39 E
Saïda 148 34.50 N 0.09 E
Saïda □5 148 33.00 N 0.30 W
Saidābād, Bngl. 126 24.18 N 89.43 E
Sa'īdābād, Īrān 267d 35.40 N 51.11 E
Saidaiji 96 34.39 N 134.02 E
Saïdia 148 35.04 N 2.15 W
Sa'īdīyeh 128 36.26 N 48.48 E
Saido 268 35.52 N 139.41 E
Saidor 164 5.35 S 146.30 E
Saidpur, Bngl. 124 25.47 N 88.54 E
Saidpur, India 124 25.33 N 83.11 E
Saidu 123 34.45 N 72.21 E
Saigawa 96 33.39 N 130.57 E
Saignelégier 58 47.15 N 7.00 E
Saignon 62 43.52 N 5.26 E
Saigō 92 36.12 N 133.20 E
Sai Gon ≃ 269c 10.45 N 106.45 E
Saigon
→ Thanh Pho Ho Chi Minh 269c 10.45 N 106.40 E
Saihaku 96 35.20 N 133.20 E
Saihan Toroi 102 41.41 N 100.26 E
Saijō, Nihon 96 33.55 N 133.11 E
Saijō, Nihon 96 34.56 N 133.07 E
Saijō ≃ 96 34.48 N 132.51 E
Saikai-kokuritsu-kōen ♦ 92 33.12 N 129.22 E
Sai Keng 271d 22.26 N 114.16 E
Saiki 96 32.57 N 131.54 E
Saiki-wan c 96 33.00 N 131.58 E
Sai Kung 271d 22.23 N 114.15 E
Saileati 85 38.57 N 74.45 E
Sailkupa 126 23.41 N 89.15 E
Saillans 62 44.42 N 5.11 E
Sailly 261 49.02 N 1.48 E
Sailmouille, Ruisseau ≃ 261 48.37 N 2.17 E
Sailolof 164 1.15 S 130.46 E
Sailor Creek ≃ 202 42.56 N 115.29 W
Sail-sous-Couzan 62 45.44 N 3.57 E
Saim 86 60.21 N 64.14 E
Saima 98 41.00 N 124.14 E
Saimaa ⊜ 26 61.15 N 28.15 E
Saimaa Canal ≍ 26 61.05 N 28.18 E
Saimbeyli 130 38.00 N 36.06 E
Sain Alto 234 23.35 N 103.15 W
Saindak 128 29.17 N 61.34 E
Ṣā'īn Dezh 128 36.40 N 46.33 E
Sainghin-en-Weppes 50 50.33 N 2.54 E
Sainjang 98 39.15 N 125.51 E
Sainō-ha'iji ⊥ 96 35.29 N 133.39 E
Sains-du-Nord 50 50.06 N 4.00 E
Sains-en-Gohelle 50 50.27 N 2.41 E
Sains-Richaumont 50 49.49 N 3.42 E
Saint Abb's Head > 46 55.54 N 2.09 W
Sainte-Adèle 206 45.57 N 74.07 W
Sainte-Adresse 50 49.30 N 0.05 E
Saint-Adrien 206 45.49 N 71.43 W
Saint-Affrique 32 43.57 N 2.53 E
Saint-Agapit 206 46.34 N 71.27 W
Saint Agatha 212 43.26 N 80.36 W
Sainte-Agathe, Mb., Can. 184 49.34 N 97.10 W
Sainte-Agathe, Fr. 62 45.49 N 3.37 E
Sainte-Agathe [-de-Lotbinière] 206 46.23 N 71.24 W
Sainte-Agathe-des-Monts 206 46.03 N 74.17 W
Sainte-Agnès, Fr. 62 43.48 N 7.28 E
Saint Agnes, Eng., U.K. 42 50.18 N 5.13 W
Saint Agnes I 42a 49.54 N 6.20 W
Saint-Agrève 62 45.01 N 4.24 E
Saint-Aignan 50 47.16 N 1.23 E
Saint-Aimé (Massueville) 206 45.55 N 72.56 W
Saint Albans, Austl. 169 37.44 S 144.48 E
Saint Albans, Austl. 170 33.17 S 150.59 E
Saint Alban's, Nf., Can. 186 47.52 N 55.51 W
Saint Albans, Eng., U.K. 42 51.46 N 0.21 W
Saint Albans, Mo., U.S. 219 38.35 N 90.46 W
Saint Albans, Vt., U.S. 188 44.48 N 73.05 W
Saint Albans, W.V., U.S. 188 38.23 N 81.50 W
Saint Albans □8 260 51.45 N 0.20 W
Saint Albans ◆8 276 40.42 N 73.46 W
Saint Albans, Cape > 168b 35.49 S 138.07 E
Saint Albans Cathedral ᵾ1 260 51.45 N 0.20 W
Saint Albert, Ab., Can. 182 53.38 N 113.38 W
Saint-Albert, P.Q., Can. 206 46.00 N 72.05 W
Saint Aldhelm's Head > 42 50.34 N 2.04 W
Saint-Alexandre-de-Kamouraska 186 47.41 N 69.38 W
Saint-Alexis-des-Monts 206 46.28 N 73.08 W
Saint-Amable 275a 45.39 N 73.18 W
Saint-Amand 56 48.49 N 4.36 E
Saint-Amand-en-Puisaye 50 47.31 N 3.04 E
Saint-Amand-les-Eaux 50 50.26 N 3.26 E
Saint-Amand-Longpré 50 47.41 N 1.01 E
Saint-Amand-Montrond 32 46.44 N 2.30 E
Saint-Amant-Roche-Savine 62 45.34 N 3.38 E
Saint-Amarin 58 47.53 N 7.01 E
Saint-Ambroix 62 44.15 N 4.11 E
Sainte-Amélie 184 50.59 N 99.21 W
Saint-Amour 58 46.26 N 5.21 E
Saint-André 157c 20.57 S 55.39 E
Saint-André, Cap > 157b 16.11 S 44.27 E
Saint-André, Ruisseau ≃ 275a 45.22 N 73.29 W
Saint-André-Avellin 206 45.43 N 75.03 W
Saint-André-de-l'Eure 50 48.54 N 1.17 E
Saint-André-de-Valborgne 62 44.09 N 3.41 E
St.-André-Est 206 45.34 N 74.20 W
Saint-André-les-Alpes 62 43.58 N 6.30 E
Saint-André-les-Vergers 50 48.17 N 4.03 E
Saint Andrew 241g 13.15 N 59.33 W
Saint Andrew, Mount ∧ 241h 13.11 N 61.13 W
Saint Andrew Lakes ⊜ 212 44.36 N 76.40 W
Saint Andrews, N.B., Can. 186 45.05 N 67.03 W
Saint Andrews, Scot., U.K. 46 56.20 N 2.48 W
Saint Andrews, S.C., U.S. 218 32.46 N 79.59 W
Saint Andrews Bay c 46 56.22 N 2.50 W
Saint Andrew's Cathedral ᵾ1 271c 1.18 N 103.51 E
Saint Andrews Channel ⋈ 186 46.03 N 60.38 W
Saint Ann 219 38.43 N 90.22 W
Sainte-Anne, Guad. 241o 16.14 N 61.23 W
Saint Anne, Guernsey 43b 49.42 N 2.12 W
Sainte-Anne, Mart. 240e 14.26 N 60.53 W
Saint Anne, Il., U.S. 216 41.01 N 87.42 W
Sainte-Anne ≃ 206 46.33 N 72.12 W
Saint Anne, Cathedral of ᵾ1 273b 4.18 S 15.19 E
Sainte Anne, Lac ⊜, Ab., Can. 182 53.43 N 114.27 W
Sainte-Anne, Lac ⊜, P.Q., Can. 186 50.05 N 67.50 W
Sainte-Anne-de-Beaupré 186 47.02 N 70.56 W
Sainte-Anne-de-Bellevue 275a 45.24 N 73.57 W
Sainte-Anne-de-la-Pérade 206 46.35 N 72.12 W
Sainte-Anne-de-Madawaska 186 47.15 N 68.02 W
Sainte-Anne-des-Chênes 184 49.40 N 96.40 W
Sainte-Anne-des-Monts 186 49.08 N 66.30 W
Sainte-Anne-des-Plaines 206 46.46 N 73.48 W
Saint Anne of the Congo ᵾ1 273b 4.16 S 15.17 E
Saint Anne's 44 53.45 N 3.02 W
Saint Ann's Bay 241q 18.26 N 77.08 W
Saint Anns Bay c 186 46.20 N 60.30 W
Saint Ann's Head > 42 51.41 N 5.10 W
Saint-Anselme 186 46.37 N 70.58 W
Saint Ansgar 190 43.22 N 92.55 W
Saint-Anthème 62 45.31 N 3.55 E
Saint Anthony, N.B., Can. 186 46.22 N 64.45 W
Saint Anthony, Nf., Can. 186 51.22 N 55.35 W
Saint Anthony, Id., U.S. 202 43.57 N 111.40 W
Saint-Antoine, P.Q., Can. 206 45.46 N 73.59 W
Saint-Antoine, Fr. 62 45.10 N 5.13 E
Saint-Antonin 32 44.09 N 1.45 E
Saint-Apollinaire (Francoeur) 206 46.37 N 71.31 W
Saint Arnaud, Austl. 166 36.37 S 143.15 E
Saint Arnaud, N.Z. 172 41.48 S 172.50 E
Saint-Arnoult, Forêt de ♦ 261 48.35 N 1.55 E
Saint-Arnoult-en-Yvelines 50 48.34 N 1.56 E
Saint Arvans 42 51.40 N 2.41 W
Saint Asaph 44 53.16 N 3.26 W
Saint-Astier 32 45.09 N 0.32 E
Saint Athan 42 51.24 N 3.25 W
Saint-Auban 62 43.51 N 6.44 E
Saint-Aubert, Mont ∧2 50 50.39 N 3.24 E
Saint Aubert Island I 219 38.40 N 91.52 W
Saint-Aubin, Fr. 50 49.53 N 0.53 E
Saint-Aubin, Fr. 58 47.02 N 5.20 E
Saint Aubin, Jersey 43b 49.11 N 2.10 W
Saint-Aubin, Schw. 58 46.54 N 6.47 E
Saint-Aubin-d'Aubigné 32 48.15 N 1.36 W
Saint-Aubin-lès-Elbeuf 50 49.18 N 1.01 E
Saint-Aubin-sur-Aire 58 48.42 N 5.27 E
Saint-Augustin 157b 23.33 S 43.46 E
Saint-Augustin ≃ 186 51.14 N 58.41 W
Saint-Augustin-Deux-Montagnes 275a 45.38 N 73.59 W
Saint Augustine 192 29.53 N 81.18 W
Saint-Augustin Nord-Ouest ≃ 186 51.16 N 58.42 W
Saint-Augustin-Saguenay 186 51.14 N 58.39 W
Saint-Aulaye 32 45.12 N 0.08 E
Saint Austell 42 50.20 N 4.48 W
Saint-Avertin 50 47.22 N 0.44 E
Saint-Avold 56 49.06 N 6.42 E
Saint-Ay 50 47.51 N 1.45 E
Saint-Aygulf 62 43.23 N 6.44 E
Saint Barbe 186 51.12 N 56.46 W
Saint Barnabas Chapel ᵾ1 174c 29.02 S 167.55 E
Saint-Barthélemy I 238 17.54 N 62.50 W
Saint-Basile 186 47.21 N 68.14 W
Saint-Basile-de-Portneuf 206 46.45 N 71.49 W
Saint-Basile-le-Grand 206 45.32 N 73.17 W
Saint Bathans, Mount ∧ 172 44.44 S 169.46 E
Sainte-Baume, Chaîne de la ⩘ 62 43.20 N 5.45 E
Saint-Béat 32 42.55 N 0.42 E
Saint Bees 44 54.30 N 3.37 W
Saint Bees Head > 44 54.32 N 3.38 W
Saint Benedict 214 40.38 N 78.44 W
Saint-Benoît, Fr. 261 48.40 N 1.55 E
Saint-Benoît, Réu. 157c 21.02 S 55.43 E
Saint-Benoît-du-Sault 32 46.27 N 1.23 E
Saint-Benoît-en-Woëvre 56 48.59 N 5.47 E
Saint Bernard 218 39.10 N 84.29 W
Saint-Bernard, Île I 275a 45.23 N 73.45 W
Saint-Bernard-de-Dorchester 206 46.30 N 71.08 W
Saint-Béron 62 45.30 N 5.43 E
Saint-Blaise, P.Q., Can. 206 45.13 N 73.17 W
Saint-Blaise, Schw. 58 47.01 N 6.59 E
Saint-Blaise-la-Roche 58 48.24 N 7.10 E
Saint Blaize, Cape > 158 34.11 S 22.10 E
Saint Blazey 42 50.22 N 4.43 W
Saint-Blin 58 48.16 N 5.25 E
Saint-Bonaventure, P.Q., Can. 206 45.58 N 72.41 W
Saint Bonaventure, N.Y., U.S. 210 42.05 N 78.28 W
Saint-Boniface-de-Shawinigan 206 46.30 N 72.49 W
Saint-Bonnet 62 44.41 N 6.05 E
Saint-Bonnet-de-Joux 58 46.29 N 4.27 E
Saint-Bonnet-le-Château 62 45.25 N 4.04 E
Saint-Bonnet-le-Froid 62 45.09 N 4.27 E
Saint Boswells 46 55.34 N 2.39 W
Saint Brendan's 186 48.52 N 53.40 W
Saint-Brice-sous-Forêt 261 49.00 N 2.21 E
Saint Bride, Mount ∧ 182 51.30 N 115.57 W
Saint Bride's 186 46.55 N 54.10 W
Saint Brides Bay c 42 51.48 N 5.15 W
Saint Bride's Major 42 51.28 N 3.38 W
Saint-Brieuc 32 48.31 N 2.47 W
Saint-Brieux 184 52.38 N 104.52 W
Saint-Broing-les-Moines, Fr. 58 47.41 N 4.50 E
Saint-Broing-les-Moines, Fr. 58 48.32 N 6.36 E
Saint-Bruno 206 45.32 N 73.21 W
Saint-Bruno, Mont ∧2 275a 45.33 N 73.19 W
Saint-Calais 50 47.55 N 0.45 E
Saint-Calixte-de-Kilkenny 206 45.57 N 73.51 W
Saint-Cannat 62 43.37 N 5.18 E
Saint-Casimir 206 46.40 N 72.08 W
Saint-Cassien, Lac de ⊜1 62 43.35 N 6.48 E
Saint Catharines 212 43.10 N 79.15 W
Saint Catharines Airport ≋ 284a 43.11 N 79.10 W
Saint Catherine 220 28.37 N 82.08 W
Saint Catherine, Monastery of
→ Qiddīsah Kātrīnā, Dayr al- ᵾ1 140 28.29 N 34.01 E
Saint Catherine, Mount ∧ 241k 12.10 N 61.40 W
Sainte-Catherine-de-Fierbois 50 47.09 N 0.39 E
Saint Catherines Island I 192 31.38 N 81.10 W
Saint Catherine's Point > 42 50.34 N 1.15 W
Saint-Célestin (Annaville) 206 46.13 N 72.26 W
Saint-Céré 32 44.52 N 1.53 E
Saint-Cergue 58 46.27 N 6.09 E
Saint-Césaire 206 45.25 N 73.00 W
Saint-Cézaire-sur-Siagne 62 43.39 N 6.48 E
Saint-Chamas 62 43.33 N 5.02 E
Saint-Chamond 62 45.28 N 4.30 E
Saint-Chaptes 62 43.58 N 4.17 E
Saint Charles, Ar., U.S. 194 34.22 N 91.08 W
Saint Charles, Id., U.S. 202 42.06 N 111.23 W
Saint Charles, Il., U.S. 216 41.54 N 88.18 W
Saint Charles, Md., U.S. 208 38.36 N 76.56 W
Saint Charles, Mi., U.S. 190 43.17 N 84.08 W
Saint Charles, Mn., U.S. 190 43.58 N 92.03 W
Saint Charles, Mo., U.S. 219 38.47 N 90.28 W
Saint Charles □6 219 38.47 N 90.43 W
Saint-Charles ≃ 275a 45.40 N 73.27 W
Saint-Charles, Lac ⊜ 206 46.55 N 71.23 W
Saint-Charles-de-Drummond 206 45.54 N 72.28 W
Saint Charles Mesa 198 38.15 N 104.32 W
Saint-Charles-sur-Richelieu 206 45.41 N 73.11 W
Saint-Chef 62 45.38 N 5.22 E
Saint-Chély-d'Apcher 32 44.48 N 3.17 E
Saint-Chéron 261 48.33 N 2.07 E
Saint-Christophe-en-Bazelle 50 47.11 N 1.43 E
Saint-Christophe-Nevis
→ Saint Kitts and Nevis □1 238 17.20 N 62.45 W
Saint Christopher (Saint Kitts) I 238 17.20 N 62.45 W
Saint Christopher-Nevis
→ Saint Kitts and Nevis □1 238 17.20 N 62.45 W
Saint-Chrysostome 206 45.06 N 73.46 W
Saint-Ciers-sur-Gironde 32 45.18 N 0.37 W
Saint Clair, Mi., U.S. 214 42.48 N 82.29 W
Saint Clair, Mo., U.S. 219 38.20 N 90.58 W
Saint Clair, Pa., U.S. 208 40.43 N 76.11 W
Saint Clair, Pa., U.S. 279b 40.16 N 79.33 W
Saint Clair □6, Il., U.S. 219 38.31 N 90.00 W
Saint Clair □6, Mi., U.S. 214 42.50 N 82.42 W
Saint Clair ≃ 214 42.37 N 82.31 W
Saint Clair, Lake ⊜ 214 42.25 N 82.41 W
Saint Clair Beach 281 42.19 N 82.51 W
Saint Clair Flats 214 42.32 N 82.37 W
Saint Clair Flats ≚ 281 42.35 N 82.36 W
Saint Clair Flats Canal ≍ 214 42.20 N 82.58 W
Saint Clair Flats State Wildlife Area ◆4 281 42.36 N 82.40 W
Saint Clair Haven 214 42.34 N 82.47 W
Saint Clair Shores 214 42.29 N 82.53 W
Saint-Clair-sur-Epte 50 49.12 N 1.41 E
Saint Clairsville, Oh., U.S. 214 40.04 N 80.54 W
Saint Clairsville, Pa., U.S. 214 40.09 N 78.31 W
Saint Clair Tunnel ◆5 214 42.57 N 82.25 W
Saint-Claud 32 45.53 N 0.23 E
Saint-Claude, Mb., Can. 184 49.40 N 98.22 W
Saint-Claude, Fr. 58 46.23 N 5.52 E
Saint-Claude, Guad. 241o 16.02 N 61.42 W
Saint-Claude, Ruisseau ≃ 275a 45.25 N 73.28 W
Saint Clears 42 51.50 N 4.30 W
Saint Clements 212 43.31 N 80.39 W
Saint Clements Bay c 208 38.17 N 76.42 W
Sainte-Clothilde 206 45.59 N 72.14 W
Sainte-Clotilde-de-Châteauguay 206 45.10 N 73.41 W
Saint-Cloud, Fr. 50 48.50 N 2.11 E
Saint Cloud, Fl., U.S. 220 28.14 N 81.16 W
Saint Cloud, Mn., U.S. 190 45.33 N 94.09 W
Saint-Cloud, Parc de ♦ 261 48.50 N 2.13 E
Saint-Colomban-des-Villards 62 45.18 N 6.14 E
Sainte-Colombe 58 47.52 N 4.32 E
Saint Columb Major 42 50.26 N 5.03 W
Saint Combs 46 57.39 N 1.54 W
Saint-Constant 206 45.22 N 73.37 W
Saint-Cosme-en-Vairais 50 48.16 N 0.28 E
Sainte-Croix, P.Q., Can. 206 46.38 N 71.44 W
Sainte-Croix, Schw. 58 46.49 N 6.31 E
Saint Croix I 241n 17.45 N 64.45 W
Saint Croix ≃, N.A. 186 45.10 N 67.10 W
Saint Croix ≃, U.S. 190 44.45 N 92.49 W
Sainte-Croix-aux-Mines 58 48.16 N 7.13 E
Saint Croix Falls 190 45.24 N 92.38 W
Saint Croix Island I 158 33.48 S 25.45 E
Saint Croix Island National Monument ♦ 188 45.08 N 67.08 W
Saint Croix National Scenic Riverway ♦ 190 46.00 N 92.25 W
Saint Croix State Park ♦ 190 46.00 N 92.40 W
Sainte-Croix-Vallée-Francaise 62 44.11 N 3.44 E
Saint-Cuthbert 206 46.09 N 73.14 W
Saint-Cyprien 32 44.52 N 1.02 E
Saint-Cyrille-de-Wendover 206 45.56 N 72.26 W
Saint-Cyr-L'École 50 48.48 N 2.04 E
Saint-Cyr-l'École, Aérodrome de ≋ 261 48.49 N 2.04 E
Saint Cyr Range ∧ 180 61.10 N 131.10 W
Saint-Cyr-sous-Dourdan 261 48.34 N 2.02 E
Saint-Cyr-sur-Loire 50 47.24 N 0.40 E
Saint-Cyr-sur-Mer 62 43.11 N 5.43 E
Saint-Dalmas-de-Tende 62 44.03 N 7.35 E
Saint-Damien-de-Brandon 206 46.20 N 73.29 W
Saint David, Az., U.S. 200 31.54 N 110.12 W
Saint David, Il., U.S. 190 40.29 N 90.02 W
Saint David's, Nf., Can. 186 48.12 N 58.52 W
Saint Davids, On., Can. 284a 43.10 N 79.06 W
Saint David's, Wales, U.K. 42 51.54 N 5.16 W
Saint Davids, Pa., U.S. 285 40.02 N 75.22 W
Saint David's Cathedral ᵾ1 42 51.54 N 5.16 W
Saint David's Head > 42 51.55 N 5.19 W
Saint David's Island I 240a 32.22 N 64.39 W
Saint Day 42 50.14 N 5.11 W
Saint-Denis, Fr. 50 48.56 N 2.22 E
Saint-Denis, Réu. 157c 20.52 S 55.28 E
Saint-Denis, Basilique ᵾ1 261 48.56 N 2.22 E
Saint-Denis-de-l'Hôtel 50 47.52 N 2.07 E
Saint-Denis-en-Bugey 58 45.57 N 5.20 E
Saint-Denis-Rivière-Richelieu 206 45.47 N 73.09 W
Saint Dennis 42 50.23 N 4.53 W
Saint-Didier-en-Velay 62 45.18 N 4.17 E
Saint-Didier-les-Bains 62 44.00 N 5.07 E
Saint-Dié 58 48.17 N 6.57 E
Saint-Disdier 62 44.44 N 5.54 E
Saint-Dizier 58 48.38 N 4.57 E
Saint Dogmaels 42 52.05 N 4.40 W
Saint-Donat-de-Montcalm 206 46.19 N 74.13 W
Saint-Donat-sur-l'Herbasse 62 45.07 N 5.00 E
Sainte-Dorothée ◆8 275a 45.32 N 73.49 W
Saint-Dyé-sur-Loire 50 47.39 N 1.29 E
Saint-Édouard-de-Maskinongé 206 46.20 N 73.09 W
Saint Edward 198 41.34 N 97.52 W
Saint-Égrève 62 45.14 N 5.41 E
Saint Eleanor's 186 46.25 N 63.49 W
Saint Elias, Cape > 180 59.52 N 144.30 W
Saint Elias, Mount ∧ 180 60.18 N 140.55 W
Saint Elias Mountains ∧ 180 60.30 N 139.30 W
Saint-Élie 250 4.50 N 53.17 W
Saint Elmo 219 39.01 N 88.50 W
Saint-Éloi 186 48.02 N 69.14 W
Saint-Émile-de-Montcalm 206 46.06 N 74.00 W
Saint-Émile-de-Québec 206 46.52 N 71.20 W
Saint-Émile-de-Suffolk 206 45.56 N 74.55 W
Sainte-Enimie 32 44.22 N 3.26 E
Saint-Épain 50 47.08 N 0.32 E
Saint-Esprit ≃ 206 45.52 N 73.27 W
Saint-Étienne 62 45.26 N 4.24 E
Saint-Étienne-de-Lugdarès 62 44.39 N 3.57 E
Saint-Étienne-de-Saint-Geoirs 62 45.20 N 5.21 E
Saint-Étienne-des-Grès 206 46.26 N 72.46 W
Saint-Étienne-de-Tinée 62 44.15 N 6.55 E
Saint-Étienne-du-Rouvray 50 49.23 N 1.06 E
Saint-Étienne-en-Dévoluy 62 44.42 N 5.56 E
Saint-Étienne-le-Laus 62 44.30 N 6.10 E
Saint-Étienne-les-Orgues 62 44.03 N 5.47 E
Saint-Étienne-lès-Remiremont 58 48.02 N 6.37 E
Saint-Eugène 206 45.30 N 74.28 W
Saint-Eustache 206 45.34 N 73.54 W
Saint-Evroult-Notre-Dame-du-Bois 50 48.48 N 0.28 E
Saint-Fabien 186 48.18 N 68.52 W
Saint Faith's 158 30.30 S 30.12 E
Saint-Fargeau 50 47.38 N 3.04 E
Saint-Fargeau-Ponthierry 261 48.33 N 2.32 E
Saint-Félicien, P.Q., Can. 176 48.39 N 72.26 W
Saint-Félicien, Fr. 62 45.05 N 4.38 E
Sainte-Félicité 186 48.54 N 67.20 W
Saint-Félix 62 45.48 N 5.58 E
Saint-Félix-de-Kingsey 206 45.48 N 72.12 W
Saint-Félix-de-Valois 206 46.10 N 73.26 W
Saint-Ferdinand (Bernierville) 206 46.06 N 71.34 W
Saintfield 48 54.28 N 5.50 W
Saint Fillans 46 56.23 N 4.07 W
Saint-Firmin 62 44.47 N 6.02 E
Saint-Firmin-sur-Loire 50 47.37 N 2.44 E
Saint-Flavien 206 46.31 N 71.36 W
Saint-Florent 36 42.41 N 9.18 E
Saint-Florentin 50 48.00 N 3.44 E
Saint-Florent-sur-Cher 32 46.59 N 2.15 E
Saint-Floris, Parc National ♦ 146 9.40 N 21.35 E
Saint-Flour 32 45.02 N 3.05 E

≃	River	Fluß	Río	Rivière	Rio			
≍	Canal	Kanal	Canal	Canal	Canal			
⌊	Waterfall, Rapids	Wasserfall, Stromschnellen	Cascada, Rápidos	Chute d'eau, Rapides	Cascata, Rápidos			
⋈	Strait	Meeresstraße	Estrecho	Détroit	Estreito			
c	Bay, Gulf	Bucht, Golf	Bahía, Golfo	Baie, Golfe	Baía, Golfo			
⊜	Lake, Lakes	See, Seen	Lago, Lagos	Lac, Lacs	Lago, Lagos			
≚	Swamp	Sumpf	Pantano	Marais	Pântano			
≋	Ice Features, Glacier	Eis- und Gletscherformen	Accidentes Glaciales	Formes glaciaires	Acidentes glaciares			
◆	Other Hydrographic Features	Andere Hydrographische Objekte	Otros Elementos Hidrográficos	Autres données hydrographiques	Outros acidentes hidrográficos			

✦	Submarine Features	Untermeerische Objekte	Accidentes Submarinos	Formes de relief sous-marin	Acidentes submarinos
□	Political Unit	Politische Einheit	Unidad Política	Entité politique	Unidade política
ᵾ	Cultural Institution	Kulturelle Institution	Institución Cultural	Institution culturelle	Instituição cultural
⊥	Historical Site	Historische Stätte	Sitio Histórico	Site historique	Sítio histórico
♦	Recreational Site	Erholungs- und Ferienort	Sitio de Recreo	Centre de loisirs	Área de Lazer
≋	Airport	Flughafen	Aeropuerto	Aéroport	Aeroporto
■	Military Installation	Militäranlage	Instalación Militar	Installation militaire	Instalação militar
◆	Miscellaneous	Verschiedenes	Misceláneo	Divers	Diversos

Name	Page	Lat.°′	Long.°′
Saint-Fons	**62**	45.42 N	4.52 E
Saint-Fortunat	**206**	45.58 N	71.36 W
Sainte-Foy	**206**	46.47 N	71.17 W
Sainte-Foy-la-Grande	**32**	44.50 N	0.13 E
Sainte-Foy-l'Argentière	**62**	45.42 N	4.28 E
Sainte-Foy-lès-Lyon	**62**	45.44 N	4.48 E
Sainte-Foy-Tarentaise	**62**	45.35 N	6.53 E
Saint Francis, Ks., U.S.	**198**	39.46 N	101.47 W
Saint Francis, S.D., U.S.	**198**	43.08 N	100.54 W
Saint Francis, Wi., U.S.	**216**	42.58 N	87.52 W
Saint Francis ≃, N.A.	**186**	47.10 N	68.57 W
Saint Francis ≃, U.S.	**194**	34.38 N	90.35 W
Saint Francis, Cape ➤, Nf., Can.	**186**	47.50 N	52.47 W
Saint Francis, Cape ➤, S. Afr.	**158**	34.14 S	24.49 E
Saint Francis, Lake ⊜	**206**	45.08 N	74.25 W
Saint Francis Bay c	**158**	34.35 S	25.10 E
Saint Francisville	**194**	30.46 N	91.22 W
Saint-François	**241o**	16.15 N	61.17 W
Saint-François ≃	**206**	46.07 N	72.55 W
Saint-François, Lac ⊜	**206**	45.55 N	71.10 W
Saint-François de Boundji	**152**	1.03 S	15.22 E
Saint-François-de-Laval ◆[8]	**275a**	45.40 N	73.34 W
Saint-François-du-Lac	**206**	46.04 N	72.50 W
Saint Francois Mountains ⋏[2]	**194**	37.30 N	90.35 W
Saint-François-sur-Bugeon	**62**	45.24 N	6.21 E
Saint-Front	**62**	44.59 N	4.08 E
Saint-Gabriel	**206**	46.17 N	73.23 W
Saint-Gabriel-de-Gaspé	**186**	48.31 N	64.32 W
Saint-Gabriel-de-Rimouski	**186**	48.25 N	68.10 W
Saint-Gall → Sankt Gallen	**58**	47.25 N	9.23 E
Saint-Galmier	**62**	45.35 N	4.19 E
Sainte-Gauburge-Sainte-Colombe	**50**	48.42 N	0.26 E
Saint-Gaudens	**32**	43.07 N	0.44 E
Saint-Gaudens National Historic Site ⊥	**188**	43.29 N	72.19 W
Saint-Gaultier	**32**	46.38 N	1.25 E
Saint-Gély-du-Fesc	**62**	43.42 N	3.48 E
Saint-Genest-Lerpt	**62**	45.27 N	4.20 E
Saint-Genest-Malifaux	**62**	45.20 N	4.25 E
Sainte-Geneviève, P.Q., Can.	**275a**	45.29 N	73.52 W
Sainte Genevieve, Mo., U.S.	**194**	37.59 N	90.03 W
Sainte-Geneviève-de-Batiscan	**206**	46.32 N	72.20 W
Sainte-Geneviève-des-Bois	**50**	48.38 N	2.20 E
Saint-Gengoux-le-National	**58**	46.37 N	4.39 E
Saint-Genis-de-Saintonge	**32**	45.29 N	0.34 W
Saint-Genis-Laval	**62**	45.41 N	4.48 E
Saint-Genis-Pouilly	**58**	46.15 N	6.01 E
Saint-Genix-sur-Guiers	**62**	45.36 N	5.38 E
Saint-Geoire-en-Valdaine	**62**	45.27 N	5.38 E
Saint George, Austl.	**166**	28.02 S	148.35 E
Saint George, Ber.	**240a**	32.22 N	64.40 W
Saint George, N.B., Can.	**186**	45.08 N	66.49 W
Saint George, On., Can.	**212**	43.15 N	80.15 W
Saint George, Pa., U.S.	**214**	41.15 N	79.47 W
Saint George, S.C., U.S.	**192**	33.11 N	80.34 W
Saint George, Ut,. U.S.	**200**	37.06 N	113.34 W
Saint George ◆[8]	**276**	40.39 N	74.05 W
Saint George, Cape ➤, Nf., Can.	**186**	48.27 N	59.15 W
Saint George, Cape ➤, Pap. N. Gui.	**164**	4.52 S	152.52 E
Saint George, Cape ➤, Fl., U.S.	**192**	29.35 N	85.04 W
Saint George, Point ➤	**204**	41.47 N	124.15 W
Saint George Island, Ak., U.S.	**180**	56.36 N	169.32 W
Saint George Island, Md., U.S.	**208**	38.07 N	76.29 W
Saint George Island I, Ak., U.S.	**180**	56.35 N	169.35 W
Saint George Island I, Fl., U.S.	**192**	29.39 N	84.55 W
Saint George's, Nf., Can.	**186**	48.26 N	58.29 W
Saint-Georges, P.Q., Can.	**188**	46.07 N	70.40 W
Saint-Georges, P.Q., Can.	**206**	46.37 N	72.40 W
Saint-Georges, Fr.	**58**	48.40 N	6.56 E
Saint George's, Gren.	**241k**	12.03 N	61.45 W
Saint-Georges, Guy. fr.	**250**	3.54 N	51.48 W
Saint Georges, De., U.S.	**208**	39.33 N	75.39 W
Saint Georges Basin c	**170**	35.07 S	150.36 E
Saint George's Bay c, Nf., Can.	**186**	48.20 N	59.00 W
Saint Georges Bay c, N.S., Can.	**186**	45.50 N	61.45 W
Saint George's Channel ʮ, Europe	**28**	52.00 N	6.00 W
Saint George's Channel ʮ, Pap. N. Gui.	**164**	4.30 S	152.30 E
Saint-Georges-de-Reneins	**58**	46.04 N	4.43 E
Saint-Georges-de-Windsor	**206**	45.42 N	71.50 W
Saint-Georges-en-Couzan	**62**	45.42 N	3.56 E
Saint Georges Head ➤	**170**	35.12 S	150.42 E
Saint George's Island I	**240a**	32.22 N	64.40 W
Saint George Sound ʮ	**192**	29.47 N	84.42 W
Saint-Gérard, Bel.	**56**	50.21 N	4.45 E
Saint-Gérard, P.Q., Can.	**206**	45.46 N	71.25 W
Saint-Germain	**32**	48.54 N	2.05 E
Saint-Germain ≃	**206**	45.55 N	72.30 W
Saint-Germain, Forêt de ♠	**261**	48.55 N	2.05 E
Saint-Germain-de-Calberte	**62**	44.13 N	3.48 E
Saint-Germain-de-Grantham	**206**	45.50 N	72.34 W
Saint-Germain-de-Joux	**58**	46.11 N	5.44 E
Saint-Germain-des-Champs	**50**	47.25 N	3.55 E
Saint-Germain-du-Bois	**58**	46.45 N	5.15 E
Saint-Germain-du-Plain	**58**	46.42 N	4.58 E
Saint-Germain-en-Laye	**50**	48.54 N	2.05 E
Saint-Germain-en-Laye, Château de ⊥	**261**	48.54 N	2.06 E
Saint-Germain-Laval	**62**	45.50 N	4.01 E
Saint-Germain-Laxis	**261**	48.35 N	2.43 E
Saint-Germain-Lembron	**32**	45.28 N	3.14 E
Saint-Germain-lès-Arlay	**58**	46.46 N	5.34 E
Saint-Germain-lès-Corbeil	**261**	48.37 N	2.29 E
Saint-Germain-l'Herm	**32**	45.28 N	3.33 E
Saint-Germain-sur-Morin	**261**	48.53 N	2.51 E
Saint Germans	**42**	50.24 N	4.18 W
Saint-Germer-de-Fly	**50**	49.27 N	1.47 E
Saint-Gervais-d'Auvergne	**32**	46.02 N	2.49 E
Saint-Gervais-les-Bains	**62**	45.54 N	6.43 E
Saint-Gervasy	**62**	43.53 N	4.29 E
Saint-Géry	**32**	44.29 N	1.35 E
Saint-Gilles, Bel.	**50**	50.49 N	4.20 E
Saint-Gilles, P.Q., Can.	**206**	46.31 N	71.22 W
Saint-Gilles, Fr.	**62**	43.41 N	4.26 E
Saint-Gilles-Croix-de-Vie	**32**	46.42 N	1.57 W
Saint-Gingolph	**58**	46.24 N	6.52 E
Saint-Girons	**32**	42.59 N	1.09 E
Saint-Gobain	**50**	49.36 N	3.23 E
Saint Gotthard Pass → San Gottardo, Passo del)(	**58**	46.33 N	8.34 E
Saint Govan's Head ➤	**42**	51.36 N	4.55 W
Saint-Gratien	**261**	48.58 N	2.17 E
Saint-Grégoire (Larochelle)	**206**	46.16 N	72.30 W
Saint Gregory, Mount ʌ	**186**	49.19 N	58.13 W
Saint-Guénolé	**32**	47.49 N	4.20 W
Saint-Guillaume-d'Upton	**206**	45.53 N	72.46 W
Saint-Héand	**62**	45.31 N	4.22 E
Saint Helena	**226**	38.30 N	122.28 W
Saint Helena □[2]	**10**	15.57 S	5.42 W
Saint Helena, Mount ʌ	**226**	38.40 N	122.38 W
Saint Helena Sound ʮ	**192**	32.27 N	80.25 W
Sainte-Hélène, Île I	**275a**	45.31 N	73.32 W
Sainte-Hélène-de-Bagot	**206**	45.44 N	72.44 W
Saint Helens, Austl.	**166**	41.20 S	148.15 E
Saint Helens, Eng., U.K.	**42**	50.42 N	1.06 W
Saint Helens, Eng., U.K.	**44**	53.28 N	2.44 W
Saint Helens, Or., U.S.	**224**	45.51 N	122.48 W
Saint Helens □[8]	**262**	53.28 N	2.45 W
Saint Helens, Mount ʌ[1]	**224**	46.12 N	122.11 W
Saint Helens Canal ≊	**262**	53.27 N	2.42 W
Saint Helier	**43b**	49.11 N	2.06 W
Saint Henry	**216**	40.25 N	84.38 W
Sainte-Hermine	**32**	46.33 N	1.04 W
Saint-Hilaire-du-Harcouët	**32**	48.35 N	1.06 W
Saint-Hilarion	**261**	48.37 N	1.44 E
Saint-Hippolyte, Fr.	**58**	47.19 N	6.49 E
Saint-Hippolyte, Fr.	**62**	43.38 N	4.45 E
Saint-Hippolyte-de-Kilkenny	**206**	45.56 N	74.01 W
Saint-Hippolyte-du-Fort	**62**	43.58 N	3.51 E
Saint-Honorat, Mont ʌ	**62**	44.05 N	6.46 E
Saint-Hubert, Bel.	**56**	50.01 N	5.23 E
Saint-Hubert, P.Q., Can.	**206**	45.30 N	73.25 W
Saint-Hubert, Étang de ⊜	**261**	48.43 N	1.51 E
Saint-Hubert-le-Roi	**261**	48.43 N	1.52 E
Saint-Hugues	**206**	45.48 N	72.52 W
Saint-Hyacinthe	**206**	45.37 N	72.57 W
Saint-Hyacinthe □[6]	**206**	45.40 N	73.05 W
Saint-Ignace, N.B., Can.	**186**	46.42 N	65.05 W
Saint Ignace, Mi., U.S.	**190**	45.52 N	84.43 W
Saint Ignace Island I	**190**	48.48 N	87.55 W
Saint Ignatius, Guy.	**246**	3.20 N	59.47 W
Saint Ignatius, Mt., U.S.	**202**	47.19 N	114.05 W
Saint-Imier	**58**	47.09 N	7.00 E
Saint-Imier, Vallon de V	**58**	47.10 N	7.00 E
Saint-Isidore	**186**	47.33 N	65.03 W
Saint-Isidore-d'Auckland	**206**	45.16 N	71.31 W
Saint-Isidore-de-Laprairie	**275a**	45.18 N	73.41 W
Saint Ives, Austl.	**274a**	33.44 S	151.10 E
Saint Ives, Eng., U.K.	**32**	50.12 N	5.29 W
Saint Ives, Eng., U.K.	**42**	52.20 N	0.05 W
Saint Ives Bay c	**42**	50.14 N	5.28 W
Saint Jacob	**219**	38.43 N	89.46 W
Saint Jacobs	**212**	43.32 N	80.33 W
Saint-Jacques	**206**	45.57 N	73.34 W
Saint-Jacques ≃	**275a**	45.26 N	73.29 W
Saint James, Il., U.S.	**219**	38.57 N	88.51 W
Saint James, Mi., U.S.	**190**	45.45 N	85.30 W
Saint James, Mn., U.S.	**198**	43.58 N	94.37 W
Saint James, Mo., U.S.	**194**	37.59 N	91.36 W
Saint James, N.Y., U.S.	**210**	40.52 N	73.09 W
Saint James, Cape ➤	**182**	51.56 N	131.01 W
Saint James City	**220**	26.29 N	82.04 W
Saint James Islands II	**240m**	18.19 N	64.50 W
Saint James Palace ʊ	**260**	51.30 N	0.08 W
Saint-Janvier	**275a**	45.43 N	73.56 W
Saint-Jean □[6]	**206**	45.15 N	73.20 W
Saint-Jean ≃, P.Q., Can.	**186**	48.46 N	64.26 W
Saint-Jean ≃, P.Q., Can.	**186**	50.17 N	64.20 W
Saint-Jean, Île I	**275a**	45.41 N	73.39 W
Saint-Jean, Lac ⊜	**176**	48.35 N	72.05 W
Saint-Jean, Rapides de ᒪ	**275a**	45.19 N	73.15 W
Saint-Jean Airport ⊠	**275a**	45.18 N	73.17 W
Saint-Jean-aux-Bois	**50**	49.21 N	2.55 E
Saint-Jean-Baptiste	**184**	49.16 N	97.21 W
Saint-Jean-Baptiste-de-Rouville	**206**	45.31 N	73.07 W
Saint-Jean-Cap-Ferrat	**62**	43.41 N	7.20 E
Saint-Jean-d'Angély	**32**	45.57 N	0.31 W
Saint-Jean-d'Assé	**50**	48.09 N	0.07 E
Saint-Jean-de-Bournay	**62**	45.29 N	5.08 E
Saint-Jean-de-Braye	**50**	47.54 N	1.58 E
Saint-Jean-de-la-Ruelle	**50**	47.55 N	1.52 E
Saint-Jean-de-Losne	**58**	47.06 N	5.15 E
Saint-Jean-de-Luz	**32**	43.23 N	1.40 W
Saint-Jean-de-Maurienne	**62**	45.17 N	6.21 E
Saint-Jean-de-Monts	**32**	46.48 N	2.03 W
Saint-Jean-des-Piles	**206**	46.41 N	72.45 W
Saint-Jean-du-Gard	**62**	44.06 N	3.53 E
Saint-Jean-en-Royans	**62**	45.01 N	5.18 E
Saint-Jean-Pied-de-Port	**32**	43.10 N	1.14 W
Saint-Jean-Port-Joli	**186**	47.13 N	70.16 W
Saint-Jean-Soleymieux	**62**	45.30 N	4.02 E
Saint-Jean-sur-Richelieu	**206**	45.19 N	73.16 W
Saint-Jeoire	**58**	46.09 N	6.28 E
Saint-Jérôme	**206**	45.47 N	74.00 W
Saint Jo	**196**	33.41 N	97.31 W
Saint Joachim	**214**	42.16 N	82.38 W
Saint Joe	**216**	41.18 N	84.54 W
Saint Joe ≃	**202**	47.21 N	116.42 W
Saint John, N.B., Can.	**186**	45.16 N	66.03 W
Saint John, Jersey	**43b**	49.15 N	2.08 W
Saint John, In., U.S.	**216**	41.27 N	87.28 W
Saint John, Ks., U.S.	**198**	38.00 N	98.45 W
Saint John, N.D., U.S.	**198**	48.56 N	99.42 W
Saint John, Wa., U.S.	**202**	47.05 N	117.34 W
Saint John I	**240m**	18.20 N	64.45 W
Saint John ≃, Liber.	**150**	6.40 N	9.10 W
Saint John ≃, N.A.	**186**	45.15 N	66.04 W
Saint John, Cape ➤	**186**	50.00 N	55.32 W
Saint John, Lake ⊜, Nf., Can.	**186**	48.23 N	54.41 W
Saint John, Lake ⊜, On., Can.	**212**	44.41 N	79.20 W
Saint John Bay c	**186**	50.54 N	57.08 W
Saint John Island I	**186**	50.49 N	57.14 W
Saint John's, Antig.	**240c**	17.06 N	61.51 W
Saint John's, Nf., Can.	**186**	47.34 N	52.43 W
Saint John's, I. of Man	**44**	54.13 N	4.38 W
Saint Johns, Az., U.S.	**200**	34.30 N	109.21 W
Saint Johns, Mi., U.S.	**216**	43.00 N	84.33 W
Saint Johns, Mo., U.S.	**219**	38.42 N	90.20 W
Saint Johns, Oh., U.S.	**216**	40.33 N	84.05 W
Saint Johns ≃, Ca., U.S.	**226**	36.25 N	119.25 W
Saint Johns ≃, Fl., U.S.	**192**	30.24 N	81.24 W
Saint Johnsburg	**210**	43.05 N	78.53 W
Saint Johnsbury	**188**	44.25 N	72.00 W
Saint Johns Creek ≃	**219**	38.34 N	91.01 W
Saint John's Jerusalem ⊥	**260**	51.25 N	0.14 E
Saint Johns Marsh ≡	**220**	27.45 N	80.40 W
Saint John's Point ➤	**48**	54.13 N	5.40 W
Saint Johns → Saint-Jean-sur-Richelieu	**206**	45.19 N	73.16 W
Saint John's University ʊ[2]	**276**	40.43 N	73.48 W
Saint Johnsville	**210**	42.59 N	74.41 W
Saint Joseph, N.B., Can.	**186**	45.59 N	64.34 W
Saint Joseph, Dom.	**240d**	15.26 N	61.26 W
Saint-Joseph, Mart.	**240e**	14.40 N	61.03 W
Saint-Joseph, N. Cal.	**175f**	20.27 S	166.36 E
Saint-Joseph, Réu.	**157c**	21.22 S	55.36 E
Saint Joseph, Il., U.S.	**194**	40.06 N	88.02 W
Saint Joseph, La., U.S.	**194**	31.55 N	91.14 W
Saint Joseph, Mi., U.S.	**216**	42.05 N	86.29 W
Saint Joseph, Mn., U.S.	**190**	45.33 N	94.19 W
Saint Joseph, Mo., U.S.	**194**	39.46 N	94.50 W
Saint Joseph, Tn., U.S.	**194**	35.02 N	87.30 W
Saint Joseph □[6], In., U.S.	**216**	41.41 N	86.15 W
Saint Joseph □[6], Mi., U.S.	**216**	41.55 N	85.31 W
Saint Joseph ≃, U.S.	**216**	42.07 N	86.29 W
Saint Joseph ≃, U.S.	**216**	41.05 N	85.08 W
Saint Joseph, East Branch ≃	**216**	41.39 N	84.34 W
Saint-Joseph, Île I	**275a**	45.41 N	73.42 W
Saint-Joseph, Lac ⊜	**206**	46.54 N	71.38 W
Saint Joseph, Lake ⊜	**176**	51.05 N	90.35 W
Saint Joseph, West Branch ≃	**216**	41.39 N	84.34 W
Saint Joseph Bay c	**192**	29.47 N	85.21 W
Saint Joseph Channel ʮ	**190**	46.19 N	84.04 W
Saint-Joseph-d'Alma → Alma	**186**	48.33 N	71.39 W
Saint-Joseph-de-Beauce	**186**	46.18 N	70.53 W
Saint-Joseph-de-Mékinac	**206**	46.55 N	72.42 W
Saint-Joseph-de-Sorel	**206**	46.02 N	73.07 W
Saint-Joseph-du-Lac	**275a**	45.32 N	74.00 W
Saint Joseph Island I	**190**	46.13 N	83.57 W
Saint Joseph's University ʊ[2]	**285**	40.00 N	75.14 W
Saint-Jouin-Bruneval	**50**	49.39 N	0.10 E
Saint-Jovite	**206**	46.07 N	74.36 W
Sainte-Julie	**206**	45.35 N	73.19 W
Saint-Julien	**58**	46.23 N	5.27 E
Saint-Julien-Chapteuil	**62**	45.02 N	4.04 E
Saint-Julien-du-Sault	**50**	48.02 N	3.18 E
Saint-Julien-du-Verdon	**62**	43.55 N	6.32 E
Saint-Julien-en-Beauchêne	**62**	44.37 N	5.42 E
Saint-Julien-en-Born	**32**	44.04 N	1.14 W
Saint-Julien-en-Genevois	**58**	46.08 N	6.05 E
Saint-Julien-en-Jarez	**62**	45.28 N	4.31 E
Saint-Julien-les-Villas	**50**	48.16 N	4.06 E
Saint-Julien-Molin-Molette	**62**	45.19 N	4.37 E
Sainte-Julienne	**206**	45.58 N	73.43 W
Saint-Junien	**32**	45.53 N	0.54 E
Saint Just, P.R.	**240m**	18.23 N	66.00 W
Saint Just, Eng., U.K.	**42**	50.07 N	5.42 W
Saint-Just-en-Chaussée	**50**	49.30 N	2.26 E
Saint-Just-en-Chevalet	**32**	45.55 N	3.50 E
Saint-Justin	**206**	46.15 N	73.05 W
Saint-Just-Malmont	**62**	45.20 N	4.19 E
Saint-Just-sur-Loire	**62**	45.29 N	4.16 E
Saint Keverne	**42**	50.03 N	5.06 W
Saint Kilda, Austl.	**168b**	34.44 S	138.32 E
Saint Kilda, Austl.	**169**	37.52 S	144.59 E
Saint Kilda, N.Z.	**172**	45.54 S	170.30 E
Saint Kilda I	**28**	57.49 N	8.36 W
Saint Kitts	**168b**	34.21 S	139.04 E
Saint Kitts and Nevis □[1], N.A.	**230**	17.20 N	62.45 W
Saint Kitts and Nevis □[1], N.A.	**238**	17.20 N	62.45 W
Saint Kitts → Saint Christopher I	**238**	17.20 N	62.45 W
Saint-Lambert, P.Q., Can.	**206**	45.30 N	73.30 W
Saint-Lambert, Fr.	**261**	48.44 N	2.01 E
Saint Landry	**194**	30.50 N	92.15 W
Saint-Laurent, Mb., Can.	**184**	50.24 N	97.56 W
Saint-Laurent, P.Q., Can.	**206**	45.30 N	73.40 W
Saint-Laurent, Fr.	**58**	48.09 N	6.27 E
Saint-Laurent-Blangy	**50**	50.18 N	2.48 E
Saint-Laurent-de-Chamousset	**62**	45.44 N	4.28 E
Saint-Laurent-du-Maroni	**250**	5.30 N	54.02 W
Saint-Laurent-du-Maroni □[8]	**250**	4.00 N	53.30 W
Saint-Laurent-du-Pont	**62**	45.23 N	5.44 E
Saint-Laurent-du-Var	**62**	43.40 N	7.11 E
Saint-Laurent-en-Caux	**50**	49.45 N	0.53 E
Saint-Laurent-en-Grandvaux	**58**	46.35 N	5.57 E
Saint-Laurent-et-Benon	**32**	45.09 N	0.49 W
Saint-Laurent-les-Bains	**62**	44.37 N	3.58 E
Saint-Laurent → Saint Lawrence ≃	**176**	49.30 N	67.00 W
Saint-Laurent-sur-Saône	**58**	46.18 N	4.50 E
Saint Lawrence, Austl.	**166**	22.21 S	149.31 E
Saint Lawrence, Nf., Can.	**186**	46.55 N	55.24 W
Saint Lawrence □[6]	**212**	44.30 N	75.27 W
Saint Lawrence ≃	**176**	49.30 N	67.00 W
Saint Lawrence, Cape ➤	**186**	47.03 N	60.37 W
Saint Lawrence, Gulf of c	**186**	48.00 N	62.00 W
Saint Lawrence, Lake ⊜	**206**	44.56 N	75.04 W
Saint Lawrence Island I	**180**	63.30 N	170.30 W
Saint Lawrence Islands National Park ♠	**212**	44.18 N	76.08 W
Saint-Lawrence Seaway ≊	**275a**	45.43 N	73.25 W
Saint-Lazare	**184**	50.26 N	101.16 W
Saint-Lazare, Gare ◆[5]	**261**	48.53 N	2.20 E
Saint-Léandre	**186**	48.44 N	67.36 W
Saint-Léger-en-Yvelines	**261**	48.43 N	1.46 E
Saint-Léger-sur-Dheune	**58**	46.51 N	4.38 E
Saint Leo	**220**	28.20 N	82.15 W
Saint Leon	**218**	39.17 N	84.57 W
Saint-Léonard, N.B., Can.	**186**	47.10 N	67.56 W
Saint-Léonard, P.Q., Can.	**206**	45.35 N	73.35 W
Saint Leonard, Md., U.S.	**208**	38.28 N	76.30 W
Saint-Léonard-d'Aston	**206**	46.06 N	72.22 W
Saint-Léonard-de-Noblat	**32**	45.50 N	1.29 E
Saint Leonards, Eng., U.K.	**42**	50.49 N	1.51 W
Saint Leonards, Eng., U.K.	**42**	50.51 N	0.34 E
Saint-Leu-d'Esserent	**50**	49.13 N	2.25 E
Saint-Leu-la-Forêt	**50**	49.01 N	2.15 E
Saint-Liboire	**206**	45.39 N	72.46 W
Saint-Lô	**32**	49.07 N	1.05 W
Saint-Louis, Sk., Can.	**184**	52.56 N	105.49 W
Saint-Louis, Fr.	**58**	47.35 N	7.34 E
Saint-Louis, Guad.	**241o**	15.57 N	61.19 W
Saint-Louis, Réu.	**157c**	21.16 S	55.25 E
Saint-Louis, Sén.	**150**	16.02 N	16.30 W
Saint Louis, Mi., U.S.	**190**	43.24 N	84.36 W
Saint Louis, Mo., U.S.	**219**	38.37 N	90.11 W
Saint Louis, Tx., U.S.	**222**	32.18 N	95.20 W
Saint-Louis □[4]	**150**	16.00 N	14.30 W
Saint Louis □[6]	**219**	38.39 N	90.25 W
Saint-Louis ≃, P.Q., Can.	**275a**	45.19 N	73.53 W
Saint Louis ≃, U.S.	**190**	46.45 N	92.06 W
Saint-Louis, Lac ⊜	**206**	45.24 N	73.48 W
Saint-Louis, Pointe ➤	**275a**	45.19 N	73.53 W
Saint Louis Crossing	**218**	39.19 N	85.51 W
Saint-Louis-de-Champlain	**206**	46.25 N	72.36 W
Saint-Louis-de-Kent	**186**	46.44 N	64.58 W
Saint Louis Park	**190**	44.56 N	93.20 W
Saint Louisville	**214**	40.10 N	82.25 W
Saint-Loup-sur-Aujon	**58**	47.53 N	5.05 E
Saint-Loup-sur-Semouse	**58**	47.53 N	6.16 E
Saint-Luc, P.Q., Can.	**206**	45.22 N	73.18 W
Saint-Luc, Schw.	**58**	46.13 N	7.36 E
Sainte-Luce	**240e**	14.28 N	60.56 W
Saint Lucia □[1], N.A.	**230**	13.53 N	60.58 W
Saint Lucia □[1], N.A.	**241f**	13.53 N	60.58 W
Saint Lucia, Cape ➤	**158**	28.25 S	32.25 E
Saint Lucia, Lake ⊜	**158**	28.05 S	32.26 E
Saint Lucia Channel ʮ	**238**	14.09 N	60.57 W
Saint Lucia Estuary	**158**	28.22 S	32.25 E
Saint Lucia Game Reserve ◆[4]	**158**	28.10 S	32.28 E
Sainte-Lucie, Fr.	**36**	41.42 N	9.22 E
Saint Lucie, Fl., U.S.	**220**	27.29 N	80.20 W
Saint Lucie □[6]	**220**	27.23 N	80.26 W
Saint Lucie Canal ≊	**220**	27.10 N	80.15 W
Saint Lucie Inlet c	**220**	27.10 N	80.10 W
Saint Lucie Lock ◆[5]	**220**	27.07 N	80.17 W
Saint-Lucien	**261**	48.39 N	1.38 E
Saint-Lupicin	**58**	46.24 N	5.47 E
Sainte-Magnance	**50**	47.27 N	4.04 E
Saint Magnus Bay c	**46a**	60.24 N	1.34 W
Saint Magnus Cathedral ʊ[1]	**46**	58.58 N	2.57 W
Saint-Malo, P.Q., Can.	**206**	45.12 N	71.30 W
Saint-Malo, Fr.	**32**	48.39 N	2.01 W
Saint-Malo, Golfe de c	**32**	48.45 N	2.00 W
Saint-Mamert-du-Gard	**62**	43.53 N	4.12 E
Saint-Mammès	**50**	48.23 N	2.49 E
Saint-Mandé	**261**	48.50 N	2.25 E
Saint-Mandrier-sur-Mer	**62**	43.04 N	5.56 E
Saint-Marc	**238**	19.07 N	72.42 W
Saint-Marc, Canal de ʮ	**238**	18.50 N	72.45 W
Saint-Marc-des-Carrières	**206**	46.41 N	72.03 W
Saint-Marcel	**58**	46.47 N	4.54 E
Saint-Marcellin	**62**	45.09 N	5.19 E
Saint-Marcelline-de-Kildare	**206**	46.07 N	73.36 W
Saint-Marc-sur-Richelieu	**275a**	45.41 N	73.12 W
Saint-Mard	**261**	49.02 N	2.42 E
Saint Margaret Bay c	**186**	51.01 N	56.58 W
Saint Margaret's at Cliffe	**42**	51.09 N	1.24 E
Saint Margarets Bay c	**186**	44.35 N	64.00 W
Saint Margaret's Hope	**46**	58.49 N	2.57 W
Sainte-Marguerite ≃	**176**	50.09 N	66.36 W
Sainte-Marguerite, Baie c	**186**	50.06 N	66.36 W
Sainte-Marguerite-sur-Mer	**50**	49.55 N	0.57 E
Sainte-Marie	**240e**	14.47 N	61.00 W
Sainte-Marie, Cap ➤	**157b**	25.36 S	45.08 E
Sainte-Marie-aux-Mines (Markirch)	**58**	48.15 N	7.11 E
Saint Maries	**202**	47.18 N	116.33 W
Saint Maries ≃	**202**	47.19 N	116.33 W
Saint-Marin → San Marino □[1]	**66**	43.56 N	12.25 E
Saint Marks, S. Afr.	**158**	32.01 S	27.22 E
Saint Marks, Fl., U.S.	**192**	30.09 N	84.12 W
Saint Marks ≃	**192**	30.08 N	84.12 W
Sainte-Marthe-de-Gaspé	**186**	49.12 N	66.10 W
Sainte-Marthe-sur-le-Lac	**275a**	45.32 N	73.56 W
Saint-Martin (Sint Maarten) I	**238**	18.04 N	63.04 W
Saint-Martin, Cap ➤	**240e**	14.52 N	61.13 W
Saint Martin, Lake ⊜	**184**	51.37 N	98.29 W
Saint-Martin-Boulogne	**50**	50.43 N	1.38 E
Saint-Martin-d'Ardèche	**62**	44.18 N	4.35 E
Saint-Martin-d'Auxigny	**50**	47.12 N	2.25 E
Saint-Martin-de-Belleville	**62**	45.23 N	6.30 E
Saint-Martin-de-Bossenay	**50**	48.26 N	3.41 E
Saint-Martin-de-Bréthencourt	**261**	48.31 N	1.56 E
Saint-Martin-de-Crau	**62**	43.38 N	4.49 E
Saint-Martin-de-Londres	**62**	43.47 N	3.44 E
Saint-Martin-de-Nigelles	**261**	48.37 N	1.37 E
Saint-Martin-d'Entraunes	**62**	44.08 N	6.46 E
Saint-Martin-des-Champs	**261**	48.53 N	1.43 E
Saint-Martin-de-Valamas	**62**	44.56 N	4.22 E
Saint-Martin-d'Hères	**62**	45.10 N	5.46 E
Saint-Martin-du-Puy	**50**	47.20 N	3.52 E
Saint-Martin-du-Tertre	**261**	49.06 N	2.21 E
Saint-Martin-du-Var	**62**	43.49 N	7.12 E
Sainte-Martine	**206**	45.15 N	73.48 W
Saint-Martin-en-Bresse	**58**	46.49 N	5.04 E
Saint-Martin-la-Garenne	**261**	49.02 N	1.41 E
Saint-Martin-la-Plaine	**62**	45.32 N	4.36 E
Saint Martins, N.B., Can.	**186**	45.21 N	65.32 W
Saint Martin's, Eng., U.K.	**42**	52.55 N	2.59 W
Saint Martin's I	**42a**	49.58 N	6.20 W
Saint Martins Keys II	**220**	28.47 N	82.44 W
Saint-Martin-Vésubie	**62**	44.04 N	7.15 E
Saint Martinville	**194**	30.07 N	91.49 W
Saint Mary	**194**	37.52 N	89.58 W
Saint Mary ≃, B.C., Can.	**182**	49.37 N	115.38 W
Saint Mary ≃, N.A.	**182**	49.37 N	112.52 W
Saint Mary, Cape ➤	**150**	13.28 N	16.40 W
Saint Mary, Mount ʌ	**164**	8.10 S	147.00 E
Saint Mary Bourne	**42**	51.16 N	1.24 W
Saint Mary Cray ◆[8]	**260**	51.23 N	0.07 E
Saint Mary Lake ⊜	**202**	48.40 N	113.30 W
Saint Marylebone ◆[8]	**260**	51.31 N	0.10 W
Saint Mary of the Lake Seminary ʊ[2]	**278**	42.17 N	88.00 W
Saint Mary Peak ʌ	**166**	31.30 S	138.33 E
Saint Mary Reservoir ⊜[1]	**182**	49.19 N	113.12 W
Saint Marys, Austl.	**166**	41.35 S	148.10 E
Saint Marys, Austl.	**170**	33.47 S	150.47 E
Saint Mary's, Nf., Can.	**186**	46.55 N	53.34 W
Saint Mary's, On., Can.	**212**	43.16 N	81.08 W
Saint Marys, Ak., U.S.	**180**	62.04 N	163.10 W
Saint Marys, Ga., U.S.	**192**	30.43 N	81.32 W
Saint Marys, Ks., U.S.	**198**	39.11 N	96.04 W
Saint Marys, Oh., U.S.	**216**	40.32 N	84.23 W
Saint Marys, Pa., U.S.	**214**	41.25 N	78.33 W
Saint Marys, W.V., U.S.	**188**	39.23 N	81.12 W
Saint Marys □[6]	**208**	38.17 N	76.38 W
Saint Mary's I	**42a**	49.55 N	6.18 W
Saint Marys ≃, N.S., Can.	**186**	45.02 N	61.54 W
Saint Marys ≃, N.A.	**190**	45.58 N	83.54 W
Saint Marys ≃, U.S.	**192**	30.43 N	81.27 W
Saint Marys ≃, U.S.	**216**	41.05 N	85.08 W
Saint Marys ≃, Md., U.S.	**208**	38.06 N	76.26 W
Saint Mary's, Cape ➤, Nf., Can.	**186**	46.49 N	54.12 W
Saint Marys, Cape ➤, N.S., Can.	**186**	44.05 N	66.13 W
Saint Marys, North Prong ≃	**192**	30.22 N	82.06 W
Saint Marys, South Prong ≃	**192**	30.22 N	82.06 W
Saint Mary's Bay	**42**	51.00 N	0.58 E
Saint Mary's Bay c, Nf., Can.	**186**	46.50 N	53.47 W
Saint Marys Bay c, N.S., Can.	**186**	44.25 N	66.10 W
Saint Marys City	**208**	38.11 N	76.26 W
Saint Mary's Hoo	**260**	51.28 N	0.36 E
Saint Marys Lake ⊜	**278**	42.17 N	87.59 W
Saint Mary's Marshes ≡	**260**	51.28 N	0.35 E
Saint-Mathieu	**32**	45.42 N	0.46 E
Saint-Mathieu, Pointe de ➤	**32**	48.20 N	4.46 W
Saint-Mathieu-de-Laprairie	**275a**	45.19 N	73.31 W
Saint Matthew Island I	**180**	60.30 N	172.45 W
Saint Matthews, Ky., U.S.	**218**	38.15 N	85.39 W
Saint Matthews, S.C., U.S.	**192**	33.39 N	80.46 W
Saint Matthias Group II	**164**	1.30 S	149.40 E
Saint-Maur-des-Fossés	**50**	48.48 N	2.30 E
Sainte-Maure-de-Touraine	**32**	47.07 N	0.37 E
Saint-Maurice, Fr.	**261**	48.49 N	2.25 E
Saint-Maurice, Schw.	**58**	46.13 N	7.00 E
Saint-Maurice □[6]	**206**	46.35 N	73.00 W
Saint-Maurice ≃	**176**	46.21 N	72.31 W
Saint-Maurice, Parc de ♠	**206**	46.52 N	73.10 W
Saint-Maurice-en-Montagne	**58**	46.34 N	5.50 E
Saint-Maurice-Montcouronne	**261**	48.35 N	2.07 E
Saint Mawes	**42**	50.09 N	5.01 W
Saint Mawgan	**42**	50.28 N	4.58 W
Saint-Max	**58**	48.42 N	6.13 E
Sainte-Maxime	**62**	43.18 N	6.38 E
Saint-Maximin-la-Sainte-Baume	**62**	43.27 N	5.52 E
Saint-Méen-le-Grand	**32**	48.11 N	2.12 W
Saint Meinrad	**194**	38.10 N	86.48 W
Sainte-Menehould	**56**	49.05 N	4.54 E
Saint-Menges	**56**	49.44 N	4.56 E
Sainte-Mère-Église	**32**	49.25 N	1.19 W
Saint Merryn	**42**	50.31 N	4.58 W
Saint-Méry	**261**	48.35 N	2.50 E
Sainte-Mesme	**261**	48.32 N	1.58 E
Saint-Mesmes	**261**	48.59 N	2.42 E
Saint Michael, Ak., U.S.	**180**	63.29 N	162.02 W
Saint Michael, Pa., U.S.	**214**	40.20 N	78.46 W
Saint Michaels	**208**	38.47 N	76.13 W
Saint-Michel, Fr.	**50**	49.55 N	4.08 E
Saint-Michel, Fr.	**62**	45.13 N	6.28 E
Saint-Michel ◆[8]	**275a**	45.35 N	73.35 W
Saint-Michel-de-Napierville	**206**	45.14 N	73.34 W
Saint-Michel-des-Saints	**206**	46.41 N	73.55 W
Saint-Michel-sur-Meurthe	**58**	48.19 N	6.54 E
Saint-Michel-sur-Orge	**261**	48.38 N	2.18 E
Saint-Mihiel	**56**	48.54 N	5.33 E
Saint Monance	**46**	56.12 N	2.46 W
Sainte-Monique-des-Deux-Montagnes	**275a**	45.40 N	74.00 W
Sainte-Montaine	**50**	47.29 N	2.19 E
Saint-Moritz → Sankt Moritz	**58**	46.30 N	9.50 E
Saint-Narcisse	**206**	46.34 N	72.28 W
Saint-Nazaire	**32**	47.17 N	2.12 W
Saint-Nazaire-en-Royans	**62**	45.04 N	5.15 E
Saint-Nazaire-le-Désert	**62**	44.34 N	5.17 E
Saint Nazianz	**190**	44.00 N	87.55 W
Saint Neots	**42**	52.14 N	0.17 W
Saint-Nicéphore	**206**	45.50 N	72.25 W
Saint-Nicolas, Bel.	**56**	50.38 N	5.32 E
Saint-Nicolas, P.Q., Can.	**206**	46.42 N	71.24 W
Saint-Nicolas-aux-Bois	**50**	49.36 N	3.25 E
Saint-Nicolas-d'Aliermont	**50**	49.53 N	1.13 E
Saint-Nicolas → Sint-Niklaas	**50**	51.10 N	4.08 E
Saint-Nizier-du-Moucherotte	**62**	45.10 N	5.38 E
Saint-Nom-la-Bretèche	**261**	48.51 N	2.01 E
Saint Nora Lake ⊜	**212**	45.08 N	78.49 W
Saint-Norbert-d'Arthabaska	**206**	46.07 N	71.50 W
Sainte-Odile ʊ[1]	**58**	48.26 N	7.24 E
Saint-Omer	**50**	50.45 N	2.15 E
Saintonge □[9]	**32**	45.30 N	0.30 W
Saint-Ouen, Fr.	**50**	50.02 N	2.03 E
Saint-Ouen, Fr.	**261**	48.54 N	2.20 E
Saint-Ouen-l'Aumône	**50**	49.03 N	2.06 E
Saint-Pacôme	**186**	47.24 N	69.57 W
Saint-Pamphile	**186**	46.58 N	69.47 W
Saint Pancras ◆[8]	**260**	51.32 N	0.07 W
Saint Pancras Station ◆[5]	**260**	51.32 N	0.08 W
Saint Paris	**218**	40.07 N	83.57 W
Saint-Pascal	**186**	47.32 N	69.49 W
Saint-Paterne	**50**	48.24 N	0.07 E
Saint-Pathus	**261**	49.04 N	2.48 E
Saint-Patrice, Lac ⊜	**190**	46.22 N	77.20 W
Saint Paul, Ab., Can.	**182**	53.59 N	111.17 W
Saint-Paul, Fr.	**62**	43.42 N	7.07 E
Saint-Paul, Fr.	**62**	44.31 N	6.45 E
Saint-Paul, Réu.	**157c**	21.00 S	55.16 E
Saint Paul, In., U.S.	**218**	39.25 N	85.28 W
Saint Paul, Ks., U.S.	**198**	37.31 N	95.10 W
Saint Paul, Mn., U.S.	**190**	44.57 N	93.05 W
Saint Paul, Ne., U.S.	**198**	41.13 N	98.27 W
Saint Paul, Or., U.S.	**224**	45.12 N	122.58 W
Saint Paul, Va., U.S.	**192**	36.54 N	82.18 W
Saint-Paul ≃, Can.	**176**	51.26 N	57.40 W
Saint Paul ≃, Liber.	**150**	6.23 N	10.48 W
Saint Paul, Cape ➤	**150**	5.49 N	0.57 E
Saint-Paul, Île I	**6**	38.43 S	77.29 E
Saint-Paul, Lac ⊜	**206**	46.18 N	72.29 W
Saint Paul Bay c	**116**	10.14 N	118.54 E
Saint-Paul-de-Chester (Chesterville)	**206**	45.57 N	71.49 W
Saint-Paul-en-Jarez	**62**	45.29 N	4.35 E
Saint-Paul-et-Valmalle	**62**	43.38 N	3.40 E
Saint-Paulien	**62**	45.08 N	3.49 E
Saint-Paulin	**206**	46.25 N	73.01 W
Saint Paul Island	**180**	57.07 N	170.17 W
Saint Paul Island I, N.S., Can.	**186**	47.15 N	60.10 W
Saint Paul Island I, Ak., U.S.	**180**	57.10 N	170.15 W
Saint Pauls	**192**	34.48 N	78.58 W
Saint Paul's Cathedral ʊ[1]	**260**	51.31 N	0.06 W
Saint Paul's Cray ◆[8]	**260**	51.24 N	0.07 E
Saint Pauls Inlet c	**186**	49.50 N	57.45 W
Saint Paul's Point ➤	**174e**	25.04 S	130.05 W
Saint-Paul-Trois-Châteaux	**62**	44.21 N	4.46 E
Saint-Péravy-la-Colombe	**50**	48.00 N	1.42 E
Saint-Péray	**62**	44.57 N	4.50 E
Saint-Père	**50**	47.28 N	3.46 E
Saint Peter, Il., U.S.	**219**	38.52 N	88.51 W
Saint Peter, Mn., U.S.	**190**	44.19 N	93.57 W
Saint Peter, Lake ⊜	**212**	45.18 N	78.02 W
Saint Peter Island I	**162**	32.17 S	133.35 E
Saint Peter Port	**43b**	49.27 N	2.32 W
Saint Peters, N.S., Can.	**186**	45.40 N	60.52 W
Saint Peters, Mo., U.S.	**219**	38.48 N	90.37 W
Saint Peters, Pa., U.S.	**285**	40.11 N	75.44 W
Saint Peters Bay	**186**	46.25 N	62.35 W
Saint Petersburg, Fl., U.S.	**220**	27.46 N	82.40 W
Saint Petersburg, Pa., U.S.	**214**	41.10 N	79.37 W
Saint Petersburg Beach	**220**	27.43 N	82.44 W
Saint Petersburg → Sankt-Peterburg	**76**	59.55 N	30.15 E
Saint Peter's College ʊ[2]	**276**	40.44 N	74.05 W
Saint-Philippe-d'Argenteuil	**206**	45.37 N	74.25 W
Saint-Philippe-de-Laprairie	**275a**	45.21 N	73.28 W
Saint-Pie	**206**	45.30 N	72.54 W
Saint-Pierre, P.Q., Can.	**275a**	45.27 N	73.39 W
Saint-Pierre, Fr.	**62**	45.40 N	3.45 E
Saint-Pierre, It.	**62**	45.42 N	7.14 E
Saint-Pierre, Mart.	**240e**	14.45 N	61.11 W
Saint-Pierre, Réu.	**157c**	21.19 S	55.29 E
Saint-Pierre, St. P./M.	**186**	46.47 N	56.11 W
Saint-Pierre I	**186**	46.47 N	56.11 W
Saint-Pierre ≃	**275a**	45.23 N	73.34 W
Saint-Pierre, Lac ⊜, P.Q., Can.	**186**	50.08 N	68.26 W
Saint-Pierre, Lac ⊜, P.Q., Can.	**206**	46.12 N	72.52 W
Saint Pierre and Miquelon (Saint-Pierre-et-Miquelon) □[2], N.A.	**176**	46.55 N	56.20 W
Saint Pierre and Miquelon (Saint-Pierre-et-Miquelon) □[2], N.A.	**186**	46.55 N	56.20 W
Saint-Pierre-d'Albigny	**62**	45.34 N	6.09 E
Saint-Pierre-de-Bœuf	**62**	45.22 N	4.45 E
Saint-Pierre-de-Broughton	**206**	46.15 N	71.12 W
Saint-Pierre-de-Chartreuse	**62**	45.20 N	5.49 E
Saint-Pierre-des-Corps	**50**	47.23 N	0.44 E
Saint-Pierre-de-Vacquière	**62**	43.52 N	4.13 E
Saint-Pierre-du-Vauvray	**50**	49.14 N	1.13 E
Saint-Pierre-Église	**32**	49.40 N	1.24 W
Saint-Pierre-en-Port	**50**	49.48 N	0.29 E
Saint-Pierre-et-Miquelon → Saint Pierre and Miquelon □[2]	**186**	46.55 N	56.20 W
Saint Pierre Island I	**138**	9.19 S	50.43 E
Saint Pierre-Jolys	**184**	49.26 N	96.59 W
Saint Pierre-le-Moûtier	**32**	46.48 N	3.07 E
Saint-Pierre-lès-Elbeuf	**50**	49.16 N	1.03 E
Saint-Pierre-sur-Dives	**28**	49.01 N	0.02 W
Saint-Pierreville	**62**	44.49 N	4.29 E
Saint-Point, Lac de ⊜	**58**	46.49 N	6.19 E
Saint-Pol-de-Léon	**32**	48.41 N	3.59 W
Saint-Pol-sur-Mer	**50**	51.02 N	2.21 E

ENGLISH: Name · Page · Lat.°′ · Long.°′ — DEUTSCH: Name · Seite · Breite°′ · Länge°′ E = Ost

Symbols in the index entries represent the broad categories identified in the key at the right. Symbols with superior numbers (⋏[1]) identify subcategories (see complete key on page *I · 1).*

Symbole im Register stellen die rechts im Schlüssel erklärten Kategorien dar. Symbole mit hochgestellten Ziffern (⋏[1]) bezeichnen Unterabteilungen einer Kategorie (vgl. vollständiger Schlüssel auf Seite *I · 1).*

Los símbolos incluídos en el texto del índice representan las grandes categorias identificadas con la clave a la derecha. Los símbolos con numeros en su parte superior (⋏[1]) identifican las subcategorías (véase la clave completa en la página *I · 1).*

Les symboles de l'index représentent les catégories indiquées dans la légende à droite. Les symboles suivis d'un indice (⋏[1]) représentent des sous-catégories (voir légende complète à la page *I · 1).*

Os símbolos incluídos no texto do índice representam as grandes categorias identificadas com a chave à direita. Os símbolos com números em sua parte superior (⋏[1]) identificam as subcategorias (veja-se a chave completa à página *I · 1).*

ʌ Mountain	Berg	Montaña	Montagne	Montanha
⋏ Mountains	Gebirge	Montañas	Montagnes	Montanhas
)(Pass	Paß	Paso	Col	Passo
V Valley, Canyon	Tal, Cañon	Valle, Cañón	Vallée, Canyon	Vale, Canhão
≚ Plain	Ebene	Llano	Plaine	Planície
➤ Cape	Kap	Cabo	Cap	Cabo
I Island	Insel	Isla	Île	Ilha
II Islands	Inseln	Islas	Îles	Ilhas
⩡ Other Topographic Features	Andere Topographische Objekte	Otros Elementos Topográficos	Autres données topographiques	Outros acidentes topográficos

ESPAÑOL

Nombre	Página	Lat.°′	Long.°′ W = Oeste
Saint-Pol-sur-Ternoise	50	50.23 N	2.20 E
Saint-Polycarpe	206	45.18 N	74.18 W
Saint-Pons	32	43.29 N	2.46 E
Saint-Pourçain-sur-Sioule	32	46.19 N	3.17 E
Saint-Prex	58	46.29 N	6.28 E
Saint-Priest	62	45.42 N	4.57 E
Saint-Priest-en-Jarez	62	45.28 N	4.22 E
Saint-Prix	261	49.01 N	2.16 E
Saint-Prosper-de-Dorchester	188	46.13 N	70.29 W
Saint-Quentin, N.B., Can.	186	47.30 N	67.23 W
Saint-Quentin, Fr.	50	49.51 N	3.17 E
Saint-Quentin, Canal de ≊	50	49.36 N	3.11 E
Saint-Quentin, Étang de ⊜	261	48.47 N	2.01 E
Saint-Rambert-d'Albon	62	45.17 N	4.49 E
Saint-Rambert-en-Bugey	58	45.57 N	5.26 E
Saint-Rambert-sur-Loire	62	45.30 N	4.15 E
Saint-Raphaël	62	43.25 N	6.46 E
Saint-Raymond	206	46.54 N	71.50 W
Saint-Rédempter-de-Lévis	206	46.42 N	71.17 W
Saint Regis	202	47.17 N	115.06 W
Saint-Régis ≃, P.Q., Can.	275a	45.24 N	73.34 W
Saint Regis ≃, N.A.	188	45.00 N	74.39 W
Saint Regis ≃, Mt., U.S.	202	47.18 N	115.05 W
Saint Regis, West Branch ≃	188	44.47 N	74.46 W
Saint Regis Falls	188	44.40 N	74.32 W
Saint Regis Indian Reservation ◈[4]	206	44.58 N	74.39 W
Saint-Rémi	206	45.16 N	73.37 W
Saint-Rémi-d'Amherst	206	46.01 N	74.46 W
Saint-Rémy (lès-Chevreuse), Fr.	50	48.42 N	2.05 E
Saint-Rémy, Fr.	58	46.46 N	4.50 E
Saint Remy, N.Y., U.S.	210	41.54 N	74.01 W
Saint-Rémy-de-Provence	62	43.47 N	4.50 E
Saint-Rémy-en-Bouzemont	58	48.38 N	4.39 E
Saint-Rémy-lès-Chevreuse	261	48.42 N	2.05 E
Saint-Rémy-l'Honoré	261	48.45 N	1.53 E
Saint-Rémy-sur-Avre	50	48.46 N	1.15 E
Saint-Renan	32	48.26 N	4.37 W
Saint-Révérien	50	47.13 N	3.30 E
Saint-Rhémy	62	45.50 N	7.11 E
Saint-Riquier	50	50.08 N	1.57 E
Saint Robert	194	37.50 N	92.09 W
Saint-Roch-de-l'Achigan	206	45.51 N	73.36 W
Saint-Romain-de-Colbosc	50	49.32 N	0.22 E
Saint-Romain-le-Puy	62	45.33 N	4.07 E
Saint-Romans	62	45.07 N	5.19 E
Saint-Romuald	206	46.45 N	71.14 W
Sainte-Rosalie	206	45.38 N	72.54 W
Sainte-Rose	241o	16.20 N	61.42 W
Sainte-Rose ◈[8]	275a	45.36 N	73.47 W
Sainte-Rose-du-Lac	184	51.03 N	99.32 W
Saintry-sur-Seine	261	48.36 N	2.30 E
Saintes, Bel.	50	50.42 N	4.10 E
Saintes, Fr.	32	45.45 N	0.38 W
Saint-Saëns	50	49.40 N	1.17 E
Saint Sampson	43b	49.29 N	2.31 W
Saint-Saturnin-d'Apt	62	43.56 N	5.23 E
Saint-Sauveur, Fr.	50	47.37 N	3.12 E
Saint-Sauveur, Fr.	58	47.48 N	6.23 E
Saint-Sauveur-des-Monts	206	45.52 N	74.10 W
Saint-Sauveur-sur-Tinée	62	44.05 N	7.06 E
Saint-Savin	32	46.34 N	0.52 E
Sainte-Savine	50	48.18 N	4.03 E
Saint-Savinien	32	45.53 N	0.41 W
Saint Saviour	43b	49.11 N	2.06 W
Saint Sebastian Bay c	158	34.25 S	21.00 E
Saint-Sébastien	206	45.07 N	73.09 W
Saint-Sébastien, Cap ›	157b	12.26 S	48.44 E
Saint-Seine-l'Abbaye	58	47.26 N	4.47 E
Saint Séverin	56	50.32 N	5.25 E
Saint Shotts	186	46.38 N	53.35 W
Sainte-Sigolène	62	45.14 N	4.15 E
Saint-Siméon	186	47.50 N	69.53 W
Saint-Simon	50	49.45 N	3.10 E
Saint Simons Island	192	31.09 N	81.22 W
Saint Simons Island I	192	31.14 N	81.21 W
Saint-Sixte ≃	206	45.39 N	75.08 W
Saintes-Maries, Golfe des c	62	43.25 N	4.31 E
Saintes-Maries-de-la-Mer	62	43.27 N	4.26 E
Sainte-Sophie-de-Mégantic	206	46.09 N	71.42 W
Saint-Soupplets	261	49.02 N	2.48 E
Saint Stanislas Bay c	174o	1.53 N	157.30 W
Saint-Stanislas-de-Kosta	206	45.11 N	74.08 W
Saint Stephen, N.B., Can.	186	45.12 N	67.17 W
Saint Stephen, S.C., U.S.	192	33.24 N	79.55 W
Saint-Sulpice-de-Favières	261	48.33 N	2.11 E
Saint-Sulpice-les-Feuilles	32	46.19 N	1.22 E
Sainte-Suzanne	58	47.30 N	6.46 E
Saint-Sylvestre	206	46.22 N	71.14 W
Saint-Symphorien, Fr.	32	44.26 N	0.30 W
Saint-Symphorien, Fr.	261	48.31 N	1.46 E
Saint-Symphorien-d'Ozon	62	45.38 N	4.52 E
Saint-Symphorien-sur-Coise	62	45.38 N	4.27 E
Sainte-Thècle	206	46.49 N	72.31 W
Saint-Théodore-d'Acton	206	45.41 N	72.35 W
Sainte-Thérèse	206	45.38 N	73.51 W
Sainte-Thérèse, Île I, P.Q., Can.	275a	45.41 N	73.28 W
Sainte-Thérèse, Île I, P.Q., Can.	275a	45.22 N	73.15 W
Saint-Thibault-des-Vignes	261	48.52 N	2.41 E
Saint Thomas, On., Can.	212	42.47 N	81.12 W
Saint Thomas, Mo., U.S.	219	38.22 N	92.13 W
Saint Thomas, N.D., U.S.	198	48.37 N	97.26 W
Saint Thomas I	240m	18.21 N	64.55 W
Saint Thomas → Charlotte Amalie	240m	18.21 N	64.56 W
Saint-Timothée	206	45.18 N	74.02 W
Saint-Tite	206	46.44 N	72.34 W
Saint-Tite-des-Caps	186	47.08 N	70.47 W
Saint-Trivier-de-Courtes	58	46.28 N	5.05 E
Saint-Trivier-sur-Moignans	58	46.04 N	4.54 E
Saint-Tropez	62	43.16 N	6.38 E
Saint Tudy	42	50.33 N	4.43 W
Sainte-Tulle	62	43.47 N	5.46 E
Saint-Ubald	206	46.45 N	72.16 W
Saint-Urbain-de-Charlevoix	186	47.33 N	70.32 W
Saint-Ursanne	58	47.22 N	7.10 E

FRANÇAIS

Nom	Page	Lat.°′	Long.°′ W = Ouest
Saint-Uze	62	45.11 N	4.52 E
Saint-Valérien	50	48.11 N	3.06 E
Saint-Valéry-en-Caux	50	49.52 N	0.44 E
Saint-Valéry-sur-Somme	50	50.11 N	1.38 E
Saint-Vallier, Fr.	58	46.38 N	4.22 E
Saint-Vallier, Fr.	62	45.10 N	4.49 E
Saint-Vallier-de-Thiey	62	43.42 N	6.51 E
Saint-Varent	32	46.53 N	0.14 W
Saint-Venant	50	50.37 N	2.33 E
Saint-Véran	62	44.42 N	6.52 E
Sainte-Victoire, Montagne ʌ	62	43.32 N	5.39 E
Saint-Victoret	62	43.25 N	5.14 E
Saint Vincent	198	48.58 N	97.13 W
Saint Vincent I	241h	13.15 N	61.12 W
Saint-Vincent, Baie de c	175f	22.00 S	166.05 E
Saint-Vincent, Cap ›	157b	21.57 S	43.16 E
Saint Vincent, Cape ›	166	43.18 S	145.50 E
Saint Vincent, Cape → São Vicente, Cabo de ›	34	37.01 N	9.00 W
Saint Vincent, Gulf c	168b	35.00 S	138.05 E
Saint Vincent and the Grenadines □[1], N.A.	230	13.15 N	61.12 W
Saint Vincent and the Grenadines □[1], N.A.	241h	13.15 N	61.12 W
Saint-Vincent-de-Paul ◈[8]	275a	45.37 N	73.39 W
Saint-Vincent-de-Tyrosse	32	43.40 N	1.18 W
Saint Vincent Passage ʯ	238	13.30 N	61.00 W
Saint Vincent's	186	46.48 N	53.38 W
Saint-Vit	58	47.11 N	5.49 E
Saint-Vith	56	50.17 N	6.08 E
Saint-Vivien-de-Médoc	32	45.26 N	1.02 W
Saint-Vrain	261	48.33 N	2.20 E
Saint Walburg	184	53.39 N	109.12 W
Saint-Wandrille-Rançon	50	49.32 N	0.46 E
Saint-Wenceslas ≃	206	46.18 N	72.23 W
Saint Williams	212	42.40 N	80.25 W
Saint-Witz	261	49.05 N	2.34 E
Saint-Yrieix-la-Perche	32	45.31 N	1.12 E
Saint-Yvon	186	49.10 N	64.48 W
Saint-Zacharie	62	43.23 N	5.43 E
Saint-Zénon	206	46.33 N	73.49 W
Sāinthiya	126	23.57 N	87.40 E
Saipan I	174n	15.12 N	145.45 E
Saipan Channel ʯ	174n	15.05 N	145.41 E
Saipan International Airport ⊠	174n	15.07 N	145.43 E
Saiqi	100	27.00 N	119.43 E
Saishu-to → Cheju-do I	90	33.20 N	126.30 E
Saita	96	34.08 N	133.49 E
Saita ≃	96	34.08 N	133.38 E
Saitama □[5]	94	36.00 N	139.30 E
Saitama University ʊ[2]	268	35.52 N	139.36 E
Saito	92	32.06 N	131.24 E
Saiwai ◈[8]	268	35.33 N	139.41 E
Saiwa Swamp National Park ♦	154	1.06 N	35.12 E
Saiyidān ◈[8]	272a	28.40 N	77.05 E
Sai Yok	110	14.07 N	99.08 E
Sajak	86	47.02 N	77.22 E
Sajam	164	0.53 S	132.41 E
Sajama	248	18.07 S	69.00 W
Sajama, Nevado ʌ	248	18.06 S	68.54 W
Sajanogorsk	86	53.08 N	91.29 E
Sajano-Šušenskoje vodochranilišče ⊜[1]	86	52.20 N	92.25 E
Sajan → Sayan Mountains ⩘	88	52.45 N	96.00 E
Sajantuj	88	51.44 N	107.30 E
Sajasan	84	43.03 N	46.17 E
Sajat	128	38.47 N	63.53 E
Sajchan	88	48.40 N	102.39 E
Sajchandulaan	102	44.40 N	109.01 E
Sajchan-Ovoo	102	45.27 N	103.54 E
Sajchin	80	48.50 N	46.47 E
Şajen	115a	7.40 S	112.31 E
Šajgino	80	57.46 N	46.51 E
Şajīd I	144	16.52 N	41.50 E
Šajmak'	120	37.27 N	74.44 E
Sajnšand	102	44.52 N	110.09 E
Sajó ≃	30	47.56 N	21.08 E
Sajószentpéter	30	48.13 N	20.44 E
Sajram	85	42.18 N	69.45 E
Sajukino	80	52.47 N	41.59 E
Sājūr (Bağırsak) ≃	130	36.40 N	38.05 E
Sak ≃	158	30.02 S	20.40 E
Saka, Kenya	154	0.09 S	39.20 E
Saka, Nihon	96	34.20 N	132.31 E
Sakado	94	35.57 N	139.24 E
Sakae, Nihon	94	35.50 N	140.15 E
Sakae, Nihon	94	36.58 N	138.35 E
Sa Kaeo	110	13.49 N	102.04 E
Sakahogi	94	35.26 N	136.59 E
Sakai, Nihon	94	36.10 N	136.14 E
Sakai, Nihon	94	36.16 N	139.15 E
Sakai, Nihon	94	36.06 N	139.48 E
Sakai, Nihon	96	34.35 N	135.28 E
Sakai, Nihon	268	35.25 N	139.22 E
Sakai ≃	94	35.18 N	139.29 E
Sakaide	96	34.19 N	133.52 E
Sakaigawa	94	35.35 N	138.37 E
Sakaiminato	96	35.33 N	133.15 E
Sakākah	128	29.59 N	40.06 E
Sakakawea, Lake ⊜[1]	198	47.50 N	102.20 W
Sakaki	94	36.28 N	138.11 E
Sakakita	94	36.25 N	138.01 E
Sakala, Pulau I	112	6.54 S	116.15 E
Sakami ≃	176	53.40 N	76.40 W
Sakami, Lac ⊜	176	53.15 N	76.45 W
Sakania	154	12.45 S	28.34 E
Sakar	128	38.56 N	63.45 E
Sakar ⩘	38	41.59 N	26.16 E
Sakaraha	157b	22.55 S	44.32 E
Sakar-Čaga	128	37.38 N	61.40 E
Sakar Island I	164	5.25 S	148.05 E
Sakartvelo → Georgia □[1]	22	42.00 N	44.00 E
Sakarya □[4]	130	40.45 N	30.35 E
Sakarya ≃	130	41.07 N	30.39 E
Sakashita	94	35.34 N	137.32 E
Sakassou	150	7.27 N	5.18 W
Sakata	92	38.55 N	139.50 E
Sakauchi	94	35.36 N	136.25 E
Sakawa	96	33.30 N	133.17 E
Sakawa ≃	94	35.15 N	139.11 E
Sakchu	98	40.23 N	125.01 E
Sakesar	123	32.33 N	71.56 E
Sakété	150	6.43 N	2.40 E
Sakhā	142	31.05 N	30.57 E
Sakhalin → Sachalin, ostrov I	89	51.00 N	143.00 E
Sākhar	120	32.57 N	65.32 E
Sakhi Sarwar	120	29.59 N	70.18 E
Sakhnin	132	32.52 N	35.17 E
Şakhrīyāt, Jabal aş- ʌ	132	31.01 N	36.21 E
Sakht Sar	128	36.53 N	50.41 E
Saki	78	45.09 N	33.35 E
Şāki ◈[8]	272c	19.06 N	72.53 E
Šakiai	76	54.57 N	23.03 E
Sākib	132	32.17 N	35.49 E
Sakiet Sidi Youssef	36	36.13 N	8.22 E
Sakijang Bendera, Pulau I	271c	1.13 N	103.51 E
Sakijang Pelepah, Pulau I	271c	1.13 N	103.52 E
Sakishima-shotō II	175d	24.46 N	124.00 E

PORTUGUÊS

Nome	Página	Lat.°′	Long.°′ W = Oeste
Sakito	92	33.02 N	129.32 E
Sakkara → Şaqqārah	142	29.51 N	31.13 E
Sakmara ≃	86	51.46 N	55.01 E
Sako	270	34.53 N	135.47 E
Sakon Nakhon	110	17.10 N	104.09 E
Sakonnet	207	41.28 N	71.12 W
Sakonnet Point ›	207	41.27 N	71.12 W
Sakoyra	150	14.17 N	1.24 E
Sakra, Pulau I	271c	1.16 N	103.42 E
Sakrand	120	26.08 N	68.16 E
Sakrivier	158	30.54 S	20.28 E
Sakrow-Paretzer Kanal ≊	264a	52.28 N	12.55 E
Saks	194	33.42 N	85.52 W
Saksagan' ≃	78	47.53 N	33.18 E
Saksauldala ◈[2]	86	44.30 N	73.00 E
Sakskøbing	41	54.48 N	11.39 E
Sakti	124	22.02 N	82.58 E
Saku, Nihon	94	36.09 N	138.30 E
Saku, Nihon	94	36.13 N	138.29 E
Sakubva	154	19.00 S	32.10 E
Sakugi	96	34.52 N	132.43 E
Sakuma	94	35.05 N	137.48 E
Sakuma-dam ◈[6]	94	35.05 N	137.47 E
Sakuma-ko ⊜[1]	94	35.08 N	137.47 E
Sakura	94	35.43 N	140.14 E
Sakura ≃	94	36.05 N	140.14 E
Sakurae	96	34.57 N	132.20 E
Sakurai	96	34.30 N	135.51 E
Sakura-tōge)(	270	34.36 N	135.53 E
Saku-shima I	94	34.43 N	137.03 E
Sakutō	96	35.01 N	134.14 E
Sakwaso Lake ⊜	184	53.01 N	91.55 W
Säkylä	26	61.02 N	22.20 E
Sakyō ◈[8]	270	35.02 N	135.48 E
Sal I	150a	16.45 N	22.55 W
Sal ≃	80	47.31 N	40.45 E
Sal, Cay I	238	23.42 N	80.24 W
Sal, Ponta do ›	266c	38.41 N	9.22 W
Sal, Punta ›	236	15.53 N	87.37 W
Šal'a, Česko.	30	48.09 N	17.52 E
Šal'a, Ross.	86	57.15 N	58.43 E
Sala, Sve.	40	59.55 N	16.36 E
Sala, Ouadi V	146	17.00 N	20.53 E
Sala Baganza	64	44.43 N	10.14 E
Salabangka, Kepulauan II	112	3.02 S	122.25 E
Salaberry, Île de I	206	45.17 N	74.07 W
Salaberry-de-Valleyfield	206	45.15 N	74.08 W
Salaca ≃	76	57.45 N	24.21 E
Salacgrīva	76	57.45 N	24.21 E
Sala Consilina	68	40.24 N	15.36 E
Salada, Laguna ⊜, Arg.	258	35.17 S	59.24 W
Salada, Laguna ⊜, Méx.	232	32.20 N	115.40 W
Saladas	252	28.15 S	58.38 W
Saladillo	252	35.38 S	59.46 W
Saladillo ≃, Arg.	252	33.25 S	63.02 W
Saladillo ≃, Arg.	252	29.05 S	63.25 W
Saladillo, Arroyo ≃	258	35.33 S	59.04 W
Saladillo de Rodríguez, Arroyo ≃	258	35.29 S	59.01 W
Saladillo Dulce, Arroyo ≃	252	31.25 S	60.33 W
Salado, Arg.	252	28.18 S	67.15 W
Salado, Tx., U.S.	222	30.57 N	97.32 W
Salado ≃, Arg.	252	38.49 S	64.57 W
Salado ≃, Arg.	252	29.13 S	66.34 W
Salado ≃, Arg.	252	31.42 S	60.44 W
Salado ≃, Arg.	252	35.44 S	57.21 W
Salado ≃, Cuba	240p	20.36 N	76.56 W
Salado ≃, Méx.	232	26.52 N	99.19 W
Salado ≃, Méx.	234	17.55 N	96.58 W
Salado ≃, Méx.	234	18.44 N	103.36 W
Salado, Arroyo ≃, Arg.	254	41.37 S	65.02 W
Salado, Arroyo ≃, Arg.	254	40.35 S	66.33 W
Salado, Rio ≃	200	34.16 N	106.52 W
Salado Creek ≃, Tx., U.S.	196	29.14 N	98.25 W
Salado Creek ≃, Tx., U.S.	222	30.59 N	97.25 W
Salaga	150	8.33 N	0.31 W
Salagle	144	1.50 N	42.17 E
Sālah	132	32.38 N	36.46 E
Şalāh ad-Dīn □[4]	128	34.15 N	43.55 E
Salahin	144	2.57 N	46.26 E
Sala'ilua	175a	13.41 S	172.34 W
Salair	86	54.13 N	85.47 E
Salairskij kr'až ʌ	86	54.15 N	85.30 E
Sălaj □[6]	38	47.15 N	23.00 E
Salak	114	2.34 N	98.20 E
Salak, Gunung ʌ	115a	6.42 S	106.44 E
Şalakas	76	55.35 N	26.08 E
Šalakuša	24	62.15 N	40.17 E
Salal	146	14.51 N	17.13 E
Salala, Chile	252	30.41 S	71.32 W
Salala, Liber.	150	6.40 N	10.05 W
Salālah, Sūd.	140	21.19 N	36.13 E
Şalālah, 'Umān	118	17.00 N	54.06 E
Salamá, Guat.	236	15.06 N	90.16 W
Salamá, Hond.	236	14.50 N	86.36 W
Salamajärven kansallispuisto ♦	26	63.20 N	24.40 E
Salaman	115a	7.35 S	110.08 E
Salamanca, Chile	252	31.47 S	70.58 W
Salamanca, Esp.	34	40.58 N	5.39 W
Salamanca, Méx.	234	20.34 N	101.12 W
Salamanca, Perú	248	15.31 S	72.50 W
Salamanca, Perú	286d	12.05 S	77.00 W
Salamanca, N.Y., U.S.	210	42.09 N	78.42 W
Salamanca □[4]	34	40.45 N	6.00 W
Salamanga	158	26.28 S	32.39 E
Salamat □[5]	146	11.00 N	20.30 E
Salamat, Bahr ≃	146	9.27 N	18.06 E
Salāmbek	120	28.18 N	65.09 E
Salamina	246	5.25 N	75.29 W
Salamínos, Órmos c	267c	37.56 N	23.27 E
Salamís	38	37.59 N	23.28 E
Salamís I	38	37.54 N	23.26 E
Salamis ⊥	130	35.10 N	33.54 E
Salamīyah	130	35.01 N	37.03 E
Salām Khān	120	31.47 N	66.45 E
Salamonia	216	40.23 N	84.52 W
Salamonie ≃	216	40.50 N	85.43 W
Salamonie Lake ⊜[1]	216	40.46 N	85.37 W
Salāmūn	142	31.04 N	31.28 E
Salandra	68	40.31 N	16.19 E
Sālang, Tūnel-e ◈[5]	120	35.19 N	69.02 E
Salani	175a	14.00 S	171.33 W
Salantai	76	56.04 N	21.32 E
Salaparuta	70	37.47 N	13.00 E
Salaquí	246	7.18 N	77.33 W
Salaquí ≃	246	7.27 N	77.07 W
Salāqūs	142	28.44 N	30.50 E
Salar	85	41.21 N	69.22 E
Salara	64	44.59 N	11.25 E
Salard	38	47.13 N	22.03 E
Salarjovo	265b	55.37 N	37.26 E
Salas	248	6.16 S	79.37 W
Salas de los Infantes	34	42.01 N	3.17 W
Salat ≃	32	43.10 N	0.58 E
Salatiga	115a	7.19 S	110.30 E
Salauš	80	55.59 N	52.53 E
Salavat	86	53.21 N	55.55 E
Salavaux	58	46.55 N	7.02 E
Salaverry	248	8.14 S	78.58 W
Salavina	252	28.48 S	63.25 W
Salawati I	164	1.07 S	130.52 E
Salawe	154	3.19 S	32.52 E
Salay	116	8.52 N	124.47 E
Salāya	120	22.19 N	69.35 E
Sala y Gómez, Isla I	18	26.28 S	105.28 W

Sala y Gomez Ridge ✣[3]	18	25.00 S	98.00 W
Salazgor'	80	54.07 N	43.09 E
Salba	88	53.14 N	92.36 E
Salbani	126	22.38 N	87.20 E
Salbohed	40	59.55 N	16.19 E
Salbosjön ⊜	40	59.50 N	14.54 E
Şalbris	50	47.26 N	2.03 E
Šalbuzdag, gora ʌ	84	41.19 N	47.48 E
Salcajá	236	14.53 N	91.27 W
Salccantay, Nevado ʌ	248	13.20 S	72.33 W
Salcedo, Pil.	116	11.09 N	125.40 E
Salcedo, Rep. Dom.	238	19.23 N	70.25 W
Salcha ≃	180	64.29 N	147.00 W
Salching	60	48.49 N	12.34 E
Şalcia	38	43.57 N	24.56 E
Šalčininkai	76	54.18 N	25.23 E
Salcombe	42	50.13 N	3.47 W
Şalda ≃	86	58.48 N	61.20 E
Šaldaj	86	51.56 N	78.48 E
Saldaña	34	42.31 N	4.44 W
Saldaña ≃	246	4.01 N	74.52 W
Saldanha	158	33.00 S	17.56 E
Şaldanhabaai c	158	33.04 S	18.00 E
Šaldež	80	56.52 N	44.46 E
Saldungaray	252	38.12 S	61.47 W
Saldus	76	56.40 N	22.30 E
Sale, Austl.	166	38.06 S	147.04 E
Sale, It.	62	44.59 N	8.48 E
Salé, Magreb	148	34.04 N	6.50 W
Sale, Eng., U.K.	44	53.26 N	2.19 W
Salebabu, Pulau I	108	3.55 N	126.40 E
Salechard	74	66.33 N	66.40 E
Sale Creek	194	35.22 N	85.06 W
Salée, Rivière ʯ	241o	16.17 N	61.33 W
Saleh, Teluk c	115b	8.34 S	117.57 E
Salelologa	175a	13.44 S	172.10 W
Salem, On., Can.	212	43.42 N	80.27 W
Salem, Dtsch.	58	47.46 N	9.16 E
Salem, India	122	11.39 N	78.10 E
Salem, S. Afr.	158	33.28 S	26.29 E
Salem, Sve.	40	59.13 N	17.44 E
Salem, Ar., U.S.	194	36.22 N	91.49 W
Salem, Il., U.S.	219	38.37 N	88.56 W
Salem, In., U.S.	218	38.03 N	86.15 W
Salem, Ia., U.S.	190	40.51 N	91.37 W
Salem, Ky., U.S.	194	37.15 N	88.14 W
Salem, Ma., U.S.	207	42.31 N	70.53 W
Salem, Mi., U.S.	281	42.24 N	83.34 W
Salem, Mo., U.S.	194	37.38 N	91.32 W
Salem, N.H., U.S.	207	42.47 N	71.12 W
Salem, N.J., U.S.	208	39.34 N	75.28 W
Salem, N.Y., U.S.	210	43.10 N	73.19 W
Salem, Oh., U.S.	214	40.54 N	80.51 W
Salem, Or., U.S.	224	44.56 N	123.02 W
Salem, S.D., U.S.	198	43.43 N	97.23 W
Salem, Ut,. U.S.	200	40.03 N	111.40 W
Salem, Va., U.S.	192	37.17 N	80.03 W
Salem, W.V., U.S.	188	39.16 N	80.33 W
Salem, Wi., U.S.	216	42.33 N	88.06 W
Salem □[6]	208	39.34 N	75.20 W
Salem ≃	208	39.34 N	75.31 W
Salem Airfield ⊠	281	42.25 N	83.34 W
Sale Marasino	64	45.43 N	10.06 E
Salem Canal ≊	285	39.41 N	75.31 W
Salem Depot	283	42.47 N	71.12 W
Salem Harbor c	283	42.31 N	70.53 W
Salem Heights	214	40.54 N	80.53 W
Salemi	70	37.49 N	12.48 E
Salem Maritime National Historic Site ⊥	207	42.31 N	70.53 W
Salem State College ʊ[2]	283	42.30 N	70.54 W
Salem Upland ⩘[1]	194	37.25 N	91.30 W
Sälen, Sve.	26	61.10 N	13.16 E
Salen, Scot., U.K.	46	56.43 N	5.47 W
Salen, Scot., U.K.	46	56.31 N	5.57 W
Salentina, Penisola ›[1]	68	40.25 N	18.00 E
Salentine, Murge ◈[1]	68	40.02 N	18.13 E
Salento	68	40.15 N	15.11 E
Salernes	62	43.33 N	6.14 E
Salerno	68	40.41 N	14.47 E
Salerno □[4]	68	40.27 N	15.16 E
Salerno, Golfo di c	68	40.32 N	14.42 E
Salers	32	45.08 N	2.30 E
Salesbury	262	53.47 N	2.30 W
Salesópolis	256	23.32 S	45.51 W
Salève, Mont ʌ	58	46.07 N	6.10 E
Salford	44	53.28 N	2.18 W
Salford □[8]	262	53.28 N	2.23 W
Şalfords	260	51.12 N	0.10 W
Šalgačova	24	62.19 N	39.35 E
Salgado	250	11.02 S	37.28 W
Salgan	80	55.14 N	45.30 E
Şalgar	246	5.58 N	75.59 W
Šalgija	86	47.35 N	70.36 E
Salgir ≃	78	45.38 N	35.01 E
Salgótarján	30	48.07 N	19.48 E
Salgueiro	250	8.04 S	39.06 W
Salher ʌ	122	20.43 N	73.56 E
Sali, Alg.	148	26.58 N	0.01 W
Şali, Cro.	36	43.56 N	15.10 E
Šali, Ross.	80	55.41 N	49.40 E
Šali, Ross.	84	43.08 N	45.54 E
Salí ≃	252	27.33 S	64.57 W
Salice Salentino	68	40.23 N	17.58 E
Salice Terme	62	44.55 N	9.01 E
Salici, Monte ʌ	70	37.44 N	14.38 E
Salida, Ca., U.S.	226	37.42 N	121.05 W
Salida, Co., U.S.	200	38.32 N	105.59 W
Salies-de-Béarn	32	43.29 N	0.55 W
Şalīf	144	15.18 N	42.40 E
Salignac-Eyvignes	32	44.59 N	1.19 E
Salihli	130	38.29 N	28.09 E
Şālikha	126	23.18 N	89.22 E
Šalikovo	82	55.30 N	36.13 E
Salim	140	12.52 N	28.40 E
Salima	154	13.47 S	34.26 E
Salīmah, Wāḥat ⫪[4]	140	21.22 N	29.19 E
Salimani	157a	11.47 S	43.17 E
Salimbatu	112	2.57 N	117.21 E
Salimgarh Fort ⊥	272a	28.40 N	77.14 E
Salimi	152	9.24 S	23.35 E
Salin	110	20.35 N	94.39 E
Salina, Ks., U.S.	198	38.50 N	97.36 W
Salina, Ok., U.S.	196	36.17 N	95.09 W
Salina, Pa., U.S.	214	40.31 N	79.30 W
Salina, Ut,. U.S.	200	38.57 N	111.51 W
Salina, Canale di ≊	70	38.32 N	14.54 E
Salina, Isola I	70	38.34 N	14.50 E
Salina Cruz	234	16.10 N	95.12 W
Salina Point ›	238	22.13 N	74.18 W
Salinas, Bra.	255	16.10 S	42.17 W
Salinas, Ec.	246	2.13 S	80.58 W
Salinas, P.R.	240m	17.59 N	66.18 W
Salinas, Ca., U.S.	226	36.40 N	121.39 W
Salinas ≃, Bra.	255	16.37 S	42.18 W
Salinas (Chixoy) ≃, N.A.	232	16.28 N	90.33 W
Salinas ≃, Ca., U.S.	226	36.45 N	121.48 W
Salinas, Pampa de las ≚	252	31.58 S	66.42 W
Salinas, Ponta das ›	152	12.50 S	12.56 E
Salinas, Sierra de ⩘	226	36.18 N	121.20 W
Salinas de Garci Mendoza	248	19.38 S	67.43 W
Salinas de Hidalgo	234	22.38 N	101.43 W
Salinas del Rey	196	27.38 N	102.24 W
Salinas Municipal Airport ⊠	226	36.40 N	121.40 W
Salinas National Monument ♦	200	34.05 N	106.14 W
Salinas Valley V	226	36.15 N	121.15 W
Salinas Victoria	196	25.53 N	100.19 W
Salin-de-Giraud	62	43.25 N	4.44 E
Salindres	62	44.10 N	4.10 E
Saline, La., U.S.	194	32.09 N	92.58 W

Saline, Mi., U.S.	216	42.10 N	83.46 W
Saline ≃, Ar., U.S.	194	33.44 N	93.58 W
Saline ≃, Ar., U.S.	194	33.10 N	92.08 W
Saline ≃, Il., U.S.	194	37.35 N	88.08 W
Saline ≃, Ks., U.S.	198	38.51 N	97.30 W
Saline ≃, Mi., U.S.	216	41.59 N	83.37 W
Saline, North Fork ≃	194	37.44 N	88.19 W
Saline Bayou ≃	194	31.45 N	92.58 W
Saline di Volterra	66	43.22 N	10.49 E
Saline Lake ⊜[1]	194	31.55 N	92.55 W
Salines, Point ›	241k	12.00 N	61.48 W
Salines, Pointe des ›	240e	14.24 N	60.53 W
Salineville	214	40.37 N	80.51 W
Salingyi	110	21.58 N	95.03 E
Salinópolis	250	0.37 S	47.20 W
Šalinskoje	86	55.43 N	93.46 E
Salins-les-Bains	58	46.57 N	5.53 E
Salins-les-Thermes	62	45.28 N	6.32 E
Salipolo	112	3.45 S	119.29 E
Salisbury, Austl.	168b	34.46 S	138.38 E
Salisbury, Dom.	240d	15.26 N	61.27 W
Salisbury, Eng., U.K.	42	51.05 N	1.48 W
Salisbury, Ct., U.S.	207	41.59 N	73.25 W
Salisbury, Md., U.S.	208	38.21 N	75.35 W
Salisbury, Ma., U.S.	207	42.50 N	70.51 W
Salisbury, Mo., U.S.	194	39.25 N	92.48 W
Salisbury, N.C., U.S.	192	35.40 N	80.28 W
Salisbury, Pa., U.S.	188	39.45 N	79.04 W
Salisbury Cathedral ʊ[1]	42	51.05 N	1.48 W
Salisbury Center	210	43.09 N	74.47 W
Salisbury Hall ⊥	260	51.43 N	0.16 W
Salisbury → Harare	154	17.50 S	31.03 E
Salisbury Island I, Austl.	162	34.21 S	123.32 E
Salisbury Island I, N.T., Can.	176	63.30 N	77.00 W
Salisbury Mills	210	41.26 N	74.08 W
Salisbury Plain ≚	42	51.12 N	1.55 W
Salisbury Plain ≃	283	42.02 N	70.58 W
Salish Mountains ⩘	202	48.15 N	114.45 W
Salito ≃	70	37.29 N	13.46 E
Salitpa	194	31.37 N	88.01 W
Salitre ≃	250	9.29 S	40.39 W
Salix	214	40.18 N	78.46 W
Şaljany	84	39.34 N	48.58 E
Šalkar, Kaz.	80	48.03 N	48.56 E
Šalkar, Kaz.	80	50.32 N	51.51 E
Šalkar, ozero ⊜	80	50.33 N	51.40 E
Šalkar-Jega-Kara, ozero ⊜	86	50.45 N	60.54 E
Salkehatchie ≃	192	32.37 N	80.53 W
Şalkhad	132	32.29 N	36.43 E
Salkhia	272b	22.35 N	88.21 E
Salkum	224	46.31 N	122.37 W
Salla	24	66.50 N	28.40 E
Salladasburg	210	41.17 N	77.14 W
Sallagriffon	62	43.53 N	6.54 E
Sallanches	58	45.56 N	6.38 E
Salland ◈[1]	52	52.20 N	6.20 E
Salles-Curan	32	44.11 N	2.47 E
Salles-sous-Bois	62	44.27 N	4.56 E
Sallgast	54	51.35 N	13.51 E
Salling ◈[1]	26	56.40 N	9.00 E
Salliqueló	252	36.45 S	62.56 W
Sallisaw	196	35.27 N	94.47 W
Sallisaw Creek ≃	194	35.23 N	94.52 W
Salluit	176	62.14 N	75.38 W
Sallūm	140	19.23 N	37.06 E
Sallūm, Khalīj as- c	146	31.41 N	25.21 E
Salm ≃, Bel.	56	50.22 N	5.52 E
Salm ≃, Dtsch.	56	49.51 N	6.51 E
Salmās	128	38.11 N	44.47 E
Salmchâteau	56	50.16 N	5.54 E
Salme	76	58.10 N	22.15 E
Salmi	24	61.22 N	31.53 E
Salmo	182	49.12 N	117.17 W
Salmon	202	45.10 N	113.53 W
Salmon ≃, B.C., Can.	182	54.05 N	122.34 W
Salmon ≃, N.B., Can.	186	46.06 N	65.56 W
Salmon ≃, On., Can.	212	44.11 N	77.15 W
Salmon ≃, N.A.	188	45.02 N	74.31 W
Salmon ≃, Ct., U.S.	207	41.29 N	72.29 W
Salmon ≃, Id., U.S.	202	45.51 N	116.46 W
Salmon ≃, N.Y., U.S.	212	43.35 N	76.12 W
Salmon ≃, Or., U.S.	224	45.03 N	124.00 W
Salmon ≃, Or., U.S.	224	45.22 N	122.02 W
Salmon, East Fork ≃	202	44.16 N	114.19 W
Salmon, Middle Fork ≃	202	45.18 N	114.36 W
Salmon, North Branch ≃	212	43.32 N	75.48 W
Salmon, South Fork ≃	202	45.23 N	115.31 W
Salmon Arm	182	50.42 N	119.16 W
Salmon-Bay	186	51.26 N	57.36 W
Salmon Creek ≃, N.Y., U.S.	210	43.16 N	77.02 W
Salmon Creek ≃, N.Y., U.S.	210	43.19 N	77.43 W
Salmon Creek ≃, Wa., U.S.	224	46.26 N	122.52 W
Salmon Creek ≃, Wa., U.S.	224	45.44 N	122.45 W
Salmon Falls Creek ≃	202	42.43 N	114.51 W
Salmon Falls Creek Reservoir ⊜[1]	202	42.08 N	114.45 W
Salmon Gums	162	32.59 S	121.38 E
Salmon Lake ⊜	212	44.49 N	78.28 W
Salmon Mountain ʌ	188	45.14 N	71.08 W
Salmon Mountains ⩘	204	41.00 N	123.00 W
Salmon Peak ʌ	196	29.28 N	100.10 W
Salmon Point ›	212	43.52 N	77.14 W
Salmon River Mountains ⩘	202	44.45 N	115.30 W
Salmon River Reservoir ⊜[1]	212	43.32 N	75.52 W
Salmon Valley	182	54.05 N	122.41 W
Salmyš ≃	86	52.01 N	55.21 E
Sal'nica	78	49.44 N	28.02 E
Salo, Centraf.	152	3.12 N	16.07 E
Salò, It.	64	45.36 N	10.31 E
Salo, Suomi	26	60.23 N	23.08 E
Salobel'ak	80	57.07 N	48.05 E
Salobra ≃	248	20.12 S	56.29 W
Salomatino	80	50.01 N	44.50 E
Salome	200	33.46 N	113.36 W
Salomon, Cap ›	240e	14.30 N	61.06 W
Salomon, Îles → Solomon Islands □[1]	175e	8.00 S	159.00 E
Salomón, Islas → Solomon Islands □[1]	175e	8.00 S	159.00 E
Salomone, Monte ʌ	267a	41.47 N	12.44 E
Salomon-Inseln → Solomon Islands □[1]	175e	8.00 S	159.00 E
Salon ≃	58	47.32 N	5.41 E
Salona	210	41.05 N	77.28 W
Salon-de-Provence	62	43.38 N	5.06 E
Salonga ≃	152	0.10 S	19.50 E
Salonga, Parc National de la ♦	152	1.45 S	21.20 E
Salonika → Thessaloníki	38	40.38 N	22.56 E
Salonta	38	46.48 N	21.40 E
Salor ≃, Esp.	34	39.39 N	7.03 W
Salor ≃, Esp.	34	39.42 N	6.28 W
Salorno (Salurn)	64	46.14 N	11.13 E
Saloslovo	265b	55.42 N	37.09 E
Şaloum ≃	150	13.50 N	16.45 W
Šalovka ≃	265b	55.47 N	38.12 E
Salpausselkä ʌ	26	61.00 N	26.30 E
Şalpazarı	130	40.59 N	39.10 E
Şalqīn	130	36.08 N	36.27 E

Sal Rei	150a	16.11 N	22.55 W
Salsacate	252	31.19 S	65.05 W
Salsette Island I	272c	19.10 N	72.53 E
Salsilgo, Qawz ♟[8]	140	10.49 N	22.54 E
Salsipuedes, Canal ʯ	232	28.37 N	113.00 W
Salsipuedes, Punta ›, C.R.	236	8.28 N	83.37 W
Salsipuedes, Punta ›, Méx.	232	32.05 N	116.53 W
Şal'sk	80	46.28 N	41.33 E
Šal'skij	24	61.48 N	35.58 E
Sal'sko-Manyčskaja gr'ada ʌ	80	46.40 N	42.30 E
Salso ≃	70	37.06 N	13.57 E
Salsomaggiore Terme	64	44.49 N	9.59 E
Salt ≃, U.S.	202	43.08 N	111.02 W
Salt ≃, Az., U.S.	200	33.23 N	112.18 W
Salt ≃, Ky., U.S.	194	38.00 N	85.57 W
Salt ≃, Mi., U.S.	281	42.39 N	82.47 W
Salt ≃, Mo., U.S.	219	39.28 N	91.04 W
Salt, Elk Fork ≃	219	39.28 N	91.53 W
Salt, Middle Fork ≃	219	39.28 N	91.49 W
Salt, North Fork ≃	219	39.30 N	91.47 W
Salt, South Fork ≃	219	39.28 N	91.49 W
Salta	252	24.47 S	65.25 W
Salta □[4]	252	25.00 S	64.30 W
Saltaim, ozero ⊜	86	56.10 N	71.45 E
Saltair	224	48.57 N	123.46 W
Saltaire	276	40.39 N	73.12 W
Saltanovka	76	52.47 N	34.17 E
Saltara	66	43.45 N	12.54 E
Salt Ash, Austl.	170	32.47 S	151.55 E
Saltash, Eng., U.K.	42	50.24 N	4.12 W
Saltbæk Vig c	41	55.43 N	11.12 E
Salt Basin ⊜	196	31.50 N	105.00 W
Saltburn-by-the-Sea	44	54.35 N	0.58 W
Salt Cay I	240b	25.06 N	77.18 W
Saltcoats, Sk., Can.	184	51.03 N	102.12 W
Saltcoats, Scot., U.K.	46	55.38 N	4.47 W
Salt Creek ≃, On., Can.	275b	43.48 N	79.42 W
Salt Creek ≃, Ca., U.S.	204	36.15 N	116.49 W
Salt Creek ≃, Il., U.S.	194	40.08 N	89.50 W
Salt Creek ≃, Il., U.S.	278	41.49 N	87.50 W
Salt Creek ≃, In., U.S.	216	41.37 N	87.09 W
Salt Creek ≃, In., U.S.	218	38.50 N	86.32 W
Salt Creek ≃, In., U.S.	218	39.27 N	85.09 W
Salt Creek ≃, Ks., U.S.	198	39.06 N	97.44 W
Salt Creek ≃, N.M., U.S.	196	33.35 N	104.23 W
Salt Creek ≃, Ok., U.S.	196	36.32 N	96.43 W
Salt Creek ≃, Or., U.S.	202	43.43 N	122.26 W
Salt Creek ≃, Or., U.S.	224	45.09 N	123.13 W
Salt Creek ≃, Wy., U.S.	202	43.41 N	106.20 W
Salt Creek, Middle Fork ≃	218	39.04 N	86.15 W
Salt Creek, North Fork ≃, Il., U.S.	216	40.13 N	88.50 W
Salt Creek, North Fork ≃, In., U.S.	218	39.08 N	86.21 W
Salt Creek, West Branch ≃	278	42.02 N	88.01 W
Salt Creek South Fork ≃	218	39.02 N	86.16 W
Salt Draw V	196	31.19 N	103.28 W
Saltee Islands II	48	52.07 N	6.36 W
Salten	41	56.05 N	9.35 E
Saltfleet	44	53.25 N	0.11 E
Saltford	42	51.24 N	2.27 W
Salt Fork Lake ⊜[1]	214	41.07 N	81.30 W
Salt Fork State Park ♦	214	40.06 N	81.29 W
Saltholm I	41	55.38 N	12.46 E
Saltillo, Méx.	232	25.25 N	101.00 W
Saltillo, Ms., U.S.	194	34.22 N	88.40 W
Saltillo, Pa., U.S.	214	40.13 N	78.01 W
Saltillo, Tn., U.S.	194	35.22 N	88.12 W
Saltillo, Tx., U.S.	222	33.11 N	95.20 W
Salt Island I	240m	18.23 N	64.31 W
Salt Lake	158	29.16 S	24.00 E
Salt Lake ⊜	196	34.05 N	103.05 W
Salt Lake City	200	40.45 N	111.53 W
Salto, Arg.	252	34.17 S	60.15 W
Salto, Ur.	252	31.23 S	57.58 W
Salto ≃	66	42.23 N	12.54 E
Salto, Lago del ⊜	66	42.15 N	13.02 E
Salto da Divisa	255	16.00 S	39.57 W
Salto de las Rosas	252	34.43 S	68.14 W
Salto del Fraile ›	286d	12.11 S	77.03 W
Salto del Guairá	252	24.03 S	54.17 W
Salto Grande	255	22.54 S	49.59 W
Salto Grande, Embalse ⊜[1]	252	31.00 S	57.55 W
Salton City	204	33.19 N	115.59 W
Salton Sea ⊜	204	33.19 N	115.50 W
Salton Sea State Recreation Area ♦	204	33.29 N	115.53 W
Saltonstall, Lake ⊜	283	42.47 N	71.04 W
Sāltora	126	23.32 N	86.56 E
Saltoro Range ⩘	123	35.17 N	77.03 E
Salto Santiago, Représa de ⊜[1]	252	25.40 S	52.30 W
Salt Pan Creek ≃	274a	33.59 S	151.02 E
Saltpeter Creek c	284b	39.20 N	76.22 W
Salt Point	210	41.44 N	73.42 W
Saltpond	150	5.12 N	1.04 W
Salt Range ⩘	123	32.40 N	72.35 E
Salt River Indian Reservation ◈[4]	200	33.31 N	111.48 W
Saltsburg	214	40.29 N	79.27 W
Saltsjöbaden	40	59.17 N	18.18 E
Salt Slough ≃	226	37.18 N	120.54 W
Saltspring Island I	224	48.47 N	123.30 W
Salt Springs Reservoir ⊜[1]	226	38.30 N	120.11 W
Saltville	192	36.52 N	81.45 W
Salt Wells Creek ≃	200	41.39 N	108.59 W
Saltykovka, Ross.	80	52.07 N	44.05 E
Saltykovka, Ross.	265b	55.46 N	37.55 E
Saluda, S.C., U.S.	192	34.00 N	81.46 W
Saluda, Va., U.S.	208	37.36 N	76.35 W
Saluda ≃	192	34.00 N	81.04 W
Saludecio	66	43.52 N	12.40 E
Saluën → Salween ≃	12	16.31 N	97.37 E
Salue Timpaus, Selat ʯ	112	1.55 S	124.00 E
Salug	116	8.07 N	122.47 E
Saluggia	62	45.14 N	8.00 E
Sālūmbar	120	24.08 N	74.03 E
Salunga	208	40.06 N	76.26 W
Saluping Island I	116	6.20 N	122.02 E
Salūq 'Atīq	130	36.36 N	39.07 E
Sālūr	122	18.32 N	83.13 E
Salurn → Salorno	64	46.14 N	11.13 E
Salussola	62	45.27 N	8.07 E
Salutaris	256	22.10 S	43.17 W
Saluzzo	62	44.39 N	7.29 E
Salvación, Bahía c	254	50.55 S	75.05 W
Salvado, Mount ʌ	162	25.15 S	121.01 E
Salvador, Bra.	255	12.59 S	38.31 W
Salvador, Pil.	116	7.54 N	123.50 E
Salvador, Ca., U.S.	226	38.20 N	122.18 W
Salvador, El → El Salvador □[1]	236	13.50 N	88.55 W
Salvador, Lake ⊜	194	29.45 N	90.15 W
Salvador Island I	116	15.31 N	119.55 E
Salvador María	258	35.18 S	59.10 W

≃ River	Fluß	Río	Rivière	Rio
≊ Canal	Kanal	Canal	Canal	Canal
⌊ Waterfall, Rapids	Wasserfall, Stromschnellen	Cascada, Rápidos	Chute d'eau, Rapides	Cascata, Rápidos
ʯ Strait	Meeresstraße	Estrecho	Détroit	Estreito
c Bay, Gulf	Bucht, Golf	Bahía, Golfo	Baie, Golfe	Baía, Golfo
⊜ Lake, Lakes	See, Seen	Lago, Lagos	Lac, Lacs	Lago, Lagos
≚ Swamp	Sumpf	Pantano	Marais	Pântano
⊓ Ice Features, Glacier	Eis- und Gletscherformen	Accidentes Glaciales	Formes glaciaires	Acidentes glaciares
⫪ Other Hydrographic Features	Andere Hydrographische Objekte	Otros Elementos Hidrográficos	Autres données hydrographiques	Outros acidentes hidrográficos

✣ Submarine Features	Untermeerische Objekte	Accidentes Submarinos	Formes de relief sous-marin	Acidentes submarinos
□ Political Unit	Politische Einheit	Unidad Politica	Entité politique	Unidade política
ʊ Cultural Institution	Kulturelle Institution	Institución Cultural	Institution culturelle	Instituição cultural
⊥ Historical Site	Historische Stätte	Sitio Histórico	Site historique	Sitio histórico
♦ Recreational Site	Erholungs- und Ferienort	Sitio de Recreo	Centre de loisirs	Area de Lazer
⊠ Airport	Flughafen	Aeropuerto	Aéroport	Aeroporto
■ Military Installation	Militäranlage	Instalación Militar	Installation militaire	Instalação militar
◈ Miscellaneous	Verschiedenes	Misceláneo	Divers	Diversos

Salvador Mazza 252 22.04 S 63.43 W
Salvage 186 48.41 N 53.38 W
Salvail ≃ 206 45.49 N 72.58 W
Salvaterra 250 0.46 S 48.31 W
Salvaterra de Magos 34 39.01 N 8.48 W
Salvatierra 234 20.13 N 100.53 W
Salve 68 39.51 N 18.17 E
Salviac 32 44.41 N 1.16 E
Salwā, Dawhat c 128 25.30 N 50.40 E
Salwā Bahrī 140 24.44 N 32.56 E
Salween ≃ 12 16.31 N 97.37 E
Salyān 124 28.22 N 82.10 E
Salyer 204 40.53 N 123.35 W
Salyersville 192 37.45 N 83.04 W
Šalygino 78 51.34 N 34.07 E
Salza ≃, Dtsch. 54 51.23 N 11.50 E
Salza ≃, Öst. 61 47.40 N 14.43 E
Salzach ≃ 30 48.12 N 12.56 E
Salza Irpina 68 40.55 N 14.53 E
Salzbergen 52 52.19 N 7.20 E
Salzböde ≃ 56 50.40 N 8.42 E
Salzbrunn 156 24.23 S 18.00 E
Salzburg 64 47.48 N 13.02 E
Salzburg □3 64 47.25 N 13.15 E
Salzgitter 52 52.10 N 10.25 E
Salzgitter-Bad ✦8 52 52.04 N 10.23 E
Salzgitter-Barum ✦8 52 52.07 N 10.25 E
Salzgitter-Immendorf ✦8 52 52.09 N 10.26 E
Salzgitter-Lebenstedt ✦8 52 52.09 N 10.20 E
Salzgitter-Thiede ✦8 52 52.11 N 10.29 E
Salzgitter-Watenstedt ✦8 52 52.06 N 10.22 E
Salzhaff c 54 54.06 N 11.36 E
Salzhausen 52 53.13 N 10.09 E
Salzhemmendorf 52 52.04 N 9.35 E
Salzkammergut ✦1 64 47.45 N 13.30 E
Salzkotten 52 51.40 N 8.36 E
Salzmünde 54 51.31 N 11.49 E
Salzwedel 54 52.51 N 11.09 E
Sam, Gabon 152 0.58 N 11.16 E
Sām, India 120 26.50 N 70.31 E
Samā 132 32.28 N 36.14 E
Sama ≃ 248 18.10 S 70.40 W
Sam A. Baker State Park ♦ 194 37.16 N 90.34 W
Samacá 246 5.29 N 73.29 W
Samacimbo 152 13.33 S 16.59 E
Sama [de Langreo] 34 43.18 N 5.41 W
Samādūn 142 30.20 N 30.57 E
Samagaltaj 88 50.36 N 95.03 E
Samah 146 28.12 N 19.09 E
Samāika ✦8 272a 28.32 N 77.05 E
Samaipata 248 18.09 S 63.52 W
Samal (Peñaplata) 116 7.05 N 125.42 E
Samalá ≃ 236 14.11 N 91.47 W
Samalanga 114 5.13 N 96.22 E
Samalayuca 200 31.21 N 106.28 W
Šamaldy-Saj 85 41.12 N 72.11 E
Samales Group II 116 6.00 N 121.45 E
Samalga Pass)(180 52.48 N 169.25 W
Samal Island I 116 7.03 N 125.44 E
Sāmalkot 122 17.03 N 82.11 E
Samālūt 142 28.18 N 30.42 E
Samambaia ≃ 255 22.45 S 53.21 W
Samāna, India 124 30.09 N 76.12 E
Samaná, Rep. Dom. 238 19.13 N 69.19 W
Samaná, Bahía de c 238 19.10 N 69.25 W
Samaná, Cabo › 238 19.18 N 69.09 W
Samana Cay I 238 23.06 N 73.42 W
Samandağı 130 36.07 N 35.56 E
Samandıra 130 40.59 N 29.13 E
Samandıra ≃ 267b 40.59 N 29.15 E
Samangān 120 36.16 N 68.01 E
Samangān □4 120 36.15 N 67.40 E
Samangwa 152 4.24 S 24.10 E
Samani 92a 42.07 N 142.56 E
Samaniego 246 1.20 N 77.35 W
Samanlı Dağları ⁂ 130 40.36 N 29.30 E
Samannūd 142 30.58 N 31.15 E
Samar 132 29.49 N 35.01 E
Samar □4 116 11.50 N 125.00 E
Samar I 116 12.00 N 125.00 E
Samara 80 53.12 N 50.09 E
Samara ≃, Ross. 80 53.10 N 50.04 E
Samara ≃, Ukr. 78 48.27 N 35.07 E
Samarai 164 10.37 S 150.40 E
Samarate 62 45.38 N 8.47 E
Samarga 89 47.17 N 138.48 E
Samarga ≃ 89 47.15 N 138.46 E
Samaria, Id., U.S. 202 42.07 N 112.20 W
Samaria, Mi., U.S. 216 41.48 N 83.35 W
Samaria (As-Sāmirah) □9 132 32.15 N 35.10 E
Samaria, Mount ∧ 169 36.52 S 146.03 E
Samaria Gorge — Farángi Samariás V 38 35.18 N 24.00 E
Samariapo 246 5.15 N 67.48 W
Samarinda 112 0.30 S 117.09 E
Samarka 89 44.44 N 134.13 E
Samarkand 85 39.40 N 66.48 E
Sāmarrā' 128 34.12 N 43.52 E
Samar Sea ⊤2 116 12.15 N 124.15 E
Samarskoje, Kaz. 86 49.00 N 83.23 E
Samarskoje, Ross. 83 46.56 N 39.41 E
Samarskoje, Ross. 86 52.02 N 58.10 E
Šamary 86 57.21 N 58.14 E
Samasata 123 29.21 N 71.33 E
Samassi 71 39.29 N 8.54 E
Samastīpur 124 25.51 N 85.47 E
Samatya ✦8 267b 41.00 N 28.56 E
Samaúna 248 7.50 S 60.02 W
Samawāri 120 28.34 N 66.46 E
Samba, Centraf. 152 6.49 N 21.12 E
Samba, India 123 32.34 N 75.07 E
Samba, Zaïre 152 0.14 N 21.19 E
Samba, Zaïre 154 4.38 S 26.22 E
Samba Caju 152 8.46 S 15.24 E
Sambaetiba 256 22.41 S 42.48 W
Sambaíba 250 7.08 S 45.21 W
Sambalpur 120 21.27 N 83.58 E
Sambar, Tanjung › 112 2.59 S 110.19 E
Sambas 112 1.20 N 109.15 E
Sambava 157b 14.16 S 50.10 E
Sambawizi 154 18.21 S 26.16 E
Şambayat 130 37.41 N 38.03 E
Sambāza 120 28.30 N 69.20 E
Sambek, Ross. 83 47.20 N 39.01 E
Sambek, Ross. 83 47.45 N 39.48 E
Sambek ≃ 83 47.16 N 39.01 E
Sambesi — Zambezi ≃ 138 18.55 S 36.04 E
Sambhal 124 28.35 N 78.33 E
Sāmbhar 120 26.55 N 75.12 E
Sāmbhar Lake ⊜ 120 26.58 N 75.05 E
Sambiase 68 38.58 N 16.17 E
Sambia — Zambia □1 154 14.30 S 27.30 E
Sambit, Pulau I 112 1.46 N 119.03 E
Sambito ≃ 250 5.40 S 42.04 W
Sambo 152 12.57 S 16.05 E
Samboan 116 9.32 N 123.18 E
Samboja 112 1.02 S 117.02 E
Sambolabbo 152 7.05 N 11.59 E
Sâmbor, Kam. 110 12.46 N 105.58 E
Sambor, Ukr. 78 49.32 N 23.11 E
Samborombón ≃ 252 35.43 S 57.20 W
Samborombón, Bahía c 252 36.00 S 57.12 W
Samborondón 246 1.57 S 79.44 W
Sambre ≃ 32 50.28 N 4.52 E
Sambre à l'Oise, Canal de la ≋ 50 49.39 N 3.20 E
Sambreville 56 50.26 N 4.37 E
Sambriāl 123 32.28 N 74.21 E
Sambú ≃ 246 8.05 N 78.18 W
Sambuca di Sicilia 70 37.39 N 13.07 E
Sambuca Pistoiese 66 44.06 N 11.00 E
Sambughetti, Monte ∧ 70 37.50 N 14.22 E
Sambungo 152 8.39 S 20.43 E
Sambusu 156 17.50 S 19.20 E
Samch'ŏk 98 37.27 N 129.10 E
Sam Chom, Khao ∧ 110 8.07 N 99.26 E
Samch'ŏnp'o 98 34.57 N 128.03 E
Šamchor 84 40.50 N 46.02 E
Samdžir, gora ∧ 88 52.32 N 93.53 E
Same 154 4.04 S 37.44 E
Same ≃ 94 36.54 N 140.49 E
Samedan 58 46.33 N 9.52 E
Samegawa 94 37.02 N 140.31 E
Šāmen 128 34.12 N 48.42 E
Samene, Oued V 148 26.49 N 7.08 E
Samer 50 50.38 N 1.45 E
Sameru Dando ∧ 124 27.02 N 90.20 E
Samet' 80 57.49 N 40.44 E
Samford 171a 27.23 S 152.53 E
Samfya 154 11.21 S 29.32 E
Samga 98 35.25 N 128.05 E
Samho 98 39.56 N 127.53 E
Saminka ≃ 265b 55.45 N 37.17 E
Samiria ≃ 246 4.42 S 74.13 W
Samish 224 48.35 N 122.33 W
Samish ≃ 224 48.38 N 122.29 W
Samish Bay c 224 48.36 N 122.28 W
Samish Lake ⊜ 224 48.39 N 122.24 W
Samj 132 32.27 N 36.30 E
Samka 110 20.09 N 96.57 E
Samlesbury 262 53.46 N 2.38 W
Samlesbury Aerodrome ≋ 262 53.47 N 2.34 W
Samlesbury Bottoms 262 53.45 N 2.34 W
Samlesbury Higher Hall ♦ 262 53.46 N 2.34 W
Şamlı 130 39.48 N 27.51 E
Sammamish, Lake ⊜ 224 47.36 N 122.06 W
Sammichele di Bari 68 40.53 N 16.57 E
Samnangjin 98 35.23 N 128.50 E
Samnaun 58 46.56 N 10.22 E
Samnaungruppe ⁂ 58 47.00 N 10.25 E
Sam Ngao 110 17.15 N 99.01 E
Samnū 146 27.17 N 14.53 E
Samnye 98 35.55 N 127.05 E
Samo 164 3.58 S 152.51 E
Samoa americane — American Samoa □2 175a 14.20 S 170.00 W
Samoa — American Samoa □2 175a 14.20 S 170.00 W
Samoa Basin ✦1 14 16.00 S 166.00 W
Samoa i Sisifo — Western Samoa □1 175a 13.55 S 172.00 W
Samoa Islands II 175a 14.00 S 171.00 W
Samo Alto 252 30.25 S 70.58 W
Samoa Occidentales — Western Samoa □1 175a 13.55 S 172.00 W
Samoa Occidental — Western Samoa □1 175a 13.55 S 172.00 W
Samoa — Western Samoa □1 175a 13.55 S 172.00 W
Samobor 36 45.48 N 15.43 E
Samoded 24 63.38 N 40.29 E
Samoëns 58 46.05 N 6.44 E
Samofalovka 80 48.57 N 44.13 E
Samoggia ≃ 64 44.41 N 11.15 E
Samojlovka 80 51.12 N 43.43 E
Samokov 38 42.20 N 23.33 E
Samolaco 58 46.15 N 9.21 E
Samora ≃ 266c 38.50 N 8.57 W
Sámos 38 37.45 N 27.00 E
Sámos I 38 37.48 N 26.44 E
Samosdelka 80 46.02 N 47.53 E
Samoset 220 27.28 N 82.32 W
Samosir, Pulau I 114 2.35 N 98.50 E
Samotevičí 76 53.13 N 31.50 E
Samothrace — Samothráki I 38 40.30 N 25.32 E
Samothráki 38 40.28 N 25.31 E
Samothráki I 38 40.30 N 25.32 E
Samouco 266c 38.43 N 9.00 W
Šamovo 76 54.12 N 31.22 E
Samovol'no-Ivanovka 80 52.33 N 50.53 E
S'amozero 24 61.54 N 33.18 E
Sampacho 252 33.23 S 64.43 W
Sampaga 112 2.19 S 119.07 E
Sampaio Correia 256 22.52 S 42.36 W
Sampalan 115b 8.41 S 115.34 E
Sampanahan 112 2.38 S 116.11 E
Sampang 115a 7.12 S 113.14 E
Sampara ≃ 112 3.49 S 122.28 E
Sampawams Creek ≃ 276 40.41 N 73.19 W
Sam Pervyj 86 45.28 N 56.06 E
Sampéyre 62 44.34 N 7.11 E
Sampford Peverell 42 50.56 N 3.22 W
Sampieri 70 36.43 N 14.44 E
Sampit 112 2.32 S 112.57 E
Sampit ≃ 112 2.44 S 112.54 E
Sampit, Teluk c 112 3.05 S 113.03 E
Sampolawa 112 5.36 S 122.43 E
Sampson 279b 40.10 N 79.53 W
Sampson State Park ♦ 210 42.44 N 76.55 W
Sampués 246 9.11 N 75.23 W
Sampur 80 52.19 N 41.37 E
Sampwe 154 9.20 S 27.26 E
Šamrajevka 78 49.46 N 29.49 E
Samrāla 123 30.51 N 76.11 E
Sam Rayburn Reservoir ⊜1 194 31.27 N 94.37 W
Samre 144 13.07 N 39.10 E
Samreboi 150 5.36 N 2.34 W
Samro, ozero ⊜ 76 58.57 N 28.49 E
Samrong, Khlong ≋ 269a 13.39 N 100.34 E
Sams 224 47.38 N 124.01 W
Samsang 120 30.31 N 82.37 E
Samsø I 41 55.52 N 10.37 E
Samsø Bælt)(41 55.48 N 10.47 E
Samson, Al., U.S. 194 31.06 N 86.02 W
Sam Son, Viet 110 19.44 N 105.54 E
Samson I 42a 49.56 N 6.22 W
Samson Indian Reserve ✦4 182 52.48 N 113.10 W
Samsonovka 85 42.44 N 70.32 E
Samsonvale, Lake ⊜1 171a 27.15 S 152.55 E
Samsonville 210 41.53 N 74.18 W
Sams Point ∧ 210 41.40 N 74.22 W
Samsu 98 41.12 N 128.00 E
Samsun 130 41.17 N 36.20 E
Samsun □4 130 41.15 N 36.00 E
Samsun Körfezi c 130 41.18 N 36.21 E
Samtens 54 54.21 N 13.17 E
Samthar 124 25.51 N 78.55 E
Samtown 194 31.16 N 92.26 W
Samtredia 84 42.10 N 42.20 E
Samu 112 2.01 S 115.57 E
Samūdragarh 126 23.21 N 88.20 E
Samuel, Mount ∧ 162 19.41 S 134.09 E
Samuel P. Taylor State Park ♦ 226 38.01 N 122.44 W
Samugheo 71 39.57 N 8.56 E
Samuhú 252 27.31 S 60.24 W
Samui, Ko I 110 9.30 N 100.00 E
Samukawa 94 35.22 N 139.23 E
Samundri 123 31.04 N 72.58 E
Samur ≃ 84 41.53 N 48.32 E
Samur-Apšeronskij kanal ≋ 84 41.38 N 48.25 E
Samurskij chrebet ⁂ 84 41.35 N 47.35 E
Samus' 86 56.46 N 84.44 E
Samusele 152 10.06 S 24.05 E
Samut Prakan 110 13.36 N 100.36 E
Samut Prakan □4 269a 13.35 N 100.35 E
Samut Sakhon 110 13.32 N 100.17 E
Samut Songkhram 110 13.24 N 100.00 E
Samuyi Shankou)(124 29.55 N 84.46 E
S'amža 76 60.01 N 41.02 E
San 150 13.18 N 4.54 W
San (Xan) ≃, Asia 110 13.32 N 105.58 E
San ≃, Europe 30 50.44 N 21.50 E
San ≃, Zhg. 100 33.02 N 119.21 E
Saña, Perú 248 6.55 S 79.35 W
San'ā', Yaman 144 15.23 N 44.12 E
Sana ≃, Bos. 36 45.03 N 16.23 E
San'a ≃, Ross. 82 54.41 N 35.55 E
Sanaag □4 144 10.30 N 47.45 E
Sanaba 150 12.25 N 3.49 W
Sanaba ≃ 150 15.06 N 10.55 W
Sanabū 142 27.30 N 30.47 E
Sanada 94 36.27 N 138.20 E
Sanae ✦3 9 70.30 S 2.30 W
Sanafā 142 30.47 N 31.21 E
Sanāfīr I 128 27.55 N 34.40 E
Sanaga ≃ 152 3.35 N 9.38 E
Sanage-yama ∧ 94 35.12 N 137.10 E
Sanagōchi 96 33.59 N 134.28 E
San Agustín, Arg. 252 38.01 S 58.21 W
San Agustín, Arg. 252 31.59 S 64.23 W
San Agustín, Bol. 248 21.05 S 67.45 W
San Agustín, Col. 246 1.53 N 76.16 W
San Agustín, Méx. 200 31.31 N 106.15 W
San Agustín, Pil. 116 16.30 N 121.45 E
San Agustín, Pil. 116 12.25 N 120.59 E
San Agustín, Cape › 116 6.16 N 126.11 E
San Agustín, Plains of ≋ 200 33.50 N 108.00 W
San Agustín Atenango 234 17.38 N 97.59 W
San Agustín de Valle Fértil 252 30.38 S 67.27 W
San Agustín Loxicha 234 16.01 N 96.38 W
San Agustín Tlaxiaca 234 20.07 N 98.53 W
Sanak Islands II 180 54.25 N 162.35 W
San Alberto 196 27.30 N 101.20 W
San Alejo 236 13.26 N 87.58 W
Sān al-Hajar, Birkat ⊜ 142 31.03 N 31.54 E
Sān al-Hajar al-Qiblīyah 142 30.58 N 31.52 E
Sanalona, Presa ⊜1 232 24.53 N 107.00 W
San Ambrosio, Isla I 244 26.21 S 79.52 W
Sanam Chai, Khlong ≋ 269a 13.38 N 100.27 E
Sanana 112 2.04 S 125.58 E
Sanana, Pulau I 112 2.12 S 125.55 E
Sānand 120 22.59 N 72.23 E
Sanandaj 128 35.19 N 47.00 E
Sanandita 248 21.40 S 63.35 W
San Andreas 226 38.11 N 120.40 W
San Andreas Lake ⊜ 282 37.36 N 122.26 W
San Andreas Rift Zone V 282 37.25 N 122.15 W
San Andrés, Col. 236 12.35 N 81.42 W
San Andrés, Col. 246 6.49 N 72.52 W
San Andrés, Méx. 232 27.14 N 114.14 W
San Andrés, Pan. 236 8.36 N 82.44 W
San Andrés, Isla de I 236 12.32 N 81.42 W
San Andrés, Laguna c 234 22.40 N 97.52 W
San Andrés Calpan 234 19.06 N 98.27 W
San Andrés Cohamiata 234 22.12 N 104.03 W
San Andrés de Giles 258 34.27 S 59.27 W
San Andres Mountains ⁂ 200 32.55 N 106.45 W
San Andrés Point › 116 13.34 N 121.52 E
San Andrés Sajcabajá 236 15.13 N 90.55 W
San Andrés Timilpan 234 19.52 N 99.45 W
San Andrés Tototepec ✦8 286a 19.15 N 99.10 W
San Andrés Tuxtla 234 18.27 N 95.13 W
San Andrés y Providencia □8 238 12.30 N 81.45 W
Sananduva 252 27.57 S 51.48 W
San Angelo 196 31.27 N 100.26 W
San Angel — Villa Obregón ✦8 286a 19.21 N 99.12 W
San Anselmo 226 37.58 N 122.33 W
San Antero 246 9.23 N 75.46 W
San Antonio, Arg. 252 28.57 S 65.20 W
San Antonio, Arg. 252 28.56 S 65.06 W
San Antonio, Belize 236 16.15 N 89.02 W
San Antonio, Bol. 248 27.53 S 70.03 W
San Antonio, Chile 252 33.35 S 71.38 W
San Antonio, Col. 246 3.55 N 75.28 W
San Antonio, C.R. 236 10.12 N 85.26 W
San Antonio, N. Mar. Is. 174n 15.08 N 145.43 E
San Antonio, Perú 248 6.22 S 76.21 W
San Antonio, Pil. 116 12.25 N 124.17 E
San Antonio, Pil. 116 14.57 N 120.05 E
San Antonio, P.R. 240m 18.30 N 67.07 W
San Antonio, Fl., U.S. 220 28.20 N 82.16 W
San Antonio, N.M., U.S. 200 35.06 N 106.22 W
San Antonio, Tx., U.S. 196 29.25 N 98.29 W
San Antonio, Ur. 252 31.22 S 57.48 W
San Antonio, Ur. 258 34.27 S 56.05 W
San Antonio □7 286b 22.55 N 82.29 W
San Antonio ≃, Méx. 196 29.13 N 103.47 W
San Antonio ≃, Méx. 232 31.00 N 116.15 W
San Antonio ≃, Ca., U.S. 226 35.52 N 120.48 W
San Antonio ≃, Tx., U.S. 196 28.30 N 96.50 W
San Antonio ≃1 288 34.24 S 58.31 W
San Antonio, Cabo › 252 36.40 S 56.42 W
San Antonio, Cabo de › 240p 21.52 N 84.57 W
San Antonio, Lake ⊜1 226 35.55 N 121.00 W
San Antonio, Mount ∧ 228 34.17 N 117.39 W
San Antonio, Punta ›, Méx. 232 29.46 N 115.42 W
San Antonio, Punta ›, Méx. 232 26.31 N 111.28 W
San Antonio, Río ≃ 200 37.11 N 105.55 W
San Antonio Bay c, Pil. 116 8.38 N 117.35 E
San Antonio Bay c, Tx., U.S. 196 28.20 N 96.45 W
San Antonio Canyon V 280 34.12 N 117.40 W
San Antonio Creek ≃ 226 38.09 N 122.33 W
San Antonio Dam ⊜6 280 34.09 N 117.41 W
San Antonio de Areco 258 34.15 S 59.28 W
San Antonio de Galipán 286c 10.33 N 66.53 W
San Antonio de los Baños 240p 22.53 N 82.30 W
San Antonio de los Cobres 252 24.11 S 66.21 W
San Antonio de Táchira 246 7.50 N 72.27 W
San Antonio de Padua, Arg. 258 34.40 S 58.42 W
San Antonio de Padua, Méx. 234 22.35 N 104.30 W
San Antonio de Padua, Mission ✦1 226 36.01 N 121.15 W
San Antonio de Tamanaco 246 9.41 N 66.03 W
San Antonio El Bravo 232 30.10 N 104.42 W
San Antonio Eloxochitlán 234 18.11 N 96.52 W
San Antonio Heights 228 34.10 N 117.40 W
San Antonio Mountain ∧ 200 36.52 N 106.02 W
San Antonio Nogalar 234 23.04 N 98.22 W
San Antonio Oeste 254 40.44 S 64.56 W
San Antonio Reservoir ⊜1 226 37.35 N 121.50 W
San Antonio Someyucan 286a 19.27 N 99.16 W
San Antonio Suchitepéquez 236 14.32 N 91.25 W
San Antonio Tecómitl ✦8 286a 19.13 N 98.59 W
San Antonio Ticino 266b 45.35 N 8.46 E
San Ardo 226 36.01 N 120.54 W
Sanaroa Island I 164 9.35 S 151.00 E
Sanary-sur-Mer 62 43.07 N 5.48 E
Sanatoga 285 40.15 N 75.36 W
Sanatoga Creek ≃ 285 40.14 N 75.36 W
Sanatorium 194 31.53 N 89.46 W
San Augustine 194 31.31 N 94.06 W
San Augustin Pass)(200 32.26 N 106.34 W
Sanaur 124 30.18 N 76.27 E
Sanāw 144 17.50 N 51.00 E
Sanāwad 120 22.11 N 76.04 E
Sanāwān 123 30.19 N 70.59 E
Sanbao, Zhg. 102 43.00 N 93.19 E
Sanbao, Zhg. 105 40.20 N 116.02 E
Sanbaoyingzi 104 41.34 N 120.56 E
San Bartolomeo in Galdo 68 41.24 N 15.01 E
San Basilio 71 39.32 N 9.11 E
San Benedetto, Alpe di ⁂ 66 43.53 N 11.43 E
San Benedetto del Tronto 66 42.57 N 13.53 E
San Benedetto in Alpe 66 43.59 N 11.41 E
San Benedetto Po 64 45.02 N 10.55 E
San Benedicto, Isla I 232 19.18 N 110.49 W
San Benigno Canavese 62 45.13 N 7.46 E
San Benito, Bol. 248 17.31 S 65.55 W
San Benito, Guat. 232 16.55 N 89.54 W
San Benito, Perú 248 7.26 S 78.56 W
San Benito, Tx., U.S. 196 26.07 N 97.37 W
San Benito □6 226 36.51 N 121.24 W
San Benito ≃ 226 36.53 N 121.34 W
San Benito Mountain ∧ 226 36.22 N 120.38 W
San Bernard ≃ 222 28.52 N 95.27 W
San Bernardino, Schw. 58 46.28 N 9.12 E
San Bernardino, Ca., U.S. 228 34.07 N 117.18 W
San Bernardino □6 228 34.40 N 117.17 W
San Bernardino, Passo del)(58 46.30 N 9.11 E
San Bernardino Mountains ⁂ 204 34.10 N 116.45 W
San Bernardino National Forest ♦ 280 34.12 N 117.38 W
San Bernardino Strait)(116 12.32 N 124.10 E
San Bernardo, Arg. 252 27.17 S 60.42 W
San Bernardo, Chile 252 33.36 S 70.43 W
San Bernardo, Méx. 232 25.59 N 105.33 W
San Bernardo, Isla I 236 11.32 N 85.06 W
San Bernardo, Islas de II 246 9.45 N 75.50 W
San Bernardo del Viento 246 9.21 N 75.57 W
Sanbe-yama ∧ 96 35.08 N 132.37 E
San Biagio 66 44.35 N 11.52 E
San Biagio di Callalta 64 45.41 N 12.22 E
San Biagio Platani 70 37.31 N 13.32 E
San Biagio Saracinisco 66 41.37 N 13.55 E
San Blas, Méx. 232 26.05 N 108.46 W
San Blas, Méx. 234 21.31 N 105.16 W
San Blas, Cape › 192 29.40 N 85.22 W
San Blas, Golfo de c 236 9.30 N 79.00 W
San Blas, Serranía De ⁂ 246 9.18 N 79.00 W
San Blas de los Sauces 252 28.24 S 67.05 W
San Bonifacio 64 45.24 N 11.16 E
San Borja 248 14.49 S 66.51 W
Sanborn, Ia., U.S. 198 43.10 N 95.39 W
Sanborn, Mn., U.S. 198 44.12 N 95.07 W
Sanborn, N.Y., U.S. 210 43.08 N 78.53 W
Sanborn, N.D., U.S. 198 46.56 N 98.13 W
San Bovio 266b 45.28 N 9.19 E
San Bruno 226 37.37 N 122.24 W
San Bruno, Point › 282 37.39 N 122.22 W
San Bruno Mountain ∧ 282 37.42 N 122.25 W
Sanbu 94 35.39 N 140.23 E
San Buenaventura, Bol. 248 14.28 S 67.35 W
San Buenaventura, Méx. 232 27.05 N 101.32 W
San Buenaventura — Ventura 228 34.17 N 119.18 W
San Buono 66 41.59 N 14.34 E
San Calogero 68 38.34 N 16.01 E
San Calogero, Monte ∧ 70 37.57 N 13.44 E
San Candido (Innichen) 64 46.44 N 12.17 E
Sancang 100 32.45 N 120.43 E
San Carlo 58 46.25 N 8.32 E
San Carlos, Arg. 252 27.45 S 55.54 W
San Carlos, Arg. 252 33.46 S 69.02 W
San Carlos, Arg. 252 25.56 S 65.56 W
San Carlos, Chile 252 36.25 S 71.58 W
San Carlos, Chile 286e 33.36 S 70.35 W
San Carlos, Méx. 232 29.01 N 100.51 W
San Carlos, Méx. 232 24.35 N 98.56 W
San Carlos, Nic. 236 11.07 N 84.47 W
San Carlos, Pan. 236 8.29 N 79.57 W
San Carlos, Para. 252 22.16 S 57.18 W
San Carlos, Pil. 116 10.30 N 123.25 E
San Carlos, Pil. 116 15.55 N 120.20 E
San Carlos, Az., U.S. 200 33.20 N 110.27 W
San Carlos, Ca., U.S. 226 37.29 N 122.15 W
San Carlos, Ur. 252 34.48 S 54.55 W
San Carlos, Ven. 246 9.40 N 68.36 W
San Carlos ≃, C.R. 236 10.47 N 84.12 W
San Carlos ≃, Az., U.S. 200 33.16 N 110.27 W
San Carlos ≃, Ven. 246 9.07 N 68.25 W
San Carlos, Riacho ≃ 252 22.51 S 57.51 W
San Carlos Airport ≋ 282 37.31 N 122.15 W
San Carlos Bay c 220 26.28 N 82.03 W
San Carlos Borromeo, Mission ✦1 226 36.34 N 121.55 W
San Carlos Centro 252 31.44 S 61.06 W
San Carlos de Bariloche 254 41.09 S 71.18 W
San Carlos de Bolívar 252 36.15 S 61.06 W
San Carlos de Chena 286e 33.35 S 70.44 W
San Carlos de Guaroa 246 3.44 N 73.14 W
San Carlos del Zulia 246 9.01 N 71.55 W
San Carlos de Río Negro 246 1.55 N 67.04 W
San Carlos Indian Reservation ✦4 200 33.23 N 110.09 W
San Carlos Reservoir ⊜1 200 33.13 N 110.24 W
San Carlos Viejo, Canal ≋ 286e 33.25 S 70.38 W
San Carpoforo Creek ≃ 226 35.47 N 121.19 W
San Casciano dei Bagni 66 42.52 N 11.53 E
San Casciano in Val di Pesa 66 43.39 N 11.11 E
San Cataldo, It. 68 40.23 N 18.17 E
San Cataldo, It. 70 37.29 N 13.59 E
San Cayetano 252 38.20 S 59.37 W
Sancergues 50 47.09 N 2.55 E
Sancerre 50 47.20 N 2.51 E
Sancerrois, Collines du ⁂2 50 47.25 N 2.45 E
San Cesario di Lecce 68 40.18 N 18.10 E
San Cesario sul Panaro 64 44.34 N 11.02 E
Sancey-le-Grand 58 47.18 N 6.35 E
Sancha, Zhg. 105 40.27 N 116.26 E
Sancha, Zhg. 106 31.52 N 119.06 E
Sancha ≃ 102 26.55 N 106.06 E
Sanchaba 107 30.19 N 104.14 E
Sanchahe 89 44.59 N 126.04 E
Sanchakou 105 39.47 N 117.19 E
Sanchang 106 31.54 N 121.15 E
Sanchazi 104 41.07 N 124.15 E
Sanchazicun 104 42.03 N 123.59 E
Sanchenglong 89 44.02 N 120.58 E
Sánchez 238 19.14 N 69.36 W
Sanchez Creek ≃ 222 32.36 N 97.50 W
Sánchez Magallanes 234 18.14 N 93.52 W
Sānchi 124 23.29 N 77.44 E
Sanchih 100 25.16 N 121.30 E
San Chirico Raparo 68 40.11 N 16.05 E
Sanch'ŏng 98 35.26 N 127.54 E
Sanchung 269d 25.04 N 121.30 E
Sanch'ungch'iao 269d 25.12 N 121.35 E
San Cipirello 70 37.58 N 13.10 E
San Cipriano Picentino 68 40.43 N 14.52 E
San Ciro de Acosta 234 21.38 N 99.49 W
San Clemente, Esp. 34 39.24 N 2.26 W
San Clemente, Ca., U.S. 228 33.25 N 117.36 W
San Clemente, Arroyo de ≃ 266d 41.20 N 2.00 E
San Clemente, Cerro ∧ 254 46.36 S 73.20 W
San Clemente a Casauria ✦1 66 42.14 N 13.55 E
San Clemente Island I 228 32.54 N 118.29 W
Sancoins 32 46.50 N 2.55 E
San Colombano al Lambro 62 45.11 N 9.29 E
San Cono 70 37.17 N 14.22 E
Sanco Point › 116 8.15 N 126.27 E
San Cosme 252 27.22 S 58.31 W
San Cosmo Albanese 68 39.35 N 16.25 E
San Costantino Albanese 68 40.02 N 16.18 E
San Cristóbal, Arg. 252 30.19 S 61.14 W
San Cristóbal, Cuba 240p 22.43 N 83.03 W
San Cristóbal, Rep. Dom. 238 18.25 N 70.06 W
San Cristóbal, Ven. 246 7.46 N 72.14 W
San Cristobal I 175e 10.36 S 161.45 E
San Cristóbal, Bahía c 232 27.23 N 114.38 W
San Cristóbal, Cerro ∧, Chile 286e 33.25 S 70.39 W
San Cristóbal, Cerro ∧, Perú 286d 12.02 S 77.01 W
San Cristóbal, Isla I 246a 0.50 S 89.26 W
San Cristóbal, Nevis — Saint Kitts and Nevis □1 238 17.20 N 62.45 W
San Cristóbal, Volcán ∧1 236 12.42 N 87.01 W
San Cristóbal de la Barranca 234 21.03 N 103.26 W
San Cristóbal de la Laguna 148 28.29 N 16.19 W
San Cristóbal de las Casas 234 16.45 N 92.38 W
San Cristóbal Totonicapán 236 14.55 N 91.26 W
San Cristobal Trench ✦1 14 11.15 S 162.45 E
San Cristóbal Verapaz 236 15.23 N 90.24 W
San Cristobal Wash V 200 32.47 N 113.44 W
San Croce, Monte ∧ 66 41.17 N 13.58 E
Sancti Spíritus 240p 21.56 N 79.27 W
Sancti Spíritus □4 240p 22.00 N 79.20 W
San Cugat, Riera de ≃ 266d 41.29 N 2.11 E
Sančursk 80 56.57 N 47.15 E
Sancy, Puy de ∧ 32 45.32 N 2.49 E
Sand, Dtsch. 56 48.32 N 7.55 E
Sand, Nor. 26 59.29 N 6.15 E
Sand ≃, Ab., Can. 184 54.22 N 111.05 W
Sand ≃, S. Afr. 156 22.25 S 30.05 E
Sand ≃, S. Afr. 158 28.05 S 26.25 E
Sanda, Nihon 96 34.53 N 135.14 E
Sanda, Nihon 268 35.39 N 139.21 E
Sandafā al-Fa'r 142 28.32 N 30.40 E
Sandai 112 1.15 S 110.31 E
Sanda Island I 44 55.18 N 5.34 W
Sandakan 112 5.50 N 118.07 E
Sandakan, Pelabuhan c 116 5.45 N 118.05 E
Sandal, Baie du c 175f 20.50 S 167.05 E
San Damián 248 12.02 S 76.24 W
San Damiano d'Asti 62 44.50 N 8.04 E
San Damiano Macra 62 44.29 N 7.16 E
Sândân 110 12.42 N 106.01 E
Sandan, Chāh ⊤4 128 28.59 N 63.27 E
Sandane 26 61.46 N 6.13 E
San Daniele del Friuli 64 46.09 N 13.00 E
Sandan-kyō ♦ 96 34.38 N 132.13 E
Sandanski 38 41.34 N 23.17 E
Sandaogang 89 46.08 N 130.05 E
Sandaogou, Zhg. 104 41.39 N 121.45 E
Sandaogou, Zhg. 105 39.33 N 115.27 E
Sandaohe 86 44.21 N 85.37 E
Sandaoliangzi 104 41.20 N 122.07 E
Sandaolingzi 104 40.58 N 124.08 E
Sandaozhen 89 47.25 N 126.25 E
Sandaré 150 14.42 N 10.18 W
Sandared 26 57.43 N 12.47 E
Sandarne 26 61.16 N 17.10 E
Sand Arroyo V 196 37.29 N 101.29 W
Sandata 80 46.16 N 41.46 E
Sandau 54 52.47 N 12.02 E
Sanday I 46 59.15 N 2.35 W
Sanday Sound c 46 59.11 N 2.31 W
Sandbach 44 53.09 N 2.22 W
Sandbank 46 55.59 N 4.58 W
Sandbanks Provincial Park ♦ 212 43.55 N 77.17 W
Sandbochum ✦8 263 51.40 N 7.41 E
Sand City 226 36.37 N 121.51 W
Sand Coulee 202 47.23 N 111.10 W
Sand Coulee Creek ≃ 202 47.27 N 111.18 W
Sand Creek ≃, U.S. 200 41.13 N 105.43 W
Sand Creek ≃, In., U.S. 218 39.03 N 85.51 W
Sand Creek ≃, Ks., U.S. 198 37.25 N 98.12 W
Sand Creek ≃, Mn., U.S. 190 45.56 N 92.39 W
Sand Creek ≃, Mt., U.S. 202 47.18 N 106.45 W
Sand Creek ≃, S.D., U.S. 198 44.02 N 98.05 W
Sand Creek ≃, Wy., U.S. 200 43.27 N 105.26 W
Sand Creek ≃, Wy., U.S. 200 41.02 N 107.52 W
Sand Creek ≃, Wy., U.S. 202 44.16 N 107.55 W
Sand Cut 220 26.56 N 80.35 W
Sande, Dtsch. 52 51.45 N 8.39 E
Sande, Dtsch. 52 53.30 N 8.01 E
Sandefjord 26 59.08 N 10.14 E
San Demetrio Corone 68 39.34 N 16.22 E
San Demetrio ne'Vestini 66 42.17 N 13.34 E
Sanders, Az., U.S. 200 35.12 N 109.19 W
Sanders, Ky., U.S. 218 38.39 N 84.56 W
Sandersdorf, Dtsch. 54 51.37 N 12.15 E
Sandersdorf, Dtsch. 60 48.54 N 11.37 E
Sandersleben 54 51.40 N 11.34 E
Sanderson 196 30.08 N 102.23 W
Sanderstead ✦8 260 51.20 N 0.05 W
Sanderston 168b 34.46 S 139.13 E
Sandersville, Ga., U.S. 192 32.58 N 82.48 W
Sandersville, Ms., U.S. 194 31.47 N 89.01 W
Sandeshkhali 126 22.22 N 88.53 E
Sandesneben 52 53.41 N 10.30 E
Sandfly Lake ⊜ 184 55.45 N 106.05 W
Sand Fork 188 38.54 N 80.45 W
Sandgate, Austl. 171a 27.20 S 153.05 E
Sandgate, Eng., U.K. 42 51.05 N 1.08 E
Sandhammaren › 26 55.23 N 14.12 E
Sandhamn 40 59.17 N 18.55 E
Sandhead 44 54.48 N 4.58 W
Sandheuwel 158 31.46 S 20.48 E
Sandhill, On., Can. 275b 43.50 N 79.49 W
Sand Hill, Ma., U.S. 207 42.13 N 70.44 W
Sand Hill ∧2 210 42.31 N 77.37 W
Sand Hill ≃ 198 47.36 N 96.52 W
Sand Hills ⁂2 198 42.00 N 101.00 W
Sandhorst 52 53.29 N 7.29 E
Sandhurst 42 51.19 N 0.48 W
Sāndi 124 27.18 N 79.57 E
Sandia 248 14.17 S 69.26 W
Sandia Crest ∧ 200 35.13 N 106.27 W
Sandia Indian Reservation ✦4 200 35.15 N 106.30 W
Sandian 100 30.56 N 114.48 E
San Diego, Ca., U.S. 228 32.42 N 117.09 W
San Diego, Tx., U.S. 196 27.45 N 98.14 W
San Diego □6 228 33.00 N 117.05 W
San Diego ≃, Cuba 240p 22.20 N 83.16 W
San Diego ≃, Ca., U.S. 204 32.46 N 117.13 W
San Diego, Cabo › 254 54.38 S 65.07 W
San Diego Aqueduct ≋1 228 32.55 N 116.55 W
San Diego Bay c 228 32.37 N 117.07 W
San Diego Creek ≃ 196 27.47 N 98.03 W
San Diego de Alcala, Mission ✦1 228 32.48 N 117.06 W
San Diego de la Unión 234 21.28 N 100.52 W
San Diego Naval Training Center ■ 228 32.44 N 117.13 W
San Dieguito ≃ 228 32.58 N 117.16 W
Sandies Creek ≃ 222 29.06 N 97.20 W
Sandıklı 130 38.28 N 30.17 E
Sandila 124 27.05 N 80.31 E
Sandilands 168b 34.31 S 137.46 E
Sandilands Village 240b 25.02 N 77.18 W
San Dimas 228 34.06 N 117.48 W
San Dimas Canyon V 280 34.10 N 117.46 W
San Dimas Reservoir ⊜1 280 34.09 N 117.43 W
San Dionisio, Nic. 236 12.45 N 85.51 W
San Dionisio, Pil. 116 11.16 N 123.06 E
Sand Island I, Mid. Is. 174g 28.12 N 177.23 W
Sand Island I, Hi., U.S. 229c 21.18 N 157.53 W
Sand Islet I 174g 28.16 N 177.23 W
Sandiway 262 53.14 N 2.36 W
Sand Key I 220 27.53 N 82.51 W
Sandkrug 54 52.53 N 13.52 E
Sandl 61 48.33 N 14.38 E
Sand Lake 210 42.38 N 73.32 W
Sand Lake ⊜, On., Can. 184 50.05 N 94.39 W
Sand Lake ⊜, On., Can. 212 44.34 N 76.15 W
Sand Lake ⊜, On., Can. 212 44.56 N 77.02 W
Sandling ∧ 64 47.39 N 13.43 E
Sandnes 26 58.51 N 5.44 E
Sandness 46a 60.17 N 1.38 W
Sandoa 152 9.41 S 22.52 E
Sandogora 80 58.12 N 40.59 E
Sandomierz 30 50.41 N 21.45 E
San Domingo Creek ≃ 226 38.07 N 120.40 W
San Domino, Isola I 66 42.07 N 15.29 E
Sandon 260 51.43 N 0.32 E
Sandoná 246 1.17 N 77.28 W
San Donaci 68 40.27 N 17.55 E
San Donà di Piave 64 45.38 N 12.34 E
San Donato di Lecce 68 40.15 N 18.10 E
San Donato di Ninea 68 39.42 N 16.03 E
San Donato Milanese 62 45.24 N 9.16 E
San Donato Val di Comino 66 41.42 N 13.49 E
Sandongo 152 15.30 S 21.28 E
San Dorligo della Valle 64 45.36 N 13.51 E
Sandouping 102 30.48 N 110.49 E
Sandoval 219 38.36 N 89.06 W
Sandovalina 255 22.27 S 51.44 W
Sandover ≃ 162 21.43 S 136.32 E
Sandovo 76 58.28 N 36.25 E
Sandoway 110 18.28 N 94.22 E
Sandown 42 50.39 N 1.09 W
Sandown Park Racecourse ♦, Austl. 274b 37.57 S 145.10 E
Sandown Park Race Course ♦, U.K. 260 51.22 N 0.22 W
Sand Point, Ak., U.S. 180 55.20 N 160.30 W
Sandpoint, Id., U.S. 202 48.16 N 116.33 W
Sandrancourt 261 49.02 N 1.39 E
Sandray I 46 56.53 N 7.30 W
Sandridge, Eng., U.K. 260 51.47 N 0.18 W
Sand Ridge, N.Y., U.S. 210 43.15 N 76.14 W
Sandrigo 64 45.39 N 11.36 E
Sandringham, Austl. 166 24.05 S 139.04 E
Sandringham, Austl. 169 37.57 S 145.00 E
Sandringham, Eng., U.K. 42 52.50 N 0.30 E
Sandringham ✦8 273d 26.09 S 28.07 E
Sandringham House ⊥ 42 52.50 N 0.30 E
Sand River Valley 158 28.28 S 29.33 E
Šandrovka 78 48.57 N 35.46 E
Sands Key I 220 25.30 N 80.11 W
Sandslån 26 63.01 N 17.47 E
Sandspit 182 53.14 N 131.50 W
Sands Point 276 40.51 N 73.43 W
Sands Point › 276 40.52 N 73.44 W
Sand Springs, Ok., U.S. 196 36.08 N 96.06 W
Sand Springs, Tx., U.S. 196 32.15 N 101.22 W
Sandspruit 158 27.18 S 29.48 E
Sandspruit ≃ 273d 26.07 S 28.04 E
Sandstedt 52 53.21 N 8.31 E
Sandston 208 37.31 N 77.18 W
Sandstone, Austl. 162 27.59 S 119.17 E
Sandstone, Mn., U.S. 190 46.07 N 92.52 W
Sandstone Creek ≃ 216 42.23 N 84.33 W
Sandu, Zhg. 100 29.46 N 120.12 E
Sandu, Zhg. 100 26.02 N 113.16 E
Sandu, Zhg. 100 29.12 N 114.40 E
Sandu, Zhg. 102 25.59 N 107.52 E
Sanduan 104 41.10 N 121.27 E
Sandu Ao c 100 26.35 N 119.40 E
Sandugan Point › 116 9.18 N 123.36 E
Sandumba 152 13.45 S 17.29 E
Sandun, Zhg. 106 31.52 N 121.50 E
Sandun, Zhg. 106 30.19 N 120.05 E
Sanduo 100 32.49 N 119.42 E
Sandusky, In., U.S. 218 39.25 N 85.29 W
Sandusky, Mi., U.S. 190 43.25 N 82.49 W
Sandusky, N.Y., U.S. 210 42.30 N 78.23 W
Sandusky, Oh., U.S. 214 41.26 N 82.42 W

Symbols in the index entries represent the broad categories identified in the key at the right. Symbols with superior numbers (⁂1) identify subcategories (see complete key on page *I · 1*).

Symbole im Register stellen die rechts im Schlüssel erklärten Kategorien dar. Symbole mit hochgestellten Ziffern (⁂1) bezeichnen Unterabteilungen einer Kategorie (vgl. vollständiger Schlüssel auf Seite *I · 1*).

Los símbolos incluídos en el texto del índice representan las grandes categorías identificadas con la clave a la derecha. Los símbolos con numeros en su parte superior (⁂1) identifican las subcategorías (véase la clave completa en la página *I · 1*).

Les symboles de l'index représentent les catégories indiquées dans la légende à droite. Les symboles suivis d'un indice (⁂1) représentent des souscatégories (voir légende complète à la page *I · 1*).

Os símbolos incluídos no texto do índice representam as grandes categorias identificadas com a chave à direita. Os símbolos com números em sua parte superior (⁂1) identificam as subcategorias (vejase a chave completa à página *I · 1*).

∧ Mountain	Berg	Montaña	Montagne	Montanha
⁂ Mountains	Gebirge	Montañas	Montagnes	Montanhas
)(Pass	Paß	Paso	Col	Passo
V Valley, Canyon	Tal, Cañon	Valle, Cañón	Vallée, Canyon	Vale, Canhão
≋ Plain	Ebene	Llano	Plaine	Planície
› Cape	Kap	Cabo	Cap	Cabo
I Island	Insel	Isla	Île	Ilha
II Islands	Inseln	Islas	Îles	Ilhas
⊥ Other Topographic Features	Andere Topographische Objekte	Otros Elementos Topográficos	Autres données topographiques	Outros acidentes topográficos

ESPAÑOL

Nombre	Página	Lat.°′	Long.°′ W = Oeste
Sandusky □[6]	214	41.21 N	83.07 W
Sandusky ≏	214	41.27 N	83.00 W
Sandusky Bay ⊂	214	41.27 N	82.52 W
Sand uul ∧	102	43.27 N	104.04 E
Sandvig	26	55.17 N	14.47 E
Sandvika	26	59.54 N	10.31 E
Sandviken	40	60.37 N	16.46 E
Sandweiler	56	49.37 N	6.13 E
Sandwich, Eng., U.K.	42	51.17 N	1.20 E
Sandwich, Il., U.S.	216	41.38 N	88.37 W
Sandwich, Ma., U.S.	207	41.45 N	70.29 W
Sandwich Bay ⊂, Nf., Can.	176	53.35 N	57.15 W
Sandwich Bay ⊂, Namibia	156	23.22 S	14.30 E
Sandwich del Sur, Islas → South Sandwich Islands II	18	57.45 S	26.30 W
Sandwick, B.C., Can.	182	49.42 N	124.59 W
Sandwick, Scot., U.K.	46a	60.00 N	1.15 W
Sand Wick ⊂	46a	60.42 N	0.52 W
Sandwīp	124	22.29 N	91.26 E
Sandwīp Channel ʮ	124	22.30 N	91.35 E
Sandwīp Island I	124	22.30 N	91.25 E
Sandy, Eng., U.K.	42	52.08 N	0.18 W
Sandy, Or., U.S.	224	45.23 N	122.15 W
Sandy, Pa., U.S.	214	41.07 N	78.47 W
Sandy, Ut,. U.S.	200	40.35 N	111.53 W
Sandy ≏, Me., U.S.	188	44.45 N	69.52 W
Sandy ≏, Or., U.S.	224	45.34 N	122.24 W
Sandy ≏, Va., U.S.	192	36.35 N	79.25 W
Sandy Bay ⊂, Nic.	236	14.28 N	83.16 W
Sandy Bay ⊂, Ma., U.S.	283	42.40 N	70.37 W
Sandy Bay Indian Reserve ◆[4]	184	50.33 N	98.40 W
Sandy Bay Mountain ∧	188	45.47 N	70.25 W
Sandy Beach	210	43.04 N	78.55 W
Sandy Branch ≏	284c	39.03 N	77.16 W
Sandy Cape ≻, Austl.	166	24.42 S	153.17 E
Sandy Cape ≻, Austl.	166	41.25 S	144.45 E
Sandy Creek	212	43.38 N	76.05 W
Sandy Creek ≏, Austl.	166	32.10 S	144.39 E
Sandy Creek ≏, U.S.	196	34.25 N	99.35 W
Sandy Creek ≏, U.S.	196	36.50 N	98.10 W
Sandy Creek ≏, Il., U.S.	219	39.34 N	90.35 W
Sandy Creek ≏, N.Y., U.S.	212	43.44 N	76.15 W
Sandy Creek ≏, N.Y., U.S.	212	43.20 N	77.55 W
Sandy Creek ≏, N.C., U.S.	192	36.08 N	78.02 W
Sandy Creek ≏, Oh., U.S.	214	40.38 N	81.26 W
Sandy Creek ≏, Pa., U.S.	214	41.18 N	79.51 W
Sandy Creek ≏, Tx., U.S.	196	30.34 N	98.26 W
Sandy Creek ≏, Tx., U.S.	222	29.02 N	96.33 W
Sandy Creek, East Branch ≏	210	43.17 N	78.03 W
Sandy Creek, North Branch ≏	212	43.51 N	75.58 W
Sandy Creek, West Branch ≏	210	43.17 N	78.03 W
Sandy Desert ◆[2]	128	28.40 N	62.30 E
Sandy Hook, Ct., U.S.	207	41.25 N	73.16 W
Sandy Hook, Ky., U.S.	192	38.05 N	83.07 W
Sandy Hook, Ms., U.S.	194	31.02 N	89.48 W
Sandy Hook ≻[2]	208	40.27 N	74.00 W
Sandy Hook Bay ⊂	276	40.26 N	74.03 W
Sandykači	128	36.33 N	62.34 E
Sandy Key I	220	25.02 N	81.01 W
Sandy Lake	214	41.20 N	80.04 W
Sandy Lake ⊜, Nf., Can.	186	49.16 N	57.00 W
Sandy Lake ⊜, On., Can.	184	53.02 N	93.00 W
Sandy Lake ⊜, On., Can.	212	44.33 N	78.24 W
Sandy Lick Creek ≏	214	41.09 N	79.05 W
Sandy Point ≻, Austl.	168b	34.16 S	138.09 E
Sandy Point ≻, Trin.	241r	11.09 N	60.50 W
Sandy Point ≻, R.I., U.S.	207	41.14 N	71.35 W
Sandy Point Town	238	17.22 N	62.50 W
Sandy Pond ⊜	283	42.26 N	71.19 W
Sandy Ridge	214	40.49 N	78.14 W
Sandy Springs	192	33.55 N	84.22 W
Sandyville, Md., U.S.	208	39.31 N	76.55 W
Sandyville, Oh., U.S.	214	40.38 N	81.23 W
Sandžak ◆[1]	38	43.10 N	19.30 E
San Eladio	258	34.46 S	59.11 W
San Elizario	200	31.35 N	106.16 W
San Emigdio Creek ≏	228	35.02 N	119.11 W
San Emilio	116	17.14 N	120.37 E
Sanen ≏	115a	8.23 S	113.37 E
San Enrique	252	35.47 S	60.22 W
San Estanislao	252	24.39 S	56.26 W
San Esteban	236	15.17 N	85.52 W
San Esteban, Isla I	232	28.42 N	112.36 W
San Esteban de Gormaz	34	41.35 N	3.12 W
San Fele	68	40.49 N	15.32 E
San Felice (Sankt Felix)	64	46.30 N	11.08 E
San Felice Circeo	66	41.14 N	13.05 E
San Felice sul Panaro	64	44.50 N	11.08 E
San Felipe, Chile	252	32.45 S	70.44 W
San Felipe, Col.	246	1.55 N	67.06 W
San Felipe, Méx.	232	31.00 N	114.52 W
San Felipe, Méx.	234	21.29 N	101.13 W
San Felipe, Pil.	116	15.04 N	120.04 E
San Felipe, Tx., U.S.	222	29.48 N	96.06 W
San Felipe, Ven.	246	10.20 N	68.44 W
San Felipe, Castillo de ⊥	236	15.39 N	89.01 W
San Felipe, Cayos de II	240p	21.58 N	83.30 W
San Felipe Aztatán	234	22.23 N	105.24 W
San Felipe Creek ≏	204	33.09 N	115.46 W
San Felipe de Vichayal	248	4.52 S	81.05 W
San Felipe Indian Reservation ◆[4]	200	35.26 N	106.26 W
San Felipe Jalapa de Díaz	234	18.04 N	96.32 W
San Felipe Nuevo Mercurio	232	24.22 N	102.06 W
San Felipe Pueblo	200	35.27 N	106.28 W
San Félix ≏	236	8.10 N	81.51 W
San Félix, Isla I	244	26.17 S	80.05 W
San Ferdinando di Puglia	68	41.18 N	16.04 E
San Fermín	196	26.20 N	104.49 W
San Fernando, Arg.	258	34.26 S	58.34 W
San Fernando, Chile	252	34.35 S	71.00 W
San Fernando, Esp.	34	36.28 N	6.12 W
San Fernando, Méx.	196	28.32 N	100.54 W
San Fernando, Méx.	200	31.16 N	110.36 W
San Fernando, Méx.	232	24.50 N	98.10 W
San Fernando, Méx.	234	16.52 N	93.13 W
San Fernando, Pil.	116	16.37 N	120.19 E
San Fernando, Pil.	116	12.30 N	123.46 E
San Fernando, Pil.	116	15.01 N	120.41 E
San Fernando, Trin.	241r	10.17 N	61.28 W
San Fernando, Ca., U.S.	228	34.16 N	118.26 W
San Fernando, Ven.	246	7.54 N	67.28 W
San Fernando □[5]	288	34.28 S	58.34 W

FRANÇAIS

Nom	Page	Lat.°′	Long.°′ W = Ouest
San Fernando, Aeródromo ⊠	288	34.27 S	58.35 W
San Fernando Airport ⊠	280	34.17 N	118.25 W
San Fernando Creek ≏	196	27.28 N	97.46 W
San Fernando de Atabapo	246	4.03 N	67.42 W
San Fernando de Henares	266a	40.26 N	3.32 W
San Fernando del Valle de Catamarca	252	28.28 S	65.47 W
San Fernando Mission ʊ[1]	280	34.16 N	118.28 W
San Fernando Point ≻	116	16.38 N	120.17 E
San Fernando Valley V	280	34.13 N	118.27 W
San Fili	68	39.20 N	16.09 E
San Filippo del Mela	70	38.10 N	15.17 E
Sånfjället ∧	26	62.17 N	13.32 E
Sånfjällets Nationalpark ♠	26	62.20 N	13.40 E
San Floriano	64	46.02 N	12.18 E
Sanford, Co., U.S.	200	37.15 N	105.54 W
Sanford, Fl., U.S.	220	28.48 N	81.16 W
Sanford, Me., U.S.	188	43.26 N	70.46 W
Sanford, Mi., U.S.	190	43.40 N	84.22 W
Sanford, N.C., U.S.	192	35.28 N	79.10 W
Sanford, Tx., U.S.	196	35.42 N	101.32 W
Sanford ≏	162	27.22 S	115.53 E
Sanford, Mount ∧	180	62.13 N	144.09 W
San Francesco, Convento ʊ[1], It.	66	42.28 N	12.45 E
San Francesco, Convento ʊ[1], It.	267a	42.03 N	12.46 E
San Francisco, Arg.	252	31.26 S	62.05 W
San Francisco, Col.	246	1.11 N	76.53 W
San Francisco, C.R.	236	9.49 N	85.15 W
San Francisco, El Sal.	236	13.42 N	88.06 W
San Francisco, Pan.	236	8.15 N	80.58 W
San Francisco, Pil.	116	8.30 N	125.56 E
San Francisco, Pil.	116	10.04 N	125.09 E
San Francisco, Ca., U.S.	226	37.46 N	122.25 W
San Francisco, Ca., U.S.	282	37.46 N	122.25 W
San Francisco □[6]	226	37.45 N	122.22 W
San Francisco ≏, Arg.	252	23.16 S	64.03 W
San Francisco ≏, U.S.	200	32.59 N	109.22 W
San Francisco, Arroyo ≏	288	34.43 S	58.19 W
San Francisco, Paso de)(	252	26.53 S	68.19 W
San Francisco, University of ʊ[2]	282	37.46 N	122.26 W
San Francisco Bay ⊂	226	37.43 N	122.17 W
San Francisco Creek ≏	196	29.53 N	102.19 W
San Francisco Culhuacán ◆[8]	286a	19.20 N	99.08 W
San Francisco de Borja	232	27.53 N	106.41 W
San Francisco de Horizonte	196	25.56 N	103.26 W
San Francisco de Lajas	234	23.07 N	105.07 W
San Francisco de la Paz	236	14.55 N	86.14 W
San Francisco del Chañar	252	29.47 S	63.56 W
San Francisco del Monte de Oro	252	32.36 S	66.08 W
San Francisco del Oro	232	26.52 N	105.51 W
San Francisco del Rincón	234	21.01 N	101.51 W
San Francisco de Macoris	238	19.18 N	70.15 W
San Francisco de Mostazal	252	33.59 S	70.43 W
San Francisco el Grande, Iglesia de ʊ[1]	266a	40.25 N	3.43 W
San Francisco International Airport ⊠	226	37.37 N	122.23 W
San Francisco Ixhuatán	234	16.22 N	94.29 W
San Francisco Libre	236	12.30 N	86.18 W
San Francisco Maritime State Historical Park ♠	282	37.48 N	122.27 W
San Francisco-Oakland Bay Bridge ◆[5]	282	37.48 N	122.22 W
San Francisco → São Francisco ≏	242	10.30 S	36.24 W
San Francisco State Fish and Game Refuge ◆[4]	282	37.35 N	122.25 W
San Francisco State University ʊ[2]	282	37.43 N	122.28 W
San Francisco Tlalcilalcalpa	234	19.18 N	99.46 W
San Francisco Tlaltenco ◆[8]	286a	19.17 N	99.01 W
San Francisco Zoological Gardens ♠	282	37.44 N	122.30 W
San Francisquito Creek ≏	282	37.28 N	122.07 W
San Franco, Cerro ∧	236	15.25 N	87.18 W
San Fratello	70	38.01 N	14.36 E
San Fratello ≏	70	38.02 N	14.34 E
Sanga, Ang.	152	11.07 S	15.22 E
Sanga, Burkina	150	11.10 N	0.10 E
Sanga, Mali	150	14.28 N	3.19 W
Sanga, Zaïre	154	7.02 S	28.21 E
San Gabriel, Ec.	246	0.36 N	77.49 W
San Gabriel, Ca., U.S.	228	34.05 N	118.06 W
San Gabriel ≏, Ca., U.S.	280	33.45 N	118.07 W
San Gabriel ≏, Tx., U.S.	222	30.46 N	97.01 W
San Gabriel, Isla I	258	34.28 S	57.54 W
San Gabriel, North Fork ≏, Ca., U.S.	280	34.15 N	117.52 W
San Gabriel, North Fork ≏, Tx., U.S.	196	30.38 N	97.41 W
San Gabriel, South Fork ≏	196	30.38 N	97.41 W
San Gabriel Arcangel, Mission ʊ[1]	280	34.06 N	118.06 W
San Gabriel Chilac	234	18.19 N	97.21 W
San Gabriel Dam ◆[6]	280	34.13 N	117.52 W
San Gabriel Mountains ⋀	228	34.20 N	118.00 W
San Gabriel Peak ∧	280	34.15 N	118.06 W
San Gabriel Reservoir ⊜[1]	228	34.13 N	117.51 W
Sangačal, mys ≻	84	40.07 N	49.30 E
San Galgano, Abbazia di ʊ[1]	66	43.10 N	11.10 E
Šangaly	24	61.08 N	43.19 E
Sangamankanda Point ≻	122	7.01 N	81.52 E
Sangamner	122	19.34 N	74.13 E
Sangamon □[6]	219	39.47 N	89.40 W
Sangamon ≏	194	40.07 N	90.20 W
Sangamon, South Fork ≏	219	39.48 N	89.32 W
Sanga Puitã	255	22.40 S	55.36 W
Sangar	74	63.55 N	127.31 E
Sangar Sarāy	120	34.24 N	70.38 E
Sangasanga-dalam	112	0.40 S	117.14 E

PORTUGUÊS

Nome	Página	Lat.°′	Long.°′ W = Oeste
Sanga Sanga Island I	116	5.04 N	119.47 E
Sangat	123	30.05 N	74.50 E
Sangatte	50	50.56 N	1.45 E
San Gavino Monreale	71	39.33 N	8.47 E
Sangay ∧[1]	246	2.00 S	78.20 W
Sangay, Parque Nacional ♠	246	1.50 S	78.20 W
Sangayán, Isla I	248	13.51 S	76.28 W
Sang Bast	128	35.59 N	59.46 E
Sangbé	152	6.03 N	12.28 E
Sangchris Lake ⊜[1]	219	39.35 N	89.30 W
Sangchris Lake State Park ♠	219	39.38 N	89.28 W
Sangchungshih	100	25.04 N	121.29 E
Sangeang, Pulau I	115b	8.12 S	119.04 E
Sang-e Māsheh	120	33.08 N	67.27 E
San Gemini	66	42.37 N	12.33 E
San Genesio Atesino	64	46.32 N	11.20 E
Sangenjaya ◆[8]	268	35.38 N	139.40 E
Sanger, Ca., U.S.	226	36.42 N	119.33 W
Sanger, Tx., U.S.	196	33.21 N	97.10 W
Sangerhausen	54	51.28 N	11.17 E
San Germán	240m	18.05 N	67.03 W
San Germano Vercellese	62	45.21 N	8.15 E
San Geronimo	226	38.01 N	122.39 W
San Gerónimo, Arroyo ≏	258	33.57 S	56.05 W
Sangerville	188	45.09 N	69.21 W
Sanggan ≏	90	40.21 N	115.21 E
Sanggar, Teluk ⊂	115b	8.20 S	118.18 E
Sanggau	112	0.08 N	110.36 E
Sangge-ri ◆[8]	271b	37.41 N	127.05 E
Sanggin Dalai	102	38.11 N	105.17 E
Sanggona	112	3.52 S	121.46 E
Sangha □[5], Centraf.	152	3.35 N	16.20 E
Sangha □[5], Congo	152	1.00 N	15.30 E
Sangha ≏	152	1.13 S	16.49 E
Sanghar	120	26.02 N	68.57 E
San Giacomo (Sankt Jakob in Pfitsch)	64	46.57 N	11.36 E
San Giacomo Filippo	58	46.20 N	9.21 E
Sangihe, Kepulauan II	112	3.00 N	125.30 E
Sangihe, Pulau I	112	3.35 N	125.32 E
Sangijn dalaj nuur ⊜	88	49.17 N	99.00 E
San Gil	246	6.33 N	73.08 W
Sangilen, chrebet ⋀	88	50.18 N	96.30 E
San Gimignano	66	43.28 N	11.02 E
San Ginesio	66	43.06 N	13.19 E
San Gion	58	46.38 N	8.50 E
San Giorgio	68	40.51 N	14.23 E
San Giorgio Canavese	62	45.20 N	7.48 E
San Giorgio della Richinvelda	64	46.03 N	12.52 E
San Giorgio del Sannio	68	41.04 N	14.51 E
San Giorgio di Lomellina	62	45.10 N	8.47 E
San Giorgio di Nogaro	64	45.50 N	13.13 E
San Giorgio di Piano	64	44.39 N	11.22 E
San Giorgio Ionico	68	40.27 N	17.23 E
San Giorgio la Molara	68	41.16 N	14.55 E
San Giorgio Lucano	68	40.07 N	16.23 E
San Giorgio Monferrato	62	45.07 N	8.23 E
San Giorgio Morgeto	68	38.23 N	16.06 E
San Giorgio Piacentino	62	44.57 N	9.44 E
San Giorgio su Legnano	266b	45.34 N	8.55 E
San Giovanni (Sankt Johann)	64	46.38 N	11.44 E
San Giovanni al Timavo (Sankt Johann in Ahrn)	64	46.58 N	11.57 E
San Giovanni a Piro	68	40.03 N	15.27 E
San Giovanni-Bianco	58	45.52 N	9.39 E
San Giovanni d'Asso	66	43.09 N	11.35 E
San Giovanni Gemini	70	37.38 N	13.39 E
San Giovanni Ilarione	64	45.30 N	11.15 E
San Giovanni in Croce	64	45.05 N	10.22 E
San Giovanni in Fiore	68	39.15 N	16.42 E
San Giovanni in Laterano ʊ[1]	267a	41.53 N	12.30 E
San Giovanni in Persiceto	64	44.38 N	11.11 E
San Giovanni la Punta	70	37.35 N	15.07 E
San Giovanni Lupatoto	64	45.23 N	11.03 E
San Giovanni Rotondo	68	41.42 N	15.44 E
San Giovanni Suergiu	71	39.07 N	8.31 E
San Giovanni Valdarno	66	43.34 N	11.32 E
San Giuliano, Lago di ⊜	68	40.37 N	16.30 E
San Giuliano Milanese	266b	45.24 N	9.17 E
San Giuliano Terme	66	43.46 N	10.26 E
San Giuseppe, It.	62	44.22 N	8.18 E
San Giuseppe, It.	70	37.58 N	13.11 E
San Giuseppe Vesuviano	68	40.50 N	14.30 E
San Giustino	66	43.33 N	12.10 E
San Giusto, Aeroporto di ⊠	66	43.11 N	10.21 E
San Giusto Canavese	62	45.19 N	7.49 E
Sangju	98	36.26 N	128.09 E
Sangkapura	115a	5.52 S	112.40 E
Sângkê ≏	110	13.13 N	103.41 E
Sangkhai	110	14.39 N	103.52 E
Sangkulirang	112	0.59 N	117.58 E
Sāngla	123	31.43 N	73.23 E
Sangley Point ≻	269f	14.30 N	120.55 E
Sāngli	122	16.52 N	74.34 E
Sanglin	100	27.54 N	114.46 E
Sangluoshu	98	37.31 N	117.43 E
Sangmélima	152	2.56 N	11.59 E
Sangngagqoiling	120	28.33 N	93.00 E
Sangnyŏng-ni	98	38.14 N	126.54 E
Sango	270	34.36 N	135.42 E
San Godenzo	66	43.55 N	11.37 E
Sāngole	122	17.26 N	75.12 E
Sangolquí	246	0.19 S	78.27 W
San Gorgonio Mountain ∧	204	34.06 N	116.50 W
San Gottardo, Passo del)(	58	46.33 N	8.34 E
Sangou	98	41.02 N	118.11 E
Sangre de Cristo Mountains ⋀	200	37.30 N	105.15 W
San Gregorio, Arg.	252	34.19 S	62.02 W
San Gregorio, It.	66	42.19 N	13.29 E
San Gregorio, Ca., U.S.	226	37.19 N	122.23 W
San Gregorio, Ur.	252	32.37 S	55.40 W
San Gregorio, Ur.	258	33.57 S	56.45 W
San Gregorio ◆[8]	286a	19.15 N	99.03 W
San Gregorio, Arroyo ≏	258	33.59 S	56.50 W
San Gregorio Creek ≏	282	37.19 N	122.25 W
San Gregorio Magno	68	40.39 N	15.24 E
San Gregorio State Beach ♠	282	37.19 N	122.24 W
Sangre Grande	241r	10.35 N	61.07 W
Sangro ≏	66	42.14 N	14.32 E
Sangrūr	123	30.14 N	75.50 E
Sangsang	120	29.25 N	86.40 E
Sangshuyuan	86	42.23 N	88.30 E
Sangsues, Lac aux ⊜	190	46.29 N	77.57 W
Sangtuda	85	38.04 N	69.04 E
Sanguandian	100	31.19 N	118.05 E
Sanguang	106	31.47 N	121.16 E
Sanguanmiao	100	32.25 N	114.04 E
Sanguanyingzi	104	41.39 N	120.44 E
Sangudo	182	53.53 N	114.54 W
Sangue, Rio do ≏	248	11.01 S	58.39 W
Sangüesa	34	42.35 N	1.17 W
Sanguinetto	64	45.11 N	11.09 E
Sanguliu	104	40.45 N	124.14 E
Sāngurli	272c	18.56 N	73.07 E
Sangutane ≏	156	24.07 S	33.47 E
Sangvor, Taj.	85	38.47 N	71.12 E
Sangvor, Taj.	85	38.53 N	71.06 E
Sangwa	154	5.30 S	26.00 E
Sangya	120	30.52 N	91.40 E
Sangyuanbao	105	40.15 N	115.32 E
Sangyuanbu	106	31.37 N	118.53 E
Sangyuanzhen	107	30.30 N	103.26 E
Sangzhi	102	29.18 N	110.02 E
Sangzidian	98	36.46 N	116.55 E
Sanhe, Zhg.	100	24.24 N	116.34 E
Sanhe, Zhg.	105	39.59 N	117.04 E
Sanhechang, Zhg.	102	31.22 N	106.48 E
Sanhechang, Zhg.	107	30.04 N	105.01 E
Sanhecun	98	42.28 N	129.39 E
Sanheji	100	32.42 N	117.55 E
Sanhekou	106	31.50 N	120.08 E
Sanhetun	104	42.38 N	123.38 E
Sanhezhan	89	52.34 N	126.02 E
Sanhezhen	100	31.30 N	117.14 E
Sanhezhuang	105	40.04 N	116.18 E
San Hipólito, Punta ≻	232	26.59 N	113.59 W
Sanhsient'ai I	100	23.08 N	121.25 E
Sanhsing	100	24.40 N	121.39 E
Sanhu	100	27.55 N	115.24 E
Sanhui, Zhg.	107	30.06 N	106.36 E
Sanhui, Zhg.	107	29.57 N	105.53 E
Sanhūr	142	29.25 N	30.46 E
Sanhūr al-Madīnah	142	31.07 N	30.44 E
Sani	100	24.25 N	120.46 E
Sanibel	220	26.26 N	82.01 W
Sanibel Island I	220	26.27 N	82.06 W
Sānī Bherī ≏	124	28.42 N	82.16 E
San Ignacio, Arg.	252	27.16 S	55.32 W
San Ignacio, C.R.	236	9.48 N	84.09 W
San Ignacio, Hond.	236	14.38 N	87.02 W
San Ignacio, Méx.	232	27.27 N	112.51 W
San Ignacio, Méx.	234	23.12 N	100.12 W
San Ignacio, Méx.	234	23.55 N	106.25 W
San Ignacio, Para.	252	26.52 S	57.03 W
San Ignacio, Perú	248	5.08 S	78.59 W
San Ignacio, Isla I	232	25.25 N	108.54 W
San Ignacio, Laguna ⊜	232	26.54 N	113.13 W
San Ignacio de Moxo	248	14.53 S	65.36 W
San Ignacio de Velasco	248	16.23 S	60.59 W
San Ildefonso, Cape ≻	116	16.02 N	121.59 E
San Ildefonso, Cerro ∧	236	15.31 N	88.17 W
San Ildefonso Indian Reservation ◆[4]	200	35.53 N	106.08 W
San Ildefonso o La Granja	34	40.54 N	4.00 W
San Ildefonso Peninsula ≻[1]	116	16.10 N	122.05 E
San Ildefonso Villa Alta	234	17.21 N	96.09 W
San'in-kaigan-kokuritsu-kōen ♠	96	35.38 N	134.38 E
Sanino	265a	59.50 N	29.54 E
Sani Pass)(	158	29.34 S	29.19 E
San Isidro, Arg.	252	28.27 S	65.44 W
San Isidro, Arg.	258	34.27 S	58.30 W
San Isidro, C.R.	236	9.22 N	83.42 W
San Isidro, Méx.	200	31.31 N	106.18 W
San Isidro, Nic.	236	12.56 N	86.12 W
San Isidro, Perú	286d	12.07 S	77.03 W
San Isidro, Pil.	116	11.24 N	124.21 E
San Isidro, Tx., U.S.	196	26.42 N	98.27 W
San Isidro □[5]	288	34.29 S	58.33 W
San Isidro el Real, Catedral de ʊ[1]	266a	40.25 N	3.42 W
Sanitaria Springs	210	42.09 N	75.46 W
Sanitatas	156	18.11 S	12.47 E
Sanitz	54	54.04 N	12.22 E
San Jacinto, Col.	246	9.50 N	75.08 W
San Jacinto, Méx.	196	25.29 N	103.44 W
San Jacinto, Pil.	116	12.34 N	123.44 E
San Jacinto, Ca., U.S.	228	33.47 N	116.57 W
San Jacinto □[6]	222	30.35 N	95.10 W
San Jacinto ≏, Ca., U.S.	228	33.43 N	117.16 W
San Jacinto ≏, Tx., U.S.	222	29.46 N	95.05 W
San Jacinto, East Fork ≏	222	30.05 N	95.09 W
San Jacinto, West Fork ≏	222	30.02 N	95.15 W
San Jacinto Monument ⊥	222	29.45 N	95.01 W
San Jacinto Peak ∧	204	33.49 N	116.41 W
San Jacinto Valley V	228	33.50 N	117.05 W
Sanjahā	142	30.50 N	31.38 E
San Javier, Arg.	252	27.53 S	55.08 W
San Javier, Arg.	252	30.35 S	59.57 W
San Javier, Bol.	248	14.34 S	64.42 W
San Javier, Bol.	248	16.20 S	62.38 W
San Javier, Méx.	196	26.16 N	99.27 W
San Javier, Ur.	252	32.41 S	58.08 W
San Javier ≏	252	31.30 S	60.20 W
San Javier de Loncomilla	252	35.35 S	71.45 W
Sanjāwi	120	30.17 N	68.21 E
Sanje	154	0.46 S	31.30 E
San Jeronimito	234	17.33 N	101.20 W
San Jerónimo, Guat.	236	15.03 N	90.12 W
San Jerónimo, Méx.	234	17.08 N	100.28 W
San Jerónimo Norte	252	31.33 S	61.05 W
Sanjiadian, Zhg.	105	40.09 N	116.36 E
Sanjiadian, Zhg.	105	39.58 N	116.06 E
Sanjiadian, Zhg.	105	39.22 N	115.58 E
Sanjiang, Zhg.	102	25.42 N	109.23 E
Sanjiang, Zhg.	107	29.33 N	104.03 E
Sanjiangzhen	107	30.31 N	103.48 E
Sanjiaocheng	102	36.47 N	104.40 E
Sanjiaopao	104	41.22 N	122.17 E
Sanjiaoshancun	104	40.42 N	122.49 E
Sanjiazhen	107	30.17 N	105.32 E
Sanjiazi, Zhg.	104	42.02 N	122.20 E
Sanjiazi, Zhg.	104	41.53 N	121.42 E
Sanjiazi, Zhg.	104	40.42 N	123.16 E
Sanjiazi, Zhg.	104	40.54 N	121.59 E
Sanjiazi, Zhg.	104	42.33 N	121.38 E
Sanjiaziyingzi	104	41.52 N	120.49 E
Sanjie, Zhg.	100	32.35 N	118.08 E
Sanjie, Zhg.	102	25.01 N	101.02 E
Sanjō	92	37.37 N	138.57 E
San Joaquín, Bol.	248	13.04 S	64.49 W
San Joaquín, Chile	286e	33.30 S	70.37 W
San Joaquín, Para.	252	24.57 S	56.07 W
San Joaquin, Pil.	116	10.35 N	122.08 E
San Joaquin, Ca., U.S.	226	36.36 N	120.11 W
San Joaquin □[6]	226	37.57 N	121.17 W
San Joaquín ≏, Bol.	248	13.08 S	63.41 W
San Joaquin ≏, Ca., U.S.	226	38.03 N	121.50 W
San Joaquin, Middle Fork ≏	226	37.32 N	119.11 W
San Joaquin, North Fork ≏	226	37.32 N	119.11 W
San Joaquin, South Fork ≏	226	37.26 N	119.14 W
San Joaquin Valley V	204	36.50 N	120.10 W
San Jon	196	35.06 N	103.19 W
San Jorge, Arg.	252	31.54 S	61.52 W
San Jorge, El Sal.	236	13.25 N	88.21 W
San Jorge, Nic.	236	11.27 N	85.48 W
San Jorge ≏	246	9.07 N	74.44 W
San Jorge, Bahía de ⊂	200	31.12 N	113.15 W
San Jorge, Cabo ≻	254	45.47 S	67.21 W
San Jorge, Canal de → Saint George's Channel ʮ	28	52.00 N	6.00 W
San Jorge, Golfo ⊂	254	46.00 S	67.00 W
San Jorge Island I	175e	8.27 S	159.35 E
San José, Arg.	252	27.46 S	55.47 W
San José, C.R.	236	9.56 N	84.05 W
San José, Méx.	196	28.16 N	100.15 W
San Jose, N. Mar. Is.	174n	15.09 N	145.43 E
San José, Para.	252	25.33 S	56.45 W
San Jose, Pil.	116	10.45 N	121.56 E
San Jose, Pil.	116	15.48 N	121.00 E
San Jose, Pil.	116	12.27 N	121.03 E
San Jose, Ca., U.S.	226	37.20 N	121.53 W
San Jose, Ca., U.S.	282	37.20 N	121.53 W
San Jose, Il., U.S.	194	40.18 N	89.36 W
San Jose, N.M., U.S.	200	35.23 N	105.28 W
San José, Ven.	286c	10.34 N	66.57 W
San José □[4]	236	9.40 N	84.00 W
San José □[5]	258	34.15 S	56.45 W
San José □[7]	286b	22.57 N	82.14 W
San Jose ≏, B.C., Can.	182	52.14 N	122.15 W
San José ≏, Ur.	258	34.38 S	56.29 W
San Jose, Arroyo ≏	282	38.03 N	122.30 W
San José, Golfo ⊂	254	42.20 S	64.18 W
San José, Isla I, Méx.	232	25.00 N	110.38 W
San José, Isla I, Pan.	246	8.15 N	79.07 W
San José, Laguna ⊂	240m	18.25 N	66.01 W
San Jose, Mission ʊ[1]	282	37.32 N	121.55 W
San Jose, Rio ≏	200	34.52 N	107.01 W
San José Ayuquila	234	17.58 N	97.57 W
San José Batuc	232	29.15 N	109.44 W
San José Buena Vista	236	13.49 N	90.19 W
San Jose Creek ≏	280	34.01 N	118.03 W
San José de Aura	196	27.34 N	101.23 W
San José de Bácum	232	27.32 N	110.09 W
San Jose de Buan	116	12.02 N	125.01 E
San José de Chiquitos	248	17.51 S	60.47 W
San José de Copán	236	14.54 N	88.44 W
San José de Feliciano	252	30.23 S	58.45 W
San José de Galipán	286c	10.35 N	66.54 W
San José de Galipán, Quebrada ≏	286c	10.37 N	66.54 W
San José de Gracia	234	20.40 N	102.35 W
San José de Guanipa	246	8.54 N	64.09 W
San José de Guaribe	246	9.52 N	65.48 W
San José de Iturbide	234	21.00 N	100.23 W
San José de Jáchal	252	30.14 S	68.45 W
San José de la Esquina	252	33.06 S	61.42 W
San José de la Parilla	234	23.44 N	104.07 W
San José de la Popa	196	26.10 N	100.47 W
San José de las Flores	234	17.20 N	95.24 W
San José de las Lajas	240p	22.58 N	82.09 W
San José de las Raíces	232	24.35 N	100.14 W
San José del Cabo	232	23.03 N	109.41 W
San José del Guaviare	246	2.35 N	72.38 W
San José de Llanetes	234	22.55 N	103.16 W
San José de los Molinos	248	13.57 S	75.41 W
San José de Lourdes	234	23.18 N	103.01 W
San José del Valle	234	23.20 N	98.24 W
San José de Mayo	258	34.20 S	56.42 W
San José de Ocuné	246	4.15 N	70.20 W
San José de Sisa	248	6.37 S	76.39 W
San José de Tiznados	246	9.23 N	67.33 W
San Jose Hills ⋀[2]	280	34.04 N	117.49 W
San Jose Island I	196	28.10 N	96.45 W
San Jose Municipal Airport ⊠	226	37.22 N	121.56 W
San Jose State University ʊ[2]	282	37.20 N	121.53 W
San Juan, Arg.	252	31.32 S	68.31 W
San Juan, Guat.	236	15.52 N	88.53 W
San Juan, Méx.	196	29.34 N	104.36 W
San Juan, Perú	248	15.21 S	75.10 W
San Juan, Pil.	116	13.50 N	121.24 E
San Juan, Pil.	116	16.40 N	120.20 E
San Juan, Pil.	116	8.25 N	126.20 E
San Juan, P.R.	240m	18.28 N	66.07 W
San Juan □[4]	252	31.00 S	69.00 W
San Juan □[6]	224	48.34 N	122.59 W
San Juan ≏, Arg.	252	32.17 S	67.22 W
San Juan ≏, B.C., Can.	224	48.34 N	124.24 W
San Juan ≏, Col.	246	4.03 N	77.27 W
San Juan ≏, Méx.	232	26.22 N	98.51 W
San Juan ≏, Méx.	234	17.59 N	99.47 W
San Juan ≏, Méx.	234	18.36 N	95.40 W
San Juan ≏, N.A.	236	10.56 N	83.42 W
San Juan ≏, Perú	248	13.27 S	76.11 W
San Juan ≏, Pil.	269f	14.35 N	121.01 E
San Juan ≏, S.A.	246	1.11 N	78.33 W
San Juan ≏, U.S.	200	37.18 N	110.28 W
San Juan ≏, Ur.	258	34.17 S	57.58 W
San Juan ≏, Ven.	246	10.14 N	62.38 W
San Juan, Bahía de ⊂	240m	18.27 N	66.07 W
San Juan, Cabezas de ≻	240m	18.23 N	65.37 W
San Juan, Cabo ≻, Arg.	254	54.44 S	63.44 W
San Juan, Cabo ≻, Gui. Ecu.	152	1.08 N	9.23 E
San Juan, Embalse de ⊜[1]	34	40.30 N	4.15 W
San Juan, Pasaje de ʮ	240m	18.24 N	65.37 W
San Juan, Pico ∧	240p	21.59 N	80.09 W
San Juan, Port ⊂	224	48.34 N	124.27 W
San Juan, Punta ≻	174z	27.03 S	109.22 W
San Juan Basin ≚[1]	200	36.15 N	108.20 W
San Juan Bautista, Méx.	196	26.58 N	101.24 W
San Juan Bautista, Para.	252	26.38 S	57.10 W
San Juan Bautista, Ca., U.S.	226	36.51 N	121.32 W
San Juan Bautista State Historical Park ♠	226	36.51 N	121.31 W
San Juan Capistrano	228	33.30 N	117.39 W
San Juan Capistrano Mission ʊ[1]	228	33.31 N	117.40 W
San Juan Cotzal	236	15.26 N	91.01 W
San Juan Creek ≏, Ca., U.S.	226	35.40 N	120.22 W
San Juan Creek ≏, Ca., U.S.	228	33.28 N	117.41 W
San Juan de Abajo	234	20.48 N	105.13 W
San Juan de Aragón, Bosque ♠	286a	19.28 N	99.04 W
San Juan de Aragón, Zoológico de ♠	286a	19.28 N	99.05 W
San Juan de Colón	246	8.02 N	72.16 W
San Juan de Dios	286c	10.35 N	66.55 W
San Juan de Guadalupe	232	24.38 N	102.44 W
San Juan [de la Maguana]	238	18.48 N	71.14 W
San Juan de la Vega	234	20.38 N	100.46 W
San Juan del César	246	10.46 N	73.01 W
San Juan del Monte	269f	14.36 N	121.02 E
San Juan del Norte	236	10.55 N	83.42 W
San Juan del Oro ≏	248	21.02 S	65.19 W
San Juan de los Cayos	246	11.10 N	68.25 W
San Juan de los Lagos	234	21.15 N	102.18 W
San Juan de los Lagos ≏	234	21.18 N	102.33 W
San Juan de los Morros	246	9.55 N	67.21 W
San Juan del Río, Méx.	232	24.47 N	104.27 W
San Juan del Río, Méx.	234	20.23 N	100.00 W
San Juan del Salado	234	23.18 N	101.56 W
San Juan del Sur	236	11.15 N	85.52 W
San Juan de Lurigancho	286d	11.59 S	77.01 W
San Juan de Micay ≏	246	3.05 N	77.32 W
San Juan de Miraflores	286d	12.11 S	76.57 W
San Juan de Payara	246	7.39 N	67.36 W
San Juan de Sabinas	196	27.55 N	101.18 W
San Juan Evangelista	234	17.54 N	95.08 W
San Juan Guichicovi	234	16.58 N	95.06 W
San Juanico	232	26.15 N	112.24 W
San Juanillo	236	10.02 N	85.44 W
San Juan Indian Reservation ◆[4]	200	36.03 N	106.04 W
San Juan Island I	224	48.32 N	123.05 W
San Juan Island National Historical Park ♠	224	48.28 N	123.00 W
San Juan Islands II	224	48.36 N	122.50 W
San Juanito, Isla I	234	21.43 N	106.38 W
San Juan Ixcaquixtla	234	18.27 N	97.49 W
San Juan Ixtayopan ◆[8]	286a	19.14 N	99.00 W
San Juan Lachao	234	16.14 N	97.09 W
San Juan Mazatlán	234	17.02 N	95.25 W
San Juan Mountains ⋀	200	37.35 N	107.10 W
San Juan Nepomuceno, Col.	246	9.57 N	75.05 W
San Juan Nepomuceno, Para.	252	26.06 S	55.58 W
San Juan Peyotán	234	22.24 N	104.21 W
San Juan Quiahije	234	16.17 N	97.20 W
San Juan Sacatepéquez	236	14.43 N	90.39 W
San Juan Teita	234	17.05 N	97.25 W
San Juan y Martínez	240p	22.16 N	83.50 W
San Julián, Méx.	234	21.01 N	102.10 W
San Julian, Pil.	116	11.45 N	125.27 E
San Julian, Quebrada ≏	286c	10.37 N	66.51 W
San Justo, Arg.	252	30.47 S	60.35 W
San Justo, Arg.	258	34.40 S	58.33 W
San Justo, Aeródromo ⊠	288	34.44 S	58.36 W
Sankanbiaiwa ∧	150	8.56 N	10.48 W
Sankarani ≏	150	12.01 N	8.19 W
Sankarankovil	122	9.10 N	77.33 E
Sankarpur	272b	22.51 N	88.27 E
Sānkdaha	126	22.46 N	89.10 E
Sankeng	100	23.36 N	112.48 E
Sankertown	214	40.28 N	78.35 W
Sankeshu	104	42.38 N	122.25 E
Sankeshwar	122	16.16 N	74.29 E
Sankey Brook ≏	262	53.22 N	2.38 W
Sankh ≏	124	22.15 N	84.48 E
Sankheda	120	22.10 N	73.35 E
Sankosh ≏	124	26.48 N	89.56 E
Sānkra	120	21.18 N	82.39 E
Sānkrāil	272b	22.34 N	88.14 E
Sankt Aegyd am Neuwalde	61	47.52 N	15.35 E
Sankt Andrä	61	46.46 N	14.49 E
Sankt Andrä vor dem Hagenthale	264b	48.19 N	16.13 E
Sankt Andreasberg	54	51.43 N	10.31 E
Sankt Anton am Arlberg	58	47.08 N	10.16 E
Sankt Antönien	58	46.58 N	9.49 E
Sankt Augustin	56	50.40 N	7.16 E
Sankt Bartholomä ʊ[1]	64	47.32 N	12.58 E
Sankt Blasien	58	47.46 N	8.07 E
Sankt Christopher-Nevis → Saint Kitts and Nevis □[1]	238	17.20 N	62.45 W
Sankt Egidien	54	50.47 N	12.36 E
Sankt Florian ʊ[1]	61	48.12 N	14.23 E
Sankt Gallen, Öst.	61	47.41 N	14.37 E
Sankt Gallen, Schw.	58	47.25 N	9.23 E
Sankt Gallen □[3]	58	47.10 N	9.08 E
Sankt Gallenkirch	58	47.01 N	9.59 E
Sankt Georgen, Dtsch.	58	48.07 N	8.20 E
Sankt Georgen, Dtsch.	58	47.59 N	7.47 E
Sankt Georgen, Öst.	61	46.43 N	14.55 E
Sankt Georgen im Attergau	64	47.56 N	13.29 E
Sankt Gertraud → Santa Gertrude	64	46.29 N	10.53 E
Sankt Gertrud ◆[8]	54	53.52 N	10.47 E
Sankt Gilgen	64	47.46 N	13.22 E
Sankt Goar	56	50.09 N	7.43 E
Sankt Goarshausen	56	50.09 N	7.44 E
Sankt Helena → Saint Helena □[2]	8	15.57 S	5.42 W
Sankt Hubert	56	51.23 N	6.26 E
Sankt Ingbert	56	49.17 N	7.06 E
Sankt Jakob im Lesachtal	64	46.41 N	12.56 E
Sankt Jakob im Rosental	61	46.33 N	14.03 E
Sankt Jakob in Defereggen	64	46.55 N	12.20 E
Sankt Jakob → San Giacomo	64	46.57 N	11.36 E
Sankt Johann am Tauern	61	47.22 N	14.29 E
Sankt Johann im Pongau	64	47.21 N	13.12 E
Sankt Johann im Walde	64	46.54 N	12.37 E
Sankt Johann in Tirol	64	47.31 N	12.26 E
Sankt Johann → San Giovanni	64	46.38 N	11.44 E
Sankt Kanzian	61	46.37 N	14.34 E
Sankt Leonhard Am Forst	61	48.09 N	15.17 E
Sankt Leonhard im Pitztal	58	47.04 N	10.51 E
Sankt Leonhard → San Leonardo	64	46.49 N	11.15 E
Sankt Lorenz ◆[8]	52	53.51 N	10.40 E
Sankt Lorenzen im Lesachtal	64	46.42 N	12.47 E
Sankt Lorenzen → San Lorenzo di Sebato	64	46.47 N	11.54 E
Sankt Lorenz-Golf → Saint Lawrence, Gulf of ⊂	186	48.00 N	62.00 W
Sankt Lorenz-Insel → Saint Lawrence Island I	180	63.30 N	170.30 W
Sankt Lorenz → Saint Lawrence ≏	176	49.30 N	67.00 W
Sankt Mang	58	47.44 N	10.21 E
Sankt Margarethen an der Raab	61	47.03 N	15.45 E
Sankt Märgen	58	48.00 N	8.05 E
Sankt Margrethen	58	47.27 N	9.36 E
Sankt Martin	64	47.28 N	13.23 E
Sankt Martin an der Raab	61	46.55 N	16.08 E
Sankt Martin in Gsies → San Martino in Casies	64	46.49 N	12.14 E

≏	River	Fluß	Río	Rivière	Rio
≊	Canal	Kanal	Canal	Canal	Canal
ʟ	Waterfall, Rapids	Wasserfall, Stromschnellen	Cascada, Rápidos	Chute d'eau, Rapides	Cascata, Rápidos
ʮ	Strait	Meeresstraße	Estrecho	Détroit	Estreito
⊂	Bay, Gulf	Bucht, Golf	Bahía, Golfo	Baie, Golfe	Baía, Golfo
⊜	Lake, Lakes	See, Seen	Lago, Lagos	Lac, Lacs	Lago, Lagos
≚	Swamp	Sumpf	Pantano	Marais	Pântano
⊓	Ice Features, Glacier	Eis- und Gletscherformen	Accidentes Glaciales	Formes glaciaires	Acidentes glaciares
⊤	Other Hydrographic Features	Andere Hydrographische Objekte	Otros Elementos Hidrográficos	Autres données hydrographiques	Outros acidentes hidrográficos

✣	Submarine Features	Untermeerische Objekte	Accidentes Submarinos	Formes de relief sous-marin	Acidentes submarinos
□	Political Unit	Politische Einheit	Unidad Politica	Entité politique	Unidade política
ʊ	Cultural Institution	Kulturelle Institution	Institución Cultural	Institution culturelle	Institução cultural
⊥	Historical Site	Historische Stätte	Sitio Histórico	Site historique	Sitio histórico
♠	Recreational Site	Erholungs- und Ferienort	Sitio de Recreo	Centre de loisirs	Area de Lazer
⊠	Airport	Flughafen	Aeropuerto	Aéroport	Aeroporto
■	Military Installation	Militäranlage	Instalación Militar	Installation militaire	Instalação militar
◆	Miscellaneous	Verschiedenes	Misceláneo	Divers	Diversos

Name	Page	Lat.	Long.
Sankt Mauritz	**52**	51.57 N	7.39 E
Sankt Michael im Lungau	**64**	47.06 N	13.38 E
Sankt Michael in Obersteiermark	**61**	47.20 N	15.01 E
Sankt Michel → Mikkeli	**26**	61.41 N	27.15 E
Sankt Moritz	**58**	46.30 N	9.50 E
Sankt Niklaus	**58**	46.11 N	7.48 E
Sankt Niklaus → San Nicolò d'Ultimo	**64**	46.30 N	10.55 E
Sankt Oswald	**60**	48.54 N	13.25 E
Sankt Paul im Lavanttal	**61**	46.42 N	14.52 E
Sankt Peter, Dtsch.	**30**	54.18 N	8.38 E
Sankt Peter, Dtsch.	**58**	48.01 N	8.01 E
Sankt Peter ♁[1]	**263**	51.37 N	7.12 E
Sankt Peter am Kammersberg	**61**	47.11 N	14.11 E
Sankt Peter am Ottersbach	**61**	46.48 N	15.45 E
Sankt-Peterburg (Saint Petersburg), Ross.	**76**	59.55 N	30.15 E
Sankt-Peterburg (Saint Petersburg), Ross.	**265a**	59.55 N	30.15 E
Sankt-Peterburg, Gorod □[7]	**265a**	59.55 N	30.15 E
Sankt Peter in der Au	**61**	48.03 N	14.37 E
Sankt Pölten	**61**	48.12 N	15.37 E
Sankt-Quirinus-Dom ♁[1]	**263**	51.12 N	6.42 E
Sankt Stefan an der Gail	**64**	46.37 N	13.31 E
Sankt Stefan im Rosental	**61**	46.54 N	15.42 E
Sankt Ulrich → Ortisei	**64**	46.34 N	11.40 E
Sankt Valentin	**61**	48.10 N	14.32 E
Sankt Veit an der Glan	**61**	46.46 N	14.21 E
Sankt Veit an der Gölsen	**61**	48.03 N	15.40 E
Sankt Veit im Pongau	**64**	47.20 N	13.09 E
Sankt-Viktors-Dom ♁[1]	**263**	51.40 N	6.27 E
Sankt Vincent → Saint Vincent and the Grenadines □[1]	**241h**	13.15 N	61.12 W
Sankt Wallburg → Santa Valburga	**64**	46.33 N	11.00 E
Sankt Wendel	**56**	49.28 N	7.10 E
Sankt-Willibrodi-Dom ♁[1]	**263**	51.40 N	6.37 E
Sankt Wolfgang im Salzkammergut	**64**	47.44 N	13.27 E
Sankuru ≃	**152**	4.17 S	20.25 E
San Lázaro	**252**	22.10 S	57.55 W
San Lázaro, Cabo ➤	**232**	24.48 N	112.19 W
San Lazaro Race Track ♠	**269f**	14.37 N	120.59 E
San Lazzaro di Savena	**64**	44.28 N	11.25 E
San Leandro	**226**	37.43 N	122.09 W
San Leandro Creek ≃	**282**	37.45 N	122.12 W
San Leo	**66**	43.54 N	12.21 E
San Leon	**222**	29.29 N	94.55 W
San Leonardo (Sankt Leonhard), It.	**64**	46.49 N	11.15 E
San Leonardo, Méx.	**196**	27.28 N	104.55 W
San Leonardo ≃	**70**	37.59 N	13.41 E
San Leone	**70**	37.16 N	13.35 E
Sanlicheng	**100**	31.48 N	114.12 E
Sanlidian	**100**	30.48 N	118.15 E
Sanlifan	**100**	30.51 N	115.15 E
Sanlintang	**106**	31.08 N	121.29 E
Sanlipu	**106**	31.46 N	119.03 E
Sanliuji	**100**	32.08 N	116.19 E
San Lope	**246**	6.12 N	71.56 W
San Lorenzo, Arg.	**252**	28.08 S	58.46 W
San Lorenzo, Arg.	**252**	32.45 S	60.44 W
San Lorenzo, Bol.	**248**	21.26 S	64.47 W
San Lorenzo, Ec.	**246**	1.17 N	78.50 W
San Lorenzo, Hond.	**236**	13.25 N	87.27 W
San Lorenzo, It.	**68**	38.01 N	15.50 E
San Lorenzo, Méx.	**196**	25.37 N	97.35 W
San Lorenzo, Méx.	**232**	25.32 N	102.11 W
San Lorenzo, Nic.	**236**	12.23 N	85.40 W
San Lorenzo, P.R.	**240m**	18.11 N	65.58 W
San Lorenzo, Ca., U.S.	**226**	37.40 N	122.07 W
San Lorenzo, Ven.	**246**	9.47 N	71.04 W
San Lorenzo ≃, Méx.	**232**	24.15 N	107.24 W
San Lorenzo ≃, Ca., U.S.	**226**	36.58 N	122.01 W
San Lorenzo, Bahía de ᑕ	**236**	13.19 N	87.30 W
San Lorenzo, Cabo ➤	**246**	1.04 S	80.56 W
San Lorenzo, Golfo del → Saint Lawrence, Gulf of ᑕ	**186**	48.00 N	62.00 W
San Lorenzo, Isla I, Méx.	**232**	28.38 N	112.51 W
San Lorenzo, Isla I, Perú	**248**	12.05 S	77.15 W
San Lorenzo, Monte (Cerro Cochrane) ∧	**254**	47.37 S	72.19 W
San Lorenzo Bellizzi	**68**	39.53 N	16.20 E
San Lorenzo Creek ≃, Ca., U.S.	**226**	36.12 N	120.38 W
San Lorenzo Creek ≃, Ca., U.S.	**282**	37.39 N	122.09 W
San Lorenzo de El Escorial	**34**	40.35 N	4.09 W
San Lorenzo de la Parrilla	**34**	39.51 N	2.22 W
San Lorenzo del Vallo	**68**	39.40 N	16.18 E
San Lorenzo di Sebato (Sankt Lorenzen)	**64**	46.47 N	11.54 E
San Lorenzo in Campo	**66**	43.36 N	12.56 E
San Lorenzo Nuovo	**66**	42.41 N	11.54 E
San Lorenzo → Saint Lawrence ≃	**176**	49.30 N	67.00 W
San Lorenzo Tezonco ◆[8]	**286a**	19.18 N	99.04 W
San Luca	**68**	38.09 N	16.04 E
Sanlúcar de Barrameda	**34**	36.47 N	6.21 W
Sanlúcar la Mayor	**34**	37.23 N	6.12 W
San Lucas, Bol.	**248**	20.06 S	65.07 W
San Lucas, Ec.	**246**	3.45 S	79.15 W
San Lucas, Méx.	**232**	22.53 N	109.54 W
San Lucas, Ca., U.S.	**226**	36.08 N	121.01 W
San Lucas, Cabo ➤	**232**	22.52 N	109.53 W
San Luis, Arg.	**252**	33.18 S	66.21 W
San Luis, Cuba	**240p**	20.12 N	75.51 W
San Luis, Cuba	**240p**	22.17 N	83.46 W
San Luis, Guat.	**236**	16.14 N	89.27 W
San Luis, Perú	**286d**	12.04 S	77.00 W
San Luis, Az., U.S.	**200**	32.04 N	111.57 W
San Luis, Co., U.S.	**200**	37.12 N	105.25 W
San Luis, Ven.	**246**	11.07 N	69.42 W
San Luis □[4]	**252**	34.00 S	66.00 W
San Luis ◆[8]	**286b**	23.05 N	82.20 W
San Luis ≃	**234**	17.13 N	100.55 W
San Luis, Arroyo ≃	**258**	34.10 S	57.44 W
San Luís, Laguna ⊜	**248**	13.45 S	64.00 W
San Luis, Sierra de ⋏	**252**	32.40 S	65.50 W
San Luis Acatlán	**234**	16.48 N	98.45 W
San Luis Creek ≃	**200**	37.42 N	105.44 W
San Luis de la Loma	**234**	17.18 N	100.55 W
San Luis de la Paz	**234**	21.18 N	100.31 W
San Luis del Cordero	**232**	25.26 N	104.18 W
San Luis del Palmar	**252**	27.31 S	58.34 W
San Luis Gonzaga	**232**	24.55 N	111.16 W
San Luis Gonzaga, Bahía ᑕ	**232**	29.48 N	114.22 W
San Luis Jilotepeque	**236**	14.39 N	89.44 W
San Luis Obispo	**226**	35.16 N	120.39 W
San Luis Obispo □[6]	**226**	35.30 N	120.30 W
San Luis Pass ᑕ	**222**	29.05 N	95.08 W
San Luis Peak ∧	**200**	37.59 N	106.56 W
San Luis Potosí	**234**	22.09 N	100.59 W
San Luis Potosí □[3]	**234**	22.30 N	100.30 W
San Luis Reservoir ⊜[1]	**226**	37.07 N	121.05 W
San Luis Rey	**228**	33.14 N	117.20 W
San Luis Rey ≃	**204**	33.12 N	117.24 W
San Luis Rey, Mission ♁[1]	**228**	33.14 N	117.20 W
San Luis Río Colorado	**232**	32.29 N	114.48 W
San Luis Soyatlán	**234**	20.12 N	103.18 W
San Luis State Recreation Area ♠	**226**	37.04 N	121.05 W
San Luis Valley V	**200**	37.25 N	106.00 W
Sanluri	**71**	39.34 N	8.54 E
San Macario	**266b**	45.36 N	8.47 E
Sanmaiden	**270**	34.34 N	135.51 E
San Mamete	**58**	46.02 N	9.04 E
San Mango d'aquino	**68**	39.03 N	16.11 E
San Manuel, Arg.	**252**	37.47 S	58.50 W
San Manuel, Méx.	**234**	17.37 N	93.24 W
San Manuel, Az., U.S.	**200**	32.35 N	110.37 W
San Marcelino	**116**	14.58 N	120.09 E
San Marcello Pistoiese	**66**	44.03 N	10.47 E
San Marcial ≃	**232**	28.04 N	110.44 W
San Marco, Capo ➤, It.	**70**	37.30 N	13.01 E
San Marco, Capo ➤, It.	**71**	39.51 N	8.26 E
San Marco Argentano	**68**	39.33 N	16.07 E
San Marco dei Cavoti	**68**	41.18 N	14.53 E
San Marco in Lamis	**68**	41.43 N	15.38 E
San Marco la Catola	**68**	41.31 N	15.00 E
San Marcos, Chile	**252**	30.56 S	71.03 W
San Marcos, Col.	**246**	8.39 N	75.08 W
San Marcos, C.R.	**236**	9.40 N	84.01 W
San Marcos, El Sal.	**236**	13.39 N	89.11 W
San Marcos, Guat.	**236**	14.58 N	91.48 W
San Marcos, Hond.	**236**	14.24 N	88.56 W
San Marcos, Hond.	**236**	15.17 N	88.23 W
San Marcos, Méx.	**234**	16.48 N	99.21 W
San Marcos, Méx.	**234**	20.02 N	99.20 W
San Marcos, Méx.	**234**	20.47 N	104.11 W
San Marcos, Ca., U.S.	**228**	33.08 N	117.09 W
San Marcos, Tx., U.S.	**196**	29.52 N	97.56 W
San Marcos □[5]	**236**	15.00 N	91.55 W
San Marcos ≃	**196**	29.29 N	97.28 W
San Marcos, Isla I	**232**	27.13 N	112.06 W
San Marcos, Laguna ⊜	**234**	20.17 N	103.33 W
San Marcos, Universidad Nacional de ♁[2]	**286d**	12.04 S	77.05 W
San Marcos Arteaga	**234**	17.45 N	97.58 W
San Marcos de Colón	**236**	13.26 N	86.48 W
San Marino, S. Mar.	**66**	43.55 N	12.28 E
San Marino, Ca., U.S.	**280**	34.07 N	118.06 W
San Marino □[1], Europe	**22**	43.56 N	12.25 E
San Marino □[1], Europe	**66**	43.56 N	12.25 E
San Martín, Arg.	**252**	29.14 S	65.46 W
San Martín, Arg.	**252**	33.04 S	68.28 W
San Martín, Col.	**246**	3.42 N	73.42 W
San Martin, Ca., U.S.	**226**	37.05 N	121.37 W
San Martín, Ur.	**258**	33.45 S	57.37 W
San Martín □[5]	**248**	7.00 S	76.50 W
San Martín ≃, Bol.	**248**	13.08 S	63.43 W
San Martín ≃, Bol.	**248**	11.50 S	67.16 W
San Martín ♁[3]	**9**	68.07 S	67.08 W
San Martín, Arroyo ≃	**258**	33.49 S	57.44 W
San Martín, Cuchilla ⋏[2]	**258**	33.45 S	57.54 W
San Martín, Lago (Lago O'Higgins) ⊜	**254**	49.00 S	72.40 W
San Martín, Volcán ∧[1]	**234**	18.33 N	95.12 W
San Martín de Bolaños	**234**	21.29 N	103.58 W
San Martín [de las Pirámides]	**234**	19.42 N	98.50 W
San Martín de las Vacas	**196**	25.30 N	101.20 W
San Martín de los Andes	**254**	40.10 S	71.21 W
San Martin de Porras	**286d**	12.04 S	77.04 W
San Martín de Valdeiglesias	**34**	40.21 N	4.24 W
San Martín → General San Martín	**258**	34.34 S	58.32 W
San Martín Hidalgo	**234**	20.27 N	103.57 W
San Martino, It.	**62**	45.27 N	8.47 E
San Martino (Sankt Martin), It.	**64**	46.47 N	11.13 E
San Martino, It.	**64**	45.25 N	10.35 E
San Martino Buon Albergo	**64**	45.25 N	11.05 E
San Martino d'agri	**68**	40.14 N	16.04 E
San Martino di Castrozza	**64**	46.16 N	11.48 E
San Martino di Lupari	**64**	45.39 N	11.51 E
San Martino in Badia (Saint Martin)	**64**	46.41 N	11.52 E
San Martino in Casies (Sankt Martin in Gsies)	**64**	46.49 N	12.14 E
San Martino in Rio	**64**	44.44 N	10.48 E
San Martino Valle Caudina	**68**	41.01 N	14.39 E
San Martín Peras	**234**	17.19 N	98.15 W
San Marzano di San Giuseppe	**68**	40.27 N	17.30 E
San Marzano sul Sarno	**66**	40.46 N	14.35 E
San Mateo, Méx.	**234**	22.59 N	103.30 W
San Mateo, Pil.	**269f**	14.42 N	121.07 E
San Mateo, Ca., U.S.	**226**	37.33 N	122.19 W
San Mateo, Fl., U.S.	**192**	29.36 N	81.35 W
San Mateo, N.M., U.S.	**200**	35.19 N	107.38 W
San Mateo, Ven.	**246**	9.45 N	64.33 W
San Mateo □[6]	**226**	37.25 N	122.20 W
San Mateo Atenco	**234**	19.16 N	99.32 W
San Mateo Bridge ◆[5]	**282**	37.36 N	122.13 W
San Mateo Canyon V	**228**	33.23 N	117.36 W
San Mateo Creek ≃	**282**	37.34 N	122.18 W
San Mateo del Mar	**234**	16.12 N	95.00 W
San Mateo Ixtatán	**236**	15.50 N	91.29 W
San Mateo Memorial Park ♠	**282**	37.17 N	122.18 W
San Mateo Point ➤	**228**	33.23 N	117.36 W
San Mateo Tecoloapan	**286a**	19.34 N	99.14 W
San Matías	**248**	16.22 S	58.24 W
San Matías, Golfo ᑕ	**254**	41.30 S	64.15 W
San Mauro Castelverde	**70**	37.55 N	14.11 E
San Mauro Forte	**68**	40.29 N	16.15 E
San Mauro la Bruca	**68**	40.07 N	15.17 E
San Mauro Marchesato	**68**	39.06 N	16.56 E
San Mauro Torinese	**62**	45.06 N	7.46 E
San Medi, Arroyo de ≃	**266d**	41.28 N	2.06 E
Sanmen	**100**	29.06 N	121.24 E
San Menaio	**68**	41.56 N	15.58 E
Sanmen Wan ᑕ	**100**	29.08 N	121.44 E
Sanmenxia (Shanxian)	**102**	34.45 N	111.05 E
San Michele, Sacra di ♁[1]	**62**	45.11 N	7.21 E
San Michele all'Adige	**64**	46.12 N	11.08 E
San Michele al Tagliamento	**64**	45.46 N	12.59 E
San Michele di Ganzaria	**70**	37.17 N	14.26 E
San Michele Mondovì	**62**	44.23 N	7.54 E
San Michele Salentino	**68**	40.38 N	17.37 E
San Miguel, Arg.	**252**	28.00 S	57.36 W
San Miguel, Bol.	**248**	16.42 S	61.01 W
San Miguel, Chile	**286e**	33.30 S	70.40 W
San Miguel, Ec.	**246**	1.44 S	79.01 W
San Miguel, El Sal.	**236**	13.29 N	88.11 W
San Miguel, Esp.	**148**	28.05 N	16.37 W
San Miguel, Méx.	**232**	29.10 N	101.28 W
San Miguel, Méx.	**234**	23.23 N	98.10 W
San Miguel, Pan.	**246**	8.27 N	78.56 W
San Miguel, Perú	**248**	13.01 S	73.58 W
San Miguel, Perú	**286d**	12.06 S	77.07 W
San Miguel, Pil.	**116**	15.09 N	120.59 E
San Miguel, Ca., U.S.	**226**	35.45 N	120.41 W
San Miguel ≃, Bol.	**248**	13.52 S	63.56 W
San Miguel (Cuilco) ≃, N.A.	**236**	15.56 N	92.10 W
San Miguel ≃, S.A.	**246**	0.08 N	75.51 W
San Miguel ≃, S.A.	**248**	19.15 S	59.20 W
San Miguel ≃, Co., U.S.	**200**	38.23 N	108.48 W
San Miguel, Cerro ∧[2]	**248**	19.19 S	60.36 W
San Miguel, Golfo de ᑕ	**246**	8.22 N	78.17 W
San Miguel, Volcán de ∧[1]	**236**	13.26 N	88.16 W
San Miguel Arcángel, Mission ♁[1]	**226**	35.44 N	120.42 W
San Miguel Bay ᑕ	**116**	13.50 N	123.10 E
San Miguel Chimalapa	**234**	16.43 N	94.41 W
San Miguel Creek ≃	**196**	28.30 N	98.25 W
San Miguel de Allende	**234**	20.55 N	100.45 W
San Miguel de Cruces	**232**	24.25 N	105.51 W
San Miguel del Monte	**258**	35.27 S	58.48 W
San Miguel de Pallaques	**248**	7.00 S	78.51 W
San Miguel de Salcedo	**246**	1.02 S	78.34 W
San Miguel de Tucumán	**252**	26.49 S	65.13 W
San Miguel El Alto	**234**	21.01 N	102.21 W
San Miguel El Grande	**234**	17.02 N	97.37 W
San Miguel → General Sarmiento	**258**	34.33 S	58.43 W
San Miguel Island I, Pil.	**116**	13.23 N	123.48 E
San Miguel Island I, Ca., U.S.	**204**	34.02 N	120.22 W
San Miguel Islands II	**116**	7.45 N	118.28 E
San Miguelito	**236**	11.24 N	84.54 W
San Miguel Ixtahuacán	**236**	15.15 N	91.45 W
San Miguel Mountain ∧	**228**	32.42 N	116.56 W
San Miguel Sola de Vega	**234**	16.31 N	96.59 W
San Miguel Talea de Castro	**234**	17.22 N	96.15 W
San Miguel Tecuixiapan	**234**	17.58 N	99.27 W
San Miguel Tenango	**234**	16.16 N	95.36 W
San Miguel Totolapan	**234**	18.08 N	100.23 W
Sanming	**100**	26.14 N	117.36 E
San Miniato	**66**	43.41 N	10.51 E
San Murezzan → Sankt Moritz	**58**	46.30 N	9.50 E
Sannahed	**40**	59.06 N	15.09 E
Sannan	**96**	35.04 N	135.02 E
Sannār	**140**	13.33 N	33.38 E
San Narciso, Pil.	**116**	13.34 N	122.34 E
San Narciso, Pil.	**116**	15.01 N	120.05 E
Sannazzaro de'Burgondi	**62**	45.06 N	8.54 E
Sannicandro di Bari	**68**	41.00 N	16.48 E
Sannicandro Garganico	**68**	41.50 N	15.34 E
Sannicola	**68**	40.05 N	18.04 E
San Nicola, Isola I	**66**	42.07 N	15.30 E
San Nicola, Monte ∧	**68**	38.35 N	16.24 E
San Nicola Arcella	**68**	39.51 N	15.48 E
San Nicola da Crissa	**68**	38.40 N	16.17 E
San Nicolás, Cuba	**240p**	22.47 N	81.55 W
San Nicolás, Esp.	**148**	27.59 N	15.46 W
San Nicolás, Hond.	**236**	15.00 N	88.45 W
San Nicolás, Méx.	**234**	16.26 N	98.32 W
San Nicolás, Perú	**248**	15.13 S	75.12 W
San Nicolas, Pil.	**116**	18.09 N	120.38 E
San Nicolás ≃	**234**	19.40 N	105.14 W
San Nicolás de los Arroyos	**252**	33.20 S	60.13 W
San Nicolás de los Garza	**196**	25.45 N	100.18 W
San Nicolas Island I	**204**	33.15 N	119.31 W
San Nicolò di Comelico	**64**	46.35 N	12.31 E
San Nicolò d'Ultimo (Sankt Nikolaus)	**64**	46.30 N	10.55 E
San Nicolò Ferrarese	**64**	44.42 N	11.42 E
San Nicolò Gerrei	**71**	39.30 N	9.18 E
Sannieshof	**158**	26.30 S	25.47 E
Sannikova, proliv Ʉ	**74**	74.30 N	140.00 E
Ṣannīn, Jabal ∧	**132**	33.57 N	35.52 E
Sannio, Monti del ⋏	**66**	41.30 N	14.45 E
Sanniquellie	**150**	7.22 N	8.43 W
Sannohe	**92**	40.22 N	141.15 E
Sannois	**261**	48.58 N	2.15 E
Sannūr, Wādī V	**142**	28.58 N	31.03 E
Sano	**94**	36.19 N	139.35 E
Sañogasta	**252**	29.18 S	67.36 W
Sanok	**30**	49.34 N	22.13 E
Sânon ≃	**58**	48.38 N	6.20 E
San Onofre	**246**	9.44 N	75.32 W
San Onofre Mountain ∧	**228**	33.22 N	117.30 W
San Pablo, Chile	**254**	40.24 S	73.01 W
San Pablo, Col.	**246**	1.40 N	77.00 W
San Pablo, Pil.	**116**	14.04 N	121.19 E
San Pablo, Pil.	**116**	7.40 N	123.27 E
San Pablo, Ca., U.S.	**226**	37.57 N	122.20 W
San Pablo ◆[8]	**286a**	19.11 N	99.04 W
San Pablo ≃, Bol.	**248**	14.52 S	63.42 W
San Pablo ≃, Méx.	**234**	18.32 N	96.01 W
San Pablo ≃, Pan.	**236**	7.51 N	81.10 W
San Pablo, Point ➤	**282**	37.58 N	122.26 W
San Pablo Autopan	**234**	19.21 N	99.40 W
San Pablo Bay ᑕ	**226**	38.06 N	122.22 W
San Pablo Creek ≃	**282**	37.58 N	122.30 W
San Pablo Huixtepec	**234**	16.50 N	96.46 W
San Pablo Reservoir ⊜[1]	**282**	37.56 N	122.15 W
San Pablo Ridge ∧	**282**	37.55 N	122.15 W
San Pablo Strait Ʉ	**282**	37.58 N	122.26 W
San Pablo Villa de Mitla	**234**	16.55 N	96.24 W
Sanpāda	**272c**	19.04 N	73.01 E
San Pancrazio Salentino	**68**	40.25 N	17.50 E
San Paolo	**64**	46.29 N	11.15 E
San Paolo di Civitate	**68**	41.44 N	15.15 E
San Pascual	**116**	13.08 N	122.59 E
San Pasqual Indian Reservation ◆[4]	**228**	33.12 N	116.58 W
San Pedro, Arg.	**252**	33.40 S	59.40 W
San Pedro, Arg.	**252**	24.14 S	64.52 W
San Pedro, Arg.	**252**	27.57 S	65.10 W
San Pedro, Chile	**252**	21.57 S	68.34 W
San Pedro, Chile	**252**	33.54 S	71.28 W
San Pedro, Col.	**246**	9.24 N	75.04 W
San Pedro, C.R.	**236**	9.56 N	84.03 W
San Pédro, C. Iv.	**150**	4.44 N	6.37 W
San Pedro, Para.	**252**	24.07 S	56.59 W
San Pedro, Tx., U.S.	**196**	27.47 N	97.40 W
San Pedro, Ur.	**258**	34.21 S	57.51 W
San Pedro, Ven.	**246**	8.50 N	71.58 W
San Pedro □[5]	**252**	24.15 S	56.30 W
San Pedro ◆[8]	**228**	33.44 N	118.18 W
San Pedro ≃, Cuba	**240p**	21.09 N	78.30 W
San Pedro ≃, Méx.	**232**	30.56 N	108.08 W
San Pedro ≃, Méx.	**234**	21.45 N	105.30 W
San Pedro ≃, N.A.	**200**	32.59 N	110.47 W
San Pedro ≃, N.A.	**232**	17.45 N	91.25 W
San Pedro ≃, Ven.	**286c**	10.35 N	66.48 W
San Pedro, Arroyo ≃	**258**	34.21 S	57.56 W
San Pedro, Point ➤, Ca., U.S.	**282**	37.35 N	122.31 W
San Pedro, Point ➤, Ca., U.S.	**282**	37.59 N	122.27 W
San Pedro, Punta ➤	**252**	25.30 S	70.38 W
San Pedro, Volcán ∧[1]	**252**	21.53 S	68.25 W
San Pedro Amuzgos	**234**	16.39 N	98.06 W
San Pedro Apóstol	**234**	16.44 N	96.44 W
San Pedro Ayampuc	**236**	14.47 N	90.27 W
San Pedro Bay ᑕ, Pil.	**116**	11.11 N	125.05 E
San Pedro Bay ᑕ, Ca., U.S.	**228**	33.45 N	118.11 W
San Pedro Breakwater ◆[5]	**280**	33.42 N	118.16 W
San Pedro Carchá	**236**	15.29 N	90.16 W
San Pedro Channel Ʉ	**228**	33.35 N	118.25 W
San Pedro Creek ≃, Ca., U.S.	**282**	37.36 N	122.30 W
San Pedro Creek ≃, Tx., U.S.	**222**	31.34 N	95.14 W
San Pedro de Arriba	**258**	34.18 S	57.47 W
San Pedro de Atacama	**252**	22.55 S	68.13 W
San Pedro de Buena Vista	**248**	18.13 S	65.59 W
San Pedro de Curahuara	**248**	17.40 S	68.02 W
San Pedro de la Cueva	**232**	29.18 N	109.44 W
San Pedro de las Colonias	**232**	25.45 N	102.59 W
San Pedro del Gallo	**232**	25.33 N	104.18 W
San Pedro de Lloc	**248**	7.26 S	79.31 W
San Pedro del Norte	**236**	13.04 N	84.33 W
San Pedro del Paraná	**252**	26.46 S	56.15 W
San Pedro de Macorís	**238**	18.27 N	69.18 W
San Pedro El Alto	**234**	16.01 N	96.28 W
San Pedro Huamelula	**234**	16.02 N	95.40 W
San Pedro Jicayán	**234**	16.25 N	97.59 W
San Pedro Juchatengo	**234**	16.21 N	97.06 W
San Pedro Mártir ◆[8]	**286a**	19.16 N	99.10 W
San Pedro Mixtepec	**234**	16.00 N	97.07 W
San Pedro Peaks ⋏	**200**	36.07 N	106.49 W
San Pedro Pinula	**236**	14.40 N	89.51 W
San Pedro Pochutla	**234**	15.44 N	96.28 W
San Pedro Sacatepéquez	**236**	14.58 N	91.46 W
San Pedro Sula	**236**	15.27 N	88.02 W
San Pedro Tabasco	**232**	17.47 N	91.10 W
San Pedro Tapanatepec	**234**	16.21 N	94.12 W
San Pedro Tututepec	**234**	16.09 N	97.38 W
San Pedro Xalostoc	**286a**	19.32 N	99.05 W
San Pedro y Miquelón → Saint Pierre and Miquelon □[2]	**186**	46.55 N	56.20 W
San Pelayo	**246**	8.58 N	75.51 W
San Pellegrino	**62**	45.50 N	9.40 E
San Piero a Grado	**66**	43.41 N	10.21 E
San Piero in Bagno	**66**	43.51 N	11.58 E
San Pierre	**216**	41.12 N	86.53 W
San Pietro (Sankt Peter)	**64**	47.01 N	12.03 E
San Pietro, Isola di I	**71**	39.08 N	8.17 E
San Pietro a Maida	**68**	38.50 N	16.20 E
San Pietro di Cadore	**64**	46.34 N	12.35 E
San Pietro in Casale	**64**	44.42 N	11.24 E
San Pietro in Gu	**64**	45.37 N	11.40 E
San Pietro in Guarano	**68**	39.20 N	16.19 E
San Pietro in Palazzi	**66**	43.20 N	10.30 E
San Pietro in Vaticano ♁[1]	**267a**	41.54 N	12.28 E
San Pietro Vara	**62**	44.20 N	9.35 E
San Pietro Vernotico	**68**	40.29 N	18.00 E
San Pitch ≃	**200**	39.03 N	111.51 W
Sanpoil ≃	**202**	47.53 N	118.41 W
San Policarpio	**116**	12.11 N	125.30 E
San Polo d'Enza	**64**	44.38 N	10.26 E
Sanpu	**98**	34.09 N	117.10 E
Sanqiao	**106**	30.35 N	119.58 E
San Quentin	**282**	37.56 N	122.29 W
San Quentin State Prison ♁	**282**	37.56 N	122.28 W
Sanquhar	**44**	55.22 N	3.56 W
Sanquianga, Parque Nacional ♠	**246**	2.30 N	78.15 W
San Quintin	**116**	16.00 N	120.50 E
San Quintín, Cabo ➤	**232**	30.21 N	116.00 W
San Quirico d'Orcia	**66**	43.03 N	11.36 E
Sanqutan	**100**	27.17 N	115.04 E
Sanquzhen	**107**	29.39 N	105.37 E
San Rafael, Arg.	**252**	34.36 S	68.20 W
San Rafael, Chile	**252**	35.19 S	71.32 W
San Rafael, Méx.	**232**	25.01 N	100.33 W
San Rafael, Méx.	**234**	20.12 N	96.51 W
San Rafael, Ca., U.S.	**226**	37.58 N	122.31 W
San Rafael, N.M., U.S.	**200**	35.06 N	107.52 W
San Rafael, Ven.	**246**	10.58 N	71.44 W
San Rafael ≃, Bol.	**248**	18.38 S	58.55 W
San Rafael ≃, Ut,. U.S.	**200**	38.47 N	110.07 W
San Rafael Bay ᑕ	**282**	37.58 N	122.28 W
San Rafael de las Tortillas	**196**	26.49 N	99.32 W
San Rafael del Norte	**236**	13.12 N	86.06 W
San Rafael del Sur	**236**	11.51 N	86.27 W
San Rafael Desert ◆[2]	**200**	38.40 N	110.30 W
San Rafael Hills ⋏[2]	**280**	34.10 N	118.12 W
San Rafael Mountains ⋏	**204**	34.45 N	119.50 W
San Rafael Oriente	**236**	13.23 N	88.21 W
San Rafael Swell ⋏[1]	**200**	38.40 N	110.45 W
San Rafael Tasajera	**236**	13.16 N	88.52 W
San Ramón, Arg.	**252**	27.42 S	64.17 W
San Ramón, Bol.	**248**	13.17 S	64.43 W
San Ramón, C.R.	**236**	10.06 N	84.28 W
San Ramón, Hond.	**236**	14.41 N	84.43 W
San Ramón, Perú	**248**	11.08 S	75.20 W
San Ramon, Pil.	**116**	13.16 N	124.05 E
San Ramon, Ca., U.S.	**282**	37.47 N	121.59 W
San Ramón, Ur.	**252**	34.18 S	55.58 W
San Ramon Creek ≃	**282**	37.54 N	122.03 W
San Ramón de la Nueva Orán	**252**	23.08 S	64.20 W
San Ramon Valley V	**282**	37.46 N	121.58 W
Sanrao	**100**	23.59 N	116.50 E
San-rei ∧	**96**	33.50 N	133.59 E
San Remigio	**116**	11.05 N	123.56 E
San Remo, Austl.	**169**	38.31 S	145.22 E
San Remo, It.	**62**	43.49 N	7.46 E
San Remo, N.Y., U.S.	**210**	40.52 N	73.13 W
San Roberto	**68**	38.18 N	15.44 E
San Rodrigo ≃	**196**	28.54 N	100.37 W
San Román ≃	**236**	16.21 N	90.22 W
San Román, Cabo ➤	**246**	12.12 N	70.00 W
San Roque, Arg.	**252**	28.34 S	58.43 W
San Roque, Arg.	**252**	30.17 S	68.41 W
San Roque, Esp.	**34**	36.13 N	5.24 W
San Roque, N. Mar. Is.	**174n**	15.15 N	145.47 E
San Roque, Pil.	**269f**	14.29 N	120.54 E
San Roque, Cabo → São Roque, Cabo de ➤	**250**	5.29 S	35.16 W
San Roque, Punta ➤	**232**	27.11 N	114.26 W
San Rosendo	**252**	37.16 S	72.43 W
San Rufo	**68**	40.26 N	15.28 E
San Saba	**196**	31.11 N	98.43 W
San Saba ≃	**196**	31.15 N	98.35 W
San Saep, Khlong ≊	**269a**	13.45 N	100.36 E
San Salvador, Arg.	**252**	29.16 S	57.31 W
San Salvador, Arg.	**252**	31.37 S	58.30 W
San Salvador, El Sal.	**236**	13.42 N	89.12 W
San Salvador (Watling Island) I	**238**	24.02 N	74.28 W
San Salvador ≃	**258**	33.37 S	58.06 W
San Salvador, Cuchilla ⋏[2]	**258**	33.56 S	57.45 W
San Salvador, Volcán de ∧[1]	**236**	13.44 N	89.17 W
San Salvador de Jujuy	**252**	24.11 S	65.18 W
San Salvador el Seco	**234**	19.08 N	97.39 W
San Salvatore, Monte ∧	**70**	37.50 N	14.03 E
San Salvatore Monferrato	**62**	44.59 N	8.34 E
San Salvatore Telesino	**68**	41.14 N	14.30 E
San Salvo	**66**	42.03 N	14.44 E
Sansanné-Mango	**150**	10.21 N	0.28 E
Sans Bois Creek ≃	**196**	35.20 N	94.50 W
San Sebastián, El Sal.	**236**	13.44 N	88.50 W
San Sebastián, Guat.	**236**	14.34 N	91.39 W
San Sebastián, Hond.	**236**	14.24 N	88.42 W
San Sebastián, Méx.	**234**	20.47 N	104.51 W
San Sebastián, P.R.	**240m**	18.20 N	66.59 W
San Sebastián, Bahía ᑕ	**254**	53.12 S	68.20 W
San Sebastián de la Gomera	**148**	28.06 N	17.06 W
San Sebastián del Álamo	**234**	21.26 N	102.21 W
San Sebastián de los Reyes	**266a**	40.33 N	3.38 W
San Sebastián de Yalí	**236**	13.18 N	86.11 W
San Sebastián → Donostia	**34**	43.19 N	1.59 W
San Sebastiano	**64**	45.38 N	10.16 E
San Sebastiano Curone	**62**	44.47 N	9.04 E
San Sebastián Tecomaxtlahuaca	**234**	17.21 N	98.02 W
San Sebastián Zinacatepec	**234**	18.20 N	97.15 W
San Secondo Parmense	**64**	44.55 N	10.14 E
Sansepolcro	**66**	43.34 N	12.08 E
San Severino Lucano	**68**	40.01 N	16.08 E
San Severino Marche	**66**	43.13 N	13.10 E
San Severo	**68**	41.41 N	15.23 E
Sansha	**100**	26.58 N	120.12 E
Sanshengchang	**89**	44.51 N	120.21 E
Sanshierzhan	**89**	53.16 N	121.49 E
Sanshijia, Zhg.	**98**	41.44 N	119.15 E
Sanshijia, Zhg.	**98**	41.05 N	119.03 E
Sanshilibao	**98**	39.15 N	121.48 E
Sanshiling	**106**	30.51 N	119.29 E
Sanshisanzhan	**89**	53.10 N	121.27 E
Sanshui	**100**	23.11 N	112.53 E
San Sigismondo (Sankt Sigmund)	**64**	46.49 N	11.46 E
San Simeon	**226**	35.39 N	121.11 W
San Simon, Méx.	**204**	30.30 N	115.58 W
San Simon, Az., U.S.	**200**	32.16 N	109.13 W
San Simón ≃, Bol.	**248**	13.13 S	63.31 W
San Simon ≃, Az., U.S.	**200**	32.50 N	109.39 W
San Simon Wash V	**200**	31.45 N	112.25 W
San Siro ◆[8]	**266b**	45.29 N	9.07 E
Sanski Most	**36**	44.46 N	16.40 E
Sanso	**150**	11.43 N	6.51 W
San Solano	**252**	31.29 S	65.55 W
Sansom Park Village	**222**	32.48 N	97.24 W
Sanson	**172**	40.13 S	175.25 E
San Sosti	**68**	39.40 N	16.02 E
San Sperate	**71**	39.21 N	9.00 E
Sans Souci	**274a**	33.59 S	151.08 E
Sans-Souci ⊥	**238**	19.37 N	72.12 W
Sanssouci, Schloss ♁	**54**	52.24 N	13.02 E
San Stefano Ticino	**266b**	45.29 N	8.55 E
Santa, Perú	**248**	8.59 S	78.36 W
Santa, Pil.	**116**	17.29 N	120.26 E
Santa ≃	**248**	8.58 S	78.39 W
Santa, Isla del I	**248**	9.02 S	78.40 W
Santa Adélia	**255**	21.16 S	48.48 W
Santa Albertina	**255**	20.02 S	50.44 W
Santa Amalia	**34**	39.01 N	6.01 W
Santa Ana, Arg.	**252**	27.22 S	55.34 W
Santa Ana, Bol.	**248**	13.45 S	65.35 W
Santa Ana, Bol.	**248**	18.43 S	58.44 W
Santa Ana, Col.	**246**	9.19 N	74.35 W
Santa Ana, Ec.	**246**	1.13 S	80.23 W
Santa Ana, El Sal.	**236**	13.59 N	89.34 W
Santa Ana, Méx.	**232**	24.04 N	100.30 W
Santa Ana, Méx.	**232**	30.33 N	111.07 W
Santa Ana, Ca., U.S.	**228**	33.44 N	117.52 W
Santa Ana, Ven.	**246**	9.19 N	64.39 W
Santa Ana ≃, Cuba	**286b**	23.04 N	82.32 W
Santa Ana ≃, Ca., U.S.	**228**	33.38 N	117.57 W
Santa Ana, Volcán de ∧[1]	**236**	13.50 N	89.38 W
Santa Ana Canyon V	**280**	33.53 N	117.43 W
Santa Ana de Chena	**286e**	33.34 S	70.47 W
Santa Ana del Alto Beni	**248**	15.31 S	67.30 W
Santa Ana Heights	**228**	33.39 N	117.54 W
Santa Ana Indian Reservation ◆[4]	**200**	35.28 N	106.37 W
Santa Ana Island I	**175e**	10.50 S	162.28 E
Santa Ana Maya	**234**	20.00 N	101.01 W
Santa Ana Mountains ⋏	**228**	33.45 N	117.35 W
Santa Ana Race Track ♠	**269f**	14.35 N	121.01 E
Santa Ana Tlacotenco ◆[8]	**286a**	19.10 N	98.59 W
Santa Anita	**234**	20.33 N	103.27 W
Santa Anita Canyon V	**280**	34.12 N	118.01 W
Santa Anita Park ♠	**280**	34.08 N	118.03 W
Santa Anna	**196**	31.44 N	99.19 W
Santa Apolonia	**196**	25.38 N	97.59 W
Santa Bárbara, Chile	**252**	37.40 S	72.01 W
Santa Barbara, Col.	**246**	5.53 N	75.35 W
Santa Bárbara, Hond.	**236**	14.53 N	88.14 W
Santa Bárbara, Méx.	**232**	26.48 N	105.49 W
Santa Bárbara, Méx.	**234**	18.52 N	101.07 W
Santa Barbara, Ca., U.S.	**204**	34.25 N	119.42 W
Santa Bárbara, Ven.	**246**	3.57 N	67.06 W
Santa Bárbara, Ven.	**246**	7.47 N	71.10 W
Santa Bárbara □[5]	**236**	15.10 N	88.20 W
Santa Barbara □[6]	**228**	33.28 N	119.02 W
Santa Bárbara ≃	**248**	16.58 S	61.39 W
Santa Bárbara, Morro de ∧	**287a**	22.57 S	43.28 W
Santa Bárbara, Túnel ◆[5]	**287a**	22.56 S	43.12 W
Santa Barbara Channel Ʉ	**204**	34.15 N	119.55 W
Santa Bárbara do Monte Verde	**256**	21.58 S	43.42 W
Santa Bárbara do Sul	**252**	28.22 S	53.15 W
Santa Barbara do Tugúrio	**256**	21.15 S	43.35 W
Santa Barbara Island I	**228**	33.28 N	119.02 W
Santa Branca	**256**	23.24 S	45.53 W
Santa Branca, Represa ⊜[1]	**256**	23.20 S	45.50 W
Santaca	**158**	26.36 S	32.32 E
Santa Catalina, Arg.	**252**	21.57 S	66.04 W
Santa Catalina, Pil.	**116**	9.20 N	122.51 E
Santa Catalina, Ur.	**258**	33.49 S	57.29 W
Santa Catalina, Arroyo ≃	**288**	34.46 S	58.27 W
Santa Catalina, Gulf of ᑕ	**228**	33.20 N	117.45 W
Santa Catalina, Isla I	**232**	25.40 N	110.47 W
Santa Catalina, Laguna ⊜	**288**	34.46 S	58.27 W
Santa Catalina Island I	**228**	33.23 N	118.24 W
Santa Catalina o Calovébora	**236**	8.47 N	81.20 W
Santa Catarina, Méx.	**204**	31.37 N	115.48 W
Santa Catarina, Méx.	**232**	25.41 N	100.28 W
Santa Catarina □[3]	**252**	27.00 S	50.00 W
Santa Catarina, Ilha de I	**252**	27.36 S	48.30 W
Santa Catarina Juquila	**234**	16.14 N	97.18 W
Santa Caterina di Pittinuri	**71**	40.06 N	8.30 E
Santa Caterina Valfurva	**64**	46.25 N	10.29 E
Santa Caterina Villarmosa	**70**	37.35 N	14.02 E
Santa Cecília	**252**	26.56 S	50.27 W
Santa Cesarea Terme	**68**	40.02 N	18.29 E
Santa Clara, Col.	**246**	2.43 S	69.43 W
Santa Clara, Cuba	**240p**	22.24 N	79.58 W
Santa Clara, Méx.	**232**	29.17 N	107.01 W
Santa Clara, Méx.	**234**	19.41 N	102.30 W
Santa Clara, Méx.	**286a**	19.34 N	99.04 W
Santa Clara, Ca., U.S.	**226**	37.20 N	121.56 W
Santa Clara, Ut,. U.S.	**200**	37.07 N	113.39 W
Santa Clara □[6]	**226**	37.20 N	121.53 W
Santa Clara ≃, Ca., U.S.	**228**	34.14 N	119.16 W
Santa Clara ≃, Ut,. U.S.	**200**	37.05 N	113.36 W
Santa Clara, Bahía de ᑕ	**240p**	23.05 N	80.30 W
Santa Clara, University of ♁[2]	**282**	37.21 N	121.56 W
Santa Clara de Olimar	**252**	32.55 S	54.58 W
Santa Clara Indian Reservation ◆[4]	**200**	35.59 N	106.10 W
Santa Clara Valley V	**226**	37.10 N	121.40 W
Santa Clarita	**286d**	12.00 S	77.01 W
Santa Clotilde	**246**	2.34 S	73.44 W
Santa Coloma de Cervelló	**266d**	41.22 N	2.01 E
Santa Coloma de Farners	**34**	41.52 N	2.40 E
Santa Coloma de Gramanet	**266d**	41.27 N	2.13 E
Santa Comba	**34**	43.02 N	8.49 W
Santa Comba Dão	**34**	40.24 N	8.08 W
Santa Cristina	**64**	46.34 N	11.43 E
Santa Cristina d'aspromonte	**68**	38.15 N	15.58 E
Santa Croce	**64**	46.05 N	12.18 E
Santa Croce, Capo ➤	**70**	37.14 N	15.15 E
Santa Croce, Lago di ⊜	**64**	46.10 N	12.20 E
Santa Croce Camerina	**70**	36.50 N	14.31 E
Santa Croce del Sannio	**68**	41.23 N	14.43 E
Santa Croce di Magliano	**66**	41.42 N	14.59 E
Santa Croce Sull'Arno	**66**	43.42 N	10.47 E
Santa Cruz, Bra.	**250**	6.13 S	36.01 W
Santa Cruz, Bra.	**255**	19.56 S	40.09 W
Santa Cruz, Chile	**252**	34.38 S	71.22 W
Santa Cruz, C.R.	**236**	10.16 N	85.36 W
Santa Cruz, Méx.	**200**	31.14 N	110.35 W
Santa Cruz, Perú	**248**	6.37 S	78.57 W
Santa Cruz, Pil.	**116**	15.46 N	119.55 E
Santa Cruz, Pil.	**116**	6.50 N	125.25 E
Santa Cruz, Pil.	**116**	14.17 N	121.25 E
Santa Cruz (Tubajon), Pil.	**116**	10.19 N	125.33 E
Santa Cruz, Pil.	**116**	13.29 N	122.02 E
Santa Cruz, Pil.	**116**	13.04 N	120.43 E
Santa Cruz, Ca., U.S.	**226**	36.58 N	122.01 W
Santa Cruz, Ven.	**246**	8.25 N	71.39 W
Santa Cruz, Ven.	**286c**	10.26 N	67.01 W
Santa Cruz □[4]	**254**	49.00 S	70.00 W
Santa Cruz □[5]	**248**	17.30 S	61.30 W
Santa Cruz □[6]	**226**	36.58 N	122.01 W
Santa Cruz ◆[8], Bra.	**256**	22.56 S	43.41 W
Santa Cruz ◆[8], India	**272c**	19.05 N	72.50 E
Santa Cruz ≃, Arg.	**254**	50.08 S	68.20 W
Santa Cruz ≃, Cuba	**286b**	23.04 N	82.29 W
Santa Cruz ≃, N.A.	**200**	32.42 N	111.33 W
Santa Cruz, Ilha I	**287a**	22.52 S	43.07 W
Santa Cruz, Isla I	**246a**	0.38 S	90.23 W
Santa Cruz, Sierra de ⋏	**236**	15.40 N	89.15 W
Santa Cruz Basin ✢[1]	**14**	12.00 S	163.00 E
Santa Cruz Cabrália	**255**	16.17 S	39.02 W
Santa Cruz da Graciosa	**148a**	39.05 N	28.01 W
Santa Cruz das Flores	**148a**	39.27 N	31.07 W
Santa Cruz de Goiás	**255**	17.19 S	48.30 W
Santa Cruz de Juventino Rosas	**234**	20.39 N	101.00 W
Santa Cruz de la Palma	**148**	28.41 N	17.45 W
Santa Cruz de la Sierra	**248**	17.48 S	63.10 W
Santa Cruz de la Zarza	**34**	39.58 N	3.10 W
Santa Cruz del Quiché	**236**	15.02 N	91.08 W
Santa Cruz del Sur	**240p**	20.43 N	78.00 W
Santa Cruz de Mudela	**34**	38.38 N	3.28 W
Santa Cruz de Tenerife	**148**	28.27 N	16.14 W
Santa Cruz de Tenerife □[4], Esp.	**34**	28.20 N	16.50 W
Santa Cruz de Tenerife □[4], Esp.	**148**	28.15 N	17.00 W
Santa Cruz do Capibaribe	**250**	7.57 S	36.12 W
Santa Cruz do Piauí	**250**	7.09 S	41.48 W
Santa Cruz do Prata	**256**	21.12 S	46.45 W
Santa Cruz do Rio Pardo	**255**	22.55 S	49.37 W
Santa Cruz do Sul	**252**	29.43 S	52.26 W
Santa Cruz International Airport ⊠	**272c**	19.05 N	72.52 E
Santa Cruz Island I	**204**	34.01 N	119.45 W
Santa Cruz Islands II	**14**	11.00 S	166.15 E

Symbols in the index entries represent the broad categories identified in the key at the right. Symbols with superior numbers (⋏[1]) identify subcategories (see complete key on page *I · 1).*

Symbole im Register stellen die rechts im Schlüssel erklärten Kategorien dar. Symbole mit hochgestellten Ziffern (⋏[1]) bezeichnen Unterabteilungen einer Kategorie (vgl. vollständiger Schlüssel auf Seite *I · 1).*

Los símbolos incluídos en el texto del índice representan las grandes categorias identificadas con la clave a la derecha. Los símbolos con numeros en su parte superior (⋏[1]) identifican las subcategorías (véase la clave completa en la página *I · 1).*

Les symboles de l'index représentent les catégories indiquées dans la légende à droite. Les symboles suivis d'un indice (⋏[1]) représentent des sous-catégories (voir légende complète à la page *I · 1).*

Os símbolos incluídos no texto do índice representam as grandes categorias identificadas com a chave à direita. Os símbolos com números em sua parte superior (⋏[1]) identificam as subcategorias (veja-se a chave completa à página *I · 1).*

∧	Mountain	Berg	Montaña	Montagne	Montanha
⋏	Mountains	Gebirge	Montañas	Montagnes	Montanhas
)(	Pass	Paß	Paso	Col	Passo
V	Valley, Canyon	Tal, Cañon	Valle, Cañón	Vallée, Canyon	Vale, Canhão
≚	Plain	Ebene	Llano	Plaine	Planície
➤	Cape	Kap	Cabo	Cap	Cabo
I	Island	Insel	Isla	Île	Ilha
II	Islands	Inseln	Islas	Îles	Ilhas
⊥	Other Topographic Features	Andere Topographische Objekte	Otros Elementos Topográficos	Autres données topographiques	Outros acidentes topográficos

ESPAÑOL

Nombre	Página	Lat.°′	Long.°′ W = Oeste
Santa Cruz Meyehualco ◆[8]	286a	19.20 N	99.03 W
Santa Cruz Mountains ⋏	226	37.15 N	122.00 W
Santa Cruz Point ≻	116	15.44 N	119.52 E
Santa Cruz Tacache de Mina	234	17.51 N	98.07 W
Santadi	71	39.05 N	8.43 E
Santa Domenica Talao	68	39.49 N	15.51 E
Santa Domenica Vittoria	70	37.55 N	14.58 E
Sant Adrià de Besòs	266d	41.25 N	2.14 E
Santa Elena, Arg.	252	30.57 S	59.48 W
Santa Elena, Ec.	246	2.14 S	80.51 W
Santa Elena, El Sal.	236	13.22 N	88.25 W
Santa Elena, Méx.	196	27.59 N	103.56 W
Santa Elena, Méx.	232	27.28 N	102.33 W
Santa Elena, Méx.	234	18.39 N	101.34 W
Santa Elena ≃	248	15.42 S	67.13 W
Santa Elena, Bahía de ⊂	246	2.06 S	80.53 W
Santa Elena, Golfo de ⊂	236	10.59 N	85.50 W
Santa Elena, Punta ≻, C.R.	236	10.54 N	85.57 W
Santa Elena, Punta ≻, Ec.	246	2.11 S	81.00 W
Santa Elena del Gomero	286e	33.29 S	70.46 W
Santa Elena de Uairén	246	4.37 N	61.08 W
Santa Elisabetta	70	37.26 N	13.33 E
Santa Eufemia	34	38.36 N	4.54 W
Santa Eugenia	34	42.33 N	9.00 W
Santa Eulalia, Esp.	34	40.34 N	1.19 W
Santa Eulalia, Guat.	236	15.45 N	91.29 W
Santa Eulària del Riu	34	38.59 N	1.31 E
Santa Fe, Arg.	252	31.38 S	60.42 W
Santa Fé, Bra.	255	15.40 S	51.16 W
Santa Fé, Bra.	255	23.01 S	51.48 W
Santa Fe, Esp.	34	37.11 N	3.43 W
Santa Fe, Hond.	236	15.55 N	86.05 W
Santa Fé, Pan.	236	8.31 N	81.05 W
Santa Fe, Pil.	116	11.09 N	123.47 E
Santa Fe, Pil.	116	16.10 N	120.57 E
Santa Fe, Pil.	116	12.10 N	122.00 E
Santa Fe, Mo., U.S.	219	39.22 N	91.49 W
Santa Fe, N.M., U.S.	200	35.41 N	105.56 W
Santa Fe □[4]	252	31.00 S	61.00 W
Santa Fé ◆[8]	286b	23.05 N	82.31 W
Santa Fe ≃, Fl., U.S.	192	29.53 N	82.53 W
Santa Fe ≃, N.M., U.S.	200	35.36 N	106.20 W
Santa Fé, Aeropuerto ⊠	286b	23.04 N	82.28 W
Santa Fe, Isla I	246a	0.49 S	90.04 W
Santa Fé, Ribeirão ≃	287b	23.24 S	46.48 W
Santa Fe Baldy ∧	200	35.50 N	105.46 W
Santa Fe Dam ◆[6]	280	34.07 N	117.58 W
Santa Fe de Bogotá	246	4.36 N	74.05 W
Santa Fe de Minas	255	16.42 S	45.26 W
Santa Fé do Sul	255	20.13 S	50.56 W
Santa Fe Flood Control Basin ⊜[1]	280	34.07 N	117.58 W
Santa Fe Springs	280	33.56 N	118.04 W
Santa Filomena	250	9.07 S	45.56 W
Santa Fiora	66	42.50 N	11.35 E
Santa Flavia	70	38.05 N	13.31 E
Sant'Agata Bolognese	64	44.40 N	11.08 E
Sant'Agata de'Goti	68	41.05 N	14.30 E
Sant'Agata del Bianco	68	38.05 N	16.05 E
Sant'Agata di Militello	70	38.04 N	14.38 E
Sant'Agata di Puglia	68	41.09 N	15.23 E
Sant'Agata Feltria	66	43.52 N	12.12 E
Sant'Agata sul Santerno	66	44.26 N	11.51 E
Santa Gertrude (Sankt Gertraud)	64	46.29 N	10.53 E
Santa Gertrudis	196	26.09 N	98.44 W
Santa Giusta, Stagno di ⊜	71	39.52 N	8.35 E
Sant'Agostino	64	44.48 N	11.23 E
Sāntāhār	124	24.48 N	88.59 E
Santa Helena	250	2.14 S	45.18 W
Santa Helena de Goiás	255	17.43 S	50.35 W
Santai, Zhg.	85	39.14 N	77.42 E
Santai, Zhg.	86	44.35 N	81.18 E
Santai, Zhg.	102	31.10 N	105.02 E
Santai, Zhg.	104	41.48 N	121.53 E
Santai, Zhg.	104	41.56 N	123.11 E
Santai, Zhg.	105	38.58 N	115.49 E
Santa Inês	255	13.17 S	39.48 W
Santa Inés, Bahía ⊂	232	26.59 N	111.59 W
Santa Inés, Isla I	254	53.45 S	72.45 W
Santa Inés Ahuatempan	234	18.25 N	98.01 W
Santa Iria de Azóia	266c	38.51 N	9.05 W
Santa Isabel, Arg.	252	36.15 S	66.56 W
Santa Isabel, Arg.	252	33.54 S	61.42 W
Santa Isabel, Bra.	256	23.19 S	46.14 W
Santa Isabel, Ec.	246	3.21 S	79.19 W
Santa Isabel, Méx.	234	23.15 N	100.52 W
Santa Isabel, P.R.	240m	17.58 N	66.24 W
Santa Isabel I	175e	8.00 S	159.00 E
Santa Isabel ≃	236	15.59 N	90.00 W
Santa Isabel, Pico de ∧	152	3.35 N	8.46 E
Santa Isabel Creek ≃	196	27.39 N	99.38 W
Santa Isabel de Sihuas	248	16.20 S	72.06 W
Santa Isabel do Araguaia	250	6.07 S	48.19 W
Santa Isabel do Rio Prêto	256	22.14 S	44.05 W
Santa Isabel → Malabo	152	3.45 N	8.47 E
Santaizi	104	41.21 N	121.36 E
Santa Josefa	116	8.02 N	125.57 E
Santa Julia	286e	33.30 S	70.38 W
Santa Juliana	255	19.19 S	47.32 W
Sant'Alberto	66	44.32 N	12.09 E
Sant'Alfio	70	37.44 N	15.08 E
Sāntalpur	120	23.45 N	71.10 E
Santa Luce	66	43.28 N	10.34 E
Santa Lucía, Arg.	252	28.59 S	59.06 W
Santa Lucía, Arg.	252	31.32 S	68.29 W
Santa Lucía, Cuba	240p	21.02 N	76.00 W
Santa Lucía, Cuba	240p	22.40 N	83.58 W
Santa Lucia, It.	64	46.28 N	10.21 E
Santa Lucía, Ur.	258	34.27 S	56.24 W
Santa Lucía, Ven.	246	8.07 N	69.46 W
Santa Lucía ≃	258	34.48 S	56.22 W
Santa Lucia, Cabo → Saint Lucia, Cape ≻	158	28.25 S	32.25 E
Santa Lucía, Cuchilla ⋏[2]	258	34.09 S	56.11 W
Santa Lucía Chico ≃	258	34.21 S	56.20 W
Santa Lucía Cotzumalguapa	236	14.20 N	91.01 W
Santa Lucia Creek ≃	226	36.13 N	121.30 W
Santa Lucia del Mela	70	38.09 N	15.17 E
Santa Lucia di Piave	64	45.51 N	12.17 E
Santa Lucia Range ⋏	226	36.00 N	121.20 W
Santa Lucía → Saint Lucia □[1]	241f	13.53 N	60.58 W
Santaluz	250	11.15 S	39.22 W
Santa Luzia, Bra.	250	6.53 S	36.56 W
Santa Luzia, Port.	34	37.44 N	8.24 W
Santa Luzia I	150a	16.46 N	24.45 W
Santa Magdalena	252	34.30 S	63.56 W
Santa-Manza, Golfu di ⊂	71	41.37 N	9.22 E
Santa Margarita	226	35.23 N	120.36 W
Santa Margarita ≃	228	33.14 N	117.25 W

FRANÇAIS

Nom	Page	Lat.°′	Long.°′ W = Ouest
Santa Margarita, Isla I	232	24.27 N	111.50 W
Santa Margarita Lake ⊜[1]	226	35.20 N	120.28 W
Santa Margarita Mountains ⋏	228	33.30 N	117.25 W
Santa Margherita di Belice	70	37.41 N	13.01 E
Santa Margherita Ligure	62	44.20 N	9.12 E
Santa María, Arg.	252	26.41 S	66.02 W
Santa Maria, Bra.	252	29.41 S	53.48 W
Santa Maria, C.V.	150a	16.36 N	22.54 W
Santa María, C.R.	236	9.39 N	83.57 W
Santa María, Méx.	196	28.02 N	101.38 W
Santa María, Pan.	236	8.07 N	80.40 W
Santa Maria, Pil.	116	17.22 N	120.29 E
Santa María, P.R.	240m	18.09 N	65.26 W
Santa Maria, Schw.	58	46.16 N	9.09 E
Santa Maria, Schw.	58	46.36 N	10.24 E
Santa Maria, Ca., U.S.	204	34.57 N	120.26 W
Santa Maria I, Port.	148a	36.58 N	25.06 W
Santa Maria I, Vanuatu	175f	14.15 S	167.30 E
Santa Maria ≃, Bra.	252	29.48 S	54.56 W
Santa Maria ≃, Bra.	252	21.50 S	54.53 W
Santa María ≃, Méx.	232	31.00 N	107.14 W
Santa María ≃, Méx.	234	21.48 N	99.10 W
Santa María ≃, Pan.	236	8.06 N	80.29 W
Santa Maria ≃, Az., U.S.	200	34.19 N	113.31 W
Santa María, Bahía ⊂	232	25.04 N	108.06 W
Santa Maria, Cabo ≻	252	34.40 S	54.10 W
Santa Maria, Cabo de ≻, Ang.	152	13.25 S	12.32 E
Santa Maria, Cabo de ≻, Port.	34	36.58 N	7.54 W
Santa Maria, Cabo → Sainte-Marie, Cap ≻	157b	25.36 S	45.08 E
Santa Maria, Cape ≻	238	23.41 N	75.19 W
Santa María, Cayo I	240p	22.40 N	79.00 W
Santa María, Cerro ∧	286d	11.56 S	76.57 W
Santa Maria, Giogo di (Pass Umbrail))(	64	46.34 N	10.25 E
Santa María, Isla I, Chile	252	37.02 S	73.33 W
Santa María, Isla I, Ec.	246a	1.17 S	90.26 W
Santa Maria, Isola I	71	41.17 N	9.22 E
Santa María, Laguna de ⊜	200	31.07 N	107.16 W
Santa Maria, Ribeirão ≃	250	7.10 S	49.13 W
Santa María, Volcán ∧[1]	236	14.45 N	91.33 W
Santa María Ajoloapan	234	19.58 N	99.03 W
Santa Maria a Monte	66	43.42 N	10.42 E
Santa María Asunción Tlaxiaco	234	17.16 N	97.41 W
Santa Maria a Vico	68	41.02 N	14.29 E
Santa María Ayoquezco	234	16.41 N	96.50 W
Santa Maria Capua Vetere	68	41.05 N	14.15 E
Santa María Chimalapa	234	16.55 N	94.41 W
Santa María Colotepec	234	15.53 N	96.55 W
Santa Maria da Boa Vista	250	8.49 S	39.49 W
Santa Maria da Vitória	255	13.24 S	44.12 W
Santa Maria degli Angeli	66	43.03 N	12.34 E
Santa María de Huazamoto	234	22.30 N	104.30 W
Santa María de Ipire	246	8.49 N	65.19 W
Santa Maria de Itabira	255	19.27 S	43.08 W
Santa Maria del Cedro	68	39.45 N	15.50 E
Santa Maria della Versa	62	44.59 N	9.18 E
Santa Maria delle Grazie ʋ[1]	266b	45.27 N	9.10 E
Santa María del Oro	232	25.56 N	105.22 W
Santa María de los Ángeles	234	22.11 N	103.14 W
Santa María del Refugio	234	23.44 N	101.14 W
Santa María del Río	234	21.48 N	100.45 W
Santa María del Valle	234	20.54 N	102.22 W
Santa Mariá de Mohovano	232	26.42 N	103.39 W
Santa Maria di Galeria ◆[8]	267a	42.01 N	12.19 E
Santa Maria di Leuca, Capo ≻	68	39.47 N	18.22 E
Santa Maria di Licodia	70	37.37 N	14.53 E
Santa Maria di Siponto ʋ[1]	68	41.40 N	15.51 E
Santa Maria do Suaçuí	255	18.12 S	42.25 W
Santa María Huazolotitlán	234	16.17 N	97.56 W
Santa María Jalapa del Marqués	234	16.30 N	95.28 W
Santa María la Real de Nieva	34	41.04 N	4.24 W
Santa Maria Madalena	255	21.57 S	42.01 W
Santa Maria Maggiore	58	46.08 N	8.28 E
Santa Maria Maggiore ʋ[1]	267a	41.53 N	12.30 E
Santa Maria Nuova	66	43.29 N	13.18 E
Santa-Maria-Siché	36	41.52 N	8.59 E
Santa María Tulpetlac	286a	19.34 N	99.03 W
Santa María Xadani	234	15.56 N	96.04 W
Santa María Zoquitlán	234	16.33 N	96.23 W
Santa Marinella	66	42.02 N	11.51 E
Santa Marta, Col.	246	11.15 N	74.13 W
Santa Marta, Guat.	236	13.58 N	91.18 W
Santa Marta, Cabo de ≻, Ang.	152	13.52 S	12.25 E
Santa Marta, Cabo de ≻, Moç.	158	26.05 S	32.58 E
Santa Marta, Cerro ∧	234	18.19 N	94.48 W
Santa Marta, Ciénaga Grande ⊂	246	10.50 N	74.25 W
Santa Marta Grande, Cabo de ≻	252	28.38 S	48.45 W
Sant'Ambrogio	64	45.31 N	10.50 E
Santa Mónica, Méx.	196	28.12 N	100.37 W
Santa Monica, Ca., U.S.	228	34.01 N	118.29 W
Santa Mónica ◆[8]	286c	10.29 N	66.53 W
Santa Monica Bay ⊂	228	33.54 N	118.25 W
Santa Monica Beach State Park ♠	280	34.01 N	118.30 W
Santa Monica Mountains ⋏	228	34.05 N	118.40 W
Santa Monica Mountains National Recreation Area ♠	228	34.05 N	118.45 W
Santa Monica Municipal Airport ⊠	280	34.01 N	118.27 W
Santan	112	0.03 S	117.28 E
Santana	255	12.59 S	44.03 W
Santana ◆[8]	287b	23.29 S	46.38 W
Santana ≃	255	19.43 S	51.02 W
Santana, Coxilha de ⋏[2]	252	31.15 S	55.15 W
Santana, Ilha de I	250	2.18 S	43.41 W
Santana, Ribeirão ≃	250	9.47 S	50.13 W

PORTUGUÊS

Nome	Página	Lat.°′	Long.°′ W = Oeste
Santana da Boa Vista	252	30.52 S	53.07 W
Santana da Vargem	256	21.15 S	45.30 W
Santana de Caldas	256	21.50 S	46.24 W
Santana de Cataguases	256	21.17 S	42.33 W
Santana de Parnaíba	256	23.27 S	46.55 W
Santana de Parnaíba □[7]	287b	23.27 S	46.54 W
Santana do Campestre	256	21.16 S	42.56 W
Santana do Capivari	256	22.14 S	44.56 W
Santana do Cariri	250	7.11 S	39.44 W
Santana do Deserto	256	21.57 S	43.11 W
Santana do Garambéu	256	21.36 S	44.06 W
Santana do Ipanema	250	9.22 S	37.14 W
Santana do Livramento	252	30.53 S	55.31 W
Santana do Matos	250	5.57 S	36.39 W
Santander, Col.	246	3.01 N	76.28 W
Santander, Esp.	34	43.28 N	3.48 W
Santander, Pil.	116	9.25 N	123.20 E
Santander □[5]	246	7.00 N	73.15 W
Santander Jiménez	232	24.13 N	98.28 W
Sant'andrea, Isola I	68	40.03 N	17.57 E
Sant'Andrea Frius	71	39.29 N	9.10 E
Sant Andreu de la Barca	266d	41.27 N	1.59 E
Santa Nella	226	37.03 N	121.02 W
Santanésia	256	22.30 S	43.49 W
Santang	100	28.44 N	116.32 E
Sant'Angelo, Castel ⊥	267a	41.55 N	12.28 E
Sant'Angelo, Monte ∧	267a	41.56 N	12.49 E
Sant'Angelo dei Lombardi	68	40.56 N	15.11 E
Sant'Angelo in Vado	66	43.40 N	12.25 E
Sant'Angelo Lodigiano	62	45.14 N	9.24 E
Sant'Angelo Muxard	70	37.28 N	13.32 E
Sant'Angelo Romano	267a	42.02 N	12.42 E
Santanghu	102	44.13 N	93.22 E
Santanilla, Islas II	238	17.25 N	83.55 W
Santa Ninfa	70	37.46 N	12.53 E
Sant'Antimo	68	40.56 N	14.14 E
Sant'antine, Nuraghe ⊥	71	40.29 N	8.46 E
Sant'Antioco	71	39.04 N	8.27 E
Sant'Antioco, Isola di I	71	39.02 N	8.25 E
Sant Antoni de Portmany	34	38.58 N	1.18 E
Sant'Antonio Abate	68	40.43 N	14.32 E
Sant'Antonio di Santadi	71	39.43 N	8.29 E
Sant'Antonio Morignone	64	46.24 N	10.21 E
Santanyi	34	39.22 N	3.07 E
Santa Panagia, Capo ≻	70	37.07 N	15.18 E
Santa Paula	228	34.21 N	119.03 W
Santa Paula Creek ≃	228	34.21 N	119.03 W
Santa Perpètua de Mogoda	266d	41.32 N	2.11 E
Santapogue Creek ≃	276	40.40 N	73.21 W
Santa Pola, Cap de ≻	34	38.12 N	0.31 W
Sant'Apollinare in Classe ʋ[1]	66	44.22 N	12.15 E
Santaquin	200	39.58 N	111.47 W
Santa Quitéria	250	4.20 S	40.10 W
Santa Quitéria do Maranhão	250	3.31 S	42.32 W
Sant'Arcangelo	68	40.15 N	16.17 E
Santarcangelo di Romagna	66	44.04 N	12.27 E
Sant'Arcangelo Trimonte	68	41.10 N	14.56 E
Santarém, Bra.	250	2.26 S	54.42 W
Santarém, Port.	34	39.14 N	8.41 W
Santarém □[5]	266c	38.50 N	8.56 W
Santaren Channel ⊻	238	24.00 N	79.30 W
Santa Rita, Bra.	250	7.08 S	34.58 W
Santa Rita, Bra.	287a	22.41 S	43.28 W
Santa Rita, Col.	246	0.33 N	73.58 W
Santa Rita, Hond.	236	15.09 N	87.53 W
Santa Rita, Méx.	196	27.29 N	100.33 W
Santa Rita, Méx.	232	28.34 N	111.42 W
Santa Rita, Pil.	116	11.27 N	124.56 E
Santa Rita, Mt., U.S.	182	48.42 N	112.19 W
Santa Rita, Ven.	246	10.32 N	71.32 W
Santa Rita, Punta ≻	258	34.28 S	57.52 W
Santa Rita de Caldas	256	22.02 S	46.20 W
Santa Rita de Catuna	252	30.57 S	66.13 W
Santa Rita de Jacutinga	256	22.09 S	44.06 W
Santa Rita del Rucio	234	23.04 N	100.19 W
Santa Rita do Araguaia	255	17.20 S	53.12 W
Santa Rita do Ibitipoca	256	21.33 S	43.55 W
Santa Rita do Sapucaí	256	22.15 S	45.42 W
Santa Rita do Weil	246	3.29 S	69.19 W
Santa Rita Park	226	37.02 N	120.35 W
Santa Rosa, Arg.	252	36.37 S	64.17 W
Santa Rosa, Arg.	252	23.22 S	64.30 W
Santa Rosa, Bol.	248	14.10 S	66.53 W
Santa Rosa, Bol.	248	10.36 S	67.25 W
Santa Rosa, Bol.	248	17.07 S	63.35 W
Santa Rosa, Bra.	252	27.52 S	54.29 W
Santa Rosa, Bra.	255	15.01 S	47.13 W
Santa Rosa, Col.	246	2.31 N	68.13 W
Santa Rosa, C.R.	236	10.51 N	85.38 W
Santa Rosa, Ec.	246	3.27 S	79.58 W
Santa Rosa, Méx.	204	31.59 N	116.45 W
Santa Rosa, Méx.	234	22.18 N	104.24 W
Santa Rosa, Para.	248	21.46 S	61.43 W
Santa Rosa, Para.	252	26.52 S	56.49 W
Santa Rosa, Ca., U.S.	226	38.26 N	122.42 W
Santa Rosa, N.M., U.S.	196	34.56 N	104.40 W
Santa Rosa, Tx., U.S.	196	26.15 N	97.50 W
Santa Rosa, Ur.	258	34.30 S	56.03 W
Santa Rosa, Ven.	246	7.03 N	68.28 W
Santa Rosa, Ven.	246	8.26 N	69.24 W
Santa Rosa, Ven.	286c	10.30 N	66.46 W
Santa Rosa □[5]	236	14.10 N	90.18 W
Santa Rosa, Mount ∧[2]	174p	13.32 N	144.55 E
Santa Rosa, Parque Nacional ♠	236	10.50 N	85.45 W
Santa Rosa, Presa ⊜[1]	234	20.58 N	103.35 W
Santa Rosa Beach	194	30.23 N	86.13 W
Santa Rosa Creek ≃	226	35.34 N	121.06 W
Santa Rosa de Aguán	236	15.57 N	85.43 W
Santa Rosa de Amanadona	246	1.29 N	66.55 W
Santa Rosa [de Copán]	236	14.47 N	88.46 W
Santa Rosa de Huechuraba	286e	33.21 S	70.41 W
Santa Rosa del Conlara	252	32.20 S	65.12 W
Santa Rosa de Leales	252	27.09 S	65.15 W
Santa Rosa de Lima	236	13.37 N	87.53 W
Santa Rosa de Locobe	286e	33.26 S	70.33 W
Santa Rosa del Palmar	248	16.54 S	62.24 W
Santa Rosa de Osos	246	6.39 N	75.28 W
Santa Rosa de Río Primero	252	31.09 S	63.23 W
Santa Rosa de Sucumbíos	246	0.22 N	77.10 W
Santa Rosa de Viterbo	246	5.53 N	72.59 W
Santa Rosa Indian Reservation ◆[4]	204	33.35 N	116.35 W
Santa Rosa Island I, Ca., U.S.	204	33.58 N	120.06 W
Santa Rosa Island I, Fl., U.S.	194	30.22 N	86.55 W
Santa Rosa Jáuregui	234	20.44 N	100.27 W
Santa Rosalía, Méx.	196	26.08 N	98.59 W
Santa Rosalía, Méx.	232	27.19 N	112.17 W
Santa Rosalía, Ven.	246	9.02 N	69.01 W
Santa Rosa Range ⋏	204	41.35 N	117.40 W
Santa Rosa Wash ∨	200	33.00 N	112.00 W
Santa Rosita	286d	12.03 S	76.59 W
Sant'Arsenio	68	40.28 N	15.29 E
Šantarskije ostrova II	74	55.00 N	137.36 E
Santa Severa	66	42.02 N	11.57 E
Santa Severina	68	39.09 N	16.55 E
Santa Sofia	66	43.57 N	11.54 E
Santa Susana	228	34.16 N	118.43 W
Santa Susana Mountains ⋏	228	34.20 N	118.42 W
Santa Sylvina	252	27.49 S	61.09 W
Santa Tecla → Nueva San Salvador	236	13.41 N	89.17 W
Santa Teresa, Bra.	255	19.55 S	40.36 W
Santa Teresa, Méx.	196	29.34 N	104.39 W
Santa Teresa, Méx.	200	30.52 N	111.33 W
Santa Teresa, Méx.	232	25.17 N	97.51 W
Santa Teresa, Méx.	234	22.28 N	104.44 W
Santa Teresa ≃	255	11.47 S	48.37 W
Santa Teresa, Embalse de ⊜[1]	34	40.40 N	5.30 W
Santa Teresa de lo Ovalle	286e	33.23 S	70.47 W
Santa Teresa di Riva	70	37.57 N	15.22 E
Santa Teresa Gallura	71	41.14 N	9.11 E
Santa Tereza de Goiás	255	13.38 S	49.01 W
Santa Terezinha	250	10.28 S	50.31 W
Santa Valburga (Sankt Wallburg)	64	46.33 N	11.00 E
Santa Venerina	70	37.41 N	15.08 E
Santa Venetia	226	38.01 N	122.31 W
Santa Vitória	255	18.50 S	50.08 W
Santa Vitória do Palmar	252	33.31 S	53.21 W
Santa Vittoria, Monte ∧	71	39.45 N	9.18 E
Santa Vittoria in Matenano	66	43.01 N	13.29 E
Santa Ynez ≃	204	34.41 N	120.36 W
Santa Ynez Canyon ∨	280	34.04 N	118.34 W
Santa Ysabel Indian Reservation ◆[4]	204	33.11 N	116.41 W
Sant Bartomeu de la Quadra	266d	41.26 N	2.02 E
Sant Boi de Llobregat	266d	41.21 N	2.03 E
Sant Carles de la Ràpita	34	40.37 N	0.36 E
Sant Climent de Llobregat	266d	41.20 N	2.00 E
Sant Cugat del Vallès	266d	41.28 N	2.05 E
Santee	228	32.50 N	116.58 W
Santee ≃	192	33.14 N	79.28 W
Santee Dam ◆[6]	192	33.24 N	80.12 W
Santee Indian Reservation ◆[4]	198	42.45 N	97.50 W
Sant'Egidio alla Vibrata	66	42.49 N	13.42 E
Sant'Elena	64	45.12 N	11.43 E
Sant'Elia a Pianisi	66	41.38 N	14.52 E
Sant'Elia Fiumerapido	66	41.32 N	13.52 E
Sant'Elpidio a Mare	66	43.14 N	13.41 E
Santena	62	44.57 N	7.45 E
Santenay	58	46.55 N	4.41 E
Santeny	261	48.43 N	2.34 E
San Teodoro, It.	70	37.51 N	14.42 E
San Teodoro, It.	71	40.46 N	9.39 E
Santermo in Colle	68	40.48 N	16.45 E
Santerno ≃	66	44.34 N	11.58 E
Santerre □[9]	50	49.40 N	2.40 E
Sant'Eufemia, Golfo di ⊂	68	38.50 N	16.00 E
Sant'Eufemia a Maiella	66	42.07 N	14.02 E
Sant'Eufemia d'Aspromonte	68	38.16 N	15.52 E
Sant'Eufemia Lamezia	68	38.55 N	16.15 E
Sant Feliu de Guíxols	34	41.47 N	3.02 E
Sant Feliu de Llobregat	266d	41.23 N	2.03 E
Sant Fost de Campsentelles	266d	41.31 N	2.14 E
Sānthia, Bngl.	126	24.03 N	89.33 E
Santhià, It.	62	45.22 N	8.10 E
Santiago, Bol.	248	18.19 S	59.34 W
Santiago, Bra.	252	29.11 S	54.53 W
Santiago, Chile	252	33.27 S	70.40 W
Santiago, Chile	286e	33.27 S	70.40 W
Santiago, Méx.	232	23.28 N	109.43 W
Santiago, Pan.	236	8.06 N	80.59 W
Santiago, Para.	252	27.09 S	56.47 W
Santiago, Perú	248	14.11 S	75.44 W
Santiago, Pil.	116	16.41 N	121.33 E
Santiago I	150a	15.05 N	23.40 W
Santiago ≃, Arg.	288	34.50 S	57.57 W
Santiago ≃, Méx.	232	25.11 N	105.26 W
Santiago ≃, S.A.	246	4.27 S	77.38 W
Santiago, Cape ≻	116	13.46 N	120.39 E
Santiago, Cerro ∧	236	8.33 N	81.44 W
Santiago, Isla I, Arg.	288	34.50 S	57.53 W
Santiago, Isla I, Ec.	246a	0.14 S	90.45 W
Santiago, Serranía de ⋏	248	18.25 S	59.25 W
Santiago Atitlán	236	14.38 N	91.14 W
Santiago Chazumba	234	18.12 N	97.40 W
Santiago Choapan	234	17.20 N	95.57 W
Santiago Creek ≃, Ca., U.S.	228	35.06 N	119.17 W
Santiago Creek ≃, Ca., U.S.	228	33.46 N	117.54 W
Santiago Dam ◆[6]	280	33.47 N	117.43 W
Santiago de Cao	248	7.58 S	79.15 W
Santiago de Chocorvos	248	13.50 S	75.16 W
Santiago de Chuco	248	8.09 S	78.11 W
Santiago de Compostela	34	42.53 N	8.33 W
Santiago de Cuba	240p	20.01 N	75.49 W
Santiago de Cuba □[4]	240p	20.10 N	75.55 W
Santiago de Huari	248	19.00 S	66.48 W
Santiago de Huata	248	16.06 S	68.53 W
Santiago de la Peña	234	20.57 N	97.24 W
Santiago de las Vegas ◆[8]	286b	22.58 N	82.23 W
Santiago del Estero	252	27.47 S	64.16 W
Santiago del Estero □[4]	252	28.00 S	63.30 W
Santiago [de los Caballeros]	238	19.27 N	70.42 W
Santiago de Machaca	248	17.05 S	69.16 W
Santiago de Méndez	246	2.43 S	78.19 W
Santiago de Surco	286d	12.09 S	77.01 W
Santiago do Cacém	34	38.01 N	8.42 W
Santiago Island I	116	16.24 N	119.56 E
Santiago Ixcuintla	234	21.49 N	105.13 W
Santiago Ixtayutla	234	16.33 N	97.39 W
Santiago Jamiltepec	234	16.17 N	97.49 W
Santiago Juxtlahuaca	234	17.20 N	98.01 W
Santiago Lachiguirí	234	16.41 N	95.32 W
Santiago Larre	258	35.34 S	59.10 W
Santiago Maravatío	234	20.10 N	101.00 W
Santiago Papasquiaro	232	25.03 N	105.25 W
Santiago Peak ∧, Ca., U.S.	228	33.42 N	117.32 W
Santiago Peak ∧, Tx., U.S.	196	29.47 N	103.25 W
Santiago Pinotepa Nacional	234	16.19 N	98.01 W
Santiago Reservoir ⊜[1]	228	33.47 N	117.43 W
Santiago → Santiago de Compostela	34	42.53 N	8.33 W
Santiago Tepalcatlapan ◆[8]	286a	19.15 N	99.08 W
Santiago Tulantepec	234	20.02 N	98.22 W
Santiago Tutla	234	17.10 N	95.26 W
Santiago Tuxtla	234	18.28 N	95.18 W
Santiago Vázquez	258	34.48 S	56.21 W
Santiago Yaveo	234	17.19 N	95.42 W
Santiago Zacatepec	234	17.11 N	95.51 W
Santiaguillo, Laguna ⊜	232	24.48 N	104.48 W
Santiam Pass)(	202	44.25 N	121.51 W
San Tian Zhu (Three Indian Temples) ʋ[1]	106	30.15 N	120.08 E
Santiao Chiao ≻	100	25.02 N	121.59 E
Santiaoqiao	106	31.36 N	121.22 E
Santi Filippo e Giacomo	70	37.51 N	12.31 E
Santiguila	150	12.42 N	7.26 W
Sant'Ilario d'Enza	64	44.46 N	10.27 E
San Timoteo	246	9.48 N	71.04 W
San Timoteo Canyon ∨	228	34.04 N	117.17 W
Säntis ∧	58	47.15 N	9.21 E
Santissima Trinita di Saccargia ʋ[1]	71	40.41 N	8.42 E
Santíssimo ◆[8]	287a	22.53 S	43.31 W
Santisteban del Puerto	34	38.15 N	3.12 W
Sant Joan de Labritja	34	39.05 N	1.30 E
Sant Joan Despí	266d	41.22 N	2.04 E
Sant Jordi, Golf de ⊂	34	40.53 N	1.00 E
Sant Just Desvern	266d	41.23 N	2.05 E
Sant Mateu del Maestrat	34	40.28 N	0.11 E
Santō, Nihon	94	35.21 N	136.22 E
Santō, Nihon	96	35.19 N	134.53 E
Santo, Tx., U.S.	196	32.36 N	98.13 W
Santo, Vanuatu	175f	15.32 S	167.08 E
Santo Aleixo	256	22.34 S	43.04 W
Santo Amaro, Bra.	250	2.33 S	43.14 W
Santo Amaro, Bra.	255	12.32 S	38.43 W
Santo Amaro ◆[8]	287b	23.39 S	46.42 W
Santo Amaro, Ilha de I	256	23.57 S	46.14 W
Santo Amaro das Brotas	250	10.47 S	37.04 W
Santo Anastácio	255	21.58 S	51.39 W
Santo André	256	23.40 S	46.31 W
Santo Ângelo	252	28.18 S	54.16 W
Santo Antão I	150a	17.05 N	25.10 W
Santo Antônio, Bra.	250	6.18 S	35.27 W
Santo António, S. Tom./P.	152	1.39 N	7.26 E
Santo Antônio ≃, Bra.	250	11.31 S	48.37 W
Santo Antônio ≃, Bra.	255	17.30 S	45.37 W
Santo Antônio ≃, Bra.	287a	22.42 S	43.37 W
Santo António, Ilha de I	156	21.58 S	35.28 E
Santo António da Charneca	266c	38.37 N	9.02 W
Santo Antônio da Patrulha	252	29.50 S	50.32 W
Santo Antônio de Jesus	255	12.58 S	39.16 W
Santo Antônio de Pádua	255	21.32 S	42.11 W
Santo Antonio de Posse	256	22.36 S	46.55 W
Santo Antônio do Amparo	255	20.57 S	44.55 W
Santo Antônio do Aventureiro	256	21.45 S	42.49 W
Santo Antônio do Içá	246	3.05 S	67.57 W
Santo Antônio do Jardim	256	22.07 S	46.41 W
Santo Antônio do Leverger	248	15.52 S	56.05 W
Santo Antônio do Pinhal	256	22.47 S	45.41 W
Santo Antônio do Rio Verde	255	17.57 S	47.27 W
Santo Antônio do Sudoeste	252	26.02 S	53.44 W
Santo Augusto	252	27.51 S	53.47 W
Santo Corazón	248	17.59 S	58.51 W
Santo Domingo, Cuba	240p	22.35 N	80.15 W
Santo Domingo, Méx.	196	25.38 N	101.05 W
Santo Domingo, Méx.	196	25.48 N	104.28 W
Santo Domingo, Méx.	232	25.32 N	112.02 W
Santo Domingo, Nic.	236	12.16 N	85.05 W
Santo Domingo, Rep. Dom.	238	18.28 N	69.54 W
Santo Domingo ≃, Méx.	234	16.41 N	93.00 W
Santo Domingo ≃, Méx.	234	17.40 N	98.07 W
Santo Domingo ≃, Méx.	234	18.10 N	96.08 W
Santo Domingo ≃, Méx.	236	16.15 N	91.17 W
Santo Domingo, Arroyo ≃	204	30.43 N	116.03 W
Santo Domingo, Isla → Hispaniola I	238	19.00 N	71.00 W
Santo Domingo de la Calzada	34	42.26 N	2.57 W
Santo Domingo de los Colorados	246	0.15 S	79.09 W
Santo Domingo Indian Reservation ◆[4]	200	35.30 N	106.25 W
Santo Domingo Nuxaá	234	17.08 N	97.02 W
Santo Domingo Pueblo	200	35.30 N	106.21 W
Santo Domingo Tehuantepec	234	16.20 N	95.14 W
Santo Domingo Teojomulco	234	16.36 N	97.14 W
Santo Domingo Zanatepec	234	16.29 N	94.21 W
Santo Estêvão	255	12.26 S	39.13 W
Sant'Olcese	62	44.30 N	8.58 E
Santolea, Embalse de ⊜[1]	34	40.47 N	0.19 W
Santo / Malo □[8]	175f	15.20 S	166.55 E
San Tomé	246	8.58 N	64.08 W
San Tommaso	66	42.11 N	13.58 E
Sant'Omobono Imagna	62	45.48 N	9.32 E
Santoña	34	43.27 N	3.27 W
Santong ≃	98	42.39 N	126.03 E
Santo Nino Island I	116	11.55 N	124.27 E
Sant' Onofrio ◆[8]	267a	41.56 N	12.25 E
Santo Onofre ≃	255	12.34 S	43.12 W
Santop, Pic ∧	175f	18.39 S	169.03 E
Sant'Oreste	66	42.14 N	12.32 E
Santorini → Thíra I	38	36.24 N	25.29 E
Santorso	64	45.44 N	11.23 E
Santos	256	23.57 S	46.20 W
Santos, Arroyo de los ≃	258	35.28 S	57.29 W
Santos, Baía de ⊂	256	24.00 S	46.21 W
Santos Dumont	256	21.28 S	43.34 W
Santos Dumont, Aeroporto ⊠	256	22.55 S	43.10 W
Santoshpur	272b	22.40 N	88.10 E
Santo Stefano, Isola I	66	40.47 N	13.27 E
Santo Stefano Belbo	62	44.43 N	8.14 E
Santo Stefano d'Aveto	62	44.35 N	9.27 E
Santo Stefano di Cadore	64	46.33 N	12.32 E
Santo Stefano di Camastra	70	38.01 N	14.21 E
Santo Stefano di Magra	64	44.10 N	9.55 E
Santo Stefano Quisquina	70	37.37 N	13.29 E
Santo Stino di Livenza	64	45.44 N	12.41 E
Santos Tomás del Norte	236	13.11 N	86.56 W
Santo Tirso	34	41.21 N	8.28 W
Santo Tomás, Col.	246	10.46 N	74.45 W
Santo Tomás, Méx.	232	31.33 N	116.24 W
Santo Tomás, Nic.	236	12.04 N	85.05 W
Santo Tomás, Perú	248	6.36 S	77.48 W
Santo Tomás, Perú	248	14.29 S	72.06 W
Santo Tomas, Pil.	116	7.29 N	125.38 E
Santo Tomás ≃, Méx.	204	31.32 N	116.40 W
Santo Tomás ≃, Perú	248	13.47 S	72.09 W
Santo Tomás, Punta ≻	232	31.34 N	116.42 W
Santo Tomas, University of ʋ[2]	269f	14.37 N	120.59 E
Santo Tomás, Volcán ∧[1]	246a	0.48 S	91.07 W
Santo Tomás y Principe → Sao Tome and Principe □[1]	152	1.00 N	7.00 E
Santo Tomé, Arg.	252	28.33 S	56.03 W
Santo Tomé, Arg.	252	31.40 S	60.46 W
Santo Tomé de Guayana → Ciudad Guayana	246	8.22 N	62.40 W
Sant' Pietro, Lago di ⊜	68	41.01 N	15.30 E
Santpoort	52	52.25 N	4.38 E
Sant Quirze de la Serra	266d	41.32 N	2.05 E
Santuanjiang	106	30.54 N	121.43 E
Santuario de Quillacas	248	19.14 S	66.58 W
Santu Lussurgiu	71	40.08 N	8.39 E
Santunying	105	40.14 N	118.12 E
Sant Vicenç dels Horts	266d	41.24 N	2.01 E
San Ubaldo	236	11.51 N	85.20 W
Sanuki	268	35.16 N	139.53 E
Sanuki-sammyaku ⋏	96	34.09 N	134.11 E
Şānūr	132	32.21 N	35.15 E
San Valentino in Abruzzo Citeriore	66	42.14 N	13.59 E
San Valentino Torio	68	40.48 N	14.36 E
San Venanzo	66	42.52 N	12.16 E
San Vendemiano	64	45.54 N	12.20 E
San Vicente, Arg.	252	28.30 S	64.09 W
San Vicente, Arg.	258	34.58 S	58.22 W
San Vicente, El Sal.	236	13.38 N	88.48 W
San Vicente □[5]	288	34.56 S	58.24 W
San Vicente, Cabo → São Vicente, Cabo de ≻	34	37.01 N	9.00 W
San Vicente, Volcán de ∧[1]	236	13.36 N	88.51 W
San Vicente Creek ≃	282	37.32 N	122.31 W
San Vicente de Alcántara	34	39.21 N	7.08 W
San Vicente de Cañete	248	13.05 S	76.24 W
San Vicente de Chucurí	246	6.54 N	73.25 W
San Vicente de la Barquera	34	43.26 N	4.24 W
San Vicente del Caguán	246	2.07 N	74.46 W
San Vicente de Tagua-Tagua	252	34.26 S	71.05 W
San Vicente Mountain ∧	280	34.08 N	118.31 W
San Vicente Reservoir ⊜[1]	228	32.55 N	116.55 W
San Vicente → Saint Vincent and the Grenadines □[1]	241h	13.15 N	61.12 W
San Vicente Tancuayalab	234	21.44 N	98.34 W
San Vigilio	64	45.34 N	10.41 E
San Vigilio ʋ[1]	64	46.37 N	11.07 E
San Vincenzo	66	43.06 N	10.32 E
San Vito, C.R.	236	8.50 N	82.58 W
San Vito, It.	71	39.26 N	9.32 E
San Vito, Capo ≻	70	38.11 N	12.44 E
San Vito, Serralta di ∧	68	38.46 N	16.22 E
San Vito al Tagliamento	64	45.54 N	12.52 E
San Vito Chietino	66	42.18 N	14.27 E
San Vito dei Normanni	68	40.39 N	17.42 E
San Vito lo Capo	70	38.10 N	12.45 E
San Vito Romano	66	41.53 N	12.59 E
San Vito sullo Ionio	68	38.43 N	16.25 E
Sanwa, Nihon	94	37.07 N	138.21 E
Sanwa, Nihon	94	36.12 N	139.49 E
Sanwa, Nihon	96	34.42 N	133.15 E
San Xavier Indian Reservation ◆[4]	200	32.05 N	111.08 W
Sanxi, Zhg.	100	30.22 N	118.25 E
Sanxi, Zhg.	100	27.42 N	120.04 E
Sanxing, Zhg.	106	31.47 N	121.35 E
Sanxing, Zhg.	106	31.58 N	121.07 E
Sanxingchang, Zhg.	107	30.19 N	104.09 E
Sanxingchang, Zhg.	107	30.32 N	104.38 E
Sanxingjie	106	32.06 N	121.01 E
Sanyang, Zhg.	100	28.37 N	116.15 E
Sanyang, Zhg.	100	31.20 N	113.10 E
Sanyang, Zhg.	100	27.57 N	114.22 E
Sanyangzhen	106	31.55 N	121.29 E
Sanyanjing	104	41.28 N	122.27 E
Sanyanqiao	100	28.39 N	113.43 E
Sanyati ≃	154	16.49 S	28.45 E
San Ygnacio	196	27.03 N	99.27 W
Sanyō, Nihon	96	34.45 N	134.01 E
Sanyō, Nihon	96	34.02 N	131.10 E
Sanyuan	102	34.35 N	108.54 E
Sanyuanpu	98	42.02 N	125.44 E
Sanyuhao	98	42.30 N	117.34 E
Sanyuzhen	106	32.08 N	121.19 E
Sanza	68	40.15 N	15.33 E
Sanzao Dao I	100	22.03 N	113.21 E
Sanza Pombo	152	7.19 S	15.59 E
Sanzar ≃	85	40.00 N	67.40 E
San Zeno di Montagna	64	45.37 N	10.43 E
Sanzha	98	41.44 N	114.39 E
Sanzhan, Zhg.	89	49.42 N	125.20 E
Sanzhan, Zhg.	89	49.36 N	126.38 E
Sanzuodian	98	41.36 N	118.49 E
São Benedito	250	4.03 S	40.53 W
São Benedito ≃	250	9.11 S	57.02 W
São Benedito das Areias	256	21.19 S	47.02 W
São Benedito do Rio Preto	250	3.20 S	43.35 W
São Bento	250	2.42 S	44.50 W
São Bento ≃	256	21.42 S	45.18 W
São Bento, Mosteiro de ʋ[1]	287a	22.54 S	43.11 W

≃ River	Fluß	Río	Rivière	Rio
≅ Canal	Kanal	Canal	Canal	Canal
⌞ Waterfall, Rapids	Wasserfall, Stromschnellen	Cascada, Rápidos	Chute d'eau, Rapides	Cascata, Rápidos
⊻ Strait	Meeresstraße	Estrecho	Détroit	Estreito
⊂ Bay, Gulf	Bucht, Golf	Bahía, Golfo	Baie, Golfe	Baía, Golfo
⊜ Lake, Lakes	See, Seen	Lago, Lagos	Lac, Lacs	Lago, Lagos
⩩ Swamp	Sumpf	Pantano	Marais	Pântano
⍓ Ice Features, Glacier	Eis- und Gletscherformen	Accidentes Glaciales	Formes glaciaires	Acidentes glaciares
⫪ Other Hydrographic Features	Andere Hydrographische Objekte	Otros Elementos Hidrográficos	Autres données hydrographiques	Outros acidentes hidrográficos

✦ Submarine Features	Untermeerische Objekte	Accidentes Submarinos	Formes de relief sous-marin	Acidentes submarinos
□ Political Unit	Politische Einheit	Unidad Politica	Entité politique	Unidade política
ʋ Cultural Institution	Kulturelle Institution	Institución Cultural	Institution culturelle	Institução cultural
⊥ Historical Site	Historische Stätte	Sitio Histórico	Site historique	Sitio histórico
♠ Recreational Site	Erholungs- und Ferienort	Sitio de Recreo	Centre de loisirs	Area de Lazer
⊠ Airport	Flughafen	Aeropuerto	Aéroport	Aeroporto
■ Military Installation	Militäranlage	Instalación Militar	Installation militaire	Instalação militar
◆ Miscellaneous	Verschiedenes	Misceláneo	Divers	Diversos

São Bento Abade 256 21.35 S 45.04 W
São Bento de Caldas 256 22.08 S 46.18 W
São Bento do Norte 250 5.04 S 36.02 W
São Bento do Sapucaí 256 22.42 S 45.43 W
São Bento do Sul 252 26.15 S 49.23 W
São Bento do Una 250 8.32 S 36.22 W
São Bernardino 287a 22.40 S 43.26 W
São Bernardo 250 3.22 S 42.24 W
São Bernardo do Campo 256 23.42 S 46.33 W
São Bernardo do Campo □7 287b 23.44 S 46.33 W
São Borja 252 28.39 S 56.00 W
São Brás 250 10.05 S 36.55 W
São Brás de Alportel 34 37.09 N 7.53 W
São Braz, Cabo de ≻ 152 9.59 S 13.19 E
São Caetano de Odivelas 250 0.45 S 48.02 W
São Caetano do Sul 256 23.36 S 46.34 W
São Caetano do Sul □7 287b 23.37 S 46.33 W
São Carlos 255 22.01 S 47.54 W
São Cristóvão 250 11.01 S 37.12 W
São Cristóvão ✈8 287a 22.54 S 43.14 W
Saodatun 104 42.02 N 123.31 E
São Domingos, Bra. 252 26.34 S 52.32 W
São Domingos, Bra. 255 13.24 S 46.19 W
São Domingos, Bra. 256 21.41 S 42.47 W
São Domingos, Gui.-B. 150 12.22 N 16.08 W
São Domingos ≃, Bra. 248 12.28 S 64.13 W
São Domingos ≃, Bra. 255 13.24 S 47.12 W
São Domingos ≃, Bra. 255 19.13 S 50.44 W
São Domingos ≃, Bra. 255 20.03 S 53.13 W
São Domingos da Bocaina 256 21.50 S 44.01 W
São Domingos do Capim 250 1.41 S 47.47 W
São Domingos do Maranhão 250 5.42 S 44.22 W
São Felipe 255 14.49 S 41.23 W
São Félix de Balsas 250 7.08 S 44.52 W
São Félix do Araguaia 250 11.36 S 50.39 W
São Félix do Piauí 250 5.56 S 42.07 W
São Filipe 150a 14.54 N 24.31 W
São Francisco 255 15.57 S 44.52 W
São Francisco ≃, Bra. 242 10.30 S 36.24 W
São Francisco ≃, Bra. 255 16.09 S 40.39 W
São Francisco ≃, Bra. 256 21.50 S 42.42 W
São Francisco ≃, Bra. 287a 22.57 S 43.20 W
São Francisco, Baía de c 252 26.10 S 48.34 W
São Francisco, Ilha de I 252 26.18 S 48.37 W
São Francisco de Assis 252 29.33 S 55.08 W
São Francisco de Goiás 255 15.55 S 49.16 W
São Francisco de Paula 252 29.27 S 50.35 W
São Francisco do Croará 287a 22.42 S 43.08 W
São Francisco do Maranhão 250 6.15 S 42.52 W
São Francisco do Piauí 250 7.15 S 42.32 W
São Francisco do Sul 252 26.14 S 48.39 W
São Francisco Xavier 256 22.54 S 45.58 W
São Gabriel 252 30.20 S 54.19 W
São Gabriel da Palha 255 19.01 S 40.32 W
São Gabriel de Goiás 255 15.12 S 47.34 W
São Gonçalo, Bra. 256 21.36 S 46.19 W
São Gonçalo, Bra. 256 22.51 S 43.04 W
São Gonçalo □7 287a 22.48 S 43.01 W
São Gonçalo do Abaeté 255 18.20 S 45.49 W
São Gonçalo do Sapucaí 256 21.54 S 45.36 W
São Gonçalo dos Campos 255 12.25 S 38.58 W
São Hill 154 8.20 S 35.12 E
São Jerônimo 252 29.58 S 51.43 W
São Jerônimo, Serra de ≁1 255 16.30 S 54.50 W
São Jerônimo da Serra 255 23.43 S 50.44 W
São João 150 11.32 N 15.26 W
São João ≃, Bra. 255 12.27 S 51.07 W
São João ≃, Bra. 256 22.33 S 42.29 W
São João da Barra 255 21.38 S 41.03 W
São João da Boa Vista 256 21.58 S 46.47 W
São João D'Aliança 255 14.42 S 47.32 W
São João da Madeira 34 40.54 N 8.30 W
São João da Mata 256 21.56 S 45.56 W
São João da Ponte 255 15.56 S 44.01 W
São João da Serra 256 21.28 S 43.27 W
São João das Lampas 266c 38.52 N 9.24 W
São João de Côrtes 250 2.12 S 44.32 W
São João del-Rei 255 21.09 S 44.16 W
São João de Meriti 256 22.48 S 43.22 W
São João de Meriti □7 287a 22.48 S 43.21 W
São João de Meriti ≃ 287a 22.48 S 43.18 W
São João do Araguaia 250 5.23 S 48.46 W
São João do Jaguaribe 250 5.16 S 38.16 W
São João do Paraíso 255 15.19 S 42.01 W
São João do Piauí 250 8.21 S 42.15 W
São João do Sabugi 250 6.43 S 37.12 W
São João dos Patos 250 6.30 S 43.42 W
São João Evangelista 255 18.32 S 42.45 W
São João Nepomuceno 256 21.33 S 43.01 W
São João Novo 256 23.33 S 47.01 W
São Joaquim 252 28.18 S 49.56 W
São Joaquim, Parque Nacional de ♦ 252 28.15 S 49.57 W
São Joaquim da Barra 255 20.35 S 47.53 W
São Jorge I 148a 38.38 N 28.03 W
São Jorge, Castelo de ⊥ 266c 38.43 N 9.08 W
São José, Bra. 252 27.38 S 48.39 W
São José, Bra. 256 22.43 S 42.36 W
São José ≃, Bra. 255 19.10 S 42.12 W
São José ≃, Bra. 287a 22.39 S 43.27 W
São José, Ponta de ≻ 152 12.36 S 13.12 E
São José da Laje 250 9.01 S 36.03 W
São José de Anauá 246 1.00 N 61.23 W
São José de Encoge 152 7.38 S 14.41 E
São José de Mipibu 250 6.05 S 35.15 W
São José do Piranhas 250 7.07 S 38.30 W
São José do Alegre 256 22.19 S 45.32 W
São José do Barreiro 256 22.38 S 44.35 W
São José do Belmonte 250 7.52 S 38.46 W
São José do Campestre 250 6.18 S 35.42 W
São José do Cedro 252 26.30 S 53.30 W
São José do Egito 250 7.28 S 37.16 W
São José do Gurupi 250 1.36 S 46.13 W
São José do Norte 252 32.01 S 52.03 W
São José do Peixe 250 7.24 S 42.34 W
São José do Piriá 250 1.17 S 46.18 W
São José do Rio Pardo 256 21.36 S 46.54 W
São José do Rio Preto, Bra. 255 20.48 S 49.23 W
São José do Rio Prêto, Bra. 256 22.10 S 42.57 W
São José dos Campos 256 23.11 S 45.53 W
São José dos Lopes 256 21.48 S 43.53 W
São José dos Pinhais 252 25.31 S 49.13 W
São José do Turvo 256 22.21 S 43.59 W
São Julião da Barra 266c 38.40 N 9.21 W
São Julião do Tojal 266c 38.51 N 9.08 W
São Leopoldo 252 29.46 S 51.09 W
São Lourenço 256 22.07 S 45.03 W
São Lourenço, Pantanal de ⊞ 248 17.30 S 56.30 W
São Lourenço da Serra 256 23.52 S 46.57 W
São Lourenço do Oeste 252 26.24 S 52.46 W
São Lourenço do Sul 252 31.22 S 51.58 W
São Luís 250 2.31 S 44.16 W
São Luís de Montes Belos 255 16.32 S 50.20 W
São Luís do Curu 250 3.40 S 39.14 W
São Luís Do Paraitinga 256 23.14 S 45.20 W
São Luís do Quitunde 250 9.20 S 35.33 W
São Luís Gonzaga 252 28.24 S 54.58 W
São Mamede 250 6.56 S 37.06 W
São Manuel 255 22.44 S 48.34 W
São Manuel ≃ 242 7.21 S 58.03 W
São Manuel do Guaiaçu 256 21.20 S 42.51 W
São Marcos ≃ 255 18.15 S 47.37 W
São Mateus, Bra. 255 18.44 S 39.51 W
São Mateus, Bra. 256 22.49 S 43.23 W
São Mateus, Port. 148a 38.26 N 28.27 W
São Mateus, Braço Norte ≃ 255 18.37 S 40.05 W
São Mateus de Minas 256 22.42 S 46.03 W
São Mateus do Sul 252 25.52 S 50.23 W
São Miguel 250 6.13 S 38.30 W
São Miguel I 148a 37.47 N 25.30 W
São Miguel ≃ 255 16.26 S 41.00 W
São Miguel do Araguaia 255 13.19 S 50.13 W
São Miguel d'Oeste 252 26.45 S 53.34 W
São Miguel do Guamá 250 1.37 S 47.27 W
São Miguel dos Campos 250 9.47 S 36.05 W
São Miguel dos Macacos 250 1.11 S 50.28 W
São Miguel do Tapuio 250 5.30 S 41.20 W
São Miguel Paulista (Baquirivu) ✈8 256 23.30 S 46.26 W
Saona, Isla I 238 18.09 N 68.40 W
Saonara 64 45.22 N 11.59 E
Saône ≃ 58 45.44 N 4.50 E
Saône-et-Loire □5 32 46.42 N 4.45 E
Saonek 164 0.28 S 130.47 E
Saoner 120 21.23 N 78.54 E
São Nicolau I 150a 16.35 N 24.15 W
São Nicolau ≃ 250 5.45 S 42.02 W
São Paulo, Bra. 256 23.32 S 46.37 W
São Paulo, Bra. 287b 23.32 S 46.37 W
São Paulo □3 255 22.00 S 49.00 W
São Paulo □7 287b 23.33 S 46.38 W
São Paulo, Ribeirão de ≃ 256 22.16 S 46.37 W
São Paulo de Olivença 246 3.27 S 68.48 W
São Paulo do Potengi 250 5.55 S 35.45 W
São Pedro 255 19.53 S 51.55 W
São Pedro ≃ 255 16.30 S 41.17 W
São Pedro de Caldas 256 21.49 S 46.16 W
São Pedro de Viseu 250 2.33 S 49.33 W
São Pedro do Estoril 266c 38.42 N 9.22 W
São Pedro do Piauí 250 5.56 S 42.43 W
São Pedro do Sul, Bra. 252 29.37 S 54.10 W
São Pedro do Sul, Port. 34 40.45 N 8.04 W
São Rafael 250 5.47 S 36.55 W
São Raimundo das Mangabeiras 250 7.01 S 45.29 W
São Raimundo Nonato 250 9.01 S 42.42 W
Saorge 62 43.59 N 7.33 E
Saori 94 35.11 N 136.44 E
São Romão 255 16.22 S 45.04 W
São Roque, Bra. 256 23.32 S 47.08 W
São Roque, Bra. 256 23.06 S 44.42 W
São Roque, Cabo de ≻ 250 5.29 S 35.16 W
São Roque da Fartura 256 21.51 S 46.45 W
São Salvador — Salvador 255 12.59 S 38.31 W
São Sebastião 256 23.48 S 45.25 W
São Sebastião, Canal de ⊻ 256 23.48 S 45.23 W
São Sebastião, Ilha de I 256 23.50 S 45.18 W
São Sebastião, Pico de ∧ 256 23.52 S 45.23 W
São Sebastião, Ponta ≻ 156 22.07 S 35.30 E
São Sebastião da Bela Vista 256 22.10 S 45.45 W
São Sebastião da Boa Vista 250 1.42 S 49.31 W
São Sebastião da Grama 256 21.43 S 46.49 W
São Sebastião da Vitória 256 21.14 S 44.25 W
São Sebastião do Barreado 256 22.04 S 43.38 W
São Sebastião do Maranhão 255 18.05 S 42.35 W
São Sebastião do Paraíso 255 20.55 S 47.00 W
São Sebastião do Rio Claro 255 15.45 S 51.30 W
São Sebastião do Rio Verde 256 22.13 S 44.58 W
São Sebastião dos Robertos 256 22.13 S 46.32 W
São Sebastião do Umbuzeiro 250 8.09 S 37.01 W
São Sepé 252 30.10 S 53.34 W
São Silvestre do Jacareí 256 23.23 S 46.01 W
São Simão, Bra. 255 18.56 S 50.30 W
São Simão, Bra. 255 21.30 S 47.33 W
São Simão, Represa de ⊜1 255 18.40 S 50.00 W
São Tiago 255 20.55 S 44.30 W
São Timóteo 255 13.51 S 42.11 W
São Tomé, Bra. 250 5.58 S 36.04 W
São Tomé, S. Tom./P. 152 0.20 N 6.44 E
São Tomé I 152 0.12 N 6.39 E
São Tomé ≃, Bra. 250 8.10 S 58.13 W
São Tomé ≃, Bra. 256 21.26 S 46.02 W
São Tomé, Cabo de ≻ 255 21.59 S 40.59 W
São Tomé, Pico de ∧ 152 0.16 N 6.33 E
Sao Tome and Principe (São Tomé e Principe) □1, Afr. 138 1.00 N 7.00 E
Sao Tome and Principe (São Tomé e Principe) □1, Afr. 152 1.00 N 7.00 E
São Tomé das Letras 256 21.43 S 44.59 W
São Tomé-et-Principe — Sao Tome and Principe □1 152 1.00 N 7.00 E
Saou 62 44.39 N 5.04 E
Saoura, Oued V 148 29.00 N 0.55 W
São Valério ≃ 250 11.20 S 48.28 W
São Vicente 256 23.58 S 46.23 W
São Vicente I 150a 16.50 N 25.00 W
São Vicente, Cabo de (Cape Saint Vincent) ≻ 34 37.01 N 9.00 W
São Vicente, Ribeirão ≃ 256 21.59 S 45.40 W
São Vicente de Minas 256 21.42 S 44.27 W
São Vicente Ferrer 250 7.35 S 35.30 W
Sa Pa 110 22.21 N 103.50 E
Sápai 38 41.02 N 25.41 E
Sapanca 130 40.41 N 30.16 E
Sapang Baho ≃ 269f 14.33 N 121.06 E
Sapao 116 10.01 N 126.02 E
Sapão ≃ 250 11.01 S 45.32 W
Saparua, Pulau I 164 3.34 S 128.40 E
Sapatgrām 124 26.20 N 90.08 E
Sapé, Bra. 250 7.06 S 35.13 W
Sape, Indon. 115b 8.34 S 118.59 E
Sapé ≃ 287a 22.52 S 43.02 W
Sape, Selat ⊻ 115b 8.39 S 119.18 E
Sapele 150 5.54 N 5.41 E
Sapello ≃ 200 35.47 N 104.59 W
Sapelo Island I 192 31.28 N 81.15 W
Saperkino 80 54.05 N 51.38 E
Şaphane 130 39.01 N 29.14 E
Sapian Bay c 116 11.33 N 122.37 E
Sapindji 152 9.39 S 23.12 E
Sapitwa ∧ 154 15.57 S 35.36 E
Šapki 76 59.36 N 31.14 E
Šapkina ≃ 24 66.44 N 52.25 E
Šapkino 80 51.42 N 42.24 E
Šapkovo, Ross. 76 55.47 N 33.20 E
Šapkovo, Ross. 82 54.34 N 39.10 E
Sa Pobla 34 39.46 N 3.01 E
Sapodilla Cays I 236 16.08 N 88.15 W
Saponara 70 38.11 N 15.26 E
Saponé 150 12.03 N 1.36 W
Sap'o-ri 98 40.49 N 129.31 E
Sap'ornaja 265a 59.46 N 30.41 E
Saporoschje — Zaporožje 78 47.50 N 35.10 E
Saposoa 248 6.56 S 76.48 W
Sapou 175c 7.18 N 151.53 E
Sapožok 80 53.56 N 40.41 E
Sappa Creek ≃ 198 40.07 N 99.38 W
Sappa Creek, Middle Fork ≃ 198 39.40 N 100.53 W
Sappa Creek, North Fork ≃ 198 39.47 N 100.35 W
Sappa Creek, South Fork ≃ 198 39.47 N 100.35 W
Sappada 64 46.34 N 12.41 E
Sapphire Mountains ≁ 202 46.20 N 113.45 W
Sappho 224 48.04 N 124.16 W
Sappington 219 38.32 N 90.22 W
Sapporo 92a 43.03 N 141.21 E
Sapri 68 40.04 N 15.38 E
Šapša 76 60.34 N 34.01 E
Sap Songkhla, Thale c 110 7.13 N 100.30 E
Šapsugskaja 78 44.45 N 38.05 E
Šaptajev 86 47.55 N 67.28 E
Saptakośī ≃ 124 26.31 N 86.58 E
Sapta-ri 271b 37.43 N 126.44 E
Sapu 152 12.29 S 19.26 E
Sapucaí 256 22.19 S 46.42 W
Sapucaí ≃ 256 21.33 S 45.46 W
Sapucaia 256 22.00 S 42.54 W
Sapucaí-Mirim 256 22.44 S 45.45 W
Sapucaí-Mirim ≃ 256 22.12 S 45.53 W
Sapudi, Pulau I 115a 7.06 S 114.20 E
Sapulpa 196 35.59 N 96.06 W
Sapulu 115a 6.54 S 113.02 E
Sapuran 115a 7.28 S 109.58 E
Sapwe 154 10.57 S 28.10 E
Sāq, Jabal ∧2 128 26.17 N 43.16 E
Sāqiat al-'Abd 140 20.48 N 30.19 E
Sāqiyat Makkī 142 30.00 N 31.13 E
Saqqārah 142 29.51 N 31.13 E
Saqqārah (Step Pyramid) ⊥ 142 29.52 N 31.13 E
Saqqez 128 36.14 N 46.16 E
Saquarema 256 22.56 S 42.30 W
Saquarema, Lagoa de c 256 22.55 S 42.33 W
Saquena 248 4.40 S 73.31 W
Saquish Neck ≻1 283 42.00 N 70.37 W
Saquisilí 246 0.51 S 78.40 W
Sāra, Bngl. 126 24.07 N 89.02 E
Sara, Burkina 150 11.43 N 3.50 W
Sara, Pil. 116 11.16 N 123.01 E
Sara, Ross. 80 54.38 N 46.46 E
Sarāb 128 37.56 N 47.32 E
Sarabia, Méx. 234 20.31 N 101.05 W
Sarabia, Méx. 234 17.03 N 95.01 W
Sarabia ≃ 234 17.11 N 94.56 W
Sarābiyūm 142 30.23 N 32.17 E
Saraburi 110 14.32 N 100.55 E
Saracena 68 39.46 N 16.09 E
Saraceno, Monte ∧ 66 41.27 N 14.44 E
Saracura ≃ 255 12.18 S 40.07 W
Saracuruna ≃ 287a 22.41 S 43.13 W
Sarafére 150 15.50 N 3.42 W
Saragosa 196 31.01 N 103.39 W
Saragossa — Zaragoza 34 41.38 N 0.53 W
Saraguay ✈8 275a 45.31 N 73.45 W
Saraguro 246 3.36 S 79.13 W
Sarai 80 53.44 N 41.00 E
Sarāi Ālamgīr 123 32.54 N 73.45 E
Saraikela 124 22.43 N 85.57 E
Sarāi Naurang 123 32.50 N 70.47 E
Sarāipāli 124 21.20 N 83.00 E
Säräisniemi 26 64.27 N 26.47 E
Sarajas de Madrid ✈8 266a 40.28 N 3.35 W
Sarajčik 80 47.30 N 51.43 E
Sarajevo 38 43.52 N 18.25 E
Saraj-Gir 80 53.36 N 53.24 E
Saraji 166 22.21 S 148.18 E
Sarajskij 80 47.19 N 40.45 E
Sarakhs 128 36.32 N 61.11 E
Saraktaš 86 51.50 N 56.22 E
Sarala 86 54.52 N 89.14 E
Saraland 194 30.49 N 88.04 W
Šaraldaj 88 51.01 N 107.38 E
Saralžinskaja 80 49.12 N 48.55 E
Saramacca □5 250 5.40 N 55.40 W
Saramacca ≃ 250 5.51 N 55.53 W
Saramaguacán ≃ 240p 21.30 N 77.17 W
Saran, Fr. 50 47.57 N 1.53 E
Saran', Kaz. 86 49.46 N 72.52 E
Šaran, Ross. 80 54.49 N 54.00 E
Saran, Gunung ∧ 112 0.25 S 111.18 E
Saranac 216 42.55 N 85.12 W
Saranac ≃ 188 44.42 N 73.27 W
Saranac Lake 188 44.19 N 74.07 W
Saranakan, gora ∧ 88 52.35 N 113.50 E
Saranap 226 37.53 N 122.06 W
Šaranbaš-Kn'azevo 80 54.58 N 54.09 E
Saranda 154 5.43 S 34.59 E
Sarandapótamos ≃ 267c 38.26 N 23.54 E
Sarandë 38 39.52 N 20.00 E
Sarandi 252 27.56 S 52.55 W
Sarandí ✈8 258 34.40 S 58.21 W
Sarandí del Yi 252 33.21 S 55.38 W
Sarandí Grande 258 33.44 S 56.20 W
Sarandira 256 21.50 S 43.11 W
Šaranga 80 57.11 N 46.34 E
Sarangani Bay c 116 5.57 N 125.11 E
Sarangani Island I 116 5.27 N 125.28 E
Sarangani Islands II 116 5.25 N 125.26 E
Sarangani Strait ⊻ 116 5.31 N 125.23 E
Sārangarh 120 21.36 N 83.05 E
Sārangpur 124 23.34 N 76.28 E
Sārankhola 126 22.18 N 89.47 E
Saranley 144 2.22 N 42.17 E
Saranpaul' 24 64.14 N 60.53 E
Saransk 80 54.11 N 45.11 E
Sarantina, Valle V 64 46.35 N 11.25 E
Sara Peak ∧ 150 9.41 N 9.17 E
Saraphi 110 18.43 N 99.03 E
Sarapiquí ≃ 236 10.43 N 83.56 W
Sarapó ≃ 287a 22.46 S 43.37 W
Šarapovo, Ross. 80 55.17 N 44.42 E
Šarapovo, Ross. 82 55.11 N 37.16 E
Sarapuí ≃ 287a 22.46 S 43.24 W
Sarapuí, Canal de ⊠ 287a 22.44 S 43.16 W
Sarapul 80 56.28 N 53.48 E
Sarapul'skaja vozvyšennost' ≁1 80 56.15 N 53.30 E
Sarapul'skoje 89 48.52 N 135.59 E
Sarāqib 130 35.52 N 36.48 E
Sarare 246 9.47 N 69.10 W
Sarare ≃ 246 7.18 N 70.41 W
Sarar Plain ⊻ 144 9.25 N 46.17 E
Sara Sara, Nevado ∧ 248 15.19 S 73.27 W
Sarasota 220 27.20 N 82.31 W
Sarasota □6 220 27.10 N 82.21 W
Sarasota Bay c 220 27.23 N 82.39 W
Sarasota-Bradenton Airport ✈ 220 27.24 N 82.33 W
Sarasota Springs 220 27.17 N 82.28 W
Saraswati ≃ 272b 22.59 N 88.22 E
Sarata 78 46.02 N 29.38 E
Sarath 126 24.14 N 86.50 E
Saratoga, Austl. 170 33.28 S 151.21 E
Saratoga, Ca., U.S. 226 37.15 N 122.01 W
Saratoga, In., U.S. 216 40.14 N 84.55 W
Saratoga, Tx., U.S. 222 30.17 N 94.31 W
Saratoga, Wy., U.S. 200 41.27 N 106.48 W
Saratoga □6 210 43.00 N 73.51 W
Saratoga Battlefield Monument ⊥ 210 43.05 N 75.36 W
Saratoga Creek ≃ 282 37.25 N 121.58 W
Saratoga Lake ⊜ 210 43.01 N 73.39 W
Saratoga National Historical Park ♦ 210 43.00 N 73.38 W
Saratoga Passage ⊻ 224 48.10 N 122.30 W
Saratoga Spa State Park ♦ 210 43.03 N 73.50 W
Saratoga Springs 210 43.04 N 73.47 W
Šara-Togot 88 51.01 N 106.43 E
Saratok 112 1.44 N 111.20 E
Saratov 80 51.34 N 46.02 E
Saratov □8 76 52.00 N 42.40 E
Saratovka 86 51.12 N 54.54 E
Saratovskoje vodochranilišče ⊜1 80 52.45 N 48.30 E
Saraurcu ∧ 246 0.06 S 77.55 W
Sarāvān, Īrān 128 27.15 N 62.40 E
Saravan, Lao 110 15.43 N 106.25 E
Sarawak □3 112 2.30 N 113.30 E
Saray 130 41.26 N 27.55 E
Saraya, Guinée 150 10.46 N 10.24 W
Saraya, Sén. 150 12.50 N 11.45 W
Sarāyān 128 33.51 N 58.31 E
Saraycık 130 40.57 N 35.08 E
Saraydüzü 130 41.20 N 34.52 E
Sarā-ye Ahmadī 128 27.56 N 56.42 E
Sarayevo — Sarajevo 38 43.52 N 18.25 E
Sarayköy 130 37.55 N 28.58 E
Sarayönü 130 38.17 N 32.25 E
Sarbaj 80 53.39 N 51.34 E
Sarbāz 128 26.39 N 61.15 E
Sarbinowo 54 52.40 N 14.40 E
Sárbogárd 30 46.53 N 18.38 E
Sarca ≃ 64 45.52 N 10.52 E
Sarce ≃ 50 48.09 N 4.18 E
Sarcee Indian Reserve ✈4 182 50.58 N 114.06 W
Sarcelle, Passe de la ⊻ 175f 22.29 S 167.12 E
Sarcelles 50 49.00 N 2.23 E
Sarche di Calavino 64 46.03 N 10.57 E
Sarcidano ✈1, It. 36 39.55 N 9.05 E
Sarcidano ✈1, It. 71 39.49 N 9.10 E
Sarčino 86 53.09 N 81.45 E
Sarclet 44 58.22 N 3.07 W
Sarcoxie 194 37.04 N 94.06 W
Sārda (Mahākālī) ≃ 124 27.22 N 81.23 E
Sard āb)(123 36.40 N 71.32 E
Sārda Canal ⊠ 124 28.08 N 80.24 E
Sardagna 64 46.03 N 11.06 E
Sardah 124 24.18 N 88.44 E
Sardāra 128 34.48 N 58.07 E
Sardara 71 39.37 N 8.49 E
Sardār Chāh 128 27.58 N 64.50 E
Sardārpur 120 22.39 N 74.59 E
Sardārshahr 120 28.26 N 74.29 E
Sar Dasht, Īrān 128 36.09 N 45.28 E
Sar Dasht, Īrān 128 32.32 N 48.52 E
Sardegna □4 71 40.00 N 9.00 E
Sardegna (Sardinia) I 71 40.00 N 9.00 E
Sardeh Band 120 33.17 N 68.39 E
Sardhana 124 29.09 N 77.37 E
Sardiha 126 22.22 N 87.09 E
Sardinal 236 10.31 N 85.39 W
Sardinata 246 8.05 N 72.48 W
Sardinia, N.Y., U.S. 210 42.32 N 78.31 W
Sardinia, Oh., U.S. 218 39.00 N 83.48 W
Sardinia — Sardegna I 71 40.00 N 9.00 E
Sardinien — Sardegna I 71 40.00 N 9.00 E
Sardis, B.C., Can. 224 49.08 N 121.57 W
Sardis, Al., U.S. 194 32.17 N 86.59 W
Sardis, Ga., U.S. 192 32.58 N 81.45 W
Sardis, Ky., U.S. 218 38.31 N 83.57 W
Sardis, Ms., U.S. 194 34.26 N 89.55 W
Sardis, Pa., U.S. 279b 40.29 N 79.42 W
Sardis, Tn., U.S. 194 35.27 N 88.18 W
Sardis Lake ⊜1 194 34.27 N 89.43 W
Sardona, Piz ∧ 58 46.55 N 9.15 E
Šardonem' 24 63.56 N 44.37 E
Sarek ∧ 24 67.25 N 17.46 E
Sareks Nationalpark ♦ 24 67.15 N 17.30 E
Sārenga, India 126 22.46 N 87.02 E
Sārenga, India 272b 22.31 N 88.13 E
Sarentino (Sarnthein) 64 46.38 N 11.21 E
Sar-e Pol 120 36.14 N 65.55 E
Sarepta 194 32.53 N 93.26 W
Sarezzo 64 45.39 N 10.12 E
Sargans 58 47.03 N 9.26 E
Sargasso Sea ⊤2 8 30.00 N 50.00 W
Sargasso Sea ⊤2 8 30.00 N 50.00 W
Sargatskoje 86 55.37 N 73.30 E
Sargé-lès-le-Mans 50 48.02 N 0.14 E
Sargent, Ga., U.S. 192 33.25 N 84.52 W
Sargent, Ne., U.S. 198 41.38 N 99.22 W
Sargent Creek ≃ 226 35.57 N 120.52 W
Sargodha 123 32.05 N 72.40 E
Šargol'džin 88 52.21 N 114.42 E
Šargorod 78 48.44 N 28.05 E
Sargou ≃ 85 43.25 N 73.50 E
Sargul', ozero ⊜ 86 54.35 N 78.51 E
Šargun 85 38.37 N 67.53 E
Sarh 146 9.09 N 18.23 E
Sarhli, Djebel ∧ 34 36.06 N 0.40 E
Sārī 128 36.34 N 53.04 E
Saría I 38 35.50 N 27.15 E
Saribi, Tanjung ≻ 164 1.36 S 135.25 E
Sarıbuğday 130 40.35 N 35.35 E
Saric 232 31.08 N 111.23 W
Saricumbe 152 12.12 S 19.46 E
Sarigan I 108 16.42 N 145.47 E
Sarıgazi ✈8 267b 41.01 N 29.12 E
Sarıgöl 130 38.14 N 28.43 E
Sarıkamış 130 40.20 N 42.35 E
Sarıkaya, Tür. 130 38.47 N 32.15 E
Sarıkaya, Tür. 130 39.30 N 35.24 E
Sarikei 112 2.07 N 111.31 E
Sarıköy 130 40.12 N 27.36 E
Sarilhos Grandes 266c 38.41 N 8.58 W

ENGLISH
Name Page Lat.°' Long.°'

Sarilhos Pequenos 266c 38.41 N 8.59 W
Sarim 154 0.23 S 40.58 E
Sarimbun, Pulau I 271c 1.26 N 103.41 E
Sarina 166 21.26 S 149.13 E
Sarine ≃ 58 46.54 N 7.14 E
Sariñena 34 41.48 N 0.10 W
Sarıoğlan 130 39.05 N 35.59 E
Saripul' 85 38.26 N 70.08 E
Sarīr 146 27.36 N 22.32 E
Sarısu 84 39.01 N 42.55 E
Sarita 196 27.13 N 97.47 W
Sariwŏn 98 38.31 N 125.44 E
Sarıyar Barajı ⊜1 130 40.02 N 31.40 E
Sarız 130 38.30 N 36.30 E
Šarja 80 58.24 N 45.30 E
Sarju (Babaī) ≃ 124 27.42 N 81.16 E
Sark I 43b 49.26 N 2.21 W
Sark ≃ 44 54.58 N 3.04 W
Sarkad 30 46.44 N 21.23 E
Šarkan 80 57.18 N 53.53 E
Sarkand 86 45.26 N 79.54 E
Şarkikaraağaç 130 38.04 N 31.23 E
Şarkışla 130 39.21 N 36.26 E
Šarkovščina 76 55.22 N 27.28 E
Şarköy 130 40.37 N 27.06 E
Sarlat-la-Canéda 32 44.53 N 1.13 E
Šarlauk 128 38.13 N 55.38 E
Sarles 198 48.56 N 98.59 W
Šarlyk 86 52.55 N 54.35 E
Sarmakovo 84 43.43 N 43.12 E
Sarmanovo 80 55.15 N 52.36 E
Sărmașu 38 46.46 N 24.11 E
Sarmathura 124 26.31 N 77.22 E
Sarmatskaja ≃ 83 47.20 N 38.48 E
Sármellék 30 46.44 N 17.10 E
Sarmi 164 1.51 S 138.44 E
Sarmiento 254 45.36 S 69.05 W
Sarmiento ≃ 288 34.25 S 58.35 W
Sarmiento de Gambia, Cerro ∧ 254 54.27 S 70.50 W
Sarmiento de Gamboa, Cerro I 9 22.48 S 43.12 W
Sarmiento de Gamboa, Lago ⊜ 254 51.04 S 72.45 W
Särna 26 61.41 N 13.08 E
Sarna, ozero ⊜ 80 48.24 N 44.38 E
Sarnano 66 43.02 N 13.18 E
Sārnāth ⊥ 124 25.24 N 83.01 E
Sarnen 58 46.54 N 8.15 E
Sărnena ≁ 38 42.35 N 25.10 E
Sarner See ⊜ 58 46.52 N 8.13 E
Sarnia 214 42.58 N 82.23 W
Sarnico 64 45.40 N 9.57 E
Sarno 68 40.49 N 14.37 E
Sarnow 54 53.45 N 13.37 E
Sarnowa 58 51.38 N 16.54 E
Sarnthein — Sarentino 64 46.38 N 11.21 E
Šarnutovskij 80 47.40 N 43.46 E
Sarny 78 51.21 N 26.36 E
Saroako 112 2.31 S 121.22 E
Saroargun 84 43.02 N 45.44 E
Sarolangun 112 2.18 S 102.42 E
Saroma-ko ⊜ 92a 44.08 N 143.50 E
Saron 158 33.11 S 19.01 E
Saronikós Kólpos c 38 37.54 N 23.12 E
Saronno 62 45.38 N 9.02 E
Saros Körfezi c 130 40.30 N 26.20 E
Sárospatak 30 48.19 N 21.34 E
Šarovka 78 50.01 N 35.27 E
Sarowbī 120 34.36 N 69.43 E
Sarpa 80 47.07 N 45.29 E
Sarpa, ozero ⊜ 80 47.18 N 45.20 E
Šarpajevka 78 48.34 N 40.59 E
Sar Passage ⊻ 175b 7.12 N 134.23 E
Šarpinskije ozera ⊜ 80 47.30 N 45.00 E
Šar Planina ≁ 38 42.05 N 20.50 E
Sarpsborg 26 59.17 N 11.07 E
Sarpy Creek ≃ 202 46.15 N 107.09 W
Sarrabus ✈1 71 39.23 N 9.21 E
Sarralbe 56 49.00 N 7.01 E
Sarras 62 45.11 N 4.48 E
Sarrath, Oued V 36 35.59 N 8.23 E
Sarratt 260 51.41 N 0.29 W
Sarre 62 45.43 N 7.15 E
Sarre (Saar) ≃ 56 49.42 N 6.34 E
Sarre Blanche ≃ 56 48.41 N 7.01 E
Sarrebourg 58 48.44 N 7.03 E
Sarrebruck — Saarbrücken 56 49.14 N 6.59 E
Sarreguemines 56 49.06 N 7.03 E
Sarre Rouge ≃ 56 48.41 N 7.01 E
Sarre-Union 56 48.56 N 7.05 E
Sarria 34 42.47 N 7.24 W
Sarriá ✈8 266d 41.24 N 2.08 E
Sarro 150 13.43 N 5.15 W
Sarroch 71 39.04 N 9.01 E
Sars 86 56.33 N 57.07 E
Sarsfield 212 45.27 N 75.21 W
Sarsina 66 43.55 N 12.08 E
Sarsol 272c 19.02 N 73.01 E
Sarstedt 52 52.14 N 9.51 E
Sarstein ∧ 64 47.36 N 13.41 E
Sarstoon (Sarstún) ≃ 236 15.53 N 88.55 W
Sarstún (Sarstoon) ≃ 236 15.53 N 88.55 W
Sarsuna 272b 22.28 N 88.18 E
Sart 56 50.31 N 5.56 E
Sartang ≃ 74 67.44 N 133.12 E
Sarteano 66 42.59 N 11.52 E
Sartell 190 45.37 N 94.12 W
Sartène 36 41.36 N 8.59 E
Sarthe □5 32 48.00 N 0.05 E
Sarthe ≃ 32 47.30 N 0.32 W
Sartičala 84 41.43 N 45.10 E
Sartilly 32 48.45 N 1.27 W
Sartirana Lomellina 62 45.07 N 8.39 E
Sartlan, ozero ⊜ 86 55.00 N 78.05 E
Sartol'gen 80 48.57 N 47.03 E
Sartrouville 261 48.57 N 2.10 E
Saru ≃ 85 42.20 N 77.55 E
Sarufutsu 92a 45.16 N 142.12 E
Saruhanlı 130 38.44 N 27.34 E
Sarūr 128 23.22 N 58.07 E
Šar Us ≃ 88 47.08 N 97.38 E
Saru-shima I 268 35.17 N 139.42 E
Sarvadyk 80 46.07 N 44.07 E
Sárvár 30 47.15 N 16.57 E
Sarver 214 40.44 N 79.45 W
Sarvestān 128 29.16 N 53.13 E
Sárvíz ≃ 30 46.24 N 18.41 E
Saryagač 85 41.27 N 69.10 E
Saryassija 85 38.25 N 67.57 E
Sarybarak 85 43.24 N 71.30 E
Sarybasat 86 46.38 N 60.27 E
Sarybulak, Kaz. 86 49.27 N 76.27 E
Sarybulak, Kyrg. 85 40.54 N 73.49 E
Saryč, mys ≻ 78 44.23 N 33.45 E
Sarychosor 85 38.32 N 69.49 E
Sarydala 85 41.11 N 70.27 E
Sary-Sep 85 41.30 N 95.36 E
Sary-Iškotrau ✈2 86 45.30 N 76.00 E
Sarykamyškoje, ozero ⊜ 72 41.56 N 57.25 E
Sarykoby 85 43.44 N 72.35 E
Sarykol'skij chrebet ≁ 120 38.00 N 74.30 E
Sarykomej 86 45.12 N 74.11 E
Sarykopa, ozero ⊜ 86 50.22 N 64.06 E
Sarymogol 85 39.55 N 72.47 E
Sarymoin, ozero ⊜ 86 51.36 N 64.30 E
Saryozek 86 44.22 N 77.59 E
Šarypovo 86 55.33 N 89.12 E
Saryšagan 86 46.07 N 73.38 E
Sarysu 86 48.23 N 69.59 E
Sarysu ≃ 86 45.12 N 66.36 E
Sary-Taš 85 39.44 N 73.15 E
Sarytau 86 49.54 N 76.41 E
Saryžaz 72 42.55 N 79.36 E
Sarzana 64 44.07 N 9.58 E
Sarzanello, Fortezza di ⊥ 64 44.08 N 9.58 E
Sarzeau 32 47.32 N 2.46 W

DEUTSCH
Name Seite Breite°' Länge°' E = Ost

S'as' ≃ 76 60.09 N 32.30 E
Sa'sa', Sūrīy. 132 33.17 N 36.02 E
Sasa, Yis. 132 33.02 N 35.24 E
Sasabe 200 31.27 N 111.31 W
Sasabe ≃ 200 30.41 N 111.56 W
Sasabeneh 144 7.55 N 43.39 E
Sasaga-mine ∧ 96 33.49 N 133.17 E
Sasaginnigak Lake ⊜ 184 51.36 N 95.40 W
Sasago-tunnel ✈5 94 35.38 N 138.47 E
Sasaguri 96 33.37 N 130.32 E
Sasak 110 0.01 S 99.42 E
Sasakwa 196 34.56 N 96.31 W
Sasamungga 175e 7.02 S 156.47 E
Sasao 270 34.57 N 135.20 E
Sasar, Tanjung ≻ 115b 9.17 S 119.56 E
Sāsarām 124 24.57 N 84.02 E
Sasayama 96 35.04 N 135.13 E
Sasa-yama ∧ 96 33.03 N 132.40 E
Sasbach 58 48.08 N 7.37 E
Sasco Brook ≃ 276 41.07 N 73.18 W
Sásd 30 46.15 N 18.06 E
Sasebo 92 33.10 N 129.43 E
Sasebo Naval Base ■ 92 33.09 N 129.45 E
Saseenos 224 48.24 N 123.40 W
Saseginaga, Lac ⊜ 190 47.06 N 78.35 W
Sashalom ✈8 264c 47.31 N 19.11 E
Sas-hegy ∧2 264c 47.23 N 19.18 E
Sashiki 174m 26.10 N 127.47 E
Sashima 94 36.08 N 139.51 E
Saskatchewan □4, Can. 176 54.00 N 105.00 W
Saskatchewan □4, Can. 184 54.00 N 105.00 W
Saskatchewan ≃ 184 53.12 N 99.16 W
Saskatoon 184 52.07 N 106.38 W
Saskylach 74 71.55 N 114.01 E
Saslaya, Cerro ∧ 238 13.45 N 85.03 W
Sasmik, Cape ≻ 180 51.36 N 177.55 W
Sāsni 124 27.43 N 78.05 E
Sasolburg 158 26.48 S 27.45 E
Sason 130 38.20 N 41.25 E
Sasovo 80 54.21 N 41.54 E
Saspamco 196 29.14 N 98.18 W
Saspul Gompa 123 34.15 N 77.09 E
Sassafras, Austl. 274b 37.52 S 145.21 E
Sassafras, Ky., U.S. 192 37.14 N 83.06 W
Sassafras ≃ 208 39.23 N 76.02 W
Sassafras Mountain ∧ 192 35.03 N 82.48 W
Sassafras Neck ≻1 208 39.25 N 75.55 W
Sassandra 150 4.58 N 6.05 W
Sassandra ≃ 150 4.58 N 6.05 W
Sassano 68 40.20 N 15.33 E
Sassari 71 40.44 N 8.33 E
Sassari □4 71 40.40 N 9.00 E
Sassbach ≃ 61 46.43 N 15.48 E
Sasse ≃ 62 44.15 N 5.55 E
Sassello 62 44.29 N 8.30 E
Sassenage 62 45.12 N 5.40 E
Sassenberg 52 51.59 N 8.02 E
Sassenheim 52 52.13 N 4.31 E
Sassnitz 54 54.31 N 13.38 E
Sassocorvaro 66 43.47 N 12.30 E
Sasso di Castalda 68 40.30 N 15.40 E
Sassoferrato 66 43.26 N 12.51 E
Sasso Marconi 64 44.24 N 11.15 E
S'as'stroj 76 60.08 N 32.34 E
Sassuolo 64 44.33 N 10.47 E
Sastobe 85 42.34 N 70.00 E
Sastown 150 4.40 N 8.26 W
Sastre 252 31.45 S 61.50 W
Sas van Gent 52 51.14 N 3.47 E
Sasyk, ozero ⊜ 78 45.12 N 33.31 E
Sasykkol', ozero ⊜ 86 46.35 N 81.00 E
Sasykoli 80 47.33 N 47.00 E
Šat ≃ 82 54.08 N 37.47 E
Satadougou 150 12.21 N 10.07 W
Satah Mountain ∧ 182 52.29 N 124.41 W
Satakunta ✈1 26 61.30 N 23.00 E
Šatalovka 78 51.09 N 38.16 E
Šatalovo 76 54.20 N 32.27 E
Sata-misaki ≻ 92 30.59 N 130.40 E
Satāna 122 20.35 N 74.12 E
Satanov 78 49.15 N 26.16 E
Satanta 198 37.26 N 100.59 W
Sátão 34 40.44 N 7.44 W
Sātāra, India 122 17.41 N 73.59 E
Satara, S. Afr. 156 24.29 S 31.47 E
Satava 175a 13.28 S 172.40 W
Sātbāria, Bngl. 126 23.52 N 89.26 E
Sātbāria, India 272b 22.25 N 88.33 E
Satélite 232 31.43 N 106.23 W
Satellite Beach 220 28.10 N 80.35 W
Satellite Channel ⊻ 224 48.43 N 123.30 W
Satema 152 4.18 N 21.42 E
Satengar, Pulau I 112 7.31 S 117.17 E
Säter 40 60.21 N 15.45 E
Sātgāchia 126 23.16 N 88.08 E
Sātghara 272b 22.44 N 88.21 E
Saticoy 228 34.17 N 119.09 W
Satilla ≃ 192 30.59 N 81.28 W
Satilpa Creek ≃ 194 31.39 N 88.03 W
Satin 222 31.21 N 97.02 W
Satipo 248 11.16 S 74.37 W
Sátiro Dias 250 11.36 S 38.36 W
Satis 80 55.02 N 43.48 E
Satīt (Tekeze) ≃ 140 14.20 N 35.50 E
Satka 86 55.03 N 59.01 E
Satkānia 120 22.04 N 92.03 E
Sātkhira 124 22.43 N 89.06 E
Sātki 80 55.11 N 44.08 E
Satla Bil ⊜ 126 22.54 N 90.04 E
Satluj — Sutlej ≃ 120 29.23 N 71.02 E
Satna 124 24.35 N 80.50 E
Sato, Cañada de ≃ 288 34.35 S 58.38 W
Satomi 94 36.43 N 140.30 E
Sátoraljaújhely 30 48.24 N 21.39 E
Šatov 61 48.48 N 16.01 E
Šatovo 82 54.56 N 37.14 E
Satow 54 53.59 N 11.51 E
Sātpura Range ≁ 122 22.00 N 78.00 E
Sätrabrunn 40 59.51 N 16.27 E
Satriano di Lucania 68 40.33 N 15.33 E
Šatrovo 86 56.31 N 64.38 E
Satrup 54 54.41 N 9.35 E
Satsop ≃ 224 47.03 N 123.30 W
Satsop, Middle Fork ≃ 224 47.05 N 123.30 W
Satsop, West Fork ≃ 224 47.02 N 123.32 W
Satsuma 194 30.51 N 88.03 W
Satsuma-hantō ≻1 92 31.25 N 130.25 E
Satsunan-shotō II 93b 29.00 N 130.00 E
Sattahip 110 12.40 N 100.54 E
Sāttānkulam 122 8.27 N 77.56 E
Satte 94 36.04 N 139.43 E
Sattel 58 47.05 N 8.42 E
Sattenapalle 122 16.24 N 80.11 E
Satthwa 110 17.46 N 94.30 E
Sattledt 60 48.04 N 14.03 E
Satui 112 3.47 S 115.27 E
Sātuli 272b 22.33 N 88.34 E
Satu Mare 38 47.48 N 22.53 E
Satu Mare □6 38 47.40 N 23.00 E
Satun 110 6.37 N 100.04 E
Šatura 80 55.34 N 39.32 E
Saturna 224 48.47 N 123.11 W
Saturna Island I 224 48.47 N 123.08 W
Saturnino M. Laspiur 252 31.42 S 62.29 W
Šaturtorf 76 55.34 N 39.26 E
Satus Creek ≃ 202 46.16 N 120.07 W
Satus Peak ∧ 224 46.15 N 120.45 W
Satyamangalam 122 11.31 N 77.15 E
Satzkorn 264a 52.29 N 12.59 E
Sau ≃ 269c 10.46 N 106.48 E
Sauble ≃ 212 44.40 N 81.17 W
Sauce, Arg. 252 30.05 S 58.46 W
Sauce, Perú 248 6.44 S 76.10 W
Sauce, Ur. 258 34.39 S 56.04 W
Sauce, Arroyo ≃ 258 34.26 S 57.28 W
Sauce, Arroyo del ≃ 288 34.35 S 58.50 W

Symbols in the index entries represent the broad categories identified in the key at the right. Symbols with superior numbers (≁1) identify subcategories (see complete key on page I · 1).

Symbole im Register stellen die rechts im Schlüssel erklärten Kategorien dar. Symbole mit hochgestellten Ziffern (≁1) bezeichnen Unterabteilungen einer Kategorie (vgl. vollständiger Schlüssel auf Seite I · 1).

Los símbolos incluídos en el texto del índice representan las grandes categorías identificadas con la clave a la derecha. Los símbolos con numeros en su parte superior (≁1) identifican las subcategorías (véase la clave completa en la página I · 1).

Les symboles de l'index représentent les catégories indiquées dans la légende à droite. Les symboles suivis d'un indice (≁1) représentent des sous-catégories (voir légende complète à la page I · 1).

Os símbolos incluídos no texto do índice representam as grandes categorias identificadas com a chave à direita. Os símbolos com números em sua parte superior (≁1) identificam as subcategorias (veja-se a chave completa à página I · 1).

∧ Mountain	Berg	Montaña	Montagne	Montanha
≁ Mountains	Gebirge	Montañas	Montagnes	Montanhas
)(Pass	Paß	Paso	Col	Passo
V Valley, Canyon	Tal, Cañon	Valle, Cañón	Vallée, Canyon	Vale, Canhão
⊻ Plain	Ebene	Llano	Plaine	Planície
≻ Cape	Kap	Cabo	Cap	Cabo
I Island	Insel	Isla	Île	Ilha
II Islands	Inseln	Islas	Îles	Ilhas
⊥ Other Topographic Features	Andere Topographische Objekte	Otros Elementos Topográficos	Autres données topographiques	Outros acidentes topográficos

ESPAÑOL — Nombre | Página | Lat.°′ | Long.°′ W = Oeste

FRANÇAIS — Nom | Page | Lat.°′ | Long.°′ W = Ouest

PORTUGUÊS — Nome | Página | Lat.°′ | Long.°′ W = Oeste

Nombre / Nom / Nome	Página / Page	Lat.°′	Long.°′ W = Oeste / Ouest
Sauce Corto, Arroyo ≃	**252**	36.55 S	61.48 W
Saucier	**194**	30.38 N	89.08 W
Saucillo	**232**	28.01 N	105.17 W
Sauda	**26**	59.39 N	6.20 E
Saudade	**256**	21.56 S	43.03 W
Sauđárkrókur	**24a**	65.46 N	19.41 W
Saúde	**250**	10.56 S	40.24 W
Saúde ◆[8]	**287b**	23.37 S	46.37 W
Saudi Arabia (Al-'Arabīyah as-Su'ūdīyah) □[1]	**118**	25.00 N	45.00 E
Saudi-Arabien → Saudi Arabia □[1]	**118**	25.00 N	45.00 E
Saudron	**58**	48.30 N	5.20 E
Sauer (Sûre) ≃, Europe	**56**	49.44 N	6.31 E
Sauer ≃, Europe	**56**	48.55 N	8.10 E
Sauerkohl-Berge ⋀[2]	**264a**	52.20 N	13.45 E
Sauerlach	**64**	47.58 N	11.38 E
Sauerland ◆[1]	**52**	51.10 N	8.00 E
Saueruiná ≃	**248**	12.00 S	58.43 W
Sauê-Uiná ≃	**248**	12.24 S	58.40 W
Saug ≃	**116**	7.27 N	125.44 E
Saugatuck, Ct., U.S.	**276**	41.08 N	73.23 W
Saugatuck, Mi., U.S.	**216**	42.39 N	86.12 W
Saugatuck ≃	**276**	41.07 N	73.22 W
Saugatuck Reservoir ◎[1]	**207**	41.16 N	73.22 W
Saugeen ≃	**190**	44.30 N	81.22 W
Saugeen Indian Reserve ◆[4]	**212**	44.33 N	81.18 W
Saugerties	**210**	42.04 N	73.57 W
Saughall	**262**	53.13 N	2.58 W
Saugor → Sāgar	**124**	23.50 N	78.43 E
Saugstad, Mount ∧	**182**	52.15 N	126.31 W
Saugus, Ca., U.S.	**228**	34.24 N	118.32 W
Saugus, Ma., U.S.	**207**	42.27 N	71.00 W
Saugus ≃	**283**	42.28 N	70.58 W
Saugus Iron Works National Historical Site ⊥	**283**	42.28 N	71.01 W
Sauh, Tanjong ≻	**114**	3.46 N	100.49 E
Saujil	**252**	28.11 S	66.14 W
Saujon	**32**	45.40 N	0.56 W
Sauk ≃, Mn., U.S.	**198**	45.36 N	94.10 W
Sauk ≃, Wa., U.S.	**224**	48.30 N	121.37 W
Sauk Centre	**198**	45.44 N	94.57 W
Sauk City	**190**	43.16 N	89.43 W
Sauk Rapids	**190**	45.35 N	94.09 W
Sauksaj ≃	**85**	39.11 N	72.15 E
Sauk Village	**216**	41.29 N	87.34 W
Saukville	**190**	43.22 N	87.56 W
Saül	**250**	3.37 N	53.12 W
Šaulape ⋀	**61**	46.55 N	14.40 E
Šaul'der	**85**	42.47 N	68.24 E
Sauldre ≃	**50**	47.16 N	1.30 E
Sauldre, Canal de la ≊	**50**	47.36 N	2.06 E
Saulgau	**58**	48.01 N	9.30 E
Saulgrub	**64**	47.40 N	11.01 E
Saulheim	**56**	49.51 N	8.09 E
Saulieu	**50**	47.16 N	4.14 E
Saulkrasti	**76**	57.17 N	24.25 E
Saulnot	**58**	47.34 N	6.38 E
Sault-au-Mouton	**186**	48.33 N	69.15 W
Sault au Récollet ◆[8]	**275a**	45.34 N	73.39 W
Sault aux Cochons, Rivière du ≃	**186**	48.44 N	69.04 W
Sault-de-Vaucluse	**62**	44.05 N	5.25 E
Saulteaux ≃	**182**	55.16 N	114.25 W
Saulteaux Indian Reserve ◆[4]	**184**	53.08 N	108.18 W
Sault-lès-Rethel	**50**	49.30 N	4.22 E
Sault Sainte Marie, On., Can.	**190**	46.31 N	84.20 W
Sault Sainte Marie, Mi., U.S.	**190**	46.29 N	84.20 W
Saulx ≃, Fr.	**56**	48.45 N	4.35 E
Saulx ≃, Fr.	**261**	48.41 N	2.19 E
Saulx-de-Vesoul	**58**	47.42 N	6.17 E
Saulx-les-Chartreux	**261**	48.42 N	2.16 E
Saulxures-sur-Moselotte	**58**	47.57 N	6.46 E
Šaum'ani	**84**	41.21 N	44.46 E
Šaum'anovsk	**84**	40.26 N	46.34 E
Saumarez Reef ⊹[2]	**166**	21.50 S	153.40 E
Saumlaki	**164**	7.57 S	131.19 E
Saumon, Rivière au ≃	**206**	45.41 N	71.27 W
Saumons, Rivíere aux ≃	**186**	49.25 N	62.15 W
Saumur	**32**	47.16 N	0.05 W
Saundatti	**122**	15.47 N	75.07 E
Saundersfoot	**42**	51.43 N	4.43 W
Saunders Island I, Falk. Is.	**254**	51.20 S	60.10 W
Saunders Island I, S. Geor.	**9**	57.47 S	26.27 W
Saunders Point ∧[2]	**162**	27.52 S	125.38 E
Saunderstown	**207**	41.30 N	71.25 W
Saunemin	**216**	40.54 N	88.24 W
Saupite	**152**	13.54 S	17.43 E
Sauquoit	**210**	43.00 N	75.16 W
Sauquoit Creek ≃	**210**	43.08 N	75.16 W
Saura	**84**	44.14 N	50.50 E
Sauran	**85**	43.29 N	67.50 E
Saurimo	**152**	9.39 S	20.24 E
Saur-Mogila ⊥	**83**	47.56 N	38.46 E
Sausalito	**226**	37.51 N	122.29 W
Sausar	**120**	21.39 N	78.47 E
Sauškin	**80**	49.30 N	43.32 E
Sausset-les-Pins	**62**	43.20 N	5.07 E
Saussy	**58**	47.28 N	4.57 E
Sausu	**112**	1.00 S	120.30 E
Saútar	**152**	11.06 S	18.27 E
Sauteurs	**241k**	12.14 N	61.38 W
Sauvas	**62**	44.19 N	4.09 E
Sauve	**62**	43.56 N	3.57 E
Sauveterre	**62**	44.02 N	4.48 E
Sauveterre-de-Béarn	**34**	43.24 N	0.56 W
Sauveterre-de-Guyenne	**32**	44.42 N	0.05 W
Sauvie Island I	**224**	45.41 N	122.49 W
Sauvo	**26**	60.21 N	22.42 E
Sauwald ◆[3]	**60**	48.28 N	13.40 E
Sauzal	**200**	31.37 N	106.18 W
Sauze di Cesana	**62**	44.56 N	6.51 E
Sauze d'Oulx	**62**	45.02 N	6.52 E
Sava, It.	**68**	40.24 N	17.34 E
S'ava, Ross.	**80**	58.01 N	46.22 E
Sava ≃	**38**	44.50 N	20.26 E
Sävaån ≃	**40**	59.45 N	17.24 E
Savage, Md., U.S.	**208**	39.08 N	76.49 W
Savage, Mt., U.S.	**198**	47.27 N	104.20 W
Savai'i I	**175a**	13.35 S	172.25 W
Savala ≃	**80**	51.03 N	41.30 E
Savalen ◎	**26**	62.15 N	10.29 E
Savalou	**150**	7.56 N	1.58 E
Savana Island I	**240m**	18.20 N	65.05 W
Savana Passage ⊔	**240m**	18.21 N	65.04 W
Savane ≃	**186**	51.08 N	71.26 W
Savanna, Il., U.S.	**190**	42.05 N	90.09 W
Savanna, Ok., U.S.	**196**	34.49 N	95.50 W
Savannah, Ga., U.S.	**192**	32.05 N	81.06 W
Savannah, Mo., U.S.	**194**	39.56 N	94.49 W
Savannah, N.Y., U.S.	**210**	43.04 N	76.45 W
Savannah, Oh., U.S.	**214**	40.57 N	82.21 W
Savannah, Tn., U.S.	**194**	35.13 N	88.14 W
Savannah ≃	**192**	32.02 N	80.53 W
Savannah River Plant ◉[3]	**192**	33.15 N	81.40 W
Savannah Sound	**192**	25.06 N	76.09 W
Savannakhét	**110**	16.33 N	104.45 E
Savanna-la-Mar	**241q**	18.13 N	78.08 W
Savanna Portage State Park ♠	**190**	46.51 N	93.10 W
Sāvantvādi	**122**	15.54 N	73.49 E
Savanūr	**122**	14.58 N	75.21 E
Sävar	**26**	63.54 N	20.34 E
Savara ≃	**62**	45.42 N	7.12 E
Savasse ≃	**62**	45.03 N	5.02 E
Savaştepe	**130**	39.22 N	27.40 E
Savat	**130**	38.21 N	40.38 E
Savcılıbüyükoba	**130**	39.14 N	33.41 E
Savé	**150**	8.02 N	2.29 E
Save (Sabi) ≃, Afr.	**156**	21.00 S	35.02 E
Save ≃, Fr.	**32**	43.47 N	1.17 E
Sāveh	**128**	35.01 N	50.20 E
Savelli	**68**	39.19 N	16.47 E
Savelugu	**150**	9.37 N	0.49 W
Savenay	**32**	47.22 N	1.57 W
Săveni	**38**	47.57 N	26.52 E
Saverdun	**32**	43.14 N	1.35 E
Savernake Forest ◆[3]	**42**	51.24 N	1.38 W
Saverne	**56**	48.44 N	7.22 E
Savery Creek ≃	**200**	41.01 N	107.27 W
Saviči, Bela.	**76**	52.25 N	29.03 E
Saviči, Bela.	**78**	51.37 N	30.17 E
Savick Brook ≃	**262**	53.49 N	2.37 W
Savièse	**58**	46.16 N	7.20 E
Savigliano	**62**	44.38 N	7.40 E
Savignano Irpino	**68**	41.14 N	15.11 E
Savignano sul Panaro	**64**	44.29 N	11.02 E
Savignano sul Rubicone	**66**	44.05 N	12.24 E
Savignone	**62**	44.34 N	8.58 E
Savigny-lès-Beaune	**58**	47.04 N	4.49 E
Savigny-le-Temple	**261**	48.35 N	2.35 E
Savigny-sur-Braye	**50**	47.53 N	0.49 E
Savigny-sur-Orge	**50**	48.40 N	2.21 E
Savill Gardens ♠	**260**	51.27 N	0.36 E
Savincy	**78**	49.24 N	37.04 E
Savines	**62**	44.32 N	6.24 E
Savinjske Alpe ⋀	**61**	46.23 N	14.35 E
Savinka, Ross.	**80**	50.06 N	47.06 E
Savinka, Ross.	**82**	54.27 N	38.52 E
Savino	**80**	56.35 N	41.13 E
Savino-Borisovskaja	**24**	62.38 N	44.34 E
Savinsk	**89**	52.10 N	140.23 E
Savinskij	**24**	62.58 N	40.08 E
Savio	**66**	44.18 N	12.18 E
Savio ≃	**66**	44.19 N	12.20 E
Saviore dell'Adamello	**64**	46.05 N	10.24 E
Săvîrşin	**38**	46.01 N	22.14 E
Şavitaipale	**26**	61.12 N	27.42 E
Šavnik	**38**	42.57 N	19.05 E
Savognin	**58**	46.36 N	9.36 E
Savoie □[5]	**32**	45.30 N	6.25 E
Savo Island I	**175e**	9.08 S	159.49 E
Savolaks ◆[1]	**26**	62.00 N	28.00 E
Sav'olovo	**82**	56.52 N	37.22 E
Sav'olovo Station ◆[5]	**265b**	55.48 N	37.35 E
Savona, B.C., Can.	**182**	50.45 N	120.50 W
Savona, It.	**62**	44.17 N	8.30 E
Savona, N.Y., U.S.	**210**	42.17 N	77.13 W
Savona □[4]	**62**	44.18 N	8.16 E
Savonlinna	**26**	61.52 N	28.53 E
Savonnières	**50**	47.21 N	0.33 E
Savonranta	**26**	62.11 N	29.12 E
Savoonga	**180**	63.42 N	170.27 W
Savory Creek ≃	**162**	23.22 S	122.37 E
Savoureuse ≃	**58**	47.31 N	6.51 E
Savoy	**196**	33.34 N	96.21 W
Savran'	**78**	48.09 N	30.04 E
Savruši	**80**	55.02 N	50.40 E
Sävsjö	**26**	57.25 N	14.40 E
S'avta	**24**	67.08 N	61.45 E
Savu Basin ⊹[1]	**14**	9.15 S	123.15 E
Savudrija	**64**	45.30 N	13.30 E
Savur	**130**	37.33 N	40.53 E
Savusavu	**175g**	16.16 S	179.21 E
Savusavu Bay ⊂	**175g**	16.45 S	179.15 E
Savu Sea → Sawu, Laut ⊤[2]	**112**	9.40 S	122.00 E
Savuto ≃	**68**	39.02 N	16.06 E
Savvatejevka	**88**	52.20 N	103.39 E
Savvino, Ross.	**82**	55.43 N	36.48 E
Savvino, Ross.	**82**	56.33 N	37.47 E
Savvo-Borz'a	**88**	50.46 N	118.18 E
Şawāb, Wādī aş- ∨	**130**	34.36 N	40.25 E
Sawabala Point ≻	**164**	10.10 S	151.15 E
Sawah	**112**	2.23 N	115.14 E
Sawahlunto	**112**	0.40 S	100.47 E
Sawai	**164**	2.58 S	129.09 E
Sawai, Teluk ⊂	**164**	2.52 S	129.12 E
Sawāi Mādhopur	**124**	25.59 N	76.22 E
Sawākin	**140**	19.07 N	37.20 E
Sawal, Gunung ∧	**115a**	7.12 S	108.16 E
Sawan, Indon.	**115b**	8.08 S	115.11 E
Sawan, Mya.	**110**	24.30 N	96.19 E
Sawang	**114**	0.45 N	103.21 E
Sawankhalok	**110**	17.19 N	99.50 E
Sawara	**94**	35.53 N	140.30 E
Sawata	**92**	38.00 N	138.16 E
Sawatch Range ⋀	**200**	39.10 N	106.25 W
Sawbridgeworth	**42**	51.50 N	0.09 E
Sawdā', Jabal as- ⋀[2]	**146**	28.40 N	15.30 E
Sawdā', Qurnat as- ∧	**130**	34.18 N	36.07 E
Sawdirī	**140**	14.25 N	29.05 E
Sawel Mountain ∧	**48**	54.49 N	7.02 W
Sawhāj	**140**	26.33 N	31.42 E
Sawi	**110**	10.14 N	99.07 E
Sawin, Lac ◎	**206**	46.32 N	73.54 W
Sawknah	**146**	29.04 N	15.47 E
Şawl	**142**	29.21 N	31.14 E
Sawla	**150**	9.17 N	2.25 W
Saw Log Creek ≃	**198**	38.07 N	99.42 W
Saw Mill ≃	**276**	40.56 N	73.53 W
Sawmill Brook ≃, Ma., U.S.	**283**	42.34 N	70.46 W
Sawmill Brook ≃, N.J., U.S.	**276**	40.28 N	74.26 W
Sawmill Creek ≃, N.J., U.S.	**276**	40.46 N	74.05 W
Sawmill Creek ≃, Pa., U.S.	**279b**	40.10 N	79.58 W
Sawmill Pond Brook ≃	**276**	41.10 N	74.23 W
Sawmill Run ≃	**285**	40.07 N	75.21 W
Sawmills	**154**	19.31 S	28.02 E
Şawqirah, Ghubbat ⊂	**118**	18.35 N	57.00 E
Sawston	**42**	52.07 N	0.10 E
Sawtayr ⊤[4]	**140**	17.03 N	30.24 E
Sawtooth National Recreation Area ♠	**202**	44.00 N	114.55 W
Sawtry	**42**	52.27 N	0.17 W
Sawu, Laut (Savu Sea) ⊤[2]	**112**	9.40 S	122.00 E
Sawu, Pulau I	**112**	10.30 S	121.54 E
Sawyer, Mi., U.S.	**216**	41.53 N	86.35 W
Sawyer, N.D., U.S.	**198**	48.05 N	101.03 W
Sawyers Hill ∧[2]	**186**	47.11 N	53.52 W
Sawyers Valley	**168a**	31.54 S	116.13 E
Sawyerville, P.Q., Can.	**206**	45.20 N	71.34 W
Sawyerville, Il., U.S.	**219**	39.05 N	89.48 W
Sawyerwood	**214**	41.02 N	81.27 W
Saxby ≃	**166**	18.25 S	140.53 E
Saxdalen	**40**	60.09 N	14.57 E
Saxen ◎	**40**	59.46 N	14.25 E
Saxike	**120**	30.44 N	86.22 E
Saxilby	**44**	53.17 N	0.40 W
Saxis	**208**	37.55 N	75.43 W
Saxmundham	**42**	52.13 N	1.29 E
Saxon, Schw.	**58**	46.09 N	7.11 E
Saxon, Wi., U.S.	**190**	46.29 N	90.24 W
Saxonburg	**214**	40.45 N	79.49 W
Saxon Woods Park ♠	**276**	40.59 N	73.45 W
Saxony → Sachsen □[9]	**30**	52.45 N	9.30 E
Saxton	**214**	40.12 N	78.14 W
Say	**150**	13.07 N	2.21 E
Sāy, Jazīrat I	**140**	20.42 N	30.20 E
Saya de Malha Bank ⊹[4]	**12**	10.30 S	61.30 E
Sayama, Nihon	**94**	35.51 N	139.24 E
Sayama, Nihon	**270**	34.31 N	135.34 E
Sayama-kyūryō ⋀[2]	**268**	35.47 N	139.24 E
Sayán	**248**	11.08 S	77.12 W
Sayan Mountains (Sajany) ⋀	**88**	52.45 N	96.00 E
Sayansk	**88**	54.02 N	102.06 E
Sayaxché	**232**	16.31 N	90.10 W
Saybrook, Il., U.S.	**216**	40.25 N	88.31 W
Saybrook, Oh., U.S.	**214**	41.50 N	80.51 W
Saybrook Manor	**207**	41.17 N	72.23 W
Sayda, Dtsch.	**54**	50.43 N	13.25 E
Şaydā (Sidon), Lubnān	**132**	33.33 N	35.22 E
Şaydā □[4]	**132**	33.15 N	35.15 E
Şaydnāyā	**132**	33.42 N	36.22 E
Sayghān	**120**	35.11 N	67.42 E
Sayḩūt	**144**	15.12 N	51.14 E
Sayil ⊥	**232**	20.16 N	89.42 W
Saylah	**142**	29.21 N	30.58 E
Saylorsburg	**210**	40.54 N	75.19 W
Saylorville Lake ◎[1]	**190**	41.48 N	93.46 W
Saylūn, Khirbat (Shiloh) ⊥	**132**	32.03 N	35.17 E
Säynätsalo	**26**	62.08 N	25.46 E
Sayō	**96**	35.00 N	134.22 E
Şayqal, Bahr ◎	**132**	33.40 N	37.06 E
Sayram Hu ◎	**86**	44.36 N	81.13 E
Sayre, Ok., U.S.	**196**	35.17 N	99.38 W
Sayre, Pa., U.S.	**210**	41.58 N	76.30 W
Sayreville	**208**	40.27 N	74.21 W
Sayula	**234**	19.52 N	103.37 W
Sayula, Laguna de ◎	**234**	20.03 N	103.31 W
Sayula de Alemán	**234**	17.52 N	94.57 W
Sayultepec	**234**	17.27 N	97.17 W
Sayville	**210**	40.44 N	73.04 W
Sayward	**182**	50.22 N	125.55 W
Saywūn	**144**	15.56 N	48.47 E
Saza	**92**	33.14 N	129.39 E
Sazanit I	**38**	40.30 N	19.16 E
Sazdy, Kaz.	**80**	46.57 N	49.19 E
Sazdy, Kaz.	**86**	47.22 N	61.48 E
Saze	**62**	43.56 N	4.41 E
Sažino	**86**	56.20 N	58.11 E
Sazlijka ≃	**38**	42.02 N	25.52 E
Şazonovo	**76**	59.04 N	35.14 E
Šazud	**120**	37.43 N	72.11 E
Sazykul', ozero ◎	**86**	55.22 N	67.34 E
Sba	**148**	28.13 N	0.08 W
Sbeïtla	**148**	35.14 N	9.08 E
Sbiba	**36**	35.33 N	9.05 E
Scaddan	**162**	33.27 S	121.43 E
Scaër	**32**	48.02 N	3.42 W
Scafati	**68**	40.45 N	14.31 E
Scafell Pikes ∧	**44**	54.27 N	3.12 W
Scaggsville	**208**	39.09 N	76.54 W
Scajaquada Creek ≃	**284a**	42.56 N	78.53 W
Scala, Teatro alla ◉	**266b**	45.28 N	9.11 E
Scala Coeli	**68**	39.27 N	16.53 E
Scalasaig	**46**	56.04 N	6.11 W
Scalby	**44**	54.18 N	0.27 W
Scalea	**68**	39.49 N	15.48 E
Scaletta Zanclea	**70**	38.03 N	15.28 E
Scalloway	**46a**	60.08 N	1.18 W
Scalpay I, Scot., U.K.	**46**	57.17 N	5.59 W
Scalpay I, Scot., U.K.	**46**	57.52 N	6.40 W
Scalp Level	**214**	40.14 N	78.50 W
Scalp Mountain ∧[2]	**48**	55.04 N	7.24 W
Scammon	**198**	37.16 N	94.49 W
Scammon Bay	**180**	61.53 N	165.38 W
Scammon Bay ⊂	**180**	61.53 N	165.54 W
Scammonden Water ◎[1]	**262**	53.38 N	1.56 W
Scampton	**44**	53.18 N	0.34 W
Scandale	**68**	39.07 N	16.57 E
Scandia	**198**	39.47 N	97.47 W
Scandiano	**64**	44.36 N	10.43 E
Scandicci	**66**	43.45 N	11.11 E
Scanlon	**190**	46.42 N	92.25 W
Scanno	**66**	41.54 N	13.53 E
Scansano	**66**	42.41 N	11.20 E
Scantic ≃	**207**	41.52 N	72.38 W
Scapa	**182**	51.52 N	111.59 W
Scapa Flow ⊂	**46**	58.55 N	3.06 W
Scapegoat Mountain ∧	**202**	47.19 N	112.50 W
Ščapino	**74**	55.19 N	159.25 E
Ščapov	**80**	51.01 N	51.11 E
Ščapovo	**82**	55.09 N	38.11 E
Scappoose	**224**	45.45 N	122.52 W
Şcar ≃	**44**	55.13 N	3.46 W
Ščara ≃	**76**	53.27 N	24.45 E
Scaramia, Capo ≻	**70**	36.47 N	14.29 E
Scarba I	**46**	56.11 N	5.43 W
Scarborough, Austl.	**168a**	31.54 S	115.45 E
Scarborough, On., Can.	**212**	43.47 N	79.15 W
Scarborough, Trin.	**241r**	11.11 N	60.44 W
Scarborough, Eng., U.K.	**44**	54.17 N	0.24 W
Scarborough Centre ◆[9]	**275b**	43.47 N	79.16 W
Scarborough Point ≻	**171a**	27.12 S	153.07 E
Scarborough Reef ⊹[2]	**116**	15.08 N	117.46 E
Scardroy	**46**	57.31 N	4.59 W
Scargill	**172**	42.56 S	172.57 E
Scarinish	**46**	56.29 N	6.48 W
Scarisbrick	**262**	53.37 N	2.56 W
Scărişoara	**38**	44.00 N	24.35 E
Scarlino	**66**	42.54 N	10.51 E
Scarp I	**46**	58.02 N	7.08 W
Scarpe ≃	**50**	50.30 N	3.27 E
Scarperia	**66**	44.00 N	11.21 E
Scarper Peak ∧	**282**	37.32 N	122.26 W
Scarriff	**48**	52.55 N	8.31 W
Scarsdale, Austl.	**169**	37.40 S	143.40 E
Scarsdale, N.Y., U.S.	**210**	40.59 N	73.49 W
Scartaglin	**48**	52.10 N	9.26 W
Scarth Hill	**262**	53.33 N	2.52 W
Ščastje	**83**	48.44 N	39.14 E
Scatarie Island I	**186**	46.00 N	59.44 W
Scatter Creek ≃	**224**	46.48 N	123.06 W
Scauri, It.	**66**	41.15 N	13.42 E
Scauri, It.	**70**	36.45 N	11.58 E
Scavaig, Loch ⊂	**46**	57.09 N	6.10 W
Scawfell Island I	**166**	20.52 S	149.36 E
Sceaux	**50**	48.47 N	2.17 E
Sceaux, Château de ⊥	**261**	48.46 N	2.18 E
Ščedrin	**76**	52.53 N	29.33 E
Ščedrovka	**83**	49.30 N	40.17 E
Ščeglovo	**265a**	60.02 N	30.46 E
Ščeljajur	**24**	65.21 N	53.21 E
Ščelkan ≃	**80**	50.47 N	43.33 E
Ščelkovo	**76**	55.55 N	38.00 E
Ščemilovo	**265b**	55.48 N	38.05 E
Scena	**64**	46.41 N	11.12 E
Scenery Hill	**214**	40.05 N	80.04 W
Sceptre	**184**	50.51 N	109.15 W
Ščerbakovo, Ross.	**74**	65.15 N	160.30 E
Ščerbakovo, Ross.	**86**	56.01 N	73.29 E
Ščerbakty	**86**	52.29 N	78.09 E
Ščerbinka	**82**	55.31 N	37.35 E
Ščerbinovka	**83**	48.26 N	37.50 E
Scerni	**66**	42.07 N	14.34 E
Scey-sur-Saône-et-Saint-Albin	**58**	47.40 N	5.58 E
Schaale ≃	**54**	53.21 N	10.49 E
Schaalsee ◎	**54**	53.35 N	10.57 E
Schaan	**58**	47.10 N	9.31 E
Schabs → Sciaves	**64**	46.46 N	11.40 E
Schachendorf	**61**	47.16 N	16.26 E
Schaefferstown	**208**	40.17 N	76.17 W
Schaephuysen	**263**	51.26 N	6.29 E
Schaerbeek	**50**	50.51 N	4.23 E
Schafberg ∧	**64**	47.47 N	13.27 E
Schäferberg ∧[2]	**264a**	52.25 N	13.08 E
Schaffhausen	**58**	47.42 N	8.38 E
Schaffhausen □[3]	**58**	47.40 N	8.35 E
Schafstädt	**54**	51.23 N	11.46 E
Schäftlarn	**64**	47.59 N	11.28 E
Schagen	**52**	52.46 N	4.47 E
Schaghticoke	**210**	42.54 N	73.35 W
Schalchen	**60**	48.07 N	13.10 E
Schale	**52**	52.26 N	7.37 E
Schalkau	**54**	50.24 N	11.00 E
Schalke ◆[8]	**263**	51.31 N	7.05 E
Schälker Heide ◆[3]	**263**	51.24 N	7.36 E
Schalksmühle	**56**	51.14 N	7.31 E
Schaller	**198**	42.30 N	95.18 W
Schanck, Cape ≻	**169**	38.30 S	144.53 E
S-Chanf	**58**	46.36 N	9.59 E
Schanfigg ∨	**58**	46.51 N	9.38 E
Schanghai → Shanghai	**106**	31.14 N	121.28 E
Schangnau	**58**	46.50 N	7.52 E
Schapbach	**58**	48.22 N	8.17 E
Schapen	**52**	52.24 N	7.33 E
Şchaprode	**54**	54.31 N	13.10 E
Šchara, gora ∧	**84**	43.00 N	43.06 E
Scharbeutz	**54**	54.03 N	10.44 E
Schardenberg	**60**	48.32 N	13.30 E
Schardenberg ∧[2]	**263**	51.27 N	6.28 E
Schärding	**60**	48.27 N	13.26 E
Scharhörn I	**52**	53.57 N	8.25 E
Schari → Chari ≃	**146**	12.58 N	14.31 E
Scharl	**263**	51.06 N	7.40 E
Scharmützelsee ◎	**54**	52.15 N	14.03 E
Scharnhorst ◆[8]	**263**	51.32 N	7.32 E
Scharnitz	**64**	47.23 N	11.17 E
Scharnitzer Klause)(	**64**	47.24 N	11.16 E
Scharrel	**52**	53.04 N	7.42 E
Scharzfeld	**52**	51.37 N	10.22 E
Schässburg → Sighişoara	**38**	46.13 N	24.48 E
Schauinsland ∧	**58**	47.55 N	7.54 E
Schaumburg	**216**	42.02 N	88.05 W
Schaut	**84**	43.43 N	42.32 E
Schebeli → Shabeelle ≃	**144**	0.12 S	42.45 E
Scheessel	**52**	53.10 N	9.29 E
Schefferville	**176**	54.48 N	66.50 W
Scheggia	**66**	43.24 N	12.40 E
Scheggino	**66**	42.43 N	12.50 E
Scheibbs	**61**	48.00 N	15.10 E
Scheiblingstein	**264b**	48.16 N	16.13 E
Scheidegg	**58**	47.35 N	9.51 E
Scheifling	**61**	47.09 N	14.24 E
Scheinfeld	**56**	49.40 N	10.27 E
Schelde (Escaut) ≃	**50**	51.22 N	4.15 E
Schelklingen	**58**	48.22 N	9.44 E
Schell Creek Range ⋀	**204**	39.10 N	114.40 W
Schellenberg ∧	**60**	48.18 N	13.03 E
Schellsburg	**214**	40.03 N	78.39 W
Schelsen ◆[8]	**263**	51.09 N	6.31 E
Schenectady	**210**	42.48 N	73.56 W
Schenectady □[6]	**210**	42.47 N	73.53 W
Schenefeld	**52**	53.36 N	9.49 E
Schenevus	**210**	42.32 N	74.49 W
Schenevus Creek ≃	**210**	42.29 N	74.59 W
Schenkendorf	**264a**	52.16 N	13.35 E
Schenkenhorst	**264a**	52.20 N	13.12 E
Schenklengsfeld	**56**	50.49 N	9.50 E
Schenley	**214**	40.41 N	79.40 W
Schenley Park ♠	**279b**	40.26 N	79.56 W
Schepsdorf-Lohne	**52**	52.30 N	7.16 E
Schererville	**216**	41.30 N	87.27 W
Scherfede	**52**	51.32 N	9.02 E
Scherlebeck	**263**	51.37 N	7.08 E
Schermbeck	**52**	51.41 N	6.52 E
Schermerhorn	**52**	52.36 N	4.52 E
Schermützelsee ◎	**54**	52.34 N	14.04 E
Scherpenheuvel	**56**	50.59 N	4.59 E
Scherpenzeel	**52**	52.05 N	5.30 E
Schertz	**196**	29.33 N	98.16 W
Schesch, Erg → Chech, Erg ◆[2]	**148**	25.00 N	2.15 W
Schesslitz	**60**	49.59 N	11.01 E
Schevelinger-Stausee ◎[1]	**263**	51.08 N	7.26 E
Scheveningen ◆[8]	**52**	52.06 N	4.18 E
Schiedam	**52**	51.55 N	4.24 E
Schieder	**52**	51.55 N	9.09 E
Schiefbahn	**56**	51.14 N	6.31 E
Schiehallion ∧	**46**	56.40 N	4.06 W
Schierke	**54**	51.46 N	10.40 E
Schierling	**60**	48.50 N	12.08 E
Schiermonnikoog	**52**	53.24 N	6.10 E
Schiermonnikoog I	**52**	53.28 N	6.15 E
Schiers	**58**	46.59 N	9.41 E
Schiessen	**58**	48.18 N	10.14 E
Schiffdorf	**52**	53.32 N	8.39 E
Schiffenensee ◎	**58**	46.50 N	7.10 E
Schifferstadt	**56**	49.23 N	8.22 E
Schiffshebewerk ◆[5]	**263**	51.37 N	7.19 E
Schihkiatschwang → Shijiazhuang	**98**	38.03 N	114.28 E
Schijndel	**52**	51.37 N	5.25 E
Schikoku → Shikoku I	**92**	33.45 N	133.30 E
Schildau	**54**	51.27 N	12.56 E
Schilde	**56**	51.14 N	4.34 E
Schilde ≃	**54**	53.26 N	10.53 E
Schildow	**54**	52.38 N	13.23 E
Schildwolde	**52**	53.14 N	6.49 E
Schiller Park	**216**	41.57 N	87.52 W
Schillingsfürst	**56**	49.17 N	10.15 E
Schillingstedt	**54**	51.14 N	11.11 E
Schilpario	**64**	46.01 N	10.09 E
Schiltach	**58**	48.17 N	8.20 E
Schiltigheim	**58**	48.36 N	7.45 E
Schimborn	**56**	50.03 N	9.11 E
Schimmert	**56**	50.55 N	5.50 E
Schinveld	**56**	50.57 N	5.59 E
Schinznach Bad	**58**	47.27 N	8.10 E
Schio	**64**	45.43 N	11.21 E
Schipbeek ≃	**52**	52.14 N	6.09 E
Schiphol, Luchthaven ⊠	**52**	52.17 N	4.40 E
Schipkau	**54**	51.31 N	13.53 E
Schirgiswalde	**54**	51.05 N	14.27 E
Schirmeck	**58**	48.29 N	7.13 E
Schirnding	**54**	50.05 N	12.13 E
Schisuoka → Shizuoka	**94**	34.58 N	138.23 E
Schjetman Reef ⊹[2]	**14**	15.10 N	178.40 W
Schkeuditz	**54**	51.24 N	12.13 E
Schkoder-See → Scutari, Lake ◎	**38**	42.12 N	19.18 E
Schkölen	**54**	51.02 N	11.49 E
Schkopau	**54**	51.23 N	11.59 E
Schladen	**52**	52.01 N	10.32 E
Schladming	**64**	47.23 N	13.41 E
Schlanders → Silandro	**64**	46.38 N	10.46 E
Schlangen	**52**	51.49 N	8.50 E
Schlangenbad	**56**	50.05 N	8.05 E
Schlänitz-See ◎	**264a**	52.27 N	12.57 E
Schlanstedt	**54**	52.00 N	11.02 E
Schlater	**194**	33.38 N	90.20 W
Schlegel Lake ◎	**276**	40.59 N	74.03 W
Schlei ⊂	**41**	54.36 N	9.51 E
Schleiden	**56**	50.31 N	6.28 E
Schleife	**54**	51.32 N	14.32 E
Schleinitz Range ⋀	**164**	3.10 S	151.40 E
Schleithal	**56**	48.59 N	8.02 E
Schleitheim	**58**	47.45 N	8.29 E
Schleiz	**54**	50.34 N	11.49 E
Schlema	**54**	50.40 N	12.40 E
Schlepzig	**54**	52.01 N	13.53 E
Schlesien → Silesia □[9]	**30**	51.00 N	16.45 E
Schlesischer (Ost) Bahnhof ◆[5]	**264a**	52.30 N	13.26 E
Schleswig, Dtsch.	**41**	54.31 N	9.33 E
Schleswig, Ia., U.S.	**198**	42.09 N	95.26 W
Schleswig-Holstein □[3]	**30**	54.20 N	9.40 E
Schlettau	**54**	50.33 N	12.56 E
Schlettstadt → Sélestat	**58**	48.16 N	7.27 E
Schleusingen	**54**	50.31 N	10.45 E
Schlicke ∧	**58**	47.31 N	10.37 E
Schlieben	**54**	51.43 N	13.23 E
Schliengen	**58**	47.46 N	7.35 E
Schlieren	**58**	47.24 N	8.27 E
Schliersee	**64**	47.44 N	11.51 E
Schlitz	**56**	50.40 N	9.33 E
Schloss Holte	**52**	51.52 N	8.35 E
Schloss Neuhaus	**52**	51.44 N	8.43 E
Schlossvippach	**54**	51.06 N	11.08 E
Schloss Zeil	**64**	47.52 N	10.00 E
Schlotheim	**54**	51.14 N	10.39 E
Schluchsee	**58**	47.49 N	8.10 E
Schluchsee ◎	**58**	47.49 N	8.10 E
Schlucht, Col de la)(	**58**	48.04 N	7.02 E
Schlüchtern	**56**	50.20 N	9.31 E
Schluderns → Sluderno	**64**	46.40 N	10.35 E
Schlüsselburg	**52**	52.29 N	9.04 E
Schlüsselfeld	**56**	49.45 N	10.37 E
Schlutup ◆[8]	**54**	53.53 N	10.48 E
Schmachtendorf ◆[8]	**263**	51.32 N	6.49 E
Schmalfeld	**52**	53.52 N	9.58 E
Schmalkalden	**54**	50.43 N	10.26 E
Schmallenberg	**56**	51.09 N	8.17 E
Schmalnau	**56**	50.27 N	9.47 E
Schmannewitz	**54**	51.24 N	12.58 E
Schmarsau	**54**	52.54 N	11.21 E
Schmelz	**56**	49.27 N	6.51 E
Schmida ≃	**61**	48.21 N	16.09 E
Schmidmühlen	**60**	49.16 N	11.56 E
Schmidt	**56**	50.39 N	6.25 E
Schmidtsdrif	**158**	28.41 S	24.02 E
Schmiedeberg	**54**	50.50 N	13.40 E
Schmiedefeld	**54**	50.37 N	10.49 E
Schmilka	**54**	50.53 N	14.14 E
Schmöckwitz ◆[8]	**264a**	52.23 N	13.39 E
Schmölln	**54**	50.53 N	12.20 E
Schmutter ≃	**58**	48.42 N	10.46 E
Schnabelwaid	**60**	49.49 N	11.35 E
Schnackenburg	**54**	53.02 N	11.32 E
Schnait	**56**	48.47 N	9.23 E
Schnaitsee	**60**	48.04 N	12.22 E
Schnaittach	**60**	49.31 N	11.19 E
Schnaittenbach	**60**	49.33 N	12.01 E
Schnakenbek	**52**	53.23 N	10.30 E
Schnecksville	**208**	40.41 N	75.36 W
Schneealpe ⋀	**61**	47.41 N	15.36 E
Schneeberg	**54**	50.36 N	12.38 E
Schneeberg ∧, Dtsch.	**54**	50.03 N	11.51 E
Schneeberg ∧, Öst.	**61**	47.47 N	15.47 E
Schneidemühl → Piła	**30**	53.10 N	16.44 E
Schneider	**216**	41.11 N	87.26 W
Schneifel ⋀[1]	**56**	50.15 N	6.25 E
Schneverdingen	**52**	53.07 N	9.47 E
Schney	**56**	50.10 N	11.04 E
Schober Gruppe ⋀	**64**	46.55 N	12.42 E
Schobüll	**41**	54.30 N	9.00 E
Schöckl ∧	**61**	47.11 N	15.28 E
Schodn'a	**82**	55.57 N	37.18 E
Schodn'a ≃	**265b**	55.50 N	37.25 E
Schœlcher	**240e**	14.37 N	61.06 W
Schoenbrunn Village State Memorial ⊥	**214**	40.27 N	81.24 W
Schofield	**190**	44.54 N	89.36 W
Schofield Barracks ■	**229c**	21.30 N	158.04 W
Schofields	**274a**	33.42 S	150.52 E
Schöftland	**58**	47.18 N	8.03 E
Schoharie	**210**	42.39 N	74.18 W
Schoharie □[6]	**210**	42.40 N	74.19 W
Schoharie Creek ≃	**210**	42.57 N	74.18 W
Schoharie Reservoir ◎[1]	**210**	42.22 N	74.26 W
Scholen	**52**	52.44 N	8.46 E
Scholes	**44**	53.49 N	1.25 W
Schollene	**54**	52.41 N	12.13 E
Schöllenen ∨	**58**	46.40 N	8.35 E
Schöller ◆[8]	**263**	51.14 N	7.01 E
Schöllkrippen	**56**	50.05 N	9.14 E
Schöllnach	**60**	48.45 N	13.11 E
Scholls	**224**	45.24 N	122.55 W
Scholven ◆[8]	**263**	51.36 N	7.01 E
Schomberg, On., Can.	**212**	44.00 N	79.41 W
Schömberg, Dtsch.	**56**	48.47 N	8.38 E
Schömberg, Dtsch.	**58**	48.13 N	8.46 E
Schonach	**58**	48.08 N	8.11 E
Schönaich	**56**	48.39 N	9.03 E
Schönau, Dtsch.	**56**	49.26 N	8.49 E
Schönau, Dtsch.	**58**	47.47 N	7.53 E
Schönau, Dtsch.	**64**	47.37 N	12.59 E
Schönbeck	**54**	53.34 N	13.34 E
Schönberg, Dtsch.	**54**	50.31 N	11.57 E
Schönberg, Dtsch.	**54**	50.11 N	12.19 E
Schönberg, Dtsch.	**54**	54.23 N	10.22 E
Schönberg, Dtsch.	**54**	53.50 N	11.38 E
Schönberg, Dtsch.	**60**	48.50 N	13.20 E
Schönberger Strand	**54**	54.25 N	10.24 E
Schönberg im Stubaital	**64**	47.11 N	11.25 E
Schönbrunn	**54**	50.32 N	10.53 E
Schönbrunn, Schloss ◉	**264b**	48.11 N	16.19 E
Schönbrunner Schlosspark ♠	**264b**	48.11 N	16.19 E
Schondra ≃	**56**	50.07 N	9.44 E
Schönebeck, Dtsch.	**54**	53.03 N	12.13 E
Schönebeck, Dtsch.	**54**	52.01 N	11.44 E
Schönebeck ◆[8]	**263**	51.28 N	6.56 E
Schöneberg ◆[8]	**264a**	52.29 N	13.21 E
Schöneck, Dtsch.	**54**	50.23 N	12.20 E
Schöneck, Dtsch.	**56**	50.13 N	8.52 E
Schönecken	**56**	50.09 N	6.27 E
Schönefeld	**264a**	52.23 N	13.30 E
Schöneiche	**54**	52.28 N	13.41 E
Schönenwerd	**58**	47.22 N	8.00 E
Schönerlinde	**264a**	52.39 N	13.27 E
Schönewalde	**54**	51.49 N	13.13 E
Schönfeld	**264a**	52.41 N	13.44 E
Schönfliess	**264a**	52.39 N	13.20 E
Schongau	**58**	47.49 N	10.54 E
Schönhagen, Dtsch.	**41**	54.38 N	10.01 E
Schönhagen, Dtsch.	**52**	51.41 N	9.33 E
Schönhausen, Dtsch.	**54**	52.35 N	12.02 E
Schönhausen, Dtsch.	**263**	51.37 N	7.38 E
Schönheide	**54**	50.30 N	12.31 E
Schönholthausen	**56**	51.11 N	8.00 E
Schöningen	**54**	52.08 N	10.58 E
Schönkirchen	**54**	54.20 N	10.15 E
Schönmünzach	**56**	48.36 N	8.22 E
Schonnebeck ◆[8]	**263**	51.29 N	7.04 E
Schönningstedt	**52**	53.32 N	10.15 E
Schönow	**54**	52.40 N	13.32 E
Schönsee	**60**	49.31 N	12.33 E
Schönthal	**60**	49.21 N	12.36 E
Schonungen	**56**	50.03 N	10.18 E
Schönwald, Dtsch.	**54**	50.12 N	12.05 E
Schönwald, Dtsch.	**58**	48.06 N	8.11 E
Schönwalde, Dtsch.	**54**	54.11 N	10.45 E
Schönwalde, Dtsch.	**54**	52.40 N	13.26 E
Schönwalde, Dtsch.	**54**	52.37 N	13.07 E
Schönwies	**58**	47.11 N	10.39 E
Schoodic Lake ◎	**188**	45.21 N	68.54 W
Schoolcraft	**216**	42.06 N	85.38 W
Schoolhouse Run ≃	**285**	40.13 N	75.27 W
Schoombee	**158**	31.28 S	25.30 E
Schoondijke	**52**	51.21 N	3.32 E
Schoonebeek	**52**	52.29 N	6.52 E
Schoonhoven	**52**	51.56 N	4.51 E
Schoorl	**52**	52.42 N	4.41 E
Schopfheim	**58**	47.39 N	7.49 E
Schopfloch	**56**	49.07 N	10.18 E
Schopp	**56**	49.21 N	7.41 E
Schöppenstedt	**54**	52.08 N	10.46 E
Schöppingen	**52**	52.05 N	7.14 E
Schorfheide	**54**	52.56 N	13.43 E
Schorfheide ◆[3]	**54**	52.55 N	13.35 E
Schörfling	**64**	47.56 N	13.36 E
Schorndorf	**56**	48.48 N	9.31 E
Schortens	**52**	53.31 N	7.56 E
Schoten	**50**	51.15 N	4.30 E
Schötmar	**52**	52.04 N	8.45 E
Schotten	**56**	50.30 N	9.07 E
Schottland → Scotland □[8]	**28**	57.00 N	4.00 W
Schouten, Kepulauan II	**164**	0.55 S	135.55 E
Schouten Island I	**166**	42.19 S	148.17 E
Schouten Islands II	**164**	3.30 S	144.40 E
Schouwen I	**52**	51.43 N	3.50 E
Schrader Creek ≃	**210**	41.43 N	76.30 W
Schrader Range ⋀	**164**	5.05 S	144.15 E
Schramberg	**58**	48.13 N	8.23 E
Schram City	**219**	39.09 N	89.27 W
Schrankogel ∧	**64**	47.02 N	11.06 E
Schraplau	**54**	51.26 N	11.40 E
Schreiber	**190**	48.48 N	87.15 W
Schrems	**61**	48.47 N	15.04 E
Schrick	**61**	48.30 N	16.37 E
Schriever	**194**	29.44 N	90.48 W
Schrobenhausen	**60**	48.33 N	11.17 E
Schröcken	**58**	47.15 N	10.05 E
Schroffenstein ∧	**158**	27.11 S	18.42 E
Schroon ≃	**188**	43.29 N	73.49 W
Schroon Lake ◎	**188**	43.47 N	73.46 W
Schrozberg	**56**	49.20 N	9.59 E
Schruns	**58**	47.04 N	9.55 E
Schulenburg, Dtsch.	**52**	52.12 N	9.47 E
Schulenburg, Tx., U.S.	**222**	29.40 N	96.54 W
Schuls → Scuol	**58**	46.48 N	10.18 E
Schultz Lake ◎	**176**	64.45 N	97.30 W
Schulzendorf	**54**	52.22 N	13.35 E
Schulzenhöhe	**264a**	52.29 N	13.47 E
Schumacher	**190**	48.28 N	81.18 W
Schüpfheim	**58**	46.57 N	8.01 E
Schüren ◆[8]	**263**	51.30 N	7.32 E
Schussen ≃	**58**	47.37 N	9.32 E
Schussenried	**58**	48.00 N	9.40 E
Schüttenberg ∧[2]	**61**	48.05 N	16.44 E
Schutter ≃	**58**	48.34 N	7.50 E
Schüttorf	**52**	52.19 N	7.13 E
Schuyler, Ne., U.S.	**198**	41.26 N	97.03 W
Schuyler, Va., U.S.	**192**	37.47 N	78.41 W
Schuyler □[6], Il., U.S.	**219**	40.07 N	90.34 W
Schuyler □[6], N.Y., U.S.	**210**	42.23 N	76.52 W
Schuyler Lake	**210**	42.47 N	75.02 W
Schuylerville	**210**	43.06 N	73.34 W
Schuylkill □[6]	**210**	40.41 N	76.12 W
Schuylkill ≃	**208**	39.53 N	75.12 W
Schuylkill Canal ≊	**285**	40.14 N	75.42 W
Schuylkill Haven	**208**	40.37 N	76.10 W
Schwaan	**54**	53.56 N	12.06 E
Schwabach	**60**	49.20 N	11.01 E
Schwaben □[5]	**58**	48.15 N	10.30 E
Schwaben □[9]	**30**	48.10 N	9.25 E
Schwabing ◆[8]	**60**	48.10 N	11.34 E
Schwäbische Alb ⋀	**58**	48.25 N	9.30 E
Schwäbisch Gmünd	**56**	48.48 N	9.47 E
Schwäbisch Hall	**56**	49.07 N	9.44 E
Schwabmünchen	**58**	48.11 N	10.45 E
Schwabstedt	**41**	54.23 N	9.11 E
Schwadorf	**264b**	48.04 N	16.35 E
Schwafheim	**263**	51.25 N	6.39 E
Schwagstorf	**52**	52.31 N	7.45 E
Schwaigern	**56**	49.08 N	9.03 E
Schwalenberg	**52**	51.52 N	9.11 E
Schwalm ≃	**56**	51.10 N	9.25 E
Schwalmstadt	**56**	50.55 N	9.11 E
Schwalmtal	**56**	51.13 N	6.16 E
Schwanden	**58**	47.00 N	9.04 E
Schwandorf	**60**	49.20 N	12.08 E
Schwanebeck, Dtsch.	**54**	52.37 N	13.32 E
Schwanebeck, Dtsch.	**54**	51.58 N	11.07 E
Schwanenstadt	**60**	48.03 N	13.46 E
Schwanenwerder ◆[8]	**264a**	52.27 N	13.10 E
Schwaner, Pegunungan ⋀	**112**	0.40 S	112.40 E
Schwanewede	**52**	53.14 N	8.35 E
Schwangau	**58**	47.35 N	10.44 E
Schwansen ◆[1]	**41**	54.35 N	9.50 E
Schwante	**264a**	52.44 N	13.05 E
Schwarme	**52**	52.54 N	9.01 E
Schwarmstedt	**52**	52.40 N	9.37 E
Schwartau ≃	**54**	53.56 N	10.41 E
Schwarza, Dtsch.	**54**	50.38 N	10.32 E
Schwarza, Dtsch.	**54**	50.41 N	11.19 E
Schwarza ≃, Dtsch.	**54**	50.41 N	11.19 E
Schwarza ≃, Öst.	**61**	47.43 N	16.13 E
Schwarzach, Dtsch.	**60**	48.55 N	12.49 E
Schwarzach, Öst.	**58**	47.27 N	9.45 E
Schwarzach ≃	**60**	49.36 N	12.08 E
Schwarzach im Pongau	**64**	47.19 N	13.09 E
Schwarzbach ≃, Dtsch.	**56**	49.16 N	7.18 E
Schwarzbach ≃, Dtsch.	**263**	51.19 N	6.44 E
Schwarzburg	**54**	50.38 N	11.12 E
Schwarze Elster ≃	**54**	51.49 N	12.51 E
Schwarze Laber ≃	**60**	49.00 N	12.03 E
Schwarzenbach am Wald	**54**	50.17 N	11.37 E
Schwarzenbach an der Saale	**54**	50.13 N	11.56 E
Schwarzenbek	**52**	53.30 N	10.29 E
Schwarzenberg	**54**	50.32 N	12.47 E
Schwarzenberg ◆[8]	**263**	51.24 N	6.42 E
Schwarzenberg Park ♠	**264b**	48.14 N	16.15 E
Schwarzenborn	**56**	50.37 N	9.58 E
Schwarzenbruck	**60**	49.21 N	11.14 E
Schwarzenburg	**58**	46.49 N	7.21 E
Schwarzenfeld	**60**	49.23 N	12.08 E
Schwarze Pumpe	**54**	51.32 N	14.20 E
Schwarzer Berg ∧[2]	**263**	51.41 N	7.12 E
Schwarzer Mann ∧	**56**	50.15 N	6.21 E
Schwarzer Regen ≃	**60**	49.10 N	12.50 E
Schwarzes Meer → Black Sea ⊤[2]	**22**	43.00 N	35.00 E
Schwarzheide	**54**	51.29 N	13.51 E
Schwarzkogel ∧	**61**	47.25 N	15.25 E
Schwarzrand ⋀	**156**	25.37 S	16.50 E
Schwarzriegel ∧	**60**	49.14 N	12.56 E
Schwarzsee	**58**	46.40 N	7.20 E
Schwarzwald (Black Forest) ⋀	**58**	48.00 N	8.15 E
Schwarzwälder Hochwald ◆[3]	**56**	49.39 N	6.55 E
Schwatka Mountains ⋀	**180**	67.25 N	157.00 W
Schwaz	**64**	47.20 N	11.42 E
Schwechat	**264b**	48.08 N	16.29 E
Schwechat ≃	**264b**	48.08 N	16.34 E
Schwedeneck	**41**	54.27 N	10.05 E
Schweden → Sweden □[1]	**24**	62.00 N	15.00 E
Schwedt	**54**	53.03 N	14.17 E
Schweez	**54**	53.53 N	12.24 E
Schweflinghausen	**263**	51.16 N	7.25 E
Schwegenheim	**56**	49.16 N	8.20 E
Schwei	**52**	53.24 N	8.21 E
Schweich	**56**	49.49 N	6.45 E
Schweidnitz → Świdnica	**30**	50.51 N	16.29 E
Schweighausen	**58**	48.13 N	7.57 E
Schweighouse-sur-Moder	**56**	48.49 N	7.44 E
Schweinfurt	**56**	50.03 N	10.14 E
Schweinitz	**54**	51.48 N	13.01 E
Schweinrich	**54**	53.10 N	12.37 E
Schweizer Nationalpark ♠	**58**	46.38 N	10.11 E
Schweizer-Reneke	**158**	27.11 S	25.18 E

Symbol	English	Deutsch	Español	Français	Português
≃	River	Fluß	Río	Rivière	Rio
≊	Canal	Kanal	Canal	Canal	Canal
∟	Waterfall, Rapids	Wasserfall, Stromschnellen	Cascada, Rápidos	Chute d'eau, Rapides	Cascata, Rápidos
⊔	Strait	Meeresstraße	Estrecho	Détroit	Estreito
⊂	Bay, Gulf	Bucht, Golf	Bahía, Golfo	Baie, Golfe	Baía, Golfo
◎	Lake, Lakes	See, Seen	Lago, Lagos	Lac, Lacs	Lago, Lagos
⋮	Swamp	Sumpf	Pantano	Marais	Pântano
⊓	Ice Features, Glacier	Eis- und Gletscherformen	Accidentes Glaciales	Formes glaciaires	Acidentes glaciares
⊤	Other Hydrographic Features	Andere Hydrographische Objekte	Otros Elementos Hidrográficos	Autres données hydrographiques	Outros acidentes hidrográficos
⊹	Submarine Features	Untermeerische Objekte	Accidentes Submarinos	Formes de relief sous-marin	Acidentes submarinos
□	Political Unit	Politische Einheit	Unidad Politica	Entité politique	Unidade política
◉	Cultural Institution	Kulturelle Institution	Institución Cultural	Institution culturelle	Instituição cultural
⊥	Historical Site	Historische Stätte	Sitio Histórico	Site historique	Sitio histórico
♠	Recreational Site	Erholungs- und Ferienort	Sitio de Recreo	Centre de loisirs	Area de Lazer
⊠	Airport	Flughafen	Aeropuerto	Aéroport	Aeroporto
■	Military Installation	Militäranlage	Instalación Militar	Installation militaire	Instalação militar
◆	Miscellaneous	Verschiedenes	Misceláneo	Divers	Diversos

Schweiz
→ Switzerland □[1] 58 47.00 N 8.00 E
Schwelm 56 51.17 N 7.17 E
Schwendi 58 48.10 N 9.58 E
Schwenke 263 51.11 N 7.26 E
Schwenksville 285 40.16 N 75.28 W
Schwepnitz 54 51.20 N 13.57 E
Schwerin, Dtsch. 54 53.38 N 11.25 E
Schwerin, Dtsch. 263 51.33 N 7.20 E
Schweriner See ⊜ 54 53.45 N 11.28 E
Schwertberg 61 48.16 N 14.35 E
Schwerte 56 51.26 N 7.34 E
Schwetzingen 56 49.23 N 8.34 E
Schweyen 56 49.10 N 7.24 E
Schwieberdingen 56 48.52 N 9.04 E
Schwielochsee ⊜ 54 52.03 N 14.12 E
Schwielowsee ⊜ 54 52.20 N 12.57 E
Schwitten 263 51.27 N 7.48 E
Schwyz 58 47.02 N 8.40 E
Schwyz □[3] 58 47.05 N 8.40 E
Sciacca 70 37.31 N 13.03 E
Sciara 70 37.55 N 13.45 E
Sciaves (Schabs) 64 46.46 N 11.40 E
Scicli 70 36.47 N 14.42 E
Scie ≃ 50 49.55 N 1.02 E
Science and Industry, Museum of ❦ 278 41.47 N 87.35 W
Sciez 58 46.20 N 6.23 E
Scigliano 68 39.08 N 16.19 E
Ščigry 78 51.53 N 36.55 E
Scilla 68 38.15 N 15.44 E
Scilly, Isles of II 42a 49.55 N 6.20 W
Ścinawa 30 51.25 N 16.27 E
Scio, N.Y., U.S. 210 42.10 N 77.59 W
Scio, Oh., U.S. 214 40.23 N 81.05 W
Scio, Or., U.S. 202 44.42 N 122.50 W
Scionzier 58 46.03 N 6.34 E
Sciota 210 40.56 N 75.19 W
Scioto □[6] 218 38.48 N 83.01 W
Scioto ≃ 188 38.44 N 83.01 W
Scioto Brush Creek ≃ 218 38.50 N 83.01 W
Scipio, In., U.S. 218 39.05 N 85.43 W
Scipio, Ut., U.S. 200 39.14 N 112.06 W
Scipio Center 210 42.47 N 76.34 W
Scippo Creek ≃ 218 39.31 N 82.59 W
Ščit ∧ 36 44.02 N 17.47 E
Ščitkoviči 76 53.13 N 27.59 E
Scituate 207 42.11 N 70.43 W
Scituate Reservoir ⊜[1] 207 41.47 N 71.36 W
Sclafani Bagni 70 37.49 N 13.51 E
Scobey 202 48.47 N 105.25 W
Scoffera, Passo della)(62 44.29 N 9.07 E
Scofield Reservoir ⊜[1] 200 39.47 N 111.09 W
Scoglitti ◂[8] 70 36.53 N 14.26 E
Ščokino 76 54.01 N 37.31 E
Scole 42 52.22 N 1.10 E
Ščolkovo 82 55.55 N 38.00 E
Scoltenna ≃ 64 44.15 N 10.50 E
Scolt Head › 42 52.58 N 0.42 E
Scone 166 32.03 S 150.52 E
Scooba 194 32.49 N 88.28 W
Scopello 62 45.46 N 8.06 E
Scordia 70 37.18 N 14.51 E
Scoresby 274b 37.54 S 145.14 E
Scorrano, It. 66 42.35 N 13.49 E
Scorrano, It. 68 40.05 N 18.18 E
Ščors 78 51.49 N 31.59 E
Ščorsk 78 48.22 N 34.06 E
Scorzè 64 45.34 N 12.06 E
Scotch ≃ 206 45.27 N 74.59 W
Scotch Plains 210 40.39 N 74.23 W
Scotchtown 210 41.29 N 74.21 W
Scotia, Ne., U.S. 198 41.27 N 98.42 W
Scotia, N.Y., U.S. 210 42.49 N 73.57 W
Scotia Lake ⊜ 190 47.05 N 81.23 W
Scotian Shelf ✢[4] 16 44.00 N 62.00 W
Scotia Ridge ✢[3] 18 54.00 S 50.00 W
Scotia Sea ⊤[2] 9 56.00 S 40.00 W
Scotland, On., Can. 212 43.01 N 80.22 W
Scotland, Pa., U.S. 208 39.58 N 77.35 W
Scotland, S.D., U.S. 198 43.08 N 97.43 W
Scotland, Tx., U.S. 196 33.40 N 98.28 W
Scotland □[8] 28 57.00 N 4.00 W
Scotland Neck 192 36.07 N 77.25 W
Scotland Run ≃ 285 39.39 N 75.03 W
Scotlandville 194 30.31 N 91.10 W
Ščot'ovo 83 48.09 N 39.04 E
Scotrun 210 41.04 N 75.19 W
Scotsburn 186 45.39 N 62.51 W
Scotstown 206 45.32 N 71.17 W
Scott, Sk., Can. 184 52.23 N 108.50 W
Scott, Ms., U.S. 194 33.35 N 91.04 W
Scott, Oh., U.S. 216 40.59 N 84.35 W
Scott □[6], Il., U.S. 219 39.38 N 90.27 W
Scott □[6], In., U.S. 218 38.41 N 85.46 W
Scott □[6], Ky., U.S. 218 38.18 N 84.35 W
Scott ≃ 204 41.48 N 123.02 W
Scott, Cape › 182 50.47 N 128.26 W
Scott, Mount ∧, Ok., U.S. 196 34.44 N 98.32 W
Scott, Mount ∧, Or., U.S. 202 42.56 N 122.01 W
Scott Air Force Base ■ 219 38.32 N 89.52 W
Scott Base ❦[3] 9 77.50 S 166.25 E
Scottburgh 158 30.19 S 30.40 E
Scott City, Ks., U.S. 198 38.28 N 100.54 W
Scott City, Mo., U.S. 194 37.13 N 89.31 W
Scott Cove ⊂ 276 41.03 N 73.28 W
Scott Creek ≃ 226 37.02 N 122.13 W
Scottdale, Mi., U.S. 216 42.03 N 86.27 W
Scottdale, Pa., U.S. 214 40.06 N 79.35 W
Scotter 44 53.29 N 0.40 W
Scott Haven 279b 40.15 N 79.47 W
Scott Island I, Ant. 9 67.24 S 179.55 W
Scott Island I, On., Can. 212 44.36 N 76.20 W
Scott Islands II 182 50.48 N 128.40 W
Scott Lake 220 25.56 N 80.13 W
Scott Mountain ∧ 202 44.11 N 115.47 W
Scott Peak ∧ 202 44.21 N 112.50 W
Scott Reef ✢[2] 160 14.00 S 121.50 E
Scott Run ≃ 284c 38.58 N 77.12 W
Scotts 216 42.11 N 85.24 W
Scottsbluff 198 41.52 N 103.40 W
Scotts Bluff National Monument ♦ 198 41.49 N 103.41 W
Scottsboro 194 34.40 N 86.02 W
Scottsburg, In., U.S. 218 38.41 N 85.46 W
Scottsburg, N.Y., U.S. 210 42.40 N 77.43 W
Scottsdale, Austl. 166 41.10 S 147.31 E
Scottsdale, Az., U.S. 200 33.30 N 111.53 W
Scotts Flat Reservoir ⊜[1] 226 39.17 N 120.55 W
Scotts Head › 240d 15.13 N 61.23 W
Scotts Hill 194 35.31 N 88.15 W
Scotts Level Branch ≃ 284b 39.22 N 76.45 W
Scottsmoor 220 28.46 N 80.53 W
Scotts Valley 226 37.03 N 122.00 W
Scottsville, Ky., U.S. 194 36.45 N 86.11 W
Scottsville, N.Y., U.S. 210 43.01 N 77.44 W
Scott Township 279b 40.32 N 80.11 W
Scottville, Il., U.S. 219 39.29 N 90.06 W
Scottville, Mi., U.S. 190 43.57 N 86.16 W
Scourie 46 58.20 N 5.08 W
Scout Lake 184 49.22 N 106.00 W
Scrabster 46 58.37 N 3.32 W
Scranton, Ia., U.S. 198 42.01 N 94.32 W
Scranton, N.Y., U.S. 210 42.44 N 78.50 W
Scranton, N.D., U.S. 198 46.08 N 103.08 W
Scranton, Pa., U.S. 210 41.24 N 75.39 W
Scremerston 44 55.44 N 1.59 W
Screven 192 31.29 N 82.01 W
Screw ≃ 164 3.55 S 142.50 E
Scribner 198 41.40 N 96.39 W
Scridain, Loch ⊂ 46 56.21 N 6.07 W
Scripps Institution of Oceanography ❦[3] 228 32.52 N 117.15 W
Scrivia ≃ 62 45.03 N 8.54 E
Scroggins 222 32.58 N 95.11 W
Scrooby 44 53.25 N 1.01 W
Scrub Island I 240m 18.28 N 64.31 W
Ščučin 76 53.36 N 24.45 E
Ščučinsk 86 52.56 N 70.12 E
Ščučje, Ross. 78 51.45 N 40.29 E
Ščučje, Ross. 80 51.46 N 40.29 E
Ščučje, Ross. 86 55.17 N 63.59 E
Ščučje Ozero 86 56.28 N 56.38 E
Scugog ≃ 212 44.24 N 78.45 W
Scugog, Lake ⊜ 212 44.10 N 78.51 W
Scugog Indian Reserve ◂[4] 212 44.11 N 78.54 W
Scugog Island I 212 44.10 N 78.53 W
Ščukino 82 54.28 N 37.01 E
Scunthorpe 44 53.36 N 0.38 W
Scuol (Schuls) 58 46.48 N 10.18 E
Scuppernong ≃ 216 42.54 N 88.42 W
Scurcola Marsicana 66 42.03 N 13.20 E
Ščurovo 82 55.03 N 38.49 E
Scurrival Point › 46 57.04 N 7.31 W
Scurry 222 32.31 N 96.23 W
Scutari, Lake ⊜ 38 42.12 N 19.18 E
Scutari → Shkodër 38 42.05 N 19.30 E
Sé ◂[8] 287b 23.33 S 46.37 W
Seabeck 224 47.38 N 122.51 W
Sea Bird Island I 224 49.15 N 121.45 W
Seabird Island Indian Reserve ◂[4] 182 49.17 N 121.42 W
Seaboard 192 36.29 N 77.26 W
Sea Bright 276 40.21 N 73.58 W
Seabrook, Md., U.S. 284c 38.58 N 76.50 W
Seabrook, N.J., U.S. 208 39.30 N 75.13 W
Seabrook, Tx., U.S. 222 29.33 N 95.01 W
Seabrook, Lake ⊜ 162 30.56 S 119.40 E
Sea Cliff 210 40.50 N 73.38 W
Seacock Swamp ≃ 208 36.48 N 76.51 W
Seacombe 262 53.25 N 3.01 W
Sea Dog Island I 276 40.36 N 73.35 W
Seadrift 196 28.30 N 96.47 W
Seaford, Eng., U.K. 42 50.46 N 0.06 E
Seaford, De., U.S. 208 38.38 N 75.36 W
Seaford, N.Y., U.S. 276 40.39 N 73.29 W
Seaford, Va., U.S. 208 37.11 N 76.26 W
Seaford Creek ≃ 276 40.38 N 73.29 W
Seaforth, Austl. 274a 33.48 S 151.15 E
Seaforth, On., Can. 190 43.33 N 81.24 W
Seaforth, Eng., U.K. 262 53.28 N 3.01 W
Seaforth, Loch ⊂ 46 57.54 N 6.40 W
Seafox Seamount ✢[3] 14 30.30 S 172.45 W
Seager Wheeler Lake ⊜ 184 54.27 N 103.30 W
Seagoville 222 32.38 N 96.32 W
Seagraves 196 32.56 N 102.33 W
Seaham 44 54.52 N 1.21 W
Seaholme 274b 37.52 S 144.50 E
Seahorse Breakers ✢[2] 112 5.30 N 112.37 E
Seahorse Point › 176 63.47 N 80.09 W
Seahouses 44 55.35 N 1.38 W
Seahurst 224 47.28 N 122.22 W
Sea Island I 224 49.12 N 123.10 W
Sea Islands II 192 31.20 N 81.20 W
Sea Isle City 208 39.09 N 74.41 W
Seal 260 51.17 N 0.14 E
Seal ≃ 176 59.04 N 94.48 W
Seal, Cape › 158 34.07 S 23.25 E
Sea Lake 166 35.30 S 142.51 E
Sealand 262 53.12 N 2.58 W
Sealark Channel ⋓ 175e 9.18 S 160.20 E
Seal Bay ⊂ 9 71.40 S 12.25 W
Seal Beach 228 33.44 N 118.06 W
Seal Beach National Wildlife Refuge ◂[4] 280 33.45 N 118.03 W
Seal Cays II 238 21.10 N 71.38 W
Seal Cove, N.B., Can. 186 44.39 N 66.51 W
Seal Cove, Nf., Can. 186 49.56 N 56.23 W
Sealdah Railroad Station ◂[5] 272b 22.34 N 88.23 E
Seale 194 32.17 N 85.10 W
Sealevel 192 34.51 N 76.23 W
Seal Island I 186 43.25 N 66.01 W
Seal Islands II 282 38.03 N 122.03 W
Seal Lake ⊜ 176 54.18 N 61.40 W
Seal Rocks II[1] 282 37.47 N 122.31 W
Sealston 208 38.15 N 77.19 W
Sealy 222 29.46 N 96.09 W
Seaman 218 38.56 N 83.34 W
Seamer 44 54.14 N 0.26 W
Seanor 214 40.13 N 78.54 W
Seara 252 27.07 S 52.17 W
Searchlight 204 35.27 N 114.55 W
Searcy 194 35.15 N 91.44 W
Searles Lake ⊜ 204 35.43 N 117.20 W
Sears Lake ⊜ 281 42.35 N 83.39 W
Searsport 188 44.27 N 68.55 W
Sears Tower ❦ 278 41.53 N 87.38 W
Searsville Lake ⊜ 282 37.24 N 122.14 W
Seascale 44 54.24 N 3.29 W
Seashore State Park ♦ 208 36.54 N 76.02 W
Seaside, Ca., U.S. 226 36.36 N 121.51 W
Seaside, Or., U.S. 224 45.59 N 123.55 W
Seaside Park 208 39.55 N 74.04 W
Seaside Park ♦ 276 41.10 N 73.12 W
Seaton, Eng., U.K. 42 50.43 N 3.05 W
Seaton, Eng., U.K. 44 54.41 N 3.33 W
Seaton, Eng., U.K. 44 53.54 N 0.14 W
Seaton ≃ 42 50.22 N 4.22 W
Seaton Delaval 44 55.04 N 1.31 W
Seaton Sluice 44 55.05 N 1.28 W
Seat Pleasant 284c 38.53 N 76.54 W
Seattle 224 47.36 N 122.19 W
Seattle, Mount ∧ 180 60.06 N 139.11 W
Seattle Heights 224 47.48 N 122.20 W
Seattle-Tacoma International Airport ⊠ 224 47.27 N 122.18 W
Seatuck National Wildlife Refuge ◂[4] 276 40.43 N 73.13 W
Seaview, Eng., U.K. 42 50.43 N 1.06 W
Sea View, Ma., U.S. 283 42.08 N 70.42 W
Seaview, N.Y., U.S. 276 40.39 N 73.09 W
Seaview, Wa., U.S. 224 46.20 N 124.03 W
Seaward Kaikoura Range ⋏ 172 42.14 S 173.39 E
Seaward Roads ⋓ 174g 28.13 N 177.25 W
Sea World ♦, Fl., U.S. 220 28.25 N 81.28 W
Sea World ♦, Oh., U.S. 214 41.21 N 81.23 W
Seba 112 10.29 S 121.50 E
Sébaco 236 12.51 N 86.06 W
Sebago Lake ⊜ 188 43.50 N 70.35 W
Se Bai ≃ 110 15.13 N 104.47 E
Sebakor, Teluk ⊂ 164 3.35 S 132.50 E
Sebakung 112 1.37 S 116.26 E
Šebalin 80 47.22 N 43.36 E
Šebalino, Ross. 80 48.16 N 43.21 E
Šebalino, Ross. 86 51.17 N 85.40 E
Sebanga 114 1.24 N 101.10 E
Sebangan, Teluk ⊂ 112 3.15 S 113.30 E
Sebangka, Pulau I 112 0.07 N 104.36 E
Sébaou, Oued ≃ 34 36.55 N 3.55 E
Sebarok, Pulau I 271c 1.13 N 103.48 E
Sebastian, Fl., U.S. 220 27.46 N 80.29 W
Sebastian, Tx., U.S. 196 26.20 N 97.47 W
Sebastian, Cape › 202 42.19 N 124.26 W
Sebastian Inlet ⊂ 220 27.51 N 80.26 W
Sebastián Vizcaíno, Bahía ⊂ 232 28.00 N 114.30 W
Sebastião de Lacerda 256 22.17 S 43.35 W
Sebastopol, Austl. 169 37.36 S 143.51 E
Sebastopol, Ca., U.S. 204 38.24 N 122.49 W
Sebastopol, Ms., U.S. 194 32.34 N 89.20 W
Sebatik, Pulau I 112 4.10 N 117.45 E
Sebba 150 13.26 N 0.32 E
Sebderat 144 15.26 N 36.40 E
Sébé ≃ 152 1.02 S 13.06 E
Sebec Lake ⊜ 188 45.18 N 69.18 W
Sebeka 198 46.38 N 95.05 W
Šebekino 78 50.25 N 36.56 E
Sébékoro 150 12.57 N 8.59 W
Šebelinka 78 49.27 N 36.30 E
Seben 130 40.24 N 31.34 E
Sebenico → Šibenik 36 43.44 N 15.54 E
Sebera, Punta ∧ 71 39.03 N 8.50 E
Seberi 252 27.29 S 53.24 W
Seberida 112 0.43 S 102.31 E
Šeberta 88 54.40 N 99.54 E
Sebeș 38 45.58 N 23.34 E
Sebesi, Pulau I 115a 5.57 S 105.30 E
Sebes Körös (Crișul Repede) ≃ 38 46.55 N 20.59 E
Sebewaing 190 43.43 N 83.27 W
Sebež 76 56.17 N 28.29 E
Sebille Manor 281 42.39 N 82.49 W
Şebinkarahisar 130 40.18 N 38.26 E
Šebiș 38 46.23 N 22.08 E
Sebnitz 54 50.58 N 14.16 E
Sebou, Oued ≃ 148 34.15 N 6.40 W
Sebree 194 37.36 N 87.31 W
Sebrell 208 36.47 N 77.07 W
Sebring, Fl., U.S. 220 27.29 N 81.26 W
Sebring, Oh., U.S. 214 40.55 N 81.01 W
Sebringville 212 43.24 N 81.04 W
Sebuku 112 4.03 N 116.56 E
Sebuku, Pulau I, Indon. 112 3.30 S 116.22 E
Sebuku, Pulau I, Indon. 115a 5.53 S 105.31 E
Sebuku, Teluk ⊂ 112 4.00 N 118.26 E
Šebunino 89 46.27 N 141.51 E
Seč 60 49.36 N 13.30 E
Seca, Ilha I 287a 22.50 S 43.11 W
Secane 285 39.55 N 75.18 W
Secang 115a 7.23 S 110.15 E
Secas, Islas II 236 7.58 N 82.02 W
Secaucus 276 40.47 N 74.03 W
Secchia ≃ 64 45.04 N 11.00 E
Sečenovo 80 55.13 N 45.54 E
Secesh ≃ 202 45.02 N 115.43 W
Séchault 56 49.16 N 4.44 E
Sechelt 182 49.28 N 123.45 W
Šechman' 76 52.32 N 40.29 E
Sechura 248 5.33 S 80.51 W
Sechura, Bahía de ⊂ 248 5.42 S 81.00 W
Sechura, Desierto de ◂[2] 248 5.50 S 80.40 W
Seckach 56 49.26 N 9.20 E
Seckau 61 47.16 N 14.47 E
Seckau ❦[1] 61 47.16 N 14.47 E
Seckauer Alpen ⋏ 61 47.20 N 14.40 E
Seckauer Zinken ∧ 61 47.20 N 14.44 E
Seclantas 252 25.18 S 66.15 W
Seclin 50 50.33 N 3.02 E
Seco ≃, Arg. 252 23.08 S 63.57 W
Seco ≃, Arg. 254 48.34 S 67.02 W
Seco ≃, Esp. 266d 41.30 N 2.09 E
Seco, Arroyo ≃, Ca., U.S. 226 36.25 N 121.20 W
Seco, Arroyo ≃, Ca., U.S. 280 34.05 N 118.13 W
Seco Creek ≃, N.M., U.S. 200 32.59 N 107.18 W
Seco Creek ≃, Tx., U.S. 196 29.02 N 99.08 W
Seco Island I 116 11.19 N 121.40 E
Second ≃ 276 40.47 N 74.09 W
Second Cliff ⏊[4] 283 42.12 N 70.43 W
Second Han-gang Bridge ◂[5] 271b 37.34 N 126.54 E
Second Herring Brook ≃ 283 42.09 N 70.47 W
Second Lake ⊜ 206 45.09 N 71.10 W
Second Mountain ∧ 208 40.33 N 76.30 W
Second San Diego Aqueduct ≊[1] 228 32.41 N 117.01 W
Second Swamp ≃ 208 37.08 N 77.12 W
Second Valley 168b 35.33 S 138.14 E
Second Watchung Mountain ∧ 276 40.55 N 74.13 W
Sečovce 30 48.43 N 21.40 E
Sečovská Polianka 30 48.47 N 21.42 E
Secretário, Ribeirão do ≃ 256 22.14 S 43.25 W
Secretary 208 38.36 N 75.56 W
Secretary Island I 172 45.15 S 166.55 E
Section 194 34.34 N 85.59 W
Secubun Island I 116 5.06 N 120.18 E
Sécure ≃ 248 15.10 S 64.52 W
Security 198 38.45 N 104.44 W
Security Square ◂[9] 284b 39.19 N 76.45 W
Séd ≃ 30 47.00 N 18.31 E
Seda, Lat. 76 57.40 N 25.46 E
Seda, Liet. 76 56.10 N 22.04 E
Seda, Zhg. 102 32.20 N 100.41 E
Seda ≃ 76 57.47 N 25.15 E
Sedah 112 10.46 S 123.12 E
Sedalia, Ab., Can. 184 51.41 N 110.40 W
Sedalia, In., U.S. 216 40.25 N 86.31 W
Sedalia, Mo., U.S. 194 38.42 N 93.13 W
Sedalia, Oh., U.S. 218 39.44 N 83.29 W
Sedan, Austl. 168b 34.35 S 139.18 E
Sedan, Fr. 56 49.42 N 4.57 E
Sedan, Ks., U.S. 198 37.07 N 96.11 W
Sedanka, Cape › 180 53.49 N 166.06 W
Sedanka Island I 180 53.50 N 166.10 W
Sedano 34 42.43 N 3.45 W
Sedano, Tanjung › 115a 7.49 S 114.27 E
Sedanovo 88 56.58 N 101.22 E
Sedari, Tanjung › 115a 5.57 S 107.18 E
Sedayu 115a 6.59 S 112.33 E
Sedbergh 44 54.20 N 2.31 W
Sedco Hills 228 33.39 N 117.24 W
Seddin 54 52.16 N 13.01 E
Seddin-Berg ∧[2] 264a 52.24 N 13.40 E
Seddinsee ⊜ 264a 52.23 N 13.41 E
Seddon 172 41.40 S 174.05 E
Seddonville 172 41.33 S 171.59 E
Sedé Boqér 132 30.52 N 34.47 E
Sedel'nikovo 86 56.57 N 75.18 E
Séderon 62 44.12 N 5.32 E
Sederot 132 31.31 N 34.35 E
Sedgefield, Eng., U.K. 44 54.39 N 1.26 W
Sedgefield, N.J., U.S. 276 40.51 N 74.28 W
Sedgefield, N.C., U.S. 192 35.10 N 80.51 W
Sedge Island I 276 40.21 N 73.59 W
Sedgewick 182 52.46 N 111.41 W
Sedgwick, Co., U.S. 198 40.56 N 102.31 W
Sedgwick, Ks., U.S. 198 37.55 N 97.25 W
Sedgwick, Mount ∧ 200 35.11 N 108.06 W
Sédhiou 150 12.44 N 15.33 W
Sedico 64 46.06 N 12.06 E
Sedilo 71 40.10 N 8.55 E
Sedini 71 40.51 N 8.49 E
Sedlčany 30 49.40 N 14.26 E
Sedley 208 36.46 N 76.59 W
Sedlice 60 49.23 N 13.56 E
Sedlitz 54 51.33 N 14.03 E
Sedlo ∧ 54 50.36 N 14.17 E
Sedn'ov 78 51.39 N 31.34 E
Šedok 84 44.13 N 40.52 E
Sedom (Sodom) ⊥ 132 31.04 N 35.23 E
Sedona 200 34.52 N 111.45 W
Sedot Yam 132 32.29 N 34.53 E
Sedova, pik ∧ 72 73.29 N 54.58 E
Sedovo 83 47.03 N 38.10 E
Sedovo-Vasiljevka 83 47.14 N 38.08 E
Sedrata 36 36.08 N 7.32 E
Sedriano 62 45.29 N 8.58 E
Sedrina 62 45.47 N 9.38 E
Sedro Woolley 224 48.30 N 122.14 W
Sedrun 58 46.41 N 8.46 E
Şedtim 24 66.25 N 56.20 E
Šeduva 76 55.46 N 23.46 E
Sędziszów 30 50.04 N 21.41 E
See, Öst. 58 47.05 N 10.28 E
See, Öst. 64 47.48 N 13.27 E
Seebad Ahlbeck 54 53.56 N 14.11 E
Seebad Bansin 54 53.57 N 14.07 E
Seebad Heringsdorf 54 53.56 N 14.08 E
Seeberg, Dtsch. 264a 52.33 N 13.41 E
Seeberg, Schw. 58 47.09 N 7.40 E
Seebergsattel)(61 47.38 N 15.18 E
Seeber Lake ⊜ 184 53.52 N 93.03 W
Seeboden 64 46.49 N 13.30 E
Seebruck 64 47.56 N 12.28 E
Seebrugg 58 47.49 N 8.13 E
Seeburg 264a 52.31 N 13.07 E
Seefeld, Dtsch. 52 53.27 N 8.21 E
Seefeld, Dtsch. 54 52.37 N 13.40 E
Seefeld in Tirol 64 47.20 N 11.11 E
Seefin ∧[2] 48 52.18 N 8.32 W
Seeg 58 47.38 N 10.36 E
Seege ≃ 54 53.04 N 11.23 E
Seehausen, Dtsch. 54 52.06 N 11.17 E
Seehausen, Dtsch. 54 52.53 N 11.45 E
Seeheim 156 26.50 S 17.45 E
Seeheim-Jugenheim 56 49.45 N 8.38 E
Seehof 264a 52.24 N 13.17 E
Seeis 156 22.29 S 17.39 E
Seekaskootch Indian Reserve ◂[4] 184 53.43 N 109.55 W
Seekoegat 158 33.03 S 22.31 E
Seekoei ≃ 158 30.18 S 25.01 E
Seekonk 207 41.48 N 71.20 W
Seelbach 58 48.18 N 7.56 E
Seeley Lake 202 47.10 N 113.29 W
Seeleys Bay 212 44.29 N 76.14 W
Seelingstädt 54 50.46 N 12.14 E
Seelow 54 52.32 N 14.23 E
Seelyville, In., U.S. 194 39.29 N 87.16 W
Seelyville, Pa., U.S. 210 41.35 N 75.17 W
Seelze 52 52.24 N 9.35 E
Seemade 144 7.10 N 48.36 E
Seemalik Butte ∧ 180 60.09 N 167.08 W
Seemenbach ≃ 56 50.17 N 8.59 E
Seemore Downs 162 30.42 S 125.15 E
Seen 58 47.29 N 8.46 E
Seengen 58 47.19 N 8.13 E
Seeon 64 47.58 N 12.26 E
Seer Green 260 51.37 N 0.36 W
Seergu 102 32.00 N 103.33 E
Seerhausen 54 51.16 N 13.15 E
Sées 50 48.36 N 0.10 E
Seesen 52 51.53 N 10.10 E
Seeshaupt 64 47.49 N 11.18 E
Seest 41 55.29 N 9.27 E
Seetal 61 47.09 N 13.57 E
Seetaler Alpen ⋏ 61 47.05 N 14.35 E
Seevetal 52 53.23 N 9.59 E
Seewalchen am Attersee 64 47.57 N 13.35 E
Seewiesen 61 47.37 N 15.16 E
Seewinkel ◂[1] 61 47.48 N 16.49 E
Seewis 58 47.00 N 9.32 E
Séez 62 45.37 N 6.48 E
Seez ≃ 58 47.07 N 9.18 E
Şefaatli 130 39.31 N 34.46 E
Šefadu 150 8.39 N 10.59 W
Sefar ⊥ 148 24.27 N 9.16 E
Sefare 156 23.02 S 27.28 E
Seferihisar 130 38.11 N 26.51 E
Séféto 150 14.08 N 9.49 W
Seffern 56 50.04 N 6.30 E
Seffner 220 27.59 N 82.17 W
Sefīd ≃ 128 37.26 N 49.55 E
Sefīd Ābeh 128 30.56 N 60.35 E
Sefrou 148 33.50 N 4.50 W
Sefton, N.Z. 172 43.15 S 172.40 E
Sefton, Eng., U.K. 262 53.30 N 2.58 W
Sefton □[8] 262 53.34 N 3.14 W
Sefton, Mount ∧ 172 43.41 S 170.03 E
Sefton Park ♦ 262 53.23 N 2.56 W
Segag 144 7.40 N 42.50 E
Segaliud ≃ 116 5.43 N 117.55 E
Segama ≃ 112 5.27 N 118.48 E
Segamat 114 2.30 N 102.49 E
Segang 100 31.58 N 114.18 E
Segangane 34 35.09 N 3.00 W
Şegarcea 38 44.06 N 23.45 E
Šegarka ≃ 86 57.16 N 84.05 E
Segbana 150 10.56 N 3.42 E
Segbwema 150 8.00 N 10.57 W
Segen ≃ 144 4.49 N 36.57 E
Segera 164 8.15 S 143.30 E
Segeri 112 4.39 S 119.33 E
Segesta ⊥ 70 37.56 N 12.50 E
Segesvár → Sighișoara 38 46.13 N 24.48 E
Segeža 24 63.44 N 34.19 E
Seggiano 66 42.56 N 11.33 E
Seggueur, Oued es V 148 31.39 N 2.26 E
Šegmas 24 64.43 N 49.14 E
Segni 66 41.41 N 13.01 E
Segno 222 30.35 N 94.41 W
Segorbe 34 39.51 N 0.29 W
Ségou 150 13.27 N 6.16 W
Ségou □[4] 150 14.00 N 5.40 E
Šegovary 24 62.23 N 42.57 E
Segovia, Col. 246 7.07 N 74.42 W
Segovia, Esp. 34 40.57 N 4.07 W
Segovia □[4] 34 41.15 N 4.00 W
Segozero, ozero ⊜ 24 63.18 N 33.45 E
Segrate 266b 45.29 N 9.19 E
Segré 32 47.41 N 0.53 W
Segre ≃ 34 41.40 N 0.43 E
Seguam Island I 180 52.17 N 172.30 W
Seguam Pass ⋓ 180 52.08 N 172.45 W
Séguédine 146 20.12 N 12.59 E
Séguéla, C. Iv. 150 7.57 N 6.40 W
Séguéla, Mali 150 14.07 N 6.44 W
Séguélon 150 9.25 N 7.09 W
Séguénéga 150 13.27 N 1.58 W
Seguí 252 31.57 S 60.08 W
Seguin 196 29.34 N 97.57 W
Seguin ≃ 212 45.21 N 80.01 W
Seguine Point › 276 40.31 N 74.12 W
Segula Island I 181a 52.01 N 178.07 E
Segundo 198 37.07 N 104.45 W
Segundo ≃ 252 31.21 S 62.59 W
Seguntur 112 1.54 N 117.47 E
Segura 34 39.50 N 6.59 W
Segura ≃ 34 38.06 N 0.38 W
Segura, Sierra de ⋏ 34 38.00 N 2.43 W
Sehāni Kalān 272a 28.41 N 77.25 E
Sehāni Khurd 272a 28.42 N 77.25 E
Sehāra Bāzār 126 23.06 N 87.49 E
Sehithwa 156 20.23 S 22.45 E
Sehlabathebe 158 29.53 S 29.05 E
Sehlabathebe National Park ♦ 158 29.53 S 29.06 E
Sehma 54 50.32 N 13.00 E
Sehnde 52 52.18 N 9.57 E
Sehnkwehn 150 5.13 N 9.12 W
Sehnkwehn ≃ 150 5.12 N 9.21 W
Sehore 124 23.12 N 77.05 E
Sehwān 120 26.26 N 67.52 E
Sehyŏn-ni 98 38.20 N 127.41 E
Seia 34 40.25 N 7.42 W
Seibert 198 39.18 N 102.52 W
Seibu 268 35.50 N 139.22 E
Seiches-sur-le-Loir 32 47.35 N 0.22 W
Seidan 96 34.19 N 134.45 E
Seidersville 210 40.35 N 75.23 W
Seiersberg 61 47.01 N 15.24 E
Seiffen 54 50.39 N 13.26 E
Seifhennersdorf 54 50.56 N 14.36 E
Seignelay 50 47.54 N 3.36 E
Seigneurial, Lac ⊜ 275a 45.33 N 73.20 W

ENGLISH — Name / Page / Lat.°′ / Long.°′

Seika 270 34.46 N 135.48 E
Seikpyu 110 20.55 N 94.47 E
Seil I 46 56.18 N 5.39 W
Seiland I 24 70.25 N 23.15 E
Seilhac 32 45.22 N 1.42 E
Seiling 196 36.08 N 98.55 W
Seillans 62 43.38 N 6.38 E
Seille ≃, Fr. 56 49.07 N 6.11 E
Seille ≃, Fr. 58 46.31 N 4.56 E
Seilo 140 12.20 N 23.50 E
Seim → Sejm ≃ 78 51.27 N 32.34 E
Sein, Île de I 32 48.02 N 4.51 W
Seinaiji 94 35.30 N 137.42 E
Seinäjoki 26 62.47 N 22.50 E
Seine □[5] 50 48.50 N 2.10 E
Seine ≃, Mb., Can. 184 49.54 N 97.07 W
Seine ≃, On., Can. 190 48.40 N 92.49 W
Seine ≃, Fr. 32 49.26 N 0.26 E
Seine, Baie de la ⊂ 32 49.30 N 0.30 W
Seine-et-Marne □[5] 50 48.30 N 3.00 E
Seine-et-Oise □[5] 50 48.45 N 2.00 E
Seine-Maritime □[5] 50 49.45 N 1.00 E
Seine-Port 50 48.33 N 2.33 E
Seine-Saint-Denis □[5] 261 48.55 N 2.30 E
Seip Mound State Memorial ⊥ 218 39.15 N 83.13 W
Seipstown 208 40.35 N 75.40 W
Seis de Septiembre → Morón 258 34.39 S 58.37 W
Seishin → Ch'ŏngjin 98 41.47 N 129.50 E
Seitenstetten 61 48.02 N 14.39 E
Seitovka 80 46.43 N 48.03 E
Seitsemisen kansallispuisto ♦ 26 61.58 N 23.20 E
Seiwa 94 34.29 N 136.30 E
Seixal 34 38.38 N 9.06 W
Seixas, Ponta do › 250 7.09 S 34.47 W
Seiz 61 47.23 N 14.55 E
Seize Îles, Lac des ⊜ 206 45.54 N 74.28 W
Sejaka 112 3.34 S 116.12 E
Sejerø I 41 55.53 N 11.09 E
Sejerø Bugt ⊂ 41 55.50 N 11.15 E
Sejm ≃ 78 51.27 N 32.34 E
Sejmčan 74 62.53 N 152.26 E
Šejno 80 53.22 N 43.12 E
Sejny 30 54.07 N 23.20 E
Sejorong 115b 9.02 S 116.48 E
Sejs 41 56.09 N 9.36 E
Sekači 80 50.30 N 43.37 E
Sekadau 112 0.01 S 110.54 E
Sekake 158 29.58 S 28.27 E
Sekampung ≃ 115a 5.36 S 105.50 E
Sekayam ≃ 112 0.07 N 110.38 E
Sekayu 112 2.51 S 103.51 E
Seke, Ityo. 144 9.56 N 38.19 E
Seke, Tan. 154 3.20 S 33.31 E
Seke-Banza 152 5.20 S 13.16 E
Sekeladi 112 2.38 S 102.14 E
Sekenke 154 4.16 S 34.10 E
Şekerli 130 37.33 N 39.22 E
Šeki (Nucha), Azer. 84 41.12 N 47.12 E
Seki, Nihon 94 35.29 N 136.55 E
Seki, Nihon 94 34.51 N 136.24 E
Seki, Tür. 130 36.24 N 29.13 E
Sekidō-san ∧ 94 36.58 N 136.59 E
Sekigahara 94 35.22 N 136.28 E
Sekigane 96 35.22 N 133.46 E
Sekijō 94 36.14 N 139.55 E
Sekima 112 1.41 S 111.31 E
Sekinomiya 96 35.22 N 134.38 E
Sekiu 224 48.15 N 124.18 W
Sekiya 270 34.27 N 135.42 E
Sekiyado 94 36.06 N 139.47 E
Seki-zaki › 96 33.15 N 131.54 E
Sekoma 156 24.41 S 23.50 E
Sekondi-Takoradi 150 4.59 N 1.43 W
Sekota 144 12.38 N 39.03 E
Sekpiegu 150 9.33 N 0.02 W
Sekretaris ≃ 269e 6.10 S 106.47 E
Şekretarka 80 52.36 N 44.11 E
Šekšema 80 58.22 N 45.11 E
Šeksna 76 59.13 N 38.30 E
Sekudai 114 1.32 N 103.40 E
Sela ≃[1] 126 21.54 N 89.39 E
Şela, Ponta da › 256 23.54 S 45.27 W
Šelabolicha 86 53.25 N 82.37 E
Şela Dingay 144 9.59 N 39.33 E
Šelagskij, mys › 74 70.06 N 170.26 E
Selah 202 46.39 N 120.31 W
Şelai ≃ 114 2.13 N 103.26 E
Šelajevo 88 56.56 N 97.42 E
Şelama 114 5.13 N 100.42 E
Šelanger 80 56.13 N 48.16 E
Selangor □[3] 114 3.20 N 101.30 E
Selangor ≃ 114 3.20 N 101.15 E
Selaön I 40 59.24 N 17.12 E
Selaphum 110 16.02 N 103.57 E
Selargius 71 39.16 N 9.10 E
Selaru, Pulau I 164 8.09 S 131.00 E
Selatan, Tanjung › 112 4.10 S 114.38 E
Sel'atin 78 47.53 N 25.12 E
Selatpanjang 114 1.00 N 102.43 E
Selawik 180 66.37 N 160.03 W
Selawik ≃ 180 66.36 N 160.20 W
Selawik Lake ⊜ 180 66.30 N 160.40 W
Selayar, Pulau I 112 6.05 S 120.30 E
Selayar, Selat ⋓ 112 5.42 S 120.28 E
Selb 54 50.10 N 12.08 E
Selbeck ◂[8] 263 51.22 N 6.52 E
Selbecke ◂[8] 263 51.20 N 7.28 E
Selbitz 54 50.19 N 11.44 E
Selborne 42 51.06 N 0.56 W
Selbu 26 63.13 N 11.02 E
Selbusjøen ⊜ 26 63.14 N 10.54 E
Selby, Austl. 274b 37.55 S 145.22 E
Selby, Eng., U.K. 44 53.48 N 1.04 W
Selby, S.D., U.S. 198 45.30 N 100.01 W
Selby ◂[8] 273d 26.13 S 28.02 E
Selbyville 208 38.27 N 75.13 W
Selchow 264a 52.21 N 13.28 E
Sel'co, Ross. 24 63.18 N 41.22 E
Sel'co, Ross. 76 53.22 N 34.06 E
Selcourt 273d 26.18 S 28.27 E
Selčuga ≃ 89 49.42 N 133.20 E
Selçuk 130 37.56 N 27.22 E
Sel'cy, Ross. 76 57.57 N 35.59 E
Sel'cy, Ross. 265a 59.57 N 30.43 E
Selden, Ks., U.S. 198 39.32 N 100.34 W
Selden, N.Y., U.S. 210 40.51 N 73.02 W
Seldovia 180 59.27 N 151.43 W
Sele ≃ 68 40.29 N 14.56 E
Sele, Piana del ⩦ 68 40.33 N 14.57 E
Sele, Selat ⋓ 164 1.10 S 131.05 E
Sele, Tanjung › 164 1.26 S 130.55 E
Selebi Phikwe 156 22.00 S 27.50 E
Selec 76 52.33 N 33.35 E
Şelec-Cholopejev 76 53.23 N 30.24 E
Šelechov 88 52.13 N 104.08 E
Selečn'a 76 52.23 N 34.23 E
Selection Park 273d 26.18 S 28.27 E
Selegas 71 39.34 N 9.06 E
Selemadeg 115b 8.29 S 115.02 E
Selembao 273b 4.22 S 15.17 E
Selemdža ≃ 89 51.42 N 128.53 E
Şelemdžinsk 89 52.36 N 131.08 E
Šelemeti 80 57.27 N 48.07 E
Selendi 130 38.45 N 28.53 E
Selenduma 88 50.55 N 106.10 E
Selenga (Selenge) ≃ 88 52.16 N 106.16 E
Selenge, Mong. 88 49.25 N 103.59 E
Selenge, Zaïre 152 1.58 S 18.11 E
Selenge □[4] 88 49.30 N 106.30 E
Selenge (Selenga) ≃ 88 52.16 N 106.16 E
Selenginsk 88 52.06 N 107.01 E
Selenicë 38 40.32 N 19.38 E
Selenn'ach ≃ 74 67.48 N 144.54 E
Selent 54 54.17 N 10.26 E
Selenter See ⊜ 54 54.17 N 10.28 E

DEUTSCH — Name / Seite / Breite°′ / Länge°′ E = Ost

Sélestat (Schlettstadt) 58 48.16 N 7.27 E
Seletar ≃ 271c 1.25 N 103.52 E
Seletar, Pulau I 271c 1.27 N 103.52 E
Seletar Airport ⊠ 271c 1.16 N 103.53 E
Seletar Hills 271c 1.23 N 103.53 E
Seletar Reservoir ⊜[1] 271c 1.24 N 103.48 E
Selety ≃ 86 53.06 N 73.22 E
Seletyteniz, ozero ⊜ 86 53.15 N 73.15 E
Selezen'ovo, Ross. 26 60.45 N 28.39 E
Selezen'ovo, Ross. 76 59.12 N 42.18 E
Selezni, Ross. 76 55.39 N 31.29 E
Selezni, Ross. 80 52.48 N 41.15 E
Selezn'ovo 76 60.45 N 28.39 E
Self Defense Fleet Headquarters ■ 268 35.18 N 139.38 E
Selfoss 24a 63.56 N 20.57 W
Selfridge 198 46.02 N 100.55 W
Selfridge Air National Guard Base ■ 281 42.36 N 82.49 W
Selghar 272c 18.57 N 73.02 E
Sel'gon 89 49.36 N 135.26 E
Sélibaby 150 15.10 N 12.11 W
Şelichino 89 50.22 N 137.38 E
Šelichova, zaliv ⊂ 74 60.00 N 158.00 E
Šelichovo 88 55.42 N 97.41 E
Selidovo 83 48.08 N 37.18 E
Seligenthal 54 50.45 N 10.28 E
Seliger, ozero ⊜ 76 57.13 N 33.05 E
Seligman, Az., U.S. 200 35.19 N 112.52 W
Seligman, Mo., U.S. 194 36.31 N 93.56 W
Selim 114 3.51 N 101.29 E
Selimbau 112 0.37 N 112.08 E
Selimiye 130 37.24 N 27.40 E
Selim River 114 3.50 N 101.24 E
Selínia 267c 37.56 N 23.32 E
Selinsgrove 208 40.47 N 76.51 W
Selinunte ⊥, It. 36 37.35 N 12.49 E
Selinunte ⊥, It. 70 37.35 N 12.49 E
Selišče, Ross. 24 64.58 N 46.18 E
Selišče, Ross. 76 56.53 N 33.16 E
Selitrennoje 80 47.11 N 47.27 E
Selivanovskaja 80 48.52 N 41.42 E
Seližarovo 76 56.51 N 33.27 E
Selje 26 62.03 N 5.22 E
Seljord 26 59.29 N 8.37 E
Selkämeri (Bottenhavet) ⊂ 26 62.00 N 20.00 E
Selke ≃ 54 51.52 N 11.14 E
Selkirk, Mb., Can. 184 50.09 N 96.52 W
Selkirk, On., Can. 212 42.49 N 79.56 W
Selkirk, Scot., U.K. 46 55.33 N 2.50 W
Selkirk, N.Y., U.S. 210 42.32 N 73.48 W
Selkirk Mountains ⋏ 182 51.00 N 117.40 W
Selkirk Provincial Park ♦ 212 42.49 N 79.58 W
Selkirk Shores State Park ♦ 212 43.33 N 76.12 W
Šelkovka 82 55.32 N 36.22 E
Šelkovskaja 84 43.30 N 46.22 E
Sella 64 46.00 N 11.25 E
Sella, Monte ∧ 64 46.40 N 12.02 E
Sella, Paso di)(64 46.30 N 11.45 E
Sella di Corno 66 42.21 N 13.14 E
Sellano 66 42.54 N 12.55 E
Selle ≃ 50 49.54 N 2.17 E
Seller Lake ⊜ 184 55.00 N 94.32 W
Sellero 64 46.03 N 10.20 E
Sellers 192 34.17 N 79.28 W
Sellersburg 218 38.23 N 85.45 W
Sellersville 208 40.21 N 75.18 W
Selles-sur-Cher 50 47.16 N 1.33 E
Sellia Marina 68 38.55 N 16.45 E
Sellières 58 46.50 N 5.34 E
Sellin 54 54.22 N 13.41 E
Sells 200 31.54 N 111.52 W
Selly Oak ◂[8] 42 52.25 N 1.52 W
Selm 52 51.42 N 7.28 E
Selma, Al., U.S. 194 32.24 N 87.01 W
Selma, Ca., U.S. 226 36.34 N 119.36 W
Selma, In., U.S. 218 40.11 N 85.16 W
Selma, N.C., U.S. 192 35.32 N 78.17 W
Selman City 222 32.11 N 94.58 W
Selmer 194 35.10 N 88.35 W
Selmigerheide ◂[8] 263 51.38 N 7.47 E
Selmont 194 32.23 N 87.01 W
Selmsdorf 54 53.48 N 10.50 E
Şelommes 50 47.45 N 1.12 E
Šelon' ≃ 76 58.14 N 30.50 E
Seloncourt 58 47.28 N 6.52 E
Selong 115b 8.39 S 116.32 E
Şelongey 58 47.35 N 5.10 E
Šelopugino 88 51.39 N 117.33 E
Selouane 34 35.04 N 2.58 W
Selous, Mount ∧ 180 62.57 N 132.31 W
Selous Game Reserve ◂[4] 154 9.10 S 37.10 E
Selsdon ◂[8] 260 51.21 N 0.04 W
Selsey 42 50.44 N 0.48 W
Selsey Bill › 42 50.43 N 0.48 W
Selsingen 52 53.22 N 9.13 E
Selston 42 53.04 N 1.20 W
Selters 56 50.32 N 7.44 E
Selty 80 57.19 N 52.10 E
Seltz 56 48.53 N 8.06 E
Selu, Pulau I 164 7.32 S 130.54 E
Selva, Arg. 252 29.46 S 62.03 W
Selva, It. 64 46.33 N 11.46 E
Sel'vačevo 82 55.25 N 37.57 E
Selva di Cadore 64 46.27 N 12.02 E
Selvagens, Ilhas II 148 30.05 N 15.55 W
Selvas ◂[3] 242 5.00 S 68.00 W
Selvino 62 45.48 N 9.45 E
Selway ≃ 202 46.08 N 115.36 W
Selwyn 166 21.32 S 140.30 E
Selwyn, Mount ∧ 182 55.59 N 123.36 W
Selwyn, Passage ⋓ 175f 16.03 S 168.12 E
Selwyn Lake ⊜ 176 59.55 N 104.35 W
Selwyn Mountains ⋏ 180 63.10 N 130.20 W
Selwyn Range ⋏ 166 21.35 S 140.35 E
Şelz ≃ 56 49.59 N 8.02 E
Šemacha, Azer. 84 40.38 N 48.39 E
Šemacha, Ross. 86 56.15 N 59.16 E
Semai, Pulau I 164 3.08 S 132.30 E
Semakau, Pulau I 271c 1.12 N 103.46 E
Seman ≃ 38 40.56 N 19.24 E
Semanggol 114 4.57 N 100.38 E
Şemangka, Teluk ⊂ 112 5.36 S 104.42 E
Šemanicha 80 57.18 N 45.24 E
Semans 184 51.25 N 104.44 W
Semanu 115a 8.00 S 110.39 E
Semarang 115a 6.58 S 110.25 E
Semaria 124 24.16 N 79.54 E
Sematan 112 1.48 N 109.46 E
Semau, Pulau I 112 10.13 S 123.22 E
Semayang, Kenohan ⊜ 112 0.14 S 116.28 E
Sembabule 154 0.05 S 31.27 E
Sembadel 62 45.16 N 3.41 E
Sembakung ≃ 112 3.47 N 117.30 E
Sembawang 271c 1.27 N 103.50 E
Sembé 152 1.39 N 14.36 E
Semberong ≃ 114 2.27 N 103.37 E
Semblançay 50 47.30 N 0.35 E
Sembo ≃ 152 7.42 S 13.01 E
Semcy 76 52.51 N 33.28 E
Şemdinli 128 37.18 N 44.35 E
Šemejkino 83 48.19 N 39.32 E
Semeliškės 76 54.40 N 24.40 E
Semenanjung Malaysia □[9] 114 4.00 N 102.00 E
Semendua 152 3.11 S 18.05 E
Semène ≃ 62 45.23 N 4.13 E
Semenicului, Munții ⋏ 38 45.05 N 22.05 E
Semenyih 114 2.57 N 101.51 E
Semertak 89 52.57 N 132.34 E
Şemeru, Gunung ∧ 115a 8.06 S 112.55 E
Šemetovo 82 54.28 N 38.30 E
Semeževo 76 52.58 N 27.00 E
Semiahmoo Bay ⊂ 224 48.58 N 122.48 W
Semibalki 83 47.00 N 39.03 E

Symbols in the index entries represent the broad categories identified in the key at the right. Symbols with superior numbers (⋏[1]) identify subcategories (see complete key on page *I · 1*).

Symbole im Register stellen die rechts im Schlüssel erklärten Kategorien dar. Symbole mit hochgestellten Ziffern (⋏[1]) bezeichnen Unterabteilungen einer Kategorie (vgl. vollständiger Schlüssel auf Seite *I · 1*).

Los símbolos incluídos en el texto del índice representan las grandes categorias identificadas con la clave a la derecha. Los símbolos con numeros en su parte superior (⋏[1]) identifican las subcategorías (véase la clave completa en la página *I · 1*).

Les symboles de l'index représentent les catégories indiquées dans la légende à droite. Les symboles suivis d'un indice (⋏[1]) représentent des sous-catégories (voir légende complète à la page *I · 1*).

Os símbolos incluídos no texto do índice representam as grandes categorias identificadas com a chave à direita. Os símbolos com números em sua parte superior (⋏[1]) identificam as subcategorias (veja-se a chave completa à página *I · 1*).

	English	Deutsch	Español	Français	Português
∧	Mountain	Berg	Montaña	Montagne	Montanha
⋏	Mountains	Gebirge	Montañas	Montagnes	Montanhas
)(	Pass	Paß	Paso	Col	Passo
V	Valley, Canyon	Tal, Cañon	Valle, Cañón	Vallée, Canyon	Vale, Canhão
⩦	Plain	Ebene	Llano	Plaine	Planície
›	Cape	Kap	Cabo	Cap	Cabo
I	Island	Insel	Isla	Île	Ilha
II	Islands	Inseln	Islas	Îles	Ilhas
⏊	Other Topographic Features	Andere Topographische Objekte	Otros Elementos Topográficos	Autres données topographiques	Outros acidentes topográficos

ESPAÑOL Nombre / FRANÇAIS Nom / PORTUGUÊS Nome	Página / Page	Lat.°′	Long.°′ W = Oeste / W = Ouest
Semibratovo	80	57.18 N	39.32 E
Semibugry	80	46.11 N	48.16 E
Semichi Islands II	181a	52.42 N	174.00 E
Semides'atnoje	78	51.21 N	38.44 E
Semidi Islands II	180	56.07 N	156.44 W
Semigorsk	88	56.42 N	104.41 E
Semijarka	86	50.54 N	78.20 E
Semikarakorsk	80	47.31 N	40.48 E
Semilej	80	53.57 N	45.21 E
Semilovo	80	55.04 N	42.10 E
Semiluki	78	51.41 N	39.02 E
Semily	30	50.36 N	15.20 E
Seminara	68	38.20 N	15.52 E
Seminary	194	31.33 N	89.29 W
Seminoe Reservoir ◎[1]	200	42.00 N	106.50 W
Seminoe State Park ♠	202	42.05 N	106.55 W
Seminole, Fl., U.S.	220	27.50 N	82.47 W
Seminole, Ok., U.S.	196	35.13 N	96.40 W
Seminole, Tx., U.S.	196	32.43 N	102.38 W
Seminole □[6]	220	28.45 N	81.13 W
Seminole, Lake ◎[1]	192	30.46 N	84.50 W
Seminole Draw V	196	32.27 N	102.20 W
Seminole Park	220	27.52 N	82.45 W
Seminskij chrebet ⋀	86	51.05 N	85.50 E
Semiozerje	88	49.52 N	110.23 E
Semioz'ornoje	86	52.22 N	64.08 E
Semioz'ornyj	88	53.44 N	120.25 E
Semipalatinsk	86	50.28 N	80.13 E
Semipolka	86	54.07 N	67.16 E
Semipolki	78	50.43 N	30.56 E
Semirara Island I	116	12.04 N	121.23 E
Semisopochnoi Island I	181a	52.00 N	179.35 E
Semitau	112	0.33 N	111.58 E
Semizbugy	86	50.12 N	74.48 E
Semizbugy, gora ∧	86	50.10 N	74.56 E
Semjany	80	56.02 N	45.59 E
Semli Kalān	124	24.10 N	76.39 E
Seml'ovo	76	55.03 N	33.58 E
Semmens Lake ◎	184	55.03 N	94.11 W
Semmering	61	47.38 N	15.49 E
Semnān	128	35.33 N	53.24 E
Semnān □[4]	128	35.30 N	54.00 E
Şemois ≃	56	49.53 N	4.45 E
Šemonaicha	86	50.39 N	81.54 E
Sem'ono-Aleksandrovka	78	51.03 N	40.12 E
Sem'onov	24	56.48 N	44.30 E
Sem'onovka, Kaz.	86	51.20 N	70.46 E
Sem'onovka, Kyrg.	85	42.43 N	77.32 E
Sem'onovka, Ukr.	78	49.36 N	33.10 E
Sem'onovka, Ukr.	78	52.10 N	32.35 E
Sem'onovskoje, Ross.	82	55.03 N	37.46 E
Sem'onovskoje, Ross.	82	55.18 N	38.21 E
Šemordan	80	56.11 N	50.26 E
Sempach	58	47.08 N	8.11 E
Sempacher See ◎	58	47.09 N	8.09 E
Sempang Mangayau, Tanjong ›	112	7.02 N	116.45 E
Semple Lake ◎	184	55.02 N	95.38 W
Sempol	115a	8.01 S	114.08 E
Semporna	112	4.28 N	118.36 E
Sempu, Pulau I	115a	8.26 S	112.42 E
Semuda	112	2.51 S	112.58 E
Semuliki ≃	154	1.14 N	30.28 E
Şemur-en-Auxois	50	47.29 N	4.20 E
Šemurša	80	54.53 N	47.32 E
Šemyšejka	80	52.54 N	45.24 E
Semža	24	66.09 N	44.08 E
Sên ≃	110	12.32 N	104.28 E
Sena, Bol.	248	11.32 S	67.11 W
Seňa, Česko.	30	48.34 N	21.15 E
Sena, Moç.	154	17.27 S	35.00 E
Senador Amaral	256	22.35 S	46.11 W
Senador Canedo	255	16.43 S	49.05 W
Senador Côrtes	256	21.48 S	42.56 W
Senador Firmino	255	20.55 S	43.06 W
Senador Guiomard	248	10.14 S	67.36 W
Senador José Bento	256	22.10 S	46.10 W
Senador José Porfírio	250	2.39 S	51.55 W
Senador Pompeu	250	5.35 S	39.22 W
Senago	266b	45.35 N	9.07 E
Senahú	236	15.24 N	89.50 W
Senai	114	1.36 N	103.39 E
Senainville	261	48.30 N	1.37 E
Senaja	112	6.45 N	117.03 E
Senaki	84	42.17 N	42.04 E
Senale	64	46.31 N	11.06 E
Senales, Val di V	64	46.45 N	10.50 E
Sena Madureira	248	9.04 S	68.40 W
Senamaninik	114	0.45 N	100.47 E
Senanayake Samudra ◎[1]	122	7.11 N	81.29 E
Senang, Pulau I	271c	1.11 N	103.44 E
Senanga	152	16.06 S	23.16 E
Sénart, Forêt de ♠	261	48.40 N	2.30 E
Sénas	62	43.45 N	5.05 E
Sena → Seine ≃	32	49.26 N	0.26 E
Senate	184	49.18 N	109.41 W
Senath	194	36.08 N	90.09 W
Şenatobia	194	34.37 N	89.58 W
Šenbertal	86	48.43 N	60.20 E
Senča	78	50.16 N	33.20 E
Send	260	51.17 N	0.31 W
Sendafa	144	9.07 N	39.00 E
Sendai, Nihon	92	31.49 N	130.18 E
Sendai, Nihon	92	38.15 N	140.53 E
Sendai ≃, Nihon	92	31.51 N	130.12 E
Sendai ≃, Nihon	96	35.32 N	134.11 E
Sendai-heiya ≚	92	38.15 N	141.00 E
Sendelingsdrif	156	28.12 S	16.53 E
Senden, Dtsch.	52	51.51 N	7.29 E
Senden, Dtsch.	58	48.19 N	10.03 E
Şendenhorst	52	51.50 N	7.49 E
Šender	86	49.46 N	66.09 E
Sendhwa	120	21.41 N	75.06 E
Sêndo	102	31.42 N	95.16 E
Sendurjana	120	21.32 N	78.17 E
Senduruhan	112	1.00 S	110.46 E
Sene ≃	150	7.30 N	0.33 W
Senebui, Tanjung ›	114	2.17 N	101.03 E
Senec	30	48.14 N	17.24 E
Seneca, Il., U.S.	216	41.18 N	88.36 W
Seneca, Ks., U.S.	198	39.50 N	96.03 W
Seneca, Md., U.S.	284c	39.04 N	77.17 W
Seneca, Mo., U.S.	194	36.50 N	94.36 W
Seneca, Or., U.S.	202	44.08 N	118.58 W
Seneca, Pa., U.S.	214	41.23 N	79.42 W
Seneca, S.C., U.S.	192	34.41 N	82.57 W
Seneca □[6], N.Y., U.S.	210	42.54 N	76.52 W
Seneca □[6], Oh., U.S.	214	41.07 N	83.11 W
Seneca ≃	210	43.12 N	76.17 W
Seneca, Mount ∧	210	42.01 N	78.49 W
Seneca Castle	210	42.53 N	77.06 W
Seneca Caverns ♁[5]	214	41.11 N	82.53 W
Seneca Creek ⊂	284b	39.19 N	76.22 W
Seneca Creek ≃	196	36.36 N	102.52 W
Seneca Falls	210	42.54 N	76.47 W
Seneca Lake ◎	210	42.40 N	76.57 W
Seneca Mall ◆[9]	284a	42.50 N	78.47 W
Seneca State Park ♠	208	39.08 N	77.15 W
Senecaville Lake ◎[1]	188	39.55 N	81.25 W
Seneffe	50	50.31 N	4.15 E
Senegal (Sénégal) □[1], Afr.	134	14.00 N	14.00 W
Senegal (Sénégal) □[1], Afr.	150	14.00 N	14.00 W
Sénégal ≃	150	15.48 N	16.32 W
Seneghe	71	40.05 N	8.36 E
Senekal	158	28.19 S	27.36 E
Senerchia	68	40.44 N	15.12 E
Senetosa, Capu di ›	71	41.33 N	8.47 E
Sénez	62	43.55 N	6.24 E
Senežskoje, ozero ◎	82	56.12 N	37.00 E
Senftenberg	54	51.31 N	14.00 E
Senga Hill	154	9.22 S	31.12 E
Sengbachstausee ◎[1]	263	51.08 N	7.09 E
Şengejskij, ostrov I	24	68.27 N	51.05 E
Šengel'šij	86	48.33 N	57.28 E
Sengés	255	24.06 S	49.29 W
Senggarang	114	1.45 N	103.03 E
Sênggê ≃	120	32.28 N	79.44 E
Senghenydd	42	51.36 N	3.16 W
Sengilej	80	53.58 N	48.46 E
Sengkamang	114	0.42 N	101.55 E
Sengsengbirge ⋀	61	47.47 N	14.15 E
Senguer ≃	254	45.32 S	68.54 W
Sengwa ≃	154	17.07 S	28.05 E
Sengwarden	52	53.35 N	8.02 E
Senhāti	126	22.53 N	89.33 E
Senhor do Bonfim	250	10.27 S	40.11 W
Senica	30	48.41 N	17.22 E
Senigallia	66	43.43 N	13.13 E
Senirkent	130	38.07 N	30.33 E
Senise	68	40.09 N	16.18 E
Senj	36	44.59 N	14.54 E
Senja I	24	69.20 N	17.30 E
Senjitu	98	41.56 N	116.25 E
Senjō-san ∧	96	35.26 N	133.36 E
Senkevičevka	78	50.32 N	25.02 E
Senkobo	154	17.38 S	25.58 E
Sen'kovo	83	49.31 N	37.43 E
Şenköy	130	36.05 N	36.05 E
Šenkursk	24	62.08 N	42.53 E
Senlac	184	52.29 N	109.41 W
Şenlikköy ◆[8]	267b	40.59 N	28.47 E
Šenlis	50	49.12 N	2.35 E
Senlisse	261	48.41 N	1.59 E
Senmonorom	110	12.27 N	107.12 E
Senn, Dahr ou ♁[4]	150	18.30 N	11.00 W
Sennaja	78	45.15 N	37.01 E
Sennan	96	34.22 N	135.17 E
Senne(Zenne) ≃	50	51.04 N	4.26 E
Sennecey-le-Grand	58	46.39 N	4.52 E
Senne II → Sennestadt	52	51.59 N	8.37 E
Sennen	42	50.04 N	5.42 W
Sennestadt	52	51.59 N	8.37 E
Senneterre	190	48.23 N	77.15 W
Senneville	275a	45.27 N	73.57 W
Sennevoy-le-Bas	50	47.48 N	4.17 E
Senno	76	54.49 N	29.43 E
Sennoj, Ross.	80	52.11 N	46.57 E
Sennoj, Ross.	80	50.16 N	43.37 E
Sennokura-yama ∧	94	36.49 N	138.50 E
Sennori	71	40.47 N	8.35 E
Sennwald	58	47.16 N	9.30 E
Sennybridge	42	51.57 N	3.34 W
Senoia	192	33.18 N	84.33 W
Senonches	50	48.33 N	1.02 E
Senones	58	48.24 N	6.59 E
Senorbì	71	39.32 N	9.08 E
Sénou	150	12.31 N	6.56 W
Sénouire ≃	62	45.16 N	3.25 E
Şenpazar	130	41.48 N	33.16 E
Šenqunyane ≃	158	30.03 S	28.10 E
Senqu → Orange ≃	156	28.41 S	16.28 E
Senriyama	270	34.47 N	135.30 E
Sens	50	48.12 N	3.17 E
Sense ≃	58	46.54 N	7.14 E
Sensée ≃	50	50.16 N	3.06 E
Sensée, Canal de la ≍	50	50.14 N	3.17 E
Sensuntepeque	236	13.52 N	88.38 W
Şenta	38	45.56 N	20.04 E
Šentala	80	54.27 N	51.29 E
Sentani, Danau ◎	164	2.36 S	140.34 E
Sentarum, Danau ◎	112	0.51 N	112.06 E
Sentas	86	49.19 N	82.28 E
Sentelek	86	51.13 N	83.44 E
Şentery	154	5.22 S	25.45 E
Šentilj	61	46.41 N	15.40 E
Sentinel	196	35.09 N	99.10 W
Sentinel Butte ∧	198	46.53 N	103.50 W
Sentinel Peak ∧	182	54.54 N	121.57 W
Sentinel Range ⋀	9	78.10 S	85.30 W
Şentino ≃	66	43.24 N	12.59 E
Šentjur	36	46.13 N	15.24 E
Sentolo	115a	7.50 S	110.13 E
Sentosa I	271c	1.15 N	103.50 E
Sento Sé	250	9.51 S	41.51 W
Sentsū-zan ∧	96	35.09 N	133.11 E
Senyavin Islands II	14	6.55 N	158.00 E
Senye	152	1.34 N	9.50 E
Şenyurt	130	37.06 N	40.40 E
Šenzaki-wan ⊂	96	34.24 N	131.15 E
Sen-zan ∧	96	34.21 N	134.51 E
Senzig	54	52.17 N	13.39 E
Senzu-dake ∧	270	34.57 N	135.52 E
Seo de Urgel	34	42.21 N	1.28 E
Seohāra	124	29.13 N	78.35 E
Seolag-san Kukrip Kongwŏn ♠	98	38.09 N	128.24 E
Seon	58	47.21 N	8.10 E
Seonāth ≃	122	21.44 N	82.28 E
Seoni	124	22.05 N	79.32 E
Seoni Mālwa	124	22.27 N	77.28 E
Seorīnārāyan	120	21.44 N	82.35 E
Seoul Bridge ◆[5]	271b	37.32 N	126.56 E
Seoul National University ⊍[2]	271b	37.28 N	126.57 E
Seoul → Sŏul	98	37.33 N	126.58 E
Seoul Stadium ♠	271b	37.35 N	127.02 E
Seoul Station ◆[5]	271b	37.34 N	126.58 E
Sepahat	114	1.34 N	101.53 E
Sepang	114	2.42 N	101.45 E
Sepanjang, Pulau I	112	7.10 S	115.50 E
Separation Creek ≃	200	41.59 N	107.28 W
Separation Point ›	172	40.47 S	173.00 E
Sepasu	112	0.43 N	117.35 E
Sepatini ≃	248	7.36 S	65.24 W
Sépeaux	50	47.57 N	3.14 E
Sepetiba ◆[8]	256	22.58 S	43.42 W
Şepetiba, Baía de ⊂	256	23.00 S	43.48 W
Šepetovka	78	50.11 N	27.04 E
Sepi	175e	8.33 S	159.50 E
Sepik ≃	164	3.51 S	144.34 E
Sepino	66	41.24 N	14.37 E
Sep'o	98	38.39 N	127.22 E
Sępólno Krajeńskie	30	53.28 N	17.32 E
Sépone → Muang Xépôn	110	16.41 N	106.14 E
Sepopa	156	18.13 S	22.13 E
Sępopol	30	54.15 N	21.00 E
Sepoti ≃	248	6.43 S	61.38 W
Sepotuba ≃	248	15.56 S	57.39 W
Seppeltsfield	168b	34.30 S	138.54 E
Seppenrade	52	51.46 N	7.23 E
Sepphoris → Ẓippori	132	32.45 N	35.17 E
Seppois-le-Bas	58	47.33 N	7.10 E
Septeuil	261	48.54 N	1.41 E
Sept Frères, Lac des ◎	206	46.20 N	75.10 W
Sept-Îles (Seven Islands)	186	50.12 N	66.23 W
Septvaux	50	49.34 N	3.23 E
Sepulga ≃	194	31.11 N	86.46 W
Sepúlveda	34	41.18 N	3.45 W
Sepulveda ◆[8]	280	34.13 N	118.28 W
Sepulveda Dam ◆[6]	280	34.10 N	118.29 W
Sepulveda Flood Control Basin ≚[1]	228	34.11 N	118.29 W
Seputih ≃	112	4.42 S	105.54 E
Sepyč	80	58.11 N	54.08 E
Sequals	64	46.10 N	12.50 E
Sequatchie ≃	192	35.02 N	85.38 W
Sequeros	34	40.31 N	6.01 W
Sequillo ≃	34	41.45 N	5.30 W
Sequim	224	48.04 N	123.06 W
Sequim Bay ⊂	224	48.03 N	123.02 W
Sequoia National Park ♠	204	36.30 N	118.30 W
Sera	96	34.36 N	133.03 E
Şera, Pulau I	164	7.40 S	131.05 E
Šerabad	128	37.40 N	67.01 E
Serachs	128	36.32 N	61.13 E
Serafettin Dağları ⋀	130	39.05 N	41.10 E
Šerafimovič	80	49.36 N	42.43 E
Šeragul	88	54.29 N	100.56 E
Seraidi	36	36.55 N	7.41 E
Seraing	56	50.36 N	5.29 E
Seraja ≃	82	56.15 N	38.45 E
Seram (Ceram) I	164	3.00 S	129.00 E
Seram, Laut (Ceram Sea) ⊤[2]	108	2.30 S	128.00 E
Serampore	126	22.45 N	88.21 E
Serang	115a	6.07 S	106.09 E
Serang ≃	115a	6.43 S	110.35 E
Serangoon	271c	1.22 N	103.54 E
Serangoon ≃	271c	1.24 N	103.56 E
Serangoon, Pulau I	271c	1.25 N	103.56 E
Serangoon Harbour ⊂	271c	1.23 N	103.57 E
Serapo	66	41.13 N	13.34 E
Serasan, Pulau I	112	2.30 N	109.03 E
Serasan, Selat ⋓	112	2.20 N	109.00 E
Seravalle Sesia	62	45.41 N	8.19 E
Seravezza	64	43.59 N	10.13 E
Seraya, Pulau I	271c	1.16 N	103.43 E
Serayevo → Sarajevo	38	43.52 N	18.25 E
Şerayu ≃	115a	7.41 S	109.06 E
Šerbakul'	86	54.38 N	72.24 E
Serbeulangit, Pegunungan ⋀	114	3.45 N	97.50 E
Serbia → Srbija □[3]	38	44.00 N	21.00 E
Serchio ≃	64	43.47 N	10.16 E
Serdce-Kamen', mys ›	180	66.57 N	171.40 W
Serdež	80	57.17 N	48.17 E
Serditoje	83	48.02 N	38.24 E
Serdo	144	11.58 N	41.18 E
Serdoba ≃	80	52.34 N	44.01 E
Serdobsk	80	52.28 N	44.13 E
Séré'ama, Mont ∧	175f	13.47 S	167.29 E
Serebr'anka, Ross.	86	57.13 N	70.42 E
Serebr'anka, Ross.	265b	55.45 N	37.55 E
Serebr'anka, Ukr.	83	48.55 N	38.08 E
Serebr'anka ≃	265b	55.47 N	37.42 E
Serebr'ansk	86	49.43 N	83.20 E
Serebr'anyj Bor ◆[8]	265b	55.48 N	37.25 E
Serebr'anyje Prudy	82	54.28 N	38.44 E
Serebrovo	88	55.24 N	97.52 E
Serechoviči	78	51.25 N	24.40 E
Sered'	30	48.17 N	17.44 E
Sereda, Ross.	76	55.54 N	35.31 E
Şereda, Ross.	80	58.00 N	40.27 E
Šeredar' ≃	82	55.56 N	39.04 E
Seredejskij	76	54.03 N	35.14 E
Seredìči	76	53.35 N	35.51 E
Seredina-Buda	78	52.11 N	34.01 E
Serednikovo, Ross.	80	55.15 N	39.40 E
Serednikovo, Ross.	265b	55.56 N	37.14 E
Seredn'ovo	265b	55.35 N	37.18 E
Seredžius	76	55.05 N	23.25 E
Şereflikoçhisar	130	38.56 N	33.33 E
Šeregeš	86	52.57 N	88.02 E
Seregno	62	45.39 N	9.12 E
Serein ≃	50	47.55 N	3.31 E
Şeremban	114	2.43 N	101.56 E
Šeremetjevka	80	55.23 N	51.32 E
Šeremetjevo, Aeroport ⊠	82	55.59 N	37.24 E
Šeremetjevskij	82	55.59 N	37.30 E
Seremuk ≃	164	1.36 S	131.46 E
Serena	216	41.29 N	88.44 W
Seren del Grappa	64	45.59 N	11.51 E
Serengeti National Park ♠	154	2.20 S	34.50 E
Serengeti Plain ≚	154	2.50 S	35.00 E
Serengka	112	1.40 S	110.40 E
Serenje	154	13.15 S	30.14 E
Şereno	256	21.19 S	42.39 W
Šereševo	76	52.33 N	24.13 E
Seret ≃	78	48.38 N	25.52 E
Serfaus	58	47.02 N	10.36 E
Ser'ga	86	57.46 N	56.52 E
Sergač	80	55.32 N	45.28 E
Sergeant	214	41.38 N	78.45 W
Sergeant Bluff	198	42.24 N	96.21 W
Sergeja Kirova, ostrova II	74	77.12 N	89.30 E
Sergejeviči	76	53.30 N	27.45 E
Sergejevka, Kaz.	86	51.39 N	68.13 E
Sergejevka, Kaz.	86	53.51 N	67.25 E
Sergejevka, Ross.	89	44.22 N	131.39 E
Sergejevka, Ross.	89	43.21 N	133.22 E
Sergejevka, Ukr.	83	48.40 N	37.22 E
Sergejevo	86	57.18 N	86.02 E
Sergen	130	41.42 N	27.42 E
Sergijevka	78	51.46 N	41.05 E
Sergijev Posad (Zagorsk)	82	56.18 N	38.08 E
Sergijevskaja, Ross.	76	60.16 N	43.54 E
Sergijevskaja, Ross.	80	50.16 N	43.47 E
Sergijevskij	80	51.56 N	51.54 E
Sergili	85	41.13 N	69.14 E
Sergines	50	48.20 N	3.15 E
Serginskij	72	62.30 N	65.38 E
Sergipe □[3]	250	10.30 S	37.30 W
Sergokala	84	42.27 N	47.40 E
Sergozero, ozero ◎	24	66.47 N	36.42 E
Seria	112	4.39 N	114.23 E
Serian	112	1.10 N	110.34 E
Seriana, Valle V	64	45.55 N	9.55 E
Seriate	62	45.41 N	9.43 E
Seribu, Kepulauan II	115a	5.36 S	106.33 E
Seribudolok, Indon.	114	2.56 N	98.37 E
Seribudolok, Indon.	114	2.51 N	99.04 E
Sericho	154	1.05 N	39.05 E
Seridó ≃	250	6.12 S	37.10 W
Sérifontaine	50	49.21 N	1.46 E
Sérifos	38	37.09 N	24.31 E
Sérifos I	38	37.11 N	24.31 E
Sérignan-du-Comtat	62	44.11 N	4.51 E
Sérigny ≃	176	56.47 N	66.00 W
Serik	130	36.55 N	31.06 E
Seringat, Pulau I	271c	1.14 N	103.51 E
Serino	68	40.51 N	14.52 E
Serinyol	130	36.24 N	36.11 E
Serio ≃	62	45.16 N	9.45 E
Seritinga	256	21.54 S	44.30 W
Serjol	24	60.02 N	48.58 E
Serkhe, Cerro ∧	248	17.22 S	69.22 W
Serkout, Djebel ∧	148	23.30 N	6.48 E
Serkovo	82	54.28 N	38.46 E
Şerles ∧	64	47.08 N	11.23 E
Šerlovaja Gora	88	50.34 N	116.15 E
Serm ◆[8]	263	51.21 N	6.42 E
Sermaise	261	48.32 N	2.05 E
Sermaises	50	48.18 N	2.12 E
Sermaize-les-Bains	56	48.47 N	4.55 E
Serman	80	53.34 N	46.22 E
Sermata, Pulau I	164	8.13 S	128.55 E
Sermide	64	45.00 N	11.18 E
Sermilik ⊂[2]	176	65.37 N	38.03 W
Sermizelles	50	47.32 N	3.48 E
Şermoneta	66	41.33 N	12.59 E
Šerna ≃	82	55.51 N	38.34 E
Sernambetiba, Pontal de ›	287a	23.02 S	43.27 W
Sernambitiba	287a	22.41 S	42.59 W
Serniki	78	51.49 N	26.14 E
Sernovodsk	80	53.56 N	51.17 E
Sernur	80	56.56 N	49.09 E
Sernyy Zavod	128	39.59 N	58.50 E
Séro	150	14.48 N	11.04 W
Serodino	252	32.37 S	60.57 W
Ser'odka	76	58.10 N	28.12 E
Seroglazka	80	47.01 N	47.29 E
Ser'ogovo	24	62.20 N	50.36 E
Serooskerke	52	51.42 N	3.50 E
Seropédica	256	22.44 S	43.43 W
Serov	86	59.29 N	60.31 E
Serovo	85	40.27 N	71.12 E
Serowe	156	22.25 S	26.44 E
Ser'oža ≃	80	55.34 N	42.29 E
Serpa	34	37.56 N	7.36 W
Serpeddi, Punta ∧	71	39.22 N	9.18 E
Serpejsk	76	54.20 N	34.59 E
Serpent, Rivière au ≃	186	49.33 N	71.14 W
Serpentine	168a	32.22 S	115.59 E
Serpentine ≃, Austl.	168a	32.33 S	115.46 E
Serpentine ≃, B.C., Can.	224	49.05 N	122.50 W
Serpentine Lakes ◎	162	28.32 S	129.09 E
Serpentine National Park ♠	168a	32.22 S	116.01 E
Serpentine Reservoir ◎[1]	168a	32.25 S	116.08 E
Serpent Mound State Memorial ⊥	218	39.02 N	83.26 W
Serpents Mouth ⋓	241r	10.00 N	62.00 W
Serpnevoje	78	46.18 N	29.02 E
Serpuchov	82	54.55 N	37.25 E
Serpukhov → Serpuchov	82	54.55 N	37.25 E
Serqo → Sark I	43b	49.26 N	2.21 W
Serra	255	20.07 S	40.18 W
Serra, Monte ∧	66	43.46 N	10.33 E
Serra Branca	250	7.29 S	36.40 W
Serracapriola	68	41.48 N	15.09 E
Serrada	64	45.53 N	11.09 E
Serra da Canastra, Parque Nacional da ♠	255	20.10 S	46.40 W
Serra da Capivara, Parque Nacionl da ♠	250	8.40 S	42.15 W
Serra d'aiello	68	39.05 N	16.08 E
Serra de'Conti	66	43.33 N	13.02 E
Serra di Corvo, Lago di ◎[1]	68	40.51 N	16.14 E
Serradifalco	70	37.27 N	13.53 E
Serra do Navio	250	0.59 N	52.03 W
Serra dos Aimorés	255	17.46 S	40.15 W
Serra do Salitre	255	19.06 S	46.41 W
Serra dos Órgãos, Parque Nacional da ♠	256	22.26 S	43.02 W
Sérrai	38	41.05 N	23.32 E
Serramanna	71	39.25 N	8.55 E
Serramazzoni	64	44.25 N	10.47 E
Serramonte Center ◆[9]	282	37.40 N	122.28 W
Serrana	255	21.14 S	47.36 W
Serrana, Cayo de ✦[4]	236	14.23 N	80.12 W
Serra Negra	256	22.36 S	46.42 W
Serra Negra do Norte	250	6.40 S	37.24 W
Serrânia	255	21.33 S	46.03 W
Serranilla, Cayo de ✦[4]	236	15.50 N	79.50 W
Serranópolis	255	18.16 S	52.00 W
Serranos	256	21.51 S	44.30 W
Serrara	68	40.42 N	13.54 E
Serra San Bruno	68	38.35 N	16.20 E
Serra San Quirico	66	43.27 N	13.01 E
Serrastretta	68	39.01 N	16.25 E
Serrat, Cap ›	36	37.14 N	9.13 E
Serra Talhada	250	7.59 S	38.18 W
Serravalle, It.	66	43.57 N	12.30 E
Serravalle, It.	66	42.47 N	13.01 E
Serravalle all'Adige	64	45.49 N	11.01 E
Serravalle Scrivia	62	44.43 N	8.51 E
Serre	68	40.35 N	15.11 E
Serre ≃	50	49.41 N	3.23 E
Serrenti	71	39.29 N	8.58 E
Serre-Ponçon, Barrage de ◆[6]	62	44.33 N	6.30 E
Serre-Ponçon, Lac de ◎[1]	62	44.30 N	6.17 E
Serres	62	44.26 N	5.43 E
Serrezuela	252	30.38 S	65.23 W
Serri	71	39.42 N	9.08 E
Serrières	62	45.19 N	4.45 E
Serrinha	250	11.39 S	39.00 W
Serriola, Bocca)(	66	43.31 N	12.21 E
Serris	261	48.51 N	2.47 E
Serrita	250	7.56 S	39.19 W
Serro	255	18.37 S	43.23 W
Şersale	68	39.01 N	16.44 E
Šerstin	76	52.39 N	31.03 E
Šerstobitovo	86	57.16 N	78.52 E
Sertã	34	39.48 N	8.06 W
Sertânia	250	8.05 S	37.16 W
Sertãozinho	256	22.19 S	46.03 W
Sertig-Dörfli	58	46.44 N	9.51 E
Sertung, Pulau I	115a	6.06 S	105.24 E
Seru	144	7.50 N	40.28 E
Şerua, Pulau I	164	6.18 S	130.01 E
Šerubaj-Nura ≃	86	49.54 N	72.31 E
Serui	164	1.53 S	136.14 E
Seruini ≃	248	7.42 S	66.42 W
Serule	156	21.58 S	27.20 E
Serutu, Pulau I	112	1.42 S	108.45 E
Seruwai	114	4.21 N	98.10 E
Sérvia	38	40.11 N	22.00 E
Servi Burnu ›	130	41.40 N	28.06 E
Servigliano	66	43.05 N	13.29 E
Servon	261	48.43 N	2.35 E
Servoz	58	45.56 N	6.46 E
Serwaru	112	8.10 S	127.42 E
Sêrxü	102	33.04 N	97.45 E
Seryševo	89	51.08 N	128.20 E
Şes, Muntele ⋀	38	47.05 N	22.30 E
Šešan	180	66.46 N	171.26 W
Sesayap ≃	112	3.36 N	117.15 E
Sesayap Lama	112	3.36 N	117.03 E
Seščа	76	53.45 N	33.23 E
Sese Islands II	154	0.20 S	32.20 E
Seseke ≃	263	51.37 N	7.32 E
Sesfontein	156	19.07 S	13.39 E
Sesheke	152	17.28 S	24.18 E
Seshu	105	39.33 N	115.37 E
Sesia ≃	62	45.05 N	8.37 E
Sesia, Val V	62	45.47 N	8.05 E
Sesibu	112	4.02 N	116.33 E
Sesimbra	34	38.26 N	9.06 W
Seskar, ostrov I	76	60.02 N	28.23 E
Şeskarö	26	65.44 N	23.44 E
Šešma ≃	80	55.27 N	51.05 E
Sesmarias ≃	256	22.28 S	44.27 W
Sesoko-jima I	174m	26.38 N	127.52 E
Sespe	228	34.23 N	118.58 W
Sespe Creek ≃	204	34.23 N	118.57 W
Sessa	152	13.56 S	20.38 E
Sessa Aurunca	68	41.14 N	13.56 E
Ses Salines, Cap de ›	34	39.16 N	3.03 E
Séssé	146	11.30 N	17.34 E
Sessenheim	56	48.48 N	7.59 E
Şesta Godano	62	44.17 N	9.40 E
Šestakovka	78	48.32 N	31.58 E
Šestakovo, Ross.	82	56.21 N	35.49 E
Šestakovo, Ross.	88	56.29 N	103.59 E
Şestao	34	43.18 N	3.00 W
Šestern'a	78	47.33 N	33.16 E
Sestino	66	43.42 N	12.18 E
Sesto (Sexten)	64	46.42 N	12.21 E
Sesto Calende	62	45.44 N	8.38 E
Sesto Fiorentino	66	43.50 N	11.12 E
Sestola	64	44.14 N	10.46 E
Sesto San Giovanni	62	45.32 N	9.14 E
Sestra ≃, Ross.	80	52.11 N	49.36 E
Sestra ≃, Ross.	82	56.43 N	37.14 E
Sestriere	62	44.57 N	6.53 E
Sestri Levante	62	44.16 N	9.24 E
Sestri Ponente	62	44.25 N	8.51 E
Sestroreck	76	60.06 N	29.58 E
Sestroreckij Razliv, ozero ◎	265a	60.04 N	30.00 E
Şestu	71	39.18 N	9.05 E
Šešupe ≃	76	55.03 N	22.12 E
Šešurga	80	57.29 N	47.35 E
Šešuvis ≃	76	55.13 N	22.15 E
Šėta, Liet.	76	55.17 N	24.15 E
Seta, Nihon	270	34.58 N	135.55 E
Seta ≃	270	34.56 N	135.54 E
Setagaya ◆[8]	268	35.39 N	139.40 E
Setail ≃	115a	8.30 S	114.21 E
Setaka	96	33.09 N	130.28 E
Setana	92a	42.26 N	139.51 E
Setapak	114	3.11 N	101.42 E
Setauket	210	40.57 N	73.07 W
Sète	62	43.24 N	3.41 E
Sete Barras	252	24.23 S	47.55 W
Sete Cidades, Parque Nacional de ♠	250	3.50 S	41.40 W
Sete de Setembro ≃	255	12.56 S	52.51 W
Sete Lagoas	255	19.27 S	44.14 W
Sete Pontes	256	22.51 S	43.05 W
Sete Quedas, Cachoeira das ↳	250	9.27 S	56.41 W
Sete Quedas, Parque Nacional de ♠	252	24.02 S	54.12 W
Sete Rios ◆[8]	266c	38.45 N	9.10 W
Setesdal V	26	59.25 N	7.25 E
Seth Ward	196	34.13 N	101.42 W
Setī □[8]	124	29.15 N	81.00 E
Setī ≃	124	28.58 N	81.06 E
Setlagodi	158	26.16 S	25.06 E
Set Net, Punta ›	236	12.28 N	83.30 W
Seto, Nihon	94	35.14 N	137.06 E
Seto, Nihon	96	33.27 N	132.15 E
Seto, Nihon	96	34.44 N	134.02 E
Setoda	96	34.18 N	133.05 E
Seto-naikai ⊤[2]	96	34.20 N	133.30 E
Seto-naikai-kokuritsu-kōen ♠	96	34.15 N	133.28 E
Seton Hall University ⊍[2]	276	40.45 N	74.15 W
Seton Lake ◎	182	50.45 N	122.05 W
Seton Portage	182	50.43 N	122.18 W
Seto-saki ›	174m	26.51 N	128.18 E
Setouchi	93b	28.10 N	129.15 E
Seto-zaki ›	96	33.40 N	135.20 E
Setraki	78	49.23 N	40.49 E
Setta ≃	64	44.22 N	11.14 E
Settat	148	33.04 N	7.37 W
Settat □[4]	148	33.05 N	7.30 W
Sette Bagni ≃	267a	42.00 N	12.31 E
Setté Cama	152	2.32 S	9.45 E
Settecamini ◆[8]	267a	41.56 N	12.37 E
Sette-Daban, chrebet ⋀	74	62.00 N	138.00 E
Settee Lake ◎	184	57.03 N	96.55 W
Settepani, Monte ∧	62	44.15 N	8.12 E
Settimo Milanese	266b	45.29 N	9.03 E
Settimo San Pietro	71	39.17 N	9.11 E
Settimo Torinese	62	45.09 N	7.46 E
Settimo Vittone	62	45.33 N	7.50 E
Settingiano	68	38.55 N	16.31 E
Setting Lake ◎	184	55.00 N	98.38 W
Settle	44	54.04 N	2.16 W
Settlement Point ›	169	38.25 S	145.25 E
Settlers	156	25.02 S	28.30 E
Settlers Cabin Regional Park ♠	279b	40.26 N	80.10 W
Settons, Lac des ◎	50	41.11 N	4.04 E
Settsu	96	34.46 N	135.33 E
Setúbal	34	38.32 N	8.54 W
Setúbal □[5]	266c	38.37 N	9.00 W
Setúbal, Baía de ⊂	34	38.27 N	8.53 W
Setun' ≃	265b	55.44 N	37.33 E
Seui	71	39.50 N	9.19 E
Seul, Lac ◎	184	50.20 N	92.30 W
Seul Choix Point ›	190	45.56 N	85.52 W
Seulimeum	114	5.22 N	95.35 E
Seulo	71	39.52 N	9.14 E
Seúl → Sŏul	98	37.33 N	126.58 E
Seumanyam	114	3.45 N	96.38 E
Seurre	58	47.00 N	5.09 E
Seuzach	58	47.32 N	8.44 E
Sev ≃	76	52.24 N	34.10 E
Sevan	84	40.34 N	44.57 E
Sevan, ozero ◎	84	40.20 N	45.20 E
Sévaré	150	14.32 N	4.06 W
Sevastopol'	78	44.36 N	33.32 E
Şevastopol'skij	86	53.08 N	65.44 E
Ševčenko	72	43.35 N	51.05 E
Ševčenkovo, Ukr.	78	49.41 N	37.10 E
Ševčenkovo, Ukr.	78	51.40 N	33.39 E
Ševčenkovo, Ukr.	78	45.33 N	29.20 E
Ševčenkovo Vtoroje	78	47.29 N	36.08 E
Sevelen, Dtsch.	52	51.29 N	6.25 E
Şevelen, Schw.	58	47.07 N	9.29 E
Ševelevskaja	24	60.52 N	44.12 E
Ševelevskij Majdan	80	54.25 N	42.15 E
Seven ≃	44	54.11 N	0.52 W
Seven Caves ♁[5]	218	39.13 N	83.23 W
Seven Creeks ≃	169	36.43 S	145.34 E
Seven Harbors	216	42.40 N	83.34 W
Sevenhill	168b	33.53 S	138.38 E
Seven Hills, Austl.	274a	33.46 S	150.57 E
Seven Hills, Oh., U.S.	214	41.23 N	81.40 W
Seven Islands → Sept-Îles	186	50.12 N	66.23 W
Seven Kings ◆[8]	260	51.34 N	0.05 E
Seven Mile	218	39.28 N	84.33 W
Seven Mile Beach National Park ♠	170	34.49 S	150.46 E
Sevenmile Bridge ◆[5]	220	24.41 N	81.11 W
Sevenmile Creek ≃	218	39.28 N	84.33 W
Sevenoaks, Eng., U.K.	42	51.16 N	0.12 E
Seven Oaks, Tx., U.S.	222	30.51 N	94.51 W
Sevenoaks □[8]	260	51.18 N	0.10 E
Sevenoaks Weald	260	51.14 N	0.12 E
Seven Palm Lake ◎	220	25.12 N	80.44 W
Seven Persons	184	49.52 N	110.54 W
Seven Sisters	42	51.46 N	3.43 W
Seven Sisters Peaks ⋀	182	54.58 N	128.10 W
Seventy Mile House	182	51.18 N	121.24 W
Seven Valleys	208	39.51 N	76.46 W
Sévérac-le-Château	32	44.19 N	3.04 E
Severance Center ◆[9]	279a	41.31 N	81.33 W
Sever'anskij les ♠	83	48.55 N	38.00 E
Severka ≃	82	55.10 N	38.45 E
Severn, S. Afr.	158	26.36 S	22.52 E
Severn, Md., U.S.	208	39.08 N	76.41 W
Severn, N.C., U.S.	208	36.30 N	77.11 W
Severn, Va., U.S.	208	37.17 N	76.24 W
Severn ≃, On., Can.	176	56.02 N	87.36 W
Severn ≃, On., Can.	212	44.52 N	79.41 W
Severn ≃, U.K.	42	51.35 N	2.40 W
Severn, Mouth of the ≃	42	51.25 N	3.00 W
Severnaja Dvina ≃	24	64.32 N	40.30 E
Severnaja Sos'va ≃	72	64.10 N	65.28 E
Severnaja Zeml'a II	74	79.30 N	98.00 E
Severna Park	208	39.04 N	76.32 W
Severn Bridge ◆[5]	42	51.39 N	2.42 W
Severn Lake ◎	184	53.54 N	90.48 W
Severnoje, Ross.	80	58.02 N	41.26 E
Severnoje, Ross.	80	54.06 N	52.32 E
Severnoje, Ross.	84	44.49 N	42.51 E
Severnoje, Ross.	86	56.21 N	78.23 E
Severnoje, Ukr.	83	48.04 N	38.44 E
Severn River ⊂, Md., U.S.	208	38.58 N	76.28 W
Severn River ⊂, Va., U.S.	208	37.19 N	76.25 W
Severn Tunnel ◆[5]	42	51.35 N	2.44 W
Severnyj, Ross.	24	67.38 N	64.06 E
Severnyj, Ross.	265b	55.56 N	37.33 E
Severnyje uvaly ⋀[2]	24	59.30 N	49.00 E
Severnyj Kommunar	80	58.23 N	54.02 E
Severnyj Prijut	84	43.16 N	41.51 E
Severnyj Ural ⋀	24	63.00 N	59.00 E
Severo-Bajkal'skoje nagorje ⋀[1]	88	57.00 N	111.00 E
Severočeský Kraj □[4]	30	50.30 N	14.00 E
Severodoneck	83	48.58 N	38.27 E
Severodvinsk	24	64.34 N	39.50 E
Severo-Dvinskij kanal ≍	76	59.45 N	38.22 E
Severo-Jenisejskij	74	60.22 N	93.01 E
Severo-Kazachstanskaja Oblast' □[8]	86	54.30 N	69.00 E
Severo-Kuril'sk	74	50.40 N	156.08 E
Severomoravský Kraj □[4]	30	49.45 N	17.50 E
Severomorsk	24	69.05 N	33.24 E
Severo-Mujskij chrebet ⋀	88	56.30 N	114.00 E
Severo-Osetinskaja Avtonomnaja Sovetskaja Socialističeskaja Respublika □[3]	84	43.00 N	44.15 E
Severo-Sibirskaja nizmennost' ≚	74	73.00 N	100.00 E
Severoural'sk	86	60.09 N	59.57 E
Severo-Zadonsk	82	54.02 N	38.24 E
Severskaja	78	44.51 N	38.42 E
Severskij Donec ≃	72	47.35 N	40.54 E
Severskij Donec-Donbass, kanal ≍	83	48.55 N	37.45 E
Severucha	86	58.28 N	63.25 E
Severy	198	37.37 N	96.13 W
Seveso	62	45.39 N	9.09 E
Şeveso ≃	266b	45.30 N	9.12 E
Ševětin	61	49.06 N	14.35 E
Sevettijärvi	24	69.26 N	28.38 E
Sevier ≃	200	39.04 N	113.06 W
Sevier, East Fork ≃	200	38.14 N	112.12 W
Sevier Bridge Reservoir ◎[1]	200	39.21 N	111.57 W
Sevier Desert ◆[2]	200	39.25 N	112.50 W
Sevier Lake ◎	200	38.55 N	113.09 W
Sevierville	192	35.52 N	83.33 W
Sevilla, Col.	246	4.16 N	75.57 W
Sevilla (Seville), Esp.	34	37.23 N	5.59 W
Sevilla □[4]	34	37.25 N	5.35 W
Sevilla, Isla I	236	8.14 N	82.24 W
Seville, Fl., U.S.	192	29.19 N	81.29 W
Seville, Oh., U.S.	214	41.00 N	81.51 W
Seville → Sevilla	34	37.23 N	5.59 W
Sevir	130	39.12 N	38.13 E
Şevketiye	130	40.05 N	27.51 E
Ševli ≃	89	54.08 N	133.04 E
Sevlievo	38	43.01 N	25.06 E
Sevran	50	48.56 N	2.32 E
Sevrej	102	43.35 N	102.12 E
Sèvres	50	48.49 N	2.12 E
Sévrier	58	45.52 N	6.08 E
Şevsk	78	52.09 N	34.30 E
Ševykan	88	54.20 N	106.49 E
Sewa ≃	150	7.18 N	12.08 W
Sewanee	194	35.04 N	85.55 W
Sewāni	123	28.55 N	75.37 E
Seward, Ak., U.S.	180	60.06 N	149.26 W
Seward, Ne., U.S.	198	40.54 N	97.05 W
Seward, N.Y., U.S.	210	42.43 N	74.37 W
Seward, Pa., U.S.	214	40.25 N	79.01 W
Seward Glacier ⌂	180	60.22 N	140.15 W
Seward Peninsula ›[1]	180	65.00 N	164.00 W
Sewaren	276	40.33 N	74.15 W
Sewekow	54	53.15 N	12.39 E
Sewell, Chile	252	34.05 S	70.23 W
Sewell, N.J., U.S.	208	39.45 N	75.08 W
Sewen	58	47.48 N	6.54 E
Sewernaja-Semlja → Severnaja Zeml'a II	74	79.30 N	98.00 E
Seweweekspoort	158	33.22 S	21.25 E
Sewickley	214	40.32 N	80.11 W
Sewickley Creek ≃	279b	40.14 N	79.47 W
Sewickley Heights	279b	40.33 N	80.09 W
Sewickley Hills	279b	40.34 N	80.08 W
Sewri ◆[8]	272c	19.00 N	72.51 E
Sexcello	152	3.58 S	11.38 E
Sexsmith	182	55.21 N	118.47 W
Sexten → Sesto	64	46.42 N	12.21 E
Sextin ≃	232	25.44 N	105.14 W
Sexton	218	39.42 N	85.27 W
Sexton Island I	276	40.39 N	73.14 W
Seya ◆[8], Nihon	268	35.29 N	139.29 E
Seya ◆[8], Nihon	268	35.27 N	139.30 E
Seybaplaya	232	19.39 N	90.40 W
Seybothenreuth	60	49.54 N	11.43 E
Seybouse, Oued ≃	148	36.54 N	7.47 E
Seychellen → Seychelles □[1]	138	4.35 S	55.40 E
Seychelles □[1]	138	4.35 S	55.40 E
Seychelles Bank ✦[4]	12	4.45 S	55.30 E
Seyches	32	44.33 N	0.18 E
Seyda	54	51.53 N	12.53 E
Seydim	130	40.33 N	34.45 E
Seydişehir	130	37.25 N	31.51 E
Seyđisfjörđur	24a	65.16 N	14.00 W
Seyfe Gölü ◎	130	39.13 N	34.23 E
Seyhan ≃	130	36.43 N	34.53 E
Seyhan Barajı ◎[1]	130	37.05 N	35.15 E
Seyitgazi	130	39.27 N	30.43 E
Seylac	144	11.21 N	43.29 E
Seymour, Austl.	169	37.02 S	145.08 E
Seymour, Ciskei	158	32.33 S	26.46 E
Seymour, Ct., U.S.	207	41.23 N	73.04 W
Seymour, In., U.S.	218	38.57 N	85.53 W
Seymour, Ia., U.S.	190	40.40 N	93.07 W
Seymour, Mo., U.S.	194	37.08 N	92.46 W
Seymour, Tx., U.S.	196	33.35 N	99.15 W
Seymour, Wi., U.S.	190	44.30 N	88.19 W
Seymour ≃	182	51.05 N	126.50 W
Seymour Inlet ⊂	182	51.03 N	127.10 W
Seymour Johnson Air Force Base ■	192	35.21 N	77.58 W
Seymour Range ⋀	224	48.40 N	124.00 W
Seymourville	194	30.27 N	91.29 W
Seyne	62	44.21 N	6.21 E
Seynod	58	45.53 N	6.05 E
Seyring	264b	48.20 N	16.29 E
Seyssel	58	45.57 N	5.49 E
Şeytan ≃	267b	41.06 N	28.59 E
Sežana	36	45.42 N	13.52 E
Sézanne	50	48.43 N	3.43 E
Şezela	158	30.24 S	30.42 E
Šežim	24	62.07 N	58.21 E
Sezimovo Ústí	30	49.23 N	14.42 E
Sezze	66	41.30 N	13.03 E
Sfax	148	34.44 N	10.46 E
Sfax □[8]	148	34.50 N	10.20 E
Sferracavallo ◆[8]	70	38.12 N	13.17 E
Sfîntu-Gheorghe	38	45.52 N	25.47 E
Sfîntu Gheorghe, Braţul ≃[1]	38	44.53 N	29.36 E
Sfîntu Gheorghe, Ostrovul I	38	45.07 N	29.22 E
Sfizef	148	35.14 N	0.15 W
Sforzesco, Castello ⊥	266b	45.28 N	9.11 E
's-Gravendeel	52	51.46 N	4.37 E
's-Gravenhage (The Hague)	52	52.06 N	4.18 E
's-Gravenzande	52	52.00 N	4.10 E
Sgritheall, Beinn ∧	46	57.08 N	5.35 W
Sgurgola	66	41.40 N	13.09 E
Sha ≃, Zhg.	98	37.31 N	117.50 E
Sha ≃, Zhg.	100	33.39 N	114.38 E
Sha ≃, Zhg.	100	26.35 N	118.02 E
Sha ≃, Zhg.	104	41.21 N	123.07 E

Symbol	English	Deutsch	Español	Français	Português
≃	River	Fluß	Río	Rivière	Rio
≍	Canal	Kanal	Canal	Canal	Canal
↳	Waterfall, Rapids	Wasserfall, Stromschnellen	Cascada, Rápidos	Chute d'eau, Rapides	Cascata, Rápidos
⋓	Strait	Meeresstraße	Estrecho	Détroit	Estreito
⊂	Bay, Gulf	Bucht, Golf	Bahía, Golfo	Baie, Golfe	Baía, Golfo
◎	Lake, Lakes	See, Seen	Lago, Lagos	Lac, Lacs	Lago, Lagos
⩩	Swamp	Sumpf	Pantano	Marais	Pântano
⌂	Ice Features, Glacier	Eis- und Gletscherformen	Accidentes Glaciales	Formes glaciaires	Acidentes glaciares
⊤	Other Hydrographic Features	Andere Hydrographische Objekte	Otros Elementos Hidrográficos	Autres données hydrographiques	Outros acidentes hidrográficos
✦	Submarine Features	Untermeerische Objekte	Accidentes Submarinos	Formes de relief sous-marin	Acidentes submarinos
□	Political Unit	Politische Einheit	Unidad Politica	Entité politique	Unidade política
⊍	Cultural Institution	Kulturelle Institution	Institución Cultural	Institution culturelle	Instituição cultural
⊥	Historical Site	Historische Stätte	Sitio Histórico	Site historique	Sitio histórico
♠	Recreational Site	Erholungs- und Ferienort	Sitio de Recreo	Centre de loisirs	Area de Lazer
⊠	Airport	Flughafen	Aeropuerto	Aéroport	Aeroporto
■	Military Installation	Militäranlage	Instalación Militar	Installation militaire	Instalação militar
◆	Miscellaneous	Verschiedenes	Misceláneo	Divers	Diversos

ENGLISH Name	Page	Lat.°′	Long.°′
Sha'alav, Har ∧	132	30.04 N	35.06 E
Sha'alvim	132	31.52 N	34.59 E
Shaanxi (Shensi) □4	102	35.00 N	109.00 E
Sha'ar HaGolan	132	32.41 N	35.36 E
Sha'ar Menashe	132	32.27 N	35.01 E
Shab'ā	132	33.21 N	35.45 E
Shaba □4	154	8.00 S	27.00 E
Shābah	142	31.11 N	30.46 E
Shabakunk Creek ≃	285	40.15 N	74.43 W
Shabās al-Milḩ	142	31.12 N	30.39 E
Shabās ash-Shuhadā'	142	31.05 N	30.45 E
Shabās 'Umayr	142	31.06 N	30.48 E
Shabbona	216	41.46 N	88.52 W
Shabeellaha Dhexe □4	144	3.00 N	46.00 E
Shabeellaha Hoose □4	144	1.30 N	44.15 E
Shabeelle (Shebele) ≃	144	0.12 S	42.45 E
Shabestar	128	38.11 N	45.42 E
Shabomeka Lake ⊜	212	44.54 N	77.09 W
Shabotik ≃	190	48.50 N	85.34 W
Shabqadar	123	34.13 N	71.34 E
Shabrāmant	142	29.56 N	31.12 E
Shabshīr al-Ḥiṣṣah	142	30.52 N	31.04 E
Shabunda	154	2.42 S	27.20 E
Shabwah	144	15.22 N	47.01 E
Shache (Yarkand)	120	38.25 N	77.16 E
Shacheng	105	40.25 N	115.31 E
Shacheng Gang c	100	27.10 N	120.24 E
Shackan Indian Reserve ◆4	182	50.17 N	121.12 W
Shackleton Ice Shelf ⊼	9	66.00 S	100.00 E
Shackleton Range ⋏	9	80.40 S	26.00 W
Shādegān	128	30.40 N	48.38 E
Shade Gap	214	40.11 N	77.52 W
Shadehill Reservoir ⊜1	198	45.45 N	102.15 W
Shade Mountain ∧	208	40.34 N	77.30 W
Shades Glen	210	41.11 N	75.42 W
Shadi	100	26.08 N	114.49 E
Shadian	98	35.30 N	114.26 E
Shading	102	31.20 N	94.40 E
Shadow Lake ⊜, On., Can.	212	44.43 N	78.48 W
Shadow Lake ⊜, Ma., U.S.	283	42.50 N	71.14 W
Shadow Lake ⊜, N.J., U.S.	276	40.21 N	74.06 W
Shado-Wood Village	214	40.35 N	79.12 W
Shadrinsk → Šadrinsk	86	56.05 N	63.38 E
Shadui	102	31.30 N	100.10 E
Shady Cove	202	42.04 N	122.36 W
Shady Grove, Fl., U.S.	192	30.17 N	83.37 W
Shady Grove, Tx., U.S.	222	32.48 N	97.01 W
Shady Hills	216	40.36 N	85.41 W
Shady Shores	222	33.10 N	97.02 W
Shadyside	188	39.58 N	80.45 W
Sha'f	132	32.38 N	36.51 E
Shafer, Lake ⊜	216	40.47 N	86.46 W
Shafer Butte ∧	202	43.47 N	116.05 W
Shafir	132	31.42 N	34.44 E
Shaft	128	37.12 N	49.24 E
Shafter	226	35.30 N	119.16 W
Shaftesbury	42	51.01 N	2.12 W
Shafton	279b	40.20 N	79.42 W
Shaftsburg	216	42.48 N	84.18 W
Shaftsbury	210	43.00 N	73.11 W
Shafu	100	22.25 N	113.01 E
Shag ≃	172	45.29 S	170.49 E
Shagamu	150	6.51 N	3.39 E
Shageluk	180	62.36 N	159.32 W
Shag Rocks II1	244	53.33 S	42.02 W
Shaguotun	104	41.10 N	120.38 E
Shāhābād, India	122	17.08 N	76.56 E
Shāhābād, India	123	30.10 N	76.53 E
Shāhābād, India	124	27.39 N	79.57 E
Shāhābād, India	272c	19.01 N	73.02 E
Shāhābād, Īrān	128	37.32 N	56.54 E
Shāhābād, Īrān	267d	35.47 N	51.31 E
Shāhāda	120	21.28 N	74.18 E
Shah Alam	114	3.04 N	101.33 E
Shahbā'	132	32.51 N	36.37 E
Shāhbandar	120	24.10 N	67.54 E
Shāhbāz Kalāt	128	26.42 N	63.58 E
Shāhbāzpur ⵡ	124	22.05 N	90.50 E
Shahdād, Namakzār-e ≚	128	30.30 N	58.30 E
Shāhdādkot	120	27.51 N	67.54 E
Shāhdādpur	120	25.56 N	68.37 E
Shāhdara, India	272a	28.30 N	77.25 E
Shāhdara, Pāk.	123	31.38 N	74.18 E
Shāhdara ◆8	272a	28.40 N	77.18 E
Shahdol	124	23.20 N	81.21 E
Shahe, Zhg.	98	36.56 N	114.30 E
Shahe, Zhg.	98	34.44 N	118.58 E
Shahe, Zhg.	98	37.01 N	119.43 E
Shahe, Zhg.	102	22.06 N	109.43 E
Shahedian	100	33.01 N	113.44 E
Shaheji	100	32.26 N	118.14 E
Shahepu	104	41.08 N	121.01 E
Shaheyi	98	39.53 N	118.31 E
Shaheying	104	40.50 N	120.46 E
Shahezhan	98	35.49 N	116.23 E
Shahezhen	105	40.08 N	116.15 E
Shahezi	89	46.05 N	129.20 E
Shāhganj	124	26.03 N	82.41 E
Shāhgarh, India	120	27.07 N	69.54 E
Shāhgarh, India	124	24.19 N	79.08 E
Shaḥḥāt	146	32.49 N	21.52 E
Shāhī Kowt	123	34.16 N	70.34 E
Shāhjahānpur	124	27.53 N	79.55 E
Shāh Jūy	120	32.31 N	67.25 E
Shāh Kot	123	31.34 N	73.29 E
Shāh Kūh ∧	128	31.37 N	59.16 E
Shāhpur, India	122	16.42 N	76.50 E
Shāhpur, Pāk.	120	28.43 N	68.25 E
Shāhpur, Pāk.	123	32.17 N	72.26 E
Shāhpura, India	120	27.23 N	75.58 E
Shāhpura, India	120	25.38 N	74.56 E
Shāhpura, India	124	23.11 N	80.42 E
Shāhpur Chākar	120	26.09 N	68.39 E
Shahrak	120	34.06 N	64.18 E
Shahr-e Bābak	128	30.07 N	55.09 E
Shahr-e Kord	128	32.19 N	50.50 E
Shahr-e Monjān	120	36.02 N	70.46 E
Shahr-e Ṣafā	128	31.50 N	66.22 E
Shahrestān	120	34.22 N	66.47 E
Shāhrūd ≃	128	36.40 N	49.26 E
Shahryār	128	35.28 N	51.05 E
Shahu	100	30.11 N	113.39 E
Shāhzādpur	126	24.10 N	89.36 E
Shā'ib al-Banāt, Jabal ∧	140	26.59 N	33.29 E
Shaighālu	120	31.11 N	68.49 E
Shaikou	100	27.19 N	117.35 E
Sha'īrah, Jabal ∧2	132	30.06 N	34.17 E
Sha'īrah, Jabal ash- ⋏	132	29.31 N	34.29 E
Shājāpur	124	23.26 N	76.16 E
Shajian	100	24.46 N	117.38 E
Shajianzi	98	41.01 N	125.26 E
Shajiazhuang	106	32.13 N	120.53 E
Shajing	100	23.36 N	114.06 E
Shajingzi	102	37.42 N	105.09 E
Shakaga-dake ∧	96	33.11 N	130.53 E
Shakaga-hana ≻	96	34.25 N	134.14 E
Shakaga-take-tunnel ◆5	96	33.27 N	130.52 E
Shakardarra	123	33.14 N	71.30 E
Shakargarh	123	32.16 N	75.10 E
Shakarpura	272a	28.46 N	77.21 E
Shakarpur Khās ◆8	272a	28.38 N	77.17 E
Shakaskraal	158	29.26 S	31.14 E
Shakawe	156	18.23 S	21.50 E
Shakeng	98	42.13 N	116.35 E
Shaker Heights	214	41.28 N	81.32 W
Shaker Heights Park ♦	279a	41.29 N	81.33 W
Shakespeare	212	43.22 N	80.49 W
Shākhen	128	33.22 N	59.32 E
Shakhty → Šachty	83	47.42 N	40.13 E
Shaki	150	8.39 N	3.25 E
Shākir, Jazīrat I	140	27.30 N	33.59 E
Shakopee	190	44.47 N	93.31 W
Shakotan-hantō ≻1	92a	43.20 N	140.30 E
Shakou	100	24.25 N	113.32 E
Shakshūk	142	29.28 N	30.42 E
Shaktoolik	180	64.20 N	161.09 W
Shakujii ◆8	268	35.45 N	139.37 E
Shakūrpur ◆8	272a	28.41 N	77.09 E
Shala, Lake ⊜	144	7.25 N	38.30 E
Shalalth	182	50.44 N	122.13 W
Shalatayn, Bi'r ⊤4	140	23.08 N	35.36 E
Shaleitian Dao I	98	39.03 N	118.44 E
Shaler Mountains ⋏	176	72.35 N	110.45 W
Shaleshanto	156	19.09 S	23.58 E
Shalford	260	51.13 N	0.34 W
Shālimah	142	31.14 N	30.52 E
Shalimar Railroad Station ◆5	272b	22.33 N	88.19 E
Shaling, Zhg.	104	41.09 N	122.22 E
Shaling, Zhg.	104	41.20 N	123.01 E
Shalingpu	104	41.47 N	123.11 E
Shalingzi	105	40.42 N	114.55 E
Shaliuhe, Zhg.	102	36.28 N	98.57 E
Shaliuhe, Zhg.	105	39.53 N	117.56 E
Shallotte	192	33.58 N	78.23 W
Shallowater	196	33.41 N	101.59 W
Shallow Brook ≃	276	40.21 N	74.35 W
Shallow Lake	212	44.36 N	81.05 W
Shaluhe	89	51.08 N	126.00 E
Shaluli Shan ⋏	102	30.45 N	99.45 E
Shām, Bādiyat ash- (Syrian Desert) ◆2	128	32.00 N	40.00 E
Shām, Jabal ash- ∧	128	23.13 N	57.16 E
Shama ≃	154	6.16 S	32.27 E
Shaman	85	38.50 N	75.36 E
Shamattawa	184	55.52 N	92.05 W
Shambe	140	7.07 N	30.46 E
Shambi	152	1.49 S	22.39 E
Shambu	144	9.40 N	37.03 E
Shambuanda	152	6.38 S	20.13 E
Shām Churasi	123	31.30 N	75.45 E
Shamei	100	24.32 N	118.25 E
Shamepūr ◆8	272a	28.45 N	77.09 E
Shamīl	128	27.30 N	56.53 E
Shāmli	124	29.27 N	77.19 E
Shammākh	132	30.30 N	35.30 E
Shamokin	208	40.47 N	76.33 W
Shamona Creek ≃	285	40.02 N	75.43 W
Shamrock, Fl., U.S.	192	29.38 N	83.08 W
Shamrock, Tx., U.S.	196	35.12 N	100.14 W
Shamsābād	124	27.01 N	78.08 E
Shamsher	272a	28.44 N	77.24 E
Shamva	154	17.18 S	31.34 E
Shan □3	110	22.00 N	98.00 E
Shanbiao	98	35.28 N	113.57 E
Shancheng	102	37.01 N	107.00 E
Shanchengzhen	98	42.23 N	125.26 E
Shandaken	210	42.07 N	74.23 W
Shandan	102	38.45 N	101.15 E
Shandatgyi	110	19.37 N	94.43 E
Shandī	140	16.42 N	33.26 E
Shandian ≃	98	42.23 N	116.21 E
Shandianhe	98	42.22 N	116.15 E
Shandīd	142	30.55 N	30.40 E
Shandon	226	35.39 N	120.22 W
Shandong	107	29.31 N	106.25 E
Shandong (Shantung) □4	98	36.00 N	118.00 E
Shandong Bandao (Shantung Peninsula) ≻1	98	37.00 N	121.00 E
Shaner	279b	40.17 N	79.47 W
Shanesville	214	40.31 N	81.39 W
Shangalume	154	10.49 S	26.34 E
Shangani	154	19.47 S	29.22 E
Shangani ≃	154	18.41 S	27.10 E
Shang'ao	106	30.41 N	119.25 E
Shangba	106	32.11 N	118.46 E
Shangbahe	100	30.40 N	115.05 E
Shangbai	106	30.29 N	119.58 E
Shangbancheng	105	40.50 N	118.03 E
Shangbatang	102	32.46 N	96.20 E
Shangcai	100	33.16 N	114.15 E
Shangcang	105	39.54 N	117.23 E
Shangchen	106	30.07 N	119.53 E
Shangcheng	100	31.48 N	115.24 E
Shangchewan	100	29.48 N	113.01 E
Shangch'iu → Shangqiu	98	34.27 N	115.42 E
Shangchuan Dao I	102	21.42 N	112.47 E
Shangdang	106	32.06 N	119.24 E
Shangdayangqi	89	51.09 N	124.02 E
Shangdian	100	34.07 N	112.23 E
Shangdianmiao	106	30.56 N	120.51 E
Shangdouying	105	40.36 N	115.33 E
Shangdu	98	41.29 N	113.34 E
Shangduichunshi	104	41.00 N	123.02 E
Shangdundu	100	27.56 N	116.15 E
Shangfu	100	28.40 N	114.59 E
Shanggaixin	102	23.25 N	100.02 E
Shanggan	100	25.56 N	119.22 E
Shanggang	100	33.30 N	120.04 E
Shanggangzi	104	42.26 N	123.03 E
Shanggao	100	28.18 N	114.54 E
Shanggecun	106	31.49 N	119.07 E
Shanggu	98	40.47 N	118.28 E
Shangguanying	98	41.18 N	117.07 E
Shanghai, Va., U.S.	208	37.37 N	76.47 W
Shanghai, Zhg.	106	31.14 N	121.28 E
Shanghai, Zhg.	106	31.07 N	121.22 E
Shanghai, Zhg.	269b	31.14 N	121.28 E
Shanghailingao	104	41.57 N	120.55 E
Shanghai Museum ✦	269b	31.13 N	121.28 E
Shanghai Shi (Shanghai Shih) □7	106	31.10 N	121.30 E
Shanghai Station ◆5	269b	31.15 N	121.28 E
Shanghang	100	25.06 N	116.25 E
Shanghe	98	37.19 N	117.07 E
Shanghekou	98	40.26 N	124.47 E
Shanghetou	105	39.12 N	116.59 E
Shanghewantun	104	41.42 N	123.23 E
Shang Hu ⊜	106	31.39 N	120.41 E
Shanghuang	106	31.33 N	119.34 E
Shanghuangqi	98	41.29 N	116.31 E
Shanghucun	105	40.45 N	115.45 E
Shangjao → Shangrao	100	28.26 N	117.58 E
Shangjiafen	104	41.18 N	121.10 E
Shangjiahe	98	41.51 N	124.28 E
Shangjiaodao	100	29.00 N	119.54 E
Shangjiatai	104	40.53 N	123.35 E
Shangjie	100	27.06 N	116.06 E
Shangjin	102	33.09 N	110.03 E
Shangjiuwu	100	33.59 N	113.01 E
Shangkasa	120	33.45 N	80.12 E
Shangkou	98	36.59 N	118.53 E
Shanglanjiagou	104	40.52 N	120.37 E
Shanglin, Zhg.	98	38.19 N	116.05 E
Shanglin, Zhg.	102	23.28 N	108.33 E
Shanglin, Zhg.	104	41.31 N	122.14 E
Shanglishi	100	27.52 N	113.46 E
Shangliuhezicun	104	41.28 N	123.32 E
Shangliulinzi	104	41.02 N	123.13 E
Shangmagushan	104	41.41 N	124.10 E
Shangmatai	105	39.22 N	117.15 E
Shangmatun	104	40.57 N	123.22 E
Shangmingdian	106	31.12 N	120.57 E
Shangmingju	105	39.41 N	115.12 E
Shangnan	102	33.31 N	110.45 E
Shangpandaoling	104	41.42 N	121.14 E
Shangpeibu	106	31.28 N	119.13 E
Shangping, Zhg.	100	25.57 N	117.33 E
Shangping, Zhg.	100	24.43 N	115.27 E
Shangping, Zhg.	100	24.29 N	114.38 E
Shangpuzi	104	41.37 N	121.35 E
Shangqianbu	106	30.27 N	120.04 E
Shangqiao	100	31.02 N	117.42 E
Shangqing, Zhg.	100	25.53 N	118.36 E
Shangqing, Zhg.	100	28.02 N	117.00 E
Shangqingshuicun	105	39.56 N	115.38 E
Shangqiu (Zhuji), Zhg.	98	34.27 N	115.42 E
Shangqiu, Zhg.	98	34.23 N	115.37 E
Shangrao	100	28.26 N	117.58 E
Shangshe	102	38.15 N	113.20 E
Shangshibatai	104	42.02 N	120.51 E
Shangshui	100	33.33 N	114.34 E
Shangsi	102	22.09 N	107.57 E
Shangtan	106	30.27 N	118.42 E
Shangtang	100	33.23 N	118.02 E
Shan Guan)(	100	27.30 N	117.06 E
Shangweiniuchang	104	40.54 N	120.44 E
Shangxian	102	33.51 N	109.54 E
Shangxingzhen	106	31.32 N	119.15 E
Shangxinhe	106	32.02 N	118.43 E
Shangxinqiu	104	42.27 N	121.37 E
Shangyangbao	98	42.30 N	124.14 E
Shangyangcun	106	30.48 N	118.40 E
Shangye	98	35.26 N	117.59 E
Shangyi (Nanhaoqian)	98	41.04 N	114.03 E
Shangying	89	44.10 N	127.17 E
Shangyinkou	102	32.52 N	103.04 E
Shangyou	100	25.51 N	114.30 E
Shangyou ≃	100	25.49 N	114.50 E
Shangyou Shuiku ⊜1	100	25.52 N	114.21 E
Shangyu	100	30.02 N	120.54 E
Shangyuan	104	41.39 N	120.55 E
Shangyun	102	23.01 N	99.50 E
Shangzhai	98	39.13 N	114.17 E
Shangzhaoshugou	104	42.12 N	121.58 E
Shangzhazi	105	40.52 N	117.42 E
Shangzhenzhuang	105	40.20 N	117.06 E
Shangzhi	89	45.13 N	127.59 E
Shangzhuangtai	105	39.41 N	115.25 E
Shanhaiguan	98	40.01 N	119.44 E
Shanhaikwan → Shanhaiguan	98	40.01 N	119.44 E
Shanhecun	89	45.38 N	128.27 E
Shanhetun	89	44.44 N	127.12 E
Shanjiazhuang	105	38.52 N	115.45 E
Shanklin	42	50.38 N	1.10 W
Shankou, Zhg.	100	26.40 N	117.46 E
Shankou, Zhg.	100	28.58 N	115.12 E
Shankou, Zhg.	100	28.48 N	114.29 E
Shankou, Zhg.	102	21.38 N	109.43 E
Shanlenggang	102	28.33 N	103.23 E
Shanli	100	29.52 N	117.21 E
Shanlian	106	30.42 N	120.19 E
Shanmenjie	106	30.40 N	118.52 E
Shanmulong	102	24.39 N	98.05 E
Shannanguan	100	31.36 N	116.52 E
Shannock	207	41.26 N	71.38 W
Shannon, Ire.	48	52.43 N	8.53 W
Shannon, N.Z.	172	40.33 S	175.25 E
Shannon, S. Afr.	158	29.08 S	26.18 E
Shannon, Ga., U.S.	192	34.20 N	85.04 W
Shannon, Il., U.S.	190	42.09 N	89.44 W
Shannon, Ms., U.S.	194	34.06 N	88.42 W
Shannon ≃	48	52.36 N	9.41 W
Shannon, Lake ⊜	224	48.37 N	121.42 W
Shannon, Mouth of the ≃1	48	52.30 N	9.50 W
Shannon Airport ⊠	48	52.41 N	8.55 W
Shannons Flat	171b	35.54 S	148.58 E
Shannontown	192	33.53 N	80.21 W
Shannonville	212	44.12 N	77.13 W
Shanpo	100	30.06 N	114.20 E
Shanrendong	89	46.50 N	123.08 E
Shanrenqiao	106	31.16 N	120.27 E
Shanshan	86	42.52 N	90.10 E
Shanshenmiao	105	40.45 N	117.11 E
Shanshūr	142	30.21 N	31.00 E
Shansi → Shanxi □4	102	37.00 N	112.00 E
Shanting	98	35.09 N	117.29 E
Shāntipur	126	23.15 N	88.26 E
Shantou (Swatow)	100	23.23 N	116.41 E
Shantung Peninsula → Shandong Bandao ≻1	98	37.00 N	121.00 E
Shantung → Shandong □4	98	36.00 N	118.00 E
Shanty Bay	212	44.25 N	79.36 W
Shanwa	154	3.10 S	33.46 E
Shanwei	100	22.47 N	115.21 E
Shanxi (Shansi) □4	102	37.00 N	112.00 E
Shanxian	98	34.48 N	116.03 E
Shanxian → Sanmenxia	102	34.45 N	111.05 E
Shanxiawu	100	28.52 N	113.52 E
Shanxu	102	22.21 N	107.58 E
Shanyang, Zhg.	100	26.43 N	119.13 E
Shanyang, Zhg.	102	33.35 N	109.49 E
Shanyang, Zhg.	106	31.19 N	120.16 E
Shanyao	100	25.13 N	118.55 E
Shanyaqiao	106	31.15 N	119.25 E
Shanyin	102	39.33 N	112.50 E
Shanzhangjiafen	105	40.37 N	116.44 E
Shanzui	105	40.48 N	118.13 E
Shanzuizi	104	41.55 N	120.30 E
Shaobo	100	32.30 N	119.32 E
Shaodenggao	104	42.13 N	121.47 E
Shaodian, Zhg.	98	34.08 N	118.25 E
Shaodian, Zhg.	100	33.10 N	114.18 E
Shaoguan	100	24.50 N	113.37 E
Shaogudian	98	36.57 N	115.32 E
Shaoguyingzi	104	41.33 N	120.27 E
Shaohing → Shaoxing	100	30.00 N	120.35 E
Shaohsing → Shaoxing	100	30.00 N	120.35 E
Shaojiaolou	106	31.05 N	121.32 E
Shaokuan → Shaoguan	100	24.50 N	113.37 E
Shaowu	100	27.20 N	117.28 E
Shaoxing	100	30.00 N	120.35 E
Shaoyang, Zhg.	102	27.15 N	111.28 E
Shaoyang, Zhg.	102	27.00 N	111.18 E
Shaoyun	107	29.30 N	105.57 E
Shaozihe	98	40.13 N	123.33 E
Shap	44	54.32 N	2.41 W
Shapinsay I	46	59.03 N	2.53 W
Shāpūr ≃	128	29.39 N	51.03 E
Shaq'ah, Ra's ash- ≻	130	34.19 N	35.41 E
Shaqqā	132	32.53 N	36.42 E
Shaqq al-Ju'ayfir, Wādī V	140	15.16 N	26.00 E
Shaqrā', Ar. Su.	128	25.15 N	45.15 E
Shaqrā, Lubnān	132	33.12 N	35.28 E
Shaqrā', Sūrīy.	132	32.54 N	36.14 E
Shaqrā', Yaman	144	13.21 N	45.42 E
Shaquan	86	44.33 N	83.25 E
Shaquzhen	107	30.33 N	103.45 E
Sharafābād	272a	28.36 N	77.23 E
Sharafkhāneh	128	38.11 N	45.29 E
Sharan Jogīzai	120	31.02 N	68.33 E
Sharatin Mountain ∧	180	57.49 N	152.41 W
Sharbatāt, Ra's ash- ≻	118	17.56 N	56.21 E
Sharbīn, Jabal ∧	132	33.43 N	36.21 E
Sharbot Lake	212	44.46 N	76.41 W
Sharbot Lake ⊜	212	44.46 N	76.41 W
Share	150	8.50 N	4.56 E
Shari	92a	43.55 N	144.50 E
Shari-dake ∧	92a	43.46 N	144.43 E
Sharīṭah, Ra's ≻	128	26.23 N	56.23 E
Shark ≃	220	25.21 N	81.05 W
Shark Bay c	162	25.30 S	113.30 E
Shark Point ≻, Austl.	274a	33.55 S	151.17 E
Shark Point ≻, Fl., U.S.	220	25.23 N	81.09 W
Shark River Hills	208	40.12 N	74.03 W
Sharktooth Mountain ∧	180	58.35 N	127.57 W
Sharm ash-Shaykh	140	27.51 N	34.17 E
Sharnbrook	42	52.13 N	0.32 W
Sharnūb	142	31.01 N	30.35 E
Sharon, On., Can.	214	42.53 N	81.22 W
Sharon, Ct., U.S.	207	41.52 N	73.28 W
Sharon, Ma., U.S.	207	42.07 N	71.10 W
Sharon, N.D., U.S.	198	47.35 N	97.53 W
Sharon, Pa., U.S.	214	41.13 N	80.29 W
Sharon, Tn., U.S.	194	36.14 N	88.49 W
Sharon, Wi., U.S.	216	42.30 N	88.43 W
Sharon Center	214	41.06 N	81.44 W
Sharon Hill	285	39.54 N	75.16 W
Sharon Park	218	39.23 N	84.35 W
Sharon Springs, Ks., U.S.	198	38.53 N	101.45 W
Sharon Springs, N.Y., U.S.	210	42.48 N	74.37 W
Sharon Valley	207	41.53 N	73.29 W
Sharonville	218	39.16 N	84.24 W
Sharpe, Lake ⊜1	198	44.05 N	99.55 W
Sharpe Lake ⊜	184	54.24 N	93.30 W
Sharpes	220	28.25 N	80.45 W
Sharp Island I	271d	22.22 N	114.17 E
Sharpley	285	39.48 N	75.33 W
Sharp Park ♦	282	37.37 N	122.29 W
Sharp Peak ∧	116	5.58 N	125.31 E
Sharpsburg, Il., U.S.	219	39.37 N	89.21 W
Sharpsburg, Ky., U.S.	218	38.12 N	83.55 W
Sharpsburg, Pa., U.S.	279b	40.29 N	79.55 W
Sharps Hill	279b	40.30 N	79.56 W
Sharps Run ≃	285	39.54 N	74.49 W
Sharpsville, In., U.S.	216	40.22 N	86.05 W
Sharpsville, Pa., U.S.	214	41.15 N	80.28 W
Sharptown, Md., U.S.	208	38.32 N	75.43 W
Sharptown, N.J., U.S.	285	39.39 N	75.21 W
Sharqī, Al-Jabal ash- (Anti-Lebanon) ⋏	132	33.35 N	36.00 E
Sharqīyah, Aṣ-Ṣaḥrā' ash- (Arabian Desert) ◆2	140	28.00 N	32.00 E
Sharqpur	123	31.28 N	74.06 E
Sharshar, Jabal ∧2	140	23.52 N	30.20 E
Shartlesville	208	40.31 N	76.06 W
Shārūnah	142	28.36 N	30.51 E
Shārūnah, Wādī V	142	28.36 N	30.52 E
Shasha	144	6.20 N	35.57 E
Shashe ≃	156	22.14 S	29.20 E
Shashemene	144	7.12 N	38.43 E
Shashi	102	30.19 N	112.14 E
Shashibu	100	25.48 N	114.54 E
Shasi → Shashi	102	30.19 N	112.14 E
Shasta	204	40.36 N	122.29 W
Shasta ≃	204	41.50 N	122.35 W
Shasta, Mount ∧1	204	41.20 N	122.20 W
Shasta Lake ⊜1	204	40.50 N	122.25 W
Shatangjiang	106	31.25 N	120.01 E
Shaṭānūf	142	30.14 N	31.04 E
Shatawī	140	14.39 N	32.06 E
Shāṭi', Wādī ash- V	146	27.30 N	13.15 E
Shatian, Zhg.	100	25.53 N	113.44 E
Shatian, Zhg.	100	23.59 N	113.56 E
Shatila	132	33.51 N	35.30 E
Sha Tin	271d	22.23 N	114.11 E
Shatt al-Arab → Arab, Shatt al- ≃	128	29.57 N	48.34 E
Shattuck	196	36.16 N	99.52 W
Shatuji	98	35.18 N	115.45 E
Shatuosi	102	31.20 N	108.51 E
Shauck	214	40.37 N	82.40 W
Shaunavon	184	49.40 N	108.25 W
Shaver Lake	226	37.09 N	119.18 W
Shaver Lake ⊜1	226	37.08 N	119.17 W
Shavertown	210	41.19 N	75.55 W
Shavé Ẕiyyon	132	32.59 N	35.05 E
Shavington	44	53.04 N	2.27 W
Shaw, Eng., U.K.	44	53.34 N	2.05 W
Shaw, Eng., U.K.	262	53.35 N	2.06 W
Shaw, Ms., U.S.	194	33.36 N	90.46 W
Shaw ≃	162	20.20 S	119.17 E
Shaw Air Force Base ■	192	33.58 N	80.29 W
Shawan, Zhg.	86	44.34 N	85.48 E
Shawan, Zhg.	100	27.52 N	119.28 E
Shawan, Zhg.	107	29.25 N	103.33 E
Shawanaga Inlet c	190	45.32 N	80.24 W
Shawangunk Kill ≃	210	41.41 N	74.10 W
Shawangunk Mountains ⋏	210	41.35 N	74.30 W
Shawano	190	44.46 N	88.36 W
Shawbury	42	52.47 N	2.39 W
Shaw Creek ≃	192	33.34 N	81.30 W
Shawhan	218	38.18 N	84.16 W
Shawinigan	206	46.33 N	72.45 W
Shawinigan ≃	206	46.32 N	72.46 W
Shawinigan, Lac ⊜	206	46.41 N	73.10 W
Shawinigan Falls → Shawinigan	206	46.33 N	72.45 W
Shawinigan-Sud	206	46.31 N	72.45 W
Shaw Island I	224	48.34 N	122.57 W
Shawmarī, Wādī ash- V	132	30.21 N	36.25 E
Shawmere ≃	190	48.20 N	82.28 W
Shawnee, Ks., U.S.	198	39.02 N	94.43 W
Shawnee, Oh., U.S.	188	39.36 N	82.12 W
Shawnee, Ok., U.S.	196	35.19 N	96.55 W
Shawnee, Lake ⊜	276	40.58 N	74.35 W
Shawnee Hills	214	40.07 N	83.09 W
Shawnee On Delaware	210	41.01 N	75.07 W
Shawnee State Park ♦	218	38.43 N	83.10 W
Shawneetown	194	37.42 N	88.11 W
Shawnī	142	30.45 N	30.55 E
Shawnigan Lake	224	48.38 N	123.35 W
Shawnigan Lake ⊜	224	48.37 N	123.37 W
Shawo, Som.	144	3.26 N	45.21 E
Shawo, Zhg.	98	34.28 N	114.37 E
Shawo, Zhg.	100	31.44 N	115.08 E
Shawo, Zhg.	100	28.52 N	114.47 E
Shawsheen ≃	283	42.42 N	71.08 W
Shawsheen Village	283	42.40 N	71.09 W
Shawtown	279b	40.20 N	79.42 W
Shawville	188	45.36 N	76.30 W
Shaxi, Zhg.	100	28.34 N	118.06 E
Shaxi, Zhg.	100	26.53 N	115.34 E
Shaxi, Zhg.	100	24.38 N	113.42 E
Shaxi, Zhg.	106	31.34 N	121.04 E
Shaxian	100	26.24 N	117.47 E
Shaxikou	100	26.33 N	118.02 E
Shaximiao	107	29.57 N	106.19 E
Shayang	100	30.42 N	112.33 E
Shaybārā I	128	25.27 N	36.48 E
Shay Gap	162	20.25 S	120.03 E
Shaykh, Jabal ash- (Mount Hermon) ∧	132	33.26 N	35.51 E
Shaykh, Wādī ash- V	142	28.48 N	30.55 E
Shaykh Al-Ḥadīd	130	36.30 N	36.35 E
Shaykh Miskīn	132	32.49 N	36.09 E
Shaykh Sa'd	128	32.34 N	46.17 E
Shaykh 'Uthmān	144	12.52 N	44.59 E
Shayuan	100	27.45 N	120.38 E
Shazhen	98	36.23 N	115.47 E
Shazhou	106	31.52 N	120.32 E
Shazihe	102	32.12 N	106.42 E
Shchekino → Ščokino	76	54.01 N	37.31 E
Shchelkovo → Ščolkovo	76	55.55 N	38.00 E
Shcherbakov → Rybinsk	76	58.03 N	38.52 E
She ≃	100	30.41 N	114.32 E
Sheaf ≃	44	53.23 N	1.26 W
Shea Island I	276	41.03 N	73.24 W
Sheakleyville	214	41.27 N	80.13 W
Shea Stadium ♦	276	40.45 N	73.51 W
Shebele	144	9.43 N	42.43 E
Shebele (Shabeelle) ≃	144	0.12 S	42.45 E
Sheberghān	120	36.41 N	65.45 E
Shebeshekong ≃	212	45.26 N	80.19 W
Sheboygan	190	43.45 N	87.42 W
Sheboygan ≃	190	43.45 N	87.42 W
Sheboygan Falls	190	43.43 N	87.48 W
Shebu	100	27.40 N	112.48 E
Shechem ⊥	132	32.13 N	35.15 E
Shechem → Nābulus	132	32.13 N	35.16 E
Shecheng	102	37.14 N	113.05 E
Shedd Canyon V	226	35.39 N	120.26 W
Shedden	214	42.44 N	81.21 W
Shediac	186	46.13 N	64.32 W
Shedin Peak ∧	182	55.55 N	127.32 W
Sheekh	144	9.56 N	45.11 E
Sheelin, Lough ⊜	48	53.48 N	7.22 W
Sheenjek ≃	180	66.45 N	144.33 W
Sheep ≃	182	50.44 N	113.51 W
Sheep Creek ≃, Ab., Can.	182	54.04 N	119.00 W
Sheep Creek ≃, U.S.	202	42.27 N	115.36 W
Sheep Creek ≃, Ut., U.S.	200	40.55 N	109.39 W
Sheep Creek ≃, Wy., U.S.	200	42.03 N	106.04 W
Sheep Haven c	48	55.10 N	7.52 W
Sheepmoor	158	26.42 S	30.13 E
Sheep Mountain ∧, Az., U.S.	200	32.32 N	114.14 W
Sheep Mountain ∧, Wy., U.S.	200	43.33 N	110.32 W
Sheep Peak ∧	196	31.14 N	104.59 W
Sheepranch	226	38.13 N	120.28 W
Sheep Range ⋏	204	36.45 N	115.05 W
Sheepshead Bay ◆8	276	40.35 N	73.56 W
's-Heerenberg	52	51.53 N	6.15 E
's-Heerenhoek	52	51.27 N	3.46 E
Sheerness	42	51.27 N	0.45 E
Sheet Harbour	186	44.55 N	62.32 W
Shefar'am	132	32.48 N	35.10 E
Sheffield, N.Z.	172	43.23 S	172.01 E
Sheffield, Eng., U.K.	44	53.23 N	1.28 W
Sheffield, Al., U.S.	194	34.45 N	87.41 W
Sheffield, Il., U.S.	190	41.21 N	89.44 W
Sheffield, Ia., U.S.	190	42.53 N	93.12 W
Sheffield, Ma., U.S.	207	42.06 N	73.21 W
Sheffield, Oh., U.S.	214	41.25 N	82.05 W
Sheffield, Pa., U.S.	214	41.42 N	79.02 W
Sheffield, Tx., U.S.	196	30.41 N	101.49 W
Sheffield Island I	276	41.03 N	73.25 W
Sheffield Island Harbor c	276	41.03 N	73.25 W
Sheffield Lake	214	41.29 N	82.06 W
Sheffield Lake ⊜	186	49.20 N	56.35 W
Shefford	42	52.02 N	0.20 W
Shefford □6	206	45.25 N	72.30 W
Shefu	100	26.11 N	115.22 E
Shegangshi	100	28.32 N	113.36 E
Shegaon	122	20.47 N	76.41 E
Sheho	184	51.38 N	103.12 W
Shehong	102	30.56 N	105.22 E
Shehongmiao	107	30.44 N	106.03 E
Shehy Mountains ⋏	48	51.48 N	9.15 W
Sheikh Hasan	144	12.04 N	35.53 E
Sheikhpura	124	25.09 N	85.51 E
Shekatika	186	51.17 N	58.20 W
Shekhūpura	123	31.42 N	73.59 E
Sheki → Šeki	84	41.12 N	47.12 E
Shekki → Zhongshan	100	22.31 N	113.22 E
Shek Kong	271d	22.26 N	114.06 E
Shek Kong Airfield ⊠	271d	22.27 N	114.05 E
Shek Kwu Chau I	271d	22.12 N	113.59 E
Shekou	100	30.44 N	114.20 E
Shek Uk Shan ∧	271d	22.27 N	114.18 E
Shelagyote Peak ∧	182	55.58 N	127.12 W
Shelbina	219	39.41 N	92.02 W
Shelbourne	169	36.52 S	144.01 E
Shelburn	194	39.11 N	87.24 W
Shelburne, N.S., Can.	186	43.46 N	65.19 W
Shelburne, On., Can.	212	44.04 N	80.12 W
Shelburne Bay c	164	11.49 S	143.00 E
Shelburne Falls	207	42.36 N	72.44 W
Shelby, In., U.S.	216	41.11 N	87.20 W
Shelby, Ia., U.S.	198	41.30 N	95.27 W
Shelby, Mi., U.S.	190	43.36 N	86.21 W
Shelby, Ms., U.S.	194	33.57 N	90.46 W
Shelby, Mt., U.S.	202	48.30 N	111.51 W
Shelby, Ne., U.S.	198	41.11 N	97.25 W
Shelby, N.C., U.S.	192	35.17 N	81.32 W
Shelby, Oh., U.S.	214	40.52 N	82.39 W
Shelby □6, Il., U.S.	219	39.24 N	88.48 W
Shelby □6, In., U.S.	218	39.31 N	85.47 W
Shelby □6, Ky., U.S.	218	38.15 N	85.13 W
Shelby □6, Mo., U.S.	219	39.49 N	92.03 W
Shelby □6, Oh., U.S.	216	40.17 N	84.09 W
Shelby Village	281	42.38 N	83.04 W
Shelbyville, Il., U.S.	219	39.24 N	88.47 W
Shelbyville, In., U.S.	218	39.31 N	85.46 W
Shelbyville, Ky., U.S.	218	38.12 N	85.13 W
Shelbyville, Mo., U.S.	219	39.48 N	92.02 W
Shelbyville, Tn., U.S.	194	35.29 N	86.27 W
Shelbyville, Lake ⊜1	219	39.30 N	88.40 W
Sheldon, Il., U.S.	216	40.46 N	87.33 W
Sheldon, Ia., U.S.	198	43.10 N	95.51 W
Sheldon, Mi., U.S.	216	42.17 N	83.28 W
Sheldon, Mo., U.S.	194	37.39 N	94.17 W
Sheldon, Tx., U.S.	222	29.52 N	95.08 W
Sheldon Brook ≃	276	41.03 N	73.52 W
Sheldon Creek ≃	212	44.07 N	79.53 W
Sheldon Point	180	62.32 N	164.52 W
Sheldon Reservoir ⊜1	222	29.52 N	95.10 W
Sheldonville	283	42.02 N	71.23 W
Sheldrake ≃	276	40.57 N	73.44 W
Sheldrake Lake ⊜, On., Can.	212	44.49 N	77.16 W
Sheldrake Lake ⊜, N.Y., U.S.	276	40.57 N	73.46 W
Shelikof Strait ⵡ	180	57.30 N	155.00 W
Shell ≃	184	50.58 N	101.24 W
Shell, Loch c	46	58.00 N	6.30 W
Shellbrook	184	53.13 N	106.24 W
Shell Brook ≃	184	53.21 N	106.00 W
Shell Creek ≃, U.S.	200	40.56 N	108.37 W
Shell Creek ≃, Ne., U.S.	198	41.27 N	96.58 W
Shell Creek ≃, N.D., U.S.	198	47.59 N	102.17 W
Shell Creek ≃, Wy., U.S.	202	44.31 N	108.03 W
Shellen	146	9.54 N	12.00 E
Shelley, B.C., Can.	182	54.00 N	122.37 W
Shelley, Id., U.S.	202	43.22 N	112.07 W
Shellharbour	170	34.35 S	150.52 E
Shell Lake, Sk., Can.	184	53.18 N	107.04 W
Shell Lake, Wi., U.S.	190	45.44 N	91.55 W
Shell Lakes ⊜	162	29.21 S	127.25 E
Shellman	192	31.45 N	84.36 W
Shellmouth Dam ◆6	184	50.58 N	101.25 W
Shellow Bowells	260	51.45 N	0.20 E
Shell Rock	190	42.42 N	92.34 W
Shell Rock ≃	190	42.38 N	92.30 W
Shellrock Peak ∧	224	46.43 N	121.14 W
Shellsburg	190	42.05 N	91.52 W
Shelocta	214	40.39 N	79.18 W
Shelter, Port c	271d	22.21 N	114.17 E
Shelter Island	207	41.04 N	72.20 W
Shelter Island I, H.K.	271d	22.20 N	114.17 E
Shelter Island I, N.Y., U.S.	207	41.04 N	72.20 W
Shelter Island Heights	207	41.05 N	72.21 W
Shelter Island Sound ⵡ	207	41.03 N	72.22 W
Shelton, Ct., U.S.	207	41.18 N	73.05 W
Shelton, Ne., U.S.	198	40.47 N	98.44 W
Shelton, Wa., U.S.	224	47.13 N	123.06 W
Shemanker ≃	150	8.12 N	9.45 E
Shemogue	186	46.09 N	64.11 W
Shemya Station	181a	52.43 N	174.05 E

DEUTSCH Name	Seite	Breite°′	Länge°′ E = Ost
Shenandoah, Ia., U.S.	198	40.45 N	95.22 W
Shenandoah, Pa., U.S.	208	40.49 N	76.12 W
Shenandoah, Va., U.S.	188	38.29 N	78.37 W
Shenandoah ≃	188	39.19 N	77.44 W
Shenandoah, North Fork ≃	188	38.57 N	78.12 W
Shenandoah, South Fork ≃	188	38.57 N	78.12 W
Shenandoah Heights	210	40.49 N	76.12 W
Shenandoah National Park ♦	188	38.48 N	78.12 W
Shenango	214	41.23 N	80.24 W
Shenango ≃	214	40.57 N	80.23 W
Shenango River Lake ⊜1	214	41.22 N	80.28 W
Shenchi	102	39.09 N	112.19 E
Shencottah	122	8.58 N	77.16 E
Shencun	106	31.04 N	118.51 E
Shendam	150	8.53 N	9.32 E
Shendang	106	30.34 N	120.49 E
Shending Shan ∧	89	46.38 N	133.28 E
Shenduncun	106	30.48 N	120.25 E
Shenfield	260	51.38 N	0.19 E
Shengang, Zhg.	100	27.20 N	116.18 E
Shengang, Zhg.	106	31.54 N	120.08 E
Shenge	150	7.55 N	12.57 W
Shengfang	105	39.04 N	116.42 E
Shenggongjing	106	31.07 N	119.48 E
Shenghongqing	100	30.12 N	114.56 E
Shengjiachi	107	30.28 N	105.03 E
Shengjiaqiao	106	31.27 N	121.24 E
Shengjiatun	104	41.14 N	121.22 E
Shengjin'gao	104	42.04 N	120.43 E
Shengou	100	34.08 N	113.13 E
Shengqing	104	41.34 N	121.36 E
Shengshan	106	30.50 N	120.15 E
Shengshui	98	35.45 N	119.39 E
Shengshuihezi	98	42.27 N	125.59 E
Shengsi Liedao II	100	30.42 N	122.20 E
Shengtian	100	27.14 N	113.06 E
Shengxian	100	29.36 N	120.48 E
Shengze	106	30.55 N	120.39 E
Shengzigou	104	41.35 N	124.04 E
Shenhu	100	24.38 N	118.39 E
Shenipsit Lake ⊜	207	41.53 N	72.26 W
Shenji	98	34.47 N	115.09 E
Shenjia	89	46.06 N	126.46 E
Shenjiadian	89	46.35 N	130.38 E
Shenjiatai	104	41.22 N	120.50 E
Shenjiawan	106	31.43 N	121.19 E
Shenjiazhuang	106	32.18 N	120.26 E
Shenjing, Zhg.	102	21.59 N	112.28 E
Shenjing, Zhg.	105	40.24 N	114.49 E
Shenjingzi	104	41.47 N	123.41 E
Shenk'eng	269d	25.00 N	121.36 E
Shenkou	100	28.42 N	116.02 E
Shenley	260	51.41 N	0.17 W
Shenmu	102	38.56 N	110.19 E
Shennan	105	38.59 N	114.56 E
Shenorock	210	41.20 N	73.44 W
Shenqiu	100	33.24 N	115.02 E
Shenquan	100	22.59 N	116.20 E
Shenquan Gang c	100	22.54 N	116.18 E
Shensi → Shaanxi □4	102	35.00 N	109.00 E
Shenton, Mount ∧	162	28.00 S	123.22 E
Shentuan	98	35.30 N	119.17 E
Shenxian, Zhg.	98	36.15 N	115.41 E
Shenxian, Zhg.	98	38.01 N	115.33 E
Shenxing	105	39.02 N	115.19 E
Shenyang (Mukden)	104	41.48 N	123.27 E
Shenze	98	38.11 N	115.11 E
Sheoganj	120	25.09 N	73.04 E
Sheokhāla	126	22.46 N	88.10 E
Sheopur	124	25.40 N	76.42 E
Shepard	182	50.57 N	113.55 W
Shepard Island I	9	74.25 S	132.30 W
Shepards Brook ≃	283	42.08 N	71.25 W
Shepaug ≃	207	41.28 N	73.19 W
Shepherd, Mi., U.S.	190	43.31 N	84.41 W
Shepherd, Tx., U.S.	222	30.30 N	95.01 W
Shepherd □8	175f	17.05 S	168.25 E
Shepherd, Îles II	175f	16.55 S	168.36 E
Shepherdstown	188	39.25 N	77.48 W
Shepherdsville	194	37.59 N	85.42 W
Sheppard Air Force Base ■	196	33.58 N	98.30 W
Sheppard Peak ∧	180	57.41 N	132.37 W
Sheppard Pond ⊜	276	41.08 N	74.13 W
Shepparton	166	36.23 S	145.25 E
Shepperd, Lake ⊜	162	29.55 S	123.09 E
Shepperton	260	51.24 N	0.27 W
Sheppey, Isle of I	42	51.24 N	0.50 E
Sheppler Hill ∧2	279b	40.09 N	79.49 W
Sheppton	210	40.53 N	76.07 W
Shepshed	42	52.47 N	1.18 W
Shepton Mallet	42	51.12 N	2.33 W
Shepway	260	51.15 N	0.33 E
Sheqi	100	33.03 N	112.57 E
Sherab	140	10.43 N	24.47 E
Sherada	144	7.21 N	36.32 E
Sheraden ◆8	279b	40.28 N	80.05 W
Sherard, Cape ≻	176	74.36 N	80.25 W
Sherborn	283	42.14 N	71.22 W
Sherborne	42	50.57 N	2.31 W
Sherborne Lake ⊜	212	45.11 N	78.47 W
Sherborne Saint John	42	51.18 N	1.07 W
Sherbro ≃	150	7.45 N	12.55 W
Sherbro Island I	150	7.45 N	12.55 W
Sherbrooke, N.S., Can.	186	45.08 N	61.59 W
Sherbrooke, P.Q., Can.	206	45.25 N	71.54 W
Sherbrooke □6	206	45.25 N	71.55 W
Sherbrooke Lake ⊜	186	44.40 N	64.35 W
Sherburn	198	43.39 N	94.43 W
Sherburne	210	42.40 N	75.29 W
Sherburne Reef ✦2	164	3.20 S	148.00 E
Sherburn in Elmet	44	53.48 N	1.15 W
Shercock	48	54.00 N	6.54 W
Shere	260	51.13 N	0.28 W
Sheridan, Ar., U.S.	194	34.18 N	92.24 W
Sheridan, Ca., U.S.	226	38.59 N	121.22 W
Sheridan, Il., U.S.	216	41.32 N	88.41 W
Sheridan, In., U.S.	218	40.08 N	86.13 W
Sheridan, Mt., U.S.	202	45.27 N	112.11 W
Sheridan, Or., U.S.	202	45.05 N	123.23 W
Sheridan, Pa., U.S.	208	40.21 N	76.14 W
Sheridan, Tx., U.S.	222	29.29 N	96.40 W
Sheridan, Wy., U.S.	202	44.47 N	106.57 W
Sheridan, Mount ∧	202	44.16 N	110.32 W
Sheridan Park ♦	284a	42.59 N	78.54 W
Sheringa	162	33.51 S	135.15 E
Sheringham	42	52.57 N	1.12 E
Sherkston	284a	42.53 N	79.08 W
Sherlock ≃	162	20.44 S	117.35 E
Sherman, Ct., U.S.	207	41.34 N	73.29 W
Sherman, Il., U.S.	219	39.54 N	89.36 W
Sherman, Ky., U.S.	218	38.44 N	84.36 W
Sherman, Ms., U.S.	194	34.21 N	88.50 W
Sherman, N.Y., U.S.	214	42.09 N	79.35 W
Sherman, Tx., U.S.	196	33.38 N	96.36 W
Sherman □6	224	45.25 N	120.49 W
Sherman Creek ≃	208	40.23 N	77.02 W
Sherman Mills	188	45.52 N	68.23 W
Sherman Mountain ∧	194	36.01 N	93.17 W
Sherman Oaks ◆8	280	34.09 N	118.26 W
Sherman Reservoir ⊜1	198	41.20 N	98.55 W
Sherman Station	188	45.53 N	68.25 W
Sherpur, Bngl.	124	24.41 N	89.25 E
Sherpur, Bngl.	124	25.01 N	90.01 E
Sher Qila	123	36.06 N	74.03 E
Sherrard	190	41.19 N	90.31 W
Sherridon	184	55.07 N	101.05 W
Sherrill	210	43.04 N	75.35 W
Sherri Park	278	42.02 N	87.51 W
Sherrodsville	214	40.29 N	81.14 W

Symbols in the index entries represent the broad categories identified in the key at the right. Symbols with superior numbers (⋏1) identify subcategories (see complete key on page *I · 1).*

Symbole im Register stellen die rechts im Schlüssel erklärten Kategorien dar. Symbole mit hochgestellten Ziffern (⋏1) bezeichnen Unterabteilungen einer Kategorie (vgl. vollständiger Schlüssel auf Seite *I · 1).*

Los símbolos incluídos en el texto del índice representan las grandes categorias identificadas con la clave a la derecha. Los símbolos con numeros en su parte superior (⋏1) identifican las subcategorías (véase la clave completa en la página *I · 1).*

Les symboles de l'index représentent les catégories indiquées dans la légende à droite. Les symboles suivis d'un indice (⋏1) représentent des sous-catégories (voir légende complète à la page *I · 1).*

Os símbolos incluídos no texto do índice representam as grandes categorias identificadas com a chave à direita. Os símbolos com números em sua parte superior (⋏1) identificam as subcategorias (veja-se a chave completa à página *I · 1).*

∧ Mountain	Berg	Montaña	Montagne	Montanha
⋏ Mountains	Gebirge	Montañas	Montagnes	Montanhas
)(Pass	Paß	Paso	Col	Passo
V Valley, Canyon	Tal, Cañon	Valle, Cañón	Vallée, Canyon	Vale, Canhão
≚ Plain	Ebene	Llano	Plaine	Planície
≻ Cape	Kap	Cabo	Cap	Cabo
I Island	Insel	Isla	Île	Ilha
II Islands	Inseln	Islas	Îles	Ilhas
⩦ Other Topographic Features	Andere Topographische Objekte	Otros Elementos Topográficos	Autres données topographiques	Outros acidentes topográficos

ESPAÑOL

Nombre	Página	Lat.°′	Long.°′ W = Oeste
Sher Shāh	123	30.06 N	71.21 E
Shertallai	122	9.42 N	76.20 E
's-Hertogenbosch	52	51.41 N	5.19 E
Sherway Centre ◆ [9]	275b	43.37 N	79.33 W
Sherwood, On., Can.	275b	43.50 N	79.31 W
Sherwood, P.E., Can.	186	46.17 N	63.08 W
Sherwood, Ar., U.S.	194	34.48 N	92.13 W
Sherwood, Md., U.S.	208	38.36 N	76.19 W
Sherwood, Mi., U.S.	216	42.00 N	85.14 W
Sherwood, N.D., U.S.	198	48.57 N	101.37 W
Sherwood, Oh., U.S.	216	41.17 N	84.33 W
Sherwood, Or., U.S.	224	45.21 N	122.50 W
Sherwood, Tn., U.S.	194	35.04 N	85.55 W
Sherwood, Lake ⊜	281	42.36 N	83.33 W
Sherwood Forest, Ca., U.S.	226	37.57 N	122.17 W
Sherwood Forest, Md., U.S.	284c	39.05 N	77.01 W
Sherwood Forest ◆ [3]	44	53.08 N	1.08 W
Sherwood Island State Park ♦	276	41.07 N	73.20 W
Sherwood Manor	207	42.01 N	72.38 W
Sherwood Park, Ab., Can.	182	53.31 N	113.19 W
Sherwood Park, De., U.S.	285	39.44 N	75.39 W
Sherwood Park, N.Y., U.S.	210	42.36 N	73.43 W
Sherwood Park ♦	275b	43.43 N	79.24 W
Sherwood Point ≻	276	41.07 N	73.20 W
Sherwood Shores	196	30.36 N	98.22 W
She Shan ∧ [2]	106	31.06 N	121.11 E
Sheshea ≃	248	9.36 S	74.10 W
Shesh Gāv	120	33.45 N	68.33 E
Shet Bandar	272c	18.58 N	72.56 E
Shetek, Lake ⊜	198	44.08 N	95.42 W
Shetland □ [4]	46a	60.30 N	1.15 W
Shetland del Sur, Islas → South Shetland Islands II	9	62.00 S	58.00 W
Shetland Islands II	46a	60.30 N	1.15 W
Shetou	106	31.39 N	119.27 E
Shetrunji ≃	120	21.19 N	72.07 E
Shetucket ≃	207	41.31 N	72.05 W
Sheva	272c	18.56 N	72.57 E
Sheva Nhava	272c	18.58 N	72.58 E
Shevaroy Hills ⋀ [2]	122	11.50 N	78.16 E
Shevington	262	53.34 N	2.42 W
Shevington Moor	262	53.35 N	2.41 W
Shewa □ [4]	144	9.00 N	39.00 E
Shewa Gimira	144	7.00 N	35.50 E
Shexian, Zhg.	98	36.33 N	113.40 E
Shexian, Zhg.	100	29.53 N	118.26 E
Sheyang, Zhg.	100	33.20 N	119.38 E
Sheyang, Zhg.	100	33.46 N	120.18 E
Sheyenne	198	47.49 N	99.07 W
Sheyenne ≃	198	47.05 N	96.50 W
Sheykhābād	120	34.05 N	68.45 E
Shey-Phoksundo National Park ♦	124	29.30 N	82.45 E
Shezhu	106	31.19 N	119.16 E
Shḥīm	132	33.37 N	35.29 E
Shi ≃, Zhg.	100	32.18 N	114.31 E
Shi ≃, Zhg.	100	32.32 N	115.52 E
Shiant, Sound of ц	46	57.55 N	6.25 W
Shiant Islands II	46	57.53 N	6.21 W
Shiawassee □ [6]	216	42.56 N	84.09 W
Shiawassee ≃	216	43.06 N	84.10 W
Shiawassee, South Branch ≃	216	42.49 N	83.56 W
Shiba	100	32.45 N	118.07 E
Shiba ≃	268	35.47 N	139.44 E
Shibadu	102	28.01 N	110.51 E
Shibakawa	94	35.13 N	138.33 E
Shibām	144	15.56 N	48.38 E
Shiban	107	30.18 N	104.28 E
Shibanxi	107	29.17 N	103.51 E
Shibaocheng	102	39.48 N	96.10 E
Shibarni	140	14.50 N	24.25 E
Shibasaki	268	35.39 N	139.34 E
Shibata	92	37.57 N	139.20 E
Shibayama	94	35.41 N	140.25 E
Shibayama-gata ⊜	94	36.21 N	136.23 E
Shibden Hall	262	53.44 N	1.51 W
Shibecha	92a	43.17 N	144.36 E
Shibetsu, Nihon	92a	43.40 N	145.08 E
Shibetsu, Nihon	92a	44.10 N	142.23 E
Shibi	100	26.43 N	120.02 E
Shibīn al-Kawm	142	30.33 N	31.01 E
Shibīn al-Qanāṭir	142	30.19 N	31.19 E
Shibing	102	26.50 N	108.04 E
Shibishan	100	29.21 N	116.45 E
Shiblanjah	142	30.28 N	31.16 E
Shibu	98	36.45 N	119.27 E
Shibukawa	94	36.29 N	139.00 E
Shibure-yama ∧	270	34.45 N	135.05 E
Shibushi	92	31.28 N	131.07 E
Shibutsu-san ∧	94	36.54 N	139.11 E
Shibuya ◆ [8]	268	35.40 N	139.42 E
Shibuzi	98	36.09 N	119.06 E
Shicha	100	28.24 N	115.50 E
Shichangyu	104	41.12 N	123.14 E
Shicheng, Zhg.	98	40.39 N	124.17 E
Shicheng, Zhg.	100	25.18 N	119.21 E
Shicheng, Zhg.	100	26.22 N	116.22 E
Shicheng Dao I	98	39.31 N	123.02 E
Shichisō	94	35.33 N	137.07 E
Shickley	198	40.25 N	97.43 W
Shickshinny	210	41.09 N	76.09 W
Shidai	100	30.20 N	117.56 E
Shidao	98	36.53 N	122.23 E
Shideng	102	26.44 N	99.11 E
Shidler	196	36.46 N	96.39 W
Shido	96	34.19 N	134.10 E
Shidong, Zhg.	107	28.59 N	105.27 E
Shidong, Zhg.	107	30.25 N	105.20 E
Shidongzigou	105	40.41 N	118.23 E
Shiel, Loch ⊜	46	56.47 N	5.35 W
Shiel Bridge	46	57.12 N	5.25 W
Shieldaig	46	57.31 N	5.39 W
Shieldhill	46	55.58 N	3.46 W
Shields ≃	202	45.43 N	110.28 W
Shiercun	106	30.31 N	119.34 E
Shi'er Shan ∧	100	29.18 N	118.08 E
Shi'erwei	106	32.15 N	119.14 E
Shifang	100	25.01 N	116.14 E
Shifnal	42	52.40 N	2.21 W
Shifo	107	29.58 N	103.50 E
Shifobao	104	41.28 N	121.27 E
Shifochang	107	30.19 N	105.07 E
Shifodian	100	32.06 N	115.46 E
Shifosi	104	42.08 N	123.20 E
Shifoya	98	40.12 N	123.10 E
Shiga, Nihon	94	36.20 N	137.59 E
Shiga, Nihon	94	35.09 N	135.55 E
Shiga □ [5]	96	35.15 N	136.00 E
Shigaib	140	15.01 N	23.36 E
Shigang, Zhg.	100	32.13 N	120.58 E
Shigang, Zhg.	106	32.14 N	121.00 E
Shigangmen	269b	31.21 N	121.17 E
Shigaopu	107	30.16 N	104.01 E
Shigar ≃, Asia	123	34.39 N	75.51 E
Shigar ≃, Pāk.	123	34.39 N	75.51 E
Shigaraki	94	34.52 N	136.03 E
Shigaraki-gū ʊ [1]	94	34.54 N	136.04 E
Shigenobu	96	33.48 N	132.50 E
Shigenobu ≃	96	33.48 N	132.41 E
Shigezhuang, Zhg.	105	38.57 N	116.19 E
Shigezhuang, Zhg.	105	38.59 N	115.36 E
Shigezhuang, Zhg.	105	39.18 N	116.53 E
Shigouyi	102	37.44 N	106.26 E
Shigu, Zhg.	100	29.27 N	117.14 E
Shigu, Zhg.	102	26.50 N	99.55 E
Shiguaigou	102	40.42 N	110.20 E
Shiguantun	104	41.38 N	123.39 E
Shigulingyu	105	40.38 N	116.54 E
Shīḥān ∧	132	31.23 N	35.44 E
Shihchiachuang → Shijiazhuang	98	38.03 N	114.28 E

FRANÇAIS

Nom	Page	Lat.°′	Long.°′ W = Ouest
Shihch'i → Zhongshan	100	22.31 N	113.22 E
Shihe	98	39.19 N	121.52 E
Shihengyuanyu	106	31.50 N	121.45 E
Shihezi	86	44.18 N	86.02 E
Shihkiachwang → Shijiazhuang	98	38.03 N	114.28 E
Shihlin ◆ [8]	269d	25.06 N	121.31 E
Shihti	269d	25.02 N	121.44 E
Shihting	269d	24.59 N	121.39 E
Shihu, Zhg.	98	41.29 N	126.18 E
Shihu, Zhg.	105	40.04 N	117.17 E
Shihuajie	102	32.20 N	111.25 E
Shihudang	106	30.58 N	121.07 E
Shihuixi	107	29.02 N	105.04 E
Shihuiyaozi	104	42.08 N	123.47 E
Shihuxia	105	40.48 N	117.22 E
Shiida	96	33.39 N	131.04 E
Shijiaba	107	30.18 N	104.46 E
Shijiagangzi	104	42.19 N	123.34 E
Shijiagou	104	42.27 N	123.28 E
Shijiao	100	23.36 N	112.59 E
Shijiaqiao, Zhg.	106	30.46 N	120.06 E
Shijiaqiao, Zhg.	106	32.18 N	119.26 E
Shijiawu	105	39.21 N	116.15 E
Shijiaxiang	107	29.38 N	104.59 E
Shijiayaozhuang	106	32.13 N	120.29 E
Shijiazhai, Zhg.	98	38.56 N	114.18 E
Shijiazhai, Zhg.	269b	31.23 N	121.30 E
Shijiazhen	106	31.51 N	121.10 E
Shijiazhuang	98	38.03 N	114.28 E
Shijiazi, Zhg.	104	42.39 N	122.06 E
Shijiazi, Zhg.	104	42.07 N	122.18 E
Shijiedu	106	30.57 N	119.13 E
Shijing, Zhg.	98	35.30 N	118.57 E
Shijing, Zhg.	100	24.40 N	118.24 E
Shijing, Zhg.	105	39.54 N	114.58 E
Shijingshan	105	39.56 N	116.07 E
Shijiu Hu ⊜	106	31.28 N	118.53 E
Shijiusuo	98	35.24 N	119.29 E
Shijiu Tuo I	98	39.11 N	118.56 E
Shijōnawate	270	34.45 N	135.39 E
Shijūmagari-tōge)(	96	35.11 N	133.32 E
Shika	94	37.01 N	136.47 E
Shikami-yama ∧	270	34.47 N	135.10 E
Shikano	96	35.28 N	134.04 E
Shikārpur, India	122	14.16 N	75.21 E
Shikārpur, India	124	28.17 N	78.01 E
Shikārpur, Pāk.	120	27.57 N	68.38 E
Shikatsu	94	35.14 N	136.53 E
Shikengkong ∧	100	24.56 N	113.00 E
Shikewusumiao	102	40.13 N	108.52 E
Shiki	94	35.50 N	139.35 E
Shikishima	94	35.41 N	138.32 E
Shikohābād	124	27.06 N	78.36 E
Shikoku I	92	33.45 N	133.30 E
Shikoku-sanchi ⋀	96	33.47 N	133.30 E
Shikoma	268	35.11 N	139.56 E
Shikotsu-ko ⊜	92a	42.45 N	141.20 E
Shikotsu-Tōya-kokuritsu-kōen ♦	92a	42.47 N	141.00 E
Shikuang	106	31.54 N	121.24 E
Shil	272c	19.09 N	73.03 E
Shilabo	144	6.05 N	44.48 E
Shilbottle	44	55.23 N	1.42 W
Shildon	44	54.38 N	1.39 W
Shiliangji	100	33.54 N	115.14 E
Shilibao	105	39.55 N	116.29 E
Shiliguri	124	26.42 N	88.26 E
Shilihe	104	41.31 N	123.22 E
Shiling	106	30.26 N	119.35 E
Shilipeng	106	31.14 N	119.35 E
Shilipu, Zhg.	105	39.29 N	116.18 E
Shilipu, Zhg.	105	39.11 N	115.59 E
Shilipu, Zhg.	105	40.15 N	117.58 E
Shiliuban	100	24.08 N	117.33 E
Shillelagh	48	52.45 N	6.32 W
Shillingstone	42	50.54 N	2.14 W
Shillington	208	40.18 N	75.57 W
Shillong	120	25.34 N	91.53 E
Shilo, Canadian Forces Base ■	184	49.49 N	99.38 W
Shiloh, Il., U.S.	219	38.34 N	89.54 W
Shiloh, N.J., U.S.	208	39.27 N	75.17 W
Shiloh, Oh., U.S.	214	40.58 N	82.36 W
Shiloh, Oh., U.S.	218	39.49 N	84.13 W
Shiloh, Oh., U.S.	218	39.49 N	84.13 W
Shiloh, Pa., U.S.	208	39.59 N	76.49 W
Shiloh National Military Park ♦	194	35.06 N	88.21 W
Shiloh → Saylūn, Khirbat ⊥	132	32.03 N	35.17 E
Shilong, Zhg.	100	23.07 N	113.48 E
Shilong, Zhg.	102	23.54 N	109.40 E
Shilong, Zhg.	107	30.15 N	106.34 E
Shilou	100	22.58 N	113.29 E
Shima, Nihon	92	34.13 N	136.51 E
Shima, Nihon	270	34.59 N	135.20 E
Shima, Zhg.	100	24.27 N	117.49 E
Shima, Zhg.	107	29.38 N	105.50 E
Shimabara	92	32.47 N	130.22 E
Shimachang, Zhg.	107	28.59 N	105.55 E
Shimachang, Zhg.	107	29.03 N	105.36 E
Shimada, Nihon	94	34.49 N	138.11 E
Shimada, Nihon	268	35.59 N	139.25 E
Shimagahara	94	34.46 N	136.03 E
Shima-hantō ≻ [1]	94	34.26 N	136.33 E
Shimamiao	106	32.08 N	119.20 E
Shimamoto	96	34.53 N	135.40 E
Shimane □ [5]	96	35.00 N	132.30 E
Shimane-hantō ≻ [1]	96	35.30 N	133.00 E
Shimantan	100	33.17 N	113.28 E
Shimanto ≃	96	32.56 N	133.00 E
Shimata ≃	96	33.57 N	131.55 E
Shimber Berris ∧	144	10.44 N	47.15 E
Shimei	106	32.14 N	120.10 E
Shimen, Zhg.	98	39.44 N	118.52 E
Shimen, Zhg.	102	29.28 N	111.17 E
Shimen, Zhg.	105	40.06 N	117.42 E
Shimen, Zhg.	106	30.37 N	120.26 E
Shimen, Zhg.	107	29.36 N	106.27 E
Shimen, Zhg.	107	29.09 N	106.02 E
Shimencun, Zhg.	106	31.21 N	119.34 E
Shimencun, Zhg.	106	30.23 N	119.41 E
Shimendong	100	28.16 N	120.07 E
Shimengou	104	40.40 N	123.43 E
Shimenjie	100	29.34 N	116.44 E
Shimenlou	100	28.58 N	114.51 E
Shimenying	105	39.54 N	116.05 E
Shimenzi	89	48.30 N	121.31 E
Shimian	102	29.18 N	102.22 E
Shimiaozi	104	40.39 N	123.31 E
Shimizu, Nihon	92	35.01 N	138.29 E
Shimizu, Nihon	92a	43.01 N	142.53 E
Shimizu, Nihon	94	36.02 N	136.09 E
Shimizu, Nihon	94	35.01 N	138.29 E
Shimizu, Nihon	96	34.05 N	135.26 E
Shimizu → Tosa-shimizu	92	32.46 N	132.57 E
Shimizu-tunnel ◆ [5]	94	36.52 N	138.55 E
Shimla	123	31.06 N	77.10 E
Shimminato	94	36.47 N	137.04 E
Shimobe	94	35.27 N	138.29 E
Shimoda	94	34.40 N	138.57 E
Shimodate	94	36.18 N	139.59 E
Shimofusa	94	35.52 N	140.21 E
Shimofusa-daichi ⋀ [1]	268	35.45 N	139.58 E
Shimofusa-kōkūkichi, Kaijō-jieitai- ■	94	35.50 N	140.05 E
Shimofusa Naval Air Base ■	268	35.48 N	140.01 E
Shimoga	122	13.55 N	75.34 E
Shimogawara	268	35.56 N	139.21 E
Shimogōri	268	35.21 N	140.03 E
Shimogyō ◆ [8]	270	34.59 N	135.45 E
Shimohōya	268	35.45 N	139.34 E
Shimoichi	96	34.22 N	135.47 E
Shimoigusa ◆ [8]	268	35.43 N	139.37 E
Shimoji	175d	24.45 N	125.16 E

PORTUGUÊS

Nome	Página	Lat.°′	Long.°′ W = Oeste
Shimoji-jima I	175d	24.49 N	125.09 E
Shimojō	94	35.24 N	137.47 E
Shimokawa	92a	44.18 N	142.39 E
Shimokita-hantō ≻ [1]	92	41.15 N	141.00 E
Shimomatsu	270	34.27 N	135.23 E
Shimomizo	268	35.31 N	139.23 E
Shimoni	154	4.39 S	39.23 E
Shimoniikura	268	35.47 N	139.38 E
Shimonita	94	36.13 N	138.47 E
Shimonoseki	96	33.57 N	130.57 E
Shimookudomi	268	35.53 N	139.26 E
Shimoryūzu-zaki ≻	96	33.30 N	133.34 E
Shimosakamoto	270	35.03 N	135.53 E
Shimosuwa	94	36.04 N	138.05 E
Shimotajiri	270	34.57 N	135.28 E
Shimotomi	268	35.50 N	139.29 E
Shimotsu	96	34.10 N	135.08 E
Shimotsuchidana	268	35.24 N	139.27 E
Shimotsui	96	34.26 N	133.47 E
Shimotsuma	94	36.11 N	139.58 E
Shimotsuruma	268	35.29 N	139.28 E
Shimoya	268	35.23 N	139.21 E
Shimoyama	94	35.02 N	137.19 E
Shimoyugi	268	35.38 N	139.23 E
Shimura ◆ [8]	268	35.46 N	139.41 E
Shin, Loch ⊜	46	58.06 N	4.34 W
Shinagawa ◆ [8]	268	35.37 N	139.45 E
Shinan	102	22.43 N	109.54 E
Shinano	94	36.48 N	138.13 E
Shinano ≃	92	37.56 N	139.03 E
Shinarā	142	28.47 N	30.46 E
Shināṣ	128	24.46 N	56.28 E
Shinawari	123	33.32 N	70.48 E
Shinbārī	273c	30.07 N	31.09 E
Shīndand	128	33.18 N	62.08 E
Shindenbaru-kichi, Kōkū-jieitai- ■	92	32.04 N	131.30 E
Shindo	268	35.21 N	139.21 E
Shiner	222	29.25 N	97.10 W
Shingbwiyang	110	26.41 N	96.13 E
Shingishū → Sinŭiju	98	40.05 N	124.24 E
Shinglehouse	214	41.57 N	78.11 W
Shingle Springs	226	38.40 N	120.56 W
Shing Mun Reservoir ⊜ [1]	271d	22.23 N	114.08 E
Shingo	96	34.59 N	133.23 E
Shingū, Nihon	92	33.44 N	135.59 E
Shingū, Nihon	96	34.55 N	134.33 E
Shingū, Nihon	96	33.56 N	133.38 E
Shingwidzi	156	23.05 S	31.25 E
Shingwidzi (Singuédeze) ≃	156	23.53 S	32.17 E
Shinichi	96	34.33 N	133.16 E
Shining Tor ∧	262	53.16 N	2.01 W
Shinīrah	132	32.22 N	36.45 E
Shinji	96	35.24 N	132.54 E
Shinji-ko ⊜	96	35.27 N	132.58 E
Shinjō, Nihon	92	38.46 N	140.18 E
Shinjō, Nihon	270	34.30 N	135.44 E
Shinjuku ◆ [8]	268	35.41 N	139.42 E
Shinkawa	94	35.09 N	136.50 E
Shīnkay	120	31.57 N	67.26 E
Shinkolobwe	154	11.02 S	26.35 E
Shinmachi	94	36.16 N	139.07 E
Shinminato ≃	270	34.38 N	135.09 E
Shinnārah, Minqār ⩡ [4]	142	28.52 N	30.38 E
Shinnayō	96	34.04 N	131.47 E
Shinnecock Bay ⊂	207	40.52 N	72.28 W
Shinnel Water ≃	44	55.13 N	3.49 W
Shinness	46	58.05 N	4.28 W
Shinnston	188	39.23 N	80.18 W
Shino-jima I	94	34.39 N	137.00 E
Shinsai-bashi ◆ [8]	270	34.40 N	135.31 E
Shinshār	130	34.36 N	36.44 E
Shinshiro	94	34.54 N	137.30 E
Shinshū-shinmachi	94	36.34 N	138.01 E
Shintone	94	35.50 N	140.20 E
Shinyanga	154	3.40 S	33.26 E
Shinyanga □ [4]	154	3.45 S	33.00 E
Shin-yōdo ≃ [1]	270	34.41 N	135.26 E
Shio	94	36.52 N	136.48 E
Shiobara	94	36.58 N	139.49 E
Shiocton	190	44.26 N	88.34 W
Shiogama	92	38.19 N	141.01 E
Shiojiri	94	36.06 N	137.58 E
Shiojiri-tōge)(	94	36.05 N	138.02 E
Shiomi-dake ∧	94	35.34 N	138.12 E
Shionoe	96	34.10 N	134.05 E
Shiono-misaki ≻	92	33.26 N	135.45 E
Shioya	94	36.46 N	139.51 E
Shioya ◆ [8]	270	34.38 N	135.06 E
Shioya-zaki ≻, Nihon	92	33.26 N	135.45 E
Shioya-zaki ≻, Nihon	94	36.59 N	140.59 E
Shiozawa	94	37.02 N	138.51 E
Shipai, Zhg.	100	23.08 N	113.21 E
Shipai, Zhg.	106	31.30 N	120.55 E
Shipanpu	107	30.28 N	104.23 E
Shipantuo	107	30.25 N	106.13 E
Ship Bottom	208	39.38 N	74.10 W
Shipbourne	260	51.15 N	0.17 E
Ship Cove	186	47.06 N	54.05 W
Shipdham	42	52.37 N	0.53 E
Shiping, Zhg.	102	28.20 N	107.42 E
Shiping, Zhg.	102	23.47 N	102.30 E
Shipley	44	53.50 N	1.47 W
Shipman, Il., U.S.	219	39.07 N	90.03 W
Shipman, Va., U.S.	192	37.43 N	78.50 W
Shippan Point ≻	276	41.01 N	73.32 W
Shippegan	186	47.45 N	64.42 W
Shippensburg	208	40.03 N	77.31 W
Shippenville	214	41.15 N	79.28 W
Shippingport	214	40.38 N	80.25 W
Shippō	94	35.10 N	136.48 E
Shiprock	200	36.47 N	108.41 W
Ship Rock ∧	200	36.42 N	108.50 W
Shipshaw ≃	186	48.27 N	71.12 W
Shipshewana	216	41.40 N	85.34 W
Shipston-on-Stour	42	52.04 N	1.37 W
Shipton-under-Wychwood	42	51.51 N	1.35 W
Shipu, Zhg.	100	29.13 N	121.55 E
Shipu, Zhg.	106	31.15 N	121.03 E
Shiqian	102	27.31 N	108.20 E
Shiqiao, Zhg.	100	33.12 N	112.36 E
Shiqiao, Zhg.	100	26.58 N	114.23 E
Shiqiao, Zhg.	106	30.30 N	119.11 E
Shiqiao, Zhg.	107	30.25 N	104.31 E
Shiqiaopu	107	30.05 N	105.23 E
Shiqiaozi	104	41.27 N	123.43 E
Shiqi → Zhongshan	100	22.31 N	113.22 E
Shiqma ≃	132	31.36 N	34.30 E
Shiquan, Zhg.	102	33.03 N	108.17 E
Shiquan, Zhg.	106	30.30 N	120.48 E
Shirahama, Nihon	94	34.54 N	139.54 E
Shirahama, Nihon	96	33.40 N	135.20 E
Shirahata-yama ∧	96	34.54 N	134.23 E
Shiraitono-taki ∟	94	35.18 N	138.38 E
Shirakami-misaki ≻	92a	41.24 N	140.12 E
Shirakawa, Nihon	94	37.07 N	140.13 E
Shirakawa, Nihon	94	35.35 N	137.12 E
Shirakawa, Nihon	94	36.16 N	136.54 E
Shirakawa-no-seki-ato ⊥	94	37.03 N	140.15 E
Shirakawa-tōge ∧ [2]	270	34.42 N	135.07 E
Shirako	94	35.26 N	140.23 E
Shirākol	126	22.18 N	88.16 E
Shirakura-yama ∧	94	35.00 N	137.46 E
Shirama-yama ∧	96	34.01 N	135.23 E
Shiramine	94	36.10 N	136.37 E
Shirane	94	35.38 N	138.28 E
Shirane-san ∧, Nihon	94	36.38 N	138.32 E
Shirane-san ∧, Nihon	94	36.48 N	139.22 E
Shirane-san (Kita-dake) ∧, Nihon	94	35.40 N	138.15 E
Shiranuka	92a	42.57 N	144.05 E
Shiraoi	92a	42.33 N	141.21 E
Shiraoka	94	36.01 N	139.40 E
Shiraone	272c	19.03 N	73.01 E
Shirasawa	94	36.40 N	139.08 E
Shirati	154	1.08 S	33.59 E
Shīrāz	128	29.36 N	52.32 E
Shirbīn	142	31.11 N	31.32 E
Shirdley Hill	262	53.36 N	2.58 W
Shire (Chire) ≃	154	17.42 S	35.19 E
Shirebrook	44	53.12 N	1.13 W
Shiremanstown	208	40.13 N	76.57 W
Shiretoko-hantō ≻ [1]	92a	44.00 N	145.00 E
Shiretoko-kokuritsu-kōen ♦	92a	44.08 N	145.10 E
Shiretoko-misaki ≻	92a	44.14 N	145.17 E
Shīrīn ≃	120	36.49 N	65.01 E
Shīr Kūh ∧	128	31.34 N	54.04 E
Shirland	216	42.27 N	89.12 W
Shirley, B.C., Can.	224	48.23 N	123.54 W
Shirley, Il., U.S.	216	40.24 N	89.04 W
Shirley, In., U.S.	218	39.53 N	85.34 W
Shirley, Ma., U.S.	207	42.32 N	71.39 W
Shirley Plantation ⊥	208	37.21 N	77.15 W
Shirleysburg	214	40.18 N	77.53 W
Shiro	222	30.37 N	95.53 W
Shiroi	94	35.48 N	140.04 E
Shiroishi	92	38.00 N	140.37 E
Shirokawa	96	33.23 N	132.46 E
Shirone	92	37.46 N	139.01 E
Shirotori, Nihon	94	35.53 N	136.52 E
Shirotori, Nihon	96	34.15 N	134.20 E
Shirouma-dake ∧	94	36.45 N	137.46 E
Shiroyama	94	35.35 N	139.19 E
Shiro-yama ∧	270	34.38 N	135.53 E
Shirpur	120	21.21 N	74.53 E
Shirrell Heath	42	50.55 N	1.12 W
Shirshābah	142	30.47 N	31.10 E
Shīrvān	128	37.24 N	57.55 E
Shisaka-jima I	96	34.07 N	133.11 E
Shisanling	105	40.19 N	116.16 E
Shi San Ling (Ming Tombs) ⊥	105	40.19 N	116.13 E
Shisanzhan	89	51.21 N	125.43 E
Shisha Hai ⊜	271a	39.57 N	116.22 E
Shishaldin Volcano ∧ [1]	180	54.45 N	163.57 W
Shishan	104	41.16 N	121.30 E
Shishi	100	24.48 N	118.38 E
Shishikui	96	33.34 N	134.18 E
Shishi Shan ∧	100	24.44 N	117.54 E
Shishmaref	180	66.14 N	166.09 W
Shishmaref Inlet ⊂	180	66.07 N	165.50 W
Shishou	102	29.43 N	112.19 E
Shisht al-An'ām	142	30.52 N	30.44 E
Shisiazhan	89	51.36 N	125.42 E
Shisixian	104	40.53 N	122.59 E
Shisler Point ≻	284a	42.52 N	79.08 W
Shisui	94	35.43 N	140.16 E
Shitai	100	30.13 N	117.27 E
Shitan, Zhg.	100	27.44 N	112.42 E
Shitan, Zhg.	100	23.10 N	113.47 E
Shitang, Zhg.	100	28.16 N	121.36 E
Shitang, Zhg.	102	25.38 N	110.50 E
Shitangwan	106	31.40 N	120.13 E
Shitara	94	35.05 N	137.35 E
Shithāthah	128	32.33 N	43.29 E
Shiting, Zhg.	100	27.36 N	113.16 E
Shiting, Zhg.	105	39.31 N	115.41 E
Shitoufangzi	89	48.38 N	126.08 E
Shitougouzi	89	49.19 N	125.55 E
Shitoumiao	102	41.41 N	106.50 E
Shitoumiaozi	104	41.38 N	121.26 E
Shitoushan	105	40.27 N	116.13 E
Shitoushuangmiao	98	41.28 N	118.55 E
Shituan	107	30.09 N	105.01 E
Shitunwei	104	41.07 N	121.31 E
Shiv	120	26.11 N	71.15 E
Shivalya	126	23.50 N	89.47 E
Shively	218	38.12 N	85.49 W
Shivering, Mount ∧	170	34.08 S	150.02 E
Shivpuri	124	25.26 N	77.39 E
Shivta, Horvot (Subeita) ⊥	132	30.53 N	34.38 E
Shivwits Plateau ⋀ [1]	200	36.15 N	113.40 W
Shiwaku-shotō II	96	34.20 N	133.45 E
Shiwan, Zhg.	100	27.17 N	112.57 E
Shiwan, Zhg.	100	28.12 N	113.49 E
Shiwan, Zhg.	100	23.01 N	113.04 E
Shiwan, Zhg.	102	37.35 N	109.01 E
Shiwenchang	104	41.43 N	123.54 E
Shiwu	89	43.48 N	124.13 E
Shixi, Zhg.	100	28.16 N	117.45 E
Shixi, Zhg.	100	28.16 N	115.36 E
Shixia	105	40.20 N	114.59 E
Shixian	89	43.05 N	129.47 E
Shixiancun	106	31.12 N	120.29 E
Shixiechang	107	29.51 N	106.41 E
Shixing	100	24.58 N	114.03 E
Shixun	100	24.44 N	118.11 E
Shiyachang	107	30.27 N	106.31 E
Shiyan, Zhg.	102	32.38 N	110.44 E
Shiyan, Zhg.	107	30.22 N	104.27 E
Shiyangchang, Zhg.	107	29.56 N	105.37 E
Shiyangchang, Zhg.	107	30.42 N	105.57 E
Shiyanqiao	107	29.19 N	105.22 E
Shiyiwei	106	31.59 N	120.43 E
Shiyizhan	89	51.13 N	125.52 E
Shiyu	107	29.46 N	106.06 E
Shizhangzi	98	40.24 N	119.48 E
Shizheng	100	24.32 N	115.50 E
Shizhenjie	100	28.51 N	116.56 E
Shizhong, Zhg.	100	24.57 N	117.06 E
Shizhong, Zhg.	106	30.44 N	120.16 E
Shizhongtan	107	30.26 N	104.35 E
Shizhu, Zhg.	100	28.48 N	120.06 E
Shizhu, Zhg.	102	29.56 N	108.09 E
Shizhuang	106	32.08 N	120.31 E
Shizhuangzi, Zhg.	104	42.24 N	122.53 E
Shizhuangzi, Zhg.	105	40.38 N	116.59 E
Shizhuzi	104	41.18 N	121.35 E
Shizichang	107	29.32 N	106.14 E
Shizigu	105	39.23 N	118.08 E
Shizikou	100	24.12 N	113.38 E
Shizilin	106	31.26 N	121.25 E
Shizipo	105	40.21 N	115.07 E
Shizipu	106	30.59 N	119.07 E
Shizuchi-kokutei-kōen ♦	96	33.45 N	133.08 E
Shizugawa	92	38.40 N	141.27 E
Shizui, Zhg.	89	43.08 N	126.06 E
Shizui, Zhg.	98	38.52 N	113.42 E
Shizuma ≃	96	35.12 N	132.28 E
Shizunai	92a	42.20 N	142.22 E
Shizuoka	94	34.58 N	138.23 E
Shizuoka □ [5]	94	35.00 N	138.00 E
Shkodër	38	42.05 N	19.30 E
Shkumbin ≃	38	41.01 N	19.26 E
Shō ≃	94	36.47 N	137.04 E
Shoal ≃	194	30.41 N	86.39 W
Shoal Cape ≻	162	33.53 S	121.07 E
Shoal Creek ≃, U.S.	194	34.50 N	87.33 W
Shoal Creek ≃, U.S.	194	37.05 N	94.42 W
Shoal Creek ≃, U.S.	194	40.28 N	92.42 W
Shoal Creek ≃, Il., U.S.	219	38.28 N	89.35 W
Shoal Creek ≃, Mo., U.S.	194	39.44 N	93.32 W
Shoal Creek, East Fork ≃	219	38.51 N	89.30 W
Shoal Creek, Middle Fork ≃	219	39.05 N	89.33 W
Shoal Creek, West Fork ≃	219	39.05 N	89.33 W
Shoal Harbour	186	48.11 N	53.59 W
Shoalhaven ≃	170	34.52 S	150.44 E
Shoalhaven Bight ⊂ [3]	170	34.52 S	150.47 E
Shoal Lake	184	50.26 N	100.34 W
Shoal Lake ⊜	184	49.32 N	95.00 W
Shoal Point ≻	276	41.08 N	73.15 W
Shoals	194	38.39 N	86.47 W
Shoals, Bay of ⊂	168b	35.37 S	137.37 E
Shoalwater Bay ⊂	166	22.02 S	150.25 E
Shōbara	96	34.51 N	133.01 E
Shōboku	96	35.06 N	134.07 E
Shobonier	219	38.52 N	89.05 W
Shōbu	94	36.04 N	139.36 E
Shōdai	270	34.51 N	135.42 E
Shōdo-shima I	96	34.30 N	134.17 E
Shoeburyness	42	51.32 N	0.48 E
Shoe Cove	186	49.55 N	55.33 W
Shoemakersville	208	40.30 N	75.58 W
Shōgawa	94	36.34 N	136.59 E
Shogunle	273a	6.35 N	3.21 E
Shohola	210	41.28 N	74.55 W
Shohola Creek ≃	210	41.28 N	74.55 W
Shokambetsu-dake ∧	92a	43.43 N	141.31 E
Shokan	210	41.58 N	74.13 W
Shōkawa	94	36.02 N	136.57 E
Sholingnur	122	13.07 N	79.25 E
Shomera	132	33.05 N	35.17 E
Shomolu	273a	6.32 N	3.23 E
Shōmyō-no-taki ∟	94	36.35 N	137.24 E
Shona, Eilean I	46	56.47 N	5.52 W
Shōnai	96	33.11 N	131.26 E
Shōnai ≃	94	35.04 N	136.50 E
Shōnan	268	35.50 N	140.02 E
Shongum	276	40.50 N	74.33 W
Shongum Lake ⊜	276	40.51 N	74.32 W
Shongwe	158	27.24 S	32.25 E
Shōō	96	35.02 N	134.08 E
Shooters Hill	170	33.54 S	149.52 E
Shooters Island I	276	40.39 N	74.10 W
Shopiere	216	42.34 N	88.57 W
Shoranūr	122	10.46 N	76.17 E
Shorāpur	122	16.31 N	76.45 E
Shoreacres, B.C., Can.	182	49.26 N	117.32 W
Shore Acres, Ca., U.S.	226	38.02 N	121.58 W
Shore Acres, Ma., U.S.	207	42.12 N	70.44 W
Shore Acres, N.J., U.S.	208	40.01 N	74.06 W
Shoreacres, Tx., U.S.	222	29.37 N	95.01 W
Shoreditch ◆ [8]	260	51.32 N	0.05 W
Shoreham, Austl.	169	38.25 S	145.03 E
Shoreham, Eng., U.K.	260	51.20 N	0.11 E
Shoreham, Mi., U.S.	216	42.03 N	86.30 W
Shoreham-by-Sea	42	50.49 N	0.16 W
Shorewood, Il., U.S.	216	41.32 N	88.12 W
Shorewood, Wi., U.S.	216	43.05 N	87.53 W
Shorewood Hills	216	43.04 N	89.26 W
Shorkot	123	30.50 N	72.04 E
Shorkot Road	123	30.47 N	72.15 E
Shorne	260	51.25 N	0.26 E
Short Acres	226	36.21 N	119.38 W
Short Beach	207	41.15 N	72.50 W
Short Creek	214	40.11 N	80.55 W
Shortland Islands II	175e	6.55 S	155.53 E
Short Mountain ∧	192	36.23 N	83.10 W
Shortsville	210	42.57 N	77.13 W
Shoshone	202	42.56 N	114.24 W
Shoshone ≃	202	44.52 N	108.11 W
Shoshone, North Fork ≃	202	44.29 N	109.18 W
Shoshone, South Fork ≃	202	44.27 N	109.14 W
Shoshone Basin ≚ [1]	202	43.05 N	108.05 W
Shoshone Lake ⊜	202	44.22 N	110.43 W
Shoshone Mountains ⋀	204	39.00 N	117.30 W
Shoshone Peak ∧	204	36.56 N	116.16 W
Shoshone Range ⋀	204	40.20 N	116.50 W
Shoshong	156	22.59 S	26.30 E
Shoshoni	200	43.14 N	108.06 W
Shostka → Šostka	78	51.52 N	33.30 E
Shotley Gate	42	51.58 N	1.15 E
Shotton	262	53.12 N	3.02 W
Shotton Colliery	44	54.44 N	1.20 W
Shotts	46	55.49 N	3.48 W
Shotwick	262	53.14 N	2.59 W
Shou'anzhen	107	30.16 N	103.37 E
Shouchang	100	29.22 N	119.13 E
Shoufeng	100	23.52 N	121.30 E
Shouguang	98	36.53 N	118.42 E
Shouning	100	27.27 N	119.30 E
Shournagh ≃	48	51.53 N	8.35 W
Shoushan	104	41.12 N	123.03 E
Shouwangfen	105	40.35 N	117.48 E
Shouxian	100	32.35 N	116.47 E
Shouyang	102	37.59 N	113.09 E
Shōwa, Nihon	94	36.37 N	139.04 E
Shōwa, Nihon	96	34.43 N	133.39 E
Showell	208	38.23 N	75.12 W
Show Low	200	34.15 N	110.01 W
Shqipëri → Albania □ [1]	38	41.00 N	20.00 E
Shreve	214	40.40 N	82.01 W
Shreveport	194	32.30 N	93.44 W
Shrevewood	284c	38.53 N	77.13 W
Shrewsbury, Eng., U.K.	42	52.43 N	2.45 W
Shrewsbury, Ma., U.S.	207	42.17 N	71.42 W
Shrewsbury, N.J., U.S.	208	40.19 N	74.03 W
Shrewsbury, Pa., U.S.	208	39.46 N	76.40 W
Shrewsbury River ⊂	276	40.21 N	74.00 W
Shrewton	42	51.12 N	1.55 W
Shri Dūngargarh	120	28.05 N	74.00 E
Shri Mohangarh	120	27.17 N	71.14 E
Shriner Mountain ∧	210	40.56 N	77.20 W
Shrīrangapattana	122	12.25 N	76.42 E
Shrivenham	42	51.36 N	1.39 W
Shropshire □ [6]	42	52.40 N	2.40 W
Shropshire Union Canal ≅	262	53.17 N	2.53 W
Shrub Oak	210	41.20 N	73.49 W
Shrule	48	53.30 N	9.08 W
Shu ≃	98	34.07 N	118.30 E
Shuajingsi	102	32.00 N	103.05 E
Shuanfeng Shan ∧	107	29.26 N	105.47 E
Shuang ≃	269d	25.00 N	121.31 E
Shuangbai	102	24.54 N	101.32 E
Shuangcheng	89	45.21 N	126.17 E
Shuangchengzi	105	40.11 N	118.03 E
Shuangdian	100	32.23 N	120.51 E
Shuangdun	106	32.13 N	121.08 E
Shuangfeng, Zhg.	102	27.24 N	112.05 E
Shuangfeng, Zhg.	106	31.31 N	121.02 E
Shuangfeng, Zhg.	106	31.31 N	121.01 E
Shuangfeng Shan ∧	100	24.28 N	114.43 E
Shuangfengyi	107	29.27 N	105.09 E
Shuangfu	105	39.48 N	117.44 E
Shuangfuchang, Zhg.	107	29.41 N	103.31 E
Shuangfuchang, Zhg.	107	30.08 N	103.32 E
Shuanggang, Zhg.	89	45.07 N	122.59 E
Shuanggang, Zhg.	100	28.11 N	117.30 E
Shuanggetun	89	48.58 N	129.57 E
Shuanggou, Zhg.	98	34.03 N	117.37 E
Shuanggou, Zhg.	100	32.12 N	112.21 E
Shuanggou, Zhg.	100	33.16 N	118.10 E
Shuanggufen	107	29.38 N	104.11 E
Shuanghe, Zhg.	100	31.33 N	116.46 E
Shuanghe, Zhg.	100	31.41 N	112.46 E
Shuanghe, Zhg.	107	29.40 N	104.48 E
Shuanghe, Zhg.	107	30.07 N	105.10 E
Shuanghe, Zhg.	107	30.15 N	104.44 E
Shuanghechang, Zhg.	107	28.51 N	104.51 E
Shuanghechang, Zhg.	107	29.25 N	106.17 E
Shuanghechang, Zhg.	107	29.12 N	105.43 E
Shuanghechang, Zhg.	107	29.18 N	105.36 E
Shuang-hsi	269d	25.01 N	121.39 E
Shuangji ≃	100	34.05 N	114.24 E
Shuangjiang, Zhg.	100	26.48 N	116.28 E
Shuangjiang, Zhg.	102	23.37 N	99.41 E
Shuangjiang, Zhg.	107	30.13 N	105.45 E
Shuangjiangqiao	102	25.19 N	98.51 E
Shuangjianji	100	33.12 N	116.40 E
Shuangjingzi	104	42.28 N	123.42 E
Shuangkou	105	39.15 N	117.02 E
Shuangliao	89	43.31 N	123.30 E
Shuanglin	106	30.47 N	120.19 E
Shuanglingzi, Zhg.	104	40.54 N	124.10 E
Shuanglingzi, Zhg.	104	40.50 N	123.06 E
Shuangliu	107	30.34 N	103.55 E
Shuangliushu	100	31.56 N	115.12 E
Shuanglongtai	104	40.56 N	122.39 E
Shuangmiao, Zhg.	100	28.24 N	120.45 E
Shuangmiao, Zhg.	100	32.09 N	116.52 E
Shuangmiaozi, Zhg.	104	42.25 N	122.17 E
Shuangmiaozi, Zhg.	104	42.02 N	121.52 E
Shuangpai	110	25.57 N	111.32 E
Shuangpaishi	106	31.24 N	118.59 E
Shuangqiao, Zhg.	100	32.29 N	116.41 E
Shuangqiao, Zhg.	105	39.54 N	116.37 E
Shuangqiao, Zhg.	106	30.59 N	118.47 E
Shuangshanzi	98	40.21 N	119.08 E
Shuangshipu	107	29.14 N	104.42 E
Shuangshiqiao, Zhg.	107	29.22 N	105.51 E
Shuangshiqiao, Zhg.	107	29.23 N	104.29 E
Shuangshu	105	39.34 N	117.01 E
Shuangshutai	89	43.50 N	121.15 E
Shuangtaizi, Zhg.	104	41.34 N	121.12 E
Shuangtaizi, Zhg.	104	42.21 N	124.10 E
Shuangtaizi, Zhg.	104	42.25 N	123.11 E
Shuangtaizi, Zhg.	104	41.00 N	122.34 E
Shuangtaizi, Zhg.	104	41.11 N	121.14 E
Shuangtaizi ≃	104	40.59 N	121.51 E
Shuangtaizihe Kou ≃ [1]	104	40.55 N	121.50 E
Shuangtang, Zhg.	100	28.01 N	116.44 E
Shuangtang, Zhg.	105	39.03 N	116.17 E
Shuangtang, Zhg.	105	38.53 N	116.54 E
Shuangtangdian	106	30.59 N	118.51 E
Shuangtuo	105	39.14 N	117.20 E
Shuangtuozhen	105	39.29 N	118.23 E
Shuangxi, Zhg.	100	27.01 N	119.03 E
Shuangxi, Zhg.	106	30.24 N	119.50 E
Shuangyang	89	43.32 N	125.42 E
Shuangyangdian	104	41.07 N	121.16 E
Shuangyaocun	105	38.55 N	117.03 E
Shuangyashan	89	46.37 N	131.22 E
Shu'ayb, Wādī V	132	31.54 N	35.38 E
Shu'ayt, Wādī V	144	18.15 N	52.00 E
Shubenacadie ≃	186	45.20 N	63.30 W
Shublik Mountains ⋀	180	69.31 N	145.40 W
Shubrā al-Khaymah	142	30.06 N	31.15 E
Shubrā Bābil	142	30.54 N	31.11 E
Shubrā Khalfūn	142	30.29 N	31.05 E
Shubrā Khīt	142	31.02 N	30.43 E
Shubuta	194	31.51 N	88.41 W
Shucheng	100	31.27 N	116.57 E
Shufu	85	39.27 N	75.52 E
Shufuka Shan ∧	89	50.28 N	123.10 E
Shugudali	89	52.47 N	124.02 E
Shuheyingzi	104	42.18 N	122.16 E
Shuhezhen	106	31.35 N	121.35 E
Shūhō	96	34.13 N	131.18 E
Shuhong	100	28.39 N	120.09 E
Shuibatang	102	28.39 N	107.03 E
Shuibei, Zhg.	100	28.04 N	115.01 E
Shuibei, Zhg.	106	31.40 N	119.39 E
Shuichaoyang	100	26.22 N	117.57 E
Shuicheng	102	26.41 N	104.50 E
Shuidao	98	37.10 N	121.33 E
Shuidiangou	89	47.43 N	122.40 E
Shuidong, Zhg.	106	31.23 N	119.37 E
Shuidong, Zhg.	106	30.47 N	118.57 E
Shuidongjie	106	31.07 N	119.33 E
Shuiduixia	106	30.17 N	118.50 E
Shuihai	100	33.02 N	120.26 E
Shuihouling	100	30.43 N	116.26 E
Shuiji	100	27.26 N	118.20 E
Shuijiahuangdi	104	42.14 N	123.28 E
Shuijian	105	40.09 N	115.58 E
Shuijing	102	26.10 N	99.09 E
Shuijingtang	102	28.50 N	108.11 E
Shuikou, Zhg.	100	26.59 N	117.41 E
Shuikou, Zhg.	100	26.22 N	118.44 E
Shuikou, Zhg.	100	26.18 N	113.46 E
Shuikou, Zhg.	100	24.00 N	115.55 E
Shuikou, Zhg.	102	25.54 N	109.06 E
Shuikou, Zhg.	107	29.29 N	103.42 E
Shuikouchang	107	29.33 N	103.40 E
Shuikouguan	102	22.30 N	106.34 E
Shuikoushan	102	26.30 N	112.30 E
Shuikouxu	100	25.09 N	114.28 E
Shuiliandong	98	42.12 N	125.09 E
Shuimenzi	98	39.36 N	122.19 E
Shuimingqiao	106	31.03 N	119.09 E
Shuimoqipan	85	39.51 N	76.42 E
Shuiquan'gou	104	41.58 N	121.50 E
Shuiquanzi, Zhg.	104	42.15 N	121.32 E
Shuiquanzi, Zhg.	104	40.53 N	121.05 E
Shuitangzi	102	29.18 N	101.10 E
Shuiting	100	29.10 N	119.14 E
Shuitou, Zhg.	100	24.43 N	118.25 E
Shuitou, Zhg.	100	23.53 N	113.37 E
Shuitou, Zhg.	100	27.38 N	120.16 E
Shuitouwei	100	26.06 N	115.28 E
Shuituzhen	107	29.47 N	106.31 E
Shuiyang	106	31.14 N	118.47 E
Shuiyang ≃	106	31.14 N	118.48 E
Shuiye	98	36.08 N	114.07 E
Shuizhai	98	36.54 N	117.24 E
Shuizhuyang	100	26.59 N	119.13 E
Shujāābād	123	29.53 N	71.18 E
Shujālpur	124	23.24 N	76.43 E
Shujiawazi	104	42.20 N	121.57 E
Shuksan, Mount ∧	224	48.50 N	121.36 W
Shulan	89	44.27 N	126.57 E
Shulaps Peak ∧	182	50.57 N	122.31 W
Shule	85	39.23 N	76.06 E
Shule ≃	102	40.50 N	94.10 E
Shūlgareh	120	36.19 N	66.53 E
Shullsburg	190	42.34 N	90.13 W
Shulu (Xinji)	98	37.54 N	115.13 E
Shumagin Islands II	180	55.07 N	159.45 W
Shumatuscacant ≃	283	42.03 N	70.51 W
Shumen → Šumen	38	43.16 N	26.55 E
Shūnah, Wādī ash- V	142	29.38 N	32.13 E
Shun'an	100	30.57 N	117.57 E
Shūnat Nimrīn	132	31.54 N	35.37 E
Shunayn, Sabkhat ⊜	146	30.30 N	21.00 E
Shunchang	100	26.50 N	117.48 E
Shunde	100	22.50 N	113.14 E
Shundian	100	34.15 N	113.20 E
Shundianqiao	106	31.24 N	120.41 E
Shunge	102	37.25 N	95.27 E
Shungnak	180	66.53 N	157.02 W
Shunhechang	107	29.57 N	104.42 E
Shunlongchang	107	30.04 N	103.27 E
Shunshanpu	104	42.08 N	122.21 E
Shuntianhu	100	24.08 N	114.48 E
Shunyi	105	40.08 N	116.38 E
Shuoduzong	102	30.48 N	95.47 E
Shuojiaji	100	33.42 N	119.44 E
Shuping	107	29.19 N	104.43 E
Shupiyan	123	33.43 N	74.50 E
Shuqayyiqah, Nafūd ⩡ [8]	128	25.45 N	43.55 E
Shuqualak	194	32.58 N	88.34 W
Shūr ≃, Īrān	128	30.57 N	57.42 E
Shūr ≃, Īrān	128	35.57 N	56.24 E
Shūr ≃, Īrān	128	31.45 N	55.15 E
Shūr ≃, Īrān	128	34.38 N	51.46 E
Shuri	174m	26.13 N	127.43 E
Shurkhua	110	22.15 N	93.38 E
Shurugwi	154	19.40 S	30.00 E
Shūsf	128	31.48 N	60.01 E
Shūsh	128	32.11 N	48.15 E
Shushan	210	43.05 N	73.21 W
Shushan Hu ⊜	98	35.36 N	116.27 E
Shūshtar	128	32.03 N	48.51 E

≃ River	Fluß	Río	Rivière	Rio	◆ Submarine Features	Untermeerische Objekte	Accidentes Submarinos	Formes de relief sous-marin	Acidentes submarinos
≅ Canal	Kanal	Canal	Canal	Canal	□ Political Unit	Politische Einheit	Unidad Politica	Entité politique	Unidade política
∟ Waterfall, Rapids	Wasserfall, Stromschnellen	Cascada, Rápidos	Chute d'eau, Rapides	Cascata, Rápidos	ʊ Cultural Institution	Kulturelle Institution	Institución Cultural	Institution culturelle	Instituição cultural
ц Strait	Meeresstraße	Estrecho	Détroit	Estreito	⊥ Historical Site	Historische Stätte	Sitio Histórico	Site historique	Sitio histórico
⊂ Bay, Gulf	Bucht, Golf	Bahía, Golfo	Baie, Golfe	Baía, Golfo	♦ Recreational Site	Erholungs- und Ferienort	Sitio de Recreo	Centre de loisirs	Area de Lazer
⊜ Lake, Lakes	See, Seen	Lago, Lagos	Lac, Lacs	Lago, Lagos	⊠ Airport	Flughafen	Aeropuerto	Aéroport	Aeroporto
≡ Swamp	Sumpf	Pantano	Marais	Pântano	■ Military Installation	Militäranlage	Instalación Militar	Installation militaire	Instalação militar
⊓ Ice Features, Glacier	Eis- und Gletscherformen	Accidentes Glaciales	Formes glaciaires	Acidentes glaciares	◆ Miscellaneous	Verschiedenes	Misceláneo	Divers	Diversos
⫪ Other Hydrographic Features	Andere Hydrographische Objekte	Otros Elementos Hidrográficos	Autres données hydrographiques	Outros acidentes hidrográficos					

Shuswap ≃ 182 50.50 N 119.00 W
Shuswap Lake ⊜ 182 50.57 N 119.15 W
Shuṭab 142 27.08 N 31.14 E
Shutendōji-yama ʌ 96 33.06 N 130.54 E
Shuteye Peak ʌ 226 37.21 N 119.25 W
Shutlingsloe ʌ 262 53.13 N 2.02 W
Shūtō 96 34.05 N 132.05 E
Shuwak 140 14.23 N 35.52 E
Shuwaykah 132 32.20 N 35.02 E
Shuya 174m 26.40 N 128.06 E
Shuyak Island I 180 58.35 N 152.30 W
Shuyang 98 34.08 N 118.47 E
Shuya
— Šuja 24 61.55 N 34.12 E
Shuyūkh Fawqānī 130 36.46 N 38.03 E
Shuzenji 94 34.58 N 138.56 E
Shwangliao
— Liaoyuan 89 42.54 N 125.07 E
Shwebo 110 22.34 N 95.42 E
Shwegun 110 17.09 N 97.39 E
Shwegyin 110 17.55 N 96.53 E
Shweli (Longchuan) ≃ 102 23.56 N 96.17 E
Shwenyaung 110 20.46 N 96.57 E
Shyamdih 126 23.47 N 86.56 E
Shyok 120 34.11 N 78.08 E
Shyok ≃ 120 35.13 N 75.53 E
Si ≃ 98 35.11 N 116.42 E
Sia 164 6.49 S 134.19 E
Siabu 114 1.01 N 99.29 E
Siachen Glacier ⊠ 123 35.30 N 77.00 E
Siād Kuh, Kavīr-e ≃ 128 32.40 N 53.52 E
Siagne ≃ 62 43.32 N 6.57 E
Siāhān Range ʌ 128 27.25 N 64.30 E
Siāh Kūh, Selseleh-ye ʌ 128 34.00 N 64.00 E
Siak ≃ 114 1.13 N 102.09 E
Siak Kecil ≃ 114 1.16 N 102.08 E
Siak Sri Indrapura 114 0.46 N 102.04 E
Sialang 114 1.31 N 99.27 E
Sialejevskaja P'atina 80 53.49 N 44.32 E
Siālkot 123 32.30 N 74.31 E
Sialsūk 120 23.24 N 92.45 E
Siam, Gulf of
— Thailand, Gulf of c 110 10.00 N 101.00 E
Siamanna 71 39.55 N 8.46 E
Siam
— Thailand □[1] 110 15.00 N 100.00 E
Si'an 106 30.54 N 119.39 E
Siangtan
— Xiangtan 100 27.51 N 112.54 E
Sianhala 150 10.03 N 6.51 W
Sianów 30 54.15 N 16.16 E
Siantan, Pulau I 112 3.10 N 106.15 E
Sian
— Xi'an 102 34.15 N 108.52 E
Sianzhuang 100 33.05 N 119.13 E
Siapa ≃ 246 2.07 N 66.28 W
Siargao Island I 116 9.53 N 126.02 E
Siari 123 34.56 N 76.44 E
Siasconset 207 41.15 N 69.58 W
Siasi 116 5.33 N 120.49 E
Siasi Island I 116 5.33 N 120.51 E
Siaškotan, ostrov I 74 48.49 N 154.06 E
Siātista 38 40.16 N 21.33 E
Siaton 116 9.04 N 123.02 E
Siaton ≃ 116 9.02 N 123.02 E
Siaton Point > 116 9.03 N 123.01 E
Siau, Pulau I 112 2.42 N 125.24 E
Siaugues-Saint-Romain 62 45.06 N 3.38 E
Šiauliai 76 55.56 N 23.19 E
Siazan' 84 41.05 N 49.06 E
Sibago Island I 116 6.45 N 122.24 E
Sibā'ī, Jabal as- ʌ 140 25.43 N 34.09 E
Sibaj 86 52.42 N 58.39 E
Sibalom 116 10.47 N 122.01 E
Sibanicú 240p 21.14 N 77.31 W
Sibao 100 25.55 N 116.42 E
Sibari, Piana di ≍ 68 39.45 N 16.25 E
Sibasa 156 22.53 S 30.33 E
Sibati 86 47.12 N 88.15 E
Sibayi ⊜ 158 27.20 S 32.40 E
Sibay Island I 116 11.51 N 121.29 E
Sibbald 184 51.23 N 110.09 W
Sibbald Point Provincial Park ♦ 212 44.19 N 79.19 W
Šibbe 85 39.53 N 72.05 E
Sibbo 26 60.22 N 25.16 E
Šibchar 126 23.21 N 90.09 E
Šibenik 36 43.44 N 15.54 E
Siberia Occidental, Llanura de
— Zapadno-Sibirskaja ravnina ≍ 72 60.00 N 75.00 E
Siberia
— Sibir' ◆[1] 74 65.00 N 110.00 E
Sibérie Occidentale, Dépression de la
— Zapadno-Sibirskaja ravnina ≍ 72 60.00 N 75.00 E
Siberut, Pulau I 108 1.20 S 98.55 E
Sibi 120 29.33 N 67.53 E
Sibiči 89 46.04 N 135.22 E
Sibidiri 164 9.00 S 142.15 E
Sibigo 114 2.51 N 95.55 E
Sibillini, Monti ⋏ 66 42.54 N 13.13 E
Sibir' (Siberia) ◆[1] 74 65.00 N 110.00 E
Sibirjakova, ostrov I 74 72.50 N 79.00 E
Sibircevo 89 44.12 N 132.26 E
Sibiti 152 3.41 S 13.21 E
Sibiti ≃ 154 3.49 S 34.46 E
Sibiu 38 45.48 N 24.09 E
Sibiu □[6] 38 46.00 N 24.15 E
Sible Hedingham 42 51.58 N 0.35 E
Sibley, Il., U.S. 216 40.35 N 88.23 W
Sibley, Ia., U.S. 198 43.23 N 95.45 W
Sibley, La., U.S. 194 32.33 N 93.18 W
Sibley, Ms., U.S. 194 31.22 N 91.23 W
Sibley Peninsula >[1] 190 48.25 N 88.45 W
Sibley Provincial Park ♦ 190 48.25 N 88.49 W
Siboa 112 0.30 N 120.02 E
Sibochang 107 28.50 N 104.32 E
Sibolga 114 1.45 N 98.48 E
Siborang 114 1.08 N 99.26 E
Siborongborong 114 2.13 N 98.59 E
Sibpur, Bngl. 124 24.02 N 90.44 E
Sibpur, India 272b 22.24 N 88.33 E
Sibpur, India 272b 22.34 N 88.19 E
Sibsa ≃[1] 126 22.01 N 89.30 E
Sibsāgar 120 26.59 N 94.39 E
Sibu 112 2.18 N 111.49 E
Sibu, Pulau I 114 2.13 N 104.04 E
Sibuatan, Gunung ʌ 114 2.56 N 98.24 E
Sibuguey ≃ 116 7.38 N 122.48 E
Sibuguey Bay c 116 7.30 N 122.40 E
Sibut 152 5.44 N 19.05 E
Sibuti 112 4.03 N 113.48 E
Sibutu Island I 112 4.46 N 119.29 E
Sibutu Passage ʁ 112 4.50 N 119.35 E
Sibuyan Island I 116 12.25 N 122.34 E
Sibuyan Sea ▾[2] 116 12.50 N 122.40 E
Siby 150 12.23 N 8.20 W
Sibyŏn 98 38.19 N 126.41 E
Sicamous 182 50.50 N 119.00 W
Sicapoo, Mount ʌ 116 18.01 N 120.56 E
Siccus ≃ 166 31.26 S 139.30 E
Šichaou 98 41.39 N 116.29 E
Šichany 80 52.07 N 47.13 E
Šichifulo ≃ 154 17.26 S 25.02 E
Si Chon 110 9.00 N 99.54 E
Sichote-Alin' ⋏ 89 48.00 N 138.00 E
Sichote-Alinskij zapovednik ♦ 89 45.15 N 136.15 E
Šichtovo 76 55.43 N 32.18 E
Sichuan (Szechwan) □[4] 102 31.00 N 105.00 E
Sichuan Pendi ≍[1] 102 30.00 N 105.00 E
Sichuanzhai 102 23.02 N 101.44 E
Sicié, Cap > 62 43.03 N 5.51 E
Sicignano degli Alburni 68 40.34 N 15.18 E
Sicilia □[4] 36 37.30 N 14.00 E
Sicilia (Sicily) I 70 37.30 N 14.00 E
Sicilia, Isla de
— Sicilia I 70 37.30 N 14.00 E
Sicily, Strait of ʁ 36 37.20 N 11.20 E
Sicily Island 194 31.50 N 91.39 W
Sicily
— Sicilia I 70 37.30 N 14.00 E
Sickingmühle 263 51.42 N 7.07 E
Sicklerville 208 39.43 N 74.58 W
Sicogon Island I 116 11.27 N 123.16 E
Sico Tinto ≃ 236 15.58 N 84.58 W
Sicuani 248 14.16 S 71.13 W
Siculiana 70 37.20 N 13.25 E
Šicun 106 31.55 N 119.18 E
Šid 38 45.08 N 19.13 E
Sīdah, Qārat ʌ[2] 142 30.16 N 29.58 E
Sidamo □[4] 144 5.00 N 39.00 E
Sidao 271a 39.51 N 116.26 E
Sidaohe 105 40.24 N 117.17 E
Sidareja 115a 7.29 S 108.47 E
Sidas 112 0.24 N 109.46 E
Sidcup ◆[8] 260 51.25 N 0.06 E
Siddeburen 52 53.25 N 6.52 E
Siddhapur 120 23.55 N 72.23 E
Siddinghausen 263 51.32 N 7.48 E
Siddington 262 53.14 N 2.14 W
Siddipet 122 18.06 N 78.51 E
Sideia Island I 164 10.35 S 150.50 E
Side'kino 80 54.32 N 51.08 E
Sidéradougou 150 10.40 N 4.15 W
Siderno 68 38.16 N 16.18 E
Šiderópolis 252 28.35 S 49.26 W
Šiderty ≃, Kaz. 80 50.10 N 52.20 E
Šiderty ≃, Kaz. 86 52.32 N 74.50 E
Sidhauli 124 27.17 N 80.50 E
Sidheros, Ákra > 38 35.19 N 26.19 E
Sidhi 124 24.25 N 81.53 E
Sidhirókastron 38 41.14 N 23.22 E
Sīdī 'Abd ar-Raḥmān 140 30.58 N 29.44 E
Sidi Aïch 34 36.37 N 4.42 E
Sidi Aïssa 148 35.53 N 3.48 E
Sidi Akacha 34 36.28 N 1.18 E
Sidi Ali 34 36.06 N 0.25 E
Sidi Ali, Oued V 148 34.07 N 2.05 W
Sidi Ali Ben Nasrallah 36 35.15 N 9.50 E
Sīdī Barrānī 140 31.36 N 25.55 E
Sidi bel Abbès 148 35.13 N 0.10 W
Sidi Bel Abbes □[5] 148 35.00 N 1.00 W
Sidi Bennour 148 32.30 N 8.30 W
Sidi Bou Zid 148 35.02 N 9.30 E
Sidi Bou Zid □[8] 148 35.00 N 9.15 E
Sidi el Hani, Sebkhet ⊜ 36 35.33 N 10.25 E
Sīdī Ghāzī 142 31.12 N 31.03 E
Sīdī Hunaysh 140 31.10 N 27.37 E
Sidi Ifni 148 29.24 N 10.12 W
Sidi Kacem 148 34.15 N 5.39 W
Sidikalang 114 2.45 N 98.19 E
Sidimo 144 2.27 N 41.58 E
Sidi Mohammed Ben Ali 34 36.09 N 0.51 E
Sidi Moussa, Oued V 148 26.58 N 3.54 E
Sidi Okba 148 34.48 N 5.54 E
Sīdī Sālim 142 31.17 N 30.48 E
Sidi Slimane 148 34.15 N 5.49 W
Sidi Smaïl 148 32.49 N 8.30 W
Sidlaghatta 122 13.23 N 77.52 E
Sidlaw Hills ⋏[2] 46 56.30 N 3.10 W
Sidley, Mount ʌ 9 77.02 S 126.00 W
Sidli 124 26.33 N 90.16 E
Sidman 214 40.20 N 78.45 W
Sidmouth 42 50.41 N 3.15 W
Sidnaw 190 46.30 N 88.42 W
Sidney, B.C., Can. 224 48.39 N 123.24 W
Sidney, Il., U.S. 194 40.01 N 88.04 W
Sidney, In., U.S. 216 41.06 N 85.45 W
Sidney, Ia., U.S. 198 40.44 N 95.38 W
Sidney, Mt., U.S. 198 47.43 N 104.09 W
Sidney, Ne., U.S. 198 41.08 N 102.58 W
Sidney, N.Y., U.S. 210 42.18 N 75.23 W
Sidney, Oh., U.S. 216 40.17 N 84.09 W
Sidney Center 210 42.17 N 75.15 W
Sidney Island I 224 48.37 N 123.18 W
Sidney Lanier, Lake ⊜[1] 192 34.15 N 83.57 W
Sido 150 11.40 N 7.36 W
Sidoan 112 0.16 N 120.12 E
Sidoarjo 115a 7.27 S 112.43 E
Sidon 194 33.24 N 90.12 W
Sidon
— Saydā 132 33.33 N 35.22 E
Sidorovo 76 58.48 N 40.58 E
Sidory 80 50.08 N 43.19 E
Sidr, Ra's as- > 142 29.36 N 32.40 E
Sidr, Wādī V 142 29.40 N 32.41 E
Sidra, Gulf of
— Surt, Khalīj c 146 31.30 N 18.00 E
Sidrolândia 255 20.55 S 54.58 W
Sidu, Zhg. 100 23.48 N 117.18 E
Sidu, Zhg. 100 24.12 N 115.15 E
Siduan 106 30.59 N 121.48 E
Siebengebirge ⋏[2] 56 50.40 N 7.14 E
Siebenlehn 54 51.01 N 13.18 E
Sieber 52 51.42 N 10.25 E
Siebnen 58 47.11 N 8.54 E
Siedenbollentin 54 53.44 N 13.23 E
Siedenburg 52 52.41 N 8.56 E
Siedlce 30 52.11 N 22.16 E
Siedlce □[4] 30 52.15 N 22.00 E
Sieg ≃ 56 50.45 N 7.05 E
Siegburg 56 50.47 N 7.12 E
Siegen 56 50.52 N 8.02 E
Siegenburg 60 48.45 N 11.51 E
Siegendorf im Burgenland 61 47.47 N 16.33 E
Siegenfeld 264b 48.02 N 16.10 E
Sieghartskirchen 61 48.15 N 16.01 E
Siegler Springs 226 38.54 N 122.39 W
Siegsdorf 64 47.46 N 12.39 E
Sielbeck 54 54.11 N 10.37 E
Sielenbach 60 48.24 N 11.16 E
Siemens, Cape > 164 1.21 S 149.34 E
Siemensstadt ◆[8] 264a 52.32 N 13.17 E
Siemianowice Śląskie 30 50.19 N 19.01 E
Siemiatycze 30 52.26 N 22.53 E
Siĕmpang 110 14.07 N 106.23 E
Siĕmréab 110 13.22 N 103.51 E
Siems-Dänischburg ◆[8] 54 53.55 N 10.44 E
Siena 66 43.19 N 11.21 E
Siena □[4] 66 43.13 N 11.21 E
Sieniawa 30 50.11 N 22.36 E
Sienna
— Siena 66 43.19 N 11.21 E
Sienyang
— Xianyang 102 34.22 N 108.42 E
Sieradz 30 51.36 N 18.45 E
Sieradz □[4] 30 51.40 N 18.45 E
Sieraków 30 52.39 N 16.04 E
Sierck-les-Bains 56 49.26 N 6.21 E
Sierksdorf 54 54.04 N 10.46 E
Sierning 61 48.03 N 14.19 E
Sierpc 30 52.52 N 19.41 E
Sierra □[6] 226 39.30 N 120.30 W
Sierra Blanca 200 31.11 N 105.21 W
Sierra Blanca Peak ʌ 200 33.23 N 105.48 W
Sierra-Bullones 116 9.51 N 124.20 E
Sierra Chica 252 36.50 S 60.13 W
Sierra City 226 39.33 N 120.37 W
Sierra Colorada 254 40.35 S 67.48 W
Sierra de Agua 232 17.32 N 88.54 W
Sierra de Outes 34 42.51 N 8.54 W
Sierra Gorda 252 22.54 S 69.19 W
Sierra Leona
— Sierra Leone □[1] 150 8.30 N 11.30 W
Sierra Leone □[1], Afr. 134 8.30 N 11.30 W
Sierra Leone □[1], Afr. 150 8.30 N 11.30 W
Sierra Leone Basin ◆[1] 10 5.00 N 17.00 W
Sierra Leone Rise ◆[3] 10 5.30 N 21.00 W
Sierra Madre 228 34.09 N 118.03 W
Sierra Mojada 196 27.17 N 103.42 W
Sierra Nevada, Parque Nacional ♦ 246 8.36 N 70.50 W
Sierra Peak ʌ 280 33.51 N 117.39 W
Sierra San Pedro Mártir, Parque Nacional ♦ 204 31.00 N 115.30 W
Sierras Bayas 252 36.57 S 60.09 W
Sierraville 226 39.35 N 120.21 W
Sierra Vista 200 31.33 N 110.18 W
Sierre 58 46.18 N 7.32 E
Siersleben 54 51.36 N 11.32 E
Siesta Key 220 27.19 N 82.34 W
Siesta Key I 220 27.16 N 82.33 W
Siete Puntas ≃ 252 23.34 S 57.20 W
Siethen 264a 52.17 N 13.13 E
Siethener See ⊜ 264a 52.17 N 13.12 E
Sietow 54 53.26 N 12.35 E
Sieve ≃ 66 43.46 N 11.26 E
Sievering ◆[8] 264b 48.15 N 16.20 E
Siezenheim 64 47.48 N 12.59 E
Sifahandra 114 1.30 N 97.21 E
Sifangtai, Zhg. 89 46.55 N 127.00 E
Sifangtai, Zhg. 104 41.33 N 121.19 E
Sifangtai, Zhg. 104 41.02 N 122.46 E
Sifangtai, Zhg. 104 41.35 N 122.57 E
Sifen 100 27.32 N 113.30 E
Sifeni 144 12.16 N 40.21 E
Sifentoudun 106 32.18 N 121.21 E
Siffu ≃ 116 17.12 N 121.48 E
Sifié 150 7.59 N 6.55 W
Sífnos I 38 36.59 N 24.40 E
Sifón Villanueva 196 27.17 N 100.17 W
Sifton 184 51.21 N 100.07 W
Sig, Alg. 34 35.32 N 0.11 W
Sig, Ross. 24 65.35 N 34.13 E
Si Galangang 114 1.15 N 99.20 E
Šigali 80 55.33 N 48.02 E
Sigean 32 43.02 N 2.59 E
Sigel 214 41.17 N 79.07 W
Sigep 110 1.02 S 98.49 E
Siggebohyttan 40 59.37 N 15.01 E
Sighetu Marmaţiei 38 47.56 N 23.54 E
Sighişoara 38 46.13 N 24.48 E
Sighty Crag ʌ 44 55.07 N 2.37 W
Sigillo 66 43.20 N 12.44 E
Sigiriya 122 7.57 N 80.45 E
Siglan 74 59.02 N 152.25 E
Siglerville 208 40.44 N 77.31 W
Sigli 114 5.23 N 95.57 E
Sigli, Cap > 34 36.54 N 4.46 E
Sigloy 50 47.50 N 2.14 E
Siglufjördur 24a 66.10 N 18.56 W
Sigmaringen 58 48.05 N 9.13 E
Sigmaringendorf 58 48.04 N 9.15 E
Signa 66 43.47 N 11.05 E
Signachi 84 41.37 N 45.54 E
Signalberg ʌ 60 49.28 N 12.32 E
Signal Hill, Ca., U.S. 280 33.47 N 118.09 W
Signal Hill, Il., U.S. 219 38.34 N 90.05 W
Signal Hill National Historic Park ♦ 186 47.35 N 52.40 W
Signal Mountain 194 35.07 N 85.20 W
Signal Mountain ʌ 188 44.12 N 72.20 W
Signal Peak ʌ 200 37.19 N 113.29 W
Signau 58 46.55 N 7.43 E
Signes 62 43.18 N 5.52 E
Signy ◆[3] 9 60.43 S 45.36 W
Signy-l'Abbaye 50 49.42 N 4.25 E
Signy-Le-Petit 50 49.54 N 4.17 E
Šigony 80 53.23 N 48.42 E
Sigourney 190 41.20 N 92.12 W
Sigre ≃ 236 15.49 N 84.38 W
Sigriswil 58 46.43 N 7.42 E
Sigsig 246 3.01 S 78.45 W
Sigtuna 40 59.37 N 17.43 E
Siguanea, Ensenada de la c 240p 21.38 N 83.05 W
Siguatepeque 236 14.32 N 87.49 W
Siguel ≃ 116 5.58 N 125.06 E
Sigüenza 34 41.04 N 2.38 W
Sigües 34 42.38 N 1.00 W
Siguiri 150 11.25 N 9.10 W
Sigulda 76 57.09 N 24.51 E
Sigurd 200 38.50 N 111.58 W
Siguri Falls ʟ 154 8.31 S 37.23 E
Sihabuhabu, Dolok ʌ 114 2.10 N 99.21 E
Sihai 105 40.33 N 116.24 E
Sihala
— Sri Lanka □[1] 122 7.00 N 81.00 E
Sihanoukville
— Kâmpóng Saôm 110 10.38 N 103.30 E
Sihecun 105 39.56 N 117.07 E
Sihepeng 114 1.06 N 99.27 E
Sihl ≃ 58 47.23 N 8.32 E
Sihlepu 158 27.42 S 32.06 E
Sihlsee ⊜ 58 47.07 N 8.47 E
Sihong 100 33.28 N 118.11 E
Sihor 120 21.42 N 71.58 E
Sihorā 124 23.29 N 80.07 E
Sihu 98 34.38 N 117.59 E
Sihuas 248 8.34 S 77.37 W
Sihuas ≃ 248 16.37 S 72.19 W
Sihui 102 23.19 N 112.40 E
Sihŭng ◆[8] 271b 37.28 N 126.54 E
Šiiči 78 52.15 N 29.14 E
Siikajoki ≃ 26 64.50 N 24.44 E
Siilinjärvi 26 63.05 N 27.40 E
Si'īr 132 31.35 N 35.09 E
Siirt 130 37.56 N 41.57 E
Siirt □[4] 128 38.00 N 42.00 E
Sija 24 63.38 N 41.38 E
Sijā ≃ 124 29.08 N 81.35 E
Sijbekarspel 52 52.43 N 4.59 E
Sijiaba 106 32.02 N 121.18 E
Sijianfang 104 42.29 N 122.17 E
Sijiao Shan I 100 30.41 N 122.28 E
Sijiazi 98 41.47 N 120.06 E
Sijing 106 31.07 N 121.16 E
Sijunjung 112 0.42 S 100.58 E
Sijupu 107 30.02 N 106.18 E
Sik 114 5.49 N 100.44 E
Sika 115b 8.45 S 122.12 E
Sikalongo 154 16.46 S 27.07 E
Sikandarābād 124 28.27 N 77.42 E
Sikandarpur, India 272a 28.42 N 77.21 E
Sikandarpur, India 272b 22.57 N 88.12 E
Sikandra 124 24.57 N 86.02 E
Sikandra Rao 124 27.42 N 78.24 E
Sikanni Chief ≃ 176 58.20 N 121.50 W
Sikao 110 7.34 N 99.21 E
Sīkar 120 27.37 N 75.09 E
Sikarpur 272b 22.36 N 88.32 E
Sikasso 150 11.19 N 5.40 W
Sikasso □[4] 150 10.55 N 7.00 W
Sikéai 38 36.46 N 22.56 E
Sikelenge 152 14.50 S 24.14 E
Sikeli 112 5.16 S 121.48 E
Sikensi 150 5.40 N 4.34 W
Sikeshu 86 44.25 N 84.14 E
Sikeston 194 36.52 N 89.35 W
Sikfors 40 59.48 N 14.35 E
Si Khiu 110 14.53 N 101.44 E
Sikiá 38 40.02 N 23.56 E
Sikiang
— Xi ≃ 102 22.25 N 113.23 E
Sikijang 114 4.22 N 98.02 E
Siking
— Xi'an 102 34.15 N 108.52 E
Síkinos 38 36.39 N 25.06 E
Síkinos I 38 36.39 N 25.06 E
Sikión ⊥ 38 37.59 N 22.44 E
Sikkim □[3] 124 27.35 N 88.35 E
Siklós ⊥ 30 45.52 N 18.28 E
Sikonge 154 5.38 S 32.46 E
Sikosi 156 17.59 S 23.19 E
Šikotan, ostrov (Shikotan-tō) I 92a 43.47 N 146.45 E
Sikrod 272a 28.43 N 77.11 E
Sikt'ach 74 69.55 N 125.02 E
Sikuati 112 6.53 N 116.40 E
Sikutu 112 0.53 N 120.37 E
Sil ≃ 34 42.27 N 7.43 W
Šila 86 56.33 N 93.02 E
Silacayoapan 234 17.30 N 98.09 W
Sila Grande ⋏ 68 39.22 N 16.30 E
Sila Greca ⋏ 68 39.30 N 16.30 E
Silai ≃ 126 22.41 N 87.46 E
Silalahi 114 2.48 N 98.32 E
Šilalė 76 55.28 N 22.12 E
Silam, Gunong ʌ 112 4.58 N 118.10 E
Silāmpur ◆[8] 272a 28.40 N 77.16 E
Silandro (Schlanders) 64 46.38 N 10.46 E
Silang 116 14.14 N 120.58 E
Silangcheng 98 42.19 N 115.43 E
Silanus 71 40.17 N 8.53 E
Silao 234 20.56 N 101.26 W
Sila Piccola ⋏ 68 39.05 N 16.35 E
Silas 194 31.45 N 88.19 W
Silat 112 0.21 N 111.47 E
Silat az-Zahr 132 32.19 N 35.11 E
Silau ≃ 114 2.58 N 99.48 E
Silaut 112 2.22 S 101.08 E
Silaw Aihagam, Gunung ʌ 114 5.25 N 95.40 E
Silay 116 10.48 N 122.58 E
Silay, Mount ʌ 116 10.47 N 123.14 E
Silba 36 44.23 N 14.42 E
Silbertal 58 47.05 N 9.59 E
Silchar 120 24.49 N 92.48 E
Šilda, India 126 22.37 N 86.49 E
Sil'da, Ross. 86 51.46 N 59.45 E
Šile 130 41.11 N 29.36 E
Šile ≃ 64 45.33 N 12.27 E
Šileby 42 52.43 N 1.06 W
Silega 24 64.03 N 44.01 E
Silenrieux 50 50.14 N 4.24 E
Silent Lake ⊜ 212 44.55 N 78.04 W
Silent Lake Provincial Park ♦ 212 44.54 N 78.05 W
Siler City 192 35.43 N 79.27 W
Sileru ≃ 122 17.47 N 81.24 E
Silesia □[9] 30 51.00 N 16.45 E
Silet 148 22.44 N 4.37 E
Siletz 202 44.43 N 123.55 W
Siletz ≃ 202 44.54 N 124.00 W
Silex 219 39.07 N 91.03 W
Silgaḍhī 124 29.16 N 80.59 E
Silghāt 120 26.37 N 92.56 E
Silhouette I 138 4.29 S 55.14 E
Siliana 148 36.05 N 9.22 E
Siliana □[8] 148 36.00 N 9.20 E
Siliana, Oued ≃ 36 36.33 N 9.25 E
Silifke 130 36.22 N 33.56 E
Şilijiang 105 39.43 N 117.28 E
Šilikty 86 47.10 N 84.32 E
Silingan, Mount ʌ 116 7.46 N 122.30 E
Siling Co ⊜ 120 31.50 N 89.00 E
Siliqua 71 39.18 N 8.48 E
Silistra 38 44.07 N 27.16 E
Şilivri 130 41.04 N 28.15 E
Šiljak ʌ 38 43.45 N 21.50 E
Siljan ⊜ 26 60.50 N 14.45 E
Şiljansnäs 26 60.45 N 14.42 E
Šilka 88 51.51 N 116.02 E
Šilka ≃ 74 53.22 N 121.32 E
Silkāripāra 126 24.14 N 87.28 E
Silkeborg 41 56.10 N 9.34 E
Silkworth 210 41.16 N 76.05 W
Sill ≃ 64 47.16 N 11.25 E
Sillamäe 76 59.24 N 27.45 E
Sillānwāli 123 31.50 N 72.33 E
Sillaro ≃ 66 44.34 N 11.51 E
Sille 130 37.56 N 32.26 E
Sillem Island I 176 70.55 N 71.30 W
Sillen ⊜ 40 58.59 N 17.22 E
Sillenstede 52 53.34 N 7.59 E
Sillery, P.Q., Can. 206 46.46 N 71.15 W
Sillery, Fr. 50 49.12 N 4.08 E
Silli 150 11.36 N 2.30 W
Sillian 64 46.45 N 12.25 E
Sillil 144 10.59 N 43.26 E
Sillon de Talbert >[1] 32 48.53 N 3.05 W
Silloth 44 54.52 N 3.23 W
Sillustani ⊥ 248 15.45 S 70.05 W
Şilly-le-Long 261 49.06 N 2.48 E
Šil'naja Balka 80 50.34 N 49.01 E
Silnice 60 48.54 N 13.44 E
Siloam Springs 194 36.11 N 94.32 W
Siloam Springs State Park ♦ 219 39.53 N 90.54 W
Şilogui 110 1.14 S 99.00 E
Šilovići 76 55.24 N 32.33 E
Šilovka 80 54.03 N 48.40 E
Šilovo, Ross. 76 55.00 N 33.46 E
Šilovo, Ross. 80 54.19 N 40.53 E
Silowana Plains ≍ 152 17.00 S 23.15 E
Silphuh 126 23.44 N 86.22 E
Silsbee 194 30.20 N 94.10 W
Silsby Lake ⊜ 184 55.29 N 95.46 W
Silschede 263 51.21 N 7.19 E
Silsden 44 53.55 N 1.55 W
Sils im Engadin 58 46.22 N 9.46 E
Silton 184 50.48 N 104.55 W
Siluas 112 1.17 N 109.51 E
Şiluko 150 6.31 N 5.09 E
Šilutė 76 55.21 N 21.29 E
Silvacane, Abbaye de ⊥[1] 62 43.44 N 5.20 E
Silvan (Miyafarkin) 130 38.08 N 41.01 E
Silvana 224 48.12 N 122.15 W
Sīlvāneh 128 37.25 N 44.51 E
Silvânia 255 16.42 S 48.38 W
Silvano d'Orba 62 44.41 N 8.40 E
Silvan Reservoir ⊜[1] 169 37.50 S 145.25 E
Silvaplana 58 46.26 N 9.47 E
Silvassa 122 20.17 N 73.00 E
Silveiras 256 22.40 S 44.52 W
Silver 196 32.04 N 100.40 W
Silverado 228 33.45 N 117.35 W
Silver Bank ✦[2] 238 20.30 N 69.45 W
Silver Bank Passage ʁ 238 20.45 N 70.15 W
Silver Bay 190 47.17 N 91.15 W
Silver Bell 200 32.23 N 111.29 W
Silver City, N.M., U.S. 200 32.46 N 108.16 W
Silver City, N.C., U.S. 192 35.00 N 79.12 W
Silver Creek, Ms., U.S. 194 31.36 N 89.59 W
Silver Creek, Ne., U.S. 198 41.18 N 97.39 W
Silver Creek, N.Y., U.S. 214 42.32 N 79.10 W
Silver Creek ≃, Az., U.S. 200 34.44 N 110.02 W
Silver Creek ≃, Ca., U.S. 226 38.47 N 120.35 W
Silver Creek ≃, Ca., U.S. 226 36.36 N 120.41 W
Silver Creek ≃, Il., U.S. 219 38.20 N 89.52 W
Silver Creek ≃, Il., U.S. 278 41.54 N 87.50 W
Silver Creek ≃, In., U.S. 218 38.17 N 85.47 W
Silver Creek ≃, In., U.S. 218 39.36 N 84.59 W
Silver Creek ≃, Ky., U.S. 192 37.48 N 84.30 W
Silver Creek ≃, Or., U.S. 202 43.16 N 119.13 W
Silver Creek ≃, Wa., U.S. 224 46.32 N 121.55 W
Silver Creek, Muddy Fork ≃ 218 38.25 N 86.44 W
Silver Creek, South Fork ≃ 226 38.49 N 120.27 W
Silverdale, B.C., Can. 224 49.09 N 122.24 W
Silverdale, N.Z. 172 36.37 S 174.40 E
Silverdale, Eng., U.K. 44 54.10 N 2.49 W
Silverdale, Pa., U.S. 208 40.21 N 75.16 W
Silverdale, Wa., U.S. 224 47.38 N 122.41 W
Silverdalen 26 57.32 N 15.44 E
Silverdome ♦ 281 42.39 N 83.15 W
Silver End 42 51.51 N 0.37 E
Silver Falls State Park ♦ 202 44.48 N 122.50 W
Silverfields 273d 26.07 S 27.49 E
Silver Fork ≃ 219 39.06 N 92.21 W
Silver Grove 218 39.02 N 84.23 W
Silver Hill 284c 38.50 N 76.56 W
Silverhope Creek ≃ 224 49.18 N 121.27 W
Silver Lake, Ca., U.S. 226 38.38 N 120.07 W
Silver Lake, In., U.S. 216 41.04 N 85.53 W
Silver Lake, Ks., U.S. 198 39.06 N 95.51 W
Silver Lake, Ma., U.S. 207 42.34 N 71.11 W
Silver Lake, Mn., U.S. 190 44.54 N 94.11 W
Silver Lake, Oh., U.S. 214 41.09 N 81.27 W
Silver Lake, Or., U.S. 202 43.07 N 121.02 W
Silverlake, Wa., U.S. 224 46.17 N 122.48 W
Silver Lake, Wi., U.S. 216 42.32 N 88.09 W
Silver Lake ⊜, Ca., U.S. 226 38.39 N 120.07 W
Silver Lake ⊜, De., U.S. 208 39.11 N 75.32 W
Silver Lake ⊜, Ma., U.S. 283 42.01 N 70.48 W
Silver Lake ⊜, N.Y., U.S. 210 42.42 N 78.02 W
Silver Lake ⊜, N.Y., U.S. 276 41.03 N 73.45 W
Silver Lake ⊜, Or., U.S. 202 43.06 N 120.53 W
Silver Lake ⊜, Or., U.S. 202 43.22 N 119.24 W
Silver Lake ⊜, Wa., U.S. 224 46.17 N 122.47 W
Silver Lake ⊜, Wa., U.S. 224 48.58 N 122.04 W
Silver Lake Park ♦ 276 41.03 N 73.45 W
Silver Lake Reservoir ⊜[1], Ca., U.S. 280 34.06 N 118.16 W
Silver Lake Reservoir ⊜[1], N.Y., U.S. 276 40.37 N 74.06 W
Silvermine ≃ 276 41.08 N 73.26 W
Silver Mine Bay c 271d 22.16 N 114.00 E
Silvermine Brook ≃ 276 41.08 N 73.27 W
Silvermine Mountains ⋏ 48 52.45 N 8.15 W
Silvermines 48 52.47 N 8.13 W
Silver Mountain ʌ 280 34.12 N 117.52 W
Silver Peak ʌ 228 33.28 N 118.35 W
Silver Peak Range ⋏ 204 37.35 N 117.45 W
Silver Spring, Md., U.S. 208 38.59 N 77.01 W
Silver Spring, Pa., U.S. 208 40.04 N 76.26 W
Silver Springs, Nv., U.S. 226 39.24 N 119.13 W
Silver Springs, N.Y., U.S. 210 42.39 N 78.05 W
Silver Springs State Park ♦ 216 41.38 N 88.32 W
Silver Star Mountain ʌ 224 48.33 N 120.35 W
Silver Star Provincial Park ♦ 182 50.22 N 119.05 W
Silverstone 42 52.05 N 1.02 W
Silver Streams 158 28.20 S 23.33 E
Silverthrone Mountain ʌ 182 51.31 N 126.06 W
Silvertip Mountain ʌ 202 47.47 N 113.15 W
Silverton, Austl. 166 31.53 S 141.13 E
Silverton, B.C., Can. 182 49.57 N 117.21 W
Silverton, Eng., U.K. 42 50.48 N 3.28 W
Silverton, Co., U.S. 200 37.48 N 107.39 W
Silverton, N.J., U.S. 208 40.00 N 74.08 W
Silverton, Oh., U.S. 218 39.12 N 84.24 W
Silverton, Or., U.S. 224 45.00 N 122.46 W
Silverton, Tx., U.S. 196 34.28 N 101.19 W
Silverwood Lake ⊜[1] 228 34.18 N 117.19 W
Silves 34 37.11 N 8.26 W
Silvi 66 42.34 N 14.05 E
Silvia 246 2.37 N 76.21 W
Silvianópolis 256 22.02 S 45.50 W
Silvícola 164 8.39 S 126.59 E
Silvies ≃ 202 43.22 N 118.48 W
Silview 285 39.42 N 75.37 W
Silvolde 52 51.54 N 6.53 E
Silvretta Gruppe ⋏ 58 46.50 N 10.10 E
Sim 86 54.59 N 57.41 E
Sim, Cap > 148 31.23 N 9.51 W
Sima, Comores 157a 12.11 S 44.17 E
Sima, Ross. 80 56.41 N 39.33 E
Simaltala 124 24.43 N 86.33 E
Simanggang 112 1.15 N 111.26 E
Simangumban 114 1.42 N 99.10 E
Şimanoviči 76 53.05 N 28.38 E
Šimanovsk 89 52.00 N 127.42 E
Simao 102 22.50 N 101.00 E
Simão Dias 250 10.44 S 37.49 W
Simão Pereira 256 21.58 S 43.19 W
Simara Island I 116 12.48 N 122.03 E
Simard, Lac ⊜ 190 47.37 N 78.41 W
Simaria Kalān 124 24.04 N 84.56 E
Simatang, Pulau I 112 1.04 N 120.23 E
Simav 130 39.05 N 28.59 E
Simav ≃ 130 40.23 N 28.31 E
Simav Gölü ⊜ 130 39.09 N 28.55 E
Simaxis 71 39.56 N 8.41 E
Simba, Kenya 154 2.10 S 37.36 E
Simba, Tan. 154 1.44 S 34.13 E
Simba, Zaïre 152 0.36 N 22.55 E
Simbach 60 48.34 N 12.45 E
Simbach am Inn 60 48.16 N 13.01 E
Simbario 68 38.37 N 16.20 E
Simberi Island I 164 2.40 S 152.00 E
Simbirsk
— Uljanovsk 80 54.20 N 48.24 E
Simbo, Tan. 154 4.53 S 29.44 E
Simbo, Tan. 154 4.40 S 33.27 E
Simbo Island I 175e 8.17 S 156.33 E
Simbruini, Monti ⋏ 66 41.55 N 13.15 E
Simcoe 212 42.50 N 80.18 W
Simcoe □[6] 212 44.25 N 79.50 W
Simcoe, Lake ⊜ 212 44.20 N 79.20 W
Simcoe Creek ≃ 224 46.22 N 120.36 W
Simcoe Island I 212 44.10 N 76.31 W
Simcoe Point > 275b 43.49 N 79.01 W
Simdega 124 22.37 N 84.31 E
Simeiz 78 44.26 N 34.01 E
Simen 104 40.44 N 123.49 E
Simeng 107 29.56 N 103.43 E
Simen Mountains National Park ♦ 144 13.08 N 38.15 E
Simenti 150 13.00 N 13.25 W
Simeri ≃ 68 38.52 N 16.43 E
Simeria 38 45.51 N 23.01 E
Simeto ≃ 70 37.24 N 15.06 E
Simeulue, Pulau I 114 2.33 N 96.05 E
Simferopol' 78 44.57 N 34.06 E
Sími 38 36.36 N 27.50 E
Sími I 38 36.35 N 27.52 E
Simi, Arroyo ≃ 228 34.16 N 118.39 W
Simiane 62 43.25 N 5.26 E
Simianshan 107 28.49 N 105.09 E
Simikot 124 29.58 N 81.50 E
Similkameen ≃ 182 48.56 N 119.26 W
Simingchang 107 29.02 N 105.45 E
Simiri 150 14.08 N 2.08 E
Simisa Island I 116 5.57 N 121.35 E
Simití 246 7.58 N 73.57 W
Simi Valley 228 34.16 N 118.47 W
Simiyu ≃ 154 2.33 S 33.25 E
Simizu
— Shimizu 94 35.01 N 138.29 E
Simla, India 272b 22.47 N 88.16 E
Simla, India 272b 22.54 N 88.22 E
Simla, Co., U.S. 198 39.08 N 104.05 W
Simla ◆[8] 272b 22.35 N 88.22 E
Simlāpāl 126 22.55 N 87.05 E
Şimleu Silvaniei 38 47.14 N 22.48 E
Šimlipālgarh 126 21.51 N 86.23 E
Simme ≃ 58 46.41 N 7.38 E
Simmelsdorf 60 49.36 N 11.21 E
Simmental V 58 46.37 N 7.25 E
Simmerath 56 50.36 N 6.18 E
Simmerberg 58 47.35 N 9.56 E
Simmering ◆[8] 264b 48.11 N 16.25 E
Simmern 56 49.59 N 7.31 E
Simmesport 194 30.59 N 91.48 W
Simmie 184 49.57 N 108.06 W
Simmons Island I 282 38.06 N 121.58 W
Simmons Point > 282 38.03 N 121.56 W
Simmonswood Moss ◆[3] 262 53.30 N 2.50 W
Simms 202 47.29 N 111.55 W
Simnas 76 54.24 N 23.39 E
Simoca 252 27.16 S 65.21 W
Simões 250 7.36 S 40.49 W
Simojärvi ⊜ 26 66.06 N 27.03 E
Simojoki ≃ 26 65.37 N 25.03 E
Simojovel 234 17.12 N 92.38 W
Simon, Lac ⊜, P.Q., Can. 206 45.58 N 75.05 W
Simon, Lac ⊜, P.Q., Can. 206 46.10 N 74.45 W
Simón Bolívar, Aeropuerto Internacional ⊠ 286c 10.37 N 66.59 W
Simoneti 84 42.14 N 42.52 E
Simonette ≃ 182 55.07 N 118.00 W
Simonhouse Lake ⊜ 184 54.30 N 101.10 W
Simonicha 80 56.31 N 53.50 E
Simoniči 78 51.53 N 28.04 E
Simonoseki
— Shimonoseki 96 33.57 N 130.57 E
Simonsbath 42 51.09 N 3.45 W
Simonson Brook ≃ 276 40.26 N 74.37 W
Simonstone 262 53.48 N 2.20 W
Simonstorp 40 58.47 N 16.09 E
Simon's Town 158 34.14 S 18.26 E
Simonton Lake 216 41.44 N 85.59 W
Şimoom Sound 182 50.45 N 126.29 W
Šimorskoje 80 55.19 N 42.02 E
Simpang, Indon. 112 1.16 S 104.05 E
Simpang, Indon. 112 1.03 S 110.06 E
Simpang, Indon. 112 0.09 N 103.15 E
Simpangampat 114 2.55 N 99.43 E
Simpang Empat 114 6.20 N 100.11 E
Simpang-kanan ≃ 114 2.21 N 97.51 E
Simpang-kiri ≃ 114 2.21 N 97.51 E
Simpang Rengam 114 1.50 N 103.19 E
Simpangtiga 114 2.23 N 99.47 E
Simpangulim 114 5.06 N 97.32 E
Simpele 26 61.26 N 29.22 E
Simplício Mendes 250 7.51 S 41.54 W
Simplon Pass)(58 46.15 N 8.02 E
Simplon Tunnel ◆[5] 58 46.15 N 8.05 E
Simpnäs 40 59.52 N 19.04 E
Simp'o-ri 98 38.36 N 127.41 E
Simpson, La., U.S. 194 31.14 N 93.00 W
Simpson, Pa., U.S. 210 41.35 N 75.29 W
Simpson ≃ 254 45.25 S 72.32 W
Simpson, Isla I 254 45.53 S 73.48 W
Simpson Desert ◆[2] 162 25.00 S 137.00 E
Simpson Desert National Park ♦ 162 25.40 S 138.15 E
Simpson Island I 190 48.48 N 87.40 W
Simpson Lake ⊜ 180 68.10 N 126.35 W
Simpson Peak ʌ 180 59.44 N 131.27 W
Simpson Peninsula >[1] 176 68.34 N 88.45 W
Simpsons Gap National Park ♦ 162 23.40 S 133.45 E
Simpson Strait ʁ 176 68.27 N 97.45 W
Simpsonville, Ky., U.S. 218 38.13 N 85.21 W
Simpsonville, Md., U.S. 208 39.11 N 76.52 W
Simpsonville, S.C., U.S. 192 34.44 N 82.15 W
Simrishamn 26 55.33 N 14.20 E
Sims 216 40.30 N 85.51 W
Şimsbury 207 41.52 N 72.48 W
Šimsk 76 58.13 N 30.43 E
Simssee ⊜ 64 47.52 N 12.14 E
Simunjan 112 1.23 N 110.45 E
Simurāli 126 23.03 N 88.30 E
Simušir, ostrov I 74 46.58 N 152.02 E
Sīnā' □[4] 142 30.15 N 32.40 E
Sīna ≃ 122 17.22 N 75.54 E
Sīnā', Shibh Jazīrat (Sinai Peninsula) >[1] 140 29.30 N 34.00 E
Sinabang 114 2.29 N 96.23 E
Sinabelkirchen 61 47.06 N 15.50 E
Sinabung, Gunung ʌ 114 3.10 N 98.24 E
Sinadhago 144 5.22 N 46.20 E
Sinagra 70 38.05 N 14.51 E
Sinai, Mount ʌ 241k 12.04 N 61.42 W
Sinai, Mount
— Mūsā, Jabal ʌ 140 28.32 N 33.59 E
Sinaia 38 45.21 N 25.33 E
Sinai Peninsula
— Sīnā', Shibh Jazīrat >[1] 140 29.30 N 34.00 E
Sin'aja ≃, Europe 76 57.10 N 28.31 E
Sin'aja ≃, Ross. 74 61.06 N 126.50 E
Sinajana 174p 13.28 N 144.45 E
Sinako, Mount ʌ 116 7.30 N 125.17 E
Sinaloa □[3] 232 25.00 N 107.30 W
Sinaloa ≃ 232 25.18 N 108.30 W
Sinalunga 66 43.12 N 11.44 E
Sinamaica 246 11.05 N 71.51 W
Sinamary ≃ 250 5.27 N 53.00 W
Sinan, Tür. 130 37.52 N 41.00 E
Sinan, Zhg. 102 27.54 N 108.18 E
Sinanju 98 39.36 N 125.36 E
Sinanpaşa 130 38.45 N 30.15 E
Sīnarū 142 29.22 N 30.45 E
Sinatle 84 42.28 N 43.04 E
Sin'avka, Bela. 76 52.58 N 26.29 E
Sin'avka, Ross. 83 47.17 N 39.17 E
Sīnāwin 146 31.02 N 10.36 E
Sinbad Creek ≃ 282 37.35 N 121.53 W
Sinbaungwe 110 19.43 N 95.10 E
Sinbo 110 24.46 N 97.03 E
Sinbokchang 98 41.01 N 128.54 E
Sincan, Tür. 130 39.28 N 37.54 E
Sincan, Tür. 130 39.59 N 32.26 E
Sincé 246 9.15 N 75.09 W
Sincelejo 246 9.18 N 75.24 W
Sinch'ang, C.M.I.K. 98 40.07 N 128.28 E
Sinch'ang, C.M.I.K. 98 40.19 N 125.27 E
Sinch'ŏn 98 38.22 N 125.28 E
Sinch'ŏn-ni 271b 37.27 N 126.48 E
Sinclair 200 41.46 N 107.06 W
Sinclair, Lake ⊜[1] 192 33.11 N 83.16 W
Sinclair, Point > 162 32.06 S 133.00 E
Sinclair Island I 224 48.37 N 122.40 W
Sinclair Mills 182 54.02 N 121.41 W
Sinclair's Bay c 46 58.30 N 3.07 W
Sinclairville 214 42.15 N 79.15 W
Sind □[4] 120 25.30 N 69.00 E
Sind ≃ 124 26.26 N 79.13 E
Sinda 89 48.57 N 136.18 E
Sindal 26 57.28 N 10.13 E
Sindangan 116 8.14 N 123.00 E
Sindangan ≃ 116 8.13 N 123.00 E
Sindangan Bay c 116 8.11 N 122.50 E
Sindangan Point > 116 8.10 N 122.40 E

Symbols in the index entries represent the broad categories identified in the key at the right. Symbols with superior numbers (⋏[1]) identify subcategories (see complete key on page *I* · *1*).

Symbole im Register stellen die rechts im Schlüssel erklärten Kategorien dar. Symbole mit hochgestellten Ziffern (⋏[1]) bezeichnen Unterabteilungen einer Kategorie (vgl. vollständiger Schlüssel auf Seite *I* · *1*).

Los símbolos incluídos en el texto del índice representan las grandes categorías identificadas con la clave a la derecha. Los símbolos con numeros en su parte superior (⋏[1]) identifican las subcategorías (véase la clave completa en la página *I* · *1*).

Les symboles de l'index représentent les catégories indiquées dans la légende à droite. Les symboles suivis d'un indice (⋏[1]) représentent des sous-catégories (voir légende complète à la page *I* · *1*).

Os símbolos incluídos no texto do índice representam as grandes categorias identificadas com a chave à direita. Os símbolos com números em sua parte superior (⋏[1]) identificam as subcategorias (veja-se a chave completa à página *I* · *1*).

	English	Deutsch	Español	Français	Português
ʌ	Mountain	Berg	Montaña	Montagne	Montanha
⋏	Mountains	Gebirge	Montañas	Montagnes	Montanhas
)(	Pass	Paß	Paso	Col	Passo
V	Valley, Canyon	Tal, Cañon	Valle, Cañón	Vallée, Canyon	Vale, Canhão
≍	Plain	Ebene	Llano	Plaine	Planície
>	Cape	Kap	Cabo	Cap	Cabo
I	Island	Insel	Isla	Île	Ilha
II	Islands	Inseln	Islas	Îles	Ilhas
⊥	Other Topographic Features	Andere Topographische Objekte	Otros Elementos Topográficos	Autres données topographiques	Outros acidentes topográficos

ESPAÑOL / FRANÇAIS / PORTUGUÊS

Nombre / Nom / Nome	Página / Page	Lat.°′	Long.°′ W = Oeste / W = Ouest
Sindangbarang	115a	7.27 S	107.08 E
Sindara	152	1.02 S	10.40 E
Sindari	120	25.35 N	71.55 E
Sindelfingen	56	48.42 N	9.00 E
Sindèr	150	14.29 N	1.22 E
Sindhnūr	122	15.47 N	76.46 E
Sindhulī Māḿdi	124	27.16 N	85.58 E
Sindi	76	58.24 N	24.40 E
Sindia	71	40.18 N	8.39 E
Sindingale	110	18.17 N	94.25 E
Sındıran	130	39.17 N	32.41 E
Sındırgı	130	39.14 N	28.10 E
Sindiyūn	142	30.15 N	31.12 E
Sin-do I	98	39.48 N	124.14 E
Sindŏk	98	36.47 N	126.10 E
Sindor	24	62.50 N	51.57 E
Sindou	150	10.40 N	5.10 W
Sindri	126	23.45 N	86.42 E
Sind Sāgar Doāb ⋏[1]	123	31.30 N	71.30 E
Sine V	150	14.10 N	16.28 W
Sinegorje	24	59.42 N	50.40 E
Sinegorsk	89	47.10 N	142.30 E
Şinegorskij	78	48.00 N	40.53 E
Šine-Ider	88	48.56 N	99.33 E
Sinekçi	130	40.16 N	27.24 E
Sinekli	130	41.14 N	28.12 E
Sinel'nikovo	78	48.20 N	35.31 E
Sinendé	150	10.21 N	2.23 E
Sinen'kije	80	51.15 N	45.46 E
Sinepuxent Bay ᑕ	208	38.16 N	75.09 W
Sines	34	37.57 N	8.52 W
Sines, Cabo de ≻	34	37.57 N	8.53 W
Sinevir	78	48.30 N	23.38 E
Sinevka	78	50.33 N	34.06 E
Sinewit, Mount ∧	164	4.40 S	152.00 E
Sinez'orki	76	53.02 N	34.26 E
Sinfra	150	6.37 N	5.55 W
Singair	126	23.49 N	90.08 E
Singako	146	9.50 N	19.29 E
Singal	123	36.06 N	73.53 E
Singalamwe	156	17.41 S	23.23 E
Singālila ∧	124	27.13 N	88.01 E
Singālila Range ⋏	124	27.25 N	88.05 E
Singaparna	115a	7.21 S	108.06 E
Singapore, Sing.	114	1.17 N	103.51 E
Singapore, Sing.	271c	1.17 N	103.51 E
Singapore □[1], Asia	108	1.22 N	103.48 E
Singapore □[1], Asia	114	1.22 N	103.48 E
Singapore I	271c	1.23 N	103.48 E
Singapore ≏	271c	1.17 N	103.51 E
Singapore, National University of ♉[2]	271c	1.18 N	103.46 E
Singapore Station ◆[5]	271c	1.17 N	103.50 E
Singapore Strait ʮ	112	1.15 N	104.00 E
Singapour → Singapore □[1]	114	1.22 N	103.48 E
Singapur → Singapore	114	1.17 N	103.51 E
Singapur → Singapore □[1]	114	1.22 N	103.48 E
Singaraja	115b	8.07 S	115.06 E
Singarka ≏	265a	59.53 N	29.54 E
Singāti	126	22.44 N	89.43 E
Singatoka	175g	18.08 S	177.30 E
Sing Buri	110	14.53 N	100.25 E
Singe	272b	22.57 N	88.26 E
Singen (Hohentwiel)	58	47.46 N	8.50 E
Singer	194	30.39 N	93.24 W
Singhi	126	23.37 N	87.48 E
Singida	154	4.49 S	34.45 E
Singida □[4]	154	5.30 S	34.30 E
Singing, India	102	28.59 N	94.50 E
Singing, India	120	28.53 N	94.47 E
Singing Tower ♠	220	27.57 N	81.34 W
Singkaling Hkāmti	110	26.00 N	95.42 E
Singkang	112	4.08 S	120.01 E
Singkawang	112	0.54 N	109.00 E
Singkep, Pulau I	112	0.30 S	104.25 E
Singkil	114	2.17 N	97.49 E
Singkuang	114	1.03 N	98.56 E
Singleton, Austl.	170	32.34 S	151.10 E
Singleton, Eng., U.K.	42	50.55 N	0.46 W
Singleton, Mount ∧, Austl.	162	29.28 S	117.18 E
Singleton, Mount ∧, Austl.	162	22.00 S	130.49 E
Singleton Ditch ≊	216	41.10 N	87.37 W
Singlewell or Ifield	260	51.25 N	0.23 E
Singö	40	60.10 N	18.44 E
Singö I	40	60.11 N	18.46 E
Singora → Songkhla	110	7.12 N	100.36 E
Şingorkai	164	5.55 S	146.55 E
Šingoža	86	47.45 N	80.40 E
Singpāra	272b	22.40 N	88.31 E
Singrāmau	124	25.57 N	82.23 E
Singuédeze (Shingwidzi) ≏	156	23.53 S	32.17 E
Singur	126	22.49 N	88.14 E
Sin'gye	98	38.36 N	126.30 E
Sinhai → Lianyungang	98	34.39 N	119.16 E
Sinh Ho	110	22.22 N	103.14 E
Sinhŭng	98	40.11 N	127.34 E
Siniaka-Minia, Réserve de ■	146	10.30 N	18.00 E
Sinicha	83	49.31 N	37.34 E
Siničká ≏	265b	55.50 N	37.19 E
Sinije gory ⋏[2]	80	51.10 N	49.25 E
Sinije Lip'agi	78	51.23 N	38.29 E
Siniloan	116	14.25 N	121.27 E
Sining → Xining	102	36.38 N	101.55 E
Siniscola	71	40.34 N	9.41 E
Sinj	36	43.42 N	16.38 E
Sinjah	140	13.09 N	33.56 E
Sinjai	112	5.07 S	120.15 E
Sinjang-ni	98	39.04 N	127.46 E
Sinjār	128	36.19 N	41.52 E
Sinjār, Jabal ⋏	130	36.25 N	41.40 E
Sinji-do I	98	34.20 N	126.50 E
Sinkan	110	24.08 N	97.01 E
Sinkāt	140	18.50 N	36.50 E
Sinkiang → Xinjiang Uygur Zizhiqu □[4]	90	40.00 N	85.00 E
Sinking ≏	48	53.37 N	8.52 W
Sinking Creek ≏	210	40.51 N	77.34 W
Sinking Spring, Oh., U.S.	218	39.04 N	83.23 W
Sinking Spring, Pa., U.S.	208	40.19 N	76.02 W
Şin'kok-ni	271b	37.37 N	126.46 E
Šinkovo, Ross.	76	56.03 N	31.31 E
Sin'kovo, Ross.	82	54.37 N	38.56 E
Sin'kovo, Ross.	82	56.26 N	36.04 E
Sin'kovo, Ross.	82	56.23 N	37.19 E
Sinks Canyon State Park ♠	200	42.45 N	108.50 W
Sin-le-Noble	50	50.22 N	3.07 E
Sinmak	98	38.25 N	126.14 E
Sinmi-do I	98	39.33 N	124.53 E
Sinn ≏	56	50.03 N	9.42 E
Sinnahwā	142	30.25 N	31.21 E
Sínnai	71	39.18 N	9.12 E
Sinnamahoning	214	41.19 N	78.06 W
Sinnamary	250	5.23 N	52.57 W
Sinnar	122	19.51 N	74.00 E
Sinnemahoning Creek ≏	210	41.15 N	77.54 W
Sinnemahoning Creek, Bennett Branch ≏	210	41.20 N	78.08 W
Sinnemahoning Creek, Driftwood Branch ≏	210	41.20 N	78.08 W
Sinnemahoning Creek, First Fork ≏	210	41.19 N	78.05 W
Sinnersdorf	56	51.01 N	6.49 E
Sinnes	26	58.56 N	6.50 E
Sinni ≏	68	40.09 N	16.42 E
Sînnicolau Mare	38	46.05 N	20.38 E
Sinntal	56	50.18 N	9.38 E
Sinnūris	142	29.25 N	30.52 E
Sinnyŏng	98	36.04 N	128.46 E
Sino, Pedra do ∧	256	22.30 S	43.03 W
Sinoie, Lacul ⊜	38	44.38 N	28.53 E
Sinop, Bra.	250	11.55 S	55.35 W
Sinop, Tür.	130	42.01 N	35.09 E
Sinop □[4]	130	41.40 N	34.50 E
Sinop Burnu ≻	130	42.02 N	35.12 E
Sinp'a	98	41.24 N	127.46 E
Sinp'o	98	40.03 N	128.12 E
Sins	58	47.11 N	8.23 E
Sinsang	98	39.38 N	127.25 E
Sinsen	263	51.40 N	7.11 E
Sinsheim	56	49.15 N	8.53 E
Sinsiang → Xinxiang	98	35.20 N	113.51 E
Sinsin	56	50.17 N	5.15 E
Sinsi-ri	98	39.59 N	124.58 E
Sinskoje	74	61.08 N	126.48 E
Sinspelt	56	49.58 N	6.19 E
Sint-Amandsberg	50	51.04 N	3.45 E
Sintana	38	46.21 N	21.30 E
Sint-Andries	50	51.12 N	3.10 E
Sintang	112	0.04 N	111.30 E
Sint Annaland	52	51.36 N	4.06 E
Sint Annaparochie	52	53.16 N	5.39 E
Sint Anthonis	52	51.37 N	5.52 E
Sint Christoffelberg ∧[2]	241s	12.20 N	69.08 W
Sint-Denijs-Westrem	50	51.01 N	3.40 E
Sint Eustatius I	238	17.30 N	62.59 W
Sint-Gillis-Waas	50	51.13 N	4.08 E
Sint Helenabaai ᑕ	158	32.43 S	18.05 E
Sint-Joris-Weert	56	50.48 N	4.39 E
Sint-Joris-Winge	56	50.55 N	4.52 E
Sint-Katelijne-Waver	56	51.04 N	4.32 E
Sint-Kruis, Bel.	50	51.13 N	3.15 E
Sint Kruis, Ned. Ant.	241s	12.18 N	69.08 W
Sint-Lenaarts	56	51.21 N	4.41 E
Sint Maarten	52	52.46 N	4.44 E
Sint Maarten (Saint-Martin) I	238	18.04 N	63.04 W
Sint Maartensdijk	52	51.33 N	4.05 E
Sint-Michiels	50	51.11 N	3.12 E
Sint Michielsgestel	52	51.38 N	5.21 E
Sint Nicolaas	241s	12.27 N	69.52 W
Sint-Niklaas (Saint-Nicolas)	50	51.10 N	4.08 E
Sint-Oedenrode	52	51.34 N	5.27 E
Sinton	196	28.02 N	97.30 W
Sintong	114	1.31 N	100.58 E
Sint Pancras	52	52.39 N	4.46 E
Sint-Pieters-Leeuw	50	50.47 N	4.14 E
Sintra	34	38.48 N	9.23 W
Sintra, Serra de ⋏[2]	266c	38.47 N	9.25 W
Sintra Granjo do Marquez, Aeroporto ⊠	266c	38.49 N	9.20 W
Sint-Truiden	56	50.48 N	5.12 E
Sint Willebrord	52	51.33 N	4.35 E
Sinú ≏	246	9.24 N	75.49 W
Sin'ucha ≏, Ross.	84	44.45 N	40.58 E
Sin'ucha ≏, Ukr.	78	48.03 N	30.51 E
Sin'uga	88	57.45 N	115.13 E
Sinŭiju	98	40.05 N	124.24 E
Sinujif	144	8.33 N	48.59 E
Sinŭp, C.M.I.K.	98	39.54 N	126.47 E
Sinŭp, Taehan	98	37.54 N	127.12 E
Sinwŏn-ni	98	38.13 N	125.44 E
Sinzig	56	50.32 N	7.15 E
Sinzing	60	49.00 N	12.02 E
Sió ≏, Magy.	30	46.20 N	18.55 E
Sio ≏, Togo	150	6.17 N	1.13 E
Siocon	116	7.42 N	122.08 E
Siófok	30	46.54 N	18.04 E
Sioma	152	16.39 S	23.30 E
Sioma Ngweze National Park ♠	152	17.15 S	23.20 E
Sion (Sitten)	58	46.14 N	7.21 E
Sionascaig, Loch ⊜	46	58.04 N	5.11 W
Sion Mills	48	54.47 N	7.29 W
Sioule ≏	32	46.22 N	3.19 E
Sioux Center	198	43.04 N	96.10 W
Sioux City	198	42.30 N	96.24 W
Sioux Falls	198	43.33 N	96.42 W
Sioux Lookout	184	50.06 N	91.55 W
Sioux Narrows	184	49.25 N	94.06 W
Sioux Rapids	198	42.53 N	95.09 W
Sipalay	116	9.45 N	122.24 E
Sipalay ≏	116	9.46 N	122.24 E
Sipaliwini □[5]	250	4.00 N	56.00 W
Sipaliwini ≏	250	2.22 N	56.50 W
Sipaozi	104	41.26 N	122.13 E
Sipapo ≏	246	5.03 N	67.48 W
Şiparia	241r	10.08 N	61.30 W
Šipčenski prohod)(	38	42.46 N	25.19 E
Şipek	130	40.14 N	41.29 E
Šipes	220	28.48 N	81.14 W
Şipesville	214	40.06 N	79.06 W
Şipicyno, Ross.	24	61.17 N	46.28 E
Şipicyno, Ross.	86	56.04 N	77.18 E
Šipilovo	82	54.49 N	37.32 E
Siping	89	43.12 N	124.20 E
Sipingjie	98	42.31 N	125.08 E
Sipirok	114	1.37 N	99.16 E
Sipitang	112	5.05 N	115.33 E
Sipiwesk	184	55.27 N	97.24 W
Sipiwesk Lake ⊜	184	55.05 N	97.35 W
Siple ♉[3]	9	75.56 S	84.15 W
Siple, Mount ∧	9	73.15 S	126.06 W
Siple Coast ⩳[2]	9	82.00 S	153.00 W
Sipocot	116	13.46 N	122.58 E
Sipofaneni	158	26.41 S	31.41 E
Sipot	114	4.31 N	96.02 E
Şipoteny	78	47.18 N	28.11 E
Šipovatoje	78	49.56 N	37.24 E
Sipplingen	58	47.47 N	9.05 E
Si Prachan	110	14.37 N	100.09 E
Sipsey ≏	194	33.00 N	88.10 W
Sipsey Creek ≏	194	33.53 N	88.17 W
Sipu	98	40.48 N	113.43 E
Şipul	164	5.50 S	148.45 E
Šipunovo	86	52.13 N	82.17 E
Šipunskij, mys ≻	74	53.06 N	160.02 E
Sipupus	114	1.25 N	99.31 E
Sipura, Pulau I	112	2.12 S	99.40 E
Siqian, Zhg.	100	22.31 N	112.52 E
Siqian, Zhg.	100	24.40 N	114.06 E
Siqueira Campos	255	23.42 S	49.50 W
Siquia ≏	236	12.09 N	84.13 W
Siquijor	116	9.13 N	123.30 E
Siquijor □[4]	116	9.11 N	123.34 E
Siquijor Island I	116	9.11 N	123.34 E
Siquirres	236	10.06 N	83.30 W
Siquisique	246	10.34 N	69.42 W
Sīra, India	122	13.45 N	76.54 E
Şira, Nor.	26	58.25 N	6.38 E
Šira, Ross.	86	54.29 N	89.56 E
Sira ≏	26	58.17 N	6.24 E
Si Racha	110	13.10 N	100.56 E
Siracuas	248	21.03 S	61.46 W
Siracusa (Syracuse)	70	37.04 N	15.17 E
Siracusa □[4]	70	37.03 N	15.00 E
Sir Adam Beck II Reservoir ⊜[1]	284a	43.08 N	79.04 W
Şirāhā	124	26.39 N	86.12 E
Šir'aj	80	49.34 N	44.07 E
Šir'ajevo	78	47.23 N	30.13 E
Sirājganj	124	24.27 N	89.43 E
Sir Alexander, Mount ∧	182	53.56 N	120.23 W
Sirāmpur	126	24.08 N	86.20 E
Şiran	130	40.12 N	39.08 E
Sirasso	150	9.16 N	6.06 W
Sirault	50	50.30 N	3.47 E
Siraway	116	7.34 N	122.08 E
Sirba ≏	150	13.46 N	1.40 E
Şīr Banī Yās I	128	24.19 N	52.37 E
Sir Colin Mackenzie Wildlife Sanctuary ◆[4]	169	37.40 S	145.32 E
Sirdalsvatn ⊜	26	58.33 N	6.41 E
Sīrdān	128	36.39 N	49.12 E
Şirdar	182	49.15 N	116.37 W
Širdkoje	78	48.08 N	34.49 E
Sir Douglas, Mount ∧	182	50.44 N	115.20 W
Sire	144	9.00 N	36.55 E
Sir Edward Pellew Group II	164	15.40 S	136.48 E
Şirega	76	60.10 N	41.15 E
Sireniki	180	64.25 N	173.57 W
Sirente, Monte ∧	66	42.09 N	13.36 E
Siret	38	47.57 N	26.04 E
Siret ≏	38	45.24 N	28.01 E
Sirevåg	26	58.30 N	5.47 E
Sir Francis Drake, Mount ∧	182	50.48 N	124.47 W
Sir Francis Drake Channel ʮ	240m	18.25 N	64.30 W
Sirghāyā	132	33.48 N	36.09 E
Sirḥān, Wādī as- V	128	30.30 N	38.00 E
Sirhind	124	30.39 N	76.23 E
Sirhind Canal ≊	123	30.47 N	76.01 E
Siria → Syria □[1]	128	35.00 N	38.00 E
Sirik, Tanjong ≻	112	2.46 N	111.19 E
Sirikit Reservoir ⊜[1]	110	17.50 N	100.30 E
Şirina I	130	36.21 N	26.42 E
Šiṙinguši	80	53.51 N	42.46 E
Sirino, Monte ∧	68	40.08 N	15.50 E
Siriya-zaki ≻	92	41.26 N	141.28 E
Sir James MacBrien, Mount ∧	180	62.07 N	127.41 W
Sīrjān	128	29.27 N	55.40 E
Sir Joseph Banks Group II	166	34.32 S	136.17 E
Sirkābād	126	23.16 N	86.12 E
Sirkeli	130	40.09 N	32.52 E
Sirmaur	124	24.51 N	81.23 E
Şirmione	64	45.30 N	10.36 E
Širmovka	78	49.34 N	29.06 E
Sirnach	58	47.28 N	9.00 E
Siro, Jabal ∧	140	14.23 N	24.23 E
Şirohi	120	24.54 N	72.51 E
Širokaja Pad'	89	50.14 N	142.09 E
Širokij	89	49.45 N	129.30 E
Širokij Bujerak	80	52.07 N	47.46 E
Širokino	83	47.06 N	37.49 E
Širokoje, Ukr.	78	47.41 N	33.14 E
Širokoje, Ukr.	83	47.58 N	38.13 E
Širokolanovka	78	47.10 N	31.24 E
Širokovo	88	55.27 N	99.23 E
Sirolo	66	43.32 N	13.37 E
Sirombu	114	0.57 N	97.25 E
Sironj	124	24.06 N	77.42 E
Síros I	38	37.26 N	24.54 E
Síros → Ermoúpolis	38	37.26 N	24.56 E
Sirotino, Bela.	76	55.23 N	29.37 E
Sirotino, Ukr.	83	48.55 N	38.31 E
Sirotinskaja	80	49.16 N	43.39 E
Siroua, Jebel ∧	148	30.41 N	7.37 W
Sırpsındığı	130	41.46 N	26.29 E
Sirrah, Nafūd as- ⩳[8]	128	23.05 N	44.25 E
Sīrrī, Jazīreh-ye I	128	25.55 N	54.32 E
Sirsa, India	123	29.32 N	75.01 E
Sirsa, India	126	22.14 N	86.38 E
Sirsāganj	124	27.03 N	78.42 E
Sirs al-Layyānah	142	30.26 N	30.58 E
Sir Sandford, Mount ∧	182	51.40 N	117.52 W
Sirsi	122	14.37 N	74.51 E
Sirsilla	122	18.23 N	78.50 E
Sirsinā, Mişr	142	30.36 N	30.54 E
Sirsinā, Mişr	142	29.24 N	30.58 E
Sirsiri	154	4.24 N	31.53 E
Sir Thomas, Mount ∧	162	27.10 S	129.45 E
Siruma	116	14.00 N	123.15 E
Sirupa ≏	232	29.10 N	108.35 W
Şirvan	130	38.02 N	42.00 E
Şīrvān (Diyālā) ≏	128	33.14 N	44.31 E
Şirvanskaja ravnina ≡	84	40.15 N	48.00 E
Širvintos	76	55.03 N	24.57 E
Sir Wilfrid Laurier, Mount ∧	182	52.47 N	119.45 W
Sir Wilfrid Laurier's Birthplace National Historic Site ⊥	206	45.51 N	73.45 W
Sirykrabet ⊥	86	44.07 N	62.35 E
Şís ≏, Guat.	236	14.09 N	91.39 W
Šiš ≏, Ross.	86	57.19 N	73.23 E
Sisa, Mount ∧	164	6.08 S	142.45 E
Sisaba ∧	154	6.09 S	29.48 E
Sisaiya Thāna	124	27.35 N	81.20 E
Sisak	36	45.29 N	16.23 E
Şi Sa Ket	110	15.07 N	104.20 E
Šišaki	78	49.53 N	34.00 E
Šišakovo	76	60.02 N	41.30 E
Şi Satchanalai	110	17.31 N	99.46 E
Šišchid (Kyzyl-Chem) ≏	88	51.21 N	96.58 E
Šiševka	76	58.52 N	38.52 E
Sishangcun	105	40.16 N	116.33 E
Sishen	158	27.55 S	22.59 E
Sishili	106	32.09 N	120.45 E
Sishilijie	100	29.08 N	116.44 E
Sishilipu	105	40.12 N	118.08 E
Sishuang Liedao II	100	26.42 N	120.24 E
Sishui	98	35.39 N	117.15 E
Sisian	84	39.32 N	46.02 E
Şisib Lake ⊜	184	52.35 N	99.22 W
Šišicy	76	53.13 N	27.32 E
Sisikon	58	46.57 N	8.42 E
Sisim ≏	88	55.09 N	91.54 E
Şisipuk Lake ⊜	184	55.45 N	101.50 W
Šiškejevo	80	54.12 N	44.45 E
Šiškino	88	52.18 N	113.35 E
Siskiyou Mountains ⋏	204	41.55 N	123.15 W
Siskiyou Pass)(	202	42.03 N	122.36 W
Şişli ◆[8]	267b	41.04 N	28.59 E
Šišlovo	82	54.14 N	38.33 E
Sison	116	9.40 N	125.31 E
Sisŏphŏn	110	13.35 N	102.59 E
Sisquoc ≏	204	34.54 N	120.18 W
Sissa ≏	115b	8.29 S	121.18 E
Sissach	58	47.28 N	7.49 E
Sissano	164	3.00 S	142.05 E
Sisséla	150	10.49 N	10.37 W
Sisseton	198	45.39 N	97.02 W
Sisseton Indian Reservation ◆[4]	198	45.40 N	97.02 W
Sissili ≏	150	10.16 N	1.15 W
Sisson Branch Reservoir ⊜[1]	186	47.16 N	67.20 W
Sissonne	50	49.34 N	3.54 E
Sissonville	188	38.31 N	81.37 W
Sīstān ◆[1]	128	30.30 N	62.00 E
Sīstān va Balūchestān □[4]	128	28.30 N	60.30 E
Sister Bay	190	45.11 N	87.07 W
Sister Lakes	216	42.05 N	86.12 W
Sisteron	62	44.12 N	5.56 E
Sisters	202	44.17 N	121.32 W
Sistersville	188	39.33 N	80.59 W
Sistig	56	50.29 N	6.30 E
Sisto ≏	66	41.18 N	13.10 E
Sistranda	26	63.43 N	8.50 E
Sit' ≏, Ross.	76	59.59 N	40.10 E
Sit' ≏, Ross.	76	58.16 N	37.54 E
Sitabamba	248	8.02 S	77.44 W
Sitai, Zhg.	85	39.23 N	77.56 E
Sitai, Zhg.	98	41.16 N	114.23 E
Sitaizi, Zhg.	104	42.29 N	123.20 E
Sitaizi, Zhg.	104	41.17 N	122.16 E
Sitaizui	105	40.49 N	115.20 E
Sitakili	150	13.07 N	11.14 W
Sitalike	154	6.38 S	31.08 E
Sitalkuchi	124	26.10 N	89.11 E
Sītāmarhi	124	26.36 N	85.29 E
Sitampiky	157b	16.41 S	46.06 E
Si Tangkay	112	4.40 N	119.24 E
Sītāpur	124	27.34 N	80.41 E
Sītāpur Branch ≊	124	28.10 N	80.25 E
Sitārāmpur	126	23.43 N	86.53 E
Siteki	158	26.32 S	31.58 E
Sites	226	39.19 N	122.20 W
Si Thep ⊥	110	15.30 N	101.10 E
Sithoniá	38	35.12 N	26.07 E
Sithoniá ≻[1]	38	40.10 N	23.47 E
Sitidgi Lake ⊜	180	68.32 N	132.42 W
Sítio D'Abadia	255	14.48 S	46.16 W
Sítio Novo	250	5.51 S	46.43 W
Sitka	180	57.03 N	135.02 W
Sitkalidak Island I	180	57.10 N	153.14 W
Sitka National Historical Park ♠	180	57.05 N	135.15 W
Sitka Point ≻	180	57.00 N	135.49 W
Sitka Sound ʮ	180	57.00 N	135.30 W
Sitkinak Island I	180	56.35 N	154.12 W
Şitkinak Strait ʮ	180	56.39 N	154.06 W
Šitkino	88	56.23 N	98.21 E
Sitkovcy	78	48.54 N	29.12 E
Sitna ≏	38	47.37 N	27.08 E
Sitn'a-Ščelkanovo	82	54.58 N	37.59 E
Sitnica ≏	38	42.45 N	21.01 E
Sitniki	80	56.27 N	44.06 E
Sitnikovo	86	56.23 N	67.53 E
Sitobela	158	26.53 S	31.36 E
Sitona	144	14.28 N	37.27 E
Sitrah	128	26.09 N	50.38 E
Sitrah ⫪[4]	140	28.42 N	26.54 E
Sittard	56	51.00 N	5.53 E
Sittendorf	264b	48.05 N	16.10 E
Sittensen	52	53.17 N	9.30 E
Sitten → Sion	58	46.14 N	7.21 E
Sitter ≏	58	47.29 N	9.14 E
Sittingbourne	42	51.21 N	0.44 E
Sittoung ≏	110	17.10 N	96.58 E
Sittwe (Akyab)	110	20.09 N	92.54 E
Situ	105	39.20 N	115.39 E
Situbondo	115a	7.42 S	114.00 E
Siufaalele Point ≻	174y	14.17 S	169.29 W
Si'ufage	174y	14.14 S	169.32 W
Siulakderas	112	1.55 S	101.18 E
Siu Lek Yuen	271d	22.23 N	114.12 E
Siumbatu	112	2.45 S	122.03 E
Siumpu, Pulau I	112	5.40 S	122.31 E
Siuna	236	13.44 N	84.46 W
Siurgus Donigala	71	39.35 N	9.12 E
Siuri	126	23.55 N	87.32 E
Siusi (Seis)	64	46.32 N	11.34 E
Siuslaw ≏	202	44.01 N	124.08 W
Siva ≏	80	56.48 N	53.55 E
Sivaganga	122	9.52 N	78.29 E
Sivakāsi	122	9.27 N	77.49 E
Sivaki	89	52.39 N	126.45 E
Sīvand ≏	128	29.51 N	52.46 E
Sivas	130	39.45 N	37.02 E
Sivas □[4]	130	39.30 N	37.15 E
Sivaš ʮ	78	46.00 N	34.30 E
Sivaslı	130	38.30 N	29.42 E
Sivašskoje	78	46.23 N	34.34 E
Şivé	150	15.42 N	13.12 W
Šiveluč, vulkan ∧[1]	74	56.39 N	161.18 E
Siverek	130	37.45 N	39.19 E
Siverskij	76	59.21 N	30.05 E
Sivkovo	82	55.26 N	35.53 E
Sivomaskinskij	24	66.40 N	62.35 E
Sivri Ada I	267b	40.54 N	28.59 E
Sivrice	130	38.27 N	39.19 E
Sivrihisar	130	39.27 N	31.34 E
Sivry-Courtry	261	48.32 N	2.45 E
Sivry-sur-Meuse	56	49.19 N	5.16 E
Sīwah	140	29.12 N	25.31 E
Sīwah, Wāḥat ⫪[4]	140	29.12 N	25.31 E
Siwalik Range ⋏	120	31.00 N	78.00 E
Siwān	124	26.13 N	84.22 E
Siwang ≏	107	29.25 N	103.50 E
Sixaola ≏	236	9.34 N	82.34 W
Six Flags Great America ♠	216	42.21 N	87.55 W
Six Flags over Mid-America ♠	219	38.31 N	90.40 W
Six Flags Over Texas ♠	222	32.45 N	97.05 W
Six-Fours-la-Plage	62	43.06 N	5.51 E
Sixian	100	33.30 N	117.56 E
Sixitou	100	27.31 N	119.57 E
Six Mile Creek ≏, On., Can.	284a	43.15 N	79.10 W
Sixmile Creek ≏, Ky., U.S.	218	38.26 N	84.58 W
Sixmile Creek ≏, N.Y., U.S.	284a	43.17 N	78.58 W
Sixmilecross	48	54.34 N	7.08 W
Six Mile Lake ⊜	212	44.55 N	79.45 W
Sixmile Run ≏	276	40.28 N	74.35 W
Six Mile Water ≏	48	54.42 N	6.14 W
Six Nations Indian Reserve ◆[4]	212	43.03 N	80.07 W
Sixshooter Draw V	196	30.51 N	102.33 W
Sixteen Mile Creek ≏, On., Can.	275b	43.27 N	79.40 W
Sixteenmile Creek ≏, Mt., U.S.	202	46.06 N	111.23 W
Sixth Cataract → Sablūkah, Ash-Shallāl as- ∟	140	16.20 N	32.42 E
Siyāl, Jazā'ir II	140	22.47 N	36.12 E
Siyāna	124	28.38 N	78.03 E
Siyang	100	33.43 N	118.41 E
Si Yat ≏	110	13.42 N	101.26 E
Siyeteb	140	18.00 N	35.01 E
Siz'absk	24	65.05 N	53.49 E
Sizaja	88	58.07 N	100.38 E
Sizhijian	98	42.25 N	114.36 E
Siziano	62	45.20 N	9.12 E
Sizilien → Sicilia I	70	37.30 N	14.00 E
Siziman	89	50.43 N	140.26 E
Siziwang Qi	102	41.33 N	111.31 E
Sizun	32	48.24 N	4.05 W
Sizuoka → Shizuoka	94	34.58 N	138.23 E
Sjælland I	41	55.30 N	11.45 E
Sjællands Odde ≻[1]	41	55.58 N	11.22 E
Själevad	26	63.18 N	18.36 E
Sjanovo	82	54.59 N	37.25 E
Sjenica	38	43.16 N	20.00 E
Sjeništa ∧	38	43.42 N	18.37 E
Sjoa ≏	26	61.41 N	9.33 E
Sjöbo	41	55.38 N	13.42 E
Sjøholt	26	62.29 N	6.48 E
Sjösa	40	58.46 N	17.04 E
Sjötorp	40	58.50 N	13.59 E
Skaby	264a	52.19 N	13.51 E
Skaby-Berge ⋏[2]	264a	52.19 N	13.49 E
Skåde	41	56.06 N	10.13 E
Skadovsk	78	46.08 N	32.54 E
Skælskør	41	55.15 N	11.19 E
Skærbæk, Dan.	41	55.31 N	9.38 E
Skærbæk, Dan.	41	55.09 N	8.46 E
Skævinge	41	55.55 N	12.10 E
Skaftafell National Park ♠	24a	64.15 N	17.00 W
Skaftung	26	62.07 N	21.22 E
Skagafjörður ᑕ	24a	65.55 N	19.35 W
Skagen	26	57.44 N	10.36 E
Skagern ⊜	40	58.59 N	14.17 E
Skagerrak ʮ	26	57.45 N	9.00 E
Skagersvik	40	58.58 N	14.06 E
Skaggs Creek ≏	194	36.54 N	86.04 W
Skagit □[6]	224	48.29 N	121.45 W
Skagit ≏	224	48.20 N	122.25 W
Skagit Bay ᑕ	224	48.19 N	122.24 W
Skagway	180	59.28 N	135.19 W
Skaidi	24	70.25 N	24.30 E
Skaistkalne	76	56.23 N	24.39 E
Skála Oropoú	38	38.20 N	23.46 E
Skala-Podol'skaja	78	48.51 N	26.12 E
Skalat	78	49.26 N	25.59 E
Skalbmierz	30	50.19 N	20.25 E
Skälderviken	41	56.17 N	12.50 E
Skälderviken ᑕ	41	56.18 N	12.38 E
Skalica	30	48.51 N	17.14 E
Skalino	76	58.32 N	40.13 E
Skalistaja, gora ∧	84	42.48 N	45.08 E
Skalistyj, gora ∧	180	68.12 N	178.10 E
Skalistyj chrebet ⋏	84	43.15 N	43.00 E
Skalistyj Golec, gora ∧	88	56.24 N	119.12 E
Skalka ⊜	24	66.50 N	18.46 E
Skalka, údolní nádrž ⊜[1]	54	50.06 N	12.19 E
Skalná	54	50.07 N	12.23 E
Skal'nyj	86	58.22 N	57.59 E
Skamania	224	45.37 N	122.02 W
Skamania □[6]	224	45.58 N	121.53 W
Skamlingsbanke ∧[2]	41	55.25 N	9.34 E
Skamokawa	224	46.16 N	123.27 W
Skanderborg	41	56.02 N	9.56 E
Skanderborg Sø ⊜	41	56.01 N	9.56 E
Skåne □[9]	41	55.59 N	13.30 E
Skaneateles	210	42.56 N	76.25 W
Skaneateles Falls	210	43.00 N	76.27 W
Skaneateles Lake ⊜	210	42.53 N	76.24 W
Skånevik	26	59.44 N	5.59 E
Skänninge	26	58.24 N	15.05 E
Skanör	26	55.25 N	12.52 E
Skara	26	58.22 N	13.25 E
Skaraborgs Län □[6]	26	58.20 N	13.30 E
Skaramagás	267c	38.01 N	23.36 E
Skärblacka	40	58.34 N	15.54 E
Skarđ	24a	64.03 N	19.50 W
Skardhø ∧	26	62.30 N	8.45 E
Skārdu	123	35.18 N	75.37 E
Skärhamn	26	58.00 N	11.33 E
Skarhult	41	55.49 N	13.23 E
Skarnes	26	60.15 N	11.41 E
Skarø I	41	55.00 N	10.29 E
Skärplinge	40	60.28 N	17.46 E
Skarszewy	30	54.05 N	18.27 E
Skårup	41	55.05 N	10.42 E
Skaryszew	30	51.19 N	21.15 E
Skarżysko-Kamienna	30	51.08 N	20.53 E
Skášov	60	49.31 N	13.26 E
Skate Creek ≏	224	46.37 N	121.41 W
Skattkärr	40	59.25 N	13.41 E
Skaudvilė	76	55.24 N	22.35 E
Skaugum	26	59.51 N	10.26 E
Skawina	30	49.59 N	19.49 E
Skebobruk	40	59.58 N	18.36 E
Skebokvarn	40	59.04 N	16.42 E
Skedviken ⊜	40	59.46 N	18.16 E
Skedvisjön ⊜	40	59.35 N	15.40 E
Skeena ≏	182	54.09 N	130.02 W
Skeena Crossing	182	55.06 N	127.49 W
Skeena Mountains ⋏	176	57.00 N	128.30 W
Skeen Peak ∧	222	32.59 N	97.48 W
Skegness	44	53.10 N	0.21 E
Skegrie	41	55.24 N	13.04 E
Skei	26	61.38 N	6.30 E
Skeikampen	26	61.20 N	10.07 E
Skelde	41	54.51 N	9.44 E
Skeleton Coast ⩳[2]	156	19.15 S	12.30 E
Skeleton Coast Park ♠	156	19.25 S	12.55 E
Skeleton Creek ≏	196	35.58 N	97.25 W
Skeleton Lake ⊜	212	45.15 N	79.27 W
Skellefteå	26	64.46 N	20.57 E
Skellefteälven ≏	26	64.42 N	21.06 E
Skelleftehamn	26	64.41 N	21.14 E
Skellig Rocks II[1]	48	51.48 N	10.31 W
Skellytown	196	35.34 N	101.11 W
Skelmersdale	44	53.33 N	2.48 W
Skelmorlie	46	55.51 N	4.53 W
Skelton, Eng., U.K.	44	54.43 N	2.51 W
Skelton, Eng., U.K.	44	54.33 N	0.59 W
Skene	26	57.29 N	12.38 E
Skene, Mount ∧	169	37.25 S	146.23 E
Skepptuna	40	59.43 N	18.05 E
Skerne ≏	44	54.29 N	1.34 W
Skerpioensdrif	158	31.05 S	21.33 E
Skerries	48	53.35 N	6.07 W
Skerryvore I[2]	46	56.19 N	7.07 W
Skewen	42	51.40 N	3.51 W
Skhíza I	38	36.44 N	21.46 E
Ski	26	59.43 N	10.50 E
Skíathos	38	39.10 N	23.29 E
Skíathos I	38	39.10 N	23.28 E
Skiatook	196	36.22 N	96.00 W
Skibbereen	48	51.33 N	9.15 W
Skibby	41	55.45 N	11.58 E
Skibotn	24	69.24 N	20.16 E
Skiddaw ∧	44	54.38 N	3.08 W
Skidegate	182	53.15 N	132.00 W
Skidegate Inlet ᑕ	182	53.14 N	132.00 W
Skidel'	76	53.34 N	24.15 E
Skidmore	196	28.15 N	97.41 W
Skien	26	59.12 N	9.36 E
Skierniewice	30	51.58 N	20.08 E
Skierniewice □[4]	30	52.10 N	20.15 E
Skiftet ʮ	26	60.15 N	21.05 E
Skihist Mountain ∧	182	50.11 N	121.54 W
Skikda (Philippeville)	148	36.50 N	6.58 E
Skikda □[5]	148	36.45 N	7.00 E
Skilak Lake ⊜	180	60.25 N	150.25 W
Skillet Fork ≏	194	38.08 N	88.07 W
Skillingaryd	26	57.26 N	14.05 E
Şkillman	276	40.25 N	74.42 W
Škin'	82	55.11 N	38.30 E
Skinnastaður	24a	66.07 N	16.24 W
Skinner Reservoir ⊜[1]	228	33.35 N	117.03 W
Skinnskatteberg	40	59.50 N	15.41 E
Skippack	285	40.14 N	75.24 W
Skippack Creek ≏	285	40.09 N	75.27 W
Skippack Creek, West Branch ≏	285	40.14 N	75.23 W
Skippers	208	36.37 N	77.38 W
Skipskop	158	34.33 S	20.25 E
Skipton, Austl.	169	37.41 S	143.22 E
Skipton, Eng., U.K.	44	53.58 N	2.01 W
Skirfare ≏	44	54.07 N	2.01 W
Skirmish Point ≻	171a	27.05 S	153.13 E
Skíros	38	38.53 N	24.33 E
Skíros I	38	38.53 N	24.32 E
Skivarp	41	55.25 N	13.34 E
Skive	26	56.34 N	9.02 E
Skjálfandafljót ≏	24a	65.57 N	17.38 W
Skjálfandi ᑕ	24a	66.08 N	17.38 W
Skjeberg	26	59.14 N	11.12 E
Skjern	26	55.57 N	8.30 E
Skjern Å ≏	41	55.57 N	8.40 E
Şklad	74	71.55 N	123.33 E
Šklov	76	54.13 N	30.18 E
Skniga ≏	82	54.53 N	37.24 E
Skobeleva, pik ∧	85	39.49 N	72.44 E
Şkoby	40	60.02 N	18.01 E
Škocjanske jame ⩳[7]	36	45.40 N	14.00 E
Skodborg	41	55.25 N	9.09 E
Skodsborg	41	55.49 N	12.34 E
Şkoenmakerskop	158	34.02 S	25.33 E
Škofije	64	45.34 N	13.48 E
Škofja Loka	36	46.10 N	14.18 E
Skoganvarre	24	69.47 N	25.06 E
Skoghall	40	59.19 N	13.26 E
Skogstorp	40	59.20 N	16.28 E
Skokholm Island I	42	51.42 N	5.16 W
Skoki	30	52.41 N	17.10 E
Skokie	216	42.02 N	87.44 W
Skokie ≏	216	42.05 N	87.46 W
Skokie Lagoons ᑕ	278	42.07 N	87.47 W
Skokloster ⊥	40	59.42 N	17.37 E
Skokomish, North Fork ≏	224	47.18 N	123.14 W
Skokomish, South Fork ≏	224	47.18 N	123.14 W
Skokomish Indian Reservation ◆[4]	224	47.21 N	123.12 W
Sköldinge	40	59.02 N	16.26 E
Skole	78	49.02 N	23.29 E
Sköllersta	40	59.09 N	15.20 E
Skolsta	40	59.40 N	17.14 E
Skolwin	54	53.32 N	14.35 E
Skomer Island I	42	51.44 N	5.17 W
Skomoroški, Ross.	82	54.05 N	36.57 E
Skomoroški, Ukr.	78	49.20 N	29.26 E
Skón	110	12.04 N	105.04 E
Skookumchuck ≏	224	46.41 N	123.00 W
Skookumchuck Reservoir ⊜[1]	224	47.47 N	122.42 W
Skoonspruit ≏	158	27.00 S	26.38 E
Skootamatta ≏	212	44.32 N	77.20 W
Skootamatta Lake ⊜	212	44.50 N	77.15 W
Skópelos, Ellás	38	39.07 N	23.43 E
Skópelos, Ellás	38	39.02 N	26.26 E
Skópelos I	38	39.10 N	23.40 E
Skopin	76	53.51 N	39.33 E
Skopje	38	41.59 N	21.26 E
Skórcz	30	53.48 N	18.32 E
Skorodnoje, Bela.	78	51.38 N	28.49 E
Skorodnoje, Ross.	78	51.05 N	37.14 E
Skørping	26	56.50 N	9.53 E
Skotfoss	26	59.12 N	9.30 E
Şkotovataja	83	48.13 N	37.54 E
Škotovo	89	43.20 N	132.21 E
Skotterud	26	59.59 N	12.07 E
Skovby	41	54.53 N	10.00 E
Skövde	26	58.24 N	13.50 E
Skovlund	41	55.44 N	8.43 E
Skovorodino	89	53.59 N	123.55 E
Skowhegan	188	44.45 N	69.43 W
Skownan	184	51.57 N	99.36 W
Skradin	36	43.49 N	15.56 E
Skreen	48	54.15 N	8.45 W
Skreia	26	60.39 N	10.56 E
Skriplivka	76	57.32 N	30.38 E
Skrīveri	76	56.39 N	25.08 E
Skromberga	41	56.00 N	12.58 E
Skrudaļiena	76	55.49 N	26.43 E
Skrunda	76	56.41 N	22.01 E
Skruv	26	56.41 N	15.22 E
Skrydstrup	41	55.14 N	9.15 E
Skudeneshavn	26	59.09 N	5.17 E
Skukuza	156	25.01 S	31.38 E
Skuleberget ∧[2]	26	63.05 N	18.21 E
Skulforp	26	58.21 N	13.49 E
Skull	48	51.32 N	9.33 W
Skull Creek ≏	222	29.32 N	96.24 W
Skull Valley	200	34.30 N	112.41 W
Skull Valley Indian Reservation ◆[4]	200	40.24 N	112.45 W
Skultuna	40	59.43 N	16.25 E
Skuna ≏	194	33.54 N	89.41 W
Şkunk ≏	190	40.42 N	91.07 W
Škunovka	86	50.45 N	55.27 E
Skuodas	76	56.16 N	21.32 E
Şkuratovskij	82	54.07 N	37.36 E
Škurinskaja	78	46.35 N	39.22 E
Skurišenskaja	80	49.52 N	42.57 E
Skurup	41	55.28 N	13.30 E
Skutskär	40	60.38 N	17.25 E
Skvira	78	49.44 N	29.40 E
Skwentna	180	61.58 N	151.11 W
Skwentna ≏	180	62.00 N	151.08 W
Skwierzyna	30	52.36 N	15.30 E
Skye, Island of I	46	57.18 N	6.15 W
Sky Harbor Airport ⊠	278	42.09 N	87.51 W
Skykomish	224	47.42 N	121.21 W
Skykomish ≏	224	47.50 N	122.03 W
Skykomish, North Fork ≏	224	47.47 N	121.33 W
Skykomish, South Fork ≏	224	47.47 N	121.33 W
Sky Lake	220	28.28 N	81.24 W
Sky Lake ⊜	212	44.48 N	81.15 W
Skyland, Nv., U.S.	226	39.01 N	119.56 W
Skyland, N.C., U.S.	192	35.29 N	82.31 W
Skylight	218	38.25 N	85.31 W
Skyline	284c	38.50 N	76.54 W
Skyline Lakes ⊜	276	41.04 N	74.16 W
Skyllberg	40	58.57 N	14.59 E
Skyring, Península ≻[1]	254	45.58 S	74.53 W
Skyring, Seno ʮ	254	52.35 S	72.00 W
Sky Sailing Airport ⊠	282	37.30 N	121.58 W
Skytop	210	41.14 N	75.15 W
Skyttorp	40	60.05 N	17.44 E
Skyway	224	47.29 N	122.14 W
Slackhall	262	53.20 N	1.53 W
Slackwood	208	40.15 N	74.44 W
Slade Green ◆[8]	260	51.28 N	0.12 E
Sladkij	80	46.10 N	42.17 E
Sladkovo	86	55.32 N	70.20 E
Slagelse	41	55.24 N	11.22 E
Slagnäs	24	65.34 N	18.05 E
Slagoviščі	76	53.57 N	35.54 E
Slaithwaite	262	53.37 N	1.53 W
Slamannan	46	55.56 N	3.50 W
Slamet, Gunung ∧	115a	7.14 S	109.12 E
Slancy	76	59.06 N	28.04 E
Slaney ≏	48	52.21 N	6.30 W
Slangerup	41	55.51 N	12.11 E
Slănic	38	45.15 N	25.57 E
Slănic Moldova	38	46.13 N	26.26 E
Slano	36	42.47 N	17.54 E
Slanské vrchy ⋏	30	48.50 N	21.30 E
Şlaný	54	50.11 N	14.04 E
Šlapanice	30	49.10 N	16.44 E
Slaščevskaja	80	49.52 N	42.21 E
Śląsk → Silesia □[9]	30	51.00 N	16.45 E
Slastucha	80	51.57 N	44.32 E
Slate Bottom Creek ≏	284a	42.53 N	78.45 W
Slate Creek ≏, Ks., U.S.	198	37.08 N	97.09 W
Slate Creek ≏, Pa., U.S.	279b	40.28 N	79.32 W
Slatedale	208	40.45 N	75.40 W
Slate Hill	210	41.23 N	74.29 W
Slater, Ia., U.S.	190	41.52 N	93.40 W
Slater, Mo., U.S.	194	39.13 N	93.04 W
Slater Creek ≏	200	40.59 N	107.23 W
Slatersville	207	42.00 N	71.34 W
Slaterville Springs	210	42.24 N	76.21 W
Slatina	38	44.26 N	24.22 E
Slatington	208	40.44 N	75.36 W
Slatino	78	50.12 N	36.11 E
Slaton	196	33.26 N	101.38 W
Slattocks	262	53.35 N	2.10 W
Slaughter	194	30.43 N	91.08 W
Slaung	115a	8.02 S	111.24 E
Slautnoje	74	63.00 N	167.59 E
Slava	89	52.08 N	129.24 E
Slav'anka, Ross.	89	42.53 N	131.21 E
Slav'anka, Ukr.	78	48.24 N	36.43 E
Slav'anka, Uzb.	85	40.40 N	68.32 E
Slav'anka ≏	265a	59.50 N	30.32 E
Slav'anogorsk	83	49.02 N	37.31 E
Slav'anoserbsk	83	48.42 N	38.59 E
Slav'ansk	83	48.52 N	37.37 E
Slav'ansk-na-Kubani	78	45.15 N	38.08 E
Slave ≏	176	61.18 N	113.39 W
Slave Coast ⩳[2]	150	6.25 N	3.00 E
Slave Lake	182	55.17 N	114.46 W
Slavgorod, Bela.	76	53.27 N	31.00 E
Slavgorod, Ross.	86	53.00 N	78.40 E
Slavgorod, Ukr.	78	50.36 N	35.21 E
Slavgorod, Ukr.	78	48.06 N	35.31 E
Slavitino	82	56.41 N	39.13 E
Slavkino	80	52.58 N	47.11 E
Slavkoviči	76	57.39 N	29.05 E
Slavkovský les ⋏	54	50.07 N	12.45 E

Symbol	English	Deutsch	Español	Français	Português
≏	River	Fluß	Río	Rivière	Rio
≊	Canal	Kanal	Canal	Canal	Canal
∟	Waterfall, Rapids	Wasserfall, Stromschnellen	Cascada, Rápidos	Chute d'eau, Rapides	Cascata, Rápidos
ʮ	Strait	Meeresstraße	Estrecho	Détroit	Estreito
ᑕ	Bay, Gulf	Bucht, Golf	Bahía, Golfo	Baie, Golfe	Baía, Golfo
⊜	Lake, Lakes	See, Seen	Lago, Lagos	Lac, Lacs	Lago, Lagos
≡	Swamp	Sumpf	Pantano	Marais	Pântano
⍓	Ice Features, Glacier	Eis- und Gletscherformen	Accidentes Glaciales	Formes glaciaires	Acidentes glaciares
⫪	Other Hydrographic Features	Andere Hydrographische Objekte	Otros Elementos Hidrográficos	Autres données hydrographiques	Outros acidentes hidrográficos
✣	Submarine Features	Untermeerische Objekte	Accidentes Submarinos	Formes de relief sous-marin	Acidentes submarinos
□	Political Unit	Politische Einheit	Unidad Politica	Entité politique	Unidade política
♉	Cultural Institution	Kulturelle Institution	Institución Cultural	Institution culturelle	Instituição cultural
⊥	Historical Site	Historische Stätte	Sitio Histórico	Site historique	Sítio histórico
♠	Recreational Site	Erholungs- und Ferienort	Sitio de Recreo	Centre de loisirs	Area de Lazer
⊠	Airport	Flughafen	Aeropuerto	Aéroport	Aeroporto
■	Military Installation	Militäranlage	Instalación Militar	Installation militaire	Instalação militar
◆	Miscellaneous	Verschiedenes	Misceláneo	Divers	Diversos

Name	Page	Lat.°'	Long.°'
Slavkov u Brna	61	49.09 N	16.52 E
Slavnoje	76	54.18 N	29.27 E
Slavonia — Slavonija □[9]	36	45.00 N	18.00 E
Slavonice	61	49.00 N	15.21 E
Slavonija □[9]	36	45.00 N	18.00 E
Slavonska Požega	36	45.20 N	17.41 E
Slavonski Brod	38	45.10 N	18.01 E
Slavsk	76	55.03 N	21.41 E
Slavskoje	78	48.49 N	23.24 E
Slavuta	78	50.18 N	26.52 E
Sława	30	51.53 N	16.04 E
Slawi	115a	6.59 S	109.08 E
Sławno	30	54.22 N	16.40 E
Slayton	198	43.59 N	95.45 W
Slea ≃	42	53.03 N	0.12 W
Sleaford	42	53.00 N	0.24 W
Slea Head >	48	52.06 N	10.27 W
Sleat, Point of >	46	57.01 N	6.02 W
Sleat, Sound of ⊔	46	57.06 N	5.49 W
Sledge	194	34.25 N	90.13 W
Sledge Island I	180	64.29 N	166.13 W
Sled Lake ◎	184	54.27 N	107.25 W
Sledmere	44	54.04 N	0.35 W
Slednevo	82	56.25 N	38.36 E
Sled'uki	76	53.35 N	30.22 E
Sleen	52	52.46 N	6.48 E
Sleeping Bear Dunes National Lakeshore ♦	190	44.50 N	86.08 W
Sleeping Giant State Park ♦	207	41.25 N	72.53 W
Sleepy Eye	198	44.17 N	94.43 W
Sleepy Hollow, Ca., U.S.	226	38.00 N	122.34 W
Sleepy Hollow, Ca., U.S.	280	33.57 N	117.47 W
Sleepy Hollow, Il., U.S.	216	42.06 N	88.24 W
Sleetmute	180	61.42 N	157.11 W
Sleidinge	50	51.08 N	3.41 E
Sleights	44	54.27 N	0.40 W
Sleman	115a	7.42 S	110.20 E
Slepino	76	59.11 N	29.02 E
Ślesin	30	52.23 N	18.19 E
Slessor Glacier ⊓	9	79.50 S	28.30 W
Slickville	214	40.27 N	79.31 W
Slidell	194	30.16 N	89.46 W
Slide Mountain ∧	210	42.00 N	74.23 W
Sliderock Mountain ∧	202	46.35 N	113.33 W
Sliedrecht	52	51.49 N	4.45 E
Slieve Aughty Mountains ⋏	48	53.05 N	8.35 W
Slieve Bloom Mountains ⋏	48	53.05 N	7.35 W
Slievekimalta ∧	48	52.45 N	8.16 W
Slievenamon ∧	48	52.25 N	7.34 W
Sligeach — Sligo	48	54.17 N	8.28 W
Sligo (Sligeach), Ire.	48	54.17 N	8.28 W
Sligo, Pa., U.S.	214	41.06 N	79.29 W
Sligo □[6]	48	54.10 N	8.40 W
Sligo Bay c	48	54.20 N	8.40 W
Sligo Creek ≃	284c	38.57 N	76.58 W
Slikkerveer	52	51.53 N	4.37 E
Slingebeek ≃	52	51.56 N	6.17 E
Slinger	190	43.20 N	88.17 W
Šlino, ozero ◎	76	57.40 N	33.23 E
Slioch ∧	46	57.41 N	5.22 W
Slippery Rock	214	41.03 N	80.03 W
Slippery Rock Creek ≃	214	40.51 N	80.15 W
Slite	26	57.43 N	18.48 E
Slīteres Rezervāts ♦	76	57.38 N	22.25 E
Sliven	38	42.40 N	26.19 E
Slivnica	38	42.51 N	23.02 E
Sloan, Ia., U.S.	198	42.13 N	96.13 W
Sloan, Nv., U.S.	204	35.56 N	115.12 W
Sloan, N.Y., U.S.	210	42.53 N	78.47 W
Sloan Peak ∧	224	48.03 N	121.20 W
Sloansville	210	42.46 N	74.20 W
Sloatsburg	210	41.09 N	74.11 W
Sloboda, Bela.	76	53.58 N	28.08 E
Sloboda, Ross.	76	55.30 N	31.51 E
Sloboda, Ross.	78	51.09 N	40.17 E
Sloboda, Ukr.	78	51.11 N	33.37 E
Slobodka, Bela.	76	55.41 N	27.11 E
Slobodka, Ross.	82	54.22 N	37.33 E
Slobodka, Ukr.	78	47.53 N	29.21 E
Slobodskoj	86	58.42 N	50.12 E
Slobodzeja	78	46.44 N	29.43 E
Slobodzeja-Mare	78	45.34 N	28.12 E
Slobozia, Rom.	38	44.34 N	27.23 E
Slobozia, Rom.	38	43.51 N	25.54 E
Slocan	182	49.46 N	117.28 W
Slocan Lake ◎	182	49.56 N	117.22 W
Slochteren	52	53.12 N	6.47 E
Slocomb	194	31.06 N	85.35 W
Slocum	207	41.32 N	71.31 W
Slocum Mountain ∧	228	35.18 N	117.13 W
Słomniki	30	50.15 N	20.06 E
Slonim	76	53.06 N	25.19 E
Slonovka	78	50.39 N	37.45 E
Słońsk	54	52.35 N	14.50 E
Sloop Channel ⊔	276	40.36 N	73.31 W
Sloping Hills	276	40.42 N	74.34 W
Slosh Indian Reserve ✦[4]	182	50.44 N	122.13 W
Sloten	52	52.54 N	5.38 E
Sloten ✦[8]	52	52.21 N	4.48 E
Slotermeer ◎	52	52.55 N	5.40 E
Slough	42	51.31 N	0.36 W
Slough □[8]	260	51.32 N	0.35 W
Slough Brook ≃	276	40.45 N	74.21 W
Sloughhouse	226	38.30 N	121.12 W
Slovakia — Slovensko □[9]	30	48.50 N	20.00 E
Slovan	214	40.21 N	80.23 W
Slovečna ≃	78	51.41 N	29.41 E
Slovečno	78	51.23 N	28.21 E
Slovenia (Slovenija) □[1]	36	46.15 N	15.10 E
Slovenija — Slovenia □[1]	36	46.15 N	15.10 E
Slovenj Gradec	61	46.31 N	15.05 E
Slovenska Bistrica	61	46.23 N	15.34 E
Slovenská Republika □[3]	30	48.30 N	20.00 E
Slovenske Gorice ⋏[2]	61	46.35 N	15.55 E
Slovenské rudohorie ⋏	30	48.45 N	20.00 E
Slovensko □[9]	30	48.50 N	20.00 E
Slovinka	80	58.02 N	43.07 E
Slowakei — Slovensko □[9]	30	48.50 N	20.00 E
Słowiński Park Narodowy ♦	30	54.40 N	17.25 E
Słubice	54	52.20 N	14.32 E
Sluč' ≃, Bela.	76	52.08 N	27.31 E
Sluč' ≃, Ukr.	78	51.37 N	26.38 E
Sluck	76	53.01 N	27.33 E
Sl'ud'anka	88	51.38 N	103.42 E
Sluderno (Schluderns)	64	46.40 N	10.35 E
Sludy	76	58.52 N	36.52 E
Sluis	52	51.18 N	3.24 E
Sluiskil	52	51.16 N	3.50 E
Šluknov	54	51.00 N	14.27 E
Slunj	36	45.07 N	15.35 E
Słupca	30	52.19 N	17.52 E
Słupia ≃	30	54.35 N	16.50 E
Słupsk (Stolp)	30	54.28 N	17.01 E
Słupsk □[4]	30	54.10 N	17.15 E
Slurry	156	25.49 S	25.52 E
Šl'uz-Mokr'aki	86	59.17 N	88.50 E
Sly, Oued ≃	34	36.04 N	1.08 E
Smachtino	82	54.51 N	36.25 E
Smackover	194	33.21 N	92.43 W
Smackover Creek ≃	194	33.22 N	92.24 W
Småland □[9]	26	57.20 N	15.00 E
Smålandsfarvandet ⊔	41	55.05 N	11.20 E
Smålandsstenar	26	57.10 N	13.24 E
Smalininkai	76	55.05 N	22.35 E
Smallbridge	262	53.38 N	2.08 W
Smalleytown	276	40.39 N	74.28 W
Smallwood	210	41.40 N	74.49 W
Smallwood Reservoir ◎[1]	176	54.05 N	64.30 W
Smallwood State Park ♦	208	38.33 N	77.12 W
Smara	148	26.44 N	11.41 W
Smartt Syndicate Dam ◎[1]	158	30.40 S	23.18 E
Smartville	226	39.12 N	121.18 W
Smeaton	184	53.30 N	104.49 W
Smeaton Bay c	182	55.20 N	130.50 W
Smečno	54	50.10 N	14.03 E
Smedby	40	58.33 N	16.16 E
Smědeč	61	48.56 N	14.09 E
Smederevo	38	44.40 N	20.56 E
Smederevska Palanka	38	44.22 N	20.58 E
Smedjebacken	40	60.08 N	15.25 E
Smela	78	49.14 N	31.53 E
Smeloje	78	50.55 N	33.36 E
Šmel'ovka	80	54.47 N	49.11 E
Smelt Brook ≃, Ma., U.S.	283	42.13 N	70.58 W
Smelt Brook ≃, Ma., U.S.	283	42.00 N	70.43 W
Smelt Pond ◎	283	41.58 N	70.43 W
Smeralda, Costa ⊥[2]	71	41.04 N	9.30 E
Smerwick Harbour c	48	52.12 N	10.24 W
Smethport	214	41.48 N	78.26 W
Smethwick	42	52.30 N	1.58 W
Smicksburg	214	40.52 N	79.10 W
Smidovič	89	48.36 N	133.49 E
Šmidta, mys >	180	68.56 N	179.30 W
Šmidta, ostrov I	74	81.08 N	90.48 E
Šmidta, poluostrov >[1]	89	54.10 N	142.40 E
Šmidta — Mys Šmidta	180	68.56 N	179.26 W
Śmigiel	30	52.01 N	16.32 E
Smilde	52	52.56 N	5.27 E
Smile	218	38.15 N	83.29 W
Smiley, Sk., Can.	184	51.37 N	109.29 W
Smiley, Tx., U.S.	222	29.16 N	97.38 W
Smiloviči	76	53.45 N	28.01 E
Smiltene	76	57.26 N	25.56 E
Smirnovskij	86	54.31 N	69.25 E
Smirnych	89	49.43 N	142.38 E
Smith	182	55.10 N	114.02 W
Smith □[6]	222	32.20 N	95.15 W
Smith ≃, U.S.	192	36.29 N	79.45 W
Smith ≃, Ca., U.S.	204	41.56 N	124.12 W
Smith ≃, Mt., U.S.	202	47.25 N	111.29 W
Smith ≃, Or., U.S.	202	43.43 N	124.05 W
Smith, Cape >	190	45.48 N	81.35 W
Smith Arm c	180	66.15 N	124.00 W
Smith Bay c	180	70.51 N	154.25 W
Smithboro, Il., U.S.	219	38.54 N	89.20 W
Smithboro, N.Y., U.S.	210	42.02 N	76.24 W
Smith Canyon V	198	37.46 N	103.26 W
Smith Center	198	39.46 N	98.47 W
Smith Creek ≃, S.D., U.S.	198	43.58 N	99.20 W
Smith Creek ≃, Wa., U.S.	224	46.45 N	123.53 W
Smithdale	279b	40.14 N	79.48 W
Smithers, B.C., Can.	182	54.47 N	127.10 W
Smithers, W.V., U.S.	188	38.10 N	81.18 W
Smithers Lake ◎[1]	222	29.29 N	95.38 W
Smithfield, Austl.	168b	34.41 S	138.41 E
Smithfield, Austl.	274a	33.51 S	150.57 E
Smithfield, On., Can.	212	44.04 N	77.41 W
Smithfield, S. Afr.	158	30.09 S	26.30 E
Smithfield, Eng., U.K.	44	54.59 N	2.52 W
Smithfield, N.C., U.S.	192	35.30 N	78.20 W
Smithfield, Oh., U.S.	214	40.16 N	80.46 W
Smithfield, Pa., U.S.	214	39.48 N	79.48 W
Smithfield, Ut,. U.S.	200	41.50 N	111.49 W
Smithfield, Va., U.S.	208	36.58 N	76.37 W
Smithflat	226	38.44 N	120.45 W
Smith Haven Mall ✦[9]	276	40.52 N	73.08 W
Smithills Hall ⊥	262	53.36 N	2.27 W
Smith Island I, B.A.T.	9	62.59 S	62.32 W
Smith Island I, N.C., U.S.	192	33.52 N	77.59 W
Smith Island I, Va., U.S.	208	37.10 N	75.51 W
Smith Island I, Wa., U.S.	224	48.19 N	122.50 W
Smith Island II	208	38.01 N	76.02 W
Smithland	194	37.08 N	88.24 W
Smithmill	214	40.46 N	78.25 W
Smith Mountain ∧	280	34.17 N	117.52 W
Smith Mountain Lake ◎[1]	192	37.10 N	79.40 W
Smith Peak ∧	202	48.50 N	116.39 W
Smith Peninsula >[1]	9	74.25 S	61.15 W
Smith Point	222	29.27 N	94.45 W
Smith Point >, N.S., Can.	186	45.51 N	63.25 W
Smith Point >, Tx., U.S.	222	29.32 N	94.46 W
Smith Point >, Va., U.S.	208	37.53 N	76.14 W
Smithport	214	40.50 N	78.52 W
Smith River	204	41.55 N	124.08 W
Smiths	194	32.32 N	85.05 W
Smithsburg	208	39.39 N	77.34 W
Smiths Creek	214	42.55 N	82.36 W
Smiths Falls	212	44.54 N	76.01 W
Smiths Fork ≃	202	41.23 N	110.12 W
Smiths Grove	194	37.03 N	86.12 W
Smiths Mills	276	41.01 N	74.22 W
Smith Sound ⊔	182	51.18 N	127.48 W
Smithton, Austl.	166	40.51 S	145.07 E
Smithton, Il., U.S.	219	38.24 N	89.59 W
Smithton, Mo., U.S.	194	38.40 N	93.05 W
Smithton, Pa., U.S.	279b	40.09 N	79.44 W
Smithtown	210	40.52 N	73.13 W
Smithtown Bay c	276	40.57 N	73.12 W
Smith Valley	218	39.36 N	86.12 W
Smithville, On., Can.	212	43.06 N	79.33 W
Smithville, Ga., U.S.	192	31.54 N	84.15 W
Smithville, In., U.S.	218	39.04 N	86.30 W
Smithville, Ms., U.S.	194	34.04 N	88.23 W
Smithville, Mo., U.S.	194	39.23 N	94.34 W
Smithville, N.J., U.S.	208	39.59 N	74.44 W
Smithville, N.J., U.S.	285	39.29 N	74.27 W
Smithville, Oh., U.S.	214	40.51 N	81.51 W
Smithville, Tn., U.S.	194	35.57 N	85.48 W
Smithville, Tx., U.S.	222	30.00 N	97.09 W
Smithville Flats	210	42.24 N	75.49 W
Smithville Lake ◎[1]	194	39.25 N	94.30 W
Smögen	26	58.21 N	11.13 E
Smoke Creek ≃, Mt., U.S.	198	48.18 N	104.41 W
Smoke Creek ≃, N.Y., U.S.	284a	42.49 N	78.52 W
Smoke Creek, South Branch ≃	284a	42.49 N	78.49 W
Smoke Creek Desert ✦[2]	204	40.30 N	119.40 W
Smoke Lake ◎	212	45.32 N	78.41 W
Smokeless	214	40.24 N	76.02 W
Smokerun	214	40.48 N	78.26 W
Smoketown	208	40.02 N	76.12 W
Smokey, Cape >	186	46.38 N	60.21 W
Smokey Dome ∧	202	43.29 N	114.56 W
Smoky ≃	182	56.10 N	117.21 W
Smoky Bay	162	32.22 S	133.56 E
Smoky Cape >	166	30.56 S	153.05 E
Smoky Hill ≃	198	39.03 N	96.48 W
Smoky Hill, North Fork ≃	198	38.55 N	101.17 W
Smoky Lake	182	54.07 N	112.28 W
Smøla I	24	63.24 N	8.00 E
Smol'anica	76	52.42 N	24.38 E
Smol'aninovo	89	43.19 N	132.28 E
Smol'any	76	54.36 N	30.04 E
Smolensk	76	54.47 N	32.03 E
Smolenskaja vozvyšennost' ⋏[1]	76	54.30 N	33.00 E
Smolenskoje	86	52.20 N	85.05 E
Smoleviči	76	54.02 N	28.05 E
Smólikas ∧	38	40.06 N	20.52 E
Smoljan	38	41.35 N	24.41 E
Smolny ʋ	265a	59.57 N	30.24 E
Smolovka	76	55.33 N	30.13 E
Smoot	200	42.37 N	110.54 W
Smoothstone ≃	184	55.20 N	106.39 W
Smoothstone Lake ◎	184	54.40 N	106.50 W
Smorgon'	76	54.29 N	26.24 E
Smorodovka	76	57.08 N	29.52 E
Smotrič	78	48.56 N	26.34 E
Smotrič ≃	78	48.34 N	26.38 E
Smuškovoje	80	47.20 N	45.55 E
Smyčka	82	56.04 N	35.56 E
Smygehamn	41	55.21 N	13.22 E
Smygehuk >	41	55.21 N	13.23 E
Smyley Island I	9	72.55 S	78.00 W
Smyrna, De., U.S.	208	39.17 N	75.36 W
Smyrna, Ga., U.S.	192	33.53 N	84.30 W
Smyrna, N.Y., U.S.	210	42.41 N	75.34 W
Smyrna, Tn., U.S.	194	35.58 N	86.31 W
Smyrna ≃	208	39.22 N	75.31 W
Smyrna — İzmir	130	38.25 N	27.09 E
Smyšl'ajevka	80	53.15 N	50.22 E
Smyth, Canal ⊔	254	52.15 S	73.40 W
Smythe, Mount ∧	176	57.54 N	124.53 W
Smythe Park ♦	275b	43.41 N	79.30 W
Smythesdale	169	37.38 S	143.41 E
Sn'adin	78	52.04 N	28.19 E
Snæfell ∧, Ísland	24a	64.48 N	15.32 W
Snaefell ∧, I. of Man	44	54.16 N	4.27 W
Snæfellness >[1]	24a	64.50 N	23.00 W
Snag	180	62.24 N	140.22 W
Snaght, Slieve ∧	48	55.12 N	7.20 W
Snagost'	78	51.21 N	34.54 E
Snahapish ≃	224	47.38 N	124.11 W
Snaith	44	53.41 N	1.02 W
Šn'ajevo	80	52.34 N	46.11 E
Snake ≃, Yk., Can.	180	65.58 N	134.10 W
Snake ≃, U.S.	202	46.12 N	119.02 W
Snake ≃, Ca., U.S.	226	39.07 N	121.43 W
Snake ≃, Mn., U.S.	190	45.49 N	92.46 W
Snake ≃, Mn., U.S.	198	48.26 N	97.07 W
Snake ≃, Ne., U.S.	198	42.47 N	100.48 W
Snake Bight c[3]	220	25.10 N	80.50 W
Snake Brook ≃	283	42.18 N	71.22 W
Snake Creek ≃, Mt., U.S.	202	48.32 N	108.53 W
Snake Creek ≃, Ne., U.S.	198	42.01 N	102.45 W
Snake Creek ≃, S.D., U.S.	198	44.58 N	98.29 W
Snake Creek, South Fork ≃	198	45.02 N	98.36 W
Snake Creek Canal ≡	220	25.57 N	80.11 W
Snake Indian ≃	182	53.11 N	118.00 W
Snake Range ⋏	204	39.00 N	114.15 W
Snake Rapids ⌞	212	45.14 N	77.20 W
Snake River Plain ≚	202	43.00 N	113.00 W
Snake Valley	169	37.37 S	143.35 E
Snake Valley V	204	39.20 N	113.55 W
Snape	42	52.11 N	1.30 E
Snaptun	41	55.49 N	10.04 E
Snares Islands II	9	48.00 S	166.30 E
Snasahögarna ∧	26	63.13 N	12.21 E
Sn'atyn	78	48.28 N	25.34 E
Snay Pôl	110	11.40 N	105.13 E
Sneads	192	30.42 N	84.55 W
Snedsted	26	56.54 N	8.32 E
Sneedville	192	36.31 N	83.13 W
Sneek	52	53.02 N	5.40 E
Sneekermeer ◎	52	53.02 N	5.45 E
Snee-osh-Beach	224	48.24 N	122.33 W
Sneeuberg ∧	158	32.25 S	19.12 E
Sneeuberg ⋏	158	31.46 S	24.20 E
Snekkersten	41	56.00 N	12.36 E
Snelgrove	275b	43.44 N	79.49 W
Snelling	204	37.31 N	120.26 W
Snettisham	42	52.53 N	0.30 E
Snežnaja ≃	88	51.28 N	104.38 E
Snežnik ∧	36	45.35 N	14.27 E
Snežnoje	83	48.01 N	38.46 E
Śniardwy, Jezioro ◎	30	53.46 N	21.44 E
Snicarte	219	40.07 N	90.14 W
Snicarte Island I	219	40.08 N	90.12 W
Snigir'ovka	78	47.06 N	32.47 E
Snina	30	48.59 N	22.07 E
Snipe Keys II	220	24.40 N	81.38 W
Snipe Lake ◎	182	55.07 N	116.46 W
Snizort, Loch c	46	57.34 N	6.28 W
Snøde	41	55.05 N	10.55 E
Snodland	42	51.20 N	0.27 E
Snoghøj	41	55.31 N	9.43 E
Snøhetta ∧	26	62.20 N	9.17 E
Snohomish	224	47.54 N	122.05 W
Snohomish □[6]	224	48.02 N	121.41 W
Snohomish ≃	224	48.01 N	122.13 W
Snønipa ∧	26	61.42 N	6.41 E
Snook	222	30.29 N	96.28 W
Snoqualmie	224	47.31 N	121.49 W
Snoqualmie ≃	224	47.50 N	122.03 W
Snoqualmie, Middle Fork ≃	224	47.31 N	121.46 W
Snoqualmie, North Fork ≃	224	47.31 N	121.46 W
Snoqualmie, South Fork ≃	224	47.31 N	121.46 W
Snoqualmie Falls	224	47.32 N	121.49 W
Snoqualmie Mountain ∧	224	47.27 N	121.25 W
Snoqualmie Pass)(	224	47.25 N	121.25 W
Snøtinden ∧	24	66.38 N	14.00 E
Snov	76	53.13 N	26.24 E
Snov ≃	78	51.45 N	31.45 E
Snover	190	43.27 N	82.58 W
Snowbird Lake ◎	176	60.41 N	103.00 W
Snow Canyon State Park ♦	200	37.11 N	113.42 W
Snow Creek ≃	224	47.59 N	122.53 W
Snowden, Sk., Can.	184	53.30 N	104.41 W
Snowden, Pa., U.S.	279b	40.16 N	79.58 W
Snowden Oaks	284c	39.04 N	76.52 W
Snowdenville	285	40.11 N	75.36 W
Snowdon ∧	44	53.04 N	4.05 W
Snowdonia National Park ♦	28	53.00 N	3.57 W
Snowdoun	194	32.14 N	86.17 W
Snowdrift	176	62.23 N	110.47 W
Snowflake	200	34.30 N	110.04 W
Snow Hill, Md., U.S.	208	38.10 N	75.23 W
Snow Hill, N.C., U.S.	192	35.27 N	77.40 W
Snowking Mountain ∧	224	48.24 N	121.17 W
Snow Lake	184	54.53 N	100.02 W
Snow Lakes ◎	224	47.29 N	120.45 W
Snowmass Mountain ∧	200	39.07 N	107.04 W
Snow Mountain ∧	226	39.23 N	122.45 W
Snow Peak ∧	202	48.35 N	118.29 W
Snows Brook ≃	283	42.47 N	71.06 W
Snow Shoe	214	41.02 N	77.57 W
Snowshoe Butte ∧	224	47.13 N	121.22 W
Snowshoe Peak ∧	202	48.13 N	115.41 W
Snowtown	166	33.47 S	138.13 E
Snow Water Lake ◎	204	41.07 N	115.00 W
Snowy ≃	166	37.48 S	148.32 E
Snowy Mountain ∧	188	43.42 N	74.23 W
Snowy Mountains ⋏	166	36.30 S	148.20 E
Snowyside Peak ∧	202	43.57 N	114.58 W
Snubba Range ⋏	171b	35.40 S	148.10 E
Snuŏl	110	12.04 N	106.26 E
Snyder, Ok., U.S.	196	34.39 N	98.57 W
Snyder, Tx., U.S.	196	32.43 N	100.55 W
Snyder □[6]	210	40.47 N	77.03 W
Snydertown	210	40.53 N	76.40 W
Soacha	246	4.35 N	74.13 W
Soahany	157b	18.42 S	44.13 E
Soaker, Mount ∧	172	45.23 S	167.15 E
Soalala	157b	16.06 S	45.20 E
Soalara	157b	23.36 S	43.44 E
Soaloka	157b	18.32 S	45.15 E
Sŏam	98	38.01 N	126.43 E
Soamanonga	157b	23.52 S	44.47 E
Soān ≃	123	33.01 N	71.44 E
Soan-do I	98	34.09 N	126.39 E
Soanierana Ivongo	157b	16.55 S	49.35 E
Soanindrariny	157b	19.54 S	47.14 E
Soap Creek ≃	190	40.55 N	92.14 W
Soap Lake	202	47.23 N	119.29 W
Soasiu — Tidore	108	0.40 N	127.26 E
Soatá	246	6.20 N	72.41 W
Soavina	157b	20.23 S	46.56 E
Soavinandriana	157b	19.09 S	46.45 E
Soay I	46	57.08 N	6.14 W
Soazza	58	46.22 N	9.13 E
Sob ≃	78	48.42 N	29.17 E
Sobaek-sanmaek ⋏	98	36.00 N	128.00 E
Sobat ≃	140	9.22 N	31.33 E
Sobernheim	56	49.47 N	7.38 E
Soběšice	60	49.12 N	13.41 E
Soběslav	30	49.15 N	14.44 E
Sobger ≃	164	3.44 S	140.20 E
Sobič	78	51.52 N	33.14 E
Sobinka	80	55.59 N	40.01 E
Soboba Indian Reservation ✦[4]	228	33.47 N	116.54 W
Soboko	140	6.49 N	24.50 E
Sobolekovo	80	55.39 N	51.53 E
Sobolev	80	51.56 N	51.43 E
Sobolevka	78	48.36 N	29.30 E
Sobolevo	82	55.31 N	38.43 E
Sobolino	88	53.23 N	119.42 E
Sobótka	30	50.55 N	16.45 E
Sobradinho	252	29.24 S	53.03 W
Sobradinho, Represa de ◎[1]	250	9.40 S	42.00 W
Sobrado	34	41.02 N	8.16 W
Sobral	250	3.42 S	40.21 W
Sobrance	30	48.45 N	22.11 E
Sobrante Ridge ∧	282	37.58 N	122.15 W
Sobrarbe ✦[1]	34	42.22 N	0.10 E
Sobue	94	35.15 N	136.43 E
Søby	41	54.56 N	10.16 E
Soča	64	46.20 N	13.39 E
Soča (Isonzo) ≃	64	45.47 N	13.32 E
Socaire	252	23.36 S	67.51 W
Socchieve	64	46.25 N	12.52 E
Soc Giang	110	22.54 N	106.01 E
Socgorodok	78	50.11 N	38.09 E
Soch	85	39.57 N	71.08 E
Soch ≃	85	40.20 N	71.02 E
Sochaczew	30	52.14 N	20.14 E
Sochaux	58	47.31 N	6.50 E
Soch'e — Shache	120	38.25 N	77.16 E
Sochi — Soči	84	43.35 N	39.45 E
Sŏch'ŏn	98	36.05 N	126.41 E
Sochondo	88	51.49 N	112.32 E
Sochondo, gora ∧	88	49.44 N	111.05 E
Soch'ŏng-do I	98	37.46 N	124.45 E
Sochor, gora ∧	88	51.18 N	105.15 E
Soči	84	43.35 N	39.45 E
Social Circle	192	33.39 N	83.43 W
Social Security Administration ʋ	284b	39.19 N	76.44 W
Sociedade Hípica Paulista ♦	287b	23.36 S	46.41 W
Société, Îles de la (Society Islands) II	14	17.00 S	150.00 W
Society Hill	192	34.30 N	79.51 W
Society Islands — Société, Îles de la II	14	17.00 S	150.00 W
Society Ridge ✢[3]	14	17.00 S	151.00 W
Soco ≃	238	18.27 N	69.12 W
Socoltenango	232	16.13 N	92.15 W
Socompa, Paso)(	252	24.27 S	68.18 W
Soconusco, Sierra de — Madre, Sierra ⋏	236	15.20 N	92.20 W
Socorro, Bra.	256	22.36 S	46.32 W
Socorro, Col.	246	6.29 N	73.16 W
Socorro, Pil.	116	9.37 N	125.58 E
Socorro, N.M., U.S.	200	34.03 N	106.53 W
Socorro, Tx., U.S.	200	31.39 N	106.18 W
Socorro ✦[8]	287b	23.39 S	46.42 W
Socorro, Isla I	232	18.45 N	110.58 W
Socota	248	6.18 S	78.44 W
Socotora, Isla — Suquṭrā I	118	12.30 N	54.00 E
Socotra — Suquṭrā I	118	12.30 N	54.00 E
Soc Trang	110	9.36 N	105.58 E
Socuéllamos	34	39.17 N	2.48 W
Soda Creek	182	52.21 N	122.18 W
Soda Creek ≃	226	38.48 N	122.29 W
Soda Lake ◎, Ca., U.S.	204	35.08 N	116.04 W
Soda Lake ◎, Ca., U.S.	226	35.15 N	119.53 W
Sodankylä	24	67.29 N	26.32 E
Soda Springs	202	42.39 N	111.36 W
Soddy-Daisy	194	35.16 N	85.10 W
Sodegaura	94	35.26 N	139.57 E
Söderälgen ◎	40	59.43 N	14.35 E
Söderåsen ⋏[2]	41	56.04 N	13.05 E
Söderbärke	40	60.05 N	15.33 E
Söderby-Karl	40	59.53 N	18.41 E
Söderfors	40	60.23 N	17.14 E
Söderhamn	26	61.18 N	17.03 E
Söderköping	26	58.29 N	16.18 E
Södermanland □[9]	41	59.12 N	16.49 E
Södermanlands Län □[6]	40	59.15 N	16.40 E
Södernmanland □[9]	40	59.12 N	16.49 E
Söderslätt □[9]	41	55.29 N	13.15 E
Södertälje	40	59.12 N	17.37 E
Södertörn >[1]	40	59.05 N	18.00 E
Sodhra	123	32.28 N	74.11 E
Sodingen ✦[8]	263	51.32 N	7.15 E
Sodium	158	30.11 S	23.09 E
Sodo	144	6.52 N	37.47 E
Sodom — Sedom ⊥	132	31.04 N	35.23 E
Sodpur	272b	22.39 N	88.23 E
Södra Björkfjärden c	40	59.18 N	17.32 E
Södra Hörken ◎	40	60.02 N	15.02 E
Södra Kvarken ⊔	26	60.15 N	19.05 E
Södra Råda	40	59.01 N	14.10 E
Södra Sandby	41	55.43 N	13.20 E
Södra Vi	26	57.45 N	15.48 E
Sodražica	36	45.46 N	14.38 E
Sodus	210	43.14 N	77.03 W
Sodus Bay c	210	43.15 N	76.58 W
Sodus Creek ≃	210	43.13 N	76.56 W
Sodus Point	210	43.16 N	76.59 W
Sŏdu-su ≃	98	42.05 N	129.00 E
Sodwalls	170	33.31 S	149.59 E
Sodwana Bay National Park ♦	158	27.30 S	32.39 E
Soe	112	9.52 S	124.17 E
Soeda	96	33.34 N	130.52 E
Soekmekaar	156	23.28 S	29.58 E
Soela väin ⊔	76	58.40 N	22.35 E
Soerabaja — Surabaya	115a	7.15 S	112.45 E
Soest, Dtsch.	52	51.34 N	8.07 E
Soest, Ned.	52	52.09 N	5.18 E
Soestdijk	52	52.11 N	5.18 E
Soestdijk, Paleis ʋ	52	52.12 N	5.15 E
Soeste ≃	52	53.10 N	7.44 E
Soesterberg	52	52.07 N	5.17 E
Soeurs, Île des I	275a	45.28 N	73.33 W
Sofádhes	38	39.20 N	22.06 E
Sofala	170	33.05 S	149.42 E
Sofala □[5]	156	19.00 S	35.00 E

ENGLISH

Name	Page	Lat.°'	Long.°'
Sofia ≃	157b	15.27 S	47.23 E
Sofia — Sofija	38	42.41 N	23.19 E
Sofiero	41	56.05 N	12.39 E
Sofija (Sofia)	38	42.41 N	23.19 E
Sofijevka, Ukr.	78	46.33 N	34.03 E
Sofijevka, Ukr.	78	48.04 N	33.52 E
Sofijevskij	83	48.12 N	38.52 E
Sofijsk, Ross.	89	51.34 N	139.52 E
Sofijsk, Ross.	89	52.15 N	133.58 E
Sofjanga	24	65.52 N	31.15 E
Sofje-Kondratjevka	83	48.18 N	38.12 E
Sofjino	82	55.30 N	38.11 E
Sofrino	82	56.09 N	37.56 E
Sofronovo	76	59.48 N	36.54 E
Sogakofe	150	6.00 N	0.36 E
Sogamoso	246	5.43 N	72.56 W
Sogamoso ≃	246	7.13 N	73.56 W
Soğanlı ≃	130	41.11 N	32.38 E
Soğanlı Geçidi)(	130	40.33 N	40.16 E
Soğanlıköy ✦[8]	267b	40.55 N	29.12 E
Sogcho — Sokch'o	98	38.12 N	128.36 E
Sogda	89	50.24 N	132.12 E
Sögel	52	52.50 N	7.31 E
Sogen	164	9.25 S	147.25 E
Sogliano al Rubicone	66	44.00 N	12.18 E
Sognafjorden c[2]	26	61.06 N	5.10 E
Søgne	26	58.05 N	7.49 E
Sogne Fjord — Sognafjorden c[2]	26	61.06 N	5.10 E
Sogn og Fjordane □[6]	26	61.30 N	6.50 E
Sogod, Pil.	116	10.45 N	124.00 E
Sogod, Pil.	116	10.23 N	124.59 E
Sogod Bay c	116	10.15 N	125.02 E
Sogo Nur ◎	102	42.18 N	101.08 E
Sogoža ≃	76	58.28 N	39.06 E
Sogri-san Kukrip Kongwŏn ♦	98	36.33 N	127.52 E
Soğuksu Milli Parkı ♦	130	40.25 N	32.35 E
Söğüt	130	40.00 N	30.11 E
Söğütalan	130	40.03 N	28.34 E
Söğüt Gölü ◎	130	37.03 N	29.53 E
Söğütlü	130	40.54 N	30.29 E
Sog Xian	120	31.50 N	93.45 E
Sohāgpur, India	124	23.19 N	81.21 E
Sohāgpur, India	124	22.42 N	78.12 E
Sohāg — Sawhāj	140	26.33 N	31.42 E
Soham	42	52.20 N	0.20 E
Sohano	175e	5.27 S	154.40 E
Soharkha	272a	28.35 N	77.24 E
Soheit-Tinlot	56	50.29 N	5.22 E
Sohland	54	51.02 N	14.25 E
Söhlde	52	52.11 N	10.14 E
Sohna	124	28.15 N	77.04 E
Sŏhŭng	98	38.27 N	126.10 E
Sŏhwa-ri	98	38.15 N	128.13 E
Soignes, Forêt de ✦[3]	56	50.47 N	4.25 E
Soignies (Zinnik)	50	50.35 N	4.04 E
Soignolles-en-Brie	261	48.39 N	2.42 E
Soin	150	12.47 N	3.49 W
Soindres	261	48.57 N	1.40 E
Soini	26	62.52 N	24.13 E
Sointula	182	50.38 N	127.01 W
Soisalo ∧	26	62.40 N	28.10 E
Soissons	50	49.22 N	3.20 E
Soisy-sous-Montmorency	261	48.59 N	2.18 E
Soisy-sur-Seine	261	48.39 N	2.27 E
Sōja	96	34.40 N	133.45 E
Sojana	24	65.48 N	43.20 E
Sojat	120	25.55 N	73.40 E
Šojda	24	61.11 N	37.40 E
Sojiji Temple ʋ[1]	268	35.31 N	139.41 E
Sojītra	120	22.33 N	72.43 E
Šojna	24	67.52 N	44.08 E
Sŏjosŏn-man c	98	39.20 N	124.50 E
Sojoton Point >	116	9.58 N	122.27 E
Sok ≃	80	53.24 N	50.08 E
Sōka, Nihon	94	35.49 N	139.48 E
Soka, Taehan	271b	37.30 N	126.48 E
Sokal'	78	50.29 N	24.17 E
Šokal'skogo, proliv ⊔	74	79.00 N	100.25 E
Sokch'o	98	38.12 N	128.36 E
Söke	130	37.45 N	27.24 E
Sokehs Passage ⊔	174r	7.01 N	158.11 E
Sokele	154	9.55 S	24.36 E
Sokhós	38	40.49 N	23.21 E
Sokir'any	78	48.27 N	27.25 E
Sokirincy	78	50.42 N	32.46 E
Sokna	26	60.14 N	9.54 E
Sokodé	150	8.59 N	1.08 E
Sokol, Ross.	74	72.24 N	126.48 E
Sokol, Ross.	76	59.28 N	40.10 E
Sokol, Ross.	89	47.14 N	142.45 E
Sokol ∧	60	49.03 N	13.31 E
Sokółka, Pol.	30	53.25 N	23.31 E
Sokolka, Ross.	80	55.34 N	51.30 E
Sokol'niki ✦[8]	265b	55.48 N	37.41 E
Sokolniki Park ♦	265b	55.48 N	37.41 E
Sokol'nikovo	82	55.21 N	35.49 E
Sokolo	150	14.44 N	6.08 W
Sokologornoje	78	46.29 N	34.58 E
Sokolov	54	50.09 N	12.40 E
Sokolova-Gora	78	50.19 N	28.36 E
Sokolova Pustyn'	82	54.51 N	38.03 E
Sokolovka	86	55.06 N	69.12 E
Sokolovo, Ross.	24	65.21 N	56.57 E
Sokolovo, Ross.	76	52.55 N	34.39 E
Sokolovo, Ross.	80	52.49 N	42.26 E
Sokolovo, Ross.	82	56.02 N	36.55 E
Sokolovo, Ross.	86	52.33 N	84.46 E
Sokolovo-Kundr'učenskij	83	47.50 N	39.57 E
Sokołów	30	50.14 N	22.07 E
Sokołów Podlaski	30	52.25 N	22.15 E
Sokol'skoje	80	57.08 N	43.13 E
Sokone	150	13.53 N	16.22 W
Sokoto	150	13.04 N	5.16 E
Sokoto □[3]	150	12.05 N	5.30 E
Sokoto ≃	150	11.20 N	4.10 E
Šokpar	85	43.49 N	74.21 E
Sŏkp'o-ri	98	37.46 N	125.27 E
Sokrutovka	80	47.54 N	46.33 E
Šokša	76	58.24 N	42.27 E
Soksa-ri	98	40.40 N	127.17 E
Sokskije jary ⋏[2]	80	54.10 N	51.30 E
Sŏk-to I	98	38.40 N	125.00 E
Sokuluk	85	42.52 N	74.18 E
Sokur, Ross.	80	52.01 N	45.48 E
Sokur, Ross.	86	55.13 N	83.13 E
Sol', Česko.	30	48.56 N	21.36 E
Sol', Ukr.	83	48.43 N	38.02 E
Sol, Costa del ⊥[2]	34	36.40 N	4.00 W
Sola, Nor.	26	58.53 N	5.36 E
Sola, Vanuatu	175f	13.53 S	167.33 E
Sola, Zaïre	154	5.09 S	27.06 E
Soła ≃	30	50.04 N	19.13 E
Solacolu	38	44.23 N	26.34 E
Solai	154	0.02 N	36.09 E
Šolaksaj	86	51.45 N	64.48 E
Solan	123	30.55 N	77.07 E
Solana	220	26.56 N	82.01 W
Solana Beach	228	32.59 N	117.16 W
Solander, Cape >	274a	34.01 S	151.14 E
Solander Island I	172	46.34 S	166.53 E
Solânea	250	6.45 S	35.39 W
Solangāri	272b	22.36 N	88.27 E
Sol'anka ≃	80	50.10 N	51.20 E
Solano	116	16.31 N	121.11 E
Solano □[6]	226	38.15 N	121.52 W
Solāpur	122	17.41 N	75.55 E
Solar, Morro ∧[2]	286d	12.11 S	77.02 W
Solarino	70	37.06 N	15.07 E
Solaro	266b	45.37 N	9.05 E
Solaro, Monte ∧	68	40.33 N	14.13 E
Solberg	26	63.47 N	17.38 E
Solbiate Arno	62	45.42 N	8.48 E

DEUTSCH

Name	Seite	Breite°'	Länge°' E = Ost
Solbiate Olona	266b	45.39 N	8.53 E
Solca, Arg.	252	30.46 S	66.28 W
Solca, Rom.	38	47.42 N	25.50 E
Solčava	61	46.25 N	14.41 E
Sol'cy	76	58.08 N	30.20 E
Solda Gölü ◎	130	37.33 N	29.42 E
Soldatskaja	84	43.48 N	43.49 E
Soldatskoje	85	40.52 N	68.56 E
Soldatsko-Stepnoje	80	49.32 N	45.30 E
Sölde ✦[8]	263	51.31 N	7.35 E
Sol de Julio	252	29.33 S	63.27 W
Sölden	64	46.58 N	11.00 E
Sölderholz ✦[8]	263	51.29 N	7.35 E
Soldier Creek ≃	198	39.04 N	95.39 W
Soldier Field ♦	278	41.52 N	87.37 W
Soldier Key I	220	25.35 N	80.10 W
Soldier Point >	240c	17.02 N	61.41 W
Soldier Pond	186	47.09 N	68.34 W
Soldiers Grove	190	43.23 N	90.46 W
Soldotna	180	60.29 N	151.04 W
Sole, Val di V	64	46.20 N	10.45 E
Solebury	208	40.23 N	75.02 W
Solec Kujawski	30	53.06 N	18.14 E
Soledad, Col.	246	10.55 N	74.46 W
Soledad, Ca., U.S.	226	36.25 N	121.19 W
Soledad, Ven.	246	8.10 N	63.34 W
Soledad, Cerro ∧	196	26.29 N	103.23 W
Soledad de Doblado	234	19.03 N	96.25 W
Soledad Díez Gutiérrez	234	22.12 N	100.57 W
Soledade	252	28.50 S	52.30 W
Soledade de Minas	256	22.04 S	45.03 W
Soledad Pass)(	228	34.30 N	118.07 W
Soleduck ≃	224	47.55 N	124.35 W
Solemar	256	24.05 S	46.36 W
Solen	198	46.23 N	100.47 W
Sølen ∧	26	61.55 N	11.30 E
Solenoje	80	46.14 N	42.32 E
Solentiname, Archipiélago de II	236	11.10 N	85.00 W
Solenzara	36	41.51 N	9.23 E
Solenzo	150	12.11 N	4.05 W
Solero	62	44.55 N	8.30 E
Solers	261	48.40 N	2.43 E
Solesmes	50	50.11 N	3.30 E
Soleure — Solothurn	58	47.13 N	7.32 E
Solferino	64	45.23 N	10.34 E
Solginskij	24	61.05 N	41.19 E
Solgne	56	48.58 N	6.18 E
Solgonskij kr'až ∧	86	55.30 N	91.00 E
Solhan	130	38.58 N	41.03 E
Solheim, Nor.	26	60.53 N	5.27 E
Solheim, S. Afr.	273d	26.11 S	28.10 E
Soliera	64	44.45 N	10.55 E
Soligalič	76	59.05 N	42.17 E
Solignac-sur-Loire	62	44.58 N	3.53 E
Soligny-la-Trappe	50	48.37 N	0.32 E
Soligorsk	76	52.48 N	27.32 E
Solihull	42	52.25 N	1.45 W
Solikamsk	86	59.39 N	56.47 E
Solila	157b	21.25 S	46.37 E
Sol'-Ileck	86	51.10 N	54.59 E
Soliman	148	36.42 N	10.30 E
Solimões — Amazon ≃	242	0.10 S	49.00 W
Solin ≃	50	48.02 N	2.43 E
Solingen	56	51.10 N	7.05 E
Solís, Arg.	258	34.18 S	59.20 W
Solís, Ur.	252	34.36 S	55.29 W
Solís, Presa ◎[1]	234	20.05 N	100.36 W
Soliseño	196	26.01 N	97.48 W
Söll	64	47.30 N	12.11 E
Šollar	84	41.40 N	48.38 E
Sollas	46	57.39 N	7.21 W
Sollefteå	26	63.10 N	17.16 E
Sollenau	61	47.53 N	16.15 E
Sollentuna	40	59.28 N	17.54 E
Sóller	34	39.46 N	2.42 E
Søllerød	41	55.49 N	12.31 E
Sollerön I	26	60.55 N	14.37 E
Søllested	41	54.49 N	11.17 E
Solliès-Pont	62	43.11 N	6.03 E
Solling ⋏	52	51.45 N	9.35 E
Söllingen	54	52.05 N	10.55 E
Solln ✦[8]	60	48.05 N	11.31 E
Sollom	262	53.40 N	2.50 W
Sollstedt	54	51.25 N	10.31 E
Solms	56	50.32 N	8.24 E
Solna	40	59.22 N	18.01 E
Solncedar	78	44.34 N	38.01 E
Solncevo	265b	55.39 N	37.24 E
Solnečnogorsk	82	56.11 N	36.59 E
Solnhofen	56	48.53 N	10.59 E
Solo ≃	115a	6.47 S	112.33 E
Šolochovskij	80	48.18 N	41.03 E
Solodča	80	49.39 N	44.17 E
Solodniki	80	48.25 N	45.16 E
Solofra	68	40.50 N	14.51 E
Sologne ✦[1]	50	47.50 N	2.00 E
Šologoncy	74	66.13 N	114.14 E
Solok	112	0.48 S	100.39 E
Sololá, Guat.	236	14.46 N	91.11 W
Solola, Som.	144	0.07 N	41.31 E
Sololá □[5]	236	14.40 N	91.15 W
Solomennikova	86	58.20 N	89.02 E
Solomennoje	24	61.51 N	34.19 E
Solomon, Az., U.S.	200	32.48 N	109.37 W
Solomon, Ks., U.S.	198	38.55 N	97.22 W
Solomon ≃	198	38.54 N	97.22 W
Solomon, North Fork ≃	198	39.29 N	98.26 W
Solomon, South Fork ≃	198	39.29 N	98.26 W
Solomon Basin ✢[1]	14	7.00 S	152.00 E
Solomon Islands □[1]	175e	8.00 S	159.00 E
Solomon Islands II	175e	8.00 S	159.00 E
Solomons	208	38.20 N	76.28 W
Solomon Sea ⊤[2]	14	8.00 S	155.00 E
Solomon's Pools — Sulaymān, Birak ⊥	132	31.41 N	35.10 E
Solon, Ia., U.S.	190	41.48 N	91.29 W
Solon, Me., U.S.	188	44.56 N	69.51 W
Solon, Oh., U.S.	214	41.23 N	81.26 W
Solon, Zhg.	89	46.36 N	121.13 E
Solonešnoje	86	51.40 N	84.21 E
Solonka	80	50.13 N	41.28 E
Sol'onoje, Ross.	84	44.03 N	40.53 E
Sol'onoje, Ukr.	78	48.13 N	34.52 E
Sol'onoje, Ukr.	83	49.18 N	37.39 E
Sol'onoje, ozero ◎	86	55.20 N	70.05 E
Sol'onoje Ozero	78	45.53 N	34.27 E
Sol'onoje Zajmišče	80	47.56 N	46.07 E
Solonópole	250	5.44 S	39.01 W
Solon Springs	190	46.21 N	91.49 W
Solopaca	68	41.11 N	14.33 E
Solor, Kepulauan II	112	8.25 S	123.30 E
Solor, Pulau I	112	8.27 S	123.05 E
Solo — Surakarta	115a	7.35 S	110.50 E
Solotča	80	54.48 N	39.51 E
Solothurn	58	47.13 N	7.32 E
Solothurn □[3]	58	47.25 N	7.35 E
Solotobe	86	44.38 N	66.05 E
Solotvin	78	48.42 N	24.25 E
Solotvina	78	47.57 N	23.52 E
Soloveckije ostrova II	24	65.07 N	35.53 E
Solovjovka	76	60.46 N	30.09 E
Solovjovsk, Ross.	88	49.55 N	115.42 E
Solovjovsk, Ross.	89	54.14 N	124.26 E
Solre-le-Château	50	50.10 N	4.05 E
Solre-sur-Sambre	50	50.18 N	4.08 E
Solrød Strand	41	55.32 N	12.14 E
Solsona	34	41.59 N	1.31 E
Solt	30	46.48 N	19.00 E
Šolta, Otok I	36	43.23 N	16.15 E
Soltānābād	128	36.23 N	58.02 E
Soltau	52	52.59 N	9.49 E
Solton	86	52.50 N	86.28 E
Soluntо ⊥	70	38.06 N	13.32 E

Symbols in the index entries represent the broad categories identified in the key at the right. Symbols with superior numbers (⋏[1]) identify subcategories (see complete key on page *I · 1*).

Symbole im Register stellen die rechts im Schlüssel erklärten Kategorien dar. Symbole mit hochgestellten Ziffern (⋏[1]) bezeichnen Unterabteilungen einer Kategorie (vgl. vollständiger Schlüssel auf Seite *I · 1*).

Los símbolos incluídos en el texto del índice representan las grandes categorias identificadas con la clave a la derecha. Los símbolos con numeros en su parte superior (⋏[1]) identifican las subcategorias (véase la clave completa en la página *I · 1*).

Les symboles de l'index représentent les catégories indiquées dans la légende à droite. Les symboles suivis d'un indice (⋏[1]) représentent des sous-catégories (voir légende complète à la page *I · 1*).

Os símbolos incluídos no texto do índice representam as grandes categorias identificadas com a chave à direita. Os símbolos com números em sua parte superior (⋏[1]) identificam as subcategorias (veja-se a chave completa à página *I · 1*).

	English	Deutsch	Español	Français	Português
∧	Mountain	Berg	Montaña	Montagne	Montanha
⋏	Mountains	Gebirge	Montañas	Montagnes	Montanhas
)(	Pass	Paß	Paso	Col	Passo
V	Valley, Canyon	Tal, Cañon	Valle, Cañón	Vallée, Canyon	Vale, Canhão
≚	Plain	Ebene	Llano	Plaine	Planície
>	Cape	Kap	Cabo	Cap	Cabo
I	Island	Insel	Isla	Île	Ilha
II	Islands	Inseln	Islas	Îles	Ilhas
⊥	Other Topographic Features	Andere Topographische Objekte	Otros Elementos Topográficos	Autres données topographiques	Outros acidentes topográficos

ESPAÑOL

Nombre	Página	Lat.°′	Long.°′ W = Oeste
Solus, Mount ∧	168a	32.28 S	116.13 E
Solutré-Pouilly	58	46.18 N	4.43 E
Solva	42	51.52 N	5.11 W
Solva ≃	42	51.52 N	5.17 W
Solvang	204	34.36 N	120.08 W
Solvarbo	40	60.24 N	15.40 E
Solvay	210	43.03 N	76.12 W
Sölvesborg	26	56.03 N	14.33 E
Sol'vyčegodsk	24	61.21 N	46.52 E
Solway Firth c[1]	44	54.50 N	3.35 W
Solwezi	154	12.11 S	26.25 E
Soly	76	54.31 N	26.11 E
Solymár	264c	47.36 N	18.56 E
Solza	24	64.33 N	39.29 E
Sōma, Nihon	92	37.48 N	140.57 E
Soma, Tür.	130	39.10 N	27.36 E
Somabula	154	19.41 S	29.41 E
Sōmahara-chūtonchi, Rikujō-jieitai- ▪	94	36.23 N	138.58 E
Somain	50	50.22 N	3.17 E
Somalia (Somaliya) □[1], Afr.	136	6.00 N	48.00 E
Somalia (Somaliya) □[1], Afr.	144	6.00 N	48.00 E
Somali Basin ✣[1]	12	0.00	52.00 E
Somalie → Somalia □[1]	144	6.00 N	48.00 E
Somaliland → Somalia □[1]	144	6.00 N	48.00 E
Somali Republic → Somalia □[1]	144	6.00 N	48.00 E
Somaliya → Somalia □[1]	144	6.00 N	48.00 E
Somalomo	152	3.23 N	12.44 E
Sŏman	98	41.20 N	128.54 E
Somanga	154	8.24 S	39.17 E
Sombernon	58	47.18 N	4.42 E
Sombo	152	8.42 S	20.57 E
Sombor	38	45.46 N	19.07 E
Sombra	214	42.43 N	82.29 W
Sombrerete	234	23.38 N	103.39 W
Sombreretillo	196	26.19 N	99.58 W
Sombrero I	238	18.36 N	63.26 W
Sombrero Channel ʮ	110	7.41 N	93.35 E
Sombrio	252	29.07 S	49.40 W
Sombrio, Lagoa do c	252	29.12 S	49.42 W
Șomcuta-Mare	38	47.31 N	23.29 E
Šomdari	120	25.49 N	72.35 E
Somenos	224	48.49 N	123.44 W
Somercotes	44	53.04 N	1.22 W
Somerdale, N.J., U.S.	208	39.50 N	75.01 W
Somerdale, Oh., U.S.	214	40.34 N	81.22 W
Someren	52	51.24 N	5.44 E
Somero	26	60.37 N	23.32 E
Sõmerpalu	76	57.51 N	26.48 E
Somers, Austl.	169	38.24 S	145.10 E
Somers, Ct., U.S.	207	41.59 N	72.26 W
Somers, Mt., U.S.	202	48.04 N	114.13 W
Somers, Wi., U.S.	216	42.38 N	87.54 W
Somersby	170	33.25 S	151.17 E
Somerset, Austl.	166	41.03 S	145.49 E
Somerset, Mb., Can.	184	49.24 N	98.39 W
Somerset, Co., U.S.	200	38.55 N	107.28 W
Somerset, Ky., U.S.	192	37.05 N	84.36 W
Somerset, Md., U.S.	284c	38.58 N	77.05 W
Somerset, Ma., U.S.	207	41.46 N	71.07 W
Somerset, N.J., U.S.	208	40.44 N	74.34 W
Somerset, Oh., U.S.	188	39.48 N	82.17 W
Somerset, Pa., U.S.	188	40.00 N	79.04 W
Somerset, Tx., U.S.	196	29.13 N	98.40 W
Somerset, Wi., U.S.	190	45.07 N	92.40 W
Somerset □[6], Eng., U.K.	42	51.08 N	3.00 W
Somerset □[6], Md., U.S.	208	38.12 N	75.41 W
Somerset □[6], N.J., U.S.	208	40.34 N	74.37 W
Somerset □[6], Pa., U.S.	214	40.09 N	79.00 W
Somerset Airport ⊠	276	40.37 N	74.40 W
Somerset Center	216	42.03 N	84.25 W
Somerset East	158	32.42 S	25.35 E
Somerset Hills Airport ⊠	276	40.41 N	74.32 W
Somerset Island I, Ber.	240a	32.17 N	64.52 W
Somerset Island I, N.T., Can.	176	73.15 N	93.30 W
Somerset Reservoir ◎[1]	171a	27.03 S	152.35 E
Somerset West	158	34.08 S	18.50 E
Somersham	42	52.23 N	0.01 E
Somers Point	208	39.19 N	74.35 W
Somersworth	188	43.15 N	70.51 W
Somerton, Eng., U.K.	42	51.03 N	2.44 W
Somerton, Az., U.S.	200	32.35 N	114.42 W
Somerton ◆[8]	285	40.06 N	75.01 W
Somerton Creek ≃	208	36.32 N	76.55 W
Somervell □[6]	222	32.15 N	97.45 W
Somerville, Austl.	169	38.13 S	145.10 E
Somerville, Ma., U.S.	207	42.23 N	71.06 W
Somerville, N.J., U.S.	210	40.34 N	74.36 W
Somerville, Oh., U.S.	218	39.33 N	84.38 W
Somerville, Tn., U.S.	194	35.14 N	89.21 W
Somerville, Tx., U.S.	222	30.20 N	96.31 W
Somerville Lake ◎[1]	222	30.18 N	96.40 W
Someș (Szamos) ≃	38	48.07 N	22.22 E
Someșu Cald ≃	38	46.44 N	23.22 E
Someșul Mare ≃	38	47.12 N	24.12 E
Someșul Mic ≃	38	47.09 N	23.55 E
Someșul Rece ≃	38	46.44 N	23.22 E
Somino	76	59.21 N	34.52 E
Somis	228	34.16 N	119.00 W
Sŏmjin-gang ≃	98	34.58 N	127.46 E
Somma	66	42.40 N	12.44 E
Sommacampagna	64	45.24 N	10.50 E
Somma Lombardo, It.	62	45.41 N	8.42 E
Somma Lombardo, It.	266b	45.41 N	8.42 E
Sommariva	166	26.24 S	146.36 E
Sommariva del Bosco	62	44.46 N	7.47 E
Sommatino	70	37.20 N	13.59 E
Somme □[5]	50	49.55 N	2.30 E
Somme ≃, Fr.	50	49.01 N	4.12 E
Somme ≃, Fr.	50	50.11 N	1.39 E
Somme, Baie de la c	50	50.14 N	1.33 E
Somme, Canal de la ≅	50	49.55 N	2.43 E
Sommedieue	56	49.05 N	5.28 E
Sommelsdijk	52	51.45 N	4.09 E
Sommen ◎	26	58.01 N	15.15 E
Sommepy-Tahure	56	49.15 N	4.33 E
Sommerberg ◆[8]	263	51.27 N	7.32 E
Sömmerda	54	51.10 N	11.07 E
Sommersdorf	54	53.17 N	14.11 E
Sommersted	41	55.19 N	9.19 E
Sommesous	50	48.44 N	4.12 E
Somme Woods ♦	278	42.09 N	87.49 W
Somnitel'nyj	89	52.12 N	139.04 E
Somo ≃	190	45.29 N	89.48 W
Somogy □[6]	30	46.25 N	17.35 E
Somonauk	216	41.38 N	88.40 W
Somonauk Creek ≃	216	41.32 N	88.41 W
Somosierra, Puerto de)(	34	41.09 N	3.35 W
Somosomo	175g	16.46 S	179.58 W
Somosomo Strait ʮ	175g	16.47 S	179.58 E
Somotillo	236	13.02 N	86.55 W
Somoto	236	13.28 N	86.35 W
Somovo, Ross.	76	52.53 N	34.58 E
Somovo, Ross.	78	51.44 N	39.23 E
Sompeta	122	18.56 N	84.36 E
Somplago	64	46.21 N	13.04 E
Sompolno	30	52.24 N	18.31 E
Somport, Puerto de)(	34	42.48 N	0.31 W
Sompuis	50	48.41 N	4.23 E
Somuncurá, Meseta de ⩘[1]	254	41.30 S	67.15 W
Somvix	58	46.44 N	8.56 E

FRANÇAIS

Nom	Page	Lat.°′	Long.°′ W = Ouest
Šomyškol'	86	46.30 N	59.53 E
Son, Ned.	52	51.31 N	5.30 E
Son, Nor.	26	59.31 N	10.42 E
Son ≃	124	25.42 N	84.52 E
Soná	236	8.01 N	81.19 W
Sona-Bata	152	4.54 S	15.09 E
Sonādugi	126	22.47 N	90.40 E
Sonaguera	236	15.38 N	86.20 W
Sonahula	124	25.05 N	87.09 E
Sonāmarg	123	34.18 N	75.18 E
Sonāmukhi	126	23.18 N	87.25 E
Sonāpur	126	23.42 N	89.30 E
Sonar	164	2.33 S	133.00 E
Sonār ≃	124	24.24 N	79.56 E
Sonari	272c	18.52 N	72.59 E
Sonarpur	272b	22.26 N	88.25 E
Sonātikri	272b	22.57 N	88.20 E
Sonceboz	58	47.11 N	7.11 E
Sonchamp	261	48.35 N	1.53 E
Sŏnch'ŏn	98	39.48 N	124.55 E
Soncino	62	45.24 N	9.52 E
Sondags ≃, S. Afr.	158	33.44 S	25.51 E
Sondags ≃, S. Afr.	158	28.43 S	30.16 E
Sondalo	64	46.20 N	10.19 E
Sønderå ≃	41	54.53 N	8.59 E
Sønderborg	41	54.55 N	9.47 E
Sønderby	41	55.47 N	10.01 E
Sønder Felding	41	55.57 N	8.47 E
Sønderhav	41	54.51 N	9.30 E
Sønderjylland □[6]	41	55.10 N	9.15 E
Sønder Nærå	41	55.18 N	10.30 E
Sønder Omme	41	55.50 N	8.54 E
Sondershausen	54	51.22 N	10.52 E
Søndersø	41	55.29 N	10.16 E
Sondi	114	2.58 N	98.52 E
Søndre Strømfjord	176	66.59 N	50.40 W
Søndre Strømfjord c[2]	176	66.30 N	52.15 W
Sondrio	64	46.10 N	9.52 E
Sondrio □[4]	58	46.10 N	10.03 E
Sonduga	76	60.08 N	41.55 E
Sone ≃	126	21.34 N	86.54 E
Sonepur	120	20.50 N	83.55 E
Sonestown	210	41.21 N	76.33 W
Song, Malay.	112	2.01 N	112.33 E
Song, Nig.	146	9.50 N	12.38 E
Song, Thai	110	18.28 N	100.11 E
Song ≃	100	27.02 N	118.18 E
Song'ao	100	29.36 N	121.41 E
Songbahutun	104	41.28 N	121.11 E
Song Bay Hap, Cua c	110	8.46 N	104.52 E
Songbu	100	31.05 N	114.48 E
Sŏngbyŏn-ni	98	38.03 N	125.18 E
Song Cau	110	13.27 N	109.13 E
Sŏng-ch'ŏn-gang ≃	98	39.48 N	127.35 E
Songcun	106	30.26 N	119.43 E
Songe	26	58.41 N	9.00 E
Songea	154	10.41 S	35.39 E
Songeons	50	49.33 N	1.52 E
Songgaizhen	107	29.03 N	105.54 E
Songgang	100	22.49 N	113.51 E
Songgato ≃	164	3.26 S	140.22 E
Songhe	100	31.10 N	113.20 E
Songhua ≃	89	47.44 N	132.32 E
Songhuahu ◎	89	43.20 N	127.07 E
Songhuajiang	89	44.46 N	125.54 E
Songhwa	98	38.21 N	125.08 E
Songino	88	48.54 N	95.54 E
Sŏngjang-ni	98	41.02 N	126.50 E
Songjiachang	107	28.47 N	104.55 E
Songjiang	106	31.01 N	121.14 E
Songjiangzhen	98	42.12 N	126.56 E
Songjiapu	107	29.38 N	104.44 E
Songjiaying	105	40.38 N	115.14 E
Sŏngjin → Kimch'aek	98	40.41 N	129.12 E
Songjŏng	98	35.10 N	126.46 E
Sŏngju	98	35.55 N	128.16 E
Songkan	102	28.27 N	106.50 E
Songkhla	110	7.12 N	100.36 E
Songkhram ≃	110	17.39 N	104.28 E
Songkou, Zhg.	100	25.48 N	118.36 E
Songkou, Zhg.	100	24.32 N	116.24 E
Songlinba	100	24.00 N	115.59 E
Songlindian	105	39.25 N	115.54 E
Songling	89	48.02 N	121.12 E
Song Ling ⩘	98	41.10 N	120.09 E
Songmen	100	28.19 N	121.34 E
Songming	102	25.24 N	102.59 E
Sŏngmo-do I	98	37.42 N	126.18 E
Sŏngnae-ri	98	39.28 N	126.59 E
Sŏngnam	98	37.26 N	127.08 E
Sŏng-ni	98	39.38 N	127.06 E
Songnim	98	38.44 N	125.38 E
Songo	152	7.22 S	14.51 E
Songololo	152	5.42 S	14.02 E
Songot ∧	154	3.59 N	34.28 E
Songpan	102	32.40 N	103.24 E
Song Phi Nong	110	14.13 N	100.03 E
Sŏngsa-ri	271b	37.38 N	126.52 E
Songshancun	104	41.02 N	121.09 E
Songshu	98	39.50 N	122.06 E
Songshugou	105	41.02 N	117.49 E
Songtangmiao	106	31.08 N	119.16 E
Songtao	102	28.06 N	109.05 E
Șongtun	98	39.54 N	123.56 E
Šonguj	24	68.47 N	33.00 E
Songu-ri	98	37.49 N	127.09 E
Songwe, Zaïre	154	3.24 S	26.16 E
Songwe, Zaïre	154	12.25 S	29.40 E
Songwe ≃	154	9.43 S	33.56 E
Songxi, Zhg.	100	27.33 N	118.46 E
Songxi, Zhg.	100	26.16 N	116.59 E
Songxia, Zhg.	100	25.44 N	119.36 E
Songxia, Zhg.	100	30.07 N	120.51 E
Songxian	102	34.10 N	112.05 E
Songyan	98	37.13 N	113.43 E
Songyin	106	30.54 N	121.13 E
Songyin ≃	100	28.18 N	119.44 E
Songzhangzi	98	41.13 N	119.08 E
Songzhuang	106	32.06 N	121.17 E
Son Ha	110	15.03 N	108.34 E
Soni, Ehi ∧	146	20.49 N	17.23 E
Sonico	64	46.10 N	10.21 E
Sonid Youqi	102	42.44 N	112.40 E
Sonid Zuoqi	102	43.58 N	113.59 E
Sonīpat	124	28.59 N	77.01 E
Sonkach	124	22.59 N	76.21 E
Sonk'ol', ozero ◎	85	41.50 N	75.08 E
Sonkovo	76	57.47 N	37.09 E
Son La	110	21.19 N	103.54 E
Sonmiāni	120	25.26 N	66.36 E
Sonmiāni Bay c	120	25.15 N	66.30 E
Sonnberg ∧	264b	48.20 N	16.15 E
Sonneberg	54	50.22 N	11.10 E
Sonnefeld	56	50.13 N	11.08 E
Sonnen	60	48.41 N	13.43 E
Sonnenberg ∧[2]	61	47.52 N	16.28 E
Sonnewalde	54	51.42 N	13.38 E
Sonning Common	42	51.31 N	0.59 W
Sonningdale	184	52.24 N	107.40 W
Sonnino	66	41.25 N	13.14 E
Sonntagberg	61	47.59 N	14.45 E
Sono	270	34.48 N	135.55 E
Sono, Rio do ≃, Bra.	250	8.58 S	48.11 W
Sono, Rio do ≃, Bra.	255	17.02 S	45.32 W
Sonobe	96	35.06 N	135.28 E
Sonogno	58	46.21 N	8.47 E
Sonoita Creek ≃	200	31.30 N	110.58 W
Sonoma	226	38.17 N	122.27 W
Sonoma □[6]	226	38.26 N	122.35 W
Sonoma Creek ≃	226	38.10 N	122.24 W
Sonoma Mountains ⩘	226	38.17 N	122.35 W
Sonoma Peak ∧	204	40.52 N	117.36 W
Sonoma State Historical Park ♦	226	38.18 N	122.28 W
Sononder	158	29.43 S	21.51 E
Sonop	158	25.39 S	27.42 E
Sonora, Ca., U.S.	226	37.59 N	120.22 W

PORTUGUÊS

Nome	Página	Lat.°′	Long.°′ W = Oeste
Sonora, Tx., U.S.	196	30.34 N	100.38 W
Sonora □[3]	232	29.20 N	110.40 W
Sonora ≃	232	28.48 N	111.33 W
Sonoran Desert ◆[2]	16	30.00 N	113.00 W
Sonora Pass)(	226	38.19 N	119.37 W
Sonostrov	24	66.09 N	34.10 E
Sonoyta	232	31.51 N	112.50 W
Sonoyta ≃	200	31.16 N	113.26 W
Sonpār Hills ⩘[2]	124	24.20 N	82.15 E
Sonqor	128	34.47 N	47.36 E
Sŏnsan	98	36.16 N	128.17 E
Sonsbeck	52	51.37 N	6.22 E
Sonseca	34	39.42 N	3.57 W
Sonskyn	158	30.47 S	26.28 E
Sonsón	246	5.42 N	75.18 W
Sonsonate	236	13.43 N	89.44 W
Sonsorol Islands II	108	5.20 N	132.13 E
Sonstorp	40	58.45 N	15.36 E
Sonstraal	158	27.07 S	22.28 E
Sontag	194	31.39 N	90.12 W
Son Tay	110	21.08 N	105.30 E
Sonthofen	58	47.31 N	10.17 E
Sontra	56	51.04 N	9.56 E
Sonwān	124	27.40 N	81.45 E
Sonyea	210	42.41 N	77.50 W
Soochow → Suzhou	106	31.18 N	120.37 E
Sooke	224	48.23 N	123.43 W
Sooke ≃	224	48.23 N	123.42 W
Sooke Basin c	224	48.23 N	123.40 W
Sooke Lake ◎	224	48.33 N	123.42 W
Sooner Lake ◎[1]	196	36.26 N	97.02 W
Soonwald ⩘	56	49.55 N	7.40 E
Soo → Sault Sainte Marie	190	46.29 N	84.20 W
Sooyaac	144	0.03 N	42.17 E
Sopa Sopa Head ›	164	1.58 S	146.35 E
Sopchoppy	192	30.03 N	84.29 W
Soperton	192	32.22 N	82.35 W
Sop Hao	110	20.33 N	104.27 E
Sophia	192	37.42 N	81.15 W
Sopki	76	57.06 N	30.55 E
Sopockin	76	53.50 N	23.39 E
Sopot	30	54.28 N	18.34 E
Sop Pong	110	22.04 N	102.03 E
Sop Prap	110	17.53 N	99.20 E
Soprabolzano	64	46.32 N	11.24 E
Sopron	61	47.41 N	16.36 E
Sopronhorpács	61	47.29 N	16.44 E
Șopronkövesd	61	47.33 N	16.45 E
Šoptykol'	86	51.16 N	75.45 E
Sopur	123	34.18 N	74.28 E
Sŏp'yŏng-ni	98	35.01 N	127.24 E
Soquel	226	36.59 N	121.57 W
Soquel Creek ≃	226	36.58 N	121.57 W
Sor, Ribeira de ≃	34	39.00 N	8.17 W
Sora	66	41.43 N	13.37 E
Sorada	122	19.45 N	84.26 E
Sorae-san ∧	271b	37.27 N	126.47 E
Soraga	64	46.22 N	11.39 E
Soragna	64	44.56 N	10.07 E
Söråker	26	62.31 N	17.30 E
Șorano	66	42.41 N	11.43 E
Šorapani	84	42.05 N	43.05 E
Soras	248	14.07 S	73.37 W
Sorata	248	15.47 S	68.40 W
Soratte, Monte ∧	66	42.15 N	12.30 E
Sorau → Żary	30	51.38 N	15.09 E
Soraya	248	14.10 S	73.19 W
Șorbas	34	37.07 N	2.07 W
Šorbas, gora ∧	86	47.25 N	84.12 E
Sorbhog	120	26.30 N	90.52 E
Sorbie	44	54.48 N	4.26 W
Sorbo ≃	85	38.45 N	69.20 E
Sorbolo	64	44.51 N	10.28 E
Sorbonne ʊ[2]	261	48.51 N	2.21 E
Sorcier, Lac au ◎	206	46.42 N	73.24 W
Sordevolo	62	45.34 N	7.59 E
Sore	32	44.20 N	0.35 W
Sorel	206	46.02 N	73.07 W
Sorell	166	42.47 S	147.33 E
Sorell, Cape ›	166	42.12 S	145.10 E
Sorel Point ›	43b	49.16 N	2.10 W
Sörenberg	58	46.50 N	8.03 E
Sorento	219	39.00 N	89.34 W
Soreq ≃	132	31.56 N	34.42 E
Soresina	64	45.17 N	9.51 E
Sörfjärden c	40	59.24 N	16.50 E
Sørfjorden c[2]	26	60.24 N	6.40 E
Sørfold	24	67.28 N	15.22 E
Sörforsa	26	61.40 N	17.00 E
Sorge ≃	41	54.21 N	9.25 E
Sorgono	71	40.01 N	9.06 E
Sorgues	62	44.00 N	4.52 E
Sorgun	130	39.49 N	35.11 E
Sori	62	44.22 N	9.06 E
Soria	34	41.46 N	2.28 W
Soria □[4]	34	41.35 N	2.35 W
Soriano	252	33.24 S	58.19 W
Soriano □[5]	258	33.45 S	57.45 W
Soriano Calabro	68	38.36 N	16.14 E
Soriano nel Cimino	66	42.25 N	12.14 E
Sorico	58	46.10 N	9.22 E
Sorido	164	1.09 S	136.03 E
Sori-do I	98	34.26 N	127.48 E
Sørli	26	64.15 N	13.45 E
Sormonne ≃	56	49.46 N	4.40 E
Sorn	46	55.30 N	4.18 W
Sorne ≃	58	47.22 N	7.22 E
Sorø, Dan.	41	55.26 N	11.34 E
Soro, India	120	21.17 N	86.40 E
Soro, Monte ∧	70	37.56 N	14.42 E
Sorocaba	255	23.29 S	47.27 W
Sorocabuçu ≃	256	23.38 S	47.13 W
Soročinka	80	47.30 N	51.44 E
Soročinsk	80	52.26 N	53.10 E
Soročkino	86	57.02 N	68.52 E
Soroco	240m	18.22 N	65.38 W
Sorok	88	52.20 N	100.12 E
Sorok ≃	61	47.07 N	16.50 E
Soroka	78	48.09 N	28.17 E
Sorokino, Ross.	86	53.45 N	84.58 E
Sorokino, Ross.	86	54.13 N	91.31 E
Sorokošiči	78	51.12 N	30.35 E
Soroksár ◆[8]	264c	47.24 N	19.07 E
Sorol I[1]	108	8.08 N	140.23 E
Soron	124	27.53 N	78.45 E
Sorong	164	0.53 S	131.15 E
Sororó ≃	250	5.24 S	49.07 W
Sorot' ≃	76	57.04 N	28.50 E
Soroti	154	1.43 N	33.37 E
Sorovskije	86	59.53 N	71.34 E
Sørøya I	24	70.36 N	22.46 E
Sorpestausee ◎[1]	56	51.20 N	7.56 E
Sorraia ≃	34	38.56 N	8.53 W
Sorrento, Austl.	169	38.20 S	144.45 E
Sorrento, It.	68	40.37 N	14.22 E
Sorrento, Fl., U.S.	220	28.48 N	81.33 W
Sorrento, La., U.S.	194	30.11 N	90.51 W
Sorris Sorris	156	20.57 S	14.50 E
Sør Rondane Mountains ⩘	9	72.00 S	25.00 E
Sorsakoski	26	62.27 N	27.39 E
Sorsatunturi ∧	24	67.24 N	29.38 E
Sorsele	24	65.30 N	17.30 E
Sorsk	86	54.01 N	90.12 E
Sorso	71	40.48 N	8.34 E
Sorsogon	116	12.58 N	124.00 E
Sorsogon □[4]	116	12.50 N	123.55 E
Sorsogon Bay c	116	12.55 N	123.55 E
Șörstafors	40	59.35 N	16.13 E
Šorsu	85	40.17 N	70.48 E
Șort	34	42.24 N	1.08 E
Šortandy	86	51.42 N	71.00 E
Sortat	46	58.33 N	3.13 W
Sortavala	24	61.42 N	30.41 E
Sortino	70	37.09 N	15.02 E
Sortland	24	68.40 N	15.20 E

Sør-Trøndelag □[6]	26	63.00 N	10.40 E
Sorunda	40	59.01 N	17.48 E
Sörup	41	54.43 N	9.40 E
Sõrve neem ›	76	57.54 N	22.03 E
Sörvik	40	60.11 N	15.09 E
Sorviži	80	57.52 N	48.32 E
Sosa, Dtsch.	54	50.30 N	12.39 E
Șosa, Taehan	271b	37.29 N	126.47 E
Šoša ≃	82	56.31 N	36.05 E
Sŏsan	98	36.47 N	126.26 E
Sösdala	41	56.02 N	13.40 E
Sos del Rey Católico	34	42.30 N	1.13 W
Sosedka	80	53.15 N	42.40 E
Sosedno	76	58.14 N	28.42 E
Sosenka ≃, Ross.	265b	55.35 N	37.23 E
Sosenka ≃, Ross.	265b	55.47 N	37.42 E
Sosenki	82	55.34 N	37.26 E
Sösetalsperre ◆[6]	52	51.44 N	10.20 E
Soshigaya ◆[8]	268	35.39 N	139.36 E
Șösjöfjällen ⩘	26	63.53 N	13.15 E
Šoška	24	62.42 N	50.40 E
Soskovo	76	52.45 N	35.23 E
Sosna ≃	76	52.42 N	38.55 E
Sosneado, Cerro ∧	252	34.45 S	69.59 W
Sosnica	78	51.32 N	32.28 E
Sosnicy	76	57.38 N	30.25 E
Sosnogorsk	24	63.37 N	53.51 E
Sosnovaja Maza	80	52.30 N	47.53 E
Sosnovaja Pol'ana ◆[8]	265a	59.50 N	30.09 E
Sosnovec	24	64.26 N	34.27 E
Sosnovica	76	60.21 N	40.50 E
Sosnovka, Kaz.	86	51.26 N	79.28 E
Sosnovka, Kyrg.	85	42.40 N	73.55 E
Sosnovka, Ross.	24	66.30 N	40.32 E
Sosnovka, Ross.	80	56.13 N	47.13 E
Sosnovka, Ross.	80	57.48 N	51.43 E
Sosnovka, Ross.	80	57.16 N	53.31 E
Sosnovka, Ross.	80	54.06 N	46.38 E
Sosnovka, Ross.	80	56.17 N	51.17 E
Sosnovka, Ross.	80	53.14 N	41.22 E
Sosnovka, Ross.	80	52.26 N	43.29 E
Sosnovka, Ross.	82	54.31 N	38.08 E
Sosnovka, Ross.	82	54.54 N	38.41 E
Sosnovka, Ross.	86	59.10 N	81.18 E
Sosnovka, Ross.	88	54.09 N	109.35 E
Sosnovo, Ross.	76	60.33 N	30.15 E
Sosnovo, Ross.	80	56.42 N	54.35 E
Sosnovoborsk	80	53.18 N	46.16 E
Sosnovoje	78	50.49 N	27.00 E
Sosnovo-Oz'orskoje	88	52.31 N	111.30 E
Sosnovskij	86	54.36 N	73.10 E
Sosnovskoje	80	55.48 N	43.10 E
Sosnovyj Bor, Bela.	76	52.32 N	29.36 E
Sosnovyj Bor, Ross.	76	59.55 N	29.07 E
Sosnovyj Bor, Ross.	86	57.07 N	55.03 E
Sosnovyj Solonec	80	53.17 N	49.33 E
Sosnowiec	30	50.18 N	19.08 E
Soso	194	31.45 N	89.16 W
Sosok	112	0.17 N	110.14 E
Sospel	62	43.53 N	7.27 E
Sospirolo	64	46.09 N	12.04 E
Șossusvlei ◎	156	24.40 S	15.23 E
Šoštanj	61	46.23 N	15.03 E
Šostka	78	51.52 N	33.30 E
Sŏsura	98	42.16 N	130.37 E
Sos'va, Ross.	72	63.40 N	62.06 E
Sos'va, Ross.	86	59.10 N	61.50 E
Sos'va ≃	86	59.32 N	62.20 E
Sosyka ≃	78	46.35 N	39.05 E
Sot' ≃	80	58.00 N	40.39 E
Sota ≃	150	11.52 N	3.24 E
Sotik	154	0.41 S	35.21 E
Sotkamo	26	64.08 N	28.25 E
Sotnicyno	80	54.17 N	41.49 E
Soto de Aldovea	266a	40.26 N	3.27 W
Soto de Pajares	266a	40.17 N	3.32 W
Soto la Marina	234	23.46 N	98.13 W
Soto La Marina ≃	234	23.45 N	97.45 W
Soto la Marina, Barra I	232	24.10 N	97.43 W
Sotomayor	248	19.18 S	65.03 W
Sotonera, Embalse de ◎[1]	34	42.05 N	0.48 W
Sotouboua	150	8.34 N	0.59 E
Sotta, Fr.	71	41.32 N	9.12 E
Sotta, Fr.	71	41.32 N	9.12 E
Sottens	58	46.39 N	6.44 E
Sottern ◎	40	59.02 N	15.29 E
Sotteville	50	49.25 N	1.06 E
Sottile, Punta ›	70a	35.30 N	12.38 E
Sottomarina	64	45.13 N	12.17 E
Sottrum	52	53.06 N	9.14 E
Sottrup	41	54.57 N	9.43 E
Sottunga I	26	60.08 N	20.40 E
Souain-Perthes-lès-Hurlus	56	49.11 N	4.32 E
Souanké	152	2.05 N	14.03 E
Soubakaniédougou	150	10.28 N	5.01 W
Soubré	150	5.47 N	6.36 W
Soudan	166	20.05 S	137.00 E
Soudan → Sudan □[1]	140	15.00 N	30.00 E
Soude ≃	50	48.52 N	4.10 E
Soudersburg	208	40.01 N	76.09 W
Souderton	208	40.18 N	75.19 W
Souesmes	50	47.27 N	2.10 E
Soufflay	152	2.01 N	14.54 E
Soufflenheim	56	48.50 N	7.58 E
Soufflot, Lac ◎	190	47.24 N	78.31 W
Souflión	38	41.12 N	26.18 E
Soufrière	241f	13.52 N	61.04 W
Soufrière ∧, Guad.	241o	16.03 N	61.40 W
Soufrière ∧, St. Vin.	241h	13.20 N	61.11 W
Soufrière Bay c, Dom.	240d	15.14 N	61.22 W
Soufrière Bay c, St. Luc.	241f	13.51 N	61.04 W
Sougahatchee Creek ≃	194	32.38 N	85.50 W
Sougne-Remouchamps	56	50.29 N	5.40 E
Souguer	148	35.12 N	1.30 E
Souhegan ≃	188	42.51 N	71.29 W
Souillac	32	44.54 N	1.29 E
Souilly	56	49.01 N	5.17 E
Souk-el-Arba-des-Beni-Hassan	34	35.16 N	5.20 W
Souk-Khemis-du-Sahel	34	35.17 N	6.05 W
Souk Larbat Gharb	148	34.43 N	6.01 W
Sŏul (Seoul), Taehan	98	37.33 N	126.58 E
Sŏul (Seoul), Taehan	271b	37.33 N	126.58 E
Sŏul □[4]	98	37.34 N	127.00 E
Soulac-sur-Mer	32	45.31 N	1.07 W
Soulaines-Dhuys	58	48.22 N	4.44 E
Soulanges □[6]	206	45.20 N	74.15 W
Soulanges, Canal de ≅	275a	45.20 N	73.58 W
Soulougou	150	13.01 N	0.23 E
Soulsbyville	226	37.59 N	120.16 W
Soultzeren	58	48.04 N	7.06 E
Soultz-Haut-Rhin	58	47.53 N	7.14 E
Soultzmatt	58	47.58 N	7.14 E
Soultz-sous-Forêts	56	48.56 N	7.53 E
Soummam, Oued ≃	34	36.45 N	5.04 E
Sound Beach	210	40.57 N	72.58 W
Sounding Creek ≃	184	52.06 N	110.28 W
Sounding Lake ◎	184	52.08 N	110.29 W
Sound View Park ♦	276	40.49 N	73.52 W
Soúnion, Ákra ›	38	37.39 N	24.02 E
Soup Harbour c	212	43.51 N	77.11 W
Souppes-sur-Loing	50	48.11 N	2.44 E
Souq Ahras	148	36.23 N	8.00 E
Sources, Mont aux ∧	158	28.46 S	28.52 E
Soure, Bra.	250	0.44 S	48.31 W
Soure, Port.	34	40.03 N	8.38 W
Sour el Ghozlane	148	36.10 N	3.45 E
Souris, Mb., Can.	184	49.38 N	100.15 W
Souris, P.E., Can.	186	46.21 N	62.15 W

Souris ≃	198	49.39 N	99.34 W
Sourlake	194	30.09 N	94.25 W
Sourland Mountain ∧[2]	208	40.29 N	74.43 W
Sourou ≃	150	12.45 N	3.25 W
Souroukaha	150	8.13 N	5.08 W
Souš	54	50.32 N	13.34 E
Sous, Oued V	148	30.27 N	9.31 W
Sousa	250	6.45 S	38.14 W
Sousânia	255	16.11 S	49.05 W
Sousas	256	22.52 S	46.59 W
Sousel	34	38.57 N	7.40 W
Sous-le-Vent, Îles → Leeward Islands II	238	17.00 N	63.00 W
Sousse	148	35.49 N	10.38 E
Sousse □[8]	148	35.40 N	10.30 E
Sout ≃, S. Afr.	158	31.35 S	18.24 E
Sout ≃, S. Afr.	158	33.03 S	23.28 E
Sout ≃, S. Afr.	158	28.56 S	20.40 E
South ≃, Ia., U.S.	190	41.29 N	93.20 W
South ≃, Ma., U.S.	283	42.10 N	70.43 W
South ≃, Mo., U.S.	219	39.52 N	91.26 W
South ≃, N.J., U.S.	208	40.29 N	74.23 W
South ≃, N.C., U.S.	192	34.20 N	78.03 W
South ≃, Va., U.S.	192	37.46 N	79.23 W
South ≃, Va., U.S.	208	38.02 N	77.23 W
South Acton	207	42.27 N	71.27 W
South Africa (Suid-Afrika) □[1], Afr.	138	30.00 S	26.00 E
South Africa (Suid-Afrika) □[1], Afr.	156	30.00 S	26.00 E
Southall ◆[8]	260	51.31 N	0.23 W
South Alligator ≃	164	12.15 S	132.24 E
Southam	42	52.15 N	1.23 W
South Amboy	208	40.28 N	74.17 W
South America ±[1]	4	15.00 S	60.00 W
South America ±[1]	18	15.00 S	60.00 W
South Amherst, Ma., U.S.	207	42.20 N	72.30 W
South Amherst, Oh., U.S.	214	41.22 N	82.14 W
Southampton, N.S., Can.	186	45.35 N	64.15 W
Southampton, On., Can.	212	44.29 N	81.23 W
Southampton, Eng., U.K.	42	50.55 N	1.25 W
Southampton, Ma., U.S.	207	42.13 N	72.43 W
Southampton, N.Y., U.S.	207	40.53 N	72.23 W
Southampton, Pa., U.S.	285	40.10 N	75.02 W
Southampton □[6]	208	36.42 N	77.05 W
Southampton (Eastleigh) Airport ⊠	42	50.57 N	1.21 W
Southampton, Cape ›	176	62.09 N	83.40 W
Southampton Island I	176	64.20 N	84.40 W
South Andaman I	110	11.45 N	92.45 E
South Anna ≃	192	37.48 N	77.25 W
South Apopka	220	28.39 N	81.31 W
Southard	208	40.08 N	74.14 W
Southards Pond ◎	276	40.43 N	73.20 W
South Ashburnham	207	42.36 N	71.56 W
South Aulatsivik Island I	176	56.45 N	61.30 W
South Australia □[3]	162	30.00 S	135.00 E
South Australian Basin ✣[1]	14	38.00 S	126.00 E
Southaven	194	34.59 N	90.02 W
South Bald Mountain ∧	200	40.45 N	105.41 W
South Baldy ∧	200	33.59 N	107.11 W
South Banda Basin ✣[1]	14	6.30 S	127.30 E
Southbank	182	54.02 N	125.46 W
South Barre	207	42.23 N	72.05 W
South Barrington	278	42.06 N	88.07 W
South Barrule ∧[2]	44	54.12 N	4.40 W
South Bass Island I	214	41.39 N	82.49 W
South Bay	220	26.39 N	80.42 W
South Bay c, Mb., Can.	184	56.43 N	99.00 W
South Bay c, N.T., Can.	176	63.58 N	83.30 W
South Bay c, On., Can.	190	45.38 N	81.50 W
South Bay c, On., Can.	212	43.55 N	77.03 W
South Bay c, On., Can.	212	44.52 N	79.47 W
South Bay c, Fl., U.S.	220	26.42 N	80.45 W
South Bay c, Va., U.S.	208	37.14 N	75.52 W
South Bay c, Wa., U.S.	224	46.53 N	124.04 W
South Baymouth	190	45.33 N	82.01 W
South Beach ♦	276	40.35 N	74.05 W
South Beacon Mountain ∧	210	41.29 N	73.57 W
South Bedias Creek ≃	222	30.54 N	95.42 W
South Bellingham	207	42.03 N	71.28 W
South Belmar	208	40.10 N	74.02 W
South Beloit	216	42.29 N	89.02 W
South Bend, In., U.S.	216	41.41 N	86.15 W
South Bend, Wa., U.S.	224	46.40 N	123.48 W
South Benfleet	42	51.33 N	0.34 E
South Bentinck Arm c	182	52.15 N	126.50 W
South Bethlehem	214	41.00 N	79.20 W
South Bihar Plains ≍	124	25.15 N	84.30 E
South Bloomfield	218	39.43 N	82.59 W
Southborough, Eng., U.K.	42	51.10 N	0.15 E
Southborough, Ma., U.S.	207	42.18 N	71.31 W
South Bosque ≃	222	31.29 N	97.16 W
South Boston	192	36.41 N	78.54 W
South Boston ◆[8]	283	42.20 N	71.03 W
South Bound Brook	276	40.33 N	74.32 W
South Bradenton	220	27.27 N	82.35 W
South Branch, Nf., Can.	186	47.55 N	59.02 W
South Branch, N.J., U.S.	276	40.33 N	74.42 W
South Brent	42	50.25 N	3.50 W
Southbridge, N.Z.	172	43.49 S	172.15 E
Southbridge, Ma., U.S.	207	42.04 N	72.02 W
South Britain	207	41.28 N	73.15 W
Southbrook, Austl.	171a	27.41 S	151.43 E
Southbrook, N.Z.	172	43.20 S	172.36 E
South Brook ≃	285	39.52 N	75.44 W
South Brookfield	186	44.23 N	64.58 W
South Brooklyn ◆[8]	276	40.41 N	73.59 W
South Bruny Island I	166	43.23 S	147.17 E
South Buganda □[5]	154	0.30 S	31.35 E
South Burlington	188	44.28 N	73.10 W
Southbury	207	41.28 N	73.12 W
South Butler	210	43.08 N	76.46 W
South Byfield	283	42.44 N	70.54 W
South Byron	210	43.03 N	78.04 W
South Cairo	210	42.17 N	73.57 W
South Canaan	210	41.30 N	75.25 W
South Cape ›	175g	17.01 S	179.55 E
South Carolina □[3], U.S.	178	34.00 N	81.00 W
South Carolina □[3], U.S.	192	34.00 N	81.00 W
South Carver	207	41.50 N	70.44 W
South Castor ≃	212	45.15 N	75.23 W
South Cave	44	53.46 N	0.35 W
South Cerney	42	51.40 N	1.56 W
South Chagrin Reservation ♦	279a	41.25 N	81.25 W
South Channel ʮ, Pil.	116	14.20 N	120.37 E

South Channel ʮ, Mi., U.S.	190	45.38 N	84.32 W
South Channel ≃[1]	281	42.32 N	82.40 W
South Chaplin	207	41.46 N	72.07 W
South Charleston, Oh., U.S.	218	39.49 N	83.38 W
South Charleston, W.V., U.S.	188	38.22 N	81.41 W
South Chatham	207	41.40 N	70.01 W
South Chelmsford	283	42.34 N	71.23 W
South Chicago ◆[8]	278	41.44 N	87.33 W
South China Basin ✣[1]	12	15.00 N	115.00 E
South China Sea Ŧ[2]	108	10.00 N	113.00 E
South Cle Elum	224	47.11 N	120.56 W
South Coast Botanic Garden ♦	280	33.47 N	118.21 W
South Coatesville	208	39.58 N	75.49 W
South Coffeyville	196	36.59 N	95.37 W
South Concho ≃	196	31.21 N	100.28 W
South Corinth	210	43.12 N	73.51 W
South Corning	210	42.07 N	77.02 W
South Cotabato □[4]	116	6.15 N	125.00 E
South Creek ≃	170	33.36 S	150.50 E
South Crest	273d	26.15 S	28.07 E
South Dakota □[3], U.S.	178	44.15 N	100.00 W
South Dakota □[3], U.S.	198	44.15 N	100.00 W
South Dandalup ≃	168a	32.35 S	115.53 E
South Dandalup Dam ◆[6]	168a	32.38 S	116.04 E
South Darenth	260	51.24 N	0.15 E
South Dartmouth	207	41.35 N	70.56 W
South Dayton	210	42.21 N	79.03 W
South Deerfield	207	42.28 N	72.36 W
South Dennis, Ma., U.S.	207	41.41 N	70.09 W
South Dennis, N.J., U.S.	208	39.10 N	74.49 W
South Dorset	210	43.13 N	73.04 W
South Dorset Downs ⩘[1]	42	50.40 N	2.25 W
South Dos Palos	226	36.57 N	120.39 W
South Downs ⩘[1]	42	50.55 N	0.25 W
South Dum Dum	126	22.37 N	88.25 E
South Duxbury	207	42.01 N	70.41 W
South East □[5]	156	25.00 S	25.45 E
Southeast Asia Treaty Organization Headquarters ʊ	269a	13.45 N	100.31 E
South East Cape ›, Austl.	166	43.39 S	146.50 E
Southeast Cape ›, Ak., U.S.	180	62.55 N	169.42 W
Southeast Indian Ridge ✣[3]	6	50.00 S	110.00 E
South Easton	207	42.02 N	71.04 W
Southeast Pacific Basin ✣[1]	6	60.00 S	115.00 W
South East Point ›, Austl.	166	39.00 S	146.20 E
South East Point ›, Kiribati	174o	1.40 N	157.10 W
South Egg Harbor	208	39.31 N	74.39 W
South Egremont	207	42.09 N	73.25 W
South Elgin	216	41.59 N	88.17 W
South Elkhorn Creek ≃	218	38.13 N	84.48 W
South El Monte	280	34.03 N	118.02 W
Southend	44	55.20 N	5.38 W
Southend Municipal Airport ⊠	42	51.34 N	0.41 E
Southend-on-Sea	42	51.33 N	0.43 E
Southend-on-Sea □[8]	260	51.33 N	0.41 E
Southend Pier ◆[5]	260	51.31 N	0.44 E
South English ≃	190	41.30 N	91.56 W
Southern □[4], Malaŵi	154	15.30 S	35.00 E
Southern □[4], S.L.	150	8.00 N	12.15 W
Southern □[4], Zam.	154	16.30 S	27.00 E
Southern □[5], Bots.	156	24.45 S	24.00 E
Southern □[5], Ug.	154	0.30 S	30.30 E
Southern Alps ⩘	172	43.30 S	170.30 E
Southern California, University of ʊ[2]	280	34.02 N	118.17 W
Southern Cook Islands II	14	20.00 S	159.00 W
Southern Cross	162	31.13 S	119.19 E
Southern Ghāts ⩘	122	9.30 N	77.00 E
Southern Highlands □[5]	164	6.00 S	143.30 E
Southern Indian Lake ◎	176	57.10 N	98.40 W
Southern Leyte □[4]	116	10.50 N	124.55 E
Southern Lueti ≃	152	16.14 S	23.13 E
Southern Pines	192	35.10 N	79.23 W
Southern Ute Indian Reservation ◆[4]	200	37.05 N	107.45 W
Southern View	219	39.46 N	89.39 W
Southern Yemen → Yemen □[1]	144	15.00 N	47.00 E
Southery	42	52.32 N	0.23 E
South Esk ≃, Austl.	166	41.25 S	147.08 E
South Esk ≃, Scot., U.K.	46	56.42 N	2.32 W
South Esk ≃, Scot., U.K.	46	55.53 N	3.04 W
Southesk Tablelands ⩘[1]	162	20.50 S	126.40 E
South Essex	207	42.38 N	70.46 W
South Euclid	214	41.31 N	81.31 W
Southey	184	50.56 N	104.30 W
South Fabius ≃	219	39.54 N	91.30 W
South Fallsburg	210	41.42 N	74.37 W
South Farmbridge	260	51.38 N	0.41 E
South Farmingdale	276	40.43 N	73.26 W
Southfield, Ma., U.S.	207	42.06 N	73.14 W
Southfield, Mi., U.S.	216	42.28 N	83.13 W
Southfields	210	41.15 N	74.11 W
South Fiji Basin ✣[1]	14	26.00 S	175.00 E
Southfleet	260	51.25 N	0.19 E
South Floral Park	276	40.43 N	73.42 W
South Foreland ›	42	51.09 N	1.23 E
South Fork, Co., U.S.	200	37.40 N	106.38 W
South Fork, Pa., U.S.	214	40.22 N	78.47 W
South Fort George	182	53.54 N	122.45 W
South Forty Foot Drain ≅	42	52.56 N	0.15 W
South Fox Island I	190	45.25 N	85.50 W
South Fulton	194	36.30 N	88.52 W
South Gate, Ca., U.S.	228	33.57 N	118.12 W
Southgate, Fl., U.S.	220	27.18 N	82.32 W
Southgate, Mi., U.S.	216	42.12 N	83.11 W
Southgate, Wa., U.S.	224	47.10 N	122.30 W
Southgate ◆[8]	260	51.38 N	0.08 W
Southgate U.S.A. ◆[9]	279a	41.25 N	81.32 W
South Georgia I	244	54.15 S	36.45 W
South Georgia and the South Sandwich Islands □[2]	244	54.00 S	38.00 W
South Gibson	210	41.44 N	75.38 W
South Glamorgan □[6]	42	51.30 N	3.25 W
South Glastonbury	207	41.40 N	72.35 W
South Glens Falls	210	43.17 N	73.38 W
South Grafton	207	42.11 N	71.42 W
South Grand ≃	194	38.18 N	93.28 W
South Grand Island Bridge ◆[5]	284a	43.00 N	78.56 W
South Green	260	51.37 N	0.26 E
South Greensburg	214	40.17 N	79.33 W
South Hackensack	276	40.51 N	74.02 W
South Hadley, Ma., U.S.	188	42.15 N	72.34 W
South Hadley, Ma., U.S.	207	42.15 N	72.34 W
South Hadley Falls	207	42.13 N	72.36 W
South Hamilton	207	42.36 N	70.52 W

Symbol	English	Deutsch	Español	Français	Português
≃	River	Fluß	Río	Rivière	Rio
≅	Canal	Kanal	Canal	Canal	Canal
ᒪ	Waterfall, Rapids	Wasserfall, Stromschnellen	Cascada, Rápidos	Chute d'eau, Rapides	Cascata, Rápidos
ʮ	Strait	Meeresstraße	Estrecho	Détroit	Estreito
c	Bay, Gulf	Bucht, Golf	Bahía, Golfo	Baie, Golfe	Baía, Golfo
◎	Lake, Lakes	See, Seen	Lago, Lagos	Lac, Lacs	Lago, Lagos
☷	Swamp	Sumpf	Pantano	Marais	Pântano
⊓	Ice Features, Glacier	Eis- und Gletscherformen	Accidentes Glaciales	Formes glaciaires	Acidentes glaciares
Ŧ	Other Hydrographic Features	Andere Hydrographische Objekte	Otros Elementos Hidrográficos	Autres données hydrographiques	Outros acidentes hidrográficos

Symbol	English	Deutsch	Español	Français	Português
✣	Submarine Features	Untermeerische Objekte	Accidentes Submarinos	Formes de relief sous-marin	Acidentes submarinos
□	Political Unit	Politische Einheit	Unidad Politica	Entité politique	Unidade política
ʊ	Cultural Institution	Kulturelle Institution	Institución Cultural	Institution culturelle	Institução cultural
⊥	Historical Site	Historische Stätte	Sitio Histórico	Site historique	Sitio histórico
♦	Recreational Site	Erholungs- und Ferienort	Sitio de Recreo	Centre de loisirs	Area de Lazer
⊠	Airport	Flughafen	Aeropuerto	Aéroport	Aeroporto
▪	Military Installation	Militäranlage	Instalación Militar	Installation militaire	Instalação militar
◆	Miscellaneous	Verschiedenes	Misceláneo	Divers	Diversos

ENGLISH — Name / Page / Lat.°′ / Long.°′
DEUTSCH — Name / Seite / Breite°′ / Länge°′ E = Ost

Name	Page	Lat.°′	Long.°′
South Hams ≍	42	50.22 N	3.50 W
South Hanningfield	260	51.39 N	0.31 E
South Hanover	283	42.05 N	70.51 W
South Harbor c	269f	14.33 N	120.58 E
South Hartford	210	43.21 N	73.25 W
South Harwich	207	41.40 N	70.02 W
South Hātia Island I	124	22.19 N	91.07 E
South Haven, In., U.S.	216	41.32 N	87.08 W
South Haven, Ks., U.S.	198	37.03 N	97.24 W
South Haven, Mi., U.S.	216	42.24 N	86.16 W
South Hayling	42	50.47 N	0.59 W
South Head >, Austl.	274a	33.50 S	151.17 E
South Head >, N.Z.	172	36.26 S	174.14 E
South Heart ≃	182	55.34 N	116.11 W
South Heights	279b	40.35 N	80.14 W
South Hempstead	276	40.41 N	73.37 W
South Henderson	192	36.17 N	78.25 W
South Henik Lake @	176	61.30 N	97.30 W
South Hero	188	44.38 N	73.18 W
South Hetton	44	54.48 N	1.24 W
South Hill, N.Y., U.S.	210	42.25 N	76.33 W
South Hill, Va., U.S.	192	36.43 N	78.07 W
South Hills ✦[8]	273d	26.15 S	28.05 E
South Hills Village ✦[9]	279b	40.21 N	80.03 W
South Hingham	207	42.11 N	70.52 W
South Hogan Creek ≃	218	39.03 N	84.54 W
South Holland	216	41.36 N	87.36 W
South Holston Lake @[1]	192	36.35 N	82.00 W
South Honcut Creek ≃	226	39.19 N	121.35 W
South Honshu Ridge ✦[3]	14	24.00 N	142.00 E
South Hopkinton	207	41.24 N	71.45 W
South Horr	154	2.06 N	36.55 E
South Houston	222	29.39 N	95.14 W
South Huntington	276	40.49 N	73.23 W
South Indian Basin ✦[1]	6	60.00 S	120.00 E
South Indian Lake	184	56.46 N	98.57 W
Southington, Ct., U.S.	207	41.35 N	72.52 W
Southington, Oh., U.S.	214	41.19 N	80.57 W
South International Falls	190	48.35 N	93.23 W
South Ionia	216	42.57 N	85.04 W
South Island I, India	122	10.03 N	72.17 E
South Island I, Kenya	154	2.38 N	36.36 E
South Island I, Micron.	175c	6.59 N	151.59 E
South Island I, N.Z.	172	43.00 S	171.00 E
South Islet I	116	8.44 N	119.49 E
South Jacksonville	219	39.42 N	90.13 W
South Kemptville Creek ≃	212	44.54 N	75.41 W
South Kenosha	216	42.32 N	87.50 W
South Kensington Museums ʊ	260	51.30 N	0.11 W
South Kent	207	41.40 N	73.28 W
South Kirkby	44	53.34 N	1.20 W
South Konkan Hills ⋏[2]	122	17.00 N	73.30 E
South Korea → Korea, South □[1]	98	36.30 N	128.00 E
South Ladder Creek ≃	198	38.41 N	101.34 W
South Laguna	228	33.30 N	117.45 W
Southlake	222	32.57 N	97.09 W
South Lake @, On., Can.	212	44.26 N	76.13 W
South Lake @, Fl., U.S.	220	28.37 N	80.52 W
South Lake Tahoe	226	38.56 N	119.58 W
South Lancaster	207	42.26 N	71.41 W
Southland, Ky., U.S.	218	38.01 N	84.31 W
Southland, Mi., U.S.	216	42.13 N	84.24 W
Southland, Tx., U.S.	196	33.22 N	101.33 W
Southland ✦[9]	282	37.39 N	122.06 W
South Laurel	284c	39.05 N	76.52 W
Southlawn, Il., U.S.	219	39.45 N	89.37 W
South Lawn, Md., U.S.	284c	38.48 N	76.59 W
South Layhill	284c	39.04 N	77.03 W
South Lebanon	218	39.22 N	84.12 W
South Lee	207	42.16 N	73.16 W
South Lima	210	42.51 N	77.41 W
South Line Island I	276	40.37 N	73.30 W
South Llano ≃	196	30.30 N	99.46 W
South Lockport	284a	43.09 N	78.42 W
South Lorain	279a	41.27 N	82.08 W
South Loup ≃	198	41.04 N	98.40 W
South Luangwa National Park ♦	154	12.50 S	31.45 E
South Luconia Shoals ✦[2]	112	5.00 N	112.42 E
South Lynnfield	283	42.31 N	71.00 W
South Lyon	216	42.27 N	83.39 W
South Macmillan ≃	180	63.03 N	133.18 W
South Magnetic Pole ✦	9	65.18 S	139.30 E
South Malosmadulu Atoll I[1]	122	5.10 N	72.58 E
South Manitou Island I	190	45.01 N	86.07 W
South Marsh Island I	208	38.06 N	76.02 W
South Medford	202	42.18 N	122.50 W
South Media	285	39.54 N	75.23 W
South Melbourne	274b	37.50 S	144.57 E
South Merrimack	207	42.48 N	71.33 W
South Miami	220	25.42 N	80.17 W
South Miami Heights	220	25.35 N	80.22 W
South Middleboro	207	41.49 N	70.49 W
South Milford	216	41.31 N	85.16 W
South Mills	192	36.26 N	76.19 W
South Milwaukee	216	42.54 N	87.51 W
South Mimms	260	51.42 N	0.14 W
Southminster	42	51.40 N	0.50 E
South Modesto	226	37.38 N	120.58 W
South Mokelumne ≃	226	38.08 N	121.35 W
South Molton	42	51.01 N	3.50 W
South Monroe	216	41.54 N	83.25 W
Southmont	214	40.18 N	78.56 W
South Montrose	210	41.48 N	75.53 W
South Moose Lake @	184	53.46 N	100.08 W
South Mountain	208	39.51 N	77.29 W
South Mountain ∧, U.S.	208	39.40 N	77.30 W
South Mountain ∧, Id., U.S.	202	42.44 N	116.54 W
South Mountain Reservation ♦	276	40.45 N	74.18 W
South Mount Vernon	214	40.23 N	82.23 W
South Nahanni ≃	176	61.03 N	123.20 W
South Naknek	180	58.43 N	157.00 W
South Nation ≃	188	45.34 N	75.06 W
South Negril Point >	241q	18.15 N	78.22 W
South New Berlin	210	42.31 N	75.23 W
South New Castle	214	40.58 N	80.21 W
South New River Canal ≊	220	26.04 N	80.12 W
South Norfolk → Chesapeake	208	36.43 N	76.15 W
South Normanton	44	53.06 N	1.20 W
South Norwalk Reservoir @[1]	276	41.11 N	73.27 W
South Norwood ✦[8]	260	51.24 N	0.04 W
South Nutfield	260	51.14 N	0.08 W
South Nyack	276	41.04 N	73.55 W
South Ockendon	42	51.32 N	0.18 E
South Ogden	200	41.11 N	111.58 W
Southold	207	41.03 N	72.25 W
South Onondaga	210	42.56 N	76.13 W
South Orange	276	40.47 N	74.15 W
South Orkney Islands II	9	60.35 S	45.30 W
South Oroville	226	39.30 N	121.33 W
South Otselic	210	42.38 N	75.46 W
Southowram	262	53.43 N	1.50 W
South Oxhey	260	51.38 N	0.23 W
South Oyster Bay c	276	40.38 N	73.28 W
South Palo Duro Creek ≃	196	36.06 N	101.29 W
South Para ≃	168b	34.36 S	138.45 E
South Para Reservoir @[1]	168b	34.42 S	138.52 E
South Paris	188	44.13 N	70.30 W
South Park	216	41.44 N	88.18 W
South Park ♦, N.Y., U.S.	284a	42.50 N	78.50 W
South Park ♦, Pa., U.S.	279b	40.19 N	80.01 W
South Pasadena, Ca., U.S.	280	34.06 N	118.08 W
South Pasadena, Fl., U.S.	220	27.46 N	82.43 W
South Pass)(	200	42.22 N	108.55 W
South Pass)(	175c	7.14 N	151.48 E
South Passage ʯ, Austl.	171a	27.22 S	153.26 E
South Passage ʯ, Oh., U.S.	214	41.35 N	82.45 W
South Patrick Shores	220	28.12 N	80.35 W
South Pekin	190	40.29 N	89.39 W
South Pender	224	48.45 N	123.09 W
South Pender Island I	224	48.45 N	123.10 W
South Perth	168a	31.59 S	115.52 E
South Petherton	42	50.58 N	2.49 W
South Philadelphia ✦[8]	285	39.56 N	75.10 W
South Philipsburg	214	40.53 N	78.13 W
South Pittsburg	194	35.00 N	85.42 W
South Plainfield	210	40.34 N	74.24 W
South Platte ≃	178	41.07 N	100.42 W
South Platte, North Fork ≃	200	39.25 N	105.10 W
South Point >, Barb.	241g	13.02 N	59.31 W
South Point >, Pil.	116	10.24 N	122.30 E
South Pole ✦	9	90.00 S	0.00
South Porcupine	190	48.28 N	81.13 W
Southport, Austl.	166	43.25 S	146.59 E
Southport, Austl.	171a	27.58 S	153.25 E
Southport, Eng., U.K.	44	53.39 N	3.01 W
Southport, Ct., U.S.	207	41.08 N	73.17 W
Southport, Fl., U.S.	194	30.17 N	85.38 W
Southport, In., U.S.	218	39.39 N	86.07 W
Southport, N.Y., U.S.	210	42.03 N	76.49 W
Southport, N.C., U.S.	192	33.55 N	78.01 W
South Portland	188	43.38 N	70.14 W
South Portsmouth	218	38.43 N	83.00 W
South Pottstown	208	40.14 N	75.39 W
South Prairie Creek ≃	224	47.08 N	122.10 W
South Raisin ≃	206	45.08 N	74.35 W
South Range	190	47.04 N	88.38 W
South Renovo	214	41.19 N	77.44 W
South Reservoir @[1]	283	42.27 N	71.07 W
South Ribble ≃[8]	262	53.45 N	2.42 W
South River, On., Can.	190	45.50 N	79.23 W
South River, N.J., U.S.	208	40.26 N	74.23 W
South River c	208	38.57 N	76.29 W
South Rockwood	216	42.04 N	83.16 W
South Ronaldsay I	46	58.46 N	2.58 W
South Roxana	219	38.50 N	90.04 W
South Royalston	207	42.37 N	72.08 W
South Rukuru ≃	154	10.46 S	34.14 E
South Russell	214	41.25 N	81.21 W
South Salmara	124	25.55 N	90.01 E
South Sand Bluff >	158	31.19 S	30.01 E
South Sandwich Islands II	18	57.45 S	26.30 W
South Sandwich Trench ✦[1]	18	56.30 S	25.00 W
South Sandy Creek ≃	212	43.43 N	76.12 W
South San Francisco	226	37.39 N	122.24 W
South San Gabriel	280	34.03 N	118.05 W
South San Jose Hills	280	34.01 N	117.55 W
South San Ramon Creek ≃	282	37.42 N	121.55 W
South Santiam ≃	202	44.41 N	123.00 W
South Saskatchewan ≃	184	53.15 N	105.05 W
South Saugeen ≃	212	44.08 N	81.02 W
South Seaville	208	39.10 N	74.45 W
South Setauket	210	40.54 N	73.06 W
South Shafter	226	35.28 N	119.17 W
South Shetland Islands II	9	62.00 S	58.00 W
South Shields	44	55.00 N	1.25 W
South Shore	218	38.43 N	82.59 W
South Shore ✦[8]	278	41.46 N	87.35 W
South Shore Mall ✦[9]	276	40.44 N	73.15 W
South Shore Plaza ✦[9]	283	42.13 N	71.01 W
Southside	174h	2.49 S	171.43 W
South Side ✦[8]	279b	40.26 N	79.58 W
Southside Place	222	29.42 N	95.26 W
South Sioux City	198	42.28 N	96.24 W
South Skunk ≃	190	41.15 N	92.02 W
South Slocan	182	49.28 N	117.32 W
South Solon	218	39.44 N	83.36 W
South Sound ʯ	48	53.02 N	9.28 W
South Spicer Island I	176	68.06 N	79.13 W
South Standard	219	39.21 N	89.47 W
South Station ✦[5]	283	42.21 N	71.04 W
South Sterling	210	41.17 N	75.21 W
South Stickney	278	41.45 N	87.46 W
South Stony Brook	276	40.53 N	73.07 W
South Stradbroke Island I	171a	27.51 S	153.25 E
South Streator	216	40.39 N	88.23 W
South Suburban → Behāla	126	22.31 N	88.19 E
South Sulphur ≃	196	33.23 N	95.18 W
South Sunday Creek ≃	202	46.27 N	105.54 W
South Superior	200	41.45 N	108.57 W
South Swansea	207	41.43 N	71.12 W
South Taranaki Bight c[3]	172	39.40 S	174.10 E
South Tasman Rise ✦[3]	6	49.00 S	148.00 E
South Temple	208	40.24 N	75.55 W
South Thompson ≃	182	50.41 N	120.21 W
South Toms River	208	39.56 N	74.12 W
South Torrington	200	42.02 N	104.11 W
South Towanda	210	41.45 N	76.27 W
South Tucson	200	32.11 N	110.58 W
South Turkeyfoot Creek ≃	216	41.25 N	83.58 W
South Turlock	226	37.29 N	120.51 W
South Twillingate Island I	186	49.37 N	54.47 W
South Tyne ≃	44	54.59 N	2.08 W
South Ubian	116	5.11 N	120.30 E
South Uist I	46	57.15 N	7.21 W
South Umpqua ≃	202	43.20 N	123.25 W
South Valley	210	42.42 N	74.43 W
South Valley Hills ⋏[2]	285	40.00 N	75.40 W
South Valley Stream	276	40.39 N	73.43 W
South Venice	220	27.03 N	82.25 W
South Ventana Cone ∧	204	36.17 N	121.38 W
South Vestal	210	42.01 N	76.00 W
South Vietnam → Vietnam □[1]	108	16.00 N	108.00 E
Southview	214	40.20 N	80.16 W
Southview Apartments	284c	38.50 N	77.00 W
South Wabasca Lake @	182	55.54 N	113.45 W
South Wales	210	42.43 N	78.35 W
South Walpole	283	42.06 N	71.15 W
Southwark ✦[8]	42	51.30 N	0.06 W
South Warren Reservoir @[1]	168b	34.43 S	138.55 E
Southwater	42	51.01 N	0.21 W
South Waverly	210	41.59 N	76.32 W
South Weald	260	51.37 N	0.16 E
Southwell	44	53.05 N	0.58 W
South Wellfleet	207	41.55 N	69.59 W
South Wellington	224	49.06 N	123.53 W
Southwest	214	40.12 N	79.32 W
South West Bay c	240b	25.00 N	77.32 W
Southwest Branch ≃	284c	38.53 N	76.48 W
South Westbury	276	40.45 N	73.35 W
South West Cape >, Austl.	166	43.34 S	146.02 E
South West Cape >, N.Z.	172	47.17 S	167.28 E
Southwest Cape >, Ak., U.S.	180	63.18 N	171.27 W
Southwest Cape >, Vir. Is., U.S.	241n	17.41 N	64.54 W
Southwest Channel ʯ	220	27.34 N	82.45 W
South West City	194	36.30 N	94.36 W
South Westerlo	210	42.27 N	74.02 W
Southwest Greensburg	214	40.17 N	79.33 W
Southwest Harbor	188	44.16 N	68.19 W
Southwest Indian Ridge ✦[3]	6	30.00 S	60.00 E
Southwest Miramichi ≃	186	46.58 N	65.35 W
Southwest Museum ʊ	280	34.06 N	118.13 W
Southwest National Park ♦	166	43.15 S	146.15 E
Southwest Pacific Basin ✦[1]	6	40.00 S	150.00 W
Southwest Point >, Ba.	238	25.51 N	77.13 W
South West Point >, Kiribati	174o	1.52 N	157.33 W
Southwest Point >, Pap. N. Gui.	164	2.14 S	146.34 E
South Weymouth	283	42.10 N	70.57 W
South Weymouth Naval Air Station ■	207	42.09 N	70.57 W
South Whitley	216	41.05 N	85.37 W
South Whittier	280	33.57 N	118.02 W
South Wichita ≃	196	33.43 N	99.29 W
Southwick, Eng., U.K.	42	50.50 N	0.13 W
Southwick, Ma., U.S.	207	42.03 N	72.46 W
South Williamson	192	37.40 N	82.17 W
South Williamsport	210	41.13 N	76.59 W
South Wilmington	216	41.10 N	88.16 W
South Windham	188	43.44 N	70.25 W
South Windsor	207	41.49 N	72.37 W
Southwold	42	52.20 N	1.40 E
Southwood	210	42.59 N	76.08 W
Southwood Acres	207	41.59 N	72.32 W
South Woodham Ferrers	42	51.39 N	0.37 E
South Woodslee	214	42.14 N	82.43 W
South Woodstock	207	41.56 N	71.57 W
Southworth	224	47.31 N	122.30 W
South Yadkin ≃	192	35.45 N	80.27 W
South Yamhill ≃	224	45.13 N	123.08 W
South Yarmouth	207	41.40 N	70.11 W
South Yarra	274b	37.51 S	145.00 E
South Yorkshire □[6]	44	53.30 N	1.15 W
South Yuba ≃	226	39.17 N	121.12 W
South Zeal	42	50.44 N	3.54 W
Soutpan	158	28.43 S	26.04 E
Soutpansberg ⋏	156	22.55 S	29.30 E
Souttouf, Adrar ⋏	148	22.15 N	15.40 W
Souvigny	32	46.32 N	3.11 E
Souzy-la-Briche	261	48.32 N	2.09 E
Sovata	38	46.35 N	25.04 E
Soverato	68	38.41 N	16.33 E
Sovere	64	45.49 N	10.01 E
Sovereign Hill Historical Park ⊥	169	37.37 S	143.51 E
Sovereign Mountain ∧	180	62.08 N	148.36 W
Soveria Mannelli	68	39.05 N	16.22 E
Sövestad	41	55.30 N	13.47 E
Sovetabad	85	40.48 N	72.58 E
Sovetašen, Haya.	84	39.50 N	45.03 E
Sovetašen, Haya.	84	40.06 N	44.33 E
Sovetka	83	47.30 N	39.15 E
Sovetsk, Ross.	76	53.56 N	37.39 E
Sovetsk, Ross.	76	55.05 N	21.53 E
Sovetsk, Ross.	80	57.37 N	48.58 E
Sovetskaja, Ross.	80	49.00 N	42.07 E
Sovetskaja, Ross.	84	44.02 N	44.03 E
Sovetskaja, Ross.	84	44.46 N	41.11 E
Sovetskaja Gavan'	89	48.58 N	140.18 E
Sovetskich Oficerov, pik ∧	85	38.26 N	73.18 E
Sovetskij, Ross.	76	60.32 N	28.41 E
Sovetskij, Ross.	80	56.46 N	48.32 E
Sovetskij, Ross.	86	51.04 N	56.29 E
Sovetskij, Taj.	85	40.11 N	71.19 E
Sovetskij, Taj.	85	38.02 N	69.35 E
Sovetskij, Ukr.	78	45.20 N	34.56 E
Sovetskoje, Kaz.	85	42.17 N	70.15 E
Sovetskoje, Ross.	78	50.21 N	39.01 E
Sovetskoje, Ross.	80	51.27 N	46.44 E
Sovetskoje, Ross.	84	42.52 N	45.41 E
Sovetskoje, Ross.	84	43.19 N	43.36 E
Šovgenovskij	78	45.02 N	40.14 E
Sovicille	66	43.17 N	11.13 E
Sovico	266b	45.39 N	9.16 E
Søvik	26	62.33 N	6.18 E
Søvind	41	55.54 N	10.01 E
Sovpolje	24	65.18 N	43.55 E
Sow ≃	42	52.48 N	2.00 W
Sowa Pan ≍	156	20.45 S	26.00 E
Sowek	164	0.49 S	135.30 E
Sowerby, Eng., U.K.	44	54.13 N	1.21 W
Sowerby, Eng., U.K.	262	53.42 N	1.56 W
Sowerby Bridge	44	53.43 N	1.54 W
Soweto	158	26.14 S	27.54 E
Sowjetisches Ehrenmal ⊥	264a	52.29 N	13.28 E
Soy	56	50.17 N	5.31 E
Sōya-kaikyō → La Perouse Strait ʯ	89	45.45 N	142.00 E
Sōya-misaki >	92a	45.31 N	141.56 E
Soyang-chŏsuji @[1]	98	37.56 N	127.53 E
Soyapango	236	13.42 N	89.09 W
Soyers Lake @	212	45.02 N	78.37 W
Soyet	124	24.12 N	76.10 E
Soyland Moor ✦[3]	262	53.40 N	2.02 W
Soyo	152	6.07 S	12.18 E
Soyons	62	44.53 N	4.51 E
Sož ≃, Europe	78	51.57 N	30.48 E
Soz' ≃, Ross.	82	56.48 N	36.44 E
Sozimskij	24	59.44 N	52.16 E
Šožma	24	61.56 N	40.15 E
Sozopol	38	42.25 N	27.42 E
Sozzago	266b	45.24 N	8.43 E
Spa	56	50.30 N	5.52 E
Spaatz Island I	9	73.12 S	75.00 W
Space Needle ʊ	224	47.38 N	122.23 W
Space Obelisk ⊥	265b	55.49 N	37.38 E
Spadafora	70	38.13 N	15.22 E
Spada Lake @[1]	224	47.57 N	121.40 W
Spaden	52	53.34 N	8.38 E
Spahl	56	50.39 N	9.55 E
Spaichingen	58	48.04 N	8.44 E
Spain (España) □[1], Europe	22	40.00 N	4.00 W
Spain (España) □[1], Europe	34	40.00 N	4.00 W
Spakenburg	52	52.15 N	5.23 E
Spalato → Split	36	43.31 N	16.27 E
Spalding, Austl.	166	33.30 S	138.37 E
Spalding, Sk., Can.	184	52.20 N	104.30 W
Spalding, Eng., U.K.	42	52.47 N	0.10 W
Spalding, Mo., U.S.	219	39.38 N	91.32 W
Spalding, Ne., U.S.	198	41.41 N	98.21 W
Spalt	56	49.10 N	10.55 E
Spam Island I	174h	2.48 S	171.43 W
Spanaway	224	47.06 N	122.26 W
Spandau ✦[8]	54	52.33 N	13.12 E
Spandau, Berliner Forst ✦[3]	264a	52.35 N	13.11 E
Spandau, Berliner Forst ♦	264a	52.35 N	13.10 E
Spang	41	54.56 N	9.50 E
Spangenberg	56	51.07 N	9.40 E
Spangler	214	40.38 N	78.46 W
Spaniard's Bay	186	47.37 N	53.17 W
Spanien → Spain □[1]	34	40.00 N	4.00 W
Spanish	190	46.12 N	82.21 W
Spanish ≃	190	46.11 N	82.19 W
Spanish Camp	222	29.23 N	96.10 W
Spanish Fork	200	40.06 N	111.39 W
Spanish Lake	219	38.47 N	90.12 W
Spanish North Africa □[2], Afr.	34	35.53 N	5.19 W
Spanish North Africa □[2], Afr.	134	35.53 N	5.19 W
Spanish Peak ∧	202	44.24 N	119.46 W
Spanish Point >	240a	32.18 N	64.48 W
Spanish Sahara → Western Sahara □[2]	134	24.30 N	13.00 W
Spanish Town, Br. Vir. Is.	240m	18.27 N	64.26 W
Spanish Town, Jam.	241q	17.59 N	76.57 W
Spannberg	61	48.27 N	16.44 E
Sparagio, Monte ∧	70	38.03 N	12.46 E
Sparbach	264b	48.04 N	16.11 E
Spargi, Isola I	71	41.14 N	9.21 E
Sparkford	42	51.02 N	2.34 W
Sparkill	276	41.02 N	73.56 W
Sparkle Lake	210	41.18 N	73.47 W
Sparkman	194	33.55 N	92.50 W
Sparks, Ga., U.S.	192	31.10 N	83.26 W
Sparks, Nv., U.S.	226	39.32 N	119.45 W
Sparland	190	41.02 N	89.26 W
Sparlingville	214	42.58 N	82.30 W
Sparneck	54	50.09 N	11.50 E
Sparreholm	40	59.04 N	16.49 E
Sparrow Bush	210	41.23 N	74.43 W
Sparrow Lake @	212	44.49 N	79.24 W
Sparrowpit	262	53.19 N	1.52 W
Sparrows Point	208	39.13 N	76.28 W
Sparrows Point >	284b	39.12 N	76.30 W
Sparta, On., Can.	212	42.42 N	81.05 W
Sparta, Ga., U.S.	192	33.16 N	82.58 W
Sparta, Il., U.S.	194	38.07 N	89.42 W
Sparta, Ky., U.S.	218	38.40 N	84.54 W
Sparta, Mi., U.S.	190	43.09 N	85.42 W
Sparta, N.J., U.S.	210	41.02 N	74.38 W
Sparta, N.C., U.S.	192	36.30 N	81.07 W
Sparta, Oh., U.S.	214	40.24 N	82.42 W
Sparta, Tn., U.S.	194	35.55 N	85.27 W
Sparta, Wi., U.S.	190	43.56 N	90.48 W
Sparta Brook ≃	276	41.08 N	73.52 W
Spartak Garden ♦	265a	59.51 N	30.30 E
Sparta Lake	210	41.03 N	74.34 W
Spartanburg, In., U.S.	218	40.03 N	84.51 W
Spartanburg, S.C., U.S.	192	34.56 N	81.55 W
Spartansburg	214	41.49 N	79.41 W
Sparta → Spárti	38	37.05 N	22.27 E
Spartel, Cap >	34	35.48 N	5.56 W
Spárti (Sparta)	38	37.05 N	22.27 E
Spartivento, Capo >, It.	68	37.55 N	16.04 E
Spartivento, Capo >, It.	71	38.53 N	8.50 E
Spas-Demensk	76	54.25 N	34.01 E
Spas-Klepiki	80	55.08 N	40.13 E
Spass	82	55.55 N	35.55 E
Spassk-Dal'nij	89	44.37 N	132.48 E
Spasskij	86	53.42 N	59.12 E
Spasskij Zavod	86	49.32 N	73.17 E
Spasskoje, Ross.	76	53.06 N	36.24 E
Spasskoje, Ross.	80	55.52 N	45.42 E
Spasskoje, Ross.	82	54.05 N	38.28 E
Spassk-R'azanskij	80	54.24 N	40.23 E
Spas-Zaulok	82	56.29 N	36.34 E
Spáta	267c	38.00 N	21.31 E
Spátha, Ákra >	38	35.42 N	23.44 E
Spaulding	219	39.52 N	89.32 W
Spaulding, Lake @[1]	226	39.20 N	120.37 W
Speaks	222	29.15 N	96.42 W
Spean, Glen V	46	56.53 N	4.45 W
Spean Bridge	46	56.53 N	4.54 W
Spear, Cape >	186	47.32 N	52.32 W
Spearfish	198	44.29 N	103.51 W
Spearman	196	36.11 N	101.11 W
Spearsville	218	39.21 N	86.11 W
Spearville	198	37.51 N	99.45 W
Spearwood	168a	32.07 S	115.47 E
Speas Artemidos (Rock Tombs) ⊥	142	27.54 N	30.52 E
Specchia	68	39.57 N	18.18 E
Spechtsbrunn	54	50.30 N	11.14 E
Spectacle Island I	283	42.19 N	70.59 W
Spectrum ♦	285	39.54 N	75.10 W
Spectrum Range ⋏	180	57.30 N	130.40 W
Spednic Lake @	186	45.36 N	67.35 W
Speed	218	38.24 N	85.45 W
Speed ≃	212	43.23 N	80.22 W
Speedway	218	39.48 N	86.16 W
Speicher	58	47.24 N	9.27 E
Speichersee @	60	48.13 N	11.45 E
Speightstown	241g	13.15 N	59.39 W
Speigletown	210	42.48 N	73.38 W
Speikkogel ∧	61	47.14 N	15.03 E
Speinshart	60	49.47 N	11.49 E
Speising ✦[8]	264b	48.10 N	16.17 E
Speke ✦[8]	262	53.21 N	2.51 W
Speke Gulf c	154	2.20 S	33.15 E
Speke Hall ⊥	262	53.20 N	2.52 W
Speldorf ✦[8]	263	51.25 N	6.52 E
Spellen	263	51.37 N	6.37 E
Spello	66	42.59 N	12.40 E
Spelthorne □[8]	260	51.25 N	0.28 W
Spelve, Loch c	46	56.22 N	5.46 W
Spenard	180	61.11 N	149.55 W
Spence Bay	176	69.32 N	93.31 W
Spencer, In., U.S.	194	39.17 N	86.45 W
Spencer, Ia., U.S.	198	43.08 N	95.08 W
Spencer, Ma., U.S.	207	42.14 N	71.59 W
Spencer, Ne., U.S.	198	42.52 N	98.42 W
Spencer, N.Y., U.S.	210	42.12 N	76.29 W
Spencer, N.C., U.S.	192	35.41 N	80.26 W
Spencer, Oh., U.S.	214	41.06 N	82.07 W
Spencer, S.D., U.S.	198	43.43 N	97.35 W
Spencer, Tn., U.S.	194	35.44 N	85.28 W
Spencer, W.V., U.S.	188	38.48 N	81.21 W
Spencer, Wi., U.S.	190	44.45 N	90.17 W
Spencer, Cape >, Austl.	166	35.18 S	136.53 E
Spencer, Cape >, N.B., Can.	186	45.12 N	65.55 W
Spencer, Cape >, Ak., U.S.	180	58.14 N	136.40 W
Spencer, Mount ∧	224	49.03 N	124.38 W
Spencer, Point >	180	65.18 N	166.50 W
Spencer Brook ≃	283	42.28 N	71.22 W
Spencer Creek ≃, On., Can.	212	43.17 N	79.54 W
Spencer Creek ≃, Mo., U.S.	219	39.33 N	91.20 W
Spencer Field ⊠	281	42.31 N	83.33 W
Spencer Gulf c	166	34.00 S	137.00 E
Spencer Lake @	224	47.16 N	122.57 W
Spencerport	210	43.11 N	77.48 W
Spencertown	210	42.20 N	73.33 W
Spencerville, On., Can.	212	44.51 N	75.33 W
Spencerville, In., U.S.	216	41.16 N	84.55 W
Spencerville, Md., U.S.	208	39.06 N	76.58 W
Spencerville, Oh., U.S.	216	40.42 N	84.21 W
Spences Bridge	182	50.25 N	121.21 W
Spenge	52	52.08 N	8.28 E
Spennymoor	44	54.42 N	1.35 W
Spenser Mountains ⋏	172	42.15 S	172.30 E
Sperenberg	54	52.08 N	13.22 E
Sperillen @	26	60.28 N	10.03 E
Sperling	224	49.08 N	122.33 W
Sperlinga	70	37.46 N	14.21 E
Sperlonga	66	41.15 N	13.26 E
Spermaceti Cove c	276	40.26 N	73.59 W
Sperone, Capo >	71	38.57 N	8.25 E
Sperrin Mountains ⋏	48	54.50 N	7.05 W
Sperry Creek ≃	279a	41.29 N	81.53 W
Sperry Rand Corporation ʊ[3]	276	40.45 N	73.42 W
Sperryville	188	38.39 N	78.13 W
Spessart ✦[1]	56	50.10 N	9.20 E
Spesutie Island I	208	39.27 N	76.05 W
Spétsai I	38	37.16 N	23.08 E
Spevakovka	83	49.03 N	38.54 E
Spexard	52	51.52 N	8.24 E
Spey ≃	46	57.40 N	3.06 W
Spey Bay c	46	57.41 N	3.00 W
Speyer	56	49.19 N	8.26 E
Speyerbach ≃	56	49.19 N	8.27 E
Speyside	241r	11.18 N	60.32 W
Spezia → La Spezia	62	44.07 N	9.50 E
Spezzano Albanese	68	39.40 N	16.19 E
Spezzano della Sila	68	39.18 N	16.20 E
Sphinx → Abū al-Hawl ⊥	142	29.59 N	31.08 E
Spiazzo	64	46.07 N	10.40 E
Spiceland	218	39.50 N	85.26 W
Spicer	198	45.13 N	94.56 W
Spicer Creek ≃	284a	43.02 N	78.53 W
Spicer Meadow Reservoir @[1]	226	38.23 N	119.59 W
Spicheren	56	49.12 N	6.58 E
Spickard	194	40.14 N	93.35 W
Spicket ≃	283	42.42 N	71.09 W
Spieka	52	53.45 N	8.35 E
Spiekeroog I	52	53.46 N	7.42 E
Spiess Seamount ✦[3]	8	54.40 S	0.15 E
Spiez	58	46.41 N	7.39 E
Spijkenisse	52	51.21 N	4.20 E
Špikov	78	48.46 N	28.35 E
Spilamberto	64	44.32 N	11.01 E
Spilimbergo	64	46.07 N	12.54 E
Spilinga	68	38.37 N	15.54 E
Spillersboda	40	59.42 N	18.51 E
Spillimacheen ≃	182	50.55 N	116.20 W
Spillville	190	43.12 N	91.57 W
Spilsby	44	53.11 N	0.06 E
Spinazzola	68	40.58 N	16.06 E
Spīn Būldak	120	31.01 N	66.24 E
Spincourt	56	49.20 N	5.40 E
Spindale	192	35.21 N	81.55 W
Spindoli	66	43.12 N	12.54 E
Spinea-Orgnano	64	45.29 N	12.10 E
Spinetta Marengo	62	44.53 N	8.41 E
Spinnerstown	208	40.26 N	75.26 W
Spinoso	68	40.16 N	15.58 E
Spires → Speyer	56	49.19 N	8.26 E
Spirit Lake, Id., U.S.	202	47.57 N	116.52 W
Spirit Lake, Ia., U.S.	198	43.25 N	95.06 W
Spirit Lake @	224	46.16 N	122.08 W
Spirit River	182	55.47 N	118.50 W
Spiritwood	184	53.22 N	107.31 W
Spiro	194	35.14 N	94.37 W
Spirovo	76	57.26 N	34.59 E
Spišská Nová Ves	30	48.57 N	20.34 E
Spitak	84	40.51 N	44.16 E
Spital am Pyhrn	61	47.39 N	14.20 E
Spithead >	42	50.45 N	1.05 W
Spit Point >	162	20.02 S	119.00 E
Spitsbergen I	12	78.45 N	16.00 E
Spitsbergen Bank ✦[4]	12	76.00 N	23.00 E
Spittal an der Drau	64	46.48 N	13.30 E
Spittal of Glenshee	46	56.48 N	3.28 W
Spitz	61	48.22 N	15.25 E
Spitzbergen und Jan Mayen → Svalbard □[2]	12	78.00 N	20.00 E
Spitzer Berg ∧[2]	264a	52.38 N	13.35 E
Spixworth	42	52.40 N	1.20 E
Spjelkavik	26	62.28 N	6.23 E
Splavnucha	80	51.05 N	45.22 E
Splendora	222	30.14 N	95.10 W
Split	36	43.31 N	16.27 E
Split, Cape >	186	45.20 N	64.30 W
Split Lake @	184	56.08 N	96.15 W
Splitrock Reservoir @[1]	276	40.58 N	74.27 W
Spluga, Passo della (Splügenpass))(	58	46.30 N	9.20 E
Splügen	58	46.33 N	9.20 E
Splügenpass (Passo della Spluga))(	58	46.30 N	9.20 E
Spodsbjerg	41	54.56 N	10.50 E
Spofford	196	29.11 N	100.25 W
Spoği	76	56.05 N	26.44 E
Spokane	202	47.39 N	117.25 W
Spokane ≃	202	47.54 N	118.20 W
Spokane, Mount ∧	202	47.55 N	117.07 W
Spokane Indian Reservation ✦[4]	202	47.55 N	118.00 W
Spokojnaja	84	44.15 N	41.25 E
Špola	78	49.01 N	31.24 E
Spoleto	66	42.44 N	12.44 E
Spoltore	66	42.27 N	14.08 E
Spondigna	64	46.38 N	10.37 E
Spondon	42	52.54 N	1.25 W
Sponds Hill ∧[2]	262	53.19 N	2.03 W
Spóng	110	13.27 N	105.34 E
Spoon ≃	194	40.18 N	90.04 W
Spooner	190	45.49 N	91.53 W
Spořice	54	50.26 N	13.25 E
Spornitz	54	53.24 N	11.43 E
Spornoje ·	74	62.20 N	151.03 E
Sporovo	76	52.25 N	25.20 E
Spørring	41	56.18 N	10.09 E
Sportforum ♦	264a	52.33 N	13.29 E
Sport Hill	207	41.14 N	73.16 W
Sporting Hill	208	40.09 N	76.26 W
Sportsman's Park Race Track ♦	278	41.50 N	87.46 W
Spotorno	62	44.14 N	8.25 E
Spot Pond @	283	42.27 N	71.06 W
Spotswood, Austl.	274b	37.50 S	144.53 E
Spotswood, N.J., U.S.	208	40.23 N	74.23 W
Spotsylvania	208	38.12 N	77.35 W
Spotsylvania □[6]	208	38.15 N	77.30 W
Spotsylvania Court House Battlefield ⊥	208	38.15 N	77.35 W
Sprague, Mb., Can.	184	49.02 N	95.38 W
Sprague, Wa., U.S.	202	47.18 N	117.58 W
Sprague ≃	202	42.34 N	121.51 W
Sprague, North Fork ≃	202	42.26 N	121.07 W
Sprague, South Fork ≃	202	42.26 N	121.07 W
Spragueville	207	41.53 N	71.32 W
Sprain Ridge Park ♦	276	40.59 N	73.51 W
Sprankle Mills	214	41.00 N	79.07 W
Spratly Islands II	108	10.00 N	114.00 E
Spratt Point >	212	44.36 N	80.01 W
Spray	202	44.50 N	119.47 W
Spray Lakes Reservoir @[1]	182	50.55 N	115.20 W
Spreča ≃	38	44.45 N	18.06 E
Spreckels	226	36.36 N	121.34 W
Spreckelsville	229a	20.53 N	156.24 W
Spree ≃	54	52.32 N	13.13 E
Spreenhagen	54	52.20 N	13.52 E
Spreeufontein	158	33.22 S	20.45 E
Spreewald ✦[1]	54	51.50 N	14.05 E
Spremberg	54	51.34 N	14.22 E
Sprendlingen	56	49.51 N	7.59 E
Spresiano	64	45.46 N	12.16 E
Spring	222	30.04 N	95.25 W
Spring ≃, U.S.	194	36.52 N	94.44 W
Spring ≃, Ar., U.S.	194	36.08 N	91.05 W
Spring, North Fork ≃	194	37.18 N	94.21 W
Spring, South Fork ≃	194	36.19 N	91.30 W
Spring Arbor	216	42.12 N	84.33 W
Spring Bay c	200	41.40 N	112.50 W
Springbok	156	29.43 S	17.55 E
Springboro, Oh., U.S.	218	39.33 N	84.14 W
Springboro, Pa., U.S.	214	41.48 N	80.22 W
Spring Branch ≃	284b	39.26 N	76.35 W
Springbrook, On., Can.	275b	43.39 N	79.47 W
Springbrook, Md., U.S.	284c	39.03 N	77.00 W
Spring Brook, N.Y., U.S.	210	42.49 N	78.40 W
Spring Brook ≃	278	41.58 N	87.59 W
Springbrook Forest	284c	39.03 N	77.01 W
Springburn	172	43.40 S	171.28 E
Spring City, Pa., U.S.	208	40.10 N	75.32 W
Spring City, Tn., U.S.	192	35.41 N	84.51 W
Spring City, Ut,. U.S.	200	39.28 N	111.29 W
Spring Coulee V	198	48.31 N	100.54 W
Spring Creek, N.Z.	172	41.28 S	173.58 E
Spring Creek, Pa., U.S.	214	41.53 N	79.32 W
Spring Creek ≃, Austl.	166	24.12 S	140.58 E
Spring Creek ≃, U.S.	198	40.30 N	101.21 W
Spring Creek ≃, Ga., U.S.	192	30.54 N	84.45 W
Spring Creek ≃, Il., U.S.	216	40.49 N	87.50 W
Spring Creek ≃, Il., U.S.	219	39.52 N	89.37 W
Spring Creek ≃, Il., U.S.	278	41.32 N	88.04 W
Spring Creek ≃, Mo., U.S.	219	38.21 N	91.10 W
Spring Creek ≃, Nv., U.S.	204	39.55 N	117.50 W
Spring Creek ≃, N.D., U.S.	198	47.15 N	101.48 W
Spring Creek ≃, Pa., U.S.	214	41.24 N	78.57 W
Spring Creek ≃, Pa., U.S.	214	40.56 N	77.47 W
Spring Creek ≃, S.D., U.S.	198	43.52 N	102.42 W
Spring Creek ≃, S.D., U.S.	198	45.54 N	100.18 W
Spring Creek ≃, Tx., U.S.	222	30.02 N	95.16 W
Springdale, Nf., Can.	186	49.30 N	56.04 W
Springdale, Ar., U.S.	194	36.11 N	94.07 W
Springdale, Oh., U.S.	218	39.17 N	84.28 W
Springdale, Pa., U.S.	214	40.32 N	79.47 W
Springdale, S.C., U.S.	192	33.57 N	81.06 W
Springdale, Ut,. U.S.	200	37.11 N	112.59 W
Springdale, Wa., U.S.	202	48.03 N	117.44 W
Spring Dale, W.V., U.S.	192	37.52 N	80.48 W
Springe	52	52.12 N	9.32 E
Springer	196	36.21 N	104.35 W
Springers Brook ≃	285	39.44 N	74.41 W
Springerville	200	34.08 N	109.17 W
Springfield, N.S., Can.	186	44.38 N	64.52 W
Springfield, On., Can.	212	42.50 N	80.56 W
Springfield, N.Z.	172	43.20 S	171.55 E
Springfield, S. Afr.	158	29.02 S	22.53 E
Springfield, Co., U.S.	198	37.24 N	102.36 W
Springfield, Fl., U.S.	194	30.09 N	85.36 W
Springfield, Ga., U.S.	192	32.22 N	81.18 W
Springfield, Il., U.S.	219	39.48 N	89.38 W
Springfield, Ky., U.S.	194	37.41 N	85.13 W
Springfield, Ma., U.S.	207	42.06 N	72.35 W
Springfield, Mi., U.S.	216	42.19 N	85.14 W
Springfield, Mn., U.S.	198	44.14 N	94.58 W
Springfield, Mo., U.S.	194	37.12 N	93.17 W
Springfield, N.J., U.S.	276	40.43 N	74.18 W
Springfield, Oh., U.S.	218	39.55 N	83.48 W
Springfield, Or., U.S.	202	44.02 N	123.01 W
Springfield, Pa., U.S.	285	39.55 N	75.19 W
Springfield, S.C., U.S.	192	33.29 N	81.16 W
Springfield, S.D., U.S.	198	42.51 N	97.53 W
Springfield, Tn., U.S.	194	36.30 N	86.53 W
Springfield, Vt., U.S.	188	43.17 N	72.28 W
Springfield, Va., U.S.	284c	38.45 N	77.13 W
Springfield, Lake @[1]	219	39.44 N	89.36 W
Springfield Center	210	42.50 N	74.53 W
Springfield Estates	284c	38.47 N	77.11 W
Springfield Lake @	285	40.11 N	75.00 W
Springfield Lake @[1]	222	31.36 N	96.33 W
Springfield Mall ✦[9]	284c	38.46 N	77.11 W
Springfield Plateau ⋏[1]	194	37.10 N	93.30 W
Springfontein	158	30.19 S	25.36 E
Spring Garden	246	6.59 N	58.31 W
Spring Garden Brook ≃	276	40.46 N	74.23 W
Spring Garden Township	208	39.57 N	76.44 W
Spring Glen, N.Y., U.S.	210	41.40 N	74.26 W
Spring Glen, Pa., U.S.	208	40.38 N	76.37 W
Spring Glen, Ut,. U.S.	200	39.39 N	110.51 W
Spring Green	190	43.10 N	90.04 W
Spring Grove, Il., U.S.	216	42.26 N	88.13 W
Spring Grove, Mn., U.S.	190	43.33 N	91.38 W
Spring Grove, Pa., U.S.	208	39.52 N	76.51 W
Springhill, N.S., Can.	186	45.39 N	64.03 W
Spring Hill, Ca., U.S.	226	39.15 N	121.03 W
Spring Hill, Fl., U.S.	220	28.33 N	82.27 W
Springhill, La., U.S.	194	33.00 N	93.28 W
Spring Hill, Pa., U.S.	214	40.23 N	78.40 W
Spring Hill, Tn., U.S.	194	35.45 N	86.55 W
Spring Hill, Tx., U.S.	222	32.34 N	94.48 W
Springhills	216	40.16 N	83.22 W
Spring Hope	192	35.56 N	78.06 W
Springhouse, B.C., Can.	182	51.55 N	122.07 W
Spring House, Pa., U.S.	285	40.11 N	75.14 W
Spring Lake, Mi., U.S.	216	43.04 N	86.11 W
Spring Lake, N.J., U.S.	208	40.09 N	74.01 W
Spring Lake, N.C., U.S.	192	35.10 N	78.58 W
Spring Lake @, Mi., U.S.	216	43.06 N	86.11 W
Spring Lake @, N.J., U.S.	276	40.35 N	74.25 W
Spring Lake Heights	208	40.09 N	74.01 W
Spring Mill, Oh., U.S.	214	40.54 N	82.36 W
Spring Mill, Pa., U.S.	285	40.04 N	75.17 W
Spring Mill Reservoir @[1]	262	53.39 N	2.13 W
Spring Mills	210	40.51 N	77.34 W
Spring Mill State Park ♦	218	38.43 N	86.25 W
Spring Mount	208	40.17 N	75.28 W
Spring Mountains ⋏	204	36.10 N	115.40 W
Spring Pond @	283	42.30 N	70.57 W
Springport, In., U.S.	218	40.03 N	85.24 W
Springport, Mi., U.S.	216	42.22 N	84.41 W
Spring Run	214	40.09 N	83.47 W

Symbols in the index entries represent the broad categories identified in the key at the right. Symbols with superior numbers (⋏[1]) identify subcategories (see complete key on page *I · 1).*

Symbole im Register stellen die rechts im Schlüssel erklärten Kategorien dar. Symbole mit hochgestellten Ziffern (⋏[1]) bezeichnen Unterabteilungen einer Kategorie (vgl. vollständiger Schlüssel auf Seite *I · 1).*

Los símbolos incluidos en el texto del índice representan las grandes categorias identificadas con la clave a la derecha. Los símbolos con numeros en su parte superior (⋏[1]) identifican las subcategorías (véase la clave completa en la página *I · 1).*

Les symboles de l'index représentent les catégories indiquées dans la légende à droite. Les symboles suivis d'un indice (⋏[1]) représentent des sous-catégories (voir légende complète à la page *I · 1).*

Os símbolos incluídos no texto do índice representam as grandes categorias identificadas com a chave à direita. Os símbolos com números em sua parte superior (⋏[1]) identificam as subcategorias (veja-se a chave completa à página *I · 1).*

English	Deutsch	Español	Français	Português
∧ Mountain	Berg	Montaña	Montagne	Montanha
⋏ Mountains	Gebirge	Montañas	Montagnes	Montanhas
)(Pass	Paß	Paso	Col	Passo
V Valley, Canyon	Tal, Cañon	Valle, Cañón	Vallée, Canyon	Vale, Canhão
≍ Plain	Ebene	Llano	Plaine	Planície
> Cape	Kap	Cabo	Cap	Cabo
I Island	Insel	Isla	Île	Ilha
II Islands	Inseln	Islas	Îles	Ilhas
± Other Topographic Features	Andere Topographische Objekte	Otros Elementos Topográficos	Autres données topographiques	Outros acidentes topográficos

ESPAÑOL — Nombre | Página | Lat.°′ | Long.°′ W = Oeste
FRANÇAIS — Nom | Page | Lat.°′ | Long.°′ W = Ouest
PORTUGUÊS — Nome | Página | Lat.°′ | Long.°′ W = Oeste

Nombre / Nom / Nome	Página / Page	Lat.°′	Long.°′
Springs	158	26.13 S	28.25 E
Springs □[5]	273d	26.14 S	28.30 E
Springs Aerodrome ⊠	273d	26.15 S	28.24 E
Springside	285	40.04 N	74.51 W
Springs Junction	172	42.19 S	172.11 E
Springsure	166	24.07 S	148.05 E
Springton	168b	34.43 S	139.05 E
Springtown	222	32.58 N	97.41 W
Springvale, Austl.	162	17.48 S	127.41 E
Springvale, Austl.	166	23.33 S	140.42 E
Springvale, Austl.	169	37.57 S	145.09 E
Springvale, Me., U.S.	188	43.28 N	70.47 W
Springvale South	274b	37.58 S	145.09 E
Spring Valley, Ca., U.S.	228	32.44 N	116.59 W
Spring Valley, Il., U.S.	190	41.19 N	89.11 W
Spring Valley, Mn., U.S.	190	43.41 N	92.23 W
Spring Valley, N.Y., U.S.	210	41.06 N	74.02 W
Spring Valley, Oh., U.S.	218	39.36 N	84.00 W
Spring Valley, Tx., U.S.	222	29.47 N	95.31 W
Spring Valley, Wi., U.S.	190	44.50 N	92.14 W
Spring Valley V	204	39.15 N	114.25 W
Spring Valley Creek ≃	204	39.20 N	114.25 W
Springview	198	42.49 N	99.44 W
Springville, Al., U.S.	194	33.46 N	86.28 W
Springville, Ca., U.S.	204	36.08 N	118.49 W
Springville, Ia., U.S.	190	42.03 N	91.26 W
Springville, N.J., U.S.	285	39.56 N	74.52 W
Springville, N.Y., U.S.	210	42.30 N	78.40 W
Springville, Pa., U.S.	210	41.42 N	75.55 W
Springville, Ut,. U.S.	200	40.09 N	111.36 W
Springwater	210	42.38 N	77.35 W
Springwood	170	33.42 S	150.33 E
Sprint ≃	44	54.22 N	2.45 W
Sprite Creek ≃	210	43.08 N	74.44 W
Sproat Lake ⊜	182	49.16 N	125.03 W
Sprockhövel	56	51.22 N	7.15 E
Sprogels Run ≃	285	40.14 N	75.37 W
Sprogø I	41	55.20 N	10.58 E
Sprötze	52	53.18 N	9.49 E
Sproul	214	40.16 N	78.28 W
Sprout Brook ≃	276	40.54 N	74.05 W
Spruce ≃	184	53.15 N	105.43 W
Spruce Brook	186	48.45 N	58.11 W
Spruce Creek	214	40.37 N	78.08 W
Spruce Creek ≃	210	43.07 N	74.46 W
Spruce Grove	182	53.32 N	113.55 W
Spruce Knob ∧	188	38.42 N	79.32 W
Spruce Knob-Seneca Rocks National Recreation Area ♠	188	38.50 N	79.20 W
Spruce Lake	184	53.32 N	109.05 W
Spruce Mountain ∧, Az., U.S.	200	34.28 N	112.24 W
Spruce Mountain ∧, Nv., U.S.	204	40.33 N	114.49 W
Spruce Pine, Al., U.S.	194	34.23 N	87.43 W
Spruce Pine, N.C., U.S.	192	35.54 N	82.03 W
Spruce Run Reservoir ⊜[1]	210	40.40 N	74.57 W
Spruce Run State Park ♠	210	40.40 N	74.56 W
Spruce Woods Provincial Park ♠	184	49.42 N	99.05 W
Spry	208	39.55 N	76.41 W
Spry Lake ⊜	212	44.44 N	81.15 W
Spulico, Capo ≻	68	39.58 N	16.39 E
Spur	196	33.28 N	100.51 W
Spurfield	182	55.13 N	114.16 W
Spurger	194	30.42 N	94.11 W
Spurn Head ≻	44	53.34 N	0.07 E
Spurr, Mount ∧	180	61.18 N	152.15 W
Sputendorf	264a	52.20 N	13.13 E
Spuzzum	182	49.41 N	121.25 W
Spy Hill	184	50.36 N	101.41 W
Spy Pond ⊜	283	42.24 N	71.09 W
Squally Channel ʮ	182	53.10 N	129.15 W
Squamish	182	49.42 N	123.09 W
Squamish ≃	182	49.45 N	123.09 W
Squam Lake ⊜	188	43.45 N	71.32 W
Square Butte Creek ≃	198	46.55 N	100.55 W
Square Lake ⊜	186	47.03 N	68.20 W
Squatec	186	47.53 N	68.43 W
Squaw Cap Mountain ∧	186	47.53 N	66.53 W
Squaw Creek ≃, Id., U.S.	202	43.51 N	116.22 W
Squaw Creek ≃, Il., U.S.	278	42.21 N	88.07 W
Squaw Creek ≃, Or., U.S.	202	44.27 N	121.20 W
Squaw Creek Lake ⊜[1]	222	32.19 N	97.47 W
Squaw Harbor	180	55.11 N	160.30 W
Squaw Hill ∧	200	41.48 N	105.02 W
Squaw Island I	284a	42.56 N	78.54 W
Squaw Peak ∧, Ca., U.S.	226	39.11 N	120.16 W
Squaw Peak ∧, Mt., U.S.	202	47.10 N	114.21 W
Squaw Rapids	184	53.41 N	103.20 W
Squaw Rapids Dam ➧[6]	184	53.40 N	103.25 W
Squaw Run ≃	279b	40.29 N	79.52 W
Squaw Valley State Recreation Area ♠	226	39.12 N	120.15 W
Squibnocket Point ≻	207	41.18 N	70.47 W
Squilax	182	50.52 N	119.35 W
Squillace	68	38.47 N	16.31 E
Squillace, Golfo di ⊂	68	38.50 N	16.50 E
Squinzano	68	40.26 N	18.03 E
Squire	192	37.14 N	81.36 W
Squires, Mount ∧	162	26.12 S	127.28 E
Squirrel ≃	180	66.57 N	160.27 W
Squirrel Hill ➧[8]	279b	40.26 N	79.55 W
Squirrel Hill Tunnel ➧[5]	279b	40.26 N	79.55 W
Squirrel's Heath ➧[8]	260	51.35 N	0.13 E
Sragen	115a	7.26 S	111.02 E
Šramkovka	78	50.10 N	32.05 E
Srbija (Serbia) □[3]	38	44.00 N	21.00 E
Srbobran	38	45.33 N	19.48 E
Srê Âmbĕl	110	11.07 N	103.46 E
Sredinnyj chrebet ⋏	74	56.00 N	158.00 E
Sredna Gora ⋏	38	42.30 N	25.00 E
Sredn'aja Achtuba	80	48.43 N	44.52 E
Sredn'aja Mokla ≃	88	55.01 N	119.37 E
Sredn'aja Nanaki, gora ∧	89	52.26 N	132.50 E
Sredn'aja Ol'okma	88	55.26 N	120.33 E
Srednegorje	76	60.34 N	29.25 E
Sredneje Kujto, ozero ⊜	24	65.08 N	31.15 E
Srednekolymsk	74	67.27 N	153.41 E
Srednerusskaja vozvyšennost' ⋏[1]	72	52.00 N	38.00 E
Srednesibirskoje ploskogorje ⋏[1]	74	65.00 N	105.00 E
Srednij Ikorec	78	51.05 N	39.45 E
Srednij Kalar	88	55.51 N	117.24 E
Srednij Ural ⋏	86	58.00 N	59.00 E
Srednij Urgal	89	51.09 N	132.59 E
Srednij Vas'ugan	86	59.16 N	78.15 E
Srednyj	83	48.09 N	39.50 E
Srê Khtŭm	110	12.10 N	106.52 E
Śrem	30	52.08 N	17.01 E
Srê Moăt	110	13.18 N	107.10 E
Sremska Mitrovica	38	44.58 N	19.37 E
Sremski Karlovci	38	45.12 N	19.57 E
Srêng ≃	110	13.21 N	103.27 E
Srêpŏk ≃	110	13.33 N	106.16 E
Sretensk	88	52.15 N	117.43 E
Sretenskoje	88	56.28 N	96.25 E
Srīdharpur	126	23.04 N	89.25 E
Sri Hargobindpur	123	31.41 N	75.39 E
Sri Jayawardenepura (Kotte)	122	6.54 N	79.54 E
Srīkākulam	122	18.18 N	83.54 E
Sri Kālahasti	122	13.45 N	79.43 E
Sri Lanka □[1], Asia	118	7.00 N	81.00 E
Sri Lanka □[1], Asia	122	7.00 N	81.00 E
Srīnagar, Bngl.	126	23.32 N	90.18 E
Srīnagar, India	123	34.05 N	74.49 E
Srīnagar, India	124	30.13 N	78.47 E
Srīnagar Airport ⊠	123	34.00 N	74.52 E
Srīpur, Bngl.	126	24.12 N	90.29 E
Srīpur, Bngl.	126	23.36 N	89.24 E
Srīrampur, India	122	19.34 N	74.34 E
Srirāmpur, India	272b	22.49 N	88.29 E
Srīrangam	122	10.52 N	78.41 E
Srīvardhan	122	18.02 N	73.01 E
Srīvilliputtūr	122	9.31 N	77.38 E
Środa Śląska	30	51.10 N	16.36 E
Środa Wielkopolski	30	52.14 N	17.17 E
Srpska Crnja	38	45.43 N	20.42 E
Ssangmun-ni ➧[8]	271b	37.39 N	127.02 E
Ssuchunghsi	100	22.06 N	120.44 E
Ssup'ing → Siping	89	43.12 N	124.20 E
Staaken ➧[8]	264a	52.32 N	13.08 E
Staaten ≃	164	16.24 S	141.17 E
Staaten River National Park ♠	164	16.40 S	143.00 E
Staatsburg	210	41.50 N	73.55 W
Staatz	61	48.40 N	16.29 E
Stabbursdalen Nasjonalpark ♠	24	70.06 N	24.30 E
Staberhuk ≻	54	54.24 N	11.19 E
Stabroek	50	51.20 N	4.22 E
Stachanov	83	48.34 N	38.40 E
Stachy	60	49.06 N	13.40 E
Stack, Loch ⊜	46	58.20 N	4.55 W
Stackpoie Head ≻	42	51.37 N	4.54 W
Stack Skerry I[2]	46	59.01 N	4.31 W
Stacksteads	262	53.41 N	2.13 W
Stacyville	190	43.26 N	92.46 W
Stad-Delden	52	52.16 N	6.42 E
Stade	52	53.36 N	9.28 E
Staden, Bel.	50	50.59 N	3.01 E
Staden, Dtsch.	56	50.20 N	8.54 E
Städjan ∧	26	61.55 N	12.52 E
Stadl an der Mur	61	47.05 N	13.58 E
Stadlandet ≻[1]	26	62.07 N	5.18 E
Stadlau ➧[8]	264b	48.14 N	16.28 E
Stadl-Paura	64	48.05 N	13.53 E
Stadskanaal	52	53.00 N	6.55 E
Stadtallendorf	56	50.50 N	9.01 E
Stadtbergen	58	48.22 N	10.50 E
Stadt Haag	30	48.07 N	14.34 E
Stadthagen	52	52.19 N	9.13 E
Stadtilm	54	50.47 N	11.05 E
Städtische Rahmede	263	51.17 N	7.40 E
Stadtkyll	56	50.21 N	6.32 E
Stadtlauringen	56	50.11 N	10.22 E
Stadtlengsfeld	56	50.47 N	10.07 E
Stadtlohn	52	51.59 N	6.55 E
Stadtoldendorf	52	51.53 N	9.37 E
Stadtprozelten	56	49.47 N	9.25 E
Stadtroda	54	50.51 N	11.44 E
Stadtsteinach	54	50.09 N	11.30 E
Stadt Wehlen	54	50.58 N	14.02 E
Stadum	41	54.44 N	9.03 E
Stäfa	58	47.15 N	8.44 E
Staffa I	46	56.25 N	6.20 W
Staffanstorp	41	55.38 N	13.13 E
Staffelberg ∧	56	50.06 N	11.02 E
Staffelde	264a	52.44 N	13.00 E
Staffelsee ⊜	64	47.42 N	11.10 E
Staffelstein	56	50.06 N	11.00 E
Staffin	46	57.37 N	6.12 W
Staffora ≃	62	45.04 N	9.01 E
Stafford, Eng., U.K.	42	52.48 N	2.07 W
Stafford, Ct., U.S.	207	41.59 N	72.17 W
Stafford, Ks., U.S.	198	37.57 N	98.36 W
Stafford, N.Y., U.S.	210	42.59 N	78.04 W
Stafford, Tx., U.S.	222	29.37 N	95.34 W
Stafford, Va., U.S.	208	38.25 N	77.24 W
Stafford □[6]	208	38.25 N	77.30 W
Staffordshire □[6]	28	52.50 N	2.00 W
Stafford Springs	207	41.57 N	72.18 W
Staffordsville	188	37.49 N	82.50 W
Staffordville	207	41.59 N	72.15 W
Stagen	112	3.18 S	116.10 E
Stag Pond ⊜	276	40.59 N	74.42 W
Stahl-Berg ∧[2]	264a	52.21 N	13.46 E
Stahlbrode	54	54.14 N	13.17 E
Stahle	52	51.50 N	9.25 E
Stahnsdorf	54	52.23 N	13.13 E
Stahringen	58	47.47 N	8.58 E
Staicele	76	57.50 N	24.45 E
Staines	42	51.26 N	0.31 W
Staines Reservoirs ⊜[1]	260	51.27 N	0.30 W
Stainforth	44	53.36 N	1.01 W
Staining	44	53.49 N	2.59 W
Stainland	262	53.40 N	1.53 W
Stainmore Forest ➧[3]	44	54.30 N	2.10 W
Stains	261	48.57 N	2.23 E
Stainz	61	46.54 N	15.16 E
Stairtown	222	29.43 N	97.44 W
Stajki	78	50.05 N	30.54 E
Staked Plain → Estacado, Llano ≚	196	33.30 N	102.40 W
Stäket	40	59.28 N	17.48 E
Stakroge	41	55.53 N	8.51 E
Stalać	38	43.40 N	21.25 E
Stalbridge	42	50.58 N	2.23 W
Stalden	58	46.14 N	7.52 E
Staletti	68	38.46 N	16.32 E
Stalham	42	52.47 N	1.31 E
Stalheim	26	60.50 N	6.40 E
Stalhofen	61	47.05 N	15.16 E
Stalinabad → Dušanbe	85	38.35 N	68.48 E
Stalin → Brașov	38	45.39 N	25.37 E
Stalin → Kuçovë	38	40.48 N	19.54 E
Stalingrad → Volgograd	80	48.44 N	44.25 E
Stalino → Doneck	83	48.00 N	37.48 E
Stalinogorsk → Novomoskovsk	82	54.05 N	38.13 E
Stalinsk → Novokuzneck	86	53.45 N	87.06 E
Stalin → Varna	38	43.13 N	27.55 E
Stallarholmen	40	59.22 N	17.12 E
Ställberg	40	59.59 N	14.55 E
Ställdalen	40	59.56 N	14.56 E
Stallwang	60	49.03 N	12.40 E
Stalowa Wola	30	50.35 N	22.02 E
Stalybridge, Eng., U.K.	44	53.29 N	2.03 W
Stalybridge, Eng., U.K.	262	53.29 N	2.04 W
Stambaugh	190	46.04 N	88.37 W
Stamford, Austl.	166	21.16 S	143.49 E
Stamford, Eng., U.K.	42	52.39 N	0.29 W
Stamford, Ct., U.S.	207	41.03 N	73.32 W
Stamford, N.Y., U.S.	210	42.24 N	74.36 W
Stamford, Tx., U.S.	196	32.56 N	99.48 W
Stamford, Vt., U.S.	207	42.45 N	73.04 W
Stamford, Lake ⊜[1]	196	33.05 N	99.35 W
Stamford Bridge	44	53.59 N	0.55 W
Stamford Brige Stadium ♠	260	51.29 N	0.11 W
Stamford Harbor ⊂	276	41.02 N	73.32 W
Stamford Museum ʊ	276	41.07 N	73.33 W
Stammbach	54	50.09 N	11.41 E
Stammersdorf ➧[8]	264b	48.18 N	16.25 E
Stammham	60	48.15 N	12.53 E
Stammheim, Dtsch.	56	48.41 N	8.46 E
Stammheim, Schw.	58	47.38 N	8.47 E
Stampede Reservoir ⊜[1]	226	39.29 N	120.07 W
Stamping Ground	218	38.16 N	84.41 W
Stampriet	156	24.20 S	18.28 E
Stamps	194	33.21 N	93.29 W
Stams	64	47.16 N	10.59 E
Stanaford	188	37.48 N	81.09 W
Stanardsville	188	38.17 N	78.26 W
Stanberry	194	40.13 N	94.32 W
Stanborough	260	51.47 N	0.13 W
Stancija-Gorčakovo	85	40.25 N	71.45 E
Stancionno-Ojašinskij	86	55.28 N	83.53 E
Standard, Ab., Can.	182	51.07 N	112.59 W
Standard, Ak., U.S.	180	64.47 N	148.32 W
Standard, Ca., U.S.	226	37.59 N	120.20 W
Standard, Pa., U.S.	214	40.10 N	79.32 W
Standard Oil Company Refinery ʊ[3]	282	37.57 N	122.24 W
Standard Shaft	279b	40.10 N	79.32 W
Standedge Canal Tunnel ➧[5]	262	53.34 N	2.00 W
Standedge Railway Tunnel ➧[5]	262	53.34 N	2.00 W
Standerton	158	26.58 S	29.07 E
Standiford Field ⊠	218	38.11 N	85.44 W
Standing Rock Indian Reservation ➧[4]	198	45.50 N	101.10 W
Standing Stone Creek ≃	214	40.30 N	78.00 W
Standing Stones ⊥	46	58.12 N	6.48 W
Standish, Eng., U.K.	44	53.36 N	2.41 W
Standish, Mi., U.S.	190	43.58 N	83.57 W
Standish Monument ⊥	283	42.01 N	70.41 W
Standon	42	51.53 N	0.02 E
Stanfield, Az., U.S.	200	32.52 N	111.57 W
Stanfield, Or., U.S.	202	45.46 N	119.12 W
Stanford, S. Afr.	158	34.26 S	19.29 E
Stanford, Ca., U.S.	226	37.25 N	122.08 W
Stanford, Ky., U.S.	192	37.31 N	84.39 W
Stanford, Mt., U.S.	202	47.09 N	110.13 W
Stanford Center ➧[9]	282	37.27 N	122.10 W
Stanford Heights	210	42.46 N	73.53 W
Stanford le Hope	42	51.31 N	0.26 E
Stanford Linear Accelerator ʊ[3]	282	37.25 N	122.12 W
Stanford Rivers	260	51.41 N	0.13 E
Stanford University ʊ[2]	282	37.26 N	122.10 W
Stanfordville	210	41.52 N	73.43 W
Stånga	26	57.17 N	18.28 E
Stångån ≃	26	58.27 N	15.37 E
Stångby	41	55.46 N	13.10 E
Stange	26	60.43 N	11.11 E
Stanger	158	29.27 S	31.14 E
Stanghella	64	45.08 N	11.45 E
Stanhope, Eng., U.K.	44	54.45 N	2.01 W
Stanhope, Ia., U.S.	190	42.17 N	93.47 W
Stanhope, N.J., U.S.	210	40.54 N	74.42 W
Stanično-Luganskoje	83	48.39 N	39.30 E
Stanislaus □[6]	226	37.39 N	121.00 W
Stanislaus ≃	226	37.40 N	121.14 W
Stanislaus, Clark Fork ≃	226	38.22 N	119.52 W
Stanislaus, Middle Fork ≃	226	38.09 N	120.21 W
Stanislaus, North Fork ≃	226	38.09 N	120.21 W
Stanislaus, South Fork ≃	226	38.04 N	120.25 W
Stanislav	78	46.34 N	32.09 E
Stanislavčik	78	48.58 N	28.07 E
Stanislav → Ivano-Frankovsk	78	48.55 N	24.43 E
Stanisławów → Ivano-Frankovsk	78	48.55 N	24.43 E
Stanke Dimitrov	38	42.16 N	23.07 E
Staňkov	60	49.34 N	13.04 E
Stanley, Austl.	166	40.46 S	145.18 E
Stanley, N.B., Can.	186	46.17 N	66.44 W
Stanley, Falk. Is.	254	51.42 S	57.51 W
Stanley, H.K.	271d	22.13 N	114.12 E
Stanley, Eng., U.K.	44	54.52 N	1.42 W
Stanley, Scot., U.K.	46	56.28 N	3.27 W
Stanley, N.Y., U.S.	210	42.49 N	77.06 W
Stanley, N.C., U.S.	192	35.21 N	81.05 W
Stanley, N.D., U.S.	198	48.19 N	102.23 W
Stanley, Va., U.S.	188	38.34 N	78.30 W
Stanley, Wi., U.S.	190	44.57 N	90.56 W
Stanley ≃	171a	27.09 S	152.32 E
Stanley, Mont ∧[2]	273b	4.19 S	15.15 E
Stanley Bay ⊂	271d	22.12 N	114.12 E
Stanley Falls ʟ	154	0.30 N	25.12 E
Stanley Mills	275b	43.46 N	79.44 W
Stanley Mound ∧	271d	22.14 N	114.12 E
Stanley Park ♠, B.C., Can.	224	49.19 N	123.09 W
Stanley Park ♠, Eng., U.K.	262	53.26 N	2.57 W
Stanley Park ♠, Eng., U.K.	262	53.49 N	3.02 W
Stanley Reservoir ⊜[1]	122	11.54 N	77.50 E
Stanleyville → Kisangani	154	0.30 N	25.12 E
Stanlow	44	53.17 N	2.52 W
Stanmore ➧[8]	260	51.37 N	0.19 W
Stannards	210	42.05 N	77.55 W
Stannington	44	55.06 N	1.40 W
Stanovoj chrebet ⋏	74	56.20 N	126.00 E
Stanovoje nagorje (Stanovoy Mountains) ⋏	88	56.00 N	114.00 E
Stanovoj Kolodez'	76	52.51 N	36.16 E
Stanovoy Mountains → Stanovoje nagorje ⋏	88	56.00 N	114.00 E
Stans	58	46.57 N	8.22 E
Stansbury	168b	34.55 S	137.47 E
Stansmore Range ⋏	162	21.23 S	128.33 E
Stansstad	58	46.59 N	8.20 E
Stanstead	206	45.01 N	72.05 W
Stanstead □[6]	206	45.10 N	72.00 W
Stanstead Abbots	42	51.47 N	0.01 E
Stansted	260	51.20 N	0.18 E
Stansted Mountfitchet	42	51.54 N	0.12 E
Stanthorpe	166	28.39 S	151.57 E
Stanton, Eng., U.K.	42	52.19 N	0.53 E
Stanton, Ca., U.S.	228	33.48 N	117.59 W
Stanton, De., U.S.	208	39.43 N	75.37 W
Stanton, Ia., U.S.	198	41.05 N	95.11 W
Stanton, Ky., U.S.	192	37.50 N	83.51 W
Stanton, Mi., U.S.	190	43.17 N	85.04 W
Stanton, Mo., U.S.	219	38.16 N	91.06 W
Stanton, Ne., U.S.	198	41.57 N	97.13 W
Stanton, N.D., U.S.	198	47.19 N	101.22 W
Stanton, Tn., U.S.	194	35.27 N	89.24 W
Stanton, Tx., U.S.	196	32.07 N	101.47 W
Stantonsburg	192	35.36 N	77.49 W
Stanwell	260	51.27 N	0.29 W
Stanwell Moor	260	51.28 N	0.30 W
Stanwood	224	48.14 N	122.22 W
Stanwood Gardens	285	40.07 N	74.57 W
Stanwyck Estates	285	39.42 N	75.33 W
Stanzach	58	47.23 N	10.34 E
Stanz im Mürztal	61	47.28 N	15.30 E
Stapelburg	54	51.53 N	10.40 E
Stapelfeld	52	53.36 N	10.13 E
Staphorst	52	52.37 N	6.12 E
Stapleford	42	52.56 N	1.16 W
Stapleford Abbotts	260	51.38 N	0.10 E
Stapleford Aerodrome ⊠	260	51.39 N	0.08 E
Stapleford Tawney	260	51.40 N	0.11 E
Staplehurst	42	51.10 N	0.33 E
Staples	198	46.21 N	94.47 W
Stapleton, Al., U.S.	194	30.44 N	87.47 W
Stapleton, Ne., U.S.	198	41.28 N	100.30 W
Stąporków	30	51.09 N	20.34 E
Star', Ross.	76	53.37 N	34.09 E
Star, Ms., U.S.	194	32.05 N	90.02 W
Star, N.C., U.S.	192	35.24 N	79.47 W
Stará Boleslav	54	50.12 N	14.42 E
Starachowice	30	51.03 N	21.04 E
Stara Fužina	64	46.17 N	13.54 E
Staraja	265a	59.55 N	30.38 E
Staraja Belica, Bela.	76	54.42 N	29.38 E
Staraja Belica, Ross.	78	51.59 N	35.13 E
Staraja Belogorka	80	52.05 N	53.17 E
Staraja Derevn'a ➧[8]	265a	59.59 N	30.15 E
Staraja Duginka	82	54.20 N	38.45 E
Staraja Kriuša	78	50.12 N	41.09 E
Staraja Kulatka	80	52.43 N	47.37 E
Staraja Kupavna	82	55.48 N	38.10 E
Staraja Majačka	78	46.30 N	33.11 E
Staraja Majna	80	54.36 N	48.57 E
Staraja Poltavka	80	50.28 N	46.28 E
Staraja Porubežka	80	52.03 N	49.11 E
Staraja Račejka	80	53.22 N	48.03 E
Staraja Rudn'a	76	52.50 N	30.17 E
Staraja Russa	76	58.00 N	31.23 E
Staraja Ruza	82	55.39 N	36.20 E
Staraja Sachča	80	54.25 N	49.58 E
Staraja Sin'ava	78	49.36 N	27.37 E
Staraja Sitn'a	82	54.56 N	38.09 E
Staraja Terizmorga	80	54.16 N	44.32 E
Staraja Toropa	76	56.17 N	31.40 E
Staraja Ušica	78	48.35 N	27.07 E
Staraja Veduga	78	51.48 N	38.31 E
Staraja Vičuga	80	57.16 N	41.53 E
Staraja Vyževka	78	51.27 N	24.24 E
Staranzano	64	45.49 N	13.30 E
Stara Pazova	38	44.59 N	20.10 E
Stara Planina (Balkan Mountains) ⋏	38	42.45 N	25.00 E
Stará Role	54	50.14 N	12.47 E
Starav, Ben ∧	46	56.32 N	5.03 W
Stará Voda	60	50.00 N	12.36 E
Stara Zagora	38	42.25 N	25.38 E
Starbejevo	265b	55.55 N	37.28 E
Starbrick	214	41.50 N	79.12 W
Starbuck, Mb., Can.	184	49.46 N	97.36 W
Starbuck, Mn., U.S.	198	45.36 N	95.31 W
Starbuck, Wa., U.S.	202	46.31 N	118.07 W
Starbuck I	14	5.37 S	155.53 W
Starčenkovo	78	47.17 N	36.59 E
Star City, Sk., Can.	184	52.53 N	104.21 W
Star City, Ar., U.S.	194	33.56 N	91.50 W
Star City, In., U.S.	216	40.58 N	86.33 W
Starcross	42	50.38 N	3.27 W
Stare Czarnowo	54	53.16 N	14.45 E
Staré Sedliště	60	49.45 N	12.42 E
Starford	214	40.42 N	78.58 W
Stargard Szczeciński (Stargard in Pommern)	30	53.20 N	15.02 E
Stargo	200	33.04 N	109.21 W
Star Harbour ⊂	175e	10.47 S	162.18 E
Stari Bar	38	42.06 N	19.08 E
Starica, Ross.	76	56.30 N	34.56 E
Starica, Ross.	76	59.04 N	29.30 E
Starica, Ross.	80	48.13 N	45.56 E
Stari Grad	36	43.11 N	16.36 E
Starij R'ad	76	58.05 N	34.54 E
Starina	76	59.37 N	44.42 E
Stari Vlah ➧[1]	38	43.35 N	20.15 E
Star Junction	214	40.04 N	79.46 W
Stark □[6]	214	40.48 N	81.22 W
Starke	192	29.56 N	82.06 W
Starke □[6]	216	41.18 N	86.37 W
Starkey	210	42.32 N	76.56 W
Starkville	194	33.27 N	88.49 W
Star Lake	224	47.22 N	122.18 W
Star Mountains ⋏	164	5.05 S	141.05 E
Starnberg	60	48.00 N	11.20 E
Starnberger See ⊜	64	47.55 N	11.18 E
Starnikovo	82	55.22 N	38.24 E
Staroalejskoje	86	51.00 N	82.01 E
Starobačaty	86	54.14 N	86.07 E
Starobaltačevo	86	56.01 N	55.56 E
Starobel'sk	83	49.16 N	38.56 E
Starobeševo	83	47.44 N	38.03 E
Starobin	76	52.44 N	27.28 E
Staročerkasskaja	83	47.15 N	40.03 E
Starocuruchajtuj	88	50.12 N	119.15 E
Staroderev'ankov-Skaja	78	46.08 N	38.58 E
Starodub	76	52.35 N	32.46 E
Starod'umejevo	80	55.16 N	54.22 E
Starogan'kino	80	53.55 N	52.15 E
Starogard Gdański	30	53.59 N	18.33 E
Staroignatjevka	83	47.32 N	37.47 E
Staroje	76	59.16 N	40.40 E
Staroje Bajsarovo	80	55.31 N	53.54 E
Staroje Drožžanoje	80	54.44 N	47.34 E
Staroje Ibrajkino	80	54.52 N	51.02 E
Staroje Jaškino	80	52.49 N	52.57 E
Staroje Jermakovo	80	54.04 N	51.59 E
Staroje Oleničevo	80	45.34 N	47.11 E
Staroje Rachino	76	58.08 N	32.39 E
Staroje Šajgovo	80	54.18 N	44.26 E
Staroje Šajmurzino	80	54.45 N	47.58 E
Staroje Selo	76	55.14 N	29.54 E
Staroje Sindrovo	80	54.25 N	44.06 E
Staroje Slavkino	80	52.34 N	45.08 E
Staroje Ustje	80	53.28 N	41.51 E
Starojurjevo	80	53.21 N	40.42 E
Starokazačje	78	46.21 N	29.59 E
Starokonstantinov	78	49.46 N	27.13 E
Starokuručevo	80	55.09 N	54.04 E
Starolaspa	83	47.34 N	37.59 E
Staroleuškovskaja	78	45.59 N	39.44 E
Staromichajlovka	83	47.58 N	37.36 E
Starominskaja	78	46.31 N	39.04 E
Staromlinovka	78	47.42 N	36.49 E
Staromušta	80	55.49 N	54.14 E
Staronikolajevo	82	55.37 N	36.16 E
Staro-Podgorodneje	82	54.46 N	38.57 E
Staropokrovka	85	42.50 N	75.18 E
Staroščerbinovskaja	78	46.37 N	38.40 E
Staroseslavino	80	53.12 N	40.25 E
Starošešminsk	80	55.22 N	51.15 E
Starosiedle	54	51.50 N	14.50 E
Starosoldatskoje	86	56.12 N	72.37 E
Starosubchangulovo	86	53.06 N	57.26 E
Starotimoškino	24	53.43 N	47.32 E
Starotitarovskaja	78	45.14 N	37.09 E
Staroutkinsk	86	57.14 N	59.20 E
Staroverovka	78	49.33 N	35.42 E
Starožilovo	80	54.14 N	39.55 E
Starožil'sk	80	56.34 N	47.17 E
Star Peak ∧	204	40.32 N	118.10 W
Starr	214	41.32 N	79.22 W
Starrucca	210	41.54 N	75.28 W
Start Bay ⊂	42	50.17 N	3.36 W
Start Point ≻	42	50.13 N	3.38 W
Startup	224	47.52 N	121.44 W
Starvation Reservoir ⊜[1]	200	40.15 N	110.30 W
Starved Rock State Park ♠	216	41.19 N	88.58 W
Staryj Ajbesi	80	54.57 N	47.03 E
Staryj-Ajdar	83	48.43 N	39.11 E
Staryj Bagr'až	80	54.54 N	51.39 E
Staryj Bir'uz'ak	84	44.47 N	46.54 E
Staryj Bol'ševik	265b	55.57 N	37.47 E
Staryj Čartorijsk	78	51.15 N	25.54 E
Staryj Chop'or	80	51.30 N	42.58 E
Staryj Čindant	88	50.33 N	115.33 E
Staryje Burasy	80	52.16 N	46.09 E
Staryje Dorogi	76	53.02 N	28.16 E
Staryje Maty	80	55.14 N	53.55 E
Staryje Popel'uchi	78	48.18 N	28.55 E
Staryje Senžary	78	49.25 N	34.27 E
Staryje Turdaki	80	53.55 N	45.29 E
Staryje Z'atcy	80	57.21 N	52.39 E
Staryj Kazangal	80	50.15 N	47.39 E
Staryj Kistruss	80	54.28 N	40.34 E
Staryj Krym, Ukr.	78	45.03 N	35.05 E
Staryj Krym, Ukr.	83	47.10 N	37.30 E
Staryj Lesken	84	43.20 N	43.55 E
Staryj Medved'	76	58.18 N	30.30 E
Staryj Merčik	78	49.58 N	35.46 E
Staryj Oskol	78	51.19 N	37.51 E
Staryj Sambor	78	49.27 N	22.59 E
Staryj Terek ≃	84	44.00 N	47.24 E
Staryj Tukšum	80	53.42 N	48.33 E
Starý Plzenec	60	49.42 N	13.28 E
Stary Sącz	30	49.34 N	20.38 E
Stassfurt	54	51.51 N	11.34 E
Staszów	30	50.34 N	21.20 E
State Center	190	42.01 N	93.09 W
State College	214	40.47 N	77.51 W
State Fair Grounds ♠	284b	39.27 N	76.38 W
Stateline, Ca., U.S.	226	38.57 N	119.57 W
State Line, Ms., U.S.	194	31.26 N	88.28 W
Stateline, Nv., U.S.	204	38.58 N	119.56 W
Staten Island I	276	40.35 N	74.09 W
Staten Island Mall ➧[9]	276	40.35 N	74.10 W
Statenville	192	30.42 N	83.01 W
State Park Place	219	38.40 N	90.03 W
State Road	192	36.19 N	80.52 W
Statesboro	192	32.26 N	81.47 W
Statesville	192	35.46 N	80.53 W
Stateville Correctional Center ʊ	278	41.35 N	88.06 W
Station Peak	162	21.10 S	118.11 E
Statte	68	40.34 N	17.12 E
Statue of Liberty National Monument ♠	210	40.41 N	74.03 W
Staubbachfall ʟ	58	46.35 N	7.55 E
Staufen	58	47.53 N	7.44 E
Staufenberg	56	50.40 N	8.43 E
Staughton Vale	169	37.51 S	144.17 E
Staunton, Il., U.S.	219	39.00 N	89.47 W
Staunton, Va., U.S.	188	38.08 N	79.04 W
Staunton → Roanoke ≃	192	35.56 N	76.43 W
Stavanger	26	58.58 N	5.45 E
Stave ≃	224	49.10 N	122.26 W
Stave Lake ⊜	182	49.15 N	122.21 W
Staveley	44	53.16 N	1.20 W
Stavelot	56	50.23 N	5.56 E
Stavely, Ab., Can.	182	50.10 N	113.38 W
Stavely, Eng., U.K.	44	54.22 N	2.49 W
Staveren	52	52.53 N	5.22 E
Stavern	26	59.00 N	10.02 E
Stavišče	78	49.23 N	30.12 E
Stavnoje	78	48.59 N	22.40 E
Stavropol'	72	45.02 N	41.59 E
Stavropol' □[8]	84	44.38 N	43.30 E
Stavropol → Toljatti	80	53.31 N	49.26 E
Stavrovo	80	56.08 N	40.00 E
Stavsnäs	40	59.17 N	18.41 E
Stawell	166	37.04 S	142.46 E
Stawell ≃	166	20.38 S	142.55 E
Stawiski	30	53.23 N	22.09 E
Stawiszyn	30	51.55 N	18.07 E
Staxigoe	46	58.28 N	3.04 W
Stayner	212	44.25 N	80.05 W
Stayton	202	44.48 N	122.47 W
Stazzema	64	43.59 N	10.19 E
Steamboat	226	39.22 N	119.44 W
Steamboat Creek ≃	226	39.31 N	119.42 W
Steamboat Mountain ∧	200	41.58 N	108.58 W
Steamboat Slough ≃	226	38.11 N	121.40 W
Steamboat Springs	200	40.29 N	106.49 W
Steamburg	210	42.07 N	78.54 W
Stearns	192	36.41 N	84.28 W
Stearns Pond ⊜	283	42.37 N	71.04 W
Stębark	30	53.30 N	20.08 E
Stebbins	180	63.32 N	162.18 W
Stebl'ov	78	49.24 N	31.06 E
Stechow	54	52.38 N	12.28 E
Steckborn	58	47.40 N	8.55 E
Stederdorf	52	52.21 N	10.15 E
Stedten	54	51.26 N	11.41 E
Stedum	52	53.18 N	6.41 E
Steeg	58	47.14 N	10.17 E
Steel ≃	190	48.46 N	86.54 W
Steel City	210	40.38 N	75.20 W
Steele, Mo., U.S.	194	36.05 N	89.49 W
Steele, N.D., U.S.	198	46.51 N	99.54 W
Steele ➧[8]	263	51.27 N	7.05 E
Steele, Mount ∧	200	41.50 N	107.00 W
Steele Creek ≃, Tx., U.S.	222	31.13 N	96.19 W
Steele Creek ≃, Tx., U.S.	222	32.01 N	97.28 W
Steeles Corners	275b	43.48 N	79.25 W
Steeleville	194	38.00 N	89.39 W
Steelhead	224	49.13 N	122.19 W
Steel's Drift	158	27.21 S	29.30 E
Steels Point ≻	174c	29.02 S	168.00 E
Steels Run ≃	279b	40.25 N	79.38 W
Steelton, N.Y., U.S.	284a	42.47 N	78.49 W
Steelton, Pa., U.S.	208	40.14 N	76.50 W
Steelville	194	37.58 N	91.21 W
Steenbergen	52	51.35 N	4.19 E
Steenburg Lake ⊜	212	44.50 N	77.41 W
Steenderen	52	52.04 N	6.11 E
Steens Mountain ⋏	202	42.35 N	118.40 W
Steenvoorde	50	50.48 N	2.35 E
Steenwijk	52	52.47 N	6.08 E
Steepbank ≃	184	57.01 N	111.28 W
Steephill Lake ⊜	184	55.58 N	103.08 W
Steep Holm I	42	51.21 N	3.07 W
Steeping ≃	44	53.06 N	0.18 E
Steeple Claydon	42	51.56 N	0.59 W
Steep Point ≻	162	26.08 S	113.08 E
Steep Rock	184	51.26 N	98.48 W
Stefanie, Lake (Chew Bahir) ⊜	144	4.40 N	36.50 E
Stefansson Island I	176	73.20 N	105.45 W
Ștefan Vodă	38	44.19 N	27.19 E
Steffisburg	58	46.47 N	7.39 E
Steg	58	47.21 N	8.56 E
Stegalovka	76	52.24 N	38.19 E
Stege	41	54.59 N	12.18 E
Stegeborg	26	58.26 N	16.35 E
Stege Bugt ⊂	41	55.01 N	12.50 E
Stegelitz	54	53.08 N	13.51 E
Steger	216	41.28 N	87.38 W
Stegersbach	61	47.10 N	16.10 E
Steglitz ➧[8]	264a	52.28 N	13.19 E
Stehag	41	55.54 N	13.23 E
Stehekin	224	48.18 N	120.39 W
Stehekin ≃	224	48.21 N	120.40 W
Steiermark □[3]	30	47.10 N	15.10 E
Steigerwald ⋏	56	49.40 N	10.20 E
Steigra	54	51.18 N	11.39 E
Steilacoom	224	47.10 N	122.36 W
Steimbke	52	52.40 N	9.22 E
Stein, Dtsch.	60	49.25 N	11.01 E
Stein, Ned.	56	50.57 N	5.46 E
Stein, Schw.	58	47.33 N	7.58 E
Steina	54	51.12 N	14.01 E
Steinach, Dtsch.	54	50.25 N	11.10 E
Steinach, Dtsch.	58	48.18 N	8.04 E
Steinach, Öst.	64	47.05 N	11.28 E
Steinach ≃	56	50.11 N	11.12 E
Steinamanger → Szombathely	61	47.14 N	16.38 E
Stein am Rhein	58	47.40 N	8.51 E
Steinau	56	50.23 N	9.27 E
Steinbach, Mb., Can.	184	49.32 N	96.41 W
Steinbach, Dtsch.	56	48.43 N	8.10 E
Steinbach-Hallenberg	54	50.42 N	10.34 E
Steinberg ∧[2]	263	51.05 N	7.27 E
Steinberger Slough ≃	282	37.33 N	122.13 W
Steinbourg	56	48.46 N	7.25 E
Steindorf	61	46.42 N	14.01 E
Steinen	58	47.38 N	7.44 E
Steinernes Meer ⋏	64	47.30 N	12.58 E
Steinfeld, Dtsch.	52	52.35 N	8.12 E
Steinfeld, Dtsch.	54	50.22 N	10.44 E
Steinfeld, Öst.	64	46.45 N	13.15 E
Steinfort	56	49.40 N	5.55 E
Steinforth	263	51.09 N	6.32 E
Steinfurt	52	52.09 N	7.21 E
Steingaden	58	47.42 N	10.51 E
Steinhagen, Dtsch.	52	52.00 N	8.24 E
Steinhagen, Dtsch.	54	54.13 N	12.59 E
Steinhatchee ≃	192	29.40 N	83.24 W
Steinhausen	156	21.49 S	18.20 E
Steinhausen ʊ[1]	58	48.01 N	9.41 E
Steinheid	54	50.28 N	11.04 E
Steinheim, Dtsch.	52	51.52 N	9.05 E
Steinheim, Dtsch.	56	48.58 N	9.16 E
Steinheim, Dtsch.	58	48.01 N	10.09 E
Steinhöfel	54	52.24 N	14.10 E
Steinhöring	60	48.05 N	12.02 E
Steinhude	52	52.27 N	9.21 E
Steinhuder Meer ⊜	52	52.28 N	9.19 E
Steinkjer	26	64.01 N	11.30 E
Steinkopf	156	29.18 S	17.43 E
Steinloge	52	52.54 N	8.19 E
Stein-Neukirch	56	50.41 N	8.03 E
Steinpass)(	64	47.39 N	12.45 E
Steinsdorf	54	52.02 N	14.40 E
Steinshamn	26	62.47 N	6.29 E
Steinstücken ➧[8]	264a	52.23 N	13.08 E
Steinwiesen	54	50.17 N	11.28 E
Stekene	50	51.12 N	4.02 E
Stekl'anka	76	59.08 N	41.37 E
Steklino	76	56.51 N	32.10 E
Steksovo	80	55.17 N	43.25 E
Stella, It.	62	44.24 N	8.30 E
Stella, S. Afr.	158	26.38 S	24.48 E
Stella, Ne., U.S.	198	40.13 N	95.46 W
Stella Niagara	210	43.12 N	79.02 W
Stella-Plage	50	50.29 N	1.35 E
Stellaquo Indian Reserve ➧[4]	182	54.03 N	124.55 W
Stellarton	186	45.34 N	62.40 W
Stelle	52	53.23 N	10.06 E
Stellenbosch	158	33.58 S	18.50 E
Steller, Mount ∧	180	60.30 N	143.02 W
Stelvio, Parco Nazionale dello ♠	58	46.30 N	10.40 E
Stelvio, Passo dello)(	58	46.32 N	10.27 E
Stemwede	52	52.25 N	8.27 E
Stenay	56	49.29 N	5.11 E
Stendal	54	52.36 N	11.51 E
Stende	76	57.09 N	22.33 E
Stenden	263	51.25 N	6.27 E
Stenhammar slott ⊥	40	59.03 N	16.31 E
Stenhouse Bay	166	35.17 S	136.56 E
Stenhousemuir	46	56.02 N	3.48 W
Stenico	64	46.03 N	10.51 E
Stenlille	41	55.32 N	11.36 E
Stenløse	41	55.46 N	12.12 E
Stenness, Loch of ⊜	46	59.00 N	3.15 W
Stenón	267c	37.58 N	22.20 E
Stenón Návstathmou ʮ	267c	37.58 N	23.33 E
Stensätra	40	60.36 N	16.44 E
Stensele	24	65.05 N	17.09 E
Stenstorp	26	58.16 N	13.43 E
Stenstrup	41	55.07 N	10.31 E
Stentrop	263	51.30 N	7.49 E
Stenungsund	26	58.05 N	11.49 E
Stepan'	78	51.10 N	26.18 E
Stepanakert	84	39.49 N	46.44 E
Stepanavan	84	41.00 N	44.23 E
Stepancevo, Ross.	80	56.08 N	41.42 E
Stepancevo, Ross.	82	56.22 N	36.10 E
Stepancy	78	49.42 N	31.18 E
Stepano-Krynka	83	47.55 N	38.21 E
Stepanovka, Ross.	80	52.04 N	53.02 E
Stepanovka, Ross.	86	57.13 N	67.26 E
Stepanovka, Ukr.	78	50.58 N	34.37 E
Stepanovo	82	55.43 N	38.28 E
Stepanovskoje	265b	55.47 N	37.10 E
Stepan Razin	84	40.24 N	49.59 E
Stepanščino	82	55.15 N	38.30 E
Stepenitz ≃	54	53.48 N	11.10 E
Stephans-Dom ʊ[1]	264b	48.12 N	16.23 E
Stephanskirchen	64	47.51 N	12.11 E
Stephen	198	48.27 N	96.52 W
Stephen A. Forbes State Park ♠	219	38.44 N	88.46 W
Stephen F. Austin State Historic Park ♠	222	29.48 N	96.05 W
Stephens	194	33.24 N	93.04 W
Stephens, Cape ≻	172	40.42 S	173.57 E
Stephens, Port ⊂	166	32.45 S	152.05 E
Stephens City	188	39.05 N	78.13 W
Stephens Creek	166	31.50 S	141.30 E
Stephens Island I	182	54.10 N	130.45 W
Stephens Knob ∧[2]	192	36.37 N	84.20 W
Stephens Lake ⊜[1]	184	56.26 N	95.07 W
Stephens Mills	210	42.23 N	77.38 W
Stephenson	190	45.24 N	87.36 W
Stephenson, Lake ⊜	222	29.35 N	94.40 W
Stephenson, Mount ∧	9	69.49 S	69.43 W
Stephens Passage ʮ	180	57.50 N	133.50 W
Stephentown	210	42.33 N	73.23 W
Stephentown Center	210	42.34 N	73.25 W
Stephenville, Nf., Can.	186	48.33 N	58.35 W
Stephenville, Tx., U.S.	196	32.13 N	98.12 W
Stephenville Crossing	186	48.30 N	58.26 W
Stepn'ak	86	52.50 N	70.50 E
Stepney ➧[8]	260	51.31 N	0.02 W
Stepnica	54	53.40 N	14.36 E
Stepnoj	80	48.56 N	45.36 E
Stepnoje, Ross.	80	51.24 N	46.52 E
Stepnoje, Ross.	84	44.17 N	44.36 E
Step Pyramid → Şaqqārah ⊥	142	29.52 N	31.14 E
Steps Point ≻	174u	14.22 S	170.45 W
Steptoe Valley V	204	39.25 N	114.45 W
Stepurino	76	56.24 N	35.16 E
Sterdyń	30	52.35 N	22.18 E
Sterkaar	158	31.05 S	23.42 E
Sterkrade ➧[8]	263	51.31 N	6.51 E
Sterkspruit	158	30.32 S	27.22 E
Sterkstroom	158	31.32 S	26.32 E
Sterlibaševo	86	53.28 N	55.15 E
Sterling, S. Afr.	158	31.16 S	21.28 E
Sterling, Ak., U.S.	180	60.32 N	150.48 W
Sterling, Co., U.S.	198	40.37 N	103.12 W
Sterling, Ct., U.S.	207	41.42 N	71.49 W
Sterling, Il., U.S.	190	41.47 N	89.41 W
Sterling, Ks., U.S.	198	38.12 N	98.12 W
Sterling, Ma., U.S.	207	42.26 N	71.45 W
Sterling, Mi., U.S.	190	44.02 N	84.01 W
Sterling, Ne., U.S.	198	40.27 N	96.22 W
Sterling, N.Y., U.S.	210	43.20 N	76.39 W
Sterling, Oh., U.S.	214	40.58 N	81.51 W
Sterling, Ok., U.S.	196	34.45 N	98.10 W
Sterling, Va., U.S.	208	39.00 N	77.25 W
Sterling City	196	31.50 N	100.59 W
Sterling Creek ≃	210	43.20 N	76.42 W
Sterling Forest Lake ⊜	276	41.10 N	74.16 W
Sterling Heights	214	42.34 N	83.01 W
Sterling Junction	207	42.24 N	71.46 W
Sterling Park	282	37.41 N	122.26 W
Sterling Run	214	41.25 N	78.12 W
Sterlington	194	32.41 N	92.05 W
Sterlitamak	86	53.37 N	55.58 E
Šternberg	54	53.43 N	11.49 E
Šternberk	30	49.44 N	17.18 E
Šternstein ∧	61	48.34 N	14.16 E
Šterovka	83	48.19 N	38.57 E
Sterup	41	54.44 N	9.44 E

≃ River	Fluß	Río	Rivière	Rio	
≚ Canal	Kanal	Canal	Canal	Canal	
ʟ Waterfall, Rapids	Wasserfall, Stromschnellen	Cascada, Rápidos	Chute d'eau, Rapides	Cascata, Rápidos	
ʮ Strait	Meeresstraße	Estrecho	Détroit	Estreito	
⊂ Bay, Gulf	Bucht, Golf	Bahía, Golfo	Baie, Golfe	Baía, Golfo	
⊜ Lake, Lakes	See, Seen	Lago, Lagos	Lac, Lacs	Lago, Lagos	
⩸ Swamp	Sumpf	Pantano	Marais	Pântano	
⍓ Ice Features, Glacier	Eis- und Gletscherformen	Accidentes Glaciales	Formes glaciaires	Acidentes glaciares	
⫪ Other Hydrographic Features	Andere Hydrographische Objekte	Otros Elementos Hidrográficos	Autres données hydrographiques	Outros acidentes hidrográficos	

⇣ Submarine Features	Untermeerische Objekte	Accidentes Submarinos	Formes de relief sous-marin	Acidentes submarinos
□ Political Unit	Politische Einheit	Unidad Política	Entité politique	Unidade política
ʊ Cultural Institution	Kulturelle Institution	Institución Cultural	Institution culturelle	Instituição cultural
⊥ Historical Site	Historische Stätte	Sitio Histórico	Site historique	Sitio histórico
♠ Recreational Site	Erholungs- und Ferienort	Sitio de Recreo	Centre de loisirs	Area de Lazer
⊠ Airport	Flughafen	Aeropuerto	Aéroport	Aeroporto
■ Military Installation	Militäranlage	Instalación Militar	Installation militaire	Instalação militar
➧ Miscellaneous	Verschiedenes	Misceláneo	Divers	Diversos

Name	Page	Lat.°′	Long.°′
Sterzing → Vipiteno	64	46.54 N	11.26 E
Stęszew	30	52.18 N	16.42 E
Štětí	54	50.25 N	14.23 E
Stetson Pond ⊜	283	42.02 N	70.50 W
Stetten am kalten Markt	58	48.07 N	9.04 E
Stettin → Szczecin	30	53.24 N	14.32 E
Stettler	182	52.19 N	112.43 W
Steuben □[6], In., U.S.	216	41.38 N	85.00 W
Steuben □[6], N.Y., U.S.	210	42.20 N	77.19 W
Steubenville	214	40.22 N	80.38 W
Stevenage	42	51.55 N	0.14 W
Stevens, N.J., U.S.	285	40.05 N	74.49 W
Stevens, Pa., U.S.	208	40.13 N	76.09 W
Stevens, Lake ⊜	224	48.01 N	122.05 W
Stevens, Mount ∧	172	40.48 S	172.27 E
Stevens Creek ≃, Ca., U.S.	282	37.26 N	122.05 W
Stevens Creek ≃, S.C., U.S.	192	33.34 N	82.03 W
Stevens Creek Park ♦	282	37.17 N	122.04 W
Stevens Creek Reservoir ⊜[1]	282	37.17 N	122.05 W
Stevens Institute of Technology ⚘[2]	276	40.44 N	74.02 W
Stevenson, Al., U.S.	194	34.52 N	85.50 W
Stevenson, Md., U.S.	284b	39.25 N	76.43 W
Stevenson, Wa., U.S.	224	45.42 N	121.53 W
Stevenson Creek ≃	162	27.06 S	135.33 E
Stevenson Entrance ʯ	180	58.45 N	152.20 W
Stevenson Lake ⊜	184	53.56 N	96.09 W
Stevens Pass)(	224	47.45 N	121.04 W
Stevens Peak ∧	202	47.27 N	115.46 W
Stevens Point	190	44.31 N	89.34 W
Stevenston	46	55.39 N	4.45 W
Stevens Village	180	66.00 N	149.05 W
Stevensville, On., Can.	284a	42.57 N	79.04 W
Stevensville, Md., U.S.	208	38.58 N	76.18 W
Stevensville, Mi., U.S.	216	42.00 N	86.31 W
Stevensville, Mt., U.S.	202	46.30 N	114.05 W
Stevensville, Pa., U.S.	210	41.46 N	76.11 W
Stevinson	226	37.20 N	120.51 W
Stevns Klint ⊥[4]	41	55.18 N	12.27 E
Steward	216	41.51 N	89.01 W
Stewardson	219	39.15 N	88.37 W
Stewart, B.C., Can.	182	55.56 N	129.59 W
Stewart, Mn., U.S.	190	44.43 N	94.29 W
Stewart ≃	180	63.18 N	139.25 W
Stewart, Cape ≻	164	11.57 S	134.45 E
Stewart, Isla I	254	54.52 S	71.12 W
Stewart, Mount ∧	166	20.12 S	145.29 E
Stewart Island I	172	47.00 S	167.50 E
Stewart Islands II	175e	8.25 S	162.52 E
Stewart Lake ⊜	219	40.09 N	90.16 W
Stewart Manor	276	40.43 N	73.41 W
Stewarton	46	55.41 N	4.31 W
Stewartstown, N. Ire., U.K.	48	54.35 N	6.41 W
Stewartstown, Pa., U.S.	208	39.45 N	76.35 W
Stewartsville, Mo., U.S.	194	39.45 N	94.29 W
Stewartsville, N.J., U.S.	208	40.41 N	75.06 W
Stewartsville, Pa., U.S.	279b	40.21 N	79.46 W
Stewart Valley	184	50.36 N	107.50 W
Stewartville	190	43.51 N	92.29 W
Stewiacke	186	45.08 N	63.21 W
Steyerberg	52	52.34 N	9.01 E
Steyning	42	50.53 N	0.20 W
Steynsburg	158	31.15 S	25.49 E
Steynsrus	158	27.58 S	27.33 E
Steyr	61	48.03 N	14.25 E
Steyr ≃	61	48.02 N	14.25 E
Steyregg	61	48.17 N	14.22 E
Steytlerville	158	33.21 S	24.21 E
Stežki	80	53.06 N	41.13 E
Stezzano	62	45.38 N	9.39 E
Sthal	126	24.12 N	89.44 E
Stia	66	43.48 N	11.42 E
Štiavnické vrchy ⩘	30	48.40 N	18.45 E
Stickle Pond ⊜	276	40.59 N	74.25 W
Stickney, Eng., U.K.	44	53.05 N	0.01 E
Stickney, Il., U.S.	216	41.49 N	87.46 W
Stickney, S.D., U.S.	198	43.35 N	98.26 W
Stidsvig	41	56.12 N	13.08 E
Stiefingbach ≃	61	46.47 N	15.35 E
Stiege	54	51.40 N	10.53 E
Stiene	76	57.26 N	24.34 E
Stienitzfliess ≃	264a	52.33 N	13.43 E
Stienitz-See ⊜	264a	52.30 N	13.49 E
Stiens	52	53.15 N	5.45 E
Stiepel ⊸[8]	263	51.25 N	7.15 E
Stif	148	36.09 N	5.26 E
Stif □[5]	148	36.15 N	5.10 E
Stiftskirche ⚘[1]	263	51.23 N	7.00 E
Stige	41	55.26 N	10.25 E
Stigler	196	35.15 N	95.07 W
Stigliano	68	40.24 N	16.14 E
Stigtomta	40	58.48 N	16.47 E
Stikine ≃	180	56.40 N	132.30 W
Stikine Ranges ⩘	180	58.45 N	130.00 W
Stiklestad	26	63.48 N	11.33 E
Stilbaai	158	34.24 S	21.26 E
Stiles	210	40.40 N	75.30 W
Stiles Pond ⊜	283	42.41 N	71.02 W
Stilesville	210	42.05 N	75.24 W
Stilfontein	158	26.50 S	26.50 E
Stilís	38	38.55 N	22.36 E
Still	148	34.20 N	5.51 E
Stillaguamish ≃	224	48.11 N	122.22 W
Stillaguamish, North Fork ≃	224	48.11 N	122.07 W
Stillaguamish, South Fork ≃	224	48.11 N	122.07 W
Stillhouse Hollow Lake ⊜[1]	222	31.00 N	97.35 W
Stilling	41	56.04 N	10.00 E
Stillman Valley	216	42.07 N	89.11 W
Stillmore	192	32.26 N	82.12 W
Still Pond	208	39.19 N	76.02 W
Still Run ≃	285	39.49 N	75.18 W
Stillwater, B.C., Can.	182	49.46 N	124.18 W
Stillwater, Mn., U.S.	190	45.03 N	92.48 W
Stillwater, N.J., U.S.	210	41.02 N	74.52 W
Stillwater, N.Y., U.S.	210	42.56 N	73.39 W
Stillwater, Oh., U.S.	214	40.20 N	81.18 W
Stillwater, Ok., U.S.	196	36.06 N	97.03 W
Stillwater, Pa., U.S.	210	41.09 N	76.22 W
Stillwater ≃, Mt., U.S.	202	45.38 N	109.17 W
Stillwater ≃, Oh., U.S.	218	39.47 N	84.12 W
Stillwater Creek ≃	214	40.25 N	81.22 W
Stillwater Range ⩘	204	39.50 N	118.15 W
Stillwell, Il., U.S.	219	40.13 N	91.11 W
Stillwell, Ok., U.S.	194	35.49 N	94.38 W
Stilo	68	38.29 N	16.28 E
Stilo, Punta ≻	68	38.28 N	16.36 E
Stimberg ∧[2]	263	51.40 N	7.15 E
Stimigliano	66	42.18 N	12.34 E
Stimson, Mount ∧	202	48.31 N	113.36 W
Stînca-Costeşti, Lacul (vodochranilišče Kostešty-Stynka) ⊜[1]	38	47.55 N	27.10 E
Stinchar ≃	44	55.06 N	5.00 W
Stinear Nunataks ⩘	9	69.42 S	64.40 E
Stine Canal ≈	226	35.15 N	119.08 W
Stine Mountain ∧	202	45.44 N	113.07 W
Stingray Point ≻	208	37.33 N	76.18 W
Stînişoarei, Munţii ⩘	38	47.10 N	26.00 E
Stinking Water Creek ≃	198	40.22 N	101.07 W
Stinnett	196	35.49 N	101.26 W
Stintino	71	40.56 N	8.13 E
Stintonville	273d	26.14 S	28.13 E
Štip	38	41.44 N	22.12 E
Stiperstones ∧	42	52.35 N	2.56 W
Stiring-Wendel	56	49.12 N	6.56 E
Stírka ∧	60	49.24 N	13.34 E
Stirling, Austl.	162	21.44 S	133.45 E
Stirling, Austl.	168a	31.54 S	115.47 E
Stirling, Austl.	168b	35.00 S	138.43 E
Stirling, Ab., Can.	182	49.30 N	112.31 W
Stirling, On., Can.	212	44.18 N	77.33 W
Stirling, Scot., U.K.	46	56.07 N	3.57 W
Stirling, N.J., U.S.	210	40.40 N	74.29 W
Stirling, Mount ∧	162	31.50 S	117.38 E
Stirling Castle ⊥	46	56.07 N	3.57 W
Stirling City	204	39.54 N	121.31 W
Stirling Range ⩘	162	34.23 S	117.50 E
Stirling Range National Park ♦	162	34.22 S	118.00 E
Stirling Reservoir ⊜[1]	168a	33.08 S	116.03 E
Stirrat	192	37.43 N	82.00 W
Stissing Mountain ∧	210	41.57 N	73.42 W
Štitary	61	48.56 N	15.51 E
Stittsville	212	45.15 N	75.55 W
Stittville	210	43.13 N	75.17 W
Stjärnhov	40	59.05 N	17.00 E
Stjärnsund, Sve.	40	60.26 N	16.12 E
Stjärnsund, Sve.	40	58.51 N	14.55 E
Stjernøya I	24	70.18 N	22.45 E
Stjørdalshalsen	26	63.28 N	10.56 E
Stöberhai ∧	54	51.39 N	10.34 E
Stochod ≃	78	51.52 N	25.38 E
Stock	260	51.40 N	0.27 E
Stock, Étang du ⊜	56	48.45 N	6.55 E
Stockach	58	47.51 N	9.00 E
Stöckalp	58	46.48 N	8.17 E
Stockamöllan	41	55.57 N	13.22 E
Stockbridge, Eng., U.K.	42	51.07 N	1.29 W
Stockbridge, Ga., U.S.	192	33.32 N	84.14 W
Stockbridge, Ma., U.S.	207	42.17 N	73.19 W
Stockbridge, Mi., U.S.	216	42.27 N	84.10 W
Stockbridge Bowl ⊜	207	42.20 N	73.19 W
Stockbridge Indian Reservation ⊸[4]	190	44.52 N	88.53 W
Stockbury	260	51.20 N	0.39 E
Stockby	40	59.20 N	17.41 E
Stockdale, Oh., U.S.	218	38.57 N	82.51 W
Stockdale, Tx., U.S.	196	29.14 N	97.57 W
Stockelsdorf	52	53.54 N	10.38 E
Stöcken	54	53.00 N	10.40 E
Stockerau	61	48.23 N	16.13 E
Stockertown	208	40.45 N	75.15 W
Stockett	202	47.21 N	111.09 W
Stockheim	56	50.19 N	9.01 E
Stockholm, Sve.	40	59.20 N	18.03 E
Stockholm, Me., U.S.	186	47.02 N	68.08 W
Stockholm, N.J., U.S.	210	41.05 N	74.31 W
Stockholm, Lake ⊜	276	41.04 N	74.32 W
Stockholms Län □[6]	40	59.30 N	18.20 E
Stock Island	220	24.34 N	81.45 W
Stockland	216	40.37 N	87.36 W
Stockport, Eng., U.K.	44	53.25 N	2.10 W
Stockport, N.Y., U.S.	210	42.19 N	73.45 W
Stockport □[8]	262	53.23 N	2.08 W
Stocksbridge	44	53.27 N	1.34 W
Stockstadt	56	49.48 N	8.28 E
Stocksund	40	59.23 N	18.04 E
Stockton, Austl.	170	32.55 S	151.47 E
Stockton, Al., U.S.	194	30.59 N	87.51 W
Stockton, Ca., U.S.	226	37.57 N	121.17 W
Stockton, Il., U.S.	190	42.20 N	90.00 W
Stockton, Ks., U.S.	198	39.26 N	99.15 W
Stockton, Md., U.S.	208	38.03 N	75.24 W
Stockton, Mo., U.S.	194	37.41 N	93.47 W
Stockton, N.J., U.S.	208	40.24 N	74.58 W
Stockton, N.Y., U.S.	214	42.19 N	79.22 W
Stockton, Ut,. U.S.	200	40.27 N	112.21 W
Stockton Heath, Eng., U.K.	44	53.22 N	2.34 W
Stockton Heath, Eng., U.K.	262	53.22 N	2.35 W
Stockton Metropolitan Airport ⊠	226	37.54 N	121.15 W
Stockton-on-Tees	44	54.34 N	1.19 W
Stockton Plateau ⩘[1]	196	30.30 N	102.30 W
Stockton Reservoir ⊜[1]	194	37.40 N	93.45 W
Stockton Springs	188	44.29 N	68.51 W
Stockum, Dtsch.	52	51.40 N	7.42 E
Stockum, Dtsch.	263	51.32 N	7.47 E
Stockum, Dtsch.	263	51.36 N	6.39 E
Stockum, Dtsch.	263	51.28 N	7.22 E
Stockum ⊸[8]	263	51.16 N	6.44 E
Stockville	198	40.31 N	100.22 W
Stockwell	216	40.17 N	86.46 W
Stockwell, Lake ⊜	285	39.51 N	74.47 W
Stoco Lake ⊜	212	44.28 N	77.18 W
Stoczek Łukowski	30	51.58 N	21.58 E
Stod	60	49.39 N	13.10 E
Stoddard Mountain ∧	228	34.42 N	117.07 W
Stöde	26	62.25 N	16.35 E
Stodoliči	78	51.44 N	28.30 E
Stodolišče	76	54.11 N	32.39 E
Stœng Trêng	110	13.31 N	105.58 E
Stoer	46	58.12 N	5.20 W
Stoer, Point of ≻	46	58.15 N	5.21 W
Stoffberg	156	25.29 S	29.49 E
Stoj, gora ∧	78	48.37 N	23.11 E
Stojba	89	52.49 N	131.43 E
Stoke	260	51.27 N	0.37 E
Stoke ≃	206	45.35 N	71.58 W
Stoke, Monts ⩘	206	45.33 N	71.42 W
Stoke D'Abernon	260	51.19 N	0.23 W
Stoke Golding	42	52.34 N	1.24 W
Stokenchurch	42	51.40 N	0.55 W
Stoke Newington ⊸[8]	260	51.34 N	0.05 W
Stoke-on-Trent	42	53.00 N	2.10 W
Stoke Poges	260	51.33 N	0.35 W
Stokes, Mount ∧	172	41.06 S	174.06 E
Stokes Inlet ⊂	162	33.50 S	121.08 E
Stokesley	44	54.28 N	1.11 W
Stokes Point ≻	166	40.10 S	143.56 E
Stokes Range ⩘[2]	164	15.46 S	130.57 E
Stokkemarke	41	54.50 N	11.23 E
Stokksnes ≻	24a	64.17 N	14.54 W
Stol ∧	38	44.13 N	22.14 E
Stolac	36	43.05 N	17.58 E
Stolbcy	76	53.29 N	26.44 E
Stolberg, Dtsch.	54	51.34 N	10.57 E
Stolberg, Dtsch.	56	50.46 N	6.13 E
Stolbišči	80	55.39 N	49.14 E
Stolboucha	86	49.59 N	84.30 E
Stolbovo	76	52.38 N	34.47 E
Stolbovoj, ostrov I	74	74.05 N	136.00 E
Stolbun	76	52.48 N	31.25 E
Stolby, zapovednik ♦	88	55.45 N	92.45 E
Stolin	78	51.53 N	26.51 E
Stollberg	54	50.42 N	12.47 E
Stöllet	26	60.24 N	13.16 E
Stol'noje	78	51.31 N	31.55 E
Stolpe	264a	52.40 N	13.16 E
Stolpen	54	51.05 N	14.04 E
Stolper Heide ⊸[3]	264a	52.39 N	13.14 E
Stolpino	80	57.24 N	42.55 E
Stolp → Słupsk	30	54.28 N	17.01 E
Stolzenau	52	52.31 N	9.04 E
Ston	36	42.50 N	17.42 E
Stondon Massey	260	51.41 N	0.18 E
Stone, Eng., U.K.	42	52.54 N	2.10 W
Stone, Eng., U.K.	260	51.27 N	0.16 E
Stoneboro	214	41.20 N	80.06 W
Stone Canyon Reservoir ⊜[1]	280	34.07 N	118.28 W
Stone Corral Creek ≃	226	39.16 N	122.06 W
Stone Creek	214	40.24 N	81.34 W
Stonecutters Island I	271d	22.19 N	114.08 E
Stonefort	194	37.37 N	88.42 W
Stoneham, Ma., U.S.	283	42.28 N	71.06 W
Stoneham, Pa., U.S.	214	41.49 N	79.07 W
Stone Harbor	208	39.03 N	74.45 W
Stonehaven	46	56.38 N	2.13 W
Stonehenge	166	24.22 S	143.17 E
Stonehenge ⊥	42	51.11 N	1.49 W
Stonehill College ⚘[2]	283	42.03 N	71.05 W
Stonehouse, Eng, U.K.	42	51.45 N	2.17 W
Stonehouse, Scot., U.K.	46	55.43 N	4.00 W
Stone Indian Reserve ⊸[4]	182	51.54 N	123.12 W
Stoneleigh	42	52.21 N	1.31 W
Stonelick Creek ≃	218	39.07 N	84.13 W
Stonelick State Park ♦	218	39.13 N	84.04 W
Stone Mountain	192	33.48 N	84.10 W
Stone Mountain ∧, Pa., U.S.	210	40.37 N	77.48 W
Stone Mountain ∧, Vt., U.S.	188	44.34 N	71.40 W
Stone Mountain Memorial State Park ♦	192	33.49 N	84.06 W
Stone Park	278	41.45 N	87.53 W
Stoner	182	53.36 N	122.40 W
Stoner Creek ≃	218	38.18 N	84.14 W
Stone Ridge	210	41.51 N	74.09 W
Stonerstown	214	40.13 N	78.16 W
Stones, East Fork ≃	194	35.59 N	86.27 W
Stones, West Fork ≃	194	35.59 N	86.27 W
Stones River National Battlefield ⊥	194	35.52 N	86.26 W
Stonestown ⊸[9]	282	37.44 N	122.28 W
Stonevilla	279b	40.18 N	79.31 W
Stoneville	192	36.27 N	79.54 W
Stonewall, Mb., Can.	184	50.09 N	97.21 W
Stonewall, La., U.S.	194	32.16 N	93.49 W
Stonewall, Ms., U.S.	194	32.07 N	88.47 W
Stonewall, Ok., U.S.	196	34.39 N	96.31 W
Stonewall Manor	284c	38.53 N	77.14 W
Stoney Creek	212	43.13 N	79.46 W
Stoney Point ≻	214	42.18 N	82.34 W
Stonington, Ct., U.S.	207	41.20 N	71.54 W
Stonington, Il., U.S.	219	39.38 N	89.11 W
Stonington, Me., U.S.	188	44.09 N	68.40 W
Stony ≃, Ak., U.S.	180	61.45 N	156.35 W
Stony ≃, Mn., U.S.	190	47.44 N	91.47 W
Stony Brook	210	40.55 N	73.08 W
Stony Brook ≃, Ct., U.S.	276	41.04 N	73.28 W
Stony Brook ≃, Ct., U.S.	276	41.08 N	73.22 W
Stony Brook ≃, Ma., U.S.	283	42.38 N	71.22 W
Stony Brook ≃, Ma., U.S.	283	42.22 N	71.16 W
Stony Brook ≃, N.J., U.S.	276	40.19 N	74.41 W
Stony Brook ≃, N.J., U.S.	276	40.56 N	74.26 W
Stony Brook Harbor ⊂	276	40.54 N	73.10 W
Stony Brook Reservation ♦	283	42.16 N	71.09 W
Stony Creek, Ct., U.S.	207	41.15 N	72.44 W
Stony Creek, Mi., U.S.	281	42.42 N	83.07 W
Stony Creek, Va., U.S.	208	36.56 N	77.24 W
Stony Creek ≃, Ca., U.S.	204	39.41 N	121.58 W
Stony Creek ≃, Il., U.S.	278	41.41 N	87.51 W
Stony Creek ≃, Mi., U.S.	216	41.57 N	83.18 W
Stony Creek ≃, Mi., U.S.	216	43.00 N	84.55 W
Stony Creek ≃, N.Y., U.S.	212	43.49 N	76.14 W
Stony Creek ≃, Pa., U.S.	285	40.07 N	75.21 W
Stony Creek ≃, Va., U.S.	208	36.56 N	77.23 W
Stony Creek, Middle Fork ≃	226	39.25 N	122.31 W
Stony Creek, North Fork ≃	226	39.22 N	122.37 W
Stony Creek, South Fork ≃	226	39.22 N	122.39 W
Stony Creek Indian Reserve ⊸[4]	182	53.57 N	124.07 W
Stony Creek Mills	208	40.21 N	75.52 W
Stonyford	226	39.22 N	122.32 W
Stony Gorge Reservoir ⊜[1]	226	39.34 N	122.31 W
Stony Indian Reserve ⊸[4]	182	51.10 N	114.55 W
Stony Island I, Mi., U.S.	281	42.07 N	83.08 W
Stony Island I, N.Y., U.S.	212	43.53 N	76.25 W
Stony Kill ≃	210	42.24 N	73.38 W
Stony Lake ⊜, Mb., Can.	176	58.51 N	98.35 W
Stony Lake ⊜, On., Can.	212	44.33 N	78.05 W
Stony Plain	182	53.32 N	114.00 W
Stony Plain Indian Reserve ⊸[4]	182	53.30 N	113.45 W
Stony Point, Austl.	169	38.22 S	145.13 E
Stony Point, Mi., U.S.	216	41.57 N	83.16 W
Stony Point, N.Y., U.S.	210	41.13 N	73.59 W
Stony Point, N.C., U.S.	192	35.51 N	81.02 W
Stony Point ≻	284a	42.50 N	78.52 W
Stony Point ≻[1]	212	43.52 N	76.15 W
Stony Prairie	214	41.21 N	83.10 W
Stony Rapids	176	59.16 N	105.50 W
Stony Ridge	214	41.30 N	83.30 W
Stony River	180	61.47 N	156.41 W
Stony Run	284b	39.11 N	76.42 W
Stony Run ≃	285	40.09 N	75.32 W
Stony Stratford	42	52.04 N	0.52 W
Stoober Bach ≃	61	47.27 N	16.35 E
Stop ≃	283	42.10 N	71.19 W
Stopnica	30	50.27 N	20.57 E
Stoppenberg ⊸[8]	263	51.29 N	7.02 E
Stör ≃	54	53.50 N	11.29 E
Storå	40	59.43 N	15.08 E
Storå ≃	26	56.19 N	8.19 E
Stora Alvaret ≚	26	56.30 N	16.30 E
Stora Gla ⊜	26	59.30 N	12.30 E
Stora Kloten ⊜	40	59.52 N	15.16 E
Stora Le ⊜	26	59.05 N	11.53 E
Stora Lulevatten ⊜	24	67.10 N	19.16 E
Stora Mellösa	40	59.13 N	15.30 E
Stora Möja I, Sve.	26	59.26 N	18.55 E
Stora Möja I, Sve.	40	59.26 N	18.55 E
Stora Norn ⊜	40	60.14 N	15.42 E
Stora Sjöfallets Nationalpark ♦	24	67.44 N	18.16 E
Stora Skedvi	40	60.24 N	15.48 E
Stora Sundby	40	59.16 N	16.07 E
Storavan ⊜	24	65.40 N	18.15 E
Stora Vika	40	58.56 N	17.48 E
Storby	26	60.13 N	19.34 E
Stord I	26	59.53 N	5.25 E
Store Andst	41	55.29 N	9.14 E
Storebælt ʯ	41	55.30 N	11.00 E
Store Heddinge	41	55.19 N	12.25 E
Store Magleby	41	55.36 N	12.38 E
Store Merløse	41	55.33 N	11.40 E
Støren	26	63.02 N	10.18 E
Store Sotra I	26	60.18 N	5.05 E
Storeton	262	53.21 N	3.03 W
Storey □[6]	226	39.28 N	119.30 W
Storfjärden ⊜	40	60.30 N	17.23 E
Storfjorden ⊂[2]	26	62.25 N	6.30 E
Storfors	40	59.32 N	14.16 E
Störitzsee ⊜	264a	52.23 N	13.51 E
Störkanal ≈	54	53.36 N	11.30 E
Storkerson Bay ⊂	176	73.00 N	124.50 W
Storkerson Peninsula ≻[1]	176	72.30 N	106.30 W
Storkow, Dtsch.	54	52.15 N	13.56 E
Storkow, Dtsch.	54	53.19 N	14.17 E
Storlien	26	63.19 N	12.06 E
Stormarn ⊸[1]	52	53.45 N	10.20 E
Storm Bay ⊂	166	43.10 S	147.32 E
Stormberg ∧	158	30.57 S	26.41 E
Stormberge ⩘	158	31.27 S	26.55 E
Storm King Mountain ∧	224	46.39 N	122.10 W
Storm Lake	198	42.38 N	95.12 W
Storm Mountain ∧	180	59.37 N	150.35 W
Stormont-Dundas and Glengarry □[6]	206	45.10 N	75.00 W
Štormovo	83	49.06 N	38.55 E
Stormsrivier	158	33.59 S	23.52 E
Stormsvlei	158	34.05 S	20.06 E
Stormville	210	41.34 N	73.45 W
Stornara	68	41.17 N	15.46 E
Stornarella	68	41.15 N	15.44 E
Stornorrforsen	26	63.52 N	20.03 E
Stornoway	46	58.12 N	6.23 W
Storo	64	45.51 N	10.35 E
Storoževaja	84	43.53 N	41.27 E
Storoževsk	24	61.57 N	52.16 E
Storožinec	78	48.10 N	25.43 E
Storrensjön ⊜	26	63.38 N	12.34 E
Storrington	42	50.55 N	0.28 W
Storrs	207	41.48 N	72.15 W
Storsjøen ⊜, Nor.	26	60.23 N	11.40 E
Storsjøen ⊜, Nor.	26	61.35 N	11.12 E
Storsjön ⊜, Sve.	26	62.48 N	13.07 E
Storsjön ⊜, Sve.	26	63.12 N	14.18 E
Storsjön ⊜, Sve.	40	60.34 N	16.44 E
Storsjön ⊜, Sve.	40	59.04 N	17.12 E
Storsteinsfjellet ∧	24	68.14 N	17.52 E
Storstrøm □[6]	41	55.00 N	11.55 E
Storstrømmen ʯ	41	54.58 N	11.55 E
Storstrømsbroen ⊸[5]	41	54.58 N	11.50 E
Stort ≃	260	51.46 N	0.01 E
Storthoaks	184	49.22 N	101.38 W
Storuman	24	65.06 N	17.06 E
Storuman ⊜[1]	24	65.14 N	16.54 E
Storuman-See → Storavan ⊜	24	65.40 N	18.15 E
Storvarts gruve	26	62.38 N	11.31 E
Storvätteshågna ∧	26	62.07 N	12.27 E
Storvik	40	60.35 N	16.32 E
Storvindeln ⊜	24	65.43 N	17.05 E
Storvreta	40	59.58 N	17.42 E
Story	202	44.34 N	106.53 W
Story City	190	42.11 N	93.35 W
Stosch, Isla I	254	49.09 S	75.26 W
Stössen	54	51.06 N	11.55 E
Stotfold	42	52.01 N	0.14 W
Stotternheim	54	51.03 N	11.02 E
Stottville	210	42.17 N	73.44 W
Stouchsburg	208	40.23 N	76.14 W
Stough Park ♦	280	34.12 N	118.18 W
Stoughton, Sk., Can.	184	49.41 N	103.03 W
Stoughton, Eng., U.K.	260	51.15 N	0.35 W
Stoughton, Ma., U.S.	207	42.07 N	71.06 W
Stoughton, Wi., U.S.	216	42.55 N	89.13 W
Stoumont	56	50.25 N	5.48 E
Stoŭng ≃	110	12.50 N	104.19 E
Stour ≃, Eng., U.K.	42	51.52 N	1.16 E
Stour ≃, Eng., U.K.	42	50.43 N	1.46 W
Stour ≃, Eng., U.K.	42	51.18 N	1.22 E
Stour ≃, Eng., U.K.	42	52.20 N	2.15 W
Stourbridge	42	52.27 N	2.09 W
Stourport-on-Severn	42	52.21 N	2.16 W
Stout Lake ⊜	184	52.08 N	94.33 W
Stoutsville	219	39.33 N	91.51 W
Stover	194	38.26 N	92.59 W
Stow, Ma., U.S.	207	42.26 N	71.30 W
Stow, N.Y., U.S.	214	42.09 N	79.25 W
Stow, Oh., U.S.	214	41.10 N	81.27 W
Stowe, Pa., U.S.	208	40.15 N	75.40 W
Stowe, Vt., U.S.	188	44.27 N	72.41 W
Stowell	194	29.47 N	94.23 W
Stowe Township	279b	40.29 N	80.04 W
Stow Maries	260	51.40 N	0.39 E
Stowmarket	42	52.11 N	1.00 E
Stow-on-the-Wold	42	51.56 N	1.44 W
Stowupland	42	52.12 N	1.01 E
Stoyoma Mountain ∧	182	49.59 N	121.13 W
Stoystown	214	40.06 N	78.57 W
Stožec	60	48.51 N	13.50 E
Stra	64	45.25 N	12.00 E
Straach	54	51.57 N	12.35 E
Strabane, N. Ire., U.K.	48	54.49 N	7.27 W
Strabane, Pa., U.S.	214	40.15 N	80.11 W
Straberg	263	51.05 N	6.45 E
Strachan	46	57.01 N	2.32 W
Strachan Island I	164	9.00 S	142.10 E
Strachur	46	56.10 N	5.04 W
Stradbally	48	53.00 N	7.08 W
Stradbroke	42	52.19 N	1.16 E
Stradeč'	78	51.56 N	23.40 E
Stradella	62	45.05 N	9.18 E
Stradone	48	53.58 N	7.14 W
Stradovn'a, ozero ⊜	82	56.53 N	36.18 E
Straelen	56	51.27 N	6.16 E
Strafford	285	40.03 N	75.25 W
Straffordville	212	42.45 N	80.47 W
Strahan	166	42.09 S	145.19 E
Straight Creek ≃	218	38.46 N	83.55 W
Strakonice	60	49.16 N	13.55 E
Stralsund	54	54.19 N	13.05 E
Strambino	62	45.23 N	7.53 E
Strand	158	34.06 S	18.50 E
Stranda	26	62.19 N	6.54 E
Strande	54	54.26 N	10.12 E
Strandhill	48	54.17 N	8.36 W
Stranger Creek ≃	198	39.00 N	95.01 W
Strangford	48	54.22 N	5.34 W
Strangford Lough ⊜	48	54.28 N	5.35 W
Strängnäs	40	59.23 N	17.02 E
Strångsjö	40	58.54 N	16.12 E
Strangways ≃	164	14.52 S	133.50 E
Strangways, Mount ∧	162	23.02 S	133.51 E
Stranorlar	48	54.48 N	7.46 W
Stranraer	44	54.55 N	5.02 W
Strasbourg, Sk., Can.	184	51.04 N	104.57 W
Strasbourg, Fr.	58	48.35 N	7.45 E
Strasbourg, Aéroport ⊠	58	48.32 N	7.38 E
Strasburg, Dtsch.	54	53.30 N	13.44 E
Strasburg, Co., U.S.	198	39.44 N	104.20 W
Strasburg, N.D., U.S.	198	46.08 N	100.09 W
Strasburg, Oh., U.S.	214	40.35 N	81.31 W
Strasburg, Pa., U.S.	208	39.58 N	76.11 W
Strasburg, Va., U.S.	188	38.59 N	78.21 W
Straševiči	76	56.49 N	34.36 E
Strašín	60	49.08 N	13.38 E
Stråssa	40	59.45 N	15.13 E
Strassburg → Strasbourg	58	48.35 N	7.45 E
Strasshof an der Nordbahn	61	48.19 N	16.39 E
Strasskirchen	60	48.50 N	12.43 E
Strata Florida Abbey ⚘[1]	42	52.16 N	3.51 W
Stratford, On., Can.	212	43.22 N	80.57 W
Stratford, N.Z.	172	39.20 S	174.17 E
Stratford, Ca., U.S.	226	36.11 N	119.49 W
Stratford, Ct., U.S.	207	41.11 N	73.08 W
Stratford, De., U.S.	285	39.40 N	75.38 W
Stratford, Ia., U.S.	190	42.16 N	93.55 W
Stratford, N.J., U.S.	208	39.49 N	75.00 W
Stratford, N.Y., U.S.	210	43.11 N	74.42 W
Stratford, Ok., U.S.	196	34.47 N	96.57 W
Stratford, Tx., U.S.	196	36.20 N	102.04 W
Stratford, Wi., U.S.	190	44.48 N	90.04 W
Stratford Centre	206	45.47 N	71.16 W
Stratford Point ≻	276	41.09 N	73.06 W
Stratford-upon-Avon	42	52.12 N	1.41 W
Strathalbyn	168b	35.16 S	138.54 E
Strathaven	46	55.40 N	4.04 W
Strathbogie Ranges ⩘	169	36.55 S	145.45 E
Strathclair	184	50.24 N	100.24 W
Strathclyde □[4]	46	56.00 N	5.15 W
Strathcona Provincial Park ♦	182	49.40 N	125.50 W
Strathdearn V	46	57.15 N	4.05 W
Strathdon	46	57.11 N	3.02 W
Strathearn V	46	56.18 N	3.45 W
Strathfield	170	33.52 S	151.06 E
Strathgordon	166	42.46 S	146.03 E
Strath Kanaird	46	57.59 N	5.11 W
Strathlorne	186	46.11 N	61.17 W
Strathminglo	46	56.16 N	3.16 W
Strathmoor ⊸[8]	281	42.23 N	83.11 W
Strathmore, Ab., Can.	182	51.03 N	113.23 W
Strathmore, Ca., U.S.	204	36.08 N	119.03 W
Strathmore, N.J., U.S.	276	40.24 N	74.13 W
Strathmore V	46	56.39 N	3.00 W
Strathpeffer	46	57.35 N	4.33 W
Strathpine	171a	27.19 S	152.59 E
Strathroy	214	42.57 N	81.38 W
Strathy ≃	46	58.34 N	4.00 W
Strathy Point ≻	46	58.35 N	4.02 W
Strattanville	214	41.12 N	79.19 W
Stratton, Eng., U.K.	42	50.50 N	4.31 W
Stratton, Eng., U.K.	42	51.44 N	1.59 W
Stratton, Co., U.S.	198	39.18 N	102.36 W
Stratton, Me., U.S.	188	45.08 N	70.26 W
Stratton, Ne., U.S.	198	40.08 N	101.13 W
Stratton, Oh., U.S.	214	40.32 N	80.38 W
Stratton Mountain ∧	188	43.05 N	72.56 W
Stratton Saint Margaret	42	51.35 N	1.45 W
Straubing	60	48.53 N	12.34 E
Strauch	263	51.09 N	6.56 E
Straumen	26	63.52 N	11.18 E
Straupitz	54	51.54 N	14.07 E
Strausberg	54	52.35 N	13.53 E
Straus-Berger Stadtforst ♦	264a	52.34 N	13.52 E
Strausberg-Vorstadt	264a	52.32 N	13.51 E
Straussberg	54	51.23 N	10.44 E
Straussee ⊜	264a	52.35 N	13.53 E
Straussfurt	54	51.09 N	10.59 E
Strausstown	208	40.30 N	76.11 W
Stravignano	66	43.05 N	12.49 E
Strawberry	226	38.13 N	118.35 W
Strawberry ≃, Ar., U.S.	194	35.53 N	91.13 W
Strawberry ≃, Ut,. U.S.	200	40.10 N	110.24 W
Strawberry Island I	284a	42.57 N	78.55 W
Strawberry Mountain ∧	202	44.19 N	118.43 W
Strawberry Point, Ca., U.S.	282	37.54 N	122.31 W
Strawberry Point, Ia., U.S.	190	42.41 N	91.32 W
Strawberry Point ≻	283	42.15 N	70.46 W
Strawberry Reservoir ⊜[1]	200	40.11 N	111.08 W
Strawberry Valley	226	39.34 N	121.06 W
Strawbridge Lake ⊜	285	39.57 N	74.57 W
Strawn	196	32.33 N	98.29 W
Straw Pump	279b	40.19 N	79.40 W
Stráž	61	49.04 N	14.54 E
Strážnice	30	48.54 N	17.18 E
Strážov	60	49.18 N	13.15 E
Strážske	30	48.53 N	21.50 E
Streaky Bay	162	32.48 S	134.13 E
Streaky Bay ⊂	162	32.36 S	134.08 E
Streamwood	216	42.01 N	88.10 W
Streatham, Austl.	169	37.41 S	143.04 E
Streatham, B.C., Can.	182	53.52 N	126.12 W
Streatham ⊸[8]	260	51.26 N	0.08 W
Streator	216	41.07 N	88.50 W
Strebersdorf ⊸[8]	264b	48.18 N	16.23 E
Středočeský Kraj □[4]	30	49.55 N	14.30 E
Stredoslovenský Kraj □[4]	30	48.50 N	19.10 E
Street	42	51.07 N	2.42 W
Streeter	198	46.39 N	99.21 W
Streetman	222	31.53 N	96.19 W
Streetsboro	214	41.14 N	81.20 W
Streets Run ≃	279b	40.23 N	79.56 W
Streetsville	212	43.35 N	79.42 W
Strehaia	38	44.37 N	23.12 E
Strehla	54	51.21 N	13.13 E
Streitberg	60	49.49 N	11.13 E
Střela ≃	60	49.55 N	13.33 E
Strelasund ʯ	54	54.20 N	13.05 E
Strel'covka	83	49.18 N	39.52 E
Streleckaja Step', zapovednik ♦	83	49.16 N	40.05 E
Streleckije Vyselki	82	54.12 N	38.57 E
Strelica	78	51.37 N	38.55 E
Střelice	61	49.09 N	16.30 E
Strelitzalt	54	53.20 N	13.05 E
Strelka	86	58.05 N	93.01 E
Strelka ≃	265a	59.52 N	30.03 E
Strelka-Čun'a	74	61.45 N	102.48 E
Strelkovo	82	55.28 N	37.37 E
Strelkovoje	78	45.54 N	34.53 E
Strel'na, Ross.	24	66.06 N	38.40 E
Strel'na, Ross.	76	59.51 N	30.02 E
Strel'na ≃	24	66.04 N	38.39 E
Strel'skaja	24	59.28 N	47.47 E
Střelské Hoštice	60	49.18 N	13.46 E
Strem ≃	61	47.00 N	16.31 E
Strembo	64	46.09 N	10.44 E
Stremilovo	82	55.09 N	37.09 E
Strenči	76	57.37 N	25.41 E
Strengen	58	47.08 N	10.27 E
Strensall	44	54.03 N	1.02 W
Stresa	62	45.53 N	8.32 E
Strešen'	78	47.08 N	28.36 E
Strešin	76	52.43 N	30.05 E
Stretford	44	53.27 N	2.19 W
Stretton, Austl.	162	32.32 S	117.41 E
Stretton, Eng., U.K.	42	52.44 N	0.35 W
Stretton, Eng., U.K.	44	53.21 N	2.35 W
Streu ≃	56	50.21 N	10.16 E
Strib	41	55.32 N	9.47 E
Striberg	40	59.33 N	14.56 E
Stříbro	60	49.46 N	13.00 E
Strichen	46	57.34 N	2.05 W
Strickherdicke	263	51.29 N	7.43 E
Strickland ≃	164	6.00 S	142.05 E
Strigno	64	46.04 N	11.31 E
Strijen	52	51.45 N	4.33 E
Striker, Lake ⊜[1]	222	31.57 N	94.59 W
Strimón (Struma) ≃	38	40.47 N	23.51 E
Stringtown	218	40.05 N	86.29 W
Striven, Loch ⊂	46	55.58 N	5.09 W
Strižament, gora ∧	84	44.46 N	42.01 E
Strižavka	78	49.19 N	28.28 E
Striži	80	58.30 N	49.13 E
Strjama ≃	38	42.10 N	24.56 E
Strobel	252	32.03 S	60.37 W
Strobel, Lago ⊜	254	48.22 S	71.12 W
Strobl	64	47.43 N	13.29 E
Strobleton	214	41.22 N	79.25 W
Strøby	41	55.23 N	12.18 E
Stroeder	254	40.11 S	62.37 W
Strofádhes, Nísoi II	38	37.15 N	21.00 E
Strogino ⊸[8]	265b	55.49 N	37.25 E
Strogonof Point ≻	180	56.53 N	158.49 W
Stroh	216	41.34 N	85.11 W
Ströhen	52	52.32 N	8.41 E
Stroitel'	78	50.47 N	36.26 E
Strokestown	48	53.47 N	8.08 W
Strom ≃	54	53.15 N	13.50 E
Stroma I	46	58.41 N	3.08 W
Stromberg, Dtsch.	52	51.48 N	8.12 E
Stromberg, Dtsch.	56	49.57 N	7.46 E
Stromboli, Isola I	70	38.47 N	15.13 E
Strome	182	52.48 N	112.04 W
Stromeferry	46	57.21 N	5.34 W
Strömkendorf	54	53.58 N	11.29 E
Stromness	46	58.57 N	3.18 W
Strömsberg	40	60.24 N	17.35 E
Strömsbro	40	60.42 N	17.10 E
Strömsbruk	26	61.53 N	17.19 E
Stromsburg	198	41.06 N	97.35 W
Strömsholm	40	59.32 N	16.15 E
Strömsnäsbruk	26	56.33 N	13.43 E
Strömstad	26	58.56 N	11.10 E
Strömsund	26	63.51 N	15.35 E
Strömsvattudal ⊜	26	63.56 N	15.28 E
Stromyn'	82	56.03 N	38.29 E
Strong	194	33.06 N	92.20 W
Strong ≃	194	31.51 N	90.08 W
Strong City	198	38.23 N	96.32 W
Stronghurst	190	40.44 N	90.54 W
Strongoli	68	39.15 N	17.03 E
Strongs Creek ≃	276	40.40 N	73.22 W
Strongs Neck ≻[1]	276	40.58 N	73.07 W
Strongstown	214	40.33 N	78.55 W
Strongsville	214	41.18 N	81.50 W
Strongsville Airport ⊠	279a	41.19 N	81.52 W
Stronsay I	46	59.07 N	2.37 W
Stronsay Firth ʯ	46	59.02 N	2.41 W
Stronsdorf	61	48.39 N	16.18 E
Strontian	46	56.41 N	5.44 W
Strood	42	51.24 N	0.28 E
Stropkov	30	49.12 N	21.40 E
Stropnice ≃	61	48.52 N	14.30 E
Stroppiana	62	45.14 N	8.27 E
Stroud, Austl.	166	32.20 S	151.56 E
Stroud, Eng., U.K.	42	51.45 N	2.12 W
Stroud, Ok., U.S.	196	35.44 N	96.39 W
Stroudsburg	210	40.59 N	75.11 W
Strövelstorp	41	56.09 N	12.49 E
Strubenvale	273d	26.16 S	28.28 E
Strücklingen	52	53.07 N	7.40 E
Struer	26	56.29 N	8.37 E
Struga	38	41.11 N	20.40 E
Strugi-Krasnyje	76	58.17 N	29.06 E
Struisbaai	158	34.49 S	20.04 E
Struisbult	273d	26.19 S	28.29 E
Strule ≃	48	54.43 N	7.25 W
Strum	190	44.32 N	91.23 W
Struma (Strimón) ≃	38	40.47 N	23.51 E
Strumble Head ≻	42	52.02 N	5.04 W
Strumica	38	41.26 N	22.38 E
Strümp	263	51.17 N	6.40 E
Strunino	82	56.23 N	38.34 E
Strupna	82	54.43 N	38.48 E
Struthers	214	41.03 N	80.36 W
Struy	46	57.24 N	4.39 W
Strydenburg	158	29.58 S	23.40 E
Strydomsvlei	158	33.10 S	23.03 E
Strydpoort	158	27.00 S	25.58 E
Stryj	78	49.15 N	23.51 E
Stryj ≃	78	49.24 N	24.13 E
Stryker, Mt., U.S.	182	48.40 N	114.46 W
Stryker, Oh., U.S.	216	41.30 N	84.24 W
Strykersville	210	42.42 N	78.27 W
Stryków	30	51.55 N	19.37 E
Stryn	26	61.55 N	6.47 E
Strynø I	41	54.54 N	10.37 E
Strypa ≃	78	48.52 N	25.26 E
Strzegom	30	50.57 N	16.21 E
Strzegowo-Osada	30	52.55 N	20.18 E
Strzelce Krajeńskie	30	52.53 N	15.32 E
Strzelce Opolskie	30	50.31 N	18.19 E
Strzelecki Creek ≃	166	29.37 S	139.59 E
Strzelecki Desert ⊸[2]	166	28.00 S	140.10 E
Strzeleckie, Mount ∧	162	21.10 S	133.53 E
Strzelecki National Park ♦	166	40.14 S	148.06 E
Strzelin	30	50.47 N	17.03 E
Strzelno	30	52.38 N	18.11 E
Strzyżów	30	49.52 N	21.47 E
Stuart, Fl., U.S.	220	27.11 N	80.15 W
Stuart, Ia., U.S.	198	41.30 N	94.19 W
Stuart, Ne., U.S.	198	42.35 N	99.08 W
Stuart, Va., U.S.	192	36.38 N	80.15 W
Stuart ≃	182	54.00 N	123.32 W
Stuart, Central Mount ∧	162	21.54 S	133.27 E
Stuart, Mount ∧	224	47.29 N	120.54 W
Stuart Channel ʯ	224	48.55 N	123.45 W
Stuart Island I, Ak., U.S.	180	63.35 N	162.30 W
Stuart Island I, Wa., U.S.	224	48.42 N	123.12 W
Stuart Lake ⊜	182	54.32 N	124.35 W
Stuart Mountains ⩘	172	45.00 S	167.37 E
Stuart Range ⩘	162	29.10 S	134.56 E
Stuarts Draft	192	38.01 N	79.02 W
Stubai V	64	47.06 N	11.19 E
Stubaier Alpen ⩘	64	47.10 N	11.05 E
Stubalpe ⩘	61	47.06 N	14.54 E
Stübbecken	263	51.23 N	7.36 E
Stubbekøbing	41	54.53 N	12.03 E
Stubbenfelde	54	54.02 N	14.01 E
Stubbenkammer	54	54.35 N	13.40 E
Stubbington	42	50.50 N	1.13 W
Stubbins	262	53.39 N	2.19 W
Stubenberg	61	47.14 N	15.48 E
Stubla ≃	78	50.50 N	26.04 E
Stubner Kogel ∧	64	47.07 N	13.06 E
Studená	61	49.11 N	15.17 E
Studenec	80	54.52 N	48.16 E
Studenica, Manastir ⚘[1]	38	43.21 N	20.35 E
Studen Kladenec, jazovir ⊜[1]	38	41.37 N	25.30 E
Studholme Junction	172	44.44 S	171.08 E
Studland	42	50.39 N	1.58 W
Studley	42	52.16 N	1.52 W
Stud'onoje, Ross.	80	51.36 N	53.10 E
Stud'onoje, Ross.	86	53.37 N	77.31 E
Stud'onok	78	51.42 N	34.07 E
Studsvik	40	58.46 N	17.23 E
Stugudal	26	62.54 N	11.52 E
Stugun	26	63.10 N	15.36 E
Stuhleck ∧	61	47.34 N	15.47 E
Stühlingen	58	47.44 N	8.26 E
Stuhlweissenburg → Székesfehérvár	30	47.12 N	18.25 E
Stuhr	52	53.01 N	8.45 E
Stuie	182	52.22 N	126.02 W
Stukely, Lac ⊜	206	45.22 N	72.15 W
Stukenbrock	52	51.54 N	8.39 E
Stull ≃	184	55.10 N	92.39 W
Stull Lake ⊜	184	54.23 N	92.34 W
Stülpe	54	52.02 N	13.19 E
Stumm	64	47.17 N	11.53 E
Stump Creek	214	41.01 N	78.50 W
Stump Creek ≃	276	40.28 N	74.16 W
Stumpf	263	51.06 N	7.13 E
Stump Lake ⊜	198	47.54 N	98.24 W
Stumsdorf	54	51.37 N	12.03 E
Stuorre Tjõure ∧	26	63.56 N	13.30 E
Stupart ≃	184	56.00 N	93.22 W
Stupava	61	48.17 N	17.02 E
Stupino	82	54.53 N	38.05 E
Stuppach	56	49.27 N	9.44 E
Stura di Ala ≃	62	45.18 N	7.24 E
Stura di Demonte ≃	62	44.40 N	7.53 E
Stura di Lanzo ≃	62	45.06 N	7.44 E
Stura di Val Grande ≃	62	45.18 N	7.24 E

Symbols in the index entries represent the broad categories identified in the key at the right. Symbols with superior numbers (⩘[1]) identify subcategories (see complete key on page *I · 1).*

Symbole im Register stellen die rechts im Schlüssel erklärten Kategorien dar. Symbole mit hochgestellten Ziffern (⩘[1]) bezeichnen Unterabteilungen einer Kategorie (vgl. vollständiger Schlüssel auf Seite *I · 1).*

Los símbolos incluídos en el texto del índice representan las grandes categorias identificadas con la clave a la derecha. Los símbolos con numeros en su parte superior (⩘[1]) identifican las subcategorías (véase la clave completa en la página *I · 1).*

Les symboles de l'index représentent les catégories indiquées dans la légende à droite. Les symboles suivis d'un indice (⩘[1]) représentent des sous-catégories (voir légende complète à la page *I · 1).*

Os símbolos incluídos no texto do índice representam as grandes categorias identificadas com a chave à direita. Os símbolos com números em sua parte superior (⩘[1]) identificam as subcategorias (veja-se a chave completa à página *I · 1).*

∧ Mountain	Berg	Montaña	Montagne	Montanha
⩘ Mountains	Gebirge	Montañas	Montagnes	Montanhas
)(Pass	Paß	Paso	Col	Passo
V Valley, Canyon	Tal, Cañon	Valle, Cañón	Vallée, Canyon	Vale, Canhão
≚ Plain	Ebene	Llano	Plaine	Planície
≻ Cape	Kap	Cabo	Cap	Cabo
I Island	Insel	Isla	Île	Ilha
II Islands	Inseln	Islas	Îles	Ilhas
⊥ Other Topographic Features	Andere Topographische Objekte	Otros Elementos Topográficos	Autres données topographiques	Outros acidentes topográficos

ESPAÑOL

Nombre	Página	Lat.°′	Long.°′ W = Oeste
Stura di Viù ≃	62	45.16 N	7.26 E
Sturbridge	207	42.06 N	72.04 W
Sturdee	162	31.52 S	132.23 E
Sturge Island I	9	67.27 S	164.18 E
Sturgeon, Mo., U.S.	219	39.14 N	92.16 W
Sturgeon, Pa., U.S.	279b	40.23 N	80.13 W
Sturgeon ≃, On., Can.	190	46.19 N	79.58 W
Sturgeon ≃, Sk., Can.	184	53.12 N	105.53 W
Sturgeon ≃, Mi., U.S.	190	45.24 N	84.38 W
Sturgeon ≃, Mi., U.S.	190	45.50 N	86.41 W
Sturgeon ≃, Mi., U.S.	190	47.02 N	88.30 W
Sturgeon Bay	190	44.50 N	87.22 W
Sturgeon Bay c	184	52.00 N	97.50 W
Sturgeon Falls	190	46.22 N	79.55 W
Sturgeon Lake ⊜, Ab., Can.	182	55.06 N	117.30 W
Sturgeon Lake ⊜, On., Can.	184	55.25 N	90.55 W
Sturgeon Lake ⊜, On., Can.	212	44.28 N	78.42 W
Sturgeon Lake ⊜, Wa., U.S.	224	45.44 N	122.48 W
Sturgeon Lake Indian Reserve ◆[4], Ab., Can.	182	55.04 N	117.29 W
Sturgeon Lake Indian Reserve ◆[4], Sk., Can.	184	53.25 N	106.05 W
Sturgeon Landing	184	54.16 N	101.49 W
Sturgeon Point ›	212	42.42 N	79.03 W
Sturgis, Sk., Can.	184	51.58 N	102.32 W
Sturgis, Ky., U.S.	194	37.32 N	87.59 W
Sturgis, Mi., U.S.	216	41.47 N	85.25 W
Sturgis, Ms., U.S.	194	33.20 N	89.02 W
Sturgis, S.D., U.S.	198	44.24 N	103.30 W
Sturla	62	44.24 N	8.59 E
Sturminster Newton	42	50.50 N	2.19 W
Štúrovo	30	47.48 N	18.49 E
Sturry	42	51.18 N	1.07 E
Sturt, Mount ʌ	166	29.33 S	141.42 E
Sturt Creek	162	19.10 S	128.10 E
Sturt Creek ≃	162	20.08 S	127.24 E
Sturtevant	216	42.41 N	87.53 W
Sturt National Park ♠	166	29.00 S	141.40 E
Sturt Stony Desert ◆[2]	166	28.30 S	141.00 E
Sturup flygplats ⊠	41	55.34 N	13.21 E
Stürzelberg	263	51.08 N	6.49 E
Stutterheim	158	32.33 S	27.28 E
Stuttgart, Dtsch.	56	48.46 N	9.11 E
Stuttgart, Ar., U.S.	194	34.30 N	91.33 W
Stuttgart □[5]	56	49.00 N	9.45 E
Stuttgart, Flughafen ⊠	56	48.41 N	9.12 E
Stützengrün	54	50.32 N	12.31 E
Stützerbach	54	50.38 N	10.51 E
Stuyvesant	210	42.24 N	73.47 W
Stuyvesant Falls	210	42.21 N	73.44 W
Stviga ≃	78	52.04 N	27.54 E
Styal	262	53.21 N	2.15 W
Stykkishólmur	24a	65.06 N	22.48 W
Styla	83	47.41 N	37.50 E
Styr' ≃	78	52.07 N	26.35 E
Styrum ◆[8]	263	51.27 N	6.51 E
Styx ≃, On., Can.	212	44.11 N	80.57 W
Styx ≃, Al., U.S.	194	30.31 N	87.27 W
Suaçuí Grande ≃	255	18.50 S	41.46 W
Suai	112	3.48 N	113.38 E
Suain	164	3.20 S	142.55 E
Suaita	246	6.07 N	73.27 W
Suakin Archipelago II	140	18.42 N	38.30 E
Sual	116	16.04 N	120.05 E
Suan	98	38.42 N	126.22 E
Suao, T'aiwan	100	24.36 N	121.51 E
Su'ao, Zhg.	100	25.38 N	119.42 E
Suapure ≃	246	6.25 N	66.23 W
Suaqui Grande	232	28.24 N	109.54 W
Suār	124	29.02 N	79.03 E
Suātala	124	23.09 N	79.02 E
Suatima	114	4.13 N	96.04 E
Šubač	76	60.22 N	38.14 E
Subačius	76	55.46 N	24.47 E
Subah	115a	6.58 S	109.52 E
Subaio	256	22.30 S	42.50 W
Subang	115a	6.34 S	107.45 E
Subansiri ≃	120	26.48 N	93.50 E
Šubarkuduk	86	49.13 N	56.34 E
Subar Laut, Pulau I	271c	1.13 N	103.50 E
Subarnapur	272b	22.58 N	88.34 E
Subarnarekha ≃	120	21.34 N	87.24 E
Šubarši	86	48.35 N	57.12 E
Subashi	85	38.22 N	74.57 E
Subasio, Monte ʌ	66	43.03 N	12.40 E
Subata	76	56.01 N	25.56 E
Subay', 'Urūq as- ◆[2]	144	22.15 N	43.05 E
Subbiano	66	43.34 N	11.52 E
Subbotino	86	53.04 N	91.55 E
Subchankulovo	80	54.34 N	53.49 E
Subei	102	39.27 N	95.03 E
Subeita → Shivta, Ḥorvot ⊥	132	30.53 N	34.38 E
Suben	60	48.25 N	13.26 E
Subhepur	272a	28.45 N	77.16 E
Subi, Pulau I	112	2.55 N	108.50 E
Subiaco	66	41.55 N	13.06 E
Subic	116	14.53 N	120.14 E
Subic Bay c	116	14.45 N	120.13 E
Subic Bay Naval Base (U.S.) ■	116	14.47 N	120.16 E
Subipur	272b	22.54 N	88.08 E
Subk al-Ahad	142	30.18 N	31.02 E
Sublette	198	37.28 N	100.50 W
Sublett Range ⋏	202	42.20 N	112.50 W
Sublime	222	29.29 N	96.48 W
Subotica	38	46.06 N	19.39 E
Suburban Airport ⊠	284c	39.05 N	76.50 W
Suburban Village	285	39.58 N	75.34 W
Suca	144	6.31 N	39.14 E
Sucarnoochee ≃	194	32.25 N	88.02 W
Succasunna	210	40.52 N	74.38 W
Succor Creek ≃	202	43.38 N	116.56 W
Suceava	38	47.39 N	26.19 E
Suceava □[6]	38	47.30 N	25.45 E
Suceava ≃	38	47.32 N	26.32 E
Sucha [Beskidzka]	30	49.44 N	19.36 E
Suchaja	88	52.32 N	107.06 E
Suchaja Volnovacha ≃	83	47.37 N	38.01 E
Suchań	30	53.17 N	15.19 E
Suchana	74	68.45 N	118.00 E
Suchang	107	30.34 N	103.34 E
Suchan → Partizansk	89	43.08 N	133.09 E
Süchbaatar	88	50.15 N	106.12 E
Süchbaatar □[4]	102	45.30 N	114.00 E
Suchdol ◆[8]	54	50.08 N	14.21 E
Suchdol nad Lužnicí	61	48.54 N	14.53 E
Suchedniów	30	51.03 N	20.51 E
Suchetgarh	123	32.34 N	74.40 E
Suchiapa	234	16.37 N	93.05 W
Suchiapa ≃	234	16.36 N	93.01 W
Súchil	234	23.38 N	103.55 W
Suchiniči	76	54.06 N	35.20 E
Suchitepéquez □[5]	236	14.25 N	91.20 W
Suchitlán	234	19.22 N	103.43 W
Suchitoto	236	13.56 N	89.02 W
Suchobezvodnoje	80	57.03 N	44.50 E
Suchoborka	24	59.06 N	49.58 E
Suchodol, Ross.	80	53.55 N	51.14 E
Suchodol, Ross.	82	54.27 N	37.22 E
Suchodol'skij	76	53.43 N	38.17 E
Suchodrev ≃	82	54.44 N	35.59 E
Suchoj	80	47.06 N	41.21 E
Suchoj Jelančik ≃	83	47.16 N	38.25 E
Suchoj Log	86	56.55 N	62.01 E
Suchoj Pit	86	58.48 N	92.49 E
Suchoj Sambek ≃	83	47.23 N	39.07 E
Suchoj Torec ≃	83	48.49 N	37.36 E

FRANÇAIS

Nom	Page	Lat.°′	Long.°′ W = Ouest
Suchona ≃	24	60.46 N	46.24 E
Suchorečka	80	52.49 N	52.27 E
Suchotinka	80	52.31 N	41.35 E
Suchou → Suzhou	106	31.18 N	120.37 E
Suchoverkovo	76	56.37 N	35.35 E
Suchov Pervyj	80	49.59 N	43.28 E
Süchow → Xuzhou	98	34.16 N	117.11 E
Süchteln	56	51.17 N	6.22 E
Suchumi	84	43.01 N	41.02 E
Sucio ≃	246	7.27 N	77.07 W
Suck ≃	48	53.16 N	8.03 W
Sucker Creek ≃	212	44.09 N	77.08 W
Sucker Creek Indian Reserve ◆[4]	182	55.28 N	116.10 W
Sucker Lake ⊜	212	44.46 N	78.16 W
Suckling, Mount ʌ	164	9.45 S	148.55 E
Sucre, Arg.	258	34.30 S	59.07 W
Sucre, Bol.	248	19.02 S	65.17 W
Sucre, Col.	246	8.49 N	74.44 W
Sucre, Ec.	246	1.16 S	80.26 W
Sucre □[3]	246	10.25 N	63.30 W
Sucre □[5], Col.	246	9.00 N	75.00 W
Sucre □[5], Ven.	286c	10.25 N	66.50 W
Sucúa	246	2.28 S	78.10 W
Sucuaro	246	4.34 N	68.50 W
Sucumbíos □[4]	246	0.06 N	76.52 W
Sucunduri ≃	248	5.50 S	59.32 W
Sucuriju	250	1.39 N	49.57 W
Sucuriú ≃	255	20.47 S	51.38 W
Sucy-en-Brie	50	48.46 N	2.32 E
Sud, Canal du ɥ	238	18.40 N	73.05 W
Sud, Grand Récif ✧[2]	175f	23.00 S	167.02 E
Sud, Pointe ›	157a	11.53 S	43.49 E
Sud, Rivière du ≃	206	45.08 N	73.15 W
Suda	76	59.09 N	37.33 E
Suda ≃	76	59.11 N	37.30 E
Südafrika → South Africa □[1]	156	30.00 S	26.00 E
Sudaj	76	58.58 N	43.08 E
Sudak	78	44.52 N	34.59 E
Südamerika → South America ⊥[1]	18	15.00 S	60.00 W
Sudan	196	34.04 N	102.31 W
Sudan (As-Sūdān) □[1], Afr.	136	15.00 N	30.00 E
Sudan (As-Sūdān) □[1], Afr.	140	15.00 N	30.00 E
Sudan ◆[1]	10	10.00 N	20.00 E
Sudañez	248	19.06 S	64.44 W
Sudarsan	272b	22.59 N	88.17 E
Südbahnhof ◆[5]	264b	48.11 N	16.23 E
Sudberg ◆[8]	263	51.11 N	7.08 E
Sudbišči	76	52.57 N	37.39 E
Sud'bodarovka	80	52.19 N	54.07 E
Südbrookmerland	52	53.29 N	7.24 E
Sudbury, On., Can.	190	46.30 N	81.00 W
Sudbury, Eng., U.K.	42	52.02 N	0.44 E
Sudbury, Ma., U.S.	207	42.23 N	71.25 W
Sudbury ≃	283	42.28 N	71.22 W
Sudbury Center	283	42.23 N	71.25 W
Sudbury Reservoir ⊜[1]	207	42.19 N	71.31 W
Südchinesisches Meer → South China Sea ⊤[2]	108	10.00 N	113.00 E
Sud Dakota → South Dakota □[3]	198	44.15 N	100.00 W
Sudd an-Na'ām, Jabal ʌ	142	29.49 N	31.43 E
Sudd → As-Sudd ◆[1]	140	8.00 N	31.00 E
Suddie	246	7.07 N	58.29 W
Sude ≃	54	53.22 N	10.45 E
Süderbrarup	41	54.38 N	9.46 E
Süderlügum	41	54.52 N	8.55 E
Suderwich	263	51.37 N	7.15 E
Sudeten → Sudety ⋏	30	50.30 N	16.00 E
Sudety ⋏	30	50.30 N	16.00 E
Süd-Georgien → South Georgia I	244	54.15 S	36.45 W
Sudi	154	10.06 S	39.57 E
Sudislavl'	80	57.53 N	41.43 E
Südkamen	263	51.35 N	7.39 E
Süd-Korea → Korea, South □[1]	98	36.30 N	128.00 E
Sudlersville	208	39.11 N	75.51 W
Südlicher Bug → Južnyj Bug ≃	78	46.59 N	31.58 E
Südlicher Indianer-See → Southern Indian Lake ⊜	176	57.10 N	98.40 W
Sudnikovo	82	55.53 N	36.02 E
Sudogda	80	55.57 N	40.50 E
Sudomskaja vozvyšennost' ⋏[1]	76	57.25 N	29.25 E
Sudong, Pulau I	271c	1.13 N	103.44 E
Süd-Orkney-Inseln → South Orkney Islands II	9	60.35 S	45.30 W
Sudost' ≃	76	52.19 N	33.24 E
Sud-Ouest □[4]	152	5.10 N	9.00 E
Sud-Ouest, Pointe du ›	186	49.23 N	63.36 W
Sudovaja Višn'a	78	49.49 N	23.22 E
Südradde ≃	52	52.41 N	7.34 E
Süd-Sandwich-Inseln → South Sandwich Islands II	18	57.45 S	26.30 W
Süd-Shetland-Inseln → South Shetland Islands II	9	62.00 S	58.00 W
Sudūd	142	30.25 N	30.54 E
Südwest-Kap → South West Cape ›	166	43.34 S	146.02 E
Sudweyhe	52	52.59 N	8.53 E
Sudža	78	51.12 N	35.16 E
Sue	96	33.35 N	130.30 E
Sue ≃	140	7.41 N	28.03 E
Sueca	34	39.12 N	0.19 W
Suecia → Sweden □[1]	24	62.00 N	15.00 E
Sue Creek c	284b	39.17 N	76.24 W
Suedberg	208	40.32 N	76.28 W
Suède → Sweden □[1]	24	62.00 N	15.00 E
Suemez Island I	182	55.17 N	133.21 W
Suèvres	50	47.40 N	1.28 E
Suez, Gulf of → Suways, Khalīj as- c	140	29.00 N	32.50 E
Suez → As-Suways	142	29.58 N	32.33 E
Suez Canal → Suways, Qanāt as- ≅	142	29.55 N	32.33 E
Sūf	132	32.19 N	35.50 E
Şufaynah	128	23.09 N	40.32 E
Suffern	210	41.06 N	74.09 W
Suffern Park	276	41.07 N	74.07 W
Suffield, Ab., Can.	184	50.12 N	111.10 W
Suffield, Ct., U.S.	207	41.58 N	72.39 W
Suffield, Oh., U.S.	214	41.01 N	81.21 W
Suffield, Canadian Forces Base ■	184	50.15 N	111.10 W
Suffolk	208	36.43 N	76.35 W
Suffolk □[6], Eng., U.K.	42	52.10 N	1.00 E
Suffolk □[6], Ma., U.S.	207	42.21 N	71.04 W
Suffolk □[6], N.Y., U.S.	210	40.55 N	72.40 W
Suffolk, Ruisseau ≃	206	45.48 N	74.59 W
Suffolk Downs Race Track ♠	283	42.23 N	71.00 W
Şūfīān	128	38.17 N	45.59 E

PORTUGUÊS

Nome	Página	Lat.°′	Long.°′ W = Oeste
Sufi-Kurgan	85	40.02 N	73.30 E
Sufu → Kashi	85	39.29 N	75.59 E
Suga-jima I	94	34.29 N	136.53 E
Sugana, Val V	64	46.00 N	11.40 E
Sugandha	272b	22.54 N	88.20 E
Sugandy	85	43.27 N	74.38 E
Sugano	268	35.44 N	139.56 E
Sugar ≃, U.S.	190	42.26 N	89.12 W
Sugar ≃, N.H., U.S.	188	43.24 N	72.24 W
Sugar ≃, N.Y., U.S.	212	43.31 N	75.19 W
Sugar City	202	43.52 N	111.44 W
Sugarcreek, Oh., U.S.	214	40.30 N	81.39 W
Sugarcreek, Pa., U.S.	214	41.25 N	79.52 W
Sugar Creek ≃, U.S.	216	40.47 N	87.45 W
Sugar Creek ≃, Il., U.S.	194	40.09 N	89.38 W
Sugar Creek ≃, Il., U.S.	219	38.28 N	89.37 W
Sugar Creek ≃, Il., U.S.	219	39.48 N	89.32 W
Sugar Creek ≃, In., U.S.	194	39.51 N	87.21 W
Sugar Creek ≃, In., U.S.	218	39.21 N	86.00 W
Sugar Creek ≃, Mi., U.S.	281	42.06 N	83.36 W
Sugar Creek ≃, N.Y., U.S.	210	42.38 N	77.09 W
Sugar Creek ≃, Oh., U.S.	214	40.31 N	81.28 W
Sugar Creek ≃, Oh., U.S.	216	40.57 N	84.11 W
Sugar Creek ≃, Oh., U.S.	218	39.27 N	83.25 W
Sugar Creek ≃, Ok., U.S.	196	35.05 N	98.10 W
Sugar Creek ≃, Pa., U.S.	210	41.47 N	76.27 W
Sugar Creek ≃, Wi., U.S.	216	42.43 N	88.19 W
Sugar Grove, Il., U.S.	216	41.45 N	88.27 W
Sugargrove, Pa., U.S.	214	41.59 N	79.21 W
Sugar Grove, Va., U.S.	192	36.46 N	81.24 W
Sugar Hill	192	34.06 N	84.02 W
Sugar Island I, On., Can.	212	44.26 N	77.17 W
Sugar Island I, Mi., U.S.	190	46.25 N	84.12 W
Sugar Land	222	29.37 N	95.38 W
Sugar Loaf	210	41.19 N	74.17 W
Sugarloaf ʌ[2]	214	41.24 N	81.06 W
Sugarloaf Hill ʌ[2]	274b	37.58 S	145.19 E
Sugarloaf Key I	220	24.40 N	81.32 W
Sugarloaf Mountain ʌ, Ky., U.S.	218	38.13 N	83.32 W
Sugarloaf Mountain ʌ, Me., U.S.	188	45.01 N	70.22 W
Sugar Loaf Mountain ʌ, Md., U.S.	208	39.16 N	77.23 W
Sugar Loaf Mountain ʌ, Ok., U.S.	194	35.02 N	94.28 W
Sugarloaf Mountain ʌ[2]	220	28.39 N	81.44 W
Sugar Loaf → Pão de Açúcar ʌ	287a	22.57 S	43.09 W
Sugarloaf Peak ʌ	280	34.14 N	117.38 W
Sugarloaf Point ›, Austl.	166	32.26 S	152.33 E
Sugar Loaf Point ›, On., Can.	284a	42.52 N	79.17 W
Sugarloaf Reservoir ⊜[1]	169	37.41 S	145.18 E
Sugarloaf Ridge State Park ♠	226	38.26 N	122.29 W
Sugar Notch	210	41.11 N	75.55 W
Sugar Pine Point State Park ♠	226	39.03 N	120.07 W
Sugartown	285	40.00 N	75.31 W
Sugauli	124	26.46 N	84.44 E
Sugbai Passage ɥ	116	5.22 N	120.33 E
Sugbay	116	7.31 N	123.19 E
Sugbuhan Point ›	116	10.04 N	126.04 E
Suggi Lake ⊜	184	54.22 N	102.47 W
Suginami ◆[8]	268	35.42 N	139.38 E
Sugita ◆[8]	268	35.23 N	139.38 E
Sugito	94	36.02 N	139.44 E
Şuğla Gölü ⊜	130	37.20 N	32.02 E
Šugnou	85	38.35 N	70.20 E
Sugod	116	12.03 N	124.09 E
Sugoj ≃	74	64.15 N	154.29 E
Šugonovo	82	54.41 N	36.41 E
Šugozero	76	59.55 N	34.12 E
Šugurovo, Ross.	80	53.25 N	46.29 E
Šugurovo, Ross.	80	54.31 N	52.06 E
Sugut ≃	112	6.26 N	117.43 E
Suguta ≃	154	2.03 N	36.33 E
Suguti	154	1.44 S	33.39 E
Suhai Hu ⊜	102	38.50 N	94.00 E
Suhaitu	102	44.50 N	93.39 E
Şuḩār	128	24.22 N	56.45 E
Suheli Island I[1]	122	10.03 N	72.17 E
Suhl	54	50.37 N	10.41 E
Suhlendorf	54	52.55 N	10.46 E
Suhopolje	36	45.48 N	17.30 E
Suhr	58	47.22 N	8.05 E
Suhr ≃	58	47.25 N	8.04 E
Suhum	150	6.05 N	0.27 W
Şuhut	130	38.32 N	30.33 E
Sūi	120	28.37 N	69.19 E
Suiá-Miçu ≃	250	11.13 S	53.15 W
Suianzhan	89	53.07 N	125.20 E
Suiattle ≃	224	48.20 N	121.33 W
Suichang	100	28.34 N	119.14 E
Suichuan	100	26.26 N	114.32 E
Suichuan ≃	100	26.30 N	114.45 E
Suid Afrika → South Africa □[1]	156	30.00 S	26.00 E
Suide	102	37.32 N	110.12 E
Suiding	86	44.03 N	80.49 E
Suido-suigenchi ⊜[1]	270	34.54 N	135.17 E
Suidvaal	158	26.52 S	29.47 E
Suifenhe	89	44.24 N	131.10 E
Suifu	94	36.37 N	140.29 E
Suifu → Yibin	107	28.47 N	104.38 E
Suigō-kokutei-kōen ♠	94	36.05 N	140.20 E
Suigō-Tsukuba-kokutei-kōen ♠	94	36.00 N	140.20 E
Suihua	89	46.37 N	127.00 E
Suijiang	102	28.31 N	104.07 E
Suileng	89	47.18 N	127.10 E
Suining, Zhg.	100	33.54 N	117.56 E
Suining, Zhg.	102	26.21 N	110.00 E
Suining, Zhg.	107	30.31 N	105.34 E
Suipacha	252	34.45 S	59.41 W
Suiping	100	33.10 N	113.57 E
Suippe ≃	50	49.25 N	3.57 E
Suippes	56	49.08 N	4.32 E
Suir ≃	48	52.15 N	7.00 W
Suisse → Switzerland □[1]	58	47.00 N	8.00 E
Suisun Bay c	226	38.06 N	122.00 W
Suisun City	226	38.14 N	122.02 W
Suisun Creek ≃	226	38.12 N	122.06 W
Suita	96	34.45 N	135.32 E
Suitland	284c	38.50 N	76.55 W
Suixi, Zhg.	100	33.56 N	116.46 E
Suixi, Zhg.	102	21.25 N	110.15 E
Suixian, Zhg.	98	34.26 N	115.05 E
Suixian, Zhg.	100	31.42 N	113.20 E
Suiyang, Zhg.	89	44.26 N	130.53 E
Suiyang, Zhg.	102	27.56 N	107.18 E
Suiyangdian	100	32.04 N	112.55 E
Suiza → Switzerland □[1]	58	47.00 N	8.00 E
Suize ≃	58	48.08 N	5.08 E

Suizhong	98	40.20 N	120.19 E
Šuja, Ross.	24	61.55 N	34.12 E
Šuja, Ross.	80	56.50 N	41.23 E
Šuja ≃, Ross.	24	61.54 N	34.15 E
Šuja ≃, Ross.	80	57.56 N	43.15 E
Sujānagar	126	23.57 N	89.25 E
Sujāngarh	120	27.42 N	74.28 E
Sujāwal	120	24.36 N	68.05 E
Suji	107	29.35 N	103.37 E
Sujiabu	100	31.38 N	116.22 E
Sujiaqiao	105	39.24 N	116.10 E
Sujiatun	104	41.40 N	123.22 E
Sujiawan	107	29.48 N	104.57 E
Sujiawu	105	39.17 N	115.55 E
Sujiazui	100	33.40 N	119.29 E
Šujskoje	76	59.22 N	40.59 E
Sujutkina Kosa, mys ›	84	44.13 N	47.15 E
Sukabihanawa	112	9.30 S	124.57 E
Sukabumi	115a	6.55 S	106.56 E
Sukadana, Indon.	112	1.15 S	109.57 E
Sukadana, Indon.	115a	5.05 S	105.33 E
Sukadana, Teluk c	112	1.24 S	109.50 E
Sukagawa	92	37.17 N	140.23 E
Sukamandi	115a	6.20 S	107.39 E
Sukamara	112	2.43 S	111.11 E
Sukanegara	115a	7.06 S	107.07 E
Sukapura	115a	7.52 S	113.03 E
Sukaraja, Indon.	112	2.21 S	110.37 E
Sukaraja, Indon.	115a	7.27 S	108.12 E
Sukaraja, Indon.	115a	7.27 S	109.17 E
Sukarno, Pegunungan → Jaya, Puncak ʌ	164	4.05 S	137.11 E
Sukau	112	5.32 N	118.17 E
Sukchar	272b	22.42 N	88.22 E
Sukch'ŏn	98	39.24 N	125.38 E
Sukematsu	270	34.31 N	135.26 E
Sukeva	26	63.52 N	27.26 E
Sukhnah, 'Ayn ⊤[4]	142	29.35 N	32.15 E
Sukhothai	110	17.01 N	99.49 E
Sukhumi → Suchumi	84	43.01 N	41.02 E
Sukkertoppen (Maniitsoq)	176	65.25 N	52.53 W
Sukkozero	24	63.11 N	32.18 E
Sukkur	120	27.42 N	68.52 E
Sukkwan Island I	182	55.05 N	132.45 W
Suklāra	126	23.11 N	86.21 E
Sukmanovka	78	51.47 N	41.34 E
Sukodadi	115a	7.06 S	112.19 E
Sukoharjo	115a	7.41 S	110.50 E
Sukovo	82	54.54 N	38.19 E
Sukroml'a	76	56.53 N	34.44 E
Sukses	156	21.01 S	16.52 E
Suksun	86	57.07 N	57.24 E
Sukumo	92	32.56 N	132.44 E
Sukun, Pulau I	115b	8.07 S	122.08 E
Sukunka ≃	182	55.37 N	121.37 W
Sul, Baía c	252	27.40 S	48.35 W
Sul, Canal do ɥ	250	0.10 S	49.30 W
Sula I	26	61.08 N	4.55 E
Sula ≃, Ross.	24	67.16 N	52.07 E
Sula ≃, Ukr.	78	49.40 N	32.41 E
Sula, Kepulauan II	112	1.52 S	125.22 E
Sulaco ≃	236	15.01 N	87.44 W
Sulaimān Khel	123	33.41 N	71.01 E
Sulaimān Range ⋏	120	30.30 N	70.10 E
Sulak, Ross.	80	51.52 N	48.21 E
Sulak, Ross.	84	43.16 N	47.32 E
Sulak ≃	84	43.20 N	47.34 E
Sulakyurt	130	40.10 N	33.44 E
Sulang	115a	6.48 S	111.23 E
Sulat	116	11.49 N	125.27 E
Sulauan Point ›	116	8.37 N	124.29 E
Sulawesi (Celebes) I	112	2.00 S	121.00 E
Sulawesi Selatan □[4]	112	3.30 S	120.00 E
Sulawesi Tengah □[4]	112	1.00 N	123.00 E
Sulawesi Tenggara □[4]	112	4.00 S	122.00 E
Sulawesi Utara □[4]	112	0.30 N	124.00 E
Sulaymān, Birak (Solomon's Pools) ⊥	132	31.41 N	35.10 E
Sulby	44	54.18 N	4.29 W
Sulcis ◆[1]	71	39.04 N	8.41 E
Suldalsvatnet ⊜	26	59.35 N	6.45 E
Sūldeh	128	36.34 N	52.01 E
Sulechów	30	52.06 N	15.37 E
Sulęcin	30	52.26 N	15.08 E
Suleja	86	55.09 N	58.50 E
Sulejów	30	51.22 N	19.53 E
Sulejówek	30	52.14 N	21.17 E
Sulen, Mount ʌ	164	3.25 S	142.15 E
Sule Skerry I[2]	46	59.05 N	4.26 W
Suleymaniye Mosque ʊ[1]	267b	41.00 N	28.57 E
Süleymanlı	130	37.54 N	36.50 E
Şülfeld	52	53.48 N	10.14 E
Šul'ginka	83	49.08 N	38.56 E
Šul'gino, Ross.	82	54.33 N	37.35 E
Sulğino, Ross.	82	55.50 N	35.55 E
Sulia	154	1.32 S	26.33 E
Suliki	112	0.06 S	100.27 E
Sulima	150	6.58 N	11.35 W
Sulin	83	48.54 N	40.07 E
Sulina	38	45.09 N	29.40 E
Sulina, Braţul ≃[1]	38	45.09 N	29.41 E
Sulincheer	102	42.41 N	109.20 E
Sulingen	52	52.41 N	8.47 E
Sulinskij	83	47.52 N	40.06 E
Sulitelma ʌ	24	67.08 N	16.24 E
Sulkava	26	61.47 N	28.23 E
Sullana	248	4.53 S	80.41 W
Sullane ≃	48	51.53 N	8.56 W
Sulligent	194	33.54 N	88.08 W
Sullivan, Il., U.S.	194	39.35 N	88.36 W
Sullivan, In., U.S.	194	39.06 N	87.24 W
Sullivan, Mo., U.S.	219	38.12 N	91.09 W
Sullivan, Oh., U.S.	214	41.02 N	82.13 W
Sullivan, Wi., U.S.	216	43.00 N	88.35 W
Sullivan □[6], N.Y., U.S.	210	41.39 N	74.42 W
Sullivan □[6], Pa., U.S.	210	41.25 N	76.29 W
Sullivan Canyon V	280	34.03 N	118.30 W
Sullivan Creek ≃	226	37.53 N	120.25 W
Sullivan Lake ⊜	182	52.00 N	112.00 W
Sullivan Stadium ♠	283	42.05 N	71.16 W
Sullivanville	210	42.14 N	76.46 W
Sully-sur-Loire	50	47.46 N	2.22 E
Sulm ≃	61	46.45 N	15.34 E
Sulmona	66	42.03 N	13.55 E
Sulot' ≃	82	56.41 N	38.01 E
Sulphur, Yk., Can.	180	63.47 N	138.53 W
Sulphur, In., U.S.	218	38.14 N	86.28 W
Sulphur, Ky., U.S.	218	38.29 N	85.16 W
Sulphur, La., U.S.	194	30.14 N	93.22 W
Sulphur, Ok., U.S.	196	34.30 N	96.58 W
Sulphur ≃, Ab., Can.	182	53.50 N	119.10 W
Sulphur ≃, U.S.	194	33.07 N	93.52 W
Sulphur Creek ≃	198	44.46 N	102.25 W
Sulphur Draw V	196	33.12 N	102.17 W
Sulphur Springs, In., U.S.	218	40.00 N	85.26 W
Sulphur Springs, Oh., U.S.	214	40.52 N	82.52 W
Sulphur Springs, Tx., U.S.	222	33.08 N	95.36 W
Sulphur Springs Draw V	196	32.12 N	101.36 W
Sulphur Springs Valley V	200	31.50 N	109.50 W
Sulsul	144	5.06 N	44.55 E
Sultan	224	47.51 N	121.48 W
Sultan ≃	224	47.52 N	121.49 W
Sultana	226	36.33 N	119.20 W
Sultanahmet Mosque ʊ[1]	267b	41.00 N	28.58 E
Sultan Alonto, Lake ⊜	116	7.53 N	124.15 E

Sultana Point ›	168b	35.08 S	137.45 E
Sulṭanatābād ◆[8]	267d	35.46 N	51.28 E
Sultançiftligi ◆[8]	267b	41.02 N	29.13 E
Sultandağı	130	38.32 N	31.14 E
Sultan Dağı ʌ	130	38.58 N	27.26 E
Sultanhanı	130	38.15 N	33.33 E
Sultanhisar	130	37.53 N	28.10 E
Sultan Kudarat	116	7.17 N	124.16 E
Sultan Kudarat □[4]	116	6.20 N	124.20 E
Sultan Mosque ʊ[1]	271c	1.18 N	103.52 E
Sultānpur, India	123	31.13 N	75.11 E
Sultānpur, India	124	26.16 N	82.04 E
Sultānpur Dabās ◆[8]	272a	28.46 N	77.03 E
Sultan sa Barongis	116	6.46 N	124.38 E
Sultan-Saly	83	47.21 N	39.35 E
Sulu	164	5.25 S	151.00 E
Sulu □[4]	116	6.00 N	121.00 E
Suluan Island I	116	10.46 N	125.57 E
Sulu Archipelago II	116	6.00 N	121.00 E
Sulu Basin ✧[1]	12	8.00 N	121.30 E
Sulu Chi ⊜	124	30.12 N	86.20 E
Sülüklü	130	39.05 N	30.58 E
Sul'ukta	85	39.56 N	69.34 E
Sululta	144	9.10 N	38.48 E
Suluntah	146	32.36 N	21.43 E
Suluova (Suluca)	130	40.47 N	35.42 E
Sulūq	146	31.39 N	20.15 E
Sulusaj	85	38.50 N	67.05 E
Sulusaray	130	40.00 N	36.06 E
Sulu Sea ⊤[2]	116	8.00 N	120.00 E
Suly	86	53.45 N	66.30 E
Sulz	58	48.18 N	7.51 E
Sulz am Neckar	58	48.21 N	8.37 E
Sulzano	64	45.41 N	10.05 E
Sulzbach	56	49.18 N	7.07 E
Sulzbach ≃	60	48.36 N	13.02 E
Sulzbach am Kocher	56	48.58 N	9.50 E
Sulzbach-Rosenberg	60	49.30 N	11.45 E
Sulzberger Bay c	9	77.00 S	152.00 W
Sulzbrunn	58	47.41 N	10.20 E
Sulzburg	58	47.50 N	7.42 E
Şülze	52	52.46 N	10.02 E
Šum, Ross.	76	59.52 N	31.46 E
Šum, Ross.	88	54.51 N	95.18 E
Šuma ◆[8]	270	34.39 N	135.08 E
Šum'ači	76	53.52 N	32.25 E
Šumadija ◆[1]	38	44.10 N	20.50 E
Sumalata	112	0.59 N	122.30 E
Sumallo ≃	224	49.14 N	121.05 W
Şumampa	252	29.22 S	63.28 W
Šumanaj	86	42.37 N	59.08 E
Sumangat, Tanjong ›	116	6.35 N	117.33 E
Sumano-ura ♠	96	34.38 N	135.08 E
Sūmār	128	33.52 N	45.39 E
Sumarokovo	82	55.46 N	35.55 E
Sumas	202	49.00 N	122.15 W
Sumas ≃	224	49.09 N	122.12 W
Sumatera (Sumatra) I	108	0.05 S	102.00 E
Sumatera Barat □[4]	112	0.30 S	100.30 E
Sumatera Selatan □[4]	112	3.00 S	104.00 E
Sumatera Utara □[4]	114	2.20 N	99.00 E
Sum'atino	82	55.00 N	36.21 E
Sumatou	107	30.28 N	104.03 E
Sumatra → Sumatera I	108	0.05 S	102.00 E
Sumava Resorts	216	41.10 N	87.26 W
Sumayh	140	12.43 N	30.50 E
Sumba I	115b	10.00 S	120.00 E
Sumba, Île I	152	1.44 N	19.32 E
Sumba, Selat ɥ	115b	9.05 S	120.00 E
Sumbar ≃	128	38.00 N	55.17 E
Sumbawa I	115b	8.40 S	118.00 E
Sumbawa Besar	115b	8.30 S	117.26 E
Sumbawanga	154	7.58 S	31.37 E
Sumbay	248	15.58 S	71.23 W
Sumbe	152	11.13 S	13.50 E
Sümber	90	46.21 N	108.20 E
Sumbilla	34	43.10 N	1.40 W
Sumbing, Gunung ʌ	115a	7.23 S	110.04 E
Sumbu National Park ♠	154	8.50 S	30.25 E
Sumburgh Head ›	46a	59.53 N	1.20 W
Sumburgh Roost ɥ	46a	59.49 N	1.19 W
Šumbut	80	55.33 N	50.41 E
Sumbuya	150	7.39 N	11.58 W
Sumdo	120	35.01 N	78.41 E
Sumé	250	7.39 S	36.55 W
Sumedang	115a	6.52 S	107.55 E
Sümeg	30	46.59 N	17.17 E
Šumek	86	48.42 N	85.32 E
Šumen	38	43.16 N	26.55 E
Sumène	62	43.59 N	3.43 E
Sumenep	115a	7.01 S	113.52 E
Šumerl'a	80	55.30 N	46.26 E
Sumgait	84	40.36 N	49.38 E
Şumgait ≃	84	40.37 N	49.37 E
Šumicha	86	55.14 N	63.19 E
Sumida ◆[8]	268	35.42 N	139.48 E
Sumida ≃	268	35.40 N	139.47 E
Sumidouro	256	22.03 S	42.41 W
Sumilao	116	8.18 N	124.57 E
Šumilino	76	55.18 N	29.37 E
Šumilinskaja	80	49.58 N	41.26 E
Suminoe ◆[8]	270	34.36 N	135.28 E
Sumisu-jima I	90	31.27 N	140.03 E
Sumiswald	58	47.02 N	7.45 E
Sumiyoshi ◆[8]	270	34.36 N	135.31 E
Sumki	86	55.03 N	65.44 E
Sumkino	86	58.09 N	68.21 E
Sumlog ≃	116	6.53 N	126.02 E
Summer Bridge	44	54.03 N	1.41 W
Summerdale	208	40.18 N	76.56 W
Summerfield, Fl., U.S.	220	29.00 N	82.02 W
Summerfield, Mo., U.S.	219	38.17 N	91.49 W
Summerfield, N.C., U.S.	192	36.12 N	79.54 W
Summerford, Nf., Can.	186	49.29 N	54.47 W
Summerford, Oh., U.S.	218	39.55 N	83.29 W
Summerhill, Ire.	48	53.29 N	6.44 W
Summerhill, Pa., U.S.	214	40.22 N	78.46 W
Summer Island I	190	45.34 N	86.39 W
Summer Isles II	46	58.02 N	5.28 W
Summer Lake ⊜	202	42.50 N	120.45 W
Summerland	182	49.36 N	119.41 W
Summerland Reserve ◆[4]	169	38.31 S	145.10 E
Sümmern	56	51.25 N	7.43 E
Summer Palace ʊ	265a	59.53 N	29.55 E
Summerseat	262	53.38 N	2.19 W
Summerside	186	46.24 N	63.47 W
Summersville, Mo., U.S.	194	37.10 N	91.39 W
Summersville, W.V., U.S.	188	38.16 N	80.51 W
Summerton	192	33.36 N	80.21 W
Summertown	194	35.26 N	87.18 W
Summerville, On., Can.	275b	43.37 N	79.34 W
Summerville, Ga., U.S.	192	34.28 N	85.20 W
Summerville, Pa., U.S.	214	41.06 N	79.11 W
Summerville, S.C., U.S.	192	33.00 N	80.11 W
Summit, Eng., U.K.	262	53.40 N	2.05 W
Summit, Ak., U.S.	180	63.20 N	149.08 W
Summit, Ca., U.S.	228	34.20 N	117.25 W
Summit, Il., U.S.	216	41.47 N	87.48 W
Summit, Ms., U.S.	194	31.17 N	90.28 W
Summit, N.J., U.S.	210	40.44 N	74.21 W
Summit, N.Y., U.S.	210	42.35 N	74.35 W
Summit, S.D., U.S.	198	45.18 N	97.02 W
Summit, Wa., U.S.	224	47.10 N	122.21 W
Summit □[6]	214	41.05 N	81.31 W
Summit Creek ≃	224	46.00 N	121.10 W
Summit Farms	284b	39.19 N	76.32 W

Summit Hill	210	40.49 N	75.52 W
Summit Lake	182	54.17 N	122.38 W
Summit Lake ⊜	224	47.04 N	123.07 W
Summit Mountain ʌ	204	39.23 N	116.28 W
Summit Park	276	41.09 N	74.03 W
Summit Park Mall ◆[9]	284a	43.05 N	78.56 W
Summit Peak ʌ	200	37.21 N	106.42 W
Summit Rock ʌ	172	45.25 S	170.04 E
Summit Station	208	40.34 N	76.12 W
Summitville, In., U.S.	216	40.20 N	85.38 W
Summitville, N.Y., U.S.	210	41.37 N	74.27 W
Summitville, Oh., U.S.	214	40.41 N	80.53 W
Summt	264a	52.41 N	13.22 E
Summter See ⊜	264a	52.42 N	13.23 E
Šumná	61	48.56 N	15.52 E
Sumnal	120	35.45 N	78.40 E
Sumner, Ia., U.S.	190	42.50 N	92.05 W
Sumner, Ms., U.S.	194	33.58 N	90.22 W
Sumner, Wa., U.S.	224	47.12 N	122.14 W
Sumner, Lake ⊜	172	42.42 S	172.13 E
Sumner, Lake ⊜[1]	196	34.38 N	104.25 W
Sumner Lake State Park ♠	196	34.38 N	104.24 W
Sumner Strait ɥ	180	56.15 N	133.45 W
Sumoto	96	34.21 N	134.54 E
Şumpangbinangae	112	4.24 S	119.36 E
Šumperk	30	49.58 N	16.58 E
Sumpiuh	115a	7.37 S	109.21 E
Sumprabum	110	26.33 N	97.34 E
Sumpter	281	42.10 N	83.29 W
Sumrall	194	31.25 N	89.32 W
Sumsar	85	41.18 N	71.19 E
Ş'umsi	80	57.07 N	51.37 E
Šumskij	88	54.48 N	99.09 E
Şumskij Posad	24	64.15 N	35.25 E
Šumskoje	78	50.07 N	26.07 E
Šumšu, ostrov I	74	50.45 N	156.20 E
Sumter	192	33.55 N	80.20 W
Sumter □[6]	220	28.38 N	82.08 W
Sumusṭā al-Waqf	142	28.55 N	30.51 E
Sumy	78	50.55 N	34.45 E
Sumy □[8]	76	52.10 N	33.40 E
Sumzom	102	29.45 N	96.10 E
S'un' ≃, Ross.	80	55.44 N	54.16 E
Sun ≃, Mt., U.S.	202	47.30 N	111.19 W
Sun ≃, Zhg.	107	29.13 N	106.21 E
Suna, Kenya	154	1.05 S	34.26 E
Suna, Ross.	80	57.51 N	50.05 E
Suna ≃	24	62.08 N	34.12 E
Sunagawa	92a	43.29 N	141.55 E
Sun al-Heteimi ⊤[4]	132	31.05 N	34.00 E
Sun' al-Menī'i ⊤[4]	132	31.07 N	34.12 E
Sunām	123	30.08 N	75.48 E
Sunāmganj	120	25.04 N	91.24 E
Sunami	94	35.25 N	136.40 E
Sunan	98	39.13 N	125.41 E
Sunapee Lake ⊜	188	43.23 N	72.03 W
Sunart, Loch ⊜	46	56.41 N	5.43 W
Sunashinden	268	35.53 N	139.30 E
Sunbāṭ	142	30.48 N	31.12 E
Sunbright	192	36.14 N	84.40 W
Sunburst	202	48.52 N	111.54 W
Sunbury, Austl.	169	37.35 S	144.44 E
Sunbury, Eng., U.K.	260	51.25 N	0.26 W
Sunbury, N.C., U.S.	192	36.26 N	76.36 W
Sunbury, Oh., U.S.	214	40.14 N	82.51 W
Sunbury, Pa., U.S.	210	40.51 N	76.47 W
Sunchales	252	30.56 S	61.34 W
Sunch'ang	98	35.23 N	127.07 E
Sunchild Indian Reserve ◆[4]	182	52.43 N	115.24 W
Sünching	60	48.53 N	12.21 E
Suncho Corral	252	27.56 S	63.27 W
Sunch'ŏn, C.M.I.K.	98	39.26 N	125.54 E
Sunch'ŏn, Taehan	98	34.57 N	127.28 E
Sun City, Az., U.S.	200	33.35 N	112.16 W
Sun City, Ca., U.S.	228	33.42 N	117.11 W
Sun City, Fl., U.S.	220	27.40 N	82.28 W
Sun City Center	220	27.43 N	82.21 W
Suncook	188	43.07 N	71.27 W
Suncook ≃	188	43.08 N	71.28 W
Sunda, Selat (Sunda Strait) ɥ	112	6.00 S	105.45 E
Sundance	198	44.24 N	104.22 W
Sundar	112	4.54 N	115.12 E
Sundar ʌ	124	28.26 N	84.20 E
Sundarbans ◆[1]	126	22.00 N	89.00 E
Sundargarh	124	22.07 N	84.02 E
Sundarnagar	123	31.32 N	76.53 E
Sunda Shelf ✧[4]	14	5.00 N	107.00 E
Sunda Strait → Sunda, Selat ɥ	112	6.00 S	105.45 E
Sunday Creek ≃	169	37.02 S	145.05 E
Sundby, Dan.	41	54.42 N	11.48 E
Sundby, Sve.	40	59.23 N	17.03 E
Sundbyberg	40	59.22 N	17.58 E
Sundbyholm	40	59.27 N	16.37 E
Sundbyholm slott ⊥	40	59.27 N	16.37 E
Sunde	26	59.50 N	5.43 E
Sunderland, On., Can.	212	44.16 N	79.04 W
Sunderland, Eng., U.K.	44	54.55 N	1.23 W
Sunderland, Ma., U.S.	207	42.28 N	72.34 W
Sunderland, Vt., U.S.	210	43.06 N	73.06 W
Sundern	56	51.20 N	8.00 E
Sünderup	41	54.46 N	9.27 E
Sundhausen	54	50.56 N	10.40 E
Sundhouse	58	48.15 N	7.36 E
Sundi-Lutete	152	4.34 S	14.14 E
Sundown, Austl.	162	26.14 S	133.12 E
Sundown, N.Y., U.S.	210	41.53 N	74.28 W
Sundown, Tx., U.S.	196	33.27 N	102.29 W
Sundra	273d	26.11 S	28.33 E
Sundre	182	51.48 N	114.38 W
Sundridge, On., Can.	190	45.46 N	79.24 W
Sundridge, Eng., U.K.	260	51.17 N	0.18 E
Sunds	41	56.12 N	9.01 E
Sundsbruk	26	62.27 N	17.22 E
Sundsvall	26	62.23 N	17.18 E
Sundwig	263	51.23 N	7.47 E
Suneori	268	35.56 N	139.24 E
Sunfield	216	42.45 N	84.59 W
Sunfish Creek ≃	218	39.01 N	83.03 W
Sunflower	194	33.32 N	90.32 W
Sunflower, Mount ʌ	198	39.04 N	102.01 W
Sungaianyar	112	2.55 S	116.18 E
Sungaiapit	114	1.09 N	102.10 E
Sungaibamban	114	3.26 N	99.09 E
Sungaibatu	112	0.48 N	110.45 E
Sungai Bayor	114	5.15 N	100.47 E
Sungaibuntu	115a	6.03 S	107.24 E
Sungaidareh	112	0.58 S	101.30 E
Sungaigerong	112	2.59 S	104.52 E
Sungaiguntung	112	0.18 N	103.37 E
Sungaikakap	112	0.04 S	109.10 E
Sungai Kolok	114	6.02 N	101.58 E
Sungailangsat	112	0.52 S	101.18 E
Sungai Lembing	114	3.55 N	103.02 E
Sungailiat	112	1.51 S	106.08 E
Sungailimau	112	0.31 S	100.03 E
Sungaimanasip	114	1.49 N	100.54 E
Sungainipah	114	0.57 N	98.57 E
Sungaipakning	114	1.20 N	102.09 E
Sungaipenuh	112	2.05 S	101.23 E
Sungaipenyu	112	0.16 N	109.04 E
Sungai Petani	114	5.39 N	100.30 E
Sungaipinang	112	0.48 S	114.04 E
Sungairampah	114	3.29 N	99.09 E
Sungairotan, Indon.	112	1.39 S	102.51 E
Sungairotan, Indon.	112	3.06 S	104.18 E
Sungaisalak	112	0.27 S	102.59 E
Sungaiselan	112	2.24 S	105.59 E
Sungai Siput	114	4.49 N	101.04 E
Sungaitampang	114	2.20 N	100.07 E
Şungaitiram	112	0.47 S	117.12 E
Šungaj	80	48.32 N	46.46 E

≃ River	Fluß	Río	Rivière	Rio	
≅ Canal	Kanal	Canal	Canal	Canal	
⌊ Waterfall, Rapids	Wasserfall, Stromschnellen	Cascada, Rápidos	Chute d'eau, Rapides	Cascata, Rápidos	
ɥ Strait	Meeresstraße	Estrecho	Détroit	Estreito	
c Bay, Gulf	Bucht, Golf	Bahía, Golfo	Baie, Golfe	Baía, Golfo	
⊜ Lake, Lakes	See, Seen	Lago, Lagos	Lac, Lacs	Lago, Lagos	
≡ Swamp	Sumpf	Pantano	Marais	Pântano	
⊓ Ice Features, Glacier	Eis- und Gletscherformen	Accidentes Glaciales	Formes glaciaires	Acidentes glaciares	
⊤ Other Hydrographic Features	Andere Hydrographische Objekte	Otros Elementos Hidrográficos	Autres données hydrographiques	Outros acidentes hidrográficos	

✧ Submarine Features	Untermeerische Objekte	Accidentes Submarinos	Formes de relief sous-marin	Acidentes submarinos
□ Political Unit	Politische Einheit	Unidad Politica	Entité politique	Unidade política
ʊ Cultural Institution	Kulturelle Institution	Institución Cultural	Institution culturelle	Institução cultural
⊥ Historical Site	Historische Stätte	Sitio Histórico	Site historique	Sitio histórico
♠ Recreational Site	Erholungs- und Ferienort	Sitio de Recreo	Centre de loisirs	Area de Lazer
⊠ Airport	Flughafen	Aeropuerto	Aéroport	Aeroporto
■ Military Installation	Militäranlage	Instalación Militar	Installation militaire	Instalação militar
◆ Miscellaneous	Verschiedenes	Misceláneo	Divers	Diversos

Name (ENGLISH) / Name (DEUTSCH)	Page / Seite	Lat.°′ / Breite°′	Long.°′ / Länge°′ E = Ost
Sungari → Songhua ≃	89	47.44 N	132.32 E
Sungchiang → Songjiang	106	31.01 N	121.14 E
Sungezhuang	105	40.15 N	116.39 E
Sungguminasa	112	5.12 S	119.27 E
Sungi ≃	115b	8.38 S	115.06 E
Sungi Point ›	116	10.55 N	125.50 E
Sungkai	114	4.00 N	101.19 E
Sung Kong I	271d	22.11 N	114.17 E
Sung Noen	110	14.54 N	101.50 E
Sungsang	112	2.22 S	104.56 E
Sungshan Domestic Airport ⊠	269d	25.04 N	121.33 E
Sungurlu	130	40.10 N	34.23 E
Sunhezhen	105	40.03 N	116.31 E
Suni	71	40.17 N	8.33 E
Suning	98	38.25 N	115.50 E
Sunjiabu	106	30.55 N	118.54 E
Sunjiadizi	104	42.09 N	124.09 E
Sunjiagou	104	40.45 N	120.39 E
Sunjiajiang	105	40.10 N	115.32 E
Sunjiakanzi	104	40.42 N	123.02 E
Sunjiawan	104	41.59 N	121.42 E
Sunjiazhai	106	30.55 N	121.52 E
Sunjikāy	140	12.20 N	29.46 E
Sunkar, gora ∧	86	44.15 N	73.50 E
Sunken Meadow State Park ♠	207	40.54 N	73.16 W
Sunkośī ≃	124	26.55 N	87.09 E
Sunland ◆[8]	280	34.16 N	118.19 W
Sunland Park	200	32.15 N	106.45 W
Sunlight Creek ≃	202	44.47 N	109.23 W
Sunlongwan	104	41.19 N	122.57 E
Sunman	218	39.14 N	85.05 W
Sunnansjö	40	60.13 N	14.57 E
Sunndalsøra	26	62.40 N	8.33 E
Sunne	26	59.50 N	13.09 E
Sunnemo	40	59.53 N	13.43 E
Sunnersta	40	59.48 N	17.39 E
Sunnī, Khawr V	140	7.09 N	28.41 E
Sunningdale	260	51.24 N	0.38 W
Sunninghill	42	51.25 N	0.40 W
Sunnybrae	186	45.24 N	62.30 W
Sunny Corner	170	33.23 S	149.53 E
Sunny Crest	278	41.33 N	87.42 W
Sunnydale	224	47.28 N	122.20 W
Sunnyland	220	27.17 N	82.29 W
Sunnylvsfjorden ⊂[2]	26	62.17 N	7.01 E
Sunnymead	228	33.56 N	117.14 W
Sunnynook	182	51.17 N	111.40 W
Sunnyridge	273d	26.10 S	28.11 E
Sunnyside, Nf., Can.	186	47.51 N	53.55 W
Sunnyside, Ca., U.S.	226	32.40 N	117.01 W
Sunny Side, Tx., U.S.	222	29.54 N	96.04 W
Sunnyside, Ut,. U.S.	200	39.33 N	110.23 W
Sunnyside, Wa., U.S.	202	46.19 N	120.00 W
Sunnyside ⊥	276	41.03 N	73.52 W
Sunnyslope, Ab., Can.	182	51.40 N	113.32 W
Sunnyslope, Wa., U.S.	224	47.30 N	122.44 W
Sunnyvale, Ca., U.S.	226	37.22 N	122.02 W
Sunnyvale, Tx., U.S.	222	32.48 N	96.33 W
Sunol	282	37.36 N	121.53 W
Sunol Ridge ∧	282	37.38 N	121.56 W
Sun Prairie	216	43.11 N	89.12 W
Sunray	196	36.01 N	101.49 W
Sunrise, Ky., U.S.	218	38.33 N	84.14 W
Sunrise, Tx., U.S.	222	31.17 N	96.53 W
Sunrise, Wy., U.S.	200	42.19 N	104.42 W
Sunrise Heights	216	42.18 N	85.09 W
Sunrise Mall ◆[9]	276	40.41 N	73.26 W
Sunrise Manor	204	36.08 N	115.04 W
Sunrise Peak ∧	224	46.20 N	121.46 W
Sun River Terrace	216	41.06 N	87.45 W
Sunset, La., U.S.	194	30.24 N	92.04 W
Sunset, Tx., U.S.	196	33.27 N	97.46 W
Sunset ◆[8]	282	37.45 N	122.30 W
Sunset Bay	214	42.11 N	79.24 W
Sunset Beach, Ca., U.S.	280	33.43 N	118.04 W
Sunset Beach, Hi., U.S.	229c	21.40 N	158.02 W
Sunset Country ◆[1]	166	35.00 S	141.30 E
Sunset Crater National Monument ♠	200	35.18 N	111.21 W
Sunset Heights	196	31.53 N	102.22 W
Sunset Hill	276	40.26 N	74.35 W
Sunset Hills	279b	40.35 N	80.15 W
Sunset Peak ∧	280	34.13 N	117.42 W
Sunset Prairie	182	55.50 N	120.48 W
Sunset Trailer Park	278	42.06 N	87.48 W
Sunset Valley	214	40.18 N	79.44 W
Sunshine, Austl.	166	37.47 S	144.50 E
Sunshine, Austl.	169	37.47 S	144.50 E
Sunshine, Ak., U.S.	180	62.10 N	150.04 W
Sunshine Island I	271d	22.16 N	114.03 E
Sunshine Point ›	281	42.36 N	82.47 W
Sunshine Skyway Bridge ◆[5]	220	27.37 N	82.39 W
Suntai ≃	146	8.05 N	10.04 E
Suntar	74	62.10 N	117.40 E
Suntar-Chajata, chrebet ⋏	74	62.00 N	143.00 E
Suntaug Lake ⊜	283	42.32 N	71.00 W
Süntel ⋏	52	52.12 N	9.25 E
Sun Temple ɷ[1]	273c	29.55 N	31.11 E
Sunter ◆[8]	269e	6.09 S	106.50 E
Sunter, Kali ≋	269e	6.07 S	106.50 E
Sunti ≃	272b	22.37 N	88.34 E
Suntrana	180	63.51 N	148.51 W
Suntsar	128	25.31 N	62.00 E
Suntu	144	8.06 N	36.57 E
Sun Valley, Id., U.S.	202	43.41 N	114.21 W
Sun Valley, Nv., U.S.	226	39.34 N	119.47 W
Sun Valley ◆[8]	280	34.14 N	118.21 W
SunValley Center ◆[9]	282	37.58 N	122.03 W
Sun Village	228	34.35 N	118.03 W
Sunwapta ≃	182	52.32 N	117.41 W
Sunwi-do I	98	37.44 N	125.15 E
Sunwu	89	49.27 N	127.20 E
Sunwui → Jiangmen	100	22.35 N	113.05 E
Sunyani	150	7.20 N	2.20 W
Sunying	98	34.30 N	114.21 E
Sunža ≃	84	43.26 N	46.08 E
Sunženskij chrebet ⋏	84	43.21 N	45.00 E
Sun Zhong Shan Ling (Tomb of Sun Yat Sen) ⊥	106	32.10 N	118.56 E
Suojarvi	24	62.05 N	32.21 E
Suolahti	26	62.34 N	25.52 E
Suomenlahti → Finland, Gulf of ⊂	26	60.00 N	27.00 E
Suomenselkä ∧	26	63.59 N	27.00 E
Suomi → Finland □[1]	24	64.00 N	26.00 E
Suomussalmi	26	64.53 N	29.05 E
Suō-nada ⊤[2]	96	33.50 N	131.30 E
Suonenjoki	26	62.37 N	27.08 E
Suontee ⊜	26	61.40 N	26.30 E
Suordach	74	66.43 N	132.04 E
Suoshu	106	31.57 N	119.00 E
Supachuy	248	19.29 S	64.31 W
Supamo ≃	246	6.48 N	61.50 W
Supaul	124	26.07 N	86.36 E
Supe	144	8.37 N	35.38 E
Superbe ≃	50	48.35 N	3.53 E
Superga, Basilica di ɷ[1]	62	45.05 N	7.46 E
Superior, Az., U.S.	200	33.17 N	111.05 W
Superior, Mt., U.S.	202	47.11 N	114.53 W
Superior, Ne., U.S.	198	40.01 N	98.04 W
Superior, Wi., U.S.	190	46.43 N	92.06 W
Superior, Laguna ⊂	234	16.20 N	94.55 W
Superior, Lake ⊜	190	48.00 N	88.00 W
Superior Lake ⊜	228	35.15 N	117.02 W
Superior Valley V	228	35.16 N	117.00 W
Supersano	68	40.01 N	18.14 E
Supetar	36	43.23 N	16.33 E
Suphan Buri	110	14.28 N	100.07 E
Suphan Buri ≃	110	13.29 N	100.17 E
Süphan Daği ∧	84	38.56 N	42.50 E
Supino	66	41.37 N	13.14 E
Supiori I	164	0.45 S	135.30 E
Sūpkhār	124	22.12 N	80.56 E
Supoj ≃	78	49.38 N	31.48 E
Suponevo	76	53.12 N	34.18 E
Supoqiao	107	30.40 N	103.59 E
Süpplingen	54	52.14 N	10.54 E
Supraśl	30	53.13 N	23.20 E
Supraśl ≃	30	53.04 N	22.56 E
Sup'ung	98	40.27 N	124.57 E
Sup'ung-chŏsuji ⊜[1]	98	40.30 N	125.05 E
Supur	126	23.01 N	86.52 E
Suputinskij zapovednik ♠	89	43.40 N	132.20 E
Sūq-ʿAbs	144	15.59 N	43.04 E
Sūq ash-Shuyūkh	128	30.53 N	46.28 E
Suqʿat al-Jamal	140	12.48 N	27.42 E
Suqian	100	33.59 N	118.18 E
Suqiao, Zhg.	100	34.08 N	113.47 E
Suqiao, Zhg.	105	39.03 N	116.29 E
Sūq Suwayq	128	24.23 N	38.27 E
Suquamish	224	47.43 N	122.33 W
Suquṭrā (Socotra) I	118	12.30 N	54.00 E
Ṣūr (Tyre), Lubnān	132	33.16 N	35.11 E
Ṣūr, ʿUmān	118	22.35 N	59.31 E
Sur, Cabo ›	174z	27.12 S	109.26 W
Sur, Campos de Hielo ⊓	254	49.10 S	73.30 W
Sur, Canal Ц	288	34.37 S	58.15 W
Sur, Point ›	226	36.18 N	121.54 W
Sura	80	53.53 N	45.45 E
Sura ◆[8]	272b	22.33 N	88.25 E
Sura ≃	80	56.06 N	46.00 E
Sura, Cape ›	144	11.10 N	47.30 E
Şūrāb, Pāk.	120	28.29 N	66.16 E
Šurab, Taj.	85	40.03 N	70.33 E
Surabaya	115a	7.15 S	112.45 E
S'urachi, Nuraghe ⊥	71	40.01 N	8.33 E
Şurad	142	30.59 N	30.54 E
Surag-san ∧	271b	37.42 N	127.04 E
Surahammar	40	59.43 N	16.13 E
Sūrak	128	25.43 N	58.48 E
Surakarta	115a	7.35 S	110.50 E
Suramana	112	0.50 S	119.33 E
Surami	84	42.01 N	43.34 E
Şūrān, Īrān	128	27.18 N	62.04 E
Šuran, Ross.	80	55.22 N	49.50 E
Şūrān, Sūrīy.	130	36.34 N	37.13 E
Şūrān, Sūrīy.	130	35.17 N	36.45 E
Şuran ≃	58	46.02 N	5.19 E
Šurany	30	48.06 N	18.14 E
Surar	144	7.27 N	40.57 E
Surat, Austl.	166	27.09 S	149.04 E
Sūrat, India	120	21.10 N	72.50 E
Sūratgarh	123	29.19 N	73.54 E
Surat Thani (Ban Don)	110	9.08 N	99.19 E
Surava	80	52.57 N	41.18 E
Suraž, Bela.	76	55.25 N	30.44 E
Suraż, Pol.	30	52.58 N	22.58 E
Suraž, Ross.	76	53.01 N	32.24 E
Surbiton ◆[8]	260	51.24 N	0.18 W
Surbo	68	40.24 N	18.08 E
Surbourg	56	48.55 N	7.51 E
Surchan	80	46.39 N	49.38 E
Surchandarja ≃	85	37.58 N	67.50 E
Surchandarjinskaja Oblast' □[8]	85	38.00 N	67.30 E
Surchdara	85	38.37 N	69.55 E
Şurchob ≃	85	38.53 N	70.03 E
Šurči	85	37.59 N	67.47 E
Surco ≃	286d	12.13 S	77.03 W
Surdulica	38	42.41 N	22.10 E
Sûre (Sauer) ≃	56	49.44 N	6.31 E
Şureanu, Munţii ⋏	38	45.38 N	23.27 E
Šureksor, ozero ⊜	86	52.16 N	75.50 E
Surendorf	41	54.28 N	10.04 E
Surendranagar	120	22.42 N	71.41 E
Suresnes	261	48.52 N	2.14 E
Suretka	236	9.34 N	82.56 W
Surf City	208	39.39 N	74.09 W
Surfers Paradise	171a	28.00 S	153.26 E
Surfside, Fl., U.S.	220	25.52 N	80.07 W
Surfside, Tx., U.S.	222	28.57 N	95.17 W
Surgères	32	46.07 N	0.45 W
Surgidero	240p	22.41 N	82.18 W
Surgijn ≃	88	47.20 N	95.50 E
Surgoinsville	192	36.28 N	82.51 W
Sürgü	130	38.01 N	37.59 E
Sürgücü	130	37.35 N	40.44 E
Surgut	74	61.14 N	73.20 E
Surhuisterveen	52	53.10 N	6.10 E
Suri	164	7.10 S	143.55 E
Suria	272b	22.51 N	88.33 E
Suriāpet	122	17.09 N	79.37 E
Suribachi-yama ∧[2]	174f	24.45 N	141.17 E
Suribao ≃	116	11.33 N	125.28 E
Surigao	116	9.45 N	125.30 E
Surigao del Norte □[4]	116	9.35 N	125.36 E
Surigao del Sur □[4]	116	9.00 N	126.00 E
Surigao Strait Ц	116	10.15 N	125.23 E
Surikova	86	56.59 N	91.31 E
Surin	110	14.53 N	103.29 E
Suriname □[1], S.A.	242	4.00 N	56.00 W
Suriname □[1], S.A.	250	4.00 N	56.00 W
Surinam → Suriname □[1]	250	4.00 N	56.00 W
Šurinda	88	55.13 N	113.23 E
Suring	190	44.59 N	88.22 W
Sūrīyah → Syria □[1]	128	35.00 N	38.00 E
S'urkum	89	50.08 N	140.31 E
Ş'urkum, mys ›	89	50.05 N	140.41 E
Šurma	80	56.58 N	50.21 E
Sūrmaq	128	31.03 N	52.48 E
Surmelin ≃	50	49.04 N	3.13 E
Surnadalsøra	26	62.59 N	8.39 E
Surodadi	115a	6.53 S	109.15 E
Surovaticha	80	55.45 N	43.56 E
Surovikino	80	48.36 N	42.51 E
Surovo	88	55.37 N	105.36 E
Surprise	200	33.37 N	112.19 W
Surprise, Lake ⊜	222	29.33 N	94.41 W
Surprise Valley V	204	41.35 N	120.05 W
Surquillo	286d	12.07 S	77.02 W
Surrency	192	31.43 N	82.11 W
Surrey	198	48.14 N	101.07 W
Surrey □[6]	42	51.10 N	0.20 W
Surrey, University of ɷ[2]	260	51.14 N	0.36 W
Surrey Heath □[8]	260	51.23 N	0.35 W
Surry	208	37.08 N	76.50 W
Surry □[6]	208	37.10 N	76.50 W
Sursee	58	47.10 N	8.06 E
Sursés V	58	46.34 N	9.38 E
Sursk	80	53.04 N	45.42 E
Surskij Majdan	80	55.01 N	46.32 E
Surskoje	80	54.30 N	46.44 E
Surt	146	31.12 N	16.35 E
Surt, Khalīj (Gulf of Sidra) ⊂	146	31.30 N	18.00 E
Surtainville	28	49.25 N	1.50 W
Surtanāhu	120	26.22 N	70.00 E
Surte	26	57.49 N	12.01 E
Surtsey I	24a	63.16 N	20.32 W
Suru	164	6.50 S	144.45 E
Suru ≃	123	34.45 N	76.12 E
Surubiú ≃	250	3.58 S	48.52 W
Sürüç	130	36.58 N	38.24 E
Suruga-wan ⊂	94	34.51 N	138.33 E
Suruí	256	22.40 S	43.07 W
Suruí ≃	287a	22.42 S	43.07 W
Surulangun	112	2.37 S	102.45 E
Suru-Lere ◆[8]	273a	6.31 N	3.22 E
Surumu ≃	246	3.22 N	60.19 W
Surveyor Creek ≃	198	40.20 N	102.38 W
Surveyor Point ›	168b	34.47 S	137.51 E
Survilliers	261	49.06 N	2.33 E
Surwold	52	53.00 N	7.30 E
Şury-le-Comtal	62	45.32 N	4.10 E
Šuryškary	74	65.54 N	65.22 E
Susa, It.	62	45.08 N	7.03 E
Susa, Nihon	96	34.37 N	131.36 E
Suså ≃	41	55.11 N	11.46 E
Susa, Valle di V	62	45.09 N	7.10 E
Sūsah	146	32.54 N	21.58 E
Susak, Otok I	36	44.31 N	14.18 E
Susaki	96	33.22 N	133.17 E
Susami	96	33.33 N	135.30 E
Susamyr	85	42.09 N	73.58 E
Susamyr ≃	85	42.08 N	74.03 E
Susamyrtau, chrebet ⋏	85	42.08 N	73.15 E
Susan	208	37.22 N	76.19 W
Susan ≃	204	40.19 N	120.17 W
Susan, Port ⊂	224	48.10 N	122.25 W
Susana Knolls	228	34.16 N	118.41 W
Sūsangerd	128	31.34 N	48.11 E
Susanino, Ross.	76	59.30 N	30.22 E
Susanino, Ross.	80	58.09 N	41.36 E
Susanino, Ross.	89	52.47 N	140.06 E
Susano	256	23.32 S	46.20 W
Susano □[7]	287b	23.35 S	46.18 W
Şusanville	204	40.24 N	120.39 W
Šušary, Ross.	265a	59.48 N	30.23 E
Šušary, Ross.	265a	59.46 N	30.21 E
Susch	58	46.46 N	10.04 E
Susegana	64	45.51 N	12.15 E
Suşehri	130	40.11 N	38.06 E
Şüsel	54	54.04 N	10.43 E
Šušenskoje	86	53.19 N	91.58 E
Sušice	60	49.14 N	13.32 E
Susitna	180	61.33 N	150.31 W
Susitna ≃	180	61.16 N	150.30 W
Susleny	78	47.25 N	28.59 E
Suslonger	80	56.18 N	48.13 E
Sušn'aki Pervoje	86	57.53 N	88.47 E
Susobana ≃	94	36.37 N	138.11 E
Susoh	114	3.43 N	96.50 E
Susong	100	30.09 N	116.06 E
Susono	94	35.09 N	138.54 E
Suspiro del Moro, Puerto del)(	34	37.04 N	3.39 W
Susquehanna	210	41.56 N	75.36 W
Susquehanna □[6]	210	41.50 N	75.50 W
Susquehanna ≃	188	39.33 N	76.05 W
Susquehanna, West Branch ≃	210	40.53 N	76.47 W
Susquehanna State Park ♠	208	39.36 N	76.09 W
Susques	252	23.25 S	66.29 W
Sussa ≃	152	7.22 S	17.05 E
Süssen	56	48.41 N	9.45 E
Süssenbrunn ◆[8]	264b	48.17 N	16.30 E
Süsser See ⊜	54	51.30 N	11.40 E
Sussex, N.B., Can.	186	45.43 N	65.31 W
Sussex, N.J., U.S.	210	41.12 N	74.36 W
Sussex, Va., U.S.	208	36.54 N	77.16 W
Sussex, Wi., U.S.	216	43.08 N	88.13 W
Sussex □[6], De., U.S.	208	38.42 N	75.23 W
Sussex □[6], N.J., U.S.	210	41.08 N	74.41 W
Sussex □[6], Va., U.S.	208	36.50 N	77.15 W
Sussex, East □[6]	42	50.55 N	0.15 E
Sussex, Vale of V	42	50.57 N	0.17 W
Sussex Inlet	170	35.11 S	150.36 E
Sussey	50	47.13 N	4.22 E
Sustenhorn ∧	58	46.42 N	8.28 E
Susten Pass)(	58	46.44 N	8.27 E
Şusteren	52	51.04 N	5.51 E
Šustikovo	82	55.17 N	35.59 E
Susu	174m	26.47 N	128.19 E
Susubona	175e	8.18 S	159.27 E
Susui	112	4.56 N	116.41 E
Susuman	74	62.47 N	148.10 E
Susurluk	130	39.54 N	28.10 E
Şusuzmüsellim	130	41.06 N	27.03 E
Šušvė ≃	76	55.10 N	23.49 E
Susz	30	53.44 N	19.20 E
Sutāhāta	126	22.08 N	88.07 E
Sutak	123	33.12 N	77.28 E
Sutama	94	35.47 N	138.25 E
Sut-Chol'	86	51.24 N	91.17 E
Sütçüler	130	37.30 N	30.59 E
Sutera	70	37.31 N	13.44 E
Sutersville	214	40.14 N	79.48 W
Suthat, Wat ɷ[1]	269a	13.45 N	100.30 E
Sutherland, Austl.	170	34.02 S	151.04 E
Sutherland, S. Afr.	158	32.24 S	20.40 E
Sutherland, Ia., U.S.	198	42.58 N	95.29 W
Sutherland, Ne., U.S.	198	41.09 N	101.07 W
Sutherland ≃	182	54.29 N	125.05 W
Sutherland, Lake ⊜	224	48.05 N	123.42 W
Sutherland Falls ∟	172	44.48 S	167.44 E
Sutherlands	168b	34.10 S	139.13 E
Sutherlin	202	43.23 N	123.18 W
Suthiāna	272a	28.31 N	77.26 E
Sutjeska Nacionalni Park ♠	38	43.22 N	18.45 E
Sutlej (Satluj) (Langqên) ≃	120	29.23 N	71.02 E
Sutri	66	42.14 N	12.13 E
Sutrio	64	46.31 N	12.59 E
Sutschou → Suzhou	106	31.18 N	120.37 E
Sütschou → Xuzhou	98	34.16 N	117.11 E
Sutter	226	39.10 N	121.45 W
Sutter □[6]	226	39.08 N	121.37 W
Sutter Buttes ∧	226	39.12 N	121.50 W
Sutter Bypass ≃	226	38.47 N	121.38 W
Sutter Creek	226	38.23 N	120.48 W
Sutter Creek ≃	226	38.22 N	120.59 W
Sutton, Austl.	171b	35.10 S	149.15 E
Sutton, P.Q., Can.	206	45.06 N	72.37 W
Sutton, Eng., U.K.	42	52.23 N	0.07 E
Sutton, Eng., U.K.	260	51.12 N	0.26 W
Sutton, Ak., U.S.	180	61.43 N	148.53 W
Sutton, Ma., U.S.	207	42.09 N	71.45 W
Sutton, Ne., U.S.	198	40.36 N	97.51 W
Sutton, W.V., U.S.	188	38.39 N	80.42 W
Sutton ◆[8]	42	51.22 N	0.12 W
Sutton, Monts ⋏	206	45.05 N	72.30 W
Sutton-at-Home	260	51.25 N	0.14 E
Sutton Bridge	42	52.46 N	0.12 E
Sutton Coldfield	42	52.34 N	1.48 W
Sutton Courtenay	42	51.39 N	1.17 W
Sutton Forest	170	34.35 S	150.19 E
Sutton in Ashfield	44	53.08 N	1.15 W
Sutton Lake ⊜[1]	188	38.40 N	80.40 W
Sutton Lane Ends	262	53.14 N	2.06 W
Sutton Leach	262	53.26 N	2.42 W
Sutton on Sea	44	53.19 N	0.17 E
Sutton on Trent	44	53.10 N	0.49 W
Sutton Park	276	40.49 N	74.42 W
Sutton Place ⊥	260	51.16 N	0.33 W
Suttons Bay	190	44.58 N	85.39 W
Sutton Scotney	42	51.10 N	1.21 W
Sutton Valence	42	51.12 N	0.36 E
Sutton Veny	42	51.11 N	2.08 W
Sutton Weaver	262	53.18 N	2.41 W
Sutton West	212	44.18 N	79.22 W
Suttor ≃	166	21.25 S	147.45 E
Suttrop	56	51.27 N	8.22 E
Suttsu	92a	42.48 N	140.14 E
Sutwik Island I	180	56.34 N	157.05 W
Suunduk ≃	86	51.46 N	58.46 E
Suurberge ⋏	158	33.18 S	25.32 E
Suurbraak	158	34.00 S	20.39 E
Suure-Jaani	76	58.33 N	25.28 E
Suur Munamägi ∧[2]	76	57.43 N	27.04 E
Suur Pakri I	76	59.20 N	23.55 E
Suva	175g	18.08 S	178.25 E
Şuvainiškis	76	56.10 N	25.17 E
Šuvalovo Oz'orki ◆[8]	265a	60.02 N	30.18 E
Suva Planina ⋏	38	43.10 N	22.10 E
Suvarlı	130	37.32 N	37.38 E
Suvasvesi ⊜	26	62.39 N	28.12 E
Šuvel'an	84	40.30 N	50.09 E
Suvereto	66	43.05 N	10.40 E
Suvo	88	53.39 N	110.00 E
Suvorka	88	56.33 N	103.24 E
Suvorov	82	54.07 N	36.30 E
Suvorovo, Ross.	82	56.07 N	35.54 E
Suvorovo, Ukr.	78	45.34 N	28.59 E
Suwa, Ityo.	144	14.17 N	41.06 E
Suwa, Nihon	94	36.02 N	138.08 E
Suwa-ko ⊜	94	36.05 N	138.05 E
Suwałki	30	54.07 N	22.56 E
Suwałki □[4]	30	54.10 N	22.15 E
Suwannaphum	110	15.33 N	103.47 E
Suwannee ≃	192	29.18 N	83.09 W
Suwannee Lake ⊜	184	56.08 N	100.10 W
Suwanose-jima I	93b	29.38 N	129.43 E
Suwanose-suidō Ц	93b	29.32 N	129.40 E
Suwarrow I[1]	14	13.15 S	163.05 W
Suwaydah	130	35.46 N	39.38 E
Şuwaylih	132	32.02 N	35.50 E
Suways, Khalīj as- (Gulf of Suez) ⊂	140	29.00 N	32.50 E
Suways, Qanāt as- (Suez Canal) ≋	142	29.55 N	32.33 E
Suwŏn	98	37.17 N	127.01 E
Suwon-dong	98	41.54 N	129.43 E
Suxi	100	29.25 N	120.07 E
Suxian	100	33.38 N	116.58 E
Suya	150	9.28 N	3.11 E
Suykbulak	86	49.48 N	80.50 E
Suyo	246	4.30 S	80.00 W
Suzak	86	44.07 N	68.28 E
Suzaka	94	36.39 N	138.19 E
Suzdal'	80	56.25 N	40.26 E
Suze ≃	58	47.08 N	7.14 E
Suze-la-Rousse	62	44.17 N	4.51 E
Suzhi	98	42.17 N	113.42 E
Suzhou (Soochow)	106	31.18 N	120.37 E
Suzhuang	105	40.04 N	116.44 E
Suzi ≃	98	41.55 N	124.17 E
Suzigou	98	40.25 N	123.25 E
S'uzikozero	24	61.48 N	37.20 E
Suz'omka	76	52.19 N	34.05 E
Suzu	92	37.25 N	137.17 E
Suzuka	94	34.51 N	136.35 E
Suzuka ≃	94	34.54 N	136.39 E
Suzuka-kokutei-kōen ♠	94	35.00 N	136.25 E
Suzuka-sammyaku ⋏	94	35.00 N	136.25 E
Suzuki	268	35.43 N	139.31 E
S'uz'um	80	58.02 N	47.32 E
Suzu-misaki ›	92	37.31 N	137.21 E
Suzun	86	53.47 N	82.19 E
Suzzara	64	45.00 N	10.45 E
Sværdborg	41	55.05 N	11.54 E
Sval'ava	78	48.33 N	22.59 E
Svalbard □[2]	12	78.00 N	20.00 E
Svalöv	41	55.55 N	13.06 E
Svaneholm	41	55.30 N	13.28 E
Svaneke	26	55.08 N	15.09 E
Svanetskij chrebet ⋏	84	42.55 N	42.42 E
Svängsta	26	56.16 N	14.46 E
Svanninge	41	55.07 N	10.15 E
Svanskog	26	59.11 N	12.33 E
Svapa ≃	78	51.44 N	34.56 E
Şvappavaara	24	67.39 N	21.04 E
Švarcevskij	82	54.06 N	37.59 E
Şvärdsjö	26	60.45 N	15.55 E
Švaricha	80	57.33 N	49.37 E
Svartå	40	59.08 N	14.31 E
Svartälven ≃	40	59.19 N	14.35 E
Svartån ≃	40	59.37 N	16.33 E
Svarte	41	55.25 N	13.43 E
Svartenhuk ›[1]	176	71.55 N	55.00 W
Svärtinge	40	58.39 N	16.00 E
Svartisen ⊓	24	66.38 N	14.00 E
Svartlöga I	40	59.34 N	19.03 E
Svartsjölandet I	40	59.22 N	17.41 E
Svataj	74	67.57 N	151.54 E
Svatava	54	50.11 N	12.35 E
Svatava ≃	54	50.32 N	12.07 E
Sv'atica ≃	80	58.22 N	51.43 E
Sv'atogorskaja	83	49.04 N	37.32 E
Sv'atoj Nos, mys ›, Ross.	24	68.10 N	39.45 E
Sv'atoj Nos, mys ›, Ross.	74	72.52 N	140.42 E
Sv'atoj Nos, poluostrov ›[1]	88	53.40 N	108.50 E
Sv'atoslavka	80	51.20 N	43.26 E
Svatovo	83	49.23 N	38.13 E
Svay Chék	110	13.48 N	102.58 E
Svay Riĕng	110	11.05 N	105.48 E
Sveafallen ∟	40	59.10 N	14.22 E
Svebølle	41	55.38 N	11.20 E
Sveča	80	58.16 N	47.32 E
Svedala	41	55.30 N	13.14 E
Svėdasai	76	55.41 N	25.22 E
Sveg	26	62.02 N	14.21 E
Şvegssjön ⊜[1]	26	62.03 N	14.10 E
Švėkšna	76	55.31 N	21.37 E
Svelgen	26	61.47 N	5.15 E
Svelvik	26	59.37 N	10.24 E
Şven'	76	53.09 N	34.21 E
Švenčionėliai	76	55.10 N	26.00 E
Švenčionys	76	55.07 N	26.10 E
Svendborg	41	55.03 N	10.37 E
Svenljunga	26	57.30 N	13.07 E
Svennevad	40	59.01 N	15.22 E
Svensen	224	46.10 N	123.39 W
Svenstorp	41	55.46 N	13.15 E
Şvenstrup	26	56.59 N	9.52 E
Šventoji	76	56.02 N	21.05 E
Šventoji ≃	76	55.06 N	24.22 E
Sverbejevo	89	53.36 N	123.15 E
Sverdlovo, Ross.	80	51.16 N	44.34 E
Sverdlovo, Ross.	82	56.38 N	36.37 E
Sverdlovsk	83	48.05 N	39.40 E
Sverdlovsk → Jekaterinburg	86	56.51 N	60.36 E
Sverdrup, ostrov I	74	74.35 N	79.30 E
Sverige → Sweden □[1]	24	62.00 N	15.00 E
Şverkestaån ≃	40	59.28 N	15.28 E
Švermov	54	50.09 N	14.05 E
Svessa	78	51.57 N	33.54 E
Sveti Arhandjel Mihajlo ɷ[1]	38	42.07 N	21.28 E
Sveti Jovan Bigorski ɷ[1]	38	41.38 N	20.37 E
Svetiloviči	76	52.48 N	31.19 E
Sveti Nikole	38	41.52 N	21.58 E
Sveti Petar u Šumi	64	45.11 N	13.52 E
Svetlaja	89	46.33 N	138.18 E
Světlá nad Sázavou	30	49.40 N	15.25 E
Svetlanovo	83	48.42 N	38.28 E
Svetlogorsk, Bela.	76	52.38 N	29.42 E
Svetlogorsk, Ross.	76	54.57 N	20.10 E
Svetlograd	72	45.20 N	42.40 E
Svetloje	80	57.03 N	53.38 E
Svetlovodsk	78	49.04 N	33.15 E
Svetlyj, Ross.	76	54.41 N	20.08 E
Svetlyj, Ross.	86	50.47 N	60.53 E
Svetlyj, Ross.	88	58.26 N	115.55 E
Svetlyj Jar	80	48.29 N	44.46 E
Svetogorsk	24	61.07 N	28.51 E
Svetozarevo	38	43.58 N	21.16 E
Svežen'kaja	80	54.01 N	42.26 E
Şvidník	30	49.18 N	21.35 E
Švihov	60	49.29 N	13.17 E
Svijaga ≃	80	55.47 N	48.40 E
Svilajnac	38	44.14 N	21.13 E
Svilengrad	38	41.46 N	26.12 E
Svindal	26	58.30 N	7.28 E
Svinecea Mare, Vîrful ∧	38	44.48 N	22.09 E
Svinesund	26	59.06 N	11.16 E
Svinninge	41	55.43 N	11.28 E
Svir'	76	54.51 N	26.24 E
Svir' ≃	76	60.30 N	32.48 E
Svirica	76	60.29 N	32.51 E
Svirsk	88	53.04 N	103.21 E
Svir'stroj	76	60.48 N	33.43 E
Sviščovka	80	52.51 N	43.44 E
Svisloč', Bela.	76	53.02 N	24.06 E
Svisloč', Bela.	76	53.26 N	28.59 E
Svisloč' ≃	76	53.26 N	28.59 E
Sviştov	38	43.37 N	25.20 E
Svistunovka	83	49.29 N	38.20 E
Svit	30	49.03 N	20.12 E
Svitávka	30	49.30 N	16.37 E
Svitavy	30	49.45 N	16.27 E
Svitino	82	54.54 N	35.49 E
Svoboda, Ross.	78	51.58 N	36.17 E
Svoboda, Ross.	78	47.12 N	40.39 E
Svobodnaja	89	46.48 N	143.23 E
Svobodnoje	83	47.32 N	37.34 E
Svobodnyj, Ross.	80	52.20 N	46.22 E
Svobodnyj, Ross.	89	51.24 N	128.08 E
Svobodnyj Port	78	46.20 N	31.51 E
Svoge	38	42.58 N	23.21 E
Svojna	82	54.09 N	36.39 E
Svol'na ≃	76	55.43 N	28.02 E
Svolvær	24	68.14 N	14.34 E
Svor	54	50.47 N	14.36 E
Svorkmo	26	63.10 N	9.45 E
Svratka ≃	61	49.11 N	16.38 E
Svržno	60	49.35 N	12.46 E
Svullrya	26	60.25 N	12.24 E
Swābi	123	34.07 N	72.28 E
Swadlincote	42	52.47 N	1.33 W
Swaffham	42	52.39 N	0.41 E
Swain	210	42.29 N	77.51 W
Swain Reefs ✦[2]	166	21.40 S	152.15 E
Swainsboro	192	32.35 N	82.20 W
Swains Island I[1]	14	11.03 S	171.05 W
Swakop ≃	156	22.38 S	14.36 E
Swakopmund	156	22.41 S	14.34 E
Swakopmund □[5]	156	23.00 S	15.00 E
Swale □[8]	260	51.21 N	0.41 E
Swale ≃	44	54.06 N	1.20 W
Swale Canyon V	224	45.49 N	121.05 W
Swale Creek ≃	224	45.49 N	121.05 W
Swaledale V	44	54.25 N	1.47 W
Swallowfield	218	38.21 N	84.51 W
Swalmen	52	51.15 N	6.02 E
Swamp City	222	32.29 N	94.56 W
Swampscott	207	42.28 N	70.55 W
Swan	222	32.26 N	95.22 W
Swan ≃, Austl.	168a	32.03 S	115.45 E
Swan ≃, Can.	184	52.30 N	100.47 W
Swan ≃, Ab., Can.	182	55.31 N	115.17 W
Swan ≃, Mn., U.S.	190	47.01 N	93.16 W
Swan ≃, Mt., U.S.	202	48.04 N	114.05 W
Swan Acres	279b	40.33 N	80.02 W
Swanage	42	50.37 N	1.58 W
Swan Bay ⊂	169	38.14 S	144.40 E
Swan Creek ≃, Austl.	171a	28.08 S	152.13 E
Swan Creek ≃, Mi., U.S.	216	41.58 N	85.19 W
Swan Creek ≃, Mi., U.S.	216	41.58 N	83.17 W
Swan Creek ≃, Oh., U.S.	216	41.39 N	83.32 W
Swan Creek ≃, S.D., U.S.	198	45.19 N	100.15 W
Swan Creek, North Branch ≃	281	42.06 N	83.23 W
Swan Creek Point ›	281	42.40 N	82.39 W
Swanee → Suwannee ≃	192	29.18 N	83.09 W
Swan Hill	166	35.21 S	143.34 E
Swan Hills	182	54.43 N	115.24 W
Swan Hills ⋏[2]	182	54.48 N	115.52 W
Swanington	216	40.35 N	87.17 W
Swan Island I	169	38.15 S	144.41 E
Swan Islands → Santanilla, Islas II	238	17.25 N	83.55 W
Swank Creek ≃	224	47.07 N	120.45 W
Swan Lake, Mb., Can.	184	49.24 N	98.46 W
Swan Lake, Mt., U.S.	202	47.55 N	113.50 W
Swan Lake, N.Y., U.S.	210	41.45 N	74.47 W
Swan Lake ⊜, Mb., Can.	184	52.30 N	100.45 W
Swan Lake ⊜, On., Can.	184	54.17 N	91.12 W
Swan Lake ⊜, Il., U.S.	219	38.57 N	90.33 W
Swan Lake ⊜, Mn., U.S.	190	44.19 N	94.15 W
Swanland	44	53.44 N	0.29 W
Swanley	42	51.24 N	0.12 E
Swanlinbar	48	54.10 N	7.42 W
Swannanoa	192	35.36 N	82.23 W
Swannanoa, Lake ⊜	276	41.01 N	74.31 W
Swan Peak ∧	202	47.43 N	113.38 W
Swanquarter	192	35.24 N	76.20 W
Swan Range ⋏	202	47.50 N	113.40 W
Swan Reach	166	34.34 S	139.36 E
Swan River	184	52.06 N	101.16 W
Swansboro	192	34.41 N	77.07 W
Swanscombe	260	51.26 N	0.18 E
Swansea, Austl.	166	42.08 S	148.04 E
Swansea, Austl.	170	33.05 S	151.38 E
Swansea, Wales, U.K.	42	51.38 N	3.57 W
Swansea, Il., U.S.	219	38.32 N	89.59 W
Swansea, Ma., U.S.	207	41.44 N	71.11 W
Swansea, S.C., U.S.	192	33.44 N	81.05 W
Swansea ◆[8]	275b	43.38 N	79.28 W
Swansea Bay ⊂	42	51.35 N	3.52 W
Swans Island I	188	44.10 N	68.25 W
Swanson Lake ⊜[1]	198	40.09 N	101.06 W
Swanton, Oh., U.S.	216	41.35 N	83.53 W
Swanton, Vt., U.S.	206	44.55 N	73.07 W
Swanville	190	45.54 N	94.38 W
Swanzey Center	207	42.49 N	72.10 W
Swartberg	158	30.15 S	29.23 E
Swarthmore	208	39.54 N	75.21 W
Swarthmore College ɷ[2]	285	39.54 N	75.21 W
Swart-Kei ≃	158	32.09 S	27.24 E
Swart-Mfolozi ≃	158	28.22 S	31.58 E
Swartplaas	158	26.08 S	26.57 E
Swartruggens	156	25.40 S	26.42 E
Swartruggens ⋏	158	33.02 S	19.35 E
Swartswood Lake	210	41.04 N	74.51 W
Swartswood State Park ♠	210	41.05 N	74.50 W
Swartz Creek	216	42.57 N	83.49 W
Swarupkāti	126	22.45 N	90.06 E
Swarupnagar	126	22.49 N	88.52 E
Swarzędz	30	52.26 N	17.05 E
Swasey Peak ∧	200	39.23 N	113.19 W
Swasey Wash V	200	39.15 N	112.53 W
Swasiland → Swaziland □[1]	158	26.30 S	31.30 E
Swāt ≃	123	34.20 N	71.34 E
Swatara Creek ≃	208	40.11 N	76.44 W
Swa-Tenda	152	7.09 S	17.07 E
Swatow → Shantou	100	23.23 N	116.41 E
Swauger Creek ≃	226	38.16 N	119.16 W
Swauk Pass)(	224	47.21 N	120.40 W
Sway	42	50.47 N	1.37 W
Swayzee	216	40.30 N	85.49 W
Swaziland □[1], Afr.	138	26.30 S	31.30 E
Swaziland □[1], Afr.	158	26.30 S	31.30 E
Swea City	190	43.23 N	94.19 W
Swede Hill	279b	40.17 N	79.34 W
Swedeland	285	40.05 N	75.20 W
Sweden (Sverige) □[1], Europe	22	62.00 N	15.00 E
Sweden (Sverige) □[1], Europe	24	62.00 N	15.00 E
Sweden Valley	214	41.45 N	77.56 W
Swede Run ≃	285	40.02 N	74.58 W
Swedesboro	208	39.44 N	75.18 W
Swedesburg	285	40.06 N	75.20 W
Swedish Knoll ∧	200	39.16 N	111.26 W
Swedru	150	5.32 N	0.43 W
Sween, Loch ⊂	46	55.59 N	5.39 W
Sweeney Plan	279b	40.11 N	79.48 W
Sweeny	222	29.02 N	95.41 W
Sweeny Park ♠	284a	43.02 N	78.52 W
Sweet Briar	192	37.33 N	79.04 W
Sweetgrass	182	49.00 N	111.57 W
Sweet Grass Creek ≃	202	45.47 N	109.47 W
Sweetgrass Hills ⋏[2]	202	48.55 N	111.30 W
Sweet Grass Indian Reserve ◆[4]	184	52.44 N	108.45 W
Sweetheart Abbey ɷ[1]	44	54.59 N	3.38 W
Sweet Home, Or., U.S.	202	44.23 N	122.44 W
Sweet Home, Tx., U.S.	222	29.21 N	97.04 W
Sweetsers	216	40.34 N	85.46 W
Sweet Springs	194	38.57 N	93.24 W
Sweet Valley	210	41.17 N	76.09 W
Sweetwater, Fl., U.S.	220	25.46 N	80.21 W
Sweet Water, Il., U.S.	219	40.03 N	89.42 W
Sweetwater, Tn., U.S.	192	35.36 N	84.27 W
Sweetwater, Tx., U.S.	196	32.28 N	100.24 W
Sweetwater ≃	200	42.31 N	107.02 W
Sweetwater Creek	220	27.59 N	82.33 W
Sweetwater Creek ≃, U.S.	196	35.18 N	99.57 W
Sweetwater Creek ≃, Tx., U.S.	196	32.40 N	100.06 W
Sweetwater Mountains ⋏	226	38.30 N	119.17 W
Swellendam	158	34.02 S	20.26 E
Swepsonville	192	36.01 N	79.21 W
Swerdlovsk → Jekaterinburg	86	56.51 N	60.36 E
Świdnica (Schweidnitz)	30	50.51 N	16.29 E
Świdnik	30	51.14 N	22.41 E
Świdwin	30	53.47 N	15.47 E
Świebodzice	30	50.52 N	16.19 E
Świebodzin	30	52.15 N	15.32 E
Świecie	30	53.25 N	18.28 E
Świerzawa	30	51.01 N	15.54 E
Świerzno	54	53.57 N	14.59 E
Święta	54	53.35 N	14.36 E
Świętokrzyskie, Góry ⋏	30	50.55 N	21.00 E
Świętokrzyski Park Narodowy ♠	30	50.55 N	21.00 E
Swift ≃, Eng., U.K.	42	52.23 N	1.16 W
Swift ≃, Ak., U.S.	180	61.53 N	156.18 W
Swift ≃, Ma., U.S.	207	42.12 N	72.22 W
Swift Creek ≃, Al., U.S.	194	32.25 N	86.38 W
Swift Creek ≃, N.C., U.S.	192	35.12 N	77.05 W
Swift Creek ≃, N.C., U.S.	192	35.57 N	77.35 W
Swift Creek ≃, Va., U.S.	208	37.17 N	77.15 W
Swift Current	184	50.17 N	107.50 W
Swift Current Creek ≃	184	50.40 N	107.44 W
Swifton	194	35.49 N	91.07 W
Swift Reservoir ⊜[1]	224	46.04 N	122.05 W
Swiftwater	210	41.06 N	75.20 W
Swilly ≃	48	54.57 N	7.42 W
Swilly, Lough ⊂	48	55.10 N	7.38 W
Swimming ≃	276	40.21 N	74.05 W
Swimming River Reservoir ⊜[1]	276	40.19 N	74.07 W
Świna ≃[1]	54	53.55 N	14.17 E
Swinburne, Cape ›	176	71.14 N	98.34 W
Swinden Reservoirs ⊜[1]	262	53.48 N	2.10 W
Swindle Island I	182	52.32 N	128.35 W
Swindon	42	51.34 N	1.47 W
Swinemünde → Świnoujście	30	53.53 N	14.14 E
Swineshead	42	52.56 N	0.09 W
Swinford	48	53.57 N	8.57 W
Swinging Bridge Reservoir ⊜[1]	210	41.37 N	74.48 W
Swinomish Indian Reservation ◆[4]	224	48.25 N	122.33 W
Świnoujście (Swinemünde)	30	53.53 N	14.14 E
Swinton, Eng., U.K.	44	53.28 N	1.20 W
Swinton, Eng., U.K.	262	53.31 N	2.20 W
Swinton, Scot., U.K.	46	55.43 N	2.15 W
Swissvale	279b	40.25 N	79.52 W
Swisttal	56	50.40 N	6.54 E
Switzerland □[6]	218	38.45 N	85.04 W
Switzerland □[1], Europe	22	47.00 N	8.00 E
Switzerland □[1], Europe	58	47.00 N	8.00 E
Swona I	46	58.45 N	3.03 W
Swordfish Seamount ✦[3]	14	18.25 N	158.25 W
Swords	48	53.28 N	6.13 W
Swords Range ⋏	166	21.57 S	141.32 E
Swormville	284a	43.02 N	78.42 W
Sworton Heath	262	53.21 N	2.28 W
Swoyerville	210	41.18 N	75.52 W
Syalach	74	66.12 N	124.00 E
Syam	58	46.42 N	5.57 E
Syāmnagar	126	22.21 N	89.07 E
Syāmpur, India	126	22.18 N	88.02 E
Syampur, India	272b	22.29 N	88.13 E
Sybille Creek ≃	198	42.07 N	105.02 W
Syburg ◆[8]	263	51.25 N	7.29 E
Sycamore, Ga., U.S.	192	31.40 N	83.38 W
Sycamore, Il., U.S.	216	41.59 N	88.41 W
Sycamore, Oh., U.S.	214	40.56 N	83.10 W
Sycamore Creek ≃, Az., U.S.	200	33.38 N	111.40 W
Sycamore Creek ≃, Mi., U.S.	216	42.43 N	84.32 W
Sycamore Creek ≃, Oh., U.S.	214	40.59 N	83.12 W
Sycamore Creek ≃, Tx., U.S.	196	29.14 N	100.48 W
Sycamore Gardens	285	39.42 N	75.42 W
Sycamore Island I	279b	40.29 N	79.52 W
Sycamore Slough ≃	226	38.48 N	121.44 W
Sycan ≃	202	42.27 N	121.15 W
Sycaway	210	42.44 N	73.39 W
Syčova	86	57.35 N	69.20 E
Syčovka	76	55.50 N	34.17 E
Syców	30	51.19 N	17.43 E
Sydenham, Austl.	274b	37.42 S	144.46 E
Sydenham, On., Can.	212	44.25 N	76.36 W
Sydenham ◆[8], S. Afr.	273d	26.09 S	28.06 E
Sydenham ◆[8], Eng., U.K.	260	51.26 N	0.03 W
Sydenham ≃, On., Can.	190	42.33 N	82.25 W
Sydenham ≃, On., Can.	212	44.35 N	80.57 W
Sydenham Lake ⊜	212	44.25 N	76.35 W
Sydenham West	274b	37.41 S	144.39 E
Sydney, Austl.	170	33.52 S	151.13 E
Sydney, Austl.	274a	33.52 S	151.13 E
Sydney, N.S., Can.	186	46.09 N	60.11 W
Sydney, Fl., U.S.	220	27.58 N	82.12 W
Sydney, University of ɷ[2]	274a	33.53 S	151.11 E
Sydney Bay ⊂, On., Can.	212	44.54 N	81.05 W
Sydney Bay ⊂, Norf. I.	174c	29.04 S	167.57 E
Sydney Bay Bluff ⊥[4]	212	44.54 N	81.07 W
Sydney Harbour Bridge ◆[5]	170	33.52 S	151.12 E

Symbols in the index entries represent the broad categories identified in the key at the right. Symbols with superior numbers (⋏[1]) identify subcategories (see complete key on page *I · 1).*

Symbole im Register stellen die rechts im Schlüssel erklärten Kategorien dar. Symbole mit hochgestellten Ziffern (⋏[1]) bezeichnen Unterabteilungen einer Kategorie (vgl. vollständiger Schlüssel auf Seite *I · 1).*

Los símbolos incluídos en el texto del índice representan las grandes categorias identificadas con la clave a la derecha. Los símbolos con numeros en su parte superior (⋏[1]) identifican las subcategorías (véase la clave completa en la página *I · 1).*

Les symboles de l'index représentent les catégories indiquées dans la légende à droite. Les symboles suivis d'un indice (⋏[1]) représentent des sous-catégories (voir légende complète à la page *I · 1).*

Os símbolos incluídos no texto do índice representam as grandes categorias identificadas com a chave à direita. Os símbolos com números em sua parte superior (⋏[1]) identificam as subcategorias (veja-se a chave completa à página *I · 1).*

	English	Deutsch	Español	Français	Português
∧	Mountain	Berg	Montaña	Montagne	Montanha
⋏	Mountains	Gebirge	Montañas	Montagnes	Montanhas
)(	Pass	Paß	Paso	Col	Passo
V	Valley, Canyon	Tal, Cañon	Valle, Cañón	Vallée, Canyon	Vale, Canhão
≚	Plain	Ebene	Llano	Plaine	Planície
›	Cape	Kap	Cabo	Cap	Cabo
I	Island	Insel	Isla	Île	Ilha
II	Islands	Inseln	Islas	Îles	Ilhas
⊥	Other Topographic Features	Andere Topographische Objekte	Otros Elementos Topográficos	Autres données topographiques	Outros acidentes topográficos

ESPAÑOL

Nombre	Página	Lat.°′	Long.°′ W = Oeste
Sydney Lake ⊜	184	50.40 N	94.24 W
Sydney Mines	186	46.14 N	60.14 W
Sydney Point ›	174d	0.53 S	169.36 E
Syferbult	158	26.00 S	27.20 E
Sygan	279b	40.21 N	80.08 W
Syke	52	52.54 N	8.49 E
Sykesville, Md., U.S.	208	39.22 N	76.58 W
Sykesville, Pa., U.S.	214	41.03 N	78.49 W
Sykkylven	26	62.24 N	6.35 E
Syktyvkar	24	61.40 N	50.46 E
Sylacauga	194	33.10 N	86.15 W
Sylarna ∧	26	63.02 N	12.13 E
Sylhet	120	24.54 N	91.52 E
Syloga	24	63.50 N	43.39 E
Sylt I	30	54.54 N	8.20 E
Sylva	192	35.22 N	83.13 W
Sylva ≃	86	57.39 N	56.54 E
Sylvan	224	45.30 N	122.41 W
Sylvan Beach	210	43.11 N	75.43 W
Sylvan Glen	285	40.11 N	75.42 W
Sylvan Grove	198	39.00 N	98.23 W
Sylvan Hills	194	34.50 N	92.13 W
Sylvania, Austl.	274a	34.01 S	151.07 E
Sylvania, Ga., U.S.	192	32.45 N	81.38 W
Sylvania, Oh., U.S.	214	41.43 N	83.42 W
Sylvania, Pa., U.S.	210	41.48 N	76.51 W
Sylvania Heights	274a	34.02 S	151.06 E
Sylvan Lake, Ab., Can.	182	52.19 N	114.05 W
Sylvan Lake, Il., U.S.	278	42.15 N	88.03 W
Sylvan Lake, Mi., U.S.	281	42.37 N	83.20 W
Sylvan Lake ⊜, Ab., Can.	182	52.21 N	114.10 W
Sylvan Lake ⊜, In., U.S.	216	41.29 N	85.20 W
Sylvan Lake ⊜, Mi., U.S.	281	42.37 N	83.20 W
Sylvan Pass)(	202	44.28 N	110.08 W
Sylvan Shores	220	28.49 N	81.41 W
Sylvensteinsee ⊜[1]	64	47.34 N	11.32 E
Sylvester, Ga., U.S.	192	31.31 N	83.50 W
Sylvester, Tx., U.S.	196	32.43 N	100.15 W
Sylvester, Mount ∧[2]	186	48.11 N	55.04 W
Sylvia	198	37.57 N	98.24 W
Sym	74	60.20 N	88.23 E
Symmes Creek ≃	188	38.26 N	82.27 W
Syn'a	24	65.22 N	57.42 E
Syndal	274b	37.53 S	145.09 E
Synkovo	82	55.21 N	37.38 E
Synnyr, chrebet ⋀	88	56.50 N	111.10 E
Syntul	80	55.00 N	41.18 E
Synžereja	78	47.38 N	28.09 E
Syon House ⊥	260	51.29 N	0.19 W
Syosset	210	40.49 N	73.30 W
Syowa ⊍[3]	9	69.00 S	39.35 E
Syracuse, In., U.S.	216	41.25 N	85.45 W
Syracuse, Ks., U.S.	198	37.58 N	101.45 W
Syracuse, Ne., U.S.	198	40.39 N	96.11 W
Syracuse, N.Y., U.S.	210	43.02 N	76.08 W
Syracuse Hancock International Airport ⊠, N.Y., U.S.	210	43.07 N	76.07 W
Syracuse Hancock International Airport ⊠, N.Y., U.S.	212	43.07 N	76.07 W
Syracuse → Siracusa	70	37.04 N	15.18 E
Syrčan	80	57.22 N	50.15 E
Syrdarja	85	40.52 N	68.38 E
Syrdarja (Syr Darya) ≃	72	46.03 N	61.00 E
Syr-Darya → Syrdarja ≃	72	46.03 N	61.00 E
Syre	46	58.22 N	4.14 W
Syre ≃	56	49.35 N	6.08 E
Syria (Sūrīyah) □[1], Asia	118	35.00 N	38.00 E
Syria (Sūrīyah) □[1], Asia	128	35.00 N	38.00 E
Syriam	110	16.46 N	96.15 E
Syrian Desert → Shām, Bādiyat ash- ✤[2]	128	32.00 N	40.00 E
Syrien → Syria □[1]	128	35.00 N	38.00 E
Syrie → Syria □[1]	128	35.00 N	38.00 E
Syrskij	76	52.34 N	39.29 E
Sysert'	86	56.29 N	60.49 E
Sysmä	26	61.30 N	25.41 E
Sysola ≃	24	61.42 N	50.53 E
Sysslebäck	26	60.44 N	12.52 E
Syston	42	52.42 N	1.04 W
Systyg-Chem	88	52.40 N	95.30 E
Syt'kovo	76	56.31 N	34.01 E
Sytykanskij, porog ∟	88	57.49 N	118.33 E
Syukunoshō	270	34.50 N	135.32 E
Syväri ⊜	26	63.16 N	28.06 E
Syzran'	80	53.09 N	48.27 E
Syzran' ≃	80	53.04 N	48.26 E
Szabadka → Subotica	38	46.06 N	19.39 E
Szabolcs-Szatmár-Bereg □[6]	30	48.00 N	22.10 E
Szada	264c	47.38 N	19.19 E
Szamocin	30	53.02 N	17.08 E
Szamos (Someș) ≃	38	48.07 N	22.20 E
Szamotuły	30	52.37 N	16.35 E
Szarvas	30	46.52 N	20.34 E
Szatmárnémeti → Satu Mare	38	47.48 N	22.53 E
Százhalombatta	264c	47.20 N	18.56 E
Szczawnica	30	49.26 N	20.30 E
Szczecin (Stettin)	30	53.24 N	14.32 E
Szczecin □[4]	30	53.45 N	15.00 E
Szczecinek (Neustettin)	30	53.43 N	16.42 E
Szczeciński, Zalew (Oderhaff) ⊂	54	53.46 N	14.14 E
Szczekociny	30	50.38 N	19.50 E
Szczuczyn	30	53.34 N	22.18 E
Szczytno	30	53.34 N	21.00 E
Szechwan Basin → Sichuan Pendi ≡[1]	102	30.00 N	105.00 E
Szechwan → Sichuan □[4]	102	31.00 N	105.00 E
Szécsény	30	48.06 N	19.31 E
Szeged	30	46.15 N	20.09 E
Szeghalom	30	47.01 N	21.11 E
Székesfehérvár	30	47.12 N	18.25 E
Szekszárd	30	46.21 N	18.42 E
Szemenyecsörnye	61	46.30 N	16.37 E
Szentendre	30	47.40 N	19.05 E
Szentendrei-Duna ≃[1]	264c	47.36 N	19.05 E
Szentendrei-sziget I	264c	47.39 N	19.07 E
Szentes	30	46.39 N	20.16 E
Szentgotthárd	61	46.57 N	16.17 E
Szentpéterfa	61	47.06 N	16.29 E
Szeping → Siping	89	43.12 N	124.20 E
Szépművészeti Museum ⊍	264c	47.31 N	19.05 E
Szerencs	30	48.09 N	21.13 E
Szigethalom	264c	47.20 N	19.00 E
Szigetszentmiklós	264c	47.21 N	19.03 E
Szilas-patak ≃	264c	47.36 N	19.06 E
Szlichtyngowa	30	51.43 N	16.15 E
Szob	30	47.50 N	18.52 E
Szolnok	30	47.10 N	20.12 E
Szombathely	61	47.14 N	16.38 E
Szprotawa	30	51.34 N	15.33 E
Sztum	30	53.56 N	19.01 E
Szubin	30	53.00 N	17.44 E
Szydłowiec	30	51.14 N	20.51 E
Szypliszki	30	54.15 N	23.05 E

FRANÇAIS

Nom	Page	Lat.°′	Long.°′ W = Ouest
T			
Ta ≃	94	36.17 N	139.54 E
Taacyn ≃	102	45.09 N	101.27 E
Taal	116	13.53 N	120.55 E
Taal, Lake ⊜	116	13.55 N	121.00 E
Taalintehdas → Dalsbruk	26	60.02 N	22.31 E
Taan ≃	100	24.24 N	120.36 E
Taancan Point ›	116	10.00 N	125.01 E
Taavetti	26	60.55 N	27.34 E
Tabacal	252	23.16 S	64.15 W
Tabacal, Quebrada ≃	286c	10.31 N	67.02 W
Tabaco	116	13.23 N	123.44 E
Tabacundo	246	0.03 N	78.12 W
Tabai ≃	164	3.01 S	135.52 E
Tabalosos	248	6.21 S	76.41 W
Tabanan	115b	8.32 S	115.08 E
Tabango	116	11.19 N	124.22 E
Tabankulu	158	30.58 S	29.19 E
Tábara	34	41.49 N	5.57 W
Tabar Island I	164	2.55 S	152.05 E
Tabar Islands II	164	2.50 S	152.00 E
Tabarka	148	36.57 N	8.45 E
Tabarz	54	50.52 N	10.31 E
Ṭabas	128	33.36 N	56.54 E
Tabasará ≃	236	8.00 N	81.39 W
Tabasco □[3]	232	18.15 N	93.00 W
Ṭabas Masīnā	128	32.48 N	60.14 E
Tabat	86	52.57 N	90.43 E
Tabatinga ≃	255	17.24 S	43.18 W
Tabayama	94	35.47 N	138.55 E
Tabayin	110	22.42 N	95.19 E
Tabb	208	37.08 N	76.29 W
Tabei	98	39.44 N	122.29 E
Tabelbala	148	29.23 N	3.15 W
Tabelbala, Kahal ⩟[8]	148	28.30 N	2.00 W
Taber	182	49.47 N	112.08 W
Taberg, Sve.	26	57.41 N	14.05 E
Taberg, Sve.	40	59.50 N	14.08 E
Taberg, N.Y., U.S.	210	43.18 N	75.37 W
Tabernacle	285	39.50 N	74.42 W
Tabi	152	8.10 S	13.18 E
Tabiang	174d	0.52 S	169.35 E
Tabiano Terme	64	44.48 N	10.21 E
Tabira	250	7.35 S	37.33 W
Tabiteuea	174t	1.25 N	173.07 E
Tabiteuea I[1]	14	1.20 S	174.50 E
Tabla	150	13.46 N	3.01 E
Tabla, Cerro de la ∧	240m	18.03 N	66.08 W
Tablada	288	34.42 S	58.32 W
Tablas, Cabo ›	252	31.51 S	71.34 W
Tablas Island I	116	12.24 N	122.02 E
Tablas Plateau ⋀[1]	116	9.43 N	122.43 E
Tablas Strait ⋓	116	12.40 N	121.48 E
Tablat	34	36.24 N	3.19 E
Table Bay ⊂	158	33.53 S	18.27 E
Table Cape ›	172	39.06 S	178.00 E
Tableland	162	17.17 S	127.00 E
Table Mountain ∧, Nf., Can.	186	47.43 N	59.13 W
Table Mountain ∧, S. Afr.	158	33.57 S	18.25 E
Table Mountain ∧, Az., U.S.	200	32.49 N	110.31 W
Table Rock	198	40.10 N	96.05 W
Table Rock Lake ⊜[1]	194	36.35 N	93.30 W
Tabletop ∧, Austl.	162	22.32 S	123.55 E
Table Top ∧, Az., U.S.	200	32.46 N	112.07 W
Tabletop Mountain ∧	171b	35.58 S	148.30 E
Tabley Mere ⊜	262	53.17 N	2.25 W
Tabligbo	150	6.35 N	1.30 E
Tablones	240m	18.15 N	65.45 W
Taboan ≃	116	17.57 N	122.11 E
Taboão, Ribeirão do ≃	287b	23.40 S	46.28 W
Taboão da Serra	256	23.38 S	46.46 W
Taboco ≃	248	19.53 S	55.58 W
Taboga	236	8.48 N	79.33 W
Tabogon	116	10.57 N	124.02 E
Tábor, Česko.	30	49.25 N	14.41 E
Tabor, Ross.	74	71.16 N	150.12 E
Tabor, Ia., U.S.	198	40.53 N	95.40 W
Tabor, N.J., U.S.	276	40.52 N	74.29 W
Tabor, S.D., U.S.	198	42.56 N	97.39 W
Tabor, Mount → Tavor, Har ∧	132	32.41 N	35.23 E
Tabora	154	5.01 S	32.48 E
Tabora □[4]	154	5.15 S	32.45 E
Tabor City	192	34.08 N	78.52 W
Tabory	86	58.31 N	64.33 E
Tabou	150	4.25 N	7.21 W
Tabrīz	128	38.05 N	46.18 E
Tábua, Riacho da ≃	250	9.12 S	44.25 W
Tabuaço	34	41.07 N	7.34 W
Tabuaeran I[1]	14	3.52 N	159.20 W
Tabuão	256	21.59 S	44.02 W
Tábuas	256	22.12 S	43.37 W
Tabu-dong	98	36.03 N	128.31 E
Tabuelan	116	10.49 N	123.52 E
Tabūk, Ar. Su.	128	28.23 N	36.35 E
Tabuk, Pil.	116	17.24 N	121.25 E
Tabuleiro	256	21.22 S	43.15 W
Tabuleiro do Norte	250	5.15 S	38.07 W
Tabuny	86	52.46 N	78.45 E
Tabuse	96	33.57 N	132.03 E
Tabuyung	114	0.51 N	99.00 E
Tabwémasana, Mont ∧	175f	15.20 S	166.44 E
Täby	40	59.30 N	18.03 E
Tacagua, Quebrada ≃	286c	10.37 N	67.02 W
Tacámbaro de Codallos	234	19.14 N	101.28 W
Tacaná	236	15.14 N	92.05 W
Tacaná, Volcán ∧[1]	236	15.08 N	92.06 W
Tacañitas	252	28.38 S	62.36 W
Tacaratu	250	9.06 S	38.10 W
Taceno	58	46.02 N	9.21 E
T'ačev	78	48.02 N	23.34 E
Taché, Lac ⊜	176	64.00 N	120.00 W
Tacheng (Qoqek)	86	46.45 N	82.57 E
Tacherting	60	48.05 N	12.34 E
Tachia	100	24.21 N	120.37 E
Tachia ≃	100	24.20 N	120.33 E
Tachiaochang Airport ⊠	107	32.01 N	118.47 E
Tachiataš	72	42.22 N	59.35 E
Tachibana, Nihon	96	33.11 N	130.36 E
Tachibana, Nihon	96	33.54 N	132.17 E
Tachie ≃	182	54.40 N	124.50 W
Tachikawa	94	35.42 N	139.25 E
Tachikawa Air Base ■	268	35.43 N	139.25 E
Tachinger See ⊜	60	47.58 N	12.45 E
Táchira □[3]	246	7.50 N	72.05 W
Tachoshui	100	24.20 N	121.44 E
Tachov	60	49.48 N	12.38 E
Tachta, Ross.	80	45.54 N	42.07 E
Tachta, Ross.	89	53.08 N	139.53 E
Tachta-Bazar	128	35.57 N	62.50 E
Tachtabrod	86	52.38 N	67.34 E
Tachtakupyr	86	43.02 N	60.17 E
Tachtamygda	89	54.06 N	123.34 E
Tacima	250	6.30 S	35.39 W
Tacina ≃	68	38.56 N	16.53 E
Tacinskij	80	48.13 N	41.17 E
Taciuã, Lago ≃	246	4.29 S	60.35 W
Tacloban	116	11.15 N	125.00 E
Taclobo	116	12.20 N	122.34 E
Tacna, Perú	248	18.01 S	70.15 W
Tacna, Az., U.S.	200	32.41 N	113.57 W
Tacna □[5]	248	17.40 S	70.20 W
Tacoignières	261	48.50 N	1.40 E
Tacoma	224	47.15 N	122.26 W
Tacoma Narrows Bridge ✤[5]	224	47.16 N	122.33 W
Taconic	207	42.02 N	73.24 W
Taconic Range ⋀	210	42.30 N	73.20 W

PORTUGUÊS

Nome	Página	Lat.°′	Long.°′ W = Oeste
Taconic State Park ⇡	210	42.05 N	73.34 W
Tacony ✤[8]	285	40.02 N	75.03 W
Tacony Creek ≃	285	40.01 N	75.06 W
Tacony Creek Park ⇡	285	40.02 N	75.07 W
Tacony Palmyra Bridge ✤[5]	285	40.01 N	75.02 W
Taco Pozo	252	25.37 S	63.17 W
Tacotalpa	234	17.36 N	92.49 W
Tacotalpa ≃	234	17.50 N	92.52 W
Tacuarembó	252	31.44 S	55.59 W
Tacuarembó ≃	252	32.25 S	55.29 W
Tacuarí ≃	252	32.46 S	53.18 W
Tacuatí	252	23.27 S	56.35 W
Tacuba ✤[8]	286a	19.28 N	99.12 W
Tacubaya ✤[8]	286a	19.25 N	99.12 W
Tacuparé, Cachoeira ∟	250	5.20 S	55.50 W
Tacurong	116	6.42 N	124.42 E
Tacuru, Bra.	252	23.43 N	55.02 W
Tacuru, Bra.	255	23.38 S	55.01 W
Tacurú, Laguna ⊜	258	34.58 S	58.25 W
Tacutu (Takutu) ≃	246	3.01 N	60.29 W
Tadain	270	34.52 N	135.24 E
Tadami	92	37.21 N	139.19 E
Tadaoka	270	34.29 N	135.24 E
Tadasuni	71	40.06 N	8.53 E
Tadcaster	44	53.53 N	1.16 W
Tademaït, Plateau du ⋀[1]	148	28.30 N	2.00 E
Tadenac Lake ⊜	212	45.03 N	79.56 W
Tādepallegūdem	122	16.50 N	81.30 E
Tadía, Ciénaga de ⊜	246	6.48 N	76.49 W
Tadine	175f	21.33 S	167.52 E
Tadio, Lagune ⊂	150	5.11 N	5.15 W
Tadjemout	148	25.37 N	3.48 E
Tadjenanet	34	36.08 N	5.59 E
Tadjeraout, Oued ∨	148	21.17 N	1.19 E
Tadjoura	144	11.47 N	42.54 E
Tadjoura, Golfe de ⊂	144	11.42 N	43.00 E
Tadley	42	51.21 N	1.08 W
Tado	94	35.08 N	136.38 E
Tadok	114	3.58 N	96.19 E
Tadotsu	96	34.16 N	133.45 E
Tadoule Lake ⊜	176	58.36 N	98.20 W
Tadoussac	186	48.09 N	69.43 W
Tādpatri	122	14.55 N	78.01 E
Taduno	112	1.55 S	123.05 E
Tadworth	42	51.17 N	0.14 W
Tadzhikistan → Tajikistan □[1]	72	39.00 N	71.00 E
Tadzhikstan → Tajikistan □[1]	72	39.00 N	71.00 E
Tadžikabad	85	39.07 N	70.50 E
T'aean	98	36.46 N	126.16 E
T'aebaek-san ∧	98	37.06 N	128.55 E
T'aebaek-sanmaek ⋀	98	37.40 N	128.50 E
Taebu-do I	98	37.15 N	126.35 E
Taech'ŏn	98	36.22 N	126.34 E
Taech'ŏng-do I	98	37.49 N	124.43 E
Taedong	98	39.05 N	125.31 E
Taedong-gang ≃	98	38.42 N	125.15 E
Taegu	98	35.52 N	128.35 E
Taegu □[4]	98	35.50 N	128.35 E
Taegwan	98	40.13 N	125.12 E
Taehan-Min'guk → Korea, South □[1]	98	36.30 N	128.00 E
Taehŭksan-do I	98	34.40 N	125.25 E
Taehŭng	98	40.06 N	126.56 E
Taehwajŏn	271b	37.36 N	126.52 E
T'aein	98	35.40 N	126.55 E
Taejin	98	36.34 N	129.24 E
Taejŏn	98	36.20 N	127.26 E
Taejujŏm	98	38.24 N	127.58 E
T'aemo-san ∧	271b	37.27 N	127.04 E
Taeng ≃	110	19.06 N	98.57 E
Taer	102	34.09 N	98.50 E
Ta'erwan	100	31.49 N	113.25 E
Taeryanghwa	98	41.14 N	129.42 E
Tafahi I	14	15.51 S	173.43 W
Tafahnā al-ʿAzab	142	30.36 N	31.15 E
Tafalla	34	42.31 N	1.40 W
Tafanlieh	100	21.58 N	120.46 E
Ṭafas	132	32.44 N	36.04 E
Tafāsīkh, Ghurd at- ⩟[8]	142	29.43 N	29.45 E
Tafassasset, Oued (Oued Tafassâsset) ∨	148	20.56 N	10.12 E
Tafassâsset, Ténéré du ✤[2]	146	21.00 N	11.00 E
Tafea □[8]	175f	19.30 S	169.00 E
Tafelbaai → Table Bay ⊂	158	33.53 S	18.27 E
Tafelberg ∧	250	3.55 N	56.10 W
Tafermaar	164	6.51 S	134.06 E
Taff ≃	42	51.27 N	3.09 W
Tafiré	150	9.04 N	5.10 W
Tafí Viejo	252	26.44 S	65.16 W
Taflan	130	41.25 N	36.09 E
Tafna, Oued ≃	34	35.17 N	1.30 W
Tafo	150	6.13 N	0.22 W
Tafraoute	148	29.40 N	8.58 W
Taft, Īrān	128	31.45 N	54.14 E
Taft, Pil.	116	11.54 N	125.25 E
Taft, Ca., U.S.	204	35.08 N	119.27 W
Taft, Fl., U.S.	220	28.23 N	81.24 W
Taft, Ok., U.S.	196	35.45 N	95.32 W
Taft, Tx., U.S.	196	27.58 N	97.23 W
Taftān, Kūh-e ∧	128	28.36 N	61.08 E
Tafton	210	41.25 N	75.11 W
Taga, Nihon	94	35.13 N	136.17 E
Taga, Nihon	270	34.49 N	135.49 E
Taga, W. Sam.	175a	13.46 S	172.28 W
Tagabukid	116	7.00 N	126.21 E
Taga Dzong	124	27.04 N	89.53 E
Tagagawik ≃	180	66.30 N	159.00 W
Tagaj	80	54.18 N	47.39 E
Tagajō	92	38.20 N	141.00 E
Tagan	86	54.57 N	77.18 E
Tagana-an	116	9.42 N	125.35 E
Taganrog	83	47.12 N	38.56 E
Taganrogskij zaliv ⊂	78	47.00 N	38.23 E
Tagant □[4]	150	18.20 N	11.30 W
Tagânt ✤[1]	150	18.00 N	12.00 W
Tagapula Island I	116	12.04 N	124.12 E
Tågarp	41	55.56 N	12.57 E
Tagauayan Island I	116	10.58 N	121.13 E
Tagawa	96	33.38 N	130.49 E
Tagaytay	116	14.06 N	120.56 E
Tagbara	152	5.56 N	21.09 E
Tagbilaran	116	9.39 N	123.51 E
Tagdempt → Tihert	148	35.28 N	1.21 E
Tage	164	6.20 S	143.20 E
Tageren Canal ≅	174q	9.33 N	138.09 E
Taggia	62	43.52 N	7.51 E
Taghit	148	30.55 N	2.02 W
Taghkanic Creek ≃	210	42.13 N	73.45 W
Taghmon	48	52.18 N	6.39 W
Tagig	269f	14.32 N	121.04 E
Tagig ≃	269f	14.31 N	121.05 E
T'aginka	78	46.47 N	33.04 E
Tagish Lake ⊜	180	59.45 N	134.15 W
Tagliacozzo	66	42.04 N	13.14 E
Tagliamento ≃	64	45.38 N	13.06 E
Tagliata, Monte della ∧	64	44.34 N	9.48 E
Taglio di Po	64	45.00 N	12.12 E
Tagna	88	53.36 N	101.54 E
Tagna ≃	88	53.38 N	101.53 E
Tago	116	9.02 N	126.13 E
Tago ≃	116	9.01 N	126.14 E
Tagoloan	116	8.32 N	124.45 E
Tagolo Point ›	116	8.44 N	123.23 E
Tagon Harbour ⊂	162	33.53 S	123.00 E
Tagounit	148	29.58 N	5.36 W
Tagourâret ⊤[4]	150	17.45 N	7.43 W
Tagow Bāy	120	35.42 N	66.03 E
Tagrina, Oued ∨	148	21.00 N	6.16 E
Taguatinga	255	12.25 S	46.26 W
Tagubanhan Island I	116	11.08 N	123.07 E
Tagudin	116	16.56 N	120.27 E
Taguedoufat ∨	150	14.50 N	7.42 E
Taguke	120	32.07 N	84.35 E
Tagul ≃	88	55.35 N	97.45 E
Tagula Island I	160	11.30 S	153.30 E
Tagum	116	7.28 N	125.48 E
T'agun	86	53.56 N	85.38 E
Tagun Bay ⊂	116	13.55 N	123.46 E
Tagus (Tejo) (Tajo) ≃	34	38.40 N	9.24 W
T'agyŏng-ni	98	38.04 N	126.03 E
Tah, Sebkha ⊜	148	27.45 N	12.42 W
Taha	89	47.33 N	124.14 E
Tahaa I	14	16.38 S	151.30 W
Tahakopa	172	46.31 S	169.23 E
Tahala	148	34.04 N	4.20 W
Tahan, Gunong ∧	114	4.38 N	102.14 E
Tahanaoute	148	31.24 N	7.54 W
Tahāneh-ye Ney Basteh	128	32.59 N	60.53 E
Tahara	94	34.40 N	137.16 E
Tahart	148	22.51 N	5.12 E
Tahat ∧	148	23.18 N	5.47 E
Taheke	172	35.27 S	173.39 E
Ṭāherī	128	27.42 N	52.21 E
Tahgong, Puntan ›	174n	15.06 N	145.39 E
Tahifet	148	22.58 N	5.55 E
Tahiryuak Lake ⊜	176	70.56 N	112.20 W
Tahiti I	174s	17.37 S	149.27 W
Tahkuna neem ›	76	59.07 N	22.36 E
Tāhlāb (Ṭālāb) ≃	128	28.09 N	62.45 E
Tahlequah	196	35.54 N	94.58 W
Ṭahmā wa Minshāt ʿAbd as-Sayyid	142	29.38 N	31.14 E
Tahmoor	170	34.13 S	150.36 E
Tahneta Pass)(	180	61.53 N	147.20 W
Tahoe, Lake ⊜	226	39.07 N	120.03 W
Tahoe City	226	39.10 N	120.08 W
Tahoe Lake ⊜	176	70.15 N	108.45 W
Tahoe Paradise	226	38.52 N	120.01 W
Tahoe Valley	226	38.55 N	120.00 W
Tahoka	196	33.10 N	101.47 W
Taholah	224	47.20 N	124.17 W
Tahoua	150	14.54 N	5.16 E
Tahoua □[5]	150	16.00 N	5.00 E
Tahquamenon ≃	190	46.34 N	85.02 W
Tahquamenon Falls State Park ⇡	190	46.29 N	85.05 W
Tahsi	100	24.57 N	121.53 E
Tahsis	182	49.55 N	126.39 W
Ṭahṭā	140	26.46 N	31.30 E
Tahtaköprü	130	39.57 N	29.39 E
Tahtsa Lake ⊜	182	53.42 N	127.26 W
Tahtsa Peak ∧	182	53.33 N	127.47 W
Tahu	100	24.26 N	120.52 E
Tahuamanu ≃	248	11.06 S	67.36 W
Tahuata I	174x	9.57 S	139.05 W
Tahulandang, Pulau I	112	2.20 N	125.25 E
Tahuna	112	3.37 N	125.29 E
Tahuofang ⊜[1]	104	41.55 N	124.07 E
Tahuya ≃	224	47.23 N	123.03 W
Ṭahwāy	142	30.22 N	30.52 E
Taï, C. Iv.	150	5.52 N	7.27 W
Tai, It.	64	46.25 N	12.20 E
Tai, Nihon	270	34.31 N	135.26 E
Tai ✤[8]	270	34.45 N	135.00 E
Taiaçupeba	256	23.40 S	46.11 W
Tai'an, Zhg.	98	36.12 N	117.07 E
Tai'an, Zhg.	104	41.23 N	122.27 E
Tai'an, Zhg.	107	30.05 N	105.47 E
Tai'angang	106	31.43 N	121.40 E
Taiarapu, Presqu'île de ›[1]	174s	17.47 S	149.14 W
Taibai	102	34.00 N	107.18 E
Taibai Shan ∧, Zhg.	98	39.19 N	114.11 E
Taibai Shan ∧, Zhg.	102	33.54 N	107.46 E
Taibilla, Sierra de ⋀	34	38.10 N	2.10 W
Taibon Agordino	64	46.18 N	12.00 E
Taibus Qi (Baochang)	98	41.56 N	115.22 E
Taicang	106	31.26 N	121.07 E
T'aichou → Taizhou	100	32.30 N	119.58 E
T'aichung	100	24.09 N	120.41 E
Taichu → T'aichung	100	24.09 N	120.41 E
Taicunzhen	106	31.27 N	119.03 E
Taiden → Taejŏn	98	36.20 N	127.26 E
Taiei	94	35.49 N	140.25 E
Taieri ≃	172	46.03 S	170.11 E
Taif → Aṭ-Ṭā'if	144	21.16 N	40.24 E
Taigu	102	37.28 N	112.30 E
Tai Hang	271d	22.17 N	114.11 E
Taihang Shan ⋀	102	38.00 N	114.00 E
Taihape	172	39.40 S	175.48 E
Taihe, Zhg.	100	33.11 N	115.36 E
Taihe, Zhg.	100	26.49 N	114.55 E
Taihe, Zhg.	107	30.10 N	105.56 E
Taihezhen, Zhg.	89	44.47 N	123.29 E
Taihezhen, Zhg.	107	30.07 N	103.50 E
Taihezhen, Zhg.	107	30.06 N	106.03 E
Taiho	174m	26.39 N	128.07 E
Taihoku → T'aipei	100	25.03 N	121.30 E
T'aihsi	100	23.42 N	120.11 E
T'aihsien → Taizhou	100	32.30 N	119.58 E
Taihu	100	30.26 N	116.16 E
Tai Hu ⊜	106	31.15 N	120.10 E
Taijiang	102	26.32 N	108.22 E
Taijimiao	98	40.55 N	113.46 E
Taijüan → Taiyuan	102	37.55 N	112.30 E
Taikang	98	34.04 N	114.50 E
Taikkyi	110	17.19 N	95.58 E
Taikou	102	31.53 N	111.07 E
Taiko-yama ∧	96	35.46 N	135.12 E
Taikyu → Taegu	98	35.52 N	128.35 E
Tailai	89	46.23 N	123.27 E
Tai Lam Chung	271d	22.22 N	114.01 E
Tai Lam Chung Reservoir ⊜[1]	271d	22.23 N	114.01 E
Tailem Bend	166	35.16 S	139.27 E
Tailfingen	58	48.15 N	9.01 E
Tai Long, H.K.	271d	22.25 N	114.22 E
Tai Long, H.K.	271d	22.13 N	113.59 E
Tai Long Bay ⊂	271d	22.24 N	114.24 E
Taima, Nihon	96	34.30 N	135.42 E
T'aima, T'aiwan	100	22.37 N	120.59 E
Taimba	74	60.18 N	98.58 E
Taimei	100	23.19 N	114.29 E
Tai Mong Tsai	271d	22.24 N	114.18 E
Tai Mo Shan ∧	271d	22.25 N	114.07 E
Taimyr-Halbinsel → Tajmyr, poluostrov ›[1]	74	76.00 N	104.00 E
Tain	46	57.48 N	4.04 W
Tainaka	270	34.36 N	135.37 E
T'ainan	100	23.00 N	120.12 E
Taínaron, Ákra ›	38	36.22 N	22.30 E
Taining	100	26.54 N	117.09 E
Tain-l'Hermitage	62	45.04 N	4.51 E
Tai O, H.K.	100	22.15 N	113.51 E
Taio, It.	64	46.20 N	11.04 E
Taiobeiras	255	15.49 S	42.14 W
Tai Pang Wan ⊂	100	22.30 N	114.24 E
T'aipei, T'aiwan	100	25.03 N	121.30 E
T'aipei, T'aiwan	269d	25.03 N	121.30 E
T'aipei □[6]	269d	25.00 N	121.40 E
Taipei Bridge ✤[5]	269d	25.04 N	121.30 E
T'aipeihsien	100	25.00 N	121.27 E
Taipei Institute of Technology ⊍[2]	269d	25.02 N	121.32 E
Taipei New Park ⇡	269d	25.03 N	121.31 E
T'aipei Shih □[7]	269d	25.05 N	121.33 E
Taiping, Malay.	114	4.51 N	100.44 E
Taiping, Zhg.	100	22.49 N	113.41 E
Taiping, Zhg.	100	30.18 N	118.12 E
Taiping, Zhg.	102	22.40 N	107.05 E
Taiping, Zhg.	107	30.24 N	103.37 E
Taipingchang, Zhg.	102	27.25 N	103.04 E
Taipingchang, Zhg.	107	29.33 N	103.33 E
Taipingchang, Zhg.	107	29.53 N	106.04 E
Taipingchang, Zhg.	107	29.55 N	103.49 E
Taipingchang, Zhg.	107	30.10 N	106.21 E
Taipingchang, Zhg.	107	30.25 N	103.46 E
Taipingchang, Zhg.	107	30.39 N	105.54 E
Taipingchuan, Zhg.	89	44.23 N	123.11 E
Taipingchuan, Zhg.	98	42.36 N	127.20 E
Taipingdian	102	32.08 N	111.45 E
Taipingkou	100	29.50 N	113.35 E
Taipingling	89	43.26 N	128.09 E
Taipingshan, Zhg.	98	40.34 N	122.25 E
Taipingshan, Zhg.	104	41.36 N	123.41 E
Taipingshao	98	40.54 N	125.08 E
Taipingsi	107	29.24 N	103.34 E
Taipingxigou	104	42.36 N	121.13 E
Taipingzhai	104	42.14 N	124.07 E
Taipingzhen, Zhg.	89	46.44 N	130.44 E
Taipingzhen, Zhg.	102	35.42 N	107.37 E
Taipingzhen, Zhg.	107	29.24 N	105.47 E
Taipingzhen, Zhg.	107	30.26 N	104.12 E
Taipingzhuang, Zhg.	104	42.38 N	123.45 E
Taipingzhuang, Zhg.	105	40.03 N	116.24 E
Taipingzhuang, Zhg.	105	40.08 N	117.36 E
Tai Po Hoi ⊂	271d	22.26 N	114.12 E
Tai Po Tsai	271d	22.21 N	114.15 E
Taipu	250	5.37 S	35.36 W
Taira	94	36.26 N	136.57 E
Taira → Iwaki	94	37.03 N	140.55 E
Tairetá	256	22.36 S	43.42 W
Tairiqiao	106	30.59 N	121.33 E
Tais	112	4.06 S	102.34 E
Taisen-zan ∧	96	33.06 N	131.17 E
Taisha	96	35.24 N	132.40 E
Taisha → Izumo	96	35.22 N	132.46 E
Taishaku-kyō ⇡	96	34.53 N	133.13 E
Taishaku-zan ∧, Nihon	94	36.58 N	139.28 E
Taishaku-zan ∧, Nihon	270	34.47 N	135.07 E
Taishan, Zhg.	98	39.01 N	113.36 E
Taishan, Zhg.	102	22.16 N	112.44 E
Taishanchang	107	30.32 N	106.42 E
Taishi, Nihon	96	34.50 N	134.33 E
Taishi, Nihon	270	34.31 N	135.39 E
Taishō	96	33.12 N	132.58 E
Taishō ✤[8]	270	34.38 N	135.27 E
Tai Shui Hang	271d	22.25 N	14.13 E
Taishun	100	27.33 N	119.43 E
Tai Tam Bay ⊂	271d	22.13 N	114.13 E
Taitao, Peninsula de ›[1]	254	46.30 S	74.25 W
Taitapu	172	43.40 S	172.33 E
Taitō ✤[8]	268	35.43 N	139.47 E
Tai Tong	271d	22.25 N	114.01 E
Taitouying	98	40.02 N	119.12 E
Taitō-zaki ›	94	35.18 N	140.25 E
T'aitung	100	22.45 N	121.09 E
Taivalkoski	26	65.34 N	28.15 E
Tai Wan	271d	22.10 N	114.15 E
Taiwan (T'aiwan) □[1], Asia	90	23.30 N	121.00 E
Taiwan (T'aiwan) □[1], Asia	100	23.30 N	121.00 E
T'aiwan I	100	23.30 N	121.00 E
Taiwan Strait ⋓	100	24.00 N	119.00 E
Tai Wan Tau	271d	22.18 N	114.17 E
Taixi	100	24.42 N	116.56 E
Taixian	100	32.31 N	120.09 E
Taixing	106	32.11 N	120.01 E
Taixizhen	106	31.03 N	119.49 E
Taiyang	100	30.12 N	119.19 E
Taiyanggong	271a	39.58 N	116.25 E
Taíyetos Óros ⋀	38	37.16 N	22.12 E
Ṭaiyiba	132	32.16 N	35.01 E
Taiyuan	102	37.55 N	112.30 E
Taizhao	120	30.01 N	93.08 E
Taizhou	100	32.30 N	119.58 E
Taizhou Liedao II	100	28.30 N	121.53 E
Taizi ≃	98	41.00 N	122.26 E
Taʿizz	144	13.38 N	44.04 E
Tāj al-ʿIzz	142	30.57 N	31.35 E
Tajarḥī	146	24.21 N	14.28 E
Tajbola	24	68.26 N	33.19 E
Tajdakovo	82	54.29 N	37.32 E
Tajerouine	36	35.54 N	8.34 E
Tajetteret, Oued ∨	148	21.20 N	7.22 E
Tajga	86	56.04 N	85.37 E
Tajgonos, mys ›	74	60.35 N	160.08 E
Tajgonos, poluostrov ›[1]	74	61.20 N	161.00 E
Tajikistan □[1], Asia	72	39.00 N	71.00 E
Tajikistan □[1], Asia	85	39.00 N	71.00 E
Tajikstan → Tajikistan □[1]	72	39.00 N	71.00 E
Tajima	94	37.12 N	139.46 E
Tajimi	94	35.19 N	137.08 E
Tajique	200	34.45 N	106.17 W
Tajiri	270	34.24 N	135.18 E
Tajitos	232	30.58 N	112.18 W
Tajlakdžegen	86	43.54 N	60.29 E
Tajlakovy	86	59.20 N	74.04 E
Tāj Mahal ⊥	124	27.10 N	78.03 E
Tajmura ≃	72	63.46 N	98.01 E
Tajmyr, ozero ⊜	74	74.30 N	102.30 E
Tajmyr, poluostrov ›[1]	74	76.00 N	104.00 E
Tajna	88	56.27 N	95.30 E
Tajninka	265b	55.54 N	37.45 E
Tajo → Tagus ≃	34	38.40 N	9.24 W
Tajožnyj, Ross.	86	56.09 N	94.29 E
Tajožnyj, Ross.	88	56.13 N	94.55 E
Tajpur, India	124	25.51 N	85.41 E
Tajpur, India	124	29.10 N	78.29 E
Tājpur, India	272b	22.44 N	88.16 E
Tajpur Khurd ✤[8]	272a	28.35 N	77.03 E
Tajšet	88	55.57 N	98.00 E
Tajsojgan	80	48.19 N	53.29 E
Tajturka	88	52.51 N	103.28 E
Tajumulco, Volcán ∧[1]	236	15.02 N	91.55 W
Tajuña ≃	34	40.07 N	3.35 W
Tājūrā', Lībiyā	146	32.53 N	13.21 E
Tajura, Ross.	88	57.00 N	106.35 E
Tajura ≃	88	57.00 N	106.35 E
Tajžina	86	53.38 N	87.28 E
Tak	110	16.52 N	99.08 E
Takāb	128	36.24 N	47.07 E
Takabanare-jima I	174m	26.22 N	127.59 E
Takabara	150	11.50 N	11.30 W
Takachiho	92	32.42 N	131.18 E
Takachu	156	22.37 S	21.58 E
Takada → Bungo-takada	96	33.33 N	131.27 E
Takada → Yamato-takada	96	34.31 N	135.45 E
Takagi	268	35.56 N	139.35 E
Takahagi	94	36.43 N	140.43 E
Takahama, Nihon	94	34.55 N	136.59 E
Takahama, Nihon	94	37.00 N	136.46 E
Takahama, Nihon	96	35.29 N	135.33 E
Takahara ≃	94	36.28 N	137.15 E
Takahashi	96	34.47 N	133.37 E
Takahashi ≃	96	34.31 N	133.42 E
Takahe, Mount ∧	9	76.16 S	112.14 W
Takaido ✤[8]	268	35.40 N	139.37 E
Takaishi	96	34.32 N	135.26 E
Takaka	172	40.51 S	172.48 E
Takakkaw Falls ∟	182	51.30 N	116.28 W
Takalaou	146	10.07 N	19.48 E
Takalar	112	5.28 S	119.24 E
Takamatsu, Nihon	94	36.46 N	136.43 E
Takamatsu, Nihon	96	34.20 N	134.03 E
Takami-shima I	96	34.19 N	133.41 E
Takamiya	96	34.47 N	132.44 E
Takami-yama ∧	94	34.25 N	136.05 E
Takamori	94	35.33 N	137.53 E
Takanabe	92	32.08 N	131.30 E
Takanawa-hantō ›[1]	96	33.58 N	132.56 E
Takanawa-san ∧	96	33.56 N	132.51 E
Takane, Nihon	94	36.02 N	137.29 E
Takane, Nihon	94	35.50 N	138.25 E
Takanezawa	94	36.37 N	139.59 E
Takano	96	35.02 N	132.55 E
Takanosu	92	40.13 N	140.22 E
Takaoka	94	36.45 N	137.01 E
Takao → Kaohsiung	100	22.38 N	120.17 E
Takao-kokutei-kōen ⇡	94	35.38 N	139.15 E
Takao-san ∧, Nihon	94	35.38 N	139.15 E
Takao-san ∧, Nihon	270	34.49 N	135.51 E
Takapau	172	40.02 S	176.21 E
Takapuna	172	36.47 S	174.47 E
Takara-jima I	93b	29.09 N	129.13 E
Takarazuka	270	34.49 N	135.21 E
Takasago	96	34.45 N	134.48 E
Takasaki	94	36.20 N	139.01 E
Takase	96	34.10 N	133.45 E
Takase ≃	94	36.28 N	137.52 E
Takashima, Nihon	92	32.39 N	129.45 E
Takashima, Nihon	94	35.18 N	136.01 E
Taka-shima I	96	34.50 N	131.50 E
Takashippu	174m	26.24 N	127.44 E
Takasu	94	35.57 N	136.53 E
Takata	96	33.06 N	130.28 E
Takata → Joetsu	94	37.06 N	138.15 E
Takata → Rikuzen-takata	92	39.01 N	141.38 E
Takatō	94	35.50 N	138.04 E
Takatomi	94	35.29 N	136.47 E
Takatori	96	34.27 N	135.48 E
Takatori-yama ∧	96	33.18 N	130.43 E
Takatori-yama ∧[2]	268	35.18 N	139.37 E
Takatsu ≃	96	34.42 N	131.49 E
Takatsuki, Nihon	94	35.28 N	136.14 E
Takatsuki, Nihon	96	34.51 N	135.37 E
Takaungu	154	3.41 S	39.51 E
Ta-kaw	110	21.36 N	98.56 E
Takayama, Nihon	94	36.08 N	137.15 E
Takayama, Nihon	94	36.37 N	138.57 E
Takayama, Nihon	94	36.40 N	138.21 E
Takayama, Nihon	270	34.45 N	135.44 E
Takayanagi, Nihon	94	37.13 N	138.38 E
Takayanagi, Nihon	268	35.25 N	139.57 E
Tak Bai	114	6.16 N	102.03 E
Takčijan	85	38.32 N	68.03 E
Takebe	96	34.52 N	133.54 E
Takefu	94	35.54 N	136.10 E
Takehara	96	34.21 N	132.55 E
Takeli	85	40.30 N	69.25 E
Takenake	120	34.11 N	81.20 E
Takengon	114	4.38 N	96.50 E
Takeno ≃	96	35.45 N	135.06 E
Takenotsuka ✤[8]	268	35.48 N	139.48 E
Takeo	92	33.12 N	130.01 E
Takeoka	268	35.12 N	139.51 E
Tåkern ⊜	26	58.21 N	14.48 E
Takeshi	94	36.17 N	138.14 E
Take-shima I	93b	30.49 N	130.26 E
Take-shima (Tok-to) II	92	37.17 N	131.53 E
Tākestān	128	36.04 N	49.43 E
Taketa	96	32.58 N	131.24 E
Taketoyo	94	34.51 N	136.55 E
Takêv	110	10.59 N	104.47 E
Take-yama ∧[2]	268	35.13 N	139.39 E
Takhādīd ⊤[4]	128	29.59 N	44.30 E
Takhār □[4]	120	36.30 N	69.30 E
Takhatpur	124	22.09 N	81.52 E
Takhli	110	15.15 N	100.21 E
Ta Khoa	110	21.13 N	104.18 E
Takht-e Jamshīd ⊥	128	29.57 N	52.52 E
Takht-i-Bhāi	123	34.17 N	71.56 E
Tāki, India	126	22.36 N	88.55 E
Taki, Nihon	94	34.30 N	136.33 E
Taki, Nihon	96	35.16 N	132.38 E
Taki, Pap. N. Gui.	175e	6.29 S	155.50 E
Takijuk Lake ⊜	176	66.15 N	113.05 W
Takikawa	92a	43.33 N	141.54 E
Takino	96	34.56 N	134.58 E
Takipur	126	24.19 N	87.58 E
Takitimu Mountains ⋀	172	45.41 S	167.53 E
Takla Lake ⊜	182	55.25 N	125.53 W
Takla Landing	182	55.29 N	125.58 W
Takla Makan → Taklimakan Shamo ✤[2]	90	39.00 N	83.00 E
Taklimakan Shamo ✤[2]	90	39.00 N	83.00 E
Tako	94	35.44 N	140.28 E
Takob	85	38.50 N	68.57 E
Tako-bana ›	96	35.36 N	133.06 E
Takolekaju, Pegunungan ⋀	112	2.00 S	121.00 E
Takoma Park	284c	38.58 N	77.00 W
Takoradi → Sekondi-Takoradi	150	4.59 N	1.43 W
Takotna	180	62.56 N	156.04 W
Takow → Kaohsiung	100	22.38 N	120.17 E
Takpochao, Okso ∧	174n	15.11 N	145.45 E
Takrouna	36	36.09 N	10.20 E
Taksimo	88	51.03 N	107.50 E
Taksino	82	56.19 N	36.10 E
Takslesluk Lake ⊜	180	61.04 N	162.55 W
Taksony	264c	47.20 N	19.04 E
Taku	92	33.17 N	130.08 E
Taku ≃	180	58.26 N	133.59 W
Takuan, Mount ∧	175e	6.27 S	155.36 E
Takua Pa	110	8.53 N	98.21 E
Taku Glacier ⍓	180	58.35 N	134.10 W
Takum	150	7.17 N	9.59 E
Takuma	96	34.13 N	133.40 E
Takundi	152	4.45 S	16.34 E
Takutea I	14	19.49 S	158.18 W
Takut Tangub Bay ⊂	116	6.33 N	122.15 E
Takutu (Tacutu) ≃	246	3.01 N	60.29 W
Takuu Islands II	14	4.45 S	157.00 E
Takysie Lake	182	53.54 N	125.53 W
Tāl	123	34.55 N	72.13 E
Tala, Bngl.	126	22.46 N	89.16 E
Tāla, India	124	23.43 N	81.02 E
Tala, Méx.	234	20.40 N	103.42 W
Talā, Mișr	142	30.41 N	30.56 E
Tala, Ur.	252	34.21 S	55.46 W
Tala, Arroyo del ≃	258	33.37 S	56.34 W
Ṭālāb (Tāhlāb) ≃	128	28.09 N	62.45 E
Talacogon	116	8.28 N	125.46 E
Talaga	112	2.11 S	125.53 E
Talagang	123	32.55 N	72.25 E
Talagante	252	33.40 S	70.56 W
Talagou	104	41.37 N	120.32 E
Ta Lai	110	11.24 N	107.23 E
Talaimannar	122	9.05 N	79.44 E
Talāja	120	21.21 N	72.03 E
Talak ✤[1]	150	18.20 N	6.00 E
Talakag	116	8.16 N	124.37 E
Talakan	89	49.38 N	133.18 E
Talakovka	83	47.10 N	37.43 E
Tālāla	120	21.02 N	70.32 E
Talalajevka	78	50.51 N	33.08 E
Talamanca, Cordillera de ⋀	236	9.30 N	83.40 W
Talamba	123	30.32 N	72.14 E
Talamone	66	42.33 N	11.08 E
Talana, It.	71	40.02 N	9.30 E
Talana, S. Afr.	158	28.10 S	30.15 E
Talandža	89	49.27 N	131.35 E
Talang, Gunung ∧	112	0.58 S	100.39 E
Talangbatu	112	4.06 S	105.29 E
Talangbetutu	112	2.53 S	104.41 E
Talangpadang	112	5.21 S	104.11 E
Talangrimbo	112	3.29 S	105.25 E
Talant	58	47.19 N	5.00 E
Talap	80	48.26 N	48.03 E

≃	River	Fluß	Río	Rivière	Rio
≅	Canal	Kanal	Canal	Canal	Canal
∟	Waterfall, Rapids	Wasserfall, Stromschnellen	Cascada, Rápidos	Chute d'eau, Rapides	Cascata, Rápidos
⋓	Strait	Meeresstraße	Estrecho	Détroit	Estreito
⊂	Bay, Gulf	Bucht, Golf	Bahía, Golfo	Baie, Golfe	Baía, Golfo
⊜	Lake, Lakes	See, Seen	Lago, Lagos	Lac, Lacs	Lago, Lagos
≡	Swamp	Sumpf	Pantano	Marais	Pântano
⍓	Ice Features, Glacier	Eis- und Gletscherformen	Accidentes Glaciales	Formes glaciaires	Acidentes glaciares
⊤	Other Hydrographic Features	Andere Hydrographische Objekte	Otros Elementos Hidrográficos	Autres données hydrographiques	Outros acidentes hidrográficos
❖	Submarine Features	Untermeerische Objekte	Accidentes Submarinos	Formes de relief sous-marin	Acidentes submarinos
□	Political Unit	Politische Einheit	Unidad Politica	Entité politique	Unidade política
⊍	Cultural Institution	Kulturelle Institution	Institución Cultural	Institution culturelle	Institução cultural
⊥	Historical Site	Historische Stätte	Sitio Histórico	Site historique	Sitio histórico
⇡	Recreational Site	Erholungs- und Ferienort	Sitio de Recreo	Centre de loisirs	Area de Lazer
⊠	Airport	Flughafen	Aeropuerto	Aéroport	Aeroporto
■	Military Installation	Militäranlage	Instalación Militar	Installation militaire	Instalação militar
✤	Miscellaneous	Verschiedenes	Misceláneo	Divers	Diversos

ESPAÑOL Nombre / FRANÇAIS Nom / PORTUGUÊS Nome	Página / Page	Lat.°′	Long.°′ W = Oeste / W = Ouest
Uč-Adži	128	38.05 N	62.48 E
Učaly	86	54.19 N	59.27 E
Učami	74	63.50 N	96.29 E
Učaral	86	46.10 N	80.56 E
Ucayali □[5]	248	9.00 S	74.00 W
Ucayali ≐	242	4.30 S	73.27 W
Uccellina, Monti dell' ⋏	66	42.38 N	11.05 E
Uccle	50	50.48 N	4.19 E
Uch	123	29.14 N	71.03 E
Uchab	156	19.47 S	17.42 E
Uchāna	124	29.28 N	76.10 E
Uchaud	62	43.45 N	4.16 E
Uchee Creek ≐	192	32.18 N	84.57 W
Uchihara	94	36.22 N	140.21 E
Uchihata	270	34.25 N	135.27 E
Uchiko	96	33.33 N	132.39 E
Uchi Lake	184	51.05 N	92.35 W
Uchinada	94	36.39 N	136.39 E
Uchinomi	96	34.30 N	134.20 E
Uchinoura	92	31.16 N	131.05 E
Uchiumi	96	33.01 N	132.30 E
Uchiura-wan ⊂	92a	42.20 N	140.40 E
Uchiza	248	8.29 S	76.23 W
Uchoa	255	20.56 S	49.13 W
Ucholovo	80	53.47 N	40.29 E
Uchra ≐	80	58.20 N	39.00 E
Uchta, Ross.	24	61.12 N	38.32 E
Uchta, Ross.	24	63.33 N	53.38 E
Uchte	52	52.30 N	8.54 E
Uchte ≐	54	52.46 N	11.45 E
Uchtoma	76	60.10 N	38.02 E
Uchtspringe	54	52.32 N	11.36 E
Učinskij Ryboučastok	86	60.02 N	65.10 E
Učinskoje vodochranilišče ⊜[1]	82	56.02 N	37.45 E
Uckange	56	49.18 N	6.09 E
Ückendorf ◆[8]	263	51.30 N	7.07 E
Uckermark ◆[1]	54	53.10 N	13.35 E
Uckfield	42	50.58 N	0.06 E
Üçköşe	130	40.13 N	41.00 E
Uckro	54	51.51 N	13.37 E
Učkupr'uk	85	40.33 N	71.04 E
Učkurgan	85	41.07 N	72.05 E
Ucluelet	182	48.57 N	125.33 W
Ucon	202	43.35 N	111.57 W
Üçpınar	130	37.08 N	32.16 E
Ucria	70	38.03 N	14.53 E
Üçtepeler ∧	130	39.39 N	42.41 E
Účterek	85	41.45 N	73.12 E
Úcua ≐	152	8.35 S	13.40 E
Učujevskij Majdan	80	54.33 N	44.30 E
Učur ≐	74	58.48 N	130.35 E
Uda ≐, Ross.	88	56.05 N	99.34 E
Uda ≐, Ross.	88	51.47 N	107.33 E
Uda ≐, Ross.	89	54.42 N	135.14 E
Udagamandalam	122	11.24 N	76.42 E
Udaipur	120	24.35 N	73.41 E
Udaj ≐	78	50.05 N	33.07 E
Udala	126	21.35 N	86.34 E
Udalguri	120	26.46 N	92.08 E
Udall	198	37.23 N	97.06 W
Udamalpet	122	10.35 N	77.15 E
Udankudi	122	8.26 N	78.01 E
Udaquiola	252	36.34 S	58.31 W
Udarnyj	89	49.07 N	142.09 E
Udaypur	124	26.56 N	86.31 E
Udbina	36	44.32 N	15.46 E
Udby	41	55.05 N	11.57 E
Uddeholm	40	60.01 N	13.37 E
Uddel	52	52.15 N	5.46 E
Uddevalla	26	58.21 N	11.55 E
Uddingston	46	55.50 N	4.06 W
Uddjaure ⊜	24	65.55 N	17.49 E
Udel'naja	82	55.38 N	38.03 E
Udel'naja ◆[8]	265a	60.01 N	30.19 E
Uden	52	51.40 N	5.36 E
Udenhout	52	51.37 N	5.08 E
Uder	56	51.22 N	10.05 E
Üdersdorf	56	50.09 N	6.49 E
Udgīr	122	18.23 N	77.07 E
Udhampur	123	32.56 N	75.08 E
Udhruḥ	132	30.20 N	35.36 E
Udi	150	6.19 N	7.25 E
Udimskij	24	61.09 N	45.52 E
Udine	64	46.03 N	13.14 E
Udine □[4]	64	46.10 N	13.00 E
Udmurtskaja Avtonomnaja Sovetskaja Socialističeskaja Respublika □[3]	80	57.00 N	53.00 E
Udokan, chrebet ⋏	88	56.20 N	118.10 E
Udoml'a	76	57.52 N	35.01 E
Udone-jima I	94	34.28 N	139.18 E
Udono	92	33.44 N	136.01 E
Udon Thani	110	17.26 N	102.46 E
Udor, Mount ∧	162	23.30 S	131.01 E
Udot I	175c	7.23 N	151.43 E
Udskaja guba ⊂	89	54.50 N	135.45 E
Udskoje	89	54.32 N	134.26 E
Udubo	146	11.57 N	10.38 E
Udupi	122	13.21 N	74.45 E
Udy	78	50.24 N	36.03 E
Udyl', ozero ⊜	89	52.06 N	139.48 E
Udža	74	71.14 N	117.10 E
Udžary	84	40.31 N	47.39 E
Uebigau	54	51.35 N	13.18 E
Uebonti	112	0.55 S	121.38 E
Uebonti, Teluk ⊂	112	0.50 S	121.45 E
Uecker ≐	54	53.45 N	14.04 E
Ueckeritz	54	54.00 N	14.02 E
Ueckermünde	54	53.44 N	14.03 E
Ueckermünder Heide ◆[3]	54	53.40 N	14.10 E
Ueda	94	36.24 N	138.16 E
Uedem	52	51.40 N	6.16 E
Uedesheim	263	51.10 N	6.48 E
Uegō	268	35.13 N	139.56 E
Ueharu	175d	24.25 N	123.46 E
Uehlfeld	56	49.40 N	10.43 E
Uele ≐	136	4.09 N	22.26 E
Uelen	180	66.10 N	169.48 W
Uel'kal'	180	65.32 N	179.17 W
Uelsen	52	52.30 N	6.53 E
Uelzen, Dtsch.	52	52.58 N	10.33 E
Uelzen, Dtsch.	263	51.33 N	7.44 E
Ueno, Nihon	94	36.05 N	138.47 E
Ueno, Nihon	94	34.45 N	136.08 E
Ueno, Nihon	270	34.53 N	135.14 E
Uenohara	94	35.37 N	139.07 E
Ueno Park ♠	268	35.43 N	139.46 E
Uenoshiba	270	34.33 N	135.28 E
Uerdingen ◆[8]	263	51.21 N	6.39 E
Uere ≐	154	3.42 N	25.24 E
Uetersen	52	53.41 N	9.39 E
Uettingen	56	49.48 N	9.43 E
Uetz	264a	52.28 N	12.56 E
Uetze	52	52.28 N	10.11 E
Ufa	86	54.44 N	55.56 E
Ufa ≐	86	54.40 N	56.00 E
Ufala, Punta ≻	70	38.22 N	14.59 E
Uffculme	42	50.54 N	3.20 W
Uffenheim	56	49.32 N	10.14 E
Ufita ≐	68	41.09 N	14.56 E
Ufra	128	40.00 N	53.02 E
Uft'uga ≐	76	59.46 N	39.21 E
Ugab ≐	156	21.08 S	13.40 E
Ugak Bay ⊂	180	57.25 N	152.45 W
Ugāle	76	57.16 N	22.02 E
Ugalla ≐	154	5.08 S	30.42 E
Ugamskij chrebet ⋏	85	42.00 N	70.20 E
Uganda □[1]	154	1.00 N	32.00 E
Uganik Island I	180	57.53 N	153.28 W
Ugârčin	38	43.06 N	24.25 E
Ugarit ⊥	130	35.35 N	35.45 E
Ugashik	180	57.32 N	157.25 W
Ugashik Bay ⊂	180	57.34 N	157.38 W
Ugatkyn ≐	180	68.24 N	171.30 E
Ugento	68	39.56 N	18.10 E
Ugep	150	5.48 N	8.05 E
Ugerløse	41	55.35 N	11.40 E
Uggiano la Chiesa	68	40.06 N	18.27 E
Ughaybish	140	10.52 N	31.05 E
Ughelli	150	5.29 N	5.59 E
Ugie	158	31.10 S	28.13 E
Ugie ≐	46	57.30 N	1.47 W
Ugíjar	34	36.57 N	3.03 W
Ugine	62	45.45 N	6.25 E
Uglegorsk, Ross.	89	49.02 N	142.03 E
Uglegorsk, Ukr.	83	48.19 N	38.17 E
Uglekamensk	89	43.13 N	133.11 E
Uglezavodsk	89	47.21 N	142.38 E
Uglič	76	57.32 N	38.19 E
Ugljan, Otok I	36	44.05 N	15.10 E
Uglovaja	80	57.01 N	52.57 E
Uglovka	76	58.14 N	33.31 E
Uglovoje	89	43.20 N	132.06 E
Uglovskoje	86	51.23 N	80.12 E
Ugly-Zavod	78	52.11 N	32.53 E
Ugnev	78	50.23 N	23.44 E
Ugodiči	80	57.10 N	39.30 E
Ugodskij Zavod	82	55.02 N	36.45 E
Ugol'naja, buchta ⊂	180	63.00 N	179.20 E
Ugolnyy	180	62.58 N	179.17 E
Ugoma ∧	154	4.00 S	28.45 E
Ugovizza	64	46.31 N	13.29 E
Ugra	76	54.47 N	34.17 E
Ugra ≐	82	54.30 N	36.07 E
Ugrojedy	78	50.52 N	35.17 E
Ugr'umovo	82	55.09 N	37.40 E
Ugtaal Cajdam	88	48.17 N	105.25 E
Uguj	86	56.02 N	76.03 E
Uğurludağ	130	40.27 N	34.28 E
Ug'ut	85	41.24 N	74.50 E
Ugyak, Cape ≻	180	58.17 N	154.04 W
Uh (Už) ≐	30	48.34 N	22.00 E
Uha-dong	98	40.41 N	125.38 E
Uḥayjibah, Jabal al- ∧	132	30.11 N	34.33 E
Uherčice	61	48.55 N	15.38 E
Uherské Hradiště	30	49.05 N	17.28 E
Uherský Brod	30	49.02 N	17.39 E
Uhingen	56	48.42 N	9.35 E
Úhlava ≐	60	49.43 N	13.23 E
Uhlenhorst	156	23.45 S	17.55 E
Ühlingen	58	47.43 N	8.19 E
Uhlman Lake ⊜	184	56.40 N	98.23 W
Uhlstädt	54	50.44 N	11.28 E
Uhrichsville	214	40.23 N	81.20 W
Uhyst, Dtsch.	54	51.11 N	14.13 E
Uhyst, Dtsch.	54	51.24 N	14.30 E
Uiche	152	12.03 S	21.02 E
Ui-do I	98	34.37 N	125.51 E
Uig	46	57.35 N	6.22 W
Uíge	152	7.37 S	15.03 E
Uíge □[5]	152	7.00 S	15.30 E
Ŭijŏngbu	98	37.44 N	127.03 E
Ŭiju	98	40.12 N	124.32 E
Uil	86	49.05 N	54.40 E
Uil ≐	80	48.36 N	52.30 E
Uilpata, gora ∧	84	42.48 N	43.48 E
Uimaharju	26	62.55 N	30.15 E
Uinebona ≐	246	5.04 N	63.01 W
Uinskoje	86	56.53 N	56.35 E
Uinta ≐	200	40.14 N	109.51 W
Uintah and Ouray Indian Reservation ◆[4]	200	40.20 N	110.20 W
Uinta Mountains ⋏	200	40.45 N	110.05 W
Uiraúna	250	6.31 S	38.25 W
Uis	156	21.08 S	14.49 E
Ŭisŏng	98	36.22 N	128.41 E
Uitenhage	158	33.40 S	25.28 E
Uitgeest	52	52.32 N	4.43 E
Uithoorn	52	52.14 N	4.50 E
Uithuizen	52	53.24 N	6.40 E
Uithuizermeeden	52	53.24 N	6.42 E
Uitspanning	158	26.46 S	29.56 E
Uj ≐, Asia	86	54.17 N	64.58 E
Uj ≐, Ross.	86	57.06 N	74.12 E
Ujae I[1]	14	9.05 N	165.40 E
Ujaly	86	44.37 N	60.57 E
Ujandina ≐	74	68.23 N	145.50 E
Ujar	86	55.48 N	94.20 E
Ujarrás ⊥	236	9.51 N	83.50 W
Ujedinenija, ostrov I	72	77.28 N	82.28 E
Ujelang I[1]	14	9.49 N	160.55 E
Ujemskij	24	64.29 N	40.50 E
Újezd, Česko.	54	50.03 N	14.44 E
Ujęzd, Česko.	60	49.26 N	13.27 E
Újezd u Brna	61	49.06 N	16.45 E
Újfehértó	30	47.48 N	21.40 E
Ujgursaj	85	40.53 N	71.03 E
Ujhāni	124	28.01 N	79.01 E
Uji	96	34.53 N	135.48 E
Uji ≐	96	34.53 N	135.42 E
Uji-guntō II	92	31.11 N	129.27 E
Ujiie	94	36.41 N	139.58 E
Ujiji	154	4.55 S	29.41 E
Uji-tawara	96	34.51 N	135.52 E
Uji-yamada → Ise	94	34.29 N	136.42 E
Ujjain	120	23.11 N	75.46 E
Újkér	61	47.28 N	16.49 E
ʻUjmān	128	25.25 N	55.27 E
Újpest ◆[8]	264c	47.34 N	19.06 E
Ujście	30	53.04 N	16.43 E
Ujskoje	86	54.22 N	60.00 E
Ujum	85	38.22 N	70.51 E
Ujung	112	7.04 S	120.46 E
Ujungbatu	114	0.43 N	100.31 E
Ujungbatu, Pulau I	114	2.20 N	97.24 E
Ujungberung	115a	6.55 S	107.42 E
Ujunggading	110	0.16 N	99.33 E
Ujunggenteng	115a	7.22 S	106.24 E
Ujungkulon, Semenanjung ≻[1]	115a	6.45 S	105.20 E
Ujungkulon National Park ♠	115a	6.40 S	105.20 E
Ujunglamuru	112	4.40 S	119.58 E
Ujungpandang (Makasar)	112	5.07 S	119.24 E
Újvidék → Novi Sad	38	45.15 N	19.50 E
Uk	88	55.04 N	98.52 E
Uka, Nihon	174m	26.48 N	128.14 E
Uka, Ross.	74	57.50 N	162.06 E
Ukamas	158	28.02 S	19.45 E
Ukara Island I	154	1.50 S	33.03 E
Ukerewe Island I	154	2.03 S	33.00 E
Ukhaydir, Wādī ∨	132	30.55 N	37.01 E
Ukhra	126	23.39 N	87.14 E
Ukhrul	120	25.07 N	94.22 E
Ukhta → Uchta	24	63.33 N	53.38 E
Ukiah, Ca., U.S.	204	39.09 N	123.12 W
Ukiah, Or., U.S.	202	45.08 N	118.55 W
Ukibaru-jima I	174m	26.18 N	128.00 E
Ukiha	96	33.19 N	130.47 E
Uki Ni Masi Island I	175e	10.15 S	161.45 E
Ukmergė	76	55.15 N	24.45 E
Ukolnoi Island I	180	55.14 N	161.34 W
Ukraina → Ukraine □[1]	22	49.00 N	32.00 E
Ukraine □[1], Europe	22	49.00 N	32.00 E
Ukraine □[1], Europe	78	49.00 N	32.00 E
Ukrainka	86	54.39 N	71.20 E
Ukrainsk	83	48.06 N	37.18 E
Ukrina ≐	36	45.05 N	17.56 E
Uks'anskoje	86	55.57 N	63.01 E
Uktuz	86	55.38 N	68.30 E
Uktym	24	62.38 N	48.52 E
Uku	152	11.24 S	14.15 E
Ukui	112	0.09 S	102.11 E
Ukurejskij	88	52.24 N	116.49 E
Ukuti	154	3.39 N	33.32 E
Ukyō ◆[8]	270	35.03 N	135.42 E
Ukyr	88	49.28 N	108.52 E
Ula, India	272b	22.43 N	88.33 E
Ula, Tür.	130	37.05 N	28.26 E
Ulaanbaatar	88	47.55 N	106.53 E
Ulaanbaatar □[8]	88	47.55 N	106.53 E
Ulaanbadrach	102	44.07 N	110.11 E
Ulaan Chus	86	49.02 N	89.23 E
Ulaangom	86	49.58 N	92.02 E
Ulaan nuur ⊜	102	44.30 N	103.35 E
Ulaan Tajga ⋏	88	50.45 N	98.30 E
Ula-Chuduk	80	47.39 N	45.34 E
Ulak Island I	181a	51.22 N	179.00 W
Ulakmedan	114	2.43 N	99.38 E
Ulamba	152	9.07 S	23.40 E
Ulamona	164	5.00 S	151.15 E
Ulan, Austl.	166	32.17 S	149.44 E
Ulan, Zhg.	102	36.59 N	98.26 E
Ulan Bator → Ulaanbaatar	88	47.55 N	106.53 E
Ulanbel'	86	44.48 N	71.10 E
Ulan Buh Shamo ◆[2]	102	40.00 N	106.30 E
Ulan-Burgasy, chrebet ⋏	88	52.45 N	109.00 E
Ulan-Erge	80	46.19 N	44.53 E
Ulang ≐	236	14.27 N	83.14 W
Ulanhot → Horqin Youyi Qianqi	89	46.05 N	122.05 E
Ulānia	126	22.12 N	90.29 E
Ulanov	78	49.42 N	28.08 E
Ulanovo	78	51.46 N	34.18 E
Ulanovskij	82	54.04 N	37.51 E
Ulanów	30	50.30 N	22.16 E
Ulansuhai Nur ⊜	102	40.56 N	108.49 E
Ulan-Ude	88	51.50 N	107.37 E
Ulan Ul Hu ⊜	120	34.45 N	90.25 E
Ulan-Ušotej	88	50.45 N	105.29 E
Ular, Pulau I	271c	1.14 N	103.45 E
Ulaş	130	39.27 N	37.03 E
Ul'ašovo	24	65.27 N	56.57 E
Ulatis Creek ≐	226	38.18 N	121.00 W
Ul'atuj	88	51.09 N	116.14 E
Ulawa Island I	175e	9.46 S	161.57 E
Ulawun, Mount ∧	164	5.03 S	151.20 E
Ulaya	154	7.04 S	36.54 E
Ułazów	30	50.17 N	23.00 E
Ul'ba	86	50.16 N	83.22 E
Ul'banskij zaliv ⊂	89	53.45 N	137.50 E
Ulchin	98	36.59 N	129.23 E
Ul'chun-Partija	88	49.56 N	112.46 E
Ulcinj	38	41.55 N	19.11 E
Ulco	158	28.21 S	24.15 E
Ulcombe	260	51.12 N	0.39 E
Ulcumayo	248	11.01 S	75.55 W
Uldum	41	55.51 N	9.36 E
Uldz ≐	88	49.56 N	115.31 E
Uleåborg → Oulu	26	65.01 N	25.28 E
Ulefoss	26	59.17 N	9.16 E
Ulen	198	47.04 N	96.15 W
Ulety	88	51.22 N	112.29 E
Ulfborg	26	56.16 N	8.20 E
Ulft	52	51.54 N	6.23 E
Ulgajsyn	86	49.38 N	60.17 E
Ulgueira	266c	38.47 N	9.28 W
Ulhās ≐	272c	19.13 N	73.01 E
Ulhāsnagar	122	19.13 N	73.07 E
Uliast	86	48.57 N	91.17 E
Uliastaj (Džavchlant)	88	47.45 N	96.49 E
Úlice	60	49.45 N	13.09 E
Ulindi ≐	154	1.40 S	25.52 E
Ulingan	164	4.30 S	145.25 E
Ulithi I[1]	108	9.58 N	139.40 E
Ulja	74	58.51 N	141.50 E
Uljanino	82	55.21 N	38.26 E
Uljanovka, Ross.	76	59.38 N	30.46 E
Uljanovka, Ukr.	78	48.20 N	30.13 E
Uljanovka, Ukr.	78	50.58 N	34.18 E
Uljanovo, Ross.	76	53.43 N	35.32 E
Uljanovo, Uzb.	85	40.07 N	68.30 E
Uljanovsk	80	54.20 N	48.24 E
Uljanovskoje, Kaz.	86	50.02 N	73.42 E
Uljanovskoje, Ross.	89	46.17 N	142.13 E
Uljuan tekojärvi ⊜	26	64.19 N	25.57 E
Ul'kajak ≐	86	48.54 N	62.00 E
Ul'kan	88	57.14 N	107.19 E
Ul'kan ≐	88	55.53 N	107.45 E
Ul'ken-Karoj, ozero ⊜	86	54.00 N	71.58 E
Ulla	76	55.14 N	29.15 E
Ulla ≐, Bela.	76	55.14 N	29.14 E
Ulla ≐, Esp.	34	42.39 N	8.44 W
Ulladulla	170	35.21 S	150.29 E
Ulladulla Head ≻	170	35.22 S	150.30 E
Ullāpāra	126	24.19 N	89.34 E
Ullapool	46	57.54 N	5.10 W
Ullastrell	266d	41.31 N	1.58 E
Üllendahl ◆[8]	263	51.19 N	7.18 E
Ullerslev	41	55.22 N	10.40 E
Ullervad	40	58.40 N	13.52 E
Ullin	194	37.17 N	89.11 W
Üllő	264c	47.23 N	19.21 E
Ullswater ⊜	44	54.34 N	2.54 W
Ullučaj ≐	84	42.18 N	48.08 E
Ullŭng-do I	92	37.29 N	130.52 E
Ullvettern ⊜	40	59.27 N	14.16 E
Ullvi	40	59.42 N	16.37 E
Ulm, Dtsch.	58	48.24 N	10.00 E
Ulm, Mt., U.S.	202	47.25 N	111.30 W
Ulma	38	47.53 N	25.18 E
Ul'ma ≐	89	51.54 N	129.18 E
Ulmarra	166	29.37 S	153.02 E
Ulmen	56	50.13 N	6.59 E
Ulmeni	38	45.04 N	26.39 E
Ulmer, Mount ∧	9	77.35 S	86.09 W
Ulmeu-Meisereich	56	50.13 N	6.58 E
Ulongué	154	14.37 S	34.19 E
Ulpur	126	23.04 N	89.50 E
Ulricehamn	26	57.47 N	13.25 E
Ulrichskirchen	61	48.24 N	16.29 E
Ulrichstein	56	50.34 N	9.11 E
Ulrum	52	53.22 N	6.20 E
Ulsan	98	35.34 N	129.19 E
Ulsta	46a	60.30 N	1.09 W
Ulsteinvik	26	62.20 N	5.53 E
Ulster	210	41.51 N	76.30 W
Ulster □[6]	210	41.56 N	74.00 W
Ulster □[9]	48	54.35 N	7.00 W
Ulster ≐	56	50.51 N	9.59 E
Ulster Canal ≍	48	54.08 N	7.22 W
Ultimo, Val d' ∨	64	46.35 N	11.00 E
Ultraoriental, Cordillera (Serra do Divisor) ⋏	248	8.20 S	73.30 W
Ulu, Indon.	112	2.45 N	125.24 E
Ulu, Ross.	74	60.19 N	127.24 E
Ulu, Süd.	140	10.43 N	33.29 E
Ulúa ≐	236	15.53 N	87.44 W
Ulubāria	126	22.28 N	88.06 E
Ulubat Gölü ⊜	130	40.10 N	28.35 E
Ulubey, Tür.	130	38.25 N	29.18 E
Ulubey, Tür.	130	40.53 N	37.43 E
Uluborlu	130	38.05 N	30.28 E
Uluçınar	130	36.27 N	35.51 E
Uludağ ∧	130	40.04 N	29.13 E
Uludāngar	272b	22.51 N	88.31 E
Uludere	128	37.27 N	42.51 E
Ulugan Bay ⊂	116	10.07 N	118.47 E
Ulugqat	85	39.48 N	74.21 E
Uluinggalau ∧	175g	16.54 S	179.59 E
Ulujul ≐	86	57.46 N	85.30 E
Ulukışla, Kıbrıs	130	35.13 N	33.37 E
Ulukışla, Tür.	130	37.33 N	34.30 E
Ulul I	14	8.35 N	149.40 E
Ulu Laho, Bukit ∧	114	5.43 N	101.27 E
Ulunchan	88	54.51 N	111.02 E
Ulundi	158	28.17 S	31.26 E
Ulunga	89	46.31 N	136.56 E
Ulungur ≐	86	46.59 N	87.27 E
Ulungur Hu ⊜	86	47.15 N	87.20 E
Ulurijskij Golec, gora ∧	88	50.12 N	111.45 E
Uluru National Park ♠	162	25.20 S	131.00 E
Ulus	130	41.35 N	32.39 E
Ulusara	126	24.16 N	90.36 E
Ulut ≐	116	12.00 N	125.27 E
Ulutau	86	48.39 N	67.01 E
Ulutau, gora ∧	86	48.39 N	66.56 E
Ulutau, gory ⋏	86	49.00 N	67.00 E
Ulu Tiram	114	1.36 N	103.49 E
Ulu Yam	114	3.27 N	101.38 E
Ulva	272c	18.59 N	73.02 E
Ulva I	46	56.29 N	6.14 W
Ulvenhout	52	51.34 N	4.48 E
Ulverston	44	54.12 N	3.06 W
Ulverstone	166	41.09 S	146.10 E
Ulvöarna II	26	63.01 N	18.40 E
Ulvshale ≻[1]	41	55.02 N	12.16 E
Ulvshyttan	40	60.18 N	15.22 E
Ulvsund ⋓	41	54.59 N	12.11 E
Ulyanovsk → Uljanovsk	80	54.20 N	48.24 E
Ulysses, Ks., U.S.	198	37.34 N	101.21 W
Ulysses, Ne., U.S.	198	41.04 N	97.12 W
Ulysses, Pa., U.S.	214	41.54 N	77.46 W
Uly-Žilanšik ≐	86	48.51 N	63.47 E
Ulzë	38	41.41 N	19.54 E
Uma	89	52.36 N	120.37 E
Umag	64	45.25 N	13.32 E
Umaji	96	33.33 N	134.03 E
Umal'tinskij	89	51.56 N	133.36 E
Umán, Méx.	232	20.53 N	89.45 W
Uman', Ukr.	78	48.44 N	30.14 E
Uman I	175c	7.18 N	151.53 E
Umanak	176	70.40 N	52.07 W
Umanak Fjord ⊂[2]	176	70.55 N	53.00 W
Umancevo	80	47.44 N	44.16 E
ʻUmān → Oman □[1]	118	22.00 N	58.00 E
Umargãon	122	20.12 N	72.45 E
Umari	250	6.38 S	38.42 W
Umari ≐	248	7.05 S	64.34 W
ʻUmarī, Qāʻ al- ⊜	132	31.42 N	36.57 E
Umaria	124	23.32 N	80.50 E
Umarizal	250	5.59 S	37.49 W
Umarkot	120	25.22 N	69.44 E
Umatac	174p	13.18 N	144.39 E
Umatilla, Fl., U.S.	220	28.55 N	81.39 W
Umatilla, Or., U.S.	202	45.55 N	119.20 W
Umatilla ≐	202	45.55 N	119.20 W
Umatilla, Lake ⊜[1]	202	45.44 N	120.35 W
Umatilla Indian Reservation ◆[4]	202	45.41 N	118.31 W
Umayan ≐	116	8.13 N	125.50 E
Umaze	270	34.57 N	135.03 E
Umba	24	66.41 N	34.15 E
Umbagog Lake ⊜	188	44.45 N	71.05 W
Umbai	114	2.10 N	102.20 E
Umbaúba	250	11.22 S	37.39 W
Umbelasha ≐	140	9.51 N	24.50 E
Umbertide	66	43.18 N	12.20 E
Umbogintwini	158	30.00 S	30.58 E
Umboi Island I	164	5.36 S	148.00 E
Umbrail, Pass (Giogo di Santa Maria))(	64	46.34 N	10.25 E
Umbria □[4]	66	43.00 N	12.30 E
Umbriatico	68	39.21 N	16.55 E
Umbroli	272c	19.11 N	73.06 E
Umbukul	164	2.30 S	150.00 E
Umbuzero, ozero ⊜	24	67.43 N	34.25 E
Ume ≐	154	16.40 S	28.26 E
Umeå	26	63.50 N	20.15 E
Umeälven ≐	24	63.47 N	20.16 E
Umedani	270	34.44 N	135.51 E
Umedpur	126	22.31 N	89.59 E
Umfolozi Game Reserve ◆[4]	158	28.19 S	31.50 E
Umfors	24	65.56 N	15.00 E
Umfreville Lake ⊜	184	50.18 N	94.45 W
Umfuli ≐	154	17.30 S	29.23 E
Umgungundhlovu ⊥	158	28.27 S	31.28 E
Umguza	154	19.25 S	27.51 E
Umhausen	64	47.08 N	10.56 E
Umhlanga Rocks	158	29.43 S	31.06 E
Umi	96	33.34 N	130.30 E
Umingan	116	15.56 N	120.50 E
Umkomaas	158	30.15 S	30.42 E
Umm ad-Daraj, Jabal ∧	132	32.19 N	35.48 E
Umm ʻAjārim ≗[8]	142	30.50 N	32.49 E
Umm al-Abīd	146	27.31 N	15.02 E
Umm al-ʻArāʼis, Wādī ∨	146	26.26 N	13.55 E
Umm al-Arānib	146	26.08 N	14.45 E
Umm al-Birak	128	23.25 N	39.13 E
Umm al-Ḥawāyā, Jabal ∧	142	28.41 N	31.06 E
Umm al-Jimāl, Khirbat ⊥	132	32.20 N	36.22 E
Umm al-Khashab	144	17.21 N	42.32 E
Umm al-Qaywayn	128	25.35 N	55.34 E
Umm al-Qiṭṭayn	132	32.19 N	36.38 E
Umm al-Quṣūr	142	27.23 N	30.54 E
Ummanz	54	54.28 N	13.10 E
Umm Artah, Wādī ∨	142	28.41 N	32.37 E
Umm as-Saʻd ⊥	132	33.16 N	36.47 E
Umm Badr	140	14.14 N	27.57 E
Umm Balad, Wādī ∨	142	27.40 N	32.39 E
Umm Bayyūʻd	140	12.05 N	31.40 E
Umm Bel	140	13.32 N	28.04 E
Umm Boim	140	11.43 N	25.57 E
Umm Dabbī	140	14.37 N	30.23 E
Umm Dam	140	13.45 N	30.59 E
Umm Dhibbān, Sūd.	140	14.14 N	29.37 E
Umm Dhibbān, Sūd.	140	15.26 N	32.51 E
Umm Digulgulaya	140	10.29 N	24.57 E
Umm Dīnār	142	30.12 N	31.04 E
Umm Durmān (Omdurman)	140	15.38 N	32.30 E
Umm el Fahm	132	32.31 N	35.09 E
Ummeln	52	51.58 N	8.27 E
Ummendorf	54	52.09 N	11.11 E
Umm Habwah, Jabal ∧[2]	142	27.23 N	31.29 E
Umm Ḥamāṭ	132	31.02 N	35.46 E
Umm Jamālah	140	11.27 N	28.12 E
Umm Kaddādah	140	13.36 N	26.42 E
Umm Khunān	273c	29.55 N	31.15 E
Umm Khushayb, Wādī ∨	142	30.24 N	32.43 E
Umm Kuwaykah	140	13.00 N	32.17 E
Umm Lajj	128	25.04 N	37.13 E
Umm Marahik, Jabal ∧[2]	140	13.40 N	26.53 E
Umm Mirdi	140	18.59 N	33.32 E
Umm Mitmān ≗[8]	142	30.41 N	32.30 E
Umm Qantur	140	14.17 N	31.22 E
Umm Qaṣr	128	30.02 N	47.56 E
Umm Qurayn	140	9.58 N	28.55 E
Umm Quṣayr	132	31.40 N	35.53 E
Umm Raqm, Jabal ∧	142	30.14 N	31.52 E
Umm Rīshah, Birkat ⊜	142	30.21 N	30.22 E
Umm Rumaylah ⫟[4]	140	16.55 N	31.40 E
Umm Ruwābah	140	12.54 N	31.13 E
Umm Saggāt, Wādī ∨	140	15.15 N	23.12 E
Umm Saysabān, Jabal ∧	132	29.45 N	35.10 E
Umm Sayyālah	140	14.25 N	31.10 E
Umm Shalīl	140	10.51 N	23.42 E
Umm Shanqah	140	13.14 N	27.14 E
Umm Shuṭūr	140	7.17 N	33.14 E
Umm Sidr, Wādī ∨	142	27.54 N	32.33 E
Umm Sughra ⫟[4]	140	15.03 N	27.12 E
Umm ʻUmayd, Raʼs ∧	142	27.50 N	32.19 E
Umm ʻUmayyid, Biʼr ⫟[4]	142	27.53 N	32.30 E
Umm ʻUmayyid, Wādī ∨	142	27.37 N	32.41 E
Umm Urūmah I	128	25.46 N	36.32 E
Umm Walad	132	32.39 N	36.26 E
Umm Zaytah, Jabal ∧[2]	142	29.49 N	32.16 E
Umnak	180	53.17 N	168.20 W
Umnak Island I	180	53.25 N	168.10 W
Umnak Pass ⋓	180	53.20 N	167.45 W
Umnäs	24	65.24 N	16.10 E
Umniati	154	18.39 S	29.49 E
Umniati ≐	154	17.30 S	29.23 E
Um'ot, Ross.	80	54.08 N	42.42 E
Um'ot, Ross.	80	52.31 N	42.58 E
Umpferstedt	54	50.59 N	11.25 E
Umpqua ≐	202	43.42 N	124.03 W
Umpulo	152	12.38 S	17.42 E
ʻUmrān	144	15.50 N	43.56 E
ʻUmrānī, Wādī al- ∨	142	27.37 N	30.53 E
Umraniye	130	39.10 N	31.15 E
Umraniye ◆[8]	267b	41.01 N	29.05 E
Umred	122	20.51 N	79.20 E
Umreth	120	22.42 N	73.07 E
Umsini, Gunung ∧	164	1.22 S	133.45 E
Ŭmsŏng	98	36.56 N	127.41 E
Umstead State Park ♠	192	35.52 N	78.47 W
Umtanum Creek ≐	224	46.52 N	120.35 W
Umtata	158	31.35 S	28.47 E
Umtentweni	158	30.42 S	30.28 E
Umuahia	150	5.33 N	7.29 E
Umuarama	255	23.45 S	53.20 W
Umurbey	130	40.14 N	26.36 E
Umurlu	130	37.50 N	27.58 E
Umzimkulu	158	30.16 S	29.56 E
Umzingwani ≐	154	22.12 S	29.56 E
Umzinto	158	30.22 S	30.33 E
Una, Bra.	255	15.18 S	39.04 W
Una, India	120	20.49 N	71.02 E
Una, India	123	31.29 N	76.17 E
Una ≐	36	45.16 N	16.55 E
Una, Mount ∧	172	42.13 S	172.35 E
Una, Ribeirão ≐	287b	23.31 S	46.18 W
Unac ≐	36	44.30 N	16.09 E
Uña de Gato	196	25.58 N	99.41 W
Unadilla, Ga., U.S.	192	32.15 N	83.44 W
Unadilla, N.Y., U.S.	210	42.19 N	75.18 W
Unadilla ≐	210	42.20 N	75.25 W
Unaí	255	16.23 S	46.53 W
Unakami	94	35.46 N	140.45 E
Unalakleet	180	63.53 N	160.47 W
Unalaska	180	53.52 N	166.32 W
Unalaska Island I	180	53.45 N	166.45 W
Unanderra	170	34.27 S	150.52 E
Unango	154	12.50 S	35.20 E
Únanov	61	48.54 N	16.04 E
Unao	124	25.35 N	78.36 E
Unare ≐	246	10.03 N	65.14 W
Unauna, Pulau I	112	0.10 S	121.35 E
Unayyir, Ḥarrat al- ≗[9]	128	25.20 N	37.45 E
ʻUnayzah, Ar. Su.	128	26.06 N	43.56 E
ʻUnayzah, Urd.	132	30.29 N	35.48 E
ʻUnayzah, Jabal ∧, Asia	128	32.12 N	39.18 E
ʻUnayzah, Jabal ∧, Urd.	132	30.30 N	35.47 E
Unazuki	94	36.49 N	137.35 E
Uncasville	207	41.26 N	72.06 W
Unchahra	124	24.23 N	80.47 E
Ŭnch'ŏn	98	38.34 N	125.26 E
Uncia	248	18.27 S	66.37 W
Uncompahgre ≐	200	38.45 N	108.06 W
Uncompahgre Peak ∧	200	38.04 N	107.28 W
Uncompahgre Plateau ⋏[1]	200	38.30 N	108.25 W
Uncukul'	84	42.42 N	46.48 E
Uncular	130	40.28 N	41.28 E
Unda	88	51.42 N	116.56 E
Unda ≐	88	51.25 N	116.05 E
Unden ⊜	40	58.47 N	14.26 E
Undenäs	40	58.39 N	14.25 E
Underberg	158	29.50 S	29.22 E
Under River	260	51.15 N	0.14 E
Undersåker	26	63.20 N	13.23 E
Underwood, In., U.S.	218	38.36 N	85.46 W
Underwood, N.D., U.S.	198	47.27 N	101.08 W
Underwood, Wa., U.S.	224	45.43 N	121.31 W
Undløse	41	55.36 N	11.35 E
Undory	80	54.37 N	48.25 E
Undu, Tanjung ≻	115b	10.05 S	120.51 E
Undu Point ≻	175g	16.08 S	179.57 W
Undva nina ≻	76	58.32 N	21.55 E
Unea Island I	164	4.55 S	149.10 E
Uneča	76	52.50 N	32.40 E
Uneča ≐	76	52.50 N	31.56 E
Uneiuxi ≐	246	0.34 S	64.58 W
Úněšov	60	49.53 N	13.09 E
Unga Island I	180	55.15 N	160.45 W
Ungama Bay ⊂	154	2.45 S	40.20 E
Ungaran	115a	7.07 S	110.24 E
Ungarie	166	33.38 S	146.58 E
Ungarn → Hungary □[1]	30	47.00 N	20.00 E
Ungava, Péninsule d' ≻[1]	176	60.00 N	74.00 W
Ungava Bay ⊂	176	59.30 N	67.30 W
Ungch'ŏn	98	35.07 N	128.44 E
Ungen'	78	47.12 N	27.48 E
Unggi	98	42.20 N	130.24 E
Ungurkuj	88	50.27 N	106.58 E
Ungvár → Užgorod	78	48.37 N	22.18 E
Unhos	266c	38.50 N	9.07 W
Unhošt'	54	50.04 N	14.08 E
Uni	80	57.46 N	51.30 E
União	250	4.35 S	42.52 W
União da Vitória	252	26.13 S	51.05 W
União dos Palmares	250	9.10 S	36.02 W
Unica	24	62.38 N	34.38 E
Unicoi	192	36.11 N	82.20 W
Unicorn Branch ≐	208	39.15 N	75.52 W
Unidad Santa Fe ◆[8]	286a	19.23 N	99.15 W
Uniejów	30	51.58 N	18.49 E
Unieux	62	45.24 N	4.16 E
Unije, Otok I	36	44.38 N	14.15 E
Unimak Island I	180	54.50 N	164.00 W
Unimak Pass ⋓	180	54.35 N	164.43 W
Unini ≐	246	1.41 S	61.31 W
Unión, Arg.	252	35.09 S	65.57 W
Union, On., Can.	212	42.42 N	81.12 W
Unión, C.R.	236	8.36 N	83.03 W
Unión, Para.	252	24.48 S	56.33 W
Union, Il., U.S.	216	42.14 N	88.33 W
Union, Ia., U.S.	190	42.14 N	93.03 W
Union, Ky., U.S.	218	38.56 N	84.40 W
Union, La., U.S.	194	30.06 N	90.54 W
Union, Ms., U.S.	194	32.34 N	89.07 W
Union, Mo., U.S.	219	38.26 N	91.00 W
Union, N.J., U.S.	210	40.41 N	74.15 W
Union, Oh., U.S.	218	39.53 N	84.18 W
Union, Or., U.S.	202	45.12 N	117.51 W
Union, S.C., U.S.	192	34.42 N	81.37 W
Union, Wa., U.S.	224	47.21 N	123.06 W
Union, W.V., U.S.	192	37.35 N	80.32 W
Union □[6], In., U.S.	218	39.38 N	84.56 W
Union □[6], N.J., U.S.	208	40.40 N	74.11 W
Union □[6], Oh., U.S.	214	40.18 N	83.19 W
Union □[6], Pa., U.S.	210	40.58 N	76.54 W
Unión ◆[8]	258	34.53 S	56.08 W
Union Bay	182	49.35 N	124.53 W
Union Beach	208	40.26 N	74.10 W
Union Bridge	208	39.34 N	77.10 W
Union Center	210	42.09 N	76.04 W
Union City, Ca., U.S.	226	37.35 N	122.04 W
Union City, Ga., U.S.	192	33.35 N	84.32 W
Union City, In., U.S.	194	40.07 N	85.05 W
Union City, Mi., U.S.	216	42.04 N	85.09 W
Union City, N.J., U.S.	276	40.46 N	74.01 W
Union City, Oh., U.S.	216	40.11 N	84.48 W
Union City, Pa., U.S.	214	41.53 N	79.50 W
Union City, Tn., U.S.	194	36.25 N	89.03 W
Union City Dam ◆[6]	214	41.55 N	79.54 W
Uniondale, S. Afr.	158	33.40 S	23.08 E
Uniondale, In., U.S.	216	40.50 N	85.15 W
Uniondale, N.Y., U.S.	276	40.42 N	73.35 W
Union Dale, Pa., U.S.	210	41.43 N	75.30 W
Unión de Reyes	240p	22.48 N	81.32 W
Unión de San Antonio	234	21.06 N	101.58 W
Union des Émirats Arabes → United Arab Emirates □[1]	128	24.00 N	54.00 E
Unión de Tula	234	19.58 N	104.16 W
Union Flat Creek ≐	202	46.50 N	117.59 W
Union Gap	202	46.33 N	120.28 W
Union Grove, Tx., U.S.	222	32.34 N	94.55 W
Union Grove, Wi., U.S.	216	42.41 N	88.03 W
Unión Hidalgo	234	16.28 N	94.50 W
Union Hill	210	43.13 N	77.23 W
Union Lake	216	42.36 N	83.26 W
Union Lake ⊜, Mi., U.S.	216	42.03 N	85.11 W
Union Lake ⊜, Mi., U.S.	281	42.37 N	83.26 W
Union Lake ⊜, N.J., U.S.	208	39.25 N	75.03 W
Union Mills	216	41.29 N	86.46 W
Union Park	220	28.30 N	81.15 W
Union Pier	216	41.49 N	86.41 W
Union Point	192	33.36 N	83.04 W
Unionport, In., U.S.	218	40.07 N	85.06 W
Unionport, Oh., U.S.	214	40.21 N	80.51 W
Union Seamount ✣[3]	16	49.35 N	132.45 W
Union Springs, Al., U.S.	194	32.08 N	85.42 W
Union Springs, N.Y., U.S.	210	42.50 N	76.41 W
Union Station ◆[5], On., Can.	275b	43.39 N	79.23 W
Union Station ◆[5], Ca., U.S.	280	34.04 N	118.14 W
Union Station ◆[5], D.C., U.S.	284c	38.54 N	77.00 W
Union Station ◆[5], Il., U.S.	278	41.53 N	87.38 W
Uniontown, Al., U.S.	194	32.26 N	87.30 W
Uniontown, Ky., U.S.	194	37.46 N	87.55 W
Uniontown, Md., U.S.	208	39.35 N	77.06 W
Uniontown, Oh., U.S.	214	40.58 N	81.24 W
Uniontown, Pa., U.S.	188	39.54 N	79.44 W
Union Valley Reservoir ⊜[1]	226	38.50 N	120.26 W
Union Village	207	41.59 N	71.32 W
Unionville, On., Can.	275b	43.52 N	79.18 W
Unionville, Ct., U.S.	207	41.45 N	72.53 W
Unionville, In., U.S.	218	39.14 N	86.25 W
Unionville, Mi., U.S.	190	43.39 N	83.27 W
Unionville, Mo., U.S.	194	40.28 N	93.00 W
Unionville, N.J., U.S.	285	40.01 N	74.46 W
Unionville, N.Y., U.S.	210	41.18 N	74.34 W
Unionville, Oh., U.S.	214	41.47 N	81.00 W
Unionville, Pa., U.S.	285	39.54 N	75.44 W
Unionville Center	214	40.08 N	83.21 W
Uniopolis	216	40.36 N	84.05 W
Unipouheos Indian Reserve ◆[4]	184	53.52 N	110.21 W
Unisan	116	13.51 N	121.59 E
United	214	40.13 N	79.29 W
United Arab Emirates (Al-Imārāt al-ʻArabīyah al-Muttaḥidah) □[1], Asia	118	24.00 N	54.00 E
United Arab Emirates (Al-Imārāt al-ʻArabīyah al-Muttaḥidah) □[1], Asia	128	24.00 N	54.00 E
United Arab Republic → Egypt □[1]	140	27.00 N	30.00 E
United Kingdom □[1], Europe	22	54.00 N	2.00 W
United Kingdom □[1], Europe	28	54.00 N	2.00 W
United Kingdom Sovereign Base Area ■	130	35.00 N	33.45 E
United Nations Headquarters ⚜	276	40.45 N	73.58 W
United States □[1]	178	38.00 N	97.00 W
United States Air Force Academy ■	200	39.00 N	104.55 W
United States Coast Guard Academy ■	207	41.22 N	72.06 W
United States Merchant Marine Academy ⚜[2]	276	40.48 N	73.46 W
United States Military Academy ■	210	41.23 N	73.58 W
United States Naval Academy ■	208	38.59 N	76.30 W
United States Steel Corporation (Lorain Plant) ⚜[3], Oh., U.S.	279a	41.27 N	82.07 W
United States Steel Corporation ⚜[3], Pa., U.S.	279b	40.20 N	79.54 W
United States Steel Corporation ⚜[3], Pa., U.S.	279b	40.25 N	79.54 W
United States Steel Corporation Fairless Works ⚜[3]	285	40.09 N	74.45 W
Unity	184	52.27 N	109.10 W
Unity Reservoir ⊜[1]	279b	40.17 N	79.30 W
Universal City	196	29.32 N	98.17 W
Universal City ⚜[3]	280	34.09 N	118.21 W
Universal Mall ◆[9]	281	42.30 N	83.05 W
Università Degli Studi ⚜[2]	266b	45.28 N	9.14 E
Universitaria, Ciudad ⚜[2]	266d	41.23 N	2.08 E
University	194	34.21 N	89.32 W
University City	219	38.39 N	90.19 W
University Gardens	276	40.46 N	73.43 W
University Heights, Ca., U.S.	226	37.26 N	122.12 W
University Heights, Oh., U.S.	279a	41.29 N	81.32 W
University Park, Il., U.S.	216	41.36 N	87.39 W
University Park, Md., U.S.	284c	38.58 N	76.57 W
University Park, N.M., U.S.	200	32.06 N	106.39 W
University Park, Tx., U.S.	222	32.52 N	96.47 W
University Place	224	47.14 N	122.32 W
University View	218	40.00 N	83.03 W
Unjha	120	23.48 N	72.24 E
Unkel	56	50.35 N	7.13 E
Unken	64	47.39 N	12.43 E
Unkurda	86	55.48 N	59.24 E
Unley	168b	34.57 S	138.35 E
Unna	52	51.32 N	7.41 E
ʻUnnāb, Jabal al- ∧	132	29.57 N	36.55 E
ʻUnnāb, Wādī al- ∨	132	30.11 N	36.39 E
Unnão	124	26.32 N	80.30 E
Uno, Canal Numero ≍	252	36.17 S	57.08 W
Uno, Ilha I	150	11.12 N	16.15 W
Unoke	94	36.43 N	136.42 E
Ŭnp'a	98	38.26 N	125.45 E
Unpenji-san ∧	96	34.02 N	133.44 E
Unqua Point ≻	276	40.39 N	73.26 W
Unquillo	252	31.14 S	64.19 W
Ŭnsan	98	39.25 N	126.01 E
Unseburg	54	51.56 N	11.30 E

≐	River	Fluß	Río	Rivière	Rio
≍	Canal	Kanal	Canal	Canal	Canal
⌊	Waterfall, Rapids	Wasserfall, Stromschnellen	Cascada, Rápidos	Chute d'eau, Rapides	Cascata, Rápidos
⋓	Strait	Meeresstraße	Estrecho	Détroit	Estreito
⊂	Bay, Gulf	Bucht, Golf	Bahía, Golfo	Baie, Golfe	Baía, Golfo
⊜	Lake, Lakes	See, Seen	Lago, Lagos	Lac, Lacs	Lago, Lagos
⩨	Swamp	Sumpf	Pantano	Marais	Pântano
⌓	Ice Features, Glacier	Eis- und Gletscherformen	Accidentes Glaciales	Formes glaciaires	Acidentes glaciares
⫟	Other Hydrographic Features	Andere Hydrographische Objekte	Otros Elementos Hidrográficos	Autres données hydrographiques	Outros acidentes hidrográficos

✣	Submarine Features	Untermeerische Objekte	Accidentes Submarinos	Formes de relief sous-marin	Acidentes submarinos
□	Political Unit	Politische Einheit	Unidad Politica	Entité politique	Unidade política
⚜	Cultural Institution	Kulturelle Institution	Institución Cultural	Institution culturelle	Institução cultural
⊥	Historical Site	Historische Stätte	Sitio Histórico	Site historique	Sitio histórico
♠	Recreational Site	Erholungs- und Ferienort	Sitio de Recreo	Centre de loisirs	Area de Lazer
⊠	Airport	Flughafen	Aeropuerto	Aéroport	Aeroporto
■	Military Installation	Militäranlage	Instalación Militar	Installation militaire	Instalação militar
◆	Miscellaneous	Verschiedenes	Misceláneo	Divers	Diversos

ENGLISH / DEUTSCH

Name	Page	Lat.°′	Long.°′
Unserfrau → Madonna	64	46.43 N	10.52 E
Unsleben	56	50.22 N	10.15 E
Unst I	46a	60.45 N	0.53 W
Unstrut ≃	54	51.10 N	11.48 E
Un't	88	49.07 N	102.50 E
Unten	174m	26.41 N	128.00 E
Unterägeri	58	47.08 N	8.35 E
Unterbach, Dtsch.	263	51.12 N	6.54 E
Unterbäch, Schw.	58	46.17 N	7.48 E
Unter dem Wind, Inseln → Windward Islands II	238	13.00 N	61.00 W
Unterelchingen	58	48.27 N	10.07 E
Unterföhring	60	48.12 N	11.38 E
Unterfranken □ 5	56	50.10 N	10.00 E
Untergermaringen	58	47.56 N	10.40 E
Unterglottertal	58	48.03 N	7.56 E
Untergriesbach	60	48.35 N	13.40 E
Untergröningen	56	48.55 N	9.53 E
Untergrüne	263	51.22 N	7.39 E
Unterhaching	60	48.04 N	11.38 E
Unterhausen	58	48.26 N	9.16 E
Unterinntal V	64	47.24 N	11.47 E
Unterjettenberg	64	47.41 N	12.49 E
Unterlaa ⊸ 8	264b	48.08 N	16.25 E
Unterlüss	52	52.50 N	10.17 E
Untermauerbach	264b	48.14 N	16.12 E
Untermünkheim	56	49.09 N	9.44 E
Untermünstertal	58	47.51 N	7.46 E
Unteröwisheim	56	49.08 N	8.40 E
Unterrath ⊸ 8	263	51.16 N	6.47 E
Unterschächen	58	46.52 N	8.47 E
Unterschwaningen	56	49.04 N	10.37 E
Unterseen	58	46.41 N	7.51 E
Untertauern	64	47.18 N	13.30 E
Unterterzen	58	47.07 N	9.15 E
Unterthingau	58	47.46 N	10.31 E
Unterueckersee ⊜	54	53.17 N	13.51 E
Unteruhldingen	58	47.43 N	9.14 E
Unterwasser	58	47.12 N	9.19 E
Unterweissbach	54	50.37 N	11.10 E
Unterwellenborn	54	50.39 N	11.26 E
Unterwössen	64	47.44 N	12.27 E
Unterzeiring	61	47.15 N	14.31 E
Untraverket	40	60.25 N	17.18 E
Unuli Horog	120	35.06 N	91.51 E
Ünye	130	41.08 N	37.17 E
Unža	80	58.01 N	44.01 E
Unža ≃	80	57.20 N	43.08 E
Unzen-Amakusa-kokuritsu-kōen ♠	92	32.45 N	130.17 E
Unzen-dake ∧	92	32.45 N	130.17 E
Unže-Pavinskaja	86	58.53 N	64.02 E
Uojan	88	56.07 N	111.38 E
Uono ≃	94	37.15 N	138.53 E
Uo-shima I	96	34.11 N	133.19 E
Uozu	94	36.48 N	137.24 E
Upa ≃	76	54.02 N	36.15 E
Upala	236	10.47 N	85.02 W
Upanema	250	5.38 S	37.15 W
Upano ≃	246	2.45 S	78.12 W
Upata	246	8.01 N	62.24 W
Upatoi Creek ≃	192	32.22 N	84.58 W
Upavon	42	51.18 N	1.49 W
Ŭpchŏ-ri	98	37.53 N	125.09 E
Upchurch	260	51.23 N	0.39 E
Upemba, Lac ⊜	154	8.36 S	26.26 E
Upemba, Parc National de l' ♠	154	9.10 S	26.35 E
Upernavik	176	72.47 N	56.10 W
Upgant-Schott	52	53.30 N	7.16 E
Uphal	140	6.58 N	34.16 E
Upham	198	48.34 N	100.43 W
Up Holland	262	53.33 N	2.44 W
Uphusen	52	53.01 N	8.58 E
Upi	116	6.57 N	124.09 E
Upía ≃	246	4.18 N	72.45 W
Upington	158	28.25 S	21.15 E
Upire ≃	246	11.27 N	68.58 W
Upland, Ca., U.S.	228	34.05 N	117.38 W
Upland, In., U.S.	216	40.28 N	85.29 W
Upland, Ne., U.S.	198	40.19 N	98.54 W
Upland, Pa., U.S.	285	39.51 N	75.23 W
Upleta	120	21.44 N	70.17 E
Upnuk Lake ⊜	180	60.21 N	158.58 W
Upolu I	175a	13.55 S	171.45 W
Upolu Point ›	229d	20.16 N	155.51 W
Uporovo	86	56.18 N	66.17 E
Upper □ 4	150	10.30 N	1.30 W
Upper Arlington	218	40.00 N	83.03 W
Upper Arrow Lake ⊜	182	50.30 N	117.55 W
Upper Artichoke Reservoir ⊜ 1	283	42.48 N	70.57 W
Upper Bay c	276	40.41 N	74.03 W
Upper Beaconsfield	274b	38.01 S	145.25 E
Upper Berkshire Valley	276	40.56 N	74.35 W
Upper Beverley Lake ⊜	212	44.37 N	76.05 W
Upper Black Eddy	210	40.35 N	75.07 W
Upper Blackville	186	46.39 N	65.52 W
Upper Brookville	276	40.51 N	73.34 W
Upper Canada Village ⊥	206	44.57 N	75.03 W
Upper Castlereagh	274a	33.43 S	150.40 E
Upperco	208	39.33 N	76.50 W
Upper Coliban Reservoir ⊜ 1	169	37.18 S	144.23 E
Upper Crystal Springs Reservoir ⊜ 1	282	37.30 N	122.20 W
Upper Darby	208	39.55 N	75.16 W
Upper Demerara-Berbice □ 4	246	5.30 N	58.20 W
Upper des Lacs Lake ⊜ 1	198	48.50 N	102.07 W
Upper Egypt → Aṣ-Ṣa'īd □ 9	140	26.00 N	32.00 E
Upper End	262	53.17 N	1.52 W
Upper Erskine Lake ⊜	276	41.06 N	74.15 W
Upper Fairmount	208	38.06 N	75.47 W
Upper Falls	284b	39.26 N	76.24 W
Upper Ferntree Gully	274b	37.54 S	145.19 E
Upper Fraser	182	54.07 N	121.56 W
Upper Ganga Canal ≋	124	29.57 N	78.12 E
Upper Gap ʊ	212	44.06 N	76.50 W
Upper Goose Lake ⊜	184	51.44 N	92.44 W
Upper Greenwood Lake	276	41.10 N	74.22 W
Upper Greenwood Lake ⊜	276	41.11 N	74.23 W
Upper Hat Creek	182	50.38 N	121.35 W
Upper Humber ≃	186	49.10 N	57.28 W
Upper Hutt	172	41.08 S	175.04 E
Upper Iowa ≃	190	43.29 N	91.14 W
Upper Island Cove	186	47.39 N	53.12 W
Upper Keechi Creek ≃	222	31.23 N	95.42 W
Upper Klamath Lake ⊜	202	42.23 N	122.55 W
Upper Lake	204	39.10 N	122.54 W
Upper Lake ⊜	204	41.44 N	120.08 W
Upper Lehigh	210	41.02 N	75.55 W
Upper Liard	180	60.02 N	128.55 W
Upper Machodoc Creek ≃	208	38.18 N	77.02 W
Upper Manitou Lake ⊜	184	49.24 N	92.48 W
Upper Marlboro	208	38.48 N	76.45 W
Upper Matecumbe Key I	220	24.55 N	80.39 W
Upper Moutere	172	41.16 S	173.00 E
Upper Musquodoboit	186	45.08 N	62.57 W
Upper Mystic Lake ⊜	283	42.27 N	71.09 W
Upper Nyack	210	41.07 N	73.55 W
Upper Peirce Reservoir ⊜ 1	271c	1.22 N	103.48 E
Upper Red Lake ⊜	198	48.10 N	94.40 W
Upper Rideau Lake ⊜	212	44.41 N	76.20 W
Upper River Rouge ≃	281	42.23 N	83.16 W
Upper Saddle River	276	41.03 N	74.05 W
Upper Saint Clair	279b	40.21 N	80.05 W
Upper Sandusky	214	40.49 N	83.16 W
Upper San Leandro Reservoir ⊜ 1	226	37.47 N	122.07 W
Upper Sheila	186	47.28 N	64.56 W
Upper Straits Lake ⊜	281	42.35 N	83.24 W
Upper Sumas	224	49.01 N	122.12 W
Upper Swan	168a	31.46 S	116.01 E
Upper Takaka	172	41.02 S	172.50 E
Upper Takutu-Upper Essequibo □ 4	246	3.00 N	59.00 W
Upper Tean	42	52.57 N	1.58 W
Upper Tooting ⊸ 8	260	51.26 N	0.10 W
Upper Ugashik Lake ⊜	180	57.40 N	156.43 W
Upper Volta → Burkina Faso □ 1	150	13.00 N	1.30 W
Upper Windigo Lake ⊜	184	52.30 N	91.35 W
Upper Yarra Reservoir ⊜ 1	169	37.41 S	145.56 E
Upper Yosemite Fall ↳	226	37.45 N	119.36 W
Uppingham	42	52.35 N	0.43 W
Uppland □ 9	40	59.59 N	17.48 E
Upplanda	40	60.14 N	17.44 E
Upplands Väsby	40	59.31 N	17.54 E
Uppsala	40	59.52 N	17.38 E
Uppsala Län □ 6	40	60.00 N	17.45 E
Upright, Cape ›	180	60.17 N	172.15 W
Upsala → Uppsala	40	59.52 N	17.38 E
Upshi	120	33.50 N	77.49 E
Upshur □ 6	222	32.45 N	94.55 W
Upstart, Cape ›	166	19.42 S	147.45 E
Upton, P.Q., Can.	206	45.39 N	72.41 W
Upton, Eng., U.K.	44	53.37 N	1.17 W
Upton, Eng., U.K.	260	51.30 N	0.35 W
Upton, Eng., U.K.	262	53.13 N	2.52 W
Upton, Eng., U.K.	262	53.23 N	3.06 W
Upton, Ky., U.S.	194	37.27 N	85.53 W
Upton, Ma., U.S.	207	42.10 N	71.36 W
Upton, Wy., U.S.	198	44.05 N	104.37 W
Upton Hill ∧ 2	169	36.52 S	145.27 E
Upton upon Severn	42	52.04 N	2.13 W
Uptown ⊸ 8	278	41.58 N	87.40 W
Upwell	42	52.36 N	0.12 E
Upwey	274b	37.54 S	145.20 E
Uquía, Cerro ∧	246	4.22 N	63.46 W
Urabá, Golfo de c	246	8.25 N	76.53 W
Urachi	84	42.21 N	47.36 E
Uracoa	246	9.00 N	62.21 W
Urad	54	52.15 N	14.45 E
Uradome-kaigan ♠	96	35.35 N	134.21 E
Urad Zhonghou Lianheqi	102	41.42 N	108.49 E
Uraga	268	35.15 N	139.43 E
Uraga-kō c	268	35.14 N	139.44 E
Uraga-suidō ʊ	94	35.13 N	139.45 E
Uragawara	94	37.09 N	138.26 E
Urahoro	92a	42.48 N	143.39 E
Uraj	86	60.08 N	64.48 E
Urakan	88	58.38 N	106.01 E
Urakawa	92a	42.09 N	142.47 E
Ural ≃	72	47.00 N	51.48 E
Uralla	166	30.39 S	151.30 E
Ural Mountains → Ural'skije gory ⋏	72	60.00 N	60.00 E
Uralo-Kl'uči	88	56.03 N	97.28 E
Uralovo	78	52.11 N	33.34 E
Ural'sk	80	51.14 N	51.22 E
Ural'skij	80	51.36 N	51.40 E
Ural'skije gory (Ural Mountains) ⋏	72	60.00 N	60.00 E
Urambo	154	5.04 S	32.03 E
Uran	272c	18.52 N	72.56 E
Urana	166	35.20 S	146.16 E
Urandangi	166	21.36 S	138.18 E
Urandi	255	14.46 S	42.38 W
Urangan	166	25.18 S	152.54 E
Urania, Austl.	168b	34.31 S	137.36 E
Urania, La., U.S.	194	31.51 N	92.17 W
Uranium City	176	59.34 N	108.36 W
Uranquinty	171b	35.12 S	147.15 E
Urarey	162	27.26 S	122.18 E
Urariá, Paraná ≃ 1	246	3.03 S	57.43 W
Uraricaá ≃	246	3.20 N	61.56 W
Uraricoera	246	3.27 N	60.59 W
Uraricoera ≃	246	3.02 N	60.30 W
Uras	71	39.42 N	8.42 E
Urasaki	174m	26.40 N	127.53 E
Urasoe	174m	26.15 N	127.43 E
Ura-T'ube	85	39.55 N	68.59 E
Uravakonda	122	14.57 N	77.16 E
Uravan	200	38.22 N	108.44 W
Urawa	94	35.51 N	139.39 E
Urayasu	94	35.39 N	139.54 E
'Urayfan Nāqah, Jabal ∧	132	30.22 N	34.27 E
'Urayyiḍah, Bi'r ⫪ 4	142	29.00 N	31.58 E
Urazmetovo	86	53.49 N	55.25 E
Urazovka	80	55.24 N	45.38 E
Urazovo	78	50.07 N	38.04 E
Urbach	56	50.53 N	7.05 E
Urban	224	48.38 N	122.40 W
Urbana, Ar., U.S.	194	33.09 N	92.26 W
Urbana, Il., U.S.	194	40.06 N	88.12 W
Urbana, In., U.S.	216	40.53 N	85.47 W
Urbana, Mo., U.S.	194	37.50 N	93.10 W
Urbana, Oh., U.S.	218	40.06 N	83.45 W
Urbancrest	218	39.53 N	83.05 W
Urbandale, Ia., U.S.	190	41.37 N	93.42 W
Urbandale, Mi., U.S.	216	44.09 N	85.11 W
Urbania	66	43.40 N	12.31 E
Urbanna	208	37.38 N	76.34 W
Urbano Noris	240p	20.36 N	76.08 W
Urbano Santos	250	3.12 S	43.23 W
Urbe	62	44.29 N	8.36 E
Urbe, Aeroporto dell' ⊠	267a	41.57 N	12.30 E
Urbiña, Peña ∧	34	43.01 N	5.57 W
Urbino	66	43.43 N	12.38 E
Urbisaglia	66	43.12 N	13.23 E
Urcos	248	13.42 S	71.38 W
Urda	80	48.47 N	47.26 E
Urdaneta	116	15.59 N	120.34 E
Urdenbach ⊸ 8	263	51.09 N	6.53 E
Urdinarrain	252	32.41 S	58.53 W
Urdoma	24	61.47 N	48.32 E
Urdžar	86	47.05 N	81.38 E
Uré	246	7.46 N	75.31 W
Ure ≃, Fr.	50	48.45 N	0.11 E
Ure ≃, Eng., U.K.	44	54.01 N	1.12 W
Urečje	76	52.57 N	27.54 E
Ûrein	142	30.58 N	30.42 E
Ureki	84	41.59 N	41.46 E
Ureliki	180	64.23 N	173.15 W
Uren'	80	57.28 N	45.49 E
Uren ⊜	40	58.59 N	16.44 E
Urén ≃	236	9.33 N	82.55 W
Ureña	246	7.55 N	72.28 W
Urenui	172	39.00 S	174.23 E
Uréparapara I	175f	13.32 S	167.20 E
Ures	232	29.26 N	110.24 W
Ureshino, Nihon	92	33.06 N	129.59 E
Ureshino, Nihon	94	34.37 N	136.29 E
Ureterp	52	53.05 N	6.10 E
Urewera National Park ♠	172	38.40 S	177.00 E
Urfa	130	37.08 N	38.46 E
Urfa □ 4	130	37.20 N	39.15 E
Urft ≃	56	50.35 N	6.30 E
Urga	86	43.35 N	58.30 E
Urgamal	88	48.29 N	94.20 E
Urga → Ulaanbaatar	88	47.55 N	106.53 E
Urgenč	72	41.33 N	60.38 E
Urgnano	62	45.35 N	9.41 E
Urgučenskij Golec, gora ∧	88	53.30 N	118.08 E
Ürgüp	130	38.38 N	34.56 E
Urgut	85	39.23 N	67.15 E
Urho	86	46.48 N	89.45 E
Urho Kekkosen kansallispuisto ♠	24	68.10 N	28.30 E
Uri, India	123	34.05 N	74.02 E
Uri, It.	71	40.38 N	8.29 E
Uri □ 3	58	46.50 N	8.40 E
Uriah	194	31.18 N	87.30 W
Uriangato	234	20.09 N	101.11 W
Uribante ≃	246	7.18 N	70.44 W
Uribe	246	3.13 N	74.24 W
Uribelarrea	258	35.09 S	58.54 W
Uribia	246	11.43 N	72.16 W
Urich	194	38.27 N	94.00 W
Urick ⊸ 8	265a	59.50 N	30.11 E
Urickij	86	53.19 N	65.34 E
Urickoje	78	52.02 N	38.11 E
Urie ≃	46	57.19 N	2.30 W
Urimba	152	10.56 S	16.32 E
Urión ≃ 1	288	34.24 S	58.31 W
Urique	232	27.13 N	107.55 W
Urique ≃	232	26.29 N	107.58 W
Uri-Rotstock ∧	58	46.52 N	8.33 E
Urituyacu ≃	246	4.45 S	75.28 W
Uriuaná ≃	250	2.47 S	50.29 W
Urizura	94	36.30 N	140.27 E
Urjala	26	61.05 N	23.32 E
Urk	52	52.39 N	5.36 E
Urkan ≃	89	53.27 N	126.56 E
Urkarach	84	42.11 N	47.38 E
Urla	130	38.18 N	26.46 E
Urlați	38	44.59 N	26.14 E
Urlingford	48	52.42 N	7.35 W
Urlings	240c	17.02 N	61.52 W
Urluk	88	50.03 N	107.55 E
Urma	126	23.10 N	86.15 E
Urman, Ross.	86	54.52 N	56.52 E
'Urmān, Sūrīy.	132	32.30 N	36.45 E
Urmary	80	55.42 N	47.57 E
Urmetan	85	39.27 N	68.17 E
Urmi ≃	89	48.44 N	134.16 E
Urmia, Lake → Orūmīyeh, Daryācheh-ye ⊜	128	37.40 N	45.30 E
Urmia → Orūmīyeh	128	37.33 N	45.04 E
Urmston	44	53.27 N	2.21 W
Urnäsch	58	47.19 N	9.17 E
Urnersee ⊜	58	46.55 N	8.37 E
Uroindo	248	21.41 S	64.41 W
Üröm	264c	47.36 N	19.01 E
Uromi	150	6.44 N	6.18 E
Uroševac	38	42.22 N	21.09 E
Uroyán, Montañas de ⋏	240m	18.14 N	67.02 W
Urožajnoje, Ross.	84	44.47 N	44.55 E
Urožajnoje, Ross.	84	43.42 N	44.13 E
Urquhart, Glen V	46	57.20 N	4.35 W
Urrao	246	6.20 N	76.11 W
Urr Water ≃	44	54.53 N	3.49 W
Ursa	219	40.04 N	91.22 W
Uršel'skij	80	55.41 N	40.13 E
Ursensollen	60	49.24 N	11.46 E
Ursk	86	54.27 N	85.24 E
Urspring	56	48.33 N	9.53 E
Ur → Tall al-Muqayyar ⊥	128	30.57 N	46.09 E
Urtazym	86	52.12 N	58.50 E
Urtigueira	252	24.12 S	50.55 W
Urt Moron	120	37.00 N	93.18 E
Uru ≃	255	15.24 S	49.36 W
Uruaçu	255	14.30 S	49.10 W
Uruana	255	15.30 S	49.41 W
Uruapan	204	31.38 N	116.15 W
Uruapan del Progreso	234	19.25 N	102.04 W
Urubamba	248	13.18 S	72.07 W
Urubamba ≃	248	10.44 S	73.45 W
Urubaxi ≃	246	0.31 S	64.50 W
Urubu ≃, Bra.	246	2.55 S	58.25 W
Urubu ≃, Bra.	250	10.51 S	49.47 W
Uruburetama	250	3.38 S	39.30 W
Urucará	250	2.32 S	57.45 W
Uruch ≃	84	43.28 N	44.06 E
Urucu ≃	246	4.11 S	63.36 W
Uruçuca	255	14.35 S	39.16 W
Uruçuí	250	7.14 S	44.33 W
Uruçuí, Serra da ⋏ 2	250	9.00 S	44.45 W
Urucuia ≃	255	16.08 S	45.05 W
Uruçuí-preto ≃	250	7.20 S	44.38 W
Urucurituba	250	2.41 S	57.40 W
Urugi	94	35.16 N	137.42 E
Uruguaiana	252	29.45 S	57.05 W
Uruguay □ 1, S.A.	244	33.00 S	56.00 W
Uruguay □ 1, S.A.	252	33.00 S	56.00 W
Uruguay (Uruguai) ≃	252	34.12 S	58.18 W
Urugudejevskij Golec, gora ∧	88	51.25 N	102.09 E
Urul'ga	88	51.45 N	114.47 E
Urul'unguj ≃	88	50.24 N	119.08 E
Ur'um, ozero ⊜	86	54.33 N	78.30 E
Urumchi → Ürümqi	90	43.48 N	87.35 E
Ur'umkan ≃	88	52.35 N	120.08 E
Ürümqi	90	43.48 N	87.35 E
Urundel	252	23.33 S	64.25 W
Ur'ung-Chaja	74	72.48 N	113.23 E
Uruoca	250	3.20 S	40.32 W
Urup	84	43.52 N	41.09 E
Urup ≃	84	44.49 N	41.10 E
Urup, gora ∧	84	43.38 N	40.58 E
Urup, ostrov I	74	46.00 N	150.00 E
Urupá ≃	248	10.54 S	61.57 W
Urupadi ≃	250	3.51 S	57.21 W
Urupês	255	21.13 S	49.17 W
Ur'upino	88	52.46 N	120.00 E
Ur'upinsk	80	50.47 N	41.59 E
Ururicaia, Ilha I	250	1.30 S	52.05 W
Uruša	89	54.03 N	122.54 E
Urus-Martan	84	43.08 N	45.32 E
Urusovo	82	54.15 N	38.26 E
Urussanga	252	28.31 S	49.19 W
Urussu	80	54.36 N	53.24 E
Urutaí	255	17.28 S	48.12 W
Urutaí, Ilha I	250	1.07 S	51.17 W
Urutaú	252	25.42 S	63.04 W
Uruti	172	38.57 S	174.32 E
Uru Uru, Lago ⊜	248	18.10 S	67.10 W
Uruwira	154	6.27 S	31.21 E
Uryl'	86	49.15 N	86.20 E
Uryū-yama ∧	270	35.03 N	135.48 E
Uryv	78	51.07 N	39.10 E
Urzajbaš	80	54.43 N	54.23 E
Urziceni	38	44.43 N	26.38 E
Ürzig	56	49.59 N	7.01 E
Urzulei	71	40.06 N	9.30 E
Uržum	80	57.08 N	50.00 E
Us	261	49.06 N	1.58 E
Us ≃	86	52.07 N	92.15 E
Usa, Nihon	96	33.31 N	131.22 E
Usa, Ross.	86	54.03 N	88.45 E
Uša ≃, Bela.	76	54.00 N	28.55 E
Usa ≃, Ross.	24	65.57 N	56.55 E
Ušač' ≃	76	55.32 N	28.30 E
Ušači	76	55.11 N	28.37 E
Usada Island I	116	6.08 N	120.33 E
Usadel	54	53.26 N	13.11 E
Uşak	130	38.41 N	29.25 E
Uşak □ 4	130	38.35 N	29.20 E
Ušaki	76	59.29 N	30.59 E
Usakos	156	22.01 S	15.32 E
Ušakovka	83	48.48 N	39.48 E
Ušakovo, Ross.	86	56.22 N	75.41 E
Ušakovo, Ross.	89	51.55 N	126.34 E
Usambara Mountains ⋏	154	4.45 S	38.30 E
Usangu Flats ≚	154	8.30 S	34.15 E
Usanovy	86	59.28 N	73.24 E
Ušaral	85	43.54 N	70.42 E
Usarp Mountains ⋏	9	71.10 S	160.00 E
Úšava	60	49.46 N	12.40 E
Usaymir, Wādī al- V	273c	30.04 N	31.23 E
Ušba, gora ∧	84	43.08 N	42.40 E
Ušbas ≃	85	43.55 N	69.39 E
Usborne, Mount ∧	254	51.41 S	58.50 W
Ušće	38	43.28 N	20.37 E
Uščerpje	76	52.43 N	31.53 E
Uscio	62	44.25 N	9.10 E
Usedom	54	53.52 N	13.55 E
Usedom (Uznam) I	54	54.00 N	14.00 E
Useldange	56	49.47 N	5.59 E
Usellus	71	39.48 N	8.51 E
Usen' ≃	80	54.44 N	53.38 E
'Usfān	144	21.55 N	39.21 E
Ushaa	152	14.55 S	23.18 E
Ushant → Ouessant, Île d' I	32	48.28 N	5.05 W
Ushashi	154	2.00 S	33.57 E
'Ushayrah	144	21.46 N	40.38 E
Ushetu	154	4.10 S	32.16 E
Ushibuka	92	32.11 N	130.01 E
Ushiku	94	35.58 N	140.08 E
Ushimado	96	34.37 N	134.10 E
Ushuaia	254	54.48 S	68.18 W
Usibelli	180	63.51 N	148.47 W
Ušica ≃	78	48.35 N	27.08 E
Usingen	56	50.20 N	8.32 E
Usini	71	40.40 N	8.32 E
Usinsk	24	65.58 N	56.39 E
Usisya	154	11.09 S	34.11 E
Usk, B.C., Can.	182	54.38 N	128.25 W
Usk, Wales, U.K.	42	51.43 N	2.54 W
Usk, Wa., U.S.	202	48.18 N	117.16 W
Usk ≃	42	51.36 N	2.58 W
Uškanij kr'až ∧	180	65.15 N	178.35 E
Uskedal	26	59.56 N	5.52 E
Usken ⊜	40	59.39 N	15.01 E
Uskovo	265b	55.56 N	37.19 E
Üsküb → Skopje	38	41.59 N	21.26 E
Uskumru ⊸ 8	267b	41.12 N	29.01 E
Uslar	52	51.39 N	9.38 E
Úslava ≃	60	49.45 N	13.24 E
Usmajac	234	19.52 N	103.34 W
Usman', Ross.	76	52.02 N	39.44 E
Usman', Ross.	89	51.29 N	134.00 E
Usmanka	80	52.49 N	51.42 E
Usmānpur ⊸ 8	272a	28.41 N	77.15 E
Usmas ezers ⊜	76	57.11 N	22.10 E
Usmat	85	39.44 N	67.40 E
Usmate Velate	62	45.39 N	9.21 E
Ušmunskij Golec, gora ∧	89	51.40 N	118.35 E
Usmyn'	76	55.52 N	31.09 E
Ušna ≃	80	55.43 N	42.12 E
Usoke	154	5.06 S	32.20 E
Usolje, Ross.	80	53.23 N	49.05 E
Usolje, Ross.	82	56.49 N	38.40 E
Usolje, Ross.	86	59.25 N	56.41 E
Usolje-Sibirskoje	88	52.47 N	103.38 E
Usolka ≃	86	57.47 N	94.35 E
Uson	116	12.13 N	123.47 E
Usoro	150	5.34 N	6.13 E
Usovo	265b	55.44 N	37.13 E
Uspallata	252	32.35 S	69.20 W
Uspanapa ≃	234	17.58 N	94.29 W
Uspenka, Kaz.	86	52.54 N	77.25 E
Uspenka, Ross.	80	50.38 N	41.28 E
Uspenka, Ukr.	83	47.43 N	38.42 E
Uspenka, Ukr.	83	48.23 N	39.10 E
Uspenovka	80	51.16 N	53.36 E
Uspenskij	86	48.42 N	72.40 E
Uspenskoje	82	55.43 N	37.04 E
Usri ≃	126	24.03 N	86.23 E
Uššaj	86	43.50 N	58.53 E
Ussassai	71	39.49 N	9.23 E
Usseglio	62	45.14 N	7.13 E
Ussel	32	45.33 N	2.18 E
Ussel ≃	56	48.44 N	11.04 E
Usshers Creek ≃	284a	43.03 N	79.02 W
Usson-en-Forez	62	45.23 N	3.56 E
Ussure	154	4.39 S	34.23 E
Ussuri (Wusuli) ≃	89	48.27 N	135.04 E
Ussurijsk	89	43.48 N	131.59 E
Ūst	123	36.56 N	72.53 E
Usta	80	57.26 N	45.40 E
Usta ≃	80	56.53 N	45.28 E
Ust'-Ajsk	86	56.07 N	57.40 E
Ustaoset	26	60.30 N	8.04 E
Ustaritz	32	43.24 N	1.27 W
Ust'-Bagar'ak	86	56.08 N	61.52 E
Ust'-Barguzin	88	53.27 N	108.59 E
Ust'-Belaja	74	65.30 N	173.20 E
Ust'-Bol'šereck	74	52.48 N	156.14 E
Ust'-B'ur'	86	53.49 N	90.15 E
Ust'-Buzulukskaja	80	50.12 N	42.10 E
Ust'-Bystr'anskaja	80	47.49 N	41.03 E
Ust'-Čaja	86	58.17 N	82.38 E
Ust'-Čaryšskaja Pristan'	86	52.24 N	83.39 E
Ust'-Čaun	74	68.47 N	170.30 E
Ust'-Choperskaja	80	49.36 N	42.24 E
Ust'-Cil'ma	24	65.27 N	52.06 E
Ust'-Čižapka	86	59.02 N	79.37 E
Ust'-Čorna	78	48.18 N	23.56 E
Ust'-Čornaja	88	52.57 N	119.02 E
Ust'-Dolyssy	76	56.09 N	29.39 E
Ust'-Doneckij	80	47.39 N	40.52 E
Ust'-Džegutinskaja	84	44.05 N	41.58 E
Úštěk	54	50.36 N	14.20 E
Ust'-Elegest	88	51.32 N	94.05 E
Uster	58	47.21 N	8.43 E
Ust'-Gr'aznucha	80	50.28 N	45.26 E
Ustica	70	38.42 N	13.11 E
Ustica, Isola di I	70	38.42 N	13.11 E
Ust'-Il'a	88	50.25 N	113.41 E
Ust'-Ilga	88	55.00 N	105.02 E
Ust'-Ilimsk	88	58.00 N	102.39 E
Ust'-Ilimskoje vodochranilišče ⊜ 1	88	57.00 N	102.15 E
Ustilug	78	50.51 N	24.09 E
Ust'-Ilyč	24	62.32 N	56.41 E
Ústí nad Labem	54	50.40 N	14.02 E
Ústí nad Orlicí	30	49.58 N	16.24 E
Ustinovka, Ukr.	78	47.57 N	32.32 E
Ustinovka, Ukr.	83	48.49 N	38.34 E
Ust'-Išim	86	57.44 N	71.10 E
Ust'-Izes	86	55.56 N	76.56 E
Ust'-Ižora	265a	59.48 N	30.36 E
Ustja ≃	24	61.30 N	42.36 E
Ust'-Javron'ga	24	63.25 N	44.21 E
Ustje, Ross.	76	60.49 N	32.49 E
Ustje, Ross.	76	59.38 N	39.43 E
Ustje, Ross.	80	57.47 N	39.47 E
Ustje, Ross.	82	55.16 N	36.20 E
Ustje, Ross.	86	57.46 N	94.42 E
Ustje-Kirovskoje	76	58.45 N	35.55 E
Ustka	30	54.35 N	16.50 E
Ust'-K'achta	88	50.32 N	106.16 E
Ust'-Kajtym	86	57.23 N	95.28 E
Ust'-Kalmanka	86	52.07 N	83.19 E
Ust'-Kamčatsk	74	56.15 N	162.30 E
Ust'-Kamenogorsk	86	49.58 N	82.38 E
Ust'-Kan, Ross.	86	50.57 N	84.45 E
Ust'-Kan, Ross.	86	56.31 N	93.48 E
Ust'-Karenga	88	54.26 N	116.30 E
Ust'-Karsk	88	52.43 N	118.48 E
Ust'-Katav	86	54.56 N	58.10 E
Ust'-Kemčug	86	57.13 N	90.30 E
Ust'-Kil'mez'	80	56.57 N	50.30 E
Ust'-Kišert'	86	57.22 N	57.15 E
Ust'-Koksa	86	50.18 N	85.36 E
Ust'-Kujda	74	70.01 N	135.36 E
Ust'-Kulom	24	61.42 N	53.40 E
Ust'-Kurd'um	80	51.39 N	46.12 E
Ust'-Kurenga	86	57.27 N	75.34 E
Ust'-Kut	88	56.46 N	105.40 E
Ust'-Labinsk	78	45.13 N	39.42 E
Ust'-Lubija	88	52.36 N	120.16 E
Ust'-Luga	76	59.40 N	28.15 E
Ust'-Lyža	24	65.44 N	56.36 E
Ust'-Maja	74	60.25 N	134.32 E
Ust'-Manja	72	62.11 N	60.20 E
Ust'-Naryk	86	54.20 N	87.25 E
Ust'-Nemda	80	57.03 N	50.22 E
Ust'-Nera	74	64.34 N	143.12 E
Ust'-Niman	89	51.23 N	132.42 E
Ust'-N'ukža	88	56.34 N	121.37 E
Uštobe	86	45.16 N	78.00 E
Ust'-Omčug	74	61.09 N	149.38 E
Ust'-Ordynskij	88	52.48 N	104.45 E
Ust'-Ordynskij Burjatskij Avtonomnyj Okrug □ 8	88	53.30 N	104.00 E
Ust'-Oz'ornaja	88	50.42 N	117.06 E
Ust'-Oz'ornoje	86	58.54 N	87.48 E
Ust'-Paden'ga	24	61.53 N	42.36 E
Ust'-Pečengskoje	76	59.47 N	42.37 E
Ust'-Pinega	24	64.11 N	41.56 E
Ust'-Pit	86	58.59 N	91.44 E
Ust'-Pogožje	80	49.28 N	44.38 E
Ustreka	76	58.38 N	34.33 E
Ust'-Reki	24	62.12 N	46.45 E
Ustroń	30	49.43 N	18.49 E
Ustrzyki Dolne	30	49.26 N	22.37 E
Ust'-Šara	76	60.13 N	33.57 E
Ust'-Ščerbedino	80	51.53 N	42.52 E
Ust'-Slav'anka ⊸ 8	265a	59.50 N	30.32 E
Ust'-Šonoša	24	61.10 N	41.18 E
Ust'-Sumy	86	54.48 N	80.26 E
Ust'-Tara	86	56.41 N	74.39 E
Ust'-Tarka	86	55.34 N	75.42 E
Ust'-Tašino	89	51.07 N	129.35 E
Ust'-Tygda	89	52.35 N	127.53 E
Ust'-Tym	86	59.26 N	80.08 E
Ust'-Tyrma	89	50.29 N	131.18 E
Ust'uckoje	76	58.32 N	35.20 E
Ust'-Uda	88	54.10 N	103.03 E
Üstükran	130	39.16 N	41.17 E
Ust'-Ulagan	86	50.38 N	87.58 E
Ust'-Umal'ta	89	51.39 N	133.18 E
Ust'-Undurga	89	53.07 N	118.04 E
Ust'-Unja	24	61.48 N	57.48 E
Ust'-Urgal	89	51.09 N	132.33 E
Ust'urt, plato ⋏ 1	72	43.00 N	56.00 E
Ust'-Us	86	52.07 N	92.17 E
Ust'-Usa	24	65.59 N	56.54 E
Ust'-Uza	80	52.58 N	45.17 E
Ust'užna	76	58.51 N	36.26 E
Ust'-Vichoreva	88	56.47 N	101.24 E
Ust'-Voja	24	64.27 N	57.40 E
Ust'-Vyjskaja	24	62.57 N	46.41 E
Ust'-Vym'	24	62.14 N	50.24 E
Ust'-Zaza	88	53.10 N	111.40 E
Ust'-Žuja	88	58.48 N	118.12 E
Usu	86	44.27 N	84.37 E
Usuchčaj	84	41.25 N	47.53 E
Usuda	94	36.12 N	138.29 E
Usugli	88	52.39 N	115.16 E
Usui	96	33.34 N	130.42 E
Usuki	96	33.08 N	131.49 E
Usuki-wan c	96	33.10 N	131.52 E
Usulután	236	13.21 N	88.27 W
Usumacinta ≃	232	18.24 N	92.38 W
Usumbura → Bujumbura	154	3.23 S	29.22 E
Ušumun	89	52.49 N	126.27 E
Ušur	80	57.47 N	52.58 E
Usuyŏng	98	34.35 N	126.18 E
Usu-zan ∧	92a	42.32 N	140.51 E
Usv'aty	76	55.45 N	30.45 E
Uta	71	39.17 N	8.57 E
Utah □ 3, U.S.	178	39.30 N	111.30 W
Utah □ 3, U.S.	200	39.30 N	111.30 W
Utah Lake ⊜	200	40.13 N	111.49 W
Utajärvi	26	64.45 N	26.23 E
Utamba	154	1.06 S	26.50 E
Utamboni ≃	152	1.00 N	9.48 E
Utan	115b	8.24 S	117.07 E
Utano	94	34.28 N	135.59 E
Utapi	156	17.31 S	15.08 E
Utashinai	92a	43.31 N	142.03 E
Utata	88	50.51 N	102.45 E
'Utaybah, Buḥayrat al- ⊜	132	33.32 N	36.37 E
Ute	198	42.03 N	95.42 W
Ute ≃	248	15.28 S	65.05 W
Ute Creek ≃	196	35.21 N	103.50 W
Utegi	154	1.20 S	34.35 E
Utelle	62	43.55 N	7.15 E
Utembo ≃	152	17.06 S	22.01 E
Ute Mountain Indian Reservation ⊸ 4	200	37.10 N	108.35 W
Utena	76	55.30 N	25.36 E
Utengule	154	8.57 S	35.50 E
Ute Reservoir ⊜ 1	196	36.21 N	103.31 W
Úterský potok ≃	60	49.48 N	13.06 E
Utersum	30	54.43 N	8.24 E
Utete	154	7.59 S	38.47 E
Utevka	80	52.57 N	50.58 E
Utfort	263	51.28 N	6.38 E
Uthai Thani	110	15.22 N	100.03 E
Uthal	120	25.48 N	66.37 E
U Thong	110	14.22 N	99.54 E
Uthumphon Phisai	110	15.05 N	104.08 E
Utiariti	248	13.02 S	58.17 W
Utica, Il., U.S.	216	41.20 N	89.00 W
Utica, In., U.S.	218	38.20 N	85.39 W
Utica, Ks., U.S.	198	38.38 N	100.10 W
Utica, Mi., U.S.	214	42.37 N	83.02 W
Utica, Ms., U.S.	194	32.06 N	90.37 W
Utica, Ne., U.S.	198	40.54 N	97.21 W
Utica, N.Y., U.S.	210	43.06 N	75.13 W
Utica, Oh., U.S.	214	40.14 N	82.27 W
Utica, Pa., U.S.	214	41.26 N	79.58 W
Utica → Utique ⊥	36	37.03 N	10.03 E
Utiel	34	39.34 N	1.12 W
Utikoomak Lake Indian Reserve ⊸ 4	182	55.57 N	115.30 W
Utikuma Lake ⊜	182	55.50 N	115.25 W
Utila	236	16.06 N	86.54 W
Utila, Isla de I	236	16.06 N	86.56 W
Utinga	287b	23.38 S	46.32 W
Utinga ≃	255	12.34 S	41.20 W
Utique	36	37.03 N	10.03 E
Utique ⊥	36	37.03 N	10.03 E
Utirik I 1	14	11.15 N	169.48 E
Utlängan I	26	56.01 N	15.47 E
Utl'ukskij liman c 1	78	46.15 N	35.12 E
Ut'ma	86	57.35 N	71.45 E
Utmānzai	123	34.11 N	71.46 E
Uto	92	32.41 N	130.40 E
Utö I	40	58.56 N	18.16 E
Utokota	156	17.50 S	20.22 E
Utonde	152	1.56 N	9.49 E
Utopia, Austl.	162	22.14 S	134.33 E
Utopia, Tx., U.S.	196	29.37 N	99.32 W
Utorgoš	76	58.17 N	30.15 E
Utraula	124	27.19 N	82.25 E
Utrecht, Ned.	52	52.05 N	5.08 E
Utrecht, S. Afr.	158	27.38 S	30.20 E
Utrecht □ 4	52	52.05 N	5.08 E
Utrera	34	37.11 N	5.47 W
Utroja ≃	76	57.23 N	28.09 E
Utsaladdy	224	48.15 N	122.30 W
Utsira	26	59.18 N	4.54 E
Utsjoki	24	69.53 N	27.00 E
Utsumi	96	34.21 N	133.17 E
Utsunomiya	94	36.33 N	139.52 E
Utta	80	46.23 N	46.01 E
Uttamapālāiyam	122	9.48 N	77.20 E
Uttaradit	110	17.38 N	100.06 E
Uttarkāshi	120	30.44 N	78.27 E
Uttarpara-Kotrung	272b	22.40 N	88.21 E
Uttar Pradesh □ 3	120	27.00 N	80.00 E
Uttendorf, Öst.	60	48.09 N	13.07 E
Uttendorf, Öst.	64	47.17 N	12.34 E
Uttenweiler	58	48.09 N	9.36 E
Ütterlingsen	263	51.15 N	7.45 E
Utting	60	48.02 N	11.05 E
Uttlesford □ 8	260	51.47 N	0.19 E
Uttoxeter	42	52.54 N	1.51 W
Utu	154	1.45 S	27.54 E
Utuado	240m	18.16 N	66.42 W
Utukok ≃	180	70.04 N	162.18 W
Utulei	174u	14.17 S	170.40 W
Utunomiya → Utsunomiya	94	36.33 N	139.52 E
Utupua I	14	11.16 S	166.29 E
Utva ≃	86	51.28 N	52.40 E
Utzenstorf	58	47.08 N	7.33 E
Uudenmaan lääni □ 4	26	60.30 N	25.00 E
Uulu	76	58.17 N	24.35 E
Üür ≃	88	50.18 N	101.54 E
Uusikaarlepyy (Nykarleby)	26	63.32 N	22.32 E
Uusikaupunki (Nystad)	26	60.48 N	21.25 E
Uusimaa ⊸ 1	26	60.30 N	25.00 E
Uvá, Bra.	255	15.53 S	50.25 W
Uva, Ross.	80	56.59 N	52.13 E
Uvá ≃	246	3.57 N	68.24 W
Uvalda	192	33.41 N	83.25 W
Uvalde	196	29.12 N	99.47 W
Úvaly	54	50.03 N	14.47 E
Uvån ≃	40	60.01 N	13.37 E
Uvaroviči	76	52.36 N	30.44 E
Uvarovka	76	55.32 N	35.37 E
Uvarovo	80	51.59 N	42.15 E
Uvas Creek ≃	226	36.58 N	121.33 W
Uvas Reservoir ⊜ 1	226	37.05 N	121.42 W
Uvat	86	59.09 N	68.54 E
'Uvda, Biq'at V	132	29.57 N	34.57 E
Uvdal	26	60.16 N	8.44 E
Uvel'skij	86	54.26 N	61.22 E
Uvernet	62	44.22 N	6.38 E
Uvero, Punta ›	241s	11.21 N	68.41 W
Uvinza	154	5.06 S	30.22 E
Uvira	154	3.24 S	29.08 E
Uvod' ≃	80	56.26 N	41.26 E
Uvongo Beach	158	30.51 S	30.23 E
Uvs □ 4	86	50.00 N	92.00 E
Uvs nuur ⊜	74	50.20 N	92.45 E
Uvworé ›	175f	18.47 S	169.16 E
Uwa	96	33.20 N	132.30 E
Uwajima	96	33.13 N	132.34 E
Uwa-kai ⫪ 2	96	33.15 N	132.15 E
'Uwaybid, Jabal ∧	142	30.06 N	32.09 E
Uwayl	140	8.46 N	27.24 E
'Uwaynāt	130	35.43 N	36.05 E
'Uwaynāt, Jabal al- ∧	140	21.54 N	24.58 E
'Uwayriḍ, Ḥarrat al- ⊻ 9	128	27.00 N	37.30 E
Uwchland	285	40.05 N	75.42 W
Uwi, Pulau I	112	1.05 N	107.24 E
Uxbridge, On., Can.	212	44.06 N	79.07 W
Uxbridge, Ma., U.S.	207	42.04 N	71.37 W
Uxbridge ⊸ 8	260	51.33 N	0.29 W
Uxmal ⊥	232	20.22 N	89.46 W
Uyak Bay c	180	57.36 N	153.57 W
Uyama	270	34.50 N	135.41 E
U-yin	110	22.53 N	95.13 E
Uyo	150	5.03 N	7.56 E
Uyu ≃	110	24.51 N	94.57 E
Uyuni	248	20.28 S	66.50 W
Uyuni, Salar de ≚	248	20.20 S	67.42 W
Už (Uh) ≃, Europe	30	48.34 N	22.00 E
Už ≃, Ukr.	78	51.15 N	30.12 E
Uza ≃, Ross.	76	57.48 N	29.31 E
Uza ≃, Ross.	80	53.02 N	45.18 E
Užanicha	86	54.41 N	81.02 E
Uzas	86	57.04 N	76.55 E
Užava	76	57.14 N	21.27 E
'Uzaym, Nahr al- ≃	128	34.01 N	44.19 E
Uzbekistan □ 1	72	41.00 N	64.00 E
Uzboj ≃	128	39.30 N	55.00 E
Uzda	76	53.27 N	27.13 E
Uzdin	38	45.12 N	20.38 E
Uzerche	32	45.26 N	1.34 E
Uzès	62	44.01 N	4.25 E
Uzgen	85	40.46 N	73.18 E
Užgorod	78	48.37 N	22.18 E
Užice → Titovo Užice	38	43.51 N	19.51 E
Uzin	78	49.50 N	30.24 E
Uzkij Lug	88	50.42 N	108.01 E
Uzkoje ⊸ 8	265b	55.37 N	37.32 E
Uzlovaja	76	53.59 N	38.10 E
Uzmorje	80	51.15 N	45.55 E
Uznach	58	47.14 N	9.00 E
Uznam (Usedom) I	54	54.00 N	14.00 E
Uzola ≃	80	56.32 N	43.38 E
Uz'ukovo	80	53.38 N	49.43 E
Üzümlü, Tür.	130	37.32 N	31.37 E
Üzümlü, Tür.	130	36.44 N	29.14 E
Uzun	85	38.22 N	68.03 E
Uzun Ada I	130	38.28 N	26.42 E
Uzunagač, Kaz.	85	43.13 N	76.20 E
Uzunagač, Kaz.	85	43.36 N	76.19 E
Uzunbulak	86	45.23 N	84.06 E
Uzunca ≃	267b	40.58 N	28.50 E
Uzunköprü	130	41.16 N	26.41 E
Uzunkuduk	85	40.33 N	67.11 E
Uzunkuyu	130	38.17 N	26.33 E
Uzunovo	82	54.32 N	38.37 E
Užur	86	55.20 N	89.50 E
Užventis	76	55.47 N	22.39 E
V			
Vä	26	55.59 N	14.05 E
Vaajakoski	26	62.16 N	25.54 E
Vääksy	26	61.11 N	25.33 E
Vaal ≃	158	29.04 S	23.38 E
Vaala	26	64.26 N	26.48 E
Vaaldam ⊜ 1	158	26.55 S	28.12 E
Vaalhartsdam ⊜ 1	158	28.06 S	24.55 E
Vaalkop ∧	158	31.21 S	26.31 E
Vaals	56	50.56 N	6.01 E
Vaalserberg ∧ 2	56	50.45 N	6.01 E
Vaalwater	156	24.20 S	28.03 E
Vaasa (Vasa)	26	63.06 N	21.36 E
Vaasan lääni □ 4	26	63.00 N	23.00 E
Vaassen	52	52.17 N	5.57 E
Vabalninkas	76	55.58 N	24.45 E
Vabkent	128	40.02 N	64.30 E
Vác	30	47.47 N	19.08 E
Vaca, Bol.	248	19.54 S	63.48 W
Vača, Ross.	80	55.48 N	42.46 E
Vaca, Mount ∧	226	38.24 N	122.06 W
Vacacaí ≃	252	29.55 S	53.06 W
Vaca Key I	220	24.43 N	81.04 W
Vacaria	252	28.30 S	50.56 W
Vacaria ≃, Bra.	255	16.39 S	42.45 W
Vacaria ≃, Bra.	255	21.55 S	53.59 W
Vacas, Arroyo de las ≃	258	34.00 S	58.18 W
Vacaville	226	38.21 N	121.59 W
Vacca, Kaap ›	158	34.21 S	21.53 E
Vaccarès, Étang de c	62	43.32 N	4.34 E
Vach ≃	74	60.45 N	76.45 E
Vacha	56	50.50 N	10.01 E
Vache, Île à I	238	18.05 N	73.38 W
Vaches, Île aux I	275a	45.41 N	73.40 W
Vaches, Rivière aux ≃	206	46.02 N	72.46 W
Vachrušev	89	48.59 N	142.58 E
Vachruševo	83	48.10 N	38.46 E
Vachš ≃	72	37.06 N	68.18 E
Vachšskij chrebet ⋏	85	38.35 N	69.45 E
Vachtan	80	57.58 N	46.42 E

Symbols in the index entries represent the broad categories identified in the key at the right. Symbols with superior numbers (⋏ 1) identify subcategories (see complete key on page *I · 1).*

Symbole im Register stellen die rechts im Schlüssel erklärten Kategorien dar. Symbole mit hochgestellten Ziffern (⋏ 1) bezeichnen Unterabteilungen einer Kategorie (vgl. vollständiger Schlüssel auf Seite *I · 1).*

Los símbolos incluídos en el texto del índice representan las grandes categorias identificadas con la clave a la derecha. Los símbolos con numeros en su parte superior (⋏ 1) identifican las subcategorías (véase la clave completa en la página *I · 1).*

Les symboles de l'index représentent les catégories indiquées dans la légende à droite. Les symboles suivis d'un indice (⋏ 1) représentent des sous-catégories (voir légende complète à la page *I · 1).*

Os símbolos incluídos no texto do índice representam as grandes categorias identificadas com a chave à direita. Os símbolos com números em sua parte superior (⋏ 1) identificam as subcategorias (veja-se a chave completa à página *I · 1).*

ENGLISH	DEUTSCH	ESPAÑOL	FRANÇAIS	PORTUGUÊS
∧ Mountain	Berg	Montaña	Montagne	Montanha
⋏ Mountains	Gebirge	Montañas	Montagnes	Montanhas
)(Pass	Paß	Paso	Col	Passo
V Valley, Canyon	Tal, Cañon	Valle, Cañón	Vallée, Canyon	Vale, Canhão
≚ Plain	Ebene	Llano	Plaine	Planície
› Cape	Kap	Cabo	Cap	Cabo
I Island	Insel	Isla	Île	Ilha
II Islands	Inseln	Islas	Îles	Ilhas
⊻ Other Topographic Features	Andere Topographische Objekte	Otros Elementos Topográficos	Autres données topographiques	Outros acidentes topográficos

ESPAÑOL / FRANÇAIS / PORTUGUÊS

Nombre / Nom / Nome	Página / Page	Lat.°′	Long.°′ W = Oeste / W = Ouest
Vači	84	42.05 N	47.13 E
Vacía Talega, Punta ≻	240m	18.27 N	65.54 W
Vacoas	157c	20.18 S	57.29 E
Vad, Ross.	80	55.32 N	44.12 E
Vad, Sve.	40	60.02 N	15.39 E
Vad ≃	80	54.33 N	42.37 E
Väddö I	40	60.00 N	18.50 E
Vădeni	38	45.22 N	27.56 E
Vader	224	46.24 N	122.57 W
Vadheim	26	61.13 N	5.49 E
Vādi	272c	18.56 N	73.06 E
Vadino	76	55.16 N	33.16 E
Vadinsk	80	53.43 N	43.04 E
Vadnagar	120	23.47 N	72.38 E
Vadodara	122	22.18 N	73.12 E
Vado de Cedillos	200	31.05 N	105.50 W
Vado de Piedra	196	29.50 N	104.40 W
Vado Hondo	200	31.09 N	111.22 W
Vado Ligure	62	44.17 N	8.27 E
Vadret, Piz ∧	58	46.41 N	9.57 E
Vadsbro	40	58.58 N	16.36 E
Vadsø	24	70.05 N	29.46 E
Vadstena	26	58.27 N	14.54 E
Vaduz	58	47.09 N	9.31 E
Vadvetjåkko Nationalpark ♦	24	68.35 N	18.20 E
Væggerløse	41	54.42 N	11.56 E
Værøy I	24	67.40 N	12.39 E
Vaga ≃	24	62.48 N	42.56 E
Vagaj	86	57.56 N	69.01 E
Vagaj ≃	86	57.59 N	69.01 E
Vågåmo	26	61.53 N	9.06 E
Vaganski Vrh ∧	36	44.22 N	15.31 E
Vaggeryd	26	57.30 N	14.07 E
Vaghena Island I	175e	7.26 S	157.46 E
Vaglia	66	43.54 N	11.17 E
Vaglio Basilicata	68	40.40 N	15.55 E
Vagney	58	48.01 N	6.43 E
Vagnhärad	40	58.55 N	17.30 E
Vagues	258	34.19 S	59.26 W
Váh ≃	30	47.55 N	18.00 E
Vaiano	66	43.58 N	11.07 E
Vaich, Loch ⊜	46	57.43 N	4.46 W
Vaiden	194	33.19 N	89.44 W
Vaigai ≃	122	9.21 N	79.00 E
Vaigat ⋓	176	70.11 N	53.00 W
Vaihingen an der Enz	56	48.56 N	8.58 E
Vaijāpur	122	19.55 N	74.44 E
Vaikam	122	9.46 N	76.24 E
Väike-Maarja	76	59.08 N	26.15 E
Väike Pakri I	76	59.20 N	24.00 E
Vail, Co., U.S.	200	39.38 N	106.22 W
Vail, Ia., U.S.	198	42.03 N	95.11 W
Vaila I	46a	60.12 N	1.37 W
Vailala ≃	164	7.25 S	145.25 E
Vaileka	175g	17.23 S	178.09 E
Vail Lake ⊜[1]	228	33.29 N	116.58 W
Vailly-sur-Aisne	50	49.25 N	3.31 E
Vailly-sur-Sauldre	50	47.27 N	2.39 E
Vail Mills	210	43.03 N	74.13 W
Vailoatai	174u	14.22 S	170.47 W
Vail Point ≻	212	44.43 N	80.45 W
Vails Gate	210	41.27 N	74.04 W
Vaimali	175f	16.34 S	168.11 E
Vaiņode	76	56.26 N	21.50 E
Vaiont, Lago di ⊜	64	46.21 N	10.21 E
Vaippār ≃	122	9.01 N	78.17 E
Vair ≃	58	48.27 N	5.42 E
Vairano Scalo	68	41.20 N	14.08 E
Vairao	174s	17.47 S	149.17 W
Vaires-sur-Marne	261	48.52 N	2.39 E
Vaison-la-Romaine	62	44.14 N	5.04 E
Vaitahu	174x	9.56 S	139.06 W
Vaîte	58	47.35 N	5.44 E
Vaitogi	174u	14.21 S	170.44 W
Vaitown	150	6.52 N	10.52 W
Vaitupu I	14	7.28 S	178.41 E
Vaja ≃	80	57.27 N	46.00 E
Vajgač	72	70.25 N	58.46 E
Vajgač, ostrov I	72	70.00 N	59.30 E
Vakaga □[5]	146	10.00 N	22.30 E
Vakaga ≃	146	9.48 N	21.32 E
Vākhān ≃	120	37.00 N	72.40 E
Vākhān ◆[1]	120	37.00 N	73.00 E
Vaklan	272c	19.07 N	73.06 E
Vaksdal	26	60.29 N	5.44 E
Vala ≃	80	56.59 N	51.16 E
Valaam	24	61.23 N	30.57 E
Valaam, ostrov I	26	61.22 N	30.57 E
Vålådalen	26	63.10 N	12.57 E
Valadeces	196	26.14 N	98.40 W
Valadim	154	12.22 S	36.10 E
Valais (Wallis) □[3]	58	46.10 N	7.30 E
Valaisannes, Alpes ⋏	58	46.00 N	7.30 E
Val-Alain	206	46.24 N	71.45 W
Valamaz	80	57.32 N	52.05 E
Valandovo	38	41.19 N	22.34 E
Valangin	58	47.01 N	6.54 E
Valap	272c	19.03 N	73.08 E
Valare, Baie ⊂	174s	17.31 S	149.46 W
Valašské Klobouky	30	49.08 N	18.01 E
Valašské Meziříčí	30	49.28 N	17.58 E
Valatie	210	42.24 N	73.40 W
Vala Ull	272c	19.02 N	73.07 E
Val-Bélair	206	46.51 N	71.26 W
Valbella	58	46.45 N	9.33 E
Vålberg	26	59.24 N	13.12 E
Valbert	56	51.07 N	7.44 E
Valbo	40	60.40 N	17.04 E
Valbondione	64	46.02 N	10.00 E
Valbonnais	62	44.54 N	5.54 E
Valcanuta ◆[8]	267a	41.53 N	12.25 E
Vâlcĕdrâm	38	43.42 N	23.27 E
Valcheta	254	40.42 S	66.09 W
Valchetta ≃	267a	41.58 N	12.30 E
Valchiusella	62	45.32 N	7.42 E
Valcivières	62	45.35 N	3.48 E
Valcourt	206	45.29 N	72.18 W
Valdagno	64	45.39 N	11.18 E
Valdahon	58	47.09 N	6.21 E
Valdai Hills → Valdajskaja vozvyšennost' ⋏[2]	76	57.00 N	33.30 E
Valdaj, Ross.	24	63.26 N	35.30 E
Valdaj, Ross.	76	57.59 N	33.14 E
Valdajskaja vozvyšennost' ⋏[2]	24	57.00 N	33.30 E
Valdarno V	66	43.45 N	11.15 E
Valdavia ≃	34	42.24 N	4.16 W
Val-David	206	46.01 N	74.12 W
Valdebeba, Arroyo de ≃	266a	41.23 N	2.10 E
Valdeblore	62	44.04 N	7.12 E
Val-de-Cães	250	1.23 S	48.29 W
Valdecañas, Embalse de ⊜[1]	34	39.45 N	5.30 W
Valdelândia	255	15.11 S	50.02 W
Val-de-Marne □[5]	261	48.47 N	2.29 E
Valdemārpils	76	57.22 N	22.35 E
Valdemarsvik	26	58.12 N	16.36 E
Valdepeñas	34	38.46 N	3.23 W
Valderaduey ≃	34	41.31 N	5.42 W
Valderas	34	42.05 N	5.27 W
Valderice	70	38.03 N	12.38 E
Valderrama	116	11.00 N	122.08 E
Valderrobres	34	40.53 N	0.09 E
Valders	190	44.03 N	87.53 W
Valdés, Península ≻[1]	254	42.30 S	64.00 W
Val-des-Bois	188	45.54 N	75.35 W
Valdese	192	35.44 N	81.33 W
Valdes Island I	224	49.04 N	123.38 W
Valdéz, Ec.	246	1.15 N	79.00 W
Valdez, Ak., U.S.	180	61.07 N	146.16 W
Valdieri	62	44.17 N	7.24 E
Val-d'Isère	62	45.27 N	6.59 E
Valdivia, Chile	254	39.48 S	73.14 W
Valdivia, Col.	246	7.11 N	75.27 W
Valdobbiadene	64	45.54 N	12.00 E
Valdoie	58	47.40 N	6.51 E
Val-d'Oise □[5]	50	49.10 N	2.10 E
Val-d'Or	190	48.07 N	77.47 W
Valdorf	52	52.09 N	8.51 E
Valdosta	192	30.49 N	83.16 W
Valdoviño	34	43.36 N	8.08 W
Valdres V	26	60.55 N	9.10 E
Valdurna (Durnholz)	64	46.44 N	11.26 E
Vale, Guernsey	43b	49.29 N	2.31 W
Vale, Or., U.S.	202	43.58 N	117.14 W
Valea lui Mihai	38	47.31 N	22.09 E
Vale de Lobos	266c	38.49 N	9.17 W
Valeene	218	38.26 N	86.24 W
Valeggio sul Mincio	64	45.21 N	10.44 E
Valehouse Reservoir ⊜[1]	262	53.29 N	1.57 W
Valemount	182	52.50 N	119.15 W
Valença, Bra.	255	13.22 S	39.05 W
Valença, Bra.	256	22.15 S	43.43 W
Valença, Port.	34	42.02 N	8.38 W
Valença do Piauí	250	6.24 S	41.45 W
Valençay	50	47.09 N	1.34 E
Valence	62	44.56 N	4.54 E
Valence → València	34	39.28 N	0.22 W
València, Esp.	34	39.28 N	0.22 W
Valencia, Hond.	236	14.47 N	85.18 W
Valencia, Pil.	116	7.57 N	125.03 E
Valencia, Ca., U.S.	228	34.26 N	118.36 W
Valencia, Pa., U.S.	214	40.40 N	79.59 W
Valencia, Ven.	246	10.11 N	68.00 W
València □[4]	34	39.30 N	0.45 W
València, Golf de ⊂	34	39.50 N	0.30 E
Valencia, Lago de ⊜	246	10.15 N	67.45 W
Valencia, Quebrada ≃	286c	10.30 N	66.46 W
Valencia de Alcántara	34	39.25 N	7.14 W
Valencia de Don Juan	34	42.18 N	5.31 W
Valencia Island I	48	51.52 N	10.20 W
Valenciennes	50	50.21 N	3.32 E
Vălenii de Munte	38	45.12 N	26.03 E
Valensole	62	43.50 N	5.59 E
Valentano	66	42.34 N	11.49 E
Valente	250	11.34 S	39.27 W
Valentigney	58	47.28 N	6.50 E
Valentin	89	43.08 N	134.17 E
Valentín Alsina ◆[8]	288	34.40 S	58.25 W
Valentine, Ne., U.S.	198	42.52 N	100.33 W
Valentine, Tx., U.S.	196	30.34 N	104.29 W
Valentine Mountain ∧	224	48.32 N	123.56 W
Valentinovka	265b	55.55 N	37.56 E
Valenton	261	48.45 N	2.28 E
Valenza	62	45.01 N	8.38 E
Valenzano	68	41.02 N	16.53 E
Valenzuela	269f	14.42 N	120.58 E
Våler	26	60.40 N	11.50 E
Valera	246	9.19 N	70.37 W
Valérien, Mont ∧[2]	261	48.53 N	2.13 E
Vale Royal □[8]	262	53.17 N	2.37 W
Valets, Lac ⊜	190	48.32 N	76.30 W
Valette, La → Valletta	36	35.54 N	14.31 E
Valfabbrica	66	43.09 N	12.36 E
Valflaunès	62	43.48 N	3.52 E
Valfurva	64	46.27 N	10.25 E
Valfurva V	64	46.26 N	10.26 E
Valga	76	57.47 N	26.02 E
Valge ≃	76	59.35 N	25.42 E
Valgorge	62	44.35 N	4.07 E
Valgrisanche	62	45.38 N	7.04 E
Valguarnera Caropepe	70	37.30 N	14.23 E
Valhalla, S. Afr.	158	25.49 S	28.08 E
Valhalla, N.Y., U.S.	210	41.04 N	73.46 W
Valhalla, Lake ⊜	276	40.56 N	74.22 W
Valiente, Península ≻[1]	236	9.05 N	81.51 W
Valiente, Punta ≻	236	9.11 N	81.55 W
Valier, Il., U.S.	194	38.01 N	89.03 W
Valier, Mt., U.S.	202	48.18 N	112.14 W
Valier, Pa., U.S.	214	40.55 N	79.03 W
Valili ∧	175g	16.39 S	179.10 E
Valinda	280	34.02 N	117.56 W
Valinhos	256	22.57 S	47.01 W
Valjevo	38	44.16 N	19.53 E
Valka	76	57.46 N	26.00 E
Valkeakoski	26	61.16 N	24.02 E
Valkenburg	56	50.52 N	5.50 E
Valkenswaard	52	51.21 N	5.28 E
V'alki, Ross.	82	55.39 N	38.05 E
Valki, Ukr.	78	49.50 N	35.37 E
Valkininkas	76	54.21 N	24.50 E
Valla	40	59.02 N	16.23 E
Valladares	196	26.53 N	100.37 W
Valladolid, Ec.	246	4.33 S	79.08 W
Valladolid, Esp.	34	41.39 N	4.43 W
Valladolid, Méx.	232	20.41 N	88.12 W
Valladolid □[4]	34	41.40 N	4.50 W
Vallage ◆[1]	58	48.24 N	5.00 E
Vallåkra	41	55.58 N	12.52 E
Vallarsa	64	45.47 N	11.07 E
Vallata	68	41.02 N	15.15 E
Vallauris	62	43.35 N	7.03 E
Vallco Fashion Park ◆[9]	282	37.19 N	122.01 W
Valldal	26	62.20 N	7.21 E
Valldoreix	266d	41.28 N	2.04 E
Valle, Esp.	34	43.14 N	4.18 W
Valle, It.	64	46.04 N	10.25 E
Valle, Lat.	76	56.30 N	24.44 E
Valle □[5]	236	13.30 N	87.35 W
Valle, Arroyo ≃	226	37.39 N	121.54 W
Vallecas ◆[8]	266a	40.23 N	3.37 W
Valle Castellana	66	42.44 N	13.29 E
Vallecillo	196	26.40 N	99.58 W
Vallecito	226	38.07 N	120.27 W
Vallecitos	200	36.05 N	106.20 W
Vallecitos Creek ≃	282	37.36 N	121.53 W
Vallecorsa	66	41.27 N	13.24 E
Valle Crucis Abbey ⌂[1]	42	52.59 N	3.12 W
Valle d'Aosta □[4]	62	45.45 N	7.25 E
Valle de Bravo	234	19.11 N	100.08 W
Valle de Guadalupe	234	21.00 N	102.37 W
Valle de Guanape	246	9.54 N	65.41 W
Valle de Juárez	234	19.53 N	102.51 W
Valle de la Pascua	246	9.13 N	66.00 W
Valle del Cauca □[5]	246	3.45 N	76.30 W
Valle de Olivos	232	27.12 N	106.17 W
Valle de Santiago	234	20.23 N	101.12 W
Valle de Zaragoza	232	27.28 N	105.49 W
Valle di Cadore	64	46.24 N	12.20 E
Valle di Sotto	64	46.25 N	10.21 E
Valledolmo	70	37.45 N	13.49 E
Valledupar	246	10.29 N	73.15 W
Valle Edén	252	31.50 S	56.09 W
Vallefiorita	68	38.46 N	16.27 E
Vallegrande	248	18.29 S	64.06 W
Valle Hermoso, Arg.	252	31.07 S	64.29 W
Valle Hermoso, Méx.	196	25.39 N	97.52 W
Vallehermoso, Pil.	116	10.20 N	123.19 E
Vallejo	226	38.06 N	122.15 W
Valle Lomellina	62	45.09 N	8.40 E
Vallelunga Pratameno	70	37.41 N	13.50 E
Valle Mosso	62	45.38 N	8.09 E
Vällen ⊜	40	60.03 N	18.20 E
Vallenar	252	28.35 S	70.46 W
Vallendar	56	50.24 N	7.37 E
Vallensbæk	41	55.38 N	12.22 E
Vallentuna	40	59.32 N	18.05 E
Vallepietra	66	41.55 N	13.14 E
Valleraugue	62	44.05 N	3.38 E
Valle Redondo	204	32.31 N	116.46 W
Vallermosa	71	39.22 N	8.48 E
Vallerotonda	66	41.33 N	13.55 E
Valleroy	56	49.12 N	5.55 E
Valles Caldera ⩡[6]	200	35.52 N	106.33 W
Valles → Ciudad de Valles	234	21.59 N	99.01 W
Vallet	32	47.10 N	1.16 W
Valletta	36	35.54 N	14.31 E
Valley, Al., U.S.	194	32.49 N	85.10 W
Valley, Ne., U.S.	198	41.18 N	96.20 W
Valley, Wa., U.S.	182	48.10 N	117.43 W
Valley ≃	184	51.21 N	99.55 W
Valley Bend	188	38.46 N	79.56 W
Valley Center, Ca., U.S.	228	33.13 N	117.02 W
Valley Center, Ks., U.S.	198	37.50 N	97.22 W
Valley City, N.D., U.S.	198	46.55 N	97.59 W
Valley City, Oh., U.S.	214	41.14 N	81.56 W
Valley Cottage	210	41.07 N	73.57 W
Valley Creek ≃, Pa., U.S.	285	40.06 N	75.28 W
Valley Creek ≃, Pa., U.S.	285	39.58 N	75.40 W
Valley Creek ≃, Tx., U.S.	196	31.43 N	100.02 W
Valleydale	280	34.06 N	117.56 W
Valley Falls, Ks., U.S.	198	39.20 N	95.27 W
Valley Falls, N.Y., U.S.	210	42.54 N	73.34 W
Valley Falls, R.I., U.S.	207	41.54 N	71.23 W
Valley Farms	200	32.59 N	111.26 W
Valleyfield	186	49.08 N	53.37 W
Valley Forge	208	40.05 N	75.28 W
Valley Forge Estates	285	40.05 N	75.26 W
Valley Forge National Historical Park ♦	208	40.06 N	75.27 W
Valley Grove	214	40.05 N	80.34 W
Valley Head, Al., U.S.	194	34.34 N	85.36 W
Valley Head, W.V., U.S.	188	38.32 N	80.02 W
Valley Home	226	37.50 N	120.55 W
Valley Mede	284b	39.17 N	76.50 W
Valley Mills	222	31.39 N	97.28 W
Valley of Desolation National Monument ♦	158	32.17 S	24.30 E
Valley of Fire State Park ♦	204	36.26 N	114.30 W
Valley of the Kings ⊥	140	25.45 N	32.37 E
Valley Park	219	38.32 N	90.29 W
Valley Plaza ◆[9]	280	34.11 N	118.24 W
Valley Springs, Ca., U.S.	226	38.12 N	120.50 W
Valley Springs, S.D., U.S.	198	43.34 N	96.28 W
Valley Station	194	38.06 N	85.52 W
Valley Stream	210	40.39 N	73.42 W
Valley Stream ≃	276	40.39 N	73.45 W
Valley Stream State Park ♦	276	40.41 N	73.42 W
Valleyview, Ab., Can.	182	55.04 N	117.17 W
Valley View, Il., U.S.	216	41.50 N	88.03 W
Valley View, Oh., U.S.	279a	41.23 N	81.37 W
Valley View, Pa., U.S.	210	40.38 N	76.32 W
Valley View, Tx., U.S.	196	33.29 N	97.10 W
Valley View Park	228	34.13 N	117.20 W
Vallgrund I	26	63.12 N	21.14 E
Valliant	196	34.00 N	95.05 W
Valli del Pasubio	64	45.41 N	11.15 E
Vallières	58	45.54 N	5.56 E
Vallimanca, Arroyo ≃	252	35.40 S	60.02 W
Vallio	64	45.38 N	10.23 E
Vallirana	266d	41.23 N	1.56 E
Vallø	41	55.24 N	12.15 E
Vallo della Lucania	68	40.14 N	15.17 E
Valloire	62	45.10 N	6.26 E
Vallombrosa	64	43.44 N	11.32 E
Vallonia	218	38.50 N	86.05 W
Vallon-Pont-d'Arc	62	44.24 N	4.24 E
Vallorbe	58	46.43 N	6.22 E
Vallorcine	58	46.02 N	6.56 E
Vallouise	62	44.51 N	6.29 E
Vallromanes	266d	41.32 N	2.18 E
Valls	34	41.17 N	1.15 E
Valluga ∧	58	47.09 N	10.12 E
Vallvidrera ◆[8]	266d	41.25 N	2.07 E
Vallvidrera, Riera de ≃	266d	41.25 N	2.01 E
Val-Marie	184	49.14 N	107.44 W
Valmaseda	34	43.12 N	3.12 W
Valmeyer	219	38.17 N	90.18 W
Valmiera	76	57.33 N	25.24 E
Valmondois	261	49.06 N	2.12 E
Valmont	50	49.44 N	0.31 E
Valmontone	66	41.46 N	12.57 E
Valmy	56	49.05 N	4.46 E
Valognes	32	49.31 N	1.28 W
Valois	210	42.32 N	76.53 W
Valois, Baie de ⊂	275a	45.26 N	73.47 W
Valok	78	45.47 N	34.57 E
Valona → Vlorë	38	40.27 N	19.30 E
Valongo	34	41.11 N	8.30 W
Valoria la Buena	34	41.48 N	4.32 W
Vālpārai	122	10.22 N	76.58 E
Valparaíso, Bra.	255	21.13 S	50.51 W
Valparaíso, Chile	252	33.02 S	71.38 W
Valparaíso, Méx.	234	22.46 N	103.34 W
Valparaiso, Fl., U.S.	194	30.29 N	86.29 W
Valparaiso, In., U.S.	216	41.28 N	87.03 W
Valparaiso, Ne., U.S.	198	41.04 N	96.49 W
Valparaíso □[4]	252	32.45 S	71.20 W
Valparaíso ≃	234	22.33 N	103.39 W
Valpelline V	62	45.50 N	7.25 E
Valpolicella ◆[1]	64	45.25 N	10.52 E
Valpovo	38	45.39 N	18.26 E
Valprato Soana	62	45.31 N	7.33 E
Valréas	62	44.23 N	4.59 E
Valrico	220	27.57 N	82.16 W
Val Roveto V	66	41.52 N	13.30 E
Vals ≃	158	27.23 S	26.30 E
Vals, Tanjung ≻	164	8.26 S	137.38 E
Val-Saint-Michel	206	46.52 N	71.27 W
Valsbaai ⊂	158	34.12 S	18.40 E
Valserine ≃	58	46.06 N	5.50 E
Valserrhein ≃	58	46.42 N	9.10 E
Valsertal V	58	46.37 N	9.10 E
Valsetz	202	44.50 N	123.39 W
Valsinni	68	40.10 N	16.26 E
Valsjöbyn	26	64.04 N	14.08 E
Valskog	40	59.27 N	15.57 E
Vals-les-Bains	62	44.40 N	4.22 E
Vals Platz	58	46.37 N	9.11 E
Vals-Près-le-Puy	62	45.01 N	3.52 E
Valstagna	64	45.51 N	11.39 E
Val-Suzon	58	47.25 N	4.54 E
Valtellina V	64	46.11 N	9.55 E
Valthermond	52	52.53 N	6.59 E
Valtice	61	48.44 N	16.45 E
Valtierrilla	234	20.32 N	101.08 W
Valtimo	26	63.40 N	28.48 E
Valtorta	58	45.59 N	9.32 E
Valtournanche	62	45.53 N	7.37 E
Valujec	76	52.46 N	33.23 E
Valujevka	80	46.44 N	43.43 E
Valujevo	265b	55.35 N	37.21 E
Valujki	78	50.13 N	38.08 E
Valvasone	64	45.59 N	12.52 E
Valverde	148	27.48 N	17.55 W
Valverde del Camino	34	37.34 N	6.45 W
Val Verde Park	228	34.27 N	118.40 W
Valyermo	228	34.26 N	117.50 W
Vamba ≃	152	7.27 S	14.17 E
Vamdrup	41	55.25 N	9.17 E
Våmhus	26	61.08 N	14.28 E
Vamizi, Ilha I	154	11.02 S	40.40 E
Vammala	26	61.20 N	22.54 E
Vamori Wash V	200	31.57 N	112.21 W
Van, Tür.	128	38.28 N	43.20 E
Van, Pa., U.S.	214	41.19 N	79.40 W
Van, Tx., U.S.	222	32.31 N	95.38 W
Van □[4]	128	39.00 N	43.45 E
Vanajavesi ⊜	26	61.09 N	24.15 E
Vanak ◆[8]	267d	35.45 N	51.23 E
Van Alstyne	196	33.25 N	96.34 W
Vanån ≃	40	60.31 N	14.14 E
Vananda	182	49.45 N	124.33 W
Vanapa ≃	164	9.05 S	147.10 E
Vanault-les-Dames	56	48.51 N	4.46 E
Vanavana I[1]	14	20.47 S	139.09 W
Vanavara	74	60.22 N	102.16 E
Van Buren, Ar., U.S.	194	35.26 N	94.20 W
Van Buren, In., U.S.	216	40.37 N	85.30 W
Van Buren, Me., U.S.	186	47.09 N	67.56 W
Van Buren, Mo., U.S.	194	36.59 N	91.00 W
Van Buren, Oh., U.S.	216	41.08 N	83.38 W
Van Buren □[6]	216	42.14 N	86.04 W
Van Buren Point	214	42.27 N	79.25 W
Vanč	85	38.23 N	71.26 E
Vanč ≃	85	38.18 N	71.19 E
Vance Air Force Base ■	196	36.21 N	97.55 W
Vanceboro	188	45.33 N	67.25 W
Vanceburg	218	38.35 N	83.19 W
Vancleave	194	30.32 N	88.41 W
Van Cortlandt Park ♦	276	40.54 N	73.53 W
Van Cortlandtville	210	41.19 N	73.54 W
Vancouver, B.C., Can.	224	49.16 N	123.07 W
Vancouver, Wa., U.S.	224	45.38 N	122.39 W
Vancouver, Cape ≻, Austl.	162	35.01 S	118.12 E
Vancouver, Cape ≻, Ak., U.S.	180	60.33 N	165.27 W
Vancouver, Mount ∧	180	60.20 N	139.40 W
Vancouver International Airport ⊠	224	48.39 N	123.26 W
Vancouver Island I	182	49.45 N	126.00 W
Vancouver Island Ranges ⋏	182	49.25 N	125.25 W
Vancouver Lake ⊜	224	45.41 N	122.44 W
Van Daalen ≃	164	3.05 S	138.09 E
Vandalia, Il., U.S.	219	38.57 N	89.05 W
Vandalia, Mi., U.S.	216	41.55 N	85.55 W
Vandalia, Mo., U.S.	219	39.18 N	91.29 W
Vandalia, Oh., U.S.	218	39.53 N	84.11 W
Vandalia Lake ⊜[1]	219	39.01 N	89.09 W
Vandam	84	40.57 N	47.57 E
Vandavāsi	122	12.30 N	79.37 E
Vandekerckhove Lake ⊜	184	57.02 N	101.25 W
Vandel	41	55.42 N	9.13 E
Vandenberg Air Force Base ■	204	34.43 N	120.33 W
Van den Bosch, Tanjung ≻	164	4.06 S	132.55 E
Vandenesse	58	47.13 N	4.37 E
Vanderbijlpark	158	26.42 S	27.54 E
Vanderbilt, Mi., U.S.	190	45.08 N	84.39 W
Vanderbilt, Tx., U.S.	196	28.49 N	96.37 W
Vanderbilt Mansion National Historic Site ⊥	210	41.47 N	73.56 W
Vanderbilt Museum ⌂	276	40.54 N	73.22 W
Vandercook Lake	216	42.11 N	84.23 W
Vandergrift	214	40.36 N	79.33 W
Vanderhoof	182	54.01 N	124.01 W
Vanderlin Island I	164	15.44 S	137.02 E
Vandervoort	194	34.22 N	94.21 W
Van Diemen, Cape ≻, Austl.	164	11.10 S	130.23 E
Van Diemen, Cape ≻, Austl.	164	16.31 S	139.41 E
Van Diemen Gulf ⊂	164	11.50 S	132.00 E
Vandling	210	41.38 N	75.29 W
Vandoeuvre-lès-Nancy	58	48.39 N	6.11 E
Vandoies (Vintl)	64	46.49 N	11.43 E
Vändra	76	58.39 N	25.02 E
Van Duzen ≃	204	40.33 N	124.08 W
Vandúzi ≃	154	18.56 S	34.01 E
Vandykpark	273d	26.16 S	28.19 E
Vandžiogala	76	55.07 N	23.58 E
Vanegas	234	23.51 N	100.52 W
Vänern ⊜	26	58.55 N	13.30 E
Vänersborg	26	58.22 N	12.19 E
Van Etten	210	42.11 N	76.33 W
Vang, Mount ∧	9	73.56 S	68.39 W
Vanga	154	4.39 S	39.13 E
Vangaindrano	157b	23.21 S	47.36 E
Vängelälven ≃	26	63.41 N	16.25 E
Van Gölü ⊜	128	38.33 N	42.46 E
Vangsnes	26	61.11 N	6.38 E
Vanguard	184	49.55 N	107.20 W
Vangunu, Mount ∧	175e	8.42 S	158.00 E
Vangunu Island I	175e	8.38 S	158.00 E
Van Hook Arm ⊂	198	47.50 N	102.25 W
Van Horn	196	31.02 N	104.49 W
Van Horne	190	42.00 N	92.05 W
Van Hornesville	210	42.54 N	74.50 W
Vani	84	42.06 N	42.30 E
Vanier	212	45.26 N	75.40 W
Vanikolo I	14	11.39 S	166.54 E
Vaniköy ◆[8]	267b	41.04 N	29.04 E
Vanimo	164	2.40 S	141.20 E
Vanino	89	49.05 N	140.15 E
Vānīvilāsa Sāgara ⊜[1]	122	13.52 N	76.26 E
Vāniyambādi	122	12.41 N	78.37 E
Vankarem	180	67.51 N	175.50 W
Vankarem ≃	180	67.42 N	176.17 W
Vankarem, laguna ⊂	180	67.40 N	176.00 W
Vankaremskaja nizmennost' ≚	180	67.30 N	176.00 W
Van Kleef Aquarium ♦	271c	1.18 N	103.51 E
Vankleek Hill	206	45.31 N	74.39 W
Vanlay	50	48.02 N	4.01 E
Van Lear	192	37.46 N	82.45 W
Vanlue	216	40.58 N	83.28 W
Vanna I	24	70.09 N	19.51 E
Vännäs	26	63.55 N	19.45 E
Vanndale	194	35.18 N	90.46 W
Vanne ≃	50	48.12 N	3.16 E
Vanne et du Loing, Aqueduc de ≅[1]	261	48.36 N	2.26 E
Vannes	32	47.39 N	2.46 W
Vannes-sur-Cosson	50	47.43 N	2.13 E
Van Ninh	110	12.42 N	109.14 E
Van Norman Lakes ⊜[1]	228	34.18 N	118.28 W
Vannovka	85	42.32 N	70.21 E
Van Nuys ◆[8]	228	34.11 N	118.26 W
Van Nuys Airport ⊠	280	34.12 N	118.29 W
Van Nuys-Sherman Oaks War Memorial Park ♦	280	34.10 N	118.27 W
Vanoi ≃	64	46.06 N	11.45 E
Vanoise, Massif de la ⋏	62	45.20 N	6.40 E
Vanoise, Parc National de la ♦	62	45.20 N	6.45 E
Van Ormer	214	40.41 N	78.30 W
Van Phong, Vung ⊂	110	12.33 N	109.18 E
Vanport	214	40.41 N	80.20 W
Van Reenen	158	28.22 S	29.24 E
Van Reenen's Plaats	158	30.55 S	21.14 E
Van Rees, Pegunungan ⋏	164	2.35 S	138.15 E
Vanrhynsdorp	158	31.36 S	18.44 E
Vanrook	166	16.57 S	141.57 E
Vanryndam ⊜[1]	273d	26.09 S	28.21 E
Vansant	192	37.13 N	82.05 W
Van Saun Mill Brook ≃	276	40.55 N	74.03 W
Vansbro	40	60.31 N	14.13 E
Van Sciver Lake ⊜	285	40.09 N	74.48 W
Van Sickle Island I	282	38.04 N	121.53 W
Vansittart Island I	176	65.50 N	84.00 W
Vansjön ⊜	40	59.59 N	16.57 E
Vanskoje	76	58.56 N	36.52 E
Vanstadensrus	158	29.59 S	27.02 E
Vantaa (Vanda)	26	60.16 N	25.03 E
Vantaa ≃	26	60.13 N	24.59 E
Vanthali	120	21.29 N	70.20 E
Vanua Lava I	175f	13.48 S	167.28 E
Vanua Levu I	175g	16.33 S	179.15 E
Vanua Mbalavu Island I	175g	17.40 S	178.57 W
Vanuatu □[1], Oc.	14	16.00 S	167.00 E
Vanuatu □[1], Oc.	175f	16.00 S	167.00 E
Vanves	261	48.50 N	2.18 E
Van Vleck	222	29.01 N	95.53 W
Van Voorhis	279b	40.10 N	79.58 W
Van Wert	216	40.52 N	84.35 W
Van Wert □[6]	216	40.52 N	84.35 W
Vanwyksdorp	158	33.46 S	21.28 E
Vanwyksvlei	158	30.18 S	21.49 E
Vanzaghello	266b	45.35 N	8.47 E
Vanzago	266b	45.32 N	9.00 E
Van Zandt □[6]	222	32.35 N	95.50 W
Vanzylsrus	158	26.52 S	22.04 E
Vao	175f	22.39 S	167.32 E
Vapn'arka	78	48.32 N	28.44 E
Vaprio d'Adda	62	45.35 N	9.31 E
Vaqueros Creek ≃	226	36.16 N	121.20 W
Var □[5]	62	43.30 N	6.20 E
Var ≃	62	43.39 N	7.12 E
Vara	26	58.16 N	12.57 E
Vara ≃	64	44.09 N	9.53 E
Varada ≃	122	14.55 N	75.40 E
Varadero	240p	23.09 N	81.16 W
Varades	32	47.23 N	1.02 W
Varages	62	43.36 N	5.58 E
Varaita ≃	62	44.49 N	7.36 E
Varaita, Valle V	62	44.35 N	7.10 E
Varaklāni	76	56.37 N	26.44 E
Varallo, It.	62	45.49 N	8.15 E
Varallo, It.	266b	45.40 N	8.38 E
Varāmīn	128	35.20 N	51.39 E
Vārānasi (Benares)	124	25.20 N	83.00 E
Varandej	24	68.48 N	58.00 E
Varangerfjorden ⊂[2]	24	70.00 N	30.00 E
Varangerhalvøya ≻[1]	24	70.25 N	29.30 E
Varangéville	56	48.38 N	6.19 E
Varano, Lago Di ⊂	68	41.53 N	15.45 E
Varano de'Melegari	64	44.41 N	10.01 E
Varapodio	68	38.19 N	15.59 E
Varaždin	36	46.19 N	16.20 E
Varazze	62	44.22 N	8.34 E
Varberg	26	57.06 N	12.15 E
Varces	62	45.05 N	5.41 E
Varciche	84	42.08 N	42.43 E
Vardak □[4]	120	34.15 N	68.00 E
Vardaman	194	33.52 N	89.10 W
Vardar (Axiós) ≃	38	40.35 N	22.50 E
Varde	26	55.38 N	8.29 E
Vardenik	84	40.08 N	45.27 E
Vardenis	84	40.11 N	45.43 E
Vardenskij chrebet ⋏	84	39.58 N	45.25 E
Vardhoúsia Óri ⋏	38	38.44 N	22.07 E
Vardø	24	70.21 N	31.02 E
Vardūj ≃	123	37.01 N	70.47 E
Varedo	62	45.36 N	9.09 E
Varegovo	80	57.47 N	39.17 E
Varel	52	53.22 N	8.10 E
Varela	252	34.07 S	66.27 W
Varėna	76	54.13 N	24.34 E
Varengeville-sur-Mer	50	49.55 N	0.59 E
Varenikovskaja	78	45.07 N	37.37 E
Varenna	58	46.01 N	9.17 E
Varenne ≃	50	49.53 N	1.08 E
Varennes	206	45.41 N	73.26 W
Varennes, Îles de II	275a	45.40 N	73.27 W
Varennes-en-Argonne	56	49.14 N	5.02 E
Varennes-Jarcy	261	48.41 N	2.34 E
Varennes-Saint-Sauveur	58	46.29 N	5.15 E
Varennes-sur-Allier	32	46.19 N	3.24 E
Varennes-sur-Amance	58	47.54 N	5.37 E
Varenovka	83	47.18 N	39.02 E
Vareš	38	44.09 N	18.19 E
Varese	62	45.48 N	8.48 E
Varese □[4]	62	45.48 N	8.40 E
Varese, Lago di ⊜	62	45.49 N	8.45 E
Varese Ligure	62	44.22 N	9.37 E
Varèze ≃	62	45.25 N	4.45 E
Varfolomejevka	80	50.01 N	48.12 E
Vårgårda	26	58.02 N	12.48 E
Vargas □[5]	286c	10.34 N	66.52 W
Vargaši	86	55.23 N	65.48 E
Vargem	256	22.53 S	46.25 W
Vargem, Riacho da ≃	250	8.42 S	39.09 W
Vargem Alegre	256	22.30 S	43.55 W
Vargem do Laje	256	22.08 S	44.49 W
Vargem Grande	250	3.33 S	43.56 W
Vargem Grande ◆[8]	287a	22.59 S	43.29 W
Vargem Grande, Ribeirão da ≃	256	22.17 S	45.40 W
Vargem Grande do Sul	256	21.50 S	46.53 W
Vargem Grande Paulista	256	23.36 S	47.01 W
Varginha	256	21.33 S	45.26 W
Vargön	26	58.22 N	12.22 E
Varigotti	62	44.11 N	8.24 E
Väringen ⊜	40	59.26 N	15.23 E
Varirata National Park ♦	164	9.20 S	147.20 E
Varjão	255	17.03 S	49.37 W
Varkallai	122	8.40 N	76.50 E
Varkaus	26	62.19 N	27.55 E
Varkhān ≃	128	32.55 N	65.30 E
Varlamovo	86	54.38 N	60.40 E
Värmdölandet I	40	59.20 N	18.33 E
Värmeln ⊜	26	59.32 N	12.54 E
Värmland □[9]	26	59.48 N	13.03 E
Värmlands Län □[6]	26	59.45 N	13.15 E
Värmlandsnäs ≻[1]	26	59.00 N	13.10 E
Varna, Blg.	38	43.13 N	27.55 E
Varna (Vahrn), It.	64	46.44 N	11.38 E
Varna, Ross.	86	53.24 N	60.58 E
Varna, N.Y., U.S.	210	42.27 N	76.26 W
Värnamo	26	57.11 N	14.02 E
Varnavino	80	57.24 N	45.04 E
Varnenski zaliv ⊂	38	43.11 N	27.56 E
Varner-Hogg Plantation State Historic Park ♦	222	29.09 N	95.37 W
Varnhem	26	58.23 N	13.39 E
Varniai	76	55.45 N	22.22 E
Varnsdorf	54	50.52 N	14.40 E
Varnville	192	32.51 N	81.04 W
Värö	26	57.16 N	12.11 E
Városliget ♦	264c	47.31 N	19.06 E
Varpaisjärvi	26	63.22 N	27.45 E
Várpalota	30	47.12 N	18.09 E
Varpan ⊜	40	60.38 N	15.36 E
Varresbeck ◆[8]	263	51.15 N	7.06 E
Vars, On., Can.	212	45.21 N	75.21 W
Vars, Fr.	62	44.37 N	6.41 E
Vars, Col de)(	62	44.32 N	6.42 E
Vâršec	38	43.12 N	23.17 E
Varsi	62	44.40 N	9.51 E
Varsinais-Suomi ◆[1]	26	60.40 N	22.30 E
Värska	76	57.58 N	27.38 E
Varsovie → Warszawa	30	52.15 N	21.00 E
Varsseveld	52	51.57 N	6.28 E
Vårsta	40	59.10 N	17.48 E
Vartašen	84	41.06 N	47.28 E
Varto	130	39.10 N	41.28 E
V'artsil'a	24	62.11 N	30.41 E
Varty Lake ⊜	212	44.23 N	76.48 W
Varuna ≃	124	25.21 N	83.03 E
Varva	78	50.31 N	32.41 E
Varvarin	38	43.43 N	21.19 E
Varvarovka, Ukr.	78	48.42 N	36.02 E
Varvarovka, Ukr.	78	49.33 N	35.12 E
Varvarovka, Ukr.	83	49.05 N	38.24 E
Varysburg	210	42.46 N	78.19 W
Várzea	256	22.30 S	44.46 W
Várzea, Rio da ≃	252	27.13 S	53.19 W
Várzea Alegre	250	6.47 S	39.17 W
Várzea da Palma	255	17.36 S	44.44 W
Varzea de Sintra	266c	38.49 N	9.24 W
Várzea Grande	248	15.39 S	56.08 W
Varzeão	252	24.34 S	49.26 W
Várzea Paulista	256	23.12 S	46.50 W
Varzi, It.	62	44.49 N	9.12 E
Varzi, Ross.	80	56.03 N	52.50 E
Varzino	24	68.19 N	38.19 E
Varzo	36	46.12 N	8.15 E
Varzob	85	38.46 N	68.49 E
Varzob ≃	85	38.30 N	68.45 E
Varzuga	24	67.24 N	36.32 E
Varzy	50	47.22 N	3.23 E
Varzyk	85	41.07 N	71.14 E
Vas	64	45.56 N	11.56 E
Vas □[6]	61	47.05 N	16.45 E
Vasai (Bassein)	122	19.21 N	72.48 E
Vasalemma	76	59.14 N	24.18 E
Vašana ≃	82	54.36 N	37.10 E
Vasar	272c	19.11 N	73.09 E
Vasa → Vaasa	26	63.06 N	21.36 E
Vascão, Ribeirão do ≃	34	37.31 N	7.31 W
Vașcău	38	46.28 N	22.28 E
Väse	40	59.23 N	13.57 E
Vāshi	272c	19.04 N	72.59 E
Vashon	224	47.26 N	122.27 W
Vashon Heights	224	47.30 N	122.28 W
Vashon Island I	224	47.24 N	122.27 W
Vasilevìči	78	52.14 N	29.49 E
Vasilija, mys ≻	180	64.34 N	178.33 E
Vasiliká	38	40.28 N	23.08 E
Vasiliški	76	53.47 N	24.51 E
Vasiljevka, Bela.	78	52.15 N	31.31 E
Vasiljevka, Ross.	89	46.52 N	134.03 E
Vasiljevka, Ukr.	78	47.26 N	35.16 E
Vasiljevo, Ross.	24	60.46 N	38.59 E
Vasiljevo, Ross.	80	55.52 N	48.42 E
Vasiljevskij, ostrov I	265a	59.56 N	30.15 E
Vasiljevskij Moch	76	57.01 N	35.55 E
Vasiljevskoje, Ross.	80	56.56 N	41.40 E
Vasiljevskoje, Ross.	80	56.31 N	45.49 E
Vasiljevskoje, Ross.	82	55.00 N	37.25 E
Vasiljevskoje, Ross.	82	56.20 N	37.54 E
Vasil'kov	78	50.12 N	30.19 E
Vasil'kovka	78	48.13 N	36.02 E
Vasil'sursk	80	56.08 N	46.01 E
Vasis	86	57.22 N	74.44 E
Vaška ≃	24	64.53 N	45.47 E
Vaskelovo	76	60.22 N	30.22 E
Vaskess Bay ⊂	174o	1.51 N	157.31 W
Vaškovci	78	48.24 N	27.08 E
Vaškovcy	78	48.23 N	25.30 E
Vaslui	38	46.38 N	27.44 E
Vaslui □[6]	38	46.30 N	27.45 E
Väsman ⊜	40	60.11 N	15.04 E
Vass	192	35.15 N	79.16 W
Vassako-Bolo, Réserve Naturelle Intégrale de la ◆[4]	146	8.10 N	19.45 E
Vassar	190	43.22 N	83.35 W
Vassdalseggi ∧	26	59.46 N	7.10 E
Vassieux-en-Vercors	62	44.53 N	5.22 E
Vassouras	256	22.25 S	43.40 W
Vassy	50	47.34 N	4.10 E
Västanfors	40	59.59 N	15.49 E
Västerås	40	59.37 N	16.33 E
Västeråsfjärden ⊂	40	59.34 N	16.34 E
Västerbotten □[9]	26	64.36 N	20.04 E
Västerbottens Län □[6]	24	64.00 N	17.30 E
Västerby	40	60.19 N	15.55 E
Västerdalälven ≃	40	60.33 N	15.08 E
Västerfärnebo	40	59.57 N	16.17 E
Västergötland □[9]	26	58.01 N	13.03 E
Västerhaninge	40	59.07 N	18.06 E
Västernorrlands Län □[6]	26	63.00 N	17.30 E
Västervik	26	57.45 N	16.38 E
Västmanland □[9]	40	59.38 N	15.15 E
Västmanlands Län □[6]	40	59.45 N	16.20 E
Vasto	66	42.07 N	14.42 E
Västra Laxsjön ⊜	40	58.54 N	14.38 E
Västra Ringsjön ⊜	41	55.53 N	13.28 E
Västra Torup	41	56.09 N	13.29 E
Vastseliina	76	57.44 N	27.17 E
Vas'ugan ≃	86	59.07 N	80.46 E
Vas'uganje ≡	86	58.00 N	77.00 E
Vas'unino	82	55.15 N	37.01 E
Vašutino	265b	55.56 N	37.26 E
Vašutkiny ozera ⊜	24	68.06 N	61.18 E
Vasvár	61	47.03 N	16.49 E
Vát	61	47.17 N	16.47 E
Vața de Jos	38	46.10 N	22.35 E
Vatan	32	47.05 N	1.48 E
Vaternish Point ≻	46	57.36 N	6.38 W
Vatersay I	46	56.55 N	7.32 W
Vaterstetten	60	48.07 N	11.47 E
Vathí	38	37.45 N	26.59 E
Vatican (Cité du) → Vatican City □[1]	267a	41.54 N	12.27 E
Vatican City (Città del Vaticano) □[1], Europe	66	41.54 N	12.27 E
Vatican City (Città del Vaticano) □[1], Europe	267a	41.54 N	12.27 E
Vaticano, Capo ≻	68	38.38 N	15.50 E
Vatikanstadt → Vatican City □[1]	66	41.54 N	12.27 E
V'atka ≃	80	55.36 N	51.30 E
V'atka → Kirov	80	58.38 N	49.42 E
Vatlirchvin, gora ∧	180	68.08 N	179.52 W
Vatnajökull ⊓	24a	64.25 N	16.50 W
Vatneyri	24a	65.38 N	23.57 W
Vätö I	40	59.49 N	18.57 E
Vatoa Island I	175g	19.50 S	178.13 W
Vatoloha ∧	157b	17.52 S	47.48 E
Vatomandry	157b	19.20 S	48.59 E
Vatra Dornei	38	47.21 N	25.21 E
V'atskije Pol'any	80	56.14 N	51.04 E
V'atskij uval ⋏[2]	80	57.20 N	49.10 E
V'atskoje, Ross.	80	57.52 N	40.16 E
V'atskoje, Ross.	89	48.44 N	135.43 E
Vattalkundu	122	10.10 N	77.46 E
Vättern ⊜	26	58.24 N	14.36 E
Vättersee → Vättern ⊜	26	58.24 N	14.36 E
Vattholma	40	60.01 N	17.44 E
Vättis	58	46.55 N	9.27 E
Vatu Ira Channel ⋓	175g	17.17 S	178.31 E
Vatukoula	175g	17.31 S	177.51 E
Vatulele I	175g	18.33 S	177.37 E
Vatulino	82	55.39 N	36.09 E
Vatutino	78	49.02 N	31.04 E
Vaubecourt	56	48.56 N	5.07 E
Vauclaix	50	47.14 N	3.49 E
Vauclin, Montagne du ∧	240e	14.33 N	60.53 W
Vaucluse	274a	33.51 S	151.17 E
Vaucluse □[5]	62	44.00 N	5.10 E
Vaucluse, Fontaine de ⊥	62	43.55 N	5.08 E
Vaucluse, Plateau de ⋏[1]	62	44.00 N	5.22 E
Vaucouleurs	58	48.36 N	5.40 E
Vaucouleurs ≃	261	48.59 N	1.44 E
Vaucresson	261	48.50 N	2.09 E
Vaud □[3]	58	46.40 N	6.30 E
Vaudherland	261	49.00 N	2.29 E
Vaudoy-en-Brie	50	48.41 N	3.05 E
Vaudreuil (Saint-Michel-de-Vaudreuil)	206	45.24 N	74.01 W
Vaudreuil □[6]	206	45.26 N	74.15 W
Vaudreuil, Baie de ⊂	275a	45.24 N	74.00 W
Vaufrey	58	47.21 N	6.55 E

Symbol	English	Deutsch	Español	Français	Português
≃	River	Fluß	Río	Rivière	Rio
≅	Canal	Kanal	Canal	Canal	Canal
∟	Waterfall, Rapids	Wasserfall, Stromschnellen	Cascada, Rápidos	Chute d'eau, Rapides	Cascata, Rápidos
⋓	Strait	Meeresstraße	Estrecho	Détroit	Estreito
⊂	Bay, Gulf	Bucht, Golf	Bahía, Golfo	Baie, Golfe	Baía, Golfo
⊜	Lake, Lakes	See, Seen	Lago, Lagos	Lac, Lacs	Lago, Lagos
≡	Swamp	Sumpf	Pantano	Marais	Pântano
⊓	Ice Features, Glacier	Eis- und Gletscherformen	Accidentes Glaciales	Formes glaciaires	Acidentes glaciares
⩡	Other Hydrographic Features	Andere Hydrographische Objekte	Otros Elementos Hidrográficos	Autres données hydrographiques	Outros acidentes hidrográficos
✣	Submarine Features	Untermeerische Objekte	Accidentes Submarinos	Formes de relief sous-marin	Acidentes submarinos
□	Political Unit	Politische Einheit	Unidad Politica	Entité politique	Unidade política
⌂	Cultural Institution	Kulturelle Institution	Institución Cultural	Institution culturelle	Instituição cultural
⊥	Historical Site	Historische Stätte	Sitio Histórico	Site historique	Sitio histórico
♦	Recreational Site	Erholungs- und Ferienort	Sitio de Recreo	Centre de loisirs	Area de Lazer
⊠	Airport	Flughafen	Aeropuerto	Aéroport	Aeroporto
■	Military Installation	Militäranlage	Instalación Militar	Installation militaire	Instalação militar
◆	Miscellaneous	Verschiedenes	Misceláneo	Divers	Diversos

ENGLISH — Name | Page | Lat.°′ | Long.°′

DEUTSCH — Name | Seite | Breite°′ | Länge°′ E = Ost

Name	Page	Lat.°′	Long.°′
Vaughan	212	43.47 N	79.36 W
Vaughn, N.M., U.S.	200	34.36 N	105.12 W
Vaughn, Wa., U.S.	224	47.21 N	122.46 W
Vaughnsville	216	40.53 N	84.09 W
Vaugneray	62	45.44 N	4.39 E
Vaugrigneuse	261	48.36 N	2.07 E
Vauhallan	261	48.44 N	2.12 E
Vaujours	261	48.56 N	2.35 E
Vaulovo	82	56.09 N	39.17 E
Vaulruz	58	46.37 N	6.59 E
Vaulx-en-Velin	62	45.47 N	4.56 E
Vaupés □[8]	246	0.45 N	70.30 W
Vaupés (Uaupés) ≃	246	0.02 N	67.16 W
Vauréal	261	49.02 N	2.02 E
Vauréal, Chute ∟	186	49.34 N	62.42 W
Vauvenargues	62	43.33 N	5.36 E
Vauvert	62	43.42 N	4.17 E
Vauvillers	58	47.55 N	6.06 E
Vauvise ≃	50	47.18 N	2.57 E
Vaux ≃	50	49.03 N	4.17 E
Vaux, Ru des ≃	261	48.42 N	2.00 E
Vauxhall	182	50.04 N	112.07 W
Vaux-le-Compte, Château de ⊥	50	48.35 N	2.42 E
Vaux-le-Pénil	261	48.32 N	2.41 E
Vaux-lès-Saint-Claude	58	46.22 N	5.44 E
Vaux-le-Vicomte, Château de ⊥	261	48.34 N	2.43 E
Vaux-Sous-Aubigny	58	47.39 N	5.17 E
Vaux-sur-Seine	261	49.00 N	1.58 E
Vavatenina	157b	17.28 S	49.12 E
Vava'u I	14	18.36 S	174.00 W
Vava'u Group II	14	18.40 S	174.00 W
Vavincourt	56	48.49 N	5.13 E
Vavoua	150	7.23 N	6.29 W
Vavož	80	56.47 N	51.55 E
Vavuniya	122	8.45 N	80.30 E
Vaxholm	40	59.24 N	18.20 E
Växjö	26	56.52 N	14.49 E
V'aža	78	49.16 N	41.01 E
Vaza-barris ≃	250	11.10 S	37.10 W
Vazante	255	18.00 S	46.54 W
Vazante Grande ≃	248	19.21 S	56.53 W
V'azemskij	89	47.32 N	134.48 E
Važgort	24	64.01 N	47.02 E
V'az'ma	76	55.13 N	34.18 E
V'az'ma ≃, Ross.	76	55.28 N	33.34 E
V'az'ma ≃, Ross.	82	56.29 N	35.49 E
V'azniki	80	56.15 N	42.10 E
Vazobe ∧	157b	18.25 S	47.18 E
V'azovaja	80	57.39 N	45.44 E
V'azovka, Ross.	80	48.19 N	45.36 E
V'azovka, Ross.	80	51.48 N	45.47 E
V'azovka, Ross.	80	50.52 N	43.57 E
V'azovka, Ross.	80	52.52 N	48.24 E
V'azovoje, Ross.	78	51.54 N	36.59 E
V'azovoje, Ross.	78	51.09 N	37.01 E
V'azovok	78	49.11 N	31.25 E
Vazuza ≃	76	56.10 N	34.35 E
Vazuzskoje vodochranilišče ⊜[1]	76	56.00 N	34.28 E
V'azyn'	76	54.25 N	27.10 E
Vazzola	64	45.50 N	12.23 E
Veachland	218	38.12 N	85.11 W
Veado, Ilha do I	287a	22.57 S	43.06 W
Veazie	188	44.50 N	68.42 W
Veberöd	41	55.38 N	13.29 E
Veblen	198	45.51 N	97.17 W
Vecchiano	66	43.47 N	10.23 E
Vechelde	52	52.16 N	10.22 E
Vecht (Vechte) ≃	52	52.35 N	6.05 E
Vechta	52	52.43 N	8.16 E
Vechte (Vecht) ≃	52	52.35 N	6.05 E
Veckerhagen	52	51.30 N	9.35 E
Vecpiebalga	76	57.08 N	25.50 E
Vecsés	30	47.25 N	19.16 E
Vecumnieki	76	56.36 N	24.31 E
Vedado ◆[8]	286b	23.08 N	82.24 W
Vedano al Lambro	266b	45.37 N	9.16 E
Vedano Olona	62	45.46 N	8.53 E
Vedāranniyam	122	10.22 N	79.51 E
Vedbæk	41	55.51 N	12.34 E
Vedder Crossing	224	49.06 N	121.57 W
Veddige	26	57.16 N	12.19 E
Vedea	38	44.47 N	24.37 E
Vedea ≃	38	43.43 N	25.32 E
Vedelago	64	45.41 N	12.01 E
Vedène	62	43.59 N	4.54 E
Vedeno	84	42.58 N	46.05 E
Vedeseta	58	45.53 N	9.32 E
Vedevåg	40	59.32 N	15.17 E
Vedi	84	39.56 N	44.42 E
Vedia	252	34.30 S	61.32 W
Vednoje	76	57.08 N	36.10 E
Vedomša	82	56.44 N	38.21 E
Vedrovo	80	57.33 N	42.52 E
Veedersburg	194	40.06 N	87.15 W
Veen	263	51.37 N	6.27 E
Veendam	52	53.06 N	6.58 E
Veenendaal	52	52.02 N	5.34 E
Veenhuizen	52	53.03 N	6.24 E
Veenoord	52	52.43 N	6.50 E
Veere	52	51.34 N	3.40 E
Veert	52	51.33 N	6.17 E
Vefsna ≃	24	65.50 N	13.12 E
Vega	196	35.15 N	102.26 W
Vega I	24	65.39 N	11.50 E
Vega, Arroyo de la ≃	266a	40.31 N	3.33 W
Vega Alta	240m	18.25 N	66.20 W
Vega Baja	240m	18.27 N	66.23 W
Vega Point >	181a	51.49 N	177.16 E
Vegår ⊜	26	58.48 N	8.47 E
Vegesack ◆[8]	52	53.10 N	8.37 E
Veghel	52	51.37 N	5.33 E
Veglie	68	40.20 N	17.58 E
Vegreville	182	53.30 N	112.03 W
Veguita	200	34.30 N	106.46 W
Vehār Lake ⊜	272c	19.09 N	72.55 E
Vehlefanz	264a	52.43 N	13.06 E
Vehnemoor ◆[3]	52	53.05 N	8.00 E
Veigné	50	47.17 N	0.44 E
Veil, Loch ⊜	46	56.20 N	4.25 W
Veilsdorf	54	50.24 N	10.48 E
Veinte de Noviembre	196	25.47 N	97.33 W
Veinticinco de Agosto	258	34.24 S	56.25 W
Veinticinco de Mayo, Arg.	252	35.26 S	60.10 W
Veinticinco de Mayo, Arg.	252	34.35 S	68.33 W
Veinticinco de Mayo, Ur.	258	34.12 S	56.22 W
Veintiocho de Mayo	246	3.50 S	78.52 W
Veintiocho de Noviembre	254	51.39 S	72.18 W
Veintisiete de Abril	236	10.15 N	85.45 W
Veio ⊥	66	42.02 N	12.24 E
Veiros	250	2.05 S	52.10 W
Veisiejai	76	54.06 N	23.42 E
Veitsbronn	56	49.31 N	10.53 E
Veitsch	61	47.35 N	15.30 E
Veitschalpe ∧∧	61	47.39 N	15.30 E
Veitshöchheim	56	49.50 N	9.52 E
Vejbystrand	41	56.19 N	12.45 E
Vejdelevka	78	50.09 N	38.27 E
Vejen	41	55.29 N	9.09 E
Vejer de la Frontera	34	36.15 N	5.58 W
Vejlby	41	56.12 N	10.13 E
Vejle	41	55.42 N	9.32 E
Vejle □[6]	41	55.45 N	9.30 E
Vejle Fjord ⊂	41	55.40 N	9.50 E
Vejprty	54	50.30 N	13.02 E
Vejrhøj ∧[2]	41	55.47 N	11.24 E
Vejrø I	41	55.02 N	11.22 E
Vekšor	24	60.33 N	49.26 E
Vel'a ≃	82	56.31 N	37.41 E
Vela Luka	36	42.58 N	16.43 E
Velapāda	272c	18.59 N	73.04 E
Velardeña	232	25.04 N	103.44 W
Velas	148a	38.41 N	28.13 W
Velas, Cabo >	236	10.22 N	85.53 W
Velázquez	252	34.02 S	54.17 W
Velbert	56	51.20 N	7.02 E
Velburg	60	49.14 N	11.41 E
Velddrif	158	32.47 S	18.11 E
Velden, Dtsch.	60	48.19 N	12.16 E
Velden, Dtsch.	60	49.37 N	11.31 E
Velden, Öst.	61	46.37 N	14.03 E
Veldhoven	52	51.24 N	5.24 E
Velebit ∧∧	36	44.38 N	15.03 E
Velebitski Kanal ⊔	36	45.00 N	14.50 E
Velegož	82	54.42 N	37.16 E
Veleka ≃	38	42.04 N	27.58 E
Velemín	54	50.33 N	13.59 E
Velen	52	51.53 N	6.59 E
Velencei-tó ⊜	30	47.12 N	18.35 E
Velesa ≃	76	56.03 N	31.58 E
Velešín	61	48.50 N	14.28 E
Velestínon	38	39.23 N	22.45 E
Velet'ma	80	55.20 N	42.25 E
Velevščina	76	54.44 N	28.35 E
Vélez	246	6.01 N	73.41 W
Velez de la Gomera, Peñón de I	34	35.11 N	4.21 W
Vélez-Málaga	34	36.47 N	4.06 W
Vélez Rubio	34	37.39 N	2.04 W
Velgast	54	54.16 N	12.48 E
Vel'gija	76	58.23 N	33.59 E
Velhas, Canal do ≋	287a	22.42 S	43.22 W
Velhas, Rio das ≃	255	17.13 S	44.49 W
Veličkovo	82	54.59 N	36.46 E
Velika Gorica	36	45.43 N	16.05 E
Velikaja, Ross.	24	59.13 N	49.04 E
Velikaja, Ross.	180	64.04 N	176.12 E
Velikaja ≃, Ross.	74	64.40 N	176.20 E
Velikaja ≃, Ross.	76	57.48 N	28.20 E
Velikaja Aleksandrovka	78	47.20 N	33.18 E
Velikaja Bagačka	78	49.47 N	33.43 E
Velikaja Beloz'orka	78	47.16 N	34.42 E
Velikaja Danilovka	78	50.04 N	36.19 E
Velikaja Dymerka	78	50.36 N	30.55 E
Velikaja Gluša	78	51.49 N	25.02 E
Velikaja Kema	89	45.30 N	137.12 E
Velikaja Kochnovka	78	49.07 N	33.27 E
Velikaja Korenicha	78	46.57 N	31.54 E
Velikaja Kosnica	78	48.09 N	28.27 E
Velikaja Lepeticha	78	47.11 N	33.56 E
Velikaja Michajlovka	78	47.04 N	29.52 E
Velikaja Novos'olka	78	47.50 N	36.50 E
Velikaja Pisarevka	78	50.26 N	35.28 E
Velikaja Rublevka	78	49.53 N	34.49 E
Velikaja Vradijevka	78	47.52 N	30.35 E
Velika Kapela ∧∧	36	45.15 N	15.00 E
Velika Morava ≃	38	44.43 N	21.03 E
Velika Plana	38	44.20 N	21.04 E
Velike Lašče	36	45.50 N	14.38 E
Veliki Bečkerek → Zrenjanin	38	45.23 N	20.24 E
Velikij Ber'oznyj	78	48.53 N	22.27 E
Velikij Bor	78	52.02 N	29.56 E
Velikij Burluk	78	50.05 N	37.24 E
Velikij Byčkov	78	47.58 N	24.03 E
Velikij Chutor	78	49.52 N	32.06 E
Velikij Dvor	82	56.46 N	37.25 E
Velikije Borki	78	49.32 N	25.45 E
Velikije Dederkaly	78	50.02 N	26.07 E
Velikije Kopani	78	46.29 N	32.59 E
Velikije Korovincy	78	49.59 N	28.17 E
Velikije Krynki	78	49.27 N	33.29 E
Velikije Lučki	78	48.26 N	22.35 E
Velikije Luki	76	56.20 N	30.32 E
Velikije Mosty	78	50.14 N	24.06 E
Velikije Soročincy	78	50.03 N	33.56 E
Velikij Gluboček	78	49.37 N	25.32 E
Velikij Log	83	48.15 N	39.33 E
Velikij Ust'ug	24	60.48 N	46.18 E
Velikij Žvančik	78	48.46 N	26.59 E
Veliki kanal ≋	38	45.45 N	18.50 E
Veliki Vitorog ∧	36	44.07 N	17.03 E
Velikoanadol'skij les ♦	83	47.42 N	37.23 E
Velikoarch-angel'skoje	78	50.51 N	40.46 E
Velikockoje	83	49.21 N	40.02 E
Velikodolinskoje	78	46.21 N	30.35 E
Velikodvorskaja	76	60.18 N	41.58 E
Velikodvorskij	80	55.15 N	40.41 E
Veliko Gradište	38	44.45 N	21.32 E
Velikoje, Ross.	76	59.32 N	36.59 E
Velikoje, Ross.	80	57.21 N	39.47 E
Velikoje, ozero ⊜, Ross.	76	57.02 N	36.34 E
Velikoje, ozero ⊜, Ross.	80	55.13 N	40.10 E
Velikonda Hills ∧∧[2]	122	14.45 N	79.10 E
Velikookt'abr'skij	76	57.26 N	33.49 E
Velikoploskoje	78	47.01 N	29.40 E
Velikorusskoje	86	54.39 N	74.38 E
Veliko Târnovo	38	43.04 N	25.39 E
Velikovisočnoje	24	67.16 N	52.01 E
Velikovo	76	59.18 N	42.08 E
Velilla de San Antonio	266a	40.22 N	3.29 W
Veli Lošinj	36	44.31 N	14.30 E
Velimče	78	51.36 N	24.44 E
Vélingara, Sén.	150	15.00 N	14.40 W
Vélingara, Sén.	150	13.09 N	14.07 W
Velingrad	38	42.04 N	24.00 E
Velino ≃	66	42.33 N	12.43 E
Velino, Monte ∧	66	42.09 N	13.23 E
Veli Stol (Hochstuhl) ∧	61	46.26 N	14.10 E
Velíž	76	55.38 N	31.12 E
Veližany	86	57.34 N	65.49 E
Vélizy-Villacoublay	261	48.47 N	2.10 E
Veljaminovo, Ross.	82	55.12 N	37.52 E
Veljaminovo, Ross.	82	55.53 N	36.52 E
Velká Bíteš	30	49.17 N	16.13 E
Vel'ké Kapušany	30	48.33 N	22.04 E
Velké Meziříčí	30	49.21 N	16.00 E
Velké Němčie	61	48.59 N	16.40 E
Velké Pavlovice	61	48.54 N	16.19 E
Velký Bor	60	49.22 N	13.42 E
Velký Šenov	54	51.00 N	14.25 E
Vellach ≃	61	46.35 N	14.29 E
Vella Gulf ⊔	175e	8.00 S	156.50 E
Vella Lavella I	175e	7.45 S	156.40 E
Vellano	66	43.57 N	10.43 E
Vellār ≃	122	11.29 N	79.46 E
Vellberg	56	49.05 N	9.53 E
Vellechevreux-et-Courbenans	58	47.33 N	6.32 E
Velletri	66	41.41 N	12.47 E
Vellinge	41	55.28 N	13.01 E
Vellmar	56	51.21 N	9.28 E
Vellore, On., Can.	275b	43.50 N	79.34 W
Vellore, India	122	12.56 N	79.08 E
Velm	264b	48.03 N	16.27 E
Velma	196	34.27 N	97.40 W
Vel'maj ≃	180	67.26 N	175.28 W
Velmede	56	51.21 N	8.22 E
Velo d'Astico	64	45.43 N	11.23 E
Velp	52	52.00 N	5.59 E
Velp ≃	56	50.58 N	5.05 E
Velpke	54	52.24 N	10.56 E
Velsen	52	52.27 N	4.39 E
Vel'sk	24	61.05 N	42.05 E
Vel't	24	68.03 N	49.55 E
Velten	54	52.41 N	13.10 E
Veltheim	52	52.11 N	8.58 E
Veltrusy	54	50.14 N	14.18 E
Veluwe ◆[1]	52	52.12 N	5.45 E
Veluwemeer ⊜	52	52.22 N	5.38 E
Velva, It.	62	44.16 N	9.33 E
Velva, N.D., U.S.	198	48.03 N	100.55 W
Velvary	54	50.15 N	14.15 E
Vémars	261	49.04 N	2.34 E
Vemdalen	26	62.27 N	13.52 E
Vemmenæs	41	54.59 N	10.40 E
Ven I	41	55.54 N	12.41 E
Venachar, Loch ⊜	46	56.13 N	4.19 W
Venaco	36	42.14 N	9.10 E
Venadillo	246	4.43 N	74.55 W
Venado	234	22.56 N	101.05 W
Venado, Isla I	241r	10.00 N	62.25 W
Venado, Isla del I	236	11.57 N	83.44 W
Venado Tuerto	252	33.45 S	61.58 W
Venafiorita, Aeroporto di ⊠	71	40.53 N	9.30 E
Venafro	66	41.29 N	14.02 E
Venalzio	62	45.09 N	7.01 E
Venâncio Aires	252	29.36 S	52.11 W
Venango	214	41.46 N	80.07 W
Venango □[6]	214	41.24 N	79.50 W
Venanson	62	44.03 N	7.15 E
Venant	261	48.30 N	2.06 E
Venarey-les-Laumes	58	47.32 N	4.26 E
Venaria	62	45.08 N	7.38 E
Venasca	62	44.33 N	7.24 E
Venasque	62	43.59 N	5.09 E
Vence	62	43.43 N	7.07 E
Venceslau Brás	256	22.31 S	45.21 W
Venceslau Braz	255	23.51 S	49.48 W
Vencimont	56	50.02 N	4.55 E
Venda □[1], Afr.	138	23.00 S	30.30 E
Venda □[1], Afr.	156	23.00 S	30.30 E
Venda Nova	34	41.40 N	7.58 W
Vendargues	62	43.39 N	3.58 E
Vendas Novas	34	38.41 N	8.28 W
Vendée □[5]	32	46.40 N	1.20 W
Vendéen, Bocage ◆[1]	32	46.40 N	1.30 W
Vendel	40	60.10 N	17.36 E
Vendelsö	40	59.12 N	18.12 E
Vendeuvre-sur-Barse	58	48.14 N	4.28 E
Vendičany	78	48.37 N	27.48 E
Vendin-lès-Béthune	50	50.32 N	2.37 E
Vendin-le-Vieil	50	50.28 N	2.52 E
Vendôme	50	47.48 N	1.04 E
Vendsyssel ◆[1]	26	57.20 N	10.00 E
Venecia	236	10.22 N	84.17 W
Venecia → Venezia	64	45.27 N	12.21 E
Venedig → Venezia	64	45.27 N	12.21 E
Venedocia	216	40.44 N	84.25 W
Venedy	219	38.24 N	89.39 W
Veneta, Laguna ⊂	64	45.25 N	12.19 E
Venetia	214	40.15 N	80.03 W
Venetian Village	216	42.24 N	88.02 W
Venetie	180	67.01 N	146.25 W
Veneto □[4]	64	45.30 N	11.45 E
Venev	82	54.21 N	38.16 E
Venezia (Venice)	64	45.27 N	12.21 E
Venezia □[4]	64	45.35 N	12.34 E
Venezuela □[1], S.A.	242	8.00 N	66.00 W
Venezuela □[1], S.A.	246	8.00 N	66.00 W
Venezuela, Golfo de ⊂	246	11.30 N	71.00 W
Venezuelan Basin ✦[1]	16	15.00 N	68.00 W
Veng	41	56.07 N	9.53 E
Vengerovka	83	48.43 N	38.24 E
Vengerovo	86	55.41 N	76.45 E
Vengurla	122	15.52 N	73.38 E
Veniaminof, Mount ∧	180	56.13 N	159.18 W
Venice, Fl., U.S.	220	27.05 N	82.27 W
Venice, Il., U.S.	219	38.40 N	90.10 W
Venice, La., U.S.	194	29.16 N	89.21 W
Venice, Oh., U.S.	214	41.27 N	82.46 W
Venice, Pa., U.S.	279b	40.19 N	80.14 W
Venice ◆[8]	228	34.00 N	118.29 W
Venice, Gulf of ⊂	64	45.15 N	13.00 E
Venice Gardens	220	27.04 N	82.26 W
Venice → Venezia	64	45.27 N	12.21 E
Venise → Venezia	64	45.27 N	12.21 E
Vénissieux	62	45.41 N	4.53 E
Venjan	26	60.57 N	13.55 E
Venjansjön ⊜	26	60.54 N	14.00 E
Venkatagiri	122	13.58 N	79.35 E
Venlo	52	51.24 N	6.10 E
Vennesla	26	58.17 N	7.59 E
Vennhausen ◆[8]	263	51.13 N	6.51 E
Venosa	68	40.57 N	15.49 E
Vénosc	62	44.59 N	6.07 E
Venosta, Val V	64	46.40 N	10.35 E
Venoste, Alpi (Ötztaler Alpen) ∧∧	64	46.45 N	10.55 E
Venray	52	51.32 N	5.59 E
Vent	64	46.52 N	10.56 E
Vent, Îles du → Windward Islands II	238	13.00 N	61.00 W
Venta ≃	76	57.24 N	21.33 E
Ventanas	246	1.23 S	79.25 W
Ventasso, Monte ∧	64	44.23 N	10.17 E
Ventersburg	158	28.09 S	27.08 E
Ventersdorp	158	26.17 S	26.48 E
Venterspos	273d	26.18 S	27.39 E
Venterstad	158	30.47 S	25.48 E
Venticano	68	41.05 N	14.50 E
Ventimiglia	62	43.47 N	7.36 E
Ventimiglia di Sicilia	70	37.55 N	13.34 E
Ventnor	42	50.36 N	1.11 W
Ventnor City	208	39.20 N	74.28 W
Ventotene	66	40.48 N	13.26 E
Ventotene, Isola I	66	40.47 N	13.25 E
Ventoux, Mont ∧	62	44.10 N	5.17 E
Ventry	48	52.08 N	10.22 W
Ventspils	76	57.24 N	21.36 E
Ventuari ≃	246	3.58 N	67.02 W
Ventura (San Buenaventura)	228	34.16 N	119.17 W
Ventura □[6]	228	34.30 N	119.00 W
Ventura ≃	228	34.16 N	119.18 W
Venturina	66	43.02 N	10.36 E
Venus, Fl., U.S.	220	27.04 N	81.21 W
Venus, Pa., U.S.	214	41.22 N	79.29 W
Venus, Tx., U.S.	222	32.26 N	97.06 W
Vénus, Pointe >	174s	17.29 S	149.29 W
Venus Bay ⊂	169	38.40 S	145.43 E
Venustiano Carranza, Méx.	232	16.21 N	92.33 W
Venustiano Carranza, Méx.	234	19.44 N	103.47 W
Venustiano Carranza, Méx.	234	20.31 N	97.38 W
Venustiano Carranza, Bahía ⊂	232	19.20 N	87.35 W
Venustiano Carranza, Presa ⊜[1]	232	27.30 N	100.40 W
Venzone	64	46.20 N	13.09 E
Véore ≃	62	44.49 N	4.49 E
Vép	61	47.14 N	16.44 E
Veprik	78	50.23 N	34.11 E
Vepsovskaja vozvyšennost' ∧∧[1]	76	60.20 N	35.15 E
Ver ≃	42	51.42 N	0.20 W
Vera, Arg.	252	29.28 S	60.13 W
Vera, Esp.	34	37.15 N	1.52 W
Vera, Il., U.S.	219	39.02 N	89.07 W
Veracruz, Méx.	200	32.25 N	115.05 W
Vera Cruz, Pa., U.S.	208	40.30 N	75.30 W
Veracruz □[3]	234	19.20 N	96.40 W
Veracruz [Llave]	234	19.12 N	96.08 W
Veraguas □[4]	236	8.30 N	81.00 W
Verano Brianza	266b	45.41 N	9.14 E
Veranópolis	252	28.57 S	51.33 W
Verāval	120	20.54 N	70.22 E
Verba	78	50.17 N	25.37 E
Verbania	58	45.56 N	8.33 E
Verbank	210	41.44 N	73.43 W
Verbeek, Pegunungan ∧∧	112	2.35 S	121.25 E
Verberg ◆[8]	263	51.22 N	6.36 E
Verberie	50	49.19 N	2.44 E
Verbicaro	68	39.45 N	15.55 E
Verbier	58	46.06 N	7.13 E
Verbilki	82	56.32 N	37.36 E
Verbinskij	83	47.53 N	40.02 E
Verbl'užka	78	48.23 N	32.54 E
Verbovskij	80	55.32 N	42.00 E
Vercelli	62	45.19 N	8.25 E
Vercelli □[4]	62	45.37 N	8.10 E
Vercel-Villedieu-le-Camp	58	47.11 N	6.24 E
Verch'aja Irmen'	86	54.35 N	82.14 E
Verchazovka	80	50.56 N	48.46 E
Vercheje Talyzino	80	55.06 N	45.49 E
Verchères	206	45.47 N	73.21 W
Verchères □[6]	206	45.45 N	73.20 W
Verchn'ačka	78	48.49 N	30.02 E
Verchn'aja Amga	74	59.30 N	126.08 E
Verchn'aja Angara ≃	88	55.42 N	109.54 E
Verchn'aja Balkarija	84	43.06 N	43.24 E
Verchn'aja Buzinovka	80	49.04 N	43.12 E
Verchn'aja Čebula	86	56.02 N	87.36 E
Verchn'aja Chava	78	51.50 N	39.56 E
Verchn'aja Chila	88	52.06 N	115.54 E
Verchn'aja Chortica	78	47.51 N	35.01 E
Verchn'aja Čuginka	83	48.55 N	39.39 E
Verchn'aja Dobrinka	80	50.46 N	45.03 E
Verchn'aja Gniluša	78	50.16 N	40.23 E
Verchn'aja Grajvoronka	78	51.41 N	37.46 E
Verchn'aja Inta	24	66.00 N	60.20 E
Verchn'aja Maza	80	52.58 N	47.56 E
Verchn'aja Orl'anka	80	53.44 N	51.04 E
Verchn'aja Pyšma	86	56.55 N	60.37 E
Verchn'aja Salda	86	58.02 N	60.33 E
Verchn'aja Serebr'akovka	80	47.21 N	42.14 E
Verchn'aja Sin'ačicha	86	57.59 N	61.40 E
Verchn'aja Sysert'	86	56.26 N	60.46 E
Verchn'aja Tajmyra ≃	74	74.15 N	99.48 E
Verchn'aja Tarka	86	56.37 N	77.30 E
Verchnaja Tereška	80	52.54 N	47.24 E
Verchn'aja Tišanka	78	51.19 N	40.32 E
Verchn'aja Tojma	24	62.13 N	45.00 E
Verchn'aja Troica	76	57.15 N	37.08 E
Verchn'aja Tura	86	58.22 N	59.49 E
Verchn'aja Zaimka	88	55.51 N	110.09 E
Verchn'aja Zima	88	53.48 N	101.47 E
Verchneaks'onovskij	80	48.21 N	42.38 E
Verchneangarskij chrebet ∧∧	88	56.20 N	111.30 E
Verchne-Anikin	83	48.09 N	39.59 E
Verchnebakanskij	78	44.52 N	37.39 E
Verchneber'ozovskij	86	50.17 N	82.13 E
Verchnebuzanskij	80	46.38 N	48.02 E
Verchnecaricynskij	80	48.23 N	43.57 E
Verchnedneprovsk	78	48.39 N	34.21 E
Verchnedneprovskij	76	54.59 N	33.21 E
Verchneduvannyj	78	48.20 N	39.48 E
Verchnedvinsk	76	55.47 N	27.56 E
Verchneimbatskoje	74	63.11 N	87.58 E
Verchnejarkejevo	80	55.27 N	54.19 E
Verchneje	78	48.53 N	38.28 E
Verchneje ◆[8]	83	48.53 N	38.28 E
Verchneje Šachlovo	82	55.02 N	37.15 E
Verchneje Sinevidnoje	78	49.06 N	23.34 E
Verchnekarabachskij kanal ≋	84	39.44 N	47.57 E
Verchnemakejevka	78	49.10 N	41.03 E
Verchnemulomskoje vodochranilišče ⊜[1]	24	68.30 N	31.05 E
Verchnesadovoje	78	44.42 N	33.42 E
Verchnesjezžeje	80	52.44 N	51.15 E
Verchnespasskoje	80	52.39 N	41.47 E
Verchne-T'oploje	83	48.51 N	39.26 E
Verchnetulomskij	24	68.38 N	31.45 E
Verchneural'sk	86	53.53 N	59.13 E
Verchneusinskoje	86	52.14 N	93.01 E
Verchnevil'ujsk	74	63.27 N	120.18 E
Verchnevolynskoje	85	40.43 N	68.51 E
Verchnij Amyl	88	53.08 N	94.30 E
Verchnij Avz'an	86	53.32 N	57.33 E
Verchnij Balyklej	80	49.34 N	45.10 E
Verchnij Baskunčak	80	48.14 N	46.44 E
Verchnij Byk	78	50.43 N	41.14 E
Verchnije Dvoriki	82	56.28 N	38.22 E
Verchnije Kigi	86	55.25 N	58.37 E
Verchnije Korobki	80	50.19 N	44.38 E
Verchnije Lipki	80	49.38 N	43.51 E
Verchnije Tatyšly	86	56.17 N	55.52 E
Verchnij Ikorec	78	51.11 N	39.46 E
Verchnij Karačan	80	51.24 N	41.46 E
Verchnij Krasnyj Pereval	89	46.33 N	134.37 E
Verchnij Kužebar	86	53.22 N	93.15 E
Verchnij Landech	80	56.51 N	42.36 E
Verchnij Leb'ažinskij	80	46.45 N	47.50 E
Verchnij Lomov	80	53.28 N	43.34 E
Verchnij Lomovec	76	52.13 N	38.37 E
Verchnij Mamon	78	50.10 N	40.23 E
Verchnij Most	76	57.31 N	28.50 E
Verchnij Nejvinskij	86	57.17 N	60.09 E
Verchnij Petr'ak	86	57.29 N	77.30 E
Verchnij Rogačik	78	47.14 N	34.21 E
Verchnij Šergol'džin	88	50.12 N	108.20 E
Verchnij Tagil	86	57.22 N	59.56 E
Verchnij Takermen'	80	55.39 N	52.43 E
Verchnij Trojanov Val (Upper Trajan's Wall) ⊥	78	46.35 N	29.00 E
Verchnij Ufalej	86	56.04 N	60.14 E
Verchnij Ul'chun	88	49.34 N	112.32 E
Verchnij Uslon	80	55.47 N	48.57 E
Verchnij Zub, gora ∧	86	53.45 N	89.15 E
Verchnyje Nikul'asy	76	60.25 N	30.45 E
Verchnyj Jenisej (Ulug-Chem) ≃	88	51.47 N	92.00 E
Verchnyj Nagol'čik	83	48.05 N	39.06 E
Verchojansk	74	67.35 N	133.27 E
Verchojanskij chrebet ∧∧	74	67.00 N	129.00 E
Vercholensk	88	54.06 N	105.35 E
Verchopuja	24	61.34 N	41.31 E
Verchošižemje	80	58.01 N	49.07 E
Verchososna	78	50.44 N	38.14 E
Verchoturje	86	58.52 N	60.48 E
Verchoturovo	86	58.22 N	95.21 E
Verchovažje	24	60.45 N	42.00 E
Verchovcevo	78	48.29 N	34.14 E
Verchovina	78	48.09 N	24.47 E
Verchovino	76	59.33 N	43.19 E
Verchovje	76	52.49 N	37.14 E
Verchovl'an'	82	55.03 N	38.21 E
Verchozim	80	52.56 N	46.23 E
Verchubinka	86	50.29 N	82.26 E
Verclause	62	44.23 N	5.26 E
Vercors ◆[1]	62	44.57 N	5.25 E
Verdalsøra	26	63.48 N	11.29 E
Verde ≃, Bra.	248	11.54 S	55.48 W
Verde ≃, Bra.	248	13.33 S	58.01 W
Verde ≃, Bra.	250	10.27 S	42.16 W
Verde ≃, Bra.	255	15.07 S	48.40 W
Verde ≃, Bra.	255	17.05 S	46.05 W
Verde ≃, Bra.	255	18.01 S	50.14 W
Verde ≃, Bra.	255	19.11 S	50.44 W
Verde ≃, Bra.	255	19.55 S	49.45 W
Verde ≃, Bra.	255	21.12 S	51.53 W
Verde ≃, Bra.	256	21.34 S	45.31 W
Verde ≃, Bra.	256	21.38 S	47.03 W
Verde ≃, Méx.	234	21.37 N	99.15 W
Verde ≃, Méx.	234	16.45 N	98.07 W
Verde ≃, Méx.	234	15.59 N	97.47 W
Verde ≃, Méx.	234	20.42 N	103.14 W
Verde ≃, Para.	252	23.09 S	57.37 W
Verde ≃, S.A.	248	13.59 S	60.24 W
Verde ≃, Az., U.S.	200	33.33 N	111.40 W
Verde, Arroyo ≃, Arg.	254	41.56 S	65.03 W
Verde, Arroyo ≃, Bol.	248	11.25 S	66.20 W
Verde, Cape >	238	22.50 N	74.52 W
Verde, Cerro ∧	234	20.30 N	104.36 W
Verde, Costa ⊥[2]	71	39.34 N	8.28 E
Verde Grande ≃	255	14.35 S	43.53 W
Verde Island I	116	13.33 N	121.05 E
Verde Island Passage ⊔	116	13.34 N	120.51 E
Verdello	62	45.36 N	9.37 E
Verden, Dtsch.	52	52.55 N	9.13 E
Verden, Ok., U.S.	196	35.05 N	98.05 W
Verde Pequeno ≃	255	14.48 S	43.31 W
Verdesela, Pinhal da ♦	266c	38.37 N	9.08 W
Verdi	226	39.31 N	119.59 W
Verdigre	198	42.35 N	98.02 W
Verdigre Creek ≃	198	42.42 N	98.03 W
Verdigris ≃	196	35.48 N	95.19 W
Verdinho ≃	255	17.29 S	50.27 W
Verdon	198	40.08 N	95.42 W
Verdon ≃	62	43.43 N	5.46 E
Verdon, Canal du ≋	62	43.43 N	5.57 E
Verdoy	210	42.46 N	73.48 W
Verduga	76	58.46 N	29.12 E
Verdugo Mountains ∧∧	280	34.13 N	118.18 W
Verdun, P.Q., Can.	206	45.27 N	73.34 W
Verdun, Fr.	32	43.52 N	1.14 E
Verdun-sur-le-Doubs	58	46.54 N	5.01 E
Verdun-sur-Meuse	56	49.10 N	5.23 E
Verdura ≃	70	37.28 N	13.12 E
Vereb'jo	76	58.41 N	32.42 E
Vereeniging	158	26.38 S	27.57 E
Veregin	184	51.35 N	102.05 W
Vereinigte Arabische Emirate → United Arab Emirates □[1]	128	24.00 N	54.00 E
Vereinigte Königreich → United Kingdom □[1]	28	54.00 N	2.00 W
Vereinigte Staaten → United States □[1]	178	38.00 N	97.00 W
Vereja, Ross.	82	55.46 N	39.06 E
Vereja, Ross.	82	55.21 N	36.11 E
Vereja, Ross.	265b	55.37 N	38.02 E
Veremejki	76	53.46 N	31.15 E
Vereščagino, Ross.	74	64.14 N	87.37 E
Vereščagino, Ross.	80	58.05 N	54.40 E
Veresegyház	264c	47.39 N	19.17 E
Veresoč'	78	51.19 N	31.46 E
Veretje	82	54.08 N	36.17 E
Véretz	50	47.22 N	0.48 E
Verga	285	39.52 N	75.10 W
Verga, Cap >	150	10.12 N	14.27 W
Vergara	252	32.56 S	53.57 W
Vergato	64	44.17 N	11.07 E
Vergel	196	25.39 N	103.32 W
Vergeletto	58	46.14 N	8.36 E
Vergemont Creek ≃	166	24.12 S	143.17 E
Vergennes	188	44.10 N	73.15 W
Verghereto	66	43.47 N	12.00 E
Vergiate	62	45.43 N	8.42 E
Vergons	62	43.55 N	6.35 E
Vergt	32	45.02 N	0.43 E
Vergulevka	83	48.24 N	38.32 E
Verigino	82	56.42 N	38.08 E
Verín	34	41.56 N	7.26 W
Veringenstadt	58	48.11 N	9.12 E
Verin Talin	84	40.23 N	43.53 E
Veriora	76	58.00 N	27.21 E
Veríssimo	255	19.42 S	48.18 W
Verkeerdevlei	158	28.48 S	26.48 E
Verkhneudinsk → Ulan-Ude	88	51.50 N	107.37 E
Verkhniy Ufaley → Verchnij Ufalej	86	56.04 N	60.14 E
Verkhnyaya Salda → Verchn'aja Salda	86	58.02 N	60.33 E
Verkhoyansk → Verchojansk	74	67.35 N	133.27 E
Verkykerskop	158	27.54 S	29.17 E
Verl (Senne I)	52	51.53 N	8.31 E
Vermaaklikheid	158	34.19 S	21.01 E
Vermaas	158	26.30 S	25.59 E
Vermand	50	49.52 N	3.09 E
Vermejo ≃	196	36.30 N	104.33 W
Vermelho ≃, Bra.	250	9.16 S	47.23 W
Vermelho ≃, Bra.	250	7.44 S	47.17 W
Vermelho ≃, Bra.	250	5.33 S	49.14 W
Vermelho ≃, Bra.	255	14.54 S	51.06 W
Vermenton	50	47.40 N	3.44 E
Vermette Lake ⊜	184	55.40 N	109.05 W
Vermezzo	266b	45.24 N	8.59 E
Vermiglio	64	46.18 N	10.42 E
Vermilion, Ab., Can.	182	53.22 N	110.51 W
Vermilion, Oh., U.S.	214	41.25 N	82.21 W
Vermilion □[6]	216	40.08 N	87.37 W
Vermilion ≃, Ab., Can.	184	53.44 N	110.18 W
Vermilion ≃, On., Can.	190	46.16 N	81.41 W
Vermilion ≃, Il., U.S.	216	41.19 N	89.04 W
Vermilion ≃, La., U.S.	194	29.46 N	92.09 W
Vermilion ≃, Mn., U.S.	190	48.16 N	92.30 W
Vermilion ≃, Oh., U.S.	214	41.26 N	82.22 W
Vermilion, Middle Fork ≃	216	40.12 N	87.45 W
Vermilion, North Fork ≃, Il., U.S.	216	40.49 N	88.30 W
Vermilion, North Fork ≃, Il., U.S.	216	40.13 N	87.39 W
Vermilion, South Fork ≃	216	40.49 N	88.30 W
Vermilion Bay	184	49.51 N	93.24 W
Vermilion Bay ⊂	194	29.40 N	92.00 W
Vermilion Lake ⊜, On., Can.	184	50.03 N	92.13 W
Vermilion Lake ⊜, Mn., U.S.	190	47.53 N	92.25 W
Vermilion Pass ⟩⟨	182	51.14 N	116.03 W
Vermillion	198	42.46 N	96.55 W
Vermillion ≃	198	42.44 N	96.53 W
Vermillion, East Fork ≃	198	43.44 N	97.03 W
Vermillion, West Fork ≃	198	43.44 N	97.03 W
Vermillion Bluffs ⊥[4]	200	40.50 N	108.30 W
Vermillion Creek ≃, U.S.	200	40.46 N	108.53 W
Vermillion Creek ≃, Ks., U.S.	198	39.12 N	96.13 W
Vermont, Austl.	274b	37.50 S	145.12 E
Vermont, Il., U.S.	194	40.17 N	90.25 W
Vermont □[3], U.S.	178	43.50 N	72.45 W
Vermont □[3], U.S.	188	43.50 N	72.45 W
Vermontville	216	42.37 N	85.01 W
Vernà, Pizzo di ∧	70	38.01 N	15.15 E
Vernaison	62	45.39 N	4.49 E
Vernal	200	40.27 N	109.31 W
Vernalis	226	37.37 N	121.17 W
Vernante	62	44.15 N	7.32 E
Vernayaz	58	46.08 N	7.02 E
Vernazza	62	44.08 N	9.41 E
Verndale	198	46.24 N	95.01 W
Verne	52	51.41 N	8.34 E
Verner	190	46.25 N	80.07 W
Verneuil	32	48.44 N	0.56 E
Verneuil-L'Étang	261	48.39 N	2.50 E
Verneuil-sur-Avre	50	48.44 N	0.56 E
Verneuil-sur-Seine	50	48.59 N	1.59 E
Verneukpan	158	30.00 S	21.00 E
Verneukpan ≌	158	30.00 S	21.10 E
Vernier	58	46.13 N	6.06 E
Verninge	41	55.18 N	10.13 E
Vernio	66	44.03 N	11.09 E
Vernole	68	40.17 N	18.18 E
Vernon, B.C., Can.	182	50.16 N	119.16 W
Vernon, On., Can.	212	45.10 N	75.28 W
Vernon, Fr.	50	49.05 N	1.29 E
Vernon, Al., U.S.	194	33.45 N	88.06 W
Vernon, Ca., U.S.	280	34.01 N	118.13 W
Vernon, Ct., U.S.	207	41.49 N	72.28 W
Vernon, Fl., U.S.	194	30.37 N	85.42 W
Vernon, Il., U.S.	219	38.48 N	89.05 W
Vernon, In., U.S.	218	38.59 N	85.36 W
Vernon, Mi., U.S.	216	42.56 N	84.02 W
Vernon, N.J., U.S.	210	41.11 N	74.29 W
Vernon, N.Y., U.S.	210	43.05 N	75.32 W
Vernon, Oh., U.S.	214	41.23 N	80.34 W
Vernon, Tx., U.S.	196	34.09 N	99.15 W
Vernon, Ut., U.S.	200	40.05 N	112.25 W
Vernon, Lake ⊜	212	45.20 N	79.17 W
Vernon Dam ◆[6]	207	42.46 N	72.31 W
Vernon Hills	278	42.13 N	87.58 W
Vernonia	224	45.51 N	123.11 W
Vernon Lake ⊜[1]	194	31.15 N	93.25 W
Vernon River	186	46.12 N	62.50 W
Vernouillet	261	48.58 N	1.59 E
Vernoux-en-Vivarais	62	44.54 N	4.39 E
Verny	56	49.01 N	6.12 E
Vero ≃	34	42.00 N	0.10 E
Vero Beach	220	27.38 N	80.23 W
Véroia	38	40.31 N	22.12 E
Verolanuova	64	45.19 N	10.04 E
Verolavecchia	64	45.19 N	10.03 E
Veroli	66	41.41 N	13.25 E
Verona, On., Can.	212	44.29 N	76.42 W
Verona, It.	64	45.27 N	11.00 E
Verona, Ky., U.S.	218	38.49 N	84.39 W
Verona, Ms., U.S.	194	34.11 N	88.43 W
Verona, N.J., U.S.	276	40.49 N	74.14 W
Verona, N.Y., U.S.	210	43.08 N	75.34 W
Verona, Oh., U.S.	218	39.54 N	84.29 W
Verona, Pa., U.S.	279b	40.30 N	79.50 W
Verona, Wi., U.S.	216	42.59 N	89.31 W
Verona □[4]	64	45.25 N	11.02 E
Verona Beach	210	43.12 N	75.44 W
Verona Beach State Park ♦	210	43.14 N	75.44 W
Verona Park	216	42.21 N	85.09 W
Verónica	258	35.22 S	57.20 W
Verperluda, ostrov I	265a	59.59 N	30.01 E
Verplanck	210	41.15 N	73.58 W
Verran	166	33.51 S	136.18 E
Verrazano-Narrows Bridge ◆[5]	210	40.36 N	74.03 W
Verrès	62	45.40 N	7.42 E
Verrettes	238	19.03 N	72.28 W
Verrey-sous-Salmaise	58	47.26 N	4.40 E
Verrières, Bois de ♦	261	48.45 N	2.15 E
Verrières-le-Buisson	261	48.45 N	2.16 E
Versa ≃	62	44.54 N	8.16 E
Versailles, Fr.	50	48.48 N	2.08 E
Versailles, Il., U.S.	194	39.53 N	90.39 W
Versailles, In., U.S.	218	39.04 N	85.15 W
Versailles, Ky., U.S.	218	38.03 N	84.43 W
Versailles, Mo., U.S.	194	38.25 N	92.50 W
Versailles, N.Y., U.S.	210	42.31 N	78.59 W
Versailles, Oh., U.S.	216	40.13 N	84.29 W
Versailles, Pa., U.S.	279b	40.21 N	79.51 W
Versailles, Château de ⊥	261	48.48 N	2.07 E
Versailles, Parc de ♦	261	48.49 N	2.06 E
Versailles State Park ♦	218	39.04 N	85.13 W
Verse ≃	263	51.15 N	7.46 E
Versec → Vršac	38	45.07 N	21.18 E
Versestausee ⊜[1]	263	51.11 N	7.41 E
Versien	158	27.05 S	27.52 E
Veršina Tei	86	53.20 N	89.36 E
Veršino-Darasunskij	88	52.20 N	115.32 E
Veršino-Šachtaminskij	88	51.21 N	117.50 E
Versmold	52	52.02 N	8.09 E
Versoix	58	46.16 N	6.10 E
Ver-sur-Launette	261	49.06 N	2.41 E
Vert	261	48.57 N	1.41 E
Vert, Cap >	150	14.43 N	17.30 W
Vert'ačij	80	48.57 N	43.53 E
Verte, Île I, P.Q., Can.	186	48.02 N	69.26 W
Verte, Île I, P.Q., Can.	275a	45.34 N	73.30 W
Vertedero	240m	18.05 N	66.15 W
Verteillac	32	45.21 N	0.22 E
Vertientes	240p	21.16 N	78.09 W
Vertijevka	78	51.10 N	31.51 E
Vertkovo	82	56.07 N	36.25 E
Vert-le-Grand	261	48.34 N	2.22 E
Vert-le-Petit	261	48.33 N	2.22 E
Vertlinskoje	82	56.14 N	36.58 E
Vertou	32	47.10 N	1.29 W
Vertova	62	45.48 N	9.50 E
Vert-Saint-Denis	261	48.34 N	2.37 E
Vertus	50	48.54 N	4.00 E
Verucchio	66	43.59 N	12.25 E
Verulam	158	29.45 S	31.02 E
Verulamium ⊥	260	51.45 N	0.22 W
Verviers	56	50.35 N	5.52 E
Vervins	50	49.50 N	3.54 E
Verwall Gruppe ∧∧	58	47.02 N	10.10 E
Verwood	42	50.53 N	1.52 W
Veryan	42	50.13 N	4.54 W
Verzasca ≃	58	46.09 N	8.52 E
Verzegnis	64	46.25 N	12.59 E
Verzenay	50	49.10 N	4.09 E
Verzino	68	39.19 N	16.51 E
Verzuolo	62	44.36 N	7.29 E
Verzy	50	49.09 N	4.10 E
Vesanto	26	62.56 N	26.25 E
Vesava ◆[8]	272c	19.08 N	72.48 E
Vescovato, Fr.	36	42.30 N	9.26 E
Vescovato, It.	64	45.10 N	10.10 E
Vescovo di Squillace, Roccelletta del ⊥	68	38.48 N	16.35 E
Vesdre ≃	56	50.37 N	5.37 E
Veseja	76	53.04 N	27.41 E
Veselí nad Lužnicí	30	49.11 N	14.43 E
Veselí nad Moravou	30	48.58 N	17.22 E
Veselinovo	78	47.21 N	31.14 E
Veselovskoje	86	54.00 N	78.43 E
Veselovskoje vodochranilišče ⊜[1]	80	47.00 N	41.18 E
Vésenaz	58	46.14 N	6.12 E
Vešenskaja	80	49.38 N	41.43 E
Vesgre ≃	50	48.48 N	1.36 E
Vesijärvi ⊜	26	61.06 N	25.32 E
Vesjegonsk	76	58.40 N	37.16 E
Veškajma, Ross.	80	54.04 N	47.02 E
Veškajma, Ross.	80	54.03 N	47.08 E
Veški	265b	55.56 N	37.37 E
Vesle ≃	50	49.23 N	3.38 E
Vešn'aki ◆[8]	265b	55.44 N	37.49 E
Ves'olaja Gora	83	48.43 N	39.16 E
Ves'olaja Rošča	86	53.47 N	76.22 E
Vesole, Monte ∧	68	40.24 N	15.10 E
Ves'oloje, Kaz.	85	43.19 N	77.06 E
Ves'oloje, Ross.	80	50.17 N	45.15 E
Ves'oloje, Ross.	83	47.10 N	38.45 E
Ves'oloje, Ukr.	78	47.01 N	34.55 E
Ves'olo-Voznesenka	83	47.09 N	38.20 E
Ves'olyj, Ross.	80	47.06 N	40.45 E
Ves'olyj, Ross.	83	47.20 N	39.18 E
Ves'olyje Terny	78	48.07 N	33.32 E
Ves'olyj Jar, Ross.	86	51.18 N	81.07 E
Ves'olyj Jar, Ross.	89	43.57 N	135.28 E
Ves'olyj Podol, Kaz.	86	53.31 N	65.54 E
Ves'olyj Podol, Ukr.	78	49.36 N	33.16 E
Ves'olyj Pos'olok ◆[8]	265a	59.54 N	30.28 E
Vesoul	58	47.38 N	6.10 E
Vespasiano	255	19.40 S	43.55 W
Vespolate	62	45.21 N	8.40 E
Vesta	236	9.43 N	83.03 W
Vest-Agder □[6]	26	58.30 N	7.10 E
Vestal	210	42.05 N	76.03 W
Vestal Center	210	42.02 N	76.01 W
Vestavia Hills	194	33.26 N	86.46 W
Vestbygd	26	58.06 N	6.35 E
Vesterålen II	24	68.45 N	15.00 E
Vester Egede	41	55.16 N	11.59 E
Vesterø Havn	26	57.18 N	10.56 E
Vester Skerninge	41	55.03 N	10.28 E

Symbols in the index entries represent the broad categories identified in the key at the right. Symbols with superior numbers (∧∧[1]) identify subcategories (see complete key on page *I · 1).*

Symbole im Register stellen die rechts im Schlüssel erklärten Kategorien dar. Symbole mit hochgestellten Ziffern (∧∧[1]) bezeichnen Unterabteilungen einer Kategorie (vgl. vollständiger Schlüssel auf Seite *I · 1).*

Los símbolos incluídos en el texto del índice representan las grandes categorias identificadas con la clave a la derecha. Los símbolos con numeros en su parte superior (∧∧[1]) identifican las subcategorías (véase la clave completa en la página *I · 1).*

Les symboles de l'index représentent les catégories indiquées dans la légende à droite. Les symboles suivis d'un indice (∧∧[1]) représentent des sous-catégories (voir légende complète à la page *I · 1).*

Os símbolos incluídos no texto do índice representam as grandes categorias identificadas com a chave à direita. Os símbolos com números em sua parte superior (∧∧[1]) identificam as subcategorias (veja-se a chave completa à página *I · 1).*

	English	Deutsch	Español	Français	Português
∧	Mountain	Berg	Montaña	Montagne	Montanha
∧∧	Mountains	Gebirge	Montañas	Montagnes	Montanhas
⟩⟨	Pass	Paß	Paso	Col	Passo
V	Valley, Canyon	Tal, Cañon	Valle, Cañón	Vallée, Canyon	Vale, Canhão
≌	Plain	Ebene	Llano	Plaine	Planície
>	Cape	Kap	Cabo	Cap	Cabo
I	Island	Insel	Isla	Île	Ilha
II	Islands	Inseln	Islas	Îles	Ilhas
⊥	Other Topographic Features	Andere Topographische Objekte	Otros Elementos Topográficos	Autres données topographiques	Outros acidentes topográficos

ESPAÑOL

Nombre	Página	Lat.°′	Long.°′ W = Oeste
Vester Sottrup	41	54.57 N	9.43 E
Vestfjorden c [2]	24	68.08 N	15.00 E
Vestfold □ [6]	26	59.15 N	10.10 E
Vestmannaeyjar	24a	63.26 N	20.12 W
Vestone	64	45.42 N	10.24 E
Vestreno	58	46.06 N	9.18 E
Vestsjælland □ [6]	41	55.35 N	11.30 E
Vestvågøya I	24	68.15 N	13.50 E
Vésubie ≃	62	43.52 N	7.12 E
Vesubio			
→ Vesuvio ∧ [1]	68	40.49 N	14.26 E
Vesuvio (Vesuvius)			
∧ [1]	68	40.49 N	14.26 E
Vesuvius Bay	224	48.53 N	123.35 W
Vesuvius			
→ Vesuvio ∧ [1]	68	40.49 N	14.26 E
Vesuv			
→ Vesuvio ∧ [1]	68	40.49 N	14.26 E
Veszprém	30	47.06 N	17.55 E
Veszprém □ [6]	30	46.50 N	17.30 E
Vésztő	30	46.55 N	21.16 E
Vet ≃	158	27.40 S	25.40 E
Vetapālem	122	15.47 N	80.19 E
Vetčin	76	52.27 N	28.10 E
Veterans Stadium ♠	285	39.54 N	75.10 W
Vétheuil	50	49.04 N	1.42 E
Vetju	24	62.57 N	50.44 E
Vetka	76	52.33 N	31.10 E
Vetlanda	26	57.26 N	15.04 E
Vetl'anka	80	52.52 N	51.09 E
Vetluga	80	57.51 N	45.47 E
Vetluga ≃	80	56.18 N	46.24 E
Vetlužskij, Ross.	80	57.11 N	45.07 E
Vetlužskij, Ross.	80	58.23 N	45.26 E
Vetoškino	80	57.18 N	49.44 E
Vetovo	38	43.42 N	26.16 E
Vetralla	66	42.19 N	12.03 E
Vetren	38	42.16 N	24.03 E
Vetrino	76	55.25 N	28.28 E
Vetriolo	64	46.02 N	11.18 E
Vetrişoaia	38	46.26 N	28.13 E
Větřni	61	48.46 N	14.17 E
Vetschau	54	51.47 N	14.04 E
Vettisfossen ∟	26	61.22 N	7.55 E
Vetto	64	44.29 N	10.20 E
Vettore, Monte ∧	66	42.49 N	13.16 E
Vetulonia	66	42.51 N	10.58 E
Veules-les-Roses	50	49.52 N	0.48 E
Veulettes-sur-Mer	50	49.51 N	0.36 E
Veurne (Furnes)	50	51.04 N	2.40 E
Vevay	218	38.44 N	85.04 W
Vevelstad	24	65.43 N	12.30 E
Veveno, Khawr V	140	6.40 N	32.58 E
Vevey	58	46.28 N	6.51 E
Vex	58	46.13 N	7.24 E
Veyle ≃	58	46.18 N	4.50 E
Veynes	62	44.32 N	5.49 E
Veyrier	62	45.53 N	6.10 E
Vézelay	50	47.28 N	3.44 E
Vézelise	58	48.29 N	6.05 E
Vézénobres	62	44.03 N	4.09 E
Vézère ≃	32	44.53 N	0.53 E
Vezirköprü	130	41.09 N	35.28 E
Vezouze ≃	58	48.35 N	6.29 E
Vezza d'Oglio	64	46.14 N	10.24 E
Vezzana, Cima della			
∧	64	46.17 N	11.50 E
Vezzano	64	46.05 N	11.00 E
Vezzano Ligure	64	44.09 N	9.52 E
Viacha	248	16.39 S	68.18 W
Viadana	64	44.56 N	10.31 E
Viadutos	252	27.34 S	52.01 W
Viale	252	31.53 S	60.01 W
Vialonga	266c	38.52 N	9.05 W
Via Mala V	58	46.40 N	9.26 E
Viamão	252	30.05 S	51.02 W
Viamonte	252	33.44 S	63.06 W
Vian	196	35.29 N	94.58 W
Viana	250	3.13 S	45.00 W
Viana, Ilha do I	287a	22.52 S	43.08 W
Viana del Bollo	34	42.11 N	7.06 W
Viana do Alentejo	34	38.20 N	8.00 W
Viana do Castelo	34	41.42 N	8.50 W
Vianden	56	49.57 N	6.11 E
Vianen	52	52.00 N	5.05 E
Viangchan (Vientiane)	110	17.58 N	102.36 E
Viangphoukha	110	20.41 N	101.04 E
Viar ≃	34	37.36 N	5.50 W
Viareggio	64	43.52 N	10.14 E
Viarmes	50	49.08 N	2.22 E
Viatka			
→ Kirov	80	58.38 N	49.42 E
Viaur ≃	32	44.08 N	2.23 E
Vibank	184	50.20 N	103.55 W
Víboras, Arroyo de			
las ≃	258	33.57 S	58.21 W
Viborg, Dan.	26	56.26 N	9.24 E
Viborg, S.D., U.S.	198	43.10 N	97.04 W
Viborg □ [6]	41	56.18 N	9.27 E
Viborg			
→ Vyborg	76	60.42 N	28.45 E
Vibo Valentia	68	38.40 N	16.06 E
Vibraye	50	48.03 N	0.44 E
Viburnum	194	37.42 N	91.08 W
Viby	41	55.33 N	12.02 E
Viby ◆ [8]	41	56.07 N	10.10 E
Vic (Vich)	34	41.56 N	2.15 E
Vic, Étang de c	62	43.29 N	3.50 E
Vicálvaro ◆ [8]	266a	40.24 N	3.36 W
Vícam	232	27.35 N	110.20 W
Vicarello	66	42.10 N	12.12 E
Vicari	70	37.49 N	13.34 E
Vicchio	66	43.56 N	11.28 E
Vicco	192	37.12 N	83.03 W
Vic-en-Bigorre	32	43.23 N	0.03 E
Vicente, Point ›	280	33.44 N	118.25 W
Vicente Casares	258	34.57 S	58.38 W
Vicente de Carvalho	256	23.56 S	46.19 W
Vicente Guerrero,			
Méx.	234	18.24 N	92.53 W
Vicente Guerrero,			
Méx.	234	19.08 N	98.10 W
Vicente Guerrero,			
Méx.	234	23.45 N	103.59 W
Vicente Guerrero,			
Presa ⊜ [1]	234	24.00 N	98.45 W
Vicente López	258	34.32 S	58.28 W
Vicente López □ [5]	288	34.32 S	58.30 W
Vicente Noble	238	18.23 N	71.11 W
Vicenza	64	45.33 N	11.33 E
Vicenza □ [4]	64	45.40 N	11.27 E
Viceroy	184	49.27 N	105.22 W
Vichada □ [5]	246	5.00 N	69.30 W
Vichada ≃	246	4.55 N	67.50 W
Vichadero	252	31.48 S	54.43 W
Vichigasta	252	29.29 S	67.31 W
Vichoreva ≃	88	56.47 N	101.22 E
Vichorevka	88	56.12 N	101.09 E
Vichra ≃	76	54.01 N	31.52 E
Vichuga			
→ Vičuga	80	57.13 N	41.56 E
Vichuquén	252	34.53 S	72.00 W
Vichy	32	46.08 N	3.26 E
Vici	196	36.08 N	99.17 W
Vickery	214	41.23 N	82.56 W
Vicksburg, Mi., U.S.	216	42.07 N	85.31 W
Vicksburg, Ms., U.S.	194	32.21 N	90.52 W
Vicksburg, Pa., U.S.	210	40.56 N	76.59 W
Vicksburg National			
Military Park ♠	194	32.24 N	90.52 W
Vico	36	42.10 N	8.48 E
Vico, Lago di ⊜	66	42.19 N	12.10 E
Vico Canavese	62	45.30 N	7.47 E
Vico del Gargano	68	41.54 N	15.57 E
Vico Equense	68	40.40 N	14.25 E
Vicoforte	62	44.21 N	7.54 E
Vicopisano	66	43.42 N	10.35 E
Viçosa, Bra.	250	9.24 S	36.14 W
Viçosa, Bra.	255	20.45 S	42.53 W
Viçosa do Ceará	250	3.34 S	41.05 W

FRANÇAIS

Nom	Page	Lat.°′	Long.°′ W = Ouest
Vicosoprano	58	46.22 N	9.37 E
Vicovaro	66	42.01 N	12.54 E
Vicq	261	48.49 N	1.50 E
Vic-Sur-Aisne	50	49.24 N	3.07 E
Vic-sur-Cère	32	44.59 N	2.37 E
Vic-sur-Seille	56	48.47 N	6.32 E
Victor, Ca., U.S.	226	38.08 N	121.12 W
Victor, Id., U.S.	202	43.36 N	111.06 W
Victor, Ia., U.S.	190	41.43 N	92.17 W
Victor, Mt., U.S.	202	46.25 N	114.08 W
Victor, N.Y., U.S.	210	42.58 N	77.24 W
Victor, Lac ⊜	186	50.35 N	61.50 W
Victorbur	52	53.29 N	7.20 E
Victor Harbor	168b	35.34 S	138.37 E
Victoria, Arg.	252	32.37 S	60.10 W
Victoria, Cam.	152	4.01 N	9.12 E
Victoria, B.C., Can.	224	48.25 N	123.22 W
Victoria, P.E., Can.	186	46.13 N	63.29 W
Victoria, Chile	252	38.13 S	72.20 W
Victoria, Gren.	241k	12.12 N	61.42 W
Victoria, Guinée	150	10.50 N	14.33 W
Victoria (Xianggang),			
H.K.	271d	22.17 N	114.09 E
Victoria, Malay.	112	5.17 N	115.15 E
Victoria, Pil.	116	13.12 N	121.15 E
Victoria, Pil.	116	15.35 N	120.41 E
Victoria, Rom.	38	45.45 N	24.41 E
Victoria, Sey.	138	4.38 S	55.27 E
Victoria, Ks., U.S.	198	38.51 N	99.08 W
Victoria, Tx., U.S.	196	28.48 N	97.00 W
Victoria, Va., U.S.	192	36.59 N	78.13 W
Victoria □ [3]	166	38.00 S	145.00 E
Victoria □ [4]	154	20.54 S	31.21 E
Victoria □ [6], On., Can.	212	44.35 N	78.50 W
Victoria □ [6], Tx., U.S.	222	28.55 N	97.00 W
Victoria ◆ [8]	288	34.28 S	58.31 W
Victoria ≃, Austl.	160	15.12 S	129.43 E
Victoria ≃, Nf., Can.	186	48.45 N	56.40 W
Victoria ≃, Méx.	234	21.02 N	99.50 W
Victoria, Isla I	254	45.18 S	73.58 W
Victoria, Lake ⊜, Afr.	154	1.00 S	33.00 E
Victoria, Lake ⊜,			
Austl.	166	34.00 S	141.16 E
Victoria, Mount ∧,			
Mya.	110	21.14 N	93.55 E
Victoria, Mount ∧,			
Pap. N. Gui.	164	8.55 S	147.35 E
Victoria, Pont ◆ [5]	275a	45.29 N	73.32 W
Victoria and Albert			
Museum ʊ	272c	18.59 N	72.50 E
Victoria Beach	184	50.43 N	96.33 W
Victoria Beach ⊥ [2]	273a	6.25 N	3.25 E
Victoria			
→ Ciudad Victoria	234	23.44 N	99.08 W
Victoria de Durango			
→ Durango	234	24.02 N	104.40 W
Victoria Falls	154	17.56 S	25.50 E
Victoria Falls ∟	154	17.55 S	25.51 E
Victoria Falls National			
Park ♠	154	17.55 S	25.40 E
Victoria Gardens ♠	272c	18.59 N	72.50 E
Victoria Harbour	212	44.45 N	79.46 W
Victoria International			
Airport ⊠	224	48.39 N	123.26 W
Victoria Island I, N.T.,			
Can.	176	71.00 N	110.00 W
Victoria Island I, Nig.	273a	6.26 N	3.26 E
Victoria Lake ⊜	273d	26.14 S	28.09 E
Victoria Lake ⊜ [1]	186	48.18 N	57.30 W
Victoria Land ◆ [1]	9	75.00 S	163.00 E
Victoria Lawn Tennis			
Association Courts			
♠	274b	37.51 S	145.02 E
Victoria Memorial Hall			
ʊ	271c	1.17 N	103.51 E
Victoria Memorial			
Museum ʊ	272b	22.33 N	88.21 E
Victoria Nile ≃	154	2.14 N	31.26 E
Victoria Park	168a	31.58 S	115.55 E
Victoria Park ♠, H.K.	271d	22.17 N	114.11 E
Victoria Park ♠, Eng.,			
U.K.	262	53.23 N	2.34 W
Victoria Peak ∧,			
Belize	232	16.48 N	88.37 W
Victoria Peak ∧, B.C.,			
Can.	182	50.03 N	126.06 W
Victoria Peak ∧, H.K.	271d	22.17 N	114.08 E
Victoria Peaks ⋀	116	9.22 N	118.20 E
Victoria Point	171a	27.35 S	153.18 E
Victoria Range ⋀,			
N.Z.	172	42.09 S	172.08 E
Victoria Range ⋀, Pil.	116	9.32 N	118.23 E
Victoria River	164	15.37 S	131.08 E
Victoria River Downs	164	16.24 S	131.00 E
Victorias	116	10.54 N	123.05 E
Victoria State Car			
Club Race Circuit ♠	274b	37.45 S	145.11 E
Victoria Station ◆ [5],			
Eng., U.K.	260	51.29 N	0.09 W
Victoria Station ◆ [5],			
Eng., U.K.	262	53.29 N	2.15 W
Victoria Strait ʯ	176	69.15 N	100.30 W
Victoria Terminus ◆ [5]	272c	18.57 N	72.50 E
Victoria University of			
Manchester ʊ [2]	262	53.28 N	2.14 W
Victoriaville	206	46.03 N	71.57 W
Victoria			
→ Vitória	255	20.19 S	40.21 W
Victoria West	158	31.25 S	23.04 E
Victorica	252	36.13 S	65.27 W
Victorino	246	2.48 N	67.50 W
Victorino de la Plaza	252	36.36 S	62.40 W
Víctor Rosales	234	22.57 N	102.42 W
Victorville	228	34.32 N	117.17 W
Victory, Mount ∧	164	9.10 S	149.05 E
Victory Gardens	276	40.52 N	74.32 W
Victory Heights	214	41.22 N	79.46 W
Victory Hills	279b	40.11 N	79.53 W
Victory Mills	210	43.05 N	73.36 W
Victory Monument ⊥	269a	13.46 N	100.33 E
Vičuga	80	57.13 N	41.56 E
Vicuña	252	30.02 S	70.44 W
Vicuña Mackenna	252	33.54 S	64.23 W
Vidal, Kaap ›	158	28.09 S	32.33 E
Vidal Gormaz, Isla I	254	52.00 S	74.45 W
Vidalia, Ga., U.S.	192	32.13 N	82.24 W
Vidalia, La., U.S.	194	31.33 N	91.25 W
Vidal Ramos	252	27.23 S	49.22 W
Vidauban	62	43.26 N	6.26 E
Videbæk	26	56.05 N	8.38 E
Videira	252	27.00 S	51.08 W
Videle	38	44.16 N	25.31 E
Vidigueira	34	38.13 N	7.48 W
Vidim, Česko.	54	50.28 N	14.31 E
Vidim, Ross.	88	56.29 N	103.09 E
Vidin	38	43.59 N	22.52 E
Vidisha	124	23.32 N	77.49 E
Vidlica	24	61.10 N	32.21 E
Vidnoje	82	55.34 N	37.41 E
Vidogošči	82	56.42 N	36.23 E
Vidor	194	30.07 N	94.00 W
Vidos ≃	267b	40.58 N	28.53 E
Vidöstern ⊜	26	57.04 N	14.01 E
Vidourle ≃	62	43.32 N	4.08 E
Vidra, Rom.	38	44.16 N	26.11 E
Vidra, Rom.	38	45.55 N	26.54 E
Vidsel	24	65.51 N	20.24 E
Vidzeme □ [9]	76	57.10 N	25.30 E
Vidzy	76	55.24 N	26.38 E
Vie ≃	50	49.05 N	0.04 E
Viecht	60	48.30 N	12.04 E
Viechtach	60	49.05 N	12.53 E
Viedma	254	40.48 S	63.00 W
Viedma, Lago ⊜	254	49.35 S	72.35 W
Viehberg ∧	61	48.33 N	14.37 E
Viehhausen	60	48.59 N	11.58 E
Vieil Armand ♠	58	47.52 N	7.10 E
Vieillard, Lac du ⊜	190	47.23 N	78.02 W
Vieille Case	240d	15.36 N	61.24 W
Vieira do Minho	34	41.39 N	8.09 W

PORTUGUÊS

Nome	Página	Lat.°′	Long.°′ W = Oeste
Viejo, Cerro ∧	248	4.49 S	79.27 W
Viekšniai	76	56.16 N	22.31 E
Vielank	54	53.15 N	11.08 E
Viella	34	42.42 N	0.48 E
Vielle-Eglise-en-			
Yvelines	261	48.40 N	1.53 E
Vielsalm	56	50.17 N	5.55 E
Viels-Maisons	50	48.54 N	3.24 E
Viena			
→ Vienne ≃	32	47.13 N	0.05 E
Vienenburg	54	51.57 N	10.34 E
Vienna, On., Can.	212	42.41 N	80.48 W
Vienna, Ga., U.S.	192	32.05 N	83.47 W
Vienna, Il., U.S.	194	37.25 N	88.54 W
Vienna, In., U.S.	218	38.39 N	85.46 W
Vienna, Md., U.S.	208	38.29 N	75.49 W
Vienna, Mo., U.S.	194	38.11 N	91.56 W
Vienna, N.J., U.S.	210	40.52 N	74.53 W
Vienna, Oh., U.S.	214	41.14 N	80.40 W
Vienna, S.D., U.S.	198	44.42 N	97.30 W
Vienna, Va., U.S.	208	38.29 N	75.49 W
Vienna, Va., U.S.	208	38.54 N	77.15 W
Vienna, W.V., U.S.	188	39.19 N	81.32 W
Vienna			
→ Wien	61	48.13 N	16.20 E
Vienne	62	45.31 N	4.52 E
Vienne □ [5]	32	46.35 N	0.30 E
Vienne ≃	32	47.13 N	0.05 E
Vienne-en-Arthies	261	49.04 N	1.44 E
Vienne-le-Château	56	49.11 N	4.53 E
Vienne			
→ Wien	61	48.13 N	16.20 E
Vientiane			
→ Viangchan	110	17.58 N	102.36 E
Vientos, Paso de los			
→ Windward			
Passage ʯ	238	20.00 N	73.50 W
Vieques	240m	18.09 N	65.27 W
Vieques, Aeropuerto			
⊠	240m	18.07 N	65.30 W
Vieques, Isla de I	240m	18.08 N	65.25 W
Vieques, Pasaje de ʯ	240m	18.11 N	65.37 W
Vieques, Sonda de ʯ	240m	18.15 N	65.23 W
Vière ≃	56	48.46 N	4.41 E
Viereck	54	53.32 N	14.02 E
Vieremä	26	63.45 N	27.01 E
Vierfontein	158	27.03 S	26.46 E
Vierhouten	52	52.20 N	5.50 E
Vieringhausen ◆ [8]	263	51.11 N	7.10 E
Vierlande ◆ [1]	52	53.26 N	10.14 E
Viernau	54	50.40 N	10.32 E
Viernheim	56	49.32 N	8.34 E
Vierraden	54	53.06 N	14.17 E
Viersen	56	51.15 N	6.23 E
Vierumäki	26	61.06 N	25.57 E
Vierwaldstättersee ⊜	58	47.00 N	8.28 E
Vierzehnheiligen ʊ [1]	56	50.08 N	11.02 E
Vierzon	50	47.13 N	2.05 E
Viesca	232	25.21 N	102.48 W
Viesecke	54	53.01 N	12.01 E
Vieselbach	54	51.00 N	11.08 E
Viesīte	76	56.21 N	25.33 E
Vieste	68	41.53 N	16.10 E
Vietgest	54	53.45 N	12.20 E
Vietnam □ [1], Asia	108	16.00 N	108.00 E
Vietnam □ [1], Asia	110	16.00 N	108.00 E
Vietnam Veterans			
Memorial ⊥	284c	38.53 N	77.03 W
Vietri di Potenza	68	40.36 N	15.30 E
Vietri sul Mare	68	40.40 N	14.44 E
Viet Tri	110	21.18 N	105.26 E
Vieux-Condé	50	50.27 N	3.34 E
Vieux-Ferette	58	47.30 N	7.18 E
Vieux-Fort, P.Q.,			
Can.	186	51.26 N	57.49 W
Vieux-Fort, Guad.	241o	15.57 N	61.43 W
Vieux Fort, St. Luc.	241f	13.44 N	60.57 W
Vieux-Fort, Pointe du			
›	241o	15.57 N	61.43 W
Vieux Fort Bay c	241f	13.44 N	60.58 W
Vieux-Habitants	241o	16.04 N	61.46 W
Vieux-Thann	58	47.48 N	7.08 E
Vievis	76	54.46 N	24.48 E
View Park	280	34.00 N	118.20 W
Vieytes	258	35.16 S	57.35 W
Vif	62	45.03 N	5.40 E
Vig	41	55.51 N	11.36 E
Viga ≃	76	59.14 N	43.41 E
Vigala	76	58.43 N	24.22 E
Vigan	116	17.34 N	120.23 E
Vigarano Mainarda	64	44.50 N	11.30 E
Vigatto	64	44.43 N	10.20 E
Vigeland	26	58.05 N	7.18 E
Vigentino ◆ [8]	266b	45.25 N	9.11 E
Vigersted	41	55.29 N	11.54 E
Vigese, Monte ∧	64	44.12 N	11.06 E
Vigésima Quinta de			
Abril, Ponte ◆ [5]	266c	38.41 N	9.11 W
Vigevano	62	45.19 N	8.51 E
Viggianello	68	39.58 N	16.05 E
Viggiano	68	40.20 N	15.54 E
Viggiù	62	45.52 N	8.54 E
Vigia	250	0.48 S	48.08 W
Vigie Airport ⊠	241f	14.01 N	60.59 W
Vignacourt	50	50.01 N	2.12 E
Vignale	62	45.01 N	8.24 E
Vignanello	66	42.23 N	12.17 E
Vigneulles-lès-			
Hattonchâtel	56	48.59 N	5.43 E
Vigneux-sur-Seine	261	48.42 N	2.25 E
Vignola	64	44.29 N	11.00 E
Vignory	58	48.17 N	5.06 E
Vignot	56	48.46 N	5.36 E
Vigny	261	49.05 N	1.56 E
Vigo	34	42.14 N	8.43 W
Vigo, Ría de c [1]	34	42.15 N	8.45 W
Vigodarzere	64	45.27 N	11.53 E
Vigo di Fassa	64	46.25 N	11.40 E
Vigolzone	62	44.55 N	9.40 E
Vigone	62	44.51 N	7.30 E
Vigonovo	64	45.23 N	12.00 E
Vigo-Rendena	64	46.05 N	10.43 E
Vigrestad	26	58.34 N	5.42 E
Viguzzolo	62	44.54 N	8.55 E
Vigy	56	49.12 N	6.18 E
Vihanti	26	64.29 N	25.00 E
Vihāri	123	30.02 N	72.21 E
Vihiers	32	47.09 N	0.32 W
Vihowa	123	31.08 N	70.30 E
Vihren ∧	38	41.46 N	23.24 E
Vihti	26	60.25 N	24.20 E
Viiala	26	61.13 N	23.47 E
Viinijärvi	26	62.39 N	29.14 E
Viinijärvi ⊜	26	62.44 N	29.17 E
Viipuri			
→ Vyborg	76	60.42 N	28.45 E
Viitasaari	26	63.04 N	25.52 E
Viivikonna	76	59.19 N	27.42 E
Vijāpur	120	23.34 N	72.45 E
Vijayawāda	122	16.31 N	80.37 E
Vijosë (Aóös) ≃	38	40.37 N	19.20 E
Vik	40	59.44 N	17.28 E
Vik ⊥	40	59.44 N	17.27 E
Vika	40	60.31 N	15.42 E
Vikajärvi	24	66.37 N	26.12 E
Vikārābād	122	17.20 N	77.54 E
Vikbolandet › [1]	40	58.32 N	16.40 E
Vikeke	112	8.52 S	126.22 E
Viken	41	56.09 N	12.34 E
Viken ⊜	26	58.39 N	14.20 E
Vikern ⊜	40	59.30 N	14.55 E
Vikersund	26	59.59 N	10.02 E
Vikhroli ◆ [8]	272c	19.07 N	72.56 E
Viking	182	53.06 N	111.46 W
Viking Village	218	39.05 N	84.18 W
Vikmanshyttan	40	60.17 N	15.49 E
Vikna	24	64.57 N	10.58 E
Vikna I	24	64.57 N	10.58 E
Vikramasingapuram	122	8.43 N	77.24 E
Viksøyri	26	61.05 N	6.35 E

Viktor	24	66.09 N	58.07 E
Viktorovka	86	52.51 N	62.32 E
Viktring	61	46.35 N	14.16 E
Vikulovo	86	56.49 N	70.37 E
Vil'a	80	55.15 N	42.13 E
Vila Alferes			
Chamusca	156	24.29 S	33.00 E
Vila Augusta	287b	23.28 S	46.32 W
Vila Babi	287a	22.42 S	43.23 W
Vila Boacaya ◆ [8]	287b	23.29 S	46.44 W
Vila Caldas Xavier	154	15.59 S	34.12 E
Vila da Maganja	154	17.18 S	37.30 E
Vila da Ribeira Brava	150a	16.37 N	24.18 W
Viladecans	266d	41.19 N	2.00 E
Viladecavalls del			
Vallès	266d	41.33 N	1.58 E
Vila de Manica	156	18.56 S	32.53 E
Vila de Rei	34	39.40 N	8.09 W
Vila Dirce	287b	23.35 S	46.48 W
Vila do Bispo	34	37.05 N	8.55 W
Vila do Conde	34	41.21 N	8.45 W
Vila do Porto	148a	36.56 N	25.09 W
Vila Embaú	256	22.37 S	45.02 W
Vila Flor	34	41.18 N	7.09 W
Vila Fontes	156	17.50 S	35.21 E
Vila Formosa ◆ [8]	287b	23.34 S	46.33 W
Vilafranca del			
Penedès	34	41.21 N	1.42 E
Vila Franca de Xira	34	38.57 N	8.59 W
Vila Galvão	287b	23.27 S	46.33 W
Vila Gamito	154	14.12 S	33.00 E
Vila Gomes da Costa	156	24.19 S	33.38 E
Vila Gouveia	156	18.03 S	33.11 E
Vila Guilherme ◆ [8]	287b	23.30 S	46.36 W
Vilaine ≃	32	47.30 N	2.27 W
Vila Isabel ◆ [8]	287a	22.55 S	43.15 W
Vila Jaguára ◆ [8]	287b	23.31 S	46.45 W
Viļaka	76	57.11 N	27.41 E
Vila Luísa	156	25.44 S	32.40 E
Vilama, Laguna de ⊜	252	22.36 S	66.55 W
Vila Machado	156	19.18 S	34.11 E
Vila Madalena ◆ [8]	287b	23.33 S	46.42 W
Vila Maria ◆ [8]	287b	23.31 S	46.34 W
Vila Mariana ◆ [8]	287b	23.35 S	46.38 W
Vila Matilde ◆ [8]	287b	23.32 S	46.31 W
Vilanculos	156	22.01 S	35.19 E
Viļāni	76	56.33 N	26.57 E
Vila Nova ≃	250	0.04 S	51.13 W
Vila Nova de			
Famalicão	34	41.25 N	8.32 W
Vila Nova de Foz			
Côa	34	41.05 N	7.12 W
Vila Nova de Gaia	34	41.08 N	8.37 W
Vilanova de la Roca	266d	41.33 N	2.17 E
Vilanova i la Geltrú	34	41.14 N	1.44 E
Vila Novo de Ourém	34	39.39 N	8.35 W
Vila Paiva de			
Andrada	156	18.44 S	34.03 E
Vila Progresso	287a	22.55 S	43.03 W
Vila Prudente ◆ [8]	287b	23.35 S	46.33 W
Vila-real, Esp.	34	39.56 N	0.06 W
Vila Real, Port.	34	41.18 N	7.45 W
Vila Real de Santo			
António	34	37.12 N	7.25 W
Vilar Formoso	34	40.37 N	6.50 W
Vilarinho do Monte	250	1.37 S	52.01 W
Vilassar de Dalt	266d	41.31 N	2.22 E
Vilassar de Mar	266d	41.30 N	2.24 E
Vila Vasco da Gama	154	14.54 S	32.14 E
Vila Velha, Bra.	250	3.13 N	51.13 W
Vila Velha, Bra.	255	20.20 S	40.17 W
Vila Velha de Ródão	34	39.38 N	7.40 W
Vila Verde, Port.	34	41.39 N	8.26 W
Vila Verde, Port.	266c	38.50 N	9.22 W
Vila Viçosa	34	38.47 N	8.13 W
Vil'ča	78	51.22 N	29.24 E
Vilcabamba,			
Cordillera de ⋀	248	12.45 S	73.20 W
Vîlcea □ [6]	38	45.19 N	24.00 E
Vildbjerg	41	56.12 N	8.46 E
Vilejka	76	54.30 N	26.53 E
Vilelas	252	27.57 S	62.38 W
Vilenki	82	54.16 N	38.55 E
Vil'gort, Ross.	24	61.35 N	50.40 E
Vil'gort, Ross.	24	60.34 N	56.24 E
Vilhelmina	26	64.37 N	16.39 E
Vilhena	248	12.43 S	60.07 W
Vilija ≃	76	54.54 N	25.35 E
Viljandi	76	58.22 N	25.36 E
Viljoensdrif	158	26.44 S	27.55 E
Viljoenshof	158	34.40 S	19.42 E
Viljoenskroon	158	27.12 S	27.00 E
Viljoenspos	158	27.35 S	30.30 E
Vilkaviškis	76	54.39 N	23.02 E
Vil'kickogo, ostrov I,			
Ross.	72	73.29 N	75.50 E
Vil'kickogo, ostrov I,			
Ross.	74	75.44 N	152.20 E
Vil'kickogo, proliv ʯ	74	77.55 N	103.00 E
Vilkija	76	55.03 N	23.35 E
Vilkovo	78	45.25 N	29.35 E
Villa Abecia	248	21.00 S	65.23 W
Villa Aberastain	252	31.39 S	68.35 W
Villa Acuña			
→ Ciudad Acuña	232	29.18 N	100.55 W
Villa Adelina ◆ [8]	288	34.31 S	58.32 W
Villa Adriana ⊥	66	41.56 N	12.45 E
Villa Alejandrina	258	33.46 S	58.21 W
Villa Alemana	252	33.03 S	71.23 W
Villa Álvarez	234	19.14 N	103.43 W
Villa Ana	252	28.29 S	59.37 W
Villa Ángela	252	27.35 S	60.43 W
Villa Atamisqui	252	28.29 S	63.48 W
Villa Atuel	252	34.50 S	67.54 W
Villaba	116	11.13 N	124.23 E
Villa Ballester ◆ [8]	258	34.32 S	58.33 W
Villabassa			
(Niederdorf)	64	46.44 N	12.10 E
Villabate	70	38.04 N	13.26 E
Villabé	261	48.35 N	2.27 E
Villa Bella	248	10.23 S	65.24 W
Villa Berthet	252	27.17 S	60.25 W
Villablino	34	42.56 N	6.19 W
Villa Borghese ʊ	267a	41.55 N	12.29 E
Villa Bosch ◆ [8]	288	34.35 S	58.34 W
Villa Bruzual	246	9.20 N	69.06 W
Villa Cañás, Arg.	252	34.00 S	61.36 W
Villacañas, Esp.	34	39.38 N	3.20 W
Villa Carlos Paz	252	31.24 S	64.31 W
Villacarriedo	34	43.14 N	3.48 W
Villacarrillo	34	38.07 N	3.05 W
Villa Castelli, Arg.	252	29.00 S	68.11 W
Villa Castelli, It.	68	40.35 N	17.28 E
Villacastín	34	40.47 N	4.25 W
Villach	64	46.36 N	13.50 E
Villacidro	71	39.27 N	8.44 E
Villa Ciudadela ◆ [8]	258	34.38 S	58.34 W
Villa Clara □ [4]	240p	22.30 N	80.00 W
Villa Comaltitlan	236	15.13 N	92.35 W
Villa Concepción del			
Tío	252	31.19 S	62.50 W
Villa Constitución	252	33.14 S	60.20 W
Villa Cortese	266b	45.34 N	8.53 E
Villa Corzo	234	16.10 N	93.15 W
Villacoublay,			
Aérodrome de ⊠	261	48.45 N	2.10 E
Villa Creek ≃	226	35.27 N	120.58 W
Villa Cuauhtémoc,			
Méx.	234	19.24 N	99.34 W
Villa Cuauhtémoc,			
Méx.	234	22.11 N	97.50 W
Villada	34	42.15 N	4.58 W
Villa de Apaseo El			
Alto	234	20.27 N	100.37 W
Villa de Arista	234	22.39 N	100.50 W
Villa de Arriaga	234	21.54 N	101.23 W
Villadeati	62	45.04 N	8.10 E
Villa de Cos	234	23.17 N	102.21 W
Villa de Cura	246	10.02 N	67.29 W
Villa de Guadalupe	234	23.22 N	100.46 W

Villa del Carmen	252	32.57 S	65.03 W
Villa del Pueblito	234	20.32 N	100.27 W
Villa del Río	34	37.59 N	4.17 W
Villa del Rosario, Arg.	252	31.35 S	63.32 W
Villa del Rosario, Arg.	252	30.47 S	57.55 W
Villa de María	252	29.54 S	63.43 W
Villa de Mayo	258	34.30 S	58.41 W
Villa de Nova Sintra	150a	14.52 N	24.43 W
Villa de Reyes	234	21.48 N	100.56 W
Villa de San Antonio	236	14.16 N	87.36 W
Villa de San			
Francisco	236	14.10 N	86.58 W
Villa de Soto	252	30.51 S	64.59 W
Villa d'Este ⊥	267a	41.57 N	12.48 E
Villa Devoto ◆ [8]	288	34.36 S	58.31 W
Villa Diamante ◆ [8]	288	34.41 S	58.26 W
Villa di Chiavenna	58	46.20 N	9.29 E
Villadiego	34	42.31 N	4.00 W
Villa Dolores	252	31.56 S	65.12 W
Villa Domínico ◆ [8]	258	34.41 S	58.19 W
Villadose	64	45.04 N	11.53 E
Villadossola	58	46.04 N	8.16 E
Villa Elisa	252	32.10 S	58.24 W
Villa Elisa ◆ [8]	258	34.50 S	58.05 W
Villa Escalante	234	19.24 N	101.39 W
Villa Flores	234	16.14 N	93.14 W
Villa Florida	252	26.23 S	57.09 W
Villafranca d'Asti	62	44.55 N	8.02 E
Villafranca del Bierzo	34	42.36 N	6.48 W
Villafranca de los			
Barros	34	38.34 N	6.20 W
Villafranca di Verona	64	45.21 N	10.50 E
Villafranca in			
Lunigiana	64	44.17 N	9.57 E
Villafranca Piemonte	62	44.47 N	7.33 E
Villafranca Sicula	70	37.35 N	13.17 E
Villafranca Tirrena	70	38.14 N	15.26 E
Villafrati	70	37.54 N	13.29 E
Villagarcía, Esp.	34	42.36 N	8.45 W
Villa García, Méx.	234	22.10 N	101.57 W
Village	196	35.33 N	97.33 W
Village Creek ≃	194	35.28 N	91.19 W
Village Green	285	39.52 N	75.26 W
Villa General Roca	252	32.39 S	66.28 W
Village of Drummond			
Hill	285	39.43 N	75.42 W
Village of the Branch	276	40.51 N	73.11 W
Villa Gesell	252	37.15 S	56.55 W
Villa Giambruno	288	34.48 S	58.13 W
Villa González Ortega	234	22.30 N	101.55 W
Villagrán, Méx.	232	24.29 N	99.29 W
Villagrán, Méx.	234	20.31 N	100.59 W
Villagrande Strisaili	71	39.58 N	9.30 E
Villa Grazia	70	38.09 N	13.10 E
Villagrazia ◆ [8]	70	38.05 N	13.20 E
Villa Grove	194	39.51 N	88.09 W
Villaguay	252	31.51 S	59.01 W
Villa Guerrero, Méx.	234	21.59 N	103.36 W
Villa Guerrero, Méx.	234	18.52 N	99.39 W
Villa Guillermina	252	28.14 S	59.28 W
Villa Hayes	252	25.06 S	57.34 W
Villahermosa	234	17.59 N	92.55 W
Villa Hernandarias	252	31.13 S	59.59 W
Villa Hidalgo, Méx.	204	30.59 N	116.10 W
Villa Hidalgo, Méx.	234	21.40 N	102.36 W
Villa Hidalgo, Méx.	234	21.44 N	105.15 W
Villa Hidalgo Yalalag	234	17.11 N	96.11 W
Villa Huidobro	252	34.50 S	64.35 W
Villaines-la-Juhel	32	48.21 N	0.17 W
Villa Insurgentes	232	25.12 N	111.44 W
Villa Iris	252	38.10 S	63.15 W
Villa Jiménez	234	19.55 N	101.35 W
Villa José L. Suárez			
◆ [8]	288	34.32 S	58.35 W
Villa Juanita	234	17.47 N	95.09 W
Villa Juárez, Méx.	232	27.10 N	109.50 W
Villa Juárez, Méx.	234	22.20 N	100.17 W
Villa Krause	252	31.34 S	68.32 W
Villa La Angostura	254	40.47 S	71.40 W
Villalago	66	41.56 N	13.50 E
Villa Larca	252	32.37 S	64.59 W
Villa La Venta	234	18.10 N	94.07 W
Villalba, Esp.	34	43.18 N	7.41 W
Villalba, It.	70	37.39 N	13.50 E
Villalba, P.R.	240m	18.08 N	66.30 W
Villaldama	232	26.30 N	100.26 W
Villa Lia	258	34.07 S	59.26 W
Villalon	116	11.31 N	124.22 E
Villalón de Campos	34	42.06 N	5.02 W
Villalonga	254	39.53 S	62.35 W
Villalpando	34	41.52 N	5.24 W
Villa Lugano ◆ [8]	288	34.41 S	58.28 W
Villalvernia	62	44.49 N	8.51 E
Villa Lynch ◆ [8]	288	34.36 S	58.31 W
Villa Madero, Arg.	288	34.42 S	58.30 W
Villa Madero, Méx.	234	19.24 N	101.16 W
Villa Mainero	232	24.32 N	99.38 W
Villamar	71	39.37 N	8.59 E
Villa María, Arg.	252	32.25 S	63.15 W
Villa Maria, Pa., U.S.	214	41.05 N	80.30 W
Villa Maria del Triunfo	286d	12.10 S	76.56 W
Villa María Grande	252	31.39 S	59.54 W
Villa Martín, Bol.	248	20.46 S	67.47 W
Villamartín, Esp.	34	36.52 N	5.38 W
Villamarzana	64	45.01 N	11.41 E
Villamassargia	71	39.16 N	8.38 E
Villa Matoque	252	25.49 S	63.49 W
Villa Mazán	252	28.40 S	66.34 W
Villa Media Agua	252	31.59 S	68.25 W
Villa Mercedes	252	30.07 S	68.42 W
Villa Minozzo	64	44.22 N	10.28 E
Villamontes	248	21.15 S	63.30 W
Villa Morelos	234	20.00 N	101.25 W
Villandraut	32	44.28 N	0.23 W
Villa Nova, Md., U.S.	284b	39.21 N	76.44 W
Villa Nova, Oh., U.S.	216	40.33 N	84.26 W
Villanova, Pa., U.S.	208	40.02 N	75.20 W
Villanova d'Asti	62	44.57 N	7.56 E
Villanova Mondovì	62	44.21 N	7.45 E
Villanova Monferrato	62	45.11 N	8.28 E
Villanova Monteleone	71	40.30 N	8.28 E
Villanova sull'Arda	64	45.01 N	10.00 E
Villanova Tulo	71	39.47 N	9.13 E
Villanova University			
ʊ [2]	285	40.02 N	75.21 W
Villa Nueva, Arg.	252	32.26 S	63.15 W
Villa Nueva, Arg.	252	32.54 S	68.47 W
Villanueva, Col.	246	10.37 N	72.59 W
Villa Nueva, Guat.	236	14.31 N	90.35 W
Villanueva, Hond.	236	15.17 N	88.00 W
Villanueva, Méx.	234	22.21 N	102.53 W
Villa Nueva, Nic.	236	12.58 N	86.49 W
Villanueva, N.M., U.S.	200	35.16 N	105.21 W
Villanueva de			
Córdoba	34	38.20 N	4.37 W
Villanueva de la			
Serana	34	38.58 N	5.48 W
Villanueva de la			
Sierra	34	40.12 N	6.24 W
Villanueva de los			
Infantes	34	38.44 N	2.59 W
Villanueva del Río y			
Minas	34	37.39 N	5.42 W
Villa Numancia	288	34.55 S	58.24 W
Villa Obregón	234	21.07 N	102.42 W
Villa Ocampo	252	28.28 S	59.22 W
Villa Ojo de Agua	252	29.31 S	63.42 W
Villa Oliva	252	26.01 S	57.53 W
Villa Opicina	64	45.40 N	13.49 E
Villa Oropeza	248	19.10 S	65.17 W
Villa Ottone			
(Uttenheim)	64	46.52 N	11.57 E
Villa Papale ʊ	267a	41.45 N	12.39 E
Villa Park, Ca., U.S.	228	33.48 N	117.48 W
Villa Park, Il., U.S.	278	41.53 N	87.59 W
Villa Park Dam ◆ [6]	280	33.48 N	117.46 W
Villa Pérez	240m	18.12 N	66.47 W
Villapiana	68	39.51 N	16.28 E
Villapiana Lido	68	39.48 N	16.29 E
Villapinzón	246	5.13 N	73.36 W

Villa Potenza	66	43.19 N	13.25 E
Villaputzu	71	39.26 N	9.34 E
Villa Quinteros	252	27.14 S	65.33 W
Villa Quintilio Varo ⊥	267a	41.58 N	12.47 E
Villa Ramírez	252	32.11 S	60.12 W
Villarcayo	34	42.56 N	3.34 W
Villar-d'Arène	62	45.02 N	6.20 E
Villard-Bonnot	62	45.14 N	5.53 E
Villard-de-Lans	62	45.04 N	5.33 E
Villardefrades	34	41.43 N	5.15 W
Villar del Arzobispo	34	39.44 N	0.49 W
Villareal	116	11.34 N	124.56 E
Villa Real ◆ [8]	288	34.37 S	58.31 W
Villa Regina	252	39.06 S	67.04 W
Villa Reynolds	252	33.43 S	65.23 W
Villa Rica	192	33.43 N	84.55 W
Villa Rivero	248	17.37 S	65.48 W
Villaroche	261	48.37 N	2.39 E
Villaroche ■	261	48.37 N	2.40 E
Villa Romana del			
Casale ⊥	70	37.22 N	14.20 E
Villa Rosa, Arg.	258	34.25 S	58.52 W
Villarosa, It.	70	37.35 N	14.10 E
Villar Pellice	62	44.48 N	7.09 E
Villar Perosa	62	44.56 N	7.15 E
Villarreales	196	26.07 N	100.20 W
Villarrica, Chile	254	39.16 S	72.13 W
Villarrica, Col.	246	3.58 N	74.37 W
Villarrica, Para.	252	25.45 S	56.26 W
Villarrica, Lago ⊜	254	39.15 S	72.06 W
Villarrobledo	34	39.16 N	2.36 W
Villarrubia de los			
Ojos	34	39.13 N	3.36 W
Villars, Arg.	258	34.50 S	58.56 W
Villars, Schw.	58	46.18 N	7.04 E
Villars-Colmars	62	44.10 N	6.36 E
Villars-en-Azois	58	48.04 N	4.45 E
Villars-les-Dombes	58	46.00 N	5.01 E
Villars-sur-Var	62	43.56 N	7.06 E
Villa Ruiz	258	34.25 S	59.15 W
Villas	208	39.01 N	74.56 W
Villa Sáenz Peña ◆ [8]	288	34.36 S	58.31 W
Villa San Andrés ◆ [8]	288	34.33 S	58.32 W
Villa Sandino	236	12.03 N	84.59 W
Villa San Giovanni	68	38.13 N	15.38 E
Villa San José	252	32.12 S	58.13 W
Villa San Martín	252	28.18 S	64.12 W
Villasanta	62	45.37 N	9.18 E
Villa Santa, Montaña			
∧	236	14.12 N	86.27 W
Villa Santa Maria	66	41.57 N	14.21 E
Villa Santina	64	46.24 N	12.55 E
Villa Santo Domingo	234	23.20 N	101.44 W
Villa Santos Lugares			
◆ [8]	288	34.36 S	58.32 W
Villasayas	34	41.21 N	2.37 W
Villa Serrano	248	19.06 S	64.22 W
Villasimius	71	39.08 N	9.31 E
Villasis	116	15.54 N	120.35 E
Villasor	71	39.23 N	8.56 E
Villa Talavera	248	19.49 S	65.25 W
Villa Tunari	248	16.55 S	65.25 W
Villa Turdera ◆ [8]	288	34.48 S	58.25 W
Villa Unión, Arg.	252	29.18 S	68.12 W
Villa Unión, Arg.	252	29.24 S	62.47 W
Villa Unión, Méx.	232	28.15 N	100.43 W
Villa Unión, Méx.	234	23.58 N	104.02 W
Villa Unión, Méx.	234	23.12 N	106.14 W
Villa Urquiza ◆ [8]	288	34.34 S	58.29 W
Villa Valeria	252	34.20 S	64.55 W
Villa Vallelonga	66	41.52 N	13.37 E
Villaverde ◆ [8]	266a	40.21 N	3.42 W
Villaverla	64	45.39 N	11.29 E
Villa Verona	226	39.28 N	121.33 W
Villavicencio	246	4.09 N	73.37 W
Villaviciosa	34	43.29 N	5.26 W
Villaviciosa de			
Córdoba	34	38.05 N	5.01 W
Villa Victoria	234	18.47 N	103.24 W
Villa Viscarra	248	17.59 S	65.36 W
Villa Vomano	66	42.37 N	13.46 E
Villazón	248	22.06 S	65.36 W
Villa Zorraquín	252	31.19 S	58.02 W
Villé	58	48.20 N	7.18 E
Villebon, Lac ⊜	190	47.58 N	77.17 W
Villebon-sur-Yvette	261	48.42 N	2.15 E
Villeconin	261	48.31 N	2.08 E
Villecresnes	261	48.43 N	2.32 E
Villecroze	62	43.35 N	6.16 E
Ville-d'Avray	261	48.50 N	2.11 E
Ville-de-Laval			
→ Laval	206	45.35 N	73.45 W
Villedieu	32	48.50 N	1.13 W
Ville-en-Tardenois	50	49.11 N	3.48 E
Villefort	62	44.26 N	3.56 E
Villefranche	58	45.59 N	4.43 E
Villefranche-de-			
Rouergue	32	44.21 N	2.02 E
Villefranche-Sur-Cher	50	47.18 N	1.46 E
Villefranche-sur-Mer	62	43.42 N	7.19 E
Villejuif	50	48.48 N	2.22 E
Villejust	261	48.41 N	2.14 E
Ville-Marie	190	47.19 N	79.26 W
Villemaur-sur-Vanne	50	48.15 N	3.44 E
Villemeux-sur-Eure	50	48.40 N	1.28 E
Villemoisson-sur-Orge	261	48.40 N	2.19 E
Villemomble	261	48.53 N	2.31 E
Villena	34	38.38 N	0.51 W
Ville Nacíonal	234	17.50 N	96.14 W
Villenauxe-la-Grande	50	48.35 N	3.33 E
Villeneuve, It.	62	45.42 N	7.14 E
Villeneuve, Schw.	58	46.24 N	6.55 E
Villeneuve-d'Ascq	50	50.37 N	3.10 E
Villeneuve-d'Aveyron	32	44.26 N	2.02 E
Villeneuve-de-Berg	62	44.33 N	4.30 E
Villeneuve-la-Garenne	261	48.56 N	2.20 E
Villeneuve-la-Guyard	50	48.20 N	3.04 E
Villeneuve-			
l'Archevêque	50	48.14 N	3.33 E
Villeneuve-le-Comte	261	48.49 N	2.50 E
Villeneuve-le-Roi	50	48.44 N	2.25 E
Villeneuve-lès-			
Avignon	62	43.58 N	4.48 E
Villeneuve-lès-			
Maguelonne	62	43.32 N	3.52 E
Villeneuve-Saint-			
Denis	261	48.49 N	2.48 E
Villeneuve-Saint-			
Georges	50	48.44 N	2.27 E
Villeneuve-sous-			
Dammartin	261	49.02 N	2.39 E
Villeneuve-sur-Lot	32	44.25 N	0.42 E
Villeneuve-sur-Yonne	50	48.05 N	3.18 E
Villennes-sur-Seine	261	48.56 N	2.00 E
Villenoy	50	48.57 N	2.52 E
Villeny	50	47.37 N	1.45 E
Villeparisis	50	48.56 N	2.37 E
Villepinte	261	48.58 N	2.32 E
Ville Platte	194	30.41 N	92.16 W
Villepreux	261	48.50 N	2.01 E
Villequier	50	49.31 N	0.40 E
Villeron	261	49.03 N	2.33 E
Villeroy	50	48.59 N	2.47 E
Villers-Bocage, Fr.	32	49.05 N	0.39 W
Villers-Bocage, Fr.	50	49.59 N	2.20 E
Villers-Bretonneux	50	49.52 N	2.31 E
Villers-Carbonnel	50	49.52 N	2.54 E
Villers-Cotterêts	50	49.15 N	3.05 E
Villers-devant-Orval	56	49.37 N	5.19 E
Villers-en-Arthies	261	49.05 N	1.44 E
Villersexel	58	47.33 N	6.26 E
Villers-Farlay	58	47.00 N	5.45 E
Villers-la-Ville	50	50.35 N	4.32 E
Villers-le-Lac	58	47.04 N	6.40 E
Villers-lès-Nancy	58	48.40 N	6.09 E
Villers-lès-Pots	58	47.13 N	5.21 E
Villers-Outréaux	50	50.02 N	3.18 E
Villers-Saint-Paul	50	49.17 N	2.29 E
Villers-Semeuse	56	49.44 N	4.45 E
Villerupt	56	49.28 N	5.56 E

	English	Deutsch	Español	Français	Português
≃	River	Fluß	Río	Rivière	Rio
≊	Canal	Kanal	Canal	Canal	Canal
∟	Waterfall, Rapids	Wasserfall, Stromschnellen	Cascada, Rápidos	Chute d'eau, Rapides	Cascata, Rápidos
ʯ	Strait	Meeresstraße	Estrecho	Détroit	Estreito
c	Bay, Gulf	Bucht, Golf	Bahía, Golfo	Baie, Golfe	Baía, Golfo
⊜	Lake, Lakes	See, Seen	Lago, Lagos	Lac, Lacs	Lago, Lagos
☷	Swamp	Sumpf	Pantano	Marais	Pântano
⊓	Ice Features, Glacier	Eis- und Gletscherformen	Accidentes Glaciales	Formes glaciaires	Acidentes glaciares
⊤	Other Hydrographic Features	Andere Hydrographische Objekte	Otros Elementos Hidrográficos	Autres données hydrographiques	Outros acidentes hidrográficos
✢	Submarine Features	Untermeerische Objekte	Accidentes Submarinos	Formes de relief sous-marin	Acidentes submarinos
□	Political Unit	Politische Einheit	Unidad Politica	Entité politique	Unidade política
ʊ	Cultural Institution	Kulturelle Institution	Institución Cultural	Institution culturelle	Institução cultural
⊥	Historical Site	Historische Stätte	Sitio Histórico	Site historique	Sitio histórico
♠	Recreational Site	Erholungs- und Ferienort	Sitio de Recreo	Centre de loisirs	Area de Lazer
⊠	Airport	Flughafen	Aeropuerto	Aéroport	Aeroporto
■	Military Installation	Militäranlage	Instalación Militar	Installation militaire	Instalação militar
◆	Miscellaneous	Verschiedenes	Misceláneo	Divers	Diversos

Villerville 50 49.24 N 0.08 E
Ville-Saint-Georges → Saint-Georges 188 46.07 N 70.40 W
Villes-sur-Auzon 62 44.03 N 5.14 E
Ville-sur-Tourbe 56 49.11 N 4.47 E
Villeta 246 5.01 N 74.28 W
Villetta Barrea 66 41.47 N 13.56 E
Villeurbanne 62 45.46 N 4.53 E
Villevaudé 261 48.55 N 2.39 E
Villeziers 261 48.40 N 2.10 E
Villiers 158 27.03 S 28.35 E
Villiers-Adam 261 49.04 N 2.14 E
Villiersdorp 158 34.00 S 19.19 E
Villiers-le-Bâcle 261 48.44 N 2.08 E
Villiers-le-Bel 261 49.00 N 2.23 E
Villiers-le-Sec 261 49.04 N 2.23 E
Villiers-Saint-Frédéric 261 48.49 N 1.54 E
Villiers-Saint-Georges 50 48.39 N 3.25 E
Villiers-sur-Marne 261 48.50 N 2.33 E
Villiers-sur-Morin 261 48.52 N 2.53 E
Villigst 263 51.26 N 7.35 E
Villingen-Schwenningen 30 48.04 N 8.28 E
Villisca 198 40.55 N 94.58 W
Villmanstrand → Lappeenranta 26 61.04 N 28.11 E
Villmergen 58 47.21 N 8.15 E
Villorba 64 45.44 N 12.14 E
Villoresi, Canale ≍ 62 45.33 N 9.31 E
Villotta 64 45.52 N 12.45 E
Vilm I 54 54.19 N 13.32 E
Vilmnitz 54 54.21 N 13.31 E
Vilna 182 54.07 N 111.55 W
Vilna → Vilnius 76 54.41 N 25.19 E
Vilnius 76 54.41 N 25.19 E
Vilosnes-sur-Meuse 56 49.20 N 5.14 E
Vilppula 26 62.01 N 24.31 E
Vils 58 47.33 N 10.38 E
Vils ≃, Dtsch. 60 49.09 N 11.58 E
Vils ≃, Dtsch. 60 48.37 N 13.11 E
Vils ≃, Europe 58 47.33 N 10.40 E
Vilsandi saar I 76 58.23 N 21.52 E
Vilsbiburg 60 48.27 N 12.12 E
Vilseck 60 49.37 N 11.48 E
Vilsheim 60 48.27 N 12.07 E
Vilshofen 60 48.39 N 13.12 E
Vil'uj ≃ 74 64.24 N 126.26 E
Vil'ujsk 74 63.45 N 121.35 E
Vil'ujskoje vodochranilišče ⊜[1] 74 62.30 N 111.00 E
Viluppuram 122 11.56 N 79.29 E
Vil'va 86 58.37 N 56.52 E
Vilvoorde 50 50.56 N 4.26 E
Vimercate 62 45.37 N 9.22 E
Vimianzo 34 43.07 N 9.02 W
Vimmerby 26 57.40 N 15.51 E
Vimodrone 266b 45.31 N 9.17 E
Vimoutiers 50 48.55 N 0.12 E
Vimpeli 26 63.09 N 23.48 E
Vimperk 60 49.03 N 13.47 E
Vimy 50 50.22 N 2.49 E
Vina 204 39.55 N 122.03 W
Vina ≃ 146 7.45 N 15.36 E
Viñac 248 12.56 S 75.47 W
Viña del Mar 252 33.02 S 71.34 W
Vinadi 58 46.55 N 10.29 E
Vinadio 62 44.18 N 7.10 E
Viñales 240p 22.37 N 83.43 W
Vinalhaven 188 44.02 N 68.49 W
Vinalhaven Island I 188 44.05 N 68.52 W
Vinantes 261 49.01 N 2.44 E
Vina Roni, Mount ∧ 175e 8.10 S 157.28 E
Vinaròs 34 40.28 N 0.29 E
Vinay 62 45.13 N 5.24 E
Vinazco ≃ 234 20.56 N 97.44 W
Vincennes, Fr. 50 48.51 N 2.26 E
Vincennes, In., U.S. 194 38.40 N 87.31 W
Vincennes, Bois de ♦ 261 48.50 N 2.25 E
Vincennes, Château de ⊥ 261 48.51 N 2.26 E
Vincennes, Étang de ⊜ 261 48.47 N 2.45 E
Vincennes Bay ⊂ 9 66.30 S 109.30 E
Vincent 194 33.22 N 86.22 W
Vincent, Point › 174c 29.00 S 167.55 E
Vincentown 208 39.56 N 74.44 W
Vinces 246 1.32 S 79.45 W
Vinchiaturo 66 41.29 N 14.35 E
Vinchina 252 28.46 S 68.10 W
Vinchos 248 13.16 S 74.21 W
Vinci 66 43.47 N 10.55 E
Vinco 214 40.25 N 78.52 W
Vindeby 41 55.03 N 10.38 E
Vindelälven ≃ 24 63.54 N 19.52 E
Vindeln 26 64.12 N 19.44 E
Vinden, Mount ∧ 162 27.01 S 115.38 E
Vinderslev 41 56.15 N 9.26 E
Vinderup 26 56.29 N 8.47 E
Vindhya Range ⋏ 120 23.00 N 77.00 E
Vinding 41 55.41 N 9.35 E
Vindinge 41 55.19 N 10.45 E
Vine Brook ≃ 283 42.27 N 71.13 W
Vinegar Hill ∧ 202 44.43 N 118.34 W
Vine Grove 194 37.48 N 85.58 W
Vine Hill 282 38.00 N 122.06 W
Vineland, Mi., U.S. 216 42.03 N 86.30 W
Vineland, N.J., U.S. 208 39.29 N 75.01 W
Vinemont 194 34.14 N 86.51 W
Vine Valley 210 42.43 N 77.20 W
Vineyard Canyon V 226 35.46 N 120.41 W
Vineyard Haven 207 41.27 N 70.36 W
Vineyard Lake ⊜ 216 42.05 N 84.13 W
Vineyard Sound ⊍ 207 41.25 N 70.46 W
Vingåker 40 59.02 N 15.52 E
Vingeanne ≃ 58 47.21 N 5.29 E
Ving Ngün 110 22.37 N 99.16 E
Vinh 110 18.40 N 105.40 E
Vinhais 34 41.50 N 7.00 W
Vinhas, Ribeira das ≃ 266c 38.42 N 9.25 W
Vinh Chau 110 9.19 N 105.59 E
Vinhedo 256 23.01 S 46.59 W
Vinh Loc 269c 10.49 N 106.34 E
Vinh Long 110 10.15 N 105.58 E
Vinh Tuy, Viet 110 9.37 N 105.22 E
Vinh Tuy, Viet 110 17.24 N 106.36 E
Vinica 36 45.28 N 15.15 E
Vinita 196 36.38 N 95.09 W
Vînju Mare 38 44.26 N 22.52 E
Vinkekuil 158 32.42 S 20.27 E
Vinkeveen 52 52.13 N 4.54 E
Vinkovci 38 45.17 N 18.49 E
Vin'kovcy 78 49.02 N 27.14 E
Vinnhorst 52 52.25 N 9.43 E
Vinnica 78 49.14 N 28.29 E
Vinnica □[8] 38 48.30 N 28.30 E
Vinniki 78 49.48 N 24.08 E
Vinnitsa → Vinnica 78 49.14 N 28.29 E
Vinnum 263 51.41 N 7.24 E
Vinogradov 78 48.09 N 23.02 E
Vinogradovo, Ross. 82 55.25 N 38.32 E
Vinogradovo, Ross. 82 55.57 N 37.32 E
Vinogrobol' 78 51.51 N 36.26 E
Vinön I 40 59.12 N 15.43 E
Vinon-sur-Verdon 62 43.43 N 5.48 E
Vinovo 62 44.57 N 7.38 E
Vinslöv 26 56.06 N 13.55 E
Vinson Massif ∧ 9 78.35 S 85.25 W
Vinstra 26 61.36 N 9.45 E
Vintilă Vodă 38 45.28 N 26.44 E
Vinto 248 17.58 S 67.04 W
Vinton, Ia., U.S. 190 42.10 N 92.01 W
Vinton, La., U.S. 194 30.11 N 93.34 W
Vinton, Va., U.S. 192 37.16 N 79.53 W
Vintondale 214 40.28 N 78.55 W
Vintrosa 40 59.15 N 14.57 E
Viñuelas, Arroyo de ≃ 266a 40.33 N 3.33 W
Viny 76 58.22 N 32.13 E
Vinzelberg 54 52.33 N 11.40 E
Vinzili 86 56.58 N 65.46 E
Viola, Il., U.S. 190 41.12 N 90.35 W
Viola, N.Y., U.S. 276 41.08 N 74.05 W
Viola, Wi., U.S. 190 43.30 N 90.40 W
Viola, Val V 64 46.27 N 10.15 E
Violín, Isla I 236 8.51 N 83.39 W
Viols-le-Fort 62 43.45 N 3.42 E
Viosne ≃ 261 49.03 N 2.06 E
Vipava 36 45.51 N 13.58 E
Vipava ≃ 64 45.54 N 13.33 E
Vipiteno (Sterzing) 64 46.54 N 11.26 E
Vipos 252 26.29 S 65.22 W
Vipperow 54 53.19 N 12.41 E
Vir, Otok I 36 44.18 N 15.04 E
Vira 58 46.08 N 8.51 E
Virac 116 13.35 N 124.15 E
Viracopos, Aeroporto de ⊠ 256 23.00 S 47.08 W
Virac Point › 116 13.31 N 124.13 E
Viradouro 255 20.53 S 48.18 W
Virago Sound ⊍ 182 54.00 N 132.36 W
Viramgām 120 23.07 N 72.02 E
Virandozero 24 64.05 N 35.58 E
Viranşehir 130 37.13 N 39.45 E
Vīrarājendrapet 122 12.12 N 75.48 E
Virbalis 76 54.38 N 22.49 E
Virden, Mb., Can. 184 49.51 N 100.55 W
Virden, Il., U.S. 219 39.30 N 89.46 W
Virden, N.M., U.S. 200 32.41 N 109.00 W
Vire 32 48.50 N 0.53 W
Vire ≃ 32 49.20 N 1.07 W
Virelles 50 50.04 N 4.20 E
Virelles, Étang de ⊜ 50 50.04 N 4.21 E
Vireux-Molhain 56 50.05 N 4.43 E
Vîrfurile 38 46.19 N 22.31 E
Virgem da Lapa 255 16.49 S 42.21 W
Virgen 64 47.00 N 12.27 E
Vírgen del San Cristóbal ♁[1] 286e 33.26 S 70.39 W
Vírgenes, Cabo › 254 52.22 S 68.20 W
Vírgenes, Islas → British Virgin Islands □[2] 240m 18.30 N 64.30 W
Vírgenes, Islas → Virgin Islands □[2] 240m 18.20 N 64.50 W
Virgen Tal V 64 47.00 N 12.25 E
Virgil, On., Can. 284a 43.13 N 79.08 W
Virgil, Ks., U.S. 198 37.58 N 96.00 W
Virgil, N.Y., U.S. 210 42.31 N 76.12 W
Virgilina 192 36.33 N 78.52 W
Virgilio 64 45.07 N 10.47 E
Virgin ≃ 200 36.31 N 114.20 W
Virgin, North Fork ≃ 200 37.10 N 113.01 W
Virginal-Samme 50 50.38 N 4.12 E
Virgin Gorda I 240m 18.30 N 64.24 W
Virgin Gorda Peak ∧ 240m 18.30 N 64.24 W
Virginia, Austl. 168b 34.40 S 138.34 E
Virgínia, Bra. 256 22.20 S 45.06 W
Virginia, Ire. 48 53.49 N 7.04 W
Virginia, S. Afr. 158 28.12 S 26.49 E
Virginia, Il., U.S. 219 39.57 N 90.12 W
Virginia, Mn., U.S. 190 47.31 N 92.32 W
Virginia □[3] 178 37.30 N 78.45 W
Virginia Beach 208 36.51 N 75.58 W
Virginia City, Mt., U.S. 202 45.17 N 111.56 W
Virginia City, Nv., U.S. 226 39.18 N 119.38 W
Virginia Creek ≃ 226 38.13 N 119.14 W
Virginia Falls ⌞ 180 61.38 N 125.42 W
Virginia Gardens 220 25.49 N 80.17 W
Virginia Hills 208 38.47 N 77.06 W
Virginia Key I 220 25.44 N 80.09 W
Virginia Peak ∧ 204 39.45 N 119.28 W
Virginia Ranch Reservoir ⊜[1] 226 39.20 N 121.19 W
Virginia Range ⋏ 226 39.18 N 119.30 W
Virginiatown 190 48.08 N 79.35 W
Virginia Water 260 51.24 N 0.34 W
Virginie occidentale → West Virginia □[3] 188 38.45 N 80.30 W
Virgin Islands □[2], N.A. 230 18.20 N 64.50 W
Virgin Islands □[2], N.A. 240m 18.20 N 64.50 W
Virgin Islands II 240m 18.00 N 64.40 W
Virgin Islands National Park ♦ 240m 18.20 N 64.45 W
Virginópolis 255 18.45 S 42.45 W
Virgin Passage ⊂[1] 240m 18.20 N 65.10 W
Virginville 208 40.31 N 75.52 W
Virgolândia 255 18.27 S 42.18 W
Virieu 62 45.29 N 5.28 E
Virieu-le-Grand 62 45.51 N 5.39 E
Virihaure ⊜ 24 67.20 N 16.35 E
Virje 36 46.04 N 16.59 E
Virkkala 26 60.12 N 24.01 E
Virklund 41 56.07 N 9.34 E
Virneburg 56 50.20 N 7.04 E
Virôchey 110 13.59 N 106.49 E
Viroflay 50 48.48 N 2.10 E
Viroin ≃ 56 50.05 N 4.43 E
Virojoki 26 60.35 N 27.42 E
Víron 267c 37.57 N 23.45 E
Vironvay 50 49.12 N 1.13 E
Viroqua 190 43.33 N 90.53 W
Virovitica 36 45.50 N 17.23 E
Virpazar 38 42.15 N 19.05 E
Virrat 26 62.14 N 23.47 E
Virsbo 40 59.52 N 16.02 E
Virserum 26 57.19 N 15.35 E
Virtaniemi 24 68.53 N 28.27 E
Virton 56 49.34 N 5.32 E
Vîrtopu 38 44.12 N 23.21 E
Virtsu 76 58.34 N 23.31 E
Virú 248 8.25 S 78.45 W
Virudunagar 122 9.36 N 77.58 E
Viru-Jaagupi 76 59.15 N 26.28 E
Virulento 196 28.52 N 104.21 W
Virunga, Parc National de ♦ 154 1.00 S 29.15 E
Virungu 154 7.04 S 29.46 E
Viru-Nigula 76 59.27 N 26.41 E
Virvyčia ≃ 76 56.13 N 22.34 E
Viry-Châtillon 50 48.40 N 2.23 E
Vis 36 43.03 N 16.12 E
Vis ≃, Fr. 62 43.56 N 3.42 E
Vis (Fish) ≃, Namibia 156 28.07 S 17.45 E
Vis ≃, S. Afr. 158 30.53 S 20.23 E
Vis, Otok I 36 43.02 N 16.11 E
Visale 175e 9.15 S 159.42 E
Visalia 226 36.19 N 119.17 W
Visalia Airport ⊠ 226 36.19 N 119.23 W
Visayan Islands II 12 11.00 N 123.30 E
Visayan Sea ⊤[2] 116 11.35 N 123.51 E
Visbek 52 52.48 N 8.19 E
Visby 26 57.38 N 18.18 E
Viscaya, Bahía de → Biscay, Bay of ⊂ 32 44.00 N 4.00 W
Viscount 184 51.57 N 105.39 W
Viscount Melville Sound ⊍ 176 74.10 N 108.00 W
Visé 56 50.44 N 5.42 E
Višegrad 38 43.47 N 19.17 E
Vis-en-Artois 50 50.15 N 2.56 E
Višera ≃ 76 58.34 N 31.24 E
Viserba 66 44.05 N 12.32 E
Viseu, Bra. 250 1.12 S 46.07 W
Viseu, Port. 34 40.39 N 7.55 W
Vișeu ≃ 38 47.55 N 24.09 E
Vișeu de Sus 38 47.44 N 24.22 E
Vishākhapatnam 122 17.42 N 83.18 E
Vishoek 158 34.08 S 18.26 E
Visim 86 57.39 N 59.30 E
Visingsö I 26 58.03 N 14.20 E
Visitation, Île de la I 275a 45.35 N 73.40 W
Viskafors 26 57.38 N 12.50 E
Viskan ≃ 26 57.14 N 12.12 E
Viškil' 80 58.05 N 48.19 E
Viskinge 41 55.40 N 11.16 E
Visl'ajevo 82 54.25 N 36.43 E
Vislanda 26 56.47 N 14.27 E
Vislinskij zaliv ⊂ 30 54.27 N 19.40 E
Vismen ⊜ 40 59.17 N 14.17 E
Visnagar 120 23.42 N 72.33 E
Višn'aki 265b 55.47 N 37.54 E
Višn'akovo 82 55.45 N 38.10 E
Višnevčik 78 49.02 N 26.28 E
Visnevo 76 54.08 N 26.14 E
Višnevoje, Ross. 80 52.38 N 43.26 E
Višnevoje, Ukr. 78 48.27 N 33.56 E
Višňové 61 48.59 N 16.09 E
Višn'ovec 78 49.54 N 25.45 E
Višn'ovka, Kaz. 86 50.49 N 72.12 E
Višn'ovka, Mol. 78 46.20 N 28.26 E
Viso, Monte ∧ 62 44.40 N 7.07 E
Visoki Dečani, Manastir ♁[1] 38 42.30 N 20.31 E
Visoko 38 43.59 N 18.11 E
Visokoi Island I 18 56.42 S 27.12 W
Visp 58 46.18 N 7.53 E
Vispa ≃ 58 46.18 N 7.52 E
Visrivier 158 31.55 S 25.25 E
Vissefjärda 26 56.32 N 15.35 E
Visselhövede 52 52.59 N 9.35 E
Vissenbjerg 41 55.23 N 10.08 E
Visso 66 42.56 N 13.05 E
Vissoie 58 46.13 N 7.36 E
Vista, Ca., U.S. 228 33.12 N 117.14 W
Vista, N.Y., U.S. 210 41.12 N 73.31 W
Vista Alegre, Arg. 252 38.45 S 68.11 W
Vista Alegre, Bra. 256 21.27 S 42.35 W
Vista Alegre, Chile 286e 33.30 S 70.43 W
Vista Alegre, Perú 286d 12.09 S 77.00 W
Vista Flores 252 33.38 S 69.09 W
Vistahermosa de Negrete 234 20.16 N 102.29 W
Vista La Mesa 228 32.35 N 117.01 W
Vista Park 228 35.21 N 118.55 W
Vistina 76 59.47 N 28.29 E
Vistre ≃ 62 43.40 N 4.15 E
Vistula → Wisła ≃ 30 54.22 N 18.55 E
Visun' ≃ 78 47.07 N 32.53 E
Vit ≃ 38 43.41 N 24.45 E
Vita, Mb., Can. 184 49.08 N 96.34 W
Vita, It. 70 37.52 N 12.49 E
Vita ≃ 246 6.11 N 67.31 W
Vitacura 286e 33.24 S 70.36 W
Vitali 116 7.22 N 122.18 E
Vitanje 36 46.23 N 15.18 E
Vitarte 248 12.02 S 76.56 W
Vit'azevka 78 48.01 N 31.53 E
Vite 122 17.17 N 74.33 E
Vitebsk 76 55.12 N 30.11 E
Vitebsk Station ◆[5] 265a 59.55 N 30.21 E
Vitel, Laguna ⊜ 258 35.32 S 58.07 W
Viterbo 66 42.25 N 12.06 E
Viterbo □[4] 66 42.25 N 12.05 E
Vitiaz Strait ⊍ 164 5.50 S 147.20 E
Vitichi 248 20.13 S 65.29 W
Vitigudino 34 41.01 N 6.26 W
Viti Levu I 175g 18.00 S 178.00 E
Vitim 74 59.28 N 112.34 E
Vitim ≃ 74 59.26 N 112.34 E
Vitimskij 88 58.14 N 113.18 E
Vitimskoje ploskogorje ⋏[1] 88 54.00 N 113.30 E
Vitinia ◆[8] 267a 41.47 N 12.24 E
Vitis 61 48.45 N 15.10 E
Vítkov 30 49.46 N 17.45 E
Vito 175e 6.02 S 155.24 E
Vítor 248 16.26 S 71.49 W
Vitor ≃ 248 16.37 S 72.19 W
Vitória, Bra. 250 2.54 S 52.01 W
Vitória, Bra. 255 20.19 S 40.21 W
Vitoria (Gasteiz), Esp. 34 42.51 N 2.40 W
Vitória, Ilha da I 256 23.45 S 45.01 W
Vitória da Conquista 255 14.51 S 40.51 W
Vitória de Santo Antão 250 8.07 S 35.18 W
Vitória do Mearim 250 3.28 S 44.53 W
Vitorino Freire 250 4.04 S 45.10 W
Vitravo ≃ 68 39.11 N 17.05 E
Vitré 28 48.08 N 1.12 W
Vitrey-sur-Mance 58 47.49 N 5.45 E
Vitry-aux-Loges 50 47.56 N 2.16 E
Vitry-en-Artois 50 50.20 N 2.59 E
Vitry-la-Ville 50 48.50 N 4.28 E
Vitry-le-François 56 48.44 N 4.35 E
Vitry [-sur-Seine] 50 48.48 N 2.24 E
Vitshumbi 154 0.41 S 29.23 E
Vittangi 24 67.41 N 21.36 E
Vitte 54 54.34 N 13.06 E
Vitteaux 58 47.24 N 4.32 E
Vittel 58 48.12 N 5.57 E
Vittinge 40 59.54 N 17.04 E
Vittoria, On., Can. 212 42.46 N 80.19 W
Vittoria, It. 70 36.57 N 14.32 E
Vittorio Veneto 64 45.59 N 12.18 E
Vittsjö 26 56.20 N 13.40 E
Vitulano 68 41.10 N 14.38 E
Vitznau 58 47.01 N 8.29 E
Viù 62 45.14 N 7.22 E
Vivarais □[9] 62 44.40 N 4.30 E
Vivarais, Monts du ⋏ 62 44.55 N 4.15 E
Viver 34 39.55 N 0.36 W
Vivero 34 43.40 N 7.35 W
Viverols 62 45.26 N 3.53 E
Viverone, Lago di ⊜ 62 45.25 N 8.02 E
Vivi ≃ 74 63.52 N 97.50 E
Vivian 194 32.52 N 93.59 W
Viviers 62 44.29 N 4.41 E
Viviers-du-Lac 62 45.39 N 5.54 E
Vivione, Passo del)(64 46.02 N 10.12 E
Vivonne 32 46.26 N 0.16 E
Vivoratá 252 37.40 S 57.39 W
Vivorillo, Cayos II 236 15.50 N 83.18 W
Viwa I 175g 17.08 S 176.54 E
Vizagapatam → Vishākhapatnam 122 17.42 N 83.18 E
Vizcaíno, Desierto de ◆[2] 232 27.40 N 113.40 W
Vizcaíno, Isla I 258 33.47 S 59.15 W
Vize 130 41.34 N 27.45 E
Vize, ostrov I 72 79.30 N 77.00 E
Vizianagaram 122 18.07 N 83.25 E
Vizille 62 45.05 N 5.46 E
Vižinada 36 45.20 N 13.46 E
Vizinga 24 61.05 N 50.04 E
Vižnica 78 48.15 N 25.12 E
Vizzini 70 37.10 N 14.53 E
Vizzola 266b 45.38 N 8.42 E
Vjulka ≃ 82 56.53 N 37.57 E
Vjunka ≃ 265b 55.42 N 38.01 E
Vjuny 86 55.31 N 82.55 E
Vlaanderen → Flanders □[9] 50 51.00 N 3.00 E
Vlaardingen 52 51.54 N 4.21 E
Vlachovo Březí 60 49.05 N 13.57 E
Vladař ∧ 54 50.05 N 13.14 E
Vlădeasa, Vîrful ∧ 38 46.45 N 22.48 E
Vlădeni 38 47.25 N 27.20 E
Vladičin Han 38 42.42 N 22.04 E
Vladikavkaz 84 43.03 N 44.40 E
Vladimir 80 56.10 N 40.25 E
Vladimir □[8] 82 56.15 N 39.00 E
Vladimirec 78 51.25 N 26.08 E
Vladimirovka, Kaz. 80 50.51 N 51.08 E
Vladimirovka, Kaz. 86 53.28 N 64.02 E
Vladimirovka, Ukr. 78 47.32 N 32.55 E
Vladimirovka, Ukr. 83 47.44 N 37.23 E
Vladimirskij Tupik 76 55.42 N 33.18 E
Vladimirskoje 80 56.49 N 45.07 E
Vladimir-Volynskij 78 50.51 N 24.20 E
Vladivostok 89 43.10 N 131.56 E
Vladyčnoje 76 58.49 N 39.29 E
Vladykino ◆[8] 265b 55.52 N 37.36 E
Vlasenica 38 44.11 N 18.56 E
Vlašim 30 49.42 N 14.54 E
Vlaskovo 82 56.11 N 36.31 E
Vlasotince 38 42.58 N 22.08 E
Vlasovo, Ross. 74 70.48 N 135.00 E
Vlasovo, Ross. 82 56.38 N 38.14 E
Vlazoviči 76 53.01 N 32.18 E
Vledder 52 52.52 N 6.12 E
Vleesbaai ⊂ 158 34.16 S 21.57 E
Vleikolk 158 29.43 S 20.50 E
Vleuten 52 52.05 N 5.02 E
Vlieland I 52 53.15 N 5.00 E
Vlijmen 52 51.42 N 5.15 E
Vlissingen (Flushing) 52 51.26 N 3.35 E
Vlodrop 52 51.08 N 6.05 E
Vloesberg → Flobecq 50 50.44 N 3.44 E
Vlonë → Vlorë 38 40.27 N 19.30 E
Vlorë 38 40.27 N 19.30 E
Vlorës, Gji i ⊂ 38 40.25 N 19.25 E
Vlotho 52 52.10 N 8.51 E
Vltava ≃ 30 50.21 N 14.30 E
Vluyn 52 51.26 N 6.32 E
Vnukovo 82 55.38 N 37.16 E
Vnukovo Airport ⊠ 265b 55.37 N 37.17 E
Voca 196 31.01 N 99.11 W
Vochrinka 82 55.24 N 38.18 E
Vochtoga 76 58.47 N 41.07 E
Vočin 36 45.37 N 17.32 E
Vöckla ≃ 64 48.00 N 13.36 E
Vöcklabruck 60 48.01 N 13.39 E
Vöcklamarkt 60 48.00 N 13.29 E
Vodla ≃ 24 61.49 N 36.00 E
Vodlozero, ozero ⊜ 24 62.20 N 36.55 E
Vodňany 30 49.09 N 14.11 E
Vodnjan 64 44.57 N 13.51 E
Vodnyj 24 63.32 N 53.18 E
Vodo 64 46.25 N 12.14 E
Vodosalma 24 64.29 N 30.44 E
Vodovatovo 80 55.24 N 43.34 E
Vodzimonje 80 56.49 N 51.38 E
Voël ≃ 158 33.07 S 25.07 E
Voerde, Dtsch. 52 51.35 N 6.41 E
Voerde, Dtsch. 263 51.18 N 7.24 E
Voesch 263 51.24 N 6.26 E
Vogelenzang 52 52.19 N 4.35 E
Vogelheim ◆[8] 263 51.29 N 6.59 E
Vogelkop → Doberai, Jazirah ›[1] 164 1.30 S 132.30 E
Vogel Peak → Dimlang ∧ 146 8.24 N 11.47 E
Vogelsang, Dtsch. 54 53.43 N 14.09 E
Vogelsang, Dtsch. 56 50.35 N 6.27 E
Vogelsberg ⋏ 56 50.30 N 9.15 E
Vogesen → Vosges ⋏ 58 48.30 N 7.10 E
Voghera 62 44.59 N 9.01 E
Vognema 76 59.59 N 38.10 E
Vogogna 58 46.01 N 8.17 E
Vogtland ◆[1] 54 50.30 N 12.05 E
Voh 175f 20.58 S 164.42 E
Vohburg an der Donau 60 48.46 N 11.37 E
Vohenstrauss 60 49.37 N 12.21 E
Vohibinany 157b 18.49 S 49.04 E
Vohilava 157b 21.04 S 48.00 E
Vohimarina 157b 13.21 S 50.02 E
Vohipeno 157b 22.22 S 47.51 E
Vohitsora 157b 23.54 S 44.17 E
Võhma 76 58.38 N 25.33 E
Vöhringen, Dtsch. 58 48.02 N 8.18 E
Vöhringen, Dtsch. 58 48.16 N 10.04 E
Vöhringen, Dtsch. 58 48.20 N 8.40 E
Vöhrum 52 52.20 N 10.10 E
Vohwinkel ◆[8] 263 51.14 N 7.09 E
Voi 154 3.23 S 38.34 E
Void 58 48.41 N 5.37 E
Voight Creek ≃ 224 47.06 N 122.10 W
Voikkaa 26 60.56 N 26.37 E
Voinești 38 47.05 N 27.26 E
Voinjama 150 8.25 N 9.45 W
Voinka 78 45.52 N 33.59 E
Voire ≃ 58 48.27 N 4.25 E
Voiron 62 45.22 N 5.35 E
Voise 50 48.24 N 1.43 E
Voise ≃ 50 48.35 N 1.35 E
Voisenon 261 48.34 N 2.40 E
Voisins-le-Bretonneux 50 48.45 N 2.03 E
Voiteur 58 46.45 N 5.37 E
Voitsberg 61 47.03 N 15.10 E
Voja ≃ 80 57.23 N 49.55 E
Vojens 41 55.15 N 9.19 E
Vojevodskoje 86 52.47 N 85.35 E
Vojkovice 54 50.15 N 13.02 E
Vojkovo, Ukr. 78 45.31 N 33.52 E
Vojkovo, Ukr. 83 48.00 N 38.02 E
Vojkovskij 83 47.46 N 38.20 E
Vojmsjön ⊜ 26 64.55 N 16.40 E
Vojnić 36 45.19 N 15.42 E
Vojnica 24 65.12 N 30.15 E
Vojnilov 78 49.08 N 24.30 E
Vojtanov 54 50.06 N 12.19 E
Vojvodina □[4] 38 45.00 N 20.00 E
Voj-Vož, Ross. 24 64.20 N 55.03 E
Voj-Vož, Ross. 24 62.56 N 54.56 E
Vokeo Island I 164 3.10 S 144.05 E
Volano 66 45.55 N 11.03 E
Volant 214 41.07 N 80.16 W
Volary 60 48.55 N 13.54 E
Volcán, Arg. 252 23.54 S 65.27 W
Volcán, Pan. 236 8.46 N 82.38 W
Volcán Isluga, Parque Nacional ♦ 248 19.30 S 68.30 W
Volčanka 80 52.33 N 49.59 E
Volcano, Ca., U.S. 226 38.26 N 120.37 W
Volcano, Hi., U.S. 229d 19.25 N 155.14 W
Volcano Island I 116 14.00 N 121.00 E
Volcano Islands → Kazan-rettō II 14 25.00 N 141.00 E
Volcán Poás, Parque Nacional ♦ 236 10.10 N 84.15 W
Volčansk, Ross. 86 59.56 N 60.04 E
Volčansk, Ukr. 78 50.18 N 36.57 E
Volčejarovka 83 48.50 N 38.22 E
Volčenskij 83 48.14 N 40.07 E
Volchonka-Zil ◆[8] 265b 55.40 N 37.37 E
Volchov 76 59.55 N 32.20 E
Volchov ≃ 76 60.08 N 32.20 E
Volčicha 86 52.02 N 80.23 E
Volčij Nos, mys › 76 60.31 N 32.35 E
Volčja ≃ 78 48.00 N 36.08 E
Volčje 78 49.14 N 22.53 E
Volčki 80 52.29 N 40.42 E
Volda 26 62.09 N 6.06 E
Volders 64 47.17 N 11.34 E
Volendam 52 52.30 N 5.04 E
Volga, Ross. 76 57.57 N 38.24 E
Volga, Ia., U.S. 190 42.48 N 91.32 W
Volga, S.D., U.S. 198 44.19 N 96.55 W
Volga ≃, Ross. 72 45.55 N 47.52 E
Volga ≃, Ia., U.S. 190 42.45 N 91.17 W
Volga-Baltic Canal → Volgo-Baltijskij kanal ≍ 24 59.00 N 38.00 E
Volgino 76 58.27 N 33.52 E
Volgo, ozero ⊜ 76 56.55 N 33.10 E
Volgo-Baltijskij kanal ≍ 24 59.00 N 38.00 E
Volgodonsk 80 47.33 N 42.08 E
Volgo-Donskoj sudochodnyj kanal imeni V.I. Lenina ≍ 80 48.40 N 43.37 E
Volgograd (Stalingrad) 80 48.44 N 44.25 E
Volgogradskoje vodochranilišče ⊜[1] 80 49.20 N 45.00 E
Volgorečensk 76 57.30 N 41.02 E
Volissós 38 38.29 N 25.58 E
Vol'ka 76 52.47 N 25.39 E
Volkach 56 49.52 N 10.13 E
Volkel 52 51.38 N 5.40 E

ENGLISH Name · Page · Lat.°′ · Long.°′

Völkermarkt 61 46.39 N 14.38 E
Völkermarkter Stausee ⊜[1] 61 46.39 N 14.38 E
Völkerschlacht-Denkmal ⊥ 54 51.18 N 12.24 E
Völklingen 56 49.15 N 6.50 E
Volkmarsen 56 51.24 N 9.07 E
Volkovincy 78 49.13 N 27.39 E
Volkovo, Ross. 76 59.15 N 41.27 E
Volkovo, Ross. 82 55.46 N 36.15 E
Volkovo Cemetery ◆ 265a 59.54 N 30.22 E
Volkovskoje 82 54.49 N 37.13 E
Volkovysk 76 53.10 N 24.28 E
Volksdorf ◆[8] 52 53.39 N 10.10 E
Völksen 52 52.13 N 9.37 E
Volksrust 158 27.24 S 29.53 E
Vollenhove 52 52.41 N 5.58 E
Vollersode 52 53.18 N 8.56 E
Vollme 263 51.10 N 7.36 E
Vollore-Montagne 62 45.47 N 3.41 E
Vollore-Ville 62 45.47 N 3.36 E
Vollsjö 41 55.42 N 13.46 E
Volma ≃ 76 53.35 N 28.19 E
Volmarstein 56 51.22 N 7.23 E
Volme ≃ 263 51.24 N 7.27 E
Volmerange-les-Mines 56 49.27 N 6.05 E
Volmerswerth ◆[8] 263 51.11 N 6.46 E
Volmunster 56 49.07 N 7.21 E
Vol'naja Gorka 76 58.43 N 30.51 E
Volnay 58 47.00 N 4.47 E
Vol'nogorsk 78 48.29 N 34.01 E
Vol'noje, Ross. 80 47.09 N 47.38 E
Vol'noje, Ross. 86 54.17 N 71.21 E
Volnovacha 83 47.36 N 37.31 E
Vol'nyj 80 45.55 N 45.14 E
Vol'nyj, ostrov I 265a 59.58 N 30.14 E
Voločajevka Vtoraja 89 48.34 N 134.34 E
Voločanka 74 71.00 N 94.28 E
Voločisk 78 49.32 N 26.11 E
Volockaja 76 60.17 N 42.59 E
Volodarka, Ross. 86 52.43 N 83.38 E
Volodarka, Ukr. 78 49.31 N 29.55 E
Volodarsk, Ross. 76 56.13 N 43.10 E
Volodarsk, Ukr. 83 48.06 N 39.35 E
Volodarskij, Ross. 80 46.24 N 48.32 E
Volodarskij, Ross. 82 55.30 N 37.57 E
Volodarskij ◆[8] 265a 59.49 N 30.05 E
Volodarskoje, Kaz. 86 53.18 N 68.08 E
Volodarskoje, Ukr. 83 47.12 N 37.20 E
Volodarsk-Volynskij 78 50.37 N 28.25 E
Volodino 86 57.06 N 83.54 E
Vologda 76 59.12 N 39.55 E
Vologda ≃ 76 59.17 N 40.13 E
Voloje 76 54.09 N 34.35 E
Volokolamsk 82 56.02 N 35.57 E
Volokonovka 78 50.29 N 37.51 E
Volokovaja 24 66.28 N 48.10 E
Volonga 24 67.07 N 47.41 E
Volonne 62 44.07 N 6.01 E
Volontirovka 78 46.26 N 29.37 E
Vólos 38 39.21 N 22.56 E
Vološino, Ross. 83 47.31 N 39.40 E
Vološino, Ross. 83 48.55 N 39.56 E
Vološka 24 61.20 N 40.06 E
Vološn'a ≃ 82 55.51 N 35.54 E
Vološno 76 58.29 N 28.29 E
Volosoviči 76 54.46 N 28.50 E
Volosovo 76 59.26 N 29.29 E
Volosskaja Balaklejka 83 49.37 N 37.20 E
Volot 76 57.56 N 30.42 E
Volovec 78 48.43 N 23.11 E
Volovo, Ross. 76 53.35 N 38.02 E
Volovo, Ross. 78 52.03 N 37.53 E
Voložin 76 54.05 N 26.32 E
Volpago del Montello 64 45.47 N 12.07 E
Volpedo 62 44.53 N 8.59 E
Volpiano 62 45.12 N 7.46 E
Völpke 54 52.08 N 11.09 E
Völs → Fiè 64 46.31 N 11.30 E
Volsini, Monti ⋏ 66 42.40 N 11.55 E
Vol'sk 80 52.02 N 47.23 E
Volstruisleegte 158 33.05 S 23.28 E
Volta □[4] 150 7.00 N 0.30 E
Volta ≃ 150 5.46 N 0.41 E
Volta, Lake ⊜[1] 150 7.30 N 0.15 E
Volta Blanche (White Volta) ≃ 150 9.10 N 1.15 W
Voltaggio 62 44.37 N 8.50 E
Voltago 64 46.16 N 12.00 E
Volta Grande 256 21.46 S 42.32 W
Voltaire, Cape › 164 14.16 S 125.35 E
Volta Mantovana 64 45.19 N 10.39 E
Volta Noire (Black Volta) ≃ 150 8.41 N 1.33 W
Volta Redonda 256 22.32 S 44.07 W
Volta Rouge ≃ 150 10.34 N 0.30 W
Volterra 66 43.24 N 10.51 E
Vol'teva 24 64.30 N 44.12 E
Voltri 62 44.26 N 8.45 E
Volturara Appula 68 41.30 N 15.03 E
Volturara Irpina 68 40.53 N 14.55 E
Volturino 68 41.28 N 15.07 E
Volturino, Monte ∧ 68 40.25 N 15.49 E
Volturno ≃ 68 41.01 N 13.55 E
Volubilis ⊥ 148 34.00 N 5.30 W
Voluntown 207 41.34 N 71.52 W
Volusia □[6] 220 28.51 N 81.05 W
Vólvi, Límni ⊜ 38 40.41 N 23.23 E
Volx 62 43.53 N 5.51 E
Volyncy, Bela. 76 55.42 N 28.11 E
Volyncy, Ross. 80 57.48 N 45.28 E
Volyně 60 49.10 N 13.53 E
Volynka 78 51.37 N 32.26 E
Volyňka ≃ 60 49.16 N 13.54 E
Volynskaja Oblast' □[8] 78 51.00 N 25.00 E
Volynskaja vozvyšennost' ⋏[1] 78 50.30 N 25.30 E
Volzhskiy → Volžskij 80 48.50 N 44.44 E
Volžsk 80 55.53 N 48.21 E
Volžskij, Ross. 80 53.27 N 50.07 E
Volžskij, Ross. 80 48.50 N 44.44 E
Vom 150 9.41 N 8.42 E
Vomano ≃ 66 42.39 N 14.02 E
Vombsjön ⊜ 41 55.41 N 13.36 E
Vomp 64 47.20 N 11.41 E
Vonavona Island I 175e 8.15 S 157.05 E
Vonda 184 52.19 N 106.06 W
Vondanka 24 59.07 N 47.49 E
Vondrozo 157b 22.49 S 47.20 E
Von Frank Mountain ∧ 180 63.33 N 154.20 W
Võnnu 76 58.17 N 27.05 E
Vonozero 76 60.22 N 34.26 E
Vonsild 41 55.27 N 9.29 E
Von Treuer Tableland ⋏[1] 162 26.38 S 122.53 E
Voorburg 52 52.05 N 4.23 E
Voordeelspan 158 29.05 S 21.32 E
Voorheesville 210 42.39 N 73.56 W
Voorne I 52 51.55 N 4.00 E
Voorschoten 52 52.07 N 4.27 E
Voorst 52 52.10 N 6.09 E
Voorthuizen 52 52.12 N 5.35 E
Vop' ≃ 76 54.56 N 32.44 E
Vopnafjörður 24a 65.47 N 14.44 W
Vopnafjörður ⊂ 24a 65.52 N 14.40 W
Vörå (Vöyri) 26 63.09 N 22.15 E
Vor'a ≃, Ross. 76 54.54 N 35.01 E
Vor'a ≃, Ross. 82 55.52 N 38.13 E
Vorarlberg □[3] 64 47.15 N 9.55 E
Vorau 61 47.25 N 15.54 E
Vorbach 60 49.49 N 11.45 E
Vorbasse 41 55.38 N 9.05 E
Vorbjovo 88 57.23 N 102.18 E
Vorchdorf 60 48.00 N 13.55 E
Vörden, Dtsch. 52 52.28 N 8.05 E
Vorden, Ned. 52 52.07 N 6.18 E
Vorder-Grauspitz ∧ 58 47.03 N 9.36 E

DEUTSCH Name · Seite · Breite°′ · Länge°′ E = Ost

Vorderkrimmi 64 47.14 N 12.12 E
Vordernberg 61 47.28 N 15.00 E
Vorderrhein ≃ 58 46.49 N 9.25 E
Vorderriss 64 47.33 N 11.26 E
Vordingborg 41 55.01 N 11.55 E
Voreifel ⋏ 56 50.15 N 7.10 E
Voreppe 62 45.18 N 5.38 E
Vorey 62 45.11 N 3.54 E
Vorga 76 53.45 N 32.45 E
Vorhalle ◆[8] 263 51.23 N 7.28 E
Vorhelm 52 51.48 N 7.56 E
Voríai Sporádhes II 38 39.17 N 23.23 E
Vøringsfossen ⌞ 26 60.26 N 7.15 E
Vórios Evvoïkós Kólpos ⊂ 38 38.40 N 23.15 E
Vorkuta 24 67.27 N 63.58 E
Vorlich, Ben ∧ 46 56.20 N 4.14 W
Vorma ≃ 26 60.09 N 11.27 E
Vormholz 263 51.24 N 7.18 E
Vormsi I 76 59.00 N 23.20 E
Vorn'any 76 54.44 N 26.01 E
Vorobjevo, Ross. 82 56.11 N 35.45 E
Vorobjevo, Ross. 86 56.08 N 76.32 E
Vorobji 82 55.09 N 36.48 E
Vorobjovka 80 50.38 N 40.56 E
Vorob'jovo, Ross. 76 59.38 N 40.55 E
Vorob'jovo, Ukr. 78 45.20 N 33.15 E
Vorochta 78 48.18 N 24.36 E
Voron' 76 55.00 N 28.39 E
Voron, porog ⌞ 88 57.05 N 98.40 E
Vorona ≃ 80 51.22 N 42.03 E
Voroncovka, Kaz. 86 48.49 N 81.32 E
Voroncovka, Ross. 78 50.37 N 40.21 E
Voroncovka, Ross. 86 59.39 N 60.14 E
Voroncovka, Ross. 88 58.51 N 112.56 E
Voroncovka, Ukr. 78 45.51 N 33.47 E
Voroncovo, Ross. 76 57.18 N 28.42 E
Voroncovo, Ross. 80 55.16 N 40.27 E
Voronej → Voronež 78 51.40 N 39.10 E
Voronež, Ross. 78 51.40 N 39.10 E
Voronež, Ukr. 78 51.46 N 33.28 E
Voronež □[8], Ross. 76 51.55 N 40.00 E
Voronež □[8], Ross. 83 49.40 N 40.00 E
Voronež ≃ 76 51.56 N 39.25 E
Voronezh → Voronež 78 51.40 N 39.10 E
Voronežskij Zapovednik ◆[4] 76 51.56 N 39.37 E
Voronino 82 56.24 N 36.52 E
Voronja ≃ 24 69.10 N 35.50 E
Voronjo, Ross. 24 68.27 N 35.21 E
Voronjo, Ross. 80 58.00 N 42.01 E
Voronki, Ross. 82 55.48 N 37.16 E
Voron'ki, Ukr. 78 50.14 N 33.02 E
Voronkovo 78 47.43 N 29.08 E
Voronok 76 52.23 N 32.40 E
Voronov, mys › 76 60.15 N 32.05 E
Voronovica 78 49.06 N 28.41 E
Voronovkova Niva 76 57.04 N 29.16 E
Voronovo, Bela. 76 54.09 N 25.19 E
Voronovo, Ross. 82 55.19 N 37.10 E
Voronovo, Ross. 86 56.01 N 83.52 E
Voropajevo 76 55.09 N 27.13 E
Voroshilovsk → Kommunarsk 83 48.30 N 38.47 E
Voroshilovsk → Stavropol' 72 45.02 N 41.59 E
Voroshilov → Ussurijsk 89 43.48 N 131.59 E
Vorošilovgrad → Lugansk 83 48.34 N 39.20 E
Vorotajevka 80 51.56 N 47.16 E
Vorotynec 80 56.04 N 45.52 E
Vorotynsk 82 54.25 N 36.05 E
Vorovskolesskaja 84 44.23 N 42.25 E
Vorožba 78 51.12 N 34.14 E
Vorožejka 86 58.12 N 90.02 E
Vorpommern □[9] 54 53.40 N 13.45 E
Vorra 60 49.33 N 11.30 E
Vorsfelde 54 52.26 N 10.49 E
Vorskla ≃ 78 48.53 N 34.06 E
Vorsma 80 55.59 N 43.16 E
Vorst, Bel. 56 51.04 N 5.01 E
Vorst, Dtsch. 56 51.18 N 6.25 E
Vørterkaka Nunatak ∧ 9 72.20 S 27.29 E
Võrtsjärv ⊜ 76 58.16 N 26.03 E
Võru 76 57.50 N 27.01 E
Voruch 85 39.52 N 70.35 E
Vorzel' 78 50.33 N 30.09 E
Vosburg 158 30.33 S 22.52 E
Voschod 80 47.24 N 41.50 E
Vösendorf 61 48.07 N 16.20 E
Vosges □[5] 58 48.10 N 6.20 E
Vosges ⋏ 58 48.30 N 7.10 E
Vosja 76 59.01 N 41.11 E
Voskresenka, Ross. 80 51.01 N 46.28 E
Voskresenka, Ross. 88 53.15 N 119.31 E
Voskresenki 82 54.57 N 38.04 E
Voskresenovskoje 265a 59.43 N 30.47 E
Voskresensk 82 55.19 N 38.42 E
Voskresenskoje, Ross. 76 53.12 N 38.43 E
Voskresenskoje, Ross. 76 58.54 N 38.36 E
Voskresenskoje, Ross. 76 59.26 N 37.56 E
Voskresenskoje, Ross. 76 57.49 N 37.40 E
Voskresenskoje, Ross. 80 56.51 N 45.26 E
Voskresenskoje, Ross. 80 51.51 N 46.56 E
Voskresenskoje, Ross. 82 54.07 N 37.07 E
Voskresenskoje, Ross. 82 56.20 N 38.29 E
Voskresenskoje, Ross. 86 53.08 N 56.10 E
Voskresenskoje, Ukr. 78 47.02 N 32.09 E
Voslapp 52 53.36 N 8.05 E
Voss 26 60.39 N 6.26 E
Vosselaar 56 51.19 N 4.53 E
Vossijatskoje 78 47.41 N 32.07 E
Vossman's Beacon 158 26.11 S 30.40 E
Vostočnaja Kambal'nica 24 68.18 N 46.00 E
Vostočno-Kazachstanskaja Oblast' □[8] 86 49.00 N 84.00 E
Vostočno-Kounradskij 86 47.02 N 75.07 E
Vostočno-Sibirskoje more (East Siberian Sea) ⊤[2] 12 74.00 N 166.00 E
Vostočnyj, Ross. 82 55.47 N 37.52 E
Vostočnyj, Ross. 86 58.48 N 61.52 E
Vostočnyj, Ross. 89 53.29 N 143.03 E
Vostočnyj, Ross. 89 48.17 N 142.34 E
Vostočnyj Sajan ⋏ 88 53.00 N 97.00 E
Vostok I 14 10.06 S 152.23 W
Vostok ♁[3] 9 78.30 S 106.50 E
Vostr'akovo 82 55.23 N 37.49 E
Vostrecovo 89 45.53 N 134.58 E
Vostrovo 86 52.09 N 80.38 E
Vosves 261 48.31 N 2.36 E
Votaw 222 30.26 N 94.41 W
Votice 30 49.38 N 14.39 E
Votkinsk 80 57.03 N 53.59 E
Votkinskoje vodochranilišče ⊜[1] 86 57.00 N 54.30 E
Vot'pa 86 60.13 N 62.57 E
Votuporanga 255 20.24 S 49.59 W
Voué 50 48.28 N 4.07 E
Vouga ≃ 34 40.41 N 8.40 W
Vougba 152 5.10 N 23.06 E
Vougeot 58 47.10 N 4.58 E
Vouillé 32 46.39 N 0.10 E
Voujeaucourt 58 47.28 N 6.46 E
Voulangis 261 48.51 N 2.54 E
Voulou 146 8.33 N 22.36 E

Symbols in the index entries represent the broad categories identified in the key at the right. Symbols with superior numbers (⋏[1]) identify subcategories (see complete key on page *I · 1*).

Symbole im Register stellen die rechts im Schlüssel erklärten Kategorien dar. Symbole mit hochgestellten Ziffern (⋏[1]) bezeichnen Unterabteilungen einer Kategorie (vgl. vollständiger Schlüssel auf Seite *I · 1*).

Los símbolos incluídos en el texto del índice representan las grandes categorias identificadas con la clave a la derecha. Los símbolos con numeros en su parte superior (⋏[1]) identifican las subcategorías (véase la clave completa en la página *I · 1*).

Les symboles de l'index représentent les catégories indiquées dans la légende à droite. Les symboles suivis d'un indice (⋏[1]) représentent des sous-catégories (voir légende complète à la page *I · 1*).

Os símbolos incluídos no texto do índice representam as grandes categorias identificadas com a chave à direita. Os símbolos com números em sua parte superior (⋏[1]) identificam as subcategorias (veja-se a chave completa à página *I · 1*).

∧ Mountain	Berg	Montaña	Montagne	Montanha
⋏ Mountains	Gebirge	Montañas	Montagnes	Montanhas
)(Pass	Paß	Paso	Col	Passo
V Valley, Canyon	Tal, Cañon	Valle, Cañón	Vallée, Canyon	Vale, Canhão
≚ Plain	Ebene	Llano	Plaine	Planície
› Cape	Kap	Cabo	Cap	Cabo
I Island	Insel	Isla	Île	Ilha
II Islands	Inseln	Islas	Îles	Ilhas
⊥ Other Topographic Features	Andere Topographische Objekte	Otros Elementos Topográficos	Autres données topographiques	Outros acidentes topográficos

ESPAÑOL

Nombre	Página	Lat.°′	Long.°′ W = Oeste
Voulx	50	48.17 N	2.58 E
Voulzie ≃	50	48.25 N	3.12 E
Voutenay-sur-Cure	50	47.33 N	3.47 E
Vouvray	50	47.25 N	0.48 E
Vouvry	58	46.20 N	6.53 E
Vouziers	56	49.24 N	4.42 E
Voves	50	48.16 N	1.38 E
Vovodo ≃	140	5.40 N	24.21 E
Vowinckel	214	41.25 N	79.14 W
Voxnan ≃	26	61.17 N	16.26 E
Voyageurs National Park ♠	190	48.30 N	93.00 W
Voyeykov Ice Shelf ⊓	9	66.20 S	124.38 E
Vöyri → Vörå	26	63.09 N	22.15 E
Voža ≃	82	54.38 N	39.10 E
Vožajol'	24	62.50 N	51.17 E
Vožd' Proletariata	76	55.26 N	39.19 E
Vozdviženka, Ross.	80	53.10 N	54.14 E
Vozdviženka, Ukr.	78	47.46 N	36.05 E
Vozdviženskoje, Ross.	80	56.58 N	45.37 E
Vozdviženskoje, Ross.	80	45.50 N	43.40 E
Vozdviženskoje, Ross.	82	56.12 N	38.04 E
Vože, ozero ⊜	24	60.30 N	39.00 E
Vožega	76	60.29 N	40.12 E
Vožega ≃	76	60.33 N	39.11 E
Vožgaly	80	58.09 N	50.11 E
Vožgora	24	64.32 N	48.25 E
Voznesenje	24	61.01 N	35.27 E
Voznesenka, Kaz.	86	52.24 N	70.12 E
Voznesenka, Ukr.	78	46.51 N	35.26 E
Voznesenovka	80	46.16 N	44.21 E
Voznesensk	78	47.34 N	31.20 E
Voznesenskoje, Ross.	80	54.54 N	42.46 E
Voznesenskoje, Ross.	80	45.49 N	43.25 E
Vozroždenija, ostrov I	86	45.03 N	59.12 E
Vozroždenije	80	52.42 N	48.12 E
Vozžajevka	89	50.44 N	128.41 E
Vrå	26	57.21 N	9.57 E
Vráble	30	48.15 N	18.19 E
Vraca	38	43.12 N	23.33 E
Vračevo	82	54.53 N	39.10 E
Vrådal	26	59.20 N	8.25 E
Vrancea □[6]	38	45.45 N	27.00 E
Vrancei, Munții ⋏	38	46.00 N	26.30 E
Vrangel'a, mys ›	89	54.17 N	138.39 E
Vrangel'a, ostrov I	74	71.00 N	179.30 W
Vranje	38	42.33 N	21.54 E
Vranov	61	48.54 N	15.49 E
Vranov [nad Topl'ou]	30	48.54 N	21.41 E
Vrbas	38	45.35 N	19.39 E
Vrbas ≃	36	45.06 N	17.31 E
Vrbovec	36	45.53 N	16.25 E
Vrbovsko	36	45.23 N	15.05 E
Vrchlabí	30	50.38 N	15.37 E
Vrede	158	27.30 S	29.06 E
Vredefort	158	27.05 S	27.16 E
Vreden	52	52.02 N	6.52 E
Vredenburg	158	32.54 S	17.59 E
Vredenburgh	194	31.49 N	87.19 W
Vredendal	158	31.41 S	18.35 E
Vreed en Hoop	246	6.48 N	58.11 W
Vreeswijk	52	52.01 N	5.05 E
Vrena	40	58.52 N	16.41 E
Vresse	56	49.52 N	4.56 E
Vreta kloster ʊ[1]	26	58.28 N	15.29 E
Vretstorp	40	59.02 N	14.52 E
Vrginmost	36	45.21 N	15.52 E
Vrhnika	36	45.58 N	14.18 E
Vriddhāchalam	122	11.30 N	79.20 E
Vriendschaps ≃	164	5.28 S	138.53 E
Vries	52	53.04 N	6.35 E
Vriezenveen	52	52.25 N	6.38 E
Vrigne-Meuse	56	49.42 N	4.51 E
Vrigstad	26	57.21 N	14.28 E
Vrilíssia	267c	38.02 N	23.50 E
Vrille ≃	50	47.31 N	2.52 E
Vrin	58	46.39 N	9.06 E
Vrin ≃	50	48.00 N	3.20 E
Vrindāvan	124	27.35 N	77.42 E
Vrlika	36	43.55 N	16.24 E
Vrnograč	36	45.10 N	15.57 E
Vroeggedeel	158	28.02 S	22.32 E
Vron	50	50.19 N	1.45 E
Vrondádhes	38	38.24 N	26.08 E
Vroomshoop	52	52.27 N	6.34 E
Vrouenspan	158	27.50 S	20.24 E
Vroutek	54	50.08 N	13.24 E
Vršac	38	45.07 N	21.18 E
Vrsar	64	45.08 N	13.37 E
Vršič)(	64	46.26 N	13.44 E
Vrubovka	83	48.44 N	38.20 E
Vrubovskij	83	48.26 N	39.07 E
Vrútky	30	49.07 N	18.55 E
Vryburg	158	26.55 S	24.45 E
Vryheid	158	27.46 S	30.48 E
Vschody	76	54.42 N	34.06 E
Vselug, ozero ⊜	76	57.03 N	32.42 E
Všepadly	60	49.28 N	13.06 E
Vsetín	30	49.21 N	17.59 E
Vsevidof, Mount ∧	180	53.07 N	168.43 W
Vsevoložsk	265a	60.01 N	30.40 E
Vtoroje Potapovo	265b	55.56 N	37.58 E
Vtoryje Levyje Lamki	80	53.17 N	41.04 E
Vuadil'	85	40.11 N	71.43 E
Vuanggava Island I	175g	18.52 S	178.54 W
Vučitrn	38	42.49 N	20.58 E
Vudor, gora ∧	85	38.13 N	71.49 E
Vue-des-Alpes)(	58	47.04 N	6.53 E
Vught	52	51.40 N	5.17 E
Vuillafans	58	47.04 N	6.13 E
Vuitebœuf	58	46.37 N	6.34 E
Vukovar	38	45.21 N	19.00 E
Vulcan, Ab., Can.	182	50.24 N	113.15 W
Vulcan, Rom.	38	45.23 N	23.17 E
Vulcan, Mi., U.S.	190	45.46 N	87.51 W
Vulcano, Bocche di Ʉ	70	38.26 N	14.57 E
Vulcano, Isola I, It.	36	38.27 N	14.58 E
Vulcano, Isola I, It.	70	38.24 N	14.58 E
Vulcano, Monte ∧	70a	35.51 N	12.52 E
Vulci ⊥	66	42.25 N	11.35 E
Vulkanešty	78	45.41 N	28.24 E
Vulkaničeskij chrebet ⋏	78	48.30 N	23.00 E
Vulture, Monte ∧	68	40.57 N	15.38 E
Vul'vyvejem ≃	180	66.58 N	179.10 W
Vung Tau	110	10.21 N	107.04 E
Vunindawa	175g	17.49 S	178.19 E
Vunisea Station	175g	19.03 S	178.09 E
Vuoggatjålme	24	66.36 N	16.22 E
Vuohijärvi	26	61.05 N	26.48 E
Vuohijärvi ⊜	26	61.12 N	26.42 E
Vuokatti ∧[2]	26	64.07 N	28.14 E
Vuoksa ≃	26	61.03 N	30.11 E
Vuoksa, ozero ⊜	76	60.40 N	29.50 E
Vuoksenniska	26	61.13 N	28.49 E
Vuotso	24	68.08 N	27.08 E
Vurnary	80	55.29 N	46.58 E
Vuturu, Pizzo ∧	70	37.56 N	14.13 E
Vuya	154	5.21 N	29.40 E
Vuyyūru	122	16.22 N	80.51 E
Vuzenica	61	46.36 N	15.10 E
Vvedenka	86	54.03 N	63.45 E
Vvedenovka	89	51.19 N	128.12 E
Vvedenskoje	82	55.42 N	36.54 E
Vyāra	120	21.07 N	73.24 E
Vyatka → Kirov	80	58.38 N	49.42 E
Vyaz'ma → V'az'ma	76	55.13 N	34.18 E
Vyazniki → V'azniki	80	56.15 N	42.10 E
Vyborg	76	60.42 N	28.45 E
Vyborgskij zaliv c	76	60.35 N	28.24 E
Výčapy	61	49.09 N	15.53 E

FRANÇAIS

Nom	Page	Lat.°′	Long.°′ W = Ouest
Vyčegda ≃	24	61.18 N	46.36 E
Vyčegodskij	24	61.16 N	46.48 E
Vychino ◆[8]	265b	55.43 N	37.48 E
Východočeský Kraj □[4]	30	50.10 N	16.00 E
Východoslovenský Kraj □[4]	30	49.00 N	21.15 E
Vydrino, Ross.	88	51.27 N	104.39 E
Vydrino, Ross.	88	56.50 N	99.02 E
Vygoda	78	48.56 N	23.55 E
Vygoniči	76	53.08 N	34.05 E
Vygoniščі	76	52.37 N	25.55 E
Vygozero, ozero ⊜	24	63.35 N	34.42 E
Vyjezdnoje	80	55.23 N	43.47 E
Vyježžij Log	86	54.58 N	93.57 E
Vyksa	80	55.18 N	42.11 E
Vylkovo	86	53.05 N	81.26 E
Vym' ≃	24	62.13 N	50.25 E
Vyntja	86	60.31 N	67.18 E
Vypolzovo	76	57.53 N	33.42 E
Vyrica	76	59.25 N	30.21 E
Vyrnwy, Lake ⊜	42	52.47 N	3.30 W
Vyša	80	53.52 N	42.24 E
Vyša ≃	80	54.02 N	42.06 E
Vyšehrad ◆[8]	54	50.01 N	14.27 E
Vyšelej	80	53.26 N	45.29 E
Vyselki	78	45.35 N	39.38 E
Vyšestеblijevskaja	78	45.12 N	37.00 E
Vyšgorodok	76	57.02 N	28.01 E
Vyška, Ross.	76	57.31 N	35.57 E
Vyška, Turk.	128	39.20 N	54.08 E
Vyskod'	76	57.46 N	30.04 E
Vyškov, Česko.	30	49.16 N	17.00 E
Vyškov, Ross.	76	52.29 N	31.41 E
Vyškovskij, pereval)(	78	48.42 N	23.38 E
Vyšná Radvaň	30	49.07 N	21.56 E
Vyšneol'šanoje	76	52.08 N	37.39 E
Vyšnevolockoje vodochranilišče ⊜[1]	76	57.35 N	34.28 E
Vyšnij Voločok	76	57.35 N	34.34 E
Vysočany ◆[8]	54	50.05 N	14.31 E
Vysock, Ross.	76	60.36 N	28.34 E
Vysock, Ukr.	78	51.43 N	26.39 E
Vysokaja, gora ∧	89	45.59 N	136.35 E
Vysokaja Gora	80	55.56 N	49.19 E
Vysoké Mýto	30	49.57 N	16.10 E
Vysoké Tatry ⋏	30	49.12 N	20.05 E
Vysokiniči	82	54.54 N	36.55 E
Vysokogornyj	89	50.09 N	139.09 E
Vysokogorsk	89	44.23 N	135.23 E
Vysokoje, Bela.	76	52.22 N	23.22 E
Vysokoje, Kaz.	85	42.30 N	70.32 E
Vysokoje, Ross.	76	56.43 N	34.55 E
Vysokoje, Ross.	76	54.02 N	33.44 E
Vysokoje, Ross.	82	54.30 N	37.03 E
Vysokoje, Ross.	265b	55.59 N	37.09 E
Vysokopolje	78	47.29 N	33.32 E
Vysokovsk	82	56.19 N	36.33 E
Vysoký kámen ∧	61	49.06 N	15.13 E
Vyssšaja Dubečn'a	78	50.44 N	30.40 E
Vyšší Brod	61	48.37 N	14.19 E
Vystupoviči	78	51.34 N	29.04 E
Vytebet' ≃	76	53.53 N	35.38 E
Vytegra	24	61.00 N	36.24 E
Vyževka ≃	78	51.41 N	24.35 E
Vzmorje	89	47.51 N	142.31 E
Vzvad	76	58.10 N	31.29 E

W

Nom	Page	Lat.°′	Long.°′ W = Ouest
W, Parc National du ♠	150	12.50 N	2.30 E
Wa	150	10.04 N	2.29 W
Waabs	41	54.32 N	9.58 E
Waackaack Creek ≃	276	40.27 N	74.08 W
Waadt → Vaud □[3]	58	46.40 N	6.30 E
Waajid	144	3.48 N	43.15 E
Waakirchen	64	47.46 N	11.40 E
Waal	58	48.00 N	10.46 E
Waal ≃	52	51.49 N	4.58 E
Waalre	52	51.24 N	5.26 E
Waalwijk	52	51.42 N	5.04 E
Waao	102	24.20 N	104.40 E
Waar, Meos I	164	2.05 S	134.23 E
Waarschoot	50	51.09 N	3.36 E
Waasmunster	50	51.06 N	4.05 E
Wabag	164	5.30 S	143.40 E
Wabamun	182	53.33 N	114.28 W
Wabamun Indian Reserve ◆[4]	182	53.30 N	114.30 W
Wabamun Lake ⊜	182	53.33 N	114.35 W
Waban	283	42.20 N	71.14 W
Waban, Lake ⊜	283	42.17 N	71.17 W
Wabana	186	47.38 N	52.57 W
Wabasca	182	56.00 N	113.53 W
Wabasca ≃	176	58.22 N	115.20 W
Wabasca Indian Reserve ◆[4]	182	55.53 N	113.32 W
Wabash, In., U.S.	216	40.47 N	85.49 W
Wabash, Oh., U.S.	216	40.33 N	84.45 W
Wabash □[6]	216	40.48 N	85.49 W
Wabash ≃	194	37.46 N	88.02 W
Wabasha	190	44.23 N	92.01 W
Wabasso, Fl., U.S.	220	27.44 N	80.26 W
Wabasso, Mn., U.S.	198	44.24 N	95.15 W
Wabatongushi Lake ⊜	190	48.26 N	84.15 W
Wabe Gestro ≃	144	4.17 N	42.02 E
Wabe Mena ≃	144	5.32 N	41.11 E
Wabeno	190	45.26 N	88.39 W
Wabera	144	6.26 N	40.42 E
Wabern	56	51.06 N	9.20 E
Wabigoon Lake ⊜	184	49.44 N	92.44 W
Wabowden	184	54.55 N	98.38 W
Wabrah ⊤[4]	128	27.26 N	47.22 E
Wąbrzeźno	30	53.17 N	18.57 E
Wabu	100	32.17 N	116.55 E
Wabu Hu ⊜	100	32.23 N	116.54 E
Wabuska	226	39.08 N	119.10 W
W.A.C. Bennett Dam ◆[6]	182	56.01 N	122.10 W
Waccamaw ≃	192	33.21 N	79.16 W
Waccamaw, Lake ⊜	192	34.17 N	78.30 W
Waccasassa Bay c	192	29.06 N	82.52 W
Wachapreague	208	37.36 N	75.41 W
Wachapreague Inlet c	208	37.35 N	75.36 W
Wachau ◆[1]	61	48.18 N	15.24 E
Wachenheim	56	49.26 N	8.10 E
Wachi	96	35.15 N	135.24 E
Wąchock, Klasztory ʊ[1]	30	51.05 N	21.01 E
Wachtberg	56	50.37 N	7.11 E
Wachtendonk	56	51.24 N	6.20 E
Wächtersbach	56	50.15 N	9.17 E
Wachusett Mountain ∧	207	42.29 N	71.53 W
Wachusett Reservoir ⊜[1]	207	42.23 N	71.43 W
Wacissa	192	30.21 N	83.59 W
Wackersdorf	60	49.19 N	12.11 E
Waco	222	31.32 N	97.08 W
Waco Lake ⊜[1]	222	31.34 N	97.13 W
Waconda Lake ⊜[1]	198	39.30 N	98.24 W
Waconia	190	44.51 N	93.47 W
Wacouno ≃	186	50.54 N	65.57 W
Wacousta	216	42.49 N	84.42 W
Wad	120	27.21 N	66.22 E
Wada, Nihon	94	35.02 N	140.01 E
Wada, Nihon	94	36.12 N	138.13 E
Wada, Nihon	268	35.12 N	139.38 E
Wada, Nihon	270	34.33 N	135.55 E
Wadagou	104	42.27 N	120.58 E
Wad Al-Ḥaddād	140	13.49 N	33.32 E
Wadamago	144	8.55 N	46.17 E
Wada-misaki ›	96	34.39 N	135.11 E
Wādat Ga	120	26.57 N	97.37 E

PORTUGUÊS

Nome	Página	Lat.°′	Long.°′ W = Oeste
Wadayama	96	35.19 N	134.52 E
Wad Bandah	140	13.06 N	27.57 E
Wad Ban Naqa	140	16.30 N	33.08 E
Wadbilliga National Park ♠	166	36.20 S	149.35 E
Waddān	146	29.10 N	16.08 E
Waddān, Jabal ⋏[2]	146	29.20 N	16.20 E
Waddeneilanden II	52	53.26 N	5.30 E
Waddenzee ⊤[2]	52	53.15 N	5.15 E
Wadderin	162	32.00 S	118.27 E
Waddesdon	42	51.51 N	0.56 W
Waddingham	44	53.27 N	0.31 W
Waddington, Eng., U.K.	44	53.10 N	0.32 W
Waddington, N.Y., U.S.	212	44.51 N	75.12 W
Waddington, Mount ∧	182	51.23 N	125.15 W
Waddinxveen	52	52.03 N	4.40 E
Waddy	218	38.08 N	85.04 W
Wade, Mount ∧	9	84.51 S	174.15 W
Wadebridge	42	50.32 N	4.50 W
Wadena, Sk., Can.	184	51.57 N	103.47 W
Wadena, In., U.S.	216	40.43 N	87.16 W
Wadena, Mn., U.S.	198	46.26 N	95.08 W
Wädenswil	58	47.14 N	8.40 E
Wadern	56	49.32 N	6.53 E
Wadersloh	52	51.44 N	8.15 E
Wadesboro	192	34.58 N	80.04 W
Wadeville	273d	26.16 S	28.11 E
Wadeye	164	14.13 S	129.32 E
Wadgassen	56	49.16 N	6.47 E
Wad Ḥāmid	140	16.30 N	32.48 E
Wadham Islands II	186	49.34 N	53.50 W
Wadhams	182	51.30 N	127.31 W
Wadhurst	42	51.04 N	0.21 E
Wadian	100	32.48 N	112.30 E
Wādī as-Sīr	132	31.57 N	35.49 E
Wādī Ḥalfā'	140	21.56 N	31.20 E
Wādī Jimāl, Jazīrat I	140	24.40 N	35.10 E
Wādī Mūsā	132	30.19 N	35.29 E
Wading ≃, Ma., U.S.	283	41.56 N	71.13 W
Wading ≃, N.J., U.S.	208	39.33 N	74.28 W
Wading, West Branch ≃	208	39.40 N	74.32 W
Wading River	207	40.57 N	72.50 W
Wādī Rashrāsh, Bi'r ⊤[4]	142	29.26 N	31.31 E
Wadley, Al., U.S.	194	33.07 N	85.33 W
Wadley, Ga., U.S.	192	32.52 N	82.24 W
Wad Madanī	140	14.25 N	33.28 E
Wadowice	30	49.53 N	19.30 E
Wadsworth, Il., U.S.	216	42.26 N	87.56 W
Wadsworth, Nv., U.S.	204	39.38 N	119.17 W
Wadsworth, N.Y., U.S.	210	42.49 N	77.54 W
Wadsworth, Oh., U.S.	214	41.01 N	81.43 W
Wadsworth Moor ◆[3]	262	53.48 N	2.02 W
Wadu I	122	5.51 N	72.58 E
Waegwan	98	35.58 N	128.24 E
Waelder	222	29.42 N	97.18 W
Waenhuiskrans	158	34.41 S	20.14 E
Wafang	98	41.44 N	118.54 E
Wafania	152	1.21 S	20.20 E
Wafrah	128	28.33 N	48.02 E
Wagadugu → Ouagadougou	150	12.22 N	1.31 W
Wāgah	123	31.36 N	74.33 E
Wagait Aboriginal Reserve ◆[4]	164	13.00 S	130.20 E
Wagang	102	28.04 N	103.10 E
Wagenborgen	52	53.15 N	6.56 E
Wagenfeld-Hasslingen	52	52.33 N	8.34 E
Wageningen, Ned.	52	51.58 N	5.40 E
Wageningen, Sur.	250	5.46 N	56.41 W
Wager Bay c	176	65.26 N	88.40 W
Wagerup	168a	32.55 S	115.54 E
Waggaman Heights	284c	38.49 N	76.57 W
Wagga Wagga	171b	35.07 S	147.22 E
Waggoner	219	39.23 N	89.39 W
Waghäusel	56	49.14 N	8.31 E
Wagin	162	33.18 S	117.21 E
Waging am See	64	47.56 N	12.43 E
Waginger See ⊜	64	47.56 N	12.47 E
Wägitaler See ⊜	58	47.06 N	8.55 E
Waglan Island I	271d	22.11 N	114.18 E
Wagna	61	46.46 N	15.34 E
Wagner	198	43.04 N	98.17 W
Wagner College ʊ[2]	276	40.37 N	74.07 W
Wagoner	196	35.57 N	95.22 W
Wagon Mound	196	36.00 N	104.42 W
Wagontire Mountain ∧	202	43.21 N	119.53 W
Wagontown	208	40.01 N	75.51 W
Wagrain	64	47.20 N	13.18 E
Wagram → Deutsch Wagram	61	48.18 N	16.34 E
Wagrien ◆[1]	54	54.15 N	10.45 E
Wągrowiec	30	52.49 N	17.11 E
Waha	146	28.16 N	19.54 E
Wahādurgañj	124	27.32 N	82.50 E
Wahai	164	2.48 S	129.30 E
Waharoa	172	37.46 S	175.46 E
Wāh Cantonment	123	33.48 N	72.42 E
Wahiawa	229c	21.30 N	158.01 W
Wāḥid	142	30.49 N	32.20 E
Wahkiakum □[6]	224	46.16 N	123.28 W
Wahlen	56	49.37 N	8.51 E
Wahlstedt	54	53.57 N	10.12 E
Wahnbachstausee ⊜[1]	56	50.48 N	7.19 E
Wahneta	220	27.57 N	81.44 W
Wahoo	198	41.12 N	96.37 W
Wahpeton	198	46.15 N	96.36 W
Wahran (Oran)	148	35.43 N	0.43 W
Wahran □[5]	148	35.30 N	0.30 E
Wahrenbrück	54	51.33 N	13.22 E
Wahrenholz	54	52.36 N	10.36 E
Währing ◆[8]	264b	48.14 N	16.21 E
Wahroonga	274a	33.43 S	151.07 E
Wahweap Creek ≃	200	37.02 N	111.35 W
Wai, India	122	17.56 N	73.54 E
Wai, Indon.	164	1.42 S	127.59 E
Waialeale ∧	229b	22.04 N	159.30 W
Waialua	229c	21.34 N	158.07 W
Waialua Bay c	229c	21.36 N	158.07 W
Waianae	229c	21.26 N	158.11 W
Waianae Range ⋏	229c	21.30 N	158.10 W
Waianapanapa State Park ♠	229a	20.47 N	156.01 W
Waiapu ≃	172	37.47 S	178.29 E
Waiatoto ≃	172	43.59 S	168.47 E
Waiau	172	42.39 S	173.03 E
Waiau ≃, N.Z.	172	42.47 S	173.22 E
Waiau ≃, N.Z.	172	46.12 S	167.38 E
Waiau ≃, N.Z.	172	38.58 S	177.24 E
Waibakul	115b	9.36 S	119.35 E
Waibeem	164	0.28 S	132.58 E
Waiblingen	56	48.50 N	9.19 E
Waibstadt	56	49.18 N	8.54 E
Waichagoumen	98	40.54 N	125.45 E
Waidbruck → Ponte Gardena	64	46.36 N	11.32 E
Waidhān	124	24.04 N	82.20 E
Waidhofen an der Thaya	61	48.49 N	15.18 E
Waidhofen an der Ybbs	61	47.58 N	14.47 E
Waidmannslust ◆[8]	264a	52.36 N	13.20 E
Waidring	64	47.35 N	12.34 E
Waiehu	229a	20.55 N	156.30 W
Waigang	106	31.22 N	121.11 E
Waigatsch → Vajgač, ostrov I	72	70.00 N	59.30 E
Waigeo, Pulau I	164	0.14 S	130.45 E
Waigoumen	98	41.24 N	116.13 E
Waihao Downs	172	44.48 S	170.55 E
Waihau Bay	172	37.37 S	177.55 E
Waihee	229a	20.56 N	156.30 W
Waihee Point ›	229a	20.57 N	156.31 W
Waiheke Island I	172	36.48 S	175.06 E
Waihi	172	37.24 S	175.51 E
Waihola	172	46.02 S	170.06 E
Waihopai ≃	172	41.31 S	173.44 E
Waihou ≃	172	37.10 S	175.32 E
Waihuantan	106	30.25 N	118.40 E
Waika	154	2.21 S	25.43 E
Waikabubak	115b	9.38 S	119.25 E
Waikaia	172	45.44 S	168.51 E
Waikaia ≃	172	45.53 S	168.48 E
Waikanae	172	40.53 S	175.04 E
Waikane	229c	21.30 N	157.51 W
Waikapu	229a	20.51 N	156.30 W
Waikare, Lake ⊜	172	37.26 S	175.13 E
Waikaremoana, Lake ⊜	172	38.46 S	177.07 E
Waikari	172	42.58 S	172.41 E
Waikato ≃	172	37.23 S	174.43 E
Waikelo	115b	9.24 S	119.14 E
Waikerie	166	34.11 S	139.59 E
Waikiki Beach ♠	229c	21.17 N	157.50 W
Waikino	172	37.25 S	175.46 E
Waikouaiti	172	45.36 S	170.41 E
Waikuatang	106	31.20 N	120.41 E
Wailo	144	9.25 N	48.55 E
Wailua	229b	22.03 N	159.20 W
Wailua River State Park ♠	229b	22.02 N	159.21 W
Wailuku	229a	20.53 N	156.30 W
Waimahaka	172	46.31 S	168.49 E
Waimakariri ≃	172	43.24 S	172.42 E
Waimamaku	172	35.33 S	173.29 E
Waimana	172	38.09 S	177.05 E
Waimana ≃	172	38.04 S	177.00 E
Waimanalo	229c	21.21 N	157.43 W
Waimangaroa	172	41.43 S	171.46 E
Waimangura	115b	9.30 S	119.14 E
Waimarama	172	39.48 S	176.59 E
Waimate	172	44.44 S	171.02 E
Waimea, Hi., U.S.	229c	21.38 N	158.03 W
Waimea, Hi., U.S.	229d	21.57 N	159.40 W
Waimea Canyon V	229b	22.04 N	159.39 W
Waimea Canyon State Park ♠	229b	22.04 N	159.40 W
Waimes	56	50.25 N	6.07 E
Wainfleet All Saints	44	53.07 N	0.14 E
Wainganga ≃	122	18.50 N	79.55 E
Waingapu	115b	9.39 S	120.16 E
Waini ≃	246	8.24 N	59.51 W
Wainscott	260	51.25 N	0.31 E
Wainstalls	262	53.45 N	1.56 W
Wainuiomata	172	41.16 S	174.57 E
Wainunu Bay c	175g	16.55 S	178.53 E
Wainwright, Ab., Can.	182	52.49 N	110.52 W
Wainwright, Ak., U.S.	180	70.38 N	160.01 W
Wainwright, Oh., U.S.	214	40.25 N	81.25 W
Waiohau	172	38.14 S	176.51 E
Waiotira	172	35.56 S	174.12 E
Waiouru	172	39.29 S	175.40 E
Waipa ≃	172	37.41 S	175.09 E
Waipahi	172	46.07 S	169.15 E
Waipahu	229c	21.23 N	158.00 W
Waipaoa	172	38.32 S	177.54 E
Waipara	172	43.04 S	172.45 E
Waipara ≃	172	43.09 S	172.48 E
Waipawa	172	39.56 S	176.36 E
Waipiata	172	45.11 S	170.10 E
Waipio Acres	229c	21.28 N	158.00 W
Waipio Bay c	229a	20.55 N	156.13 W
Waipiro	172	38.01 S	178.20 E
Waipu	172	35.59 S	174.27 E
Waipukurau	172	40.00 S	176.34 E
Wairakei	172	38.38 S	176.06 E
Wairarapa, Lake ⊜	172	41.13 S	175.15 E
Wairau ≃	172	41.30 S	174.04 E
Wairau Valley	172	41.34 S	173.32 E
Wairio	172	46.00 S	168.02 E
Wairoa	172	39.02 S	177.25 E
Wairoa ≃	172	39.04 S	177.26 E
Waisanzao	106	30.57 N	121.52 E
Waischenfeld	60	49.51 N	11.21 E
Waïsisi	175f	19.30 S	169.22 E
Waitahanui	172	38.47 S	176.05 E
Waitahuna	172	45.59 S	169.46 E
Waitakaruru	172	37.15 S	175.23 E
Waitaki ≃	172	44.57 S	171.09 E
Waitara, Austl.	274a	33.43 S	151.07 E
Waitara, N.Z.	172	39.00 S	174.13 E
Waitara ≃	172	38.59 S	174.14 E
Waitarere	172	40.33 S	175.12 E
Waita Reservoir ⊜[1]	229b	21.55 N	159.27 W
Waitati	172	45.45 S	170.34 E
Waita-zan ∧	96	33.08 N	131.10 E
Waite Hill	214	41.37 N	81.22 W
Waitemata	172	36.56 S	174.42 E
Waite Park	190	45.33 N	94.13 W
Waitoa	172	37.37 S	175.38 E
Waitotara	172	39.48 S	174.44 E
Waitotara ≃	172	39.51 S	174.41 E
Waitpinga	168b	35.37 S	138.29 E
Waitsburg	202	46.16 N	118.09 W
Waitzen → Vác	30	47.47 N	19.08 E
Waiuku	172	37.15 S	174.45 E
Waiuta	172	42.18 S	171.49 E
Waiwera South	172	46.13 S	169.30 E
Waiwo	164	0.56 S	131.03 E
Waiya	164	3.13 S	128.55 E
Waizenkirchen	60	48.20 N	13.52 E
Wajiki	96	33.51 N	134.30 E
Wajima	92	37.24 N	136.54 E
Wajir	154	1.45 N	40.04 E
Waka, Ityo.	144	7.07 N	37.26 E
Waka, Tx., U.S.	196	36.17 N	101.03 W
Waka, Zaïre	152	1.01 N	20.13 E
Wakajabi	164	5.38 S	134.24 E
Wakakusa	94	35.36 N	138.29 E
Wakakusa-yama ∧[2]	270	34.42 N	135.52 E
Wakamatsu → Aizu-wakamatsu	92	37.30 N	139.56 E
Wakami ≃	190	47.43 N	82.22 W
Wakami Lake ⊜	190	47.29 N	82.51 W
Wakamiya	96	33.44 N	130.37 E
Wakano-ura ♠	96	34.11 N	135.11 E
Wakarusa	216	41.32 N	86.03 W
Wakarusa ≃	198	38.57 N	95.05 W
Wakasa	96	35.20 N	134.24 E
Wakasa-wan c	92	35.45 N	135.40 E
Wakasa-wan-kokutei-kōen ♠	96	35.35 N	135.30 E
Wakatipu, Lake ⊜	172	45.05 S	168.34 E
Wakatomika Creek ≃	214	40.07 N	82.00 W
Wakato-ōhashi ◆[5]	96	33.54 N	130.49 E
Wakaw	184	52.39 N	105.44 W
Wakaw Lake ⊜	184	52.40 N	105.35 W
Wakayama	96	34.13 N	135.11 E
Wakayama □[5]	96	34.00 N	135.20 E
Wakayanagi	92	38.46 N	141.08 E
Wake, Nihon	96	34.48 N	134.08 E
Wake, Zaïre	152	0.48 S	20.10 E
WaKeeney	198	39.01 N	99.53 W
Wakefield, N.Z.	172	41.24 S	173.03 E
Wakefield, Eng., U.K.	44	53.42 N	1.29 W
Wakefield, Ks., U.S.	198	39.12 N	97.00 W
Wakefield, Ma., U.S.	207	42.30 N	71.04 W
Wakefield, Ne., U.S.	198	42.16 N	96.51 W
Wakefield, Oh., U.S.	218	38.59 N	83.01 W
Wakefield, R.I., U.S.	207	41.26 N	71.30 W
Wakefield, Va., U.S.	192	36.58 N	76.59 W
Wakefield ≃	168b	34.10 S	138.10 E
Wakefield Forest	284c	38.50 N	77.14 W
Wake Forest	192	35.58 N	78.30 W
Wake Island □[2], Oc.	14	19.17 N	166.36 E
Wake Island □[2], Oc.	174a	19.17 N	166.36 E
Wake Island I[1]	174a	19.18 N	166.38 E
Wake Island Air Force Base ■	174a	19.17 N	166.37 E
Wake Lagoon c	174a	19.18 N	166.36 E
Wakema	110	16.36 N	95.11 E
Wakeman	214	41.15 N	82.23 W
Wakeman ≃	182	51.00 N	126.30 W
Wakenda Creek ≃	194	39.19 N	93.16 W
Wake Village	194	33.26 N	94.07 W
Wakhān → Vākhān ◆[1]	120	37.00 N	73.00 E
Waki	96	34.04 N	134.09 E
Wakis	164	6.13 S	150.17 E
Wakita	196	36.53 N	97.55 W
Wakkanai	92a	45.25 N	141.40 E
Wakkerstroom	158	27.24 S	30.10 E
Wakō, Nihon	268	35.47 N	139.37 E
Wako, Pap. N. Gui.	164	6.05 S	149.05 E
Wakomata Lake ⊜	190	46.34 N	83.22 W
Wakonassin ≃	190	46.28 N	81.51 W
Wakonda	198	43.00 N	97.06 W
Wakre	164	0.19 S	131.09 E
Waku Kundo	152	11.25 S	15.07 E
Wakunai	175e	5.52 S	155.13 E
Wakusimi ≃	190	49.08 N	82.17 W
Wala ≃	154	5.46 S	32.04 E
Walamba	154	13.29 S	28.45 E
Walanae ≃	112	4.08 S	119.58 E
Walang	102	28.33 N	100.54 E
Wal Athiang	140	7.42 N	29.40 E
Walawe ≃	122	6.06 N	81.01 E
Walbeck	52	51.30 N	6.15 E
Walberswick	42	52.19 N	1.39 E
Walbran Creek ≃	224	48.34 N	124.40 W
Walbridge	214	41.35 N	83.29 W
Wałbrzych (Waldenburg)	30	50.46 N	16.17 E
Walburg	222	30.44 N	97.35 W
Walbury Hill ∧[2]	42	51.21 N	1.30 W
Walcha	166	30.59 S	151.36 E
Walchensee ⊜	64	47.36 N	11.20 E
Walcheren I	52	51.33 N	3.35 E
Walcheren, Kanaal door ≋	50	51.26 N	3.35 E
Walchsee	64	47.39 N	12.19 E
Walcott, B.C., Can.	182	54.31 N	126.51 W
Walcott, Ia., U.S.	190	41.35 N	90.46 W
Walcott, N.D., U.S.	198	46.32 N	96.56 W
Walcott, Lake ⊜[1]	202	42.40 N	113.23 W
Walcourt	50	50.15 N	4.25 E
Wałcz	30	53.17 N	16.28 E
Wald	58	47.17 N	8.55 E
Wald ◆[8]	263	51.11 N	7.03 E
Waldaist ≃	61	48.19 N	14.34 E
Waldai → Valdajskaja vozvyšennost' ⋏[2]	24	57.00 N	33.30 E
Wald am Schoberpass	61	47.27 N	14.40 E
Waldbauer ◆[8]	263	51.18 N	7.28 E
Waldbillig	56	49.47 N	6.18 E
Waldböckelheim	56	49.49 N	7.43 E
Waldbröl	56	50.53 N	7.37 E
Waldbronn	56	48.56 N	8.29 E
Waldburg	58	47.45 N	9.43 E
Waldeck, Dtsch.	56	51.12 N	9.04 E
Waldeck, Dtsch.	60	49.52 N	11.57 E
Walden, Co., U.S.	200	40.43 N	106.16 W
Walden, N.Y., U.S.	210	41.33 N	74.11 W
Walden, Lake ⊜	281	42.39 N	83.46 W
Waldenbuch	56	48.38 N	9.07 E
Waldenburg, Dtsch.	54	50.52 N	12.36 E
Waldenburg, Dtsch.	56	49.11 N	9.38 E
Waldenburg, Schw.	58	47.23 N	7.45 E
Waldenburg → Wałbrzych	30	50.46 N	16.17 E
Walden Pond ⊜, Ma., U.S.	283	42.26 N	71.20 W
Walden Pond ⊜, Ma., U.S.	283	42.28 N	71.00 W
Walden Ridge ∧	194	35.30 N	85.15 W
Waldershof	60	49.59 N	12.04 E
Walderslade	260	51.21 N	0.32 E
Waldfischbach	56	49.17 N	7.40 E
Waldheim, Sk., Can.	184	52.37 N	106.38 W
Waldheim, Dtsch.	54	51.04 N	13.01 E
Waldighoffen	58	47.33 N	7.19 E
Wald im Pinzgau	64	47.15 N	12.14 E
Waldkappel	56	51.08 N	9.52 E
Waldkirch	58	48.05 N	7.57 E
Waldkirchen	60	48.44 N	13.37 E
Waldkirchen am Wesen	60	48.26 N	13.49 E
Waldkraiburg	60	48.12 N	12.28 E
Waldmohr	56	49.23 N	7.20 E
Waldmünchen	60	49.23 N	12.43 E
Waldnaab ≃	60	49.36 N	12.08 E
Waldo, B.C., Can.	182	49.13 N	115.13 W
Waldo, Ar., U.S.	194	33.21 N	93.17 W
Waldo, Oh., U.S.	214	40.27 N	83.04 W
Waldoboro	188	44.05 N	69.22 W
Waldo Lake ⊜	283	42.07 N	71.03 W
Waldo Lake ⊜[1]	202	43.44 N	122.03 W
Waldon ≃	42	50.51 N	4.15 W
Waldorf	208	38.37 N	76.56 W
Waldport	202	44.25 N	124.04 W
Waldron, Sk., Can.	184	50.51 N	102.30 W
Waldron, Ar., U.S.	194	34.53 N	94.05 W
Waldron, In., U.S.	218	39.27 N	85.40 W
Waldron, Mi., U.S.	216	41.43 N	84.25 W
Waldron Island I	224	48.43 N	123.02 W
Waldsassen	60	50.00 N	12.18 E
Waldshut	58	47.37 N	8.13 E
Waldstatt	58	47.21 N	9.17 E
Waldthurn	60	49.40 N	12.20 E
Waldviertel ◆[1]	61	48.40 N	15.40 E
Waldwick	276	41.00 N	74.07 W
Walea, Selat Ʉ	112	0.40 S	122.00 E
Walembele	150	10.30 N	1.58 W
Walensee ⊜	58	47.07 N	9.12 E
Walenstadt	58	47.07 N	9.19 E
Wales, Ak., U.S.	180	65.36 N	168.05 W
Wales, Ma., U.S.	207	42.04 N	72.13 W
Wales, Wi., U.S.	216	43.00 N	88.23 W
Wales □[8]	28	52.30 N	3.30 W
Wales Center	210	42.46 N	78.32 W
Wales Island I, B.C., Can.	182	54.45 N	130.30 W
Wales Island I, N.T., Can.	176	68.00 N	86.43 W
Walewale	150	10.21 N	0.48 W
Walgett	166	30.01 S	148.07 E
Walgreen Coast ✦[2]	9	75.15 S	105.00 W
Walhachin	182	50.45 N	120.59 W
Walhalla, N.D., U.S.	198	48.55 N	97.55 W
Walhalla, S.C., U.S.	192	34.45 N	83.03 W
Walhalla ⊥	60	49.03 N	12.14 E
Walheim	56	50.42 N	6.10 E
Walhonding	214	40.22 N	82.09 W
Walhonding ≃	214	40.18 N	81.53 W
Wali	105	39.42 N	118.20 E
Walia	164	3.47 S	138.32 E
Walikale	154	1.25 S	28.03 E
Walincourt	50	50.04 N	3.20 E
Walis Island I	164	3.15 S	143.20 E
Walkaway	162	28.57 S	114.48 E
Walkden	44	53.32 N	2.24 W
Walkenried	54	51.35 N	10.37 E
Walker, Ia., U.S.	190	42.17 N	91.46 W
Walker, Mi., U.S.	216	43.00 N	85.46 W
Walker, Mn., U.S.	190	47.06 N	94.35 W
Walker, N.Y., U.S.	210	43.18 N	77.52 W
Walker □[6]	222	30.42 N	95.35 W
Walker ≃	204	38.54 N	118.47 W
Walker, Lac ⊜	186	50.16 N	67.09 W
Walker, Mount ∧[2]	171a	27.48 S	152.34 E
Walker Basin Creek ≃	228	35.20 N	118.47 W
Walker Bay c	158	34.30 S	19.20 E
Walker Creek ≃, Az., U.S.	200	36.58 N	109.42 W
Walker Creek ≃, Ma., U.S.	283	42.38 N	70.44 W
Walker Creek ≃, Wy., U.S.	198	43.09 N	104.52 W
Walker Lake ⊜, Mb., Can.	184	54.42 N	96.57 W
Walker Lake ⊜, Ak., U.S.	180	67.10 N	154.26 W
Walker Lake ⊜, Nv., U.S.	204	38.44 N	118.43 W
Walker Lake ⊜[1]	210	40.48 N	77.11 W
Walker Point ›	158	34.05 S	22.57 E
Walker River Indian Reservation ◆[4]	204	39.00 N	118.40 W
Walkers Mill	279b	40.24 N	80.08 W
Walkersville	208	39.29 N	77.21 W
Walkerton, On., Can.	212	44.07 N	81.09 W
Walkerton, In., U.S.	216	41.28 N	86.28 W
Walkerton, Va., U.S.	208	37.43 N	77.01 W
Walkertown	192	36.10 N	80.09 W
Walker Valley	210	41.38 N	74.23 W
Walkerville	202	46.02 N	112.32 W
Walk Mill	262	53.46 N	2.12 W
Wall, Pa., U.S.	279b	40.24 N	79.47 W
Wall, S.D., U.S.	198	43.59 N	102.14 W
Wallace, Ca., U.S.	226	38.12 N	120.59 W
Wallace, Id., U.S.	202	47.28 N	115.55 W
Wallace, Ne., U.S.	198	40.50 N	101.09 W
Wallace, N.Y., U.S.	210	42.26 N	77.28 W
Wallace, N.C., U.S.	192	34.44 N	77.59 W
Wallaceburg	214	42.36 N	82.23 W
Wallace Lake ⊜	279a	41.22 N	81.52 W
Wallaceton	214	40.57 N	78.17 W
Wallacetown	214	42.38 N	81.28 W
Wallach	263	51.35 N	6.34 E
Wallachia □[9]	38	44.00 N	25.00 E
Wallacia	170	33.52 S	150.39 E
Wallal Downs	162	19.47 S	120.40 E
Wallam Creek ≃	166	28.40 S	147.20 E
Wallan	169	37.25 S	144.59 E
Wallangarra	166	28.56 S	151.56 E
Wallaroo	168b	33.56 S	137.38 E
Wallaroo Mines	168b	33.57 S	137.41 E
Wallasey	44	53.26 N	3.03 W
Wallau	56	50.56 N	8.28 E
Walla Walla	202	46.03 N	118.20 W
Walldorf, Dtsch.	54	50.36 N	10.23 E
Walldorf, Dtsch.	56	49.18 N	8.38 E
Walldürn	56	49.35 N	9.22 E
Walled Lake	216	42.32 N	83.28 W
Walled Lake ⊜	281	42.31 N	83.29 W
Wallen	216	41.09 N	85.09 W
Wallend	260	51.27 N	0.42 E
Wallenfels	54	50.16 N	11.28 E
Wallenhorst	52	52.21 N	8.01 E
Wallenpaupack, Lake ⊜	210	41.25 N	75.12 W
Waller	222	30.04 N	95.56 W
Waller □[6]	222	30.00 N	96.00 W
Wallerawang	170	33.25 S	150.04 E
Wallern im Burgenland	61	47.43 N	16.56 E
Wallers	50	50.22 N	3.24 E
Wallersdorf	60	48.44 N	12.45 E
Wallersee ⊜	64	47.55 N	13.11 E
Wallerstein	56	48.53 N	10.28 E
Wallgau	64	47.31 N	11.16 E
Wallgrove	274a	33.47 S	150.51 E
Wallhead Airport ⊠	279a	41.21 N	82.09 W
Wallingford, Eng., U.K.	42	51.37 N	1.08 W
Wallingford, Ct., U.S.	207	41.27 N	72.49 W
Wallingford, Pa., U.S.	285	39.54 N	75.22 W
Wallingford, Vt., U.S.	188	43.28 N	72.58 W
Wallington	276	40.51 N	74.06 W
Wallington ◆[8]	260	51.21 N	0.09 W
Wallis	222	29.37 N	96.03 W
Wallis, Îles II	14	13.18 S	176.10 W
Wallis and Futuna □[2]	14	14.00 S	177.00 W
Wallisellen	58	47.25 N	8.36 E
Wallis → Valais □[3]	58	46.10 N	7.30 E
Wallisville	222	29.50 N	94.44 W
Wallisville Lake ⊜[1]	222	29.50 N	94.45 W
Wallkill	210	41.36 N	74.11 W
Wallkill ≃, U.S.	210	41.51 N	74.03 W
Wallkill ≃, U.S.	276	41.11 N	74.35 W
Wallkill, Wildcat Branch ≃	276	41.07 N	74.36 W
Wall Lake, Ia., U.S.	198	42.16 N	95.05 W
Wall Lake, Mi., U.S.	216	42.31 N	85.24 W
Wall Lake ⊜	216	42.31 N	85.23 W
Wallmer Bridge	262	53.43 N	2.48 W
Wallmerod	56	50.29 N	7.56 E
Wallops Island I	208	37.52 N	75.27 W
Wallowa	202	45.34 N	117.31 W
Wallowa ≃	202	45.43 N	117.47 W
Wallowa Mountains ⋏	202	45.10 N	117.30 W
Walls, Scot., U.K.	46a	60.14 N	1.35 W
Walls, Ms., U.S.	194	34.57 N	90.09 W
Wallsbüll	41	54.47 N	9.14 E
Wallsend, Austl.	170	32.55 S	151.40 E
Wallsend, Eng., U.K.	44	55.00 N	1.31 W
Wallstawe	54	52.47 N	11.01 E
Wall Town Drainage Ditch ≋	216	40.26 N	88.10 W
Wallula, Lake ⊜[1]	202	46.00 N	119.00 W
Walmer, S. Afr.	158	33.59 S	25.36 E
Walmer, Eng., U.K.	42	51.13 N	1.24 E
Walmersley	262	53.37 N	2.18 W
Walney, Isle of I	44	54.07 N	3.15 W
Walnut, Ca., U.S.	228	34.01 N	117.51 W
Walnut, Il., U.S.	190	41.33 N	89.35 W
Walnut, Ia., U.S.	198	41.28 N	95.13 W
Walnut, Ks., U.S.	198	37.36 N	95.04 W
Walnut, Ms., U.S.	194	34.56 N	88.53 W
Walnut, N.C., U.S.	192	35.50 N	82.44 W
Walnut ≃	198	37.03 N	97.00 W
Walnut Canyon National Monument ♠	200	35.10 N	111.31 W
Walnut Canyon Reservoir ⊜[1]	280	33.50 N	117.45 W
Walnut Cove	192	36.17 N	80.08 W
Walnut Creek, Ca., U.S.	226	37.54 N	122.03 W
Walnut Creek, Oh., U.S.	214	40.33 N	81.43 W
Walnut Creek ≃, Ca., U.S.	280	34.03 N	118.01 W
Walnut Creek ≃, Ca., U.S.	282	37.54 N	122.03 W
Walnut Creek ≃, Ks., U.S.	198	38.21 N	98.41 W
Walnut Creek ≃, Oh., U.S.	188	39.41 N	82.59 W
Walnut Creek ≃, Tx., U.S.	222	32.38 N	97.00 W
Walnut Creek, Middle Fork ≃	198	38.32 N	100.08 W
Walnut Creek, South Fork ≃	198	38.25 N	99.53 W
Walnut Grove, B.C., Can.	224	49.11 N	122.39 W
Walnut Grove, Ca., U.S.	226	38.15 N	121.31 W
Walnut Grove, Mn., U.S.	198	44.13 N	95.28 W
Walnut Grove, Ms., U.S.	194	32.35 N	89.27 W
Walnut Heights	282	37.53 N	122.08 W
Walnut Hill	219	38.29 N	89.03 W
Walnut Lake	281	42.33 N	83.19 W
Walnut Lake ⊜	281	42.33 N	83.20 W
Walnut Park	280	33.58 N	118.13 W
Walnutport	208	40.45 N	75.35 W
Walnut Ridge	194	36.04 N	90.57 W
Walnut Springs	222	32.03 N	97.45 W
Walpert Ridge ∧	282	37.38 N	122.00 W
Walpeup	166	35.08 S	142.02 E

Symbol	English	Deutsch	Español	Français	Português
≃	River	Fluß	Río	Rivière	Rio
≋	Canal	Kanal	Canal	Canal	Canal
ʟ	Waterfall, Rapids	Wasserfall, Stromschnellen	Cascada, Rápidos	Chute d'eau, Rapides	Cascata, Rápidos
Ʉ	Strait	Meeresstraße	Estrecho	Détroit	Estreito
c	Bay, Gulf	Bucht, Golf	Bahía, Golfo	Baie, Golfe	Baía, Golfo
⊜	Lake, Lakes	See, Seen	Lago, Lagos	Lac, Lacs	Lago, Lagos
⩸	Swamp	Sumpf	Pantano	Marais	Pântano
⊓	Ice Features, Glacier	Eis- und Gletscherformen	Accidentes Glaciales	Formes glaciaires	Acidentes glaciares
⊤	Other Hydrographic Features	Andere Hydrographische Objekte	Otros Elementos Hidrográficos	Autres données hydrographiques	Outros acidentes hidrográficos

Symbol	English	Deutsch	Español	Français	Português
✦	Submarine Features	Untermeerische Objekte	Accidentes Submarinos	Formes de relief sous-marin	Acidentes submarinos
□	Political Unit	Politische Einheit	Unidad Politica	Entité politique	Unidade política
ʊ	Cultural Institution	Kulturelle Institution	Institución Cultural	Institution culturelle	Instituição cultural
⊥	Historical Site	Historische Stätte	Sitio Histórico	Site historique	Sitio histórico
♠	Recreational Site	Erholungs- und Ferienort	Sitio de Recreo	Centre de loisirs	Area de Lazer
⊠	Airport	Flughafen	Aeropuerto	Aéroport	Aeroporto
■	Military Installation	Militäranlage	Instalación Militar	Installation militaire	Instalação militar
◆	Miscellaneous	Verschiedenes	Misceláneo	Divers	Diversos

Name	Page	Lat.°′	Long.°′
Walpole, Austl.	162	34.57 S	116.44 E
Walpole, Ma., U.S.	207	42.08 N	71.15 W
Walpole, N.H., U.S.	188	43.04 N	72.25 W
Walpole Island I	214	42.34 N	82.30 W
Walpole Island Indian Reserve ◆[4]	214	42.32 N	82.37 W
Walpole Saint Peter	42	52.42 N	0.15 E
Walsall	42	52.35 N	1.58 W
Walschleben	54	51.04 N	10.56 E
Walsden	262	53.42 N	2.06 W
Walsenburg	200	37.37 N	104.46 W
Walsh, Austl.	164	16.39 S	143.54 E
Walsh, Ab., Can.	184	49.57 N	110.03 W
Walsh, Co., U.S.	198	37.23 N	102.16 W
Walsh, Ky., U.S.	218	38.41 N	82.58 W
Walsh ≃	164	16.31 S	143.42 E
Walshaw Dean Reservoirs ⊜[1]	262	53.48 N	2.03 W
Walshville	219	39.04 N	89.37 W
Walsingham	212	42.41 N	80.32 W
Walsoorden	52	51.23 N	4.02 E
Walsrode	52	52.52 N	9.35 E
Walston	214	40.58 N	79.01 W
Walsum	52	51.32 N	6.41 E
Walt Disney World ♠	220	28.26 N	81.35 W
Waltenhofen	64	47.40 N	10.17 E
Walterboro	192	32.54 N	80.40 W
Walter F. George Lake ⊜[1]	192	31.49 N	85.08 W
Walter Reed Army Medical Center ⛉	284c	38.58 N	77.02 W
Walters	196	34.21 N	98.18 W
Waltersdorf, Dtsch.	54	50.52 N	14.38 E
Waltersdorf, Dtsch.	264a	52.22 N	13.35 E
Waltershausen	54	50.53 N	10.33 E
Waltershofen	58	47.46 N	9.55 E
Waltersville	194	32.22 N	90.52 W
Walthall	194	33.36 N	89.16 W
Waltham, Eng., U.K.	44	53.31 N	0.06 W
Waltham, Ma., U.S.	207	42.22 N	71.14 W
Waltham Abbey	42	51.42 N	0.01 E
Waltham Forest ◆[8]	42	51.35 N	0.01 W
Waltham on the Wolds	42	52.49 N	0.49 W
Walthamstow ◆[8]	260	51.35 N	0.01 W
Walthill	198	42.08 N	96.29 W
Walton, N.S., Can.	186	45.14 N	64.00 W
Walton, Eng., U.K.	42	51.24 N	0.25 W
Walton, Eng., U.K.	42	51.58 N	1.21 E
Walton, Fl., U.S.	220	27.17 N	80.15 W
Walton, In., U.S.	216	40.39 N	86.14 W
Walton, Ky., U.S.	218	38.52 N	84.36 W
Walton, N.Y., U.S.	210	42.10 N	75.07 W
Walton Hills	214	41.22 N	81.32 W
Walton-le-Dale	44	53.45 N	2.39 W
Walton on the Hill	260	51.17 N	0.15 W
Walton-on-the-Naze	42	51.51 N	1.16 E
Walton Run ≃	285	40.05 N	74.59 W
Waltonville	219	38.13 N	89.02 W
Waltrop	52	51.37 N	7.23 E
Walt Whitman Bridge ◆[5]	285	39.54 N	75.08 W
Walt Whitman Homes	285	39.52 N	75.11 W
Walt Whitman House State Historic Site ⊥	276	40.49 N	73.25 W
Walt Whitman Mall ◆[9]	276	40.50 N	73.25 W
Waltz	216	42.06 N	83.23 W
Walupt Lake ⊜	224	46.25 N	121.28 W
Walvisbaai (Walvis Bay)	156	22.59 S	14.31 E
Walvisbaai ᑕ	156	22.57 S	14.30 E
Walvis Bay □[8]	156	22.59 S	14.31 E
Walvis Bay → Walvisbaai	156	22.59 S	14.31 E
Walvis Ridge ✢[3]	10	28.00 S	3.00 E
Walwa	171b	35.58 S	147.45 E
Walwen	262	53.14 N	3.15 W
Walworth, N.Y., U.S.	210	43.08 N	77.17 W
Walworth, Wi., U.S.	216	42.31 N	88.35 W
Walworth □[6]	216	42.41 N	88.32 W
Walyunga National Park ♠	168a	31.44 S	116.04 E
Walyungup, Lake ⊜	168a	32.21 S	115.47 E
Walze	263	51.16 N	7.31 E
Walzin, Château de ⊥	56	50.13 N	4.55 E
Wama	152	12.14 S	15.33 E
Wamac	219	38.31 N	89.08 W
Wamba, Kenya	154	0.59 N	37.19 E
Wamba, Nig.	150	8.58 N	8.36 E
Wamba, Zaïre	154	2.09 N	28.00 E
Wamba (Uamba) ≃	152	3.56 S	17.12 E
Wambel ◆[8]	263	51.32 N	7.32 E
Wamego	198	39.12 N	96.18 W
Wamel	52	51.53 N	5.28 E
Wamesit	283	42.37 N	71.15 W
Wami ≃	154	6.08 S	38.49 E
Wamiao	100	30.49 N	113.02 E
Wamic	224	45.13 N	121.16 W
Wamma ≃	164	3.23 S	135.13 E
Wamme ≃	56	50.10 N	5.16 E
Wamplers Lake ⊜	216	42.05 N	84.09 W
Wampool ≃	44	54.54 N	3.14 W
Wampsville	210	43.04 N	75.42 W
Wampú	236	15.01 N	85.02 W
Wampú ≃	236	14.59 N	85.03 W
Wampum	214	40.53 N	80.20 W
Wampus ≃	276	41.07 N	73.43 W
Wampus Lake Reservoir ⊜[1]	276	41.09 N	73.43 W
Wamsasi	112	3.33 S	126.10 E
Wamsutter	200	41.40 N	107.58 W
Wamuran	171a	27.02 S	152.52 E
Wanaaring	166	29.42 S	144.09 E
Wanaka	172	44.42 S	169.09 E
Wanaka, Lake ⊜	172	44.30 S	169.08 E
Wanakah	210	42.45 N	78.54 W
Wanamassa	208	40.14 N	74.02 W
Wanamie	210	41.10 N	76.02 W
Wanamingo	190	44.18 N	92.47 W
Wan'an, Zhg.	100	26.56 N	117.22 E
Wan'an, Zhg.	100	26.30 N	114.49 E
Wan'an ≃	100	25.20 N	117.21 E
Wan'anchang	107	30.39 N	104.25 E
Wanapiri	164	4.33 S	135.59 E
Wanapitei ≃	190	46.02 N	80.51 W
Wanapitei Lake ⊜	190	46.45 N	80.45 W
Wanapum Lake ⊜[1]	202	47.00 N	120.00 W
Wanaque	210	41.02 N	74.17 W
Wanaque ≃	276	40.58 N	74.17 W
Wanaque Reservoir ⊜[1]	210	41.05 N	74.17 W
Wanatah	216	41.25 N	86.53 W
Wanau	164	1.22 S	132.42 E
Wanbaoshan	89	44.12 N	125.11 E
Wanbi	166	34.46 S	140.19 E
Wanblee	198	43.34 N	101.40 W
Wanborough	42	51.33 N	1.42 W
Wanchangchang	107	29.43 N	104.19 E
Wanchese	192	35.50 N	75.38 W
Wanda	158	29.36 S	24.28 E
Wandai	164	3.41 S	136.41 E
Wandana	162	32.04 S	133.49 E
Wandawega	216	42.45 N	88.40 W
Wande	98	36.21 N	116.56 E
Wanderer	154	19.37 S	29.59 E
Wandering	168a	32.40 S	116.40 E
Wandering ≃	182	55.05 N	112.30 W
Wanderup	41	54.41 N	9.20 E
Wandhofen	263	51.26 N	7.33 E
Wandingzhen	102	24.05 N	98.04 E
Wandlitz	54	52.45 N	13.26 E
Wandlitzer See ⊜	264a	52.46 N	13.27 E
Wando	98	34.18 N	126.47 E
Wan-do I	98	34.21 N	126.42 E
Wandoan	166	26.08 S	149.57 E
Wandsbek ◆[8]	52	53.34 N	10.04 E
Wandsworth ◆[8]	42	51.27 N	0.11 W
Waneta Lake ⊜	210	42.27 N	77.06 W
Wanette	196	34.57 N	97.01 W
Wanfang	104	41.57 N	122.52 E
Wanfoxia	102	40.04 N	95.55 E
Wanfried	56	51.10 N	10.10 E
Wanfu ≃	98	35.10 N	116.35 E
Wang ≃	110	17.08 N	99.02 E
Wanga	154	2.58 N	29.13 E
Wangal	164	6.10 S	134.12 E
Wanganderry, Mount ∧	170	34.20 S	150.15 E
Wanganui	172	39.56 S	175.03 E
Wanganui ≃	172	39.56 S	175.00 E
Wang'anzhen	105	39.19 N	114.54 E
Wangaratta	166	36.22 S	146.20 E
Wangary	166	34.33 S	135.29 E
Wangbaotaicun	104	41.10 N	123.18 E
Wangbenying	105	40.28 N	116.06 E
Wangbintun	104	41.58 N	123.43 E
Wangchang, Zhg.	107	28.52 N	105.55 E
Wangchang, Zhg.	107	29.05 N	104.40 E
Wangchangtuizigou	104	41.14 N	120.32 E
Wangcheng	100	28.23 N	112.48 E
Wang Chin	110	17.53 N	99.37 E
Wangcun	98	36.41 N	117.41 E
Wangcunkou	100	28.22 N	118.59 E
Wangdain	124	29.02 N	89.15 E
Wangdalong	102	29.25 N	99.03 E
Wangdian	106	30.37 N	120.44 E
Wangdu	98	38.43 N	115.09 E
Wangdu Phodrang	124	27.29 N	89.54 E
Wange	154	2.00 S	40.55 E
Wangels	54	54.16 N	10.45 E
Wangen an der Aare	58	47.14 N	7.39 E
Wangenbourg	58	48.37 N	7.19 E
Wangen im Allgäu	58	47.41 N	9.50 E
Wangerooge	52	53.48 N	7.54 E
Wangerooge I	52	53.46 N	7.55 E
Wangersen	52	53.22 N	9.25 E
Wangfu	104	42.05 N	121.29 E
Wanggameti, Gunung ∧	115b	10.07 S	120.14 E
Wanggangpu	104	41.38 N	123.09 E
Wanggao	102	24.38 N	111.30 E
Wanggezhuang	105	40.00 N	117.52 E
Wanggil-li	271b	37.36 N	126.39 E
Wanggoutun	104	41.40 N	121.53 E
Wanghai	98	40.26 N	120.30 E
Wanghai Shan ∧	104	41.37 N	121.41 E
Wanghechenggou	104	41.52 N	121.13 E
Wang Hin, Khlong ≚	269a	13.48 N	100.35 E
Wanghu	98	39.47 N	113.54 E
Wanghuzhuang	105	38.50 N	117.05 E
Wāngi	58	47.30 N	8.57 E
Wangingsha	100	22.44 N	113.33 E
Wangi Wangi	170	33.04 S	151.35 E
Wangiwangi, Pulau I	112	5.20 S	123.35 E
Wangji, Zhg.	100	33.52 N	118.44 E
Wangji, Zhg.	100	34.00 N	117.46 E
Wangjia, Zhg.	106	32.07 N	120.59 E
Wangjia, Zhg.	106	31.59 N	121.13 E
Wangjiadian, Zhg.	100	31.26 N	113.58 E
Wangjiadian, Zhg.	105	40.03 N	117.29 E
Wangjiagou	104	42.33 N	123.16 E
Wangjiajing, Zhg.	98	37.49 N	115.23 E
Wangjiajing, Zhg.	98	39.56 N	122.11 E
Wangjiang	100	30.09 N	116.41 E
Wangjiangjing	106	30.53 N	120.43 E
Wang Jian Mu (Tomb of Wang Jian) ⊥	107	30.38 N	104.04 E
Wangjiaputun	104	40.39 N	122.50 E
Wangjiapuzi, Zhg.	104	40.41 N	122.24 E
Wangjiapuzi, Zhg.	104	41.05 N	123.34 E
Wangjiaqiao	106	30.50 N	119.18 E
Wangjiashan	105	40.19 N	114.45 E
Wangjiashao	102	23.57 N	102.18 E
Wangjiatai	105	39.17 N	117.29 E
Wangjiaying, Zhg.	105	40.36 N	116.34 E
Wangjiaying, Zhg.	105	39.06 N	115.59 E
Wangjiazhai	106	31.21 N	121.37 E
Wangjiazui	106	31.16 N	120.18 E
Wangkantou	100	29.12 N	120.09 E
Wangkou	105	38.56 N	116.44 E
Wangkui	89	46.50 N	126.30 E
Wanglanzhuang	105	39.26 N	118.01 E
Wangling	100	27.13 N	113.26 E
Wangliu	100	32.25 N	115.40 E
Wangmiao	100	26.50 N	112.52 E
Wangmulazi	104	41.42 N	124.02 E
Wang Noi	110	14.13 N	100.44 E
Wangong	89	49.10 N	118.53 E
Wangpan Shan II	106	30.30 N	121.15 E
Wangpan Yang ᑕ	100	30.30 N	121.46 E
Wangpingchang	107	29.17 N	105.45 E
Wangqing	89	43.20 N	129.48 E
Wangqingmen	98	41.42 N	125.23 E
Wangqingtuo	105	39.11 N	116.53 E
Wangqinzhuang	105	39.15 N	117.05 E
Wangqucun	106	31.22 N	120.19 E
Wangs	58	47.02 N	9.26 E
Wang Saphung	110	17.18 N	101.46 E
Wangshanhutun	104	42.03 N	122.37 E
Wangshi	100	33.11 N	116.04 E
Wangsi	98	38.00 N	116.55 E
Wangsim-ni ◆[8]	271b	37.36 N	127.03 E
Wangsiying	107	30.34 N	103.29 E
Wangtai, Zhg.	98	36.05 N	119.59 E
Wangtai, Zhg.	100	26.39 N	117.57 E
Wangtan	100	29.45 N	120.40 E
Wang Thong	110	16.50 N	100.26 E
Wangtian	100	25.59 N	116.04 E
Wangting	106	31.26 N	120.26 E
Wangtongshitai	104	42.05 N	123.11 E
Wangtuan, Zhg.	98	37.32 N	116.08 E
Wangtuan, Zhg.	98	37.17 N	122.04 E
Wangtuanji	100	33.12 N	116.21 E
Wangu	107	30.19 N	106.05 E
Wanguzhen	107	29.41 N	105.57 E
Wangwenzhuang	105	38.53 N	117.15 E
Wangxiangshang	106	31.29 N	120.15 E
Wangxiangtai	105	40.02 N	115.09 E
Wangxiuqiao	106	31.38 N	121.03 E
Wangyangzhen	107	29.44 N	104.14 E
Wangyedian	98	41.36 N	118.17 E
Wangyefu	98	41.50 N	118.23 E
Wangyehmiao → Horqin Youyi Qianqi	89	46.05 N	122.05 E
Wangyiguantun	104	42.36 N	123.19 E
Wangzhai	98	34.09 N	116.47 E
Wangzhimawo	105	39.39 N	117.40 E
Wangzhong	98	35.08 N	116.58 E
Wangzhuang	100	33.07 N	117.29 E
Wangzhuangbu	98	39.27 N	113.56 E
Wangzhuangji	98	34.09 N	118.23 E
Wangzhuangzi	105	39.17 N	118.14 E
Wanham	182	55.44 N	118.24 W
Wanhedian	100	32.16 N	113.16 E
Wanheimerort ◆[8]	263	51.24 N	6.46 E
Wanhsien → Wanxian	102	30.52 N	108.22 E
Wanhuyu	102	38.24 N	110.40 E
Wani	122	20.04 N	78.57 E
Wani, Gunung ∧	112	4.29 S	123.01 E
Wanica □[5]	250	5.50 N	55.10 W
Wanie-Rukula	154	0.15 N	25.32 E
Wanigela	164	9.22 S	149.10 E
Wanipigow ≃	184	51.11 N	96.18 W
Wanjiabu	100	28.51 N	115.39 E
Wanjiaqiao	106	30.25 N	119.07 E
Wanjiatun	98	40.03 N	119.51 E
Wanjindian	100	32.50 N	114.46 E
Wānkāner	120	22.37 N	70.56 E
Wankendorf	54	54.07 N	10.13 E
Wankum	56	51.24 N	6.20 E
Wanle Weyne	144	2.37 N	44.54 E
Wanli, T'aiwan	269d	25.11 N	121.41 E
Wanli, Zhg.	106	31.06 N	120.16 E
Wanna	52	53.44 N	8.46 E
Wanna Lakes ⊜	162	28.30 S	128.27 E
Wān Namton	110	22.03 N	99.33 E
Wanne-Eickel	52	51.32 N	7.09 E
Wanneroo	168a	31.45 S	115.48 E
Wannery Creek ≃	162	22.47 S	115.43 E
Wannian	100	28.42 N	117.03 E
Wanning	110	18.53 N	110.26 E
Wannsee ◆[8]	264a	52.25 N	13.09 E
Wanon Niwat	110	17.38 N	103.46 E
Wanouchi	94	35.17 N	136.38 E
Wānow	120	32.38 N	65.54 E
Wanparti	122	16.22 N	78.04 E
Wanquan	98	40.52 N	114.45 E
Wansdorf	264a	52.38 N	13.05 E
Wan-See → Van Gölü ⊜	128	38.33 N	42.46 E
Wanshan	107	30.23 N	106.06 E
Wanshouchang	107	29.26 N	105.55 E
Wanstead	172	40.08 S	176.32 E
Wanstead ◆[8]	260	51.34 N	0.02 E
Wantage	42	51.36 N	1.25 W
Wantagh	210	40.41 N	73.30 W
Wantan	102	30.03 N	110.18 E
Wantirna	274b	37.51 S	145.14 E
Wantirna South	274b	37.52 S	145.14 E
Wanxian, Zhg.	102	30.52 N	108.22 E
Wanxian, Zhg.	105	38.50 N	115.09 E
Wanyuan	102	32.04 N	108.02 E
Wanzai	100	28.06 N	114.27 E
Wanzarīk	146	27.31 N	13.29 E
Wanzhuang	105	39.34 N	116.36 E
Wanzleben	54	52.03 N	11.26 E
Wapack Range ⩘	207	42.48 N	71.52 W
Wapakoneta	216	40.34 N	84.11 W
Wapanucka	196	34.22 N	96.25 W
Wapato	202	46.26 N	120.25 W
Wapawekka Hills ⩘[2]	184	54.45 N	104.20 W
Wapawekka Lake ⊜	184	54.55 N	104.40 W
Wapella, Sk., Can.	184	50.15 N	102.00 W
Wapella, Il., U.S.	219	40.13 N	88.58 W
Wapello	190	41.10 N	91.11 W
Wapenamanda	164	5.35 S	143.55 E
Wapesi Lake ⊜	184	50.34 N	92.21 W
Wāpi	122	20.22 N	72.54 E
Wapinda	152	3.41 N	22.48 E
Wapinitia Pass)(	224	45.14 N	121.42 W
Wapisu Lake ⊜	184	55.47 N	99.11 W
Wapiti ≃	182	55.08 N	118.18 W
Wapizagonke, Lac ⊜	206	46.43 N	73.02 W
Waples	222	32.29 N	97.43 W
Wapoga ≃	164	2.42 S	136.06 E
Wappapello, Lake ⊜[1]	194	36.58 N	90.20 W
Wapping	207	41.50 N	72.33 W
Wappinger Creek ≃	210	41.35 N	73.57 W
Wappingers Falls	210	41.35 N	73.54 W
Wapsipinicon ≃	190	41.44 N	90.20 W
Waptus Lake ⊜	224	47.30 N	121.10 W
Wapus ≃	190	47.11 N	76.06 W
Wapus Lake ⊜	184	56.27 N	102.12 W
Waqf aṣ-Ṣawwān, Jibāl ⩘	132	30.53 N	36.48 E
Wāqid	142	30.42 N	30.44 E
Waqqāṣ	132	32.33 N	35.36 E
War	192	37.18 N	81.41 W
Wara	94	35.45 N	137.05 E
Warabi	94	35.49 N	139.41 E
Wārāh	120	27.27 N	67.48 E
Warakaraket I	164	2.15 S	130.36 E
Waramaug, Lake ⊜	207	41.42 N	73.22 W
Warangal	122	18.00 N	79.35 E
Wararisbari, Tanjung ›	164	1.05 S	136.23 E
Wārāseoni	120	21.45 N	80.02 E
Waratah, Austl.	166	41.27 S	145.32 E
Waratah, Austl.	170	32.54 S	151.44 E
Waratah Bay ᑕ	166	38.51 S	146.04 E
Warboys	42	52.24 N	0.04 W
Warbreccan	166	24.18 S	142.51 E
Warburg	52	51.29 N	9.08 E
Warburton, Austl.	162	26.07 S	126.35 E
Warburton, Austl.	169	37.46 S	145.41 E
Warburton, Pāk.	123	31.33 N	73.50 E
Warburton, Eng., U.K.	262	53.24 N	2.27 W
Warburton Aboriginal Reserve ◆[4]	162	24.00 S	128.15 E
Warburton Bay ᑕ	176	63.50 N	111.30 W
Warburton Creek ≃	166	27.55 S	137.28 E
Warchha	123	32.25 N	71.59 E
Ward, N.Z.	172	41.50 S	174.08 E
Ward, Pa., U.S.	285	39.53 N	75.31 W
Ward ≃	166	26.32 S	146.06 E
Ward, Mount ∧	172	43.52 S	169.50 E
Warda	222	30.03 N	96.55 W
Wardcliff	216	42.43 N	84.28 W
Ward Cove	182	55.24 N	131.44 W
Warden, S. Afr.	158	27.56 S	29.00 E
Warden, Wa., U.S.	202	46.58 N	119.02 W
Wardenburg	52	53.04 N	8.11 E
Warder	54	53.59 N	10.22 E
Wardersee ⊜	54	53.58 N	10.26 E
Wardha	122	20.45 N	78.37 E
Wardha ≃	122	19.38 N	79.48 E
Ward Hill ∧[2], Scot., U.K.	46	58.54 N	3.20 W
Ward Hill ∧[2], Scot., U.K.	46	58.57 N	3.09 W
Ward Hunt, Cape ›	164	8.05 S	149.55 E
Ward Hunt Strait ⋓	164	9.25 S	149.55 E
Wardle	44	53.39 N	2.08 W
Wardlow	182	50.54 N	111.33 W
Ward Mountain ∧	202	46.10 N	114.17 W
Wardner	182	49.25 N	115.26 W
Wardour, Vale of V	42	51.05 N	2.00 W
Wards Chapel	284b	39.24 N	76.52 W
Wards Island I	276	40.47 N	73.56 W
Ward's Stone ∧	44	54.02 N	2.38 W
Wardsville, On., Can.	214	42.39 N	81.45 W
Wardsville, Mo., U.S.	219	38.29 N	92.10 W
Wardswell Draw V	196	32.39 N	102.35 W
Wardt	52	51.41 N	6.25 E
Ware, Eng., U.K.	42	51.49 N	0.02 W
Ware, Ma., U.S.	207	42.15 N	72.14 W
Ware ≃	207	42.11 N	72.22 W
War Eagle Creek ≃	194	36.14 N	94.00 W
Waregem	50	50.53 N	3.25 E
Wareham, Eng., U.K.	42	50.41 N	2.07 W
Wareham, Ma., U.S.	207	41.45 N	70.43 W
Warehouse Point	207	41.55 N	72.37 W
Waremme	56	50.41 N	5.15 E
Waren, Dtsch.	54	53.31 N	12.40 E
Waren, Indon.	164	2.16 S	136.20 E
Warenai ≃	164	2.52 S	135.55 E
Warenda	166	22.37 S	140.32 E
Warendorf	52	51.57 N	7.59 E
Ware River ᑕ	208	37.23 N	76.27 W
Ware Shoals	192	34.23 N	82.14 W
Waretown	208	39.47 N	74.11 W
Warffum	52	53.23 N	6.34 E
Warfusée-Abancourt	50	49.52 N	2.35 E
Warga	52	53.08 N	5.51 E
Wargalo	144	6.17 N	47.31 E
Wargla	148	31.59 N	5.25 E
Wargla □[5]	148	29.00 N	8.00 E
Warialda	166	29.32 S	150.34 E
Wariap	164	1.34 S	134.11 E
Warilau	164	5.24 S	134.30 E
Warilau, Pulau I	164	5.23 S	134.33 E
Warin	54	53.48 N	11.42 E
Warinanco Park ♠	276	40.39 N	74.14 W
Warin Chamrap	110	15.12 N	104.53 E
Waring Mountains ⩘	180	66.50 N	159.00 W
Wāris Alīganj	124	25.01 N	85.38 E
Warka	30	51.47 N	21.10 E
Warkopi	164	1.08 S	134.07 E
Warks Burn ≃	44	55.03 N	2.08 W
Warkworth, On., Can.	212	44.12 N	77.53 W
Warkworth, N.Z.	172	36.24 S	174.40 E
Warkworth, Eng., U.K.	44	55.21 N	1.36 W
Warland, Eng., U.K.	262	53.41 N	2.05 W
Warland, Mt., U.S.	182	48.30 N	115.17 W
Warland Reservoir ⊜[1]	262	53.41 N	2.04 W
Warley Moor Reservoir ⊜[1]	262	53.47 N	1.57 W
Warley → Smethwick	42	52.30 N	1.58 W
Warlingham	42	51.19 N	0.04 W
Warlington	42	51.39 N	1.01 W
Warman	184	52.20 N	106.34 W
Warmandi	164	0.22 S	132.39 E
Warmbad, Namibia	156	28.29 S	18.41 E
Warmbad, S. Afr.	156	24.55 S	28.15 E
Warm Baths → Warmbad	156	24.55 S	28.15 E
Warm Beach	224	48.10 N	122.21 W
War Memorial Cross ⊥	169	37.20 S	144.36 E
Warmenhuizen	52	52.43 N	4.44 E
Warmensteinach	60	49.59 N	11.47 E
Warmeriville	50	49.21 N	4.13 E
Warmington	42	52.08 N	1.24 W
Warminster, Eng., U.K.	42	51.13 N	2.12 W
Warminster, Pa., U.S.	208	40.12 N	75.06 W
Warminster Naval Air Development Center ■	285	40.12 N	75.09 W
Warm Springs, Ga., U.S.	192	32.53 N	84.40 W
Warm Springs, Mt., U.S.	202	46.11 N	112.48 W
Warm Springs, Or., U.S.	202	44.45 N	121.15 W
Warm Springs, Va., U.S.	192	38.02 N	79.47 W
Warm Springs ≃	202	44.52 N	121.04 W
Warm Springs Indian Reservation ◆[4]	224	45.00 N	121.25 W
Warm Springs Reservoir ⊜[1]	202	43.37 N	118.14 W
Warnbro Sound ⋓	168a	32.20 S	115.40 E
Warnemünde ◆[8]	54	54.10 N	12.04 E
Warner, Ab., Can.	182	49.17 N	112.12 W
Warner, N.H., U.S.	188	43.16 N	71.49 W
Warner, Ok., U.S.	196	35.29 N	95.18 W
Warner Lakes ⊜	202	42.25 N	119.50 W
Warner Mountains ⩘	204	41.40 N	120.20 W
Warner Peak ∧	202	42.27 N	119.44 W
Warner Ranch	228	33.56 N	117.13 W
Warner Robins	192	32.37 N	83.36 W
Warners	210	43.05 N	76.20 W
Warners Pond ⊜	283	42.28 N	71.24 W
Warnerville	210	42.34 N	74.30 W
Warnes, Arg.	252	34.55 S	60.31 W
Warnes, Bol.	248	17.30 S	63.10 W
Warnes Brook ≃	276	40.25 N	74.18 W
Warneton	50	50.45 N	2.57 E
Warngau	64	47.50 N	11.41 E
Warnicken → Primorje	76	54.57 N	20.02 E
Warnkenhagen	54	54.00 N	11.04 E
Warnow ≃	54	54.06 N	12.09 E
Warns	52	52.52 N	5.25 E
Warnsveld	52	52.08 N	6.13 E
Waroona	168a	32.50 S	115.55 E
Warpath ≃	184	52.21 N	98.26 W
Warra	166	26.56 S	150.55 E
Warrabri Aboriginal Reserve ◆[4]	162	21.00 S	134.20 E
Warracknabeal	166	36.15 S	142.24 E
Warr Acres	196	35.31 N	97.37 W
Warragamba Dam ◆[6]	170	33.54 S	150.36 E
Warragul	169	38.10 S	145.56 E
Warrandyte	274b	37.45 S	145.13 E
Warrandyte South	274b	37.46 S	145.14 E
Warrāq al-ʿArab	273c	30.06 N	31.12 E
Warrāq al-Ḥaḍar, Jazīrat I	273c	30.07 N	31.13 E
Warrāq al-Hadar wa Ambūtbah wa Mīt an-Naṣārā	273c	30.06 N	31.13 E
Warrawagine	162	20.51 S	120.42 E
Warrawee	274a	33.44 S	151.07 E
Warrawolong, Mount ∧	170	33.03 S	151.15 E
Warrawong	170	34.29 S	150.53 E
Warrego ≃	166	30.24 S	145.21 E
Warrego Range ⩘	166	25.00 S	146.30 E
Warren, Austl.	166	31.42 S	147.50 E
Warren, Eng., U.K.	262	53.14 N	2.10 W
Warren, Ar., U.S.	194	33.36 N	92.03 W
Warren, Il., U.S.	190	42.29 N	89.59 W
Warren, In., U.S.	216	40.40 N	85.25 W
Warren, Ma., U.S.	207	42.12 N	72.11 W
Warren, Mi., U.S.	216	42.28 N	83.01 W
Warren, Mn., U.S.	198	48.11 N	96.46 W
Warren, Mo., U.S.	219	39.47 N	91.45 W
Warren, N.J., U.S.	276	40.37 N	74.30 W
Warren, Oh., U.S.	214	41.14 N	80.49 W
Warren, Or., U.S.	224	45.49 N	122.50 W
Warren, Pa., U.S.	214	41.50 N	79.08 W
Warren, R.I., U.S.	207	41.43 N	71.16 W
Warren □[6], In., U.S.	216	40.21 N	87.17 W
Warren □[6], Mo., U.S.	219	38.45 N	91.09 W
Warren □[6], N.J., U.S.	210	40.49 N	75.05 W
Warren □[6], N.Y., U.S.	210	43.26 N	73.43 W
Warren □[6], Oh., U.S.	218	39.26 N	84.13 W
Warren □[6], Pa., U.S.	214	41.51 N	79.08 W
Warren ≃	162	34.35 S	115.50 E
Warren City	222	32.33 N	94.54 W
Warrendale	214	40.39 N	80.04 W
Warren Dunes State Park ♠	216	41.56 N	86.36 W
Warren H. Manning State Park ♠	283	42.34 N	71.18 W
Warren Park	218	39.46 N	86.03 W
Warren Peaks ⩘	198	44.29 N	104.28 W
Warrenpoint	48	54.06 N	6.15 W
Warren Point ›	180	69.44 N	132.30 W
Warrens	190	44.07 N	90.29 W
Warrensburg, Il., U.S.	219	39.56 N	89.04 W
Warrensburg, Mo., U.S.	194	38.45 N	93.44 W
Warrensburg, N.Y., U.S.	188	43.29 N	73.46 W
Warrensville	210	41.19 N	76.57 W
Warrensville Heights	214	41.26 N	81.32 W
Warrenton, S. Afr.	158	28.09 S	24.47 E
Warrenton, Ga., U.S.	192	33.24 N	82.39 W
Warrenton, Mo., U.S.	219	38.48 N	91.08 W
Warrenton, N.C., U.S.	192	36.23 N	78.09 W
Warrenton, Or., U.S.	224	46.09 N	123.55 W
Warrenton, Tx., U.S.	222	30.01 N	96.44 W
Warrenton, Va., U.S.	188	38.42 N	77.47 W
Warrenville	216	41.49 N	88.10 W
Warrenzin	54	53.54 N	12.57 E
Warri	150	5.31 N	5.45 E
Warriedar Hill ∧[2]	162	29.06 S	117.06 E
Warriewood	274a	33.42 S	151.18 E
Warrill Creek ≃	171a	27.39 S	152.44 E
Warrington, N.Z.	172	45.43 S	170.35 E
Warrington, Eng., U.K.	44	53.24 N	2.37 W
Warrington, Fl., U.S.	194	30.23 N	87.16 W
Warrington, Pa., U.S.	285	40.15 N	75.08 W
Warrington □[8]	262	53.24 N	2.33 W
Warrington Airport ⊠	285	40.16 N	75.09 W
Warrior	194	33.48 N	86.48 W
Warrior Creek ≃	192	31.15 N	83.34 W
Warrior Reefs ✢[2]	164	9.35 S	143.10 E
Warriors Mark	214	40.42 N	78.08 W
Warrnambool	166	38.23 S	142.29 E
Warroad	198	48.54 N	95.18 W
Warrumbungle National Park ♠	166	31.20 S	149.00 E
Warsak	123	34.10 N	71.25 E
Warsaw, Il., U.S.	190	40.21 N	91.26 W
Warsaw, In., U.S.	216	41.14 N	85.51 W
Warsaw, Ky., U.S.	218	38.47 N	84.54 W
Warsaw, Mo., U.S.	194	38.14 N	93.22 W
Warsaw, N.Y., U.S.	210	42.44 N	78.07 W

ENGLISH

Name	Page	Lat.°′	Long.°′
Warsaw, N.C., U.S.	192	34.59 N	78.05 W
Warsaw, Oh., U.S.	214	40.20 N	82.00 W
Warsaw, Va., U.S.	208	37.57 N	76.45 W
Warsaw Station ◆[5]	265a	59.54 N	30.19 E
Warsaw → Warszawa	30	52.15 N	21.00 E
Warschau → Warszawa	30	52.15 N	21.00 E
Warscheneck ∧	61	47.39 N	14.14 E
Warshiikh	144	2.18 N	45.48 E
Warsop	44	53.13 N	1.09 W
Warspite	182	54.06 N	112.37 W
Warstein	56	51.26 N	8.21 E
Warszawa (Warsaw)	30	52.15 N	21.00 E
Warszawa □[4]	30	52.15 N	21.00 E
Warta	30	51.42 N	18.38 E
Warta ≃	30	52.35 N	14.39 E
Wartburg, S. Afr.	158	29.25 S	30.35 E
Wartburg, Tn., U.S.	192	36.06 N	84.35 W
Wartburg ⊥	54	50.58 N	10.18 E
Wartenberg	60	48.24 N	11.59 E
Wartenberg ◆[8]	264a	52.34 N	13.31 E
Warth	58	47.15 N	10.11 E
Warthan Creek ≃	226	36.08 N	120.20 W
Warthe → Warta ≃	30	52.35 N	14.39 E
Wartin	54	53.15 N	14.09 E
Warton, Eng., U.K.	44	54.09 N	2.47 W
Warton, Eng., U.K.	262	53.45 N	2.54 W
Warton Aerodrome ⊠	262	53.45 N	2.54 W
Wartrace	194	35.31 N	86.20 W
Wartsberg ∧[2]	263	51.25 N	6.29 E
Waru	164	3.24 S	130.40 E
Warud	120	21.28 N	78.16 E
Warunta, Laguna de ⊜	236	15.23 N	84.05 W
Waruta ≃	164	3.18 S	140.08 E
Warwick, Austl.	171a	28.13 S	152.02 E
Warwick, P.Q., Can.	206	45.56 N	71.59 W
Warwick, Eng., U.K.	42	52.17 N	1.34 W
Warwick, Md., U.S.	208	39.25 N	75.46 W
Warwick, N.Y., U.S.	210	41.15 N	74.21 W
Warwick, R.I., U.S.	207	41.41 N	71.22 W
Warwick ≃	208	37.05 N	76.33 W
Warwick Castle ⊥	42	52.17 N	1.34 W
Warwick Channel ⋓	164	13.51 S	136.16 E
Warwick Farm Racecourse and Motor Race Track ♠	274a	33.55 S	150.57 E
Warwickshire □[6]	42	52.13 N	1.37 W
Warza	54	51.00 N	10.41 E
Wasaga Beach	212	44.31 N	80.01 W
Wasagu	150	11.25 N	5.49 E
Wasatch Mountain State Park ♠	200	40.33 N	111.31 W
Wasatch Plateau ⩘[1]	200	39.20 N	111.30 W
Wasatch Range ⩘	200	40.40 N	111.35 W
Wasāwewāla	123	30.28 N	73.40 E
Wasbank	158	28.24 S	30.05 E
Wasbister	46	59.10 N	3.07 W
Wascana Creek ≃	184	50.39 N	104.55 W
Wäschenbeuren	56	48.46 N	9.41 E
Wasco, Ca., U.S.	226	35.35 N	119.20 W
Wasco, Or., U.S.	224	45.35 N	120.41 W
Wasco □[6]	224	45.10 N	121.12 W
Wase	150	9.06 N	9.59 E
Wase ≃	146	8.27 N	10.06 E
Waseca	190	44.04 N	93.30 W
Waseda University ⛉[2]	268	35.42 N	139.43 E
Wasekamio Lake ⊜	184	56.45 N	108.45 W
Wasen	58	47.03 N	7.48 E
Wasgomuwa National Park ♠	122	7.40 N	80.45 E
Washademoak Lake ⊜	186	45.48 N	65.58 W
Washago	212	44.45 N	79.20 W
Washburn, Il., U.S.	190	40.55 N	89.17 W
Washburn, Me., U.S.	186	46.47 N	68.09 W
Washburn, N.D., U.S.	198	47.17 N	101.01 W
Washburn, Wi., U.S.	190	46.40 N	90.53 W
Washburn ≃	44	53.54 N	1.39 W
Washburn, Mount ∧	202	44.48 N	110.25 W
Washburn Lake ⊜	176	70.03 N	106.50 W
Washdyke	172	44.21 S	171.14 E
Washicoutai	186	50.17 N	60.42 W
Washiga-take ∧	94	35.56 N	136.58 E
Wāshīm	122	20.06 N	77.09 E
Washimiya	94	36.06 N	139.40 E
Washington, Eng., U.K.	44	54.55 N	1.30 W
Washington, Ca., U.S.	226	39.22 N	120.48 W
Washington, Ct., U.S.	207	41.37 N	73.18 W
Washington, D.C., U.S.	208	38.53 N	77.02 W
Washington, D.C., U.S.	284c	38.53 N	77.02 W
Washington, Ga., U.S.	192	33.44 N	82.44 W
Washington, Il., U.S.	190	40.42 N	89.24 W
Washington, In., U.S.	194	38.39 N	87.10 W
Washington, Ia., U.S.	190	41.17 N	91.41 W
Washington, Ks., U.S.	198	39.49 N	97.03 W
Washington, Ky., U.S.	218	38.36 N	83.48 W
Washington, La., U.S.	194	30.36 N	92.03 W
Washington, Mi., U.S.	214	42.44 N	83.02 W
Washington, Mo., U.S.	219	38.33 N	91.01 W
Washington, N.J., U.S.	210	40.45 N	74.58 W
Washington, N.C., U.S.	192	35.31 N	77.01 W
Washington, Pa., U.S.	214	40.10 N	80.14 W
Washington, Tx., U.S.	222	30.20 N	96.10 W
Washington, Ut,. U.S.	200	37.07 N	113.30 W
Washington, Va., U.S.	188	38.42 N	78.09 W
Washington □[6], Il., U.S.	219	38.21 N	89.23 W
Washington □[6], In., U.S.	218	38.36 N	86.06 W
Washington □[6], N.Y., U.S.	210	43.15 N	73.27 W
Washington □[6], Or., U.S.	224	45.33 N	123.07 W
Washington □[6], Pa., U.S.	214	40.10 N	80.15 W
Washington □[6], R.I., U.S.	207	41.28 N	71.35 W
Washington □[6], Tx., U.S.	222	30.15 N	96.20 W
Washington □[6], Wi., U.S.	216	43.14 N	88.15 W
Washington □[3], U.S.	178	47.30 N	120.30 W
Washington □[3], U.S.	202	47.30 N	120.30 W
Washington, Lake ⊜, Fl., U.S.	220	28.07 N	80.45 W
Washington, Lake ⊜, Wa., U.S.	224	47.37 N	122.15 W
Washington, Mount ∧	188	44.15 N	71.15 W
Washington Court House	218	39.32 N	83.26 W
Washington Crossing	208	40.17 N	74.52 W
Washington Crossing State Historic Site ⊥	208	40.17 N	74.53 W
Washington Depot	207	41.38 N	73.18 W
Washington Heights ◆[8]	276	40.52 N	73.56 W
Washington Island	190	45.23 N	86.55 W
Washington Island I	190	45.23 N	86.55 W
Washington Memorial Chapel ⛉[1]	285	40.06 N	75.26 W
Washington Mills	210	43.03 N	75.16 W

DEUTSCH

Name	Seite	Breite°′	Länge°′ E = Ost
Washington Monument ♠	284c	38.53 N	77.03 W
Washington Monument State Park ♠	208	39.30 N	77.38 W
Washington National Airport ⊠	208	38.51 N	77.02 W
Washington-on-the-Brazos State Historic Park ♠	222	30.20 N	96.09 W
Washington Park	219	38.38 N	90.05 W
Washington Park ♠, Il., U.S.	278	41.48 N	87.37 W
Washington Park ♠, Oh., U.S.	279a	41.27 N	81.40 W
Washington Pass)(	224	48.32 N	120.39 W
Washington Place	218	39.47 N	86.01 W
Washington Rock State Park ♠	276	40.37 N	74.28 W
Washington's Headquarters ⊥	285	40.06 N	75.28 W
Washington Terrace	200	41.10 N	111.58 W
Washington Township	276	40.54 N	74.00 W
Washington Valley	276	40.48 N	74.32 W
Washington Valley Reservoir ⊜[1]	276	40.36 N	74.34 W
Washingtonville, N.Y., U.S.	210	41.26 N	74.10 W
Washingtonville, Oh., U.S.	214	40.54 N	80.46 W
Washingtonville, Pa., U.S.	210	41.03 N	76.40 W
Washita ≃	196	34.12 N	96.50 W
Washoe □[6]	226	39.22 N	119.43 W
Washoe Lake ⊜	226	39.16 N	119.48 W
Washougal	224	45.34 N	122.21 W
Washougal ≃	224	45.35 N	122.23 W
Washow Bay ᑕ	184	51.22 N	96.47 W
Washtenaw □[6]	216	42.15 N	83.50 W
Washtucna	202	46.45 N	118.18 W
Wāshuk	128	27.44 N	64.48 E
Wasian	164	1.54 S	133.17 E
Wasilków	30	53.12 N	23.12 E
Wasilla	180	61.35 N	149.26 W
Wasior	164	2.43 S	134.30 E
Wasiri	112	7.35 S	126.38 E
Wāsiṭ □[4]	128	32.45 N	45.25 E
Waskada	184	49.06 N	100.46 W
Waskaganish	176	51.30 N	78.45 W
Waskahigan ≃	182	54.45 N	117.12 W
Waskaiowaka Lake ⊜	184	56.30 N	96.20 W
Waskatenau	182	54.07 N	112.47 W
Waskesiu Lake ⊜	184	53.56 N	106.10 W
Waskom	194	32.29 N	94.04 W
Wąsosz	30	51.34 N	16.42 E
Waspam	236	14.44 N	83.58 W
Waspuk ≃	236	14.38 N	84.26 W
Wasquehal	50	50.40 N	3.09 E
Wassaic	210	41.48 N	73.35 W
Wasselonne	58	48.38 N	7.27 E
Wassen	58	46.42 N	8.36 E
Wassenaar	52	52.07 N	4.24 E
Wassenberg	56	51.06 N	6.08 E
Wasseralfingen	56	48.52 N	10.06 E
Wasserbillig	56	49.44 N	6.30 E
Wasserburg am Inn	60	48.04 N	12.13 E
Wasserkuppe ∧	56	50.30 N	9.56 E
Wasserkurl	263	51.33 N	7.38 E
Wasserleben	54	51.55 N	10.44 E
Wassertrüdingen	56	49.02 N	10.35 E
Wassigny	50	50.01 N	3.36 E
Wass Lake ⊜	184	53.40 N	95.25 W
Wassmannsdorf	264a	52.22 N	13.28 E
Wassou	150	10.02 N	13.39 W
Wassy	58	48.30 N	4.57 E
Wast Water ⊜	44	54.26 N	3.18 W
Wasu	164	6.00 S	147.15 E
Wasum	164	6.05 S	149.20 E
Wasungen	54	50.40 N	10.22 E
Watabeag Lake ⊜	190	48.14 N	80.32 W
Watampone (Bone)	112	4.32 S	120.20 E
Watamu Marine National Park ♠	154	3.23 S	40.00 E
Waṭan, Wādī al- V	142	30.26 N	31.49 E
Watansopeng	112	4.21 S	119.53 E
Watapi Lake ⊜	184	55.18 N	109.35 W
Watarai	94	34.26 N	136.37 E
Watarase ≃	94	36.13 N	139.42 E
Wataru I	122	5.43 N	73.23 E
Watatic, Mount ∧	207	42.42 N	71.53 W
Watauga	222	32.51 N	97.15 W
Watchet	42	51.12 N	3.20 W
Watch Hill	207	41.18 N	71.51 W
Watchung	276	40.38 N	74.27 W
Watchung Reservation ♠	276	40.41 N	74.23 W
Water	262	53.44 N	2.14 W
Waterbeach	42	52.16 N	0.11 E
Waterberg	156	20.28 S	17.13 E
Waterberge ⩘	156	24.30 S	28.00 E
Waterberg Plateau Park ♠	156	20.30 S	17.00 E
Waterbury, Ct., U.S.	207	41.33 N	73.02 W
Waterbury, Vt., U.S.	188	44.20 N	72.45 W
Waterdale	158	30.40 S	24.02 E
Wateree ≃	192	33.45 N	80.37 W
Wateree Lake ⊜[1]	192	34.25 N	80.50 W
Waterend, Eng., U.K.	260	51.47 N	0.30 W
Water End, Eng., U.K.	262	53.41 N	2.15 W
Waterfall, Austl.	170	34.08 S	151.00 E
Waterfall, Pa., U.S.	214	40.08 N	78.04 W
Waterford, On., Can.	212	42.56 N	80.17 W
Waterford (Port Láirge), Ire.	48	52.15 N	7.06 W
Waterford, S. Afr.	158	33.05 S	25.00 E
Waterford, Ca., U.S.	226	37.38 N	120.46 W
Waterford, Ct., U.S.	207	41.20 N	72.09 W
Waterford, In., U.S.	216	41.40 N	86.50 W
Waterford, Mi., U.S.	216	42.42 N	83.24 W
Waterford, N.Y., U.S.	210	42.47 N	73.40 W
Waterford, Pa., U.S.	214	41.56 N	79.59 W
Waterford, Wi., U.S.	216	42.45 N	88.12 W
Waterford □[6]	48	52.10 N	7.40 W
Waterford Harbour ᑕ	48	52.10 N	6.55 W
Waterford Mills	216	41.33 N	85.50 W
Waterford Works	208	39.43 N	74.50 W
Watergate Bay ᑕ	42	50.27 N	5.05 W
Watergrasshill	48	52.01 N	8.21 W
Watergrove Reservoir ⊜[1]	262	53.39 N	2.08 W
Waterhen ≃	184	54.38 N	107.47 W
Waterhen Lake ⊜, Mb., Can.	184	52.06 N	99.34 W
Waterhen Lake ⊜, Sk., Can.	184	54.28 N	108.25 W
Waterhouse Range ⩘	162	24.01 S	133.25 E
Wateringbury	260	51.15 N	0.25 E
Wateringen	52	52.02 N	4.16 E
Water Island	276	40.41 N	73.02 W
Waterkloof	158	30.19 S	25.18 E
Waterloo, Austl.	164	16.38 S	129.18 E
Waterloo, Austl.	168a	33.20 S	115.47 E
Waterloo, Austl.	168b	33.59 S	138.53 E
Waterloo, Bel.	50	50.43 N	4.23 E
Waterloo, On., Can.	212	43.28 N	80.31 W
Waterloo, P.Q., Can.	206	45.21 N	72.31 W
Waterloo, S.L.	150	8.20 N	13.04 W
Waterloo, Eng., U.K.	44	53.28 N	3.02 W
Waterloo, Al., U.S.	194	34.55 N	88.03 W
Waterloo, Il., U.S.	219	38.20 N	90.08 W
Waterloo, In., U.S.	216	41.25 N	85.01 W
Waterloo, Ia., U.S.	190	42.29 N	92.20 W
Waterloo, N.Y., U.S.	210	42.54 N	76.51 W
Waterloo, Wi., U.S.	216	43.11 N	88.59 W
Waterloo □[6]	212	43.30 N	80.30 W
Waterloo Bay ᑕ	168b	35.08 S	137.26 E
Waterloo State Recreation Area ♠	216	42.22 N	84.20 W
Waterloo Station ◆[5]	260	51.30 N	0.07 W

Symbols in the index entries represent the broad categories identified in the key at the right. Symbols with superior numbers (⩘[1]) identify subcategories (see complete key on page *I · 1).*

Symbole im Register stellen die rechts im Schlüssel erklärten Kategorien dar. Symbole mit hochgestellten Ziffern (⩘[1]) bezeichnen Unterabteilungen einer Kategorie (vgl. vollständiger Schlüssel auf Seite *I · 1).*

Los símbolos incluídos en el texto del índice representan las grandes categorias identificadas con la clave a la derecha. Los símbolos con numeros en su parte superior (⩘[1]) identifican las subcategorías (véase la clave completa en la página *I · 1).*

Les symboles de l'index représentent les catégories indiquées dans la légende à droite. Les symboles suivis d'un indice (⩘[1]) représentent des sous-catégories (voir légende complète à la page *I · 1).*

Os símbolos incluídos no texto do índice representam as grandes categorias identificadas com a chave à direita. Os símbolos com números em sua parte superior (⩘[1]) identificam as subcategorias (veja-se a chave completa à página *I · 1).*

∧ Mountain	Berg	Montaña	Montagne	Montanha
⩘ Mountains	Gebirge	Montañas	Montagnes	Montanhas
)(Pass	Paß	Paso	Col	Passo
V Valley, Canyon	Tal, Cañon	Valle, Cañón	Vallée, Canyon	Vale, Canhão
≚ Plain	Ebene	Llano	Plaine	Planície
› Cape	Kap	Cabo	Cap	Cabo
I Island	Insel	Isla	Île	Ilha
II Islands	Inseln	Islas	Îles	Ilhas
✢ Other Topographic Features	Andere Topographische Objekte	Otros Elementos Topográficos	Autres données topographiques	Outros acidentes topográficos

ESPAÑOL

Nombre	Página	Lat.°′	Long.°′ W = Oeste
Waterlooville	42	50.53 N	1.02 W
Waterman, Il., U.S.	216	41.46 N	88.46 W
Waterman, Wa., U.S.	224	47.34 N	122.35 W
Waterman Mountain ∧	228	34.20 N	117.56 W
Waterman Wash V	200	33.21 N	112.31 W
Water Mill	207	40.55 N	72.21 W
Waterport	210	43.20 N	78.16 W
Waterport Pond ⊜[1]	212	43.19 N	78.16 W
Waterproof	194	31.48 N	91.23 W
Waterside	214	40.11 N	78.23 W
Waterside Park	276	40.56 N	73.20 W
Watersmeet	190	46.16 N	89.10 W
Waterton ≃	182	49.32 N	113.16 W
Waterton-Glacier International Peace Park ♠	202	48.47 N	113.45 W
Waterton Lakes National Park ♠	182	49.05 N	113.50 W
Watertown, Ct., U.S.	207	41.36 N	73.07 W
Watertown, Ma., U.S.	207	42.22 N	71.11 W
Watertown, N.Y., U.S.	212	43.58 N	75.54 W
Watertown, S.D., U.S.	198	44.53 N	97.06 W
Watertown, Wi., U.S.	216	43.11 N	88.43 W
Waterval-Boven	156	25.40 S	30.20 E
Watervale	168b	33.57 S	138.38 E
Water Valley, Ms., U.S.	194	34.09 N	89.37 W
Water Valley, N.Y., U.S.	284a	42.42 N	78.51 W
Water View	208	37.43 N	76.36 W
Waterville, N.S., Can.	186	45.03 N	64.41 W
Waterville, P.Q., Can.	206	45.16 N	71.54 W
Waterville, Ire.	48	51.49 N	10.13 W
Waterville, Ks., U.S.	198	39.41 N	96.44 W
Waterville, Me., U.S.	188	44.33 N	69.37 W
Waterville, Ma., U.S.	207	42.40 N	72.04 W
Waterville, Mn., U.S.	190	44.13 N	93.34 W
Waterville, N.Y., U.S.	210	42.55 N	75.22 W
Waterville, Oh., U.S.	216	41.30 N	83.43 W
Waterville, Pa., U.S.	210	41.19 N	77.22 W
Waterville, Wa., U.S.	202	47.38 N	120.04 W
Watervliet, Mi., U.S.	216	42.11 N	86.15 W
Watervliet, N.Y., U.S.	210	42.43 N	73.42 W
Watervliet Reservoir ⊜[1]	210	42.43 N	73.58 W
Wates, Indon.	114	1.00 N	100.16 E
Wates, Indon.	115a	7.55 S	112.07 E
Wates, Indon.	115a	7.51 S	110.10 E
Watford, On., Can.	214	42.57 N	81.53 W
Watford, Eng., U.K.	42	51.40 N	0.25 W
Watford □[8]	260	51.40 N	0.25 W
Watford City	198	47.48 N	103.16 W
Wa'th	140	8.10 N	32.07 E
Wathaman ≃	184	57.16 N	102.52 W
Wathaman Lake ⊜	184	56.55 N	103.43 W
Wathena	198	39.45 N	94.56 W
Watheroo	162	30.17 S	116.04 E
Watheroo National Park ♠	162	30.14 S	115.52 E
Wathlingen	52	52.32 N	10.09 E
Wath upon Dearne	44	53.29 N	1.20 W
Wati	120	28.02 N	96.59 E
Watino	182	55.43 N	117.37 W
Watkins Glen	210	42.22 N	76.52 W
Watkins Glen International Raceway ♠	210	42.20 N	76.55 W
Watkins Glen State Park ♠	210	42.22 N	76.55 W
Watkins Island I	284c	39.02 N	77.17 W
Watkins Lake ⊜	281	42.40 N	83.22 W
Watkinsville	192	33.51 N	83.24 W
Watlaar	164	5.28 S	133.07 E
Watling Island → San Salvador I	238	24.02 N	74.28 W
Watlington	42	51.37 N	1.00 W
Watoga State Park ♠	188	38.07 N	80.05 W
Watonga	196	35.50 N	98.24 W
Watonwan ≃	198	44.04 N	94.07 W
Watopeka ≃	206	45.34 N	72.00 W
Watou	50	50.51 N	2.37 E
Wat Phai Tan, Khlong ≊	269a	13.48 N	100.33 E
Watrous, Sk., Can.	184	51.40 N	105.28 W
Watrous, N.M., U.S.	200	35.47 N	104.58 W
Watsa	154	3.03 N	29.32 E
Watseka	216	40.46 N	87.44 W
Watsi Kengo	152	0.48 S	20.33 E
Watson, Austl.	162	30.29 S	131.31 E
Watson, Sk., Can.	184	52.07 N	104.31 W
Watson, In., U.S.	218	38.22 N	85.41 W
Watsonia	274b	37.43 S	145.05 E
Watson Lake	180	60.07 N	128.48 W
Watsons Bay	274a	33.51 S	151.17 E
Watsons Creek	274b	37.40 S	145.13 E
Watsons Creek ≃	274b	37.43 S	145.16 E
Watsontown	210	41.05 N	76.51 W
Watsonville	226	36.54 N	121.45 W
Watt	222	31.39 N	96.51 W
Watten	50	50.50 N	2.13 E
Watten, Loch ⊜	46	58.29 N	3.19 W
Wattens	64	47.17 N	11.36 E
Wattenscheid	56	51.29 N	7.08 E
Wattenwil	58	46.46 N	7.30 E
Wattignies	50	50.35 N	3.03 E
Wattiwarriganna ≃	162	28.57 S	136.10 E
Wattle Flat	170	33.08 S	149.41 E
Wattle Glen	274b	37.40 S	145.11 E
Wattle Park ♠	274b	37.50 S	145.07 E
Watt Mountain ∧	240d	15.19 N	61.19 W
Watton	42	52.35 N	0.48 E
Wattrelos	50	50.42 N	3.13 E
Watts ◆[8]	280	33.56 N	118.15 W
Watts Bar Lake ⊜[1]	192	35.48 N	84.39 W
Watts Branch ≃	284c	39.03 N	77.15 W
Wattsburg	214	42.00 N	79.49 W
Watts Island I	208	37.48 N	75.53 W
Watts Mills	192	34.31 N	82.02 W
Wattville	273d	26.13 S	28.18 E
Wattwil	58	47.18 N	9.06 E
Watu	152	3.18 S	20.03 E
Watubela, Kepulauan II	164	4.35 S	131.40 E
Wat Wat	164	4.29 S	152.21 E
Watzekopf ∧	58	46.59 N	10.48 E
Watzmann ∧	64	47.33 N	12.55 E
Wau	164	7.20 S	146.45 E
Waubach	56	50.55 N	6.03 E
Waubaushene	212	44.45 N	79.42 W
Waubaushene Channel ʯ	212	44.46 N	79.45 W
Waubay	198	45.19 N	97.18 W
Waubay Lake ⊜	198	45.25 N	97.25 W
Waubesa, Lake ⊜	216	43.01 N	89.20 W
Waubra	169	37.21 S	143.39 E
Waubuno Creek ≃	212	42.58 N	81.08 W
Wauchope, Austl.	162	20.36 S	134.15 E
Wauchope, Austl.	166	31.27 S	152.44 E
Wauchula	220	27.32 N	81.48 W
Wauconda, Il., U.S.	216	42.15 N	88.08 W
Wauconda, Wa., U.S.	182	48.43 N	119.00 W
Wauconda, Wa., U.S.	202	48.43 N	119.00 W
Waugh	184	49.40 N	95.13 W
Waugh Mountain ∧	202	45.29 N	114.47 W
Waukara, Bukit ∧	112	1.15 S	119.42 E
Waukaringa	166	32.18 S	139.26 E
Waukarlycarly, Lake ⊜	162	21.25 S	121.50 E
Waukegan	216	42.21 N	87.50 W
Waukena	226	36.08 N	119.31 W
Waukesha	216	43.00 N	88.13 W
Waukesha □[6]	216	43.02 N	88.20 W
Waukomis	196	36.16 N	97.53 W
Waukon	190	43.16 N	91.28 W
Waulsort	56	50.13 N	4.52 E
Wauna	224	47.22 N	122.38 W
Waunakee	216	43.11 N	89.27 W

FRANÇAIS

Nom	Page	Lat.°′	Long.°′ W = Ouest
Wauneta	198	40.25 N	101.22 W
Waupaca	190	44.21 N	89.05 W
Waupecan Creek ≃	216	41.20 N	88.28 W
Waupoos Island I	212	43.59 N	76.58 W
Waupun	190	43.38 N	88.43 W
Wauregan	207	41.44 N	71.54 W
Waurika	196	34.10 N	97.59 W
Waurika Lake ⊜[1]	196	34.15 N	98.05 W
Wausa	198	42.29 N	97.32 W
Wausau	190	44.57 N	89.37 W
Wausaukee	190	45.22 N	87.57 W
Wauseon	216	41.32 N	84.08 W
Waushakum Pond ⊜	283	42.16 N	71.26 W
Wautoma	190	44.04 N	89.17 W
Wauwa	154	3.27 N	27.21 E
Wauwatosa	216	43.02 N	88.00 W
Wauzeka	190	43.05 N	90.52 W
Wave Hill	162	17.29 S	130.57 E
Waveland, Ma., U.S.	283	42.17 N	70.53 W
Waveland, Ms., U.S.	194	30.17 N	89.22 W
Waveney ≃	42	52.28 N	1.45 E
Waver ≃	44	54.52 N	3.17 W
Waverley, Austl.	169	37.53 S	145.10 E
Waverley, Austl.	274a	33.54 S	151.16 E
Waverley, N.Z.	172	39.46 S	174.38 E
Waverley, S. Afr.	158	31.58 S	26.28 E
Waverley, Ma., U.S.	283	42.23 N	71.11 W
Waverley ◆[8]	273d	26.08 S	28.04 E
Waverly, Al., U.S.	194	32.44 N	85.35 W
Waverly, Fl., U.S.	220	27.59 N	81.37 W
Waverly, Il., U.S.	219	39.35 N	89.57 W
Waverly, Ia., U.S.	190	42.43 N	92.28 W
Waverly, Ks., U.S.	198	38.23 N	95.36 W
Waverly, Mi., U.S.	216	42.44 N	84.33 W
Waverly, Mn., U.S.	190	45.04 N	93.57 W
Waverly, Mo., U.S.	194	39.12 N	93.31 W
Waverly, Ne., U.S.	198	40.55 N	96.31 W
Waverly, N.Y., U.S.	210	42.00 N	76.31 W
Waverly, Oh., U.S.	218	39.07 N	82.59 W
Waverly, Pa., U.S.	210	41.32 N	75.42 W
Waverly, Tn., U.S.	194	36.05 N	87.47 W
Waverly, Va., U.S.	208	37.02 N	77.05 W
Waverly Hall	192	32.41 N	84.44 W
Wavre	56	50.43 N	4.37 E
Wavrin	50	50.34 N	2.55 E
Wāw	140	7.42 N	28.00 E
Wāw ≃	140	7.03 N	27.13 E
Wawa, On., Can.	190	47.59 N	84.47 W
Wawa, Nig.	150	9.55 N	4.25 E
Wawa, Sūd.	140	20.26 N	30.21 E
Wawa ≃	236	13.53 N	83.28 W
Wawaka	216	41.27 N	85.28 W
Wāw al-Kabīr	146	25.20 N	16.43 E
Wawanesa	184	49.36 N	99.41 W
Wawarsing	210	41.46 N	74.21 W
Wawasee, Lake ⊜	216	41.24 N	85.41 W
Wawayanda State Park ♠	276	41.11 N	74.26 W
Wawiag ≃	190	48.25 N	91.07 W
Wawoi ≃	164	8.01 S	143.33 E
Waworada, Teluk c	115b	8.44 S	118.51 E
Wawota	184	49.55 N	102.00 W
Waxahachie	222	32.23 N	96.50 W
Waxahachie, Lake ⊜[1]	222	32.20 N	96.49 W
Waxhaw	192	34.55 N	80.44 W
Waxuecun	106	31.07 N	121.38 E
Waxweiler	56	50.05 N	6.22 E
Way, Lake ⊜	162	26.48 S	120.18 E
Waya I	175g	17.18 S	177.08 E
Wayabula	108	2.17 N	128.12 E
Wayaopu	106	30.33 N	118.53 E
Waycross	192	31.12 N	82.21 W
Wayi	154	5.11 N	30.10 E
Wayland, Ia., U.S.	190	41.08 N	91.39 W
Wayland, Ky., U.S.	192	37.26 N	82.48 W
Wayland, Ma., U.S.	283	42.21 N	71.21 W
Wayland, Mi., U.S.	216	42.40 N	85.38 W
Wayland, N.Y., U.S.	210	42.34 N	77.35 W
Wayland, Oh., U.S.	214	41.10 N	81.04 W
Waylyn	192	32.51 N	79.59 W
Waymansville	218	39.04 N	86.03 W
Waymart	210	41.34 N	75.24 W
Wayne, Ab., Can.	182	51.23 N	112.39 W
Wayne, Mi., U.S.	216	42.16 N	83.23 W
Wayne, Ne., U.S.	198	42.13 N	97.01 W
Wayne, N.J., U.S.	210	40.55 N	74.16 W
Wayne, N.Y., U.S.	210	42.28 N	77.06 W
Wayne, Oh., U.S.	214	41.18 N	83.28 W
Wayne, Ok., U.S.	196	34.55 N	97.18 W
Wayne, Pa., U.S.	208	40.02 N	75.23 W
Wayne, W.V., U.S.	188	38.13 N	82.26 W
Wayne □[6], Il., U.S.	219	38.25 N	88.40 W
Wayne □[6], In., U.S.	218	39.50 N	84.54 W
Wayne □[6], Mi., U.S.	216	42.14 N	83.12 W
Wayne □[6], N.Y., U.S.	210	43.04 N	77.00 W
Wayne □[6], Oh., U.S.	214	40.48 N	81.56 W
Wayne □[6], Pa., U.S.	210	41.34 N	75.16 W
Wayne City	194	38.20 N	88.35 W
Wayne Lakes	218	40.01 N	84.39 W
Waynesboro, Ga., U.S.	192	33.05 N	82.00 W
Waynesboro, Ms., U.S.	194	31.40 N	88.38 W
Waynesboro, Pa., U.S.	208	39.45 N	77.34 W
Waynesboro, Tn., U.S.	194	35.19 N	87.45 W
Waynesboro, Va., U.S.	192	38.04 N	78.53 W
Waynesburg, Oh., U.S.	214	40.40 N	81.15 W
Waynesburg, Pa., U.S.	188	39.53 N	80.10 W
Waynesfield	216	40.36 N	83.59 W
Wayne State University ∪[2]	281	42.21 N	83.04 W
Waynesville, Il., U.S.	194	40.15 N	89.08 W
Waynesville, Mo., U.S.	194	37.49 N	92.12 W
Waynesville, N.C., U.S.	192	35.29 N	82.59 W
Waynesville, Oh., U.S.	218	39.32 N	84.05 W
Waynoka	196	36.34 N	98.52 W
Waynoka, Lake ⊜[1]	218	38.55 N	83.47 W
Wayoh Reservoir ⊜[1]	262	53.39 N	2.24 W
Waza	146	11.25 N	14.34 E
Waza, Parc National de ♠	146	11.20 N	13.40 E
Wazah	120	33.22 N	69.26 E
Wāzah Khwāh	120	32.12 N	68.21 E
Waziers	50	50.23 N	3.07 E
Wāzin	146	31.57 N	10.40 E
Wazīrābād	123	32.27 N	74.07 E
Wazīrābād ◆[8]	272a	28.43 N	77.14 E
Wāzīrpur ◆[8]	272a	28.41 N	77.10 E
Wazuka	96	34.47 N	135.55 E
Wazuka ≃	270	34.45 N	135.53 E
Wda ≃	30	53.25 N	18.29 E
We, Pulau I	114	5.51 N	95.18 E
Wea Creek ≃	216	40.24 N	86.57 W
Weagamow Lake ⊜	184	52.53 N	91.22 W
Weald Park ♠	260	51.38 N	0.14 E
Wealdstone ◆[8]	260	51.36 N	0.20 W
Weam	164	8.40 S	141.08 E
Wear ≃	44	54.55 N	1.22 W
Wearhead	44	54.45 N	2.13 W
Wearyan ≃	164	15.57 S	136.51 E
Weatherford, Ok., U.S.	196	35.31 N	98.42 W
Weatherford, Tx., U.S.	222	32.45 N	97.47 W
Weatherford, Lake ⊜[1]	222	32.47 N	97.41 W
Weatherly	210	40.56 N	75.50 W
Weatogue	207	41.51 N	72.49 W
Weaubleau	194	37.53 N	93.32 W
Weaver, Austl.	168b	34.56 S	137.40 E
Weaver, Al., U.S.	194	33.45 N	85.48 W

PORTUGUÊS

Nome	Página	Lat.°′	Long.°′ W = Oeste
Weaver, Tx., U.S.	222	33.10 N	95.25 W
Weaver ≃	44	53.19 N	2.44 W
Weaver ≊	262	53.19 N	2.45 W
Weaverham	44	53.16 N	2.35 W
Weaver Lake ⊜	184	52.45 N	96.35 W
Weavertown	279b	40.16 N	80.11 W
Weaverville, Ca., U.S.	204	40.43 N	122.56 W
Weaverville, N.C., U.S.	192	35.41 N	82.33 W
Webau	54	51.10 N	12.04 E
Webb, Sk., Can.	184	50.11 N	108.12 W
Webb, Ms., U.S.	194	33.56 N	90.20 W
Webb Brook ≃	283	42.32 N	71.14 W
Webb City	194	37.08 N	94.27 W
Webber Lake ⊜	184	54.28 N	94.00 W
Webberville	216	42.40 N	84.10 W
Webbwood	190	46.16 N	81.53 W
Weber ≃	200	41.13 N	112.16 W
Weber, Mount ∧	182	55.32 N	128.31 W
Weber City	192	36.37 N	82.33 W
Weber Creek ≃	226	38.46 N	121.00 W
Weber Hill	219	38.27 N	90.34 W
Weberi Bekera	144	9.39 N	39.03 E
Webster, Ab., Can.	182	55.26 N	118.42 W
Webster, Fl., U.S.	220	28.36 N	82.03 W
Webster, In., U.S.	218	39.54 N	84.57 W
Webster, Ma., U.S.	207	42.03 N	71.52 W
Webster, N.Y., U.S.	210	43.12 N	77.25 W
Webster, Pa., U.S.	214	40.11 N	79.50 W
Webster, S.D., U.S.	198	45.19 N	97.31 W
Webster, Wi., U.S.	190	45.52 N	92.22 W
Webster City	190	42.28 N	93.48 W
Webster Crossing	210	42.40 N	77.38 W
Webster Groves	219	38.35 N	90.21 W
Webster Lake ⊜	216	41.19 N	85.41 W
Websters Corners, B.C., Can.	224	49.13 N	122.30 W
Websters Corners, N.Y., U.S.	284a	41.47 N	78.45 W
Webster Springs	188	38.28 N	80.24 W
Weches	222	31.33 N	95.14 W
Wechmar	54	50.53 N	10.47 E
Wechselburg	54	51.00 N	12.47 E
Weda	108	0.21 N	127.52 E
Wedau ◆[8]	263	51.24 N	6.48 E
Wedau, Sportpark ♠	263	51.25 N	6.47 E
Weddell Island I	254	51.55 S	61.00 W
Weddell Sea ⊤[2]	9	72.00 S	45.00 W
Wedderburn	166	36.25 S	143.37 E
Wedding ◆[8]	264a	52.33 N	13.22 E
Weddinghofen	263	51.36 N	7.37 E
Wedel	52	53.35 N	9.41 E
Wedemark	52	52.33 N	9.44 E
Wedge, Central Mount ∧	162	22.51 S	131.50 E
Wedge Mountain ∧	182	50.10 N	122.50 W
Wedgeport	186	43.44 N	65.59 W
Wedgewood	219	38.47 N	90.17 W
Wedmore	42	51.14 N	2.49 W
Wedowee	194	33.18 N	85.29 W
Wedron	216	41.26 N	88.46 W
Weduar, Tanjung ›	164	6.00 S	132.50 E
Wedweil	140	9.00 N	27.12 E
Wedza	154	18.35 S	31.35 E
Weebo	162	28.01 S	121.03 E
Weed	204	41.25 N	122.23 W
Weed Heights	226	38.59 N	119.12 W
Weedon	206	45.42 N	71.28 W
Weedon Beck	42	52.14 N	1.05 W
Weedon Island I	220	27.51 N	82.36 W
Weed Patch	228	35.19 N	118.55 W
Weed Patch Hill ∧[2]	218	39.10 N	86.13 W
Weedsport	210	43.02 N	76.33 W
Weedville	214	41.17 N	78.30 W
Weehawken	276	40.46 N	74.01 W
Weeim, Pulau I	164	1.29 S	130.14 E
Wee Jasper	171b	35.09 S	148.41 E
Weekapauq	207	41.20 N	71.45 W
Weeki Wachee Spring ♠	220	28.32 N	82.35 W
Weeki Wachee Swamp ≡	220	28.31 N	82.37 W
Weeks Point ›	276	40.53 N	73.39 W
Weekstown	208	39.35 N	74.36 W
Weelde	56	51.25 N	5.00 E
Weeley	42	51.51 N	1.07 E
Weel Shimbirro	144	2.23 N	44.16 E
Weems	208	37.39 N	76.26 W
Weende	52	51.33 N	9.55 E
Weenen	158	28.57 S	30.03 E
Weener	52	53.10 N	7.21 E
Weeney Bay c	274a	34.01 S	151.10 E
Weeping Water	198	40.52 N	96.08 W
Weequahic Lake ⊜	276	40.42 N	74.12 W
Weert	52	51.15 N	5.43 E
Weesatche	222	28.51 N	97.27 W
Weesby	41	54.50 N	9.08 E
Weesow	264a	52.39 N	13.43 E
Weesp	52	52.17 N	5.02 E
Weetfeld ◆[8]	263	51.38 N	7.49 E
Weethalle	166	33.53 S	146.38 E
Weeting	42	52.27 N	0.37 E
Weeton	262	53.48 N	2.56 W
Weetulta	168b	34.15 S	137.38 E
Wee Waa	166	30.14 S	149.26 E
Weeze	52	51.37 N	6.12 E
Wefensleben	54	52.11 N	11.09 E
Weferlingen	54	52.19 N	11.02 E
Wegberg	56	51.08 N	6.16 E
Wegdraai	158	28.50 S	21.52 E
Wegeleben	54	51.53 N	11.10 E
Wegendorf	264a	52.36 N	13.45 E
Wegenstedt	54	52.23 N	11.11 E
Wegeringhausen	56	51.02 N	7.45 E
Weggis	58	47.02 N	8.26 E
Węgliniec	30	51.17 N	15.13 E
Węgorzewo	30	54.14 N	21.44 E
Węgorzyno	30	53.32 N	15.33 E
Węgrów	30	52.25 N	22.01 E
Wegscheid	60	48.36 N	13.48 E
Wehdel	52	53.30 N	8.48 E
Wehebach Stausee ⊜[1]	56	50.45 N	6.20 E
Wehingen	58	48.08 N	8.47 E
Wehofen ◆[8]	263	51.32 N	6.46 E
Wehr	58	47.37 N	7.54 E
Wehringhausen ◆[8]	263	51.21 N	7.27 E
Wehrsdorf	54	51.03 N	14.22 E
Wei ≃, Zhg.	98	37.05 N	119.28 E
Wei ≃, Zhg.	98	36.51 N	115.43 E
Wei ≃, Zhg.	102	34.30 N	110.20 E
Weichang (Zhuizishan)	98	42.00 N	117.32 E
Weichselboden	61	47.40 N	15.10 E
Weichsel → Wisła ≃	30	54.22 N	18.55 E
Weichuan	98	34.17 N	113.58 E
Weicun	106	31.59 N	119.55 E
Weida	54	50.45 N	12.04 E
Weida ≃	54	50.47 N	12.06 E
Weiden am See	61	47.55 N	16.52 E
Weidenberg	60	49.57 N	11.43 E
Weiden in der Oberpfalz	60	49.41 N	12.10 E
Weidenstetten	56	48.33 N	9.59 E
Weiding	60	49.16 N	12.46 E
Weidling	264b	48.17 N	16.19 E
Weidlingau ◆[8]	264b	48.13 N	16.13 E
Weidlingbach	264b	48.16 N	16.15 E
Weidlingerbach ≃	264b	48.18 N	16.20 E
Weifang	98	36.42 N	119.04 E
Weigelstown	208	39.59 N	76.49 W
Weihai	98	37.28 N	122.07 E
Weihaiwei → Weihai	98	37.28 N	122.07 E
Weihmichl	60	48.36 N	12.03 E
Weihnachtsinsel → Christmas Island □[2]	112	10.30 S	105.40 E
Wei Island I	164	3.20 S	144.25 E
Weijiagou	105	40.28 N	115.08 E
Weijiatang	106	31.25 N	118.55 E
Weijiazhuang	105	39.37 N	116.22 E
Weijiazui	100	30.29 N	117.20 E
Weijingtang	106	31.27 N	120.39 E
Weikersheim	56	49.29 N	9.54 E
Weil ≃	56	50.28 N	8.16 E
Weil am Rhein	58	47.37 N	7.38 E
Weilburg	56	50.29 N	8.15 E
Weil der Stadt	56	48.45 N	8.52 E
Weiler	58	47.36 N	9.55 E
Weilerbach	56	49.29 N	7.37 E
Weilerswist	56	50.45 N	6.50 E
Weilheim	64	47.50 N	11.08 E
Weilheim an der Teck	56	48.37 N	9.32 E
Weilmoringle	166	29.15 S	146.51 E
Weilmünster	56	50.26 N	8.22 E
Weimar, Dtsch.	54	50.59 N	11.19 E
Weimar, Dtsch.	56	51.22 N	9.23 E
Weimar, Ca., U.S.	226	39.02 N	120.58 W
Weimar, Tx., U.S.	222	29.42 N	96.46 W
Weinan	102	34.29 N	109.29 E
Weinböhla	54	51.10 N	13.34 E
Weinel Cross Roads	279b	40.37 N	79.37 W
Weiner	194	35.37 N	90.53 W
Weinfelden	58	47.34 N	9.06 E
Weingarten, Dtsch.	56	49.05 N	8.31 E
Weingarten, Dtsch.	58	47.48 N	9.38 E
Weinheim	56	49.33 N	8.39 E
Weining, Zhg.	102	26.43 N	104.18 E
Weining, Zhg.	104	41.21 N	123.49 E
Weinsberg	56	49.10 N	9.17 E
Weinsberger Wald ◆[3]	61	48.30 N	14.50 E
Weinviertel ◆[1]	61	48.38 N	16.25 E
Weipa	164	12.41 S	141.52 E
Weippe	202	46.22 N	115.56 W
Weir, India	124	27.01 N	77.11 E
Weir, Ks., U.S.	198	37.18 N	94.46 W
Weir, Ms., U.S.	194	33.16 N	89.17 W
Weir ≃, Austl.	166	28.50 S	149.06 E
Weir ≃, Mb., Can.	184	56.54 N	93.21 W
Weir ≃, Ma., U.S.	283	42.16 N	70.53 W
Weir, Lake ⊜	220	29.00 N	81.57 W
Weir River	184	56.49 N	94.04 W
Weirsdale	220	28.58 N	81.55 W
Weirton	214	40.25 N	80.35 W
Weisberg → Monguelfo	64	46.45 N	12.06 E
Weisburd	252	27.18 S	62.36 W
Weisburg	218	39.13 N	85.03 W
Weischlitz	54	50.26 N	12.02 E
Weisendorf	56	49.37 N	10.49 E
Weiser	202	44.15 N	116.58 W
Weiser ≃	202	44.15 N	116.59 W
Weishan (Xiazhen), Zhg.	98	34.52 N	117.09 E
Weishan, Zhg.	100	29.20 N	120.25 E
Weishan, Zhg.	100	29.41 N	120.48 E
Weishan, Zhg.	102	25.15 N	100.20 E
Weishancheng	100	32.34 N	113.24 E
Weishanhe	104	40.47 N	123.31 E
Weishan Hu ⊜	98	34.40 N	117.15 E
Weishanzhuang	105	39.40 N	116.25 E
Weishi	98	34.25 N	114.11 E
Weismain	54	50.05 N	11.14 E
Weisner Mountain ∧	194	34.02 N	85.40 W
Weissach	56	48.50 N	8.55 E
Weissbriach	64	46.41 N	13.15 E
Weisse Elster ≃	54	51.26 N	11.57 E
Weissenbach	264b	48.05 N	16.13 E
Weissenbach am Lech	58	47.26 N	10.39 E
Weissenberg	54	51.11 N	14.40 E
Weissenborn	54	50.52 N	13.25 E
Weissenbrunn	54	50.12 N	11.20 E
Weissenburg	58	46.39 N	7.28 E
Weissenburg in Bayern	56	49.01 N	10.58 E
Weissenfels	54	51.12 N	11.58 E
Weissenhorn	58	48.18 N	10.09 E
Weissensee	54	51.11 N	11.04 E
Weissensee ◆[8]	264a	52.33 N	13.27 E
Weissensee ⊜	64	46.42 N	13.22 E
Weissenstadt	54	50.06 N	11.53 E
Weissenstein, Dtsch.	56	48.42 N	9.53 E
Weissenstein, Öst.	64	46.41 N	13.44 E
Weissenstein ∧	58	47.15 N	7.31 E
Weissenstein Tunnel ◆[5]	58	47.12 N	7.23 E
Weissenthurm	56	50.24 N	7.27 E
Weisser Main ≃	54	50.04 N	11.24 E
Weisser Nil → White Nile ≃	140	15.38 N	32.31 E
Weisser See → Beloje, ozero ⊜	76	60.11 N	37.37 E
Weisser Stein ∧	56	50.23 N	6.20 E
Weisses Meer → Beloje more ⊤[2]	24	65.30 N	38.00 E
Weisse Spitze ∧	64	46.52 N	12.21 E
Weissfluh ∧	58	46.50 N	9.48 E
Weisshorn ∧	58	46.06 N	7.42 E
Weissig	54	51.05 N	13.52 E
Weisskugel (Palla Bianca) ∧	64	46.48 N	10.44 E
Weiss Lake ⊜[1]	192	34.15 N	85.35 W
Weissmeer-Ostsee Kanal → Belomorsko-Baltijskij kanal ≊	24	62.48 N	34.48 E
Weissport	210	40.50 N	75.42 W
Weisstannen	58	46.59 N	9.21 E
Weisswasser	54	51.30 N	14.38 E
Weisweiler	56	50.50 N	6.19 E
Weitang	105	40.24 N	117.24 E
Weitang ≃	104	42.19 N	122.18 E
Weitendorf	54	53.54 N	12.16 E
Weitensfeld	61	46.51 N	14.11 E
Weiterstadt	56	49.54 N	8.35 E
Weitian	100	27.43 N	118.46 E
Weitin	54	53.34 N	13.12 E
Weiting	106	31.22 N	120.47 E
Weitmar ◆[8]	263	51.27 N	7.12 E
Weitnau	58	47.38 N	10.07 E
Weitou	100	24.34 N	118.34 E
Weitra	61	48.42 N	14.54 E
Weituo	107	30.03 N	106.08 E
Weitzgrund	54	52.11 N	12.32 E
Weiwan	98	36.43 N	115.54 E
Weixdorf	54	51.09 N	13.48 E
Weixi, Zhg.	102	27.14 N	99.12 E
Weixi, Zhg.	107	30.12 N	106.39 E
Weixian, Zhg.	98	36.57 N	115.15 E
Weixian, Zhg.	98	36.22 N	114.56 E
Weixian (Hanting), Zhg.	98	36.52 N	119.07 E
Weixin	102	27.48 N	105.06 E
Weiyuan	107	29.33 N	104.39 E
Weiyuan ≃	102	22.50 N	100.20 E
Weiyuankou	100	30.09 N	115.15 E
Weiyuanpu	98	42.39 N	124.16 E
Weiz	61	47.13 N	15.37 E
Weizhen	98	37.17 N	114.44 E
Weizhou Dao I	102	21.03 N	109.04 E
Weizhou Wan c	100	24.34 N	118.30 E
Weizhuang	105	39.02 N	115.20 E
Weizi	98	40.04 N	123.10 E
Weizigou, Zhg.	104	42.25 N	122.47 E
Weizigou, Zhg.	104	41.05 N	120.38 E
Weizigou, Zhg.	104	42.05 N	120.34 E
Weizigoumen	98	41.58 N	116.49 E
Weiziyu	98	41.29 N	124.31 E
Wejherowo	30	54.37 N	18.15 E
Wekiva ≃	220	28.52 N	81.23 W
Wekiwa Springs State Park ♠	220	28.43 N	81.27 W
Wekoewa Punt ›	241s	12.14 N	68.24 W
Wekusko Lake ⊜	184	54.45 N	99.50 W
Welaka	192	29.28 N	81.40 W
Welbourn Hill	162	27.21 S	134.06 E
Welch, Ok., U.S.	196	36.52 N	95.05 W
Welch, Tx., U.S.	196	32.56 N	102.08 W
Welch, W.V., U.S.	192	37.25 N	81.35 W
Welch Creek ≃	282	37.32 N	121.51 W
Welches	224	45.19 N	121.57 W
Welch Peak ∧	224	49.10 N	121.36 W
Welcome, On., Can.	212	43.58 N	78.21 W
Welcome, Mn., U.S.	198	43.40 N	94.37 W
Welcome, S.C., U.S.	192	34.49 N	82.26 W
Welcome Lake ⊜	212	45.25 N	78.25 W
Welcome Monument ⊥	269e	6.11 S	106.49 E
Welden	58	48.27 N	10.40 E
Weldiya	144	11.50 N	39.41 E
Weldon, Sk., Can.	184	53.00 N	105.08 W
Weldon, Il., U.S.	219	40.07 N	88.45 W
Weldon, N.C., U.S.	192	36.25 N	77.35 W
Weldon, Tx., U.S.	222	31.01 N	95.34 W
Weldon ≃	194	40.06 N	93.38 W
Weldona	198	40.20 N	103.58 W
Weldon Brook ≃	276	40.58 N	74.35 W
Weleetka	196	35.20 N	96.08 W
Welega □[4]	144	9.40 N	35.50 E
Weleri	115a	6.58 S	110.04 E
Welfare Island I	276	40.45 N	73.57 W
Welgedag	273d	26.12 S	28.30 E
Welhamgreen	260	51.44 N	0.13 W
Welheim ◆[8]	263	51.32 N	6.59 E
Weligama	122	5.58 N	80.25 E
Welikaja → Velikaja ≃	76	57.48 N	28.20 E
Welkenraedt	56	50.40 N	5.59 E
Welker Seamount ✦[3]	16	55.07 N	140.20 W
Welkite	144	8.15 N	37.50 E
Welkom	158	27.59 S	26.45 E
Well	52	51.34 N	6.06 E
Welland	212	42.59 N	79.15 W
Welland ≃, On., Can.	212	43.04 N	79.03 W
Welland ≃, Eng., U.K.	42	52.53 N	0.02 E
Welland Canal ≊	212	43.03 N	79.13 W
Welland Junction	284a	42.57 N	79.14 W
Wellard	168a	32.19 S	115.50 E
Wellaune	54	51.34 N	12.33 E
Wellborn, Fl., U.S.	192	30.13 N	82.49 W
Wellborn, Tx., U.S.	222	30.32 N	96.18 W
Wellerode	56	51.14 N	9.34 E
Wellers Bay c	212	44.00 N	77.34 W
Wellers Creek ≃	278	42.03 N	87.53 W
Wellesbourne	42	52.12 N	1.35 W
Welles Harbor c	174g	28.12 N	177.26 W
Wellesley, On., Can.	212	43.28 N	80.45 W
Wellesley, Ma., U.S.	207	42.17 N	71.17 W
Wellesley ≃	168a	33.17 S	115.44 E
Wellesley College ∪[2]	283	42.18 N	71.19 W
Wellesley Hills	283	42.19 N	71.17 W
Wellesley Island I	212	44.19 N	75.58 W
Wellesley Islands II	164	16.42 S	139.30 E
Wellesley Island State Park ♠	212	44.19 N	76.01 W
Wellesley Lake ⊜	180	62.30 N	139.50 W
Wellfleet	207	41.56 N	70.02 W
Well Hill	260	51.21 N	0.09 E
Wellin	56	50.05 N	5.07 E
Welling ◆[8]	260	51.28 N	0.07 E
Wellingborough	42	52.19 N	0.42 W
Wellinghofen ◆[8]	263	51.28 N	7.29 E
Wellington, Austl.	166	32.33 S	148.57 E
Wellington, B.C., Can.	224	49.13 N	124.01 W
Wellington, On., Can.	212	43.57 N	77.21 W
Wellington, N.Z.	172	41.18 S	174.47 E
Wellington, S. Afr.	158	33.38 S	18.57 E
Wellington, Eng., U.K.	42	52.43 N	2.31 W
Wellington, Eng., U.K.	42	50.59 N	3.14 W
Wellington, Co., U.S.	200	40.42 N	105.00 W
Wellington, Il., U.S.	216	40.32 N	87.41 W
Wellington, Ks., U.S.	198	37.15 N	97.22 W
Wellington, Mo., U.S.	194	39.08 N	93.58 W
Wellington, Nv., U.S.	226	38.45 N	119.22 W
Wellington, Oh., U.S.	214	41.10 N	82.13 W
Wellington, Tx., U.S.	196	34.51 N	100.12 W
Wellington, Ut,. U.S.	200	39.32 N	110.44 W
Wellington □[6]	212	43.50 N	80.30 W
Wellington, Isla I	254	49.20 S	74.40 W
Wellington Bay c, N.T., Can.	176	69.30 N	106.30 W
Wellington Bay c, On., Can.	212	43.56 N	77.21 W
Wellington Channel ʯ	176	75.00 N	93.00 W
Wellington Point	171a	27.29 S	153.15 E
Wellington Reservoir ⊜[1]	168a	33.24 S	116.01 E
Wellington Station	186	46.27 N	64.00 W
Wellman, Ia., U.S.	190	41.27 N	91.50 W
Wellman, Tx., U.S.	196	33.03 N	102.26 W
Wells, B.C., Can.	182	53.06 N	121.34 W
Wells, Eng., U.K.	42	51.13 N	2.39 W
Wells, Mi., U.S.	190	45.47 N	87.04 W
Wells, Mn., U.S.	190	43.44 N	93.43 W
Wells, Nv., U.S.	204	41.06 N	114.57 W
Wells, N.Y., U.S.	210	43.24 N	74.17 W
Wells, Tx., U.S.	222	31.29 N	94.56 W
Wells □[6]	216	40.44 N	85.11 W
Wells, Lake ⊜	162	26.43 S	123.10 E
Wells, Mount ∧	168a	32.42 S	116.20 E
Wells, Mount ∧[2]	162	17.26 S	127.14 E
Wellsboro	210	41.44 N	77.18 W
Wells Bridge	210	42.22 N	75.15 W
Wellsburg, Ia., U.S.	190	42.27 N	92.56 W
Wellsburg, N.Y., U.S.	210	42.00 N	76.43 W
Wellsburg, W.V., U.S.	214	40.16 N	80.36 W
Wells Cathedral ∪[1]	42	51.13 N	2.39 W
Wellsford	172	36.17 S	174.31 E
Wells Gray Provincial Park ♠	182	52.20 N	120.00 W
Wells Lake ⊜	184	57.15 N	101.00 W
Wells-next-the-Sea	42	52.58 N	0.51 E
Wells Point ›	284b	39.17 N	76.23 W
Wells State Park ♠	207	42.09 N	72.05 W
Wells Tannery	214	40.05 N	78.10 W
Wellston, Oh., U.S.	188	39.07 N	82.31 W
Wellston, Ok., U.S.	196	35.41 N	97.03 W
Wellsville, Ks., U.S.	198	38.43 N	95.04 W
Wellsville, Mo., U.S.	219	39.04 N	91.34 W
Wellsville, N.Y., U.S.	210	42.07 N	77.56 W
Wellsville, Oh., U.S.	214	40.36 N	80.38 W
Wellsville, Pa., U.S.	208	40.03 N	76.56 W
Wellsville, Ut,. U.S.	200	41.38 N	111.55 W
Wellton	200	32.40 N	114.08 W
Welmel ≃	144	5.38 N	40.47 E
Welmen	263	51.39 N	6.41 E
Welney	42	52.31 N	0.15 E
Welo □[4]	144	11.50 N	40.20 E
Welper	263	51.25 N	7.12 E
Wels	61	48.10 N	14.02 E
Welschbillig	56	49.51 N	6.34 E
Welse ≃	54	53.10 N	14.18 E
Welsford	186	45.27 N	66.20 W
Welsh	194	30.14 N	92.49 W
Welshpool, Austl.	169	38.39 S	146.26 E
Welshpool, Wales, U.K.	42	52.40 N	3.09 W
Welsickendorf	54	51.54 N	13.08 E
Welsleben	54	52.00 N	11.38 E
Weltenburg	60	48.54 N	11.50 E
Welver	52	51.38 N	7.57 E
Welverdiend	158	26.23 S	27.16 E
Welwitschia	156	20.21 S	14.57 E
Welwyn Garden City	42	51.50 N	0.13 W
Welwyn Hatfield □[8]	260	51.47 N	0.12 W
Welzheim	56	48.53 N	9.38 E
Welzow	54	51.34 N	14.10 E
Wem	42	52.51 N	2.44 W
Wema	152	0.26 S	21.38 E
Wembere ≃	154	4.10 S	34.11 E
Wembley	182	55.09 N	119.08 W
Wembley ◆[8]	260	51.33 N	0.18 W
Wembley Stadium ♠, S. Afr.	273d	26.14 S	28.03 E
Wembley Stadium ♠, Eng., U.K.	260	51.33 N	0.17 W
Wembury	42	50.19 N	4.05 W
Wemding	56	48.52 N	10.43 E
Wemeldinge	52	51.31 N	4.00 E
Wemme	224	45.20 N	121.57 W
Wemperhardt	56	50.09 N	6.05 E
Wemyss Bay	46	55.53 N	4.54 W
Wen ≃, Zhg.	98	36.38 N	119.22 E
Wen ≃, Zhg.	98	35.28 N	118.32 E
Wen'an	105	38.52 N	116.28 E
Wen'an Wa ≡	105	38.54 N	116.37 E
Wenas Creek ≃	224	46.42 N	120.35 W
Wenatchee	202	47.25 N	120.18 W
Wenatchee ≃	202	47.27 N	120.19 W
Wenatchee, Lake ⊜	224	47.49 N	120.47 W
Wenatchee Mountains ⋀	202	47.20 N	120.45 W
Wenchang	110	19.41 N	110.48 E
Wencheng	100	27.50 N	120.05 E
Wenchi	150	7.42 N	2.07 W
Wenchow → Wenzhou	100	28.01 N	120.39 E
Wendaohezi	104	41.46 N	124.09 E
Wendel	279b	40.18 N	79.41 W
Wendell, Id., U.S.	202	42.46 N	114.42 W
Wendell, N.C., U.S.	192	35.46 N	78.22 W
Wendelsheim	56	49.46 N	7.59 E
Wendelstein	60	49.21 N	11.08 E
Wendelstein ∧	64	47.42 N	12.00 E
Wendelville	284a	43.04 N	78.47 W
Wenden, Dtsch.	52	52.19 N	10.30 E
Wenden, Dtsch.	56	50.57 N	7.51 E
Wenden, Az., U.S.	200	33.49 N	113.32 W
Wendeng	98	37.12 N	122.04 E
Wendesi	164	2.25 S	134.13 E
Wendilou	104	41.13 N	121.08 E
Wendisch Rietz	54	52.13 N	14.01 E
Wendish Baggendorf	54	54.04 N	12.56 E
Wendji	152	0.04 S	18.10 E
Wendland ◆[1]	54	53.00 N	11.10 E
Wendo	144	6.38 N	38.27 E
Wendover, Eng., U.K.	42	51.46 N	0.46 W
Wendover, Ut,. U.S.	200	40.44 N	114.02 W
Wenduine	50	51.18 N	3.05 E
Wenebegon ≃	190	46.53 N	83.12 W
Wenebegon Lake ⊜	190	47.24 N	83.08 W
Wenfang	100	28.02 N	117.19 E
Weng	60	48.40 N	12.23 E
Weng ≃	100	24.10 N	113.24 E
Weng'an	102	26.53 N	107.22 E
Wengbo	120	31.23 N	86.40 E
Wengcheng	100	24.23 N	113.51 E
Wengdang	124	28.50 N	90.03 E
Wenge	152	0.03 N	24.01 E
Wengen, Dtsch.	58	47.41 N	10.09 E
Wengen, Schw.	58	46.36 N	7.56 E
Wengern	263	51.24 N	7.21 E
Wengjiabu	106	30.23 N	120.21 E
Wengong	107	30.11 N	104.09 E
Wenguantun	104	41.53 N	123.30 E
Wengyang	100	28.03 N	120.58 E
Wengyuan	100	24.21 N	114.08 E
Wenham	207	42.36 N	70.53 W
Wenham Lake ⊜	283	42.35 N	70.53 W
Wenham Swamp ≡	283	42.37 N	70.55 W
Wenheng	100	25.42 N	116.45 E
Wenī	124	28.21 N	83.34 E
Wenigzell	61	47.26 N	15.47 E
Wenjiachang	107	30.41 N	103.55 E
Wenjiang	107	30.42 N	103.49 E
Wenjiangban	100	26.01 N	117.51 E
Wenjiazhen	100	28.20 N	116.05 E
Wenling	100	28.22 N	121.20 E
Wenlock	164	13.06 S	142.58 E
Wenlock ≃	164	12.02 S	141.55 E
Wenlock Edge ⋀[4]	42	52.30 N	2.40 W
Wenlong	100	24.48 N	114.54 E
Wenmingsi	100	25.33 N	113.20 E
Wennigsen	52	52.16 N	9.34 E
Wenning ≃	44	54.07 N	2.39 W
Wennington ◆[8]	260	51.30 N	0.13 E
Wenniu	102	24.18 N	104.31 E
Wenns	58	47.10 N	10.44 E
Wenona, Il., U.S.	216	41.03 N	89.03 W
Wenona, Md., U.S.	208	38.08 N	75.57 W
Wenonah	208	39.47 N	75.08 W
Wenquan, Zhg.	86	44.59 N	81.04 E
Wenquan, Zhg.	100	23.37 N	113.43 E
Wenquansi	104	41.20 N	124.04 E
Wenshan	102	23.30 N	104.20 E
Wenshang	98	35.44 N	116.29 E
Wenshui, Zhg.	102	28.28 N	106.30 E
Wenshui, Zhg.	102	37.28 N	112.01 E
Wensickendorf	264a	52.45 N	13.23 E
Wensleydale V	44	54.19 N	2.00 W
Wensum ≃	42	52.37 N	1.19 E
Went ≃	44	53.39 N	0.59 W
Wentorf	52	53.30 N	10.15 E
Wentworth, Austl.	166	34.07 S	141.55 E
Wentworth, N.C., U.S.	192	36.24 N	79.46 W
Wentworth, S.D., U.S.	198	43.59 N	96.57 W
Wentworth Falls	170	33.43 S	150.22 E
Wentworth Park	273d	26.07 S	27.48 E
Wentworthville	274a	33.48 S	150.58 E
Wentzville	219	38.48 N	90.51 W
Wenxi	102	35.26 N	111.11 E
Wenxian	102	32.58 N	104.46 E
Wenxingchang	107	29.52 N	106.29 E
Wenyu ≃	105	39.56 N	116.40 E
Wenzenbach	60	49.05 N	12.12 E
Wenzhou	100	28.01 N	120.39 E
Wenzhu	100	27.01 N	113.58 E
Wenzhuangzicun	104	42.16 N	123.51 E
Weobley	42	52.09 N	2.51 W
Weohyakapka, Lake ⊜	220	27.49 N	81.25 W
Wepener	158	29.46 S	27.00 E
Wépion	56	50.25 N	4.52 E
Weppersdorf	61	47.35 N	16.26 E
Wequetequock	207	41.21 N	71.52 W
Wera ≃	115b	8.20 S	120.43 E
Werbellin	54	52.53 N	13.41 E
Werbellinsee ⊜	54	52.54 N	13.40 E
Werben	54	52.52 N	11.58 E
Werbomont	56	50.23 N	5.41 E
Werchojansker Gebirge → Verchojanskij chrebet ⋀	74	67.00 N	129.00 E
Werda	156	25.15 S	23.16 E
Werdau	54	50.44 N	12.22 E
Werden ◆[8]	263	51.23 N	7.00 E
Werder, Dtsch.	54	52.23 N	12.56 E
Werder, Ityo.	144	6.58 N	45.20 E
Werder ◆[1]	54	53.40 N	13.25 E
Werdohl	56	51.15 N	7.45 E
Were Ilu	144	10.37 N	39.28 E
Werfen	64	47.28 N	13.11 E
Weri	164	3.12 S	132.38 E
Werkel	56	51.09 N	9.18 E
Werkendam	52	51.49 N	4.53 E
Werl	52	51.33 N	7.54 E
Werlaburgdorf	54	52.04 N	10.31 E
Werl-Aspe	52	52.04 N	8.43 E
Werleshausen	56	51.19 N	9.54 E
Werlte	52	52.51 N	7.41 E
Wermelskirchen	56	51.08 N	7.13 E
Wermsdorf	54	51.17 N	12.56 E
Wern ≃	56	50.02 N	9.44 E
Wernadinga	166	18.07 S	139.58 E
Wernberg, Dtsch.	60	49.32 N	12.10 E
Wernberg, Öst.	64	46.37 N	13.56 E
Werne	52	51.40 N	7.38 E
Werne ◆[8]	263	51.29 N	7.18 E

≃	River	Fluß	Río	Rivière	Rio
≊	Canal	Kanal	Canal	Canal	Canal
∟	Waterfall, Rapids	Wasserfall, Stromschnellen	Cascada, Rápidos	Chute d'eau, Rapides	Cascata, Rápidos
ʯ	Strait	Meeresstraße	Estrecho	Détroit	Estreito
c	Bay, Gulf	Bucht, Golf	Bahía, Golfo	Baie, Golfe	Baía, Golfo
⊜	Lake, Lakes	See, Seen	Lago, Lagos	Lac, Lacs	Lago, Lagos
≡	Swamp	Sumpf	Pantano	Marais	Pântano
⊓	Ice Features, Glacier	Eis- und Gletscherformen	Accidentes Glaciales	Formes glaciaires	Acidentes glaciares
⊤	Other Hydrographic Features	Andere Hydrographische Objekte	Otros Elementos Hidrográficos	Autres données hydrographiques	Outros acidentes hidrográficos
✦	Submarine Features	Untermeerische Objekte	Accidentes Submarinos	Formes de relief sous-marin	Acidentes submarinos
□	Political Unit	Politische Einheit	Unidad Politica	Entité politique	Unidade política
∪	Cultural Institution	Kulturelle Institution	Institución Cultural	Institution culturelle	Instituição cultural
⊥	Historical Site	Historische Stätte	Sitio Histórico	Site historique	Sitio histórico
♠	Recreational Site	Erholungs- und Ferienort	Sitio de Recreo	Centre de loisirs	Area de Lazer
⊠	Airport	Flughafen	Aeropuerto	Aéroport	Aeroporto
■	Military Installation	Militäranlage	Instalación Militar	Installation militaire	Instalação militar
◆	Miscellaneous	Verschiedenes	Misceláneo	Divers	Diversos

Werneck, Bra. 256 22.13 S 43.19 W
Werneck, Dtsch. 56 49.59 N 10.05 E
Werneuchen 54 52.38 N 13.44 E
Wernigerode 54 51.50 N 10.47 E
Wernitz 264a 52.34 N 12.55 E
Wernsdorf 264a 52.22 N 13.43 E
Wernsdorfer See ⊜ 264a 52.23 N 13.42 E
Wernshausen 54 50.43 N 10.21 E
Wernstein 60 48.30 N 13.28 E
Werra ≃ 30 51.26 N 9.39 E
Werribee 169 37.54 S 144.40 E
Werribee ≃ 169 37.59 S 144.41 E
Werribee Gorge State Park ♦ 169 37.40 S 144.21 E
Werribee South 169 37.56 S 144.42 E
Werries 52 51.41 N 7.53 E
Werrington 274a 33.45 S 150.46 E
Werris Creek 166 31.21 S 150.39 E
Werschweiler 56 49.27 N 7.13 E
Wersten ◆[8] 263 51.11 N 6.49 E
Wertach 58 47.36 N 10.25 E
Wertach ≃ 58 48.24 N 10.53 E
Wertheim 56 49.46 N 9.31 E
Werther, Dtsch. 52 52.04 N 8.24 E
Werther, Dtsch. 54 51.29 N 10.46 E
Wertingen 56 48.34 N 10.41 E
Wervershoof 52 52.44 N 5.09 E
Wervik 50 50.47 N 3.02 E
Wervin 262 53.15 N 2.52 W
Werwaru 164 8.13 S 128.11 E
Weschnitz ≃ 56 49.43 N 8.24 E
Weseke 52 51.54 N 6.51 E
Wesel 52 51.40 N 6.38 E
Wesel-Datteln-Kanal ≋ 263 51.38 N 6.36 E
Wesenberg 54 53.17 N 12.58 E
Wesendahl 264a 52.36 N 13.49 E
Wesendorf 52 52.35 N 10.31 E
Weser ≃ 52 53.32 N 8.34 E
Weser-Elbe-Kanal (Mittellandkanal) ≋ 54 52.16 N 11.41 E
Weser-Ems □[6] 52 52.45 N 8.00 E
Wesergebirge ⋀⋀ 52 52.15 N 9.10 E
Wesham 262 53.48 N 2.53 W
Wesickaman Creek ≃ 285 39.44 N 74.43 W
Wesī Śahar 124 28.15 N 84.23 E
Weskan 198 38.52 N 101.57 W
Weslaco 196 26.09 N 97.59 W
Weslemkoon Lake ⊜ 212 45.02 N 77.25 W
Wesley, Dom. 240d 15.34 N 61.19 W
Wesley, Ia., U.S. 190 43.05 N 93.59 W
Wesleyville, Nf., Can. 186 49.09 N 53.34 W
Wesleyville, Pa., U.S. 214 42.08 N 80.00 W
Wessel, Cape ➤ 164 10.59 S 136.46 E
Wesseling 56 50.49 N 6.58 E
Wessel Islands II 164 11.30 S 136.25 E
Wesselsbron 158 27.50 S 25.23 E
Wesselsvlei 158 27.23 S 23.47 E
Wessington 198 44.27 N 98.41 W
Wessington Springs 198 44.04 N 98.34 W
Wessobrunn 64 47.52 N 11.01 E
Wesson 194 31.42 N 90.23 W
Wessum 52 52.05 N 6.58 E
West, Ms., U.S. 194 33.11 N 89.46 W
West, Tx., U.S. 222 31.48 N 97.05 W
West ≃, N.Y., U.S. 210 42.41 N 77.22 W
West ≃, Vt., U.S. 188 42.52 N 72.33 W
West Abington 207 42.05 N 70.58 W
Westacres 216 42.35 N 83.26 W
West Acton 207 42.28 N 71.28 W
West Alexander 214 40.06 N 80.31 W
West Alexandria 218 39.44 N 84.31 W
Westall, Point ➤ 162 32.55 S 134.04 E
West Allen ≃ 44 54.55 N 2.19 W
West Allis 216 43.01 N 88.00 W
Westalton 219 38.51 N 90.13 W
West Amityville 276 40.41 N 73.26 W
West Andover 207 42.39 N 71.09 W
West Athens 280 33.55 N 118.18 W
West Atlantic City 208 39.23 N 74.28 W
West Babylon 210 40.43 N 73.21 W
Westbahnhof ◆[5] 264b 48.11 N 16.20 E
West Baines ≃ 164 15.36 S 129.58 E
West Bangor 210 40.52 N 75.14 W
Westbank 182 49.50 N 119.38 W
West Bank □[9] 132 31.40 N 35.15 E
West Barnstable 207 41.42 N 70.22 W
West Barrington 207 41.44 N 71.20 W
West Bay, N.S., Can. 186 45.43 N 61.10 W
Westbay, Fl., U.S. 194 30.17 N 85.52 W
West Bay ⊂, Fl., U.S. 194 30.16 N 85.47 W
West Bay ⊂, Tx., U.S. 222 29.15 N 94.57 W
West Bay Shore 276 40.42 N 73.16 W
West Belmar 208 40.10 N 74.02 W
West Bend, Ia., U.S. 198 42.57 N 94.26 W
West Bend, Wi., U.S. 190 43.25 N 88.11 W
West Bengal □[3] 124 24.00 N 88.00 E
West Bergholt 42 51.55 N 0.51 E
West Berlin 208 39.48 N 74.56 W
West-Berlin □[3] 264a 52.30 N 13.15 E
West Bernard Creek ≃ 222 29.23 N 95.58 W
Westbevern 52 52.01 N 7.47 E
West Bhāgīrath Plain ≚ 126 23.30 N 88.00 E
West Bijou Creek ≃ 198 39.51 N 104.08 W
West Billerica 283 42.33 N 71.19 W
West Blocton 194 33.07 N 87.07 W
West Bloomfield 210 42.54 N 77.32 W
West Bolivar 214 40.23 N 79.10 W
Westborough 207 42.16 N 71.37 W
Westbourne 184 50.09 N 98.35 W
West Bow Creek ≃ 198 42.46 N 97.08 W
West Boxford 283 42.42 N 71.04 W
West Boylston 207 42.22 N 71.47 W
West Bradenton 220 27.30 N 82.37 W
West Branch, Ia., U.S. 190 41.40 N 91.20 W
West Branch, Mi., U.S. 190 44.16 N 84.14 W
West Branch Reservoir ⊜[1] 210 41.25 N 73.42 W
West Branch State Park ♦ 214 41.07 N 81.05 W
Westbridge 182 49.10 N 118.59 W
West Bridgewater 207 42.01 N 71.00 W
West Bridgford 42 52.56 N 1.08 W
West Bristol 285 40.06 N 74.53 W
West Bromwich 42 52.31 N 1.56 W
Westbrook, Austl. 171a 27.36 S 151.52 E
Westbrook, On., Can. 212 44.16 N 76.38 W
Westbrook, Ct., U.S. 207 41.17 N 72.26 W
Westbrook, Me., U.S. 188 43.40 N 70.22 W
Westbrook, Mn., U.S. 198 44.02 N 95.26 W
Westbrook, Tx., U.S. 196 32.21 N 101.01 W
West Brook ≃ 276 41.04 N 74.18 W
West Brookfield 207 42.14 N 72.08 W
Westbrookville 210 41.30 N 74.34 W
West Burlington, Ia., U.S. 190 40.49 N 91.09 W
West Burlington, N.Y., U.S. 210 42.42 N 75.11 W
West Burra I 46a 60.05 N 1.21 W
Westbury, Eng., U.K. 42 52.41 N 2.57 W
Westbury, Eng., U.K. 42 51.16 N 2.11 W
Westbury, N.Y., U.S. 276 40.45 N 73.35 W
Westbury-on-Severn 42 51.50 N 2.24 W
West Butte ∧ 202 48.57 N 111.32 W
Westby, Austl. 171b 35.30 S 147.25 E
Westby, Mt., U.S. 198 48.52 N 104.03 W
Westby, Wi., U.S. 190 43.39 N 90.51 W
West Cache Creek ≃ 196 34.13 N 98.23 W
West Caicos I 238 21.39 N 72.28 W
West Calder 46 55.52 N 3.35 W
West Caldwell 276 40.50 N 74.18 W
West Cameron 208 40.45 N 76.41 W
West Camp 210 42.07 N 73.56 W
West Canada Creek ≃ 188 43.01 N 74.58 W
West Cape ➤ 172 45.54 S 166.26 E
West Cape Howe ➤ 162 35.08 S 117.36 E
West Cape May 208 38.56 N 74.56 W
West Carlisle 196 33.35 N 101.56 W
West Caroline Basin ✦[1] 14 4.00 N 138.00 E
West Carrollton 218 39.40 N 84.15 W
West Carson 280 33.57 N 118.23 W
West Carthage 212 43.58 N 75.36 W
West Catfish Creek ≃ 212 42.46 N 81.04 W
West Channel ≃[1] 180 68.51 N 136.10 W
West Chelmsford 283 42.37 N 71.23 W
Westchester, Il., U.S. 216 41.51 N 87.52 W
West Chester, Pa., U.S. 208 39.57 N 75.36 W
Westchester, Va., U.S. 284c 38.51 N 77.16 W
Westchester □[6] 210 41.02 N 73.46 W
Westchester ◆[8], Ca., U.S. 280 33.55 N 118.25 W
Westchester ◆[8], N.Y., U.S. 276 40.51 N 73.52 W
West Chester Airport ⊠ 285 39.59 N 75.35 W
Westchester County Airport ⊠ 207 41.04 N 73.43 W
Westchester Creek ≃ 276 40.48 N 73.51 W
Westchester Estates 284c 38.47 N 76.55 W
Westchester Station 186 45.37 N 63.40 W
West Chester University of Pennsylvania ♜[2] 285 39.57 N 75.36 W
West Chicago 216 41.53 N 88.12 W
West Clandon 260 51.15 N 0.30 W
West Clarksville 210 42.08 N 78.15 W
West Clear Creek ≃ 200 34.34 N 111.51 W
West Cleddau ≃ 42 51.46 N 4.54 W
Westcliffe 200 38.08 N 105.27 W
Westcliffe ◆[8] 273d 26.11 S 28.02 E
Westcliff-on-Sea 260 51.32 N 0.41 E
West College Corner 218 39.34 N 84.48 W
West Collingswood Heights 285 39.59 N 75.07 W
West Columbia, S.C., U.S. 192 33.59 N 81.04 W
West Columbia, Tx., U.S. 222 29.08 N 95.38 W
West Concord, Ma., U.S. 207 42.27 N 71.23 W
West Concord, Mn., U.S. 190 44.09 N 92.53 W
West Conshohocken 285 40.04 N 75.19 W
West Cote Blanche Bay ⊂ 194 29.40 N 91.45 W
Westcott 260 51.13 N 0.22 W
Westcott Cove ⊂ 276 41.02 N 73.30 W
West Covina 228 34.04 N 117.56 W
West Creek 208 39.38 N 74.18 W
West Creek ≃, In., U.S. 216 41.12 N 87.30 W
West Creek ≃, Pa., U.S. 214 41.30 N 78.15 W
Westdale, Ma., U.S. 283 42.01 N 70.59 W
Westdale, N.Y., U.S. 210 43.23 N 75.49 W
West Danby 210 42.19 N 76.32 W
West Davenport 210 42.27 N 74.58 W
West Deane Park ♦ 275b 43.40 N 79.34 W
West Decatur 214 40.56 N 78.17 W
West Delaware Aqueduct ≋[1] 210 41.52 N 74.31 W
Westdene ◆[8] 273d 26.11 S 27.59 E
West Dennis 207 41.39 N 70.10 W
West Derby ◆[8] 262 53.26 N 2.54 W
West Derry 214 40.20 N 79.20 W
West Des Moines 190 41.34 N 93.42 W
West Ditch ≋ 276 40.56 N 74.19 W
West Dolores ≃ 200 37.35 N 108.21 W
West Drayton ◆[8] 260 51.30 N 0.29 W
West Duffins Creek ≃ 212 43.51 N 79.04 W
West Duxbury 283 42.03 N 70.47 W
West Easton 210 40.41 N 75.14 W
West Eaton 210 42.51 N 75.39 W
Westecunk Creek ≃ 208 39.37 N 74.16 W
West Edmeston 210 42.46 N 75.17 W
West Edmondale 284b 39.18 N 76.43 W
West Elizabeth 279b 40.17 N 79.54 W
West Elk Mountains ⋀⋀ 200 38.40 N 107.15 W
West Elk Peak ∧ 200 38.43 N 107.13 W
West Elkton 218 39.35 N 84.33 W
West Ellicott 214 42.05 N 79.16 W
West Elmira 210 42.04 N 76.50 W
West End, Ba. 238 26.41 N 78.58 W
West End, Eng., U.K. 260 51.44 N 0.04 W
West End, Eng., U.K. 260 51.20 N 0.38 W
West End, Ar., U.S. 194 34.13 N 92.03 W
West End, Il., U.S. 216 42.17 N 89.09 W
West End, N.Y., U.S. 210 42.28 N 75.05 W
West End, N.C., U.S. 192 35.14 N 79.34 W
West End ◆[8], Eng., U.K. 260 51.32 N 0.24 W
West End ◆[8], Pa., U.S. 279b 40.27 N 80.02 W
Westende, Bel. 50 51.10 N 2.46 E
Westende, Dtsch. 263 51.25 N 7.24 E
Westendorf 64 47.26 N 12.13 E
Westenfeld ◆[8] 263 51.28 N 7.09 E
Westenholz 52 51.45 N 8.28 E
Westenschouwen 52 51.41 N 3.42 E
Westerbauer ◆[8] 263 51.20 N 7.23 E
Westerblokker 52 52.39 N 5.08 E
Westerbönen 263 51.36 N 7.46 E
Westerbork 52 52.51 N 6.37 E
Westerburg 56 50.33 N 7.58 E
Westercelle 52 52.36 N 10.05 E
Westerdale 46 58.27 N 3.30 W
Westeregeln 54 51.57 N 11.23 E
Westerham 42 51.16 N 0.05 E
Westerhausen 54 51.48 N 11.03 E
Westerholt 52 51.36 N 7.05 E
Westerholz ◆[3] 263 51.32 N 7.28 E
Westerich □[9] 56 49.15 N 7.20 E
Westerkappeln 52 52.18 N 7.52 E
Westerland 30 54.54 N 8.18 E
Westerlo, Bel. 56 51.05 N 4.55 E
Westerlo, N.Y., U.S. 210 42.31 N 74.03 W
Westerly 207 41.22 N 71.49 W
Western 198 40.23 N 97.11 W
Western □[4], Ghana 150 5.30 N 2.30 W
Western □[4], Kenya 154 0.30 N 34.35 E
Western □[4], Sol.Is. 175e 8.00 S 157.00 E
Western □[4], Zam. 152 16.00 S 24.00 E
Western □[5], Pap. N. Gui. 164 7.00 S 142.00 E
Western □[5], Ug. 154 1.00 N 31.00 E
Western ≃ 166 22.22 S 142.25 E
Western Area □[4] 150 8.20 N 13.00 W
Western Australia □[3] 160 25.00 S 122.00 E
Western Branch ≃ 284c 38.55 N 76.48 W
Western Canal ≋ 226 39.28 N 121.35 W
Western Channel ⊔ 98 34.40 N 129.00 E
Western Cove ⊂ 168b 35.43 S 137.38 E
Western Desert → Gharbīyah, Aṣ-Ṣaḥrā' al- ◆[2] 140 27.00 N 27.00 E
Western Division □[5] 175g 18.00 S 177.30 E
Western Ghāts ⋀⋀ 122 14.00 N 75.00 E
Western Highlands □[5] 164 5.45 S 144.30 E
Western Isles □[4] 46 57.40 N 7.00 W
Westernport 188 39.29 N 79.02 W
Western Port ⊂ 169 38.22 N 145.20 E
Western Port Bay ⊂ 169 38.15 S 145.20 E
Western Sahara □[2], Afr. 134 24.30 N 13.00 W
Western Sahara □[2], Afr. 148 24.30 N 13.00 W
Western Samoa □[1], Oc. 14 13.55 S 172.00 W
Western Samoa □[1], Oc. 175a 13.55 S 172.00 W
Western Sayans → Zapadnyj Sajan ⋀⋀ 74 53.00 N 94.00 E
Western Shore 186 44.32 N 64.19 W
Western Springs 278 41.48 N 87.54 W
Westernville 210 43.18 N 75.23 W
Westerschelde ⊂[1] 52 51.25 N 3.45 E
Westerstede 52 53.15 N 7.55 E
Westervelt 219 39.29 N 88.52 W
Westerville 214 40.07 N 82.55 W
Westerwald ⋀⋀ 56 50.40 N 7.55 E
West European Basin ✦[1] 10 47.00 N 15.00 W
West Exeter 210 42.48 N 75.09 W
West Fairview 208 40.16 N 76.54 W
Westfalen □[9] 52 51.50 N 7.30 E
Westfalenhalle ♜ 263 51.30 N 7.27 E
West Falkland I 254 51.50 S 60.00 W
West Falls 210 42.42 N 78.41 W
West Falmouth 207 41.36 N 70.38 W
West Fargo 198 46.52 N 96.54 W
West Farleigh 260 51.15 N 0.27 E
West Farmington 214 41.23 N 80.58 W
Westfield, Eng., U.K. 42 50.55 N 0.35 E
Westfield, Il., U.S. 194 39.27 N 88.01 W
Westfield, In., U.S. 218 40.02 N 86.07 W
Westfield, Ma., U.S. 207 42.07 N 72.45 W
Westfield, N.J., U.S. 210 40.39 N 74.20 W
Westfield, N.Y., U.S. 214 42.19 N 79.34 W
Westfield, Pa., U.S. 210 41.55 N 77.32 W
Westfield, Tx., U.S. 222 30.01 N 95.24 W
Westfield, Wi., U.S. 190 43.53 N 89.29 W
Westfield ≃ 207 42.05 N 72.35 W
Westfield, Middle Branch ≃ 207 42.16 N 72.52 W
Westfield, West Branch ≃ 207 42.13 N 72.52 W
Westfield Center 214 41.01 N 81.55 W
West Fiord ⊂[2] 176 76.02 N 90.00 W
Westford, Ma., U.S. 283 42.34 N 71.26 W
Westford, N.Y., U.S. 210 42.39 N 74.48 W
West Fork 194 35.55 N 94.11 W
West Foxboro 283 42.05 N 71.17 W
West Frankfort 194 37.53 N 88.55 W
West Friesland ◆[1] 52 52.45 N 4.50 E
West Frisian Islands → Waddeneilanden II 52 53.26 N 5.30 E
West Fulton 210 42.34 N 74.28 W
Westgate, Austl. 166 26.35 S 146.12 E
Westgate, Mi., U.S. 216 43.03 N 85.42 W
Westgate on Sea 42 51.23 N 1.21 E
West Genesee Terrace 210 43.03 N 76.16 W
West-Ghats → Western Ghāts ⋀⋀ 122 14.00 N 75.00 E
West Gilgo Beach 276 40.37 N 73.25 W
West Glacier 202 48.29 N 113.58 W
West Glamorgan □[6] 42 51.35 N 3.35 W
West Glens Falls 210 43.18 N 73.43 W
West Glenville 210 42.56 N 74.04 W
West Goshen 207 41.49 N 73.15 W
West Granby 207 41.57 N 72.50 W
West Grand Lake ⊜ 188 45.15 N 67.50 W
West Groton 207 42.36 N 71.37 W
West Grove 208 39.49 N 75.49 W
Westham 208 37.35 N 77.32 W
West Ham ◆[8] 260 51.31 N 0.01 E
West Hamburg 208 40.33 N 76.00 W
West Ham Football Club ♦ 260 51.32 N 0.02 E
Westham Island I 224 49.05 N 123.10 W
West Hamlin 188 38.17 N 82.11 W
Westhampton, N.Y., U.S. 207 40.49 N 72.39 W
Westhampton, Va., U.S. 284c 38.54 N 77.11 W
West Hanningfield 260 51.40 N 0.30 E
West Hanover 283 42.07 N 70.53 W
West Harbor ⊂ 276 40.54 N 73.32 W
West Harrison 218 39.15 N 84.49 W
West Hartford 207 41.45 N 72.44 W
West Hartland 207 42.00 N 72.58 W
Westhausen 56 48.53 N 10.11 E
Westhaven, Ca., U.S. 204 41.03 N 124.06 W
West Haven, Ct., U.S. 207 41.16 N 72.57 W
Westhaven, Il., U.S. 278 41.35 N 87.51 W
West Haverstraw 210 41.12 N 73.59 W
West Hazleton 210 40.57 N 75.59 W
Westhead 262 53.34 N 2.51 W
West Hebron 210 43.14 N 73.22 W
West Heidelberg 274b 37.45 S 145.02 E
Westheim 56 49.03 N 9.44 E
West Helena 194 34.33 N 90.38 W
Westhemmerde 263 51.33 N 7.47 E
West Hempstead 276 40.42 N 73.39 W
West Henrietta 210 43.02 N 77.40 W
West Hickory 214 41.34 N 79.25 W
Westhill 46 57.09 N 2.17 W
West Hill ◆[8] 275b 43.46 N 79.11 W
Westhofen 263 51.25 N 7.31 E
Westhoff 222 29.12 N 97.28 W
Westhoffen 58 48.36 N 7.26 E
West Hollywood, Ca., U.S. 228 34.05 N 118.21 W
West Hollywood, Fl., U.S. 220 26.01 N 80.10 W
Westholme 224 49.52 N 123.42 W
West Homestead 279b 40.24 N 79.55 W
Westhope, N.D., U.S. 198 48.54 N 101.01 W
Westhope, Oh., U.S. 216 41.18 N 83.57 W
West Horndon 260 51.34 N 0.21 E
West Horsley 260 51.16 N 0.27 W
Westhoughton 262 53.33 N 2.32 W
West Hoxton 274a 33.55 S 150.49 E
West Humber ≃ 212 43.44 N 79.33 W
West Humble 260 51.15 N 0.20 W
West Huntington 276 40.42 N 73.18 W
West Hurley 210 42.00 N 74.06 W
Westhuyzen 158 27.30 S 25.27 E
West Hyde 260 51.37 N 0.30 W
West Ice Shelf ⊓ 9 67.00 S 85.00 E
Westick 263 51.35 N 7.38 E
Westig 263 51.22 N 7.45 E
West Indies II 230 19.00 N 70.00 W
Westindische Inseln → West Indies II 230 19.00 N 70.00 W
West Irian → Irian Jaya □[4] 164 5.00 S 138.00 E
West Island I, Austl. 164 15.36 S 136.34 E
West Island I, Ma., U.S. 207 41.36 N 70.50 W
West Islip 210 40.42 N 73.18 W
West Jan Mayen Ridge ✦[3] 10 71.00 N 13.00 W
West Jefferson, N.C., U.S. 192 36.24 N 81.29 W
West Jefferson, Oh., U.S. 218 39.56 N 83.16 W
West Jordan 200 40.36 N 111.56 W
Westkapelle, Bel. 50 51.19 N 3.18 E
Westkapelle, Ned. 52 51.32 N 3.27 E
West Keansburg 276 40.27 N 74.09 W
West Kettle ≃ 182 49.07 N 119.00 W
West Kilbride 46 55.42 N 4.51 W
West Kill 210 42.13 N 74.31 W
West Kingsdown 42 51.21 N 0.17 E
West Kingston 207 41.28 N 71.33 W
West Kirby 44 53.22 N 3.10 W
Westkirchen 52 51.53 N 8.02 E
West Kittanning 214 40.49 N 79.32 W
West Lafayette, In., U.S. 216 40.25 N 86.54 W
West Lafayette, Oh., U.S. 214 40.16 N 81.45 W
Westlake, La., U.S. 194 30.15 N 93.15 W
Westlake, Oh., U.S. 214 41.27 N 81.55 W
Westlake, Tx., U.S. 222 32.59 N 97.12 W
West Lake ⊜, On., Can. 212 43.56 N 77.17 W
West Lake ⊜, Fl., U.S. 220 25.12 N 80.49 W
West Lake ⊜, N.J., U.S. 276 40.58 N 74.22 W
West Lamma Channel ⊔ 271d 22.13 N 114.04 E
West Lancashire □[8] 262 53.35 N 2.50 W
Westland, Mi., U.S. 216 42.19 N 83.24 W
Westland, Pa., U.S. 214 40.17 N 80.16 W
Westland Center ◆[9] 281 42.20 N 83.23 W
Westland National Park ♦ 172 43.30 S 170.10 E
Westlands 207 42.37 N 71.20 W
West Lanham Hills 284c 38.57 N 76.53 W
West Laramie 200 41.18 N 105.37 W
West Lawn 284c 38.52 N 77.11 W
West Lebanon, In., U.S. 216 40.16 N 87.23 W
West Lebanon, Pa., U.S. 214 40.35 N 79.22 W
West Leechburg 214 40.37 N 79.37 W
Westleigh, S. Afr. 158 27.31 S 27.21 E
Westleigh, Eng., U.K. 262 53.30 N 2.31 W
West Leipsic 216 41.07 N 84.00 W
Westley 226 37.33 N 121.12 W
West Leyden 212 43.28 N 75.28 W
West Liberty, Ia., U.S. 190 41.34 N 91.15 W
West Liberty, Ky., U.S. 192 37.55 N 83.15 W
West Liberty, Oh., U.S. 216 40.15 N 83.45 W
West Liberty, Pa., U.S. 214 41.00 N 80.03 W
West Liberty, W.V., U.S. 214 40.10 N 80.35 W
West Liberty ◆[8] 279b 40.24 N 80.01 W
Westliche Sahara → Western Sahara □[2] 148 24.30 N 13.00 W
Westliche Sierra Madre → Madre Occidental, Sierra ⋀⋀ 232 25.00 N 105.00 W
Westline 214 41.47 N 78.46 W
West Linn 224 45.21 N 122.36 W
West Linton 46 55.46 N 3.22 W
West Little Owyhee ≃ 202 42.28 N 117.15 W
Westlock 182 54.09 N 113.52 W
West Lorne 214 42.36 N 81.36 W
West Los Angeles ◆[8] 280 34.03 N 118.28 W
West Lulworth 42 50.38 N 2.15 W
West Lunga ≃ 154 13.06 S 24.39 E
West Lunga National Park ♦ 154 12.55 S 25.10 E
West Malling 42 51.18 N 0.25 E
West Malling Aerodrome ⊠ 260 51.16 N 0.24 E
West Manayunk 285 40.01 N 75.14 W
West Manchester 218 39.54 N 84.37 W
West Mansfield, Ma., U.S. 207 41.59 N 71.14 W
West Mansfield, Oh., U.S. 216 40.24 N 83.32 W
West Mariana Basin ✦[1] 14 15.00 N 137.00 E
West Mayfield 214 40.47 N 80.20 W
West Meadowview 216 41.08 N 87.52 W
Westmeath □[6] 48 53.30 N 7.30 W
West Medway 207 42.08 N 71.25 W
West Melbourne 220 28.04 N 80.39 W
West Memphis 194 35.08 N 90.11 W
West Meon 42 51.01 N 1.05 W
Westmere 210 42.41 N 73.52 W
West Mersea 42 51.47 N 0.55 E
West Miami 220 25.45 N 80.17 W
West Middlesex 214 41.10 N 80.27 W
West Middletown 214 40.15 N 80.25 W
West Midlands □[6] 42 52.30 N 2.00 W
West Mifflin 214 40.22 N 79.52 W
West Milford 210 41.07 N 74.22 W
West Millbury 207 42.11 N 71.48 W
West Mill Creek ≃ 222 29.55 N 96.17 W
West Milton, Oh., U.S. 218 39.57 N 84.19 W
West Milton, Pa., U.S. 210 41.01 N 76.52 W
West Milwaukee 216 43.00 N 87.58 W
West Mineola 222 32.41 N 95.31 W
Westminster, Ca., U.S. 228 33.45 N 118.02 W
Westminster, Co., U.S. 200 39.50 N 105.02 W
Westminster, Md., U.S. 208 39.34 N 76.59 W
Westminster, Ma., U.S. 207 42.32 N 71.54 W
Westminster, Oh., U.S. 216 40.42 N 83.58 W
Westminster, S.C., U.S. 192 34.39 N 83.05 W
Westminster Abbey ♜[1] 260 51.30 N 0.07 W
Westminster Mall ◆[9] 280 33.45 N 118.01 W
West Modesto 226 37.37 N 121.02 W
West Monroe 194 32.31 N 92.08 W
Westmont, Ca., U.S. 280 33.56 N 118.18 W
Westmont, Il., U.S. 278 41.47 N 87.58 W
Westmont, N.J., U.S. 285 39.54 N 75.02 W
Westmont, Pa., U.S. 214 40.18 N 78.57 W
West Monterey 214 41.03 N 79.39 W
West Montreal ≃ 190 47.56 N 80.39 W
West Moors 42 50.49 N 1.55 W
Westmoreland, Ks., U.S. 198 39.23 N 96.24 W
Westmoreland, N.Y., U.S. 210 43.07 N 75.24 W
Westmoreland, Tn., U.S. 194 36.33 N 86.14 W
Westmoreland, Va., U.S. 208 38.04 N 76.34 W
Westmoreland □[6], Pa., U.S. 214 40.18 N 79.33 W
Westmoreland □[6], Va., U.S. 208 38.10 N 76.50 W
Westmoreland City 214 40.20 N 79.41 W
Westmoreland State Park ♦ 208 38.09 N 76.50 W
Westmorland 204 33.02 N 115.37 W
Westmount 206 45.29 N 73.36 W
West Mountain ∧ 188 43.51 N 74.43 W
West Mud Creek ≃ 222 32.07 N 95.10 W
West Mustang Creek ≃ 222 29.04 N 96.26 W
West Nab ∧ 262 53.35 N 1.53 W
West Nanticoke 210 40.13 N 76.01 W
West New Britain □[5] 164 5.45 S 149.30 E
West Newbury 207 42.48 N 70.59 W
West Newton, Ma., U.S. 283 42.21 N 71.14 W
West Newton, Pa., U.S. 214 40.12 N 79.46 W
West New York 276 40.47 N 74.00 W
West Nicholson 154 21.06 S 29.25 E
West Nishnabotna ≃ 198 40.39 N 95.37 W
West Nodaway ≃ 194 40.38 N 95.01 W
West Norriton 208 40.08 N 75.22 W
West Norwood ◆[8] 260 51.26 N 0.06 W
West Novaya Zemlya Trough ✦[1] 10 73.30 N 50.00 E
West Nueces ≃ 196 29.16 N 99.56 W
West Nyack 210 41.06 N 73.58 W
West Okaw ≃ 219 39.32 N 88.42 W
Weston, Austl. 170 32.49 S 151.28 E
Weston, Malay. 112 5.13 N 115.36 E
Weston, Eng., U.K. 262 53.19 N 2.44 W
Weston, Co., U.S. 200 37.07 N 104.50 W
Weston, Ct., U.S. 207 41.12 N 73.22 W
Weston, Id., U.S. 202 42.02 N 111.58 W
Weston, Ma., U.S. 207 42.22 N 71.18 W
Weston, Mi., U.S. 216 41.46 N 84.06 W
Weston, Mo., U.S. 194 39.24 N 94.54 W
Weston, Ne., U.S. 198 41.11 N 96.44 W
Weston, Oh., U.S. 216 41.20 N 83.47 W
Weston, Or., U.S. 202 45.48 N 118.25 W
Weston, Pa., U.S. 210 40.57 N 76.09 W
Weston, W.V., U.S. 188 39.02 N 80.28 W
Weston □[8] 275b 43.43 N 79.31 W
Westonaria 273d 26.19 S 27.39 E
West Oneonta 210 42.28 N 75.07 W
Westönnen 52 51.33 N 7.58 E
Weston Reservoir ⊜[1] 283 42.21 N 71.18 W
Westons Mill Pond ⊜ 276 40.28 N 74.25 W
Westons Mills 210 42.04 N 78.23 W
Weston-super-Mare 42 51.21 N 2.59 W
Weston upon Trent 42 52.45 N 2.02 W
West Orange, N.J., U.S. 276 40.47 N 74.14 W
West Orange, Tx., U.S. 194 30.05 N 93.46 W
Westover, Md., U.S. 208 38.07 N 75.42 W
Westover, Pa., U.S. 214 40.45 N 78.40 W
Westover, Tn., U.S. 194 35.36 N 88.52 W
Westover, W.V., U.S. 188 39.38 N 79.58 W
Westover Air Force Base ■ 207 42.12 N 72.33 W
Westoverledingen 52 53.10 N 7.28 E
Westowne 284b 39.17 N 76.43 W
West Palm Beach 220 26.42 N 80.03 W
West Palm Beach Canal ≋ 220 26.38 N 80.03 W
West Paris 188 44.19 N 70.34 W
West Park 210 41.48 N 73.58 W
West Paterson 276 40.53 N 74.11 W
West Pawlet 210 43.21 N 73.15 W
West Peckham 260 51.15 N 0.22 E
West Pensacola 194 30.25 N 87.16 W
Westphalia, Ks., U.S. 198 38.10 N 95.29 W
Westphalia, Mi., U.S. 216 42.55 N 84.47 W
Westphalia, Mo., U.S. 219 38.26 N 91.59 W
West Pittsburg, Ca., U.S. 226 38.01 N 121.56 W
West Pittsburg, Pa., U.S. 214 40.55 N 80.21 W
West Pittston 210 41.19 N 75.47 W
West Plains 194 36.43 N 91.51 W
West Point, Ca., U.S. 226 38.23 N 120.31 W
West Point, Ga., U.S. 192 32.52 N 85.11 W
Westpoint, In., U.S. 216 40.21 N 87.03 W
West Point, Ia., U.S. 190 40.43 N 91.27 W
West Point, Ky., U.S. 194 37.59 N 85.56 W
West Point, Ms., U.S. 194 33.36 N 88.39 W
West Point, Ne., U.S. 198 41.50 N 96.42 W
West Point, N.Y., U.S. 210 41.23 N 73.57 W
West Point, Oh., U.S. 214 40.43 N 80.42 W
West Point, Pa., U.S. 285 40.12 N 75.18 W
West Point, Va., U.S. 208 37.31 N 76.47 W
West Point ∧ 180 64.57 N 144.40 W
West Point ➤, Austl. 166 35.01 S 135.57 E
West Point ➤, P.E., Can. 186 46.37 N 64.25 W
West Point Lake ⊜[1] 192 33.00 N 85.10 W
West Pond ⊜ 276 40.53 N 73.38 W
Westport, Nf., Can. 186 49.47 N 56.38 W
Westport, N.S., Can. 186 44.16 N 66.21 W
Westport, On., Can. 212 44.41 N 76.26 W
Westport, Ire. 48 53.48 N 9.32 W
Westport, N.Z. 172 41.45 S 171.36 E
Westport, Ct., U.S. 207 41.08 N 73.21 W
Westport, In., U.S. 218 39.10 N 85.34 W
Westport, Ky., U.S. 218 38.28 N 85.28 W
Westport, Ma., U.S. 207 41.37 N 71.04 W
Westport, Or., U.S. 224 46.07 N 123.22 W
Westport, Pa., U.S. 214 41.18 N 77.51 W
Westport, Wa., U.S. 224 46.53 N 124.06 W
West Portland 224 45.25 N 122.45 W
West Portland Park 224 45.21 N 122.37 W
Westport Point 207 41.31 N 71.04 W
West Portsmouth 218 38.45 N 83.01 W
West Prairie ≃ 182 55.30 N 116.31 W
West Puente Valley 280 34.04 N 117.59 W
West Pullman ◆[8] 278 41.41 N 87.39 W
Westpunt ➤ 241s 12.37 N 70.03 W
West Pymble 274a 33.46 S 151.08 E
West Quoddy Head ➤ 188 44.49 N 66.57 W
West Rand 273d 26.07 S 27.45 E
Westray I 46 59.18 N 3.00 W
Westray Firth ⊔ 46 59.12 N 2.55 W
West Redding 207 41.19 N 73.26 W
Westrem 50 50.58 N 3.52 E
West Richfield 214 41.14 N 81.39 W
West Richland 202 46.18 N 119.20 W
West River ⊂ 208 38.52 N 76.31 W
West Road ≃ 182 53.19 N 122.52 W
West Rosebud Creek ≃ 202 45.29 N 109.27 W
West Roxbury ◆[8] 283 42.17 N 71.09 W
West Rupert 210 43.14 N 73.14 W
West Rutland 188 43.35 N 73.02 W
West Ryde 274a 33.48 S 151.05 E
West Sacramento 226 38.34 N 121.31 W
West Saint Marys ≃ 186 45.15 N 62.04 W
West Saint Modeste 186 51.36 N 56.42 W
West Salem, Il., U.S. 194 38.31 N 88.00 W
West Salem, Oh., U.S. 214 40.58 N 82.06 W
West Salem, Wi., U.S. 190 43.53 N 91.04 W
West Salt Creek ≃ 200 39.13 N 108.54 W
Westsamoa → Western Samoa □[1] 175a 13.55 S 172.00 W
West Sand Lake 210 42.39 N 73.37 W
West Saugerties 210 42.07 N 74.03 W
West Sayville 276 40.43 N 73.05 W
West Sayville County Park ♦ 276 40.43 N 73.06 W
West Scenic Park 220 27.55 N 81.39 W
West Scotia Basin ✦[1] 18 57.00 S 53.00 W
West Seneca 210 42.50 N 78.45 W
West Sepik □[5] 164 4.00 S 141.30 E
West Shoal Lake ⊜ 184 50.20 N 97.41 W
West Siberian Plain → Zapadno-Sibirskaja ravnina ≚ 72 60.00 N 75.00 E
Westsibirisches Flachland → Zapadno-Sibirskaja ravnina ≚ 72 60.00 N 75.00 E
West Side Canal ≋ 226 35.19 N 119.23 W
West Side Tennis Club ♦ 276 40.43 N 73.51 W
West Simsbury 207 41.52 N 72.51 W
West Slope 224 45.29 N 122.45 W
West Spanish Peak ∧ 200 37.23 N 104.59 W
West Springfield, Ma., U.S. 207 42.06 N 72.37 W
West Springfield, Pa., U.S. 214 41.57 N 80.29 W
West Springfield, Va., U.S. 208 38.46 N 77.13 W
West Stewartstown 206 44.59 N 71.31 W
West Stockbridge 207 42.20 N 73.22 W
West Stony Creek ≃ 210 43.15 N 74.13 W
West Suffield 207 41.59 N 72.41 W
West Sunbury 214 41.00 N 79.54 W
West Sussex □[6] 42 50.55 N 0.35 W
West Swanzey 207 42.52 N 72.20 W
West Terre Haute 194 39.27 N 87.27 W
West-Terschelling 52 53.21 N 5.13 E
West Thompson Lake ⊜[1] 207 41.57 N 71.54 W
West Thurrock 260 51.29 N 0.16 E
West Tiana 207 40.52 N 72.33 W
West Tilbury 260 51.29 N 0.24 E
West Tisbury 207 41.22 N 70.40 W
West Toodyay 168a 31.33 S 116.27 E
West Torrens 168b 34.56 S 138.32 E
Westtown, N.Y., U.S. 210 41.20 N 74.32 W
Westtown, Pa., U.S. 285 39.56 N 75.33 W
West Townsend 207 42.40 N 71.44 W
West Turffontein ◆[8] 273d 26.16 S 28.02 E
West Union, Ia., U.S. 190 42.57 N 91.48 W
West Union, Oh., U.S. 218 38.47 N 83.32 W
West Union, W.V., U.S. 188 39.17 N 80.46 W
West Union Creek ≃ 282 37.25 N 122.16 W
West Unity 216 41.35 N 84.26 W
West University Place 222 29.43 N 95.26 W
West Upton 207 42.10 N 71.37 W
Westvale 210 43.02 N 76.13 W
West Valley, Mt., U.S. 202 46.08 N 113.01 W
West Valley, N.Y., U.S. 210 42.24 N 78.37 W
West Valley City 200 40.42 N 111.57 W
West Vancouver 182 49.22 N 123.12 W
West View 214 40.31 N 80.02 W
West View Amusement Park ♦ 279b 40.31 N 80.02 W
Westview Heights 207 41.33 N 73.05 W
Westville, N.S., Can. 186 45.34 N 62.43 W
Westville, In., U.S. 216 41.32 N 86.54 W
Westville, N.H., U.S. 207 42.49 N 71.07 W
Westville, N.J., U.S. 285 39.52 N 75.07 W
Westville, Oh., U.S. 218 40.07 N 83.51 W
Westville, Ok., U.S. 194 35.59 N 94.34 W
Westville, Pa., U.S. 214 41.13 N 78.50 W
Westville Center 206 44.57 N 74.24 W
Westville Grove 285 39.51 N 75.07 W
Westville Lake ⊜[1] 207 42.05 N 72.05 W
Westville Oaks 285 39.51 N 75.08 W
West Virginia □[3], U.S. 178 38.45 N 80.30 W
West Virginia □[3], U.S. 188 38.45 N 80.30 W
West-Vlaanderen □[4] 50 51.00 N 3.00 E
West Walker ≃ 226 38.53 N 119.10 W
West Wallsend 170 32.54 S 151.35 E
Westward Ho90 42 51.02 N 4.15 W
West Wareham 207 41.47 N 70.45 W
West Warren 207 42.12 N 72.14 W
West Warwick 207 41.42 N 71.31 W
West Water ≃ 46 56.47 N 2.38 W
West Webster 210 43.12 N 77.29 W
Westwego 194 29.54 N 90.08 W
West Wellow 42 50.58 N 1.35 W
West Whittier 280 33.59 N 118.03 W
West Wickham ◆[8] 260 51.22 N 0.01 W
West Willington 207 41.52 N 72.18 W
West Willow 216 42.14 N 83.34 W
West Windsor 210 42.06 N 74.46 W
West Winfield, N.Y., U.S. 210 42.53 N 75.11 W
West Winfield, Pa., U.S. 214 40.48 N 79.42 W
Westwold 182 50.28 N 119.45 W
Westwood, Ca., U.S. 204 40.18 N 121.00 W
Westwood, In., U.S. 218 39.55 N 85.25 W
Westwood, Ma., U.S. 207 42.12 N 71.14 W
Westwood, Mi., U.S. 216 42.18 N 85.38 W
Westwood, N.J., U.S. 210 40.59 N 74.01 W
Westwood, Pa., U.S. 214 40.18 N 78.56 W
Westwood ◆[8] 280 34.04 N 118.27 W
Westwood Lakes 220 25.44 N 80.22 W
Westworth Village 222 32.45 N 97.25 W
West Wyalong 166 33.55 S 147.13 E
West Wycombe 42 51.39 N 0.49 W
West Yarmouth 207 41.39 N 70.14 W
West Yegua Creek ≃ 222 30.20 N 96.52 W
West Yellow Creek ≃ 194 39.38 N 93.04 W
West Yellowstone 202 44.39 N 111.06 W
West York 208 39.57 N 76.45 W
West Yorkshire □[6] 44 53.45 N 1.40 W
Wetan, Pulau I 164 7.54 S 129.32 E
Wetar, Pulau I 112 7.48 S 126.18 E
Wetar, Selat ⊔ 112 8.20 S 126.30 E
Wetaskiwin 182 52.58 N 113.22 W
Wete 154 5.04 S 39.43 E
Wethau 54 51.08 N 11.52 E
Wetherby 44 53.56 N 1.23 W
Wetherill Park 274a 33.51 S 150.54 E
Wethersfield 207 41.43 N 72.40 W
Wethmar 263 51.37 N 7.33 E
Wetiko Hills ⋀⋀[2] 184 54.30 N 92.20 W
Wetluga → Vetluga ≃ 80 56.18 N 46.24 E
Wetmore 198 39.38 N 95.48 W
Wet Mountains ⋀⋀ 200 38.00 N 105.10 W
Weto 152 7.57 N 7.50 E
Wetten 52 51.34 N 6.17 E
Wetter, Dtsch. 56 50.54 N 8.43 E
Wetter, Dtsch. 56 51.23 N 7.23 E
Wetter ≃ 56 50.18 N 8.49 E
Wetterau □[9] 56 50.15 N 8.50 E
Wetteren 50 51.00 N 3.53 E
Wetterhorn ∧ 58 46.39 N 8.08 E
Wetterstein Gebirge ⋀⋀ 64 47.25 N 11.05 E
Wettigan 110 18.57 N 95.21 E
Wettin 54 51.35 N 11.48 E
Wettingen 58 47.28 N 8.19 E
Wettringen 52 52.12 N 7.19 E
Wetumka 196 35.14 N 96.14 W
Wetumpka 194 32.32 N 86.12 W
Wetwang 44 54.01 N 0.34 W
Wetzikon 58 47.19 N 8.47 E
Wetzlar 56 50.33 N 8.29 E
Wetzstein ∧[2] 54 50.27 N 11.27 E
Wevelgem 50 50.48 N 3.10 E
Wevelinghoven 56 51.06 N 6.37 E
Wewahitchka 192 30.06 N 85.12 W
Wewak 164 3.35 S 143.40 E
Wewelsfleth 52 53.50 N 9.24 E
Wewer 52 51.41 N 8.42 E
Wewoka 196 35.09 N 96.29 W
Wexford, Ire. 48 52.20 N 6.27 W
Wexford, Pa., U.S. 214 40.38 N 80.03 W
Wexford □[6] 48 52.20 N 6.40 W
Wexford ◆[8] 275b 43.45 N 79.18 W
Wexford Harbour ⊂ 48 52.20 N 6.24 W
Wey ≃ 42 51.23 N 0.28 W
Weyakwin Lake ⊜ 184 54.30 N 106.00 W
Weyanoke 284c 38.48 N 77.09 W
Weyarn 64 47.51 N 11.48 E
Weyauwega 190 44.19 N 88.56 W
Weybridge 42 51.23 N 0.28 W
Weyburn 184 49.41 N 103.52 W
Weyer ◆[8] 263 51.10 N 7.01 E
Weyer Markt 61 47.52 N 14.41 E
Weyersheim 56 48.43 N 7.48 E
Weyhausen 52 52.47 N 10.23 E
Weyhe 52 52.59 N 8.52 E
Weymouth, N.S., Can. 186 44.25 N 66.00 W
Weymouth, Eng., U.K. 42 50.36 N 2.28 W
Weymouth, Ma., U.S. 207 42.13 N 70.56 W
Weymouth, N.J., U.S. 208 39.30 N 74.46 W
Weymouth, Cape ➤ 164 12.37 S 143.27 E
Weymouth Back ≃ 283 42.15 N 70.55 W
Weymouth Fore ≃ 283 42.16 N 70.56 W
Weymouth Great Pond ⊜ 283 42.12 N 71.02 W
Wezemaal 56 50.57 N 4.46 E
Wezep 52 52.27 N 6.00 E
Whakatane 172 37.58 S 177.00 E
Whakatane ≃ 172 37.57 S 177.00 E
Whalan 274a 33.45 S 150.49 E
Whale Creek ≃ 276 40.27 N 74.13 W

Symbols in the index entries represent the broad categories identified in the key at the right. Symbols with superior numbers (⋀⋀[1]) identify subcategories (see complete key on page *I · 1).*

Symbole im Register stellen die rechts im Schlüssel erklärten Kategorien dar. Symbole mit hochgestellten Ziffern (⋀⋀[1]) bezeichnen Unterabteilungen einer Kategorie (vgl. vollständiger Schlüssel auf Seite *I · 1).*

Los símbolos incluídos en el texto del índice representan las grandes categorias identificadas con la clave a la derecha. Los símbolos con numeros en su parte superior (⋀⋀[1]) identifican las subcategorías (véase la clave completa en la página *I · 1).*

Les symboles de l'index représentent les catégories indiquées dans la légende à droite. Les symboles suivis d'un indice (⋀⋀[1]) représentent des sous-catégories (voir légende complète à la page *I · 1).*

Os símbolos incluídos no texto do índice representam as grandes categorias identificadas com a chave à direita. Os símbolos com números em sua parte superior (⋀⋀[1]) identificam as subcategorias (veja-se a chave completa à página *I · 1).*

	English	Deutsch	Español	Français	Português
∧	Mountain	Berg	Montaña	Montagne	Montanha
⋀⋀	Mountains	Gebirge	Montañas	Montagnes	Montanhas
)(	Pass	Paß	Paso	Col	Passo
V	Valley, Canyon	Tal, Cañon	Valle, Cañón	Vallée, Canyon	Vale, Canhão
≚	Plain	Ebene	Llano	Plaine	Planície
➤	Cape	Kap	Cabo	Cap	Cabo
I	Island	Insel	Isla	Île	Ilha
II	Islands	Inseln	Islas	Îles	Ilhas
⊥	Other Topographic Features	Andere Topographische Objekte	Otros Elementos Topográficos	Autres données topographiques	Outros acidentes topográficos

Whaley Bridge 44 53.20 N 1.59 W
Whaley Lake 210 41.33 N 73.40 W
Whaleysville 208 38.23 N 75.18 W
Whaleyville 208 36.37 N 76.41 W
Whalley 44 53.50 N 2.24 W
Whalom 207 42.34 N 71.44 W
Whalsay I 46a 60.20 N 0.59 W
Whangaehu ≃ 172 40.03 S 175.06 E
Whangamata 172 37.12 S 175.52 E
Whangamomona 172 39.09 S 174.44 E
Whanganui National Park ♦ 172 39.20 S 175.00 E
Whangara 172 38.34 S 178.13 E
Whangarei 172 35.43 S 174.19 E
Whangaruru Harbour c 172 35.22 S 174.21 E
Whaplode 42 52.48 N 0.02 W
Wharfe ≃ 44 53.51 N 1.07 W
Wharfedale V 44 54.01 N 1.56 W
Wharles 262 53.49 N 2.50 W
Wharton, N.J., U.S. 210 40.53 N 74.34 W
Wharton, Oh., U.S. 214 40.52 N 83.21 W
Wharton, Tx., U.S. 222 29.18 N 96.06 W
Wharton, W.V., U.S. 188 37.54 N 81.40 W
Wharton □6 222 29.17 N 96.13 W
Wharton Basin ≁1 12 21.00 S 100.00 E
Wharton Lake ⊜ 176 64.00 N 99.55 W
Wharton State Forest ♦ 285 39.45 N 74.40 W
Whataroa 172 43.17 S 170.25 E
Whatatutu 172 38.23 S 177.50 E
What Cheer 190 41.24 N 92.21 W
Whatcom □6 224 48.48 N 121.59 W
Whatcom, Lake ⊜ 224 48.43 N 122.20 W
Whately 207 42.26 N 72.38 W
Whatley 194 31.39 N 87.42 W
Whatshan Lake ⊜ 182 50.00 N 118.03 W
Whauphill 44 54.49 N 4.29 W
Wheao ≃ 172 38.34 S 176.39 E
Wheatfield 216 40.33 N 87.06 W
Wheathampstead 42 51.49 N 0.17 W
Wheatland, Ca., U.S. 226 39.00 N 121.25 W
Wheatland, Ia., U.S. 190 41.49 N 90.50 W
Wheatland, In., U.S. 214 41.12 N 80.28 W
Wheatland, Wy., U.S. 200 42.03 N 104.57 W
Wheatland Hills 208 40.02 N 76.21 W
Wheatland Reservoir ⊜1 200 41.52 N 105.36 W
Wheatley, On., Can. 214 42.06 N 82.27 W
Wheatley, Eng., U.K. 42 51.44 N 1.08 W
Wheatley, Ar., U.S. 194 34.54 N 91.06 W
Wheatley Hill 44 54.45 N 1.23 W
Wheaton, Il., U.S. 216 41.51 N 88.06 W
Wheaton, Md., U.S. 208 39.02 N 77.03 W
Wheaton, Mn., U.S. 198 45.48 N 96.29 W
Wheaton Plaza ≁9 284c 39.02 N 77.03 W
Wheaton Regional Park ♦ 284c 39.03 N 77.02 W
Wheat Ridge 200 39.45 N 105.04 W
Wheelbarrow Peak ∧ 204 37.27 N 116.05 W
Wheeler, In., U.S. 216 41.30 N 87.10 W
Wheeler, Ms., U.S. 194 34.34 N 88.36 W
Wheeler, Tx., U.S. 196 35.26 N 100.16 W
Wheeler ≃, P.Q., Can. 176 57.02 N 67.13 W
Wheeler ≃, Sk., Can. 184 57.20 N 105.30 W
Wheeler Air Force Base ■ 229c 21.29 N 158.03 W
Wheeler Dam ≁6 283 42.48 N 71.12 W
Wheeler Island I 282 38.05 N 121.56 W
Wheeler Lake ⊜1 194 34.40 N 87.05 W
Wheeler Peak ∧, Ca., U.S. 226 38.25 N 119.17 W
Wheeler Peak ∧, Nv., U.S. 204 38.59 N 114.19 W
Wheeler Peak ∧, N.M., U.S. 200 36.34 N 105.25 W
Wheeler Ridge 228 35.06 N 119.01 W
Wheelersburg 218 38.43 N 82.51 W
Wheelers Hill 274b 37.55 S 145.11 E
Wheeling, Il., U.S. 216 42.08 N 87.55 W
Wheeling, W.V., U.S. 214 40.03 N 80.43 W
Wheeling Creek ≃ 214 40.03 N 80.41 W
Wheelock 222 30.54 N 96.24 W
Wheelock ≃ 44 53.12 N 2.26 W
Wheelton 262 53.41 N 2.36 W
Wheelwright, Arg. 252 33.47 S 61.13 W
Wheelwright, Ky., U.S. 192 37.19 N 82.43 W
Wheelwright Park ♦ 283 42.15 N 70.49 W
Wheeny Creek ≃ 170 33.26 S 150.50 E
Whela Creek ≃ 162 26.17 S 116.50 E
Whelan, Mount ∧2 166 23.25 S 138.54 E
Whelpeyhill 260 51.44 N 0.33 W
Whernside ∧ 44 54.14 N 2.23 W
Whetstone Creek ≃ 214 40.23 N 83.03 W
Whetstone Gulf State Park ♦ 212 43.44 N 75.27 W
Whickham 44 54.56 N 1.41 W
Whidbey Island I 224 48.15 N 122.40 W
Whidbey Island Naval Air Station ■ 224 48.17 N 122.37 W
Whiddon Down 42 50.43 N 3.51 W
Whigham 192 30.52 N 84.19 W
Whigville 207 41.43 N 72.56 W
Whim Creek 162 20.50 S 117.50 E
Whinham, Mount ∧ 162 26.04 S 130.15 E
Whippany 210 40.49 N 74.25 W
Whippany ≃ 276 40.51 N 74.21 W
Whirl Creek ≃ 212 43.28 N 81.12 W
Whirlwind Reefs ≁2 164 4.42 S 148.16 E
Whiskey Peak ∧ 200 42.18 N 107.35 W
Whiskeytown-Shasta-Trinity National Recreation Area ♦ 204 40.45 N 122.15 W
Whisky Chitto Creek ≃ 194 30.31 N 92.55 W
Whiston 262 53.25 N 2.50 W
Whitacres 207 41.48 N 72.29 W
Whitaker 279b 40.24 N 79.53 W
Whitakers 192 36.06 N 77.42 W
Whitbourne 186 47.25 N 53.32 W
Whitburn, Eng., U.K. 44 54.57 N 1.22 W
Whitburn, Scot., U.K. 46 55.52 N 3.42 W
Whitby, On., Can. 212 43.52 N 78.56 W
Whitby, Eng., U.K. 44 54.29 N 0.37 W
Whitby, Eng., U.K. 262 53.17 N 2.54 W
Whitby Abbey ⊥1 44 54.28 N 0.38 W
Whitchurch, Eng., U.K. 42 51.53 N 0.51 W
Whitchurch, Eng., U.K. 42 51.14 N 1.20 W
Whitchurch, Eng., U.K. 42 51.52 N 2.39 W
Whitchurch, Eng., U.K. 42 52.58 N 2.41 W
Whitchurch-Stouffville 212 43.58 N 79.15 W
Whitcombe, Mount ∧ 172 43.13 S 170.55 E
White, Ga., U.S. 192 34.16 N 84.44 W
White, S.D., U.S. 198 44.26 N 96.38 W
White □6 216 40.45 N 86.46 W
White ≃, B.C., Can. 182 50.23 N 115.35 W
White ≃, On., Can. 190 48.33 N 86.16 W
White ≃, N.A. 180 63.11 N 139.36 W
White ≃, U.S. 194 33.53 N 91.03 W
White ≃, U.S. 198 43.45 N 99.30 W
White ≃, U.S. 200 40.04 N 109.41 W
White ≃, Az., U.S. 200 33.44 N 110.13 W
White ≃, In., U.S. 194 38.25 N 87.44 W
White ≃, Mi., U.S. 190 43.25 N 86.21 W
White ≃, Nv., U.S. 204 37.42 N 115.10 W
White ≃, Or., U.S. 224 45.14 N 121.04 W
White ≃, Tx., U.S. 196 33.14 N 100.56 W
White ≃, Vt., U.S. 188 43.37 N 72.20 W
White ≃, Wa., U.S. 224 47.12 N 122.15 W
White ≃, Wa., U.S. 224 47.50 N 120.49 W
White ≃, Wi., U.S. 190 46.36 N 90.42 W
White ≃, Wi., U.S. 216 42.41 N 88.17 W
White, East Fork ≃, Az., U.S. 200 33.47 N 110.00 W
White, East Fork ≃, In., U.S. 194 38.33 N 87.14 W
White, Lake ⊜ 162 21.05 S 129.00 E
White, Lake ⊜1 218 39.07 N 83.02 W
White, North Fork ≃, Az., U.S. 200 33.47 N 110.00 W
White, North Fork ≃, Co., U.S. 200 39.58 N 107.38 W
White, South Fork ≃ 200 39.58 N 107.38 W
White, West Fork ≃ 224 47.07 N 121.37 W
White Bay c 186 50.00 N 56.30 W
White Bear Indian Reserve ≁4 184 49.45 N 102.15 W
White Bear Lake 190 45.03 N 93.00 W
Whitebear Lake ⊜ 184 51.05 N 108.05 W
White Bluff 194 36.06 N 87.13 W
White Breast Creek ≃ 190 41.24 N 93.02 W
White Butte ∧ 198 46.23 N 103.19 W
Whitecap Lake ⊜ 184 56.54 N 95.14 W
White Cap Mountain ∧ 188 45.35 N 69.13 W
White Castle 194 30.10 N 91.08 W
White Center 224 47.31 N 122.21 W
White Chuck ≃ 224 48.11 N 121.27 W
White City, Fl., U.S. 220 29.53 N 85.13 W
White City, Ks., U.S. 198 38.47 N 96.44 W
White City Stadium ♦ 260 51.31 N 0.14 W
White Clay Creek ≃, U.S. 198 43.12 N 102.48 W
White Clay Creek ≃, U.S. 285 39.42 N 75.37 W
White Cliffs, Austl. 162 28.26 S 122.57 E
White Cliffs, Austl. 166 30.51 S 143.05 E
White Cloud 190 43.33 N 85.46 W
White Cloud Island I 212 44.50 N 80.58 W
Whitecombe ∧, N.Z. 172 45.36 S 169.05 E
White Coomb ∧, Scot., U.K. 44 55.26 N 3.20 W
Whitecourt 182 54.09 N 115.41 W
White Creek 210 42.58 N 73.18 W
White Creek ≃, In., U.S. 218 38.58 N 86.01 W
White Creek ≃, Wa., U.S. 224 46.01 N 121.08 W
White Deer, Pa., U.S. 210 41.05 N 76.52 W
White Deer, Tx., U.S. 196 35.26 N 101.10 W
White Deer Creek ≃ 210 41.05 N 76.53 W
White Earth ≃ 198 48.09 N 102.42 W
White Earth Indian Reservation ≁4 198 47.18 N 95.50 W
White Esk ≃ 44 55.12 N 3.10 W
Whiteface 196 33.36 N 102.37 W
Whiteface ≃ 190 46.58 N 92.48 W
Whiteface Mountain ∧ 188 44.22 N 73.54 W
Whitefield, Eng., U.K. 44 53.33 N 2.18 W
Whitefield, Eng., U.K. 262 53.33 N 2.18 W
Whitefield, N.H., U.S. 188 44.22 N 71.36 W
Whitefish 202 48.24 N 114.20 W
Whitefish ≃ 190 45.55 N 86.57 W
Whitefish Bay 216 43.06 N 87.54 W
Whitefish Bay c, On., Can. 184 49.26 N 94.14 W
Whitefish Bay c, N.A. 190 46.40 N 84.50 W
Whitefish Lake ⊜, Ab., Can. 182 54.22 N 111.55 W
Whitefish Lake ⊜, Mb., Can. 184 55.34 N 93.13 W
Whitefish Lake ⊜, N.T., Can. 176 62.41 N 106.48 W
Whitefish Lake ⊜, On., Can. 190 48.03 N 84.29 W
Whitefish Lake ⊜, On., Can. 212 45.18 N 79.47 W
Whitefish Lake ⊜, On., Can. 212 44.31 N 76.14 W
Whitefish Lake ⊜, Ak., U.S. 180 61.21 N 160.00 W
Whitefish Lake ⊜, Mt., U.S. 202 48.27 N 114.22 W
White Fish Lake Indian Reserve ≁4 182 54.20 N 111.45 W
Whitefish Point 190 46.45 N 84.59 W
Whitefish Point ▶ 190 46.45 N 85.00 W
Whitefish Range ∧ 202 48.40 N 114.26 W
Whiteford 208 39.42 N 76.20 W
Whiteford Point ▶ 42 51.38 N 4.14 W
White Fox 184 53.27 N 104.05 W
White Fox ≃ 184 53.32 N 104.00 W
Whitegate 48 51.50 N 8.14 W
White Gull Creek ≃ 184 53.44 N 104.20 W
Whitehall (Paulstown), Ire. 48 52.41 N 7.01 W
Whitehall, Scot., U.K. 46 59.07 N 2.37 W
White Hall, Ar., U.S. 194 34.16 N 92.05 W
White Hall, Il., U.S. 219 39.26 N 90.24 W
White Hall, Md., U.S. 208 39.37 N 76.37 W
Whitehall, Mi., U.S. 190 43.24 N 86.20 W
Whitehall, Mt., U.S. 202 45.52 N 112.05 W
Whitehall, N.Y., U.S. 188 43.33 N 73.24 W
Whitehall, Oh., U.S. 218 39.58 N 82.53 W
Whitehall, Pa., U.S. 214 40.21 N 79.59 W
Whitehall, Wi., U.S. 190 44.22 N 91.18 W
Whitehaven, Eng., U.K. 44 54.33 N 3.35 W
White Haven, Pa., U.S. 210 41.03 N 75.46 W
Whitehead 48 54.46 N 5.43 W
White Holme Reservoir ⊜1 262 53.41 N 2.02 W
Whitehorse, Yk., Can. 180 60.43 N 135.03 W
White Horse, N.J., U.S. 208 40.11 N 74.42 W
White Horse, Vale of V 42 51.37 N 1.37 W
Whitehorse Hill ∧2 42 51.34 N 1.34 W
Whitehouse, Scot., U.K. 46 57.13 N 2.37 W
Whitehouse, N.J., U.S. 210 40.37 N 74.46 W
Whitehouse, Oh., U.S. 216 41.31 N 83.48 W
White House, Tn., U.S. 194 36.35 N 86.49 W
Whitehouse, Tx., U.S. 222 32.13 N 95.14 W
White House ≁ 284c 38.54 N 77.02 W
White House Station 210 40.36 N 74.46 W
White Island I, Ant. 9 66.44 S 48.35 E
White Island I, N.T., Can. 176 65.50 N 84.50 W
White Island I, N.Z. 172 37.31 S 177.11 E
White Lake, Mi., U.S. 281 42.41 N 83.33 W
White Lake, N.Y., U.S. 210 41.40 N 74.50 W
White Lake, S.D., U.S. 198 43.43 N 98.42 W
White Lake, Wi., U.S. 190 45.09 N 88.45 W
White Lake ⊜, On., Can. 190 48.48 N 85.36 W
White Lake ⊜, On., Can. 212 44.47 N 76.45 W
White Lake ⊜, On., Can. 212 44.27 N 77.03 W
White Lake ⊜, On., Can. 212 45.18 N 76.31 W
White Lake ⊜, La., U.S. 194 29.45 N 92.30 W
White Lake ⊜, Mi., U.S. 281 42.40 N 83.34 W
Whiteland 218 39.33 N 86.05 W
Whitelaw 182 56.07 N 118.04 W
Whiteley Village 260 51.21 N 0.26 W
White Lick Creek ≃ 218 39.30 N 86.23 W
White Lick Creek, East Fork ≃ 218 39.35 N 86.22 W
White Lick Creek, West Fork ≃ 218 39.38 N 86.23 W
Whiteman Air Force Base ■ 194 38.44 N 93.34 W
Whiteman Airpark ≋ 280 34.15 N 118.25 W
Whiteman Range ∧ 164 5.50 S 149.55 E
Whitemans Creek ≃ 212 43.10 N 80.21 W
Whitemark 166 40.07 S 148.01 E
White Marsh 284b 39.23 N 76.26 W
Whitemarsh Run ≃ 284b 39.22 N 76.25 W
White Meadow Lake 210 40.55 N 74.31 W
White Meadow Lake ⊜ 276 40.55 N 74.31 W
White Mills 210 41.32 N 75.12 W
White Mountain 180 64.41 N 163.24 W
White Mountain Peak ∧ 204 37.38 N 118.15 W
White Mountains ∧, U.S. 204 37.30 N 118.15 W
White Mountains ∧, Az., U.S. 200 33.45 N 109.40 W
White Mountains ∧, N.H., U.S. 188 44.10 N 71.35 W
Whitemouth 184 49.57 N 95.59 W
Whitemouth ≃ 184 50.07 N 96.02 W
Whitemouth Lake ⊜ 184 49.14 N 95.40 W
Whitemud ≃ 184 50.15 N 98.37 W
Whiten Head ▶ 46 58.34 N 4.36 W
White Nile (Al-Bahr al-Abyaḍ) ≃ 140 15.38 N 32.31 E
White Nile Dam — Jabal al-Awliyā', Khazzān ≁6 140 15.14 N 32.29 E
White Oak, Md., U.S. 284c 39.02 N 77.00 W
White Oak, Pa., U.S. 279b 40.20 N 79.48 W
White Oak, Tx., U.S. 222 32.32 N 94.52 W
White Oak ≃ 192 34.40 N 77.07 W
White Oak Creek ≃, Oh., U.S. 218 38.47 N 83.57 W
White Oak Creek ≃, Tx., U.S. 194 33.16 N 94.39 W
White Oak Creek, East Fork ≃ 218 39.00 N 83.53 W
White Oak Creek, North Fork ≃ 218 39.00 N 83.53 W
White Oak Lake ⊜1 194 33.40 N 93.10 W
White Oak Regional Park ♦ 279a 40.21 N 79.47 W
White Pass ⤫, N.A. 180 59.38 N 135.05 W
White Pass ⤫, Wa., U.S. 224 46.38 N 121.24 W
White Pigeon 216 41.47 N 85.38 W
White Pine, Mi., U.S. 190 46.45 N 89.35 W
Whitepine, Mt., U.S. 182 47.45 N 115.29 W
White Pine, Tn., U.S. 192 36.06 N 83.17 W
White Pines, Ca., U.S. 226 38.18 N 120.21 W
White Pines, Il., U.S. 278 41.57 N 87.57 W
White Plains, Md., U.S. 208 38.35 N 76.56 W
White Plains, N.Y., U.S. 210 41.02 N 73.45 W
White Plains, N.C., U.S. 192 36.26 N 80.38 W
White Pond ⊜ 283 42.26 N 71.23 W
White River, On., Can. 190 48.35 N 85.15 W
Whiteriver, Az., U.S. 200 33.50 N 109.57 W
White River, S.D., U.S. 198 43.34 N 100.44 W
White River Junction 188 43.38 N 72.19 W
White Rock 224 49.02 N 122.49 W
White Rock Creek ≃, Ks., U.S. 198 39.55 N 97.51 W
White Rock Creek ≃, Tx., U.S. 222 30.54 N 95.16 W
White Rock Creek ≃, Tx., U.S. 222 32.43 N 96.44 W
White Rock Lake ⊜1 222 32.50 N 96.44 W
White Rocks ∧ 192 36.40 N 83.27 W
Whiterocks ≃ 200 40.26 N 109.55 W
White Roding 260 51.48 N 0.16 E
White Russia — Belarus □1 22 53.50 N 28.00 E
Whitesail Lake ⊜ 182 53.30 N 127.00 W
White Salmon 224 45.43 N 121.29 W
White Salmon ≃ 224 45.43 N 121.31 W
Whitesand ≃ 184 51.34 N 101.55 W
White Sands Beach 207 41.18 N 72.09 W
White Sands Missile Range ■ 200 32.23 N 106.28 W
White Sands National Monument ♦ 200 32.46 N 106.20 W
Whitesboro, N.J., U.S. 208 39.02 N 74.51 W
Whitesboro, N.Y., U.S. 210 43.07 N 75.17 W
Whitesboro, Tx., U.S. 196 33.39 N 96.54 W
Whitesburg 192 37.07 N 82.49 W
White Sea — Beloje more ▾2 24 65.30 N 38.00 E
White Settlement 222 32.45 N 97.27 W
Whiteshell Provincial Park ♦ 184 50.00 N 95.25 W
Whiteside 219 39.11 N 91.01 W
Whiteside, Canal ⵍ 254 53.55 S 70.15 W
White's Landing 214 41.25 N 82.54 W
White Springs 192 30.19 N 82.45 W
White Stone 208 37.38 N 76.23 W
Whitestone ≁8 276 40.47 N 73.49 W
White Stone Lake ⊜ 184 56.25 N 97.31 W
Whitestown 218 39.59 N 86.20 W
White Sulphur Springs, Mt., U.S. 202 46.32 N 110.54 W
White Sulphur Springs, N.Y., U.S. 210 41.48 N 74.50 W
White Sulphur Springs, W.V., U.S. 192 37.47 N 80.17 W
Whites Valley 210 41.42 N 75.22 W
Whitesville, Ky., U.S. 194 37.40 N 86.52 W
Whitesville, N.Y., U.S. 210 42.02 N 77.45 W
Whitesville, W.V., U.S. 188 37.58 N 81.31 W
White Swan 224 46.22 N 120.43 W
Whiteswan Lakes ⊜ 184 54.05 N 105.10 W
Whiteside 212 44.23 N 79.09 W
White Valley 214 40.25 N 79.36 W
Whiteville, N.C., U.S. 192 34.20 N 78.42 W
Whiteville, Tn., U.S. 194 35.19 N 89.08 W
White Volta (Volta Blanche) ≃ 150 9.10 N 1.15 W
Whitewater, Ks., U.S. 198 37.57 N 97.08 W
Whitewater, Mt., U.S. 202 48.45 N 107.37 W
Whitewater, Wi., U.S. 216 42.50 N 88.43 W
Whitewater ≃, In., U.S. 218 39.10 N 84.47 W
Whitewater ≃, Ca., U.S. 204 33.30 N 116.03 W
Whitewater ≃, Mo., U.S. 194 37.01 N 89.43 W
Whitewater, Dry Fork ≃ 218 39.11 N 84.47 W
Whitewater, East Fork ≃ 218 39.24 N 85.01 W
Whitewater, Greens Fork ≃ 218 39.45 N 85.07 W
Whitewater, Nolands Fork ≃ 218 39.41 N 85.07 W
Whitewater Baldy ∧ 200 33.20 N 108.39 W
Whitewater Bay c 220 25.16 N 81.00 W
Whitewater Creek ≃, N.A. 202 48.30 N 107.11 W
Whitewater Creek ≃, Ga., U.S. 192 32.21 N 84.03 W
Whitewater Creek ≃, Wi., U.S. 216 42.52 N 88.45 W
Whitewater Lake ⊜, Mb., Can. 184 49.15 N 100.20 W
Whitewater Lake ⊜, Wi., U.S. 216 42.47 N 88.42 W
Whitewater State Park ♦ 218 39.36 N 84.58 W
White Woman Creek ≃ 198 38.25 N 100.54 W
Whitewood, Austl. 166 21.28 S 143.36 E
Whitewood, Sk., Can. 184 50.20 N 102.15 W
Whitewood, S.D., U.S. 198 44.27 N 103.38 W
Whitewood, Lake ⊜ 198 44.20 N 97.18 W
Whitewright 196 33.30 N 96.23 W
Whitfield 42 51.09 N 1.18 E
Whithorn, Jam. 241q 18.15 N 78.02 W
Whithorn, Scot., U.K. 44 54.44 N 4.25 W
Whitianga 172 36.50 S 175.42 E
Whiting, In., U.S. 216 41.40 N 87.29 W
Whiting, Ia., U.S. 198 42.07 N 96.08 W
Whiting, Ks., U.S. 198 39.35 N 95.36 W
Whiting, N.J., U.S. 208 39.57 N 74.22 W
Whiting, Wi., U.S. 190 44.29 N 89.33 W
Whiting Bay 44 55.29 N 5.06 W
Whiting Field Naval Air Station ■ 194 30.43 N 87.02 W
Whitingham 207 42.47 N 72.53 W
Whitinsville 207 42.06 N 71.40 W
Whitland 42 51.50 N 4.37 W
Whitley □6 216 41.10 N 85.29 W
Whitley Bay 44 55.03 N 1.25 W
Whitley City 192 36.43 N 84.28 W
Whitley Row 260 51.15 N 0.06 E
Whitman 207 42.04 N 70.56 W
Whitman Mission National Historic Site ⊥ 202 46.01 N 118.30 W
Whitmans Pond ⊜ 283 42.12 N 70.57 W
Whitman Square 208 39.45 N 75.03 W
Whitmire 192 34.30 N 81.36 W
Whitmore Lake 216 42.25 N 83.46 W
Whitmore Lake ⊜ 281 42.26 N 83.45 W
Whitmore Mountains ∧ 9 82.35 S 104.30 W
Whitmore Village 229c 21.30 N 158.01 W
Whitney Heights 226 36.37 N 119.32 W
Whitney, On., Can. 212 45.30 N 78.14 W
Whitney, Pa., U.S. 214 40.15 N 79.24 W
Whitney, Tx., U.S. 222 31.57 N 97.19 W
Whitney, Lake ⊜1 222 31.55 N 97.23 W
Whitney, Mount ∧ 204 36.35 N 118.18 W
Whitney Point 210 42.19 N 75.58 W
Whitney Point Lake ⊜1 210 42.25 N 75.55 W
Whitney Woods Reservation ♦ 283 42.13 N 70.51 W
Whitstable 42 51.22 N 1.02 E
Whitsunday Island I 166 20.17 S 148.59 E
Whittaker 216 42.08 N 83.36 W
Whittemore, Ia., U.S. 198 43.03 N 94.25 W
Whittemore, Mi., U.S. 190 44.14 N 83.48 W
Whittier, Ak., U.S. 180 60.47 N 148.42 W
Whittier, Ca., U.S. 228 33.58 N 118.01 W
Whittier, N.C., U.S. 192 35.26 N 83.22 W
Whittier Narrows Dam ≁6 280 34.01 N 118.04 W
Whittier Narrows Flood Control Basin ⊜1 280 34.02 N 118.04 W
Whittingham 44 55.24 N 1.54 W
Whittington 42 52.52 N 3.00 W
Whittle, Cap ▶ 186 50.11 N 60.08 W
Whittle Hill ∧2 262 53.40 N 2.16 W
Whittle-le-Woods 262 53.41 N 2.38 W
Whittlesea, Austl. 169 37.31 S 145.07 E
Whittlesea, Ciskei 158 32.10 S 26.50 E
Whittlesey 42 52.34 N 0.08 W
Whittlesey, Mount ∧2 190 46.18 N 90.37 W
Whitwell 194 35.12 N 85.31 W
Whitwick 42 52.44 N 1.21 W
Whitworth 262 53.40 N 2.10 W
Whitworth Peak ∧ 224 49.05 N 121.13 W
Wholdaia Lake ⊜ 176 60.43 N 104.10 W
Whonock 224 49.11 N 122.28 W
W. Howard Frankland Bridge ≁5 220 27.56 N 82.35 W
Whyalla 166 33.02 S 137.35 E
Whycocomagh 186 45.59 N 61.07 W
Whymper, Mount ∧ 224 48.57 N 124.10 W
Wiang Pa Pao 110 19.22 N 99.30 E
Wiang Phan 110 20.26 N 99.53 E
Wiarton 212 44.45 N 81.09 W
Wiasi 150 10.21 N 1.20 W
Wiau Lake ⊜ 182 55.23 N 111.18 W
Wiawso 150 6.12 N 2.29 W
Wiay I 46 57.23 N 7.13 W
Wiązów 30 50.49 N 17.11 E
Wibaux 198 46.59 N 104.11 W
Wiblingen ≁8 58 48.21 N 9.58 E
Wichian Buri 110 15.39 N 101.07 E
Wichita 198 37.41 N 97.20 W
Wichita ≃ 196 34.07 N 98.10 W
Wichita Falls 196 33.54 N 98.29 W
Wichita Mountains ∧ 196 34.45 N 98.40 W
Wichlinghofen ≁8 263 51.27 N 7.30 E
Wick 46 58.26 N 3.06 W
Wick ≃ 46 58.27 N 3.05 W
Wickatunk 276 40.21 N 74.14 W
Wickede 52 51.29 N 7.52 E
Wickede ≁8 263 51.32 N 7.37 E
Wickenburg 200 33.58 N 112.43 W
Wickepin 162 32.46 S 117.30 E
Wicker Memorial Park ♦ 278 41.34 N 87.28 W
Wickett 196 31.34 N 102.59 W
Wickford 42 51.38 N 0.31 E
Wickham, Austl. 162 20.31 S 117.08 E
Wickham, P.Q., Can. 206 45.45 N 72.30 W
Wickham, Eng., U.K. 42 50.54 N 1.10 W
Wickham ≃ 164 16.22 S 131.06 E
Wickham, Cape ▶ 166 39.36 S 143.57 E
Wickham Bishops 260 51.47 N 0.40 E
Wickham Market 42 52.09 N 1.22 E
Wickiup Reservoir ⊜1 202 43.40 N 121.43 W
Wickliffe, Ky., U.S. 194 36.58 N 89.05 W
Wickliffe, Oh., U.S. 214 41.06 N 80.43 W
Wickliffe, Oh., U.S. 214 41.36 N 81.27 W
Wicklow 48 52.59 N 6.03 W
Wicklow □6 48 53.00 N 6.30 W
Wicklow Head ▶ 48 52.58 N 6.00 W
Wicklow Mountains ∧ 48 53.02 N 6.24 W
Wickrath 56 51.07 N 6.24 E
Wicksteed Lake ⊜ 190 46.46 N 79.40 W
Wicomico 208 37.17 N 76.31 W
Wicomico □6 208 38.22 N 75.36 W
Wicomico ≃ 208 38.13 N 75.55 W
Wicomico Church 208 37.49 N 76.23 W
Wiconisco 208 40.34 N 76.41 W
Wiconisco Creek ≃ 208 40.32 N 76.58 W
Wid ≃ 262 51.45 N 0.27 E
Widas ≃ 115a 7.30 S 112.08 E
Widden Brook ≃ 170 32.32 S 150.22 E
Widdern 56 49.19 N 9.25 E
Widdert ≁8 263 51.08 N 7.04 E
Widdop Reservoir ⊜1 262 53.48 N 2.06 W
Widdrington Station 44 55.15 N 1.36 W
Wide Bay c, Pap. N. Gui. 164 5.05 S 152.05 E
Wide Bay c, Ak., U.S. 180 57.20 N 156.25 W
Widecombe in the Moor 42 50.35 N 3.48 W
Widemouth Bay 42 50.47 N 4.32 W
Widen 188 38.27 N 80.51 W
Widener College ⊥2 285 39.52 N 75.21 W
Wide Open 44 55.03 N 1.38 W
Wideree, Mount ∧ 9 72.08 S 23.30 E
Wide Ruin Wash V 200 35.13 N 109.52 W
Widford 260 51.43 N 0.27 E
Widgeegoara Creek ≃ 166 27.30 S 145.55 E
Widgiemooltha 162 31.30 S 121.34 E
Widnes 44 53.22 N 2.44 W
Wi-do I 98 35.36 N 126.17 E
Widodaren 115a 7.25 S 111.14 E
Widuchowa 54 53.10 N 14.25 E
Widur 124 27.55 N 85.10 E
Wiebelskirchen 56 49.22 N 7.11 E
Więcbork 30 53.22 N 17.30 E
Wieck 54 54.06 N 13.26 E
Wied ≃ 56 50.26 N 7.27 E
Wieda 54 51.38 N 10.34 E
Wiederitzsch 54 51.24 N 12.22 E
Wiedlisbach 58 47.15 N 7.39 E
Wiefelstede 52 53.15 N 8.07 E
Wiehe 54 51.16 N 11.25 E
Wiehengebirge ∧ 52 52.20 N 8.40 E
Wiehengebirge, Naturpark ♦ 52 52.20 N 8.20 E
Wiehl 56 50.57 N 7.31 E
Wiek 54 54.37 N 13.17 E
Wieleń 30 52.54 N 16.10 E
Wielichowo 30 52.08 N 16.21 E
Wieliczka 30 49.59 N 20.04 E
Wielkopolska ≁1 30 51.50 N 17.20 E
Wielkopolski Park Narodowy ♦ 30 52.15 N 16.50 E
Wieluń 30 51.14 N 18.34 E
Wiemelhausen ≁8 263 51.28 N 7.13 E
Wien (Vienna), Öst. 61 48.13 N 16.20 E
Wien (Vienna), Öst. 264b 48.13 N 16.20 E
Wien □3 264b 48.12 N 16.22 E
Wien ≃ 264b 48.12 N 16.23 E
Wien, Universität ⊥2 264b 48.13 N 16.22 E
Wiener Berg ∧2 264b 48.10 N 16.22 E
Wienerherberg 264b 48.03 N 16.33 E
Wiener Neudorf 61 48.05 N 16.19 E
Wiener Neustadt 61 47.49 N 16.15 E
Wiener Neustädter Kanal ≡ 61 48.05 N 16.22 E
Wienerwald ∧ 61 48.10 N 16.00 E
Wienhagen ∧2 263 51.08 N 7.33 E
Wienhausen 52 52.35 N 10.11 E
Wien-Schwechat, Flughafen ≋ 264b 48.07 N 16.33 E
Wiepke 54 52.36 N 11.20 E
Wieprz ≃ 30 51.34 N 21.49 E
Wieprza ≃ 30 54.26 N 16.22 E
Wieprz-Krzna, Kanał ≡ 30 51.56 N 22.56 E
Wiera ≃ 56 50.55 N 9.10 E
Wierden 52 52.22 N 6.35 E
Wieren 52 52.53 N 10.39 E
Wiergate 194 31.00 N 93.42 W
Wieringermeer ≁1 52 52.45 N 5.00 E
Wieringerwerf 52 52.51 N 5.02 E
Wieruszów 30 51.18 N 18.08 E
Wierzyca ≃ 30 53.51 N 18.50 E
Wies 61 46.43 N 15.16 E
Wies ⊥1 58 47.40 N 10.53 E
Wiesa 54 50.36 N 13.01 E
Wiesau 60 49.55 N 12.11 E
Wiesbaden 56 50.05 N 8.14 E
Wiesbaden □5 56 50.20 N 8.20 E
Wiescheid ≁8 263 51.08 N 6.59 E
Wiescherhöfen ≁8 263 51.39 N 7.46 E
Wiese ≃ 58 47.35 N 7.35 E
Wiesede 52 53.27 N 7.46 E
Wieselburg 61 48.08 N 15.09 E
Wiesen 58 46.43 N 9.43 E
Wiesenburg 54 52.07 N 12.26 E
Wiesenfeld 56 51.16 N 10.06 E
Wiesensteig 58 48.34 N 9.37 E
Wiesent ≃ 60 49.42 N 11.05 E
Wiesentheid 56 49.47 N 10.20 E
Wieseth ≃ 56 49.10 N 10.39 E
Wiesloch 56 49.17 N 8.42 E
Wiesmoor 52 53.25 N 7.43 E
Wieting 61 46.52 N 14.32 E
Wietmarschen 52 52.31 N 7.07 E
Wietze 52 52.39 N 9.50 E
Wietzen 52 52.43 N 9.04 E
Wigan 44 53.33 N 2.38 W
Wigan □8 262 53.32 N 2.35 W
Wiggensbach 58 47.44 N 10.14 E
Wigger ≃ 58 47.18 N 7.53 E
Wiggington 260 51.47 N 0.38 W
Wiggins, Co., U.S. 198 40.13 N 104.04 W
Wiggins, Ms., U.S. 194 30.51 N 89.08 W
Wiggins Fork ≃ 202 43.27 N 109.28 W
Wigglesworth 44 54.01 N 2.17 W
Wight, Isle of I 42 50.40 N 1.20 W
Wigmore, Eng., U.K. 42 52.19 N 2.51 W
Wigmore, Eng., U.K. 260 51.21 N 0.35 E
Wignehies 50 50.01 N 4.00 E
Wigston 42 52.36 N 1.05 W
Wigton 44 54.49 N 3.09 W
Wigtown 44 54.52 N 4.26 W
Wigtown Bay c 44 54.46 N 4.15 W
Wijalpurā 124 26.55 N 85.51 E
Wijchen 52 51.48 N 5.43 E
Wijhe 52 52.24 N 6.07 E
Wijk aan Zee 52 52.29 N 4.36 E
Wijk bij Duurstede 52 51.58 N 5.20 E
Wil 58 47.27 N 9.03 E
Wilbarger Creek ≃ 222 30.11 N 97.23 W
Wilber 198 40.28 N 96.57 W
Wilberforce, Austl. 170 33.33 S 150.50 E
Wilberforce, Oh., U.S. 218 39.42 N 83.52 W
Wilberforce Falls ▾ 176 67.07 N 108.47 W
Wilbraham 207 42.07 N 72.25 W
Wilbur 202 47.45 N 118.42 W
Wilburton 196 34.55 N 95.18 W
Wilcannia 166 31.34 S 143.23 E
Wilcock, Peninsula ▾1 254 50.40 S 74.00 W
Wilcox, Sk., Can. 184 50.07 N 104.44 W
Wilcox, Ne., U.S. 198 40.21 N 99.10 W
Wilcox, Pa., U.S. 214 41.34 N 78.41 W
Wilcox, Tx., U.S. 222 30.27 N 96.22 W
Wilcox, Mount ∧ 207 42.15 N 73.15 W
Wildalpen 61 47.39 N 14.59 E
Wildau 54 52.19 N 13.38 E
Wildbad im Schwarzwald 56 48.45 N 8.32 E
Wildberg, Dtsch. 54 52.52 N 12.37 E
Wildberg, Dtsch. 56 48.37 N 8.44 E
Wildboarclough 262 53.13 N 2.02 W
Wildcat Canyon Regional Park ♦ 282 37.56 N 122.17 W
Wildcat Creek ≃, Ca., U.S. 282 37.57 N 122.23 W
Wildcat Creek ≃, In., U.S. 216 40.28 N 86.52 W
Wildcat Creek, Middle Fork ≃ 216 40.25 N 86.46 W
Wildcat Creek, South Fork ≃ 216 40.26 N 86.48 W
Wildcat Hill ∧2 184 53.17 N 102.30 W
Wild Coast ∧2 158 32.30 S 28.45 E
Wilde ≁8 288 34.42 S 58.20 W
Wildegg 58 47.25 N 8.11 E
Wildeman ≃ 164 5.33 S 139.13 E
Wildemann 52 51.49 N 10.17 E
Wildenbruch 264a 52.17 N 13.04 E
Wildenfels 54 50.40 N 12.35 E
Wildenstein 58 47.59 N 6.58 E
Wildenthal 54 50.27 N 12.37 E
Wilder 202 43.40 N 116.54 W
Wilderness 158 34.00 S 22.36 E
Wilderness of Judaea (Midbar Yehuda) ≁2 132 31.30 N 35.18 E
Wilderness State Park ♦ 190 45.42 N 84.57 W
Wildersville 194 35.46 N 88.21 W
Wildervank 52 53.04 N 6.51 E
Wildeshausen 52 52.54 N 8.26 E
Wildfield 212 43.49 N 79.44 W
Wildflecken 56 50.23 N 9.54 E
Wildfontein 158 31.04 S 24.50 E
Wildhaus 58 47.12 N 9.22 E
Wildhay ≃ 182 54.02 N 117.20 W
Wildhorn ∧ 58 46.21 N 7.22 E
Wildhorse Creek ≃, U.S. 198 40.36 N 102.00 W
Wildhorse Creek ≃, Ok., U.S. 196 34.32 N 97.10 W
Wild Horse Creek ≃, Wy., U.S. 198 44.39 N 106.08 W
Wild Horse Draw V 196 31.11 N 104.50 W
Wild Horse Hill ∧2 168a 33.12 S 116.40 E
Wild Horse Lake ⊜ 202 48.58 N 110.00 W
Wild Horse Plains 168b 34.22 S 138.17 E
Wildnest Lake ⊜ 184 55.00 N 102.20 W
Wildon 61 46.53 N 15.31 E
Wild Rice ≃, Mn., U.S. 198 47.20 N 96.50 W
Wild Rice ≃, N.D., U.S. 198 46.45 N 96.47 W
Wild Rice, South Branch ≃ 198 47.12 N 96.38 W
Wildrose, N.D., U.S. 198 48.37 N 103.11 W
Wild Rose, Wi., U.S. 190 44.10 N 89.14 W
Wildseeloder ∧ 64 47.26 N 12.32 E
Wildspitze ∧ 58 46.53 N 10.52 E
Wildstrubel ∧ 58 46.24 N 7.32 E
Wildwood, Ab., Can. 182 53.37 N 115.14 W
Wildwood, Fl., U.S. 220 28.51 N 82.02 W
Wildwood, Il., U.S. 216 42.21 N 88.00 W
Wildwood, N.J., U.S. 208 38.59 N 74.48 W
Wildwood, Pa., U.S. 214 40.36 N 79.58 W
Wildwood, Lake ⊜ 276 41.09 N 74.32 W
Wild Wood Beach 284b 39.15 N 76.25 W
Wildwood Canyon Park ♦ 280 34.13 N 118.17 W
Wildwood Crest 208 38.58 N 74.50 W
Wiley 224 46.33 N 120.39 W
Wilfersdorf 61 48.35 N 16.38 E
Wilge ≃, S. Afr. 158 27.03 S 28.20 E
Wilge ≃, S. Afr. 158 25.34 S 29.10 E
Wilgena 162 30.46 S 134.44 E
Wilgespruit ≃ 273d 26.07 S 27.52 E
Wilhelm, Lake ⊜1 214 41.23 N 80.08 W
Wilhelm, Mount ∧ 164 5.45 S 145.05 E
Wilhelmina Gebergte ∧ 250 3.45 N 56.30 W
Wilhelminakanaal ≡ 52 51.47 N 4.51 E
Wilhelminaoord 52 52.53 N 6.10 E
Wilhelmina Peak — Trikora, Puncak ∧ 164 4.15 S 138.45 E
Wilhelmsburg 61 48.06 N 15.36 E
Wilhelmsburg ≁8 52 53.30 N 10.00 E
Wilhelmshaven 52 53.31 N 8.08 E
Wilhelmshöhe, Schloss ⊥ 56 51.21 N 9.22 E
Wilhelmshorst 54 52.19 N 13.03 E
Wilhelmstadt ≁8 264a 52.31 N 13.11 E
Wilhelmstal 156 21.54 S 16.19 E
Wilhelmstein, Schloss ⊥ 52 52.28 N 9.18 E
Wilis, Gunung ∧ 115a 7.52 S 111.48 E
Wilkau-Hasslau 54 50.40 N 12.31 E
Wilkerson Pass ⤫ 200 39.02 N 105.32 W
Wilkes-Barre 210 41.14 N 75.52 W
Wilkes-Barre Scranton Airport ≋ 210 41.20 N 75.45 W
Wilkesboro 192 36.08 N 81.09 W
Wilkes Island I 174a 19.18 N 166.34 E
Wilkes Land ≁1 9 69.00 S 120.00 E
Wilkeson 224 47.06 N 122.02 W
Wilket Creek ≃ 275b 43.43 N 79.21 W
Wilket Creek Park ♦ 275b 43.43 N 79.21 W
Wilkhaven 46 57.52 N 3.45 W
Wilkie 184 52.25 N 108.43 W
Wilkinsburg 279b 40.26 N 79.51 W
Wilkinson 218 39.53 N 85.36 W
Wilkinson Lakes ⊜ 162 29.40 S 132.39 E
Wilkins Sound ⵍ 9 70.15 S 73.00 W
Wilkins Township 279b 40.25 N 79.50 W
Will □6 216 41.32 N 88.05 W
Will, Mount ∧ 180 57.31 N 128.46 W
Willacoochee 192 31.20 N 83.02 W
Willamette ≃ 202 45.39 N 122.46 W
Willamette, Middle Fork ≃ 202 44.01 N 123.01 W
Willamette, North Fork ≃ 202 43.46 N 122.32 W
Willamina 224 45.04 N 123.29 W
Willamina Creek ≃ 224 45.05 N 123.28 W
Willandra Billabong Creek ≃ 166 33.08 S 144.06 E
Willapa 224 46.40 N 123.39 W
Willapa ≃ 224 46.42 N 123.50 W
Willapa Bay c 224 46.37 N 124.00 W
Willard, Mo., U.S. 194 37.18 N 93.25 W
Willard, N.M., U.S. 200 34.35 N 106.01 W
Willard, N.Y., U.S. 210 42.40 N 76.52 W
Willard, Oh., U.S. 214 41.03 N 82.44 W
Willard, Ut., U.S. 200 41.24 N 112.02 W
Willard, Wa., U.S. 224 45.48 N 121.38 W
Willard, Punta ▶ 232 28.50 N 113.15 W
Willards 208 38.23 N 75.20 W
Willaston, Austl. 168b 34.36 S 138.45 E
Willaston, Eng., U.K. 262 53.18 N 3.00 W
Willaumez Peninsula ▾1 164 5.05 S 150.05 E
Willcox 200 32.15 N 109.49 W
Willcox Playa ⊜ 200 32.08 N 109.51 W
Willebadessen 52 51.37 N 9.02 E
Willebroek 50 51.04 N 4.22 E
Willem Pretorius Game Reserve ≁4 158 28.16 S 27.13 E
Willemsoord 52 52.49 N 6.05 E
Willemstad, Ned. 52 51.42 N 4.26 E
Willemstad, Ned. Ant. 241s 12.06 N 68.56 W
Willenhall 42 52.36 N 2.02 W
Willerburn Acres 284c 39.03 N 77.10 W
Willeroo 164 15.17 S 131.35 E
Willer-sur-Thur 58 47.51 N 7.05 E
Willersvalde 54 54.07 N 13.08 E
Willesden ≁8 260 51.33 N 0.14 W
Willet 210 42.28 N 75.55 W
Willett Pond ⊜ 283 42.11 N 71.14 W
Willey Creek ≃ 279a 41.25 N 81.25 W
Willi, Lac ⊜ 206 46.07 N 71.34 W
William, Mount ∧, Austl. 166 37.17 S 142.36 E
William, Mount ∧, Austl. 169 37.13 S 144.47 E
William, Mount ∧2 168a 32.57 S 116.07 E
William "Bill" Dannelly Reservoir ⊜1 194 32.10 N 87.10 W
William Boyce Regional Park ♦ 279b 40.28 N 79.45 W
William Girling Reservoir ⊜1 260 51.37 N 0.02 W
William H. Harsha Lake ⊜1 218 39.02 N 84.07 W
William Lake ⊜ 184 53.50 N 99.25 W
Williamnagar 124 25.30 N 90.35 E
William Patterson College ⊥2 276 40.56 N 74.12 W
William P. Gleason Park ♦ 278 41.33 N 87.21 W
William Preston Lane Jr. Memorial Bridge ≁5 208 39.00 N 76.28 W
Williams, Austl. 168a 33.01 S 116.52 E
Williams, Az., U.S. 200 35.14 N 112.11 W
Williams, Ca., U.S. 226 39.09 N 122.08 W
Williams, Ia., U.S. 190 42.29 N 93.32 W
Williams, Mn., U.S. 198 48.46 N 94.57 W
Williams □6 216 41.35 N 84.32 W
Williams ≃, Austl. 166 20.04 S 141.08 E
Williams ≃, Austl. 168a 32.59 S 116.24 E
Williams ≃, Austl. 170 32.45 S 151.45 E
Williams, Cape ▶ 9 70.29 S 164.05 E
Williams Air Force Base ■ 200 33.18 N 111.40 W
Williams Bay 216 42.34 N 88.32 W
Williamsburg, On., Can. 212 44.58 N 75.15 W

ENGLISH — Name | Page | Lat.°′ | Long.°′

DEUTSCH — Name | Seite | Breite°′ | Länge°′ E = Ost

Williamsburg, In., U.S. 218 39.57 N 84.59 W
Williamsburg, Ia., U.S. 190 41.39 N 92.00 W
Williamsburg, Ky., U.S. 192 36.44 N 84.09 W
Williamsburg, Ma., U.S. 207 42.23 N 72.43 W
Williamsburg, Mo., U.S. 219 38.55 N 91.42 W
Williamsburg, Oh., U.S. 218 39.03 N 84.03 W
Williamsburg, Pa., U.S. 214 40.27 N 78.12 W
Williamsburg, Va., U.S. 208 37.16 N 76.42 W
Williamsburg ◆[8] 276 40.42 N 73.57 W
Williamsburg Bridge ◆[5] 276 40.43 N 73.58 W
Williams Center 216 41.26 N 84.36 W
Williams Creek ≃, Austl. 274a 33.57 S 150.58 E
Williams Creek ≃, In., U.S. 218 39.36 N 85.09 W
Williamsdale 171b 35.35 S 149.09 E
Williamsfield 214 41.32 N 80.32 W
Williams Fork ≃ 200 40.26 N 107.39 W
Williams Lake 182 52.08 N 122.09 W
Williams Lake Indian Reserve ◆[4] 182 52.07 N 122.00 W
Williams Mountain ∧[2] 194 34.15 N 94.33 W
Williamson, N.Y., U.S. 210 43.13 N 77.11 W
Williamson, W.V., U.S. 192 37.40 N 82.16 W
Williamson □[6] 222 30.40 N 97.32 W
Williamson ≃ 202 42.28 N 121.57 W
Williamson Head ≻ 9 69.09 S 157.49 E
Williamsport, Nf., Can. 186 50.32 N 56.19 W
Williamsport, In., U.S. 216 40.17 N 87.17 W
Williamsport, Oh., U.S. 214 39.35 N 83.07 W
Williamsport, Pa., U.S. 210 41.14 N 77.00 W
Williamston, Mi., U.S. 216 42.41 N 84.16 W
Williamston, N.C., U.S. 192 35.51 N 77.03 W
Williamston, S.C., U.S. 192 34.37 N 82.28 W
Williamstown, Austl. 168b 34.40 S 138.53 E
Williamstown, Austl. 169 37.52 S 144.54 E
Williamstown, On., Can. 206 45.08 N 74.35 W
Williamstown, Ky., U.S. 218 38.38 N 84.33 W
Williamstown, Ma., U.S. 207 42.42 N 73.12 W
Williamstown, N.J., U.S. 208 39.41 N 74.59 W
Williamstown, N.Y., U.S. 212 43.26 N 75.54 W
Williamstown, Pa., U.S. 208 40.34 N 76.37 W
Williamstown, Vt., U.S. 188 44.07 N 72.32 W
Williamstown, W.V., U.S. 188 39.24 N 81.27 W
Williamstown Junction 285 39.45 N 74.56 W
Williamstown Lake ⊜[1] 218 38.41 N 84.32 W
Williamsville, Il., U.S. 219 39.57 N 89.32 W
Williamsville, N.Y., U.S. 210 42.57 N 78.44 W
Williamtown 170 32.49 S 151.50 E
Willich 56 51.16 N 6.33 E
Willikies 240c 17.05 N 61.42 W
Willimantic 207 41.42 N 72.12 W
Willimantic ≃ 207 41.43 N 72.12 W
Willingale 260 51.44 N 0.19 E
Willingboro 208 40.01 N 74.52 W
Willingdon, Ab., Can. 182 53.50 N 112.08 W
Willingdon, Eng., U.K. 42 50.47 N 0.15 E
Willingdon, Mount ∧ 182 51.45 N 116.15 W
Willingen 56 51.17 N 8.37 E
Willingham 42 52.19 N 0.04 E
Willington, Eng., U.K. 42 52.50 N 1.33 W
Willington, Eng., U.K. 44 54.43 N 1.41 W
Willis, Mi., U.S. 216 42.09 N 83.33 W
Willis, Tx., U.S. 222 30.25 N 95.28 W
Willis ≃ 192 37.41 N 78.07 W
Willisau 58 47.07 N 8.00 E
Willis Group II 164 16.18 S 150.00 E
Willis Island I 186 48.48 N 53.42 W
Williston, S. Afr. 158 31.20 S 20.53 E
Williston, Fl., U.S. 192 29.23 N 82.26 W
Williston, N.D., U.S. 198 48.08 N 103.38 W
Williston, Oh., U.S. 214 41.36 N 83.20 W
Williston, S.C., U.S. 192 33.24 N 81.25 W
Williston Lake ⊜[1] 176 55.40 N 123.40 W
Williston Park 276 40.45 N 73.38 W
Willisville 194 37.59 N 89.35 W
Willis Wharf 208 37.30 N 75.48 W
Williton 42 51.10 N 3.20 W
Willits 204 39.24 N 123.21 W
Willmar 198 45.07 N 95.02 W
Willmersdorf 264a 52.40 N 13.41 E
Willmore Wilderness Provincial Park ♠ 182 53.45 N 119.00 W
Willoughby, Austl. 170 33.48 S 151.12 E
Willoughby, Oh., U.S. 214 41.38 N 81.25 W
Willoughby, Cape ≻ 166 35.51 S 138.07 E
Willoughby Bay ⊂ 240c 17.02 N 61.44 W
Willoughby Hills 214 41.35 N 81.25 W
Willow, Ak., U.S. 180 61.45 N 150.03 W
Willow, Mi., U.S. 216 42.07 N 83.24 W
Willow, N.Y., U.S. 210 42.05 N 74.14 W
Willow ≃, Ab., Can. 182 55.58 N 113.55 W
Willow ≃, B.C., Can. 182 54.03 N 122.21 W
Willow ≃, Mn., U.S. 190 46.40 N 93.35 W
Willow ≃, Wi., U.S. 190 44.59 N 92.46 W
Willowbrook, Sk., Can. 184 51.13 N 102.47 W
Willow Brook, Ca., U.S. 280 33.54 N 118.13 W
Willowbrook, Il., U.S. 278 41.46 N 87.56 W
Willowbrook, Md., U.S. 284c 39.02 N 77.11 W
Willow Brook ≃, On., Can. 212 43.53 N 80.16 W
Willow Brook ≃, Eng., U.K. 42 52.32 N 0.24 W
Willow Brook ≃, N.J., U.S. 276 40.20 N 74.10 W
Willowbrook Mall ◆[9] 276 40.53 N 74.15 W
Willowbrook Park ♠ 276 40.36 N 74.09 W
Willow Bunch 184 49.24 N 105.37 W
Willow Bunch Lake ⊜ 184 49.27 N 105.28 W
Willow City 198 48.36 N 100.17 W
Willow Creek, Ca., U.S. 204 40.56 N 123.38 W
Willow Creek, Mt., U.S. 202 45.49 N 111.38 W
Willow Creek ≃, Ab., Can. 182 49.46 N 113.21 W
Willow Creek ≃, On., Can. 212 44.25 N 79.53 W
Willow Creek ≃, Ca., U.S. 226 37.09 N 119.27 W
Willow Creek ≃, Ca., U.S. 226 39.22 N 122.05 W
Willow Creek ≃, Il., U.S. 216 41.42 N 89.10 W
Willow Creek ≃, In., U.S. 216 41.15 N 85.08 W
Willow Creek ≃, Mi., U.S. 281 42.20 N 83.25 W
Willow Creek ≃, Mt., U.S. 202 48.10 N 111.11 W
Willow Creek ≃, Mt., U.S. 202 48.09 N 106.38 W
Willow Creek ≃, Mt., U.S. 202 46.28 N 108.28 W
Willow Creek ≃, Nv., U.S. 204 38.10 N 116.35 W
Willow Creek ≃, N.D., U.S. 198 48.34 N 100.27 W
Willow Creek ≃, Oh., U.S. 279a 41.20 N 82.03 W
Willow Creek ≃, Or., U.S. 202 44.00 N 117.13 W
Willow Creek ≃, Or., U.S. 202 45.48 N 120.01 W
Willow Creek ≃, Ut,. U.S. 200 40.02 N 109.45 W
Willow Creek, North Fork ≃ 226 37.13 N 119.30 W
Willow Creek, South Fork ≃ 226 39.32 N 122.10 W
Willowdale ◆[8] 275b 43.47 N 79.26 W
Willowdale State Forest ♠ 283 42.40 N 70.54 W
Willowdene 273d 26.18 S 29.57 E
Willowemac 210 41.55 N 74.41 W
Willowemoc Creek ≃ 210 41.53 N 74.48 W
Willow Glen ◆[8] 282 37.18 N 121.53 W
Willow Grove 208 40.08 N 75.06 W
Willow Grove Naval Air Station ■ 208 40.12 N 75.08 W
Willow Grove Park ♠ 285 40.08 N 75.08 W
Willow Hill 214 40.06 N 77.48 W
Willowick 214 41.37 N 81.28 W
Willow Lake 198 44.37 N 97.38 W
Willow Lake ⊜, N.T., Can. 176 62.11 N 119.10 W
Willow Lake ⊜, N.Y., U.S. 276 40.43 N 73.50 W
Willowlake ≃ 176 62.52 N 123.08 W
Willow Metropolitan Park ♠ 281 42.08 N 83.22 W
Willowmore 158 33.17 S 23.29 E
Willow Park 222 32.45 N 97.39 W
Willowra 162 21.15 S 132.35 E
Willowra Aboriginal Reserve ◆[4] 162 21.15 S 132.35 E
Willow Reservoir ⊜[1] 190 45.45 N 89.50 W
Willow Ridge Estates 284a 43.01 N 78.49 W
Willow River 182 54.04 N 122.28 W
Willow Run, De., U.S. 285 39.44 N 75.37 W
Willow Run, Mi., U.S. 216 42.14 N 83.35 W
Willow Run, Va., U.S. 284c 38.49 N 77.10 W
Willow Run Airport ⊠ 281 42.14 N 83.32 W
Willows 226 39.31 N 122.11 W
Willow Springs, Ca., U.S. 228 34.53 N 118.18 W
Willow Springs, Il., U.S. 278 41.44 N 87.51 W
Willow Springs, Mo., U.S. 194 36.59 N 91.58 W
Willow Springs, Pa., U.S. 279b 40.19 N 79.44 W
Willow Street 208 39.59 N 76.17 W
Willowvale 158 32.16 S 28.30 E
Willow Woods 284c 38.50 N 77.16 W
Will Rogers Beach State Park ♠ 280 34.01 N 118.30 W
Will Rogers State Park ♠ 280 34.03 N 118.31 W
Willroth 56 50.34 N 7.31 E
Wills, Lake ⊜ 162 21.25 S 128.51 E
Wills Creek ≃, Austl. 166 22.43 S 140.02 E
Wills Creek ≃, Oh., U.S. 188 40.09 N 81.55 W
Wills Creek Lake ⊜[1] 214 40.08 N 81.45 W
Willseyville 210 42.17 N 76.23 W
Willshire 216 40.45 N 84.48 W
Wills Point 222 32.43 N 96.01 W
Willston 284c 38.52 N 77.09 W
Willunga 168b 35.17 S 138.33 E
Wilmar 194 33.37 N 91.55 W
Wilmer, Al., U.S. 194 30.49 N 88.21 W
Wilmer, Pa., U.S. 285 40.07 N 75.32 W
Wilmer, Tx., U.S. 222 32.35 N 96.41 W
Wilmerding 279b 40.23 N 79.48 W
Wilmersdorf ◆[8] 264a 52.30 N 13.19 E
Wilmette 216 42.04 N 87.43 W
Wilmington, Austl. 166 32.39 S 138.07 E
Wilmington, Eng., U.K. 260 51.26 N 0.12 E
Wilmington, De., U.S. 208 39.44 N 75.32 W
Wilmington, Il., U.S. 216 41.18 N 88.08 W
Wilmington, Ma., U.S. 207 42.32 N 71.10 W
Wilmington, N.C., U.S. 192 34.13 N 77.56 W
Wilmington, Oh., U.S. 218 39.26 N 83.49 W
Wilmington, Vt., U.S. 188 42.52 N 72.52 W
Wilmington ◆[8] 280 33.47 N 118.16 W
Wilmington Manor 285 39.41 N 75.35 W
Wilmington Manor Gardens 285 39.40 N 75.34 W
Wilmore, Ky., U.S. 192 37.51 N 84.39 W
Wilmore, Pa., U.S. 214 40.23 N 78.43 W
Wilmot, Ar., U.S. 194 33.03 N 91.34 W
Wilmot, Oh., U.S. 214 40.39 N 81.38 W
Wilmot, S.D., U.S. 198 45.24 N 96.51 W
Wilmot, Wi., U.S. 216 42.31 N 88.11 W
Wilmot Woods ♠ 278 42.18 N 87.56 W
Wilmslow 44 53.20 N 2.15 W
Wilna — Vilnius 76 54.41 N 25.19 E
Wilnecote 42 52.36 N 1.40 W
Wilnsdorf 56 50.49 N 8.09 E
Wilpattu National Park ♠ 122 8.20 N 80.00 E
Wilpen 214 40.17 N 79.12 W
Wilpshire 262 53.47 N 2.28 W
Wilsall 202 45.59 N 110.39 W
Wilsdruff 54 51.05 N 13.32 E
Wilseder Berg ∧[2] 52 53.10 N 9.56 E
Wilseyville 226 38.23 N 120.31 W
Wilshamstead 42 52.05 N 0.27 W
Wilson, Austl. 166 32.00 S 138.22 E
Wilson, Ar., U.S. 194 35.34 N 90.02 W
Wilson, Ct., U.S. 207 41.48 N 72.38 W
Wilson, Il., U.S. 278 42.21 N 87.54 W
Wilson, Ks., U.S. 198 38.49 N 98.28 W
Wilson, La., U.S. 194 30.55 N 91.06 W
Wilson, N.Y., U.S. 210 43.18 N 78.49 W
Wilson, N.C., U.S. 192 35.43 N 77.54 W
Wilson, Ok., U.S. 196 34.09 N 97.25 W
Wilson, Pa., U.S. 208 40.41 N 75.14 W
Wilson, Tx., U.S. 196 33.19 N 101.44 W
Wilson ≃, Austl. 164 16.47 S 128.17 E
Wilson ≃, Austl. 166 27.38 S 141.24 E
Wilson ≃, Or., U.S. 224 45.28 N 123.53 W
Wilson, Cape ≻ 176 66.59 N 81.28 W
Wilson, Mount ∧, Az., U.S. 200 35.59 N 114.37 W
Wilson, Mount ∧, Ca., U.S. 280 34.13 N 118.04 W
Wilson, Mount ∧, Co., U.S. 200 37.51 N 107.59 W
Wilson, Mount ∧, Nv., U.S. 204 38.15 N 114.23 W
Wilson, Mount ∧, Or., U.S. 224 45.04 N 121.39 W
Wilson, Mount ∧[2], Austl. 162 20.14 S 127.39 E
Wilson, Mount ∧[2], Austl. 168b 35.13 S 138.38 E
Wilson, Point ≻, Austl. 169 38.05 S 144.30 E
Wilson, Point ≻, Wa., U.S. 224 48.08 N 122.45 W
Wilson Cliffs ⊥[4] 162 22.03 S 127.09 E
Wilson Creek ≃, Tx., U.S. 222 33.07 N 96.35 W
Wilson Creek ≃, Wa., U.S. 202 47.25 N 119.07 W
Wilson Lake ⊜[1], Al., U.S. 194 34.49 N 87.30 W
Wilson Lake ⊜[1], Ks., U.S. 198 38.57 N 98.40 W
Wilson Range ⋏ 162 28.50 S 124.25 E
Wilson Run ≃, De., U.S. 285 39.48 N 75.35 W
Wilson Run ≃, Pa., U.S. 279b 40.13 N 79.37 W
Wilsons Beach 186 44.56 N 66.56 W
Wilson's Creek National Battlefield ♠ 194 37.06 N 93.27 W
Wilsons Promontory ≻ 166 38.55 S 146.20 E
Wilsons Promontory National Park ♠ 166 39.00 S 146.25 E
Wilsonville, Il., U.S. 219 39.04 N 89.51 W
Wilsonville, Ne., U.S. 198 40.06 N 100.06 W
Wilsonville, Or., U.S. 224 45.18 N 122.46 W
Wilster 52 53.55 N 9.22 E
Wilthen 54 51.06 N 14.24 E
Wilton, Eng., U.K. 42 51.05 N 1.52 W
Wilton, Ct., U.S. 207 41.11 N 73.26 W
Wilton, Me., U.S. 188 44.35 N 70.13 W
Wilton, N.H., U.S. 207 42.50 N 71.44 W
Wilton, N.Y., U.S. 210 43.11 N 73.45 W
Wilton, N.D., U.S. 198 47.09 N 100.46 W
Wilton, Wi., U.S. 190 43.48 N 90.31 W
Wilton ≃ 164 14.45 S 134.33 E
Wilton Creek ≃ 212 44.12 N 76.56 W
Wilton Farm Acres 284b 39.18 N 76.50 W
Wilton Manors 220 26.09 N 80.08 W
Wiltshire □[6] 42 51.15 N 1.50 W
Wiltz 56 49.48 N 5.55 E
Wiluna 162 26.36 S 120.13 E
Wimapedi ≃ 184 55.27 N 99.07 W
Wimauma 220 27.42 N 82.17 W
Wimberley 196 30.00 N 98.06 W
Wimbleball Reservoir ⊜[1] 42 51.04 N 3.28 W
Wimbledon 198 47.10 N 98.27 W
Wimbledon ◆[8] 260 51.25 N 0.12 W
Wimbledon Common ♠ 260 51.26 N 0.14 W
Wimborne Minster 42 50.48 N 1.59 W
Wimereux 50 50.46 N 1.37 E
Wimmelburg 54 51.31 N 11.30 E
Wimmenau 56 48.55 N 7.25 E
Wimmera ≃ 169 36.55 S 142.56 E
Wimmis 58 46.41 N 7.38 E
Winagami Lake ⊜ 182 55.38 N 116.45 W
Winam ⊂ 154 0.15 S 34.35 E
Winamac 216 41.03 N 86.36 W
Winburg 158 28.37 S 27.00 E
Winburne 214 40.57 N 78.08 W
Wincanton 42 51.04 N 2.25 W
Wincham 262 53.16 N 2.29 W
Winchcombe 42 51.57 N 1.58 W
Winchelsea, Austl. 169 38.15 S 143.59 E
Winchelsea, Eng., U.K. 42 50.55 N 0.42 E
Winchendon 207 42.41 N 72.02 W
Winchester, On., Can. 212 45.06 N 75.21 W
Winchester, N.Z. 172 44.12 S 171.17 E
Winchester, Eng., U.K. 42 51.04 N 1.19 W
Winchester, Ca., U.S. 228 33.42 N 117.05 W
Winchester, Id., U.S. 202 46.14 N 116.37 W
Winchester, Il., U.S. 219 39.37 N 90.27 W
Winchester, In., U.S. 218 40.10 N 84.58 W
Winchester, Ky., U.S. 192 37.59 N 84.10 W
Winchester, Ma., U.S. 283 42.27 N 71.08 W
Winchester, N.H., U.S. 207 42.46 N 72.23 W
Winchester, Oh., U.S. 218 38.56 N 83.39 W
Winchester, Tn., U.S. 194 35.11 N 86.06 W
Winchester, Tx., U.S. 222 30.01 N 97.01 W
Winchester, Va., U.S. 188 39.11 N 78.10 W
Winchester Cathedral ʊ[1] 42 51.04 N 1.19 W
Winchmore Hill 260 51.39 N 0.39 W
Winchmore Hill ◆[8] 260 51.38 N 0.06 W
Wind ≃, Yk., Can. 180 65.49 N 135.18 W
Wind ≃, Wa., U.S. 224 45.43 N 121.47 W
Wind ≃, Wy., U.S. 202 43.35 N 108.13 W
Windang 170 34.32 S 150.53 E
Windau — Ventspils 76 57.24 N 21.36 E
Windber 214 40.14 N 78.50 W
Wind Cave National Park ♠ 198 43.32 N 103.25 W
Windeck 56 50.48 N 7.37 E
Winder 192 33.59 N 83.43 W
Winder, Lake ⊜ 220 28.15 N 80.51 W
Windera 166 26.03 S 151.50 E
Windermere, B.C., Can. 182 50.30 N 115.58 W
Windermere, Eng., U.K. 44 54.23 N 2.54 W
Windermere, Fl., U.S. 220 28.30 N 81.32 W
Windermere ⊜ 44 54.22 N 2.56 W
Windermere Lake ⊜ 190 47.56 N 83.47 W
Winder Village 285 40.06 N 74.52 W
Windfall, Ab., Can. 182 54.11 N 116.15 W
Windfall, In., U.S. 216 40.21 N 85.57 W
Windgap 210 40.51 N 75.18 W
Windham, Ct., U.S. 207 41.41 N 72.09 W
Windham, N.H., U.S. 283 42.48 N 71.18 W
Windham, N.Y., U.S. 210 42.19 N 74.15 W
Windham, Oh., U.S. 214 41.14 N 81.02 W
Windham □[6], Ct., U.S. 207 41.55 N 71.55 W
Windham □[6], Vt., U.S. 207 42.50 N 72.43 W
Windham Manor 284c 39.04 N 77.00 W
Windhoek 156 22.34 S 17.06 E
Windhoek □[5] 156 22.30 S 17.00 E
Windigo ≃ 184 53.22 N 91.48 W
Windigo Lake ⊜ 184 52.35 N 91.32 W
Windisch 58 47.29 N 8.13 E
Windischeschenbach 60 49.48 N 12.09 E
Windischgarsten 61 47.44 N 14.20 E
Wind Lake 216 42.49 N 88.09 W
Wind Lake ⊜ 216 42.50 N 88.09 W
Windlass Run ≃ 284b 39.24 N 76.24 W
Windleite ∧ 54 51.22 N 10.56 E
Windlesham 260 51.22 N 0.40 W
Windley Key I 220 24.57 N 80.35 W
Windmill Point ≻, On., Can. 284a 42.52 N 79.01 W
Windmill Point ≻, Mi., U.S. 281 42.22 N 82.55 W
Windmill Point ≻, Va., U.S. 208 37.37 N 76.17 W
Windom, Mn., U.S. 198 43.51 N 95.07 W
Windom, N.Y., U.S. 210 42.47 N 78.48 W
Windom Peak ∧ 200 37.37 N 107.35 W
Windorah 166 25.26 S 142.39 E
Windorf, Dtsch. 60 48.37 N 13.13 E
Windorf, Öst. 61 48.27 N 14.02 E
Window Rock 200 35.40 N 109.03 W
Wind Point 216 42.47 N 87.45 W
Wind River Indian Reservation ◆[4] 202 43.26 N 109.00 W
Wind River Peak ∧ 200 42.42 N 109.07 W
Wind River Range ⋏ 200 43.05 N 109.25 W
Windrush ≃ 42 51.42 N 1.25 W
Windsbach 56 49.14 N 10.50 E
Windsor, Austl. 168b 34.25 S 138.20 E
Windsor, Austl. 170 33.37 S 150.49 E
Windsor, Nf., Can. 186 48.57 N 55.40 W
Windsor, N.S., Can. 186 44.59 N 64.08 W
Windsor, On., Can. 214 42.18 N 83.01 W
Windsor, On., Can. 281 42.18 N 83.01 W
Windsor, P.Q., Can. 206 45.34 N 72.00 W
Windsor, Eng., U.K. 42 51.29 N 0.38 W
Windsor, Ca., U.S. 204 38.33 N 122.49 W
Windsor, Co., U.S. 200 40.28 N 104.54 W
Windsor, Ct., U.S. 207 41.51 N 72.38 W
Windsor, Il., U.S. 194 39.26 N 88.35 W
Windsor, In., U.S. 218 40.09 N 85.12 W
Windsor, Mo., U.S. 194 38.31 N 93.31 W
Windsor, N.J., U.S. 208 40.15 N 74.35 W
Windsor, N.Y., U.S. 210 42.05 N 75.39 W
Windsor, N.C., U.S. 192 35.59 N 76.56 W
Windsor, Oh., U.S. 214 41.32 N 80.56 W
Windsor, Pa., U.S. 208 39.54 N 76.35 W
Windsor, Vt., U.S. 188 43.29 N 72.23 W
Windsor, Va., U.S. 208 36.48 N 76.44 W
Windsor, Wi., U.S. 216 43.13 N 89.20 W
Windsor, Gare ◆[5] 275a 45.30 N 73.34 W
Windsor, University of ʊ[2] 281 42.18 N 83.04 W
Windsor Airport ⊠ 214 42.17 N 82.58 W
Windsor and Maidenhead □[8] 260 51.28 N 0.37 W
Windsor Castle ⊥ 42 51.29 N 0.36 W
Windsor Forest 192 31.58 N 81.07 W
Windsor Forest ◆[3] 42 51.27 N 0.43 W
Windsor Great Park ♠ 260 51.27 N 0.37 W
Windsor Heights 214 40.12 N 80.40 W
Windsor Hills 280 33.59 N 118.21 W
Windsor Locks 207 41.55 N 72.37 W
Windsor Race Course ♠ 260 51.29 N 0.39 W
Windsor Raceway ♠ 281 42.15 N 83.05 W
Windsor Terrace 284b 39.19 N 76.43 W
Windsorton 158 28.16 S 24.44 E
Windsorville 207 41.53 N 72.32 W
Windthorst 196 33.34 N 98.26 W
Windward Islands II 238 13.00 N 61.00 W
Windward Passage ʉ 238 20.00 N 73.50 W
Windy Hills 285 39.48 N 75.35 W
Windy Lake ⊜ 184 54.22 N 102.35 W
Windy Peak ∧, Co., U.S. 200 38.21 N 106.16 W
Windy Peak ∧, Wa., U.S. 202 48.56 N 119.58 W
Windy Run ≃ 284c 38.54 N 77.05 W
Winefred ≃ 184 56.02 N 110.36 W
Winefred Lake ⊜ 182 55.30 N 110.35 W
Winejok 140 9.01 N 27.34 E
Winesburg 214 40.37 N 81.42 W
Winfield, Ab., Can. 182 52.58 N 114.26 W
Winfield, Al., U.S. 194 33.55 N 87.49 W
Winfield, Il., U.S. 216 41.52 N 88.10 W
Winfield, Ia., U.S. 190 41.07 N 91.26 W
Winfield, Ks., U.S. 198 37.14 N 96.59 W
Winfield, Mo., U.S. 219 38.59 N 90.44 W
Winfield, N.J., U.S. 276 40.38 N 74.17 W
Winfield, Tx., U.S. 222 33.10 N 95.07 W
Winfield, W.V., U.S. 188 38.31 N 81.53 W
Wing 198 47.08 N 100.16 W
Wing ≃ 198 46.29 N 94.58 W
Wingate, Eng., U.K. 44 55.44 N 1.23 W
Wingate, Md., U.S. 208 38.16 N 76.04 W
Wingate, N.C., U.S. 192 34.59 N 80.26 W
Wingate Mountains ⋏ 164 14.29 S 130.42 E
Wingates 262 53.34 N 2.32 W
Wingdale 210 41.39 N 73.34 W
Wingecarribee ≃ 170 34.23 S 150.07 E
Wingecarribee Reservoir ⊜[1] 170 34.34 S 150.30 E
Wingello 170 34.42 S 150.09 E
Wingene 50 51.04 N 3.16 E
Wingen-sur-Moder 56 48.55 N 7.22 E
Wingerworth 44 53.12 N 1.26 W
Wingham, Austl. 166 31.52 S 152.22 E
Wingham, On., Can. 212 43.53 N 81.19 W
Wingham, Eng., U.K. 42 51.17 N 1.13 E
Wing Lake Shores 281 42.33 N 83.17 W
Wingles 50 50.29 N 2.51 E
Wingo 194 36.38 N 88.44 W
Wings Field ⊠ 285 40.08 N 75.16 W
Wingst 52 53.43 N 9.03 E
Winhole Channel ʉ 276 43.37 N 73.48 W
Winhöring 60 48.16 N 12.39 E
Winifred 202 47.33 N 109.22 W
Winifreda 252 36.15 S 64.14 W
Winisk 176 55.15 N 85.12 W
Winisk ≃ 176 55.17 N 85.05 W
Winisk Lake ⊜ 176 52.55 N 87.22 W
Wink 196 31.45 N 103.06 W
Winkana 110 15.44 N 98.01 E
Winkelman 200 32.59 N 110.46 W
Winkelpos 158 27.35 S 26.49 E
Winkler, Mb., Can. 184 49.11 N 97.56 W
Winkler, Tx., U.S. 222 31.56 N 96.13 W
Winklern 64 46.52 N 12.52 E
Winlaw 182 49.37 N 117.34 W
Winlock 224 46.29 N 122.56 W
Winneba 150 5.25 N 0.36 W
Winnebago, Il., U.S. 190 42.15 N 89.14 W
Winnebago, Mn., U.S. 190 43.46 N 94.09 W
Winnebago, Ne., U.S. 198 42.14 N 96.28 W
Winnebago □[6] 216 42.17 N 89.06 W
Winnebago ≃ 190 43.03 N 92.57 W
Winnebago, Lake ⊜ 190 44.00 N 88.25 W
Winnebago Indian Reservation ◆[4], Ne., U.S. 198 42.15 N 96.31 W
Winnebago Indian Reservation ◆[4], Wi., U.S. 190 44.15 N 90.38 W
Winnecke, Mount ∧[2] 162 18.47 S 130.20 E
Winnecke Creek ≃ 162 18.35 S 131.34 E
Winneconne 190 44.06 N 88.42 W
Winneconnet 283 41.59 N 71.08 W
Winneconnet Pond ⊜ 283 41.58 N 71.08 W
Winnekendonk 52 51.36 N 6.17 E
Winnekenni Park ♠ 283 42.47 N 71.04 W
Winnemucca 204 40.58 N 117.44 W
Winnemucca Lake ⊜ 204 40.09 N 119.20 W
Winnenden 56 48.53 N 9.24 E
Winner 198 43.22 N 99.51 W
Winnetka 216 42.06 N 87.44 W
Winnetka ◆[8] 280 34.13 N 118.35 W
Winnett 202 47.00 N 108.21 W
Winnfield 194 31.55 N 92.38 W
Winnibigoshish, Lake ⊜ 190 47.27 N 94.12 W
Winnie 194 29.49 N 94.23 W
Winning 162 23.09 S 114.32 E
Winningen, Dtsch. 54 51.49 N 11.26 E
Winningen, Dtsch. 56 50.18 N 7.31 E
Winnipeg 184 49.53 N 97.09 W
Winnipeg ≃ 184 50.38 N 96.19 W
Winnipeg, Lake ⊜ 184 52.00 N 97.00 W
Winnipeg Beach 184 50.31 N 96.58 W
Winnipegosis 184 51.39 N 99.56 W
Winnipegosis, Lake ⊜ 184 52.30 N 100.00 W
Winnipesaukee, Lake ⊜ 188 43.35 N 71.20 W
Winnsboro, La., U.S. 194 32.09 N 91.43 W
Winnsboro, S.C., U.S. 192 34.22 N 81.05 W
Winnsboro, Tx., U.S. 222 32.57 N 95.17 W
Winnsboro, Lake ⊜[1] 222 32.55 N 95.21 W
Winnsboro Mills 192 34.21 N 81.05 W
Winnweiler 56 49.34 N 7.51 E
Winona, Ks., U.S. 198 39.03 N 101.14 W
Winona, Mi., U.S. 190 46.52 N 88.55 W
Winona, Mn., U.S. 190 44.03 N 91.38 W
Winona, Ms., U.S. 194 33.28 N 89.43 W
Winona, Mo., U.S. 194 37.00 N 91.19 W
Winona, Oh., U.S. 214 40.50 N 80.54 W
Winona, Tx., U.S. 222 32.29 N 95.10 W
Winona Lake, In., U.S. 216 41.13 N 85.49 W
Winona Lake, N.Y., U.S. 210 41.31 N 74.03 W
Winona Lake ⊜ 216 41.13 N 85.50 W
Winooski 188 44.29 N 73.11 W
Winooski ≃ 188 44.30 N 73.15 W
Winooski, North Branch ≃ 188 44.15 N 72.35 W
Winschoten 52 53.08 N 7.02 E
Winscombe 42 51.18 N 2.50 W
Winsen, Dtsch. 52 52.41 N 9.54 E
Winsen, Dtsch. 52 53.22 N 10.12 E
Winsford, Eng., U.K. 42 51.06 N 3.33 W
Winsford, Eng., U.K. 44 53.12 N 2.32 W
Winshill 42 52.48 N 1.36 W
Winside 198 42.10 N 97.10 W
Winslow, Eng., U.K. 42 51.57 N 0.54 W
Winslow, Az., U.S. 200 35.01 N 110.41 W
Winslow, Me., U.S. 188 44.32 N 69.37 W
Winslow, N.J., U.S. 285 39.39 N 74.52 W
Winslow Reef ⊹[2] 14 1.36 S 174.57 W
Winsted, Ct., U.S. 207 41.55 N 73.03 W
Winsted, Mn., U.S. 190 44.57 N 94.02 W
Winston, Fl., U.S. 220 28.01 N 82.00 W
Winston, Or., U.S. 202 43.07 N 123.24 W
Winston Churchill Memorial ʊ 219 38.52 N 91.58 W
Winston Creek ≃ 224 46.30 N 122.40 W
Winston-Salem 192 36.05 N 80.14 W
Winsum 52 53.19 N 6.31 E
Wintego Lake ⊜ 184 55.33 N 102.52 W
Winter 190 45.49 N 91.00 W
Winter Beach 220 27.43 N 80.25 W
Winterberg, Dtsch. 56 51.11 N 8.32 E
Winterberg, Dtsch. 263 51.17 N 7.18 E
Winterberg ∧[2] 263 51.20 N 7.13 E
Winterberge ⋏ 158 32.28 S 26.15 E
Winterbourne Abbas 42 50.43 N 2.34 W
Winter Creek ≃ 280 34.12 N 118.02 W
Winterfeld 54 52.44 N 11.14 E
Winter Garden 220 28.33 N 81.35 W
Winter Gardens 228 32.50 N 116.56 W
Winter Harbor 188 44.23 N 68.05 W
Winter Harbour 182 50.31 N 128.02 W
Winterhaven, Ca., U.S. 204 32.44 N 114.38 W
Winter Haven, Fl., U.S. 220 28.01 N 81.43 W
Winter Hill ∧[2] 262 53.38 N 2.31 W
Wintering ≃ 198 48.12 N 100.34 W
Wintering Lake ⊜ 184 55.24 N 97.42 W
Winter Island I, N.T., Can. 176 66.14 N 83.04 W
Winter Island I, Ca., U.S. 282 38.03 N 121.51 W
Winter Island I, Ma., U.S. 283 42.32 N 70.52 W
Winterlingen 58 48.11 N 9.07 E
Winter Park, Fl., U.S. 220 28.35 N 81.20 W
Winter Park, N.C., U.S. 192 34.12 N 77.53 W
Winterport 188 44.38 N 68.51 W
Winters, Ca., U.S. 226 38.31 N 121.58 W
Winters, Tx., U.S. 196 31.57 N 99.57 W
Winters Bayou ≃ 222 30.22 N 95.06 W
Winters Canal ≅ 226 38.32 N 121.58 W
Wintersdorf 54 51.03 N 12.21 E
Winterset, Ia., U.S. 190 41.19 N 94.00 W
Winterset, Oh., U.S. 214 40.06 N 81.25 W
Winter Springs 220 28.41 N 81.18 W
Winters Run ≃ 208 39.26 N 76.18 W
Winterstown 208 39.50 N 76.37 W
Wintersville 214 40.22 N 80.42 W
Winterswijk 52 51.58 N 6.44 E
Winterthur, Schw. 58 47.30 N 8.43 E
Winterthur, De., U.S. 285 39.48 N 75.35 W
Winterthur Museum ʊ 285 39.48 N 75.36 W
Winterton, Nf., Can. 186 47.58 N 53.20 W
Winterton, S. Afr. 158 28.46 S 29.35 E
Winterton, Eng., U.K. 44 53.39 N 0.36 W
Winterton-on-Sea 42 52.43 N 1.42 E
Winterville, Ga., U.S. 192 33.58 N 83.16 W
Winterville, Ms., U.S. 194 33.30 N 91.03 W
Winterville, N.C., U.S. 192 35.31 N 77.24 W
Winthrop, Ct., U.S. 207 41.21 N 72.29 W
Winthrop, Ia., U.S. 190 42.28 N 91.44 W
Winthrop, Me., U.S. 188 44.18 N 69.58 W
Winthrop, Ma., U.S. 283 42.22 N 70.59 W
Winthrop, Mn., U.S. 190 44.32 N 94.21 W
Winthrop, Wa., U.S. 182 48.28 N 120.11 W
Winthrop, Lake ⊜ 283 42.11 N 71.25 W
Winthrop Harbor 216 42.28 N 87.49 W
Wintinna 162 27.44 S 134.07 E
Wintinna Creek ≃ 162 27.47 S 134.14 E
Winton, Austl. 166 22.23 S 143.02 E
Winton, N.Z. 172 46.09 S 168.20 E
Winton, S. Afr. 158 27.29 S 22.34 E
Winton, Ca., U.S. 226 37.23 N 120.37 W
Winton, N.C., U.S. 192 36.23 N 76.55 W
Winton, Wa., U.S. 224 47.44 N 120.44 W
Wintzenheim 58 48.04 N 7.17 E
Winwick 262 53.26 N 2.36 W
Winz 263 51.23 N 7.09 E
Winzenberg 263 51.06 N 7.38 E
Winzer 60 48.44 N 13.04 E
Winzermark 263 51.23 N 7.08 E
Wipper ≃, Dtsch. 54 51.47 N 11.42 E
Wipper ≃, Dtsch. 54 51.17 N 11.10 E
Wipper ≃, Dtsch. 263 51.07 N 7.24 E
Wipperdorf 54 51.28 N 10.42 E
Wipperfeld 263 51.05 N 7.19 E
Wipperfürth 56 51.07 N 7.23 E
Wippra 54 51.34 N 11.16 E
Wirāṭnagar 124 26.29 N 87.17 E
Wīrendranagar 124 28.35 N 81.38 E
Wireton, Il., U.S. 278 41.40 N 87.42 W
Wireton, Pa., U.S. 279b 40.34 N 80.14 W
Wīrgañj 124 27.00 N 84.52 E
Wiriagar ≃ 164 2.17 S 132.52 E
Wirksworth 44 53.05 N 1.34 W
Wirosari 115a 7.05 S 111.05 E
Wirral □[8] 262 53.22 N 3.05 W
Wirral ≻[1] 44 53.20 N 3.03 W
Wirraminna 166 31.12 S 136.15 E
Wirrulla 162 32.24 S 134.31 E
Wisbech 42 52.40 N 0.10 E
Wisby — Visby 26 57.38 N 18.18 E
Wiscasset 188 44.00 N 69.39 W
Wische ◆[1] 54 52.50 N 11.55 E
Wischhafen 52 53.46 N 9.19 E
Wisconsin □[3], U.S. 178 44.45 N 89.30 W
Wisconsin □[3], U.S. 190 44.45 N 89.30 W
Wisconsin ≃ 190 43.00 N 91.10 W
Wisconsin, Lake ⊜[1] 190 43.24 N 89.43 W
Wisconsin Dells 190 43.37 N 89.46 W
Wisconsin Dells V 190 43.41 N 89.49 W
Wisconsin Rapids 190 44.23 N 89.49 W
Wiscoy 210 42.30 N 78.05 W
Wisdom 202 45.37 N 113.27 W
Wisdom, Lake ⊜ 164 5.20 S 147.05 E
Wise 192 36.58 N 82.34 W
Wise □[6] 222 33.07 N 97.40 W
Wise ≃ 202 45.48 N 112.57 W
Wiseman 180 67.25 N 150.06 W
Wisemans Ferry 170 33.24 S 150.59 E
Wises Landing 218 38.35 N 85.25 W
Wishart 184 51.34 N 104.00 W
Wishaw 46 55.47 N 3.56 W
Wishek 198 46.16 N 99.33 W
Wishkah ≃ 224 46.58 N 123.45 W
Wishram 224 45.39 N 120.57 W
Wisła 30 49.40 N 18.52 E
Wisła ≃ 30 54.22 N 18.55 E
Wisley Aerodrome ⊠ 260 51.18 N 0.28 W
Wisley Gardens ♠ 260 51.19 N 0.29 W
Wisłok ≃ 30 50.13 N 22.32 E
Wisłoka ≃ 30 50.27 N 21.23 E
Wismar, Dtsch. 54 53.53 N 11.28 E
Wismar, Guy. 246 6.00 N 58.18 W
Wismarbucht ⊂ 54 53.57 N 11.25 E
Wisner, La., U.S. 194 31.58 N 91.39 W
Wisner, Ne., U.S. 198 41.59 N 96.54 W
Wissahickon Creek ≃ 285 40.01 N 75.12 W
Wissant 50 50.53 N 1.40 E
Wissembourg 56 49.02 N 7.57 E
Wissen 56 50.47 N 7.43 E
Wissenkerke 52 51.35 N 3.45 E
Wissey ≃ 42 52.33 N 0.21 E
Wissinoming ◆[8] 285 40.01 N 75.04 W
Wissmar 56 50.38 N 8.41 E
Wissous 261 48.44 N 2.20 E
Wister 194 34.58 N 94.43 W
Wisznice 30 51.48 N 23.12 E
Witbank 158 25.56 S 29.07 E
Witberge ⋏ 158 30.45 S 27.32 E
Witbooisvlei 156 25.04 S 18.27 E
Witchekan Lake ⊜ 184 53.25 N 107.35 W
Witches Falls National Park ♠ 171a 27.56 S 153.10 E
Witch Hazel 224 45.30 N 122.46 W
Witdraai 158 26.58 S 20.45 E
Witfield 273d 26.11 S 28.12 E
Witham 42 51.48 N 0.38 E
Witham ≃ 44 53.06 N 0.13 W
Withamsville 218 39.03 N 84.16 W
Withens Clough Reservoir ⊜[1] 262 53.42 N 2.02 W
Witheridge 42 50.55 N 3.42 W
Withernsea 44 53.44 N 0.02 E
Witherspoon, Mount ∧ 180 61.23 N 147.12 W
Withington ◆[8] 262 53.26 N 2.14 W
Withington Green 262 53.14 N 2.18 W
Withlacoochee ≃, U.S. 192 30.24 N 83.10 W
Withlacoochee ≃, Fl., U.S. 192 29.00 N 82.45 W
Withnell 262 53.42 N 2.34 W
Withokspruit ≃ 273d 26.19 S 28.21 E
Witjira National Park ♠ 162 26.25 S 135.40 E
Wit-Kei ≃ 158 32.09 S 27.24 E
Witkoppies ∧ 158 27.44 S 29.20 E
Witkowo 30 52.27 N 17.47 E
Witless Bay 186 47.16 N 52.50 W
Witley 42 51.09 N 0.38 W
Wit-Mfolozi ≃ 158 28.22 S 31.58 E
Witney 42 51.48 N 1.29 W
Witnica 30 52.40 N 14.55 E
Wit Nossob ≃ 156 23.05 S 18.45 E
Witpoort 158 27.10 S 26.08 E
Witrivier 156 24.40 S 31.00 E
Witry-lès-Reims 50 49.18 N 4.07 E
Witsand 158 34.24 S 20.50 E
Witt 219 39.15 N 89.20 W
Wittabrenna Creek ≃ 166 29.20 S 142.43 E
Witteberg ⋏ 158 28.40 S 28.02 E
Witteberge ⋏ 158 33.18 S 20.36 E
Wittelsheim 58 47.49 N 7.15 E
Witten 56 51.26 N 7.20 E
Wittenau ◆[8] 264a 52.35 N 13.20 E
Wittenberg, Dtsch. 54 51.52 N 12.39 E
Wittenberg, Wi., U.S. 190 44.49 N 89.10 W
Wittenberge 54 53.00 N 11.44 E
Wittenburg 54 53.31 N 11.04 E
Wittenheim 58 47.49 N 7.20 E
Wittenoom 162 22.17 S 118.19 E
Wittensee ⊜ 41 54.23 N 9.45 E
Wittering 42 52.37 N 0.27 W
Wittgensdorf 54 50.53 N 12.52 E
Wittichenau 54 51.23 N 14.14 E
Wittingen 54 52.43 N 10.44 E
Wittislingen 56 48.37 N 10.25 E
Wittlaer 56 51.19 N 6.44 E
Wittlich 56 49.59 N 6.53 E
Wittman 208 38.47 N 76.17 W
Wittmar 54 52.07 N 10.38 E
Wittmund 52 53.34 N 7.47 E
Witton Park ♠ 262 53.45 N 2.31 W
Wittow ≻[1] 54 54.38 N 13.19 E
Wittstock 54 53.10 N 12.29 E
Witu 154 2.23 S 40.26 E
Witu Islands II 164 4.40 S 149.25 E
Witvlai 156 22.23 S 18.32 E
Witwatersrand, University of the ʊ[2] 273d 26.12 S 28.02 E
Witwatersrand Gold Mine ◆[7] 273d 26.12 S 28.11 E
Witwatersrant ◆[1] 158 26.00 S 27.00 E
Witzenhausen 56 51.20 N 9.51 E
Witzhelden 263 51.07 N 7.06 E
Witzputz 156 27.25 S 17.43 E
Wiveliscombe 42 51.03 N 3.19 W
Wivenhoe 42 51.52 N 0.58 E
Wivenhoe Reservoir ⊜[1] 171a 27.20 S 152.35 E
Wiwa Creek ≃ 184 50.02 N 106.31 W
Wixom 216 42.31 N 83.32 W
Wiżajny 30 54.23 N 22.51 E
Wizernes 50 50.43 N 2.14 E
Wjatka — V'atka ≃ 80 55.36 N 51.30 E
W. Kerr Scott Reservoir ⊜[1] 192 36.07 N 81.15 W
Wkra ≃ 30 52.27 N 20.44 E
Wladiwostok — Vladivostok 89 43.10 N 131.56 E
Władysławowo 30 54.49 N 18.25 E
Wleń 30 51.01 N 15.40 E
Wlingi 115a 8.05 S 112.19 E
Włocławek 30 52.39 N 19.02 E
Włocławek □[4] 30 52.30 N 19.05 E
Włodawa 30 51.34 N 23.32 E
Włoszczowa 30 50.52 N 19.59 E
Wnion ≃ 42 52.45 N 3.54 W
Woady Yaloak ≃ 169 38.06 S 143.33 E
Wobaer 85 39.19 N 75.32 E
Wöbbelin 54 53.24 N 11.30 E
Woburn 207 42.28 N 71.09 W
Woburn ◆[8] 275b 43.46 N 79.13 W
Woburn Sands 42 52.01 N 0.39 W
Woden, Austl. 171b 35.22 S 149.08 E
Woden, Tx., U.S. 222 31.30 N 94.32 W
Wodgina 162 21.11 S 118.40 E
Wodonga 166 36.07 S 146.54 E
Wodzisław Śląski 30 50.00 N 18.28 E
Woensdrecht 52 51.26 N 4.18 E
Woerdeke 85 39.41 N 77.53 E
Woerden 52 52.05 N 4.54 E
Woerth 56 48.56 N 7.45 E
Woëvre ◆[1] 56 49.05 N 5.40 E
Wofosi 105 40.09 N 115.18 E
Wo Fo Si (Temple of the Sleeping Buddha) ʊ[1] 105 40.01 N 116.12 E
Wognum 52 52.41 N 5.01 E
Wohlde 41 54.24 N 9.17 E
Wohlen 58 47.21 N 8.17 E
Wohlensee ⊜ 58 46.58 N 7.20 E
Wohlford, Lake ⊜[1] 228 33.10 N 116.59 W
Wohlthat Mountains ⋏ 9 71.35 S 12.20 E
Wohra ≃ 56 50.49 N 8.55 E
Woi 140 7.53 N 31.10 E
Woincourt 50 50.04 N 1.32 E
Woippy 56 49.09 N 6.09 E
Wojcieszów 30 50.58 N 15.56 E
Wokalup 168a 33.06 S 115.53 E
Wokam, Pulau I 164 5.37 S 134.30 E
Wokha 120 26.06 N 94.16 E
Woking, Ab., Can. 182 55.35 N 118.46 W
Woking, Eng., U.K. 42 51.20 N 0.34 W
Woking □[8] 260 51.19 N 0.32 W
Wokingham 42 51.25 N 0.51 W
Wokingham Creek ≃ 166 22.19 S 142.30 E
Wolbach 198 41.24 N 98.24 W
Wolbeck 52 51.55 N 7.43 E
Wolbrom 30 50.24 N 19.46 E
Wolcott, Ct., U.S. 207 41.36 N 72.59 W
Wolcott, In., U.S. 216 40.45 N 87.02 W
Wolcott, N.Y., U.S. 210 43.13 N 76.48 W
Wolcott Creek ≃ 210 43.17 N 76.50 W
Wolcottsburg 210 43.04 N 78.38 W
Wolcottsville 210 43.07 N 78.31 W
Wolcottville 216 41.32 N 85.22 W
Wołcza ≃ 54 53.58 N 14.53 E
Wołczenica ≃ 54 53.52 N 14.44 E
Wołczyn 30 51.01 N 18.03 E
Woldberg ⋏[1] 52 52.25 N 5.55 E
Woldegk 54 53.27 N 13.35 E
Woldingham 260 51.17 N 0.02 W

Symbols in the index entries represent the broad categories identified in the key at the right. Symbols with superior numbers (⋏[1]) identify subcategories (see complete key on page *I · 1).*

Symbole im Register stellen die rechts im Schlüssel erklärten Kategorien dar. Symbole mit hochgestellten Ziffern (⋏[1]) bezeichnen Unterabteilungen einer Kategorie (vgl. vollständiger Schlüssel auf Seite *I · 1).*

Los símbolos incluídos en el texto del índice representan las grandes categorias identificadas con la clave a la derecha. Los símbolos con numeros en su parte superior (⋏[1]) identifican las subcategorías (véase la clave completa en la página *I · 1).*

Les symboles de l'index représentent les catégories indiquées dans la légende à droite. Les symboles suivis d'un indice (⋏[1]) représentent des sous-catégories (voir légende complète à la page *I · 1).*

Os símbolos incluídos no texto do índice representam as grandes categorias identificadas com a chave à direita. Os símbolos com números em sua parte superior (⋏[1]) identificam as subcategorias (veja-se a chave completa à página *I · 1).*

∧	Mountain	Berg	Montaña	Montagne	Montanha
⋏	Mountains	Gebirge	Montañas	Montagnes	Montanhas
)(	Pass	Paß	Paso	Col	Passo
V	Valley, Canyon	Tal, Cañon	Valle, Cañón	Vallée, Canyon	Vale, Canhão
≚	Plain	Ebene	Llano	Plaine	Planície
≻	Cape	Kap	Cabo	Cap	Cabo
I	Island	Insel	Isla	Île	Ilha
II	Islands	Inseln	Islas	Îles	Ilhas
⊥	Other Topographic Features	Andere Topographische Objekte	Otros Elementos Topográficos	Autres données topographiques	Outros acidentes topográficos

ESPAÑOL

Nombre	Página	Lat.°′	Long.°′ W = Oeste
Wolds, The ⋏[2]	44	53.20 N	0.10 W
Woleai I[1]	108	7.21 N	143.52 E
Woleu-Ntem □[4]	152	1.30 N	12.00 E
Wolf ≃, On., Can.	190	48.49 N	88.30 W
Wolf ≃, U.S.	194	35.09 N	90.04 W
Wolf ≃, Ks., U.S.	198	39.54 N	95.11 W
Wolf ≃, Ms., U.S.	194	30.21 N	89.18 W
Wolf ≃, Wi., U.S.	190	44.11 N	88.48 W
Wolf, Isla I	246a	1.23 N	91.49 W
Wolf, Volcán ∧[1]	246a	0.02 N	91.20 W
Wolfach	58	48.17 N	8.13 E
Wolf-Bay	186	50.16 N	60.08 W
Wolf Creek, Mt., U.S.	202	47.00 N	112.04 W
Wolf Creek, Or., U.S.	202	42.41 N	123.23 W
Wolf Creek ≃, U.S.	196	36.35 N	99.30 W
Wolf Creek ≃, Ca., U.S.	226	39.02 N	121.08 W
Wolf Creek ≃, Co., U.S.	200	40.12 N	108.29 W
Wolf Creek ≃, In., U.S.	216	41.15 N	87.07 W
Wolf Creek ≃, Ia., U.S.	190	42.20 N	92.09 W
Wolf Creek ≃, Mt., U.S.	198	48.05 N	105.40 W
Wolf Creek ≃, Mt., U.S.	202	47.37 N	109.38 W
Wolf Creek ≃, Oh., U.S.	214	41.16 N	83.11 W
Wolf Creek ≃, Pa., U.S.	214	41.03 N	80.07 W
Wolf Creek ≃, S.D., U.S.	198	43.21 N	97.37 W
Wolf Creek ≃, S.D., U.S.	198	44.42 N	98.40 W
Wolf Creek Lake ⊜[1]	198	38.14 N	95.41 W
Wolf Creek Pass)(	200	37.29 N	106.48 W
Wolf Creek State Park ♠	219	39.30 N	88.41 W
Wolfdale	214	40.12 N	80.17 W
Wolfe □[6]	206	45.45 N	71.30 W
Wolfeboro	188	43.35 N	71.12 W
Wolfe City	196	33.22 N	96.04 W
Wolfegg	58	47.49 N	9.47 E
Wolfe Island	212	44.12 N	76.26 W
Wolfe Island I	212	44.12 N	76.20 W
Wolfe Lake ⊜	212	44.40 N	76.30 W
Wolfen	54	51.40 N	12.16 E
Wolfenbüttel	52	52.10 N	10.32 E
Wolfenden, Mount ∧	182	50.26 N	127.33 W
Wolfenschiessen	58	46.55 N	8.24 E
Wolfertschwenden	58	47.53 N	10.16 E
Wolfforth	196	33.30 N	102.01 W
Wolfgangsee ⊜	64	47.44 N	13.26 E
Wolfhagen	56	51.19 N	9.10 E
Wölfis	54	50.48 N	10.46 E
Wolf Island I	212	44.33 N	78.15 W
Wolflake, In., U.S.	216	41.20 N	85.30 W
Wolf Lake, Mi., U.S.	216	43.15 N	86.06 W
Wolf Lake ⊜, Ab., Can.	182	54.42 N	110.59 W
Wolf Lake ⊜, On., Can.	212	44.44 N	78.11 W
Wolf Lake ⊜, Yk., Can.	180	60.40 N	131.40 W
Wolf Lake ⊜, U.S.	278	41.40 N	87.31 W
Wolf Lake ⊜, N.J., U.S.	276	40.57 N	74.42 W
Wolf Mountain ∧	180	65.17 N	154.02 W
Wolfpassing	264b	48.19 N	16.11 E
Wolf Point	202	48.05 N	105.38 W
Wolframs-Eschenbach	56	49.14 N	10.43 E
Wolfratshausen	64	47.54 N	11.25 E
Wolf Rock I[2]	28	49.57 N	5.49 W
Wolf Run	214	40.30 N	80.54 W
Wolfsberg	61	46.51 N	14.51 E
Wolfsberg ∧[2]	263	51.38 N	6.27 E
Wolfsburg	54	52.25 N	10.47 E
Wolf's Castle	42	51.54 N	4.58 W
Wolfsegg am Hausruck	60	48.06 N	13.40 E
Wolfstein	56	49.35 N	7.36 E
Wolftrap Creek ≃	284c	38.58 N	77.17 W
Wolf Trap Farms for the Performing Arts ♠	284c	38.56 N	77.16 W
Wolfurt	58	47.28 N	9.45 E
Wolfville	186	45.05 N	64.22 W
Wolgan ≃	170	33.12 S	150.28 E
Wolgast	54	54.03 N	13.46 E
Wolga → Volga ≃	72	45.55 N	47.52 E
Wolgograder Stausee → Volgogradskoje vodochranilišče ⊜[1]	80	49.20 N	45.00 E
Wolgograd → Volgograd	80	48.44 N	44.25 E
Wolhusen	58	47.04 N	8.04 E
Wolin	30	53.50 N	14.35 E
Wolin I	54	53.55 N	14.31 E
Woliński Park Narodowy ♠	30	53.55 N	14.30 E
Wolkenstein	54	50.39 N	13.04 E
Wolkersdorf	61	48.23 N	16.31 E
Wölkisch	54	51.13 N	13.21 E
Wolkramshausen	54	51.25 N	10.44 E
Wollangambe ≃	170	33.21 S	150.35 E
Wollaston	42	52.15 N	0.40 W
Wollaston, Islas II	254	55.40 S	67.30 W
Wollaston Beach ≛[2]	283	42.17 N	71.01 W
Wollaston Lake ⊜, On., Can.	212	44.50 N	77.50 W
Wollaston Lake ⊜, Sk., Can.	176	58.15 N	103.20 W
Wollaston Peninsula ≻[1]	176	70.00 N	115.00 W
Wollemi Creek ≃	170	33.13 S	150.31 E
Wollemi National Park ♠	166	32.50 S	150.30 E
Wollogorang	166	17.13 S	137.57 E
Wollombi	170	32.56 S	151.09 E
Wollombi Brook ≃	170	32.33 S	151.04 E
Wollondilly ≃	170	33.57 S	150.26 E
Wollongong	170	34.25 S	150.54 E
Wöllstein	56	49.49 N	7.58 E
Wolmaransstad	158	27.12 S	26.13 E
Wolmirsleben	54	51.57 N	11.29 E
Wolmirstedt	54	52.15 N	11.37 E
Wolnzach	60	48.36 N	11.37 E
Wołomin	30	52.21 N	21.14 E
Wołów	30	51.21 N	16.39 E
Wolowaru	115b	8.46 S	121.54 E
Wolseley, Sk., Can.	184	50.25 N	103.19 W
Wolseley, S. Afr.	158	33.26 S	19.12 E
Wolsey	198	44.24 N	98.28 W
Wolsingham	44	54.44 N	1.52 W
Wolsztyn	30	52.08 N	16.06 E
Wolterdingen	52	53.02 N	9.50 E
Woltersdorf, Dtsch.	54	52.24 N	12.22 E
Woltersdorf, Dtsch.	54	52.26 N	13.45 E
Woluogu	105	39.40 N	117.46 E
Wolvega	52	52.53 N	6.00 E
Wolverhampton	42	52.36 N	2.08 W
Wolverine	190	45.16 N	84.36 W
Wolverine Lake	281	42.33 N	83.29 W
Wolverine Loon Lake ⊜	281	42.33 N	83.30 W
Wolverine Mountain ∧	180	65.20 N	149.51 W
Wolvertem	50	50.57 N	4.18 E
Wolverton	42	52.04 N	0.50 W
Wolwehoek	158	26.55 S	27.48 E
Wölzerbach ≃	61	47.08 N	14.23 E
Wolziger See ⊜	54	52.16 N	13.50 E
Woman ≃	190	47.57 N	82.19 W
Wombarra	170	34.16 S	150.58 E
Wombat, Mount ∧	169	36.51 S	145.40 E
Wombeyan Caves ≛[5]	170	34.18 S	149.56 E

FRANÇAIS

Nom	Page	Lat.°′	Long.°′ W = Ouest
Wombourne	42	52.32 N	2.11 W
Wombwell	44	53.31 N	1.24 W
Womelsdorf	208	40.22 N	76.11 W
Women's Rights National Historical Park ♠	210	42.54 N	76.47 W
Wommels	52	53.06 N	5.36 E
Wompatuck State Park ♠	283	42.13 N	70.51 W
Wonarah	162	19.55 S	136.20 E
Wondai	166	26.19 S	151.52 E
Wondelgem	50	51.05 N	3.43 E
Wonderfonteinspruit ≃	273d	26.16 S	27.42 E
Wonderkop	158	27.50 S	27.26 E
Wonder Lake	216	42.25 N	88.21 W
Wonderland	204	40.24 N	121.19 W
Wonderland Center ◆[9]	281	42.22 N	83.20 W
Wonderland Dog Track ♠	283	42.25 N	71.00 W
Wondinong	162	27.52 S	118.25 E
Wŏndong-ni	98	34.23 N	126.40 E
Wonersh	260	51.12 N	0.33 W
Wonewoc	190	43.39 N	90.13 W
Wong ≃	124	27.10 N	89.30 E
Wongan Hills	162	30.53 S	116.42 E
Wonga Park	274b	37.44 S	145.16 E
Wonga-Wongué, Parc National de ♠	152	0.30 S	9.30 E
Wonggarasi	112	0.33 N	121.36 E
Wong Ka Wai	271d	22.24 N	113.58 E
Woniushi	104	42.31 N	123.03 E
Wŏnjang-ni	98	39.05 N	125.32 E
Wŏnju	98	37.22 N	127.58 E
Wonogiri	115a	7.49 S	110.55 E
Wonokromo	115a	7.18 S	112.44 E
Wonosari	115a	7.58 S	110.35 E
Wonosegoro	115a	7.18 S	110.39 E
Wonosobo	115a	7.22 S	109.54 E
Wonotobo Vallen ⌊	250	4.22 N	57.58 W
Wonreli	112	8.05 S	127.09 E
Wŏnsan	98	39.09 N	127.25 E
Wonthaggi	169	38.36 S	145.35 E
Woocalla	166	31.42 S	137.13 E
Wood, Pa., U.S.	214	40.10 N	78.08 W
Wood, S.D., U.S.	198	43.29 N	100.28 W
Wood □[6], Oh., U.S.	216	41.22 N	83.39 W
Wood □[6], Tx., U.S.	222	32.48 N	95.20 W
Wood ≃, B.C., Can.	182	52.10 N	118.30 W
Wood ≃, Sk., Can.	184	50.08 N	106.10 W
Wood ≃, U.S.	207	41.26 N	71.43 W
Wood ≃, Ak., U.S.	180	64.35 N	148.41 W
Wood ≃, Ne., U.S.	198	41.02 N	98.05 W
Wood ≃, Wy., U.S.	202	44.07 N	108.58 W
Wood, Mount ∧, Yk., Can.	180	61.14 N	140.31 W
Wood, Mount ∧, Mt., U.S.	202	45.17 N	109.49 W
Woodacre	226	38.05 N	122.36 W
Woodall Mountain ∧[2]	194	34.45 N	88.11 W
Wood Bay ⊂	180	69.45 N	129.00 W
Woodberry Forest	284c	38.48 N	76.56 W
Woodbine, Ga., U.S.	192	30.57 N	81.43 W
Woodbine, Ia., U.S.	198	41.44 N	95.42 W
Woodbine, Md., U.S.	208	39.21 N	77.03 W
Woodbine, N.J., U.S.	208	39.14 N	74.48 W
Woodbourne, N.Y., U.S.	210	41.45 N	74.35 W
Woodbourne, Oh., U.S.	218	39.38 N	84.10 W
Woodbourne, Pa., U.S.	285	40.12 N	74.53 W
Woodbridge, Eng., U.K.	42	52.06 N	1.19 E
Woodbridge, Ca., U.S.	226	38.09 N	121.18 W
Woodbridge, Ct., U.S.	207	41.21 N	73.00 W
Woodbridge, N.J., U.S.	210	40.33 N	74.17 W
Woodbridge, Va., U.S.	208	38.39 N	77.15 W
Woodbridge Center ◆[9]	276	40.33 N	74.18 W
Woodbridge Creek ≃	276	40.32 N	74.15 W
Woodbridge Island I	283	42.48 N	70.50 W
Woodburn, Il., U.S.	219	39.03 N	90.00 W
Woodburn, In., U.S.	216	41.07 N	84.51 W
Woodburn, Or., U.S.	224	45.08 N	122.51 W
Woodbury, Eng., U.K.	42	50.41 N	3.24 W
Woodbury, Ct., U.S.	207	41.32 N	73.12 W
Woodbury, Ga., U.S.	192	32.59 N	84.34 W
Woodbury, Mi., U.S.	216	42.46 N	85.05 W
Woodbury, N.J., U.S.	208	39.50 N	75.09 W
Woodbury, N.Y., U.S.	276	40.49 N	73.28 W
Woodbury, Pa., U.S.	214	40.14 N	78.22 W
Woodbury, Tn., U.S.	194	35.49 N	86.04 W
Woodbury Creek ≃	285	39.52 N	75.11 W
Woodbury Heights	285	39.49 N	75.09 W
Woodchester	168b	35.13 S	138.57 E
Woodchopper	180	65.18 N	143.25 W
Woodchurch	42	51.05 N	0.46 E
Woodcliff Lake	276	41.01 N	74.04 W
Woodcliff Lake ⊜	276	41.01 N	74.03 W
Woodcock	214	41.45 N	80.05 W
Woodcock, Mount ∧	162	19.16 S	134.02 E
Woodcrest, Ca., U.S.	228	33.52 N	117.21 W
Woodcrest, Pa., U.S.	285	39.59 N	75.35 W
Wood Dale	278	41.57 N	87.58 W
Woodenbong	166	28.23 S	152.37 E
Woodend	169	37.22 S	144.32 E
Woodfibre	182	49.40 N	123.15 W
Woodfield ◆[9]	278	42.03 N	88.03 W
Woodford, Austl.	171a	26.57 S	152.47 E
Woodford, Ire.	48	53.03 N	8.23 W
Woodford, Eng., U.K.	262	53.21 N	2.10 W
Woodford □[6], Il., U.S.	216	40.43 N	89.16 W
Woodford □[6], Ky., U.S.	218	38.06 N	84.15 W
Woodford ◆[8]	260	51.36 N	0.02 E
Woodford Aerodrome ⊠	262	53.20 N	2.09 W
Woodford Bridge ◆[8]	260	51.36 N	0.04 E
Woodford Halse	42	52.10 N	1.12 W
Wood Green ◆[8]	260	51.36 N	0.07 W
Woodhall Spa	44	53.09 N	0.13 W
Woodham	260	51.21 N	0.30 W
Woodham Ferrers	260	51.40 N	0.36 E
Woodham Mortimer	260	51.43 N	0.37 E
Woodham Walter	260	51.44 N	0.37 E
Woodhaven	216	42.08 N	83.14 W
Woodhaven ◆[8]	276	40.41 N	73.51 W
Woodhead Reservoir ⊜[1]	262	53.30 N	1.52 W
Woodhill	275b	43.45 N	79.41 W
Wood Hill ∧[2]	283	42.39 N	71.13 W
Woodhull, Il., U.S.	190	41.10 N	90.18 W
Woodhull, N.Y., U.S.	210	42.05 N	77.25 W
Woodinville	224	47.45 N	122.09 W
Wood Islands	186	45.58 N	62.45 W
Woodlake, Ca., U.S.	204	36.25 N	119.06 W
Wood Lake, Ne., U.S.	198	42.38 N	100.14 W
Woodlake, Tx., U.S.	222	31.01 N	95.02 W
Wood Lake ⊜, On., Can.	212	45.01 N	79.05 W
Wood Lake ⊜, Sk., Can.	184	55.17 N	103.17 W
Woodland, Ca., U.S.	226	38.40 N	121.46 W
Woodland, Ga., U.S.	192	32.47 N	84.33 W
Woodland, Il., U.S.	216	40.43 N	87.44 W
Woodland, Me., U.S.	188	45.09 N	67.24 W
Woodland, Mi., U.S.	216	42.43 N	85.08 W
Woodland, N.C., U.S.	192	36.19 N	77.12 W
Woodland, Pa., U.S.	214	40.59 N	78.20 W
Woodland, Wa., U.S.	224	45.54 N	122.44 W
Woodland Beach	216	41.57 N	83.19 W
Woodland Heights	214	41.25 N	79.43 W

PORTUGUÊS

Nome	Página	Lat.°′	Long.°′ W = Oeste
Woodland Hills ◆[8]	280	34.11 N	118.35 W
Woodland Hills Park ♠	279a	41.28 N	81.36 W
Woodland Park, Co., U.S.	200	38.59 N	105.03 W
Woodland Park, Pa., U.S.	210	41.18 N	77.03 W
Woodlands, N.Z.	172	46.22 S	168.33 E
Woodlands, Sing.	271c	1.27 N	103.46 E
Woodlands, N.Y., U.S.	276	41.01 N	73.50 W
Woodlawn, Il., U.S.	219	38.20 N	89.02 W
Woodlawn, Ky., U.S.	194	37.02 N	88.34 W
Woodlawn, Md., U.S.	284b	39.19 N	76.43 W
Woodlawn, Md., U.S.	284c	38.57 N	76.53 W
Woodlawn, Wa., U.S.	224	47.01 N	123.48 W
Woodlawn ◆[8]	278	41.47 N	87.36 W
Woodlawn Beach	210	42.48 N	78.51 W
Woodlawn Heights	284b	39.11 N	76.39 W
Woodley	42	51.28 N	0.54 W
Woodlyn	285	39.52 N	75.20 W
Woodlynne	285	39.55 N	75.05 W
Woodmansey	44	53.50 N	0.29 W
Woodmansterne	260	51.19 N	0.10 W
Woodmere, N.Y., U.S.	210	40.37 N	73.42 W
Woodmere, Oh., U.S.	279a	41.28 N	81.29 W
Woodmoor	284b	39.20 N	76.44 W
Wood Mountain ∧	184	49.14 N	106.20 W
Wood Mountain Indian Reserve ◆[4]	184	49.21 N	106.24 W
Woodplumpton	262	53.48 N	2.47 W
Woodport	276	40.59 N	74.36 W
Woodrarung Range ⋏	162	27.10 S	115.30 E
Woodridge, Austl.	171a	27.38 S	153.06 E
Woodridge, Mb., Can.	184	49.17 N	96.09 W
Woodridge, Il., U.S.	216	41.44 N	88.03 W
Wood-Ridge, N.J., U.S.	276	40.50 N	74.05 W
Woodridge, N.Y., U.S.	210	41.43 N	74.34 W
Wood River, Ak., U.S.	180	59.04 N	158.26 W
Wood River, Il., U.S.	219	38.51 N	90.05 W
Wood River, Ne., U.S.	198	40.49 N	98.35 W
Wood River Lakes ⊜	180	59.30 N	158.45 W
Wood River Mountains ⋏	180	59.32 N	159.30 W
Woodroffe ≃	166	21.28 S	137.58 E
Woodroffe, Mount ∧	162	26.20 S	131.45 E
Woodrow	192	35.08 N	77.05 W
Woodrow Wilson Memorial Bridge ◆[5]	284c	38.48 N	77.02 W
Woodruff, Az., U.S.	200	34.46 N	110.02 W
Woodruff, S.C., U.S.	192	34.44 N	82.02 W
Woodruff, Wi., U.S.	190	45.53 N	89.41 W
Woodruff Creek ≃	281	42.21 N	83.43 W
Woods	168b	34.15 S	138.31 E
Woods, Lake ⊜	162	17.50 S	133.30 E
Woods, Lake of the ⊜	184	49.15 N	94.45 W
Woods Bay ⊂	212	45.08 N	80.00 W
Woodsboro, Md., U.S.	208	39.31 N	77.18 W
Woodsboro, Tx., U.S.	196	28.14 N	97.19 W
Woodsburgh	276	40.37 N	73.42 W
Woods Creek ≃, N.Y., U.S.	276	40.39 N	73.24 W
Woods Creek ≃, N.Y., U.S.	284a	43.04 N	78.58 W
Woodsfield	188	39.45 N	81.06 W
Woods Hole	207	41.31 N	70.40 W
Woodside, Austl.	166	38.31 S	146.52 E
Woodside, Austl.	168b	34.57 S	138.52 E
Woodside, Eng., U.K.	260	51.45 N	0.11 W
Woodside, Ca., U.S.	226	37.25 N	122.15 W
Woodside, De., U.S.	208	39.04 N	75.34 W
Woodside, Pa., U.S.	285	40.13 N	74.53 W
Woodside ◆[8]	276	40.45 N	73.55 W
Woodside National Historic Park ♠	212	43.26 N	80.08 W
Woodson, Il., U.S.	219	39.38 N	90.13 W
Woodson, Tx., U.S.	196	33.01 N	99.03 W
Woods Point	169	37.35 S	146.15 E
Woods Reservoir ⊜[1]	194	35.20 N	86.00 W
Woodstock, Austl.	166	22.15 S	141.57 E
Woodstock, N.B., Can.	186	46.09 N	67.34 W
Woodstock, On., Can.	212	43.08 N	80.45 W
Woodstock, Eng., U.K.	42	51.52 N	1.21 W
Woodstock, Ct., U.S.	207	41.56 N	71.58 W
Woodstock, Il., U.S.	216	42.18 N	88.26 W
Woodstock, Md., U.S.	284b	39.19 N	76.52 W
Woodstock, N.Y., U.S.	210	42.02 N	74.07 W
Woodstock, Oh., U.S.	218	40.10 N	83.32 W
Woodstock, Vt., U.S.	188	43.37 N	72.31 W
Woodstock, Va., U.S.	188	38.52 N	78.30 W
Woodstown	208	39.39 N	75.19 W
Wood Street	260	51.15 N	0.38 W
Woodsville	188	44.09 N	72.02 W
Woodvale Airfield ⊠	262	53.35 N	3.03 W
Woodview Manor	278	42.06 N	87.53 W
Wood Village	224	45.32 N	122.19 W
Woodville, Austl.	168b	34.53 S	138.32 E
Woodville, On., Can.	212	44.24 N	78.59 W
Woodville, N.Z.	172	40.20 S	175.52 E
Woodville, Al., U.S.	194	34.38 N	86.16 W
Woodville, Ca., U.S.	226	36.06 N	119.12 W
Woodville, Fl., U.S.	192	30.20 N	84.15 W
Woodville, Ga., U.S.	192	33.40 N	83.06 W
Woodville, Ma., U.S.	207	42.14 N	71.33 W
Woodville, Mi., U.S.	216	43.39 N	85.40 W
Woodville, Ms., U.S.	194	31.06 N	91.17 W
Woodville, N.Y., U.S.	210	42.40 N	77.22 W
Woodville, Oh., U.S.	214	41.27 N	83.21 W
Woodville, Tx., U.S.	194	30.46 N	94.24 W
Woodward, Ia., U.S.	190	41.51 N	93.55 W
Woodward, Ok., U.S.	196	36.26 N	99.23 W
Woodward, Pa., U.S.	210	40.54 N	77.21 W
Woodward Reservoir ⊜[1]	226	37.51 N	120.52 W
Woodway, Tx., U.S.	222	31.30 N	97.12 W
Woodway, Wa., U.S.	224	47.47 N	122.23 W
Woodworth, Oh., U.S.	214	40.59 N	80.40 W
Woodworth, Wi., U.S.	216	42.34 N	88.00 W
Woody ≃	184	52.30 N	100.51 W
Woody Creek ≃	202	47.27 N	106.21 W
Woody Head ≻	166	29.22 S	153.22 E
Woody Island	180	57.47 N	152.22 W
Wool	42	50.41 N	2.14 W
Woolacombe	42	51.10 N	4.13 W
Woolamai, Cape ≻	169	38.34 S	145.21 E
Wool Bay	168b	35.00 S	137.45 E
Wooldridge	158	33.13 S	27.15 E
Wooler	44	55.33 N	2.01 W
Woolford	208	38.30 N	76.11 W
Woolgangie	162	31.10 S	120.32 E
Woolgoolga	166	30.07 S	153.12 E
Woollahra	274a	33.53 S	151.15 E
Woolmarket	194	30.28 N	88.59 W
Woolooware Bay ⊂	274a	34.02 S	151.09 E
Woolpit	42	52.13 N	0.54 E
Woolrich	210	41.12 N	77.23 W
Woolsey Peak ∧	200	33.10 N	112.53 W
Woolston	262	53.24 N	2.32 W
Woolton ◆[8]	262	53.23 N	2.52 W
Woolwich ◆[8]	260	51.29 N	0.04 E
Woomargama	171b	35.50 S	147.15 E
Woomera	166	31.31 S	137.10 E
Woomera Prohibited Area ◆[4]	162	29.45 S	134.30 E
Woonona	170	34.21 S	150.55 E
Woonsocket, R.I., U.S.	207	42.00 N	71.30 W
Woonsocket, S.D., U.S.	198	44.03 N	98.16 W
Woorabinda	166	24.08 S	149.28 E
Wooramel	162	25.44 S	114.17 E
Wooramel ≃	162	25.47 S	114.10 E
Woorim	171a	27.08 S	153.12 E
Wooroloo	168a	31.48 S	116.19 E
Wooster	214	40.48 N	81.56 W
Wootton	42	52.11 N	0.53 W
Wootton Bassett	42	51.33 N	1.54 W
Wootton Wawen	42	52.16 N	1.47 W
Woqooyi Galbeed □[4]	144	10.00 N	44.00 E
Worb	58	46.56 N	7.34 E
Worbis	54	51.25 N	10.21 E
Worcester, S. Afr.	158	33.39 S	19.27 E
Worcester, Eng., U.K.	42	52.11 N	2.13 W
Worcester, Ma., U.S.	207	42.15 N	71.48 W
Worcester, N.Y., U.S.	210	42.35 N	74.45 W
Worcester, Pa., U.S.	285	40.12 N	75.21 W
Worcester □[6], Md., U.S.	208	38.11 N	75.24 W
Worcester □[6], Ma., U.S.	207	42.16 N	71.48 W
Worcester Municipal Airport ⊠	207	42.16 N	71.52 W
Worden, Il., U.S.	219	38.55 N	89.50 W
Worden, Mt., U.S.	202	45.57 N	108.09 W
Worden Pond ⊜	207	41.26 N	71.35 W
Wördern	61	48.20 N	16.13 E
Wörgl	64	47.29 N	12.04 E
Workai, Pulau I	164	6.40 S	134.40 E
Work Channel ʊ	182	54.30 N	130.15 W
Workers' Stadium ♠	271a	39.55 N	116.27 E
Workington	44	54.39 N	3.35 W
Worksop	44	53.18 N	1.07 W
Workum	52	52.57 N	5.26 E
Worland	202	44.01 N	107.57 W
World End Pond ⊜	283	42.45 N	71.12 W
Worli ◆[8]	272c	19.01 N	72.50 E
Wörlitz	54	51.50 N	12.25 E
Wormerveer	52	52.28 N	4.46 E
Wormhoudt	50	50.53 N	2.28 E
Wormit	46	56.25 N	2.59 W
Wormley	260	51.44 N	0.01 W
Worms	56	49.38 N	8.22 E
Worms Head ≻	42	51.34 N	4.20 W
Wormshill	260	51.17 N	0.42 E
Wörnitz ≃	56	48.42 N	10.45 E
Woronesch → Voronež	78	51.40 N	39.10 E
Woronoco	207	42.09 N	72.49 W
Woronora	274a	34.01 S	151.03 E
Woronora ≃	274a	34.00 S	151.04 E
Woronora Reservoir ⊜[1]	170	34.08 S	150.56 E
Worplesdon	260	51.16 N	0.37 W
Worpswede	52	53.13 N	8.56 E
Wörrstadt	56	49.50 N	8.07 E
Wörsbach ≃	56	50.22 N	8.09 E
Worsbrough	44	53.31 N	1.29 W
Worsley	262	53.30 N	2.23 W
Worsthorne	262	53.47 N	2.11 W
Wörth, Dtsch.	56	49.48 N	9.09 E
Worth, Dtsch.	263	51.13 N	7.39 E
Worth, Il., U.S.	216	41.41 N	87.47 W
Worth, Lake ⊜[1]	222	32.48 N	97.28 W
Wortham	222	31.47 N	96.27 W
Wörth am Rhein	56	49.03 N	8.16 E
Wörth an der Donau	60	49.00 N	12.25 E
Wörth an der Isar	60	48.37 N	12.24 E
Worthen	42	52.38 N	3.00 W
Wörther See ⊜	61	46.37 N	14.10 E
Worthing	42	50.48 N	0.23 W
Worthington, In., U.S.	194	39.07 N	86.58 W
Worthington, Md., U.S.	284b	39.14 N	76.47 W
Worthington, Mn., U.S.	198	43.37 N	95.35 W
Worthington, N.Y., U.S.	276	41.02 N	73.50 W
Worthington, Oh., U.S.	214	40.05 N	83.01 W
Worthington, Pa., U.S.	214	40.50 N	79.37 W
Worthington Peak ∧	204	37.55 N	115.37 W
Wörthsee ⊜	60	48.03 N	11.10 E
Worthville, Ky., U.S.	218	38.36 N	85.04 W
Worthville, Pa., U.S.	214	41.02 N	79.08 W
Worton	208	39.16 N	76.05 W
Wŏrun-dong	98	39.36 N	125.20 E
Wosimi	164	2.54 S	134.31 E
Wostok → Vostok ⊍[3]	9	78.30 S	106.50 E
Wosu	112	2.21 S	121.50 E
Wotap, Pulau I	164	7.21 S	131.16 E
Wotho I[1]	14	10.06 N	165.59 E
Wotje I[1]	14	9.27 N	170.02 E
Wotton, P.Q., Can.	206	45.44 N	71.48 W
Wotton, Eng., U.K.	260	51.13 N	0.23 W
Wotton-under-Edge	42	51.39 N	2.21 W
Wotu	112	2.35 S	120.48 E
Woudenberg	52	52.05 N	5.25 E
Woudrichem	52	51.49 N	5.00 E
Woudsend	52	52.56 N	5.36 E
Wouldham	260	51.21 N	0.28 E
Wounded Knee	198	43.08 N	102.21 W
Wounded Knee Creek ≃	198	43.26 N	102.32 W
Wounta	236	13.33 N	83.32 W
Wounta, Laguna de ⊂	236	13.38 N	83.34 W
Wour	146	21.21 N	15.57 E
Wouri ≃	152	4.06 N	9.43 E
Woutchaba	152	5.13 N	13.05 E
Wouw	52	51.32 N	4.24 E
Wowan	166	23.55 S	150.12 E
Wowoni, Pulau I	112	4.08 S	123.06 E
Woyla ≃	114	4.18 N	95.56 E
Woy Woy	170	33.30 S	151.20 E
Woźniki	30	50.36 N	19.03 E
Wragby	44	53.18 N	0.19 W
Wrangel Island → Vrangel'a, ostrov I	74	71.00 N	179.30 W
Wrangell	180	56.28 N	132.23 W
Wrangell, Cape ≻	181a	52.50 N	172.26 E
Wrangell, Mount ∧	180	62.00 N	144.06 W
Wrangell Island I	180	56.15 N	132.10 W
Wrangell Mountains ⋏	180	62.00 N	143.00 W
Wrangell-Saint Elias National Park ♠	180	61.00 N	142.00 W
Wrath, Cape ≻	46	58.37 N	5.01 W
Wray	198	40.04 N	102.13 W
Wraysbury	260	51.27 N	0.33 W
Wrea Green	262	53.46 N	2.55 W
Wreck Bay ⊂	170	35.11 S	150.40 E
Wreck Island I	208	37.16 N	75.48 W
Wreck Reef ✦[2]	166	22.13 S	155.17 E
Wrecks, Bay of ⊂	174o	1.52 N	157.17 W
Wredenhagen	54	53.17 N	12.31 E
Wremen	52	53.39 N	8.30 E
Wren	216	40.48 N	84.46 W
Wrens	192	33.12 N	82.23 W
Wrentham, Ab., Can.	182	49.32 N	112.10 W
Wrentham, Eng., U.K.	42	52.23 N	1.40 E
Wrentham, Ma., U.S.	207	42.04 N	71.19 W
Wrentham State Forest ♠	283	42.02 N	71.20 W
Wrexham	44	53.03 N	3.00 W
Wriezen	54	52.43 N	14.08 E
Wright	278	41.31 N	87.21 W
Wright, Mount ∧, Austl.	166	31.12 S	142.26 E
Wright, Mount ∧, Mt., U.S.	202	47.58 N	112.49 W
Wright Brothers National Memorial ⊥	192	35.55 N	75.50 W
Wright City, Mo., U.S.	219	38.49 N	91.01 W
Wright City, Ok., U.S.	194	34.03 N	95.00 W
Wright City, Tx., U.S.	222	32.12 N	94.59 W
Wrightington Bar	262	53.37 N	2.42 W
Wright Patman Lake ⊜[1]	194	33.16 N	94.14 W
Wright-Patterson Air Force Base ■	218	39.49 N	84.03 W
Wright Peak ∧	204	38.59 N	122.46 W
Wrights	219	39.23 N	90.18 W
Wrightsboro	222	29.22 N	97.34 W
Wrights Corners	210	43.13 N	78.46 W
Wrightson, Mount ∧	200	31.42 N	110.50 W
Wrightstown, N.J., U.S.	208	40.02 N	74.37 W
Wrightstown, Pa., U.S.	208	40.17 N	74.58 W
Wrightstown, Wi., U.S.	190	44.19 N	88.09 W
Wrightsville, Ga., U.S.	192	32.43 N	82.43 W
Wrightsville, Pa., U.S.	214	40.01 N	76.31 W
Wrightsville Beach	192	34.12 N	77.47 W
Wrightwood	228	34.21 N	117.37 W
Wrigley, N.T., Can.	180	63.16 N	123.37 W
Wrigley, Tn., U.S.	194	35.54 N	87.20 W
Wrigley Field ♠	278	41.57 N	87.39 W
Wrigley Gulf ⊂	9	74.00 S	129.00 W
Writtle	42	51.44 N	0.26 E
Wrocław (Breslau)	30	51.06 N	17.00 E
Wrocław □[4]	30	51.15 N	17.00 E
Wrong Lake ⊜	184	52.38 N	96.10 W
Wronki	30	52.43 N	16.23 E
Wrotham	42	51.19 N	0.19 E
Wrotham Heath	260	51.18 N	0.21 E
Wrottesley, Cape ≻	176	74.33 N	121.32 W
Wroughton	42	51.31 N	1.46 W
Wroxham	42	52.42 N	1.24 E
Wroxton	184	51.14 N	101.53 W
Września	30	52.20 N	17.34 E
Wschowa	30	51.48 N	16.19 E
Wu ≃, Zhg.	98	34.25 N	117.55 E
Wu ≃, Zhg.	100	28.57 N	116.39 E
Wu ≃, Zhg.	100	24.48 N	113.35 E
Wu ≃, Zhg.	102	29.43 N	107.24 E
Wu ≃, Zhg.	102	27.12 N	109.48 E
Wu ≃, Zhg.	102	27.03 N	109.53 E
Wu'an	98	36.40 N	114.12 E
Wubaozhen	107	29.14 N	104.29 E
Wubin	162	30.06 S	116.38 E
Wubu	102	37.33 N	110.39 E
Wuchagou	89	46.46 N	120.16 E
Wuchang	89	44.54 N	127.08 E
Wuchang Hu ⊜	100	30.17 N	116.47 E
Wuchang → Wuhan	100	30.36 N	114.17 E
Wucheng, Zhg.	98	37.09 N	115.53 E
Wucheng (Jiucheng), Zhg.	98	37.13 N	116.02 E
Wucheng, Zhg.	100	29.36 N	118.10 E
Wucheng, Zhg.	100	33.28 N	113.44 E
Wucheng, Zhg.	100	29.10 N	115.59 E
Wuch'i	100	24.16 N	120.31 E
Wuchin → Changzhou	106	31.47 N	119.57 E
Wuch'iu Yü I	100	25.00 N	119.27 E
Wuchow → Wuzhou	102	23.30 N	111.27 E
Wuchuan, Zhg.	102	21.25 N	110.40 E
Wuchuan, Zhg.	102	28.25 N	107.56 E
Wuchuan, Zhg.	102	41.05 N	111.23 E
Wuchung → Wuzhong	102	37.57 N	106.10 E
Wucun	105	38.57 N	115.19 E
Wuda	102	39.30 N	106.40 E
Wudao	98	39.28 N	121.28 E
Wudaogou, Zhg.	98	41.43 N	127.05 E
Wudaogou, Zhg.	98	42.08 N	125.51 E
Wudaoliang	120	35.11 N	93.35 E
Wudaolianggou	104	40.59 N	120.35 E
Wudi	98	37.44 N	117.35 E
Wudian, Zhg.	100	32.42 N	117.18 E
Wudian, Zhg.	100	31.57 N	112.46 E
Wuding	102	25.32 N	102.23 E
Wuding ≃	102	37.05 N	110.20 E
Wudinna	166	33.03 S	135.28 E
Wudu, Zhg.	100	27.37 N	119.00 E
Wudu, Zhg.	100	28.23 N	118.14 E
Wudu, Zhg.	102	33.24 N	104.50 E
Wuduhe	102	31.03 N	111.03 E
Wuerqihan	89	49.37 N	121.45 E
Wufeng	102	30.11 N	110.33 E
Wufeng Shan I	106	31.07 N	120.16 E
Wufengxi	107	30.37 N	104.29 E
Wufu	100	30.06 N	120.58 E
Wugang	102	26.44 N	110.38 E
Wugong	102	34.20 N	108.04 E
Wugong Shan ∧	100	27.35 N	114.18 E
Wugong Shan ⋏	100	27.21 N	113.50 E
Wugouying	100	33.28 N	114.08 E
Wugunuoer	89	49.10 N	119.19 E
Wuhai	102	39.39 N	106.41 E
Wuhan	100	30.36 N	114.17 E
Wuhe, Zhg.	100	33.10 N	117.54 E
Wuhe, Zhg.	100	24.26 N	115.25 E
Wuhle ≃	264a	52.29 N	13.34 E
Wuhsing → Huzhou	106	30.52 N	120.06 E
Wuhsi → Wuxi	106	31.35 N	120.18 E
Wuhu, Zhg.	100	31.21 N	118.22 E
Wuhu, Zhg.	100	31.11 N	118.35 E
Wuhua	100	23.57 N	115.48 E
Wuhuanchi	104	42.20 N	121.51 E
Wuhuang	107	29.58 N	104.46 E
Wuhudongmiao	102	38.19 N	107.20 E
Wüjang	120	33.38 N	79.50 E
Wuji, Zhg.	98	38.13 N	114.57 E
Wuji, Zhg.	98	34.12 N	119.02 E
Wujia ≃	102	41.10 N	108.45 E
Wujiabeigou	104	40.57 N	123.50 E
Wujiang, Zhg.	100	31.52 N	118.28 E
Wujiang, Zhg.	100	27.14 N	115.15 E
Wujiang, Zhg.	106	31.10 N	120.38 E
Wujiangdu	102	27.16 N	106.48 E
Wujianpu	107	29.10 N	105.50 E
Wujiapai	105	39.32 N	117.18 E
Wujiapu	105	38.52 N	117.07 E
Wujiazhen	107	29.38 N	105.24 E
Wujiazhuang, Zhg.	105	40.35 N	115.20 E
Wujiazhuang, Zhg.	106	32.18 N	120.10 E
Wujiazi, Zhg.	89	46.27 N	123.34 E
Wujiazi, Zhg.	104	42.13 N	122.08 E
Wujiazi, Zhg.	104	42.30 N	121.10 E
Wujing	100	25.16 N	114.36 E
Wukang	106	30.33 N	119.58 E
Wukari	150	7.51 N	9.47 E
Wukeshu, Zhg.	89	46.02 N	123.45 E
Wukeshu, Zhg.	89	44.48 N	126.08 E
Wulai	100	24.52 N	121.33 E
Wulajia	89	48.23 N	129.58 E
Wulanheduojia	102	42.40 N	113.20 E
Wulanhutong	98	41.44 N	114.49 E
Wulanmutou	104	42.23 N	121.21 E
Wulanwusu, Zhg.	86	44.20 N	85.50 E
Wulanwusu, Zhg.	102	41.39 N	107.48 E
Wular Lake ⊜	123	34.20 N	74.33 E
Wulasitai, Zhg.	89	43.15 N	121.27 E
Wulasitai, Zhg.	89	43.28 N	122.44 E
Wulateqianqi	102	40.39 N	109.05 E
Wulaxi	102	28.38 N	101.40 E
Wuleidao Wan ⊂	98	36.55 N	122.00 E
Wulfen	52	51.43 N	7.00 E
Wülfrath	56	51.17 N	7.02 E
Wulfsen	52	53.18 N	10.08 E
Wulfsode	52	53.04 N	10.13 E
Wulften	52	51.40 N	10.10 E
Wulian (Hongning)	98	35.47 N	119.15 E
Wulian Feng ⋏	102	28.03 N	103.57 E
Wuliangdian	104	41.52 N	122.16 E
Wuliang Shan ⋏	102	24.30 N	100.45 E
Wuliaru, Pulau I	164	7.27 S	131.04 E
Wulichuan	102	33.49 N	111.08 E
Wulie ≃	105	40.54 N	117.55 E
Wuling	98	35.53 N	114.36 E
Wuling Shan ∧	105	40.36 N	117.29 E
Wulitaizi	104	41.28 N	123.21 E
Wulizhuang	100	33.49 N	118.57 E
Wulka ≃	61	47.52 N	16.40 E
Wüllen	52	52.04 N	6.58 E
Wullwye Creek ≃	171b	36.30 S	148.49 E
Wulong, Zhg.	102	29.20 N	107.43 E
Wulong, Zhg.	104	41.39 N	124.13 E
Wulong ≃	98	36.35 N	120.56 E
Wulongbei	98	40.21 N	124.16 E
Wulsdorf ◆[8]	52	53.30 N	8.35 E
Wultschau	61	48.42 N	14.50 E
Wulu ≃	85	39.38 N	74.38 E
Wuluhan	115a	8.21 S	113.33 E
Wuluhayingzi	104	42.20 N	121.34 E
Wulumuch'i → Ürümqi	90	43.48 N	87.35 E
Wulumuqi → Ürümqi	90	43.48 N	87.35 E
Wuluo	102	26.09 N	108.15 E
Wulur	164	7.09 S	128.39 E
Wulu Station ◆[5]	271a	39.56 N	116.16 E
Wum	152	6.23 N	10.04 E
Wumang Dao I	98	39.14 N	123.03 E
Wumiaoxiang	107	30.23 N	104.17 E
Wuming	102	23.10 N	108.18 E
Wümme ≃	52	53.10 N	8.44 E
Wunamu	86	46.06 N	85.44 E
Wundowie	168a	31.46 S	116.22 E
Wundwin	110	21.05 N	96.02 E
Wuneba	154	4.50 N	30.20 E
Wungong Brook ≃	168a	32.06 S	115.59 E
Wuning	100	29.17 N	115.06 E
Wünnenberg	52	51.31 N	8.42 E
Wunnummin Lake ⊜	176	52.55 N	89.10 W
Wun Rog	140	9.00 N	28.21 E
Wünschendorf	54	50.48 N	12.05 E
Wünsdorf	54	52.10 N	13.28 E
Wunsiedel	60	50.02 N	12.01 E
Wunstorf	52	52.25 N	9.26 E
Wuntho	110	23.54 N	95.41 E
Wunuer	89	48.53 N	121.15 E
Wupaowan	107	29.50 N	103.59 E
Wupatki National Monument ♠	200	35.24 N	111.14 W
Wuping	100	25.08 N	116.06 E
Wupper ≃	263	51.05 N	7.00 E
Wuppertal, Dtsch.	56	51.16 N	7.11 E
Wuppertal, Dtsch.	263	51.16 N	7.11 E
Wuppertal, S. Afr.	158	32.15 S	19.15 E
Wuqi, Zhg.	100	27.10 N	120.23 E
Wuqi, Zhg.	102	37.08 N	108.10 E
Wuqia	85	39.42 N	75.13 E
Wuqiang (Xiaofan)	98	38.03 N	115.58 E
Wuqing (Yangcun)	105	39.23 N	117.04 E
Wuraming	168a	32.48 S	116.16 E
Wurarga	162	28.25 S	116.17 E
Würenlingen	58	47.32 N	8.16 E
Wurgwitz	54	51.01 N	13.37 E
Wurm ≃, Dtsch.	56	51.08 N	6.10 E
Würm ≃, Dtsch.	56	48.53 N	8.42 E
Würm ≃, Dtsch.	60	48.10 N	11.28 E
Wurmannsquick	60	48.21 N	12.47 E
Wurmberg ∧	54	51.45 N	10.37 E
Wurno	150	13.17 N	5.24 E
Wurong	164	6.07 S	140.47 E
Würselen	56	50.49 N	6.08 E
Wurtsboro	210	41.35 N	74.29 W
Wurtsboro Hills	210	41.36 N	74.30 W
Wurtsmith Air Force Base ■	190	44.27 N	83.23 W
Wuruf	164	6.43 S	146.25 E
Wuryantoro	115a	7.54 S	110.51 E
Wurzbach	54	50.28 N	11.32 E
Würzburg	56	49.48 N	9.56 E
Wurzen	54	51.22 N	12.44 E
Wusanga	152	3.22 S	22.50 E
Wusha	100	30.39 N	117.18 E
Wushan, Zhg.	100	32.04 N	117.03 E
Wushan, Zhg.	102	34.38 N	105.04 E
Wushan, Zhg.	102	31.05 N	109.48 E
Wushan, Zhg.	106	31.44 N	118.58 E
Wusheng, Zhg.	100	29.56 N	119.25 E
Wusheng, Zhg.	107	30.21 N	106.17 E
Wushengchang	107	29.00 N	103.43 E
Wushenqi	102	38.58 N	109.01 E
Wushi, Zhg.	102	22.11 N	110.11 E
Wushi, Zhg.	106	31.44 N	120.59 E
Wushishi	150	9.46 N	6.07 E
Wushu	100	26.20 N	114.56 E
Wusi	175f	15.22 S	166.36 E
Wusih → Wuxi	106	31.35 N	120.18 E
Wuskwatim Lake ⊜	184	55.32 N	98.32 W
Wusong	106	31.23 N	121.29 E
Wusong ≃	106	31.15 N	121.29 E
Wust	54	52.33 N	12.07 E
Wüsten	52	52.06 N	8.47 E
Wüstensachsen	56	50.30 N	10.00 E
Wusterhausen	54	52.54 N	12.28 E
Wusterhusen	54	54.07 N	13.37 E
Wustermark	54	52.33 N	12.56 E
Wüstermarke	54	51.49 N	13.36 E
Wusterwitz	54	52.22 N	12.18 E
Wüsting	52	53.07 N	8.20 E
Wustrow, Dtsch.	54	52.55 N	11.07 E
Wustrow, Dtsch.	54	54.05 N	11.34 E
Wustrow ≻[1]	54	54.05 N	11.34 E
Wusuli (Ussuri) ≃	89	48.27 N	135.04 E
Wusuo	100	25.02 N	116.02 E
Wuta	106	31.31 N	120.39 E
Wutach ≃	58	47.37 N	8.15 E
Wutai, Zhg.	85	39.28 N	78.09 E
Wutai, Zhg.	86	44.36 N	82.06 E
Wutai, Zhg.	98	41.18 N	113.59 E
Wutai, Zhg.	102	38.44 N	113.17 E
Wutai Shan ∧	98	39.04 N	113.35 E
Wutai Shan ⋏	98	39.13 N	113.45 E
Wutaizi	104	42.27 N	123.17 E
Wutan	102	28.29 N	111.40 E
Wutanchang	107	29.15 N	106.04 E
Wutang	106	31.31 N	119.10 E
Wutangdun	106	30.38 N	120.08 E
Wutangjie	100	29.59 N	122.22 E
Wuteve, Mount ∧	150	8.09 N	9.56 W
Wutianzhen	100	30.23 N	117.12 E
Wutong	102	25.18 N	110.01 E
Wutonghaolai	89	42.55 N	120.15 E
Wutongqiao	107	29.26 N	103.51 E
Wutongwozi	102	42.27 N	95.17 E
Wutsin → Changzhou	106	31.47 N	119.57 E
Wutun	100	27.51 N	118.04 E
Wut'ungch'iao → Wutongqiao	107	29.26 N	103.51 E
Wutungkiao → Wutongqiao	107	29.26 N	103.51 E
Wutuohuo	102	40.51 N	101.48 E
Wuustwezel	50	51.23 N	4.36 E
Wuvulu Island I	164	1.45 S	142.50 E
Wuwei, Zhg.	100	31.18 N	117.54 E
Wuwei (Liangzhou), Zhg.	102	37.58 N	102.49 E
Wuxi, Zhg.	102	31.25 N	109.34 E
Wuxi (Wuhsi), Zhg.	106	31.35 N	120.18 E
Wuxi, Zhg.	106	31.20 N	118.39 E
Wuxi ≃	100	29.00 N	118.56 E
Wuxiang	102	36.51 N	113.00 E
Wuxingchang	106	31.13 N	119.23 E
Wuxuan	102	23.36 N	109.42 E
Wuyang, Zhg.	100	33.26 N	113.34 E

Symbol	English	Deutsch	Español	Français	Português
≃	River	Fluß	Río	Rivière	Rio
≍	Canal	Kanal	Canal	Canal	Canal
⌊	Waterfall, Rapids	Wasserfall, Stromschnellen	Cascada, Rápidos	Chute d'eau, Rapides	Cascata, Rápidos
ʊ	Strait	Meeresstraße	Estrecho	Détroit	Estreito
⊂	Bay, Gulf	Bucht, Golf	Bahía, Golfo	Baie, Golfe	Baía, Golfo
⊜	Lake, Lakes	See, Seen	Lago, Lagos	Lac, Lacs	Lago, Lagos
☷	Swamp	Sumpf	Pantano	Marais	Pântano
⌂	Ice Features, Glacier	Eis- und Gletscherformen	Accidentes Glaciales	Formes glaciaires	Acidentes glaciares
≛	Other Hydrographic Features	Andere Hydrographische Objekte	Otros Elementos Hidrográficos	Autres données hydrographiques	Outros acidentes hidrográficos

Symbol	English	Deutsch	Español	Français	Português
✦	Submarine Features	Untermeerische Objekte	Accidentes Submarinos	Formes de relief sous-marin	Acidentes submarinos
□	Political Unit	Politische Einheit	Unidad Politica	Entité politique	Unidade política
⊍	Cultural Institution	Kulturelle Institution	Institución Cultural	Institution culturelle	Institução cultural
⊥	Historical Site	Historische Stätte	Sitio Histórico	Site historique	Sitio histórico
♠	Recreational Site	Erholungs- und Ferienort	Sitio de Recreo	Centre de loisirs	Area de Lazer
⊠	Airport	Flughafen	Aeropuerto	Aéroport	Aeroporto
■	Military Installation	Militäranlage	Instalación Militar	Installation militaire	Instalação militar
◆	Miscellaneous	Verschiedenes	Misceláneo	Divers	Diversos

ENGLISH — Name | Page | Lat.°′ | Long.°′

DEUTSCH — Name | Seite | Breite°′ | Länge°′ E = Ost

Wuyang, Zhg. **100** 25.41 N 115.55 E
Wuyang, Zhg. **102** 26.41 N 110.20 E
Wuyi, Zhg. **98** 37.49 N 115.54 E
Wuyi, Zhg. **100** 32.13 N 118.26 E
Wuyi, Zhg. **100** 28.54 N 119.48 E
Wuying **89** 48.05 N 129.15 E
Wuyi Shan ∧∧ **90** 27.52 N 117.40 E
Wuyuan, Zhg. **100** 29.15 N 117.49 E
Wuyuan, Zhg. **102** 41.06 N 108.29 E
Wuyun **89** 49.16 N 129.37 E
Wuyunqiao **100** 26.02 N 114.52 E
Wuyur ≃ **89** 47.00 N 124.10 E
Wuzaizi **104** 42.28 N 123.57 E
Wuzhai **102** 38.58 N 111.55 E
Wuzhan **89** 45.51 N 126.17 E
Wuzhen **106** 30.46 N 120.29 E
Wuzhi Shan ∧, Zhg. **105** 40.29 N 118.00 E
Wuzhi Shan ∧, Zhg. **110** 18.57 N 109.43 E
Wuzhong **102** 38.00 N 106.10 E
Wuzhou (Wuchow) **102** 23.30 N 111.27 E
Wuzong **106** 32.14 N 121.03 E
Wyaaba Creek ≃ **164** 16.27 S 141.35 E
Wyaconda **194** 40.23 N 91.55 W
Wyaconda ≃ **194** 40.04 N 91.30 W
Wyalkatchem **162** 31.10 S 117.22 E
Wyalusing **210** 41.40 N 76.15 W
Wyalusing Creek ≃ **210** 41.40 N 76.16 W
Wyandanch **276** 40.45 N 73.21 W
Wyandot **214** 40.44 N 83.08 W
Wyandot □[6] **214** 40.50 N 83.17 W
Wyandotte **216** 42.12 N 83.09 W
Wyandotte Cave ≛[5] **218** 38.14 N 86.18 W
Wyandotte National Wildlife Refuge ◆[4] **281** 42.14 N 83.08 W
Wyandra **166** 27.15 S 145.59 E
Wyangala, Lake ⊜[1] **166** 33.58 S 148.55 E
Wyano **214** 40.12 N 79.42 W
Wyatt, In., U.S. **216** 41.31 N 86.10 W
Wyatt, Mo., U.S. **194** 36.54 N 89.13 W
Wycheproof **166** 36.05 S 143.14 E
Wychwood **273d** 26.12 S 28.08 E
Wyckoff **210** 41.00 N 74.10 W
Wydgee **162** 28.51 S 117.49 E
Wydgelee **158** 34.23 S 20.26 E
Wy-Dit-Joli-Village **261** 49.06 N 1.50 E
Wye **42** 51.11 N 0.56 E
Wye ≃, On., Can. **212** 44.44 N 79.52 W
Wye ≃, U.K. **42** 51.37 N 2.39 W
Wye ≃, Eng., U.K. **44** 53.12 N 1.37 W
Wyee **170** 33.11 S 151.29 E
Wye Lake ⊜ **212** 44.43 N 79.52 W
Wyemandoo ∧ **162** 28.31 S 118.32 E
Wyeville **190** 44.01 N 90.23 W
Wyhl **58** 48.09 N 7.39 E
Wyhra ≃ **54** 51.09 N 12.27 E
Wyk **30** 54.42 N 8.34 E
Wyke Regis **42** 50.36 N 2.29 W
Wykoff **190** 43.42 N 92.16 W
Wylandville **279b** 40.12 N 80.08 W
Wyleswood Lake ⊜ **279a** 41.20 N 81.55 W
Wylie, Pa., U.S. **279b** 40.27 N 79.59 W
Wylie, Tx., U.S. **222** 33.01 N 96.32 W
Wylie, Lake ⊜[1] **192** 35.07 N 81.02 W
Wylye ≃ **42** 51.04 N 1.52 W
Wymah **171b** 36.02 S 147.17 E
Wymark **184** 50.07 N 107.44 W
Wymeswold **42** 52.47 N 1.06 W
Wymondham **42** 52.34 N 1.07 E
Wymore **198** 40.07 N 96.39 W
Wynantskill **210** 42.42 N 73.39 W
Wynberg **158** 34.02 S 18.28 E
Wynbring **162** 30.33 S 133.32 E
Wyncote **285** 40.05 N 75.08 W
Wyndham, Austl. **164** 15.28 S 128.06 E
Wyndham, N.Z. **172** 46.20 S 168.51 E
Wyndmere **198** 46.16 N 97.07 W
Wyndmoor **285** 40.04 N 75.11 W
Wynigen **58** 47.06 N 7.40 E
Wynndel **182** 49.11 N 116.33 W
Wynne **194** 35.13 N 90.47 W
Wynnewood, Ok., U.S. **196** 34.38 N 97.09 W
Wynnewood, Pa., U.S. **285** 40.00 N 75.16 W
Wynniatt Bay c **176** 72.55 N 110.30 W
Wynnum **171a** 27.27 S 153.10 E
Wynona **196** 36.32 N 96.19 W
Wynoochee ≃ **224** 46.58 N 123.35 W
Wynoochee Lake ⊜[1] **224** 47.25 N 123.35 W
Wynot **198** 42.44 N 97.10 W
Wynyard, Austl. **166** 40.59 S 145.41 E
Wynyard, Sk., Can. **184** 51.47 N 104.10 W
Wyocena **190** 43.29 N 89.18 W
Wyodak **198** 44.17 N 105.22 W
Wyola Lake ⊜ **162** 29.08 S 130.17 E
Wyoming, On., Can. **190** 42.57 N 82.07 W
Wyoming, De., U.S. **208** 39.07 N 75.33 W
Wyoming, Il., U.S. **190** 41.03 N 89.46 W
Wyoming, Ia., U.S. **190** 42.03 N 91.00 W
Wyoming, Mi., U.S. **216** 42.54 N 85.42 W
Wyoming, N.Y., U.S. **210** 42.49 N 78.05 W
Wyoming, Oh., U.S. **218** 39.13 N 84.27 W
Wyoming, Pa., U.S. **210** 41.18 N 75.50 W
Wyoming, R.I., U.S. **207** 41.30 N 71.42 W
Wyoming □[6], N.Y., U.S. **210** 42.44 N 78.08 W
Wyoming □[6], Pa., U.S. **210** 41.32 N 75.57 W
Wyoming □[3] **178** 43.00 N 107.30 W
Wyoming Peak ∧ **200** 42.36 N 110.37 W
Wyomissing **208** 40.19 N 75.57 W
Wyong **170** 33.17 S 151.25 E
Wyong ≃ **170** 33.18 S 151.28 E
Wyperfield National Park ♦ **166** 35.30 S 142.00 E
Wyre ≃ **44** 53.55 N 3.00 W
Wyreema **171a** 27.39 S 151.52 E
Wyre Forest ◆[3] **42** 52.23 N 2.23 W
Wyrzysk **30** 53.10 N 17.15 E
Wyśmierzyce **30** 51.38 N 20.49 E
Wysoka **30** 53.11 N 17.05 E
Wysokie Mazowieckie **30** 52.56 N 22.32 E
Wysox **210** 41.46 N 76.24 W
Wyszków **30** 52.36 N 21.28 E
Wyszogród **30** 52.23 N 20.11 E
Wythenshawe ◆[8] **262** 53.24 N 2.17 W
Wythenshawe Hall ⊥ **262** 53.24 N 2.17 W
Wytheville **192** 36.56 N 81.05 W
Wytschegda → Vyčegda ≃ **24** 61.18 N 46.36 E
Wyvis, Ben ∧ **46** 57.42 N 4.35 W

X

Xaafuun **144** 10.25 N 51.16 E
Xàbia **34** 38.47 N 0.10 E
Xabregas ◆[8] **266c** 38.44 N 9.07 W
Xá-Cassau **152** 9.02 S 20.14 E
Xaclbal ≃ **236** 16.06 N 90.58 W
Xaidulla **120** 36.21 N 78.02 E
Xainza **120** 30.57 N 88.38 E
Xaitongmoin **124** 29.22 N 88.15 E
Xai-Xai **156** 25.02 S 33.34 E
Xalapa **234** 19.32 N 96.55 W
Xalin **144** 9.06 N 48.37 E
Xalisco **234** 21.27 N 104.54 W
Xalostoc **234** 19.24 N 98.03 W
Xalpatlahuac **234** 17.01 N 99.18 W
Xaltianguis **234** 17.04 N 99.50 W
Xam (Chu) ≃ **110** 19.53 N 105.45 E
Xambioá **250** 6.25 S 48.40 W
Xambrê ≃ **255** 24.02 S 53.59 W
Xam Nua **110** 20.25 N 104.02 E
Xá-Muteba **152** 9.34 S 17.50 E
Xan (San) ≃ **110** 13.32 N 105.58 E
Xang ≃ **124** 29.22 N 89.09 E
Xangongo **152** 16.43 S 15.01 E
Xanten **52** 51.39 N 6.26 E
Xánthi **38** 41.08 N 24.53 E
Xanxerê **252** 26.53 S 52.23 W
Xapecó ≃ **252** 27.06 S 53.01 W
Xapuri **248** 10.39 S 68.31 W
Xapuri ≃ **248** 10.39 S 68.30 W
Xarardheere **144** 4.39 N 47.51 E
Xar Moron ≃, Zhg. **90** 43.25 N 121.41 E
Xar Moron ≃, Zhg. **102** 43.02 N 111.20 E
Xarrama ≃ **34** 38.14 N 8.20 W
Xàtiva (Játiva) **34** 38.59 N 0.31 W
Xau, Lake ≚ **156** 21.15 S 24.38 E
Xauen → Chaouen **148** 35.10 N 5.16 W
Xavante ≃ **250** 11.23 S 49.41 W
Xavantes ≃ **250** 10.40 S 50.41 W
Xavantina **255** 21.15 S 52.48 W
Xa Vo Dat **110** 11.09 N 107.31 E
Xaxim **252** 26.56 S 52.31 W
Xcalak **232** 18.16 N 87.50 W
X-Can **232** 20.50 N 87.43 W
Xelva **34** 39.45 N 0.59 W
Xenia, Il., U.S. **219** 38.38 N 88.38 W
Xenia, Oh., U.S. **218** 39.41 N 83.55 W
Xénô **110** 16.35 N 104.50 E
Xercavins, Arroyo de ≃ **266d** 41.30 N 2.02 E
Xerém **256** 22.33 S 43.18 W
Xeres → Jerez de la Frontera **34** 36.41 N 6.08 W
Xertigny **58** 48.03 N 6.24 E
Xeruã ≃ **248** 6.03 S 67.50 W
Xhumo **156** 21.07 S 24.42 E
Xi ≃, Zhg. **100** 25.14 N 118.03 E
Xi ≃, Zhg. **100** 30.21 N 115.06 E
Xi ≃, Zhg. **100** 24.34 N 117.30 E
Xi ≃, Zhg. **102** 42.20 N 100.20 E
Xi ≃, Zhg. **102** 22.25 N 113.23 E
Xi ≃, Zhg. **104** 41.15 N 123.32 E
Xi ≃, Zhg. **104** 41.30 N 121.26 E
Xi ≃, Zhg. **107** 30.26 N 103.48 E
Xiaang **106** 30.45 N 120.07 E
Xiaba **100** 24.54 N 116.06 E
Xiabai, Zhg. **106** 31.12 N 119.50 E
Xiabai, Zhg. **106** 30.29 N 120.00 E
Xiabanghu **100** 30.31 N 112.38 E
Xiabian **104** 40.51 N 120.30 E
Xiabuji **100** 28.19 N 116.20 E
Xiacang **105** 39.47 N 117.24 E
Xiache **100** 24.40 N 115.08 E
Xiachengzi **89** 44.41 N 130.27 E
Xiachuan Dao I **102** 21.40 N 112.37 E
Xiacun **105** 40.21 N 116.14 E
Xiadao **100** 26.34 N 118.16 E
Xiadian, Zhg. **98** 37.06 N 120.19 E
Xiadian, Zhg. **100** 31.26 N 114.17 E
Xiadian, Zhg. **105** 39.57 N 116.55 E
Xiadianjie **100** 25.13 N 118.27 E
Xiafeidi **98** 42.18 N 124.21 E
Xiafu, Zhg. **100** 25.01 N 113.41 E
Xiafu, Zhg. **100** 23.52 N 115.45 E
Xiagaixin **102** 22.36 N 99.59 E
Xiagang **106** 31.55 N 120.13 E
Xiagezhuang **98** 36.41 N 120.25 E
Xiaguan, Zhg. **98** 39.07 N 114.09 E
Xiaguan, Zhg. **102** 25.34 N 100.14 E
Xiaguan, Zhg. **106** 32.06 N 118.44 E
Xiaguanjunchang **104** 41.28 N 121.40 E
Xiaguanpi **100** 24.04 N 117.06 E
Xiagucheng **102** 36.47 N 102.53 E
Xiagucun **106** 30.56 N 119.09 E
Xiahada **104** 41.58 N 124.08 E
Xiahailangzhai **104** 41.35 N 123.46 E
Xiahe **102** 35.18 N 102.30 E
Xiahuangjintun **104** 41.57 N 123.48 E
Xiahuayuan **105** 40.29 N 115.17 E
Xiajiabaozi **98** 42.16 N 124.37 E
Xiajialou **104** 42.25 N 123.39 E
Xiajiang **100** 27.32 N 115.08 E
Xiajiangdun **106** 31.14 N 120.24 E
Xiajiangwu **106** 30.29 N 119.00 E
Xiajiayuan **106** 32.13 N 120.38 E
Xiajiezi **102** 27.28 N 101.35 E
Xiajin **98** 36.55 N 115.57 E
Xiakou **100** 28.28 N 118.31 E
Xialianggang **105** 39.14 N 115.07 E
Xialufang **102** 31.11 N 103.38 E
Xiamaguan **102** 37.14 N 106.28 E
Xiamen (Amoy) **100** 24.28 N 118.07 E
Xiamen Gang c **100** 24.19 N 118.10 E
Xiamianzhen **107** 30.08 N 106.32 E
Xiamin'ansutai **104** 41.54 N 120.53 E
Xiamocun **106** 31.09 N 119.22 E
Xi'an (Sian) **102** 34.15 N 108.52 E
Xian ≃ **107** 29.22 N 104.44 E
Xianchenggu **98** 36.53 N 115.17 E
Xiandu **100** 25.04 N 117.44 E
Xianfeng, Zhg. **100** 25.42 N 117.53 E
Xianfeng, Zhg. **102** 29.41 N 109.02 E
Xiang ≃, Zhg. **100** 25.35 N 115.49 E
Xiang ≃, Zhg. **102** 29.00 N 112.56 E
Xiang'an **100** 31.12 N 117.46 E
Xiangcheng, Zhg. **100** 33.28 N 114.53 E
Xiangcheng, Zhg. **100** 33.53 N 113.29 E
Xiangcheng, Zhg. **102** 28.59 N 99.45 E
Xiangcheng, Zhg. **106** 31.29 N 120.44 E
Xiangfan **102** 32.03 N 112.01 E
Xiangfuguan **100** 28.30 N 115.26 E
Xiangfusi **107** 30.06 N 104.24 E
Xianggang → Victoria **271d** 22.17 N 114.09 E
Xianggongshi **100** 28.25 N 113.32 E
Xianggongzhuang **105** 39.48 N 118.19 E
Xianghe **105** 39.46 N 116.59 E
Xiangheguan **100** 33.08 N 113.26 E
Xianghuazhen **106** 31.31 N 121.43 E
Xiangjia, Zhg. **106** 31.20 N 120.31 E
Xiangjia, Zhg. **106** 31.19 N 120.23 E
Xiangjiachang **107** 30.08 N 104.18 E
Xiangkhoang **110** 19.20 N 103.22 E
Xiangkhoang, Plateau de ∧∧[1] **110** 19.30 N 103.10 E
Xiangning **102** 36.01 N 110.45 E
Xiangride **102** 36.02 N 98.08 E
Xiangshan, Zhg. **100** 29.28 N 121.51 E
Xiangshan, Zhg. **105** 39.59 N 116.12 E
Xiangshan Gang c **100** 29.38 N 121.48 E
Xiangshizhen **107** 29.17 N 105.09 E
Xiangshui, Zhg. **100** 23.15 N 114.10 E
Xiangshui, Zhg. **100** 34.12 N 119.34 E
Xiangtan **100** 27.51 N 112.54 E
Xiangtang **100** 28.26 N 115.58 E
Xiangxiang **102** 27.43 N 112.27 E
Xiangyang **105** 39.13 N 115.25 E
Xiangyangkou **105** 40.06 N 115.47 E
Xiangyin **100** 28.40 N 112.53 E
Xiangyuan **102** 36.32 N 113.00 E
Xiangyun **102** 25.30 N 100.30 E
Xiangzhenpu **100** 30.52 N 117.21 E
Xiangzhou, Zhg. **98** 36.12 N 119.24 E
Xiangzhou, Zhg. **102** 23.55 N 109.49 E
Xiangzhu **100** 29.02 N 120.04 E
Xianinggang **100** 28.20 N 112.56 E
Xianjiang **100** 27.48 N 120.30 E
Xianju **100** 28.51 N 120.44 E
Xianning **100** 29.53 N 114.13 E
Xiannongtan Stadium ♦ **271a** 39.52 N 116.23 E
Xiannübu **100** 25.36 N 114.40 E
Xianru **89** 43.11 N 128.02 E
Xianshichang **107** 28.43 N 105.44 E
Xianshui ≃ **102** 30.05 N 110.59 E
Xianshuigu **105** 38.59 N 117.23 E
Xiantan, Zhg. **107** 29.21 N 104.53 E
Xiantan, Zhg. **107** 28.50 N 106.12 E
Xiantang **100** 23.48 N 114.46 E
Xianxia Ling ∧∧ **100** 28.30 N 118.46 E
Xianxian **98** 38.13 N 116.06 E
Xianyang, Zhg. **100** 28.02 N 118.30 E
Xianyang, Zhg. **102** 34.22 N 108.42 E
Xianyou **100** 25.23 N 118.40 E
Xianzhong **100** 28.36 N 113.48 E
Xiao ≃ **100** 28.11 N 120.14 E
Xiao'an ≃ **107** 29.59 N 106.13 E
Xiao'ao **100** 26.14 N 119.39 E
Xiaoazhang **102** 23.42 N 104.58 E
Xiaobangniulu **104** 41.34 N 122.46 E
Xiaobeigou **104** 41.55 N 120.46 E
Xiaobeihe, Zhg. **104** 42.39 N 123.58 E
Xiaobeihe, Zhg. **104** 41.22 N 122.50 E
Xiaocaohu **86** 43.06 N 88.30 E
Xiaochangshan Dao I **98** 39.12 N 122.41 E
Xiaocheng **100** 26.20 N 119.47 E
Xiaochengdu **106** 30.59 N 120.04 E
Xiaochengzi, Zhg. **89** 46.33 N 122.54 E
Xiaochengzi, Zhg. **89** 42.56 N 123.12 E
Xiaochi **100** 30.33 N 116.23 E
Xiaochikou **100** 29.46 N 115.59 E
Xiaodanyang **106** 31.38 N 118.43 E
Xiaodong **102** 22.14 N 108.39 E
Xiao'ergou **89** 49.12 N 123.42 E
Xiaofangshen **104** 42.13 N 123.54 E
Xiaofanshan **105** 40.16 N 115.19 E
Xiaofen **106** 31.45 N 119.39 E
Xiaofeng **106** 30.36 N 119.32 E
Xiaogan **100** 30.55 N 113.54 E
Xiaogangkou **100** 28.14 N 115.50 E
Xiaogaojiatun **104** 41.02 N 121.59 E
Xiaogencaigangzi **104** 41.48 N 122.42 E
Xiaogu **107** 29.08 N 104.01 E
Xiaoguai **86** 45.13 N 85.02 E
Xiaogushan **98** 39.49 N 123.12 E
Xiaohaizhen **106** 31.58 N 120.59 E
Xiaohaladaokou **98** 42.37 N 119.32 E
Xiaohan **98** 35.48 N 114.52 E
Xiaohe **106** 32.01 N 119.52 E
Xiaohei Shan ∧ **102** 24.42 N 98.55 E
Xiaohekou **102** 33.19 N 107.25 E
Xiaoheyan **98** 42.26 N 119.38 E
Xiaoheying **102** 32.37 N 104.23 E
Xiao Hinggan Ling (Lesser Khingan Range) ∧∧ **89** 48.45 N 127.00 E
Xiaohongmen **271a** 39.49 N 116.26 E
Xiaohu **100** 27.20 N 118.14 E
Xiaohuying **98** 41.09 N 117.13 E
Xiaoji, Zhg. **98** 36.45 N 121.01 E
Xiaoji, Zhg. **100** 27.08 N 113.15 E
Xiaoji, Zhg. **100** 32.38 N 119.48 E
Xiaojiachang **107** 30.18 N 106.28 E
Xiaojiagang **100** 31.06 N 113.55 E
Xiaojialing **100** 29.35 N 116.32 E
Xiaojiang **100** 25.08 N 114.59 E
Xiaojianji **100** 33.23 N 116.29 E
Xiaojiawu **105** 39.36 N 116.36 E
Xiaojiayingzi **98** 40.17 N 118.47 E
Xiaojieling **100** 31.36 N 115.09 E
Xiaojin **102** 31.00 N 102.21 E
Xiaojingfang **105** 39.22 N 116.34 E
Xiaojiu **89** 45.15 N 127.47 E
Xiaokaoshantun **104** 42.10 N 123.53 E
Xiaokuli **89** 50.18 N 120.20 E
Xiaokunshan **106** 31.02 N 121.07 E
Xiaolan **100** 22.41 N 113.14 E
Xiaoliangshan **104** 42.05 N 122.32 E
Xiaoling, Zhg. **89** 45.20 N 127.18 E
Xiaoling, Zhg. **104** 42.18 N 123.23 E
Xiaoling ≃ **104** 41.06 N 121.07 E
Xiaolingzi **104** 41.07 N 123.19 E
Xiaolinzhuang **104** 41.36 N 124.01 E
Xiaolipu **98** 36.24 N 116.35 E
Xiaolongtan **102** 23.51 N 103.10 E
Xiaoluan ≃ **98** 41.36 N 117.05 E
Xiaolüzhuang **106** 31.57 N 119.25 E
Xiaomei **100** 27.50 N 118.58 E
Xiaomei Guan)(**100** 25.17 N 114.17 E
Xiaomiaozi **98** 41.24 N 114.25 E
Xiaonanhai **107** 29.23 N 106.27 E
Xiaopikou **98** 35.47 N 115.53 E
Xiaopingyang **102** 23.22 N 109.13 E
Xiao Qaidam He ⊜ **102** 37.30 N 95.12 E
Xiaoqiao **100** 26.57 N 118.30 E
Xiaoqiaotou **106** 30.43 N 119.27 E
Xiaoqing ≃ **98** 37.17 N 118.52 E
Xiaoqingchuizi **104** 42.30 N 123.39 E
Xiaoquandong **102** 41.14 N 95.26 E
Xiaosanjiazi **104** 42.34 N 123.23 E
Xiaosha ≃ **104** 41.13 N 122.45 E
Xiaoshakou **100** 29.58 N 113.16 E
Xiaoshan **106** 30.10 N 120.15 E
Xiaoshangqiao **100** 33.43 N 113.58 E
Xiaoshi **100** 27.27 N 116.49 E
Xiaoshixiang **100** 30.36 N 116.38 E
Xiaoshu **106** 30.48 N 119.46 E
Xiaoshun **100** 29.11 N 119.51 E
Xiaosigou **98** 40.53 N 118.33 E
Xiaosijia **104** 42.24 N 120.46 E
Xiaotang **98** 41.38 N 119.33 E
Xiaotanghe **98** 42.04 N 127.10 E
Xiaotao **100** 25.46 N 117.08 E
Xiaotazi **104** 42.17 N 123.08 E
Xiaotian **100** 31.12 N 116.33 E
Xiaotianji **100** 32.45 N 115.36 E
Xiaotun **104** 42.24 N 123.44 E
Xiaotunzicun **104** 41.14 N 123.20 E
Xiaowa **104** 41.03 N 122.04 E
Xiaowan **100** 26.53 N 116.36 E
Xiaowangmiao **100** 29.41 N 121.21 E
Xiaowutai Shan ∧ **105** 39.51 N 115.09 E
Xiaowutai Shan ∧∧ **105** 39.50 N 115.00 E
Xiaoxi **100** 25.48 N 115.21 E
Xiaoxi ≃ **106** 32.15 N 120.24 E
Xiaoxian **98** 34.11 N 116.56 E
Xiaoxincheng **105** 39.24 N 115.11 E
Xiaoxintian **271a** 39.58 N 116.22 E
Xiaoxizhen **106** 30.51 N 119.50 E
Xiaoyangjiadian **104** 42.23 N 122.24 E
Xiaoyangqi **89** 50.48 N 124.12 E
Xiaoyantai **104** 41.26 N 123.10 E
Xiaoyaozhen **100** 33.46 N 114.16 E
Xiaoyi **102** 37.10 N 111.46 E
Xiaoying, Zhg. **98** 37.18 N 118.04 E
Xiaoying, Zhg. **105** 40.12 N 116.33 E
Xiaoyingcun **105** 39.28 N 116.41 E
Xiaoyuan **107** 30.00 N 104.56 E
Xiaozhan **105** 38.55 N 117.25 E
Xiaozhang ≃ **105** 39.47 N 117.22 E
Xiaozhongdian **102** 27.40 N 99.46 E
Xiaozhuang **104** 41.30 N 121.27 E
Xiaozhujiawan **106** 31.24 N 121.01 E
Xiapu, Zhg. **100** 26.52 N 120.01 E
Xiapu, Zhg. **100** 27.49 N 114.26 E
Xiaqialafangzi **104** 41.48 N 121.44 E
Xiaqi Dao I **100** 29.42 N 122.15 E
Xiaqiubao **98** 37.01 N 119.54 E
Xiasantumen **105** 38.50 N 114.48 E
Xiashe **106** 30.33 N 120.11 E
Xiashesi **100** 27.46 N 112.57 E
Xiashi → Haining **106** 30.32 N 120.41 E
Xiashu **106** 32.11 N 119.10 E
Xiashuerfowei **89** 50.23 N 120.47 E
Xiashuiquan **104** 41.52 N 123.38 E
Xiataizi **105** 40.37 N 117.45 E
Xiatang, Zhg. **100** 33.45 N 112.39 E
Xiatang, Zhg. **106** 31.29 N 118.41 E
Xiatangtian **106** 30.55 N 120.12 E
Xiataohuatu **104** 41.42 N 120.36 E
Xiawa **98** 42.39 N 120.35 E
Xiawajiang **106** 30.59 N 121.51 E
Xiawaziyu **104** 41.15 N 123.38 E
Xiaxi **106** 31.43 N 119.45 E
Xiaxian **102** 35.11 N 111.15 E
Xiaxiangcheng **102** 28.42 N 99.59 E
Xiaxikou **100** 26.15 N 118.59 E
Xiaxinhe **106** 31.40 N 119.31 E
Xiayang, Zhg. **100** 28.48 N 119.41 E
Xiayang, Zhg. **100** 24.39 N 116.52 E
Xiayang, Zhg. **100** 26.46 N 117.59 E
Xiayi **98** 34.14 N 116.06 E
Xiaying, Zhg. **98** 37.03 N 119.25 E
Xiaying, Zhg. **105** 40.10 N 117.25 E
Xiayunling **105** 39.43 N 115.44 E
Xiazhang **98** 36.08 N 116.57 E
Xiazhen **100** 28.39 N 118.21 E
Xiazhuang, Zhg. **98** 35.28 N 118.43 E
Xiazhuang, Zhg. **100** 27.22 N 119.01 E
Xiazhuang, Zhg. **105** 39.54 N 117.01 E
Xiazhuang, Zhg. **105** 39.38 N 115.26 E
Xiazikou **105** 39.01 N 115.25 E
Xiban **107** 30.32 N 106.12 E
Xibaqianmou **104** 40.59 N 121.35 E
Xibeiyingzi **104** 41.55 N 121.38 E
Xibo ≃ **98** 42.17 N 118.57 E
Xibu **100** 31.46 N 118.17 E
Xicang **106** 31.34 N 120.29 E
Xichang, Zhg. **102** 27.58 N 102.13 E
Xichang, Zhg. **104** 42.15 N 124.12 E
Xicheng **89** 48.10 N 125.29 E
Xichong **102** 31.00 N 105.52 E
Xicicun **105** 39.29 N 116.08 E
Xico **234** 19.25 N 97.00 W
Xicoténcatl **234** 23.00 N 98.56 W
Xicotepec de Juárez **234** 20.17 N 97.57 W
Xictle, Volcán ∧[1] **286a** 19.14 N 99.14 W
Xicun **100** 27.46 N 114.14 E
Xidachuan **98** 41.46 N 127.34 E
Xidapo **89** 43.12 N 130.02 E
Xidaying **105** 39.41 N 116.14 E
Xidian **100** 29.32 N 121.26 E
Xiditou **105** 39.16 N 117.23 E
Xidongting Shan ∧ **106** 31.07 N 120.16 E
Xié ≃ **246** 0.54 N 67.11 W
Xiecun **105** 39.00 N 115.31 E
Xiedian **100** 33.27 N 113.28 E
Xiefang **100** 26.12 N 116.41 E
Xieji **98** 34.32 N 115.29 E
Xiejia **98** 42.24 N 125.42 E
Xiejiagangzi **104** 41.55 N 122.20 E
Xiejiapu **106** 31.15 N 119.09 E
Xiejunmiao **107** 30.15 N 103.40 E
Xielipuke **120** 31.30 N 82.45 E
Xiemachang **107** 29.46 N 106.22 E
Xiemata Shan ∧ **89** 50.28 N 120.47 E
Xiepu **100** 30.02 N 121.37 E
Xieqiao, Zhg. **106** 32.03 N 120.22 E
Xieqiao, Zhg. **106** 30.29 N 120.34 E
Xietang **106** 31.18 N 120.44 E
Xiexi **106** 31.54 N 118.54 E
Xiexinggou **104** 41.51 N 121.05 E
Xifei ≃ **100** 32.38 N 116.39 E
Xifeng, Zhg. **98** 42.43 N 124.40 E
Xifeng, Zhg. **102** 27.02 N 106.30 E
Xifengkou **105** 40.24 N 118.19 E
Xifocun **104** 41.26 N 122.33 E
Xigangzi **89** 49.58 N 127.20 E
Xigaolizhuangzi **104** 41.40 N 122.55 E
Xigaotan **98** 38.18 N 116.13 E
Xigaotun **98** 40.27 N 122.36 E
Xigazê **120** 29.17 N 88.53 E
Xiguanjiatun **104** 42.35 N 123.10 E
Xiguanyingzi **104** 41.50 N 120.37 E
Xihaikou **104** 40.50 N 121.05 E
Xihan ≃ **102** 33.30 N 106.02 E
Xihe, Zhg. **100** 31.01 N 118.28 E
Xihe, Zhg. **100** 31.41 N 113.27 E
Xihe, Zhg. **102** 34.01 N 105.17 E
Xiheying **105** 39.53 N 114.42 E
Xihezhuang **105** 39.20 N 118.02 E
Xi Hu ⊜ **106** 30.15 N 120.08 E
Xihua **100** 33.47 N 114.31 E
Xihuangcang **106** 31.43 N 121.40 E
Xihuanzidong **104** 41.31 N 122.28 E
Xihuashan, Zhg. **100** 25.28 N 114.20 E
Xihuashan, Zhg. **105** 40.07 N 116.54 E
Xihuishan **104** 41.41 N 122.38 E
Xiis **144** 10.53 N 46.54 E
Xiji, Zhg. **102** 35.58 N 105.44 E
Xiji, Zhg. **105** 39.49 N 116.52 E
Xijialong **102** 23.31 N 103.51 E
Xijiang **100** 25.50 N 115.49 E
Xijianshanzi **104** 40.47 N 120.48 E
Xi Jiao Airfield ⊠ **271a** 39.58 N 116.15 E
Xijiapuzitun **104** 41.26 N 123.50 E
Xijir Ulan Hu ⊜ **120** 35.12 N 90.18 E
Xikou, Zhg. **89** 46.40 N 120.40 E
Xikou, Zhg. **100** 28.52 N 119.11 E
Xikou, Zhg. **100** 25.26 N 118.45 E
Xikou, Zhg. **100** 29.11 N 114.23 E
Xikou, Zhg. **100** 29.14 N 114.24 E
Xikou, Zhg. **100** 29.44 N 118.02 E
Xikou, Zhg. **106** 30.40 N 118.41 E
Xikouxu **100** 25.24 N 117.03 E
Xikouzi **89** 53.06 N 120.40 E
Xilai **107** 30.20 N 103.29 E
Xilaiqiao **106** 32.03 N 119.54 E
Xilaizhen **106** 32.07 N 120.25 E
Xilin **120** 28.33 N 87.48 E
Xi Ling (Western Tombs) ⊥ **105** 39.24 N 115.18 E
Xilintuo **120** 30.08 N 88.04 E
Xilitla **234** 21.20 N 98.58 W
Xiliuhe **105** 38.58 N 116.32 E
Xiliushuyingzi **104** 42.25 N 121.54 E
Xilókastron **38** 38.05 N 22.38 E
Xiluga ≃ **98** 42.21 N 118.38 E
Xiluncun **89** 47.08 N 126.26 E
Ximagou **105** 40.16 N 117.50 E
Ximakou **100** 30.33 N 113.47 E
Ximalatu **89** 47.00 N 122.01 E
Ximalin **98** 40.48 N 114.29 E
Ximiao **102** 41.09 N 100.17 E
Ximucheng **104** 40.42 N 122.54 E
Xin ≃ **100** 28.37 N 116.40 E
Xin'an, Zhg. **89** 43.46 N 125.40 E
Xinan, Zhg. **100** 25.26 N 117.35 E
Xin'an, Zhg. **100** 23.02 N 114.56 E
Xin'an, Zhg. **100** 26.44 N 116.13 E
Xin'an, Zhg. **105** 39.09 N 116.38 E
Xin'an, Zhg. **106** 31.47 N 120.09 E
Xin'an, Zhg. **106** 31.30 N 120.22 E
Xin'an ≃ **100** 29.33 N 118.58 E
Xin'andian **100** 32.37 N 114.03 E
Xin'andu **100** 30.52 N 116.53 E
Xin'anji **100** 33.22 N 115.13 E
Xin'anjiang Shuiku ⊜[1] **100** 29.27 N 119.06 E
Xin'anpu **104** 42.39 N 123.27 E
Xin'anqiao **106** 32.16 N 121.07 E
Xin'ansuo **102** 23.16 N 103.27 E
Xin'anzhen, Zhg. **89** 44.06 N 123.46 E
Xin'anzhen, Zhg. **105** 39.45 N 117.32 E
Xi'nanzhuang **105** 40.48 N 118.23 E
Xinavane **156** 25.02 S 32.47 E
Xinba, Zhg. **98** 34.27 N 119.09 E
Xinba, Zhg. **100** 30.24 N 116.52 E
Xinba, Zhg. **106** 32.08 N 120.39 E
Xinba, Zhg. **106** 32.16 N 119.45 E
Xinbao'an **105** 40.27 N 115.24 E
Xin Barag Youqi (Altan Emel) **88** 48.41 N 116.53 E
Xin Barag Zuoqi (Amgalang) **88** 48.14 N 118.18 E
Xinbin, Zhg. **98** 41.42 N 125.02 E
Xinbin, Zhg. **106** 30.56 N 121.04 E
Xinbo **98** 42.19 N 117.44 E
Xincai **100** 32.44 N 114.59 E
Xincang, Zhg. **106** 30.25 N 120.42 E
Xincang, Zhg. **106** 30.44 N 121.11 E
Xinchang, Zhg. **100** 29.30 N 120.53 E
Xinchang, Zhg. **102** 28.03 N 103.46 E
Xinchang, Zhg. **102** 25.10 N 104.18 E
Xinchang, Zhg. **106** 31.42 N 121.46 E
Xinchang, Zhg. **106** 31.02 N 121.38 E
Xinchang, Zhg. **107** 30.29 N 106.21 E
Xinchang, Zhg. **107** 30.16 N 104.29 E
Xinchang, Zhg. **107** 29.20 N 104.15 E
Xinchang, Zhg. **107** 29.38 N 104.33 E
Xinchangzi **107** 29.40 N 103.46 E
Xincheng, Zhg. **100** 25.34 N 114.36 E
Xincheng, Zhg. **102** 24.09 N 108.46 E
Xincheng (Gaobeidian), Zhg. **105** 39.20 N 115.51 E
Xincheng, Zhg. **105** 38.59 N 117.33 E
Xincheng, Zhg. **106** 32.17 N 119.14 E
Xincheng, Zhg. **106** 30.48 N 120.36 E
Xinchengzi **104** 42.03 N 123.30 E
Xinchepaizi **86** 44.55 N 84.30 E
Xincunji **100** 32.53 N 115.31 E
Xindai **106** 30.49 N 121.05 E
Xindi **104** 42.21 N 120.31 E
Xindian, Zhg. **89** 45.55 N 127.50 E
Xindian, Zhg. **98** 37.07 N 114.49 E
Xindian, Zhg. **98** 37.29 N 118.28 E
Xindian, Zhg. **100** 33.07 N 112.38 E
Xindian, Zhg. **100** 31.33 N 115.16 E
Xindian, Zhg. **100** 33.38 N 113.51 E
Xindian, Zhg. **100** 29.40 N 113.40 E
Xindian, Zhg. **105** 40.11 N 116.11 E
Xindian, Zhg. **105** 40.47 N 116.49 E
Xindian, Zhg. **105** 39.10 N 116.27 E
Xindian, Zhg. **107** 29.19 N 105.40 E
Xindianbu **100** 32.24 N 116.22 E
Xindianzi, Zhg. **105** 40.04 N 118.01 E
Xindianzi, Zhg. **107** 28.49 N 103.35 E
Xindianzi, Zhg. **107** 29.03 N 103.46 E
Xindianzi, Zhg. **107** 29.52 N 106.06 E
Xindianzi, Zhg. **107** 29.46 N 105.11 E
Xindianzi, Zhg. **107** 29.43 N 104.01 E
Xindu **102** 23.59 N 111.46 E
Xinfatuncun **104** 41.13 N 122.28 E
Xinfeng, Zhg. **100** 25.24 N 114.56 E
Xinfeng, Zhg. **100** 27.26 N 116.40 E
Xinfeng, Zhg. **100** 24.04 N 114.12 E
Xinfeng, Zhg. **100** 33.19 N 120.30 E
Xinfeng, Zhg. **100** 24.05 N 116.53 E
Xinfeng, Zhg. **106** 31.09 N 118.40 E
Xinfeng, Zhg. **106** 32.05 N 119.34 E
Xinfeng, Zhg. **106** 30.43 N 120.55 E
Xinfeng ≃ **100** 23.42 N 114.42 E
Xinfeng Shuiku ⊜[1] **100** 23.52 N 114.30 E
Xing'an, Zhg. **89** 48.49 N 121.45 E
Xing'an, Zhg. **102** 25.37 N 110.31 E
Xin'gang, Zhg. **106** 31.56 N 120.57 E
Xingang, Zhg. **106** 32.03 N 120.25 E
Xing'antun **89** 51.31 N 120.08 E
Xingcheng **104** 40.37 N 120.43 E
Xingguo **100** 26.21 N 115.19 E
Xinghai **102** 35.31 N 99.36 E
Xinghe **98** 40.48 N 113.58 E
Xinghua **100** 32.57 N 119.50 E
Xinghua Wan c **100** 25.20 N 119.20 E
Xingjing **102** 29.43 N 102.59 E
Xingkai Hu (ozero Chanka) ⊜ **89** 45.00 N 132.24 E
Xingliu **100** 33.04 N 115.41 E
Xinglong, Zhg. **100** 32.05 N 112.51 E
Xinglong, Zhg. **102** 35.38 N 106.08 E
Xinglong, Zhg. **105** 40.26 N 117.34 E
Xinglong, Zhg. **107** 30.36 N 106.20 E
Xinglong, Zhg. **107** 30.20 N 106.07 E
Xinglongchang, Zhg. **107** 30.25 N 104.06 E
Xinglongchang, Zhg. **107** 29.34 N 106.09 E
Xinglongchang, Zhg. **107** 29.54 N 105.26 E
Xinglongcun **89** 49.50 N 125.12 E
Xinglongdian, Zhg. **104** 42.16 N 124.00 E
Xinglongdian, Zhg. **104** 41.59 N 123.03 E
Xinglonggou, Zhg. **104** 41.46 N 120.38 E
Xinglonggou, Zhg. **104** 40.45 N 123.08 E
Xinglongpao **89** 46.27 N 125.47 E
Xinglongtai **104** 42.30 N 123.48 E
Xingning **100** 24.09 N 115.45 E
Xingou, Zhg. **100** 30.41 N 113.57 E
Xingou, Zhg. **100** 30.08 N 112.56 E
Xingren **102** 25.27 N 105.13 E
Xingrenbu **102** 37.06 N 105.12 E
Xingshanbao **89** 45.30 N 125.45 E
Xingtai **98** 37.04 N 114.29 E
Xingtan **100** 22.46 N 113.07 E
Xingtang **98** 38.26 N 114.33 E
Xingtian **100** 27.30 N 118.02 E
Xingu ≃ **242** 1.30 S 51.53 W
Xinguan **100** 33.38 N 118.05 E
Xingwenping **102** 29.24 N 103.23 E
Xingxian **102** 38.36 N 111.15 E
Xingxing **106** 30.39 N 121.09 E
Xingyi, Zhg. **98** 38.18 N 115.01 E
Xingyi, Zhg. **102** 25.06 N 104.58 E
Xingzhuangzi **105** 40.34 N 115.00 E
Xingzi **100** 29.28 N 116.01 E
Xinhe, Zhg. **98** 37.32 N 115.14 E
Xinhe, Zhg. **100** 28.30 N 121.27 E
Xinhe, Zhg. **105** 39.03 N 117.37 E
Xinhe, Zhg. **106** 31.59 N 121.21 E
Xinhekou **89** 48.22 N 130.45 E
Xinheng **100** 23.38 N 116.18 E
Xinhezhen **106** 31.35 N 121.31 E
Xinhezhuang **106** 31.10 N 118.46 E
Xinhua **102** 27.37 N 111.02 E
Xinhuai ≃ **100** 34.23 N 120.05 E
Xinhuang **106** 30.37 N 120.55 E
Xinhui **100** 22.32 N 113.02 E
Xining (Sining) **102** 36.38 N 101.55 E
Xiniu, Zhg. **100** 24.10 N 113.07 E
Xiniu, Zhg. **106** 31.25 N 120.07 E
Xiniuguchengzi **104** 41.01 N 122.24 E
Xinji, Zhg. **98** 35.19 N 115.36 E
Xinji, Zhg. **100** 33.24 N 114.44 E
Xinji, Zhg. **105** 39.52 N 117.10 E
Xinji, Zhg. **105** 40.04 N 118.21 E
Xinjiaji **98** 36.56 N 116.59 E
Xinjian, Zhg. **100** 28.46 N 120.02 E
Xinjian, Zhg. **100** 28.34 N 115.47 E
Xinjian, Zhg. **106** 31.33 N 119.39 E
Xinjiang, Zhg. **100** 24.29 N 113.52 E
Xinjiang, Zhg. **102** 35.40 N 111.11 E
Xinjiang, Zhg. **106** 32.05 N 120.40 E
Xinjianglang **106** 30.58 N 120.54 E
Xinjiang Uygur Zizhiqu (Sinkiang) □[4] **90** 40.00 N 85.00 E
Xinjiapu **105** 40.32 N 115.57 E
Xinjiazhuang **105** 40.31 N 114.58 E
Xinjie **102** 26.48 N 101.15 E
Xinjieji **89** 52.08 N 126.24 E
Xinjin (Pulandian), Zhg. **98** 39.24 N 121.58 E
Xinjin, Zhg. **107** 30.25 N 103.49 E
Xinjingzi **86** 42.13 N 87.36 E
Xinjuntun **105** 39.39 N 117.57 E
Xinkai ≃ **89** 43.37 N 123.36 E
Xinkaigang **106** 31.55 N 120.56 E
Xinkengdong **100** 26.09 N 113.46 E
Xinle (Dongchangshou) **98** 38.24 N 114.47 E
Xinli **89** 44.41 N 126.45 E
Xinlitun, Zhg. **89** 43.34 N 125.18 E
Xinlitun, Zhg. **104** 42.15 N 122.51 E
Xinlitun, Zhg. **104** 42.00 N 122.09 E
Xinlizhuang **105** 39.17 N 116.10 E
Xinmin **104** 42.00 N 122.48 E
Xinmintun **104** 41.39 N 123.02 E
Xinning **102** 26.19 N 110.45 E
Xinping **102** 24.06 N 101.58 E
Xinpu **100** 24.31 N 116.08 E
Xinqianhu **98** 37.59 N 118.15 E
Xinqiao, Zhg. **106** 31.32 N 119.04 E
Xinqiao, Zhg. **106** 31.04 N 121.18 E
Xinqiao, Zhg. **107** 29.32 N 106.28 E
Xinqiao, Zhg. **107** 30.10 N 103.50 E
Xinqiao, Zhg. **107** 30.33 N 105.33 E
Xinqiaotou **106** 31.00 N 119.24 E
Xinqiaozhen **107** 29.36 N 103.39 E
Xinqiu **98** 41.53 N 119.41 E
Xinqizhou **100** 28.56 N 115.50 E
Xinqu **86** 44.57 N 85.15 E
Xinquan **100** 25.23 N 116.38 E
Xinsanyu **106** 31.58 N 120.07 E
Xinshao **102** 27.11 N 111.20 E
Xinshengzhen **107** 29.29 N 104.39 E
Xinshi, Zhg. **106** 30.37 N 120.19 E
Xinshi, Zhg. **106** 32.04 N 120.02 E
Xinshizhen, Zhg. **102** 28.39 N 104.02 E
Xinshizhen, Zhg. **107** 30.20 N 104.35 E
Xinshu ≃ **98** 34.41 N 119.12 E
Xintai **98** 35.54 N 117.44 E
Xintaimen **98** 40.50 N 120.23 E
Xintaizi, Zhg. **104** 41.06 N 122.42 E
Xintaizi, Zhg. **104** 42.07 N 123.36 E
Xintang, Zhg. **100** 23.08 N 113.36 E
Xintang, Zhg. **102** 30.13 N 109.30 E
Xintang, Zhg. **106** 31.02 N 119.59 E
Xintangcun **106** 31.53 N 119.31 E
Xintanpu **100** 29.43 N 114.54 E
Xintian **102** 25.53 N 112.05 E
Xintun **104** 42.11 N 123.45 E
Xinvi **105** 40.04 N 118.21 E
Xinwei **100** 25.21 N 115.48 E
Xinwen (Suncun) **98** 35.53 N 117.40 E
Xinxian, Zhg. **100** 31.38 N 114.51 E
Xinxian, Zhg. **102** 38.25 N 112.48 E
Xinxiang **98** 35.20 N 113.51 E
Xinxim ≃ **250** 7.57 S 53.20 W
Xinxing, Zhg. **89** 43.16 N 129.48 E
Xinxing, Zhg. **100** 22.40 N 112.52 E
Xinxing, Zhg. **102** 19.57 N 109.32 E
Xinxu, Zhg. **100** 24.57 N 117.34 E
Xinxu, Zhg. **100** 22.52 N 114.20 E
Xinyang **100** 32.08 N 114.04 E
Xinyao **100** 27.39 N 118.52 E
Xinye **100** 32.33 N 112.21 E
Xinyi (Xin'anzhen), Zhg. **98** 34.22 N 118.21 E
Xinyi (Dongzhen), Zhg. **102** 22.13 N 110.50 E
Xinyi ≃ **100** 34.29 N 119.49 E
Xinying **102** 36.03 N 105.35 E
Xinyu **100** 27.49 N 114.57 E
Xinyuan **86** 43.08 N 82.31 E
Xinzao **100** 23.02 N 113.26 E
Xinzha **102** 23.41 N 101.09 E
Xinzhai, Zhg. **98** 39.24 N 118.46 E
Xinzhai, Zhg. **98** 36.24 N 118.37 E
Xinzhai, Zhg. **102** 24.33 N 99.08 E
Xinzhan **100** 33.33 N 114.50 E
Xinzhang **105** 39.05 N 116.46 E
Xinzhangzi **105** 40.45 N 117.50 E
Xinzhao **102** 39.32 N 107.52 E
Xinzhazhen **106** 31.50 N 119.52 E
Xinzhen, Zhg. **98** 35.37 N 114.03 E
Xinzhen, Zhg. **105** 39.01 N 116.22 E
Xinzhen, Zhg. **106** 31.24 N 121.24 E
Xinzheng **100** 34.25 N 113.43 E
Xinzhou, Zhg. **100** 30.50 N 114.47 E
Xinzhou, Zhg. **102** 19.48 N 109.18 E
Xinzhuang, Zhg. **98** 35.05 N 117.56 E
Xinzhuang, Zhg. **271a** 39.56 N 116.31 E
Xinzhuangtou **105** 39.25 N 115.45 E
Xinzhuangzi, Zhg. **104** 41.05 N 121.23 E
Xinzhuangzi, Zhg. **105** 40.14 N 116.59 E
Xinzhuangzi, Zhg. **105** 40.32 N 115.10 E
Xinzhuangzi, Zhg. **105** 38.52 N 117.21 E
Xinzhuangzi, Zhg. **105** 39.20 N 118.25 E
Xinzo de Limia **34** 42.03 N 7.43 W
Xiongdi Yu II **100** 23.33 N 117.40 E
Xiongjiachang **102** 26.31 N 105.39 E
Xiongxian **105** 38.59 N 116.05 E
Xiongyuecheng **98** 40.10 N 122.08 E
Xipamanu (Chipamanu) ≃ **248** 10.43 S 67.50 W
Xiping, Zhg. **100** 28.27 N 119.29 E
Xiping, Zhg. **100** 33.23 N 114.02 E
Xiping'anhe **104** 40.47 N 122.01 E
Xiqia **106** 31.03 N 119.37 E
Xiqilichiquan **89** 49.59 N 119.27 E
Xiqin **100** 26.33 N 118.06 E
Xiqing Shan ∧∧ **102** 35.30 N 101.30 E
Xique-Xique **250** 10.50 S 42.44 W
Xisanshilipu **100** 32.40 N 117.31 E
Xisantai **98** 39.38 N 121.37 E
Xishan, Zhg. **100** 28.34 N 115.37 E
Xishan, Zhg. **105** 39.38 N 118.10 E
Xishanqiao **106** 31.57 N 118.43 E
Xishanxicun **105** 40.01 N 116.50 E
Xisha Qundao (Paracel Islands) II **108** 16.30 N 112.15 E
Xishijiazi **104** 41.46 N 120.55 E
Xishiqiao **106** 31.53 N 120.06 E
Xishu **98** 36.41 N 113.49 E
Xishui **100** 30.27 N 115.13 E
Xishuiyu **105** 40.25 N 116.16 E
Xisuhupu **104** 41.41 N 123.14 E
Xitai **98** 40.37 N 120.12 E
Xitan **100** 23.47 N 117.08 E
Xitang **106** 30.57 N 120.53 E
Xitangqiao, Zhg. **106** 31.49 N 120.38 E
Xitangqiao, Zhg. **106** 30.37 N 121.01 E
Xitaoyuan **104** 40.57 N 122.11 E
Xiti **120** 33.27 N 82.48 E
Xitianmu Shan ∧ **106** 30.21 N 119.25 E
Xitiao ≃ **106** 30.57 N 120.10 E
Xiting **106** 32.07 N 121.00 E
Xitole **150** 11.43 N 14.50 W
Xituan **105** 39.29 N 115.47 E
Xiu ≃ **100** 29.13 N 115.56 E
Xiujiangpu **104** 41.17 N 123.02 E
Xiuning **100** 29.47 N 118.10 E
Xiushan **102** 28.29 N 108.52 E
Xiushui **100** 29.04 N 114.33 E
Xiushui ≃ **104** 42.03 N 122.58 E
Xiushuihe **104** 42.22 N 123.01 E
Xiuyan **98** 40.17 N 123.18 E
Xiva **34** 39.28 N 0.43 W
Xiwei **100** 25.22 N 117.46 E
Xiweizigou **104** 42.01 N 121.59 E
Xiwenquan **107** 29.42 N 106.07 E
Xiwu **100** 29.40 N 121.30 E
Xiwukou **106** 30.24 N 118.54 E
Xixabangma Feng ∧ **124** 28.22 N 85.50 E
Xixi **100** 26.45 N 118.42 E
Xixia **102** 33.22 N 111.28 E
Xixian, Zhg. **100** 32.21 N 114.44 E
Xixian, Zhg. **102** 36.43 N 110.52 E
Xixiang **102** 32.48 N 107.55 E
Xixiangyang **105** 39.33 N 116.02 E
Xixiaojie **104** 40.42 N 122.12 E
Xixiashu **106** 31.57 N 119.49 E
Xixing **106** 30.11 N 120.13 E
Xixona **34** 38.32 N 0.30 W
Xiyang, Zhg. **98** 37.37 N 113.42 E
Xiyang, Zhg. **100** 25.50 N 117.25 E
Xiyang, Zhg. **106** 31.49 N 120.43 E
Xiyang, Zhg. **106** 31.52 N 119.23 E
Xiyang Dao I **100** 26.32 N 120.04 E
Xiyangji **100** 33.25 N 116.22 E
Xiyangjiao **106** 31.43 N 120.23 E
Xiyangshugou **104** 40.41 N 122.44 E
Xiyangzhuang **106** 31.50 N 119.22 E
Xiyingzi **104** 41.55 N 122.34 E
Xiyou **98** 37.24 N 119.56 E
Xiyushi **106** 30.36 N 119.26 E
Xizang Zizhiqu (Tibet) □[4] **90** 32.00 N 88.00 E
Xizhi ≃ **100** 23.04 N 114.31 E
Xizhimen Station ◆[5] **271a** 39.56 N 116.21 E
Xizhong Dao I **98** 39.26 N 121.17 E
Xizhou **100** 29.29 N 121.39 E
Xizi **98** 41.48 N 119.16 E
Xochiapa **234** 17.39 N 95.46 W
Xochicalco ⊥ **234** 18.48 N 99.19 W
Xochimilco ◆[8] **286a** 19.16 N 99.06 W
Xochimilco, Lago de ⊜ **286a** 19.16 N 99.06 W
Xochipala **234** 17.48 N 99.39 W
Xochistlahuaca **234** 16.47 N 98.15 W
Xochitlán **234** 19.59 N 97.36 W
Xoka **120** 29.58 N 93.48 E
Xom Binh Phuoc **269c** 10.40 N 106.47 E
Xom Xoai Minh **269c** 10.42 N 106.50 E
Xu ≃ **100** 28.17 N 116.05 E
Xuancheng **106** 30.58 N 118.45 E
Xuan'en **102** 30.00 N 109.20 E
Xuanfeng **100** 27.42 N 114.08 E

Symbols in the index entries represent the broad categories identified in the key at the right. Symbols with superior numbers (∧∧[1]) identify subcategories (see complete key on page *I · 1*).

Symbole im Register stellen die rechts im Schlüssel erklärten Kategorien dar. Symbole mit hochgestellten Ziffern (∧∧[1]) bezeichnen Unterabteilungen einer Kategorie (vgl. vollständiger Schlüssel auf Seite *I · 1*).

Los símbolos incluídos en el texto del índice representan las grandes categorias identificadas con la clave a la derecha. Los símbolos con numeros en su parte superior (∧∧[1]) identifican las subcategorías (véase la clave completa en la página *I · 1*).

Les symboles de l'index représentent les catégories indiquées dans la légende à droite. Les symboles suivis d'un indice (∧∧[1]) représentent des sous-catégories (voir légende complète à la page *I · 1*).

Os símbolos incluídos no texto do índice representam as grandes categorias identificadas com a chave à direita. Os símbolos com números em sua parte superior (∧∧[1]) identificam as subcategorias (veja-se a chave completa à página *I · 1*).

English	Deutsch	Español	Français	Português
∧ Mountain	Berg	Montaña	Montagne	Montanha
∧∧ Mountains	Gebirge	Montañas	Montagnes	Montanhas
)(Pass	Paß	Paso	Col	Passo
V Valley, Canyon	Tal, Cañon	Valle, Cañón	Vallée, Canyon	Vale, Canhão
≚ Plain	Ebene	Llano	Plaine	Planície
› Cape	Kap	Cabo	Cap	Cabo
I Island	Insel	Isla	Île	Ilha
II Islands	Inseln	Islas	Îles	Ilhas
≛ Other Topographic Features	Andere Topographische Objekte	Otros Elementos Topográficos	Autres données topographiques	Outros acidentes topográficos

ESPAÑOL — Nombre | Página | Lat.°′ | Long.°′ W = Oeste

Xuang ≃ 110 19.58 N 102.15 E
Xuanhan 102 31.24 N 107.43 E
Xuanhua 105 40.37 N 115.03 E
Xuanhuadian 100 31.42 N 114.29 E
Xuanhui ≃ 98 38.07 N 117.45 E
Xuanjiabao 106 32.17 N 120.01 E
Xuanjiangying 98 41.25 N 116.45 E
Xuan Loc 110 10.56 N 107.14 E
Xuantan 107 29.12 N 105.34 E
Xuan Thoi Thuong 269c 10.52 N 106.34 E
Xuanwei 102 26.07 N 104.05 E
Xuanzhuang 105 39.29 N 118.07 E
Xubu 98 40.02 N 113.43 E
Xuchang, Zhg. 100 34.03 N 113.49 E
Xuchang, Zhg. 107 29.06 N 104.31 E
Xucheng 98 35.56 N 116.27 E
Xuchilquitongo 234 17.15 N 96.53 W
Xucun 106 30.27 N 120.22 E
Xudazhuang 100 33.44 N 117.53 E
Xuddun 144 9.09 N 47.28 E
Xuddur 144 4.07 N 43.54 E
Xueao 100 29.27 N 121.30 E
Xuebu 106 31.43 N 119.22 E
Xuecheng 98 34.50 N 117.16 E
Xuedian, Zhg. 100 34.04 N 113.04 E
Xuedian, Zhg. 100 34.30 N 113.44 E
Xuefanggou 104 41.57 N 121.01 E
Xuefeng 100 33.21 N 118.22 E
Xuehu 98 34.08 N 116.27 E
Xueshan Zhang ∧ 100 24.24 N 113.37 E
Xueshuiwen 89 49.10 N 129.45 E
Xuetangpuzi 104 40.38 N 123.53 E
Xueyanqiao 106 31.30 N 120.06 E
Xuezhen 106 31.35 N 118.38 E
Xuguanzhen 106 31.23 N 120.30 E
Xuguichenxiaodian 106 32.07 N 121.20 E
Xuguit Qi (Yakeshi) 89 49.17 N 120.41 E
Xuji 100 31.50 N 116.22 E
Xujiabu 100 29.27 N 116.18 E
Xujiadong 100 25.54 N 113.02 E
Xujiadu 100 28.18 N 114.44 E
Xujiagou 104 42.17 N 124.04 E
Xujiapuzi 104 40.44 N 123.18 E
Xujiatou 106 31.19 N 119.25 E
Xujiazhai, Zhg. 106 31.11 N 121.46 E
Xujiazhai, Zhg. 269b 31.23 N 121.17 E
Xuliying 105 39.28 N 116.02 E
Xun ≃, Zhg. 89 49.27 N 128.55 E
Xun ≃, Zhg. 102 23.28 N 111.18 E
Xungru 120 29.15 N 84.49 E
Xunhe 89 49.18 N 128.04 E
Xunhua 102 35.49 N 102.26 E
Xunjiansi 105 40.50 N 116.04 E
Xunke 89 49.35 N 128.25 E
Xunle 102 25.17 N 108.12 E
Xunmukou 98 34.03 N 114.42 E
Xunshansuo 98 37.10 N 122.29 E
Xunwu 100 24.58 N 115.38 E
Xunwu ≃ 100 24.28 N 115.26 E
Xunxian 98 35.43 N 114.31 E
Xupu, Zhg. 102 27.44 N 110.24 E
Xupu, Zhg. 106 31.45 N 120.54 E
Xushe 106 31.24 N 119.39 E
Xushi 106 31.40 N 120.57 E
Xushui 105 39.02 N 115.39 E
Xutian 98 34.10 N 114.03 E
Xuwan 100 27.55 N 116.31 E
Xuwen 102 20.21 N 110.11 E
Xuxiandai 106 30.40 N 120.47 E
Xuxiang 106 31.33 N 120.13 E
Xuyen Moc 110 10.34 N 107.25 E
Xuyi 100 33.01 N 118.29 E
Xuyong 102 28.10 N 105.24 E
Xuzhou (Süchow) 98 34.16 N 117.11 E
Xuzhuang 106 31.09 N 120.32 E

Y

Yaak 182 48.50 N 115.42 W
Yaan 102 30.03 N 103.02 E
Yaapeet 166 35.46 S 142.03 E
Yaaq-Baraawe 144 1.57 N 43.11 E
Yaba ◆[8] 273a 6.30 N 3.23 E
Yaba College of Technology ʊ[2] 273a 6.32 N 3.23 E
Ya'bad 132 32.27 N 35.10 E
Yabakei 96 33.27 N 131.07 E
Yabassi 152 4.28 N 9.58 E
Yabe 96 33.09 N 130.49 E
Yabe ≃ 96 33.06 N 130.26 E
Yabelo 144 4.54 N 38.05 E
Yablis 236 14.10 N 83.49 W
Yablonovy Range → Jablonovyj chrebet ⋏ 88 53.30 N 115.00 E
Yabrīn ⊤[4] 128 23.17 N 48.58 E
Yabrūd 130 33.58 N 36.40 E
Yabu, Nihon 96 35.22 N 134.47 E
Yabu, Nihon 174m 26.36 N 127.57 E
Yabucoa 240m 18.03 N 65.53 W
Yabuki 94 37.12 N 140.19 E
Yabuli 89 44.55 N 128.35 E
Yacambu, Parque Nacional ♦ 246 9.40 N 69.42 W
Yacaré Norte, Riacho ≃ 252 22.43 S 58.14 W
Yacheng 110 18.25 N 109.11 E
Yachi ≃ 102 27.18 N 107.15 E
Yachimata 94 35.39 N 140.19 E
Yachiyo, Nihon 94 35.43 N 140.07 E
Yachiyo, Nihon 94 36.10 N 139.53 E
Yacimiento Río Turbio 254 51.32 S 72.18 W
Yaco 248 17.09 S 67.24 W
Yaco (Iaco) ≃ 248 9.03 S 68.34 W
Yacolt 224 45.51 N 122.24 W
Yacuiba 248 22.02 S 63.45 W
Yacuma ≃ 248 13.38 S 65.23 W
Yacyretá, Isla I 252 27.25 S 56.30 W
Yada ≃ 96 35.38 N 134.37 E
Yādgīr 122 16.46 N 77.08 E
Yadkin ≃ 192 35.23 N 80.03 W
Yadkinville 192 36.08 N 80.39 W
Yad Mordekhay 132 31.35 N 34.34 E
Yadong 124 27.29 N 88.55 E
Yādūdah 132 32.40 N 36.04 E
Yaenengu 152 2.28 N 23.15 E
Yaeyama-rettō II 175d 24.20 N 124.00 E
Yāfā 132 32.41 N 35.17 E
Yafran 146 32.04 N 12.31 E
Yaftābād 267d 35.39 N 51.19 E
Yafuquan 85 39.12 N 76.09 E
Yagachi-shima I 174m 26.40 N 128.01 E
Yağcılar 130 39.25 N 28.23 E
Yageg 144 3.16 N 44.00 E
Yagi 96 35.04 N 135.32 E
Yagishiri-tō I 92a 44.26 N 141.25 E
Yağlıca Dağı ∧ 84 40.18 N 43.18 E
Yago 234 21.50 N 105.04 W
Yagonde 152 0.02 N 22.41 E
Yagoona 274a 33.55 S 151.02 E
Yagoua 146 10.20 N 15.14 E
Yagradagzê Shan ∧ 120 35.12 N 95.20 E
Yaguachi Nuevo 246 2.07 S 79.41 W
Yaguajay 240p 22.19 N 79.14 W
Yaguala ≃ 236 15.25 N 86.40 W
Yaguará 246 2.40 N 75.31 W
Yaguaraparo 246 10.34 N 62.49 W
Yaguarí 252 31.31 S 54.58 W
Yaguarón (Jaguarão) ≃ 252 32.39 S 53.12 W
Yaguas ≃ 246 2.45 S 70.04 W
Yagur 132 32.44 N 35.04 E
Yahagi ≃ 94 34.50 N 136.59 E
Yahagong 102 28.24 N 99.11 E
Yahara ≃ 190 42.48 N 89.07 W
Yahata → Kitakyūshū 96 33.53 N 130.50 E

FRANÇAIS — Nom | Page | Lat.°′ | Long.°′ W = Ouest

Yahe, Zhg. 89 45.24 N 130.24 E
Yahe, Zhg. 106 31.44 N 119.52 E
Yahila 152 0.13 N 24.28 E
Yahk 182 49.05 N 116.05 W
Yahmūm al-Asmar, Jabal ∧ 142 29.56 N 31.38 E
Yaho 268 35.41 N 139.27 E
Yahōga-take ∧ 96 33.04 N 130.50 E
Yahongqiao 105 39.45 N 117.51 E
Yahualica 234 21.08 N 102.51 W
Yahuma 152 1.05 N 23.13 E
Yahyalı 130 38.07 N 35.22 E
Yai ≃ 114 5.02 N 101.47 E
Yai, Khao ∧, Asia 110 12.27 N 99.26 E
Yai, Khao ∧, Thai 110 15.25 N 99.20 E
Yainax Butte ∧ 202 42.20 N 121.16 W
Yaita, Nihon 94 36.48 N 139.56 E
Yaita, Nihon 268 35.57 N 140.03 E
Yaitopya → Ethiopia □[1] 144 9.00 N 39.00 E
Yaizu 94 34.52 N 138.20 E
Yajiang 102 30.02 N 101.05 E
Yaka 130 41.15 N 34.01 E
Yakacık 130 36.47 N 36.10 E
Yakacık ◆[8] 267b 40.55 N 29.13 E
Yakage 96 34.37 N 133.35 E
Yakak, Cape › 180 51.38 N 177.00 W
Yakapınar 130 37.00 N 35.36 E
Yakarta → Jakarta 115a 6.10 S 106.48 E
Yake-dake ∧ 94 36.14 N 137.35 E
Yake-yama ∧ 94 36.55 N 138.03 E
Yakhchāl, Afg. 120 31.47 N 64.41 E
Yakhchāl, Afg. 128 31.47 N 64.41 E
Yakima 202 46.36 N 120.30 W
Yakima □[6] 224 46.34 N 121.03 W
Yakima ≃ 202 46.15 N 119.02 W
Yakima Firing Center ■ 202 46.44 N 120.10 W
Yakima Indian Reservation ◆[4] 224 46.16 N 121.03 W
Yakkan ≃ 96 33.34 N 131.22 E
Yakmach 128 28.45 N 63.51 E
Yako 150 12.58 N 2.16 W
Yakō ◆[8] 268 35.32 N 139.41 E
Yakobi Island I 180 58.00 N 136.30 W
Yakoma 152 4.05 N 22.27 E
Yakou 100 24.46 N 118.46 E
Yakuendai 268 35.43 N 140.03 E
Yakuluku 154 4.20 N 28.48 E
Yakumo 92a 42.15 N 140.16 E
Yakuno 96 35.19 N 135.00 E
Yakushi-dake ∧ 94 36.28 N 137.33 E
Yakushi-ji ʊ[1] 94 36.25 N 139.53 E
Yaku-shima I 93b 30.20 N 130.30 E
Yakutat 180 59.33 N 139.44 W
Yakutat Bay ⊂ 180 59.40 N 140.00 W
Yakutat Seamount ✢[3] 16 35.15 N 48.00 W
Yakutsk → Jakutsk 74 62.00 N 129.40 E
Yala, Ghana 150 10.07 N 1.52 W
Yala, Thai 110 6.33 N 101.18 E
Yalaha 220 28.44 N 81.48 W
Yalahau, Laguna ⊂ 232 21.30 N 87.15 W
Yalakdere 130 40.36 N 29.33 E
Yalata 162 31.29 S 131.52 E
Yalata Aboriginal Reserve ◆[4] 162 31.30 S 131.45 E
Yalca, Laguna ◎ 258 35.34 S 57.55 W
Yalding 260 51.13 N 0.26 E
Yale, B.C., Can. 182 49.34 N 121.26 W
Yale, Mi., U.S. 190 43.07 N 82.47 W
Yale, Ok., U.S. 196 36.06 N 96.41 W
Yale, Va., U.S. 208 36.50 N 77.17 W
Yale, Lake ◎ 220 28.54 N 81.45 W
Yale, Mount ∧ 200 38.51 N 106.18 W
Yale Lake ◎[1] 224 46.00 N 122.12 W
Yalgar ≃ 162 26.09 S 117.57 E
Yalgoo 162 28.20 S 116.41 E
Yalgorup National Park ♦ 168a 32.55 S 115.41 E
Yali 152 0.04 N 21.03 E
Yaliji 98 36.06 N 114.56 E
Yalikamba 152 1.17 S 22.30 E
Yalinga 152 6.31 N 23.15 E
Yalisere 152 0.11 N 22.33 E
Yalleroi 166 24.04 S 145.45 E
Yallourn 169 38.11 S 146.21 E
Yallourn North 169 38.09 S 146.22 E
Yalnızçam Dağları ⋏ 84 41.10 N 42.25 E
Yalobusha ≃ 194 33.33 N 90.10 W
Yaloká 152 5.19 N 17.05 E
Yalong ≃ 102 26.37 N 101.48 E
Yaloupi ≃ 250 2.47 N 52.28 W
Yalova 130 40.39 N 29.15 E
Yalta → Jalta 78 44.30 N 34.10 E
Yalu 89 48.34 N 122.09 E
Yalu (Amnok-kang) ≃, Asia 98 39.55 N 124.22 E
Yalu ≃, Zhg. 89 46.56 N 123.30 E
Yalufi 152 0.45 N 24.26 E
Yalvaç 130 38.17 N 31.11 E
Yalwal Creek ≃ 170 34.50 S 150.23 E
Yamachiche 206 46.16 N 72.50 W
Yamachiche ≃ 206 46.16 N 72.48 W
Yamada, Nihon 92 39.28 N 141.57 E
Yamada, Nihon 94 35.49 N 140.36 E
Yamada, Nihon 94 36.34 N 137.05 E
Yamada, Nihon 96 33.33 N 130.47 E
Yamada, Nihon 174m 26.26 N 127.47 E
Yamada, Nihon 270 34.31 N 135.39 E
Yamada, Nihon 270 34.48 N 135.32 E
Yamada ≃ 270 34.47 N 135.04 E
Yamada → Tosa-yamada 96 33.36 N 133.41 E
Yamaga, Nihon 96 33.01 N 130.41 E
Yamaga, Nihon 96 33.27 N 131.30 E
Yamagata, Nihon 92 38.15 N 140.20 E
Yamagata, Nihon 94 36.38 N 140.24 E
Yamagata, Nihon 94 36.10 N 137.52 E
Yamagawa 92 31.12 N 130.39 E
Yamaguchi, Nihon 94 35.33 N 137.33 E
Yamaguchi, Nihon 96 34.10 N 131.29 E
Yamaguchi, Nihon 270 34.50 N 135.15 E
Yamaguchi □[5] 96 34.20 N 131.30 E
Yamaguchi-chosuichi ◎[1] 268 35.46 N 139.25 E
Yama-Hita-Hiko-san-kokutei-kōen ♦ 96 33.25 N 131.02 E
Yamakawa 96 34.04 N 134.15 E
Yamakita 94 35.21 N 139.05 E
Yamakuni 96 33.24 N 131.02 E
Yamakuni ≃ 96 33.37 N 131.12 E
Yamām, Jabal al- ∧ 132 30.02 N 35.28 E
Yamamoto, Nihon 96 34.07 N 133.44 E
Yamamoto, Nihon 270 34.38 N 135.38 E
Yamanaka 94 36.15 N 136.22 E
Yamanakako 94 35.24 N 138.52 E
Yamanaka-ko ◎ 94 35.25 N 138.52 E
Yamanashi 94 35.40 N 138.40 E
Yamanashi □[5] 94 35.30 N 138.30 E
Yamanouchi 94 36.44 N 138.25 E
Yamasaki 96 35.00 N 134.33 E
Yamashina ◆[8] 270 34.58 N 135.49 E
Yamashiro, Nihon 94 34.45 N 135.49 E
Yamashiro, Nihon 96 33.57 N 133.45 E
Yamaska (Saint-Michel) 206 46.00 N 72.55 W
Yamaska □[6] 206 46.00 N 72.45 W
Yamaska ≃ 206 46.06 N 72.56 W
Yamaska, Mont ∧[2] 206 45.27 N 72.52 W
Yamaska Nord ≃ 206 45.17 N 72.51 W
Yamaska Sud-Est ≃ 206 45.17 N 72.55 W
Yamate 270 34.30 N 135.27 E
Yamatengwumulu 102 38.38 N 97.05 E
Yamato, Nihon 94 35.48 N 136.54 E
Yamato, Nihon 94 35.29 N 139.29 E
Yamato, Nihon 94 37.10 N 138.56 E

PORTUGUÊS — Nome | Página | Lat.°′ | Long.°′ W = Oeste

Yamato, Nihon 96 33.08 N 130.26 E
Yamato ≃ 96 34.36 N 135.26 E
Yamato-Aogaki-kokutei-kōen ♦ 94 34.40 N 135.50 E
Yamato-kōriyama 96 34.38 N 135.47 E
Yamato-takada 96 34.31 N 135.45 E
Yamatsuri 94 36.52 N 140.25 E
Yamazaki 268 35.56 N 139.54 E
Yamba 166 29.26 S 153.22 E
Yambata 152 2.26 N 21.58 E
Yambéring 150 11.49 N 12.21 W
Yambio 154 4.34 N 28.23 E
Yambol → Jambol 38 42.29 N 26.30 E
Yamboyo 152 0.40 N 22.18 E
Yambrasbamba 248 5.45 S 77.54 W
Yambuya 154 1.16 N 24.33 E
Yamdena, Pulau I 164 7.36 S 131.25 E
Yame 96 33.28 N 130.34 E
Ya Men ⊂ 100 22.09 N 113.05 E
Yamenkou 105 39.53 N 116.12 E
Yamenying 89 43.25 N 122.19 E
Yamethin 110 20.26 N 96.09 E
Yamhill 224 45.21 N 123.11 W
Yamhill □[6] 224 45.15 N 123.20 W
Yamhill ≃ 224 45.14 N 123.00 W
Yamia 150 13.24 N 10.18 E
Yamizo-san ∧ 94 36.56 N 140.17 E
Yamma Yamma, Lake ◎ 166 26.20 S 141.25 E
Yamoussoukro 150 6.49 N 5.17 W
Yampa 200 40.09 N 106.54 W
Yampa ≃ 200 40.32 N 108.59 W
Yampa Plateau ⋏[1] 200 40.25 N 109.00 W
Yamparaez 248 19.10 S 65.10 W
Yamsay Mountain ∧ 202 42.56 N 121.22 W
Yamu 102 43.48 N 94.48 E
Yamuna ≃ 120 25.25 N 81.50 E
Yamuna Bridge ◆[5] 272a 28.40 N 77.14 E
Yamunānagar 124 30.07 N 77.18 E
Yamzho Yumco ◎ 120 28.58 N 90.44 E
Yan 114 5.48 N 100.22 E
Yan ≃, S. Lan. 122 8.55 N 81.01 E
Yan ≃, Zhg. 102 36.24 N 110.28 E
Yanac 166 36.08 S 141.26 E
Yanacachi 248 16.23 S 67.43 W
Yanachaga-Chemillen, Parque Nacional ♦ 248 10.10 S 75.20 W
Yanadani 96 33.32 N 133.01 E
Yanagawa 96 33.10 N 130.24 E
Yanagi 270 34.25 N 135.56 E
Yanagimoto 270 34.34 N 135.51 E
Yanahara 96 34.55 N 134.05 E
Yanaha-shima I 174m 26.54 N 127.56 E
Yanahuara 248 16.24 S 71.33 W
Yanai 96 33.58 N 132.07 E
Yanaka 268 35.24 N 140.01 E
Yanam 122 16.44 N 82.13 E
Yan'an 102 36.36 N 109.28 E
Yanaoca 248 14.13 S 71.26 W
Yanarsu 130 38.02 N 41.33 E
Yanbian 102 26.55 N 101.30 E
Yanbu 100 23.05 N 113.10 E
Yanbu' al-Baḥr 128 24.05 N 38.03 E
Yanbutou 100 29.52 N 115.04 E
Yanceyville 192 36.24 N 79.20 W
Yanchang 102 36.31 N 110.08 E
Yancheng, Zhg. 100 33.36 N 113.57 E
Yancheng, Zhg. 100 33.24 N 120.09 E
Yanchep 168a 31.33 S 115.41 E
Yanchep National Park ♦ 168a 31.32 S 115.40 E
Yanchi, Zhg. 102 37.52 N 107.22 E
Yanchi, Zhg. 105 40.02 N 115.53 E
Yanchuan 102 36.56 N 110.05 E
Yanco 166 34.36 S 146.25 E
Yanco Creek ≃ 166 35.16 S 145.07 E
Yanda Creek ≃ 166 30.28 S 145.45 E
Yandal 162 27.33 S 121.07 E
Yandama Creek ≃ 166 30.00 S 140.10 E
Yandé, Île I 175f 20.03 S 163.49 E
Yande Aboriginal Reserve ◆[4] 162 21.35 S 118.45 E
Yandev 150 7.20 N 9.01 E
Yandina 175e 9.07 S 159.13 E
Yandja 152 1.41 S 17.43 E
Yandongi 152 2.51 N 22.16 E
Yandoon 110 17.02 N 95.39 E
Yandua Island I 175g 16.49 S 178.18 E
Yandun 102 42.20 N 94.09 E
Yanfeng 102 25.53 N 101.01 E
Yanfolila 150 11.11 N 8.09 W
Yang ≃, Thai 110 15.44 N 104.00 E
Yang ≃, Zhg. 105 40.24 N 115.20 E
Yangambi 154 0.47 N 24.28 E
Yangan, Austl. 171a 28.12 S 152.13 E
Yang'an, Zhg. 98 37.38 N 117.09 E
Yan'gang 100 26.02 N 116.22 E
Yangarakata 154 3.01 N 30.28 E
Yangasa Levu I 175g 18.57 S 178.26 W
Yangbajain 120 30.06 N 90.33 E
Yangce 100 32.58 N 113.14 E
Yangcha 98 41.11 N 126.15 E
Yangchang 107 30.22 N 103.42 E
Yangcheng, Zhg. 102 35.29 N 112.25 E
Yangcheng, Zhg. 106 31.24 N 120.47 E
Yangcheng Hu ◎ 106 31.26 N 120.47 E
Yangchiang → Yangjiang 102 21.51 N 111.56 E
Yangch'ŏn ◆[8] 271b 37.34 N 126.51 E
Yangchow → Yangzhou 100 32.24 N 119.26 E
Yangchu 98 37.11 N 120.47 E
Yangch'üan → Yangquan 98 37.52 N 113.36 E
Yangchun 102 22.10 N 111.46 E
Yangcun, Zhg. 100 28.07 N 117.40 E
Yangcun, Zhg. 100 23.26 N 114.30 E
Yangcun, Zhg. 105 39.09 N 115.50 E
Yangcunqiao 100 29.36 N 119.28 E
Yangdachengzi 89 43.59 N 124.25 E
Yangdalinzi 98 42.38 N 125.07 E
Yangdang 100 32.23 N 112.39 E
Yangdian 106 31.08 N 119.45 E
Yang'erzhuang 98 38.18 N 117.30 E
Yangfang 105 40.07 N 116.07 E
Yangfangpu 105 40.48 N 115.01 E
Yangfengang 105 39.07 N 116.52 E
Yangfenzhen 106 30.28 N 120.03 E
Yanggang Do □[4] 98 41.15 N 128.00 E
Yangganzhen 106 31.00 N 119.15 E
Yanggao 98 40.25 N 113.44 E
Yanggezhuang 105 40.09 N 116.48 E
Yanggong-ni 271b 37.39 N 126.37 E
Yanggu, Taehan 98 38.06 N 127.59 E
Yanggu, Zhg. 98 34.44 N 114.48 E
Yanggu, Zhg. 98 36.08 N 115.48 E
Yangguanpu 100 32.13 N 115.31 E
Yanghang 106 31.22 N 121.26 E
Yanghe 100 33.47 N 118.23 E
Yanghexi 102 29.39 N 108.40 E
Yanghu 100 32.34 N 116.30 E
Yanghua 107 30.11 N 104.45 E
Yanghua ≃ 107 30.09 N 104.42 E
Yangi-Yul' → Jangijul' 85 41.07 N 69.03 E
Yangji, Zhg. 98 36.44 N 113.56 E
Yangji, Zhg. 98 34.25 N 116.06 E
Yangji, Zhg. 100 34.19 N 119.28 E
Yangjia, Zhg. 98 34.19 N 119.28 E
Yangjia, Zhg. 106 30.41 N 120.15 E
Yangjiachang, Zhg. 107 29.23 N 104.21 E
Yangjiachang, Zhg. 107 29.45 N 105.21 E
Yangjiafeng 100 30.49 N 112.47 E
Yangjiagou 105 39.18 N 117.54 E
Yangjiajie 107 30.18 N 104.39 E
Yangjian 106 31.39 N 120.33 E
Yangjiang 102 21.51 N 111.56 E
Yangjiaogou 98 37.16 N 118.50 E
Yangjiaqiao, Zhg. 100 27.44 N 112.46 E
Yangjiaqiao, Zhg. 106 31.53 N 121.42 E
Yangjiaqiao, Zhg. 106 32.02 N 121.26 E
Yangjiatao 105 39.49 N 117.51 E
Yangjiawopu 104 42.21 N 122.57 E
Yangjiazeng 105 40.12 N 117.04 E
Yangjiazhangzi 104 40.48 N 120.33 E
Yangjie 102 24.49 N 100.22 E
Yangjishi 100 26.39 N 113.14 E
Yangkou 100 26.47 N 117.51 E
Yangkoushi 100 28.39 N 118.53 E
Yanglinjie 100 29.07 N 113.27 E
Yangliupu, Zhg. 100 30.52 N 118.37 E
Yangliupu, Zhg. 107 30.09 N 104.03 E
Yangliuqing 105 39.08 N 117.01 E
Yangloudong 100 29.31 N 113.44 E
Yanglousi 100 29.30 N 113.38 E
Yangluo 100 30.41 N 114.34 E
Yangluomayu 104 40.47 N 122.54 E
Yangmachang 107 30.39 N 103.45 E
Yangma Dao I 98 37.28 N 121.37 E
Yangmahe 107 30.29 N 104.31 E
Yangmeisi 100 25.42 N 114.30 E
Yangmiao, Zhg. 98 34.11 N 114.53 E
Yangmiao, Zhg. 106 30.51 N 120.49 E
Yangmingshan ◆[8] 269d 25.09 N 121.33 E
Yangming Shan ∧ 102 26.03 N 111.56 E
Yangmugou, Zhg. 98 40.36 N 124.28 E
Yangmugou, Zhg. 104 41.11 N 123.50 E
Yangmulin 105 40.06 N 115.12 E
Yangon (Rangoon) 110 16.47 N 96.10 E
Yangon □[8] 110 16.50 N 96.10 E
Yangor 174b 0.31 S 166.54 E
Yangpingguan 102 32.51 N 106.09 E
Yangpu 100 27.14 N 119.08 E
Yangp'yŏng 98 37.30 N 127.29 E
Yangp'yŏng-ni 98 40.53 N 127.58 E
Yangqi 106 31.23 N 119.57 E
Yangquan 98 37.52 N 113.36 E
Yangriwan 102 31.37 N 110.49 E
Yangsan 98 35.21 N 129.03 E
Yangshan, Zhg. 98 41.13 N 120.24 E
Yangshan, Zhg. 98 35.13 N 116.13 E
Yangshan, Zhg. 102 24.28 N 112.38 E
Yangshigangzi 104 41.42 N 122.59 E
Yangshitun 104 42.06 N 123.44 E
Yangshu 106 31.39 N 120.08 E
Yangshugemen 105 40.55 N 118.18 E
Yangshugoudonggou 104 41.43 N 120.41 E
Yangshuling 98 41.02 N 118.47 E
Yangshuo 102 24.45 N 110.24 E
Yangtan 106 30.42 N 119.11 E
Yangtian Zhang ∧ 100 24.37 N 115.38 E
Yangting 98 37.24 N 122.07 E
Yangtou 100 23.26 N 115.24 E
Yangtze → Chang ≃ 90 31.48 N 121.10 E
Yanguan 106 30.26 N 120.32 E
Yangwan, Zhg. 100 28.22 N 116.46 E
Yangwan, Zhg. 106 31.03 N 120.22 E
Yangxi, Zhg. 100 30.11 N 118.39 E
Yangxi, Zhg. 100 27.18 N 114.10 E
Yangxian 102 33.03 N 107.47 E
Yangxiang, Zhg. 106 31.29 N 119.35 E
Yangxiang, Zhg. 106 31.12 N 121.01 E
Yangxiangtun 104 40.58 N 122.48 E
Yangxiaodian 100 31.46 N 116.45 E
Yangximu ≃ 104 42.04 N 123.00 E
Yangxin, Zhg. 98 37.39 N 117.34 E
Yangxin, Zhg. 100 29.51 N 115.12 E
Yangxiudian 271a 39.44 N 116.32 E
Yangyang 98 38.04 N 128.36 E
Yangyuan (Xicheng) 98 40.01 N 114.10 E
Yangze 100 26.57 N 118.23 E
Yangzhong 106 32.16 N 119.49 E
Yangzhou 100 32.24 N 119.26 E
Yangzhuang 100 33.36 N 118.58 E
Yangzhujuanzi 104 41.38 N 122.46 E
Yangzi 100 31.19 N 112.36 E
Yangzishao 98 42.28 N 126.09 E
Yanhaiyingzi 104 41.52 N 123.05 E
Yanhe, Zhg. 100 31.16 N 115.07 E
Yanhe, Zhg. 102 28.37 N 108.35 E
Yanhecheng 105 40.04 N 115.43 E
Yanheying 98 40.02 N 119.03 E
Yanhui 98 37.54 N 113.51 E
Yanina → Ioánnina 38 39.40 N 20.50 E
Yanji, Zhg. 98 34.41 N 115.27 E
Yanji, Zhg. 98 42.57 N 129.32 E
Yanji, Zhg. 98 34.17 N 115.39 E
Yanji (Longjing), Zhg. 98 42.47 N 129.26 E
Yanjia 104 40.57 N 121.41 E
Yanjiabao 106 32.19 N 120.07 E
Yanjiadian 98 39.48 N 121.49 E
Yanjiahe 100 31.48 N 114.50 E
Yanjiajie 104 41.02 N 121.32 E
Yanjiao 105 39.56 N 116.48 E
Yanjiapu 105 39.52 N 118.00 E
Yanjiatuozi 104 42.27 N 123.47 E
Yanjiawopeng 104 40.59 N 121.17 E
Yanjin 98 35.11 N 114.11 E
Yanjing, Zhg. 102 29.00 N 98.34 E
Yanjing, Zhg. 107 29.56 N 106.21 E
Yankalilla 168b 35.28 S 138.21 E
Yankalilla Bay ⊂ 168b 35.28 S 138.15 E
Yankari Game Reserve ◆[4] 146 9.45 N 10.30 E
Yankdök 98 39.14 N 126.41 E
Yankee Lake 210 41.35 N 74.33 W
Yankee Springs State Recreation Area ♦ 216 42.38 N 85.30 W
Yankee Stadium ♦ 276 40.50 N 73.56 W
Yankeetown 220 29.01 N 82.42 W
Yankton 198 42.52 N 97.23 W
Yankton Indian Reservation ◆[4] 198 43.10 N 98.22 W
Yanling, Zhg. 98 34.07 N 114.11 E
Yanling, Zhg. 106 31.54 N 119.30 E
Yanliumiao 100 32.01 N 116.52 E
Yanmeimeizi 105 39.42 N 115.03 E
Yanna 166 26.56 S 146.03 E
Yannarie ≃ 162 22.28 S 114.48 E
Yanqi 90 42.00 N 86.15 E
Yanqian, Zhg. 100 24.54 N 116.14 E
Yanqian, Zhg. 100 26.15 N 117.28 E
Yanqianhu 104 42.16 N 123.12 E
Yanqiao 106 31.41 N 120.17 E
Yanqidoumen 106 31.17 N 118.42 E
Yanqing 105 40.28 N 115.58 E
Yanque 248 15.39 S 71.39 W
Yanrey 162 22.31 S 114.48 E
Yanshan, Zhg. 98 38.05 N 117.13 E
Yanshan, Zhg. 100 28.18 N 117.41 E
Yanshan, Zhg. 102 23.41 N 104.21 E
Yan Shan ⋏ 105 40.20 N 117.40 E
Yanshankou 105 39.59 N 117.42 E
Yanshi 100 25.17 N 117.10 E
Yanshi ≃ 100 25.20 N 117.17 E
Yanshou 89 45.28 N 128.20 E
Yansi 100 29.48 N 118.20 E
Yanṭā 132 33.36 N 35.57 E
Yantabulla 166 29.21 S 145.00 E
Yantai (Chefoo), Zhg. 98 37.33 N 121.20 E
Yantai, Zhg. 105 39.47 N 116.38 E
Yantan, Zhg. 100 28.28 N 120.44 E
Yantan, Zhg. 100 28.55 N 120.11 E
Yantan, Zhg. 107 29.17 N 104.52 E
Yantian, Zhg. 100 26.53 N 119.53 E
Yantian, Zhg. 100 27.21 N 114.22 E
Yantic ≃ 207 41.31 N 72.05 W
Yantietang ≋ 106 31.49 N 120.46 E
Yanting 102 31.19 N 105.23 E
Yantis 222 32.56 N 95.35 W
Yantongshan, Zhg. 89 43.17 N 126.00 E
Yantongshan, Zhg. 105 40.42 N 115.06 E
Yanu 164 9.57 S 148.25 E
Yanwangshan 104 41.36 N 123.57 E
Yanweigang 98 34.30 N 119.48 E
Yanxi 100 24.46 N 117.47 E
Yanxia 100 29.34 N 114.50 E
Yanxidu 100 26.51 N 114.58 E
Yanxing 102 25.23 N 101.42 E
Yan Yean Reservoir ◎[1] 169 37.33 S 145.08 E
Yanyegongsi 106 32.02 N 121.41 E
Yanyuan 102 27.29 N 101.32 E
Yanzhou 98 35.33 N 116.50 E
Yanziji 106 32.09 N 118.49 E
Yanzijiao 102 23.38 N 100.12 E
Yanzikou 102 27.31 N 105.21 E
Yao, Centraf. 152 5.19 N 19.36 E
Yao, Nihon 96 34.37 N 135.36 E
Yao, Tchad 146 12.51 N 17.34 E
Yao Airport ⊠ 270 34.36 N 135.36 E
Yao'an 102 25.32 N 101.12 E
Yaoba 107 28.45 N 105.39 E
Yaocun, Zhg. 98 36.12 N 113.50 E
Yaocun, Zhg. 98 35.41 N 116.57 E
Yaocun, Zhg. 105 39.09 N 115.32 E
Yaodafangshen 104 42.27 N 122.59 E
Yaoerwan 105 40.49 N 115.27 E
Yaogongbu 100 29.51 N 120.18 E
Yaohongcaopao 104 40.55 N 122.26 E
Yaohuamen 106 32.08 N 118.52 E
Yaohuangdi 104 41.32 N 122.48 E
Yaojiaji 100 31.14 N 114.22 E
Yaojiaqiao 106 32.10 N 119.46 E
Yaojiatun 104 41.18 N 121.57 E
Yaojiawopeng 104 41.47 N 122.25 E
Yaojie 102 36.26 N 102.59 E
Yaoling 100 24.49 N 113.58 E
Yaolugou 98 40.34 N 119.24 E
Yaoluzi 104 41.26 N 121.34 E
Yaopi 100 26.52 N 113.38 E
Yaopu 100 32.14 N 118.20 E
Yaoqianhutun 104 41.32 N 123.36 E
Yaoshizhen 107 30.11 N 105.30 E
Yaotou 100 26.38 N 114.48 E
Yaotsu 94 35.28 N 137.09 E
Yaotun, Zhg. 89 49.28 N 127.30 E
Yaotun, Zhg. 104 40.59 N 122.18 E
Yaotutun 104 42.06 N 123.29 E
Yaoundé 152 3.52 N 11.31 E
Yaowan 98 34.12 N 118.03 E
Yaowangmiao 98 40.47 N 120.10 E
Yaoxian 102 34.56 N 108.53 E
Yaoya ≃ 236 13.28 N 84.14 W
Yao Yai, Ko I 110 8.00 N 98.35 E
Yaozhan 89 52.53 N 125.13 E
Yap I 174q 9.31 N 138.06 E
Yapacaní 248 16.45 S 64.18 W
Yapacani ≃ 248 16.00 S 64.25 W
Yapakopra 164 4.24 S 135.05 E
Yapehe 152 0.13 S 24.27 E
Yapei (Tamale Port) 150 9.10 N 1.10 W
Yapen, Pulau I 164 1.45 S 136.15 E
Yapen, Selat ⊔ 164 1.30 S 136.10 E
Yapero 164 4.59 S 137.11 E
Yapeyú 252 29.28 S 56.49 W
Yaphank 207 40.50 N 72.56 W
Yappar ≃ 166 18.22 S 141.16 E
Yapraklı 130 40.46 N 33.47 E
Yap Trench ✢[1] 14 8.30 N 138.00 E
Yaqian 100 26.38 N 114.30 E
Ya'qūb 140 12.29 N 25.11 E
Yaque del Norte ≃ 238 19.51 N 71.41 W
Yaqui ≃ 232 27.37 N 110.39 W
Yaquina ≃ 202 44.37 N 124.04 W
Yara 240p 20.16 N 76.57 W
Yaracuy □[3] 246 10.20 N 69.10 W
Yaraka 166 24.53 S 144.04 E
Yaratuar 164 2.58 S 134.40 E
Yarbasan 130 38.59 N 28.49 E
Yarcombe 42 50.52 N 3.05 W
Yardea 166 32.23 S 135.32 E
Yardımcı 130 37.00 N 38.59 E
Yardımcı Burnu › 130 36.13 N 30.25 E
Yardley 208 40.14 N 74.50 W
Yardville 208 40.10 N 74.39 W
Yare ≃ 42 52.35 N 1.44 E
Yarí ≃ 246 0.23 S 72.16 W
Yariga-take ∧ 94 36.20 N 137.39 E
Yārik 123 32.06 N 70.47 E
Yarīm 144 14.29 N 44.21 E
Yaring 110 6.52 N 101.22 E
Yaritagua 246 10.05 N 69.08 W
Yarkand → Shache 120 38.25 N 77.16 E
Yarkand → Yarkant ≃ 90 40.28 N 80.52 E
Yarkant (Yarkand) ≃ 90 40.28 N 80.52 E
Yarker 212 44.23 N 76.46 W
Yarkhūn ≃ 123 36.17 N 72.30 E
Yarlarweelor 162 25.35 S 117.59 E
Yarle Lakes ◎ 162 30.15 S 131.27 E
Yarloop 168a 32.57 S 115.54 E
Yarlung → Brahmaputra ≃ 120 24.02 N 90.59 E
Yarma 130 37.49 N 32.54 E
Yarmouth, N.S., Can. 186 43.50 N 66.07 W
Yarmouth, Eng., U.K. 42 50.42 N 1.29 W
Yarmouth, Me., U.S. 188 43.48 N 70.11 W
Yarmouth, Ma., U.S. 207 41.42 N 70.13 W
Yarmouth → Great Yarmouth 42 52.37 N 1.44 E
Yarmu 164 4.18 S 142.17 E
Yarmūk, Nahr al- ≃ 132 32.38 N 35.34 E
Yarra ≃ 169 37.51 S 144.54 E
Yarra Bend Park ♦ 274b 37.48 S 145.01 E
Yarra Glen 169 37.40 S 145.23 E
Yarragon 169 38.12 S 146.04 E
Yarra Junction 169 37.47 S 145.37 E
Yarraloola 162 21.34 S 115.52 E
Yarram 166 38.33 S 146.41 E
Yarraman 171a 26.50 S 151.59 E
Yarrangobilly 171b 35.39 S 148.28 E
Yarrangobilly ≃ 171b 35.48 N 148.23 E
Yarrangobilly Caves ⊥[5] 171b 35.44 S 148.29 E
Yarraville 274b 37.49 S 144.53 E
Yarrawonga 166 36.01 S 146.00 E
Yarra Yarra Lakes ◎ 162 29.40 S 115.47 E
Yarrow, B.C., Can. 224 49.05 N 122.02 W
Yarrow, Scot., U.K. 46 55.32 N 3.01 W
Yarrow ≃ 262 53.40 N 2.49 W
Yarrowee ≃ 169 37.48 S 143.56 E
Yarrow Point 224 47.39 N 122.13 W
Yarrow Reservoir ◎[1] 262 53.38 N 2.34 W
Yarrow Water ≃ 44 55.34 N 2.51 W
Yarrunga, Lake ◎[1] 170 34.45 S 150.20 E
Yarty ≃ 42 50.47 N 3.01 W
Yarumal 246 6.58 N 75.24 W
Yasa 152 3.42 S 21.24 E
Yasaka, Nihon 96 35.39 N 135.07 E
Yasaka, Nihon 96 34.46 N 132.04 E
Yasa-Lokwa 152 5.15 S 19.24 E
Yasato 94 36.14 N 140.12 E
Yasawa I 175g 16.47 S 177.31 E
Yasawa Group II 175g 17.00 S 177.23 E
Yasendu 152 0.27 N 24.20 E
Yashanjie 106 30.51 N 119.03 E
Yashbum 144 14.19 N 46.56 E
Yashi 150 12.23 N 7.54 E
Yashikera 150 9.46 N 3.28 E
Ya-shima I 96 33.44 N 132.09 E
Yashima ♦ 96 34.23 N 134.08 E
Yashio 268 35.49 N 139.51 E
Yashiro 96 34.55 N 134.58 E
Yashiro-jima I 96 33.55 N 132.15 E
Yāsīn 123 36.21 N 73.19 E
Yasku 146 12.20 N 12.30 E
Yasothon 110 15.45 N 104.08 E
Yass 166 34.50 S 148.55 E
Yassıada I 267b 40.51 N 29.00 E
Yassy → Iași 38 47.10 N 27.35 E
Yasu, Nihon 94 35.03 N 136.01 E
Yasu, Nihon 96 33.32 N 133.45 E
Yasuda 96 33.26 N 133.59 E
Yasugi 96 35.26 N 133.15 E
Yāsūj 128 30.40 N 51.36 E
Yasun Burnu › 130 41.08 N 37.41 E
Yasuní ≃ 246 0.56 S 75.23 W
Yasuni, Parque Nacional ♦ 246 0.50 S 76.15 W
Yasuoka 94 35.22 N 137.50 E
Yasuura 96 34.17 N 132.45 E
Yasuzuka 94 37.08 N 138.28 E
Yata 248 13.20 S 66.35 W
Yata ≃, Bol. 248 10.29 S 65.26 W
Yata ≃, Centraf. 146 10.23 N 22.45 E
Yatabe 94 36.02 N 140.04 E
Yatağan 130 37.20 N 28.09 E
Yatakala 150 14.48 N 0.22 E
Yata-Ngaya, Réserve de Faune de la ◆[4] 146 9.15 N 23.30 W
Yāṭar 132 33.09 N 35.20 E
Yatate-yama ∧ 92 34.10 N 129.10 E
Yaté 175f 22.09 S 166.57 E
Yates □[6] 210 42.40 N 77.03 W
Yatesboro 214 40.48 N 79.20 W
Yates Center 198 37.52 N 95.43 W
Yates City 190 40.46 N 90.00 W
Yathata Island I 175g 17.15 S 179.32 W
Yathkyed Lake ◎ 176 62.41 N 98.00 W
Yating 102 25.03 N 106.05 E
Yatomi 94 35.06 N 136.43 E
Yatsuga-take ∧ 94 35.59 N 138.23 E
Yatsuga-take-chūshin-kōgen-kokutei-kōen ♦ 94 36.03 N 138.20 E
Yatsuka 96 35.17 N 133.42 E
Yatsuo 94 36.34 N 137.08 E
Yatsushiro 92 32.30 N 130.36 E
Yatsushiro-kai ⊂ 92 32.20 N 130.25 E
Yaṭṭah 132 31.27 N 35.05 E
Yatta Plateau ⋏[1] 154 2.00 S 38.00 E
Yatton 42 51.24 N 2.49 W
Yatuá ≃ 246 1.43 N 66.30 W
Yatusiro → Yatsushiro 92 32.30 N 130.36 E
Yauca 248 15.40 S 74.32 W
Yauca ≃ 248 15.41 S 74.31 W
Yauco 240m 18.02 N 66.51 W
Yauco ≃ 240m 17.59 N 66.48 W
Yauco, Embalse de ◎[1] 240m 18.07 N 66.50 W
Yauli 248 11.41 S 76.06 W
Yaundé → Yaoundé 152 3.52 N 11.31 E
Yaupi 246 2.59 S 77.50 W
Yauri 248 14.47 S 71.29 W
Yautepec 234 18.53 N 99.04 W
Yau Tong 271d 22.18 N 114.13 E
Yauyos 248 12.24 S 75.57 W
Yāval 120 21.10 N 75.42 E
Yavarí (Javari) ≃ 242 4.21 S 70.02 W
Yavari Mirim ≃ 246 4.31 S 71.44 W
Yavaros 232 26.42 N 109.31 W
Yavatmāl 122 20.24 N 78.08 E
Yaven Yaven Creek ≃ 171b 35.06 S 147.46 E
Yavero ≃ 248 12.06 S 72.57 W
Yavi 130 39.48 N 36.13 E
Yaví, Cerro ∧ 246 5.32 N 65.59 W
Yavita 246 2.55 N 67.26 W
Yaviza 246 8.11 N 77.41 W
Yavne 132 31.53 N 34.45 E
Yavuzeli 130 37.20 N 37.33 E
Yavuzkemal 130 40.43 N 38.21 E
Yaw ≃ 110 20.55 N 94.49 E
Yawahara 268 35.59 N 140.01 E
Yawata, Nihon 96 34.52 N 135.42 E
Yawata, Nihon 268 35.32 N 140.08 E
Yawatahama 96 33.27 N 132.24 E
Yawata → Kitakyūshū 96 33.53 N 130.50 E
Yaxchilán ⊥ 232 16.54 N 90.58 W
Yaxi 102 27.32 N 106.45 E
Yaxian 110 18.20 N 109.30 E
Yaxigang 106 31.23 N 119.10 E
Yaxley 42 52.31 N 0.16 W
Yayama 152 1.16 S 23.07 E
Yayladağı 130 35.56 N 36.01 E
Yayladere 130 39.14 N 40.03 E
Yaylak 130 37.23 N 38.20 E
Yayouta 150 8.11 N 8.30 W
Yayuan 98 41.47 N 126.11 E
Yazd 128 31.53 N 54.25 E
Yazd □[4] 128 32.00 N 54.30 E
Yazi 98 37.04 N 121.17 E
Yazichangcun 104 41.16 N 122.26 E
Yazıhan 130 38.36 N 38.11 E
Yazmān 123 29.08 N 71.45 E
Yazoo ≃ 194 32.22 N 91.00 W
Yazoo City 194 32.51 N 90.24 W
Ybbs ≃ 61 48.10 N 15.06 E
Ybbs an der Donau 61 48.11 N 15.05 E
Ybbsitz 61 47.56 N 14.53 E
Ybor City 220 27.57 N 82.27 W
Ybycuí 252 26.01 S 57.03 W
Yding Skovhøj ∧[2] 41 56.00 N 9.48 E
Ydstebøhavn 26 59.08 N 5.15 E
Ydžid Parma ⋏ 24 63.06 N 58.15 E
Ye 110 15.15 N 97.51 E
Yea 169 37.13 S 145.26 E
Yea ≃ 169 37.11 S 145.23 E
Yeading ◆[8] 260 51.32 N 0.24 W
Yeadon, Eng., U.K. 44 53.52 N 1.41 W
Yeadon, Pa., U.S. 285 39.56 N 75.15 W
Yeagertown 208 40.38 N 77.34 W
Yealm ≃ 42 50.18 N 4.03 W
Yealmpton 42 50.21 N 3.59 W
Yebawgyi 110 18.40 N 94.35 E
Yebbi-Bou 146 20.58 N 18.04 E
Yébigué, Enneri ∨ 146 22.04 N 17.49 E
Yèbles 261 48.38 N 2.46 E
Yebyu 110 14.15 N 98.12 E
Yecapixtla 234 18.53 N 98.52 W
Yecheng 120 37.54 N 77.25 E
Yech'ŏn 98 36.40 N 128.26 E
Yecla 34 38.37 N 1.07 W
Yécora 232 28.20 N 108.58 W
Yedashe 110 19.09 N 96.21 E
Yedi Göller Milli Parkı ♦ 130 40.50 N 31.30 E
Yedikule ◆[8] 267b 40.59 N 28.55 E
Yedikule ⊥ 267b 40.59 N 28.55 E
Yédinga, Ouadi ∨ 146 15.46 N 20.05 E
Yedseram ≃ 146 12.30 N 14.05 E
Yeed 144 4.33 N 43.02 E
Yeeda 162 17.36 S 123.39 E
Yeelanna 166 34.09 S 135.45 E
Yeelirrie 162 27.17 S 120.06 E
Yeernuozha Hu ◎ 120 32.30 N 89.30 E
Yegor'yevsk → Jegorjevsk 82 55.23 N 39.02 E
Yegros 252 26.24 S 56.25 W
Yegua Creek ≃ 222 30.23 N 96.18 W
Yeguas, Punta › 258 34.55 S 56.19 W
Yeguas, Río de las ≃ 34 37.22 N 4.45 W
Yehliu 269d 25.12 N 121.41 E
Yehliu Chia › 269d 25.13 N 121.42 E
Yehud 132 32.02 N 34.53 E
Yei 154 4.05 N 30.40 E
Yei ≃ 140 6.15 N 30.13 E
Yeji, Ghana 150 8.13 N 0.39 W
Yeji, Zhg. 100 31.52 N 115.55 E
Yekaterinburg → Jekaterinburg 86 56.51 N 60.36 E
Yekaterinodar → Krasnodar 78 45.02 N 39.00 E
Yekaterinoslav → Dnepropetrovsk 78 48.27 N 34.59 E
Yekokora ≃ 152 1.20 N 20.21 E
Yekumbo 152 1.02 S 23.27 E
Ye Kyun I 110 18.37 N 93.47 E
Yela Island I 160 11.21 S 154.09 E
Yelarbon 166 28.34 S 150.45 E

≃ River	Fluß	Río	Rivière	Rio	✢ Submarine Features	Untermeerische Objekte	Accidentes Submarinos	Formes de relief sous-marin	Acidentes submarinos
≋ Canal	Kanal	Canal	Canal	Canal	□ Political Unit	Politische Einheit	Unidad Politica	Entité politique	Unidade política
⌊ Waterfall, Rapids	Wasserfall, Stromschnellen	Cascada, Rápidos	Chute d'eau, Rapides	Cascata, Rápidos	ʊ Cultural Institution	Kulturelle Institution	Institución Cultural	Institution culturelle	Institução cultural
⊔ Strait	Meeresstraße	Estrecho	Détroit	Estreito	⊥ Historical Site	Historische Stätte	Sitio Histórico	Site historique	Sitio histórico
⊂ Bay, Gulf	Bucht, Golf	Bahía, Golfo	Baie, Golfe	Baía, Golfo	♦ Recreational Site	Erholungs- und Ferienort	Sitio de Recreo	Centre de loisirs	Area de Lazer
◎ Lake, Lakes	See, Seen	Lago, Lagos	Lac, Lacs	Lago, Lagos	⊠ Airport	Flughafen	Aeropuerto	Aéroport	Aeroporto
≣ Swamp	Sumpf	Pantano	Marais	Pântano	■ Military Installation	Militäranlage	Instalación Militar	Installation militaire	Instalação militar
⊓ Ice Features, Glacier	Eis- und Gletscherformen	Accidentes Glaciales	Formes glaciaires	Acidentes glaciares	◆ Miscellaneous	Verschiedenes	Misceláneo	Divers	Diversos
⊤ Other Hydrographic Features	Andere Hydrographische Objekte	Otros Elementos Hidrográficos	Autres données hydrographiques	Outros acidentes hidrográficos					

Yelcho, Lago ⊜ 254 43.18 S 72.18 W
Yele 150 8.25 N 11.50 W
Yelets → Jelec 76 52.37 N 38.30 E
Yélimané 150 15.08 N 10.34 W
Yell I 46a 60.36 N 1.06 W
Yellandu 122 17.36 N 80.20 E
Yellow ≏, U.S. 194 30.33 N 87.00 W
Yellow ≏, In., U.S. 216 41.16 N 86.50 W
Yellow ≏, Ia., U.S. 190 43.05 N 91.11 W
Yellow ≏, Wi., U.S. 190 44.58 N 91.18 W
Yellow ≏, Wi., U.S. 190 43.59 N 90.03 W
Yellow ≏, Wi., U.S. 190 46.01 N 92.22 W
Yellow Breeches Creek ≏ 208 40.13 N 76.51 W
Yellow Creek ≏, U.S. 194 33.34 N 88.20 W
Yellow Creek ≏, Co., U.S. 200 40.10 N 108.24 W
Yellow Creek ≏, Oh., U.S. 214 40.34 N 80.40 W
Yellow Creek ≏, Tn., U.S. 194 36.26 N 87.34 W
Yellow Creek, North Fork ≏ 214 40.33 N 80.42 W
Yellow Creek State Park ♦ 214 40.35 N 79.02 W
Yellowdine 162 31.18 S 119.39 E
Yellow Grass 184 49.49 N 104.08 W
Yellowhead Pass)(182 52.53 N 118.28 W
Yellow House Draw V 196 33.35 N 101.50 W
Yellow → Huang ≏ 90 37.32 N 118.19 E
Yellowknife 176 62.27 N 114.21 W
Yellowknife ≏ 176 62.31 N 114.19 W
Yellow Lake ⊜ 212 44.20 N 75.36 W
Yellow Medicine ≏ 198 44.44 N 95.25 W
Yellow Mountain ∧ 166 32.30 S 146.51 E
Yellow Sea ▿[2] 90 36.00 N 123.00 E
Yellow Springs 218 39.48 N 83.53 W
Yellowstone ≏ 178 47.58 N 103.59 W
Yellowstone, Clarks Fork ≏ 202 45.39 N 108.43 W
Yellowstone Falls ʟ 202 44.43 N 110.30 W
Yellowstone Lake ⊜ 202 44.25 N 110.22 W
Yellowstone National Park 202 44.59 N 110.42 W
Yellowstone National Park ♦ 202 44.30 N 110.35 W
Yellowtail Dam ◆[6] 202 45.12 N 107.57 W
Yell Sound ʮ 46a 60.32 N 1.15 W
Yellville 194 36.13 N 92.41 W
Yelm 224 46.56 N 122.36 W
Yelma 162 26.30 S 121.40 E
Yelvertoft 166 20.13 S 138.53 E
Yelverton 42 50.30 N 4.05 W
Yelwa 150 10.51 N 4.46 E
Yema ≏ 102 41.25 N 95.10 E
Yemadu 86 43.36 N 81.50 E
Yemagong 124 29.28 N 89.06 E
Yemaotai 104 42.20 N 122.53 E
Yemassee 192 32.41 N 80.51 W
Yematan 102 34.40 N 98.16 E
Yemen (Al-Yaman) □[1], Asia 118 15.00 N 47.00 E
Yemen (Al-Yaman) □[1], Asia 144 15.00 N 47.00 E
Yemen, People's Democratic Republic of → Yemen □[1] 144 15.00 N 47.00 E
Yemen, República Popular Democrática del → Yemen □[1] 144 15.00 N 47.00 E
Yémen, République démocratique populaire du → Yemen □[1] 144 15.00 N 47.00 E
Yen 152 2.27 N 12.41 E
Yenagoa 150 4.55 N 6.19 E
Yenakiyevo → Jenakijevo 83 48.14 N 38.13 E
Yenangyaung 110 20.28 N 94.52 E
Yenanma 110 19.46 N 94.48 E
Yen Bai 110 21.42 N 104.52 E
Yen Chau 110 21.03 N 104.18 E
Yench'eng → Yancheng 100 33.24 N 120.09 E
Yenchi → Yanji 98 42.57 N 129.32 E
Yenda 166 34.15 S 146.11 E
Yende Millimou 150 8.53 N 10.11 W
Yendéré 150 10.12 N 4.58 W
Yendi 150 9.26 N 0.01 W
Ye-ngan 110 21.09 N 96.27 E
Yenge ≏ 152 0.55 S 20.40 E
Yengema 150 8.43 N 11.10 W
Yengisar 85 38.57 N 76.03 E
Yengo 152 0.22 N 15.29 E
Yengo, Mount ∧ 170 32.59 S 150.51 E
Yéni 150 13.26 N 2.59 E
Yeniçağa 130 40.46 N 32.02 E
Yenice, Tür. 130 39.45 N 28.55 E
Yenice, Tür. 130 39.55 N 27.18 E
Yenice, Tür. 130 36.59 N 35.03 E
Yenice, Tür. 130 41.11 N 32.19 E
Yenice ≏ 130 41.35 N 32.03 E
Yenicekale 130 37.37 N 36.37 E
Yeniceoba 130 38.53 N 32.48 E
Yenierenköy 130 35.32 N 34.11 E
Yenifoça 130 38.44 N 26.51 E
Yenikapı ◆[8] 267b 41.00 N 28.57 E
Yeniköy 130 39.46 N 28.00 E
Yeniköy ◆[8] 267b 40.59 N 28.53 E
Yenimehmetli 130 39.26 N 32.10 E
Yenipazar, Tür. 130 37.48 N 28.12 E
Yenipazar, Tür. 130 40.11 N 30.31 E
Yenişehir 130 40.16 N 29.39 E
Yenisey → Jenisej ≏ 72 71.50 N 82.40 E
Yennadon 224 49.14 N 122.34 W
Yenne 62 45.42 N 5.46 E
Yennora 274a 33.52 S 150.58 E
Yenshuichen 100 23.20 N 120.16 E
Yentna ≏ 180 61.34 N 150.28 W
Yeo ≏ 42 51.02 N 2.49 W
Yeola 122 20.02 N 74.29 E
Yeo Lake ⊜ 162 28.04 S 124.23 E
Yeoman 216 40.40 N 86.43 W
Yeoval 166 32.45 S 148.40 E
Yeovil 42 50.57 N 2.39 W
Yeoville ◆[8] 273d 26.12 S 28.04 E
Yepachic 232 28.26 N 108.23 W
Yeppoon 166 23.08 S 150.45 E
Yerba Buena, Montaña ∧ 236 14.05 N 87.26 W
Yerba Buena Island I 282 37.48 N 122.22 W
Yères ≏ 50 50.02 N 1.19 E
Yerevan → Jerevan 84 40.11 N 44.30 E
Yerilla 162 29.28 S 121.49 E
Yering 274b 37.41 S 145.23 E
Yerington 226 38.59 N 119.09 W
Yerington Indian Reservation ◆[4] 226 39.05 N 119.12 W
Yerkes 285 40.10 N 75.27 W
Yerkes Astronomical Observatory ʊ[3] 216 42.34 N 88.34 W
Yerkesik 130 37.07 N 28.17 E
Yerköy 130 39.38 N 34.29 E
Yerlisu 130 40.46 N 26.39 E
Yermasóyia 130 34.43 N 33.05 E
Yermenonville 261 48.33 N 1.37 E
Yermo 204 34.54 N 116.49 W
Yeroḫam 132 31.00 N 34.55 E
Yerolimín 38 36.28 N 22.24 E
Yèrre ≏ 50 48.01 N 1.16 E
Yerres 50 48.43 N 2.30 E
Yerres ≏ 50 48.43 N 2.27 E
Yerseke 52 51.29 N 4.02 E
Yerupaja, Nevado ∧ 248 10.16 S 76.54 W
Yerushalayim (Al-Quds) (Jerusalem) 132 31.46 N 35.14 E
Yerushalayim □[5] 132 31.45 N 35.00 E
Yerville 50 49.40 N 0.54 E
Yesa, Embalse de ⊜[1] 34 42.36 N 1.09 W
Yesan 98 36.41 N 126.50 E
Yeshenpu 104 40.51 N 122.32 E
Yeshiva University ʊ[2] 276 40.51 N 73.55 W
Yeshvi 272c 18.55 N 73.03 E
Yeşil ≏ 130 41.24 N 36.35 E
Yeşilçonlu 130 40.13 N 28.06 E
Yeşildere 130 37.09 N 33.31 E
Yeşilhisar 130 38.21 N 35.06 E
Yeşilkent 130 36.59 N 36.10 E
Yeşilköy 130 40.57 N 28.49 E
Yeşilköy Burnu > 267b 40.57 N 28.50 E
Yeşilova 130 37.30 N 29.46 E
Yeşiltepe 130 37.12 N 33.02 E
Yeşilyazı 130 39.20 N 39.05 E
Yeşilyurt 130 38.18 N 38.15 E
Yeso 196 34.26 N 104.36 W
Yeso Creek ≏ 196 34.13 N 104.15 W
Yesŏng-gang ≏ 98 37.53 N 126.24 E
Yessentuki → Jessentuki 84 44.03 N 42.51 E
Yeste 34 38.22 N 2.18 W
Yes Tor ∧ 42 50.42 N 4.00 W
Yesud HaMa'ala 132 33.03 N 35.36 E
Yetholme 170 33.27 S 149.49 E
Yetman 166 28.54 S 150.46 E
Yetminster 42 50.53 N 2.33 W
Yetsou I 152 2.08 S 10.42 E
Yettem 226 36.29 N 119.16 W
Yetti 164 3.00 S 140.53 E
Yetti ◆[1] 148 26.10 N 7.50 W
Ye-u 110 22.46 N 95.26 E
Yeu, Île d' I 32 46.42 N 2.20 W
Yevpatoriya → Jevpatorija 78 45.12 N 33.22 E
Yexian, Zhg. 98 37.13 N 119.54 E
Yexian, Zhg. 100 33.37 N 113.20 E
Yexie 106 30.56 N 121.19 E
Yextla ≏ 234 18.00 N 100.06 W
Yeysk → Jejsk 78 46.42 N 38.16 E
Yeyuan 98 36.22 N 118.27 E
Yeywa 110 21.41 N 96.24 E
Yezd → Yazd 128 31.53 N 54.25 E
Yeze Hu ⊜ 106 31.08 N 120.40 E
Yezhuang 105 39.10 N 116.18 E
Yezhuhe 105 40.53 N 118.13 E
Ygatimí 252 24.05 S 55.30 W
Ygnacio Canal ≖ 282 37.55 N 122.03 W
Yguazú ≏ 252 25.20 S 55.00 W
Yhú 252 24.59 S 55.59 W
Yi 98 42.08 N 118.48 E
Yi ≏, Ur. 252 33.07 S 57.08 W
Yi ≏, Zhg. 98 34.07 N 118.15 E
Yi ≏, Zhg. 100 34.10 N 112.10 E
Yi ≏, Zhg. 105 39.14 N 115.46 E
Yi'an 89 47.55 N 125.20 E
Yiannitsá 38 40.48 N 22.25 E
Yibao 106 30.25 N 119.53 E
Yibin (Ipin) 107 28.47 N 104.38 E
Yibug Caka ⊜ 120 33.00 N 86.25 E
Yibutan 107 28.54 N 104.40 E
Yicanghe 100 32.47 N 120.43 E
Yichang (Ichang) 102 30.42 N 111.17 E
Yicheng, Zhg. 98 34.46 N 117.37 E
Yicheng, Zhg. 98 36.48 N 114.17 E
Yicheng, Zhg. 102 31.43 N 112.07 E
Yichexun 102 26.50 N 103.28 E
Yichuan, Zhg. 100 34.26 N 112.24 E
Yichuan, Zhg. 102 36.04 N 110.06 E
Yichun, Zhg. 90 47.42 N 128.55 E
Yichun, Zhg. 100 27.50 N 114.23 E
Yicun 105 38.57 N 115.37 E
Yidan 89 43.24 N 125.25 E
Yidie 102 37.08 N 110.30 E
Yidu, Zhg. 98 36.41 N 118.28 E
Yidu, Zhg. 102 30.22 N 111.22 E
Yidun 102 29.56 N 99.22 E
Yiewsley ◆[8] 260 51.31 N 0.28 W
Yifag 144 12.02 N 37.44 E
Yifeng, Zhg. 100 33.19 N 113.47 E
Yifeng, Zhg. 100 28.26 N 114.46 E
Yigaolou 106 30.56 N 120.20 E
Yığılca 130 40.58 N 31.27 E
Yiğitler 130 39.52 N 26.37 E
Yigou 98 35.51 N 114.20 E
Yihe 100 23.50 N 114.53 E
Yihechang 107 30.23 N 106.24 E
Yi He Yuan (Summer Palace) ʊ 105 40.00 N 116.16 E
Yihezhuang, Zhg. 98 37.53 N 118.23 E
Yihezhuang, Zhg. 104 41.15 N 122.57 E
Yihuang 100 27.34 N 116.10 E
Yihuang ≏ 100 28.05 N 116.18 E
Yijiangzhen 100 30.55 N 118.28 E
Yijiawan 100 27.58 N 113.01 E
Yijiazi 104 42.29 N 122.41 E
Yijingpu 105 40.08 N 117.47 E
Yijinqiao 100 30.54 N 117.12 E
Yijun 102 35.24 N 109.00 E
Yikengaolu 102 42.17 N 98.19 E
Yikou 100 26.45 N 117.00 E
Yilaha 89 48.50 N 125.10 E
Yilan 89 46.19 N 129.34 E
Yilaxi 89 43.47 N 126.08 E
Yıldız Dağı ∧ 130 40.08 N 36.56 E
Yıldız Dağları ⋀ 130 41.50 N 27.30 E
Yıldızeli 130 39.52 N 36.38 E
Yilehuli Shan ⋀ 89 51.20 N 124.30 E
Yili 107 30.45 N 105.58 E
Yiliang, Zhg. 102 24.58 N 103.07 E
Yiliang, Zhg. 102 27.35 N 104.01 E
Yiliekede 89 48.51 N 121.37 E
Yilin 100 33.36 N 119.37 E
Yiling 100 32.30 N 119.46 E
Yiliping 120 37.55 N 93.30 E
Yilliminning 162 32.54 S 117.22 E
Yilong, Zhg. 89 47.28 N 125.23 E
Yilong, Zhg. 102 31.34 N 106.19 E
Yilong, Zhg. 102 25.20 N 103.14 E
Yimachi 104 42.11 N 122.15 E
Yimatu 104 41.55 N 121.25 E
Yimen, Zhg. 100 33.39 N 116.02 E
Yimen, Zhg. 102 24.43 N 102.10 E
Yimuhe 89 52.45 N 120.07 E
Yin ≏, Mya. 110 20.04 N 95.01 E
Yin ≏, Zhg. 98 42.19 N 118.37 E
Yinan (Jiehu) 98 35.37 N 118.30 E
Yinbaing 110 17.25 N 97.46 E
Yinchuan 102 38.30 N 106.18 E
Yindarlgooda, Lake ⊜ 162 30.45 S 121.55 E
Yindi 154 1.35 N 27.40 E
Yinfang 105 39.07 N 114.52 E
Ying ≏ 100 32.30 N 116.32 E
Yingcheng 100 30.57 N 113.32 E
Yingchengzi, Zhg. 89 44.08 N 125.56 E
Yingchengzi, Zhg. 98 38.58 N 121.23 E
Yingchengzi, Zhg. 104 41.50 N 124.04 E
Yingchengzi, Zhg. 104 42.22 N 124.14 E
Yingde 100 24.12 N 113.24 E
Yingen 102 41.09 N 104.45 E
Yingfang 105 40.14 N 116.17 E
Yinggehai 110 18.31 N 108.44 E
Yinghe 100 32.16 N 116.31 E
Yingjin ≏ 98 42.20 N 119.19 E
Yingkoshih ≏ 269d 25.06 N 121.43 E
Yingkou, Zhg. 104 40.40 N 122.14 E
Yingkou (Dashiqiao), Zhg. 104 40.38 N 122.30 E
Yingpan, Zhg. 102 25.48 N 106.18 E
Yingpan, Zhg. 102 24.44 N 99.38 E
Yingpanjie 102 25.27 N 98.24 E
Yingqiao 100 33.58 N 113.39 E
Yingshan, Zhg. 100 30.45 N 115.39 E
Yingshan, Zhg. 100 31.38 N 113.50 E
Yingshan, Zhg. 102 31.08 N 106.31 E
Yingshang 100 32.38 N 116.15 E
Yingshouyingzi, Zhg. 105 40.33 N 117.38 E
Yingshouyingzi, Zhg. 105 40.49 N 117.55 E
Yingtan 100 28.14 N 117.00 E
Yingtaogou 104 42.08 N 121.57 E
Yingtaoyuan 104 41.10 N 123.05 E
Yingtian 100 28.50 N 112.56 E
Yingxiangjie 107 29.24 N 105.11 E
Yingxianpu 104 41.20 N 121.31 E
Yining (Kuldja) 86 43.54 N 81.21 E
Yinjiadai 106 32.03 N 120.07 E
Yinjiang 102 28.02 N 108.28 E
Yinjiawopeng 104 42.34 N 121.01 E
Yinkeng 100 26.14 N 115.34 E
Yinliu 105 39.59 N 117.23 E
Yinmabin 110 22.05 N 94.54 E
Yinmahe 89 44.07 N 125.44 E
Yinmatu ≏ 98 40.57 N 117.43 E
Yinnietharra 162 24.39 S 116.11 E
Yinnyein 110 16.48 N 97.23 E
Yinong 102 30.19 N 101.01 E
Yinping 98 34.15 N 118.39 E
Yinqiaotou 106 31.52 N 119.13 E
Yin Shan ⋀ 102 41.48 N 109.00 E
Yinshanzhen 107 29.41 N 104.58 E
Yinwogou 98 41.55 N 117.55 E
Yinxian 100 29.50 N 121.38 E
Yinxiang 106 31.55 N 118.49 E
Yinxianji 100 32.07 N 116.32 E
Yinyangjie 104 42.16 N 121.23 E
Yinyuan 102 23.26 N 101.54 E
Yinzhan'ao 100 23.33 N 113.07 E
Yio Chu Kang 271c 1.23 N 103.51 E
Yi'ong 102 30.17 N 94.51 E
Yi'ong ≏ 120 29.56 N 95.10 E
Yi Pak 271d 22.19 N 114.00 E
Yipinchang 107 29.17 N 106.34 E
Yipinglang 102 25.11 N 101.51 E
Yiqian 100 26.34 N 116.11 E
Yirba Muda 144 6.12 N 38.42 E
Yirga Alem 144 6.52 N 38.22 E
Yirkā 132 32.57 N 35.13 E
Yirol 140 6.33 N 30.30 E
Yirrkala 164 12.14 S 136.56 E
Yirshi 89 47.20 N 119.45 E
Yirwa 140 7.47 N 27.15 E
Yisaduo 102 28.50 N 96.44 E
Yishan, Zhg. 100 27.32 N 120.32 E
Yishan, Zhg. 102 24.40 N 108.35 E
Yishui 98 35.50 N 118.41 E
Yishun 271c 1.26 N 103.50 E
Yisikan 89 49.09 N 124.47 E
Yisra'el → Israel □[1] 132 31.30 N 35.00 E
Yisuhe 100 27.46 N 112.54 E
Yitajing 102 42.32 N 94.12 E
Yitang, Zhg. 98 35.10 N 118.16 E
Yitang, Zhg. 100 31.06 N 113.42 E
Yíthion 38 36.45 N 22.34 E
Yiting 100 29.15 N 119.57 E
Yitm, Wādī al- V 132 29.34 N 35.01 E
Yitong 89 43.20 N 125.17 E
Yitong ≏ 98 42.40 N 125.58 E
Yitulihe 89 50.38 N 121.34 E
Yiwu, Zhg. 100 29.18 N 120.04 E
Yiwu, Zhg. 102 43.15 N 94.45 E
Yiwu, Zhg. 102 22.00 N 101.28 E
Yiwulü Shan ⋀ 104 41.42 N 121.42 E
Yixi 100 23.45 N 116.38 E
Yixian, Zhg. 100 29.55 N 117.56 E
Yixian, Zhg. 104 41.32 N 121.15 E
Yixian, Zhg. 105 39.21 N 115.29 E
Yixiken 89 52.57 N 125.40 E
Yixing 106 31.22 N 119.50 E
Yixingbu 105 39.12 N 117.12 E
Yixingchang 107 30.37 N 106.38 E
Yixu 100 26.02 N 119.16 E
Yixun ≏ 98 41.16 N 117.35 E
Yiyang, Zhg. 100 28.23 N 117.25 E
Yiyang, Zhg. 102 28.36 N 112.20 E
Yiyang, Zhg. 102 34.30 N 112.10 E
Yiyuan (Nanma) 98 36.11 N 118.08 E
Yiyuankou 98 40.10 N 119.35 E
Yizhang 100 25.26 N 112.56 E
Yizheng 106 32.16 N 119.12 E
Yizikong 102 25.38 N 104.28 E
Yizre'él 132 32.33 N 35.20 E
Yizre'el, 'Émeq ≚ 132 32.36 N 35.14 E
Ylakiai 76 56.17 N 21.51 E
Yläne 26 60.53 N 22.55 E
Ylihärmä 26 63.09 N 22.47 E
Yli-Kitka ⊜ 26 66.08 N 28.30 E
Ylimarkku → Övermark 26 62.38 N 21.30 E
Ylistaro 26 62.57 N 22.31 E
Ylivieska 26 64.05 N 24.33 E
Ylöjärvi 26 61.33 N 23.36 E
Ymeray 261 48.31 N 1.42 E
Ymir 182 49.17 N 117.13 W
Yndin 24 61.24 N 55.10 E
Yngaren ⊜ 40 58.52 N 16.35 E
Yngen ⊜ 40 59.44 N 14.18 E
Yntaly 86 48.58 N 70.55 E
Ynykčanskij 74 60.15 N 137.43 E
Yoakum 222 29.17 N 97.09 W
Yobi, Indon. 164 1.43 S 138.04 E
Yobi, Indon. 164 1.42 S 136.27 E
Yockanookany ≏ 194 32.40 N 89.40 W
Yoco 246 10.36 N 62.24 W
Yocona ≏ 194 34.11 N 90.11 W
Yōda 268 35.24 N 139.25 E
Yoder 216 40.55 N 85.10 W
Yodo ≏ 96 34.41 N 135.25 E
Yodoe 96 35.28 N 133.26 E
Yodogawa ◆[8] 270 34.42 N 135.28 E
Yoe 208 39.55 N 76.39 W
Yōga ◆[8] 268 35.38 N 139.38 E
Yogo 94 35.33 N 136.12 E
Yog Point > 116 14.06 N 124.12 E
Yoğuntaş 130 41.50 N 27.04 E
Yogyakarta 115a 7.48 S 110.22 E
Yogyakarta □[4] 115a 7.45 S 110.30 E
Yoho National Park ♦ 182 51.26 N 116.30 W
Yoichi 92a 43.12 N 140.41 E
Yojoa, Lago de ⊜ 236 14.50 N 88.00 W
Yŏju 98 37.18 N 127.37 E
Yōka 96 35.24 N 134.46 E
Yokadouma 152 3.31 N 15.03 E
Yōkaichi 94 35.06 N 136.12 E
Yōkaichiba 94 35.42 N 140.33 E
Yokamba 152 0.01 N 22.17 E
Yokana 152 0.45 N 22.53 E
Yokawa 96 34.52 N 135.06 E
Yokchi-do I 98 34.38 N 128.15 E
Yokkaichi, Nihon 94 34.58 N 136.37 E
Yokkaichi, Nihon 96 33.32 N 131.20 E
Yoko 152 2.36 S 20.06 E
Yokoate-jima I 93b 28.48 N 129.00 E
Yokohama, Nihon 94 35.27 N 139.39 E
Yokohama, Nihon 268 35.27 N 139.39 E
Yokohama-kō c 268 35.27 N 139.39 E
Yokohama National University ʊ[2] 268 35.25 N 139.36 E
Yokohama Park Baseball Ground ♦ 268 35.26 N 139.39 E
Yokolo 152 0.36 S 23.04 E
Yokonuma 268 35.58 N 139.27 E
Yokoshiba 94 35.40 N 140.28 E
Yokosuka 94 35.18 N 139.40 E
Yokosuka District Naval Headquarters ■ 268 35.17 N 139.39 E
Yokosuka-kō c 268 35.18 N 139.39 E
Yokosuka Naval Base ■ 94 35.18 N 139.41 E
Yokota, Nihon 96 35.10 N 133.06 E
Yokota, Nihon 268 35.23 N 140.01 E
Yokota, Nihon 270 34.40 N 135.55 E
Yokota Air Base ■ 268 35.45 N 139.21 E
Yokote 92 39.18 N 140.34 E
Yola 146 9.12 N 12.29 E
Yolaina, Serranías de ⋀ 236 11.40 N 84.20 W
Yolboyu 130 37.55 N 40.00 E
Yolo 226 38.44 N 121.48 W
Yolo □[6] 226 38.41 N 121.46 W
Yolo ≏ 273b 4.19 S 15.20 E
Yolo Bypass ≏ 226 38.25 N 121.40 W
Yolombó, Col. 246 6.36 N 75.01 W
Yolombo, Zaïre 152 1.32 S 23.15 E
Yolonga 152 1.36 S 23.12 E
Yom ≏ 110 15.52 N 100.16 E
Yombi 152 1.26 S 10.37 E
Yomou 150 7.34 N 9.16 W
Yona 174p 13.25 N 144.47 E
Yonabaru 174m 26.12 N 127.45 E
Yonago 96 35.26 N 133.20 E
Yonaguni 175d 24.27 N 122.57 E
Yonaguni-shima I 175d 24.27 N 123.00 E
Yonaha-dake ∧[2] 174m 26.43 N 128.13 E
Yŏnan 98 37.55 N 126.10 E
Yoncalı 130 39.01 N 38.15 E
Yoncalla 202 43.35 N 123.16 W
Yŏnch'on ◆[8] 271b 37.38 N 127.04 E
Yoneshiro ≏ 92 40.13 N 140.01 E
Yonezawa 92 37.55 N 140.07 E
Yŏngam 98 34.48 N 126.40 E
Yongamp'o 98 39.55 N 124.24 E
Yŏngan, C.M.I.K. 98 41.15 N 129.30 E
Yong'an, Zhg. 100 25.58 N 117.22 E
Yongan, Zhg. 107 30.44 N 106.16 E
Yong'an, Zhg. 107 29.13 N 104.46 E
Yong'an ≏ 100 28.52 N 121.04 E
Yonganbao 98 40.15 N 119.52 E
Yong'anchang 107 30.24 N 103.58 E
Yong'anshi 100 28.13 N 113.19 E
Yŏngbyŏn 98 39.49 N 125.48 E
Yongchang, Zhg. 100 29.13 N 119.20 E
Yongchang, Zhg. 102 38.17 N 101.59 E
Yongchangzhen 106 31.42 N 121.44 E
Yongcheng 100 33.58 N 116.21 E
Yongch'ŏn, C.M.I.K. 98 39.59 N 124.28 E
Yŏngch'ŏn, Taehan 98 38.07 N 127.05 E
Yŏngch'ŏn, Taehan 98 35.58 N 128.56 E
Yongch'ŏn-dong 98 41.18 N 129.40 E
Yongchuan 107 29.21 N 105.54 E
Yongchun 100 25.21 N 118.21 E
Yongdeng 102 36.48 N 103.14 E
Yongdian 98 40.34 N 124.48 E
Yongding 100 24.46 N 116.43 E
Yongding ≏, Zhg. 100 24.42 N 116.34 E
Yongding ≏, Zhg. 105 39.20 N 117.04 E
Yongdingmen Station ◆[5] 271a 39.52 N 116.23 E
Yŏngdŏk 98 36.26 N 129.23 E
Yŏngdong 98 36.10 N 127.48 E
Yŏngdŭngp'o ◆[8] 271b 37.32 N 126.54 E
Yongfeng, Zhg. 100 29.44 N 116.49 E
Yongfeng, Zhg. 100 27.19 N 115.24 E
Yongfengchang 107 30.33 N 105.05 E
Yongfu 100 25.05 N 117.20 E
Yonggang 98 38.52 N 125.21 E
Yonggangonch'ŏn 98 38.53 N 125.14 E
Yonggi 98 36.24 N 128.24 E
Yongguzhai 98 34.05 N 116.50 E
Yonghe 100 28.18 N 113.51 E
Yongheshi 100 28.18 N 113.51 E
Yonghŭng 98 39.32 N 127.13 E
Yŏnghŭng-do I 98 37.16 N 126.28 E
Yŏnghŭng-man c 98 39.15 N 127.30 E
Yongi 89 43.40 N 126.30 E
Yŏngil-man c 98 36.02 N 129.26 E
Yongji 102 34.51 N 110.29 E
Yongjia, Zhg. 100 28.11 N 120.42 E
Yongjia, Zhg. 107 29.34 N 106.01 E
Yŏngjong-do I 98 37.30 N 126.31 E
Yŏngju 98 36.50 N 128.37 E
Yongkang, Zhg. 100 32.32 N 117.24 E
Yongkang, Zhg. 100 28.53 N 120.02 E
Yongkou 100 26.16 N 118.19 E
Yongle, Zhg. 89 45.45 N 125.12 E
Yongle, Zhg. 105 39.32 N 115.59 E
Yongle ≏ 100 26.54 N 113.12 E
Yongledian 105 39.43 N 116.46 E
Yonglong 106 31.34 N 121.48 E
Yonglonghe 100 30.46 N 112.48 E
Yŏngmi-dong 98 39.40 N 125.31 E
Yongnian (Linmingguan) 98 36.47 N 114.30 E
Yongnianchang 107 29.08 N 104.51 E
Yongning, Zhg. 100 24.43 N 118.42 E
Yongning, Zhg. 102 38.20 N 106.17 E
Yongning, Zhg. 102 22.42 N 108.50 E
Yongning, Zhg. 102 27.47 N 100.38 E
Yongningcheng 105 40.34 N 116.11 E
Yongningjian 98 39.56 N 121.48 E
Yong Peng 114 2.01 N 103.04 E
Yongping, Zhg. 100 28.12 N 117.45 E
Yongping, Zhg. 102 25.28 N 99.33 E
Yongqing, Zhg. 105 39.19 N 116.29 E
Yongqing, Zhg. 107 30.00 N 105.27 E
Yongquan 100 28.46 N 121.19 E
Yongren 102 26.08 N 101.40 E
Yŏngsan-gang ≏ 98 34.54 N 126.32 E
Yongsan-ni 98 38.52 N 125.56 E
Yŏngsanp'o 98 34.58 N 126.44 E
Yongshan 102 28.15 N 103.24 E
Yongshanqiao 100 29.06 N 117.17 E
Yongsheng 102 26.42 N 100.43 E
Yongshou 102 34.43 N 108.05 E
Yongshun 102 28.57 N 109.41 E
Yongshunchang 107 30.06 N 105.26 E
Yongtai 100 25.54 N 118.58 E
Yŏngwŏl 98 37.12 N 128.28 E
Yŏngwŏn 98 39.49 N 126.32 E
Yongwŏn-ni 98 40.41 N 128.42 E
Yongxin, Zhg. 100 26.56 N 114.18 E
Yongxin, Zhg. 107 28.59 N 106.32 E
Yongxing, Zhg. 98 40.11 N 123.52 E
Yongxing, Zhg. 100 26.08 N 113.06 E
Yongxing, Zhg. 102 39.08 N 110.31 E
Yongxing, Zhg. 106 31.56 N 120.55 E
Yongxing, Zhg. 107 30.34 N 105.35 E
Yongxing, Zhg. 107 30.13 N 105.06 E
Yongxingchang, Zhg. 107 29.02 N 104.34 E
Yongxingchang, Zhg. 107 29.37 N 106.23 E
Yongxingchang, Zhg. 107 30.20 N 103.44 E
Yongxiu 100 29.04 N 115.49 E
Yŏngyang, Taehan 98 36.40 N 129.07 E
Yongyang, Zhg. 100 26.57 N 114.46 E
Yŏngyn 98 39.18 N 125.34 E
Yongyŏn-ni 98 40.44 N 126.09 E
Yongzhai 100 27.59 N 115.26 E
Yŏnhŭi-ri 271b 37.33 N 126.41 E
Yŏnhwa-san ∧ 98 40.46 N 127.23 E
Yonibana 150 8.26 N 12.14 W
Yonkers 210 40.55 N 73.53 W
Yonkers Raceway ♦ 276 40.55 N 73.52 W
Yonne □[5] 50 47.55 N 3.45 E
Yonne ≏ 32 48.23 N 2.58 E
Yono 94 35.53 N 139.38 E
Yŏnp'yŏng-yŏlto II 98 37.38 N 125.40 E
Yonsei University ʊ[2] 271b 37.34 N 126.56 E
Yoo, Enneri V 146 19.24 N 16.38 E
Yoontow 144 0.08 S 42.34 E
Yopal 246 5.21 N 72.23 W
Yop'o-ri 98 38.50 N 125.33 E
Yopurga 85 39.15 N 76.45 E
Yoqne'am 132 32.39 N 35.07 E
Yorba Linda 228 33.53 N 117.48 W
Yorii 94 36.07 N 139.12 E
Yorishima 96 34.29 N 133.35 E
York, Austl. 168a 31.53 S 116.46 E
York, On., Can. 212 43.41 N 79.29 W
York, S.L. 150 8.17 N 13.11 W
York, Eng., U.K. 44 53.58 N 1.05 W
York, Al., U.S. 194 32.29 N 88.17 W
York, In., U.S. 216 41.41 N 84.49 W
York, Ne., U.S. 198 40.52 N 97.35 W
York, N.Y., U.S. 210 42.52 N 77.53 W
York, N.D., U.S. 198 48.18 N 99.34 W

ENGLISH — Name | Page | Lat.°′ | Long.°′

York, Pa., U.S. 208 39.57 N 76.43 W
York, S.C., U.S. 192 34.59 N 81.14 W
York □[6], On., Can. 212 43.55 N 79.25 W
York □[6], Pa., U.S. 208 39.58 N 76.44 W
York □[6], Va., U.S. 208 37.15 N 76.40 W
York ≏, On., Can. 212 45.20 N 77.35 W
York ≏, P.Q., Can. 186 48.49 N 64.34 W
York ≏, Va., U.S. 208 37.15 N 76.23 W
York, Cape > 164 10.42 S 142.31 E
York, Kap > 16 75.53 N 66.12 W
York, Vale of V 44 54.10 N 1.20 W
Yorkana 208 39.59 N 76.35 W
York Center, Il., U.S. 278 41.52 N 87.59 W
York Center, Oh., U.S. 216 40.24 N 83.27 W
Yorkdale Centre ◆[9] 275b 43.44 N 79.27 W
Yorke Peninsula >[1] 166 35.00 S 137.30 E
Yorketown 168b 35.02 S 137.36 E
York Factory 184 57.00 N 92.18 W
Yorkfield 278 41.52 N 87.56 W
York Haven 208 40.06 N 76.42 W
Yorklyn 285 39.48 N 75.40 W
York Minster ʊ[1] 44 53.57 N 1.04 W
York New Salem 208 39.54 N 76.47 W
Yorkshire, N.Y., U.S. 210 42.31 N 78.28 W
Yorkshire, Pa., U.S. 208 39.59 N 76.41 W
Yorkshire, Va., U.S. 208 38.47 N 77.27 W
Yorkshire Dales National Park ♦ 44 54.13 N 2.10 W
Yorkshire Wolds ⋀[2] 44 54.00 N 0.40 W
York Sound ʮ 160 14.50 S 125.05 E
York Springs 208 40.00 N 77.07 W
Yorkton 184 51.13 N 102.28 W
Yorktown, In., U.S. 218 40.10 N 85.29 W
Yorktown, Tx., U.S. 222 28.58 N 97.30 W
Yorktown, Va., U.S. 208 37.14 N 76.30 W
Yorktown ◆[9] 278 41.51 N 88.01 W
Yorktown Battlefield ⊥ 208 37.13 N 76.31 W
Yorktown Heights 210 41.16 N 73.46 W
Yorktown Manor 207 41.38 N 71.26 W
York Township Airport ⊠ 278 41.51 N 88.02 W
York University ʊ[2] 275b 43.47 N 79.30 W
Yorkville, Il., U.S. 216 41.38 N 88.26 W
Yorkville, Mi., U.S. 216 42.23 N 85.24 W
Yorkville, N.Y., U.S. 210 43.06 N 75.16 W
Yorkville, Oh., U.S. 214 40.09 N 80.43 W
Yorkville ◆[8] 275b 43.40 N 79.24 W
Yoro, Hond. 236 15.09 N 87.07 W
Yoro, Mali 150 14.17 N 2.08 W
Yōrō, Nihon 94 35.18 N 136.33 E
Yoro □[5] 236 15.15 N 87.15 W
Yōrō ≏ 94 35.32 N 140.04 E
Yoroi-zaki > 94 34.24 N 136.55 E
Yoron-jima I 93b 27.02 N 128.26 E
Yōrō-no-taki ʟ 94 35.17 N 136.32 E
Yorosso 150 12.22 N 4.47 W
Yosemite Creek ≏ 226 37.44 N 119.36 W
Yosemite National Park 226 37.45 N 119.35 W
Yosemite National Park ♦ 226 37.51 N 119.33 W
Yoshida, Nihon 94 36.02 N 139.02 E
Yoshida, Nihon 94 34.46 N 138.15 E
Yoshida, Nihon 96 33.16 N 132.33 E
Yoshida, Nihon 96 34.40 N 132.42 E
Yoshida, Nihon 96 35.10 N 132.51 E
Yoshida ≏ 96 34.03 N 131.02 E
Yoshii, Nihon 94 36.15 N 138.59 E
Yoshii, Nihon 96 33.20 N 130.45 E
Yoshii, Nihon 96 34.38 N 133.26 E
Yoshii, Nihon 96 34.55 N 134.06 E
Yoshii, Nihon 270 34.53 N 135.03 E
Yoshii ≏ 96 34.36 N 134.03 E
Yoshikawa, Nihon 94 37.13 N 138.25 E
Yoshikawa, Nihon 94 35.53 N 139.51 E
Yoshikawa, Nihon 270 34.55 N 135.28 E
Yoshimi 94 36.02 N 139.27 E
Yoshino, Nihon 96 34.21 N 135.51 E
Yoshino, Nihon 96 34.06 N 134.23 E
Yoshino ≏, Nihon 94 34.22 N 135.40 E
Yoshino ≏, Nihon 96 34.05 N 134.36 E
Yoshinodani 94 36.17 N 136.39 E
Yoshino-Kumano-kokuritsu-kōen ♦ 92 34.07 N 135.55 E
Yoshioka 94 36.27 N 139.01 E
Yoshiumi 96 34.09 N 133.03 E
Yoshiwa 96 34.29 N 132.09 E
Yoshkar-Ola → Joškar-Ola 80 56.38 N 47.52 E
Yosowilangun 115a 8.15 S 113.18 E
Yos Sudarso, Pulau (Frederik Hendrikeiland) I 164 7.50 S 138.30 E
Yŏsu 98 34.46 N 127.44 E
Yotausito 248 16.03 S 63.03 W
Yōtei-zan ∧ 92a 42.49 N 140.49 E
Yotsukaidō 94 35.39 N 140.10 E
Yotvata 132 29.53 N 35.03 E
You ≏, Zhg. 100 26.23 N 118.27 E
You ≏, Zhg. 102 22.50 N 108.06 E
You ≏, Zhg. 102 28.27 N 110.24 E
Youanmi 162 28.37 S 118.49 E
Youbou 224 48.53 N 124.13 W
Youcheng 100 29.14 N 116.48 E
Youfang 106 32.09 N 119.50 E
Youghal 48 51.51 N 7.50 W
Youghal Bay c 48 51.52 N 7.50 W
Youghiogheny ≏ 214 40.22 N 79.52 W
Yougoslavie → Yugoslavia □[1] 22 44.00 N 19.00 E
Youhe 100 32.19 N 113.50 E
Youjidong 104 42.12 N 121.07 E
Youkounkoun 150 12.32 N 13.08 W
Youlan 100 28.34 N 116.10 E
Young, Austl. 166 34.19 S 148.18 E
Young, Sk., Can. 184 51.47 N 105.46 W
Young, Az., U.S. 200 34.06 N 110.57 W
Young, Ur. 252 32.41 S 57.38 W
Young America 216 40.34 N 86.20 W
Younghusband Peninsula >[1] 166 36.00 S 139.30 E
Youngs ≏ 224 46.10 N 123.49 W
Youngs, Lake ⊜ 224 47.25 N 122.07 W
Youngs Creek 218 38.29 N 86.30 W
Youngs Creek ≏ 219 39.21 N 91.51 W
Youngs Rock I[2] 174e 25.03 S 130.07 W
Youngstown, Ab., Can. 182 51.32 N 111.13 W
Youngstown, Fl., U.S. 192 30.21 N 85.26 W
Youngstown, N.Y., U.S. 210 43.14 N 79.03 W
Youngstown, Oh., U.S. 214 41.05 N 80.38 W
Youngstown Municipal Airport ⊠ 214 41.15 N 80.41 W
Youngsville, La., U.S. 194 30.05 N 91.59 W
Youngsville, N.Y., U.S. 210 41.48 N 74.54 W
Youngsville, N.C., U.S. 192 36.01 N 78.28 W
Youngsville, Pa., U.S. 214 41.51 N 79.19 W
Youngwood 214 40.14 N 79.34 W
Youngwood Park ♦ 279b 40.14 N 79.36 W
Yountville 226 38.24 N 122.22 W
Youshashan 120 38.08 N 91.10 E
Youssoufia 148 32.16 N 8.33 W
Youtingpu 107 29.26 N 105.45 E
Youville ◆[8] 275a 45.33 N 73.39 W
Youxi, Zhg. 100 28.45 N 121.06 E
Youxi, Zhg. 100 26.11 N 118.09 E
Youxi, Zhg. 107 29.12 N 106.09 E
Youxian 100 27.00 N 113.21 E
Youxizhen 107 30.35 N 106.18 E
Youyang 102 28.58 N 108.41 E
Youyi 89 46.44 N 131.44 E
Youyu 102 40.09 N 112.32 E
Youzhagou 106 31.04 N 118.46 E
Youzhou 105 40.09 N 115.42 E

DEUTSCH — Name | Seite | Breite°′ | Länge°′ E = Ost

Yoweragabbie 162 28.13 S 117.39 E
Yŏyang-ni 98 37.30 N 128.43 E
Yozgat 130 39.50 N 34.48 E
Yozgat □[4] 130 39.40 N 35.10 E
Ypacaraí 252 25.23 S 57.16 W
Ypané ≏ 252 23.29 S 57.19 W
Ypé Jhú 252 23.54 S 55.20 W
Yport 50 49.44 N 0.19 E
Ypres → Ieper 50 50.51 N 2.53 E
Ypsilanti 216 42.14 N 83.36 W
Ypsilanti East 216 42.15 N 83.35 W
Yreka 204 41.44 N 122.38 W
Yrgajty ≏ 85 43.03 N 74.43 E
Yron ≏ 56 49.10 N 5.52 E
Ysabel Channel ʮ 164 2.00 S 150.00 E
Ysbyty Ystwyth 42 52.20 N 3.48 W
Yser (IJzer) ≏ 50 51.09 N 2.43 E
Ysieux, Ruisseau l' ≏ 261 49.09 N 2.22 E
Yssche ≏ 56 50.49 N 4.38 E
Yssel → Issel ≏ 52 52.00 N 6.10 E
Ysselmeer → IJsselmeer ▿[2] 52 52.45 N 5.25 E
Yssingeaux 62 45.08 N 4.07 E
Ystad 41 55.25 N 13.49 E
Ystalyfera 42 51.47 N 3.47 W
Ysterfonteinpunt > 158 33.22 S 18.09 E
Ystrad ≏ 44 53.13 N 3.20 W
Ystrad Aeron 42 52.11 N 4.11 W
Ystradfellte 42 51.48 N 3.34 W
Ystradgynlais 42 51.47 N 3.45 W
Ystwyth ≏ 42 52.24 N 4.05 W
Ytambey ≏ 252 24.46 S 54.24 W
Ythan ≏ 46 57.18 N 2.00 W
Ytre Arna 26 60.26 N 5.30 E
Ytterharnäs 40 60.39 N 17.21 E
Ytterhogdal 26 62.12 N 14.51 E
Yttermalung 40 60.35 N 13.50 E
Ytterselö 40 59.23 N 17.15 E
Yttre Hållsfjärden c[2] 40 59.08 N 17.40 E
Yttygran, ostrov I 180 64.36 N 172.40 W
Yū 96 34.02 N 132.13 E
Yu ≏ 102 23.24 N 110.05 E
Yu, Pulau I 164 0.03 S 129.36 E
Yu'alliq, Jabal ∧ 140 30.22 N 33.31 E
Yuam ≏ 110 17.47 N 97.45 E
Yuan ≏, Zhg. 100 28.09 N 115.34 E
Yuan ≏, Zhg. 102 28.58 N 111.49 E
Yuan'an 102 31.04 N 111.26 E
Yuanao 100 26.29 N 119.48 E
Yuanbachang 107 29.44 N 105.27 E
Yuanhua 106 30.25 N 120.46 E
Yuanjiang 102 23.34 N 102.03 E
Yuankeng 100 26.48 N 117.44 E
Yüanli 100 24.27 N 120.39 E
Yüanlin 100 23.58 N 120.34 E
Yuanling 102 28.20 N 110.16 E
Yuanmou 102 25.38 N 101.54 E
Yuan → Red ≏ 110 20.17 N 106.34 E
Yuanshancun 106 31.08 N 120.20 E
Yuanshi 98 37.45 N 114.32 E
Yuantan, Zhg. 100 32.47 N 112.53 E
Yuantan, Zhg. 100 23.39 N 113.12 E
Yuantongsi 107 30.13 N 104.15 E
Yuantouzhu 106 31.32 N 120.14 E
Yuanxiang 98 34.14 N 115.19 E
Yuanxiangzhen 106 31.39 N 119.15 E
Yuanxing 107 30.36 N 104.59 E
Yuanyang (Yangwu), Zhg. 98 35.04 N 113.57 E
Yuanyang, Zhg. 102 23.12 N 102.52 E
Yuanyangpu 107 30.10 N 105.15 E
Yuanyangqiao 107 29.41 N 106.33 E
Yuasa 96 34.02 N 135.11 E
Yuat ≏ 164 4.25 S 143.55 E
Yuba 102 29.27 N 97.42 E
Yuba □[6] 226 39.16 N 121.17 W
Yuba ≏ 226 39.07 N 121.36 W
Yuba City 226 39.08 N 121.36 W
Yubara 96 35.12 N 133.45 E
Yubara-chosuichi ⊜ 96 35.13 N 133.43 E
Yūbari 92a 43.04 N 141.59 E
Yūbari-sanchi ⋀ 92a 43.15 N 142.20 E
Yubdo 144 9.00 N 35.22 E
Yūbetsu 92a 44.14 N 143.37 E
Yūbetsu ≏ 92a 44.14 N 143.37 E
Yucaipa 228 34.02 N 117.02 W
Yucatán □[3] 232 20.50 N 89.00 W
Yucatán, Canal de ʮ 238 21.45 N 85.45 W
Yucatan Peninsula (Península de Yucatán) >[1] 232 19.30 N 89.00 W
Yucca 200 34.52 N 114.08 W
Yucca Lake ⊜ 204 36.59 N 116.01 W
Yucca Valley 204 34.07 N 116.35 W
Yuchaozhuang 105 39.35 N 117.50 E
Yucheng, Zhg. 98 36.56 N 116.39 E
Yucheng, Zhg. 106 30.32 N 120.51 E
Yuci 102 37.45 N 112.41 E
Yuda 92 39.20 N 140.50 E
Yudaokou 98 42.14 N 116.48 E
Yudi Shan ∧ 89 52.17 N 121.52 E
Yudong 106 32.02 N 121.22 E
Yudu 100 25.59 N 115.24 E
Yue ≏ 107 28.50 N 104.21 E
Yuebo 107 29.03 N 104.12 E
Yuecheng 100 32.39 N 114.49 E
Yuechi 107 30.33 N 106.26 E
Yuejiatun 104 41.10 N 120.43 E
Yuejiawopeng 104 41.35 N 122.20 E
Yuekou 100 30.32 N 113.03 E
Yuelai 106 31.56 N 121.27 E
Yuelaichang, Zhg. 107 29.44 N 106.32 E
Yuelaichang, Zhg. 107 28.53 N 106.22 E
Yuemenpu 107 30.28 N 106.34 E
Yuendumu 162 22.16 S 131.49 E
Yuendumu Aboriginal Reserve ◆[4] 162 22.20 S 131.47 E
Yuen Long 271d 22.26 N 114.02 E
Yuepu 106 31.25 N 121.26 E
Yueqing 100 28.08 N 120.58 E
Yuewang 106 31.33 N 121.09 E
Yuexi, Zhg. 100 30.50 N 116.24 E
Yuexi, Zhg. 102 28.42 N 102.28 E
Yueyang 100 29.23 N 113.06 E
Yuezi 100 24.54 N 115.02 E
Yufa 105 39.31 N 116.19 E
Yufeng 107 30.37 N 105.11 E
Yufu-dake ∧ 96 33.17 N 131.24 E
Yufuin 96 33.15 N 131.20 E
Yugan 100 28.41 N 116.41 E
Yugawara 94 35.09 N 139.04 E
Yuge 96 34.15 N 133.12 E
Yugoslavia (Jugoslavija) □[1] 22 44.00 N 19.00 E
Yugou 100 33.42 N 118.55 E
Yuguan 98 39.56 N 119.22 E
Yuguo 104 41.52 N 123.15 E
Yuhang (Linping) 106 30.25 N 120.18 E
Yuhebu 102 38.01 N 109.37 E
Yuhu 100 27.53 N 120.08 E
Yuhuaizhuang 105 39.24 N 117.40 E
Yuhuan 100 28.10 N 121.12 E
Yuhuan Dao I 100 28.08 N 121.12 E
Yuhuang Ding ∧ 98 36.50 N 121.21 E
Yui 94 35.06 N 138.34 E
Yuin 162 27.58 S 116.02 E
Yujiachang 107 29.57 N 104.04 E
Yujiacun 106 31.45 N 121.48 E
Yujiang 100 28.11 N 116.47 E
Yujiaqiao 106 31.30 N 119.25 E
Yujiawan 86 44.32 N 86.45 E
Yukarıbey 130 39.15 N 27.06 E
Yukarıdudullu ◆[8] 267b 41.02 N 29.09 E
Yuke 98 37.58 N 115.39 E
Yūki, Nihon 94 36.18 N 139.53 E
Yuki, Nihon 96 34.29 N 132.16 E
Yuki, Nihon 96 34.46 N 133.17 E
Yuki, Nihon 96 33.46 N 134.36 E

Symbols in the index entries represent the broad categories identified in the key at the right. Symbols with superior numbers (⋀[1]) identify subcategories (see complete key on page *I · 1*).

Symbole im Register stellen die rechts im Schlüssel erklärten Kategorien dar. Symbole mit hochgestellten Ziffern (⋀[1]) bezeichnen Unterabteilungen einer Kategorie (vgl. vollständiger Schlüssel auf Seite *I · 1*).

Los símbolos incluídos en el texto del índice representan las grandes categorias identificadas con la clave a la derecha. Los símbolos con numeros en su parte superior (⋀[1]) identifican las subcategorías (véase la clave completa en la página *I · 1*).

Les symboles de l'index représentent les catégories indiquées dans la légende à droite. Les symboles suivis d'un indice (⋀[1]) représentent des sous-catégories (voir légende complète à la page *I · 1*).

Os símbolos incluídos no texto do índice representam as grandes categorias identificadas com a chave à direita. Os símbolos com números em sua parte superior (⋀[1]) identificam as subcategorias (veja-se a chave completa à página *I · 1*).

	English	Deutsch	Español	Français	Português
∧	Mountain	Berg	Montaña	Montagne	Montanha
⋀	Mountains	Gebirge	Montañas	Montagnes	Montanhas
)(	Pass	Paß	Paso	Col	Passo
V	Valley, Canyon	Tal, Cañon	Valle, Cañón	Vallée, Canyon	Vale, Canhão
≚	Plain	Ebene	Llano	Plaine	Planície
>	Cape	Kap	Cabo	Cap	Cabo
I	Island	Insel	Isla	Île	Ilha
II	Islands	Inseln	Islas	Îles	Ilhas
⊥	Other Topographic Features	Andere Topographische Objekte	Otros Elementos Topográficos	Autres données topographiques	Outros acidentes topográficos

ESPAÑOL Nombre	Página	Lat.°′	Long.°′ W = Oeste
FRANÇAIS Nom	Page	Lat.°′	Long.°′ W = Ouest
PORTUGUÊS Nome	Página	Lat.°′	Long.°′ W = Oeste

Yukon, Ok., U.S. 196 35.30 N 97.45 W
Yukon, Pa., U.S. 214 40.13 N 79.41 W
Yukon □[4], Can. 176 64.00 N 135.00 W
Yukon □[4], Can. 180 64.00 N 135.00 W
Yukon ≐ 180 62.33 N 163.59 W
Yukon Flats ≡ 180 66.30 N 146.00 W
Yukou 105 40.12 N 117.00 E
Yukuhashi 96 33.44 N 130.59 E
Yulan 210 41.31 N 74.56 W
Yulao 102 23.31 N 111.46 E
Yulara 162 25.14 S 131.04 E
Yule ≐ 162 20.41 S 118.17 E
Yule Bay c 9 70.44 S 166.40 E
Yule Island I 164 8.50 S 146.30 E
Yuli, Nig. 146 9.42 N 10.17 E
Yüli, T'aiwan 100 23.20 N 121.18 E
Yuli, Zhg. 98 37.00 N 121.25 E
Yuliang 100 29.52 N 118.30 E
Yuliangpu 89 43.26 N 121.55 E
Yulin, Zhg. 102 22.36 N 110.07 E
Yulin, Zhg. 102 38.20 N 109.29 E
Yulin, Zhg. 110 18.16 N 109.32 E
Yulincun 105 40.12 N 116.42 E
Yul-li 98 38.52 N 126.13 E
Yulong 107 29.58 N 104.22 E
Yuma, Az., U.S. 200 32.43 N 114.37 W
Yuma, Co., U.S. 198 40.08 N 102.43 W
Yuma, Bahía de c 238 18.21 N 68.35 W
Yuma Marine Corps Air Station ■ 200 32.40 N 114.38 W
Yuma Proving Ground ■ 204 33.05 N 114.25 W
Yumare 246 10.37 N 68.41 W
Yumbel 252 37.08 S 72.32 W
Yumbi, Zaïre 152 1.53 S 16.32 E
Yumbi, Zaïre 154 1.14 S 26.14 E
Yumbo 246 3.35 N 76.28 W
Yumen (Laojunmiao) 102 39.56 N 97.51 E
Yumenzhen 102 40.17 N 97.07 E
Yumesaki 96 34.58 N 134.42 E
Yumezaki ≐ 96 34.47 N 134.39 E
Yumin 86 46.02 N 82.37 E
Yumurtalık 130 36.49 N 35.45 E
Yun ≐ 100 30.43 N 114.04 E
Yuna, Austl. 162 28.20 S 115.00 E
Yuna, Nihon 174m 26.46 N 128.12 E
Yuna ≐ 238 19.12 N 69.37 W
Yunak 130 38.49 N 31.45 E
Yunan (Ducheng) 102 23.11 N 111.29 E
Yunaska Island I 180 52.40 N 170.50 W
Yuncao 100 31.26 N 118.04 E
Yuncheng, Zhg. 98 35.35 N 115.54 E
Yuncheng, Zhg. 102 35.00 N 110.59 E
Yundamindra 162 29.07 S 122.02 E
Yundanyingzi 104 42.00 N 121.34 E
Yunderup 168a 32.35 S 115.46 E
Yunfeng Ding ∧ 106 30.56 N 120.02 E
Yungas ◆[1] 248 16.00 S 67.45 W
Yungay, Chile 252 37.07 S 72.01 W
Yungay, Perú 248 9.09 S 77.44 W
Yungchia → Wenzhou 100 28.01 N 120.39 E
Yungchi → Jilin 89 43.51 N 126.33 E
Yungho 269d 25.01 N 121.31 E
Yungning → Nanning 102 22.48 N 108.20 E
Yung Shue Wan 271d 22.14 N 114.06 E
Yunhe 100 28.06 N 119.34 E
Yunhe → Peixian 98 34.21 N 117.59 E
Yunjin 107 29.06 N 105.40 E
Yunkai Dashan ⋀ 102 22.30 N 111.00 E
Yun Ling ⋀ 102 27.20 N 99.20 E
Yunlong, Zhg. 102 25.50 N 99.17 E
Yunlong, Zhg. 107 30.31 N 104.46 E
Yunluchang 107 29.45 N 105.57 E
Yunmeng 100 31.02 N 113.41 E
Yunmenling 100 25.15 N 115.49 E
Yunmenzhen 107 30.06 N 106.20 E
Yunnan □[4] 102 24.00 N 101.00 E
Yunnanfu → Kunming 102 25.05 N 102.40 E
Yunotani 94 37.14 N 139.01 E
Yunotsu 96 35.05 N 132.21 E
Yunta 166 32.35 S 139.33 E
Yunting 106 31.53 N 120.19 E
Yunwu Shan ∧ 98 41.07 N 116.34 E
Yunxi, Zhg. 100 29.28 N 113.16 E
Yunxi, Zhg. 102 32.49 N 110.13 E
Yunxian, Zhg. 102 24.30 N 100.03 E
Yunxian (Yunyang), Zhg. 102 32.49 N 110.49 E
Yunxiao 100 24.04 N 117.20 E
Yunyan ≐ 100 34.39 N 119.18 E
Yunyang, Zhg. 100 33.28 N 112.42 E
Yunyang, Zhg. 102 30.58 N 109.02 E
Yunzalin ≐ 110 17.23 N 97.40 E
Yunzhong 100 29.13 N 117.40 E
Yunzhou 98 41.01 N 115.44 E
Yuping 102 27.07 N 108.47 E
Yuqi 106 31.43 N 120.11 E
Yuqia 102 38.07 N 94.35 E
Yuqian'gou 104 41.41 N 121.28 E
Yuqiao Shuiku ◎[1] 105 40.02 N 117.33 E
Yuqing 102 27.05 N 107.44 E
Yura, Nihon 96 33.57 N 135.07 E
Yura, Perú 248 16.11 S 71.40 W
Yura ≐ 96 35.31 N 135.17 E
Yurano-hana ≻ 96 33.01 N 132.23 E
Yurécuaro 234 20.20 N 102.18 W
Yurga → Jurga 86 55.42 N 84.51 E
Yuri-jima I 96 33.51 N 132.32 E
Yurimaguas 248 5.54 S 76.05 W
Yuriria 234 20.12 N 101.09 W
Yuriria, Laguna de ◎ 234 20.15 N 101.06 W
Yuruarí ≐ 246 6.44 N 61.40 W
Yurubi, Parque Nacional ♣ 246 10.25 N 68.42 W
Yürük 130 40.56 N 27.04 E
Yurumanguí ≐ 246 3.27 N 77.21 W
Yurungkax ≐ 120 37.00 N 79.55 E
Yuryev → Tartu 76 58.23 N 26.43 E
Yusala, Laguna ◎ 248 14.05 S 67.12 W
Yuşa Tepesi ∧[2] 267b 41.09 N 29.05 E
Yuscarán 236 13.55 N 86.51 W
Yushan, Zhg. 100 26.54 N 118.36 E
Yushan, Zhg. 100 28.41 N 118.15 E
Yushan, Zhg. 100 33.19 N 113.41 E
Yü Shan ∧, T'aiwan 100 23.28 N 120.57 E
Yu Shan ∧, Zhg. 100 26.06 N 115.20 E
Yushanzhen 102 29.38 N 108.19 E
Yushu, Zhg. 89 44.46 N 126.34 E
Yushu (Jiegu), Zhg. 102 33.01 N 97.00 E
Yushugou 86 44.07 N 87.05 E
Yushulinzi, Zhg. 98 41.30 N 119.07 E
Yushulinzi, Zhg. 98 40.59 N 125.57 E
Yushupu 104 41.10 N 122.08 E
Yushutai, Zhg. 89 43.30 N 124.17 E
Yushutai, Zhg. 104 41.42 N 123.26 E
Yushuwan 105 40.04 N 115.35 E
Yusichang 107 29.14 N 105.25 E
Yūsofābād ◆[8] 267d 35.44 N 51.25 E
Yuste, Monasterio de ʊ[1] 34 40.08 N 5.45 W
Yūsuf, Baḥr ≍ 142 29.18 N 30.50 E
Yusufeli 130 40.50 N 41.33 E
Yusuhara 96 33.23 N 132.55 E
Yusuhara ≐ 96 33.11 N 132.58 E
Yutai (Guting) 98 35.02 N 116.40 E
Yutian, Zhg. 100 26.27 N 114.36 E
Yutian, Zhg. 105 39.53 N 117.45 E
Yutian, Zhg. 120 36.51 N 81.40 E
Yuting 100 29.50 N 117.57 E
Yūtō 94 34.42 N 137.38 E
Yutou 100 28.36 N 118.30 E
Yuty 252 26.32 S 56.18 W
Yutz 56 49.21 N 6.11 E
Yütz'u → Yuci 102 37.45 N 112.41 E
Yüwan-dake ∧ 93b 28.18 N 129.21 E
Yuwangcheng 100 31.31 N 114.29 E
Yüweng Tao I 100 23.36 N 119.30 E
Yuwŏnjin 98 40.18 N 126.37 E
Yuxi, Zhg. 100 25.36 N 119.18 E
Yuxi, Zhg. 102 24.23 N 102.34 E
Yuxi, Zhg. 106 32.03 N 121.11 E
Yuxi, Zhg. 107 30.19 N 105.47 E
Yuxian, Zhg. 98 39.48 N 114.33 E
Yuxian, Zhg. 100 34.10 N 113.28 E
Yuxian, Zhg. 102 38.09 N 113.25 E
Yuxiangpu 98 34.27 N 114.57 E
Yuxiangtou 106 31.14 N 120.53 E
Yuxikou 100 31.26 N 118.17 E
Yuyao 100 30.04 N 121.10 E
Yuya-wan c 96 34.23 N 130.56 E
Yuyŏn-ni 98 38.42 N 127.10 E
Yuyuan Tan ◎ 271a 39.55 N 116.18 E
Yuza 92 39.01 N 139.54 E
Yuzawa, Nihon 92 39.10 N 140.30 E
Yuzawa, Nihon 94 36.56 N 138.49 E
Yuzhno-Sakhalinsk → Južno-Sachalinsk 89 46.58 N 142.42 E
Yuzovka → Doneck 83 48.00 N 37.48 E
Yuzuruha-san ∧ 96 34.14 N 134.49 E
Yvelines □[5] 50 48.50 N 1.50 E
Yvelines, Forêt des ♣ 261 48.40 N 1.55 E
Yverdon 58 46.47 N 6.39 E
Yvetot 50 49.37 N 0.46 E
Yvette 261 48.43 N 1.55 E
Yvette ≐ 50 48.40 N 2.20 E
Yvoir 56 50.20 N 4.53 E
Yvoire 58 46.22 N 6.20 E
Yvonand 58 46.48 N 6.45 E
Yvron ≐ 50 48.39 N 2.56 E
Ywamun 110 20.31 N 95.25 E
Ywathagyi 110 22.18 N 95.42 E
Ywathit 110 19.10 N 97.30 E
Yxlan I 40 59.38 N 18.52 E
Yxsjöberg 40 60.03 N 14.46 E
Yzeron 62 45.42 N 4.35 E
Yzeure 32 46.34 N 3.21 E

Z

Za, Oued ≐ 148 34.34 N 3.03 W
Zaachila 234 16.57 N 96.45 W
Zaaimansdal 158 33.35 S 23.22 E
Zaajatskaja 86 52.53 N 61.35 E
Zaalajskij chrebet ⋀ 85 39.20 N 72.30 E
Zaamin 85 39.58 N 68.24 E
Zaanstad 52 52.26 N 4.49 E
Žabaj ≐ 86 51.42 N 68.22 E
Žabajkal'sk 88 49.38 N 117.19 E
Zăbala ≐ 38 45.51 N 26.46 E
Žabalj 38 46.01 N 21.55 E
Zabari 38 44.21 N 21.13 E
Zabarjad, Jazīrat I 140 23.37 N 36.12 E
Žabasak 86 50.21 N 61.40 E
Zāb-e Küchek → Little Zab ≐ 128 35.12 N 43.25 E
Zaberfeld 56 49.03 N 8.55 E
Zabīd 144 14.10 N 43.17 E
Zabīd, Wādī V 144 14.07 N 43.06 E
Žabinka 76 52.12 N 24.01 E
Zabituj 88 53.16 N 102.50 E
Ząbkowice Śląskie 30 50.36 N 16.53 E
Žabljak 38 43.09 N 19.07 E
Zabłudów 30 53.01 N 23.20 E
Zābol 128 31.02 N 61.30 E
Zābol □[4] 120 32.00 N 67.15 E
Zābolī 128 27.07 N 61.40 E
Zabolotje, Bela. 76 52.40 N 28.34 E
Zabolotje, Bela. 76 53.56 N 24.46 E
Zabolotje, Ross. 82 56.40 N 38.06 E
Zabolotje, Ross. 82 54.24 N 38.54 E
Zabolotje, Ross. 82 55.32 N 38.12 E
Zabolotje, Ukr. 78 51.38 N 24.15 E
Zabolotov 78 48.29 N 25.16 E
Zaborje, Bela. 76 55.55 N 29.19 E
Zaborje, Ross. 76 55.24 N 31.32 E
Zaborje, Ross. 76 54.51 N 32.41 E
Zaborje, Ross. 76 53.06 N 31.42 E
Zaborje, Ross. 82 55.23 N 37.47 E
Zabory 76 55.58 N 32.17 E
Zabré 150 11.10 N 0.38 W
Zábřeh 30 49.53 N 16.52 E
Zabrze (Hindenburg) 30 50.18 N 18.46 E
Zaburunje 80 46.44 N 50.09 E
Zabyčanje 76 53.25 N 31.52 E
Zabzugu 150 9.17 N 0.22 E
Zacapa 236 14.58 N 89.32 W
Zacapa □[5] 236 15.00 N 89.30 W
Zacapoaxtla 234 19.53 N 97.35 W
Zacapu 234 19.50 N 101.43 W
Zacata 208 38.07 N 76.47 W
Zacatecas 232 22.47 N 102.35 W
Zacatecas □[3] 232 23.00 N 103.00 W
Zacatecoluca 236 13.30 N 88.52 W
Zacatepec 234 18.39 N 99.12 W
Zacatlán 234 19.56 N 97.58 W
Zacatongo 234 20.49 N 104.33 W
Začepilovka 78 49.12 N 35.14 E
Zacharias Creek ≐ 285 40.11 N 75.23 W
Zacharkovo 265b 55.47 N 37.19 E
Zacharovo, Ross. 76 54.22 N 39.17 E
Zacharovo, Ross. 82 56.31 N 36.44 E
Zacharvan' 82 56.18 N 55.48 E
Zachary 194 30.38 N 91.09 W
Zachidnoje 78 51.29 N 31.15 E
Zachmet 128 37.43 N 62.30 E
Zachožje 265a 59.44 N 30.51 E
Zachrebetnoje 24 69.00 N 36.25 E
Začistje 76 54.25 N 28.45 E
Zacks Bay c 276 40.36 N 73.29 W
Zacoalco de Torres 234 20.14 N 103.35 W
Zacualpa 236 15.05 N 90.50 W
Zacualpan, Méx. 234 21.15 N 105.10 W
Zacualpan, Méx. 234 20.28 N 98.22 W
Zacualtipan 234 20.39 N 98.36 W
Zaculeu ⊥ 236 15.21 N 91.29 W
Zadar 36 44.07 N 15.14 E
Zadetkale Kyun I 110 10.08 N 98.12 E
Zadetkyi Kyun I 110 9.58 N 98.13 E
Zadi (Inkisi) ≐ 152 4.46 S 14.52 E
Zadní Chodov 60 49.54 N 12.44 E
Zadoi 120 33.10 N 95.05 E
Zadonsk 76 52.23 N 38.57 E
Zadorra ≐ 34 42.40 N 2.54 W
Žadovo 78 52.03 N 32.39 E
Zaerap 76 59.18 N 36.37 E
Zafarabad 85 40.11 N 68.51 E
Ẓafar al-Qadīmah 142 30.58 N 31.37 E
Za'farānah, Bi'r ⊤[4] 142 29.07 N 32.33 E
Za'farānah, Ra's ≻ 142 29.06 N 32.40 E
Zafarwāl 123 32.21 N 74.54 E
Zafer Burnu ≻ 130 35.42 N 34.35 E
Zafferana Etnea 70 37.41 N 15.06 E
Zafferano, Capo ≻ 70 38.06 N 13.30 E
Zafirovo 38 44.00 N 26.50 E
Zafra 34 38.25 N 6.25 W
Žaga 64 46.18 N 13.29 E
Zagabria → Zagreb 36 45.48 N 15.58 E
Żagań 30 51.37 N 15.19 E
Žagare 76 56.21 N 23.15 E
Zagarise 68 39.00 N 16.39 E
Zagarolo 66 41.50 N 12.50 E
Zagazig → Az-Zaqāzīq 142 30.35 N 31.31 E
Zaghouan 148 36.24 N 10.09 E
Zaghouan, Jebel ∧ 36 36.21 N 10.08 E
Zagnanado 150 7.16 N 2.21 E
Zagnitkov 78 48.03 N 28.54 E
Zagora 148 30.22 N 5.50 W
Zagora ⋀ 36 43.40 N 16.15 E
Zagor'anskij 265b 55.55 N 37.55 E
Zagórów 30 52.11 N 17.55 E
Zagorskij 89 47.19 N 142.28 E
Zagórz 30 49.31 N 22.17 E
Zagreb 36 45.48 N 15.58 E
Zāgros, Kūhhā-ye ⋀ 128 33.40 N 47.00 E
Zagros Mountains → Zāgros, Kūhhā-ye ⋀ 128 33.40 N 47.00 E
Zagryzovo 83 49.31 N 37.43 E
Žagubica 38 44.13 N 21.48 E
Zagustaj 88 51.58 N 110.45 E
Za'gya ≐ 120 31.55 N 88.58 E
Zagyva ≐ 30 47.10 N 20.13 E
Zahana 34 35.32 N 0.25 W
Zāhedān 128 29.30 N 60.52 E
Zahīrābād 122 17.41 N 77.37 E
Zaḥlah 130 33.51 N 35.53 E
Zahna 54 51.54 N 12.47 E
Zahns Airport ⊠ 276 40.42 N 73.24 W
Záhony 30 48.25 N 22.11 E
Záhorská Ves 61 48.23 N 16.51 E
Zahrān 144 17.40 N 43.30 E
Zahrensdorf 54 53.45 N 11.40 E
Zaidpur 124 26.50 N 81.20 E
Zaigrajevo 88 51.50 N 108.16 E
Zaijiafangzi 104 41.17 N 122.39 E
Zailijskij-Alatau, chrebet ⋀ 85 43.00 N 77.00 E
Žailma, Kaz. 85 43.46 N 69.47 E
Žailma, Kaz. 86 51.32 N 61.37 E
Zaimka 88 58.41 N 100.40 E
Zaimokuza 268 35.18 N 139.33 E
Zainsk 80 55.18 N 52.06 E
Zaire □[5] 152 7.00 S 13.30 E
Zaire (Zaïre) □[1] 138 4.00 S 25.00 E
Zaïre → Congo ≐ 138 6.04 S 12.24 E
Zaizhuangzi 105 40.02 N 117.43 E
Zaj ≐ 80 55.36 N 51.40 E
Zajarsk 88 56.10 N 102.52 E
Zajcevka 83 49.41 N 40.00 E
Zajcevo, Ross. 82 54.08 N 37.26 E
Zajcevo, Ross. 265b 55.39 N 37.11 E
Zajcevo, Ukr. 83 48.32 N 38.04 E
Zajcevo, Ukr. 83 48.24 N 38.02 E
Zaječar 38 43.54 N 22.17 E
Zajkany 78 47.59 N 27.22 E
Zaj-Karataj 80 54.42 N 52.22 E
Zajmo-Obryv 83 47.02 N 39.19 E
Zajsan 86 47.28 N 84.55 E
Zajsan, ozero ◎ 86 48.00 N 84.00 E
Žajsk 80 55.54 N 42.32 E
Zajukovo 84 43.37 N 43.19 E
Zaka 154 20.20 S 31.29 E
Zakamensk 88 50.23 N 103.17 E
Zakarpatskaja Oblast' □[8] 78 48.30 N 23.00 E
Zákas 38 40.02 N 21.16 E
Zakatal'skij zapovednik ♣ 84 41.48 N 46.38 E
Zakataly 84 41.38 N 46.39 E
Zakatnyj 80 46.32 N 44.04 E
Zakfero 140 12.10 N 27.35 E
Zākhū 128 37.08 N 42.41 E
Zákinthos 38 37.47 N 20.53 E
Zákinthos I 38 37.52 N 20.44 E
Zakínthou, Porthmós ꓵ 38 37.50 N 21.00 E
Zakīyah 132 33.20 N 36.08 E
Zakliczyn 30 49.51 N 20.48 E
Zaklików 30 50.47 N 22.06 E
Zákolany 54 50.10 N 14.14 E
Zakopane 30 49.19 N 19.57 E
Zakotnoje, Ukr. 83 49.28 N 38.58 E
Zakotnoje, Ukr. 83 48.54 N 37.58 E
Zakouma 146 10.54 N 19.49 E
Zakouma, Parc National de ♣ 146 10.45 N 19.30 E
Zakroczym 30 52.26 N 20.37 E
Žaksy 86 51.55 N 67.20 E
Žaksybaj ≐ 80 49.24 N 53.18 E
Zákupy 54 50.42 N 14.40 E
Zala 144 6.28 N 37.20 E
Zala □[6] 61 46.45 N 16.50 E
Zala ≐ 61 46.43 N 17.16 E
Zalaegerszeg 30 46.51 N 16.51 E
Zalai-dombság ⋀[2] 61 46.37 N 16.48 E
Zalalövő 61 46.51 N 16.35 E
Zalamea de la Serana 34 38.39 N 5.39 W
Žalanaš 86 51.12 N 65.02 E
Zalanga 150 10.37 N 10.10 E
Žalany 54 50.35 N 13.55 E
Zalari 88 53.34 N 102.32 E
Zalaszentgrót 30 46.59 N 17.02 E
Zalatárnok 61 46.42 N 16.46 E
Zalau, Nig. 150 10.20 N 9.00 E
Zalău, Rom. 38 47.11 N 23.03 E
Žalauly, ozero ◎ 86 52.53 N 74.10 E
Zaldívar, Laguna ◎ 286b 22.58 N 82.27 W
Žalec 36 46.15 N 15.10 E
Zalegošč' 76 52.56 N 36.53 E
Zaleščiki 78 48.38 N 25.44 E
Zalesje, Ross. 76 54.51 N 21.32 E
Zalesje, Ross. 76 58.42 N 36.10 E
Zalesovo 86 54.00 N 84.47 E
Zalingei 140 12.54 N 23.29 E
Zalizničnoje 78 47.53 N 33.29 E
Založcy 78 49.48 N 25.24 E
Zalṭan 146 32.57 N 11.52 E
Zaltbommel 52 51.48 N 5.15 E
Žaltyr 86 51.40 N 69.50 E
Žaltyr, ozero ◎ 80 47.24 N 51.07 E
Zalučje 76 57.40 N 31.46 E
Zalukokoaže 84 43.54 N 43.13 E
Zalun 110 17.29 N 95.34 E
Zama, Nihon 268 35.29 N 139.24 E
Zama, Ms., U.S. 194 32.58 N 89.22 W
Zama, Camp ■ 268 35.30 N 139.24 E
Zama-iriya 268 35.29 N 139.24 E
Zamakh 144 16.30 N 47.35 E
Zamālik, Jazīrat az- I 273c 30.03 N 31.13 E
Žaman-Akkol', ozero ◎ 86 48.58 N 63.30 E
Žamankak 80 48.56 N 48.45 E
Žamantau, gora ∧[2] 80 48.20 N 51.50 E
Zamantı ≐ 130 37.36 N 35.35 E
Zamarino 82 54.18 N 37.11 E
Žambaj 80 47.11 N 50.34 E
Zambales □[4] 116 15.20 N 120.05 E
Zambales Mountains ⋀ 116 15.45 N 120.05 E
Žamberk 30 50.05 N 16.28 E
Zambezi 152 13.33 S 23.06 E
Zambezi (Zambeze) ≐ 138 18.55 S 36.04 E
Zambézia □[5] 154 16.15 S 37.30 E
Zambezi Escarpment ⩲[4] 154 16.10 S 30.30 E
Zambia □[1], Afr. 138 14.30 S 27.30 E
Zambia □[1], Afr. 154 14.30 S 29.00 E
Zambie → Zambia □[1] 154 14.30 S 27.30 E
Zamboanga 116 6.54 N 122.04 E
Zamboanga del Norte □[4] 116 8.15 N 123.00 E
Zamboanga del Sur □[4] 116 7.50 N 123.00 E
Zamboanga Peninsula ≻[1] 116 7.32 N 122.16 E
Zamboanguita 116 9.06 N 123.12 E
Zambrano 246 9.45 N 74.49 W
Zambrone 68 38.42 N 15.59 E
Zambrów 30 53.00 N 22.15 E
Zâmbuè 154 15.10 S 30.50 E
Zambujal 266c 38.52 N 9.07 W
Zamch 30 50.20 N 23.00 E
Zamežnaja 24 65.02 N 51.50 E
Zamfara ≐ 150 12.05 N 4.02 E
Zamglaj 78 51.49 N 31.13 E
Zami ≐ 110 16.09 N 97.58 E
Zamjany 80 46.50 N 47.40 E
Zamkova, gora ∧[2] 76 53.30 N 25.43 E
Zamora, Ec. 246 4.04 S 78.58 W
Zamora, Esp. 34 41.30 N 5.45 W
Zamora, Ca., U.S. 226 38.48 N 121.53 W
Zamora □[4] 34 41.45 N 6.00 W
Zamora ≐ 246 2.59 S 78.13 W
Zamora-Chinchipe □[4] 246 4.15 S 78.50 W
Zamora de Hidalgo 234 19.59 N 102.16 W
Zamość 30 50.44 N 23.15 E
Zamość □[4] 30 50.35 N 23.20 E
Zamožnoje 83 47.19 N 37.49 E
Zams 58 47.09 N 10.35 E
Zamševa 86 59.07 N 89.14 E
Zamuro, Punta ≻ 246 11.26 N 68.50 W
Zamzam, Wādī V 146 31.26 N 15.27 E
Zamzor 88 55.21 N 98.35 E
Zana ⊥ 34 35.45 N 6.05 E
Žanadarja 86 44.45 N 64.40 E
Zanaga 152 2.51 S 13.50 E
Zanapa ≐ 234 17.58 N 94.06 W
Žanašu 80 47.27 N 48.31 E
Žanatalap, Kaz. 86 47.11 N 61.52 E
Žanatalap, Kaz. 86 47.06 N 84.13 E
Žanatarlyk 86 44.16 N 73.12 E
Žanatas 85 43.34 N 69.45 E
Záncara ≐ 34 39.18 N 3.18 W
Zanda 120 31.30 N 79.30 E
Žandov 54 50.44 N 14.24 E
Zandvoort 52 52.22 N 4.32 E
Zandvoort, Circuit Autorace ♣ 52 52.24 N 4.32 E
Zane Hills ⋀[2] 180 66.10 N 156.00 W
Zanesfield 216 40.20 N 83.41 W
Zanesville, In., U.S. 216 41.02 N 85.00 W
Zanesville, Oh., U.S. 188 39.56 N 82.00 W
Zanevka 265a 59.56 N 30.31 E
Zangasso 150 12.09 N 5.37 W
Zangelan 84 39.06 N 46.39 E
Zangenstein 60 49.24 N 12.19 E
Zangezurskij chrebet ⋀ 84 39.30 N 45.54 E
Zanggezhuang 98 37.28 N 120.57 E
Zangguy 120 37.22 N 78.48 E
Žangiztobe 86 49.16 N 81.18 E
Zangji 100 33.01 N 113.52 E
Zangmār ≐ 84 39.17 N 44.50 E
Zânguè ≐ 154 17.52 S 35.20 E
Zangwan 100 29.27 N 117.23 E
Zanhuang 98 37.38 N 114.26 E
Zanjān 128 36.40 N 48.29 E
Zanjān □[4] 128 36.30 N 49.00 E
Zanjān ≐ 128 37.08 N 47.47 E
Zanjón 252 27.55 S 64.15 W
Zanjón ≐ 252 31.16 S 67.41 W
Žankala ⊥ 86 44.29 N 64.05 E
Žannetty, ostrov I 74 76.43 N 158.00 E
Zannone, Isola I 66 40.58 N 13.03 E
Zanpa-misaki ≻ 174m 26.26 N 127.43 E
Zanri 102 28.58 N 100.50 E
Žanterek 86 47.57 N 54.21 E
Zante → Zákinthos I 38 37.52 N 20.44 E
Zanthus 162 31.02 S 123.34 E
Zantiébougou 150 11.24 N 7.15 W
Zanyang 98 34.00 N 116.13 E
Zanzibar 154 6.10 S 39.11 E
Zanzibar I 154 6.10 S 39.20 E
Zanzibar Channel ꓵ 154 6.00 S 39.00 E
Zaohe 98 34.03 N 118.07 E
Zaoheshi 100 26.53 N 114.41 E
Zaojiang 98 37.30 N 115.43 E
Zaojiaochang 107 29.58 N 106.11 E
Zaojiatuo 105 39.23 N 118.11 E
Zaokskij 82 54.44 N 37.24 E
Zaolin 100 26.24 N 114.24 E
Zaorosongou 152 5.02 N 16.13 E
Zaoshi, Zhg. 100 26.22 N 112.50 E
Zaoshi, Zhg. 100 30.51 N 113.20 E
Zaostroviči 76 52.54 N 26.47 E
Zaostrovje, Ross. 24 60.50 N 30.22 E
Zaostrovje, Ross. 76 60.38 N 33.16 E
Zaouiet Azmour 36 36.55 N 11.01 E
Zaouiet el Mgaïz 36 36.56 N 10.50 E
Zaoxi 100 30.13 N 119.30 E
Zaoyang 100 32.10 N 112.43 E
Zaō-zan ∧ 92 38.08 N 140.26 E
Zaozhuang 98 34.53 N 117.34 E
Zaoz'orje, Ross. 76 57.12 N 38.15 E
Zaoz'orje, Ross. 265b 55.34 N 38.02 E
Zaoz'ornyj 86 55.58 N 94.42 E
Zap 198 47.17 N 101.55 W
Zapadnaja Dvina 76 56.16 N 32.04 E
Zapadnaja Dvina (Daugava) ≐ 76 57.04 N 24.03 E
Zapadna Morava ≐ 38 43.42 N 21.23 E
Zapadno-Sibirskaja ravnina ≚ 72 60.00 N 75.00 E
Zapadnyj Alamedin, pik ∧ 85 42.32 N 74.34 E
Zapadnyj chrebet ⋀ 89 50.00 N 142.25 E
Zapadnyj Karakol ≐ 85 42.08 N 74.05 E
Zapadnyj Sajan ⋀ 74 53.00 N 94.00 E
Západočeský Kraj □[4] 30 49.45 N 13.00 E
Západoslovenský Kraj □[4] 30 48.20 N 18.00 E
Zapala 252 38.54 S 70.04 W
Zapaleri, Cerro ∧ 252 22.49 S 67.11 W
Zapardiel ≐ 34 41.29 N 5.02 W
Zapata 196 26.54 N 99.16 W
Zapata, Península de ≻[1] 240p 22.20 N 81.35 W
Zapatera, Isla I 236 11.45 N 85.50 W
Zapatoca 246 6.49 N 73.17 W
Zapato Chino Creek ≐ 226 36.09 N 120.11 W
Zapatosa, Ciénaga de ◎ 246 9.05 N 73.50 W
Zapfendorf 56 50.01 N 10.56 E
Zapiola 258 35.03 S 59.03 W
Zaplavnoje, Ross. 80 52.58 N 51.44 E
Zaplavnoje, Ross. 80 48.43 N 45.01 E
Zapl'usje 76 58.26 N 29.43 E
Zapokrovskij 88 50.50 N 119.05 E
Zapol'arnyj, Ross. 24 69.26 N 30.48 E
Zapol'arnyj, Ross. 24 67.30 N 63.42 E
Zapolje 76 58.23 N 29.41 E
Zapopan 234 20.43 N 103.24 W
Zaporojie → Zaporožje 78 47.50 N 35.10 E
Zaporozh'ye → Zaporožje 78 47.50 N 35.10 E
Zaporožje, Ukr. 78 47.50 N 35.10 E
Zaporožje, Ukr. 83 48.14 N 38.41 E
Zaporožskaja 78 45.23 N 36.52 E
Zapotán 234 18.41 N 103.39 W
Zapotillo 246 4.25 S 80.31 W
Zapotiltic 234 19.37 N 103.26 W
Zapotitlán 234 19.31 N 103.44 W
Zapotlán, Laguna ◎ 234 19.45 N 103.30 W
Zapotlanejo 234 20.38 N 103.04 W
Zapovednoje 76 55.04 N 21.24 E
Zapovednyj 89 42.52 N 133.45 E
Zaprudn'a 82 56.34 N 37.26 E
Zaqqūṭ 146 28.29 N 19.37 E
Zara 130 39.55 N 37.46 E
Zarāf, Baḥr az- ≐ 140 9.25 N 31.10 E
Zaragoza, Col. 246 7.30 N 74.52 W
Zaragoza, Esp. 34 41.38 N 0.53 W
Zaragoza, Méx. 232 31.39 N 106.20 W
Zaragoza, Méx. 232 28.29 N 100.55 W
Zaragoza, Méx. 234 23.58 N 99.46 W
Zaragoza, Méx. 234 19.46 N 97.33 W
Zaragoza, Méx. 234 22.02 N 100.44 W
Zaragoza □[4] 34 42.30 N 1.00 W
Zarajsk 82 54.46 N 38.53 E
Zaramag 84 42.43 N 43.57 E
Zarand 128 30.48 N 56.35 E
Zaranda Hill ∧[2] 150 10.15 N 9.35 E
Zarand-e Kohneh 128 35.17 N 50.30 E
Zarandului, Munții ⋀ 38 46.10 N 22.15 E
Zaranj 128 31.06 N 61.53 E
Zarasai 76 55.44 N 26.15 E
Zárate 258 34.06 S 59.02 W
Zarautz 34 43.17 N 2.10 W
Zaraza 246 9.21 N 65.19 W
Zara → Zadar 36 44.07 N 15.14 E
Žarbulak 86 46.05 N 82.04 E
Zarcero 236 10.11 N 84.23 W
Zardaly 85 39.38 N 70.57 E
Zard Kūh ∧ 128 32.22 N 50.04 E
Zardob 84 40.13 N 47.43 E
Zarečensk 24 66.40 N 31.23 E
Zarečje, Ross. 24 63.08 N 44.46 E
Zarečje, Ross. 76 56.52 N 33.50 E
Zarečje, Ross. 76 58.56 N 39.40 E
Zarečje, Ross. 265b 55.41 N 37.23 E
Zarečnoje 78 51.48 N 26.06 E
Zarečnyj, Ross. 76 53.45 N 39.35 E
Zarečnyj, Ross. 80 57.28 N 42.18 E
Zarečnyj, Ross. 80 53.13 N 45.13 E
Zarembo Island I 180 56.20 N 132.50 W
Zarephath 276 40.32 N 74.35 W
Zaresskoje, ozero ◎ 85 38.13 N 72.45 E
Zargān 128 29.46 N 52.43 E
Zarghūn Shahr 120 32.51 N 68.25 E
Zari 146 13.04 N 12.43 E
Zaria 150 11.07 N 7.44 E
Žarinskaja 86 53.43 N 84.58 E
Žarkamys 86 47.56 N 56.26 E
Żarki 30 50.38 N 19.22 E
Žarkova 86 58.00 N 87.17 E
Žarkovskij 76 55.52 N 32.17 E
Žarma 86 48.48 N 80.50 E
Zarnān 267d 35.41 N 51.09 E
Zărnești 38 45.34 N 25.19 E
Zarow ≐ 54 53.46 N 14.02 E
Zarqā', Nahr az- ≐ 132 32.07 N 35.33 E
Zarqā', Raqabat az- V 140 9.14 N 29.44 E
Zarqā' Mā'īn, Wādī V 132 31.37 N 35.34 E
Zarqūn 142 31.07 N 30.28 E
Zarrentin 54 53.35 N 10.55 E
Zarrīneh ≐ 128 37.05 N 45.54 E
Zarrīn Shahr 128 32.32 N 51.23 E
Žarsuat 86 46.27 N 80.48 E
Zarten 58 47.58 N 7.56 E
Zarubino, Ross. 76 58.44 N 33.28 E
Zarubino, Ross. 89 42.40 N 131.04 E
Zaruma 246 3.41 S 79.37 W
Zarumilla 246 3.30 S 80.16 W
Żary (Sorau) 30 51.38 N 15.09 E
Žaryk 86 48.52 N 72.51 E
Žaryn' 76 53.47 N 33.04 E
Zarzaïtine 148 28.18 N 9.48 E
Zarzal 246 4.24 N 76.04 W
Zarzis 148 33.30 N 11.07 E
Zarzuela, Arroyo de la ≐ 266a 40.29 N 3.45 W
Zarzuela, Hipodromo de la ♣ 266a 40.28 N 3.45 W
Zasa 76 56.17 N 25.58 E
Zaschendorf 54 53.42 N 11.37 E
Zaschwitz 54 51.10 N 13.02 E
Zašejek 24 67.25 N 32.28 E
Zasenbeck 54 52.40 N 10.51 E
Zasieki 54 51.43 N 14.43 E
Zāskār ≐ 123 34.10 N 77.20 E
Zāskār Mountains ⋀ 120 33.00 N 78.00 E
Žaškov 78 49.15 N 30.06 E
Zaslavl' 76 54.01 N 27.15 E
Zaslavl'skoje vodochranilišče ◎[1] 76 53.58 N 27.22 E
Zasosna 78 50.37 N 38.23 E
Žastalap 80 49.11 N 50.24 E
Zastava 24 59.12 N 46.46 E
Zastávka 61 49.11 N 16.23 E
Zastavna 78 48.31 N 25.50 E
Zastron 158 30.18 S 27.07 E
Zasulje, Bela. 76 53.34 N 26.50 E
Zasulje, Ross. 24 64.41 N 47.48 E
Za'tarī, Wādī az- V 132 32.09 N 36.15 E
Žatec 54 50.18 N 13.32 E
Zaterečnyj 84 44.48 N 45.11 E
Zatišje 78 47.19 N 29.51 E
Z'at'kovo 86 53.36 N 80.20 E
Zatobol'sk 86 53.12 N 63.43 E
Zaton 86 53.18 N 83.49 E
Zauche ◆[1] 54 52.15 N 12.35 E
Zauchwitz 54 52.12 N 13.02 E
Zauel 144 3.33 N 43.45 E
Zaural'skoje plato ⋀[1] 86 53.00 N 62.00 E
Zavalje 78 48.13 N 30.01 E
Zavalla 194 31.09 N 94.26 W
Zaval'noje 76 52.02 N 39.51 E
Zave 154 17.13 S 30.02 E
Zaventem 50 50.53 N 4.28 E
Zavet 38 43.46 N 26.40 E
Zavetnoje 80 47.07 N 43.52 E
Zavety Iljiča 89 49.02 N 140.17 E
Zavidoviči 38 44.27 N 18.09 E
Zavidovka 82 54.16 N 38.49 E
Zavidovo 82 56.32 N 36.32 E
Zavitinsk 89 50.07 N 129.27 E
Zavjalovo, Ross. 80 56.47 N 53.23 E
Zavjalovo, Ross. 86 54.30 N 82.27 E
Zavlekov 60 49.20 N 13.30 E
Zavod Michajlovskij 80 56.32 N 54.17 E
Zavodo-Petrovskij 86 56.50 N 66.45 E
Zavodoukovsk 86 56.33 N 66.32 E
Zavodouspenskoje 86 56.51 N 65.00 E
Zavodovski Island I 18 56.20 S 27.35 W
Zavodskoj, Ross. 78 48.24 N 40.19 E
Zavodskoj, Ross. 86 53.04 N 84.25 E
Zavolžje 80 56.37 N 43.26 E
Zavolžsk 80 57.30 N 42.10 E
Zavolžskoje 80 46.59 N 47.37 E
Zavoronežskoje 80 52.53 N 40.33 E
Zavorovo 82 55.20 N 38.13 E
Zāwa 120 28.04 N 66.23 E
Zawadzkie 30 50.37 N 18.29 E
Zawichost 30 50.49 N 21.52 E
Zawiercie 30 50.30 N 19.25 E
Zawīlah 146 26.10 N 15.07 E
Zāwiyat 'Abd al-Qādir 142 31.02 N 29.49 E
Zāwiyat Abū Musallum 273c 29.56 N 31.10 E
Zāwiyat al-Amwāt 142 28.04 N 30.50 E
Zawiyat al-Judhāmī 142 28.42 N 30.54 E
Zāwiyat al-Mukhaylā 146 32.09 N 22.17 E
Zāwiyat Masūs 146 31.33 N 21.03 E
Zāwiyat Nābit 273c 30.07 N 31.09 E
Zāwiyat Razīn 142 30.25 N 30.51 E
Zāwiyat Saqr 142 30.56 N 30.12 E
Zawiyat Shammās 140 31.31 N 26.24 E
Zāwiyat Sīdī Ghāzī 142 31.03 N 30.05 E
Zāwiyet an-Najjār 273c 30.11 N 31.17 E
Zawr, Ra's az- ≻, Ar. Su. 128 27.25 N 49.20 E
Zawr, Ra's az- ≻, Kuwayt 128 28.44 N 48.24 E
Zāyandeh ≐ 128 32.16 N 52.53 E
Zaydābād 120 34.17 N 69.07 E
Zayü 102 28.48 N 97.27 E
Zayü ≐ 102 28.28 N 97.03 E
Zaza ≐ 240p 21.37 N 79.32 W
Zaza, Presa ◎[1] 240p 21.50 N 79.23 W
Zaza del Medio 240p 22.00 N 79.23 W
Zazafotsy 157b 22.13 S 46.26 E
Zāzamt, Wādī V 146 30.58 N 14.49 E
Zazir, Oued V 148 20.25 N 5.30 E
Zban 86 48.53 N 63.58 E
Zbaraž 78 49.39 N 25.47 E
Zbąszyń 30 52.16 N 15.55 E
Zbąszynek 30 52.15 N 15.50 E
Zbečno 60 50.03 N 13.56 E
Zbiroh 60 49.52 N 13.47 E
Zborov 78 49.39 N 25.08 E
Zborovy 60 49.23 N 13.31 E
Zbraslav 30 49.59 N 14.24 E
Zbruč ≐ 78 48.32 N 26.26 E
Zbůch 60 49.41 N 13.14 E
Ždanova 86 58.37 N 88.58 E
Ždanov → Mariupol' 83 47.06 N 37.33 E
Ždanovo 78 48.14 N 34.44 E
Ždany 78 50.12 N 33.13 E
Žd'ár 60 50.03 N 13.28 E
Žd'ár nad Sazavou 30 49.34 N 15.57 E
Ždiar 30 49.17 N 20.16 E
Zdice 60 49.55 N 13.59 E
Zdikovec 60 49.05 N 13.42 E
Zdolbunov 78 50.31 N 26.15 E
Zdroje ◆[8] 54 53.20 N 14.40 E
Zduńska Wola 30 51.36 N 18.57 E
Zduny 30 51.39 N 17.24 E
Zdviž ≐ 78 51.01 N 30.02 E
Ze ≐ 105 38.50 N 115.13 E
Zealandia 184 51.37 N 107.45 W
Zearing 190 42.09 N 93.17 W
Zēbāk 120 36.32 N 71.21 E
Zeballos 182 49.59 N 126.51 W
Zeballos, Monte ∧ 254 47.01 S 71.42 W
Zebediela 156 24.19 S 29.21 E
Zebila 150 10.56 N 0.29 W
Žebl'aki 80 58.23 N 45.45 E
Žebrák 60 49.52 N 13.56 E
Zebulon, Ga., U.S. 192 33.06 N 84.20 W
Zebulon, N.C., U.S. 192 35.49 N 78.18 W
Zechlinerhütte 54 53.09 N 12.51 E
Zeda, Monte ∧ 58 46.03 N 8.32 E
Zedang 120 29.16 N 91.46 E
Zeddine, Oued ≐ 34 36.15 N 1.48 E
Zedelgem 50 51.09 N 3.08 E
Zederhaus 64 47.09 N 13.30 E
Zeebrugge 50 51.20 N 3.12 E
Zeehan 166 41.53 S 145.20 E
Zeeland, Ned. 52 51.42 N 5.40 E
Zeeland, Mi., U.S. 216 42.48 N 86.01 W
Zeeland, N.D., U.S. 198 45.58 N 99.49 W
Zeeland □[4] 52 51.27 N 3.45 E
Zeelandbrug ◆[5] 52 51.37 N 3.53 E
Zeerust 156 25.33 S 26.06 E
Zeesen 54 52.16 N 13.38 E
Zeestow 264a 52.34 N 12.58 E
Zeeuws-Vlaanderen □[9] 52 51.19 N 3.45 E
Zefat (Safad) 132 32.58 N 35.30 E
Žegalovo, Ross. 80 54.43 N 43.25 E
Žegalovo, Ross. 265b 55.54 N 37.59 E
Žegdoči 89 53.20 N 120.49 E
Zege 144 11.42 N 37.23 E
Zegher, Ḥamādat ≚ 146 27.18 N 11.30 E
Zégoua 150 10.30 N 5.40 W
Zegrir, Oued V 148 32.43 N 5.00 E
Zeguo 100 28.32 N 121.20 E
Zehdenick 54 52.59 N 13.20 E
Zehlendorf 54 52.47 N 13.23 E
Zehlendorf ◆[8] 264a 52.26 N 13.15 E
Zeigler 194 37.53 N 89.03 W
Zeil 56 50.01 N 10.35 E
Zeil, Mount ∧ 162 23.24 S 132.23 E
Zeiselmauer 264b 48.20 N 16.11 E
Zeist 52 52.05 N 5.15 E
Zeithain 54 51.19 N 13.19 E
Zeitlarn 60 49.05 N 12.06 E
Zeitz 54 51.03 N 12.08 E
Zeja 89 53.45 N 127.15 E
Zeja ≐ 89 50.13 N 127.35 E
Zejskoje vodochranilišče ◎[1] 89 54.28 N 127.45 E
Zekeriyaköy ◆[8] 267b 41.11 N 29.01 E
Zekiah Swamp Run ≐ 208 38.25 N 76.57 W
Žel'abino 265b 55.52 N 37.11 E
Žel'abužskaja 82 54.36 N 36.32 E
Želannoje 83 48.13 N 37.25 E
Zelaya 258 34.21 S 58.52 W
Zelaya □[5] 236 13.00 N 84.00 W
Želča ≐ 76 58.19 N 27.40 E
Žel'dyadyr ◆[1] 86 49.30 N 68.30 E
Želdybino 82 56.14 N 39.02 E
Zele 50 51.04 N 4.02 E
Żelechów 30 51.49 N 21.54 E
Zelee, Cape ≻ 175e 9.45 S 161.34 E
Zelená Lhota 60 49.14 N 13.10 E
Zelencovo 76 59.52 N 44.59 E
Zelenčukskaja 84 43.52 N 41.36 E
Zelenec 24 62.29 N 55.16 E
Zelenga 80 46.11 N 48.37 E
Zelengora ⋀ 38 43.15 N 18.45 E
Zelenoborskij 24 66.49 N 32.18 E
Zelenogorsk 76 60.12 N 29.42 E
Zelenograd 82 56.01 N 37.11 E
Zelenogradsk 76 54.58 N 20.29 E
Zelenokumsk 84 44.24 N 43.53 E
Zelenovka 78 46.59 N 36.14 E
Želetava 61 49.09 N 15.38 E
Zeletin ≐ 38 46.03 N 27.23 E
Železinka 86 53.32 N 75.18 E
Železn'a 82 54.31 N 37.28 E
Železná Ruda 60 49.09 N 13.14 E
Železnik 38 44.43 N 20.23 E
Železnodorožnyj, Ross. 24 62.35 N 50.55 E
Železnodorožnyj, Ross. 76 54.22 N 21.19 E
Železnodorožnyj, Ross. 82 55.45 N 38.01 E
Železnodorožnyj, Uzb. 86 43.04 N 58.50 E
Železnogorsk 76 52.22 N 35.23 E
Železnogorsk-Ilimskij 88 56.37 N 104.08 E
Železnoje 83 48.19 N 37.51 E
Železnovodsk 84 44.08 N 43.02 E
Zelienople 214 40.47 N 80.08 W
Zelina 36 45.58 N 16.15 E
Zell, Dtsch. 56 50.01 N 7.10 E
Zell, Dtsch. 58 47.42 N 7.51 E
Zell, Schw. 58 47.09 N 7.55 E
Zella-Mehlis 54 50.39 N 10.39 E
Zell am Harmersbach 58 48.21 N 8.04 E
Zell am Moos 64 47.54 N 13.19 E
Zell am See 64 47.19 N 12.47 E
Zell am Ziller 64 47.14 N 11.53 E
Zellersee c 58 47.42 N 9.03 E
Zeller See ◎ 64 47.19 N 12.48 E
Zellingen 56 49.53 N 9.43 E
Zellwood 220 28.44 N 81.36 W
Želnava 61 48.50 N 13.57 E
Želon' ≐ 78 51.33 N 29.51 E
Zel'onaja Rošča, Ross. 76 60.10 N 29.08 E
Zel'onaja Rošča, Ross. 80 54.29 N 52.02 E
Zel'onaja Rošča, Ross. 83 47.07 N 40.13 E
Zel'onodol'sk 80 55.51 N 48.33 E
Zel'onoje 78 47.43 N 33.12 E
Zel'onoje Ozero 88 53.40 N 116.36 E
Zel'onyj, Kaz. 80 48.07 N 51.31 E
Zel'onyj, Kaz. 80 51.10 N 50.41
Zel'onyj, ostrov (Shibotsu-Tō) I 92a 43.30 N
Zel'onyj Bor 76 54.0
Zelo Surrigone 266b
Zelów 3
Žel'tau Ajtau ⋀
Zeltweg
Želudok
Zel'va, Bela.

≐ River	Fluß	Río	Rivière	Rio
≍ Canal	Kanal	Canal	Canal	Canal
⟓ Waterfall, Rapids	Wasserfall, Stromschnellen	Cascada, Rápidos	Chute d'eau, Rapides	Cascata, Rápidos
ꓵ Strait	Meeresstraße	Estrecho	Détroit	Estreito
c Bay, Gulf	Bucht, Golf	Bahía, Golfo	Baie, Golfe	Baía, Golfo
◎ Lake, Lakes	See, Seen	Lago, Lagos	Lac, Lacs	Lago, Lagos
≡ Swamp	Sumpf	Pantano	Marais	Pântano
ℵ Ice Features, Glacier	Eis- und Gletscherformen	Accidentes Glaciales	Formes glaciaires	Acidentes glaciares
⊤ Other Hydrographic Features	Andere Hydrographische Objekte	Otros Elementos Hidrográficos	Autres données hydrographiques	Outros acidentes hidrográficos

◆ Submarine Features	Untermeerische Objekte	Accidentes Submarinos	Formes de relief sous-marin	Aci
□ Political Unit	Politische Einheit	Unidad Politica	Entité politique	Un
ʊ Cultural Institution	Kulturelle Institution	Institución Cultural	Institution culturelle	In
⊥ Historical Site	Historische Stätte	Sitio Histórico	Site historique	S
♣ Recreational Site	Erholungs- und Ferienort	Sitio de Recreo	Centre de loisirs	
⊠ Airport	Flughafen	Aeropuerto	Aéroport	
■ Military Installation	Militäranlage	Instalación Militar	Installation militaire	D.
✦ Miscellaneous	Verschiedenes	Misceláneo	Divers	

ENGLISH

Name	Page	Lat.°′	Long.°′
Želva, Liet.	76	55.13 N	25.06 E
Zel'v'anka ≃	76	53.24 N	24.32 E
Zelzate	50	51.12 N	3.49 E
Žemaičių Naumiestis	76	55.22 N	21.42 E
Žemaitija □[9]	76	55.45 N	23.00 E
Žembejtinskij	80	50.30 N	52.39 E
Zembin	76	54.22 N	28.13 E
Zembla Septentrional → Severnaja Zeml'a II	74	79.30 N	98.00 E
Zembra, Île I	36	37.08 N	10.48 E
Žemčug	88	51.41 N	102.24 E
Zemcy	76	56.15 N	32.23 E
Zemetčino	80	53.30 N	42.38 E
Zemgale □[9]	76	56.30 N	25.00 E
Zémio	154	5.02 N	25.08 E
Zeml'ansk	78	51.54 N	38.44 E
Zemmer	56	49.53 N	6.41 E
Zemmora	34	35.44 N	0.45 E
Zemmour ◆[1]	148	24.50 N	12.15 W
Zemo-Kedi	84	41.26 N	46.24 E
Zémongo, Réserve de Faune de ◆[4]	140	6.45 N	25.15 E
Zemoul, Oued V	148	29.12 N	7.52 W
Žemovo	82	54.45 N	38.49 E
Zempin	54	54.04 N	13.57 E
Zempoala	234	19.24 N	96.24 W
Zempoala ≃	234	20.16 N	97.27 W
Zempoala ⊥	234	19.27 N	96.23 W
Zempoala, Punta ›	234	19.28 N	96.19 W
Zemst	50	50.59 N	4.28 E
Zemun	38	44.50 N	20.24 E
Zenas	218	39.07 N	85.29 W
Zendeh Jān	128	34.21 N	61.45 E
Zeneta	184	50.44 N	102.02 W
Zeng ≃	100	23.09 N	113.46 E
Zengcheng	100	23.19 N	113.49 E
Zengjiawan	105	39.22 N	118.24 E
Zengkou ≃	105	39.19 N	117.37 E
Zenica	38	44.12 N	17.55 E
Zenifim, Har ∧[2]	132	30.06 N	34.51 E
Zenith	224	47.23 N	122.19 W
Zen'kov	78	50.13 N	34.22 E
Zenn ≃	56	49.31 N	10.58 E
Zenna	58	46.06 N	8.45 E
Zenne (Senne) ≃	50	51.04 N	4.26 E
Zenon Park	184	53.04 N	103.45 W
Zenon Videla Dorna	258	35.33 S	58.53 W
Zenson di Piave	64	45.41 N	12.29 E
Zentralafrikanische Republik → Central African Republic □[1]	136	7.00 N	21.00 E
Zentral-Friedhof ◆	264b	48.09 N	16.27 E
Zentral-Massiv → Central, Massif ⋏	32	45.00 N	3.10 E
Zentsūji	96	34.14 N	133.47 E
Zenza do Itombe	152	9.16 S	14.13 E
Zenzeli	80	45.56 N	47.03 E
Zepernick	54	52.39 N	13.32 E
Zephyr	196	31.41 N	98.48 W
Zephyr Cove	226	39.00 N	119.57 W
Zephyrhills	220	28.14 N	82.10 W
Zepu	120	38.13 N	77.16 E
Zérab, Ouadi V	146	11.03 N	19.47 E
Zeralda	34	36.41 N	2.53 E
Zeravšan	85	39.11 N	68.40 E
Zeravšan ≃	72	39.22 N	63.45 E
Zeravšanskij chrebet ⋏	85	39.15 N	68.30 E
Zerbst	54	51.58 N	12.04 E
Žerdevka	80	51.51 N	41.28 E
Žerebec ≃	83	48.57 N	38.03 E
Zereh, Gowd-e ⊥[7]	128	29.45 N	61.50 E
Zerenda	86	52.55 N	69.10 E
Žerev ≃	78	51.12 N	29.04 E
Zerf	56	49.36 N	6.41 E
Zerga, Merja ⊂	34	34.51 N	6.17 W
Zergenta	80	47.42 N	45.12 E
Zeri	62	44.21 N	9.46 E
Zerind	38	46.37 N	21.31 E
Żerków	30	52.05 N	17.34 E
Zermatt	58	46.02 N	7.45 E
Zernez	58	46.43 N	10.05 E
Zernograd	78	46.50 N	40.19 E
Žernovka	82	54.49 N	37.46 E
Zernsdorf	54	52.18 N	13.41 E
Zero ≃	64	45.32 N	12.22 E
Zeroud, Oued V	36	35.50 N	10.13 E
Zerqan	38	41.30 N	20.21 E
Žešart	24	62.05 N	49.34 E
Zestafoni	84	42.07 N	43.02 E
Žest'anka	80	51.36 N	49.24 E
Žestoki	82	56.19 N	36.22 E
Žestylevo	82	56.24 N	37.39 E
Zetel	52	53.25 N	7.58 E
Žetybaj	80	48.51 N	48.04 E
Žetykol', ozero ⊜	86	51.02 N	60.54 E
Zeulenroda	54	50.39 N	11.58 E
Zeuthen	54	52.20 N	13.37 E
Zeuthener See ⊜	264a	52.21 N	13.39 E
Zeven	52	53.18 N	9.16 E
Zevenaar	52	51.56 N	6.05 E
Zevenbergen	52	51.38 N	4.36 E
Zevenbergschen Hoek	52	51.41 N	4.40 E
Zevenwouden ◆[1]	52	52.57 N	6.00 E
Zevio	64	45.22 N	11.08 E
Zeyādah Kot	272b	22.27 N	88.20 E
Zeyawadi	110	18.33 N	96.26 E
Zeytinbağı	130	40.23 N	28.47 E
Zeytinburnu ◆[8]	267b	40.59 N	28.54 E
Zeytindağ	130	38.58 N	27.04 E
Zeyveh	84	39.07 N	47.42 E
Zeze	270	35.00 N	135.54 E
Zêzere ≃	34	39.28 N	8.20 W
Zghartā	130	34.24 N	35.54 E
Zgierz	30	51.52 N	19.25 E
Zgornje Hoče	61	46.29 N	15.38 E
Zgorzelec	30	51.12 N	15.01 E
Zgurovka	78	50.31 N	31.46 E
Zhabuchaka Hu ⊜	120	31.30 N	84.00 E
Zhage	102	26.20 N	103.51 E
Zhagenasongduo	102	33.12 N	94.33 E
Zhag'yab	102	30.32 N	98.00 E
Zhahasutai	86	42.58 N	85.20 E
Zhai ≃	100	32.19 N	115.02 E
Zhaihe	100	32.08 N	114.54 E
Zhaili	100	27.42 N	117.22 E
Zhailing	98	41.00 N	116.53 E
Zhaiqiao	106	31.35 N	119.55 E
Zhaitang	105	39.57 N	115.42 E
Zhaitun	104	41.46 N	122.06 E
Zhakou, Zhg.	102	29.59 N	112.10 E
Zhakou, Zhg.	106	30.23 N	120.47 E
Zhakou, Zhg.	106	30.13 N	120.08 E
Zhalantun → Butha Qi	89	48.02 N	122.43 E
Zhalanyingzi	104	41.29 N	120.37 E
Zhalun	120	32.25 N	81.35 E
Zhaluomude	89	49.13 N	120.22 E
Zhancheng	98	37.41 N	117.46 E
Zhang ≃, Zhg.	100	31.05 N	113.11 E
Zhang ≃, Zhg.	100	25.51 N	114.46 E
Zhang ≃, Zhg.	102	36.10 N	115.05 E
Zhangbei	98	41.04 N	114.48 E
Zhangcang	98	35.54 N	119.57 E
Zhangcun, Zhg.	100	33.20 N	115.59 E
Zhangcun, Zhg.	100	28.50 N	117.57 E
Zhangcun, Zhg.	106	30.28 N	119.22 E
Zhangcun, Zhg.	106	30.40 N	119.57 E
Zhangdang	104	41.54 N	124.05 E
Zhangde	100	34.07 N	113.27 E
Zhangdiyingzi	89	50.30 N	127.16 E
Zhangdu	100	30.38 N	118.13 E
Zhangdu Hu ⊜	100	30.40 N	114.42 E
…hangfang	105	39.35 N	115.41 E
…angfengji	98	35.14 N	116.01 E
…nggang	100	30.34 N	112.51 E
Zhanggezhuang, Zhg.	98	36.47 N	119.47 E
Zhanggezhuang, Zhg.	105	40.08 N	116.56 E
Zhanggou	104	42.07 N	124.06 E
Zhangguangcai Ling ⋏	89	45.25 N	129.20 E
Zhangguizhuang	105	39.07 N	117.18 E
Zhanggutai	98	42.40 N	122.28 E
Zhanghezhuang	105	38.56 N	114.56 E
Zhanghuang	102	22.01 N	109.27 E
Zhanghuanggang	106	32.07 N	120.30 E
Zhanghuban	100	26.23 N	118.29 E
Zhangji	98	34.08 N	117.24 E
Zhangjiachang, Zhg.	107	29.26 N	104.34 E
Zhangjiachang, Zhg.	107	29.33 N	104.54 E
Zhangjiachang, Zhg.	107	29.57 N	103.48 E
Zhangjiadian	105	39.44 N	114.54 E
Zhangjiagou	100	30.18 N	113.22 E
Zhangjiaji	100	32.09 N	112.23 E
Zhangjiajie	104	41.28 N	124.08 E
Zhangjiakou (Kalgan)	105	40.50 N	114.53 E
Zhangjiapang	100	30.25 N	115.47 E
Zhangjiapu	104	41.18 N	122.02 E
Zhangjiaqiao, Zhg.	106	31.36 N	120.36 E
Zhangjiaqiao, Zhg.	107	30.02 N	104.15 E
Zhangjiatou	106	31.38 N	119.05 E
Zhangjiatun, Zhg.	104	41.05 N	121.44 E
Zhangjiatun, Zhg.	105	40.37 N	114.57 E
Zhangjiawa	105	40.10 N	117.52 E
Zhangjiawan	105	39.51 N	116.41 E
Zhangjiawopu	104	41.10 N	122.17 E
Zhangjiayingzi	104	42.04 N	120.57 E
Zhangjingqiao	106	31.39 N	120.27 E
Zhangjinhe	100	30.14 N	112.35 E
Zhangliangdian	100	33.42 N	113.02 E
Zhangliantang	106	31.01 N	121.02 E
Zhangling	98	36.32 N	119.29 E
Zhanglu	98	36.16 N	115.33 E
Zhangmang	100	32.03 N	114.32 E
Zhangming	102	31.49 N	104.51 E
Zhangmuqiao	100	31.26 N	116.44 E
Zhangmushi	100	27.01 N	112.38 E
Zhangmutou	100	22.55 N	114.05 E
Zhangping	100	25.19 N	117.25 E
Zhangpu, Zhg.	100	24.09 N	117.36 E
Zhangpu, Zhg.	106	31.17 N	120.57 E
Zhangqiangzhen	98	42.39 N	122.59 E
Zhangqiao	100	32.21 N	117.38 E
Zhangqiu (Mingshui)	98	36.43 N	117.30 E
Zhangsanta	102	39.37 N	110.14 E
Zhangsanying	98	41.34 N	117.39 E
Zhangshitai	104	41.50 N	122.51 E
Zhangshuping	102	31.20 N	111.02 E
Zhangshuxia	100	25.54 N	112.45 E
Zhangtaitai	104	40.59 N	121.05 E
Zhangtaizi	104	41.22 N	123.16 E
Zhangting	100	30.02 N	121.19 E
Zhangwan	100	26.43 N	119.36 E
Zhangwenpu	105	40.26 N	116.04 E
Zhangwu, Zhg.	104	42.22 N	122.31 E
Zhangwu, Zhg.	106	30.47 N	119.33 E
Zhangwutaimen	104	42.16 N	122.42 E
Zhangxinliuji	100	33.43 N	115.48 E
Zhangyan, Zhg.	106	31.48 N	119.44 E
Zhangyan, Zhg.	106	30.48 N	121.16 E
Zhangyangongtun	104	40.58 N	120.46 E
Zhangye	102	38.56 N	100.27 E
Zhangze	106	30.55 N	121.15 E
Zhangzhishan	106	31.56 N	121.01 E
Zhangzhou (Longxi)	100	24.33 N	117.39 E
Zhangzhu	106	31.16 N	119.37 E
Zhangzhuang, Zhg.	98	37.03 N	116.32 E
Zhangzhuang, Zhg.	98	36.02 N	118.01 E
Zhangzhuang, Zhg.	106	31.57 N	119.52 E
Zhangzi Dao I	98	39.00 N	122.44 E
Zhanhua (Fuguo)	98	37.42 N	118.08 E
Zhanji	98	34.14 N	115.52 E
Zhanjiajing	107	29.15 N	104.55 E
Zhanjiang	102	21.16 N	110.28 E
Zhanjiaqiao, Zhg.	100	29.19 N	113.34 E
Zhanjiaqiao, Zhg.	106	30.25 N	120.08 E
Zhanyang	100	25.30 N	119.28 E
Zhanyi	102	25.38 N	103.43 E
Zhanyu	89	44.31 N	122.37 E
Zhao'an	100	23.47 N	117.12 E
Zhao'an Wan ⊂	100	23.38 N	117.19 E
Zhaobeikou	105	38.55 N	116.06 E
Zhaochuan	105	40.41 N	115.18 E
Zhaocun	105	39.35 N	116.14 E
Zhaodong	89	46.05 N	125.59 E
Zhaogezhuang, Zhg.	98	37.27 N	120.37 E
Zhaogezhuang, Zhg.	105	39.45 N	118.24 E
Zhaoguang	89	48.07 N	126.43 E
Zhaohe	100	33.12 N	112.49 E
Zhaohuazhen	107	29.02 N	105.08 E
Zhaojiagou	104	40.47 N	123.27 E
Zhaojiapuzi	104	40.51 N	123.49 E
Zhaojiaqiao	106	30.44 N	121.12 E
Zhaojiatangfang	104	42.07 N	122.57 E
Zhaojiatun	104	41.24 N	121.53 E
Zhaojiawopeng	104	42.30 N	123.06 E
Zhaojiaying	105	38.58 N	116.42 E
Zhaojue	102	28.15 N	102.50 E
Zhaomaozhuang	105	39.28 N	117.59 E
Zhaomutun	104	41.10 N	121.38 E
Zhaoping	102	24.03 N	110.52 E
Zhaoqiao	100	28.42 N	114.45 E
Zhaoqing (Gaoyao)	102	23.03 N	112.27 E
Zhaosu	86	43.06 N	81.08 E
Zhaotan	100	29.42 N	116.48 E
Zhaotong	102	27.19 N	103.48 E
Zhaotun	104	41.54 N	121.59 E
Zhaoxian, Zhg.	98	37.45 N	114.46 E
Zhaoxian, Zhg.	98	35.44 N	118.55 E
Zhaoxing	89	47.43 N	131.19 E
Zhaoya	107	29.00 N	105.35 E
Zhaoyi	105	39.55 N	116.43 E
Zhaoyuan, Zhg.	89	45.31 N	125.09 E
Zhaoyuan, Zhg.	98	37.22 N	120.24 E
Zhaozhou	89	45.41 N	125.21 E
Zhaozhuang, Zhg.	98	34.45 N	116.27 E
Zhaozhuang, Zhg.	98	34.14 N	116.38 E
Zhaozhuangzi	105	39.10 N	117.20 E
Zhapu	106	30.36 N	121.05 E
Zhari Namco ⊜	120	31.05 N	85.35 E
Zhashui	102	33.40 N	109.01 E
Zhaxi Co ⊜	120	32.10 N	85.05 E
Zhaxigang	120	32.32 N	79.41 E
Zhayi	102	28.34 N	99.09 E
Zhaze	106	32.09 N	119.29 E
Zhdanov → Mariupol'	83	47.06 N	37.33 E
Zhecheng	98	34.06 N	115.19 E
Zhegao	100	31.46 N	117.45 E
Zhegu	120	28.43 N	91.43 E
Zhêhor	102	31.41 N	100.24 E
Zhejiang (Chekiang) □[4]	100	29.00 N	120.00 E
Zhelang	100	22.43 N	115.32 E
Zhelin, Zhg.	100	29.14 N	115.30 E
Zhelin, Zhg.	100	23.36 N	117.06 E
Zhelin, Zhg.	106	30.50 N	121.29 E
Zhen ≃	100	24.55 N	113.44 E
Zhen'an	102	33.27 N	109.01 E
Zhenbeikou	102	39.15 N	106.17 E
Zhenbiancheng	105	40.10 N	115.49 E
Zhenchang, Zhg.	105	39.47 N	115.24 E
Zhenchang, Zhg.	106	32.04 N	121.02 E
Zhenfeng	102	25.23 N	105.41 E
Zheng'an	102	28.31 N	107.29 E
Zheng'anpu	104	41.43 N	121.56 E
Zhengcun	105	39.13 N	115.40 E
Zhengding	98	38.10 N	114.34 E
Zhengdongyu	106	31.59 N	120.10 E
Zhengfang	100	28.42 N	117.53 E
Zhengguanchang	107	29.54 N	106.35 E
Zhengguo	100	23.25 N	113.53 E
Zhenghe	100	27.22 N	118.50 E
Zhengji	98	34.26 N	117.01 E
Zhengjiadiancun	104	41.05 N	122.20 E
Zhengjiawu	100	29.29 N	120.05 E
Zhenglan Qi (Dund Hot)	98	42.16 N	115.49 E
Zhengning	102	35.22 N	108.24 E
Zhengping	100	25.22 N	114.46 E
Zhen'guosi	271a	39.51 N	116.21 E
Zhengxiangbai Qi (Qagan Nur)	98	42.16 N	114.52 E
Zhengyang	100	32.37 N	114.23 E
Zhengyangguan	100	32.28 N	116.32 E
Zhengyi	106	31.23 N	120.52 E
Zhengzhou (Chengchow)	102	34.48 N	113.39 E
Zhengzhuang	100	28.11 N	119.01 E
Zhengzi	107	29.22 N	104.16 E
Zhengzichang	107	29.08 N	106.38 E
Zhenhai, Zhg.	100	29.57 N	121.42 E
Zhenhai, Zhg.	100	24.16 N	118.06 E
Zhenhai, Zhg.	102	21.53 N	112.25 E
Zhenjiang, Zhg.	98	40.44 N	125.28 E
Zhenjiang, Zhg.	106	32.13 N	119.26 E
Zhenjiangguan	102	32.25 N	103.35 E
Zhenjiaqiao	106	32.08 N	120.49 E
Zhenjinqiao	107	30.12 N	104.22 E
Zhenkang	102	24.06 N	99.16 E
Zhenlai	89	45.52 N	123.14 E
Zhenning	102	26.05 N	105.46 E
Zhenping	102	33.08 N	112.19 E
Zhenru	106	31.15 N	121.24 E
Zhentou	100	27.04 N	114.56 E
Zhentou ≃	100	32.58 N	114.24 E
Zhentoudian	100	29.10 N	117.29 E
Zhentoushi	100	28.01 N	113.20 E
Zhenxi	107	29.29 N	104.33 E
Zhenxiaguan	100	27.12 N	120.28 E
Zhenxing	98	42.38 N	124.53 E
Zhenxiong	102	27.27 N	104.50 E
Zhenyu	100	27.08 N	120.18 E
Zhenyuan, Zhg.	102	35.46 N	107.18 E
Zhenyuan, Zhg.	102	26.53 N	108.19 E
Zhenze	106	30.55 N	120.30 E
Zhenzhumen	98	41.53 N	126.45 E
Zhenzichang, Zhg.	107	29.59 N	105.11 E
Zhenzichang, Zhg.	107	29.52 N	104.12 E
Zhenzichang, Zhg.	107	30.38 N	104.20 E
Zhenzijie	107	28.48 N	106.40 E
Zhenziling	104	42.10 N	124.12 E
Zhenzizhen	105	39.50 N	118.20 E
Zheqiao	100	26.27 N	112.48 E
Zherong	100	27.16 N	119.54 E
Zheshan	106	30.15 N	120.24 E
Zhetang	106	31.45 N	118.55 E
Zhidan	102	37.00 N	108.40 E
Zhidoi	102	33.08 N	94.50 E
Zhierling	98	40.26 N	114.16 E
Zhigou	98	35.55 N	119.13 E
Zhijiang	102	27.27 N	109.41 E
Zhijin	102	26.41 N	105.37 E
Zhili	106	30.52 N	120.16 E
Zhitan	100	29.35 N	117.16 E
Zhitang, Zhg.	106	31.33 N	121.01 E
Zhitang, Zhg.	106	31.36 N	120.58 E
Zhitomir → Žitomir	78	50.16 N	28.40 E
Zhitouji	100	33.28 N	118.18 E
Zhiwucun	106	30.38 N	119.47 E
Zhixi	100	23.57 N	114.33 E
Zhixia	100	29.42 N	119.36 E
Zhixiqiao	106	31.49 N	119.29 E
Zhiyang	100	33.47 N	113.07 E
Zhizushan	104	41.50 N	121.24 E
Zhob	120	31.20 N	69.27 E
Zhob ≃	120	32.04 N	69.50 E
Zhonganpu	104	41.37 N	121.58 E
Zhong'aozhen	107	29.46 N	105.41 E
Zhongba, Zhg.	100	23.43 N	115.22 E
Zhongba, Zhg.	120	29.38 N	84.13 E
Zhongbu, Zhg.	100	31.25 N	117.45 E
Zhongbu, Zhg.	100	31.40 N	117.45 E
Zhongbu, Zhg.	100	28.50 N	117.16 E
Zhongchuan	100	26.58 N	119.27 E
Zhongcun	102	33.27 N	110.05 E
Zhongdai	106	30.46 N	120.59 E
Zhongdian	102	27.50 N	99.40 E
Zhongdu, Zhg.	100	24.56 N	116.26 E
Zhongdu, Zhg.	100	33.04 N	118.46 E
Zhongdu, Zhg.	107	28.46 N	103.58 E
Zhongduan	100	25.17 N	116.41 E
Zhongerchong	104	41.58 N	123.58 E
Zhonggang	100	32.38 N	115.45 E
Zhonggong	98	36.30 N	117.01 E
Zhonggoumen	98	41.00 N	116.26 E
Zhonggu	104	42.27 N	124.00 E
Zhongguan	106	30.39 N	120.11 E
Zhongguo → China □[1]	90	35.00 N	105.00 E
Zhonghe	102	27.11 N	103.52 E
Zhonghechang	107	30.12 N	104.49 E
Zhongheying	102	23.48 N	103.36 E
Zhonghezhen	107	30.34 N	104.06 E
Zhonghuamen	106	32.01 N	118.46 E
Zhonghuopu	100	29.44 N	113.59 E
Zhongjianchang	107	28.46 N	106.13 E
Zhongjiang	102	31.00 N	104.18 E
Zhongjiatai	104	40.48 N	122.46 E
Zhonglou	98	35.24 N	119.02 E
Zhongluotan	100	23.23 N	113.23 E
Zhongluyantai	104	41.32 N	123.17 E
Zhongmeihe	100	31.19 N	116.45 E
Zhongmou	98	34.46 N	114.01 E
Zhongning	102	37.27 N	105.38 E
Zhongpingchang	102	31.15 N	110.10 E
Zhongqiao	106	31.11 N	119.11 E
Zhongsha	100	26.24 N	116.36 E
Zhongshan, Zhg.	100	26.12 N	117.26 E
Zhongshan (Shiqizhen), Zhg.	100	22.31 N	113.22 E
Zhongshan ʊ[3]	9	69.22 S	76.23 E
Zhongshan Park ♠	269b	31.13 N	121.25 E
Zhongtiao Shan ⋏	102	35.12 N	111.35 E
Zhongting ≃	105	39.03 N	116.46 E
Zhongtou	100	34.00 N	113.21 E
Zhongwei	102	37.33 N	105.10 E
Zhongwopu	102	38.30 N	102.59 E
Zhongxian, Zhg.	100	27.17 N	116.47 E
Zhongxian, Zhg.	102	30.29 N	108.05 E
Zhongxiang	100	31.11 N	112.33 E
Zhongxiangzhen	107	29.50 N	104.08 E
Zhongxin, Zhg.	100	23.16 N	113.38 E
Zhongxin, Zhg.	100	24.14 N	114.44 E
Zhongxin, Zhg.	104	40.47 N	124.08 E
Zhongxing, Zhg.	106	32.17 N	119.34 E
Zhongxing, Zhg.	107	30.12 N	103.32 E
Zhongxingchang	107	29.07 N	105.18 E
Zhongxinzhen, Zhg.	107	30.16 N	106.15 E
Zhongxinzhen, Zhg.	107	30.30 N	104.03 E
Zhongyangqu	104	40.47 N	122.05 E
Zhongyaozhan	89	50.46 N	125.54 E
Zhongyi	100	31.08 N	114.52 E
Zhongying	105	39.38 N	117.06 E
Zhongzangcun	105	38.52 N	115.38 E
Zhongzhan	100	25.16 N	114.24 E
Zhongzhuang	105	39.25 N	114.47 E
Zhou ≃	105	39.47 N	117.23 E
Zhouba	107	29.06 N	103.43 E
Zhoubachang	107	28.59 N	103.52 E
Zhoucun	98	36.47 N	117.48 E
Zhoudangfan	100	31.54 N	114.31 E
Zhoujiachang	107	30.33 N	104.25 E
Zhoujiadai	106	32.12 N	120.26 E
Zhoujiadu	106	31.11 N	121.29 E
Zhoujiagou	107	30.08 N	104.30 E
Zhoujiatun, Zhg.	104	41.34 N	121.05 E
Zhoujiatun, Zhg.	104	41.29 N	121.50 E
Zhoujiatun, Zhg.	104	41.04 N	120.47 E
Zhoujiatun, Zhg.	104	41.16 N	120.58 E
Zhoujiawopu	104	42.31 N	122.45 E
Zhoujiayao	104	41.19 N	122.48 E
Zhoujingxiang	106	31.32 N	120.23 E
Zhoukoudianzhen	105	39.41 N	115.56 E
Zhoulichang	107	29.55 N	105.09 E
Zhouning	100	27.16 N	119.12 E
Zhoupo	107	29.48 N	104.01 E
Zhoupu	106	31.07 N	121.34 E
Zhouqu	102	33.43 N	104.10 E
Zhouquan	106	30.35 N	120.21 E
Zhoushan Dao I	100	30.05 N	122.10 E
Zhoushan Qundao II	100	30.00 N	122.00 E
Zhoushu	106	31.28 N	120.59 E
Zhoushuizi	98	38.57 N	121.34 E
Zhoutieqiao	106	31.26 N	120.00 E
Zhouwangmiao	106	30.28 N	120.29 E
Zhouxi	100	29.13 N	116.20 E
Zhouxiang	100	30.10 N	121.08 E
Zhouxinzhen	106	31.30 N	120.18 E
Zhouzhai	106	32.02 N	121.31 E
Zhouzhi	102	34.12 N	108.10 E
Zhouzhuang, Zhg.	105	39.09 N	115.18 E
Zhouzhuang, Zhg.	106	31.06 N	120.51 E
Zhouzhuang, Zhg.	106	32.15 N	120.08 E
Zhuanghang	106	30.54 N	121.23 E
Zhuanghe	98	39.43 N	123.01 E
Zhuangji	98	34.20 N	115.15 E
Zhuanglang	102	34.58 N	106.07 E
Zhuangtou	105	40.55 N	117.57 E
Zhuangtouyingzi, Zhg.	104	41.43 N	120.32 E
Zhuangtouyingzi, Zhg.	104	41.50 N	120.43 E
Zhuangxi	107	30.33 N	104.31 E
Zhuangyuanqiao	100	27.54 N	120.48 E
Zhuanping Shan ∧	107	29.07 N	103.37 E
Zhuanqiao	106	31.04 N	121.23 E
Zhuantouwan	100	31.29 N	112.24 E
Zhuanwantai	104	41.20 N	122.22 E
Zhuao	100	29.05 N	121.16 E
Zhucang	102	27.18 N	107.26 E
Zhucheng	98	36.00 N	119.24 E
Zhudi	269b	31.12 N	121.18 E
Zhudian	100	30.33 N	115.12 E
Zhuergan	89	52.04 N	120.48 E
Zhufengzhen	106	30.35 N	118.56 E
Zhufuo	107	29.02 N	105.51 E
Zhugan ≃	100	32.18 N	114.42 E
Zhuganpu	100	32.13 N	114.39 E
Zhugao	107	30.37 N	104.40 E
Zhuge, Zhg.	98	36.00 N	118.32 E
Zhuge, Zhg.	100	29.15 N	119.18 E
Zhugentan	107	29.25 N	103.50 E
Zhugou	98	36.52 N	120.15 E
Zhugouzhen	100	32.47 N	113.42 E
Zhugusi	102	37.01 N	102.27 E
Zhuhe	100	29.44 N	113.06 E
Zhuhongyu	104	40.48 N	123.00 E
Zhuji	100	29.43 N	120.14 E
Zhujiabeng	106	31.21 N	120.41 E
Zhujiabian	106	31.38 N	119.11 E
Zhujiachang, Zhg.	107	29.48 N	104.20 E
Zhujiachang, Zhg.	107	30.03 N	104.13 E
Zhujiafang	104	41.20 N	122.40 E
Zhujiahang	106	30.51 N	121.19 E
Zhujiahe	106	31.08 N	120.53 E
Zhujia Jian I	100	29.54 N	122.24 E
Zhujiajiao	106	31.06 N	121.02 E
Zhujiajiaotou	106	31.24 N	121.11 E
Zhujiang Kou ⊂[1]	100	22.36 N	113.44 E
Zhujiangqing	100	27.18 N	114.44 E
Zhujiaqiao	106	30.26 N	119.03 E
Zhujiawan, Zhg.	100	32.28 N	117.29 E
Zhujiawan, Zhg.	100	30.56 N	114.10 E
Zhujiawan, Zhg.	105	40.08 N	114.56 E
Zhujiawopeng	104	42.27 N	122.13 E
Zhujiesi	102	33.34 N	97.21 E
Zhukeng	100	23.49 N	112.55 E
Zhukou, Zhg.	98	34.07 N	115.04 E
Zhukou, Zhg.	100	27.41 N	118.53 E
Zhukou, Zhg.	100	26.58 N	117.16 E
Zhukovskiy → Žukovskij	82	55.35 N	38.08 E
Zhulanbu	100	25.36 N	115.46 E
Zhulin, Zhg.	100	32.20 N	113.38 E
Zhulin, Zhg.	106	31.45 N	119.27 E
Zhulong ≃	98	38.47 N	115.59 E
Zhulongqiao	100	32.21 N	118.09 E
Zhuluke	98	41.36 N	119.54 E
Zhumadian	100	32.58 N	114.03 E
Zhuolu	105	40.22 N	115.12 E
Zhuoni	102	34.32 N	103.24 E
Zhuotian	100	25.38 N	116.13 E
Zhuoxian	105	39.30 N	115.58 E
Zhuozi	102	40.52 N	112.33 E
Zhuqianzongpuzi	104	42.17 N	123.18 E
Zhuqiao, Zhg.	98	37.22 N	120.05 E
Zhuqiao, Zhg.	106	31.07 N	121.44 E
Zhuqiao, Zhg.	106	30.26 N	120.36 E
Zhurushan	100	30.26 N	113.48 E
Zhushan	102	32.10 N	110.19 E
Zhusigang	100	31.14 N	118.23 E
Zhutan	100	28.04 N	114.10 E
Zhutang, Zhg.	106	31.06 N	118.39 E
Zhutang, Zhg.	106	31.47 N	120.24 E
Zhutian	100	28.43 N	117.01 E
Zhuting, Zhg.	100	27.24 N	113.04 E
Zhuting, Zhg.	100	27.48 N	114.02 E
Zhuwo	105	40.02 N	115.48 E
Zhuwotuo	107	30.31 N	104.34 E
Zhuwumiao	100	30.54 N	116.19 E
Zhuxi, Zhg.	100	28.10 N	118.53 E
Zhuxi, Zhg.	102	32.09 N	109.42 E
Zhuxi, Zhg.	107	29.32 N	105.40 E
Zhuxianzhen	98	34.37 N	114.16 E
Zhuxichang	100	28.58 N	114.06 E
Zhuya	98	36.38 N	118.12 E
Zhuyang	98	36.16 N	117.22 E
Zhuyangxi	107	29.03 N	105.57 E
Zhuyangzhen	102	34.20 N	110.44 E
Zhuyuan	107	29.34 N	104.08 E
Zhuzeqiao	106	31.34 N	119.20 E
Zhuzhenji	100	32.31 N	118.42 E
Zhuzhou (Chuchow)	100	27.50 N	113.09 E
Zhuzikou	100	29.17 N	112.41 E
Zi ≃, Zhg.	98	37.12 N	118.34 E
Zi ≃, Zhg.	102	28.41 N	112.43 E
Zi ≃, Zhg.	102	31.59 N	96.53 E
Zia Indian Reservation ◆[4]	200	35.30 N	106.43 W
Zia International Airport ⊠	126	23.46 N	90.23 E
Ziama Mansouria	34	36.40 N	5.29 E
Ziano	64	46.17 N	11.34 E
Ziārat	120	30.23 N	67.43 E
Ziārat-e Shāh Maqṣūd	120	31.59 N	65.30 E
Ziārat Gali Chāh ⊤[4]	128	28.20 N	63.38 E
Žiar nad Hronom	30	48.36 N	18.52 E
Zibdīn	132	33.22 N	35.28 E
Zibo (Zhangdian)	98	36.47 N	118.01 E
Zicapa	234	17.57 N	99.02 W
Zicavo	36	41.54 N	9.08 E
Zichang	102	37.19 N	109.33 E
Žichovice	60	49.16 N	13.37 E
Zichuan	98	36.38 N	117.55 E
Žičicy	76	55.07 N	31.17 E
Zickhusen	54	53.45 N	11.25 E
Židačov	78	49.23 N	24.08 E
Ziddi	85	39.03 N	68.48 E
Žideli	86	48.40 N	70.29 E
Zid'ki	78	49.42 N	36.21 E
Židlochovice	61	49.02 N	16.37 E
Ziębice	30	50.37 N	17.00 E
Ziegelroda	54	51.20 N	11.28 E
Ziegendorf	54	53.18 N	11.49 E
Ziegenhain	56	50.55 N	9.15 E
Ziegenhals	264a	52.21 N	13.40 E
Ziegenrück	54	50.37 N	11.38 E
Zielona Góra (Grünberg)	30	51.56 N	15.31 E
Zielona Góra □[4]	30	52.00 N	15.20 E
Ziemetshausen	58	48.18 N	10.31 E
Zierenberg	56	51.22 N	9.18 E
Zierikzee	52	51.38 N	3.55 E
Ziersdorf	61	48.31 N	15.55 E
Ziesar	54	52.16 N	12.17 E
Ziesendorf	54	54.00 N	12.02 E
Ziethen	54	53.53 N	13.40 E
Žiežmariai	76	54.48 N	24.27 E
Ziftā	142	30.43 N	31.15 E
Žigajlovka	78	50.38 N	35.07 E
Žigalgan	84	44.36 N	50.46 E
Žigalovo	88	54.48 N	105.08 E
Žigansk	74	66.45 N	123.20 E
Zigazinskij	86	53.50 N	57.20 E
Zigong (Tzukung)	107	29.24 N	104.47 E
Ziguéy	146	14.43 N	15.47 E
Zigui	102	31.00 N	110.31 E
Ziguinchor	150	12.35 N	16.16 W
Ziguinchor □[4]	150	12.45 N	16.20 W
Žigulevsk	80	53.25 N	49.27 E
Žiguli	80	53.22 N	49.19 E
Žiguli ⋏	80	53.20 N	49.40 E
Zigutaicun	104	42.01 N	121.16 E
Zig Zag, Cerro ∧[2]	286d	12.12 S	76.59 W
Zihedian	98	36.48 N	118.22 E
Zihuatanejo	234	17.38 N	101.33 W
Zihukou, Zhg.	100	28.44 N	112.33 E
Zihukou, Zhg.	100	28.55 N	118.08 E
Ziiyang	102	32.31 N	108.48 E
Žijančurino	86	51.33 N	56.55 E
Žijenkum	85	42.50 N	69.00 E
Zijiao	98	37.21 N	117.25 E
Zijin	100	23.40 N	115.11 E
Zijingguan	105	39.23 N	115.12 E
Zijin Shan ∧[2]	106	32.04 N	118.51 E
Zikejevo	76	53.44 N	34.52 E
Zikhron Ya'aqov	132	32.34 N	34.57 E
Zikoufang	100	26.22 N	117.24 E
Zilair	86	52.14 N	57.30 E
Žilaja Kosa	80	46.49 N	53.12 E
Žilaja Tambica	24	62.32 N	36.09 E
Zile	130	40.18 N	35.54 E
Zili	102	26.50 N	100.27 E
Žilina	30	49.14 N	18.46 E
Žilino	76	54.54 N	21.56 E
Zillah, Lībiyā	146	28.33 N	17.35 E
Zillah, Wa., U.S.	202	46.24 N	120.15 W
Ziller ≃	64	47.24 N	11.50 E
Zillertal V	64	47.20 N	11.50 E
Zillertaler Alpen (Alpi Aurine) ⋏	64	47.00 N	11.55 E
Zillis	58	46.38 N	9.27 E
Zillisheim	58	47.41 N	7.16 E
Zilly	54	51.56 N	10.49 E
Zilme	144	16.25 N	43.49 E
Žiloj, ostrov I	84	40.19 N	50.36 E
Žiloj Bor	76	59.06 N	34.37 E
Žil'ovo	82	54.59 N	38.02 E
Ziltendorf	54	52.12 N	14.37 E
Zilupe	76	56.23 N	28.07 E
Zilwaukee	190	43.28 N	83.55 W
Zima	88	53.55 N	102.04 E
Zima ≃	88	53.52 N	102.02 E
Žima, gora ∧	88	53.18 N	107.38 E
Zimapán	234	20.45 N	99.21 W
Zimatlán	234	16.52 N	96.47 W
Zimba	154	17.19 S	26.13 E
Zimbabwe □[1], Afr.	138	20.00 S	30.00 E
Zimbabwe □[1], Afr.	154	20.00 S	30.00 E
Zimbor	38	47.00 N	23.16 E
Zimella	64	45.20 N	11.22 E
Zimi	150	7.19 N	11.18 W
Zimljansker-Stausee → Ciml'anskoje vodochranilišče ⊜[1]	80	48.00 N	43.00 E
Zimmara, Monte ∧	70	37.45 N	14.16 E
Zimn'ackij	80	49.44 N	42.53 E
Zimnicea	38	43.39 N	25.21 E
Zimogorje	83	48.35 N	38.56 E
Zimonino	76	53.47 N	31.52 E
Zimovniki	80	47.08 N	42.28 E
Zimovskoje	86	57.31 N	86.52 E
Zin, Naḥal V	132	30.57 N	35.19 E
Zinal	58	46.08 N	7.38 E
Zinapécuaro [de Figueroa]	234	19.52 N	100.49 W
Zinave, Parque Nacional de ♠	156	21.35 S	33.35 E
Zinder	150	13.48 N	8.59 E
Zinder □[5]	146	15.00 N	10.30 E
Zinga	152	3.43 N	18.35 E
Zinga Mulike	154	9.09 S	38.44 E
Zingaro, Passo dello)(	70	37.43 N	14.50 E
Zingst	54	54.26 N	12.41 E
Zingst ›[1]	54	54.25 N	12.50 E
Zingwanda	140	7.10 N	27.56 E
Ziniaré	150	12.35 N	1.18 W
Žiniške ≃	85	43.14 N	78.30 E
Zinkgruvan	40	58.49 N	15.05 E
Zin'kov	78	49.04 N	27.04 E
Zinnik → Soignies	50	50.35 N	4.04 E
Zinnowitz	54	54.04 N	13.55 E
Zinswiller	56	48.55 N	7.35 E
Zion, Il., U.S.	216	42.26 N	87.49 W
Zion, Md., U.S.	208	39.40 N	75.57 W
Zionhill	208	40.29 N	75.24 W
Zion National Park ♠	200	37.10 N	113.00 W
Zionsville	218	39.57 N	86.15 W
Zionz Lake ⊜	184	51.25 N	91.52 W
Zipaquirá	246	5.02 N	74.00 W
Žipkovšino	88	51.52 N	112.59 E
Zippori	132	32.45 N	35.17 E
Zipsendorf	54	51.02 N	12.16 E
Ziqlāb, Wādī V	132	32.30 N	35.34 E
Zir	130	39.59 N	32.31 E
Zīra	123	30.58 N	74.59 E
Žir'akovo	86	57.53 N	65.37 E
Zirándaro	234	18.27 N	100.59 W
Zirāpur	124	24.01 N	76.22 E
Žir'atino	76	53.15 N	33.44 E
Zirbitzkogel ∧	61	47.04 N	14.34 E
Zirchow	54	53.53 N	14.08 E
Zirgan	86	53.14 N	55.55 E
Žirje, Otok I	36	43.40 N	15.39 E
Zirl	64	47.17 N	11.14 E
Zirndorf	56	49.26 N	10.58 E
Žirnov	80	48.13 N	41.06 E
Žirnovsk	80	51.00 N	44.46 E
Ziro	120	27.38 N	93.42 E
Žiroškino	82	55.22 N	38.03 E
Žirovnice	30	49.15 N	15.11 E
Zishan	100	25.57 N	115.35 E
Zistersdorf	61	48.32 N	16.45 E
Zisterzienserabtei ʊ[1]	56	49.01 N	8.47 E
Zisuntang	106	30.38 N	118.42 E
Zitadelle ⊥	264a	52.33 N	13.13 E
Žiteli	24	65.04 N	47.26 E
Žitenice	54	50.35 N	14.08 E
Žitjevo	76	59.54 N	41.06 E
Žitkoviči	78	52.14 N	27.54 E
Žitkovo	76	60.42 N	29.20 E
Žitkur	80	48.57 N	46.17 E
Zitlala	234	17.38 N	99.05 W
Zitlaltepec	234	19.12 N	97.54 W
Žitnoje	80	45.49 N	47.41 E
Žitomir	78	50.16 N	28.40 E
Zitong	102	31.43 N	105.10 E
Zittau	54	50.54 N	14.47 E
Zitundo	156	26.45 S	32.50 E
Ziwa Magharibi □[4]	154	2.00 S	31.30 E
Ziway, Lake ⊜	144	8.00 N	38.50 E
Ziwuji	100	32.55 N	115.58 E
Zixi, Zhg.	100	27.42 N	117.02 E
Zixi, Zhg.	100	28.01 N	117.46 E
Zixing	100	25.58 N	113.24 E
Ziya ≃	105	39.09 N	117.10 E
Ziyamet	130	35.28 N	34.08 E
Ziyang	107	30.07 N	104.39 E
Ziyuan	102	26.01 N	110.31 E
Ziyun	102	25.43 N	106.05 E
Ziz, Oued V	148	30.39 N	4.26 W
Žizdra	76	53.45 N	34.44 E
Žizdra ≃	82	54.14 N	36.12 E

DEUTSCH

Name	Seite	Breite°′	Länge°′ E = Ost
Zizers	58	46.56 N	9.34 E
Zizhong	107	29.48 N	104.50 E
Zizhou	102	37.37 N	109.41 E
Žižica	76	56.17 N	31.21 E
Žižickoje, ozero ⊜	76	56.14 N	31.15 E
Žižma ≃	76	53.54 N	25.36 E
Zlarin	36	43.42 N	15.50 E
Zlatá Koruna ʊ[1]	61	48.52 N	14.22 E
Zlatar	36	46.06 N	16.05 E
Zlaté Moravce	30	48.25 N	18.24 E
Zlatica	38	42.43 N	24.08 E
Zlatograd	38	41.23 N	25.06 E
Zlatoust	86	55.10 N	59.40 E
Zlatoustovsk	89	52.58 N	133.38 E
Zlín	30	49.13 N	17.41 E
Zlītan	146	32.28 N	14.34 E
Žlobin	76	52.54 N	30.03 E
Złocieniec	30	53.33 N	16.01 E
Złoczew	30	51.25 N	18.36 E
Zlonice	54	50.15 N	14.07 E
Złotoryja	30	51.08 N	15.55 E
Złotów	30	53.22 N	17.02 E
Žlutice	54	50.03 N	13.10 E
Zlydnev	80	48.46 N	45.48 E
Zlynka, Ross.	76	52.25 N	31.44 E
Zlynka, Ukr.	78	48.28 N	31.32 E
Zmeinogorsk	86	51.10 N	82.13 E
Zmeinyj, ostrov I	78	45.15 N	30.12 E
Žmerinka	78	49.02 N	28.06 E
Żmigród	30	51.29 N	16.55 E
Zmijev	78	49.40 N	36.19 E
Žminj	36	45.09 N	13.55 E
Zmi'ovka	76	52.40 N	36.23 E
Zna → Cna ≃	80	54.32 N	42.05 E
Znaim → Znojmo	61	48.52 N	16.02 E
Znamenka, Kaz.	86	50.05 N	79.32 E
Znamenka, Ross.	76	54.54 N	34.34 E
Znamenka, Ross.	80	52.24 N	41.26 E
Znamenka, Ross.	86	53.10 N	79.30 E
Znamenka, Ross.	86	53.32 N	91.54 E
Znamenka, Ross.	88	54.42 N	104.50 E
Znamenka, Ukr.	78	48.43 N	32.40 E
Znamenka, Ukr.	83	48.51 N	37.22 E
Znamenka Vtoraja	78	48.43 N	32.35 E
Znamensk	76	54.37 N	21.13 E
Znamenskoje, Ross.	76	53.17 N	35.41 E
Znamenskoje, Ross.	80	53.19 N	42.57 E
Znamenskoje, Ross.	86	57.08 N	73.55 E
Znamenskoje, Ross.	265b	55.45 N	37.09 E
Žnin	30	52.52 N	17.43 E
Znob'-Novgorodskoje	78	52.16 N	33.36 E
Znojmo	61	48.52 N	16.02 E
Zoagli	62	44.20 N	9.16 E
Zoar	158	33.30 S	21.28 E
Zoar Village State Memorial ⊥	214	40.36 N	81.27 W
Zoarville	214	40.35 N	81.24 W
Zobia	154	2.58 N	25.56 E
Zöblitz	54	50.39 N	13.14 E
Zóbuè	154	15.38 S	34.26 E
Zocca	64	44.21 N	10.59 E
Žochova, ostrov I	74	76.04 N	152.40 E
Zod	84	40.12 N	45.52 E
Žodino	76	54.06 N	28.21 E
Žodiški	76	54.38 N	26.26 E
Zoétélé	152	3.15 N	11.53 E
Zoetermeer	52	52.03 N	4.30 E
Zofingen	58	47.18 N	7.57 E
Zogang	102	29.55 N	97.44 E
Zogno	62	45.48 N	9.40 E
Zográfos	267c	37.59 N	23.46 E
Zohar	132	31.36 N	34.42 E
Zohar, Mizpé ∧[2]	132	31.13 N	35.14 E
Zohreh ≃	128	30.04 N	49.31 E
Zola Predosa	64	44.29 N	11.12 E
Zolder	56	51.01 N	5.18 E
Zoldo Alto	64	46.22 N	12.06 E
Zolfo Springs	220	27.29 N	81.47 W
Zolka ≃	84	44.17 N	43.51 E
Żółkiewka	30	50.55 N	22.51 E
Zollhaus	56	50.17 N	8.04 E
Zollikofen	58	47.00 N	7.28 E
Zollikon	58	47.20 N	8.35 E
Zolling	60	48.27 N	11.46 E
Zol'noje	80	53.27 N	49.48 E
Zoločov, Ukr.	78	50.17 N	35.59 E
Zoločov, Ukr.	78	49.47 N	24.52 E
Zolotaja Gora	89	54.16 N	126.36 E
Zolotaja Lipa ≃	78	48.59 N	25.04 E
Zolotari	80	49.46 N	46.21 E
Zolotar'ovka	80	53.04 N	45.20 E
Zolotkovo	80	55.32 N	41.06 E
Zolotniki	78	49.17 N	25.23 E
Zolotoje, Ross.	80	50.51 N	45.53 E
Zolotoje, Ukr.	83	48.41 N	38.31 E
Zolotoj Kolodec	83	48.32 N	37.15 E
Zolotoj Potok	78	48.54 N	25.20 E
Zolotonoša	78	49.40 N	32.02 E
Zolotucha	80	47.49 N	46.44 E
Zolotuchino	78	52.05 N	36.23 E
Žoltoje, Ukr.	78	48.30 N	33.31 E
Žoltoje, Ukr.	78	47.47 N	33.50 E
Ž'oltoje, Ukr.	83	48.39 N	39.07 E
Žoltyje Vody	78	48.21 N	33.31 E
Žolymbet	86	51.45 N	71.44 E
Zomba	154	15.23 S	35.18 E
Zomergem	50	51.07 N	3.33 E
Zone Point ›	42	50.08 N	5.00 W
Zongchang	107	28.52 N	104.36 E
Zongjiaxiang	269b	31.12 N	121.22 E
Zongo	152	4.21 N	18.36 E
Zonguldak	130	41.27 N	31.49 E
Zonguldak □[4]	130	41.30 N	32.15 E
Zongwe	154	5.05 S	27.55 E
Zongyang	100	30.42 N	117.12 E
Zonhoven	56	50.59 N	5.21 E
Zonnebeke	50	50.52 N	2.59 E
Zons	56	51.07 N	6.50 E
Zonza	36	41.45 N	9.10 E
Zoo, Bahnhof ◆[5]	264a	52.30 N	13.20 E
Zooafskolk	158	29.56 S	20.24 E
Zoom ≃	52	51.30 N	4.14 E
Zoppot → Sopot	30	54.28 N	18.34 E
Zopui	120	23.39 N	92.14 E
Zörbig	54	51.37 N	12.07 E
Zorge	54	51.38 N	10.38 E
Zorge ≃	54	51.27 N	10.54 E
Zorgo	150	12.15 N	0.36 W
Zorgongo	150	12.16 N	0.48 W
Zorinsk	83	48.25 N	38.34 E
Zorita	34	39.17 N	5.42 W
Zorkul', ozero ⊜	120	37.27 N	73.40 E
Zorn ≃	56	48.45 N	7.55 E
Zorneding	60	48.05 N	11.49 E
Zornica	38	42.23 N	26.56 E
Zorra, Arroyo de la ≃	196	29.31 N	101.13 W
Zorritos	246	3.40 S	80.40 W
Zorzor	150	7.46 N	9.28 W
Zöschen	54	51.21 N	12.07 E
Zossen	54	52.13 N	13.27 E
Zoti	84	41.53 N	42.28 E
Zottegem	50	50.52 N	3.48 E
Zou □[5]	150	8.00 N	2.15 E
Zou ≃	150	6.28 N	2.25 E
Zouan-Hounien	150	6.55 N	8.13 W
Zouar	146	20.27 N	16.32 E
Zouérat	148	22.42 N	12.30 W
Zoug → Zug	58	47.10 N	8.31 E
Zoulabot	152	3.17 N	14.02 E
Zoumagang	107	29.28 N	106.18 E
Zoumayi	98	39.07 N	114.34 E
Zouping	98	36.53 N	117.42 E
Zourma	150	11.22 N	0.49 W
Zousfana, Oued V	148	30.29 N	2.17 W
Zoutelande	52	51.30 N	3.30 E
Zoutkamp	52	53.20 N	6.18 E
Zouxian	98	35.24 N	117.00 E

…**ls** in the index entries represent the broad …es identified in the key at the right. Symbols …rior numbers (⋏[1]) identify subcategories (see …ey on page *I · 1).*

… Register stellen die rechts im …ärten Kategorien dar. Symbole mit … Ziffern (⋏[1]) bezeichnen Unterab… …tegorie (vgl. vollständiger Schlüssel

Los símbolos incluídos en el texto del índice representan las grandes categorias identificadas con la clave a la derecha. Los símbolos con numeros en su parte superior (⋏[1]) identifican las subcategorías (véase la clave completa en la página *I · 1).*

Les symboles de l'index représentent les catégories indiquées dans la légende à droite. Les symboles suivis d'un indice (⋏[1]) représentent des sous-catégories (voir légende complète à la page *I · 1).*

Os símbolos incluídos no texto do índice representam as grandes categorias identificadas com a chave à direita. Os símbolos com números em sua parte superior (⋏[1]) identificam as subcategorias (veja-se a chave completa à página *I · 1).*

∧ Mountain	Berg	Montaña	Montagne	Montanha
⋏ Mountains	Gebirge	Montañas	Montagnes	Montanhas
)(Pass	Paß	Paso	Col	Passo
V Valley, Canyon	Tal, Cañon	Valle, Cañón	Vallée, Canyon	Vale, Canhão
≚ Plain	Ebene	Llano	Plaine	Planície
› Cape	Kap	Cabo	Cap	Cabo
I Island	Insel	Isla	Île	Ilha
II Islands	Inseln	Islas	Îles	Ilhas
⊥ Other Topographic Features	Andere Topographische Objekte	Otros Elementos Topográficos	Autres données topographiques	Outros acidentes topográficos

ESPAÑOL · FRANÇAIS · PORTUGUÊS

Nombre / Nom / Nome	Página / Page	Lat.°′	Long.°′ W = Oeste / W = Ouest
Zova	**132**	31.48 N	35.06 E
Zovka	**76**	58.26 N	28.52 E
Žovnino	**78**	49.23 N	32.41 E
Žovten', Ukr.	**78**	49.03 N	24.45 E
Žovten', Ukr.	**78**	47.14 N	30.20 E
Žovtnevoje, Ukr.	**78**	46.52 N	32.02 E
Žovtnevoje, Ukr.	**78**	49.39 N	34.09 E
Žovtnevoje, Ukr.	**78**	50.57 N	34.22 E
Žovtnevoje, Ukr.	**78**	51.15 N	28.07 E
Zozov	**78**	49.19 N	29.01 E
Zrenjanin	**38**	45.23 N	20.24 E
Zriba	**36**	36.20 N	10.16 E
Zrmanja ≃	**36**	44.15 N	15.32 E
Zruč nad Sázavou	**30**	49.45 N	15.07 E
Zscherndorf	**54**	51.36 N	12.15 E
Zschieren ◆ 8	**54**	51.00 N	13.52 E
Zschopau	**54**	50.44 N	13.04 E
Zschopau ≃	**54**	51.08 N	13.03 E
Zschorlau	**54**	50.34 N	12.38 E
Zschornewitz	**54**	51.43 N	12.25 E
Zschortau	**54**	51.28 N	12.21 E
Žuanbalyk	**86**	45.04 N	61.51 E
Žuantobe	**86**	44.45 N	68.54 E
Zuarungu	**150**	10.47 N	0.48 W
Zuata ≃	**246**	7.52 N	65.22 W
Zubaydīyah, Jabal az- ʌ	**132**	33.48 N	37.02 E
Zubayr, Jazā'ir az- II	**144**	15.05 N	42.08 E
Zubayr, Wādī V	**142**	27.27 N	32.41 E
Zubcov	**76**	56.10 N	34.34 E
Zubkoviči	**78**	51.02 N	27.41 E
Zubova Pol'ana	**80**	54.04 N	42.51 E
Zubovka	**80**	54.16 N	51.06 E
Zubovo, Ross.	**76**	54.33 N	35.29 E
Zubovo, Ross.	**76**	60.19 N	36.57 E
Zubovo, Ross.	**80**	56.52 N	44.08 E
Zuccarello	**62**	44.07 N	8.07 E
Zuccone, Monte ʌ	**62**	44.26 N	9.37 E
Zuchwil	**58**	47.12 N	7.33 E
Zuckerhütl ʌ	**64**	46.58 N	11.09 E
Zudar	**54**	54.15 N	13.20 E
Z'udev, ostrov I	**80**	45.35 N	47.58 E
Zuel	**64**	46.31 N	12.08 E
Zuénoula	**150**	7.26 N	6.03 W
Zuera	**34**	41.52 N	0.47 W
Ẓufār ◆ 1	**118**	17.00 N	54.10 E
Zufaytat Mashtūl	**142**	30.20 N	31.21 E
Zug	**58**	47.10 N	8.31 E
Zug □ 3	**58**	47.00 N	8.30 E
Zugdeli	**88**	55.03 N	111.10 E
Zugdidi	**84**	42.30 N	41.53 E
Zugersee ◎	**58**	47.08 N	8.30 E
Zug Island I	**281**	42.17 N	83.07 W
Zugló ◆ 8	**264c**	47.31 N	19.08 E
Zugres	**83**	48.01 N	38.15 E
Zugspitze ʌ	**64**	47.25 N	10.59 E
Zugurma Game Reserve ◆ 4	**150**	9.55 N	5.00 E
Zühlsdorf	**264a**	52.44 N	13.24 E
Zui	**76**	57.06 N	31.37 E
Zuid-Beijerland	**52**	51.45 N	4.22 E
Zuid-Beveland I	**52**	51.25 N	3.45 E
Zuidbroek	**52**	53.10 N	6.52 E
Zuidelijk Flevoland ◆ 1	**52**	52.22 N	5.20 E
Zuiderzee → IJsselmeer ⫧ 2	**52**	52.45 N	5.25 E
Zuid-Holland □ 4	**52**	52.00 N	4.30 E
Zuidhorn	**52**	53.14 N	6.24 E
Zuidlaren	**52**	53.05 N	6.41 E
Zuid-Willemsvaart ≅	**52**	51.12 N	5.52 E
Zuidwolde	**52**	53.15 N	6.35 E
Zuja	**78**	45.03 N	34.20 E
Žuja ≃	**88**	58.45 N	118.11 E
Zújar ≃	**34**	39.01 N	5.47 W
Zújar, Embalse del ◎ 1	**34**	38.50 N	5.20 W
Zujevka, Ross.	**80**	58.25 N	51.10 E
Zujevka, Ukr.	**83**	48.04 N	38.15 E
Z'ukajka	**80**	58.12 N	54.43 E
Žukopa	**76**	56.33 N	32.42 E
Žukopa ≃	**76**	56.54 N	32.46 E
Žukovka, Ross.	**76**	53.32 N	33.44 E
Žukovka, Ross.	**86**	56.05 N	91.42 E
Žukovka, Ross.	**265b**	55.44 N	37.15 E
Žukovskaja	**80**	47.37 N	42.28 E
Žukovskij	**82**	55.35 N	38.08 E
Žukovskoje	**80**	46.05 N	41.21 E
Żukowo	**30**	54.21 N	18.22 E
Zula	**144**	15.11 N	39.41 E
Zula ≃	**234**	20.21 N	102.46 W
Žulanka	**86**	54.22 N	80.36 E
Zulayl, Wādī az- V	**132**	32.09 N	36.03 E
Žuldyz	**80**	49.16 N	49.30 E
Žulebino	**265b**	55.42 N	37.51 E
Zuli ≃	**102**	36.35 N	104.35 E
Zulia □ 3	**246**	10.00 N	72.10 W
Zulia ʌ	**154**	4.07 N	33.58 E
Zulia ≃	**246**	9.04 N	72.18 W
Zülpich	**56**	50.41 N	6.39 E
Zulueta	**240p**	22.22 N	79.34 W
Zululand □ 9	**158**	28.10 S	32.00 E
Z'ul'z'a	**88**	52.33 N	116.13 E
Žumala	**80**	50.29 N	49.47 E
Zumar, Tur'at az- ≅	**273c**	29.58 N	31.15 E
Zumarraga	**116**	11.38 N	124.50 E
Zumba	**246**	4.52 S	79.09 W
Zumbo	**154**	15.36 S	30.25 E
Zumbro ≃	**190**	44.18 N	91.56 W
Zumbro, North Fork ≃	**190**	44.15 N	92.29 W
Zumbro, South Fork ≃	**190**	44.15 N	92.29 W
Zumbrota	**190**	44.17 N	92.40 W
Zumpango del Río	**234**	17.39 N	99.30 W
Zumpango de Ocampo	**234**	19.48 N	99.06 W
Zundert	**52**	51.28 N	4.40 E
Zundi	**152**	10.28 S	16.48 E
Zune	**156**	18.59 S	35.18 E
Zungeru	**150**	9.48 N	6.09 E
Zungri	**68**	38.39 N	15.59 E
Zungur	**150**	9.58 N	9.47 E
Zungwini	**158**	27.34 S	30.53 E
Zunhua	**105**	40.12 N	117.58 E
Zuni, N.M., U.S.	**200**	35.04 N	108.51 W
Zuni, Va., U.S.	**208**	36.51 N	76.49 W
Zuni ≃	**200**	34.39 N	109.40 W
Zuni Indian Reservation ◆ 4	**200**	35.15 N	108.20 W
Zunsuzhi	**102**	44.40 N	112.50 E
Zunyi	**102**	27.39 N	106.57 E
Zuo ≃	**102**	22.50 N	108.06 E
Zuo'an	**100**	26.10 N	114.16 E
Zuodeng	**102**	23.27 N	106.57 E
Zuogezhuang	**105**	39.01 N	116.37 E
Zuomaozigou	**104**	42.12 N	120.41 E
Zuomuchedong Hu ◎	**120**	28.25 N	88.15 E
Zuoquan	**102**	37.03 N	113.30 E
Zuosuo	**102**	27.45 N	100.54 E
Zuotema	**120**	35.50 N	80.45 E
Zuowei	**105**	40.41 N	114.43 E
Zuoxiunulemiao	**88**	48.08 N	115.38 E
Zuoyun	**102**	40.02 N	112.54 E
Zuoz	**58**	46.36 N	9.58 E
Županja	**38**	45.04 N	18.42 E
Zūq Muṣbīḥ	**132**	33.58 N	35.37 E
Žura, Mol.	**78**	47.31 N	29.04 E
Zura, Ross.	**80**	57.37 N	53.26 E
Zūrābād	**128**	38.49 N	44.35 E
Žuraviči, Bela.	**76**	53.15 N	30.33 E
Žuraviči, Ukr.	**78**	50.59 N	25.43 E
Žuravl'ovka, Kaz.	**86**	51.57 N	69.56 E
Žuravl'ovka, Ukr.	**83**	48.13 N	38.58 E
Zurayghiṭ	**128**	26.29 N	40.33 E
Žurban	**89**	54.12 N	127.56 E
Zurich, On., Can.	**190**	43.26 N	81.37 W
Zurich, Ned.	**52**	53.06 N	5.23 E
Zürich, Schw.	**58**	47.23 N	8.32 E
Zürich □ 3	**58**	47.25 N	8.40 E
Zürich, Flughafen ⊠	**58**	47.27 N	8.33 E
Zurich, Lake ◎	**278**	42.12 N	88.06 W
Zürichsee ◎	**58**	47.13 N	8.45 E
Zurigo → Zürich	**58**	47.23 N	8.32 E
Zurmi	**150**	12.46 N	6.48 E
Żuromin	**30**	53.04 N	19.55 E
Zurq, Al-Qārāt az- ʌ 2	**142**	29.00 N	29.55 E
Zürs	**58**	47.10 N	10.10 E
Zuru	**150**	11.27 N	5.12 E
Zurzach	**58**	47.35 N	8.18 E
Zuša ≃	**76**	53.27 N	36.23 E
Zusam ≃	**56**	48.42 N	10.45 E
Žusandala ◆ 2	**86**	44.20 N	75.00 E
Zushi	**94**	35.18 N	139.35 E
Zusmarshausen	**58**	48.24 N	10.35 E
Züssow	**54**	53.59 N	13.32 E
Žut, Otok I	**36**	43.52 N	15.19 E
Zutiua ≃	**250**	3.43 S	45.29 W
Žutovo Vtoroje	**80**	47.49 N	43.51 E
Zutphen	**52**	52.08 N	6.12 E
Zützen	**54**	51.57 N	13.38 E
Zuwārah	**146**	32.56 N	12.06 E
Zuwayzā	**132**	31.42 N	35.55 E
Z'uzel'skij	**86**	56.29 N	60.07 E
Žužemberk	**36**	45.50 N	14.56 E
Z'uzino	**265b**	55.40 N	38.07 E
Z'uzino ◆ 8	**265b**	55.39 N	37.35 E
Žuzymdyk	**85**	43.05 N	69.08 E
Zv'agino	**265b**	55.59 N	37.48 E
Zvannoje	**78**	51.23 N	34.33 E
Zvenigorod	**82**	55.44 N	36.51 E
Zvenigorodka	**78**	49.04 N	30.57 E
Zvenigovo	**80**	55.58 N	48.02 E
Zverevo	**83**	48.01 N	40.07 E
Zverinogolovskoje	**86**	54.28 N	64.50 E
Zvezdec	**38**	42.07 N	27.25 E
Zvezdnyj	**88**	56.49 N	106.27 E
Zvíkovec	**60**	49.56 N	13.42 E
Zvishavane	**154**	20.20 S	30.02 E
Zvolen	**30**	48.35 N	19.08 E
Zvon ʌ	**60**	49.33 N	12.39 E
Zvornik	**38**	44.23 N	19.06 E
Zwaag	**52**	52.40 N	5.05 E
Zwaagwesteinde	**52**	53.15 N	6.04 E
Zwadība	**152**	3.04 N	14.02 E
Zwanenburg	**52**	52.23 N	4.45 E
Zwartemeer	**52**	52.43 N	7.03 E
Zwarte Meer ◎	**52**	52.37 N	5.57 E
Zwartsluis	**52**	52.37 N	6.04 E
Zweckel ◆ 8	**263**	51.36 N	6.59 E
Zwedru	**150**	6.04 N	8.08 W
Zweibrücken	**56**	49.15 N	7.21 E
Zweifall	**56**	50.43 N	6.15 E
Zweisimmen	**58**	46.33 N	7.22 E
Zweite Wiener Hochquellenleitung ≅ 1	**61**	48.10 N	16.14 E
Zwenkau	**54**	51.13 N	12.19 E
Zwentendorf	**61**	48.21 N	15.55 E
Zwesten	**56**	51.03 N	9.10 E
Zwettl	**61**	48.37 N	15.10 E
Zwevegem	**50**	50.48 N	3.20 E
Zwevezele	**50**	51.02 N	3.12 E
Zwickau	**54**	50.44 N	12.29 E
Zwickauer Mulde ≃	**54**	51.10 N	12.48 E
Zwiefalten	**58**	48.14 N	9.28 E
Zwiefaltendorf	**58**	48.13 N	9.31 E
Zwierzyniec	**30**	50.37 N	22.58 E
Zwiesel	**60**	49.01 N	13.14 E
Zwieselstein	**64**	46.56 N	11.02 E
Zwijndrecht	**52**	51.49 N	4.39 E
Zwillbrock	**52**	52.04 N	6.42 E
Zwingenberg, Dtsch.	**56**	49.25 N	9.02 E
Zwingenberg, Dtsch.	**56**	49.43 N	8.37 E
Zwischenahner Meer ◎	**52**	53.12 N	8.01 E
Zwochau	**54**	51.28 N	12.16 E
Zwoleń	**30**	51.22 N	21.35 E
Zwölfaxing	**264b**	48.06 N	16.28 E
Zwolle, Ned.	**52**	52.30 N	6.05 E
Zwolle, La., U.S.	**194**	31.37 N	93.38 W
Zwönitz	**54**	50.38 N	12.49 E
Zwota	**54**	50.21 N	12.25 E
Żychlin	**30**	52.15 N	19.39 E
Zymoetz ≃	**182**	54.33 N	128.26 W
Zyr'anka	**74**	65.45 N	150.51 E
Zyr'anovsk	**86**	49.43 N	84.20 E
Zyr'anovskij	**86**	57.46 N	61.42 E
Zyr'anskoje	**86**	56.50 N	86.38 E
Żyrardów	**30**	52.04 N	20.25 E
Zyryanovsk → Zyr'anovsk	**86**	49.43 N	84.20 E
Żyrzyn	**30**	51.30 N	22.07 E
Żywiec	**30**	49.41 N	19.12 E

≃ River	Fluß	Río	Rivière	Rio
≅ Canal	Kanal	Canal	Canal	Canal
Waterfall, Rapids	Wasserfall, Stromschnellen	Cascada, Rápidos	Chute d'eau, Rapides	Cascata, Rápidos
Strait	Meeresstraße	Estrecho	Détroit	Estreito
Bay, Gulf	Bucht, Golf	Bahía, Golfo	Baie, Golfe	Baía, Golfo
◎ Lake, Lakes	See, Seen	Lago, Lagos	Lac, Lacs	Lago, Lagos
Swamp	Sumpf	Pantano	Marais	Pântano
Ice Features, Glacier	Eis- und Gletscherformen	Accidentes Glaciales	Formes glaciaires	Acidentes glaciares
⫧ Other Hydrographic Features	Andere Hydrographische Objekte	Otros Elementos Hidrográficos	Autres données hydrographiques	Outros acidentes hidrográficos

Submarine Features	Untermeerische Objekte	Accidentes Submarinos	Formes de relief sous-marin	Acidentes submarinos
□ Political Unit	Politische Einheit	Unidad Politica	Entité politique	Unidade política
Cultural Institution	Kulturelle Institution	Institución Cultural	Institution culturelle	Instituição cultural
Historical Site	Historische Stätte	Sitio Histórico	Site historique	Sitio histórico
Recreational Site	Erholungs- und Ferienort	Sitio de Recreo	Centre de loisirs	Area de Lazer
⊠ Airport	Flughafen	Aeropuerto	Aéroport	Aeroporto
Military Installation	Militäranlage	Instalación Militar	Installation militaire	Instalação militar
◆ Miscellaneous	Verschiedenes	Misceláneo	Divers	Diversos